THE
INTERNATIONAL
WHO'S WHO
1968—69

THE
INTERNATIONAL
WHO'S WHO

THIRTY-SECOND EDITION

1968–69

LONDON

EUROPA PUBLICATIONS LTD.

18 BEDFORD SQUARE, W.C.1.

R/CT
120
I5
1968-69
c.1

Made and printed in England by
STAPLES PRINTERS LIMITED
at their Rochester, Kent, establishment

FOREWORD TO THE 32nd EDITION

Each new edition of THE INTERNATIONAL WHO'S WHO is the result of a complete and thorough revision of its predecessor. Not only are daily records of changes to existing entries maintained, but there is also continuous research directed towards the selection of new names for inclusion in the next edition. More than six hundred new biographies have been added to this latest volume and they will, we believe, still further enhance the value of THE INTERNATIONAL WHO'S WHO as a source of international biographical reference.

We are continuing to add where possible the full date of birth and telephone number of each entry, and although we do not give family details, we have tried to state close family relationships between individuals listed in this book.

An obituary list of persons whose deaths have been noted since the preparation of the previous edition appears at the end of the book.

We would once again like to express our thanks to all those who, by completing questionnaires or by correcting proofs sent to them, have enabled us to bring our information up-to-date. We would particularly like to emphasise the necessity for proofs of entries to be returned to us without delay, as only in this way can we be certain that every entry is as accurate and as up-to-date as possible.

July 1968.

FOREWORD TO THE FIRST EDITION
(1935)

THE INTERNATIONAL WHO'S WHO has been compiled to meet a need which has for long been noticeable to all who are brought into contact with the world of affairs. Business men, traders, bankers, politicians, journalists, writers, librarians, in every country are familiar with the existing reference books in which they can find short biographical details of the prominent figures in the life of the country. Anyone whose work leads to the handling of numbers of names of his eminent contemporaries knows by experience what an inestimable assistance it is to him to be able to find out, in a second or two, exactly "Who's Who".

But hitherto there has been a gap—an irritating, unnecessary gap—in this field of reference. Biographical reference books have been almost exclusively national. Names could be verified, addresses ascertained, past careers scrutinised, only if the subjects of the enquiry were of the same nationality as the searcher. Any attempt to have readily at hand similar information for citizens of foreign countries involved the possession of an array of different reference books. The inconvenience of this is obvious. The expense is too great for all but the tiny minority. The net result has been that biographical references for foreigners have not been available for the great majority of those who needed them.

THE INTERNATIONAL WHO'S WHO fills this need. It does not claim to include all those who find a place in the national reference books, nor does it give as many biographical details of those included as may be found elsewhere. But it does claim to include more names and more information than in any other international reference book of this kind.

THE INTERNATIONAL WHO'S WHO does not wish to supersede or to compete with the national reference books; it desires to supplement and co-ordinate them.

The compilation has necessitated both selection and compression; both are subject to the fallibility of judgment, but the compilers have attempted to include everyone whose name is known outside his own country, and to make mention of all those biographical details which are likely to be of value to foreigners. In compiling this information every attempt has been made to ensure accuracy. In the majority of cases the facts have been ascertained from the best possible source—to wit, the subject himself. In the remainder, information has been secured from authoritative sources, such as embassies, government offices, institutions, etc. Should any inaccuracies have crept in or any noteworthy names have been omitted, correction will be made in later editions, and the publishers will be grateful for any corrections or supplementary information forwarded to them by the kindness of users of the volume.

It is the wish of the compilers and publishers that THE INTERNATIONAL WHO'S WHO will have made a humble contribution to the cause of international understanding, without which permanent peace will be impossible.

ABBREVIATIONS

A.A.A.	..	Agricultural Adjustment Administration
A.A.A.S.	..	American Association for the Advancement of Science
A.A.F.	..	Army Air Force
A.B.	..	Bachelor of Arts
A.C.A.	..	Associate of the Institute of Chartered Accountants
Acad.	..	Academy
Accad.	..	Accademia
Accred.	..	Accredited
A.C.I.S.	..	Associate of the Chartered Institute of Secretaries
A.C.S.	..	American Chemical Society
Act.	..	Acting
A.C.T.	..	Australian Capital Territory
A.D.C.	..	Aide-de-camp
Adm.	..	Admiral
Admin.	..	Administrative, Administration, Administrator
A.E.R.E.	..	Atomic Energy Research Establishment
A.F.	..	Air Force
A.F.C.	..	Air Force Cross
affil.	..	affiliated
A.F.L.	..	American Federation of Labor
A.G.	..	Aktiengesellschaft (Joint Stock Company)
A.H.A.	..	American Historical Association
a.i.	..	ad interim
A.I.A.	..	Associate of Institute of Actuaries; American Institute of Architects
A.I.B.	..	Associate of the Institute of Bankers
A.I.C.C.	..	All-India Congress Committee
A.I.C.E.	..	American Insitute of Civil Engineers
A.I.Ch.E.	..	American Institute of Chemical Engineers
A.I.E.E.	..	American Institute of Electrical Engineers
A.I.F.	..	Australian Imperial Forces
A.(I.)I.A.L.	..	Associate of the (International) Institute of Arts and Letters
A.I.M.E.	..	American Institute of Mining Engineers; Associate of the Institution of Mining Engineers
A.I.Mech.E.	..	Associate of the Institution of Mechanical Engineers
A.I(nst.)C.E.	..	Associate of the Institution of Civil Engineers
A.I.R.	..	All-India Radio
Akad.	..	Akademie
A.K.C.	..	Associate of King's College (London)
Ala.	..	Alabama
A.L.S.	..	Associate of the Linnæan Society
Alt.	..	Alternate
A.M.	..	Master of Arts; Alpes Maritimes
Amb.	..	Ambassador
A.M.I.C.E.	..	Associate Member of the Institution of Civil Engineers
A.M.I.E.E.	..	Associate Member of the Institution of Electrical Engineers
A.M.I.Mech.E.	..	Associate Member of the Institution of Mechanical Engineers
A.P.	..	Andhra Pradesh
Approx.	..	Approximately
Apptd.	..	Appointed
A.R.A.	..	Associate of the Royal Academy
A.R.A.M.	..	Associate of the Royal Academy of Music
A.R.C.A.	..	Associate of the Royal College of Art
A.R.C.M.	..	Associate of the Royal College of Music
A.R.C.S.	..	Associate of the Royal College of Science
A.R.I.B.A.	..	Associate of the Royal Institute of British Architects

A.R.I.C.	..	Associate of the Royal Institute of Chemistry
Ariz.	..	Arizona
Ark.	..	Arkansas
A.R.S.A.	..	Associate of the Royal Scottish Academy; Associate of the Royal Society of Arts
A.S.C.E.A.	..	American Society of Civil Engineers and Architects
A.S.M.E.	..	American Society of Mechanical Engineers
Asoc.	..	Asociación
Ass.	..	Assembly
Asscn.	..	Association
Assoc.	..	Associate
A.S.S.R.	..	Autonomous Soviet Socialist Republic
Asst.	..	Assistant
Aug.	..	August
b.	..	born
B.A.	..	Bachelor of Arts
B.A.A.S.	..	British Association for the Advancement of Science
B.Agr.	..	Bachelor of Agriculture
B.A.O.	..	Bachelor of Obstetrics
B.Arch.	..	Bachelor of Architecture
Bart.	..	Baronet
B.A.S.	..	Bachelor in Agricultural Science
B.B.A.	..	Bachelor of Business Administration
B.B.C.	..	British Broadcasting Corporation
B.C.	..	British Columbia
B.Ch., B.Chir.	..	Bachelor of Surgery
B.C.L.	..	Bachelor of Civil Law; Bachelor of Canon Law
B.Com(m).	..	Bachelor of Commerce
B.C.S.	..	Bachelor of Commercial Sciences
B.D.	..	Bachelor of Divinity
Bd.	..	Board
B.D.S.	..	Bachelor of Dental Surgery
B.E.	..	Bachelor of Engineering; Bachelor of Education
B.E.A.	..	British European Airways
Beds.	..	Bedfordshire
B.E.F.	..	British Expeditionary Force
B.Eng.	..	Bachelor of Engineering
Berks.	..	Berkshire
B.F.A.	..	Bachelor of Fine Arts
B.I.S.	..	Bank of International Settlements
B.L.	..	Bachelor of Laws
Bldg.	..	Building
B.Lit(t).	..	Bachelor of Letters
B.LL.	..	Bachelor of Laws
B.L.S.	..	Bachelor in Library Science
B.M.	..	Bachelor of Medicine
B.M.A.	..	British Medical Association
B.Mus.	..	Bachelor of Music
Bn.	..	Battalion
B.O.A.C.	..	British Overseas Airways Corporation
Brig.	..	Brigadier
B.S.	..	Bachelor of Science; Bachelor of Surgery
B.S.A.	..	Bachelor of Scientific Agriculture
B.Sc.	..	Bachelor of Science
Bt.	..	Baronet
Bucks.	..	Buckinghamshire
B.W.I.	..	British West Indies
c.	..	circa
C.A.	..	Chartered Accountant
Cabt.	..	Cabinet
Calif.	..	California

Cambs.	..	Cambridgeshire
Cantab.	..	Of Cambridge University
Capt.	..	Captain
C.B.	..	Companion of the (Order of the) Bath
C.B.C.	..	Canadian Broadcasting Corporation
C.B.E.	..	Commander of (the Order of) the British Empire
C.B.S.	..	Columbia Broadcasting System
C.C.	..	Companion of Canada
C.C.P.	..	Chinese Communist Party
C.D.U.	..	Christliche Demokratische Union
C.E.	..	Civil Engineer
cen.	..	central
C.Eng.	..	Chartered Engineer
CENTO	..	Central Treaty Organisation
CERN	..	Conseil (now Organisation) Européen (ne) pour la Recherche Nucléaire
CGT	..	Confédération Générale du Travail
C.H.	..	Companion of Honour
Chair.	..	Chairman
Ch.B.	..	Bachelor of Surgery
Chem.	..	Chemistry
Ch.M.	..	Master of Surgery
C.I.	..	Channel Islands
C.I.A.	..	Central Intelligence Agency
Cía.	..	Compagnía (Company)
C.I.D.	..	Criminal Investigation Department
C.I.E.	..	Companion of (the Order of) the Indian Empire
Cie.	..	Compagnie (Company)
C.I.E.E.	..	Companion of the Institution of Electrical Engineers
C.-in-C.	..	Commander-in-Chief
C.I.O.	..	Congress of Industrial Organisations
C.L.D.	..	Doctor of Civil Law (U.S.A.)
C.Lit.	..	Companion of Literature
C.M.	..	Master in Surgery
C.M.G.	..	Companion of (the Order of) St. Michael and St. George
Co.	..	Company; County
C.O.	..	Commanding Officer
C.O.I.	..	Central Office of Information
Col.	..	Colonel
Coll.	..	College
Colo.	..	Colorado
COMECON		Council for Mutual Economic Aid
Comm.	..	Commission
Commdg.	..	Commanding
Commdr.	..	Commander, Commandeur
Commdt.	..	Commandant
Commr.	..	Commissioner
Conf.	..	Conference
Conn.	..	Connecticut
Cons.	..	Conservative
Contrib.	..	Contributor; contribution
C.P.A.	..	Certified Public Accountant
Corpn.	..	Corporation
Corresp.	..	Correspondent; Corresponding
C.P.	..	Communist Party
C.P.P.	..	Convention People's Party (Ghana)
C.P.P.C.C.	..	Chinese People's Political Consultative Conference
C.P.S.U.	..	Communist Party of the Soviet Union
cr.	..	created
C.S.I.R.(O.)	..	Council for Scientific and Industrial Research (re-named Commonwealth Scientific and Industrial Research Organisation)
C.St.J.	..	Commander of (the Order of) St. John of Jerusalem
Cttee.	..	Committee
C.V.	..	Commanditaire Vennootschap
C.V.O.	..	Commander of the (Royal) Victorian Order

D.Arch.	..	Doctor of Architecture
D.B.	..	Bachelor of Divinity
D.B.E.	..	Dame Commander of (the Order of) the British Empire
D.C.	..	District of Columbia
D.C.L.	..	Doctor of Civil Law
D.C.M.	..	Distinguished Conduct Medal
D.Cn.L.	..	Doctor of Canon Law
D.Comm.	..	Doctor of Commerce
D.C.S.	..	Doctor of Commercial Sciences
D.C.T.	..	Doctor of Christian Theology
D.D.	..	Doctor of Divinity
D.D.R.	..	Deutsche Demokratische Republik (German Democratic Republic)
D.D.S.	..	Doctor of Dental Surgery
Dec.	..	December
D.Econ.	..	Doctor of Economics
D. en D.	..	Docteur en Droit
D. en Med.	..	Doctor of Medicine
D.Eng.	..	Doctor of Engineering
Del.	..	Delegate, delegation, Delaware
Dem.	..	Democratic
Dep.	..	Deputy
Dept.	..	Department
D. ès L.	..	Docteur ès Lettres
D. ès Sc.	..	Docteur ès Sciences
Devt.	..	Development
D.F.	..	Distrito Federal
D.F.A.	..	Doctor of Fine Arts
D.F.C.	..	Distinguished Flying Cross
D.H.	..	Doctor of Humanities
D.H.L.	..	Doctor of Hebrew Literature
D.Hum.Litt.		Doctor of Humane Letters
Dip.Agr.	..	Diploma in Agriculture
Dip.Ed.	..	Diploma in Education
Dip(l).Eng.	..	Diploma in Engineering
Dir.	..	Director
Dist.	..	District
D.Iur.	..	Doctor of Law
D. Iur. Utr.		Doctor of both Civil and Canon Law
Div.	..	Division
D.L.	..	Deputy Lieutenant
D.Lit(t).	..	Doctor of Letters; Doctor of Literature
D.L.S.	..	Doctor of Library Science
D.M.	..	Doctor of Medicine (Oxford)
D.M.D.	..	Doctor of Dental Medicine
D.Mus.	..	Doctor of Music
D.M.V.	..	Doctor of Veterinary Medicine
D.O.	..	Doctor of Ophthalmology
D.P.H.	..	Diploma in Public Health
D.Phil.	..	Doctor of Philosophy
Dr. Agr.	..	Doctor of Agriculture
Dr.Ing.	..	Doctor of Engineering
Dr.Iur.	..	Doctor of Laws
D(r).Med.	..	Doctor of Medicine
Dr.Oec.(Publ.)		Doctor of (Public) Economy
Dr.Rer.Nat.	..	Doctor of Natural Sciences
Dr.rer.Pol.	..	Doctor of Political Science
D.S.	..	Doctor of Science
D.S.C.	..	Distinguished Service Cross
D.Sc.	..	Doctor of Science
D.Sc.S.	..	Doctor of Social Science
D.S.I.R.	..	Department of Scientific and Industrial Research
D.S.M.	..	Distinguished Service Medal
D.S.O.	..	Distinguished Service Order
D.S.T.	..	Doctor of Sacred Theology
D.Theol.	..	Doctor of Theology
D.T.M.(& H.)		Diploma in Tropical Medicine (and Hygiene)
D.U.P	..	Diploma of the University of Paris
E.	..	East
ECA	..	Economic Co-operation Administration; Economic Commission for Africa

ECAFE	..	Economic Commission for Asia and the Far East
ECE	..	Economic Commission for Europe
ECITO	..	European Central Inland Transport Organization
ECLA	..	Economic Commission for Latin America
Econ(s).	..	Economic(s)
ECOSOC	..	Economic and Social Council
ECSC	..	European Coal and Steel Community
ed.	..	educated
Ed.D.	..	Doctor of Education
Ed.M.	..	Master of Education
E.D.	..	Doctor of Engineering (U.S.A.)
Ed.	..	Editor
Edin.	..	Edinburgh
Edn.	..	Edition
Educ.	..	Education
E.E.	..	Electrical Engineer(ing) (U.S.A.)
EEC	..	European Economic Community
e.h.	..	Ehrenhalben (Honorary)
EIB	..	European Investment Bank
E.M.	..	Master of Engineering (U.S.A.)
Em(e)r.	..	Emeritus
Eng.	..	Engineering, England
Eng.D.	..	Doctor of Engineering
est.	..	establishments
E.T.H.	..	Eidgenössische Technische Hochschule (Swiss Federal Institute of Technology)
Ets.	..	Etablissements
EURATOM		European Atomic Energy Commission
Exec.	..	Executive
Exhbn.	..	Exhibition
Exp.	..	Experimental

f.	..	founded
F.A.A.	..	Fellow of Australian Academy of Science
F.A.C.C.A.	..	Fellow of the Association of Certified and Corporate Accountants
F.A.C.P.	..	Fellow of American College of Physicians
F.A.C.S.	..	Fellow of the American College of Surgeons
F.A.I.A.	..	Fellow of the American Institute of Architects
F.A.I.A.S.	..	Fellow of the Australian Institute of Agricultural Science
F.A.M.S.	..	Fellow Indian Academy of Medical Sciences
FAO	..	Food and Agriculture Organisation
F.A.S.E.	..	Fellow of Antiquarian Society, Edinburgh
F.B.A.	..	Fellow of the British Academy
F.B.I.	..	Federal Bureau of Investigation; Federation of British Industries
F.C.A.	..	Fellow of the Institute of Chartered Accountants
F.C.G.I.	..	Fellow of the City and Guilds of London Institute
F.C.I.C.	..	Fellow of the Chemical Institute of Canada
F.C.I.S.	..	Fellow of the Chartered Institute of Secretaries
F.C.T.	..	Federal Capital Territory
F.C.W.A.	..	Fellow of the Chartered Institute of Cost and Works Accountants
F.D.G.B.	..	Freier Deutscher Gewerkschaftsbund
Feb.	..	February
Fed.	..	Federation; Federal
F.G.S.	..	Fellow of the Geological Society
F.I.A.	..	Fellow of the Institute of Actuaries
F.I.B.	..	Fellow of the Institute of Bankers
F.I.D.	..	Fellow of the Institute of Directors
Fil.Lic.	..	Licentiate in Philosophy
F.I.M.	..	Fellow of the Institute of Metallurgists
F.Inst.F.	..	Fellow of the Institute of Fuel
F.Inst.P.	..	Fellow of the Institute of Physics
F.Inst.Pet.	..	Fellow of the Institute of Petroleum

F.I.R.E.	..	Fellow of the Institution of Radio Engineers
F.J.I.	..	Fellow of the Institute of Journalists
F.K.C.	..	Fellow of King's College (London)
Fla.	..	Florida
F.L.A.	..	Fellow of the Library Association
F.L.N.	..	Front de Libération Nationale
F.L.S.	..	Fellow of the Linnæan Society
F.M.	..	Field Marshal
fmr.	..	former
fmrly.	..	formerly
F.N.I.	..	Fellow of the National Institute of Sciences of India
FOA	..	Foreign Operations Administration
F.R.A.C.P.	..	Fellow of the Royal Australasian College of Physicians
F.R.A.C.S.	..	Fellow of the Royal Australasian College of Surgeons
F.R.A.I.	..	Fellow of the Royal Anthropological Institute
F.R.A.I.A.	..	Fellow of the Royal Australian Institute of Architects
F.R.A.I.C.	..	Fellow of the Royal Architectural Institute of Canada
F.R.A.M.	..	Fellow of the Royal Academy of Music
F.R.A.S.	..	Fellow of the Royal Astronomical Society; Fellow of the Royal Asiatic Society
F.R.Ae.S.	..	Fellow of the Royal Aeronautical Society
F.R.B.S.	..	Fellow of the Royal Society of British Sculptors; Fellow of the Royal Botanic Society
F.R.C.M.	..	Fellow of the Royal College of Music
F.R.C.O.	..	Fellow of the Royal College of Organists
F.R.C.O.G.		Fellow of the Royal College of Obstetricians and Gynaecologists
F.R.C.P.(E.)		Fellow of the Royal College of Physicians (Edinburgh)
F.R.C.S.(E.)		Fellow of the Royal College of Surgeons (Edinburgh)
F.R.Econ.S.		Fellow of the Royal Economic Society
F.R.E.S.	..	Fellow of the Royal Entomological Society
F.R.F.P.S.	..	Fellow of Royal Faculty of Physicians and Surgeons
F.R.G.S.	..	Fellow of the Royal Geographical Society
F.R.Hist.S.	..	Fellow of the Royal Historical Society
F.R.Hort.S.		Fellow of the Royal Horticultural Society
F.R.I.B.A.	..	Fellow of the Royal Institute of British Architects
F.R.I.C.	..	Fellow of the Royal Institute of Chemistry
F.R.Met.Soc.		Fellow of the Royal Meteorological Society
F.R.S.	..	Fellow of the Royal Society
F.R.S.A.	..	Fellow of the Royal Society of Arts
F.R.S.C.	..	Fellow of the Royal Society of Canada
F.R.S.E.	..	Fellow of the Royal Society of Edinburgh
F.R.S.L.	..	Fellow of the Royal Society of Literature
F.R.S.M.	..	Fellow of the Royal Society of Medicine
F.R.S.S.	..	Fellow of the Royal Statistical Society
F.S.A.	..	Fellow of the Society of Antiquaries
F.S.I.A.	..	Fellow of the Society of Industrial Artists
F.T.I.	..	Fellow of the Textile Institute
F.Z.S.	..	Fellow of the Zoological Society

Ga.	..	Georgia
G.A.T.T.	..	General Agreement on Tariffs and Trade
G.B.	..	Great Britain
G.B.E.	..	Knight (or Dame) Grand Cross of (the Order of) the British Empire
G.C.B.	..	Knight Grand Cross of (the Order of) the Bath
G.C.I.E.	..	Knight Grand Commander of the Indian Empire
G.C.M.G.	..	Knight Grand Cross of (the Order of) St. Michael and St. George

G.C.S.I.	..	Knight Grand Commander of the Star of India
G.C.V.O.	..	Knight Grand Cross of the (Royal) Victorian Order
Gen.	..	General
G.H.Q.	..	General Headquarters
Glos.	..	Gloucestershire
G.m.b.H.	..	Gesellschaft mit beschränkter Haftung (Limited Liability Company)
G.O.C. (in C.)		General Officer Commanding (in Chief)
Gov.	..	Governor
Govt.	..	Government
G.P.O.	..	General Post Office
G.S.O.	..	General Staff Officer
Hants.	..	Hampshire
h.c.	..	honoris causa
H.E.	..	His Eminence; His Excellency
Herts.	..	Hertfordshire
Hist.	..	History
H.H.	..	His (or Her) Highness
H.L.D.	..	Doctor of Humane Letters
H.M.	..	His (or Her) Majesty
H.M.S.	..	His (or Her) Majesty's Ship
Hon.	..	Honourable; Honorary
Hons.	..	Honours
H.Pk.	..	Hilali-i-Pakistan
H.Q.	..	Headquarters
H.R.H.	..	His (or Her) Royal Highness
Hunts.	..	Huntingdonshire
Ia.	..	Iowa
IAEA	..	International Atomic Energy Agency
IATA	..	International Air Transport Association
IBRD	..	International Bank for Reconstruction and Development (World Bank)
ICAO	..	International Civil Aviation Organisation
ICC	..	International Chamber of Commerce
ICE	..	Institute of Civil Engineers
ICFTU	..	International Confederation of Free Trade Unions
I.C.I.	..	Imperial Chemical Industries
ICOM	..	International Council of Musicians
I.C.S.	..	Indian Civil Service
Ida.	..	Idaho
IDA	..	International Development Association
IFC	..	International Finance Corporation
IGY	..	International Geophysical Year
Ill.	..	Illinois
ILO	..	International Labour Organisation
IMF	..	International Monetary Fund
Inc.	..	Incorporated
Ind.	..	Indiana; Independent
Insp.	..	Inspector
Inst.	..	Institute; Institution
Inst.C.E.	..	Institution of Civil Engineers
Inst.E.E.	..	Institution of Electrical Engineers
Inst.Mech.E		Institution of Mechanical Engineers
Int.	..	International
I.N.T.U.C.	..	Indian National Trades Union Congress
I.T.A.	..	Independent Television Authority
I.T.V.	..	Independent Television
IUPAC	..	International Union of Pure and Applied Chemistry
IUPAP	..	International Union of Pure and Applied Physics
Jan.	..	January
J.C.B.	..	Bachelor of Canon Law
J.C.D.	..	Doctor of Canon Law
J.D.	..	Doctor of Jurisprudence

Jhr.	..	Jonkheer
J.P.	..	Justice of the Peace
Jr.	..	Junior
Jt.	..	Joint
J.U.D.	..	Juris utriusque Doctor (Doctor of both Civil and Canon Law)
Ju.D.	..	Doctor of Law
Kan.	..	Kansas
K.B.E.	..	Knight Commander of (the Order of) the British Empire
K.C.	..	King's Counsel
K.C.B.	..	Knight Commander of (the Order of) the Bath
K.C.I.E.	..	Knight Commander of (the Order of) the Indian Empire
K.C.M.G.	..	Knight Commander of (the Order of) St. Michael and St. George
K.C.V.O.	..	Knight Commander of the Royal Victorian Order
K.G.	..	Knight of (the Order of) the Garter
K.L.M.	..	Koninklijke Luchtvaart Maatschappij (Royal Dutch Airlines)
K.P.	..	Knight of (the Order of) St. Patrick
K.St.J.	..	Knight of (the Order of) St. John of Jerusalem
K.T.	..	Knight of (the Order of) the Thistle
Kt.	..	Knight
Ky.	..	Kentucky
La.	..	Louisiana
Lancs.	..	Lancashire
L.C.C.	..	London County Council
L.D.S.	..	Licentiate in Dental Surgery
Leics.	..	Leicestershire
L. ès D.	..	Licencié ès Droit
L. ès L.	..	Licencié ès Lettres
L.H.D.	..	Doctor of Humane Letters
L.I.	..	Long Island
Lic. en Der.		Licenciado en Derecho
Lic. en Fil.	..	Licenciado en Filosofía
Lic.Med.	..	Licentiate in Medicine
Lieut.	..	Lieutenant
Lincs.	..	Lincolnshire
Litt.D.	..	Doctor of Letters
LL.B.	..	Bachelor of Laws
LL.D.	..	Doctor of Laws
LL.L.	..	Licentiate of Laws
LL.M.	..	Master of Laws
L.M.	..	Licentiate of Medicine; or Midwifery
L.M.S.S.A.	..	Licentiate in Medicine and Surgery of the Society of Apothecaries
L.N.	..	League of Nations
Lond.	..	London
L.R.C.P.	..	Licentiate of the Royal College of Physicians
L.R.C.S.	..	Licentiate of the Royal College of Surgeons
Ltd(a).	..	Limited; Limitada
M.A.	..	Master of Arts
M.Agr.	..	Master of Agriculture (U.S.A.)
Maj.	..	Major
Man.	..	Manager, Managing; Manitoba
M.Arch.	..	Master of Architecture
Mass.	..	Massachusetts
M.B.	..	Bachelor of Medicine
M.B.A.	..	Master of Business Administration
M.B.E.	..	Member of (the Order of) the British Empire

M.C.	..	Military Cross	Nat.	..	National
M.C.C.	..	Marylebone Cricket Club	NATO	..	North Atlantic Treaty Organisation
M.Ch.	..	Master of Surgery	Naz.	..	Nazionale
M.Ch.D.	..	Master of Dental Surgery	N.B.	..	New Brunswick
M.C.L.	..	Master of Civil Law	N.B.C.	..	National Broadcasting Corporation
M.Com(m)...		Master of Commerce	N.C.	..	North Carolina
Md.	..	Maryland	N.C.N.C.	..	National Council of Nigeria and the
M.D.	..	Doctor of Medicine			Cameroons
M.D.S.	..	Master of Dental Surgery	N.D.	..	North Dakota
M.E.	..	Mechanical Engineer	N.E.	..	North East
Me.	..	Maine	Neb.	..	Nebraska
M.E.F.	..	Middle East Force	Nev.	..	Nevada
mem.	..	member	N.G.O.	..	Non-Governmental Organisation
M.Eng.	..	Master of Engineering (Dublin)	N.H.	..	New Hampshire
Mfg.	..	Manufacturing	N.J.	..	New Jersey
Mgr.	..	Monseigneur; Monsignor	N.M.	..	New Mexico
M.I.	..	Marshall Islands	Northants.	..	Northamptonshire
M.I.C.E.	..	Member of the Institution of Civil Engineers	Notts.	..	Nottinghamshire
M.I.Chem.E.	..	Member of the Institute of Chemical	Nov.	..	November
		Engineers	N.P.C.	..	National People's Congress
Mich.	..	Michigan	nr.	..	near
Middx.	..	Middlesex	N.R.C.	..	Nuclear Research Council
M.I.E.E.	..	Member of the Institution of Electrical	N.S.W.	..	New South Wales
		Engineers	N.V.	..	Naamloze Vennootschap
Mil.	..	Military	N.W.	..	North West
M.I.Mar.E...		Member of the Institute of Marine Engineers	N.Y.	..	New York
M.I.Mech.E.	..	Member of the Institution of Mechanical	N.Y.C.	..	New York City
		Engineers	N.Z.	..	New Zealand
M.I.Min.E...		Member of the Institution of Mining			
		Engineers	O.	..	Ohio
Min.	..	Minister; Ministry	OAS	..	Organization of American States
Minn.	..	Minnesota	O.B.E.	..	Officer of (the Order of) the British Empire
M.Inst.T.	..	Member of the Institute of Transport	O.C.	..	Officer Commanding
Miss.	..	Mississippi	Oct.	..	October
M.I.Struct.E.	..	Member of the Institution of Structural	OECD	..	Organisation for European Co-operation
		Engineers			and Development
M.I.T.	..	Massachusetts Institute of Technology	OEEC	..	Organisation for European Economic Co-
M.J.	..	Master of Jurisprudence			operation
M.L.A.	..	Member of the Legislative Assembly	O.F.S.	..	Orange Free State
M.L.C.	..	Member of the Legislative Council	Okla.	..	Oklahoma
M.M.	..	Military Medal	O.M.	..	Member of the Order of Merit
Mo.	..	Missouri	O.P.	..	Ordo Praedicatorum (Dominicans)
M.O.H.	..	Medical Officer of Health	OPEC	..	Organisation of Petroleum Exporting
M.O.I.	..	Ministry of Information			Countries
Mont.	..	Montana	O.P.M.	..	Office of Production Management
M.P.	..	Member of Parliament; Madhya Pradesh	Ore.	..	Oregon
		(India)	Org.	..	Organisation
M.P.A.	..	Master of Public Administration (Harvard)	O.S.B.	..	Order of St. Benedict
M.P.E.	..	Master of Physical Education	O.S.R.D.	..	Office of Scientific Research and Develop-
M.Ph.	..	Master of Philosophy (U.S.A.)			ment
M.R.A.S.	..	Member of the Royal Asiatic Society	O.W.I.	..	Office of War Information
M.R.C.P.(E.)	..	Member of the Royal College of Physicians	Oxon.	..	Of Oxford University; Oxfordshire
		(Edinburgh)			
M.R.C.S.(E.)	..	Member of the Royal College of Surgeons	Pa.	..	Pennsylvania
		(Edinburgh)	Paed.	..	Paediatrics
M.R.C.V.S...		Member of the Royal College of Veterinary	Parl.	..	Parliament; Parliamentary
		Surgeons	P.C.	..	Privy Councillor
M.R.I.	..	Member of the Royal Institution	P.C.C.	..	Provincial Congress Committee
M.R.I.A.	..	Member of the Royal Irish Academy	Pd.B.	..	Bachelor of Pedagogy
M.R.P.	..	Mouvement Républicain Populaire	Pd.D.	..	Doctor of Pedagogy
M.R.S.A.	..	Member of the Royal Society of Arts	Pd.M.	..	Master of Pedagogy
M.R.S.L.	..	Member of the Royal Society of Literature	P.E.I.	..	Prince Edward Island
M.S.	..	Master of Science; Master of Surgery	P.E.N.	..	Poets, Playwrights, Essayists, Editors and
M.S.A.	..	Mutual Security Agency			Novelists (Club)
M.Sc.	..	Master of Science	Perm.	..	Permanent
Mus.Bac. or B.		Bachelor of Music	Ph.B.	..	Bachelor of Philosophy
Mus.Doc. or D.		Doctor of Music	Ph.D.	..	Doctor of Philosophy
Mus.M.	..	Master of Music (Cambridge)	Pharm.D.	..	Docteur en Pharmacie
M.V.D.	..	Master of Veterinary Medicine	Phil.	..	Philosophy
M.V.O.	..	Member of the Royal Victorian Order	Phila.	..	Philadelphia
			P.L.A.	..	Port of London Authority
N.	..	North	P.O.(B.)	..	Post Office (Box)
N.A.S.A.	..	National Aeronautics and Space Adminis-	P.P.R.A.	..	Past President of the Royal Academy
		tration			

P.Q.	..	Province of Quebec
P.R.	..	Public Relations
P.R.A.	..	President of the Royal Academy
Prep.	..	Preparatory
Pres.	..	President
P.R.I.	..	President of the Royal Institute (of Painters in Water Colours)
P.R.I.B.A.	..	President of the Royal Institute of British Architects
Priv.Doz.	..	Privat Dozent (recognised teacher not on the regular staff)
P.R.O.	..	Public Relations Officer
Prof.	..	Professor
Propr.	..	Proprietor
P.R.S.	..	President of the Royal Society
P.R.S.A.	..	President of the Royal Scottish Academy
P.T.T.	..	Postes, Télégraphes et Téléphones
Pty.	..	Proprietary
Publ(s).	..	Publication(s)
P.W.D.	..	Public Works Department
P.W.P.	..	Polish Workers' Party
Q.C.	..	Queen's Counsel
Q.M.G.	..	Quartermaster-General
R.A.	..	Royal Academy; Royal Academician
R.A.C.	..	Royal Armoured Corps
R.A.C.P.	..	Royal Australian College of Physicians
R.A.F.	..	Royal Air Force
R.A.F.V.R.	..	Royal Air Force Volunteer Reserve
R.A.M.	..	Royal Academy of Music
R.A.M.C.	..	Royal Army Medical Corps
R.B.A.	..	Royal (Society of) British Artists
R.C.	..	Roman Catholic
R.C.A.	..	Royal College for Art; Royal Canadian Academy; Radio Corporation of America
Rep.	..	Representative; Represented
Repub.	..	Republic
resgnd.	..	resigned
retd.	..	retired
Rev.	..	Reverend
R.F.A.	..	Royal Field Artillery
R.F.C.	..	Royal Flying Corps
R.G.S.	..	Royal Geographical Society
R.Hist.S.	..	Royal Historical Society
R.I.	..	Rhode Island; Royal Institute (of Painters in Water Colours); Royal Institution
R.I.B.A.	..	Royal Institute of British Architects
R.M.P.A.	..	Royal Medico-Psychological Association
R.N.	..	Royal Navy
R.N.V.R.	..	Royal Naval Volunteer Reserve
R.O.I.	..	Royal Institute of Oil Painters
R.P.	..	Member Royal Society of Portrait Painters
R.S.A.	..	Royal Scottish Academy; Royal Society of Arts
R.S.F.S.R.	..	Russian Soviet Federative Socialist Republic
Rt. Hon.	..	Right Honourable
Rt. Rev.	..	Right Reverend
R.V.O.	..	Royal Victorian Order
R.W.S.	..	Royal Society of Painters in Water Colours
S.	..	South
S.A.	..	South Africa; Société Anonyme, Sociedad Anonima
S.B.	..	Bachelor of Science (U.S.A.)
S.C.	..	South Carolina; Senior Counsel (Republic of Ireland)
SCAP	..	Supreme Command Allied Powers
Sc.B.	..	Bachelor of Science

Sc.D.	..	Doctor of Science
S.Dak.	..	South Dakota
S.E.	..	South East
SEATO	..	South East Asia Treaty Organisation
Sec.	..	Secretary
S.E.C.	..	Securities and Exchange Commission
Secr.	..	Secretariat
S.E.D.	..	Sozialistische Einheitspartei Deutschlands (Socialist Union Party of the German Democratic Republic)
Sept.	..	September
S.-et-O.	..	Seine-et-Oise
S.F.I.O.	..	Société Française de l'Internationale Ouvrière (French Socialist Party)
SHAEF	..	Supreme Headquarters Allied Expeditionary Force
SHAPE	..	Supreme Headquarters Allied Powers in Europe
S.J.	..	Society of Jesus (Jesuits)
S.J.D.	..	Doctor of Juristic Science
S.M.	..	Master of Science
Soc.	..	Society
S.p.A.	..	Società per Azioni
S.P.D.	..	Sozialdemokratische Partei Deutschlands
S.Pk.	..	Star of Pakistan
Spl.	..	Special
S.S.R.	..	Soviet Socialist Republic
Staffs.	..	Staffordshire
S.T.B.	..	Bachelor of Sacred Theology
S.T.D.	..	Doctor of Sacred Theology
S.T.M.	..	Master of Sacred Theology
Supt.	..	Superintendent
S.W.	..	South West
T.A.	..	Territorial Army
TAA	..	Technical Assistance Administration
TAB	..	Technical Assistance Board
T.D.	..	Territorial Decoration; Tealta Dáil (Mem. of the Dáil)
Temp.	..	Temporary
Tenn.	..	Tennessee
Tex.	..	Texas
Th.B.	..	Bachelor of Theology
Th.D.	..	Doctor of Theology
Th.M.	..	Master of Theology
Tit.	..	Titular
Trans.	..	Translation; translator
Treas.	..	Treasurer
T.U.(C.)	..	Trades Union (Congress)
T.V.A.	..	Tennessee Valley Authority
U.A.R.	..	United Arab Republic
U.K.	..	United Kingdom (of Great Britain and Northern Ireland)
UN(O)	..	United Nations (Organisation)
UNA	..	United Nations Association
UNEF	..	United Nations Emergency Force
UNESCO	..	United Nations Educational, Scientific and Cultural Organisation
UNICEF	..	United Nations International Children's Emergency Fund
Univ.	..	University
UNKRA	..	United Nations Korean Relief Administration
UNRRA	..	United Nations Relief and Rehabilitation Administration
UNRWA	..	United Nations Relief and Works Agency
UNSCOB	..	United Nations Special Commission on the Balkans
U.P.	..	United Provinces, Uttar Pradesh (India)
U.S.A.	..	United States of America

ABBREVIATIONS

U.S.A.F.	..	United States Air Force	WEA	..	Workers' Educational Association
U.S.N.	..	United States Navy	WEU	..	Western European Union
U.S.S.	..	United States Ship	WFTU	..	World Federation of Trade Unions
U.S.S.R.	..	Union of Soviet Socialist Republics	WHO	..	World Health Organisation
			Wilts.	..	Wiltshire
			Wis.	..	Wisconsin
			WMO	..	World Meteorological Organisation
Va.	..	Virginia	Worcs.	..	Worcestershire
V.C.	..	Victoria Cross	W.R.A.C.	..	Women's Royal Army Corps
V.D.	..	Volunteer Decoration	W.R.N.S.	..	Women's Royal Naval Service
V.G.	..	Vicar-General	WUS	..	World University Service
Vol(s).	..	Volume(s)	W.Va.	..	West Virginia
Vt.	..	Vermont	Wyo.	..	Wyoming
W.	..	West	Y.M.C.A.	..	Young Men's Christian Association
W.A.	..	Western Australia	Yorks.	..	Yorkshire
Wash.	..	Washington	Y.W.C.A.	..	Young Women's Christian Association

REIGNING ROYAL FAMILIES

Biographical entries of most of the reigning monarchs and of certain other members of the reigning royal families will be found in their appropriate alphabetical order in the biographical section of this book.

AFGHANISTAN

Reigning King

MOHAMMED ZAHIR SHAH; b. October 15, 1914; succeeded his father, Mohammed Nadir Shah, who was assassinated, November 8, 1933; married, November 4, 1931, his cousin, HUMAIRA, daughter of Sardar Ahmad Shah.

Children of the King

Princess Bulqis; b. 1932.
Prince Ahmad Shah; b. 1934.
Princess Maryam; b. 1936.
Prince Mohammed Nadir; b. 1941.
Prince Shah Mahmud; b. 1946.
Prince Mohammed Daoud Pashtoonyar; b. 1949.
Prince Mirwais; b. 1957.

Sisters of the King

Princess Zohra.   Princess Sultana.
Princess Zainab.   Princess Bulqis.

BELGIUM

Reigning King

KING BAUDOUIN; b. September 7, 1930; succeeded to the throne July 17, 1951, after abdication of his father, King Léopold III; married December 15, 1960, doña Fabiola de Mora y Aragon (b. June 11, 1928).

Father of the King

King Léopold III; b. November 3, 1901; married (1) November 4, 1926, Princess Astrid of Sweden (b. November 17, 1905, died August 29, 1935); (2) September 11, 1941, Mlle. Mary Liliane Baels (three children).

Brother of the King

Prince Albert, Prince of Liège; b. June 6, 1934; married, July 2, 1959, Donna Paola Ruffo di Calabria (two sons, one daughter).

Sister of the King

Joséphine Charlotte, Princess of Belgium; b. October 11, 1927; married, April 9, 1953, Prince Jean of Luxembourg (b. January 5, 1921) (five children).

CAMBODIA

NORODOM SIHANOUK, Ex-King of Cambodia, was nominated Head of State, June 12th, 1960, and, on this occasion, took an oath of fidelity to the vacant throne. Prince Norodom Sihanouk will cease to be Head of State when the Crown Council designates a new King chosen from the Princes of the Royal Family.

DENMARK

Reigning King

KING FREDERIK IX; b. March 11, 1899; succeeded to the throne April 20, 1947, on the death of his father, King Christian X; married, May 24, 1935, PRINCESS INGRID OF SWEDEN (b. March 28, 1910).

Children of the King

Princess Margrethe; b. April 16, 1940; married, June 10, 1967, Count Henri de Laborde de Monpezat; son Prince Frederik André Henrik Christian, b. May 26, 1968.

Princess Benedikte; b. April 29, 1944; married, February 3rd, 1968, Prince Richard zu Sayn-Wittgenstein Berleburg.

Princess Anne-Marie; b. August 30, 1946; married September 18, 1964, King Constantine of the Hellenes.

Parents of the King

King Christian X; b. September 26, 1870; son of King Frederik VIII and Queen Louise; married, 1898, Princess Alexandrine of Mecklenburg-Schwerin (b. December 24, 1879; died December 28, 1952); died April 20, 1947.

Brother of the King

Prince Knud; b. July 27, 1900; married, September 8, 1933, Princess Caroline-Mathilde of Denmark, b. April 27, 1912.

Children

Princess Elisabeth; b. May 8, 1935
Prince Ingolf; b. February 17, 1940.
Prince Christian; b. October 22, 1942.

ETHIOPIA

Reigning Emperor

EMPEROR HAILE SELLASSIE I; b. July 23, 1892; crowned King (Negus) October 7, 1928, proclaimed Emperor April 2, 1930, after the death of the Empress Zauditu; crowned November 2, 1930; married WOIZERO MENEN in 1911 (died February 1962).

Children of the Emperor

Asfa Wossen; b. July 26, 1916; proclaimed Crown Prince and heir to the throne November 2, 1930; married (1) Princess Wolete Israel Seyoum, daughter of Ras Seyoum Mengesha (Governor of Tigré Province), whom he divorced in 1945; (2) Princess Medferiash-Worq, daughter of General Ababa Damtew.

Prince Makonnen, Duke of Harar; b. 1923; died 1957; married Princess Sara Gizaw.

Prince Sahle Selassie; b. 1931; married, June 14, 1959, Princess Mahtsente Habte-Mariam (died April 23, 1962).

Princess Tenagne-Worq; b. 1913.

Princess Zannaba-Worq; b. 1917; died 1933.

Princess Tsahai; b. 1919; died 1942.

Parents of the Emperor

Ras Makonnen, late Governor of Harar, and Woizero Yeshimebet.

GREECE

Reigning King

KING CONSTANTINE; b. June 2, 1940; succeeded to the throne March 6, 1964 on the death of his father King Paul I; married, September 18, 1964, PRINCESS ANNE-MARIE of Denmark; left Greece 14 Dec. 1967.

Children of the King

Princess Alexia; b. July 10, 1965.
Prince Paul; b. May 20, 1967.

Parents of the King

King Paul I; b. December 14, 1901; succeeded to the throne April 1, 1947, on the death of his brother King George II; married January 8, 1938, Princess Frederika Louise, daughter of the Duke of Brunswick; died March 6, 1964.

Sisters of the King

Princess Sophia; b. November 2, 1938; married May 14, 1962, Don Juan Carlos, Prince of Asturias; two daughters.
Princess Irene; b. May 11, 1942.

IRAN

Reigning Shah

MOHAMMAD REZA PAHLAVI ARYAMCHR, Shahanshah of Iran; b. October 26, 1919; succeeded to the throne September 16, 1941, on the abdication of his father, Reza Shah Pahlavi; married (1) March 15, 1939, PRINCESS FAWZIEH, daughter of King Fouad I of Egypt (divorced November 19, 1948); (2) February 12, 1951, SORAYA ESFANDIARI-BAKHTIARI (divorced March, 1958); (3) December 21, 1959, FARAH DIBA.

Children of the Shah

Princess Shahnaz; b. October 27, 1940.
Prince Reza; b. October 31, 1960 (Crown Prince).
Princess Maasoumeh Farahnaz; b. March 12, 1963.
Prince Ali Reza; b. April 28, 1966.

Father of the Shah

Reza Shah Pahlavi the Great; b. March 15, 1878; elected Shah of Persia December 13, 1925, abdicated September 16, 1941; died July 26, 1944.

Brothers and Sisters of the Shah

Princess Shams.	Prince Ahmad Reza.
Princess Ashraf.	Prince Mahmood Reza.
Prince Gholam Reza.	Princess Fatemeh.
Prince Abdul Reza.	Prince Hamid Reza.

JAPAN

Reigning Emperor

EMPEROR HIROHITO; b. April 29, 1901; succeeded his father December 25, 1926; married, January 26, 1924, PRINCESS NAGAKO KUNI (b. March 6, 1903), daughter of Prince Kuni.

Children of the Emperor

Princess Shigeko (Terunomiya); b. December 6, 1925 (married); died July 1961.
Princess Kazuko (Takanomiya); b. September 30, 1929 (married).
Princess Atsuko (Yorinomiya); b. March 7, 1931 (married).
Prince Akihito (Tsugunomiya); b. December 23, 1933; married, April 10, 1959, Michiko Shoda; sons, Prince Naruhito Hironomiya; b. February 23, 1960; Prince Fumihito (Ayanomiya); b. November 30, 1965.

Prince Masahito (Yoshinomiya); b. November 28, 1935; married, October 1964, Hanako Tsugaru.
Princess Takako (Suganomiya); b. March 2, 1939; married, March 10, 1960, Hisanaga Shimazu.

Parents of the Emperor

Emperor Yoshihito; b. August 31, 1879; married, May 10, 1900, died 1926; Princess Sadako (b. June 25, 1884, died May 1951), daughter of Prince Kujo.

Surviving Brothers of the Emperor

Prince Nobuhito (Takamatsunomiya); b. January 3, 1905.
Prince Takahito (Mikasanomiya); b. December 2, 1915.

JORDAN

Reigning King

KING HUSSEIN; b. November 14, 1935; succeeded to the throne on the abdication of his father, August, 1952; ascended the throne May 2, 1953; married, April 19, 1955, PRINCESS DINA, daughter of Abd-el-Hamid Aoun of Saudi Arabia (now divorced); married May 25, 1961, Muna El Hussein.

Children of the King

Princess Alya; b. February 13, 1956.
Prince Abdullah; b. January 30, 1962.
Prince Feisal; b. October 11, 1963.
Princess Zein; b. April 26, 1968.
Princess Ayeshia; b. April 26, 1968.

Parents of the King

King Talal; b. February 26, 1907; married, November 27, 1933, Queen Zein Al Sharaf.

Brothers and Sister of the King

H.R.H. Prince Mohammed.
H.R.H. Prince Hassan (named as Crown Prince, April 1, 1965).
H.R.H. Princess Basmah.

LAOS

King

SAVANG VATTHANA; King of Laos; b. 07; eldest son of King Sisavang Vong; succeeded King Sisavang Vong Oct. 59.

Heir Apparent

Crown Prince Vong Savang; b. September 27, 1931.

LIBYA

Reigning King

KING IDRIS I; b. March 12, 1890; former Emir of Cyrenaica; proclaimed King of Libya December 2, 1950; ascended the throne December 24, 1951; married his cousin, EMIRA FATIMA.

Father of the King

Sayed Mohammed al Mahdi es Senussi; b. 1844; died 1894; son of Sayed Mohammed Ali es Senussi, the Grand Senussi, b. 1788, died 1860.

LIECHTENSTEIN

Reigning Prince

FRANZ JOSEPH II; b. August 16, 1906; succeeded his great-uncle, July 25, 1938; married, March 7, 1943, COUNTESS GINA VON WILCZEK (PRINCESS GEORGINE).

Children of the Prince

Prince Hans Adam; married Countess Marie Kinsky, July 30, 1967.

Prince Philip.

Prince Nicolaus.

Princess Nora.

Prince Franz Joseph Wenzel Georg Maria.

Brothers and Sisters of the Prince

Princess Maria Theresia (Countess Strachwitz).

Prince Karl Alfred.   Prince Ulrich.

Prince Georg.   Princess Henriette (Countess Eltz.)

Prince Aloys.

Prince Heinrich.

LUXEMBOURG

Reigning Monarch

GRAND DUKE JEAN; b. January 5, 1921; succeeded November 12, 1964, on the abdication of his mother, Grand Duchess Charlotte; married, April 9, 1953, JOSEPHINE CHARLOTTE, PRINCESS OF BELGIUM (b. October 11, 1927).

Children of the Grand Duke

Princess Marie-Astrid; b. February 17, 1954.

Prince Henri; b. April 16, 1955.

Prince Jean; b. May 15, 1957.

Princess Margaretha; b. May 15, 1957.

Prince Guillaume; b. May 1, 1963.

Parents of the Grand Duke

Grand Duchess Charlotte, Duchess of Nassau; b. January 23, 1896; succeeded January 15, 1919; abdicated in favour of her son, Grand Duke Jean, November 12, 1964; married, November 6, 1919, Prince Félix of Bourbon Parma (b. September 28, 1893).

Brother and Sisters of the Grand Duke

Princess Elisabeth; b. December 22, 1922; married, May 9, 1956, Prince François Ferdinand of Hohenberg (b. September 13, 1927).

Princess Marie-Adelaide; b. May 21, 1924; married, April 10, 1958, Count Charles Joseph Henckel de Donnersmarck (b. November 7, 1928).

Princess Marie-Gabrielle; b. August 2, 1925; married, November 6, 1951, Count Knud de Holstein-Ledreborg (b. October 2, 1919).

Prince Charles; b. August 7, 1927; married, March 1, 1967, Joan Douglas Dillon.

Princess Alix; b. August 24, 1929; married, August 17, 1950, H.H. Prince Antoine de Ligne (b. March 8, 1925).

MALAYSIA

Supreme Head of State (The Yang di-Pertuan Agong)

HIS MAJESTY TUANKU ISMAIL NASIRUDDIN SHAH IBNI AL-MARHUM SULTAN ZAINAL ABIDIN, Sultan of Trengganu; b. January 24, 1907; elected Yang di-Pertuan Agong August 19, 1965, installed April 11, 1966.

MONACO

Reigning Prince

PRINCE RAINIER III; b. May 31, 1923; succeeded his grandfather, Prince Louis II, May 9, 1949; married, April 18, 1956, Miss GRACE PATRICIA KELLY, daughter of the late Mr. John Brendan Kelly and Mrs. John Brendan Kelly, of Philadelphia, U.S.A.

Children of the Prince

Prince Albert Alexander Louis Peter; born March 14, 1958.

Princess Caroline Louise Marguerite; born January 23, 1957.

Princess Stéphanie Marie Elisabeth; born February 1, 1965.

Parents of the Prince

Princess Charlotte, Duchess of Valentinois (b. September 30, 1898); married, March 19, 1920, Comte Pierre de Polignac, who assumed the style and title of Prince Pierre of Monaco; died November 10, 1964.

MOROCCO

Reigning King

KING HASSAN II, (formerly Crown Prince Moulay Hassan); b. July 9, 1929; son of King Mohammed V (died February 26, 1961); became King and Prime Minister of Morocco when he succeeded his father, February 1961.

Children of the King

Princess Myriam; b. August 26, 1962.

Prince Mohamed; b. August 21, 1963.

Princess Asma; b. 1965.

Princess Hasna; b. 1967.

Brother and Sisters of the King

Prince Moulay Abdallah; married, September 8, 1959, Lamia Solh.

Princess Lalla Aicha.

Princess Lalla Malika.

Princess Lalla Nezha.

Princess Lalla Amina.

Princess Lalla Fatima.

Uncles of the King

Prince Moulay Hassan.

Prince Moulay Abdeslam.

NEPAL

Reigning Sovereign

KING MAHENDRA BIR BIKRAM SHAH DEVA; b. June 11, 1920; succeeded his father March 14, 1955.

Heir-Apparent

Crown Prince Birendra Bir Bikram Shah Deva.

NETHERLANDS

Reigning Queen

QUEEN JULIANA LOUISE EMMA MARIE WILHELMINA, Princess of Orange Nassau, Duchess of Mecklenburg; Princess of Lippe-Biesterfeld, etc.; b. April 30, 1909; succeeded to the throne on the abdication of her mother, September 4, 1948; inaugurated September 6, 1948; married, January 7, 1937, PRINCE BERNHARD LEOPOLD FREDERIK EVERHARD JULIUS COERT KAREL GODFRIED PIETER OF LIPPE-BIESTERFELD (b. June 29, 1911).

Children of the Queen

Princess Beatrix Wilhelmina Armgard; b. January 31, 1938; married Herr Claus von Amsberg, March 10, 1966; son, Prince Willem-Alexander Claus Georg Ferdinand, b. April 27, 1967.

Princess Irene Emma Elisabeth; b. August 5, 1939; married Prince Carlos Hugo of Bourbon Parma, April 29, 1964.

Princess Margriet Francisca; b. January 19, 1943; married January 10, 1967, Pieter van Vollenhoven; son, Prince Maurits Willem Pieter van Orange Nassau van Vollenhoven, b. April 17, 1968.

Princess Maria Christina; b. February 18, 1947.

Parents of the Queen

Princess Wilhelmina Helena Pauline Maria; b. August 31, 1880; daughter of King Willem III and his second wife, Princess Adelheid Emma Wilhelmina Theresia of Waldeck and Pyrmont; succeeded to the throne November 23, 1890; married, February 7, 1901, Prince Hendrik Wladimir Albrecht Ernst of Mecklenburg-Schwerin (b. April 19, 1876, died July 3, 1934); abdicated September 4, 1948; died November 28, 1962.

NORWAY
Reigning King

KING OLAV V; b. July 2, 1903; succeeded to the throne on the death of his father, King Haakon VII, September 21, 1957; married March 21, 1929, Princess Martha of Sweden (b. March 28, 1901, died April 5, 1954), daughter of Prince Carl (third son of King Oscar II of Norway and Sweden).

Children of the King

Crown Prince Harald; b. February 21, 1937; engaged to be married to Miss Sonja Haraldson.

Princess Ragnhild Alexandra; b. June 9, 1930; married, May 15, 1953, Hr. Erling Lorentzen.

Princess Astrid Maud Ingeborg; b. February 12, 1932; married January 12, 1961, Hr. Johan Martin Ferner.

Parents of the King

King Haakon VII of Norway; b. August 3, 1872, died September 21, 1957; elected King of Norway by the Storting, November 18, 1905; married July 22, 1896, Princess Maud (b. November 27, 1869, died November 20, 1938), third daughter of King Edward VII of Great Britain.

SAUDI ARABIA
Reigning King

KING FAISAL IBN ABDUL-AZIZ IBN ABDUL-RAHMAN AL FAISAL AL SAUD, Imam of the Moslems, Head of the Council of Ministers; b. 1905; acceded November 2, 1964.

Children of the King include
Seven sons.
Brothers of the King include

King Saud ibn Abdul Aziz; b. 1902; acceded November 9, 1953, relinquished throne November 2, 1964.

Prince Khaled ibn Abdul Aziz (heir-apparent); Crown Prince and Deputy Premier; b. 1909.

Amir Mohammed; b. 1910.

Amir Fahad; b. 1922; Deputy Prime Minister.

Amir Sultan; b. 1924; Minister of Defence.

Amir Talal; b. 1930.

SWEDEN
Reigning King

KING GUSTAF VI ADOLF; b. November 11, 1882; succeeded to the throne October 29, 1950, on the death of his father; married (1) June 15, 1905, PRINCESS MARGARET (b. January 15, 1882; died May 1, 1920), daughter of Prince Arthur, Duke of Connaught; (2) November 3, 1923, LADY LOUISE MOUNTBATTEN, daughter of the Marquess of Milford Haven (b. July 13, 1889, died March 7, 1965).

Children of the King (of first marriage)

Prince Gustaf Adolf, Duke of Västerbotten; b. April 22, 1906, died January 26, 1947; married, October 20, 1932, Sibylla, Princess of Saxe-Coburg and Gotha (b. January 18, 1908).

Children

Crown Prince Carl Gustaf, Duke of Jämtland; b. April 30, 1946.

Princess Margaretha; b. October 31, 1934; married June 30, 1964, Mr. John Ambler; daughter, Sybilla Louise, b. April 14, 1965; son, Charles Edward, b. July 14, 1966.

Princess Birgitta; b. January 19, 1937; married May 25, 1961, Prince of Hohenzollern Johann Georg; sons, Carl Christian, b. 1963; Hubertus, b. June 9, 1966; daughter, Desirée, b. 1965.

Princess Désirée; b. June 2, 1938; married June 5, 1964, Baron Niclas Silfverschiöld; son, Carl Edmund, b. 1965; daughter, Christina Louise Madeleine, b. 1966.

Princess Christina; b. August 3, 1943.

Sigvard (Count Sigvard Bernadotte); b. June 7, 1907; relinquished Royal rights and privileges on his marriage; son, Carl Edmund, b. 1965; daughter, Christina Louise Madeleine, b. June 29, 1966.

Queen Ingrid; b. March 28, 1910; married, May 24, 1935, Crown Prince Frederik of Denmark (now King Frederik IX).

Prince Bertil, Duke of Halland; b. February 28, 1912.

Carl Johan (Count Carl Johan Bernadotte); b. October 31, 1916; relinquished Royal rights and privileges on his marriage.

Parents of the King

King Gustav V; b. June 16, 1858, died October 29, 1950; married September 20, 1881, Princess Victoria of Baden (b. August 7, 1862, died April 4, 1930).

Brother of the King

Prince Wilhelm, Duke of Södermanland; b. June 17, 1884; married, May 3, 1908, Grand Duchess Maria Pavlovna (b. April 18, 1890), daughter of Grand Duke Paul Alexandrovitch of Russia (divorced May 17, 1914; died June 5, 1965).

THAILAND
Reigning King

KING BHUMIBOL ADULYADEJ; b. December 5, 1927; succeeded to the throne on the death of his brother, King Ananda Mahidol, June 9, 1946; married, April 28, 1950, PRINCESS SIRIKIT KITIYAKARA (born August 12, 1932), daughter of H.H. Prince Nakkhatra Mongkol, Krommun Chandaburi Suranat.

Children of the King

Princess Ubol Ratana; b. April 5, 1951.

Prince Vajiralongkorn; b. July 28, 1952.

Princess Sirindhorn; b. April 2, 1955.

Princess Chulabhorn; b. July 4, 1957.

Parents of the King

Prince Mahidol of Songkhla and Princess Sri Sangwalya.

Sister of the King

Princess Kalyani Vadhana.

UNITED KINGDOM

Reigning Queen

QUEEN ELIZABETH II; b. April 21, 1926; succeeded to the throne February 6, 1952, on the death of her father, King George VI; crowned June 2, 1953; married, November 20, 1947, H.R.H. The Prince Philip, DUKE OF EDINBURGH, K.G. (b. June 10, 1921), son of Prince Andrew of Greece and Princess Alice of Battenberg (Mountbatten).

Children of the Queen

Prince Charles Philip Arthur George, Prince of Wales, Duke of Cornwall and Rothesay, Earl of Chester and Carrick, Baron of Renfrew, Lord of the Isles and Great Steward of Scotland, K.G. (heir-apparent); b. November 14, 1948.

Princess Anne Elizabeth Alice Louise; b. August 15, 1950.

Prince Andrew Albert Christian Edward; b. February 19, 1960.

Prince Edward Antony Richard Louis; b. March 10, 1964.

Parents of the Queen

King George VI; b. December 14, 1895; son of King George V and Queen Mary (b. May 26, 1867); married, April 26, 1923, Lady Elizabeth Angela Marguerite Bowes-Lyon (b. August 4, 1900); succeeded to the throne December 11, 1936; died February 6, 1952.

Sister of the Queen

Princess Margaret Rose; b. August 21, 1930; married, May 6, 1960, the Earl of Snowdon; son, Viscount Linley, b. November 3, 1961; daughter, Lady Sarah Frances Elizabeth Armstrong-Jones, b. May 1, 1964.

The full titles of Queen Elizabeth II are as follows:

United Kingdom
"Elizabeth the Second, by the Grace of God, of the United Kingdom of Great Britain and Northern Ireland and of her other Realms and Territories, Queen, Head of the Commonwealth, Defender of the Faith."

Canada
"Elizabeth the Second, by the Grace of God, of the United Kingdom, Canada, and her other Realms and Territories, Queen, Head of the Commonwealth, Defender of the Faith."

Australia
"Elizabeth the Second, by the Grace of God, of the United Kingdom, Australia, and her other Realms and Territories, Queen, Head of the Commonwealth, Defender of the Faith."

New Zealand
"Elizabeth the Second, by the Grace of God, of the United Kingdom, New Zealand, and her other Realms and Territories, Queen, Head of the Commonwealth, Defender of the Faith."

Ceylon
"Elizabeth the Second, Queen of Ceylon and of her other Realms and Territories, Head of the Commonwealth."

Sierra Leone
"Elizabeth the Second, Queen of Sierra Leone and of her other Realms and Territories, Head of the Commonwealth."

Jamaica
"Elizabeth the Second, by the Grace of God, of Jamaica and of her other Realms and Territories, Queen, Head of the Commonwealth.

Trinidad and Tobago
"Elizabeth the Second, by the Grace of God, Queen of Trinidad and Tobago and of her other Realms and Territories, Head of the Commonwealth."

Malta
"Elizabeth the Second, by the Grace of God, Queen of Malta and of her other Realms and Territories, Head of the Commonwealth."

Gambia
"Elizabeth the Second, Queen of Gambia and of her other Realms and Territories, Head of the Commonwealth."

Guyana
"Elizabeth the Second, by the Grace of God, Queen of Guyana and of her other Realms and Territories, Head of the Commonwealth."

Barbados
"Elizabeth the Second, by the Grace of God, Queen of Barbados and of her other Realms and Territories, Head of the Commonwealth."

The Republics of India, Pakistan, Ghana, Cyprus, Tanzania, Uganda, Kenya, Zambia, Malawi, Nigeria and Botswana, together with the Kingdom of Malaysia and the Independent Sovereign State of Lesotho, recognise the Queen as "Head of the Commonwealth".

YEMEN

Reigning Imam

The Commander of the Faithful SAIF-AL-ISLAM MOHAM-MED AL-BADR, the Imam, b. 1926; succeeded his father, the Imam Ahmad bin Yahia bin Mohammed Hamid ud-Din, King of Yemen, September 19, 1962.

INTERNATIONAL WHO'S WHO

1968-69

A

Aalberse, Petrus Josephus Mattheus; Netherlands lawyer and politician; b. 10; ed. Gymnasium St. Aloysius and Univ. of Leiden.
Secretary Building Industry Asscn. 42–47; Adviser, social orgs. 47–62; mem. Wassenaar Town Council 45-54; Sec. and later Pres. Landelijk Comité Rechtszekerheid 47-52; Sec. Catholic Social Advice and "Raad van Overleg" 55-62; Pres. Catholic People's Party 62-; mem. Second Chamber of States General; Commander, Order of Gregory the Great.
Dedelstraat 28, The Hague, Netherlands.
Telephone: 070-112697.

Aalto, (Hugo) Alvar Henrick; Finnish architect; b. 3 Feb. 1898; ed. Jyväskylän Lyseo and Univ. of Technology, Helsinki.
Graduated as architect 21, owner of architectural practice 23-; Prof. at Mass. Inst. of Technology 46-48; mem. Acad. of Finland 55-, Pres. 63-; Hon. mem. Royal Coll. of Arts, London, Assoc. per l'Architettura Organica, Rome, Instituto de Arquitetos do Brasil, Södra Sveriges Byggnastdekniska Samfund 57-, Accad. di Belle Arti, Venice, American Acad. of Arts and Sciences 57-, Asscn. of Finnish Architects 58-, Norske Arkitekters Lansforbund, Norway 59-, Colegio de Arquitectos del Peru 65-, V-Dala Nation, Uppsala 65-; mem. or corresp. mem. numerous other acads.; Chevalier Légion d'Honneur, Akademisk Arkitektførenings Aeresmedaille, Denmark, Prins Eugen Medal, Sweden, Royal Gold Medal of Architecture (U.K.) 57, Commdr. Order of Dannebrog (Denmark), Gold Medal American Inst. of Architects 63, Gold Cube, Svensk Arkitekters Riksförbund 63, Cordón del Calli de Oro, Soc. de Arquitectos Mexicanos 63, Bronzeplakette, Freie Akad. der Künste in Hamburg 65, Suomen Leijonan ritarikunta suurrrusti 65, Diplome des Palmes d'Or du Mérite de l'Europe 66, Thomas Jefferson Medal, Univ. of Virginia 67; numerous hon. degrees.
Principal works: Finnish Pavilions at Paris Int. Exhbn. 37, New York World Fair 39, Paimio Sanatorium, Oulu and Jyväskyla Univ. buildings, Viipuri Library, flats in Berlin, Domitory Block for Mass. Inst. of Technology, Catania (Sicily) City Centre, government and office buildings, Helsinki.
Tiilimaki 20, Helsinki, Finland.

Aartsen, Dr. J. Van; Netherlands politician; b. 09.
Former mem. The Hague City Council; Minister of Transport and Waterways 58–59; Minister of Housing and Building 59–63; Minister of Transport and Waterways 63-65; Anti-Revolutionary Party.
Van Alkemadelaan 203, The Hague, Netherlands.

Abbado, Claudio; Italian conductor; b. 33; ed. Conservatorio Giuseppe Verdi, Milan, and Musical Acad. in Vienna.
Guest conductor of principal orchestras in Europe and America; conductor at the Vienna Festival 61-, Salzburg Festival 65-, Edinburgh Festival 66-, Prague Spring 66-, Lucerne Festival 66-, Sergei Koussewitzky Prize, Berkshire Music Festival (U.S.A.) 58, and Dimitri Mitropoulos Prize 63.
Via Speronari 8, 20123, Milan, Italy.
Telephone: 890411.

Abbas, Ferhat; Algerian politician; b. 90; ed. Algiers Univ.
Formerly a chemist at Sétif; took part in organization of the Algerian People's Union 38; published "Manifesto of the Algerian People" 43; founded Amis du Manifeste et de la Liberté (A.M.L.) 44 and took part in the formation of the Union Démocratique du Manifeste Algérien (U.D.M.A.) 46; elected representative to French Constitutional Assembly 46, later member of French Union Assembly; elected to Algerian Assembly 48 and 54; Leader of U.D.M.A. 46-56; joined Nat. Liberation Front (F.L.N.) 55; mem. F.L.N. delegation to 11th Gen. Assembly of UN 57; leader del. to North African Conf., Tangier 58; Prime Minister of "Provisional Government of the Algerian Republic" (in Tunisia) 58-61; Pres. of the Chamber of the independent state of Algeria 62-63; under detention July 64-June 65.
Publ. *La Nuit coloniale* 63.
Fetis, Algeria.

Abbas, Sayed Mekki, B.LITT.; Sudanese international official; b. 1 Jan. 1911; ed. Gordon Memorial Coll., Khartoum, Univ. Coll. of the South West (Exeter, England) and Oxford Univ.
Sudan Ministry of Education 31-46 (chiefly with Bakht er Ruda Inst. of Education); mem. Local Govt. Advisory Board, Advisory Council for N. Sudan, Sudan Constitution Drafting Cttee.; Editor *El Baid* (political and social weekly); mem. Board of Dirs. Sudan Gezira Board 50-58, Man. Dir. 55-58; Exec. Sec. UN Econ. Comm. for Africa (ECA), Addis Ababa 58-62; Special Rep. in the Congo of UN Sec.-Gen. March-May 61; Sudan Commercial Bank 62-63; Asst. Dir.-Gen., Food and Agriculture Organization, United Nations 63-; Hon. LL.D. (Exeter).
Publ. *The Sudan Question* 52.
Food and Agriculture Organization of the United Nations, Viale delle Terme di Caracalla, Rome, Italy.
Telephone: 5797, Extension 3001, 3002.

Abbott, Hon. Douglas Charles, P.C., Q.C., B.C.L., LL.D.; Canadian lawyer; b. 29 May 1899; ed. Bishop's Coll., Lennoxville; McGill Univ.; and Dijon Univ. (France).
Member of Parl. 40-54; Parl. Asst. to the Minister of Finance 43-45, to Minister of Nat. Defence 45; Minister of Nat. Defence for Naval Services, later Minister of Nat. Defence 45; Minister of Finance 46-54; Puisne Justice, Supreme Court of Canada 54-; Chancellor, Bishop's Univ. 58-.
124 Springfield Road, Ottawa, Ontario, Canada.

Abbott, Very Rev. Eric Symes, K.C.V.O., M.A.; British ecclesiastic; b. 26 May 1906; ed. Nottingham High School and Jesus Coll., Cambridge.
Curate, St. John's, Smith Square, London, S.W.1, 30-32; Chaplain, King's Coll., London 32-36, Lincoln's Inn 34-36; Warden, Lincoln Theological Coll. 36-45; Dean,

King's Coll., London 45-55; Warden, Keble Coll., Oxford 55-60; Dean of Westminster 60-; Chaplain to H.M. The King 48-52, to H.M. The Queen 52-60; Hon. D.D. The Deanery, Westminster, London, S.W.1, England.

Abboud, Gen. Ibrahim; Sudanese army officer and politician; b. 26 Oct. 1900; ed. Gordon Coll., Khartoum, and Military Coll., Khartoum.
Commissioned 17, joined Sudan Defence Force 25, served Eritrea, Ethiopia and North Africa in Second World War; Deputy C.-in-C. Sudanese Army 54-56, C.-in-C. 56-64; Pres. Supreme Council of the Armed Forces, Prime Minister and Minister of Defence 58-64.
Suakin, Sudan.

Abdel-Rahman, Aisha, PH.D. (*pen name* **Bint el-Shati**); United Arab Republic (Egyptian) writer and university professor; ed. Cairo Univ.
Assistant Lecturer, Cairo Univ. 39-; Literary Critic, *Al Ahram* 42-; Inspectress in Arabic Languages and Literature, Ministry of Educ. 42; Lecturer in Arabic, Ain Shams Univ. 50-57, Asst. Prof. 57-62, Prof. of Arabic Literature and Chair. Univ. Coll. for Women 62-; mem. Higher Council of Arts and Letters 60-; State Prize 36; Acad. of Arabic Language Award for Textual Studies 50, for Short Story 54.
Publs. *Rissalet el Ghofram by Abul Ala'a* 50, *New Values in Arabic Literature* 61, *The Koran: Literary Interpretation* 62, *Ibn Seeda's Arabic Dictionary* 62, *Contemporary Arab Women Poets* 63; six books on illustrious women of Islam; two novels; four vols. of short stories.
13 Agam Street, Heliopolis, Cairo, U.A.R.

Abdel-Rahman, Ibrahim Helmi, PH.D.; United Arab Republic United Nations official; b. 5 Jan. 1919; ed. Univs. of Cairo, London, Edinburgh, Cambridge and Leiden.
Lecturer in Astronomy and Astrophysics, later Asst. Prof., Cairo Univ. 42-54; Sec.-Gen. Council of Ministers 54-58; Dir. Egyptian Atomic Energy Comm. 54-59; mem. and Sec.-Gen. Nat. Science Council 56-58; mem. Nat. Planning Comm. 57-60; Dir. Inst. of Nat. Planning 60-63; UN Commr. for Industrial Devt. 63-66; Exec. Dir. UN Industrial Devt. Org. (UNIDO) 67-; Exec. Egyptian Del. UNESCO Gen. Conf. 48, 52, 54; mem. U.A.R. Del. to Int. Atomic Energy Agency, Vienna 57; mem. numerous UN Missions.
United Nations Industrial Development Organization, Felderhaus, Rathausplatz 2, A-1010 Vienna, Austria.

Abdoh, Djalal, LL.D.; Iranian diplomatist; b. 10; ed. Teheran and Paris Univs.
Asst. Dir. Ministry of Justice 37-39; Public Prosecutor, Court of Govt. Employees, Teheran 41-43; Dir.-Gen. Ministry of Justice 43-44; mem. Parl. 44-49; mem. Iranian Del. to UN 46-53, 54-59; Dep. Perm. Rep. Iranian Mission to UN 49-53; Dir.-Gen. of Political Affairs, Ministry of Foreign Affairs 54-55; Ambassador and Perm. Rep. to UN 55-59; Minister of Foreign Affairs 59; UN Plebiscite Commr. British Cameroons 59-61; Roving Ambassador of Iran 61-62; Prof. Int. Law and Pol. Science, Teheran Univ. 61; Admin.UN Temporary Exec. Authority (UNTEA, West New Guinea) Oct. 62-May 63; mem. Iranian Del. to UN 63-65; Amb. to India 65-.
Publs. *Civil Procedure of Iran, Comparative Law, International Private Law, Eléments psychologiques dans les Contrats, Le Ministère public, Le Régime pénitentiaire en Iran, The Political Situation in the Middle East* (Persian), *The Political Situation in Africa* (Persian).
Imperial Iranian Embassy, 5 Barakhamba Road, New Delhi, India.

Abdraziakov, Abdulkhak Asyanovich; Soviet politician; b. 1915; ed. Mokhshan Agricultural Coll. and Higher Party School.
Veterinary surgeon 34-38; mem. C.P.S.U. 39-; Soviet work 39-42; party work 42-47; Adviser to Central Cttee.

of C.P.S.U. 47-59 ;Chair. Council of Ministers of Tatar Autonomous Republic 59-.
Council of Ministers of Tatar Autonomous Republic, Kazan, Tatar Autonomous Republic, U.S.S.R.

Abdul Jamil, tan Sri, P.M.N., P.J.K.; Malaysian diplomatist; b. 14 Jan. 1912; ed. Clifford School and Oxford Univ., England.
Joined Admin. Service 32; State Sec. Perlis 51-52; State Financial Officer, Selangor 54-55, State Sec. 56; Chief Minister, State of Selangor 57-59; Deputy Sec. to the Treasury 59-61; Sec. to the Treasury (Federal) 61-64; Chief Sec. to Malaysian Govt., Head of Home and Foreign Service, Sec. to the Cabinet 64-67; High Commr. for Malaysia in U.K. Nov. 67-; fmr. Vice-Chair. Malaysian Red Cross; fmr. Chair. Malaysian Boy Scout Asscn; fmr. Pres. Malaysian Lawn Tennis Asscn.
45 Belgrave Square, London, S.W.1, England.
Telephone: 01-245-9221.

Abdul Maliki, Alhaji, C.B.E.; Nigerian civil servant; b. 14; ed. Katsina Training Coll.
Teacher, Okene Middle School 34-35; Supervisor, Native Administration Works 36-39; Provincial Clerk 39-40; Chief Exec. Officer, Igbirra Administration 40-55, Admin. Sec. 55; mem. House of Assembly and House of Reps. 52-55; Commr. of Northern Nigeria in the United Kingdom 55-58, of Federation of Nigeria 58-60, High Commr. 60-66; Amb. to France 66-; mem. Nigerian Port Authority, Northern Region Production Board and King's Coll. Advisory Board.
Nigerian Embassy, 49 avenue Kléber, Paris 16e, France.

Abdul Rahman, Tunku ibni Al-Marhum Sultan Abdul Hamid Halim Shah, C.H., B.A.; Malaysian politician; b. 8 Feb. 1903; ed. St. Catharine's Coll., Cambridge, and Inner Temple, London.
Appointed to Executive and Legislative Councils, as unofficial mem. 52; Leader, Fed. Legislative Council; Chief Minister and Minister for Home Affairs 55; first Prime Minister and Minister of External Affairs, Federation of Malaya Aug. 57-Feb. 59, Aug. 59-Sept. 63; Prime Minister and Minister of External Affairs, Malaysia Sept. 63-; Minister of Information and Broadcasting 63-64; Minister of Culture, Youth and Sports 64-; Dir. and scripted film *Raja Bersiong* 68; leader successively of United Malay National Organization and Alliance Party; numerous foreign honours.
Office of the Prime Minister, Jalan Dato Onn, Kuala Lumpur, Malaya, Malaysia.

Abdulgani, Roeslan; Indonesian diplomatist, civil servant and politician; b. 1914; ed. Teacher Training Coll., Surabaya.
Active in Nat. Youth Movement seeking independence from Dutch; active in anti-Japanese underground during Japanese occupation; Editor *Bakti* (in East Java) 45; Sec.-Gen. Ministry of Information 47-53; Sec.-Gen. Ministry of Foreign Affairs 53-56; Del. to UN 51, 56, 66; Sec.-Gen. Afro-Asian Conf., Bandung 55; headed Del. to Suez Conf. 56; Minister of Foreign Affairs 56-57; mem. Constituent Assembly 57-; Vice-Chair Nat. Council 57-59; Vice-Chair. Supreme Advisory Council 59-62; Co-ordinating Minister and Minister of Information 63-65; Deputy Prime Minister for Political Institutions 66; Perm. Rep. to UN 67-; Indonesian medals; several hon. degrees; mem. P.N.I. (Indonesian Nat. Party).
Publs. *In Search of Indonesian Identity, The Bandung Spirit, Indonesian and Asian-African Nationalism, Pantjasila: The Prime Mover of the Indonesian Revolution, Hero's Day: In Memory of the Fighting in Surabaya on 10 November 1945, Impact of Utopian-Scientific and Religious Socialism on Indonesian Socialism,* etc.
Office of the Permanent Representative of Indonesia to the United Nations, 866 United Nations Plaza, New York, N.Y. 10017, U.S.A.
Telephone: 212-755-2600.

Abdullah, Sheikh Mohammad; Indian politician; b. 05; ed. Kashmir and Aligarh (U.P.).
Founder of Kashmir Muslim Conf., later Kashmir Nat. Conf. for representative govt. in Kashmir 38; Pres. All-India States People's Conf. 46; sentenced to 9 years' imprisonment for leading peoples of Jammu and Kashmir State in struggle against Maharajah of Kashmir for constitutional govt. and civil liberties Aug. 46 (sentence not carried out); Head of Interim Govt. Nov. 47; mem. Indian Del. to U.N. Jan. 48; Prime Minister of Jammu and Kashmir Mar. 48-53; in detention 53-58, April 58-April 64 and May 65-Jan. 68; mem. Indian Constituent Assembly June 49.
New Delhi, India.

Abdurazakov, Malik Abdurazakovich; Soviet politician; b. 1919; ed. Namangan Teachers' Training Coll. and Higher Party School of C.P.S.U. Central Cttee.
Young Pioneer leader, teacher, school director, Insp. for Namangan Dept. of Educ. 33-40; mem. C.P.S.U. 40-; Young Communist League and C.P. work in Uzbekistan 40-; First Sec. Tashkent Regional Cttee. of C.P. of Uzbekistan 61-; mem. Central Cttee. of C.P. of Uzbekistan; Alt. mem. Central Cttee. of C.P.S.U. 61-; Alt. mem. Bureau of Central Cttee. of C.P. of Uzbekistan; Deputy to U.S.S.R. Supreme Soviet.
Tashkent Regional Committee, Communist Party of Uzbekistan, Tashkent, U.S.S.R.

Abe, Kobo; Japanese novelist and playwright; b. 7 March 1924; ed. Tokyo Univ.
25th Akutagawa Prize 51, Post-War Literature Prize 49, Yomiuri Literary Prize 62, Kishida Prize for Drama 58.
Publs. *Owarishi Michino Shirubenni* (The Road Sign at the End of the Road), *Akai Mayu* (Red Cocoon) 49, *Kabe-S. Karumashi No Hanzai* (The Crimes of S. Karma, Esq.) 51, *Gaki Domei* (Hunger Union) 54, *Seifuku and other plays* (The Uniform) 55, *Doreigari* (Hunt for a Slave) 55, *Kemonotachi wa Kokyo o Mezasu* (Animals are Forwarding to Their Natives) 57, *Dai Yon Kanpyoki* (The Fourth Unglacial Period) 59, *Yurei wa Kokoni Iru* (Here is a Ghost) 59, *Ishi no Me* (Eyes of Stone) 60, *Suna no Onna* (The Woman in the Dunes) 62, *Tanin no Kao* (The Face of Another) 64, *Omaenimo Tsumi Ga Aru* (You are Guilty, Too) 65, *Enomoto Buyo* (Buyo Enomoto) 65.
1-22, Wakaba Cho, Chofu City, Tokyo, Japan.

Abe, Kojiro; Japanese industrialist; b. 3 Jan. 1897; ed. Kyoto Imperial Univ.
Entered Toyo Spinning Co. Ltd. 21, Dir. 42, Man. Dir. 46, Pres. 47-62, Chair. 62-; Chair. All-Japan Cotton Spinners' Asscn. 50-61.
21-4 Ushigamimae, Sumiyoshicho, Higashinadaku, Kobe, Japan.

Abegg, Carl Julius; Swiss businessman; b. 91.
Dir. Nestlé Alimentana, S.A. 37-; Chair. 48-62, Hon. Chair. 62-; Chair. Zürich Insurance Co.
Nestlé Alimentana, S.A., Vevey, Vaud, Switzerland.

Abel, I(orwith) W(ilbur); American union official; b. 11 Aug. 1908.
With American Sheet and Tin Plate Co. (now sub. U.S. Steel Corpn.) 25-33; mem. staff United Steelworkers of America, Dir. Canton-Massillon 42, Sec.-Treasurer Nat. Org. 53-65, Pres. 65-; mem. War Manpower Comm., War Labor Board, Second World War.
United Steelworkers of America, Commonwealth Building, Pittsburgh 22; and 3216 Apache Road, Pittsburgh 34, Pa., U.S.A.

Abel Smith, Sir Alexander, Kt., T.D., J.P.; British merchant banker and business executive; b. 18 Sept. 1904; ed. Eton and Magdalen Coll., Oxford.
Military Service 39-45; Dir. J. Henry Schroeder Wagg & Co. Ltd. 47-; Chair. Provident Mutual Life Assurance Asscn. 67-; Dir. other companies; Deputy Chair.

Export Council for Europe 64; Legion of Merit (U.S.A.) 45; Knight Order of Dannebrog (Denmark) 64.
Hounsdell Place, Mark Cross, Crowborough, Sussex, England.
Telephone: Rotherfield 347.

Abelson, Philip Hauge, B.S., M.S., PH.D.; American physicist and editor; b. 27 April 1913; ed. Washington State Coll. and Univ. of California at Berkeley.
Assistant Physicist, Dept. of Terrestrial Magnetism, Carnegie Inst. of Washington 39-41, Staff mem. (of Dept.) 46-53, Dir. of Geophysical Laboratory 53-; Principal Physicist and Civilian-in-Charge, Naval Research Laboratory Branch, Navy Yard, Philadelphia 41-46; Co-Editor *Journal of Geophysical Research* 59-65; Editor *Science* 62-; mem. Nat. Insts. of Health Biophysics and Biophysical Chemistry Study Section 56-59, Gen. Advisory Cttee. to Atomic Energy Comm. 60-63, Cttee. on Science and Public Policy of Nat. Acad. of Sciences 62-63; Consultant to Nat. Aeronautics and Space Admin. 60-63; mem. Nat. Acad. of Sciences, American Acad. of Arts and Sciences, American Philosophical Soc. and many other learned socs.; U.S. Navy Distinguished Civilian Service Medal 45, Physical Sciences Award, Washington Acad. of Sciences 50, Distinguished Alumnus Award, Washington State Univ. 62, Hillebrand Award, Chemical Soc. of Washington 62, *Modern Medicine* Award 67; Hon. D.Sc., Yale Univ.; work includes identification of uranium fission products 39-40, co-discovery of Neptunium 40, separation of uranium isotopes 43, biosynthesis in micro-organisms 53, amino acids in fossils 55, fatty acids in rocks 56.
Publ. (edited) *Researches in Geochemistry* vols. 1 and 2 59, 67.
Geophysical Laboratory, Carnegie Institution of Washington, 2801 Upton Street, N.W., Washington, D.C. 20008, U.S.A.
Telephone: 202-966-0334.

Abendroth, Walter; German composer and critic; b. 29 May 1896.
Military service 16-18; Critic and Ed. Cologne *Allgemeine Musikzeitung* 29-30; Critic and Chief Ed. Berlin *Allgemeine Musikzeitung* 30-34; Musical Adviser *Berliner Lokalanzeiger* 34-44; Magazine Dir. *Die Zeit*, Hamburg 45-55; Cultural Corresp. *Die Zeit*, Munich 55-; mem. Hamburg Freie Akad. der Künste.
Compositions incl. five symphonies; Concerto for Orchestra; Viola, Violin, Cello and Piano Concertos; Divertimento for Chamber Orchestra, Fantasy Concerto for Small Orchestra and Harpsichord Obbligato; five string quartets and other chamber music especially for viola; songs.
Publs. Biographies of H. Pfitzner and A. Bruckner; *Deutsche Musik der Zeitwende Die Symphonien Anton Bruckners, Vom Werden und Vergehen der Musik, Vier Meister der Musik, Selbstmord der Musik? Bildbiographie Anton Bruckner, Kleine Geschichte der Musik, Ich warne Neugierige* (autobiography), *Arthur Schopenhauer*.
Belgradstrasse 156, Munich 23, German Federal Republic.
Telephone: 362758.

Abenius, Håkan Wilhelm; Swedish business man; b. 5 July 1902; ed. Royal Technical Univ. of Stockholm.
Managing Dir. Stora Kopparbergs Bergslags A.B., Falun 48-66; fmr. Chair. Fed. of Swedish Industries; mem. Jernkontoret 48-, Chair. 62-; mem. Board of Stockholms Superfosfat Fabriks A.B., Nitroglycerin A.B.
Magasinsgatan 2-4, Falun, Sweden.

Aberconway, 3rd Baron, of Bodnant; Charles Melville McLaren; British business executive; b. 16 April 1913; ed. Eton Coll., and New Coll., Oxford.
Barrister, Middle Temple 37; Army service 39-45; Chair.

John Brown & Co. Ltd., Sheepbridge Engineering Ltd., English China Clays Ltd.; Dep. Chair. Westland Aircraft Ltd.; Sub. Gov. London Assurance; Dir. Nat. Provincial Bank Ltd.; Pres., Royal Horticultural Soc. 61-.
25 Egerton Terrace, London, S.W.3, England; and Bodnant, Tal-y-cafn, North Wales.

Abercrombie, Nigel James, M.A., D.PHIL.; British public servant; b. 5 August 1908; ed. Haileybury and Oriel Coll., Oxford.
Lecturer in French, Magdalen Coll., Oxford 31-36; Prof. of French and Head of Modern Languages Dept., Univ. Coll., Exeter 36-40; Secretary's Dept., Admiralty 40-62; Cabinet Office 62-63; Sec.-Gen. Arts Council of Great Britain 63-; Paget-Toynbee Prize 34.
Publs. *The Origins of Jansenism* 36, *Saint Augustine and French Classical Thought* 38, *Life and Work of Edmund Bishop* 59.
Baldy's Garden, Lewes, Sussex, England.
Telephone: Lewes 3833.

Aberdeen and Temair, 3rd Marquis; **Dudley Gladstone Gordon,** D.S.O., M.I.MECH.E.; British industrialist; b. 6 May 1883; ed. Cargilfield and Harrow.
Apprenticeship Hall, Russell & Co., shipbuilders, Aberdeen, and W. H. Allen, Son & Co. Bedford; mem. staff J. & E. Hall 07, Chair. 36-60; served Gordon Highlanders, First World War; Pres. British Engineers' Asscn. 36-39; Pres. British Asscn. of Refrigeration 24-27, 56-58; Pres. Fed. of British Industries 40-43; Chair. Hadfields Ltd., Sheffield 45-61; Dir. Barclay's Bank 44-58, Phoenix Assurance Co. Ltd. 60, Industrial and Commercial Finance Corpn. 45-61; mem. Exec. Cttee. British Iron and Steel Fed. 45-62; Pres. Inst. of Mechanical Engineers 47-48; Pres. Engineering section, British Asscn. for Advancement of Science 53, and British Iron and Steel Research Asscn. 53; Hon. LL.D. (Aberdeen).
Bullards, East Grinstead, Sussex, England.

Abernethy, Roy; American motor car executive; b. 29 Sept. 1906; ed. Carnegie Inst. of Technology.
Mechanic, car distributor, salesman, District Man. Packard Distributorship 25-32, Wholesale Man. Packard Motor Car Co., Pittsburgh 32-43, Packard Regional Man. 43-45, Zone Man. 45-48, Vice-Pres. and Packard Eastern Regional Man. 48, Owner, Packard Dealership 48-50, Gen. Man. Packard 50-51, Asst. Gen. Sales Man. Packard 51-53; Vice-Pres. and Gen. Sales Man. Kaiser-Frazer Sales Corpn., and Willys Motors Inc. 53-54; Vice-Pres. Nash Sales, American Motors Corpn. 54, Vice-Pres. Automotive Distribution 55, Exec. Vice-Pres. 60, Gen. Man. 61, Pres. and Chief Operations Officer Feb. 62-67, Pres. and Chief Exec. Officer Nov. 62-67; dir. other companies.
1919 Rathmore Drive, Bloomfield Hills, Michigan, U.S.A.

Abetti, Giorgio, C.B.E. (Hon.), D.SC.; Italian astronomer; b. 5 Oct. 1882.
Dir. Arcetri Observatory 21-52; Astronomer Roman Coll. Rome 10-19; mem. De Filippi Asiatic expedition 13-14; Prof. of Astronomy Florence Univ. 21-, Rector 36; mem. Accad. Naz. dei Lincei; fmr. Vice-Pres. Int. Astronomical Union; mem. Royal Astronomical Society; Chief Italian Acad. expeditions to Siberia and Sudan for Solar eclipses 36, 52; fmr. Pres. Int. Cttee. for Study of Solar and Terrestrial Relationships; Pres. Italian Astronomical Soc. 53-64; awarded Silver Medal of Royal Italian Geographical Society, Lincei Prize 25, Janssen Medal 37, Gold Medal of Ministry of Public Instruction 57, Gold Medal Italian Astronomical Soc. 64; mem. Royal Society of Edinburgh; Pres. Nat. Inst. of Optics 52, Italian Fulbright Asscn. 59.
Publs. *Il Sole* 63 (English trans. 63), *Stelle e Pianeti* 56 (English trans. 66), *Amici e nemici di Galileo* 45, *Scienza d'oggi* 46, *Storia dell' Astronomia* 48 (English trans. 52)

64, *Kepler* 51; *Esplorazione dell'Universo* 59, 65, *Le Nebulose e gli Universiisole* (with M. Hack) 59, (English trans. 65), *Solar Research* 62, *Unità del Cosmo* 64; Ed. *Osserv. e Mem. Oss. Arcetri* (22-53).
Istituto Nazionale di Ottica, Largo Enrico Fermi 6, 50125 Florence, Italy.
Telephone: 221180; 221179.

Abid, Ali; Indian politician and trade unionist; b. 1900.
Trade Unionist since working in Kanpur Mills at the age of 13; participated in nationalist struggles; arrested about a dozen times; one of the founders of the I.N.T.U.C. 47; Pres. Bombay I.N.T.U.C. 48-51; represented Indian workers in Int. Confs. 46, 48, 50, 63, 64 and 65; Leader, Indian Delegation to ILO Confs. 53, 54, 57 and 61, mem. ILO Governing Body, mem. ICFTU Exec. Board; Dep. Minister for Labour 52-57 and 57-62; Vice-Pres. Nat. Trade Union Congress.
Mazdoor Manzil, Parel Tank Road, Parel, Bombay 1, India.

Abidia, Fathi, B.A.; Libyan diplomatist; b. 21 March 1922; ed. Cairo Univ.
Special Sec. to King Idris I 50-54; Under-Sec. of Royal Divan 54-55; Counsellor, Washington, D.C. 55-57, London 57-61; Chargé d'Affaires, Jeddah 61-62; Dir. of Political Dept., Ministry of Foreign Affairs 62-63; Under-Sec. Ministry of Foreign Affairs 63; Ambassador to U.S.A. 63-67, to Brazil 67.
Embassy of Libya, Rio de Janeiro, Brazil.

Abou Nosseir, Mohamed, B.A.; United Arab Republic (Egyptian) lawyer and politician; b. 15.
Legal practice 36-39; Advocate, State Legal Dept. 39-44; Advocate, Legal Dept. of Cabinet 44-46; Asst. Councillor and Sec.-Gen. State Council 52; Councillor, State Council, Public Works Section 53; Supervisor, Admin. Contracts Section, State Council 54; Dep. Minister of Commerce and Industry 54; Head of trade mission to Indonesia and Japan 54; mem. official del. to Bandung Conf. for Afro-Asian Countries 55; Head of Trade Missions to China 55, to U.K. 56, and of Econ. Mission to Syria 56; Minister of Commerce and Industry 56-58, of Municipal and Rural Affairs 58-61 (Egyptian Regional Govt.); Chair. Board of Dirs., Gen. Egyptian Housing and Urbanism Org. 61-; Minister of Housing and Public Utilities 64-66; mem. Gen. Secr. of Arab Socialist Union 66-, Chair. of Preparatory Cttee. for New Perm. Constitution 66-; Minister of Justice 68-.
4 El Saleh Ayoub Street, Zamalek, Cairo, U.A.R.
Telephone: 833360 (Office); 804739 (Home).

Abou-Richeh, Omar, B.A.; Syrian diplomatist; b. 10 April 1910; ed. American Univ. of Beirut.
Gen. Dir. Nat. Library of Aleppo; mem. Arab Academy, Damascus; educational rep. of Syria in League of Arab States; Del. to UNESCO 49; Minister to Brazil 50-53, to Argentina 53; Minister to India 54-58; Ambassador of the U.A.R. to India 58-59, to Austria 59-61; Ambassador of Syrian Arab Republic to U.S.A. 61-64, to India 64-.
Publs. *Selected Poems* (2 vols.), *Zikar*, *The Deluge*.
Embassy of the Syrian Arab Republic, 10 Panch Sheel Marg, Chanakyapuri, New Delhi, India.

Abraham, Ato Emmanuel; Ethiopian educationist, diplomatist and politician; b. 1913; ed. Tafari Makonnen School, Addis Ababa.
Headmaster, Asba-Tafari School, Harar Province 31-35; Sec. Ethiopian Legation, London 35-42; Dir.-Gen. Ministry of Foreign Affairs 43-44, Ministry of Education 44-47; Del. to San Francisco Conf. on Int. Organisation 45; Del. to U.N., New York 47, 49 and 50, special mission to Iran and Indonesia 49; Minister to India 49-52; Ambassador to Italy 52-55, to the United Kingdom 55-59, concurrently Minister to the Netherlands

56-59; Chief of Political Affairs, Private Imperial Cabinet 59-61; Minister of Posts, Telegraphs and Telephones 61-66, of Communications 66-.
P.O. Box 1329, Addis Ababa, Ethiopia.

Abramov, Alexander Nikitich, M.SC.; Soviet diplomatist; b. 13 Aug. 1905.
Diplomatic Service 44-, Minister in Helsinki 46-48, Ambassador to Israel 53-58, to Cambodia 59-62, to Laos 60-62, to Algeria 62-64; Ministry of Foreign Affairs 64-66; Ambassador to Dahomey 66-; Order of Red Banner of Labour (twice).
U.S.S.R. Embassy, Cotonou, Dahomey.

Abramov, Grigorii Grigorievich; Soviet politician; b. 18; ed. Bauman Technical Inst., Moscow.
Engineer 41-47; party work 47-49; Second Sec. Mytishchi Town Cttee., Communist Party, First Sec. Shchelkovsk Town Cttee. 49-55; Section Leader, Moscow City Party Cttee. 55-59, Second Sec. 59-60, First Sec. 60-63; First Dep. Chair. Econ. Council 63-65; Dep. Minister Chemical and Oil Machine Building 65-; mem. Central Cttee. C.P.S.U. 61-66; Dep. to U.S.S.R. Supreme Soviet; mem. Presidium of Supreme Soviet 62-66.
Ministry of Chemical and Oil Machine Building, 25 Bezbohny per., Moscow, U.S.S.R.

Abramovitz, Max, B.S., M.S.; American architect; b. 23 May 1908; ed. Illinois and Columbia Univs., Ecole des Beaux Arts, Paris.
Member of Harrison, Fouilhoux & Abramovitz 41-45, Harrison & Abramovitz 45-; U.S. Army (Corps of Engineers) 42-45; Deputy Dir. of Planning, U.N., New York City 47-52; U.S. Air Force (Colonel) 50-52; Fellow, American Inst. of Architects; mem. Architectural League of New York, American Soc. of Civil Engineers, Century Asscn.; Dir. Regional Plan Asscn. Inc.; Trustee, Mount Sinai Hospital; Legion of Merit 45; Dr. of Fine Arts, Univ. of Pittsburgh 61; Award of Achievement, Univ. of Illinois Alumni Asscn. 63; Fellow, Brandeis Univ. 63.
Works include: Corning Glass Center (Corning, N.Y.) 51, Mellon Nat. Bank, U.S. Steel Building, Alcoa Building (Pittsburgh), U.S. Embassy (Rio de Janeiro) 52, U.S. Embassy (Havana) 53, Republic Nat. Bank Building (Dallas) 54, Three Chapels at Brandeis Univ. 55, Socony Mobil Building (New York City) 56, Commercial Investment Trust Building (New York City) 57, Wachovia Bank and Trust Co. Building (Charlotte, N.C.) 58, Corning Glass Building (New York City) 59, Gateway No. 4 (Pittsburgh) 60, Philharmonic Hall, Lincoln Center for the Performing Arts (New York City), Columbia Univ. Law School and Library (New York City) 62, Univ. of Illinois Assembly Hall (Champaign, Ill.) 63, Phoenix Mutual Life Insurance Bldg. (Hartford, Conn.) 64.
630 Fifth Avenue, New York 20, N.Y., U.S.A.

Abrams, Gen. Creighton Williams, Jr.; American army officer; ed. West Point and Cavalry School, Fort Bliss, Texas.
In 4th Armoured Div. during Second World War; after war served Washington, Fort Knox, Korea and Europe; attended Command and Gen. Staff School, Fort Leavenworth, Kansas, and Army War Coll., Carlisle Barracks, Pennsylvania; Brig.-Gen. 56, Commanding Gen. of a Corps 63; Vice-Chief of Staff of the Army 64-67; Deputy Commdr. U.S. Forces in Viet-Nam April 67-April 68, Commdr. April 68-; numerous decorations.
U.S. Military Assistance Command, Saigon, Republic of Viet-Nam.

Abrard, (Marie) René (Jean), D. ÈS S.; French geologist; b. 25 June 1892.
Asst. in Muséum National d'Histoire Naturelle, Paris 21; Asst. Dir. of the Laboratory 22; Prof. in Museum 41-; Asst. in French Geological Map Service 21; Head of Geological Map Service 41-; Pres. of French Geological Society 47; Officier Légion d'Honneur.
Publs. include *Le Lutétien du Bassin de Paris* 25, *Faciès et associations paléontologiques* 28, *Mollusques pléistocènes de la côte française des Somalis* 41, *Fossiles néogènes et quaternaires des Nouvelles-Hébrides* 47, *Géologie de la France* 48, *Géologie régionale du Bassin de Paris* 50, *Histoire géologique du Bassin de Paris* 50, *Carte hydrogéologique de la Région Parisienne* 61.
61 rue de Buffon, Paris 5e, France.

Abrassimov, Pyotr Andreevich; Soviet diplomatist; b. 1912; ed. Byelorussian State Univ.
Electrician 28-31; Soviet Army 41-42; Party work 42-46, 50-52, 55-56; Perm. Rep. Byelorussian S.S.R. Council of Ministers at U.S.S.R. Council of Ministers 46-48; First Vice-Chair. Byelorussian S.S.R. Council of Ministers 48-50, 52-55; Minister-Counsellor, Soviet Embassy, Peking 56-57; Ambassador to Poland 57-61; First Sec. Smolensk Regional Cttee. of C.P.S.U. 61-62; Ambassador to the German Democratic Republic 62-; mem. Central Cttee. C.P.S.U.; Dep. Supreme Soviet of U.S.S.R.; Order of Lenin (twice), Red Banner, Red Banner of Labour.
Embassy of the U.S.S.R., Berlin, Germany.

Abrikosov, Alexei Alexeyevich; Soviet physicist; b. 1928; ed. Moscow Univ.
Post-graduate Research Assoc., Inst. of Physical Problems, U.S.S.R. Acad. of Sciences 48-65; Head of Dept., Inst. of Theoretical Physics, U.S.S.R. Acad. of Sciences 65-; Research Assoc., Asst. Prof., Prof. Moscow Univ. 51-; Corresp. mem. U.S.S.R. Acad. of Sciences 64-; Lenin Prize 66.
Publs. include works on theory of superconductors, application of theory of field statistical physics.
U.S.S.R. Academy of Sciences, 14 Lenin Prospekt, Moscow, U.S.S.R.

Abs, Hermann J.; German banker; b. 15 Oct. 1901; ed. part-time studies, Univs. of Bonn and Cologne.
Joined staff of Delbrück Schickler & Co., bankers, Berlin 29, Partner 35-37; mem. Management Board, Deutsche Bank, Berlin 37; mem. Management Board, Reconstruction Loan Corpn., Frankfurt 48-59, Chair. 59-; Head, German Del. on German External Debts 51-53; mem. Management Board Süddeutsche Bank A.G. 52-67, now Deutsche Bank A.G., Frankfurt, mem. Supervisory Board 67-; mem. Advisory Board Int. Finance Corpn. 62-; Hon. Chair. Supervisory Board Deutsche Überseeische Bank, Hamburg-Berlin, Pittler Maschinenfabrik A.G., Langen bei Frankfurt (Main); Chair. Supervisory Board Bergwerksgesellschaft Dahlbusch, Gelsenkirchen, Daimler-Benz A.G., Stuttgart, Deutsche Libbey-Owens-Gesellschaft für maschinelle, Glasherstelling A.G. (Delog), Gelsenkirchen-Rotthausen, Deutsche Lufthansa A.G., Cologne, Dortmund-Hörder Hüttenunion A.G., Dortmund, Philipp Holzmann A.G., Frankfurt (Main), Kali-Chemie A.G., Hanover, Phoenix Gummiwerke A.G., Hamburg-Harburg, Rheinisch-Westfälisches Elektrizitätswerk A.G., Essen, Salamander A.G., Kornwestheim, Gebr. Stumm G.m.b.H., Brambaur, Suddeutsche-Zucker-A.G., Mannheim, Vereinigte Glanzstoff-Fabriken A.G., Wuppertal-Elberfeld, Zellstoffabrik Waldhof, Wiesbaden, Fried. Krupp G.m.b.H.; Deputy Chair. Supervisory Board A.G. der Dillinger Hüttenwerke, Dillingen, BASF Badische Anilin-& Soda-Fabrik A.G., Deutsche Shell A.G., Hamburg, Klöckner-Humboldt-Deutz A.G., Cologne, Neunkirchener Eisenwerk A.G., Neunkirchen, H. Albert de Bary & Co., N.V., Amsterdam, Siemens A.G., Berlin and Munich; mem. Supervisory Board Gelsenkirchener Bergwerks A.G., Essen, Metallgesellschaft A.G., Frankfurt (Main); Chair. Admin. Board Kreditanstalt für Wiederaufbau, Deutsche Bundesbahn; mem. Admin. Board Banco Comercial

Transatlántico, Barcelona, Banco Español en Alemania; Dr. h.c. (Univ. of Göttingen, Wirtschaftshochschule, Mannheim, etc.).
Junghofstrasse 5-11, Frankfurt/Main, German Federal Republic.

Abusch, Alexander; German politician; b. 14 Feb. 1902.
Former sales employee; edited Communist Press 21-39; interned French prison camp 39-40; Resistance Movement, S. France 40-41; Ed. *Freies Deutschland* (Mexico) 41-45; mem. Socialist Unity Party (SED) 46-; Sec. German League of Culture; mem. German Writers Union 52-; Sec. of State for Culture of the D.D.R. 54-58; Minister of Culture 58-60; Dep. Chair. (Culture and Education) Council of Ministers 61-.
Council of Ministers, Berlin, Germany.

Abushady, Mohamed Mahmoud, B.COM., A.C.I.P.; United Arab Republic (Egyptian) banker; b. 15 Aug. 1913; ed. Cairo Univ., Chartered Inst. of Patent Agents, and American Univ., Washington.
Controller-Gen. Insurance Dept., Ministry of Finance 49-52; Dir.-Gen. Govt. Insurance and Provident Funds 53; Chair. and Man. Dir. Development and Popular Housing Co. 54-55; Sub-Gov. Nat. Bank of Egypt 55-60, Man. Dir. 61-67, Chair. and Man. Dir. 67-; Chair. Social Insurance Org. 56-57; Chair. and Man. Dir. Cairo Insurance Co. 56-57; Man. Dir. Cairo Bank 56-57; Order of the Republic, 2nd Class.
Publs. *The Art of Central Banking and its Application in Egypt* 52, *Central Banking in Egypt* 52.
20 Dr. Halim Abou Seif, Heliopolis, Cairo, U.A.R.

Achard, Marcel; French playwright; b. 5 July 1899.
Awarded Prix de l'Humour Français in 24; responsible for scenario and dialogue of over eighty films; mem. Acad. Française 59-.
Publs. *La Messe est dite* 23, *Voulez-vous jouer avec moi?* 23, *Malborough s'en va-t-en guerre* 24, *La femme silencieuse* 25, *Je ne vous aime pas* 26, *La vie est belle* 28, *Jean de la Lune* 29, *La belle Marinière* 29, *Mistigri* 30, *Domino* 31, *La Femme en blanc* 32, *Petrus* 33, *Noix de Coco* 35, *Le Corsaire* 38, *Adam* 39, *Mlle. de Panama* 42, *Colinette* 43, *Auprès de ma blonde* 48, *Nous irons à Valparaiso* 49, *La Demoiselle de petite vertu* 49, *Le Moulin de la Galette* 51, *Les Compagnons de la Marjolaine* 53, *Le Mal d'amour* 55, *Patate* 57, *Noix de coco, L'Idiote, La Polka des Lampions, Turlututu, Eugène le Mystérieux, Machin-Chouette.*
8 rue de Courty, Paris 7e, France.

Acharya, Bejoy Krishna; Indian civil servant and diplomatist; b. 1 May 1912; ed. Calcutta Univ. and Univ. Coll. London.
Joined I.C.S. 36; Chief Minister, Tripura State 48-49; Deputy Sec. in Ministries of Industry, External Affairs 49-51; Deputy High Commr. for India in East Pakistan 51-54; Minister and Political Rep. to Cambodia 55-56, Foreign Service Inspector, External Affairs 56, Joint Sec. External Affairs 57-59; Ambassador to Czechoslovakia and Rumania 59-62, to Morocco and Tunisia 62-64, High Commr. in Canada 64-66; Amb. to Brazil, Bolivia and Venezuela 66-.
c/o Department of External Affairs, New Delhi, India.

Achebe, Chinua, B.A.; Nigerian writer; b. 16 Nov. 1930; ed. Government Coll., Umuahia, and Univ. Coll., Ibadan.
Producer, Nigerian Broadcasting Corpn., Lagos 54-58, Regional Controller, Enugu 58-61, Dir. *Voice of Nigeria*, Lagos 61-66; Rockefeller Fellowship 60-61; UNESCO Fellowship 63; Foundation mem. Soc. of Nigerian Authors; Editorial Adviser African Writers' Series (Heinemann); Chair. Citadel Books Ltd. (Publishers), Enugu 66-; Nigerian Nat. Trophy 60; Margaret Wrong Memorial Prize 59; Jock Campbell *New Statesman* Award 65.

Publs. *Things Fall Apart* 58, *No Longer at Ease* 60, *Arrow of God* 64, *A Man of the People* 66, *Chike and the River* 66.
P.M.B. 1122, Enugu, Eastern Nigeria.

Acheson, Dean Gooderham, A.B., LL.B.; American lawyer and politician; b. 11 April 1893; ed. Yale and Harvard Univs.
U.S. Navy, First World War; Private Sec. to Louis D. Brandeis, Associate Justice U.S. Supreme Court 19-21; with firm Covington, Burling and Rublee 21-33; Under-Sec. of Treasury May-Nov. 33, resigned; mem. firm Covington, Burling, Rublee, Acheson and Shorb 34-41 and July 47-Jan. 49; Asst. Sec. State Dept. 41-45; Under-Sec. of State 45-47; Sec. of State 49-53; private law practice 53-; Head, Advisory Group, NATO 61; Hon. M.A. (Yale Univ.), Hon. LL.D. (Wesleyan and Harvard Univs.), Hon. D.C.L. (Oxon.), Hon. LL.D. (Cantab.), 58 (Yale), 62 (Johns Hopkins); Democrat.
Publs. *An American Vista* 56, *A Citizen Looks at Congress* 57, *Power and Diplomacy* 58, *Sketches from Life of Men I Have Known* 61, *Morning and Noon* 65.
2805 P Street, Washington, D.C., U.S.A.

Achille, Jean-Claude; French public administrator; b. 6 June 1926; ed. Ecole Polytechnique and Ecole des Mines, Paris.
Engineer, Coal mines Bassin de Blanzy 50-51; Engineer of Mines, Valenciennes, then Asst. to Chief Engineer, Douai Mines 51-56; Technical Councillor and Dir. of Offices at Ministry of Industry and Commerce 56-59; Asst. Dir.-Gen. Gaz de France 59-63; Dir.-Gen. Charbonnages de France 63-; Dir. Houillères du bassin du Nord et du Pas-de-Calais, Houillères du bassin de Lorraine, and other companies; mem. Econ. and Social Cttee. European Community.
Charbonnages de France, 9 avenue Percier, Paris 8e, France.

Achkar, Marof; Guinean diplomatist; b. 5 July 1930; ed. elementary and secondary schools, Guinea, and Bréguel Engineering School, Paris.
Director *Ballets Africains* 57-59; fmr. Correspondent, Information Service of Guinea; Attaché, Perm. Mission of Guinea to UN 59-60, Second Sec. 60-61, First Sec. 61-62, Minister-Counsellor 62-63, Ambassador 63-64, Ambassador and Perm. Rep. 64-; Chair. UN Special Cttee. on Policies of *apartheid* of Govt. of Republic of South Africa 64.
Permanent Mission of Guinea to the United Nations, 17 East 73rd Street, New York, N.Y., U.S.A.

Acker, Achille H. Van; Belgian politician; b. 98.
Mem. Chamber of Representatives 27; Questeur de l'Assemblée 36; Prime Minister Feb. 45-March 46; Min. of Economic Affairs March 46; Prime Min. and Min. for Coal Production March-July 46; Min. of Communications March 47-49; Prime Minister 54-58; Pres. Chamber of Reps. 61-.
Westmeersch, Bruges, Belgium.

Acker, Sven Hermann; Danish public servant; b. 27 Feb. 1911; ed. Ordrup Gymnasium and Københavns Universitet.
Secretary to Minister of Public Works 46-48; Del. UN Transport Cttee., Geneva 47-50, 52-56; Chair. UN Cttee. on Road Transport, Geneva 54-56; Dir.-Gen. Nat. Travel Asscn. of Denmark 57-67, Danish Tourist Board 67-; Chair. Regional Comm. for Europe, Int. Union of Official Travel Orgs. 64-67; mem. Exec. Cttee. for Preservation of Natural Amenities in Denmark; Vice-Chair. Cttee. Royal Danish Music and Ballet Festival 57-58; Knight 1st Class Order of Dannebrog.
Hostrups Have 1, Copenhagen V; Summer: Nordre Strandvej 408, Hornbaek, Denmark.

Ackeret, Jakob; Swiss scientist; b. 17 March 1898; ed. Fed. Inst. of Technology, Zürich and Göttingen Univ.

Asst. to Prof. Stodola, Zürich 20; Head of Department, Kaiser Wilhelm Inst., Göttingen 21-27; Chief Engineer Escher Wyss Ltd., Zürich 28-32; Prof. and Dir. Inst. of Aerodynamics, Swiss Fed. Inst. of Technology, Zürich 32-; Hon. Fellow New York Inst. of Aeronautical Sciences; hon. mem. American Society of Mechanical Engineers; Dr. h.c. (Vienna and Karlsruhe Univs.); Hon. Fellow Royal Aeronautical Soc.
Publs. include *Fluid Mechanics in General, High-Speed Aerodynamics, Rockets.*
Eidgenössische Technische Hochschule, Sonneggstrasse 3, Zürich 6; and Schützenweg 3, Küsnacht, Zürich, Switzerland.

Ackley, (Hugh) Gardner, PH.D.; American educationalist, economist and diplomatist; b. 30 June 1915; ed. Western State Teachers' Coll. and Univ. of Michigan.
Instructor, Ohio State Univ. 39-40, Univ. of Michigan 40-41; Office of Price Administration, Washington 41-43, 44-46; Office of Strategic Services 43-44; Asst. Prof. Univ. of Michigan 46-47, Assoc. Prof. 47-52, Prof. 52-68; Econ. Adviser and Asst. Dir. Office of Price Stabilization 51-52; mem. Board of Editors, *American Economic Review* 53-56; Dir. Social Science Research Council 59-62; Vice-Pres. American Econ. Asscn. 63; mem. Council of Econ. Advisers, Exec. Office of the Pres. of U.S. 62-68, Chair. 64-68; Amb. to Italy 68-; Hon. LL.D. (Western Michigan Univ.) 64, (Kalamazoo Coll.) 67.
Publs. *Macroeconomic Theory* 61, *Un Modello Econometrico dello Sviluppo Italiano nel Dopoguerra* 63.
American Embassy, Via Vittorio Veneto 119-A, Rome, Italy.

Acutt, Sir Keith (Courtney), K.B.E.; British mining executive; b. 6 Oct. 1909.
War service 39-45; fmr. Chair. Hudson Bay Mining and Smelting Co. Ltd., now Dir; Joint Deputy Chair. Anglo-American Corpn. of South Africa Ltd.; Chair. Orange Free State Investment Trust, Wankie Colliery Co.; Dir. numerous finance and mining companies.
44 Main Street, Johannesburg, South Africa.

Adachi, Tadashi; Japanese businessman; b. 28 Feb. 1883; ed. Higher Commercial School, Tokyo.
With Mitsui Bussan Kaisha Ltd. 05-11; with Oji Paper Co. 11-46, Pres. 42-46; Pres. of other paper firms concurrently; Dir. Tokyo Metropolitan Council of Commerce, Industry and Economy; Chair. Kanto Management Council; Dir. Nissan Asscn.; Man. Dir. Japan Industry Club 46-; Chair. Radio Tokyo 51-; Pres. Japan Chamber of Commerce and Industry; Chair. Hotel New Japan 59-; Pres. Japan Nat. Tourist Org.; Hon. K.B.E.
522 8-chome, Kamimeguro, Meguro-ku, Tokyo, Japan.

Adair, Charles Wallace, Jr., A.B.; American diplomatist and international civil servant; b. 26 Jan. 1914; ed. Wisconsin Univ., American Institute of Banking, George Washington Univ., Princeton Univ.
Chase National Bank 35-38; Woodward and Lothrop 38-40; U.S. Foreign Service 40-, Mexico 40-41, Bombay 42-46, Rio de Janeiro 48; Nat. War Coll. 51-52; Adviser NATO 52-54; Economic Counsellor, Embassy, Brussels 55-58; Dep. Asst. Sec. for Economic Affairs 59-61; Dep. Sec.-Gen. OECD 61-63; U.S. Minister-Counsellor, Buenos Aires 63-65; Ambassador to Panama 65-.
American Embassy, Panama, Republic of Panama.

Adam, Kenneth, C.B.E., M.A.; British television official; b. 1 March 1908; ed. Nottingham High School and St. John's Coll., Cambridge.
Manchester Guardian 30-34; Home News Editor, B.B.C. 34-36; Chief Correspondent, *The Star* 36-40; Press Officer, British Airways 40-41; Dir. Publicity, B.B.C. 41-49, Controller, Light Programme 49-55; Joint Gen.

Man. Hulton Press 55-57; Controller, Television Programmes, B.B.C. 57-61, Dir. Television June 61-.
14 Bickenhall Mansions, London, W.1, England.
Telephone: WELbeck 2609.

Adam, Gen. Sir Ronald Forbes, G.C.B., D.S.O., O.B.E.; British army officer; b. 30 Oct. 1885; ed. Eton and Royal Military Acad. Woolwich.
Served Great War 14-18; Gen. Staff Officer Staff Coll. Camberley 32-35, Commandant 37; Gen. Staff Officer War Office 35-36; British Del. Gen. Staff conversations between Great Britain, France and Belgium 35; Commander 1st Div. Royal Artillery 36-37; Deputy Chief Imperial Gen. Staff 37-40; Gen. Officer Commanding Northern Command 40-41; Adjutant Gen. to Forces 41-46; mem. Army Council 42-46; Chair. British Council 46-55, Pres. 55-; Pres. Nat. Inst. Adult Education; mem. Miners' Welfare Comm. 46-54; mem. Exec. Board UNESCO 50-52, Chair. 52-54; Principal, Working Men's Coll. 56-61; Chair. Council of Inst. of Education, London Univ.; Gov. Birkbeck Coll.; Trustee, Nat. Central Library; Pres. United Nations Asscn.; Hon. LL.D. (Aberdeen); Hon. Fellow, Worcester Coll., Oxford.
Carylls Lea, Faygate, Sussex, England.

Adamov, Arthur; French (b. Russian) playwright; b. 23 Aug. 1908.
Publs. include *La Parodie, L'Invasion, Le Ping-Pong, Le Professeur Taranne, Tous contre Tous, Paolo Paoli, En Fiacre, Printemps 71, Ici et maintenant;* translations of Russian authors, particularly Gorki, Chekhov and Gogol.
52 rue de Seine, Paris 6e, France.

Adamowicz, Antoni Karol, M.IUR.; Polish administrator; b. 22 Aug. 1914; ed. Jagiellonian Univ., Cracow.
Barrister at law 35-39; Polish Resistance and prisoner, Auschwitz and Leitmeritz concentration camps 41-45; Admin. of Recovered Territories, Wrocław 47; Dir. Prime Minister's Office 47-57; Vice-Pres. Polish Chamber of Foreign Trade 57-58, Pres. 58-; Labour Banner (2nd Class), Commdr. of the Order "Polonia Restituta", Gold Cross of Merit.
Polish Chamber of Foreign Trade, Trebacka 4, Warsaw, Poland.
Telephone: 26-02-21.

Adams, Arthur Stanton, M.A., SC.D.; American educationist; b. 1 July 1896; ed. U.S. Naval Acad. and Submarine School, Univ. of Calif., and Colorado School of Mines.
Served in U.S. Navy 18-21; Teacher, Mathematics and Science, public and private schools, Denver 21-25; Asst. Prof. of Metallurgy and Mathematics, Assoc. Prof. of Mechanics, and Prof. of Metallurgy and Mathematics, Colorado School of Mines 27-40, Asst. to Pres. 38-40; Asst. Dean of Engineering and Dir. Engineering, Science and Management, War Training Programme, Cornell Univ. 40-42; Bureau of Naval Personnel 41-45; Provost of Cornell Univ. 46-48; Pres. Univ. of New Hampshire 48-50; Pres. American Council on Education 51-61; Pres. Salzburg Seminar in American Studies 61-65; Consultant to Pres., Univ. of New Hampshire 65-; Regents Lecturer, Univ. of California 61; Pres. Asscn. of Land-Grant Colls. and Univs. 49-50; Visiting Prof. of Higher Education, Univ. of Colorado 62; mem. American Society of Mechanical Engineering, American Asscn. for the Advancement of Science, etc.; Legion of Merit; Hon. degrees from 36 U.S. colls. and univs.
Publs. *The Development of Physical Thought* (with Leonard B. Loeb) 33, *Fundamentals of Thermodynamics* (with George D. Hilding) 45.
Cedar Point Road, Durham, N.H. 03824, U.S.A.
Telephone: 603-742-3050.

Adams, Charles Francis, A.B.; American industrialist; b. 2 May 1910; ed. Harvard Univ.
Joined Jackson & Curtis (Investment Banking) 34,

Partner 37; served with U.S. Navy (Commdr.) 40-46; with Jackson & Curtis 46-47; Exec. Vice-Pres. Raytheon Manufacturing Co. (now Raytheon Co.) 47, Pres. 48-60, 62-, Chair. 60-62; Dir. Bath Iron Works Corpn. 50-, Liberty Mutual Insurance Co. 53-, Sheraton Corpn. of America 58-63, First Nat. Bank of Boston 59-, The Gillette Co. 60-, A. C. Cossor Ltd. 61-; hon. degrees, Bates Coll., Northeastern and Suffolk Univs.
Raytheon Company, Lexington, Mass. 02173, U.S.A.
Telephone: 617-862-6600.

Adams, Sir Grantley Herbert, Kt., C.M.G., Q.C., M.P.; British politician; b. 28 April 1898; ed. Harrison Coll., Barbados and Oxford Univ.
Premier of Barbados 54-58; fmr. Leader of Assembly and mem. of the Exec. Cttee., Barbados; Prime Minister of the Federation of the West Indies 58-62; Chair. Barbados Labour Party.
Tyrol Cot, Codrington Hill, St. Michael, Barbados, West Indies.

Adams, John Bertram, C.M.G., F.R.S., D.SC., M.I.E.E.; British scientist; b. 24 May 1920; ed. Eltham Coll.
Worked at Atomic Energy Research Establishment, Harwell 45-52; joined European Org. for Nuclear Research (CERN) 53, Dir. of Proton Synchrotron Div. 54-60, Dir.-Gen. 60-61; Dir. Culham Laboratory, U.K. Atomic Energy Authority 60-67, concurrently Controller, Minister of Technology 65-66; mem. for Research, U.K. Atomic Energy Authority 66-; Röntgen Prize (Univ. of Giessen) 60, Duddell Medal, Physical Soc. 61; Hon. D.Sc. Univ. of Geneva 60, Univ. of Birmingham 61, Univ. of Surrey 66.
The Grey House, Lincombe Lane, Boars Hill, Oxford, England.

Adams, Kenneth Stanley; American business executive; b. 31 Aug. 1899; ed. Kansas City High School and Kansas Univ.
Phillips Petroleum Co. 20-, production and accounting depts. 22-32, Asst. to Pres. 32-35, Dir. and mem. Exec. Cttee. 35-, Treas. and Asst. to Pres. 35-38, Exec. Vice-Pres. 38, Pres. 38-51, Chair. of Board 51-67; Dir. First Nat. Bank in Bartlesville, OKC Corpn.; LL.D. Drury Coll., Oklahoma Baptist Univ. 59.
Post Office Drawer A, Bartlesville, Okla. 74003, U.S.A.
Telephone: 918-336-6600.

Adams, Leonie (Mrs. William Troy), B.A., D.LITT.; American poet and teacher; b. 9 Dec. 1899; ed. Barnard Coll.
Editorial work Wilson Publishing and Metropolitan Co. Museum of Art 22-28; Guggenheim Fellowship for Creative Writing 28-30; Instructor in Literature, New York Univ. 30-32, Sarah Lawrence Coll. 33-34, in Literature and Writing, Bennington Coll. 35-37, 41-45, in Writing, New Jersey Coll. for Women 46-47, Columbia Univ. 47-; Consultant in Poetry, Library of Congress 48-49; Fellow in American Letters, Library of Congress 48-55; mem. Nat. Inst. of Arts and Letters (Sec. 59-61), Acad. American Poets 59; D.Litt. (New Jersey Coll. for Women) 50; Harriet Monroe Award 54; Shelley Memorial Award 54; Bollingen Prize in Poetry 54 (jointly); Acad. of American Poets Award 59; Fulbright Lecturer in American Studies, France 55-56; Sabbatical Grant, Nat. Council on the Arts 66-67; Visiting Prof., Univ. of Washington, Seattle 68-69.
Publs. *Those Not Elect* (and other poems) 25, *High Falcon* 29, *Lyrics of François Villon* (edited, with translation) 33, *Poems, A Selection* 54.
Candlewood Mountain Road, R.D.2, New Milford, Conn., U.S.A.
Telephone: 201-354-9550.

Adams, Robert; British sculptor; b. 5 Oct. 1917; ed. Northampton School of Art.
Works in wood, stone, bronze, steel and concrete;

Instructor Central School of Art, London 49-59; one-man exhibitions at Gimpel Fils, London, between 47 and 62, in Paris 49, New York 50, 63, Dublin 55, New Jersey 55, Wuppertal 57, Düsseldorf 57, Bonn 57, Dortmund 57; represented at Biennali: São Paulo 50-57, Antwerp 51, 53, 59, Venice 52-62; other group exhibitions: Holland Park, London 54-57 and Documenta III Kassel 65; works in various permanent collections including Arts Council, British Council, Museum of Modern Art, New York, Museum of Modern Art, Turin, São Paulo Museum, Univ. of Michigan, Tate Gallery, London.
Major works include sculptures: Kings Heath School, Northampton; Municipal Theatre Gelsenkirchen, B.P. Building London, P. & O. Liner *Canberra*, Union Castle Liner *Transvaal Castle;* Heathrow Airport, London; Sekers Showrooms, London.
Rosslyn Studio, Pilgrims Lane, Hampstead, London, N.W.3, England.
Telephone: HAMpstead 9617.

Adams, Roger, PH.D.; American chemist; b. 2 Jan. 1889; ed. Harvard, Univ. of Berlin and Kaiser Wilhelm Inst.
Instructor, Harvard Univ. 13-16; mem. Board of Overseers 50-52; Asst. Prof. Univ. of Illinois 16-18, Prof. 19-26, Prof. of Organic Chemistry and Head of Chemistry and Chemical Engineering Dept. 26-54, Research Prof. 53-57, Emeritus 57-; Major, Chemical Warfare Service 18; mem. Nat. Defence Research Cttee. 41-46; Scientific Adviser to Deputy Military Gov. of Germany 45; Chair. Scientific Advisory Mission to Military Govt. of Japan 47; Fellow of American Inst. of Chemists; American Asscn. for Advancement of Science (Exec. Cttee. 41-46, 48-, Chair. of Chemical Section 27, Pres. 50); mem. of American Chemical Society (Dir. 31-35, 40-46, Pres. 35, Chair. of Board 44-50), Society of Chemical Industry, Harvey Society, Nat. Inventors' Council, Nat. Acad. of Sciences (Council 31-37, 59-62, Chair. of Chemical Section 38-41, Foreign Sec. 50-54), American Acad. of Arts and Sciences, American Philosophical Society; Hon. mem. numerous foreign societies; Vice-Pres. Int. Union of Pure and Applied Chemistry 51-55; Editor-in-Chief of *Organic Reactions* 41-; Board of Directors, Nat. Science Foundation 54-60; holder of several medals, including Elliot Cresson Medal 44 and Davy Medal 45, Richards Medal 46, Priestley Medal 46, Medal for Merit 48, Midwest Medal Award 53, A. W. Hofmann Medal 53, Perkin Medal 54, Franklin Medal 60, American Inst. of Chemists Medal 64, Nat. Medal of Science 64; Order of Lincoln 67; Hon. C.B.E. (U.K.); Hon. Sc.D. (Harvard, Yale, Pa., Rochester, Northwestern Univs., Brooklyn Polytechnic Inst., Drexel Inst. of Technology, Univ. of Illinois, Bridgeport Univ.); Hon. LL.D. (Univ. of Michigan).
Publs. *Laboratory Experiments in Organic Chemistry* (with J. R. Johnson) 28, 33, 39, 49, 63.
603 W. Michigan Avenue, Urbana, Ill., U.S.A.
Telephone: 344-5515.

Adams, Sherman; American politician and public servant; b. 8 Jan. 1899; ed. Dartmouth Coll.
Treasurer Black River Lumber Co. 21-22; Manager timber and lumber operations, Parker-Young Co., Lincoln, New Hampshire (N.H.) 28-45; mem. N.H. House of Reps. 41-44; Chair. Comm. of Labor 41-42, Speaker 43-44; mem. 79th Congress, Second N.H. District 45-47; Gov. of New Hampshire 49-53; Chief of White House Staff and Asst. to the President 53-58; Lecturer in Govt. Dartmouth Coll., Wooster Coll., Princeton Univ. and other American institutions; Pres. Loan Mountain Corpn.; served with U.S. Marine Corps 18; Hon. LL.D. (Dartmouth Coll., Univ. of N.H., Center Coll., Univ. of St. Lawrence, Univ. of Maine, Middlebury

Coll., Bates Coll., Bryant Coll.), C.L.D. (New England Coll.); Republican.
Publ. *First Hand Report* 61.
Pollard Road, Lincoln, N.H., U.S.A.

Adams, Walter, C.M.G., O.B.E., B.A.; British university administrator; b. 16 Dec. 1906; ed. Univ. Coll., London.
Lecturer in History, Univ. Coll., London 27-33; Sec. Academic Assistance Council (Soc. for the Protection of Science and Learning) 33-38, The Refugee Survey (Royal Inst. of Int. Affairs) 37-38, The London School of Economics and Political Science 38-45; with Political Intelligence Dept., Foreign Office, and later Deputy Head, British Political Warfare Mission, Washington 41-45; Sec. Inter-University Council for Higher Education in the Colonies 46-55; Principal. Univ. Coll. of Rhodesia and Nyasaland 55-67; Dir. London School of Econs. 67-; Hon. LL.D. (Malta and Melbourne Univs.).
Publ. *The Diary of Robert Hooke, 1672-80* (with H. W. Robinson) 35.
London School of Economics, Houghton Street, London, W.C.2, England.
Telephone: 01-405-7686.

Adan, Ahmed Mohamed; Somali diplomatist; b. 27 Dec. 1927; ed. Edinburgh and Oxford Univs.
Former Clerk of Legislative Assembly, Somaliland Protectorate and Sec. Council of Ministers; Del. of Somalia to UN Gen. Assembly 60-61, 64-65; Chargé d'Affaires to U.S.S.R. 61-62, Amb. 62-65; Amb. to U.S.A. 65-68.
Ministry of Foreign Affairs, Mogadishu, Somalia.

Adarkar, Bhaskar Namdeo, M.B.E., M.A.; Indian economist; b. 18 May 1910; ed. Wilson Coll., Bombay and Gonville and Caius Coll., Cambridge.
Agent, Bank of India Ltd., Bombay 38; Research Officer to the Economic Adviser to the Govt. of India 38-40; Chief Research Officer 40-41; Under-Sec. to the Govt. Commerce Dept. 41-43; Asst. Economic Adviser to the Govt. 43-45, Deputy Economic Adviser 45-49; mem. Indian Tariff Board 49 and 50-52; Sec. Reconstruction Cttees. 41-43, mem. Tariff Comm. 52-57; Exec. Dir. Int. Monetary Fund 57-61; Jt. Sec. Ministry of Commerce and Industry 61-62; Additional Sec. Ministry of Economic and Defence Co-ordination Feb.-Aug. 63, Additional Sec. Ministry of Finance Sept. 63-65; Deputy Gov. Reserve Bank of India 65-.
Publs. include *Indian Tariff Policy, Devaluation of the Rupee, The Gold Problem, History of the Indian Tariff.*
Reserve Bank of India, Bombay, India.

Addams, Charles Samuel; American cartoonist; b. 7 Jan. 1912; ed. Colgate Univ., Univ. of Pennsylvania, and Grand Central School of Art.
Artist for *The New Yorker* 33-.
Publs. *Drawn and Quartered* 42, *Addams and Evil* 48, *Monster Rally* 51, *Home Bodies* 54, *Night Crawlers* 57, *Dear Dead Days* 59, *The Groaning Board* 64, *The Charles Addams Mother Goose* 67.
25 West 43rd Street, New York City, N.Y., U.S.A.

Addis, John Mansfield, C.M.G.; British diplomatist; b. 11 June 1914; ed. Rugby and Christ Church, Oxford.
Third Sec. Foreign Office 38; with Allied Force H.Q. (Mediterranean) 42-44; Junior Private Sec. to Prime Minister 45-47; First Sec., Nanking 47-50; Peking 50, Counsellor, Peking 54-57; Counsellor, Foreign Office 57-60; Ambassador to Laos 60-62; Fellow Harvard Center for Int. Affairs 62-63; Ambassador to Philippines 63-.
British Embassy, Manila, Philippines; and Woodside, Frant, Sussex, England.

Adeane, Sir Robert, Kt., O.B.E., J.P.; British business executive; b. 1905; ed. Eton and Trinity Coll., Cambridge.

Chairman, Cochran & Co. (Annan) Ltd., City & Foreign Investment Trust Ltd., Municipal Trust Co. Ltd., New York & General Trust Ltd., London & Overseas Investment Co. Ltd., Securities Agency, Consolidated Trust and Int. Financial Soc.; Man. Dir. and Dir. of other companies; Trustee, Tate Gallery 55-62.
18 Cheyne Walk, Chelsea, London, S.W.3; and Quendon Hall, Essex, England.

Adebayo, Col. Robert; Nigerian army officer; b. 1928; ed. Christ's School, Ado-Ekiti, and Eko Boys' High School, Lagos.
Joined Army 48; commissioned in England 53, returned to Nigeria 54, Capt. 57, Maj. 60, Lieut.-Col. 62, Col. 64; A.D.C. to Gov.-Gen. 57-58; served in UN Peace Keeping Force (Congo) 61-63; Chief of Staff of Nigerian Army 64-65; Mil. Gov. of W. Nigeria 66-; mem. Fed. Exec. Council.
Office of the Military Governor of Western Nigeria, Lagos, Nigeria.

Adebo, Simeon Olaosebikan; Nigerian lawyer and diplomatist; b. 5 Oct. 1913; ed. King's Coll., Lagos, London Univ. and Gray's Inn, London.
Permanent Sec. to Ministry of Finance, W. Nigeria 57-59, to Treasury 59-60; Head of Civil Service and Chief Sec. to Govt. of W. Nigeria 61-62; Perm. Rep. of Nigeria to the United Nations 62-67; UN Under-Sec.-Gen. and Exec. Dir. of UN Inst. for Training and Research 68-; Pres. Soc. for Int. Devt. 66-67, 67-68; six honorary degrees.
c/o UNITAR, UN Headquarters, New York, N.Y., U.S.A.
Telephone: 212-PL4-1234, Ext. 4285.

Adeel, Omer Abdel Hamid, LL.B.; Sudanese diplomatist; b. 23; ed. Sudan Schools and King's Coll., London Univ.
Entered Govt. Service 42; Customs Officer 45-48; joined Sudan Police 48, studied in England 52-54; Barrister-at-Law (Gray's Inn) 55; Superintendent of Police (C.I.D.), Sudan 55; Private Sec. to Supreme Council of Republic 56; Ambassador to Italy 56-59; Perm. Rep. to UN 59-64; appointed by UN Secretariat to supervise elections in Cook Islands 65; Consultant for implementation of UN Gen. Assembly and Security Council Resolutions on Non Self-Governing Territories 65-66; Resident Rep. of UN Devt. Programme (UNDP) in Iraq Oct. 66-.
c/o United Nations, New York City, U.S.A.

Ademola, Rt. Hon. Sir Adetokunbo Adegboyega, P.C., K.B.E., C.F.R.; Nigerian lawyer; b. 1 Feb. 1906; ed. St. Gregory's Grammar School, Lagos, King's Coll., Lagos, Cambridge Univ. and Middle Temple, London.
In Crown Law Office, Lagos 34-35; Admin. officer, Enugu 35; in private practice as barrister and solicitor, Lagos 36-39; Magistrate in Nigeria 39-49; Puisne Judge, Nigeria 49-55; Chief Justice, Western Region 55-58; Chief Justice, Supreme Court 58-; mem. Int. Comm. of Jurists; Hon. Bencher, Middle Temple 59.
Supreme Court, Lagos, Nigeria.

Aderemi, Sir Adesoji, the Oni of Ife, K.C.M.G.; Nigerian administrator; b. 89; ed. St. Philip's School, Ife.
Served with Nigeria Railway Dept. 09-21; Oni of Ife 30-; mem. Nigerian Legislative Council 47; Del. African Conf., London 48; Pres. Western Region House of Chiefs 51-63; mem. Nigerian House of Reps. 51-54; Central Minister without Portfolio 51-55; Del. to Nigerian Constitution Conf. 57 and 58; Gov. Western Region of Nigeria 60-62; mem. Nigerian Cocoa Marketing Board 47-51; Dir. Nigerian Produce Marketing Co. Ltd. 47-51.
The Afin, Ife, Western Region, Nigeria.

Adermann, Rt. Hon. Charles Frederick, P.C.; Australian politician; b. 3 Aug. 1896.
Member of Federal House of Representatives 43-; Chair.

of Cttees. 50-58; Minister for Primary Industry 58-67; Chair. Queensland Peanut Marketing Board 24-52, Kingaroy Shire Council 39-46, Australian Agricultural Council; Country Party.
Box 182 P.O., Kingaroy, Queensland, Australia.
Telephone: Kingaroy 410.

Adiseshiah, Malcolm Sathianathan, M.A., PH.D.; Indian educationist and UNESCO official; b. 18 April 1910; ed. Madras, London and Cambridge Univs.
Professor of Econs., Calcutta, and Madras Univs. 30-46; Assoc. Gen. Sec. Int. Student Service 46-48; Dep. Dir. Exchange of Persons Service, UNESCO 48-50; Dir. Dept. of Tech. Assistance, UNESCO 50-54; Asst. Dir.-Gen. UNESCO 55-63, Dep. Dir.-Gen. 63-.
Publs. *Demand for Money* 38, *Agricultural Economic Development* 41, *Handicraft Industries* 42, *Rural Creidt* 43, *Planning Industrial Development* 44, *Restless Nations* 62, *War on Poverty* 63, *Non-political UN* 64, *Welfare and Wisdom* 65, *Economics of Indian Natural Resources* 66.
6 rue Eugène Labiche, Paris 16, France; Pallavaram, South India.

Adjie, Lieut.-Gen. Ibrahim; Indonesian army officer and diplomatist; b. 24 Feb. 1923; ed. Acad. for Officers, Indonesian Volunteer Army, Fort Benning, Staff and Command Coll.
Commanding Officer, Indonesian Volunteer Army 42-45, People's Security Forces 45; Battalion Commdr. 46, Chief-of-Staff 2nd Regiment, West Java Territory 47; Deputy Commdr. Sub-Territory VII (Sumatra) 48; Mil. Gov. South Tapanuli 49; Chief of Staff 1st Div., North Sumatra 54; Mil. Attaché, Yugoslavia 56-59; Chief of Staff, Siliwangi Corps 59, Commdg. Gen. 60-66; Chair. Nat. Front, West Java 60-66; Amb. to the U.K. 66-; numerous awards including 12 mil. honours.
Publs. *Doctrines of Total People's Defence and Territorial Warfare* 60, *Doctrines of Territorial Management* 60, *National Alertness* 66.
Nusantara, Bishop's Grove, The Bishop's Avenue, London, N.2, England.

Adler, John Hans, PH.D., D.IUR., M.A.; American economist; b. 16 Nov. 1912; ed. German Univ., Prague, Czechoslovakia, and Yale Univ.
Research Asst., Yale Inst. of Int. Studies 41-42; Instructor in Economics, Oberlin Coll. 42-44; Economist, Board of Govs., Fed. Reserve System 44-45; Dep. Chief, Finance Div., U.S. War Dept., Vienna 45-47; Economist, Fed. Reserve Bank, N.Y.C. 47-50; Economist Int. Bank for Reconstruction and Devt. 50-57, Econ. Adviser 57-61, Dir. Econ. Devt. Inst., Int. Bank for Reconstruction and Devt. 62-67; Senior Adviser Int. Bank for Reconstruction and Devt. 67-; Chief, or Chief Economist, several World Bank Missions, Latin America, Africa, Far East.
Publs. *Public Finance in a Developing Country—El Salvador: A Case Study* (with H. C. Wallich) 49, *Public Finance and Economic Development in Guatemala* (with E. R. Schlesinger and E. C. Olsen) 52, *The Pattern of U.S. Import Trade since 1923* (with E. R. Schlesinger and E. Van Westerborg) 52, *Recursos Financieros y Reales para el Dasarrollo* 61, 65.
5620 Western Avenue, Chevy Chase, Maryland 20015, U.S.A.

Adler, Kurt Herbert; American conductor and opera impresario; b. 2 April 1905; ed. Acad. of Music, Vienna, Conservatoire and Music-Historical Inst. of Univ. of Vienna.
Conducted in Max Reinhardt Theatres, Vienna 25-28, in Germany, Italy and Czechoslovakia 28-37; Asst. Conductor to Toscanini and Instructor at Mozarteum Salzburg Festivals 36 and 37; went to U.S.A. 38; Conductor Chicago Opera Company 38-42, Conductor New York Opera Company 45; joined San Francisco Opera Company 43, Artistic and Musical Dir. 53-56, Gen. Dir. 56-; Producer, Spring Opera, San Francisco; Gen. Dir. Western Opera Theater; Head, Merola Opera Program; Artistic Adviser, San Francisco Conservatory of Music 49-51; Guest Conductor with various orchestras in U.S.A., and in Italy 38-58; Hon. Mus.D. (Coll. of Pacific) 56; Star of Solidarity (Italy); Order of Merit, German Fed. Rep. 59; Grand Order of Merit, Austria 61.
The San Francisco Opera Association, War Memorial Opera House, San Francisco 2, Calif., U.S.A.

Ado, Andrei Dmitrievich; Soviet physiologist; b. 1909; ed. Kazan Medical Inst.
Member C.P.S.U. 43-; Assoc., Prof., Head of Chair, Kazan Medical Inst. 31-52, Head of Chair, Second Moscow Medical Inst. 52-; Corresp. mem. U.S.S.R. Acad. of Medical Sciences 45-65, mem. 65-; Dir. Research Allergological Laboratory, U.S.S.R. Acad. of Medical Sciences 61-; Vice-Chair. Board U.S.S.R. and Moscow Socs. of Patologicophysiologists; Asst. Editor *Patologicheskaya fiziologa;* Chair. Problem Comm. on Allergy; Order of Lenin, Badge of Honour, etc.
Publs. Over 200 works on inflammation, allergy and immunity.
Allergological Laboratory, U.S.S.R. Acadamy of Medical Sciences, 10 Lenin Prospekt, Moscow, U.S.S.R.

Adomakoh, Albert, M.A.; Ghanaian banker, economist and lawyer; b. 8 April 1924; ed. Downing Coll., Cambridge.
Barrister-at-Law; Sec. Bank of Ghana 57-62; Postgraduate, London School of Econ. 61-62; Man. Dir. and Chair. Nat. Investment Bank 62-65; Gov. Bank of Ghana 65-68; Commr. (Minister) for Agriculture March 68-; mem. Econ. Cttee. of Nat. Liberation Council; mem. Univ. Council, Legon, Volta River Authority, Nat. Advisory Cttee.
Publ. *The History of Currency and Banking in West African Countries* 62.
P.O.B. 4104, Accra, Ghana.
Telephone: 26979.

Adorno, Theodor W., DR. PHIL.; German philosopher, sociologist and musicologist; b. 11 Sept. 1903; ed. Kaiser Wilhelm Gymnasium, Frankfurt-am-Main, and Frankfurt Univ.
Editor musical periodical *Anbruch*, Vienna 28-31; philosophical studies at Oxford 34; Musical Dir. Princeton Radio Research Project, U.S.A. 38-41; Co-Dir. Research Project on Social Discrimination, Berkeley Univ., Calif. 44-48; returned to Germany 49; Reader in Philosophy and Sociology, Frankfurt Univ. 50-53, Extra Prof. 53-56, Prof. 56-; Dir. Inst. for Social Research, Frankfurt; Pres. Deutsche Gesellschaft für Soziologie 63-; Arnold Schoenberg Medal 54; German Critics' Prize for Literature 59; Goetheplakette der Stadt Frankfurt.
Publs. *Kierkegaard* 33, *Philosophie der neuen Musik* 49, *Minima Moralia* 51, *Versuch über Wagner* 52, *Prismen* 55, *Dissonanzen* 56, *Zur Metakritik der Erkenntnistheorie* 56, *Noten zur Literatur I-III* 58, 61, 65, *Klangfiguren* 59, *Mahler* 60, *Einleitung in die Musiksoziologie* 62, *Eingriffe* 63, *Der getreue Korrepetitor* 63, *Drei Studien zu Hegel* 63, *Moments musicaux* 64, *Jargon der Eigentlichkeit* 64, *Negative Dialektik* 66.
Kettenhofweg 123, Frankfurt-am-Main, German Federal Republic.

Adoula, Cyrille; Congolese politician; b. 13 Sept. 1921. Formerly a Trade Union official; Minister of Interior Sept. 60-Aug. 61; Prime Minister Aug. 61-July 64, Minister of Foreign Affairs 63-July 64; Ambassador to Belgium, Luxembourg and EEC 66, to U.S.A. 66-.
Embassy of the Democratic Republic of the Congo, 1800 New Hampshire Avenue, N.W., Washington, D.C 20009, U.S.A.
Telephone: 234-7690.

Adrian, 1st Baron, cr. 55, of Cambridge; **Edgar Douglas Adrian,** O.M., M.A., M.D., F.R.S., F.R.C.P.; British physiologist; b. 30 Nov. 1889; ed. Westminster and Trinity Coll., Cambridge.

Became Fellow of Trinity Coll., Cambridge 13; Foulerton Research Prof., Royal Society 29-37; Prof. of Physiology, Cambridge Univ. 37-51; Master of Trinity Coll., Cambridge 51-65; Vice-Chancellor Cambridge Univ. 57-59 and Chancellor 67-; Chancellor Leicester Univ. 58-; Pres. Royal Soc. 50-55, Brit. Asscn. for the Advancement of Science 54, Royal Soc. of Medicine 60-62; mem. Acad. des Sciences and Acad. de Médecine, Paris, Accad. dei Lincei, Rome, Royal Acads. of Science, Netherlands, Denmark and Sweden, Royal Flemish Acad. of Medicine, American Philosophical Society, Nat. Acad. of Sciences, etc.; Hon. F.R.S.M., F.R.S.E., etc.; awarded Baly Medal 29; Nobel Prize for Medicine 32; Royal Medal of Royal Society 34; Copley Medal 47; Hon. D.Sc. (Pa., Oxford, Harvard, Lyons, London, Manchester, Durham, Belfast, Johns Hopkins, New York, Sheffield and Hull, Brazil, Bologna, Freiburg, Paris, etc.), Hon. LL.D. (McGill, St. Andrews, Glasgow, Wales, Liverpool, Dalhousie), Hon. M.D. (Brussels, Louvain, Montreal). Publs. *The Basis of Sensation* 28, *The Mechanism of Nervous Action* 32, *The Physical Background of Perception* 47.

Trinity College, Cambridge, England.
Telephone: Cambridge 58201.

Adu, Amishadai Larson, C.M.G., O.B.E., M.A.; Ghanaian public servant; b. 14; ed. Achimota School, Ghana, Queens' Coll. Cambridge and Imperial Defence Coll., London.

Science Master, Achimota School 39-42; joined Colonial Admin. Service, Gold Coast 42, Joint Sec. Cttee. on Constitutional Reform (Coussey Cttee.) 49; Commr. for Africanisation, Gold Coast Civil Service 50-52, Dir. of Recruitment and Training 52-55; Sec. for External Affairs Gold Coast 55-57, Perm. Sec. Ministry of External Affairs, Ghana 57-59; Sec. to Cabinet, Ghana 59-61; Sec. Nat. Council for Higher Education and Research, Ghana 61-62; Sec.-Gen. East African Common Services Organisation 62-63; Regional Rep. UN Technical Assistance Board and Dir. Special Fund Programmes in E. Africa 64-65; Deputy Sec.-Gen. Commonwealth Secretariat, London 66-.

Publ. *The Civil Service in New African States* 65.
Office: Commonwealth Secretariat, Marlborough House, London, S.W.1, England; Home: P.O.B. 20, Aburi, Ghana.
Telephone: 01-839-1071 (Office).

Advani, Tillumal Menghraj, M.A., LL.B.; Indian educationist; b. 26 March 1888; ed. Univ. of Bombay.

Sind Scholar D. J. Sind Coll. 04, Dakshna Fellow 09; Prof. of English D.A.V. Coll. Lahore 12-13, S.P. Coll. Srinagar 14, D. J. Sind Coll. Karachi 14-45; Dean, Faculty of Arts, D. J. Sind Coll. 45-47, Principal 47-48; Founder-Principal Jai Hind Coll. Bombay 48-64; Vice-Chancellor Univ. of Bombay 57-60; Vice-Chancellor Jammu and Kashmir Univ. 63-; Fellow Univ. of Bombay 30-, mem. Acad. Council 36-; mem. Central Advisory Board of Education; Pres. Indian Nat. Theatre 58-61.

University of Jammu and Kashmir, Srinagar, Jammu, India.

Adzhubei, Aleksei Ivanovich; Soviet journalist; b. 24; ed. Moscow Univ. Inst. of Journalism.

Army service in Second World War; Student Editor, Art Editor, Editor *Komsomolskaya Pravda* 53-59; Editor-in-Chief *Izvestia* 59-64; Editorial staff *Soviet Union* Nov. 64-; fmr. Ed. *Sovietskaya Pechat* (organ of Union of Soviet Journalists); Deputy to Supreme Soviet of the U.S.S.R. from Kropotkin District, Krasnodar Prov.; mem. Central Cttee. of C.P.S.U. 61-64; Lenin Prize 60.

Soviet Union Journal, 1-8 Moskvin Ulitsa, Moscow, U.S.S.R.

Afanasenko, Yevgeni Ivanovich; Soviet politician; b. 14; ed. Herzen Pedagogical Inst., Leningrad.

Secondary school teacher 38-41; Soviet Army 41-46; mem. C.P.S.U. 43-; Head of Education Dept., Frunze Reg., Moscow 48-50; party work 50-56; Head of Org. Dept., Moscow City Cttee., C.P.S.U. 54-55, Sec. City Cttee. 55-56; Minister of Education for the R.S.F.S.R. 56-66; Amb. to Rwanda 66-; Candidate mem. Central Cttee. of C.P.S.U. 61-66; Deputy to U.S.S.R. Supreme Soviet; Order of Lenin, Order of Red Banner of Labour, Order of Red Star.

U.S.S.R. Embassy, Kigali, Rwanda.

Afanasiev, Georgii Dimitriyevich; Soviet geologist; b. 06; ed. Leningrad State Univ.

Research work, Inst. of Petrology 30; Head of Dept. of Gen. Petrography, U.S.S.R. Acad. of Sciences Inst. of Geology of Ore Deposits, Petrography, Mineralogy and Geochemistry 50-; Learned Sec., Dept. of Geological and Geographical Sciences, U.S.S.R. Acad. of Sciences 48-53; Dep. Chief Learned Sec., U.S.S.R. Acad. of Sciences 58-; Asst. to Chief Ed. of *Proceedings of the U.S.S.R. Acad. of Sciences, Geological Series* 54-59, Chief Editor 59-; Vice-Pres. Comm. for Absolute Dating of Geological Formations 62-63, Pres. 63-; Pres. of the Petrographic Cttee. 62-; Order of Red Banner of Labour, Badge of Honour, Order of Patriotic War, Order of Lenin.

U.S.S.R. Academy of Sciences, 14 Lenin Prospekt, Moscow, U.S.S.R.

Afanasiev, Pavel Yakovlevich; Soviet politician; b. 05; ed. C.P.S.U. Party School.

Member C.P.S.U. 25-; party work 27-; Sec. Nizhne Amur Regional Cttee. C.P.S.U. 45-47; Chair. Exec. Cttee. Council of Workers' Deputies, Nizhne Amur 47-50; Chair. Khabarovsk Territorial Exec. Cttee. 50-53, Magadan Regional Cttee. of Councils of Workers' Deputies 53-58; First Sec. Magadan Regional Cttee., C.P.S.U. 58-68; Cand. mem. Central Cttee. C.P.S.U. 61-; Deputy to U.S.S.R. Supreme Soviet.

c/o Regional Committee of C.P.S.U., Magadan, U.S.S.R.

Afanasiev, Sergei Alexandrovich; Soviet politician; b. 18; ed. Bauman Technical Inst., Moscow.

Engineer, Ministry of Armaments 41-46; Dep. Head, Dept. Ministry of Armaments of U.S.S.R. 46-53; Head of Technological Board, U.S.S.R. Ministry of Defence Industries 53-57; Deputy Chair. Leningrad Council of Nat. Economy 58-61; Chair. R.S.F.S.R. Council of Nat. Economy, Deputy Chair. Council of Ministers R.S.F.S.R. 61-65; U.S.S.R. Minister of General Machine Building 65-; mem. Central Cttee. C.P.S.U. 61-; Deputy to U.S.S.R. Supreme Soviet.

Ministry of General Machine Building, Moscow, U.S.S.R.

Aflak, Michel; Syrian politician; b. 10; ed. Univ. of Paris.

Former teacher, Damascus Lycée; Founder and Sec.-Gen. Baath Party 42-65; arrested Feb. 66.

c/o Baath Party Headquarters, Damascus, Syrian Arab Republic.

Afrifa, Brig. Akwasi Amankwa; Ghanaian army officer and politician; b. 1936; ed. Royal Military Acad., Sandhurst, England.

Second Lieut. 60; in command of rifle platoon, Congo 60; Lieut. 61, Platoon Commdr. 5th Infantry Battalion, Tamale, Ghana 61; infantry courses in U.K. 61, later served again in Congo; 1st Brigade H.Q., Ghana 62, then 2nd Brigade, Kumasi; Maj. Aug. 65; mem. Nat. Liberation Council 66-, in charge of Finance.

Publ. *The Ghana Coup.*
National Liberation Council, Accra, Ghana.

Afro; (see **Basaldella, Afro**).

Aga Khan IV, H.H. Shah Karim; leader of the Ismaili Muslims; b. 13 Dec. 1936; ed. Le Rosey (Switzerland) and Harvard Univ.
Succeeded to title July 57 on death of Grandfather Mohamed Shah Aga Khan; granted title His Highness by the Queen 57, His Royal Highness by Shah of Iran 59; Commdr. Ordre du Mérite Mauritanien 60; Grand Croix de l'Ordre du Croissant Vert des Comores 66; Grand Croix de l'Ordre National Malgache 66.
1 rue des Ursins, Paris 4e, France.

Aga Khan, Prince Sadruddin; British and Iranian UN official; b. 33; ed. Harvard Univ. and Harvard Univ. Graduate School for Arts and Sciences.
UNESCO Consultant for Afro-Asian Projects 58; Head of Mission and Adviser to UN High Commr. for Refugees 59-60; UNESCO Special Consultant to Dir.-Gen. 61; Exec. Sec. Int. Action Cttee. for Preservation of Nubian Monuments 61; UN Dep. High Commr. for Refugees 62-65, High Commr. 65-; Publ. *The Paris Review*; Founder and Sec. Harvard Islamic Asscn.; Pres. Council on Islamic Affairs, New York City; mem. Inst. of Differing Civilizations, Brussels.
Château de Bellerive, Collonge-Bellerive, Geneva, Switzerland.

Agagianian, H.E. Cardinal Gregory Peter, PH.D., S.T.D., J.C.D.; Armenian-born Vatican ecclesiastic; b. 18 Sept. 1895; ed. schools in Tiflis and Pontifical Urban Athenaeum "De Propaganda Fide", Rome.
Came to Rome to begin studies 06; ordained priest 17; exercised ministry in Tiflis 19-21; Vice-Rector Pontifical Armenian Coll., Rome 21, Rector 32; Prof. of Cosmology and Dogmatic Theology, Pontifical Urban Athenaeum "De Propaganda Fide" 21; Chamberlain of Pope Pius XI 32; Titular Bishop of Comana in Armenia 35; elected Patriarch of the Armenians 37; created Cardinal by Pope Pius XII 46; Pro-Prefect Sacred Congregation "De Propaganda Fide" 58-60, Prefect 60-; mem. Sacred Congregations pro Doctrina Fidei, of the Sacraments, of Rites, of the Consistory, for the Oriental Church and for Extraordinary Ecclesiastical Affairs; mem. Pontifical Comm. for Authentic Interpretation of Code of Canon Law; Pres. Pontifical Comm. for Codification of Oriental Canon Law.
Palazzo di Propaganda Fide, Piazza di Spagna 48, Rome, Italy.

Agaltsov, Marshal Filipp Alexandrovich; Soviet air force officer; b. 1900; ed. Military-Political Academy.
Soviet Forces 19-; Spanish Civil War 37-38; successively Commdr. Air Regiment. Air Division, Air Corps, Second World War; later Dep. C-in-C. Soviet Air Forces; Commdr. Soviet Long Range Air Force 62-; mem. C.P.S.U. 42-; Order of Lenin (three times), Order of Suvorov (twice), Order of Red Banner (four times), Order of Red Star, Order of Patriotic War, etc.
Ministry of Defence, 34 Maurice Thorez Embankment, Moscow, U.S.S.R.

Agar, Herbert Sebastian, A.B., A.M., PH.D., LITT.D., LL.D.; American writer and journalist; b. 29 Sept. 1897; ed. Columbia and Princeton Univs.
Served with U.S. Naval Reserve 17-18; London corresp. *Louisville Courier-Journal* and *Louisville Times* 29-34; author syndicated daily newspaper column *Time and Tide*; Editor *Louisville Courier-Journal* 40-42; joint Editor (with Allen Tate) of symposium *Who Owns America?* 36; Lt.-Commdr. U.S. Navy 42; Special Asst. Ambassador Winant, London 43-45; Counsellor for Public Affairs, U.S. Embassy, London 45-46; British Isles Editor *Freedom and Union* Jan. 47; Pres. Freedom House, New York 41-42; Dir Rupert Hart-Davis Ltd. 53-64; Dir. T.W.W. Ltd. (Independent T.V. South Wales and West of England) 57-.
Publs. *Fire and Sleet and Candlelight* (with Willis Fisher and Eleanor Carroll Chilton) 28, *Milton and Plato* 28, *The Garment of Praise* (with Eleanor Carroll Chilton) 29, *Bread and Circuses* 30, *The People's Choice* 33 (Pulitzer Prize for American History), *Land of the Free* 35, *Pursuit of Happiness* 38, *Beyond German Victory* (with Helen Hill Miller) 40, *A Time for Greatness* 43, *The Price of Union* 50, *Declaration of Faith* 52, *Abraham Lincoln* 52, *The Price of Power* (British edition, *The Unquiet Years*) 57, *The Saving Remnant* 60, *The Perils of Democracy* 65.
Beechwood, Petworth, Sussex, England.
Telephone: Graffham 213.

Agnelli, Giovanni; Italian industrialist; b. 12 March 1921.
Grandson of Giovanni Agnelli, founder of F.I.A.T. (manufacturers of land, sea and air engines and vehicles); Chair. F.I.A.T. 66-; Chair. of R.I.V. (Factory at Villar Perosa).
10 Corso Marconi, Turin, Italy.
Telephone: 6565.

Agnon, Shmuel Yosef; Israeli writer; b. 8 Aug. 1888; ed. privately.
Lived in Galicia 88-07, in Palestine 07-13, in Germany 13-24, in Jerusalem 24-; Nobel Prize for Literature 66; State of Israel Prize (twice); Bialik Prize (twice); Ussishkin Prize; Literary Prize, New York Univ.; Fellow of Bar-Ilan Univ., Hon. Fellow Weizmann Inst. of Science 67; D.Lit. Jewish Theological Seminary of America, Hon. D.Phil. Hebrew Univ., Hon. Lit.D. Columbia Univ. N.Y. 67, Yeshivah Univ., N.Y. 67; Medal of City of New York 67; Pres. Mekitzei Nirdamim (Soc. for publication of ancient manuscripts).
Publs. include eight vols. stories and novels, *Hakhnasat Kallah* (Bridal Canopy), *Eilu VeEilu* (Both These and the Other Things), *Al Kappot HaMan'ul* (Upon the Handle of the Lock), *Oreakh Natah Lalun* (A Guest for the Night), *Temol Shilshom* (In Times Past), *Samukh VeNir'eh* (Nigh and Visible), *Ad Henah* (Thus Far), *HaEsh VeHa'etzim* (The Fire and the Wood), *Days of Awe* (anthology of traditional lore and observances), *You Have Seen* (collection of writings on the Divine revelation at Mount Sinai), *Book, Author and Story*.
Talpioth, Jerusalem, Israel.

Ago, Roberto, C.B.E., LL.D., P.S.D.; Italian university professor; b. 26 May 1907; ed. Univ. of Naples.
Lecturer in Int. Law, Univ. of Cagliari 30-33, Univ. of Messina 33-34; Prof. of Int. Law, Univ. of Catania 34, Univ. of Genoa 35, Milan Univ. 38, Rome Univ. 56-; Pres. Italian Society for Int. Organisation; Italian Del. to ILO Conf. 45-; to UNESCO 49-50, Law of Sea Conf. 58-60, Vienna Conf. 61; mem. Comm. for drafting European Constitution 52; Chair. Governing Board ILO 54-55, 67-68; mem. and Pres. Int. Law Comm. of UN 57-; mem. Perm. Court of Arbitration 57-; Hon. Pres. World Fed. of UN Asscns.; Judge *ad hoc*, Int. Court of Justice 59-60; Pres. Arbitration Tribunal France-Germany, France-U.S.A.; mem. and Pres. numerous other int. tribunals and conciliation comms.; mem. Inst. de Droit Int.; mem. Curatorium Hague Acad. of Int. Law, American Acad. of Political and Social Sciences, Inst. Hellénique Droit Int.; Hon. mem. Indian Soc. Int. Law; Grand Officer, Order of Merit (Italy), Officier Légion d'Honneur, Hon. C.B.E.
Publs. *Teoria del diritto internazionale privato* 34, *Il requisito dell'effettività dell'occupazione in diritto internazionale* 34, *Règles générales des conflits de lois* 36, *La Responsabilità indiretta in diritto internazionale* 36, *Lezioni di diritto internazionale privato* 39, *Le délit international* 39, *Lezioni di diritto internazionale* 43, *Scienza giuridica e diritto internazionale* 50, *Diritto positivo e diritto internazionale* 56, *International Organisations and their Functions in the Field of Internal Activities of States* 57, *Positive Law and International*

Law 57, *Il Trattato istitutivo dell' Euratom* 61, *The State and International Organisation* 63, *La responsabilité internationale des Etats* 63, *La qualité de l'Etat pour agir en matière de protection diplomatique des sociétés* 64, *Le Nazioni Unite per il diritto internazionale* 65, *La coopération internationale dans le domaine du droit international public* 66, *La codification du droit international et les problèmes de sa réalisation* 68.
143 Via della Mendola, Rome, Italy.
Telephone: 324-231.

Agoshkov, Mikhail Ivanovich; Soviet mining specialist, b. 05; ed. Far East Polytechnic Inst., Vladivostock.
Lecturer, Far East Polytechnic Inst. 31-33; Dean, North Caucasian Inst. of Minse and Metallurgy 33-41; Asst. Dir. Inst. of Mines, U.S.S.R. Acad. of Sciences 41-58; Head, Laboratory of Mining Inst., U.S.S.R. Acad. of Sciences 54-; Prof. Inst. of Nonferrous Metals 51-; Dep. Chief Learned Sec., U.S.S.R. Acad. of Sciences 57-; Corresp. mem. U.S.S.R. Acad. of Sciences 53.
Publs. *Mining of Ore Deposits* 45, *Methods of Estimating Output of Metal Mines* 49, *Research of Technological Processes of Underground Mining* 59, *Mining Methods of Vein Type Deposits* 60, *Mining of Ore and Placer Deposits* 62.
14 Lenin Prospekt, Moscow, U.S.S.R.

Agranat, Simon, LL.D.; Israeli judge; b. 06; ed. Chicago Univ.
Settled in Palestine 30; law practice 31-40; Magistrate 40-48; Pres. District Court, Haifa 48-50; Judge Supreme Court 50-, Deputy Pres. 51-66, Pres. 66-.
The Supreme Court, Jerusalem, Israel.

Agrawala, Vasudeva Sharan, M.A., PH.D., D.LITT.; Indian university professor and writer; b. Aug. 1904; ed. Banaras Hindu Univ. and Lucknow Univ.
Curator, Mathura Museum 31-39, Lucknow Museum 40-45; Supt. Nat. Museum and Nat. Museum Branch of Archaeological Survey of India, New Delhi 46-51; Prof. and Head of Dept. of Art and Architecture, Coll. of Indology, Banaras Hindu Univ. 51-; Pres. Museums Asscn. of India and other historical asscns.; Pres. All-India Prakrit Text Soc. 64-.
Publs. *A Revised Catalogue of Mathura Museum* 50, *India as Known to Panini* 53, *Paninikalina Bharatavarsha* 55, *Jayasi's Padamavata* 55, *Kadambari: A Cultural Study* 58, *Prithiviputra, or Essays on Indian Culture* 60, *Sparks from the Vedic Fire* 62, *The Thousand-Syllabled Speech of Vedic Symbolism, Vol. I* 63, *Vidyapati's Kirtilata* 62, *Matsya Purana: A Study* 63, *Devi Mahatmya: Glorification of the Great Goddess* 63, *Solar Symbolism of the Boar* 63, *Vedic Lectures* 63, *Harshacharita: A Cultural Commentary* 64, *Vamana Purana: A Study* 64, *Bharata Savitri, Vol. I* 57, *Vol. II* 64, *Chakradhvaja: The Wheel Flag of India* 64, *Ancient Indian Folk-Cults* 64, *Divyavadana* 65, *Indian Art* 65.
Department of Art and Architecture, College of Indology, Banaras Hindu University, Varanasi 5, India.

Agricola, Rudolf, DR.RER.POL.; German economist and politician; b. 1900.
Joined Communist Party of Germany 24; lecturer in economics 27-33; dismissed for political reasons; illegal anti-Fascist activity 33-45, incl. eight years' imprisonment; Chair. Heidelberg branch Communist Party 45; publr. and editor *Rhein-Neckar-Zeitung* 45-48; Chair. *DENA* news agency; Prof. of Political Economy, Univ. of Halle-Wittenberg 48; Dir. Inst. of Political Economy, Halle 49-53; Rector, Univ. of Halle 51-53; Departmental Dir. Inst. of Econs. 53-56; mem. Volkskammer of German Democratic Republic 49-58; Consul-Gen. and Commercial Rep. to Finland 56-62; Minister Plenipotentiary 61; Prof. Political Econ. and Nordistics and Dir. Inst. of Nordistics, Univ. of Greifswald 63-.
Am Treptower Park 35, Berlin-Treptow, Germany.

Agudelo Villa, Dr. Hernando; Colombian economist and international official; b. 23; ed. University of Antioquía, and London School of Economics.
Former Congressman, Colombia; Minister of Finance 58-61; fmr. Exec. Dir. Inter-American Development Bank; mem. Cttee. of Nine, Alliance for Progress.
c/o Inter-American Development Bank, Washington, D.C., U.S.A.

Aguirre Palancares, Norberto; Mexican agricultural engineer; ed. Escuela Nacional de Agricultura.
Agrarian reform work, rising to Dir. for Agrarian Law 29-43; Dir. Nat. Comm. for Maize; Rector Univ. of Sonora 53-56; Sec.-Gen. Govt. of Oaxaca; Federal Deputy at 39th, 41st and 45th Sessions of Congress; Sec. for Agricultural Affairs 64-; Rep. of Mexico at numerous confs. on land problems.
Publs. on Mexican agricultural problems.
Secretaría de Asuntos Agrarios, Mexico, D.F., Mexico.

Ahanda, Vincent de Paul; Cameroon diplomatist and politician; b. 24 June 1918; ed. Mission Catholique de Mvolyé, Yaoundé, Petit Séminaire St. Joseph, Akono and Grand Seminaire St. Laurent, Yaoundé.
Civil Servant, Cameroon 40-56; Deputy to Legis. Assembly 56; Minister of Youth and Sport and Nat. Educ. 57; Ambassador to German Fed. Repub. 60-62; Ambassador to Belgium, Luxembourg and Netherlands and Perm. Rep. to EEC 62-65; Prime Minister of East Cameroon 65-66; Chevalier de l'Ordre National de la Valeur Camerounaise; Grand Croix de l'Ordre de Mérite du Grand Duché de Luxembourg.
Yaoundé, Cameroon.

Ahdab, Ibrahim El; Lebanese engineer and diplomatist; b. 04; ed. Paris.
Former engineer, Beirut; mem. and Pres. Council of Jt. Economic Affairs, Lebanon and Syria 44; Minister to Turkey 47-53, to Switzerland 54-55; Ambassador to U.K. 55-60; Dir. of Political Affairs, Ministry of Foreign Affairs 60-62; Ambassador to U.S.A. 62-.
Lebanese Embassy, 2560 28th Street, N.W., Washington, D.C., U.S.A.

Ahidjo, Ahmadou; Cameroon politician; b. Aug. 1924; ed. Ecole Supérieure d'Administration, Yaoundé.
Began his career in radio administration; elected as Rep. to Representative Assembly of Cameroon 47; fmr. Sec. of Assembly, Pres. Admin. Affairs Comm., Vice-Pres.; Counsellor Assembly of the French Union 55-58, fmr. Sec.; Pres. Territorial Assembly of Cameroon 56-57; Minister of the Interior 57-59; Deputy Prime Minister 57-58; Prime Minister 58-59; Prime Minister and Minister of the Interior, independent state of Cameroon Jan.-May 60; Pres. of Cameroon May 60-61, of the Fed. of Cameroon 61-; Pres. Groupe d'Union Camerounaise; Titulaire Etoile Noire du Bénin.
Présidence de la République, Yaoundé, Cameroon.

Ahlberg, Hakon; Swedish architect; b. 10 June 1891; ed. Stockholm Technical Univ. and Acad. of Art.
Pres. Royal Acad. of Arts, Stockholm 54-62.
Works include churches at St. Sköndal, Mälarhöjden and Malmberget; building at Gothenburg exhibition; Masonic home for children; Horticultural Hall, Stockholm; St. Olof's Hospital, Visby; Sidsjoe Psychiatric Hospital, Sundsvall; Children's Hospital, Oslo; industrial buildings, offices and housing for LKAB Ltd., Kiruna; Univ. Hospital, Maracaibo, Venezuela; Courthouse, Gothenburg, Museum and theatre, Falun, etc.
Publs. *Modern Swedish Architecture* 24, *Gunnar Asplund, Architect* 50.
Blasieholmstorg 11 C, Stockholm C, Sweden.

Ahlmann, Hans Jakob Konrad Wilhelmsson, PH.D.; Swedish geographer and diplomatist; b. 14 Nov. 1889.
Asst. Prof. of Geography, Uppsala Univ. 21; Prof. of Geography, Stockholm Univ. 29-50; Swedish Ambassador in Oslo 50-56; leader of Swedish-Norwegian expedition

to the North-Eastland 31, to Spitzbergen 34; leader Swedish-Icelandic investigations of Vatnajökull 36-38; leader Swedish-Norwegian expedition to N.E. Greenland 39-40; Swedish leader of Norwegian-British-Swedish Antarctic Expedition 49-52; Pres. Int. Geographical Union 56-60.
Publs. *Sommar vid Polhavet* (with S. Malmberg), *Nutida Sverige, Land of Ice and Fire, Norge, natur och näringsliv, Glaciological Research on the North Atlantic Coasts, Glacier Variations and Climatic Fluctuations* 53.
Fregattvägan 6, Stockholm Sv, Sweden.
Telephone: 197401.

Ahmed, Aziz, O.B.E.; Pakistani civil servant and diplomatist; b. 06; ed. Cambridge Univ.
Sub-Divisional Officer, Bengal 34-37; Dir. Debt Conciliation, Bengal 37-39; District Magistrate, Raj Shahi District 39-41; Registrar Co-op Socs., Bengal 41-43; Dir. Procurement, Dept. of Civil Supplies, Bengal 43-44, Jt.-Sec. (Planning) 44-46; Dep. Sec. Indian Dept. of Agriculture 46-47; Chief Sec. to Govt. of E. Pakistan 47-52; Sec. to Cabinet, Central Govt., Pakistan 52-56; Sec. to various Ministries, then Sec.-Gen. to Govt. of Pakistan 56-59; Ambassador to U.S.A. 59-63; Sec. to Govt. of Pakistan, Ministry of Foreign Affairs 63-; Hilali-i-Pakistan, Sitara-i-Pakistan.
Office: Ministry of Foreign Affairs, Islamabad; Home: 55 Clifton, Karachi, Pakistan.

Ahmed, Fakhruddin Ali, B.A.; Indian barrister and politician; b. 13 May 1905; ed. St. Stephen's Coll., Delhi, St. Catharine's Coll., Cambridge, and Inner Temple, London.
Called to Bar; went to Assam 28; joined Indian Nat. Congress 31; mem. Assam Pradesh Congress Cttee. 36-, All-India Congress Cttee. 36-; Minister of Finance and Revenue, Assam 38-39; detained 42-45; Advocate-Gen. of Assam 46; mem. Rajya Sabha 52-53; Minister of Finance, Law, Community Devt., and Panchayat 57-66, of Local Self-Government 57-62; Union Minister for Irrigation and Power 66-Nov. 66, of Education Nov. 66-March 67, of Industrial Devt. and Company Affairs March 67-; mem. All-India Congress Working Cttee. 64-.
Ministry of Industrial Development, New Delhi, India.

Ahmed, Ghulam; Pakistani diplomatist.
Trade Commr. to Italy 47-48; Head, Pakistan Civil Intelligence Agency 48-49; mem. Cabinet Secr., Govt. of Pakistan 49-51; Sec. Ministry of Interior 51, later Ministry of Information and Broadcasting and States and Frontier Regions 51-55; Perm. Rep. of Pakistan to UN 57-58; Chair. Water and Power Devt. Authority, W. Pakistan 57-58; Chair. Nat. Planning Comm., Pakistan 58-61; Amb. to U.S.A. 63-66.
c/o Ministry of Foreign Affairs, Karachi, Pakistan.

Ahmed, Jamal Mohamed, B.LITT.; Sudanese diplomatist; b. 17; ed. Gordon Coll., Khartoum, Univ. Coll., Exeter, Devon, and Balliol Coll., Oxford.
Teacher, Sudan Govt. Schools 39-44; mem. Publications Bureau, Ministry of Education, Sudan 46-49; Warden, Univ. Coll., Khartoum 50-56; Sudan Foreign Service 56-, Ambassador to Iraq 56-59, to Ethiopia 59-64; Perm. Rep. to UN 64-65; Ambassador to U.K. 65-.
Publ. *Intellectual Origins of Egyptian Nationalism* 61.
Embassy of Sudan, 3 Cleveland Row, St. James's, London, SW.1, England.

Ahmed, Rashid, M.A.; Pakistani radio administrator; b. 11; ed. Govt. Coll. Lahore (Panjab Univ.).
Lecturer in English, Govt. Coll. and Islamia Coll. Lahore 33-35; Asst. Master, Doon School 35-36; Dir. of Programmes, All-India Radio 36-37, Asst. Station Dir. 37-38, Station Dir. 38-47; Deputy Dir.-Gen. Radio Pakistan 47-59, Dir.-Gen. 59-63; Editor Planning Comm., Govt. of Pakistan 63-.
Pakistan Planning Commission, Rawalpindi, Pakistan.

Ahmed, S. Habib, B.A.; Pakistani United Nations official; b. 1 April 1915; ed. Univ. of Delhi.
Admin., Cent. Govt., India 35-41; Finance and Budget Officer, Tata Iron & Steel Co., India 41-47; Budget Officer, UN 49-50; Pub. Admin. Adviser UN Commr., Libya 50; Adviser on Public Admin., Ethiopia and Iraq 51-54; Chief, Office for Asia and the Far East, UN Technical Assist. Admin. 55-59; Dep. Dir. Bureau of Tech. Assist. Operations UN Headquarters 59-60; Chief Admin. Officer, UN Mission in the Congo 60-62; Chief, Civilian Operations UN Operations in the Congo 60-62; Resident Rep. of Tech. Assist. Board, and Dir. of Special Fund Programme, Congo 62-64, Resident Rep. of UN Development Programme, Somalia 64-67, Libya 68-.
c/o United Nations UNDP, P.O.B. 20, Grand Central Station, New York, N.Y. 10017, U.S.A.

Aho, Lauri Emil, M.A.; Finnish politician and journalist; b. 18 July 1901; ed. Helsinki Univ.
Literary Dir., K. J. Gummerus Publishing Co. 31-34; Asst. Editor-in-Chief *Uusi Suomi* 34-37; Official, Employers' Asscn. 37-40; Editor-in-Chief *Uusi Suomi* 40-56; Chair. Helsinki City Council 53-56; Mayor of Helsinki 56-; Pres. Asscn. of Finnish Cities 58-67; mem. Int. Press Inst.; numerous Finnish and foreign decorations.
Aleksanterinkatu 14, Helsinki, Finland.
Telephone: 666-383.

Ahomadegbe, Justin Tometin; Dahomeyan politician; b. 17; ed. William Ponty School, Dakar, and School of Medicine, Dakar.
Medical work, Cotonou, Porto-Novo 44-47; mem. Gen. Council, Dahomey 47, Sec.-Gen. Bloc Populaire Africain; Sec.-Gen. Union Démocratique Dahoméenne (U.D.D.) 56; mem. Grand Council, A.O.F. 57; mem. Dahomey Legislative Assembly 59, Pres. 59-60; medical work 60-61; imprisoned 61-62; Minister of Health, Public Works and Nat. Education 63; Vice-Pres. of Dahomey, Pres. of Council of Ministers and Minister in Charge of Interior, Defence, Security and Information 64-65, also in charge of the Plan 65.
Cotonou, Dahomey.

Ahuja, V. K.; Indian diplomatist; b. 23; ed. Bombay Univ.
Attaché, later Second Sec., Moscow 51; Under-Sec. Ministry of Education 52-54; Second Sec., Paris 54-55, First Sec. 55-56; First Sec., Moscow 56-59, Bangkok 59-62; First Sec. (Commercial), Wellington 62, Counsellor 62-63; High Commr. in New Zealand 63-66.
c/o Ministry of Foreign Affairs, New Delhi, India.

Ah-ying (Chien Hsing-tsun); Chinese author and literary historian; b. 05.
Co-founder *Sun* monthly; mem. League of Left Writers; editor *Sea Breeze* monthly; undertook research on modern and Ch'ing literature; Dean Ta-t'ung Univ.; Ed. *Readers' Digest* (Shanghai); mem. All-China Fed. of Literary and Art Circles 49, later Sec.-Gen.; mem. Council, Chinese Writers' Union; has published plays, poems, novels and criticism.
Chinese Writers' Union, Peking, China.

Aibek (Musa Tashmukhamedov); Soviet writer and poet; b. 05; ed. Tashkent Univ.
Chair. Uzbek Writers' Union 45-50; mem. Presidium of the Uzbek Acad. of Sciences 45-; Deputy to U.S.S.R. Supreme Soviet until 66; mem. C.P.S.U. 47-; awarded the Order of Lenin three times, State Prize, Badge of Honour 51, Order of Red Banner of Labour 55.
Publs. Verse: *Feelings* 26, *The Flutes of the Heart* 29, *The Torch* 32; Poems: *Dilbar, a daughter of the times* 32, *Bakhtigul and Sagindik* 34, *The Girls* 47, *Selected Poems* 49, *Songs of the Sun* 45, *Zafaz and Zakhza* 51, *Lovers of Truth* 57; Novels: *Sacred Blood* 39, *Navoi* 46, *The Wind*

of the Golden Valley 49, *In Search of Light* 56, *The Sun Will Not Darken* 58, *Childhood* 62; Selected Works (5 vols.) 62-63.
Union of Writers of Uzbek S.S.R., Tashkent, Uzbek S.S.R., U.S.S.R.

Aichi, Ki-ichi; Japanese politician; b. 07; ed. Tokyo Imperial Univ.
Ministry of Finance 31-50, Dir. Minister's Secretariat 46-47, Dir. Banking Bureau 47-50; mem. House of Councillors 50-54; Minister for Int. Trade and Industry and Dir. of Economic Council Board 54; mem. House of Representatives 55-; Dir.-Gen. Cabinet Secretariat 57-58; Minister of Justice 58-59; Minister of Education 64-66; Chief Cabinet Sec. 66-; Liberal Democrat.
3-17-1, Yushima, Bunkyo-ku, Tokyo, Japan.
Telephone: 831-5637.

Aichinger, Ilse (Frau Günter Eich); German and Austrian writer; b. 1 Nov. 1921; ed. high school and Universität Wien.
Formerly worked with Inge Scholl at Hochschule für Gestaltung, Ulm; later worked as a reader for S. Fischer (publishers), Frankfurt and Vienna; Förderungspreis des Österreichischen Staatspreises 52, Preis der *Gruppe 47* 52, Literaturpreis der Freien und Hansestadt Bremen 54, Immermannpreis der Stadt Düsseldorf 55, Literaturpreis der Bayerischen Akademie 61.
Publs. *Die Grössere Hoffnung* (novel) 48, *Knöpfe* (radio play) 52, *Der Gefesselte* (short stories) 54, *Zu keiner Stunde* (dialogues) 57, *Besuch im Pfarrhaus* (radio play) 61, *Wo ich wohne* (stories, dialogues, poems) 63, *Eliza, Eliza* (stories) 65.
Lenggries/Obb., Lindenweg 12, German Federal Republic.

Aiken, Conrad Potter, A.B.; American poet; b. 5 Aug. 1889; ed. Harvard Univ.
Contributing editor *Dial*; awarded Pulitzer prize 29; Consultant in Poetry, Library of Congress 50-52; mem. American Acad. of Arts and Letters; Nat. Book Award 54; Bollingen Award for *A Letter from Li-Po* 56; Acad. of American Poets Award 57; Gold Medal for Poetry of Nat. Inst. of Arts and Letters 58; Huntington Hartford Foundation Award 61; St. Botolph Club Award 64; Brandeis Univ. Gold Medal for Poetry 67.
Publs. *Earth Triumphant and Other Tales* 14, *Turns and Movies* 16, *The House of Dust* 20, *Punch, the Immortal Liar* 21, *Blue Voyage* 27, *Costumes by Eros* 28, *Scepticisms: Notes on Contemporary Poetry* 19, *Bring! Bring! and Other Stories* 25, *Preludes for Memnon* 31, *The Coming Forth by Day of Osiris Jones* 31, *Great Circle* 33, *King Coffin* 35, *Landscape West of Eden* 35, *Time in the Rock* 36, *A Heart for the Gods of Mexico* 39, *The Conversation* 40, *And in the Human Heart* 40, *Brownstone Eclogues* 42, *The Soldier* 44, *A Comprehensive Anthology of American Poetry* 45, *Twentieth Century American Poetry* 45, *The Kid* 47, *The Divine Pilgrim* 49, *Skylight One* 49, *Mr. Arcularis* (play) 49, *The Short Stories of Conrad Aiken* 50, *Ushant: an essay* (autobiography) 52, *Collected Poems* 53, *A Letter from Li-Po and Other Poems* 55, *Sheepfold Hill and Other Poems* 58, *A Reviewer's A.B.C. (Collected Criticism)* 58, *Collected Short Stories of Conrad Aiken* 60, *Selected Poems* 61, *The Morning Song of Lord Zero, Poems Old and New* 63, *Collected Novels* 64, *A Seizure of Limericks* 64, *Cats and Bats and Things with Wings* 65, *Poets on Poetry* (contributor) 65, *Preludes* 66, *Tom, Sue, and the Clock* 66.
Brewster, Mass., U.S.A.

Aiken, Frank; Irish politician; b. 13 Feb. 1898; ed. Christian Brothers' School, Newry.
Active in Volunteers and Gaelic League 13-; Commander Northern Div. I.R.A. 21; participated in negotiations resulting in Collins-de Valera pact; Chief of Staff I.R.A. 23-25; mem. Dail for Co. Louth 23-; Minister for Defence 32-39; Minister for Co-ordination of Defence 39-45;

Minister for Finance 45-48; Minister for External Affairs 51-54 and 57-; Tánaiste (Deputy Prime Minister) 65-; Grand Cross of Pian Order, Grand Cross Order of Merit (German Federal Republic), Grand Officer Order of St. Charles; Hon. LL.D. (Nat. Univ. of Ireland); Fianna Fáil.
"Dúngaoithe", Sandyford, Co. Dublin, Ireland.

Aiken, George David, LL.D. (Vermont); American agriculturist and politician; b. 20 Aug. 1892; ed. High School.
Member Vermont Horticultural Soc. 10-, Pres. 17-18; owner of nursery at Putney, Vt.; mem. Vermont House of Reps. 31-35 and Speaker 33-35; Lieut.-Gov. of Vermont 35-37, Gov. 37 and 39; Senator from Vermont 41-; Chair. Senate Cttee. on Expenditures in the Exec. Depts. Jan. 47-49, Agriculture and Forestry 53-55; Hon. Sc.D. (Norwich); Republican.
Publs. *Pioneering with Wildflowers* 33, *Pioneering with Fruits and Berries* 36, *Speaking from Vermont* 38.
Putney, Vermont, U.S.A.

Aiken, Howard Hathaway, M.S., PH.D.; American mathematician; b. 1900; ed. Harvard, Wisconsin and Chicago Univs.
Industrial positions with Madison Gas and Electric Co. and Westinghouse Electric Co.; Instructor in Physics and Communication Engineering 37-39; Faculty Instructor in Physics and Communication Engineering, Harvard Univ. 39-41, Assoc. Prof. of Applied Mathematics 41-46, Prof. of Applied Mathematics 46-61, Dir. Computation Laboratory 46-; served 39-45 war as Commdr. U.S. Navy, on leave from Harvard Univ., Prof. Emer. of Applied Mathematics, Harvard Univ. 61-; Distinguished Service Prof. of Information Technology, Univ. of Miami 61; Fellow, American Acad. of Arts and Sciences; mem. Asscn. for Advancement of Science, Econometric Society, etc.; decorations and honours include: Palmes de l'Acad. Française and Chevalier de la Légion d'Honneur (France); Dr. Ing. e.h. (Technische Hochschule, Darmstadt), etc.
P.O. Box 8245, University of Miami, Florida, U.S.A.

Ailes, Stephen; American lawyer; b. 25 March 1912; ed. Episcopal High School, Alexandria, Virginia, Princeton Univ., and West Virginia Univ. Law School.
Asst. Prof. of Law, West Virginia Univ. 37-40; private legal practice 40-42; Legal Staff, Office of Price Admin. and Asst. Gen. Counsel, Consumer Price Div. 42-46; law firm Steptoe and Johnson, Washington, D.C. 46-47, 48-61; Counsel, American Economic Mission to Greece 47-48; Under-Sec. of Army 61-64; Sec. of the Army 64-65; private legal practice, Steptoe & Johnson 65-.
Office: Steptoe & Johnson, 1250 Connecticut Ave., Washington, D.C. 20036; Home 4521 Wetherill Road, N.W., Washington, D.C. 20016, U.S.A.

Ailleret, Pierre Marie Jean; French engineer; b. 10 March 1900; ed. Ecole Polytechnique.
Former Director General (Studies and Research) Electricité de France, Dep. Dir.-Gen. 59-; Pres. Union Technique de l'Electricité; Prof. Ecole Nat. des Ponts et Chaussées; mem. Comité de l'Energie Atomique, Admin. Council Conservatoire Nat. des Arts et Métiers; Soc. d'Energie Nucléaire Franco-Belge des Ardennes; Commdr. Légion d'Honneur.
34 rue des Vignes, Paris 16e, France.

Aitken, Sir (John William) Max, Bart., D.S.O., D.F.C.; British newspaper executive; b. 15 Feb. 1910; ed. Westminster School and Pembroke Coll., Cambridge.
Royal Air Force 39-45; Conservative M.P. 45-50; Chair. of Board Beaverbrook Newspapers Ltd.; Dir. The Price Co. Ltd., Assoc. Television Ltd.; renounced peerage but succeeded to the Baronetcy of Sir Max Aitken (later Lord Beaverbrook) June 64.
The Garden House, Cherkley, Leatherhead, Surrey, England.

Aitken, Sir Robert Stevenson, M.D., D.PHIL., F.R.C.P., F.R.C.P.E., F.R.A.C.P.; British physician; b. 16 April 1901; ed. New Zealand Schools, Univs. of Otago and Oxford. London Hospital 26-34; Reader in Medicine, British Postgraduate Medical School, Univ. of London 35-38; Regius Prof. of Medicine Univ. of Aberdeen 39-48; Vice-Chancellor, Univ. of Otago, N.Z. 48-53; Vice-Chancellor Univ. of Birmingham 53-Sept. 68; Chair. Birmingham Repertory Theatre; Hon. LL.D. (Dalhousie, Melbourne, Panjab, McGill, Pennsylvania, Aberdeen, Newfoundland, Leicester), Hon. D.C.L. (Oxon.), Hon. D.Sc. (Sydney, Liverpool).
University of Birmingham, Birmingham 15, England. Telephone: 021-472-1301.

Aitmatov, Chingiz; Soviet (Kirghiz) writer; b. 1928; ed. Kirghiz Agricultural Inst.
Writer 52-; First Sec. of Cinema Union of Kirghiz S.S.R.; Candidate mem. Central Cttee. of C.P. of Kirghiz S.S.R.; Lenin Prize for *Tales of the Hills and the Steppes* 63.
Publs. include: stories: *Face to Face, Short Stories, Melody* 61, *Tales of the Hills and the Steppes* 63; novels: *Djamilya* 59, *My Poplar in a Red Kerchief* 60, *Camel's Eye, The First Teacher, Farewell Guilsari.*
Kirghiz Branch of Union of Writers of U.S.S.R., Ulitsa Pushkina 52, Frunze, Kirghiz S.S.R., U.S.S.R.

Aitmuratov, Erezhep; Soviet politician; b. 1929; ed. Central Asia Polytechnical Inst.
Electrical engineer, Chief Power Engineer of Takhia-Tash Power Undertaking of Kara-Kalpak A.S.S.R. 52-57; mem. C.P.S.U. 55-; party official, Vice-Chair. Council of Ministers of Kara-Kalpak A.S.S.R. and Uzbek Farming Equipment Asscn., Sec. Khodzheili Industrial Production Party Cttee. 57-63; Chair. Council of Ministers of Kara Kalpak A.S.S.R. 63-; mem. Central Cttee. Communist Party of Uzbekistan; Deputy to U.S.S.R. Supreme Soviet.
Council of Ministers of Kara-Kalpak A.S.S.R., Nukus, U.S.S.R.

Ajavon, Robert; Togolese physician and diplomatist; b. 10; ed. Univ. of Paris.
Representative of Togo, French Senate 52-56; Pres. Chamber of Deputies, Togo 56-58; Pres. Cttee. on Foreign Affairs and Defence, Togo National Assembly 58-64; Ambassador to United States and Perm. Rep. to United Nations 64-67.
c/o Ministry of Foreign Affairs, Lomé, Togo.

Ajtai, Miklos; Hungarian government official; b. 19 May 1914; ed. Budapest Univ. of Sciences.
Chemist, Chinoin factory; in resistance movement during Second World War; entered State service 45, successively Chief Departmental Leader, Ministry of Welfare, Section Head, Ministry of Industry, First Deputy Minister of Light Industry; Deputy Pres., State Planning Office 56-61, Pres. 61-67; Deputy Prime Minister 67-; mem. Central Cttee. Hungarian Socialist Workers' Party; mem. Political Cttee. of Hungarian Socialist Workers' Party 62-.
Office of the Deputy Prime Minister, Budapest, Hungary.

Akagi, Munenori; Japanese politician; b. 04; ed. Univ. of Tokyo.
Farmer; Vice-Chair. Ibaragi Prefecture; Vice-Chair. Farmer's Asscn.; Consultant, Ministry of Commerce and Industry; Parl. Vice-Minister of Education; mem. House of Reps.; Vice-Sec. Liberal Democratic Party 57; Minister of Agriculture and Forestry 57, 63-66; Sec.-Gen. of Cabinet 58-59; State Minister, Defence Agency 59-60.
c/o Ministry of Agriculture, Tokyo, Japan.

Akasaka, Takeshi; Japanese business executive; b. 28 Jan. 1900; ed. Tohoku Univ.
Nippon Kokan Kabushiki Kaisha (Japan Steel and Tube Corpn.) 34-, Dir. 49-, Managing Dir. 59-63, Pres. 63-.
Nippon Kokan Kabushiki Kaisha, Otemachi, Chiyoda-ku, Tokyo, Japan.

Ake, Siméon; Ivory Coast lawyer and diplomatist; b. 4 Jan. 1932; ed. Univs. of Dakar and Grenoble.
Chef de Cabinet to Minister of Public Service, Ivory Coast 59-61; First Counsellor, Ivory Coast Mission to UN 61-63; Dir. of Protocol, Ministry of Foreign Affairs 63-64; Amb. to U.K., Sweden, Denmark and Norway 64-66; Perm. Rep. of Ivory Coast to UN Sept. 66-; Officer of Nat. Order of Republic of Ivory Coast.
Permanent Mission of Ivory Coast to United Nations, 46 East 74th Street, New York, N.Y. 10021, U.S.A.

Akhmadulina, Bella; Soviet poet of Tatar origin; b. 1937; ed. Gorky Inst. of Literature.
Poems include: *The Rope* 62, *The Rain* 63, *My Ancestry* 64.
Union of Soviet Writers, Moscow, U.S.S.R.

Akhokhov, Aslanbi Nakhovich; Soviet politician; b. 1912; ed. Higher Party School of C.P.S.U. Central Committee.
Young Communist League, later trade union official 31-41; mem. C.P.S.U. 41-; Soviet Army 41-46; party official 46-57; Chair. of Council of Ministers of Kabardino-Balkar Autonomous S.S.R. 57-; Deputy to U.S.S.R. Supreme Soviet; mem. Budget Cttee., Soviet of Nationalities, U.S.S.R. Supreme Soviet.
Council of Ministers of Kabardino-Balkar A.S.S.R., Nalchik, U.S.S.R.

Akhundov, Veli Yusufovich; Soviet (Azerbaijan) politician; b. 16; ed. Azerbaijan Medical Inst.
Member C.P.S.U. 39-; Soviet Army 41-46; Chair. Central Cttee. Azerbaijan Medical Workers Union 46-49; Minister of Public Health, Azerbaijan S.S.R. 54-58; Chair. Council of Ministers, Azerbaijan S.S.R. 58-59; Sec. Central Cttee. Communist Party of Azerbaijan S S.R. 58, First Sec. 59-; mem. Central Cttee. C.P.S.U. 61-; Dep. to Supreme Soviet of U.S.S.R.
Central Committee of the Communist Party of Azerbaijan, Baku, Azerbaijan S.S.R., U.S.S.R.

Akhunova, Tursunoy; Soviet agricultural worker and politician; b. 1937; ed. school of mechanization of agriculture.
Driver-mechanic of cotton picking machine, S.M. Kirov Collective Farm, Chinaz District, Tashkent Region, Uzbek S.S.R.; mem. C.P.S.U. 62-; mem. Supreme Soviet of U.S.S.R.; mem. Central Cttee. Komsomol of Uzbekistan, Central Cttee. of C.P. of Uzbekistan; Hero of Socialist Labour.
Kirov Collective Farm, Chinaz District, Tashkent Region, Uzbek S.S.R., U.S.S.R.

Akilandam, Perungalur Vaithialingam (*pseudonym* Akilon); Indian Tamil writer; b. 7 Feb. 1923; ed. Maharaja's Coll., Pudukkottai.
Writer 40-; in Indian Post & Telegraph Dept. 45-58; freelance writer 58-; Sec. Tamil Writers' Asscn., Tiruchy 53-57; Sec. Gen. Fed. of All-India Tamil Writers 62-; Dir. Tamil Writers' Co-op. Soc. 63-; mem. Tamil Advisory Board, Sahitya Akademi 64-; Producer, Spoken Word in Tamil, All-India Radio, Madras 65-; Pres. Tamil Writers Asscn. 67; Kalai Magai Prize for *Penn* 46, Tamil Akademi Award for *Nenjin Alaigai* 53, Sahitya Akademi Award for *Vengaiyin Maindan* 63.
Publs. include: novels: *Penn* 46, *Snehithi* 50, *Nenjin Alaigai* 53, *Pavai Vilakku* 58, *Vengaiyin Maindan* 61, *Ponmalar* 64, *Kayalvizhi* 64, *Chittirap Paavai* 67; short stories: *Sakthivel* 47, *Nilavinilay* 50, *Vazhi Pirandhadu* 52, *Sahodara Andro?* 63, *Nellore Arisi* 67.
171 Lloyds Road, Madras 14, India.
Telephone: 81968.

Akimov, Nikolai Pavlovich; Soviet producer and artist; b. 1901; ed. Art School.
Stage designer 22-; Producer 32-; Chief Producer Leningrad Comedy Theatre 35-49, 55-; Chief Producer, Lensovet Theatre 51-55; produced *Krechinsky's Wedding*, Paris 66; People's Artist of U.S.S.R. 61-.
Leningrad Comedy Theatre, Nevsky Prospekt 56, Leningrad, U.S.S.R.

Aklilou Abte-Wold, Teshafi Teezaz, L. en D.; Ethiopian politician; b. 12 March 1912; ed. French Lycée, Alexandria, Univ. of Paris and Ecole des Sciences politiques, Paris.
Chargé d'Affaires, Ethiopian Legation, Paris 36-40; Vice-Minister of the Pen 42-43; Vice-Minister (and acting Minister) for Foreign Affairs 43-49; Minister for Foreign Affairs 49; Acting Chief Del., San Francisco Conf. 45 and Ethiopian signatory U.N. Gen. Assembly from 1st to 7th session and 10th session; mem. Consultative Cttee. for Legislation 43-; Pres. Board of Education 47-; mem. Board of Dirs. State Bank of Ethiopia; Chief Del. of Ethiopia, Suez Conf., London 56; Deputy Prime Minister and Minister for Foreign Affairs (with the title of Blattenguetta) 58-60; Prime Minister and Minister of the Pen 61-63; Prime Minister 63-; awards include Grand Officier Légion d'Honneur; Grand Officer of Trinity (Ethiopia); Grand Cordon of Menelik II (Ethiopia), Ismail (Egypt), El Sol del Peru, Order of Orange Nassau, Flag of Yugoslavia, St. George (Greece) and the Aztec Eagle (Mexico); Grand Cross Orders of the North Star (Sweden), Dannebrog (Denmark), St. Olav (Norway), Merit (Germany); Hon. G.C.V.O.
Prime Minister's Office, P.O. Box 1031, Addis Ababa, Ethiopia.

Aknazarov, Zekeriya Sharafutdinovich; Soviet politician; b. 1924; ed. Sverdlovsk Inter-Regional Party School and Bashkirian Pedagogical Inst.
Soviet Army 42-45; mem. C.P.S.U. 45-; Second Sec. Baimak District Cttee. of Lenin Young Communist League; Young Communist League official 48-51; First Sec. Bashkir Regional Cttee. of Young Communist League 51-54; official of Bashkir Regional Cttee. of C.P.S.U. 54-60; Research student at Acad. of Social Sciences of C.P.S.U. Central Cttee. 60-62; Chair. Council of Ministers of Bashkir Autonomous S.S.R. 62-; mem. Central Auditing Comm. of C.P.S.U.; Deputy to U.S.S.R. Supreme Soviet.
Council of Ministers of Bashkir A.S.S.R., Ufa, U.S.S.R.

Aksenov, Vassily Pavlovich; Soviet writer; b. 20 Aug. 1932; ed. Leningrad Medical Inst.
Physician 56-60; professional writer 60-; mem. Union of Soviet Writers; mem. Editorial Board *Yunosti* (magazine).
Publs. Novels: *Colleagues* 60, *Starry Ticket* 61, *Oranges from Morocco* 63, *Time, My Friend, Time* 64; collected stories: *Catapult* 64, *Half Way to the Moon* 66; screenplay for films; *Colleague, My Young Friend, When they Raise the Bridges, Travelling* 67; play: *Always Sell* 65.
Union of Soviet Writers, 52 Vorovsky Street, Moscow, U.S.S.R.

Aksyonov, Alexander Nikiforovich; Soviet politician; b. 1924; ed. Higher Party School of C.P.S.U. Central Committee.
Collective farmer 41-42; Soviet Army 42-43; Young Communist League official 43-57; Minister of Public Order of Byelorussian S.S.R. 60-65; First Sec. Vitebsk Regional Cttee. of C.P. of Byelorussia 65-; mem. Central Cttee. C.P. of Byelorussia; Deputy to U.S.S.R. Supreme Soviet.
Vitebsk Regional Committee of Communist Party of Byelorussia, Vitebsk, U.S.S.R.

Akufo-Addo, Edward, M.O.V., M.A.; Ghanaian lawyer; b. 1906; ed. Presbyterian Church Seminary, Akropong, Achimota School, St. Peter's Coll., Oxford, and Middle Temple, London.
Member Legis. Council, Ghana 49-50; mem. Coussey Constitutional Comm., Ghana 49; Judge of Ghana Supreme Court 62-64; Chair. Political Cttee. of Nat. Liberation Council 66; Chair. Board of Dirs. Ghana Commercial Bank 66; Chair. Constitutional Comm., Ghana 66-; Chief Justice of Ghana Sept. 66-; Chair. Gen. Legal Council, Ghana 66-; Chair. Council of Univ. of Ghana 66-; mem. London Inst. of World Affairs; Hon. Fellow St. Peter's Coll., Oxford.
Chief Justice's Chambers, Supreme Court, Accra; Home: Yeboaa Buw, 46/5 Nima Road, Ringway Central, Accra, Ghana.
Telephone: 63951, Ext. 256 (Chambers); Home: 63534.

Alaini, Muhsin; Yemeni diplomatist; b. 1932; ed. Cairo Univ. and Univ. de Paris.
Schoolteacher, Aden 58-60; Int. Confed. of Arab Trade Unions 60-62; Minister of Foreign Affairs, Yemen Arab Repub. Sept.-Dec. 62, 65; Perm. Rep. to UN Dec. 62-65, 65-67, 68-; Amb. to U.S.A. 63-65, 65-67, 68-; Prime Minister Nov.-Dec. 67.
Permanent Mission of Yemen Arab Republic to the United Nations, 211 East 43rd Street, 19th Floor, New York, N.Y., U.S.A.

Alam, Assadollah; Iranian agriculturalist and politician; b. 19; ed. Karaj Agricultural College, Univ. of Teheran.
Gov.-Gen. of Baluchistan 45-48; Minister of the Interior 48, of Agriculture 49, of Labour 50; Superintendent of the Pahlavi Estates and mem. of the High Council for their disposal 51; fmr. Dir. Pahlavi Foundation; Minister of the Interior 55-57; Leader People's Party 56-; Prime Minister July 62-March 64; Chancellor Pahlavi Univ.; Minister of the Imperial Court 66-.
Ministry of the Imperial Court, Teheran, Iran.

Alami, Musa; Jordanian agronomist; b. c. 1895; ed. American Univ. of Beirut and England.
Practised law in Palestine; propaganda for Arab claims to Palestine; founded Arab Development Soc. 43; left Palestine 48; lived in Jericho and began farming in desert 48-.
Arab Development Society, P.O.B. 16, Jericho, Jordan.

Alamuddin, Najib Salim, B.A.; Lebanese airline executive; b. 9 March 1909; ed. American Univ. of Beirut and Coll. of South West, Exeter, England.
Teacher of Engineering and Mathematics, American Univ. of Beirut 29-33; Insp. of Mathematics, Education Dept., Govt. of Trans-Jordan; Insp.-Gen. of Customs, Trade and Industry, Trans-Jordan 33-40; Chief Sec. Govt. of Trans-Jordan 40-42; founded Near East Resources Co. 42; Gen. Man. Middle East Airlines 52-56, Chair. and Pres. 56-; Minister of Tourism and Information 65; Minister of Public Works 65-66; mem. Supreme Econ. Council of Lebanon, Exec. Cttee. of Int. Air Transport Asscn.; dir. several Lebanese companies.
Middle East Airlines Airliban, Beirut International Airport, Beirut, Lebanon.
Telephone: 270080.

Alarcón de Quesada, Ricardo; Cuban diplomatist; b. 21 May 1937; ed. Univ. de Habana.
Head of Student Section, Provincial Office of 26 July Revolutionary Movement 57-59; Pres. Univ. Students' Fed., Sec. Union of Young Communists; Dir. for Regional Policies (Latin America), Ministry of Foreign Affairs 62-66; mem. Governing Council of Inst. for Int. Politics, Ministry of Foreign Affairs; Perm. Rep. of Cuba to the UN 66-.
Permanent Mission of Cuba to the United Nations, 6 East 67th Street, New York, N.Y. 10021, U.S.A.

Alatriste Abrego, Sealtiel; Mexican civil servant; ed. Universidad Nacional Autónoma de México and Escuela Nacional de Comercio y Administración.
Former Public Accountant, Treas. Fed. District, and Under-Sec. for Nat. Patrimony; Dir.-Gen. Instituto Mexicano del Seguro Social; articles on accountancy and economics.
Instituto Mexicano del Seguro Social, Mexico D.F., Mexico.

Albarranc, Adrien; French scientist and journalist; b. 6 March 1913; ed. Ecole Nationale Supérieure d'Electrotechnique and Faculté des Sciences, Grenoble. Sometime Asst. at the Ecole Française de Papeterie de Grenoble and engineer and technical adviser to the Papeteries Navarre; now Man.-Dir. of Editions M.P. and Impacar; Admin. Impression des Documents multiples, Nouvelles Messageries de la Presse Parisienne, Precilec; Pres. of "Le Modèle Réduit", and "Albaco" and "Coopérative de la Presse Périodique"; Officier de la Légion d'Honneur; Croix de Guerre 39-45; Médaille de la Résistance; Legion of Merit; King's Medal; Croix de Guerre Belge; Médaille de la Résistance Polonaise.
154 rue du Faubourg, Saint-Denis, Paris 10e, France; Home: 3 rue de Logelbach, Paris 17e, France.

Albee, Edward; American playwright; b. 12 March 1928; ed. Lawrenceville and Choate Schools, Washington, and Columbia Univ.
Has written a number of plays, including: *The Death of Bessie Smith, The American Dream, The Sand Box* 61, *The Zoo Story* 61, *Who's Afraid of Virginia Woolf* 62, stage adaptation of *The Ballad of the Sad Café* (Carson McCullers) 63, *Tiny Alice* 64, *Malcolm* (from novel by James Purdy) 66, *A Delicate Balance* (Pulitzer Prize 67) 66, *Everything in the Garden* (after a play by Giles Cooper) 67, two one-act plays: *Box* and *Quotations from Chairman Mao Tse-tung* 68.
c/o The William Morris Agency, 1470 Broadway, New York, N.Y., U.S.A.

Albers, Josef; American (b. German) painter and art teacher; b. 19 March 1888; ed. Teachers' Seminary, Royal Art School, Berlin, Art Acad., Munich, Bauhaus, Weimar.
Teacher in public schools 08-13, 15-19; Prof. at Bauhaus, Weimar, Dessau, Berlin 23-33; Prof. of Art, Black Mountain Coll., N.C., U.S.A. 33-49; Prof. of Art and Chair. Yale Univ. School of Art 50-58, Prof. Emeritus 58-, Visiting Critic 58-60; mem. Nat. Inst. of Arts and Letters 68-; paintings in numerous American, Australian and European museums and galleries; Ada S. Garret Prize 54; William Clark Prize 57; Award for Painting, Pittsburgh Int. Exhbn. 67; D.F.A. h.c. Univ. of Hartford, Conn. 57, Yale Univ. 62, California Coll. of Arts and Crafts 64, Univ. of Chapel Hill 67; Hon. LL.D. (Univ. of Bridgeport) 66; Hon. Dr. Phil. (Ruhr Univ., Bochum) 67; Officers' Cross of Order of Merit, German Fed. Rep. 57, Ford Foundation Grant 59, 1964 Gold Medal, American Inst. of Graphic Arts, Grosse Verdienstkreuz des Verdienstordens der Bundesrepublik Deutschland 68, etc.
8 North Forest Circle, New Haven, Conn. 06515, U.S.A. Telephone: New Haven (Conn.) 387-5300.

Albert, A(braham) Adrian, M.S., PH.D.; American mathematician; b. 9 Nov. 1905; ed. Univ. of Chicago.
Nat. Research Council Fellow 28-29; Instructor in Mathematics, Columbia Univ. 29-31; Asst. Prof. in Mathematics, Univ. of Chicago 31-37, Associate Prof. 37-41, Prof. 41-60, E. H. Moore Distinguished Service Prof. 60-; Associate Dir. Applied Mathematics Group, Northwestern Univ. 44-45; Editor *Bulletin of American Mathematical Society* 39-43 and of Colloquium Publications of A.M.S. 51-57; Man. Editor *Transactions* 43-49; Editor *Mathematical Surveys* 41-45; *Toronto Mathematical Series* 43-; Chair. Div. of Mathematics, Nat. Research Council 52-55; mem. Nat. Acad. of

Sciences, Mathematical Asscn. of America, Brazilian Acad. of Sciences, São Paulo Mathematical Society, Argentine Acad. of Sciences, American Asscn. for the Advancement of Science; mem. Gen. Sciences Advisory Panel (to Director of Defense for Research and Development) 54-; Advisory Cttee. to U.S. Commr. of Education 63-; Vice-Pres. American Mathematical Soc. 56-58, Pres. 65-66; Chair. Dept. of Mathematics, Univ. of Chicago 58-62, Dean, Div. of Physical Sciences 62-; Chair. Section of Mathematics, Nat. Acad. of Sciences 58-61; Dir. Communications Research Div. Inst. for Defense Analyses 61-62; Hon. mem. Argentine Mathematical Soc. and Mexican Mathematical Soc. 65-; Hon. LL.D. (Notre Dame) 65.
Publs. *Modern Higher Algebra* 36, *Structure of Algebras* 39, *Introduction to Algebraic Theories* 40, *College Algebra* 46, *Solid Analytic Geometry* 49, *Fundamental Concepts of Modern Algebra* 56; Ed. *Studies in Modern Algebra* 63. 1359 E. Park Place, Chicago, Illinois 60637, U.S.A.

Albert, Calvin; American sculptor; b. 19 Nov. 1918; ed. Inst. of Design, Chicago, Art Inst. of Chicago and Archipenko School of Sculpture.
Teacher, New York Univ. 49-52, Brooklyn Coll. 47-49, Inst. of Design 42-46; Teacher Pratt Inst. 49-, Head of Graduate Sculpture Program 65-; first one-man exhbn. Theobald Gallery, Chicago 41, other exhbns. in the U.S. and Galleria George Lester, Rome; sculpture and drawings in collections of Whitney Museum, Metropolitan Msueum, Jewish Museum, Art Inst. of Chicago, Detroit Inst. of Arts, Univ. of Nebraska, Chrysler Museum of Art and William Rockhill Nelson Gallery of Art; Fulbright Advanced Research Grant to Italy 61; Tiffany Grants 63, 65; Guggenheim Fellowship 66. Publ. *Figure Drawing Comes to Life* (with Dorothy Seckler).
222 Willoughby Avenue, Brooklyn, New York 11205, U.S.A.

Albert, Carl Bert, A.B., B.A., B.C.L., LL.D.; American lawyer and politician; b. 10 May 1908; ed. Univ. of Oklahoma and Oxford Univ.
Admitted to Oklahoma Bar 36; Legal Clerk, Federal Housing Admin. 35-37; practised law, Oklahoma City 37; attorney and accountant Sayre Oil Co. 37-38; law practice, Mattoon, Ill. 38-39; legal dept., Ohio Oil Co 39-40; served army 41-46; practised law McAlester, Oklahoma 46-47; mem. House of Reps. 47-, Democratic Whip 55; Majority Leader 62-; Bronze Star.
827 E. Osage, McAlester, Oklahoma, U.S.A.
Telephone: 918-GA3-6318; 202-225-4565.

Albertz, Heinrich; German politician; b. 22 Jan. 1915; ed. theological studies in Berlin, Halle and Breslau.
Curate in Berlin 37, arrested during Second World War as active member of Protestant Church; Head of Refugee Office, City of Celle 46; mem. Social Democrat Party (S.P.D.) 46-; Rep. for Refugees, Lower Saxony Landtag 47; mem. Refugee Council, Exec. Cttee. of S.P.D. 47; Dir. of Senate Cttee. for People's Welfare, West Berlin 55-59; Head of Senate Chancellery, West Berlin 61-63; Senator for Internal Affairs, West Berlin 61-63; Deputy Mayor and Senator for Internal Affairs 65-66; Mayor of West Berlin Dec. 66-67; Niedersächsische Landesmedaille, Grosses Verdienstkreuz mit Stern und Schulterband.
1 Berlin 33, Taubertstrasse 19, Germany.
Telephone: 891119.

Albery, Sir Bronson James, Kt., B.A.; British theatre director; b. 6 March 1881; ed. Uppingham and Balliol Coll., Oxford.
Barrister-at-Law 05; Lieut. R.N.V.R. 17-19; Pres. Society of West End Theatre Managers 41-45 and 52-53; Chair. Theatres' War Service Council 42-45; Joint-Admin. of Old Vic and Sadler's Wells 42-44; Chair. Old

Vic Trust 51-59; Chair. British Council Drama Advisory Cttee. 54-61; Man. Dir. The Wyndham Theatres Ltd. 25-62, Chair. 62-65; Gov. Old Vic.
8 Lees Place, London, W.1, England.

Albrecht, Jerzy; Polish politician; b. 14; ed. Warsaw Acad. of Political Sciences.
One of the organizers of the Polish Workers' Party during Nazi occupation; imprisoned in concentration camp 42-45; mem. Cen. Cttee. Polish United Workers' Party 45-, Sec. 56-59; Chair. Presidium, Warsaw Nat. Council (municipal council) 49-56; Deputy Chair. Council of State 57-59; Minister of Finance 61-.
12 Swiętokrzyska, Warsaw, Poland.

Albright, William F., PH.D., LITT.D., D.H.L., TH.D., LL.D., D.H.C., D.C.L., L.H.D., H.H.D.; American orientalist and archaeologist; b. 24 May 1891; ed. Upper Iowa and Johns Hopkins Univs.
Thayer Fellow, American School of Oriental Research in Jerusalem 19-20, Acting Dir. 20-21, and Dir. 21-29 and 33-36; W. W. Spence Prof. of Semitic Languages, Johns Hopkins Univ. 29-58; Vice-Pres. American Schools of Oriental Research 37-66; Dir. Excavations at Gibeah of Saul, Tell Beit Mirsim and Bethel; Chief Archaeologist, Sinai 47-48, Beihan (South Arabia) 50-51; mem. Nat. Acad. of Sciences (Washington), American Philosophical Society (Vice-Pres. 56-59), American Acad. Arts and Sciences; foreign mem. Royal Danish, Flemish and Irish Acads.; corresp. mem. Inst. de France and Austrian Acad. of Sciences; Corresp. Fellow, British Acad.; Hon. Fellow, German Archaeological Inst.; mem. (hon.) Société Asiatique, Glasgow Oriental Society, British Society for Old Testament Study; Pres. Int. Org. of Old Testament Scholars 56-59; American Council Learned Socs. prize for research in humanities; Gold Medal of Archaeological Inst. of America 67.
Publs. *Excavation at Gibeah of Benjamin* 24, *The Spoken Arabic of Palestine* 27, *The Archæology of Palestine and the Bible* 32, *The Excavation of Tell Beit Mirsim* 32-41, *The Vocalisation of the Egyptian Syllabic Orthography* 34, *Recent Discoveries in Bible Lands* 36, *From the Stone Age to Christianity* 40, *Archæology and the Religion of Israel* 42, *Archaeology of Palestine* 49, *Recent Discoveries in Bible Lands* 56, *The Biblical Period from Abraham to Ezra* 63, *History, Archaeology and Christian Humanism* 64, *Yahweh and the Gods of Canaan* 68.
Johns Hopkins Univ., Baltimore, Md. 21218; Home: 3401 Greenway, Baltimore, Maryland 21218, U.S.A.
Telephone: 301-467-9859 (Home).

Alcobre Ares, Manuel; Argentine writer; b. 7 June 1900; ed. Commercial Secondary School.
Editor daily *Crítica* 30-38, review *Estampa* 38-41; Sec.-Gen. Asscn. Argentine Writers 49-51; Prof. of Castillian and Literature in Technical Schools; Municipal Poetry Prize, Buenos Aires; Nat. Poetry Prize of Nat. Cultural Comm.
Publs. Poetry: *Paisajes Civiles* 28, *Poemas de Media Estación* 31, *Espuma en la Arena* 37, *Hogar y Paisajes Nuevos* 40, *Acento Forestal* 43, *El Arbol Solariego* 46, *Canción en Sol de Despedida* 49, *Silvas de la Tierra que Fué Mar* 55, *Estación Terminal* 57, *Epístola al Cielo* 60, *Patria! Argentina!* 60; prose: *Luces a la Distancia* 34, *Bajo el Paraguay* 35.
Calle Joaquin V. Gonzales 4292, Buenos Aires, Argentina.

Alcock, Frederick James, B.A., PH.D., F.R.S.C.; Canadian geologist; b. 16 Nov. 1888; ed. Yale Univ. and Univs. of Toronto and Wisconsin.
With Geological Survey of Canada 16-47; Chief Curator, Nat. Museum of Canada 47-56; Fellow Royal Society of Canada 25- (Pres. of Section IV 47-48, Hon. Sec. 44-49); Fellow Geological Society of America, mem. of Council 42-45; Fellow Royal Canadian Geographical Soc., mem. Editorial Board 42-; mem. Canadian Inst. of Mining and Metallurgy.

Publs. 38 Geological Maps; over 100 papers on the geology and geography of Canada.
398 Third Avenue, Ottawa, Ont., Canada.
Telephone: 234-5790.

Alconada Aramburú, Carlos Román Santiago; Argentine lawyer and politician; b. 20; ed. Colegio San Luis, La Plata, Colegio Nacional and Universidad Nacional, La Plata.
Member Judicial Authority, Prov. of Buenos Aires 43-52, Public Prosecutor 55-57; Minister of Interior 57-58, of Educ. and Justice 63-66; Prof. of Commercial Law and of Private Law, Universidad Nacional, La Plata; Unión Cívica Radical del Pueblo.
Publs. *Código de Comercio Anotado* (3 vols.) 54-60, *Cuestiones Institucionales* 62, *Arbitraje y Abogacía* 62.
Universidad Nacional de la Plata, Calle 7 entre 47 y 48, La Plata, Argentina.

Alcorn, (Hugh) Meade, A.B., LL.B.; American politician; b. 20 Oct. 1907; ed. Dartmouth Coll. and Yale Univ.
Admitted to Connecticut Bar 33; Asst. State's Attorney, Hartford County, 35-42, State's Attorney 42-48; mem. Connecticut House of Reps. 37, 39 and 41, Majority Leader 39, Speaker 41; Republican Chair. Suffield, Conn. 38-53; del. Republican Nat. Convention 40, 48, 52, 56 (Chair.); alt. del. 44; Seventh District Committeeman; Nat. Committeeman from Conn. 53-61; Vice-Chair. Cttee. on Arrangements for 1956 Republican Nat. Convention 56; Chair. Republican Nat. Cttee. 57-59; mem. Hartford County, Conn. State (Pres. 50-51) and American Bar Asscns., American Judicature Soc.; Vice-Pres. and Dir. First Nat. Bank of Suffield; Dir. United Bank & Trust Co., Hartford, Conn.
49 Russell Avenue, Suffield, Conn., U.S.A.
Telephone: 668-7306.

Alcover y Sureda, José Felipe; Spanish diplomatist; b. 26 May 1903; ed. Univs. of Barcelona, Madrid, Paris and London.
Entered Foreign Service 29, Vice-Consul, New York 30-33, served Bogotá, Bucharest and Rome 33-39; in Ministry of Foreign Affairs 40 and 44; Consul in Casablanca 43; served Rome 45-51, Paris 52; Dir. Middle East Dept., Ministry of Foreign Affairs 53; Consul-Gen. Rabat 54-56; Amb. to Morocco 56-58; Amb. to U.A.R. 58-62; Amb. to Algeria 62-64, to Sweden 64-; Gran Cruz del Mérito Civil, Caballero de la Orden de Carlos III, Comendador con placa de la Orden de Isabel La Católica, and other Spanish and foreign decorations.
Spanish Embassy, F.d. Prins Carls Palats, Djurgården, Stockholm No, Sweden.

Aldenham, Baron; **Walter Durant Gibbs;** British company director; b. 11 Oct. 1888; ed. Eton and Trinity Coll., Cambridge.
Served First World War Gallipoli, Palestine and Persia 14-18; Chair. Antony Gibbs & Sons, Merchant Bankers 39-65, Dir. 65-, Australian Pastoral Co. Ltd.; Chair. Westminister Bank Ltd. 50-61, Dir. 61-; fmr. mem. Cttee. of London Clearing Bankers; Dir. Commercial Union Assurance Co. Ltd., English, Scottish, Australian Bank Ltd., etc.; Pres. British Asscn. of Bankers 54-55.
Briggens, Ware, Herts., England.

Alderton, George Edwin Lisle, C.M.G.; New Zealand lawyer and diplomatist; b. 11 Jan. 1888; ed. Grammar School and Univ. Coll., Auckland.
Former barrister and solicitor, Lisle, Alderton & Kingston; served Navy 15-18 and 39-42; mem. Transport Appeal Board and Co-ordination Board 34-36; Dir. Devonport Ferry Co. and North Shore Transport Co.; Chair. Auckland Div. Nat. Party 36-37; Vice-Pres. New Zealand Nat. Party 38; High Commr. for New Zealand in Australia 50-58.
33 Portland Road, Auckland, New Zealand.

Aldewereld, Siem; Netherlands banker; b. 09; ed. Amsterdam Univ.

Entered service of Rotterdam Bank, Amsterdam 30; Govt. Dir. of Foreign Exchange Control, Curaçao 40; during the war, Supervisor of Netherlands East Indies assets in Western Hemisphere, New York 42; Financial Adviser for Netherlands Indies affairs, Netherlands Embassy, Washington; Asst. to Treas. Int. Bank for Reconstruction and Development 46-52, Asst. Dir. 52-55, Dir. Department of Technical Operations 55-65, Vice-Pres. Int. Bank for Reconstruction and Development 65-.

International Bank for Reconstruction and Development, Washington, D.C.; Home: 2801 New Mexico Avenue, N.W., Apartment 1407, Washington, D.C. 20007, U.S.A.

Telephone: 965-3136.

Aldington, 1st Baron (cr. 62); **Toby Austin Richard William Low,** P.C., K.C.M.G., C.B.E., D.S.O., T.D.; British banker and industrialist; b. 25 May 1914.

Called to Bar 39; Army Service 39-45; Conservative M.P. 45-62; Parl. Sec. to Ministry of Supply 51-54; Minister of State, Board of Trade 54-57; Dep. Chair. Conservative Party Org. 59-63; Chair. National and Grindlays Bank Ltd.; Chair. General Electric Co. Ltd.; Chair. Associated Electrical Industries Ltd.; Chair. Exporters Refinance Corpn. Ltd.; Dir. John Brown & Co. Ltd., English China Clays Ltd., The London Assurance, Sun Alliance and London Insurance Ltd., United Power Co. Ltd. (Chair.), Nat. Discount Co. Ltd., Wm. Brandt's Sons & Co. Ltd., Lloyds Bank Ltd.

Knoll Farm, Aldington, nr. Ashford, Kent; and 19 Cadogan Gardens, London, S.W.3, England.

Aldrich, Hulbert Stratton, PH.B.; American banker; b. 3 April 1907; ed. Phillips Acad. and Yale Univ.

Joined New York Trust Co. 30, Asst. Treas. 39-43, Vice-Pres. 43-52, Pres. 52-59 (co. merged with Chemical Corn Exchange Bank to form Chemical Bank New York Trust Co.); Vice-Chair. Chemical Bank New York Trust Co. 59-; Dir. numerous other companies.

Home: 1088 Park Avenue, New York City; Office: 20 Pine Street, New York City, N.Y., U.S.A.

Telephone: 770-1511.

Aldrich, Winthrop Williams, A.B., LL.B., LL.D., D.SC.; American banker and diplomatist; b. 2 Nov. 1885; ed. Harvard Univ. Law School.

U.S. Ambassador to Great Britain 53-57; fmr. Chair. Board of Dirs., Chase Manhattan Bank; mem. Bar, State of New York.

Room 5600, 30 Rockefeller Plaza, New York 20, N.Y., and 960 Fifth Avenue, New York 21, N.Y., U.S.A.

Alegría, Ciro; Peruvian writer; b. 1909; ed. Colégio de San Juan.

One of leaders of *aprista* movement; imprisoned 31-33; exiled to Chile for pro-Indian socialist agitation 34.

Publs. include: *La serpiente de oro* 35, *Los perros hambrientos* 39, *El mundo es ancho y ajeno* 41, *Duelo de caballeros* 63, *Novelas completas* 64.

c/o Editorial Losada, S.A., Alsina 1131, Buenos Aires, Argentina.

Aleixandre, Vicente; Spanish writer; b. 1898; ed. Univ. of Madrid.

Member Spanish Acad., Hispanic Soc. of America, Monde Latin Paris Acad.; corresp. mem. Sciences and Arts, Puerto Rico Acad. Arts, Malaga Acad., Hipano-american Bogotá Acad.; awarded Nat. Prize of Literature.

Publs. *Ambito* 28, *Espadas como Labios* 32, *Pasión de la Tierra* 35, *La Destrucción o el Amor* 35, *Sombra del Paraiso* 44, *Mundo a Solas* 50, *Vida del Poeta: El amor y la poesía* 50, *Poemas Paradisiacos* 52, *Nacimiento Ultimo* 53, *Historia del Corazón* 54, *Algunos Caracteres de la Nueva Poesía Española* 55, *Ocho Poemas de Aleixandre* 55, *Mis Poemas Mejores* 57, *Los Encuentros* 58, *Poemas Amorosos* 60, *Poesías Completas* 60, *Picasso* 61, *Antigua Casa Madrileña* 61, *En Un Vasto Dominio* 62, *María la Gorda* 63, *Retratos con Nombre* 65, *Presencias* 65, *Dos Vidas* 67.

Velintonia 3 (Parque Metropolitano), Madrid 3, Spain.

Aleixo, Pedro; Brazilian politician; b. 1 Aug. 1901; ed. Univ. de Minas Gerais.

Councellor, Deliberative Council of Minas Gerais; Dir. Estado de Minas; Sec., later Pres. of Consultative Council of Minas Gerais 31; Pres. of Admin. Reform Comm. of Minas Gerais 33; Deputy to Nat. Constituent Assembly 33; Fed. Deputy 34-37, 59-66, Majority Leader 35-36, 64; Pres. of Chamber of Deputies 37; Pres. Inst. of Lawyers 38; Dir. Banco Hypotecário do Estado de Minas Gerais 38-43; Law Posts, Univ. of Minas Gerais and Univ. Católica de Minas Gerais 49-; Deputy to Minas Gerais Constituent Assembly 47; Sec. of Interior and Justice, Minas Gerais 47-50; Fed. Minister of Educ. and Culture 66; Vice-Pres. of Brazil 66-; Aliança Renovadora Nacional (ARENA).

Office of the Vice-President, Brasilia, Brazil.

Alejos Arzu, Carlos; Guatemalan diplomatist; b. 18; ed. Instituto Modelo, Guatemala, and Economic Univ., Guatemala.

Assistant Accountant, Packard Agency; Accountant, Eichenberg and Guatemala Bookstore; Partner, sub-Man. Cia. Automotrix Guatemalteca; Partner, Helvetia Plantation, San Sebastian; Owner, Zambe Plantation; Ambassador to United States 60-63.

c/o Ministry of Foreign Affairs, Guatemala City, Guatemala.

Alekperov, Aziz Aga-Aga-baba; Soviet foreign trade official; b. 1916; ed. Inst. of Foreign Trade, Moscow.

Has worked in foreign trade 38-; various posts in All-Union *Vostokintorg* (Eastern Foreign Trade) Asscn., Chair. 65-.

All-Union *Vostokintorg* Association, 32-34 Smolenskaya-Sennaya Ploshchad, Moscow, U.S.S.R.

Alekseev, Mikhail Pavlovich; Soviet (Russian) professor of literature; b. 1896; ed. Univ. of Kiev.

Lecturer, Kiev Univ. 19-20, Odessa Univ. 21-27; Prof. Leningrad Univ 32-60, Head of Dept. of Philology 45-47, 50-53; corresp. mem. U.S.S.R. Acad. of Sciences, 46-58, mem. 58-; mem. Inst. of Russian Literature of Acad. of Sciences, Leningrad; Head Sector of Interrelations of Russian and foreign literatures; Chair. Pushkin Comm., U.S.S.R. Acad. of Sciences; Hon. Ph.D. (Univ. of Rostock); Hon. D.Litt. (Univ. of Oxford), Hon. D. ès L. (Bordeaux and Paris); Hon. D.Phil. (Univ. of Budapest).

Publs. *Siberia in the References of European Travellers and Writers,* 2 vols. 32, 36, 2nd. edn. 46, *History of English Literature* 43, 60, *The Russian Language in England* 44, *The English Language in Russia* 46, *Pushkin and the Science of his Time* 56, *Hogarth and his Analysis of Beauty* 58, *Byron MSS in the U.S.S.R.* 58, *Letters of Turgenev* 61, *Hispano-Russian Literary Relations* 64, *Shakespeare and Russian Culture* 65, *Pushkin's "Monument"* 67.

Institute of Russian Literature (Pushkin House), 4 nab. Makarova, Leningrad, U.S.S.R.

Alemaiyehou, Haddis; Ethiopian diplomatist and politician; b. 17 Oct. 1913; ed. Taffari Makonnen School, Addis Ababa and American Univ., Washington.

Ministry of Education 32-35; Ethiopian Army 35-36; Resistance Forces 36-37, exiled in Italy 37-43; Dep. Dir. Press and Information Dept. 44-45; Consul, Jerusalem 45-47, First Sec., Washington 47-50; Dir.-Gen. Ministry of Foreign Affairs 50-52, Vice-Minister 52-56; Perm. Rep. to UN 56-59; Minister of State for Foreign Affairs 60-61, Minister of Education 61,

Ambassador to U.K. 61-66, to the Netherlands 62-66; Minister of Planning and Development 66-.
Ministry of Planning and Development, Addis Ababa; Ethiopia.

Alemán, Miguel; Mexican government official; b. 05; ed. Universidad Nacional Autónoma de Mexico.
Private law practice, later Magistrate, High Court of Justice 28-35; Senator 35-36; Gov. of Veracruz 36-40; Sec. for Govt. under President Camacho 40-45; President of Mexico 46-52; later Pres. Nat. Council for Tourism.
c/o Consejo Nacional de Turismo, Mexico City, Mexico.

Alemann, Roberto Teodoro; Argentine diplomatist and economist; b. 22 Dec. 1922; ed. National Univ. of Buenos Aires, Univ. of Berne.
Financial Counsellor, London 56; Treasury Dir., Adviser to Ministry of Economy 58; Under-Sec. of Economy, Financial Counsellor, Washington 59; Minister of Economy 61; Ambassador to United States 62-63; Prof. of Econs., Law School, Univ. of Buenos Aires 62.
Melian 1831, Buenos Aires, Argentina.

Alende, Oscar Eduardo; Argentine politician; b. 6 July 1909; ed. Universidad Nacional de La Plata and Univ. de Buenos Aires.
Educational Inspector, La Plata 26-30; Doctor at Banfield Hospital; Provincial Govt. Buenos Aires 48-55; mem. Constituent Assembly 57-; Gov. Buenos Aires 58-62; Presidential candidate of Unión Cívica Radical Intransigente (U.C.R.I.); Pres. U.C.R.I.
Maipú 295, Banfield, Province of Buenos Aires, Argentina.

Aler, Lieut.-Gen. Izaak Alphonse; Netherlands company director and Air Force officer; b. 3 May 1896; ed. Royal Military Acad., Breda.
Air Force Pilot 18-25; K.L.M. Pilot 26-39; recalled to Air Force as Staff Captain 39-40; prisoner of war in Stanislau and Neu Brandenburg 42-45; returned to active service 45-53; Knight in the Order of Orange-Nassau 48; mem. of Air Advisory Cttee. of European Defence Community 48; Chief of Air Staff 50; Knight in the Order of the Netherlands Lion 51; Commander in the Legion of Merit 51; mem. Board of Royal Netherlands Aircraft Factories "Fokker" 53; Grand Officer in the Order of Orange-Nassau and awarded "General Snijders" Gold Medal 53; Pres. K.L.M. (Royal Dutch Airlines) 54-61.
Huzarenlaan 18, Gorssel, Netherlands.
Telephone: 05759-1504.

Alessandri Rodríguez, Jorge; Chilean businessman and politician; b. 96; ed. Nat. Univ. of Chile.
Deputy from Santiago 25; fmr. Prof. School of Engineering, Santiago; fmr. mem. Public Works Comm.; Dir. of a number of paper factories and sugar refineries; Vice-Pres. Bank of South America; Minister of Finance 48-50; Senator 57; President of Chile 58-64.
Santiago, Chile.

Alessandrini, Adolfo; Italian diplomatist; b. 02; ed. Univ. of Bologna.
Entered Diplomatic Service 25, served Cairo, Klagenfurt, Belgrade 26-35; at Foreign Office, Rome 35-37; at Peking, Berne 37-41; Chief of Liaison Service with Allied Armies, Rome 44-46; Minister in Beirut 46-50; Ambassador to Greece 50-54; Perm. Rep. to NATO 54-58, 60-67; Sec.-Gen. Ministry of Foreign Affairs, Rome 58; Ambassador to Canada 59; Grand Cross of the Italian Order of Merit, Hon. K.B.E. (U.K.), Grand Officier de la Légion d'Honneur.
c/o Ministry of Foreign Affairs, Rome, Italy.

Alessandro, Victor; American conductor; b. 27 Nov. 1915; ed. Univ. of Rochester, N.Y., Mozarteum Acad., Salzburg, and Accad. Santa Cecilia, Rome.
Musical Dir. Oklahoma Symphony 38-51, San Antonio Symphony Orchestra and San Antonio Grand Opera Festival 51-; Alice M. Ditson Award, Columbia 56; Nat. Music Council Award 64.
San Antonio Symphony Orchestra, South Texas Building, San Antonio, Texas 78205, U.S.A.

Alewyn, Richard, PH.D.; German professor of German literature; b. 24 Feb. 1902; ed. Lessing-Gymnasium, Frankfurt, and Univs. of Frankfurt, Marburg, Munich and Heidelberg.
Privatdozent, Univ. of Berlin 31; Assoc. Prof. Univ. of Heidelberg 32-33; Visiting Prof. Sorbonne, Paris 33-35; Assoc. Prof. Queens Coll., New York 39-48, Prof. 48-49; Prof. Univ. of Cologne 49-55, Free Univ. of Berlin 55-59; Prof. of German Literature, Univ. of Bonn 59-; Ed. *Euphorion* 56-62; hon. mem. Modern Language Asscn. of America; Guest Lecturer, Univ. of Calif., Davis 68; mem. Akad. der Wissenschaften zu Göttingen, Arbeitsgemeinschaft für Forschung des Landes Nordrhein Westfalen, PEN Club.
Publs. *Vorbarocker Klassizismus* 26, 2nd edn. 62, *Johann Beer* 32, *Über Hugo Hofmannsthal* 58, 3rd ed. 63, *Das Grosse Welttheater* 59, French trans. *L'Univers du Baroque* 64.
11 Wurzerstrasse, Bad Godesberg, German Federal Republic.

Alexander, David; British banker; b. 26 April 1906; ed. The White House School, Brampton, Cumberland.
National Bank of Scotland 23, Gen. Manager 55, Dir. 58; Dir. and Gen. Manager, National Commercial Bank of Scotland Ltd. 59-67, Vice-Chair. 67-; Vice-Pres. British Bankers' Asscn. 65; Dir. Scottish Agricultural Securities Corpn., Lloyds & Scottish Ltd., Lloyds & Scottish Finance Ltd., Life Asscn. of Scotland Ltd., Beneficial Finance Corpn. Ltd., Adelaide, Australia.
The Shieling, Whitehouse Road, Edinburgh 4, Scotland.

Alexander, Henry Clay, A.B., LL.B.; American banker; b. 1 Aug. 1902; ed. public schools, Murfreesboro (Tenn.), Vanderbilt Univ. and Yale Univ. Law School.
Associated with law firm of Davis, Polk, Wardwell, Gardiner & Reed, New York 25-39; partner J. P. Morgan & Co. 39-40, Dir. and Vice-Pres. 40-48, Exec. Vice-Pres. 48-50, Pres. and Chief Exec. Officer 50-55, Chair. and Chief Exec. Officer 55-59; Chair. and Chief Exec. Officer Morgan Guaranty Trust Co. 59-65, Chair. Exec. Cttee. 65-67; Dir. Gen. Motors Corpn., Johns-Manville Corpn., Standard Brands Inc.; Trustee Consolidated Edison Co. of New York Inc.; mem. Business Council; Vice-Pres. Board of Trustees, Presbyterian Hospital; Trustee, Metropolitan Museum of Art, Alfred P. Sloan Foundation, United States Churchill Foundation; Vice-Chair. U.S. Strategic Bombing Survey in Second World War; Medal for Merit.
23 Wall Street, New York City, N.Y. 10015, U.S.A.

Alexander, Rt. Hon. Sir Ulick, P.C., G.C.B., G.C.V.O., C.M.G., O.B.E.; British company director; b. 10 Feb. 1889; ed. Eton and Sandhurst.
Coldstream Guards 09; served France, Egypt. Palestine, First World War, Egyptian Army 15-21; Military Sec. Egyptian Army 20-21; Political Sec. to Gov.-Gen. of South Africa 23-25; Comptroller of the Household, Duke and Duchess of Kent 28-36; Keeper of Privy Purse and Treasurer to the King 36-52, to the Queen 52; Receiver-Gen. to Duchy of Lancaster 36-52; Trustee Ascot Authority 42-52; Sec. Royal Victorian Order 42-52; Extra-Equerry to the King 37-52, to the Queen 52-; Chair. Tanganyika Concessions Ltd. 52-57, Dir. 57-63; Chair. Rhodesian Board, Standard Bank of S. Africa 53-57; Dir. Benguela Railway Co. (Angola) 52-64, Union Minière du Haut Katanga 54-63, Banque Belge Ltd., London 57-.
Flat B, 3 Cadogan Gardens, London, S.W.3, England.
Telephone: 01-730-6767.

Alexander, William Gemmell, M.B.E., M.A.; British co-operative official; b. 19 Aug. 1918; ed. Sedbergh School and Brasenose Coll., Oxford.

Army Service 39-45; Co-operative Societies Officer, Gilbert and Ellice Islands 46-51; Registrar of Co-operative Societies, Mauritius 51-55; Co-operative posts, Cyprus 55-60; Manager, Agricultural Dept., Co-operative Wholesale Society 60-63; Dir. Int. Co-operative Alliance 63-.

International Co-operative Alliance, 11 Upper Grosvenor Street, London, W.1; Home: Sheepcote, North Park, Gerrards Cross, Bucks., England.

Telephone: 01-499-5991 (Office); Gerrards Cross 84040 (Home).

Alexander of Tunis, 1st Earl, cr. 52; **Field-Marshal Harold Rupert Leofric George Alexander**, K.G., G.C.B., O.M., G.C.M.G., C.S.I., D.S.O., M.C., LL.D.; British officer; b. 10 Dec. 1891; ed. Harrow and Sandhurst.

Served First World War France 14-18; Loe-Agra Operations NW. Frontier 35, Mohmand Operations 35; commanded regiment and regimental district of Irish Guards 28-30; Gen. Staff Officer, 1st Grade Northern Command 32-34; Commander Nowshera Brigade, Northern Command India 34-38; A.D.C. to the King 36-37; Commander 1st Div. 38-40; Gen. Officer Commanding-in-Chief Southern Command 40-42; Officer Commanding Burma 42; C.-in-C. Middle East 42-43; Deputy C.-in-C. N. Africa 43; Military Gov. of Sicily 43; C.-in-C. Allied Armies in Italy 44-45; Supreme Allied Commander 44-45; Awarded Order of Suvorov 44 and Grand Cross of Merit of Knights of Malta 45; Gov.-Gen. of Canada 46-52; Minister of Defence 52-54; recipient of many City Freedoms and Hon. Degrees; Chancellor, Order of St. Michael and St. George 56, Grand Master 60.

Publ. *Memoirs* 62.

Winkfield Lodge, Windsor Forest, Berks., England.

Alexandris, Vice-Admiral Constantine; Greek naval officer; b. 14 Dec. 1894; ed. Naval Coll.

Served Balkan Wars 12-13, First World War 17-18, Greco-Turkish War 18-22; Lieut.-Commdr. 21, Commdr. 26, Capt. 36, Rear-Admiral 43; Chief of Naval Comm. Great Britain 27-28; Staff Coll. 28-30; Chief of Comm. to Italy 32-33; Dir. Operations Div. Naval Staff 33-35; Naval and Air Attaché Great Britain 41-43; Commdr.-in-Chief Greek Naval Forces 43-44; Chief of Naval Personnel Greek Admiralty Dec. 45-46, retd. 46; Pres. Naval Officers Pension Fund 51, Maritime Museum 57; Hellenic Atlantic Treaty Asscn.; Hon. C.B. 44; Commdr. Legion of Merit 46; Knight Commdr. Order of Phoenix; Knight Commdr. Order of Cruzeiro do Sol (Brazil); Hon. C.-in-C. of the Fleet 64.

Publ. *Sea Power in the History of Ancient Greece* 50, *Our Navy during the War Period 1941-45* 52, *Sea Power in the History of the Byzantine Empire* 57, *The Revival of our Sea Power during the Turkish Rule* 60.

15 Odos Stessichorou, Athens 138, Greece.

Alexandrov, Alexandr Danilovich; Soviet mathematician; b. 12.

Former Rector Leningrad Univ.; specialised in subject of convex bodies and general surfaces in geometry; mem. Acad. of Sciences of U.S.S.R. 65-; State prizewinner.

Institute of Mathematics, Novosibirsk 90, U.S.S.R.

Alexandrov, Alexandr Mikhailovich; Soviet diplomatist; b. 1907; ed. Kharkov Mechanical Engineering Inst. Member Communist Party of the Soviet Union 26-; Head of Central European Dept., Ministry of Foreign Affairs 39-40; Counsellor, Embassy in Bulgaria 40-42, in Australia 42-44; at Ministry of Foreign Affairs, Moscow 44-46, Head of Fourth European Dept. at Ministry 46-49; Minister to New Zealand 49-53; Deputy Head of Consular Dept., Ministry of Foreign Affairs 53-58; Amb. to Iceland 58-64; at Ministry of Foreign Affairs 64-66; Amb. to Sierra Leone 66-; Badge of Honour (thrice), Red Banner of Labour, etc.

U.S.S.R. Embassy, Freetown, Sierra Leone.

Alexandrov, Anatoly Nikolaevich, D.SC.; Soviet composer; b. 25 May 1888; ed. Moscow Conservatoire. Professor of Composition at Moscow Conservatoire 23-; Order of Red Banner of Labour 43, State Prize 51, Order of Lenin 53; Merited Arts Worker R.S.F.S.R. 46; People's Artist R.S.F.S.R. 64.

Works include *Bela* (opera in 4 acts), *Wild Bara* (opera in 3 acts); Symphony in C Major (4 movements); 13 piano sonatas, and numerous other works for piano; 4 string quartets; over 100 songs and many other compositions; film music.

Moscow State Conservatoire, 13 Ulitsa Herzena, Moscow, U.S.S.R.

Alexandrov, Anatoly Petrovich; Soviet physicist; b. 13; ed. Kiev Univ.

Work devoted to physics of dielectrics, mechanical and electrical properties of high polymeric compounds; developed widely-used static theory of strength of solids; invented relaxation theory of elasticity in polymers, etc.; State prizewinner; mem. Acad. of Sciences of U.S.S.R.; Dir. Inst. of Atomic Energy, U.S.S.R. Acad. of Sciences.

Atomic Energy Institute, U.S.S.R. Academy of Sciences, 46 Ulitsa Kurchatov, Moscow, U.S.S.R.

Alexandrov, Col. Boris Alexandrovich; Soviet composer and conductor; b. 1905; ed. Moscow State Conservatoire.

Conductor, Central Theatre of Soviet Army 29-37; Deputy Chief, Soviet Army Song and Dance Co. 37-46, Chief 46-; Asst. Prof., Moscow Conservatoire 33-; People's Artist of R.S.F.S.R. 48, of U.S.S.R. 58; Order of Lenin 49, 67, Order of Red Banner of Labour 64.

Principal works: *Marriage in Malinovka* (operetta) 37, *A Year Later* (operetta) 40, *A Girl of Barcelona* (operetta) 42, *My Guzel* (orchestral) 46, *Left-hander* (ballet) 55, *October Soldier Defending Peace* (oratorio) 66; also songs and choral works.

Soviet Army House, Ploshchad Kommuny, Moscow, U.S.S.R.

Alexandrov, Grigory Vasilievich; Soviet film director; b. 1903.

Began career as actor in the Central Workers' Studio of Proletkult 21; began film work 24; worked with S. Eisenstein as director of *Strike*, as actor and assistant in *Battleship Potemkin*, and co-director of *October* 27, *Old and New* 28-29, *Mexico* 31; worked in Paris 29, Hollywood and Mexico 29-30; People's Artist of the U.S.S.R.; mem. Lenin Int. Peace Prize Cttee.; State prizes 41, 50; Order of Lenin (twice), Order of Red Banner of Labour. Made films: *Jolly Fellows* 34, *Circus* 36, *Volga-Volga* 38, *Bright Path* 39, *Spring* 47, *Meeting on the Elbe* 49, *Composer Glinka* 52, *Russian Souvenir* 60; produced *Dear Liar* (Kilthy) in Mossoviet Theatre.

Mosfilm Studio, Moscow, U.S.S.R.

Alexandrov, Konstantin Ivanovich, M.SC; Soviet diplomatist; b. 1912; ed. Gorky Inst. of Water Transport Engineers.

Member C.P.S.U. 37-; Diplomatic Service 56-; Counsellor, Counsellor-Minister, Prague 56-62; at U.S.S.R. Foreign Ministry 62-63; Counsellor-Minister, Belgrade 63-65; Amb. to Afghanistan 65-; Order of Red Banner of Labour, etc.

U.S.S.R. Embassy, Kabul, Afghanistan.

Alexandrov, Pavel Sergeevich; Soviet mathematician; b. 96; ed. Moscow Univ.

Prof. of Mathematics at Moscow Univ.; founded Soviet Topological School; Pres. Moscow Mathematical School; Academician, Acad. of Sciences of the U.S.S.R.; foreign assoc. U.S. Nat. Acad. of Sciences 47; mem. American Philos. Soc., Polish Acad. of Sciences, corresp. mem. Acad. of Sciences, Berlin, Göttingen, Halle.

Publs. *Combinatorial Topology* 47, *Untersuchungen über*

Gestalt und Lage abgeschlossener Mengen beliebiger Dimension (Annals of Mathematics, Princeton, N.Y., 29, vol. 30), *Topologische Dualitätssätze I, II* (59, 62), *Einführung in die Gruppentheorie von P.S.* 60, *Nichtabgeschlossene Mengen* 62.

Moscow State University, Leninskiye Gory, Moscow, U.S.S.R.

Alexanyan, Arto Bogdanovich; Soviet epidemiologist; b. 1892; ed. Odessa Univ.
Army Surgeon 16-20; epidemiologist in Armenia 20-31; Head of Dept., Sanitary and Hygiene Inst. 30-36; Chief Sanitary Insp., Head of Dept., Public Health Commissariat, Armenian S.S.R. 35-40; Head of Chair, Erevan Medical Inst. 35-; Army Surgeon 41-45; Corresp. mem. U.S.S.R. Acad. of Medical Sciences 45-60, mem. 60-; mem. Board U.S.S.R. Soc. of Hygienists, Epidemiologists, Microbiologists and Infectionists; Order of Lenin, Red Star, Badge of Honour, Red Banner of Labour; Merited Scientist of Armenian S.S.R.
Publs. Over 120 works on regional pathology, treatment and prevention of diptheria, dysentery, etc.
Erevan State Medical Institute, 2 Kirov Street, Erevan, U.S.S.R.

Alexeyev, Alexander Ivanovich; Soviet (Russian) diplomatist; b. 13; ed. Moscow Univ.
Diplomatic Service 41-; First Sec. Buenos Aires 54-58; Head of Dept. for Latin American Countries, State Cttee. of U.S.S.R. Council of Ministers for Cultural Relations with Foreign Countries 59-60; Counsellor, Havana 60-62, Ambassador to Cuba 62-67.
c/o Ministry of Foreign Affairs, Moscow, U.S.S.R.

Alexeyev, Nikolai Borisovich; Soviet diplomatist; b. 1912; ed. Moscow State Univ.
Diplomatic Service 43-; Chargé d'Affaires, Uruguay 49-54; Dept. Head, U.S.S.R. Ministry of Foreign Affairs 54-57; Counsellor, UN 59; Ambassador to Argentina 59-66; on staff of U.S.S.R. Ministry of Foreign Affairs 66-67; Amb. to Chile 67-.
U.S.S.R. Embassy, Santiago, Chile.

Alexeyev, Pyotr Fyodorovich; Soviet journalist; b. 1913; ed. Tashkent Pedagogical Inst. and Higher Party School of the C.P.S.U.
Young Communist League Official, Uzbek S.S.R. 31-32; journalistic work 32-62; Editor-in-Chief *Selskaya Zhizn* (Country Life); mem. Central Auditing Comm. of the C.P.S.U. 66; mem. C.P.S.U. 40-.
Editorial Board, *Selskaya Zhizn*, Pravda Street No. 24, Moscow, U.S.S.R.

Alexeyevsky, Evgeny Evgenyevich; Soviet politician; b. 1906.
Deputy People's Commissar for Agriculture, Tajikstan 31; Commissar Cavalry Div., Second World War; in charge of agriculture in various regions of Ukraine 46; Deputy Minister of Agriculture, Ukraine in 'fifties; fmr. Chair. U.S.S.R. State Cttee. for Irrigated Farming and Water Conservancy; Minister of Reclamation and Water Conservancy 65-.
Ministry of Reclamation and Water Conservancy, Moscow; Home: Orlikov per. 1/11, Moscow, U.S.S.R.

Alexiadis, George; Greek lawyer and public official b. 18 Dec. 1911; ed. Athens Univ.
Practising lawyer 33-; Legal Adviser to Nat. Bank of Greece 40; head of a resistance organisation and publisher of an underground newspaper 41-45; Counsellor to Athens Municipality 50; publ. *Perspective* 60-; fmr. Dir.-Gen. Hellenic Nat. Broadcasting Inst.; Medal of Nat. Resistance; Progressive Party.
Publs. include: *Legal and Social Aspect of the Idea of the State* 39, *Introduction to Land Allotment* 41, *Geo-Economy and Geo-Policy of Greek Countries* 45 and 46, *The Reform of Criminal Law in Soviet Russia* 57, *Political History of Modern Greece* 60-63.

National Bank of Greece, 86 Aeolou Street, Athens; Home: 166 St. Sophia Street, Athens 202, Greece. Telephone: 876-497; 318-930.

Alexius, Patriarch **(Sergei Vladimirovich Simansky);** Russian ecclesiastic; b. 77; ed. Law Faculty Moscow Univ. and Moscow Ecclesiastical Academy.
Deacon 02; Priest 03; Insp. Pskov Ecclesiastical Seminary 04-06; Rector and Archimandrite Tula Ecclesiastical Seminary 06-11; Rector Novgorod Ecclesiastical Seminary and Prior St. Antony Monastery 11-13; Bishop of Tikhvin and Vicar of Novgorod 13-21; Bishop of Yamburg and Vicar of Petrograd 21-26; Archbishop of Novgorod 26-32, Metropolitan 32; Metropolitan of Leningrad 33-43; Metropolitan of Leningrad and Novgorod 43-45; perm. mem. Holy Synod 43-; Acting Patriarch of Orthodox Church 44-45; Patriarch of Moscow and All Russia 45-; Leningrad Defence Medal 44, Order of Red Banner of Labour 46, 52, 62 and 67.
5 Chisty pereulok, Moscow G-34, U.S.S.R.

Alfaro Polanco, José Maria; Spanish writer and diplomatist; b. 06.
Dir. of magazines *Vértice, Escorial, Fe,* and daily *Arriba*; Vice-Pres. of Cortes; Ambassador to Argentina 59-.
Publs. *Versos de un invierno, Leoncio Pancorbo, La última farsa, El molinero y el diablo, Fue en una venta.*
Embajada de España, 2720 Mariscal Ramón Castilla, Buenos Aires, Argentina.

Alfaro Siqueiros, David; Mexican mural painter; b. 29 Dec. 1896; ed. Mexican Acad. of Fine Arts, and Europe.
Served in Mexican Revolutionary Army 14-21, Spanish Republican Army 36; initiated modern mural painting in Mexico with Diego Rivera, José Clemente-Orozco and others 22; founded *El Machete*, weekly organ of Syndicate of Painters, Writers and Engravers of Mexican Revolution, of which he is Sec.-Gen.; Pres. of Anti-Fascist League 34; founded experimental workshop, N.Y. 35; worked in Mexico 39-; murals for Palace of Fine Arts, Mexico 48-50; second prize for foreign painters in Venice Biennale 50; elected mem. of jury of First Genoa Biennale 52; Lenin Peace Prize 67.
Works include: *Retrato de la burguesía, Muerto al Invasor, Alegoría de la Igualdad racial, Cuauhtamoc contra el mito, Nueva Democracia, Por Una Seguridad Social Integral, Porfirsmo y la Revolución,* mural for Hotel Casino de la Selva, Cuernavaca Morelos State 65, for Chapultepec Castle, Mexico City.
Publs. *No hay más ruta que la nuestra* 45, *Como se pinta un mural* (in the monograph *Siqueiros*) 51, *La Significación de la Pintura mexicana moderna* 51.
Mexico City, Mexico.

Alföldi, András; Hungarian archæologist and historian; b. 27 Aug. 1895; ed. Budapest Univ.
Prof. of Roman History, Inst. for Advanced Study, Princeton; mem. Institut de France, British, Royal Swedish, Lincei, Göttingen, Bavarian, Danish, Hungarian, Austrian, Bulgarian and other Acads.; Hon. Ph.D. (Utrecht. Bonn, Paris and Ghent Univs.); Gold Medal City of Rome.
Publs. *Der Untergang der Römerherrschaft in Pannonien* 24-26, *Studies on the World Crisis of the Third Century A.D., The Huns, Studies on the Monarchical Representation in Rome* 34-35; contrib. to *Cambridge Ancient History* 35-38, *Festivals of Isis in Rome in the IVth Century* 37, *Studies on the Social Morphology, Art and Archæology of the Nomads of Eurasia* 36-37, *Die Kontorniaten* 41-43, *Daci e Romani in Transilvania* 40, *A History of Aquincum* 42, *Zu den Schicksalen Siebenbürgens* 44, *The Conversion of Constantine and Pagan Rome* 48, *Valentinian I and the Senate* 50, *Studies on Zoomorphic Headgear* 50, *The Origins of the Roman Patriciate* 51, *The Birth of Imperial Symbolism* 52-53, *Caesar's Monarchy* 53, *The Tragic Costume* 54,

The Trojan Legend in Rome 57, *The Roman Surname* 66, *The Domination of Cavalry in Greece and Rome after the Kings* 66, *Early Rome and the Latins* 65, *Imperial vows and Alexandrine Gods* 66, *The Role of the Cavalry in Greece and Rome* 67.

272 Mercer Street, Princeton, N.J. 08540, U.S.A. (winter) and Spiez, Switzerland (summer).
Telephone: 921-6127 (U.S.A.).

Alfozan, Yusuf; Saudi Arabian diplomatist; b. 13; ed. Arabia and Bombay, India.
Editor *Shubban's Voice* 36-38; Personal Agent in Bombay to H.M. King Abdulaziz Ibn Saud 38; Consul-Gen. Palestine 39-41, Bombay 49-55; Minister to India 55-57, Amb. 57-65, to Iran 66-.
Embassy of Saudi Arabia, Villa Avenue, Nasser Street, Teheran, Iran.

Alfrink, H.E. Cardinal Bernardus Johannes; Netherlands ecclesiastic; b. 5 July 1900; ed. Aartsbisschoppelijk Seminarie, Culemborg, Groot-Seminarie, Rijsenburg, Pauselijk Bijbel-Instituut, Rome, and Jerusalem.
Prof. of Holy Scripture, Aartsbisschoppelijk Groot-Seminarie, Rijsenburg 33-45; Prof. for Old Testament and Hebrew Language, Univ. of Nijmegen 45-51; tit. Archbishop of Tyana and Coadjutor of the Archdiocese of Utrecht 51-55; Archbishop of Utrecht 55-; created Cardinal by Pope John XXIII 60.
Publs. *Het Boek Prediker, Het Boek Ecclesiasticus, Epistels en Evangelien volgens het Romeins Missaal, Het Passiverhaal der vier Evangelisten, Het Boek Josue.*
40 Maliebaan, Utrecht, Netherlands.

Alfvén, Hannes Olof Gösta, PH.D.; Swedish professor of plasma physics; b. 30 May 1908; ed. Universitet i Uppsala.
Professor of Theory of Electricity, Royal Inst. of Technology, Stockholm 40-45, of Electronics 45-63, of Plasma Physics 63-; mem. Swedish Science Advisory Council; mem. Swedish Acad. of Sciences, Swedish Acad. of Eng. Sciences; Foreign Assoc. U.S. Acad. of Sciences; mem. other foreign Acads.; Gold Medal, Royal Astronomical Soc. (U.K.) 67.
Publs. papers in physics and astrophysics and: *Cosmical Electrodynamics* 50, *On the Origin of the Solar System* 54, *Cosmical Electrodynamics: Fundamental Principles* (with C.-G. Fälthammar) 63, *Worlds-Antiworlds* 66.
Royal Institute of Technology, Stockholm 7, Sweden.

Ali, Amjad; Pakistani politician and diplomatist; ed. Govt. Coll. of Lahore.
Delegate to various world conferences; Chief Whip of the Govt. of Punjab 42; mem. of Constituent Assembly of India 46; Minister of Economic Affairs. Pakistani Embassy in Washington, and alternate governor of the International Monetary Fund 50; Pres. of ECOSOC 52; Ambassador to U.S.A. 53; Minister of Finance and Economic Affairs 55-56; Minister of Finance 56-58; Chair. Investment Promotion Bureau 61-63; Perm. Rep. to UN 64-67, Chair. UN Cocoa Conf. 66.
c/o Ministry of Foreign Affairs, Karachi, Pakistan.

Ali, Anwar, M.A.; Pakistani civil servant; b. 13; ed. Islamia Coll., Lahore.
With Govt. of India 43-47; Dep. Sec. Ministry of Finance, Govt. of Pakistan 47-52, Joint Sec. 52-54; Dir. National Bank of Pakistan 49-53; Dir. State Bank of Pakistan 52-54; Dir. Middle Eastern Dept. Int. Monetary Fund, Washington 54; Gov. Saudi Arabian Monetary Agency 58-; decorated Sitara-e-Quaid-e-Azam 61.
Office: Saudi Arabian Monetary Agency, Jeddah; Home: 25 Sharia Ali Ibn Abi Talib Sharafia, Jeddah, Saudi Arabia.

Ali, (Chaudhri) Mohamad, M.SC.; Pakistani politician; b. 15 July 1905; ed. Lahore and Univ. of Punjab.
Lecturer in chemistry, Islamia Coll., Lahore 27-28; joined Indian Accounts and Audit Service 28; Ac-

countant-Gen., Bahawalpur 32-36; entered Govt. of India service 36; Under-Sec. Finance Dept. 38-39; Deputy Financial Adviser 39-43; Joint Financial Adviser, Ministry of Supply 43-45; Financial Adviser War and Supply 45-47; mem. Steering Cttee. of Partition Council 47; Sec.-Gen. to Govt. of Pakistan 47-51; Minister of Finance 51; Minister of Finance and Econ. Affairs 54-55; Prime Minister and other portfolios 55-56; Leader Nizam-E-Islam Party.
Publ. *The Emergence of Pakistan* 67.
86-D/1, Gulberg III, Lahore, Pakistan.
Telephone: 81434.

Ali, Sadiq, B.A.; Indian politician; b. 11; ed. Allahabad Univ.
Perm. Sec., All India Congress Cttee. 38-48; mem. Lok Sabha 50-58, Rajya Sabha 58-; Gen. Sec. Indian Congress Party 58-65.
Publs. *Know Your Country, Congress Ideology and Programme, Culture in India, General Elections 1957, Towards Socialist Thinking in Congress.*
6 Jandar Mandar Road, New Delhi, India.

Ali, Salman Ahmed; Pakistani diplomatist; b. 29 Sept. 1913; ed. Oxford Univ.
Government Service 41-; Ministry of Commerce, later Ministry of Information and Broadcasting 47-49; Press Attaché, Pakistani High Comm., London 49-53; served Canada, Netherlands, Turkey 53-58; Counsellor, Moscow 58-61, Washington 61-63; Dir.-Gen., Ministry of Foreign Affairs 63-66; Amb. to U.S.S.R. Nov. 66-.
Embassy of Pakistan, Sadova-Kudrinskaya ul. 17 Moscow, U.S.S.R.

Ali Khan, Begum Liaquat (widow of late Liaquat Ali Khan, fmr. Prime Minister of Pakistan), M.A., B.T.; Pakistani diplomatist; ed. Univs. of Lucknow and Calcutta.
Founder Pres. All-Pakistan Women's Asscn., Nat. Guard, Naval Reserve and Cottage Industry Projects; chair. various educational, hospital and social work groups; del. to U.N. General Assembly 52; mem. I.L.O. Expert Cttee. on Recommendations 55; Ambassador to the Netherlands 54-61, to Italy 61-66, to Tunisia 61-64.
Quaid-i-Millat House, Bath Island, Karachi, Pakistan.

Ali Khan, Sadath; Indian diplomatist; b. 16; ed. Nizam Coll., Hyderabad.
Hyderabad Govt. Service 45; Mem. of Parliament (Lok Sabha) 52-57, 57-61; Parl. Sec. to Prime Minister 53-61; Alternate Del. to Trusteeship Council and to UN Gen. Assembly 54; Prime Minister's Rep. in the Middle East 54-59; Parl. Sec. 61; Amb. to Iraq 61-66, to Turkey 66-.
Publs. *Projects for Prosperity, Brief Thanksgiving,* Tibor Mende's *Conversation with Nehru* (Urdu trans.).
Indian Embassy, Kızılırmak Cad. 50, Ankara, Turkey.

Ali Mohammed Khan, Sardar-i-Ala; Afghan politician; b. 91; ed. Habibia Coll., Kabul.
Insp. of Schools 22; Vice-Minister of Education 24; Minister to Rome 26-27; Minister of Commerce 28; Minister of Education and Acting Foreign Minister 29; Minister of Foreign Affairs 47-53; Dep. Prime Minister 53-63; Minister of Court 63-.
Shahr-i-Nao, Kabul, Afghanistan.

Alican, Ekrem; Turkish politician; b. 5 May 1916; ed. Univ. of Ankara.
Inspector, Ministry of Finance 43; mem. Democratic Party 50-55; Co-founder Freedom Party 55; Minister of Finance May-Dec. 60; founded New Turkey Party 61, leader; mem. Grand Nat. Assembly 61-; Dep. Prime Minister June 62-63.
Grand National Assembly, Ankara; Home: Küfükesat, dört yol, Marmara 7, Ankara, Turkey.

Aliger, Margarita Iosifovna; Soviet poetess; b. 7 Oct. 1915; ed. Gorky Literary Inst.
Member C.P.S.U. 42-; State prizewinner 43; Order of Red Banner of Labour 65.
Publs. *Year of Birth* 38, *The Railway* 39, *Stones and*

Grasses 40, *To the Memory of the Brave* 42, *Zoya* 42, *Lyrics* 43, *Your Victory* 46, *Selected Poems* 47, *A Tale of Truth* 47, *First Thunder* 47, *First Signs* 48, *The Lenin Hills* 53, *The Beautiful Metcha-River* 53, *Man on His Way* 54, *Lyrics* 55, *From a Notebook* 57, *Lyrics and Poems* 59, *A Few Steps* 64, *Russia: My Native Country* 67, *Stronger than Death* 68; Essays: *Chilean Summer* 65, *Return to Chile* 66; trans. poems of Aragon, Pablo Neruda, Bagriana, etc.

Writers' Union, 52 Vorovsky Street, Moscow, U.S.S.R.

Alikhani, Ali Naghi; Iranian economist and politician; b. 29; ed. Alborz Coll., Teheran, Univ. of Teheran and Univ. of Paris.

Former Econ. Adviser to Nat. Iranian Oil Co. and other orgs.; Minister of Economy 63-.

Publ. *Factors Proportion* (French).

Ministry of Economy, Teheran, Iran.

Alikhanov, Abram Isaakovich; Soviet physicist; b. 04; ed. Leningrad Polytechnic Institute.

Began research into radio-activity and radio-active radiation 34; together with brother A. I. Alikhanyan and the scientist Kozodaev discovered the phenomenon of the emission of "couples" (positron and electron) by charged nuclei; started research in the sphere of cosmic rays and continued work on nuclear physics 39; one of the authors of the first Soviet reactor with heavy water delay 49; Hon. mem. Czechoslovak Acad. of Sciences 62; mem. Soviet Acad. of Sciences 43; State prizewinner for work on nuclear physics, 41, 48; mem. Bureau of Nuclear Physics, U.S.S.R. Acad. of Sciences.

14 Leninski Prospekt, Moscow, U.S.S.R.

Alikhanov, Enver Nazarovich; Soviet politician; b. 17; ed. Azerbaijan Industrial Inst.

Soviet Army 41-42; Industrial Geologist 42-45; mem. C.P.S.U. 43-; Apparatus of Central Cttee. of Azerbaijan C.P. 45-51; Azerbaijan oil industry 51-59; Minister of Oil Industry, Azerbaijan 58-59; Sec. Central Cttee. of Azerbaijan C.P. 59-62; Chair. Council of Ministers of Azerbaijan 62-; Alt. mem. Central Cttee. of C.P.S.U.; mem. Central Cttee. C.P. of Azerbaijan; Deputy to U.S.S.R. Supreme Soviet; Lenin Prize 61.

Council of Ministers of Azerbaijan S.S.R., Baku, Azerbaijan S.S.R., U.S.S.R.

Alikhanyan, Artemi Isaakovich; Soviet physicist; b. 08; ed. Leningrad Univ.

Began research work 31; discovered with his brother (Alikhanov, A. I.) and Kozodaev emission of "couples" (positron and electron) by agitated nuclei 34; discovered with brother and Nikitin varitrons 41; Corresp. mem. U.S.S.R. Acad. of Sciences 45; mem. Armenian S.S.R. Acad. of Sciences 43; State Prize 41, 48.

Institute of Physics of the U.S.S.R. Academy of Sciences, 53 Leninsky Prospekt, Moscow, U.S.S.R.

Alimarin, Ivan Pavlovich; Soviet chemist; b. 1903.

At All-Union Research Inst. of Mineral Raw Materials 23-53; Prof. Moscow Inst. of Fine Chemical Technology 50-53, Moscow Univ. 53-; at Inst. of Geochemistry and Analytical Chemistry, U.S.S.R. Acad. of Sciences 49-; Corresp. mem. U.S.S.R. Acad. of Sciences 53-66, mem. 66-.

U.S.S.R. Academy of Sciences, 14 Lenin Prospekt, Moscow, U.S.S.R.

Alioto, Joseph; American lawyer and politician; b. 1917; ed. Roman Catholic coll.

Former govt. lawyer, Washington, specializing in anti-trust cases; returned to private practice in Calif.; Sec. Rice Growers Asscn. of Calif.; Mayor of San Francisco Jan. 68-; Democrat.

Office of the Mayor, San Francisco, California, U.S.A.

Aliyeva, Sakina; Soviet (Azerbaijan) philologist and politician; b. 1925; ed. Azerbaijan State Univ. and Higher Party School.

Minister of Education, Nakhichevan Republic 60-61;

Sec. Nakhichevan Regional Cttee., C.P. of Azerbaijan 62-63; Pres. of Presidium of Supreme Soviet of Nakhichevan A.S.S.R. 63-.

Presidium of Supreme Soviet of Nakhichevan A.S.S.R., Nakhichevani, Nakhichevan A.S.S.R., U.S.S.R.

Alkhimov, Vladimir Sergeyevich; Soviet foreign trade official; b. 1919; ed. Leningrad Financial and Economic Inst., and Acad. of Foreign Trade.

Member C.P.S.U. 42-; Chief of Dept., later Deputy Dir., Research Inst. of Commercial Exchange 50-57; Commercial Counsellor, U.S.A. 57-60; Deputy Chief, later Chief of Dept., Ministry of Foreign Trade 61-67; Deputy Minister of Foreign Trade 67-; Hero of Soviet Union; and other decorations.

U.S.S.R. Ministry of Foreign Trade, 32/34 Smolenskaya-Sennaya ploshchad, Moscow, U.S.S.R.

Alkmim, José Maria; Brazilian lawyer, university professor and politician; b. 01; ed. Univ. of Belo Horizonte.

Prof. of Philosophy, Univ. of Minas Gerais; Dir. of Nat. Press of State of Minas; elected deputy 34 and appointed Sec. to the Ministry of the Interior; founder of the Penitenciária das Neves, and its Dir. until 45; elected Federal deputy 45, 50, 54; Sec. of Finance for the State of Minas Gerais 50-53; Dir. Banco do Brasil 53; Minister of Finance 56; Deputy for State of Minas Gerais; Vice-Pres. of Brazil April 64-67.

Brasilia, Brazil.

Allais, Maurice; French economist; b. 31 May 1911; ed. Ecole Polytechnique and Ecole Nationale Supérieure des Mines de Paris.

Department of Mines and Quarries 37-43; Dir. Bureau de Documentation et de Statistique Minière 43-48; econ. research 48-; Prof. of Gen. Economy, Ecole Nationale Supérieure des Mines de Paris 44-; Prof. of Econ. Theory, Inst. of Statistics, Univ. of Paris 47-; Dir. of Research, Centre Nat. de la Recherche Scientifique 54-; Prof. Graduate Inst. of Int. Studies, Geneva 67-; Chevalier Légion d'Honneur; Officier Palmes Académiques and other awards; Dr. h.c. (Groningen).

Publs. *Abondance ou Misère* 46, *Economie et Intérêt* 47, *Traité d'Economie Pure* 52, *La gestion des houillières nationalisées et la théorie économique* 53, *Les fondements comptables de la macroéconomique* 54, *Le pendule paraconique* 57-59, *L'Europe Unie, route de la prospérité* 60, *Manifeste pour une Société Libre* 58, *Le Tiers-Monde au Carrefour—Centralisation autoritaire ou planification concurrentielle* 62, *L'Algérie d'Evian* 62, *The Role of Capital in Economic Development* 63, *Reformulation de la théorie quantitative de la monnaie* 65, *L'Impôt sur le Capital* 66.

15 rue des Gâte-Ceps, (92) Saint Cloud, France.

Allal El Fassi, Mohammed; Moroccan politician; b. 06; ed. Univ. of Fez.

Work with Moroccan nationalists 20-; imprisoned briefly 30; Prof. Univ. of Fez 32, forced to leave Morocco (for nationalist activities) 33; returned 34, presented plans for reform and independence to French authorities; imprisoned 35-36; presided first meeting Comité d'Action Marocaine 36; exiled to French Equatorial Africa 36; returned to Morocco 46, became a leader of Istiqlal Party (formed 43); lived abroad 47-53; leader, Istiqlal (Independent Party) 56-; Minister for Muslim Affairs 61.

Publ. *The Independence Movements in Arab North Africa* 54.

Parti Istiqlal, Rabat, Morocco.

Allamanis, Stelios; Greek lawyer and politician; b 10; ed. Univs. of Athens, Göttingen and Grenoble.

Lawyer, Karditsa 32-45, Athens 45-; fmr. E.P.E.K. Party M.P., Democratic Working People's Party 56-61; Centre Union Party 61-; Minister of Agriculture 51-52; Minister of Public Works Nov. 63-Feb. 64, of Communications Feb. 64-65, of Educ. 65-66.

c/o Ministry of Education, Athens, Greece.

Allard, Sven; Swedish diplomatist; b. 6 July 1896.
Attaché Foreign Office 21; Warsaw Legation 22; Riga,
Reval, Kovno 23; Second Sec. Brussels and The Hague
25; First Vice-consul London 30; First Sec. Warsaw 32,
Rome 33, Paris 34; Commercial Counsellor 34;
Counsellor of Legation and Chargé d'Affaires Athens 38,
Ankara 39-40, Sofia 41; Rep. Gov. for relief in Greece
42-43; Minister to China 43-47; Minister to Rumania
(also accredited to Hungary and Bulgaria) 49-51;
Minister to Czechoslovakia (also accredited to Hungary)
51-54, to Austria 54-56; Ambassador to Austria 56-64;
Rep. to FAO, Rome 64-.
Publ. *Diplomat in Vienna* (in Swedish and German) 65.
Via Marco Besso 11, Rome, Italy.

Allardt, Helmut, DR. JUR.; German diplomatist; b.
20 March 1907; ed. Univs. of Berlin and Göttingen.
Asst. in Political Science, Göttingen Univ. 31-32; en-
tered Foreign Service 36; served Teheran, Copenhagen
and Ankara, Commercial Relations Div. in the Ministry
of Foreign Affairs; Ambassador to Indonesia 56-59;
Dir.-Gen. EEC Development Fund 59; Ministerial Dir.
Ministry of Foreign Affairs 61-63; Ambassador to
Spain 63-.
German Embassy, calle Fortuny 8, Madrid, Spain.
Telephone: 2-240140.

Allégret, Marc, L. en D.; French film director; b. 23
Dec. 1900.
Sec. *Soirées de Paris* Ballet; accompanied André Gide
to Congo where he made documentary film 26; directed
Marcel Pagnol's production of *Fanny* and a number of
other films including *Lac aux Dames* 34, *Gribouille,
Orage, Les Beaux Jours, Razumov, Entrée des Artistes,
Les Petites du Quai aux Fleurs,* and *Félicie Nanteuil*; has
directed two English films: *Blanche Fury* and *The
Naked Heart.*
11 *bis* rue Lord Byron, Paris 8e, France.

Allegro, John Marco; British philologist and archæo-
logist; b. 17 Feb. 1923; ed. Wallington County Grammar
School and Univ. of Manchester.
Royal Navy 41-46; Manchester Univ. 47-52; research in
Hebrew dialects, Magdalen Coll., Oxford 52-53; British
rep. on Int. Editing Team for Dead Sea Scrolls, Jerusa-
lem 53; Lecturer in Comparative Semitic Philology and
Hebrew, Univ. of Manchester 54-62, in Old Testament
and Intertestamental Studies 62-; Adviser to Jordanian
Govt. on Dead Sea Scrolls 61-; Trustee and Hon. Sec.
Dead Sea Scrolls Fund 62-.
Publs. *The Dead Sea Scrolls* 56, 64, *The People of the
Dead Sea Scrolls* 58, *The Treasure of the Copper Scroll*
60, 64, *Search in the Desert* 64, *The Shapira Affair* 65,
Discoveries in the Judaean Desert of Jordan V 68.
"Elmwood", Reservoir Road, Whaley Bridge, nr.
Stockport, Cheshire, England.
Telephone: Whaley Bridge 2657.

Allen, Charles, Jr.; American investment banker; b.
1 Jan. 1903; ed. New York Public Schools and Commerce
High School.
Founder, Allen & Co. (investment bankers) 22; Chair.
of Board Allen Ranches, Pres. Bayou Interests Inc.;
Dir Colorado Fuel & Iron Corpn. (now C. F. and I.
Steel Corpn.), Warner Bros.—Seven Arts Ltd., Pepsico
Inc., American Bosch Arma Corpn., Ogden Corpn.;
official of numerous other companies.
Allen and Company, 30 Broad Street, New York, N.Y.
10004, U.S.A.
Telephone: HA2-2600.

Allen, Sir (William) Denis, K.C.M.G., C.B.; British
diplomatist; b. 24 Dec. 1910; ed. Wanganui Collegiate
School, New Zealand, and Pembroke Coll., Cambridge.
Foreign Service 34-, China, Foreign Office, Washington
38-50; Head of German Political Dept., Foreign Office
50-53, Asst. Under-Sec. Sec. of State (Far East) 53-56,
Deputy Under-Sec. of State (Admin.) 56-59; Deputy

Commr.-Gen. for South East Asia, Singapore 59-63;
Amb. to Turkey 63-67; Deputy Under Sec. of State
(Political) 67-.
Foreign Office, London S.W.1, England.
Telephone: 01-930-8440.

Allen, Florence Ellinwood, M.A., LL.B., HON. LL.D.;
American attorney and judge; b. 23 March 1884; ed.
Western Reserve Univ., Chicago, and N.Y. Univ. Law
Schools.
Asst. County Prosecutor 18; elected Judge, Court of
Common Pleas, Cuyahoga Co., Ohio 20; elected Judge,
Supreme Court of Ohio 22; re-elected 28; appointed
Judge of U.S. Circuit Court of Appeals for Sixth Circuit
(Ohio, Michigan, Kentucky, Tennessee) 34, Chief Judge
58-59; awarded hon. degrees of LL.D. by twenty-five
Univs. and Colls., including Western Reserve, New
York, Ohio State, Rutgers, Washington and N.
Carolina and Utah Univs.; Albert Gallatin Medal.
Publs. *This Constitution of Ours, The Treaty as an
Instrument of Legislation* 52.
c/o U.S. Court of Appeals, 112 Federal Bldg., Cleveland
14, Ohio, U.S.A.

Allen, Rt. Rev. Geoffrey Francis, M.A.; British ecclesi-
astic; b. 25 Aug. 1902; ed. Rugby, Univ. Coll., Oxford
and Ripon Hall, Oxford.
Sec. Student Christian Movement, Liverpool 26; Curate
St. Saviour's, Liverpool 27; Chaplain Ripon Hall, Oxford
28; Fellow and Chaplain Lincoln Coll., Oxford 30-35;
Union Theological College, Canton 35; Deputy Provost
Birmingham Cathedral 41; Nat. Christian Council of
China 42; Archdeacon of Birmingham 44-47; Bishop in
Egypt 47-52; Principal Ripon Hall, Oxford 52-59;
Bishop of Derby 59-.
Publs. *Tell John* (joint author) 32, *He that Cometh* 32,
Christ the Victorious 35, *The Courage to be Real* 38,
Law with Liberty 42.
Bishop's House, Turnditch, Derby, DE5 2LH, Derby-
shire, England.
Telephone: Cowers Lane 464.

Allen, George Cyril, C.B.E., M.COM., PH.D., F.B.A.;
British university professor Emeritus; b. 28 June 1900;
ed. King Henry VIII School, Coventry, and Univ. of
Birmingham.
Lecturer Nagoya Commercial Coll. Japan 22-25;
Research Fellow and Lecturer, Univ. of Birmingham
25-29; Prof. of Economics and Commerce, Univ. Coll.,
Hull 29-33; Prof. of Economic Science, Univ. of Liver-
pool 33-47; Prof. of Political Economy, Univ. Coll.,
London Univ. 47-67; Temp. Asst. Sec. Board of Trade
40-44, Temp. Counsellor, Foreign Office Sept. 45-April
46; mem. various Govt. Cttees. 44- (mem. Monopolies
and Restrictive Practices Comm. 50-62); Pres. Economic
Section, British Asscn. 50; Dir. Anglo-Nippon Trust;
mem. Acad. Planning Board, new Univ. of Ulster 65-;
Order of the Rising Sun 3rd Class (Japan); Fellow
British Acad.
Publs. *Modern Japan and its Problems* 28, *The Industrial
Development of Birmingham and the Black Country* 29,
British Industries and their Organisation 33, (revised
35, 39, 45, 51, 59), *Japan, The Hungry Guest* 38, *A Short
Economic History of Japan* 46 (revised 62), *Japan's Eco-
nomic Recovery* 58, part-author of *The Industrialisation
of Japan and Manchukuo* 40, *Western Enterprise in Far
Eastern Economic Development* 54, and of *Western
Enterprise in Indonesia and Malaya* 57, *The Structure
of Industry in Britain* 61 (revised 66), *Japan's Economic
Expansion* 65, *Japan as a Market and Source of Supply*
67.
Quinces, Beech Close, Cobham, Surrey, England.
Telephone: Cobham (Surrey) 4744.

Allen, George Venable, A.M.; American diplomatist;
b. 3 Nov. 1903; ed. Duke Univ., Durham N.C., and
Harvard Univ.
Newspaper reporter 26-28; American Vice-Consul,

Kingston, Jamaica 30, Shanghai 31-34, Patras, Greece 34-36; Consul and Diplomatic Sec., Cairo 36-38; Dept. of State, Washington 38-46; U.S. Ambassador to Iran April 46-48; Asst. Sec. of State for Public Affairs 48-49; Ambassador to Yugoslavia 49-53; Ambassador to India and Nepal 53-54; Asst. Sec. for Near Eastern, South Asian and African Affairs 54-56; Ambassador to Greece July 56-Nov. 57; Dir. U.S. Information Agency Nov. 57-60; Pres. Tobacco Inst. 61-66; Dir. Foreign Service Inst. 66-.
4730 Quebec Street, N.W., Washington, D.C., U.S.A. Telephone: EM2-3010.

Allen, James Lawrence; Australian diplomatist; b. 5 Jan. 1913; ed. Prince Alfred Coll., Adelaide, Adelaide Univ. and London Univ.
Professor of English, Christian Coll., Bankura, West Bengal 38-41; Indian Army 42-45; Indian Civil Service 45-46; Australian Foreign Service 46-, New Delhi 46-47, Canberra 47-52, Washington 53-55, Manila 56-57, Canberra 58-59, New Delhi 60-61, Canberra 62-63; Dir. Colombo Plan Bureau, Colombo 64-65.
Department of External Affairs, Canberra, A.C.T., Australia.

Allen, Sir Peter Christopher, Kt., M.A., B.SC.; British industrial chemist and business executive; b. 8 Sept. 1905; ed. Harrow School and Trinity Coll., Oxford.
Joined Brunner, Mond and Co. (now Mond Div. of I.C.I.) 28; Man. Dir. Plastics Div., Imperial Chemical Industries (I.C.I.) 42-48, Chair. Plastics Div. 48-51, Dir. of I.C.I. 51-, Dep. Chair. 63-68, Chair. 68-; Pres. Canadian Industries Ltd. 59-62, Chair. 62-68; Pres. and Chair. I.C.I. of Canada Ltd. 61-68; Dir. Royal Trust Co., Canada 61-64; mem. Export Council for Europe 62-65; Vice-Chair. of Asscn. of British Chemical Manufacturers 63-65; Pres. British Plastics Federation 63-65; mem. Iron & Steel Holding and Realisation Agency 63-67; mem. British National Export Council and Chair. Cttee. for Exports to Canada 64-67; mem. National Economic Development Cttee. for Chemical Industry 64-67; Commonwealth Export Council 64-67; Pres. Chemical Industries Asscn. Ltd. 65-67; mem. Council of Confederation of British Industry 65-67.
Publs. *The Railways of the Isle of Wight* 28, *Locomotives of Many Lands* 54, *On the Old Lines* 57, *Narrow Gauge Railways of Europe* (with P. B. Whitehouse) 59, *Steam on the Sierra* (with R. A. Wheeler) 60, *Round the World on the Narrow Gauge* (with P. B. Whitehouse) 66, *The Curve of Earth's Shoulder* (with Consuelo Allen) 66, *Rails in the Isle of Wight* (with A. B. MacLeod) 67.
Imperial Chemical Industries Ltd., Imperial Chemical House, Millbank, London S.W.1, England.
Telephone: 01-834-4444.

Allen, Raymond Bernard, M.D., PH.D.; American educationist; b. 7 Aug. 1902; ed. Univ. of Minnesota and the Mayo Foundation.
Assoc. Dean in charge of Graduate Studies, Coll. of Physicians and Surgeons, Columbia Univ. 34-36; Assoc. Dir. N.Y. Post-Graduate Medical School and Hospital, Columbia Univ. 33-36; Dean, Wayne Univ. Coll. of Medicine 36-39; Exec. Dean, Chicago Colls. of Univ. of Illinois 39-46, Dean, Coll. of Medicine 43-46; Pres. Univ. of Washington, Seattle 46-52; Dir. Psychological Strategy Board 52; Chancellor, Univ. of California, Los Angeles 52-59; Dir. U.S. Operations Mission to Indonesia 59-61; Chief, Office of Research Co-ordination, Pan American Health Org., Washington 62-65, Office of Health and Population Dynamics 65-67; Consultant, Health-Education, Population Dynamics 67-.
Publs. include *Medical Education and the Changing Order*.
2700 Que Street N.W., Washington, D.C. 20007, U.S.A. Telephone: 202-338-9458.

Allen, Sir Roger, K.C.M.G.; British diplomatist; b. 17 Aug. 1909; ed. Repton and Corpus Christi Coll., Cambridge.
Called to the Bar (Inner Temple) 37; employed temporarily in Foreign Office 40; transferred to Moscow 46; apptd. Foreign Service Officer Jan. 46; Foreign Office 48; Head U.N. (Political) Dept. 49; Head of African Dept. 50-53; Asst. Under-Sec. of State 53-54; Deputy U.K. High Commr. in Germany 54-55, Minister in Bonn 55-56; Ambassador to Greece 57-61, to Iraq 61-65; Deputy Under-Sec. Foreign Office 65-67, Amb. to Turkey 67-.
British Embassy, Ankara, Turkey.

Allen, William McPherson, A.B., LL.B.; American lawyer and businessman; b. 1 Sept. 1900; ed. Montana and Harvard Univs.
Member of law firm Donworth, Todd and Higgins (name changed to Holman, Sprague and Allen) 30-45; Pres. The Boeing Co. 45-; Dir. Pacific Nat. Bank of Seattle, Standard Oil Co., Calif., Weyerhaeuser Co.; Hon. LL.D. Montana and Seattle Univs.
Office: The Boeing Co., P.O. Box 3707, Seattle, Washington 98124; Home: The Highlands, Seattle, Washington 98177, U.S.A.

Allende, Dr. Salvador; Chilean physician and politician; b. 09.
Leader Popular Action Front; Candidate for Presidency of Chile 58, Sept. 64, now Pres. of Senate.
Providencia, Santiago; and Algarrabo, Chile.

Allerslev Jensen, Erik; Danish library director; b. 22 May 1911; ed. Danish Library School.
Assistant Librarian, Frederiksberg Public Library 33-37; Head of Dept. of Printed Catalogue Cards, State Inspectorate for Public Libraries 37-42; Dir. Danish Library Bureau 42-46; Dep. Dir. State Inspectorate for Public Libraries 46-59, Dir. 60-; Dir. Danish Library School 46-56; Dir. School of Advanced Library Studies, Gothenburg 58-; Pres. Public Libraries Section, Int. Fed. of Library Asscns.
Publs. *Dansk Bogfortegnelse* (The Danish National Bibliography) 35-60, *Decimal-Klassedeling* (Decimal Classification), 4th Edition, 54, *Lærebog i Biblioteksteknik* (Manual of Library Economy), 4th Edition, 59, *Dansk bibliotekslitteratur* (Danish Library Literature: A Bibliography) 50, *Biblioteker og Læsning* (Libraries and Reading) 6 vols. 56-64, *Skrifter udsendt af den Nordiske Fortsættelsesskole for Bibliotekarer* (Publs. from the Scandinavian Library School in Gothenburg) 4 vols. 60-62, *Biblioteksstudier* (Library Studies) 3 vols. 63.
State Inspectorate for Public Libraries, Gammel Kongevej 60, Copenhagen V, Denmark.
Telephone: 01-31-38-25.

Alley, Col. Alphonse; Dahomeyan army officer and politician; b. 9 April 1930; ed. primary schools at Lome, Togo, and Military School in Ivory Coast.
Joined 5th Senegalese Rifle Regt., Dakar; served in Indo-China 50-53, Morocco 55-56, Algeria 59-61; returned to Dahomey 61; Second-Lieut. Dahomeyan Army 61, Capt. 62, Major 64, Lieut.-Col. 67, Chief of Staff 67; Pres. of Dahomey Dec. 67-.
Office of the President, Porto Novo, Dahomey.

Alliali, Camille; Ivory Coast lawyer and diplomatist; b. 23 Nov. 1926; ed. Dakar Lycée and Lycée Champollion, Grenoble.
Former Advocate, Court of Appeal, Abidjan; Vice-Pres. Nat. Assembly, Ivory Coast 59; Senator of French Community 59-61; Ambassador to France 61-63; Minister of Foreign Affairs 63-66; Keeper of the Seals and Minister of Justice 66-; Commandeur, Légion d'Honneur and other decorations.
Ministry of Justice, Abidjan, Ivory Coast.

Allibone, Thomas Edward, C.B.E. PH.D., D.SC., M.I.E.E., F.R.S.; British scientist; b. 11 Nov. 1903; ed. Sheffield and Cambridge Univs.

High Voltage Laboratory, Metropolitan Vickers Co. 30-44; Univ. of California (British team, Atomic Bomb) 44-45; Dir. Research Laboratory, Associated Electrical Industries, Aldermaston 46-63; Scientific Adviser to A.E.I. Ltd. 63-; Dir. Assoc. Elec. Industries (Woolwich) Ltd.; Chief Scientist, Central Electricity Generating Board 63-; Extraordinary Prof. of Electrical Engineering, Leeds Univ. 67-; Vice-Pres. Inst. Physics 48-52; Chair. Research Cttee., Electrical Research Asscn. 55-62; Vice-Pres. Royal Inst. 55-57; mem. Council, Physical Soc. 53-57, Advisory Council, Royal Military Coll., Shrivenham; Pres. Section A British Asscn. 58.
Publs. *High Voltage Electrical Phenomena and Thermonuclear Reactions, Release and Use of Atomic Energy.*
Round Hill, Enborne, Newbury, Berkshire, England.

Allimadi, E. Otema; Ugandan diplomatist; b. 11 Feb. 1929; ed. in Uganda.
N.C.O. in E. African Army Medical Corps. 47-53; mem. Uganda Nat. Congress 53, Nat. Admin. and Organizing Sec. 56-59, Sec.-Gen. 59, later Vice-Chair. Uganda People's Congress; Deputy Perm. Rep. to UN 64-66; Amb. to U.S.A. 66-, concurrently Perm. Rep. to UN 67-.
Permanent Mission of Uganda to the United Nations, 801 Second Avenue, New York, N.Y. 10017, U.S.A.

Allis, William P.; American physicist; b. 15 Nov. 1901; ed. Massachusetts Inst. of Technology, Univ. of Nancy (France), Princeton Univ. and Univ. of Munich.
Member of Physics Faculty, Massachusetts Inst. of Technology 25-, Prof. of Physics 50-; on staff, Radiation Laboratory, Office of Scientific Research and Development 40-42; Consultant, Los Alamos Scientific Laboratory 52-; Asst. Sec.-Gen. for Scientific Affairs, NATO 62-64; Vice-Pres. American Acad. of Arts and Sciences 60-62; U.S. Army 42-45; Visiting Prof. Harvard Univ. 60; Visiting Fellow Oxford Univ. 68; Fellow American Physical Soc., Physical Soc. of London.
Publs. *Thermodynamics and Statistical Mechanics* 52, *Nuclear Fusion* 60, *Waves in Anisotropic Plasmas* 63, *Electrons, Ions and Waves* 67.
Massachusetts Institute of Technology, Cambridge, Mass. 01239; Home: 33 Reservoir Street, Cambridge, Mass. 01238, U.S.A.

Allison, Rt. Rev. Sherard Falkner, D.D.; British ecclesiastic; b. 19 Jan. 1907; ed. Jesus Coll. and Ridley Hall, Cambridge.
Curate, St. James's, Tunbridge Wells 31-34; Chaplain, Ridley Hall, Cambridge 34-36; Vicar, Rodbourne Cheney, Swindon 36-40, Erith 40-45; Principal, Ridley Hall 45-50; Bishop of Chelmsford 51-61, of Winchester and Prelate of the Order of the Garter 61-.
Wolvesey, Winchester, Hants., England.

Allon, Brig. Gen. Yigal; Israeli soldier, agriculturalist and politician; b. 10 Oct. 1918; ed. Kaduri Agricultural Coll., Univs. of Jerusalem and Oxford.
Joined Hagana 31, Commdr. of Palmach Company 41, in Syria and Lebanon with Allies, Dep. Commdr., Palmach 43, Commdr.-in-Chief, Palmach 45-48; charged with Hagana operations in Palestine 45-47, in command, Upper Galilee, Central Israel, Jerusalem Corridor, the Negev and N. Sinai 47-48; Mem. and Co-Founder Kibbutz Genossar 37-; Minister of Labour 61-; mem. Exec. Cttee. Hakibbutz Hameuchad; fmr. Sec. Gen. Achduth Ha-avodah Socialist Party; mem. 3rd and 4th Knessets.
Publs. *The Story of Palmach* 51, *Curtain of Sand* 60.
Kibbutz Genossar, Israel.

Allott, Gordon Llewellyn, B.A., LL.B.; American lawyer and politician; b. 2 Jan. 1907; ed. Univ. of Colorado.
Admitted to Colorado Bar 29; practised law in Lamar, Colorado; District Attorney, Prowers County 46-48; active in Young Republican League of Colorado 35-40; Gen. Counsel, Young Republican Nat. Fed. 38-41;

Chair. 41-46, mem. Exec. Cttee. 46-49; served army 42-46; Lieut.-Gov. of Colorado 50-54; U.S. Senator from Colorado 55-.
Lamar, Colorado, U.S.A.

Allyn, Stanley Charles, A.B.; American business executive; b. 20 July 1891; ed. Univ. of Wisconsin.
Accountant, Asst. Comptroller, Comptroller, Treas., Vice-Pres. and Gen. Manager The National Cash Register Co., Dayton, Ohio 13-40, Dir. 18, Pres. 40-57, Chair. 57-61, Chair. Exec. Cttee., 62-64; Dir. Emeritus 64-; Dir. Mead Corpn., Western Allegheny R.R. Co.; Trustee, Northwestern Mutual Life Insurance Co., Cttee. for Economic Development Inst. of Int. Education, Ohio State University; Vice-Pres. and Trustee Grand Central Art Galleries; U.S. Representative Economic Comm. for Europe 56-57; Chair. U.S. Del. UNESCO Conf., New Delhi 56; Chair. Cttee. U.S. Nat. Comm. for UNESCO, San Francisco 57; Hon. Trustee, Inst. of Int. Education, N.Y.C. 54-59; mem. Board of Trustees, Ohio State Univ.; Trustee, Logistics Management Inst., Washington; Trustee, Dir. Ohio State Univ. Research Foundation; Dir. Dayco Corpn., Master Consolidated Inc.; Hon. LL.D. (Wisconsin, Miami, Ohio, Oxford); L.H.D. (Dayton, Cincinnati); Officier Légion d'Honneur; Presidential Certificate of Merit, etc.
Office: 1016 Talbott Tower, Dayton 45402, Ohio; Home: 2021 Ridgeway Road, Dayton, Ohio 45419, U.S.A.

Almeida, Dr. Bernardo V.M. de, Count of Caria, C.B.E., DR.IUR.; Portuguese business executive; b. 1912; ed. Pedro Nuñes High School and Univ. of Lisbon.
Vice-President, C. Santos S.A.R.L. 34-, Vidago, Melgaço & Pedras Salgadas S.A.R.L.36-; Man. Dir. Supersumos Lda. 59-; mem. Board Siderurgia Nacional S.A.R.L. 60-, Banco Pinto & Sotto Mayor 60-; mem. Fiscal Board Companhia de Papel do Prado 60-; mem. Board Associação Industrial Portuguesa 58-; Pres. Associação Commercial de Lisboa 59-64; mem. Conselho Superior de Minas 63-.
Rua Rosa Araújo 8-20, Lisbon, Portugal.

Almeida, Gen. Pedro Geraldo de; Brazilian army officer and administrator; b. 01; ed. Military School, Realengo.
Assistant Instructor Realengo Military School 32-36. Head of Artillery Section 37-38; Brazilian Military Attaché Uruguay 38-41; Asst. to Dep. Chief of Army Staff 41-44; Cavalry Commdr. and mem. War Ministry Cabinet 44-50; Head of Military Comm. to U.S. 51-53; Commdr. Artillery School Regiment 53-55; Head of Chief Army Staff Cabinet 55-59; Commdr. Artillery Div. 59-60; Head Rio de Janeiro Military Coll. 60-61; Head Military Cabinet of the Presidency and Commder Military Region 61; Head Agulhas Negras Military Acad. 62; Exec. Dir. Brazilian Section of Interamerican Council for Commerce and Production (CICYP) 63-.
Home: Avenue Copacabana, 300-Ap. 703, Rio de Janeiro, Brazil.
Telephone: 23-50-55 (Office); 37-96-16 (Home).

Almeida, Romulo; Brazilian economist; b. 14; ed. Univ. of Bahia.
Worked as lawyer, newspaperman and teacher; Dir. Statistics, Federal Territory of Acre; Head of Economic Dept., Nat. Confederation of Manufacturers 45-51; Lecturer, Nat. School of Economics, Adviser to Pres. of Brazil 51-54; Organiser, First Pres. Banco Nordeste Brasil 54; Dep. 55-59; Sec. of Treasury, Bahia State 55-57, Sec. of Development 59-61; Exec. Sec., Latin American Free Trade Asscn. (LAFTA) 61-62; mem. Comm. of Nine of Inter-American Econ. and Social Council 62-; Rep. and Adviser to many int. econ. confs.
Publ. Transl. Marshall's *Principles of Economics* 45.
Pan American Union, Washington 6, D.C., U.S.A.

Almond, Gabriel Abraham; American educator; b. 1 Dec. 1911; ed. Univ. of Chicago.
Fellow, Social Science Research Council 35-36, 46;

Instructor, Political Science, Brooklyn Coll. 39-42; Office of War Information, Washington 42-45, War Dept., European Theatre of Operations 45; Research Assoc., Inst. of Int. Studies, Yale Univ. 47-49, Assoc. Prof. of Political Science 49-51; Assoc. Prof. of Int. Affairs, Princeton Univ. 51-54, Prof. 54-57, Prof. of Politics 57-59; Prof. of Political Science, Yale 59-63; Prof. of Political Science, Stanford Univ. 63-, Exec. Head, Dept. of Political Science, Stanford Univ. 64-; Consultant, Air Univ. 48, Dept. of State 50, Office of Naval Research 51, Scientific Advisory Board, U.S. Air Force 60-; Fellow, American Acad. of Arts and Sciences; Pres. American Political Science Asscn. 65-66; mem. Social Science Research Council.
Publs. *The American People and Foreign Policy* 50, *The Appeals of Communism* 54; editor *The Struggle for Democracy in Germany* 49, *The Politics of the Developing Areas* 60; co-author *The Civic Culture* 63.
Stanford University, Stanford, California; Home: 4147 Old Trace Road, Palo Alto, California, U.S.A.

Almond, James Lindsay, Jr., LL.B.; American politician and lawyer; b. 15 June 1898; ed. Univ. of Virginia. Asst. Commonwealth's Attorney, Roanoake, Va. 30-33; Judge, Roanoake Hustings Court 33-46; mem. U.S. House of Representatives (Dem.) 46-48; Attorney-Gen. of Virginia 48-57; Gov. of Virginia 58-62; Judge, U.S. Court of Customs and Patent Appeals 63-.
United States Court of Customs and Patent Appeals, Internal Revenue Building, Washington 25, D.C., U.S.A.

Aloisi Masella, H.E. Cardinal Benedetto; Vatican ecclesiastic; b. 29 June 1879.
Ordained priest 02; Titular Archbishop of Caesarea in Mauritania 19; created Cardinal by Pope Pius XII 46; Bishop of Palestrina 48-66; Archpriest of the Lateran Patriarchal Archbasilica (St. John Lateran); Prefect Sacred Congregation of Sacramental Discipline; Chamberlain of the Holy Roman Church; mem. Sacred Congregations of the Consistory, for the Oriental Church, of Religious, De Propaganda Fide, of Rites, of Seminaries and of Extraordinary Ecclesiastical Affairs; mem. Supreme Tribunal of the Apostolic Signatura; mem. Pontifical Comm. for the authentic interpretation of the Code of Canon Law, Cardinalicial Comm. for the Sanctuary of Pompeii and Loreto.
Via della Scrofa 70, Rome, Italy.

Alonso, Dámaso, PH.D.; Spanish university professor and writer; b. 98; ed. Univ. Madrid.
Former Lecturer in Spanish at Univs of Berlin, Cambridge, Stanford, California; Hunter College, N.Y.; Inst. of Int. Education, N.Y.; Columbia Univ. New York; Visiting Prof. at Yale, Johns Hopkins Univ., Harvard; Prof. at Centre of Historical Studies, Madrid 23-36; Prof. of Spanish Language and Literature, Valencia Univ. 33-39; Prof. of Romance Philology, Madrid Univ. 39-; Dr. h.c. (Univs. of Lima, Bordeaux, Rome, Hamburg, Oxford, Freiburg and Costa Rica); mem. Royal Spanish Acad., Royal Acad. of History, Madrid, Modern Humanities Research Asscn. (Pres. 60); foreign mem. Arcadia and Lincei, Rome, American Philosophical Soc.; Corresp. mem. British Acad.; Pres. Int. Asscn. of Hispanists 62-65.
Publs. Criticism: *Temas gongorinos* 27, *La Lengua poética de Góngora* 35, 50, 61, *La Poesía de San Juan de la Cruz* 46, 58, 67 (Italian trans.), *Ensayos sobre Poesía española* 44, *Vida y obra de Medrano* 48, Pt. II (with S. Reckert) 58, *Poesía Española* 50, 53, 57, 62, 68 (Portuguese, German and Italian trans.), *Seis cales en la expresión literaria española* (co-author) 51, 56, 63, *Poetas españoles contemporáneos* 52, 58, *La Primitiva Epica francesa a la luz de una "Nota Emilianense"* 45, *Estudios y Ensayos gongorinos* 55, 60, *Menéndez Pelayo, Crítico literario, De los siglos oscuros al de oro* 58, 64, *Primavera temprana de la literatura europea* 61, *Góngora y el Polifemo* 60, 61, 67, *Dos españoles del Siglo de Oro* 60, *Cuatro poetas españoles* 62, *Del Siglo de Oro a este Siglo de siglas* 62, 68; Poetry: *Poemas Puros* 21, *Oscura Noticia* 44, 59, *Hijos de la Ira* 44, 46, 58 (German and Italian trans.), *Hombre y Dios* 55, 59 (Italian trans.); translations of James Joyce, G. M. Hopkins and von Wartburg into Spanish.
Avenida A. Alcocer 33, Madrid 16, Spain.

Alonso-Fueyo, Sabino; Spanish university professor and newspaper editor; b. 09.
Journalist 30-; fmr. Ed. *Levante*, Valencia; fmr. Prof. of Philosophy and Political Doctrine, Valencia Univ.; Ed. *Arriba* 62-; mem. Falange.
Arriba, Avda. del Generalisimo 142, Madrid, Spain.

Alonso Vega, Camilo; Spanish army officer and politician; b. 89.
Retired as Lieut.-Gen. 55; Minister of Home Affairs 56-; numerous military decorations.
Ministry of Home Affairs, Madrid, Spain.

Alpatov, Mikhail Vladimirovitch, D.HIST. ART.; Soviet art historian; b. 10 Dec. 1902; ed. St. Michael Secondary School, Moscow and Moscow Univ.
Prof. Moscow Inst. of Fine Arts 25-; mem. Acad. of Fine Arts 54.
Publs. *Denkmäler der Ikonenmalerei* (with Oskar Wulff) 25, *Geschichte der altrussischen Kunst* (with N. Brunov) (two vols.) 32 (both in German), *Italian Art at the Time of Dante and Giotto* 39, *Essays on the History of Western Art* 64, *History of Art* (three vols.) 48-55 (all in Russian), *Russian Impact on Art* 50 (in English), *Alexander Ivanov, his Life and Work* (two vols.) 56 (in Russian), *Geschichte der Kunst* Vol. I 60, II 64 (in German), *Andrej Rublev* 62, *Il Maestro del Cremlino* 63 (both in Italian), *Die Dresdner Galerie* 66 (in German).
Institute of Fine Arts, Moscow, U.S.S.R.

Alphand, Hervé; French economist and diplomatist; b. 31 May 1907; ed. Lycée Janson de Sailly and Ecole des Sciences Politiques.
Insp. of Finances and Dir. Trade Agreements Div., Min. of Commerce 37-38; Sec.-Gen. Ministerial Cttee. of Nat. Economy 38; Financial Counsellor to Embassy Washington 40-41; Dir. of Economic Affairs, French Nat. Cttee. 41-44; Dir.-Gen. French Foreign Office 45; French Ambassador to OEEC; French Deputy to the Atlantic Council 50; French mem. NATO Permanent Council 52-54; Ambassador to UN 55, to U.S.A. 56-65; Sec.-Gen. French Foreign Office 65-.
122 rue de Grenelle, Paris 7e, France.
Telephone: 468-44-59.

Alport, 1st Baron, cr. 61, of Colchester; **Cuthbert James McCall Alport,** P.C., T.D.; British politician; b. 22 March 1912; ed. Haileybury, Cambridge Univ.
President, Cambridge Union Soc. 35; Tutor Ashridge Coll. 35-37; called to Bar; War Service 39-45; Dir. Conservative Political Centre 45-50; Conservative M.P. for Colchester 50-61; Chair. Joint East and Central African Board 53-55; Asst. Postmaster-Gen. 55-57; Parl. Under-Sec. of State, Commonwealth Relations Office 57-59, Minister of State 59-61; High Commr. to Fed. of Rhodesia and Nyasaland 61-June 63; U.K. Del. to Council of Europe, Strasbourg 64-65; Prime Minister's Special Envoy to Rhodesia 67; Fellow British Inst. of Management 67; High Steward of Colchester 67.
Publs. *Kingdom in Partnership* 37, *Hope in Africa* 52, *The Sudden Assignment* 65.
The Cross House, Layer de la Haye, Colchester, Essex, England.
Telephone: Layer de la Haye 217.

Alsogaray, Alvaro C. (brother of Julio Alsogaray, *q.v.*); Argentine politician; b. 1913; ed. Argentine Mil. Acad. Service in Air Force 31-47; in private business 47-55; Minister of Industry in provisional govt. 55; resigned and founded Civil Independent Party; Minister of Economic Affairs July 59-61; Acting Minister of Labour

and Welfare July 59-61; Minister of Economy 62; re-founder of Civil Independent Party 65; Special Amb. responsible for co-ordination of Argentina's foreign econ. policy 66; Amb. to U.S.A. 66-.
Embassy of Argentina, 1600 North Hampshire Avenue, N.W., Washington, D.C., U.S.A.
Telephone: DE2-7100.

Alsogaray, General Julio Rodolfo (brother of Alvaro Alsogaray, *q.v.*); Argentine army officer; b. 25 Jan. 1918; ed. Colegio Militar de la Nación.
Military Attaché in Mexico 60; Commdr., Second Cavalry Div. 61-62; Dir. Colegio Militar, Commdr. Armoured Div. 62; Under Sec. of War 62-66; Commdr.-in-Chief of Argentine Army Dec. 66-.
Aráoz 2876, Buenos Aires, Argentina.

Alsop, Joseph Wright, B.A. (brother of Stewart Alsop, *q.v.*); American journalist and author; b. 11 Oct. 1910; ed. Groton School and Harvard Univ.
Mem. *New York Herald Tribune* staff, New York 32-35, Washington 36-37; author (with Robert Kintner) of syndicated column *The Capital Parade* (North American Newspaper Alliance) 37-40; Lieut. Commdr. U.S. Navy 40, later joined Volunteer Air Force as aide to Gen. Chennaut; captured by Japanese at Hong Kong, exchanged and returned to U.S.; Dir. Lend-Lease Mission to China, Chungking 42; author (with brother Stewart Alsop) of column *Matter of Fact* (*New York Herald Tribune* Syndicate) 46-58, sole author 58; Legion of Merit, Order of Cloud Banner (China).
Publs. *The 168 Days, Men Around the President* (with Robert Kintner) 38, *The American White Paper* (with Robert Kintner) 40, *We Accuse* (with Stewart Alsop) 54, *The Reporter's Trade* (with Stewart Alsop) 60, *From the Silent Earth* 64.
2720 Dumbarton Ave., N.W., Washington 7, D.C., U.S.A.

Alsop, Stewart Johonnot Oliver, B.A. (brother of Joseph Alsop, *q.v.*); American journalist and author; b. 17 May 1914; ed. Groton School and Yale Univ.
Editor of Doubleday Doran 36; enlisted in King's Royal Rifle Corps 42, transferred to U.S. Army 43, parachuted into France to join Resistance; author (with brother Joseph Alsop) of column *Matter of Fact* (*New York Herald Tribune* Syndicate) 46-58; Washington Ed. *Saturday Evening Post* 58-; Croix de Guerre avec Palmes.
Publs. *Sub Rosa* (with Thomas Braden) 45, *We Accuse* 54, *The Reporter's Trade* 60 (both with Joseph Alsop), *Nixon and Rockefeller, The Center: People and Power in Political Washington* 68; numerous contributions to *Saturday Evening Post, Atlantic Monthly, Harpers, Readers' Digest.*
3520 Springland Lane, N.W., Washington, D.C., U.S.A.

Alter, Gerald M., PH.D.; American banking official; b. 15 Dec. 1919; ed. Harvard Univ. and Harvard Univ. Graduate School.
Former economist, U.S. Treasury, U.S. Bureau of the Budget, Commerce Dept., and Federal Reserve Board; Int. Bank for Reconstruction and Development 51-, Asst. to Economic Dir. and Chief of General Studies Div. 51-58, Economic Adviser, Dept. of Operations, W. Hemisphere 58-64, Dir. W. Hemisphere Dept. 64-.
International Bank for Reconstruction and Development, Washington, D.C. 20433, U.S.A.

Altmeier, Peter; German politician; b. 12 Aug. 1899 in the Saar; ed. Koblenz.
Mem. Zentrum (Catholic) Party during Weimar Republic; mem. Koblenz City Council 29-33; State Chair. C.D.U. 46- and Minister-Pres. of Rhineland-Palatinate 47-; Pres. Bundesrat 65-; Grand Cross, Order of Merit (Fed. Germany), Commdr. Légion d'Honneur.
Office of the Minister-President, Mainz, Rhineland; Home: 5400 Koblenz, Moselufer 34, German Federal Republic.

Alty, Thomas, PH.D., D.SC., D.C.L., LL.D., F.INST.P., F.R.S.C., F.R.S.E.; British university official; b. 30 Sept. 1899; ed. Liverpool and Cambridge Univs.
Lecturer in Physics, Univ. of Durham 24-25; Prof. of Physics, Univ. of Saskatchewan 25-35; Cargill Prof. of Natural Philosophy, Univ. of Glasgow 35-48; Master of Rhodes Univ. Coll. 48-51, Principal and Vice-Chancellor 51-63; Chair. South African Cttee. of Univ. Principals 58-60; Chair. Asscn. of Univs. of British Commonwealth 58-60; Deputy Principal, Univ. of Birmingham 63-.
The University, Birmingham 15, England.

Alva, Mrs. Violet, M.A., LL.B., M.P.; Indian lawyer, journalist and politician; b. 24 April 1908; ed. St. Xavier's Coll. and Govt. Law Coll., Bombay.
Founder editor of *Indian Woman;* Prof. of English, Indian Women's Univ. 36; mem. Bombay Municipal Corpn. 46, Bombay Legal Council 47-52; Dep., Press Delegation to Egypt 50; mem. Standing Cttee. All-India Newspapers Editors' Conf. 52; mem. Rajya Sabha 52-, Public Accounts Cttee. of Parl. 54-55; Dep. Minister for Home Affairs 57-62; Pres. Int. Fed. of Women Lawyers 62-64; Deputy Chair. Rajya Sabha 62-; Pres. YWCA of India 64-67.
3 Ashoka Road, New Delhi, India.

Alvarado, Carlos Alberto, M.D.; Argentine physician; b. 04; ed. Univ. of Buenos Aires, Scuola di Malariologia, Rome and London School of Tropical Medicine and Hygiene.
In national health service 31-54, rose to Regional Dir. of Health, N. Zone 51-54; Asst. Prof. of Hygiene, Univ. of Tucumán 41-47, Prof. of Epidemiology and Public Health Administration 48-54; Chief, Malaria Eradication Branch, Pan American Health Org. 55-58; Dir. Div. of Malaria Eradication, WHO 58-64.
Publ. *The Treatment of Malaria* 41.
c/o WHO, Geneva, Switzerland.

Alvarado Garaicoa, Teodoro, DR.JUR.; Ecuadorean lawyer and diplomatist; b. 03; ed. Hamburg, and Univ. of Guayaquil, Ecuador.
Sec. of Presidency; later Under-Sec., Ministry of the Interior; mem. Consultative Board for Foreign Affairs 46-48; Minister-Counsellor, Washington, D.C. 48, Organization of American States (O.A.S.) 48; mem. Chamber of Reps.; Senator; Minister of Foreign Relations Sept. 52-53; Ambassador to the U.S.A. 56-57; Minister of Superior Court of Justice 57-58; Ambassador to O.A.S. 60-63; Pres. Lawyer Coll.; Dean, Int. Law Inst., Univ. of Guayaquil; decorations from Ecuador, Bolivia, Chile, Colombia, etc.; Liberal Party.
Publs. *El Imperialismo y la Democracia a través de la Doctrina Monroe, Principios Normativos del Derecho Internacional Público, La Doctrina Internacional de Franklin D. Roosevelt, La Trascendencia de las Reuniones Interamericanas, El Río de las Amazonas, Sinopsis del Derecho Territorial Ecuatoriano, Doce Hombres, La Plataforma Submarina y el Mar Territorial, La responsabilidad del Estado en los daños causados a los extranjeros, Los principios de Nulidad y Revisión en los Tratados Internacionales.*
P.O. Box 661, Guayaquil, Ecuador.

Alvarez, Luis Walter, S.B., S.M., PH.D., SC.D.; American physicist; b. 13 June 1911; ed. Univ. of Chicago.
Research Associate, Instructor, Asst. Prof., and Assoc. Prof., Univ. of California 36-45, Prof. of Physics 45-; Assoc. Dir. Lawrence Radiation Laboratory 54-59; Vice-Pres. American Physical Soc. 68; Collier Trophy 46, Medal for Merit 47, John Scott Medal and Prize 53, Einstein Medal 61, Pioneer Award of American Inst. of Electrical Engineers 63, Nat. Medal of Science 64, Michelson Award 65.
Lawrence Radiation Laboratory, University of California, Berkeley, Calif. 94720, U.S.A.
Telephone: 415-843-2740.

Alvárez Amezquita, José; Mexican physician and politician; b. 11; ed. Colego Francés Morelos, Mexico City, and Medical School, National Univ., Mexico City. Secretariat of Health and Welfare, Mexico City 49-52; Titular Prof. Clínica Propédeutica Quirúrgica 42-53, Prof. of Gastroenterology 57; Dir.-Gen. of Medical Sciences, Dept. of Labour and Social Services, Mexico City 56-58; Sec. of Health and Welfare 58-65; Pres. of Council of General Health, Mexico City 58-65; Pres. several medical orgs.; mem. numerous medical institutes.
Office; Varsovia 36, Mexico, D.F.; Home: Heroes del 47 No. 113, Mexico, D.F., Mexico.
Telephone: 11-89-15 (Office); 49-16-01 (Home).

Alvarez Tabio, Fernando; Cuban judge and diplomatist; b. 15 July 1907; ed. Universidad de Habana. Municipal Judge, Cuba 33-47; Court Magistrate, Province of Las Villas 47-50; Magistrate, Court of Justice, Havana 50-57, Magistrate Pres. 57-58, dismissed for political reasons 58; Justice of Supreme Court 59, and Head of Court of Constitutional and Social Guarantees 59-; Dir. Inst. for Int. Affairs and Prof. of Comparative Constitutional Law and Govt., School of Political Sciences, Univ. of Havana 62-; Perm. Rep. of Cuba to UN 64.
Supreme Court of Justice, Havana, Cuba.

Alvera, Pierluigi; Italian diplomatist; b. 14.
Consul, Berne 43-44, then Basle, Glasgow; First Sec., Bonn 49-51, later Council of Europe; Consul-General, San Francisco 55, later Economic Service, Ministry of Foreign Affairs; Ambassador to Libya 63-67.
c/o Ministry of Foreign Affairs, Rome, Italy.

Alverny, Marie-Thérèse d', DR.PHIL.; French palaeographical archivist; b. 25 Jan. 1903; ed. Univ. de Strasbourg and Univ. de Paris à la Sorbonne, Ecole nat. des Chartes and Ecole pratique des Hautes Etudes, Paris.
Librarian Bibliothèque nationale 28, Asst. Keeper of MSS. 47-62; Prof. Centre of Higher Studies of Mediaeval Civilization, Univ. of Poitiers 57-; Maître de Recherche, Centre national de la Recherche scientifique (CNRS) 63-, Dir. of Research 67-; Gen. Sec. Bibliographical Comm., Int. Union of the History of Sciences; Co.-Dir. *Archives d'Histoire doctrinale et littéraire du Moyen-Age* 54; mem. Editorial Cttee. *Scriptorium* 66-; mem. Soc. of the School of Charters (Pres. 65-66), Society of Latin Studies and Int. Cttee. of Palaeography; Corresp. mem. Mediaeval Acad. of America, Acad. of Humanities of Barcelona and British Acad.; Chevalier Légion d'Honneur; Dr. h.c., Oxford.
Publs. *Catalogue général des manuscrits latins de la Bibliothèque nationale,* vol. 3, 54, vol. 4, 58, *Deux traductions latines du Coran au Moyen Age* 48, *Marc de Tolède, Traducteur d'Ibn Tumart* 50-51, *Avicenna latinus* vols. I-VII 61-67, *Alain de Lille, Textes inédits, avec une introduction sur sa vie et ses oeuvres* 65, *La Sagesse et ses sept filles: Recherches sur les Allégories de la Philosophie et des Arts libéraux IXe-XIIe siècle* 46.
Centre National de la Recherche Scientifique, 15 Quai Anatole France, Paris 7e; Homes: 58 rue de Vaugirard, Paris 6e; and Clérac, par Meyrannes (Gard), France.
Telephone: 548-09-03 (Paris home).

Alves de Souza, Carlos; Brazilian diplomatist; b. 01.
Second Sec. 24; Chargé d'Affaires, Montevideo 25; First Sec. 26; Chargé d'Affaires, Paris 29, Vienna 34-35, Mexico City 35-37; Counsellor 36; Minister (Second Class) 38; Head, Dept. of Admin. of Minister for Foreign Relations 43-45; Minister (First Class) 44; Ambassador to Cuba 45; Govt. Rep. at inauguration of Pres. of Cuba 48; Head of Del. to Second Session of Economic Comm. of Latin America 49; Ambassador to Italy 50-55, to France 55-64, to U.K. 64-66.
c/o Ministry of Foreign Affairs, Rio de Janeiro, Brazil.

Al Wu; Chinese author; b. 04.
Casual labourer in Burma and Yunnan Province; proofreader in newspaper offices; schoolteacher; obliged to leave Burma for political reasons 31; began his career as a writer in Shanghai; during the war was head of the Kweilin branch of the Nat. Writers' Resistance Society. Publs. Numerous novels and short stories about Southwestern China; critical essays.
Chinese Writers' Union, Peking, China.

Amachree, Godfrey Kio Jaja, Q.C., LL.B.; Nigerian lawyer and United Nations official; b. 18; ed. Govt. Coll., Umuahia; King's Coll., Lagos; Higher Coll., Yaba; Univ. Coll., London; Pembroke Coll., Cambridge and Gray's Inn, London.
Nigerian Legal Dept. 49-55, Senior Crown Counsel 55; Acting Legal Sec., S. Cameroons 55; Acting Solicitor-Gen., Fed. of Nigeria 57, Solicitor-Gen. 58-62; Perm. Sec., Fed. Ministry of Justice 58-62; Under-Sec. in charge of UN Civilian Operations in the Congo 62-63, Under-Sec. Dept. of Trusteeship and Non Self-Governing Territories 63-66.
187 Overlook Road, New Rochelle, N.Y. 10804, U.S.A.

Amadeo, Mario; Argentine diplomatist; b. 15 Jan. 1911; ed. Univ. of Buenos Aires.
Lawyer, Buenos Aires 34-39, Banco Hipotecario Nacional 47-48; Diplomatic Service 39-, served Vatican, Uruguay, Chile 39-44; Head, Political Dept. Argentine Ministry of Foreign Affairs 41-45; Prof. of Int. Law, Buenos Aires Law School 47-53; Minister of Foreign Affairs 55; Perm. Rep. to UN 58-62; Prof. Univ. of Buenos Aires 62-.
Publ. *Por una convivencia internacional* 54.
Paraná 1195, Buenos Aires, Argentina.

Amado, Jorge; Brazilian novelist.
Publs. include: *Mar Morto, Jubiabá, The Violent Land, São Jorge dos Ilheus, Cacau, Suor, Capitães da Areia, ABC de Castro Alves, Bahia de Todos os Santos, O Amor do Soldado, Seara Vermelha, O Cavaleiro da Esperança, O Mundo da Paz, Os subterrâneos da Liberdade, Gabriela Cravo e Canela, Os velhos marinheiros, Os pastores da noite, Dona Flor e seus dois maridos!.*
Rua Alagoinhas, 33-Salvador, Bahía, Brazil.

Amaldi, Edoardo, PH.D.; Italian physicist; b. 5 Sept. 1908; ed. Rome Univ.
Professor, Gen. Physics Rome Univ.; Vice-Pres. Istituto Nazionale di Fisica Nucleare; mem. Accademia Naz. dei Lincei, Royal Soc. of Sciences of Uppsala, U.S.S.R Acad. of Sciences; Hon. mem. Royal Inst. of Great Britain, Nat. Acad. of Sciences of U.S.A., Royal Soc. (U.K.), etc.
Publs. various papers on atomic and nuclear problems.
Istituto di Fisica, Città Universitaria, Rome, Italy.

Amano, Teiyu; Japanese philosopher; b. 30 Sept. 1884; ed. Kyoto Univ.
Professor Seventh High School, Kagoshima, and Peers' School; Prof. Kyoto Univ. 31-44, Emer. 44-; fmr. Dir. First High School; Minister of Education 50-52; Principal, Dokkwo Gakuen 55-; Pres. Dokkyo Univ. 64-; Pres. Central Education Council 55-62, mem. 62-67.
567 Kichijoji, Musashino-shi, Tokyo, Japan.

Amatayakul, Manu, DR. PHIL., DR. RER. POL.; Thai diplomatist; b. 12; ed. Chulalongkorn Univ., Univ. of Berlin and Univ. of Berne.
Lecturer in Public Finance, Econs., Journalism, Chulalongkorn Univ., lecturer in Int. Law, Thammasat Univ. 42-47; Deputy Chief Thai Perm. Del. to UN 49-50; Dir. of UN Dept., Ministry of Foreign Affairs 53-59; Prof. of Int. Relations, Chulalongkorn Univ. 55-58; mem. Thai Del. to UN Gen. Assembly 47-49, 53, 58, 61; mem. Civil Aviation Board of Thailand 53-59; Amb. to U.S.S.R. 59-63, to Spain 63-65; Dir.-Gen. of Treaty and Legal Dept., Ministry of Foreign Affairs 65-;

Special Grand Cordon of Most Noble Order of Crown of Thailand 65, and other decorations.
Publs. *Umwandlung der Währungspolitik Europas von 1918–1939, Kreditpolitik Europas, United Nations*, and other works.
Office: Treaty and Legal Department, Ministry of Foreign Affairs, Bangkok; Home: 69 Prongchai Road, Mahamek, Bangkok, Thailand.
Telephone: 32873; 20347.

Amaury, Emilien; French editor and advertising manager; b. 5 March 1909; ed. Univ. de Paris.
Founder, Office de Publicité Générale; creator of resistance movement called Groupe de la Rue de Lille during occupation; Perm. mem. Féd. de la Presse Clandestine during occupation; Dir. Agence Havas after liberation; Founder and Man. *Carrefour*; Pres. and Founder *Parisien Libéré* and several provincial journals; Pres. Syndicat de la Presse Hebdomadaire Parisienne, Comité National Intersyndical de la Presse Périodique Française; Grand Officier de la Légion d'Honneur, Croix de Guerre, Rosette de la Résistance.
114 Champs Elysées, Paris 8e, France.

Ambartsumyan, Ruben Sergeyevich; Soviet structural scientist; b. 1911; ed. Moscow Inst. of Non-Ferrous Metals.
Member C.P.S.U. 42-; Research Assoc., U.S.S.R. Inst. of Aircraft Materials 33-; specialist in structural materials and their processing; Prof. 55; Corresp. mem. U.S.S.R. Acad. of Sciences 66-; Merited Scientist of R.S.F.S.R.
U.S.S.R. Academy of Sciences, 14 Lenin Prospekt, Moscow, U.S.S.R.

Ambartsumyan, Victor Amazaspovich; Soviet astrophysicist; b. 18 Sept. 1908; ed. Leningrad Univ. and Pulkovo Observatory.
Lecturer and research worker Leningrad Univ. 31-43; Prof. Astrophysics Erivan Univ. 47-; Corresp. mem. U.S.S.R. Acad. of Sciences 39-53, mem. 53-; founder and Dir. Byurakan Observatory 45-; Pres. Armenian Acad. of Sciences 47-; Vice-Pres. Int. Astronomical Union 48-55, Pres. 61-64; Dep. Supreme Soviet U.S.S.R. 50-; mem. Central Cttee. Communist Party of Armenia; specialist on problems of stellar cosmogony; corresp. mem. French Acad. of Sciences; German Acad. of Sciences (Berlin); Hon. mem. American Acad. of Arts and Sciences; foreign assoc. U.S. Nat. Acad. of Sciences 59; State prize 46, 50; two Orders of Lenin; two Orders of Red Banner.
Publs. *Teoroticheskaya astrofizika* 39, *Evolyutsiya zvezd i astrofizika* 47, *Novyi sposob rascheta rassejania sveta v mutnoi srede* 42, *O rasseyaniis sveta atmosferami planet* 42, *K. voprosu o diffusnom otrazhenii sveta mutnoi sredoi* 43, *Nautchnye Trudy* (2 vols.) 60.
Academy of Sciences of Armenian S.S.R., Barekamutyan Street 24, Erevan, Armenia, U.S.S.R.

Ambrière, Francis; French writer and journalist; b. 27 Sept. 1907; ed. Univs. of Dijon and Paris.
Before Second World War was Ed. *Nouvelles Littéraires* and dramatic critic *Mercure de France*; served in French Army in Second World War; prisoner in Germany and Poland; Dir. of *Guides Bleus* May 45-; Prés.-Dir. Gén. of *L'Université des Annales* May 47-; dramatic critic of monthly *Les Annales*; Dir. *Connaissance du Monde* 58; Officier Légion d'Honneur, Commdr. des Arts et Lettres.
Publs. *La Vie Secrète des Grands Magasins* 32 (revised 38), *Le Favori de François Ier* 36, *Les Grandes Vacances* (Prix Goncourt 46), *Le Solitaire de La Cervara* 47, *La Galerie Dramatique* 49, *Le Maroc* 52.
79 boulevard Saint-Germain, Paris 6e, France.

Amelko, Admiral Nikolai Nikolayevich; Soviet naval officer; b. 1914; ed. Frunze Higher Naval School and Acad. of General Staff.
Naval service 33-; Commdr. of ships, Baltic Fleet

37-41; Commdr. of ship formation 41-46; Chief of Staff, Pacific Fleet 56-62; Commdr. Pacific Fleet 62-; Alt. mem. Central Cttee. of C.P.S.U.
U.S.S.R. Ministry of Defence, Maurice Thorez Embankment, Moscow, U.S.S.R.

Amerasinghe, Hamilton Shirley; Ceylonese diplomatist; b. 18 March 1913; ed. Royal Coll., Colombo and Ceylon Univ. Coll.
Ceylon Civil Service 37; Sec. to Minister of Health, Ceylon 41-46; Resident Manager, Gal Oya Development Board 50-52; Counsellor, Washington 53-55; Controller of Establishments, General Treasury, Ceylon 55-57; Alt. Del. Ceylon Del. to UN 57; Controller of Supply, Cadre and Finance, General Treasury, Ceylon 58; Perm. Sec. to Ministry of Nationalised Services and Chair. Port (Cargo) Corpn., Colombo 58; Sec. to Treasury and Perm. Sec. Ministry of Finance 61-63; Dir. Bank of Ceylon 62-63; High Commr. of Ceylon in India 63-67; Perm. Rep. to UN 67-.
Permanent Mission of Ceylon to the United Nations, 630 Third Avenue, New York, N.Y. 10017, U.S.A.

Amery, Rt. Hon. Julian; British politician; b. 27 March 1919; ed. Eton and Oxford Univ.
War Correspondent, Spanish Civil War 38-39; Attaché H.M. Legation, Belgrade, and on special missions 39-40; Sergeant R.A.F. 40-41; commissioned and transferred to Army; active service, Egypt, Palestine, Adriatic 41-42; liaison officer to Albanian Resistance 44; on the staff of Mr. Churchill's personal mission to Generalissimo Chiang Kai-Shek 45; M.P. 50-66; Under-Sec. of State for War 57-58, for Colonies 58-60; Sec. of State for Air 60-62; Minister for Aviation 62-64; Conservative.
Publs. *Sons of the Eagle, The Life of Joseph Chamberlain, Joseph Chamberlain and the Tariff Reform Campaign.*
112 Eaton Square, London, S.W.1, England.

Amiel, Denys; French dramatist; b. 5 Oct. 1884.
Fmr. Vice-Pres. Société des Auteurs et Compositeurs Dramatiques; Hon. Sec. Int. Confed. of Authors and Composers; Grand Prix du Théâtre.
Publs. *La Souriante Madame Beudet* 21, *Le Couple* 23, *Café-Tabac* 23, *Le Voyageur* 23, *La Carcasse* 26, *M. et Mme. Un Tel* 25, *L'Image* 27, *L'Age de Fer* 30, *Décalage* 31, *Trois et une* 31, *L'Homme* 34, *La femme en fleur* 35, *Ma liberté* 37, *Famille* 38, *La Maison Monestier* 39, *Mon Ami* 43, *"1939"* 40, *Le nouvel amour* 46, *Le Manoir de Gers* 49, *La Dormeuse éveillée* 50, *Pardonnez-leur* 51, *Vivre Ensemble* 51, *Le paysan du Danube* 51, *Les Naufragées* 52, *L'Age du Feu* 53, *Nature* 54, *Le Portrait* 55, *Vedettes* 57, *Terre, Confession, Confidences* 58, *Elle et Elle* 59, *Duplicata* 60.
Domaine de la Condamine, La Gaude, Alpes Maritimes, France.
Telephone: 32-40-09.

Amies, (Edwin) Hardy; British dressmaker and designer; b. 17 July 1909; ed. Brentwood School.
Trainee, W. & T. Avery, Birmingham 30-34; Man. Designer Lachasse, Farm Street, London W.1 34-39; Intelligence Corps 39-45; Man. Dir. Hardy Amies Ltd. 46-; opened Hardy Amies Boutique Ltd. 50; Dir. Hardy Amies Ready-to-Wear 50-; Dressmaker to the Queen 55-; Design Consultant to Michelsons Ltd. 57, Bryan Manufacturing Co. Ltd. 61, J. Hepworth & Son Ltd. 60-, C. & J. Clark (Men's Shoe Div.) 63-, D. Byford & Co. Ltd. 63-, Dent Allcott & Co. Ltd. 65-, Bonsoir Ltd. 66-, Tern-Consulate Ltd. 66-, Alexandra Overalls Ltd. 66-; Overseas: Park Lane Neckwear (Canada) 62-, B. Smuts-Kennedy Ltd. (New Zealand) 65-, Ernest Hiller Apparel Pty. Ltd. (Australia) 65-, Cambridge Clothing Co. (New Zealand) 66-, John W. Shackelford & Son Ltd. (New Zealand) 66, Genesco Inc. (U.S.A.) 67; Vice-Pres. Clothing Inst. 57-; Chair. Inc. Soc. of London Fashion Designers 59-60; Officier de

l'Ordre de la Couronne (Belgium) 46; Royal Designer for Industry 64; numerous design awards.
Publs. *Just So Far* 54, *ABC of Men's Fashions* 64.
Hardy Amies Ltd., 14 Savile Row, London, W.1, England.
Telephone: 01-734-2436.

Amin, Mohamed El Amir: Sudanese airways official; b. 1 June 1919; ed. Gordon Memorial Coll., Khartoum.
Attached to Office of Civil Sec. (now Ministry of Interior) 38-48; Chief of Booking and Freight Office, Sudan Airways 48-54, Sales Supt. Sudan Airways 54-66; Gen. Man. Sudan Airways 66-.
Office: Sudan Airways, P.O. Box 253, Khartoum, Sudan; Home: Khartoum North, Sudan.

Amin, Moustafa; United Arab Republic (Egyptian) publisher; b. 14; ed. Cairo and Georgetown Univ., Washington, D.C., U.S.A.
Editor *Akher Saa* 38-41, *Al-Etnein* 41-44; publisher *Akhbar El-Yom* 44-65, *Akher Saa* 46-65, *Al-Guil* 50-65, *Al-Akhbar* (daily) 52-65; mem. of Parl. 44-49; arrested 65, sentenced to life imprisonment Aug. 66.
c/o *Akhbar El-Yom*, Sharia Sahafa, Cairo, U.A.R.

Amin, Osman Mohammad, D. ÈS L.; United Arab Republic (Egyptian) university professor; b. 05; ed. Saïdia School, Giza, and Univs. of Cairo and Paris.
Member Egyptian Univ. Mission, Paris 31-39; Lecturer, Faculty of Arts, Cairo 39; Asst. Prof. Faculty of Arts Cairo 48; Prof. of Philosophy, Cairo Univ., Cairo 54-56; Head of Dept. 57; Sec. Egyptian Philosophical Society; Pres. Asscn. Muhammad Abduh.
Publs. *L'Humanisme de F. C. S. Schiller* (French) 39, *Muhammad Abduh* (French) 44, *Towards Better Universities* (Arabic) 52, *Philosophical Essays* (Arabic) 53, *The Pioneer of Egyptian Thought* (Arabic) 55, *Descartes* (Arabic), 4th edn. 57, *Lights on Contemporary Moslem Philosophy* (English) 58, *Schiller* (Arabic) 58, *Stoic Philosophy* (Arabic), 2nd edn. 59; Editor: *Les Classiques de la Philosophie* (Arabic) 42, *Les Chefs-d'oeuvre de la Philosophie Occidentale* (Arabic) 46, *Al-Fārābī* (Classification of Sciences) 49, *Ibn Rushd* (Compendium of Metaphysics) 58; translations of Kant and Descartes.
22A Sharia Mohammad Said, Cairo, U.A.R.

Amini, Ali, D.ECON. ET IUR; Iranian politician; b. 05; ed. Ecole de Droit, Grenoble, and Faculté de Droit, Paris, France.
Alternate Judge, Court of First Instance, and Penal Branch, Court of Appeal, Teheran 31; Dir.-Gen. Dept. of Customs and Monopolies 33, Economic Section, Ministry of Finance 39; Asst. Prime Minister 40; Dir. Foreign Exchange Comm.; Deputy, 15th Legislative Session of the Majlis; Head of Narcotics Del. to Geneva and U.S.A.; Minister of Nat. Economy; Head of Iranian Trade Del. to Germany and France; Minister of Economy 52; Minister of Finance 53, of Justice 55; Ambassador to U.S.A. 56-58; Leader of Independents in general election 60; Prime Minister 61- July 62.
Publ. *L'institution du monopole de commerce extérieur en Perse.*
Park Aminodoleh, Teheran, Iran.

Amis, Kingsley, M.A.; British author; b. 16 April 1922; ed. City of London School and St. John's Coll., Oxford.
Lecturer in English, Univ. Coll. of Swansea 49-61; Fellow of Peterhouse, Cambridge 61-63; Visiting Fellow in Creative Writing, Princeton Univ. 58-59; Somerset Maugham Award 55.
Publs. *A Frame of Mind* 53, *Lucky Jim* 54, *That Uncertain Feeling* 55, *A Case of Samples* 56, *I Like it Here* 58, *New Maps of Hell* 60, *Take a Girl Like You* 60, *My Enemy's Enemy* 62, *One Fat Englishman* 63, *The James Bond Dossier* 65, *The Egyptologists* (with Robert Conquest) 65, *The Anti-Death League* 66, *A Look*

Around the Estate (poems 1957-1967) 67; (as Robert Markham) *Colonel Sun* 68.
108 Maida Vale, London, W.9, England.

Ammar, Abbas Moustafa, PH.D.; United Arab Republic (Egyptian) international civil servant; b. 07; ed. Cairo, Manchester, Cambridge and Columbia Univs.
Lecturer in Socio-Economics, Intermediate Coll. of Commerce, Cairo 31-37; Research Work in Social and Cultural Anthropology, Manchester and Cambridge Univs. 37-42; Lecturer and Asst. Prof. of Social Anthropology and Socio-Economics, Cairo Univ. 42-47; Head, Petitions Div., Trusteeship Dept. of UN 48-50, 51-52; Dir.-Gen. Rural Welfare Dept., Egyptian Ministry of Social Affairs 50-51, Minister of Social Affairs 52-54, Minister of Education 54; Asst. Dir-Gen. Int. Labour Office, Geneva 54-64, Deputy Dir.-Gen. 64-.
Publs. Arabic: *Anthropological Study of the Arabs* 46, *Report on Adult Education and People's University for Workers* 47, *Report on Population Situation in Egypt* 53, *Re-organisation of the Egyptian Village in a Decentralised Administration* 54; English: *The Peoples of Sharqia: An Anthropo-Socio-Economic Study of the Eastern Province of the Nile Delta* (2 vols.) 46.
2 rue Crespin, 1200 Geneva, Switzerland.

Ammoun, Fouad; Lebanese politician; b. 26 Nov. 1899; ed. Beirut School of Law and Univ. de Paris à la Sorbonne.
President, Court of Appeal and of Cassation, Lebanon 35-42, Attorney-Gen. 42-43; Commr. of Govt. attached to Council of State 43-44; Joined Ministry of Foreign Affairs 44, Legal Expert 44-45 Gen. Sec. 45-56, 60-63; mem. Cttee. drafting Covenant of League of Arab States and numerous int. treaties 44-; Minister for Planning and Nat. Economy Feb.-March 64; Minister for Foreign Affairs 64-65; Judge Int. Court of Justice 65-; Chair. Lebanese Nat. Comm. UNESCO 45-55, 60-63, and Cttee. Int. Econ. Relations 60-63; mem. del. to UN seven sessions between 48-63; Cordon of the Phoenix (Greece).
Publs. several juridical articles, notably an explanation of the *Code Correctionnel Libanais* (with Ph. N. Boulos and W. El Kassar).
International Court of Justice, The Hague, Netherlands.

Amory, 1st Viscount, cr. 60, of Tiverton in the County of Devon; **Derick Heathcoat Amory,** K.G., P.C.; British politician and public official; b. 26 Dec. 1899; ed. Eton Coll. and Christ Church, Oxford.
Served 39-45 war; Conservative M.P. for Tiverton Div. Devon 45-60; Minister of Pensions 51-53; Minister of State, Board of Trade 53-54; Minister of Agriculture and Fisheries July 54; Minister of Agriculture, Fisheries and Food Oct. 54-Jan. 58; Chancellor of the Exchequer 58-60; High Commr. for U.K. in Canada 61-63; Chair. Royal Comm. on Penal Reform 64-; Chair. Medical Research Council 65-; Dir. Lloyds Bank, John Heathcoat & Co. Ltd., I.C.I.; Dep. Gov. Hudson's Bay Co. 64-65, Gov. 65-; Chair. John Heathcoat and Co. 66-; Hon. LL.D. (Exeter, McGill, Mount Allison and Bishop's).
Chevithorne Barton, Tiverton, Devon, England.

Amosov, Nikolai Mikhailovich; Soviet surgeon, cybernetician and novelist; b. 6 Dec. 1913; ed. Archangel Medical Inst. and Inst. of Technology.
Doctor of Medical Sciences 53, Prof. 54; Corresp. mem. Acad. of Medical Sciences of U.S.S.R. 61-; Chief of Dept. of Thoracic Surgery, Kiev Inst. for Advanced Medical Training; Chief of Clinic for Cardiovascular Surgery, Kiev Inst. of Thoracic Surgery; Chief of Dept. of Biocybernetics, Inst. of Cybernetics; Merited Scientist of Ukraine; Lenin Prize for evolving original methods in pulmonary surgery.
Publs. *Surgical Treatment of Suppurated Disease of Lung* 54, *Pneumonectomy and Resection of Lung with TBC* 57, *Essays on Thoracic Surgery* 58, *Heart Operation with*

Use of Artificial Circulation of Blood 62, *Control of Vital Functions and Cybernetics* 64, *Simulation of Thinking and Mental Processes* 65; novel: *Thoughts and Heart* 65 (*Russian Surgeon*, English trans. 66).
Institute of Thoracic Surgery, Kiev 38, U.S.S.R.

Amsinck, Ove; Danish shipowner; b. 14 Oct. 1901; ed. Østre Borgerdyd School, Copenhagen.
Progress Steamship Co. and Marius Nielsen and Son 19-, Asst. Manager 32-45; Asst. Dir. Progress Steamship Co. 45-50, Managing Dir. 50-; Chair. Danish Shipowners' Asscn. 61-65; Chair. Maritime Council 61-65; mem. Board of Dirs. Baltic and Int. Maritime Conference, fmr. mem. Presidium Shipbrokers' Asscn.; mem. Board of H. H. Andersen and Co., and Procator A./S., Copenhagen; mem. several shipping societies and asscns.; Knight First Class, Order of Dannebrog.
Steamship Company Progress, 28 Christians Brygge, DK-1559 Copenhagen V; Home: Damgaardsvej 32, DK-2930 Klampenborg, Denmark.
Telephone: 11-20-20 (Office); Ordrup 2040 (Home).

Amsterdam, Gustave G.; American financier; b. 18 Aug. 1908; ed. Univ. of Pennsylvania.
Vice-Pres. Albert M. Greenfield & Co. 38-56; Vice-Pres. Bankers' Securities Corpn. 46-51, Exec. Vice-Pres. 51-55, Pres. 55-, Chair. 59-; Chair. City Stores Co., Diversified Stores Co. Inc.; Pres. Benjamin Franklin Hotel Corpn.. Albert M. Greenfield Foundation; Vice-Pres. Bankers' Realty Corpn., Lit Bros. Foundation.
Home: 5209 Woodbine Avenue, Philadelphia 31; Office: 1315 Walnut Street, Philadelphia 7, Pa., U.S.A.

Amstutz, Walter Hermann, D.PHIL.; Swiss publisher; b. 5 Dec. 1902; ed. Berne City Grammar School, Univs. of Berne, Zurich, Munich and London School of Economics.
Director of Publicity, St. Moritz 30-38; Co-Founder *Graphis* 45, Nature Method Publishing Co. (language correspondence courses) 48-; Editor *Who's Who in Graphic Art* 61; cttee. mem. Swiss Foundation for Alpine Research; founder and hon. mem. Swiss Univ. Ski Club, etc.
Im Schilf, 8708 Männedorf/Zürich, Switzerland.
Telephone: 74-01-63.

Amuzegar, Jahangir, PH.D.; Iranian economist and politician; b. 13 Jan. 1920; ed. Univs. of Teheran, Washington and California.
Teaching Asst., Univ. of California, Los Angeles 51-53; Lecturer, Whittier Coll. 53, Univ. of Michigan 53-55; Asst. Prof. Pomona Coll., Claremont, California 55-56; Asst. Prof. Michigan State Univ., E. Lansing, Mich. 56-58; Assoc. Prof. Occidental Coll., Los Angeles 58-60; Brookings Research Prof. 60-61; Econ. Adviser, Plan Org., Govt. of Iran 56-57; Minister of Commerce, Iran 61-62; mem. Iranian Parl. 60; mem. Council of Money and Credit 61-62, High Econ. Council 61-62; mem. Board of Dirs. Bank Melli Iran 61-62; Chair. Board, Foreign Trade Co. (Iranian Govt. Org.) 61-62; Minister of Finance 62; Chair. High Council of Nat. Iranian Oil Co. 62; Ambassador-at-Large, Chief of Iranian Econ. Mission, Washington, D.C. 63-.
Publ. *Technical Assistance in Theory and Practice: The Case of Iran* 66.
Iranian Economic Mission, 2233 Wisconsin Avenue, N.W., Washington, D.C. 20007, U.S.A.

Anand, Bal Krishan, M.B., B.S., M.D.; Indian physiologist; b. 19 Sept. 1917; ed. Government Coll. and K.E. Medical Coll. Lahore.
Prof. of Physiology, Lady Hardinge Medical Coll., New Delhi 49-57, All India Inst. of Medical Sciences, New Delhi 57-; Rockefeller Foundation Fellow at Yale Univ. School of Medicine 50-51; Fellow, Indian Acad. of Medical Sciences, Nat. Inst. of Sciences (F.N.I.); Indian Council of Medical Research Senior Research Award 62; Watumull Foundation Award in Medicine

61; Sir Shanti Swaroof Bhatnagar Memorial Award for Scientific Research in Medicine 63.
All India Institute of Medical Sciences, Ansari Nagar, New Delhi 16, India.

Anand, Mulk Raj, PH.D.; Indian author and critic; b. 12 Dec. 1905; ed. Punjab and London Univs.
Active in Nationalist and Gandhi movements; lecturer, London County Council; B.B.C. broadcaster; film script writer, British Ministry of Information; edited (56) various magazines, Leverhulme Fellow for Research in Hindustani literature; Editor *Marg* magazine, India; mem. India Nat. Acad. of Letters, Indian Nat. Acad. of Arts, Indian Nat. Book Trust; Tagore Prof. of Art and Literature, Univ. of Chandigarh, Punjab; Padma Bhushan 67.
Publs. Novels: *Private Life of an Indian Prince, The Big Heart, The Sword and the Sickle, Across the Black Waters, Untouchable, Coolie, The Barbers' Trade Union, Seven Summers,* etc.; Essays: *Apology for Heroism, Lines Written to an Indian Air,* etc.
Jassim House, 25 Cuffe Parade, Colaba, Bombay 5, India.

Ananian, Vakhtang Stepanovich; Soviet writer; b. 05. Correspondent and later Editor *Matchkal;* full-time writing 30-; Order of Red Banner of Labour.
Publs. include: *A Chrestomathy of Hunters Stories* (5 vols.) 48-59, *At the Shore of Lake Sevan* 50 (translated into eighteen languages), *Steep Paths* 55 (translated into eight languages), *The Childhood in Mountains* 54, *The Prisoners of Leopard's Valley* 56 (translated into eight languages), *Animal World of Armenia* Vol. I 61, II 62, III 65, *Fatherland Mountains* 63, *The Rain* (novel) 64, *Death Enemies* (novel) 66.
Writers' Union, Erevan, Armenian S.S.R., U.S.S.R.

Ančerl, Karel; Czechoslovak conductor; b. 11 April 1908; ed. Státni konservator, Prague.
Conductor, Liberated Theatre, Prague 30-33, Prague Radio Orchestra 33-39; imprisoned in concentration camps during Nazi occupation; Chief Conductor, Grand Opera House, Prague 45-48; Prof. Acad. of Music, Prague 48-52; Chief Conductor Czech Philharmonic Orchestra 50-; conducts concerts all over the world; Klement Gottwald State Prize 58; Charles Cross Acad. Prize 60, 64; Honoured Artist 65, Nat. Artist 67.
Prague 1, 25 Národni tř., Czechoslovakia.

Anda, Geza; Swiss (b. Hungarian) pianist; b. 19 Nov. 1921; ed. Budapest Acad. of Music.
Début with Mengelberg 39; since then has appeared with Berlin Philharmonic, Vienna Philharmonic, New York Philharmonic, Amsterdam Concertgebouw, Philharmonia (London). Paris Conservatoire, Santa Cecilia (Rome), Philadelphia, Chicago, San Francisco Symphony Orchestras and many others; frequent soloist at Salzburg, Lucerne, Edinburgh, Vienna, Montreux and Besançon Festivals; annual appearances Royal Festival Hall, London; numerous recordings; Chevalier Ordre des Arts et des Lettres; Franz Liszt Prize 40; Grand Prix des Disques 61, 62, 63; Grand Prix des Discophiles 66; Preis der Deutschen Schallplattenkritik 66.
Zollikerstrasse 178, 8008 Zürich, Switzerland.
Telephone: O & I-31-54-04.

Andersch, Alfred; German writer; b. 4 Feb. 1914; ed. Wittelsbacher Gymnasium, Munich.
Spent six months in Dachau Concentration Camp as Communist Youth Leader 33; fmr. industrial worker; Editor of newspapers after Second World War (*Der Ruf, Texte und Zeichen, Studio Frankfurt*); now broadcaster and freelance writer; mem. Group 47; Deutscher Kritiker-Preis 58; Nelly Sachs-Preis 68.
Publs. *Deutsche Literatur in der Entscheidung* (essays) 48, *Europäische Avantgarde* (anthology) 48, *So begann meine Hoffnung* (narrative) 48, *Die Kirschen der Freiheit* (autobiog.) 52, *Die bitteren Wasser von Lappland* (feature) 53, *Sansibar oder der letzte Grund* (novel)

57, *San Gaetano* (narrative) 57, *Mit dem Chef in Chenon-
ceaux* (narrative) 57, *Geister und Leute* 58, *Wanderungen
im Norden* 62, *Ein Liebhaber des Halbschattens* (stories)
63, *Aus einem römischen Winter* 66, *Efraim* (novel) 67.
For radio: *Strahlende Melancholie* 53, *Die Bürde des
weissen Mannes*, *Brennpunkt Indochina* 53, *Die letzen
vom schwarzen Mann* 54, *Die Feuerinsel oder Die
Heimkehr des Kapitän Tizzoni* 55, *Fahrerflucht* 58,
Synnöves Halsband 58, *Aktion ohne Fahnen* (adapted
from *Sansibar oder der letzte Grund*) 58, *Der Tod des
James Dean* 60, *Der Albino* 60, *Von Ratten und Evan-
gelisten* 60, *In der Nacht der Giraffe* 60, *Biologie und
Tennis* (with H. Krapp) 58, *Russisches Roulette* 61.
Berzona (Valle Onsernone), Ticino, Switzerland.
Telephone: Locarno (Switzerland) 90233.

Andersen, Einar Anton, D.SC., M.SC.; Danish geodesist,
mathematician and astronomer; b. 16 Sept. 1905; ed.
Østre Borgerdyd School and Univ. of Copenhagen.
Geodesist, Royal Danish Geodetic Inst. 26-40, state
geodesist 40-55, Dir. 55-; Privatdocent Univ. of Copen-
hagen 47-50, Asst. Prof. 50-56, Prof. 56-; Pres. Nat.
Cttee. of Int. Union of Geodesy and Geophysics 55,
Nat. Cttee. Int. Council of Scientific Unions 62, Danish
Map Comm. 56, Scandinavian Geodetic Comm. 57-60,
Danish Comm. for Glaciology 62, Man. Cttee. for Int.
Glaciological Expedition to Greenland 63-66, Danish
Cttee. for Upper Mantle Project 65, Danish Photogram-
metric Soc. 65; Pres. Nat. Cttee. for COSPAR 66; Treas.
Int. Union of Geodesy and Geophysics 60-; mem.
numerous int. cttees.; mem. Danish Acad. of Technical
Sciences 56, Royal Danish Acad. of Sciences and
Letters 58; Commdr. Order of Dannebrog, Iceland
Falcon.
Publs. *Des étalonnages fondamentaux* 46, *Gravity
Measurements in Sjaelland, Møen, Falster, and Lolland*
47, *Solution of Great Systems of Normal Equations* 47,
Determination of Latitude at Budinge 48, *Practical
Formulas for Accurate Calculation of Geographical
Coordinates* 53, *Mesures des Bases 1932–34* 53, *C.C.G.
Andrae* 55, *L'Institut Géodésique de Danemark de
1928–55* 56, *Geodetic Tables* 56, *Deux cents ans de
travaux géodésiques scientifiques au Danemark* 57,
*Transfer of Geographical Coordinates by means of
Clarke's Curve of Alignment* 59, *Gravimétrie, La géo-
physique en Danemark* 59.
Geodetic Institute, Proviantgaarden, Copenhagen K;
and 8 Serridslevvej, Copenhagen Ø, Denmark.
Telephone: ØBRO 7568 and 01-11-60-17.

Andersen, Hans George, LL.B., LL.M.; Icelandic
diplomatist; b. 19; ed. Univ. of Iceland and Harvard
Univ.
Legal Adviser, Ministry of Foreign Affairs, Lecturer,
Univ. of Iceland 48-54; Ambassador to NATO 54-62,
to OEEC 56-62, to France 61-62, to Sweden 62-63, to
Norway 63-; Commdr. of the Order of the Falcon.
Icelandic Embassy, 30 Stortingsgaten, Oslo, Norway.

Andersen, Knud Børge, M.ECON.; Danish politician;
b. 1 Dec. 1914.
Danmarks Radio 40-50; Teacher, Krogerup Folk High
School 46-50; Headmaster, Workers' Folk High School,
Roskilde 50-57, Scandinavian Folk High School,
Geneva 53, 58; Adviser, Prison Education Dept. 57-64;
mem. Danish Nat. Comm. for UNESCO 49-; mem.
Econ. Comm. of Labour Movement 52-; mem. Folketing
57-; Minister of Educ. 64-68; mem. Nordic Council
62-64, 68-; mem. Rask Ørstad Foundation 57-64; Co-
Editor *Verdens Gang* 53-58; Social Democrat.
Urbansgade 2, Copenhagen Ø, Denmark.

Andersen, Magnus; Norwegian politician; b. 20
March 1916.
Fisherman 31-55; Acting Chairman, Norwegian Fisher-
men's Union 55-63; fmr. Chair. local Tax Assessment

Comm.; Chair. Lofoten Fishing Comm. 61-63; Minister
of Fisheries Sept. 63-65; Labour.
Oslo, Norway.

Andersen, Mogens; Danish painter; b. 8 Aug. 1916;
ed. in Copenhagen under art master P. Rostrup
Boyesen.
Art teacher Copenhagen 52-59, Académie de la Grande
Chaumière, Paris 63; mem. cttee. Danish Art Exhbn.
Arrangement 56-58; mem. Royal Acad. of Fine Arts 65;
Eckersberg Medal 49, and other awards.
Exhibitions: Copenhagen 35-40, 42-50, 53-66, 67; Paris
50-66; Private Exhbns.: Copenhagen 53, 63 and 66,
Paris and Ålborg (Denmark) 54, Lund (Sweden) 59,
Paris 59, 63, 66 and 67; Group Exhbns. in Europe and
the U.S.A.; Venice Biennale 68.
Major works: Composition in Niels Bohr Inst., Copen-
hagen 55, Mural, Central Library, Copenhagen 58-59,
Composition in Central Library, Århus 64, *October*,
State Art Museum 64.
Publs. *Moderne fransk malerkunst* 48, *Omkring Kilderne*
67.
Strandagervej 28, Copenhagen 2900 Hellerup, Denmark.
Telephone: Hellerup 266.

Andersen, Oluf, M.D.; Danish pediatrician; b. 24 June
1901; ed. Københavns Universitet.
Assistant, Research Inst. of Hygiene and Immunisation
Study, Berlin 29-30; Asst. Doctor, Univ. Children's
Clinic, Rigshospital, Copenhagen 33-44; Queen Louise's
Children's Hospital 34-36, 37-39; Head of Hospital 40;
Clinical Prof., Univ. of Copenhagen 40-, Regular Prof.
and mem. Faculty 61-; Scientific Adviser in Pediatrics,
Nat. Health Service of Denmark 40; Chair. or Del.
numerous cttees.; Vice-Pres. Exec. Board World Health
Org. (WHO) 54-55; Knight Order of Dannebrog.
Gammel Vartovvej 14, Copenhagen-Hellerup, Denmark.

Andersen, Rolf; Norwegian diplomatist; b. 25 July
1897.
Entered foreign service 23; served Paris 23-25, Oslo
25-31 (Private Sec. to Minister 27-31), London 31-35;
Adviser Norwegian Del. to L.N. 31-34, concurrently
Asst. to Norwegian Judge at Hague Int. Court 32-33;
served Paris 35-37; Ministry of Foreign Affairs 37-45;
Dir.-Gen. Ministry of Foreign Affairs 45-48; Minister to
Switzerland 48-50 (and concurrently to Austria 49-50),
to Spain 50-53; Minister to Italy 53-55, Ambassador
55-58; Amb. to Denmark 58-63, to France 63-67.
c/o Ministry of Foreign Affairs, Oslo, Norway.

Andersen, Svend, M.POL.ECON.; Danish banker; b. 26
Sept. 1915; ed. Københavns Universitet.
Economist, Nat. Bank of Denmark 40, Chief of Secr.
50-61, Man. 61-62, Deputy Gov. 62-63, mem. Board of
Govs. 63-; Economist, Int. Bank for Reconstruction
and Devt. (World Bank) 46-50; mem. Boards, Deputy
Chair. The Ship Credit Fund of Denmark 63-, War
Risk Insurance of Danish Ships of Copenhagen and
Danish War Risk Cargo Insurance of Copenhagen 63-,
Nordic Cttee. for Financial Matters 66-, Nat. Econ.
Soc.; Knight Order of Dannebrog.
Danmarks Nationalbank, Holmens Kanal 17, DK 1093
Copenhagen K; Home: Viggo Rothes Vej 31, DK 2920
Charlottenlund, Denmark.

Anderson, Sir Austin Innes, Kt., M.A.; British ship-
owner; b. 16 March 1897; ed. Harrow School and King's
Coll., Cambridge.
Dir. of Anderson Green & Co. (Managers of Orient Line)
24-63; Asst. Dir. Ministry of War Transport 40-45; Pres.
of Chamber of Shipping of U.K. 55; Dir. Westminster
Bank 50-; Chair. Orient Line 52-60; Dir. Peninsular &
Oriental Steam Navigation Co. 55-62.
Summers, West Clandon, Surrey, England.

Anderson, Axel Ivar, PH.D.; Swedish newspaper editor
and politician; b. 91; ed. Uppsala Univ., Sweden, and in
England, France and Germany.

Mem. staff of *Stockholms Dagblad* 14-17; Chief Editor *Ostgöta Correspondenten* 17-30; Proprietor and Chief Editor *Ostergölands Dagblad* 30-40; mem. Riksdag 24-48; Chair. Financial Comm. of Riksdag 37-40; Editor-in-Chief *Svenska Dagbladet* 40-55; mem. Board of Dirs. Sveriges Riksbank 40-47; Pres. Swedish Publicists' Club 44-58; Chair. Tidn. Telegrambyrå 47-56; Chair. Royal Thaatre 53-61; mem. Board of Sveriges Radio 47-53; Chair. Swedish Press Archives 55-66.
Bragevagen 8, Stockholm, Sweden.
Telephone: 08-105210.

Anderson, Carl David, B.S., PH.D., SC.D., LL.D.; American physicist; b. 3 Sept. 1905; ed. California Inst. of Technology.
Teaching Fellow in Physics 27-30, Research Fellow 30-33, Asst. Prof. of Physics 33-37, Assoc. Prof. California Inst. of Technology 37-39, Prof. 39-; Chair. Div. of Physics, Mathematics and Astronomy 62-; awarded gold medal of American Inst. 35, Nobel Prize for Physics 36, Elliott Cresson Medal of Franklin Inst. 37; John Ericsson Medal of American Soc. of Swedish Engineers 60; engaged in research on gamma rays and cosmic rays 30-; mem. Nat. Acad. of Sciences, American Acad. of Arts and Sciences and American Philosophical Soc.
California Institute of Technology, Pasadena, Calif. 91109, U.S.A.
Telephone: 213-795-6841.

Anderson, Clinton Presba; American politician; b. 23 Oct. 1895; ed. Dakota Wesleyan Univ. and Univ. of Michigan.
Newspaper reporter and editor in Albuquerque, N.M. 18-22; engaged in insurance business 22-62; Treas. State of New Mexico 33-34; Administrator N.M. Relief Admin. 35; Chair. and Exec. Dir. Unemployment Compensation Comm. of N.M. 36-38; mem. U.S. Congress 41-45; Sec. of Agriculture 45-48; Senator from New Mexico 48-; Democrat; several Hon. Degrees.
Home: 3621 Camino Alameda, S.W., Albuquerque, N.M.; Office: 215-5th Street S.W., Albuquerque, N.M., U.S.A.

Anderson, Sir Colin (Skelton), Kt. (brother of Sir Donald Anderson, *q.v.*); British shipowner; b. 15 July 1904; ed. Eton and Trinity Coll., Oxford.
Director, P. & O. Steam Navigation Co. 60-; Chair. Gray Dawes, Westray 60-, Anderson Green & Co. Ltd. 63-, Ocean Travel Devt. 61-; Dir. Australia & N.Z. Bank 51-, Midland Bank Ltd. 50-, Marine Insurance Co. Ltd. 50-, Orient S.N. Co. Ltd. 50-; Dir. Royal Opera House, Covent Garden Ltd. 61-, City Arts Trust Ltd. 62-; Chair. Nat. Asscn. of Port Employers 47-48, 50-54, I.C.C. Comm. on Sea Transport 65-67, Int. Chamber of Shipping 49-63, Hon. Pres. 63-; Chair. London Shipowners' Dock Labour Cttee. 44-45, London Port Employers (and mem. London Board of Nat. Dock Labour Board) 45-47; Pres. British Employers' Confed. 56-58 (Vice-Pres. 52-56), Chamber of Shipping of U.K. 49; mem. Royal Fine Art Comm. 59-; Chair. Trustees of Tate Gallery 60-67 (Vice-Chair. 53-59); Trustee Nat. Gallery 63-67; Chair. Contemporary Art Soc. 56-60; Provost, Royal Coll. of Art 67- (Chair. 52-56); mem. British Transport Comm. Design Panel 62-; Officer Order of Orange Nassau (Neths.); Hon. Designer of Royal Coll. of Art, Hon. Assoc. of Royal Inst. of British Architects; Hon. LL.D., Aberdeen; Hon. Fellow, Trinity Coll., Oxford.
Admiral's House, Hampstead Grove, London, N.W.3.

Anderson, Sir Donald Forsyth, Kt. (brother of Sir Colin Anderson, *q.v.*); British businessman; b. 3 Sept. 1906; ed. Eton Coll. and Trinity Coll., Oxford.
Joined Peninsular and Oriental Steam Navigation Co. 34, Chair. and a Man. Dir. 60-; service with Ministries of Shipping and War Transport 39-43; Chair. Shipping Fed.; Pres. Int. Shipping Fed. and a Joint Chair. Nat. Maritime Board 50-62; Pres. Shipping Fed. 63-; Pres. Chamber of Shipping of U.K. and Chair. Gen. Council of British Shipping 53-54; Chair. British Liner Cttee. 56-58; Pres. Inst. of Export 61-63; mem. Minister of Transport's Shipping Advisory Panel 62-65; Dir. of numerous Companies.
The Manor, Notgrove, Gloucestershire, England.
Telephone: Guiting Power 239.

Anderson, Eugenie Moore; American diplomatist; b. 26 May 1909; ed. Stephens Coll., Simpson Coll., Carleton Coll., Inst. of Musical Art, New York City.
Chairman, Minnesota State Comm. for Fair Employment Practices 55-60; mem. Board, U.S. Cttee. for Refugees 59-60; mem. Democratic Nat. Advisory Cttee. on Foreign Policy 57-60; mem. Board of Dirs. American Asscn. for the United Nations 59-61; Vice-Chair. Citizens' Cttee. for Int. Devt. 61-62; Trustee, American Freedom from Hunger Foundation 62; Minister to Bulgaria 62-64; U.S. Rep. to UN Trusteeship Council 65-.
Tower View, Red Wing, Minn., U.S.A.

Anderson, Major-Gen. Frederick L.; American diplomatist; b. 4 Oct. 1905; ed. U.S. Mil. Acad.
Commissioned as Second Lieut. 28; served at various stations in U.S. and abroad; assigned to U.K. 41; commd. 3rd Bombardment Div., Britain 43; Commdg. Gen. VIII Bomber Commd. July 43; Major-Gen. Aug. 43; Deputy Commdg. Gen. U.S. Strategic Air Forces in Europe 44; Asst. Chief of Air Staff for Personnel 45-47; retd. from Air Force 47; served as officer and dir. of various companies in N.Y., Calif. and Texas, and as gen. business consultant in Tex.; Deputy U.S. Special Rep. in Europe (rank of Ambassador) Mar. 52; Dir. of U.S. Leasing Corpn., Porter Int. Co., Lear Siegler Inc., Royal Industries Inc., Federal Petroleum Inc., Trustee, Rand Corpn., D.F.C., D.S.M. (with oak leaf clusters), Silver Star and Legion of Merit (U.S.); Hon. C.B. (U.K.); Officier de la Légion d'Honneur and Croix de Guerre (France), and other decorations.
168 Eleanor Drive, Woodside, Calif., U.S.A.

Anderson, George W., Jr., B.S.; American diplomatist; b. 15 Dec. 1906; ed. U.S. Naval Acad., National War Coll.
Naval Aviator 30; Squadron and Ships Officer; C.O. 35-43; Joined Bureau of Aeronautics, Washington, as Plans Officer, Commdr. Aircraft, U.S. Pacific Fleet 43-44, Asst. to Dep. Commdr. in Chief, 44-45, Aviation Officer, Strategic Plans Section 45-48; C.O. U.S.S. *Mindoro* 48-49; Fleet Operations Officer, 6th Fleet 50; with SHAPE 50-52; C.O. U.S.S. *Franklin D. Roosevelt* 52-53; Special Asst. to Chair. Joint Chiefs of Staff, Washington 53-55; Chief of Staff, Joint Staff, Commdr. in Chief, U.S. Pacific Command 56-57, Vice-Admiral and Aide to Commdr. in Chief 57-58; Commdr Carrier Div. Six 58-59; Commdr. Sixth Fleet and Commdr. Naval Striking and Support Forces, S. Europe 58-61; Chief of Naval Operations 61-63; Ambassador to Portugal 63-66; Legion of Merit, Bronze Star Medal and many other American citations; Hon. O.B.E.
5907 Frazier Lane, McLean, Va. 22101, U.S.A.

Anderson, Lindsay Gordon, M.A.; British film and theatre director; b. 17 April 1923; ed. St. Ronan's School, Cheltenham Coll., and Wadham Coll., Oxford.
Co-Founder and Editor Film Review *Sequence* 47-52; Co-Founder Free Cinema Group, Nat. Film Theatre 56-59; Pres. Jury, Canadian Nat. Film Festival 63; Jury mem. Int. Festivals Delhi 65, Venice 66.
Films produced: *Wakefield Express* 53, *Thursday's Children* (with Guy Brenton) 54, *O Dreamland* 54, *Every Day Except Christmas* 57, *This Sporting Life* 63, *The White Bus* 65/66, *Raz, Dwa, Trzy* (The Singing Lesson) for Documentary Studio, Warsaw 67.
Stage productions: *The Long and the Short and the Tall*

59, *Serjeant Musgrave's Dance* 59, *The Lily White Boys* 60, *Billy Liar* 60, *The Fire Raisers* 61, *The Diary of a Madman* 63, *Andorra* 64, *Julius Caesar* 64, *The Cherry Orchard* 66; directed Polish production of *Inadmissible Evidence* (Nit Do Obrony), Teatr Wspolczesny,Warsaw 66.

Publ. *Making a Film* 62.

57 Greencroft Gardens, London, N.W.6, England.

Telephone: 01-624-3143.

Anderson, Marian; American singer; ed. Philadelphia public school.

Studied with Agnes Reifsneider, Giuseppe Boghetti and Frank La Forge; concerts in U.S.A., Europe, Africa, S. America, Japan and W. Indies 26-53; operatic début 55; operatic tours 55-; U.S. Del. to UN 58; U.S. Presidential Medal of Freedom Award 62, and numerous overseas awards.

Publ. *My Lord, What a Morning!* (autobiography) 56.

c/o Hurok Attractions, 730 5th Avenue, New York City 19, N.Y., U.S.A.

Anderson, O. Kelley, B.A., M.B.A.; American insurance executive; b. 07; ed. Univ. of Iowa and Harvard Graduate School of Business Admin.

Dir. and officer of financial and industrial companies 31-; founder Boston Fund, Inc. (open-end investment co.), Pres. 39-50; Pres. Consolidated Investment Trust 39-50; Dir. New England Mutual Life Insurance Co. 47-, Pres. 51-66, Chair. and Chief Exec. Officer 66-; Dir. Boston Edison Co., Boston Fund Inc., Canada Gen. Fund Inc., Gillette Co., Diversification Fund Inc., United Fruit Co., S. D. Warren Co., Exchange Fund of Boston Inc., Depositors Fund of Boston Inc., Fiduciary Exchange Fund Inc.; Trustee, Century Shares Trust, Consolidated Investment Trust, Real Estate Investment Trust of America, Boston Univ.; Fellow, American Acad. of Arts and Sciences.

501 Boylston Street, Boston 02117, Mass., U.S.A.

Anderson, Robert Bernard; American lawyer and public servant; b. 4 June 1910; ed. Godley High School, Weatherford Coll. and Univ. of Texas.

Taught in Burleson High School 27-30; studied Univ. of Texas Law School 30-32, was meanwhile elected to the Texas legislature; practised law 32; Asst. Attorney Gen. of Texas and Prof. of Law at Univ. of Texas 33; State Tax Commissioner 34-37, and Chair. and Exec. Dir. Texas Unemployment Comm. 36; Gen. Counsel for the Waggoner Estate (oil and ranching empire) 37-, Gen. Man. 41-53; U.S. Sec. of Navy 53-54; Deputy Sec. of Defense 54-55; Sec. of Treasury 57-61; Special Envoy of Pres. of U.S. to U.A.R. Oct. 67; Served as Pres. of Texas Board of Education, Dir. of the Reserve Bank of Texas and on many other public bodies; fmr. Pres. Ventures Ltd., mem. Board of Dirs.; Chair. Exec. Cttee. Dresser Industries; mem. Board of Dirs. Greenwich Trust Co., Webb & Knapp (Canada) Ltd., Missouri Pacific Railroad Co., N.Y. Capital Fund of Canada Ltd.; partner Carl M. Loeb, Rhoades & Co. 61-.

1 Deerpark Court, Greenwich, Conn., U.S.A.

Anderson, Robert Orville, B.A.; American cattle rancher and business exec.; b. 17; ed. Univ. of Chicago.

Founder and Pres. Hondo Oil and Gas Co. (fmrly. Malco Refineries Inc.) 41-63; Founder and Owner, Lincoln County Livestock Co., Texas and New Mexico; Chair. Federal Reserve Bank of Dallas 59-65; Dir. Northern Natural Gas Co. 60-63; Chair. of Exec. Cttee. and Dir. The Atlantic Refining Co. 63-65, Chair. of Board 65-; mem. Nat. Petroleum Council 54-; Chair. Aspen Inst. for Humanistic Studies 59-, The Aspen Co.; Chair. Lovelace Foundation 62-, Kennedy Center for the Performing Arts; Trustee, Univ. of Chicago 63-; mem. Washington Inst. for Foreign Affairs 63-; official of numerous civic and business orgs.

Box 1000, Roswell, New Mexico 88201, U.S.A.

Anderson, Captain William R., U.S.N. (retd.); American naval officer; b. 17 June 1921; ed. Columbia Military Acad. and U.S. Naval Acad.

Commissioned 42; service in submarines 42-59; Idaho Univ. Inst. of Naval Tactics 51; Naval Reactors Branch, Atomic Energy Comm. 56-57, 59; Commdr. *Nautilus*, the world's first atomic submarine 57-59 (in which he achieved the first totally submerged transit of the North Pole and N.W. Passage 58); Freedoms Foundation 62-64; mem. U.S. House of Reps. 64-; Bronze Star Combat "V", various war and campaign medals; Legion of Merit 58, Christopher Columbus Int. Medal (Italy) 58, Patron's Medal, Royal Geographical Soc. 59, Freedom Leadership Award 60; Democrat.

Publs. *Nautilus 90 North* 59, *First under the North Pole* 59, *The Useful Atom* 66.

3006 P. Street, N.W., Washington, D.C., U.S.A.

Telephone: 333-3938.

Anderson-Imbert, Enrique, PH.D.; Argentine university professor; b. 12 Feb. 1910; ed. Universidad Nacional de Buenos Aires.

Professor, Univ. of Cuyo, Argentina 40-41, Univ. of Tucumán, Argentina 41-46, Univ. of Michigan 47-65; First Victor S. Thomas Prof. of Hispanic American Literature, Harvard Univ. 65-; mem. Academia de Artes y Ciencias de Puerto Rico 65; Prize from Buenos Aires City for novel *Vigilia* 34.

Publs. *Tres novelas de Payró con pícaros en tres miras* 42, *Ibsen y su tiempo* 46, *Ensayos* 46, *El arte de la prosa en Juan Montalvo* 48, *Estudios sobre escritores de América* 54, *La crítica literaria contemporánea* 57, *Los grandes libros de Occidente* 57, *¿Qué es la prosa?* 58, *El cuento español* 59, *Crítica interna* 61, *El grimorio* 61, *Vigilia-Fuga* 63, *Los domingos del profesor* 65, *El gato de Cheshire* 65, *Historia de la literatura hispanoamericana* 5th edition (2 vols.) 65, *Genio y figura de Sarmiento* 67.

Department of Romance Languages, 201 Boylston Hall, Harvard University, Cambridge, Massachusetts 02138, U.S.A.

Telephone: 489-2378.

Andersson, Bibi; Swedish actress; b. 11 Nov. 1935; ed. Terserus Drama School and Royal Dramatic Theatre School, Stockholm.

Malmö Theatre 56-59, Royal Dramatic Theatre, Stockholm 59-; appearances at Uppsala Theatre 62-.

Plays acted in include: *Erik XIV* 56, *Tre systrar* 61, *King John* 61, *Le Balcon* 61, *La Grotte* 62, *Uncle Vanya* 62, *Who's Afraid of Virginia Woolf* 63, *As You Like It* 64, *After the Fall* 64-65.

Films acted in include: *Sjunde inseglet* (Seventh Seal) 56, *Smultronstället* (Wild Strawberries) 57, *Nära livet* (The Brink of Life) 58, *Sommarnöje Sökes* (Summer House Wanted) 58, *Djävulens öga* (Eye of the Devil) 61, *Älskarinnen* (The Mistress) 62, *För att inte tala om alla dessa kvinnor* (All those Women) 64, *Juninatt* (June Night) 65, *Ön* (The Island) 65, *Syskonbädd* (My Sister, My Love) 66, *Persona* 66, *Duel at Diablo* 66.

c/o Svenska Filminstitutet, Kungsgatan 48, Stockholm C; Home: Tykö Vägen 28, Lidingo, Sweden.

Telephone: 7663801.

Andersson, Sven Olof Morgan; Swedish politician; b. 5 April 1910; ed. Gothenburg.

Carpenter and instructor in W.E.A., Gothenburg 32-35; mem. of Board of Socialist Youth Movement 34-40; Rep. of Workers' Federation, Gothenburg 35-45; Sec. Social Democrat Party 47-; Minister of Communications 51-57; Minister of Defence 57-.

Försvarsdepartementet, Regeringsgatan 1-3, Stockholm 16, Sweden.

Telephone: 08-22-40-70.

Andics, Erzsébet, PH.D.; Hungarian historian and university professor; b. 02.

Prof. of Modern Hungarian History, Eötvös Lóránt

Univ., Budapest; Deputy Minister for Education 53-56; awarded Kossuth Prize.

Publs. include *Kossuth Lajos harca az árulók és megalkuvókellen a reformkorban és a forradalom idején* (Lajos Kossuth's Struggle Against the Traitors and Opportunists during the Reform Era and the Time of the Revolution), *A Magyarországi munkásmozgalom az 1848-49-es forradalomtol és Szabadságharctól az 1917-es Nagy Októberi Szocialista Forradalomig* (The Hungarian Working Class Movement from the 1848-49 Revolution and The War of Independence up to the 1917 Great October Revolution) 55.

Eötvös Lóránd Tudományegyetem, Budapest V, Egyetem-Tér 1; and Budapest II, Orsó-utca 19, Hungary.

Telephone: 364-106.

Andrade, Edward Neville da Costa, D.SC., PH.D., LL.D., F.R.S.; British physicist; b. 27 Dec. 1887; ed. London, Heidelberg, Cambridge and Manchester Univs.

Fellow Univ. Coll. London 15; Prof. of Physics Artillery Coll. Woolwich 20-28; Quain Prof. of Physics London Univ. 28-50, Emeritus Prof. 50; Dir. Royal Institution and Davy Faraday Laboratory 50-52; mem. Advisory Council, Ministry of Supply 40; Pres. Physical Society 43, Foreign Sec. 45-60; Holweck Prize 47; Grande Medaille Osmond 51; corresp. mem. Académie des Sciences; hon. mem. Soc. Française de Physique, Inst. of Metals 66; Chevalier Légion d'Honneur; Royal Soc. Hughes Medal 58.

Publs. *The Structure of the Atom, The Atom, Engines, The Mechanism of Nature, The New Chemistry, Viscosity and Plasticity, The Atom and its Energy, Isaac Newton, From Small Beginnings, Poems and Songs, An Approach to Modern Physics, Rutherford and the Nature of the Atom.*

Department of Metallurgy, Imperial College of Science, Prince Consort Road, London, S.W.7; Home: Flat 3, 19 The Boltons, London, S.W.10, England.

Telephone: 01-589-5111 (Office); 01-373-4241 (Home).

Andreazza, Mario David; Brazilian army officer and politician; b. 20 Aug. 1918; ed. Escola Militar.

Second Lieut. 41, Lieut. 43, Capt. 45, Maj. 53, Lieut.-Col. 60, Col. 65; Brazilian Mil. Mission in Paraguay 52; fmr. Sec. of Council of Nat. Security, later at Fed. Dept. of Information, later with Dept. of Armed Forces; on staff of Minister of War 64; Minister of Transport 67-; numerous decorations.

Ministry of Transport, Brasilia, Brazil.

Andreev, Alexander Nikitovich; Soviet politician; b. 1917; ed. Uman Inst. of Agriculture and Higher Party School of Central Committee of C.P. of Ukraine.

Education service 33-42; Soviet Army 42-45; mem. C.P.S.U .,44-; party official 45-54; Sec., Second Sec. Cherkassy Regional Cttee. of C.P. of Ukraine 54-65, First Sec. 65-; mem. Central Cttee. C.P. of Ukraine; Deputy to U.S.S.R. Supreme Soviet.

Cherkassy Regional Committee, Communist Party of the Ukraine, Cherkassy, U.S.S.R.

Andreev, Andrei Andreevich; Soviet politician; b. 95; Mem. Communist Party 14; mem. Central Cttee. of Metal Workers 19; Chair. Central Cttee. of Railwaymen 20; mem. Central Cttee. of Communist Party 20 and Sec. 24-25; Sec. Communist Party in N. Caucasus 28-30; Chair. Central Control Comm. 22-27, People's Commissar of Workers' and Peasants' Inspection, and Dep. Chair. U.S.S.R. Council of People's Commissars 30-31; Commr. Transport 31-35; Sec. Central Cttee. of Communist Party 35-46; Deputy to Supreme Soviet U.S.S.R. 37-; Chair. Council for Collective Farm Affairs 46; Chair. Council of Union, U.S.S.R. Supreme Soviet 38-45; mem. Politburo 32-53; mem. Cttee. for Economic Rehabilitation Liberated Areas 43; Commissar for Agriculture 43-46; Deputy Chair. Council of Ministers 46-53; mem.

Praesidium of Supreme Soviet of U.S.S.R. 53-62; Orders of Lenin and other decorations.

Soviet-China Friendship Society, 14 Prospekt Kalinina, Moscow, U.S.S.R.

Andreev, Nikolai Nikolaevich; Soviet physicist; b. 80; ed. Univ. of Basle.

Instructor and research worker at higher educational establishments and research centres 17-; Corresp. mem. U.S.S.R. Acad. of Sciences 33-53, mem. 53-; Head, Acoustics Lab. Lebedev Physics Inst. U.S.S.R. Acad. of Sciences 40-; Order of Lenin (three times), Order of Red Banner of Labour.

Publs. *Lattice, Prism and Resonator* 18, *Electrical Oscillations and their Spectra* 17, *Equilibrium and Oscillations of a Piezoelectric Crystal* 28, *Acoustics of Moving Medium* 34, *Acoustic Measurements* 39, *Problems of Modern Acoustics* 63.

Presidium, U.S.S.R. Academy of Sciences, 14 Leninsky Prospekt, Moscow, U.S.S.R.

Andreev, Victor Georgiyevich; Soviet foreign trade official; b. 1912; ed. Moscow Metallurgical Inst.

Member C.P.S.U. 44-; Engineer 34-51; Deputy Dir., later Dir. of Office, then Vice-Chair. Mashinoexport 61-65, Chair. 65-; Order of Red Banner of Labour.

Mashinoexport, 35 Mosfilmovskaya ul., Moscow, U.S.S.R.

Andreev, Vyacheslav Stepanovich; Soviet trade unionist; b. 1926; ed. Moscow Power Engineering Secondary School and All-Union Power Engineering Correspondence Inst.

Turner 42-46; technician, later Senior Laboratory Worker, Lebedev Physics Inst., U.S.S.R. Acad. of Sciences 47-51; Engineering Plant 51-62; Chair. Central Cttee. of Power and Electrical Workers' Trade Union 62-; mem. All-Union Central Council of Trade Unions 68-; mem. C.P.S.U. 54-; two medals.

Central Committee of the Power and Electrical Workers' Trade Union, 42 Lenin Prospekt, Moscow, U.S.S.R.

Andreotti, Giulio; Italian journalist and politician; b. 14 Jan. 1919; ed. Univ. of Rome.

Pres. Fed. of Catholic Univs. in Italy 42-45; Deputy to the Constituent Assembly 45 and to Parl. 47-; Under-Sec. in the Govts. of De Gasperi and Pella 47-53; Minister for the Interior in Fanfani Govt. 54; Minister of Finance 55-July 58, of Treasury July 58-Feb. 59, of Defence Feb. 59-Feb. 60, Mar. 60-66, of Industry and Commerce 66-; Christian Democrat.

Ministry of Industry and Commerce, Rome, Italy.

Andres, Stefan; German writer; b. 26 June 1906; ed. Univs. of Cologne, Jena and Berlin.

In Southern Italy 33, 37-50; in Rome 62-; mem. P.E.N. 49-, Deutsche Akademie für Sprache und Dichtung; numerous prizes; Grosses Bundesverdienstkreuz, Commendatore dell'Ordine al Merito della Repubblica Italiana.

Publs. inc. novels: *Utopia* (trans. in 13 languages), *Knabe im Brunnen, Mann von Asteri, Hochzeit der Feinde, Ritter der Gerechtigkeit, Reise nach Portiuncula, Der Mann im Fisch, Der Taubenturm*; trilogy: *Sintflut*; verse: *Granatapfel*; history: *The History of the Bible* (trans. in 10 languages) 65, *Die italienischen Romane.*

Via Domenico Silveri 30, 00165 Rome, Italy.

Telephone: 6370342.

Andrewes, Sir Christopher Howard, M.D., LL.D., F.R.S., F.R.C.P.; British physician; b. 7 June 1896; ed. Highgate School and St. Bartholomew's Hospital, London.

Surgeon Sub-Lieut. Royal Naval Volunteer Reserve 18-19; House Physician and Chief Asst. to Medical Professorial Unit, St. Bartholomew's Hospital 21-23, 25-26; Asst. Resident Physician, Hospital of Rockefeller Inst., New York City 23-25; William Julius Mickle Fellow, Univ. of London 31; Oliver-Sharpey Lecturer Royal Coll. of Physicians 34; mem. Nat. Inst. for

Medical Research 27-61, Deputy Dir. 52-61; in charge of WHO World Influenza Centre, Mill Hill, London 59-61.
Publs. *Viruses of Vertebrates* 64, *The Common Cold* 65, *The Natural History of Viruses* 67.
Overchalke, Coombe Bissett, Salisbury, Wilts., England.
Telephone: Coombe Bissett 201.

Andrews, Eamonn; Irish radio and television commentator and official; b. 19 Dec. 1922; ed. Synge School, Dublin.
Insurance Clerk, Dublin; boxing commentaries, Radio Eireann 40; *Irish Independent* 45; studied acting under Abbey Theatre actress Ria Mooney, wrote play *The Moon is Black*; came to England 50; radio and television appearances include Sports Programmes, Children's Programmes, *What's My Line* and *This is Your Life*; Chair. Irish Television Authority (Radio Eireann) 60-66, joined ABC Television 64, presents *The Eamonn Andrews Show* and *World of Sport;* Knight Order of St. Gregory the Great.
Publ. *This is My Life* 63.
4 Golden Square, London W.1, England.

Andrews, Sir (William) Linton, Kt.; British journalist; b. 27 May 1886; ed. Hull Grammar School and Christ's Hospital.
Reporter, *Eastern Morning News,* Hull 02; later journalist at Huddersfield, Sheffield, Portsmouth, Dundee, London and Paris; served in Black Watch, First World War 14-19; sub-Editor *Daily Mail* 19-23; Editor *Leeds Mercury* 23, *Yorkshire Post and Leeds Mercury* (combined paper) 39-60; Dir. Yorkshire Post Newspapers, Yorkshire Radio and Television Co., and Brontë Parsonage Museum; Pres. Guild of British Newspaper Editors 52-53; Chair. British Press Council 55-59; mem. of Court, Leeds Univ.; Chair. of Council of Brontë Soc.; Fellow, Royal Soc. of Arts; Fellow, Inst. of Journalists, Pres. 46; Hon. LL.D. (Leeds), Hon. D.Litt. (Emerson Coll., Boston, U.S.A.); Vice-Chair. Leeds Centenary Musical Festival 58, 61, 64.
Publs. *Haunting Years* 30, *Yorkshire Folk* 32, *Wayside Pageant* 33, *Newspaper English* 56, *Problems of an Editor* 62, *Autobiography of a Journalist* 64; contributor to *Has the Church Failed?* 48, and *If I Had My Time Again* 50; edited *The Yorkshire Post: Two Centuries* 54.
28 North Parade, West Park, Leeds 16, England.
Telephone: Leeds 52973.

Andrianov, Kuzma Andrianovich; Soviet chemist; b. 1904; ed. Moscow Univ.
All-Union Electro-Technical Inst. 30; Instructor, Moscow Chemico-Technological Inst. 30-41, Moscow Power Eng. Inst. 41-46; Prof. Moscow Power Eng. Inst. 46-; Assoc. Inst. of Elemental Organic Compounds, U.S.S.R. Acad. of Sciences 54-; Corresp. mem. U.S.S.R. Acad. of Sciences 53-64, mem. 64-; three State Prizes; Lenin Prize.
U.S.S.R. Academy of Sciences, 14 Leninsky Prospekt, Moscow, U.S.S.R.

Andric, Ivo; Yugoslav novelist; b. 10 Oct. 1892; ed. Zagreb, Vienna, Cracow and Graz Univs.
In his youth was a mem. of revolutionary nat. movement; in the period between the World Wars served in the diplomatic service (Amb. to Germany); mem. Serbian Acad.; Nobel Prize for Literature 61.
Publs. include: *The Spinster, A Bosnian Story* (English translation 59), *The Bridge on the Drina* (English translation 59), *Devil's Yard* (English trans. 62), *The Woman from Sarajevo* (English trans.) 66.
Ulica Proleterskih Brigada 2-a, Belgrade, Yugoslavia.

Andriessen, Jacobus Eye; Netherlands economist and business executive; b. 25 July 1928; ed. Netherlands School of Economics, Rotterdam and Amsterdam Free Univ.
Director Dept. of Gen. Econ. Policy, Ministry of Econ.

Affairs 55-59; Prof., Legal Faculty, Univ. of Amsterdam 59; Adviser to Ministry of Economic Affairs 59; mem. Economic and Social Cttee. of European Economic Community (E.E.C.) 62; Minister of Economic Affairs 63-65; mem. Management Council Van Leer Group of Companies; Christian Historical Union.
Publs. *Development of Modern Price Theory* 55, *Anticycle Policy in a Western European Context* 59, *Theory and Practice of Economics* 64, *The Field of Force between Economics and Politics* 64.
Waldeck Pyrmontlaan 16, Wassenaar, Netherlands.
Telephone: 01751-9019.

Andrieu, René Gabriel, B.P., L.-ès-L.; French journalist; b. 24 March 1920; ed. Toulouse Univ.
Diplomatic Editor *Ce Soir* 46-58; Chief Editor *L'Humanité* 58-; Croix de Guerre, Médaille de la Résistance; mem. Central Cttee. French Communist Party 61-.
6 Boulevard Poissonnière, Paris, France.

Andriyashev, Anatoly Petrovich; Soviet zoologist; b. 1910; ed. Leningrad Univ.
Post-graduate, Research Assoc., Asst. Prof. Leningrad Univ. 33-39; Research Assoc. Inst. of Zoology, U.S.S.R. Acad. of Sciences 39-; Corresp. mem. U.S.S.R. Acad. of Sciences 66-.
Publ. works on ichthyology.
U.S.S.R. Academy of Sciences, 14 Lenin Prospekt, Moscow, U.S.S.R.

Andropov, Yuri Vladimirovich; Soviet politician; b. 1914; ed. Inland Water Ways Transport Coll., Petrozavodsk State Univ. and Higher Party School.
Young Communist League, Yaroslavl Region and Karelo-Finnish Republic 36-44; mem. C.P.S.U. 39-; Counsellor, later Ambassador to Hungary 53-57; official responsible for party relations with other Communist countries 57-62; mem. Central Cttee. C.P.S.U. 61-; Deputy to U.S.S.R. Supreme Soviet; mem. Secretariat, Central Cttee. of C.P.S.U. 62-; Candidate mem. Politburo, Central Cttee. of C.P.S.U. June 67-; Chair. State Security Cttee. of U.S.S.R. Council of Ministers 67-.
State Security Committee of U.S.S.R. Council of Ministers, Moscow, U.S.S.R.

Androvskaya, Olga Nikolaevna; Soviet actress; b. 98; ed. Moscow Art Theatre Studio School.
Has played many parts in Moscow Art Theatre since 24; People's Artist of U.S.S.R.; State prizewinner.
Moscow Art Theatre, 3 Proyezd Khudozhestvennogo Teatra, Moscow, U.S.S.R.

Andrycz, Nina; Polish actress; b. 15; ed. Warsaw.
Début, Teatr Nowy, Warsaw 34; now mem. Teatr Polski Co.; has played leading roles in a large number of productions, including Solange (*Summer in Nohant*), Chimène (*Le Cid*), Lucretia Borgia, St. Joan (Shaw's *St. Joan*), Maria Stuart (*Slowacki*); guest appearances in Moscow.
Karasia 2, Warsaw, Poland.

Andrzejewski, Jerzy; Polish writer; b. 09.
Publs. Novels: *Ład serca* (*Harmony of the Heart*) (Young Writers Prize, Polish Acad. of Literature) 39, *Popiólmm i dia* (*Ashes and Diamonds*) (Odrodzenie Award) 48, *Ciemności kryja ziemie* (*Darkness Covers the Earth*) 57, *Bramy raju* (*The Gates of Paradise*) 61; stories: *Drogi nieuniknione* (*The Inevitable Ways*) 37, *Noc* (*Night*) 45, *Złoty lis* (*The Golden Fox*) 55, *Idzie skeczac po górach* (*He Cometh Leaping upon the Mountains*) 63; also *Ksiazka dla Marcina* (*A Book for Martin*) (reminiscences) 54, and *Swieto Winkelrieda* (*Winkelreid's Day*) (play written in collaboration with J. Zagórski) 45.
Krakowskie Przedmieście 87, Warsaw, Poland.

Aneizi, Dr. A. N.; Libyan economist and diplomatist; b. 1904; ed. Pescia, Florence and Naples Univs. and Oriental Inst. of Naples.

Secretary, Cyrenaica Govt. 31-33; Councillor, Benghazi 34; Dir. Auqaf Benghazi 35-40; Political work in Egypt 41-51; mem. Libya House of Reps. 52-55; Finance Minister 53-55; Founder and First Gov. Central Bank of Libya 55-61; Amb. to Lebanon and Jordan 61-62; Petroleum Minister 63-64; Chair. Sahara Bank, Libyan Insurance Co., Nat. Navigation Co. May 64-; Pres. Intellectual Soc. of Libya 65-, Libyan Olympic Cttee. 67-; Highest Libya Independence Decoration 54; High Lebanon and Jordan Decoration 62.
P.O. Box 270, Tripoli, Libya.
Telephone: 32771; 32127 (Home).

Angami, T. N.; Indian politician; b. 1913.
Served in Indian Army overseas during Second World War; in Indian Civil Service 46-50; Chair. *De facto* Nagaland Legislative Assembly 61-63; Speaker Nagaland Legislative Assembly 64-66; Chief Minister Nagaland 66-.
P.O. Kohima, Nagaland, India.

Angelloz, Joseph-François; French retired university rector; b. 7 Oct. 1893; ed. Univs. of Leipzig and Lyon. Teacher of German, Lycées of Rochefort, Düsseldorf, Laon and Paris 20-42; Prof. of German Language and Literature, Univ. of Caen 42-50; Rector, Univ. of the Saar 50-56; Rector, Montpellier Acad. 56-58; Rector, Acad. of Strasbourg 58-64; Officier, Légion d'Honneur, Commdr. des Palmes Académiques.
Publs. translations of Goethe, Rilke, Thomas Mann and H. Mann, Stefan Zweig and A. Zweig.
Marie de Thônes, Haute-Savoie, France.

Ångström, Anders, M.SC., PH.D.; Swedish meteorologist; b. 28 Feb. 1888; ed. Univs. of Uppsala, Cornell and Jena.
Fellow of Physics, Cornell Univ., N.Y. 12-13; Chair. Met. Section Swedish National Comm. for Geodesy and Geophysics 34-56; Asst. Prof. Meteorology Uppsala Univ. 16-18; First State Meteorologist 34; Chief Swedish Weather Bureau 40; Dir.-in-Chief Swedish Meteorological and Hydrological Inst. 49-54; mem. Smithsonian Inst. expedition to Algeria 12; leader expedition to Mount Whitney, California 13, to Switzerland 29; Pres. Int. Radiation Comm. 36-45; Pres. Swedish Society for Anthropology and Geography 39-40 and 50-52; mem. Royal Swedish Acad. of Agriculture 43, Royal Swedish Acad. of Military Sciences 46, Royal Swedish Acad. of Sciences 48, Int. Meteorological Cttee. 49-51, Permanent Rep. of Sweden at World Meteorological Organisation 51-54, Council Int. Union for Geodesy and Geophysics 49-60, Meteorological Expert of U.N. to Iceland Govt. 56, Vice-Pres. Int. Climatological Comm. of U.N. 53-57; Fellow Eppley Foundation for Research 58; Int. Meteorological Org. Prize 62; Rossby Prize, Swedish Geophysical Soc. 68.
Publs. on meteorology and solar and terrestrial radiation.
Stavgårdsgatan 57, Stockholm-Bromma, Sweden.
Telephone: 08-250773.

Anguiano, Raul; Mexican painter; b. 26 Feb. 1915; studied under Jose Vizcarra and Ixca Farias.
Concerned in Modern Art movement, Mexico 34; founder mem. Taller de Gráfica Popular; studied at Art Students' League, New York 40-41; 28 one-man exhbns. in Mexico, Paris 52-65, San Francisco 53-65, Havana 56, Chile 59-60, Moscow 62, Rome 65, Miami 65, San Antonio (Texas) 66; has exhibited in collective exhbns. in London, Warsaw, Tokyo, Berlin, Prague, Peking, Lille, Los Angeles, Lugano, etc.; works include murals for the Hormona Laboratories, Onyx-Mex Industries and the Nat. Museum of Anthropology, Mexico City; has completed series of works about *lacandones* of Lacandona Jungle; numerous prizes.
Pestalozzi 1242, Mexico 12, D.F., Mexico.
Telephone: 43-30-13.

Angulo-Iñiguez, Diego; Spanish art historian; b. 01; ed. Univs. of Seville, Madrid, Berlin.
Prof. of History of Modern Art, Granada Univ. 25-26, Univ. of Seville 27-40, Madrid Univ. 40-; Deputy Curator, Museo del Prado 42-47; Dir. Inst. de Arte Diego Velázquez; mem. Real Academia de la Historia, Real Academia de Bellas Artes de San Fernando.
Publs. *La Arquitectura Mudéjar Sevillana* 35, *La Escultura en Andalucia* (3 vols.) 27-39, *Planos de Monumentos de América* (7 vols.) 33-39, *Historia del Arte Hispano Americano* (3 vols.) 45, *Velázquez* 47, *Historia del Arte* (2 vols.) 53, *Pintura del Renacimiento* 54.
Instituto Diego Velázquez, Medinaceli 4, Madrid 14, Spain.

Anichkov, Sergei Victorovich; Soviet physiologist; b. 1892; ed. First Leningrad Medical Inst.
Junior Assoc., Asst. Prof. First Leningrad Medical Inst. 22-24; Head of Chair, Leningrad Mil. Medical Acad. 24-37; Prof. Kirov Mil. Medical Acad. 37-44; Head of Chair, Second Leningrad Medical Inst. 45-; Head of Dept. of Experimental Medicine, U.S.S.R. Acad. of Medical Sciences 46; Corresp. mem. U.S.S.R. Acad. of Medical Sciences 47-50, mem. 50-; mem. C.P.S.U. 62-; mem. Central Council U.S.S.R. Physiol. Soc.; Hon. mem. Rome Medical Acad.; mem. Int. Brain Research Org.; mem. Council Int. Pharmacological Asscn.; Order of Lenin, State Prize, etc.; Dr. h.c. Charles Univ., Prague, Helsinki Univ.
Publs. Over 120 works on pharmacology of endocrine glands, physiology and pharmacology of carotid haemoreceptors, reflectory dystrophy and its pharmacotherapy, pharmacology of nervous system and new original nerotropic preparations (antiphens).
Institute of Experimental Medicine, U.S.S.R. Academy of Medical Sciences, 69/71 Kirov Prospekt, Leningrad, U.S.S.R.

Anikin, Alexandr Sergeevich; Soviet diplomatist; b. 26 Sept. 1917.
Ministry of Foreign Affairs 46-; First Sec. Brussels 51-52, Paris 52-54; Counsellor Paris 54-56; Amb. to Cambodia 56-59; Deputy Head of Dept., Ministry of Foreign Affairs 59-65; Amb. to Chile 65-68; on staff, Ministry of Foreign Affairs 68-.
Ministry of Foreign Affairs, Moscow, U.S.S.R.

Anin, Patrick Dankwa, M.A., LL.B.; Ghanaian lawyer and politician; b. 27 July 1928; ed. Prince of Wales Coll., Achimota, Selwyn Coll., Cambridge, and London School of Economics.
Called to Bar, Middle Temple 56, Called to Gold Coast Bar 56; fmr. Dir. Bank of Ghana; mem. Electoral Comm. 66-67; Commr. for Communications July 67-Feb. 68, Commr. for External Affairs Feb. 68-; fmr. mem. Board of Govs. Sunyani Secondary School, Bechem St. Joseph's Coll.
Ministry of External Affairs, P.O. Box M-53, Accra, Ghana.

Ankrah, Maj.-Gen. Joseph Arthur; Ghanaian army officer; b. 18 Aug. 1915; ed. Wesley Methodist School, Accra, and Accra Acad.
Comes from Ga tribe, S. Ghana; fmr. mission-school teacher; supply duties as Warrant Officer, Second World War; commissioned 49; Battalion Commdr., later Brigadier, Kasai Province, Congo 60-61, awarded Ghana Mil. Cross; Chief of Defence Staff, Ghana 61-July 65; Chair. Nat. Liberation Council, Ghana, March 66-.
National Liberation Council, Accra, Ghana.

Ankudinov, Vladimir Mikhailovich; Soviet government official; b. 26 July 1908; ed. Foreign Trade Acad.
Financial Inspector 25-29; People's Commissariat of Internal and Foreign Trade 29-31; Ministry of Foreign Trade 31-47; Chair. Board Intourist Foreign Travel Agency 47-64; Chair. Board of Foreign Tourism for Council of Ministers of U.S.S.R. 64-; Order of Lenin,

two Orders of the Red Banner of Labour, and medals. Board of Foreign Tourism, Marx Prospekt 16, Moscow, U.S.S.R.

Annadurai, Conjeevaram Natarajan, M.A.; Indian politician and journalist; b. 15 Sept. 1909; ed. Conjeevaram and Pachaiappa's Coll., Madras.
Active in Justice Party; Sub-Editor *Justice*; several times courted jail; Editor *Dravidanadu* 42; fmr. Editor *Viduthalai*; Editor *Kanchi* (Tamil weekly) until March 67; founded *Homeland* (English weekly) 57, also *Homerule*; mem. Rajya Sabha 62, Lok Sabha 67-; Chief Minister of Madras March 67-.
Publs. Books, plays, stories, political articles, and scripts for Tamil films.
Avenue Road, Nungambakkam, Madras 34; Fort St. George, Madras 9, India.

Annan, Baron (Life-Peer) cr. 65, of Royal Burgh of Annan; **Noel Gilroy Annan,** O.B.E., M.A.; British university official; b. 25 Dec. 1916; ed. King's Coll., Cambridge.
Served in War Office 40-42, Staff Coll., Camberley 42, War Cabinet Offices 43-44, Joint Intelligence Staff and later France and Germany 44-45; Gen. Staff Officer, Political Division, British Control Comm. 46; Fellow, King's Coll., Cambridge 46, Asst. Tutor 46-56, Provost 56-66; Provost of Univ. Coll., London 66-; Gov. of Stowe School 45-66; Senior Fellow, Eton Coll. 56-66; mem. Gulbenkian Cttee. for Art in U.K. 58-64; mem. Academic Planning Board, Univ. of East Anglia; Chair. Academic Planning Board, Univ. of Essex; mem. Academic Advisory Board Brunel Univ., mem. Cttee. on Social Studies 64-; mem. Public Schools Comm. 66-; Trustee, British Museum 63-; Le Bas Prize 48, James Tait Black Memorial Prize 51.
Publs. *Leslie Stephen: His Thought and Character in Relation to his Time* 51, *The Intellectual Aristocracy* (in *Studies in Social History*, edited by J. H. Plumb) 55, *Roxburgh of Stowe* 65.
University College, Gower Street, London, W.C.1, England.
Telephone: 01-387-7050.

Annenkov, Nikolai Alexandrovich; Soviet theatre and film actor; b. 1899; ed. Higher Theatre School of Maly Theatre, Moscow.
Actor of Maly Theatre 24-; mem. C.P.S.U. 42-; People's Artist of U.S.S.R. 60; State Prize (thrice).
Main roles include: Mitya (*Poverty is no Vice* by A. N. Ostrovsky), Cherkun (*Barbarians* by Maxim Gorky), Sintsov (*Enemies* by Gorky), Nil (*Lower Middle Classes* by Gorky), Plakun (*The Eternal Source* by Zorin), Ognev (*Front* by A. Korneichuk), Motylev (*Glozy* by V. Gusev).
Maly Theatre, 1/6 Ploshchad Sverdlova, Moscow, U.S.S.R.

Annigoni, Pietro; Italian painter; b. 7 June 1910; ed. Accademia di Belle Arti, Florence.
First exhibition held in Florence 32; exhibition, Milan 36; helped found group of modern realistic painting, which exhibited in Milan 47, and subsequently in Rome and Florence; exhbns. Wildenstein's (London 50, New York 57), Paris, London 54; mem. Accademia di S. Luca, Rome, Arti del Disegno, Florence; mem. Royal Soc. of Portrait Painters, London.
Works include portraits of The Duchess of Devonshire, Miss Margaret Rawlings, Lord and Lady Howard de Walden, Dame Margot Fonteyn; *Say You This is Man?* 53, *Way to the Sermon on the Mount* 54, Portrait of H.M. Queen Elizabeth II 55, Portrait of H.R.H. the Prince Philip, Duke of Edinburgh 57, Portrait of H.R.H. Princess Margaret 58, *Life* 61, Portrait of President Kennedy 61; fresco *Crucifix* in S. Martino Castagno, Florence; Portrait of Pope John XXIII; *The Immaculate Heart of Mary* 62; Portrait of H.M. Queen

Elizabeth, the Queen Mother 63; altarpiece Church of S. Lorenzo, Florence 64; *Resurrection* fresco in Church of S. Michele, Ponte Buggianese (Montecatini) 67; Portraits of Shah of Iran and Queen Fara Diba 68.
Borgo degli Albizi 8, Florence, Italy.

Annorkwei II, Nene, Q.M.C.; Ghanaian chief; b. 1900; ed. Wesleyan School, Accra.
Entered Nigerian civil service as Treasury Clerk 19; transferred to Gold Coast 30; promoted to Accountant 44; elected Manche of Prampram 48; appointed Treas. of Provincial Council, Eastern Province, and mem. Council's Standing Cttee. 48; later Pres. Joint Provincial Council of Chiefs (representing Eastern and Western Regions); Chair. Ghana Museum and Monuments Board 57-; Queen's Medal for Chiefs 56.
Manche of Prampram, Prampram, Ghana.

Anokhin, Peter Kuzmich; Soviet physiologist; b. 27 Jan. 1898; ed. Leningrad State Medical Inst.
Graduated in medicine 26; Lecturer 28; Laboratory work with Bachterev and Pavlov 20-30; Prof. Physiology, Nizhni Novgorod 30-35; Head Dept. of Gen. Physiology, All-Union Inst. of Experimental Medicine 34-46; mem. U.S.S.R. Acad. of Medical Sciences 45-; Dir. Inst. Normal and Pathological Physiology, Moscow 48-53; Chief, Physiological Laboratory 53-58; Prof. and Head of Faculty, First Moscow Medical Inst. 55-; mem. U.S.S.R. Acad. of Sciences 66-.
Publs. *The Problem of Centre and Periphery in the Physiology of Nervous Activity* 35, *Problems of Higher Nervous Activity* 49, *Internal Inhibition as the Problem of Physiology* 58, *Electroencephalographic Analysis of the Conditioned Reflex* 58, *A New Conception of the Architecture of the Conditioned Reflex* 61, *The Multiple ascending influences of the subcortical centres on cerebral cortex* 61, *The Theory of the Functional System as a Premise to the Construction of Physiological Cybernetics* 62, *The Electroencephalogram as a Result of Ascending Influences on the Cells of the Cortex* 63, *Systemogenesis as a General Regulator of Brain Development* 64, *Key Mechanisms of the Functional System as Units of Self-Regulation* 64, *The Hypothesis of the Convergent Locking of the Conditioned Reflex* 65, *Cybernetics and Integrative Brain Activity* 66, *Cybernetics, Neurophysiology and Psychology* 66.
I. M. Sechenov Institute of Physiology, Karl Marx av. 18, Moscow; Kutuzowsky av. 18, ap. 38, Moscow G-151, U.S.S.R.
Telephone: G-3-15-61; B-9-68-66.

Anouilh, Jean Marie Lucien Pierre; French playwright; b. 23 June 1910; ed. Collège Chaptal and Univ. of Paris.
Plays include: *L'Ermine* (The Ermine) 34, *Y'avait un prisonnier* 35, *Le Voyageur sans bagages* 37, *Le Bal des Voleurs* (Thieves' Carnival) 38, *La Sauvage* (Restless Heart) 38, *Cavalcade d'Amour* 41, *Le Rendez-vous de Senlis* 42, *Léocadia* (Time Remembered) 42, *Euridice* (Point of Departure) 42, *Oreste* 45, *Antigone* 46, *Roméo et Juliette* (Fading Mansion) 46, *Medea* 46, *L'invitation au château* (Ring Round the Moon) 48, *Ardèle ou la Marguerite* 49, *La Répétition, ou l'amour puni* 50, *Colombe* 50, *La Valse des toréadors* (Waltz of the Toreadors) 52, *L'Alouette* (The Lark) 53, *Ornifle* 55, *Pauvre Bitos* (Poor Bitos) 56, *L'Hurluberlu* 58, *Beckett ou l'amour de Dieu* (Becket) 59, *Foire d'Empoigne* 60, *La Grotte* 61, *l'Orchestre* 62, *Monsieur Barnett* (TV play).
Films include: *Monsieur Vincent, Pattes Blanches, Caprice de Caroline, Becket.*
c/o Les Editions de la Table Ronde, 40 rue du Bac, Paris 7e.

Ansermet, Ernest Alexandre, LIC. SC. PHYS. ET MATH.; Swiss musician; b. 83; ed. Univs. of Lausanne and Paris; musical studies in Switzerland and Paris.
Professor Maths., Lausanne 03-09; conductor orchestra Kursaal, Montreux 10-14; conductor symphony con-

certs Geneva 15-18; founder and conductor Orchestre de la Suisse Romande de Genève 18-67; chief conductor Orchestra Radio Geneva; conductor Russian ballet of Serge Diaghilev 15-23; concerts in S. America, Mexico, N. America, Europe; mem. various int. examination boards, Commdr. Légion d'Honneur and Etoile Belge, Grand Croix Ordre du Phénix (Greece); Dr. h.c. (Univs. of Lucerne and Neuchâtel).
Numerous musical publications incl. *Les fondements de la musique dans la conscience humaine* (2 vols.) 61.
11 Rue Bellot, Geneva, Switzerland.

Ansett, Reginald Myles; Australian aviation, road transport and television company administrator; b. 13 Feb. 1909.
Managing Dir. Ansett Transport Industries Ltd. and subsidiaries, Ansett Transport Industries (Operations) Pty. Ltd. (Trading as Ansett-ANA, Airlines of New South Wales, Airlines of South Australia, Ansett Freight Express and Ansett Flying Boat Services, Ansett Pioneer, Aviation Engineering Supplies, N.I.C. Instrument Co.), Ansett Airlines of Papua, New Guinea Ltd., Ansett Hotels Pty. Ltd., Ansett Gen. Aviation Pty. Ltd., Ansair Pty. Ltd., Barrier Reef Islands Pty. Ltd., Ansett Motors Pty. Ltd., Mildura Bus Lines Pty. Ltd., Provincial Motors Bendigo Pty. Ltd., Austarama Television Pty. Ltd.; Dir. MacRobertson Miller Airlines Ltd., Cathay Holdings Ltd., Cathay Pacific Airways Ltd. (Hong Kong), Pacific Air Maintenance and Supplies Co. Ltd. (Hong Kong), Woolcord Fabrics Ltd., Universal Telecasters Queensland Ltd.
489 Swanston Street, Melbourne, Victoria, Australia.

Ansiaux, Hubert-Jacques-Nicolas; Belgian banker; b. 24 Nov. 1908; ed. Univ. Libre de Bruxelles.
Director, Nat. Bank of Belgium 41-54, Deputy Gov. 54-57, Gov. 57-; Chair. Inst. Belgo-Luxembourgeois du Change 57-; Dir. Bank for Int. Settlements 57-; Gov. for Belgium, Int. Monetary Fund 57-; Chair. Conseil des Institutions publiques de Crédit 57-; mem. Conseil général de la Caisse Générale d'Epargne et de Retraite 57-; Chair. Conseil d'Admin. de l'Office Central de la Petite Epargne 57-; mem. Man. Board and Chair. Standing Finance Cttee. of Carnegie Hero Fund 57-; mem. Conseil d'Administration de l'Université Libre de Bruxelles 59-; First Vice-Chair. Nat. Council on Scientific Policy 59-; Alt. Gov. for Belgium of Int. Bank for Reconstruction and Devt. 60-; Alt. Gov. for Belgium Int. Finance Corpn. 60-; mem. Man. Board Fondation Nationale pour le Financement de la Recherche Scientifique 60-, Comité Consultatif des Finances du Fonds Nat. de la Recherche Scientifique 60-; Pres. Cttee. of Govs. of Central Banks of European Econ. Community; Officer Order of Leopold and Grand Officer Order of Crown (Belgium) and decorations from Netherlands, Luxembourg, Syria, Norway, Italy, Greece, France, Great Britain and U.S.A.
Banque Nationale de Belgique, 5 boulevard de Berlaimont, Brussels; Home: Le Bois Sauvage, 158 avenue Circulaire, Brussels 18, Belgium.
Telephone: 17-63-00 (Office); 74-58-93 (Home).

Antelava, Nikolai Vardenovich; Soviet surgeon; b. 1893; ed. Rostov Univ.
Intern Tbilisi Medical Inst. 20-23; Bier and Saderbruch Clinic 23-24; Surgeon Zugdidi District Hospital 24-28; Leningrad Mil. Medical Acad. 28-29; Head of Dept., consulting surgeon, Sukhumi 29-39; Prof. 39; Head of clinic Daghestan Medical Inst. 39-41; Head of Chair Tbilisi Refresher Medical Inst. 41-; Senior Assoc. Inst. of Experimental Surgery 46-51; Chief Surgeon Ministry of Public Health Georgian S.S.R. 49-54; Corresp. mem. U.S.S.R. Acad. of Medical Sciences 50-63, mem. 63-; mem. C.P.S.U. 46-; mem. of Board, U.S.S.R. Surgeons' Soc.; Hon. mem. U.S.S.R. and Georgian Phthisiatrists; mem. Int. Soc. of Surgeons; Hon. mem. Italian Surgeons' Soc., Czechoslovak Medical Soc.; Order of Lenin,

Red Star, S. P. Fedorov Prize 56, Lenin Prize 61, Merited Scientist of Georgian S.S.R.
Publs. About 160 works on thoracic surgery, particularly treatment of tuberculosis and brucellosis, cardiovascular and cardiac surgery.
Refresher Medical Institute, 12 Lunacharski Street, Tbilisi, U.S.S.R.

Anthony, Hon. John Douglas; Australian farmer and politician; b. 31 Dec. 1929; ed. Murwillumbah High School, The King's School, Paramatta, and Queensland Agricultural Coll.
Member House of Reps. 57-, Exec. Council 63-, Minister for the Interior 64-67, of Primary Industry 67-; Deputy Leader Australian Country Party 66-.
Parliament House, Canberra, A.C.T., Australia.

Anthony, Seth Kwabla; Ghanaian diplomatist; b. 16 June 1915; ed. Achimota Coll., Ghana.
Former teacher, Achimota Coll.; Ghanaian Army 39-45; Admin. Service, Gold Coast 46, District Officer in Ashanti 46-51; Asst. Sec. Ministry of Defence and External Affairs, Gold Coast 52-54; Senior Asst. Sec. Ministry of Interior 54-56; Counsellor and Chargé d'Affaires, Ghana Embassy, Washington 56-59; Acting Perm. Rep. of Ghana to UN 56-57; Counsellor, Paris 59, then Perm. Rep. to UN, Geneva, and Consul-Gen., Switzerland; High Commr. in India 62-66, concurrently accred. to Afghanistan 62-66, in U.K. 66-.
Ghana High Commission, 13 Belgrave Square, London, S.W.1, England.

Antokolsky, Pavel Grigorievich; Soviet poet; b. 96; ed. Moscow Univ. Law Faculty.
State prizewinner for *My Son* 43; Order of Red Banner of Labour (twice).
Publs. *Robespierre and Gorgon* 28, *1871 Commune* 31, *François Villon* 34, *Great Distances* 35, *Pushkin's Year* 38, *Half a Year* 42, *Iron and Fire* 42, *The Third Book of the War* 43, *My Son* 43, *A Lane in Arbat* 54, *Ocean* 55, *The Studio* 58, *The Strength of Vietnam* 60, *Pushkin* 60, *High Tension* 62, *Picasso* 63, *Adopted Brothers* 63, *Selected Poems* (2 vols.) 64, *Fourth Dimension* 64, *Les voies des poètes* 65, *Poèmes* (2 vols.) 66; trans. of French poets.
Union of Soviet Writers, Vorovsky 52, Moscow, U.S.S.R.

Antoniewicz, Wlodzimierz, PH.D.; Polish archæologist; b. 93; ed. Lemberg, Cracow, Poznań, Paris and Vienna Univs.
Keeper, Wawel Castle Museum 16-19; Prof. of Prehistory, Polish Free Univ. 19-39; Prof. Warsaw Univ. 20-, Dean, Faculty of Humanities 34-36, Rector 36-45; during German occupation Prof. and mem. Acad. Senate, clandestine Univ. of Warsaw; Prof. Polish Archæology, Univ. of Warsaw; Deputy Dir. State Museum of Archaeology; mem. Polish Acad. of Sciences, Swedish Acad. of Sciences, German Leopoldina Acad.; Hon. Fellow Soc. of Antiquaries of London; Hon. mem. Prehistory Soc., London; mem. Prehistory Inst., Florence, Anthropological Soc. Vienna, Archaeological Soc. of Helsinki, Finno-Ugrian Soc. Helsinki; Dr. h.c. (Riga Univ.).
Publs. Over 350 works, including *U podstaw archeologii przedhistorycznej w Polsce (Foundations of Pre-Historic Archæology in Poland)* 26, *Archeologia Polski (Polish Archæology)* 28, *Sprawy muzealne (Museum Affairs)* 33, *Historia Sztuki Pierwotnej (History of Primitive Art)* 58, *Pastoral and Shepherds' Life in the Tatra Mountains and Podhale* (Vols. I-VIII) 59-68.
Krakowskie Przedmiescie 32/4, Warsaw, Poland.
Telephone: 26-85-44.

Antonio (Antonio Ruiz Soler); Spanish dancer; b. 21.
Danced with Rosario under name *Los Chavalillos Sevillanos*, later *Rosario and Antonio* until 52; with own company, *Antonio, Ballet Español* 52- and *Antonio y sus Ballets de Madrid*, 64; Cross of Isabel la Católica; Gold

Medal of Swedish Dance Acad.; Medal of Ministry of Information 63; Cross of Commdr. of Civil Merit; Gold Plate of Spanish Artists Syndicate; Silver Plate of Ministry of Information to First Dancer of Spain; Medal of Work.
Coslada 7, Madrid, Spain.
Telephone: Madrid 256-24-01.

Antonioni, Michelangelo, L. ECON. and COMM.; Italian film director; b. 29 Sept. 1912; ed. Univ. of Bologna.
Film critic *Corriere Padano* and *L'Italia Libera.*
Films: *Gente del Po* 45, *Amorosa Menzogna* 46, *N.U.* 48, *Sette Canne un Vestito, La Villa dei Mostri, Superstizione* 49 (documentaries); *Cronaca di un Amore* 50, *La Signora Senza Camelie* 52-53, *I Vinti* 53, *Le Amiche* 55, *Il Grido* 57, *L'Avventura* 59, *La Notte* 61, *L'Eclisse* 62, *Il Deserto Rosso* 64, *Blow Up* 66 (Golden Palm, Cannes Film Festival 67).
Via Vincenzo Tiberio 18, Rome, Italy.

Antoniu, Costache; Romanian actor; b. 26 Feb. 1900; ed. Jassy Coll. of Dramatic Arts.
Actor in provincial theatres until 35; mem. Romanian Nat. Theatre Co., Bucharest 35-; Rector and Prof. Theatre Inst. "I. L. Caragiale" 54-; Deputy to Grand Nat. Assembly; mem. Nat. Peace Cttee.; Pres. Artistes' Asscn.; notable roles include Scapin, title role in *Les Fourberies de Scapin* (Molière), Nenea Iancu in *Acolo departe* (*There Far Away*, Stefănescu) and, in recent years, Prof. Andronic in *Ultima oră* (*Stop Press,* Sebastian), Spiridon Hampu in *Ziua cea mare* (*The Great Day*, Banus), Profirel in *Hagi Tudose* (Delavrancea), Udrea in *Steaua fără nume* (*The Nameless Star*, Sebastian), title role in Chekov's *Uncle Vanya*, Prozorov in Chekhov's *Three Sisters*, Muromschi in *Nunta lui Crecinschi* (*Crecinshi's Wedding*, Suhovo-Cobylin), Micola in *Fericirea furată* (*Stolen Happiness*, Franco), Dr. Prell in *Institutorii* (Ernst), Cernogubov in *Personal Matter* (Stein), Pristanda, the Candidate in *D'Ale Carnavalului* (*Carnival Scenes*) and the tipsy citizen in *O Scrisoare Pierdută* (*A Lost Letter*, Caragiale), title role in *Conu Leonida* (Caragiale), Spirache in *Titanic Vals* (Muşatescu), etc.; Film roles include: Gounod in *Darclée*, Priest in *Pădureo Spînzuratilor* (*The Forest of the Hanged*), *Vacanta la Mare* (*Holiday at the Seaside*), *Streînul* (*The Stranger*); Artist of the People, three State Prizes, Order of Labour Second Class, Star of Romanian People's Repub.
Publ. *From the Past of the Rumanian Theatre* (memoirs) 53.
B-dul Schitu Magureanu 1, Bucharest, Romania.
Telephone: 15-33-95.

Antoniutti, H.E. Cardinal Ildebrando; Vatican ecclesiastic; b. 3 Aug. 1898.
Ordained 20; Titular Archbishop of Synnada in Phrygia 36-; Papal Diplomatic Service 27-; Papal Nuncio in Spain 53-62; cr. Cardinal 62; Prefect of Sacred Congregation for Religious and Secular Insts.
Via Rusticucci 13, Rome, Italy.

Antonov, Alexei Konstantinovich; Soviet politician; b. 12; ed. Leningrad Polytechnic Inst.
Engineer, later Chief Factory Engineer 35-57; econ. work, Leningrad Regional Econ. Cttee. 57-59, Dep. Chair. Leningrad Regional Econ. Cttee. 59-61, Chair. 61-65; Candidate mem. Central Cttee. of C.P.S.U. 61-; Minister of Electro-Technical Industry (U.S.S.R.) 65-; Deputy to U.S.S.R. Supreme Soviet.
Ministry of Electro-Technical Industry, 12 Bolshaya Gruzinskaya ulitsa, Moscow, U.S.S.R.

Antonov, Nikolai Afanasyevich; Soviet politician; b. 1921; ed. Leningrad Industrial Inst.
Member C.P.S.U. 44-; Soviet Army 41-45; Dir. Borovichi Mechanical Plant 45-55; Chair. Exec. Cttee. of Borovichi City Soviet of Workers' Deputies 55-56; Chief

of Section, Novgorod Regional Cttee. of C.P. 56-60; Sec. Novgorod Regional Cttee. of C.P. 60-66; Chair. Exec. Cttee. Novgorod Regional Soviet of Workers' Deputies 66-; Deputy to R.S.F.S.R. Supreme Soviet.
Novgorod Regional Soviet of Workers' Deputies, Novgorod, U.S.S.R.

Antonov, Oleg Konstantinovich; Soviet aircraft designer; b. 1906; ed. Leningrad Polytechnical Inst.
Member C.P.S.U. 45-; Head Experimental Design Dept. 46-; Chief Designer for Aircraft Industry 62-; gliders and aeroplanes designed under his direction include: AN-10, AN-24, AN-22 (ANTEI); Corresp. mem. Ukrainian Acad. of Sciences; Deputy to Supreme Soviet of U.S.S.R.; State Prize 52; Lenin Prize 62; Hero of Socialist Labour 66; numerous Soviet Orders.
Ministry of Aircraft Industry, Moscow, U.S.S.R.

Antonov, Sergei Fyodorovich; Soviet engineer, diplomatist and politician; b. 1911.
Worked formerly in agencies and ministries of meat and milk industry; Minister of Milk and Dairy Products Industry 54-57; Ambassador to Afghanistan 60-65; Minister of Meat and Milk Industry 65-.
Ministry of Meat and Milk Industry, Moscow, U.S.S.R.

Antonova, Irina Alexandrovna; Soviet art historian; b. 20 March 1922; ed. Moscow Lomonosov Univ.
Scientist and Post-Graduate Student, State A.S. Pushkin Museum 46-49, Senior Scientific Worker 49-61; Dir. 61-; specialist in Italian art; contributor on ancient and modern Western art in journals *Iskusstvo* (Art), *Tvorchestvo* (Creative Work) and *Khudozhnik* (Artist); Dir. Soviet Art Exhbn. in Czechoslovakia 57, Austria 59; Head Soviet Pavilion, Venice 60; mem. C.P.S.U. 54-. Publs. *Venetian Painting of the 16th Century* 56, *Veronese* 63; script for film *Pictures in the Dresden Gallery.*
State A.S. Pushkin Museum of Fine Arts, Volkhonka 12, Moscow, U.S.S.R.
Telephone: 94-79-26.

Antunovic, Rista; Yugsolav politician; b. 25 June 1917; ed. Belgrade Univ.
Former Sec. District Cttee. Yugoslav Communist Youth Fed.; fmr. mem. C.P. District Cttee. for Leskovac; mem. Communist Party 40-; a leader of liberation movement in S. Serbia, Second World War; later Sec. C.P. District Cttees. for Vranje and Leskovac; Commdr. First Div. Nat. Liberation Army, S. Serbia; mem. Central Cttee. C.P. of Serbia 45-; Central Cttee. of Yugoslav C.P. 52-; mem. Exec. Cttee. Central Cttee. of Serbian C.P. 48-; later Sec. Serbian C.P. City Cttee. for Belgrade, later Org. Sec. Central Cttee. Serbian C.P.; also Minister of Trade and Minister of Agriculture for Serbia, and mem. Exec. Council for Serbia; mem. Fed. Assembly 45-; later mem. Fed. Exec. Council, mem. Fed. Chamber of Fed. Assembly; decorations include Order of People's Hero, Order of Nat. Liberation, Order of Repub. with Gold Wreath, Partisan Memorial Order.
c/o Federal Executive Council, Belgrade, Yugoslavia.

Anzai, Masao; Japanese chemical executive; b. 12 Nov. 1904; ed. Tokyo Univ.
With Showa Denko 32-, Dir. 53, Man. Dir. 54-59, Pres. 59-; Pres. Showa Neoprene 60-, Japan Olefin Chemicals 65-, Tokuyama Petrochemical 65-; Dir. SKY Aluminium 64-; Acting Chair. Govt. Admin. Management and Inspection Comm.; Dir. Fed. of Econ. Orgs., Japan Fed. of Employers Asscns., Japan Chemical Industry Asscn.
Showa Denko K.K., 34 Shiba Miyamoto-cho, Minato-ku, Tokyo; Home: 10 Taira-cho, 1-chome, Meguro-ku, Tokyo, Japan.

Ao, P. Shilu, B.A.; Indian (Naga) politician; b. 15 Dec. 1916; ed. St. Edmund's Coll., Shillong.
Assam Civil Service 51-60; Co-organiser Naga Nat.

Council; fmr. Chief Exec. Councillor, Nagaland; Chief Minister of Nagaland 61-66, 67.
Kohima, Nagaland, India.

Aoki, Kinichi; Japanese business executive; b. 14 Feb. 1898; ed. Tokyo Coll. of Commerce.
Former Pres. White Brick Manufacturing Co.; formerly with Tokyo Woollen Fabric Manufacturing Co., later Nihon Steel Tube Co. Ltd.; Pres. Tokyo Electric Power Co. 59, now Chair.; Chair. Shinagawa Fire Brick.
15 Toyowachamachi, Shibuya-ku, Tokyo, Japan.

Apel, Willi, DR.PHIL.; American (b. German) musicologist; b. 1893; ed. Univs. of Bonn, Munich, Berlin.
Piano studies with Leonid Kreutzer, Edwin Fischer; lecturer on music 26-36; went to U.S.A. 36; taught at Longy School of Music 36-43, Harvard Univ. and Radcliffe Coll. 38-42, Boston Center for Adult Education 37-50; Prof. of Music, Indiana Univ. 50-63, Emeritus Prof. 64-; Fellow, Medieval Acad. of America.
Publs. *The Notation of Polyphonic Music 800-1600* 42, *Harvard Dictionary of Music* 44, *Historical Anthology of Music* (with A. T. Davison, 2 vols.) 46, 50, *Masters of the Keyboard* 47, *French Secular Music of the Late 14th Century* 50, *Gregorian Chant* 58, *Harvard Brief Dictionary of Music* 60, *Geschichte der Orgel-und Klaviermusik bis 1700* 67.
1018 East Second Street, Bloomington, Ind., U.S.A.
Telephone: 33-2-1655.

Apithy, Sourou Migan; Dahomeyan politician; b. 8 April 1913; ed. Ecole Libre des Sciences Politiques, Ecole Nat. d'Organisation Economique et Sociale.
Deputy of Dahomey to French Constituent Assemblies 45-46; mem. Nat. Assembly 46-58; del. to seventh and eighth sessions UN 53; mem. Grand Council French West Africa 47-57; Pres. Gen. Council Dahomey 55-57; Prime Minister Provisional Govt. 58-59; Minister without Portfolio 60; Vice-Pres. and Minister of the Plan and Development 60; Ambassador of Dahomey to France, U.K., and Switzerland to 63; Minister of Finance, Economy and the Plan 63-64; Pres. of the Republic of Dahomey 64-Nov. 65; Commdr. de la Grande-Comore.
Publ. *Au Service de mon Pays.*
Porto Novo, Dahomey, West Africa.

Apostel, Hans-Erich; Austrian composer; b. 01; studied music under Schönberg and Berg.
Professor 43-52, Lector 52-; mem. Austrian Arts Council 60-; City of Vienna Prize 48, Austrian State Prize 57.
Compositions: Songs, piano pieces, choral works, three string quartets, *Haydn Variations*, Op. 17, *Rondo Ritmico*, Op. 27, piano concerto, Op. 30, works for woodwind, *Ode for Full Orchestra and Alto Solo*, Op. 36, *Tryptic for Boys' Choir*, Op. 37, *Little Chamber Concerto*, Op. 38, *Symphony for Chamber Orchestra*, Op. 41.
Krongasse 11, 1050 Vienna, Austria.

Apostol, Gheorghe; Rumanian politician; b. 13.
Member, Communist Party of Rumania 34-48, Central Cttee. of Communist Party of Rumania 45-48, Political Bureau of Central Cttee. of Rumanian Workers' Party 48-; First Sec. Central Cttee. of Rumanian Workers' Party 54-55; Pres. Central Council of Trade Unions 55-61; First Deputy Chair. Council of Ministers 61-Dec. 67; Chair. Central Council of Trade Unions and mem. Council of Ministers Dec. 67-.
Council of Ministers, Bucharest, Rumania.

Apostolakos, Christos; Greek civil servant and politician; b. 1913; ed. Athens Univ. Law School.
Civil Servant, Ministry of Nat. Economy 29, Ministry of Labour 36-61; mem. Exec. Cttee. Supreme Civil Servants Comm. 57, Pres. 58-61, Life Pres. 61-; Publisher *Laconian Voice* 32, *Labour Law Bulletin* 51; Editorial Staff *Embros* (newspaper) 44-53; Publisher *People's Struggle* (newspaper) 63; Nat. Radical Union

Deputy 61-62, Centre Union Deputy 62-; Minister of Social Welfare July 65, of Public Order Oct. 65-66; Commander Order of Phoenix; Gold Cross of Holy Sepulchre.
Publs. *Wages—Salaries—Collective Labour Agreements* (2 vols.) 47, *Compendium of Wages* (2 vols.) 52, *The State and the Civil Servant* 57.
c/o Ministry of Public Order, Athens, Greece.

Appel, André, D.D., L.H.D.; French ecclesiastic; b. 20 Dec. 1921.
Former Chaplain Univ. of Paris; Sec.-Gen. French Protestant Fed. 56-64; Pastor Temple Neuf, Strasbourg 64-65; Sec.-Gen. Lutheran World Fed. 65-.
150 route de Ferney, 1211 Geneva 20, Switzerland.
Telephone: 33-3400.

Appel, Karel Christian; Netherlands painter; b. 25 April 1921; ed. Rijksakademie van Beeldende Kunsten, Amsterdam.
Began career as artist 38; exhibitions in Europe, America and Japan 50-; has executed murals in Amsterdam, The Hague, Rotterdam, Brussels and Paris; UNESCO Prize, Venice Biennale 53; Lissone Prize, Italy 58; Acquisition Prize, São Paulo Bienal 59; Graphique Int. Prize, Ljubljana, Yugoslavia 59; Guggenheim Nat. Prize, Netherlands 51; Guggenheim Int. Prize 61.
Office: c/o Galerie Statler, 51 rue de Seine, Paris; Home: 7 rue Brézin, Paris 14e, France.

Apró, Antal; Hungarian politician; b. 13.
Joined Communist Party 31; Pres. of Building Workers' Asscn. 45; Gen. Sec. Trade Union Council 48-51; Minister of Building Materials Industry 52-53; Deputy Prime Minister 53-56, 61-; Minister of Industry 56-57; First Deputy Prime Minister 58-61; Perm Rep. to Council for Mutual Econ. Aid 62-; Pres. Nat. Council, Patriotic People's Front 56-57; mem. Politburo, Socialist Workers' Party.
c/o Council of Ministers, Budapest, Hungary.

Apryatkin, Semyon Semyonovich; Soviet politician; b. 1911; ed. Azerbaijan Oil Inst.
Executive positions in oil industry 34-57; mem. C.P.S.U. 48-; First Vice-Chair. Checheno-Ingushetia Council of Nat. Econ. 57-58; Sec. Checheno-Ingushetia Regional Cttee. of C.P.S.U. 58-66, First Sec. 66-; Deputy to U.S.S.R. Supreme Soviet; mem. Central Auditing Comm. C.P.S.U.; Hero of Socialist Labour 48; State Prize 49.
Checheno-Ingushetia Regional Committee of C.P.S.U., Grozny, U.S.S.R.

Aquarone, Stanislas Raoul Adrien, B.A., A.M., PH.D.; Australian international civil servant; b. 13 Nov. 1915; ed. Univ. of Toronto Schools, Univ. of Toronto, and Columbia Univ., N.Y.
Former teacher of French language and literature, Hamilton Coll. and in Columbia, Panama and Toronto Univs.; Sec. Int. Court of Justice 48-51, First Sec 51-60, Deputy Registrar 60-66, Registrar 66-.
Publ. *The Life and Works of Emile Littré (1801-1881)* 58.
International Court of Justice, Peace Palace, The Hague; Home: Benoordenhoutsweg 93, The Hague, Netherlands.

Aragon, Louis; French novelist, poet and essayist; b. 3 Oct. 1897.
One of founders and fmr. leader Surrealist Movement, now leader Socialistic Realism Movement; Sec. French section of Int. Asscn. of Writers for Defence of Culture; mem. Cttee. of Dirs. *Europe* review; Dir. fmr. Paris daily *Ce Soir*; Editor *Les Lettres Françaises* (weekly); mem. Communist Party; mem. Lenin Int. Peace Prize Cttee.; served with Tank Div. 39-40, prisoner of war, escaped to unoccupied France, worked in the Resistance movement.
Publs. Novels: *Anicet, Le Libertinage, Le Paysan de*

Paris, Les cloches de Bâle, Les Beaux Quartiers (awarded Prix Renaudot), *Les voyageurs de l'Impériale, Aurélien, La Semaine Sainte, La mise à mort, l'Oubli;* essays: *Traité du Style, Les aventures de Télémaque, Pour un réalisme socialiste;* poems: *Feu de joie, Le Mouvement perpétuel, La grande Gaîté, Persécuté persécuteur, Hourra l'Oural, Le Crève-Coeur, Les Yeux d'Elsa, La Diane française;* history: *Histoire de l'U.R.S.S. de 1917–1960.*
Saint-Arnoult-en-Yvelines (Seine-et-Oise), France.

Aragones Vila, José; Spanish diplomatist; b. 15; ed. Universidad de Madrid.
Foreign Service 43-; Vice-Consul, San Francisco, and Consul, Galveston, U.S.A. 44-48; General Sec., Ministry of Foreign Affairs 48-51; Commercial Attaché, Washington, later Santiago 51-59; Administrator, Int. Bank for Reconstruction and Development 59-63; Minister (Economic Affairs), Paris 63-65; Chief of Spanish Del. to Org. for Economic Co-operation and Development (O.E.C.D.) 65-.
Organisation for Economic Co-operation and Development, Château de la Muette, 2 rue André-Pascal, Paris 16e, France.

Aram, Abbas; Iranian diplomatist; b. 1906.
Entered diplomatic service 31; Asst. Chief, Third Political Div., Foreign Ministry 43; First Sec. Berne 45; First Sec., Counsellor, and Chargé d'Affaires, Washington 46, 49 and 50; Dir. Fourth Political Div., Foreign Ministry 51; Counsellor, Embassy, Baghdad 53; Chargé d'Affaires and Minister, Washington 53 and 54-56; Dir.-Gen. Political Affairs, Foreign Ministry 58; Ambassador to Japan 58, concurrently to Republic of China; Minister of Foreign Affairs 59-60; Ambassador to Iraq 60-62; Minister of Foreign Affairs 62-67; Amb. to U.K. 67-.
Imperial Iranian Embassy, 26 Princes Gate, London, S.W.7, England.

Arámburu, Gonzalo N. de; Peruvian diplomatist; b. 1899; ed. Lima Inst., Universidad Nacional Mayor de San Marcos, Lima and Central Univ. of Madrid, Spain.
Ministry of Foreign Affairs, Lima 20; Second Sec., Washington, Berlin, Rome 22-29, First Sec., Madrid, Rio de Janeiro 29-36, Counsellor, London 36-40; Dir. of Protocol, Lima 40-43; Del. to French Cttee. of Nat. Liberation, Algiers 43-44; Minister in Paris 44-46; successively Ambassador to Colombia, Ecuador, German Federal Republic, Uruguay and Netherlands 46-62, to Great Britain 62-; Grand Officier Légion d'Honneur, Grand Cross of the Order "Al Mérito por Servicios Distinguidos", Peru and numerous other decorations.
Embassy of Peru, 52 Sloane Street, London, S.W.1., England.

Arámburu, Pedro Eugenio; Argentine army officer and politician; b. 21 May 1903.
Entered Nat. Military Coll. 19 and Infantry School 27; held a number of military administrative posts in various provinces; entered Escuela Superior de Guerra 33, graduated as General Staff Officer 35; sent on study mission to Europe 39, appointed permanent Prof. of the Staff Coll. 43; Military Attaché in Brazil 51; General and Dir. of Staff Coll. 54; provisional Pres. of the Repub. 55-58; Pres. Unión del Pueblo Argentino (UDELPA).
Montevideo 1053, Buenos Aires, Argentina.

Aranne, Zalman; Russian-born Israeli politician; b. 1 March 1899; ed. Agricultural Univ. Kharkov.
Joined admin. staff of the Histadrut (Gen. Fed. of Jewish Labour), posts held include: Sec. Organisation Dept., Treasurer, Dir. of Public Information Bureau and Dir. of the Histadrut Workers' Coll. 36-48; Sec.-Gen. of Tel-Aviv Labour Council and of Israel Labour Party 48-51; mem. Knesset 49-; fmr. Chair. Foreign Affairs and Security Cttees.; mem. Israel Del. to UN

50; Minister without Portfolio 54, of Education 55-60, of Education and Culture 63-.
16 Hagedud Ha'ivri, Jerusalem, Israel.

Araoz de Lamadrid, Aristobulo Donato; Argentine judge; b. 12 Dec. 1908; ed. Universidad de Buenos Aires.
Teacher 36-47; Pres. Nat. Institute of Social Welfare 56-57; mem. Supreme Court of Justice 58-67, Pres. 65-67.
Palacio de Justicia, Plaza Lavalle, Buenos Aires, Argentina.

Arapov, Boris Alexandrovich; Soviet composer; b. 1905; ed. Leningrad Conservatoire.
Professor Leningrad Conservatoire 40; Exec. mem. Leningrad Composers Section, Soviet Composers' Union; Honoured Worker of Arts of Uzbek S.S.R. 44, of R.S.F.S.R. 57; Order of Red Banner of Labour 53.
Compositions include: *Negro Protest Songs for Voice and Jazz Orchestra* 40, *Hodja Nasreddin* (Uzbek opera) 43, *Russian Suite for Symphony Orchestra* 50, *The Frigate "Victory"* (opera) 58, Third Symphony 63, *Rain* (Chamber opera) 65.
R.S.F.S.R. Composers' Union, Ulitsa Nezhdanovoi, Moscow, U.S.S.R.

Arberry, Arthur John, M.A., LITT.D. (Cantab.), F.B.A.; British orientalist; b. 12 May 1905; ed. Portsmouth Grammar School and Pembroke Coll., Cambridge.
Fellow of Pembroke Coll. Cambridge 31; Head of Classics Dept. Cairo Univ. 32-34; Asst. Librarian India Office London 34-44; War Service with War Office and Min. of Information 39-44; Prof. of Persian, London Univ. 44-46; Prof. of Arabic London Univ., and Head of Middle East Dept. School of Oriental and African Studies 46-47; Sir Thomas Adams' Prof. of Arabic Univ. of Cambridge 47-, Chair. Middle East Centre, Univ. of Cambridge; Hon. D.Litt. (Malta), Nishan-i Danish (Iran).
Publs. *Mawaqif and Mukhatabat of Niffari* 35, *Doctrine of the Sufis* 35, *Introduction to the History of Sufism* 43, *British Orientalists* 43, *Fifty Poems of Hafiz* 47, *Immortal Rose* 48, *Ruba'iyat of Rumi* 49, *Omar Khayyam* 50, *Modern Arabic Poetry* 50, *Sufism* 51, *Omar Khayyam: a new version* 52, *Moorish Poetry* 53, *Scheherezade* 53, *Persian Poems* 54, *The Koran Interpreted* 55, *Fitzgerald's Salaman and Absal* 56, *The Seven Odes* 57, *Classical Persian Literature* 58, *Romance of the Rubaiyat* 59, *Oriental Essays, Maltese Anthology* 60, *Discourses of Rumi* 61, *Dun Karm* 61, *Tales* and *More Tales from the Masnavi* 61, *Aspects of Islamic Civilization* 64, *Arabic Poetry* 65, *Muslim Saints and Mystics* 66, *Javid-nama* 66, *Poems of al-Mutanabbi* 67, *The Koran Illuminated* 67.
Pembroke College, Cambridge; Home: 12 Gurney Way, Cambridge, England.
Telephone: Cambridge 57484.

Arboussier, Gabriel Marie D'; Senegalese politician; b. 14 Jan. 1908; ed. Collège des Dominicains, Sorèze, Lycée de Toulouse and Faculty of Law, Univ. of Paris.
Governor's Office, Dakar 37-41, Head of Office, Yako 41-43; Head of Political Office for Ivory Coast 43-44; Dep. for French Equatorial Africa to French Constituent Assembly 45-47; organiser of Conf. at Bamako, which formed R.D.A. (Rassemblement Démocratique Africain) 46, Gen. Sec. 49-50; Rep. for Ivory Coast in Assembly of French Union 47-53, Vice-Pres. 47-50; Rep. of Niger at Grand Council of French West Africa 56-60, Vice-Pres., later Pres.; Minister of Justice and Keeper of The Seals, Senegal 60-62; Ambassador to France 63-64, concurrently Perm. Del. to UNESCO, Exec. Dir. UN Inst. for Training and Research 65-68; Consultant to Pontifical Comm. for Studies on Justice and Peace 67; Grand Croix de l'Ordre National du Sénégal, Commdr. Légion d'Honneur and other decorations; Hammarskjöld Prize 67.

1245 Park Avenue, New York, N.Y., U.S.A.; 102 avenue des Champs-Elysées, Paris 8e, France; and 32 rue Victor Hugo, Dakar, Senegal.

Arbus, André; French designer, architect and sculptor; b. 17 Nov. 1903; ed. Lycée Toulouse and Ecole des Beaux-Arts, Toulouse.
Professor, Ecole Nationale Supérieure des Arts Décoratifs and Ecole Nationale Supérieure des Beaux-Arts; Artistic Counsellor for Marseille; retrospective exhibition Maison de la Pensée française 59, Musée Galierra 65; mem. Institut de France; Officier Légion d'Honneur, Officier de l'Ordre National du Mérite, Officier des Arts et Lettres; Prix Blumenthal 34, Grand Prix de l'Exposition internationale de Bruxelles 58.
Major works: Interior decoration: Elysée Palace, Chateau de Rambouillet, state room of Gen. Eisenhower, Marnes-la-Coquette, steamships *Provence, Bretagne, Viet-Nam, France* and *Pasteur*; designed Chain of Légion d'Honneur; Architectural works: bridge at de Martigues, Château St. Nom la Breteche; Sculpture: *The Wounded Warrior, The Sea-horse*, and monuments at Brest and Marseille; Busts of Jacques Jaujard, Louis Süe, Pierre Bertin, Georges Rouault, la Toulousaine.
14 avenue du Maine, Paris 15e, France.
Telephone: 633-89-93.

Arbuzov, Alexei Nikolaevich; Soviet playwright; b. 08; ed. Leningrad Theatrical School.
Actor in theatres in Leningrad and Moscow 23-; mem. Union of Soviet Writers; Literary work 30-; Order of Red Banner of Labour 58; Lenin Prize 61.
Publs. plays: *Six Favourites* 35, *The Long Road* 35, *Tanya* 39, *The Year of the Tsar* 41, *Little House on the Outskirts* 43, *The Wandering Years* 54, *They are Waiting for us Somewhere* 53, *Irkutsk Story* 59, *The Twelfth Hour* 59, *The Prodigal Son* 61, *My Poor Marat* 64, *The Promise* 66, *Confessions at Night* 67.
Union of Soviet Writers, 52 Vorovsky Street, Moscow, U.S.S.R.

Arbuzov, Boris Alexandrovich; Soviet chemist; b. 4 Nov. 1903; ed. Inst. of Agriculture and Forestry, Kazan, and Univ. of Kazan.
Docent Prof., Inst. of Chemical Technology, Kazan 30-38; Prof. of Organic Chemistry, Univ. of Kazan 38-, Dean of Chemistry Div. 40-50; Dir. Inst. of Organic Chemistry in Kazan, U.S.S.R. Acad. of Sciences 58-65; Dir. Arbuzov Inst. of Organic and Physical Chemistry 65-; mem. U.S.S.R. Acad. of Sciences 53-.
Publs. *Investigations in the Field of Isomeric Rearrangements of Bicyclic Terpens and their Epoxydes* 36, *The Arbuzov Transformation*, etc.
Arbuzov Institute of Organic and Physical Chemistry, Kazan, U.S.S.R.

Archambault, Pierre; French journalist; b. 24 June 1912.
Préfet (Acting) Indre-et-Loire 44; Dir.-Gen. "Nouvelle République du Centre Ouest" 45-; Pres. Syndicat Nat. de la Presse Quotidienne Régionale 52; Pres. Confédération de la Presse Française 53-.
4 rue de la Préfecture, Tours, Indre-et-Loire, France.

Arciniegas, Germán, D.L.; Colombian professor and diplomatist; b. 6 Dec. 1900; ed. Univ. Nacional, Bogotá.
Vice-Consul, London 29; Chargé d'Affaires, Buenos Aires 40; Minister of Education, Republic of Colombia 42-46; Visiting Prof. Univ. of Chicago 44, Univ. of Calif. 45, Columbia Univ. 47; Prof. Columbia Univ. 54-59; Amb. to Italy 59-62; Editor *Cuadernos*, Paris 62, now Colombian Amb. to Venezuela; mem. Acad. of History and Letters of Colombia; corresp. mem. acads. in Spain, Argentina, Mexico, Cuba, etc.; Hammarsjköld Prize 67.
Publs. *El Estudiante de la Mesa Redonda* 32, *América Tierra Firme* 37, *Los Comuneros* 38, *The Knight of El*

Dorado 42, *Germans in the Conquest of America* 43, *The Green Continent* 44, *Este Pueblo de América* 45, *Caribbean, Sea of the New World* 46, *The State of Latin America* 52, *Amerigo and the New World* 55, *Italia, Guía para Vagabundos* 59, *América Mágica* 59, *América Mágica II* 61, *Cosas del Pueblo* 62, *El Mundo de la Bella Simoneta* 62, *Entre el Mar Rojo y el Mar Muerto* 64, *Latin America: A Cultural History* 66, *Genio y Figura de Jorge Isaacs* 67.
Embassy of Colombia, Urbanización Campo Alegre, Avenida El Parque 18, Caracas, Venezuela.
Telephone: 33-16-98.

Arcy, Baron Jean D'; French television administrator; b. 10 June 1913; ed. Ecole des Hautes Etudes Commerciales, Paris, Faculté de Droit, Paris, and Ecole d'Application d'Artillerie, Fontainebleau.
Artillery officer 34-45; asst. dir. in Ministry of Deported Prisoners and Refugees 44-45; private sec. to Minister of Armies 45-46; Dir. of office of Minister of Youth, Arts and Letters 47; technical adviser to Minister of Information 48-49; seconded for special duties with Radiodiffusion-Télévision française 50-52, Television Programme Dir. 52-59, Dir. of Int. Relations of R.T.F. 59-61; Dir. Radio and Visual Services Div., UN 61-; Vice-Pres. Programme Comm. of Eurovision and Int. Cinema and Television Council; Chevalier Légion d'Honneur; Croix de Guerre; Resistance Medal.
Homes: 65 Seaview Avenue, New Rochelle, N.Y., U.S.A.; 4 square Mignot, Paris 16e, France.

Arden, John; British playwright; b. 26 Oct. 1930; ed. Sedbergh School, King's Coll., Cambridge, and Edinburgh Coll. of Art.
Fellow in Playwriting, Bristol Univ. 59-60; Visiting Lecturer (Politics and Drama), New York Univ. 67.
Plays: *All Fall Down* 55, *The Life of Man* 56, *The Waters of Babylon* 57, *Live Like Pigs* 58, *Sergeant Musgrave's Dance* 59, *Soldier, Soldier* 60, *The Business of Good Government* 60, *Wet Fish* 62, *The Workhouse Donkey* 63, *Ironhand* 63, *Ars Longa Vita Brevis* (with Margaretta D'Arcy) 64, *Armstrong's Last Goodnight* 64, *Left Handed Liberty* 65, *Friday's Hiding* (with Margaretta D'Arcy) 66, *The Royal Pardon* (with Margaretta D'Arcy) 66.
c/o Margaret Ramsay Ltd., 14A Goodwin's Court, London, W.C.2, England.

Ardizzone, Edward, A.R.A., F.S.I.A.; British artist; b. 16 Oct. 1900; ed. Clayesmore School, Westminster School of Art.
Clerk in London 18-26; freelance artist 26-; served in Royal Artillery 39-40; full-time official War Artist 40-45; Tutor, Royal Coll. of Art, London; has illustrated more than 100 books for British and American publishers; works purchased by the Tate Gallery, the Arts Council of Great Britain and various provincial art galleries; Kate Greenaway Medal; Hon. A.R.C.A.
Publs. A series of children's books, with original illustrations, including *Little Tim and the Brave Sea Captain Tim All Alone, Diana and Her Rhinoceros*, etc., and numerous book illustrations.
130 Elgin Avenue, London, W.9, England.

Ardon, Mordechai; Israeli (b. Polish) artist; b. 13 July 1896; ed. Bauhaus, Weimar and Munich Acad. of Fine Arts.
After working in Berlin and teaching in the Itten School of Art, emigrated to Israel 33; Adviser on Art to Ministry of Education and Culture, Jerusalem.
Ardon House, Yefeh Nof Quarter, Jerusalem, Israel.

Aref, Maj.-Gen. Abdul Rahman Mohammed (brother of late President Abdul Salam Aref); Iraqi army officer and politician; b. 1916; ed. Baghdad Military Acad.
Head of Armoured Corps until 62; Commdr. 5th Div. Feb. 63-Nov. 63; assisted in overthrow of Gen. Kassem 63; mem. Regency Council 65; Asst. Chief of Staff Iraqi

Armed Forces Dec. 63-64; Acting Chief of Staff 64, Chief of Staff 64-; Pres. of Iraq April 66-, also Prime Minister May 67.
Office of the President, Baghdad, Iraq.

Areilza, José María de, Count of Motrico; Spanish diplomatist; b. 3 Aug. 1909; ed. Bilbao Univ. and Univ. of Salamanca.
Joined Franco Party 36; Mayor of Bilbao 37; Dir.-Gen. of Industry, Franco Cabinet 38-40; mem. Cortes 43; Amb. to Argentina 47-50; industrial and banking activities 50-54; Amb. to U.S.A. 54-60, to France 60-64.
Castellana 61, Madrid, Spain.
Telephone: 2241675.

Arenales Catalán, Emilio; Guatemalan diplomatist; b. 10 May 1922; ed. Univ. of San Carlos, Guatemala.
Participated Students' Movement during overthrow of Jorge Ubico 44; Pres. El Derecho Asscn. and mem. Univ. Council of San Carlos 45 (represented Students at Int. Confs. London and Prague); Legal Counsellor, UNESCO Preparatory Comm. 46, External Relations Counsellor to UNESCO 47-48; Sec.-Gen. Int. Hylean Amazon Conf. 48; Permanent Rep. to U.N. 55-58; Pres. Cttee. on Information from Non-Self-Governing Territories 56-58; Chair. Guatemalan Del. to Trusteeship Council 56, 57, 58; Vice-Pres. Trusteeship Council 57; Chair. Del. to XI and XXII sessions of UN Gen. Assembly; Pres. Special Political Cttee. of Gen. Assembly 57; Vice-Pres. Trusteeship Council 57-58; Pres. Trusteeship Council 58; Minister of Foreign Affairs 66-.
Ministry of Foreign Affairs, Guatemala City; Home: 9 Avenida 15-28, Guatemala City 10, Republic of Guatemala.
Telephone: 21212 and 680525.

Arendt, Hannah; American (b. German) writer; b. 14 Oct. 1906; ed. Univs. of Marburg, Freiburg and Heidelberg.
Social Worker, Paris 33-40; went to U.S. 41; Research Dir., Conf. on Jewish Relations 44-46; Chief Ed. Schocken Books Inc.; Exec. Dir. Jewish Cultural Reconstruction, New York City 49-52; Rockefeller Fellow 58-60; Prof. Univ. of Chicago 63-; Sigmund Freud Prize for Scientific Prose, German Acad. for Language and Literature 67; Hon. Litt.D. (Western Coll. for Women).
Publs. *The Origins of Totalitarianism* 51, *The Human Condition* 58, *Between Past and Future* 61, *On Revolution* 63, *Eichmann in Jerusalem* 63, *Die Kontroverse* 65.
370 Riverside Drive, New York City 25, N.Y., U.S.A.

Arespacochaga y Felipe, Juan de; Spanish civil servant; b. 1920; ed. Univ. of Madrid.
Former civil engineer and economist; Dir. Gen. for Tourist Promotion.
Publs. *Las Obras Hidráulicas y la decadencia económica de España* 48, *El aceite de Oliva, moneda mediterránea* 49, *El multiplicador económico en las obras de riego* 56, *Los transportes españoles y la integración europea* 59, *Las inversiones del O.P. en la Plan Nacional.*
García de Paredes 63 4 dcha., Madrid 3, Spain.

Arfa, Hassan; Iranian army officer, politician and diplomatist; b. 1895; ed. Military colls., Turkey, Switzerland and France, Ecole Supérieure de Guerre, Paris.
Commissioned 14; Military Attaché in London 26; Commander 1st Guards Cavalry and A.D.C. to His Majesty Reza Shah 31; Commander Military Acad. 32; Inspector Gen. of Cavalry 36; Lecturer, Staff College 36; Commdr. 1st Army Division 42; A.D.C. to H.M. Mohammed Reza Shah 42; Deputy Chief of Staff 42; Chief, Intelligence Dept. of Army 42; Commdr. Teheran Training Centre 42; Gov. of roads, railways and ports 43; Chief of Staff, Iranian Army 43-46; rtd. 47; Leader of Asiatic Group 47; Leader of Nat. Movement Party 51;

Minister of Communications 51; Ambassador to Turkey 58-61, to Pakistan 62-63; Order of Homayun, 1st class; Royal Greek Order of Phoenix (1st class).
Publs. *Under Five Shahs* 64, *The Kurds* 66.
c/o Ministry of Foreign Affairs, Teheran, Iran.

Argod, Hubert Aymard, DIP. SC. POL.; French diplomatist; b. 28 Aug. 1914; ed. Ecole des Roches, Ecole Libre des Sciences Politiques, Paris.
Diplomatic Service 41-; French Provisional Govt., Algiers; First Sec. French Del. to UN, New York 46; First Sec., Beirut 47-50, High Comm. in Germany 51; European Affairs Dept., Ministry of Foreign Affairs 52, Tunisian and Moroccan Affairs Dept. 56-58, Head, Levant Desk 58-61; First Counsellor, Tunis 61; Ambassador to Chad 61-62; Minister-Counsellor, Algiers 62; Deputy High Rep. Algiers 63; Ambassador to Cambodia 64-; Officier, Légion d'Honneur, Croix de Guerre (39-45).
French Embassy, Phnom-Penh, Cambodia.

Arguedas, José María; Peruvian ethnologist and writer; b. 18 Jan. 1911; ed. Univ. Nacional de San Marcos, Lima.
Spent early life among Quechuan Indians; teacher of Spanish, Colegio Nacional "Mateo Pumacahua", Sicuani 39; Head of Folklore Section, Ministry of Educ. 45; Head of Instituto de Estudios Etnológicos, Museo de la Cultura 51; Professor of Regional Cultures of Peru, Univ. of San Marcos 59-; Dir. Casa de la Cultura 63; Dir. Museo Nacional de Historia 64-; Prof. of Quechua at Univ. Agraria 63-; Nat. Novel Prize and other awards.
Publs. Stories: *Agua* 35, *Diamantes y Pedernales* 53; novels: *Yawar Fiesta* 40, *Los Ríos Profundos* 59, *El Sexto* 61, *Todas las Sangres* 65; bi-lingual Quechuan songs: *Tupac Amaru Taytanchisman* 62, *Jetman* 66; essays; *La evolución de las comunidades Indígenas* 56, *Puquio, una comunidad en proceso de cambio* 55.
Apartado Postal 43, Lima, Peru.

Arias, Arnulfo; Panamanian coffee planter and politician; b. 02.
Ambassador to Italy 32; President of Panama 39-40, 49-50; Candidate for President 64; Leader, Partido Panameñista.
Partido Panameñista, Panama City, Panama.

Arias, Dame Margot Fonteyn de, D.B.E. (wife of Roberto Arias, *q.v.*); British ballerina; b. 18 May 1919; ed. U.S.A. and China.
As prima ballerina of the Royal Ballet Company, London, has danced all principal classical roles as well as leading roles in many modern ballets, and has appeared in many countries all over the world; Pres. Royal Acad. of Dancing 54-; Order of Finnish Lion; several hon. degrees.
c/o Royal Opera House, Covent Garden, London, W.C.2, England.

Arias, Roberto Emilio, B.A. (husband of Dame Margot Fonteyn de Arias, *q.v.*); Panamanian lawyer, editor and diplomatist; b. 18; ed. Peddie School, New Jersey, and St. John's Coll. Cambridge.
Called to Panamanian Bar 39; Editor *El Panamá-America* 42-46; Publisher *La Hora* 48-; Del. to UN Assembly 53; Amb. to U.K. 55-58, 60-62; Deputy to Nat. Assembly of Panama 64-.
Apartado 6307, Panama City, Republic of Panama.

Arias E., Ricardo M.; Panamanian diplomatist, politician and businessman; b. 12; ed. Colegio La Salle, Panama, Shenandoah Valley Acad., Virginia, George-town Univ., Washington, U.S.A. and Univ. Católica, Santiago, Chile.
Mem. Nat. Electoral Jury 44-48; Minister of Agriculture, Commerce and Industries 49-51, of Labour, Health and Social Welfare 52-55; Second Vice-Pres. of the Republic 52-55; Acting Pres. Sept. 54; Minister of Foreign Affairs Jan. 55; Pres. of the Republic 55-56; fmr.

Ambassador to U.S. and to Organization of American States; Rep. to Int. Bank for Reconstruction and Development 56; defeated candidate, Presidential election May 60; Ambassador to United States 64-; Leader, Coalición Patriótica Nacional; Pres. Sociedad Ganadera (Cattle Asscn.), Compañía Panameña de Aviación; Hon. LL.D. (Rockhurst Coll.); numerous Panamanian and foreign orders.
Embassy of Panama, 2862 McGill Terrace, N.W., Washington D.C., U.S.A.

Arias Robledo, Eduardo, LL.D., D. RER. POL.; Colombian banker and businessman; b. 18; ed. Instituto Lasalle, Bogotá and Bolivar Catholic Univ., Medellín.
Delegate, Antiquia Assembly; mem. Council of Medellín; formerly Minister of Finance, Medellín; formerly Dep. Dir. Banco de la República, now Gen. Man.; formerly Dep. Man. Agrarian, Industrial and Mining Bank, and of Central Loans Bank.
Publ. *Derecho minero colombiano* (with Dr. G. Arias Mejia).
Carrera 12, 91-09, Bogotá, Colombia.

Arifov, Ubai Arifovich; Soviet nuclear physicist; b. 1909; ed. Samarkand Pedagogical Inst.
Dir. Physico-Technical Inst., Uzbek Acad. of Sciences 45-56; mem. Acad. of Sciences of Uzbekistan 56-, Pres. 62-66; Dir. Inst. of Nuclear Physics, of Uzbek Acad. of Sciences 56-62, Dir. Physico-Technical Inst. 64-; Editor Doclady Acad. Nauk Uzbekskej S.S.R.
Academy of Sciences of Uzbekistan, Tashkent, Uzbek S.S.R., U.S.S.R.

Arismendi, José Loreto; Venezuelan lawyer and politician; b. 98; ed. Universidad Central de Venezuela and Paris Univ.
Legal Counsellor for the Federal District 24-36; Prof. of Mercantile Law, Central Univ., until 53; Minister of Education 53, of Foreign Affairs 56-58; awarded Gran Cordón de la Orden del Libertador and various foreign decorations; edited second edition of *Tratado de las Sociedades Civiles y Mercantiles.*
c/o Ministry of Foreign Affairs, Caracas, Venezuela.

Aristov, Averky Borisovich, M.SC.; Soviet politician and diplomatist; b. 1903; ed. Leningrad Polytechnic Inst.
Engineer, Tsentrolit Works, Leningrad 32-34; Scientific activity 34-39; Sec. Sverdlovsk Regional Cttee. of C.P.S.U. 40-43, Kemerovo 43-44, Krasnoyarsk 44-50, Chelyabinsk 50-52; Sec. C.P.S.U. Central Cttee. 52-53, 55-60; Deputy Chair. C.P.S.U. Central Cttee. Bureau for R.S.F.S.R. 57-61; mem. C.P.S.U. Central Cttee. 52-, mem. Presidium 57-61; Amb. to Poland 61-; Orders of Lenin, Red Banner of Labour, Red Star, etc.
U.S.S.R. Embassy, Warsaw, Poland.

Arkadev, Georgy Petrovich; Soviet diplomatist; b. 05; ed. Economic Inst.
Publishing and pedagogical activities 19-36; joined Russian diplomatic service 36; People's Commissariat for Foreign Affairs 37-44; Ministry of Foreign Affairs 44-47; Soviet Mil. Administration, Germany 47-49; Counsellor, U.S.S.R. Diplomatic Mission to D.D.R. 49-51; Foreign Ministry U.S.S.R. 51-52, Chief U.S.A. Dept. 52-53; Ambassador to Norway 54-56; Dep. Perm. U.S.S.R. Rep. to UN 56-60; Under-Sec. UN, Head Dept. of Political and Security Council Affairs 60, Adviser to Sec.-Gen. 62; resigned 62; Head, Dept. of Int. Econ. Orgs. of Ministry of Foreign Affairs 62-66; Perm. Rep. of U.S.S.R. to IAEA, Vienna 66; Perm. U.S.S.R. Rep. at Int. Orgs. in Vienna 68-.
International Atomic Energy Agency, Vienna, Austria.

Arkhangelsky, Alexandr Alexandrovich; Soviet aircraft designer; b. 1892; ed. Moscow Higher Technical School.
Research work in aerodynamic laboratory of Moscow Higher Technical School and under N. E. Zhukovsky;

worked in Central Aerohydrodynamic Inst. 18-36; took part in constructing first metal aeroplanes; in aircraft industry 36-; works with A. N. Tupolev in his Designing Office, supervised design and construction of all his planes; State Prize; Merited Worker of Science and Technology of R.S.F.S.R. 47; Hero of Socialist Labour and other decorations.
c/o Ministry of Aircraft Engineering, Moscow, U.S.S.R.

Arkhurst, Frederick Siegfried; Ghanaian journalist and diplomatist; b. 13 Oct. 1920; ed. Mfantsipim School, Cape Coast, and Univ. of Aberdeen, Scotland.
Eisenhower Fellowship in U.S.A. 54; Attaché, British Embassy, Rome 55-56; Public Relations Officer, Gold Coast Office, London 56-57; Second Sec. Ghana High Comm., London 57; First Sec. Perm. Mission of Ghana to UN 57-59, Counsellor 59-60; mem. Secr. UN Econ. Comm. for Africa 60-62; Principal Sec. Ministry of Foreign Affairs 62-65; Faculty Fellow, Center for International Affairs, Harvard Univ. 62-63; Perm. Rep. to UN 65-.
Permanent Mission of Ghana to the United Nations, 144 East 44th Street, New York, N.Y. 10017, U.S.A.

Arland, Marcel; French novelist and essayist; b. 5 July 1899.
Winner Goncourt Prize 29, Grand Prix de Littérature de l'Académie Française 52, Grand Prix Nat. des Lettres 60; Dir. of *La Nouvelle Revue Française.*
Publs. Novels: *Terres étrangères* 24, *Etienne* 25, *Monique* 26, *Les Ames en peine* 27, *L'Ordre* 29 (Goncourt Prize), *Antarès* 32, *Les Vivants* 33, *La Vigie* 35, *Les plus beaux de nos jours* 38, *Terre Natale* 38, *La Grace* 39, *Zélie dans le désert* 44, *Il faut de tout pour faire un monde* 47, *La Consolation du Voyageur* 52, *L'Eau et le Feu* 56, *A perdre Haleine* 60, *Le Grand Pardon* 65; Essays: *Étapes, Édith, La Route obscure* 25, *Où le cœur se partage* 27, *Essais critiques* 31, *Le promeneur* 44, *Les échanges* 45, *Pascal* 47, *Marivaux* 49, *Anthologie de la Poésie française* 41, *La Prose française: Anthologie, histoire et critique d'un art* 51, *Je vous écris . . .* 60, *La Nuit et les Sources* 62, *Carnets de Gilbert* 67, *La Musique des Anges* 67.
5 rue Sébastien-Bottin, Paris 7e, France.

Arletty (*pseudonym* of Léonie Bathiat); French actress; b. 15 May 1898.
On stage has played in *Le Bonheur Mesdames, Fric-Frac* and *Un Tramway nommé Désir, La descente d'Orphée* (Tennessee Williams) 59, *Un Otage* at Théâtre de France 62, *Les monstres sacrés* 66; played title role in *Phèdre* on radio; has made a number of films including *Hôtel du Nord* 38, *Le Jour se Leve* 39, *Fric-Frac* 39, *Circonstances Atténuantes* 39, *Madame Sans-Gêne* 41, *Les Visiteurs du Soir* 42, *Les Enfants du Paradis* 44, *Maxime* 59, *Huis Clos* 59, *L'Etouffe-Chrétien* 60, *La Gamberge* 61, *Le Jour le Plus Long* 61, *Tempo di Roma* 62, *Le Voyage à Biarritz* 62, *Gibier de potence.*
31 rue Raynouard, Paris 16e, France.
Telephone: AUT 91-63.

Arley, Niels Henrik, DR. PHIL.; Danish physicist and mathematician; b. 7 Feb. 1911; ed. Københavns Universitet.
Mathematics teacher, Royal Danish Naval Acad. 35-55; Research Fellow, Inst. for Theoretical Physics, Univ. of Copenhagen 36-40, Asst. Prof. 40-54, Assoc. Prof. 54-; Dir. Geophysics Research Inst., Univ. of Copenhagen 47-53; mem. cttee. Danish Deep-sea Expedition 50-52; Assoc. Editor *Journal for Geophysical Research* 52-58; External Examiner Technical Univ. of Denmark 54-; Visiting Scientist, Norsk Hydro's Inst. Cancer Research, Oslo 54-; Visiting Prof. to numerous Univs.; Pres. Danish Soc. Protection Scientific Work 51-52; Knight Order of Dannebrog.
Publs. *Introduction to the Theory of Probability and Statistics* 40, *Theory of Stochastic Processes and their*

Application to the Theory of Cosmic Radiation 43, *Atomic Power: An Introduction to the Technical, Military, Medical and Biological Problems of the Atomic Age* (with H. Skov) 59.
The Niels Bohr Institute, University of Copenhagen; Department of Biophysics, Norsk Hydro's Institute for Cancer Research, Oslo 3, Norway; and Polarvej 12, Hellerup, Denmark.
Telephone: Søborg 3001.

Armagh, Protestant Episcopalian Archbishop of, and Primate of All Ireland (*see* McCann, Most Rev. James).

Armagh, Roman Catholic Archbishop of, and Primate of all Ireland (*see* Conway, H.E. Cardinal William).

Armah, Kwesi, F.C.I.; Ghanaian diplomatist and politician; b. 21 Sept. 1929; ed. Ghana Coll., Cape Coast, Ghana and the Inst. of Commerce, England.
Regional Sec. Central Region Branch, Convention People's Party until 57; Chair. Cttee. of African Orgs., London 59-61; Political Attaché, Ghana High Comm., London May 60-Dec. 60, Dep. High Commr. Dec. 60-Oct. 61, High Commr. Oct. 61-65, concurrently Overseas Rep., Convention People's Party Feb. 64-65; Minister of Overseas Trade 65-66; arrested in London April 66; imprisoned Nov. 66; allowed to stay in U.K. Jan. 67, arrested again Feb. 67.
Publ. *Africa's Golden Road* 65.

Armand, Louis; French administrator; b. 17 Jan. 1905; ed. Annecy and Lyon Lycées, Ecole Polytechnique and Ecole Nationale Supérieure des Mines.
Began career as mining engineer; joined railway staff (P.L.M.) 34; worked in Resistance during Occupation, organising Résistance-Fer group; Dir. Gen. of S.N.C.F. (French Nat. Railways) 49, Pres. Board of Dirs. 55; Hon. Pres. and Sec.-Gen. Union Int. des Chemins de Fer; Pres. Bureau d'Organisation des Ensembles Industriels Africains 54-58; fmr. mem. Atomic Energy Comm. Scientific Council and Pres. of Industrial Equipment Cttee. within Atomic Energy Comm.; Pres. Euratom Comm. 58-59; Pres. Asscn. française de normalisation (Afnor), and La Protectrice; Dir. Cie. Int. des Wagons-Lits, Union des Banques, Cie. Pétrofina, Publicis, and other companies; mem. Cttee. of Studies for Channel Tunnel, mem. of Institut 60; mem. Académie Française 63-; Prés. du Conseil de l'Ecole Polytechnique; Prof. Ecole Nationale d'Administration; several French decorations, including Grand Officier Légion d'Honneur, Croix de Guerre (39-45), etc.; Medal of Freedom (U.S.), Hon. K.B.E.
Office: 14 rue Jean Rey, Paris 15e; Home: 30 avenue de Villiers, Paris 17e, France.
Telephone: Bretagne 01-20 (Office).

Armand Ugon, Enrique C., D.IUR.; Uruguayan lawyer; b. 93; ed. Univ. of Montevideo.
Provincial Attorney 18; Judge, Court of First Instance 20, Court of Appeal 38; Pres. High Court 49; del. to 12th Session of League of Nations, Geneva 31, to 2nd Inter-American Conf. of Lawyers, Rio de Janeiro 43; Pres. del. to 3rd Session of U.N. Gen. Assembly, Paris 48, to 5th Session 50; del. of Uruguay and Costa Rica to Inter-American Council of Jurists 50; Judge, Int. Court of Justice 52-61; mem. Comm. of Inquiry (Ghana, Portugal) 61; Pres. Comm. of Inquiry (Portugal, Liberia) 62; Judge *ad hoc* of the Int. Court of Justice 63.
Publs. *Las Leyes Inconstitucionales* 16, *El Derecho de Resistencia* 50; (co-author) *Compilación de Leyes y Decretos del Uruguay* 30.
Rio Branco 1345, Montevideo, Uruguay.

Armeladze, Ilya Davydovich; Soviet politician; b. 1911; ed. Moscow Textile Inst.
Member, C.P.S.U. 43-; mem. staff Tbilisi Inst. of Silk Industry 35-40; at Ministry of Textile Industry of Georgian S.S.R. 40-47; First Deputy Minister of Textile Industry of Georgian S.S.R. 47-52, Minister 54-58; First Vice-Chair. State Planning Cttee. of Georgian S.S.R. 52-54; Perm. Rep. of Council of Ministers of Georgian S.S.R. to U.S.S.R. Council of Ministers 58-; Deputy to Supreme Soviet of Georgian S.S.R.; awards include Order of Red Banner of Labour.
Permanent Representation of the Georgian Council of Ministers to the U.S.S.R. Council of Ministers, Ulitsa Paliashvili 6, Moscow, U.S.S.R.

Armendariz, Antonio; Mexican lawyer and diplomatist; b. 29 Sept. 1905; ed. National Univ. of Mexico.
Fmr. Prof. of Sociology and Economy, Nat. Univ. of Mexico; Dir.-Gen. of Secondary Education 41-43; private law practice 43-53; Pres. Nat. Comm. on Securities 49-52; Under-Sec. of Finance and Public Credit 53-59; Ambassador to United Kingdom 60-64; Pres. Nat. Bank for Foreign Trade 65-; mem. and fmr. Pres. Anglo-Mexican Cultural Inst.; Hon. K.B.E. (U.K.).
Nat. Bank for Foreign Trade, Venustiano Carranza 25-2°, Mexico 1, D.F.; Home: Calle del Arbol 21, San Angel, Mexico 20, D.F., Mexico.
Telephone: 48-25-28 (Home); 10-97-02, 12-33-37 (Office).

Armitage, Kenneth; British sculptor; b. 18 July 1916; ed. Leeds Coll. of Art and Slade School, London.
Teacher of Sculpture, Bath Acad. of Art 47-56; Gregory Fellowship, Leeds Univ. 53; British Council Visitor in Sculpture to Venezuela 63-64; One-man exhibitions London 52, 57, 62, 65, New York 54, 56, 58, 62, Retrospective exhibition Whitechapel Art Gallery, London 59, represented at Venice Biennale 58; many group exhibitions in America and Europe; works in public collections in Belgium, France, Germany, Italy, Netherlands, Switzerland, U.K., U.S.A., Venezuela; David Bright Prize Venice Biennale 58.
22A Avonmore Road, London, W.14, England.
Telephone: 01-603-5800.

Armour, Frank Ralph, Jr.; American business executive; b. 30 Dec. 1908; ed. Pittsburgh Univ.
H. J. Heinz Co. (Pittsburgh) 27-, Vice-Pres. 49-57, Dir. 47-, Exec. Vice-Pres. 57-59, Pres. and Chief Operating Officer 59-66, Vice-Chair. of Board 66-; Dir. Pittsburgh Nat. Bank, Consolidated Natural Gas Co. and numerous orgs.; mem. American Management Asscn.
H. J. Heinz Co., P.O.B. 57, Pittsburgh, Pa. 15230, U.S.A.

Armstrong, Anthony (Anthony Armstrong Willis), O.B.E., M.C.; British writer; b. 2 Jan. 1897; ed. Uppingham and Trinity Coll., Cambridge.
Served Royal Engineers 15-25; Squadron Leader R.A.F. Volunteer Reserve 40-46; creator and Editor *Tee Emm*, R.A.F. Training Magazine; *Punch* writer (as "AA") for many years, various work with B.B.C., including *Over to You* series, and many radio plays.
Publs. Novels: *Patrick Undergraduate, Patrick Engaged, Patrick Helps, No Dragon, No Damsel*; vols. humorous articles: *Warriors at Ease, Warriors Still at Ease, Selected Warriors, Easy Warriors, Percival and I, Percival at Play, How To Do It, Me and Frances, Livestock in Barracks, Apple and Percival, Britisher on Broadway, While You Wait, Warriors Paraded, Nothing to do with the War, Prangmere Mess, My Friend Serafin, Prune's Progress, Nice Types* (with Raff), etc.; crime novels: *The Trail of Fear, The Trail of the Black King, The Poison Trail*, etc.; other books: *The Prince who Hiccupped, Laughter Omnibus, Laughter Parade, The Naughty Princess, Cottage into House, We Like the Country, Village at War, We Keep Going, The Year at Margarets, No Higher Mountain, He was Found in the Road, Spies in Amber, The Strange Case of Mr. Pelham, Saying Your Prayers*; plays: *Well Caught, Sitting on a Fence, Ten-Minute Alibi, Mile-Away Murder, Orders are Orders* (with Ian Hay), *Without Witness* (with Harold Simpson), *The Three Pigeons* (with Roland

Crossley), *Eleventh Hour, Here we Come Gathering* (with Philip King), *The Running Man, Bellamy* (with Arnold Ridley), *Stephanie Stays a Week, Jumble Warfare*, etc.
The Knapp, Grayswood Road, Haslemere, Surrey, England.

Armstrong, Hamilton Fish, A.B.; American editor and writer; b. 7 April 1893; ed. Princeton Univ.
Military Attaché U.S. Legation Belgrade 18; mem. Editorial Staff *New York Evening Post* 19-21, special corresp. in Eastern Europe 21-22; Managing Editor *Foreign Affairs* quarterly 22-28, Editor 28-; mem. President's Advisory Cttee. on Political Refugees 38-42; mem. Comm. on Post-war Problems, U.S. State Dept. 42-44; special asst., with rank of Minister, to American Ambassador London 44; Special Adviser to Sec. of State 45; Adviser to U.S. Del. San Francisco Conference; Hon. LL.D. (Brown Univ. 42, Columbia Univ. 63), Hon. Litt.D. (Yale Univ. 57), Dr. h.c. (Basel Univ. 60), Hon. Litt.D. (Princeton Univ. 61, Harvard 63).
Publs. *The New Balkans* 26, *Where the East Begins* 29, *Hitler's Reich* 33, *Europe Between Wars* 34, *Can We Be Neutral?* (with Allen W. Dulles) 36, *We or They* 37, *When There is No Peace* 39, *Can America Stay Neutral?* 39, *Chronology of Failure* 40, *The Calculated Risk* 47, *Tito and Goliath* 51, *Those Days* 63.
58 East 68th Street, New York, N.Y. 10021, U.S.A.
Telephone: 212-LEhigh 5-3300.

Armstrong, James Shelley Phipps; Canadian business executive and public official; b. 28 Dec. 1899; ed. Ashbury Coll., Univ. of Toronto Schools.
Supt. of Agencies, Norwich Union Fire Insurance Society 22-29; Agency Man. Dominion of Canada Gen. Insurance Co. and Casualty Co. of Canada 30-39; fmr. Man. Dir. Lambton Creamery & Packing Co.; Past Pres. Life Underwriters' Asscn. of Toronto, etc.; Past Pres. Canadian Chamber of Commerce in U.K.; Past Pres. Canadian Veterans' Asscn. in U.K.; Agent-Gen. for Ontario in United Kingdom.
13 Charles II Street, London, S.W.1., England.
Telephone: 01-930-6404.

Armstrong, Louis; American musician; b. 4 July 1900.
Joined Kid Ory's Band 17, King Oliver's 22; own band in Chicago 25; tour of U.S. and Great Britain; tour of Holland and Scandinavia 33-34, Australia and Europe 54-55, Ghana 56, Europe 58 and 59; has appeared in the films *Every Day's a Holiday, Going Places, Cabin in the Sky, Jam Session, Doctor Rhythm, Glory Alley, The Strip, The Glen Miller Story, High Society, The Five Pennies*; numerous recordings; composer of a large number of songs.
c/o Associated Booking Corporation, 50 West 57th Street, New York City, N.Y., U.S.A.

Armstrong, Sir Thomas Henry Wait, M.A., D.MUS., F.R.C.M.; British musician; b. 15 June 1898; ed. Keble Coll., Oxford and Royal Coll. of Music.
Organist Thorney Abbey 14; Sub-Organist, Peterborough Cathedral 15; served R.G.A. 17-19; Sub-Organist, Manchester Cathedral 22; Organist, St. Peter's, Eaton Square 23; Organist, Exeter Cathedral 28; Cramb Lecturer in Music, Univ. of Glasgow 49; Student of Christ Church, Oxford 39-55; Student Emeritus 55-; Choragus of the Univ. and Lecturer in Music 37-54; Conductor of Oxford Bach Choir and Oxford Orchestral Soc.; Organist, Christ Church, Oxford 53-55; Principal, Royal Acad. of Music 55-68; Hon. F.R.C.O.; Hon. R.A.M.
Royal Academy of Music, York Gate, Marylebone Road, London, N.W.1, England.

Armstrong, Sir William, G.C.B., M.V.O.; British civil servant; b. 3 March 1915; ed. Bec School, London and Exeter Coll., Oxford.
Assistant Principal, Bd. of Educ. 38; Asst. Private Sec. to Pres. of Bd. of Educ. 40; Private Sec. to Sec. of War

Cabinet 43-46; Principal Private Sec. to successive Chancellors of Exchequer 49-53; Under-Sec. Overseas Finance Div., H.M. Treasury 53-57, Home Finance Div. 57-58, Third Sec. and Treasury Officer of Accounts 58-62, Joint Perm. Sec. 62-68; Head of Home Civil Service 68-; Hon. Fellow, Exeter Coll., Oxford 63; Visiting Fellow, Nuffield Coll., Oxford 64.
54 Bilton Towers, Great Cumberland Place, London, W.1, England.
Telephone: 01-262-1750.

Arnall, Ellis Gibbs; American politician and lawyer; b. 20 March 1907; ed. Univ. of the South, Sewanee and Georgia Univ.
Mem. Georgia legislature; Asst. Attorney-Gen. 37-39; Attorney-Gen. 39-43; Gov. of Georgia 43-47. Pres. Soc. of Ind. Motion Picture Producers; Senior mem. Law Firm Arnall, Golden and Gregory; mem. U.S. Del. to 4th annual conf. UNESCO, Paris 49; U.S. Del. Anglo-American Film Conf., London 50; Trustee Univ. of the South, Mercer Univ.; Dir. U.S. Office of Price Stabilization 52; Pres. Ind. Film Producers' Export Asscn. 56-; Chair. Board of Dirs. Nat. Asscn. of Life Insurance Companies; Chair. Board of Dir. Coastal States Life Insurance; Dir. Manufacturers Nat. Bank; Dir. of numerous other companies; mem. U.S. Nat. Comm. for UNESCO 63-.
Publs. *The Shore Dimly Seen* 46, *What the People Want* 47.
Residence: 213 Jackson Street, Newnan, Ga. 30263; Office: 10th Floor, Fulton Federal Building, Atlanta, Ga. 30303, U.S.A.
Telephone: 404-577-5100.

Arnaud, Claude; French diplomatist; b. 9 Nov. 1919; ed. Univs. de Dijon, Lyon et Paris à la Sorbonne.
Attaché, Washington 45-46; Office of Resident-Gen. in Morocco 46-51; First Sec. Bonn 52-55; Econ. Dept., Foreign Office, Paris 55-59; Counsellor, Chargé d'Affaires, Belgrade 59-62; Minister-Counsellor, Perm. Mission to UN 62-65; Amb. to Laos Jan. 66-68, to Kenya 68-; Chevalier Légion d'Honneur, Croix de Guerre 39-45.
French Embassy, Nairobi, Kenya.

Arnaudi, Carlo; Italian microbiologist and politician; b. 23 May 1899; ed. Univ. of Milan.
Pres. of Agricultural Sciences Faculty, Milan Univ.; fmr. Pres. Nat. Cttee. for Agriculture, Nat. Research Council, fmr. mem. Admin. Cttee., Nat. Research Council; mem. Socialist Party 21-; City Councillor, Milan 51-; mem. Senate 58-; Minister of Scientific Research and Technology 63; mem. Accademia Nazionale dei Lincei.
The Senate, Rome; and Via Ippolito Nievo 2, Milan, Italy.
Telephone: 462911 (Rome); 4697262 (Milan).

Arnold, Malcolm; British composer; b. 21 Oct. 1921; ed. Royal Coll. of Music, London.
Principal Trumpet, London Philharmonic Orchestra 42-44 and 46-48; served army 44-46; full-time composer and conductor 48-; awarded Cobbett Prize 41, Mendelssohn Scholarship 48.
Works include *Beckus the Dandipratt* (overture) 43, 1st Symphony 49, 2nd Symphony 53, 3rd Symphony 57, 4th Symphony 60, 5th Symphony 61, 6th Symphony 67, ten concertos, *Homage to the Queen*, Coronation Ballet performed at Covent Garden 53; film music *Bridge on the River Kwai* 58 (Hollywood Oscar), *Inn of the Sixth Happiness* (Ivor Novello Award) 59.
Primrose Cottage, St. Merryn, Padstow, Cornwall, England.

Arnold, M. L. (Melvin Luxton); American publisher; b. 23 Aug. 1913.
Editorial Staff, *The News-Telegram*, Portland, Ore. 30-35; Field Staff, Exec. Office of Pres. of U.S. 43-44;

Head, Publications Group, Standard Oil Co. (N.J.), N.Y. 44-45; Dir., Editor-in-Chief, Beacon Press, Boston 45-55; various positions with Harper & Row, including Editor of Religious Books, Editor (Founding) of Harper Torchbook Series, Exec. Vice-Pres., Head of School Text Div. 56-67, Pres. and Dir. Harper & Row, Publishers Inc. 67-.

Publs. Co-author *The Africa of Albert Schweitzer* 48 (revised 58).

Harper & Row, Publishers Inc., 49 East 33rd Street, New York, N.Y. 10016, U.S.A.

Telephone: 889-7500.

Arnoul, Françoise (Françoise Gautsch); French actress; b. 9 June 1931; ed. Lycée de Rabat, Lycée Molière (Paris) and Paris Conservatoire.

Films include *Nous irons à Paris, La Maison Bonnadieu, Le Désir et l'Amour, La Plus Belle Fille du Monde, Les Compagnons de la Nuit, Les Amants du Tage, French-Cancan, Des Gens sans Importance, Thérèse Etienne, La Chatte, Asphalte, La Bête à l'Affût, Le Bal des Espions, La Chatte sort ses Griffes, La Morte-Saison des Amours, le Testament d'Orphée, les Parisiennes, Vacances portugaises, A couteaux tirés, Lucky Joe*; theatre debut in *les Justes* (Camus) Versailles 66.

c/o Agence Bernheim, 55 avenue Georges V, Paris 8e; and 32 rue Monsieur-le-Prince, Paris 6e, France.

Arnould, Reynold; French artist; 7 Dec. 1919; ed. Lycée Corneille, Rouen, Ecole des Beaux-arts, Rouen and Ecole nationale supérieure des Beaux-arts.

Information mission in U.S.A. 45-46; Dir. School of Art, Baylor Univ., Texas 49-52, Baylor Univ. Summer Arts School, Paris 52; Dir. Museum Maison de la Culture, Le Havre 52-65; Curator of Grand Palais 65-; numerous exhbns. in Paris; exhbn. by Musée des arts décoratifs at Louvre called *Reynold Arnould, forces et rythmes de l'industrie*; works in Musée nationale d'art moderne, Paris, and museums and art galleries in U.S.A., Britain, Belgium, Switzerland, Italy and Norway; Chevalier Légion d'Honneur, Chevalier Ordre Nat. du Mérite, Officier Ordre des Arts et Lettres.

Grand Palais, avenue Winston Churchill, Paris 8e, France.

Telephone: ELY. 32-98.

Arnoux, Alexandre; French writer; b. 27 Feb. 1884; ed. Paris Univ.

Novelist and essayist; awarded Renaissance prize 21; mem. of Académie Goncourt March 47.

Publs. Novels: *Abisag ou L'Eglise transportée par la foi* 18, *Le Cabaret* 19, *Indice 33* 20, *Ecoute s'il pleut* 23, *Suite variée* 24, *Chiffre* 26, *Les Gentilshommes de Ceinture* 28, *Carnet de route du Juif Errant* 31, *Ki-Pro-Ko* 36, *Le rossignol napolitain* 37; *Rencontres avec Richard Wagner* 24, *Poésie du Hasard* 34, *Paris-sur-Seine* 39, *Rêveries d'un policier amateur* 42, *Rhône, mon fleuve* 44, *Hélène et les Guerres* 45, *Calendrier de Flore* 46, *Algorithme* 48, *Paris ma grand' ville, Contacts allemands* 50, *Les Crimes Innocents* 52, *Etudes et Caprices* 53, *Royaume des Ombres* 54, *Faut-il Brûler Jeanne?* 54, *Roi d'un jour* 56, *Pour solde tout compte* 58, *Zulma l'Infidèle* 60, *Visite à Mathusalem* 61, *Le Siège de Syracuse* 62, *Flamenca* 64, *La double Hélène* 67.

3 rue Debrousse, Paris 16e, France.

Telephone: 553-0130.

Arnshtam, Leo Oskarovich; Soviet film director and scenario writer; b. 1905; ed. Leningrad Conservatoire.

Started work in films 29; State prizewinner.

Directed films: *Girl Friends* 35, *Friends* 38, *Zoya* 44, *Glinka* 49, *Romeo and Juliet* 54 (Cannes Festival Award), *Lesson in History* 57 (Co-production with Bulgaria; award at Carlovy Vary Festival), *Five days—five nights* 60 (Co-production with D.D.R.)

Mosfilm Studio, Mosfilmovskaya ulitsa, Moscow, U.S.S.R.

Arnstein, Karl, DR.TECH.; American engineer; b. 24 March 1887; ed. Prague.

Engineer Zeppelin Co., Friedrichshafen 14-24, designed about 70 military and commercial airships; Vice-Pres. and Chief Engineer Goodyear-Zeppelin Co. 24-39; Vice-Pres. and Chief Engineer Goodyear Aircraft Corpn. (now Goodyear Aerospace Corpn.) 40-57; designed American dirigibles *Akron* and *Macon* and numerous non-rigid airships, also stratosphere balloons, heavier-than-air craft, and a streamlined train; Consultant 57-59; independent consultant 59-; U.S. Navy Distinguished Service Award 57; Hon. Dr. Ing. (Aachen), Hon. D.Sc. (Akron).

817 Delaware Avenue, Akron, Ohio 44303, U.S.A.

Telephone: 864-5417.

Aron, Raymond Claude Ferdinand, LITT.D.; French journalist and university professor; b. 14 March 1905; ed. Univ. of Paris.

Lecturer, Univ. of Cologne 30-31; on staff, French Inst., Berlin 31-33; Prof. Lycée du Havre 33-34; Sec. Centre of Social Information, Ecole Normale Supérieure 34-39; Prof. Univ. of Toulouse 39; Editor *La France Libre*, London 40-44; on staff *Combat* 46, and *Figaro* 47-; Prof. Inst. d'Etudes politiques and Sorbonne; Prof.-at-Large, Cornell Univ.; mem. Académie des Sciences morales et politiques 63-; Foreign Hon. mem. American Acad. Arts and Sciences 61-; mem. American Philosophical Soc.; Chevalier Légion d'Honneur; Prix des Ambassadeurs 62; Hon. Ph.D. (Harvard, Basle, Brussels and Columbia Univs.).

Publs. *Introduction à la Philosophie de L'Histoire* 38, *La Sociologie allemande contemporaine* 35, *Le grand schisme* 48, *Les guerres en chaîne* 51, *L'Opium des intellectuels* 55, *La Tragédie algérienne* 57, *Paix et guerre entre les nations* 62, *Dix-Huit Leçons sur la Société Industrielle* 63, *La lutte des classes* 64, *Démocratie et totalitarisme* 65, *Trois Essais sur L'Age industriel* 66, *Les Etapes de la pensée sociologique* 67.

Office: 6 rue de Tournon, Paris 6e; Home: 34 avenue du Président Kennedy, Paris 16e, France.

Telephone: MED. 3900.

Aron, Robert; French writer; b. 25 May 1898; ed. Lycée Condorcet and the Sorbonne, Paris.

Founder, with Arnaud Dandieu, of the "Ordre Nouveau" personalist movement 30; arrested by occupation forces 41; escaped to Algeria 43; worked with Giraud and de Gaulle Govts. 43-44; Dir. of Theoretical Studies Mouvement Fédéraliste Français and La Fédération 46-; Chevalier Légion d'Honneur, Croix de Guerre (1914-18), Prix Femina 61.

Publs. *La Révolution Nécessaire* (with A. Dandieu) 33, *Victoire à Waterloo* 37, *Histoire de Vichy* 54, *Ce que je crois* 55, *Histoire de la Libération de la France* 59, *Les Années obscures de Jésus* 60, *Les grands dossiers de l'histoire contemporaine* 62, *Jesus of Nazareth: The Hidden Years* (trans.) 62, *Les origines de la guerre d'Algérie* 62, *Les Grands Dossiers de l'Histoire Contemporaine, Les Nouveaux Grands Dossiers de l'Histoire Contemporaine, Le Dieu des Origines des cavernes du Sinai, Charles de Gaulle, La France avait deux capitales: Vichy, Alger, Histoire de l'épuration* 67.

2 rue Michel-Ange, Paris 16, France.

Arosemena Gómez, Otto, LL.D.; Ecuadorean lawyer and politician; b. 1922.

Former lawyer in Guayaquil; Leader of Coalición Institucionalista Democrática; Provisional Pres. of Ecuador Nov. 66-.

Office of the President, Quito, Ecuador.

Arosemena Monroy, Carlos Julio, D.IUR.; Ecuadorean politician; b. 20.

Counsellor, Ecuadorean Embassy, Washington 46-52; Chair. Chamber of Deputies 52; Minister of Defence 52-53; Vice-Pres. 60-61; Pres. of Ecuador 61-63.

Quito, Ecuador.

Arpino, Giovanni; Italian writer; b. 27 Jan. 1927; ed. Univ. degli Studi, Turin.

Has worked as Editor for Einaudi and Editoriale Zanichelli; has contributed to *Il Giorno, Paese sera, Paese, Stasera* (dailies), *Il Mondo, Vie nuove, Mondo Nuovo, Le Ore, Tempo, Illustrazione italiana* (periodicals), *Botteghe Oscure, Il contemporaneo, Il Ponte, Paragone, Tempo presente, Nuova corrente, Europa letteraria, Itinerari, Cinema nuovo, Questo e altro* (cultural magazines); Strega Prize 64.

Publs. *Sei stato felice* (novel) 52, *Barbaresco* (poems) 54, *Il prezzo dell'oro* (poems) 55, *Gli anni del giudizio* (novel) 58, *La suora giovane* (novel) 59, *Rafé e Micropiede* (for children—Bancarellino Prize) 60, *Mille e una Italia* (for children) 61, *Una nuvola d'ira* (novel) 62, *L'ombra delle colline* (novel—Strega Prize) 64, *Un'anima persa* (novel) 66.

Via Leopardi 15, Milan, Italy.

Arrango, Augusto Guillermo; Panamanian economist and diplomatist; b. 08; ed. Univ. of Pennsylvania.

Assistant Comptroller, later Gen. Comptroller, Republic of Panama 37-42, Econ. Adviser, Ministry of Foreign Affairs 44-46; Officer and Dir. Panama Bank and Trust Co., Panama Coca-Cola Co., Hoteles Interamericanos S.A., Blokmigon S.A., Cold Lake Pipe Line Co. Ltd., Montreal, Central Financiera S.A., Panama-North American Asscn.; Ambassador of Panama to United States and to Organization of American States (OAS) 61-64.

c/o Ministry of Foreign Affairs, Panama City, Panama.

Arrau, Claudio; Chilean pianist; b. 6 Feb. 1903; ed. privately.

Gave first concert at age of five in Santiago; went to Berlin to study with Martin Krause, a pupil of Liszt (on subsidy paid by Chilean Govt.) 10-20; awarded Liszt and Ibach prizes; Int. Congress of Pianists (Switzerland) Award 25; gave first American concert 23, returned 41, and annual tours since; tours include Russia 31, 32, Australia 47, South Africa 49, 52 and 56, South and North America, Europe, and Israel 51 and 53, India, Ceylon and Singapore 55 and 56, World Tour 58.

c/o Columbia Artists Management Inc., 113 57th Street, New York 19, N.Y., U.S.A.

Arriaga Ochoa, Antonio; Mexican historian and museum curator; b. 11; ed. Colegio Primitivo y Nacional de San Nicolás de Hidalgo and Universidad Michoacana.

History Master, Colegio Primitivo y Nacional de San Nicolás de Hidalgo and other schools 35-52; Head, Colegio Primitivo de San Nicolás 38-41; Dir. of Museo Michoacado 38; Dir. of Summer School, Universidad Michoacana; Dir. Nat. Museum of History, Nat. Inst. of Anthropology and History.

Inst. of Anthropology and History.

Publs. *Organización Social de los Tarascos* (5 Vols.), *Notas y Documentos de Don José María Morelos, Derroteros sobre el Caudillo Don José María Morelos, Documentos sobre el nacimiento de Don Miguel Hidalgo.* Museo Nacional de Historia, Castillo de Chapultepec, Mexico, D.F., Mexico.

Arriba y Castro, H.E. Cardinal Benjamin de; Spanish ecclesiastic; b. 8 April 1886; ed. Spanish Coll. of San José, Pontifical Gregorian Univ., Pontifical Acad. of St. Thomas, Pontifical Biblical Inst. (all Rome), Pontifical Univ. of Toledo.

Successively Prof. of Methodology and Historical Criticism, Greek, Hebrew and Fundamental Theology, Madrid Seminary; Canon of Madrid Cathedral 20; Diocesan Sec. Madrid 21-31, Provisor and Deputy Vicar-Gen. 31-35; Bishop of Mondoñedo 35-44, of Oviedo 44-49; Archbishop of Tarragona 49-; nominated and created Cardinal 53; Grand Cross of Naval Merit, of

Isabel the Catholic, of Carlos III and of Alfonso X the Wise, Cruz San Raimundo de Penyafort.

Publ. *Catecismo de Acción Católica.*
Palacio Arzobispal, Tarragona, Spain.

Arrupe, Father Pedro, S.J.; Spanish ecclesiastic; b. 14 Nov. 1907; ed. with Fathers of Escuelas Pias, Bilbao, Univ. of Madrid (Medicine), and Jesuit studies in Spain, Belgium, Netherlands and U.S.A.

Entered Society of Jesus 27; in Japan 38-65, engaged in parish ministries, training of Novices, Provincial Superior 54-65; was in Hiroshima when first atomic bomb exploded; Superior-Gen. of Soc. of Jesus 65-.

Publs. eight spiritual books (Japanese); autobiography (Spanish).

Superiore Generale della Compagnia di Gesù, Borgo Santo Spirito 5, Rome, Italy.

Artobolevsky, Ivan Ivanovich; Soviet scientist; b. 9 Oct. 1905; ed. Moscow Timiriazev Acad.

Worked in field of machines, mechanisms and automatics; invented classification of dimensional mechanisms; Prof. of Applied Mechanics, Inst. of Machine Research, Moscow; mem. Acad. of Sciences of U.S.S.R.; Honoured Scientific and Technical worker of R.S.F.S.R.; James Watt Medal.

Publs. *Theory of Dimensional Mechanisms* 37, *Theory of Mechanisms and Machines* 53, *Theory of Mechanisms for the Generation of Plane Curves* 59, *Synthesis of Plane Mechanisms* 59, *Theory of Mechanisms* 65.

Institute of Machine Research, 4 Ulitsa Griboyedova, Moscow, U.S.S.R.

Artsikhovsky, Artemy Vladimirovich; Soviet archæologist; b. 26 Dec. 1902; ed. Moscow Univ.

Professor of Archæology at Moscow Univ., head of Dept. of Archæology 39-; carried on excavations at Novgorod for thirty years; Corresp. mem. U.S.S.R. Acad. of Sciences 60-.

Publs. *Ancient Russian Miniatures as Historical Source* 44, *Introduction to Archæology* 47, *Foundations of Archæology* 54, *Birch Bark Rolls of Novgorod* 54-63, etc. Moscow University, Flat 113, Leninskigory, Moscow, U.S.S.R.

Telephone: AV9-19-53.

Artsimovich, Lev Andreevich; Soviet physicist; b. 1909; ed. Byelorussian Univ.

Researcher and lecturer in higher educational and scientific establishments 30-; mem. Acad. of Sciences of U.S.S.R. 53-, mem. Presidium; Lenin Prizewinner 58; Order of Lenin (twice); Order of Red Banner, etc.

Publs. include: *Inhibiting radiation for electrons of High Energies* 38, *Angular Distribution of Fast Electrons Dispersed by Nuclei of Aluminium* 46, *Radiation of Fast Electrons in the Magnetic Field* (in English) 46, *Investigation of Pulse Discharges of High Amperage* 56, *Rigid Radiation of Pulse Discharges* 56, *Controlled Thermonuclear Reactions* 61.

Academy of Sciences of U.S.S.R., 14 Leninsky Prospekt, Moscow, U.S.S.R.

Arup, Ove Nyquist, C.B.E., M.ING.F., M.I.C.E., M.I.STRUCT.E., M.I.C.E.I., M.S.A.I.C.E.; British and Danish consulting engineer; b. 16 April 1895; ed. Preparatory School, Hamburg, Germany, Public School, Sorø, Denmark, and Univ. of Copenhagen.

Designer, Christiani & Nielsen G.m.b.H., Hamburg 22; Chief Designer, Christiani & Nielsen Ltd., London 25-34 (Designer 23-25); Dir. and Chief Designer, J. L. Kier & Co. Ltd., London 34-38; Dir. Arup Designs Ltd., Arup & Arup Ltd., Pipes Ltd. 38-45; Senior Partner, Ove Arup and Partners, London, Dublin, W. Africa, S. Africa and Australia 49-; Consulting Engineer for schools, flats, air raid shelters, industrial projects, marine work (Air Ministry), hospitals, universities, cathedrals, bridges; Chair. Soc. of Danish Civil Engineers in Great Britain and Ireland 55-59; Visiting

Lecturer, Harvard Univ. 55; Knight First Class, Order of Dannebrog (Denmark); Royal Gold Medal, Royal Inst. of British Architects 66; Hon. D.Sc. (Durham Univ.).
Publs. *Design, Cost, Construction and Relative Safety of Trench, Surface, Bombproof and other Air Raid Shelters* 39, *Safe Housing in Wartime* 41.
Office: 13 Fitzroy Street, London W.1; Home: 6 Fitzroy Park, Highgate, London, N.6, England.
Telephone: 01-636-1531 (Office); 01-340-3388 (Home).

Arutyunov, Alexandr Ivanovich; Soviet neurosurgeon; b. 1904; ed. North Caucasian Univ.
Head Doctor of Hospital, Mari Autonomous Republic 29-30; Intern at clinic 30-32; Postgraduate, Senior Assoc. Central Neurosurgical Inst. 32-41; Army Surgeon 41-45; Head of clinic, Kiev Psychoneurological Inst. 45-50; Dir. Ukrainian Inst. 50-64; Corresp. mem. U.S.S.R. Acad. of Medical Sciences 61-67, mem. 67-; Dir. Burdenko Inst. of Neurosurgery; Head of Chair Central Medical Refresher Inst. 64-; mem. C.P.S.U. 40-; Deputy Academic Sec., Dept. of Clinical Medicine, U.S.S.R. Acad. of Medical Sciences; Chair. U.S.S.R. Soc. of Neurosurgeons; First Vice-Pres. Int. Fed. of Neurosurgical Socs.; Vice-Pres. Int. Neurosurgical Asscn.; Order of Lenin, Red Banner of Labour, Red Star, Red Banner (twice).
Publs. About 120 works on traumas of central nervous system, treatment of consequences of cerebral and spinal inflammation, perfection of neurosurgical technique.
Burdenko Institute of Neurosurgery, 13/5 First Tverskoy-Yamskoy by-street, Moscow, U.S.S.R.

Arutyunyan, Alexandr Grigoryevich; Soviet composer; b. 1920; ed. Erevan Conservatoire.
Executive mem. Armenian Composers' Union, Soviet Composers' Union; State Prize 49; Honoured Worker of Arts for Armenian S.S.R. 56; Red Banner of Labour 56; People's Artist of Armenia 62.
Compositions include: Concerto for piano and orchestra 41, Overture No. 1 *Our Just Cause* 42, Overture No. 2 *Concert Overture* 44, Polyphonic partita for piano 45, *Motherland Cantata* 47, Symphonic poem *In Memory of Collective Farmer Zakiyan* (with E. Mirzoyan) 48, Overture No. 3 *Festive Overture* 49, *Lenin Cantata* (with E. Mirzoyan) 50, Concerto for voice and orchestra, Concerto for trumpet and orchestra 50, Concertino for piano and orchestra 51, Dance suite for symphony orchestra 53, Symphony 58, *Lay of the Armenian People* (vocal symphonic poem) 61, *Sayat-Nova* (opera) 65.
Armenian Composers' Union, 25 Ulitsa Demirchyana, Erevan, U.S.S.R.

Arutyunyan, Nagush Khachaturovich; Soviet mechanical engineer and politician; b. 1912; ed. Erevan Polytechnic Inst., Moscow Military Engineering Acad.
Former Hydrological Engineer; Researcher, Armenian S.S.R. Acad. of Sciences 45-50; Prof. Erevan Univ. 50-, Rector 61-63; mem. Armenian Acad. of Sciences 50-, Vice-Pres. 60-61; mem. Communist Party 42-; Chair. of Presidium of Supreme Soviet of Armenian S.S.R. 63-; Deputy Chair. Supreme Soviet of U.S.S.R. 63-; mem. Central Auditing Cttee. of C.P.S.U.; mem. Central Cttee. of Armenian C.P.
Presidium of Supreme Soviet of U.S.S.R., Moscow, U.S.S.R.

Arze Quiroga, Eduardo; Bolivian lawyer and diplomatist; b. 07; ed. Sucre and Bolivar National Colls., and Univ. of San Simón, Cochabamba.
On staff of *El Republicano*, Cochabamba 22-32; Bolivian Army 32-36; Prof. of Political Economy and Sec.-Gen. of Univ., Univ. of Cochabamba 36-40; Private Sec. to Pres. of Republic 40; Sec., Bolivian Embassy, Vatican 40-42; Dir. Econ. Dept., Ministry of Foreign Affairs

43-44, Under-Sec. of Foreign Affairs 44-45, 46-51; Senator 51; Perm. Rep. to UN 52-54; Ambassador to Colombia 57-58; Minister of Foreign Affairs, Bolivia 60-62; Ambassador to Argentina 62-; numerous decorations.
Publs. *Introducción a los Apuntes de la Teoría del Valor de Daniel Salamanca* 37, *Valor, Moneda, Crédito y Desarrollo* 57.
Embassy of Bolivia, Buenos Aires, Argentina.

Asafu-Adjaye, Sir Edward Okyere, Kt.; Ghanaian lawyer and diplomatist; b. 03; ed. Adisadel Coll., and University Coll., London.
Studied Philosophy and Law; called to the Bar in England and Gold Coast 27; practised in Accra courts 27-34, in Kumasi courts 34-; served on Gold Coast dels. to Sec. of State for the Colonies, London 34, to Coronation of H.M. King George VI 37, to Centennial celebrations of Liberia 47, to Commonwealth Parl. Conf., Ottawa 49, and to Coronation of H.M. Queen Elizabeth II 53; nominated to Legislative Council by Asanteman Council 46; re-nominated to Legislative Assembly 51; returned to Assembly as C.P.P. rep. 54; Minister of Local Govt. 51-55; Minister of Trade and Labour 55-56; resumed legal practice 56-57; Ghana High Commr. in United Kingdom 57-61; Ambassador to France 57-61; Fellow, Univ. Coll. London 61-; mem. Ghana Board, Barclays Bank D.C.O. 61-; Dir. Consolidated African Selection Trust 61-66; mem. UN Cttee. to examine methods of resolving the situation in S. Africa 64.
c/o Bank of West Africa Ltd., P.O. Box 564, 37 Gracechurch Street, London, E.C.3, England.

Asakai, Koichiro; Japanese diplomatist; b. 06; ed. Univ. of Commerce, Tokyo.
Entered diplomatic service 29; Dir. of Gen. Affairs Bureau, Ministry of Foreign Affairs 46; Dir.-Gen. Central Liaison Office of Cabinet 48; Dean of Foreign Service Training Inst., Tokyo 49; Minister of Embassy, London 52; Ambassador to Philippines 56; Ambassador to U.S.A. 57-63.
Katase, Fujisawa-shi, Japan.

Asamov, Salakhitdin; Soviet politician; b. 1930; ed. Moscow Veterinary Acad.
Member C.P.S.U. 56-; zoo-technician, Dir. Nishan State Stud Farm, Karshi District, Surkhandarya Region 55-61; party official and Minister of Agriculture of Uzbek S.S.R. 61-64, also Chair. Samarkand Regional Soviet of Working People's Deputies; First Sec. Kashkadarya Regional Cttee. of C.P. of Uzbekistan 64-; mem. Central Cttee. C.P. of Uzbekistan; Deputy to U.S.S.R. Supreme Soviet.
Kashkadarya Regional Committee of C.P. of Uzbek S.S.R., Karshi, U.S.S.R.

Asbeck, Werner, DR. ING.; German business executive; b. 3 Jan. 1908; ed. Technische Hochschule, Aachen.
Superintendent, Leipziger Leichtmetallwerk Bernhard Berghaus, Rackwitz 39-43; Asst. to Pres. Vereinigte Stahlwerke, Düsseldorf 43-50; Dir. Investment Dept., Stahl-Treuhänder-Vereinigung, Düsseldorf 50-53; Asst. to Technical Board of Dirs., Dortmund-Hörder-Hütten-union A.G., Dortmund 53-54; mem. Board of Dirs. Klöckner-Werke A.G. (now Chair. Management Board), Hütte Bremen, Bremen 54-61, Klöckner-Werke A.G., Duisburg 61-.
Am Est 2, 4035 Breitscheid Bez. Düsseldorf, German Federal Republic.

Asbrink, Per Valfrid; Swedish banker; b. 12; ed. Univ. of Stockholm.
Co-operative Union 34-38; Editor *Social Yearbook*, Asscn. for Social Work 38-42; Sec. Stockholm Town Council 43-45; Sec. on 1946 Comm. on Education 46-47; Ministry of Communications 48-55, Under Sec. 51-55; Governor, Sveriges Riksbank (Bank of Sweden) 55-;

Chair. Board of Luossavaara-Kiirunavaara A.B. (iron mining) 57-, A.B. Aerotransport 62-, A.B. Tumba bruk (papermaking) 63-; mem. Board Scandinavian Airlines System 52-, Bank for Int. Settlements, Basle 55-.
Lessebovägen 143-145, Enskede, Stockholm, Sweden.

Aschengreen, (Julius) Christian; Danish business executive; b. 17 Jan. 1896.
East Asiatic Co. Ltd. 11-, Managing Dir. 52-61, now Dep. Chair.; Pres. Danish Shipowners' Asscn. 59-61; Chair. Nakskov Shipyard, Steamship Co. Myren, S.A.S. Invest A/S, Danish Airlines Ltd.; Alternating Chair. Nordic Tankship Ltd., Scandinavian Airlines System; mem. Board, Port of Copenhagen Authority, Copenhagen Freeport Co.; Vice-Pres. General Transport Comm., Int. Chamber of Commerce; Commdr. Order of Dannebrog, and other decorations.
Det Danske Luftfartselskab A/S, Ved Stranden 14, Copenhagen K, Denmark.

Asea, Soloman Bayo, M.B., CH.B., D.T.M. (& H.), D.P.H.; Ugandan diplomatist and doctor; b. 24; ed. Makerere Coll., Liverpool School of Tropical Medicine, and London School of Hygiene and Tropical Medicine. Medical Officer, Uganda 52-62, Senior Medical Officer 62, Principal Medical Officer 63; Ambassador to the U.S.A. 64-66; High Commr. in U.K. 66-; Prize B.M.A. Essay for Medical Students 51.
Uganda House, P.O. Box 257, 58/59 Trafalgar Square, London, W.C.2, England.
Telephone: 01-839-1963.

Asfia, Safi; Iranian mining engineer and politician; ed. Polytechnic Inst., Paris.
Professor of Mining Engineering, Teheran Univ. 38-; fmr. Chief, Irrigation Dept., Iranian Govt.; Dep. Dir. Plan Organisation 54-61, Dir. 61-.
Ministry of the Development Plan, Teheran, Iran.

Ásgeirsson, Ásgeir; Icelandic politician; b. 13 May 1894; ed. Univs. of Iceland, Copenhagen and Uppsala.
Sec. to the Bishop of Iceland 15-16; Sec. Nat. Bank of Iceland 17-18; Teacher, Icelandic Teachers' Coll. 18-27; Dir. of Education 26-31 and 34-38; Man. Icelandic Fisheries Bank 38-52; mem. of Althing (Icelandic Parl.) 23-52, Speaker 30; Minister of Finance 31-34; Prime Minister 32-34; mem. Foreign Affairs Cttee. 28-31 and 38-52; Icelandic Del. to Bretton Woods Economic and Monetary Conf. 44; Gov. Int. Monetary Fund 46-52; Pres. of Iceland 52-; Grand Master, Order of Icelandic Falcon, and other Icelandic and foreign decorations.
Bessastadir, Iceland.

Ash, Roy Lawrence, M.B.A.; American industrialist; b. 20 Oct. 1918; ed. Harvard Univ.
Bank of America 36-42, 47-49; Chief Financial Officer, Hughes Aircraft Co. 49-53; Litton Industries Inc. 58-, Exec. Vice-Pres. 58-61, Pres. 61-; mem. Board of Dirs., Bank of America, Global Marine Inc., Pacific Mutual Life Insurance Co.; Dir. Los Angeles World Affairs Council, Calif. Inst. Assocs.; mem. Board of Trustees, Calif. Inst. of Technology; official of educational orgs.
Litton Industries Inc., 9370 Santa Monica Boulevard, Beverly Hills, California, U.S.A.

Asha, Rafik; Syrian diplomatist; b. 10; ed. Beirut and New York Univs.
Teacher 32-42; Dep. Dir.-Gen. of Supplies, Syrian Ministry of Supplies 41-44; Consul-Gen., New York 45-52; Del. to UN 46-60; Chargé d'Affaires, Washington 52-57; Dir.-Gen. Political Dept., Ministry of Foreign Affairs 57-59; U.A.R. Deputy Perm. Rep. at UN 59-61; Syrian Ambassador to U.S.S.R. 61-62; Sec. Gen. Ministry of Foreign Affairs 62-64; Perm. Rep. to UN 64-65.
c/o Ministry of Foreign Affairs, Damascus, Syrian Arab Republic.

Ashanti, King of the (see Prempeh II).

Ashby, Sir Eric, M.A., D.SC., SC.D , LL.D., D.LITT., D.C.L., A.R.C.S., D.I.C., F.R.S.; British botanist and university administrator; b. 24 Aug. 1904; ed. City of London School, Imperial Coll. of Science, London, and Univ. of Chicago.
Commonwealth Fund Fellow, U.S.A. 29-31; lecturer in Botany, Imperial Coll. 31-35; Prof. of Botany, Univ. of Bristol 35-37; Prof. of Botany, Univ. of Sydney, Australia 38-46; Harrison Prof. of Botany, Manchester Univ. 46-50; Pres. and Vice-Chancellor, The Queen's Univ. Belfast 50-59; Counsellor and Chargé d'Affaires Australian Legation, Moscow 45; mem. Exec. Council Scientific and Industrial Research 56-60; Master of Clare Coll. Cambridge 58-; Chair. Int. Comm. on Higher Education in Nigeria 59-61; Vice-Chair. Asscn. of Univs. of British Commonwealth 59-61; Vice-Chair. Commonwealth Scholarships Comm. 59-62; mem. Univ. Grants Cttee. 60-67; Chair. Cttee. of Award, Commonwealth Fund of N.Y. 63-; Hon. Adviser, Nigerian Nat. Univ. Comm. 62-; Pres. British Asscn. for Advancement of Science 63; Council Royal Soc. 64-65; Trustee Ciba Foundation 66-; mem. Central Advisory Council for Science and Technology 67-; Vice-Chancellor, Univ. of Cambridge 67-.
Publs. *Environment and Plant Development* 31, *English-German Botanical Terminology* 38, *Challenge to Education* 46, *Scientist in Russia* 47, *Science and the People* 53, *Technology and the Academics* 58, *Community of Universities* 63, *African Universities and Western Tradition* 64, *Universities, British, Indian, African* 66.
The Master's Lodge, Clare College, Cambridge, England.
Telephone: Cambridge 58681.

Ashcroft, Dame Peggy (Dame Edith Margaret Emily Hutchinson), D.B.E.; British actress; b. 22 Dec. 1907; ed. Croydon and Central School of Speech Training, Albert Hall, London.
First appeared at Birmingham Repertory Theatre 26; rôles include: Constance Neville (*She Stoops to Conquer*), Naemi (*Jew Süss*) 29, Desdemona (with Paul Robeson) 30, Irina (*The Three Sisters*) 37-38, Cecily Cardew (*The Importance of Being Ernest*) 39-40, 42, Catherine (*The Dark River*) 43, Haymarket Repertory Season 44-45, Evelyn Holt (*Edward My Son*) 47, Catherine Sloper (*The Heiress*) 49, Hester Collyer (*The Deep Blue Sea*) 52, Hedda Gabler 54, Miss Madrigal (*The Chalk Garden*), Shen Te (*The Good Woman of Setzuan*) 56, Rebecca West (*Rosmersholm*) 59, title role *Duchess of Malfi* 61, Madame Ranevsky (*The Cherry Orchard*) 62, and numerous Shakespearian performances at The Old Vic, London, and as mem. Royal Shakespeare Company, Stratford and London 60-64; in *The Seagull* 64, *Days in the Trees* 66, *Ghosts* 67 (all in London).
Films inc. *The Wandering Jew, Thirty Nine Steps, The Nun's Story;* King's Gold Medal (Norway); Hon. D.Litt. (Oxon.) 61, Leicester 64; Hon. D.Lit., London 65.
Manor Lodge, Frognal Lane, London, N.W.3, England.

Ashenheim, Sir Neville Noel, Kt., C.B.E.; Jamaican lawyer, business executive and diplomatist; b. 18 Dec. 1900; ed. Jamaica Coll. and Wadham Coll., Oxford.
Chairman, Jamaican Board Standard Life Assurance 58-61, House of Myers Ltd. 44-61, Fred. L. Myers & Son (Produce) Ltd. 44-61, Gleaner Co. Ltd. 44-67, Consolidated Int. Corpn. Ltd. 58-, Jamaica Chemical Industries Ltd. 44-, Blinds and Furnishings Ltd. 49-, Jamaica Industrial Development Corpn. 52-57, Caribbean Cement Co. 66; official of other companies; mem. Legislative Council 59; Minister without Portfolio and Leader of Govt. Business in Legislative Council, Jamaica 62; Amb. to United States 62-67; Minister without Portfolio and Leader of Govt. Business in Senate 67-.
11 Waterloo Road, Kingston 10, Jamaica.

Ashihara, Yoshinobu, B.A., M.ARCH., D.ENG.; Japanese architect; b. 7 July 1918; ed. Univ. of Tokyo and Harvard Univ. Graduate School.
Worked in architectural firms, Tokyo 46-52; in Marcel Breuer's firm, New York 53; visited Europe on Rocke-feller Travel Grant 54; Head, Yoshinobu Ashihara and Assocs. 55-; Lecturer in Architecture, Hosei Univ., Tokyo 55-59, Prof. of Architecture 59-65; visited Europe and U.S.A. to study exterior space in architecture 60; Prof. of Architecture, Musashino Art Univ., Tokyo 64-; Visiting Prof., School of Architecture and Building, Univ. of New South Wales, Australia 66-; Award of Architectural Inst. of Japan for Chuo-Koron Building 60; Special Award of Architectural Inst. of Japan for Komazawa Olympic Gymnasium 65.
Works include: Chuo-Koron Building, Sony Building, Komazawa Olympic Gymnasium 65, Japanese Pavilion, Expo 67, Montreal.
Publ. *Exterior Space in Architecture: From the Building to the City* 62.
Y. Ashihara Architectural Design Office, 7th Floor, Sumitomo-seimei Shibuya Building, 107 Ohwada-cho, Shibuya-ku, Tokyo; Home: 47 Nishihara-3, Shibuya-ku, Tokyo, Japan.

Ashiotis, Costas; Cypriot diplomatist; b. 1908; ed. Pancyprian Gymnasium, Nicosia, and London School of Economics.
Former journalist and editor; Govt. Service 42-; Asst. Commr. of Labour 48; Dir.-Gen. Ministry of Foreign Affairs 60; mem. Cypriot Dels. to UN and Int. Confs.; High Commr. in U.K. 66-; Hon. M.B.E.
Publ. *Labour Conditions in Cyprus During the War Years 1939–45.*
Cyprus High Commission, 93 Park Street, London, W.1, England.

Ashiwara, Yoshishige; Japanese electricity executive; b. 4 March 1901; ed. Kyoto Univ.
President, Kansai Electric Power Co.; Vice-Pres. Expo 70.
1049 Ikeda, Tomatsu, Higashi, Amagasaki City, Hyogo Prefecture, Japan.

Ashkenazy, Vladimir; Soviet concert pianist; b. 6 July 1937; ed. Central Music School, Moscow, and Moscow Conservatoire.
Second Prize, Int. Chopin Competition, Warsaw 55; Gold Medal, Queen Elizabeth Int. Piano Competition, Brussels 56; Joint winner (with John Ogdon) Tchaikov-sky Piano Competition, Moscow 62; concerts in many countries.
29 Cedars Close, London, N.W.4, England.

Ashmole, Bernard, C.B.E., M.C., M.A., B.LITT., F.B.A.; British archaeologist; b. 22 June 1894; ed. Hertford Coll., Oxford.
Craven Fellow, Athens and Rome British Schools 20-22; Asst. Curator of Coins, Ashmolean Museum, Oxford 23-25; Dir. British School at Rome 25-28; Yates Prof. Archaeology, London Univ. 29-48; Keeper, Greek and Roman Antiquities, British Museum 39-56; Lincoln Prof. of Classical Archaeology and Art, Oxford Univ. 56-61; Geddes-Harrower Prof. of Greek Archaeology and Art, Aberdeen Univ. 61-62; Fellow, Lincoln Coll., Oxford, Hon. Fellow, Hertford Coll., Oxford.
Publs. *Catalogue of Ancient Marbles at Ince Blundell Hall, Greek Sculpture and Painting* (with Sir J. D. Beazley), *Olympia: The Sculptures of the Temple of Zeus* (with N. Yalouris and A. Frantz).
The Mill House, Iffley, Oxford, England.

Ashton, Sir Frederick, C.B.E.; British choreographer and dancer; b. 17 Sept. 1906; ed. Dover Coll. and Dominican Fathers, Lima, Peru.
Principal choreographer and Dir. Royal Ballet; Flight-Lieut., R.A.F., during Second World War; Queen Elizabeth II Coronation Award; Legion of Honour

(France); Commdr. of the Order of the Dannebrog; Hon. D.Litt. (Durham).
Choreography for *Symphonic Variations, Cinderella, Les Patineurs, Rendezvous, Façade, Scènes de Ballet, Wedding Bouquet, Capriol Suite, Sylvia, Romeo and Juliet, Ondine, La Fille Mal Gardée, Jazz Calendar,* etc.
Royal Opera House, Covent Garden, London, W.C.2, England.

Ashton, Thomas Southcliffe, M.A., F.B.A.; British economic historian; b. 11 Jan. 1889; ed. Manchester Univ.
Asst. Lecturer in Economics Sheffield Univ. 12-19; Lecturer and Tutor in Economics and Political Science Birmingham Univ. 19-21; Senior Economics Lecturer 21, Reader in Currency and Public Finance 27, Dean Faculty of Commerce and Administration 39-44, Man-chester Univ.; Pres. Manchester Statistical Soc. 38-40; Prof. Economic History, London Univ. 44-54. Prof. Emeritus 54-; Pres. Economic History Soc. 60-63; Hon. Vice-Pres. Royal Historical Soc. 61-, Royal Economic Soc. 64-; Hon. D.Litt. (Nottingham), Hon. Litt.D. (Manchester), Hon. Fil.D. (Stockholm).
Publs. *Iron and Steel in the Industrial Revolution* 24, *The Coal Industry of the 18th century* (with J. Sykes) 29, *Economic and Social Investigations in Manchester 1833-1933* 34, *An Eighteenth-Century Industrialist: Peter Stubs of Warrington* 39, *The Industrial Revolution* 48, Edited (jointly with R. S. Sayers) *Papers in English Monetary History* 53, *An Economic History of England: The Eighteenth Century* 55, *Economic Fluctuations in England 1700–1800* 59.
Tredwells, Blockley, Gloucestershire, England.
Telephone: Blockley 334.

Asimov, Isaac, B.S., M.A., PH.D.; American bio-chemist and science fiction writer; ed. Columbia Univ.
Instructor in Biochemistry, Boston Univ. School of Medicine 49-51, Asst. Prof. 51-55, Assoc. Prof. 55-; professional writer 38-; various awards.
Publs. Eighty-seven books including *The Human Body* 63, *The Human Brain* 64, *New Intelligent Man's Guide to Science* 65, *Asimov's Biographical Encyclopedia of Science and Technology* 64, *Understanding Physics* 66, *The Universe* 66.
Home: 45 Greenough Street, West Newton, Mass. 02165, U.S.A.
Telephone: 617-527-9072.

Askarov, Asanbai; Soviet politician; b. 1922; ed. Frunze Teachers' Training Coll. and Higher Party School of C.P.S.U. Central Cttee.
In Educational Service 39-42; Soviet Army 42-46; Party Official 46-51, 54-58; Chair. Djambul Regional Soviet of Working People's Deputies 58-59; First Sec., Djambul Regional Cttee., Communist Party of Kazakhstan 59-65; First Sec. Alma Ata Regional Cttee., C.P. of Kazakhstan; mem. Central Cttee. of C.P.S.U. and of Central Cttee. of Kazakhstan C.P. 65-; Alt. mem. Bureau of Central Cttee., C.P. of Kazakhstan; Deputy to U.S.S.R. Supreme Soviet; mem. Mandate Cttee., Soviet of Nationalities of U.S.S.R. Supreme Soviet; mem. C.P.S.U. 44-.
Alma Ata Regional Committee, Communist Party of Kazakh S.S.R., Alma Ata, U.S.S.R.

Askenase, Stefan; Belgian (b. Polish) concert pianist; b. 10 July 1896; ed. Coll. in Lemberg and Acad. of Music, Vienna.
War service, Austrian officer 15-18; Teacher, Cairo Conservatoire 22-25; resident in Brussels 25-; Prof. Royal Conservatoire of Music, Brussels 57-61; concert tours all over Europe and overseas; records for Deutsche Grammophon Gesellschaft.
Hotel Astoria, Brussels, Belgium.

Askin, Hon. Robin William; Australian politician; b. 1908; ed. Sydney Technical High School, New South Wales.

Former bank official; with Australian Imperial Forces, Second World War; mem. New South Wales Parl. 50-; Deputy Leader of Liberal Party 54-59, Leader 59-; Premier and Treas. of New South Wales 65-.
Parliament House, Sydney; and "Avon", Oyama Avenue, Manly, Sydney, New South Wales, Australia.

Asmodi, Herbert Christian Ernst; German playwright; b. 30 March 1923; ed. Ruprecht-Karl Universität, Heidelberg.
War service 42-45; studies at Heidelberg 47-52; freelance writer, Munich 52-; Gerhard Hauptmann-Preis der Freien Volksbühne Berlin 54.
Publs. comedies: *Pardon wird nicht gegeben, Nachsaison, Die Menschenfresser, Mohrenwäsche; Stirb & Werde* (two episodes from the German recovery).
Munich 23, Germaniastrasse 5, German Federal Republic.
Telephone: 348436.

Asnag, Abdallah Al-Majid Al-; Aden trade union official and politician; b. 1933.
Senior Reservation Officer, Aden Airways 51-62; Leader, People's Socialist Party, Gen. Sec. Aden Trade Union Congress until Dec. 62, 63-65; imprisoned Dec. 62-Dec. 63; now Head of Political Bureau, Front for Liberation of Occupied South Yemen (FLOSY).
c/o People's Socialist Party, Steamer Point, Aden.

Aspinall, Arthur, C.V.O., M.A., D.LITT.; British university professor; b. 11 July 1901; ed. Manchester Univ.
Lecturer in History, Univ. of Rangoon 25-31; Lecturer in Modern History, Univ. of Reading 31-47, Prof. of Modern History 47-65, Prof. Emeritus 65-.
Publs. *Lord Brougham and the Whig Party* 27, *Cornwallis in Bengal* 31, *The Formation of Canning's Ministry* 37, *The Letters of King George IV, 1812-1830*, 3 vols. 38, *Lady Bessborough and her Family Circle* (with the Earl of Bessborough) 40, *The Correspondence of Charles Arbuthnot* 41, *The Diary of Henry Hobhouse* 47, *Politics and the Press* 49, *The Letters of Princess Charlotte* 49, *The Early English Trade Unions* 49, *Mrs. Jordan and her Family* 51, *Three Early Nineteenth Century Diaries* 52, *The Cabinet Council 1783-1835* (Raleigh Lecture on History) 52, *English Historical Documents, 1783-1832* (with E. A. Smith) 59, *Parliament through seven centuries: Reading and its M.P.s* (co-author) 62, *The Later Correspondence of George III*, Vol. I 62, Vol. II 63, Vol. III 67, Vol. IV 68, *The Early Correspondence of George, Prince of Wales, 1770–1812*, Vol. I 63, Vol. II 64, Vol. III 65, Vol. IV 67, Vol. V 68.
Highlands, Belle Vue, Maughold, Ramsey, Isle of Man, England.
Telephone: Ramsey 3343.

Aspinall, Wayne Norviel; American lawyer and politician; b. 3 April 1896; ed. Univ. of Denver and Denver Law School.
Admitted to Colorado Bar 25-; also engaged in peach orchard industry; mem. Colorado House of Reps. 31-38, Speaker 37, 38; State Senator 39-48; mem. U.S. House of Reps. 48-, now Chair. of House Interior and Insular Affairs Cttee.; Democrat.
Old House Office Building, Washington, D.C., U.S.A.

Aspling, Sven; Swedish politician; b. 28 Aug. 1912.
Journalist 37-42; Constituency Organiser, Social Democrat Party 42-46, Asst. Sec.-Gen. 46-48, Sec.-Gen. 48-62; mem. Parl. 56-; Minister of Social Affairs 62-.
Ministry of Social Affairs, Stockholm 2, Sweden.

Asplund, Karl, B.A., PH.D.; Swedish poet and art historian; b. 27 April 1890; ed. Uppsala Univ.
Sec. Art History Society 15-16; Correspondent *Dagens Nyheter* 14-21 and *Svenska Dagbladet* 22-34; Man. Dir. Bukowski Co. 29-53; Pres. Bellman Soc. 43-64; mem. Architects Acad., Stockholm.
Publs. *Egron Lundgren* 14-15, *Katalog öv. utst. av äldre*

svenska Porträttminiatyrer i Stockholm 15, *Den svenska porträttminiatyrens hist.* 16, *Vers från väster, Anders Zorn, his Life and Work* 21, *Zorn's Engraved Work* 20, *Ivar Arosenius* 28, *Borta bra* 32, *Orient* 37, *Axel Fridell* 37. *Selected Poems* 38, *Carl Eldh* 43, *Livets Smultronsställen* 45, *Att overleva* 48, *Augusti* 52, *En Stenhammarkrönika* 54, *Septemberskyar* 57, *De Ijusa timmarna* 59, *Konst, Kännare, Köpmän* 62, Ed. *P. A. Hall, Sa correspondance de famille* 55, *Nils Dardel* 57, etc.
Rådmansg. 17, Stockholm, Sweden.

Asquini, Alberto; Italian university professor; b. 12 Aug. 1889.
Prof. of Commercial Law, Univ. of Urbino 15-20, Sassari 20-21, Trieste 21-25, Pavia 25, Padua 26-35, Rome 35-68; mem. Accad. Naz. dei Lincei, Rome.
Publs. *Il Contratto di Trasporto* 35, *Scritti giuridici*, Vol. I 36, II 39, III 61, *Titoli di Credito* 65, *Rivista diritto Commerciale* 38-67, *Rivista società* (misc. articles) 56-67.
Via N. Porpora 9, 00198 Rome, Italy.
Telephone: 860-355; 867-669.

Asquith of Yarnbury, Baroness (Life Peeress) cr. 64; **(Helen) Violet Bonham Carter,** D.B.E.; British politician; b. 15 April 1887; ed. privately.
Elder daughter of Rt. Hon. H. H. Asquith, 1st Earl of Oxford and Asquith; Pres. Women's Liberal Fed. 23-25, 39-45; mem. Winston Churchill's Focus in Defence of Freedom and Peace 36-39; mem. Exec. League of Nations Union until 41; Gov. of B.B.C. 41-46; Pres. Liberal Party Org. 45-47, Vice-Pres. 47-; Gov. of Old Vic 45-; Vice-Chair. United Europe Movement 47-48; Hon. Pres. UN Asscn. 45-57, Patron 57-; Pres. Royal Inst. of International Affairs 64-; Trustee Glyndebourne Arts Trust 55-; Hon. LL.D. (Sussex).
Publ. *Winston Churchill as I Knew Him* 65.
21 Hyde Park Square, London, W.2, England.

Asratyan, Ezras Asratovich; Soviet physiologist; b. 31 May 1903; ed. Erevan State Univ.
Asst. State Univ. Erevan 25-30; scientific worker in Physiological Inst. U.S.S.R. Acad. of Sciences 30-38; Head of Neuro-Physiological Laboratory, Leningrad Brain Research Inst. 35-41; Head of Physiological Dept. Pedagogical Inst. Leningrad 36-41; Prof. of Physiology, Tashkent Medical Institute 41-43; Professor, Medical Inst. Moscow 43-50; Head of Physiological Laboratory U.S.S.R. Acad. of Sciences 44-60; Head of Physiological Dept. Moscow Second State Medical Inst. 50-60; Head, Inst. of Higher Nervous Activity and Neurophysiology 60-; mem. Armenian Acad. of Sciences; corresp. mem. U.S.S.R. Acad. of Sciences; Pavlov Prize 50; Order of Lenin, Order of Red Star, Order of Red Banner; Pavlov Gold Medal 61.
Publs. *Essays on Etiology, Functional Pathology and Therapy of the Traumatic Shock* 45, *Physiology of the Central Nervous System* 53, *Lectures on Some Problems of Neurophysiology* 58, *Reliability of Brain* 63, *Compensatory adaptations, Reflex Activity and the Brain* 65.
Apartment 89, 13 Leninsky Prospekt, Moscow, U.S.S.R.
Telephone: B-1-08-81; B-2-08-65.

Assmann, Arno; German theatre producer and manager; b. 30 July 1908; ed. Gymnasium und Realschule zum heiligen Geist, Breslau, and Musikhochschule, Breslau.
At Schauspielhaus, Hamburg 46-47, Thalia-Theater, Hamburg 47-52, Schauspielhaus, Frankfurt/Main 52-55, Kammerspiele, Munich 55-58; Dir. Theater am Gärtnerplatz, Munich 59-63; Dir. Bühnen der Stadt Köln (Cologne City Theatres) Jan. 64-Sept. 64, Gen. Dir. Sept. 64-.
Productions include: *Der Schulfreund* (Kammerspiele, Munich) 59, *Fiesko* (Residenztheater, Munich) 59, *Hoffmanns Erzählungen* (Staatsoper, Munich) 60, *Julius Caesar* (Bühnen der Stadt Köln) 64, *Don Carlos* (Opera,

Cologne) 64, *Dantons Tod* (Cologne) 65, *Billy Budd* (Opera, Cologne) 65.

5 Köln-Marienburg, Parkstrasse 24, German Federal Republic.

Astaikin, Ivan Pavlovich; Soviet politician; b. 1917; ed. Higher Party School of C.P.S.U. Central Cttee.

Teacher and Dir. of secondary school 34-39; Official, Young Communist League 39-48; Sec., Second Sec., Mordvinian Regional Cttee. of C.P.S.U. 48-54; Chair. Council of Ministers of Mordvinian S.S.R. 54-; Deputy to U.S.S.R. Supreme Soviet; mem. C.P.S.U. 39-.

Council of Ministers, Mordvinian Autonomous S.S.R., Saransk, U.S.S.R.

Astaire, Fred; American actor and dancer; b. 10 May 1899.

Co-starred with his sister as Fred and Adele Astaire 16-32; has appeared in numerous musical comedies and films, television dramas and Fred Astaire Specials (musical), including: *Lady Be Good, The Bandwaggon, Gay Divorce, Top Hat, Holiday Inn, The Sky's the Limit, The Ziegfield Follies, The Belle of New York, Daddy Long Legs, Silk Stockings, On the Beach, Pleasure of his Company, Finian's Rainbow, The Midas Run.*

Publ. *Steps in Time* 60 (autobiography).

c/o Lambs Club, New York, N.Y., U.S.A.

Astaurov, Boris Lvovich; Soviet biologist; b. 1904; ed. Moscow Univ.

Associate Inst. of Experimental Biology, now Inst. of Animal Morphology 35-55; Head, Laboratory of Experimental Embryology, Severtsov Inst. of Animal Morphology, U.S.S.R. Acad. of Sciences 55-; Corresp. mem. U.S.S.R. Acad. of Sciences 58-66, mem. 66-.

U.S.S.R. Academy of Sciences, 14 Leninsky Prospekt, Moscow, U.S.S.R.

Astin, Allen V(arley), M.S., PH.D.; American physicist; b. 12 June 1904; ed. Univ. of Utah and New York Univ.

Nat. Research Council Fellow, Johns Hopkins Univ. 28-30; Research Assoc., Utilities Research Cttee., Nat. Bureau of Standards 30-32, Physicist 32, Asst. Chief Ordnance Development Div. 44-48, Chief Electronics and Ordnance Div. 48-50, Assoc. Dir. 51-52, Dir. 52-; Fellow American Physical Soc.; Fellow, Inst. of Electrical and Electronic Engineers; mem. Nat. Acad. of Sciences, American Philosophical Soc., Int. Cttee. of Weights and Measures, American Ordnance Assocn., etc.; Presidential Certificate of Merit.

5008 Battery Lane, Bethesda, Md. 20014, U.S.A.

Aston, James William, B.S.; American banker; b. 6 Oct. 1911; ed. Texas A. & M. Coll.

Served U.S.A.A.F. 41-45; Vice-Pres. Repub. Nat. Bank of Dallas 45-55, Exec. Vice-Pres. 55-57, Pres. 57-61, Pres. and Chief Exec. Officer 61-65, Chair. and Chief Exec. Officer 65-; official of numerous civic and philanthropic orgs.

Republic National Bank of Dallas, P.O. Box 5961, Dallas 22, Texas, U.S.A.

Astor, Hon. Francis David Langhorne; British journalist; b. 5 March 1912; ed. Eton and Balliol Coll., Oxford.

Staff, *Yorkshire Post* 36; served Second World War 39-45; Foreign Editor *The Observer* 46-48, Editor 48-; Croix de Guerre.

12 Elm Tree Road, London, N.W.8; and Manor House, Sutton Courtenay, Berkshire, England.

Telephone: 01-286-0223 (London).

Astor, Hon. Gavin (son of Lord Astor of Hever, *q.v.*); British company director; b. 1 June 1918; ed. Eton and New Coll., Oxford.

Served in Army in Second World War 39-45; prisoner-of-war 44-45; Pres. Times Newspapers Ltd. 67-; Chair. Commonwealth Press Union 59-; Dir. Monotype Corpn. Ltd. 52-, Alliance Assurance Co. Ltd. 54-, Electrolux Ltd. 59-.

11 Lyall Street, London, S.W.1, England.

Telephone: 01-235-4755.

Astor of Hever, Baron, cr. 56, of Hever Castle in the County of Kent; **Col. John Jacob Astor,** HON. D.LIT. (Lond.) (father of Hon. Gavin Astor, *q.v.*); British newspaper proprietor; b. 20 May 1886; ed. Eton and New Coll., Oxford.

Mem. Post Office Advisory Council 33-39; Chair. Westminster Employment Cttee. 24-25; mem. Broadcasting Cttees. 23 and 35; mem. B.B.C. Gen. Advisory Council 37-39; fmr. Co-Chief Propr. and Dir. The Times Publishing Co. Ltd., Chair. 23-59; Conservative M.P. for Dover 22-45; fmr. Chair. Phoenix Assurance Co., London Guarantee and Accident Corpn.; Pres. Commonwealth Press Union.

Les Terres Blanches, Pegomas, Grasse, France.

Astrom, C. Sverker; Swedish diplomatist; b. 15; ed. Univ. of Uppsala.

Foreign Service 39-, Moscow 40-43, Ministry of Foreign Affairs 43-46, Washington 46-48, Ministry of Foreign Affairs 48-53, London 53-56; Head of Political Dept., Min. of Foreign Affairs 56-63; Perm. Rep. to UN 64-.

Permanent Mission of Sweden to the United Nations, 757 Third Avenue, New York 17, N.Y., U.S.A.

Astsatryan, Egish Tevosovich; Soviet politician; b. 1914; ed. Tbilisi Industrial Inst.

Member C.P.S.U. 44-; Deputy Chief Engineer of mine, Chief Engineer, Mining Trust 38-50; Sec. Erevan Territorial Cttee. of C.P. of Armenia, and Chief of Section, Central Cttee. of Armenian C.P. 50-60; Chair. Econ. Council of Armenian S.S.R. 60-65; Chair. Cttee. of People's Control of Armenian S.S.R. 66-; mem. Central Cttee. of Armenian C.P.

Council of Ministers of Armenian S.S.R., Erevan, U.S.S.R.

Asturias, Miguel Angel; Guatemalan writer; b. 19 Oct. 1899; ed. Instituto Nacional de Guatemala, Universidad de Guatemala and Univ. de Paris à la Sorbonne.

Founder of Gen. Students Asscn., Guatemala, also Universidad Popular de Guatemala; founder of periodical *El Diario del Aire;* Cultural Attaché, Guatemalan Embassy, Mexico 46-47; Minister-Counsellor, Guatemalan Embassy, Buenos Aires 47-52; Minister, Paris 52-53; Ambassador to El Salvador 53; now lives in France; Amb. of Guatemala to France 66-; has lectured on literature in univs. in S. America and Europe; Prix Sylla Monsegur, Paris 31; Prix du Meilleur Roman Etranger, Paris, for *Monsieur le Président* 52; Lenin Peace Prize 66; Nobel Prize for Literature 67.

Publs. *El Problema Social del Indio* 23, *Arquitectura de la Vida Nueva* (lectures) 28, *Leyendas de Guatemala* 30, *El Señor Presidente* 46, *Sien de Alondra* (anthology of poetry 1918-1948) 48, *Hombres de Maiz* 49, *Viento Fuerte* 50, *El Papa Verde* 53, *Week-End en Guatemala* 55, *Los Ojos de los Enterrados* 60, *El Alha Jadito* 61, *Mulata de Tal* 63, *Antología Teatral* 64, *Clarivigilia Primaveral* (poems) 65, *Le Miroir de Lida Sal* 67.

Ambassade de Guatemala, rue de Courcelles 73, Paris 8e, France.

Atalla, Anton Abden-Nur; Jordanian lawyer, banker and politician; b. 97; ed. American Univ. of Beirut and Univ. of Jerusalem.

Crown Counsel 24-27, Magistrate 28-31, Senior Magistrate 32-37, Judge of District Court, Palestine 37-43; Senior Partner A. H. Atalla and Co. (law firm) 43-48; Regional Gen. Manager, Arab Land Bank, Jordan 48-60, Dep. Gen. Manager 60-63; mem. Jordan House of Reps. and Chair. House Finance Cttee. 54-56; Minister of Foreign Affairs 63-64; Gen. Man. Arab Land Bank, Jordan 64-; mem. Jordan Senate 64-.

The Senate, Amman, Jordan.

Atassi, Nureddin, M.D.; Syrian politician; b. 1929; ed. Damascus Univ.

Minister of the Interior Aug. 63; Deputy Prime Minister Oct. 64; mem. Syrian Presidential Council May 64-Dec.

65; Chief of the Syrian State Feb. 66-; Sec.-Gen. Syrian Baath Party 66-.
Office of the Chief of State, Damascus, Syrian Arab Republic.

Athanasiadis-Novas, George; Greek politician; b. 93; ed. Athens Univ.
Former journalist and lawyer; mem. Parl. 26-39, 50-; Minister of Interior 45, of Education 45, 50-51; Minister in charge of Prime Minister's Office 51-52, 63; Pres. of Chamber of Deputies 64-65; Prime Minister 65; Deputy Prime Minister Sept. 65-66; mem. Athens Acad. 55-; Centre Union.
Publs. (under pseudonym George Athanas) *Time of War, Sequence, Lyric Poetry, The Education of the Citizen.*
Aristeidou 12, Athens, Greece.

Athenagoras I; Archbishop of Constantinople and Oecumenical Patriarch; b. 86; ed. Theological School of Halki, Istanbul.
Metropolitan of Corfu 24-30; Archbishop of North and South America 30-48; Archbishop of Constantinople, New Rome, and Oecumenical Patriarch 48-.
Rum Ortodoks Patrikhanesi, Fener, Istanbul, Turkey.

Athens and All Greece, Archbishop of (*see* Kotsonis, Archbishop Ieronymos).

Atiya, Aziz Suryal, M.A., PH.D., LITT.D.,; United Arab Republic (Egyptian) historian and writer; b. 98; ed. Univs. of Liverpool and London.
Charles Beard Fellow and Univ. Fellow, Univ. of Liverpool 30-32; History Tutor, School of Oriental Studies, Univ. of London 33-34; Prof. of Medieval and Oriental History, Univ. of Bonn 35-38; Prof. Medieval History, Cairo 38-42, Alexandria 42-54; consultant to Library of Congress, Washington, D.C. 50-51; visiting lecturer U.S. univs., Univ. of Zürich and Swiss Inst. of Int. Affairs 50-51; Pres. Inst. of Coptic Studies, Cairo 54-56; Medieval Acad. Visiting Prof. of Islamic Studies, Univ. of Michigan, Ann Arbor 55-56; Luce Prof. of World Christianity, Union Theological Seminary, and Visiting Prof. of History, Columbia Univ., New York 56-57; Visiting Prof. of Arabic and Islamic History, Princeton Univ. 57-58; mem. Inst. for Advanced Study, Princeton 58-59; Dir., Middle East Center, Utah Univ. 59-67; Distinguished Prof. of History, Utah 67-; corresp. mem. UNESCO Int. Comm. for the Scientific and Cultural History of Mankind; corresp. mem. Coptic Archaeological Soc.; mem. Medieval Acad. of America, Mediterranean Acad., Rome; Hon. D.H.L.
Publs. *The Crusade of Nicopolis* 34, *The Crusade in the Later Middle Ages* 38, *Egypt and Aragon—Embassies and Diplomatic Correspondence between 1300 and 1330* 38, *Kitab Qawanin al-Dawawin by Saladin's Wazir ibn Mammati* 43, *History of the Patriarchs of the Egyptian Church,* 2 Vols. 48-59; *Monastery of St. Catherine in Mt. Sinai* 49, *The Mt. Sinai Arabic Microfilms* 54, *Coptic Music* 60, *Crusade, Commerce and Culture* 62, *The Crusades—Historiography and Bibliography* 62, *History of Eastern Christianity* 68, etc. (all books in either English or Arabic).
8 Sharia Wadi el-Nil, Maadi, near Cairo, U.A.R.; 1335 Perry Avenue, Salt Lake City, Utah, U.S.A.
Telephone: Cairo 34134; Salt Lake City 328-1086.

Atkinson, Joseph Story, B.A.; Canadian journalist; b. 8 April 1904; ed. Univ. of Toronto Schools and Univ. of Toronto.
Joined staff of *Toronto Star* 26, Sec.-Treas. 34, Vice-Pres. 40, Chair. of Board of Dirs. 48, 66-, Pres. 57; Chair. Atkinson Charitable Foundation.
4 Old Forest Hill Road, Toronto, Ontario, Canada.
Telephone: HU9-6210.

Atkinson, Justin Brooks, A.B., L.H.D. (Hon.); American writer; b. 28 Nov. 1894; ed. Harvard Univ.
Literary Editor *New York Times* 22-25, Dramatic Critic 25-42, War Correspondent in China 43-44; Cor-

respondent in Russia 45-46; dramatic critic 46-60; columnist 60-64; Pulitzer Prize 47.
Publs. *Henry Thoreau, the Cosmic Yankee* 27, *East of the Hudson* 31, *Cingalese Prince* 35, *Once Around the Sun* 51, *Tuesdays and Fridays* 63, *Brief Chronicles* 66.
Durham, N.Y., U.S.A.

Atkinson, William Christopher, M.A.; British university professor; b. 9 Aug. 1902; ed. Univs. of Belfast and Madrid.
Lecturer in Spanish, Durham 26-32; Stevenson Prof. of Hispanic Studies, Univ. of Glasgow 32-, Dir. Inst. of Latin-American Studies 66-; Head of Spanish and Portuguese Sections, Foreign Office Research Dept. 39-43; Hon. Sec. Modern Humanities Research Asscn. 29-36; British Council Lecturer, Latin America 46, 60; Chair. First Scottish Cultural Del. to U.S.S.R. 54; Carnegie Fellow visiting American univs. 55; Rockefeller Fellow visiting Latin-American univs. 57; Visiting Prof. Univ. Coll. of Rhodesia and Nyasaland 63; mem. Hispanic Society of America; Hon. Prof. Nat. Univ. of Colombia, Bogotá.
Publs. *Spain, A Brief History* 34, *The Lusiads of Camoens* 52, *The Remarkable Life of Don Diego* 58, *A History of Spain and Portugal* 60, *The Conquest of New Granada* 61.
Andorra, Bearsden, Glasgow, Scotland.
Telephone: Bearsden (Glasgow) 0368.

Atta, William Ofori; Ghanaian cocoa executive; b. 10 Oct. 1910; ed. Achimota School, Gold Coast, Queen's Coll., Cambridge, London School of Economics, and Gray's Inn, London.
Taught history, Achimota School 39-43; State Sec. Akim Abuakwa, later State Treas. 43-47; Head of Abuakwa State Coll. 47; mem. Ghana Congress Party after 47; mem. Volta River Project Del. to Canada 55; mem. Nat. Cttee. of Volta River Project; politically detained 59, 63, 64; mem. Political Cttee. Nat. Liberation Council; Chair. Cocoa Marketing Board 66-.
Cocoa Marketing Board, P.O. Box 933, Accra, Ghana.

Attar, Mohamed Said Al-; Yemeni economist; b. 26 Nov. 1927; ed. Ecole Pratique des Hautes Etudes à la Sorbonne, Inst. d'Etude du Développement Econ. et Social (I.E.D.E.S.), Univ. de Paris.
Research I.E.D.E.S. 60-62; Dir.-Gen. Yemen Bank for Reconstruction and Devt. 62-65; Minister of Econ. March-Aug. 65; Pres. Econ. Comm. Oct. 65-Feb. 66; Pres. Board Yemen Bank and Pres. of Econ. High Comm. March 66-.
Publs. *L'Industrie du gant en France* 61, *L'épicerie à Paris* 61, *Etude sur la croissance économique de l'Afrique Occidentale* 62, *Le marché industriel et les projets de l'Arabie Séoudite* 62, *Le sous-développement économique et social du Yemen* (*Perspectives de la Révolution Yemenite*) 64, Arabic edition 65.
Yemen Bank for Reconstruction and Development, Sana'a, Yemen; Home: 5 square Neuilly-Château, Neuilly-sur-Seine, France.

Attassi, Lt.-Gen. Louai; Syrian army officer and politician; b. 26; ed. Syrian Military Acad., and Staff Officers' Coll., Homs.
Took part in Palestinian war 48; opposed Syrian break with Egypt 61; Garrison Commdr., Aleppo April 62; Military Attaché, Syrian Embassy, Washington 62-63; C.-in-C. of Syrian Armed Forces and Pres. of Revolutionary Council March 63-July 63.
Damascus, Syrian Arab Republic.

Atterberg, Kurt; Swedish musician; b. 12 Dec. 1887; ed. Royal Technical High School, Stockholm.
Dir. Section Royal Patent Office 37; Hon. Pres. Int. Confed. Authors' and Composers' Societies; Music Critic *Stockholms Tidningen* 19-57; Pres. Asscn. of Swedish Composers 24-47; Hon. Pres. 47-; Sec. Council

for Int. Collaboration with Composers 35-39; Sec. Acad. of Music Stockholm 40-53.
Works include nine symphonies, five operas, five concertos, chamber music, choral works.
Rindögatan 25, Stockholm, NO, Sweden.

Attiyia, Mahmoud Ibrahim, B.SC.; United Arab Republic (Egyptian) geologist; b. 1900; ed. Cairo and Imperial Coll. of Science and Technology, London. Asst. Lecturer, School of Engineering, Giza 23-25; Geologist, Geological Survey of Egypt 29, Asst. Dir. 39, Dir. 49; Dir.-Gen. Mines and Quarries Dept. 54-56; Tech. Dir. Mineral Wealth Co. and Sinai Manganese Co., Cairo 56-; delegated Prof. of Geology, Cairo Univ.; A.R.C.S. London 29; F.G.S. London 30; mem. Inst. d'Egypte 46; mem. Board of the Desert Inst. of Egypt 50; mem. Egyptian Acad. of Sciences 50; mem. Conseil d'Administration de la Société de Géographie d'Egypte 51; State Prize in Geological and Chemical Sciences; Order of the Republic (Egypt).
Publs. *Notes on the Underground Water in Egypt* 42, *The Barramiya Mining District* 48, *New Mode of Occurrence of Iron-Ore Deposits* 49, *Iron-Ore Deposits of Egypt* 50, *Ground-Water in Egypt* 53, *Deposits in the Nile Valley and the Delta* 54, *Iron-Ore Deposits of the District East of Aswan* 55.
13 Sharia el-Malek el-Mozaffar, Geziret el-Rada, Cairo, U.A.R.

Attwood, William, B.A.; American journalist and diplomatist; b. 14 July 1919; ed. Choate School, Princeton Univ.
U.S. Army 41-45; Correspondent *New York Herald Tribune* 46-48, *Collier's Magazine* 49-51; European Editor *Look Magazine* 51-55, National Editor 55-57, Foreign Editor 57-61; Special Adviser to U.S. UN Del. 63-64; Ambassador to Guinea 61-63, Ambassador to Kenya 64-66; Editor-in-Chief Cowles Communications Inc.; Alumni Trustee Princeton Univ.; Democrat.
Publs. *The Man Who Could Grow Hair* 49, *Still the Most Exciting Country* 55, *The Reds and the Blacks* 67.
423 Carter Street, New Canaan, Conn., U.S.A.
Telephone: 203-966-5831.

Attygalle, Sir Nicholas, F.R.C.S., F.R.C.O.G., D.L.O., L.M.S., D.SC.; Ceylonese university official; b. 14 July 1898; ed. Royal Coll., and Ceylon Medical Coll., Colombo, Univ. Coll., London, and Middlesex Hospital, Medical School.
Gynæcologist, General Hospital, Colombo 35-44; Prof. of Obstetrics and Gynæcology, Univ. of Ceylon 44-53; Dean, Faculty of Medicine 45-53; Pres. of Senate 53-55; Vice-Chancellor, Univ. of Ceylon 55-66; Pres. Inter-Univ. Board of India and Ceylon 60; Pres. Ceylon Medical Council 64.
108 Horton Place, Colombo 7, Ceylon.
Telephone: Colombo 9334.

Atwood, John Leland, A.B., B.S.; American engineer; b. 26 Oct. 1904; ed. Hardin Simmons Univ. and Univ. Texas.
Junior Engineer, Army Air Corps, Wright Field, Ohio 28; Design Engineer, Douglas Aircraft Co. 30-32; Vice-Pres. and Chief Engineer, North American Aviation Inc. 34, Pres. 48-, Chief Exec. Officer 60-, Chair. of the Board 62-; Fellow, Inst. Aeronautical Sciences, Pres. 54-; mem. Soc. Automotive Engineers.
Office: North American Aviation Inc., 1700 E. Imperial Highway, El Segundo, Calif., U.S.A.
Telephone: 213-670-9151.

Aubert, Jacques, D. ès D.; French administrator and politician; b. 6 Aug. 1913; ed. Lycée de Brest and Faculté de droit de Paris.
Legal Adviser Ministry of Foreign Affairs 39-40; Asst. to Sec.-Gen. of Comm. on Cotton Imports 41-42; Chef du Cabinet of Prefect 42; Asst. Prefect, Dir. of Security

for French Occupation Zone in Austria 47, Sec.-Gen., Vienna 51; Asst. Prefect, Dreux 53; Asst. Dir. Private Office of Pierre Voizard, Resident Gen. of France at Tunis 54, Sec.-Gen. Martinique, Constantine 55; Dir. Private Office of Abdelkadar Barakok, Sec.-of-State for Algeria, and Private Offices of Bourgès-Manoury and Félix Gaillard 57-58; Prefect and Technical Adviser, Private Office of Prefect of Police 58; Dir. Sûreté Nationale in Algeria 60-61; Prefect of Loir-et-Cher 61; Dir. Private Office of R. Frey, Minister of the Interior 62-66; Sec.-Gen. of the Police 66-; Chevalier Légion d'Honneur, Croix de la Valeur Militaire.
33 rue Poussin, Paris 16e, France.

Aubinière, Gen. Robert Joseph; French air force officer and astronautical specialist; b. 24 Sept. 1912; ed. Ecole Polytechnique, and air force training.
War service, North Africa 42, Chief of Operations, N. Region of France 43, then sent to a concentration camp; Vice-Commdt., Ecole de l'Air de Salon-de-Provence 45-48, Commdt. 60; Air Force Staff Colleges 49; Deputy Chief-of-Staff 5th Airborne Region 50-53; Commdt., Ground Staff Training School Rochefort 54-57, Centre Interarmées d'Essais d'Engins Spéciaux, Colomb-Béchar 57-58; promoted Gén. de Brigade Aérienne 58; Technical and Industrial dir. of Aeronautics 60; promoted Gén. de Division Aérienne 61; Dir.-Gen. Centre National d'Etudes Spatiales 62-; Grand Officier Légion d'Honneur, Croix de Guerre, Médaille de l'Aéronautique.
Centre National d'Etudes Spatiales, 129 rue de l'Université, Paris 7e, France.

Auboin, Roger; French banker; b. 15 May 1891; ed. Paris Univ.
Mem. Council of State 19; Adviser Nat. Bank of Rumania 29-35; Sec.-Gen. for Nat. Economy 37; mem. Gen. Council Bank of France 37; Gen. Man. Bank for International Settlements, Basle, 38-58; Commandeur de la Légion d'Honneur, Grand Officer Order of Orange Nassau, Commdr. Order of Leopold, Commdr. Order of Merit of Republic of Italy.
1 avenue de Budé, Geneva, Switzerland; 25 bis rue de Constantine, Paris 7e, France.

Aubrun, Charles Vincent; French university professor; b. 4 April 1906; ed. Univ. of Paris.
Prof., Univ. of Poitiers 39-45, Univ. of Bordeaux 45-51, Univ. of Paris 51-, Dir. Inst. of Hispanic Studies 53-.
Publs. *Bolivar: choix de lettres, discours, proclamation* 34, *Lope de Vega, Peribáñez* 43, *Le Chansonnier espagnol d'Herberay des Essarts, 15e siècle* 51, *L'Amérique Centrale* 52, 62, 67, *Histoire des Lettres hispano-américaines* 54, *Calderón, La estatua de Prometeo* 65, *Calderón, Eco y Narciso* 61, *Bolivar, Cuatro cartas y una memoria* 61, *Lope de Vega, La Circe* 62, *Histoire du théâtre espagnol* 65, *La comédie espagnole (1600-1680)* 66, *L'espagnol à l'Université* (2 vols.) 67.
31 rue Gay-Lussac, Paris 5e, France.
Telephone: 633-55-37.

Auchincloss, Louis Stanton, LL.B.; American lawyer and author; b. 27 Sept. 1917; ed. Groton School, Yale Univ. and Univ. of Virginia.
Admitted to New York bar 41, Assoc. Sullivan and Cromwell 41-51, Hawkins, Delafield and Wood, New York City 54-58, partner 58-; Lieut. U.S. Navy 41-45.
Publs. *The Indifferent Children* 47, *The Injustice Collectors* 50, *Sybil* 52, *A Law for the Lion* 53, *The Romantic Egoists* 54, *The Great World and Timothy Colt* 56, *Venus in Sparta* 58, *Pursuit of the Prodigal* 59, *House of Five Talents* 60, *Reflections of a Jacobite* 61, *Portrait in Brownstone* 62, *Powers of Attorney* 63, *The Rector of Justin* 64, *Pioneers and Caretakers* 65, *The Embezzler* 66, *Tales of Manhattan* 67.
1111 Park Avenue, New York City 28, N.Y., U.S.A.

Auchinleck, Field Marshal Sir Claude John Eyre,
G.C.B., G.C.I.E., C.S.I., D.S.O., O.B.E.; British army officer;
b. 21 June 1884; ed. Wellington Coll. and Royal Mil.
Coll., Sandhurst.
Commissioned Indian Army 03; joined 62nd Punjabis
04; served Egypt 14-15, Aden 15, Mesopotamia 16-19;
Imperial Defence Coll. 27; commanded 1st Battalion
1st Punjab Regt. 29-30; Instructor Staff Coll. Quetta
30-33; Commander Peshawar Brigade 33-36; Deputy
Chief of Gen. Staff Army Headquarters India 36-38,
Commander Meerut District 38; mem. Expert Cttee.
on Indian Defence 38; Commdr. Allied Land Forces in
Northern Norway 40; Commdr.-in-Chief Southern
Command 40; Commdr.-in-Chief India 41, Middle
East 41-42, India 43-47; Chair. Dowsett Holdings
Ltd. 54; Chair. Murrayfield Real Estate Co. Ltd. 58;
Hon. LL.D. (Aberdeen, St. Andrews); Virtuti Militari
(Poland) 44; War Cross (Czechoslovakia) 44; Order of
Chief Commdr., Legion of Merit (U.S.A.) 45; Order of
Star of Nepal (1st Class) 45; Grand Cross, Order of St.
Olaf (Norway) 47; Order of Cloud and Banner (China)
47; Légion d'Honneur 49.
Oswald House, Northgate, Beccles, Suffolk, England.

Auden, Wystan Hugh; American poet (British by
birth); b. 21 Feb. 1907; ed. Gresham's School, Holt, and
Christ Church, Oxford.
U.S. national 46; awarded King's Poetry Medal 37 and
$1,000 prize by American Acad. of Arts and Letters 45;
Pulitzer Prize 48; mem. American Acad. of Arts and
Letters 54; Prof. Poetry, Oxford Univ. 56-61; Alexander
Droutzkoy Gold Medal, Poetry Soc. of America 59,
Guinness Poetry Award 59; Nat. Medal for Literature
(U.S.A.) 67; Hon. Litt.D. (Swarthmore Coll.).
Publs. *Poems* 30, *The Orators* 32, *The Dance of Death*
33, *The Dog Beneath the Skin* (with Christopher Isher-
wood) 35, *The Poet's Tongue* (with John Garrett) 35,
The Ascent of F.6 (with Christopher Isherwood) 36,
Look Stranger 36, *Letters from Iceland* (with Louis Mac-
Neice) 37, *Spain* 37, *On the Frontier* (with Christopher
Isherwood) 38, *Oxford Book of Light Verse* (Editor) 38,
Journey to a War (with Christopher Isherwood) 39,
Selected Poems 40, *Another Time* 40, *New Year Letter* 41,
For the Time Being 44, *Selections from Tennyson* 46,
The Age of Anxiety 47, *Greek Reader* 48, *Nones* 51,
Libretto of *The Rake's Progress* (with Chester Kallman)
51, *Poets of the English Language*, 5 vols. (Editor) 52,
The Knights of the Round Table (from French play by
Jean Cocteau) 54, *Kierkegaard* 55, *The Shield of Achilles*
56, *Homage to Clio* 60, Libretto of *Elegy for Young
Lovers* (with Chester Kallman) 61, *The Dyer's Hand*
(collection of prose) 63, Libretto of *Die Bessariden* (with
Chester Kallman) 65, *About the House* (poems) 65;
Editor Yale series *Younger Poets* 47-59, *Nineteenth
Century Minor Poets* 67.
c/o Random House, Madison Avenue, New York, N.Y.,
U.S.A.

Audenhove, Omer Van; Belgian politician; b. 3 Dec.
1913.
Member Resistance, Second World War; mem. Munici-
pal Council, Diest 46-, Mayor 47-58; mem. Belgian
Senate 54-; Minister of Public Works and Reconstruc-
tion 55-58, 58-61; Président Parti Libéral de Belgique
May-Oct. 61, Président-fondateur, Parti de la Liberté
et du Progrès 61-; Officier de l'Ordre de la Couronne;
Officier Ordre de Léopold II avec Palmes; Chevalier de
l'Ordre de Léopold; Croix de Guerre avec Palmes;
Grand Croix de l'Ordre Orange-Nassau (Netherlands).
Publ. *Deux lois indispensables.*
Parti de la Liberté et du Progrès, 39 rue de Naples,
Brussels, Belgium.

Audry, Colette; French writer; b. 6 July 1906; ed.
Ecole Normale Supérieure, Sèvres.
Professor of Literature, Lycée Molière, Paris 45-65;
Literary Critic *Les Temps Modernes* 45-55; on staff
Editions Gonthier 63-; film-set designer and script-
writer; Prix Medicis for *Derrière la Baignoire* 62.
Publs. novels: *On joue perdant, Aux yeux du souvenir,
Léon Blum ou la politique du Juste, Connaissance de
Sartre, Sartre ou la Réalité humaine* 66; screen-plays:
*Les malheurs de Sophie, La Bataille du rail, Olivia,
Absence, Liberté surveillée, Derrière la Baignoire*; play:
Soledad.
20 rue du Ranelagh, Paris 16e, France.

Auer, Väinö, PH.D.; Finnish geologist and geographer;
b. 7 Jan. 1895; ed. Helsinki Univ.
Mem. Forest Research Inst. 18-29; Geologist, Geological Survey of Canada 26; Lecturer in Geography,
Helsinki Univ. 22-29 and Prof. 29-63; Rockefeller
scholarship 26; leader of geographical expedition to
Patagonia and Tierra del Fuego 28-29; Pres. Finnish
Geographical Society and Finnish Forestry Asscn. 35-36;
leader geographical expeditions to Patagonia 37-38,
47-53 and 57; Hon. Dir. Forestry Research of Argentina
47; President Finnish Acad. of Science 59; mem.
Finnish Scientific Acad., etc.; highest award of honour
of Finnish Culture Foundation, Finnish Acad. of
Sciences, Kordelin Foundation; Fennia Gold Medal
50; Kairamo Silver Medal 50; Cajander Medal 55;
Martin Behaim Silver Medal 59; Rueppell Silver Medal
61; Helsinki Univ. Medal; war medals; Commdr. (First
Class) Order of Lion, Finland; Commdr. of White Rose,
Finland; mem. numerous foreign socs.; hon. degree
(Univ. of Bonn).
Publs. *Verschiebungen der Wald- und Steppengebiete
Feuerlands in post-glazialer Zeit, Las Capas Volcánicas
como Base de la Cronología Postglacial de Fuegopata-
gonia, Consideraciones científicas sobre la conservación
de los naturales de la Patagonia, Nuevos Aspectos de la
Sequía en la Patagonia, The Pleistocene of Fuego-
Patagonia: I The Ice and Inter-Glacial Ages, II History
of the Flora and Vegetation, III Shoreline Displacements,
IV Bog Profiles,* etc.
Rakuunantie 4, B, 14, Helsinki 33, Finland.
Telephone: Helsinki 486433.

Auger, Pierre Victor, D.ès-s.; French university professor; b. 14 May 1899; ed. Ecole Normale Supérieure,
and Univ. of Paris.
Assistant, Faculty of Sciences, Univ. of Paris 27, Dir. of
Studies 32, Prof. 37-; Research Assoc. Univ. of Chicago
41-44; Dir. of Higher Educ., Ministry of Educ., Paris
45-48; Dir. Dept. of Natural Sciences UNESCO 48-59;
Chair. French Cttee. for Space Research 59-62; mem.
Anglo-Canadian team on Atomic Energy, Canada
42-44; French del. to UN Atomic Energy Comm. 46-48;
Dir.-Gen. European Space Research Org. 62-67; Com-
mandeur Légion d'Honneur, Commandeur des Palmes
Académiques; Int. Feltrinelli Prize 61.
Publs. *Les rayons cosmiques* 41, *What are Cosmic Rays?*
44, *L'Homme Microscopique* 52, *Main Trends in
Scientific Research* 61.
12 rue Emile Faguet, Paris 14e; and 23 Rue Laperouse,
Paris 16e, France.
Telephone: 225-2118 (Office); 402-9634 (Home).

Augstein, Rudolf; German magazine publisher; b.
5 Nov. 1923; ed. High School.
Lieutenant, Second World War; Publisher and Chief
Ed. *Der Spiegel* (weekly) 46-; under arrest (for alleged
political offence) Oct. 62-Jan. 63.
Publ. *Konrad Adenauer* 64.
Der Spiegel, Pressehaus, Hamburg 1, German Federal
Republic.

Auguste, Carlet R.; Haitian economist and diplo-
matist; b. 03.
Professor of Econs., Cap Haitien School of Law 44-59;
Sec. of State for Commerce 47-48, for Finance and
Commerce 50; mem. Legislative Assembly 50-54; Perm.

Rep. to UN 59-67; Amb. to German Fed. Repub. 67-. Embassy of Haiti, Bad Godesberg, Rheinallee 33, German Federal Republic.

Augustincic, Antun; Yugoslav sculptor; b. 1900. Joined Partisan movement 43; Vice-Pres. Anti-Fascist Council for Nat. Liberation of Yugoslavia.
Works include memorial in front of U.N. H.Q., New York, busts of Pres. Tito, Memorial to Red Army at Batina Skela on the Danube and Memorial to Pilsudski; Memorial to Miner, Geneva Memorial to Victims of Fascism, Addis Ababa Memorial to Ras Makonen; mem. Yugoslav Acad. Sciences and Arts.
Yugoslav Academy of Sciences and Arts, Braće, Kavurćia 1, Zagreb, Yugoslavia.

Aujaleu, Eugéne Jean Yves; French physician; b. 29 Oct. 1903; ed. Toulouse Faculty of Medicine.
Inspector-Gen. of Health 41; Dir. Health Service, Free French Govt. Algiers 42-44; Dir. of Social Hygiene, Ministry of Health 45; Dir.-Gen. of Public Health 56; Dir.-Gen. Nat. Inst. of Health and Medical Research 64; Councillor of State 66; Chair. WHO Exec. Board 59-60.
144 boulevard du Montparnasse, Paris 14e, France.

Aulaqi, Sheikh Mohammed Farid Al-; South Arabian politician; b. 1929; ed. Aden Protectorate Coll. for Sons of Chiefs, Government Secondary School, Aden, and Queen's Coll., Oxford.
Joined Protectorate Govt. Service as Asst. Political Officer 50; Political Officer 56-59; Minister of Finance, Fed. of S. Arabia 59-63, Minister of External Affairs 63-67.
Aden, People's Republic of South Yemen.

Aulie, Andreas, O.B.E.; Norwegian attorney-general; b. 97.
Superintendent of Police 22; Chief C.I.D. 30; Public Prosecutor 39; Gen. Chief Norwegian Police 43; Attorney-Gen. 46-67; Norwegian rep. UN European consultative group for prevention of crime and treatment of offenders.
H. Ibsensgt 7, Oslo, Norway.

Aung, Htin, B.A., LL.B., B.LITT., PH.D.; Burmese educationalist; b. 09; ed. Univs. of Rangoon, London, Dublin, Cambridge, Paris and Leyden.
Called to the Bar (Lincoln's Inn) 32; apptd. to Senior Service, Univ. of Rangoon 36, Prof. of English 46, Prof. of Anthropology 57; Rector, Univ. of Rangoon Dec. 46-59; Ambassador to Ceylon 59-; Sec. Council of Nat. Educ., Burma 36-46; Vice-Chair. UNESCO Nat. Comm.; Leader Burmese Del., UNESCO Gen. Confs., Florence 50, Paris 51; mem. Inter-Univ. Board of India. Publs. *Burmese Drama* 37, *Burmese Folk-Tales* 47.
Burmese Embassy, Colombo, Ceylon.

Auric, Georges; French composer; b. 15 Feb. 1899; ed. Paris Conservatoire and Schola Cantorum, Paris.
Mem. "Les Six" movement in France; Music Critic, *Marianne* 36, and later *Paris-Soir*; Gen. Administrator, Paris Opera 62-; mem. Acad. des Beaux-Arts; Commandeur Légion d'Honneur, and other decorations.
Compositions include songs and piano music; film music, e.g. for René Clair's *A Nous la Liberté* 32 and Jean Cocteau's *L'Aigle à deux Têtes* 48; ballet music includes *Le Peintre et son Modèle* 49, *Phèdre* 50, *Chemin de Lumière* 52, *Coup de Feu* 52; *Le Masque* (opera); sonata for piano and violin 37; *Quatre Chansons Françaises* (work for unaccompanied four-part chorus) 50.
90 rue du Faubourg-Saint-Honoré, Paris 8e, France.

Austin, (John) Paul; American business executive; b. 14 Feb. 1915; ed. Harvard Univ., Harvard Law School and Culver Military Acad.
Legal practice, New York 40-41, 45-49; U.S. Navy 42-45; Legal Dept., The Coca-Cola Co. 49-50, Asst. to Pres. The Coca-Cola Export Corpn. 50-58, Pres. and Dir. The Coca-Cola Export Corpn. 59-62, Exec. Vice-Pres. The Coca-Cola Co. 61-62, Pres. and Dir. The Coca-Cola Co.

62-, Chief Exec. Officer 66-; Dir. Morgan Guaranty Trust Co. of New York, Gen. Electric Co., Trust Co. of Georgia, and Continental Oil Co.; Legion of Merit.
P.O.B. 1734, Atlanta, Ga. 30301, U.S.A.

Austregésilo de Athayde, Belarmino Maria; Brazilian journalist; b. 25 Sept. 1898; ed. Seminário de Prainha, Fortaleza, Liceu do Ceará and Univ. of Rio de Janeiro.
Teacher 17-18; Dir. Sec. *A Tribuna* 18-21; on staff of *Correio da Manhã* 21; Dir. *O Jornal* (with Diarios Asociados) 24-32; exiled for political reasons 31; Dir. *Diário da Noite*; Editor-in-Chief *O Jornal*; mem. Brazilian Del. UN Gen. Assembly, Paris 48; mem. Brazilian Acad. of Letters 31-, Pres. 59-; Ordem do Mérito Naval Aeronáutico 57, Militar 63, Jornalístico 65; numerous foreign decorations.
Publs. *Histórias Amargas* 21, *Quando as Hortencias Florescem* 21, *A Influência Espiritual Americana* 38, *Fora da Imprensa* 48, *Mestre de Liberismo* 52, *Na Academia* 53, *Discurso de recepção a José Lins do Rego* 56, *Vanaverba* 66.
Rua Cosme Velho 599, Rio de Janeiro, Brazil.

Autant-Lara, Claude; French film director and author; b. 5 Aug. 1901; ed. Lycée Janson de Sailly, Mill Hill School, London, Ecole des Arts Décoratifs, and Ecole des Beaux-Arts.
Entered French film industry 20; directed first short picture *Faits-Divers* 23; Hon. Pres. Syndicat des Techniciens du Cinéma Français; Pres. Fédération Nationale du Spectacle.
Principal films: *Le Diable au Corps, Douce, The Red Inn, Game of Love, Le Rouge et le Noir, Seven Sins, Marguerite de la Nuit, La Traversée de Paris, En cas de malheur, La Jument verte, Le Bois des Amants, Tu ne tueras point, Vive Henri-IV, Vive l'amour, Le Comte de Monte-Cristo, Le Meurtrier, Le Magot de Joséfa, Le Journal d'une femme en blanc, le Nouveau Journal d'une femme en blanc.*
6 rue Ballu, Paris 9e, France.

Aveline, Claude; French writer; b. 19 July 1901.
Hon. Pres. Soc. Anatole France; Pres. of Jury for Prix Jean-Vigo (Cinema); Officier de la Légion d'Honneur; Médaille de la Résistance (with rosette), etc.; Grand Prix Société des Gens de Lettres 52, Prix Italia 55.
Publs. Novels: *Le Point du Jour* 28, *La vie de Philippe Denis* (*Madame Maillart* 30, *Les amours et les haines* 52, *Philippe* 55), *Le prisonnier* 36, *Le temps mort* 44, *Suite policière* (*La double mort de Frédéric Belot* 32, *Voiture 7 Place 15* 37, *L'Abonné de la ligne U* 47, *Le jet d'eau* 47), *Pour l'amour de la nuit* 56, *Le poids de feu* 59, *C'est vrai . . .* 60; Essays and Travel Books: *La merveilleuse légende du Bouddha* 28, *La promenade égyptienne* 34, *Les devoirs de l'esprit* 45, *Anatole France* 49, *Et tout le reste n'est rien* 51, *Les Mots de la Fin* 57, *Le Code des jeux* 61, *Avec toi-même,* etc. 63, *Les réflexions de Monsieur F.A.T.* 63, *Célébration du lit* 67; Play: *Brouart et le désordre* 64; Poetry: *Portrait de l'Oiseau-Qui-N'Existe-Pas* 65, *De* 68.
19 rue Servandoni, Paris 6e, France.

Averoff-Tossizza, Evangelos; Greek economist, journalist and politician; b. 10; ed. Univ. of Lausanne.
Began career as journalist, worked in Switzerland and Greece; active in resistance movement during 39-45 war, imprisoned in Northern Italy, later escaped and continued resistance work until end of war; mem. of Parl. 46-; fmr. Minister of Supply, National Economy and Commerce, and Under-Sec. for Foreign Affairs; Minister of Agriculture Feb.-May 56, of Foreign Affairs May 56-63; sentenced to five years imprisonment Aug. 67, later pardoned; mem. Nat. Radical Union.
c/o Ministry of Foreign Affairs, Athens, Greece.

Avidom (Mahler-Kalkstein), Menahem, B.A.; Israeli composer; b. 6 Jan. 1908; ed. American Univ., Beirut, and in Paris.

Lecturer on theory of music, Hebrew Conservatoire of Music, Tel-Aviv 36-, and Music Teachers' Training Coll. Tel-Aviv 45-; Sec.-Gen. Israel Philharmonic Orchestra 46-; Vice-Pres. Board of Dirs. Acum Ltd. (Composers and Authors Asscn.), Dir.-Gen. 56-; Dir. Arts Dept. Jerusalem Convention Centre 52; Art Adviser, Govt. Tourist Centre, Ministry of Commerce and Industry 54-; Pres. League of Composers; Fellow Int. Inst. for Arts and Letters, Bodensee 58; mem. Nat. Arts Council 62; Israel State Prize 61.
Compositions include *A Folk Symphony* 47, *Symphony No. 2 David* 48, *Sinfonietta* 51, 2 Piano Sonatinas 49, *Concertino* for violinist Jascha Heifetz, *Concertino* for cellist Gregor Piatigorsky 51, *Alexandra Hashmonaïth* (opera in 3 acts) 52, *Jubilee Suite*, *Triptyque Symphonique*, concerto for strings and flute, music for strings, symphonies 3, 4, 5 and 6, psalms and cantatas, *12 Preludes Variés* for piano, *Metamorphoses* for string quartet 60, *Symphony No. 7* (25th anniversary of Israel Philharmonic Orchestra), *Enigma*, septet for 5 wood instruments, piano and percussion, Quartet for brass, Reflexions for 2 flutes, Triptyque for Solo violin, "B-A-C-H" Suite for Chamber Orchestra, *Festival Sinfonietta* (Symphony No. 8) 66, *The Crook* (comic opera) 66/67, *Symphonie Variée* (Symphony No. 9) for Chamber Orchestra 68.
Office: ACUM House, Rothschild Boulevard 118, Tel-Aviv; Home: Samadar Street, Ramat-Gan, Israel.
Telephone: 240105 (Office); 725512 (Home).

Avila, Rev. Fernando Bastos de; Brazilian ecclesiastic and sociologist; b. 17 March 1918; ed. Univs. of Nova Friburgo (Brazil), Louvain and Gregorian Univ., Rome.
Professor of Sociology, Catholic Pontifical Univ. of Rio de Janeiro 57-; Social Dir. Nat. Catholic Immigration Comm. 54-; mem. Council, Nat. Fed. of Trade 60-; Dir. *Spes—Sintese Política, Econômica, Social.*
Publs. *Economic Impacts of Immigration* 56, *L'Immigration au Brésil* 57, *Introdução a Sociología* 62, *Solidarismo* 65.
Rua Marquês de S. Vicente 209, Rio de Janeiro, Brazil.
Telephone: 476030.

Avinoam (Grossman), Reuben, B.A.; Israeli writer and educationist; b. 12 Aug. 1905; ed. New York Univ.
Lecturer in English, Herzlia Hebrew Coll., Tel Aviv 29, Head of Dept. of English 46-49; Hon. Sec. P.E.N. Centre in Israel 42-56; del. of Hebrew P.E.N. to Int. P.E.N. Congress, Zürich 47, Venice 49, Dublin 53; Inspector-Gen. of English Studies, Department of Education, Ministry of Education and Culture 50-52; Editor-in-Chief of literary publs. in memory of heroes of Israel's wars 52-; mem. Exec. of Hebrew Writers' Asscn. 53-56, 60-63.
Publs. *Arbaa Iyim (Four Islands)*, *Av Ubito (Father and Daughter)* 34, Poetry: *Shirim* 31, *Idiliyoth (Idylls)* 34, *Aley Dvai (Leaves of Woe)* 48, *Shirath Enayim Velevav (Song of Eyes and Heart)* 49, *Hebrew Anthology of English Verse* 44, *Collected Poems (1930-50)* 50, *Hebrew Anthology of American Verse* 53, *Hebrew Anthology of English Verse* (revised and complete edition) 56, *Images of Yore* 64; *Etz Shatalti (A Tree I Planted)* 58; *Hebrew-English Dictionary*, many translations of English works into Hebrew; Tchernichowsky prize (awarded by Municipality of Tel Aviv for Translation) 58; Editor Hebrew version of Shakespeare's Tragedies (trans. three); Editor anthology of works of heroes of Israel's wars (*Gvile Esh*—Parchments of Fire, appeared in 3 vols. 52, 58, 61); editor and author series of booklets *Feats of Valour* (heroic battles in Israeli Wars).
103 Rothschild Boulevard, Tel Aviv, Israel.
Telephone: 226752.

Avon, Earl of, cr. 61 and **Eden,** 1st Viscount, cr. 61, of Royal Leamington Spa in the County of Warwick; **(Robert) Anthony Eden,** K.G., P.C., M.C.; British poli-

tician; b. 12 June 1897; ed. Eton and Christ Church, Oxford.
Conservative M.P. for Warwick and Leamington 23-57; Parliamentary Private Sec. to Sir Austen Chamberlain 26-29; Under-Sec. of State for Foreign Affairs in Nat. Govt. Sept. 31-33; Lord Privy Seal without seat in Cabinet, assigned to special work at Foreign Office 34-35; Sec. for L.N. Affairs June-Dec. 35; Sec. of State for Foreign Affairs Dec. 35-Feb. 38, resgnd.; conducted diplomatic missions to Moscow, Warsaw and Prague 35; Trustee Nat. Gallery 35-49; Sec. of State for the Dominions with special access to the War Cabinet Sept.-39-April 40; Sec. of State for War 40, for Foreign Affairs Dec. 40-July 45; Leader House of Commons 42-45; Chair. Conservative Foreign Affairs Cttee. 45, and Army Cttee. 45; Chancellor Birmingham Univ. 45; Dir. Westminster Bank Ltd. 46-51; Chair. O.E.E.C. 52-54; Deputy Prime Minister and Sec. of State for Foreign Affairs 51-55; Prime Minister 55-Jan. 57; Pres. Royal Shakespeare Theatre, Stratford-upon-Avon 58-66; Hon. D.C.L. (Oxford, Durham), Hon. LL.D. (Cambridge, Leeds, Sheffield, Belfast, Toronto, California, Birmingham).
Publs. *Places in the Sun* 26, *Foreign Affairs* 39, *Freedom and Order* (Selected Speeches) 47, *Days for Decision* 49, *Full Circle* (memoirs) 60, *Facing the Dictators* (memoirs) 62, *The Reckoning* (memoirs) 65, *Towards Peace in Indo-China* 66.
Manor House, Alvediston, Salisbury, Wilts., England.

Avramenko, Stepan Stepanovich; Soviet politician; b. 1918; ed. Belotserkov Inst. of Agriculture.
Veterinary surgeon 41-49; Local Govt. and Party work 49-55; First Sec., Barabinsk Town Cttee. of C.P.S.U. (Novosibirsk Region) 55-59; Chair. Novosibirsk Regional Soviet 59-64; First Sec. Amursk Regional Cttee. of C.P.S.U. 64-; Alt. mem. C.P.S.U. Central Cttee.; Deputy to U.S.S.R. Supreme Soviet; mem. Mandate Comm., Soviet of Union, U.S.S.R. Supreme Soviet; mem. C.P.S.U. 50-.
Amursk Regional Committee, Communist Party of Soviet Union, Blagoveschensk, U.S.S.R.

Avramovic, Dragoslav; Yugoslav international bank official; ed. Univ. of Belgrade.
Former Asst. Prof., Law Faculty, Belgrade Univ.; fmr. Adviser to Yugoslav Nat. Bank on Credit and Foreign Policy; fmr. Consultant on External Economics, Yugoslav State Secretariat for Int. Affairs; Dir. of Special Economic Studies, World Bank 53-.
International Bank for Reconstruction and Development (World Bank), Washington 25, D.C., U.S.A.

Avriel, Ehud; Israeli diplomatist; b. 19 Oct. 1917; ed. High School, Vienna.
Israeli Minister to Czechoslovakia 48, concurrently to Hungary 49; Minister to Rumania 50; Dir.-Gen. Prime Minister's Office, Jerusalem 51-57; Ambassador to Ghana and Liberia 57-61, to Congo (Léopoldville) 60-61; Deputy Dir. Gen. Ministry of Foreign Affairs 61-66; Ambassador to Italy and Malta 66-.
Ministry of Foreign Affairs, Jerusalem; and Neoth Mordechai, Hagalil Haelyon, Upper Galilee, Israel.

Avtsin, Alexander Pavlovich; Soviet pathologist; b. 1908; ed. First Moscow Medical Institute.
Associate, Inst. of Neuropsychiatric Prophylaxis 33-38; Asst. Prof. Third Moscow Medical Inst. 37-41; Asst. Prof. First Moscow Medical Inst. 42-43; Army Surgeon 43-46; Head of Dept., Inst. of Normal and Pathological Morphology, U.S.S.R. Acad. of Medical Sciences 45-61; Corresp. mem. U.S.S.R. Acad. of Medical Sciences 61-65, mem. U.S.S.R. Acad of Medical Sciences 65-; Dir. Inst. of Human Morphology, U.S.S.R. Acad. of Medical Sciences 61-; Vice-Chair. Moscow Soc. of Pathologicoanatomists, Vice-Chair. U.S.S.R. Soc. of Pathologicoanatomists; mem. Editorial Board *Arkhiv*

patologii, Co-Editor Big Medical Encyclopaedia; Order of Lenin, Order of Red Banner of Labour and Bulgarian Red Banner of Labour.

Publs. Over 100 works on pathological anatomy of cerebral tumours, hormonotherapy of cerebral neoplasms, infectious diseases and military pathology.

Institute of Morphology, U.S.S.R. Academy of Medical Sciences, Block 18, 61/2, Shchepkin Street, Moscow, U.S.S.R.

Awolowo, Chief Obafemi, B.COM. (HONS.), LL.B. (Lond.), B.L., LL.D. (Ashiwaju of Ijebu Remo, Losi of Ikenne, Lisa of Ijeun, Apesin of Oshogbo, Odole of Ife, Ajagunla of Ado Ekiti, Odofin of Owo and Obong Ikpan Isong of Ibibioland); Nigerian politician; b. 6 March 1909; ed. London Univ.

Teacher 28-29; Stenographer 30-34; Newspaper Reporter 34-35; engaged in motor transport and produce buying 36-44; Solicitor and Advocate, Supreme Court of Nigeria 47-51; Minister of Local Govt. and Leader of Govt. Business Western Region 52-54; co-founder and first Gen. Sec. of Egbe Omo Oduduwa, a Yoruba cultural movement; founder and Fed. Pres. of the Action Group; Premier, Govt. of the Western Region of Nigeria 54-59; Leader of the Opposition in Federal Parliament 60-May 62, detained May 62-Nov. 62, on trial for treasonable felony and conspiracy Nov. 62-Sept. 63; sentenced to 10 years imprisonment Sept. 63; given free pardon and released Aug. 66; elected Leader of Yorubas Aug. 66; Chancellor of Univ. of Ife, Nigeria 67-; Vice-Chair. Federal Exec. Council and in charge of Ministry of Finance June 67-.

Publs. *Path to Nigerian Freedom, Awo* (autobiography), *Thoughts on Nigerian Constitution.*

c/o P.O. Box 136, Ibadan, Nigeria.

Axen, Hermann; German journalist; b. 6 March 1916. Mem. Communist Youth League 32; emigrated to France; imprisoned in concentration camps 40-45; mem. Central Cttee. Socialist Unity Party (S.E.D.) 50; Chief Editor *Neues Deutschland* 56-67; Candidate mem. of Politburo of Central Cttee. of Socialist Unity Party 67-; mem. Volkskammer; Silver Medal Vaterländischer Verdienstorden.

Sozialistische Einheitspartei Deutschlands, 102 Berlin, Am Marx-Engels-Platz 2, Germany.

Axer, Erwin; Polish theatre producer and director; b. 1 Jan. 1917; ed. Lwów, and Nat. Acad. of Theatrical Art, Warsaw.

Assistant Producer, Nat. Theatre, Warsaw 38-39; Actor-Producer, Polish State Drama Theatre, U.S.S.R. 39-41; Art Dir., Teatr Kameralny, Łódź 46-49; Dir. and producer Teatr Wspolczesny (Contemporary Theatre) Warsaw 49-; Dir. and Chief Producer, Nat. Theatre, Warsaw 55-57; Prof. Extraordinary Producers Dept. Acad. of Theatre, Warsaw 57-66, Prof. Ordinary 66-; State Awards for Artistic Achievement 51, 53, 55, 62, Nagroda Krytyki im Boya-Zelenskiego (Critics Award) 60; Commanders Cross, Sztandar Pracy (Second Class), Polonia Restituta.

Productions include: *Major Barbara* (Shaw) 47, *Niemcy* (Kruczkowski) 55, *Kordjan* (Slowacki) 56, *Pierwszy dzien wolnosci* 59, *Iphigenia in Tauris* 61, *Karjera Arturo Ui* (Brecht) Warsaw 62, Leningrad 63, *Three Sisters* (Chekhov) 63, Düsseldorf 67, *Androcles and the Lion* (Shaw) Warsaw 64, *Tango* (Mrozek) Warsaw 65, Düsseldorf 66, *Die Ermittlung* (Weiss) Warsaw 66, *Le Piéton de l'Air* (Ionesco) Warsaw 67.

Publs. include: *Listy ze sceny I* (Letters from the Stage) 55, *Listy ze sceny II* 57, *Sprawy Teatralne* (Things Theatrical) 66.

27/11 Odynca, Warsaw, Poland.
Telephone: 44-01-16.

Axisa, John F., M.B.E.; Maltese diplomatist; b. 20 Nov. 1906.

Malta Civil Service; Dir. of Emigration 47-56; Dir. of Technical Education 56-59; Dir. of Emigration, Labour and Social Welfare 59-60, Under-Sec. 60-61; Commr.-Gen. for Malta in London 61-64; High Commr. of Malta in U.K. 64-, also Amb. to France 66-, Libya 66-, German Fed. Repub. 67-, Belgium 67-.

High Commission of Malta, Malta House, 24 Haymarket, London, S.W.1, England.
Telephone: 01-839-5033.

Aydalot, Maurice, D. en D.; French judge; b. 22 June 1905; ed. Faculté de Droit de Paris.

Magistrate, Ministry of Justice 30; Deputy Public Prosecutor, Paris 37, Public Prosecutor 51, Prosecutor-Gen., Court of Appeal, Paris 57-62; Prosecutor-Gen., Court of Cassation 62-67; First Pres. Court of Cassation 67-; Commandeur de la Légion d'Honneur.

Publs. *Les atteintes au crédit de l'Etat, L'expertise comptable judiciaire, Droit Pénal des Affaires.*

Palais de Justice, 5 quai de l'Horloge, Paris 1er, France.

Ayer, Alfred Jules, M.A., F.B.A.; British university professor; b. 29 Oct. 1910; ed. Eton Coll. and Christ Church, Oxford.

Lecturer in Philosophy, Christ Church, Oxford 32-35, Research Student of Christ Church 35-44; Fellow of Wadham Coll. Oxford 44-46, Dean of Wadham 45-46; Grote Prof. of the Philosophy of Mind and Logic, Univ. of London 46-Oct. 59; Wykeham Prof. of Logic, Oxford Oct. 59-; served in Welsh Guards and on Intelligence Duties during Second World War; Attaché British Embassy Paris 45; Fellow of New Coll., Oxford; Hon. Fellow of Wadham Coll., Oxford 57-; Hon. mem. American Acad. of Arts and Sciences 63; Dr. h.c. Univ. of Brussels 62.

Publs. *Language, Truth and Logic* 36, *The Foundations of Empirical Knowledge* 40, *Thinking and Meaning* 47, *British Empirical Philosophers* (editor, with Raymond Winch) 52, *Philosophical Essays* 54, *The Problem of Knowledge* 56, *Privacy* 60, *Philosophy and Language* 60, *The Concept of a Person and Other Essays* 63; Editor *Logical Positivism* 60, *The Origins of Pragmatism* 68.

New College, Oxford; Home: 10 Regents Park Terrace, London, N.W.1, England.

Aykroyd, Wallace Ruddell, C.B.E., M.D., SC.D.; British nutritionist; b. 30 July 1899; ed. The Leys School, Cambridge, and Univ. of Dublin.

Beit Memorial Research Fellow 28-30; mem. Health Section, League of Nations 30-35; Dir. Nutrition Research Laboratories, Coonoor, India 35-45; mem. Indian Famine Inquiry 44-45; Dir. Nutrition Div. F.A.O. 46-60; Senior Lecturer, Dept. of Human Nutrition, London School of Hygiene and Tropical Medicine 61-66; Hon. Fellow American Public Health Assen., American Inst. of Nutrition.

Publs. *Vitamins and Other Dietary Essentials* 32, *Three Philosophers* 35, *Human Nutrition and Diet* 38, *Sweet Malefactor—Sugar, Slavery and Human Society* 67.

Queen Anne House, Charlbury, Oxford, England.
Telephone: Charlbury 441.

Aylestone, Baron (Life Peer), cr. 67, of Aylestone in the City of Leicester; **Herbert William Bowden,** P.C., C.B.E.; British politician and television executive; b. 20 Jan. 1905.

President Leicester Labour Party 38; M.P. 45-67; Parl. Private Sec. to Postmaster-Gen. 47-49; Asst. Govt. Whip 49-50, Deputy Opposition Whip 51-55, Chief Opposition Whip 55-64; Lord Pres. of the Council 64-66; Sec. of State for Commonwealth Affairs 66-67; Chair. Independent Television Authority (I.T.A.) 67-.

House of Lords, London, S.W.1, England.

Aylmer, Sir Felix, Kt. (*Pseudonym* of Sir Felix Aylmer Jones), O.B.E., B.A.; British actor; b. 21 Feb. 1889; ed. Magdalen Coll. School and Exeter Coll., Oxford.

First stage appearance at the Coliseum with

Seymour Hicks 11; Birmingham Repertory Theatre 13; served in R.N.V.R. First World War 14-18; Pres. British Actors' Equity Association; principal stage appearances in London: *R. E. Lee* 23, *The Terror* 27, *The Nelson Touch* 31, *The Voysey Inheritance*, *St. Joan*, *Bird in Hand* 34, *Heroes Don't Care*, *Waste* 36, *Yes and No* 37, *The Flashing Stream* 38, *Scandal at Barchester* 44, *Daphne Laureola* 49, *First Person Singular* 52, *Spider's Web* 54-56, *The Chalk Garden* 56; appeared on N.Y. stage, 22, 25, 39 and 53-54; principal films: *Tudor Rose*, *Victoria the Great*, *The Demi-Paradise*, *Henry V*, *Mr. Emmanuel*, *The Ghosts of Berkeley Square*, *Hamlet*, *Prince of Foxes*, *Quo Vadis*, *Ivanhoe*, *Knights of the Round Table*, *St. Joan*, *Captain Dreyfus*, *Separate Tables*, *The Doctor's Dilemma*, *Never Take Sweets from a Stranger*, *From the Terrace*, *Exodus*, *The Boys*, *Becket*, *The Chalk Garden*.
Publs. *Dickens Incognito* 59, *The Drood Case* 64.
6 Painshill House, Cobham, Surrey, England.
Telephone: Cobham (Surrey) 2463.

Aymond, Alphonse Henry, A.B., J.D.; American lawyer and public utilities official; b. 27 Sept. 1914; ed. Northwestern Univ. and Univ. of Michigan.
Admitted to Illinois Bar 39, Michigan Bar 47; with Miller, Gorham, Wescott and Adams, Chicago; 39-44 Commonwealth and Southern Corpn., New York City 46-47; Attorney, Consumers Power Co., Jackson, Mich. 46-51, Gen. Attorney 51-55, Vice-Pres. and Gen. Counsel 55-57, Exec. Vice-Pres. and Dir. 57-60, Chair. of Board and Dir. 60-; Pres. and Dir. Michigan Gas Storage Co. 60-; Dir. City Bank and Trust Co., Nat. Bank of Detroit, American Seating Co., Kellogg Co., Edison Electric Inst.,; Trustee W. K. Kellogg Foundation.
Consumers Power Co., 212 W. Michigan Avenue, Jackson, Mich., U.S.A.

Ayre, Sir Wilfred, Kt.; British business executive; b. 12 April 1890; ed. South Shields and King's Coll., Newcastle upon Tyne.
Founder (with brother) Burntisland Shipbuilding Co. Ltd. 18; fmr. Pres., The Burntisland Shipbuilding Group; Chair. Burntisland Shipbuilding Co. Ltd.; Vice-Chair. and Dir. Nat. Commercial Bank of Scotland; Dir. Allen Lithographic Co. Ltd.
Priory House, Aberdour, Fife, Scotland.
Telephone: Aberdour 396.

Ayrton, Michael; British sculptor, painter and writer; b. 20 Feb. 1921; ed. London, Vienna and Paris.
Designed production John Gielgud's revival of *Macbeth* 42; taught life-drawing and theatre design, Camberwell School of Art 42-44; Art Critic of *The Spectator* 44-46; Biennial exhbns., Redfern Gallery, London 43-59; designed ballet *Le Festin de L'Araignée* (Sadlers Wells Co.) 44, opera-masque *The Fairy Queen*, Covent Garden 46, 51; Retrospective Exhbns.: Wakefield 49, Whitechapel 55; One-man Exhbns.: Milan and Rome 50, Zürich 51, Paris 52, Chicago 60, 67, Johannesburg 65, Buffalo (U.S.A.) 65, Nat. Gallery of Canada (tour) 65-67, Toronto 66, Santa Barbara 67; London: Matthieson Gallery 61, Grosvenor Gallery 64, 66.
Publs. *Golden Sections* 57, *The Testament of Daedalus* 61, *Drawings and Sculpture by Michael Ayrton* 61, 66, *The Maze Maker* 67.
Films: *The Drawings of Leonardo da Vinci* 52, *Greek Sculpture* 59.
Bradfields, Toppesfield, nr. Halstead, Essex, England.
Telephone: Great Yeldham 228.

Ayub Khan: (*see* Khan).

Ayub, Muhammad, B.A., Barrister-at-law; Pakistani diplomatist; b. 15 June 1914; ed. Univ. Coll., London, London School of Economics and Gray's Inn.
Joined Indian Civil Service 36, Asst. Commr., Punjab 36-41; Under Sec. and Dep. Sec., Dept. of Supply and Commerce, Govt. of India 42-47; Dep. Sec. and Jt. Sec., Ministries of Commerce, Kashmir Affairs and Finance, Govt. of Pakistan 47-54; Sec. Adviser, Pakistan Del. to UN 47-52; Eisenhower Exchange Fellowship 54-55; Dir. Pakistan Industrial Development Corpn. 55-60; Sec. Ministry of Finance, Govt. of Pakistan 60-61; Ambassador to Fed. Germany 61-64, to European Econ. Community 62-67, to Belgium and Luxembourg 64-67, to European Coal and Steel Community 64-67; Perm. Rep. to European Office of UN and specialized Agencies in Geneva 65-67; Exec. Dir. World Bank 67-; All-India Table Tennis Champion 35-36; M.B.E., Star of the Quaid-i-Azam.
Publ. *United Nations at Work* 52.
International Bank for Reconstruction and Development, 1818 H Street, N.W., Washington, D.C., U.S.A.
Home: Piracha Street, Bhera, West Pakistan.

Ayyanger, M. Ananthasayanam, B.A., B.L.; Indian politician; b. 4 Feb. 1891; ed. Pachiappa's Coll., Madras and Madras Law Coll.
Mathematics Teacher 12-13; Advocate, Madras High Court and Supreme Court of India 15-52; Editor *Shri Venkatesa Patrika* 18-30; imprisoned at various times for political activities, involved in "Quit India" Movement 42-44; mem. Municipal Council, Chittoor District, Fiscal Commission, Central Advisory Board of Education, Andhra Provincial Congress Cttee.; Dir. District Co-operative Central Bank, Chittoor; Chair. Criminal Tribes Enquiry Cttee. and Cttee. for the Establishment of an All-India Trades Certificate Board; Pres. Harijan Sevak Sangh, Chittoor, Chittoor District Congress Cttee., Chittoor Bar Asscn.; former mem. Constituent Assembly, Deputy Speaker and mem. Steering Cttee.; Dep. Speaker, Lok Sabha 52-56, Speaker 56-62; Gov. of Bihar 62-67; Chair. Estimates Cttee. 50-54; Pres. Indian Asscn. for a World Fed. Govt.; Del. to Commonwealth Parl. Conf. Ottawa 52; Leader Indian Parl. Del. to China 56; Chair. Commonwealth Parl. Conf. 57-59; Leader Parl. del. East Europe 59, Commonwealth Parl. Conf. 59.
Publ. *Our Parliament*, *Kamala Lectures on Indian Culture*.
Tirupati, Andhra, India.

Azcárate y Flórez, Pablo de, M.A., LL.D.; Spanish jurist and diplomatist; b. 30 July 1890; ed. Institución Libre de Enseñanza, Madrid and Univs. of Madrid, Zaragoza and Paris.
Prof. of Administrative Law Santiago de Compostela Univ. 13, Granada 15; mem. Spanish Parl. 18-19; mem. staff L.N. 22; Dir. Administrative and Minorities Section of Secretariat 29-33; Deputy Sec.-Gen. 33-36; Ambassador to Great Britain 36-39; Chair. Servicio para la Emigración de Republicanos Españoles 39-40; Hon. Sec. Juan Luis Vives Scholarship Trust 42; Dir. and Founder Instituto Español 42; Chief of U.N. Palestine Mission 48; U.N. Municipal Comm. for Jerusalem; Sec. Truce Cttee. U.N. Palestine Comm.; Principal Sec. U.N. Conciliation Comm. for Palestine 49-52.
Publs. *El Régimen Parroquial en Inglaterra* 12, *La Intervención Administrativa del Estado en los Ferrocarriles* 17, *La Guerra y los Servicios Públicos de Carácter Industrial* (Vol. 1 and 2) 21; Report on Minorities in *Encyclopædia Britannica*, *League of Nations and National Minorities, an Experiment* (Carnegie Endowment for International Peace, Washington) 44, etc., *La Intervención nazi-fascista en la guerra de España* 57, *Memoria sobre las "Vaughan Papers"* 57, *La Guerra hispano-americana de 1898* 60, *Wellington y España* 60, *Protection of Minorities* 66, *Mission to Palestine 1948-1952* 66.
19 rue Ferdinand Hodler, 1207 Geneva, Switzerland.
Telephone: 36-98-81.

Azevedo, Carlos de, M.A.; Portuguese museum administrator; b. 18; ed. Lisbon Univ.
Lecturer in Portuguese, Oxford Univ. 45-47; at Lisbon Museum of Ancient Art 48-50; carried out official survey of Portuguese monuments in India 51; Curator, Lisbon Museum of Contemporary Art 55-; Exec. Sec. Fulbright Comm. in Portugal 60-; rep. of *The Connoisseur* in Portugal 54-; mem. Acad. Int. de la Céramique; Fellow Royal Soc. of Arts (London).
Publs. Two books on Portuguese colonial architecture.
Rua Alexandre Herculano 17-3°, D, Lisbon, Portugal.

Azgur, Zair Isaakovich; Soviet monumental and portrait sculptor; b. 08; ed. Leningrad Acad. of Arts and Kiev Arts Inst.
Known for his busts of revolutionary figures (*F. Dzerzhinsky, Gracchus Baboeuf*) 31-33, of figures of the Second World War and leading Soviet statesmen, workers, artists and scientists; mem. Acad. of Arts of the U.S.S.R.; State prizewinner; People's Artist of the Byelorussian S.S.R.; Gold Medal, Exhibition to celebrate 40th anniversary of the Soviet Revolution; Brussels Int. Exhibition 58.
Byelorussian Artists' Union, Minsk, U.S.S.R.

Azhaev, Vasilii Nikolaevich; Soviet writer; b. 15; ed. Writers' Union Literature Inst. 44.
Editor *Soviet Literature*; State prizewinner, Order of Red Banner of Labour 65.
Publs. *Gold* 48, *Far from Moscow* 48, *Foreword to Life* 62, *In Search of Happiness* (stories) 65, *The Third is Superfluous* 67, and other novels.
(*Died, April* 1968.)

Azhari, Ismail al-; Sudanese politician; b. 1900; ed. Gordon Coll., Khartoum, and American Univ. of Beirut. Grandson of Sayed Ismail al-Azhari, Mufti of the Sudan; served Dept. of Education, Sudan Govt. 21-46; Sec. Graduates Congress 39, Pres. 40; visited U.S. 47 concerning dispute between U.K. and Egypt raised with UN; Pres. Nat. Unionist Party 52- (fmrly. Ashiqqa Party 43); First Prime Minister of the Sudan and Minister of Interior 54-56; Minister of Defence 54-56; Pres. Supreme Council June 65-.
P.O.B. 319, Omdurman, Sudan.

Azhari, Yusuf Omar; Somali diplomatist; b. 15 May 1936; ed. law studies.
Served in various Govt. Depts.; joined Ministry of Foreign Affairs 60; First Sec., Bonn 62, Counsellor, Bonn 65; Counsellor, Washington 66-68; Amb. to U.S.A. March 68-.
Somali Embassy, 1875 Connecticut Avenue, N.W., Suite 1109, Washington, D.C., U.S.A.

Azikiwe, Rt. Hon. Nnamdi, P.C., M.A., M.SC., LL.D., D.LITT.; Nigerian politician; b. 16 Nov. 1904; ed. Lincoln and Pennsylvania Univs.
Fmr. Instructor in History and Political Science Lincoln Univ. Pa.; fmr. Gov. Dir. African Continental Bank Ltd.; Chair. Associated Newspapers of Nigeria Ltd., African Book Co. Ltd.; Pres. Nat. Council of Nigeria and the Cameroons; Vice-Pres. Nigerian Nat. Democratic Party; elected mem. of Legislative Council of Nigeria 47-51; mem. Brooke Arbitration Tribunal 44, Nigerianisation Comm. 48, MacDonald Arbitration Tribunal 48; mem. Western House of Assembly 52-53, Eastern House 54-59; former Minister of Local Govt., Eastern Region, and Minister of Internal Affairs 55-57; Premier, Eastern Nigeria 54-59; Pres. Fed. Senate 60; Gov.-Gen. and C.-in-C. Fed. of Nigeria 60-63, President of Nigeria 63-66; Chancellor and Chair. Council of the Univ. of Nigeria 61-66.
Publs. *Liberia in World Politics* 34, *Renascent Africa* 37, *The African in Ancient and Medieval History* 38, *Land Tenure in Northern Nigeria* 42, *Political Blueprint of Nigeria* 43, *Economic Reconstruction of Nigeria* 43,
Economic Rehabilitation of Eastern Nigeria 55, *Zik: a Selection of Speeches* 61.
Onuíyi Haven, P.O.B. 7, Nsukka, Nigeria.

Azimov, Pigam Azimovich; Soviet specialist in Turkmenian language and literature; b. 1915; ed. Ashkhabad Pedagogic Inst.
Member C.P.S.U. 39-; at Ashkhabad Pedagogic Inst. 48-50; at Turkmenian State Univ. 50-63; mem. Turkmenian Acad. of Sciences 51-, Pres. 66-; several U.S.S.R. decorations.
Presidium of the Turkmenian Academy of Sciences, 15 Ulitsa Gogolya, Ashkhabad, U.S.S.R.

Azkoul, Karim, PH.D.; Lebanese diplomatist and writer; b. 15 July 1915; ed. Jesuit Univ. of St. Joseph, Beirut, and Univs. of Paris, Berlin, Bonn and Munich. Professor of History, Arab and French Literature, and Philosophy in various colls. in Lebanon 39-46; Dir. of an Arabic publishing house and monthly Arabic review *The Arab World*, Beirut 43-45; mem. Lebanese Del. to UN 47-50, Acting Perm. Del. to UN 50-53; Head of UN Affairs Dept., Ministry of Foreign Affairs 53-57; Head, Perm. Del. of Lebanon to UN 57-59; Consul-Gen. in Australia 59-61; Ambassador to Ghana, Guinea and Mali 61-64, to Iran and Afghanistan 64-66; Order of Cedar (Lebanon), Order of Holy Sepulchre (Jerusalem), Order of St. Marc (Alexandria), Order of the Brilliant Star (Republic of China), Order of Southern Star (Brazil), Order of St. Peter and Paul (Damascus).
Publs. *Reason and Faith in Islam* (in German) 38, and *Reason in Islam* (in Arabic) 46; trans. into Arabic *Consciencism* (Nkrumah) 64.
c/o Journal *Al-Safa*, Beirut, Lebanon.
Telephone: 252390.

Aznar Zubigaray, Manuel; Spanish journalist and diplomatist; b. 18 Nov. 1894; ed. Univ. de Madrid.
War Corresp. 14-18; Co-Founder and Editor *El Sol* (newspaper); Diplomatic Service 40-, served France 40-45, Washington 45-48; Ambassador to Dominican Republic 48-51, to Argentina 51-55; Editor *La Vanguardia*, Barcelona 60-63, also Int. Columnist *Blanco y Negro*, Madrid, Dir. Spanish News Agency "Efe", Pres. Press Nat. Council, Madrid; Ambassador to Morocco 63-64; Perm. Rep. to United Nations 64-.
Publs. *Military History of the Spanish Civil War* 40, *The Battle of France* 44, *Diplomatic Antecedents of the Second World War* 44, *The Alcazar will not Surrender* 42.
Permanent Mission of Spain to the United Nations, 820 Second Avenue, New York 17, N.Y., U.S.A.

Aznavour, Charles (*pseudonym* for Aznavourian, Varenagh); French singer and film star; b. 22 May 1924; ed. Ecole centrale de T.S.F., Centre de spectacle, Paris. With Jean Dasté Company 41; with Pierre Roche in *Les Fâcheux* and *Arlequin* 44; numerous song recitals in France, Europe and U.S.A.; actor in numerous films including: *La tête contre les murs* 59, *Tirez sur le pianiste* 60, *Un taxi pour Tobrouk, Le testament d'Orphée, Le Diable et les Dix Commandements, Haute-Infidélité* 64, *la Métamorphose des cloportes* 65, *Paris au mois d'août* 66, *Le facteur s'en va-t-en guerre* 66.
Film music includes: *Soupe au lait, l'Île du bout du monde, Ces dames préfèrent le mambo, Le cercle vicieux, De quoi tu te mêles Daniela, Douce Violence, Les Parisiennes;* also author and singer of numerous songs; composer of operetta *Monsieur Carnaval* 65.
124 rue La Boétie, Paris 8e, France.

Azuma, Ryotaro, M.D.; Japanese administrator; b. 93; ed. Tokyo Univ.
Studied medicine in Japan and England; Prof. Tokyo Univ. 34-53; Dir. Physical Culture School 37; Dir. Medical Affairs Bureau, Ministry of Welfare 46-51; Pres. Ibaraki Univ. 53-58; Gov. Tokyo Metropolis 59-67; Fellow, Univ. Coll., London.
1217, 2-chome, Shimoshakujii, Nerima-ku, Tokyo, Japan.

B

Ba, Ousmane; Mali politician; b. 1919; ed. African School of Medicine and Pharmacy, Dakar.
Minister of Civil Service in Govt. Council of Upper Volta 57-58; Minister Del. to Presidency in Provisional Govt. of Soudan 58-59; Minister of Labour, Civil Service and Social Affairs, Mali 59-62; Minister of the Interior, of Information and of Tourism 62-64; Minister of State for Foreign Affairs Sept. 64-Sept. 66; Minister of Foreign Affairs Sept. 66-.
Ministry of Foreign Affairs, Bamako, Mali.

Baako, Kofi; Ghanaian politician; b. 26; ed. Saltpond Roman Catholic School and St. Augustine's Coll., Cape Coast.
Teacher 45-46; pupil surveyor in Civil Service 47; subsequently Editor, Cape Coast *Daily Mail*; imprisoned for his part in "Positive Action" 50; released 51; elected Councillor, Cape Coast Town Council 52; mem. Legislative Assembly 54-; former Minister without Portfolio and Govt. Chief Whip; fmr. Minister of Information, African Affairs, Education; Minister of Establishments and Presidential Affairs 60-61; Minister of State for Parl. Affairs and Leader of the Nat. Assembly May 61-Oct. 61; Minister of Defence Oct. 61-65.
c/o Ministry of Defence, Accra, Ghana.

Baba, Corneliu; Romanian artist; b. 1906; ed. Bucharest Univ. and Inst. of Fine Arts, Jassy.
Teacher Inst. of Fine Arts, Jassy, and N. Grigorescu Inst. of Fine Arts, Bucharest; First official exhbn. 40; numerous official exhbns. in Romania, Moscow, Venice, Vienna, Prague, Warsaw, Rome, Sofia, etc. 44-; Hon. mem. U.S.S.R. Acad. of Art 58-; Corresp. mem. Acad. Socialist Republic of Romania 63, Acad. of Arts, Berlin 64; People's Artist 62, State Prizewinner 53, 54.
Major works: *Odihna la Cimp* (Homecoming from the Fields) 54, *Intoarcerea de la Sapă* (Coming Back from Maize Hoeing) 42, *Tǎranii* (Peasants) 58, *Otelaru* (Steelworkers) 60, portraits of M. Sadoveanu, Lucia Sturza Bulandra, Tudor Arghezi and his wife, and book illustrations.
Uniunea Artistilor Plastici Bucureşti, Calea Victoriei 155, Bucharest, Romania.

Babaevsky, Semyon Petrovich; Soviet writer; b. 09; ed. Moscow Literary Inst.
Member Communist Party of Soviet Union 39-, war corresp. 41-45; Deputy to Supreme Soviet 50, 54; mem. Board U.S.S.R. Union of Writers; State Prizewinner 48, 49, 50; Order of Red Banner of Labour 59.
Publs. Novels: *Cavalier of the Golden Star, Geese Island* 47, *Light over the Earth* 49, *Well-Spring Grove* 56, *White Mosque, Sukhaya Buivola* 58, *Along Paths and Roads* 59, *Son's Mutiny* 61, *Native Land* 65.
U.S.S.R. Union of Writers, 52 Vorovsky Street, Moscow, U.S.S.R.

Babajanyan, Arno Arutyunovich; Soviet composer; b. 1921; ed. Erevan and Moscow Conservatoires.
Assistant Prof. at Erevan Conservatoire 56; State Prize 51, Honoured Worker of Arts of Armenian S.S.R. 56, People's Artist of Armenian S.S.R. 62.
Principal works: Variations for Piano 37, Prelude 39, Sonata for Piano 43, *Dance Vagarshapat* 44, Polyphonic Sonata for Piano 46, Heroic Ballade for Piano and Orchestra 42, Sonata for Violin and Piano 59, *My Heart is in the Mountains* (operetta) 62; variety, jazz, film and theatre music.
Armenian Composers' Union, Ulitsa Demerchana, Erevan, U.S.S.R.

Babanova, Mariya Ivanovna; Soviet actress; b. 1900.
Started work at M.E. Meyerhold theatre later known as Mayakovsky Theatre 20; People's Artist of the Soviet Union; State prize; most important parts Polina (*Profitable Post*—A. N. Ostrovsky), Goga (*A Man with a Portmanteau*—A. M. Faiko), Juliet (*Romeo and Juliet*), Countess Diana (*A Dog on the Loft*—Lope de Vega), Tanya (*Tanya*—A. N. Arbuzov), Sofia (*Zykovy*—M. Gorky), Ranevskaya (*The Cherry Orchard*—Chekhov), Maggy (*What Every Woman Knows*—Barrie), Kay (*A Woman's Life*—K. Morimoto), Mary (*Mary October*—Duvilie).
Moscow Mayakovsky Theatre, 19 Ulitsa Herzena, Moscow, U.S.S.R.

Babarin, Evgeny Ivanovich; Soviet foreign trade official; b. 1907; ed. Moscow Textile Inst.
Member C.P.S.U. 30-; Deputy Commercial Rep., later Commercial Rep. of U.S.S.R. in Germany 39-41; Chair. *Exportlyon* 41-45, 47-48; official, Ministry of Foreign Trade 45-47; U.S.S.R. Commercial Rep. in Poland 48-52, 61-; Comecon Counsellor 52-53, 60-61; Counsellor, Soviet Embassy, Poland 53-58; Chair. *Tekhnopromexport* 58-60; Order of Lenin, Order of Red Banner of Labour, Badge of Honour.
U.S.S.R. Commercial Representation, Warsaw, Poland.

Babayev, Sabir; Soviet composer; b. 1920; ed. Tashkent Conservatoire.
Executive mem. Uzbek Composers' Union; Sec. Soviet Composers' Union.
Principal works: Two Suites for Symphony Orch. 46-48, Two Poems and *Festival Overture* for folk instrument orch. 50-52; Concerto for chang (Uzbek folk instrument) and orch. of folk instruments 52; Cantata, *Cotton Farmers of Uzbekistan* 55, *Segokh* (symphonic poem on folk themes) 56; *Love of Motherland* (musical drama) 57, *During the Festival* (symphonic poem) 58, *Khamza* (opera) 61, *Uzbek Poetic Songs* 66.
Uzbek Composers' Union, Tashkent, U.S.S.R.

Babcock, Horace W., PH.D.; American astronomer; b. 13 Sept. 1912; ed. California Inst. of Technology and Univ. of California.
Instructor, Yerkes and McDonald Observatories 39-41; Staff mem. Radiation Laboratory, Mass. Inst of Technology 41-42; Staff mem. Office of Scientific Research and Devt. Project, Calif. Inst. of Technology 42-45; Staff mem. Mount Wilson and Palomar Observatories 46-, Asst. Dir. 57-64, Dir. 64-; mem. Nat. Acad. of Sciences, American Philosophical Soc., American Acad. of Arts and Sciences; Draper Medal 57, Eddington Medal, Royal Astronomical Soc. 57; Hon. Sc.D.
Publs. Articles in scientific and technical journals, mainly on magnetic fields of the sun and stars, theory of the sun's magnetic field, rotation of the spiral galaxy in Andromeda, ruling of diffraction gratings, astronomical instrumentation.
Mount Wilson and Palomar Observatories, 813 Santa Barbara Street, Pasadena, Calif. 91106, U.S.A.

Babics, Antal, DR. MED.; Hungarian surgeon and urologist; b. 1902.
Lecturer, Urological Clinic, Budapest Medical Univ. 40, Prof. and Dir. of Clinic 45-; Corresp. mem. Hungarian Acad. of Sciences 49-50, mem. 50-; Sec. Medical Dept., Hungarian Acad. of Sciences; mem. Presidium Int. Urological Soc.; Hon. mem. Soviet Soc. of Surgeons, Urological Soc. of Italy and Romania, Purkinje Soc. of Czechoslovakia, Soviet Medical Acad.; Kossuth Prize 51.
Publs. include: *Urology* 52, *The Theory and Clinical Aspects of Kidney Necrosis* 52.
Medical University, Budapest; and Budapest II, Gyergyó-utca 5, Hungary.
Telephone: 355-109.

Babin, Jean; French professor; b. 26 Feb. 1905; ed. Univ. de Nancy.
High School teacher 27-29, Lycée Asst. 29-33, Prof. 33-41; School Inspector 41-47; Dir. of Education in the Saar 47-48; Prof. Faculty of Letters, Lille Univ. 48-55; Rector, Acad. de Strasbourg 55-58, Acad. de Bordeaux 60-; Dir. du Centre Nat. des Œuvres Univs. 58-60; Officier de la Légion d'Honneur, Commdr. Ordre des Palmes Acad.
Publs. (with A. Babin) *Du Français au latin et aux langues vivantes par l'analyse* 36, *Les lieux-dits de la Commune de Boureuilles (Meuse)* 52, *Le toponymiste dans la mine* 53, *Les lieux-dits de la mer* 54, *Les parlers de l'Argonne* 55.
29 Cours D'Albret, Bordeaux, France.
Telephone: 52-44-75.

Babington Smith, Michael James, C.B.E.; British banking executive; b. 20 March 1901; ed. Eton and Trinity Coll., Cambridge.
Director, Glyn, Mills & Co. (fmr. Deputy Chair.), Bank of England, Bank for Int. Settlements, Associated Electrical Industries Ltd., and other companies; Sheriff of London 53.
10 Chester Row, London, S.W.1, England.

Baboin, Robert; French industrialist; b. 11 Oct. 1901; ed. Ecole Polytechnique de Paris.
Vice-Pres. Union Sidérurgique Lorraine (Sidélor), D.A.V.U.M., Soc. des Forges et Laminoirs de Jemmapes, Soc. Métallurgique de Champagne, Charbonnages de Beeringen; Dir. Groupement de l'Industrie Sidérurgique (GIS), Charbonnages Limbourg-Meuse, Hauts Fournaux et Forges d'Allevard, Comptoir des Combustible d'Alsace et de Lorraine, Soc. Alsacienne de Navigation Rhénane, Actuma, Cie. des Tubes de Normandie, Soc. Int. de la Moselle, Cie. Générale d'Electricité.
1 rue Georges-Berger, Paris 17e, France.

Babotchkin, Boris Andreevich; Soviet theatre and cinema actor and director; b. 1904; ed. Moscow Youth Studio.
Acted in provincial theatres 21-27, Leningrad theatres 27-40, Moscow theatres 40-48, Maly Theatre, Moscow 48-51, 55-; leading roles: Khlestakov in *The Inspector General* by Gogol, and Chatsky in *Wit Works Woe* by Griboedov; mem. C.P.S.U.; film roles include: *Chapaev* (Chapaev), etc.; State prizewinner for work in films 41, 57, Order of Lenin, Order of the Red Banner of Labour, People's Artist of the U.S.S.R.
Maly Theatre, 1/6 Ploshchad Sverdlova, Moscow, U.S.S.R.

Bacall, Lauren; American actress; b. 16 Sept. 1924.
Films since 42 include *To Have and Have Not, The Big Sleep, Confidential Agent, Dark Passage, Key Largo, Young Man with a Horn, Bright Leaf, How to Marry a Millionaire, Woman's World, The Cobweb, Blood Alley, Written on the Wind, Designing Woman, The Gift of Love, Flame over India, Sex and the Single Girl.*
c/o John Springer Assoc. Inc., 667 Madison Avenue, New York City 21, U.S.A.

Bacchelli, Riccardo; Italian writer; b. 19 April 1891.
Member Accad. Naz. dei Lincei, Accademia della Crusca, Florence, Accademia delle Scienze, Bologna, Accademia delle Scienze, Ferrara; Grand Officer of Italian Republic 53, Dott. h.c. Univs. of Bologna and Milan.
Publs. *Poemi lirici* 14, *Lo sa il tonno* 24, *Il diavolo al Pontelungo* 27, *Amore di poesia* 30, *La Congiura di Don Giulio d'Este* 31, *Oggi, domani e mai* 32, *Mal d'Africa* 34, *Iride* 37, *Il Mulino del Po* 38-40, *Gioacchino Rossini* 41, *Il Fiore della Mirabilis* 42, *Il Pianto del Figlio di Lais* 45, *Lo Sguardo di Gesù* 48, *L'Alba dell'Ultima Sera* 49, *La Cometa* 51, *Italia per terra e per mare* 52, *L'incendio di Milano* 52, *Memorie del Tempo Presente* 53, *Il Figlio*

di Stalin 53, *Tre giorni di passione* 55, *Nel fiume della Storia* 55, *Amleto* 56, *I tre schiavi di Giulio Cesare* 57, *Viaggio in Grecia* 59, *Non ti chiamerò più padre* 59, *Leopardi e Manzoni* 60, *Viaggi all'estero e vaggabondaggi di fantasia* 66, *Giorno per giorno 1912-1922* 66, *America in confidenza* 66, *Rapporto segreto* 67.
Borgonuovo 20, Milan, Italy.

Bacci, H.E. Cardinal Antonio; Vatican ecclesiastic; b. 4 Sept. 1885.
Former Secretary of Briefs to Princes; Protonotary Apostolic 54; created Cardinal by Pope John XXIII 60.
The Vatican, Rome, Italy.

Bacewicz, Grazyna; Polish composer and violinist; b. 13.
Studied in Warsaw and Paris; Prof. Łódź Conservatoire 34-35, 45-46; Vice-Pres. Union of Polish Composers 59-; Warsaw City Musical Prize 49; two State prizes 50, 52; prizes at I and II Festivals of Polish Music 51, 55; 1st prize International Composers Competition, Liège 51, 2nd prize 56, UNESCO Prize 60, Union of Polish Composers Prize 60, State Prize 62, Prix du Gouvernement Belge and Gold Medal, Brussels 65.
Compositions include four symphonies 45, 50, 52, 53, overture for symphony orchestra 43, concerto for string orchestra 48, seven violin concertos 38, 45, 52, 54, 56, 65, piano concerto 49, seven string quartets 38, 42, 47, 51, 55, 60, 65, two quintets for piano and string quartet 52, 65, piano studies 57, radio comic opera 59, music for strings, trumpets and percussion 59, *Pensieri Notturni* for orchestra 61, five sonatas for violin and piano, concerto for orchestra 62, two concertos for cello and orchestra, quartet for four cellos 63, cantata for celebrations of 600th Anniversary of Jagiellonian Univ., Cracow 64; *Musica* in three movements for symphony orchestra 64; comic ballet *Esik in Ostende* 64, *Contradizione* (ensemble for 15 persons) 66, concerto for two pianos and orchestra 66; *In una parte* for orchestra 67; Concerto for viola and orchestra 67.
Mochnackiego 4, Warsaw, Poland.
Telephone: 22-08-82.

Bach, Wilhelm Franz-Josef, DR. ING.; German engineer and diplomatist; b. 4 Feb. 1917; ed. Technical Univs. of Aachen, Berlin and Brunswick.
Assistant Prof. of Aerodynamics, Technical Univ., Aachen 42-45; Deputy Chief Editor *Aachener Volkszeitung* 47-50; Diplomatic Service 51-, Canberra, Washington 52-57; Personal Asst. to German Chancellor (Dr. Adenauer) 57-61; Consul-Gen., Hong Kong 61-64; Ambassador to Iran 64-; numerous decorations.
Publ. *Pressure distribution on objects flying with supersonic velocity.*
Embassy of the German Federal Republic, P.O. Box 48, Teheran, Iran.

Bachauer, Gina; British (b. Greek) pianist; b. 21 May 1913; ed. Athens Coll., Athens Conservatoire of Music, and Ecole Normale, Paris under Cortot and Rachmaninov.
Debut Athens Symphony Orchestra, conductor Mitropoulos 35; more than 600 concerts for Allied Forces 40-46; Debut in London 47 and in New York 50; annual concert tours in America 51-, also in Australia, Belgium, Canada, Cuba, Cyprus, Finland, France, Greece, Ireland, Israel, Italy, Netherlands, New Zealand, Norway, Portugal, Romania, South Africa, Spain, Sweden, Switzerland, U.K., Venezuela and Yugoslavia; Order of Golden Phoenix and Commdr. Order of Welfare (Greece); Prize, Vienna Int. Piano Competition 33.
41 Highgate West Hill, London, N.6, England.

Bachawat, Ranadhir Singh; Indian judge; b. 18 July 1907; ed. St. Xavier's Coll., Calcutta, Calcutta Univ., and Inner Temple, London.
Called to Bar, Inner Temple, London 31; Advocate,

Calcutta High Court 31; Judge, Calcutta High Court 50-64; Judge, Supreme Court of India 64-.
Supreme Court, New Delhi, India.

Bacher, Robert Fox, B.S., PH.D.; American physicist; b. 31 Aug. 1905; ed. Univ. of Michigan.
Nat. Research Fellow Physics, Calif. Inst. of Technology 30-31; Mass. Inst. of Technology 31-32; Alfred Lloyd Fellow Univ. of Michigan 32-33; Instr. Columbia Univ. 34-35; Instructor to Prof., Cornell Univ. 35-49; Radiation Laboratory, Mass. Inst. of Technology 40-45 (on leave 43-45); Los Alamos Laboratory, Atomic Bomb Project 43-Jan. 46; Dir. of Laboratory of Nuclear Studies, Cornell Univ. 46; mem. U.S. Atomic Energy Comm. 46-49; Prof. of Physics, Calif. Inst. of Technology 49-, Chair. Div. of Physics, Mathematics and Astronomy 49-62, Provost 62-; mem. President's Science Advisory Cttee. 57-60, Consultant 60-; Trustee Carnegie Corpn., Inst. for Defense Analyses, Universities Research Asscn. Inc., Atoms for Peace Awards, Rand Corpn. 50-60; Dir. Detroit Edison Co., Bell & Howell Co., TRW Inc., Power Reactor Devt. 60; mem. Nat. Acad. of Sciences, American Philosophical Soc., American Acad. of Arts and Sciences, American Physical Soc. (Pres. 64), American Asscn. for Advancement of Science, American Asscn. of Univ. Profs.; awarded Medal for Merit by Pres. Truman Jan. 46.
Publ. *Atomic Energy States* (with S. Goudsmit) 32.
California Institute of Technology, Pasadena, Calif. 91109; and 345 South Michigan Avenue, Pasadena, Calif. 91106, U.S.A.

Bachmann, Ingeborg; Austrian writer; b. 1926; ed. in Innsbruck, Graz and Vienna.
Worked for Rot-Weiss-Rot radio station, Vienna, in early 'fifties; lived in Rome 53-57, Naples 54; travelled to Paris and U.S.A.; lived in Munich 57-58, later in Zürich; Visiting Prof. of Poetry, Univ. of Frankfurt 59-60; lived in Berlin 63-64; Büchner Preis 64.
Publs. *Die gestundete Zeit* (poetry) 53, *Zikaden* (radio play) 54, *Anrufung des grossen Bären* (poetry—awarded Bremer Literature Prize) 56, *Der gute Gott von Manhattan* (radio play—awarded Hörspielpreis der Kriegsblinden) 58, *Das dreissigste Jahr* (short stories—awarded Deutscher Kritikerpreis) 61, *Ein Ort für Zufälle* 65, librettos for ballet *Der Idiot* (Henze) 52, opera *Der Prinz von Homburg* (Henze) 60, opera *Der Junge Lord* (Henze) 64.
c/o R. Piper & Co. Verlag, 8 Munich 13, Georgenstrasse 4, German Federal Republic; Via Bocca di Leone 60, Rome, Italy.

Backhaus, Wilhelm; German pianist; b. 26 March 1884; ed. Leipzig Conservatoire.
Studied with Reckendorf, d'Albert and von Siloti; numerous tours in Europe, North and South America and Australia 02-; Prof. Manchester (England) Royal Coll. of Music 05-08; Hon. mem. Konzerthaus-Gesellschaft, Gesellschaft der Musikfreunde, Vienna and Accad. Filarmonica, Rome; numerous recordings; Rubinstein Prize, Paris 05, Bösendorfer Ring 53.
Villa Wellingtonia, Lugano, Switzerland.

Backstrand, Clifford J., A.B., B.S.; American business executive; b. 21 July 1897; ed. Riverside Polytechnic High School, Pomona Coll. and Univ. of Pennsylvania.
Joined Armstrong Cork Co. as student salesman 21, Dir. 35-, Vice-Pres. 38-42, Vice-Pres. attached to President's Office 42-45, First Vice-Pres. 45-50, Pres. 50-62, Chair. 62-68; Dir. Hamilton Watch Co. 45-65, Bell Telephone Co. of Pa. 53-, Pittsburgh Plate Glass Co. 58-65, Nat. Asscn. of Manufacturers 59-66; Hon. LL.D. Elizabethtown Coll., Pomona Coll., Bucknell Univ.; Hon. D.C.S., Franklin and Marshall Coll., Lancaster. 1267 Wheatland Avenue, Lancaster, Pa. 17603, U.S.A.
Telephone: 392-5017.

Backus, John Warner, A.M.; American computer programmer and mathematician; b. 3 Dec. 1924; ed. Columbia Univ.
Research Staff mem., Thomas J. Watson Research Center 59-63; I.B.M. Fellow 63-; W. W. McDowell Award, Inst. of Electrical and Electronics Engineers 67.
Publs. *Systems Design of the IBM 704 Computer* (with G. M. Amdahl) 54, *The Fortran Automatic Coding System* (with others) 57, *The Syntax and Semantics of the Proposed International Algebraic Language of the Zürich ACM-GAMM Conference* 59, *Report on the Algorithmic Language ALGOL 60* (with others) 60.
400 Upper Terrace, San Francisco, California 94117, U.S.A.
Telephone: 415-731-8155.

Bacon, Edmund Norwood, B.ARCH.; American architect and planner; b. 5 Feb. 1910; ed. Cornell Univ. and Cranbrook Acad.
Architectural Designer, Shanghai, China 34; housing projects for W. Pope Barney, Architect, Philadelphia 35; Supervisor of City Planning, Flint (Michigan) Inst. of Research and Planning; Man. Dir. Philadelphia Housing Asscn. 40-43; Co-Designer Better Philadelphia Exhibition and Senior Land Planner, Philadelphia City Planning Comm.; Exec. Dir. Philadelphia City Planning Comm. 49-; Professional Adviser, Franklin Delano Roosevelt Memorial Competition 59; mem. President's Citizens' Advisory Cttee. on Recreation and Natural Beauty 66; numerous awards.
Publ. *Design of Cities* 67.
Philadelphia City Planning Commission, 13th Floor, City Hall Annex, S.E. Corner Juniper and Filbert Streets, Philadelphia, Pennsylvania 19107, U.S.A.
Telephone: MUnicipal 6-4600.

Bacon, Francis; Irish painter; b. 10.
Began to teach himself to paint 30; first One-Man Shows London 49, New York 53; exhibited at Venice Biennale 54; rep. at Brussels Int. Exhbn. 58; important works include: *Studies for a Larger Composition* 45, *Study after Velasquez* 51, *Mad Dog* 52 (all in Tate Gallery, London); *Painting* 46, *Dog* 52 (both in New York Museum of Modern Art); *Studies of the Human Body* 49 (Nat. Gallery of Victoria, Melbourne, Australia); Retrospective Exhibition Tate Gallery, London 62; exhibition New London Gallery 63, Solomon Guggenheim Museum, N.Y. 63, Galerie Maeght, Paris 66, Marlborough New London Gallery 67; Rubens Prize, City of Siegen 66.
c/o Marlborough Fine Art Ltd., 39 Old Bond Street, London, W.1, England.

Bacon, Francis Thomas, O.B.E., M.A., A.M.I.MECH.E.; British mechanical engineer; b. 21 Dec. 1904; ed. Eton and Trinity Coll., Cambridge.
With C. A. Parsons & Co., Newcastle-on-Tyne 25-40; anti-submarine work for Admiralty in Second World War; research on Hydrox Fuel Cell, Cambridge Univ. 46-56; consultant to Nat. Research Development Corpn. on development of Hydrox Fuel Cells, Cambridge 57-62; consultant to Energy Conversion Ltd. 62-; S. G. Brown Award (Royal Soc.) 65.
Westfield, Little Shelford, Cambs., England.
Telephone: Shelford 2244.

Bacon, Paul; French politician; b. 1 Nov. 1907; ed. Ecole Professionnelle de Pau.
Began career as furniture designer 23-27; mem. Gen. Secrétariat Jeunesse Ouvrière Chrétienne 27-37; Chief Editor of *Monde Ouvrier* 37-39; served French Army 39-40; Dir. of *Syndicalisme* (organ of Confédération Française des Travailleurs Chrétiens) 45; Deputy (M.R.P.) 46-; Sec. to Presidency of Council 49-50; Minister of Labour and Social Security, Bidault, Queuille, Pleven, Queuille, Pleven, Faure Cabinets 50-52, Mayer Cabinet 53, Laniel Cabinet 53-54, Faure Cabinet 55-56, Gaillard Cabinet 57-58; Minister without Portfolio, subsequently Minister of Labour, de Gaulle

Cabinet 58; Minister of Labour, Debré Cabinet 59-May 62, Pompidou Cabinet 62; mem. Conseil Economique et Social 63; Dir. Turin Int. Centre for Advanced Technical and Vocational Training, Int. Labour Org. (I.L.O.) 64-67; Chair. Centre d'Etude des Revenus et des Coûts (Commissariat-Gén. du Plan) 67-.
Publs. *La Naissance de la Classe Ouvrière, Vers la Réforme de l'Entreprise Capitaliste, La Démocratie Economique et Sociale.*
23 avenue Balzac, La Varenne-St.-Hilaire (Val de Marne); and C.E.R.C., 30 rue Las Cases, Paris 7e, France.

Badeau, John Stothoff, B.SC., S.T.M., LL.D., D.D.; American educationist; b. 24 Feb. 1903; ed. Union, Rutgers and Columbia Univs. and Union Theological Seminary.
Teacher, Long Island 24-25; ordained, Reformed Church in America 28; Missionary, United Mission in Mesopotamia, Mosul, Iraq 28-35; Asst. Prof. of Philosophy and Dean, Faculty of Arts and Sciences, American Univ. at Cairo 36; Regional Chief, Middle East, O.W.I. 43; Pres. American Univ. at Cairo 45-53; Pres. Near East Foundation 53-61; Ambassador to United Arab Republic 61-64; Dir. Near and Middle East Inst., Columbia Univ. 64-.
Publs. *East and West of Suez* 43, *Emergence of Modern Egypt* 53, *The Lands Between* 58.
Columbia Univ., New York, N.Y., U.S.A.

Baden-Powell, Olave, Lady (Olave St. Clair), G.B.E.; British Chief Guide; b. 22 Feb. 1889; ed. privately.
Chief Guide of the British Commonwealth 17; World Chief Guide 30-; widow of Lord Baden-Powell, the founder of the Boy Scout and Girl Guide Movements; Grand Cross of the British Empire, Order of the Phoenix of Greece, Order of White Rose of Finland, decorations from Haiti, Peru and Panama, Order of the Sacred Treasure of Japan.
Publ. *Baden-Powell* 64.
Hampton Court Palace, East Molesey, Surrey, England.

Badings, Henk, Prof. Ing.; Netherlands composer; b. 17 Jan. 1907; ed. Tech. Univ., Delft.
Asst. in Palaeontology, Tech. Univ., Delft 31; first symphony performed in Amsterdam 30; Prof. of Composition, Rotterdam Conservatoire 34-37; Co.-Dir. Musical Lyceum, Amsterdam 37-41; Dir. State Conservatoire, The Hague 41-45; musical composition 45-; Dir. Electronic Music Studio, Univ. of Utrecht 61-64, Prof. of acoustics and information 64-; Prof. of Musical Composition, Musikhochschule, Stuttgart 62-; Paganini Prize 53, Italia Prize 54; Marzotto Prize 64; mem. Royal Flemish Acad. of Art; Hon. Citizen of New Martinsville, W. Virginia, U.S.A.
Compositions: twelve symphonies, chamber music, choral works, operas, etc., as well as electronic music.
Einsiedelstrasse 14, 7405 Dettenhausen, German Federal Republic.
Telephone: 0711-246041; 07157-2887.

Badura-Skoda, Paul; Austrian pianist; b. 6 Oct. 1927; ed. Realgymnasium der Schottenbastei, Konservatorium der Stadt Wien, and Edwin Fischer's Master Class in Lucerne.
Regular concerts since 48; tours all over the world as soloist and with leading orchestras; yearly master classes with Vienna and Edinburgh Festivals -66; artist in residence, Univ. of Wisconsin, master classes in Madison, Wisconsin 66-; First Prize Austrian Music Competition 47, Second Prize Budapest 48.
Compositions: *A Mass in D, Cadenzas to Piano and Violin Concertos by Mozart and Haydn.*
Publ. Co-author *Interpreting Mozart on the Keyboard;* Editions of Schubert.
1217 Seminole Highway, Madison, Wis. 53711, U.S.A.

Baer, Francis Shaw, B.A.; American banker; b. 9 March 1893; ed. Occidental Coll., Calif.
Vice-Pres. Hunter Dulin Co., Los Angeles 22-24; Pres. Baer-Brown-Parsons Co., Los Angeles 24-29; Vice-Pres. Security-First Nat. Co., Los Angeles 29-30; Pres. Pacific Co., Los Angeles 30-34, Pacific Finance Co., Los Angeles 34-42; Vice-Chair. Bank of America Nat. Trust and Savings Asscn. 42-45; Senior Vice-Chair. Bd., Bank of America 45-49; Senior Vice-Pres. and mem. Exec. Cttee., Bankers Trust Co., N.Y. 49-55, Exec. Vice-Pres. 55-56, Chair. Exec. Cttee. 56-58; Chair. Bd., First Western Bank & Trust Co., San Francisco 59-61, United Calif. Bank 61-68, Hon. Chair. 68-.
405 Montgomery Street, San Francisco, Calif. 94104, U.S.A.

Baerdemaeker, Adolphe de, D. en D.; Belgian diplomatist; b. 28 Oct. 1920; ed. Univ. Catholique de Louvain.
Economic Surveys Branch, Ministry of Econ. Affairs 43; Attaché, Econ. and Financial Affairs, Belgian Embassy, London 45; Deputy Sec.-Gen. Brussels Treaty Org., London 50; Deputy Sec. NATO Council, London, and Sec. of Econ. and Financial Bureau, Paris 51-52; Counsellor, Private Office of Minister of Econ. Affairs 52-54; Counsellor, Econ. Questions, Vice-Chair. OEEC Econ. Cttee., Belgian Dels. to NATO and OEEC, Paris 54-58; Dir., Gen. Directorate of External Relations, European Econ. Community 58; Perm. EEC Del. to OECD 66-.
129 avenue Malakoff, Paris 16e, France.

Baeyens, Jacques Ferdinand Marcel Georges; French diplomatist; b. 14 April 1905; ed. Ecole Libre des Sciences Politiques.
Diplomatic Service, Bucharest 30-33, Tokyo 33-38, Washington 38-43, Tunis 43-45; Counsellor, San Francisco 45-46, Shanghai 46-47; Ministry of Foreign Affairs 47-52; Ambassador to Chile 52-53; Chief of Press and Information, Ministry of Foreign Affairs 53-54; Ambassador to Ethiopia 55-56; Consul-Gen., New York 57-58; Dir. of American Affairs, Ministry of Foreign Affairs 58-60; Ambassador to Brazil 60-64, to Greece 64-.
French Embassy, 7 Léoforos Vassilissis Sofias, Athens, Greece.

Baez-Camargo, Gonzalo; Mexican teacher; b. 13 Nov. 1899; ed. Methodist Mexican Inst., Union Evangelical Seminary, Mexico, and Nat. Univ., Mexico.
Vice-President Methodist Mexican Inst., Puebla 27; Exec. Sec. and Gen. Sec. on Christian Education, Evangelical Council of Mexico 29-41; Manager Union Publishing House 31-46; Prof. Christian Literature and Journalism 41-61, Old Testament 62, Hebrew 63-, Union Evangelical Seminary; Sec. Cttee. on Literature, Cttee. on Co-operation in Latin America 46-60; Prof. Modern Ideologies, Presbyterian Seminary 63; Prof. Spanish, Iberoamerican Univ. 64-; Prof. Old Testament, Baptist Seminary 64; Prof. Old Testament, Lutheran Seminary 66; mem. Editorial Cttee., New Spanish Version of the Bible 60-.
Publs. *Hacia la Renovación Religiosa en Hispano-américa* 30, *Principios y Método de la Educación Cristiana* 32, *Religion in the Republic of Mexico* (co-author) 35, *Baltasar Gracián y Morales* 44, *El Artista y Otros Poemas* 46, *Biografía de un templo* 53, *Tres poemas* 51, *La Nota Evangélica en la Poesía Hispanoamericana* 60, *Protestantes enjuiciados por la Inquisición en Iberoamérica* 60, *El Comunismo el cristianismo y los cristianos* 60, *Genio y espíritu del metodismo wesleyano* 62; under pseudonym of "Pedro Gringoire": *La Superstición de la Sangre "Aria"* 42, *Martin Niemoeller* 38, *Un Prefacio a la Educación para la Libertad* 46, *Las manos de Cristo* 50, *Los manuscritos de Qumrán* 57, *El materialismo zoológico* 63, *El doctor Mora, impulsor de la causa*

biblica en México 63, *Galería de retratos literarios* 67.
Ave. Nevado 133, Mexico 13, D.F., Mexico.
Telephone: 39-54-40.

Baffour, Robert Patrick, O.B.E.; Ghanaian university
official; b. 12; ed. Mfantsipim School and London Univ.
Gold Coast Railway 35-41; Lecturer in Engineering,
Achimota 41-46; Mechanical Engineer, Accra Municipal
Council 46-53; Chief Transport Officer, later Perm. Sec.
Ministry of Communications 53-60; Ghana Supply
Comm. 60-61; Principal, Kumasi Coll. of Technology
60-61, Vice-Chancellor, Kwame Nkrumah Univ. 61-
(now Univ. of Science and Technology, Kumasi);
Chair. Ghana Atomic Energy Comm. 63; Pres. Int.
Atomic Energy Agency (I.A.E.A.) 63.
University of Science and Technology, Kumasi, Ghana.

Bafile, Monsignor Corrado; Vatican diplomatist; b.
1903; ed. State Univ., Rome, and Lateran Univ., Rome.
Ordained priest 36; Vatican Secretariat of State 39-;
Privy Chamberlain to Pope John XXIII 58-60; Papal
Nuncio to Germany 60-; Titular Archbishop of Antiochia
in Pisidia 60-.
Papal Nunciature, Turmstrasse 29, Bad Godesberg,
German Federal Republic.

Bagramian, Marshal Ivan Kristoforovich; Soviet army
officer and politician; b. 97; ed. Frunze Military Acad.,
and General Staff Acad., Soviet Army.
Member, C.P.S.U. 41-; South West and Western Fronts
41-43; Commdr. First Baltic Front 43-45; Military
Commdr. Baltic Military Area 45-54; Chief Insp.
U.S.S.R. Ministry of Defence 55-56; Marshal of Soviet
Union 55-; Chief, Rear Admin. and Supply Services of
Soviet Army; Deputy Minister of Defence of U.S.S.R.
58-; Head of Gen. Staff, Mil. Acad. 56-58; mem. Central
Cttee. of C.P.S.U. 61-; Deputy to U.S.S.R. Supreme
Soviet; Hero of Soviet Union; Order of Lenin (four
times), Order of Suvorov (twice), Order of Kutuzov,
Order of Red Banner (three times), etc.
Publs. include: *Fighting Traditions of the Soviet Armed
Forces, Warrior City on the Dnieper* 65.
Ministry of Defence, Maurice Thorez 34, Moscow,
U.S.S.R.

Bagrit, Sir Leon, Kt.; British business executive;
b. 13 March 1902; ed. St. Olave's School, London, and
London Univ.
Founder, B. P. Swift Ltd., Engineers 35, amalgamated
with Elliott Bros. (London) Ltd. 47; Man. Dir. Elliott
Bros. (London) Ltd. 47-57; Man. Dir. Elliott-Automa-
tion Ltd. 57-, Chair. 62-; Dir. and Deputy Chair. English
Electric 67-; B.B.C. Reith Lecturer Nov.-Dec. 64;
Chair. Friends of Covent Garden; Albert Medal, Royal
Soc. of Arts 65.
Publ. *The Age of Automation* (Reith Lectures) 64.
Upper Terrace House, Hampstead, London, N.W.3,
England.

Baguidy, Fern D.; Haitian lawyer and diplomatist;
b. 20; ed. Lycée Nord Alexis, Jérémie, and Lycée
Alexandre Pétion, Law School, and Inst. of Ethnology,
Port-au-Prince.
Assistant Chief of Immigration and Emigration Service
47-51; Pan-American World Airways 51-57; First Sec.
Haitian Del. to Organization of American States (OAS)
57-58, Minister-Counsellor 58-59; Minister-Counsellor,
Embassy of Haiti in United States 60, 61-62; Chargé
d'Affaires of Haiti to OAS 61, Ambassador to OAS 62-.
Representation of Haiti at Organization of American
States, 4400 Seventeenth St., N.W., Washington, D.C.
20011, U.S.A.

Bahadur K. C., Kaisher; Nepalese educationist and
diplomatist; b. 28 Jan. 1907; ed. St. Paul's Mission
School, St. Xavier's Coll., Calcutta, and Univ. Coll.,
Calcutta.
Translator and Lecturer, Tri-Chandra Coll. 30-32;
research in MS., inscriptions and sculpture, Nepal 32-
45; Nepalese Resident in Tibet 46-50; Sec. Ministry of

Educ., Health and Local Self Govt. 56-61; Del. to UN
56-57, UNESCO 60; Ambassador to People's Repub.
of China, concurrently to Mongolian People's Repub.
and Burma 61-65, also to Repub. of Indonesia and
Kingdom of Laos 62-65; Chair. Nepal Public Service
Comm. 66-; awarded Italian Order of Merit 53; Order
of the Ghurkas (1st Class) of King Mahendra 62.
Publs. *Countries of the World* 35, *Ancient and Modern
Nepal* 53, *Materials for the Study of Nepalese History
and Culture* 58, *Judicial Customs of Nepal, Part I* 58,
Eroticism in Nepalese Art 60, *Introduction to Kathmandu
and Patan* 61, *Universal Value of Nepalese Aesthetics,
Part I and II* 61-62.
Public Service Commission, Singh Durbar, Katmandu,
Home: Kamal Pokhari, Katmandu, Nepal.
Telephone: 11696.

Bahadur, Raj, B.SC., M.A., LL.B.; Indian lawyer and
politician; b. 21 Aug. 1912; ed. Agra Coll. and St.
John's Coll., Agra.
Mem. Cen. Advisory Cttee. Bharatpur State 39-42,
Municipal Comm. 41-42; resigned from these posts in
connection with "Quit India" Movement; mem. Rep.
Assembly 43; Sec. Assembly Praja Parishad Party 43-
48, Gen. Sec. Matsya Union Congress Cttee. 48-49; Pres.
Bharatpur Bar Asscn. 48-51; elected to Constituent
Assembly of India from Bharatpur Nov. 48; mem. of
Union Parl. 48-; Sec. Congress Party in Parl. 50-52;
Dep. Min., later Min. of State for Communications
51-56; led Indian Del. to 10th Session of Int. Civil
Aviation Organisation, Caracas; Minister of Communi-
cations Dec. 56-April 57; Minister of State for Transport
and Communications 57-62; Minister of State for
Transport 62-64, Minister of Transport 64-66; Minister
of Information and Broadcasting 66-67; Advocate,
Supreme Court of India 67-Dec. 67; Amb. to Nepal
Jan. 68-; mem. Rajasthan P.C.C. and All-India Con-
gress Cttee.; Congress Party.
Embassy of India, P.O. Box 292, Katmandu, Nepal.
Telephone: 11300.

Baharoon, Zain Abdu; Aden politician; ed. locally.
Managing Partner, Brothers Trading Co.; Vice-Pres.,
Aden Chamber of Commerce; mem. Aden Legislative
Council 62-63; Minister of Finance, First Aden National
Govt. Jan.-July 63; Chief Minister of Aden State
July 63-65.
Aden, People's Republic of Southern Yemen.

Bahnini, Ahmed; Moroccan lawyer and politician;
b. 1909.
Interpreter 32-42; Called to Bar, Fez 42; Pres. of
Supreme Court 56; later Sec.-Gen. of Ministry of the
Interior; Minister of Justice Jan.-Nov. 63; Prime
Minister Nov. 63-June 65; Pres. Social Democratic
Party 64-; Pres. Supreme Court 66-.
The Supreme Court, Rabat, Morocco.

Baibakov, Nikolai Konstantinovich; Soviet politician;
b. 1911; ed. Azerbaijan Industrial Inst.
Oil-mining engineer in Azerbaijan oil field 32-37; Chief
Engineer and Manager of Leninneft Oil Trust in Baku
37; Dir. Vostokneft in Soviet East 38-39; Dir. Central
Management Board for oil extraction in Eastern districts of the People's Commissariat of Oil Industry
39-40; Deputy People's Commissar of the Oil Industry
of U.S.S.R. 40-44; Minister of Oil Industry of U.S.S.R.
44-45; Chair. of U.S.S.R. State Planning Comm. 55-57,
65-; first Deputy Chair. of Council of Ministers of
R.S.F.S.R. and Chair. of State Planning Comm. of
R.S.F.S.R. 57; Vice-Chair. U.S.S.R. Council of Ministers 66-; Chair. State Cttee. of the Chemical and Oil
Industry 63-64; Chair. State Cttee. of Oil Production
Industry 64-65; mem. Central Cttee. of C.P.S.U.;
awarded three Orders of Lenin, two Orders of Red
Banner of Labour, Lenin Prize, and medals.
State Planning Committee, 4 1st Dyakovsky per.,
Moscow, U.S.S.R.

Baijal, Dharan Chand; Indian engineer and railway executive; b. 8 Aug. 1906; ed. Univ. of Allahabad and Thomason Coll. of Civil Engineering, Roorkee.

Indian Railway, Service of Engineers 30, later with E. Bengal Railway; Defence of India Corps (Railways) 42-46; Deputy Dir. (Projects) Railway Board 46-47, Joint Dir. Civil Engineering 47-52, Div. Superintendent, N. Railway 52-55, Dir. Efficiency Bureau, Railway Board 55-56; Sec. Railway Board 56-57, special duty 57-58; Gen. Manager, Northeast Frontier Railway 58-59; mem. (Staff) Railway Board 59-62, Chair. 62-65; Chair. Bharat Heavy Electricals Ltd. 65-.

Bharat Heavy Electricals Ltd., 5 Parliament Street, New Delhi 1, India.
Telephone: 45683.

Bailey, Clyde H., M.S., PH.D.; American bio-chemist; b. 87; ed. North Dakota Agricultural Coll., and Minnesota and Maryland Univs.

Scientific Asst. U.S. Dept. Agriculture 07-11; at Minnesota Univ. as Instructor 13-14; Asst. Prof. 14-16; Assoc. Prof. 17-20, Prof. 20-; Vice-Dir. Minnesota Agricultural Experiment Station 38-41; Dean of the Dept. Agriculture, Minnesota Univ. 41-52, Dean Emeritus 53-; mem. Advisory Cttee. on Food Processing, Agricultural Research Admin., U.S. Dept. of Agriculture and Adviser, Research and Development Branch of Office of Quartermaster-Gen., War Dept.; awarded Thomas Burr Osborne Medal 32, Nicolas Appert Medal 46, Neumann Medal 55, Spencer Medal 60; Hon. Pres. Int. Assoc. Cereal Chemists 58; Hon. D.Sc.

Publs. Monographs on *Chemistry of Wheat Flour* 25, *Constituents of Wheat and Wheat Flour* 44; *Physical Tests of Flour Quality* 40.

Home: 2304 Doswell Avenue, St. Paul, Minn. 55108; Office: Institute of Agriculture, University of Minnesota, St. Paul 1, Minnesota, U.S.A.

Bailey, Sir Kenneth Hamilton, C.B.E., Q.C., M.A., B.C.L., LL.M.; Australian jurist and diplomatist; b. 3 Nov. 1898; ed. Melbourne and Oxford Univs.

Rhodes Scholar 18; Vice-Master, Queen's Coll., Melbourne Univ. 24-27; Prof. of Jurisprudence, Melbourne Univ. 28-30, Prof. of Public Law 31-46, and Dean of Law Faculty 28-42; Adviser Australian Del. Imperial Conf. 37; Del. L.N. Assembly 37, 46; mem. Aliens Tribunal 41; served as Consultant Commonwealth Attorney General's Dept. 43-45; mem. Aust. Del. San Francisco 45, UN Gen. Assembly 46, 56, 58, 62-67; Sec. Commonwealth Attorney-General's Dept. 46-64; Solicitor-Gen. 46-64; High Commr. in Canada 64-; Hon. LL.D. (Dalhousie).

90 Sparks Street, Ottawa, Ontario, Canada.
Telephone: 236-0841 (Ottawa).

Bailly, Gen. Paul; French air force officer; b. 2 Sept. 1903; ed. Ecole Spéciale de St. Cyr.

Commissioned 24, pilot 26, posted to the Levant; test pilot 29-31; staff course 35-37; commanded a reconnaissance group 40; joined French forces in U.K. 42; commanded a bomber group attached to the R.A.F. 43-45; A.O.C. French Air Forces in Morocco and Air Training in North Africa 45-47; Deputy Chief of Staff 47-49; in command of Air Defence 49-53; Chief of Staff to C.-in-C. Central Europe 53-55, of the French Air Force 55-58, Inspector-Gen. 58-59; mem. management Soc. Lorraine-Escaut 61-; Grand Officier Légion d'Honneur, Croix de Guerre and other French and foreign decorations.

8 Avenue Mozart, Paris 16e, France.

Bainbridge, Kenneth Tompkins, S.M., M.A., PH.D.; American physicist; b. 27 July 1904; ed. Mass. Inst. of Technology and Princeton Univ.

Nat. Research Council Fellow 29-31; Bartol Research Foundation Fellow 31-33 Guggenheim Memorial Foundation Fellow 33-34; Asst. Prof. Harvard Univ. 34-38,

Assoc. Prof. 38-46, Prof. of Physics 46, Chair. Dept. of Physics 53-56; George Vasmer Leverett Prof. of Physics, Harvard 61-; Div. Leader, Nat. Defense Research Cttee., Radiation Laboratory 40-43; Group and Division Leader, Los Alamos Laboratory 43-46; awarded Levy Medal, Franklin Inst. 33; elected American Acad. Arts and Sciences 38, Nat. Acad. Sciences 46; dir. first atomic bomb "Trinity" test Feb.-Sept. 45; awarded Presidential Certificate of Merit for war research work on radar 48; Trustee Assoc. Univs. Inc. 58-59.

Lyman Laboratory of Physics, Harvard University, Cambridge, Mass. 02138, U.S.A.

Baines, Rt. Rev. Henry Wolfe, M.A.; British ecclesiastic; b. 7 Feb. 1905; ed. Repton, Oxford Univ., Cuddesdon Theological Coll.

Travelling Sec., Student Christian Movement 27-29; St. Mary the Virgin, Oxford 30-31; St. John's Cathedral, Hong Kong 34-38; St. Nicholas, Radford 38-41; Rector of Rugby 41-49; Bishop of Singapore 49-60; Bishop of Wellington, New Zealand 60-.

Bishopscourt, Eccleston Hill, Wellington, N.I., New Zealand.
Telephone: Wellington 41-495.

Bainton, Roland Herbert; American educationist; b. 94 (England); ed. Whitman Coll. and Yale Univ.

Emigrated to U.S.A. 02; Instructor in Church History, Yale Univ. 20-23, Asst. Prof. 23-32, Assoc. Prof. 32-36, Titus Street Prof. of Ecclesiastical History 36-62, Emer. 62-.

Publs. include *Here I Stand* (A Life of Martin Luther) 50, *The Travail of Religious Liberty* 51, *The Reformation of the Sixteenth Century* 52, *Hunted Heretic: A Study of Michael Servetus* 53, *The Age of the Reformation* 56, *What Christianity Says about Sex, Love and Marriage* 57, *Yale and The Ministry* 57, *Pilgrim Parson, The Life of James Herbert Bainton* 58, *Christian Attitudes to War and Peace* 60, *Collected Papers* (3 vols.) 62, 63, 64, *Horizon History of Christianity* 64, and numerous paperbacks.

409 Prospect Street, New Haven, Conn. 06510, U.S.A.

Bairamov, Nurbedi; Soviet politician; b. 12; ed. Marysk Pedagogical Inst.

Served in Soviet Army 34-36; mem. Communist Party 39-; in charge of Central Cttee. Dept. Turkmen Communist Party 48-50; Chair. Presidium Turkmen Supreme Soviet 59-64; Head of Supreme Board for Communal Services, Council of Ministers of Turkmenian S.S.R. 64-; Deputy Chair. Presidium U.S.S.R. Supreme Soviet 59-66.

16 Nadsonovsky ul., Ashkabad, Turkmenian S.S.R., U.S.S.R.

Baird, Tadeusz; Polish composer, b. 28.

Studied in Warsaw; awarded State Prize for First Symphony 51, Olympics Prize for Second Piano Sonatina 52, City of Cologne Music Prize 63, State Prize 64, Prize of the Union of Polish Composers 65, three First Prizes, Tribune Int. des Compositeurs, UNESCO, Paris, for *Four Essays, Variations without Theme,* and *Four Dialogues,* etc.

Compositions include: Sinfonietta 49, Symphonies 50, 52, Piano Concerto 49, *Colas Breugnon* (suite for string orchestra and flute) 51, Concerto for orchestra 53, *Lyric Suite* (text by J. Tuwim) 53, Cassazione for orchestra 56, *Four Essays for Orchestra* 58, *Divertimento* (for four wind instruments) 57, String Quartet 58, *Espressioni Varianti* (for violin and orchestra) 59, *Egzorta* (for speaker, choir and orchestra) 60, *Erotiques* (for soprano and orchestra) 61, *Etude* (for voices, orchestra, piano and percussion) 61, *Variations without theme* (for orchestra) 62, *Epiphany Music* (for orchestra) 63, *Four Dialogues for Oboe and Chamber Orchestra* 64, *Tomorrow* (one-act opera after Conrad), *Four Songs* (for mezzosoprano and chamber orchestra) 66, *Four Novellettes* (for chamber orchestra) 67; chamber pieces, works for flute, oboe, piano, clarinet, and bassoon, choral and solo songs, incidental music for stage and films.

Lipska 11 m.4, Warsaw and c/o Union of Polish Composers, Rynek Starego Miasta 27, Warsaw, Poland. Telephone: 17-43-12.

Bakarić, Vladimir, LL.D.; Yugoslav politician; b. 8 March 1912.

Helped organise uprising in Croatia 41; mem. of Presidium of Anti-Fascist Council for Yugoslav Nat. Liberation; mem. Nat. Cttee. for the Liberation of Yugoslavia; Pres. Govt. of the Nat. Republic of Croatia, later Pres. of the Exec. Council 45-53; Pres. Assembly of the Nat. Republic of Croatia 53-; mem. Yugoslav Acad. of Sciences and Arts; mem. Presidency of Cen. Cttee. of Yugoslav League of Communists; Orders of Nat. Hero, Partisan Star (1st Class), Brotherhood and Unity (1st Class), Bravery, Partisan Commemoration Medal 41.

Publs. Books and articles on economics and social science.

Zagreb, Radićev trg. br. 2, Yugoslavia.

Bakatselos, George; Greek lawyer and politician; b. 1906; ed. Univ. of Salonika.

Member Directing Cttee. of resistance movement EDES in N. Greece during Second World War; wounded 44; elected Liberal Deputy for Salonika 46, 50, 51, 56 and 58, Centre Union Deputy 61, 63 and 64; Sec.-Gen. Gen. Admin. for Macedonia 45-46; Under-Sec. for Health and Social Welfare, Building and Reconstruction 50; Minister of Labour 51, 63-66, of Agriculture Sept. 51; Greek and foreign decorations.

9 Aristoteles Street, Salonika, Greece.

Bakayev, Victor Georgievich, DR.TECH.SC.; Soviet politician; b. 02; ed. Moscow Inst. of Transport Communications.

Started working as blacksmith's apprentice at Berdjansk port workshop; graduated Moscow Inst. of Transport Communications 29; lecturer in insts. of Moscow and Leningrad 37-42; Deputy Minister of Merchant Marine 45-54; Minister of Merchant Marine of U.S.S.R. 54-; Dep. to Supreme Soviet of U.S.S.R.; Alt. mem. Central Cttee. of C.P.S.U. 61-; awards inc. three Orders of Lenin, two Orders of the Red Banner of Labour.

Publs. *Organisation of Handling Operations in Sea Ports* 39, *Organisation of Scheduled Shipping* 47, *The Principles of Exploitation of Sea Transport* 50, *The History of Russian Navigation in the First Half of the XIII Century* 54, *Sea Transport of the U.S.S.R. for the Past Forty Years* 57, *World Shipping and Maritime Traffic of Capitalist Countries* 64, *Operations of Merchant Marine* 65; and other works.

Ministry of Merchant Marine, 1-3 Ulitsa Zhdanova, Moscow, U.S.S.R.

Bakema, Jakob B.; Netherlands architect; b. 8 March 1914; ed. Technical High School, Groningen, Acad. of Building, Amsterdam, and Technical Univ. Delft.

Formerly worked in architectural offices of Van Tijen and Van Eesteren; Assoc. with Prof. Ir. J. H. Van Den Broek in architectural office of Van Den Broek & Bakema; Extraordinary Prof. in Architectural Design, Technical Univ., Delft 63-; Officer Order of Orange Nassau; Officer Order of Crown (Belgium).

Major works: Social Centre, Cinema 't Venster, Shopping Centre Lijnbaan, Rotterdam; Montessori School, Rotterdam; church in Nagele; Town Hall, Marl (Fed. Germany); housing block, Hansaviertel, Berlin; Regional Plan, North-Kennemerland (North Holland); town planning for cities of Leeuwarden, Hengelo, Eindhoven and Amsterdam; Netherlands Pavilion, Brussels Int. Exhbn. (with other); World Broadcasting Building, Hilversum; building and laboratories for Technical Univ., Delft.

Posthornstraat 12b, Rotterdam, Netherlands.

Baker, Carlos; American educator and writer; b. 5 May 1909; ed. Dartmouth Coll., Harvard Univ. and Princeton Univ.

Teacher of English, Thornton Acad. 33-34, Nichols School, Buffalo 34-36; Princeton Univ. 38-, Prof. of English 51-54, Woodrow Wilson Prof. of Literature 54-, Dept. Chair. 52-58; Guggenheim Fellowship 65-66.

Publs. inc. *Shelley's Major Poetry* 48, *Hemingway: The Writer as Artist* 52, *A Friend in Power* (novel) 58, *The Land of Rumbelow* (novel) 63, *A Year and a Day* (poems) 63.

34 Allison Road, Princeton, New Jersey, U.S.A.

Baker, Crowdus; American merchandising executive; b. 27 Feb. 1906; ed. Terrill Prep. School, Staunton Military Acad. and Austin Coll., Texas.

Sears, Roebuck & Co. 29-, Operating Supt. Mail Order Plant, Seattle 35-39, Boston 39-42, Philadelphia 42-45, Gen. Man. New England Operations 45-51, Treas. 51-54, Dir. 52-, Chair. Finance Cttee. 57-, mem. Exec. Cttee. 57-, Vice-Pres. and Comptroller 54-63, Pres. 63-; Dir. Allstate Insurance Co., Sears Bank and Trust Co., Calcasieu Chemical Co., Bethlehem Steel Corpn., official of several business and civic orgs.; Hon. D.Iur. Austin Coll. and Villanova Univ.

2298 Drury Lane, Northfield, Illinois, U.S.A.

Baker, Edgar Robey; American publisher; b. 16 Oct. 1920; ed George Washington Univ.

On staff of Time Inc. 45-; Asst. to publisher of *Life* 45-46; Man. *Life* 46-48; Gen. Man. Time-Life Int. 48-49, Managing Dir. 49-65; Publisher *Life en Español* 52-65; Vice-Pres. Time Inc. 57-, Dir. Corporate Devt. 66-; Dir. Time-Life Int., London, Ltd., General Learning Companies, Chase (Manhattan) Int. Investment Corpn., Selected Risk Investments, Editorial Abril (Argentina); Co-Chair. Inter-American Investment Conf. 55; Co-Dir. Int. Industrial Development Conf. 57; Trustee Cordell Hull Foundation; Dir. Nat. Foreign Trade Council, Far East American Council.

Office: Rockefeller Center, New York City 20; Home: 15 East 91st Street, New York, N.Y.; also White Pines, Sharon, Conn., U.S.A.

Baker, Gen. Sir Geoffrey Harding, G.C.B., C.M.G., C.B.E., M.C.; British army officer; b. 20 June 1912; ed. Wellington Coll., Royal Military Acad., Woolwich.

Commissioned into Royal Artillery 32; India, with 11th Field Brigade 35; "F" (Sphinx) Battery, R.H.A. 37, Egypt 39; Middle East Staff Coll. 40; Brigade Maj. R.A. 4th Indian Div., Western Desert and Eritrea 40, 41; Instructor M.E. Staff Coll. 42; G.S.O. 1, H.Q. Eighth Army 42-43; C.O. 127th Field Regt., R.A., Sicily 43; B.G.S., H.Q. 21st Army Group, North-West Europe 44; Deputy Dir. War Office 47; C.O. 3rd Regt., R.H.A. 50-52; Dir. War Office 52-53; Dir. of Operations and Chief of Staff to Gov. of Cyprus Nov. 55-Feb. 57; C.R.A., 7th Armoured and 5 Divs. B.A.O.R. 57-59; Asst. Chief of Staff, H.Q. Northern Army Group, Germany 59; Chief of Staff, H.Q. Southern Command 60-61; Chief of Staff Contingencies Planning, Supreme H.Q. Allied Powers Europe 61-63; Col. Commdt., R.A. 64-; Vice-Chief of Gen. Staff 63-66; G.O.C.-in-C. H.Q. Southern Command 66-68; Chief of Gen. Staff 68-; U.S. Legion of Merit (Cmdr.) 46.

c/o National & Grindlay's Bank, 26 Bishopsgate, London, E.C.2, England.

Baker, George Pierce, A.M., PH.D.; American educationist; b. 1 Nov. 1903; ed. Harvard Univ.

Instructor in Economics and Tutor in Div. of Economics, History and Govt., Harvard Coll. 28-36; Asst. Prof. of Transportation, Harvard Business School 36-39; Associate Prof. of Transportation 39-46; mem. Civil Aeronautics Board 40-42, Vice-Chair. 42; Lieut.-Col. Quartermaster Corps 42, Col.-Gen. Staff Corps 43-45; Dir. Office of Transport and Communications Policy,

State Dept. 45-46; Prof. of Int. Transport and Communications, Fletcher School of Law and Diplomacy 46-47; James J. Hill Prof. of Transportation, Harvard Univ. 46-63; George Fisher Baker Prof. of Admin. 63-; U.S. mem. UN Transport and Communications Comm. 46-56; Pres. Transport Asscn. of America 54-62, Chair. of Board 62-; Dean of Faculty, Harvard Business School 62-; Pres. Transportation Research Foundation 61-64; Dir. Mobil Oil Corpn., Lockheed Aircraft Corpn., First Nat. Bank of Boston; Fellow American Acad. of Arts and Sciences; Legion of Merit; several hon. degrees. Publs. *The Formation of the New England Railroad Systems* 37, *Case Problems in Transportation Management* (with G. E. Germane) 57.
Dean's House, Harvard Business School, Soldier's Field, Boston, Mass. 02163, U.S.A.

Baker, Howard Henry, Jr., LL.B.; American politician; b. 15 Nov. 1925; ed. The McCallie School, Chattanooga, Univ. of the South, Sewanee, Tennessee, Tulane Univ. of New Orleans, and Univ. of Tennessee Coll. of Law.
U.S. Naval Reserve 43-46; Practising Attorney 49-; Chair. Board First Nat. Bank, Oneida, Tenn.; Dir. Stearns Coal and Lumber Co.; fmr. Pres. Colonial Natural Gas Co.; fmr. Dir. Scott County Hospital, Oneida; fmr. Chair. Scott Municipal Airport Authority; Senator from Tennessee, Jan. 67-; Republican.
U.S. Senate, Washington, D.C.; Home: Huntsville, Tenn., U.S.A.

Baker, Sir John (**Fleetwood**), Kt., O.B.E., F.R.S., M.A., SC.D., D.SC., D.ENG., LL.D., M.INST.C.E., M.I.STRUCT.E., M.I.MECH.E.; British engineer; b. 19 March 1901; ed. Rossall School and Clare Coll., Cambridge.
Technical Asst. Royal Airship Works 25; Asst. Lecturer Univ. Coll. Cardiff 26; Scientific Asst. Building Research Station Dept. of Scientific and Industrial Research 28; Technical Officer to Steel Structures Research Cttee. 31-36; Prof. of Civil Engineering Bristol Univ. 33-43; mem. Civil Defence Research Cttee. 39-48; Scientific Adviser and Head of Design Section, A.R.P. Dept., Ministry of Home Security 39-43; Fellow Clare Coll. 43; Prof. of Mechanical Sciences and Head of Dept. of Engineering, Cambridge Univ. 43-68; mem. Council, Inst. of Civil Engineers 47-56, 58-66; mem. of Council British Welding Research Asscn. 46-63, Univ. Grants Cttee. 54-64; Dir. John Brown and Co. Ltd., Technical Devt. Capital Ltd., I.D.C. Ltd., Cambridge Fender and Engineering Co. Ltd.
Publs. *Differential Equations of Engineering Science* 29, *Analysis of Engineering Structures* 36, *The Steel Skeleton*, Vol. I 54, Vol. II 56, *Plastic Design of Frames* 69.
100 Long Road, Cambridge, England.
Telephone: Trumpington 2152.

Baker, Joséphine; American-born French singer; b. 3 June 1906.
Has appeared in numerous revues and operettas at the Folies Bergères, Casino de Paris, La Créole, etc.; films include *Zouzou* and *Princess Tam-Tam*; Chevalier Légion d'Honneur.
Publs. *Les Mémoires de Joséphine Baker, La Tribu Arc-en-Ciel.*
Les Milandes, par Castelnaud-Fayrac (Dordogne), France.

Baker, Richard Edward St. Barbe; British silviculturist; b. 9 Oct. 1889; ed. Dean Close School, Cheltenham, Saskatchewan Univ., Gonville and Caius Coll., Cambridge, and Imperial Forestry Inst., Oxford Univ.
Student, farmer and lumber camp employee, Canada 09-13; Army Service 14-19; Asst. Conservator of Forests, Kenya 20-23, Nigeria 24-29; founded Men of the Trees, Kenya 22, Great Britain 24, Palestine 29, as a world-wide society 32, Junior Men of the Trees 56, settled in New Zealand and established Commonwealth and Overseas Headquarters of Men of the Trees 59; lectured and conducted forestry planning in U.S.A.,

Canada, South America; Convenor, World Forestry Charter Gatherings 45-56; founded Friends of Sahara (U.S.A. and U.K.); prepared report and launched Sahara Reclamation Programme 63-64; has organized several exhbns. of Portraits of Trees; Founder and Editor *Trees and Life* (Journal of Men of the Trees) 34-59.
Publs. *Tree Lovers' Calendar* 29-67, *Trees—Book of the Seasons* 40, *Africa Drums* 42, *The Redwoods* 43, 59, *I Planted Trees* 44, *Green Glory—Forests of the World* 47, *New Earth Charter* 49, *Famous Trees* 53, *Sahara Challenge* 54, *Kabongo* 55, *Land of Tane* 56, *British Isles Section of World Geography of Forest Resources* 56, *Dance of the Trees* 57, *Kamiti—A Forester's Dream* 58, *Horse Sense* 61, *Trees of Bible Lands* 62, *Trees of New Zealand* 65, *True Book of Trees* 65, *Sahara Conquest* 66.
Mount Cook Station, P.O.B. 3, Lake Tekapo, New Zealand.
Telephone: Lake Tekapo 842.

Bakhrakh, Lev Davidovich; Soviet physicist; b. 1921; ed. Zhukovsky Air Force Engineering Acad.
Research Assoc. Zhukovsky Air Force Engineering Acad. 45-; Corresp. mem. U.S.S.R. Acad. of Sciences 66-.
Publs. Works on radiophysics and radio engineering.
U.S.S.R. Academy of Sciences, 14 Lenin Prospekt, Moscow, U.S.S.R.

Bakhshi, Ghulam Mohammad; Indian politician; b. 21 July 1907; ed. C.M.S. School, Srinagar, Kashmir.
Began his career as a school teacher in Ladakh; worked in Srinagar for All India Spinners' Asscn.; joined Muslim Conf. 31; organised Bilcha Party 33-34, youth movement 36; imprisoned for eighteen months; active in organising Nat. Conf. Cttees. in Kashmir 38-; fled to then British India during "Quit Kashmir" movement 46-47; Deputy Prime Minister, Kashmir 48-53, Prime Minister 53-63; Pres. All Jammu and Kashmir Nat. Conf.; mem. Legislative Assembly, Jammu and Kashmir 67-.
Srinagar, Kashmir, India.

Bakhtov, Konstantin Konstantinovich; Soviet foreign trade official; b. 1912; ed. Inst. of Foreign Trade.
Chief of Section, *Exportkhleb* 37-39; mem. C.P.S.U. 39-; official, U.S.S.R. Trade Representation in France 39-41; Chief, Section, People's Commissariat for Foreign Trade 41-44; Commercial Attaché, later Deputy Commercial Rep. of U.S.S.R. in France 44-47; Chief of Section, later Chief of Dept., Ministry of Foreign Trade 47-49; U.S.S.R. Commercial Rep. in France 49-53; Chief of Dept., Ministry of Foreign Trade 53-65; U.S.S.R. Commercial Rep. in Italy 65-; Order of Red Banner of Labour (twice), Badge of Honour.
U.S.S.R. Commercial Representation, Rome, Italy.

Bakic, Vojin; Yugoslav sculptor; b. 15; ed. Zagreb Acad. of Fine Arts.
Has executed numerous monuments in Yugoslavia; rep. at Brussels Int. Exhibition 58.
c/o Zagreb Acad. of Fine Arts, Zagreb, Yugoslavia.

Bakker, J. A.; Netherlands politician; b. 27 May 1921; ed. Netherlands School of Economics, Rotterdam.
Town Councillor, Bolsward 49-55; Mayor of Andijk 55; Mayor of Hoogeveen 59; Crown mem. Social Econ. Council 56; State Sec. Ministry of Econ. Affairs 63-66; Minister of Econ. Affairs 66-67; Minister for Traffic and Waterways 67-.
Ministry of Traffic and Waterways, Binnenhof 20, The Hague, Netherlands.
Telephone: 070-659810.

Bakr, Brig. Ahmed Hassan; Iraqi army officer and politician.
Forced to retire from Iraq Army 59; Prime Minister of Iraq Feb. 63-Nov. 63; Vice-Pres. of Iraq Nov. 63-64.
Baghdad, Iraq.

Bakri, Bashir El-; Sudanese diplomatist; b. 18; ed. Univs. of Cairo, Oxford and Paris.
Mem. of many Sudanese dels. to U.N. and other international centres; Foreign Ministry 56; Ambassador to France 57, Belgium 57, Netherlands 59, Spain 60-61, Nigeria 61-65; Dir. El Nilein Bank 65-.
El Nilein Bank, P.O. Box 466, Khartoum, Sudan.

Bălăceanu, Petre; Romanian diplomatist; b. 14 Nov. 1906; ed. Craiova Secondary School and Bucharest Commercial Acad.
On the staff of the Nat. Bank 28; Econ. Counsellor, Romanian Embassy, Washington; Minister to Argentina 47-48; Vice-Pres. State Planning Cttee. 48-53; Pres. State Bank, First Deputy Minister of Finance 53-57; Minister to U.K. 57-61, U.S.A. 61-64, Ambassador to U.S.A. 64-67; Prof. of Econ. Sciences, Lenin Inst. of Econs., Bucharest.
c/o Ministry of Foreign Affairs, Bucharest, Romania.

Balafrej, Ahmed; Moroccan politician; b. 08; ed. Univs. of Paris and Paris.
Sec.-Gen. in Istiqlal (Independence) Party 44-; later exiled by French, returned to Morocco 55; Minister of Foreign Affairs 55-58; Prime Minister May-Dec. 58; Ambassador-at-Large 60-61; Dep. Prime Minister June 61; Minister of Foreign Affairs 61-Nov. 63; Personal Rep. of King with rank of Minister 63-.
The Royal Palace, Rabat, Morocco.

Balaguer, Joaquín; Dominican diplomatist and politician; b. 1 Sept. 1907; ed. Univ. de Santo Domingo and Univ. de Paris à la Sorbonne.
Served Madrid 32-35; Under-Sec. of Foreign Affairs 36-40; Minister to Colombia 40-46; Alt. Rep. to UN 47; Minister of Foreign Affairs 54-55, of Educ. and Arts 55-57; Vice-Pres. of Dominican Repub. 57-60, Pres. 60, 66-; voluntary exile in U.S. 62-65; Founder-Leader Reformist Party 62-.
Office of the President, Santo Domingo, Dominican Republic.

Balanchine, George; Russian-born American choreographer; b. 9 Jan. 1904; ed. Imperial Ballet School and Conservatoire, St. Petersburg.
With Ballets Russes (Diaghileff) 24; Dir. Copenhagen Royal Theatre 29; founder mem. Ballets Russes de Monte Carlo 32; at Metropolitan Opera, New York 34-37; co-founder School of American Ballet 34; Artistic Dir., New York City Ballet Co. 48-; ballets include *The Nightingale, Pastorale, Triumph of Neptune, Apollon, Bal, Cotillon, Mozartfina, Song of Norway, Agon, Monumentum pro Gesualdo, Movements,* choreography for films and plays include *On Your Toes, Goldwyn Follies, The Boys from Syracuse, Cabin in the Sky, I Married an Angel, House of Flowers.*
Publ. *Balanchine's Complete Stories of the Great Ballets* 54.
2291 Broadway, New York 24, N.Y., U.S.A.

Balanchivadze, Andrei Melitonovich; Soviet composer; b. 06; ed. Tiflis and Leningrad Conservatories.
Wrote music to ballet *Heart of the Mountains* 38, and to twenty films, including *Georgy Saakadze, David Guramishvili, Lost Paradise, They Descended from the Mountains, Mameluk,* etc.; State prizewinner for symphony 44, and second concerto for piano and orchestra 46; People's Artist of Georgian S.S.R.; Compositions include *Mzia* (opera) 49, third concerto for piano and string orchestra 53, concerto for bassoon and orchestra 54, *Ruby Stars* (ballet) 51; orchestral works: *Lake Ritza, The Sea, The Dnieper, Solemn Overture, On the Tbilisi Sea, Rhapsody, Ballade;* second symphony (with piano) 59, *Stranitsy Zhizni* (Pages of Life) (ballet) 61, Fourth Concerto for *Piano and Orchestra* 62, *Vecher* (Evening), Miniature for string quartet 64, *Fantasia* for piano 64, *Muvri* (ballet) 65.
Georgian Composers' Union, 22 Prospekt Rustaveli, Tbilisi, Georgia, U.S.S.R.

Balandin, Anatoli Nikiforovich; Soviet politician; b. 1927; ed. Orenburg Inst. of Agriculture.
Agronomist, and Dir. of machine and tractor station 52-57; Official, Agricultural Dept. of Orenburg Regional Cttee. of C.P.S.U., and First Sec. Chkalovsk District Cttee. of C.P.S.U. 57-62; Head Sorochinsk Collective State Farm Production Dept., Head of Agricultural Dept. of Orenburg Regional Cttee. of C.P.S.U., then Sec. 62-66; Chair. Orenburg Regional Soviet, and Deputy to U.S.S.R. Supreme Soviet 66-; mem. C.P.S.U. 54-.
Orenburg Regional Soviet of Working People's Deputies, Orenburg, U.S.S.R.

Balasanyan, Sergei Artemyevich; Soviet composer; b. 1902; ed. Moscow Conservatoire.
Secretary R.S.F.S.R. Composers' Union; Exec. mem. U.S.S.R. Composers' Union; Asst. Prof. 61-65, Prof. 65-; Honoured Worker of Tadjik S.S.R. 39, State Prize 49, People's Artist of Tadjik S.S.R. 57, Honoured Worker of Arts of R.S.F.S.R. 64; orders and medals of Soviet Union.
Principal works: *The Vose Uprising* (opera) 39, *Kova the Blacksmith* (opera) 41, *Leili and Medjnun* (ballet) 47, Two Sonatinas for Piano 48, Tadjik Suite (for symphony orchestra) 48, *Bakhtior and Nisso* (opera) 54, *Seven Armenian Songs* (symphonic suite) 55, *Afghan Suite* 56, Nine Songs by Komitas for Voice and Symphony Orchestra 57, Three Songs by Sayat-Nova for Voice and Symphony Orchestra 57, *Islands of Indonesia* (six symphonic pictures for orchestra) 59, 61, Rhapsody on a Theme of Rabindranath Tagore, Four Songs of Africa, Two Songs of Latin America, *Shakuntala* (ballet) 61.
Moscow Section of R.S.F.S.R. Composers' Union, 4-6 Tretya Miusskaya ulitsa, Moscow, U.S.S.R.

Balay, Georges, L. ès D.; French diplomatist; b. 25 May 1903.
Diplomatic posts, Moscow, Bucharest, Rio de Janeiro, Sofia and Rome; London 42, Algiers 43, Paris 44; Chargé d'Affaires, Rome 46-47; Minister, Baghdad 48-49; Mission in Libya 50-51; Ambassador to Lebanon 52-56, to South Africa 58-; Commandeur Légion d'Honneur.
French Embassy, Pretoria, South Africa.

Balbin, Ricardo; Argentine politician; b. 29 July 1904; ed. Universidad de la Plata.
Deputy 31-52; imprisoned by Perón; anti-Perónist candidate for Presidency 51; founder and Pres. Unión Cívica Radical del Pueblo (U.C.R.P.); U.C.R.P. candidate for Presidency 58-62.
544 calle 49, La Plata, Argentina.

Balcer, Hon. Leon, B.A., LL.L.; Canadian lawyer and politician; b. 17; ed. Laval Univ., Quebec.
Admitted Quebec Bar 41; active service Royal Canadian Navy 41-45; practising law 46-; Sec.-Treas. town of Three Rivers 46-49; mem. House of Commons 49-; Pres. Young Conservatives of Canada 50-53; Canadian Govt. del. to 6th Session, U.N., Paris 52; Pres. Conservative Asscn. of Canada 57; Solicitor-Gen. 57, acting Minister of Mines and Technical Surveys 57-58, Min. 58-59; Minister of Transport 60-63.
1635 Royale, Three Rivers, P.Q.; and The Savoy, 140 Slater, Ottawa, Canada.

Balchin, Brig. Nigel Marlin; British author; b. 3 Dec. 1908; ed. Dauntsey's School and Peterhouse, Cambridge.
Publs. *Darkness Falls from the Air* 42, *The Small Back Room* 44, *Mine Own Executioner* 45, *Lord, I Was Afraid* 47, *The Borgia Testament* 48, *A Sort of Traitors* 49, *A Way Through the Wood* 50, *Sundry Creditors* 53, *Last Recollections of my Uncle Charles* 54, *The Fall of a Sparrow* 55, *The Leader of the House* 60, *Seen Dimly before Dawn* 62, *In the Absence of Mrs. Petersen* 66, *Kings of Infinite Space* 67.
48 Regent's Park Road, London, N.W.1, England.
Telephone: 01-722-5754.

Balcon, Sir Michael, Kt.; British film producer; b. 19 May 1896.
Founder and Dir. Gainsborough Pictures Ltd. 28; Dir. of Production, Gaumont-British Picture Corpn. Ltd. 31; Dir. and Producer Ealing Films Ltd. 38-59; Chair. British Lion Films (Holdings) Ltd. until 65; Gov. British Film Inst.; Dir. Border Television Ltd.; mem. Court of Royal Coll. of Art, London Acad. of Music and Dramatic Art; Fellow British Film Acad.; Hon. Fellow British Kinematograph Soc.; Knight (1st Class) Order of St. Olav (Norway); Hon. D.Litt. (Birmingham). Productions include: *The Good Companions, Evergreen, I Was a Spy, Man of Arran, A Yank at Oxford, The Foreman Went to France, Next of Kin, Dead of Night, The Captive Heart, The Overlanders, Hue and Cry, Scott of the Antarctic, Whisky Galore, Kind Hearts and Coronets, The Blue Lamp, The Lavender Hill Mob, The Man in the White Suit, Where No Vultures Fly, Mandy, The Cruel Sea, The Divided Heart, The Night My Number Came Up, Touch and Go, The Ladykillers, The Long Arm, The Shiralee, Dunkirk, The Scape-goat, The Siege of Pinchgut, The Long and the Short and the Tall, Sammy Going South.*
Upper Parrock, Hartfield, Sussex; and 10/23 Down Street, London, W.1, England.
Telephone: Forest Row 2370; 01-499-8908 (London).

Balderston, C. Canby, B.S., A.M., PH.D.; American banker; b. 1 Feb. 1897; ed. Westtown School, Pennsylvania and Univ. of Pennsylvania.
Assistant Prof. of Industry, Univ. of Pennsylvania 25-31, Prof. 31-54; Dean, Wharton School of Finance and Commerce, Univ. of Pennsylvania 41-54; mem. Board of Dirs. Federal Reserve Bank of Philadelphia 43-53, Dep. Chair. 49-53; Chief, War Dept., Wage Administration Agency and Wage Administration Section, H.Q. Army Service Forces 42-45; mem. Board of Governors Fed. Reserve System 54-65, Vice-Chair. 55-65; Pres. Leeds and Lippincott 50-; official of several business and educational orgs.
Publs. *Managerial Profit Sharing* 28, *Profit-Sharing for Wage-Earners* 37, *Group Incentives* 30, *Executive Guidance of Industrial Relations* 35, *Wage Setting* 40.
Penncrest, 45 Rose Tree Road, Media, Pennsylvania, U.S.A.

Baldinger, Ernst, D.SC.; Swiss physicist; b. 5 Jan. 1911; ed. in Basle and Fed. Inst. of Technology, Zürich.
Professor of Applied Physics, Basle Univ. 48-.
Publs. numerous works in the fields of electronics and nuclear physics.
Weidengasse 35, Basle, Switzerland.

Baldini, Gabriele, M.A., PH.D.; Italian professor; b. 29 Aug. 1919; ed. Liceo Visconti, Rome and Cambridge Univs.
Professor of English, Trieste Univ. 50-51, Rome Univ. 51, Istituto Orientale, Naples 53; Full Prof., Rome Univ. 55-59, 61-; Dir. Istituto Italiano di Cultura, London 59-61; Contributor to *Il Corriere della sera* 63-.
Publs. *Melville o le Ambiguità* 52, *John Webster e il Linguaggio della Tragedia* 53, *Teatro Inglese della Restaurazione e del '700* 55, *Le tragedie di Shakespeare* 57, *La tradizione letteraria dell'Inghilterra Medioevale* 58, *Le più belle pagine della letteratura Inglese dalle origini all'età di Shakespeare* 60, *Il dramma elisabettiano* 62, *Opere Complete di W. Shakespeare nuovamente tradotte e annotate* 63, *Manualetto shakespeariano* 64, *La fortuna di Shakespeare* 65, *Le rondini dell' Orfeo* 65, *Le acque rosse del Potomac* (autobiog. Vol. I, 67).
Piazza Campo Marzio 3, Rome, Italy.
Telephone: 651-786.

Baldwin, Charles F., B.S.; American diplomatist; b. 21 Jan. 1902; ed. Georgetown Univ.
U.S. Foreign Commerce Service 27, Sydney 27-30, Oslo 46-48; U.S. Political Adviser, Trieste 48-49; Counsellor (Econ. Affairs), London 50-51; Consul-Gen. Singapore 52-53; Deputy Asst. Sec. of State for Far East Econ. Affairs 54-55; Ambassador to Fed. of Malaya 61-63, to Malaysia 63-64; Diplomat in Residence, Univ. of Virginia 64-.
Falcon Drive, Colthurst, Charlottesville, Va., U.S.A.

Baldwin, James A.; American writer; b. 2 Aug. 1924; ed. DeWitt Clinton High School.
First professional publication *Nation* book review 46; articles and stories in *Nation, Reporter, Harper's Bazaar, Partisan Review, Commentary, Mademoiselle, The New Leader, Esquire, The New Yorker* 46; stories included in Martha Foley's *Best Short Stories* 58, 61, and O. Henry's *Best Short Stories of 1959*; play *Amen Corner* produced at Howard Univ. 55; mem. Dramatists' Guild, New Dramatists' Cttee., Actors' Studio; Eugene F. Saxton Fellowship 45, Rosenwald Fellowship 48, Guggenheim Fellowship 54, Partisan Review Fellowship and Nat. Inst. of Arts and Letters Award 56, Ford Foundation Grant 59.
Publs. *Go Tell It On The Mountain* (novel; published in U.S.A., Great Britain, Italy, France, Germany, Japan, Denmark and Sweden) 53, *Notes of a Native Son* (essays; U.S.A. and Sweden) 55, *Giovanni's Room* (novel; U.S.A., Great Britain, France, Germany, Sweden and Denmark) 56, *Nobody knows my Name* (essays; U.S.A. and Sweden) 61, *Another Country* (novel; U.S.A. and Great Britain) 62, *The Fire Next Time* (essays) 63, *Blues for Mr. Charlie* (play) 63, (with Richard Avedon) *Nothing Personal* 64, *Going to Meet the Man* 65, *Tell Me How Long the Train's Been Gone* (novel) 67.
470 West End Avenue, New York, N.Y., U.S.A.

Balenciaga, Cristóbal; Spanish couturier; b. 95.
Opened fashion house, San Sebastian 16, Madrid 32, Paris 37, Barcelona 38; Cross of Knight of Order of Isabel la Católica (Spain).
Office: 10 avenue George V, Paris 8e, France.

Balke, Siegfried; German chemist and politician; b. 1 June 1902; ed. Technical Coll. of Munich.
Industrial chemist 25-53, 63-; Fed. Minister for Posts and Telecommunications 53-56; mem. Bundestag 57-; Fed. Minister for Nuclear Energy 56-62; Chair. Deutsches Museum, Munich; Hon. Prof. Munich Univ.; Senator, Max Planck Gesellschaft; Pres. German Employers' Asscn.
8 Munich 22, Lerchenfeldstrasse 9, German Federal Republic.

Balkow, Julius; German politician; b. 26 Aug. 1909; ed. primary school and Univ. of Leipzig.
Former locksmith; mem. Sozialistische Einheitspartei Deutschlands 31-; student at Univ. of Leipzig 46-49; Ministry of Foreign and Inner-German Trade 51-, Deputy Minister of Foreign and Inner-German Trade 56-61, Minister 61-65; Deputy Chair. Council of Ministers; mem. Central Cttee. Sozialistische Einheitspartei Deutschlands 63-; mem. Volkskammer 63-; several decorations.
Ministerrat der Deutschen Demokratischen Republik, Berlin, Germany.

Ball, Eric Glendinning, B.S., M.A., PH.D.; American university professor; b. 12 July 1904; ed. Haverford Coll. and Univ. of Pennsylvania.
Asst., School of Medicine, Univ. of Pa. 26-28; Nat. Research Fellow, Johns Hopkins Medical School 29-30, Instructor in Physiological Chemistry 30-33, Associate in Physiological Chemistry 33-40; Int. Physiological Congress Fellow, Rome 32; Guggenheim Memorial Foundation Fellow, Berlin-Dahlem 37-38; Asst. Prof. of Biological Chemistry, Harvard Medical School 40-41, Associate Prof. 41-46, Prof. 46-, Chair. Div. of Medical Sciences 52-; Acting Head of the Department of Biological Chemistry 43-46, 58-59, Edward S. Wood Prof. of Biological Chemistry 62-; Guggenheim Memorial Foundation Fellow and Visiting Investigator, Scripps

Clinic and Research Foundation, La Jolla, Calif. 63-; Eli Lilly Prize in Biochemistry 40; Fellow American Asscn. for Advancement of Science; mem. of Nat. Acad. U.S.A., Society of Biological Chemists, American Chemical Society, American Acad. of Arts and Sciences, Biochemical Society of Great Britain, etc.; Hon. M.A. (Harvard Univ.) 42; Hon. D.Sc. (Haverford Coll.) 49; holder of Southern Cross, Brazil 45, Certificate of Merit, U.S.A. 48; mem. Editorial Board *Journal of Biological Chemistry* 50-60 and *Biochemical Preparations* 48-56 (Editor-in-Chief Vol. 2), *Biochemistry* 60-.
Harvard Medical School, 25 Shattuck Street, Boston, Mass. 02115, U.S.A.

Ball, George Wildman; American lawyer and government official; b. 21 Dec. 1909; ed. Northwestern Univ. Admitted to Illinois Bar 34, D.C. Bar 46; law practice Chicago 35-42, Washington 46-61; Assoc. Gen. Counsel Lend-Lease Admin. 42-43, Foreign Econs. Admin. 43-44; Dir. U.S. Strategic Bombing Survey, London 44-45; Political Adviser to Adlai Stevenson; Under-Sec. of State for Econ. Affairs Feb.-Dec. 61; Under-Sec. of State Dec. 61-Sept. 66; Pres. of Board of Dirs. of Lehmann Brothers Int. Ltd. Oct. 66-May 68; Perm. Rep. to UN June 68-; Hon. LL.D. (Northwestern Univ.); Democrat.
Publ. *The Discipline of Power* 68.
c/o Dept. of State, Washington 25, D.C., U.S.A.

Ball, Lucille; American actress.
Film actress 34-; TV actress; Pres. Desilu Productions Inc. 62-.
Films include: *Roberta, Chatterbox, Follow the Fleet, Stage Door, Having a Wonderful Time, Affairs of Annabell, Room Service, Valley of the Sun, Seven Days Leave, DuBarry was a Lady, Best Foot Forward, Meet the People, Thousands Cheer, Without Love, Love from a Stranger, Her Husband's Affairs, Long, Long Trailer, Forever Darling, Facts of Life*; TV Shows: *I Love Lucy, The Lucy Show.*
Beverly Hills, California, U.S.A.

Ball, William, A.B., M.A.; American actor and theatrical director; b. 31; ed. Fordham Univ. and Carnegie Inst. of Technology.
Oregon Shakespeare Festival 50-53; Antioch Shakespeare Festival 54; Group 20 Players 55; San Diego Shakespeare Festival 56; Arena Stage, Washington D.C. 57-58; *Back to Methuselah*, Broadway, New York and tour 58; *Six Characters in Search of an Author, Così Fan Tutte* 59, *The Inspector General* 60, *Porgy and Bess* 61, *Midsummer Night's Dream* 63, New York City Center Opera Co. off-Broadway: *The Misanthrope, The Lady's Not for Burning, The Country Wife, Ivanov, A Month In The Country* 56-58, *Under Milk Wood* 56-61, *Six Characters In Search of an Author* 63, *The Tempest*, Stratford, Conn. Shakespeare Festival; *Yeoman of the Guard* (Stratford, Canada) 64; Librettist and Dir. *Natalia Petrovna* (New York City Center Opera Co.) 64; *Tartuffe* (Lincoln Center Repertory Co.) 65; Founder and Gen. Dir. American Conservatory Theatre (A.C.T.) initiated at Pittsburgh Playhouse in 66 with a 16-play double repertory theatre; performing in San Francisco and Chicago on alternating seasonal basis with 23-play repertory 67; Fulbright Scholarship to Great Britain, NBC/RCA Fellowship to Carnegie Inst. of Technology, Ford Foundation Director's Grant 59, Ford Foundation Comm. for opera libretto *Natasha.*
450 Geary Street, San Francisco, Calif., U.S.A.

Ballantine, Duncan Smith, A.B., PH.D.; American college president; b. 5 Nov. 1912; ed. Amherst Coll. (Mass.), and Harvard Univ.
Held various teaching appointments 36-42; served with U.S.N.R. 42-46; Assoc. Prof. History, Mass. Inst. Technology 47-52; Pres. Reed Coll. 52-55; Pres. Robert Coll. 55-62; Research Assoc. Harvard Univ. Center for International Affairs 62; now Chief, Education Division,

International Bank for Reconstruction and Development; mem. American Hist. Asscn., Econ. History Asscn., Asscn. American Colls., American Council Education; hon. LL.D.
Publ. *U.S. Naval Logistics in the Second World War* 47.
Home: 5110 38th St. NW, Washington 16, D.C., U.S.A.; Office: International Bank for Reconstruction & Development 1818 H Street, N.W., Washington, D.C., U.S.A.
Telephone: EM3-1969.

Ballard, Bristow Guy, O.B.E.; Canadian electrical engineer; b. 19 June 1902; ed. Queen's Univ.
Member, Engineering Design Dept., Westinghouse Mfg. Co. 24-30; mem. Nat. Research Council of Canada, in charge of Electrical Engineering Branch 30-45; development of anti-magnetic mine equipment 39-45; Officer-in-Charge Electrical Engineering and Radio Branch, Nat. Research Council of Canada 46-48, Dir. Radio and Electrical Engineering Div. 48-63, Vice-Pres. (Scientific) Nat. Research Council of Canada 54-63, Pres. 63-67; Pres. Canadian Patents and Devt. Ltd. 67-.
Publs. Papers on high-voltage research, and precision electrical control.
Office: National Research Building, Montreal Road, Ottawa 7; Home: 390 Cloverdale Road, Ottawa 2, Ontario, Canada.
Telephone: 993-9022 (Office); 749-9744 (Home).

Ballinger, Margaret Livingstone, B.A., M.A.; South African (b. Scottish) politician; b. 94; ed. Holy Rosary Convent (Port Elizabeth), Huguenot Coll. (Wellington), Rhodes Univ. (Grahamstown) and Somerville Coll., Oxford.
Settled in South Africa 04; elected to Union Parl. 37, returned unopposed 42, re-elected 48, returned unopposed 54 as Native Rep. for Cape Eastern; parliamentary seat abolished by Bantu Self-Government Act 59; mem. South African Liberal Party 53- (1st Pres.); Dyason Memorial Lecturer, Inst. Int. Affairs, Australia 60; Assoc. Fellow, Nuffield Coll., Oxford 61; fmr. Senior Lecturer in History, Witwatersrand Univ.
Publs. *Influence of Holland on Africa, Britain in South Africa, Bechuanaland and Basutoland* (with W. G. Ballinger) and articles on race and economic problems.
8 Firdale Road, Newlands, Cape, South Africa.

Ballinger, William George; South African (b. British) politician; b. 94; ed. Glasgow Univ. and Elsinore Coll., Denmark.
Town and Parish Councillor, Motherwell (Scotland) 22-28; Adviser on African Trade Union, Industrial and Co-operative Organisations; Adviser British Workers' Del. I.L.O. Confs. Geneva 35 and 36; Senator (Rep. of Transvaal Natives) 48-60; seat abolished by Bantu Self-Government Act 60; Research student, Queen Elizabeth House, Oxford 61; Hon. Sec. Non-European Progress Trust, Cape Town.
Publs. *Race and Economic Contacts, Britain in South Africa, Bechuanaland and Basutoland* (with Margaret Ballinger).
8 Firdale Road, Newlands, Cape, South Africa.

Balluseck, Daniel J. von; Netherlands journalist and diplomatist; b. 8 March 1895; ed. School of Economics, Rotterdam, and Univs. of Geneva and Amsterdam.
Correspondent of *Algemeen Handelsblad* in London, Paris, Geneva, Indonesia, Mexico, U.S.A. and Amsterdam 18-28, chief editor 28-41 and 45-49; civilian prisoner during occupation; Permanent Rep. to U.N. (with rank of Ambassador) 50-55; Ambassador to U.S.S.R. 55-57, to Canada 58-60; delegate of Ministry of Foreign Affairs in Defence Coll., The Hague 61-; Knight Order of Netherlands Lion; Officer Order of Orange Nassau.
Publs. *Holland's House: A Nation Building a Home,* by Peter Bricklayer (pen-name) 39; *Wij deelgenooten*

(story of the Netherlands-Indonesian relationship) by Pieter Schakel (pen-name) 45.
96B Koninginnegracht, The Hague, Netherlands.
Telephone: The Hague 553774.

Balmain, Pierre Alexandre; French couturier; b. 18 May 1914; ed. Lycée de Chambéry and Ecole des Beaux Arts.
Designed for Molyneux 34-39, Lucien Lelong 41-45; began own business 46; opened branch in New York 51, Caracas 54; Chevalier de la Légion d'Honneur, etc.
Publ. *My Years and Seasons* (memoirs) 64.
44 rue François Ier, Paris 8e, France.
Telephone: BAL 6804.

Balogh, Thomas, M.A., DR. RER. POL. (cr. Life Peer June 68); British political economist; b. 2 Nov. 1905; ed. Gymnasium, Univs. of Budapest, Berlin and Harvard.
Fellow, Hungarian Coll., Berlin 27-28; Rockefeller Fellow 28-30; banking 31-39; Lecturer, Balliol Coll., Oxford 39-45, Fellow 45-, Reader in Econs., Oxford Univ. 60-; mem. Econ. and Financial Sub-cttee. of Labour Party Exec. Cttee. 50-; Consultant or Adviser to Reserve Bank of Australia, Govts. of Malta, India, Jamaica, British Guiana, Mauritius and Algeria, FAO and UN Econ. Comms. for Latin America and Africa; Visiting Prof., Minneapolis, Madison, Harvard and Delhi; Econ. Adviser to British Cabinet 64- (on part-time basis Oct. 67-).
Publs. *Studies in Financial Organisation* 47, *The Dollar Crisis* 49, *Fabian Essays* (Int. and Colonial), co-author *The Establishment, Economic Future of Malta* (with Seers) 55, *Planning and Monetary Organisation in Jamaica* 56, *The Economic Development of the Mediterranean* (with Ergas) 57, *Development Plans in Africa* (with Ergas) 59, *Economic Policy in Underdeveloped Areas and the Price Mechanism* 62, *Aspects of Development* 63, *Unequal Partners* 63, *Planning for Prosperity* 63, *The Economics of Poverty* 66.
The Cabinet Office, Whitehall, London, S.W.1; and Balliol College, Oxford, England.
Telephone: Oxford 49601.

Balogun, Kolawole, Chief **Jagun of Otan,** LL.B.; Nigerian lawyer, politician and diplomatist; b. 26; ed. Govt. Coll., Ibadan.
On staff of *Nigerian Advocate,* later radio announcer, then Asst. Editor *West African Pilot;* legal studies in London 48-51, called to the Bar 51; Sec. London branch National Council of Nigeria and the Cameroons (NCNC) 51; Nat. Sec. NCNC 51-57; mem. of Fed. Parl. 54; Fed. Minister without Portfolio, later Fed. Minister of Information; resigned from govt. 58; Nigerian Commr. in Ghana 59-60, High Commr. 60-61; mem. of Ministry of Foreign Affairs 61-; Chair. Nigerian Nat. Shipping Line 62-.
P.O. Box 617, Lagos, Nigeria.

Balsis, Edwardas Kosto; Soviet composer; b. 1919; ed. Kaunas Conservatoire.
Chairman Lithuanian Composers' Union; Sec., Exec. mem. U.S.S.R. Composers' Union; Asst. Prof. 60-; Honoured Worker of the Arts of Lithuanian S.S.R. 59; People's Artist of Lithuanian S.S.R. 65.
Principal works: Piano Sonata 49, *Vilnius* (poem for symphony orchestra) 50, *Heroic Poem* (for symphony orchestra) 52, String Quartet in G-minor 53, First Concerto for Violin and Orchestra 54, *Dance Suite* of Lithuanian folk dances for symphony orchestra 57, Second Concerto for Violin and Orchestra 58, *Egle, Queen of the Snakes* (ballet) 60, Cantata for Choir and Symphony Orchestra 61; Film music: *The Bridge, Blue Roads* 57, *Adonas Wants to Become a Man* 59, *Living Heroes* 60, *The Cannonade* 61, *Old Sailor's Song, Going on a Long Sea Voyage* 64.
Lithuanian Composers' Union, 6 Ulitsa Reshitoyu, Vilnius, Lithuanian S.S.R., U.S.S.R.

Baltadzis, Alexander; Greek politician; b. 04; ed. Athens Univ.
President, Panhellenic Confederation of Farm Co-operatives Union, State Lands Management Dept., Tobacco Trades Asscn. 45; Founder and Leader, Farmers and Workers Party; mem. Parliament 50-; mem. Exec. Cttee. Centre Union 61-; Minister of Agriculture Nov. 63-65.
5 Pandoras Street, Ekeli, Athens, Greece.

Balthus (Balthasar Klossowski de Rola); French artist; b. 29 Feb. 1908.
Exhibited Galerie Pierre, Paris 34, Pierre Matisse Gallery, New York City 38, 39, 49, 56, Moos Gallery, Geneva 43, Wildenstein Galleries, Paris 46, 56, Dunn Int. Exhbn., London 63; Dir. Villa Medici, Rome 61-.
Works include: Frescoes, Church of Beatenberg, Switzerland 28, Costumes and Sets for Artaud's *The Cenci* 35, for *Cosi Fan Tutte,* Aix-en-Provence 50, numerous paintings.
Villa Medici, Rome, Italy.

Baltra, Alberto; Chilean lawyer and economist; b. 12.
Professor of Political Economy and Director of School of Economics 35; Vice-Pres. Int. Exchange Comm. 39; Dir.-Gen. of Trade at Ministry of National Economy 42; Under-Sec. of State, Ministry of Nat. Economy 46; accompanied Pres. on trade missions to Brazil and the Argentine 47; Minister of Nat. Economy and Trade 47; mem. of Import Licensing Comm. 47; Pres. Radical Party 58; Prof. of Economic Theory and Dir. of Dept. of Social Sciences, Univ. of Chile, Santiago; Consultant to UN Econ. Comm. for Latin America (ECLA).
Publs. *Economía Dirigida, El principio orgánico biológico en la economía, Organización económica de la U.R.S.S., Crecimiento económico de América Latina* (trans. Polish and Russian), *La desnacionalización del petróleo chileno, Tres países del mundo socialista, Pedro Aguirre Cerda, Teoría Económica, Nuestra América y sus Problemas, Problemas del Subdesarrollo Latinoamericano.*
Avenida Antonio Varas 475, Santiago, Chile.

Baltzer, Fritz, PH.D.; Swiss zoologist; b. 12 March 1884; ed. Univ. of Würzburg.
Former Prof. of Zoology, Würzburg and Freiburg (Germany); Prof. Univ. of Berne 21-, Rector 38-39; Visiting Prof. of Embryology, State Univ. of Iowa 48-49; work on sea urchins, physiology of the senses in spiders, experimental embryology, merogony and chimeras of amphibians; Foreign Assoc. Nat. Acad. of Sciences, U.S.A. 67; Dr. h.c. (Strasbourg, Freiburg-im-Breisgau).
Berne, Finkenhubelweg 6, Switzerland.

Balzhinnyam, Delegjunain; Mongolian politician and diplomatist; b. 13.
Minister of Livestock Breeding 49-57; Sec. Mongolian People's Revolutionary Party (in charge of Agricultural Affairs) until 62; Ambassador to Bulgaria, also accred. to U.K. 63-.
Embassy of the Mongolian People's Republic, 16 boulevard Tolbukhin, Sofia, Bulgaria.

Bam, Arvind Shankar, B.SC.; Indian civil servant and United Nations official; b. 12 March 1918; ed. Fergusson Coll., Poona, and King's Coll., London.
Entered Civil Service 41, Asst. Collector, Dharwar 42-44; Special Officer, Civil Supplies, Darjeeling 44-45; District Controller of Civil Supplies, Jalpaiguri 45-46; Asst. Collector, Broach 46-47; Under-Sec., Home Dept., Govt. of Bombay April-Aug. 47, Deputy Sec. 47-49; First Collector and District Magistrate, Kolhapur 49-52; Dep. Sec. Ministry of Rehabilitation, Calcutta 52-57; Controller for Iron and Steel 57-61; Chair. Tea Board, Govt. of India 61-65; Gen. Man. Indian Airlines Corpn. Dec. 65-Nov. 66, Chair. and Gen. Man. Dec. 66-June 67; Resident Rep. of UN Devt. Programme in Yugoslavia 67-; Leader, Indian Steel Del. to ECAFE 60;

Leader, Indian Tea Del. to U.S., Canada, Australia, New Zealand and Singapore 62.
Resident Representative of United Nations Development Programme, Svetozara Markovica 58, P.O. Box 644, Belgrade, Yugoslavia.
Telephone: 644-463.

Bambang Sugeng, Maj.-Gen. Raden; Indonesian army officer and diplomatist; b. 31 Oct. 1913; ed. High School and Law Univ., Indonesia.
Regimental Commdr. 45-46; Chief of Staff 6th Div. 46-47; Commdr. 18th Brigade 47-48; Military Gov. of Jogjakarta 48-49; First Dep. Chief of Staff of Army 49-51; Commdr. 1st Div. and Regional Military Gov. of East Java 51-54; Commdr. and Chief of Staff of Army 54-55; Indonesian Minister to the Vatican 56-60; Ambassador to Japan 60-64, to Brazil 64-.
Indonesian Embassy, Rua Toneleros 338, Copacabana, Rio de Janeiro, Brazil.

Bancroft, Anne; American actress; b. 17 Sept. 1931; ed. Christopher Columbus High School, New York City.
Theatre: Broadway debut in *Two for the Seesaw* 58; played Anne Sullivan in *The Miracle Worker* 59-60, *The Devils* 65, *The Little Foxes* 67.
Films: *The Miracle Worker, Don't Bother to Knock, Tonight we Sing, Demetrius and the Gladiators, The Pumpkin Eater, Seven Women, The Graduate* 68.
Numerous TV appearances including *Mother Courage and her Children*; Academy Award for film *The Miracle Worker* 62.
c/o David J. Cogan, 350 Fifth Avenue, New York, N.Y., U.S.A.

Bancroft, Harding Foster; American newspaper executive; b. 29 Dec. 1910; ed. Williams Coll. and Harvard Law School.
Lawyer 36-41; Office of Price Admin., Washington 41-43; Lend-Lease Admin. 43; U.S. Navy 43-45; Chief Div. UN Political Affairs, Dept. of State 45; U.S. Dep. Rep., UN Collective Measures Comm. 50-53; Legal Adviser, Int. Labour Org. (ILO), Geneva 53-56; Sec. *The New York Times* 57-63, Dir. 61-, Exec. Vice-Pres. 63-; mem. U.S. Del. UN Gen. Assembly 66.
The New York Times, Times Square, N.Y.C. 36; and 214 East 70th Street, New York, N.Y. 10021, U.S.A.
Telephone: 212-RH4-3485.

Banda, Aleke Kadonaphani; Malawi journalist and politician; b. 19 Sept. 1939; ed. United Missionary School, Que Que and Inyati School, Bulawayo.
Secretary Nyasaland African Congress (N.A.C.), Que Que Branch 54; Gen. Sec. S. Rhodesia African Students Asscn. 57-59; arrested and detained in Rhodesia 59, deported to Nyasaland; Founder-mem. Malawi Congress Party (M.C.P.), Sec.-Gen. 59; Editor Nyasaland Trade Union Congress newspaper *Ntendere Pa Nchito* and mem. T.U.C. Council 59-60; Personal Political Sec. to Dr. Hastings Banda 60-; Sec. M.C.P. Del. to Lancaster House Conf. resulting in self-govt. for Malawi 60; Sec. to subsequent confs. 60, 62; Man. Editor *Malawi News* 59-66; Dir. Malawi Press Ltd. 60; Dir.-Gen. Malawi Broadcasting Corpn. 64-66; Nat. Chair. League of Malawi Youth and Commdr. Malawi Young Pioneers 63-; Dir. Reserve Bank of Malawi 65-66; Minister of Devt. and Planning 66-67, of Econ. Affairs (incorporating Natural Resources, Trade and Industry, and Devt. and Planning), and Minister of Works and Supplies 67-.
Ministry of Economic Affairs, Blantyre, Malawi.

Banda, Hastings Kamuzu, PH.B., B.SC., M.B., CH.B.; M.D., L.R.C.S.; Malawi doctor and politician; b. 05, ed. mission school, Edinburgh Univ. and in U.S.A.
Worked in gold mine; spent twelve years in U.S. in study and medical practice; medical practice in Willesden, England, until 54, in Kumasi, Ghana 54-58; returned to Nyasaland to take up leadership of Malawi Congress Party 58-; detained during declared state of emergency March 59-April 60; Minister of Natural

Resources, Survey and Local Govt. 61-63, Prime Minister of Nyasaland 63-July 64, of Malawi July 64-, also Minister of Special Services and Health Dec. 63-; Pres. of Repub. of Malawi July 66-; Chancellor, Univ. of Malawi 65-.
Office of the President, Zomba, Malawi.

Bandaranaike, Sirimavo; Ceylonese politician; b. 17 April 1916; ed. St. Bridget's Convent, Colombo.
Widow of the late S. W. R. D. Bandaranaike (Prime Minister of Ceylon 56-59); Pres. of Sri Lanka Freedom Party 60-; Prime Minister, Minister of Defence and External Affairs July 60-65; mem. Senate until 65.
Horagolla, Nittambuwa, Ceylon.

Bandeira, Manuel; Brazilian poet and writer; b. 19 April 1886; ed. Colégio Pedro II and Escola Politecnica de São Paulo.
Inspector of Secondary Educ., Colégio Pedro II 35-38; Prof. of Universal Educ., Colégio Pedro II 38-43; Prof. of Hispano-American Literature, Universidade do Brasil 43-56; travelled in Europe 57; mem. Consultative Council of Nat. Historical and Artistic Heritage 38-; mem. Brazilian Acad. of Letters 40-; Prêmio da Sociedade Felipe d'Oliveira 37; Prêmio da Instituto Brasileiro de Educação e Cultura 46.
Publ. poems: *A Cinza das Horas* 17, *Carnaval* 19, *O Ritho Dissoluto* 24, *Libertinagem* 30, *Estrêla da Mañhá* 36, *Lira dos Cinquent'anos* 44, *Poemas Traduzidos* 45, *Mafuá do Malungo* 48, *Belo Belo* 48, *Opus 10* 52, *Estrêla da Tarde* 63, *Preparação para a Morte* 65; prose: *Guia de Ouro Petro* 38, *Apresentação da Poesia Brasileira* 57, *Itinerário de Pasárçada* 57.
Avenida Beira Mar 406, Apartamento 806, Rio de Janeiro, Brazil.

Bandeira de Mello, Lydio Machado, DR. JUR.; Brazilian university professor; b. 19 July 1901; ed. Univ. of Brazil.
Professor of Criminal Law, Univ. of Minas Gerais 52-54, Comparative Criminal Law 54-.
Publs. *O Problema do Mal* (The Problem of Evil) 35, *A Procura de Deus* (Research of God) 38, *Responsabilidade Penal* (Criminal Liability) 41, *Prova Matemática da Existência de Deus* (Mathematical Proof of God's Existence) 42, *Teoria do Destino* (Theory of Fate) 44, *A Predestinação Para O Bem* (The Predestination for Good) 48, *Metafísica do Número* (Metaphysics of Numbers) 46, *Tabu, Pecado e Crime* (Taboo, Sin and Crime) 49 *O Real e o Possível* (Real and Possible) 53, *Manual de Direito Penal* (Handbook of Criminal Law) Vols. 1-4, 53-58, *A Origem dos Sexos* (The Origin of Sex) 55, *Filosofia do Direito* (The Philosophy of Law) 57, *Ontologia e Lógica da Contradição* (Ontology and Logic of Contradiction) 59, *Metafísica do Tempo* 61, *O Direito Penal Hispano-Luso Medievo* (Spanish-Portuguese Medieval Criminal Law) 2 vols. 61, *Tratado de Direito Penal* (Treatise on Criminal Law), *Crime e Exclusão de Criminalidade* (Crime: Justifiable Acts) 62, *Da Responsabilidade Penal e Da Isenção de Pena* (Criminal Liability and its Variations) 62, *Da Capitulação dos Crimes e da Fixação das Penas* (The Art of Sentencing) 63, *Metafísica da Gravitação* (Gravitation), *Memória, Espaço e Tempo* (Memory, Space and Time) 2 vols. 63, *Cosmologia do Movimento* (Cosmology of Motion) 65, *Teologia Matemática* 65, *Metafísica do Espaço* 66, *A Pluralidade de Consciências* (Monism or Pluralism?) 67, *Crítica Cosmológica da Física Quântica* (Cosmological Critique of Quantum Theory) 68.
Rua Alvarenga Peixoto 1603, Belo Horizonte, Minas Gerais, Brazil.

Bandio, Jean Arthur; Central African Republic politician; b. June 1923; ed. Edouard-Renard Coll., Brazzaville.
Teacher, Brazzaville until 53, then advanced studies in France; returned to Congo (Brazzaville) and became Asst. District Chief for Sibiti; later District Officer, many parts of Central African Repub.; Dir. of Admin.

Affairs, Central African Repub. 59; Minister of Interior 60-67, of Foreign Affairs Jan. 67-.
Ministère des Affaires Etrangères, Bangui, Central African Republic.

Banerji, Shishir Kumar, B.A., I.C.S.; Indian diplomatist; b. 21 Oct. 1913; ed. Univ. of Allahabad and New Coll., Oxford.
Deputy Commr. Central Provinces 37-46; Sec. Civil Supplies, Central Provinces Govt. 46-47; First Sec. and later Chargé d'Affaires, Tehran 47-49; Deputy Sec. Ministry of External Affairs 49-51; Deputy High Commr., Lahore 51-54; Consul-Gen. San Francisco 54-56; Chair. UN Visiting Mission to British and French Togolands 55; Envoy to Syria 56, Ambassador 57-58; High Commissioner to Malaya 58-59; Joint Sec., Ministry of External Affairs 60-61; Chief of Protocol 61-64; Chief Inspector of Indian Missions abroad 64; Ambassador to German Federal Republic 64-67; Sec. Ministry of Foreign Affairs 67; Amb. to Japan 67-.
Indian Embassy, 1, 2-chome, Kodan, Chiyoda-ku, Tokyo, Japan.

Bangerter, Hans Ernst; Swiss sports official; b. 10 June 1924; ed. Technical Coll., Bienne.
Assistant Sec. Int. Fed. of Football Asscns. (FIFA), Zürich 53-59; Sec.-Gen. Union of European Football Asscns. (UEFA), Berne 60-.
Office: UEFA, P.O. Box 16, Berne; Home: Hubelgasse 25, 3065 Bolligen, BE, Switzerland.

Bangoura, Karim; Guinean diplomatist; b. 22.
Military service 42-45; Dep. to Territorial Assembly 46-57; Counsellor, French Union Assembly 54-58; Administrator, Guinean Press Agency 60; Dir. of Cabinet of Ministry of Information and Tourism 61-62; Ambassador to U.S.A., Canada, Mexico 63-.
Embassy of Guinea, 2112 Leroy Place, N.W., Washington 8, D.C., U.S.A.

Bank-Anthony, Sir Mobolaji, K.B.E.; Nigerian business executive; b. 11 June 1907; ed. Methodist Boys High School, Lagos, Church Missionary Society Grammar School, Lagos, and Ibeju-Ode Grammar School.
Postal Clerk, Nigerian Post and Telegraph Dept. 24; later built up palm oil business and after Second World War built up construction, haulage and cinema companies; Fellow Inst. of Directors, London.
Executive House, 2A Mill Street, P.O.B. 75, Lagos, Nigeria.

Bannerman, David Armitage, O.B.E., B.A., M.A., SC.D., F.R.S.E.; Scottish ornithologist and farmer; b. 27 Nov. 1886; ed. Wellington Coll. and Pembroke Coll., Cambridge.
Zoological Dept. British Museum 10-52; served in France, First World War; Asst. Censor, Second World War; stock-breeder of Pedigree Galloway Cattle and Border Cheviots; Gold Medallist British Ornithological Union; Hon. Pres. Scottish Ornithologists; Vice-Pres., Royal Society for the Protection of Birds; Order of St. John; Hon. LL.D. (Glasgow).
Publs. *The Canary Islands: Their History, Natural History and Scenery* 22, *The Birds of Tropical West Africa* (8 vols.) 30-51, *The Birds of West and Equatorial Africa* (2 vols.) 53, *The Birds of the British Isles* (13 vols.) 53-64, *The Birds of Cyprus* (with W. Mary Bannerman) 59, *The Birds of the Atlantic Islands* (vol. 1) 62, (vol. 2) 65 (with W. Mary Bannerman), vol. 3 (*Azores*) 66.
Shambellie, New Abbey, Scotland.

Bannikov, Nikolai Vasilyevich; Soviet politician; b. 1914; ed. Kuibyshev Industrial Inst.
Shop Mechanic, then Man., later Chief Mechanic, then Dep. Dir. of factory, and Party Organizer of C.P.S.U. Central Cttee. at a Kuibyshev factory 37-45; Party Official 45-59; Second Sec., Karaganda Regional Cttee.

of Communist Party of Kazakhstan 59-62, Second Sec. 63-; also mem. Central Cttee. of C.P. of Kazakhstan, Alt. mem. of C.P.S.U. Central Cttee., and Deputy to U.S.S.R. Supreme Soviet; mem. C.P.S.U. 40-.
Karaganda Regional Committee, Communist Party of Kazakhstan, Karaganda, U.S.S.R.

Bansal, Ghamandi Lal, M.A., LL.B.; Indian commercial executive; b. 3 Dec. 1914; ed. A.V. Mission School, Ranikhet, Government Intermediate Coll., Almora, and Lucknow Univ.
Former Dir. State Bank of India; mem. Indian Parl. 52-57; Sec.-Gen. Fed. of Indian Chambers of Commerce and Industry, All-India Organisation of Industrial Employers, Indian Nat. Cttee. of Int. Chamber of Commerce 57-; Chair. Governing Body of Shri Ram Coll. of Commerce.
Publ. *India and Pakistan—An Analysis of Economic, Agricultural and Mineral Resources.*
28 Ferozeshah Road, New Delhi 1, India.

Banzar, Jhambalyn; Mongolian diplomatist; b. 10 July 1922; ed. Mongolian State Univ., Ulan-Bator.
Secondary school teacher 46-48; local govt. posts 48-50; First Sec., Moscow 50-54; Head of Dept., Ministry of Foreign Affairs 54-56; First Sec., Prague 56-58; Head of Dept., Ministry of Foreign Affairs, and Deputy Foreign Minister 58-60; Amb. to Hungary 60-64; Permanent Rep. of Mongolian People's Repub. to UN 66-.
Permanent Mission of Mongolian People's Republic to the United Nations, 6 East 77th Street, New York, N.Y. 10021, U.S.A.
Telephone: UN1-9464.

Bao-Dai, H. M.; Viet-Namese ex-Monarch; b. 11; ed. in Viet-Nam and in France.
Son of Emperor Khai-Din, acknowledged Heir-Apparent 22; assumed throne 32; signed treaty with France 49 recognising legitimacy of nat. aspirations; withdrew to Hong Kong 50, and later to France; deposed 55.
Nice, Alpes Maritimes, France.

Barák, Rudolf; Czechoslovak politician; b. 11 May 1915.
Chair. Regional Nat. Cttee. in Brno; fmr. mem. of the Political Bureau of the Cen. Cttee. of the Communist Party of Czechoslovakia; Minister of the Interior 53-61; Head, Comm. for the Direction of Nat. Cttees. 61-62; Vice-Premier 59-62.
Prague, Czechoslovakia.

Baranov, Vasily Gavrilovich; Soviet physiologist; b. 1899; ed. Leningrad Military Medical Acad.
Army Surgeon 23-24, 41-45; Intern 25-32; Senior Assoc. Inst. of Experimental Medicine 32-40; Head of Dept., First Leningrad Medical Inst. 38-41, 45-46; Senior Research Assoc. 46-54; Head of Laboratory, Inst. of Physiology 54-, Prof. 54; Corresp. mem. U.S.S.R. Acad. of Medical Sciences 52-60, mem. 60-; mem. Board U.S.S.R. Soc. of Therapeutists; Chair. Leningrad Soc. of Endocrinologists; Orders of Red Banner of Labour and Red Star.
Publs. Over 75 works on endocrinology, including pathogenesis and treatment of toxic goitre, diabetes mellitus, physiology and pathology of ageing and climax.
Institute of Physiology, U.S.S.R. Academy of Sciences, Makarov Embankment, Leningrad, U.S.S.R.

Barański, Leon Józef, LL.D.; Polish banker; b. 95; ed. Cracow and Vienna Univs.
Entered Civil Service 19; Head Foreign Exchange Section of Treasury 24; Dir. Financial Dept. Treasury 26; Commr. Bank of Poland 24, mem. Board 30, Man. 31, Gen. Man. 35, Dir. 45; Del. int. financial and economic Confs. The Hague 29, London 33; mem. Preparatory Comm. of Experts Geneva; Del. of Polish Govt. to U.N. Monetary and Financial Conf., Bretton Woods 44;

Exec.-Dir. Int. Bank of Reconstruction and Development, Washington 46-50; Man. Dir. Development Bank of Ethiopia 51-53; Financial Adviser, Govt. of Indonesia 54-58; Chief Adviser, Bank of Sudan 58-62; Adviser, Int. Bank for Reconstruction and Development (I.B.R.D.) 62-, I.B.R.D. Adviser in Ghana 62.
8 Parkway, Woodford Green, Essex, England.

Barbagelata y Figari, Hugo David; Uruguayan historian and journalist; b. 87; ed. Montevideo Univ. and Ecole des Sciences Politiques, Paris.
Co-editor *La Razón* 07; Hon. Asst. to Uruguayan Legation, Paris 08-10; Editor *La Revista de América*, Paris 11-13; founded *Biblioteca Latino-Americana* in Paris, and edited *La Gaceta de América* 21; Co-editor *L'Amérique Latine*, Paris 23-30; Uruguayan del. to Int. Inst. for Intellectual Co-operation 24-46, to UNESCO 46-64; Officier de la Légion d'Honneur; Gran Oficial de la Orden del Sol del Peru.
Publs. *Páginas Sudamericanas* 09, *Bolívar y San Martín* 11, *Artigas y la Revolución Americana* 14, *Histoire de l'Amérique espagnole* 36, *La Révolution Française et l'Amérique latine* 37, *La novela y el cuento en Hispano-América* 47, *El Doctor Don Carlos de Castro en la Diplomacia de la América del Sur* 53, *Rubén Darío et José Enrique Rodó* 58, *Les grands romantiques français et le Modernisme en Amérique Latine* 61, *Quatre Héros Uruguayens* 64, *Universalité actuelle de la renomé d'Artigas* 66, *A propos du cinquantenaire du décès de José Enrique Rodó* 67; Editor *Pages choises de José Enrique Rodó* 18, *Una Centuria Literaria* 24, *La touffe sauvage de Juana de Ibarbourou* 25, *La Literatura Hispano-Americana* 38.
20 rue du Colonel Moll, Paris 17e, France.
Telephone: ETOile 77-63.

Barber, Rt. Hon. Anthony Perrinot Lysberg, P.C., T.D., M.P.; British politician; b. 4 July 1920; ed. Retford School and Oriel Coll., Oxford.
Army Service 39-40, Royal Air Force 40-45; Member of Parliament 51-64, 65-; Parl. Private Sec., Air Ministry 52-54; Govt. Whip 55-57; Lord Commissioner of the Treasury 57-58; Parl. Private Sec. to Prime Minister 58-59; Econ. Sec. to the Treasury 59-62, Financial Sec. to the Treasury 62-63; Minister of Health 63-64; Chair. Conservative Party Sept. 67-; Financial Dir. and Deputy Chair. Redfearn Brothers Oct. 54-; Dir. British Ropes Nov. 64-, Chartered Bank 66-; Conservative.
15 Montpelier Square, London, S.W.7, England.
Telephone: 01-589-9517.

Barber, Samuel, DR. MUS.; American composer; b. 9 March 1910; ed. Curtis Inst. of Music, Philadelphia.
Works include: String Quartet 36, Symphony 36, Adagio for Strings 36, Essay for Orchestra 37, Concerto for Violin and Orchestra 40, Second Essay 42, Second Symphony 44, *Capricorn Concerto* 44, 'Cello Concerto 46, Ballet Suite, *Medea* 46, *Knoxville: Summer of 1915* (voice and orchestra) 47, *Piano Sonata* 49, *Souvenir* 53, *Prayers of Kierkegaard* (for chorus, soprano and orchestra) 54, *Vanessa* 58, *Die Natale* 60, *Piano Concerto* 62, *Andromache's Farewell* 63, *Antony and Cleopatra* (opera) 66; Hon. D.Mus. (Harvard); mem. Nat. Inst. of Arts and Letters, U.S.A.; American Soc. of Composers, Authors and Publishers; Pulitzer Prize 63.
Capricorn, Mount Kisco, N.Y., U.S.A.

Barberot, Roger; French diplomatist; b. 20 Jan. 1915; ed. Naval Coll., Brest.
Naval Service, Second World War in Africa and Italy; left the Army with rank of Lt.-Col. 47; work for R.P.F. Movement of Gen. de Gaulle 47-51; engaged in private business and travelled to the Middle and Far East and S. America; Commdr. of a brigade, Algeria 56-57, resigned 57; joined supporters of Gen. de Gaulle 58; Technical Counsellor, Ministry of Nat. Education 59; Ambassador to the Central African Repub. 60-65, to Uruguay 65-; decorations include Grand Officier de la Légion d'Honneur, Croix de la Liberation, Officier de la Médaille de la Résistance, Croix de Guerre (10 palms), D.S.C. (U.S.A.), Grand Officier du Mérite Centrafricain, Commandeur du Nicham-el-Anouar, Merite agricole.
Publ. *Malaventure en Algérie* 57.
French Embassy, Montevideo, Uruguay; Home: 9 Louis Félix Faure, La Flotte-en-Ré, Charente Maritime, France.
Telephone: 77 La Flotte-en-Ré.

Barbieri, H.E. Cardinal Antonio Maria; Uruguayan ecclesiastic; b. 92.
Joined the Capuchin Order; ordained priest 21; Titular Bishop of Macra 36; Archbishop of Montevideo 40-; created Cardinal by Pope John XXIII Dec. 58.
Calle Treinta y Tres 1368, Montevideo, Uruguay.

Barbieri, Fedora; Italian singer; b. 4 June 1919; ed. Trieste High School and Conservatoire.
Scholarship to Teatro Lirico, Florence 40; début as Fidalma in Cimarosa's *The Secret Marriage*, Teatro Comunale, Florence 40; has appeared in leading roles at La Scala, Milan 42-, Teatro Colon, Buenos Aires 47-, Metropolitan Opera House, New York and Royal Opera House, Covent Garden, London 50-; has also appeared at numerous important festivals and opera seasons in Italy, Germany, U.S.A., France, Spain, Portugal, Brazil, Austria, etc.; has sung leading roles in recordings of *Aida*, *Il Trovatore*, *Requiem*, *Falstaff*, *Un Ballo in Maschera* (Verdi), *La Gioconda* (Ponchielli), *La Favorita* and *Linda di Chamonix* (Donizetti), *Suor Angelica* (Puccini).
Viale Belfiore 9, Florence, Italy.

Barbieri, Lázaro; Argentine politician; b. 11; ed. Univ. Nacional de Tucumán.
Former Prof. of Sociology, Univ. Nacional de Tucumán; Prof. of Argentine History and Social Thought, Univ. Nacional de Tucumán; Governor of Tucumán Province.
Publs. *La Integración de Latinoamerica—Su Problemática Sociológica*, *La Reforma Religiosa y la Formación de la Conciencia Moderna*, *Sociología de la Educación y la Problemática del Sistema Educativo*.
Universidad Nacional de Tucumán, San Miguel de Tucumán, Argentina.

Barbieri, Bishop Sante Uberto, B.A., M.A., B.D.; Argentine Methodist ecclesiastic; b. 2 Aug. 1902 (in Italy); ed. schools and univs. in Brazil and U.S.A.
Methodist Minister, Brazil 26-29; theological studies in U.S.A. 29-33; Dir. Theological School Porto Alegre Brazil 34-38; Minister Montevideo 39; Prof., Dir. Evangelical Faculty Buenos Aires 40-41; Minister, Buenos Aires Central Methodist Church 42-46; Prof. Evangelical Faculty and Evangelistic Exec. Sec. 47-48; Elected Bishop Methodist Church of Argentina, Bolivia and Uruguay 49; re-elected for fifth time 64; Joint Pres. World Council of Churches, 54-61, mem. Exec. and Central Cttees. 61; Joint Vice-Pres. World Council of Christian Education and Sunday Schools.
Publs. in Portuguese, Spanish, Italian, English.
Casilla 5296, Correo Central, Buenos Aires, Argentina.

Barbirolli, Sir John, Kt., F.R.A.M., F.T.C.L.; British conductor; b. Dec. 1899; ed. Royal Acad. of Music, London.
Fmr. mem. Int. String Quartet; founded and conducted Barbirolli Chamber Orchestra 25; Conductor British Nat. Opera Co. 26, Scottish Orchestra 33; Perm. Conductor and Music Dir. New York Philharmonic Symphony Orchestra 36-42, Hallé Orchestra 43-58, Conductor-in-Chief and Musical Adviser Hallé Orchestra 59-68, Conductor Laureate 68-; Conductor-in-Chief, Houston Symphony Orchestra 61-67; Musical Adviser, Assoc. Rediffusion Ltd.; Gold Medal of Royal Philharmonic Soc. 50; Hon. Mus.D. (Manchester 50, Dublin 52, Sheffield 57, London 61); Hon. Freeman Dyers' Co.; Freeman City of Manchester 58; Hon. Academician,

Accademia Nazionale di Santa Cecilia 60; Commdr. Order of Merit, Italian Republic.
8 St. Peter's Square, Manchester 2, England.

Barbour, Walworth, A.B.; American diplomatist; b. 4 June 1908; Harvard Univ.
Served Naples 31, Athens 33, Baghdad 36, Sofia 39, Cairo 41, Baghdad and Cairo 42, with American Rep. to exiled Greek and Yugoslav Govts., Cairo 43, Athens 44; Asst. Chief, Div. of Southern European Affairs, Dept. of State, Washington 45; Chief, Div. of Southeast European Affairs 47; Counsellor (with rank of Minister), Moscow 49; Dir. Office of Eastern European Affairs 51; Deputy Asst. Sec. of State for European Affairs 54-55; Minister and Deputy Chief of Mission, American Embassy, London 55-61; Ambassador to Israel 61-.
American Embassy, Tel-Aviv, Israel.

Barclay, Sir Roderick Edward, G.C.V.O., K.C.M.G.; British diplomatist; b. 22 Feb. 1909; ed. Harrow School and Trinity Coll., Cambridge.
Entered Foreign Service 32; served Brussels, Paris and Washington; Principal Private Sec. to Sec. of State for Foreign Affairs 49-51; rose to be an Asst. Under-Sec. of State 51 and a Deputy Under-Sec. of State 53; Ambassador to Denmark 56-60; Dep. Under-Sec. of State for Foreign Affairs 60-63; Ambassador to Belgium 63-.
British Embassy, Brussels, Belgium.

Barclay, Theodore David; British banker; b. 6 Sept. 1906; ed. Harrow and Trinity Coll., Cambridge.
Barclays Bank Ltd. 27, Local Director 34, Dir. 48-, Dir. Barclays (France) Ltd., British Linen Bank; Chair. Alliance Assurance Co. Ltd. 56-; Chair. Sun Alliance Insurance Ltd. 59; High Sheriff of Suffolk 59.
Desnage Lodge, Higham, Bury St. Edmunds, Suffolk, England.

Barcs, Sándor; Hungarian journalist; b. 10 Nov. 1912.
Editor, Hungarian Telegraphic Agency 45-50, Gen. Man. 50-; mem. Council Patriotic People's Front, Parl. and Presidential Council; Chair. Hungarian Football Association 49-63; Vice-Pres. European Football Union (UEFA) 62-; mem. Council Inter-parliamentary Union 63-; Chair. Nat. Fed. of Hungarian Journalists 65-.
Hungarian Telegraphic Agency, Fém utca 5/7, Budapest 1, Hungary.
Telephone: 159-490.

Barcsay, Jenö; Hungarian artist; b. 14 Jan. 1900; ed. Acad. of Fine Arts, Budapest.
Studied on state scholarship in Paris 26-27, 29-30, and in Italy; mem. artists' colony at Szentendre 29-; Prof. of Anatomy and Perspective, Acad. of Fine Arts, Budapest 45-; principal works include paintings, drawings and mosaics; numerous exhbns. in Hungary and abroad; exhibited at Venice Biennale 64; Kossuth Prize 53; Honoured Artist Award 64; Gold Medal Pro Arte 67.
Publs. *Anatomy for the Artist* 53, *Man and Drapery* 58, *Form und Raum* 66.
Budapest VI, Népköztásaság u. 87-89, Hungary.
Telephone: 229-480.

Bard, Philip, A.B., A.M., PH.D.; American physiologist; b. 25 Oct. 1898; ed. Thacher School, Ojai, Calif., Princeton and Harvard Univs.
Teaching Fellow in Physiology, Harvard 25-26, instructor 26-28; Asst. Prof. Biology, Princeton Univ. 28-31; Asst. Prof. Physiology and Tutor Normal Medical Sciences, Harvard Medical School 31-33; Prof. Physiology and Dir. Physiology Dept., Johns Hopkins Univ. 33-64, Prof. Emeritus 64-; Dean of Medical Faculty 53-57; mem. and fmr. Pres. American Physiological Soc., mem. Nat. Acad. Sciences, American Acad. Arts and Sciences, Asscn. of American Physicians, American Philosophical Soc., American Neurological Asscn., Soc. for Experimental Biology and Medicine (Pres. 59-61), Asscn. Research in Nervous and Mental Diseases

(Pres. 50); served as mem. of Cttee. on Aviation Medicine; Chair. Sub-Cttee. on Motion Sickness; mem. Cttee. on Shock and Transfusions, Div. Medical Sciences, Nat. Research Council, Washington, D.C., during Second World War; Trustee, Rockefeller Univ. 57-; Lashley Award for Work in Neurobiology, American Philosophical Soc. 62; American Coll. of Physicians Award for Achievement in Science of Medicine 68; Hon. Sc.D. (Princeton 47, Washington and Lee Univ. 49), Dr. h.c. (Univ. Católica de Chile and Univ. Nacional Mayor de San Marcos de Lima).
Office: Johns Hopkins Medical School, Baltimore, Md. 21205; Home: 6 Meadow Road, Baltimore, Md. 21212, U.S.A.
Telephone: 301-955-3881.

Bardeen, John, PH.D., D.SC.; American physicist; b. 23 May 1908; ed. Univs. of Wisconsin and Princeton.
Geophysicist with Gulf Research and Development Corpn. 30-33; Junior Fellow, Harvard Univ. 35-38; Asst. Prof. of Physics, Univ. of Minnesota 38-41; Physicist at U.S. Naval Ordnance Laboratory 41-45; Research Physicist, Bell Telephone Laboratory 45-51; Prof. of Electrical Engineering and Physics, Univ. of Illinois 51-; Fellow, American Physical Society, mem. Nat. Acad. of Sciences; Stuart Ballantine Medal (with W. H. Brattain) 52, Buckley Prize 54, John Scott Medal (with W. H. Brattain) 55, Nobel Prize for Physics (with W. Shockley and W. H. Brattain) 56 for research leading to the invention of the transistor, U.S. Nat. Medal of Science 65.
55 Greencroft, Champaign, Illinois, U.S.A.

Bardot, Brigitte; French actress; b. 28 Sept. 1934; ed. Paris Conservatoire.
Stage and film career 52-; films include *Manina: la Fille sans Voile, Le Fils de Caroline Chérie, Futures Vedettes, Les Grandes Manoeuvres, La Lumière d'en Face, Cette Sacrée Gamine, La Mariée est trop Belle, Et Dieu Créa la Femme, En Effeuillant la Marguerite, Une Parisienne, Les Bijoutiers du Clair de Lune, En Cas de Malheur, La Femme et le Pantin, Babette s'en va-t-en Guerre, Voulez-vous Danser avec Moi?, La Vérité, Please not now?, Le Mépris, Le Repos du guerrier, Une Ravissante Idiote, Viva Maria, A coeur joi 67, Two Weeks in September 67.*
71 avenue Paul Doumer, Paris 16e; and La Madrague, Saint-Tropez (Var.), France.

Bardyadayev, Konstantin Lavrentyevich; Soviet politician; b. 1917; ed. Buryat Veterinary Inst.
Accountant, Economist, and Instructor, Buryat Co-operative Alliance 35-38; Chair. of a district consumers' co-operative union 38-39; Chair. Exec. Cttees. numerous District Soviets of Working People's Deputies 39-47; Business Man., Council of Ministers, Buryat Autonomous S.S.R. 47-55; Chair. of a collective farm, and First Sec. of a District Cttee. of C.P.S.U. 55-61; Dir. Buryat State Farm Trust, and Head of a collective and state farm production management board 61-62; Chair. Council of Ministers, Buryat Autonomous S.S.R. 62-, and Deputy to U.S.S.R. Supreme Soviet; mem. C.P.S.U. 40-.
Council of Ministers of the Buryat Autonomous S.S.R., Ulan-Ude, U.S.S.R.

Bargellini, Piero; Italian writer; b. 5 Aug. 1897.
Founder *Calendario dei pensieri e delle pratiche solari* 23, *Frontespizio* 29; Mayor of Florence 66-67; articles for numerous newspapers and magazines including the *Corriere della Sera*; Christian Democrat.
Publs. include: *Scritti a maggio* 31, *Fra Diavolo* 32, *San Bernardino da Siena* 33, *G. Carducci* 34, *Architettura con fregio polemico* 35, *David* 36, *Città di pittori* 39, *Via Larga* 41, *S. Francesco* 41, *Volti di pietra* 43, *Caffé Michelangiolo* 44, *Il Ghirlandaio del bel mondo fiorentino* 45, *La fiaba pittorica di Benozzo Gozzoli* 46, *Amor profano* 46, *Il sogno nostalgico di Sandro Botticelli* 46,

La pittura ascetica del Beato Angelico 48, *La dolce mestizia del Perugino* 50, *Vedere e capire Firenze* 50, *Lui* 50, *Lei* 50, *Pian dei Giullari* (12 vols.) 50, *Nostalgico di Sandro Botticelli* 51, *Chiodi solari* 52, *Santa Chiara* 52, *Canto alle rondini* 53, *Sant'Antonino da Firenze* 54, *Tivurzi* 55, *Ghirlanda per Firenze* 56, *In Lizza per l'arte* 57, *Santi come uomini* 57, *Belvedere: arte Greca, arte etrusca* (2 vols.) 57-59, *I santi del giorno* 58, *Il Natale nella storia, nella leggenda e nell'arte* 59, *Assisi città santa* 60.
Via della Pinzochere 3, Florence, Italy.

Barger, Thomas C.; American oil executive; b. 30 Aug. 1909; ed. Univ. of North Dakota, U.S.A.
Joined Arabian American Oil Co. (Aramco) as geologist 37; Dir. Local Govt. Relations; Rep. to Saudi Arabian Govt.; Vice-Pres. Aramco 58, Pres. 59-, Chief Exec. Officer 61-.
Arabian American Oil Company, 505 Park Avenue, New York 22, N.Y., U.S.A.

Barghoorn, Frederick Charles, PH.D.; American university professor; b. 4 July 1911; ed. Amherst Coll. and Harvard Univ.
Press Attaché, American Embassy, Moscow 43-47; Department of Political Science, Yale Univ. 47-, Prof. of Political Science 56-.
Publs. *The Soviet Image of the United States* 50, *Soviet Russian Nationalism* 56, *Soviet Foreign Propaganda* 64.
Department of Political Science, Yale University, New Haven, Connecticut, U.S.A.

Bargmann, Wolfgang L., DR. MED.; German anatomist; b. 27 Jan. 1906; ed. Frankfurt, Munich, Vienna and Berlin Univs.
Privat Dozent, Zürich Univ. 35-38; Prosector, Leipzig Univ. 38-42; Prof. Extraordinary, Königsberg Univ. 42-45, Göttingen 45; Prof. Ordinary, Kiel Univ. 46-; Dir. Anatomical Inst. Kiel Univ. 45-; Rector, Kiel Univ. 49-50, 65-66; Vice-Pres. German Research Asscn. 55-61, mem. Wissenschaftsrat 58-64; Pres. Anatomical Soc. 58-61; mem. Royal Swedish Acad. 53, Deutsche Akad. Naturforscher Leopoldina 58; Hon. mem. Japanese Anatomical Soc. 59; mem. Norwegian Acad. 61-; Corresp. mem. Mainz Acad. 63-, Finnish Acad. 65; Senator Max-Planck Gesellschaft 66; Schleiden Medal (Leopoldina) 67; Dr. med. vet. h.c. (Giessen) 67.
Publs. *Histologie und Mikroskopische Anatomie des Menschen* (6th edition) 67, *Das Zwischenhirn-Hypophysensystem* 54, Editor, *Handbuch der Mikroskopischen Anatomie des Menschen, Zeitschrift für Zellforschung*.
Niemannsweg 81, Kiel, German Federal Republic.
Telephone: Kiel 46239.

Barich, Karl; German steel executive; b. 20 Oct. 1901; ed. Wirtschaftshochschule Mannheim.
Head Management Clerk, Geisweider Eisenwerke A.G. 41-45, mem. Management Board 45-47; mem. Management Board Hüttenwerk Geisweid A.G. (formed by merger) 47-51; mem. Management Board Stahlwerke Südwestfalen A.G. 51-54, Chair. 54-; Chair. Wirtschaftsvereinigung Eisen-und Stahlindustrie 48-49, and later until 54, now mem. Management Cttee.; mem. Boards of scientific, cultural and other insts.; Dr.rer.pol. h.c. (Wirtschaftshochschule Mannheim) 57.
Stahlwerke Südwestfalen A.G., 5903 Geisweid, Postfach 6, German Federal Republic.

Barkatt, Reuven; Israeli politician; b. 5 June 1906; ed. Paris and Strasbourg Univs.
Settled in Palestine 26; Gen.-Sec. Soldiers' Welfare Cttee. 40-46; Head Int. Cultural and Arab Departments, Histadrut 46-60; Ambassador to Norway 60-61; Sec.-Gen. Mapai 62-66; mem. Knesset 66-.
56 Arlossoroff Street, Holon, Israel.

Barke, (James) Allen; British motor executive; b. 16 April 1903; ed. technical school.

General engineering 22-32; Ford Motor Co. 32-; Chaser, Purchase Dept. 33-38; Buyer, Purchase Dept. 39-47; Chief Buyer (Tractors) 47-48; Man. Leamington Foundry 48-53; Exec. Dir. and Gen. Man. Briggs Motor Bodies Ltd. 53-59; Dir. Product Divs. Ford Motor Co. 59-61; Asst. Man. Dir. 61-62, Man. Dir. 62-63, Chief Exec. Officer and Man. Dir. 63-65, Vice-Chair. 65-May 68.
Thurlestone, Mill Green, Ingatestone, Essex, England.
Telephone: Fryerning 549.

Barker, George Granville; British writer; b. 26 Feb. 1913; ed. Marlborough Road School, Chelsea, London.
Prof. of English Literature, Imperial Tohoku Univ., Japan 39-41; lived in America 41-43; returned to England 44; in Italy 60-; Arts Fellow, York Univ. 66.
Publs. *Poems* 33, *Alanna Autumnal* 33, *Calamiterror, Janus* 35, *Lament and Triumph* 40, *News of the World, The True Confession of George Barker* 50, *Collected Poems* 57, *Two Plays, The View from a Blind I* 62, *The New Confession* 63, *Dreams of a Summer Night* 65, *The Golden Chains* 68, *Essays* 68.
c/o Faber and Faber, 24 Russell Square, London, W.C.1; and Bintry House, Itteringham, Aylsham, Norfolk, England.
Telephone: Saxthorpe 240.

Barker, Robinson Franklin, A.B.; American glass executive; b. 20 Dec. 1913; ed. Harvard Univ.
Served U.S. Naval Reserve 42-45; with P.P.G. Industries Inc. 35-; various managerial positions, then Asst. to Pres., and Gen. Man. (Planning) Glass Div. 55-57, Vice-Pres., Gen. Man. Glass Div. 57-62, Vice-Pres. Glass and Fiber Glass Group 62-66, Pres. 66-, also Dir. of Co.; Dir. Pennitalia, S.p.A., P.P.G. Industries Foundation, S.A. les Glaces de Courcelles, Canadian Pittsburgh Industries Ltd. and other companies.
Office: 1 Gateway Center, Pittsburgh 22; Home: 8 Woodland Road, Sewickley, Pa., U.S.A.

Barker, Sir William, K.C.M.G., O.B.E.; British diplomatist; b. 19 July 1909; ed. Univs. of Liverpool and Prague.
Foreign Office 43; First Sec., Prague 45-47, transferred Moscow 47; Counsellor and Chargé d'Affaires, Oslo 51-54; Consul-General, Boston, Mass. 54; Counsellor, Washington 55-60; Minister, Moscow 60-63; Fellow, Center for Int. Affairs, Harvard Univ. 63-64; Asst. Under-Sec. of State, Foreign Office 65-66; Amb. to Czechoslovakia 66-.
British Embassy, Thunovská 14, Malá Strana, Prague, Czechoslovakia.

Barkovsky, Anatoli Alexandrovich; Soviet diplomatist; b. 1921; ed. Moscow Inst. of Historical Archives.
Diplomatic Service 51-; Sec., Cairo 52-58; First Sec., Dept. of Near Eastern Countries of U.S.S.R. Ministry of Foreign Affairs 58-59; Counsellor, Cairo 59-61; Consul-Gen., Damascus 61; Ambassador to Syrian Arab Republic 61-67; on staff of Ministry of Foreign Affairs 67-.
Ministry of Foreign Affairs, 32-34 Smolenskaya-Sennaya Ploshchad, Moscow, U.S.S.R.

Barlog, Boleslaw; German theatre director and producer; b. 28 March 1906; ed. Oberrealschule, Berlin.
Assistant Producer, Volksbühne, Berlin 30-33; Asst. Dir. UFA and TERRA films 35-39, Dir. 39-45; Dir.-Gen. Berlin Municipal Theatres 45- (Schlosspark Theatre 45-, Schiller Theatre 51-, Schiller-Theatre Workshop 58-); Fed. German Grand Order of Merit 50; mem. Acad. of Arts, Berlin.
Spindelmühler Weg 7, 1 Berlin 45, Germany.

Barmin, Vladimir Pavlovich; Soviet engineer; b. 1909; ed. Moscow Higher Technical School.
At Compressor plant, U.S.S.R. Acad. of Sciences 30-, Chief Designer 40-46; Instructor, Moscow Higher Tech-

nical School 31-; mem. C.P.S.U. 44-; Corresp. mem. U.S.S.R. Acad. of Sciences 58-66, mem. 66-.
U.S.S.R. Academy of Sciences, 14 Leninsky Prospekt, Moscow, U.S.S.R.

Barnard, Christiaan Neethling, M.D., M.S., PH.D.; South African heart surgeon; b. 1922; ed. Univ. of Cape Town.
Graduated as doctor 46; intern, Groote Schuur Hospital, Cape Town 47; then spent two years in general practice in Ceres; then Senior Resident Medical Officer, City Fever Hospital, Cape Town; returned to Groote Schuur Hospital; then Charles Adams Memorial Scholar, Univ. of Minnesota, concentrating on cardio-thoracic surgery; on return to Groote Schuur Hospital concentrated on open-heart operations and cardiac research; Head of Cardiac Research and Surgery, Univ. of Cape Town; developed the Barnard Valve, for use in open-heart surgery; performed first successful open-heart operation in South Africa; performed first successful heart transplant operation in world 67; Hon. Dr. Univ. of Cape Town.
Groote Schuur Hospital, Cape Town, South Africa.

Barnard, Lance Herbert; Australian politician; b. 1 May 1919; ed. Launceston Technical Coll.
Qualified as teacher and served in Educ. Dept.; mil. service in Second World War 40-45, Australian Cadet Corps, with rank of Captain 45-54; mem. Parliament 54-; State Pres. Tasmanian Branch, Australian Labor Party 63-; Dep. Leader, Parl. Labor Party 67-; mem. Joint Public Accounts Cttee. 56-58, Fed. Parl. Labor Party Exec. 58-61; Del., Parl. Asscn. Group Conf., London 62; mem. Commonwealth Immigration Advisory Council.
8 Lantana Avenue, Launceston, Tasmania, Australia.

Barnes, Charles Edward; Australian grazier and politician; b. 13 Nov. 1901; ed. Mowbray House and Sydney Grammar School.
Member, House of Representatives 58-; Minister of State for Territories 63-68; Minister of State for External Territories 68-; mem. Cabinet 65-66; Country Party.
Parliament House, Canberra, A.C.T. 2600, Australia.

Barnes, Edward Larrabee, B.S., B.A.; American architect; b. 22 April 1915; ed. Milton Acad., Harvard Univ. and Graduate School of Design.
Sheldon Travelling Fellowship 42; architectural practice in New York City 49-; Critic of Architectural Design, Pratt Inst., Brooklyn 53-54, Yale School of Architecture 56-; work exhibited at Museum of Modern Art (New York) and published in architectural magazines; Fellow American Inst. of Architects; Dir. Municipal Art Soc. of New York 60; Trustee American Acad. in Rome 63; Yale Award for Distinction in the Arts, Arnold Brunner Prize, Nat. Inst. of Arts and Letters 59; Silver Medal, Architectural League, N.Y. 60, Progressive Architecture Design Award 63, F.H.A. First Honor Award 63.
Works include: Prefabricated aluminium house for Consolidated Vultee Aircraft Corpn. 48, private houses, series of camps for *Herald Tribune* Fresh Air Fund, urban renewal housing projects in Sacramento, Calif., and San Juan, Puerto Rico, jet plane interiors and other work for Pan American Airways, U.S. Consulate, Tabriz, Iran; also office buildings, shopping centre, coll. and univ. campus planning and buildings.
Office: 410 East 62nd Street, New York, N.Y. 10021; Home: Wood Road, Mount Kisco, N.Y., U.S.A.
Telephone: 212-838-8500.

Barnes, Harry Elmer, A.M., PH.D.; American historian and sociologist; b. 15 June 1889; ed. Syracuse, Columbia and Harvard Univs.
Instructor in Historical Sociology, Syracuse Univ. 13-15; Lecturer in History, Columbia Univ. 17-18; Assoc. Prof.

of History, Clark Univ. 18-19; Prof. of History, New School for Social Research 19-20 and Lecturer 23-24, 26 and 37; Prof. of History, Clark Univ. 20-23, of Historical Sociology, Smith Coll. 23-30, and of Economics, Amherst Coll. 23-25; Lecturer Teachers' Coll., Columbia Univ. 37-38; with Scripps-Howard Newspapers 29-40; Consultant and Historian, War Productivity Board 43-44, Smaller War Plants Corpn. 45-46; Prof. of Sociology, Temple Univ. 46, Univ. of Colorado 48-49, Indiana Univ. 51, Washington State Univ. 54-55.
Publs. *Sociology and Political Theory* 23, *New History and the Social Studies* 25, *History and Social Intelligence* 26, *Genesis of the World War* 26, *Living in the Twentieth Century* 28, *Twilight of Christianity* 29, *World Politics* 30, *Story of Punishment* 30, *History of Western Civilization* 35, *Economic History of the Western World* 37, *Intellectual and Cultural History of the Western World* 37, 65, *History of Historical Writing* 37, 63, *Social Thought from Lore to Science* (with Howard Becker) 38, 61, *Society in Transition: Problems of a Changing Age* 39, 52, *Social Institutions* 42, *American Way of Life* 42, *New Horizons in Criminology* (with N. K. Teeters) 43, 51, 59, 68, *Prisons in Wartime* 44, *Pennsylvania Penology* 44, *Survey of Western Civilisation* 47, *An Introduction to the History of Sociology* 48, *Historical Sociology* 48, *Perpetual War for Perpetual Peace* (with C. C. Tansill *et al.*) 53, *The People versus Caryl Chessman* (with N. K. Teeters *et al.*) 68, etc.
31509 Pacific Coast Highway, Malibu, Calif. 90265, U.S.A.
Telephone: 213-457-2331.

Barnes, Henry A.; American traffic engineer; b. 16 Dec. 1906; ed. Univ. of Michigan, Michigan State Coll. Extension School, and General Motors Inst. of Technology.
Maintenance Engineer, Chevrolet Motor Co. 33-37; Traffic Engineer, Capt. of Police, City of Flint, Michigan 37-47; Traffic Dir. City and County of Denver 47-53; Dir. of Traffic, City of Baltimore 53-57, Commr. of Transit and Traffic 57-62; Commr. of Traffic for New York City 62-; consultant for Traffic American and European cities; mem. I.E.E.E.; Hon. D.P.A. Susquehanna Univ.
Publ. *The Man with the Red and Green Eyes*.
Office: 28-11 Bridge Plaza N., Long Island, N.Y. 11101; Home: 79-33 215th Street, Bayside, N.Y., U.S.A.

Barnes, Nathan; Liberian diplomatist; b. 14 April 1914; ed. Cape Palmas Seminary.
Liberian Revenue Service 37-44; County Attorney, Maryland County, Liberia 44, Circuit Judge 45-56; Minister to Italy 56; Ambassador to Italy 56-60; Perm. Rep. to UN 60-; Knight, Grand Band Humane Order African Redemption; Grand Commdr. Star of Africa.
Permanent Mission of Liberia to the United Nations, 235 East 42nd Street, New York, N.Y., U.S.A.

Barnes, Robert Henry, B.S., M.D. (son of Harry Elmer Barnes, *q.v.*); American psychiatrist; b. 4 Nov. 1921; ed. Union Coll., Schenectady, New York, Duke Univ. and Univ. of Colorado.
Instructor, Psychosomatic Medicine, Univ. of Colorado 52-53, Asst. Prof. of Psychiatry, Duke Univ. 53-56; Assoc. Prof., Prof. and Chair., Dept. of Psychiatry, Univ. of Missouri in Kansas City 56-58; Exec. Dir. Greater Kansas City Mental Health Foundation 56-58; Acting Dir. Epidemiological Field Station, Kansas City, Missouri 67-68; Prof. of Psychiatry, Univ. of Texas School of Medicine, San Antonio 68-; Fellow, American Psychiatric Asscn.; Consultant Nat. Inst. of Mental Health in Community Mental Health Programs and Epidemiology 62-.
Publs. *A Community Concern* (with Epps and McPartland) 65; and 30 articles on geriatrics, psychosomatic medicine, electroencephalography, cerebral circulation,

psychiatric education, group therapy and community psychiatry.
The University of Texas Medical School at San Antonio, 7703 Floyd Curl Drive, San Antonio, Texas 78229, U.S.A.
Telephone: 512-826-6045.

Baron, Jean-Jacques; French engineer; b. 11 May 1909; ed. Ecole Centrale des Arts et Manufactures, Paris.
Engineer, later Technical Dir. L'Aluminium Français 33-57; Dir. Div. of Atomic Energy and its Applications, Compagnie Péchiney 58-; Pres. Fonderie de Précision, Upsil Ltd.; Dir. Ecole Centrale des Arts et Manufactures, Paris; Chevalier Légion d'Honneur, Ordre des Palmes Académiques.
Office: 23 rue Balzac, Paris 8e; Home: 31 avenue Georges-Mandel, Paris 16e, France.
Telephone: 227-54-72 (Office); 727-55-15 (Home).

Baroum, Jacques; Chad politician; b. 13 July 1932; ed. Coll. de Bongor, Ecole des cadres supérieurs, Lycée Savorgnan-de-Brazza, Brazzaville, and Université de Paris à la Sorbonne.
Doctor, Hospital of Fort-Lamy 62-64; Minister of Public Health and Social Affairs 64-65; Minister of Foreign Affairs 65-; mem. Political Office of the Progressive Party 63-.
P.O. Box 784, Fort-Lamy, Chad.

Baroyan, Oganes Vagarshakovich; Soviet health official; b. 24 Dec. 1906; ed. First Medical Inst. of Moscow.
Professor of Epidemiology and Microbiology; Dir., Dept. of Epidemiology, Ivanovski Virology Inst. of Acad. of Medical Sciences; Dir. Gamaleya Inst. of Epidemiology and Microbiology, Acad. of Medical Sciences 64-; Asst. Dir.-Gen. World Health Organization, Geneva 61-64; Prof. and Academician Acad. of Medical Sciences of U.S.S.R.; mem. Int. Epidemiological Asscn.; Hon. mem. Soc. of Czechoslovak Epidemiologists and Microbiologists of Purkyně Medical Soc. of Czechoslovakia.
N. F. Gamaleya Institute of Epidemiology and Microbiology, Gamaleya Street 2, Moscow, U.S.S.R.
Telephone: D 4-62-49.

Barpal, Josef; Israeli shipping executive; b. 98; ed. University, Russia.
Zionist, Rumania; settled in Palestine 25; mem. of Kibbutz Ramat David; assisted illegal immigration; co-founder and fmr. Man. Dir. ZIM Israel Navigation Co. Ltd. 45 and subsidiary Shohum.
ZIM Israel Navigation Co. Ltd., 7-9 Ha'atsmaut Road, Haifa, Israel.

Barr, Alfred Hamilton, Jr., PH.D.; American museum official and art historian; b. 28 Jan. 1902; ed. Boys' Latin School, Baltimore, Maryland, and Princeton and Harvard Univs.
Instructor, History of Art, Vassar Coll. 23-24, Princeton Univ. 25-26; Assoc. Prof. of Art, Wellesley Coll. 26-29; Dir., Museum of Modern Art, New York 29-43, Trustee 39-, Dir. of Museum Collections 47-67; Editor of several periodicals on art; Hon. Litt.D. (Princeton), Hon. Ph.D. (Bonn); several foreign decorations.
Publs. *Cubism and Abstract Art* 36, *What is Modern Painting?* 43, *Picasso: Fifty Years of his Art* 46, *20th Century Italian Art* (with J. T. Soby) 49, *Matisse: His Art and His Public* 51.
Home: 49 East 96th Street, New York, N.Y., U.S.A.

Barr, John Andrew, LL.B.; American lawyer, business executive and educator; b. 10 Sept. 1908; ed. De Pauw and Indiana Univs.
With law firm of Wildermuth and Force (Gary, Ind.) 30-33; Attorney Montgomery Ward & Co. 33-35; Partner Wildermuth, Force and Barr 35-38; rejoined

Montgomery Ward legal staff 38, Asst. Sec. 40-49, Vice-Pres. and Sec. 49-55, Dir. 50-65, Chair. 55-65; Dean, Graduate School of Business, Northwestern Univ. 65-; Dir. Northern Trust Co., Swift & Co., Commonwealth Edison Co., S. C. Johnson and Son Inc.
Graduate School of Business, Northwestern Univ., 339 East Chicago Ave., Chicago, Ill., U.S.A.

Barr, Joseph Walker; American government official; b. 17 Jan. 1918; ed. De Pauw Univ. and Harvard Univ.
Former Exec. Vice-Pres. Merz Engineering, Indianapolis; fmr. Sec.-Treas. Barr Devt. Corpn., Indianapolis; fmr. Treas. O. L. Barr Grain Co., Indianapolis; fmr. mem. U.S. House of Reps., mem. Banking and Currency Comm.; Asst. to Sec. (Congressional Relations), Dept. of Treasury 61-64; Chair. Board Fed. Deposit Insurance Corpn. 64-65; Under-Sec. of Treasury 65-; U.S. Navy 42-45; Hon. LL.D. Vincennes Univ. 66, DePauw Univ. 67.
U.S. Treasury Dept., Washington 20220, D.C.; Home: 11001 Glen Road, Potomac, Maryland, U.S.A.

Barr, Morris; Australian international official; ed. Scotch Coll., Melbourne Univ. and Melbourne Conservatorium of Music.
Member editorial staff Melbourne *Argus*; served with Australian Imperial Forces; Head, Melbourne Conservatorium of Music 48; with English-Speaking Union 51-, Dir. of Programmes 59-64; Dir.-Gen. 64-.
English-Speaking Union, 37 Charles Street, London W.1, England.
Telephone: 01-629-7400.

Barrachin, Edmond; French journalist and politician; b. 12 Jan. 1900.
Deputy 34-36, 46, 51, 56-58; Senator 59-; volunteer 39, prisoner 40, escaped and joined Free French; founder *Action* group; Minister-in-charge of Constitutional Reform 53-56; mem. Constitutional Consultative Cttee. 58; fmr. Pres. of Independent group in Senate; Médaille Militaire, Croix de Guerre.
15 rue du Cirque, Paris 8e, France

Barran, David Haven; British oil executive; b. 23 May 1912; ed. Winchester Coll. and Trinity Coll., Cambridge.
Asiatic Petroleum Co. 34-61, served Egypt, Sudan, Red Sea, India, London 34-58, Pres. Asiatic Petroleum Corpn., New York 58-61; Managing Dir. The Shell Petroleum Co., Shell Int. Petroleum Co. 61-64; Principal Dir. Bataafse Petroleum Mij. N.V. 61-64; Dir. Shell Transport and Trading Co. Ltd. 61-64, Deputy Chair. and Managing Dir. 64-67, Chair. and Managing Dir. 67-; Dir. Shell Oil Co. 64-; Dir. Shell Caribbean Co. 64-.
Brent Eleigh Hall, Sudbury, Suffolk; and 36 Kensington Square, London, W.8, England.
Telephone: 01-937-5664 (London).

Barratt, Sir Sydney, Kt.; British business executive; b. 11 Aug. 1898; ed. Clifton Coll., Bristol, and Balliol Coll., Oxford.
Lecturer in Chemistry, Univ. of Leeds 22-24, Univ. Coll., London 24-32; Asst. Dir. of Research, Albright and Wilson Ltd. 32, Dir. 38, Chair. 58-67; Dir. Joseph Lucas Ltd. 59-; Chair., Clifton Coll. Council; Hon. Fellow, Univ. Coll., London 60.
Crowe Hall, Widcombe, Bath, Somerset, England.

Barrault, Jean-Louis (husband of Madelaine Renaud, *q.v.*); French actor and producer; b. 8 Sept. 1910; ed. Collège Chaptal.
Master at Collège Chaptal 31; began stage career in rôle of servant in *Volpone* 31; produced and acted in a number of plays, including: *Autour d'une Mère* 35, *Hamlet, Tandis que j'agonise, Numance* 37, *La Faim*; with the Comédie-Française, 40-47: *Antoine et Cléopâtre, Le Soulier de Satin*; founded Compagnie M. Renaud-J.-L. Barrault 47: *Les Nuits de la Colère, les Fausses Confidences, Amphitryon, Baptiste, Occupe-toi d'Amélie,*

Le Procès, Partage de Midi, Le Bossu, Christophe Colomb, Pour Lucrèce, La Cerisaie 54, *Le Songe des Prisonniers* 55, (Théâtre Marigny) *Le Personnage Combattant, Madame Sans-Gêne, La Vie Parisienne* 58; Dir. Théâtre de France (fmr. Odéon) 59, Théâtre des Nations 65-; Officier, Légion d'Honneur.

Has also made numerous films including *Les Beaux Jours, Hélène* 36, *Mademoiselle Docteur, Drôle de Drame, Un Grand Amour de Beethoven, Le Puritain* 37, *L'Or dans la Montagne* 39, *La Symphonie Fantastique* 42, *Les Enfants du Paradis* 44, *Le Cocu magnifique* 46, *La Ronde* 50, *Versailles* 55.

Publs. *Réflexions sur le Théâtre* 49, *Nouvelles Réflexions sur le Théâtre* 59.

Editor: *Cahiers de la Compagnie M. Renaud-J.-L. Barrault.*

18 avenue du Président Wilson, Paris 16e, France.

Barre, Raymond; French international civil servant; b. 12 April 1924; ed. Faculté de Droit, Paris, and Inst. d'Etudes politiques, Paris.

Professor at Inst. des Hautes Etudes, Tunis 51-54; Prof. at Faculté de Droit et de Sciences économiques, Caen 54-63; Prof. Inst. d'Etudes politiques, Paris 61-, Faculté de Droit et Sciences économiques, Paris 62-; Dir. du Cabinet to Minister of Industry 59-62; mem. Cttee. of Experts (Comité lorrain) studying financing of investments in France 63-64; mem. Comm. of Gen. Econ. and Financing of Fifth Plan and other govt. cttees.; Vice-Pres. of Comm. of European Communities, responsible for Econ. and Financial Affairs.

Commission des Communautés Européennes, 23–27 avenue de la Joyeuse Entreé, Brussels, Belgium; Home: 6 rue de Bagatelle, 92 Neuilly sur Seine, France.

Barreiros Rodríguez, Eduardo; Spanish business executive; b. 19.

Chairman of Board of Dirs. Barreiros Diesel S.A., Rheinstahl Hanomag Barreiros, S.A., David Brown Engranajes S.A., Barreiros A.E.C., S.A., Barreiros Empresa Constructora S.A., Financiera Barreiros S.A., Comercial Internacional Barreiros S.A., Cía. Portuguesa de Motores y Camiones S.A.

Princesa 1, Madrid, Spain.

Barrenechea, Norberto M., PH.D.; Argentine business executive and diplomatist; b. 20 Aug. 1924; ed. Universidad de Buenos Aires.

President of Board of Dirs. and Gen. Attorney Pedro D. Duhalde y Cia. (agricultural firm) 58-; Pres. Board of Dirs. El Brasero, S.A.; Vice-Pres. Board of Dirs. Indal S.A.; Dir. Emaluar S.A., Maldonado S.A., Martin B. Lanz S.A., S.A.A.G. San Luis Comercial; Trustee Eugenio Cozzarin S.A.; Amb. of Argentina in U.S.A. 64-66; Technical mem. Comm. for Promotion of Econ. Devt. in Argentina; mem. American-Argentine Univ. Asscn., Corporación Argentina de Aberdeen Angus, Jockey Club.

Publs. *Treatise on Auditing, Treatise on Financial Mathematics.*

Sarmiento 329, Buenos Aires, Argentina.

Telephone: 71-5710; 31-6030.

Barrett, Charles S., B.S., PH.D.; American physicist and metallurgist; b. 28 Sept. 1902; ed. Univs. of S. Dakota and Chicago.

Div. of Physical Metallurgy, Naval Research Laboratory, Anacostia, D.C. 28-32; Metals Research Laboratory and Dept. of Metallurgy, Carnegie Inst. of Technology, Pittsburgh 32-46; Prof., Inst. tor the Study of Metals, Univ. of Chicago 46-; consulting metallurgist 44-; Eastman Visiting Prof., Oxford Univ. 65-66; Editor Metals and Alloys Section of *Structure Reports* for Int. Union of Crystallography 49-51; Pres. American Society for X-ray and Electron Diffraction 47; mem. Exec. Cttee. American Inst. for Mining and Metallurgical Engineers 43-45, 54-57 (Mathewson Medal 34, 44, 50),

Dir. 62-, Fellow 65-; mem. Nat. Acad. of Sciences 67-; Hon. mem. American Soc. of Metals (Howe Medal 39); mem. Ship Steel Cttee. of Nat. Research Council 48-62, Advisory Cttee., Office of Ordnance Research 56-59; Fellow American Physical Soc., American Crystallographic Asscn., Inst. of Metals, U.S.A., Nat. Cttee. of Int. Union of Crystallography 50-55; Clamer Medal of Franklin Inst. 50.

Publs. *Structure of Metals* 43, 53, 66; papers on research in metallurgy, crystallography and physics.

University of Chicago, Chicago 60637, Ill., U.S.A.

Barrett, Edward Ware, A.B.; American journalist; b. 3 July 1910; ed. Princeton Univ. and Univ. of Dijon.

On staff of *Birmingham* (Ala.) *News* 30-31; with Columbia Broadcasting System 32-33; with *Newsweek* 33-50, Washington Corresp. 35-36, National Affairs Editor 36-37, assoc. Editor 37-42, Editorial Dir. 46-50; with Office of War Information 42-43, with Psychological Warfare Branch of Allied Force H.Q. 43-44; Exec. Dir. of O.W.I. overseas operations, then Dir. of overseas branch 44-45; U.S. Asst. Sec. of State for Public Affairs 50-52; Editor, Consultant, N.Y. 52-54; Pres. Edward W. Barrett and Associates 52-56; Exec. Vice-Pres. Hill and Knowlton 55-56; Dean, Graduate School of Journalism, Columbia Univ. 56-; Trustee Inst. of Int. Educ. 52-60, Atlantic Council of the U.S. 62-, Asia Soc. 61-; Dir. UN Asscn. 64-, American Research Bureau 64-; Pres. Asscn. for Educ. in Journalism 65.

Home: Hawkwood Lane, Greenwich, Conn.; Office: 2960 Broadway, New York 27, N.Y., U.S.A.

Barrie, Sir Walter; British business executive; b. 31 May 1901; ed. Merchiston Castle, Edinburgh, and Gonville and Caius Coll., Cambridge.

Entered Lloyd's 26; mem. Cttee. of Lloyd's 46; Deputy Chair. of Lloyd's 51-52; Chair. of Lloyd's 53, 54, 57, 58; Pres. Insurance Inst. of London 55-56, Pres. Chartered Insurance Inst. 62-63; Dir. Westminster Bank Ltd., John Ferguson & Sons (Glasgow) Ltd., The English Asscn. of American Bond and Share Holders Ltd., The Ulster Bank Ltd., The English Asscn. Investment Trust Co. Ltd., Robt. Bradford (Holdings) Ltd., Joseph W. Hobbs & Co. Ltd.

Compton Elms, Pinkneys Green, Berkshire, England.

Barrientos Ortuño, General René; Bolivian air force officer and politician; b. 20; ed. flight training at Randolph Field, Texas, U.S.A.

Commander-in-Chief of Bolivian Air Force; Head of Military Junta in Bolivia Nov. 64-65, Co-Head 65-Jan. 66; President of Bolivia Aug. 66-.

Office of the President, La Paz, Bolivia.

Barrios, Dr. Gonzalo; Venezuelan lawyer and politician; b. 03.

Former lawyer; Chair. Acción Democrática Party; Minister of Interior March 64-Nov. 66.

c/o Ministry of the Interior, Caracas, Venezuela.

Barros, Adhemar de; Brazilian physician and politician; b. 1901.

Governor, São Paulo State 63-66; Candidate for Pres. of Brazil 55, 60, 65; Pres. Partido Social Progresista (P.S.P.).

c/o Palácio do Gobierno, São Paulo, Brazil.

Barros Barreto, Frederico de, LL.B.; Brazilian judge; b. 1895; ed. Colegio Pedro II and Univ. of Rio de Janeiro.

Barrister, Fed. District 16-28; substituting judge in civil cases 21; Subpretor 22; Criminal Judge, Second Court of First Instance 28; Electoral Judge, Second and Fifth Zones 32-36; State Emergency Judge, Fed. District 35; Civil Judge, Fourth Court of First Instance 35; Judge for wills and legacy cases 36; Pres. Court of Nat. Security 36-45; Lecturer on Commercial Maritime Law, Faculty of Law, Petropolis, State of Rio de Janeiro 36-39; Judge, Court of Appeal, Fed. District 37;

Lecturer on Constitutional Law 39-40; member of Supreme Court 39-, Vice-Pres. 49-51, Pres. (Chief Justice) 60-62; Pres. Supervisory Comm. for Mil. Law.
Avenida Epitácio Pessôa, 1 840 (Lagôa), Rio de Janeiro, Brazil.

Barros Câmara, H. E. Cardinal Jaime de; Brazilian ecclesiastic; b. 94; ed. Ginásio Catarinense and Seminário Cen. de São Leopoldo.
Former Rector, Archdiocenal Seminary, Florianopolis; Bishop of Mossoró 35-41, Archbp. of Belém do Pará 41-43, of Rio de Janeiro 43-; created Cardinal 46; Ordinary of the Oriental Church in Brazil; Hon. D.Phil. (Rio Grande do Sul Univ.); Hon. Grand Master Order of the Holy Sepulchre; Commdr. Order of Isabel the Catholic (Spain), Order of Boiacá (Colombia), Order of the Cedar of Lebanon, Grand Cross of Naval Merit (Brazil), Grand Officer of Brazilian Army and Air Force.
Palácio São Joaquim, Rua da Gloria 446, Rio de Janeiro, Brazil.

Barrow, Errol Walton, B.SC. (Econ.); Barbadian barrister and politician; b. 21 Jan. 1920; ed. Combermere School, Harrison Coll., Lincoln's Inn, London, and London Univ.
Flying duties, Royal Air Force 40-47; Founder-mem. Dem. Labour Party 55, Chair. 58-; Prime Minister of Barbados 61-, Prime Minister of independent Barbados Nov. 66-, also Minister of Finance and External Affairs; Hon. LL.D.
Culloden Farm, St. Michael, Barbados.

Barrowclough, Major-Gen. The Rt. Hon. Sir Harold Eric, P.C., K.C.M.G., C.B., D.S.O., M.C., E.D., LL.B.; New Zealand lawyer; b. 23 June 1894; ed. Otago Univ.
Served in army 14-19 and 39-45; Chief Justice of New Zealand 53-65; former Vice-Pres. Royal Empire Soc.; former Chair. Consultative Cttee. on Hospital Reform; Croix de Guerre; Greek Military Cross; Legion of Merit.
29 Salamanca Road, Kelburn, Wellington W.1, New Zealand.

Barrows, Leland, A.M.; American government official and diplomatist; b. 27 Oct. 1906; ed. Univ. of Kansas.
Teacher, newspaper reporter, broadcaster 28-34; U.S. Dept. of Agriculture 34-42; Asst. Dir. War Relocation Authority 42-44; Office of Price Admin., Fed. Public Housing Authority, Dept. of State 44-48; Exec. Asst. to Special Rep. in Europe, Econ. Co-op. Admin. 49-53; Dir. Mission to Greece, Foreign Operations Agency 52-54, Mission to Vietnam 49-58; Regional Dir., Near and South Asia Operations, Int. Co-op. Admin. 58-61; Amb. to Repub. of Cameroon 61-67.
c/o Department of State, Washington, D.C., U.S.A.

Barry, Sir Gerald Reid, Kt.; British journalist; b. 20 Nov. 1898; ed. Marlborough and Corpus Christi Coll., Cambridge.
Served European War, Royal Flying Corps and Royal Air Force 16-19, Capt. 18; Asst. Editor *Saturday Review* 21-24, Editor 24-30; Founder 30 and Editor 30-34 *Week-End Review;* Dir. *New Statesman and Nation and Week-End Review;* Manager Editor and Dir. *News Chronicle* 36-47, Dir. 47-60; contrib. to daily and weekly press, broadcast talks; Editor *The Week-End Calendar* 33, *This England* 34; mem. Exec. Anglo-Soviet Public Relations Cttee. 41; Vice-Pres. Nat. Council Civil Liberties; Hon. A.R.I.B.A.; co-founder P.E.P. (Political and Economic Planning); Fellow Nat. Inst. Journalists; Dir. Festival of Britain 1951; Co-editor *The Week-end Book* 55; Educational Adviser Granada T.V. Network; Fellow Royal Soc. of Arts.
4 Mount Street, London, W.1, England.

Barsacq, André; French theatre producer; b. 24 Jan. 1909; ed. Ecole des Arts Décoratifs.
Founded "Troupe des Quatre Saisons"; Dir. of Théâtre de l'Atelier 40-; has directed the following plays (and created décor and costumes): *Le Bal des Voleurs,*

Antigone, L'Invitation au Château, Colombe, La Tête des Autres, L'œuf, La Bonne Soupe, Château en Suède, La Fourmi dans le Corps, Les Cailloux, Frank V, Le Satyre de la Villette, Un Mois à la Campagne, Le Monstre Turquin 64, *Ce soir on improvise* 65, *L'Idiot* 66, *Les Trois Soeurs* 66, etc.; has also directed films; *Le Rideau Rouge;* Pres. Union of Stage Managers; contrib. *Art Vivant, Art et Décoration, La Revue Théâtrale;* Chevalier Légion d'Honneur.
Publs. *Agrippa* (comedy); translations one-act plays by Chekhov and plays by Gogol and Turgenev.
1 place Charles Dullin, Paris 18e, France.

Barshai, Rudolf Borisovich; Soviet conductor; b. 24; ed. Moscow Conservatoire.
Performed in chamber ensembles with Shostakovich, Richter, Oistrakh, Rostropovich; founded Moscow Chamber Orchestra 55; numerous tours abroad; composer of orchestrations and arrangements for chamber orchestra of old and contemporary music.
State Philharmonic Society, 31 Ul. Gorkogo, Moscow, U.S.S.R.

Barszczewska, Elzbieta; Polish actress; b. 13; ed. Warsaw.
Début, Teatr Nowy 34; now mem. Teatr Polski Co. major roles include Ophelia (*Hamlet*), Infanta (*Le Cid*), Nora (*The Doll's House*), Lilla Weneda; guest appearances in Moscow.
Teatr Polski, Warsaw, Poland.

Bart, Lionel; British composer and lyricist; b. 1 Aug. 1930.
Ivor Novello Awards as song writer 57 (three), 59 (four), 60 (two); Variety Club Silver Heart as Show Business Personality of the Year, Broadway, U.S.A. 60; Antoinette Perry Award (Tony) for *Oliver!* 62.
Principal works: Lyrics for *Lock Up Your Daughters* 59, music and lyrics for *Fings Ain't Wot They Used T'be* 59, music, lyrics and book for *Oliver!* 60, music, lyrics and direction of *Blitz!* 62, music and lyrics of *Maggie May* 64; film scores include: *Serious Charge, In the Nick, Heart of a Man, Let's Get Married, Light Up the Sky, The Tommy Steele Story, The Duke Wore Jeans, Tommy the Toreador, Sparrers Can't Sing, From Russia with Love, Man in the Middle;* many individual hit songs.
Apollo Music Ltd., 164 Shaftesbury Avenue, London, W.C.2, England.

Barth, Karl, DR. THEOL., D.D., LL.D.; Swiss theologian; b. 10 May 1886; ed. Berne, Berlin, Tübingen and Marburg Univs.
Hon. Prof. Göttingen 21; Prof. Münster i. W. 25; Prof. Bonn 30-34, Basle 35-62; Leader of German Church Opposition to "Nazification" for which he was retired 35; Foreign Assoc., Acad. des sciences morales et politiques; Hon. Dr. Theol. Münster 22, deprived of degree 39, restored 45.
Publs. *Suchet Gott so werdet ihr leben* 18, *Der Römerbrief* 18, *Das Wort Gottes und die Theologie* 25, *Die Auferstehung der Toten* 25, *Prolegomena zur Dogmatik* 27, *Die Theologie und die Kirche* 28, *Zur Lehre vom Heiligen Geist* 30, *Anselms Beweis der Existenz Gottes* 31, *Kirchliche Dogmatik* 32-59, *Theologische Existenz Heute* 33, *Credo* 35, *Theologische Studien* 38, *A Letter from Switzerland to Great Britain* 41, *The Church and the War* 44, *Eine Schweizer Stimme* 45, *Die protestantische Theologie im* 19. *Jahrhundert* 47, *Dogmatik im Grundriss* 47, *Die Christliche Lehre nach dem Heidelberger Katechismus* 48, *Fürchte dich nicht!* 49, *Against the Stream* 54, *Wolfgang Amadeus Mozart* 56, *Theologische Fragen und Antworten* 57, *Den Gefangenen Befreiung* 59, *Einführung in die Evangelische Theologie* 62, *Rufe mich an!* 65.
Bruderholzallee 26, Basle, Switzerland.

Barth, T(homas) F(redrik) W(eiby), DR. PHIL.; Norwegian university professor; b. 18 May 1899; ed. Universitas Regia Fredericiana, Oslo.

Assistant, Univ. of Oslo, Technische Hochschule, Berlin, Univ. of Leipzig; Staff mem. Geophysical Laboratory, Carnegie Inst., Washington, D.C. 29-36; Prof. Univ. of Oslo 36-46, 49-, also Dir. of Mineralogisk-Geologisk Museum, Univ. of Oslo; Prof. Univ. of Chicago 46-49; Pres. Int. Union of Geological Sciences 64-; Royal Order of St. Olav (Norway); Reusch Medal 28, Roebling Medal 60, Eskola Medal 68; Hon. Dr. (Univs. of Copenhagen, Nancy, Kiel, Liège and Zürich). Publs. *Eruptivgesteine* in Part I of *Die Entstehung der Gesteine, ein Lehrbuch der Petrologie* (Barth-Correns-Eskola) 39, 60, *Volcanic Geology, Hot Springs, and Geysers of Iceland* 50, *Theoretical Petrology* 52, 62.
Rödkleivfaret 6, Voksenkollen, Oslo, Norway.
Telephone: 686960; 699356.

Bartha, Dénes, DR. PHIL. HABIL.; Hungarian musicologist; b. 2 Oct. 1908; ed. High School of Music, Budapest, and Berlin Univ.
Librarian, Music Dept. Nat. Library 30; joined staff Budapest High School of Music 35-42, Prof. of Musicology 42 (Deputy Chair. 51-); Music Critic *Pester Lloyd* 39-44; Editor monthly journal *Magyar Zenei Szemle* 41-44; Music Adviser to Budapest Municipal Orchestra 47-48; Editor *Zenei Szemle* 47-48, *Zenetudományi Tanulmányok* (with B. Szabolcsi) (Vols. 1-10) 53-62; *Studia Musicologica* (with B. Szabolcsi) 61-; mem. Directorium Int. Soc. of Musicology, New York; Neilson Prof. Smith Coll., Northampton, Mass.; Visiting Prof. Harvard Univ. 64-65, Cornell Univ. 65-66, Univ. of Illinois 66, Univ. of Pittsburgh 66-67; Dent Medal 63. Publs. include *Egyetemes Zenetörténet* (General History of Music) (2 vols.) 35, *Musik, Musikgeschichte, Musikleben in Ungarn* 40, *Die ungarische Musik* (with Zoltán Kodály) 43, *A Zenetörténet Antológiája* 48, *Ötödfélszáz Énekek* 53, *The Nine Symphonies of Beethoven* 56, *J. S. Bach* 56, 60, *Haydn als Opernkapellmeister* 60, *J. Haydn, Ges. Briefe und Dokumente Krit. Ausgabe* 65, *Zenei Lexikon* (3 vols.) 65.
Attila u. 87, Budapest, Hungary.
Telephone: 360-431.

Barthel, Max; German writer; b. 17 Nov. 1893.
Publs. Verse: *Verse aus den Argonnen, Freiheit, Die Faust, Arbeiterseele, Sonne, Mond und Sterne, Botschaft und Befehl, Hutzlibum, Danksagung, Die Lachparade, Lobgesang, Roter Mohn, Das Lied vom Walde, Spielzeuglieder, Von Ostern bis Pfingsten, Lasset uns die Welt gewinnen, Überfluss des Herzens, An den Mond, Morgenblau und Nachtmusik, Sachen zum Lachen (Kinderlieder), Wir spielen Zirkus (Kindersingspiel), Die Sonne krönt das Jahr* (cantata), *Das lachende Paradies, Tänzerische Lieder, Frühling am Bodensee* (song cycles), *Das Lied vom Leben* (cantata); novels: *Das Spiel mit der Puppe, Das Land auf den Bergen, Die Strasse den ewigen Sehnsucht, Das Haus an der Landstrasse, Kein Bedarf an Weltgeschichte* (autobiography); short stories: *Der Bund der Drei, Das vergitterte Land 13 Indianer*; reports: *Deutschland, Erde unter den Füssen.*
5484 Bad Niederbreisig, Rhein, German Federal Republic.

Bartholomew, Frank H., LL.D.; American journalist; b. 5 Oct. 1898; ed. Oregon State Univ.
Began newspaper career 18; joined United Press 21, Pacific Div. Man. 24-30, Vice-Pres. (Pacific Area) 30; Pres. and Gen. Man. United Press Int. 58-62, Chair. of the Board, United Press Int. 62-, Int. K.K. (Japan), Int. of Canada Ltd., United Feature Syndicate Wire Service Supply Co., United Radio Shows, Metropolitan Newspaper Feature Syndicate, British United Press Ltd.; Chair. Planet News Ltd.; Dir. Pacific Nat. Bank, San Francisco, San Francisco Fed. Savings and Loan Asscn.; Pres. Buena Vista Winery Inc., Sonoma, Calif.; war corresp. in Pacific 42-45, China 49, Korea 50, Indo-China 54.
United Press International, 220 East 42nd Street, New York City 17, N.Y.; Home: Glenbrook, Nevada, U.S.A. Telephone: MU2-0400 (New York); 588-6408 (Glenbrook).

Bartlett, (Charles) Vernon (Oldfeld), C.B.E.; British author, politician and publicist; b. 30 April 1894.
Formerly Reuter's correspondent at Peace Conf.; subsequently *The Times* corresp. in Switzerland and Rome; London Dir. L.N. Secretariat 22-32; speaker on international affairs for B.B.C. 28-34; Diplomatic Commentator *News Chronicle* 34-54; Editor *World Review* 34-40; Independent M.P. for Bridgwater 38-50; Political Commentator *Straits Times*, Singapore 55-61.
Publs. *Journey's End* (with R. C. Sherriff); *Topsy Turvy, Calf Love, This is my Life, Go East, Old Man, East of the Iron Curtain, Struggle for Africa, Report from Malaya, And now To-morrow, Tuscan Retreat, A Book About Elba, Introduction to Italy,* etc.
Villa Ferrante, San Ginese di Compito, Lucca, Italy.
Telephone: Capannori 34125.

Bartlett, E. L. (Bob); American politician; b. 20 April 1904; ed. Univs. of Washington and Alaska.
Fmr. staff mem. of *Fairbanks* (Alaska) *News-Miner*; Sec. to Delegate from Alaska 33-35; gold miner 36-39; Sec. of Alaska under presidential appointment 39-44; Del. to Congress from Alaska 44-59; Senator from Alaska 59-; Democrat.
Senate Office Building, Washington, D.C., and P.O. Box 740, Juneau, Alaska, U.S.A.

Bartlett, Sir Frederic, C.B.E., F.R.S., M.A.; British psychologist; b. 20 Oct. 1886; ed. St. John's Coll., Cambridge.
Asst. to Dir. Psychological Laboratory Cambridge 14; Reader in Experimental Psychology Cambridge Univ. 22, Dir. Psychological Laboratory 22-52; Editor *British Journal of Psychology* 24-48; Pres. Section J, British Asscn. 29; Prof. of Experimental Psychology Cambridge Univ. 31-52; Fellow St. John's Coll. Cambridge; mem. Medical Research Council 41-47, 49-52; foreign hon. mem. American Acad. Arts and Sciences, Int. Asscn. Applied Psychology, American Philosophical Society, Société de Psychologie de France, American Nat. Acad. of Sciences; Hon. Fellow British Psychological Society and hon. mem. numerous foreign psychological socs.; Hon. D.Phil. (Athens Univ.), Hon. D.Sc. (Princeton, Oxford and London Univs.), Hon. Dr. Psych. (Louvain Univ.), Hon. LL.D. (Edinburgh), Hon. D.Ed. (Padua).
Publs. *Exercises in Logic* 13, *Psychology and Primitive Culture* 23, *Textbook of Experimental Psychology* (Part II) (with Dr. C. S. Myers) 25, *Psychology and the Soldier* 27, *Remembering: An Experimental and Social Study* 32, *The Problem of Noise* 34, *The Study of Society* 39, *Political Propaganda* 40, *The Mind at Work and Play* 50, *Thinking: an Experimental and Social Study* 58.
161 Huntingdon Road, Cambridge, England.
Telephone: Cambridge 53909.

Bartlett, Vernon (*see* Bartlett (C.) V. (O.)).

Bartok, Eva; British (b. Hungary) actress; b. 1934.
Joined Drama Centre, Budapest 47, then made stage debut in *Time and the Conways* (Priestley); film debut in *The Prophet of the Fields*, Budapest 48; came to England 50; two painting exhibitions.
Stage roles in *Time and the Conways, The Lovers, Woman with Red Hair, Paint Myself Black, Lady of the Moon,* and *Rain,* etc.; film roles in *The Prophet of the Fields, 12 Heures d'Orologe, Orient Express, I'll Wait for You in Hell, The Last Waltz, Fantastic Holiday, Madeleine, A Tale of Five Cities, Carnival Stories, Operation Amsterdam, 10,000 Bedrooms,* etc.; also British television appearances.
Publ. *Worth Living For* 58.
c/o Theo Cowan Ltd., 45 Clarges Street, London, W.1, England.

Barton, Derek Harold Richard, F.R.S., F.R.S.E.; British organic chemist; b. 8 Sept. 1918; ed. Tonbridge School and Imperial Coll., Univ. of London.

Lecturer, Imperial Coll. 45-59; Visiting Prof., Harvard Univ. 49-50; Reader in Organic Chemistry, Birkbeck Coll., Univ. of London 50-53, Prof. 53-55; Regius Prof. of Chemistry, Glasgow Univ. 55-57; Prof. of Organic Chemistry, Imperial Coll. of Science and Technology, Univ. of London 57-; Pedler Lecturer, Chem. Soc. 67; Hon. Fellow Deutsche Akad. der Naturforscher Leopoldina 67; Hon. D.Sc. Univ. of Montpellier 62, Univ. of Dublin 64; numerous medals.

Department of Chemistry, Imperial College, London, S.W.7, England.

Telephone: 01-589-5111.

Barton, Henry Askew, B.S.E.E., M.A., PH.D.; American physicist; b. 98; ed. Princeton Univ.

Engineer with American Telephone and Telegraph Co. 21-23; Nat. Research Fellow, Harvard Univ. 25-27; Fellow Bartol Research Laboratory 27-29; Asst. Prof. Cornell Univ. 29-31; Dir. American Inst. of Physics 31-57, Admin. Consultant 57-; Vice-Chair. Div. Physical Sciences of Nat. Research Council 33-45.

335 East 45 Street, New York 17, N.Y., U.S.A.

Barwick, Rt. Hon. Sir Garfield Edward John, P.C., G.C.M.G., B.A., LL.B.; Australian lawyer and politician; b. 22 June 1903; ed. Sydney Univ.

Admitted to N.S.W. Bar 27, Victoria Bar 45, Queensland Bar 58; Pres. N.S.W. Bar Asscn. 50-52, 54-55, Law Council of Australia 52-54; mem. Fed. House of Reps. for Parramatta 58-64; Attorney-Gen. 58-64; Acting Minister for External Affairs Mar.-Apr., Aug.-Nov. 59, Apr.- June 60, Minister for External Affairs Dec. 61-64; Chief Justice of Australia 64-; Chancellor Macquarie Univ., Sydney, March 67-.

Office of the Chief Justice, High Court of Australia, Sydney; and Mundroola, Mahers Road, Beecroft, Sydney, Australia.

Barzel, Rainer, DR. IUR.; German lawyer, civil servant and politician; b. 20 June 1924; ed. Gymnasium, Braunsberg (East Prussia), Berlin, and Univ. of Cologne.

Air Force, Second World War; Civil Service, North Rhine-Westphalia, Ministry for Fed. Affairs 49-56, resigned 56; Exec. mem. Christian Democrat Party (CDU), First Deputy Chair. CDU and Chair. CDU in Bundestag 66-; mem. Bundestag 57-; Fed. Minister for All-German Affairs 62-63.

Publs. *Die geistigen Grundlagen der politischen Parteien* 47, *Souveränität und Freiheit* 50, *Die deutschen Parteien* 51.

Ferdinandstrasse 4, Paderborn, German Fed. Republic.

Barzini, Luigi, B.LITT.; Italian journalist and writer; b. 21 Dec. 1908; ed. School of Journalism, Columbia Univ., New York.

Special Correspondent *Corriere della Sera* 30-40; Editor and Publisher *Il Globo*, Rome 44-47; contributor to Italian and other magazines including *Encounter*, *Harper's Magazine*, *Preuves*, *Der Monat*; mem. Italian Chamber of Deputies 58-; Liberal.

Publs. *Americans are Alone in the World* 53, *Mosca Mosca* 61, *The Italians* 64.

1055 Via Cassia, Tomba di Nerone, Rome, Italy.

Telephone: 307-1925.

Barzun, Jacques; American (b. French) teacher and writer; b. 30 Nov. 1907; ed. Lycée Janson de Sailly and Columbia Univ.

Instructor in History, Columbia Univ. 29, Asst. Prof. 38, Assoc. Prof. 42, Prof. 45-, Dean of Graduate Faculties 55, Dean of Faculties and Provost 58-67, Univ. Prof. 67-, Seth Low Prof. 60; mem. Acad. Delphinale (Grenoble), American Nat. Inst. of Arts and Letters, American Historical Asscn., Royal Soc. of Arts,

American Arbitration Asscn.; Chevalier de la Légion d'Honneur; Extraordinary Fellow, Churchill Coll., Cambridge 61.

Publs. *The French Race* 32, *Race: A Study in Modern Superstition* 37, *Of Human Freedom* 39, *Darwin, Marx, Wagner* 41, *Teacher in America* 45, *Berlioz and the Romantic Century* 50, *God's Country and Mine* 54, *The Energies of Art* 56, *Music in American Life* 56 (with H. Graff), *The Modern Researcher* 57, *The House of Intellect* 59, *Classic, Romantic and Modern* 61, *Science, the Glorious Entertainment* 64; Editor: *Pleasures of Music* 51, *The Selected Letters of Lord Byron* 53, *New Letters of Berlioz* (and trans.) 54, *The Selected Writings of John Jay Chapman* 57, *Modern American Usage* (with others); Trans.: *Diderot: Rameau's Nephew* 52, *Flaubert's Dictionary of Accepted Ideas* 54, *Evenings with the Orchestra* 56, *Courteline: A Rule is a Rule* 60, *Beaumarchais: The Marriage of Figaro* 61.

110 Low Library, Columbia University, New York, U.S.A.

Telephone: 280-2841.

Basaldella, Afro (brother of Mirko Basaldella, *q.v.*); Italian painter; b. 1912; ed. Acad. of Fine Arts, Venice.

Works under the name of Afro; represented in the most important museums of U.S.A. and Europe; executed design for *Ritratto di Don Chisciotte* Rome 57; first prize Venice Biennale 56, second prize Pittsburgh Int. 59, UNESCO Award, Paris.

Via Tartaglia 3, Rome, Italy.

Basaldella, Mirko; Italian sculptor and painter; b. 28 Sept. 1910; ed. Acads. of Fine Arts of Venice, Florence, Rome and Monza.

One-man shows in Italy and U.S.A. before Second World War; one-man shows at Knoedler Gallery, New York 47, Galleria dell' Obelisco, Rome 47, and subsequent shows in New York, Milan and Rome; Second Prize in Int. Competition for monument to Unknown Political Prisoner 53; First Prize for Sculpture, São Paulo Biennale 55; recent one-man exhbns. include Viviano Gallery, New York, Fogg Museum, Harvard Univ. 58, Providence Museum, R.I. School of Design 59, Obelisk Gallery, Washington, D.C. 61, La Nuova Pesa, Rome 63, Inst. of Contemporary Art, Boston 64, Ward-Nasse Gallery, Boston 65, Galleria Don Chisciotte, Rome 66, De Cordova Museum, Boston 67; mem. American Acad. of Arts and Sciences 62; Gold Medal from Pres. of Repub. of Italy 64; First Prize Nat. Exhbn. Quadriennale D'Arte, Rome 66; First Prize Int. Exhbn. "Premio Del Fiorino", Florence; Moretti Prize for Distinguished Contribution to Arts; Dir. of Design Workshop, Harvard Univ. 57-.

Principal works include: bronze memorial gates for Ardeatine caves; ceiling decoration of Hall of Honour in FAO Building, Rome; memorial to Italian dead at Mauthausen, Austria; large bronze sculpture for front of Krannert Art Museum, Urbana, Ill.; mosaic fountain in Piazza Benedetto Brin, La Spezia; bas-relief for Chapel of Sisters of St. Anne, Arlington, Mass. 66; bas-relief for Int. Anthropology Soc. Centre, Austria.

Via del Babuino 29, Rome, Italy; and 244 Brattle Street, Cambridge 38, Mass., U.S.A.

Bashev, Ivan Hristov; Bulgarian journalist and politician; b. 16; ed. Univ. of Sofia.

Editor *Narodna Mladej* 44-46; Bulgarian Rep. to World Fed. of Democratic Youth, Paris 46-51; Dep. Minister of Education 56; Dep. Minister of Foreign Affairs 62, Minister of Foreign Affairs 62-; mem. Communist Party 46-; mem. Central Cttee. of Bulgarian Communist Party.

Ministry of Foreign Affairs, Sofia, Bulgaria.

Basiev, Oleg Alexandrovich; Soviet politician; b. 1919; ed. Novocherkassk Veterinary Inst.

Soviet Army 41-48; Lecturer, Horsebreeding Dept.,

Novocherkassk Veterinary Inst., and Sec. of Party Bureau at the Inst. 49-54; Second Sec., Tselina District Cttee. (Rostov Region) of C.P.S.U. 54-58; First Sec., Dubovskoye District Cttee. (Rostov Region) of C.P.S.U. and Official at Central Cttee. of C.P.S.U. 58-62; Chair. Council of Ministers of North Osetian Autonomous S.S.R. 62-, and Deputy to U.S.S.R. Supreme Soviet; mem. C.P.S.U. 47-.
Council of Ministers of the North Osetian Autonomous S.S.R., Ordjonikidze, U.S.S.R.

Baskakov, Sergei Alexeyevich; Soviet politician; b. 1911; ed. Industrial Inst. of the Urals.
Member C.P.S.U. 31-; technologist, later Senior Engineer, U.S.S.R. Ministry of Armament 35-43; party and trade union work 43-51; Deputy Minister of Medium Machine Building, U.S.S.R. 53-54; on staff, Central Cttee. of C.P.S.U. 54-, Dept. Chief 56-, mem. Central Auditing Comm. 61-.
Central Auditing Commission of the Communist Party of the Soviet Union, Moscow, U.S.S.R.

Basnayake, Hema Henry, Q.C.; Ceylonese judge; b. 3 Aug. 1902; ed. St. Aloysius Coll., Galle, and St. Joseph's Coll., Colombo.
Admitted to the Bar 27; Crown Counsel 32; Cttee. for preparing new revised edition of Legislative Enactments of Ceylon 37-38; Asst. Legal Draughtsman 39; Senior Crown Counsel 44; Acting Solicitor-Gen. 45, Jan. 46; Acting Attorney-Gen. 46, 47; mem. Local Govt. Service Comm. 45-47; Solicitor-Gen. 46; Puisne Justice 47-51; Attorney-Gen. 51-55; Acting Chief Justice 55; Chief Justice 56-64; Chair Board of Trustees, Ceylon Univ. Sangharama and Vihara Trust, Musaeus Girls Coll., Kalutara Bodhi Trust; Pres. Child Protection Soc., Crippled Children's Aid Asscn.; Vice-Pres. St. John Ambulance Asscn.; Man. Trustee, A. B. Gomes Trust; Pres. Ceylon Farmers' Asscn., Maha Bodei Soc. of Ceylon.
Publ. *Legislative Enactments of Ceylon* 38, 56.
Elibank House, Elibank Road, Colombo 5, Ceylon.

Basov, Alexandr Vasilievich, M.SC.; Soviet politician and diplomatist; b. 1912; ed. Vologda Agricultural Inst. Veterinary Inst. 30-42; teacher 42-54; Sec. Rostov Regional Cttee., C.P.S.U. 54-55; Chair. Rostov District Exec. Cttee. 55-60; First Sec. Rostov District Cttee., C.P.S.U. 60-62; mem. Central Cttee. C.P.S.U. 61-, Counsellor, Cuba 62-65; Minister of Agriculture of R.S.F.S.R. 65; Ambassador to Romania 65-.
U.S.S.R. Embassy, Bucharest, Romania.

Basov, Nikolai Gennadievich; Soviet physicist; b. 14 Dec. 1922; ed. secondary school and Moscow Inst. of Physical Engineers.
P. N. Lebedev Physical Inst. 48-, Vice-Dir. 57-, also Head of Laboratory of Quantum Physics; Prof., Moscow Inst. of Physical Engineers; works particularly in field of quantum radio physics; Corresp. mem. U.S.S.R. Acad. of Sciences 62-66, Academician 66-; Editor *Priroda* (Nature)—Popular Science Magazine 68-; Lenin Prize 59; Nobel Prize for Physics 64.
P. N. Lebedev Physical Inst. of the Acad. of Sciences of the U.S.S.R., 53 Leninsky Prospekt, Moscow, U.S.S.R.
Telephone: AB7-21-57.

Bass, Lawrence Wade, PH.D.; American chemical engineer; b. 18 June 1898; ed. Tulane, Yale, Lille and Paris Univs. and Pasteur Inst., Paris.
Rockefeller Inst. 25-29; Exec. Staff Mellon Inst. 29-31; Dir. of Research Borden Co., New York 31-36; Asst. Dir. Mellon Inst. 37-42; Dir. New England Ind. Research Foundation 42-44; Dir. Chemical Research Air Reduction Co. Inc. 44-48; Research and Development U.S. Indus. Chemicals Inc. 44-48, Vice-Pres. 48-52; Exec. Arthur D. Little Inc. 52-54, Vice-Pres. 54-64, Consultant 64-; Pres. American Inst. Chemical Engs. 45.

Publs. *Chemistry of the Inorganic Complex Compounds* 23, *Nucleic Acids* 31, *Management of Technical Programs* 65, *Formulation of Research Policies* 67.
Office: 630 Fifth Avenue, New York City 10020; Home: 220 Madison Avenue, New York City 10016, U.S.A.

Bassani, Giorgio; Italian writer; b. 1916; ed. Univ. of Bologna.
Chief Editor *Botteghe Oscure* 48-61, Dir. of Literary Series with Feltrinelli including *Il Gattopardo*, G. di Lampedusa 57-63; Teacher History of Theatre, Acad. d'Arte Drammatica 57-; Vice-Pres. Radio Televisione Italiana 64-65; Strega Prize 56, Viareggio Prize 62.
Publs. *Cinque storie ferraresi* 56, *Gli occhiali d'oro* (novel) 58, *Il giardino dei Finzi-Contini* (novel) 62, *L'alba ai vetri* (poems) 63, *Dietro la porta* (novel) 64, *Le parole preparate* (essays) 66.
Via G. B. De Rossi 33, Rome, Italy.

Basson, Jacob Daniel du Plessis ("Japie"); South African politician; b. 1918; ed. Stellenbosch Univ.
Political sec. and journalist in Repub. and S.W. Africa 39-50; mem. S. African Parl. for Namib, S.W. Africa 50-59 (Nat. Party of S.W.A.); expelled from Nat. Party Caucus over differences concerning Govt.'s race policies 59; Independent M.P., leading extra-Parl. Political Group (The Nat. Union) 59-61; merger of Nat. Union with United Party (official opposition party) 61; M.P. (United Party) for Bezuidenhout, Johannesburg 61-; Shadow Minister of Foreign Affairs, Immigration and State Information.
House of Assembly, Cape Town; Home: Unitas, 123 Kitchener Avenue, Bezuidenhout Valley, Johannesburg, South Africa.
Telephone: 24-5040 (Johannesburg).

Bastian, Paul Henri, LIC. EN DROIT; Luxembourg government official; b. 9 Sept. 1896; ed. Luxembourg Athénée, Munich and Montpellier Univs.
Sec. Gen. Luxembourg Branch Soc. Gén. Alsacienne de Banque 22-29; Dir. Agence Economique et Financière, Luxembourg 29-39; Pres. Asscn. des Journalistes Luxembourgeois 36-38; Dir. Luxembourg city food services 40-41; Dir. Gewerbebank, Deputy Dir. Banque Gén. de Luxembourg 41-44; Hon. Commissaire du Gouvernement, Ministry of Finance 44-; mem. Council, Inst. Belgo-Luxembourgeois du Change; mem. Monetary Cttee. E.E.C. 58-; mem. Benelux Cttee. Econ. Policy 60-; mem. Luxembourg Del. to O.E.C.D.; Dir. of several companies; Commdr. Ordre Adolphe de Nassau, Officier Ordre de la Couronne de Chêne, Ordre de la Couronne de Belgique, Commdr. Ordre de Léopold II, Commdr. Ordre de St. Grégoire le Grand, Légion d'Honneur, Commdr. Order of Merit (Germany and Italy).
Publs. *La Fortune Nationale du Grand-Duché de Luxembourg* 34, *Le Système Monétaire du Grand-Duché de Luxembourg* 36, *Le Commerce Extérieur du Grand-Duché de Luxembourg* 39.
15 Rue Guillaume Schneider, Luxembourg.
Telephone: 23038.

Bastid, Paul Raymond Marie; French politician; b. 17 May 1892; ed. Ecole Normale Supérieure, Faculté des Lettres et Faculté de Droit de Paris.
Deputy for Cantal 24-45, Paris 46-51; Radical Socialist; Sec. of the Chamber 25; Del. to the L.N. 26-28, 32-36; President of Foreign Affairs Cttee. of the Chamber 34; Minister of Commerce in Blum Cabinet June 36; Prof. Law Faculty, Paris Univ. 54-65; Joint Vice-Pres. French British Parl. Cttee. 39-40; Del. to Council of Europe Assembly 49-51; mem. C.N.R., mem. A.C.P., Pres. Constitutional Cttee; mem. of Constituent Assembly 46, and of National Assembly; mem. Acad. of Moral and Political Sciences 46.
Publs. *Les communautés taisibles de l'ancien droit* 16, *L'hypothèque grecque et sa signification historique* 17, *Sieyès et sa pensée* 39, *Les discours de Sieyès dans les débats constitutionnels de l'an III* 39, *Doctrines et*

institutions politiques de la Seconde République, 2 vols. 45, *Cormenin* 47, *Notes sur les Amériques* 48, *La Révolution de 1848 et le droit international* 48, *Les institutions politiques de la Monarchie parlementaire française* 54, *Le gouvernement d'assemblée* 57, *Les grands procès politiques de Socrate à Pétain* 62, *Benjamin Constant et sa Doctrine* (2 vols.) 66; fiction *Frédérique* 46, *Ironies amoureuses* 48, poems: *Le Florilège de Primus* 46, *La Lanterne magique* 56, *En marge des jours* 62.
88 rue de Grenelle, Paris 7e, France.

Bastid, Suzanne; French lawyer; b. 15 Aug. 1906; ed. Lycée de Grenoble, Lycée Fénelon, Paris, and Univ. de Paris à la Sorbonne.
Professor, Faculty of Law, Lyon 33-46, Paris 46-; Prof. Inst. d'études politiques, Univ. de Paris 46-; Pres. Admin. Tribunal, UN 52-; Sec.-Gen. Inst. of Int. Law 63-; mem. then Pres. Political and Juridical Studies Section, Nat. Council of Scientific Research; mem. French Del. to UN Gen. Assembly (4th to 13th Sessions); Chevalier Légion d'Honneur; Commdr. Royal Order of Sahametrei (Cambodia).
Publs. include: *Les fonctionnaires internationaux, Jurisprudence de la Cour internationale de Justice, Les Tribunaux administratifs internationaux et leur jurisprudence, Les questions territoriales devant la C.I.J.*
88 rue de Grenelle, Paris 7e, France.

Basyn, Thomas, LL.D.; Belgian banker; b. 98; ed. Univ. of Louvain and Columbia Univ.
Practised as lawyer 22-26; associated with Nat. City Bank of New York (Brussels branch) 29-36; Asst. Man. Office de Liquidation des Interventions de Crise 36-39; Man. Banque Nationale de Belgique, Antwerp 41; Gen. Sec. Banque Nationale de Belgique, Brussels 41; Exec. Dir. Int. Bank for Reconstruction and Development; Foreign Rep. Banque Nat. de Belgique 52; Lecturer on Credit and Money, St. Louis High School, Brussels 27-39; corresp. of *Journal de Genève* 32-40; Financial Counsellor, Belgian Embassy, Wash., D.C., April 49-; adviser to Nat. Bank of Belgium 60-; Chevalier de l'Ordre de Léopold, Officier de l'Ordre de la Couronne, Officier de l'Ordre du Chêne (Luxembourg).
The Westchester, 4000 Cathedral Avenue N.W., Washington, D.C., U.S.A.

Bata, Thomas John; Canadian shoe executive; b. 17 Sept. 1914; ed. privately and business college in Europe.
President Bata Ltd.; Chair. of Bata Shoe Co. of Canada Ltd. 39-, British Bata Shoe Co. Ltd. 46-, Dir. and officer several companies connected with Bata Group; Dir. American Management Asscn. 58-61; Founder mem. Planning Council President's Professional Asscn. (U.S.A.) 61.
Batawa, Ontario, Canada.

Bataillon, Marcel Edouard, D. ès L.; French university professor; b. 20 May 1895; ed. Lycée Carnot, Dijon, Lycée Louis-le-Grand, Paris, Ecole Normale Supérieure, Paris, and Ecole des Hautes Etudes Hispaniques, Madrid.
Artillery Officer, First World War 14-18, Prof. Univ. of Lisbon 22-26, Lycée de Bordeaux 26-29, Univ. of Algiers 29-37, Univ. of Paris 37-45, Collège de France 45-65, Hon. Prof. Collège de France 65-; Dir. Collège de France 55-65; mem. Acad. des Inscriptions et Belles Lettres 52-; Pres. Fédération Int. des Langues et Littératures Modernes, Modern Humanities Research Asscn.; mem. Royal Acads. of Belgium, Netherlands and Sweden, Accad. dei Lincei, Rome, Bavarian Acad. of Sciences; Corresp. mem. Spanish Acad., and Acad. of History, Madrid; Commandeur Légion d'Honneur; Commandeur des Palmes Académiques; Croix de Guerre; Dr. h.c. (Louvain, Turin and Montevideo).
Publs. *Erasme et l'Espagne* 37, *Etudes sur le Portugal au temps de l'humanisme* 52, *Le Docteur Laguna auteur du*

"Voyage en Turquie" 58, *La Celestine selon F. de Rojas* 61, *Varia lección de clasicos españoles* 64, *Etudes sur Bartolomé de las Casas* 66.
14 rue de l'Abbé de l'Epée, Paris 5e, France.

Bateman, Ralph Melton, M.A., F.C.I.S.; British business exec.; b. 15 May 1910; ed. Epsom Coll. and Univ. Coll. Oxford.
Turner and Newall Ltd. 31-, Dir. 57-, Deputy Chair. and Joint Man. Dir. 59-67, Chair. 67-.
Turner and Newall Ltd., Asbestos House, 77–79 Fountain Street, Manchester 2; Home: Highfield, Styal, Wilmslow, Cheshire, England.
Telephone: Wilmslow 22745.

Bates, Harry C.; American trade unionist; b. 22 Nov. 1882; ed. Denton.
Pres. Bricklayers Local Union, Dallas, Texas 10-14; Pres. Texas Bricklayers Unions 12-20; rep. Bricklayers, Masons and Plasterers Int. Union of America 14-22, Vice-Pres. 20-24, Treas. 24-28, Pres. 36-; Vice-Pres. and mem. Exec. Cttee. American Fed. of Labor 34-; mem. Amalgamation Cttee. A.F.L.-C.I.O. 54, Vice-Pres. and mem. Exec. Cttee. 55-; del. to numerous European trade union confs.
815 15th Street, Washington 5, D.C., U.S.A.

Bates, Herbert Ernest; British writer; b. 16 May 1905; ed. Kettering Grammar School.
Publs. *The Two Sisters, Catherine Foster, Charlotte's Row, The Fallow Land, The Poacher, A House of Women, Spella Ho, Fair Stood the Wind for France, The Purple Plain* 47, *The Jacaranda Tree* 49, *Scarlet Sword* 51, *Love for Lydia* 52, *The Feast of July* 54, *The Sleepless Moon, Death of a Huntsman, The Darling Buds of May* 58, *The Cruise of the Breadwinner, The Nature of Love, A Breath of French Air* 59, *An Aspidistra in Babylon* 60, *When the Green Woods Laugh* 60, *The Day of the Tortoise, The Golden Oriole* 62, *A Crown of Wild Myrtle* 62, *Oh! to be in England* 63, *Seven by Five* 63, *A Moment in Time* 64, *The Wedding Party* 65, *The Distant Horns of Summer* 67, *The Four Beauties* 68 (novels); *The Black Boxer, Cut and Come Again, Something Short and Sweet, The Bride Comes to Evensford, Dear Life, The Flying Goat, Colonel Julian, The Woman Who Had Imagination, Beauty of the Dead, The Daffodil Sky, The Watercress Girl, The Fabulous Mrs. V* 64 (short stories); *Country Tales*, 30 *Tales, My Uncle Silas, Sugar for the Horse, Now Sleeps the Crimson Petal* (collected stories); *Flowers and Faces, Through the Wood, Down the River, The Seasons and the Gardener, The Heart of the Country, O! Happy Countryman, The Country Heart, The Country of White Clover, Edward Garnett: A Memoir* (essays); *Modern Short Story* (criticism); as "Flying Officer X" *The Greatest People in the World, How Sleep the Brave.*
The Granary, Little Chart, Ashford, Kent, England.

Bath and Wells, Bishop of (*see* Henderson, Rt. Rev. E. B.).

Batista y Zaldivar, Gen. Fulgencio; Cuban politician; b. 01.
Formerly teacher, tailor's and carpenter's apprentice, agricultural worker, mechanic and railway employee; soldier in Nat. Army 21-23; entered Guardia Rural 23, later clerk at Staff Headquarters and Sergeant-clerk; took part in rising against Gen. Machado's Govt. 31-33; Col. and Chief-of-Staff of Constitutional Army appointed by Revolutionary Govt. 33-39; Pres. of the Republic 40-44, 52-54, re-elected 54; fled to Dominican Republic on success of Castro Revolution Jan. 59; settled in Madeira Sept. 59.
Funchal, Madeira.

Batitsky, Gen. Pavel Fyodorovich; Soviet army officer and politician; b. 1910; ed. Frunze Military Acad., and Acad. of General Staff.
Soviet Army 24-; mem. C.P.S.U. 38-; Chief of Div. Staff, then Div. and Corps Commdr. 41-45; Area

Mil. Commdr. 48-50; Chief of Gen. Staff, Soviet Army Air Force 50-53; First Deputy Commdr. Area Anti-Aircraft Defence 53-54, Commdr. 54-65; First Deputy Chief Gen. Staff Soviet Armed Forces 65-66; C.-in-C. U.S.S.R. Anti-Aircraft Defence, Deputy Minister of Defence 66-; Cand. mem. Central Cttee. of C.P.S.U. 61-66, mem. 66-; Deputy to U.S.S.R. Supreme Soviet; Hero of the Soviet Union; Order of Lenin (four times), Order of Kutuzov (twice), Order of Suvorov, Order of Red Banner (four times).
Ministry of Defence, 34 Maurice Thorez Embankment, Moscow, U.S.S.R.

Batliner, Gerard, D.IUR.; Liechtenstein lawyer and government official; b. 9 Dec. 1928; ed. Grammar School, Schwyz, Switzerland, and Univs. of Zürich, Fribourg, Paris, and Freiburg im Breisgau.
Practice at County Court of Principality of Liechten-stein 54-55; lawyer, Vaduz 61; Vice-Pres. Progressive Burgher Party 58; Vice-Mayor of Eschen 60; Pres. Asscn. of Liechtenstein Lawyers 62; Head of Govt. of Principality of Liechtenstein 62-.
Chief of Government, Government Building, 9490 Vaduz, Liechtenstein.

Batov, Gen. Pavel Ivanovich; Soviet army officer; b. 14 June 1897.
Tsarist Army 15-17, Red Army 17-; mem. Communist Party 29-; Corps Commdr. E. Poland 39; Div. Commdr. Finland 39; Garrison Commdr. Tbilisi, Georgia 41; served E. Germany, later Commdr. Kaliningrad Mil. District 45-55; Commdr. Carpathian Mil. District 55-58, Baltic Mil. District 58-60, U.S.S.R. Southern Army Group (Hungary) 60-62; Chief of Staff, Jt. Armed Forces of Warsaw Pact Org. 62-65; First Deputy Chief of Staff Soviet Armed Forces 62-66; Insp.-Gen. Ministry of Defence 66-; Deputy to Supreme Soviet of U.S.S.R.; Order of Lenin (five times); Hero of the Soviet Union (twice); Order of Suvorov (three times); Order of Kutuzov; Order of Red Banner (three times), etc.
Publs. include: *In Battles and On the March, The Oder Operation.*
Ministry of Defence, 34 Maurice Thorez Embankment, Moscow, U.S.S.R.

Batten, Harry Albert; American advertising execu-tive; b. 30 Jan. 1897; ed. Philadelphia public schools.
N. W. Ayer and Son 11-, Vice-Pres. (Copy) 29, Dir. 31-, Pres. 36-51, Chair. Board 51-65, Exec. Cttee. 65-; U.S. Navy, First World War; Dir. Philadelphia Orchestra and official of numerous civic and philanthropic orgs.; Hon. Dr. of Law, Temple Univ.
The Barclay, Rittenhouse Square, Philadelphia, Pa., U.S.A.

Batten, Jean Gardner, C.B.E.; New Zealand aviator; b. 09; ed. Cleveland House Coll., Auckland.
Obtained flying licence 30, commercial pilot's licence 32; made solo flights England-India 33, England-Australia (woman's record) 34, Australia-England (first woman to complete return flight) 35, England-Brazil (world record 61½ hours; fastest crossing of S. Atlantic 13½ hours: first England-S. America and solo S. Atlantic flight by woman) 36, England-New Zealand (first direct flight, establishing record England-Australia solo 5 days 21 hours, Australia-New Zealand over Tasman Sea 9 hours 29 minutes) 37, Australia-England (solo record 5 days 18 hours 15 minutes) 37; many Trophies and Medals; Chevalier Légion d'Honneur; Officer Order of Southern Cross of Brazil.
Publ. *My Life* 38.
c/o Barclays Bank D.C.O., Gibraltar.

Batten, William Milfred, B.S.; American business executive; b. 4 June 1909; ed. Parkersburg High School (W.Va.) and Ohio State Univ.
Salesman, Section Man., Asst. Man., J. C. Penney Co.

store, Lansing, Mich. 35-40; Training Dir. Personnel Dept. J. C. Penney Co., New York 40-42; consultant in Organisation Planning & Control Div. Office of Q.M.G., Washington 42; military service, Office of Q.M.G., U.S. Army as Lieut.-Col. 42-45; Zone Personnel Rep. (Eastern Zone), J. C. Penney Co., New York 45-51, Asst. to Pres. 51, 53, Vice-Pres. 53-58, Pres. 58-64, Chair of Board 64-; Hon. LL.D. (Morris Harvey Coll. and West Virginia Univ.); Hon. L.H.D. (Marietta Coll.).
235 Trumbull Road, Manhasset, Long Island, N.Y., U.S.A.

Battista, Archie J.; American banker; b. 1 Aug. 1907; ed. Univ. of Pennsylvania, Rutgers Univ. and Harvard Univ. Graduate School.
Manager, Foreign Dept. and Credit Dept., J. P. Morgan and Co. Inc. 29-48; Vice-Pres. Union Bank of Com-merce, Cleveland, Ohio 48; Gen. Financial Man. and Assoc. Vice-Pres. Geo. H. McFadden and Bro. Inc. 49-60; Vice-Pres. and Gen. Man. Int. Banking Dept., The First Pennsylvania Banking and Trust Co., Philadelphia 60-; Pres. and Dir. First Pennsylvania Overseas Finance Corpn.; Vice-Chair. First Pennsyl-vania Overseas Devt. Corpn. Ltd., Nassau, Bahamas; Treas. and Dir. Drexel Inst., Council on Int. Relations.
Office: The First Pennsylvania Banking and Trust Co., Philadelphia, Pa. 19101; Home: 421 Great Springs Road, Bryn Mawr, Pa., U.S.A.

Battle, Lucius Durham, A.B., LL.B.; American govern-ment official; b. 1 June 1918; ed. Univ. of Florida.
Manager of student staff, Univ. of Florida Library 40-42; Assoc. Admin. Analyst, War Dept. 42-43; U.S. Naval Reserve 43-46; Foreign Affairs Specialist, Dept. of State, Washington 46-49; Special Asst. to Sec. of State 49-53, 61-64, also Exec. Sec. Dept. of State 61-62; First Sec., Copenhagen 53-55; Deputy Exec. Sec. NATO, Paris 55-56; Asst. Sec. of State for Educational and Cultural Affairs 62-64; Amb. to United Arab Repub. 64-67; Asst. Sec. of State for Near Eastern and S. Asian Affairs, Washington 67-; Chair. UNESCO Gen. Conf., Paris 62; Vice-Pres. Colonial Williamsburg Inc., Williamsburg Restoration Inc.; mem. Board of Trustees John F. Kennedy Center for Performing Arts, Washing-ton Gallery of Modern Art 62-64; mem. American Foreign Service Asscn. (Pres. 62-63).
Department of State, Washington, D.C.; Home: 3200 Garfield Street, N.W., Washington, D.C., U.S.A.

Baudet, Philippe French diplomatist; b. 29 Aug. 1901; ed. Lycée Condorcet, Faculty of Law and Ecole des Sciences Politiques, Paris.
Entered diplomatic service 28, occupied posts in Con-stantinople, Washington, Peking, Paris, Mexico and Chungking; Free French Forces in London 42; Wash-ington 42-45; Dir. Asian Affairs, Ministry of Foreign Affairs 45-47; Minister-Counsellor, London 47-50; Ambassador to Yugoslavia 50-54, to Argentina 55-57, to Turkey 56-57; Diplomatic Counsellor to French Govt. 57-62; Civil Asst. to Sec. of State for Defence 59-62; Ambassador to Switzerland 62-64, to U.S.S.R. 64-66; Ambassadeur de France (Hon.); Commdr. de la Légion d'Honneur, Hon. K.C.V.O. (U.K.), Grand Officer Order of Orange Nassau (Neths.), etc.
31 *bis* boulevard Suchet, Paris 16e, France.
Telephone: 288-65-62.

Baudouin; King of the Belgians; b. 7 Sept. 1930.
Son of King Leopold III; became Prince Royal Aug. 50; ascended Belgian throne July 51; m. 1960, Doña Fabiola de Mora y Aragón, b. 11 June 1928; K.G.
Royal Palace, Laeken, Brussels 2, Belgium.

Bauer, Peter Thomas, M.A.; British economist; b. 6 Nov. 1915; ed. Scholae Piae (Budapest) and Gonville and Caius Coll., Cambridge.
Fellow Gonville and Caius Coll. Cambridge 46-60; Reader, Agricultural Economics, Univ. of London 47-

48; Univ. Lecturer in Economics, Cambridge Univ. 48-56, Smuts Reader in Commonwealth Studies 56-60; Prof. of Economics (with special reference to economic development and underdeveloped countries), Univ. of London 60-.

Publs. *The Rubber Industry* 48, *West African Trade* 54, *The Economics of Under-developed Countries* (with B. S. Yamey) 57, *Economic Analysis and Policy in Under-developed Countries* 58, *Indian Economic Policy and Development* 61; numerous articles on economic subjects. London School of Economics and Political Science, Houghton Street, London W.C.2, England.

Bauman, John Nevin, B.S., M.S.; American automobile executive; b. 11 March 1899; ed. Bucknell Univ. and Michigan Univ.

Standard Steel Car Co., Pittsburgh 21; joined White Motor Co. 22, Vice-Pres. 36-56, Pres. 56-, Chief Exec. Officer 60-; mem. Soc. Automotive Engineers; Dir. North American Coal Co., Cleveland Trust Co., Sherwin-Williams Co.

White Motor Company, 842 E. 79th Street, Cleveland 1, Ohio, U.S.A.

Baumel, Jacques; French politician; b. 6 March 1918; ed. Univ. d'Aix-Marseille.

Sec.-Gen., Mouvements Unis de la Résistance 40-44; mem. Consultative Assembly 44-45, Deputy 46-51; Editor of *Voici Pourquoi* and publisher of *Panoramas* 52-58; Senator 59-; Sec.-Gen. Union pour la Nouvelle République—Union Démocratique du Travail (UNR-UDT) 62-67; Chevalier Légion d'Honneur, Compagnon de la Libération, Croix de Guerre, Médaille de la Résistance.

14 rue Marguerite, Paris 17e, France.

Baumgartner, Wilfrid Siegfried, D. EN D.; French financial administrator; b. 21 May 1902; ed. Ecole des Sciences Politiques and Univ. of Paris.

Inspector of Finance 25-30; Chef du Cabinet of Min. of Finance 30; Deputy Dir. of Treasury at Min. of Finance 30-34, Asst. Dir. 34-35, Dir. 35-37; Dir.-Gen. and Pres. of Conseil d'Administration du Crédit National 37-49; mem. Gen. Council of Banque de France 37-49; Gov. of Bank 49-60; Minister of Finance 60-62; Président Directeur Général Rhône-Poulenc S.A. 63-; Prés. Alliance Française 66-; Pres. Financial Comm. Int. Chamber of Commerce 65-; mem. Acad. des Sciences morales et politiques 65-; Hon. LL.D. Law School of Paris; Hon. Gov. Banque de France; Grand Officier, Légion d'Honneur.

98 Rue de Grenelle, Paris 7e, France; 22 avenue Montaigne, Paris 8e, France.

Baumont, Maurice Edmond Marie, D. ès L.; French historian; b. 26 Feb. 1892; ed. Ecole Normale Supérieure, Univ. of Paris.

With Reparations Comm. in Berlin 20-27, with L.N. 27-39; Hon. Prof. Inst. Universitaire des Hautes Etudes Internationales (Geneva); Historical Adviser, Ministry of Foreign Affairs; Editor (France) Wilhelmstrasse documents (publ. in 10 vols. since 50); Hon. Prof. Univ. of Paris; Curator Musée de Chantilly; mem. Acad. des sciences morales et politiques.

Publs. include *L'Allemagne, Lendemain de Guerre et de Révolution* 22, *Quinze Ans d'Histoire Universelle 1914-1929*, *L'Abdication de Guillaume II* 30, *L'Affaire Eulenburg* 33, *L'Essor Industriel et l'Impérialisme Colonial (1878-1904)* 49, *La Faillite de la Paix (1918-1939)* 51, *Histoire de la France pour tous les Français: Vol. II, 1878 à nos Jours* 50, *Gloires et Tragédies de la IIIe République* 56, *Aux sources de l'Affaire Dreyfus* 59, *La Grande Conjuration Contre Hitler* 63, *L'Europe de 1900 à 1914* 67.

10 avenue Emile Acollas, Paris 7e, France.
Telephone: SUFfren 90-26.

Baunsgaard, Hilmar Tormod Ingolf; Danish businessman and politician; b. 26 Feb. 1920; ed. commercial schools.

Dep.-Man. grocery firm 44-47; Business Man. Købmaendenes Indkøbscentral A/S HOKI, Odense 47-61; Pres. Social-Liberal Party Youth 48-50; mem. Exec. Social-Liberal Party 48-57 (Vice-Pres. 54-57); mem. of Parl. 57-; Minister of Commerce 61-64; Prime Minister Feb. 68-; Marketing Man. at WA Reklame-Marketing S/I 64-68; mem. Board Nat. Bank of Denmark; political writer on *Berlingske Tidende* and *Aktuelt.*

Blidanpark 34, Hellerup, Denmark.

Bautista de Lavalle, Juan; Peruvian lawyer and diplomatist; ed. Universidad Mayor de San Marcos de Lima.

Secretary, Chargé d'Affaires, Peruvian Legation, Bolivia 19; First Sec. Peruvian Legation, France; Judge, Higher Court, Lima 30-38, Substitute Judge, Supreme Court 38-45, Judge 45; Peruvian Ambassador to Organization of American States (OAS) 46-; Pres. of Council of OAS 47-48, 63-64.

Pan American Union, Washington 6, D.C., U.S.A.

Bawden, Edward, C.B.E., R.A., R.D.I.; British artist; b. 03; ed. Cambridge School of Art and Royal Coll. of Art.

Tutor, Royal Coll. of Art 32-; Official War Artist, Middle East 40-45; work represented in Tate Gallery, London, and in other London, provincial and Commonwealth galleries; Trustee, Tate Gallery 51-58.

Royal College of Art, Exhibition Road, London, S.W.7; and Brick House, Great Bardfield, Braintree, Essex, England.

Baxter, Sir John Phillip, K.B.E., C.M.G., B.SC., PH.D., M.I.CHEM.E., F.R.A.C.I., M.I.E. (Aust.), F.A.A.; Australian chemical engineer and educationalist; b. 7 May 1905; ed. Hereford, and Birmingham Univ.

Research Dir.-Gen. Chemicals Division I.C.I. and Dir. Thorium Ltd. -49; Prof. of Chemical Engineering N.S.W. Univ. of Technology 49-53, Dir. 53-54, Vice-Chancellor (now Univ. of New South Wales) 55-; Chair. Atomic Energy Comm. 57-.

1 Kelso Street, Enfield, N.S.W., Australia.
Telephone: 744261.

Bayani, Mehdi, PH.D.; Iranian librarian; b. 06; ed. Univ. of Teheran.

Librarian, Nat. Teachers' Coll., and Lecturer, Faculty of Literature, Teheran Univ. 33; Head of Education Dept., Ispahan Province 40; Special Inspector and Asst. Dir. of Education Dept., Min. of Art and Industry 41; Gen. Dir. Nat. Library of Teheran 42-; Dir. Imperial Library and Dir.-Gen. The Nat. Library 57-; Prof. Nat. Teachers' Coll. 61-, Faculty of Art 63-.

Editor: *Nimuneh-Sukhan-i-Farsi* 38, *Rahnemaye Ganjineh Koran* 48, *Specimens of Fine Writing from the National Library, Teheran* 48, *Specimens of Fine Writing from the Imperial Library of Iran* 51, *Ahval va Athare mir Emad* 52.

Publs. *Three Essays of Sheikh Shahabod-din Suhrawardi* 38-40; *Essay Sawanih-fel-Eshq Ahmad Ghazzali* 43; *Badaya ol-Azman* (Tarikhe Afzal) 47.

Imperial Library, Teheran, Iran.

Bayar, Celâl; Turkish politician.

Minister of Nat. Economy 21; Minister of Reconstruction and Settlement (when Turkish and Greek populations were exchanged in accordance with Treaty of Lausanne) 23; founded Ish Bank 24; Minister of Nat. Economy 32; Prime Minister 37-39; Vice-Pres. Republican People's Party during Presidency of Kemal Atatürk; undertook leadership of new Democratic Party founded 46; Pres. of the Republic May 50-60; detained on Yassiada Island 60-61; sentenced to life imprisonment Sept. 61, released on grounds of health

63; imprisoned again 63-64; released again on health grounds Nov. 64; granted full pardon July 66.
Ankara, Turkey.

Bayero, Alhaji Mohammadu Kabiru; Nigerian diplomatist; b. 26; ed. Kano Judicial School, School for Arabic Studies, police training, Inst. of Administration, Zaria, and Univ. of Manchester.
Tax Scribe, Kano Native Administration 46-50; Chief of Native Administration (Police), Kano 53-56; District Head, Garki District 56-64; mem. Nigerian Parliament 59; Ambassador to Guinea 64-.
Embassy of Nigeria, B.P. 54, Conakry, Guinea.

Bayet, Jean Alexis, D.LITT.; French Latin scholar; b. 12 Nov. 1892.
Mem. French Academy in Rome 17-20; Prof. Caen Univ. 26-32; Prof. of Latin Poetry at the Sorbonne 32-; mem. Institut de France 48; Dir. French Acad. in Rome 52-60; mem. Pont. Accad. Romana di Archeologia 54; mem. Accad. Naz. dei Lincei 56; Commdr. Légion d'Honneur, Palmes Académiques, Order of Merit (Italy).
Publs. *Les origines de l'Hercule Romain* 26, *Herclé* 26, *La Sicile Grecque* 26, *Architecture et Poésie* 32, *Littérature Latine* 34 (new ed. 65, Spanish ed. 66), *Histoire Romaine* 40, *Tite-Live* I-VII 40-68, *Cicéron, Correspondence* IV, V 49, 64, *Histoire Politique et Psychologique de la Religion Romaine* 57 (Ital. ed. 59), *Lettres de Gaelius* 65, *Mélanges de Littérature latine* 67.
135 Boulevard St. Michel, Paris 5e, France.
Telephone: 033-66-48.

Bayh, Birch Evans, Jr.; American lawyer, farmer and politician; b. 22 Jan. 1928; ed. Purdue Univ. and Indiana Univ.
Former farmer, later in legal practice, Terre Haute; mem. Indiana House of Reps. 55-62, Minority Leader 57-58, 61-62, Speaker 59-60; U.S. Senator from Indiana 63-; Democrat.
United States Senate, Washington, D.C.; 1445 Woodacre Drive, MacLean, Va., U.S.A.

Bayne, Right Rev. Stephen Fielding, Jr., S.T.D.; American bishop; b. 21 May 1908; ed. Trinity School, New York, Amherst Coll. and General Theological Seminary.
Fellow and Tutor, New York Gen. Theological Seminary 32-34; ordained 33; Rector, Trinity Church, St. Louis, Mo. 34-39, St. John's, Northampton, Mass. 39-42; Chaplain, Columbia Univ. 42-47, U.S.S. *Salerno Bay* 44-46; Bishop of Olympia, Wash. 47-59; Exec. Officer, Anglican Communion 60-64; Director of Overseas Dept., Episcopal Church of U.S. 64-; numerous hon. degrees.
Publs. *The Optional God* 53, *Christian Living* 57, *In the Sight of the Lord* 58, *Enter with Joy* 61, *Mindful of the Love* 62, *An Anglican Turning Point* 64.
Episcopal Church Center, 815 Second Avenue, New York 17, N.Y., U.S.A.

Bayramoğlu, Fuat; Turkish diplomatist; b. 12; ed. School of Political and Administrative Sciences, Istanbul, and Univ. of Liège.
Entered Diplomatic Service 39; mem. Gen. Directorate of Press and Publication Cttee. 43; Head of Secretariat Prime Minister's Office 44-46; Chair. Press Dept. Cttee. 46; Dir. in Foreign Ministry 48; Consul, Cyprus 49; Consul Gen., Jerusalem 51-53; Dir.-Gen. Consular and Claims Dept., Ministry of Foreign Affairs, Ankara 53-57; Ambassador to Norway 57-59, to Iraq 59-60, to Iran 60-62, to Italy 62-63; Sec.-Gen. Ministry of Foreign Affairs 63-65; Ambassador to Belgium 65-.
Turkish Embassy, 74 rue Jules Lejeune, Brussels 6, Belgium.

Bayülken, Ümit Halûk; Turkish diplomatist; b. 7 July 1921; ed. Lycée of Haydarpaşa, Istanbul, and Univ. of Ankara (Political Sciences).
Ministry of Foreign Affairs 44-; Reserve Officer in

Army 45-47; Vice-Consul, Frankfurt (Main) 47-49; First Sec., Bonn 50-51; Ministry of Foreign Affairs 51-53; First Sec. Turkish Perm. Mission to UN 53-57, Counsellor 57-59; Turkish Rep. to London Joint Cttee. on Cyprus 59-60; Dir.-Gen., Policy Planning Group, Ankara 60-63; Deputy Sec.-Gen. for Political Affairs 63-64, Sec.-Gen. 64-66; Amb. to U.K. 66-; Leader or mem. various Turkish Dels. to int. confs. and meetings; Hon. G.C.V.O. (U.K.); Order of Isabel la Católica (Spain); Grosses Bundesverdienstkreuz (German Fed. Repub.).
Publs. lectures, articles, studies and essays on minorities, Cyprus, principles of foreign policy, int. relations and disputes.
Turkish Embassy, 43 Belgrave Square, London, S.W.1, England.
Telephone: 01-235-5252.

Bazaine, Jean, L. ès L.; French painter; b. 1904.
Executed stained glass windows for church at Assy 46, at Saint Severin, Paris 66, ceramic mural and windows at Audincourt 51-54, ceramic mural at UNESCO 60, and Maison de la Radio, Paris 63; exhibited Galerie Carré, Galerie Maeght, Paris; Retrospective Exhbns., Berne 58, Eindhoven 59, Hanover 63, Zürich 63, Oslo 63, Paris 65; Rep. at Biennali of Venice, São Paulo and Carnegie; Grand Prix Nat. des Arts 64.
Publ. *Notes sur la peinture d'aujourd'hui* 48.
36 rue Pierre Brossolette, 92-Clamart, France.

Bazarov, Semyon Tarasovich; Soviet diplomatist; b. 1914; ed. Saratov Juridical Inst.
Diplomatic Service 39-, Counsellor Sweden, Iran; Head, Middle East Dept., Ministry of Foreign Affairs 46-49, Head, European Dept. 59-62; Ambassador to Mexico 62-67; on staff of Ministry of Foreign Affairs 67-.
Ministry of Foreign Affairs, 32–34 Smolenska-Sennaya ploshchad, Moscow, U.S.S.R.

Bazelaire de Ruppierre, Mgr. Louis de, L. ès L., DR. en Théologie; French ecclesiastic; b. 4 Jan. 1893; ed. Grand Séminaire d'Issy, Institut Catholique Paris, and Collège Angélique Rome.
Ordained Priest 16; Army Chaplain 17-18; Prof. of Philosophy, Prof. of Theology, and then Superior, Grand Séminaire de Nancy 20-47; Protonotary Apostolic 47; Archbishop of Chambéry 47-66.
Publ. *Les laïcs aussi sont l'Eglise.*
10 boulevard de la Colonne, Chambéry, France.

Bazelon, David Lionel; American judge; b. 3 Sept. 1909; ed. Univ. of Ill. and Northwestern Univ.
Private practice, Illinois 32-35; Asst. U.S. Attorney, Northern District of Illinois 35-40; senior mem. Gottlieb and Schwartz 40-46; Asst. Attorney-Gen. U.S. Lands Div. 46-47, Office of Alien Property 47-49; Judge, U.S. Court of Appeals, District of Columbia circuit 49-, Chief Judge 62-; Lecturer, Law and Psychiatry, Univ. of Pennsylvania Law School 57-58, 58-59; Sloan Visiting Prof., Menninger Clinic, Topeka, Kansas 60-61, Regent's Lecturer, Univ. of Calif. at Los Angeles 64; Lecturer in Psychiatry, The Johns Hopkins Univ. School of Medicine 64-; Clinical Prof. of Psychiatry (Socio-legal aspects), George Washington Univ. 66-; Chair. Task Force on Law, President's Panel on Mental Retardation 61-62; Isaac Ray Award, American Psychiatric Asscn. 60-61; mem. Board of Dirs. American Orthopsychiatric Asscn. 65-, Pres. Elect 68; mem. Board of Dirs. Joint Comm. on Mental Health of Children Inc. 65-; mem. Nat. Advisory Mental Health Council, Public Health Service 67-71; mem. Board of Trustees, Salk Inst. for Biological Studies 61-; mem. Cttee. on Ethics, American Heart Asscn. 68-; Hon. LL.D. (Colby Coll.) 66.
U.S. Court of Appeals; Home: 3020 University Terrace N.W., Washington D.C. 20001, U.S.A.
Telephone: ST3-5700, Extension 7118.

Bazhan, Mikola Platonovich; Soviet poet; b. 1904; ed. Inst. of Foreign Relations, Kiev.

Editor-in-Chief, Ukrainian Soviet Encyclopedia; mem. C.P.S.U. 40-; mem. Acad. of Sciences of Ukrainian S.S.R.; mem. Board of U.S.S.R. Union of Writers; Vice-Pres. European Community of Writers; State prizewinner; awarded five Orders.

Publs. *17th Patrol* 26, *Immortality* 37, *Fathers and Sons* 38, *Mother* 39, *Tambi* 40, *Daniil Galitsky* 42, *The Stalingrad Notebook* 43, *Impressions of England* 48, *Mickiewicz in Odessa* 56, *By the Saviour's Tower* 52, *Italian Meetings* 61, *A Flight through the Storm* 63, *Immortality of the Stone* 67.

5/5 Repina, Kiev, Ukrainian S.S.R., U.S.S.R.

Bazin, Germain (René Michel), D. ès L., L. en D.; French museum curator (Chief Curator of Museum of Louvre); ed. Coll. Ste. Croix, Neuilly, Coll. de Pontlevoy and Univ. de Paris.

Professor, Brussels Free Univ. 34; began Museum career in Dept. of Drawings, Ecole des Beaux Arts; Keeper of Paintings, Louvre 37, Dir. of Paintings and Drawings 51-65 (Museum of Louvre), Dir. of Restoration, Paintings of French Museums 65; Prof. of Museum Studies at Ecole Louvre 41; Infantry Capt. 39-40; active work in protection of French art treasures 40-45; organized 30 exhbns. in France and abroad; has frequently lectured in Europe, U.S.A., S. America; has made film on *Impressionism*, Art Adviser for film *The Louvre* (N.B.C., New York); Del. to numerous UNESCO Cttees.; mem. Central Inst. of Conservation, Rome; mem. numerous acads.; Officier Légion d'Honneur; Officier Arts et Lettres; Grand Officier Ordre de Léopold (Belgium); Commandeur de la Couronne (Belgium), and Orders from Italy, Portugal, Sweden and Brazil; Dr. h.c. (Univ. do Brasil).

Publs. *Le Mont St. Michel* 32, *Le Louvre* 33, *Les Trésors de la Peinture française* 41, *Fra Angelico* 43, *Corot* 43, *L'époque impréssionniste* 44, *Le Crépuscule des Images* 46, *Les grands Maîtres hollandais* 49, *Histoire générale de l'art (de la Préhistoire à nos jours)* 53, *L'Art religieux baroque au Brésil* 56, *Les Trésors de la Peinture au Louvre* 58, *L'Aleijadinho* 59, *Les Maîtres des Ecoles etrangères au Musée de l'Ermitage* 60, *Baroque Gallery of Flowers* 60, *Les Trésors du Musée du Jeu de Paume* 61, *Le Message de l'Absolu* 64, *Baroque et Rococo* 65, *Le Temps des Musées* 67.

Palais du Louvre, Paris 1er; 29 avenue Georges Mandel, Paris 16e, France.

Bazin, Hervé (*see* **Hervé-Bazin, Jean-Pierre Marie**).

Bazovsky, Vladimir Nikolayevich; Soviet politician; b. 17; ed. Leningrad Refrigeration Inst.

Soviet Army 41-46; mem. C.P.S.U. 42-; party work 46-; on staff of Central Cttee. of C.P.S.U. 60-61; First Sec. Novgorod Regional Cttee., C.P.S.U. 61-; Cand. mem. Central Cttee. C.P.S.U. 61-; Deputy to U.S.S.R. Supreme Soviet.

Novgorod District Cttee. of C.P.S.U., Novgorod, U.S.S.R.

Bazzaz, Abdul Rahman Al-; Iraqi politician and oil administrator; b. 20 Feb. 1913; ed. Baghdad Univ. and King's Coll., London.

Judge 45-55; Dean of Law Coll., Baghdad 55-59; Prof. Arab Nationalism, Arab League Inst. of Higher Arabic Studies, then Dir. 59-63; Ambassador to United Arab Republic 63, to U.K. 63-65; Sec.-Gen. Org. of Petroleum Exporting Countries (OPEC) 64-65; Deputy Prime Minister, Minister of Foreign Affairs and Acting Minister of Oil 65; Prime Minister 65-66, also Minister of Interior 66.

Baghdad, Iraq.

Bea, His Eminence Cardinal Augustin, S.J.; German ecclesiastic; b. 28 May 1881.

Ordained priest in the Soc. of Jesus 12; Jesuit Provincial for Upper Germany 21-24; Dir. Higher Studies Jesuit Coll., Rome 24-28; Rector Rome Biblical Inst. 30-49; Confessor to Pope Pius XII; Editor *Biblica* 30-51; created Cardinal by Pope John XXIII 59; Chair. Secretariat for the promotion of Christian unity 60-, and of Neo-Volgata Comm.; Hon. LL.D. (Harvard).

Publs. Numerous works on Biblical subjects.

Via Aurelia 527, 00165 Rome 6, Italy.

Telephone: 6223092.

Beadle, George Wells, M.SC., PH.D.; American biologist; b. 22 Oct. 1903; ed. Univ. of Nebraska and Cornell Univ.

Nat. Research Fellow, Calif. Inst. of Technology 31-33, Research Fellow and Instructor 33-36; Asst. Prof. of Genetics, Harvard Univ. 36-37; Prof. of Biology and Chair. Division of Biology, Calif. Inst. of Technology 46-61; Pres. American Asscn. for the Advancement of Science 56-57; Eastman Visiting Prof., Oxford 58-59; Pres. Chicago Univ. 61-; Lasker Award 50, Dyer Award 51, Emil C. Hansen Prize 53, Nobel Prize for Medicine (with Lederberg and Tatum) 58; Albert Einstein Award 58; Nat. Award, American Cancer Soc. 59, Kimber Genetics Award, Nat. Acad. of Sciences 60; D.Sc. (Hon.) Yale, Nebraska, Northwestern, Rutgers, Kenyon, Wesleyan, Oxford, Birmingham.

Publ. *An Introduction to Genetics* (jointly) 39, *The Language of Life* (with Muriel Beadle) 66.

University of Chicago, Chicago 37, Ill., U.S.A.

Beadle, Rt. Hon. Sir Thomas (Hugh William), P.C., Kt., C.M.G., O.B.E., Q.C.; Rhodesian politician and judge; b. 6 Feb. 1905; ed. Univ. of Capetown and Queen's Coll., Oxford.

Advocate, Bulawayo 30-39; Royal West African Frontier Force, Gold Coast 39-40; Deputy Judge Advocate-Gen. S. Rhodesian Forces, and Parl. Sec. to Prime Minister 40-46; M.P. 39-50; Minister of Justice, Internal Affairs, Health, Education, S. Rhodesia 46-50; Judge of High Court, S. Rhodesia 50-61, Chief Justice 61-; Hon. Fellow Queens Coll., Oxford 66.

Chief Justice's Chambers, High Court, Bulawayo, Rhodesia.

Beal, Orville Ellsworth, B.A., M.B.A.; American insurance executive; b. 11 March 1909; ed. Rutgers Univ.

Prudential Insurance Co. of America 26-, Senior Vice-Pres. (District Agencies) 47-51, Senior Vice-Pres. (Public Relations) 51-53, Senior Vice-Pres. (North Central Operations) 53-57, Exec. Vice-Pres. 57-62, Pres. 62-; Trustee, Past Pres. Life Underwriters Training Council; Dir. Life Insurance Medical Research Fund; Dir., Past Chair. Inst. of Life Insurance; official of numerous other business, civic and cultural orgs.

Prudential Insurance Co. of America, Newark, N.J. 07101, U.S.A.

Telephone: 201-336-4401.

Beale, Sir Howard, K.B.E., Q.C.; Australian lawyer, diplomatist and company director; b. 1898; ed. Univ. of Sydney.

Called to the Bar 25; Lecturer, Workers' Educational Asscn. 27, Army Educational Dept. 40; R.A.N. 42-45; Liberal mem. for Parramatta, House of Reps. 46-58; mem. Commonwealth Parl. Public Works Cttee. 47-49; Minister for Information and Transport 49-50, for Supply 50-58, and of Defence Production 56-58 and Minister-in-charge of Atomic Energy Comm. and Aluminium Production Comm. 50-58; Acting Minister for Immigration 51-52, 53, 54; Minister for Nat. Development 52-53, for Air 52, for Defence 57; mem. Australian Defence Council, Cabinet Defence Preparations Cttee., Cabinet Cttee. on Uranium and Atomic Energy 50-58; Ambassador to U.S.A. 57-64; Alternate Gov. Int. Monetary Fund 60, 62 and 64; Pres. Arts Council of Australia 64-66; Regents' Visiting Prof., Univ. of California 66; Hon. LL.D., Kent Univ., Ohio, Hon. D.H. Lit., Nebraska.

2 Aston Gardens, Bellevue Hill, Sydney, Australia.

Beals, Carleton, M.A.; American writer; b. 13 Nov. 1893; ed. Calif., Columbia, Madrid, Rome and Mexico Univs.

Principal American High School Mexico City 19-20; Editor Latin-American Press Syndicate 34-36; Pres. Editorial Board *Latin-American Digest* 33-34; special corresp. Europe, Mexico, Central America, Spain, N. Africa, Italy, Turkey, U.S.S.R. and Germany 20-23, 34, 37, 46, 57, 61; mem. expeditions to Indian Regions Mexico 30-31, Peru, Bolivia, Ecuador, Amazon, Patagonia 46, 61; Nat. Acad. of Recording Arts Award 65.

Publs. *Rome or Death—the Story of Fascism* 23, *Mexico—an Interpretation* 23, *Brimstone and Chili* 27, *Con Sandino en Nicaragua* 28, *Destroying Victor* 29, *Mexican Maze* 31, *Banana Gold* 32, *Porfirio Diaz, Dictator of Mexico* 33, *The Crime of Cuba, Fire on the Andes* 34, *Black River* 35, *The Story of Huey P. Long* 35, *The Stones Awake* 36, *America South* 37, *The Coming Struggle for Latin-America, Glass Houses* 38, *American Earth* 39, *The Great Circle* 41, *Pan America, A Program for the Western Hemisphere* 41, *Dawn Over the Amazon* 43, *Rio Grande to Cape Horn* 43, *Lands of the Dawning Morrow* 48, *The Long Land: Chile* 48, *Our Yankee Heritage: The Making of New Haven* 51, *Stephen Austin: Father of Texas* 53, *Our Yankee Heritage: The Making of Bristol* 54, *Our Yankee Heritage: New England's Contributions to American Civilisation* 55, *Adventure of the Western Sea: The Story of Robert Gray* 56, *Taste of Glory* 56, *John Elliot: The Man who loved the Indians* 58, *House in Mexico* 58, *Brass-Knuckle Crusade, The Great Know-nothing Conspiracy* 60, *Nomads and Empire Builders* 61, *Cyclone Carry: The Story of Carry Nation* 62, *Latin America: World in Revolution* 63, *Eagles of the Andes* 63; jointly: *The Mexican Genius* 31, *Cohtemporary Opinion* 33, *Rifle Rule in Cuba* (with Clifford Odets) 35, *The Writer in a Changing World* 37, *We Testify* 41, *New Invitation to Learning* 44, *What South Americans Think of Us* 45, *The Price of Liberty* 47, *Bits of Silver* 61, *Under the Fifth Sun, Mexico Old and New* 64, *Arévalo, Anti-communism in Latin America* 64, *War within a War* 65, *Land of the Mayas, Past and Present* 66, *The Great Revolt and its Leaders* 68, *Stories Told by the Aztecs Before the Spaniards Came* 68.

RFD2 Box 25, Killingworth, Conn., U.S.A.

Beam, Jacob D., B.A.; American diplomatist; b. 24 March 1908; ed. Princeton and Cambridge Univs.

Vice-Consul, Geneva 31-34; Third Sec., Berlin 34-40; Second Sec., London 41-45; Asst. Political Adviser, U.S. Forces, Germany 45-47; Chief, Central European Div., Dept. of State 47-49; Consul-Gen., Djakarta 49-51; Acting U.S. Rep., U.N. Comm. for Indonesia 51; Counsellor, Belgrade 51-52; Minister-Counsellor, Moscow 53; Deputy Asst. Sec. of State 53-57; Ambassador to Poland 57-61; in charge of political and negotiating affairs, Arms Control and Disarmament Agency 61-66; Amb. to Czechoslovakia 66-68.

American Embassy, Prague, Czechoslovakia.

Beament, Brigadier George Edwin, O.B.E., K.ST.J., E.D., Q.C., B.A.SC.; Canadian officer and lawyer; b. 12 April 1908; ed. Royal Military Coll. Kingston, Toronto Univ., Osgoode Hall Law School, Staff Coll., Camberley.

Called to Ontario Bar 34; Partner Beament and Beament, Ottawa 37; mobilised 2nd Field Battery R.C.A., Major 39; proceeded to England in command 2/14 Field Battery R.C.A. 40; Brigade Major 1st Canadian Armoured Brigade 41; C.O. 6 Canadian Field Regiment R.C.A.; Lieut.-Col. 42; Col. Gen. Staff First Canadian Army 43; Brigadier Gen. Staff First Canadian Army 45; mentioned in despatches; awarded Croix de Guerre avec Palme, Order of the White Lion, 3rd Class, Czechoslovak Military Cross; Pres. Khaki Univ. of Canada in the U.K. 45-46; now Counsel Beament, Fyfe, Ault, Hutton and Wilson, Barristers and Solicitors; Pres.

Royal Mil. Coll. Club of Canada 53-54; Pres. Ottawa Community Chests 53-55; Pres. United Services Inst. 55-56; Pres. Ottawa Y.M.C.A. 58-60; Gov. Carleton Univ.; mem. Nat. Capital Comm. 60-66; Bencher Law Soc. Upper Canada 64-; Vice-Chancellor, Ven. Order of St. John (Canada); Knight of Grace Ven. Order of St. John 64; Gov. Corps of Commissionaires (Ottawa); Dir. Ottawa Charitable Foundation.

Office: Suite 816, 56 Sparks Street, Ottawa 4, Ontario; Home: 200 Rideau Terrace, Ottawa, Ontario, Canada. Telephone: 235-6736 (Office); 745-1146 (Home).

Beams, Jesse Wakefield, A.B., M.A., PH.D., SC.D. (Hon.); American physicist; b. 25 Dec. 1898; ed. Fairmount Coll., Kansas, Wisconsin Univ., Virginia Univ.

Instructor of Physics and Mathematics, Alabama Polytechnic Inst. 22-23; Nat. Research Fellow in Physics, Virginia and Yale Univs. 25-27; Instructor in Physics Yale Univ. 27-28; Assoc. Prof. Physics, Virginia Univ. 28-30; Prof. Physics 30-; Chair. Dept. of Physics 48-62; mem., Gen. Advisory Cttee. Atomic Energy Comm., 54-60, Nat. Acad. Sciences, American Phil. Soc., Optical Soc. of America, American Asscn; Univ. Professors, American Physics Teachers' Asscn.. awarded Potts Medal of Franklin Inst.; Fellow American Physical Soc., American Acad. of Arts and Sciences; A.A.A.S. Chair., Section B 42; Pres. Virginia Acad. of Science 47; Francis H. Smith Prof. of Physics 53; Naval Ordinance Development Award 46; Jefferson Award 55; Scott Award 56; Pres. American Physical Society 58-59; Lewis Prize 58, Alumni Award Wichita Univ. 59; Nat. Medal of Science 67.

Publs. Numerous researches in field of electrical discharge in gases; electro-optical Kerr effect; studies of phenomena which occur in short intervals of time; studies of phenomena which occur in high centrifugal fields; the development of high speed centrifuges; the acceleration of ions to high energies; measurement of particle and molecular weights; low temperature physics; strength of materials; isotope separation.

Department of Physics, University of Virginia, Charlottesville, Va. 22903, U.S.A.

Telephone: Charlottesville (Va.) 2952166, Extension 3128.

Bearsted, 3rd Viscount, cr. 25, of Maidstone; **Marcus Richard Samuel;** British business executive; b. 1 June 1909; ed. Eton Coll. and New Coll., Oxford.

Army Service 39-45; Chair. Hill Samuel and Co. until 66 (mem. Board of Dirs. 66-), The 1928 Investment Trust Ltd., Tanker Finance Ltd.; Dir. other companies; Trustee and Chair. Whitechapel Art Gallery.

1 Eaton Close, London, S.W.1, England.

Beaton, Cecil Walter Hardy; British photographer and designer; b. 14 Jan. 1904; ed. Harrow and Cambridge.

Portrait photographer, stage and film designer; settings and costumes for *Black Vanities, Kipps, Pitt the Younger, Anna Karenina, An Ideal Husband, Gigi, The Doctor's Dilemma*; stage productions: *Lady Windermere's Fan* (London and New York), *The Second Mrs. Tanqueray, Quadrille* (London and New York), *Portrait of a Lady* (New York), *The Chalk Garden, My Fair Lady* (New York and London), *Vanessa* (New York), *Turandot.*

Publs. *The Book of Beauty* 30, *Cecil Beaton's Scrapbook* 37, *Cecil Beaton's New York* 39, *My Royal Past* 39, *History Under Fire* (with James Pope Hennessey) 41, *Time Exposure* (with Peter Quennell) 41, *Winged Squadrons* 42, *Near East* 43, *British Photographers* 44, *Far East* 45, *Chinese Album* 46, *Ashcombe* 49, *Photobiography* 51, *Ballet* 51, *Persona Grata* (with Kenneth Tynan) 53, *The Glass of Fashion* 54, *It Gives me Great Pleasure* 55, *The Face of the World* 57, *Japanese* 59, *Cecil Beaton's Diaries 1922-1939* 61, *Quail in Aspic* 62, *My Fair Lady* 64, *Diaries: The Years Between* 65.

8 Pelham Place, London, S.W.7; Reddish House, Broadchalke, nr. Salisbury, Wilts., England.

Beattie, (John) Robert, B.A.; Canadian economist and banker; b. 30 May 1910; ed. Univ. of Manitoba and Oxford Univ.
With Manufacturers' Life Insurance Co., Toronto 33-35; entered Bank of Canada, Ottawa 35, Deputy Chief of Research Dept. 40, Chief of Research Dept. 44, Executive Asst. to Govs. 50, Deputy Gov. 55-.
252 Buena Vista Road, Rockcliffe Park, Ottawa, Canada.

Beaudoin, Hon. Louis René, P.C., Q.C.; Canadian barrister and solicitor; b. 12; ed. Montreal Coll., Coll. Ste-Marie, Seminary of Ste-Thérèse, Coll. St-Laurent, Univ. of Montreal.
Mem. Board of Dirs. Global Life Insurance Co., Global Gen. Insurance Co., Global Reinsurance Co., Laurentide Acceptance Corpn., Paquette & Paquette Inc., etc.; mem. Canadian House of Commons 45-58; Deputy Chair. of Cttees. 49-52; Deputy Speaker 52-53; Speaker 53-57; Vice-Pres. Nat. Liberal Federation 49-51; Canadian Del. to Second Session of U.N. Gen. Assembly in New York 49; Del. Commonwealth Parl. Conf., Wellington (N.Z.) and Canberra 50; Pres. Exec. Cttee. Canadian Branch, Commonwealth Parl. Asscn. 47-54, Hon. Pres. 53-57; mem. Gen. Council C.P.A. 51-54; Q.C. 52; mem. Bar of Montreal and P.Q.
Suite 910, Aldred Building, 507 Place d'Armes, Montreal, Canada.

Beaumont, Sir Richard Ashton, K.C.M.G., O.B.E.; British diplomatist; b. 29 Dec. 1912; ed. Repton and Oriel Coll., Oxford.
Entered Consular Service 36, served Beirut 36, Damascus 38; war service 41-44; joined Foreign Office 45, served Mosul 46-47; Chargé d'Affaires, Damascus, 47; Consul, Jerusalem 48-49, Caracas 49-53, Baghdad 53-57; Imperial Defence Coll. 58; Head of Arabian Dept. Foreign Office 59-61; Amb. to Morocco 61-65, to Iraq 65-.
British Embassy, Karradat Mariam, Baghdad, Iraq.

Beaupre, Robert S.; American banker; b. 14 Feb. 1911; ed. Lewis and Clark High School, Spokane, Washington, and Univ. of Washington.
Seattle First Nat. Bank 29-, Pres. and Dir. 61-; Dir. and Chair. Exec. Cttee. Pacific Coast Banking School 58-59; Dir. Chamber of Commerce of United States; mem. Board of Trustees, Seattle Chamber of Commerce; official of numerous business, civic and philanthropic orgs.
Seattle First National Bank, P.O. Box 3586, Seattle, Washington 98124, U.S.A.

Beaupre, Thomas Norbert, B.SC., M.SC.; Canadian business executive; b. 17 Aug. 1917; ed. McGill Univ.
Served in Second World War with Royal Canadian Army Service Corps; in Trade and Commerce Dept., Govt. of Canada, Ottawa; later in Defence Production as Asst. Deputy Minister and Dir. of Aircraft Production; Vice-Pres. and Sec. Canadian Chemical and Cellulose Co. Ltd. 53-57; Exec. Vice-Pres. Columbia Cellulose Co. Ltd. and Celgar Ltd., Vancouver 57-58, Pres. 58-61; Pres. Brit. Columbia Forest Products Ltd. 61-, Chair. of Board 64-; Chair. of Board and Pres. Domtar Ltd. 66-; Dir. Argus Corpn., Royal Bank of Canada, CAE Industries Ltd., B.C. Air Lines Ltd., Hudson's Bay Co., Hudson's Bay Oil and Gas Co. Ltd., Canadian Corpn. for 1967 World Exhbn., Montreal; Governor Canadian Export Asscn.
Office: 2240 Sun Life Building, Montreal 2; Home: 3207 The Boulevard, Westmount, Quebec, Canada.

Beausse, Jean Ulric Marie de; French diplomatist; b. 10 April 1903; ed. Ecole Libre des Sciences Politiques.
Attaché, French Embassy, Vatican 31; Sec., Santiago 35-37, Helsinki 40-43, Stockholm 43-45, Warsaw 45-49; Consul-Gen., Monaco 49-56; Minister to Bulgaria 56-61; Ambassador to Cambodia 61-64, to Kenya 64-.
French Embassy, P.O. Box 1784, Nairobi ,Kenya.

Beauvoir, Simone Lucie Ernestine Marie Bertrand de; French writer; b. 9 Jan. 1908; ed. Paris Univ.
Taught in various lycées 31-43; awarded Prix Goncourt for *Les Mandarins* 45; Hon. LL.D. (Cantab.).
Publs. Novels: *L'Invitée* 43 (English edition *She Came to Stay* 49, American ed. 54), *Le Sang des Autres* 45 (English and American eds. *The Blood of Others* 48), *Les Mandarins* 45 (American ed. *The Mandarins* 56, English ed. 57), *Tous les Hommes sont Mortels* 47 (American ed. *All Men are Mortal* 55); Play: *Les Bouches Inutiles* 54; non-fiction: *Pyrrus et Cinéas* 44, *Pour une Morale de l'Ambiguité* (American ed. *The Ethics of Ambiguity*) 48, *L'Amérique du Jour au Jour* 48 (English ed. *America Day by Day* 52, American ed. 53), *Le Deuxième Sexe* 49 (American ed. *The Second Sex* 52, English ed.), *Faut-il Brûler Sade?* 51 (English and American eds. *Must We Burn Sade?* 53), *Privilèges* 57, *La Longue Marche* 51 American and English eds. *The Long March* 58), *Mémoires d'une Jeune Fille Rangée* 58, *Brigitte Bardot* 60, *The Prime of Life* 62, *La Force des Choses* 63, *Une Mort très Douce* 64, *Les Belles Images* 66.
11 bis rue Schoelcher, Paris 14e, France.

Beavan, John; British journalist; b. 10; ed. Manchester Grammar School.
With *Evening Chronicle*, Manchester 28-30, *Manchester Evening News* 30-40; Diarist, Leader Writer *Evening Standard* 40-42; News Editor and Chief Sub-Editor, *The Observer* 42-43; Editor, *Manchester Evening News*; Dir. Manchester Guardian and Evening News Ltd. 43-46; London Editor, *Manchester Guardian* 46-55; Asst. Dir. Nuffield Foundation 55-60; Editor, *Daily Herald* Oct. 60-62; Political Adviser, *Daily Mirror* Group 62-.
Flat 5, 156 Sloane Street, London S.W.1., England.

Beavogui, Louis Lansana; Guinean politician; b. 1923; ed. West African Medical School, Dakar.
Former Asst. Medical Officer, Gueckedou, S. Guinea; later Medical Officer, Kissidougou, later becoming Mayor; Minister of Trade, Industry and Mining, Guinea 57-58, of Econs. 58-61, of Foreign Affairs 61-.
Ministry of Foreign Affairs, Conakry, Guinea.

Beazley, Sir John Davidson, Kt., C.H., M.A., D.LITT., F.B.A.; British archæologist; b. 13 Sept. 1885; ed. Christ's Hospital and Balliol Coll., Oxford.
Student and Tutor of Christ Church, Oxford 07-25; Prof. of Classical Archæology, Oxford 25-56; Hon. Fellow of Lincoln Coll.. Oxford; Hon. Fellow, Balliol Coll.; Hon. Student of Christ Church; Antonio Feltrinelli Foundation Prize 65; Hon. Litt.D., D.Litt., Ph.D., LL.D., D.-ès-L.
Publs. *Attic Red-figured Vases in American Museums* 18, *The Lewes House Collection of Ancient Gems* 20, *Greek Vases in Poland* 28, *Campana Fragments in Florence* 33, *Attic Red-figure Vase-Painters* 42, 63, *Etruscan Vase-painting* 47, *The Development of Attic Black-figure* 51, 64, *Attic Black-figure Vase-Painters* 56.
100 Holywell, Oxford, England.

Beb a Don, Philémon, L.B.; Cameroonian diplomatist; b. 15 Aug. 1925; ed. Lycée d'Aix en Provence and Univ. d'Aix en Provence et Toulouse.
With local civil and financial admin. 45-54; studied law, Paris 54-57; Principal Civil Administrator, Acad. of Int. Law, The Hague 57; Chief of Staff of Ministry of Econ. Affairs 57-58; Cameroonian mem. of French Del. to Int. Conf. on Coffee, Rio de Janeiro 58; Chief of Office of Legal Affairs, Ministry of Interior 58-60; with Ministry of Foreign Affairs 60-61; Counsellor, Cameroon Embassy in France 61-62, Amb. to France 62-67.
c/o Ministry of Foreign Affairs, Yaoundé, Cameroon.

Bebler, Ales, LL.D.; Yugoslav politician and diplomatist; b. 07; ed. Coll. and Univ. of Ljubljana and Univ. of Paris.
Deputy Minister of Foreign Affairs 49; Permanent Rep.

U.N. 50-51; Under-Sec. Foreign Affairs 52-55; Ambassador to France 55-58; elected to Parliament 58; Chair. Foreign Relations Cttee. of the House of the Union 58-61; Amb. to Indonesia 61-; mem. Rann of Kutch Tribunal; mem. Central Cttee. C.P.
Yugoslav Embassy, Djakarta, Indonesia.

Becerra de la Flor, Dr. Daniel; Peruvian surgeon and politician; b. 23 Jan. 1906; ed. Colegio Nacional de la Libertad, Moquegua and Univ. Nacional Mayor, San Marcos.
Assistant Lecturer, Surgery, San Marcos Univ. to 61; Principal Lecturer and Head of Surgery Dept., Cayetano Heredia School of Medicine; Senator 62-, Prime Minister and Minister of Public Health 65-; Founder-Pres. Peruvian Soc. of Gastroenterology; Vice-Pres. Peruvian Acad. of Surgeons; Accion Popular Party.
Office of the Prime Minister, Lima, Peru.

Bech, Joseph, LL.D.; Luxembourg politician; b. 17 Feb. 1887; ed. Univs. of Fribourg and Paris.
Deputy 14; Minister of Justice and Home Affairs 21-25; Minister of State, Pres. of Govt. and Minister of Foreign Affairs 26-37; Hon. Minister of State, Minister of Foreign Affairs 37-40; in London 40-44; Minister of State, Pres. of Govt. and Minister of Foreign Affairs 53; Prime Minister and Minister for Foreign Affairs, and External Commerce 53-58; mem. European Economic Community Council of Ministers 58; Pres. Chamber of Deputies 59, Hon. Pres. 64; fmr. Pres. NATO, North Atlantic Council; Robert Schuman Prize, Bonn. Univ. 67; Charlemagne Prize, Aachen.
34 Avenue Monterey, Luxembourg, Grand Duchy of Luxembourg.

Becher, Ulrich; Austrian-Swiss (b. German) writer; b. 2 Jan. 1910; ed. Werner-Siemens-Gymnasium, Berlin, Freie Schulgemeinde Wickersdorf, and Univs. of Geneva, Berlin and Leipzig.
Former mem. Georg Grosz circle, Berlin; went to Vienna 33; newspaper corresp. Paris and Switzerland; escaped to Zürich 38; in Rio de Janeiro 41-43, Brazilian interior 44, New York City 45-48, Basle 49-; Drama Prize, German Stage Club, Cologne 55.
Publs. *Männer machen Fehler* (short stories) 32, *Die Eroberer* (short stories) 36, *Nachtigall will zum Vater fliegen* (novel) 50, *Kurz nach 4* (novel) 57, *Männer machen Fehler, Geschichten der Windrose* (collected short stories) 58, *Das Herz des Hais* (novel) 60, *Brasilianischer Romanzero* 62, plays: *Niemand* 34, *Der Bockerer* (with Peter Preses) 48, *Samba* 51, *Feuerwasser* 52, *Mademoiselle Löwenzorn* 54, *Die Kleinen und die Grossen* 57, *Der Herr kommt aus Bahia* 58, *Makumba* 65.
Spalenring 95, Basle, Switzerland.

Bechtel, Stephen Davison; American engineer-constructor; b. 24 Sept. 1900; ed. Univ. of Calif.
Joined W. A. Bechtel Co., Vice-Pres. 25-36, Pres. 36-46; First Vice-Pres. Six Companies Inc. (constructors of Hoover Dam) 31-35; Dir. Bechtel-McCone Corpn. 37-46; during Second World War Chair. Calif. Shipbuilding Corpn.; now Senior Dir. Bechtel Corpn.; Dir. various Bechtel engineering and construction corporations and international affiliates; Dir. Stanford Research Inst. 49-; Pres. Lakeside Corpn.; Dir. Industrial Indemnity Co. and Southern Pacific Co.; Trustee Ford Foundation 60-; mem. Business Advisory Council U.S. Dept. of Commerce 50-61 (Chair. 58-59), The Business Council 61-; Hon. LL.D., D.Eng.; John Fritz Medal 61; Nat. Defense Transportation Award 60; Order of Cedar (Lebanon), Knight Order of St. Sylvester (Holy See), Kt. Commdr. Court of Honour.
Home: 244 Lakeside Drive, Oakland, California 94612; Office: 155 Sansome Street, San Francisco, California 94104, U.S.A.

Bechtolf, Erich; German banker; b. 8 April 1891.
Deutsche Bank A.G. 22-, fmr. mem. Management Board, Chair. Supervisory Board 59-.
Hamburg 20, Heilwigstrasse 93, German Federal Republic.

Beck, Béatrix Marie; Swiss writer; b. 30 July 1914; ed. Lycée de St. Germain-en-Laye and Université de Grenoble.
Former Sec. to André Gide; journalist; mem. Jury, Prix Fémina; Prix Goncourt for *Léon Morin, prêtre*; Prix Félix Fénéon.
Publs. *Barny, Une Mort irrégulière, Léon Morin, prêtre, Des accommodements avec le ciel, le Premier Mai Abram Krol, Le Muet, Cou coupé court toujours.*
c/o MM. Cailler (Editeurs), Geneva, Switzerland.

Beck, Conrad; Swiss composer; b. 16 June 1901; ed. Konservatorium, Zürich.
Further musical studies in Paris with Ibert, Honegger and Roussel 23-32; Ludwig Spohr Prize, City of Brunswick; Composers Prize of Asscn. of Swiss composers; Kunst preis, City of Basle.
Principal works: Seven symphonies, many other symphonic works, concertos, two oratorios, cantatas, chamber music, etc., including *Der Tod zu Basel* (Miserère), *Die Sonnenfinsternis.*
St. Johann Vorstadt 7, Basle, Switzerland.
Telephone: 230450.

Beck, Most Rev. George Andrew; British (Roman Catholic) ecclesiastic; b. 28 May 1904; ed. Clapham Coll., London, and St. Michael's Coll., Hitchin.
Priest 27; Staff St. Michael's Coll., Hitchin until 41, Headmaster 41-44; Headmaster, The Becket School, Nottingham 44-48; Titular Bishop of Tigia and Coadjutor Bishop of Brentwood 48-51, Bishop of Brentwood 51-55; Bishop of Salford 55-64; Archbishop of Liverpool 64-; Chair. Catholic Education Council 48.
Publs. *Assumptionist Spirituality* 36, *The Family and the Future* 48.
Archbishop's House, Woolton, Liverpool 25, England.
Telephone: GATeacre 1233.

Becker, Aharon; Israeli (b. Russia) Secretary-General of Histadrut (General Federation of Labour); b. 1906.
Went from Russia to Israel 24; mem. Kibbutz 25; building worker 26-28; Sec. Ramat Gan Labour Council 29-32; Sec. Union of Textile Workers 33-34; mem. Exec. of Labour Council in Tel-Aviv 34-43; Man. Dir. Industrial Dept., Co-operative Wholesale Soc. 43-47; Head of Supply Mission, Ministry of Defence 48-49; Head of Trade Union Dept. and mem. Exec. Bureau, Gen. Fed. of Labour in Israel 49-61; Deputy mem. Governing Body of ILO 54-; mem. Knesset; mem. Secr. of Israel Labour Party; mem. Council of Dirs., Bank of Israel.
Publs. Numerous articles in Hebrew and British press; various booklets and publications on economic and labour problems.
Histadrut Building, Arlosoroff Street, Tel-Aviv, Israel.

Becker, Carl Johan; Danish archaeologist; b. 3 Sept. 1915; ed. Metropolitanskolen, Københavns Universitet.
Assistant, National Museum 34-41, Asst.-Keeper 41-52; Prof. of Prehistoric Archaeology, Univ. of Copenhagen 52-, Dean Faculty of Arts 63-64, mem. Konsistorium 64-; Chief Editor *Acta Archaeologica* 48-; mem. Royal Danish Acad. of Sciences and Letters; mem. numerous European Prehistoric and Archaeological societies.
Publs. *Enkeltgravkulturen på de danske Øer* 36, *Mosefundne Lerkar fra Yngre Stenalder* 48, *Die Mittel-Neolithischen Kulturen in Südskandinavien* 55, *Förromersk Jernalder i Syd-og Midtjylland* 61.
23 Egernvej, Copenhagen F., Denmark.
Telephone: FA. 5711.

4

Becker, Hans Detlev; German publisher and journalist; b. 11 June 1921; ed. Univ. of Münster.
Managing Editor *Der Spiegel* 50-58, Chief Editor 59-61, Publisher 62-.
c/o Spiegel-Verlag, 2 Hamburg 1, Speersort 1; Home: 2057 Wentorf, Bez. Hamburg, Am Buchenhain 3, German Federal Republic.
Telephone: 0411-3395-9337 (Office).

Beckett, Samuel, M.A.; Irish author; b. 13 April 1906; ed. Portora Royal School and Trinity Coll., Dublin.
Lecturer Ecole Normale Supérieure, Paris, 28-30, Trinity Coll., Dublin 30-32; now lives in Paris; Prix Formentor 61.
Publs. Verse: *Whoroscope* 30, *Echo's Bones* 35; Novels: *Murphy* 38, *Watt* 44, *Molloy* 51, *Malone meurt* 52, *L'Innommable* 53, (English edition) 57, *Molloy* (English edition) 56, *Malone Dies* (English edition) 56, *Comment C'est* (English edition 63), *Imagination Dead Imagine* 66; Short Stories: *More Pricks than Kicks* 34, *Nouvelles et textes pour rien* 55; Stage Plays: *En attendant Godot* 52 (English version *Waiting for Godot*), *Fin de Partie* 57 (English version *End Game*), *Krapp's Last Tape* 59, *Happy Days* 60, *Play* 63; Radio Plays: *All that Fall* 57, *Embers* 59, *Words and Music* 61, *Cascando* 64; Essay: *Proust* 65, *No's Knife: Collected Shorter Prose 1945-66* 67.
c/o Editions de Minuit, 7 rue Bernard Palissy, Paris 6e, France.

Beckman, Nils Arvid Teodor; Swedish judge; b. 30 Oct. 1902; ed. Univ. of Stockholm.
Court of Appeal, Stockholm 41-47; Vice-Attorney-Gen. 44-47; mem. Comm. for Criminal Law Reform 37-53; Pres. Comm. for Rent Law Reform 57-61; Judge of Supreme Court 47-63, Pres. of Supreme Court 63-; Pres. Swedish Asscn. of Criminologists.
Publs. *Swedish Criminal Law, Criminality and Social Defence in Sweden, Cases in Swedish Family Law, Cases in International Law.*
Sveavägen 35-37, Stockholm, Sweden.

Becu, Omer Lieven; Belgian trade union official; b. 02; ed. Primary and Secondary Schools in Ostend.
Merchant Navy 20-29; Asst. Gen. Sec. Int. Mercantile Marine Officers' Asscn. 29-32; Gen. Sec. Int. Mercantile Marine Officers' Asscn. and Gen. Sec. Belgian Merchant Navy Officers' Asscn. 32-45; Gen. Sec. Belgian Transport Workers' Union and mem. Executive Cttee. of Belgian T.U.C. 45, Int. Transport Workers' Fed. 46; Pres. Int. Transport Workers' Fed. and Gen. Sec. Belgian Seafarers' and Dockers' Sections 47-50; Gen. Sec. Int. Transport Workers' Fed. 50-; Pres. Int. Confed. of Free Trade Unions 53-57, Gen. Sec. 60-67; mem. Belgian Socialist Party; King's Medal, U.K.; Medal of Freedom, U.S.A.; Chevalier Ordre de Léopold II.
c/o 37-41 rue Montagne aux Herbes Potagères, Brussels 1, Belgium.

Beddington-Behrens, Sir Edward, Kt., C.M.G., PH.D.; British economist; ed. Charterhouse, Royal Military Acad., Woolwich, Christ Church, Oxford, and London Univ.
Army service 15-18, 39-45; Permanent Secretariat, League of Nations 21-24; Chief Organiser, Commonwealth Conf. of European League for Econ. Co-operation 51, Central and Eastern European Conf. 52; Chair., European Industrial Conf. 58; Chair. Political and Econ. Conf. of the Seven 60, Conf. on Central and E. Europe, Brussels 63, Conf. on European Co-operation in Advanced Technology 65; mem. U.K. Cttee. of Fed. of Commonwealth and British Chambers of Commerce; Pres. Army League; Founder mem. European Movement; Chair. Jeremiah Ambler Ltd., Ocean Trust Co. Ltd., etc.

Publs. *Look Back, Look Forward* 63, *Why Britain Must Join Europe* 66.
Chesham House, Chesham Place, London S.W.1, England.

Bedell, Ralph Clairon, A.M., PH.D.; American university professor and public servant; b. 4 June 1904; ed. Univ. of Missouri.
Prof. of Educational Psychology, Northeast Missouri State Teachers Coll. 33-37; Dean of Faculty, Central Missouri State Coll. 37; Prof. of Educational Psychology and Measurements, Univ. of Nebraska 38-50; served Navy 43-46; Prof. of Psychology and Education, The American Univ., Washington, D.C. 50-52; with U.S. Office of Education, Dept. of Health, Education and Welfare 52-66; on leave 55-58; Sec.-Gen. South Pacific Comm. Nouméa, New Caledonia 55-58; Prof. of Education, Univ. of Missouri, Columbia 67-.
Publs. *General Science for To-day* (co-author) 36, *Pre-Flight Aeronautics* (co-author) 42, *Basic Guidance for Nebraska Schools* (Editor) 48.
201 Mark Twain Hall, University of Missouri, Columbia, Missouri 65201, U.S.A.
Telephone: 314-449-9749.

Bedregal Gutiérrez, Guillermo, LL.D., DR. POL. and ECON. SC.; Bolivian lawyer and economist; b. 26; ed. Univ. of San Simon, Cochabamba, Univ. of San Andres, La Paz, Univ. of Salamanca and Central Univ. of Madrid.
Former Statutory Prof. History of Law, Univ. of San Andres, La Paz; fmr. Under-Sec. of State for Finance, Bolivia; fmr. Minister-Sec., Presidency of the Rep.; Congressman for Potosí; Minister of State and Pres. Corporación Minera de Bolivia (COMIBOL) 59-64; Dep. Gov., Inter-American Development Bank 62-64, Exec. Dir. 63.
Publs. *The Historic Route of the Bolivian Revolution* 58, *The Mining Nationalization and the Responsibilities of the Labour Unions* 59, *Latin-American Socialism and the National Revolution* 60, *The Recovery of Nationalized Mining* 61, *The Bolivian Revolution—Its Perspectives within the Cycle of Latin-American Liberation* 62, *Infrastructure, Monetary System and Economic Development* 62, *The Integration of Bolivia's Tin Mining Industry* 62, *National Economy and Latin-America's Defence* 63, *Tin Smelting in Bolivia* 64.
c/o Corporación Minera de Bolivia, P.O. Box 349, La Paz, Bolivia.

Beebe, Frederick Sessions; American lawyer and publishing executive; b. 20 Feb. 1914; ed. Dartmouth Coll. and Yale Univ.
Associated with law firm Cravath, Swaine and Moore 38-61, mem. 50-61; U.S. Naval Reserve, Second World War; Chair. of Board The Washington Post Co. 61-, Newsweek Inc. 62-; Dir. Allied Chemical Corporation, Bowaters Mersey Paper Co. Ltd., Tri-Continental Corporation.
Newsweek, Inc., 444 Madison Avenue, New York City, New York 10022, U.S.A.
Telephone: HA1-1234.

Beeby, Clarence Edward, C.M.G., M.A., PH.D.; New Zealand educationist and administrator; b. 16 June 1902; ed. Christchurch Boys' High School, Canterbury Coll., Univ. of New Zealand, University Coll., London, and Univ. of Manchester.
Lecturer in Philosophy and Education, Canterbury Univ. Coll., Univ. of N.Z. 23-34; Dir. N.Z. Council for Educational Research 34-38; Asst. Dir. of Education, Education Dept., N.Z. 38-40, Dir. of Education 40-60 (on leave of absence 48-49); Asst. Dir.-Gen. of UNESCO 48-49; Ambassador to France 60-63; leader N.Z. Dels. to Gen. Confs. of UNESCO 46, 47, 50, 53, 54, 56, 58, 60, 63; Hon. Counsellor of UNESCO 50; mem. of UNESCO Exec. Board 60-63, Chair. 63; Research Fellow,

Harvard Univ. 63-67; Commonwealth Visiting Prof., Univ. of London 67-68.

Publs. *The Intermediate Schools of New Zealand* 38, *Entrance to University* (with W. Thomas and M. H. Oram) 39, *The Quality of Education in Developing Countries* 66.

73 Barnard Street, Wellington, New Zealand.

Beeching, Baron (Life Peer), cr. 65; **Richard Beeching,** A.R.C.S., B.SC., D.I.C., PH.D.; British business executive and transport administrator; b. 21 April 1913; ed. Maidstone Grammar School and Imperial Coll. of Science and Technology, London.

Fuel Research Station, Greenwich 36-37; Mond Nickel Co. 37-43; Armaments Design Dept., Fort Halstead 43-48; joined I.C.I. 48, "Terylene" Council 51-53, Vice Pres. I.C.I. (Canada) Ltd. 53, Chair. Metals Div. 55, Dir. I.C.I. 57; Dir. British Nylon Spinners Ltd. 59; Dir. I.C.I. (Australia and New Zealand) Ltd. 60; Chair. British Transport Comm. 61-62, Chair. British Railways Board 62-65; rejoined I.C.I. 65, Deputy Chair. 66-March 68; Chair. Royal Comm. on Assizes and Quarter Sessions 66-; mem. Nat. Econ. Devt. Council (N.E.D.C.) 62-64; Fellow of Imperial Coll.; Hon. LL.D. (London Univ.), Hon. D.Sc. (Nat. Univ. of Ireland).

Little Manor, Lewes Road, East Grinstead, Sussex, England.

Telephone: East Grinstead 25477.

Beeghly, Charles Milton, A.B.; American steel executive; b. 6 Oct. 1908; ed. Ohio Wesleyan Univ.

Metal Carbides Co., Newark 31; Goff-Kirby Co., Cleveland 32-33; Buffalo Slag Co. 34; Cold Metal Products Co., Youngstown 35-38, Production Man. 39-42, Sales Man. 39-50, Vice-Pres. and Dir. 46-, Gen. Man. 52-; Pres. Jones & Laughlin Steel Corpn. (strip steel division) 57-, Exec. Vice-Pres. Corpn. 58-60, Pres. 60-63, Chair. and Chief Exec. Officer 63-, Dir. 57-; mem. Exec. Cttee. American Iron and Steel Inst.

Jones & Laughlin Steel Corporation, 3 Gateway Center, Pittsburgh 30, Pa., U.S.A

Beel, L. J. M.; Netherlands politician; b. 12 April 1902.

Head of administrative service of the town council of Eindhoven, resgnd. on the nomination of a Nazi Burgomaster; practised as consulting lawyer at Eindhoven 42-45; Minister of Home Affairs in Gerbrandy Govt. Feb. 45; in Schermerhorn Govt. 45-46; Prime Minister 46-48; mem. Parl. 48; Royal Comm. for Indonesia 48-49; Prof. Univ. of Nijmegen and Tilburg 49-52; Minister of the Interior 51-56; Dep. Prime Minister 52-56; Minister of State 56, Councillor of State April-Dec. 58; Prime Minister Dec. 58-May 59; Vice-Pres. Council of State 59-.

Rijksstraatweg 596, Wassenaar, Netherlands.

Telephone: 01751-9208.

Beeley, Sir Harold, K.C.M.G., C.B.E., M.A.; British diplomatist; b. 15 Feb. 1909; ed. Highgate School and Queen's Coll., Oxford.

Lecturer at Univs. of Sheffield, London, Oxford and Leicester 30-39; entered Foreign Service 46; Counsellor, Copenhagen 49-50, Baghdad 50-53, Washington 53-55; Ambassador to Saudi Arabia 55; Asst. Under-Sec. Foreign Office 56-58; Deputy Perm. Rep. to UN 58-61; Amb. to United Arab Republic 61-64, 67-; Perm. Rep. of U.K. to Disarmament Conf., Geneva 64-67.

Publ. *Disraeli* 36.

c/o Foreign Office, London S.W.1, England.

Beer, (Georges) Henrik (Teodor W:son), M.A.; Swedish Red Cross official; b. 22 Nov. 1915; ed. Univ. of Stockholm.

Sec. Nat. Defence League 42-44; Dir. Swedish Govt. Comm. for Int. Relief 44-47; Sec.-Gen. Swedish Red Cross 47-60; Sec.-Gen. League of Red Cross Societies

60-; Sec.-Gen. XVII Int. Red Cross Conf. 48; Exec. Dir. Folke Bernadotte Memorial Foundation 51-62.

17 Chemin des Crets, Petit-Saconnex, 1211 Geneva 19, Switzerland.

Beer, Otto F., DR. PHIL.; Austrian writer and journalist; b. 8 Sept. 1910; ed. Univ. of Vienna.

Editor *Neues Wiener Journal* and *Neues Wiener Tagblatt* until 39; Chief Editor *Salzburger Nachrichten* 45; Drama Critic, *Welt am Abend* 46-48, *Der Standpunkt,* Merano 48-52, *Neues Österreich*, Vienna 52-, Österreichischer Rundfunk 67-.

Publs. Novels: *Zehnte Symphonie* 52, *Wiedersehen in Meran* 52, *Ich-Rodolfo-Magier* 65, *Christin-Theres* 67; comedies: *Man ist nur zweimal jung* 55, *Operette* 60, *Die Eintagsfliege* 61.

Laudongasse 29, Vienna VIII, Austria.

Beer, Samuel Hutchison, PH.D.; American university professor; b. 28 June 1911; ed. Staunton Military Acad., Univ. of Michigan, and Oxford and Harvard Univs.

Writer, Resettlement Admin. and Democratic Nat. Cttee. 35-36; Reporter *New York Post* 36-37; *Fortune* magazine 37-38; Instructor in Government, Harvard Univ. 38-42, Asst. Prof. 46-48, Assoc. Prof. 48-53, Prof. of Govt. 53-, Chair. Dept. of Govt. 54-58; Nat. Chair. Americans for Democratic Action 59-; U.S. Army 42-45.

Publs. *The City of Reason* 49, *Treasury Control: The Coordination of Financial and Economic Policy in Great Britain* 56, *Modern British Politics* 65.

87 Lakeview Avenue, Cambridge, Mass., U.S.A.

Beernink, H. K. J., LL.D.; Netherlands lawyer and politician; b. 2 Feb. 1910; ed. Rijksuniversiteit te Utrecht.

Worked at various municipal offices 32-45; Town Clerk of Rijswijk 45; mem. Second Chamber of States-Gen. 46-; Chair. Christian-Historical Union; Minister for Home Affairs 67-.

Ministry for Home Affairs, The Hague; Home: Rembrandtkade 65, Ryswyk, Netherlands.

Beevor, J. G., O.B.E.; British lawyer and financial administrator; b. 1 March 1905; ed. Winchester Coll. and Oxford Univ.

Adviser, British Del. Marshall Plan Conf., Paris 47; Man.-Dir. Commonwealth Development Finance Co. Ltd. 54-56; Vice-Pres. Int. Finance Corpn. 56-64; fmr. partner Slaughter and May, Solicitors (London); financial adviser and Dir. of several British companies.

51 Eaton Square, London, S.W.1, England.

Telephone: 01-235-7987.

Begg, Admiral Sir Varyl, G.C.B., D.S.O.; British naval officer; b. 1 Oct. 1908; ed. St. Andrews School, Eastbourne, and Malvern Coll.

Royal Navy 26-, Gunnery Officer 33, H.M.S. *Glasgow* 39-40, H.M.S. *Warspite* 40-43; commanded H.M. Gunnery School, Chatham 48-50, 8th Destroyer Flotilla 50-52, H.M.S. *Excellent* 52-54, H.M.S. *Triumph* 55-56; Chief of Staff to C.-in-C. Portsmouth 57-58; Flag Officer Commanding Fifth Cruiser Squadron and Flag Officer, Second-in-Command, Far East Station 58-60; a Lord Commr. of Admiralty and Vice-Chief of Naval Staff 61-63; C.-in-C. British Forces in Far East and U.K. Mil. Adviser to SEATO 63-65; C.-in-C. Portsmouth and Allied C.-in-C. Channel Aug. 65-Feb. 66; Chief of Naval Staff and First Sea Lord Feb. 66-68.

c/o Ministry of Defence, Whitehall, London, S.W.1, England.

Begin, Menachem, M.J.; Israeli lawyer and politician; b. 1913; ed. Univ. of Warsaw.

Head of Betar Zionist Youth Movement in Poland 39; arrested and held in concentration camp in Siberia 40-41; C.-in-C. of Irgun Zvai Leumi in Israel 42; founded (now Chair.) Herut (Freedom) Movement in Israel 48; mem. of first, second and third Knessets; Minister without Portfolio 67-.

Publs. *The Revolt: personal memoirs of the Commander of Irgun Zvai Leumi* 49, *The White Nights.*
1 Rosenbaum Street, Tel-Aviv, Israel.

Begmatova, Sakin Begmatovna; Soviet politician; b. 1921; ed. All-Union Financial and Economic Inst. Teacher 39-41; Deputy People's Commissar for Food Industry of Kirghiz S.S.R. 41-49; Chief of Section, Frunze City Cttee. of Communist Party, Kirghizia 49-52; Deputy Minister of Finance, Kirghiz S.S.R. 52-61; Vice. Chair. Council of Ministers and Minister of Foreign Affairs, Kirghiz S.S.R. 61-; mem. C.P.S.U. 43-; mem. Central Cttee. of C.P., Kirghiz S.S.R.
Council of Ministers of Kirghiz S.S.R., Frunze, U.S.S.R.

Begougne de Juniac, Gontran; French diplomatist; b. 28 July 1908; ed. Ecole Montalambert, Limoges, Ecole libre des Sciences politiques, Paris, and Univ. de Paris à la Sorbonne.
Deputy Consul 35; Sec. of Embassy, Berlin 36-37, Moscow 37-41; Ministry of Foreign Affairs 41; Sec. of Embassy, Dublin 45-47; Div. of Cultural Relations, Ministry of Foreign Affairs 47-49, Sec.-Gen. of Four Powers Conf. 49; Counsellor, Washington 49-55; Minister and Minister-Counsellor, London 55-60; Ambassador to Ethiopia 60-65, to Turkey 65-; Officier Légion d'Honneur, etc.
Ambassade de France, 70 Paris caddesi, Ankara, Turkey; Home: boulevard du Général Koenig, Neuilly/Seine, France.

Begtrup, Mrs. Bodil Gertrud; Danish diplomatist; b. 12 November 1903; ed. Københavns Universitet.
Member of Danish delegation to League of Nations 38, and to U.N. 46-52; Film Censor 39-48; Minister to Iceland 49-55, Ambassador 55; Ministry of Foreign Affairs 56; Perm. Rep. Council of Europe 56-59; Ambassador to Switzerland 59-, and accredited Minister to Austria 59-60; mem. board Danish National Council of Women 29, Vice-Pres. 31, Pres. 46-49; Pres. U.N. Comm. on the Status of Women 46-47, mem. 48-49; Pres. Danish Society for the U.N. 56-59; Dr. Iur. h.c. Smith Coll. Massachusetts.
Danish Embassy, Thunstrasse 95, Berne, Switzerland.

Béguin, Bernard, L. ès L.; Swiss journalist; b. 14 Feb. 1923; ed. Geneva High School, Geneva Univ. and Graduate Inst. of Int. Studies.
Swiss Sec. World Student Relief 45-46; corresp. at U.N. European Headquarters; *Journal de Genève* 46-, Foreign Editor 47, Editor-in-Chief 59-; Diplomatic Commentator, Swiss Broadcasting System 54-59, Swiss T.V. 59-; Central Pres. Swiss Press Asscn. 58-60; mem. Federal Comm. on Cartels 64-.
41 Avenue de Budé, Geneva, Switzerland.
Telephone: 25-03-50; 33-75-30.

Béguin, Olivier Pierre; Swiss church official; b. 2 Jan. 1914; ed. Univ. of Geneva.
Secretary, Ecumenical Comm. for Chaplaincy Aid to War Prisoners 40-45; Sec. for Europe, United Bible Socs. 47-49, Gen. Sec. 49-; Hon. D. Hum. (Rikkyo Univ.).
Publ. *Roman Catholicism and the Bible, Directory of Bible Societies.*
101 Queen Victoria Street, London, E.C.4, England.
Telephone: 01-236-1616.

Beharrell, Sir George Edward; British industrialist; b. 26 May 1899; ed. Wellingborough School.
Received early training in shipping business in England and S. Africa; Dunlop Rubber Co., Dir. of Equipment Sales 32, Dir. of main board of company 42, Joint Man. Dir. 43, Man. Dir. 45, Deputy Chair. and Man. Dir. 49-57, Chair. 57-Dec. 67, Pres. 68-; and Dir. or Chair. of many Dunlop subsidiary and assoc. companies; Chair. Internat. Synthetic Rubber Co. Ltd.; Pres. Fed. of British Rubber Manufacturers' Asscn. 48-50; Pres. Tyre Manufacturers' Conf. 47-55; Pres. Society of

Motor Manufacturers and Traders 51-52; Pres. Inst. of Rubber Industry 62-64.
Dunlop House, 25 Ryder Street, St. James's, London, S.W.1, England.

Beheiry, Mamoun, B.A.; Sudanese banker; b. 25; ed. Victoria Coll., Alexandria and Brasenose Coll., Oxford. Former Dep. Perm. Under-Sec. Ministry of Finance and Econs.; fmr. Chair. Sudan Currency Board; Gov. Central Bank of Sudan 59-63; Minister of Finance and Econs. 63-64; Pres. African Development Bank 65-; Chair. Nat. Technical Planning Cttee. 62.
African Development Bank, B.P. 1387, Abidjan, Ivory Coast.

Behnia, Abdolhossein; Iranian civil servant and politician; b. 07; ed. Univ. of Paris.
Ministry of Finance, successively Dir. of Ministerial Office, Dir. Iranian Tobacco Monopoly, Dir.-Gen. of Distribution, of Production, Dir.-Gen. of Ministry of Finance, Dir. of Currency Comm., Dir. of Foreign Trade, Dir. Iranian Credit Bank; mem. Supreme Chamber of Bank Melli; Minister of Finance 61-64; Chair. Iranian Credit Bank 64-.
11 Dey Street, Soheil Avenue, Teheran, Iran.
Telephone: 42292; 36055.

Běhounek, František, DR. RER. NAT., D.SC.; Czechoslovak radiologist; b. 27 Oct. 1898.
Mem. Czechoslovak Acad. of Sciences and Accad. Nuovi Lincei; Prof. of Radiology, Charles Univ., Prague; mem. Gen. Nobile's North Pole Expedition; Order of Labour 55; Paris Silver Medal 57; Silver Plaque, Czechoslovak Acad. of Sciences.
Publs. *The Problems of Potassium, Artificial Disintegration of Radioactive Bodies, Atmospheric Electricity and Radioactivity in the Region of the North Pole, Radioactivity of Pitchblend District of Jáchymov, Ionisation in Air-conditioned Buildings, Radioactivity of Czechoslovak Thermal Springs*, etc.
Prague 4-Podolí, Sinkulova 24, Czechoslovakia.

Behrens, Leonard Frederick, C.B.E., J.P., M.COM.; British retired businessman; b. 15 Oct. 1890; ed. Manchester Grammar School, Rugby School and Manchester Univ.
Entered family firm of Sir Jacob Behrens & Sons, Bradford and Manchester 11, Partner 20, Dir. 48, retd. 54; Acting Pres. Liberal Party Sept. 55-Sept. 56, Pres. Sept. 56-57, Chair. Exec. 59-61; Hon. Pres. World Fed. of UN Asscns. (Acting Pres., Stockholm 51, New York 63); Chair. Hallé Concerts Soc. 52-59; Deputy Chair. Royal Manchester Coll. of Music; Hon. Treas. Manchester Inst. of Contemporary Arts; served with Serbian Relief Fund 15-18; Chair. Manchester Information Cttee. and Lecturer to H.M. Forces 40-45; Royal Observer Corps 41-52; Yugoslav Order of St. Sava, Chinese Order of Brilliant Star.
Netherby, 119 Barlow Moor Road, Didsbury, Manchester, England.
Telephone: 061-DID-3600.

Behrman, Samuel Nathaniel, A.B., A.M.; American journalist and dramatist; b. 9 June 1893; ed. Clarke Coll., Harvard and Columbia Univs.
Publs. Plays: *The Second Man* 27, *Serena Blandish* 28, *Meteor* 29, *Brief Moment* 32, *Biography* 33, *Love Story* 34, *Rain from Heaven* 35, *End of Summer* 36, *Amphitryon* (adapted from French) 37, *Wine of Choice* 38, *No Time for Comedy* 39, *The Talley Method* 41, *The Pirate* 42, *Jacobowsky and the Colonel* (with Franz Werfel) 44, *Fanny* (with Joshua Logan) 54, *Dunnigan's Daughter* 45, *Jane* (from Somerset Maugham) 46, *I Know My Love* (from Achard) 49, *The Cold Wind and the Warm* 59, *Lord Pengo* 62, *But for Whom Charlie* 64. Films: *Queen Christina, Anna Karenina, Tale of Two Cities, Me and the Colonel*; Prose works: *Duveen* 52,

The Worcester Account 54, *Portrait of Max* 60, *The Suspended Drawing Room* 65.
1185 Park Avenue, New York, N.Y. 10028, U.S.A.

Beier, Max Walter Peter, DR. PHIL.; Austrian museum curator and professor; b. 6 April 1903; ed. Univ. of Vienna.
Natural History Museum, Vienna 27-; Dir. Zoological Dept.; corresp. mem. Argentine Entomological Soc., Finland Entomological Soc.; Hon. mem. Netherlands Entomological Soc.; Fabricius Medal 66.
Publs. Over 300 scientific publications.
Naturhistorisches Museum, Zoologische Abteilung, A-1010 Vienna 1, Burgring 7, Austria.
Telephone: 93-27-12, Ext. 267.

Beinecke, William Sperry; American lawyer and business executive; b. 22 May 1914; ed. Phillips Acad., Andover, Westminster School, Connecticut, Yale Univ. and Columbia Univ., New York.
Admitted to New York Bar 41; Assoc. Chadbourne, Wallace, Parke and Whiteside 40-41, 46-48; U.S. Navy 41-46; Partner, Casey, Beinecke and Chase 48-51; Gen. Counsel, The Sperry and Hutchinson Co. 52-54, Gen. Counsel and Vice-Pres. 54-60, Pres. 60-; Pres. The Sperry and Hutchinson Co. Ltd., Sept. 62-; Dir. of other companies.
Sperry and Hutchinson Building, 330 Madison Avenue, New York City, N.Y. 10017, U.S.A.

Beise, S. Clark, B.S.; American banker; b. 13 Oct. 1898; ed. Univ. of Minnesota School of Business.
Regimental supply sergeant in First World War; worked with Minneapolis Trust Co. 22-24, with Nat. Bank Examiners Minneapolis Office (covering Ninth Fed. Reserve District) 24-27; with People's Nat. Bank Jackson (Mich.) rising to Vice-Pres. 27-33; Nat. Bank Examiner, Twelfth Fed. Reserve District 33-36; Vice-Pres. Bank of America 36-45, Exec. Vice-Pres. 45-51, Senior Vice-Pres. 51-54, Pres. 54-63, Chair. Exec. Cttee. 63-; mem. Cttee. for Econ. Devt. Nat. Industrial Conf. Board 54-; Dir. Stanford Research Inst., Walt Disney Productions, Fruehauf Corpn.; Chair. San Francisco Foundation; mem. Business Council.
420 El Cerrito Avenue, Hillsborough, Calif. 94010, U.S.A.

Beisebaev, Massimkhan; Soviet politician; b. 1908; ed. Agricultural Coll., Alma Ata, and Higher Party School, Moscow.
People's Commissariat for Agriculture, Kazakhstan 31-36; mem. C.P.S.U. 32-; Apparatus of Central Cttee. of Kazakh C.P., later Alma Ata Regional Cttee., Kazakh C.P. 36-41; Soviet Army 41-42; Chair. Exec. Cttee. Alma Ata Regional Council of Workers' Deputies 42-43; First Deputy Rep. Purchases Cttee. U.S.S.R. 43-46; Second Sec. Akmolinsk Regional Cttee., First Sec. Kokchetav Regional Cttee., Kazakh C.P. 46-54; Dep., later First Dep. Chair. Council of Ministers of Kazakh S.S.R. 54-58, 63-64, Chair. 64-; First Sec. Alma Ata Regional Cttee., Kazakh C.P. 58-64; Cand. mem. Central Cttee. of C.P.S.U. 61-66, mem. 66-; mem. Central Cttee. Kazakh C.P.; Deputy to Supreme Soviets of Kazakh S.S.R. and U.S.S.R.
Council of Ministers of the Kazakh S.S.R., Alma Ata, Kazakh S.S.R., U.S.S.R.

Beith, John Greville Stanley, C.M.G.; British diplomatist; b. 4 April 1914; ed. Eton and King's Coll., Cambridge.
Diplomatic Service 37-, Athens, Buenos Aires, Foreing Office 40-49; Head of U.K. Del. to UN, Geneva 49-53; First Sec. and Head of Chancery, Prague 53-54; Counsellor and Head of Chancery, Paris 54-59; Head of Levant Dept., Foreign Office 59-61, North and East African Dept. 61-63; Ambassador to Israel 63-66; Asst. Sec.-Gen. NATO 66-.
NATO, Brussels 39, Belgium.

Beitz, Berthold; German industrialist; b. 26 Sept. 1913; ed. Secondary School.
Bank apprentice; employment in Shell, Hamburg; in charge of the Galician oilfields, Poland 39-44; Deputy Chair. British Zonal Insurance Control Dept. 46; Dir.-Gen. Iduna Germania Insurance Co. 49-53; General-bevollmächtigter Dr. Alfried Krupp von Bohlen und Halbach 53-67; Chair. Board of Curators, Alfried Krupp von Bohlen und Halbach-Stiftung; Vice-Chair. Supervisory Board, Fried Krupp G.m.b.H., Essen.
Hügel 14, 43 Essen-Bredeney, German Federal Republic.
Telephone: 22001.

Béjart, Maurice Jean; French choreographer and stage director; b. 1 Jan. 1927.
Director, Ballet de l'Etoile, Paris 53-57; Dir., Ballet Théâtre de Paris 57-59; Dir. Ballet du XXe. Siècle, Brussels 59-, Brussels Opera, Théâtre Royal de la Monnaie.
Productions include: *Orphée, Le Voyage, Le Sacré du Printemps, Les Noces, Don Juan, Boléro, Symphonie pour un Homme seul* (ballets); *The Merry Widow, Tales of Hoffmann, Ode à la Joie* (IXe symphonie), *La damnation de Faust, Messe pour le temps présent, Romeo et Juliétte, Prospective, Baudelaire, Ni Fleurs—ni couronnes, La Tentation de St-Antoine.*
Publs. *Mathilde ou le temps perdu* (novel), *La Reine verte* (play).
Théâtre de la Monnaie, Brussels, Belgium.

Bek, Alexandr Alfredovich; Soviet writer; b. 3 Jan. 1903; ed. Moscow Univ.
Volunteer in Red Army and Editor of divisional paper 19; worked in a Moscow tannery 22-24; contributor to *Pravda*; subsequently engaged in literary criticism; worked in Siberia on construction of Kuznetsk metallurgical works 33; published first story *Kurako* 34; mem. Writers' Union of U.S.S.R.
Publs. include *Volokolamshoe shosse* (The Road to Volokolamsk) (novel) 43, 44, *Domenshchiki* (The Blast-Furnace Workers) (stories) 46, *Timofei—Otkrytoe Serdtse* (Timothy Open-Heart) 47, *Molodye Lyudi* (Young People) (with Nataliya Loiko) 54, *Zhizn Berezhkova* (Berezhkov's Life) 56, *Stchastlivaya Ruka* (The Lucky Hand) 59, *Neskolko Dnei* (Several Days) (sequel to *Volokolamskoe shosse*) 60, *Rezerv Generala Panfilova* (General Panfilov's Reserve) 61, *Moi geroi* (My Heroes) 67.
U.S.S.R. Union of Writers, 52 Vorovsky Street, Moscow, U.S.S.R.

Belafonte, Harry; American singer; b. 1 March 1927; ed. George Washington High School, New York.
In Jamaica 35-39; service with U.S. Navy 43-45; stagehand and actor American Negro Theater; student at Manhattan New School for Social Research Dramatic Workshop 46-48; first engagement at the Vanguard, Greenwich Village; later at the Black Orchid, Chicago, Chase Hotel, St. Louis, Five O'Clock Club, Miami, etc.; European tour 58; Pres. Belafonte Enterprises Inc.; Broadway appearances in *Three For Tonight, Almanac, Belafonte At The Palace*, and in films *Bright Road, Carmen Jones, Island In the Sun, The World, the Flesh and the Devil, Odds Against Tomorrow*; numerous recordings.
c/o Mike Merrick, 1414 6th Avenue, New York, N.Y., U.S.A.

Belaúnde Terry, Fernando; Peruvian architect and politician; b. 7 Oct. 1913; ed. France and U.S.A.
Member Chamber of Deputies 45-48; Dean in School of Architecture, Lima 48-56; Leader Popular Action Party (Partido Acción Popular) 56-; Presidential Candidate 56, 62; Pres. of Peru 63-.
Publ. *Peru's Own Conquest* (autobiography).
Office of the President, Lima, Peru.

Belcher, Taylor Garrison; American diplomatist; b. 1 July 1920; ed. Brown Univ., Providence, R.I. U.S. Navy 42-45; U.S. Foreign Service 45-, Mexico City 45-49, Consul, Glasgow 50-54; International Affairs Officer, Dept. of State 54-57; Consul and Consul-Gen. Nicosia, Cyprus 57-60; Canadian National Defense Coll. 60-61; Dir. Office of West Coast Affairs, Bureau of Inter-American Affairs, Dept. of State 61-64; Ambassador to Cyprus 64-.
American Embassy, Nicosia, Cyprus.

Belfrage, Leif Axel Lorentz; Swedish diplomatist; b. 1 Feb. 1910; ed. Stockholm Univ.
Practised law at Stockholm Magistrates Court 33, subsequently joined Ministry of Commerce; Dir. Swedish Clearing Office 40; Dir. Swedish Trade Comm. 43-45; entered Foreign Office 45, Head of Section in Commercial Dept. 45-46; Commercial Counsellor, Washington 46-49; Head of Commercial Dept., Foreign Office, Stockholm 49-53; Asst. Under-Sec. of State at Foreign Office 53-56, Perm. Under-Sec. of State 56-57; Amb. to U.K. Dec. 67-; Hon. G.B.E. (U.K.).
Royal Swedish Embassy, 29 Portland Place, London, W.1, England.
Telephone: 01-580-2080.

Belgium, King Baudouin I of (*see* Baudouin).

Belgium, Archbishop Primate of (*see* Suenens, Cardinal Joseph).

Belgodère, Paul Louis; French mathematician; b. 25 Feb. 1921; ed. Ecole Normale Supérieure.
Sec.-Gen. Intermédiaire des Recherches Mathématiques 43-49; Technical Assoc. Centre National de la Recherche Scientifique 44-; Sec. Mathematical Society of France 46-; Mathematical Librarian, Ecole Normale Supérieure 50-54; Gen.-Sec. Inst. Henri Poincaré 54-.
Institut Henri Poincaré, 11 rue Pierre et Marie Curie, Paris 5e, France.
Telephone: 033-42-10.

Belin, Roger, D.IUR.; French civil servant; b. 21 March 1916; ed. Univ. of Paris Law Faculty, Paris School of Political Sciences.
Auditeur Conseil d'Etat 43; Chargé de Mission, Présidence du Conseil 44; Maître des Requêtes, Conseil d'Etat 49; mem. Atomic Energy Cttee. 51; Dir. Présidence du Conseil 55; Sec.-Gen. of the Government 58-; Pres. Régie autonome des transports parisiens 64-; Conseiller d'Etat 65-; Officier Légion d'Honneur.
9 Boulevard Flanolain, Paris 16e, France.
Telephone: TRO 14-09.

Beliy, Victor Arkadyevich; Soviet composer; b. 1904; ed. Moscow Conservatoire.
Member Board of U.S.S.R. Composers' Union; State Prize 52, Honoured Artist of Byelorussian S.S.R. 55, Honoured Worker of the Arts of R.S.F.S.R. 56; Order of Red Banner of Labour 47; Badge of Honour 64.
Principal compositions: Instrumental works: Lyric Sonatina 29, Sonata for Piano 41, Sonata for Piano No. 4 46, Sixteen Preludes on Folk Themes of the U.S.S.R. 47, Two Pieces for Piano on Byelorussian Themes 50, Sonata for Violin and Piano 53; Works for Voice and Piano: *26 Works* 26, *War Cycle* (words by E. Toller) 29, *Ten Chuvash Songs* 33, *Leavetaking* 35, *Song of the Partisan Girl* 35, *The Little Airman* 35, *Winter Road* 36, *Sea Songs* 39, *Ballade of Captain Gastello* 41, *Lenin's Birthday* 49; Choral works: *Hunger March* 30, Suite on Chuvash Themes 36, Two Fragments from the poem *V. I. Lenin* 38, *Three Roads* 39, *Slav Suite* 42, Two Choral Works on Russian Folk Themes 45; Songs: *Workers of All Lands Unite* 30, *Song of the 30th Division* 33, *Eaglet* 36, *Song of the Brave* 41, *Boldly, Red Navymen* 41, *October Song* 49, *In Defence of Peace* 49.
Composers' Union of the U.S.S.R., 8-10 Nezhdanova Street, Moscow, U.S.S.R.

Bell, David E.; American economist; b. 20 Jan. 1919; ed. Pomona Coll., and Harvard Univ.
Joined Budget Bureau 39; served U.S. Marine Corps, Second World War; Budget Bureau 45-47; Asst. in White House 47-51; Admin. Asst. to Pres. Truman 51; Head, Stevenson's Research Staff, Pres. Election Campaign 52; Head, Littauer Center Economic Mission to Pakistan 54-57; Lecturer in Economics, Littauer Center (Harvard Graduate School of Public Admin.) 57, Sec. (Chief Admin. Officer) 59-61; Dir. U.S. Budget Bureau 61-62; Administrator, Agency for Int. Devt. 62-66; Vice-Pres. (Int. Activities), Ford Foundation 66-.
Publs. *Allocating Development Resources: Some Observations Based on Pakistan Experience* 59.
Ford Foundation, 320 East 43rd Street, New York, N.Y. 10017, U.S.A.

Bell, Elliott Vallance, A.B.; American publisher; b. 25 Sept. 1902; ed. Columbia University.
Financial writer *N.Y. Herald-Tribune* 29, *New York Times* 29-39; First Pres. N.Y. Financial Writers' Asscn. 38-39; economic adviser to Thomas E. Dewey 39-40; research consultant to Wendell Wilkie 40; mem. Editorial Board *New York Times* 41-42; Supt. of Banks New York State 43-49; Chair. Exec. Cttee. McGraw-Hill Inc. 50-67; Editor *Business Week* 51-64, now Editor Emer.; Dir. McGraw Hill Inc., Tri-Continental Corpn., N.Y. Life Insurance Co., New York Telephone Co., etc.; Trustee John Simon Guggenheim Memorial Foundation; mem. Emer. President's Advisory Cttee. on Labor-Management Policy; Trustee Emer., Council on Foreign Relations, Brookings Inst.; Trustee, R. W. Strauss Memorial Foundation; Hon. LL.D. Bard Coll., St. Lawrence Univ., Hon. D.C.S. Pace Coll.
Publs. *We Saw It Happen* (with other correspondents *New York Times*) 38.
Home: 200 E. 66th Street, New York 10021; Office: 330 W. 42nd Street, New York 10036, U.S.A.

Bell, Sir Gawain (Westray), K.C.M.G., C.B.E.; British administrator; b. 21 Jan. 1909; ed. Winchester Coll. and Hertford Coll., Oxford.
Sudan Political Service 31; seconded to Govt. of Palestine 38; Military Service, Middle East 41-45, Lt.-Col. Arab Legion 42-45; Deputy Sudan Agent, Cairo 49-51; Deputy Civil Sec., Sudan Govt. 53-54; Perm. Under-Sec., Ministry of Interior 54-55; H.M. Political Agent, Kuwait 55-57; Gov., Northern Region of Nigeria 57-62; Sec.-Gen. Council for Middle East Trade 63-64; Joint Constitutional Adviser to Govt. of Fed. of South Arabia 65-66; Sec.-Gen. South Pacific Comm. 67-; K.St.J. 58; Order of Independence 3rd Class (Trans Jordan).
South Pacific Commission, Noumea, New Caledonia; and Hidcote Bartrim Manor, Chipping Campden, Glos., England.

Bell, James Dunbar, PH.D.; American diplomatist; b. 1 July 1911; ed. Univs. of Chicago and New Mexico.
Reporter *Albuquerque Journal*, New Mexico 33-34; Chief Statistician, New Mexico Dept. of Public Welfare 36-37; Instructor Gary Coll. 39-41; Analyst, Office of Co-ordinator, Inter-American Affairs 41-42; Special Asst., Dept. of Justice 43-44; Prof. Hamilton Coll. 46-47; Dept. of State 44-, Bogotà, Santiago, Manila 44-52; Officer-in-Charge, Philippine Affairs, Washington 53-54; Deputy Dir. Philippine and Southeast Asian Affairs 54-55; Dir. Office of Southwest Pacific Affairs 56-57, 60-64; Deputy Chief of Mission and Counsellor, Djakarta 57-59; Ambassador to Malaysia 64-.
American Embassy, Kuala Lumpur, Malaysia.

Bell, John Oscar, B.S., J.D.; American diplomatist; b. 4 Oct. 1912; ed. George Washington Univ. and Nat. War Coll.
Joined Dept. of State 31, Counselor, Copenhagen 52-54;

Dir. U.S. Operations Mission, Pakistan 55-57; Regional Dir. N.E. and S. Asia, Int. Cooperation Admin. 57-58; Dep. Co-ordinator, Mutual Security Program 59-61; Ambassador to Guatemala 61-65; Political Adviser to Strike Command, U.S. Armed Forces 65-.
c/o Department of the Army, Washington 25, D.C., U.S.A.

Bell, Marie (*pseudonym of* Marie Bellon); French actress; b. 23 Dec. 1905; ed. Lycée de Bordeaux, Bordeaux and Paris Conservatoires.
Pensionnaire and later Sociétaire, Comédie Française 21-53; founded own company La Compagnie Marie Bell 53; Dir. Théâtre du Gymnase 59-; principal theatre roles in *Phèdre, Le Misanthrope, Cyrano de Bergerac, Ruy Blas,* etc.; produced and acted in *Madame Princesse* 65-66; films include *Carnet de Bal* and *Le colonel Chabert;* Officier Légion d'Honneur.
32 avenue des Champs-Elysées, Paris 8e, France.

Bell, Ralph Pickard. O.B.E., B.A., D.C.L.; Canadian industrialist.
Chancellor, Mount Allison Univ.; Pres. Pickard Investments Ltd.; Hon. Dir. Bank of Nova Scotia; during Second World War Aircraft Controller and Dir.-Gen. Aircraft Production Branch of Dept. of Munitions and Supply, Ottawa and mem. U.S.-Canadian Joint War Production Cttee.
High Head, Murder Point, Mahone Bay, Nova Scotia, Canada.
Telephone: 902-624-8818.

Bellanger, Claude; French journalist; b. 2 April 1910. Sec.-Gen. of the Ligue Française de l'Enseignement 36-39; Dir. Centre d'Entraide aux Etudiants Prisonniers 40-44; active with resistance and clandestine press, 40-44; now Dir.-Gen. of *Le Parisien libéré;* Hon. Pres. Syndicat de la Presse Parisienne; Vice-Pres. Féd. Nationale de la Presse Française; Pres. Féd. Int. des Editeurs de Journaux; Vice-Pres. l'Institut Français de Presse, Conseil d'Administration de L'Agence France-Presse; mem. Admin. Council *Courrier de L'Ouest* (Angers), *Maine Libre* (Le Mans); Officier de la Légion d'Honneur, Médaille de la Résistance, Croix de Guerre, etc.
Publs. *Vers la Guerre ou Vers La Paix* 36, *Nouvelles Chroniques Interdites, Les Bannis* 44, *Poètes Prisonniers* 44, *La Presse des Barbelés* 51, *Presse Clandestine 1940–1944* 61, *Les débuts d'Emile Zola dans la presse* 64.
124 rue Réaumur, Paris 2e, France.

Bellmon, Henry, B.S.; American farmer and politician; b. 3 Sept. 1921; ed. Oklahoma State Univ.
U.S. Marine Corps 42-46; mem. Oklahoma Legislature 46-48; Farmer 45-; State Chair. Republican Party 60-62; Gov. of Oklahoma 63-67; Chair. Nixon for President Cttee. 68; Candidate for U.S. Senate 68.
Route One, Red Rock, Oklahoma, U.S.A.

Bellow, Saul, B.S.; American writer; b. 10 June 1915; ed. Northwestern Univ.
Professor, Univ. of Minn. 46-48; Prof. Princeton Univ. 52-53; Prof. Univ. of Chicago 64-; Nat. Book Award, Inst. of Arts and Letters 53, Ford Foundation Grant 59, Prix Int. de Littérature 65.
Publs. include contributions to numerous magazines and journals; also *Dangling Man* 44, *The Victim* 47, *The Adventures of Augie March* 53, *Seize the Day* 56, *Henderson the Rain King* 59, *Great Jewish Short Stories* 63, *Herzog* 64, *The Last Analysis* 64.
c/o University of Chicago, Chicago 37, Ill., U.S.A.

Belluschi, Pietro, DOTT.ING.; American architect; b. 18 Aug. 1899; ed. Univ. of Rome and Cornell Univ.
Draftsman for A. E. Doyle, Architect, Portland, Ore. 25-28; chief designer A. E. Doyle & Assoc. 28-33, partner 33-43; own architectural practice 43-; Dean, School of Architecture and Planning, Mass. Inst. of Technology 51-65; Hon. Sc.D., Christian Brothers Coll. 57; Hon. LL.D., Reed Coll. 50; Hon. Dr. of Fine Arts, Univ. of Rhode Island 63.
Principal works: Portland Art Museum, Equitable Building, Oregonian Publishing Plant (all Portland, Ore.); Library for Bennington Coll., Vt. 59; many churches and temples in U.S.A.
1 Fairfield Street, Boston 16, Mass., U.S.A.

Belmondo, Jean-Paul; French comedian film star; b. 9 April 1933; ed. Ecole Alsacienne, Paris, Cours Pascal and Conservatoire national d'art dramatique.
Started career on the stage; mainly film actor since 57; Pres. French Union of Actors 63-66.
Plays acted in include: *L'Hôtel du Libre-Echange, Oscar, Trésor-Party, Médée, La mégère apprivoisée;* Films acted in include: *Sois belle et tais-toi, A pied, à cheval et en voiture, Les Tricheurs, Charlotte et son Jules, Drôle de dimanche* 58, *Les Copains du dimanche, Mademoiselle Ange, A double tour, Classe tous risques, A bout de souffle, l'Amour, La Novice, La Ciociara, Moderato Cantabile, Léon Morin Prêtre, Le Doulos* 62, *Dragées au poivre, L'Aîné des Ferchaux, Peau de banane, 100,000 dollars au soleil* 63, *Echappement libre* 64, *Les tribulations d'un Chinois en Chine, Pierrot le Fou* 65, *Paris, brûle t'il?* 66, *Le Voleur* 66, *Casino Royale* 67.
Cimura, 2 rue Paul Cézanne, Paris 8e, France.

Beloff, Max, B.LITT., M.A., F.R.HIST.S.; British historian; b. 2 July 1913; ed. St. Paul's School and Corpus Christi Coll. and Magdalen Coll., Oxford.
Asst. Lecturer in History, Manchester Univ. 39-46; Nuffield Reader in Comparative Study of Institutions, Oxford Univ. 46-57; Fellow of Nuffield Coll. 47-57; Gladstone Prof. of Govt. and Public Admin. Univ. of Oxford and Fellow of All Souls Coll. 57-; Hon. LL.D. (Univ. of Pittsburgh).
Publs. *Public Order and Popular Disturbances 1660-1714* 38, *The Foreign Policy of Soviet Russia* 47-49, *Thomas Jefferson and American Democracy* 48, *Soviet Policy in the Far East 1944-51* 53, *The Age of Absolutism 1660-1815* 54, *Foreign Policy and the Democratic Process* 55, *Europe and the Europeans* 57, *The Great Powers* 59, *The American Federal Government* 59, *New Dimensions in Foreign Policy* 61, *The United States and the Unity of Europe* 63, *Europe du XIX et XX Siècles* 60-66 (Joint Editor), *The Balance of Power* 68.
All Souls College, Oxford, England.
Telephone: Oxford 49641.

Belokhvostikov, Nikolai Dmitrievich; Soviet diplomatist; b. 1918.
Diplomatic Service 42-, Canada 44-45, Chargé d'Affaires 45-49; Ministry of Foreign Affairs 49-52; Counsellor U.K. 52-56; Dep. Head Second European Dept., Ministry of Foreign Affairs 56-58, Head 58-62; Amb. to Sweden 62-67; Head, Scandinavian Dept., Ministry of Foreign Affairs 67-.
Ministry of Foreign Affairs, 32-37 Smolenskaya-Sennaya ploshchad, Moscow, U.S.S.R.

Belokurov, Vladimir Vyacheslavovich; Soviet actor; b. 04; ed. A. M. Gorky Higher Inst. of Public Education, Kazan.
Pevtsov Company, Kazan 18-19; Kazan Theatre 19-23; Moscow Theatre of Revolution 24-36; Moscow Art Theatre Company 36-; has starred in films 32-; mem. All-Russian Theatrical Soc.; People's Artist of U.S.S.R.; State Prize; Order of Red Banner of Labour and medals.
Principal Roles: Kostylev (*Lower Depths,* **Gorky**), Yasha (*Cherry Orchard,* Chekhov), Kudryash (*The Storm,* Ostrovsky), Belogubov (*A Lucrative Post,* Ostrovsky), Mercutio (*Romeo and Juliet,* Shakespeare), Chichikov (*Dead Souls,* Gogol), Molchalin (*Woe from Wit,* Gribyedov), Grigory (*Fruits of Enlightenment,* Tolstoy), Alesha (*Land,* Virta), Veretennikov (*Officer*

of the Fleet, Kron), Gvozdilin (*Third Pathétique*, Pogodin), Gavriil Nechai (*Over the Dnieper*, Korneichuk).
Moscow Art Theatre, 3 Proyezd Khudozhestvennogo Teatra, Moscow, U.S.S.R.

Belov, Nicolai Vassilevich; Soviet crystallographer; b. 14 Dec. 1891; ed. Warsaw Gymnasium and St. Petersburg Polytechnic Inst.
Head, X-Ray Dept., Inst. of Crystallography of U.S.S.R. Acad. of Sciences 38-; Prof. of Crystallography, Gorky Univ. 46-, Moscow Univ. 53-; Vice-Pres. Int. Union of Crystallography 57-66, Pres. 66-; Pres. Scientific Comm. of Soviet Crystallographers; Corresp. mem. U.S.S.R. Acad. of Sciences 46-53, mem. 53-; State Prize (1st Class) 52, Order of Red Banner of Labour 53, Order of Lenin 61, Lomonosov Medal 66.
Publs. *Structure of Ionic Crystals and Metallic Phases* 47, *Structural Crystallography* 51, *A Class-Room Method of Deriving 230 Space Groups of Symmetry* 51, *Crystal Chemistry of Silicates with Large Cations* 61, *Essays in Structural Mineralogy 1959-1967* 67.
Institute of Crystallography, Academy of Sciences of U.S.S.R., 59 Lenin Prospekt, Moscow, U.S.S.R.
Telephone: B-2-58-95.

Belozersky, Andrei Nicolaevich; Soviet biochemist; b. 1905; ed. Tashkent State Univ.
Postgraduate, Tashkent State Univ. 27-30; Asst. to Prof. of Plant Biochemistry, Moscow State Univ. 30-32, Asst. Prof. 32-43, Prof. 43-60, Head of Dept. of Plant Biochemistry 60-, Head of Laboratory of Organic Biochemistry 65-; Corresp. mem. U.S.S.R. Acad. of Sciences 60-62, Academician 62-; Lomonossoff Prize 48, Order of Lenin (twice), Order of Red Banner of Labour.
Publs. more than 200 papers and books on biochemistry.
Biological Faculty, Moscow State University, Moscow, U.S.S.R.

Belsky, Igor Dmitrievich; Soviet choreographer; b. 1925; ed. Leningrad Ballet School.
Dancer with Leningrad Kirov Theatre of Opera and Ballet 43-62; Teacher of folk character dance at Leningrad Choreography School 46-; Producer and Choreographer, Leningrad Kirov Theatre of Opera and Ballet 59-62, Chief Choreographer 62-; People's Artist of the R.S.F.S.R.
Principal roles: Rotbart (*Swan Lake*), Nurali (*Fountain of Bakhchiserai*), Tybalt (*Romeo and Juliet*), Shurale (Yarushllin's *Shurale*), Severyan (Prokofiev's *Stone Flower*), Mako (Karayev's *Thunder Road*).
Chief productions: *Shores of Hope* (Petrov) 59, *Leningrad Symphony* (Shostakovich) 61, *Humpbacked Horse* (Shchedrin) 63.
Leningrad Kirov Theatre of Opera and Ballet, 1 Ploshchad Iskusstv 1, Leningrad, U.S.S.R.

Beltrami, H.E. Cardinal Giuseppe; Vatican ecclesiastic; b. 17 Jan. 1889.
Ordained 16; Bishop 40; Titular Bishop of Damascus; Apostolic Nuncio in Netherlands 59-67; cr. Cardinal 67.
The Vatican, Rome, Italy.

Beltrán, Pedro G.; Peruvian newspaper publisher.
Fmr. Pres. Nat. Agricultural Society; fmr. Chair. of Board, Central Reserve Bank of Peru; Peruvian Ambassador to Washington 44-45; mem. Advisory Board of Int. Bank for Reconstruction and Development 48-50; Peruvian del. to Economic, Financial and other Int. Confs. (Bretton Woods 44, Inter-American, Mexico 45, U.N., San Francisco 45, etc.); Prime Minister and Minister of Finance 59-61; headed the political Alianza Nacional in Peru; Publisher of morning daily *La Prensa*, Lima; Hon. LL.D. Yale and California Univs.; Hon. Fellow, London School of Economics and Political Science.
Belaochaga 590, Lima, Peru.

Beltrán, Washington; Uruguayan newspaper executive and politician; b. 14; ed. Universidad de la República, Montevideo.
Joined *El País* 39, Sub-Dir. 49-61, Co- Dir. 61-, mem. House of Representatives 46; founded Reconstrucción Blanca group 54, and Union Blanca Democratica group within National Party 50; Senator 50-; Nat. Counsellor of Govt. 62-65; Pres. of National Council of Govt. 65-66.
c/o Consejo Nacional de Gobierno, Montevideo, Uruguay.

Beltrão, Alexandre Fontana; Brazilian coffee executive.
Former Chair. World Coffee Promotion Council; fmr. Chair. Pan-American Coffee Bureau; Exec. Dir. Int. Coffee Org. April 68-.
International Coffee Organisation, 22 Berners Street, London, W.1, England.

Beltrão, Hélio Marcos Penna; Brazilian lawyer, economist and politician; b. 15 Oct. 1916; ed. Faculdade Nacional de Direito and New York Univ.
President of Social Security Agency (IAPI) 45; Pres. Brazilian Petroleum Inst. 54; Dir. of PETROBRAS (Govt. Oil Co.) 54-56; Sec. of Planning, State of Guanabara 60-61; Man. Dir. Mesbla Merchandising Co., Rio de Janeiro 62-67; Minister of Planning and Gen. Co-ordination (Brazil) March 67-.
Ministry of Planning and General Co-ordination, Av. Presidente Antonio Carlos 375, 6th Floor, Brasília; Home: Rua Venancio Flores 198, apt. 203, Brasília, Brazil.
Telephone: 22-8892, 42-7941, 42-0083 (Office); 47-4180 (Home).

Belukha, Nikolai Andreyevich; Soviet politician; b. 1920; ed. Moscow Bauman Higher Technical School.
Design Engineer, Chelyabinsk factory and research inst. in Leningrad 45-48; Party Official 48-63; Second Sec., Central Cttee., Communist Party of Latvia 63-; mem. Bureau, Central Cttee., C.P. of Latvia; mem. Central Auditing Comm. of C.P.S.U. 66-; Deputy Supreme Soviet of U.S.S.R.; mem. C.P.S.U. 48-.
Central Committee, Communist Party of Latvia, Riga, U.S.S.R.

Belyaev, Col. Pavel Ivanovich; Soviet cosmonaut; b. 1925; ed. Eisk Air Force School for Marine Pilots and Krasnoznameny Acad. for Aerial Warfare.
Turner in factory 42; fighter pilot 45; mem. Communist Party of Soviet Union 49-; cosmonaut training 60-; Commander of space craft *Voskhod II*, March 18 and 19 65; Hero of the Soviet Union; Pilot-Cosmonaut of U.S.S.R.
Zvezdny Gorodok, Moscow, U.S.S.R.

Belyayev, Prof. Victor Mikhailovich; Soviet musicologist; b. 1888; ed. Petersburg Conservatoire.
Principal publs. *A. K. Glazunov* Vol. I 22, *S. V. Rakhmaninov* 24, *Turkmenian Music* 28, *Music of Ferghana* 33, *Byelorussian Folk Music* 41, *Rhythm of Uzbek Folk Music* 41, *Outline of the Development of Uzbek Musical Culture* 43, *Treatise on the Music of Abdurahman Djami* 44, *Murataly Kurenkeyev* 45, *The Work of N. I. Peiko* 47, *Outlines of the History of the Music of the Peoples of the U.S.S.R.* 56; articles on M. P. Mussorgsky 30, *Composers of Soviet Georgia* 40.
Composers' Union of the R.S.F.S.R., Nezhdanova Street No. 8/10 (Block 2), Moscow K-9, U.S.S.R.

Bembinov, Grigori Badmayevich; Soviet politician; b. 1923; ed. Alma Ata State Inst. of Agriculture.
Agronomist 41-42; Soviet Army 42-45; Agronomist and First Deputy Chief of Semipalatinsk Regional Dept. of Agriculture 45-57; Deputy Head, Agricultural Dept. of Kalmyk Regional Cttee. of C.P.S.U., Deputy Minister, later Minister, of Agriculture of Kalmyk Autonomous

S.S.R. 57-62; Chair. Council of Ministers of Kalmyk Autonomous S.S.R., and Deputy to U.S.S.R. Supreme Soviet 62-; mem. C.P.S.U. 46-.
Council of Ministers of the Kalmyk Autonomous S.S.R., Elista, U.S.S.R.

Ben Baruch (Schwartz), Shalom; Israeli journalist; b. 29 Nov. 1886; ed. Odessa Univ., Russia.
Dir. Palestine Telegraphic Agency until 35; fmr. Dir. *Palestine Bulletin* and Jerusalem branch of daily *Haboker* 22-36; Founder *Echo of Jerusalem.*
Publs. *The Arab Question, The Poetry of Saul Tchernichovsky, The Jewish Question at the Peace Conference, The Shekel, The Zionist Organisation, Herzl in His Diaries, Herzl in His Letters* 40, *Jabotinsky the Nation's Fighter* 42, 43, *Max Nordau in His Letters* 44, *Diaspora and Palestine* 45, *Ussishkin in His Letters* 49, *Jerusalem in the New Hebrew Poetry* 54; edited *The United Nations Organisation* (essays) 52.
18 Histadruth Street, Jerusalem, Israel.

Ben Bella, Mohammed; Algerian politician; b. 16.
Warrant Officer in Moroccan regiment during Second World War (decorated); Chief O.A.S. rebel military group in Algeria 47; imprisoned 49-52 (escaped); directed Algerian national movement from exile in Libya 52-56; arrested Oct. 56; held in France 59-62; Vice-Premier, Algerian Nationalist Provisional Govt., Tunis 62, Leader, Algerian Political Bureau, Algeria 62, Premier of Algeria Sept. 62-65, Pres. of Algeria Sept. 63-65; Lenin Peace Prize 63.
Algiers, Algeria.

Ben Gurion, David; Israeli politician; b. 16 Oct. 1896; ed. privately and Istanbul Univ.
Settled in Palestine 06; exiled by Turks as Zionist 15; went to U.S., where one of organisers of Jewish Legion, in which he himself served under Gen. Allenby; mem. Gen. Council Zionist Organisation 20; one of organisers of Jewish Labour Party (Mapai) and Gen. Fed. of Jewish Labour (Histadruth), and Sec.-Gen. of Fed. 21-35; Chair. Jewish Agency for Palestine 35-48; proclaimed Independence of Israel May 14th, 1948; Head of Provisional Govt. and Minister of Defence from then until March 49; Frime Minister and Minister of Defence 49-53, 55-63; Leader of Mapai (Labour) Party; Hon. Degrees Jewish Theological Seminary of America and Hebrew Univ. of Jerusalem; Bialik Literary Prize for Judaica 52, Hadassah Henrietta Szold Award 58; Hon. LL.D. (Brandeis Univ.) 60.
Publs. *Self-Government of Villayets* 14, *Eretz Israel* 18, *We and our Neighbours* 20, *The Labour Movement and Revisionism* 33, *From Class to Nation* 33, *Mishmarot* (essays on Labour Zionism) 35, *The Struggle* (5 vols.) 47-50, *Israel at War* 50, *Vision and Implementation* (5 vols.) 51-57, *Mima-amad Leam* 55, *Rebirth and Destiny of Israel* 54, *Nezach Israel* (Yiddish) 53, *En la Patria Libre, The Sinai Campaign* 59, *Israel: Years of Challenge* (English) 63, *Ben Gurion looks back, Dvarim Kehavayatam* and many essays and articles.
Sdeh Boker, Israel.

Ben Haim, Paul; German-born Israeli composer; b. 5 July 1897; ed. State Acad. of Music and Univ. of Munich.
Active as conductor, composer and pianist in Germany until 33; settled in Tel-Aviv permanently 33; composer and teacher since 33; Hon. Pres. League of Composers in Israel; Israel State Prize 57.
Compositions: *5 Pieces for Piano* 48, *Sonatina for Piano* 49, *Melody and Variations* 53, *Three Songs without Words* 54, *Concerto for Strings* 57, *The Sweet Psalmist of Israel* 59, two symphonies and many other works.
11 Aharonovitz Street, Tel-Aviv, Israel.
Telephone: 221238.

Ben-Natan, Asher; Israeli diplomatist; b. 15 Feb. 1921; ed. Z. P. Hayut Hebrew Coll., Vienna, and Institut des Hautes Etudes Internationales, Geneva.

Co-founder and mem. Kibbutz Mederot-Zeraim 38-44, latterly Sec. and Treas.; Political Dept., Jewish Agency 44-45; on mission to Europe to organize rescue of Jews and illegal immigration to Palestine; attached to office of Head of Jewish Agency 47-48; Ministry of Foreign Affairs 48-51; studies in Geneva 51-53; Govt. Rep. on Board of Red Sea Inkodeh Co. 53-56, Gen. Man. 55-56; Rep. of Ministry of Defence in Europe 56-58; Dir.-Gen. Ministry of Defence 59-65; Ambassador to German Fed. Republic 65-; Officier Légion d'Honneur; Commandeur de l'Ordre National (Ivory Coast); Commandeur de l'Ordre de l'Etoile Equatoriale (Gabon).
89 University Street, Tel-Aviv, Israel; Embassy of Israel, Bad Godesberg, Ubierstrasse 78, German Federal Republic.
Telephone: Bad Godesberg 56-061.

Bénard, André Pierre Jacques; French oil executive; b. 19 Aug. 1922; ed. Lycée Janson de Sailly, Lycée Georges Clémenceau, Nantes, Lycée Thiers, Marseilles, Ecole Polytechnique.
Entered Société Anonyme des Pétroles Jupiter 46; Head of Bitumen services, Société des Pétroles Shell Berre 50-58, Head of Nat. Activities Dept. 58-59; Asst. Dir.-Gen. Société pour l'Utilisation Rationnelle des Gaz 60-61, Pres., Dir.-Gen. 62-64; Asst. Dir.-Gen. of Shell Française 64-67; Pres., Dir.-Gen. Soc. des Pétroles Shell Berre 67-; Pres., Dir.-Gen. Shell Française 67-; Dir. Compagnie Française des Produits Chimiques Shell, Compagnie des Pétroles d'Algérie, Compagnie de Raffinage Shell Berre, Shell Gabon, Société Maritime Shell, Société pour l'Utilisation Rationnelle des Gaz; Médaille des Evadés; Médaille de la Résistance; Chevalier du Mérite Agricole; Chevalier dans l'Ordre National du Mérite.
Shell Française, 27 rue de Berri, 75- Paris 8ème, France.
Telephone: Paris 256-82-82.

Bénard, Jean Pierre, L. ès L.; French diplomatist; b. 29 Feb. 1908; ed. Lycée Janson-de-Sailly and Univ. de Paris à la Sorbonne.
Journalist, Agence Havas, Washington 34-36, Chief, News Service, Middle East and Cairo 36-39; Diplomatic Service 45-, Counsellor, U.S.A. 45-54; Dep. Dir. NATO Information Div. 55-57; Minister, Tunisia 57-60; Ambassador, Fed. Republic of Cameroon 60-65, to Ethiopia 65-; Officier, Légion d'Honneur.
French Embassy, B.P. 1464, Addis Ababa, Ethiopia.

Benawa, Abdul Raouf; Afghan writer and administrator; b. 13; ed. Ganj Public School, Kandahar.
Mem. Language Dept. Afghan Acad. 39; mem. Words Dept. Afghan Acad. and Asst. Information Dept. 40; Dir. Publication Dept. Afghan Acad. 41; Gen. Dir. *Pusthu Tolana;* Sec. Afghan Acad. and Dir. *Kabul* magazine; proprietor of weekly magazine *Hewad;* mem. History Dept. 50, Dir. Internal Publ. Dept. 51, Gen. Dir. 52; Press Attaché India 53-56; Pres. Radio Kabul 56-63; Press and Cultural Counsellor, Cairo 63-.
Publs. *Women in Afghanistan, Mir Wiess Neeka, Literary Sciences, Pusthu Songs, De Ghanamo Wazhai, Pushtoonistan, A Survey of Pushtoonistan, Rahman Baba, Pir mohammad-Kakar, Khosh-hal Khan se Wai, Pushtoo Killi,* Vol. 4, *Kazim Khan-e-Shaida;* translations: *Mosa-fir Iqbal, Geetan-Jali Tagoor, Da Darmista-tar Pushtoo Seerane, Leaders of Pashtoonistan, History of Hootaki, Preshana afkar* (poem), *Da zra khwala, Pashto writers today* (2 vols.), *Pashto reader for schools, Pachakhan* (A leader of Pashtoni), *Landei* (public poems); plays: *I-Zoor gonahgar* (Old criminal), *Ishtebah* (confusion), *Kari bar asal, Aashyanae aqab, Zarang, Chaoki der khater, Hakoomat baidar.*
Afghan Embassy, Cairo, United Arab Republic; and Ministry of Information and Culture, Kabul, Afghanistan.

Benda, Ernst; German lawyer and politician; b. 15 Jan. 1925; ed. Kant-Gymnasium, Berlin-Spandau, Humboldt Univ., Freie Univ. Berlin, Univ. of Wisconsin.

War service; prisoner-of-war; Humboldt Univ. 46-48; Freie Univ., Berlin 48-51; Univ. of Wisconsin 49-55; District appointment, Spandau 51-54; mem. Berlin House of Reps. 55-57; Chair. Berlin Christian Democratic Union Youth Dept. 52-54; mem. Fed. Govt. 66; Under-Sec. in Interior Ministry; Minister of the Interior 68-.

Publs. *Notstandsverfassung und Arbeitskampf* 63, *Rechtsstaat und Verjährung* 65, *Industrielle Herrschaft und sozialer Staat* 66, *Die Notstandsverfassung* 66.

1 Berlin, 20, Adickestrasse 65, Federal German Republic.

Telephone: 38-25-78.

Bender, Albert F., Jr.; American lawyer and United Nations official; b. 5 July 1914; ed. Princeton Univ. and Columbia Univ. Law School.

Admitted to New Jersey Bar 39; private law firm 38-42; Attorney, Anti-Trust Div. of Dept. of Justice 42; U.S. Army 43-45; Chief of External Assets and Intelligence Branch, later Exec. Officer of Finance Div., Office of Mil. Govt. of U.S. 45-48; U.S. mem. German External Property Comm. 47-48; mem. U.S. Dels. to UN 48-66, mem. UNACABQ 60-66; lately Senior Adviser on Legal and Int. Org. Affairs of U.S. Mission to UN, New York; UN Deputy High Commr. for Refugees 66-.

United Nations High Commission for Refugees, Palais des Nations, Geneva, Switzerland; Home: 61 Commodore Road, Chappaqua, New York, U.S.A.

Telephone: Central 8-8140 (New York); (022)-8-46-83 (Geneva).

Bendetsen, Karl Robin, A.B., LL.B.; American lawyer and business executive; b. 11 Oct. 1907; ed. Leland Stanford Univ.

Law practice 34-40; U.S. Army 40-46; Management Counsel 46-47; Special Counsel to Sec. of Defense 48; Asst. Sec. of Army 50-52, Under Sec. of Army 52; Chair. Board Panama Canal Co. 50; Dir.Gen. U.S. Railroads 50-52; Champion Paper and Fiber Co. (now Champion Papers Inc.) 52-, Pres. and Chief Exec. Officer 60-, Chair. 65-67, Chair. of Board, Dir., Chief Exec. Officer, U.S. Plywood-Champion Papers Inc. 67-; Special Asst. to Sec. of Defense for German Affairs, also for Philippines 56; Chair. Advisory Council on Non-Military Instruction, Office of Sec. of Defense 62.

U.S. Plywood-Champion Papers Inc., 777 Third Avenue, New York, N.Y. 10017, U.S.A.

Benedek, Marcell; Hungarian writer, critic and translator; b. 1885.

University Lecturer under Repub. of Councils 19, later discharged; Reader at Dante Publishing House, later Dir. Uj Idök Inst. of Literature; Prof. at Bolyai Univ. of Kolozsvár, Cluj 45-47; returned to Hungary 47; Prof. of Literature, Budapest Univ. 47-62; Chief Editor *Hungarian Encyclopedia of Literature* 63-65; Kossuth Prize 63.

Publs. include: *The Art of Reading, Modern Hungarian Literature, Modern World Literature, Shakespeare, Selected Novels, First in My Life* 57.

c/o Eötvös Lóránd University, Egyetem-tér 1, Budapest V; Home: Vércse-utca 246, Budapest XII, Hungary.

Telephone: 180-820 (Office); 259-949 (Home).

Benedetti, Jean Baptiste Antoine; French public servant; b. 3 June 1902; ed. Lycée d'Alger, Collège de Bône, Univ. de Paris and Inst. des Sciences Politiques, Paris.

Local Government 29-55; Inspector-Gen. Third Military Region 49-55, Second Military Region 55-58; Prefect, Seine 58-63; Pres. Prefectoral Body Asscn. 61-

65; Pres. Admin. Council, Charbonnages de France 63-, Economic and Social Counsellor 64-; Grand Officier Légion d'Honneur, Grand Officier Ordre National du Mérite, Croix de Guerre and other decorations.

Charbonnages de France, 9 avenue Percier, Paris 8e; and Le Mas, Villelongue-de-la-Salanque, Pyr.-Or.; and 60 rue de l'Hotel de Ville, Paris 4e, France.

Telephone: ARC 79-11.

Benedetti, Mario; Uruguayan writer; b. 14 Sept. 1920; ed. Colegio Alemán.

Journalist on *Marcha* (weekly) and Literary, Film and Theatre Critic on *El Diario, Tribuna Popular* and *La Mañana*; visited Europe 57, 66-67.

Publs. Fiction: *Esta mañana* 49, *El último viaje y otros cuentos* 51, *Quién de nosotros* 53, *Montevideanos* 59, *La Tregua* 63, *Gracias por el Fuego* 65; plays: *Ustedes por ejemplo* 53, *El Reportaje* 58, *Ida y Vuelta* 58; poetry: *La víspera indeleble* 45, *Sólo mientras tanto* 50, *Poemas de la Oficina* 56, *Poemas del Hoyporhoy* 65, *Inventario* 65, *Contra los puentes levadizos* 66; essays: *Peripecia y novela* 48, *Marcel Proust y otros ensayos* 51, *Literatura uruguaya siglo XX* 63.

c/o Editorial Alfa, Ciudadela 1389, Montevideo, Uruguay.

Benedictos (Vassilios Papadopoulos); Greek orthodox ecclesiastic; b. 1892; ed. Greek Orthodox Hieratic School, Jerusalem, and Athens Univ.

Clerk, Patriarchal Offices, Jerusalem 14; ordained deacon 14; accompanied the then Patriarch to Damascus during World War I; studies in Law and Theological Schools, Athens Univ. 21-25; Rep. of Patriarch of Jerusalem at World Christian Conf. of Faith and Order, Geneva 27; Exarch of the Holy Sepulchre in Athens 29-46; ordained priest and Archimandrite 46; mem. Holy Synod, Jerusalem Patriarchate 46-; Legal Adviser and Chair. Pending Property Cttee. 47; Chair. Financial Cttee. 50; rep. of Patriarch, Internationalisation of Jerusalem Trusteeship Conf. 50; Archbishop of Tiberias 51; Greek Orthodox Patriarch of Jerusalem 57-; Grand Cross of King George of Greece, Grand Cross and Cordon of Patriarchate of Antioch, Jordanian and Lebanese orders.

Greek Orthodox Patriarchate, P.O. Box 4074, Jerusalem, Jordan.

Benediktov, Ivan Alexandrovich; Soviet politician and diplomatist; b. 02; ed. Timiryazev Agricultural Acad., Moscow.

Began work in Vichugsk Textile Mills, Ivanovo Region 17; studied workers' faculty until before 23; agronomist and economist in Uzbek People's Commissariat of Agriculture and Collective Farm Centre 23-30; served Soviet Army 30-31; Deputy-Dir. later Dir. Moscow Regional Trust of State Market Gardens 31-37; People's Commissar of State Farm of R.S.F.S.R. 37-38; Vice-Chair. R.S.F.S.R. Council of People's Commissars 37-38; 1st Deputy Commissar for Agriculture of U.S.S.R. 38, 43-46; People's Commissar of Agriculture 38-43, 46-47; Chair. All-Union Agricultural Exhibition 38-53; Minister of Agriculture 47-53, 53-55; Ambassador to India 53, 59-67, to Yugoslavia 67-; Minister of State Farms 55-57; Deputy Chair. State Planning Comm. and Minister of Agriculture of R.S.F.S.R. 57-59; mem. Communist Party 30-, candidate-mem. Central Cttee. 39-52, mem. Central Cttee. 52-; Deputy to Supreme Soviet 46-55; four Orders of Lenin; two Orders of Red Banner of Labour.

U.S.S.R. Embassy, Belgrade, Yugoslavia.

Benediktsson, Bjarni, PH.B., LL.B.; Icelandic lawyer and politician; b. 08; ed. Univs. of Iceland and Berlin.

Prof. of Law, Univ. of Iceland 32; Mayor of Reykjavik 40, re-elected 42, 45; M.P. 42-; Icelandic Del. to UN Gen. Assembly 46; Minister of Foreign Affairs and Minister of Justice 47-53, Justice and Education 53-56; Chief Editor *Morgunbladid* 56-59; Pres. Althing

(Icelandic Parl.) 59; Minister of Justice and Industries 59-61, 62-63; Prime Minister Sept.-Dec. 61, Nov. 63-; mem. Central Cttee. Independence Party 36-, Pres. 61. Háahlíd 14, Reykjavík, Iceland.

Benediktsson, Jakob, M.A., PH.D.; Icelandic philologist; b. 20 July 1907; ed. Univ. of Copenhagen.
Asst. Editor *Old-Icelandic Dictionary* (Copenhagen) 39-46; Librarian Univ. of Copenhagen 43-46; Editor-in-Chief *Icelandic Dictionary* Univ. of Iceland 48-.
Publs. *Gísli Magnússon* 39, *Chronologie de deux listes des prêtres kamiréens* 40, *Jardabók Árna Magnussonar og Páls Vídalíns* (vols. VII, X, XI) 40-43, *Skardsbók* (Corpus codicum Islandicorum XVI) 43, *Two Treatises on Iceland* 43, *Veraldar saga* 44, *Ferdabók Tómasar Sæmundssonar* 47, *Ole Worm's Correspondence with Icelanders* 48, *G. Andrésson, Deilurit* 48, *Persius rímur* 49, *Arngrími Jonae Opera I-IV* 50-57, *Arngrímur Jónsson and his Works* 57, *Skardsárbók* 58, *Sturlunga Saga* (Early Icelandic Manuscripts I) 58, *Islenzk-dönsk ordabók, Vidbaetir* 63, *Islendingabók, Landnámabók* 68.
2 Stigahlíd, Reykjavík, Iceland.
Telephone: 30987.

Benediktsson, Pétur, LL.D.; Icelandic banker; b. 06; ed. Reykjavik Grammar School and Univ.
Minister to Great Britain and to Norwegian Govt. in London 42-44, to U.S.S.R. 44-51, to Czechoslovakia 46-51, to Poland 46-51, to France 46-56, to Belgium 46-56, to Italy 47-56, to Switzerland 49-56, to Spain 49-56, to Portugal 49-56, to Ireland 51-56; Permanent Del. to OEEC 48-56; Dir. Nat. Bank of Iceland 56-.
National Bank of Iceland, Austurstraeti 11, Reykjavík, Iceland.

Bénézit, Jacques Charles Victor; French oil executive; b. 7 Oct. 1913; ed. Ecole Polytechnique, Ecole des Mines.
Mining Engineer, Nancy, Paris; Dir. Exploration/Production Dept. 55; Dir. Compagnie Française des Pétroles; Pres. and Dir.-Gen. Compagnie Française des Pétroles (Algeria); Vice- Pres. Compagnie Générale de Géophysique; Dir. French Petroleum Co. of Canada Ltd., Compagnie des Pétroles Total Libye, Société d'étude des marchés européens du gaz d'Hassi R'Mel transporté par canalisations (Somarel) and several other companies; Chevalier, Légion d'Honneur.
Compagnie Française des Pétroles, 5 rue Michel-Ange, Paris 16e; and 89 avenue de Villiers, Paris 17e, France.

Bengelloun, Ali, L. ès D.; Moroccan diplomatist; b. 27; ed. Collège Moulay Idriss de Fes and Faculté de Droit de l'Université de Paris à la Sorbonne.
Casablanca Court of Justice 50; Ministry of Justice (Civil Affairs Dir. and Sec.-Gen.) 55-62; Chair. Cttees. establishing Supreme Court and Nationality Code; Vice-Chair. Constitutional Council; Govt. Lawyer to Int. Comm. of Conciliation and Arbitration, Geneva 57; Amb. to U.S. and Canada 62-65; private business 65-67; Minister of Justice 67, of Royal Cabinet July 67-.
Ministry of Royal Cabinet, Rabat, Morocco.

Bengsch, H.E. Cardinal Alfred Bernhard, DR.THEOL.; German ecclesiastic; b. 10 Sept. 1921; ed. grammar school, Berlin, Philosophical-Theological Coll., Fulda, Ludwig Maximilians Universität, Munich.
Ordained 50; Chaplain in Berlin; further study and Asst. at Theological Coll., Erfurt 54-56; Lecturer in Dogma and Rhetoric at Theological Coll., Neuzelle 56-59; Titular Bishop of Tubia and Asst. Bishop of Berlin 59; Bishop of Berlin and Pres. of Berlin Seminar on Holy Orders 61; Archbishop 62-; created Cardinal 67.
Publs. *Heilsgeschichte und Heilswissen* 57, *Unterwegs zum Herrn* 59, *Heiligung, Umkehr, Vollendung* 59, *Berufung und Bewährung* 60, *Der Glaube an die Auferstehung* 62, *Den Glauben Leben* 65, *Konzil für Dich* 66, *In Erwartung der Wiederkunft* 66, *Den Glauben leben* Vol. II 67.
Berlin W 8, Hinter der Kath. Kirche 3 (East Berlin); Berlin 19, Wundtstrasse 48/50 (West Berlin), Germany.
Telephone: 56-30-97 (East Berlin); 302-04-61 (West Berlin).

Bengzon, Cesar, B.A., LL.B.; Philippine judge; b. 29 May 1896; ed. Ateneo de Manila and Univ. of the Philippines.
Law Clerk, Bureau of Justice 19, Special Attorney, then Asst. Attorney 20, Solicitor-Gen. 31; Dean and Prof. of Law, Univ. of Manila 28-32; Under-Sec. of Justice and Chair. Board of Pardons 33; Assoc. Justice, Court of Appeals 36; Assoc. Justice, Supreme Court 45; Prof. of Law, Univ. of Santo Tomas and Philippine Law School 48-54; Chair. Senate Electoral Tribunal 50-57; Chief Justice Supreme Court 61; Judge, Int. Court of Justice, The Hague 66-; mem. Philippine Acad. of Sciences and Humanities 64-; Pres. Philippine Section, Int. Comm. of Jurists 64, 66; mem. Nat. Research Council 64-, American Judicature Soc. 65, Philippine Soc. of Int. Law 65-; LL.D. *h.c.* Univ. of Manila 57, Ateo de Manila Univ. 64, Univ. of the Philippines 64.
International Court of Justice, The Hague, Netherlands.

Benhima, Ahmed Taiba (brother of Dr. Mohamed Benhima, *q.v.*); Moroccan diplomatist; b. 13 Nov. 1927; ed. Univs. of Nancy and Paris.
Chargé d'Affaires, Paris 56-57, Ambassador to Italy 57-59; Sec.-Gen. of Ministry of Foreign Affairs 59-61; Perm. Rep. to UN 61-64; Minister of Foreign Affairs 64-66; Dir. Cabinet of King 66-67; Perm. Rep. to UN 67-.
Permanent Mission of Morocco to the United Nations, 757 Third Avenue, New York, N.Y. 10017, U.S.A.

Benhima, Mohamed, M.D. (brother of Ahmed Benhima, *q.v.*); Moroccan physician and politician; b. 25 June 1924; ed. Faculté de Médecine de Nancy, France.
Chief Medical Officer, Had Court District 54-56; Chief of Central Service for Urban and Rural Hygiene 56-57; Head of Personal Office of Minister of Public Health 57-60; Sec.-Gen. Ministry of Public Health Jan.-June 60; Gov. of Provinces of Agadir and Tarfaya 60-61; Minister of Public Works 61-62, 63-65, 67-, of Commerce, Industry, Mines, Handicrafts and Merchant Marine 62-63; Minister of Nat. Educ. 65-67; Prime Minister July 67-; decorations from Govts. of Morocco, Sweden, Ethiopia, Tunisia, Liberia and United Arab Republic.
Km. 5,500, Route des Zaërs, Rabat, Morocco.

Benidickson, William Moore, M.P.; Canadian lawyer and politician; b. 8 April 1911; ed. Univ. of Manitoba.
M.P. 45-; Parl. Asst. to Minister of Transport 51-53, to Minister of Finance 53-57; Minister of Mines and Technical Surveys 63-65; Liberal-Labour.
House of Commons, Ottawa, Canada.

Benites, Leopoldo, DR. RER. POL.; Ecuadorean diplomatist; b. 17 Oct. 1905; ed. Univ. of Guayaquil.
Minister to Uruguay 47-52; Alt. Rep. of Ecuador to UN 53-54; Ambassador to Bolivia 54-56, to Argentina 56, to Uruguay 56-60; Perm. Rep. to UN 60-.
Permanent Mission of Ecuador to the United Nations, 820 Second Avenue, New York City, N.Y., U.S.A.

Benitez, Jaime, LL.M., LL.D.; Puerto Rican university president; ed. Georgetown Univ. and Univ. of Chicago.
Instructor in Political Science, Univ. of Puerto Rico 31-41, Assoc. Prof. 41-42, Chancellor of Univ. 42-66, Pres. 66-; Head Hearings Officer, Nat. War Labor Board, Washington; Del. to UNESCO Conf., Paris 51; mem. U.S. Nat. Comm. UNESCO 51-55; Pres. Cttee. of Bill of Rights, Puerto Rico Constitutional Convention 51; mem. Housing Cttee., U.S. Federal Housing Agency 57; U.S. Del., Conf. of Univs., Utrecht, Holland 48;

Fellow American Acad. of Arts and Sciences, American Acad. of Political and Social Sciences, Federal Bar Asscn., Nat. Asscn. of State Univs. (Pres. 58), Colegio de Abogados de Puerto Rico.

Publs. *The Concept of the Family in Roman and Common Law Jurisprudence* 31, *Political and Philosophical Theories of Jose Ortega y Gasset* 39, *Reflexiones Sobre el Presente* 50, *La Iniciación Universitaria y las Ciencias Sociales* 52, *The United States, Cuba, and Latin America* 61, *Junto a la Torre* 63, *Discurso en Salamanca* 65, *Sobre el Futuro Cultural y Político de Puerto Rico* 65.

President's Residence, University of Puerto Rico, Rio Piedras, Puerto Rico.

Beniuc, Mihai, D.PHIL.; Romanian writer; b. 20 Nov. 1907; ed. Arad High Schools, Cluj Univ. and in Germany.

Professor, Cluj Univ. 30; now Prof. of Psychology, Chair. Parhon Univ.; Bucharest; revolutionary poet 26-; mem. Grand Nat. Assembly; Chair. Writers' Union of the Romanian People's Republic until 65; mem. Romanian Acad., State Prizes 51 and 54; Order of Labour (First Class), Star of the Republic (Second Class), etc.

Publs. Verse: *Songs of Desolation* 38, *New Songs* 40, *Poems* 43, *The Lost City* 43, *A Man is Waiting for the Sunrise* 46, *Selected Poems* 49, *Banners* 52, *The Apple Tree near the Road* 54, *Durability* 55, *The Heart of the Old Vesuvius, Journeys Through Constellations* 57, *An Hour before Sunset* 59, *Songs of the Heart* 61, *The Matter and the Dreams* 61, *Colours of the Autumn* 62, *Strings of Time* 63, *Headlights* 64, *Rock Flowers* 65, *Day by Day* 65, *Other Ways* 67 (many translated); Prose: *Personal Hate, On the Edge of the Knife* 59, *An Ordinary Man has Disappeared* 64, *Learning and Intelligence in Animals* 34, *The Roundabout Path of the Fighting Fish* 38, *Territoriality* 39, *The Reciprocal Influence of Behaviour Patterns Learnt by Betta Splendens Regan*; Plays: *In the Cucu Valley* 59, *The Return* 60; Criticism: *Our Poetry* 56, *Mason Manole* 57.

Str. Grădina Bordei 51, Bucharest, Romania.

Telephone: 33-12-33.

Benjamin, Curtis G.; American publisher; b. 13 July 1901; ed. Univ. of Kentucky, Univ. of Chicago and Univ. of Arizona.

McGraw-Hill Book Co. 28-, Manager, College Dept. 32-42, Vice-Pres. 42-46, Pres. 46-60, Chair. of Board 60-; Dir. McGraw-Hill Inc. 44-, McGraw-Hill Co. of Canada Ltd. 47-, McGraw-Hill Publishing Co. Ltd. (London) 47-; Pres. American Book Publishers Council 58-60; Chair. Govt. Advisory Cttee. on Int. Book Programs 62-64; mem. Science Information Council, Nat. Science Foundation 59-60, 64-; Hon. LL.D. (Kentucky), Hon. Litt. D. (Arizona).

McGraw-Hill Book Company, 330 West 42nd Street, New York, N.Y. 10036; Home: Kellogg Hill Road, Weston, Conn., U.S.A.

Benjamin, Hilde, DR. h.c.; German lawyer and politician; b. 5 Feb. 1902; studied law.

Practising lawyer until 33; joined Communist Party 27; commercial employment during Nazi régime; State lawyer in Berlin 45; joined Sozialistische Einheitspartei Deutschlands (S.E.D.) 46; Vice-Pres. Supreme Court 49; Minister of Justice 53-67; Prof. of History of Admin. of Justice, Deutsche Akad. für Staats-und Rechtswissenschaft "Walter Ulbricht" 67-; mem. Central Cttee. S.E.D. 53; mem. Volkskammer; Clara-Zetkin Medal, two Distinguished Service Orders, Order of the Banner of Labour, medal for Fighters against Fascism, Order of Merit (Gold).

Deutsche Akademie für Staats-und Rechtswissenschaft "Walter Ulbricht", Potsdam-Babelsberg, German Democratic Republic.

Benkei, András; Hungarian politician; b. 23.

Former mechanic; Sec. Szabolcs-Szatmár County Cttee. of Food Industry Trade Union 49; Head, Industrial Dept., Szabolcs-Szatmár County Party Cttee. 51-54; First Sec. Nyiregyháza Municipal Cttee., Hungarian Socialist Workers Party 54-57; First Sec. Szabolcs-Szatmár County Party Cttee. 57-63; Minister of Internal Affairs 63-; mem. Central Cttee. Hungarian Socialist Workers Party; mem. National Assembly.

Ministry of Internal Affairs, Budapest, Hungary.

Benn, Rt. Hon. Anthony Neil Wedgwood, P.C., M.P.; British politician; b. 3 April 1925; ed. Westminster School and New Coll., Oxford.

R.A.F. Pilot 43-45; Oxford Univ. 46-49; Producer, B.B.C. 49-50; M.P. 50-60, compelled to leave House of Commons on inheriting peerage 60, re-elected and unseated 61, renounced peerage and re-elected 63; Nat. Exec. Labour Party 59-; Chair. Fabian Soc. 64; Postmaster-Gen. 64-66; Minister of Technology 66-.

Publ. *The Regeneration of Britain* 65.

House of Commons, London, S.W.1; Home: 12 Holland Park Avenue, London, W.11, England.

Telephone: 01-727-5503.

Bennani, Khalil; Libyan bank governor; b. 20; ed. privately.

Acting Mayor of Benghazi 52; Councillor of Interior and Education 52, of Public Health 53, of Education 53; Deputy Chief of Royal Cabinet 54-61; Governor of Nat. Bank of Libya 61-.

National Bank of Libya, P.O. Box 1103, Tripoli, Libya.

Bennecke, Gen. Jürgen; German army officer; b. 12 Sept. 1912.

Entered *Reichswehr* as Cadet 30, Lieut. 33; Unit Officer and Adjutant until Second World War; served Western Front, Balkans and Eastern Front during Second World War; Deputy First Gen. Staff Officer (Ops.), Central Army Group at end of Second World War; Prisoner-of-war in England for two years, later managed a farm in S. Baden; Joined *Amt Blank* (later Ministry of Defence) 52; Head of Org. and Training Div., *Bundeswehr*; Commdr. 16th Panzergrenadier Brigade, Flensburg 58-60, 7th Panzergrenadier Div., Unna 63-64; Commdt. Gen. Staff Coll., Hamburg 64-66; Commanding Gen. I Corps 66-68; C.-in-C. Allied Forces, Central Europe April 68-.

H.Q. Allied Forces Central Europe, Brunssum, Netherlands.

Benner, Thomas Eliot, A.M., ED.D.; American university professor; b. 11 Feb. 1894; ed. Harvard Univ.

Public Schools of Mass., Md., and Me. 14-19; State Dept. of Educ. Ala. 19-22; Dean Ala. Polytechnic Inst. 23-24; Chancellor Univ. of Puerto Rico 24-29; Visiting Prof. Columbia Univ. 29-31; Dean Coll. of Education, Univ. of Illinois 31-45; Chief Educ. Div., U.S. Element of Allied Council Austria 46-47; educational consultant in Korea for UNESCO and UNKRA 51-52, to Turkish Ministry of Education, Ankara 54-57; to office of Prime Minister, Israel 57; Prof. of Education, Univ. of Ill. 47-62; Adviser to the Pres., Univ. of Puerto Rico 62-; Dir. Inst. for Training in Univ. Librarianship 68-; photographer and editor of colour documentary films on Korea, Turkey, Cuba, Puerto Rico; Hon. mem. Univ. of Vienna 47; Hon. LL.D., Univ. of Puerto Rico 53.

Office of the President, University of Puerto Rico, Rio Piedras, Puerto Rico 00931; and c/o Finfrock Law Offices, Race Street, Urbana, Ill., U.S.A.

Telephone: 765-6590 (San Juan).

Bennett, Lt.-Col. Charles Moihi To Arawaka, D.S.O., M.A., DIP.ED., DIP.SOC.SC.; New Zealand diplomatist; b. 1913; ed. Univ. of N.Z. and Exeter Coll., Oxford.

Schoolmaster 37; Staff mem. New Zealand Broadcasting Service 38-39; service with New Zealand Army in U.K., Greece, Crete, North Africa, commanding Maori Battalion from Alamein to Tunis, 39-46; Staff mem. War

Histories Section, Internal Affairs Dept., mem. Ngarimu Scholarship Fund Board 47-50; Asst. Controller Maori Welfare Division, Maori Affairs Dept. 51-57, Dir. 57-58; mem. State Literary Advisory Cttee., New Zealand Parole Board 51; New Zealand High Commr. to Malaya (the first Maori to lead an overseas Mission) 59-63; Asst. Sec. Dept. of Maori Affairs, Wellington 63-.
P.O. Box 2390, Wellington, C.1, New Zealand.

Bennett, Emmett Leslie, M.A., PH.D.; American classical scholar; b. 12 July 1918; ed. Univ. of Cincinnati.
Research analyst, U.S. War Dept. 42-45; taught in Dept. of Classics, Yale Univ.47-58; Fulbright Research Scholar, Athens 53-54, Cambridge 65; mem. Inst. for Advanced Study, Guggenheim Fellow, Visiting Lecturer in Greek, Bryn Mawr Coll. 55-56; Dept. of Classical Languages, Univ. of Texas 58-59; Univ. of Wisconsin Inst. for Research Humanities 59-, Dept. of Classics 60-; corresp. mem. German Archaeological Inst., Visiting Prof. Univ. of Colorado 67; mem. Comité Int. Permanent pour les Etudes Mycéniennes, Archaological Inst. of America, American Philogical Asscn.
Publs. *The Pylos Tablets* 51 and 56, *The Mycenae Tablets* 53 and 58, *Mycenaean Studies* 64, Editor, *Nestor* 57-, etc.
University of Wisconsin, Madison, Wis. 53706, U.S.A.
Telephone: 608-257-3162.

Bennett, James V., A.B., LL.B.; American prisons administrator; b. 28 Aug. 1894; ed. Brown and George Washington Univs.
Air Service First World War; Investigator U.S. Bureau of Efficiency 19, Sec. Personnel Classification Board; Commr. of Prison Industries 30; Dir. Bureau of Prisons, Dept. of Justice 37-65; in charge of Prison Branch, American Occupation Zone 45; Dr. of Humanistics, Springfield Coll. 55; Pres. Award for Distinguished Fed. Civilian Service 59; Hon. LL.D. (Brown Univ.).
Publs. *Prison Labor at the Cross-Roads* 34, *The Kind of Prisons We Deserve* 48, *Inside U.S.P.* 48, *Correctional Institution Design and Construction* 49, *Verdict Guilty—Now What* 53, *Enter Prisoner—Exit Citizen* 57, *Law and Corrections Open New Vistas for the Psychiatrist* 57, *A Prison Administrator Views Today's Narcotics Problem* 58, *The Last Full Ounce* 59, *Gearing Contemporary Architecture to Contemporary Penology* 59, *Reconciling Legal and Correctional Values* 60, supplement to *Correctional Institution Design and Construction* 60.
5840 Marbury Road, Bethesda, Maryland, U.S.A.

Bennett, John Coleman, M.A., D.D., S.T.D.; American theologian; b. 22 July 1902; ed. Phillips Exeter Acad., Williams Coll., Oxford Univ. and Union Theological Seminary.
Mem. of Faculty, Auburn Theological Seminary 30-38; Prof. of Theology, Pacific School of Religion 38-43; Prof. of Christian Theology and Ethics, Union Theological Seminary 43-57, Dean of Faculty 55-, William E. Dodge Jr. Prof. of Applied Christianity 57-61, Reinhold Niebuhr Prof. of Social Ethics 61-, Pres. 63-; Pres. American Theological Soc. 54, American Soc. for Christian Social Ethics 61; Co-Editor *Christianity and Crisis*; several honorary degrees.
Publs. *Social Salvation* 35, *Christian Realism* 41, *Christian Ethics and Social Policy* 46, *Christianity and Communism* 48 (new ed. *Christianity and Communism Today* 60), *Christians and the State* 58, Ed. *Nuclear Weapons and the Conflict of Conscience* 62, *Foreign Policy in Christian Perspective* 66.
606 W. 122nd Street, New York City, N.Y. 10027, U.S.A.

Bennett, Richard Rodney, A.R.A.M., F.R.A.M.; British composer; b. 29 March 1936; ed. Leighton Park School, Reading, Royal Acad. of Music, London and under Pierre Boulez, Paris.
Commissioned to write two operas by Sadler's Wells 62;

Prof. of Composition, Royal Acad. of Music 63-65; Arnold Bax Soc. Prize for Commonwealth Composers 64.
Compositions: *The Approaches of Sleep* 59, *Journal, Calendar, Winter Music for Orchestra* 60, *The Ledge, Suite Française, Oboe Sonata* 61, *Nocturnes, London Pastoral "Fantasy"* 62, *Aubade, Jazz Calendar, String Quartet No. Four, Five Studies* 64, *Symphony* 65, *Epithalamion* 66, *Symphony No. 2* 67, *Wind Quartet, Piano Concerto* 68; Opera: *The Mines of Sulphur* 64, *A Penny for a Song* 66; Television Music: *Stephen D. Hamlet, Malatesta, The Midnight Thief, Hereward the Wake, The Order*; Film Music: *Indiscreet, Devil's Disciple, Blind Date, The Mark, Only Two Can Play, Wrong Arm of the Law, Heavens Above, Billy Liar, One Way Pendulum, The Nanny, The Witches, Far from the Madding Crowd, Billion Dollar Brain.*
c/o London International, Park House, Park Street, London, W.1, England.

Bennett, Wallace Foster; American politician; b. 13 Nov. 1898; ed. Univ. of Utah.
Pres. Bennett's (Paint and Glass) Co. and Bennett's Motor Co., Salt Lake City till 50, now Chair. of both; Pres. Nat. Glass Distributors Asscn. 37, Salt Lake Rotary Club 40, Salt Lake Community Chest 44-45; Nat. Asscn. of Manufacturers 49; mem. LDS (Mormon) Church; Republican Senator from Utah 50-; mem. Senate Banking and Currency Cttee. and Senate Finance Cttee., Joint Cttee. on Atomic Energy, Joint Cttee. on Defence Production.
Publs. *Faith and Freedom* 50, *Why I am a Mormon* 58.
P.O. Box 1320, Salt Lake City, Utah, U.S.A.

Bennett, Hon. William Andrew Cecil; Canadian businessman and politician; b. 1900; ed. in New Brunswick and Alberta.
Pres. Bennett's Stores Ltd. (estbd. 1930) operating chain of five stores (hardware, electrical appliances, etc.) in the Okanagan valley; B.C. Legislature 41-, Prime Minister of British Columbia 52-, and also Pres. of Exec. Council and Minister of Finance 55-; leader of the Social Credit movement in B.C.; Freeman of the City of Kelowna.
2768 Satellite Street, Victoria, B.C., Canada.

Bennett, William John, O.B.E., LL.D., B.A.; Canadian administrator; b. 3 Nov. 1911; ed. Fort William Collegiate Coll. and Univ. of Toronto.
Private Sec. to Minister of Transport 35-39; Chief Exec. Asst. to Minister of Munitions and Supply 39-46; Pres. and Man. Dir. Eldorado Mining and Refining Ltd. (the Govt. agency responsible for uranium procurement) 47-58; Pres. Northern Transportation Co. Ltd. 47-58; Eldorado Aviation Ltd. 53-58, Pres. Atomic Energy of Canada Ltd. 53-58, Exec. Vice-Pres. and Gen. Man. Canadian British Aluminium Co. Ltd. 58-, Pres. and Gen. Manager 59-.
216 Clemow Avenue, Ottawa, Ont., Canada.

Bennett, William Tapley, Jr.; American diplomatist; b. 1 April 1917; ed. Univ. of Georgia, Univ. of Freiburg, Germany, and George Washington Univ.
Instructor in Political Science, Univ. of Georgia 37; with Nat. Inst. of Public Affairs 39-40; Dept. of Agriculture 40; Asst. to Co-ordinator, Office of Defense Housing 40-41; with State Dept. 41-, officer in charge Central American and Panama Affairs 49-51, Caribbean Affairs 51, Deputy Dir. South American Affairs 51-54; Nat. War Coll. 54-55; Special Asst. to Deputy Under-Sec. of State 55-57; Counsellor, Vienna 57-61, Rome 61; Counsellor (with rank of Minister), Athens 61-64; Amb. to Dominican Republic 64-66, to Portugal 66-.
American Embassy, Lisbon, Portugal.

Benny, Jack; American entertainer; b. 14 Feb. 1894; ed. Waukegau High School, Illinois.
Violinist 12, film star 29-, radio entertainer 32-, also TV entertainer.

Films inc. *To Be or Not to Be, George Washington Slept Here, The Horn Blows at Midnight.*
1002 N. Roxbury Drive, Beverly Hills, California, U.S.A.

Benoit, Balla; Cameroonian government official; b. 1924; ed. Coll. Turgot, Paris, Lycée Louis-le-Grand, Paris, Institut d'Etudes Politiques and Institut des Hautes Etudes d'Outre-Mer, Paris.
Director of Cabinet, Ministry of Finance 59; Prefect, Dept. of Ntem 59-60; Dir. of Cabinet, Prime Minister's Office 60-62; Federal Inspector of Admin. and Prefect of Nyong and Sanaga 62-Sept. 63; Minister of Foreign Affairs, Federal Republic of Cameroon Sept. 63-67.
c/o Ministry of Foreign Affairs, Yaoundé, Cameroon.

Benoit, Jean Paul, L.PH.; French ecclesiastic; b. 8 Jan. 1898; ed. Univ. de Paris à la Sorbonne.
Director Société Centrale d'Evangélisation de L'Eglise Reformée de France 47-63; Prés. Alliance Evangelique Française 45-; Médaille Militaire, Croix de Guerre.
Publs. *Enquête sur les valeurs spirituelles à Paris* 45, *Puissance du Seigneur, Trois aventuriers pour Dieu, J. F. Oberlin, pasteur d'hommes* 56, *Combats d'apôtres* 57.
47 rue de Clichy, Paris 9e, France.

Bensah, Emmanuel Korbla; Ghanaian politician; b. 12; ed. Keta Basel Mission Senior School.
Joined Gold Coast Civil Service 31, qualified as nurse and pharmacist 36; in business 48-49; entered politics 49; Foundation Mem. Convention People's Party (C.P.P.); Regional Chair. C.P.P. (Central Region); M.P. 51-; Dep. Minister of Commerce and Industry 53, of Trade and Labour 54, of Finance 56; Minister of Works 57, of Works and Housing 57-62, of Communications and Works 62-65, of Works 65-66; Chief of State Protocol 62-66; mem. Central Cttee. of C.P.P.
Accra, Ghana.

Benson, Rt. Hon. Edgar John, P.C., M.P.; Canadian chartered accountant and politician; b. 23; ed. Queen's Univ., Kingston, Ontario.
Joined firm England, Leonard and Macpherson (chartered accountants), Kingston, Ontario 52; Asst. Prof. of Commerce, Queen's Univ., Kingston 52-62; M.P. 62-; Parl. Sec. to Minister of Finance 63-64; Minister of National Revenue 64-66; Pres. of Treasury Board 66-April 68; Minister of Finance April 68-; Head of Central Mortgage and Housing Corpn. 68-; Liberal.
119 McMichael Street, Kingston, Ontario, Canada.

Benson, Ezra Taft, M.S.; American agriculturist and religious leader; b. 4 Aug. 1899; ed. Brigham Young Univ., Iowa State Coll., and Univ. of Calif.
Missionary of Church of Jesus Christ of Latter-day Saints in U.K. 21-23; County Agricultural Agent, Univ. of Idaho Extension Service 29, Extension Economist and Marketing Specialist 30-39, Head Dept. of Agricultural Economics and Marketing 31; Sec. Idaho Cooperative Council 33-38; Exec. Sec. Nat. Council of Farmer Co-operatives 39-43; served on several advisory cttees. and nat. boards in field of agriculture 39-; mem. Exec. Cttee. American Inst. of Co-operation 42-52; Chair. Board of Trustees 52; mem. Farm Foundation 46, 50; mem. Nat. Agricultural Advisory Cttee. during Second World War; mem. Nat. Farm Credit Cttee. 40-43; U.S. del. Int. Conf. of Farm Organisations, London 46; U.S. Sec. of Agriculture Jan. 53-61; Dir. Corn Products Inc. 61-; mem. Council of Twelve, Church of Jesus Christ of Latter-day Saints 43-, Pres. Mormon Church European Mission 63-; Republican.
1907 Quincy Street, N.W., Washington, D.C., U.S.A.

Benthall, Michael Pickersgill, C.B.E.; British theatrical producer; b. 8 Feb. 1919; ed. Eton Coll. and Christ Church, Oxford.
Actor 38; Old Vic and Open Air Theatre, London 39; Royal Artillery, rising to rank of Major 39-46; Old Vic tours of Australia 55, U.S.A. and Canada 55, 58, 60, arranged tours to Europe, Middle East and U.S.S.R. 61, Australia 61, North and South America 62; Dir. Old Vic 53-62, Gov. Old Vic Trust 62-; Dir. Bird and Co. (London) Ltd., Trevor Productions Ltd., Popinjay Ltd. Principal productions include *Hamlet* 44, 48, 53, 59, *The Merchant of Venice* 47, *King John, The Taming of the Shrew, Aida* 48, *A Midsummer Night's Dream* 49, 54, *Cymbeline* 49, *As You Like It* 50, *Antony and Cleopatra, Caesar and Cleopatra, The Tempest* 51, *The Millionairess* 52, all plays in Shakespeare Folio, Old Vic 53-58, *Macbeth, Henry V, Twelfth Night, Sganarelle, Tartuffe, The Cenci, The Double Dealer, The Importance of Being Earnest* 59, *Man and Boy* 63, *Macbeth* (Lisbon) 64, *Romeo and Juliet* (Tokyo) 65; wrote scenarios for ballets *Miracle in the Gorbals* 44 and *Adam Zero* 46.
Flat 11, 72 Eaton Square, London, S.W.1, England.

Bentinck, Baron Adolph Willem Carel; Netherlands diplomatist; b. 3 Sept. 1905; ed. State Univ. of Utrecht.
Netherlands Trading Society and Ministry of Finance; Ministry of Foreign Affairs 37-; Chargé d'Affaires, Budapest 39-40, Cairo 40-45; Minister-Counsellor, London 45-50; Minister, Berne 51-56; Netherlands mem. European Comm. for the Saar Referendum; Dep. Sec.-Gen. NATO 56-58; Ambassador to United Kingdom and Iceland 58-63, to France 63-; Netherlands and foreign awards.
Royal Netherlands Embassy, 85 rue de Grenelle, Paris 7e, France.

Bentley, Nicolas Clerihew; British artist and author; b. 14 June 1907; ed. Univ. Coll. School, Heatherley School of Art.
Son of E. C. Bentley; Dir. André Deutsch Ltd.
Publs. *The Tongue-Tied Canary* 48, *The Floating Dutchman* 50, *Third Party Risk* 53, *A Version of the Truth* 60, *The Victorian Scene* 68, etc.
7 Hobury Street, London, S.W.10, England.

Bentley, Phyllis Eleanor, B.A., D.LITT.; British novelist. b. 19 Nov. 1894; ed. Halifax, Cheltenham Ladies' Coll.
Member North Regional B.B.C. Advisory Council 47-53; Fellow Royal Soc. of Literature; Vice-Pres. English centre, P.E.N.; mem. Cttee. of Royal Literary Fund.
Publs. *The World's Bane* 18, *Pedagomania* 18, *Environment* 22, *Cat-in-the-Manger* 23, *The Spinner of the Years* 28, *The Partnership* 28, *Carr* 29, *Trio* 30, *Inheritance* 32, *A Modern Tragedy* 34, *The Whole of the Story* 35, *Freedom, Farewell!* 36, *Sleep in Peace* 38, *Take Courage* 39, *Manhold* 40, *Here is America* 42, *Regional Novel* 42, *The Rise of Henry Morcar* 46, *Some Observations on the Art of Narrative* 46, *The Brontës* 47, *Colne Valley Cloth* 47, *Life Story* 48, *Quorum* 50, *Panorama* 52, *The House of Moreys* 53, *Noble in Reason* 55, *Love and Money* 57, *Crescendo* 58, *Kith and Kin* 60, *The Young Brontës* 60, *Committees* 62, *O Dreams, O Destinations* 62, *Public Speaking* 64, *Enjoy Books* 64, *The Adventures of Tom Leigh* 64, *Tales of the West Riding* 65, *A Man of his Time* 66, *Ned Carver in Danger* 67.
The Grange, Warley, Halifax, Yorks., England.
Telephone: Halifax 81624.

Benton, Thomas Hart; American painter; b. 15 April 1889; ed. Western Military Acad., Acad. Julien, Paris, and Chicago Art Inst.
Began career as newspaper cartoonist; began painting 07; since 17 has specialised as a painter of the American scene and of American history; works include numerous murals on historical subjects at New Britain Museum, New York, Univ. of Indiana, Lincoln Univ., Jefferson City, New York Power Authority, etc.; hon. mem. Argentine Nat. Acad. of Fine Arts, Florence Acad. of Design Arts, etc.; Gold Medal, New York Architectural League 33; D.F.A. (Missouri Univ.), D.Litt. (Lincoln Univ.).
Publ. *An Artist in America.*
3616 Belleview Avenue, Kansas City, Mo., U.S.A.

Benton, William, A.B.; American publishing executive; b. 1 April 1900; ed. Carleton Coll. and Yale Univ. With advertising firm of Lord & Thomas until 29; founder Benton & Bowles, advertising agency, N.Y., Pres. 29-35, Chair. Board until 36, retd.; Vice-Pres. Univ. of Chicago 37-45, Asst. to Chancellor 45, Trustee 46; Asst. Sec. of State for Public Affairs, Dept. of State 45-47; Chair. of Board, *Encyclopaedia Britannica* and Encyclopaedia Britannica Films 42-, Muzak Corpn.; Senator from Conn. 49-52; mem. U.S. del. Inter-American Conf. on War and Peace, Mexico City 45, Constitutional Conf., UNESCO, London 45; Chair. U.S. dels. UNESCO Gen. Confs., Paris 46, Mexico City 47; U.N. Conf. on Freedom of Press, Geneva 48; U.S. mem. Exec. Board, UNESCO 63-; Vice-Chair. Cttee. for Econ. Development 42-45, Trustee 58-; Democrat.
Publs. *This is the Challenge* 58, *The Voice of Latin America* 63.
342 Madison Avenue, New York City 17, N.Y., U.S.A.

Bentov, Mordechai; Israeli journalist and politician; b. 28 March 1900; ed. Inst. of Technology, Warsaw Univ. and Jerusalem Law Classes.
Settled in Palestine 20; Founder and Chief Editor *Al Hamishmar* 43-48 and 49-55; signed Declaration of Independence of Israel 48; mem. Knesset 49-; Minister of Labour and Reconstruction, Provisional Govt. 48-49; Minister of Development 55-61; mem. Jewish Agency Del. to U.N., Lake Success 47; Del. to Zionist Congresses, Round Table Conf. London 39, World Jewish Congress, U.S.A. 44, Geneva 53; mem. Secretariat, United Workers Party (MAPAM); Chair. Economic Affairs Cttee. of the Knesset 51-55; Minister of Housing 66-; mem. World Exec. Hashomer Hatzair, Exec. *Histadrut* and Zionist Action Cttee.; mem. Exec. World Jewish Congress.
Publs. *The Case for Bi-National Palestine* 46, *Israel's Economy at the Crossroads* 65.
Kibbutz Mishmar Haemek, Israel.

Bentwich, Norman, O.B.E., M.C.; British jurist and barrister; b. 28 Feb. 1883; ed. St. Paul's School and Trinity Coll., Cambridge.
Called to the Bar 08; Lecturer Khedivial School of Law 13-15; with British Army (E.E.F.) 15-20; Senior Judicial Officer Occupied Territories Admin. 18-20; Legal Sec. and Attorney-Gen. Palestine 20-31; Dir. LN High Commr. for Refugees from Germany 33-36; with Ministry of Information 40-41; with Air Ministry 42; on mission to Emperor of Ethiopia 43; Prof. Int. Relations Hebrew Univ. of Jerusalem 32-51; Vice-Chair. Jewish Cttee. for Relief Abroad; Chair. United Restitution Office 48-, Nat. Peace Council 44-46, Friends of Hebrew Univ. 46-; Lecturer Hague Acad. of Int. Law, 29, 34, 54; Hon.. LL.D. (Aberdeen and Melbourne Univs.); Hon. Ph.D. (Hebrew Univ. of Jerusalem); Labour.
Publs. *Palestine of the Jews* 18, *England in Palestine* 32, *Palestine* 33 (2nd edn. 47), *The Mandates System* 31, *The Religious Foundations of Internationalism* 33, *Wanderer Between Two Worlds* 42, *Judea Lives Again* 44, *Wanderer in War* 46, *I Understand the Risks* 50, *Israel* 52, *The Rescue and Achievement of Refugee Scholars* 53, *Life of Judah Magnes* 54, *Israel and her Neighbours* 55, *They Found Refuge* 56, *The Jews in Our Time* 60, *Israel Resurgent* 60, *New-Old Land of Israel* 61, *77 Years* 62, *Mandate Memories* 65, *Life of Brigadier Frederick Kisch* 66.
Hollycot, Vale of Health, London, N.W.3; University of Jerusalem, Jerusalem, Israel.

Bentz van den Berg, Pieter Rudolph; Netherlands iron and steel executive; b. 21 Feb. 1901; ed. Nederlandsche Economische Hoogeschool, Rotterdam.
Koninklijke Nederlandsche Hoogovens en Staalfabrieken N.V. (Royal Netherlands Blast Furnaces and Steelworks), Ijmuiden 24-67, Gen. Proxy 31-46, Man. Dir. 46-65, Senior Man. Dir. 65-, mem. Board 67-; Vice-Pres. Economic League for European Co-operation, Pres. Dutch Section; Pres. Central Org. for Economic Relations with Foreign Countries; Dir. various other companies; Commdr. Order of Vasa (Sweden), Knight of the Order Nederlandsche Leeuw.
Van Lennepweg 5, Oosterbeek, Netherlands.

Bentzon, Niels Viggo; Danish composer; b. 24 Aug. 1919; ed. Danish Royal Conservatory.
Musical works: Twelve symphonies, seven piano concertos, opera *Faust*, choral works, five ballets, pieces for chamber orchestra, string quartet and piano.
Solsortvej 33, Copenhagen, Denmark.
Telephone: Fasan 24.

Benya, Anton; Austrian trade union official; b. 12; ed. occupational school.
Electromechanic, shop steward; mem. Exec. Cttee. Metal Workers and Miners Union 48, Chair. 62-; Sec. Austrian Trade Union Fed. 48, Vice-Pres. 59, Pres. 63-; mem. Parl. 56; mem. Exec. Cttee. Socialist Party.
1130 Vienna XIII, Wattmanngasse 68, Austria.

Benz, Ernst Wilhelm, DR. PHIL., LIC. THEOL., D.D. (Marburg); German university professor; b. 17 Nov. 1907; ed. Univs. of Tübingen, Berlin and Rome.
Docent Univ. of Halle-Wittenberg 32-35; Extraordinary Prof. of Church History Univ. of Marburg 35-37; Ordinary Prof. 37-; mem. Acad. of Sciences, Mainz 49, Acad. Septentrionale, Paris 58, American Acad. of Arts and Sciences, Boston 65.
Publs. *Das Todesproblem in der Stoa* 29, *Marius Victorinus und die Entwicklung der abendländischen Willensmetaphysik* 32, *Ecclesia Spiritualis, Die Geschichtsanschauung und Kirchenidee der franziskanischen Reformation* 34, *Der vollkommene Mensch, nach Jakob Boehme* 37, *Nietzsches Ideen zur Geschichte des Christentums* 38, *Emanuel Swedenborg* 48, *Swedenborg in Deutschland* 48, *Leibniz und Peter der Grosse* 48, *Wittenberg und Byzanz* 48, *Die Ost-Kirche und die russische Christenheit* 49, *Die abendländische Sendung der östlichorthodoxen Kirche* 50, *Indische Einflüsse auf die frühchristliche Theologie* 51, *Paulus als Visionär* 52, *Russische Heiligenlegenden* 53, *Bischofsamt und apostolische Sukzession* 53, *Die Ostkirche* 53, *Augustins Lehre von der Kirche* 54, *Schelling, Werden und Wirken seines Denkens* 55, *Schellings Theologische Geistesahnen* 55, *Adam, Der Mythus von Urmenschen* 56, *Geist und Leben der Ostkirche* 57, *Die christliche Kabbala* 58, *Der Prophet Jakob Boehme* 59, *Die Bedeutung der griechischorthodoxen Kirche für das Abendland* 59, *Ideen zu einer Theologie der Religionsgeschichte* 60, *Das Christentum und die nichtchristlichen Hochreligionen, Eine internationale Bibliographie* 60, *Kirchengeschichte in ökumenischer Sicht* 61, *Der Übermensch, Eine Diskussion* 61, *Zen in europäischer Sicht* 62, *Asiatische Begegnungen* 63, *Buddhas Wiederkehr und die Zukunft Asiens* 63, *The Eastern Orthodox Church: Its Thought and Life* 63, *Die protestantische Thebais* 63, *Patriarchen und Einsiedler: der tausendjährige Athos und die Zukunft der Ostkirche* 64, *Schöpfungsglaube und Endzeiterwartung* 65, *Buddhism or Communism, Which holds the Future of Asia?* 65, *Russische Kirche und abendländisches Christentum* 66, *Evolution and Christian Hope* 65, *Les Sources Mystiques de la Philosophie Romantique Allemande* 68; Edited *Sonderhefte Z.R.G.G.*, *Reinkarnation, Moderne Aktivität der nichtchristlichen Hochreligionen, Christliche Brüderschaften, Messianische Kirchen, Sekten und Bewegungen im heutigen Afrika*.
Lutherstrasse 7a, 355 Marburg (Lahn), Hessen, German Federal Republic.
Telephone: 2675.

Benzer, Seymour, B.A., M.S., PH.D.; American biologist; b. 15 Oct. 1921; ed. Brooklyn Coll. and Purdue Univ.

Assistant Prof. of Physics Purdue Univ. 47-53, Assoc. Prof. of Biophysics 53-58, Prof. 58-61, Stuart Distinguished Prof. 61-67; Biophysicist Oak Ridge Nat. Laboratory 48-49; Research Fellow California Inst. of Technology 49-51, Visiting Assoc. 65-67, Prof. of Biology 67-; Fulbright Research Scholar, Pasteur Inst., Paris 51-52; Senior Nat. Science Foundation Research Fellow Cambridge 57-58; Fellow American Asscn. for the Advancement of Science; mem. Nat. Acad. of Sciences, Harvey Soc., Biophysical Soc.; Awards include Sigma Xi Research Award 57 and McCoy Award 65, Purdue Univ. and Gairdner Award of Merit (Canada) 64, Ricketts Award, Univ. of Chicago.
Publs. *The Elementary Units of Heredity* 57, *Induction of Specific Mutations with 5-bromouracil* 58, *Topology of the Genetic Fine Structure* 59, *Topography of the Genetic Fine Structure* 61, *A Change from Nonsense to Sense in the Genetic Code* 62, *On the Role of Soluble Ribonucleic Acid in Coding for Amino Acids* 62, *A Physical Basis for Degeneracy in the Genetic Code* 62, *Adventures in the r11 Region* 66.
Division of Biology, California Institute of Technology, Pasadena, Calif. 91109, U.S.A.
Telephone: 795-7697.

Beran, H.E. Cardinal Joseph, D.D.; Czechoslovak ecclesiastic; b. 29 Dec. 1888; ed. Pilsen and Rome.
Rector of Seminary 33-46; Prof. of Pastoral Theology at Univ. of Prague 39; in Dachau concentration camp June 42-April 45; Archbishop of Prague Nov. 46-; living elsewhere in Czechoslovakia until 63; created Cardinal 65, living in Rome 65-.
Publs. *Ritus missae in libris liturgicis saec. XIII-XVI* 31, *Gabriel Schneider, Founder of the Notre-Dame Congregation of Bohemia* 33, *Psychology and Confessional* 30, *Celibacy of Priests* 41, *Staroplzenské kostely* 47.
Pontificio Collegio Nepomuceno, Via Concordia 1, Rome, Italy.
Telephone: 77-67-61.

Bérard, Armand; French diplomatist; b. 2 May 1904; ed. Ecole Normale Supérieure, Paris and Heidelberg Univ., and French School for Advanced Spanish Studies, Madrid.
Served Berlin 31, Office of Under-Sec. of Foreign Affairs 36, Office of Prime Minister 36-37, Washington 38, Rome (Quirinal) 39; mem. French Del. to Armistice Comm. Wiesbaden 40-42; mem. Underground Foreign Affairs Study Bureau 42; escaped to Algiers 44; Minister-Counsellor in Washington 45; Deputy High Commr. in Germany 49; Diplomatic Adviser to Prime Minister 55; Ambassador to Japan 56-59; Perm. Rep. to UN 59-62, Amb. to Italy 62-67; Perm. Rep. to UN 67-; Commdr. Légion d'Honneur.
740 Park Avenue, New York, N.Y. 10021, U.S.A.
Telephone: RE 4-60-51.

Bérard, Maurice Robert Georges; French banker; b. 17 March 1891; ed. Paris Univ.
Hon. Pres. Bank of Syria and Lebanon, of Radio Orient; Dir. Bank of Paris and the Netherlands; Pres. Friends of Nat. Museum of Modern Art; Vice-Pres. Friends of the Louvre; Pres. Assoc. Léonard de Vinci; Vice-Pres. Amis d'Eugène Delacroix; Gold Medal Aero Club of America and Aero Club of France; Officer Legion of Honour; Croix de Guerre 14-18; D.C.M.; Mérite Agricole.
Publs. *Renoir à Wargemont, Une Famille du Dauphiné.*
7 rue Alfred Dehodencq, Paris 16e, France.
Telephone: TRO 16-94.

Bercher, Harry O.; American business executive; b. 06; ed. Univ. of Illinois.
International Harvester Co. 28-, Vice-Pres. 53-56, Exec. Vice-Pres. 56-62, Pres. 62-; Dir. other companies.
International Harvester Co., 401 N. Michigan Avenue, Chicago, Ill. 60611, U.S.A.

Berchtold, Walter, LL.D.; Swiss transport executive; b. 10 Oct. 1906; ed. Univs. of Zürich, Paris and Nottingham, and in Italy.
At District Court, Winterthur 30; Operating Staff, Swiss Fed. Railways, Richterswil and Wettingen 31, Morges, Chiasso and Bellinzona 32; Personnel Dept. and Secr.-Gen. of Swiss Fed. Railways, Berne 33-38; Financial Editor *Neue Zürcher Zeitung* 38-45; District Man. Swiss Fed. Railways, Zürich 46-50; Pres. of Management Board, Swissair 50-.
Swissair, Balsberg-Kloten, Zürich, Switzerland.

Bercot, Pierre, D. en D.; French businessman; b. 12 July 1903; ed. Lycée Henri IV, Faculté de Droit, Paris, Ecole Nationale des Langues Orientales.
Pres. and Gen. Man. Soc. Anonyme André Citroën 58-.
Home: 45 boulevard Suchet, Paris 16e; Office: 133 Quai André Citroën, Paris 15e, France.

Berenblum, Isaac, M.D., M.SC.; Israeli pathologist and experimental biologist; b. 26 Aug. 1903; ed. Bristol Grammar School and Leeds Univ.
Riley-Smith Research Fellow, Dept. Experimental Pathology and Cancer Research, Leeds Univ. Medical School 27-36; Beit Memorial Research Fellow, Dunn School of Pathology, Oxford Univ. 36-40; Departmental and Univ. Demonstrator in Pathology, Oxford Univ. 40-48; in charge of Oxford Univ. Research Centre of British Empire Cancer Campaign 40-48; Special Research Fellow, Nat. Cancer Inst., Bethesda, Md., U.S.A. 48-50; Visiting Prof. of Oncology, Hebrew Univ., Jerusalem 51-57; Jack Cotton Prof. of Cancer Research, Head of Dept. of Experimental Biology, The Weizmann Inst. of Science, Rehovoth, Israel 50-; Hon. Life mem. New York Acad. of Sciences 58, mem. Israel Nat. Acad. Sciences and Humanities, World Acad. Arts and Sciences.
Publs. *Science versus Cancer* 46, *Man against Cancer* 52, *Cancer Research Today* 67.
Weizmann Institute of Science, Rehovoth, Israel.

Berès, Pierre; French publisher; b. 13; ed. Sorbonne.
Founded Maison Berès 30; published *La Fée Electricité* by Raoul Dufy 42; founded *Sciences* 59, *Art de France* 60; Managing Dir. Hermann Publishing Co.; Croix de Guerre; Chevalier Légion d'Honneur.
40 Avenue Foch, Paris 16e, France.

Bereza, Veniamin Grigorievich; Soviet mining engineer and politician; b. 11; ed. Northern Caucasus Mining and Metallurgical Inst.
Mining engineer 37-45; mem. C.P.S.U. 45-; Chief Engineer, then Dir. Leninogorsk Polymetallurgical Plant 45-54; Dep. Minister of Non-Ferrous Metallurgy, Kazakh S.S.R. 54-57; Chair. South Kazakhstan Regional Econ. Cttee. 57-60; First Dep. Chair. Kazakh Regional Econ. Cttee. 60-65; Minister of Non-Ferrous Metallurgy, Kazakh S.S.R. 65-; mem. Central Cttee. of C.P. of Kazakh S.S.R. 51-; Lenin Prize 61.
Ministry of Non-Ferrous Metallurgy, Alma Ata, Kazakh S.S.R., U.S.S.R.

Berezowski, Cezary, LL.D.; Polish jurist; b. 1898; ed. Warsaw Univ.
Professor of Int. Law, Warsaw Univ. 37-, and Inst. of Law, Polish Acad. of Sciences 56-; Lecturer, Acad. of Int. Law, The Hague 38; mem. Warsaw Scientific Soc.
Publs. *Les sujets non-souverains du droit international* 39, *Organizacja Narodów Zjednoczonych (Organisation of the United Nations)* 46, *Prawo międzynarodowe (International Law)*, *Zagadnienia zwierzchnictwa terytorialnego (Problems of Territorial Authority)* 57, *Międzynarodowe prawo lotnicze (International Air Law)* 64, *La reconnaissance internationale de différents régimes de propriété* 61, *Prawo międzynarodowe publiczne Cz. I (International Public Law Vol. I)* 66, and numerous other works on international law.
Dąbrowskiego 82 m.38, Warsaw, Poland.

Berg, Axel Ivanovich; Soviet scientist; b. 1893; ed. Military Naval Acad.
Specialist in field of radio engineering; Instructor, Naval Engineering School 25-, Leningrad Electrical Engineering Inst. 26-, Mil. Naval Acad., Leningrad 27-; Head, All Union A. S. Popov Soc. of Radio Engineering and Electrical Communications and All Union Scientific Council for Radio-physics and Radio Engineering, U.S.S.R. Acad. of Sciences; Chair. Scientific Council for Complex Problem of Cybernetics, U.S.S.R. Acad. of Sciences 59-; Editor-in-Chief Encyclopedia *Automation in Production and Industrial Electronics*; mem. C.P.S.U. 44-; Hero of Socialist Labour, Order of Lenin, etc.
Publs. include: *Theory of Vacuum Alternating-Current Generators* 25, *Theory of Calculation of Thermionic Generators* 32, *Selected Works* 64.
U.S.S.R. Academy of Sciences, 14 Leninsky Prospekt, Moscow, U.S.S.R.

Berg, Cornelis C.; Netherlands orientalist; b. 1900; ed. Univ. of Leiden.
Teacher, Oriental Coll., Surakarta, Java 27-28; Prof. of Javanese, Univ. of Leiden 29-49, Prof. of Austronesian Linguistics, Univ. of Leiden 49-; Prof. of Bahasa Indonesia, Univ. of Amsterdam 51-; Pres. Union Académique Internationale, Brussels 59-62; mem. Royal Acad. of Netherlands 47-.
Publs. Several books in field of oriental studies, particularly Javanese historiography and Indonesian linguistics.
Gerecht 8, Leiden, Netherlands.

Berg, Fritz; German manufacturer; b. 27 Aug. 1901; ed. Univ. of Cologne.
Pres. Bundesverband der Deutschen Industrie, Cologne, Union des Industries de la Communauté Européenne (UNICE) Brussels, Wirtschaftsverband Eisen-, Blech- und Metallwaren, Düsseldorf, South Westphalian Chamber of Commerce.
Lüdenscheiderstrasse 16, Altena in Westfalen, German Federal Republic.

Berg, Paal Olav; Norwegian jurist; b. 18 Jan. 1873.
Mem. Supreme Court 13; Pres. of Industrial Court 16; Min. of Social Affairs 19-20; Min. of Justice 24-26; Pres. Supreme Court 29-40, 45-46; mem. Governing Body I.L.O. 37-45; Pres. 38-39; mem. Council of Europe Comm. of Human Rights 54-60; mem. Acad. of Sciences, Oslo 34; hon. mem. American Acad. of Arts and Sciences; Hon. LL.D. (Copenhagen and Helsinki Univs.); Grand Cross Norwegian St. Olav's Order 46, Swedish Polar Star Order 48, Finnish White Rose Order 49, Medal for Civil Deed.
Publs. *Arbeidsrett* (Treatise on Labour Legislation) 30, *The Right to Employment* 45, *The Constitution of Norway and Human Rights* 45, *For Godvilje og Rett* (For Good Will and Justice) 46.
(*Died*, 24 *May* 1968.)

Berganza, Teresa; Spanish mezzo-soprano singer; b. 16 March 1935.
Debut in Madrid 55, in England, Glyndebourne 58; has sung in Vienna, Milan, Aix-en-Provence, Netherlands, Edinburgh, Israel, America; has appeared in London at Royal Festival Hall 60, 61, 62, 67, and Royal Opera House, Covent Garden 59, 60, 63, 67; appeared as Rosina in *Il Barbiere di Siviglia*, Covent Garden 67.
Joaquín Maria Lopez 29, Madrid 15, Spain.
Telephone: 2336359.

Bergen, William Benjamin, B.S. AERO.E.; American space engineer and business exec.; b. 29 March 1915; ed. Mass. Inst. of Technology.
Glenn L. Martin Co., Baltimore, Md. (now Martin Co.) 37-; Dir., Special Weapons Dept. 48-49, Chief Engineer 49-51, Vice-Pres. and Chief Engineer 51-53, Exec. Vice-Pres. 53-55, Pres. 59; now Vice-Pres. (Space Div.)

North American Aviation Inc. 67-; mem. American Inst. of Aerospace Sciences; mem. Corpn. of M.I.T.; Dir. Black and Decker Mfg. Corpn. and Maryland Nat. Bank; winner of Lawrence Sperry Award 43.
Merrymans Mill Road, Phoenix P.O., Maryland, U.S.A.

Bergenström, Stig Gullmar, LL.D.; Swedish administrator; b. 3 Dec. 1909; ed. Univ. of Uppsala.
Judiciary service at Court of Justice 34-37; Sec.-Gen. Group of the Swedish Employers' Confed. 37, Asst. Dir. 41, Vice-Dir. 44, Dir. 49-; mem. Employers' Group of Governing Body of ILO 50-; Vice-Pres. Exec. Cttee. of Int. Org. of Employers 52-62, Pres. Exec. Cttee. of Int. Org. of Employers 63-; Chair. Int. Council of Danish, Finnish, Norwegian and Swedish Employers' Confederations.
Swedish Employers' Confederation, S. Blasieholmshamn 4a, Stockholm 16, Sweden.
Telephone: Stockholm 22-56-20.

Berger, Hans, DR. JUR.; German lawyer and diplomatist; b. 29 Sept. 1909; ed. Cologne Univ.
Asst. judge, Cologne 37-39; Adviser to Commr. for Price-Control, Berlin 39-44; Judge, Cologne 45-47, Supreme Court of British Zone of Germany, Cologne 48-49; Pres. Court, Düsseldorf 49-53; Ministerial Dir., Ministry of the Interior, Bonn 53-54; Head, Legal Dept., Foreign Office, Bonn 54-59; Ambassador to Denmark 59-63, to Netherlands 63-65; Sec. of State to the President of the German Fed. Republic 65-.
53 Bonn, Kaiser Friedrichstrasse 16, German Federal Republic.
Telephone: 2-01-01.

Berger, Samuel D., PH.B.; American diplomatist; b. 6 Dec. 1911; ed. Univ. of Wisconsin and London School of Economics.
Served U.K. 42-50; Special Asst. to Director for Security 51-53; Counsellor Tokyo, Wellington (N.Z.), Athens 53-61; Ambassador to Republic of Korea 61-64; Dep. Commdt. Foreign Affairs, Nat. War Coll., Washington, D.C. 64-65; Deputy Asst. Sec. of State for Far Eastern Affairs 65-68; Deputy Amb. to Repub. of Viet-Nam 68-.
2911 33rd Place, N.W., Washington, D.C. 20008, U.S.A.; American Embassy, Saigon, Viet-Nam (A.P.O. San Francisco 96243).

Bergeron, André Louis; French printer and trade unionist; b. 1 Jan. 1922.
Secretary-Gen. of Typographical Union, Belfort 46-47; Force-Ouvrière 47-48, Perm. Sec. Belfort Area 48; Sec.-Gen. Fédération Force Ouvrière du Livre 48-50; Regional Del. Force Ouvrière and mem. Exec. Cttee. 50-56, mem. Bureau de la Confédération 56-63, Sec.-Gen. Force Ouvrière 63-.
Force Ouvrière, 198 avenue du Maine, Paris 14e, France.

Bergeron, Tor Harold Percival, D.SC.; Swedish meteorologist; b. 15 Aug. 1891; ed. Univ. of Stockholm and at Bergen and Leipzig.
Junior meteorologist, Stockholm 20-22, Bergen 22-23; Senior meteorologist, Bergen 25-28, Oslo 29-35; Consultant and Visiting Lecturer, Malta 28, 29, Moscow 30, 32; Senior meteorologist, Swedish Meteorological and Hydrological Inst. 35-41, Chief of Synoptic Section 41-47; Asst. Prof. of Meteorology, Stockholm Univ. 41-47; Prof. of Meteorology Uppsala Univ. 47-60, Emeritus 60-; Leader Project Pluvius, Uppsala Univ. 61-; Consultant/Visiting Prof. Univ. of Calif. (Los Angeles) 47, 57, 59, 61, 63; mem. Royal Swedish Acad. of Sciences, Royal Scientific Soc., Uppsala, Norwegian Acad. of Sciences; Hon. mem. American Meteorological Soc., Royal Meteorological Soc. (London), Swedish Geophysical Soc.; Dr. h.c. (Uppsala); several decorations including Int. Meteorological Org. Prize 66.
Publs. *Wellen und Wirbel an einer quasistationären*

Grenzfläche über Europa (with G. Swoboda) 24, *Über die dreidimensional verknüpfende Wetteranalyse (I & II)* 28, 34, *Richtlinien einer dynamischen Klimatologie* 30, *Physikalische Hydrodynamik* (with others) 33, *On the Physics of Clouds and Precipitation* 35, *Sechssprachiges Meteorologisches Wörterbuch* 39, *General Effects of Ice-Nuclei in Clouds* 39, *The Coastal Orographic Maxima of Precipitation in Autumn and Winter* 39, *A General Survey in the Field of Cloud Physics* 53, *The Problem of Tropical Hurricanes* 54, *Dynamic Meteorology and Weather Forecasting* (with others) 57, *Methods in Scientific Weather Analysis and Forecasting* 59, *Problems and Methods of Rainfall Investigation* 60, *Preliminary Results of Project Pluvius* 61, *The possible role of snow-drift in building up high inland ice-sheets* 65, *On the low-level redistribution of atmospheric water caused by orography* 65.
Meteorologiska Institutionen, Uppsala, Sweden.

Bergersen, Birger Martin, DR.PHIL.; Norwegian teacher and public servant; b. 25 July 1891; ed. Oslo Univ.
Curator Paleontological Museum 21; Asst. at Zoological Laboratory 22; lecturer Norwegian Coll. of Dentistry 25, Dir. of Anatomy Department 29, Prof. of Anatomy 32, Vice-Rector 33-37, Rector 39-42 and 45; on staff of Ministry of Supply and Reconstruction in London 42-45; Minister to Sweden 46, Ambassador 47; Minister of Ecclesiastical Affairs and Educ. 53-60; mem. Oslo City Council 35-45; Chair. Whaling Council 36-54; Pres. Int. Whaling Comm., Chair. Joint Cttee. Norwegian Research Councils 49-54, 60-65; mem. Board of Dirs. Maritime Museum 28-67, Vice-Chair. Oslo Municipal Art Collection 45-64, etc.; mem. Norwegian Acad. of Science in Oslo and Trondheim; Dr. (h.c.) Stockholm Univ.
Publs. Many papers on zoology, comparative anatomy, dental anatomy and pedagogy.
Anton Schjöth's gt. 13, Oslo 4, Norway.
Telephone: Oslo 460373.

Bergesen, d.y., Sigval; Norwegian shipowner; b. 27 April 1893; ed. Oslo Commercial Coll.
Joined firm Sigval Bergesen, Stavanger 16; partner and Head, Shipowning Dept. 18-35; established Sig. Bergesen d.y. & Co., Oslo and Stavanger (of which he is now Senior Partner) 35; co-Dir. A. P. Møller, Copenhagen and Odense Staalskibsvaerft, Odense 34-39; returned to Norway 39; Chair. and Dir. Skibsaktieselskapet Snefonn, Skipsaksjeselskapet Bergehus, A/S Rosenberg Mekaniske Verksted, Stavanger; Chair. of Board, Stavanger Preserving Co. A/S. Teknisk Bureau A/S, A/S Sigmalm, A/S Sigbulk, A/S Sigship, A/S Siganka; mem. Board of Trustees Norges Skipshypotek A/S; Commdr. Order of St. Olav, Commdr. Order of Dannebrog, Légion d'Honneur, Médaille de l'Alliance Française, Les Palmes d'Officier de L'Instr. Publique (France), Knight's Cross of the Order of the Redeemer (Greece), Royal Order of George I.
Home: Huk Avenue 15, Bygdøy Oslo; Office: Berghus, Drammensveien 106, Oslo, Norway.

Berggolts, Olga Fedorovna; Soviet poetess; b. 1910; ed. Leningrad Univ.
Member Communist Party 40-; Order of Red Banner of Labour 60; Order of Lenin 67; State Prize 50.
Publs. *Poems* 34, *February Diary* 42, *Leningrad Poem* 42, *Leningrad Notebook* 44, *In Memory of the Defenders* 45, *Your Path* 46, *Verses and Poems* 48, *Pervorrossiisk* 50; Plays: *They Lived in Leningrad* 44, *On Our Earth* 47, *Loyalty* 54; Biography: *Day Stars* 59, *This is Leningrad Calling . . .* 64.
U.S.S.R. Writers Union, Leningrad Branch, Leningrad, U.S.S.R.

Berggren, Thommy; Swedish actor; b. 37; ed. The Pickwick Club (private dramatic school), Atelierteatern, Stockholm, and Gothenburg Theatre.

Gothenburg Theatre 59-63; Royal Dramatic Theatre, Stockholm 63-.
Plays acted in include: *Gengangaren* (Ibsen) 62, *Romeo and Juliet* 62, *Chembalo* 62, *Who's Afraid of Virginia Woolf* 64.
Films acted in include: *Pärlemor* 61, *Barnvagnen* (The Pram) 62, *Kvarteret Korpen* (Ravens End) 63, *En söndag i september* (A Sunday in September) 63, *Karlek 65* (Love 65) 65, *Elvira Madigan* 67.
c/o Svenska Filminstitutet, Kungsgatan 48, Stockholm C., Sweden.

Berghes, Ferry von; German business executive; b. 15 Nov. 1910; ed. Gymnasium, Düsseldorf, and Univs. of Cologne, Cambridge, Heidelberg and Bonn.
Prussian State Admin. 35-39; war service 39-45; mem. Board of Dirs. Deutsche Erdöl-AG 39-62, Pres. 62-; mem. Board of Dirs. Mannesmann AG 39-; management of family forestry estate 45-59; Sec. of State, Ministry of Econs. and Transport, Rheinland-Pfalz 59-62; mem. Board of Dirs. Albingia 64-.
Office: DEA-Haus, Hamburg 13, Mittelweg 180; Home: Hamburg 39, Leinpfad 22, German Federal Republic.

Bergman, Ingmar; Swedish theatrical and film producer; b. 14 July 1918; ed. Stockholm Univ.
Producer Royal Theatre, Stockholm 40-42; script-writer and producer Swedish Film Co. 40-44; Theatre Dir. Helsingborg 44-46, Gothenburg 46-49, Malmö 54-63; Chief, Royal Dramatic Theatre, Stockholm 63-66; Erasmus Prize 65; freelance producer of several films, including *Port of Call* 48, *Summer Interlude* 50, *Waiting Women* 52, *Summer with Monika* 52, *Sawdust and Tinsel* 53, *A Lesson in Love* 53, *Journey into Autumn* 54, *Smiles of a Summer Night* 55, *The Seventh Seal* 56-57, *Wild Strawberries* 57, *The Face* 58, *The Devil's Eye* 61, *As in a Glass* 61, *Winter Light* 63, *The Silence* 63, *A Proposito di tutte queste Donne* 64, *The Cannibals* 65, *Persona* 66, *The Hour of the Wolf* 67, and also *Prison Thirst, So Close to Life* and *The Virgin Spring*; author of plays *A Painting on Wood, The City.*
c/o Royal Dramatic Theatre, Stockholm, Sweden.

Bergman, Ingrid; Swedish actress and film star; b. 29 Aug. 1915; ed. Stockholm.
Starred in Swedish, German, American, Italian, British and French films, including *Intermezzo, Edna Natt, Casablanca, Bells of St. Mary's, Stromboli, Anastasia, Indiscreet, Inn of Sixth Happiness, The Road to Rome, Goodbye Again, The Visit, The Yellow Rolls-Royce*; has also appeared on the stage in New York, Rome, Paris and London, including *A Month in the Country* (London) 65, *More Stately Mansions* (Eugene O'Neill), Los Angeles, New York 67-68; Order of Vasa.
Choisel, Seine-et-Oise, France.

Bergman, Samuel Hugo, PH.D.; Israeli philosopher; b. 25 Dec. 1883.
Philosopher and critic; Dir. Jewish Nat. and Univ. Library in Jerusalem until 35; Prof. of Philosophy Hebrew Univ., Rector 35-38, Dean Faculty of Humanities 52-53; hon. mem. Inst. Int. de Philosophie; hon. D.Phil. (Hebrew Univ.); mem. Israel Academy of Sciences and Humanities.
Publs. *Untersuchungen zum Problem der Evidenz der inneren Wahrnehmung* 08, *Das philosophische Werk Bolzanos* 10, *Das Unendliche und die Zahl* 13, *Jawne und Jerusalem* 19, *The Philosophy of Kant* 27, *Der Kampf um das Kausalgesetz in der jüngsten Physik* 29, *The Philosophy of Maimon* 32, 67, *Present-day Thinkers* 35, *Theory of Knowledge* 41, *Pensadores Judíos Contempordneos* 44, *Science and Belief* 45, *Judiska Religionsfilosofer i vdr generation* 50, *Introduction to Logic* 53, *God and Man in Modern Thought* 56, *Thinkers and Believers* 59, *Faith and Reason* 61, *Men and Ways, Philosophical Essays* (Hebrew) 67.
51 Ramban Road, Jerusalem, Israel.
Telephone: 3-2534.

Bergmans, Pieter; Netherlands publisher; b. 9 Nov. 1908; ed. Coll. "Ruwenberg", St. Michielsgestel, Netherlands.
W. Bergmans (publishers and booksellers), Tilburg 28-46; Managing Dir. Elsevier Publishing Co., Amsterdam 46-.
Van Merlenlaan 30, Heemstede, Netherlands.

Bergquist, Kenneth Paul, B.S.; American air force officer; b. 21 Nov. 1912; ed. U.S. Military Acad. and National War Coll.
Air Attaché, Athens 47-49; Dir. of Operations, Air Defence Command, Colorado 50-55; Dir. of Operations, Air Force H.Q., Washington, D.C. 55-58; Commdr. Electronic Systems Div., Hanscom Field, Mass. 58-62; Commdr. Air Force Communications Service 62-65; Legion of Merit, Air Medal, Bronze Star Medal, Greek Order of the Phoenix.
H.Q.s A.F.C.S., Scott Air Force Base, Illinois, U.S.A.

Berinson, Zvi, SC. DIP., B.A.; Israeli judge; b. 07; ed. Scots Coll., Safad, Israel, Jesus Coll., Cambridge, and Gray's Inn, London.
Lecturer, Scots Coll. 29-31; Legal Adviser and Dir. Municipal Dept. Gen. Fed. of Jewish Labour, Palestine 36-49; Dir.-Gen. Ministry of Labour, Israel Govt. 49-53; Judge, Supreme Court 54-; Lecturer on Labour Law and Social Insurance, Hebrew Univ. 53-; Chair. Israel Soc. of Criminology and League of Socs. for the Rehabilitation of Offenders; Pres. Public Council for the Prevention of Noise and Air Pollution in Israel; Vice-Chair. Int. Prisoners' Aid Asscn.; head of Israel Del. to ILO 49-53, 58-59.
The Supreme Court of Israel, Jerusalem, Israel.

Berio, Luciano; Italian composer; b. 24 Oct. 1925; ed. Liceo Classico and Conservatorio G. Verdi, Milan.
Founder of Studio de Fonologia Musicale, Italian Radio; Teacher of Composition and Lecturer at Mills Coll. (Calif.), Darmstadt, and Harvard Univ.; now Prof. of Composition, Juilliard School of Music, N.Y.
Compositions include: *5 Variazioni* 51, *Nones for Orchestra* 54, *Alleluyah I and II* 55-57, *Thema (Omaggio a Joyce)* 58, *Circles* 60, *Visage* 61, *Epifanie* 63, *Passagio* 62, *Laborintus* 65.
53 Potter Place, Weehawken, N.J., U.S.A.
Telephone: 201-863-8283.

Beriosova, Svetlana; British ballerina; b. 24 Sept. 1932.
With Grand Ballet de Monte Carlo 47, Metropolitan Ballet 48-49, Sadler's Wells Theatre Ballet 50-52, Sadler's Wells Ballet (now Royal Ballet) 52-; leading roles in *Swan Lake, The Sleeping Beauty, Giselle, Coppélia, Trumpet Concerto, Pastorale, The Shadow, Rinaldo and Armida, The Prince of the Pagodas, Antigone, Baiser de la Fée, Diversions, Perséphone, Images of Love* and other ballets.
Royal Opera House, Covent Garden, London, W.C.2, England.

Beritashvili, Ivane Solomonovich; Soviet physiologist; b. 1884; ed. Tbilisi Seminary and St. Petersburg Univ.
Experimental work under Prof. N. Wedensky 10-14; Prof. Physiology State Univ. Tbilisi 19-61; Dir. Inst. of Physiology, Georgian Acad. of Sciences 39-51, Scientific Leader; mem. U.S.S.R. Acad. of Sciences 39-, Georgian Acad. of Sciences 41-, U.S.S.R. Acad. of Medical Sciences 44-; Hon. mem. N.Y. Acad. of Sciences 59-; Pres. Physiological Soc., Georgian S.S.R.; State prize-winner; U.S.S.R. Acad. of Sciences Pavlov Prize; Order of Lenin; Order of Red Banner of Labour (twice).
Publs. *Zur Erregungsrhythmik des Nerven- und Muskelsystems* 13, *Labyrinth and Neck Tonic Reflexes* 15, *Allg. Charakteristik der Tätigkeit des Z.N.S.* 22, *The Individually-acquired Activity of the Central Nervous System* 32, *Studies of Individual Behaviour in Dogs* 34-35, *The Main Forms of Nervous and Psycho-nervous Activity* 47,

General Physiology of Nervous and Muscle Systems Vols. 1 and 2 47-48, *Nervous Mechanisms of Spatial Orientation of Mammals* 59, *Nervous Mechanisms of Behaviour of the Higher Vertebrates* 61, *Studies on the Nature of Man in Ancient Georgia* (Chaps. IV-XIV) 61, *Neural Mechanisms of Higher Vertebrate Behavior* 65.
Presidium of Georgian Academy of Sciences, Tbilisi, Georgian S.S.R., U.S.S.R.

Berkeley, Lennox, B.A.; British composer; b. 12 May 1903; ed. Gresham's School, Holt, and Merton Coll., Oxford.
Studied music in Paris with Mlle. Nadia Boulanger 27-31; mem. B.B.C. Music Dept. staff 42-45; awarded Collard Fellowship in Music 46; now Composition Prof. Royal Acad. of Music London.
Principal works incl.: Orchestra: two Symphonies, *Divertimento, Nocturne,* Concerto for piano and orchestra, Concerto for two pianos and orchestra, Concerto for violin and chamber orchestra, Five Pieces for violin and orchestra, *The Winter's Tale* (suite); Chamber Music: Two string quartets, string trio, Sonata for viola and piano, Trio for violin, horn and piano, Sextet for clarinet, horn and string quartet, Piano: Sonata, six Preludes, four Concert studies; Vocal: *Four Poems of St. Teresa* for contralto and strings, *Stabat Mater* for six soloists and twelve instruments, *Five Poems of W. H. Auden, Autumn Legacy,* Song Cycle for voice and piano, *Mass* for five voices, *Songs of the Half-Light* for high voice and guitar; Opera: *Nelson, A Dinner Engagement, Ruth, Castaway.*
8 Warwick Avenue, London, W.2, England.
Telephone: AMBassador 3922.

Berkin, John Phillip, C.B.E., M.A.; British oil executive; b. 23 Oct. 1905; ed. Taunton School and Sidney Sussex Coll., Cambridge.
Joined Royal Dutch/Shell Group 27 and served in Far East, London and U.S.A.; Vice-Pres. Asiatic Petroleum Corpn. New York 42-46; Dir. Shell Petroleum Co. Ltd. 53-, Man. Dir. 57-66; Dir. Bataafse Petroleum Maatschappij N.V. 57-; Dir. "Shell" Transport and Trading Co. Ltd. 57-; Dir. Industrial Reorganisation Corpn. 66-, National & Grindlays Bank Ltd. 66-.
Greenhill, Hurstwood Lane, Haywards Heath, Sussex, England.

Berle, Adolf Augustus, Jr., A.M., LL.B.; American lawyer and diplomatist; b. 29 Jan. 1895; ed. Harvard.
Attorney 16-; 2nd Lt. U.S. Infantry 17-19; Expert, American Comm. to Negotiate Peace 18-19; Prof. Law, Columbia Univ. 27-; Chamberlain, New York City 34-37; Asst. Sec. of State 38-44; Ambassador to Brazil 45-46; senior partner, Berle & Berle 47-; Lecturer Air War Coll. 51-; Chair. Pres. Kennedy's Task Force on Latin America Jan.-July 61; Consultant to Sec. of State 61-; Chair. American Molasses Co. 46-61; Democrat.
Publs. *Studies in Corporation Finance* 38, *Modern Corporation and Private Property* 32, *The 20th Century Capitalist Revolution* 54, *Tides of Crisis* 57, *Power without Property* 59, *Latin America: Diplomacy and Reality* 62, *The American Economic Republic* 63.
70 Pine Street, New York, N.Y., U.S.A.

Berliet, Paul; French industrialist; b. 5 Oct. 1918; ed. Lycée Ampère, Lyon.
Deputy Dir.-Gen. Société Automobiles M. Berliet 54-58, Admin. Dir.-Gen. 58-62, Pres. Dir.-Gen. 62-; Pres. Société Africaine des Automobiles M. Berliet 58-; Chevalier Légion d'Honneur.
La Cerisaie, rue Carnot, 69 Saint-Cyr-au-Mont-d'Or, France.

Berlin, Irving, D.MUS.; American composer and song writer; b. 11 May 1888 in Russia; ed. public schools in New York City.
Went to U.S.A. 93; Pres. Irving Berlin Music Corpn.; Medal of Merit for *This is the Army,* special gold medal for *God Bless America.*

Songs include: *Alexander's Ragtime Band, Oh, How I Hate to get up in the morning, Always, Reaching for the Moon, White Christmas, God Bless America, Blue Skies, What'll I do, All Alone, Remember, Everybody's Doing It, There's No Business Like Show Business, How Deep is the Ocean,* among hundreds of others; musicals: *This is the Army* (comedy), *Easter Parade* (film), *Annie Get Your Gun, Miss Liberty* and *Call Me Madam* (stage musicals).

Irving Berlin Music Corporation, 1650 Broadway, New York City, N.Y., U.S.A.

Berlin, Sir Isaiah, Kt., C.B.E., M.A., F.B.A.; British university teacher; b. 6 June 1909; ed. St. Paul's School and Corpus Christi Coll., Oxford.

Lecturer in Philosophy, New Coll., Oxford 32; Fellow of All Souls Coll., Oxford 32-38; Fellow and Tutor New Coll. 38-50; attached to British Information Service N.Y. 41; First Sec., British Embassy, Washington 42-46, Moscow 45; Lecturer, Oxford Univ. 47-; Sub-Warden New Coll. 49-50; Research Fellow, All Souls Coll. 50-57; Chichele Prof. of Social and Political Theory, Oxford Univ. 57-67; Visiting Lecturer, Harvard 49, 51, 53, Ford Research Prof. 62, Mellon Lecturer, Washington, D.C. 65; Mary Flexner Lecturer, Bryn Mawr Coll. 52-53; Auguste Comte Memorial Lecturer, London School of Economics 53; Northcliffe Lecturer, University Coll., London; Alexander White Prof., Chicago Univ. 55; Gov. Univ. of Jerusalem; Prof. of Humanities, City Univ. of New York 66-67; Pres. Wolfson Coll., Oxford 66-.

Publs. *Karl Marx* 39, *The Hedgehog and the Fox* 53, *The Inevitability of History* 54, *The Age of Enlightenment* 56, *Two Concepts of Liberty* 58, *The Life and Opinions of Moses Hess* 59, *Studies in the Philosophy of History* 68. Wolfson College, Oxford, England.

Bernabei, Ettore; Italian journalist and broadcasting executive; b. 21; ed. Univ. of Florence.

Director *Il Giornale del Mattino* (Florence) 51-56, *Il Popolo* (Rome) 56-60; Editor *La Nazione del Popolo* (Florence); Dir.-Gen. Radiotelevisione Italiana 61-. Radiotelevisione Italiana, Viale Mazzini 14, Rome, Italy.

Bernabò-Brea, Luigi; Italian archaeologist; b. 27 Sept. 1910; ed. Univs. of Genoa and Rome and Italian School of Archaeology, Athens.

Inspector, Archaeological Museum, Taranto 38; Supt. of Antiquities for Liguria 39-41, for Eastern Sicily 41-; Dir. Archaeological Museum, Syracuse 41-; founder and Dir. Aeolian museum, Lipari; Dir. Italian archaeological mission to Poliochni, Lemnos; Dr. h.c. Clermont Ferrand.

Publs. *Corpus vasorum Antiquorum, Museo Civico Genova-Pegli* 42, *Gli scavi nella Caverna delle Arene Candide di Finale Ligure,* Vol. I 46, Vol. II 56, *La scultura funeraria tarantina* 52, *L'Athenaion di Gela e le sue terrecotte architettoniche* 52, *Akrai* 56, *Sicily before the Greeks* 58, *Poliochni, città preistorica nell' Isola di Lemnos,* Vol. I 64, and other books in collaboration with M. Cavalier.

Museo Archeologico Nazionale, Piazza del Duomo 14, Syracuse, Sicily, Italy.

Bernadotte, Count Sigvard Oscar Fredrik (son of King Gustav VI of Sweden, *q.v.*); Swedish industrial designer; b. 7 June 1907; ed. Uppsala Univ., Royal Acad. of Arts, Stockholm and Munich.

Designed silverware, textiles, bookbindings, glass, porcelain 29-; Partner, Bernadotte & Bjørn (Industrial Design) 49, own firm Bernadotte Design AB 64-; Awarded Gold Medal, Silver Medal and Diploma at the Milan Triennale.

Villagatan 10, Stockholm, Sweden.

Bernal, John Desmond, M.A., F.R.S.; British physicist; b. 10 May 1901; ed. Stonyhurst Coll., Bedford School and Emmanuel Coll., Cambridge.

Research Davy Faraday Laboratory 23-27; Lecturer in Structural Crystallography Cambridge 27-34, Asst. Dir. Research in Crystallography 34-38; Prof. of Physics Birkbeck Coll. 38-63, Prof. of Crystallography, Univ. of London 63-; gave scientific advice to Min. of Home Security 39-42; Scientific Adviser to Chief of Combined Operations 42-45; Chair. of Scientific Advisory Cttee. at Ministry of Works 45-47; mem. Govt. Advisory Cttee. for Scientific and Technical Information 65-66; Royal Medal of Royal Soc. 45; Lenin Peace Prize 53; Grotius Silver Medal 59; mem. Acad. of Sciences of Poland 54; mem. Acad. of Sciences of Hungary 54; mem. Romanian Acad. of Sciences 54; mem. Lenin Peace Prize Cttee.; Hon. Prof. Moscow Univ. 57; mem. U.S.S.R. Acad. of Sciences 58; mem. Acad. of Science, Bulgaria 58; Hon. Dr. Humboldt Univ. 59; regular mem. Czechoslovak Acad. of Sciences 60; Corresp. mem. German Acad. of Sciences 62; Fellow, Emmanuel Coll., Cambridge 65; mem. Norwegian Acad. of Sciences 66.

Publs. *The World, The Flesh, and the Devil* 29, *The Social Function of Science* 39, *The Freedom of Necessity* 49, *The Physical Basis of Life* 51, *Marx and Science* 52, *Science and Industry in the Nineteenth Century* 53, *Science in History* 54 (3rd edition 65), *World Without War* 58 (2nd ed. 61), *Origin of Life* 67. Birkbeck College, Malet Street, London, W.C.1., England.

Bernal y Garcia Pimentel, Ignacio, PH.D.; Mexican anthropologist; b. 13 Feb. 1910; ed. Loyola Coll., Montreal, Canada, National Univ. and National School of Anthropology, Mexico.

Director, Dept. of Anthropology, Mexico City Coll. 48-59; Prof., National Univ. of Mexico 49-; Sec. Soc. Mexicana de Antropología 54-62; Perm. Del. to UNESCO, Mexico 55-56; Dir., Nat. Museum of Anthropology, Mexico 62-68, Nat. Inst. of Anthropology and History, Mexico 68-, Teotihuacan Project 73-; Regular mem. Academia Mexicana de la Historia, Foreign Fellow, American Acad. of Arts and Science; mem. other Mexican and foreign anthropological orgs.; decorations from Netherlands, France, Italy, Belgium, Denmark and German Fed. Repub.

Publs. *Introduction to Archaeology* 52, *Mesoamerica* 53, *Huitzilopochtli Vivo* 57, *Pintura Precolombina* 58, *Tenochtitlan en una Isla* 59, *Correspondencia de Bandelier* 60, *Toynbee y Mesoamérica* 60, *Bibliografía y Etnografía* 62, *Mexico before Cortez* 63, *Teotihuacan* 63, *Mexican Wall Paintings* 63, *Mexican Art* 63; various sections *Handbook of Middle American Indians* 65, *El Museo de Antropología* 67, *La Cerámica de Monte Alban* 67. Tres Picos 65, Mexico City 5, D.F., Mexico.

Bernard, Sir Dallas Gerald Mercer, Baronet, cr. 54; British banker; b. 22 March 1888.

Man. Dir. Jardine Matheson & Co. Ltd., Hong Kong, China and Japan 22-28; mem. Legislative Council, Hong Kong 26-28, Exec. Council 27-28; Chair. Hong Kong Gen. Chamber of Commerce 23, 26-27; Chair. Court of Dirs. Hong Kong and Shanghai Banking Corpn. 24, 26-27; Dir. Matheson & Co. Ltd. 28-42, Alliance Assurance Co. Ltd. 31-42, British and Chinese Corpn. Ltd. 28-42, Chinese Central Railways 28-42; mem. London Consultative Cttee., Hong Kong and Shanghai Banking Corpn. 59-64; Dir. Bank of England 36-49, Deputy Gov. Bank of England 49-54; Dir. Courtaulds Ltd. 54-62, 64-65, Chair. 62-64; Chair. British Bank of the Middle East 54-65, Dir. 65-67; Chair. Jordan Currency Board 54-57.

Sandylands, Englefield Green, Surrey, England.

Bernard, Jean Jacques; French playwright and novelist; b. 30 July 1888; ed. Lycée Carnot and Univ. of Paris.

Publs. *Le Voyage à deux* 09, *La Joie du Sacrifice* 12, *La Maison épargnée* 19, *Le Feu qui reprend mal* 21,

Martine 22, *Le Printemps des autres* 24, *L'Invitation au voyage* 24, *Denise Marette* 25, *L'Ame en peine* 26, *Le Secret d'Arvers* 26, *Le Roy de Malousie* 28, *A la recherche des coeurs* 31, *La Louise* 31, *Les Soeurs Guédonec* 31, *Jeanne de Pantin* 33, *Nationale 6* 35, *Deux hommes* 37, *Le Jardinier d'Ispahan* 39, *Marie Stuart, Reine d'Ecosse* 42, *Louise de la Vallière* 43, *La Librairie Jalin* 45, *Notre-Dame d'en haut* 51, *La Route de France* 51, *Mon grand ami* 51, *De Tarse, en Citicie* 61 (plays); *L'Epicier* 14, *Les Enfants jouent . . .* 19, *Les Tendresses menacées* 24, *Le Roman de Martine* 29, *Madeleine Landier* 33, *Le Pain rouge* 47, *Marie et le Vagabond* 49 (novels); *Témoignages* 33, *Le Camp de la mort lente* 45, *Mon Père Tristan Bernard* 55 (essays), *Mon Ami le Théâtre* (essays) 58, *Saint-Paul ou la fidélité* 62.
22 rue Eugène Flachat, Paris 17e, France.

Bernard, Karl; German lawyer and banker; b. 8 April 1890; ed. classical school and Univs. of Freiburg, Grenoble, Paris, Munich, Berlin, and Halle.
Junior Judge 16-20; Judge in Supreme Court for Economic Affairs 20-29; Permanent Head of Ministerial Dept. in Reich Board of Trade 29-35; dismissed by Hitler for political reasons; Man. Dir. Frankfurt Mortgage Bank 36-48; Pres. Board of Dirs. Bank Deutscher Länder 48-57; Hon. Dr. of Laws 54.
Im Burgfeld 237, 6 Frankfurt am Main 21, German Federal Republic.
Telephone: Frankfurt 571293.

Bernard, Lucien, M.D.; French public health official; b. 30 Nov. 1913; ed. Faculté de Paris and Inst. Pasteur, Paris.
Director of Health Services and Prof. of Microbiology, School of Medicine, Rheims 41-44; Chief of Mobile Laboratory for Epidemics, Paris 45; Chief of Communicable Diseases branch and Int. Health at Ministry of Public Health 46-56; Asst. to Dir.-Gen. of Public Health 56-58; Dir. of Health Services, Regional Office for South East Asia, World Health Org. (WHO) 58-63, Dir. in the office of the Dir.-Gen., Geneva and Personal Rep. of the Dir.-Gen. at Regional Office for Africa 63-64; Asst. Dir.-Gen. WHO Feb. 64-; Lauréat, Acad. nationale de Médicine.
Publs. on microbiology, epidemiology and public health administration.
World Health Organization, avenue Appia, 1211 Geneva, Switzerland.
Telephone: 34-60-61.

Bernardes, Carlos Alfredo; Brazilian diplomatist; b. 16; ed. Univ. of Rio de Janeiro.
Brazilian Foreign Service 39-, Lisbon 44-46, Paris 48-51, Washington 59-61; mem. Brazilian Mission to U.N. 52-59; Pres. of Board of Governors of Int. Atomic Energy Agency (IAEA) 58; Secretary-Gen. Brazilian Ministry of External Affairs 62-63; Perm. Rep. of Brazil to UN July 63-64; Personal Rep. of UN Sec.-Gen. in Cyprus 65-67.
c/o Ministry of Foreign Affairs, Rio de Janeiro, Brazil.

Bernardini, Gilberto, DR. PHYS.; Italian physicist; b. 20 Aug. 1906; ed. Univs. of Pisa and Florence and Kaiser Wilhelm Inst., Berlin-Dahlem.
Prof. of Physics, Univ. of Bologna 39, Univ. of Rome 45; Research Prof. of Physics, Univ. of Ill., U.S.A. 50; Visiting Prof., Columbia Univ. 48-49 and 49-50; Dir. of Research in S.C. Div. European Org. for Nuclear Research (CERN), Geneva 57-; Dir. of S.C. Div. CERN, Geneva 58-59; Dir. of Research CERN 60-62, Univ. of Rome 63-64; Dir. Scuola Normale Superiore, Pisa 64-; Vice-Pres. Italian Inst. for Nuclear Studies; Pres. Italian Physical Soc.; Nat. mem. Accad. Nazionale dei XL, Accad. Pugliese delle Scienze 67; Fellow American Physical Soc.; mem. Accad. Bologna, Modena and Bari; awarded Int. Medal Augusto Righi, Somaini Prize 55,

Presidential Gold Medal (Italy); hon. degree, Univ. of Rochester.
Scuola Normale Superiore, Pisa, Italy.
Telephone: 43554.

Bernáth, Aurél; Hungarian painter and writer on art; b. 13 Nov. 1895; ed. grammar school, Budapest, Nagybánya Art School, Vienna, Berlin, Italy, France, U.K., etc.
Prof. Coll. of Fine Arts.
Works in many public and private collections in Hungary and abroad; Kossuth Prize 48; Outstanding Artist of Hungarian People's Republic 64. Most prominent works: *Riviera, Morning, Mother and Child, Violin, The Luncheon, The Kovács Family, On the Balcony, Portrait of Lőrinc Szabó*.
Publs. *Irások a művészetről, A Múzsa Körül* (essays on art), *Igy Éltünk Pannoniában* (novel), *Utak Pannoniából* (novel) 60.
Stollár Béla u. 4, Budapest V, Hungary.
Telephone: 125-524.

Bernbaum, Maurice Marshall; American diplomatist; b. 15 Feb. 1910; ed. Harvard Univ. and Univ. of Chicago.
Social work, Chicago 32-35; Economist, U.S. Tariff Comm., Washington 35-36; served Foreign Service Vancouver, Singapore, Caracas, Managua, Quito, Washington, Caracas 36-55; Dir. Office of South American Affairs. Dept. of State 55-59; Minister-Counsellor, Buenos Aires 59-60; Ambassador to Ecuador 60-65, to Venezuela 65-.
American Embassy, Caracas, Venezuela.

Berner, Endre Qvie, DR. TECHN.; Norwegian chemist; b. 24 Sept. 1893; ed. State Univ. of Technology at Trondheim.
Lecturer in Organic Chemistry, Trondheim 22-23; Prof. of Chemistry, Univ. of Oslo 34-61; mem. Norwegian Chemical Society (Chair. Trondheim Div. 31-33, Chair. Oslo Div. 39-40; Pres. 46-50, Hon. mem. 66), Royal Norwegian Society of Sciences, Norwegian Acad. of Science, Royal Swedish Acad. of Engineering Sciences; hon. foreign mem. Society of Chemical Industry; Vice-Pres. Int. Union of Chemistry 51-55.
Publ. *Textbook of Organic Chemistry* (in Norwegian) 6th edn. 64, and many scientific papers.
Gyldenlovesgate 13, Oslo 2, Norway.

Bernet Kempers, Karel Phillipus, DR.PHIL.; Netherlands musicologist; b. 97; ed. Univ. of Munich.
Prof. History of Music, Royal Conservatory, The Hague 29-49; Prof. Amsterdam Conservatory 34-53; Lecturer in Musicology, Univ. of Amsterdam 37-46, Prof. 46-65; Sec. Royal Dutch Society of Musicians 34-41, Chair. 45-65, Hon. Pres. 65-; Vice-Pres. Netherlands Council of Musicians 50-65; mem. Council of Concertgebouw Orchestra 56-; Editor *Preludium-Concertgebouwniews* 45-; Pres. Consulting Cttee. Int. Musicological Soc., Dutch Soc. of Musical History; Officer of Order of Orange-Nassau.
Publs. *Jacobus Clemens von Papa und seine Motetten* 28, *De Italiaanse Opera van Peri tot Puccini* 29, *Muziekgeschiedenis* 32 (6th edition 65), *Muziek in den Ban der letteren* 35, *Beknopte Geschiedenis van het Kerklied* (with Prof. Dr. G. v. d. Leeuw) 48, *Meesters der Muziek* (5th edition) 55, *Panorama der Muziek* 48, *Complete Works of Clemens von Papa* (Editor).
Harmoniehof 221, Amsterdam, Netherlands.

Bernhard, Leopold Frederik Everhard Julius Coert Karel Godfried Pieter, H.R.H. Prince; Prince of the Netherlands; b. Germany 29 June 1911; ed. Gymnasiums at Zuellichau and Berlin, and Univs. of Lausanne, Munich and Berlin.
Studied law for six years, graduated 34; worked in executive capacity with I.G. Farben, Paris, and with Netherlands Trading Co.; married Princess Juliana of

the Netherlands 37, assuming Netherlands nationality and rank of Captain in Netherlands Army; studied at Netherlands Staff Coll.; appointed mem. State Council; resisted German invasion of Holland, May 40; evacuated family to England and returned to Continent, with army until fall of France; returned to England and qualified as pilot; appointed Hon. Air Commodore R.A.F.V.R. 41; subsequently Chief Netherlands Liaison Officer with British Forces, Col., later Major-Gen. and Chief of Netherlands Mission to War Office; visited war fronts in North Africa and Normandy; maintained liaison throughout the war between Netherlands Underground and the Allied Govts.; appointed Supreme Commdr. (Lieut.-Gen.) Netherlands Armed Forces 44, and played important part in liberation of Holland; decorated for his services in this operation by H.M. King George VI (G.B.E.); subsequently resigned from office of Supreme Commdr.; appointed Chair. Joint Chiefs of Staff, mem. Council for Mil. Affairs of the Realm, and mem. Joint Defence, Army, Admiralty and Air Force Councils; also Inspector-Gen. of Army, Navy and Air Force; Admiral, General R. Neths. A.F., General (Army) 55; Hon. Air Vice-Marshal R.A.F. 55-; Dir. Netherlands Trade and Industries Fair, Royal Blast Furnaces (Ijmuiden), Royal Dutch Airlines (K.L.M.), Netherlands Bank for Nat. Recovery and of Royal Fokker Aircraft Industries; has made business and goodwill visits to North, South and Central America, West and South Africa, Canada, and Netherlands Antilles, and has greatly contributed to post-war expansion of Netherlands trade; founder and Dir. Prince Bernhard Fund for the Advancement of Arts and Sciences in the Netherlands; Cttee. Int. Equestrian Fed.; Pres. European Cultural Foundation; Regent Praemium Erasmianum Foundation; Hon. mem. Royal Aeronautical Soc., Royal Inst. Naval Architects; Hon. mem. Aeromedical Soc.; Hon. degrees Univs. of Utrecht, Delft, Montreal, British Columbia, Amsterdam and Michigan; many decorations.
Palace of Soestdyk, Baarn, Netherlands.

Bernhard, Wilhelm; French (b. Swiss) scientist; b. 8 Nov. 1920; ed. Grammar School, Berne, Univs. of Berne and Geneva.
Assistant to Prof. C. Oberling 48-60; worked with Profs. Leroux and Pasteur Vallery-Radot, Dir. of Research Centre Nat. de la Recherche Scientifique 61-; Head of Electronic Microscopy Lab., Inst. de Recherches sur le Cancer, Villejuif 48-; mem. Conseil Nat. de la Recherche Scientifique 60-; Dir. Inst. de Recherche sur le Cancer, Villejuif; Grand prix scientifique de la ville de Paris 64; Ehrlich Prize 67.
Institut de Recherche sur le Cancer, Villejuif (Val-de-Marne), France.

Bernshteyn, Sergey Natanovich; Soviet mathematician; b. 80; ed. Paris Univ. and Göttingen Univ., Germany.
Instructor, Kharkov Inst. 07-20, Prof. 20-33; Corresp. mem. U.S.S.R. Acad. of Sciences 24-29, mem. 29-; Prof. Leningrad Polytechnic Inst. 33-41, Prof. Leningrad Univ. 34-41; Hon. mem. Moscow Mathematical Soc. 40-; Foreign mem. Bulgarian and French Acads. of Sciences; State Prize 41; Hon. Dr. Algiers Univ. 44, Paris Univ. 45.
Publs. *Probability Theory* 46, *Collected Works* 4 vols. 52-61, *The Analytical Nature of Solutions of Differential Equations of Ecliptical Type* 56.
Institute of Mathematics, U.S.S.R. Academy of Sciences, Ul. Vavilova 28, Moscow, U.S.S.R.

Bernstein, Leonard; American conductor, composer and pianist; b. 25 Aug. 1918; ed. Boston Latin School, Harvard and Curtis Inst. of Music.
Assistant at Berkshire Music Center 42, mem. of Faculty 48-55, Head, Conducting Dept. 51-55; Asst. Conductor N.Y. Philharmonic Orchestra 43-44; Dir.

N.Y. City Symphony 45-48; Musical Adviser Israel Philharmonic Orchestra 48-49; Prof. of Music, Brandeis Univ. 51-56; Co-conductor N.Y. Philharmonic 57-58, Musical Dir. 58-; conducted with leading orchestras of America and in the capitals of Europe; music lectures on "Omnibus" television programme 55-; Dir. N.Y. Phil. Young People's Concerts on nationwide television 58-; tours in S. America, Europe, Near East and U.S.S.R.
Compositions: *Clarinet Sonata* 42, *Jeremiah* (symphony) 42, *On the Town* 45, *Symphony No. 2, The Age of Anxiety* 49, *Trouble in Tahiti* (one-act opera) 52, *Wonderful Town* 53, *On the Waterfront* 54, *Serenade for Violin, Strings and Percussion* 54, *Candide* 56, *West Side Story* 57, *Symphony No. 3—Kaddish* 63, *Chichester Psalms* for chorus and orchestra 65, and other scores for stage and songs.
Publs. *The Joy of Music* 59, *Leonard Bernstein's Young People's Concerts* 62, *The Infinite Variety of Music.*
c/o N.Y. Philharmonic Orchestra, Philharmonic Hall, New York, N.Y. 10023, U.S.A.

Bernstein, Peretz; Israeli businessman, journalist and politician; b. 12 June 1890; ed. Meiningen Gymnasium.
Businessman in the Neths. 13-35; Sec. Neths. Zionist Organisation 22, Pres. 30-34; Editor Neths. *Zionist Weekly* 24-30; Chief Editor *Haboker*, Tel-Aviv 37-45, and 58-64; mem. Exec. Jewish Agency and Head of Dept. of Trade and Industry 46-48; Minister of Trade, Industry and Commerce, Provisional Govt. of Israel 48-49; Minister of Commerce and Industry Dec. 52-55; Pres. Gen. Zionist Org. in Israel 44-47 and 49-61, Liberal Party 61-; mem. Knesset (Israel Parl.) 49-64.
Publs. *Der Antisemitismus als Gruppenerscheinung* 26 (publ. in English as *Jew-Hate as a Sociological Problem* 51), *Der Zionistische Gedanke auf Irrwegen* 31, *Over Joodsche Problematiek* 35.
25 Ben Maimon Boulevard, Jerusalem, Israel.
Telephone: 36152.

Bernstein, Robert Louis; American publisher; b. 1 Jan. 1923; ed. Harvard Univ.
U.S. Army Air Force 43-46; with Simon & Schuster (book publishers) 46-57, Gen. Sales Man. 50-57; Random House Inc. 58-, Vice-Pres. (Sales) 61-63, First Vice-Pres. 63-65, Pres. 65-.
Office: Random House, Inc., 457 Madison Avenue, New York, N.Y. 10022; Home: 20 Murray Hill Road, Scarsdale, N.Y., U.S.A.

Bernstein, Sidney Lewis, LL.D.; British television executive; b. 30 Jan. 1899.
Films Adviser, Ministry of Information 40-45; Liaison, British Embassy, Washington 42; Chief, Film Section, Allied Forces Headquarters, N. Africa 42-43; Chief, Film Section, SHAEF 43-45; Chair., Granada Group Ltd., Granada Television Ltd., Granada Theatres Ltd., Granada Publishing Ltd.; Hon. LL.D.
36 Golden Square, London, W.1, England.

Berrill, Norman John, F.R.S., F.R.S.C., PH.D., D.SC.; Canadian zoologist; b. 28 April 1903; ed. Bristol and London Univs.
Lecturer in Zoology, Univ. of London 25-27; Lecturer in Physiology, Univ. of Leeds 27-28; Asst. Prof. in Zoology, McGill Univ. Montreal 28-31, Assoc. Prof. 31-46, Chair. Dept. of Zoology 37-47, Strathcona Prof. of Zoology 47-65, Research Assoc. 65; now Lecturer in Biology, Swarthmore Coll., Pennsylvania.
Publs. *The Tunicata* 51, *The Living Tide* 51, *Journey into Wonder* 52, *Sex and the Nature of Things* 53, *Man's Emerging Mind* 55, *The Origin of Vertebrates* 55, *You and the Universe* 57, *Growth, Development and Pattern* 61, *Worlds Apart* 65, *Biology in Action* 66, *Inherit the Earth* 66, *Life of the Ocean* 66.
Home: 410 North Swarthmore Avenue, Swarthmore, Pa. 19081, U.S.A.
Telephone: 215-544-1762 (Swarthmore).

Berro, Pedro P.; Uruguayan lawyer, journalist and diplomatist; b. 29 June 1903.
Former Prof. of Int. Law, Naval Coll. of Uruguay; fmr. mem. Faculty for Labour Law, Uruguayan Coll. of Law and Social Sciences; fmr. Sec. Uruguayan National Party; fmr. Editor *Diarios de la Democracia* (daily), *El País* (daily); fmr. Editor-in-Chief *El Debate*; fmr. Chief Political Editor *Tribuna*; Perm. Rep. of Uruguay to UN 66-.
Permanent Mission of Uruguay to the United Nations, 301 East 47th Street, New York, N.Y. 10017, U.S.A.

Berry, Walter (husband of Christa Ludwig, *q.v.*); Austrian baritone singer; b. 8 April; ed. Vienna School of Engineering and Vienna Music Acad.
Student mem. Vienna State Opera 50-53, ordinary mem. 53-; awarded title *Kammersinger* by Austrian Govt. 63; Guest singer at openings of opera houses in Vienna, Munich, Berlin, Tokyo, New York (Metropolitan Opera), at festivals in Salzburg, Munich, Aix-en-Provence, Lucerne, Netherlands, Stockholm, Saratoga; appearances in New York, Chicago, Buenos Aires, Tokyo, Paris, Berlin, Munich, etc.; Prizes from Music Concourses in Vienna, Verviers and Geneva.
Roles include: Wozzeck, Ochs von Lerchenau, Barak, Olivier, Escamillo, Pizarro, Telramund, Klingsor, Wotan, Sachs, Amonasro, Scarpia, Figaro, Guglielmo, Leporello.
Office: Klosterneuburg, Gschwendt 21, Niederösterreich, Austria; Home: Lucerne, Seefeldstrasse 11, Switzerland.

Berryman, John; American author; b. 25 Oct. 1914; ed. South Kent School, Columbia Univ., and Clare Coll., Cambridge.
Member Faculty, Wayne Univ., Detroit 39-40, Harvard 40-43; Instructor in English, Lecturer, Fellow in Creative Writing, Princeton Univ., intermittently 43-49; Lecturer, Univ. of Washington 50; Rockefeller Fellow in Humanities 44-46; Hodder Fellow, Princeton Univ. 50-51; Guggenheim Fellow 52-53; Elliston Lecturer in Poetry, Univ. of Cincinnatti 52; numerous prizes including Shelley Memorial Award 49, American Acad. Award 50, Harriet Monroe Poetry Prize, Univ. of Chicago 57.
Publs. include: *Poems* 42, *The Dispossessed* (poems) 48, *Stephen Crane* 50, *Unfortunate Traveller*, *77 Dream Songs* 64, *Berryman's Sonnets* 67.
272 Nassau Street, Princeton, N.J., U.S.A.

Bersell, Petrus Olof Immanuel, A.B., B.D., D.D., L.H.D., LL.D., TH.D.; American church executive; b. 6 May 1882; ed. Augustana Coll., Illinois, Augustana Theological Seminary.
Coll. Instructor and teacher 99-05; ordained Ministry 06; Pastor various Lutheran churches 06-35; Gen. Sec. American Lutheran Conference 30-34, Vice-Pres. 34-36, mem. Exec. Cttee. 30-; Pres. Nat. Lutheran Council 41-45; Vice-Pres. Lutheran Brotherhood of America 18-22; Vice-Pres. and Dir. Lutheran Brotherhood Inst. 27-43; Dir. Augustana Coll. and Theological Seminary 33-51; Pres. Lutheran Augustana Church Home Missions Board 38-48; mem. Board Foreign Missions, United Lutheran Church, etc.; Chair. Service Comm. Nat. Lutheran Council 41-48, Service Bureau 48-; Chair. Lutheran Service Comm.; Pres. Augustana Lutheran Church 35-51, Emeritus 51-; mem. Exec. Cttee. Lutheran World Federation 48-52; Chair. U.S. Admin. Cttee. 47-53; mem. Central Cttee. World Council of Churches 48-61; del. World Council of Churches Assembly, Amsterdam 48, Evanston 54, New Delhi 61; mem. General Board, Nat. Council of Churches 51-56; Assoc. Editor official organ of Lutheran Brotherhood, *The Bond*; knighted by King of Sweden 48; Commdr. Royal Order of North Star, Commdr. Order of the Lion of Finland.

Publs. *Christmas Voices, At the Dawn of Day, The Home Altar.*
5320 Brookview Avenue, Minneapolis, Minn. 55424, U.S.A.
Telephone: Minneapolis 926-5264.

Bertaux, Pierre, DR. ès L.; French civil servant; b. 8 Oct. 1907; ed. Ecole Normale Supérieure and Paris Univ.
Dir. of Spoken Word, Radiodiffusion d'Etat 34-36; Personal Sec. at Ministries of Foreign Affairs and Education 36-37; Prof. Faculty of Arts, Rennes; Prof. Faculty of Arts, Toulouse 38-39; served French Army 39-40; active in Resistance Movement; Commr. of the Republic, Toulouse 44-46; Dir. of Secretariat of Minister of Transport and Public Works 46-47; Prefect of Rhone 47-48; Inspector-Gen. of Administration 48-49; Dir.-Gen. of Sûreté Nationale 49-51; Senator of French Sudan 53-55; Pres. and Dir.-Gen. Acrow-France 55-58; Prof. Univ. Lille 58-64, Prof. Sorbonne, Paris 64-; Officier de la Légion d'Honneur, Compagnon de la Libération.
Publs. *Hoelderlin* 36, *Allemagne de Guillaume II* 62, *Geschichte Afrikas* 62, *Mutation der Menschheit* 63, Bertaux-Lepointe Dictionaries 67-68.
106 rue Brancas, 92 Sèvres, France.
Telephone: Paris 027-0023.

Bertelsen, Hans Valdemar; Danish diplomatist; b. 5 Feb 1906; ed. Univ. of Copenhagen.
Entered Foreign Service 31; has served Political, Legal, Admin. and Economic Sections, Ministry of Foreign Affairs, and served Danish Del. to L.N. 32 and 33; served Brussels 37-38, Rome 40-42; Head Labour Office, Danish Consulate-Gen. in Hamburg 42-44 (arrested 44-45); served Stockholm 45 and Washington 46-49; Chief of Section, Ministry of Foreign Affairs 49-54, concurrently Chair. dels. for trade and payment agreements with France, Belgium, Netherlands, Indonesia, Norway, Sweden and Britain; Minister to Mexico 54-58, Ambassador 58-59, concurrently Minister to Costa Rica, Cuba, Dominican Republic, El Salvador, Haiti, Honduras, Nicaragua and Panama; Ambassador to China 59-62; special assignment, Ministry of Foreign Affairs 64; Amb. to Lebanon 67-, also accredited to Syria, Jordan, Saudi Arabia, Kuwait, and Cyprus.
Royal Danish Embassy, Immeuble Minkara, Rue Clemenceau, P.O. Box 5190, Beirut, Lebanon.
Telephone: 251-397, 251-398, 296-070.

Berthoin, Jean; French politician; b. 12 Jan. 1895.
Served 14-18 war; entered civil service 19, served in Tunisia, Algeria and in various districts in France; Dir. to Cabinet (Colonies, Marine, Interior), Sarraut Govt. 32-36, Inspector-Gen. 36-38; Sec.-Gen. Ministry of the Interior 38-40; Treas., Dept. de l'Isère (and active in Resistance during 39-45 war) 40-47, Dept. de la Seine 47-48; mem. Parti Radical Socialiste; Senator for Isère 48-; Minister of the Interior, Queuille Govt. 50, of Education, Mendès-France Govt. 54-55, Faure Govt. 55-56, de Gaulle Govt. 58-59; Minister of Interior Jan. 59; mem. European Parl.; Grand Officier Légion d'Honneur, Croix de Guerre and nine citations.
67 avenue Niel, Paris 17e, France.

Bertinelli, Virginio; Italian lawyer and politician; b. 31 Aug. 1901; ed. Univ. of Pavia.
Fmr. lawyer; Prefect of Como 45-46; Ed. *Il Popolo Comasco* 47; mem. Chamber of Deps. 48-; fmr. Under Sec. of Educ.; Under Sec. of Defence 55-58, Under Sec. Ministry of Transport 58-62; Minister of Labour and Social Security 62-63; Minister without Portfolio 66-; Pres. Social Democrat Parl. Group, Pres. Foreign Parl. Cttee.
Via XX Settembre 30, Como, Italy.
Telephone: 24005.

Bertoli, Monsignor Paolo; Vatican diplomatist; b. 1 Feb. 1908.
Ordained priest 30; Sec. Apostolic Nunciature, Belgrade 33-38, France 38-42; fmr. Head of Mission for Emigration to South America; Chargé d'Affaires a.i., Apostolic Nunciature, Port-au-Prince, Haiti 44-46; Counsellor, Apostolic Nunciature, Berne 46-52; Titular Archbishop of Nicomedia 52-; Apostolic Del. in Turkey 52-53, Apostolic Nuncio in Colombia 53-59, in Lebanon 59-60; France 60-.
Nonciature Apostolique, avenue Président Wilson 10, Paris 16e, France.
Telephone: 727-58-34.

Bertrand, Alfred; Belgian trade union official and politician; b. 26 May 1913.
Worked in mines at Waterschei for eight years; active in youth section of Christian Workers' Union, later becoming Pres.; involved in other trade union work; M.P. for Hasselt-Saint-Trond; Minister of Communications 61-65, of Public Health 65-66, of Communications 66-; Christian Social Party.
Bevingensteenweg, 4 Sint Truiden, Brussels, Belgium.

Berzegov, Nukh Aslancherievich; Soviet politician; b. 1925; ed. Krasnodar Pedagogic Inst.
Member Communist Party of Soviet Union 44-; various posts in education in Adygeisk Autonomous Region 48-52; Head, Adygeisk Regional Dept. of Education 52-57; Vice-Chair. Adygeisk Regional Soviet 57-58; Sec. Adygeisk Regional Cttee. of C.P.S.U. 58-60, First Sec. 60-; Deputy to U.S.S.R. Supreme Soviet.
Adygeisk Regional Committee, Communist Party of the Soviet Union, Maikop, U.S.S.R.

Beschev, Boris Pavlovich; Soviet politician; b. July 1903; ed. Leningrad Inst. of Railway Engineers.
Engineer on October Line 35-36; Dir. Orjonikidze Line (Northern Caucasus) 37-40; Dir. October Line (Leningrad) 40; Dir. Dept. of N.W. Lines and Dir. Kuibyshev Line 41-44; Deputy People's Commissar and subsequently Deputy Minister of Railways 44-48; Minister of Railways of U.S.S.R. 48-; Deputy, U.S.S.R. Supreme Soviet; mem. Central Cttee. of C.P.S.U. 52-; awarded Order of Lenin (six times), Order of the Red Banner of Labour, Hero of Socialist Labour and other decorations.
Ministry of Railway Transport, 2 Novo-Basmannaya ulitsa, Moscow B-174, U.S.S.R.

Bessemoulin, Jean; French meteorologist; b. 18 March 1913; ed. Univ. de Paris à la Sorbonne and Univ. de Nancy.
National Meteorological Office 35-; Head successively of Banne d'Ordanche, Nancy and Clermont-Ferrand Meteorological Stations; Head South East Meteorological Region 42-45; Head, Forecast Division, Service Météorologique Métropolitain 45-48, Asst. Dir. 58-61; Asst. to Dir. of National Meteorology 61-64, Dir. of National Meteorology 64-; Principal Del. of France to the Fourth Congress of the World Meteorological Org.; mem. numerous W. M. O. Cttees. and Meteorological Societies; Officier Légion d'Honneur, Croix de Guerre avec palme, and other decorations.
Météorologie Nationale, 1 quai Branly, Paris 7e, France.

Bessis, Marcel Claude; French hematologist; b. 15 Nov. 1917; ed. Lycée Janson de Sailly and Univ. de Paris (School of Medicine).
Head of Research Laboratory of Nat. Centre for Blood Transfusions 47-65; Dir. Inst. of Cell Pathology, Bicêtre Hospital 65-; mem. Nat. Cttee. for Scientific Research 64-; Laureate Acad. des Sciences et de Médecine; Editor *Nouvelle Revue française d'Hématologie* 46-; Hon. mem. Harvey Soc. 63, Hon. Fellow American Coll. of Physicians; Chevalier Légion d'Honneur.
Publ. *Cytology of Blood and Blood-forming Organs* 56.
Institut de Pathologie Cellulaire, Hôpital Bicêtre, 94

Kremelin-Bicêtre; Home: 2 rue Saint Simon, Paris 7e, France.
Telephone: Littré 48-74 (Home); RAM 6195 (Office).

Bessmertnova, Natalya Igorevna; Soviet ballet dancer; b. 19 July 1941; ed. Bolshoi Theatre Ballet School.
Artiste of Bolshoi Theatre Ballet 61-.
Important roles include: Mazurka and 7th Valse (*Chopiniana*), Pas de trois (*Swan Lake*), variations (*Baiadere*), Giselle (*Giselle*), The Muse (*Paganini*, music by Rachmaninov), Florin (*Sleeping Beauty*), Leila (*Leila and Medjnun*, by Balasanyan), Shirin (*Legend of Love*), Odette-Odile (*Swan Lake*), Girl (*Le Spectre de la Rose*), Maria (*The Fountain of Bakhtchisaray*).
State Academic Bolshoi Theatre of U.S.S.R., 1 Ploshchad Sverdlova, Moscow, U.S.S.R.

Best, Charles Herbert, C.B.E., M.A., M.D., D.SC., F.R.C.P., F.R.C.P.(C.), F.R.C.P.(E.), F.R.S.C., F.R.S.; Canadian physiologist; b. 27 Feb. 1899; ed. Toronto and London Univs.
Fellow Physiology Dept. Toronto Univ. 20-21; Research mem. Connaught Laboratories 22-32; Asst. Prof. of Physiological Hygiene 26-29, Acting Dir. of Dept. 29-41; Prof. of Physiology and Dir. of Dept. 29-; Assoc. Dir. Connaught Laboratories 32-41; Consultant 41-; Research Assoc. 23-41 and Dir. and Prof. Banting-Best Dept. of Medical Research 41-; a Scientific Dir. Int. Health Div. of Rockefeller Foundation 41-43 and 46-48; Surgeon-Capt. R.C.N.V.R. and Dir. R.C.N. Medical Research Unit; co-discoverer of Insulin with Dr. Banting; Vice-Pres. British Diabetic Asscn. 34-; First Hon. Pres. Canadian Diabetic Asscn. 52; Hon. mem. American Diabetes Asscn. 40-, Pres. 48-49, mem. of Council, Hon. Pres. 60-; mem. American Philosophical Soc.; Dir. Roscoe B. Jackson Laboratory 55-; Pres. Int. Union of Physiological Sciences 53-, Asscn. of American Physicians 54, Pontifical Acad. of Sciences 55; Foreign Assoc. Nat. Acad. of Sciences; Foreign mem. The Royal Swedish Acad. of Science 61; mem. Advisory Cttee. on Medical Research of WHO; hon. mem. European Asscn. for the Study of Diabetes; Flavelle Medal Royal Soc. of Canada 50; Dale Medal of Soc. for Endocrinology 59; Joslin Medal, New England Diabetes Asscn. 65; Hon. D.Sc. (Chicago, Oxford, Laval, Maine, Northwestern), Hon. Sc.D. (Cambridge), Dr. h.c. (Paris), Hon. M.D. (Amsterdam, Louvain, Liège, Caracas, Thessaloniki, Freie Univ. of Berlin), Hon. LL.D. (Dalhousie, Queen's, Melbourne and Edinburgh); Hon. mem. Acad. of Medicine of Toronto 66; Legion of Merit (U.S.), and many other awards.
Publs. *The Human Body* (with N. B. Taylor) 32, *The Physiological Basis of Medical Practice* (with N. B. Taylor) 37, *Selected Papers of Charles H. Best* 63.
Charles H. Best Institute, 112 College Street, Toronto; and 105 Woodlawn Avenue W., Toronto 7, Ont., Canada.
Telephone: 928-2586.

Beste, Niklot, D.THEOL. h.c., DR.PHIL., D.D.; German theologian; b. 30 June 1901; ed. Univs. of Marburg, Innsbruck, Breslau and Rostock.
Curate and later Pastor in Benthen bei Lübz 27-32; Pastor to the *Volksmission* in Schwerin 32-33; Pastor in Neubukow 33-46; Bishop of the Evangelical-Lutheran Church of Mecklenburg 46-; Deputy Administrator United Evangelical-Lutheran Church of Germany.
Schleifmühlenweg 4, Schwerin (Mecklenburg), German Democratic Republic.

Besterman, Theodore Deodatus Nathaniel, D.LITT., LL.D., D.ès L.; British scholar; b. 18 Sept. 1904; ed. Lycée de Londres, and Oxford Univ. (extra-mural).
Investigation Officer and Editor, Society for Psychical Research 27-35; special lecturer, London School of

Librarianship 31-38; Joint Editor, Oxford Books on Bibliography, Gen. Editor Asscn. of Special Libraries 42-46; founder and editor *Journal of Documentation* 44-47; Editor and Exec. Officer *British Union Catalogue of Periodicals* 44-46; Editor *Studies on Voltaire and the Eighteenth Century* 55-; successively Counsellor, World Bibliographical and Library Centre, and Head, Dept. for the Exchange of Information, UNESCO 46-49; Hon. Treas. Folk Lore Society 28-29; mem. of Council 26-37; Dir. Inst. et Musée Voltaire, Les Délices, Geneva 52-; Pres. Int. Congress on the Enlightenment 63-67, Int. Soc. for Eighteenth-century Studies 68-; Chevalier Légion d'Honneur.

Publs. *The Beginnings of Systematic Bibliography* 35 (3rd edn. 52), *A World Bibliography of Bibliographies* (2 vols.) 39-40, 4th edn. (5 vols.) 65, *Early Printed Books to the End of the Sixteenth Century: a Bibliography of Bibliographies* 40, 2nd edn. 61, *British Sources of Reference and Information* 47, *Index Bibliographicus* (2 vols.) 51, 52, *Voltaire's Notebooks* (2 vols.) 52, *Voltaire's Correspondence* (107 vols.) 52-65, *St. Jean de Brébeuf, les Relations de ce qui s'est passé au pays des Hurons* 57, *Lettres de la Marquise du Châtelet* (2 vols.) 57, *Lettres d'amour de Voltaire à sa nièce* 57, *Voltaire on Shakespeare* 67, and many other works.
68 Pall Mall, London, S.W.1, England.

Bestor, Arthur Eugene; M.A., PH.D., LL.D.; American historian; b. 20 Sept. 1908; ed. Yale Univ.
Instructor, Yale 30-31, 34-36, Asst. Prof. Columbia Univ. 37-42; Asst. Prof. Humanities, Stanford Univ. 42-45, Assoc. Prof. History 45-46; Assoc. Prof. of History, Univ. of Illinois 47-51, Prof. 51-62; Harmsworth Prof. of American History, Oxford Univ. 56-57; Prof. of History, Univ. of Washington 62-; Fulbright Visiting Prof., Univ. of Tokyo 67.
Publs. *Education and Reform at New Harmony* 48, *Backwoods Utopias* 50, *Educational Wastelands* 53, *The Restoration of Learning* 55.
Department of History, University of Washington; and 4553 55th Avenue, N.E., Seattle, Wash. 98105, U.S.A. Telephone: 206-LA4-4202.

Betancourt, Rómulo; Venezuelan politician; b. 22 Feb. 1908; ed. Caracas Univ.
Imprisoned while still a student by the Vicente Gómez régime; exiled to Colombia; returned to Venezuela to lead anti-Communist underground left-wing movement 36; again in exile 39-41; organised Acción Democrática 41-; Pres. Revolutionary Governing Junta on overthrow of Medina Angarita 45; forced again into exile by Pérez Jiménez régime 48-58; President of Venezuela Feb. 59-64.
Berne, Switzerland.

Betancur-Mejía, Dr. Gabriel; Colombian international civil servant; b. 26 April 1918; ed. Javeriana Univ., Bogotá, Syracuse Univ., U.S.A., and School of Advanced International Studies, Washington.
Former Sec. of Technical and Econ. Affairs to Pres. of Colombia; fmr. Founder and Dir. Colombia Inst. for Advanced Training Abroad (ICETEX); Prof. of Finance and Int. Trade; fmr. Chair. Special Comm. for Programming and Devt. of Education, Science and Culture in Latin America, Org. of American States; fmr. Dir.-Gen. Colombian Asscn. of Univs.; Asst. Dir-Gen. of UNESCO (in charge of educational activities) 63-66; Minister of Education, Colombia 55-56, 66-.
Apartado Aéreo 6113, Bogotá, Colombia.

Beteta, Ramón, PH.D.; Mexican lawyer, economist, diplomatist and writer; b. 01; ed. Univ. of Texas and National Univ. of Mexico.
Professor of Econs., Nat. Univ. of Mexico 25-42; Gen. Dir. Statistics Dept., Ministry of Economy 33-35; Under-Sec. for Foreign Affairs 36-40, of the Treasury 41-45; Pres. Board of Dirs. Nacional Financiera 41-52, Nat. Railways of Mexico 46-52; Sec. of Treasury 46-52;

Gov. from Mexico of Int. Monetary Fund and World Bank 46-52; Ambassador to Italy 53-58; Minister to Greece 55-58; Editor *Novedades, Diario de la Tarde,* and *The News* 58-64; weekly TV programme; numerous awards.
Publs. *Tierra del Chicle* 29, 51, *La Mendicidad en México* 31, *Programa Económico y Social de México* 34, *En Defensa de la Revolución* 35, *Tres Años de Política Hacendaria* 49, *Pensamiento y Dinámica de la Revolución Mexicana* 50, 51, *El Desarrollo Económico de México en los Ultimos Años* 55, *Disertaciones sobre México desde Europa* 55, *Entrevistas y Pláticas* 61, *Camino a Tlaxcalantongo* 61.
Campos Eliseos 204, Mexico 5, D.F., Mexico.

Bethe, Hans Albrecht, PH.D.; Alsatian-born American physicist; b. 2 July 1906; ed. Goethe Gymnasium (Frankfurt/Main) and Frankfurt/Main and Munich Univs.
Lecturer German Univs. 28-33, Manchester and Bristol Univs. (England) 33-35; Asst. Professor Cornell Univ. 35-37, Prof. 37-; Dir. Theoretical Physics Div. Los Alamos Scientific Laboratory 43-46; mem. President's Science Advisory Cttee. 56-59; mem. American Philosophical Soc., Nat. Acad. of Sciences, American Physical Soc. (Pres. 54), American Astronomical Soc.; foreign mem. Royal Soc. (London); Draper Medal 48, Max Planck Medal 55; Presidential Medal of Merit 46, Enrico Fermi Award 61; Nobel Prize for Physics 67.
Publs. *Mesons and Fields* 55; contributions to *Handbuch der Physik* 33, *Review of Modern Physics* 36-37, etc., and to scientific journals.
Laboratory of Nuclear Studies, Cornell University, Ithaca, N.J., U.S.A.

Betjeman, John, C.B.E.; English poet and author; b. 06; ed. Marlborough and Magdalen Coll., Oxford.
Heinemann Award; Duff Cooper Award; William Foyle Poetry Prize (twice); Queen's Medal for Poetry 60.
Publs. *Mount Zion, Ghastly Good Taste, Continual Dew, An Oxford University Chest, Antiquarian Prejudice, Old Lights for New Chancels, Selected Poems, First and Last Loves, A Few Late Chrysanthemums, The English Town in the Last Hundred Years, Collected Poems, Summoned by Bells* (autobiog. in verse), *English Churches* (with Rev. Basil Clarke), *High and Low*; *Guides* to Cornwall, Devon and (with John Piper) Shropshire, Buckinghamshire and Berkshire.
The Mead, Wantage, Berkshire, England.

Bettelheim, Charles, DR. en D., L. ès L.; French economist; b. 20 Nov. 1913; ed. Paris Univ.
Dir. Centre for Social Studies and Int. Relations, Ministry of Labour, Paris 44-48; French rep. Conf. on Trade and Employment 47; Prof. of Political Economy at Ecole Pratique des Hautes Etudes 48-; Head of U.N. Mission for Technical Assistance to Indian Govt. 55-56; Prof. at Ecole Nationale d'Administration; Prof. at Inst. d'Etudes du Développement Economique et Social 58-64; mem. French Sociological Inst.; Dir. of the review *Problèmes de Planification* and Centre d'Etudes de Planification Socialiste.
Publs. *La Planification Soviétique* 39, *Les Problèmes théoriques et pratiques de la Planification* 46, *L'Economie Allemande sous le Nazisme* 46, *Bilan de l'Economie Française de 1918 à 1946* 47, *Esquisse d'un Tableau Economique de l'Europe* 48, *Initiations aux recherches sur les idéologies économiques et les réalités sociales* 48, *Emploi et Chômage devant la Théorie Economique* 49, *L'Economie Soviétique* 50, *Auxerre en 1950* 50, *Théories contemporaines de l'emploi* 51, *Nouveaux aspects de la théorie de l'emploi* 52, *Long-Term Planning Problems* 56, *Foreign Trade and Planning for Economic Development* 56, *Studies in the Theory of Planning,* Bombay 59, *Some Basic Planning Problems* 60, *Teoría de la Planificación* 61, *Problemas Teóricos y Prácticos de la Planificación* 62, *L'Inde Indépendante* 62, *Planification et Croissance*

accélérée 64, *La construction du socialisme en Chine* 65, *Los Marcos Socioeconómicos y la organización de la planificación Social* 66, *Problèmes Théoriques et Pratiques de la Planification* 66, *La Transition vers l'Economie Socialiste* 68.
17 rue des Feuillantines, Paris 5e, France.
Telephone: 633-36-38.

Bettencourt, André; French politician; b. 21 April 1919.
General Counsellor for Lillebonne 46-; mem. Chamber of Deputies 51-; Vice-Pres. Foreign Affairs Comm. Nat. Assembly; Sec. of State to Presidency of the Council 54-55; Sec. of State for Transport 66-67; Sec. of State, Ministry of Foreign Affairs 67-May 68, Minister of Posts and Telecommunications May 68-; Chevalier Légion d'Honneur, Croix de Guerre.
Assemblée Nationale, Paris 7e, France.

Beue Tann, DIPL.ING.; Chinese politician; b. 5 Dec. 1900; ed. Technische Hochschule, Dresden.
Commercial Counsellor and Counsellor, Chinese Embassy, Berlin 33-41; Sec.-Gen. Chinese Defence Supplies Inc., Washington 42-43; Vice-Minister, Ministry of Econs., Nat. Govt. of China; Dir. Bank of Communications 43-46; Vice-Minister, Ministry of Communications; Chair. Board of Dirs., Postal Remittance and Savings Bank 46-49; Exec. Dir. Int. Monetary Fund (IMF) 50-.
Int. Monetary Fund, Washington, D.C. 20431, U.S.A.

Beugel, Ernst Hans van der; Netherlands business executive; b. 2 Feb. 1918; ed. Univ. of Amsterdam.
Government service 45-60; Sec., Econ. Cttee. of the Cabinet, Ministry of Econ. Affairs; Dir. Bureau of the Marshall Plan, Ministry for Foreign Affairs 47, Dir. Gen. Econ. and Mil. Aid Programme 52; Sec. of State (Ministry of Foreign Affairs) for Foreign Affairs 57-58; Ambassador and Special Consultant to the Minister for Foreign Affairs 59; Deputy Pres. KLM Royal Dutch Airlines 60-61, Pres. 61-63; Dir. of several companies 63-; Professor of Int. Relations, Leiden Univ. 66-; Vice-Chair., Netherlands Inst. for Int. Affairs; Grand Cross of the Oak Crown (Luxembourg), Grand Cross of the Order of Leopold II (Belgium), Knight Commdr. of the Order of St. Michael and St. George (U.K.), Grand Officer of Dannebrog (Denmark), Commdr. Légion d'Honneur (France), Knight Netherlands Lion, Officer, Orange Nassau.
Office: Smidswater 1, The Hague; Home: Van Ouwenlaan 50, The Hague, Netherlands.
Telephone: 241848 (Home); 113567 (Office).

Beus, J. G. de, LL.D.; Netherlands diplomatist; b. 09; ed. Univ. of Leyden.
Entered foreign service; served Brussels 36-38, Copenhagen 38-39, Berlin 39-40; Sec. to Foreign Office and to Prime Minister (London) 40-45; Counsellor, Washington 45-49; Permanent Del. to U.N. 48-49; Alternative Del. to Third General Assembly of U.N.; Head Far-Eastern Office 49; Deputy High Commr., Djakarta 50; Minister, Washington 50-54; Ambassador to Pakistan 55-57; Ambassador to the U.S.S.R. 57-60; Ambassador to Australia 60-63; Perm. Rep. of Netherlands to UN 64-67; Amb. to Fed. Repub. of Germany 67-; Officer Order of Orange-Nassau, Knight Order of Netherlands Lion.
Publs. *The Jurisprudence of the General Claims Commission, U.S.A. and Mexico* 38, *De Wedergeboorte van het Koninkrijk* 43, *The Future of the West* 53, *In Rusland* 64.
Netherlands Embassy, Bonn, Federal Republic of Germany.

Beuve-Méry, Hubert, L. és L., D. en D.; French journalist; b. 5 Jan. 1902; ed. Paris Univ.
Dir. Legal and Economic Section, Institut Français de Prague 28-39; diplomatic corresp. of *Temps*, Prague 34-38; with Inst. Français, Lisbon 40-42; Dir. Nat.

School, Uriage; Dir.-Gen. (Man. Editor) *Le Monde* 44-; writes under pseudonym "Sirius".
Publs. *La Théorie des Pouvoirs Publics d'après François de Vittoria et ses rapports avec le droit public contemporain* 28, *Vers la plus grande Allemagne* 39, *Réflexions politiques* 51, *Suicide de la IVe République* 58.
107 boulevard Raspail, Paris 6e, France; and *Le Monde*, 5 rue des Italiens, Paris 9e, France.

Beverloo, Cornelis Van; Netherlands painter; b. 22; ed. Amsterdam Acad. of Fine Arts.
Co-founder, with Appel and Constant, of the experimental "Reflex" group; co-founder of "Cobra" group 48; rep. at numerous exhibitions, including Brussels Int. Exhibition 58, Dunn Int. Exhibition, London 63; works under the name of "Corneille".
c/o Société des Artistes Indépendants, Grand Palais des Champs-Elysées, Cours la Reine, Paris 8e, France.

Bexelius, Tor Alfred, Juris Kandidat; Swedish lawyer; b. 25 April 1903; ed. Stockholm Univ.
Appeal Court Judge 37-48, Presiding Judge 48-54; Chair. or mem. numerous Legislative Cttees. 42-; Chair. Näringsfrihetsråd (Nat. Anti-Cartel Board) 54-56; Chair. Nat. Employees' Inventions Board 55-; Justitieombudsman (Parliamentary Commr. for Justice) 56-.
Publs. Numerous treatises on law and legislation.
Svalnäsvägen 37, Djursholm, Sweden.

Beyen, Johan Willem; Netherlands banker and diplomatist; b. 2 May 1897; ed. Utrecht Univ.
Mem. staff Treasury Dept. 21-23; Legal Adviser Philips Incandescent Lamp Co. 24-25; Man. Amsterdam Office, Javasche Bank 25-27; Joint Man. Dir. Rotterdamsche Bankvereniging 27-35; Alternate Pres. Bank Int. Settlements Basle 35-37, Pres. 37-40; Adviser Netherlands Govt. London 40-45; Dir. Lever Bros., Unilever 40-46; Exec. Dir. Int. Bank for Reconstruction and Development, Washington, D.C. 46, Head of World Bank Mission to Morocco 64; Exec. Dir. Int. Monetary Fund 48; Minister of Foreign Affairs 52-56; Govt. Commr. for Netherlands-German Relations; Ambassador to France 58-63; Chair. Amsterdam-Rotterdam Bank 64-; awards include Knight of the Order of the Netherlands Lion, Grand Officer of the Order of Orange Nassau, Grand Cross of the Légion d'Honneur.
Publ. *Money in a Maelstrom* 49.
Ridderlaan 14, Wassenaar, Netherlands.
Telephone: 01751-5510.

Beyer, Hans Hermann Max, DR. PHIL.; German chemist; b. 6 Oct. 1905; ed. Humboldt-Universität zu Berlin.
Lecturer in Chemistry, Humboldt-Univ., Berlin 39; Prof. Univ. of Greifswald 47, Full Prof. 50-, Dir. of Inst. for Organic Chemistry 50-, Rector, Univ. of Greifswald 50-54, Pro-Rector for Research Affairs 58-65; mem. Deutsche Akademie der Wissenschaften, Berlin 64-; Nationalpreis; Vaterländischer Verdienstorden in Silber; Ernst-Moritz-Arndt-Medaille; August-Kekule-Medaille; Alexander-von-Humboldt Medaille; mem. American Chem. Soc., Chem. Soc. of London, Swiss Chem. Soc., Gesellschaft Deutscher Naturforscher und Ärzte.
Publs. *Lehrbuch der organischen Chemie* 53 (14 editions 53-67) and numerous scientific articles.
22 Greifswald, Steinbeckerstrasse 15, German Democratic Republic.

Bezençon, Marcel, L. ès L.; Swiss broadcasting official; b. 1 May 1907; ed. Lausanne and Vienna Univs.
Journalist; Dir. Société Romande de Radiodiffusion, Radio-Lausanne 39-50; Dir.-Gen. Société Suisse de Radiodiffusion et Télévision (Swiss Broadcasting Corpn.) 50-; Pres. E.B.U. Television Programme Cttee.
Giacomettistrasse 1, 3000 Berne 16, Switzerland.
Telephone: 031-44-55-55.

Beznosov, Pavel Alexandrovich; Soviet politician; b. 1922; ed. Higher Party School of C.P.S.U. Central Cttee.
Soviet Army 41-42; Sub-Editor, then Editor, district newspaper 42-44; Young Communist League Official, then Party Official 44-56; First Sec., Inta Town Cttee. of C.P.S.U. 56-58; Official at C.P.S.U. Central Cttee. 58-62; Second Sec., Komi Regional Cttee. of C.P.S.U. 62-63; Chair. Council of Ministers, Komi Autonomous S.S.R., and Deputy to U.S.S.R. Supreme Soviet 63-; mem. C.P.S.U. 43-.
Council of Ministers of Komi Autonomous S.S.R., Syktyvkar, U.S.S.R.

Bezombes, Roger; French painter; b. 17 Jan. 1913. Has exhibited in Paris since 37 and taken part in most overseas exhibitions of French art; work shown in Musée d'Art Moderne and Musée des Beaux Arts (Paris) and in museums in Paris, Menton, Algiers, Oran, Rabat, Athens, Jerusalem, etc.; Prix Nat. de Peinture. Works include paintings, illustrations for *Le grain de Sable* 55, lithographs; mural decorations for the steamer *Ile de France* and for the liner *France*; apartments at the official residence of the Pres. of the Republic, etc.; tapestries executed at Aubusson, including the collection for the Maison d'Outre Mer, Univ. of Paris; Brussels Exhibition 58; Metropolitan Opera N.Y. 58; Nouvelle Maison de la Radio de Paris; Chevalier de la Légion d'Honneur; Prof. Académie Julian.
Publ. *L'Exotisme dans l'Art et la Pensée* 54.
3 quai Saint-Michel, Paris, France.
Telephone: Odéon 95-73.

Bhabha, Cooverji Hormusji, M.A., B.COM., J.P.; Indian businessman; b. 22 July 1910; ed. St. Xavier's Coll. and Sydenham Coll. of Commerce, Bombay.
Fellow St. Xavier's Coll. 32-34; Fellow and Lecturer in Banking Law and Practice, Sydenham Coll. of Commerce 32-33; J.P. 38-; Commerce mem. Govt. of India Sept. 48; mem. Works, Mines and Power Nov. 46; Minister of Commerce, Govt. of India, Aug. 47-April 48; Leader Indian del. to World Trade Conf. Havana 47 (elected Vice-Pres. of Conf.); Chair. Indian Banks Asscn. 55-61; Vice-Chair. Central Bank of India Ltd.; Dir. Investment Corpn. of India, Andra Valley Power Supply Co. Ltd., Swadeshi Co. Ltd., Tata Engineering & Locomotive Co. Ltd., Spencer & Co. Ltd.
49 Cuffe Parade, Colaba, Bombay 5, India.

Bhagat, Bali Ram; Indian politician; b. 22; ed. Patna Coll.
Secretary Bihar Provincial Congress Cttee. 49; mem. Provisional Parl. 50-52, Lok Sabha 52-; Parl. Sec. Ministry of Finance 52-55; Dep. Minister for Finance 55-63; Minister of State for Planning Sept. 63-67, for Defence 67-Nov. 67, for External Affairs Nov. 67-.
Ministry of External Affairs, New Delhi, India.

Bhagat, Dhanraj; Indian sculptor; b. 20 Dec. 1917; ed. Khalsa High School and Mayo School of Arts, Lahore.
Teacher, Mayo School of Arts 39 and 44; Lecturer in Sculpture, Delhi Polytechnic Art Dept. 46-60, Senior Lecturer 60-62, Asst. Prof. 62-; numerous commissions throughout India; works in stone, wood, plaster, cement, and metal-sheet; eight one-man sculpture shows in India 50-66; exhibitions abroad in London and Paris 48, East European countries 55 and 58, U.S.A. 54, German Federal Republic 58, São Paulo 62, South Africa 65.
College of Art, 22 Harding Avenue, New Delhi; and H 20, New Delhi South Extension Part 1, New Delhi, India.

Bhagavantam, Suri, M.SC.; Indian scientist and university professor; b. 1909; ed. Nizam Coll., Hyderabad and Madras Univ.
Professor of Physics, Andhra Univ. until 48; Scientific

Liaison Officer, B.C.S.O. and Scientific Adviser to Indian High Commr. in U.K., London 48-49, Prof. of Physics, Osmania Univ. 49-52, Vice-Chancellor and Dir. Physical Laboratories 52-57; Dir. Indian Inst. of Science, Bangalore 57-62; Scientific Adviser to Minister of Defence 61-; Chair. Bharat Electronics Ltd.; Dir. Aeronautics India Ltd.; Hon. D.Sc., F.N.I. and F.A.Sc.
Publs. *Scattering of Light and Raman Effect* 40, *Theory of Groups and Its Application to Physical Problems* 52, *Crystal Symmetry and Physical Properties* 66.
Office of the Scientific Adviser to the Minister of Defence, 177 South Block, New Delhi 11, India.
Telephone: 31519.

Bhagwati, Natwarlal Harilal, M.A., LL.B.; Indian lawyer; b. 21 Dec. 1921; ed. Elphinstone Coll., Bombay.
Fmr. Prof., Govt. Law Coll., Bombay; fmr. Advocate, High Court, Bombay; fmr. mem. Bar Council, Bombay; Vice-Chancellor, Bombay Univ. 49-51, Banaras Hindu Univ. 60-66; Puisne Judge, High Court of Judicature, Bombay 44-52; Judge of the Supreme Court 52-59.
Anand Bhuwan, Babranath 2nd X Road, Chowpatty, Bombay 7, India.

Bhaktavatsalam, M.; Indian politician; b. 97.
Legal Practice until 27; Deputy Mayor, Madras Corpn. 36; mem. and Vice-Pres. Chingleput District Board 32-38; Vice-Pres. Tamil Nad Congress Cttee. 35, fmr. Sec. Tamil Nad Congress Cttee; mem. All-India Congress Cttee; Minister for Public Works, Madras 46-62, for Agriculture and Community Projects 53-54, for Home Affairs 57-62, for Finance 62-63, Chief Minister of Madras 63-67.
"Mallika", Mylapore, Madras, India.

Bhatia, Prem Narain; Indian journalist and diplomatist; b. 1911; ed. Government Coll., Lahore, and Punjab Univ.
Army Service, Second World War; Dir. of Public Information, Bengal Government 45-46; Political Correspondent *The Statesman* (Calcutta and New Delhi) 46-58; Public Relations Adviser, Indian Embassy, Moscow 48; Editor *The Tribune*, Ambala 59; Resident Editor *The Times of India*, Delhi 60-62; Delhi Editor *The Indian Express* 63-67; High Commr. in Kenya 67-; India Corresp. *The Guardian* (Manchester and London).
Indian High Commission, P.O. Box 30074, Nairobi, Kenya.

Bhattacharyya, Bhabani, PH.D.; Indian author and journalist; b. 10 Nov. 1906; ed. Patna and London.
Press Attaché at Indian Embassy in Washington 49-50; Asst. Ed. *The Illustrated Weekly of India*, Bombay 50-52; mem. Nat. Acad. of Literature.
Publs. *Some Memorable Yesterdays, Indian Cavalcade, The Golden Boat,* and the novels *So Many Hungers, Music for Mohini, He Who Rides A Tiger, A Goddess Named Gold, Shadow from Ladareh* (novels translated into 16 European languages), *Towards Universal Man.*
Godhuli, Bezon Bagh, Nagpur, India.

Bhattachryya, Birendra Kumar, B.SC., M.A.; Indian journalist and writer; b. 16 March 1924; ed. Jorhat Government High School, Cotton Coll., Gauhati, Calcutta Univ. and Gauhati Univ.
Former Science Teacher, Ukrul High School, Manipur; Editor *Ramdhenu* 51-61, *Sadiniya Navayung* 63-; Exec. mem. Sanjukta Socialist Party, Assam; Sahitya Akademi Award for Assamese Literature 61.
Publs. novels: *Iyaruingam* (won Akademi Award), *Rajpathe Ringiai* (Call of the Main Street), *Mother, Sataghai* (Killer); collections of short stories: *Kolongajioboi* (Still Flows the Kolong), *Satsari* (Necklace).
Kharghuli Development Area, Gauhati 1, Assam, India.

Bhave, Acharya Vinoba; Indian philosopher and savant; b. 11 Sept. 1895.
Co-worker and disciple of late Mahatma Gandhi;

Founder and Leader of *Bhoodan* (Land Gift) Movement, the purpose of which is to bring about fundamental social and economic change in society by peaceful means. The movement began by way of a collection of gifts of land from landowners to be distributed among the landless, later developing into voluntary renunciation of ownership of land in favour of village communities, or *Gramdan*; more than four million acres of land were collected by *Bhoodan* and about 18,000 villages have declared *Gramdan* or common ownership (March 1966). Leader of *Shanti Sena* (Peace Volunteers) a movement for conflict resolution and socio-economic reform.
Publs. *Talks on the Gita* 60, *Democratic Values* 63, *Steadfast Wisdom* 66.
Sarva Seva Sangh, Rajghat, Varanasi, India.

Bhumibol Adulyadej; King of Thailand; b. 5 Dec. 1927; ed. Bangkok and Lausanne, Switzerland.
Youngest son of Their Royal Highnesses Prince and Princess Mahidol of Songkhla; succeeded his brother, the late King Ananda Mahidol, June 46; married Her Majesty the present Queen Sirikit, daughter of H.H. the late Prince Chandapuri Suranath, 28th April 50; formal Coronation 5th May 50; three daughters, H.R.H. Princess Ubol Ratana, b. 51, H.R.H. Princess Sirindhorn, b. 55, H.R.H. Princess Chulabhorn, b. 57; one son, H.R.H. Prince Vajiralongkorn, b. 52.
Chitralada Villa, Bangkok, Thailand.

Bhutto, Zulfikar Ali; Pakistani lawyer and politician; b. Jan. 1928; ed. Univ. of California (Berkeley), Christ Church, Oxford, and Lincoln's Inn, London.
Lecturer in Int. Law, Univ. of Southampton 52-53; Teacher of Constitutional Law, Sind Muslim Law Coll., and private legal practice 53-58; Minister for Commerce 58-60, of Minority Affairs, Nat. Reconstruction and Information Jan. 60-62, of Fuel, Power and Natural Resources, and Kashmir Affairs April 60-62, of Industries and Natural Resources 62-65, of Foreign Affairs 63-June 66; formed People's Party Nov. 67; mem. and leader Pakistan Dels. to UN; several decorations.
Al-Murtaza, Larkana, Pakistan.

Biaggi, Francantonio; Italian consulting engineer; b. 99; ed. Politecnico, Milan, and Pavia Univ.
Operation engineer, Società Orobia, Milan 24-46, Engineering Man. 46, later Deputy Gen. Man.; Gen, Man., later Man. Dir. Società Elettrica Bresciana, Brescia 48-; Man. Dir. Società Energia Elettrica (SENEL), Rome, Società Elettrica Valle Camonica; Vice-Pres. Società Lago d'Idro, Brescia; Dir. Rezzato-Vobarno Railway, Brescia; Appointee for Foreign Relations, Società Edison, Milan; expert OEEC Cttee. for Tariffs; Councillor, Federazione Nazionale Imprese Elettriche (FENIEL), Associazione Imprese Elettriche Lombarde Trentine Emiliane (AIELTE); fmr. mem. Italo-Austrian Cttee. for East Tyrol Hydro-Electric Plants; Italian Govt. del. to European Technical Comm. of ECA for study of interconnection problems in U.S.A. 49; Councillor Associazione Nazionale Imprese Produttrici e Distributrici di Energia Elettrica (ANIDEL); Dir. Società Italiana Autotrasporti (SIA).
Publs. *L'elettricità in Diritto* 46, *Ordnungsprobleme der elektrischen Energiewirtschaft im Rahmen der Erfahrungen in Italien* 51, *Report on the Tecaid Mission in the United States* (with Marin) 49, *Wechselwirkungen zwischen Tarifpolitik und Ausbauplanung der Energieerzeugung* (with Boselli) 52.
Piazza Vittoria 7, Brescia, Italy.

Bianchi, Bruno; Italian government official; b. 30 Jan. 1901; ed. Polytechnic, Bologna.
Former Central Dir. of Società Romana di Elettricità; fmr. Pres. and Gen. Man. of Finelettricà; now Pres. Soc. per lo Sirluppo dell'Edilizia Industrializzata S.p.A. (EDINA); Ordine al Merito della Repubblica Italiana.
Via Aniene 14, Rome, Italy.

Bianchi-Bandinelli, Ranuccio, D.LIT.; Italian university professor; b. 19 Feb. 1900; ed. Rome Univ.
Prof. of Classical Archæology, Univ. of Cagliari, Sardinia 29 and 47-49, Univ. of Groningen, Neths. 31-33, Univ. of Pisa 34-37, Univ. of Florence 38-45, 50-56, Univ. of Rome 57-64; Dir. Gen. of Fine Arts, Italy 45-47; Nat. mem. Accad. dei Lincei; Foreign mem. U.S.S.R. Acad. of Sciences 58; mem. Acad. of Sciences of Poland 62; corresp. mem. Deutsche Akad. der Wissenschaften zu Berlin 62, Nederlandse Akad. van Wetenschappen 66, Acad. Inscriptions et belles-lettres 67, Pontificia Accad. di Archeologia 39; Dr. h.c. Univs. Jena, Berlin, Brussels; Chevalier de la Légion d'Honneur (France); Dir. of art magazine *La Critica d'Arte* 35-42; co-editor reviews, *Società*, Rome 45-61, *Archaeologia Classica*, Rome 57-64; Dir. magazine *Dialoghi di Archaeologia*, Rome 67; Editor *Enciclopedia d. Arte Antica Classica e Orientale* (Inst. d. Enciclopedia Italiana, Rome) 58-67.
Publs. *Clusium* 25, *Sovana* 29 (studies in Etruscan art and topography), *Le pitture delle tombe etrusche di Chiusi* 39, *Storicità dell'arte classica* I 43, II 50, *Diario di un borghese* (memoirs) I 48, II 62, *Hellenistic-Byzantine Miniatures of the Iliad* 55, *Organicità e Astrazione* 56, *Archeologia e Cultura* 61, *Leptis Magna* 64.
21 Via Arenula, Rome; Villa Geggiano, Siena, Italy.
Telephone: Rome 65-55-78; Siena 33-0-24.

Bianchi Gundian, Dr. Manuel; Chilean lawyer and diplomatist; b. 95; ed. Pedagogical Institute and Univ. of Chile.
Joined Foreign Service 11, served Germany, Brazil, Panama, Venezuela, Cuba, Bolivia and Mexico; Minister of Foreign Affairs 40; Ambassador to U.K. 41-53; Co-founder *La Nación*, Santiago; mem. Inter-American Commission on Human Rights, Chair. 62-.
Inter-American Commission on Human Rights, c/o Pan American Union, Washington 6, D.C., U.S.A.

Biancini, Angelo; Italian sculptor; b. 11; ed. Accademia di Santa Luca.
Professor and Artistic Dir. Istituto d'Arte, Faenza; Regular Exhibitor Venice Biennali and Rome Quadriennali 34-58; international exhibitor throughout the world; Prize, Milan Triennale 40, Venice Biennale 58.
Major Works: three statues, Galleria d'Arte Moderna, Rome, Canadian Temple Rome, Mosaic Marist Fathers' International Coll. etc.
Istituto d'Arte di Ceramica, Faenza, Italy.

Bibby, Sir (Arthur) Harold, Bt., D.S.O., D.L.; British shipowner and banker; b. 18 Feb. 1889; ed. Rugby.
Joined Bibby Bros. & Co. 07; served in First World War, France and Flanders 15-18; Chair. Liverpool Steam Ship Owners' Asscn. 27, 58 (centenary year); High Sheriff of Cheshire 34-35, apptd. Deputy Lieut. 35; Chair. Liverpool Sailors' Home 21-51, Pres. 51-; Chair. *Indefatigable* and Nat. Sea Training School for Boys 31-51, Pres. 51-; Chair. Bibby Line Ltd.; Dir. Martins Bank 29-67, Chair. 47-62; Dir. The Sea Insurance Co. Ltd. 22-68, Chair. 30-56; Gov. Rugby School 32-67; Hon. LL.D. (Liverpool Univ.).
Tilstone Lodge, Tarporley, Cheshire; and Martins Bank Building, Water Street, Liverpool, England.

Bible, Alan, LL.D.; American lawyer and politician; b. 20 Nov. 1909; ed. Univ. of Nevada and Georgetown Law School, Washington.
Admitted to Nevada Bar 35; assoc. Law Partner with P. A. McCarran, Reno 35-38; District Attorney, Storey County, Nevada 35-38; Deputy Attorney-Gen. for Nevada 38-43, Attorney-Gen. 43-53; Senator from Nevada 54-; mem. American Bar Asscn.; Democrat.
125 North Center Street, Reno, Nevada, U.S.A.

Bibo, Istvan, DR. POL. and JUR.; Hungarian scholar and politician; b. 7 Aug. 1911; ed. Grammar schools at Budapest and Szeged, Piarist Coll., Szeged Univ., Vienna, Geneva.

Called to the Bar 40; Lecturer Szeged Univ. 40; in Ministry of Justice 41-45; Counsellor, later departmental chief, Ministry of Interior 45-46; Prof. of Political Sciences Szeged Univ. 46-50; Deputy Pres. of East European Research Inst. Budapest 47-49; Librarian, Univ. of Budapest 51-56; Minister of State Oct. 56; imprisoned 56-63; Librarian, Central Statistical Office 63-.

Publs. *A szankciók kérdése a nemzetközi jogban, Kényszer, jog, szabadság, Jogszerü közigazgatás, eredményes közigazgatás, erös végrehajtóhatalom, A magyar demokrácia válsága, A keleteurópai kisnépek nyomorusága, Zsidókérdés Magyarországon 1944 után.*

Berkenye-u. 4, Budapest II, Hungary.

Bićanić, Rudolf; Yugoslav economist; b. 05; ed. Zagreb Univ. and Ecole des Hautes Etudes Commerciales, Paris.

Dir. Peasants Co-operative Zagreb and Economic and Social Research Inst. 35-40; Vice-Pres. Croatian Electric Co. 39-40; Dir. Foreign Trade Dept. Min. of Commerce and Industry 40; Vice-Gov. Nat. Bank of Yugoslavia 41-44; arrived Great Britain Aug. 41; mem. Allied Post-War Requirements Cttee., UNRRA Council 44-45; Rep. in London of Yugoslav Nat. Cttee. of Liberation; Dir. Office of Foreign Trade, Belgrade 45-46; Prof. of Applied Economics, Univ. of Zagreb 46-; Dean, Faculty of Law 52-53; Visiting Prof. Univ. of Texas 58.

Publs. *Kako živi narod, Agrarna kriza 1873-1895, Ekonomska podloga hrvatskog pitanja, Pogled iz svjetske perspektive i nasa ekonomska orientacija, Agrarna prenapučenost u Hrvatkoj, Hrvatska ekonomika na prijelazu iz feudalizma u kapitalizam I 51, Počeci kapitalizma u hrvatskoj ekonomici i politici 53, Predavanja iz ekonomike FNRJ, I, II, Problemi vanjske trgovine.*

Brace Kavurića 25, Zagreb, Yugoslavia.

Bickmore, Lee Smith; American food executive; b. 5 June 1908; ed. Utah State Univ. and Harvard School of Business Admin.

Joined Nat. Biscuit Co. (Nabisco) 33, District Sales Man., Newark (N.J.) 46-49, Admin. Asst. to Vice-Pres. (Sales), General Office 49-50, Vice-Pres (Sales, Advertising and Marketing) 50-57, Senior Vice-Pres. and mem. Exec. Dept. 57, Exec. Vice-Pres. and mem. Board of Dirs. 59, Pres. 60-, Chief Exec. Officer 61-; official of numerous Nabisco subsidiaries and other companies.

National Biscuit Company, 425 Park Avenue, New York, N.Y. 10022, U.S.A.

Bidault, Georges; French politician; b. 5 Oct. 1899; ed. Coll. des Jésuites de Turin, Univ. de Paris.

Served First World War 17-18, subsequently Prof. at Valenciennes, Rheims and Paris Univs.; adviser and leader writer for *L'Aube* until 39; mobilised 39, prisoner 40, released, apptd. Prof. Univ. of Lyons; resistance leader; Minister of Foreign Affairs under de Gaulle 44; Deputy (Loire) 45-62; Prime Minister of Provisional Govt. 46; Minister of Foreign Affairs 47; Pres. M.R.P. 49; Prime Minister 49-50, Deputy Prime Minister (Queuille Govt.) 51, Minister of Nat. Defence (Pleven Govt.) 51-52; Minister of Foreign Affairs (Mayer and Laniel Govts.) 53-54; Pres. of temporary Council April 58; exile in Brazil 63-67, Belgium 67-68; returned to France June 68; Lecturer, Univ. of Guanabara 65; Grand Cross Légion d'Honneur etc.

Publ. *D'une Resistance a l'autre* (autobiographical) 65. Paris, France.

Biddle, Eric H.; American administrator; b. 27 April 1898; ed. Univ. of Pennsylvania and Oxford Univ.

Industrial Management and Finance 22-32; Relief Administrator of Pennsylvania 32-35; Exec. Dir. Community Fund of Philadelphia 35-40; Exec. Vice-Pres. U.S. Cttee. for Care of European Children from the war zones 40-41; mission to U.K. 41, Head Special Mission to U.K. and missions to European, Middle East and Occupied Territories 42-46 for various U.S. Govt. Depts.; Adviser U.S. Del. UNRRA 45, UNESCO 46, UN 45-46; Chair. Advisory Group of Experts on Admin., Personnel and Budgetary questions to UN Gen. Assembly 45-47; Special Asst. to Sec.-Gen. UN 46; Special Asst. to Dir. of OIC, Consultant to Asst. Sec. of State for Public Affairs and special missions to Europe 47; Special Asst. for Overseas Admin. ECA, Acting Chief ECA Mission to Korea and Asst. to U.S. Ambassador to Korea 48; Consultant, ECA Mission to Italy and Special Asst. to Dir. of German and Austrian Affairs, Dept. of State 49; Consultant to Chair., Nat. Sec. Resources Board, Exec. Office of the Pres. 49-51, and to various ECA and MSA officials 51-52; Special Consultant to Exec. Chair. Tech. Assistance Board (UN); Management Consultant 53-57, Vice-Pres. and Dir. Porter Int. Co. 57-65; Vice-Pres. United States Leasing Corpn. 58-61; Pres. Biddle Associates 61-.

1200 N. Nash Street, Arlington, Va. 22209, U.S.A. Telephone: 522-4766.

Biddle, Francis, B.A., LL.D.; American lawyer; b. 9 May 1886; ed. Haverford and Groton Schools and Harvard Univ.

Private Sec. to Mr. Justice Holmes 11-12; admitted to Pennsylvania Bar 12; associated Biddle, Paul and Jayne 12-15; practised with Barnes, Biddle and Myers 17-39; partner 22-39; special asst. U.S. Attorney Eastern District Pennsylvania 22-26; admitted to practice before U.S. Supreme Court 27; Judge Circuit Court of Appeals 39; Solicitor-Gen. 40-41, Attorney-Gen. 41-45; Chair. Nat. Labor Relations Board 34-35; American mem. Int. Military Tribunal to try major German War Criminals 45-46; Nat. Chair. Americans for Democratic Action 50-53; mem. Permanent Court of Arbitration 51-57; mem. Franklin Delano Roosevelt Memorial Comm. 56; Trustee Twentieth Century Fund; Four Freedoms Award 42; Order of Merit (Italy) 54; Hon. LL.D. (La Salle, Hobart and William Smith Colls., Drexel Inst. and Boston Univ.); Hon. Bencher Inner Temple (London); Democrat.

Publs. *Llanfear Pattern* 27, *Mr. Justice Holmes* 42, *Democratic Thinking and the War* 44, *The World's Best Hope* 50, *The Fear of Freedom* 52, *A Casual Past* 61, *In Brief Authority* 62, *Justice Holmes, Natural Law and the Supreme Court.*

1669 31st Street, N.W., Washington, D.C., U.S.A.

Biddle, George, A.B., LL.D.; American artist; b. 24 Jan. 1885; ed. Harvard Univ., Paris and Pennsylvania Art Schools.

Ninety-five exhibitions in Europe, Japan, India, Americas; instrumental in creation of Fed. Art Projects; Pres. Mural Painters of America 35; Vice-Pres. Painters, Gravers and Sculptors 34; Pres. Mural Artists Guild 37-39; finished 5 large frescoes for Dept. of Justice, Washington 36, murals for New Brunswick N.J., Post Office 39; frescoes for National Library, Rio de Janeiro 42; Chair. War Dept. Art Cttee.; official war artist in Tunisia, Sicily and Italy 43; frescoes for Supreme Court Mexico City 45; mem. Art Advisory Cttee., Dept. of State; mem. Nat. Fine Arts Comm. 52-55; artist in residence American Acad., Rome 51-52; Vice-Pres. Nat. Inst. of Arts and Letters 62-; Art Editor and Dir. of *1948 Magazine of Year.*

Publs. *American Artist's Story* 39, *Artist at War* 44, *Green Islands, Coward McCann, Adolphe Borie* 38, *Boardman Robinson* 38, *George Biddle's War Drawings* 44, *The Yes and No of Contemporary Art* 57, *Indian Impressions* 60.

Croton-on-Hudson, N.Y. 10520, U.S.A. Telephone: CR1 4666.

Bieber, Margarete, PH.D.; American (b. German) archaeologist; b. 31 July 1879.

Prof. of Archæology Giessen Univ. and Dir. of the

Archæological Inst. of the Univ. until 33; Hon. Fellow Somerville Coll. Oxford 33-34; Lecturer Barnard Coll. 34-36; Associate Prof. of Fine Arts and Archæology Columbia Univ. New York 36-48; (retd. 48); Special Lecturer Barnard Coll. 48-50, Princeton Univ. 48-50, Inst. of Gen. Studies, Columbia Univ. 48-54; Hon. D.Litt., Columbia Univ. 54; Hon. Senator, Giessen Univ. 59.

Publs. *Katalog der Skulpturen in Kassel* 16, *Die Denkmäler zum Theaterwesen im Altertum* 20, *Griechische Kleidung* 28, *Entwicklungsgeschichte der griechischen Tracht* 34, 67, *The History of the Greek and Roman Theatre* 39, 61, *Laocoon: the Influence of the Group since its Re-discovery* 42, 67, *German Readings in the History and Theory of Fine Arts* 46, *German Readings, A Survey of Greek and Roman Art* 58, *The Sculpture of the Hellenistic Age* 55, 61, *A Bronze Statuette in Cincinnati* 57, *Romani Palliati* 59, *The Copies of the Herculaneum Women* 62, *Alexander the Great in Greek and Roman Art* 64, *New Trends in the New Books on Ancient Art* 65.

605 W. 113th Street, Apt. 33, New York, N.Y. 10025, U.S.A.

Telephone: MO3-4454.

Bieberbach, Ludwig, PH.D.; German mathematician; b. 4 Dec. 1886; ed. Heidelberg and Göttingen Univs.
Lecturer Königsberg Univ. 10; Prof. Basle 13, Frankfurt 15, and Berlin 21-45; mem. Prussian Acad. of Science 24-45.

Publs. *Differential-und Integralrechnung, Lehrbuch der Funktionentheorie, Theorie der Differentialgleichungen, Algebra, Analytische Geometrie, Projektive Geometrie, Differentialgeometrie, Höhere Geometrie, Konforme Abbildung, Theorie der geometrischen Konstruktionen, C. F. Gauss, Galilei und die Inquisition, Analytische Fortsetzung, Theorie der gewöhnlichen Differentialgleichungen auf funktiontheoretischer Grundlage, Theorie der gewöhnlichen Differentialgleichungen im reellen Gebiet.*

Bahnhofstrasse 5, (8203) Oberaudorf, German Federal Republic.

Telephone: 08033-661.

Bienkowski, Wladyslaw; Polish politician and journalist; b. 06; ed. Warsaw Univ.
Joined Polish Workers' Party 42, mem. Cen. Cttee. 45-48; mem. Polish United Workers' Party 48-; mem. Seym (Parliament) 47-52, 57-; Dir. Polish Nat. Library 49-56; Minister of Education 56-59; Dep. Chair. State Nature Conservation Board 59-.

3/5 Reja, Warsaw, Poland.

Biermann, Ludwig Franz Benedikt, DR. PHIL.; German astrophysicist; b. 13 March 1907; ed. Univs. of Hanover, Munich, Freiburg and Göttingen.
Assistant Univ. of Göttingen 33; Scholarship, Univ. of Edinburgh 34; at Univ. of Jena 34-36; Lecturer (Dozent) Univ. of Berlin 38, Univ. of Hamburg 45-47, Assoc. Prof. 47-48; Assoc. Prof. Univ. of Göttingen 48; Head of Astrophysics Dept., Max-Planck-Inst. for Physics and Astrophysics 47-58, Dir. of Inst. 58-; Prof. of Astronomy Univ. of Munich 59-; mem. Bayerische Akad. der Wissenschaften; Corresp. mem. Soc. Royale des Sciences, Liège; Assoc. Royal Astronomical Soc., London; Visiting Prof. Calif. Inst. of Technology, Haverford Coll., Princeton Univ. 55, Univ. of Calif. (Berkeley) 59-60, Univs. of Sydney and Canberra 60, Inst. for Advanced Studies, Princeton 61; Visiting Fellow, Univ. of Colorado, Boulder 67; Copernicus Prize 43; Bruce Gold Medal of Astronomical Soc. of the Pacific 67.
Major work includes: Investigation on stellar evolution and stellar structure 31-39, theoretical work on the solar atmosphere and corona 46-, problems of cosmic radiation and interstellar magnetic fields 50-, physics of comets and problems related to interplanetary matter and the solar wind 51-, plasma physics and its relation to astrophysics 56-, problems of space research 63-.

Office: Max-Planck-Institut für Physik und Astrophysik, 8000 Munich 23, Föhringer Ring 6; Home: 8000 Munich 23, Rohmederstrasse 12, German Federal Republic.

Bierwirth, John E.; American business executive; b. 21 April 1895; ed. Yale Univ.
Vice-President and Dir. Thompson-Starrett Co. Inc. 19-29; Vice-Pres. New York Trust Co. 29-41, Pres. and Trustee 41-; Pres. Nat. Distillers and Chemical Corpn. 49-58, Chair. and Chief Exec. Officer 58-, now Chair. and Chief Exec. Officer.
National Distillers and Chemical Corporation, 99 Park Avenue, New York City, N.Y. 10016; Home: Briarwood Crossing, Cedarhurst, Long Island, N.Y., U.S.A.

Biesheuvel, Barend William; Netherlands agriculturalist and politician; b. 5 April 1920; ed. Free Univ. of Amsterdam.
Ministry of Agriculture 45-47; Sec. for Foreign Relations, Fed. of Agriculture 47-52; Gen. Sec. Nat. Protestant Farmers' Union 52-59, Pres. 59-63; mem. Parl. 57-61, 63-; mem. European Parl.; Deputy Prime Minister, Minister of Agriculture and Fisheries 63-67; Anti-Revolutionary Party.
Overste den Oudenlaan 8, Aerdenhout, Netherlands.

Biggar, Frank; Irish diplomatist; b. 17; ed. Blackrock Coll., Dublin.
Third Sec. Dept. of External Affairs 41-43; Third Sec. and Vice-Consul, New York, Washington, San Francisco 43-46; Second Sec., Rome 46-48; First Sec., then Counsellor, Econ. Div., Dublin 48-54; Counsellor, London 54-59; Minister to Portugal 59-60; Ambassador to Belgium 60-, Head of Irish Mission to EEC 61-, ECSC 63-; Grande Croix de la Couronne (Belgium).
Irish Embassy, 51 Avenue Victor Emmanuel, Brussels, Belgium.

Biggers, John David, LL.D.; American industrialist; b. 19 Dec. 1888; ed. Washington Univ. and Michigan Univ.
Associated automobile and glass industries 14-30; Pres. Libbey Owens Ford Glass Co. 30-53, Chair. and Chief Exec. Officer 53-60, Chair. Finance Cttee. 60-64; Admin. U.S. Unemployed Census 37-38; Dir. of War Production 40-41; Minister to Gt. Britain (in charge of co-ordination of war production) 41; Chair. Business Advisory Council, Dept. of Commerce, 53; New York Stock Exchange, Public Gov. 57-60; Dir. several companies; Pres. Toledo Museum of Art 52-57; President's Medal of Merit 46, Commdr's Cross, Order of Orange Nassau 56.
112 Rockledge Circle, Perrysburg, Ohio 43552, U.S.A.

Biggs, Edward George Power; American (b. British) organist; b. 29 March 1906; ed. Hurstpierpoint Coll., and Royal Acad. of Music, London.
Organist and Soloist Sir Henry Wood's Festival Orchestra at Queen's Hall; freelance concert organist in America; many organ recital recordings on historic organs, and recordings first for R.C.A. Victor then Columbia Recording Companies; Fellow American Acad. of Arts and Sciences; D.Mus. (Hon.), Acadia Univ., Nova Scotia and New England Conservatory, Boston.
53 Highland Street, Cambridge 38, Mass., U.S.A.

Biggs, Norman Parris; British oil executive; b. 23 Dec. 1907; ed. John Watson's School, Edinburgh.
Bank of England 27-46; Dir. Kleinwort, Sons & Co. Ltd. 47-52; Dir. Esso Petroleum Co. 52-57, Man. Dir. 57-64, Vice-Chair. 64-66; Vice-Pres. (Finance) Esso Europe Inc. 66-67; Chair. Esso Petroleum Co. Ltd. 68-; Dir. The Nat. Bank Ltd., Gillett Bros. Discount Co. Ltd.; Chair. Council of Hansard Soc. for Parl. Govt.
Esso Petroleum Co. Ltd., Victoria Street, London, S.W.1; Home: Higham House, Northiam, Rye, Sussex, England.

Bignami, Enrico; business executive; b. 24 Aug. 1905. Vice-Chair. and Man. Dir. Nestlé Alimentana S.A.; Dr. h.c. Lausanne Univ.; mem. Board of Trustees, IMEDE, Management Devt. Inst., Lausanne.

Nestlé Alimentana S.A., Avenue Nestlé, Vevey, Switzerland.

Bihalji-Merin, Oto; Yugoslav critic, essayist and novelist; b. 3 Jan. 1904; ed. Belgrade and Berlin Acads. of Fine Art.

Began his career as a painter; now works as an author, editor and art critic; also writes under the pseudonyms Peter Merin and Peter Thoene; Editor-in-Chief *Jugoslavia* 49-58; mem. Selection Cttee., Art Exhibition, Brussels Int. Exhbn. 58; Order of People's Merit, 1st Class, Chevalier Ordre de Léopold (Belgium), Herder Prize 64.

Publs. *Conquest of the Skies* 37 (English, French, German, Dutch and Swedish translations), *Spain Between Death and Birth* 38 (English and German translations), *Modern German Art* (English edn. 38, Serbo-Croat edn. 55), *Au Revoir in October* (novel) 47, *Thoughts and Colours* (essays), *The Foundry* (play) 50, *Yugoslavia, a Small Country between the Worlds* 54 (German edn. 55, Dutch edn. 56), *Yugoslav Sculpture of the XX Century* 55 (English, French and German translations), *Peter Lubarda and the Painting "The Battle of Kossovo", The Invisible Door* (play) 56, *Rencontres in Our Days* (essays) 57, *Icons and Frescoes in Serbia and Macedonia* (French, English and German translations), *Primitive Arts of the XX Century in Europe and America* 59; chapter on Yugoslav and Polish art in *Neue Kunst nach 1945* 58, *The Adventure of Modern Art,* 62, 64, 68, *Bogosav Zivkovic, World of a Primitive Sculptor* 62, 63, *Bogomil Sculpture* 62, 64 (*The Bogomils* in English 63), *Architects of Modern Thought* 65, *Primitive Artists of Yugoslavia* 65, *Die Welt von oben* 66, *Thousands of Years of Art in Yugoslavia* (Editor and preface) 67, *Man and his World* 68.

Nemanjina ul. 3, Belgrade, Yugoslavia.
Telephone: 641-571.

Bilac Pinto, Olavo; Brazilian lawyer and politician; b. 08; ed. Instituto Moderno de Educação, Minas Gerais, and Universidade de Minas Gerais.

Criminal lawyer, Belo Horizonte 31-33; Police Instructor, Minas Gerais 33-34; Deputy of Constituent and Legislative Assemblies, Minas Gerais 34; Dir. *Revista Forense* 35; Prof. Faculty of Law, Univ. of Minas Gerais 39-41; fmr. Prof. of Administrative Law, Univ. of Brazil; Fed. Deputy 50-; Financial Sec. State of Minas Gerais 61; Leader of União Democrática National (U.D.N.) in Chamber of Deputies 62-63; Pres. of Nat. Cttee. U.D.N. 63-; Del. to UN 64; Pres. Brazilian Chamber of Deputies 65-66; Ambassador to France 66-.

Publs. *Contribuição de Melhoria* 37, *Ministério Público* 37, *Regulamentação Efetiva dos Serviços de Utilidade Pública* 41, *Estudos de Direito Público* 53, *Le Financement de l'Hotellerie Touristique* 64, *Guerra Revolucionaria* 64.

Brazilian Embassy, avenue Montaigne 45, Paris 8e, France; and Av. Vieira Souto 550, Rio de Janeiro, GB, Brazil.

Bilak, Vasil, D.SC.S.; Czechoslovak politician; b. 8 Nov. 1917; ed. School of Political Studies at Central Committee of Communist Party of Czechoslovakia, Prague.

Took part in Slovak Nat. Rising 44; full-time party official, Regional Cttee., C.P. of Slovakia, Bratislava 50-51; Dept. Head, Central Cttee., C.P. of Slovakia 53; Sec. and Chief Sec. Regional Cttee., C.P. of Slovakia, Presov 54-58; Minister-Commr., Comm. for Educ. and Culture of Slovak Nat. Council 59-62, Minister 60-62; Deputy Chair. Slovak Nat. Council 60-63; Sec. Central Cttee. C.P. of Slovakia 62-68, First Sec. 68-; mem. Central Cttee. C.P. of Czechoslovakia 54-; mem.

Presidium Central Cttee. C.P. of Czechoslovakia 68-; Deputy to Slovak Nat. Council 54-64; mem. Central Cttee. of C.P. of Slovakia 55-; Deputy to Nat. Assembly 60-; mem. Presidium, Central Cttee. of C.P. of Slovakia 62-; mem. Presidium Nat. Assembly 63-; mem. Central Cttee. of Nat. Front 63-; Order of Labour 67.

Central Committee of Communist Party of Slovakia, Bratislava, Hlboká 2, Czechoslovakia.

Bilbao, Esteban; Spanish lawyer and politician.
Ministry of Justice 39-43; Pres. Cortes 43-65; Pres. Council of the Kingdom; mem. Royal Spanish Acad. of Moral and Political Science 43-; Pres. Royal Acad. of Jurisprudence 44-; Gran Cruz de Isabel la Católica, de Carlos III, del Merito Naval, de Santiago y la Espada, and numerous other decorations from Iraq, the Vatican; Hijo Predilecto de Bilbao and Benemérito de Viscaya.

Real Academia de Jurisprudencia y Legislación, Marqués de Cubas 13, Madrid, Spain.

Bilgehan, Cihat; Turkish judge and politician; b. 1923.
Deputy for Balikesir 61-; Minister of Educ. Jan.-Nov. 65; Minister of State Nov. 65-66; Minister of Finance 66-; Justice Party.

Ministry of Finance, Ankara, Turkey.

Bilheimer, Rev. Robert Sperry, B.A., B.D., D.D.; American ecclesiastic; b. 28 Sept. 1917; ed. Phillips Exeter Acad., Yale Univ., Yale Divinity School.

Minister, Westminster Presbyterian Church 46-48; Sec., The Inter-Seminary Movement 45-48; Programme Sec., World Council of Churches, New York 48-54, Assoc. Gen. Sec., Dir. of the Division of Studies, Geneva 54-63; Senior Minister, Central Presbyterian Church, Rochester, N.Y. 63-66; Dir. Int. Affairs Programs, The Nat. Council of Churches of Christ in the U.S.A. 66-.

Publs. *What Must the Church Do?* 47, *The Quest for Christian Unity* 52.

Office: Room 566, 475 Riverside Drive, New York, N.Y. 10027; Home: 80 East Hartsdale Avenue, Apt. 317, Hartsdale, N.Y. 10530, U.S.A.
Telephone: 914-761-9454 (Home).

Bilibin, Alexander Fedorovich; Soviet infectionist; b. 1897; ed. Kiev Univ.

Physician, Head of Section in hospital 22-24; Head of Chair, Third Moscow Medical Inst. 44-50, Second Moscow Medical Inst. 50-; Corresp. mem. U.S.S.R. Acad. of Medical Sciences 50-60, mem. 60-; Hon. mem. Czechoslovak Purkinye Scientific Soc.; Order of Lenin, Red Banner of Labour; Merited Scientist of U.S.S.R.

Publs. About 150 works on acute infectious diseases (dysentery, salmonellosis, Botkin disease).

Second Medical Institute, 1 Malaya Pirogovskaya Street, Moscow, U.S.S.R.

Bilkenroth, Georg, D.ENG.; German mining engineer; b. 24 Feb. 1898; ed. Bergakademie, Clausthal.

Technical Dir. and mem. of Board, Braunkohlenwerke Salzdetfurt A.G.; technical and scientific mem. Coal Admin., German Economic Comm. 47-; Scientific Dir. Nationalized Coal Industry, Berlin 55-; Sec. Technical-Scientific Council for Coal, Ministry of Heavy Industry; mem. Research Council, German Democratic Republic, Deutsche Akad. der Wissenschaften; Chief, Int. Bureau for Rock Mechanics, Int. Asscn. of Mining Engineers, Int. Mining Cttee.; Dr. rer. oec. h.c.; Nat Prize.

102 Berlin, Inselstrasse 12; Home: 1233 Storkow/Mark, Hubertushöhe, German Democratic Republic.
Telephone: Storkow 2051 (Home).

Bill, Max; Swiss architect, sculptor, painter and writer; b. 22 Dec. 1908; ed. Zürich School of Art and Craft and Dessau Bauhaus.

Professor at Zürich 44-45; Dir. Inst. for Design, Ulm, Germany 51-56; Prof. of Environmental Design, Staats Inst. for Fine Arts, Hamburg 67-; rep. at Triennale

Milan 36 and 51, grand prix 53, 56, Biennale São Paulo 51 (1st Int. Sculpture prize) and 57, Biennale Venice 58, Pittsburgh Carnegie 58, 61, 64, 67, Brussels Int. Exhbn. 58, Documenta Kassel 55, 59, 64, Sculpture Biennale Antwerp 55, 57, 59, 61, 63, 65, 67; Int. Sculpture Exhbn. Paris 61; Montreal Int. Exhbn. 67; mem. Fed. of Swiss Architects; mem. Swiss Fine Art Comm.; mem. Zürich City Council 61-, Swiss Fed. Council 67-; Hon. Fellow American Inst. of Architects 64; Arch. Sec. Educ. and Creation, Swiss Nat. Exhbn., Lausanne 64. Publs. include *Die mathematische Denkweise in der Kunst unserer Zeit* 49, *Form* 52.
Home: Rebhusstrasse 50, 8126 Zumikon, Switzerland; Office: Albulastrasse 39, 8048 Zürich, Switzerland.

Billanovich, Giuseppe; Italian philologist; b. 6 Aug. 1913; ed. Univ. degli Studi, Padua.
Senior Research Fellow Warburg Inst, London 48-50; Prof. Italian Literature Fribourg Univ., Switzerland 50-60; Prof. Mediaeval and Humanistic Philology, Catholic Univ. of Milan; Antonio Feltrinelli Prize for Philology 65; Co-Dir. *Thesaurus Mundi* and annual *Italia Medioevale e Umanistica*.
Publ. *I primi umanisti e le tradizioni dei classici latini* 53.
Corso Magenta 48, Milan, Italy.

Bill-Belotserkovsky, Vladimir Naumovich; Soviet playwright; b. 30 Sept. 1885.
Honoured Art Worker; mem. C.P.S.U. 17-; Orders of Badge of Honour 39, of Red Banner of Labour 55.
Publs. *Bifshteks s krovyu* (Underdone Steak), *Etapy* (Stages), *Echo*, *Lievo Rulya* (Left Rudder), *Shtil* (Calm), *Golos Niedr* (The Voice of the Womb), *Luna Sleva* (The Moon on the Left), *Zhizn Zovet* (Life is Calling), *Poedinok* (The Duel), *Zapad Nervnichaet* (The West is Nervous), *Pogranichniki* (The Frontier Guards), *Vokrug Ringa* (Around the Ring), *Shturm* (The Storm), *Put Zhizni* (Way of Life), *Stories and Essays*.
U.S.S.R. Union of Writers, 52 Vorovsky Street, Moscow, U.S.S.R.

Billeskov-Jansen, Frederik Julius, DR.PHIL.; Danish professor; b. 30 Sept, 1907; ed. Københavns Universitet.
Assistant Lecturer in Danish, Univ. of Copenhagen 35-38, Prof. 41-; Lecturer, Univ. de Paris à la Sorbonne 38-41; Editor *Orbis Litterarum* 43-50; mem. Royal Danish Acad. of Sciences and Letters, mem. Int. Asscns. of Comparative Literature and of German Language and Literature, mem. Danish Acad.
Publs. *Danmarks Digtekunst I-III* 44-58, 2nd edition 64, *Holberg som Epigrammatiker og Essayist* 39, Editions of Holberg: *Moralske Tanker* 43, *Epistler* 54, *Memoirer* 63, *Søren Kierkegaards Litterære Kunst* 51, *Søren Kierkegaards: Vaerker i Udvalg* 50, *Poetik* (Vols. I and II) 41-48, *Den Danske Lyrik* 61-66, *Esthétique de l'œuvre d'art littéraire* 48, *L'Age d'or* 53, *Anthologie de la Littérature danoise* (bilingual edition) 64.
Frydendalsvej 20, 1809 Copenhagen V, Denmark.
Telephone: 01-316369.

Billetdoux, François-Paul; French writer, actor, director and producer; b. 7 Sept. 1927; ed. Ecole d'Art Dramatique Charles Dullin and Institut des Hautes Etudes Cinématographiques.
Producer and Dir. Radiodiffusion Française 46-, in Caribbean 49-50, Gen. Overseas Service 57-58; journalist 51; cabaret actor and disc jockey 51-53; work for theatre, radio, television and films 59-; numerous prizes.
Publs. *L'Animal* (novel) 55, *Une rose pour Charles Cros* 57, *Royal Garden Blues* 57, *Brouillon d'un bourgeois* 61; Plays: *Treize pièces à louer* 51, *A la nuit la nuit* 55, *Tchin-Tchin* 59, *Le comportement des époux Bredburry* 60, *Va donc chez Törpe* 62, *Pour Finalie* 62, *Comment va le monde, Môssieu?, Il tourne, Môssieu!* 64, *Il faut passer par les nuages* 64; Television: *Pitchi Poï ou la parole donnée* 67, *Silence! L'arbre remue encore!* 67.
31 square Montsouris, Paris 14e, France.

Billotte, Gen. Pierre; French army officer and politician; b. 8 March 1906; ed. Ecole Militaire de Saint-Cyr.
Military Rep. of Free French in Moscow 41-42; Chief of Staff to Gen. de Gaulle in London 42-44, Sec. of Cttee. for Nat. Defence; Commdr. Brigade under Gen. Leclerc 44-45; Asst. Gen. Chief of Staff Nat. Defence 45-46; French Mil. Rep. to UN 46-50; retired from army 50; mem. Chamber of Deputies 51-55, 62-; Minister of Nat. Defence and of the Armed Forces 55; Rep. of France on various UN Cttees. 55-62; Vice-Pres. U.N.R. Group in Nat. Assembly 62-; Minister of State Overseas Depts. and Territories 66-68; Mayor of Créteil 65: Commdr. Légion d'Honneur; Compagnon de la Libération.
Publs. *Fatalité de la defaite allemande* 41, *Le Temps du choix* 50, *L'Europe est Nèe* 55, *Considération sur la Strategie Mondiale* 57, *Du Pain sur la Planche* 65.
39 Boulevard du Commandant Charcot, Neuilly-sur-Seine, France.

Billoux, François; French politician; b. 21 May 1903; ed. Ecole pratique de Commerce et d'Industrie de Roanne (Loire).
Communist Deputy; Town Councillor, Marseille; Commr. of State French Cttee. Nat. Liberation 44; Minister for Public Health 44-45; Minister for Nat. Economy 45-46; Minister for Reconstruction 46; Minister for Nat. Defence Jan.-May 47; mem. Politbureau of French Communist Party; political dir. *France Nouvelle*.
44 rue Le Peletier, Paris 9e, France.
Telephone: PRO-42-22.

Billy, André; French author and journalist; b. 13 Dec. 1882; ed. Petit Séminaire and Coll. des Jésuites.
Literary critic and writer in *Paris-Midi*, *L'Homme Libre*, *L'Œuvre*, and *Le Figaro*; mem. Acad. Goncourt, Soc. des Gens de Lettres.
Publs. Over fifty works including novels, biographies, etc.
La Chevrette, Barbizon, Seine-et-Marne, France.

Bilsland, 1st Baron; cr. 50; **Alexander Steven Bilsland,** Bt., K.T., M.C., D.L., LL.D., J.P.; British company director; b. 13 Sept. 1892; ed. Glasgow Acad. and Cambridge Univ.
President Glasgow Chamber of Commerce 33-35; Chair. Bilsland Bros. Ltd., Bilsland (Holdings) Ltd., Glasgow Stockholders Trust Ltd., Scottish Nat. Trust Ltd., Second Scottish Nat. Trust Ltd., Third Scottish Nat. Trust Ltd.; Pres. Scottish Amicable Life Assurance Soc., The Building Centre (Scotland) Ltd., and other companies; fmr. Gov. Bank of Scotland; mem. Royal Co. of Archers (H.M. Bodyguard for Scotland); Hon. A.R.I.B.A., Hon. mem. American Acad. of Arts and Sciences, U.S. Medal of Freedom.
Kinrara, Aviemore, Inverness-shire; Office: 89 West Campbell Street, Glasgow, C.2, Scotland.

Binaghi, Walter; Argentine civil engineer and international official; b. 13 July 1919; ed. Colegio Nacional de Buenos Aires and Buenos Aires Univ.
Asst. at Buenos Aires Univ. 43; Aerodrome designer, Directorate of Infrastructure 43, Dir. Runways Section 45, Aerodrome Planning 46; rep. I.C.A.O. Air Navigation Cttee. 47-49, Chair. Air Navigation Comm. 49-57; Pres. 8th Assembly, I.C.A.O. 54, Pres. of Council of I.C.A.O. 57-; Hon. Dr. Eng. School of Mines and Engineering, South Dakota 59.
Home: 1460 McGregor Street, Montreal; Office: International Aviation Building, 1080 University Street, Montreal 3, Quebec, Canada.

Binder, Paul, DR. SC. POL.; German economist; b. 29 July 1902; ed. Technical High School, Stuttgart, and Univs. of Tübingen, Rostock, Dijon.
Deputy Dir. of Dresdner Bank, Berlin 37-40; Provincial

Dir., later State Sec. and Dir. of the Finance Ministry and Deputy Prime Minister of Württemberg-Hohenzollern; mem. of Parl. Council, Bonn 49; mem. Council of Economic Advisers for the Appraisal of General Econ. Devt. 64-68; mem. Board European Cttee. for Econ. and Social Progress (CEPES), and Dir. its German Board; mem. Board of Dirs. Econ. Cttee. of C.D.U. (Pres. Sub-Cttee. on Finance); Hon. Senator Tubingen Univ.; Grosses Verdienstkreuz mit Stern.
Publs. *Schalthebel der Konjunktur* 39, *Die Stabilisierung der Wirtschaftskonjunktur* 56, *U.S.A. und Wir* 56, *Kaufkraft, Produktivität, freie Kapitalbildung* 56, *Die Bundesbahn und ihre Konkurrenten* 61.
Home: Hermann Kurz-strasse 24, Stuttgart-N, Office: Königstrasse 48, Stuttgart-N., German Federal Republic.

Binder, Theodor, M.D.; Peruvian physician; b. 19; ed. Hebel-Gymnasium Lörrach, Univs. of Freiburg, Strasbourg, and Basle, and Swiss Tropical Inst., Basle.
Clinic Chief, Swiss Tropical Inst. 47-48; Public Health Officer, Oxapampa, Peru 48-50; Staff, Medical School, Univ. of San Marcos, Lima 51-56; Founder of Clinic for the Poor, and constructor of Hospital, Pucallpa 56-60, Inauguration Hospital Amazónico Albert Schweitzer, Yarinacocha, Pucallpa 60, Director 60-; Founder and Dir. Instituto Tropical Amazónico 63-.
Publs. Philosophy; *Friedrich Nietzsche* 50, *Goethe's Iphigenia and the Ethics* 51, *A. Schweitzer as a Philosopher* 54, *Heroism as an Attitude towards Life* 56, *Personal Ethics in a Depersonalizing age* 63, Medicine: *Congenital Malaria* 50, *Treatment of Hypertension* 52, *Latin-America: Nonanalytical Psychotherapy* 58, *Histoplasmosis in Eastern Peru* 64, *Dermotomycosis and Deep Mycosis in Eastern Peru* 65.
Hospital Amazónico Albert Schweitzer, P.O. Box 78, Pucallpa, Peru.

Bindzi, Benoit; Cameroonian civil servant and diplomatist; b. 1924; ed. St. Joseph Seminary, Ekok.
On staff of Customs, Civil Customs Admin. 44-58; Sec.-Gen. Union of Customs Workers, Sec.-Gen. Fed. of Cameroon Civil Servants 44-58; Sec.-Gen. Le Bloc Démocratique Camerounais 55-58; Chef de Cabinet, Ministry of Econ. Affairs 58-59; Nat. School of Admin., Paris 59, Chef de Cabinet, later Chief of Protocol, Cameroon Ministry of Foreign Affairs 60-61; Dep. Perm. Rep., later Perm. Rep. *ad interim* to UN 61-62, Perm. Rep. 62-65; Minister of Information and Tourism, Cameroon June 65-66, of Foreign Affairs 66-67.
Ministry of Foreign Affairs, Yaoundé, Cameroon.

Bing, Rudolf, C.B.E.; British impresario; b. 9 Jan. 1902.
Hessian State Theatre, Darmstadt 28-30; Civic Opera, Berlin-Charlottenburg 30-33; Gen. Man. Glyndebourne Opera, England 35-49; Artistic Dir. Edinburgh Int. Festival 47-49; Gen. Man. Metropolitan Opera, N.Y. 50-; Hon. D.Mus. (Lafayette Coll., Pa.), Hon. D.Litt. (Dickinson Coll., Pa.); Chevalier Légion d'Honneur.
c/o Metropolitan Opera, Lincoln Center, New York, N.Y., U.S.A.

Bingen, Sir Eric Albert, Kt.; British business executive; b. 1898; ed. Cheltenham Coll. and St. John's Coll., Oxford.
Served First World War; Solicitor 24; Legal Dept., Imperial Chemical Industries Ltd. 27-51, Dir. 51-63, Dep. Chair. 59-63; Chair. Remploy Ltd. 63-.
Flat 1, 25 Princes Gate, Kensington S.W.7, England.

Binger, James Henry, A.B., LL.B.; American lawyer and business executive; b. 16 May 1916; ed. Yale Univ. and Univ. of Minnesota.
Associate, Fletcher, Dorsey, Barker, Colman and Barber 41-43; Minneapolis-Honeywell Regulator Co.

(Honeywell Inc. 64) 43-, Asst. Sec. 45-46, Asst. Vice-Pres. 46-50, Vice-Pres. and Gen. Man. Valve Div., Philadelphia 50-52, Vice-Pres. 52-61, Dir. 59-, Pres. 61-65, Chair. 65-; Dir. Northwestern Bell Telephone Co., Northwest Airlines, Northwest Bancorporation.
Honeywell Inc., 2701 Fourth Avenue South, Minneapolis, Minnesota, U.S.A.

Bingham, Commdr. Barry; American journalist; b. 10 Feb. 1906; ed. Harvard Univ.
Pres. *Louisville Courier-Journal, Louisville Times,* WHAS Inc., Standard Gravure Corpn.; Chief E.C.A. Mission to France 49-50; Commdr. de la Légion d'Honneur; Trustee Rockefeller Foundation, Berea Coll.; Dir. Asia Foundation; Chair. Int. Press Inst., American Press Inst.; Hon. C.B.E. (U.K.).
Glenview, Kentucky, U.S.A.

Bingham, Colin William Hugh; Australian journalist; b. 10 July 1898; ed. Townsville Grammar School and Queensland Univ.
Foreign Corresp. *Sydney Morning Herald* 43-48, Assoc. Ed. 57-61, Acting Ed. 57-58, Ed. 61-65; Ford Memorial Prize for Verse, Queensland Univ.
Publ. *Men and Affairs* 67.
30 Arnold Street, Killara, Sydney, Australia.
Telephone: 492970 (Sydney).

Bingham, Jonathan Brewster; American diplomatist; b. 24 April 1914; ed. Yale Univ.
Member, New York Bar; U.S. Army 43-45; private legal practice 39-41, 46-51, 53-54, 59-61; Office of Price Admin. 41-42; Dept. of State 45-46; Asst. Dir. Office of Int. Security Affairs, Dept. of State 51; Dep. Administrator, Tech. Co-op. Admin. 51-53; Sec. to State Gov. 55-58; U.S. Rep. UN Trusteeship Council 61-63, Pres. 62-63; U.S. Rep. UN Econ. and Social Council 63-64; Rep. 23rd District New York, U.S. House of Reps. 65-.
5000 Independence Avenue, Bronx, N.Y. 10471, U.S.A.

Bingham, Wheelock Hayward; American businessman; b. 28 Nov. 1907; ed. Harvard Univ.
Pres. and Dir. R. H. Macy & Co. Inc.; Dir. Bank of America.
Home: 100 East 50th Street, New York 22, N.Y.; Office: R. H. Macy & Co. Inc., Herald Square, New York City, N.Y., U.S.A.

Binoche, Jean André; French diplomatist; b. 19 Aug. 1903; ed. Ecole Libre des Sciences Politiques.
Clerk, Ministry of Finance 34-36; Asst. Dir. Moroccan Office, Paris 36-41; Sec.-Gen., Tunisian Govt. 41-44, Fighting French in Levant 44-45; First Counsellor Beirut 46; Asst. Dir., Central Admin. 46-50; Chargé d'Affaires East Africa 50-52, Minister 52; Ambassador to Peru 52-55; Chargé d'Affaires Washington 55-57; Ambassador to Norway 57-61, to Yugoslavia 61-62, 62-65, to Brazil 65-; Officier Légion d'Honneur.
French Embassy, Avenida Presidente Antonio Carlos 58, Rio de Janeiro, Brazil; and 36 boulevard Suchet, Paris 16e, France.

Biobaku, Saburi Oladeni, C.M.G., B.A., M.A., PH.D.; Nigerian historian and university official; b. 16 June 1918; ed. Government Coll., Ibadan, Higher Coll., Yaba, University Coll. Exeter, Trinity Coll. Cambridge, and Inst. of Historical Research, London.
Master, Govt. Coll., Ibadan 41-44; Educ. Officer 47-50; Asst. Liaison Officer for Nigerian Students in U.K., Colonial Office, London 51-53; Registrar, Univ. Coll., Ibadan 53-57; Sec. to Premier and Exec. Council, W. Nigeria 57-61; Pro-Vice-Chancellor, Univ. of Ife and Dir. Institutes of African Studies and of Public Admin. 61-65; Vice-Chancellor Designate, Univ. of Zambia Feb.-March 65; Vice-Chancellor Univ. of Lagos 65-, Prof. and Dir. of African Studies 65-; Dir. Yoruba Historical Research Scheme 56-; Chair. Cttee. of Vice-Chancellors, Nigeria 67-; Vice-Chair. Standing Cttee., *Encyclopaedia Africana* 67-; mem. Exec. Board Asscn.

of African Univs. 67-; Pres. Historical Soc. of Nigeria 68-; created Are of Iddo, Abeokuta 58; Hon. Fellow, W. African Asscn. of Surgeons 68.
Publs. *The Origin of the Yoruba* 55, *The Egba and their Neighbours* 57, *African Studies in an African University* 63.
Vice-Chancellor's Office, University of Lagos, Lagos; Vice-Chancellor's Lodge, 10 James George Street, Alagbon Close, Ikoyi, Lagos; The Chalet, Mile 2, Owode Road, Abeokuta, Nigeria.
Telephone: Lagos 43761 (Office); 21860 (Home); Abeokuta 206.

Birane, Wane Mamadou; Mauritanian politician; b. 1929; ed. St. Louis, Senegal, and Federal School for Posts and Telecommunications, Dakar.
Meteorological Services, Mauritania 46; later civil servant, Niger, Senegal; Dir. Posts and Telecommunications, Mauritania 60; Perm. Sec. Ministry of Transport, Posts and Telecommunications 61-63; Dir.-Gen. of Transportation 63-66; Minister for the Plan 66; Minister for Foreign Affairs and Planning Oct. 66-.
Ministry of Foreign Affairs, Nouakchott, Mauritania.

Birecki, Henryk; Polish diplomatist; b. 16.
Permanent Rep. to U.N. Gen. Assembly 51-56; Dir. Ministry of Foreign Affairs 56-; mem. Economic and Social Council 13th-16th Sessions, Vice-Chair. and Pres. Economic Cttee. Session; Polish Rep. Comm. on Human Rights, Comm. on Int. Commodity Trade; Chair. Polish del. to the Diplomatic Conf., Vienna 61.
Ministry of Foreign Affairs, Warsaw, Poland.

Birgi, Muharrem Nuri; Turkish diplomatist; b. 08; ed. School of Political Sciences, Paris, and Faculty of Law, Geneva.
Joined the Foreign Ministry 32; held diplomatic posts in Warsaw, Vichy and Madrid; since 44 has held many posts at the Ministry of Foreign Affairs (finally Sec.-Gen.) representing Turkey at int. confs.; Amb. to Great Britain 57-60; Turkish Perm. Rep. to NATO 60-.
NATO Headquarters, Brussels 39, Belgium.
Telephone: 41-00-40.

Biris, Stavros Ioannou; Greek politician and publisher; b. 21; ed. Pandeian School, Athens.
Former teacher and publisher; resistance in Crete in Second World War, published three clandestine newspapers; Gen. Sec. Governmental Del. to Crete 44-45; mem. Parl. 52-58, 63-; Minister of the Merchant Marine 64-65; Founder and Chair. Biris Publishing House; Centre Union.
Karaiskou III, Piraeus, Greece.

Biriukov, Dmitry Andreyevich; Soviet physiologist; b. 1904; ed. Rostov Univ.
Junior Research Assoc., Asst. Prof. Rostov Univ. 27-35; Prof. 35; Head of Chair., Pedagogical and Medical Insts., Rostov, Second Moscow Medical Inst. 35-50; Dir. Voronezh Medical Inst. 39-44; corresp. mem. U.S.S.R. Acad. of Medical Sciences 50-62, mem. 62-; Dir. Inst. of Experimental Medicine, Leningrad 50-; Order of Lenin, Red Banner of Labour, Badge of Honour; Dr. h.c. Charles Univ., Prague.
Publs. Over 200 works on reflectory regulation of cardiovascular system, inter-relation of cardiovascular and respiratory systems.
Institute of Experimental Medicine, 69/71 Kirov Prospekt, Leningrad, U.S.S.R.

Birkelund, Palle; Danish librarian; b. 29 Jan. 1912; ed. Københavns Universitet and Aarhus Universitet.
Library Asst., State Library, Aarhus and Univ. Library, Copenhagen, Asst. Librarian 44; UNESCO Fellowship, U.S.A. 49; Nat. Librarian 52-; Vice-Chair. Danish Library Asscn.; Chair. Danish Asscn. of Research Libraries, Danish Asscn. for Bookcraft, Danish Circle of Book Collectors.

Publs. Co-editor: *Nordisk leksikon for bogvaesen* 47-62, and library and bibliographical reviews.
The Royal Library, Copenhagen; and 6 Strandgade, Copenhagen, Denmark.
Telephone: SU 189.

Birket-Smith, Kaj, M.SC., PH.D.; Danish ethnologist; b. 20 Jan. 1893; ed. Univ. of Copenhagen.
Asst. Curator Nat. Museum of Denmark 29-34, Curator 34-40, Head Curator Ethnological Dept. 40-63; Reader in Ethnology, Univ. of Copenhagen 45-63; ethnological and archæological field work in Greenland, Arctic Canada, Alaska, Philippines, and British Solomon Islands; Hon. D.Sc. Philadelphia, Hon. Ph.D. Oslo and Basle.
Publs. Numerous works, mainly on the ethnology of the Arctic and of Oceania.
25 Drosselvej, Copenhagen F, Denmark.

Birksted, Kaj, D.S.O., O.B.E., D.F.C.; Danish air force officer; b. 2 March 1915.
Chief of Staff, Danish Air Force 50-; SHAPE 54-60; NATO Headquarters 60-; awards Commdr. of St. Olav (Norway), Norwegian War Cross, Haakon VII comm. Medal, Knight of Dannebrog, etc.
NATO Headquarters, Brussels, Belgium.

Birla, B. M.; Indian industrialist; b. 04.
One of the founders of the Indian Chamber of Commerce and Pres. in 36 and 44; founder and Pres. Indian Sugar Mills Asscn. and Indian Paper Mills Asscn.; mem. Fiscal Comm., Govt. of India; Pres. Fed. of Indian Chambers of Commerce and Industry 54; fmr. Dir. Central Board Reserve Bank of India and Chair. of Local Board, Eastern Area; Chair. West Bengal Financial Corpn., Hindustan Motors Ltd., Ruby Gen. Insurance Co. Ltd., India Exchange Ltd.; Man. Dir. Birla Bros. Private Ltd.; Dir. The Atul Products Ltd., and various other concerns.
Office: 15 India Exchange Place, Calcutta 1; Home: Birla House, 8/9 Alipore Road, Calcutta 27, India.

Birla, Ghanshyandas; Indian business man and philanthropist; b. 94.
Pres. Indian Chamber of Commerce, Calcutta 24; founded and maintained a large number of educational and other public institutions; mem. Indian Fiscal Comm., Bengal Legislative Council, Royal Comm. on Labour; Del. Labour Conf., Geneva 27; unofficial Indian adviser Indo-British Trade Negotiations 36-37; Pres. All-India Harijan Sevak Sangh; Man. Dir. Birla Bros. Ltd.; Padma Vibhushan 57; Hon. LL.D. (Banaras Hindu Univ.) 67.
15 India Exchange Place, Calcutta, India.

Birladeanu, Alexandru; Romanian economist and politician; b. 21 Jan. 1911; ed. Univ. of Jassy.
Member Romanian C.P. 43-; Prof., Head of Dept. of Political Economy, Inst. of Econ. Sciences, Bucharest 46-51; Sec.-Gen., then Deputy Minister, Ministry of Nat. Economy 46-48; Minister of Foreign Trade 48-54; First Deputy Chair., then Chair. State Planning Cttee. 55; mem. Central Cttee. Romanian C.P. 55-, Alt. mem. Political Bureau 62-65, mem. Political Bureau 65-; Deputy Chair. Council of Ministers 55-65, 67-, First Deputy Chair. 65-67; Chair. Nat. Council for Scientific Research 67-; mem. Exec. Cttee. and Perm. Presidium Central Cttee. of Romanian C.P. 65-; mem. Romanian Acad.of Sciences 55-; Deputy to Grand Nat. Assembly; Hero of Socialist Labour 64.
Council of Ministers of Socialist Republic of Romania, Bucharest; and B-dul Ana Ipătescu No. 50, Bucharest, Romania.

Birley, Sir Robert, K.C.M.G., M.A.; British university professor; b. 14 July 1903; ed. Rugby and Balliol Coll., Oxford.
Asst. master, Eton Coll. 26-35; Headmaster of Charterhouse 35-47; Educational Adviser, British Zone of

Germany 47-49; Headmaster of Eton Coll. 49-63; Visiting Prof. of Educ., Univ. of Witwatersrand 63-66; mem. Fleming Cttee. 44; Burge Memorial Lecturer 47, Reith Lecturer 49; Gresham Prof. of Rhetoric; Head Prof. Dept. Social Studies and the Humanities, City Univ., London; Grosses Bundesverdienstkreuz 57; Hon. Dr. Ing. Berlin Technical Univ., Hon. LL.D. Edinburgh, Witwatersrand, Leeds and Liverpool Univs., Hon. D.Phil. Frankfurt/Main Univ.
Publs. *Speeches and Documents in American History* (4 vols.), *The English Jacobins, Sunk Without Trace* 62. 38 Trinity Church Square, London, S.E.1, England. Telephone: 01-253-4399.

Biró, József; Hungarian politician; b. 13 Feb. 1921; ed. Economic and Technical Academies, Univ. of Law. Former instrument maker, fitter and welder; fmr. Head of Wages Dept., Technical Dept., Imports Dept., Ministry of Foreign Trade; Managing Dir. foreign trade enterprise 55-57; Head Commercial Dept., Hungarian Legation, London 57-60; Sec., Party Cttee. of Ministry of Foreign Trade 60-62, Dep. Minister of Foreign Trade 62-63, Minister of Foreign Trade 63-; mem. Central Cttee. Hungarian Socialist Workers' Party 66-.
Ministry of Foreign Trade, Budapest, Hungary.

Biros, Casimir Marc; French government official; b 25 April 1905; ed. Lycée de Foix, American Univ. of Beirut, and Faculty of Law, Univ. of Lyon.
Former Govt. Official, Indo-China, then successively Provincial Head, and Dir. of High Commissioner's Office; later Sec.-Gen. Govt. of New Caledonia; Gov. of Dahomey; attached to Ministry of Armed Forces 60-62; French High Commr. in the Pacific and to New Hebrides, Gov. of New Caledonia 62-65; Dir. Office Ministry of the Army 65-; Officier, Légion d'Honneur, several foreign decorations.
14 *bis*, rue de la Flèche, Sceaux, Seine, France.

Birrenbach, Kurt, D.IUR.; German business executive; b. 2 July 1907; ed. Paulinum Grammar School, Münster, and Univs. of Geneva, Paris, Munich, Berlin and Münster.
Adviser for financial affairs and foreign exchange transactions 35-39; importer and exporter of steel and steel products, S. America and Germany 39-54; Chair. Thyssen Vermögensverwaltung GmbH, Düsseldorf 55-; Chair. of Supervisory Board, August Thyssen-Hütte A.G., Duisburg-Hamborn 62-; Vice-Chair. Handelsunion A.G., Düsseldorf; Chair. Fritz Thyssen Stiftung, Cologne; mem. of the Bundestag; Chair. of Policy Cttee., Atlantic Inst., Paris; official of other firms and int. orgs.; Christian Democrat.
Publ. *The Future of the Atlantic Community* 63.
Düsseldorf, Berliner Allee 33, German Federal Republic. Telephone: 81176.

Bishop, Elizabeth; American poetess and writer; b. 8 Feb. 1911; ed. Walnut Hill School, New England, and Vassar Coll., Poughkeepsie, New York.
Consultant in Poetry, Library of Congress, Washington D.C. 49-50; Howard Mifflin Literary Fellowship, Guggenheim Fellowship, Shelley Memorial Award, Amy Lowell Fellowship, Partisan Review Fellowship, etc.; mem. American Inst. of Arts and Letters; Pulitzer Prize for Poetry 56.
Publs. *North and South* (poems), *A Cold Spring* 55, *Poems* 55, *The Diary of Helena Morley* (trans. from Portuguese) 57, *Questions of Travel* 65.
Caixa Postal 279, Petrópolis, Brazil.

Bishti, Ahmed; Libyan politician; ed. Italian School, Tripoli and Cairo Univ.
Doctor in Tripoli 55-61; Joined Ministry of Health 61; Dir. of Govt. Hospitals, Tripoli 62-63; Minister of Health 63-64; Ambassador to the Lebanon 64-65; Minister of Foreign Affairs 65-.
Ministry of Foreign Affairs, Tripoli, Libya.

Bismarck, Klaus von; German radio executive and ecclesiastical official; b. 6 March 1912; ed. High School, Doberan, agricultural education (training).
Army training 34-38; continued agricultural studies 38-39; Second World War service rising to Lieut.-Col. and commdr. of infantry regt. 39-45, prisoner-of-war 45; Dir. Juvenile Welfare Office, Herford 45-46, Jugenddorf (Youth Leader Training Centre) Vlotho a.d. Weser 46-49; Dir.-Gen. Westdeutscher Rundfunk 61-; mem. Cen. Cttee. Ecumenical Council of Churches, All German Synod, Presidium German Evangelical Church Council; Co-editor *Evangelische Ethik* (newspaper); Pres. Soc. for Social Progress; Hon. D.Theol. (Münster Univ.); mem. Senate, Max Planck-Gesellschaft.
Publs. Editor with Prof. Dr. Friedrich Karrenberg of series *Kirche im Volk*; papers on sociology and theology.
Wallrafplatz 5, Köln, German Federal Republic. Telephone: 20701.

Bisplingoff, Raymond Lewis; American aeronautical engineer; b. 7 Feb. 1917; ed. Eidgenössische Technische Hochschule, Zürich, and Univ. of Cincinnati.
Engineer, Aeronca Aircraft Corpn. 37-40, Wright Field 40-41; Instructor, Univ. of Cincinnati 41-43; Engineer, Bureau of Aeronautics, Navy Dept., Washington 43-46; Asst. Prof. Massachusetts Inst. of Technology 46-48, Assoc. Prof. 48-53, Prof. 53-; mem. Scientific Advisory Board, United States Air Force; mem. Cttee. of N.A.S.A. (Nat. Aeronautics and Space Admin.), Dir., Office of Advanced Research and Technology, N.A.S.A. until Nov. 63, Assoc. Administrator for Advanced Research and Technology Nov. 63-, Special Asst. to Administrator 65-; mem. Nat. Acad. of Engineering 65; Consultant to Admin., Fed. Aviation Agency 65-; Prof. and Head, Dept. of Aeronautics and Astronautics, Massachusetts Inst. of Technology 66-; Pres. American Inst. of Aeronautics and Astronautics 66; Chair. N.A.S.A. Research and Technology Advisory Council; Vice-Chair. Aeronautics and Space Engineering Board, Nat. Acad. of Engineers; Vice-Chair. Sonic Boom Cttee., Nat. Acad. of Sciences; mem. Nat. Acad. of Sciences; Fellow American Acad. Arts and Sciences, Royal Aeronautical Soc.; Hon. Fellow, American Inst. of Aeronautics and Astronautics; various hon. degrees; N.A.S.A. Distinguished Service Medal 67.
Publs. Three books and many papers in the field of aeronautics and astronautics.
Department of Aeronautics and Astronautics, Massachusetts Institute of Technology, Cambridge, Massachusetts 02139; Home: 15 Fife Road, Wellesley 82, Massachusetts 02181, U.S.A.
Telephone: 617-235-8478 (Home); 617-864-6900 (Office).

Bissell, Claude T(homas), M.A., PH.D.; Canadian university administrator; b. 10 Feb. 1916; ed. Runnymede Collegiate Inst., Toronto, Toronto and Cornell Univs.
Reuben Wells Leonard Fellowship 36, Cornell Fellowship 37; Instructor in English, Cornell Univ. 38-41; Lecturer in English, Toronto Univ. 41-42; served in Canadian Army in Europe 42-45; on staff of Khaki Coll. England 45-46; Asst. Prof. of English, Dean in Residence, Univ. Coll. Toronto Univ. 47; Asst. to Pres. Toronto Univ. 48, Assoc. Prof. 51, Vice-Pres. of Univ. 52-56; Pres. Carleton Univ. Ottawa 56-58; Pres. Univ. of Toronto 58-; Chair. Canada Council 60-62; Pres. Nat. Conf. Canadian Univs. and Colls. 62-63; Chair. Canadian Univs. Foundation 62-63; Pres. World Univ. Service of Canada 62-63; Hon. D.Litt. (Manitoba), Hon. LL.D. (McGill, Queen's, New Brunswick, Carleton, Montreal, St. Lawrence, British Columbia, Michigan and Columbia Univs.).
Publs. Edited and contributed to *University College: A Portrait, 1853-1953, Canada's Crisis in Higher Education, Our Living Tradition*; numerous articles.

Simcoe Hall, University of Toronto, Toronto 5; Home: 93 Highland Avenue, Toronto 5, Ontario, Canada.

Bista, Kirti Nidhi, M.A.; Nepalese politician; b. 1927; ed. Tri-Chandra Coll., Katmandu and Lucknow Univ.
Assistant Minister for Education 61-62, Minister for Educ. 62-64, for Foreign Affairs 64; Vice-Chair. Council of Ministers and Minister for Foreign Affairs and Educ. 64-66; Vice-Chair. Council of Ministers and Minister for Foreign Affairs and Econ. Planning 66-67; Deputy Prime Minister and Minister for Foreign Affairs and Educ. Jan. 67-; Leader Nepalese Dels. to UN Gen. Assemblies 64, 65, 66, and to UNESCO Gen. Confs. 62, 64, 66, and to various other confs.; accompanied H.M. the King on many State Visits; Order of the Right Hand of Gurkhas (First Class), Fed. German Order of Merit, French Legion of Honour.
Kshetra Pati, Katmandu, Nepal.

Biswas, Charu Chandra, C.I.E., M.A., LL.B.; Indian lawyer and politician; b. 88; ed. Hindu School, Presidency Coll. and Ripon Law Coll. (Univ. of Calcutta).
Advocate, Calcutta High Court 10-; Fellow and Syndicate mem. Univ. of Calcutta 17-22 and 26-51; Comm. Calcutta Corpn. 21-24, Councillor 25-37; mem. Calcutta Improvement Trust 26-37; mem. Indian Legislative Assembly 30-37; Judge, Calcutta High Court 37-48; Dean, Faculty of Law, Calcutta Univ. 38-50; Vice-Chancellor 49-50; mem. Indian Parl. Congress Party 50-; Minister for External Affairs 50-52, for Law and Minority Affairs 52-56; mem. Council of States 52-.
5 Queen Victoria Road, New Delhi, India; and 58 Puddopukur Road, Elgin Road P.O., Calcutta, India.

Biszku, Béla; Hungarian politician; b. 13 Sept. 1921.
Joined Communist Party 44 and worked as a Communist Party official; Minister of Home Affairs 57-61; Dep. Prime Minister 61-62; mem. Political Cttee., Hungarian Socialist Workers' Party 57-, Sec. Central Cttee. 62-.
Hungarian Socialist Worker's Party, Szécheny Rakpart, 19, Budapest, Hungary.

Bitar, Salah El-; Syrian politician; b. 12; ed. Damascus and Univ. of Paris.
Secondary school teacher in Damascus 34-42; entered politics 42; co-founder, with Michel Aflaq, of Arab Resurrection Party and Editor of party organ; left Syria after Shishekly coup 52; later returned and took part in merging of Renaissance and Socialist parties to form Baath Party; elected to Parliament after overthrow of Shishekly 54; Minister of Foreign Affairs 56; head of Syrian Del. to U.N. Gen. Assembly 57; Minister of Culture and Nat. Guidance, U.A.R. 58-59; Prime Minister of Syrian Arab Republic March-11 May 63, 13 May 63-Nov. 63, May 64-Oct. 64, Dec. 65-66; concurrently Minister of Foreign Affairs May 63-Nov. 63; Vice-Pres. Council of Revolutionary Command Nov. 63-66.
Beirut, Lebanon.

Bitossi, Renato; Italian trade unionist; b. 31 March 1899.
Former steelworker; fmr. Pres. Lucca Nat. Liberation Cttee.; fmr. Sec. Florence Chamber of Commerce; mem. Italian Socialist Party, later Italian Communist Party; Senator; Pres. World Fed. of Trade Unions (W.F.T.U.) 62-.
Via Milazzo 7, Florence, Italy.

Bitsios, Dimitri S.; Greek diplomatist; ed. Univ. of Athens.
Entered Diplomatic Service 39, served Cairo, London and New York; Head, Economic Section, Ministry of Foreign Affairs; Head, 4th Political Dept., Ministry of Foreign Affairs; Del. to UN 56-61, Perm. Rep. 61-65, 67-; Head, 1st Political Dept., Ministry of Foreign Affairs 65-66; Private Sec. to King of the Hellenes; Order of the Phoenix; Distinguished Service Medal.

Publs. *Egypt and the Middle East, Greek Diplomatic History.*
Permanent Mission of Greece to UN, 69 East 79th Street, New York, N.Y. 10021, U.S.A.

Bittner, Horst; German diplomatist.
Leader of German Trade Mission, Moscow 57-65; Ambassador to U.S.S.R. 65-; Vaterländischer Orden in Bronze 65.
Embassy of German Democratic Republic, Ul. Stanislavskovo 10, Moscow, U.S.S.R.

Biyogho, Jacques; Gabon diplomatist; b. 1932; ed. Libreville, Gabon, and training in timber industry, Mouchard, France.
Instructor, Technical School, Libreville 60-61; Deputy in Gabon Nat. Assembly 61-64; First Counsellor, Paris 64-66; Perm. Rep. to UN 66-67.
c/o Ministry of Foreign Affairs, Libreville, Gabon.

Bizot, Henry; French banker; b. 27 Aug. 1901; ed. Inst. Sainte-Croix, Neuilly-sur-Seine.
Inspector of Finances 25; Asst. Sec.-Gen. Comptoir national d'escompte de Paris 30-59, Dir.-Gen. 59-62, Admin. Dir.-Gen. 62-63, Vice-Pres. Dir.-Gen. 63-64, Pres. 64-; Pres. Banque nationale de Paris 66-; Chair. Unival; Dir. numerous companies including Banque industrielle de l'Afrique du Nord, Didot-Botton, Idéal-Standard; Commdr. Légion d' Honneur.
76 avenue Raymond-Poincaré, Paris 16e, France.

Bjerknes, Jakob Aall Bonnevie; Norwegian meteorologist; b. 2 Nov. 1897; ed. Oslo and Leipzig Univs.
Meteorologist Bergen Observatory 18-; Dir. Weather Service for Western Norway 20; Prof. Geophysical Inst. Bergen 31-40; Prof. Univ. of Calif., Los Angeles 40-; hon. mem. Royal Meteorological Society, London, awarded its Symons Gold Medal 40; Bowie Medal, American Geophysical Union 42, Royal Order of St. Olav 46, Vega Medal of Swedish Assoc. of Geography 58; elected to Nat. Acad. Washington, D.C. 47; mem. Royal Swedish Acad. of Sciences; foreign mem. Royal Norwegian Acad. of Sciences, Hon. Fellow Indian Acad. of Sciences; Hon. mem. American Meteorological Soc. 58; Pres. Meteorological Asscn. of the Int. Union of Geodesy and Geophysics 48-51, Vice-Pres. I.U.G.G. 51-54; Int. Meteorological Org. Prize 59; Rossby Award from American Meteorological Soc. 60; Nat. Medal of Science from Pres. of U.S. 66; mem. American Acad. of Arts and Sciences 60.
Department of Meteorology, University of California, Los Angeles, Calif. 90024, U.S.A.

Bjerve, Petter Jakob, CAND. ŒCON. D.PHIL.; Norwegian economist and politician; b. 27 Sept. 1913; ed. Univ. of Oslo.
Research Asst. Economics Inst., Oslo Univ. 39-40; Research Fellow, Oslo Univ. 45-49; Chief of Div. Ministry of Finance 45-49; Dir.-Gen. Central Bureau of Statistics of Norway 49-60, 63-; Minister of Finance 60-63; mem. Labour Party.
Publs. *Hva krigen kosten Norge* (What the War Cost Norway) 45, *Government Economic Planning and Control* 50, *Planning in Norway 47-56* 59.
Central Bureau of Statistics, Oslo, Norway.

Björk, Anita; Swedish actress; b. 25 April 1923; ed. Royal Dramatic Theatre School, Stockholm.
Numerous stage appearances at Royal Dramatic Theatre, Stockholm, including *Miss Julie* 48.
Principal theatre roles at Royal Dramatic Theatre, Stockholm, include: Agnes (*Brand*, Ibsen), Celia (*The Cocktail Party*, Eliot), Rosalind (*As You Like It*, Shakespeare), Juliet (*Romeo and Juliet*, Shakespeare), Eliza (*Pygmalion*, Shaw), Solange (*Les Bonnes*, Genet), The girl (*Look Back in Anger*, Osborne), Johanna (*Les séquestrés d'Altona*, Sartre).
Films acted in include: *Himlaspelet* 42, *Räkna de*

lyckliga stunderna blott (Count Your Blessings) 44, *Hundra dragspel och en flicka* (One Hundred Concertinas and a Girl) 46, *Ingen väg tillbaka* (No Return) 47, *Kvinna utan ansikte* 47, *Det kom en gäst* (There Came a Guest) 47, *På dessa skuldror* (On these Shoulders) 48, *Människors rike* (The Realm of Men and Women) 49, *Kvartetten som sprängdes* (The Quartet that was Broken) 50, *Fröken Julie* 50-51, *Han glömde henne aldrig* 52, *Night People* 53, *Die Hexe* 54, *Giftas* 55, *Der Cornet* 55, *Moln över Hellesta* (Dark Clouds over Hellesta) 56, *Sången om den eldröda blommen* 56, *Gäst i eget hus* (Guest in One's Own House) 57, *Mannekäng i rött* 58, *Tärningen är kastad* 60, *Goda vänner trogna grannar* 60, *Vita frun* 62, *Älskade par* 64.
Jagarestigen 7, Saltsjo-Duvnäs, Stockholm, Sweden.

Björnsson, Henrik Sv., LL.B.; Icelandic diplomatist; b. 2 Sept. 1914; ed. Univ. of Iceland.
Graduated in law and joined Foreign Service 39, served Copenhagen, Reykjavík, Washington 39-44; Head of Dept. Ministry of Foreign Affairs, Reykjavík 44-47; Sec. Oslo 47-49; Counsellor, Paris 50-52; Sec. to Pres. of Iceland 52-56; Sec.-Gen. Ministry of Foreign Affairs 56-61; Amb. to Great Britain and Netherlands and Minister to Spain and Portugal 61-65; Amb. to France and Luxembourg, Minister to Yugoslavia 65; Amb. to Belgium and Perm. Rep. to NATO 65-67, OECD 65-, Council of Europe 68-; Kt. Commdr. Order of Icelandic Falcon, Hon. K.B.E. and other foreign decorations.
Ambassade d'Islande, 124 boulevard Haussmann, Paris 8e, France.
Telephone: LABorde 81-54.

Bjørnvig, Thorkild Strange, DR. PHIL.; Danish poet and writer; b. 2 Feb. 1918; ed. Cathedral School, Aarhus, and Univ. of Aarhus.
Publisher's Reader, Gyldendalske Boghandel, Nordisk Forlag; mem. Danish Acad. 60; several prizes.
Publs. poetry: *Stjaernen bag gavlen* 47, *Anubis* 55, *Figur og Ild* 59; essays: *Rilke og tysk Tradition* 59, *Begyndelsen* 60, *Kains Alter* 64.
Dauglykkevej 16, Humlebaek, Denmark.

Blacher, Boris; German composer; b. 19 Jan. 1903; ed. Technische Hochschule Berlin, Hochschule für Musik, Berlin, and Universität Berlin.
Spent early years in China and Siberia; in Berlin 22-; freelance composer until 38; teacher at Konservatorium Dresden 38-39; teacher at Musikhochschule Berlin 48; Dir. Hochschule für Musik, Berlin 53-; Lecturer, Technical Univ., Berlin 60-; Guest Lecturer, Bryanston, U.K. 49-50, Mozarteum Salzburg 55, Tanglewood, U.S.A. 66; mem. Akademie der Künste, Berlin; numerous music prizes.
Works include 9 operas, 9 ballets, compositions for orchestra, choir and chamber music, notably operas: *Preussisches Märchen* 52, *Rosamunde Floris* 60, *Zwischenfälle bei einer Notlandung* (electronic opera) 65; ballets: *Hamlet* 49, *Der Mohr von Venedig* 55, *Tristan* 65; oratorios: *Der Grossinquisitor* 42, *Requiem* 58; orchestra: *Concertante Musik* 37, *Paganini Variationen* 47, *Orchester-Ornament* 53, *Orchester-Fantasie* 56, 3 piano concertos, violin concertos, viola concerto, 'cello concerto.
Hochschule für Musik, Berlin-Charlottenburg, Fasanenstrasse 1; and Berlin 37, Kaunstrasse 6, Germany.

Black, Eugene R., B.A.; American banker; b. 1 May 1898; ed. Univ. of Georgia.
Served First World War; later associated with Harris, Forbes & Co. N.Y. investment bankers; Man. Atlanta Office Chase-Harris, Forbes Corpn. 31, Asst. Vice-Pres. 33; Second Vice-Pres. Chase Nat. Bank N.Y. 33, Vice-Pres. 37-47, now Dir. and consultant; Exec. Dir. for U.S. Int. Bank for Reconstruction and Development 47-49; Senior Vice-Pres. Chase Nat. Bank N.Y. March-June 49; Pres. and Chair. Int. Bank for Reconstruction and

Development July 49-63, Int. Finance Corpn. Oct. 61-63; Special Financial Consultant to Sec-Gen. of UN 63-; Dir. American Express, Royal Dutch Petroleum Co. and numerous other companies 63-; Special Adviser to Pres. of U.S.A. on S.E. Asia Devt.; Financial Adviser to Sheikh of Kuwait and mem. Kuwait Investment Advisory Cttee.; many nat. and int. awards.
Publ. *The Diplomacy of Economic Development*.
Office: 1 Chase Manhattan Plaza, New York 5, N.Y.; Home: 178 Columbia Heights, Brooklyn 1, N.Y., U.S.A.

Black, Hugo La Fayette; American lawyer; b. 27 Feb. 1886; ed. Univ. of Alabama.
Began practice in Birmingham 07; police judge 10-11; served World War 15-18; solicitor, Jefferson County, Ala. 15-17; gen. practice, Birmingham 19-27; U.S, Senator from Alabama, two terms, 27-37; Assoc. Justice, U.S. Supreme Court 37-; Democrat.
Supreme Court Building, Washington, D.C., U.S.A.

Black, Misha, O.B.E.; British architect and industrial designer; b. 16 Oct. 1910.
Partner in Industrial Design Partnership 32-39; Principal Exhibition Architect to Ministry of Information 40-45; Exhibition Consultant to UNESCO 47 and 54; Co-ordinating Architect, Festival of Britain 1951; Consultant to Ceylon Govt., Colombo Exhibition 52 and 56; Industrial Design Consultant to B.O.A.C. 51-56; Senior Partner, Design Research Unit and Black, Bayes and Gibson, Architects; mem. MARS Group 38-57; mem. Council of Soc. of Industrial Artists 38-58, Pres. 54-56; Advisory Council, Inst. of Contemporary Art 51-67; mem. Council of Industrial Design 55-64; Design Consultant to British Transport Comm. 56-66; Royal Designer to Industry 58; Joint Interior Architect to Orient Line 57-60; Prof. of Industrial Design (Eng.) Royal Coll. of Art 59-; Architect to Zoological Soc. of London for Small Mammal House 62-67; Pres. Int. Council of Socs. of Industrial Design 59-62; Design Consultant to London Transport Board 64-; Vice-Pres. Modular Soc. 66-; Gold Medal, Soc. of Industrial Artists 65; mem. Advisory Council, Science Museum 66-.
Designs for Spanish-American Exhibition, Seville 28, Int. Exhibition Paris 37, Empire Exhibition Glasgow 38, N.Y. World's Fair 39, Brussels International Exhbn. 58, Montreal Int. Exhbn. 67; and for public and private companies.
37 Duke Street, London, W.1, England.
Telephone: 01-486-1681.

Black, Robert Fager; American executive; b. 2 Nov. 1889; ed. Harrisburg High School, Mercersburg Acad. and Princeton Univ.
Pres. Brockway Motor Co., N.Y. 30-35, The White Motor Co., Cleveland 35-45, Chair. and Chief Exec. Officer 56-60, Chair. 60-; Distinguished Service Medal, Ohio State Univ.
13901 Shaker Boulevard, Cleveland 20, Ohio, U.S.A.

Black, Sir William Rushton, Kt. (cr. Life Peer June 68); British business executive; b. 12 Jan. 1893; ed. Barrow Secondary School, Barrow Technical Coll.
With Vickers Ltd. 08-28; Man. Weymanns Motor Bodies 28; Gen. Man. Park Royal Vehicles Ltd. 34-39, Man. Dir. 39; Dir. Associated Commercial Vehicles Ltd. 49, Man. Dir. 57; Chair. A.E.C. Ltd. 58; Chair. Leyland Motor Corpn. 63-67.
Birchwood Grange, Ruxley Cres., Claygate, Surrey, England.

Blackburn, Lieut.-Col. Sir Charles Bickerton, K.C.M.G., O.B.E., B.A., M.D., CH.M., F.R.C.P., F.R.S.M., F.R.A.C.P.; Australian physician; b. 74; ed. Univs. of Adelaide and Sydney.
Lecturer in Clinical Medicine Univ. of Sydney 12- and Dean Faculty of Medicine 33; mem. Senate, Univ. of Sydney 19-; hon. Physician Royal Prince Alfred

Hospital 11-34; hon. Consulting Physician 34; Chancellor Univ. of Sydney 41-64.
Publs. include articles in Australian Medical Journal.
229 Macquarie Street, Sydney, N.S.W., Australia.

Blackett, Patrick Maynard Stuart, O.M., C.H., P.R.S., M.A.; British physicist; b. 18 Nov. 1897; ed. Royal Naval Colls., Osborne and Dartmouth, Magdalene Coll., Cambridge.
Served Royal Navy 14-19; Fellow King's Coll. 23-33; Prof. of Physics, Birkbeck Coll. 33-37; Langworthy Prof. of Physics Manchester Univ. 37-53; Pro-Vice-Chancellor 50-52; Prof. of Physics, Imperial Coll. of Science and Technology, Univ. of London 53-65, Fellow 65-; mem. Board of Nat. Research Development Corpn. 49-65; mem. Scientific Policy Cttee. European Org. for Nuclear Research 54-58; mem. Council of Dept. of Scientific and Industrial Research 55-60; mem. Governing Board of Nat. Inst. for Research in Nuclear Science 57-60; mem. Council of Inst. for Strategic Studies 58-60; mem. Council, Royal Inst. Int. Affairs 56-60; Pres. British Asscn. for the Advancement of Science 57-58; Dep. Chair. Advisory Council, Ministry of Technology 65-; Pres. Royal Soc. 65-; mem. Board of Trustees, British Museum 63-; mem. Council and Exec. Cttee., Overseas Devt. Inst.; Royal Soc. Medal 40 for study of cosmic rays, share in discovery of positive electron, work on mesons, etc.; fmr. Pres. Asscn. Scientific Workers; American Medal for Merit 46; Royal Soc. Copley Medal 56 for studies of cosmic ray showers and heavy mesons and in field of palaeomagnetism; corresp. mem. Acad. of Sciences (Physics Section), France; Foreign mem. U.S.S.R. Acad. of Sciences 66; Assoc. mem. Nat. Acad. of Sciences (U.S.A.); Nobel Prize for Physics 48; numerous honorary degrees.
Publs. *The Military and Political Consequences of Atomic Energy* 48, *Lectures on Rock Magnetism* 56, *Atomic Weapons and East-West Relations* 56, *Studies of War* 62.
Imperial College of Science and Technology, London, S.W.7, England.

Blackie, William; American business executive; b. 1 May 1906; ed. Scotland.
Apprenticed to chartered accountant, Glasgow, Scotland 24-29; Price, Waterhouse & Co., Chicago 30-39; Controller, Caterpillar Tractor Co., Peoria, Illinois 39-43, Vice-Pres. 43-54, Exec. Vice-Pres. 54-62, Dir. 58-, Pres. 62-66, now Chair. and Chief Exec. Officer; Pres. other companies.
Caterpillar Tractor Co., Peoria; Home: 493 E. High Point Drive, Peoria, Illinois, U.S.A.

Blackwell, Sir Basil Henry, Kt., M.A., J.P.; British bookseller and publisher; b. 29 May 1889; ed. Magdalen Coll. School and Merton Coll., Oxford.
Chairman, Basil Blackwell and Mott Ltd. 21-, B. H. Blackwell Ltd. 24-, and Blackwell Scientific Publications Ltd. 39-; Pres. Antiquarian Booksellers Asscn. 25 and 26, Pres. Associated Booksellers of Great Britain and Ireland 34 and 35, Pres. The Classical Asscn. 65; Officier d'Académie; Hon. Fellow, Merton Coll., Oxford; Hon. LL.D. (Manchester Univ.) 65.
49 Broad Street, Oxford; and Osse Field, Appleton, Berkshire, England.

Blagonravov, Anatoly Arkadievich; Soviet scientist; b. 1894; ed. Artillery Faculty, Military Technical Acad.
Instructor and research scientist, F. E. Dzezhinsky Mil. Artillery Acad. 29-46, Prof. 38-; Pres. Acad. of Artillery Sciences 46-64; mem. U.S.S.R. Acad of Sciences 43-; Dir. Inst. for Study of Machines, Moscow 53-; Academician-Sec. U.S.S.R. Acad. of Sciences Dept. of Engineering 57-63; Editor-in-Chief *Mashinovedenie* (Study of Machines); Chair. U.S.S.R. Acad. of Sciences Comm. on Study and Use of Space; Vice-Pres. Cttee. on Space Research (COSPAR); mem. Czechoslovak Acad. of Sciences; Hero of Socialist Labour,

State Prize, Order of Lenin (thrice), Order of Red Banner of Labour (thrice).
Publs. *Foundations of Design of Automatic Armaments* 31, *Material of Small Arms* 45-56, *Study of Upper Layers of Atmosphere with Use of Rockets* 57, *Study of Space and Upper Layers of Atmosphere* 63.
Academy of Sciences of U.S.S.R., 14 Leninsky Prospekt, Moscow, U.S.S.R.

Blair, Clay Drewry, Jr.; American writer and editor; b. 1 May 1925; ed. Tulane Univ. and Columbia Univ.
Time Magazine 48-55; Military Correspondent, *Life* Magazine 55-57; Associate Editor *The Saturday Evening Post* 57-61, Asst. Managing Editor 61-62, Man. Editor 62-63, Editor-in-Chief 63-64; Senior Vice-Pres, Exec. Vice-Pres. and Dir. and Editor-in-Chief The Curtis Publishing Co. 62-64.
Publs. *The Atomic Submarine and Admiral Rickover* 54, *The Hydrogen Bomb* (with James Shepley) 54, *Beyond Courage* 55, *Valley of the Shadow* 55, *Nautilus 90, North* (with Commander William R. Anderson) 59, *Diving for Pleasure and Treasure* 60, *Always Another Dawn* (with A. Scott Crossfield) 60.
Copper Beech Road, Greenwich, Connecticut, U.S.A.

Blair, William McCormick, Jr., A.B., LL.B.; American lawyer and diplomatist; b. 24 Oct. 1916; ed. Stanford Univ. and Univ. of Virginia.
U.S. Air Force (Capt.) 42-46; admitted to Illinois Bar 48; with Wilson & McIlvaine, Chicago 47-50; Admin. Asst. to Adlai E. Stevenson 50-56; Partner Stevenson, Rifkind and Wirtz, Chicago 57-61; Ambassador to Denmark 61-64, to Philippines 64-68; Bronze Star; Order of Officer of the Crown (Belgium).
c/o Department of State, Washington, D.C., U.S.A.

Blais, Marie-Claire; Canadian writer; b. 5 Oct. 1939; ed. Quebec, Paris and United States.
Guggenheim Foundation Fellowship, New York 63; Prix de la langue française 61, Prix France-Quebec 64, Prix Médicis 66.
Publs. *La Belle Bête* 59, *Tête blanche* 60, *Jour est noir* 62, *Une saison dans la vie d'Emmanuel* 65, *L'Insoumise* 66 (novels); *Pays Voiles, Existences* (poems) 62-63.
Wellfleet, Mass., U.S.A.

Blaisse, Pieter Alfons, LL.D.; Netherlands politician; b. 11; ed. Univ. of Amsterdam and Technische Hochschule, Hanover.
Secretary Philip's Glowlamp Works 35-43; Dir. of Foreign Trade, Netherlands Ministry of Econ. Affairs 45-52; M.P. 52-; mem. European Parl.; several decorations; Catholic People's Party; Pres. of Cttee. for Foreign Trade.
Publ. *The Trade Policy of the Netherlands.*
218 Ruychrocklaan, The Hague, Netherlands.

Blaizot, Jean P. M. L. F., D. ès sc.; French university official; b. 14 Jan. 1915; ed. Lycée de Versailles, Sorbonne, Paris.
Teacher, Evreux 40-44, Paris 44-45; worked for Nat. Centre of Scientific Research 45-48, Tutor, then Prof. Toulouse Univ. 48-60, Dean 65-; Rector, Poitiers Univ. 61-64; fmr. Dir. Inst. of Physiology, Toulouse; mem. Asscn. of French Speaking Physiologists, Soc. of Biological Chemistry; Commdr. Palmes Académiques 61; Chevalier Légion d'Honneur 62.
Publs. *Les Relations physiologiques entre la glande thyroide et la vitamine B1, Journal de Physiologie, Annales de la Nutrition, Bulletin de la Société de Chimie Biologique.*
Office: 4 Grande rue St. Michel, 31 Toulouse 04; Home: 14 rue des Frênes, 31 Toulouse 04, France.

Blake, Rev. Eugene Carson, A.B., TH.B.; American church official; b. 7 Nov. 1906; ed. Princeton Univ., Edinburgh Univ., and Princeton Theological Seminary.
Teacher, Forman Christian Coll., Lahore, India 28-29; Asst. Pastor, Collegiate Church of St. Nicholas, New

York 32-35; Pastor, First Presbyterian Church, Albany, N.Y. 35-40, Pasadena (Calif.) Presbyterian Church 40-51; Stated Clerk, The United Presbyterian Church in the U.S.A. 51-66 (The Presbyterian Church in the U.S.A. until 58); Gen. Sec. World Council of Churches 66-; Pres. Nat. Council of Churches (U.S.A.) 54-57; Trustee, Princeton Univ. 57-61; Hon. Rector, Univ. of Dubuque 63-64; Chair. Div. of Inter-Church Aid, Refugee and World Service, World Council of Churches; official and mem. numerous other religious, civic and educational orgs.; 19 honorary degrees.

Publ. *He is Lord of All, The Church in the Next Decade.* World Council of Churches, 150 Route de Ferney, Ch. 1211, Geneva 20, Switzerland.

Telephone: 33-34-00.

Blakenham, 1st Viscount (cr. 63) of Little Blakenham, in the County of Suffolk; **John Hugh Hare,** P.C., O.B.E.; British politician; b. 22 Jan. 1911; ed. Eton Coll.
Lieut.-Colonel, Suffolk Yeomanry 39-45; Alderman London County Council 37-52; M.P. 50-63; Vice-Chair. Conservative Party Org. 51-55, Chair. 63-65; Minister of State for Colonial Affairs 55-56; Sec. of State for War 56-58; Minister of Agriculture 58-59, of Labour 60-63; Chancellor of Duchy of Lancaster and Dep. Leader, House of Lords 63-64.

10 Holland Park, London, W.11, England.

Blamont, Philippe Lucien, DIPL.SC.POL.; French international official; b. 17 Nov. 1927; ed. Faculté de Droit de Paris, Inst. d'Etudes politiques de Paris, Cambridge Univ. and Georg-August-Universität zu Göttingen.
Secretary of conf. of Advocates at Council of State and Court of Cassation 51; mem. office of Dir.-Gen., Int. Labour Office (ILO), Geneva 52-53, Int. Organizations Div. 53-57, Liaison Office with UN, New York 57-59, Exec. Asst. to Dir.-Gen., Geneva 60-64, Dir. Liaison Office with UN 64-66; Dir., Int. Centre for Advanced Technical and Vocational Training, Turin 66-.

International Centre for Advanced Technical and Vocational Training, Corso Unità d'Italia 140, Turin, Italy.

Turin 633-733.

Blancard, Jean Raymond Edouard; French engineering administrator; b. 18 Aug. 1914; ed. Ecole Polytechnique.
Engineer, then Chief Engineer of Mines; Dir. of Carburettors, Central Admin. of Industry and Commerce until 60; mem. Admin. Council Gaz de France 59-; Ministerial Del. for Air Force 59-61; Pres. Bureau de recherches de pétrole (B.R.P.) 59-65; Vice-Pres. Entreprise de recherches et d'activités pétrolières (ERAP) 65-; Pres. Dir.-Gen. Soc. auxiliare de l'Erap (AUXERAP) 65, Soc. française de recherches et d'exploitation petrolières (SOFREP) 66-; Pres. Industrial Equipment Cttee., Atomic Energy Comm. 61-; Vice-Pres. Régie nat. des Usines Renault 61-65; Pres. Dir.-Gen. SNECMA 64-68; Perm. Under Sec. for Armaments 68-; Dir. Turboméca, Nord-Aviation, Sud-Aviation; Vice-Pres. Union Syndicale des industries aéronautiques et spatiales 65-; Officier Légion d'Honneur.

19 boulevard Flandrin, Paris 16e, France.

Blanchard, Francis; French international civil servant; b. 21 July 1916; ed. Univ. of Paris.
French Home Office; Int. Org. for Refugees, Geneva 47-51; Int. Labour Office, Geneva 51-, Asst. Dir.-Gen. 56-, Deputy Dir.-Gen. Mar. 68-.
International Labour Office, 154 rue de Lausanne, Geneva, Switzerland; Home: Prébailly, Gex (Ain), France.

Blancke, Harold; American textile executive.
Chairman and Chief Exec. Officer, Celanese Corpn.of America and Pres., Chair. and Dir. of subsidiaries; Dir. Canadian Celanese Ltd., Montreal.

Celanese Corpn. of America, 180 Madison Avenue, New York City, N.Y.; Home: Harlee Farm, Blairstown, N.J., U.S.A.

Blanco-Cervantes, Dr. Raúl; Costa Rican chest specialist and politician; b. 03; ed. Liceo de Costa Rica and Luis Maximilian Univ., Munich.
Medical Director, Sanatorio Carlos Durán 33-; Dir. of Anti-Tuberculosis Dept., Ministry of Public Health 37-; Minister of Public Health 48-49; Pres. College of Physicians and Surgeons of Costa Rica 46, 47; Dir.-Gen. of Assistance, Ministry of Public Health 50, 51; First Vice-Pres. of Costa Rica 53-58, 62-66; Acting Pres. of Costa Rica 55; Dir. Hospital Nacional para Tuberculosis 58-; several decorations.
Hospital Nacional para Tuberculosis, San José, Costa Rica.

Blanco Villalta, Jorge Gastón; Argentine diplomatist and writer; b. 09.
Vice-Consul Istanbul 34-35; First Sec. Ministry of Foreign Affairs 46; Head of U.N. Div., Political Dept., Ministry of Foreign Affairs 46; in charge of liaison with Nat. Congress 47; Sec.-Gen. Argentine del. U.N. Assemblies 47, 48; Counsellor 48; Dir. Intellectual Co-operation and Counsellor attached to Presidency 48-53; Sec.-Gen. and Del. Inter-American Conf. 54; Dir. Middle East and East Europe Dept. Ministry of Foreign Affairs 54- (Minister 54, Ambassador 55-); Royal Order of Phoenix (Greece), Order of the Cedar (Lebanon).
Publs. *El Pueblo Turco* 36, *Cuadros de la Estambul Actual* 37, *Literatura turca* 39, *Kemal Ataturk* 39, *Literatura turca contemporánea* 40, *El Milagro Turco* 40, *Conquista del Rio de la Plata* 43, *Historia de la Conquista del Rio de la Plata* 46, *Antropofagía ritual americana* 48, *Montoya, apóstol de los guaraníes* 55, *Organización de los Estados Americanos* 57, *La Organización de la Comunidad Internacional* 60.
Las Heras 4095, Buenos Aires, Argentina.

Blancpain, Marc; French writer; b. 29 Sept. 1909; ed. Collèges d'Hirson et de Laon, Université de Nancy, Univ. de Paris à la Sorbonne and Ecole Normale supérieure, Saint-Cloud.
Teacher, Ecole Internationale de Genève 31-35, Lycée Français, Cairo 35-39; Sec.-Gen. of Alliance Française 45-; mem. P.E.N. Club, Soc. des Gens de Lettres, Acad. Stanislas, Acad. des Sciences d'Outre-Mer; Officier Légion d'Honneur, Croix de Guerre 39-45, Commandeur des Palmes Académiques, Commandeur Ordre National du Mérite, and orders from Peru, Chile, Brazil and Belgium; Grand Prix du Roman, Acad. Française 45, Prix Courteline 46, Prix Scarron 55, Prix Engelmann (Belgium) 56, Grand Prix du Rayonnement Français (Acad. Française) 61.
Publs. include: *Le Solitaire* (novel) 45, *Les Contes de la Lampe à Graisse* (novel) 46, *Le Carrefour de la Désolation* (novel) 51, *Voyages et Verres d'Eau* (essay) 52, *La Femme d'Arnaud vient de mourir* (novel) 58, *Contes de Vermeil* (for children) 58, *Les Peupliers de la Prétentaine* 61, *Vincennes Neuilly* (short stories) 63, *Grandes Heures d'un Village de la Frontière* 64, *Les Truffes du Voyage* 65, *Aujourd'hui, l'Amérique latine* 66, *Alla des Antipodes* (novel) 67, *Les Lumières de la France* (essay). Prof.: 101 blvd. Raspail, Paris VIe; Home: 12 blvd. Jean Mermoz, Neuilly-sur-Seine, France.
Telephone: 624-87-21 (Home).

Blandford, John, M.E.; American administrator; b. 19 Aug. 1897; ed. Stevens Inst. of Technology, Hoboken, N.J.
Engineer, The Texas Co. 20-22; staff mem. Nat. Inst. Public Admin. 22-23; Asst. to City Man., Petersburg, Va. 23-24; Dir. Research, Newark, N.J., Chamber of Commerce 24-26: Dir. Cincinnati Bureau Governmental Research 26-31; mem. President's Cttee. for Employment 31; Dir. Public Safety, City of Cincinnati 31-33; Asst. to Chair. Tenn. Valley Authority 33-34, Co-

ordinator and Sec. of Board 34-37, Gen. Man. 37-39; Asst. Dir. U.S. Bureau of the Budget 39-42; Admin. Nat. Housing Agency 42-46; Adviser to Govt. of China 46-47; consultant on govt. relations 47-48; Deputy Chief ECA Mission to Greece 48-50; U.S. rep. (rank of Ambassador) Advisory Comm. U.N. Relief and Works Agency for aid to refugees in Palestine and the Middle East 50-51, Dir. 51-53; Consultant to Govt. of Puerto Rico 53-54; Pub. Admin. Clearing House on survey of pub. admin. in 20 Latin American Republics 54-55; Exec. Dir. New York State, New York City Fiscal Relations Committee 55-56; chief rep. in Iran, Development and Resources Corp., New York City 56-58; U.N. Adviser on pub. admin. govt. of Venezuela 58-59; U.N. Adviser on rationalization, Govt. of Argentina 60; Consultant Inter-American Planning Soc. 61, Agency for Int. Devt. 62-64; Operations Evaluation Staff, AID 64-; Hon. Dr. Eng. (Stevens Inst. of Technology).
Potomac House, 612 Chainbridge Road, McLean, Va., U.S.A.

Blanding, Sarah Gibson, LL.D.; American educationist; b. 22 Nov. 1898; ed. New Haven Normal School of Gymnastics; Kentucky and Columbia Univs., and London School of Economics.
Instructor in physical education, Kentucky Univ. 19-22; Acting Dean of Women 23-24; Dean of Women and Asst. Prof. 26-36; Dean of Women and Associate Prof. 37-41; Dir. New York State Coll. of Home Economics. Cornell Univ. 41-42; Dean 42-46; Pres. Vassar Coll. 46-64, Pres. Emer. 64-; mem. Governor's Cttee. on Educ. and Employment of Women; Board of Trustees, The Edward W. Hazen Foundation, Wykeham Rise School, Chatham Coll.; Cttee. for Econ. Devt., mem. Acad. Freedom Cttee., American Civil Liberties Union; mem. Comm. on Independent Colls. and Univs of the Asscn. of Colls. and Univs. of N.Y. State; mem. Nat. Advisory Council, American Asscn. for UN; mem. Board of Trustees, Helen Dwight Reid Educational Foundation Inc.
Lakeville, Conn., U.S.A.

Blaney, Neil Terence, T.D.; Irish politician; b. 29 Oct. 1922; ed. National School and St. Eunan's Coll., Letterkenny.
Member outdoor staff, Irish Tourist Asscn. 42-44; Insp. Irish Tourist Board 45; Civil Servant 45-47; mem. Dail 48-; Provincial Organizer, later Dublin City Organizer, Irish Vintners and Grocers' Asscn. 49-51; mem. Donegal County Council 49-57, Deputy Vice-Chair. 50-54, Chair. 55-57; Minister for Posts and Telegraphs 57, for Local Govt. 57-66, of Agriculture and Fisheries Nov. 66-; mem. Nat. Exec. Fianna Fáil Party 49-51, Joint Hon. Treas. 56-.
Rossnakill, Letterkenny, Co. Donegal, Ireland.

Blank, Theodor; German politician; b. 19 Sept. 1905; ed. Univ. of Münster and Technische Hochschule, Hanover.
Carpentry apprenticeship after *Volksschule*; Sec. Central Cttee. Christian Factory and Transport Workers' Union 30, dismissed 33; resumed studies 33-36; served 39-45 war; joint founder, German Fed. of Trades Union 45-50; Town Councillor in Dortmund 45, mem. *Land* Parl. of Nordrhein-Westfalen 46, mem. Economic Council 47; C.D.U. mem. *Bundestag* 49-; Chief Dept. for questions concerned with Allied Troops and Defence 50-55; Minister of Defence 55-56; Minister of Labour and Social Affairs 57-66.
Breslauer Str. 20, Bad Godesberg/Rhein, German Federal Republic.

Blankenhorn, Herbert; German diplomatist; b. 15 Dec. 1904; ed. Gymnasiums in Strasbourg, Berlin and Karlsruhe, and Univs. of Munich, London, Heidelberg and Paris.
Entered Foreign Service 29; served Athens 32-35, Washington 35-39, Helsinki 40, Berne 40-43; Foreign Office, Berlin (Protocol Section) 43-45; Deputy Sec.-Gen. Zonal Advisory Council, Hamburg 46-48; Sec.-Gen. Christian Democratic Party (British Zone) 48; Private Sec. to Pres. of the Parl. Council, Bonn (Dr. Adenauer) 48-49; Chief of Liaison Office with Allied High Commission 49; Political Dir. Foreign Office 50-55; Ambassador to NATO 55-58; Ambassador to France 58-63, to Italy 64-65, to U.K. 65-.
Embassy of the German Federal Republic, 23 Belgrave Square, London, S.W.1, England.
Telephone: 01-235 5033.

Blanzat, Jean; French writer; b. 1905; ed. Collège de Bellac and Ecole normale d'instituteurs de Versailles. Literary Dir. Editions Grasset 45-53; mem. Publisher's Readers' Cttee. Editions Gallimard 53-; Grand Prix du roman de l'Académie française 42; Prix Fémina 65.
Publs. novels: *Enfance* 30, *A moi-même, ennemi* 33, *Septembre* 36, *l'Orage du matin* 42, *la Gartempe* 57, *le Faussaire* 65, *L'Iguane* 66.
7 rue de Navarre, Paris 5e, France.

Blašković, Dionýz, M.D., D.SC.; Czechoslovak virologist; b. 2 Aug. 1913; ed. Charles Univ., Prague.
Research work, Inst. of Bacteriology and Immunology, Charles Univ.; bacteriological research 34-46; Rockefeller Foundation Fellow, United States 46-47; Head, Dept. of Epidemiology and Microbiology, State Health Inst., Bratislava 45-52; Prof. Med. Faculty, Comenius Univ., Bratislava 54-; Dir. Inst. of Virology, Slovak Acad. of Sciences, Bratislava 53-; Sec.-Gen. Int. Council of Scientific Unions (ICSU) 63-66; First Vice-Pres. Slovak Acad. of Sciences; mem. Presidium Slovak Acad. of Sciences; Editor-in-Chief *Acta Virologica*; Hon. mem. All-Union Soc. of Hygienists, Epidemiologists, Microbiologists and Infectionists of U.S.S.R. 56; WHO expert; mem. New York Acad. of Sciences 60; Hon. mem. Polish Microbiological Soc. 63, Austrian Microbiological Soc. 63; Foreign mem. U.S.S.R. Acad. of Sciences 65; mem. Int. Org. for Cell Research, London; mem. Soc. Gen. Microbiology, London; mem. Deutsche Akad. Naturforscher Halle/Saale 67; State Prize for Science 51; Purkyně Medal in Medical Sciences 56; Order of Labour 63.
Virological Institute, Bratislava, Czechoslovakia.

Blattný, Ctibor, DR.ING., DR.SC.; Czechoslovak botanist; b. 8 Sept. 1897; ed. Coll. of Agricultural Engineering, Prague.
Director Inst. for Experimental Botany, Czechoslovak Acad. of Sciences 60-; Prof. Agric. Coll., Prague 67-; State Prize 58; Dr. h.c., Schiller Univ., Jena.
Publs. Scientific papers on plant viruses, especially agricultural plant viruses.
Institute for Experimental Botany, Na Karlovce 1, Prague 6-Dejvice, Czechoslovakia.

Blaustein, Jacob; American executive; b. 30 Sept. 1892; ed. Lehigh Univ.
Co-founder American Oil Co. 10, Pres. 33-37, Dir. 37-; Dir. Mexican Petroleum Corpn., Pan-American Petroleum and Transport Co., etc.; Pres. American Trading and Production Corpn.; Consultant, U.S. del. UN Conf. San Francisco 45, mem. del. Tenth Session UN Gen. Assembly; Dir. Baltimore Symphony Orchestra.
Office: American Building, Baltimore 3; Home: Alto Dale, Pikesville, Md., U.S.A.

Blazer, Rexford S., A.B.; American oil executive; b. 1 Sept. 1907; ed. Univ. of Illinois.
Joined Allied Oil Co., Cleveland as Sales Trainee 28, Dir. 35-59, Vice-Pres. 38-48, Pres. 48-59; Dir. Ashland Oil and Refining Co., Kentucky 49-, Pres. 51-57, Chair. Board 57-; mem. Exec. Cttee., American Petroleum Inst.; Dir., mem. of Exec. and Finance Cttees., Nat. Petroleum Refiners Asscn.; Dir. Asphalt Inst., Third Nat. Bank, Ashland; Trustee, Kentucky Independent Coll. Foundation; Trustee & Co.-Vice-Chair. Exec.

Cttee. Automotive Safety Asscn.; mem. numerous other Oil Industry and other Orgs.
Ashland Oil and Refining Co., 1409 Winchester Ave., Ashland, Kentucky; Home: 2711 Seminole Ave., Ashland, Kentucky, U.S.A.
Telephone: 606-324-9115 (Home); 606-324-1111 (Office).

Blech, Harry; British conductor; b. 2 March 1910; ed. Central London Foundation, Trinity Coll. of Music and Manchester Coll. of Music.
Violin soloist 28-30; with B.B.C. Symphony Orchestra 30-36; Founder-mem. Blech Quartet 33-50, London Wind Players 42, London Mozart Players 49, Haydn-Mozart Soc. 49, London Mozart Choir 52; Hon. R.A.M.
The Owls, 70 Leopold Road, Wimbledon, London, S.W.19, England.

Blegen, Carl William, B.A., PH.D.; American archaeologist; b. 27 Jan. 1887; ed. Minnesota and Yale Univs., American School of Classical Studies, Athens.
Sec. American School of Classical Studies, Athens 13-20, Asst. Dir. 20-26, Act. Dir. 26-27; Prof. of Classical Archæology Cincinnati Univ. Graduate School of Arts and Sciences 27-57, Prof. Em. 57-; Dir. Dept. of Classics 50-57; attached to Office of Strategic Services, Washington 42-45; Cultural Attaché American Embassy, Athens 45-46; Dir. American School of Classical Studies, Athens 48-49; mem. American Philosophical Soc., American Philological Asscn., Archæological Inst. of America, German Archæological Inst. and other foreign acads. and insts.; corresp. Fellow British Acad.; Fellow Amer. Acad. of Arts and Sciences; hon. degrees from Oslo, Salonika, Oxford, Cambridge, Athens, Jerusalem and Cincinnati Univs.; First Gold Medal of Archaeological Inst. of America 66.
Publs. *Korakou: A Prehistoric Settlement near Corinth* 21, *Zygouries: A Prehistoric Settlement in the Valley of Cleonae* 28, *Acrocorinth* (in collaboration) 30, *Prosymna* (with Elizabeth Blegen) 37, *Troy* (in collaboration) Vol. I 50, Vol. II 51, Vol. III 53, Vol. IV 58, *Troy and the Trojans* 63, *The Palace of Nestor at Pylos* (Vol. I) (with Marion Rawson) 66.
9 Plutarchou, Athens 139, Greece.

Blessing, Karl; German banker and businessman; b. 5 Feb. 1900; ed. High School of Economics, Berlin.
Official in Reichsbank 20-29; Asst. to Dr. Schacht, Paris, Hague and Baden-Baden Confs. 29; Dept. Head Bank for Int. Settlements, Basle 30-34; Sec. Basle Reparation Experts Conf. 31, Preparatory Cttee. World Economy Conf. 32, World Economy Conf. 33; rejoined Reichsbank 34, Dir. 37-39 (dismissed Feb. 39); Adviser Ministry of Economic Affairs 34-37; Dir. German Unilever Group 39-41 (dismissed); worked in mineral oil business 42-45; Dir. German Unilever Group 48-, Chair. 52-; Dir. Daimler Benz A.G., Dresdner Bank A.G., Vereinigte Elektrizitäts- und Bergwerksaktiengesellschaft, Deutsche Unionbank, etc. 48-57, Kreditanstalt für Wiederaufbau 48-; Pres. Deutsche Bundesbank 58-, Dir. Bank for Int. Settlements 58-; Gov. for German Fed. Republic Int. Monetary Fund 58-.
Deutsche Bundesbank, Taunusanlage 4-6, 6 Frankfurt am Main 1, German Federal Republic.
Telephone: 2681.

Blesson, Jacques de, L. ès sc.; French diplomatist; b. 21 Jan. 1902.
Attaché 25; Third Sec. London 28; Second Sec. The Hague 33, First Sec. 39; Deputy Chief of Div. of Ministry of Foreign Affairs 40; Counsellor Vatican 41; in charge of special mission to Ethiopia for Provisional Govt. 44; Minister to Ethiopia 45-50; Deputy Resident-Gen. in Morocco 50; Dir. Dept. of American Affairs, Ministry of Foreign Affairs 53; Ambassador to Ireland 55-61; Diplomatic Adviser to the Govt. 61-64; Ambassador to Sweden 64-67.
55 rue de Verneuil, Paris 7e, France.

Bleuler, Manfred Eugen; Swiss physician; b. 4 Jan. 1903; ed. Univs. of Geneva and Zürich.
Various hospital posts in Switzerland and U.S.A. 27-32; Senior Medical Officer, St. Pirminsberg Hospital, Pfäfers 33-36; Senior Medical Officer, Univ. Psychiatric Clinic, Friedmatt, Basle 37-42; Prof. of Psychiatry and Dir. Psychiatric Clinic, Univ. of Zürich 42-; Hon. mem. Vienna Society of Doctors.
Publs. *Krankheitsverlauf, Persönlichkeit und Verwandtschaft Schizophrener* 41, *Endokrinologische Psychiatrie* 54, and other works.
Burghölzli, Zürich, 8, Switzerland.

Bleustein-Blanchet, Marcel; French advertising executive; b. 21 Aug. 1906.
Founded Société Publicis 27, now Pres.; founded Radio-Cité 35, Société Régie-Presse 38, now Dir.-Gen.; founding Co-Pres. Confédération de la Publicité Française; founder and Pres. Fondation de la Vocation; Commdr. Légion d'Honneur, Croix de Guerre, Médaille de la Résistance, etc.
Publ. *Sur mon Antenne* 48.
Office: 133 avenue des Champs-Elysées, Paris 8e; Home: 23 rue Albéric-Magnard, Paris 16e, France.

Blind, Adolf, DR.RER.POL.; German university professor and business executive; b. 16 Oct. 1906; ed. Univ. of Frankfurt.
Privat Dozent, Univ. of Frankfurt 34-36; Head of Statistical Office, Saarland, and City of Saarbrücken 36-42; Extra-Mural Prof., Univ. of Heidelberg 42-49; Prof., Univ. of Saarbrücken 49; Minister of Finance, Saarland 55-57; Prof. of Statistics, Univ. of Frankfurt 57-; Chair. of Advisory Board Saarbergwerke 57-; mem. Int. Statistical Inst.; Dep. Chair. German Statistical Asscn.; Grosses Verdienstkreuz.
Publs. *Die Heimarbeit in der Schweiz* 29, *Beiträge zur deutschen Statistik* 36, *Wesen und Eigentümlichkeit sozialstatistische/Erkenntnis* 53, *Das derzeitige Verhältnis zwischen Statistik und Nationalökonomie* 63, *Wirtschaftsstatistik in Forschung und Lehre* 66.
Passavantstrasse 10, Frankfurt am Main, German Federal Republic.

Bliss, Sir Arthur, Kt.; British composer; b. 2 Aug. 1891; ed. Rugby and Pembroke Coll., Cambridge.
Prof. of Music Royal Coll. and Royal Acad. of Music; Dir. of Music B.B.C. 42-44; Master of the Queen's Musick 52-; Hon. Mus.D. Edinburgh 45, London 47, Bristol 63, Cambridge 64; Hon. LL.D. (Glasgow) 49; Hon. Fellow, Pembroke Coll., Cambridge 54; Commdr. Order Leopold II; Gold Medal, Royal Phil. Soc. 63; Chair. Music Cttee., British Council 46-50.
Works include *Colour Symphony* 22, *Introduction and Allegro* 24, *Hymn to Apollo* 26, *Oboe Quintet* 27, *Pastoral* 28, *Morning Heroes* 30, *Clarinet Quintet* 32, *Viola Sonata* 33, *Piano Concerto* 39, *String Quartet* 40, *Miracle in the Gorbals* (ballet) 44, *Adam Zero* (ballet) 46, *The Olympians* (opera), libretto J. B. Priestley 48, *2nd String Quartet* 50, *Scena, The Enchantress, Piano Sonata* 51, *Song of Welcome* 54; film music for *Things to Come, Conquest of the Air, Music for Strings* 35, *Checkmate* (ballet) 37, *Christopher Columbus* 49, *Beggar's Opera* 52, *Meditations on a Theme of John Blow* 53, *Violin Concerto* 55, *Discourse for Orchestra* 57, *Lady of Shalott* (ballet), *Tobias and the Angel* (television opera) 58, cantata, *The Beatitudes* 61, cantata, *Mary of Magdala* 63, *The Golden Cantata* 64.
8 The Lane, Marlborough Place, London, N.W.8, England.
Telephone: 01-624 8441.

Bliss, Ray Charles, A.B.; American insurance executive and politician; b. 16 Dec. 1907; ed. Univ. of Akron, Ohio.
Secretary, Treas. Wells & Bliss Inc. 33-37; Pres. Tower Agencies Inc. (general insurance) 47-; mem. Summit County Board of Elections 36-, Chair. 49-50; Chair.

Summit County Republican Central Cttee. 42-64; Chair. Ohio Republican State Central and Exec. Cttee. 49-65; mem. Republican Nat. Cttee. 52-, mem. Exec. Cttee. 52-, Vice-Chair. Republican Nat. Cttee. 60-65, Chair. 65-; Univ. of Akron Alumni Award 66.
Home: 2535 Addyston Road, Akron, Ohio 44313; Office: Republican National Committee, 1625 Eye Street, N.W., Washington, D.C. 20006, U.S.A.

Blitz, Gérard; French (b. Belgian) business executive; b. 28 Feb. 1912; ed. Collège d'Anvers.
Diamond cutter 32-50; Founder, Pres., Dir.-Gen., Club Méditerranée (holiday org.) 50-; Vice-Pres. Sodecotour 66-; Croix de Guerre.
Office: 8 rue de la Bourse, Paris 2e; Home; 6 rue du Printemps, Paris 17e, France.

Bliven, Bruce, A.B.; American journalist; b. 27 July 1889; ed. Stanford Univ.
Dir. Dept. of Journalism Southern California Univ. 14-16; mem. editorial staff *Printers' Ink* 16-18; mem. Editorial Board, *N.Y. Globe* 19-23, *The New Republic* 23-54; New York corresp. *The Manchester Guardian* 27-47; mem. Nat. Asscn. of Science Writers 40-; Lecturer in Communication and Journalism, Stanford Univ. 57-; Trustee, Twentieth Century Fund (emeritus). Publs. *The Men Who Make the Future* 42, *What the Informed Citizen Needs to Know* (co-editor) 45, *Twentieth Century Unlimited* (Editor) 50, *Preview for Tomorrow: The Unfinished Business of Science* 53, *The World Changers* 65.
Kingscote Gardens, Stanford, Calif. 94305, U.S.A.
Telephone: 415-328-0497.

Bloch, Ernst, DR. PHIL.; German professor of philosophy; b. 8 July 1886; ed. Munich and Würzburg Univs. In Switzerland, France, Czechoslovakia and U.S.A. 33-49; Prof. of Philosophy Leipzig Univ. 49-57, Visiting Prof. Tübingen Univ. 61-; Peace Prize of German Booksellers 67.
Publs. *Geist der Utopie* 18, 23, 64, *Thomas Münzer als Theologe der Revolution* 21, 62, *Spuren* 30, 59, *Erbschaft dieser Zeit* 35, 62, *Subjekt-Objekt, Erläuterungen zu Hegel* 51, 62, *Avicenna und die Aristotelische Linke* 52, *Das Prinzip Hoffnung* 54, 59, *Zur Ontologie des Noch-Nicht-Seins* 61, *Naturrecht und menschliche Würde* 61, *Verfremdungen* I and II 62, 64, *Tübinger Einleitung in die Philosophie* I and 2, 63, 64, *Literarische Aufsätze* 65.
Im Schwanzer 35, Tübingen, German Federal Republic.

Bloch, Felix, PH.D.; American university professor; b. 23 Oct. 1905; ed. Fed. Inst. of Technology, Zürich, and Univ. of Leipzig.
Lecturer, Univ. of Leipzig 32-33; Acting Assoc. Prof., Stanford Univ. 34-36, Prof. of Physics 36-; Dir.-Gen. European Council for Nuclear Research, Geneva 54-55; mem. Nat. Acad. of Sciences; Pres. American Physical Soc. 65-; Fellow, Churchill Coll., Cambridge 67; Nobel Prize for Physics 52.
Department of Physics, Stanford University, Stanford, Calif., U.S.A.

Bloch, Konrad, PH.D.; American (b. German) biochemist; b. 21 Jan. 1912; ed. Technische Hochschule, Munich, and Columbia Univ.
Emigrated to U.S.A. 36, naturalised 44; Instructor and Research Assoc., Columbia Univ. 39-46, Asst. Prof. of Biochemistry, Univ. of Chicago 46-50, Prof. 50-54; Higgins Prof. of Biochemistry, Harvard Univ. 54-; Fellow American Acad. of Sciences; mem. Nat. Acad. of Sciences; Fritzsche Award, American Chemical Soc. 64; Nobel Prize for Medicine with Prof. Theodor Lynen for discoveries concerning the mechanism and regulation of cholesterol and fatty acid metabolism 64.
Publ. *Lipide Metabolism* 61.
Harvard University, Cambridge 38, Mass., U.S.A.

Block, Joseph Leopold, A.B.; American steel company executive; b. 6 Oct. 1902; ed. Harvard School (Chicago) and Cornell Univ.
Joined Inland Steel Co. 22, sales dept. 23-27, Asst. Vice-Pres. 27-30, Vice-Pres. and Dir. 30-49, Vice-Pres. in charge of sales 36-51, Vice-Chair. 49-52, Vice-Pres. and Chair. Finance Cttee. 52-53, Pres. 53-56, Pres. and Chief Exec. Officer 56-59, Chair. and Chief Exec. Officer 59-67, Chair. Exec. Cttee. and Dir. 67-; Chair. Steel Production Cttee., War Production Board 41-43, Asst. Dir. 43-44, Deputy Dir. 44; Pres. Chicago Asscn. of Commerce and Industry 57-59; Dir. Commonwealth Edison Co., First Nat. Bank of Chicago, Community Fund of Chicago, Vice-Pres. 50-61, Pres. 61-63; Dir. Jewish Fed. of Chicago 31-52, Pres. 47-50; Trustee Cttee. for Economic Development, Ill. Inst. of Technology; Hon. LL.D. St. Joseph's Coll. (Collegeville, Ind.) and Bradley Univ., etc.
Office: 30 W. Monroe St., Chicago; Home: 1325 Astor St., Chicago, Ill., U.S.A.

Block, Leo E. de; Netherlands politician; b. 14 Aug. 1904; ed. Rijksuniversiteit te Leiden.
Various posts in Dutch and foreign banks 23-45; Ministry of Finance 47-59; Ministry of Econ. Affairs 59-63; Dir. K.L.M. (Royal Dutch Airlines); State Sec. Ministry of Foreign Affairs 63-66; State Sec. for Transport and Waterways 66-67; Minister of Econ. Affairs 67-.
Ministry of Economic Affairs, The Hague, Netherlands.

Block, Philip D., Jr., B.S.; American steel executive; b. 25 June 1906; ed. Phillips Acad., Andover, Mass. and Sheffield Science School, Yale.
With Inland Steel Co., Chicago 28-, Asst. Vice-Pres. 34-48, Dir. 42-, Vice-Pres. in Charge of Raw Materials 48, later Senior Vice-Pres., then Vice-Chair. 59-67, Chair. 67-; Dir. Continental-Illinois Nat. Bank and Trust Co. of Chicago; Trustee Univ. of Chicago 57-.
Office: 30 West Monroe Street, Chicago 3; Home: 1540 Lake Shore Drive, Chicago 10, Illinois, U.S.A.

Blokhin, Nikolai Konstantinovich; Soviet politician; b. 1915; ed. Astrakhan River School, Leningrad Inst. of Water Transport Engineers, and Higher Party School.
Teacher 35-40; Chief Mechanic, Astrakhan Ship Repair Plant 40-41; Soviet Army 41-44; Chief of Section, Volgotanker Shipping Co. 44-45; Deputy First Sec. Astrakhan Regional Cttee. of C.P. 53-59; First Deputy Chair. Astrakhan Econ. Council 59-61; First Sec. Astrakhan City Cttee., of C.P. 61-63; Chair. Exec. Cttee., Astrakhan Regional Soviet of Workers' Deputies 63-; mem. C.P.S.U. 42-; Deputy to R.S.F.S.R. Supreme Soviet.
Astrakhan Regional Soviet of Workers' Deputies, Astrakhan, U.S.S.R.

Blokhin, Nikolai Nikolayevich, M.D.; Soviet surgeon and cancer specialist; b. 4 May 1912; ed. Gorky State Medical Inst.
Intern at Gorky Medical Inst. 34-37, Asst. Prof. in Surgical Clinic 37-47, Prof. and Chief of Surgical Clinic 47-52, Dir. of Inst. 51-52; Dir. Inst. of Experimental and Clinical Oncology of U.S.S.R. Acad. Medical Sciences 52-; Pres. and full member U.S.S.R. Acad. Medical Sciences 60-68; Deputy to U.S.S.R. Supreme Soviet; Pres. Inst. of Soviet-American Relations; Pres. Int. Union against Cancer 66-; Foreign mem. Polish Acad. Sciences; Hon. mem. Purkině" Czech Med. Soc.; Life mem. N.Y. Acad. of Sciences; Order of Lenin (twice), Order of Red Star.
Publs. *Skinplastic* 56, *Problems of Chemiotherapy of Malignant Tumours* (Editor) 60, *Modern Diagnostic Methods in Malignant Tumours* (Editor) 67, and numerous other publications on surgery and cancer research.
Academy of Medical Sciences of the U.S.S.R., 14 Solyanka, Moscow.
Telephone: 97-20-75.

Blokhintsev, Dmitri Ivanovich; Soviet physicist; b. 1908; ed. Moscow Univ.

Instructor, Moscow Univ. 30-, Prof. 36-; Scientific Worker, P. M. Lebedev Physical Inst., U.S.S.R. Acad. of Sciences 35-56; Dir. Joint Inst. for Nuclear Research 56-64, Head of Dept. 65-; Corresp. mem. U.S.S.R. Acad. of Sciences 58-, Ukrainian S.S.R. Acad. of Sciences 39-; mem. Hungarian Acad. of Sciences, German Leopoldina Acad.; Vice-Pres. Int. Union of Pure and Applied Physics; mem. C.P.S.U. 43-; State and Lenin prizewinner; Hero of Socialist Labour, Order of Lenin, etc.

Publs. *On the Theory of Phosphorescence* 34, *On the theory of Solid Rectifiers* 38, *Spectra fluorescences and absorptions of various molecules* 39, *Bases of Quantum Mechanics* 49, 63, *Elementary Particles and Field* 50, *Reactor of Atomic Power Station* (with others) 58, *Collection of Scientific Works and Articles* 58, 60, *Diffusion of the Signal inside a Telemetric Particle* 62.

Joint Institute for Nuclear Research, Dubna, Moscow Region, U.S.S.R.

Blomdahl, Karl-Birger; Swedish composer; b. 19 Oct. 1916; studied in Stockholm and abroad.

Studied counterpoint, composition and orchestration with Hilding Rosenberg, conducting at Royal High School of Music with Tor Mann; now composing in Stockholm; mem. Swedish Royal Acad. of Music 53-; Head of Music, Swedish Radio and TV 65-.

Compositions: Operas: *Aniara* 59, *Herr von Hancken* 64; Ballets: *Sisyphos* 57, *Minotauros* 58, *Game for Eight* 62; Oratorios: *In the Hall of Mirrors* 53, *Anabase* 56; Orchestral: Symphony No. 3 51, Chamber Concerto for piano, wind instruments and percussion 53, *Fioriture* 60, *Forma Ferritonans* 61, *Altisonans, Voyage in this Night* 66, and other symphonic and chamber music.

Drottninggatan 106, Stockholm, Sweden.

Blond, Neville, C.M.G., O.B.E.; British company director; b. 11 Feb. 1896; ed. Manchester Grammar School.

Served First World War; liaison officer with Ministère de la Guerre 18-21; joined family firm in Manchester 21; served in R.A.F. 39-41; Deputy Regional Controller, Min. of Production 42-45; Hon. Trade Adviser, Board of Trade 45-47; on Central Economic Planning Staff 47; U.K. Trade Adviser in U.S.A. 48-49; fmr. Adviser to High Commr. in Canada; late Hon. Trade Adviser on North American Exports to Board of Trade; Chair. Emu Wool Industries Ltd.; Chair. English Stage Co. Ltd.; Officier, Légion d'Honneur.

Gotwick Manor, East Grinstead, Sussex, England.

Blondin, Antoine, L. ès L.; French writer; b. 11 April 1922; ed. Lycée Louis-le-Grand and Univ. de Paris à la Sorbonne.

Contributor to *Paris-Presse, Arts, La Parisienne,* etc.; wrote scenarios for the films *La Route Napoléon, Obsession, La Foire aux Femmes;* Prix des Deux-Magots 49, Prix Interallié for *Un Singe en Hiver* 59.

Publs. *L'Ecole Buissonnière, Les Enfants du Bon Dieu, L'Humeur Vagabonde, Un Singe en Hiver, Un Garçon d'honneur.*

33 quai Voltaire, Paris 7e, France.

Blough, Roger M(iles), A.B., LL.B.; American lawyer and industrialist; b. 19 Jan. 1904; ed. Susquehanna Univ. Penn. and Yale Law School.

Taught in Penn. High School 25-28; studied law 28-31; with law firm of White & Case, N.Y. 31-42; Gen. Solicitor for U.S. Steel Corpn. of Delaware 42-51; Exec. Vice-Pres. (Law) U.S. Steel Co. (in 53 merged into U.S. Steel Corpn.) 51, Vice-Chair. Board of Dirs. 52, Dir. 52, Gen. Counsel 53, Chair. 55-; mem. Gen. Advisory Cttee., U.S. Arms Control and Disarmament Agency, Dir. Susquehanna Univ., The Commonwealth Fund; Chase Manhattan Bank, Equitable Life Assurance Soc. of the U.S.A., American Iron & Steel Inst., Business Cttee.

for the Arts, Int. Asscn. for Promotion & Protection of Private Foreign Investments, Int. Iron & Steel Inst.; Trustee Nat. Industrial Conf. Board, Cttee. for Econ. Development, Presbyterian Hospital in the City of New York, U.S. Council of Int. Chamber of Commerce; mem. and fmr. Chair. The Business Council; Hon. mem. Yale Law School Asscn. Exec. Cttee.; mem. New York State Bar Asscn., Asscn. of Bar of City of New York, The Pilgrims of the U.S., The English-Speaking Union, American and Allegheny County Bar Asscns., American Foreign Service, Council on Foreign Relations, Metropolitan Museum of Art, Legal Aid Soc., Exec. and Finance Cttees. U.S. Steel Corpn.; Assoc. mem. Center for Inter-American Relations; Sponsor, Atlantic Council; Honor Award of Stevens Inst. of Technology; numerous honorary degrees.

71 Broadway, New York 6, N.Y., U.S.A.

Blucher, Walter Harold, LL.B.; American planning executive; b. 29 April 1901; ed. Detroit Coll. of Law.

Assoc. with Detroit City Plan Comm. 19-34, City Planner and Sec. 25-34; Consultant Nat. Resources Board 33-34, Housing Div. Public Works Admin. 34-35; Consultant Economist to Bureau of Reclamation; Consultant to Mich. State Planning Comm. and to Nat. Cttee. on Urban Transportation; American Soc. Planning Official 34-53, Consultant 54-59, and of Asscn. of State Planning and Development Agencies since creation 46-53; mem. Bureau and Exec. Cttee. Int. Fed. for Housing and Town Planning 48-53, Alfred Bettmann Foundation, Southern Regional Education Board. Advisory Cttee. and Hon. mem. Community Planning Asscn. of Canada; Pres. American Inst. Planners 56-57; Northeastern Illinois Metropolitan Area Planning Commission 57; Prof. Planning Illinois Univ. 58; Advisory Cttee. Div. of Slum Clearance and Urban Redevelopment, H.H.F.A., Advisory Board Inst. for Urban Land and Housing Studies, Columbia Univ., Advisory Board Program for Planning, Univ. of Chicago, Board of Govs., Metropolitan Housing and Planning Council, Chicago, etc.; Hon. Corresp. mem. Town Planning Inst. of G.B.; Prof. Univ. of Chicago and other univs.; fmr. Dir. S. E. Michigan Metropolitan Comm. Res. Corpn. 60-62; Planning Consultant 62.

Francis Palms Buildings, Detroit, Mich., U.S.A.

Telephone: 802-375-2371.

Blume, Peter; American painter; b. 27 Oct. 1906; ed. New York Educational Alliance Art School.

Exhibited Daniel Gallery New York 26-31, Julien Levy Gallery 37, Durlacher Bros. 47, Kennedy Gallery 68, Retrospective Exhibition, Paintings and Drawings 26-65, Manchester N.H., and Hartford, Conn. 64, and museums throughout U.S.; works in Museum of Modern Art, Whitney, Metropolitan, Newark, Boston, Columbus, Cleveland, Philadelphia and Fogg Museums, Wadsworth Atheneum, Williams, Randolf-Macon Colls., Art Inst. Chicago; prizeman Carnegie Int. Exhibition, Pittsburgh 34, and Artists for Victory Exhibition 42, Guggenheim Fellowship 32, renewal 36; awarded grant of American Acad. of Arts and Letters and Inst. of Arts and Letters 47; elected Assoc. Nat. Acad. of Design 48; mem. Nat. Inst. of Arts and Letters 50, American Acad. of Arts and Letters 60.

Works: *South of Scranton, Parade, Light of the World, The Eternal City, The Rock, Passage to Etna, Tasso's Oak, Winter, Summer,* etc.

Sherman, Conn., U.S.A.

Blumenthal, W(erner) Michael, PH.D.; American (b. German) business executive; b. 3 Jan. 1926; ed. Univ. of California at Berkeley and Princeton Univ.

Went to U.S. 47, naturalized 52; Research Assoc., Princeton Univ. 54-57; Labor Arbitrator, State of New Jersey 55-57; Vice-Pres., Dir. Crown Cork Int. Corpn. 57-61; Deputy Asst. Sec. of State for Econ. Affairs, Dept. of State 61; President's Deputy Special Rep. for

Trade Negotiations (with rank of Amb.) 63; Chair. U.S. Del. to Kennedy Round tariff talks; Pres. Bendix Int. Aug. 67-.

c/o Bendix Corporation, Fisher Building, Detroit, Mich. 48202, U.S.A.

Blundell, Sir Michael, K.B.E.; British farmer and politician; b. 7 April 1907; ed. Wellington Coll.
Emigrated to Kenya 25; served in Royal Engineers (Col.) 39-45; Comm. for European Settlement 46-47; Chair. Pyrethrum Board of Kenya 49-54, Allsopps African Investments 49-54; mem. Kenya Legislative Council for Rift Valley Constituency 48-58, 61-62; specially selected mem. under Lennox-Boyd Constitution for Kenya, April 58-61; Acting Leader, European Elected mems. 51, Leader 52; Minister on Emergency War Council 54; Minister of Agriculture 55-59, 61-62; Leader New Kenya Party 59-63; Chair. E. A. Breweries Ltd. 64-, Uganda Breweries Ltd. 65-.
Publ. *So Rough a Wind* 64.
P.O.B. 100, Nakuru, Kenya.
Telephone: Bahati 219 and Nairobi 20962.

Blunden, Edmund C., C.B.E., M.C., M.A., F.R.S.L.; British writer; b. 1 Nov. 1896; ed. Christ's Hospital and Queen's Coll., Oxford.
Professor of English Literature Tokyo Univ. 24-27; Fellow and Tutor in English Literature Merton Coll., Oxford 31-43; with U.K. Liaison Mission, Tokyo 47-50; Prof. of English, Hong Kong Univ. 53-64; Oxford Prof. of Poetry 66-; awarded Hawthornden Prize 22; Queen's Poetry Medal 56; Hon. mem. Japan Acad.; Hon D.Litt. (Leeds, Leicester); C.Lit. 62; Order of Rising Sun (Japan) 63.
Publs. *Poems 1914-1930, Undertones of War* (new ed. 65), *Life of Leigh Hunt, The Face of England, Votive Tablets, The Mind's Eye, Keats's Publisher, Poems 1930-1940, Thomas Hardy, Cricket Country, Shelley, a biography* 46, *Poems of Many Years* 57, *A Hong Kong House* (poems) 62, *Eleven Poems* 66.
c/o A. D. Peters, 10 Buckingham Street, London, W.C.2; Home: Hall Mill, Long Melford, Suffolk, England.

Blunt, Sir Anthony (Frederick), K.C.V.O., M.A., PH.D., F.B.A., F.S.A.; British art historian; b. 26 Sept. 1907; ed. Marlborough and Trinity Coll., Cambridge.
Fellow of Trinity Coll., Cambridge 32-36; on staff of Warburg Inst., London 37-39; Reader in History of Art London Univ. and Deputy Dir. Courtauld Inst. of Art 39; war service, France 39-40, War Office 40-45; Surveyor of the Pictures of King George VI 45-52, of the Queen's Pictures 52-; Prof. of History of Art London Univ. and Dir. Courtauld Inst. of Art 47-; Slade Prof. of Fine Art, Univ. of Cambridge 65-66; Commdr. of Order of Orange-Nassau 48, of Legion of Honour 58; Hon. D.Litt. (Bristol) 61, (Durham) 63.
Publs. *Artistic Theory in Italy* 40, *François Mansart* 41, *French Drawings at Windsor Castle* 45, *Rouault's Miserere* 51, *The Drawings of Nicholas Poussin* (with Walter Friedlaender) 39-, *Art and Architecture in France 1500-1700* 53, *The Drawings of G. B. Castiglione and Stefano Della Bella at Windsor Castle* 54, *Venetian Drawings at Windsor Castle* 57, *Philibert de l'Orme* 58, *The Art of William Blake* 59, *Roman Drawings at Windsor Castle* (with H. L. Cooke) 60, *Picasso, The Formative Years* (with Phoebe Pool) 62, *Seurat* (introduction and notes) 65, *The Paintings of Nicholas Poussin* 67, *Picasso's Guernica* 67.
20 Portman Square, London, W.1, England.

Blunt, Wilfrid Jasper Walter, A.R.C.A.; British schoolmaster and writer; b. 19 July 1901; ed. Marlborough Coll., Worcester Coll., Oxford, Royal Coll. of Art.
Art Master, Haileybury Coll. 23-38; Drawing Master, Eton Coll. 38-59; Curator of the Watts Gallery 59-; Veitch Gold Medal, Royal Horticultural Society.
Publs. include: *The Haileybury Buildings* 36, *Desert*

Hawk 47, *The Art of Botanical Illustration* 50, *Tulipomania* 50, *Black Sunrise* 51, *Sweet Roman Hand* 52, *Japanese Colour Prints* 52, *Flower Drawings by Georg Dionysius Ehret* 53, *Pietro's Pilgrimage* 53, *Sebastiano* 56, *Great Flower Books* (with Sacheverell Sitwell) 56, *Van Spaendonck* 57, *A Persian Spring* 57, *Lady Muriel* 62, *Of Flowers and a Village* 63, *Cockerell* 64, *Isfahan, Omar* 66, *John Christie of Glyndebourne* 68.
The Watts Gallery, Compton, Guildford, England.
Telephone: Puttenham 235.

Bluyssen, Most Rev. Johannes Wilhelmus Maria; Netherlands ecclesiastic; b. 10 April 1926; ed. St. Michielsgestel and Haaren Episcopal Seminaries.
Curate Veghel 50-52; Vice-Prefect Seminary St. Michielsgestel 52-54; studied in Rome 54-57; Spiritual Dir. Seminary St. Michielsgestel 57-61; Joint Bishop of 's-Hertogenbosch 61-.
Graafsebaan 170, Rosmalen, Netherlands.

Bo, Giorgio; Italian politician; b. 4 Feb. 1905.
Taught at Univs. of Moderna and Ferrara until 34, Prof. of Civil Law, Univ. of Genoa 34-; mem. Italian Resistance and of Comitato di Liberazione Nazionale of Christian Democrat Party during fascist period; mem. Nat. Council and Central Cttee. of Christian Democrat Party, Regional Sec. for Liguria 46-48; mem. Senate 48-, Vice-Pres. 53-57; Minister of State Participations May 57-July 58; Minister of Industry and Commerce 58; Minister of Public Admin. Reform 59-60; Minister of State Participations 60-; mem. Ligurian Acad. of Science and Letters.
Publs. *Verso lo State Moderno* 60, *Il Nuovo Ciclo* 63.
Ministry of State Participations, Via Sallustriana 53, Rome; Home: Viale Padre Santo 5, Genoa, Italy.
Telephone: 893-459 (Home).

Bô, Marcel; French industrialist; b. 31 July 1892; ed. Ecole Polytechnique de Paris.
Honorary Pres. Rhône-Poulenc S.A.; Pres. Société des Usines Chimiques Rhône-Poulenc; Hon. Pres. Rhodiaceta; Dir. Crédit Lyonnais, Soc. normande de produits chimiques; Commdr. Légion d'Honneur.
Home: 4 Square Lamartine, Paris 16e; Office: 22 avenue Montaigne, Paris 8e, France.

Boase, Thomas Sherrer Ross, M.C., M.A., F.B.A.; British art historian; b. 31 Aug. 1898; ed. Rugby and Magdalen Coll., Oxford.
Fellow and Tutor Hertford Coll., Oxford 22 -37; Prof. of History of Art, Univ. of London; Dir. Courtauld Inst. of Art 37-47; Pres. Magdalen Coll., Oxford 47-68; Vice-Chancellor Univ. of Oxford 58-60; Hon. D.C.L. Oxford and Melbourne; Hon. D.Litt. Durham and Reading; Hon. LL.D. Rockefeller Inst.
Publs. *Oxford History of English Art*, Vols. 3 and 10.
6 Atherton Drive, Wimbledon, London, S.W.19, England.
Telephone: 01-946 1131.

Bobba, Franco, DR. JUR., DR. RER. POL.; Italian diplomatist; b. 2 Oct. 1913; ed. Univ. of Pavia, Acad. of Int. Law, The Hague, Univs. of Berlin and Poitiers.
Entered Ministry of Foreign Affairs 38; Sec. Bône and Berlin 39-43; Ministry of Foreign Affairs 50, concerned with matters relating to European integration and economic co-operation; mem. Italian Del. to Brussels Conf. for negotiation of Rome Treaties and to Interim Cttee. of Rome Treaties; Dir.-Gen. Econ. and Financial Affairs Section, Comm. of EEC; Dir. European Investment Bank: Ministerial rank 62-.
European Investment Bank, 85 blvd. de Waterloo, Brussels, Belgium.

Bobbio, Norberto, DR. JUR. ET PHIL.; Italian professor; b. 18 Oct. 1909; ed. Univ. of Turin.
Prof. of Legal Philosophy, Univs. of Camerino 35-38, Siena 38-40, Padua 40-48 and Turin 48-; Ordinary Fellow, Accad. dei Lincei.

Publs. *L'analogia nella logica del diritto* 38, *La consuetidine come fatto normativo* 42, *La filosofia del decadentismo* 44, *Studi di teoria generale del diritto* 55, *Politica e cultura* 55, *Italia civile* 64, *Da Hobbes a Marx* 65, *Giusnaturalismo e positivismo giuridico* 65.
Via Sacchi 66, Turin, Italy.
Telephone: 59-70-56.

Bobosadykova, Guldjichon; Soviet politician; b. 1937; ed. Tadjik State Univ.
First Sec., Dushanbe City Cttee. of Young Communist League, Tadjikistan, Sec. Central Cttee. of Y.C.L. 59-61; First Sec. Central Cttee. of Y.C.L., Tadjikistan 61-; mem. C.P.S.U. 60-, Central Cttee. of C.P., Tadjikistan; Deputy to U.S.S.R. Supreme Soviet.
Central Committee of Young Communist League of Tadjikistan, Dushanbe, U.S.S.R.

Bobrowski, Czeslaw, LL.M.; Polish economist and politician; b. 04; ed. Warsaw Univ. and Ecole des Sciences Politiques, Paris.
Dir. Dept. of Economics, Ministry of Agriculture and Agrarian Reform 35; Pres. Cen. Planning Bureau, Vice-Chair. Economic Cttee., Council of Ministers 45-47; Deputy Chair. Economic Council, Council of Ministers 57-; Prof. of Economic Planning, Warsaw Univ. 59-.
1/3 Aleja Ujazdowskie, Warsaw, Poland.

Bochenski, Joseph, O.P., D.D., PH.D.; Swiss (b. Polish) philosopher; b. 30 Aug. 1902; ed. Univs. of Lwow and Poznan.
Lecturer, Angelicum, Rome 34-36; Prof. 37-40; Docent Univ. of Cracow 38; served Polish Army Great Britain 40-44; Italy 44-45; Extr. Prof. Univ. of Fribourg 45-48, Prof. 48-, Dean. Faculty of Arts 50-52; Visiting Prof. Univ. of Notre Dame, Ind. 55-56, Univ. of Pittsburgh 58, Univ. of Calif. 58-59; Univ. of Kansas 60; Dir. East-European Study Centre, Fribourg 58-, Ost-Kolleg, Cologne 62; Rector, Univ. of Fribourg 64-66, Vice-Rector 66-68.
Publs. *De cognitione Exist. Dei* 36, *Elementa logicae Graecae* 37, *Nove Lezioni di Logica Simbolica* 38, *S. Thomae Aq. De modalibus* 40, *La Logique de Théophraste* 47, *Petri Hispani Summulae Logicales* 47, *Europäische Philosophie der Gegenwart* 47, *On Analogy* 48, *Précis de logique mathématique* 49, *Diamat* 50, *Ancient Formal Logic* 51, *Die Zeitgenössischen Denkmethoden* 54, *Formale Logik* 56, *Handbuch des Weltkommunismus* (ed.) 58, *Wege zum philosophischen Denken* 60, *Die dogmatischen Grundlagen der sowjetischen Philosophie* 60, *Logic of Religion* 65, Editor *Studies in Soviet Thought* and *Sovietica*.
1 Place Georges Python, CH-1700 Fribourg, Switzerland.

Bocher, Main Rousseau (Mainbocher); American couturier; b. 24 Oct. 1890.
Began his career as a musician, studying piano and singing; art studies in Chicago, New York and Munich; illustrator for *Harper's Bazaar*, Paris 22-23; Editor *Vogue* (Paris) 23-29; Founder Pres. Mainbocher, Paris 30, Mainbocher, Inc., New York 40-; designed uniforms for W.A.V.E.S., Women's Marine Corps, Girl Scouts, Red Cross, etc.
609 Fifth Avenue, New York City 22, N.Y., U.S.A.

Bochkarev, Alexandr Pankratievich; Soviet politician; b. 08; ed. Higher Party School of Central Cttee. of C.P.S.U.
Member C.P.S.U. 31-; party and Soviet work 32-53; Chair. Saratov Regional Exec. Cttee., Soviet of Workers' Deputies 55-63, 64-; First Sec. Saratov Regional Cttee., C.P.S.U., for Agriculture 63-64; Cand. mem. Central Cttee. of C.P.S.U. 61-; Deputy to U.S.S.R. Supreme Soviet.
Saratov Regional Executive Committee of Soviet of Workers' Deputies, Saratov, U.S.S.R.

Bochvar, Andrey Anatolevich; Soviet metallographer; b. 02; ed. Moscow Higher Technical School.
Instructor, Moscow Higher Technical School 23-30;

Instructor, Moscow Kalinin Inst. of Non-Ferrous Metals and Gold 30-34, Prof. 34-60; mem. U.S.S.R. Acad. of Sciences 46-; Bureau mem. Physical Chemistry and Technology of Inorganic Materials, U.S.S.R. Acad. of Sciences 63-; State Prize 41, Hero of Socialist Labour and other awards.
Publs. *Study of Mechanism and Kinetics of Alloy Crystallisation of Eutectic Types* 35, *Principles of Hot Working of Alloys* 40, *On Different Mechanisms of Plasticity in Metallic Alloys* 48, *Metallography* 56, *On the Development of Doubles by Deforming Metals* 64.
Academy of Sciences of U.S.S.R., Leninsky Prospekt 14, Moscow, U.S.S.R.

Bock, Fritz, LL.D.; Austrian politician; b. 11; ed. Univ. of Vienna.
Co-founder Fed. of Austrian Workers and Employees (Austrian People's Party) 45, Head 47-; Head of section of Social Policy, Austrian People's Party 47; Gen. Counsellor Austrian Nat. Bank 47-51; M.P. 49-; Sec. of State, Fed. Ministry of Commerce and Reconstruction 52-55, Fed. Ministry of Finance 55-56; Fed. Minister of Commerce and Reconstruction 56-66; Vice-Chancellor and Minister of Trade 66-68; Vice-Pres. Austrian Econ. Fed.; numerous decorations.
Braungasse 47, Vienna XVII, Austria.

Boden, Dr. Hans August Constantin; German industrialist; b. 28 July 1893; ed. Univs. of Würzburg and Oxford.
Served with Ministry of Reconstruction and at Finance Ministry; German rep. Reparations Comm. Paris 25-29; Gen. Sec. German Del. to Young Plan Conf. Paris and The Hague 29; Man. Finance Dept. Allgemeine Elektricitäts-Gesellschaft Berlin 29; mem. German Negotiating Cttee. to Schuman Plan Conf. Paris June 50; Chair. Allgemeine Elektricitäts-Gesellschaft AEG-Telefunken; Dir. of the following: Dresdner Bank A.G. (Frankfurt/M.), Hamburgische Elektricitäts-Werke A.G. (Hamburg), Hochtief A.G. für Hoch- und Tiefbauten vorm. Gebr. Helfmann (Essen), Kreditanstalt für Wiederaufbau, Frankfurt/M., Mannesmann A.G. (Düsseldorf); Hon. Pres. I.C.C., Paris 61.
Kurhessenstrasse 44, 6, Frankfurt/Main, German Federal Republic.
Telephone: 0611-600-3598.

Bodman, Henry Taylor, B.S.; American banker; b. 26 Jan. 1906; ed. Hotchkiss School (Lakeville, Conn.) and Princeton Univ.
With Nat. Bank of Detroit 33-, Vice-Pres. 45-49, Vice-Pres. and Asst. to Pres. 49, Gen. Vice-Pres. 50-58, Pres. 58-, Chair. 65-; Dir. Michigan Bell Telephone Co., Nat. Steel Corpn. and numerous other concerns; Legion of Merit.
National Bank of Detroit, P.O. Box 116, Detroit, Michigan 48226, U.S.A.
Telephone: 965-6000, Extension 3124/5.

Bodnaras, Gen. Emil; Romanian army officer and politician; b. 04; ed. Law Faculty, Iaşi Univ., Military School of Timişoara and Special Artillery School.
Member, Communist Party of Romania 40-48, Central Cttee. of Communist Party of Romania 45-48, Central Cttee. of Romanian Workers' Party 48-, Political Bureau 48-; Sec.-Gen., later Under-Sec. of State, Presidency of Council of Ministers 45-47; Minister of the Armed Forces 47-57, of Transport and Telecommunications 57-59; Deputy Chair. Council of Ministers 54-65, First Deputy Chair. 65-67.
Executive Committee of Central Committee of Romanian C.P., Bucharest, Romania.

Bodrov, Mikhail Fyodorovich; Soviet diplomatist; b. 1903; ed. Moscow Inst. of Finance and Economics.
Member C.P. of Soviet Union 28-; Financial work 27-38; Deputy People's Commissar for Finance of U.S.S.R. 38-46; Counsellor, Soviet Embassy, Prague 46-48;

Amb. to Bulgaria 48-54; Deputy Head of Dept., Ministry of Foreign Affairs 54-58; Amb. to Israel 58-64; at Ministry of Foreign Affairs 64-66 (Consultant Expert for Middle East Countries 65-66); Amb. to Kuwait 66-; Order of Lenin, Red Banner of Labour, Badge of Honour, etc.
U.S.S.R. Embassy, Al-Kuwayt, Kuwait.

Bodson, Victor Hubert Joseph, LL.D.; Luxembourg Common Market official; b. 24 March 1902; ed. Athénée de Luxembourg and Univs. of Strasbourg, Algiers and Montpellier.
Member Luxembourg Socialist Labour Party 30; mem. Chamber of Deputies 34-61, Communal Council 34-40; Minister of Justice, of Transport and of Public Works 40-47, 51-59; Vice-Pres. Chamber of Deputies 37-40, 48-51, 59-61, Pres. 64-67, Hon. Pres. 67-; Councillor of State 61-64, Hon. Councillor of State 64-; Pres. Int. Asscn. of French-language Parliamentarians 67; mem. Comm. of European Communities 67-; mem. for Luxembourg (Socialist) of Action Cttee. for United States of Europe; numerous foreign decorations.
Commission of the European Communities, Brussels, Belgium; Home: Villa Malpaartes, Mondorf-les-Bains, Grand Duchy of Luxembourg.
Telephone: 35-00-40 (Office); 689-15 (Home).

Bodyul, Ivan Ivanovich; Soviet politician; b. 18; ed. Moscow Military Veterinary Acad. and Higher Party School, Central Committee of C.P.S.U.
Veterinary Surgeon, Soviet Army 42-46; Asst. Chief. Agricultural Group, Moldavian Council of Ministers 46-48; Govt. Controller of State Farms, Moldavian S.S.R. 48-51; econ. work 52-54; party work 51-52, 54-56; Apparatus of Central Cttee. of C.P.S.U. 58-59; Second Sec. Communist Party of Moldavian S.S.R. 59-61, First Sec. 61-; mem. Central Cttee. of C.P.S.U. 61-; Deputy to Supreme Soviets of U.S.S.R. and Moldavian S.S.R.
Central Committee of the Communist Party of Moldavia, Kishinev, Moldavian S.S.R., U.S.S.R.

Bøe, Johannes, PH.D.; Norwegian archaeologist; b. 17 Jan. 1891; ed. Univ. of Oslo and Bergen Museum.
Lecturer, Bergen 15; Keeper of Antiquities Bergen Museum 21; attached to Musée des Antiquités Nationales, Paris 23-24; Prof. Univ. of Bergen and Dir. Historical Museum, 42-60; Chair. Norwegian section, Int. Council of Museums; Gen.-Sec. Int. Congress of Prehistoric and Protohistoric Sciences 32-50; Hon. LL.D. Glasgow 55.
Publs. *Jernalderens keramikk i Norge* 31, *Felszeichnungen im westlichen Norwegen* 32, *Boplassen i Skipshelleren* 34, *Le Finnmarkien* 36, *Norse Antiquities in Ireland* 40, *Til høgfjellets forhistorie* 42, etc.
Roavn. 2, Lillehammer, Norway.

Boegner, Jean-Marc; French diplomatist; b. 3 July 1913; ed. Lycée Janson-de-Sailly, Ecole Libre des Sciences Politiques and the Faculty of Letters, Paris.
Attaché, Berlin, Ankara, Beirut, Stockholm, The Hague; Ministry of Foreign Affairs, Paris 52-55; Minister to the Presidency of the Council 55-58; Technical Counsellor to Charles de Gaulle (Pres. of the Council) 58-59; Technical Counsellor to Sec.-Gen., Presidency of the Republic 59; Ambassador to Tunisia 59-61; Ambassador to EEC and Euratom 61-; Officier Légion d'Honneur.
Permanent Mission of France to EEC and Euratom, 42 Boulevard du Régent, Brussels, Belgium.

Boegner, Marc, DR. THEOL. LIC. EN D.; French ecclesiastic; b. 21 Feb. 1881; ed. Orléans and Paris.
Ordained Pastor Reformed Church of France 05; Pastor Aouste 05-11; Prof. of Theology Coll. of Society of Evangelical Missions, Paris 11-18; Pastor Church Passy 18-53; Pres. French Fed. of Student Christian Asscns. 22-39; Pres. Fed. of French Protestant Churches

29-61; Pres. Nat. Council of Reformed Church of France 38-50; Pres. World Council of Churches 48-54; Membre de l'Institut 46, de l'Académie Française 62-; Grand Officier Légion d'Honneur; Hon. D.D. (Univs. of Edinburgh, Toronto and Aberdeen, and Northwestern Univ.), Dr. Theol. (Univs. of Prague, Bonn and Geneva).
Publs. *La Vie et la Pensée de T. Fallot* (2 vols.) 14-26, *Dieu, l'éternel tourment des hommes* 29, *Jésus-Christ* 30, *Qu'est-ce que l'Eglise* 31, *L'Eglise et les questions du temps présent* 32, *La Vie chrétienne* 33, *Le Christ devant la souffrance et la joie* 35, *Le Problème de l'Unité chrétienne* 47, *La Prière de l'Eglise universelle* 51, *La Vie Triomphante* 54, *Le Chrétien et la Souffrance* 57, *Notre Vocation à la Sainteté* 58.
34 avenue d'Eylau, Paris 16e, France.

Boël, Baron René; Belgian industrialist; b. 27 Oct. 1899; ed. Univ. Libre de Bruxelles.
Army Service, First and Second World Wars; Pres. of Admin. Council, Solvay & Cie, S.A., Brussels; Pres. de la Gérance de la Mutuelle Solvay, Solvay, Boël & Cie., Brussels; Pres. of Admin. Council of Soc. de Participations et d'Opérations relatives à l'Industrie Chimique (Swiss); Dir. S. A. Usines Gustave Boël, Brussels, S.A. Union Financière Boël; Pres. European League of Econ. Co-operation; mem. Exec. Bureau of European Movement, Pres. Financial Cttee.; mem. Hon. Cttee. of Eurospace; mem. Belgian Cttee. of European Foundation for Culture and Finance for Culture of Council of Europe; Dir. Maison de la Chimie, Paris; mem. Man. Cttee. of Fed. of Belgian Industries; mem. Admin. Council of Univ. of Brussels; Pres. Admin. Council of Orchestre Nat. de Belgique; Pres. of Friends of Musées Royaux des Beaux-Arts de Belgique; mem. Conseil Nat. de la Politique Scientifique; Pres. Belgo-American Asscn.; Hon. Prof., Univ. of Brussels; Hon. Citizen of State of New York 64; Grand Officier de l'Ordre de la Couronne; Commandeur de l'Ordre de Léopold; Officier Légion d'Honneur (France), and decorations from Brazil and German Fed. Repub.
Solvay & Cie., S.A., 33 Rue du Prince Albert, Brussels 5, Belgium.

Boerma, Addeke Hendrik; Netherlands agricultural engineer; b. 3 April 1912; ed. Agricultural Univ., Wageningen.
Netherlands Farmers' Organisation 34-38; Adviser to Food Office, Ministry of Agriculture 38-41; Dir. Crop Marketing Board 41-44; Govt. Commr. for Food and Agriculture, liberated parts of Netherlands 44; Acting Dir.-Gen. of Food 45; Govt. Commr. for Foreign Agricultural Relations 46; Regional Rep. for Europe, Food and Agriculture Organization of the United Nations (FAO) 48-51, Dir. Econs. Div. FAO 51-58, Head of Program and Budgetary Service, FAO 58-62, Asst. Dir.-Gen. FAO 60-67, Dir.-Gen. Jan. 68-, Exec. Dir., World Food Program, FAO 62-67; Knight, Order of Lion (Netherlands), etc.
"La Pergola", Via Erodoto 11, Casal Palocco, Via Cristoforo Colombo (Km. 22), Rome, Italy.

Boesch, Hans H., PH.D.; Swiss university professor; b. 24 March 1911; ed. Universität Zürich and Clark Univ., U.S.A.
Professor of Geography, Zürich Univ. 41-, Dir. Geography Inst., Zürich Univ. 42-; Vice-Pres. Int. Geographical Union 49-56, Sec.-Gen. 56-; Vice-Pres. Int. Council of Scientific Unions 65-; Hon. D.Sc. (Clark).
Publs. scientific works in field of physical, regional and economic geography.
8006 Zürich, 10 Blümlisalpstrasse, Switzerland.

Boeschenstein, Harold; American business executive; b. 21 July 1896; ed. Univ. of Illinois.
Edwardsville (Ill). National Bank 20; Illinois Terminal Railroad 21; Illinois Glass Co. 21-29, merged with

Owens Bottle Co. 29, Vice-Pres., General Manager, Dir.
34-38; Pres., Dir. Owens-Corning Fiberglas Corpn.
38-63, Chair. of Board 63-; also Chair. Fiberglas Canada
Ltd.; Dir. Dow Jones & Co. Inc., Ford Motor Co., Inter-
national Paper Co., Nat. Distillers & Chemical Corpn.,
Ohio Bell Telephone Co., American Electric Power Co.,
Edwardsville (Ill.) Nat. Bank and Trust Co.; mem.
Business Council, U.S. Govt. 51-, Chair. 54-56; Trustee,
Toledo Museum of Art, Univ. of Ill. Foundation,
American Museum of Natural History (N.Y.), Ruther-
ford B. Hayes Foundation, Midwest, Southwest and
Stanford Research Insts.
Office: P.O. Box 901, Toledo 43601, Ohio; and 717 Fifth
Avenue, New York City 10022, U.S.A.

Boeschenstein, William Wade; American glass execu-
tive; b. 7 Sept. 1925; ed. Phillips Acad. and Yale Univ.
Owens-Corning Fiberglas Corpn., Detroit 50-, Branch
Man. 55-59, Vice-Pres. (Central Region) 59-61, Vice-
Pres. (Sales Branch Operations) 61-63, Vice-Pres.
(Marketing) 63-67, Exec. Vice-Pres. Oct. 67-.
Owens-Corning Fiberglas Corporation, P.O.B. 901,
Toledo, Ohio 43601, U.S.A.

Boëthius, Carl Axel, D.PHIL.; Swedish archaeologist;
b. 18 July 1889; ed. Uppsala Univ., Berlin Univ., and
British School in Athens.
Lecturer, Uppsala Univ. 18; Dir. Swedish Archæological
Inst. 26-35, 52-53, 55-57; Prof. of Classical Archæology
and History, Göteborg Univ. 35-55; Rector Göteborg
Univ. 46-51; Sec. Cttee. of Swedish Archæological Inst.;
corresp. Fellow British Acad.; mem. Archæological Inst.
of America. American Philosophical Soc., Soc. for Pro-
motion of Roman Studies, Danish, Italian, Finnish,
Norwegian, Pontifical and Swedish acads. and asscns.;
Pres. Centro Int. delle Arti e del Costume, Venice 60.
Publs. *Die Pythaïs* 18, *Kalender des Dorischen Argos,
Roman Architecture from its Classical to its Late Imperial
Phase* 41, *Greek and Roman Town Architecture* 48,
Three Roman Contributions to World Architecture 48;
*The Golden House of Nero, Some Aspects of Roman
Architecture* 60, *The Etruscan Centuries in Italy* 62, and
several other studies on Roman archæology and history
in various languages.
Viale delle Mura Gianicolensi 80, Rome, Italy.
Telephone: Rome 502462.

Boeynants, Paul Vanden; Belgian politician; b. 22
May 1919; ed. Collège Saint-Michel.
Former butcher; mem. Chamber of Reps. 49-; Minister
of Middle Classes 58; Dir. 1958 Exhbn., Brussels; Chair.
Social Christian Party 61-; Prime Minister 66-68.
Chamber of Representatives, Brussels, Belgium.

Bogaers, Petrus Clemens Wilhelmus Maria, DR.ECON.;
Netherlands trade unionist and politician; b. 2 July
1924; ed. Episcopal Coll. Grammar School, Roermond,
and Tilburg School of Economics.
Assistant to Prof. v.d. Brink 47; Econ. Adviser to
Roman Catholic Worker's Union 48, Head, Scientific
Advisory Section, Roman Catholic Workers' Union
57-63; Dep. mem. Socio-Economic Council 54; mem.
Econ. and Social Cttee. European Economic Com-
munities 58; mem. Second Chamber, Netherlands Parl.
59; Minister of Housing and Building 63-65; Minister of
Housing and Physical Planning 65-66; Commdr., Order
of Orange Nassau.
Lingenskamp 25, Laren, North Holland, Netherlands.

Bogaerts, Theo; Belgian journalist; b. 93; ed. Coll.
Damiaan, Aarschot.
Journalist, writer and lecturer; Pres. Foreign Press
Union in Belgium; fmr. Pres. Asscn. of Catholic Writers
in Belgium; fmr. Pres. Asscn. of Catholic Journalists in
Belgium; numerous Belgian and foreign decorations;
Prix littéraire du Brabant.
Publs. 15 books, incl. novels, short stories, and travel
books.
613 Boulevard de Smet de Naeyer, Brussels 2, Belgium.

Bogan, Louise; American poet and critic; b. 11 Aug.
1897; ed. Girls' Latin School, Boston and Boston Univ.
Poetry reviewer for *The New Yorker* 31-; Consultant
in poetry, Library of Congress 45-46; is now Ad-
junct Prof., Department of General Education, New
York Univ.; has also lectured at Washington (Seattle),
Chicago and Columbia Univs.; mem. Nat. Inst. of Arts
and Letters, Advisory Board John Simon Guggenheim
Foundation 55-58; Dir. Edward MacDowell Asscn. Inc.;
Harriet Monroe Award (Univ. of Chicago) 48, Bollingen
Prize for poetry 55.
Publs. Poetry: *Body of this Death* 23, *Dark Summer* 29,
The Sleeping Fury 37, *Poems and New Poems* 41,
Collected Poems (1923-1953) 54; *Achievement in
American Poetry* 51, *Collected Criticism* 54, *The Blue
Estuaries* (poems 1923-1968); also poems, critical
articles and fiction in *New Republic, Nation, Poetry*
(Chicago), *Atlantic Monthly, New Yorker*; co-translator
The Glass Bees 61, *The Journal of Jules Renard* 64.
709 West 169th Street, New York, N.Y. 10032, U.S.A.

Bogarde, Dirk (Van den Bogaerde, Derek Niven);
British actor; b. 28 March 1921; ed. Allan Glen's
School, Glasgow, Univ. Coll. School, London, and
Chelsea Polytechnic.
Army Service 40-46.
Roles in plays include Cliff in *Power without Glory* 47,
Orpheus in *Point of Departure* 50, Nicky in *The Vortex*
53, Alberto in *Summertime* 55-56, *Jezebel* 58.
Films include *Hunted, Appointment in London, They
Who Dare, The Sleeping Tiger, Doctor in the House,
Doctor at Sea, Doctor at Large, The Spanish Gardener,
Cast a Dark Shadow, Ill Met by Moonlight, A Tale of
Two Cities, The Wind Cannot Read, The Doctor's
Dilemma, Libel, Song Without End, The Angel Wore Red,
The Singer Not the Song, Victim, H.M.S. Defiant,
Password is Courage, The Mind Benders, I Could Go On
Singing, The Servant, Doctor in Distress, Hot Enough for
June, High Bright Sun, King and Country, Darling . . . ,
Modesty Blaise, Accident, Our Mother's House, Sebastian,
The Fixer.*
London International Artistes, Park House, Park
Street, Mayfair, London, W.1, England.

Boggs, James Caleb, B.A., LL.B.; American lawyer and
politician; b. 15 May 1909; ed. Dover High School,
Delaware, Univ. of Delaware and Georgetown Univ.
Law School.
Practised law in Delaware 38-41 and 46; served in
U.S. Army in European campaigns (colonel); mem.
U.S. House of Representatives 46-52, mem. House
Cttees. on Exec. Expenditures, Admin., and Judiciary;
Gov. of Delaware 53-60; Senator from Delaware 61-;
mem. American Bar Asscn., Delaware Bar Asscn.,
Acad. of Political Science; fmr. Nat. Dir. Junior
Chamber of Commerce; Legion of Merit, Croix de
Guerre avec Palmes, Bronze Star with Cluster; Repub-
lican.
1203 Corinnell Road, Green Acres, Wilmington C,
Del., U.S.A.

Boggs, Jean Sutherland, B.A., M.A., PH.D.; Canadian
art gallery director; b. 11 June 1922; ed. Trinity Coll.,
Univ. of Toronto, and Radcliffe Coll., Harvard Univ.
Assistant Prof. of Art, Skidmore Coll. 48-49, Mount
Holyoke Coll. 49-52; Assoc. Prof. of Art, Univ. of Calif.
at Riverside 54-62; Curator, The Art Gallery of Toronto
62-64; Steinberg Prof. of History of Art, Washington
Univ. 64-66; Dir. Nat. Gallery of Canada 66-; Hon.
LL.D. Univ. of Toronto 67, Laurentian Univ., Sudbury
67; Hon. D.U.C. Univ. of Calgary 67.
Publs. *Portraits by Degas* 62; Exhbn. Catalogues:
Picasso the Man (The Art Gallery of Toronto) 64,
Drawings by Degas (City Art Museum of St. Louis) 67.
National Gallery of Canada, Lorne Building, Ottawa;
Home: 69 Mackay Street, Ottawa 2, Canada.
Telephone: 992-3110 (Office); 745-1434 (Home).

Boggs, Thomas Hale; American politician; b. 15 Feb. 1914; ed. Tulane Univ., New Orleans.

Admitted to Louisiana Bar 37, practice of civil law 43-46; mem. U.S. House of Reps. 41-; U.S. Naval Reserve 43-46; mem. House Cttee. of Ways and Means 49-, of Joint Econ. Cttee. 57-; Vice-Chair. Democratic Nat. Convention 56-; mem. President's Comm. on Assassination of Pres. Kennedy; Parliamentarian, Democratic Nat. Convention 64; Asst. Majority Leader House of Reps. 62-; Hon. LL.D. (Loyola Univ.).

1304 First Street, New Orleans 13, La., U.S.A.

Bognár, József; Hungarian politician; b. 17; ed. in Szombathely.

Studied literature and philosophy; taught in a grammar school; joined the "March Front" Resistance Movement during 39-45 war; joined Smallholders Party; mem. of Parl. 45 and organiser and secretary of the Smallholders Party; Minister of Information 46; Mayor of Budapest 47-48; Vice-Pres. Smallholders Party 48-49; Minister of Internal Trade 48-53; of Internal and Foreign Trade 53-54, of External Trade 54-56; Prof. of Trade Econs., Karl Marx Univ. of Econ. Science, Budapest 57-; Pres. Inst. for Cultural Relations 61-; mem. Presidium Hungarian-Soviet Friendship Soc.; Assoc. mem. Hungarian Acad. of Sciences; Econ. Adviser to Ghanaian Govt. 62; Dep. Hungarian Parl.; mem. Presidium Patriotic Popular Front; Chair. Hungarian World Alliance.

Institute for Cultural Relations, Budapest V, Dorottya-utca 8, Hungary.

Telephone: 183-890.

Bogoliubov, Mikhail Nikolayevich; Soviet philologist; b. 1918; ed. Leningrad Univ.

Service in the Army 41-45; Lecturer and Researcher Leningrad Univ. 44-60; Dean Oriental Dept. 60-; Corresp. mem. U.S.S.R. Acad. of Sciences 66-.

U.S.S.R. Academy of Sciences, 14 Lenin Prospekt, Moscow, U.S.S.R.

Bogolyubov, Nikolai Nikolaevich; Soviet mathematician; b. 1909.

Professor, Kiev and Moscow Univs. 36-; mem. U.S.S.R. Acad. of Sciences 53-, Academician-Sec. Dept. of Mathematics 63-; mem. Presidium U.S.S.R. Acad. of Sciences; mem. Ukrainian S.S.R. Acad. of Sciences 48-; Foreign mem. Bulgarian and Polish Acads. of Sciences; Foreign mem. German Acad. of Science, Berlin 66, American Acad. of Sciences and Arts, Boston; Dir. Joint Inst. for Nuclear Research 65-; Deputy to U.S.S.R. Supreme Soviet 66-; State and Lenin prizewinner. Publs. *New Methods in Calculus of Variations* 32, *Introduction into Non-Linear Mechanics* 37, *Basic Theory of Measuring in Non-Linear Mechanics* 37, *On Some Statistical Methods in Mathematical Physics* 45, *Problems of Dynamic Theory in Statistical Physics* 46, *New Method in Theory of Superconductivity* 58, *On the Problem of Hydrodynamics of Superfluid Liquids* 63, *Quasimeans in Problems of Statistical Mechanics* 63, *Asymptomatic Methods in the Theory of Non-Linear Oscillations* 63.

Joint Institute for Nuclear Research, Dubna, Moscow Region, U.S.S.R.

Bogomolov, Alexei Federovich; Soviet physicist; b. 1913; ed. Moscow Power Inst.

Postgraduate, Research Assoc. Moscow Power Inst. 37-41; Army Service 41-45; mem. C.P.S.U. 44; Asst. Prof., Head of Chair, Moscow Power Inst. 45-; Doctor of Tech. Sciences, Prof. 56; Merited Scientist of R.S.F.S.R.; Corresp. mem. U.S.S.R. Acad. of Sciences 66-.

Publs. Works on radiophysics and radio engineering.

U.S.S.R. Academy of Sciences, 14 Lenin Prospekt, Moscow, U.S.S.R.

Bogush, Lev Konstantinovich; Soviet surgeon; b. 1905; ed. Nizhni Novgorod Univ.

Head of Dept. at hospital, Gorky Region 29-40; Master of Medicine 37, Doctor 43; Army Surgeon 40-46; Senior Research Assoc., Inst. of Tuberculosis 46-51; Head of Dept., Central Inst. of Tuberculosis 56; Prof., Corresp. mem. U.S.S.R. Acad. of Medical Sciences 57, mem. 63-; mem. Board U.S.S.R. and Moscow Soc. of Phthisiatrists; Order of Red Banner of Labour, Red Star, Patriotic War; Lenin Prize 61.

Publs. Over 160 works on surgery of pulmonary tuberculosis.

Central Institute of Tuberculosis, Yauza Railway Stop, Moscow, U.S.S.R.

Bohan, Marc; French couturier; b. 22 Aug. 1926; ed. Lycée Lakanal, Sceaux.

Assistant with Piguet 45, later with Molyneux and Patou; Dior organisation London 58, later Paris; Artistic Dir. Soc. Christian Dior 60-.

Office: 30 avenue Montaigne, Paris 8e; Home: 4 rue Fabert, Paris 7e, France.

Boheman, Erik; Swedish diplomatist, politician and business executive; b. 19 Jan. 1895; ed. Stockholm High School and Univ. of Stockholm.

Army Service 15-18, Foreign Service 18-60, served Paris, London, Foreign Office, Turkey, Bulgaria, Greece, Poland and Romania 18-37; Sec.-Gen., Foreign Office 38-45; Amb. to France 45-47, to U.K. 47-48, to U.S.A. 48-60; Senator for City of Gothenburg 59-, Vice-Chair. Parl. Foreign Relations Cttee. and Chief Rep. Opposition 59-, Speaker of First Chamber of Parl. 65-; Chair. Board Svenska Aeroplan AB (SAAB), AB Svenska Järnvägsverkstäderna (ASJ), Nymoella Paper Mill Co., ARA Companies; Vice-Chair. Board Swedish Match Co., L. M. Ericsson Telephone Co., Papyrus Co.; Dir. Stockholm Enskilda Bank, Holmens Bruks & Fabriks AB, Swedish American Line, Scandinavian Airlines System (SAS); Grand Cross Order of Vasa; Grand Cross Order of Dannebrog; Grand Cross Finnish White Rose; Grand Officier Légion d'Honneur; Hon. K.B.E. (U.K.) and numerous other foreign decorations; Hon. LL.D. (Tufts Coll., Augustana Coll., Gustav Adolphus Coll., Upsala Coll.).

Publ. *På Vakt* (memoirs—2 vols.) 63, 64.

Office: Stockholms Enskilda Bank, Stockholm 16; Homes: Hovslagargatan 5b, Stockholm C; and Anneberg, Oerserumsbrunn, Sweden.

Bohlen, Charles Eustis, A.B.; American diplomatist; b. 30 Aug. 1904; ed. Harvard Univ.

Entered Foreign Service 29; Vice-Consul, Prague 29-31, Paris 31-34; Moscow 34; Dept. of State 36; Second Sec., Moscow 37; Consul, Moscow 38; Second Sec., Tokyo 41; Dept. of State 42; Asst. Chief, Div. of European Affairs 43; First Sec., Moscow 43-44; Chief, Div. of Eastern European Affairs 44; Asst. to Sec. of State for White House Liaison 44; Special Asst. to Sec. of State 46; Counsellor, Dept. of State 47; Minister, U.S. Embassy, Paris 49; Counsellor, Dept. of State 51-53, Amb. to U.S.S.R. 53-57, to Philippines 57-59; Special Asst. to Sec. of State 59-62; Amb. to France 62-67; Deputy Under-Sec. of State for Political Affairs 67-; Sec. U.S. dels., Int. Sugar Conf., London 37, Brussels Conf. 37; accompanied Sec. of State, Moscow Conf. 43; attended Teheran Conf. 43; accompanied Pres. Roosevelt, Crimea Conf. 45; Political and Liaison Officer, U.S. del., San Francisco Conf. 45; Political Adviser, U.S. del., Berlin Conf. 45; Asst. to U.S. mem., Council of Foreign Ministers, London 45; detailed to Meeting of Foreign Secs., Moscow 45; Political Adviser, U.S. dels., 2nd session, Conf. of Foreign Ministers, Paris, and Paris Conf. 46, and 4th session, Conf. of Foreign Ministers, Moscow 47; Adviser, U.S. dels., Conf. of

Foreign Ministers, London 47, and U.N. Gen. Assembly, Paris 48, etc.
Department of State, Washington, D.C., U.S.A.

Böhm, Karl, D.IUR.; Austrian musician; b. 28 Aug. 1894; ed. Graz Classical Secondary School, Karl-Franzens Univ., Graz, and under Eusebius Mandyczewski, Vienna.
Conductor, Graz City Theatre 17-21; at Munich State Opera 21-27; Gen. Music Dir., Darmstadt 27-31; at Hamburg 31-33; Dir. Dresden State Opera 34-42; Dir. Vienna State Opera 43-45, 54-56; Conductor, Vienna Philharmonic Orchestra 33-, Berlin Philharmonic Orchestra, New York Philharmonic Orchestra etc.; Guest Conductor Teatro San-Carlo, Naples, Teatro alla Scala, Milan, Teatro Colon, Buenos Aires, Metropolitan Opera, New York, etc.; Conductor at Salzburg Festival, Bayreuth Festival, etc.; Hon. mem. Mozarteum, Salzburg, Music Acad., Graz, Music Soc. of Steiermark, Soc. for Music Theatre, Vienna, Concerthouse Soc., Vienna, Cultural Circle, Vienna, German Opera, Berlin, Vienna Philharmonic Orchestra; Hon. Senator Karl-Franzens Univ., Graz; Hon. Ring of Vienna, Graz, Bayreuth, Steiermark, Vienna Philharmonic Orchestra; Bruckner-Ring of Vienna Symphonic Orchestra; Schalk Medal, Vienna Philharmonic Orchestra; Schmidt Medal, Soc. of Friends of Music, Vienna; Mozart Medal, Mozarteum, Salzburg and Mozart Soc., Prague; Brahms Medal, Hamburg; Great Badge of Honour in Silver; Great Distinguished Service Cross in Gold with Star, etc.; Hon. Citizen of Salzburg, Hon. Prof., Gen. Music Dir. of Austria, Hon. Conductor of Vienna Philharmonic Orchestra; Music Prize of Steiermark, Prize of Art, Berlin, and other awards.
1190 Vienna, Himmelstrasse 41, Austria.

Bohr, Aage, DR.PHIL., D.SC. (son of late Nils Bohr); Danish physicist; b. 19 June 1922; ed. Univ. of Copenhagen.
Associate D.S.I.R., London 43-45; research asst., Inst. of Theoretical Physics, Copenhagen 46; Prof. of Physics, Univ. of Copenhagen 56-; Dir. Niels Bohr Inst.; mem. Danish Acad. of Sciences, Norwegian Acad. of Sciences, Royal Physiographical Soc. of Lund, Sweden, American Acad. of Arts and Sciences, American Philosophical Soc.; Dannie Heineman prize 60, Pius XI Medal 63.
Publ. *Rotational States of Atomic Nuclei* 54.
Granhöjen 10, Hellerup, Copenhagen, Denmark.

Boichenko, Viktor Kuzmich; Soviet government official; b. 21 July 1925; ed. Foreign Trade Inst.
Red Army 42-46; Soviet Trade Mission, Peking 54-55; Dep. Consul, U.S.S.R. Gen. Consulate, Shanghai 55-57, First Sec. Soviet Embassy, Peking 57-59; Dep. Chair. *Intourist* 59-62, First Dep. Chair. 62-64, Chair. 64-; Vice-Pres. Int. Fed. of Nat. Tourist Asscns. 64-66; mem. Joint Temporary Man. Cttee., Universal Fed. of Travel Agents' Asscns. (UFTAA) 66-67; Hero of Soviet Union, Order of Lenin, Order of Red Banner of Labour, Order of Red Star, etc.
Intourist Foreign Travel Agency, 16 Marx Prospekt, Moscow, U.S.S.R.

Boikova, Anna Petrovna; Soviet politician; b. 28 Nov. 1918; ed. Pskov Pedagogical Inst.
Member C.P.S.U. 40-; Teacher, later Headmistress and Education Officer 40-43; party work 43-54; First Sec. Kuibyshev District Cttee. of C.P.S.U. (Leningrad) 54-56; Second Sec. Leningrad City Cttee. C.P.S.U. 56-63; Deputy Chair. Leningrad City Council of Workers' Deputies 63-64, First Deputy Chair. 64-; mem. Central Auditing Comm. C.P.S.U. 56-61; mem. Presidium R.S.F.S.R. Supreme Soviet.
Leningrad City Council of Workers' Deputies, Leningrad, U.S.S.R.
Telephone: A-9-14-25.

Boisdeffre (Néraud le Mouton de), Pierre Jules Marie Raoul; French writer, diplomatist and broadcasting official; b. 11 July 1926; ed. Lycée Condorcet, Collège Stanislas, Univ. de Paris à la Sorbonne, Ecole Libre des Sciences Politiques, Ecole Nationale d'Administration and Harvard Univ.
Civil Servant, Ministry of Nat. Educ. 50-55; Deputy Dir. of Press Affairs, Ministry of Foreign Affairs 58-63; Dir. of Sound Broadcasting, Office de Radiodiffusion et Télévision Française (O.R.T.F.) 63-; Chevalier de l'Ordre National du Mérite, Officier des Arts et Lettres, Chevalier des Palmes Académiques, Officier de l'Etoile Polaire, Chevalier de l'Ordre de la Couronne, Commdr. de l'Ordre Nat. du Cèdre, Commdr. de l'Ordre du Christ; Grand Prix de la Critique (for *Métamorphose de la Littérature*) 50.
Publs. *Métamorphose de la Littérature* (Vol. I *de Barrès à Malraux*, Vol. II *de Proust à Sartre*) 50, *Où va le Roman?* 62, *Les Ecrivains français d'aujourd'hui* 63, 65, *Une histoire vivante de la littérature d'aujourd'hui (1939-64)* 64, *Une anthologie vivante de la littérature d'aujourd'hui* I 65, II 66, *La Cafetière est sur la table* 67; critical portraits: *Barrès parmi nous* 52, *André Malraux* 52, *Kafka* (with R. M. Albérès) 60, *Barrès* 62, *Giono* 65.
Office: Maison de l'O.R.T.F., 116 avenue du Président Kennedy, Paris 16e; Home: 5 cité Vaneau, Paris 7e, France.
Telephone: BA6-26-01.

Boissard, Adéodat Louis; French banker; b. 21 Nov. 1901; ed. Ecole Saint-François-de-Sales, Dijon, Lycée de Dijon, and Univ. de Paris à la Sorbonne.
Inspector of Finances 27; Dir.-Gen. of Estates, Ministry of Finance 40; Gov. Crédit Foncier de France 55-67; Pres. Service d'exploitation industrielle des tabacs et des allumettes (S.E.I.T.A.); Grand Officier Légion d'Honneur.
1 boulevard Beauséjour, Paris 16e, France.

Boisseson, Robert Barbara de Labelotterie, Baron de, L. ès D.; French diplomatist; b. 23 Dec. 1905; ed. Ecole des Sciences Politiques.
Served Warsaw 30, European section Ministry of Foreign Affairs, Paris 35, Peking 39; 1st. Counsellor, Tokyo 44; Dep. Dir. Office for Asian Affairs 50; Del. at Residence General, Tunisia 51, Minister Plenipotentiary 52; Chargé d'Affaires, Consulate-Gen., Tangier 54-57; Ambassador to Chile 57-60, to Lebanon 60-64, to Spain 64-; Commdr. Légion d'Honneur.
French Embassy, Calle Villalar, 2-Madrid, Spain; Chateau de Roquerperlic, 14 Noailhac, Tarn, France.
Telephone: Madrid 225-78-40.

Boissier, Léopold, LL.D.; Swiss jurist; b. 16 June 1893; ed. Geneva and Zürich Univs.
Mem. diplomatic missions to Italy and Great Britain 17-20; Lecturer Geneva Univ. 21, Prof. 37-; Sec. Inter-Parl. Bureau 21, Sec.-Gen. Inter-Parl. Union 33-53; Pres. Swiss L.N. Union 33-36; Pres. Fed. of Int. Organisations; Pres. Swiss Peace Council; mem. Int. Cttee. Red Cross, Pres. 55-64; mem. Institut de France; Grotius Silver Medal 59; Editor *L'Annuaire interparlementaire, Bulletin interparlementaire, L'Année politique,* etc.
Publs. *La séparation des pouvoirs en droit suisse, Le contrôle parlementaire de la politique étrangère, Regards vers la Paix, Nouveaux Regards vers la Paix,* etc.
6 rue des Granges, Geneva, Switzerland.

Boissier-Palun, Léon Louis; Senegalese lawyer and diplomatist; b. 29 June 1916; ed. Lycée Faidherba and Bordeaux Univ.
Officer Troupes Colonials, Second World War; Deputy Senegal Assembly; Senator French Community; Pres. Comm. for Economic Affairs and Planning of Senegalese Legislative Assembly; High Counsellor, Pres. Grand Council 52-57; Minister for Econ. Affairs responsible

for inter-territorial relations in Senegal 57; Administrator of the Banking Inst. for the issue of French currency in French West Africa and Togoland; Amb. to United Kingdom 60-66, to Austria, Norway, Sweden and Denmark 61-66, to Switzerland 64-66, to France 66; Pres. Econ. and Social Council, Dakar 64-; co-founder Bloc Démocratique Sénégalais; Commdr. Légion d'Honneur, Grand Officier, l'Ordre nat. du Sénégal, Hon. K.B.E.

25 avenue Pasteur, Dakar, Senegal.

Boissieu, Charles-Albert de; French banker; b. 13 Dec. 1896; ed. Ecole Polytechnique.
President Société des Forces Motrices de Chancy-Poughny, Société des Charbonnages de Winterslag; Hon. Pres. Société des Forges et Ateliers du Creusot; Vice-Pres. Union Européenne Industrielle et Financière; Dir. Banque de l'Afrique Occidentale, Gaz de France, Banque de l'Indochine, Schneider S.A., Compagnie Industrielle de Travaux, West Canadian Magnetic Ores, Asscn. Nat. des Sociétés par Actions, North American Holdings Ltd., S.A. Française de Réassurances etc.
12 bis avenue Bosquet, Paris 7e, France.

Boitsov, Vassily Vassilevich; Soviet technologist and politician; b. 08; ed. Moscow Higher Technical School.
Engineering posts 37-46; Dir. of Scientific Research of technological institute 47-63; Chair. State Cttee. of Standards, Measures and Measuring Instruments 63-; mem. Communist Party of Soviet Union; Dep. to Supreme Soviet of R.S.F.S.R.
State Committee for Standards, Measures and Measuring Instruments, 9 Lenin Prospekt, Moscow, U.S.S.R.

Bojart Ortega, Rafael; Argentine university professor; ed. Univs. of Buenos Aires, El Salvador, Barcelona and Columbia Univ., New York.
Founder Academia de Estudios Históricos Bartolomé Mitre 58, Univ. of Morón 60, Instituto Enrique Larreta 64, Academia Internacional de Historia 65; Pres. Academia de Estudios Históricos Bartolomé Mitre, Rector, Univ. of Morón; mem. Real Academia Hispano-americana de Cádiz, Academia Argentina de Diplo-macia, Academia de Estudios Parlamentarios y Legislativos Internacionales, Instituto de Cultura Americana de Madrid, Instituto Argentino Hispánico.
Publs. *Introducción a la filosofía, Filosofía de la Historia, La Poesía Epica Medieval, La Estética Contemporánea, La Esencia de la Poesía, El Motivo de la Angustia en el Existencialismo, La Poesía de Carlos Obligado, La Inteligencia en el Gobierno de los Pueblos, Ricardo Rojas y el Futuro de América, El Hispanismo en Larreta, Borges Escritor, La Fuerza de Occidente*; novels *La Música de la Montaña, El Hombre Nuevo, Una Aventura en el Año 2000*; plays: *Polichinela, Los Hijos que no Nacieron.*
San Martín 933, piso 7°, Depto. 51, Buenos Aires, Argentina.
Telephone: TE-31-2052.

Bokassa, Col. Jean Bedel; Central African Republic army officer and politician; b. 22 Feb. 1921; ed. Ecole Sainte Jeanne-d'Arc, M'Baiki, Ecole Missionnaire, Bangui, and Ecole Missionnaire, Brazzaville.
Joined French Army 39, rose to Captain 61; organized army of Central African Republic; Commdr.-in-Chief, Central African Republic Army Jan. 63; President, Prime Minister, Minister of Defence and Justice, Central African Republic Jan. 66-; Légion d'Honneur, Croix de Guerre.
Office of the President, Bangui, Central African Republic.

Bokhorst, Matthys, LITT.D., D.PHIL.; South African art historian; b. Netherlands 28 Aug. 1900; ed. Rotterdam, Leyden Univ. and Switzerland.
Prof. of Netherlands Cultural History and Dir. Neths. Inst. Pretoria Univ. 29-51; Editor *Nederlandse Post* 51-; Pres. South African Asscn. of Arts 51-58; Chair. Govt.

Art Advisory Comm. 52-68; Dir. Michaelis Art Gallery 56-64; Dir. South African National Gallery 62-; mem. Exec. Council of South African Museums Asscn. 58-, Nat. Arts Council 68-.
Publs. *Nederlands-Zwitserse Betrekkingen voor en na 1700* 30, *Kultuur van een Waterland* 37, *Handvest der Vryheid* 44, *Die Kuns van'n Kwarteeu* 54, *Art at the Cape* 64, *The S.A. National Gallery* 65.
"Het Trappenhuis", Talma Road, Muizenberg, Cape Town, South Africa.
Telephone: 85345.

Boland, Frederick Henry, B.A., LL.B.; Irish diplomatist; b. 04; ed. Clongowes Wood Coll., Trinity Coll., Dublin, King's Inn, Dublin, Harvard and Chicago Univs.
Third Sec. Irish Foreign Service 29; First Sec. Paris 32; Head of L.N. Section, Dublin 34; Head of Div., Dept. of Industry and Commerce 36; Asst. Sec. Dept. of External Affairs 38, Permanent Sec. 46; Ambassador to Great Britain 50-56; Rep. to U.N. 56-64; Chancellor, Dublin Univ. 64-; Chair Nat. Industrial Economic Council 64-; Chair. Esso Ireland; Dir. Nat. Bank Ltd. 64-, Arthur Guinness Son & Co. 64-, John Power & Son, Dublin 64-; Pres. 15th Session, UN Gen. Assembly; Knight Commdr. Order of St. Gregory (Holy See), Grand Cross, Order of North Star (Sweden); Hon. LL.D.
60 Ailesbury Road, Dublin, Ireland.

Boland, Kevin; Irish politician; b. 15 Oct. 1917; ed. St. Joseph's Christian Brothers' Schools, Marino, Dublin, O'Connell Schools, Dublin, and Univ. Coll., Dublin.
Member Dublin Corpn, Grangegoram Mental Hospital Board and Dublin Fever Hospital Board 55-57; mem. Parl. Dublin 57-; Minister for Defence 57-61, for Social Welfare 61-66, for Local Govt. 66-.
Red Gap, Rathcoole, Co. Dublin, Ireland.

Boldizsár, Iván; Hungarian writer and journalist; b. 30 Oct. 1912; ed. Budapest Univ.
An early member of the progressive village research movement in Hungary; Editor-in-Chief of Information, Peace Conf. Del. 46; Del. for UNESCO 46; Sec. of State in Hungarian Ministry of Foreign Affairs 47-51; Editor *Magyar Nemzet* 51-55, *Hetfoi Hirlap* 56, *Tukor (Mirror)* 57-58, *The New Hungarian Quarterly* 60-; Pres. Hungarian PEN Club 64-.
Publs. *A nyugati kapu, Tiborc, A gazdag parasztok orszaga, Fortocska, Téli parbaj, Magyarorszagi Napló, A toll fegyverével, A reménység uzenete, Reggeltől reggelig, Tiborc uj arca, Balatoni Kaland, Magyarország Utikönyv, Szuletésnap, Az ejszaka vegen, Rokonok és idegenek, Zsiráffal Angliában, Királyalma, Tulélók* (play).
Balogh Adám-utca 29, Budapest II, Hungary.
Telephone: Budapest 136-857.

Boldrini, Marcello; Italian statistician and business executive; b. 9 Feb. 1890; ed. Univ. Commerciale Luigi Bocconi, Milan.
With League of Nations as Editor *Bulletin Mensuel de Statistique* 19-22; fmr. Prof. of Statistics, Univs. of Messina, Padua, Milan Univ. of the Sacred Heart and Luigi Bocconi Univ.; Prof. of Statistics at Rome Univ. until 65; Vice-Chair. Ente Nazionale Idrocarburi (E.N.I.) 53-62, Chair. 62-67; mem. Higher Council for Statistics 60-63, Pres. Int. Inst. for Statistics; has formed school of statisticians producing a *Treatise of Statistics* in several volumes, Vol. I (Boldrini's *Teoria della Statistica*) appeared 65; mem. Accad. dei Lincei, Pontifical Acad. of Sciences and other learned socs.; Gran Croce, Ordine al Merito.
Publs. *Statistica, Teoria e metodi, Statistiche Letterarei, Alla ricerca del tempo nell'Arte.*
c/o Ente Nazionale Idrocarburi (E.N.I.), Viale dell'Arte 72 (EUR), Rome; and Piazza della Repubblica 23, Milan, Italy.

Bolduman, Mikhail Panteleimonovich; Soviet actor; b. 98.
Zhmerinka Drama Group, Ukraine 23; Kiev Russian Drama Theatre 24-31; Moscow Korsh Theatre 31-33; Moscow Art Theatre of the U.S.S.R. 33-; also films; State Prize of the U.S.S.R. (twice), People's Actor of R.S.F.S.R. and other awards.
Moscow Art Theatre of the U.S.S.R., 3 Proyezd Khudozhestvennogo Teatra, Moscow, U.S.S.R.

Bolikango, Jean; Congolese politician; b. 09; ed. Père de Scheut Mission School, Léopoldville.
Teacher 26-59; Pres. Front d'Unité Bangala (FUB) and later its successor, Parti de l'Unité Nationale (Puna); Runner-up in election for Head of State 60; Minister of Information 60-61; Deputy Prime Minister 62; Minister of Public Works Nov. 65-66.
Parti de l'Unité Nationale, Kinshasa, Democratic Republic of Congo.

Bolitho, Henry Hector; British (b. New Zealand) writer; b. 28 May 1898.
Publs. include: *Solemn Boy* 27, *Judith Silver* 29 (novels); *The Letters of Lady Augusta Stanley* 27, *A Victorian Dean* (with Very Rev. A. V. Baillie) 30, *Albert the Good* 32, *Victoria the Widow and her Son* 35, *The House in Half-Moon Street* 36, *Older People* 36, *Edward VIII* 37, *Royal Progress* 37, *George VI* 37, *Later Letters of Queen Victoria* 38, *Victoria and Albert* 38, *The Emigrants* 39, *Rumania under King Carol* 39, *America Expects* 40, *War in the Strand* 42, *Combat Report* 43, *No Humour in My Love* 46, *Task for Coastal Command* 46, *The Reign of Queen Victoria* 48, *A Biographer's Notebook* 50, *A Century of British Monarchy* 51, *Without the City Wall* (with Derek Peel) 52, *Jinnah, Creator of Pakistan* 54, *A Penguin in the Eyrie* 55, *The Angry Neighbours, A Diary of Palestine and Transjordan* 56, *No. 10 Downing Street* 57, *My Restless Years* 62, *The Galloping Third* 63, *A Summer in Germany* 63, *Albert, Prince Consort* 64.
1 St. Nicholas Road, Brighton, Sussex, England.
Telephone: Brighton 27964.

Bolkiah Mu'izuddin Waddaulah, H.H. Sultan Hassanal, D.K., P.S.P.N.B., P.S.N.B., P.S.L.J., S.P.M.B., P.A.N.B.; Sultan of Brunei; b. 15 July 1946; ed. privately, and Victoria Inst., Kuala Lumpur, Malaysia, and Royal Military Acad., Sandhurst.
Eldest son of former Sultan Sir Muda Omar Ali Saifuddin, K.C.M.G. (*q.v.*); appointed Crown Prince and Heir Apparent 61; Ruler of State of Brunei Oct. 67-; Hon. Capt. Coldstream Guards 68; Sovereign and Chief of Royal Orders instituted by Sultans of Brunei.
Istana Darul Hana, Brunei.

Böll, Heinrich Theodor; German writer; b. 21 Dec. 1917.
Publs. *Der Zug war pünktlich* 49, *Wanderer, kommst du nach Spa?* 50, *Wo wärst du, Adam?* 51, *Und sagte kein einziges Wort* 52, *Haus ohne Hüter* 54, *Das Brot der frühen Jahre* 55, *So war Abend und Morgen* 56, *Tal der donnernden Hufe, Irisches Tagebuch* 57, *Dr. Murkes Gesammeltes Schweigen* 58, *Billard um Halbzehn* 59, *Ein Schluck Erde* 62, *Ansichten eines Clowns* 63, *Entfernung von der Truppe* 64, *Als der Krieg ausbrach* (stories) 65, *Frankfurter Vorlesungen* 66, *Ende einer Dienstfahrt* 66.
Belvederestrasse 35, Köln-Müngersdorf, German Federal Republic.

Bollnow, Otto Friedrich, DR. PHIL.; German philosopher; b. 14 March 1903; ed. Univs. of Berlin, Greifswald and Göttingen.
Teacher of Philosophy and Education, Göttingen 31-39; Prof. of Psychology and Education, Giessen 39-46; Prof. of Philosophy and Education, Mainz 46-53, Univ. of Tübingen 53-.
Publs. *Dilthey* 36, *Das Wesen der Stimmungen* 41, *Existenzphilosophie* 43, *Einfache Sittlichkeit* 47, *Rilke* 51, *Die Pädagogik der deutschen Romantik* 52, *Neue*

Geborgenheit: Das Problem einer Überwindung des Existenzialismus 55, *Die Lebensphilosophie* 58, *Wesen und Wandel der Tugenden* 58, *Existenzphilosophie und Pädagogik* 59, *Mass und Vermessenheit des Menschen* 62, *Mensch und Raum* 63, *Die Pädagogische Atmosphäre* 64, *Französischer Existentialismus* 65, *Krise und neuer Anfang* 66, *Sprache und Erziehung* 66.
Waldeckstrasse 27, D74 Tübingen, German Federal Republic.
Telephone: 4076.

Bolshakov, Ivan Grigorevich; Soviet politician; b. 02; ed. Moscow Economic Inst.
U.S.S.R. Council of People's Commissars; Chair. Union Cttee. for Cinema Affairs 39-46; Minister of Cinematography 46-53; Dep. Minister of Culture 53-54; Dep. Minister of Trade 54-60; Dep. Chair. State Cttee. for Cultural Relations with Foreign Countries 60-63; scientific work in technical aesthetics, All-Union Research Inst. of Technical Aesthetics 63-; two Orders of Lenin, Red Banner of Labour.
All-Union Research Institute of Technical Aesthetics, Exhibition of National Economy Achievements, 115 Building, Moscow; Home: Gorky Street 9, ap. 47, Moscow, U.S.S.R.
Telephone: 2-9-96-29.

Bolt, Robert Oxton; British playwright; b. 15 Aug. 1924; ed. Manchester Grammar School and Manchester Univ.
Office Boy, Insurance Office, Manchester 41-42; Manchester Univ. 43; R.A.F. and W. African Frontier Force 43-46; Manchester Univ. 46-49, Exeter Univ. 49-50; Teacher, Bishopsteignton Village School 50-51, Millfield School, Somerset 51-58; freelance writer 58-; Oscar for *A Man for All Seasons* (film) 67.
Plays: *Flowering Cherry* 57, *The Tiger and the Horse* 59, *A Man for all Seasons* 61 (film 67), *Gentle Jack* 63, *The Thwarting of Baron Bolligrew* (for children) 66, *Brother and Sister* 67; Filmscripts: *Lawrence of Arabia* 62, *Dr. Zhivago* 64.
15 Chelsea Embankment, London, S.W.3, England.

Bolte, Hon. Sir Henry Edward, K.C.M.G.; Australian farmer and politician; b. 1908; ed. Ballarat Church of England Grammar School.
Served Second World War in Australian Imperial Forces; mem. Victoria Legislative Assembly for Hampden 47-; Minister of Water Supply, Mines and Conservation 48-50; Premier, Treasurer 55-, and Minister for Conservation (Victoria) 55-61; Leader, Liberal and Country Party of Victoria 53-; Hon. LL.D. Melbourne Univ. 65, Monash Univ. 67.
"Kialla", Meredith, Victoria, Australia.

Bolton, Sir George Lewis French, K.C.M.G.; British banker; b. 16 Oct. 1900.
Société Générale de Paris 17; Helbert, Wagg & Co. Ltd. 20; Bank of England to assist in management of Exchange Equalisation Fund 33; Tripartite Monetary Agreement 36; Adviser to Bank of England 41-48; Exec. Dir. of Bank of England 48-57, Dir. 57-68; Dir. Bank for Int. Settlements 49-57; Exec. Dir. Int. Monetary Fund 46-52, Alternate Gov. 52-57; Chair. Bank of London and South America 57-; Chair. Commonwealth Devt. Finance Co. Ltd., Bank of London and Montreal Ltd.; Chair. Int. Banking Services 68-; Dir. Balfour Williamson Investment Co. Ltd., Canadian Pacific Railway Co., Canadian Pacific Steamships Ltd., Canadian Pacific Air Services Ltd., Canadian Pacific Oil & Gas of Canada Ltd., Sun Life Assurance Co., of Canada.
Pollards Cross, Hempstead, Essex, England.

Bolz, Lothar, DR. JUR.; German lawyer and politician; b. 3 Sept. 1903; ed. Univs. of Munich, Kiel and Breslau.
Held various legal positions 26-30; law practice 30-33;

in exile in Poland and U.S.S.R. 33-47; Minister for Construction 49-53, Deputy Prime Minister 50-67 and Minister of Foreign Affairs 53-65 in Govt. of German Democratic Republic; Chair. Nat. Democratic Party of Germany 48-; Vaterländischer Verdienstorden in Gold, Orden Banner der Arbeit and other awards.
Friedrichstrasse 65, Berlin, W.8, Germany.

Bomani, Paul; Tanzanian politician; b. 1 Jan. 1925; ed. locally.
Employee, Williamson Diamonds Ltd. 45-47; Asst. Sec., later Sec. Mwanza African Traders' Co-operative Soc.; Organiser, Lake Province Growers' Asscn. 52; studied Co-operative Development at Loughborough Coll. 53-54; mem. Legislative Council 55; Manager Victoria Fed. of Co-operative Unions Ltd. 55; Minister of Agriculture, Tanganyika 60-62, Minister of Finance 62-64, Minister of Finance of Tanzania 64-65; Minister for Econ. Affairs and Devt. Planning 65-67, June 67-, of Commerce 67.
Ministry of Economic Affairs, Dar es Salaam, Tanzania.

Bombassei Frascani de Vettor, Giorgio; Italian diplomatist; b. 29 June 1910; ed. Universitá degli Studi, Florence and Inst. of Political and Social Sciences "Cesare Alfieri", Florence.
Italian Diplomatic Service 33-, served Egypt, U.S.A., France, Ceylon, U.S.S.R., Switzerland, Brazil 33-52; Deputy Dir. of Int. Co-operation, Ministry of Foreign Affairs 52-56, Deputy Dir.-Gen. of Political Affairs 56-57; Perm. Rep. of Italy to Council of Europe 57-61; Ambassador to Luxembourg 61-67; Perm. mem. Italian Del. to Special Council of Ministers of European Coal and Steel Community (ECSC) 61-; Ambassador to the Netherlands 65-67; Perm. Rep. of Italy to the European Communities 67-; Grand Officer Order of Merit (Italy), Medal of Freedom (U.S.A.) and other decorations.
Italian Permanent Delegation to the European Communities, 62 rue Belliard, Brussels, Belgium.
Telephone: 134070.

Bomboko, Justin; Congolese politician; ed. Brussels Univ.
Member, Union Mongo Party, Equator Province; Minister of Foreign Affairs, Lumumba cabinet, June 60, Ileo cabinet, Sept. 60; mem., Congolese Comm. set up to co-operate with U.N., July 60; Leader, Col. Mobutu's governing College of High Commissioners, with responsibility for Foreign Affairs, Sept. 60; Minister of Foreign Affairs 61-63, 65-, of Justice 63-65, of Foreign Trade Oct. 67-.
Ministry of Foreign Affairs, Kinshasa, Democratic Republic of Congo.

Bomholt, Julius; Danish educationalist and politician; b. 11 June 1896; ed. Univ. of Copenhagen.
Teacher, Silkeborg 21, Askov Folk High School 21-22; Teacher, Workers' High School, Esbjerg 22, Head 24-29; M.P. (Social Democrat) 29-; mem. Radio Council 34-50. Chair. 40-Feb. 50 and Dec. 50-53; Chair. Lower House of Parl. 45-50, 64-68; Minister of Educ. 50, 53-57, of Social Affairs 57-61, for Cultural Affairs 61-64.
Publs. *Danish Literature from the Industrial Revolution to the Present Day* 30, *Workers' Culture* 32, *Modern Authors* 33, *Expeditions* 35, *Harald Bergstedt* 38, *The Danish Folk High School* 38, *Longing I-II* (novel) 44, *Scandinavian Profiles* 45, *Culture Problems* 45, *Before the Storm* 47, *Flowering Boughs* 47; in co-operation with Peder Norgaard: *New Signals* (radio play) 32, *Greenland at the Beginning of a New Epoch* 50, *Humanity in the Centre* 53, *Idea and Work* 53, *The Essential* 53, *Reform of the Primary School* 53, *From Pocket-book to Television* 54, *Bound for Life* 54; in co-operation with H. C. Hansen: *Hans Hedtoft: Life and Work* 55, *Winter Light* 56, *The Port of Heaven* 56, *The Swallows* 56, *From No. 21* (speeches) 57, *Ephemera and Eternity* 58, *Beyond the Mountain* 59, *Unknown Friend* 60, *The Book on H. C. Hansen* (with Viggo Kampmann) 60, *Solstice* 61, *M.P.*

62, *The Third Phase of the Revolution* 63, *Where are you?* 63, *The Fairy-Tale about the Poorhouse* 64, *Tales of the Old Tiles* 65, *The Knight of God* 66, *In the Centre of the Kingdom* 67, *Visions* (poems) 67.
Sønderho, Fanø, Denmark.
Telephone: 051-6-4-86.

Bonami, Charles Victor; French broadcasting official; b. 16 May 1908.
Posts, Telegraphs and Telecommunications Services 26-34; Radiodiffusion Télévision Française 35-, successively Asst. Head of Section, Head of Section, Asst. Dir., Head of Service, Head of Department, now Head of Department of Gen. Affairs and Public Relations; founder *RTF Information-Documentation* 47-64; Founder-mem. European Broadcasting Union (EBU) 50-; mem. Admin. Council, Office de Coopération Radiophonique (O.C.O.R.A.); Officier, Légion d'Honneur. Chevalier du Mérite postal.
2 rue Henri Duchène, Paris 15e, France.

Bondarchuk, Sergei Fedorovich; Soviet film actor and director; b. 1920; ed. All Union State Inst. of Cinematography.
Principal roles: Othello, Shevchenko (*Taras Shevchenko*), Valko (*The Young Guard*), Dymov (*The Grasshopper*), Yershov (*An Unfinished Tale*), Ivan Franko (*Ivan Franko*), Matvei Krylov (*The Soldiers Go On*), Sokolov (*Destiny of a Man*), Kozostylov (*Seryozha*), Pierre Bezukhov (*War and Peace*); Dir. and played in film *Destiny of a Man*; directed *War and Peace* 62-67; Order of Lenin; People's Artist of U.S.S.R.; Lenin and State Prizes.
"Mosfilm" Studio, 1 Mosfilmovskaya ul., Moscow, U.S.S.R.

Bondarenko, Ivan Afansyevich; Soviet politician; b. 1926; ed. Azov Agricultural Inst.
Checker with collective farm field crop team 42-43; Soviet Army service 43-45; Sectional Agronomist for Machine and Tractor Station, then Chief Agronomist for Forest-Shelterbelt Station 45-56; Dir. Educational-Experimental Farm and Lecturer at Azov Black Sea Inst. of Agriculture 56-59; Party Official, and Sec. of Rostov Regional Cttee. of C.P.S.U. 59-64; Chair. Rostov Regional Soviet 64-66; First Sec., Rostov Regional Cttee. of C.P.S.U. and Deputy to U.S.S.R. Supreme Soviet 66-; mem. C.P.S.U. 50-.
Rostov Regional Committee of Communist Party of the Soviet Union, Rostov-on-Don, U.S.S.R.

Bonde, Gen. Count Thord; Swedish army officer; b. 17 March 1900.
Entered army 20, Capt. 33, Major 41, Lieut.-Col. 43, Col. 46, Major-Gen. 55, Lieut.-Gen. 57, Gen. 63; Mil. Attaché to Washington 43-45; Chief of National Defence Coll. 53-55; C.-in-C. Swedish Army 57-63; Chief of Staff to H.M. the King of Sweden 63-.
Skärkiksvägen 22, Djursholm, Sweden.

Bondevik, Kjell, M.A.; Norwegian politician; ed. Universitetet i Oslo.
Schoolteacher 27-37; Headmaster Sauda High School 37-64; Senior Lecturer in Social History Univ. of Bergen 65-; Chair. Christian People's Party in Rogaland 39-50; mem. Nat. Board of Party 49-61; mem. Storting 50-65, Chair. of its Social Affairs Cttee. 54-61; Parl. Leader Christian People's Party 61-65; Minister of Social Affairs Aug.-Sept. 63, Ecclesiastical Affairs and Educ. 65-.
Publs. works on Norwegian folklore and traditions.
Ministry of Ecclesiastical Affairs and Education, Oslo, Norway.

Bondeville, Emmanuel; French composer; b. 29 Oct. 1898.
Dir. des Emissions artistiques, Radiodiffusion Française 35-45; Dir. Opéra de Monte-Carlo 45-49; Dir. Théâtre National de l'Opéra-Comique 49-52; Dir. du Théâtre

National de l'Opéra 52-63; mem. Académie des Beaux Arts 56-64, Perm. Sec. 64-, Pres. then Hon. Pres. (64-) Comité nat. de la musique; Grand Prix de la musique, Soc. des auteurs 66.
Works: *Le Bal des Pendus* 30, *L'Ecole des Maris* 35, *Illuminations, Sonate pour Piano, La Cloche Fêlée, Trois Pochades, La Rhapsodie Foraine, Le Pardon de Saint-Anne, Illustrations pour Faust* 42, *Madame Bovary* 51, *Gaultier-Garguille* 53, *Symphonie Lyrique* 57, *Symphonie Choréographique* 65.
Palais Mazarin, 25 Quai de Conti, Paris 6, France.

Bondi, Hermann, M.A., F.R.S.; British mathematician; b. 1 Nov. 1919; ed. Real Gymnasium, Vienna and Trinity Coll., Cambridge.
Fellow, Trinity Coll. Cambridge 43-49, 52-54; Lecturer in Mathematics, Cambridge Univ. 48-54; Prof. of Applied Mathematics, Univ. of London (King's Coll.) 54-, on leave of absence 67-; Dir.-Gen. European Space Research Org. (ESRO), Paris 67-; Research Assoc. Cornell Univ. 51, Harvard Coll. Observatory 53; Visiting Prof. Cornell Univ. 60; Fellow, Royal Society 59, Royal Astronomical Soc. (Sec. 56-64), Cambridge Philosophical Soc.; Chair. Nat. Cttee. for Astronomy 64-67.
Publs. *Cosmology* 52, (2nd edn. 60), *The Universe at Large* 61, *Relativity and Common Sense* 64, numerous papers.
European Space Research Organisation (ESRO), 114 avenue de Neuilly, 92 Neuilly-sur-Seine, France.
Telephone: 637-74-00, Ext. 321.

Bondor, József; Hungarian building engineer and politician.
Former mason's apprentice; joined workers movement 40, Communist Party 45; directed reconstruction of Lenin Foundry Works in County Borsod; one of founders and builders of town of Dunaujváros; Chief Engineer, later Vice-Pres. of Budapest Metropolitan Council 61-65; Deputy Minister of Building Construction and City Planning 65-68, Minister 68-.
Ministry of Building and City Planning, Budapest V, Beloiannisz-utca 2-4, Hungary.
Telephone: 112-200.

Bongo, Albert Bernard; Gabonese politician; b. 30 Dec. 1935; ed. primary school at Bacongo (Congo-Brazzaville) and technical coll., Brazzaville.
Civil servant; served Air Force 58-60; entered Ministry of Foreign Affairs 60; Dir. of Private Office of Pres. Léon Mba 62, in charge of Information 63-64, Nat. Defence 64-65; Minister-Del. to Presidency in charge of Nat. Defence and Co-ordination, Information and Tourism 66-67; Vice-Pres. of Repub. March-Dec. 67; Pres. of Repub. of Gabon Dec. 67-; Founder and Sec.-Gen. Parti Démocratique Gabonais 68; High Chancellor, Ordre Nat. de l'Etoile Equatoriale; Grand Cross, Ordre Nat. de Côte d'Ivoire, Ordre Nat. du Niger; High Officer, Ordre Nat. Centrafricain; Commdr., Ordre Nat. Français du Mérite; Officier du Mérite Combattant.
Boîte Postale 546, Libreville, Gabon.
Telephone: 26-90.

Bonhomme, Albert; French public servant; b. 7 July 1913; ed. Faculty of Law, Paris and Toulouse.
Army service 39-45; Dep. Prefect of Tiaret 45-47, of Oran 47-49; Sec.-Gen. of Guadeloupe 49-51; Dep. Prefect of Tlemcen 51-56; Prefect of Medea 56-58, of Aveyron 58-60, of Guadeloupe 60-65; Prefect without Portfolio 65-; Advisor to Govt. of Panama 67; Public Security 68; Officier, Légion d'Honneur.
Publs. *Monsieur Aimé Lafleur* 57, *Adieu Foulards, Adieu Madras* 61.
Ministère de l'Intérieur, 1 place Beauvau, Paris 8e, France.
Telephone: Maillat 1888.

Bönisch, Peter H.; German journalist; b. 4 May 1927; ed. Dr. Hugo Eckner Coll., Berlin Univ.
Political Editor *Die Neue Zeitung* 45-49; Editor *Tagespost* 49-52; Special Asst. to Pres. Nordwest-Deutsche-Rundfunk 52-55; Editor Kindler Publishing Co. 55-59, Springer Publishing Corpn. 59-, *Berliner Illustrierte;* Editor *Bild-Zeitung, Bild am Sonntag;* Order of Merit (German Fed. Republic).
Verlag Axel Springer, Kaiser-Wilhelm-Strasse 6, 2 Hamburg 36, German Federal Republic.
Telephone: Hamburg 34-91-9-424.

Bonjour, Edgar Conrad, DR. PHIL.; Swiss university professor; b. 21 Aug. 1898; ed. Univs. of Berne, Geneva, Paris and Berlin.
High school teacher 21-32; Deputy Director of Federal Archives 32; Priv. Doz. Univ. of Berne 33-35; Prof. of History, Univ. of Basle 35-, Dean of the Faculty of Philosophy 40, Rector and Pres. of Assembly of Swiss univ. rectors 46; Pres. of Basle Historic Society 46-49; mem. of Polish Acad., Bavarian Acad.; Dr. h.c. Univ. of Neuchâtel 59.
Publs. *Geschichte der Schweiz* 38, *Schillers Historische Schriften* 44, *Geschichte der schweizerischen Neutralität* 46, *Das Schicksal des Sonderbundes in zeitgenössischer Darstellung* 47, *Die Gründung des schweizerischen Bundesstaates* 48, *Theodor Kocher* 50, *Basel im Schweizerbund* 51, *Johannes von Müller* 52, *Der Neuenburger Konflikt* 56, *Studien zu Johannes von Müller* 57, *Die Schweiz und Europa* 58, *Die Universität Basel* 60, *Die Schweiz und Europa II* 61, *Die Geschichtsschreibung der Schweiz* (2 vols.) 62 (in collaboration with R. Feller), *Geschichte der schweizerischen Neutralität* (revised, enlarged edition, 3 vols.) 67.
Benkenstrasse 56, Basle, Switzerland.
Telephone: 061-3826-10.

Bonneau, Gabriel; French diplomatist; b. 12 May 1904; ed. Ecole des Langues Orientales.
Attaché, Teheran 31-34; Sec., Kabul 34-40, Chargé d'Affaires 37-38, 39-40; joined Free French Forces 40, Brigade Française d'Orient, Massawah 41; Head, Middle East Section, Free French H.Q., London 42; Del. of French Nat. Cttee. in Canada 43-44; Dir. of Middle East Dept., Ministry of Foreign Affairs, Paris 45-49; Ambassador to Mexico 49-55, to Sweden 55-58, to Uruguay 58-65, to Switzerland 65-; Grand-Officier du Mérite, Commandeur Légion d'Honneur, Croix de Guerre, Médaille de la Résistance.
Ambassade de France, Berne, Switzerland.

Bonnefous, Edouard; French politician; b. 24 Aug. 1907; ed. Ecole des Sciences Politiques and Inst. des Hautes Etudes Internationales.
Fmr. Pres. Comm. on Foreign Affairs, Nat. Assembly; Minister of Commerce, Faure Cabinet 52; Minister of State, Mayer Cabinet Jan. 53; Minister of Posts and Telegraphs until 56; Minister of Transport and Public Works 57-58; Deputy from Seine-et-Oise 46-58, Senator 59-; mem. Consultative Assembly, Council of Europe; del. to UN 48-52, Pres. French Cttee., Ligue Européenne de Coopération Economique; Prof. Inst. des Hautes Etudes Internationales; Pres. Soc. of Political Economy, Asscn. Nat. de Protection des Eaux, Asscn. professionnelle de la Presse Républicaine; Vice-Pres. Inst. Océanographique, Institut des Hautes Etudes de l'Amerique; Pres. Cttee. of *Revue Politique et Parlementaire;* mem. de l'Institut de France; Pres. Acad. des Sciences Morales et Politiques.
Publs. *Le Corporatisme, Devant et derrière le Rideau de Fer, A travers l'Europe Mutilée, L'Idée Européenne et sa Réalisation, L'Europe en face de son destin, Encyclopédie de l'Amérique Latine, La reforme administrative, Les grands Travaux, Histoire Politique de la IIIe République* (7 vols.), *La Terre et la Faim des Hommes, L'Année Politique* (19 vols.), *Les milliards qui s'envolent, Le monde est-il surpeuplé?*
6 rue de l'Elysée, Paris, France.

Bonnelly, Dr. Rafael; Dominican politician; b. 05. Fmr. teacher and lawyer; Dep. in Nat. Assembly 39-41, Senate 41; Minister of Interior and Police 41-42; Teacher of Law, Univ. of Ciudad Trujillo 42-46; Minister of Labour and Nat. Economy 46; Ambassador to Spain and later to Venezuela; fmr. Rector, Univ. of Ciudad Trujillo (now Univ. of Santo Domingo); Founder, Nat. Civic Union 61; Head, Council of State 61-63; Movimiento de Integración Nacional.
Santo Domingo, Dominican Republic.

Bonnet, Henri; French scholar and diplomatist; b. 26 May 1888; ed. Ecole Normale Supérieure and Paris Univ. Mem. L.N. Secretariat 20-31; Dir. Inst. of Intellectual Co-operation 31-40; Commr. and Minister for Information Provisional Govt. of the French Republic 43-44; Ambassador to U.S.A. 44-55; Vice-Pres. Franco-American Cttee.; mem. Board Dirs. Centre of Studies of Foreign Policy; Pres. Franco-American Cttee. for Industrial Co-operation; Grand Officier de la Légion d'Honneur, Croix de Guerre (14-18), Médaille de Résistance.
23 rue Verneuil, Paris 7e, France.
Telephone: 222-31-39.

Bonnier, Kaj; Swedish publisher; b. 16 March 1901. Chairman of Board Dagens Nyheters AB, publishers of daily newspapers; Man. Dir. AB Kaj Bonnier and Co.
Drottninggatan 71D, Stockholm, Sweden.

Bono, Gaudenzio, DR. ENG.; Italian industrialist; b. 17 May 1901; ed. Politecnico of Turin.
Sole Man. Dir. and Gen. Man. FIAT, Turin; Chair. "Galileo Ferraris" Nat. Electrical Eng. Inst.; Dir. several Italian companies; Cavaliere del Lavoro, Knight Grand Cross of the Italian Republic.
10 Corso Marconi, Turin, Italy.

Bonow, (Karl Daniel) Mauritz, LIC. PHIL.; Swedish co-operative official; b. 5 Sept. 1904; ed. Uppsala Univ. and London School of Economics.
Asst. Chief of Sec., Kooperativa förbundet 31-39; Chief of Research Bureau, State Food Comm. 40-41; Gen. Sec. and Dir., Kooperativa förbundet 41-; Vice-Pres. Int. Co-operative Alliance 55-60, Pres. 60-.
Publs. *Staten och jordbrukskrisen* (The State and the Agricultural Crisis) 35, *Staten och näringslivet* (The State and Economic Life) 43, *Kooperationen och folk-försörjningen* (Co-operation and the Structure of Society) 36, *Producer and Consumer* 54, *Co-operation in a Changing World* 60.
Björn Trädgårdsgränd 3, Stockholm, Sweden.
Telephone: 40-97-83.

Bonvin, Roger; Swiss public servant; b. 12 Sept. 1907; ed. Sion and Einsiedeln Colls.
Constructed tunnels for Dixence S.A. 32-34; Fed. Topography Service 34-35; Local Govt. Depts. 36-49; Collaborator in Elektrowatt S.A. 49-55, Mayor of Sion 55-62; Nat. Councillor 55-; Fed. Councillor 62-; Head of Finance Dept. Swiss Fed. Council 65-67; Minister of Transport 68-; Vice-Pres. of Swiss Confederation 66, Pres. 67.
Grand Pont 29, Sion, Switzerland.

Bonvoisin, Baron Pierre de, D. en D., M.A.; Belgian banker; b. 03; ed. Liège and Princeton Univs.
Hon. Chair. of Board, Banque de la Société Générale de Belgique, Brussels; Extraordinary Prof. of Money and Banking, Univ. of Louvain; Hon. Chair. Belgian American Banking Corpn., N.Y., Belgian American Bank & Trust Co., N.Y.; Chair. Crédit Foncier International; Hon. Chair. Banque Belge Ltd. (London); Chair. Banque Italo-Belge, Brussels; Dir. Banque de l'Union Parisienne, C.F.C.B. Paris, Compagnies Belges d'assurances Générales, Agence Maritime Internationale, Antwerp.
Home: 30 Boulevard Saint Michel, Brussels 4; Office: 3 Montagne du Parc, Brussels, Belgium.

Booher, Edward E.; American publisher; b. 29 June 1911; ed. Antioch Coll.
McGraw-Hill Book Company, Vice-Pres. 44-54, Exec. Vice-Pres. 54-60, Pres. 60-; Trustee, Antioch Coll.; Dir. Cttee. for a Nat. Trade Policy, McGraw-Hill, Inc.; Chair. of the Board Franklin Book Programs Inc., of Board of Higher Education of New Jersey; Dir. and Vice-Pres. American Book Publishers Council; mem. Board of Foreign Scholarships, Advisory Cttee. on Mexican-American Education.
McGraw-Hill Book Co., 330 West 42nd Street, New York, N.Y., U.S.A.
Telephone: 212-971-2033.

Böök, Klas Erik, FIL. LIC.; Swedish banker and diplomatist; b. 10 March 1909.
Sec. Bank of Sweden 37; Head of Research Dept., Bank of Sweden 40; Deputy Man. Foreign Exchange Control Office 40; Man. Bank of Sweden 43; Deputy Gov. 44; mem. Foreign Trade Comm. Board 44; Envoy Extraordinary and Min. Plen.; Head of Commercial Dept. Foreign Office 47; Deputy Chair. Export Credit Guarantee Board; Chair. Foreign Exchange Control Board, mem. Foreign Funds Control Board; Gov. Bank of Sweden 48-51; Swedish Minister in Canada 51-55; Ambassador to China and Thailand 55-61, to India, Ceylon and Nepal 61-65, to Switzerland 65-.
Swedish Embassy, Marienstrasse 30, Berne, Switzerland.

Boom, Dr. Geert; Netherlands scientific officer; b. 8 Dec. 1933; ed. High School, Rijksuniversiteit Groningen.
Scientific Officer, Univ. of Groningen 60-65, Senior Scientific Officer 65-; Gen. Sec. Int. Union of Crystallography 66-.
Publs. various scientific papers.
Laboratorium Voor Fysiche Metaalkunde der Rijksuniversiteit, Westersingel 34, Groningen, The Netherlands.
Telephone: Groningen 36141.

Boon, Henrik Nicolaas, LL.D.; Netherlands diplomatist; b. 23 Aug. 1911; ed. Univs. of London, Paris and Leyden and Geneva School of Int. Studies.
Served Ministry of Foreign Affairs 36-39; served in Madrid, Brussels, Washington, Tsjoengking, Batavia and Nanking 39-47; Deputy and later Chief of Diplomatic Affairs Division, Ministry of Foreign Affairs 47-49; Sec.-Gen. Ministry of Foreign Affairs 49-52, Minister later Amb. to Italy 52-58, Amb. to Venezuela 58-61; Amb. on Special Mission; Perm. Rep. to NATO 61-; Knight Order of Netherlands Lion, Officer Order of Orange Nassau, Grand Cross Order of Adolf van Nassau of Luxembourg, Grand Officer Order of the Crown of Belgium, Commdr. Légion d'Honneur.
Publ. *Rêve et réalité dans l'oeuvre économique et social de Napoléon III.*
6 rue Nisard, Boisfort, Brussels 17, Belgium.
Telephone: 73-70-85.

Boorstin, Daniel J., M.A., LL.D.; American educator and author, b. 1 Oct. 1914; ed. Harvard Coll., Balliol Coll. Oxford, and Yale Univ.
Harvard Coll. and Harvard Law School 38-42; Office of Lend-Lease Admin., Washington 42; Asst. Prof., Swarthmore Coll. 42-44; Prof. of American History, Univ. of Chicago 44-; Prof. of American History, Univ. of Paris 61-62: Pitt Prof. American History and Institutions, Cambridge 64-65, Preston and Stirling Morton Distinguished Service Prof. of History; Fellow Trinity Coll., mem. American Revolution Bicentennial Commission; several prizes.
Publs. *The Mysterious Science of the Law* 41, *Delaware Cases 1792-1830* (3 vols.) 43, *The Lost World of Thomas Jefferson* 48, *The Genius of American Politics* 53, *The Americans: The Colonial Experience* 58, *America and the Image of Europe* 60, *The Image* 62, *The Americans:*

The National Experience 65, *An American Primer* 66.
c/o Department of History, University of Chicago,
Chicago 60637; Home: 5609 South Woodlawn Avenue,
Chicago, Illinois 60637, U.S.A.
Telephone: 312-Plaza 2-3161.

Boothby, Baron, **of Buchan and Rattray Head** (Life
Peer), **Robert J. G. Boothby,** K.B.E., LL.D.; British politi-
cian; b.1900; ed. Eton and Magdalen Coll., Oxford.
Unionist M.P. for East Aberdeenshire 24-58; Parl.
Private Sec. to Mr. Winston Churchill (Chancellor of
the Exchequer) 26-29; Parl. Sec. to Ministry of Food
40-41; British del. to Consultative Assembly of Council
of Europe 49-57, Vice-Chair. Cttee. on Economic Affairs
52-56; Rector of St. Andrews Univ. 58-61; Pres. Anglo-
Israel Asscn.; Officier de la Légion d'Honneur 50.
Publs. *The New Economy* 43, *I Fight to Live* 47, *My
Yesterday, Your Tomorrow* 62.
House of Lords, London, S.W.1, England.

Boothe, Clare (*see* **Luce, Mrs. Clare**).

Borch, Fred J.; American business executive; b.
28 April 1910; ed. Western Reserve Univ.
General Electric Co. 31-, Vice-Pres. (Marketing) 54-59;
Vice-Pres. and Group Executive (Consumer Products)
59-61, Executive Vice-Pres. (Operations) 61-63, Pres.
and Chief Executive Officer 63-.
General Electric Co., 570 Lexington Avenue, New York,
N.Y. 10022, U.S.A.

Borch, Otto Rose; Danish diplomatist; b. 1 Sept.
1921; ed. Københavns Univ. and Columbia Univ., New
York.
Joined Ministry of Foreign Affairs, Copenhagen;
Danish Embassy, Bonn 54-58; Ministry of Foreign
Affairs 58; Head of Political Affairs Dept. 61-64;
Deputy Perm. Rep. to NATO 64-67; Perm. Rep. to
UN 67-.
Permanent Mission of Denmark to the United Nations,
235 East 42nd Street, New York, N.Y. 10017, U.S.A.

Bord, André; French politician; b. 30 Nov. 1922.
Member of Chamber of Deputies 58-; a French Deputy
at European Parliament; mem. Strasbourg Munici-
pality 59-; Sec. of State for Interior 66-; Médaille
Militaire, Croix de Guerre.
Assemblée Nationale, Paris 7e, France.

Borda, Guillermo Antonio; Argentine lawyer and
politician; b. 22 Sept. 1914; ed. Univ. de Buenos Aires.
Professor of Argentine History, School of Commerce
No. 6 41-46; Prof. in Faculty of Law and Social Sciences,
Univ. of Buenos Aires 47-56; Prof. of Civil Law, Univ.
of Salvador 57-, Catholic Univ. of Buenos Aires 58-;
Minister of Finance, Public Works and Agriculture,
Province of San Luis 45; Sec. of Public and Urban
Works, City of Buenos Aires 58; mem. Court of Civil
Appeals 59-62, Vice-Pres. 62-63, Pres. 63-66; Minister
of Interior Dec. 66-.
Publs. *Error de hecho y de derecho* 46, *Historia Argentina*
46, *Retroactividad de la ley y derechos adquiridos* 51,
Tratado de Derecho Civil Argentino, Parte General 53,
Familia 55.
Montevideo 471, Buenos Aires, Argentina.

Bordaz, Robert; French government official; b. 6 July
1908.
Communications and Merchant Marine Office, Algiers
43; Ministry of Public Works, Paris; Master of Petitions,
Council of State 44; Ministry of Nat. Economy 45;
Govt. Commr., Banque de Paris et des Pays Bas 46-48;
Head of Private Office of Minister of Construction
48-51; Dir. Broadcasting Inst. of Cambodia, Laos and
Viet-Nam 51-54; Deputy Commr. Indo-China 54-56;
Commercial Counsellor and Head of Dept. of Econ.
Expansion, Moscow 56-58; Counsellor of State 58-;
Dir.-Gen. Radiodiffusion-Télévision Française 62-64;
mem. Board of Agence France-Presse, Commr.-Gen.

French section 1967 World Exhbn. of Montreal 64-;
Officier Légion d'Honneur; Rosette de la Résistance;
Commdr. des Arts et Lettres.
Publ. *La nouvelle Economie Soviétique 1953-1960* 60.
15 rue Gay-Lussac, Paris 5e, France.

Bordeaux Le Pecq, Andrée; French painter and
engraver; b. 3 Oct. 1910; ed. Convent of the Sacred
Heart, Weymouth and Univ. of Oxford.
Member of Paris painting salons; Founder-Pres. Musée
d'Art Naïf; Founder-Pres. Comparaisons Salon; Pres.
Nat. Fine Arts Section, Women's Business Asscn.; ten
one-man exhbns. in Paris, also in Rome, New York,
Mexico, Guadalajara, Tokyo, Vienna, Rio de Janeiro,
Brussels and San Francisco; represented in Musée Nat.
d'Art Moderne, Paris and numerous French museums,
also hung in Galleries at Djakarta, Tel-Aviv, Vienna,
Reykjavík, Phoenix (Arizona) and Tokyo; numerous
prizes include Grande Médaille de Vermeil de la Ville
de Paris 64; Chevalier Légion d'Honneur.
Major works: numerous book illustrations include 36
pen and ink plates for *Les Pierres m'ont dit,* Théophile
Briant, and *Les Tentations,* Grazia Deledda; drawings
for tapestries for Mobilier National; monumental works
in lava.
36 rue de la Pompe, Paris 16e, France.

Bordier, Paul; French Inspector of Finances; b.
16 Jan. 1921; ed. Rochefort-sur-Mer and Bordeaux
Lycées, Ecole Nat. de la France d'Outre-Mer.
Service in Morocco, French colonies and in Ministry of
Overseas France; Dir.-Gen. of Economic Affairs, French
Equatorial Africa until 56; Gov. Niger 56-58; High
Commr. Central African Republic 58-60; Technical
Adviser, Ministry of Co-operation 61; Inspector of
Finances 62-; Pres. Groupe Foncier du Plan 65-66;
Pres. Chambre Syndicale Commerce et Industrie des
Eaux Minérales 68.
1 rue de Sfax, Paris 16e; and 24 rue du IV Septembre,
Paris 1er, France.
Telephone: PAS 65-91; RIC 79-51.

Bordier, Roger; French writer; b. 5 March 1923; ed.
secondary school.
Journalist in the provinces, later in Paris; Contributor
to *Nouvelles Littéraires* and *Aujourd'hui*; radio and
television writer; Prix Renaudot 61.
Publs. poems: *Les Epicentres* 51; novels: *La Cinquième
Saison* 59, *Les Blés* 61, *Le Mime* 63, *L'Entracte* 65;
Un âge d'or 67; Play: *Les Somnambules* 63.
8 rue Geoffrey St. Hilaire, Paris 5e, France.
Telephone: 535-22-56.

Borel, Jacques; French writer, teacher and critic;
b. 17 Dec. 1925; ed. Lycée Henri IV, Paris, and Univ.
de Paris à la Sorbonne.
Teacher, Lycée de Clermont-Ferrand 52-56, Lycée
Rodin, Paris 56-67; contributes poems and essays to
*Nouvelle Revue française, Critique, Mercure de France,
Botteghe Oscure, Cahiers du Sud, Figaro,* etc.; Prix
Goncourt 65.
Publs. Editor Verlaine's *Complete Works* 59-60; *Poetical
Works* 62, *L'Adoration* (novel) 65, *Tata ou de l'Education*
(play) 67; Trans. James Joyce's *The Cat and the Devil*
66, *Collected Poems* 67, Prefaces to *Romanciers au Travail*
67, Du Bellay's *Poetical Works* 67.
22 rue de Chevreuse, 91 Bures-sur-Yvette, Essonne,
France.
Telephone: 928-57-29.

Borel, Jacques Paul; French restaurant executive; b.
9 April 1927; ed. Lycées Condorcet and Carnot, Paris,
Ecole des Hautes Etudes Commerciales.
Commercial engineer, IBM France 50-57, Manager
Saigon (Viet-Nam) Branch Office IBM; Pres. Soc.
française de distribution de produits alimentaires
(Sofradipa) 57-, Dir. 60-; Pres. Jacques-Borel Restau-
rants Co. 60-; Pres. Soc. Centrale d'Achats de produits

alimentaires (Scapa) 61-, then Dir.; Pres. Econ. Restaurant Asscn., Soc. de Promotion Touristique des Autoroutes 66, later Dir.; Dir. Soc. Wimpy de France (Seor); Pres. Ticket-Restaurant Co.
60 avenue de Saxe, Paris 15e; Home: Le Villefreux, 47 avenue de Villefreux, 92 Vaucresson, Hauts de Seine, France.
Telephone: 273-17-20 (Office); 970-10-20 (Home).

Boreskov, Georgy Konstantinovich; Soviet chemist; b. 1907; ed. Odessa Chemical Inst.
At Ukrainian Chemico-Radiological Inst., Odessa 28-37; Instructor, Odessa Inst. of Chemical Technology 30-37, Odessa Univ. 34-37; Dir. Catalysis Lab., Moscow Ferti-lizer, Insecticide and Fungicide Research Inst. 37-49; Assoc. Karpov Physico-Chemical Inst. 46-; Prof. Moscow Inst. of Chemical Technology 49-; Corresp. mem. U.S.S.R. Acad. of Sciences 58-66, mem. 66-; Dir. Inst. of Catalysis, Siberian Dept., U.S.S.R. Acad. of Sciences 61-; State Prize 42; Hero of Socialist Labour 67.
Institute of Catalysis, Siberian Department of U.S.S.R. Academy of Sciences, Novosibirsk, U.S.S.R.

Borg, Kim, M.TECH.; Finnish singer; b. 19; ed. Helsinki Inst. of Technology and Sibelius-Acad. Helsinki.
Début, Helsinki 47; Royal Theatre, Copenhagen 52-57; Finnish National Opera 52-; Munich State Opera 56-57; Glyndebourne Opera Co. 56 and 59; Metropolitan Opera Co., New York 59-62; Royal Theatre, Stockholm 65-; Hamburg State Opera 65-; tours in Europe, North America, Asia and Australia; numerous re-cordings.
Office: Konsertbolaget, Hamngatan, Stockholm, Sweden; Home: Österbrogade 158, Copenhagen, Denmark.

Borg Olivier, Dr. George, LL.D.; Maltese politician; b. 5 July 1911; ed. Lyceum and Royal Univ. of Malta.
Elected to Council of Govt. 39, to Legislative Assembly 47; Minister of Works and Reconstruction and Minister of Education 50; Prime Minister and Minister of Works and Reconstruction 50-55; Leader of Opposition 55-58; Prime Minister and Minister of Economic Planning and Finance 62-, also Minister of Commonwealth and Foreign Affairs 65-; Hon. D.Litt.; Knight Grand Cross Order of St. Sylvester and Order of Pius IX (Vatican); Leader Nationalist Party.
Auberge d'Aragon, Valetta, Malta.

Borge, Victor; Danish-born American entertainer; b. 3 Jan. 1909; ed. Borgerdydskolen and Copenhagen Conservatoire.
Concert pianist 22-34; revue, theatre and film career as composer, actor and musical comedian 34-; settled in U.S.A. 40, U.S. citizen 48; Order of Dannebrog.
Field Point Park, Greenwich, Conn., U.S.A.

Borgeaud, Maurice Camille; French metals executive; b. 5 Oct. 1909; ed. Ecole Polytechnique.
Former Vice-Pres. of USINOR (Union sidérurgique du Nord de la France), Pres., Dir.-Gen. 66-; Vice-Pres. Soc. métallurgique de Pont-à-Vendin; Dir. Groupement de l'industrie sidérurgique, and other companies; Officier Légion d'Honneur.
USINOR, 14 rue d'Athènes, Paris 9e; Home: 14 avenue de l'Observatoire, Paris 14e, France.

Borges, Jacobo; Venezuelan painter; b. 28 Nov. 1931; ed. Escuela de Artes Plásticas Cristóbal Rojas, Caracas and Ecole des Beaux Arts, Paris.
Member of Young Painters' Group and Illustrator of magazines and record covers while in Paris 51-56, also exhibited in French Nat. Exhbns.; Prof. of Scenography and Plastic Analysis, Escuela de Artes Plásticas Cristóbal Rojas, Caracas 58-65; Prof. of Scenography, Theatre School of Valencia and Dir. Experimental Art Centre, Univ. of Venezuela 66-; one-man exhbns. in Caracas at Galeria Lauro 56, Museo de Bellas Artes 56, Galería G 63 and Galería Techo 65; represented in

numerous group exhbns. including São Paulo Bienal 57, 63, 65, Venice Biennale 58, Brussels World Fair 58, and Int. Exhbns. at Guggenheim Museum, New York 64, 65; Nat. Painting Prize 63, Armando Reverón Bienal Prize 65.
Major works: *La Lámpara y la Silla* 51, *La Pesca* 57, *Sala de Espera* 60, *Todos a la Fiesta* 62, *Ha Comenzado el Espectáculo* 64, *Altas Finanzas* 65; series of *Las Jugadoras* and *Las Comedoras de Helados* 65-66.
c/o Museo de Bellas Artes, Avenida los Caobos, Caracas, Venezuela.

Borges, Jorge Luis; Argentine author and university professor; b. 24 Aug. 1899; ed. in Switzerland, Cam-bridge and Buenos Aires Univs.
Director Nat. Library of Buenos Aires, and fmr. Prof. of English and North American Literature, Buenos Aires Univ.; mem. Acad. Argentina de Letras; Hon. K.B.E.; Premio de Honor, Prix Formentor 61 (with Samuel Beckett), Fondo de las Artes 63.
Publs. many short stories, poems and essays, including *Luna de Enfrente, Cuaderno San Martín, Historia de la Eternidad, Antología Clásica de la Literatura Argentina, El Martín Fierro* (with Margarita Guerrero), *La Poesía Gauchesca, El Aleph, El Jardín de Desiderios que se bifurcan, Inquisiciones, Otras Inquisiciones, Historia de la Eternidad, Historia Universal de la Infamia, Fervor de Buenos Aires, Ficciones, Labyrinthe, Libro de Cielo y del Infierno* (poems) 60, *El Hacedor* 60, *Antología personal* 61.
México 564, Buenos Aires, Argentina.

Borgnine, Ernest; American actor; b. 24 Jan. 1917; ed. New Haven public schools.
Films include *From Here to Eternity, Bad Day at Black Rock, Marty, Violent Saturday, Square Jungle, Three Brave Men, Hell Below, The Rabbit Trap, Man on String, Barabbas*; Oscar for Best Performance 56.
9390 Brighton Way, Beverly Hills, Calif., U.S.A.

Borila, Petre; Romanian politician; b. 06.
Member, Union of Communist Youth 22-24, Com-munist Party of Romania 24-48, Central Cttee. of Romanian Workers' Party 48-, Political Bureau 52-; Dep. Minister of Armed Forces, later Minister of Con-struction, later Pres. State Control Comm., later Minister of Food Industry 49-54; Dep. Chair. Council of Ministers 54-65; mem. Exec. Council Romanian Communist Party 65-; mem. of the State Council.
State Council, Bucharest; Home: Bulvardul Aviatorilor 86, Bucharest, Romania.

Borin, Vadim Ivanovich; Soviet trade corporation official; b. 14 Jan. 1926; ed. Steel Inst., Moscow, and All-Union Acad. for Foreign Trade, Moscow.
Senior Engineer, Chief of Dept., U.S.S.R. Trade Del. in U.K. 55-60; Dir. *Promsyrioimport* 60-62; Deputy Trade Rep. of U.S.S.R. in Finland 62-66; Pres. *Sojuzchim-export* (export and import of chemical products) 66-.
Vsesojuznoje Objedinenije Sojuzchimexport, Ministry of Foreign Trade, 32-34 Smolenskaya-Sennaya plosh-chad, Moscow, U.S.S.R.

Boring, Edwin Garrigues, M.E., A.M., PH.D., American psychologist; b. 23 Oct. 1886; ed. Cornell Univ.
Instructor in Psychology, Cornell Univ. 13-18; Capt., psychological service, U.S. Army 18-19; Prof. of Experi-mental Psychology, Clark Univ. 19-22; Associate Prof. of Psychology, Harvard Univ. 22-28; Dir. Psychological Laboratory 24-49; Prof. Psychology 28-56; Edgar Pierce Prof. of Psychology 56-57, Emeritus 57-; Lowell Tele-vision Lecturer 56-57; Editor *Contemporary Psychology* 56-61; Consulting Editor Basic Books 61-; mem. Nat. Acad. of Sciences, American Philosophical Soc., American Acad. of Arts and Sciences; Foreign Assoc. British, French, Italian and Spanish Psychological Socs.; Hon. Sc.D. (Univ. of Pa., Clark Univ.); Gold Medal American Psychological Foundation 59.

Publs. Works on research in psychology of sensation and perception and research in history of experimental psychology; *History of Experimental Psychology* 29 (revised edn. 50), *Physical Dimensions of Consciousness* 33, *Sensation and Perception in the History of Experimental Psychology* 42, *Psychologist at Large* 61, *History, Psychology and Science* 63; (joint editor) *Psychology, a Factual Textbook* 35, *Introduction to Psychology* 38, *Psychology for the Fighting Man* 43, *Psychology for the Armed Services* 45, *Foundations of Psychology* 48, *A Source Book in the History of Psychology* 65.
21 Bowdoin Street, Cambridge, Mass. 02138, U.S.A.
Telephone: 617-454-0852.

Borisenko, Nikolai Mikhailovich; Soviet politician; b. 1918; ed. Kharkov Veterinary Inst.
Veterinary technician 39-41; Soviet Army 41-45; mem. C.P.S.U. 43-; State farm dir. and Man. of Ukrainian agricultural trust 45-55; Chair. of local Soviet, Chair. Chernigov Regional Soviet of Working People's Deputies 55-63; First Sec. Chernigov Regional Cttee· of C.P. of Ukraine 63-; mem. Central Cttee. C.P. of Ukraine; Deputy to U.S.S.R. Supreme Soviet.
Chernigov Regional Committee, Communist Party of Ukraine, Chernigov, U.S.S.R.

Borisov, Alexandr Vasilyevich; Soviet politician; b. 1913; ed. Gorky Inst. of Agriculture.
Agronomist 36, 38-41; Soviet Army 36-38, 41-46; Chief Agronomist, Krasnoufimsk District Dept. of Agriculture 46-59, later Head Sverdlovsk Regional Dept. of Agriculture; Vice-Chair. Sverdlovsk Regional Soviet 59-64, Chair. 64-; mem. C.P.S.U. 45-; Deputy to U.S.S.R. Supreme Soviet.
Sverdlovsk Regional Soviet of Working People's Deputies, Sverdlovsk, U.S.S.R.

Borisov, Mikhail Ivanovich; Soviet trade union official; b. 13; ed. Saratov Highway Construction Inst.
Road Building Dept., Central Board of Highways, later Central Board of Aviation Construction 36-50; Chair. Central Cttee. of Trade Union of Workers of Construction of Heavy Industry Works 50-56, of Building Workers' Trade Union 56-57, of Trade Union of the Workers of the Building Trades and Building Materials Industry 57-64; in U.S.S.R. State Cttee. for Construction 64-; mem. C.P.S.U., All-Union Central Council of Trade Unions; Order of Red Star, Red Banner of Labour, etc.
U.S.S.R. State Cttee. for Construction, Marx Prospekt, Moscow, U.S.S.R.

Borkh, Inge; Swiss soprano opera singer; b. 26 May 1921; ed. Drama School, Vienna, and Vienna Acad.
Theatre performances (dancing, piano) in Vienna and Milan, then in Switzerland in German version of *Konsul* (Menotti); int. career 51-, Bayreuth, Paris, Vienna, Edinburgh Festival; first visit to U.S.A. 53; World Première of *Irische Legende* (Egk) 55; appeared as Salome and Elektra, Carnegie Hall, New York 58; Bavarian Court Singer 63; appeared at opening of Nationaltheater, Munich, in *Die Frau ohne Schätten* Nov. 63; Grand Prix du Disque for *Elektra, Antigone* (Orff), and Schönberg's *Gurrelieder*.
Haus Weitblick, CH 9405 Wienacht, Switzerland.
Telephone: Heiden 912091.

Born, Jorge; Argentine industrial, commercial and financial company director; b. 24 July 1900; ed. Athenée Royal, Antwerp, Belgium, and Univ. de Bruxelles, Belgium.
Director, Bunge y Born S.A. 26-, Pres. and Chair. 56-; Vice-Pres. Molinos Rio de la Plata S.A. 51-, Bunge y Born Foundation 64-; breeder of pedigree cattle (Hereford) and controls ownership of ranches in several Argentine provinces; Knight Order of Leopold, Officer Order of Crown (Belgium).
25 de Mayo 501, Buenos Aires, Argentina.

Born, Max, M.A., PH.D., F.R.S.; British (b. German) physicist; b. 11 Dec. 1882.
Lecturer in Physics, Göttingen Univ. 09; Prof. of Theoretical Physics, Berlin 15, Frankfurt 19, and Göttingen 21-33; Stokes Lecturer, Cambridge 33-36; Tait Prof. of Natural Philosophy, Edinburgh Univ. 36-53; acquired British nationality 39; Nobel Prize for Physics with (Walter Bothe) 54; Hon. D.Sc., Hon. LL.D., Hon. Dr.rer.nat., Hon. Dr. Ing., Hon. Ph.D.
Publs. *Dynamik der Kristallgitter* 15, *Die Relativitätstheorie Einsteins* 20, *Atomtheorie des festen Zustandes* 23, *Probleme der Atomdynamik* 26, *Elementare Quantenmechanik* (with P. Jordan) 30, *Optik* 33, *Atomic Physics* 35, *The Restless Universe* 35, *Experiment and Theory in Physics* 43, *Natural Philosophy of Cause and Chance* 49, *Kinetic Theory of Liquids* (with H. S. Green) 49, *Dynamical Theory of Crystal Lattices* (with Kun Huang) 54, *Physics in my Generation* 56, *Principles of Optics* (with E. Wolf) 59, *Physics and Politics* 62, *Collected Papers* (2 vols.) 63, and about 200 divers papers.
Marcardstrasse 4, Bad Pyrmont, German Federal Republic.
Telephone: Bad Pyrmont 05281-577.

Borna, Bertin; Dahomeyan politician; b. 30; ed. Université de Dakar.
Secretary-General Parti Démocratique Dahoméen (P.D.D.) 59-60; Asst. Sec.-Gen. Parti Dahoméen de l'Unité (P.D.U.) 60; mem. National Assembly 59-; Minister for Public Functions and Works 60-67, for Finance and Econ. Affairs 66-67; Commdr. Légion d'Honneur, and Commdr. du Mérite Dahoméen.
P.O. Box. 312, Cotonou, Dahomey.

Bornet, Charles Ange Emile; French judge; b. 14 Oct. 1897; ed. Lycées, Caen and Lille, Université de Lille.
Magistrate 22-; Attorney, Lille 44-46, Attorney-Gen., Nancy 46-48; Pres. Civil Court Seine 54-58; Court of Cassation, Counsellor 48-54, Pres. of Chamber 58-62, First Pres. 63-67; Commdr. Légion d'Honneur.
38 rue des Ecoles, Paris 5e, France.

Borodin, Andrei Mikhailovich; Soviet veterinary surgeon and politician; b. 1912; ed. Alma Ata Zoo-Veterinary Inst.
Acting Veterinary Surgeon on state farm, and Veterinary Surgeon for an agricultural combine in Kazakhstan 32-39; exec. post, Agricultural Dept., Kustanai Region, Kazakh S.S.R. 39-42; exec. Party and local govt. posts 42-45; Asst. Head of Dept., Central Cttee., C.P. of Kazakhstan, then First Deputy Minister of Agriculture and Procurements, Kazakhstan S.S.R. 45-53; Rep. of U.S.S.R. Ministry of Procurements for Kazakh S.S.R. 53-56; First Sec., Akmolinsk Regional Cttee., C.P. of Kazakhstan 56-57; Minister of Agriculture, then Vice-Chair., State Planning Cttee., Kazakh Council of Ministers 57-58; at H.Q. of Central Cttee., C.P. of Kazakhstan 58-59; First Sec., Kustanai Regional Cttee., C.P. of Kazakhstan; mem. Central Cttees. of C.P.S.U. and of C.P. of Kazakhstan 59-; Deputy to U.S.S.R. Supreme Soviet; mem. C.P.S.U. 41-.
Kustanai Regional Committee, Communist Party of Kazakhstan, Kustanai, U.S.S.R.

Borodin, Victor Petrovich; Soviet politician; b. 1924; ed. Volgograd Inst. of Agriculture.
Soviet Army 42-52; Official, Volgograd Regional Cttee., C.P.S.U., Head of Dept. of Agriculture, then Second Sec., Volgograd Regional Cttee. of C.P.S.U. 52-65; Chair. Volgograd Regional Soviet 65-; mem. C.P.S.U. 46-; Deputy to Supreme Soviet; mem. Budget Cttee., Soviet of Union.
Volgograd Regional Soviet of Working People's Deputies, Volgograd, U.S.S.R.

Borotra, Jean (Robert); French civil engineer and company director; b. 13 Aug. 1898; ed. Lycées Saint Louis and Michelet, Paris, Univ. de Paris à la Sorbonne and Ecole Polytechnique.

Civil Engineer 22; Commercial Man. Satam 24-30, Dir. 30-; Commissar-Gen. Gen. Educ. and Sport in Marshal Pétain's Govt. 40-42, deported by Gestapo 42-45; Vice-Pres. French Lawn Tennis Asscn. 30-; Pres. Comm. *Doctrine of Sport*, High Cttee. of Sport, Paris 62-; Pres. Int. Lawn Tennis Fed. 60-61, Vice-Pres. 61-; Vice-Pres. Int. Council for Sport and Physical Educ. (ICSPE) 60-; Pres. and Dir. several French and foreign companies; Commdr. Légion d'Honneur, Croix de Guerre (14-18, 39-45) and several other decorations; winner of numerous lawn tennis prizes, including six Wimbledon Championships (two for singles, three for doubles, and one for mixed doubles), and mem. French Davis Cup Team 22-47.

35 avenue Foch, Paris 16e; and Domaine de Pouy, Arbonne près Biarritz, Basses Pyrénées, France.

Borov, Todor; Bulgarian bibliographer and librarian; b. 01; ed. Sofia and Berlin Univs.
Prof. in Library Science Univ. of Sofia; Editor *Bǎlgarska kniga* (the Bulgarian book), *Yearbook of Bulgarian Bibliographical Inst.* 45-63.
Publs. *Knigi, biblioteki, bibliografija* (Books, libraries, bibliography) 41, *Pǎtija kǎm knigite* (The Road to the Books) 42, *Cehov i Bǎlgarija* 55, *Bulgarische Bibliographie* 60, *Die Bibliographie als Universitätslehrfach* 63, *Ausbildung von Bibliothekaren* 64.
Zar Krǔm 15, Sofia, Bulgaria.
Telephone: 87-52-40.

Borovik-Romanov, Victor-Andrei Stanislavovich; Soviet physicist; b. 1920; ed. Moscow Univ.
Research Assoc. Inst. of Physical Problems U.S.S.R. Acad. of Sciences 47-48; Research Assoc. Moscow Inst. of Measures and Measuring Instruments 48-55; Inst. of Physico-Technical and Radio Measurements, U.S.S.R. Cttee. of Standards, Measures and Measuring Instruments 55-56; Assoc. Deputy Dir. Inst. of Physical Problems U.S.S.R. Acad. of Sciences; Corresp. mem. U.S.S.R. Acad. of Sciences 66-.
Publs. Works on experimental and theoretical physics.
U.S.S.R. Academy of Sciences, 14 Lenin Prospekt, Moscow, U.S.S.R.

Borovkov, Alexander Alexeyevich; Soviet mathematician; b. 1931; ed. Moscow Univ.
Postgraduate, Research Assoc. Moscow Univ. 54-60; Assoc. Head of Dept. Inst. of Mathematics, Siberian Branch U.S.S.R. Acad. of Sciences 60-; Lecturer, Head of Chair Novosibirsk Univ. 61-; Corresp. mem. U.S.S.R. Acad. of Sciences 66.
Publs. Works on problems of theory probabilities.
U.S.S.R. Academy of Medical Sciences, 14 Lenin Prospekt, Moscow, U.S.S.R.

Borrelli, Rev. Mario, L.S.T.; Italian ecclesiastic; b. 22; ed. Major Archdiocesan Seminary, Naples.
One of the founders of O.N.A.R.M.O., Naples 46; founder of first J.O.C. in Naples 47, of I.R.P., Naples 48, of "Casa dello Scugnizzo", Naples 50; Founder-Dir. *Lo Scugnizzo* (monthly magazine) 50-.
Publ. *La Concezione Copernico Galileiana e la Filosofia di Tomaso D'Aquino* 61, *La Relazione tra il Conservatorio dei Poveri di Gesù Cristo e l'Oratorio di Napoli* 61, *A Streetlamp and the Stars* 63, *Il Largo dei Girolamini* 62, *Memorie Baroniane dell'Oratorio di Napoli* 63, *Opere e Documenti sul Baronio presso la British Museum Library* 64, *I Documenti dell'Oratorio Napoletano* 64, *Le Testimonianze Baroniane dell'Oratorio di Napoli, Documenti sul Baronio presso la Bodleian Library, L'Epistolario del Giuato Calvino nei suoi Rapporti col Baronio* 65.
Largo San Gennaro a Materdei, Naples; Oratory of St. Philip, Via Duomo 142, Naples, Italy.

Borrie, Wilfred David, M.A.; British (b. New Zealand) demographer; b. 2 Sept. 1913; ed. Waitaki Boys High School, Oamaru, New Zealand, Univ. of Otago, N.Z. and Cambridge Univ.

Lecturer, Social History and Econs., Sydney Univ. 44-46, Senior Lecturer 46-47; Research Fellow, Research School of Social Sciences, Australian Nat. Univ. 49-52, Reader 52-57, Prof. and Head of Dept. of Demography 57-; Vice-Pres. Int. Union for Scientific Study of Population 61-63; Pres. Social Science Research Council of Australia 62-64, Australian Council of Social Services 63-64; Chair. Population Comm., UN 65-; mem. Immigration Planning Council of Australia 65-.
Publs. *Population Trends and Policies* 47, *Immigration* 48, *Italians and Germans in Australia* 54, *The Cultural Integration of Immigrants* (Part I and General Editor) 59, *Australia's Population Structure and Growth* (with G. Spencer) 65.
Department of Demography, Australian National University, P.O.B. 4, Canberra, A.C.T., Australia.
Telephone: 49-2306.

Borschette, Albert, D. ès L.; Luxembourg diplomatist; b. 14 June 1920; ed. Univs. of Aix-en-Provence, Innsbruck, Munich, Erlangen and Paris.
Press Attaché, Ministry of State, Luxembourg 45-47; Head of Luxembourg Mission to French Zone of Germany 47-49; mem. Luxembourg Mission to Allied Control Comm., Berlin 49-50; Sec. Luxembourg Legation, Bonn 50-53, Sec., later Counsellor, Brussels 53-56; Deputy Head of Del. to Intergovernmental Cttee. for the Common Market and Euratom 56-57, to Interim Cttee. 57-58; Luxembourg Rep. to Euratom 58-59, Amb., Perm. Rep. to European Communities 58-; numerous decorations.
Publs. *Journal Russe* 46, *Literatur und Politik* 51, *Itinéraires I* 52; novel: *Continuez à mourir* 57.
73 avenue de Cortenbergh, Brussels, Belgium.
Telephone: 35-20-60.

Borten, Per; Norwegian agronomist and politician; b. 3 April 1913; ed. Norwegian Agricultural Univ., Ås.
Head, Technical Section, Provincial Agricultural Admin., Sör-Tröndelag 46-65; Chair. Fla Municipal Council 45, Provincial Council, Sör-Tröndelag 48; fmr. Head of Youth Movement of Agrarian Movement, Sör-Tröndelag; Regional Sec. Norwegian Farmers' Union 45-47; mem. Storting 50-, Pres. Odelsting 61-65; Chair. Agrarian Party 55-, Parl. Leader 57; Prime Minister 65-; Deputy Chair. Housing Bank 55-; mem. Council of Farmers' Bank 65-; Chair. Council of United Life Insurance Cos. in Norway 59-.
Office of the Prime Minister, Oslo, Norway.

Borůvka, Josef; Czechoslovak agriculturalist and politician; b. 18 Dec. 1911; ed. School of Political Studies, Central Cttee. of Communist Party of Czechoslovakia.
Farmer, mem. agricultural co-operative 27-49; Regional Cttee., C.P. of Czechoslovakia, Hradec Králové, Official, Head of Agricultural Dept., Sec. 49-56; Chief Sec. Regional Cttee. Nat. Front, Hradec Králové 56-60; Chair. of Co-operative Farm 60-68; Minister of Agriculture and Food 68-; Alt. mem. Central Cttee. C.P. of Czechoslovakia 49-54, mem. 54-; Deputy to Nat. Assembly 46-, Chair. Agricultural Cttee. of Nat. Assembly 58-64; numerous decorations.
Ministry of Agriculture and Food, Prague 1, Těšnov, Czechoslovakia.

Bosch, Baron Jean van den, LL.D.; Belgian diplomatist; b. 27 Jan. 1910; ed. Université Catholique de Louvain.
Diplomatic Service 34-; Sec., Peking 37-40, Ottawa 40-42; Chargé d'Affaires to Luxembourg Govt. in London 42-44; Counsellor 44, attached to Household of Prince Charles, Regent of Belgium, later served Cairo, Paris; Minister 53; Consul-Gen., Hong Kong 54-55; Ambassador to Egypt and Minister to Libya 55-59; Perm. Under-Sec. of State, Ministry of Foreign Affairs and Foreign Trade 59-60, 60-65; Ambassador to

Congo July and Aug. 60; Ambassador to U.K. 65-; numerous decorations.

Belgian Embassy, 103 Eaton Square, London, S.W.1, England.

Bosch, Juan; Dominican writer and politician; b. 09; ed. La Vega and Santo Domingo.

Founded literary group *Las Cuevas* (The Caves); exile in Puerto Rico and Cuba, travelled extensively in Latin America 37-61; founded Dominican Revolutionary Party 39, Pres. until Oct. 66; fmr. Prof. of Inst. of Political Science of Costa Rica; Pres. of Dominican Repub. 63; unsuccessful candidate for Presidency 66; voluntary exile in Spain.

Publs. *Camino Real* (Royal Path—short stories), *Indios* (Indians), *La Mañosa* (The Shrew—novel), *Mujeres en la Vida de Hostos* (Women in the life of Hostos), *Hostos —El Sembrador* (Hostos, the Sower), *Dos Pesos de Agua* (Two Pesos worth of Water), *Ocho Cuentos* (Eight Tales), *La Muchacha de la Guaira* (The Girl from La Guaira), *Cuba, la Isla Fascinante* (Cuba, the Fascinating Island), *Cuentos de Navidad* (Christmas Stories), *Life of Bolivar, Cuentos escritos en el Exilio* (Tales written in Exile), *Trujillo: Causas de una tiranía sin Ejemplo* (Trujillo: Causes of a Tyranny without Equal), *The Unfinished Experiment: Democracy in the Dominican Republic* 65, *David* 66.

c/o Dominican Revolutionary Party, Santo Domingo, Dominican Republic.

Bosch-Gimpera, Pere, PH.D., Mexican (born Spanish) historian and archæologist; b. 22 March 1891; ed. Barcelona, Madrid and Berlin Univs.

Dir. Catalan Archæological Service 15-, and of Archæological Museum 21-; Prof. of Prehistory and Ancient History Barcelona Univ. 16-39, Dean Philosophical Faculty 31-33, Rector of the Univ. 33-39; Pres. conf. for foundation of Congress of Prehistorical and Protohistorical Science, Berne 31; Minister of Justice, Catalan Autonomous Govt. 37-38; Prof. Univ. of Mexico 40-48, Univ. of Guatemala 45-46; Chief of the Div. of Philosophy and Humanities, UNESCO 48-52; Sec.-Gen. Int. Union for Anthropological and Ethnological Sciences 53-; Prof. Univ. of Mexico and School of Anthropology, Mexico 53-; Dr. h.c. (Heidelberg).

Publs. *Prehistoria catalana* 19, *Études sur le néolithique et l'énéolithique de France* (with J. Serra-Ràfols) 27, *Etnología de la Península ibérica* 32, *La conquista romana de España* (with P. Aguado) 35, *España* 37, *L'art grec à Catalunya* 37, *Two Celtic Waves in Spain* 42, *España un mundo en formación* 43, *El poblamiento y la formación de los pueblos de España* 45, *Historia de Catalunya* (with F. Soldevila) 45, *Historia de Oriente* 47-51, *Los Iberos* 48, *Phéniciens et Grecs dans l'extrême Occident* 51, *Mouvements Celtiques* 50-55, *Ibères, Basques, Celtes* 56-57, *Todavía el problema de la cerámica ibérica* 58, *Asia y América en el paleolítico inferior, Supervivencias* 58, *L'Amérique: Paléolithique et Mésolithique, Néolithique et Pré-Colombien* 59, *El Problema Indo-europeo* 60, *Les Indoeuropéens* 61, *Civilisation mégalithique portugaise et civilisations espagnoles (L'Anthropologie)* 67, *L'Amerique avant Christophe Colomb* 67.

Office: Instituto de Investigaciones Históricas (sección de Antropología), Facultad de Ciencias, planta baja, Ciudad Universitaria, Mexico 20, D.F.; Home: Callejón de Olivo 84-4, Colonia Agrícola, Mexico City 20, D.F. Mexico.

Telephone: 24-29-37.

Bosco, Giacinto; Italian lawyer and politician; b. 25 Jan. 1905.

Former Prof. of Int. Law, Rome Univ.; fmr. Editor *Rivista di Studi Politici Internazionali*, Florence and *Rivista di Studi europei*, Milan; fmr. Legal Adviser, Ministry of Foreign Affairs; mem. Senate 48-, Pres. 58-60; Under-Sec. of State for Defence 53-58, Minister for Educ. 60-62, of Justice 62-63, of Labour and Social

Security Dec. 63-July 64, 66-; mem. European Parl.; Christian Democrat.

Il Senato, Rome, Italy.

Bose, Satyendra Nath, D.SC., F.N.I., F.R.S., D.R.S., Desikottama; Indian educationist; b. 1 Jan. 1894; ed. Presidency Coll., Calcutta and Univ. of Calcutta.

Lecturer, Calcutta Univ. 16-21; Reader, Dacca Univ. 21-26, Prof. 27-45; Prof. Calcutta Univ. 45-56, Nat. Prof. of Physics 58; mem. Rajya Sabha 52-58; Vice-Chancellor, Visva-Bharati 56-58; fmr. Pres. Indian Science Congress 43; fmr. Pres. Nat. Inst. of Sciences; Fellow Royal Soc. 58; Padma Vibhushan, Govt. of India; Meghnath Saha Memorial Gold Medal (Nat. Inst. of Sciences).

Publs. *Light Quanta Statistics, Affine Connection Coefficients*, etc.

22 Iswar Mill Lane, Calcutta 6, India.

Bose, Vivian, B.A., LL.B.; Indian jurist; ed. Dulwich Coll., England, and Pembroke Coll., Cambridge.

Called to Bar, Middle Temple, London 13; practised at Nagpur Bar, India 13-36; Principal, Univ. Coll. of Law 24-30; Govt. Advocate and Standing Counsel to Govt. of Central Provinces and Berar 30-36; Additional Judicial Commr., Nagpur 31-36; Puisne Judge, Nagpur High Court 36-49, Chief Justice, Nagpur High Court 49-51; Puisne Judge, Supreme Court of India 51-56, retd. 56, ad. hoc. Judge 58-59; mem. Int. Comm. of Jurists 58-, Pres. 59-66, Hon. Pres. 66-; Chief Commr. for India, Boy Scouts Asscn. 48-49, Nat. Commr. 59-62.

Henessy Road, Nagpur 1, Maharashtra, India.

Boshgens, Georgy Sergeyevich; Soviet scientist (mechanics); b. 1916; ed. Moscow Aviation Inst.

Research Assoc. Central Airhydrodynamic Inst. 40; mem. C.P.S.U. 63-; Corresp. mem. U.S.S.R. Acad. of Sciences.

U.S.S.R. Academy of Sciences, 14 Lenin Prospekt, Moscow, U.S.S.R.

Boskovsky, Willi; Austrian conductor; b. 16 June 1909; ed. Akad. für Musik, Vienna.

Conductor of New Year Concerts of Vienna Philharmonic Orchestra 54-; Founder of Vienna Octet; Leader of Philharmonic Orchestra of Vienna State Opera; soloist in chamber music; numerous decorations including Mozart Medal, Salzburg and Vienna; Österreichisches Ehrenkreuz; Kreisler Prize.

1030 Vienna 3, Jacquingasse 51, Austria.

Telephone: 72-6459.

Bosquet, Alain, M.A. (*pseudonym* of Anatole Bisk); American (b. Russian) writer and critic; b. 28 March 1919; ed. Athéenée d'Uccle, Univ. Libre de Bruxelles and Univ. de Paris à la Sorbonne.

Served with Belgian, French and U.S. Armies 40-45; Editorial Sec. *la Voix de France*, New York 42-43; served with Allied Control Council, Berlin, then with Dept. of State 45-51; Prof. of French Literature, Brandeis Univ., U.S.A. 58-59; Prof. of American Literature, Univ. of Lyons 59-60; Columnist, *Combat* 53-; critic, French Nat. Broadcasting System 56-; Literary Dir. Editions Calmann-Lévy 56-; Literary Critic Radio Canada 56-; columnist, *Le Monde* 61-; Prix Guillaume Apollinaire for *Langue Morte* 52; Prix Sainte-Beuve for *Premier Testament* 57; Prix Max Jacob for *Deuxième Testament* 59; Prix Femina-Vacaresco for *Verbe et Vertige* 62; Prix Interallié for *la Confession Mexicaine* 65.

Publs. poems: *La vie est clandestine* 45, *A la mémoire de ma planète* 48, *Langue morte* 51, *Quel royaume oublié* 55, *Premier Testament* 57, *Deuxième Testament* 59, *Maître Objet* 62, Selected Poems, translated by Samuel Beckett, Charles Guenther, and Edouard Roditi 63; essays: *Saint-John Perse, Pierre Emmanuel, Emily Dickinson, Walt Whitman, Anthologie de la poésie américaine* 56, *35 jeunes poètes américaines* 61, *Verbe et Vertige* (on contemporary poetry) 61, *Entretiens avec Salvador Dali* 67, *Dorothea Tanning, Le Middle West* 67; novels: *la Grande Eclipse* 52, *Ni Singe, ni Dieu* 53, *Le Mécréant* 60, *Un besoin de malheur* 63, *les Petites Eternités* 64, *la Confession mexicaine* 65.

32 rue de Laborde, Paris 8e, France.

Bossman, J. E., M.B., CH.B.; Ghanaian physician and diplomatist; b. 20 Sept. 1916; ed. Mfantsipim School, Cape Coast, King's Coll., London, Univ. of Edinburgh, and Scotland School of Medicine of Royal Coll. of Physicians and Surgeons.

Medical Officer, Medical Inst., Peterborough, England 44-46; Medical Officer, Korle Bu Hospital, Accra, Orphanage Home, Accra, Kumasi Coll. of Technology 46-58; Perm. Rep. to European Office of UN 58-60; Ambassador to Tunisia 60-61, Morocco 61-63, Algeria 63-65; Ambassador to France and Perm. Del. to UNESCO 64-65; High Commr. in U.K. 65-66.

c/o Ghana High Commission, 13 Belgrave Square, London, S.W.1, England.

Bost, Pierre, L. de Philosophie; French writer; b. 5 Sept. 1901; ed. Lycée Henri IV and Sorbonne.

Secretary Editions Bernard Grasset and *Nouvelle Revue Française* 24-26; Sec.-Editor at Senate 27-33; Chief Editor of *Marianne* 33-35; Vice-Pres. Asscn. of Screen-writers 65-; has written scripts for many films often with Jean Aurenche), including *Patrie, La Symphonie Pastorale, Le Diable au Corps, Occupe toi d'Amélie*, etc.

Publs. include Novels: *Hercule et Mademoiselle, Un An dans un Trou, Monsieur L'Amiral va bientôt mourir, La Haute Fourche, Dieu a besoin des hommes*; plays: *L'Imbécile, Deux paires d'amis*; Films: *La Maison du Silence* 52, *Jeux Interdits* 52, *La Puissance et la Gloire* 53, *Le blé en herbe, Les orgueilleux, Le Rouge et le Noir, Chiens perdus sans collier, La Traversée de Paris, Gervaise, Œil pour œil, En cas de malheur*, etc.

12 rue de L'Abbaye, Paris 6e, France.

Bot, Theodorus; Netherlands politician; b. 11; ed. State Univ., Utrecht.

Former civil servant 36-59; East Asiatic Affairs Bureau Indonesia 36-42; Japanese P.O.W. Burma-Thailand 42-45; General Political Adviser The Hague and Djakarta 46-54; Dir. Western Co-operation Foreign Affairs The Hague 54-59; State Sec. for Interior (Netherlands New Guinea Affairs) 59-63; Minister of Education, Arts and Sciences 63-65; Minister without Portfolio for the Under-Developed Countries 65-67; Knight Order Netherlands Lion, Knight Grand Cross St. Olav of Norway and other foreign decorations; Catholic People's Party.

c/o Ministry for the Under-Developed Countries, The Hague, Netherlands.

Botashev, Magomet Abdurzakovich; Soviet politician; b. 1921; ed. Tashkent Inst. of Railway Engineering and Higher Party School.

Soviet Army 39-45; Railway Engineer, Frunze 52-57; Second Sec., Karachayevo Regional Cttee. of C.P. 57-58; Chair. Planning Comm. Exec. Cttee. Karachayevo-Cherkessk Regional Soviet of Workers' Deputies 58-62; Chief of Section, later Sec., Karachayevo-Cherkessk Regional Cttee. of C.P. 64-65; Chair. Exec. Cttee. Karachayevo-Cherkessk Regional Soviet of Workers' Deputies 66-; Deputy to R.S.F.S.R. Supreme Soviet.

Karachayevo-Cherkessk Regional Soviet of Workers' Deputies, Cherkessk, U.S.S.R.

Botelho, Carlos; Portuguese painter; b. 18 Sept. 1899; ed. Lisbon and Paris Acads. of Fine Arts.

Decorated Portuguese pavilion, Colonial Exhibition, Paris 31, Universal Exhibition, Paris 37; rep. XXV Venice Biennale 50, São Paulo Biennale 51-53, 55, 57, Brussels Int. Exhibition 58; Grand Prix, Paris Int;

Exhibition; Sousa Cardoso Prize 39, Columbano Prize 40, S. Paulo Biennale: Prix d'Acquisition 51, Mention d'Honneur 53; Hallmark Award Prix, New York 52. Silver Medal Brussels Exhibition 58; Exhibited at 50 Years of Modern Art Exhibition Brussels and Art and Work Exhibition Charleroi 58; organized in conjunction with British Council Henry Moore Exhibition in Lisbon 59; retrospective exhibition Lisbon 59; "Promotion of Architecture" Exhibition, Barcelona 60; Rep., XXX Biennale, Venice 60; Exhibition, Madrid 61; one-man Exhbn., New York 63, Lisbon 64, New York 65; Exhbns. São Paulo, London, Rio de Janeiro 65, Madrid 66; Gulbenkian Prize, Lisbon 61.

Atelier Buzano, Parede, Portugal.

Botha, Matthys Izak, B.A., LL.B.; South African diplomatist; b. 13; ed. Selborne Coll., East London and Univ. of Pretoria.

Department of Finance 31-44; Dept. of Foreign Affairs 44-, Washington 44-51, New York 51-54; Head of Political Div., Dept. of Foreign Affairs, Pretoria 55-58; Minister to Switzerland 59-60; Minister, London 60-62; Perm. Rep. to UN 62-.

South African Mission to the United Nations, 300 East 42nd Street, New York 17, N.Y., U.S.A.

Botha, Michiel Coenraad; South African politician; b. 14 Dec. 1912; ed. Univ. of Stellenbosch, Pretoria Univ. and Univ. of Cape Town.

Teacher, Transvaal schools 35-36; Lecturer, Pretoria Technical Coll. 37-43; Sec. Afrikaanse Taal-en Kultuurvereniging 43-53; later Deputy Minister of Bantu Admin. and Devt.; Minister of Bantu Admin. and Devt., and Minister of Bantu Educ. 66-; Nat. Party.

Ministry of Bantu Education, Pretoria, South Africa.

Botha, Pieter Willem, M.P.; South African politician; ed. Univ. of the Orange Free State.

Mem. of Parl.; fmr. Dep. Minister of the Interior; Minister of Community Development, Public Works and Coloured Affairs 61-66, of Defence 66-.

Ministry of Defence, Pretoria, South Africa.

Bothereau, Robert; French trade unionist; b. 22 Feb. 1901.

Metal worker; Sec. State Workers' Trade Union, Orleans 26-28; Sec.-Gen. Loiret Département Union 28-33; Sec. Gen. Confederation of Labour (C.G.T.) 33-48; Sec.-Gen. Gen. Confederation of Labour—Force Ouvrière (G.C.T.F.O.) 47-64; mem. French Econ. and Social Council 48-63; mem. Gen. Council Banque de France 63, Counsellor of State 64-67.

21 rue du Puits de Roussy, 45-Beaugency, France.

Telephone: (38): 89-22-55.

Botsio, Kojo; Ghanaian politician; b. 16; ed. Adisadel Coll., Achimota Coll., Accra, Fourah Bay Coll., Sierra Leone, and Brasenose Coll., Oxford.

Fmr. Treas. W. African Nat. Secr. London; fmr. Vice-Principal Akim Abuakwa State Coll., Kibi; Gen. Sec. Convention People's Party 49-60; mem. Legislative Ass. 51-57, Nat. Ass. 57-62; Leader of the House 65-; Minister of Educ. and Social Welfare 51-54, of State 56-57, of Trade and Industries May-Nov. 58, of Foreign Affairs Dec. 58-March 59, for Economic Affairs 59-60; Minister of Agriculture and Minister of State for Parl. Affairs 60-61; Dir. of Ideological Studies, C.P.P. 60-61; Chair. Nat. Council for Higher Educ. 62-63; Minister for Foreign Affairs 63-65; Chair. State Planning Comm. 65-66, under house arrest 66, released June 66.

c/o State Planning Commission, Accra, Ghana.

Bottomley, Rt. Hon. Arthur George, P.C., O.B.E., M.P.; British politician; b. 7 Feb. 1907; ed. elementary schools and University Extension Classes, Toynbee Hall.

Organiser, Nat. Union of Public Employees 35-41, 59-62; Dep. Regional Commr. for S.E. England 41-45; M.P. 45-59, 62-; Parl. Under-Sec. of State for Dominions 46-47, Sec. for Overseas Trade 47-51; Sec. of State for

Commonwealth Relations 64-66, Minister for Overseas Devt. 66-67; Labour.
Publs. *Two Roads of Colonialism, Why Britain Should Join the Common Market, The Use and Abuse of Trade Unions.*
19 Lichfield Road, Woodford Green, Essex, England.

Bottrall, Francis James Ronald, O.B.E., F.R.S.L.; British poet and literary historian; b. 2 Sept. 1906; ed. Redruth County School and Pembroke Coll., Cambridge.
Lecturer in English Helsinki Univ. 29-31; Commonwealth Fund Fellowship Princeton Univ. U.S.A. 31-33; Johore Prof. of English Language and Literature Raffles Coll. Singapore 33-37; Asst. Dir. and Prof. of English Literature British Inst. Florence 37-38; Sec. London Univ. School of Oriental and African Studies 39-45; seconded to Air Min., Priority Officer 40; British Council Rep. Sweden 41-44, Italy 45-50; Controller Education Div. British Council 50-54; Rep. Brazil 54-56, Greece 57-59, Japan 59-61; Chief, Fellowships and Training Branch, Food and Agriculture Org. (FAO) of UN 63-65; Syracuse Int. Poetry Prize 54.
Publs. *The Loosening and Other Poems* 31, *Festivals of Fire* 34, *The Turning Path* 39, *T. S. Eliot: Dikter i Urval* 42, *Farewell and Welcome* 45, *Zephyr Book of English Verse* 45, *Selected Poems* 46, *The Palisades of Fear* 49, *Adam Unparadised* 54, *Collected Poems* 61, *Rome* (Art Centres of the World) 68.
Villa Cornubia, Via Miramare 11/12, Albano Laziale, Rome, Italy.
Telephone: 931417.

Botvinnik, Mikhail Moiseevich; Soviet chess player; b. 17 Aug. 1911; ed. Leningrad M.I. Kalinin Polytechnic Inst.
Chess Champion of U.S.S.R. 31, 33, 39, 41, 44, 45, 52; World Champion 48-57, 58-60, 61-63; Chess Grandmaster of U.S.S.R.; Senior Scientific Official All-Union Scientific Research Inst. of Electrical Energy 55-; Int. Grand Master; Order of Lenin; Order of Red Banner of Labour 61, Order of Honour (twice).
All Union Scientific Research Institute of Electrical Energy, Bezsenevskaja Embankment 16, Moscow; U.S.S.R.

Bouattoura, Tewfik; Algerian politician and diplomatist; b. 31 Jan. 1936.
Officer, National Liberation Army 57-58; diplomatist 58-62; Ambassador of Provisional Republic of Algeria to Ghana 62; Deputy Dir. of Cabinet of Minister of Foreign Affairs, Algiers 62, Dir. of Political Affairs 63-64; Perm. Rep. of Algeria to UN 64-; Pres. Econ. and Social Council (ECOSOC) for 1966; Rep. of Algeria at Special Cttee. on Peacekeeping Operations; Head of Algerian Del. to 38th and 39th sessions of ECOSOC; Perm. Rep. UN Security Council 68.
Permanent Mission of Algeria to the United Nations, 750 Third Avenue, New York City, N.Y. 10017, U.S.A.

Bouchard, Marcel Félix; French university professor; b. 30 June 1898; ed. Ecole Normale Supérieure.
Prof. Lycée de Vesoul 20, Belfort 22, Dijon 25; Lecturer in French Classical Literature, Faculty of Letters Nancy 33, Prof. 37, Dean of Faculty 45-46; Rector of Académie de Dijon and Pres. of the Univ. Council 46-; served in both World Wars; fmr. Pres. Académie des Sciences, Arts et Belles-Lettres de Dijon 62; fmr. Pres. Perm. Conf. of Rectors and Vice-Chancellors of European Univs.; fmr. Vice-Pres. of Asscn. of French Speaking Univs.; Vice-Pres. Int. Asscn. of Univs.; Officier Légion d'Honneur; Officier Mérite Agricole; Commdr. Ordre des Palmes Académiques; Grand Cross, Order of Merit of Germany; Dr. h.c. Univ. of Montreal, Univ. of Manchester.
Publs. *De l'Humanisme à l'Encyclopédie* 30, *Les caractères véritables de Pierre Legouz* 30, *Lamartine ou le sens de l'amour* 40, *L'histoire des oracles de Fontenelle* 46,

L'Académie de Dijon et le premier Discours de Rousseau 50.
Académie de Dijon, 51 rue Monge, 21 Dijon, France.
Telephone: 30-31-00.

Bouda, François; Upper Voltan politician; b. 16; ed. William Ponty School.
Former Archivist, Nigerian Govt.; fmr. Personnel Officer, Ivory Coast; elected Dep. Upper Volta 59; fmr. Minister of Public Affairs; Minister of Planning and Economic Affairs 61-62, of Finances 62-63; mem. Rassemblement Démocratique Africain (R.D.A.).
Sec. Gen. l'Ecole Nationale d'Administration, Ouagadougou, Upper Volta, West Africa.

Boukar, Abdoul; Chad diplomatist; b. 1934; ed. Chad and Ecole Nationale d'Administration, Paris.
Teacher and mem. business firm, Chad 53-59; First Sec., Kano (Nigeria) 60-61; Ambassador to Nigeria 61-64, to U.S.A. 64-; Perm. Rep. to UN 65-.
Permanent Mission of Chad to the United Nations, 150 E. 52nd Street, New York 22, N.Y., U.S.A.
Telephone: PL-2-0920.

Bouladoux, Maurice; French trade unionist; b. 16 July 1907.
Accountant, textile factory 22-23; Founder, Constitution of Young Christian Trade Unionists, Pres. of Paris Region 29-; Sec.-Gen. French Confederation of Christian Workers 37; Head Buyer, Chemical Industry 40-45; Sec.-Gen. French Confederation of Christian Workers 48-53, Pres. 53-61; Pres. Int. Federation of Christian Trade Unions 61-; mem. Admin. Council, Int. Labour Org. (ILO) 60-; mem. Econ. and Social Cttee. of European Econ. Community and Euratom 58-; Counsellor of State 64-.
26 rue Montholon, Paris 9e, France.

Boulanger, Nadia (Juliette); French composer, conductor and music teacher; b. 16 Sept. 1887; ed. Paris Conservatoire.
Hon. Prof. Paris Conservatoire, Prof. Ecole Normale de Musique, Dir. and Prof. American Conservatory of Music, Fontainebleau 49-; Maître de Chapelle of H.H. the Prince of Monaco; compositions include orchestral and instrumental pieces and songs; Officier Légion d'Honneur.
36 rue Ballu, Paris 9e, France.

Boulding, Kenneth Ewart, M.A.; American university professor; b. 18 Jan. 1910; ed. Liverpool Collegiate School, New Coll., Oxford, and Univ. of Chicago.
Commonwealth Fellow 32-34; Asst. Edinburgh Univ. 34-37; Instructor, Colgate Univ., U.S.A. 37-41; Economist, L.N. 41-42; Prof. Fisk Univ. 42-43; Assoc. Prof. Iowa State Coll. 43-46; Angus Prof. of Political Economy and Chair. of Dept., McGill Univ. 46-47; Prof. Iowa State Coll. 47-49; Prof. of Economics, Univ. of Michigan 49-; Fellow, Center for Advanced Study in Behavioral Science, Stanford, Calif. 54-55; John Bates Clark Medal, American Economic Asscn. 49, Prize for Distinguished Scholarship in the Humanities 62.
Publs. *Economic Analysis* 41 (fourth edn. 65), *The Economics of Peace* 45, *The Naylor Sonnets* 45, *A Reconstruction of Economics* 50, *The Organizational Revolution* 53, *The Image* 56, *Principles of Economic Policy* 58, *The Skills of the Economist* 58, *Conflict and Defense* 62, *The Meaning of the Twentieth Century* 64.
Department of Economics, Univ. of Michigan, Ann Arbor, Mich., U.S.A.

Boulez, Pierre; French composer; b. 26 March 1925; ed. Paris Conservatoire.
Studied with Messiaen, Vaurabourg-Honegger and Leibowitz; Dir. of Music to Jean-Louis Barrault theatre company 48; has conducted concerts at Amsterdam, the Donaueschingen Festival and elsewhere.
Works: First Piano Sonata 46, Sonata for Two Pianos 46, Sonatina for Flute and Piano 46, *Le Visage Nuptial*

(5 poems of René Char for 2 solo voices, female choir and orch.) 46-50, Second Piano Sonata 48, *Le Soleil des Eaux* (2 poems of René Char for voice and orch.) 48, *Livre pour Quattuor* (string quartet) 49, *Symphonie Concertante* (piano and orch.) 50, *Le Marteau sans Maître* (cantata for voice and instruments to texts by René Char, also ballet 65) 55, *Structures* (2 pianos) 56, Third Piano Sonata 57-58, *Improvisations sur Mallarmé* (soprano and chamber ensemble) 58, *Doubles* (orch.) 58, *Poésie pour Pouvoir* (orch. and eight-track tape-recorder) 58, *Tombeau* (soprano and orch.) 59, *Pli selon Pli* 60, *Eclat*.
Publs. *Penser la musique aujourd'hui* 66, *Relevés d'apprenti* (essays) 67.
Weidestrasse 24, Baden-Baden, German Fed. Republic.

Boulin, Robert; French lawyer and politician; b. 20 July 1920.
Lawyer 46-; U.N.R. (Union pour la Nouvelle République) Dep. 58-61, 62-; mem. Central Cttee. U.N.R.; Sec. of State for Repatriation Jan.-Sept. 62; Sec. of State for the Budget Sept. 62-May 68; Minister of Civil Service May 68-; Mayor of Libourne 65-.
10 rue de Géraud, Libourne, Gironde, France.

Boulloche, André François Roger Jacques, L. en DR.; French politician; b. 7 Sept. 1915; ed. Ecole Polytechnique, Paris.
Dir. du Cabinet of Paul Ramadier 47; Minister of Nat. Defence 48-49; Dir. Service de l'Infrastructure, Sec. of State for Air 53-55; Dir. of Public Works and Urbanisation, Morocco 55; Minister without Portfolio, de Gaulle Cabinet July 58-Jan. 59; Minister of Education, Debré Cabinet Jan. 59-Dec. 59; Counsellor of State 60-63; Mayor of Montbéliard 65-; Deputy from Doubs 67-; Commdr. Légion d'Honneur, Compagnon de la Libération, Médaille de la Résistance, Croix de Guerre.
87 avenue Paul Doumer, Paris 16e, France.
Telephone: JAS 44-25.

Boult, Sir Adrian C., Kt., M.A., D.MUS., F.R.C.M.; British musician; b. 8 April 1889; ed. Westminster School, Christ Church, Oxford, and Leipzig Conservatorium.
Fmr. Conductor British Symphony Orchestra; has conducted in London, Vienna, Munich, Prague, Barcelona, Boston, Brussels, Zürich, Paris and New York; Dir. Birmingham City Orchestra 24-30; Dir. of Music B.B.C. 30-42; Conductor B.B.C. Symphony Orchestra until 50; Chief Conductor London Phil. Orch. 50-57, Birmingham Symphony Orchestra 59-60; on staff of Royal Coll. of Music 19-30, 62-66 (Vice-Pres.); Royal Phil. Soc. Gold Medallist 44, hon. mem. Royal Acad. of Sweden; Hon. LL.D. (Birmingham, Liverpool), Hon. Mus. Doc. (Edinburgh and Cambridge), Hon. R.A.M.; Hon. G.S.M.
Publ. *Thoughts on Conducting* 63.
36 Wigmore Street, London, W.1, England.
Telephone: 01-935-1387.

Boumedienne, Houari (real name: **Mohammed Boukharouba**) Algerian army officer and politician; b. 1927; ed. Islamic Inst., Constantine, and Cairo.
Former teacher, Guelma; promoted rebel activities in Oran area, Algeria 55; Commdr. of Wilaya 55-57; Chief of Staff, F.L.N. 60-62; Minister of Defence 62-; First Deputy Premier 63-65; Chair. of Revolutionary Council 65-; Prime Minister 65-.
Office of the Prime Minister, Algiers, Algeria.

Boumendjel, Ahmed; Algerian politician; b. 08.
Former lawyer; fmr. mem. Democratic Union of the Algerian Manifesto (U.D.M.A.); Political Adviser to Provisional Govt. of the Algerian Republic; Head, Algerian Del. Melun Conf. June 60, mem. Algerian Del. Evian Conf. May 61; fmr. mem. Algerian Nat. Revolutionary Cttee.; Minister of Reconstruction, Works and Transport Sept. 62-65.
Assemblée Nationale, Palais Carnot, Algiers, Algeria.

Boun Oum (Na Champassak), Prince; Laotian politician; b. 11; ed. Saigon.
Member of resistance movt. against Japanese 41-45; Pres. Nat. Assembly 48-49; Prime Minister and Minister of Nat. Defence 49-50; resigned 50; Prime Minister Dec. 60-62; Minister of Religion 66-.
Ministry for Religion, Vientiane, Laos.

Bourdet, Claude; French journalist; b. 28 Oct. 1909; ed. Coll. de Normandie, Lycée Hoche (Versailles), Fed. Inst. of Technology (Zürich).
Attached to Cabinet of Minister of Nat. Economy 36-39; Man. La Manda (soap and oil firm) 40-41; mem. Dir. Cttee. "Combat" Movement and Manager of secret paper 42; mem. Conseil Nat. de la Résistance; arrested and imprisoned in Oranienburg and Buchenwald concentration camps 44; Vice-Pres. Consultative Ass. 45; Dir.-Gen. Radiodiffusion Française 45; Manager *Combat* 47-50; Founder and Editor *L'Observateur* (now *France-Observateur*) 50-63; founder Centre d'Action des Gauches Indépendants 52; mem. Municipal Council of Paris, Gen. Council of Seine 59-, Nat. Cttee. Parti Socialiste Unifié 60-; Editor *L'Action* 64-; Ligue des Droits de l'Homme; Compagnon de la Libération.
47 Avenue d'Iéna, Paris 16e, France.

Bourgeois, Paul, D.PHIL.; Belgian astronomer; b. 13 Feb. 1898; ed. Univ. Libre, Brussels.
Assistant Belgian Royal Observatory 24, Assoc. Astronomer 36, Astronomer 38, Dir. 47, Hon. Dir. 63; Extraordinary Prof. Université Libre, Brussels 54; fmr. Pres. Abstracting Board, Int. Council of Scientific Unions; Vice-Pres. Centre Nat. de calcul mécanique; corresp. mem. Bureau des Longitudes; mem. Int. Astronomical Union; fmr. mem. Conseil Nat. de la Politique scientifique; Vice-Pres. Inst. pour la Recherche Scientifique en Afrique Centrale; Assoc. mem. Académie Royale des Sciences d'Outre-Mer; Quinquennial Prize for Statistics 29-33; Officier, Ordre de Léopold, Commdr., Ordre de la Couronne, Grand Officier Ordre de Léopold II.
Publs. Numerous scientific papers on meridian astronomy, astrometry, astrophysics and stellar statistics.
31 Rue Paul Hankar, Brussels 18, Belgium.
Telephone: 02-743058.

Bourges, Yvon; French overseas administrator and politician; b. 29 June 1921; ed. Univ. de Rennes.
High Commr.-Gen. African Equatorial Union 58-60; Deputy of Ille and Vilaine (St. Malo); Mayor of Dinard 62-65; State Sec. for Scientific Research 65-66, for Information 66-67, for Co-operation 67-; Chevalier Légion d'Honneur.
Mairie de Dinard, Dinard, Brittany; Assemblée Nationale, Paris 7e, France.

Bourgès-Maunoury, Maurice; French politician; b. 19 Aug. 1914.
Active with Resistance Movement 41-44; mem. Constituent Assembly 46; Radical Socialist Dep. for Haute Garonne 56-58; Sec. of State (Budget) in Schuman Cabinet Nov. 47-July 48; Sec. of State (Armed Forces) in Marie rnd Schuman Cabinets July-Sept. 48; returned to Govt. as Minister of Public Works July 50; Sec. of State, Présidence du Conseil July 50-July 51; Deputy Minister of Nat. Defence, Pleven Cabinet Aug. 51-Jan. 52; Minister of Armaments, Faure Cabinet Jan.-Feb. 52; French delegate to 7th Session of the U.N. 52; Minister of Finance, Mayer Cabinet Jan.-July 53; Minister of the Interio. until 56, of Nat. Defence 56-57; Prime Minister 57; Minister of Interior 57-58; Pres. Société Industrielle et financière de l'Artois et des Mines de Kali; Chevalier Légion d'Honneur, etc.
67 rue La Boétie, Paris 8e, France.

Bourget, Maurice; Canadian engineer and politician; b. 20 Oct. 1907.
Member of Parl. 40-62; fmr. Parl. Asst. to Minister of

Public Works; Speaker of Senate 63-66; Dir. British Newfoundland Corpn. 63-; Liberal.
59 St. Etienne Street, Lévis, Quebec, Canada.

Bourguiba, Habib Ben Ali; Tunisian politician; b. 3 Aug. 1903; ed. Univ. of Paris, Ecole Libre des Sciences Politiques.
Active in politics and journalism since 28; mem. Destour Party 21, broke away and formed Neo-Destour Party (outlawed by the French) 34; imprisoned by the French 34-36 and 38-43; escaped to Middle East 45, travelled to promote Tunisian independence 45-49, world tour during Tunisian negotiations with French Govt. 51; arrested 52, placed under surveillance at Tabarka (Jan.), imprisoned at Remada (March), in solitary confinement, Ile de la Galite (May) until 54; released 54, under surveillance in France 54-55, during negotiations; returned to Tunisia following Franco-Tunisian Agreements 55; Pres. Tunisian Nat. Assembly, Prime Minister, Pres. of the Council, Minister of Foreign Affairs and of Defence 56-57; Pres. Tunisian Repub. and Head of Cabinet 57-; Pres. Neo-Destour; Ordre du Sang, Ordre de la confiance en diamants.
Publs. *Le Destour et la France* 37, *La Tunisie et la France* 55.
Office of the President, Tunis, Tunisia.

Bourguiba, Habib, Jr., L. ès D.; Tunisian diplomatist; b. 9 April 1927; ed. Collège Sadiki, Law School, France.
Collaborated in national liberation movement, especially 51-54; lawyer in training, Tunis 54-56; Counsellor, Tunisian Embassy, Washington 56-57; Ambassador to Italy 57-58, to France 58-61, to U.S.A. 61-63, to Canada 61-62; Perm. Rep. to UN 61-62; Ambassador to Mexico 62-63; Sec.-Gen. to Presidency of Republic Dec. 63-64; in charge of Dept. of Youth and Sports, Dept. of Tourism, Nat. Office of Artisanship and Information Dept. Dec. 63-64; Sec. of State for Foreign Affairs 64-.
Ministry of Foreign Affairs, Tunis; Villa Al Mahroussa, Colline Notre Dame, Le Belvédère, Tunis, Tunisia.
Telephone: 260-531 (Home).

Bouri, Wahbi El-; Libyan politician and diplomatist; b. 23 Jan. 1916; ed. Univs. of Naples and Siena.
Deputy Chief of Royal Cabinet, later Master of Ceremonies of Royal Palace, Libya 48-53; Counsellor of Embassy, Cairo 53-56; Under-Sec. of Foreign Affairs 56-57; Minister of Foreign Affairs 57-59; Minister of State for Parliamentary Affairs 59-61; Minister of Justice 61-62; Minister of Petroleum Affairs 62-63; Perm. Rep. of Libya to UN 63-65, 65-; Minister o Foreign Affairs 65.
Permanent Mission of Libya to the United Nations, 866 United Nations Plaza, New York, N.Y. 10017, U.S.A.

Bourlière, François (Marie Gabriel), M.D., L. ès S.; French biologist and university professor; b. 21 Dec. 1913; ed. Univ. of Paris.
Research Asst., School of Medicine, Paris Univ. 42; Prof. of Physiology, School of Medicine, Rouen 46-49; Prof. of Gerontology, Univ. of Paris 59-; Editor of *La Terre et la Vie*; co-editor *Gerontologia*; Fellow, New York Acad. of Sciences 62; Pres. Int. Union for Conservation of Nature and Natural Resources 63-66; Convener Int. Biological Programme (Terrestrial Ecology) 64-; Dir. Nat. Foundation of Gerontology 68-; mem. Int. Ethological Cttee. 68-.
Publs. *Eléments d'un Guide Bibliographique du Naturaliste* (2 vols.) 40-41, *Formulaire technique du Zoologiste* 41, *Vie et Moeurs des Mammifères* 51, *Le Monde des Mammifères* 54, *The Natural History of Mammals* 54, *Sénescence et Sénilité* 58, *Introduction à l'écologie des Ongulés* 60, *The Land and Wildlife of Eurasia* 64; co-author: *Traité de Zoologie,* Vol. 15 *Oiseaux,* and Vol. 17 *Mammifères, Précis de Gérontologie* (in collabora-

tion) 56, *Problèmes de Production Biologique* 67, *Progrès en Gérontologie* 68.
45 rue des Saints Pères, Paris 6, France.
Telephone: BAB 00-71.

Bourne, Geoffrey Howard, D.SC., D.PHIL.; British professor and anatomist; b. 17 Nov. 1909; ed. Univs. of Western Australia and Melbourne.
Biologist, Australian Inst. of Anatomy 34-36; Biochemist, Commonwealth of Australia Advisory Council on Nutrition 36-38; Beit Memorial Fellow for Medical Research at Oxford 38-41; Mackenzie Mackinnon Research Fellow of the Royal Coll. of Surgeons and Royal Coll. of Physicians 41-43; Demonstrator in Physiology, Oxford 40-43 and 46-47; in charge of Research and Development, Rations and Biological Problems, Special Forces in S.E. Asia (Major) 44; Nutritional Adviser, British Mil. Admin. of Malaya (Lieut.-Col.) 45-46; Reader in Histology, Univ. of London, London Hospital 47-57; Prof. and Chair. Anatomy Dept., Emory Univ., Ga., U.S.A. 57-63; Dir. Yerkes Regional Primate Research Center, Emory Univ. 63-.
Publs. include *Starvation in Europe* 43, *The Mammalian Adrenal Gland* 49, *An Introduction to Functional Histology* 55, 61, *Division of Labour in Cells* 61, *Structure and Function of Muscle* 63, *Muscular Dystrophy in Man and Animals* 63, *Atherosclerosis and its Origins* 63, *International Review of Dietetics* vols. 1-10 continuing.
Yerkes Primate Center, Emory University, Atlanta, Georgia, U.S.A.
Telephone: 939-2489.

Boussac, Marcel; French industrialist; b. 17 April 1889.
Textile entrepreneur 17; Dir.-Gen. Comptoir de l'Industrie Cotonnière; Founder and owner of the House of Christian Dior; racehorse owner; Chevalier de la Légion d'Honneur.
21 rue Poissonnière, Paris 2e, France.

Boustany, Fouad Emile, DR.-ès-LETTRES; Lebanese scholar; b. 15 Aug. 1906; ed. Deir-el-Kamar Coll. and Univ. St. Joseph, Beirut.
Teacher in Arab Literature, Islamic Insts. and History of Arab Civilization, Institut des Lettres Orientale 33-45; Dir. Ecole Normale 42-53; Prof. of Near Eastern History and Civilizations, Inst. des Sciences Politiques 45-55; Prof. of Arab Literature, Islamic Philosophy and Arab History, Acad. Libanaise des Beaux-Arts 47-53; Rector Univ. Libanaise 53-; Sec.-Gen. Lebanese Nat. Comm. for UNESCO 48-55; Sec.-Gen. Int. Comm. for Translation of Classic Works 49-; Dr. h.c. Univs of Lyon 57, Austin, Texas 58, Georgetown, Washington, D.C. 58; Lebanese, French, Vatican and other decorations.
Publs. *Au temps de l'Emir* 26, *Ar-Rawae* (critical studies) 27, *Pourquoi* 30, *Histoire du Liban sous les Chéhab* of Emir Haïdar Chéhab (with Dr. A. Rustem) 33-35, *Bagdad, capitale des lettres abbassides* 34, *Le rôle des chrétiens dans l'établissement de la Omayyade* 38, *Le style orale chez les Arabes préislamiques* 41, *Al-Magani al Haditah* (5 vols.) 46-50, *Cinq jours à travers la Syrie* 50, *Encyclopaedia Arabica* (6 vols.) 56-66.
Université Libanaise, Beirut, Lebanon.

Boustead, Col. Sir John Edmund Hugh, K.B.E., C.M.G., D.S.O., O.B.E., M.C. and bar; British political agent; b. 14 April 1895; ed. Royal Naval Colls., Osborne and Dartmouth, H.M.S. *Cornwall* and Oxford Univ.
Midshipman and Acting Sub-Lieut. 13-15; Royal Navy, German East and German South-West Africa and Cape Station; S. African Brigade, Egypt, Western Desert and France 15-19; Capt. S. African Brigade attached to Gen. Denikin's Army in South Russia 19; apptd. Gordon Highlanders, Malta, Constantinople, Chanak and Eastern Thrace 21-24; led Kanchenjunga Expedition 26;

Sudan Camel Corps 24-29; Gen. Staff S.D.F. Khartoum 30; commdr. Sudan Camel Corps 31; mem. Everest Expedition 33; retd. from Army to Sudan Political Service 35; District Commr. Western District, Darfur 35-40; recalled to service 40; raised and trained Sudan Frontier Battn. S.D.F. and commanded it Jan.-July 41; served in Central Abyssinia; S.D.F. Brigade in Eritrea 43; commd. 2nd S.D.F. Brigade 45; recalled to Political Service Aug. 45; Resident Adviser to the Hadhramaut States and British Agent Eastern Aden Protectorate 49-58; Devt. Sec., Muscat 58-61; Political Agent, Abu Dhabi 61-65; several foreign orders; F.R.G.S.
c/o Diplomatic Service Administration Office, Great George Street, London, S.W.1, England.

Bouteflika, Abdul Aziz; Algerian politician; b. 1935; ed. Morocco.
Former Captain, Nat. Liberation Army; fmr. Minister of Sports; Minister of Foreign Affairs Sept. 63-; mem. F.L.N. Political Bureau 64-.
Ministry of Foreign Affairs, Algiers, Algeria.

Boutin, Bernard Louis, PH.B.; American business executive; b. 2 July 1923; ed. St. Michael's Coll., Winooski, Vermont, and Catholic Univ. of America, Washington, D.C.
President and Treas., Boutin Insurance Agency Inc., Laconia, New Hampshire 48-63; Proprietor, Boutin Real Estate Co., Laconia 55-63; Mayor of Laconia 55-59; Deputy Admin., Gen. Services Admin., Washington D.C. Feb.-Nov. 61; Admin. of Gen. Services 61-64; Exec. Vice-Pres. Nat. Asscn. Home Builders 64-65; Admin. of Small Business Admin. 66-67; Deputy Dir. Office of Econ. Opportunity 65-66; Exec. Sanders Assoc. Inc. 67-; Democratic Candidate for Gov. of New Hampshire 58, 60; numerous awards; Hon. LL.D., St. Michael's Coll.
2 Rockland Street, Nashua, New Hampshire 03060, U.S.A.

Boutros, Fouad; Lebanese lawyer and politician; b. 1920; ed. Coll. des Frères, Beirut.
Judge, Civil and Mixed Commercial Court, Beirut 44-47; Judge Mil. Tribunal and Court Lawyer 47-50; Govt. Lawyer 51-57; Minister of Nat. Educ. and of the Plan 59-60; mem. Chamber of Deputies 60-; Minister of Justice 61-64; Vice-Pres. of the Council, Minister of Educ. and Defence 66-67; numerous decorations.
c/o Ministry of Education, Beirut, Lebanon.

Boutteville, Roger; French businessman; b. 25 Sept. 1892; ed. Ecole Polytechnique de Paris.
Pres. and Gen. Man. Soc. Alsacienne de Constructions Mécaniques; Pres. Maisons Phénix; Vice-Pres. Soc. Gén. de Constructions Electriques et Mécaniques (Als-Thom); Dir. Soc. Lyonnaise des Eaux et de l'Eclairage, Soc. de Force et Lumière Electrique, Crédit Industriel et Commercial, Soc. Nat. d'Investissement, etc.; Commdr. Légion d'Honneur, Croix de Guerre.
Home: 47 rue de Bellechasse, Paris 7e; Office: 32 rue de Lisbonne, Paris 8e, France.

Bouziri, Nejib; Tunisian diplomatist; b. 1925; ed. School of Law, Paris, and Inst. d'Etudes Politiques, Paris.
Former advocate, Court of Appeals, Tunis; later worked in Ministry of State and Ministry of Interior; later Chef de Cabinet, Ministry of Foreign Affairs; Chargé d'Affaires, Rome 57-58; Amb. to Italy 58-61, to German Fed. Rep. 61-64; Sec. of State for Posts and Telecommunications 64; Vice-Pres. Nat. Assembly 64-65; Amb. to U.S.S.R. 65-; Chair. Admin. and Budgetary Cttee. of UN Gen. Assembly 65.
Tunisian Embassy, Ul. Kachalova 28, U.S.S.R.

Boveri, Theodore, Dipl. Ing.; Swiss electrical engineer, b. 27 Nov. 1892; ed. Kantonschule, Aarau, Switzerland, and Technische Hochschule, Karlsruhe.
Design of electrical motors and Asst. to Works Man.,

Brown, Boveri & Cie. Ltd., Baden, Switzerland 17-26; American Brown Boveri Corpn., Camden, N.J. 26-28; Man. Railway Dept., Brown, Boveri & Co. Ltd. 28-34; Man. Dir. (Electrical Engineering) 34-46; Exec. Vice-Pres. Brown, Boveri and Co. Ltd. 46-; Hon. mem. Swiss Asscn. of Electrical Engineers.
Brown, Boveri & Company Ltd., 5401 Baden, Switzerland.

Boveri, Walter E., D.RER.COM.; Swiss banker and industrialist; b. 6 Dec. 1894; ed. Oxford, Geneva and Zürich Univs.
Member of Board, Brown Boveri and Co. Ltd., Baden, Switzerland 30; founded Private Bank and Trust Co., Zürich 32; Chair. Board, Swiss American Electric Co., South American Electric Co. 32; Chair. Brown Boveri and Co. 38-66; Founder-Chair. Reactor Ltd., Würenlingen (private company constructing research atomic reactors) 55; mem. of Board, Swiss Credit Bank, Electro-Watt Ltd., Motor-Columbus Ltd., Farbwerke Hoechst A.G., Frankfurt/Main, Gen. Finance Co. and S. American electrical firms; Austrian Great Golden Hon. Medal, Grand Officer Peruvian Order of Merit, Commdr. "Cruzeiro do Sol" (Brazil); Dr. (h.c.) Berne Univ., Zürich Fed. Inst. of Technology.
Publs. *Ansprachen und Betrachtungen* 54, *Atomic Energy in a Small Country* 57, *Ethics in the Atomic Age* 58, *Auf der Suche nach einem Sinn des Daseins* 59.
Bärengasse 29, Zürich 8, Switzerland.

Bovet, Daniel, DR.SC.; Italian physiologist; b. 07; ed. Univ. of Geneva.
Assistant in Physiology, Univ. of Geneva 28-29; Asst. Inst. Pasteur, Paris 29-39, Dir. of Laboratory 39-47; Dir. of Laboratories of Therapeutical Chemistry, Istituto Superiore di Sanità, Rome 47-64; Prof. of Pharmacology, Univ. of Sassari 64-; Nobel Prize for Physiology and Medicine 57; mem. Accad. Naz. dei Lincei; Grand Officer of the Order of the Italian Republic; Hon. Doctorates Palermo, Geneva, Rio de Janeiro, etc.
Publs. *Structure chimique et activité pharmacodynamique des médicaments du système nerveux végétatif* (with F. Bovet-Nitti) 48, *Curare and Curare-like Agents* (with F. Bovet-Nitti and G. B. Marini-Bettolò) 59.
Istituto di Farmacologia, Via Rolando 1, Sassari; Home: Via G.B. de Rossi 30, Rome, Italy.

Bowden, Baron (Life Peer), cr. 63, of Chesterfield, **Bertram Vivian Bowden,** M.A., PH.D., M.SC.TECH., M.I.E.E.; British college principal and politician; b. 18 Jan. 1910; ed. Chesterfield Grammar School, Emmanuel Coll., Cambridge, and Univ. of Amsterdam.
Schoolmaster, The Collegiate School, Liverpool 35-37; Chief Physics Master, Oundle School 37-40; Telecommunications Research Establishment, Swanage and Malvern 40-43; Naval Research Laboratory, Washington 43-45; Mass. Inst. of Technology (M.I.T.) 45-46; Atomic Energy Research Establishment, Harwell 46; Partner, Sir Robert Watson-Watt and Partners 46-50; Ferranti Ltd. (in charge of application of digital computers) 50-53; Principal, Manchester Municipal Coll. of Technology (now Univ. of Manchester Inst. of Science and Technology) 53-64, 65-; Minister of State, Dept. of Educ. and Science 64-65.
Publs. *Faster than Thought—A Symposium on Digital Computers* 53, *The Proposals for the Development of the Manchester College of Science and Technology* 56.
Roxana, Park Road, Hale, Cheshire, England.
Telephone: RINgway 2476.

Bowen, Elizabeth Dorothea Cole (Mrs. Alan Cameron), C.B.E.; British writer; ed. Downe House, Downe, Kent. Hon. D.Litt. (Trinity Coll. Dublin and Oxford Univ.); C.Lit.
Publs. *The Hotel* 27, *The Last September* 29, *Friends and Relations* 31, *To the North* 32, *The House in Paris* 35, *The Death of the Heart* 38, *Bowen's Court* 42, *Seven Winters* 43, *The Heat of the Day* 49, *The Shelbourne* 51;

short stories: *Encounters* 23, *Ann Lee's* 26, *Joining Charles* 29, *The Cat Jumps* 34. *Look at All those Roses* 41, *The Demon Lover* 45, *Collected Impressions* (essays) 50, *A World of Love* (novel) 55, *A Time in Rome* 60, *Afterthought* 62, *The Little Girls* (novel) 64, *A Day in the Dark* (short stories) 65.
Carbery, Church Hill, Hythe, Kent, England.

Bowen, Ira Sprague, A.B., PH.D., SC.D.; American astronomer; b. 21 Dec. 1898; ed. Oberlin Coll. and Calif. Inst. of Technology.
Instructor Calif. Inst. of Tech. 21-26, Asst. Prof. 26-28, Assoc. Prof. 28-31, Prof. 31-45; Dir. Mount Wilson Observatory 46-64, Palomar Observatory 48-64, Distinguished Service Staff mem. 64-; Draper Medal Nat. Acad. of Sciences; Rumford Medal, American Acad. of Arts and Sciences; Potts Medal, Franklin Inst.; Ives Medal, Optical Society of America; Bruce Medal, Astronomical Society of the Pacific; Gold Medal, Royal Astronomical Soc.
Publs. Numerous articles on spectra, optics, nebulae and cosmic rays.
Home: 2388 N. Altadena Drive, Altadena, Calif.; Office: Mount Wilson and Palomar Observatories, 813 Santa Barbara Street, Pasadena, Calif., U.S.A.
Telephone: Sy 7-2608 (Home); Sy 6-4351 (Office).

Bowie, Robert Richardson; American lawyer and university professor; b. 24 Aug. 1909; ed. Gilman School, Baltimore, Maryland, Princeton Univ. and Harvard Law School.
Admitted to Maryland Bar 34, mem. firm Bowie and Burke, Baltimore 34-42; Reporter, Maryland Comm. on Civil Procedure 39-41; Asst. Dir. Maryland Legis. Council 40-41; Asst. Attorney-Gen., Maryland 41-42; U.S. Army 42-46; Special Asst. to Dep. Military Governor for Germany 45-46; Prof. of Law, Harvard Univ. 45-55; Gen. Counsel, Special Adviser U.S. High Commissioner for Germany 50-51; Dir. Policy Planning Staff, Dept. of State 53-55; Asst. Sec. of State for Policy Planning 55-57; Prof. of International Relations, Dir. Center for International Affairs, Harvard Univ. 57-; Legion of Merit with Oak Leaf Cluster.
Publs. various books, and *Shaping the Future: Foreign Policy in an Age of Transition* 64.
170 Coolidge Hill, Cambridge 38, Massachusetts 02138, U.S.A.

Bowles, Chester, B.S.; American diplomatist; b. 5 April 1901; ed. Yale Univ.
Business in N.Y., Chair. of Board, Benton and Bowles Inc. 25-40; Dir. Price and Rationing Controls, State of Conn. 41-43; Administrator of Wartime Price, Rent and Rationing Controls for the U.S., mem. Production Board 43-46; Dir. of Economic Stabilisation 46; U.S. Del. UNESCO Conf. Paris 46; Consultant to Trygve Lie, U.N., Int. Chair. U.N. Appeal for Children 47-48; Gov. State of Conn. 49-51; U.S. Ambassador to India and Nepal 51-53; U.S. Congressman 59-61; mem. Foreign Affairs Cttee. 59-60; Under-Sec. of State Jan.-Nov. 61; Special Rep. and Adviser to the Pres. for African, Asian and Latin American Affairs Dec. 61-63; Amb. to India 63-; numerous hon. degrees; Democrat.
Publs. *Tomorrow Without Fear* 46, *Ambassador's Report* 54, *The New Dimensions of Peace* 55, *Africa's Challenge to America* 56, *American Politics in a Revolutionary World* 56, *Ideas, People and Peace* 58, *The Coming Political Breakthrough* 60, *Conscience of a Liberal* 62, *Makings of a Just Society* 63.
Hayden's Point, Essex, Conn., U.S.A.

Bowles, Paul; American composer and writer; b. 30 Dec. 1910; ed. Univ. of Va. and in Berlin and Paris.
Music Critic for *New York Herald-Tribune* 42-45.
Compositions of music for films, for the theatre: *Doctor Faustus, Twelfth Night, The Glass Menagerie, Cyrano de Bergerac, Watch on the Rhine, Summer and Smoke,*

Sweet Bird of Youth, The Milk Train Doesn't Stop Here Any More, etc.; scores for ballets: *Yankee Clipper, Pastorela* (American Ballet Company), *Colloque Sentimental* (Marquis de Cuevas); operas: *Denmark Vesey, The Wind Remains, Yerma*; and a number of sonatas, concertos, etc.; also wrote novels, *The Sheltering Sky, Let it come Down, The Spider's House, Up Above the World, A Life Full of Holes* (with Driss ben Hamed Charhadi), *Love With a Few Hairs* (with Mohammed Mrabet); short stories, collections, *A Little Stone, The Hours after Noon, A Hundred Camels in the Courtyard, Pages from Cold Point*; non-fiction, *Their Heads are Green, Yallahi*
2137 Tanger Socco, Tangier, Morocco.
Telephone: 17883.

Bowman, Sir James, Bt., K.B.E., D.C.L.; British coal-mining administrator; b. 8 March 1898.
J.P. 35; Gen. Sec. Northumberland Miners Asscn. (later Nat. Union of Mine Workers, Northumberland Area) 35-49; Vice-Pres. Nat. Union of Mine Workers 38-49; mem. Gen. Council of T.U.C. 45-49; Chair. Nat. Coal Board, Northumberland Division 50-55; Deputy Chair. Nat. Coal Board 55-56, Chair. 56-61; fmr. mem. Nat. Miners' Welfare Joint Council, D.S.I.R., Royal Comm. on the Press.
"Woodlands", Killingworth Station, Forest Hall, Newcastle upon Tyne 12, England.

Bowra, Sir (Cecil) Maurice, Kt., M.A., D.LITT., F.B.A.; British educationist; b. 8 April 1898; ed. Cheltenham Coll. and New Coll., Oxford.
Served in France, First World War 17-18; Fellow and Tutor, Wadham Coll., Oxford 22-38, Warden of Wadham Coll. 38-; Prof. of Poetry 46-51; Vice-Chancellor of Oxford Univ. 51-54; Hon. Fellow, New Coll., Oxford 46; Pres. English Asscn. 58, 59, British Acad. 59, 60-61; Commdr. Légion d'Honneur; Commdr. Royal Order of the Phoenix of Greece; Kenyon Medal for Classical Studies, British Acad. 67; Hon. LL.D. (St. Andrews), Hon. Litt.D. (Dublin, Harvard, Wales, Hull), Dr. h.c. (Paris, Aix).
Publs. *Tradition and Design in the Iliad* 30, *Ancient Greek Literature* 33, *Pindari Carmina* 35, *Greek Lyric Poetry* 36, *Early Greek Elegists* 38, *The Heritage of Symbolism* 43, *A Book of Russian Verse* 43, *Sophoclean Tragedy* 44, *From Virgil to Milton* 45, *The Creative Experiment* 49, *The Romantic Imagination* 50, *Heroic Poetry* 52, *Problems of Greek Poetry* 54, *Primitive Song* 62, *In General and in Particular* 64, *Pindar* 64; trans. *Pindar's Pythian Odes* (with H. T. Wade-Gery) 28; co-editor; *Oxford Book of Greek Verse* 30, *Oxford Book of Greek Verse in Translation* 37, *Inspiration and Poetry* 55, *The Greek Experience* 57, *Landmarks in Greek Literature* 66, *Poetry and Politics, 1900-1966* 66, *Memories* 66.
Wadham College, Oxford, England.

Boyd, Alan S.; American government official; b. 20 July 1922.
Legal practice 48-57; mem. Florida Railroad and Public Utilities 55-59; mem. Civil Aeronautics Board 59, Chair. 60-65; Under-Sec. of Commerce for Transportation 65-66; Sec. Dept. of Transportation 67-; Democrat.
Department of Transportation, Washington 25, D.C., U.S.A.

Boyd, Aquilino Edgardo; Panamanian lawyer and diplomatist; b. 21; ed. La Salle, Panama City, Holy Cross Coll., U.S.A., Univs. of Havana and Panama.
First Sec. Cuba 46-47, Washington 47-48; Congressman, Panama Nat. Assembly 48-52, 56-60; Pres. Nat. Assembly 49; Minister of Foreign Affairs 56-58; Perm. Rep. to UN 62-67; Pres. Nationalist Party of Panama.
c/o Ministry of Foreign Affairs, Asuncion, Paraguay.

Boyd, Arthur Merric Bloomfield; Australian painter; b. 24 July 1920; ed. State School, Murrumbeena, Victoria.

Taught painting and sculpture by parents and grand-father; painted and exhibited in Australia 44-59, in England 59-; designed for theatre, Melbourne 55-57, ballet, Edinburgh Festival and Sadler's Wells 61, Covent Garden 63; Retrospective Exhibition, White-chapel Gallery, London 62, Adelaide 64; rep. at Dunn Int. Exhibition London 63.
c/o Commercial Bank of Australia Ltd., 34 Piccadilly, London, W.1, England.

Boyd, Howard Taney; American business executive; b. 5 June 1909; ed. Georgetown Univ.
Admitted D.C. Bar 34, Texas Bar; Sec. to Attorney-Gen. of U.S. 34; Asst. U.S. Attorney, D.C. 35-39; Partner, law firm Hogan and Hartson, Washington 39-52; Vice-Pres., Asst. Gen. Counsel, El Paso Natural Gas Co. 52-57, Dir. 53-, Exec. Vice-Pres. 57-60, Pres. 60-65, Chair. 65.
2727 Allen Parkway, Houston, Texas; and 2929 Buffalo Speedway, Houston, Texas, U.S.A.

Boyd, Martin à Beckett; British author; b. 10 June 1893; ed. in Australia.
Publs. include *The Lemon Farm* 35, *A Single Flame* 39, *Lucinda Brayford* 46, *The Cardboard Crown* 52, *A Difficult Young Man* 55, *Outbreak of Love* 57, *Much Else in Italy* 58, *When Blackbirds Sing* 62, *Day of my Delight* 66.
c/o Australia and New Zealand Bank, 71 Cornhill, London, E.C.3, England.

Boyd, Virgil Edward; American automobile executive; b. 8 July 1912; ed. American Business Coll., Omaha, Neb.
Assistant to Pres., American Motors Corpn. 54-56, Field Sales Man., then Dir. of Sales Operations, Automotive Div. 56-61, Vice-Pres. Automotive Sales 61-62; Vice-Pres. and Gen. Sales Man. Chrysler Corpn. 62-63, Vice-Pres. and Group Exec., Automotive Sales 63-64, Group Vice-Pres. Domestic Automotive 64-66, mem. Board of Dirs. 64-, Pres. Jan. 67-.
Chrysler Corporation, 341 Massachusetts Ave., Detroit 31, Michigan; Home: 376 Dunstan Road, Bloomfield Hills, Michigan, U.S.A.

Boyd of Merton, 1st Viscount cr. 60, of Merton-in-Penninghame in the county of Wigtown; **Alan Tindal Lennox-Boyd,** P.C., C.H.; British politician; b. 18 Nov. 1904; ed. Sherborne and Christ Church, Oxford.
President of the Union, Oxford 26; Conservative M.P. for Mid-Beds. 31-60; Parl. Sec., Ministries of Labour 38, of Home Security 39, of Food 39-40, and of Aircraft Production 43-45; served R.N.V.R. 40-43; Minister of State for Colonial Affairs 51-52; Minister of Transport and Civil Aviation 52-54; Sec. of State for Colonies 54-59; Exec. Dir. Arthur Guinness Son & Co. Ltd. 59-61, Man. Dir. 61-67, Joint Vice-Chair. 67-; Dir. Tate and Lyle 66-, Imperial Chemical Industries 67-; Trustee, British Museum 62-; D.L. Cornwall 65-.
5 Eaton Close, London, S.W.1; and Ince Castle, Saltash, Cornwall, England.

Boyd-Carpenter, Rt. Hon. John Archibald, P.C., M.P.; British politician; b. 2 June 1908; ed. Stowe School and Balliol Coll., Oxford.
Called to Bar 34; practised S.E. Circuit; joined Scots Guards 39, served until 45; M.P. 45-; Financial Sec. to Treasury 51-54; Minister of Transport and Civil Aviation 54-55, of Pensions and Nat. Insurance 55-62, Chief Sec. to Treasury and Paymaster-Gen. 62-64; Chair. Public Accounts Cttee. House of Commons 64-; Dir. London County Freehold and Leasehold Properties Ltd. 64-, J. F. Thomasson and Co. 66-, City and Int. Investment Trust 66-; Conservative.
Publ. *The Conservative Case* 50.
12 Eaton Terrace, London, S.W.1, England.

Boyd Orr, 1st Baron, cr. 49, of Brechin; **John Boyd Orr,** C.H., Kt., D.S.O., M.C., F.R.S., F.R.S.E., LL.D., D.SC., M.D.; British physiologist; b. 23 Sept. 1880; ed. Glasgow Univ.
Served Royal Army Medical Corps 14-18; Dir. Rowett Research Inst. on Animal Nutrition to 45, resgnd.; Imperial Bureau of Animal Nutrition; mem. Min. of Health Advisory Cttee. on Nutrition, Min. of Agriculture Cattle Cttee., Colonial Advisory Council on Agriculture and Animal Health; mem. Fat Stock Reorganisation Comm. 32, Milk 35-36; Prof. of Agriculture Aberdeen Univ. 42-45; Joint Editor *Nutrition Abstracts and Reviews*; Chair. Scottish Scientific Advisory Cttee. 39-; mem. L.N. Technical Comm. on Nutrition; mem. War Cabt. Scientific Cttee. on Food Policy 40; M.P. Scottish Univs. 45-46; Dir.-Gen. Food and Agriculture Org. 45-48; Chancellor, Glasgow Univ. 46-; Pres. World Acad. of Science and Art, Jerusalem 61-; Nobel Peace Prize 49; Commdr. Légion d'Honneur.
Publs. *Minerals in Pastures and their Relation to Animal Nutrition* 28, *The National Food Supply* 34, *Food, Health and Income* 36, *Food and the People* 43, *Fighting for What?* 44, *The White Man's Dilemma* 53, *As I Recall* 66.
Newton, by Brechin, Angus, Scotland.

Boye, Ibrahima; Senegalese judge; b. 29 March 1924; ed. Univ. de Montpellier.
Attorney-at-Law, Court of Appeals, Nîmes, France; later mem. Public Prosecutor's Office at Court of Appeals of Montpellier; later French Judge, Guinea, Pres. of Colonial Court of Appeals, Dahomey; Examining Magistrate, Cotonou and Abidjan; Justice of the Peace, Agbonville, Ivory Coast; Technical Adviser in Ministry of Justice, Senegal 60, later Dir. of Cabinet and Justice of Supreme Court; Attorney-Gen., Senegal 61-; Chair. UN Comm. on Human Rights 68-.
UN Commission on Human Rights, c/o Economic and Social Council of the United Nations, New York City, U.S.A.

Boyer, Hervé, D. en D.; Haitian economist and politician; b. 22; ed. Univs. of Port au Prince and Paris.
National Bank of Haiti 41-45; Dir. Econ. Affairs, Secr. of State for Foreign Affairs 49-57; Counsellor, Treasury 57-59; Under-Sec. of State for Finance 59; Sec. of State for Commerce and Industry 59-60, for Finance and Econ. Affairs 61-64; Chevalier Légion d'Honneur, Commdr. Al Mérito, Grand Officier Honneur et Mérite.
Publ. *Economie Comparée d'Haiti, de la République Dominicaine et de Cuba.*
Montagnes Noirées, Petion-Ville, Haiti.

Boyesen, Jens Mogens; Norwegian diplomatist; b. 9 Oct. 1920; ed. Oslo Univ.
Active in Resistance 40-45; degree in law 47; Asst. Judge 48; entered Foreign Service 49; Under-Sec. Ministry of Foreign Affairs 51-54, Ministry of Defence 54-55; Ambassador to NATO 55-63, to OEEC 55-61, to OECD 61-63; Under-Sec. of State for Foreign Affairs 64-65; Assoc., Norwegian Defence Research Establishment Jan. 67-.
Havna Allé 9, Oslo, Norway.
Telephone: 69-73-10 (Oslo).

Boyko, Hugo, PH.D.; Israeli botanist; b. 6 Oct. 1892; ed. Army Officers' School and Univ. of Vienna.
Served as Austrian officer in First World War; later Man. in industrial firm; lecturer in Systematic Botany and Plant Geography, Univ. of Vienna; went to Palestine 35; private scientist until appt. as Ecologist to Govt. of Palestine 44, apptd. by Govt. of Israel as Ecological Adviser 48, retd. 62; Chair. Int. Comm. for Applied Ecology 47-61, Int. Cttee. for Desert Ecology (IUBS), Int. Cttee. on Ecological Climatography 56-64; Fellow and Hon. Sec.-Gen. World Acad. of Art and Science 60-65, Pres. World Acad. of Art and Science 65-; numerous Hon. memberships and awards.

Publs. About 100 scientific publs. including *The Geo-ecological Law* 47, *Saline and Seawater Irrigiation* 59, Editor *Science and the Future of Mankind* 61, *Principles of Climate Classification* 62, *Salinity and Aridity* 66, *Saline Irrigation for Agriculture and Forestry* 68, *Farming the Deserts* 68.
1 Ruppin Street, Rehovot, Israel.

Boyland, Eric, D.SC., PH.D.; British university professor; b. 24 Feb. 1905; ed. Univs. of Manchester and London.
Lister Inst. for Preventive Medicine 28-30; Kaiser Wilhelm Inst. für Medizinische Forschung, Heidelberg 30-31; Physiological Chemist to Royal Cancer Hospital, London 31; Reader in Biochemistry, Univ. of London 35-47, Prof. of Biochemistry in Univ. of London, at the Chester Beatty Research Inst. of the Royal Cancer Hospital 48-; Judd Award for Cancer Research, N.Y. 48; Medal of Société de Chimie biologique 56.
Office: Chester Beatty Research Institute, Fulham Road; Home: 42 Bramerton Street, London, S.W.3, England.
Telephone: 01-352-2601 (Home); 01-352-8133 (Office).

Boyle, Marshal of the R.A.F. Sir Dermot Alexander, G.C.B., K.C.V.O., K.B.E., A.F.C.; British officer; b. 2 Oct. 1904; ed. St. Columba's Coll., Ireland, and R.A.F. Coll., Cranwell.
Commissioned R.A.F. 24; 17 Squadron, Hawkinge 25, 1 Squadron, Hinaidi 26; 6 Squadron, Mosul 27; C.F.S; Wittering 27-29; Cranwell 30; 601 Squadron 30-33; Staff Officer, H.Q., R.A.F. India 33-35; Staff Coll. Andover 36; Chief Flying Instructor, Cranwell 37-39; H.Q. Advanced Air Striking Force 39-40; 83 Squadron. Scampton 40-41; Asst. Sec. War Cabinet Office 41; Commanding Officer, Stradishall 42; Senior Air Staff Officer, H.Q. No. 83 Group 43-45; A.D.C. to the King 43; Air Commodore 44; A.O.C. No. 11 Group 45; Imperial Defence Coll. 46; Asst. Commdt. Bracknell 47; Dir.-Gen. of Personnel, Air Ministry 48, of Manning 49-51; Air Vice-Marshal 49; A.O.C. No. 1 Group, Bomber Command 51-53; C.-in-C. Fighter Command 53-55; Air Marshal 54; Air Chief Marshal 56; Chief of Air Staff 56-59; Vice-Chair. British Aircraft Corpn. 62-.
Pauls Place, Sway, Lymington, Hants., England.

Boyle, Rt. Hon. Sir Edward (Charles Gurney), Bt., P.C., M.P.; British politician; b. 31 Aug. 1923; ed. Eton Coll. and Christ Church, Oxford.
Member of Parl. 50-; Parl. Private Sec. to Under-Sec. for Air 51-52, and to Parl. Sec. to Ministry of Defence 52-53; Parl. Sec., Ministry of Supply 54-55; Econ. Sec. to Treasury 55-56; Parl. Sec. Ministry of Education 57-59; Financial Sec. to Treasury 59-62; Minister of Education 62-64; Minister of State under Sec. of State for Educ. and Science April 64-Oct. 64; Pro-Chancellor Sussex Univ. 65-; Dir. Penguin Publishing Co. Ltd. 65- (now Deputy Chair.), Penguin Books Ltd. 66-; Man. Dir. Allen Lane the Penguin Press Ltd. 67 (now Dir.); mem. Arts Council 65-; Hon. LL.D. (Leeds and Southampton), Hon. D.Sc. (Univ. of Aston in Birmingham); Conservative.
Ockham House, Hurst Green, Sussex, England.

Braadland, Erik; Norwegian diplomatist and politician; b. 21 Nov. 1910; ed. Univ. of Oslo.
Entered Foreign Service 34; held various appointments in Oslo and abroad; Deputy Head of Norwegian Mil. Mission, Berlin 47, Acting Head 49; Minister to Yugoslavia 52-54; Ambassador to U.S.S.R. 54-59, to U.K. 59-61; M.P. 61-; Centre Party.
Ør pr. Halden, Norway.
Telephone: Halden 97199.

Brace, Lloyd D.; American banker; b. 26 Feb. 1903; ed. Dartmouth Coll.
Joined First Nat. Bank of Boston 25, Dir. 42-, Pres. 47-, Chair. of the Board 59-66, of Exec. Cttee. 66-; Dir.,

mem. Exec. Cttee. United Shoe Machinery Corpn., Dir. American Telephone and Telegraph Co., The Gillette Co., John Hancock Mutual Life Insurance Co., Gen. Motors Corpn., Stone and Webster.
First National Bank of Boston, 67 Milk Street, Boston, Mass. 02110, U.S.A.
Telephone: 617-444-0906.

Bracher, Karl Dietrich, DR. PHIL.; German political scientist and historian; b. 13 March 1922; ed. Gymnasium, Stuttgart, Univ. of Tübingen and Harvard Univ.
Research Asst. and Head of Dept., Inst. of Political Science, Berlin 50-58; Lecturer, German Hochschule für Politik, Berlin; Privatdozent and Prof. Free Univ., Berlin 55-58; Prof. of Political Science and Contemporary History, Univ. of Bonn, and Dir. Seminar of Political Science, Bonn 59-; Pres. Comm. for History of Parl. and Political Parties, Bonn 62-; Fellow, Center for Advanced Study in the Behavioral Sciences, Stanford, U.S.A. 63-64; Pres. German Asscn. of Political Science 65-67; mem. Inst. for Advanced Study, Princeton, U.S.A. 67-68; mem. Board, Institut für Zeitgeschichte, Munich, German Asscn. of Foreign Policy, Germania Judaica, Asscn. of German Scientists; mem. Editorial Board, *Politische Vierteljahresschrift*, *Neue Politische Literatur*, *Bonner Historische Forschungen*, *Journal of Contemporary History, Government and Opposition*, *Modern Constitutionalism and Democracy* (joint editor) 2 vols. 66.
Publs. *Conscience in Revolt* (with others) 54, *National-sozialistische Machtergreifung und Reichskonkordat* 56, *Die Auflösung der Weimarer Republik* 55, *Staat and Politik* (with E. Fraenkel) 57, *Die Nationalsozialistische Machtergreifung* (with others) 60, *The Foreign Policy of the Federal Republic of Germany* 63, *Problems of Parliamentary Democracy in Europe* 64, *Adolf Hitler* 64, *Deutschland zwischen Demokratie und Diktatur* 64, *Theodor Heuss und die Wiederbegründung der Demokratie in Deutschland* 65, *Staatsbegriff und Demokratie in Deutschland* 68.
Am Hofgarten 15, Bonn, German Federal Republic.

Brachet, Jean Louis Auguste, M.D.; Belgian biologist; b. 19 March 1909; ed. Univ. Libre de Bruxelles.
Assistant in Anatomy, Faculty of Medicine, Univ. of Brussels 34-38, Dir. of Studies 38, Prof. 42-, Dir. of Dept. of Animal Morphology; also Dir. of Laboratory of Molecular Embryology, Int. Lab. for Genetics and Biophysics, Naples; Rockefeller Fellow, Princeton 37; Visiting Prof. Inst. Pasteur, Paris 46, Univ. of Pa. 47, Indian Cancer Research Centre, Bombay 56, Rockefeller Inst. 58, Weizmann Inst., Israel 60, Univ. of Texas 65, Univ. of Jerusalem 66; Francqui Prof., Univs. of Liège, Ghent and Louvain; mem. Acad. royale des Sciences de Belgique, Acad. royale de Médicine de Belgique, Royal Danish Acad., Nat. Acad. of Sciences, Washington, American Acad. of Arts and Sciences, Royal Soc., London, Royal Soc., Edinburgh, Deutsche Akad. der Naturforscher Leopoldina, Halle, Yugoslav Acad. of Sciences, Istituto Lombardo, Milan, Soc. français de Biologie, Inst. grand-ducal de Luxembourg; Dr. h.c. (Univs. of Strasbourg, Poitiers, Turin, Palermo, Edinburgh, Weizmann Inst., Israel, and Inst. agronomique de Gembloux.).
Publs. *Embryologie chimique* 44, 45 (trans. English, Russian and Chinese), *Biochemical Cytology* 57 (trans. Russian and Polish), *The Biological Role of Ribonucleic Acids* 60; Co-Editor *The Cell* (6 vols.); over 300 publications on the biochemical bases of embryonic development, the role of nucleic acids in the synthesis of proteins, the role of the nucleus in the differentiation and synthesis of macromolecules.
Faculté des Sciences, Université Libre de Bruxelles, 67 rue des Chevaux Rhode-St.-Genèse, Brussels, Belgium.

Bradbury, Norris Edwin, B.A., PH.D.; American physicist; b. 30 May 1909; ed. Pomona Coll., Calif., Univ. of Calif. and Mass. Inst. of Technology.
Asst. Prof. of Physics 34-37, Assoc. Prof. 37-42, Prof. 42-51, Stanford Univ.; Prof. Univ. of Calif. 51-; Dir. Los Alamos Scientific Laboratory, New Mexico 45-; Captain U.S. Naval Reserve 41-61; Fellow of the Nat. Acad. of Sciences and of the American Physical Soc.
Box 1663, Los Alamos; Home: 1451 47th Street, Los Alamos, New Mexico 87544, U.S.A.

Bradford, Robert Davis, B.S., M.S.; American metallurgist and business executive; b. 29 April 1903; ed. Univ. of Utah.
Research Chemist, Utah Copper Co. 25-26; American Smelting and Refining Co. (ASARCO) 26-, Asst. to Gen. Manager Western Dept. 29-30, New York Ore Dept. 30-36, Asst. Manager Southwestern Dept. 36-40, Manager East Helena Plant (Montana) 40-42, Manager Southwestern Dept. 42-47, Manager Selby Plant (Calif.) 47-49, Manager Utah Dept. 49-51, Gen. Manager Western Dept. 51-52, Vice-Pres. American Smelting and Refining Co. (Head of Federated Metals Division) 57-63, Exec. Vice-Pres. 59-63, Pres. 63-; Dir. ASARCO subsidiaries and other companies; mem. various scientific societies.
American Smelting and Refining Company, 120 Broadway, New York, N.Y. 10005; Home 20 Church Street, Greenwich, Conn. 06830, U.S.A.

Bradley, Gen. of the Army Omar Nelson; American army officer; b. 12 Feb. 1893; ed. U.S. Military Acad., West Point.
Second-Lieut. of infantry 15; advanced through grades to Gen. of the Army Sept. 50; Prof. of Mil. Science and Tactics, S. Dakota State Coll. Sept. 19-20; Instructor in Hawaii 25-28; graduated from Command and Gen. Staff School, Fort Leavenworth, Kan. July 29; Instructor at Infantry School, Fort Benning, Ga. 29-33; graduated from War Coll., Washington June 34; Instructor in Tactics, later Plans and Training Officer, West Point 34-38; Asst. Sec., Gen. Staff July 39-Feb. 41; Commandant of Infantry School, Fort Benning Feb. 41-Feb. 42; commanded 82nd Infantry Div. Feb. 42; commanded U.S. Second Corps in Tunisia and in invasion of Sicily 43; commanded First U.S. Army during invasion of Europe 44; later commanded 12th Army Group; Administrator of Veterans' Affairs 45-47; Chief of Staff U.S. Army 48-49; Chair. Joint Chiefs of Staff U.S. Dept. of Defence 49-53; U.S. Rep., NATO Military Cttee. (Chair. 49-50) and Standing Cttee. 49-53; Chair. Bulova Research Devt. Labs., N.Y. 53-58, Bulova Watch Co. 58-; decorations incl. D.S.M. (3 Oak Leaf Clusters), D.S.M. of U.S. Navy, Legion of Merit with Oak Leaf Clusters, Silver Star, Bronze Star Medal, Hon. K.C.B. (Great Britain), Grand Cross of the Legion of Honour and Croix de Guerre with Palm (France), Order of Suvorov 1st degree and of Kutuzov 1st degree (U.S.S.R.), and many other awards.
Publ. *A Soldier's Story* 51.
Office: 630 Fifth Avenue, New York, N.Y. 10020; Home: 1720 Carla Ridge, Beverly Hills, California, 90210, U.S.A.

Bradshaw, Thornton F.; American business executive; b. 4 Aug. 1917; ed. Phillips Exeter Acad., Harvard Coll. and Harvard Graduate School of Business Admin.
Associate Prof., Harvard Business School 42-52; Partner, Cresap, McCormick and Paget, New York 52-56; Dir. The Atlantic Refining Co., Philadelphia (now Atlantic Richfield Co.) 56-, Vice-Pres. 56-62, Exec. Vice-Pres. 62-64, Pres. 64-, Chair. Exec. Cttee. 66-; Dir. Atlas Chemical Industries Inc. 60-, First Pennsylvania Banking and Trust Co. 61-, Penn Mutual Life Insurance Co. 62-.

Publs. *Controllership in Modern Management* 49, *Developing Men for Controllership* 50.
326 Grays Lane, Haverford, Pennsylvania, U.S.A.

Braga, Ney; Brazilian politician; b. 25 July 1917; ed. in Curitiba and Escola Militar de Realengo.
Second Lieut. 38, rising to Reserve Brig.-Gen. in 63 on retirement from army; Chief of Police for Paraná 52-54, Prefect 54-58; Fed. Deputy 58; Gov. of Paraná 60-65; responsible for the creation of various companies during his governorship including Companhia de Desenvolvimento Econômico do Paraná (CODEPAR) and Companhia Paranaense de Energia Elétrica (COPEL); mem. Senate; Pres. Council for the Extreme South (CODSEUL) 63; Christian Democrat (Nat. Pres.); Dr. h.c. Univ. of Paraná; numerous honours and awards.
The Senate, Brasilia, Brazil.

Braga, Ruben; Brazilian journalist and diplomatist; b. 12 Jan. 1913; ed. Univ. de Minas Gerais.
Professional journalist in Brazil 32-; roving correspondent for Brazilian newspapers in America and Europe; covered elections of Peron and Eisenhower; War Correspondent for *Diarios Associados*, Brazilian Revolution 32, with Brazilian Expeditionary Force in Italy 44-45; Head of Commercial Writers in Brazil 35; Ambassador to Morocco 61-63.
Publs. *O Conde e o Passarinho* 36, *O Morro do Isolamento* 44, *Com a FEB na Itália* 45, *Um Pé de Milho* 48, *O Homem Rouco* 49, *50 Crônicas Escolhidas* 51, *Três Primitivos* 54, *A Borboleta Amarela* 55, *A Cidade e a Roça* 57, *100 Crônicas Escolhidas* 58, *Ai de ti, Copacabana* 60, *Chroniques de Copacabana de Paris et d'Ailleurs* 63.
Rua Prudente Morais 599, Rio de Janeiro, Brazil.

Braga da Cruz, Guilherme, DR. JUR.; Portuguese university professor; b. 11 June 1916; ed. Lyceum of Braga, Univ. of Coimbra, Univ. of Paris.
Vice-Pres. Centro Académico de Democracia Cristã, Coimbra 36-37; Asst. Prof. Faculty of Law, Coimbra Univ. 42-47, Prof. 47-, Dean, Faculty of Law 58-61, Rector 61-62; mem. "Câmara Corporativa" 53-57, 57-61, Vice-Pres. 55-57; Portuguese mem. Int. Court of Justice, Right of Passage over Indian Territory case 57-59; Academician, Portuguese Acad. of History 51-, Acad. of Sciences 62-, Acad. Int. des Sciences Politiques 63-, Acad. de Législation, Toulouse 64-, and Int. Acad. of Portuguese Culture 67-; Dr. h.c. Faculty of Law, São Paulo Univ. 62, Navarra Univ. (Pamplona) 67; several national and foreign decorations.
Publs. *Algumas Considerações Sôbre a "Perfiliatio"* 38, *O Direito de Troncalidade,* 2 vols. 41, 47, *O Problema da Sucessão dos Ascendentes no Antigo Direito Grego* 47, *A Posse de Ano e Dia* 49, *O Direito de Superfície no Direito Romano* 49, *S. Martinho de Dume e a Legislação Visigótica* 50, *Direitos e Deveres do Estado na Educação* 52, *Origem e Evolução da Universidade* 53, *A Sucessão Legítima no Código Euricano* 53, *Formação Histórica do Moderno Direito Português e Brasileiro* 55, *O Problema do Regime de Bens Supletivo* 56, *Regimes de Bens do Casamento* 57, *Capacidade Patrimonial dos Cônjuges* 57, *O Problema da Universidade* 61, *Afinidade (Subsistência do vínculo após a dissolução do casamento)* 62, *Le Code Napoléon dans la formation du droit civil portugais moderne* 63, *Les pactes successoraux dans l'ancien droit portugais* 63, *Casamento: Contrato e Sacramento* 64, *Propriedade da Farmácia* 64.
Avenida Dias da Silva, 6, Coimbra, Portugal.
Telephone: 2-32-45.

Bragg, Sir (William) Lawrence, Kt., C.H., O.B.E., M.C., F.R.S.; British physicist; b. 31 March 1890; ed. Adelaide Univ. and Trinity Coll., Cambridge.
Fellow and Lecturer in Natural Sciences Trinity Coll. Cambridge 14; Nobel Prizeman (in conjunction with his

father, Sir W. H. Bragg) for research work on X-rays and crystal structures 15; Langworthy Prof. of Physics Victoria Univ. Manchester 19-37; Dir. Nat. Physical Laboratory 37-38; Cavendish Prof. of Physics Cambridge Univ. 38-53; Prof. Natural Philosophy Royal Inst. 38-53; Fullerian Prof. of Chemistry, Royal Inst. 53-, Resident Prof. and Dir. Royal Inst. 54-66, Prof. Emer. 66-; Pres. Inst. of Physics 39-43; Privy Council Cttee. Scientific and Industrial Research 42-47; Commdr. Order of Leopold of Belgium.
6A The Boltons, London, S.W.10, England.
Telephone: 01-370-5189.

Braham, Maloum Ould; Mauritanian politician; b. 1930; ed. Rosso and William Ponty School.
Teacher at Nema 51-54, Boutilimit 54-56; Headmaster Tidjikja and Kiffa 57-63; Inspector for Primary Educ. 63-66; Minister of Foreign Affairs Feb. 66-Oct. 66; Minister of Rural Economy 66-67, of Commerce, Transport and Tourism 67-.
Ministry of Commerce, Nouakchott, Mauritania.

Brahimi, Lakhdar; Algerian diplomatist; b. 34; ed. Medersa Algiers, Faculté de Droit et Institut des Sciences Politiques, Algiers then Paris.
Student Leader 53-56; Algerian Front of Nat. Liberation (F.L.N.) to 56; Perm. Rep. of F.L.N. and later of Provisional Govt. of Algeria in South East Asia 56-61; Gen. Secretariat Ministry of External Affairs 61-63; Ambassador to U.A.R. and Sudan 63-; Perm. Rep. to Arab League.
Algerian Embassy, Garden City, Cairo, United Arab Republic.

Braibant, Charles, L. en D., L. ès L.; French writer and archivist; b. 31 March 1889; ed. Lycées Janson-de-Sailly and Louis-le-Grand and Paris Univ.
Served French Army 14-18; Curator of Naval Archives 19-44; Inspector-Gen. of Archives of France 44-48; Dir.-Gen. of Archives of France 48-59, Hon. Dir.-Gen. 59-; Pres. Int. Archives Council 50-53, Hon. Pres. 53-; Grand Officier, Légion d'Honneur, Commandeur des Palmes Académiques and other decorations.
Publs. *Le Roi Dort, Le Soleil de Mars, Le Rive des Dieux, Irène Soubeyran, Resplendine et autres Victimes, Lumière bleue, La Guerre à Paris, Le Métier d'Ecrivain, Mer franque, Le Secret d'Anatole France, Un Bourgeois sous trois Républiques, Félix Foure à l'Elysée, Histoire de la tour Eiffel.*
7 rue Louis-Boilly, Paris 16e, France.

Braidwood, Robert J.; American archaeologist and anthropologist; b. 29 July 1907; ed. Michigan, Berlin and Chicago Univs.
Field archaeology in Iraq, Illinois, Syria, New Mexico, Turkey and Iran; Prof. of Anthropology and Old World Pre-history, Univ. of Chicago 54-; Fellow, American Acad. of Arts and Sciences, Nat. Acad. of Sciences, American Philosophical Soc.; Corresp. mem. Deutsches Archäologisches Institut, Österreichische Akademie der Wissenschaft and various other academies.
Publs. *Excavations in the plain of Antioch I* (with Linda Braidwood), *Prehistoric investigations in Iraqi Kurdistan* (with Bruce Howe, *et al.*).
Oriental Institute, University of Chicago, Chicago, Illinois 60637, U.S.A.
Telephone: 312-643-0800.

Brain, Hugh Gerner, C.B.E., M.S.M., HON. M.AUST.I.M.M.; Australian company secretary and director; b. 3 Dec. 1890; ed. State School, and Univ. High School, Melbourne.
Clerical employment in Victoria Public Service 07-13, Commonwealth Public Service 13-15; abroad with Australian Imp. Force 15-19; discharged as Capt. and D.A.A.G.; Chair. Australasian Temperance and Gen. Mutual Life Assurance Soc. Ltd. 56-; Asst. Hon. Sec. Dept. of Defence Co-ordination 40; business mem.

(hon.) Australian Naval Board 41-46; mem. of Examinations Board and Appointments Board, Univ. of Melbourne; mem. Soldiers' Children's Education Board, Colonial Service Appts. Board; Chair. The Baillieu Educational Trusts 36-51.
Office: 390 Lonsdale Street, Melbourne 3000; Home: 415 Kooyong Road, Elsterwick 3185, Victoria, Australia.
Telephone: 60-0591 (Office); 53-5158 (Home).

Braine, John Gerard, A.L.A.; British author; b. 13 April 1922; ed. St. Bede's Grammar School, Bradford and Leeds School of Librarianship.
Assistant Librarian, Bingley Public Library 40-51; Branch Librarian, Northumberland County Library 54-56, Yorkshire West Riding County Library 56-57; mem. B.B.C. North Region Advisory Council 60-64.
Publs. *Room at the Top* 57, *The Vodi* 59, *Life at the Top* 62, *The Jealous God* 64, *The Crying Game* 68.
The Holt, Pyrford Heath, Pyrford, Woking, Surrey, England.
Telephone: Byfleet 43155.

Braithwaite, Eustace Adolphe, M.SC.; Guyanan diplomatist; b. 27 June 1912; ed. New York Univ. and Cambridge Univ.
Royal Air Force, Second World War; schoolteacher, London 50-57; Welfare Officer, London County Council 58-60; Human Rights Officer, World Veterans Foundation, Paris 60-63; Lecturer and Educ. Consultant, UNESCO, Paris 63-66; Perm. Rep. of Guyana to UN 67-68; Amb. to Venezuela 68-; Ainsfield Wolff Literary Award for *To Sir, With Love.*
Publs. *To Sir, With Love* 59 (film 67), *A Kind of Homecoming* 61, *Paid Servant* 62, *A Choice of Straws* 65.
Embassy of Guyana, Caracas, Venezuela.

Branca, Vittore (Felice Giovanni), D.LITT.; Italian educationist; b. 9 July 1913; ed. Univ. of Pisa.
Prof. Accad. della Crusca Florence 37-48; Prof. of Italian Literature, Maria Assunta Univ., Rome 48-50; Prof. of Italian Literature, Univ. of Catania 50-53, Univ. of Padua 53-60; Head of Div. of Arts and Letters, UNESCO 50-53; Sec.-Gen. Int. Asscn. for Study of Italian Literature and Fondazione Giorgio Cini; mem. Cttee. Int. Asscn. of Modern Language and Literature; adviser to publishing houses; Editor *Lettere Italiane* and *Studi sul Boccaccio* (magazines) and of numerous series of classical texts and essays; mem. Int. P.E.N., Accad. Arcadia, 1st Ven. Scienze Lettere, Accad. del Mediterraneo, Nat. Comm. of UNESCO.
Publs. Editions and critical studies of San Francesco, Boccaccio, Petrarch, Alfieri, Manzoni, Poliziano and other classical authors.
San Marco 1957, Venice, Italy.
Telephone: 89-819.

Branch, Harllee, Jr., B.A., LL.B.; American business executive; b. 21 June 1906; ed. Boys High School, Atlanta, Davidson Coll., N. Carolina, and Lamar School of Law, Emory Univ., Atlanta.
Director, Fed. Reserve Bank of Atlanta 53-55; Pres. Southeastern Electric Exchange 54-55, Edison Electric Inst. 55-56, The Southern Co. 57-, Chair. Board 63-; Vice-Pres. and Dir. Georgia, Alabama, Gulf and Mississippi Power Co. 57-; mem. U.S. Business Advisory Council 62-; dir. of other cos. and official of educ. orgs.
3106 Nancy Creek Road, N.W., Atlanta, Georgia 30327, U.S.A.

Brand, The Hon. David, M.L.A.; Australian politician; b. 12; ed. Government School, Mullewa, Western Australia.
Mem. Western Australian Legislative Assembly for Greenough 45-; Hon. Minister for Housing, Forests and Local Govt. 49; Minister for Works, Water Supply and Housing 50; Leader of the Opposition and Parliamentary Leader, Liberal and Country League 57-59;

Premier, Treasurer and Minister for Tourists, Govt. of Western Australia 59-.
Home: 24 Ednah Street, Como; and Parliament House, Perth, Western Australia.

Brandi, Cesare, PH.D.; Italian author and art critic; b. 8 April 1906; ed. Univs. of Siena, Pisa and Florence. Inspector for the Superintendence of the Monuments and Galleries of Siena 33-39; founder and Dir. Central Restoration Inst., Rome 39; started publishing *Immagine* (a review) 48, and the *Bollettino* of the Inst. 50; Superintendent, Dept. of Antiquities and Fine Arts 53-; Commendatore dell'Ordine al Merito della Repubblica 54. Publs. *Rutilio Manetti* 32, *La R. Pinacoteca di Siena* 33, *Mostra della pittura riminese del '300* 35, *Giotto* 38, *Carmine o della pittura con due saggi su Duccio e Picasso* 47, *Morandi* 42, *Giovanni di Paolo* 47, *Quattrocentisti senesi* 49, *La fine dell'avanguardia* 50, *La fine dell' avanguardia e l'arte di oggi* 52, *Duccio* 51, *Celso o della poesia* 57, etc.
Piazza S. Francesco di Paola 7, Rome, Italy.

Brandi, Hermann Theodor, DR. MONT.; German businessman; b. 25 Dec. 1908; ed. Aachen, Berlin-Charlottenburg and Leoben Insts. of Technology.
Member Management Board, August Thyssen-Hütte A.G., Verein Deutscher Eisenhüttenleute, Wirtschaftsvereinigung Eisen-und Stahlindustrie, Vereinigung Industrieller Kraftwirtschaft, Gesellschaft für Wasserwirtschaft; Chair. of Board Arbeitgeberverband Eisen-und Stahlindustrie, Düsseldorf, Gesellschaft zur Förderung der Spektrochemie und angewandten Spektroskopie e.V.; Chair. Board of Dirs. Emscher-Lippe-Bergbau A.G., Martin & Pagenstecher A.G.; Deputy Chair. Board of Dirs. Friedrich Thyssen Bergbau A.G., Linde A.G., Rheinische Kalksteinwerke G.m.b.H.; Deputy mem. Management Board Ruhrverband und Ruhrtalsperrenverein; mem. Board of Dirs. Dolomitwerke G.m.b.H., Barbara Erzbergbau G.m.b.H., Brown, Boverie & Cie. A.G., and of several other cos.; Pres. Gesellschaft von Freunden der Aachener Hochschule; Chair. Stromausschuss der Gesellschaft für Stromwirtschaft m.b.H.; mem. German Atomic Energy Comm.; Dr.-Ing. E.h.
August Thyssen-Hütte A.G., 4 Düsseldorf, August Thyssen-Strasse 1; Home: 433 Mülheim-Ruhr-Speldorf, Wichernstrasse 4, German Federal Republic.
Telephone: 8241.

Brando, Marlon, Jr.; American actor; b. 3 April 1924; ed. Shattuck Military Acad.
Has appeared in the plays *I Remember Mama*, *Candida*, *A Flag is Born*, *The Eagle has Two Heads*, *A Streetcar Named Desire*, etc., and the films *The Men*, *A Streetcar Named Desire*, *Viva Zapata*, *Julius Caesar*, *The Wild Ones*, *Desirée*, *On the Waterfront*, *Guys and Dolls*, *Teahouse of the August Moon*, *Sayonara*, *The Young Lions*, *The Fugitive Kind*, *The Ugly American*, *Bedtime Story*, *Morituri*, *Southwest to Sonora* 66, *Reflections in a Golden Eye* 67; Dir. the film *The One-Eyed Jacks*, etc.; Acad. Award for the best actor of the year 54.
Hawley Road, Mundelein, Ill., U.S.A.

Brandt, Cornelis J.; Netherlands journalist; b. 14 Feb. 1913; ed. Netherlands Inst. of Chartered Accountants. Began career as accountant and Sec. to agricultural and banking organisations; Acting Editor-in-Chief *Amsterdamsche Effectenblad* and *Het Financieele Dagblad* 43-49; Financial Editor *De Telegraaf* 49-52, Editor-in-Chief 52-, Man. Dir. 64-.
Publ. *Preference Shares* 46.
Hartelstein 3, Amsterdam-Buitenveldert, Netherlands.

Brandt, Karl, DR. AGR.; American economic adviser and agriculturalist; b. Germany 9 Jan. 1899; ed. Berlin and Württemberg Univs.
Dir. German Farm Tenants Bank 25-27; Agricultural

Adviser Central Co-operative Bank Berlin 28-29; Prof. Coll. of Agriculture Berlin Univ. 29-33; mem. Graduate Faculty of Political and Social Sciences, New School for Social Research New York 33-38; Visiting Research Prof. Louisiana State Univ. 37-38; Economic Adviser to Sec. of Agriculture 42; Consultant to War Food Admin. 44; Economic Adviser on Food and Agriculture to U.S. Military Govt. in Germany 45-46; Guest Prof. Univ. Heidelberg 48-49; Prof. Economic Policy and Dir. Food Research Inst. Stanford Univ. Calif. 38-; mem. Joint Technical Mission to Uruguay of Int. Bank for Reconstruction and Development and F.A.O. 50; Consultant to Ford Foundation 51-55; mem. of the President's Council of Economic Advisers, Washington 58-61; Exchange Prof. Free Univ. of Berlin 54-55; Hon. Dr. Phil. (Heidelberg); Hon. mem. Soc. Royale d'Economie Politique de Belgique; mem. Acad. d'Agriculture, Paris.
Publs. *Reconstruction of World Agriculture* 45, *Germany's Agricultural and Food Policy in World War II* 53.
221 Kingsley Avenue, Palo Alto, Calif., U.S.A.

Brandt, Willy; German politician; b. 18 Dec. 1913; ed. Lübeck and Oslo Univ.
Emigrated to Norway 33; journalistic and political activity in Norway and Sweden 33-45; corresp. in Berlin for Scandinavian newspapers 45-47; represented Exec. Cttee. of Sozialdemokratische Partei Deutschlands (S.P.D.) in Berlin 48-49; mem. Exec. Cttee. Berlin S.P.D. 50-, Dep. Chair. 54-58, Chair. 58-63; Chair. Social Democratic Party of Federal Germany (S.P.D.) 64-; Chief Editor *Berliner Stadtblatt* 50-51; mem. Berlin Chamber of Deputies 50, Pres. 55-57; mem. German Federal Parl. (Bundestag) 49-57; Ruling Mayor of West Berlin 57-66; Minister of Foreign Affairs, German Fed. Repub. 66-; Pres. German Bundesrat 57-58, 66-; Vice-Chancellor, Federal Republic of Germany 66-; Pres. German Nat. Day; Senator Max-Planck Asscn.; Hon. Dr. Pennsylvania Univ. 58, Maryland 60, Harvard 63, School for Social Research 64; Social Democrat (S.P.D.); numerous hon. degrees and foreign decorations.
Publs. include *Krigen i Norge* 45, *Ernst Reuter* (with R. Lowenthal) 57, *Von Bonn nach Berlin* 57, *My Road to Berlin* 60, *The Ordeal of Co-existence* 63, *Begegnung mit Kennedy* 64, *Draussen* (with G. Struve) 66.
Auswärtiges Amt, 53 Bonn/Rhein, German Federal Republic.
Telephone: Bonn 2071.

Brandys, Kazimierz; Polish writer; b. 16.
Co-Editor *Odrodzenie* after war (weekly), Cracow; mem. Exec. Cttee. Polish Writers' Union; State Literary Prize (twice); Premio Elba (Italy) 64.
Publs. novels: *The Invincible City* 46, *The Wooden Horse* 46, *Between the Two Wars* (4 vols.) 48, *The Citizens* 54, *The Red Cap* 56, *Defence of Granada* (apology for writers and actors) 56, *Matka Królów* (Sons and Comrades) 57, *Listy do pani Z.* (Letters to Mrs. Z.) 58-61, *Romantycznośc* (Romanticism) 60, *Sposób bycia* (The Way to be) 64, *Dżoker* (Joker) 66.
Nowomiejska 5, Warsaw 40, Poland.

Branigin, Roger Douglas, A.B., LL.B.; American lawyer and politician; b. 26 July 1902; ed. Franklin Coll. and Harvard Univ.
Deputy Prosecuting Attorney, Franklin, Indiana 26-29; Counsel, Federal Land Bank and Farm Credit Administration, Louisville 30-38, Gen. Counsel 32-38; private legal practice 38-42, 46-64; U. S. Army 42-46; Pres. Indiana State Bar Asscn.; Dir. several companies; Gov. of Indiana 65-; mem. Newcomen Soc.; Hon. LL.D., Butler Univ. and Franklin Coll.; Democrat.
State Capitol, Indianapolis; Home: 611 South Seventh Street, Lafayette, Indiana, U.S.A.
Telephone: 742-8747.

Branscomb, B. Harvie, B.A., PH.D., D.LITT., LL.D., D.H.L.; American educationist; b. 25 Dec. 1894; ed. Birmingham-Southern Coll., Oxford and Columbia Univs.

Asst. Prof. Southern Methodist Univ. 19-25; Prof. Duke Univ. 25-46; Dir. Univ. Libraries, Duke Univ. 32-37; Dean Divinity School 44-46; Chancellor Vanderbilt Univ. 46-63; Consultant to World Bank on Educational Policy 62-63; Trustee Gen. Education Board 47; Chair. U.S. Educational Exchange Advisory Comm. 47-51; Chair. Comm. on Education and Int. Affairs, American Council of Education 58; Chair. U.S. Nat. Comm. for UNESCO; Delegate General Conference, World Health Org. 65 and 66; Chair. U.S. Del., World Conf. on Illiteracy 65, Conf. of Ministers of Educ. of Latin American countries 66; mem. U.S. Nat. Advisory Health Council 63-67; Consultant. Acad. Educational Devt. 67-; Trustee, several educational orgs.
Publs. *The Message of Jesus* 25, *Jesus and the Law of Moses* 30, *The Teachings of Jesus* 31, *The Gospel according to Mark* 37, *Teaching with Books* 40.
1620 Chickering Road, Nashville 15, Tenn., U.S.A.
Telephone: 269-6821.

Brassens, Georges; French musician; b. 22 Oct. 1921; ed. Coll. de Sète, Lycée de Montpellier.
Composer and singer of songs in cabarets and music halls 52-; acted in and composed music and songs for the film *Porte des Lilas* 56; large number of songs include *La Mauvaise Réputation, Le Gorille, Le Fossoyeur, Hécatombe,* etc., Grand prix du Disque 64; Prix de poésie, Acad. Française 67.
Publs. *La Tour des Miracles* (novel), *La Mauvaise Réputation* (collection of songs).
18 rue Pigalle, Paris 9e, France.

Brasseur, Maurice Paul; Belgian politician; b. 09.
Teacher, Namur and Mons; served with Resistance 40-45; Burgomaster, Loverval 41-65; Minister of the Interior 50-52; mem. Chamber of Reps. 49-65, Vice-Pres. 58-61; Minister of Foreign Trade and Technical Assistance to under-developed countries 61; Gov. for Province of Luxembourg 65-; mem. of many Belgian missions abroad; numerous Belgian and foreign decorations, including Grand Croix de l'Ordre de Léopold II; Christian Socialist.
Palais Provincial, Arlon, Belgium.

Brasseur, Pierre; French actor and playwright; b. 22 Dec. 1905.
Made cinema debut in silent films *Madame sans-Gêne* and *Feu* 27; has since appeared in numerous films, including *Quai des Brumes, Lumière d'Eté, Adieu Léonard, Les Enfants du Paradis, Les Portes de la Nuit, Les Amants de Vérone, Les Mains Sales, La Vie à Deux, The Possessors, Les Yeux sans Visage, Candide, Les Amours célèbres, La Vie de Château.*
Publs. include *Folies Bout de Bois, Notre Femme qui êtes aux Cieux, Le Marchand d'Etoiles* (plays).
1 bis boulevard Richard-Wallace, Neuilly-sur-Seine, Hauts-de-Seine, France.

Bratby, John, A.R.A., A.R.C.A., R.B.A., F.I.A.L.; British painter; b. 19 July 1928; ed. Tiffin Boys School, Kingston Art School, Royal Coll. of Art, London.
Works in Tate Gallery, London, Nat. Gallery of Canada, Nat. Gallery of New South Wales, New York Museum of Modern Art, Walker Art Gallery, Arts Council, Glasgow Museum of Art, etc.; rep. at Pittsburgh Int. Festival 55, 57, Venice Biennale 56; executed painting for the film *The Horse's Mouth* 58; Editorial Adviser *Art Quarterly*; Guggenheim Nat. Award 56 and 58.
Publs. *Breakdown* 60, *Breakfast and Elevenses* 61, *Brake-Pedal Down* 62, *Break 50 Kill* 63.
7 Hardy Road, Blackheath, London, S.E.3, England.
Telephone: 01-858-6288.

Bratchenko, Boris Fedorovich; Soviet mining engineer, economist and politician; b. 1912; mem. C.P.S.U. 40-.
Has worked at coal mines in Rostov Region 35-49, at big combine in Karaganda, Kazakhstan 49-53; Govt. posts 53-; fmr. Vice-Chair. Council of Ministers of Kazakh Planning Cttee.; Minister of Coal Industry 65-; Candidate mem. Central Cttee. of C.P.S.U.; Deputy to U.S.S.R. Supreme Soviet.
Ministry of Coal Industry, 11 Sadovo-Sukha revskaya ulitsa, Moscow, U.S.S.R.

Bratschi, Robert; Swiss trade union official; b. 91.
Mem. staff Fed. Railways until 17; entered Swiss Railway Workers' Asscn. 18, Gen. Sec. 20-54; Pres. Swiss Public Employers' Asscn. 22-54; Pres. Swiss Confed. of Trade Unions 34-54; Pres. Int. Transport Workers' Fed.; mem. Admin. Council Swiss Fed. Railways 21-; mem. Council Swiss Nat. Bank 45; mem. Swiss Nat. Council and of Berne Cantonal Council 22-, Pres. 41-42; mem. Swiss Parliament 22-, Pres. 57-58; Man. Berne-Lötschberg-Simplon Railway until 54.
Genfergasse 11, Berne, Switzerland.

Bratsiotis, Panayotis, D.TH.; Greek university professor; b. 89; ed. Athens, Leipzig and Jena Univs.
Prof. Pedagogical Acad. of Piraeus 15-22; Prof. of Biblical Science, Athens Univ. 25-29, Prof. of Old Testament 29, Rector of Univ. 55-56; mem. Acad. of Athens 55, Pres. 60; foreign mem. Royal Flemish Acad. of Brussels; Hon. D.D. (Glasgow Univ.).
Publs. *St. John Baptist* 21, *Christianity and Culture* 40, *Humanism and Christianity, Social Thought of the Old Testament, Commentary to the Apocalypse of St. John* 50, *Commentary to the Ecclesiastes* 52, *Introduction to the Old Testament* 55, *Commentary to Isaiah, Chap. 1-12* 56-, *Meaning of Christian Agape* 56, *Die Orthodoxe Kirche in griechischem Licht* 59-60, *Ein orthodoxes Bekenntnis* 66.
Akidimia Athinon, Odos Panepistimiou, Athens, Greece.

Brattain, Walter H., B.S., M.A., D.PHIL.; American research physicist; b. 10 Feb. 1902; ed. Whitman Coll., Oregon and Minnesota Univs.
Research physicist Radio Section, Bureau of Standards 28-29, Bell Telephone Laboratories Inc. 29-41, 44-67; Columbia Univ. War Research Div. 42-43; Visiting Lecturer, Harvard Univ. 52-53; Visiting Prof. of Physics, Whitman Coll., Walla Walla, Washington; mem. Nat. Acad. of Sciences; Stuart Ballantine Medal 52, John Scott Medal 55 (both with Dr. John Bardeen), Nobel Prize in Physics 56 (with Dr. John Bardeen and Dr. William Shockley); Fellow American Physical Soc., American Acad. of Arts and Sciences; mem. Franklin Inst.; Hon. D.Sc. (Minnesota and Portland Univs., Whitman, Gustavus Adolphus and Union Colls.).
1019 Alvarado Terrace, Washington 99362, U.S.A.
Telephone: 529-4627.

Bratteli, Trygve Martin; Norwegian journalist and politician; b. 11 Jan. 1910; ed. public elementary school.
Editor Socialist newspaper *Folkets Frihet* 34; Editor fortnightly journal *Arbeider-Ungdommen*; Sec. Labour League of Youth 34-40; Vice-Chair. Norwegian Labour Party 45-65, Chair. 65-; Chair. Defence Comm. 46-49; M.P. 50-; Minister of Finance Nov. 51-55 and 56-60, of Communications 60-64; Chair. Labour Party Parliamentary Group 64-.
The Storting, Oslo; Home: Ullevålsvegen 58, Oslo, Norway.
Telephone: 603525.

Brauer, Jerald Carl, A.B., B.D., PH.D.; American church historian and educator; b. 16 Sept. 1921; ed. Carthage Coll., Northwestern Lutheran Theological Seminary and Univ. of Chicago.
Minister, United Lutheran Church of America 51-;

Instructor, Church History and History of Christian Thought, Union Theological Seminary, New York City 48-50; Asst. Prof. of Church History, Federated Theological Faculty, Univ. of Chicago 50-54, Assoc. Prof. 54-60, Dean, Federated Theological Faculty 55-60; Visiting Prof. Univ. of Frankfurt 61; mem. Board of Dirs. Inst. for Advanced Pastoral Educ. and Augustana Coll.; mem. Board of Theological Educ., Lutheran Church in America (Pres. 62); Del. of Lutheran Church in America to Lutheran World Fed. Assembly, Helsinki 63; Observer to Vatican Council Sessions 64, 65.

Publs. *Protestantism in America* 53, rev. edn. 66, *Luther and the Reformation* (with Jaroslav Pelikan) 53, *Basic Questions for the Christian Scholar* 54; Editor: *The Future of Religions* by Paul Tillich 66, *Essays in Divinity* 8 vols. 67.

5620 Blackstone Avenue, Chicago 37, Illinois, U.S.A. Telephone: HY3-6886.

Brauer, Max; German politician; b. 3 Sept. 1887; ed. elementary school.

Employed by Produktion co-operative society 10-14; served First World War 14-18; Provisional Senator Altona 18, Second Burgomaster and Town Treas. 19, Chief Burgomaster 24; mem. Prussian Privy Council, Schleswig-Holstein Provincial Council and Provincial Cttee. 24; left Germany 33; delegated by L.N. as adviser on local govt. and admin. affairs to Gen. Chiang Kai-shek; lecturer U.S.A. 36; U.S. citizen 39; Chair. German Labour Del. to American Fed. of Labour 39; returned to Germany as Chair. A.F.L. Study Comm. 46; mem. of Senate and First Burgomaster of Hansestadt Hamburg Nov. 46-54, Pres. 58; rep. of Hamburg, Frankfurter Länderrat 48; mem. Deutscher Bundestag 61-65, Council of Europe, Western European Union; mem. Board Alte Volksfürsorge; Pres. Deutscher Bühnenverein; Social Democratic Party.

Publs. *State Policy of Hamburg* 47, *Public Economy—yesterday, today and tomorrow* 51.

Neuer Wall 41, 2 Hamburg 39, German Federal Republic.

Braun, Baron Sigismund von; German diplomatist; b. 15 April 1911; ed. Univs. of Hamburg, Berlin, and Cincinnati, Ohio.

Counsellor, German Embassy, London 53-58; Chief of Protocol, Foreign Office, Bonn 58-62; Observer (with rank of Ambassador) of German Federal Republic to the United Nations 62-; Dr. h.c. and numerous decorations.

119 East 65th Street, New York City 21, N.Y., U.S.A.

Braun, Wernher von, B.S., PH.D.; American scientist (b. German, naturalized American 55); b. 23 March 1912; ed. Federal Inst. Technology, Zürich, Inst. Technology, Berlin, and Univ. of Berlin.

Research on Liquid Fuels since 30; research with German Ordnance Dept. on liquid fuel rocket development 32; tested successful launchings of two rudimentary liquid fuel rockets of the A-2 type which reached altitudes of 1.6 miles 34; Technical Dir. of Peenemuende Rocket and Devt. Centre 37; Project Dir. Research and Devt. Service, U.S. Army Ordnance Corps, Fort Bliss, Texas 45; Adviser for V-2 test firings at White Sands Proving Grounds, New Mexico; Dir. Devt. Operations Div., Army Ballistic Missile Agency, Redstone Arsenal, Ala. 56- (responsible for Jupiter IRBM and Explorer series of Satellites); Dir. George C. Marshall Space Flight Center, Nat. Aeronautics and Space Admin. 60- (responsible for devt. of Saturn launch vehicles for American Lunar Landing Program); Fellow American Inst. of Aeronautics, American Astronautical Soc.; Hon. Fellow Norwegian Interplanetary Soc.; Hon. Fellow Brit. Interplanetary Soc.; Hon. mem. of numerous foreign socs.; Space Flight Award, American Astronautical Soc. 57, Dr. Robert H. Goddard Memorial Trophy 58, Pres. Award for Distinguished Fed. Civilian

Service 59, and others; Hon. D.Sc. (Alabama, St. Louis, Clark, Pittsburgh, Emory and Berlin Univs., Nat. Univ. of Cordoba, Argentina and Canisius, Iowa, Butler, Bradley, D'Youville, Wesleyan and Wagner Colls.); Hon. LL.D. (Univ. of Chattanooga, Adelphi and Iona Colls., N.Y., Penn. Mil. and William Jewell Colls.).

Publs. include *The Mars Project* 52, *Across the Space Frontier* 52, *Space Medicine* 52, co-author *Physics and Medicine of the Upper Atmosphere* 52, *Conquest of the Moon* 53, *Exploration of Mars* 56, *Project Satellite* 58, *First Men to the Moon* 60, *A Journey Through Space and the Atom* 62, (with Frederick I. Ordway) *History of Rocketry and Space Travel* 67, *Space Frontier* 68.

P.O. Box 6822, Huntsville, Ala. 35812, U.S.A.

Braunshteyn, Alexander Yevseevich; Soviet biochemist; b. 1902; ed. Kharkov Medical Inst.

Biochemical Inst., U.S.S.R. People's Commissariat of Health until 36; All-Union Inst. of Experimental Medicine 36-45; Head of Laboratory, Inst. of Biological and Medical Chemistry, U.S.S.R. Acad. of Medical Sciences 45-; mem. U.S.S.R. Acad. of Medical Sciences; Corresp. mem. U.S.S.R. Acad. of Sciences 60-66, mem. 66-; State Prize.

Institute of Biological and Medical Chemistry, U.S.S.R. Academy of Medical Sciences, Pogodinskaya 10, Moscow, U.S.S.R.

Bray, Gen. Robert Napier Hubert Campbell, G.B.E., K.C.B., D.S.O.; British army officer; b. 14 June 1908; ed. Gresham's School, Holt, and Royal Military Coll., Sandhurst.

Second Lieutenant, Duke of Wellington's Regt. 28; Norway, Middle East and North Western Europe 39-45; Brigadier, General Staff, British Army of the Rhine 50-52, Korea 54; Dir. of Land Air Warfare, and Dir. of NATO Standardisation, War Office 54-57; Major-Gen. 54; General Officer Commanding, 56th Infantry Div. (T.A.) 57-59; Commander, Land Forces, Arabian Peninsula 59-61; G.O.C. in C. Southern Command 61-63; Commdr.-in-Chief Allied Forces, N. Europe 63-67; Deputy Supreme Allied Commdr. Europe (SACEUR), North Atlantic Treaty Org. (NATO) 67-.

North Atlantic Treaty Organization, Brussels, Belgium; and c/o Army and Navy Club, Pall Mall, London, S.W.7, England.

Brdička, Rudolf, DR.RER.NAT.SC.; Czech physico-chemist; b. 25 Feb. 1906; ed. Charles Univ., Prague.

Asst., Physico-Chemistry Inst., Charles Univ. 28; Rockefeller Fellowship to Univ. of Calif. 34-35; research work in medical chemistry, Univ. of Würzburg 36; cancer research, Research Dept., Radiotherapeutical Inst., Bulovka Hospital, Prague 39-45; Doc. of Physical Chemistry, Charles Univ. 34, Assoc. Prof. 48, Full Prof. 49, Academician 52; Chief of the Laboratory of Physico-Chemistry, Acad. of Sciences, Prague 52-, Dir. Physico-Chemical Inst. 54-; has taken part in many int. confs. on polarographic research and lectured on that subject abroad; mem. Leopoldina Acad., German Democratic Repub.; awards include Order of Labour 59, State Prize 54.

Publ. *Textbook on Physical Chemistry* (in Czech) 52 (German edn. 58, 61, 62, 63, 65, Bulgarian edn. 65).

Lazarská 5, Prague I, Czechoslovakia.

Bream, Julian, O.B.E.; British guitarist and lutanist; b. 15 July 1933; ed. Royal Coll. of Music.

Began professional career Cheltenham 46, London début 50; tours in Europe and America, appeared at festivals at Aldeburgh, Three Choirs, King's Lynn, Holland, Ansbach, Berlin, and Stratford (Canada); research into Elizabethan Lute music which led to revival of interest in that instrument; has encouraged contemporary English compositions for the guitar; Founder, int. summer school, Wiltshire 65.

c/o Basil Douglas Ltd., 8 St. George's Terrace, London, N.W.1, England.

Breder, Charles M.; American ichthyologist; b. 25 June 1897; ed. High School, Newark.
Scientific Asst. and Fishery Expert with U.S. Bureau of Fisheries 19-21; aquarist N.Y. Aquarium 21-25, Research Assoc., Asst. Dir., Acting Dir., Dir. 25-43; Chair. and Curator Dept. of Fishes and Aquatic Biology, American Museum of Natural History, Ichthyology Dept. 44-65, Curator Emeritus 65-; Visiting Prof. New York Univ. 41-50; Dir. Lerner Marine Laboratory, Bimini, Bahamas 47-57; Advisory Board Cape Haze Marine Laboratory, Florida (now the Mote Marine Laboratory) 57-66, mem. Board of Dirs. 67-; Research Assoc., Bingham Oceanographic Laboratory, Yale Univ. 33-60; Fellow, New York Zoological Soc.; Hon. D.Sc. (Newark Univ.).
Publs. *Field Book of the Marine Fishes of the Atlantic Coast from Labrador to Texas* 29, *Modes of Reproduction in Fishes* (with D. E. Rosen) 66, and technical papers.
Englewood, Florida, RFD 1, Box 452, U.S.A.
Telephone: 813-474-1810.

Breech, Ernest; American industrialist; b. 24 Feb. 1897; ed. Drury Coll., Springfield, and Walton School of Commerce, Univ. of Illinois.
Accountant, Fairbanks, Morse & Co. 17-20; Auditor, Adams and Westlake 20-22; Comptroller, Yellow Cab Manufacturing Co. 23-29; Dir. Yellow Truck and Coach Manufacturing Co., Chicago 27-33; Gen. Asst. Treasurer, Gen. Motors Corpn. N.Y. 29-33, mem. Admin. Cttee. 39-42; Chair. Board North American Aviation Inc. 33-42, Dir. 33-36; Pres. and Dir. Bendix Aviation Corpn. 42-46; Dir. Lehman Corpn., One William Street Fund; Exec. Vice-Pres. and Dir. Ford Motor Co. 46-55, Chair. and Alternate Chief Exec. 55-60, Chair. Finance Cttee. 60-61; Chair. Trans World Airlines 61-; mem. Business Advisory Council, Dept. of Commerce; Hon. LL.D. (Drury Coll., Springfield, Univs. of Missouri, Detroit and Michigan), Dr. Business Admin. (Bowling Green State Univ.).
Trans World Airlines Inc., 10 Richards Road, Kansas City, Missouri, U.S.A.

Breit, Gregory, A.M., PH.D.; American physicist; b. 14 July 1899; ed. Johns Hopkins Univ., Univ. of Leyden (Nat. Research Fellow), and Harvard Univ.
Asst. Prof. of Physics, Minnesota Univ. 23-24; Mathematical Physicist, Dept. of Terrestrial Magnetism, Carnegie Inst. of Washington 24-29; Prof. of Physics, New York Univ. 29-34, Wisconsin Univ. 34-47, Yale Univ. 47-58, Donner Prof. of Physics 58-; Research Assoc., Carnegie Inst. 29-44; Visiting mem. Inst. for Advanced Study, Princeton, New Jersey 35-36; on leave of absence as mem. of Uranium Cttee. (Section S), Office of Scientific Research and Development and other war work 40-45; mem. Nat. Acad. of Sciences; Fellow American Acad. of Arts and Sciences, American Physical Soc., Inst. of Electronic and Electrical Engineers, Geophysical Union; Assoc. Editor. *Physical Review* 27-29, 39-41, 54-56, 61-63, Assoc. Editor, *Proceedings of National Academy of Sciences* 58-60, *Il Nuovo Cimento* 64-; Councillor American Physical Soc. 35-38; mem. Div. of Physical Sciences, Nat. Research Council 32-33, 38-41; Franklin Medal 64; Nat. Medal of Science 67; Hon. D.Sc. (Univ. of Wisconsin).
Publs. *A Test of the Existence of the Conducting Layer* (with M. A. Tuve) 26, *The Effect of Retardation on the Interaction of Two Electrons* 29, *Quantum Theory of Dispersion*, Parts I-V 32, Parts VI and VII 33, *Capture of Slow Neutrons* (with E. Wigner) 36, *Theory of Scattering of Protons by Protons* 36, *Handbuch der Physik*, Vol. 42, part I, *Nuclear Reactions: II, Theory* (with others); and other publications on kindred subjects.
Sloane Physics Laboratory, 2014 Yale Station, Yale University, New Haven, Connecticut 06520, U.S.A.
Telephone: 203-787-3131, Extension 794.

Brekhov, Konstantin Ivanovich; Soviet engineer and politician; b. 07; ed. Kharkov Machine Building Inst.
Engineer, machine-building factories 31-42; mem. C.P.S.U. 31-; Dir. Irkutsk Heavy Machine-Building Works 44-54; Dep. Minister of Building and Road Machine Building, U.S.S.R. 54-57; econ. work, Moscow Region 57-59; Chair. Moscow Regional Econ. Cttee. 59-63; Chair. State Cttee. for Building of Machinery for Chemical and Oil Industries 64-65; Minister for Chemical and Oil Engineering 65-; Cand. mem. Central Cttee. of C.P.S.U. 61-; Deputy to Supreme Soviet of U.S.S.R.
Ministry for Chemical and Oil Engineering, Moscow, U.S.S.R.

Bremer, Fédéric; Belgian physiologist; b. June 1892; ed. Univ. of Brussels.
Honorary Prof. and Dir. Laboratory of Physiopathology, Univ. of Brussels 32-; Pres. Nat. Centre for Neurophysiological and Muscular Research 54; mem. Belgian Acad. of Medicine, Sciences Div. Belgian Royal Acad.; Hon. mem. American Physiological Soc., Biology Soc., Paris, American Acad. of Arts and Sciences, Int. Brain Research Org.; mem. Physiological Soc. of Great Britain; Assoc. mem. Nat. Acad. Medicine of France, and other medical orgs.; Corresp. mem. Inst. de France; Dr. h.c. Univs. of Aix-Marseille, Montpellier, Strasbourg and Utrecht; Grand Officier de l'Ordre de Léopold; Croix de Guerre and Croix du Feu 14-18.
Publs. *L'activité électrique de l'écorce cérébrale* 38, *Some Problems in Neurophysiology* 53.
115 boulevard de Waterloo, Brussels, Belgium.
Telephone: 380844.

Brennan, H.E. Cardinal Francis J.; American ecclesiastic; b. 7 May 1894.
Dean of the Sacred Rota 40-; Prefect of Sacred Congregation for the Sacraments 68-; created Cardinal by Pope Paul VI 67.
Via Donizetti 7, Rome, Italy.

Brennan, Joseph; Irish politician; b. 14 Feb. 1913; ed. primary and technical schools.
Member Donegal County Council and subsidiary Cttees. 45-59; mem. Parl. for Donegal West 51-61, S.W. Donegal 61-; Parl. Sec. to Taoiseach and to Minister for Defence 61-65; Minister for Posts and Telegraphs 65-66, of Social Welfare 66-.
Dunkineely, Co. Donegal; and Ballinclea House, Ballinclea Road, Killiney, Co. Dublin, Ireland.

Brennan, William Joseph, Jr., B.S., LL.B.; American judge; b. 25 April 1906; ed. Pennsylvania and Harvard Univs.
Admitted to New Jersey Bar 31; practised in Newark, N.J. 31-49; Superior Court Judge 49-50, Appellate Division Judge 50-52; Justice, Supreme Court of New Jersey 52-56; Assoc. Justice, Supreme Court of the U.S. 56-; served as Colonel, General Staff Corps, U.S. Army in Second World War; Legion of Merit; Hon. D.C.L. (New York and Colgate Univs.), Hon. S.J.D. (Suffolk Univ.), Hon. LL.D. (Wesleyan, St. John's, Pennsylvania and Rutgers Univs.).
Supreme Court of the United States, Washington, D.C. 20543; and 3037 Dumbarton Avenue, N.W., Washington, D.C., U.S.A.

Brenner, Otto; German trade union official; b. 8 Nov. 1907; ed. elementary school.
Training and occupation as electrician until 33; arrested and sentenced for anti-Nazi activity 33; Founder-mem. of trade union and Social Democrat Party in Hanover 45; District Head, Industriegewerkschaft (IG) Metall für die Bundesrepublik Deutschland, Hanover 47-52, Chair. 52-, First Chair. 56-; mem. Management Board of Fed. of German Trade Unions 54-; Pres. Int. Fed. of Metalworkers 61-; mem. Commercial and Social Council of EEC and Euratom.
Industriegewerkschaft Metall für die Bundesrepublik

Deutschland, Frankfurt, Untermainkai 70-76; Home: 6 Frankfurt am Main, Hammarsköldring 85, German Federal Republic.

Brenner, Sydney, M.B., D.PHIL., F.R.S.; British scientist; b. 13 Jan. 1927; ed. Univ. of the Witwatersrand, Johannesburg, and Oxford Univ.
Lecturer in Physiology, Univ. of Witwatersrand 55-57; mem. Scientific Staff of Medical Research Council at M.R.C. Laboratory of Molecular Biology, Cambridge 57-; Fellow of King's Coll., Cambridge 59-; Foreign Hon. mem. American Acad. of Arts and Sciences; Hon. D.Sc. (Dublin).
Medical Research Council Laboratory of Molecular Biology, Cambridge; Home: 7 Long Road, Cambridge, England.

Bresson, Robert; French film producer; b. 25 Sept. 1907.
Started as painter; made first film 34; awarded many prizes for *Journal d'un Curé de Campagne*.
Films produced include: *Anges du Péché* 43, *Les Dames du Bois de Boulogne* 45, *Journal d'un Curé de Campagne* 51, *Un Condamné à Mort s'est echappé* 56, *Pickpocket* 59, *Le Procès de Jeanne d'Arc* 62, *Lancelot du Lac* 65, *Au Hasard, Balthasar* 66, *Mouchette* 66.
49 Quai Bourbon, Paris 4e, France.

Bret, Paul Louis, B.A., D.PHIL.; French journalist and writer; b. 26 Sept. 1893.
Sub-editor Havas News Agency Paris 28; Asst. Man. Havas London 29, Man. 30; Man. Havas Algiers 42; Man. France-Afrique News Agency Algiers 43; London corresp. *Le Parisien Libéré* 44; Gen. Man. French Press Agency (Agence France-Presse) Paris 47-50; Head Press Div. UNESCO Paris 50; Technical Adviser Société Générale de Presse, Paris 52, Chair. 55-; Chevalier Légion d'Honneur, Croix de Guerre, Chevalier Ordre Léopold, Order Polonia Restituta; Hon. C.B.E.; Commandeur de la Grande Comore.
Publs. *Information et Démocratie* 53, *Au Feu des Evénements: Mémoires d'un Journaliste* 60.
24 rue Henri Heine, Paris 16e, France.
Telephone: 288-68-88.

Bretscher, Willy; Swiss journalist; b. 26 Oct. 1897; ed. District School, Olten, Secondary School, Winterthur, Commercial School of Swiss Merchants' Asscn. and Univ. of Zürich.
Journalist *Neues Winterthurer Tagblatt* 14; Editor *Neue Zürcher Zeitung* 17, Berlin Corresp. 25-29 and Chief Editor 33-67; Vice-Pres. Exec. Cttee. Liberal International; mem. Nat. Council 51-67; Pres. of its Foreign Affairs Cttee. 54-55, 62-63; Pres. Swiss Winston Churchill Foundation.
Publs. *Geschichte der Sozialistischen Bewegung in der Schweiz* 24, *Siebzig Leitartikel* 44, *Die politische Lage der Schweiz am Kriegsende* 45, *Schweizerische Aussenpolitik in der Nachkriegszeit* 51, *Russia by Twilight* 56, *The Defence of the West* 57, *Der Kampf um Berlin* 61, etc.
Freiestrasse 29, 8032 Zürich, Switzerland.

Breuer, Marcel Lajos, M.A., F.A.I.A.; American (b. Hungarian) architect; b. 22 May 1902; ed. Hungarian Public School, and Bauhaus, Weimar.
Teacher Bauhaus, Dessau 25-28; architect Berlin 28-31; travels and architectural comms. Spain, Morocco, Switzerland, Germany, Hungary, Greece, England, Haiti, Pakistan, Japan, Mexico, Venezuela, Brazil, Argentina, Peru 31-35; architect London 35-37; Assoc. Prof. Graduate School of Design Harvard Univ. 37-46; fmr. Partner Walter Gropius and Marcel Breuer, Cambridge, Mass; Vice-Pres. Nat. Inst. Arts and Letters; Fellow, American Acad. Arts and Sciences; Hon. mem. of Architectural Socs. in Colombia, Peru, Argentina; Hon. Dr. Govt. of Hungary; AIA Medal of Honor 65; T. Jefferson Foundation Medal 68; AIA Gold Medal 68.

Publ. *Sun and Shadow* 56 (in Japanese) 57, *Marcel Breuer 1921-1961*.
Office: 635 Madison Avenue, New York 22, N.Y., U.S.A.; and 48 rue Chapon, Paris 3e, France; Home: 628 West Road, New Canaan, Conn., U.S.A.
Telephone: 212-PL8-1766 (Office); 203-WO6-9735 (Home).

Brewer, Gene Cedric; American business executive; b. 17 Oct. 1913; ed. Univ. of Oregon.
U.S. Plywood Corpn. 37-, Supt. Orangeburg, S.C. 43-45, Asst. Man. 46-49; Gen. Man. Shasta Plywood Inc. (subsid. of U.S. Plywood) 49-51, Pres. 51-54; Vice-Pres. (W. Coast Operations) U.S. Plywood Corpn. 54-58; Pres. 58- (now Pres. of U.S. Plywood—Champion Papers); dir. other companies.
Office: 777 3rd Avenue, New York City, N.Y. 10017, U.S.A.

Brewer, George Tilman; Liberian diplomatist; b. 03; ed. Feeder Govt. School, Cuttington Coll. and Liberia Coll.
Commr. Harper Commonwealth District 35-43; Supervisor Maryland County 44-52; Ambassador to Haiti 52-56, to Spain 56-59, to Great Britain 59-64; several times del. to UN.
c/o State Department, Monrovia, Liberia.

Brewster, Daniel Baugh, A.B., LL.B.; American farmer, lawyer and politician; b. 23 Nov. 1923; ed. Gilman School, Baltimore, St. Paul's School, Concord, Princeton Univ., Johns Hopkins Univ. and Univ. of Maryland Law School.
U.S. Marine Corps, rising to Col. 42-; Lawyer 49-; Maryland House of Delegates 50-58; U.S. House of Reps. 59-62, mem. House Armed Services Cttee. 59-62; U.S. Senator from Maryland 63-; mem. Senate Armed Services Cttee., and other Senate cttees.; Democrat.
U.S. Senate, Washington, D.C. 20510 U.S.A.

Brewster, Kingman, Jr.; American educator; b. 17 June 1919; ed. Yale Univ. and Harvard Univ.
Chairman *Yale Daily News* 40-41; Special Asst. Co-ordinator, Inter-American Affairs 41; Research Assoc.; Dept. of Economics, Mass. Inst. of Technology 49-50, Asst. Prof. of Law, Harvard Univ. 50-53, Prof. 53-60; Provost, Yale Univ. 60-63, Pres. 63-; U.S. Naval Reserve 42-46; Hon. LL.D. from numerous Univs.
Publs. *Antitrust and American Business Abroad* (with M. Katz) 59, *Law of International Transactions and Relations* 60.
43 Hillhouse Avenue, New Haven, Connecticut, U.S.A.

Breycha-Vauthier, Arthur, D.IUR., DR.RER. POL.; Austrian librarian and diplomatist; b. 1 July 1903; ed. Theresianum, Vienna, and Univs. of Vienna, Louvain, London and Innsbruck.
Law Librarian, League of Nations Library 28, Asst. Librarian 34-37, Acting Librarian 37-45; Prof. Geneva Library School 39-64; Asst. Sec. Int. Fed. of Library Asscns. 29-, Treas. 58-; Chief Librarian, UN Library, Geneva 46-64, Librarian Emeritus 64-; Ambassador to Lebanon, concurrently to Syria, Jordan, Saudi Arabia, Iraq and Kuwait 64-68; Dir. Diplomatic Academy.
Publs. *Sources of Information—a Handbook of the Publications of the League of Nations* 39, *La Stirpe trentina di Giovanni Segantini* 59, *Le fonctionnaire international* 59, *Internationale Bibliotheksarbeit* 60, *Die Zeitschriften der Oesterreichischen Emigration* 60, *Tantur* 61, *Metternich-Maximen* 62, *Documentación internacional* 62; Editor *Actes du Conseil de la F.I.A.B.*, Vols. I-XXVII, *Vital Problems of International Libraries* 65.
Favoritenstrasse 15, Vienna IV, Austria.

Brezhnev, Leonid Ilyich; Soviet politician; b. 19 Dec. 1906; ed. secondary school for Land Organization and Reclamation, Kursk, and Dnieprodzerzhinsk Metallurgical Inst.

Chief of District Land Dept., Deputy Chair. of District Exec. Cttee., later Deputy Chief, Urals Regional Land Dept. 27-30; Engineer, Dnieprodzerzhinsk Metallurgical Plant 31-35; Soviet Army 35-36; Deputy Chair. Exec. Cttee. Dnieprodzerzhinsk City Council, Chief of Dept., Dniepropetrovsk Regional Party Cttee. 37-39, Sec. 39-41; Political Officer, Soviet Army 41-46; First Sec. Zaporozhye Regional Party Cttee., Ukraine C.P. 46-47, Dniepropetrovsk Regional Party Cttee. 47-50; First Sec. Central Cttee., C.P. of Moldavia 50-52; mem. Central Cttee. of C.P.S.U. 52-, Alt. mem. Presidium 52-53, Sec. Central Cttee. of C.P.S.U. 52-53; Deputy Chief Central Political Dept., Soviet Army and Navy 53-54; Second Sec. Central Cttee. of Kazakh C.P. 54, First Sec. 55-56; Alt. mem. Presidium Central Cttee. of C.P.S.U. 56-57, mem. 57-66, mem. Politburo 66-; Sec. Central Cttee. of C.P.S.U. 56-60; Chair. of Presidium of Supreme Soviet of U.S.S.R. 60-64, mem. Sept. 65-; Sec. Central Cttee. of C.P.S.U. 63, First Sec. 64-66, Gen. Sec. 66-; Hero of Socialist Labour 61, Hero of the Soviet Union, three Orders of Lenin, two Orders of Red Banner, and other decorations.
Central Committee of the Communist Party of the Soviet Union, 4 Staraya ploshchad, Moscow, U.S.S.R.

Bridge, George Wilfred, F.C.I.I.; British company director; b. 1 Jan. 1894; ed. Westoe Road Secondary School, South Shields.
Legal and General Assurance Soc. Ltd. 19-, Gen. Manager 46-59, Dep. Chair. 59-; Dep. Chair., Gresham Life Assurance Soc. Ltd. 58-, Gresham Fire and Accident Insurance Soc. Ltd. 58-; Chair. City Centre Properties 63-; Pres. Insurance Inst. of London 51-52, Chartered Insurance Inst. 54-55.
8 Heath Rise, Kersfield Road, Putney, S.W.15, England. Telephone: 01-788-1703.

Bridgeford, Lt.-Gen. Sir William, K.B.E., C.B., M.C.; Australian army officer; b. 28 July 1894; ed. Ballarat High School and Duntroon Royal Military Coll.
Served Army in Egypt and France; Brigade Major, 12th and 18th Infantry Brigades and 3rd Cavalry Brigade 19-24; Instructor, Duntroon Royal Mil. Coll. 25, Staff Coll., Quetta, India 26-27; Brigade Major, 6th Cavalry Brigade, Adelaide 28-31; Training Directorate, Army H.Q. 32-34; G.S.O. 2nd Cavalry Division, Victoria 34-38; Instructor, Army Command and Staff School 38; Imperial Defence Coll., London 39; Colonel 39, Mil. Liaison Officer, London; Brigadier 40; Commdr. 25th Infantry Brigade; Deputy Adjutant and Q.M.G. 1st Australian Corps, Middle East 40; Major-Gen. 42; Commdr. 3rd Australian Armoured Division 43; Deputy Adjutant and Q.M.G., New Guinea Force 43-44; Commdr. 3rd Australian Division, A.I.F. 44-45; Q.M.G., Army H.Q., Melbourne 46-51, C.-in-C., British Commonwealth Forces in Korea 51-53; G.O.C., Eastern Command 51-53; Chief Exec. Officer, Olympic Games, Melbourne 53-56; Greek Military Cross, U.S. Legion of Merit.
c/o Naval and Military Club, Alfred Place, Melbourne, Australia.

Bridgeman, Hon. Sir Maurice Richard, K.B.E., K.ST.J.; British businessman; b. 26 Jan. 1904; ed. Eton Coll. and Trinity Coll., Cambridge.
Joined Anglo-Iranian Oil Co. 26; Adviser Ministry of Economic Warfare 39; Sec. Oil Control Board 40; Adviser Govt. of India 42; Principal Asst. Sec. (Petroleum Div.) Ministry of Fuel and Power 44-46; mem. Advisory Council on Middle East Trade 58-61; Chair. and Managing Dir. British Petroleum Co. 60-; Dir. Nat. Provincial Bank.
10 Kylestrome House, Ebury Street, London, S.W.1; The Glebe House, Selham, Petworth, Sussex, England. Telephone: Lodsworth 205.

Bridges, 1st Baron, cr. 57, of Headley; **Edward Bridges,** K.G., P.C., G.C.B., G.C.V.O., M.C., F.R.S.; British civil servant (retd.); b. 4 Aug. 1892; ed. Eton and Magdalen Coll., Oxford.
Served with 4th Oxford and Bucks. Light Infantry, Great War; entered Treasury 19, Principal Asst. Sec. 37-38; Sec. of the Cabinet 38-Dec. 46; Permanent Sec. to the Treasury 45-56 (retd.); Chair. Pilgrim Trust; Chancellor of Reading Univ. 59-; Fellow of All Souls Coll., Oxford 20-27 and 54; Chair. of Govs., London School of Economics; Hon. Fellow Magdalen Coll., Oxford, University Coll., Cambridge; Hon. LL.D. (Bristol, London, Cambridge, Leicester, Liverpool and Hong Kong); Hon. D.Litt. (Reading), Hon. D.C.L. (Oxford).
Publ. *The Treasury* 64.
Goodman's Furze, Headley, Epsom, Surrey, England. Telephone: Headley 265.

Briggs, Asa, M.A., B.SC.; British historian; b. 7 May 1921; ed. Keighley Grammar School and Sidney Sussex Coll., Cambridge.
Fellow, Worcester Coll., Oxford 45-55, Reader in Recent Social and Econ. History, Univ. of Oxford 50-55; Prof. of Modern History, Leeds Univ. 55-61; Pro-Vice Chancellor, Prof. of History, Univ. of Sussex 61-, Dean of Social Studies 61-65, Vice-Chancellor 67-; Deputy Pres. Workers Educational Asscn. 54-58, Pres. 58-67; mem. Univ. Grants Cttee. 58-67; Hon. D.Litt.
Publs. *Patterns of Peacemaking* (with D. Thomson and E. Meyer) 45, *History of Birmingham, 1865-1938* 52, *Victorian People* 54, *Friends of the People* 56, *The Age of Improvement* 59, Ed. *Chartist Studies* 59, *History of Broadcasting*, Vol. I 61, Vol. II 65, *Victorian Cities* 63.
Ashcombe House, Lewes, Sussex, England. Telephone: Lewes 4794.

Briggs, Ellis Ormsbee, A.B.; American diplomatist and writer; b. 1 Dec. 1899; ed. Dartmouth Coll.
Instructor, Robert Coll., Constantinople 21-23; contrib. to magazines 23-25; joined Foreign Service 25 and began career as Vice-Consul, Callao-Lima 26; later became Asst. Chief, Div. of American Republics, State Dept. 37; First Sec. Santiago 40, Havana 41; Counsellor Havana 44; Chief of Div. of Caribbean and Central American Affairs, State Dept. 44; Ambassador to Dominican Republic 44; Counsellor and later Minister of Embassy, Chungking 45; Dir. Office of American Republic Affairs, State Dept. 45-47; Ambassador to Uruguay 47-49; Ambassador to Czechoslovakia 49-52; Ambassador to Korea 52-55; Ambassador to Peru 55-56; Ambassador to Brazil 56-59, to Greece 59-62, to Spain 62; Visiting Prof. of Int. Studies, Univ. of South Carolina 65; Hon. LL.D. (Dartmouth Coll., Bowdoin Coll., Colby Coll., Ricker Coll.); Medal of Freedom 55.
Publs. *Shots Heard Round World* 57, *Farewell to Foggy Bottom* 64, *Anatomy of Diplomacy* 68.
3 Pleasant Street, Hanover, New Hampshire, U.S.A.

Briggs, Sir (Alfred) George Ernest, Kt.; British businessman; b. 12 Feb. 1900; ed. Oundle School.
Deputy Controller Ministry of Supply 42-45, 51-52; Chair. Gen. Refractories Ltd.; Dir. Thomas Tilling Ltd., Payne Products Int. Ltd., Package Deal Construction Ltd., Court Line, London Electricity Board.
Courtyard House, Lavershot Hall, London Road, Sunningdale, Berkshire, England.

Brilej, Joža, LL.D.; Yugoslav lawyer and diplomatist; b. 10; ed. Univ. of Ljubljana.
Barrister in Ljubljana until 41; Organiser of Liberation Movement in Slovenia; Colonel, Nat. Liberation Army until 45; mem. Slovene Nat. Assembly; mem. Nat. Council of Slovenia 43; Head of Political Dept., Ministry of Foreign Affairs until 50, when apptd. Asst. Foreign Minister; Ambassador to Great Britain 50-53;

Perm. Rep to UN 54-57; fmr. Counsellor of State for Foreign Affairs; Ambassador to United Arab Repub. 62-63; Pres. Cttee. for Economic Relations with Foreign Countries and mem. Federal Exec. Council 63-; Deputy to Federal Assembly; Yugoslav Orders for Bravery, of Brotherhood and Unity (1st Class), of Merit for the People (2nd Class), of Labour (1st Class), of Partisan Star (1st Class), etc.
Federal Executive Council, Belgrade, Yugoslavia.

Brillouin, Léon, D.SC.; French physicist; b. 7 Aug. 1889; ed. Paris Ecole Normale Supérieure.
Dir. Laboratory of Coll. de France 23-28; Prof. Science Faculty of Paris Univ. 28-32; Prof. of Theoretical Physics, Coll. de France 32-48; Prof. Columbia Univ., New York 43-45; Dean of Faculty of Science, Ecole Libre des Hautes Etudes, New York; Prof. Harvard Univ. 46-49; Int. Business Machines Corpn. 49-54; Adj. Prof. Columbia Univ. 54-; mem. Nat. Acad. of Sciences, Washington, D.C.
Publs. *Les mesures en haute fréquence* 23, *La théorie des quanta et l'atome de Bohr* 23, *Selected papers on wave mechanics* 28, *Statistiques quantiques* 30, *L'atome de Bohr* 31, *Quantenstatistik* 33, *Notions de Mathématiques pour les sciences expérimentales* 35, *Les tenseurs en Mécanique et en Elasticité* 38, *Wave Propagation in Periodic Structures* 46, *Propagations des Ondes* 55, *Science and Information Theory* 56, 60, *Wave propagation and group velocity* 60, *Vie Matière et Observation* 60.
88 Central Park West, New York, N.Y. 10023, U.S.A.

Brimelow, Sir Thomas, K.C.M.G., O.B.E.; British diplomatist; b. 25 Oct. 1915; ed. New Mills Grammar School and Oriel Coll., Oxford.
Probationer Vice-Consul, Danzig 38; Consulate, Riga 39, Acting Consul 40; served in Consulate-Gen., New York 40; in charge of Consular Section of Embassy, Moscow 42-45; Foreign Office 45; First Sec. (Commercial) and Consul, Havana 48, Chargé d'Affaires 48, 49, 51; in Moscow 51-54; Counsellor (Commercial) Ankara 54-56; Head of Northern Dept., Foreign Office 56-60; Counsellor, Washington 60-63; Minister, Moscow 63-66; Ambassador to Poland 66-.
British Embassy, Warsaw, Poland.
Telephone: 281001.

Brimmer, Andrew Felton, M.A., PH.D.; American economist and government official; b. 13 Sept. 1926; ed. Univ. of Washington, Univs. of Delhi and Bombay (India), and Harvard Univ.
Teaching Fellow, Harvard Univ. 54-55; Economist, Fed. Reserve Bank of New York 55-58; Asst. Prof. of Econs. Michigan State Univ. 58-61, Asst. Prof. of Finance, Wharton School, Univ. of Pa. 61-63; Deputy Asst. Sec. for Econ. Affairs, U.S. Dept. of Commerce 63-65, Asst. Sec. 65-66; mem. Board of Govs. Fed. Reserve System March 66-; Govt. Man of Year, Nat. Business League 63; Arthur S. Flemming Award 66; Russwurm Award 66.
Publs. *Life Insurance Companies in the Capital Market* 62, *Survey of Mutual Fund Investors* (with Arthur Freedman) 63.
Office: Board of Governors, Federal Reserve System, 20th and Constitution Avenue, N.W., Washington, D.C. 20551; Home: 4611-29th Place, N.W., Washington, D.C. 20008, U.S.A.

Brinckerhoff, Charles M.; American mining executive; b. 15 March 1901; ed. Columbia Coll. and Columbia School of Mines.
Phelps-Dodge Corpn., Arizona, Inspiration Consolidated Copper Co., Andes Copper Mining Co. 25-48; Gen. Man. Chile Exploration Co., Chile 48-56, Exec. Vice-Pres. 57-58; Pres. and Dir. Anaconda Co. 58-64, Vice-Chair. and Chief Exec. Officer 64-65, Chair. and Chief Exec. Officer 65-; official of other companies.
Anaconda Co., 25 Broadway, New York City 4, N.Y., U.S.A.

Brink, Rt. Rev. Cornelius Bertie, B.A.; South African ecclesiastic; b. 01; ed. Univ. of Stellenbosch and Theological Seminary, Stellenbosch.
Ordained Minister 28; Moderator for the Transvaal Province, South African Dutch Reformed Church 45; mem. Council of Univ. of Witwatersrand, Exec. Council of the South African Bureau for Racial Affairs, Central Cttee. of the World Council of Churches, Exec. Cttee. of the World Presbyterian Alliance; Transvaal Editor *Die Kerkbode*; mem. Die Suid-Afrikaanse Akademie vir Wetenskap en Kuns.
49 Milner Street, Waterkloof, Pretoria, Republic of South Africa.

Brink, Johannes Roelof Maria van den, DR. ECON.; Netherlands banker and politician; b. 15; ed. Catholic High School, Tilburg.
With Ministry of Commerce and Industry 40-42; Prof. Roman Catholic Univ., Nijmegen 45-48; mem. First Chamber, States-Gen. 45-48; Minister of Economic Affairs 48-52; Gen. Adviser Amsterdam-Rotterdam Bank, N.V., and Incasso-Bank, N.V. 52-53, Gen. Man. 54-; Chair. Supervisory Board, Algemene Kunstzijde Unie N.V. (AKU).
Herengracht 595, Amsterdam, Netherlands.

Brinckmann, Rudolf, D.IUR.; German banker; b. 8 Feb. 1889; ed. Goethe-Gymnasium, Frankfurt am Main, and School for Oriental Languages, Berlin.
Deutsche Bank, Constantinople 15-18, Hamburg 18-19; with M. M. Warburg & Co. 20-, Gen. Partner 38-, name changed to Brinckmann, Wirtz & Co., Hamburg 41; Chair. Board C. H. F. Müller G.m.b.H.; Dir. Nord-Deutsche Versicherungs-Gesellschaft, Deutsche Gesellschaft für Wertpapiersparen m.b.H., Hemmor Zement A.G., Bank for Int. Settlements; Pres. German-Iranian Chamber of Commerce; Chair. Budget Comm. of Int. Chamber of Commerce, Paris; Grosses Verdienstkreuz mit Stern; Order of Homayoun (Iran).
c/o Brinckmann, Wirtz & Co., 2 Hamburg 1, Ferdinandstrasse 75, German Federal Republic.
Telephone: Hamburg 33-99-91.

Brinton, (Clarence) Crane; American historian; b. 2 Feb. 1898; ed. Harvard and Oxford Univs.
Instructor and Tutor, Harvard Univ. 23-28, Asst. Prof. and Tutor 28-35, Assoc. Prof. and Tutor 35-42, Prof. 42-; Senior Fellow, Soc. of Fellows 39-, Chair. 42-; Special Asst. Office of Strategic Services, European Theatre of Operations, U.S. Army 42-45; mem. American Historical Assen., Royal Historical Soc., Int. Inst. of Arts and Letters, etc.; Chevalier Légion d'Honneur (France).
Publs. include: *The United States and Britain* 45, *From Many One* 48, *Ideas and Men* 50, *The Temper of Western Europe* 53, *The Shaping of the Modern Mind* 53, *A History of Civilisation* (with others) 55, revised 60, *A History of Western Morals* 59, *The Fate of Man* 61, *Anatomy of Revolution, Nietzsche* (revised edn.) 65, *The Political Ideas of the English Romanticists* 67.
60 Buckingham Street, Cambridge, Mass 02138, U.S.A.
Telephone: 354-1432.

Brion, Marcel; French writer; b. 21 Nov. 1895; ed. Collège Champittet, Lausanne and Faculty of Law, Aix-en-Provence.
Lawyer 20-24; writer 25-; mem. Académie Française 64-; Grand Prix de Littérature, Académie Française 53, Prix des Ambassadeurs 55, Prix littéraire de Monaco 56; Officier, Légion d'Honneur, Officier, Couronne d'Italie, Officier, Ordre du Mérite Italien.
Publs. include *Château d'Ombres* 43, *Goethe* 50, *Léonard de Vinci* 54, *Robert Schumann et l'âme romantique* 56, *Romantic Art* 58, *La chanson de l'oiseau étranger* 60, *La ville de sable* 62, *L'Art abstrait, L'Art fantastique, L'Allemagne romantique* (2 vols.) 63, *La Folie Céladon*

63, *La Rose de cire* 64, *L'enchanteur, Les escales de la haute nuit* 65, *De l'autre côté de la forêt* 66, *La Peinture romantique* 66.
32 rue de Bac, Paris 7e, France.

Brisac, Gen. Pierre, B. es sc., B. es L.; French army officer and administrator; b. 3 April 1897; ed. Lycée Henri IV, Paris, Lycées, Avignon, Nîmes; Ecole Polytechnique; Ecole d'Artillerie de Fontainebleau; Ecole de Cavalerie de Saumur; Ecole Supérieure de Guerre. Joined Artillery 15, Sub-Lieut. 16, Lieut. 18, Capt. 26; Syria 27-30, Morocco 35-37; Staff Officer 39-40, Lieut.-Col. 41, Col. 42; Chief of Staff, Org. of Army Resistance 44; Gen. of Brigade 44; Commdt. Ecole Polytechnique 45-50, 2nd Div. Infantry 50-53; Dep. C.-in-C. French Army in Germany 53-54; Gen. de Corps d'Armée 55; Dep. Chief of Gen. Staff (Logistics and Admin.) SHAPE 55-57; Dep. Sec.-Gen. WEU and Head of Secr., Perm. Cttee. on Armaments 59-64; Grand Officier, Légion d'Honneur; Croix de Guerre 14-18, 39-45; Médaille de la Résistance; Médaille de l'Aéronautique.
26 Parc de la Bérengère, 92 St. Cloud, S.-et-O., France.

Brittain, Vera, M.A. (wife of George Catlin, *q.v.*); British writer; ed. St. Monica's, Kingswood, Surrey, and Somerville Coll., Oxford.
President, Married Women's Asscn.; Hon. Life Pres. Soc. of Women Writers and Journalists; Vice-Pres. Women's Int. League for Peace and Freedom, Nat. Peace Council; Chair. Emeritus Board Peace News Ltd.; Fellow Royal Soc. of Literature; mem. P.E.N.; numerous overseas lecture tours.
Publs. Testament of Youth 33, *Honourable Estate* 36, *Thrice a Stranger* 38, *Testament of Friendship* 40, *England's Hour* 41, *Humiliation with Honour* 42, *Account Rendered* 45, *On Becoming a Writer* 47, *Born 1925: A Novel of Youth* 49, *Valiant Pilgrim* 50, *Lady into Woman* 53, *Testament of Experience* 57, Editor *Letters of Winifred Holtby and Vera Brittain* 60, *Pethick-Lawrence: A Portrait* 63, *The Rebel Passion: A Short History of some Pioneer Peacemakers* 64, *Envoy Extraordinary: An impression of Vijaya Lakshmi Pandit* 65, *Radclyffe Hall—A Case of Obscenity?* 68.
4 Whitehall Court, London, S.W.1, England.
Telephone: 01-829-5250.

Britten, (Edward) Benjamin, O.M., C.H.; British composer; b. 22 Nov. 1913; ed. Gresham's School, Holt, and Royal Coll. of Music, London.
Hon. D.Mus. (Belfast, Cambridge, Nottingham, Hull, Oxford, Manchester, London, Leicester); Hanseatic Goethe Prize 62, Aspen Award and Royal Philharmonic Soc. Gold Medal 64, Sibelius Prize 65.
Works include: *Simple Symphony* 23-26, *Sinfonietta* 32, *Phantasy* 32, *A Boy Was Born* 32-33, *Suite for Violin and Piano* 34-35, *Friday Afternoons* 35, *Our Hunting Fathers* 36, *Soirées Musicales I* 36, *II* 41, *Variations on a Theme of Frank Bridge* 37, *On This Island* 37, *Mont Juic* (with Lennox Berkeley) 38, *Piano Concerto No. 1 in D Major* 38, *Violin Concerto No. 1 in D Minor* 39, *Kermesse Canadienne* 39, *Ballad of Heroes* 39, *Les Illuminations* 39, *Diversions* 40, *Seven Sonnets of Michelangelo* 40, *Sinfonia de Requiem* 40, *String Quartet No. 1 in D Major* 41, *Scottish Ballad* 41, *Hymn to St. Cecilia* 42, *A Ceremony of Carols* 42, *Rejoice in the Lamb* 43, *Prelude and Fugue* 43, *Serenade* 43, *Festival Te Deum* 45, *String Quartet No. 2 in C* 45, *Peter Grimes* 44-45, *Holy Sonnets of John Donne* 45, *Young Person's Guide to the Orchestra* 45, *The Rape of Lucretia* 46, *Albert Herring* 47, *Canticle I* (Francis Quarles) 47, *A Charm of Lullabies* 47, *Saint Nicolas* (cantata) 48, *The Beggars' Opera* (new version) 48, *Let's Make an Opera* 49, *Spring Symphony* 49, *Billy Budd* 51, *Canticle II* (Abraham and Isaac) 52, *Gloriana* 53, *Winter Words* (Hardy) 53, *Turn of the Screw* 54, *Canticle III* (Sitwell) 54, *Prince of the Pagodas* (ballet) 56, *Six Chinese Songs* 58, *Noye's Fludde* (opera) 58, *Nocturne* 58, *6 Hölderlin Fragments* 58-59, *Cantata*

Academica 59, *Missa Brevis* 59, *A Midsummer Night's Dream* (opera) 60, *Sonata in C* (cello and piano) 61, *War Requiem* 62, *Psalm 150* 63, *Cantata Misericordium* 63, *Symphony for Violoncello and Orchestra* 64, *Curlew River* (church parable) 64, *Cello Suite* 64, *Songs and Proverbs by William Blake, Voices for Today, Poet's Echo* 65, *The Burning Fiery Furnace* (church parable) 66, *The Golden Vanity* (Vaudeville for boys voices and piano), *The Building of the House* (overture with chorus), *Second Suite for Solo Cello, The Prodigal Son* (church parable) 68.
The Red House, Aldeburgh, Suffolk, England.

Britton, Cedric John Charles, M.D., CH.B., D.P.H., F.C. PATH.; British consulting physician; b. 04; ed. Nelson Coll. N.Z., Univ. of Otago, and Middlesex Hospital, London.
Bacteriologist, Univ. of Otago 31; Asst. Pathologist, The Middlesex Hospital 32-33 and 37-46, Christchurch Hospital, N.Z. 34-36; now Physician-in-charge Dept. Allergy and Hon. Hæmatologist, Prince of Wales's Hospital, London; Pathologist and Allergist, St. Andrew's Hospital, London; Hon. Pathologist, Finchley Memorial Hospital and Hendon District Hospital; Treas., Asscn. British Allergists; Councillor British Medical Asscn.; mem. Int. Soc. of Allergy, Int. Soc. of Haematology, British and European Socs. of Haematology, Pathology Soc. of Great Britain and Ireland, Asscn. Clinical Pathologists, American Acad. of Sciences; hon. mem. Argentine and French Allergy Societies.
Publs. *Disorders of the Blood* (10th edn.) 68, *Bone Marrow Biopsy* 49.
35 Harley Street, London, W.1, England.

Brizola, Leonel Moura; Brazilian politician; b. 22; ed. Engineering School of Rio Grande do Sul.
State Dep. 47-51, 51-58; fmr. Sec. of Public Works; Lord Mayor of Pôrto Alegre 55; Gov. of Rio Grande do Sul 58-62; Fed. Dep. to Nat. Assembly for Rio Grande do Sul, expelled from Nat. Assembly April 64; fmr. Leader of Labour Party.
Montevideo, Uruguay.

Broad, Charlie Dunbar, LITT.D., F.B.A.; British philosopher; b. 30 Dec. 1887; ed. Dulwich Coll. and Trinity Coll., Cambridge.
Fellow Trinity Coll. 11-17; Lecturer in Philosophy Univ. Coll. Dundee 14-20; Prof. of Philosophy Bristol Univ. 20-23; Fellow and Lecturer in Moral Science Trinity Coll., Cambridge 23-33; Knightbridge Prof. Moral Philosophy, Cambridge Univ. 33-53, Prof. Emeritus 53-; Visiting Prof. Univ. of Michigan 53-54; Flint Prof. of Philosophy, Univ. of California 54; Fellow, Royal Swedish Acad. of Sciences, American Acad. Arts and Sciences, Société Royale des Lettres de Lund; Hon. LL.D. (Aberdeen, Bristol Univs. and Trinity Coll., Dublin), Hon. Dr. Phil. (Uppsala).
Publs. *Perception, Physics and Reality, Scientific Thought, Mind and its Place in Nature, The Philosophy of Francis Bacon, Five Types of Ethical Theory, Examination of McTaggart's Philosophy, Ethics and History of Philosophy, Religion, Philosophy and Psychical Research, Lectures on Psychical Research.*
Trinity College, Cambridge, England.
Telephone: Cambridge 58201.

Broadley, Sir Herbert, K.B.E.; British international civil servant; b. 23 Nov. 1892; ed. King Edward VI Grammar School, Louth and Birkbeck Coll., Univ. of London.
Entered British Civil Service 12; served in India Office (Mil. Dept.) 12-20; Board of Trade 20-26; Sec. Imperial Customs Conf. 21, German (Reparations) Act Cttee. 21, and Imperial Economic Cttee. 25-26; resigned from Civil Service 26, and joined firm of W. S. Crawford Ltd. (Advertising Agents) 27; Dir. W. S. Crawford Ltd. and Managing Dir. of Berlin Branch 27-32, in charge of

Distribution and Research Dept. London 32-39; Ministry of Food 39, Asst. Sec. Nov. 39, Principal Asst. Sec. 40, Deputy Sec. 41, Second Sec. 45-48, Leader U.K. Dels. Int. Wheat Conferences 47, 48; Deputy Dir.-Gen. FAO of UN 48-58, Acting Dir. Gen. 56; Rep. for the U.K., UN Children's Fund 58-; Gov. Birkbeck Coll. 64-; Commdr. Order of the Crown (Belgium) 48.
Publ. *The People's Food* (with the late Sir William Crawford) 38.
c/o United Nations' Children's Fund, Stratford Place, London, W.1; Home: Hollingsworth, Redlands Lane, Ewshot, Farnham, Surrey, England.
Telephone: Crondall 437 (Home); 01-629-1880 (Office).

Broches, Aron, LL.D.; Netherlands lawyer; b. 2 March 1914; ed. Univ. of Amsterdam and Fordham Univ. Law School.
Legal adviser, Netherlands Economic Mission and Netherlands Embassy, New York and Washington, D.C., 42-46; Sec. Neths. Del. to U.N. Monetary and Financial Conf., Bretton Woods 44; Sec. and Legal Adviser, Neths. Del. to Inaugural Meeting, Int. Monetary Fund and Int. Bank for Reconstruction and Development 46; Attorney in Legal Dept., I.B.R.D. 46-51, Asst. Gen. Counsel 51-56, Dir. Legal Dept. and Assoc. Gen. Counsel 56-59, Gen. Counsel 59-; mem. President's Council 65-; Sec.-Gen. Int. Centre for Settlement of Investment Disputes 67-; Chief I.B.R.D. Econ. Survey Mission to Nigeria 53-54.
2600 Tilden Place, Washington, D.C. 20008, U.S.A.
Telephone: EM2-3335.

Brøchner- Mortensen, Knud, M.D.; Danish physician; b. 4 July 1906; ed. Univ. of Copenhagen.
Professor of Medicine and Dir. of Medical Dept. A., Univ. Hospital of Copenhagen; Dean of Medical Faculty, Univ. of Copenhagen 56-57, mem. Konsistorium 63, Chair. Medical Educ. Cttee. 62-64; mem. Danish State Research Foundation 63; Chair. Medical Council, Univ. Hospital of Copenhagen 58-64, mem. Building Cttee. 58; mem. W.H.O. Expert Advisory Panel on Chronic Degenerative Diseases 63; Hon. mem. American Rheumatism Asscn., Sociedad Argentina de Reumatologia, Swedish Rheumatism Asscn.; mem. Norwegian Medical Soc.; Heberden Oration Medal 57.
Publ. *Uric Acid in Blood and Urine* 37.
Frederick d. V's Vej 1, Copenhagen Ø, Denmark.
Telephone: 391610.

Brock, Baron (Life Peer), cr. 65, of Wimbledon; **Russell Claude Brock,** Kt., M.D., M.S., F.R.C.S., F.R.A.C.S., F.A.C.S.; British surgeon; b. 24 Oct. 1903; ed. Christ's Hospital and Guy's Hospital (Univ. of London).
Surgeon to Guy's Hospital 36-, to the Brompton Hospital 36-; Hunterian Prof., Royal Coll. of Surgeons 38; Exchange Prof. of Surgery, Johns Hopkins Hospital 49; mem. Council Royal Coll. of Surgeons 49-, Vice-Pres. 57-58, Pres. 63-; numerous medals and prizes.
Publs. *Anatomy of the Bronchial Tree* 46, *Life and Work of Astley Cooper* 52, *Lung Abscess* 52, *Anatomy of Pulmonary Stenosis* 57.
2 Harley Street, London, W.1, England.
Telephone: 01-580-1441.

Brockett, Ernest Delwin, Jr.; American oil executive; b. 16 April 1913; ed. Texas Agricultural and Mechanical Univ.
Gulf Oil Corpn. 34-, Asst. Supt. of Production, Fort Worth 48-49, Staff Asst. Production Dept. 49-52, Vice-Pres. and Man. Houston Production Div. 55-57, Vice-Pres. and Co-ordinator Production Dept., Pittsburgh 57-58, Exec. Vice-Pres. and Dir. 60, Pres. 60-65, Chair. and Chief Exec. Officer 65-; Asst. to Pres. Mene Grande Oil Co., Caracas 52-55; Pres. and Chief Exec. Officer, British American Oil Co. Ltd., Toronto 58-59; U.S. Army 40-45.
Gulf Oil Corporation, Gulf Building, Pittsburgh, Pa. 15230, U.S.A.

Brocklebank, Sir John Montague, Bt.; British businessman; b. 3 Sept. 1915; ed. Eton Coll.
Honorary Pres. and Past. Chair. Cunard Steamship Co. Ltd., Cunard White Star Ltd., Thomas and John Brocklebank Ltd.; Deputy Chair. B.O.A.C.-Cunard Ltd. 62-, Martins Bank Ltd.
Bryn Coch Hall, Mold, Flintshire, Wales.

Brockway, Baron (Life Peer), cr. 64, of Eton and Slough; **(Archibald) Fenner Brockway;** British politician; b. 1 Nov. 1888; ed. Eltham Coll.
Leader War Resisters' Movement during First World War; journalist; Chair. No More War Movement and War Resisters' Int. 23-28; Gen. Sec. Independent Labour Party 23-26 and 33-39, Political Sec. 39-46, and Editor *New Leader* 26-29 and 31-46; Chair. Congress of Peoples against Imperialism 48-54; Chair. The Movement for Colonial Freedom 54-; Labour M.P. 29-31, 50-64.
Publs. *The Devil's Business* 15, *Socialism and Pacifism* 17, *The Government of India* 20, *English Prisons To-day* (with Stephen Hobhouse) 21, *A New Way with Crime* 28, *The Indian Crisis* 30, *Bloody Traffic* 33, *Hungry England* 32, *Will Roosevelt Succeed?* 34, *Purple Plague* (novel) 35, *Workers' Front* 38, *Inside the Left* 42, *Death Pays a Dividend* (with F. Mullaly) 44, *German Diary* 46, *Socialism over Sixty Years: Life of Jowett of Bradford* 46, *Bermondsey Story: Life of Alfred Salter* 49, *Why Mau-Mau?* 53, *African Journeys* 55, *1960—Africa's Year of Destiny* 60, *Red Liner* 62, *Outside the Right* 62, *African Socialism* 63, *Immigration* (with Norman Pannell) 65, *This Shrinking Explosive World: A Study in Race Relations* 67.
House of Lords, London, S.W.1, and 67 Southway, London, N.20, England.
Telephone: 01-445-3054 (Home).

Brod, Max, LL.D.; German writer; b. 27 May 1884.
Novelist, poet, dramatist, essayist and composer; fmr. Editor *Prager Tagblatt*; now with Habima Theatre.
Publs. *The Redemption of Tycho Brahe, Reubeni, Three Loves, The Kingdom of Love, Die Frau, die nicht enttäuscht, Annerl, Galilei in Gefangenschaft, Beinahe ein Vorzugsschüler, Der Meister, Der Sommer, den man zurückwünscht* 53, *Armer Cicero* 55, *Rebellische Herzen* 57, *Mira* 58, *Jugend im Nebel* 59, *Die Rosenkoralle* 61, *Die verkaufte Braut, Durchbruch ins Wunder* 62 (novels); *Heidentum, Christentum, Judentum, Diesseits und Jenseits* (essays); *Lord Byron* (play); *Das Schloss* (*nach Kafka*) (play) 64; *Heinrich Heine, L. Janáček, Franz Kafka, Johannes Reuchlin, Der Prager Kreis* 66 (biographies); *King Saul* (play), *Streitbares Leben* (autobiography) 60; *Requiem Hebraicum* (for orchestra); *The Mediterranean Sea* (fantasy for piano); *Yemenite Songs* (voice and piano); *Zwei Israelische Bauerntanze* (for orchestra), *Zwei Lieder nach Texten von Kafka* (voice and orchestra); Editor Franz Kafka's works.
16 Hayarden Street, Tel Aviv, Israel.

Brodal, Alf, M.D.; Norwegian neuroanatomist; b. 25 Jan. 1910; ed. Univ. of Oslo.
Asst. Dept. of Anatomy, Odontological High School of Norway, Oslo 37-43; Prosector of Anatomy, Univ. of Oslo 43-50, Prof. of Anatomy 50-, Dean Medical Faculty 64-, Pro-Rector 67-; Co-Editor *Ergebn. Anat. Entwickl. gesch.*; Rockefeller Fellowship, Dept. of Human Anatomy, Oxford Univ. 46-47; Fellow, Norwegian Acad. of Sciences 44; mem. Royal Soc. of Medicine, London 46; Assoc. mem. Nordic Neurological Asscn. 47; Corresp. mem. American Neurological Asscn. 53; mem. Deutsche Akad. Naturforsch Leopoldina 64-; Fridtjof Nansen Prize 52, Monrad-Krohn Prize 41 and 60; Barany Medal (Uppsala) 63-; Anders Jahre's Medical Prize 66; Dr. h.c. Univ. of Uppsala.
Publs. (Monographs) *The Reticular Formation of the Brain Stem* 57 (Russian ed. 60), (with Jan Jansen) *Aspects of Cerebellar Anatomy* 54, (with Jan Jansen) *Das Kleinhirn* 58, (with Pompeiano and Walberg)

The Vestibular Nuclei and their Connections 62, (Textbooks) *Neurological Anatomy in Relation to Clinical Medicine* 48 (Japanese ed. 61), *The Cranial Nerves* 59.
Anatomical Institute, University of Oslo, Karl Johans gt 47, Oslo 1, Norway.
Telephone: 41-02-90.

Brodie, Rabbi Israel, B.A., B.LITT.; British Rabbi; b. 10 May 1895; ed. Jews' Coll., London, Univ. Coll., London and Balliol Coll., Oxford.
Jewish Chaplain to the Forces 17-19 and 40-48; Senior Jewish Chaplain 44-48; Minister, Melbourne Hebrew Congregation 22-37; Tutor and Lecturer in Homiletics, Jews' Coll. London 38-48; Chief Rabbi, United Hebrew Congregations of the British Commonwealth 48-65, Emer. Chief Rabbi; Fellow Univ. Coll., London; D.D. (Hon.); Hon. D.C.L. (Durham).
Flat 15, 9B Portland Place, London, W.1, England.

Broek, J. H. van den; Netherlands architect; ed. Technological Univ.
Private architect, Rotterdam 27-37; assoc. with Ir. J. A. Brinkman (Brinkman & Van der Vlugt) 37; assoc. with Prof. J. B. Bakema (Van den Broek & Bakema) 47-; mem. Exec. Cttee. Int. Union of Architects; Chair. Good Living Foundation; mem. Efficient Housing Foundation; Hon. mem. American Inst. of Architects; Hon. Corresp. mem. Royal Inst. of British Architects; Officer Order of Orange Nassau; Chevalier Légion d'Honneur; Officier Ordre du Couronne (Belgium).
Principal works: Dutch Pavilion, World Exhbn., Paris 37, Brussels 58; Deaconesses' Hospital, Rotterdam 39; housing in Rotterdam, Amsterdam, 's-Gravenhage, Hengelo, Eindhoven, Leeuwarden; department stores in Rotterdam, Arnheim and Eindhoven; shopping centre "Lijnbaan", Rotterdam 53; Montessori Lyceum, Rotterdam 58; Town Hall, Marl, German Fed. Republic (First Prize in Int. Competition) 58; churches at Schiedam and Nagele 59; World Broadcasting Building, Hilversum 61; buildings, laboratories, auditorium for Technological Univ., Delft 50-65.
Publs. *Woonmogelijkheden in het Nieuwe Rotterdam* (Living in New Rotterdam) (with Van Tijen and Maaskant), *Creatieve krachten in de architectonische conceptie* (Creative Forces in Architectural Conception) 48, *Guide to Dutch Architecture* 55, *Habitation* 45-65.
Van den Broek & Bakema Architecten, Posthoornstraat 12B, Rotterdam, Netherlands.

Brofoss, Erik, Cand. jur., Cand. œcon.; Norwegian banker; b. 21 June 1908; ed. Oslo Univ.
Asst. Judge West Telemark 33-35; employed by State Insurance Service 35-37, by Oslo Tax Assessment Office 37-41; escaped to Sweden Dec. 41, where employed by Norwegian Refugee Office; travelled to London April 42, mem. staff Norwegian Ministry of Finance until Oct. 42; Dir. Ministry of Supply (London); fmr. Vice-Chair. Economic Co-ordinating Council; Minister of Finance Nov. 45-47; Minister of Trade Dec. 47-54; Gov. Bank of Norway (Central Bank) 54-; Chair. Joint Consultation Council 54-65; Chair. Regional Devt. Fund 62-; Lecturer, Univ. of Oslo 57-66; Gov. Int. Monetary Fund; mem. Labour Party.
Bank of Norway, Bankplassen 4, Oslo, Norway.

Brogan, Sir Denis William, Kt., M.A., F.B.A., HON. LL.D. (Glasgow); British political scientist; b. 11 Aug. 1900; ed. Glasgow, Balliol Coll., Oxford, Harvard Univ.
Fmr. Lecturer Univ. Coll. London, London School of Economics; Fellow and Tutor Corpus Christi Coll. Oxford; now Prof. of Political Science and Fellow of Peterhouse Cambridge; Dir. Hamish Hamilton Ltd.; Chevalier de la Légion d'Honneur (France), Commdr. Order of Orange Nassau (Neths.); Fellow of British Acad.; Hon. Fellow, London School of Economics; foreign mem. Institut de France; Benjamin Franklin Medal, Royal Soc. of Arts 66.

Publs. *American Political System* 33, *Proudhon* 34, *Abraham Lincoln* 35, *Development of Modern France* 40, *U.S.A., Is Innocence Enough, Politics and Law in the United States* 41, *The English People* 43, *The American Problem* 44, *The Free State* 45, *French Personalities and Problems* 46, *American Themes: The Era of Franklin D. Roosevelt* 48, *The Price of Revolution* 52, *Introduction to American Politics* 54, *The French Nation* 57, *Citizenship Today* 60, *The United States in the Modern World* 60, *American Aspects* 64, *Worlds in Conflict* 67.
Peterhouse, Cambridge, England.

Broglie, Prince Jean de, D. en D.; French politician; b. 21 June 1921; ed. Ecole des Sciences Politiques.
Auditor, Council of State 46; Conseiller-Gen., Rugles 51-58, 58-; Master of Petitions, Council of State 54-; Ind. Deputy for Eure 58-65; Mayor of Broglie; Sec. of State for the Sahara and Overseas Territories and Depts. 61-62, for Public Functions 62, for Algerian Affairs Dec. 62-66, for Foreign Affairs 66-; Chevalier, Légion d'Honneur, Croix de Guerre, Médaille de la Résistance.
9 rue Adolphe-Yvon, Paris 16e, France.

Broglie, Prince Louis de, D.SC.; French scientist; b. 15 Aug. 1892; ed. Univ. of Paris.
Professor of Theoretical Physics Paris Univ. (Inst. Henri Poincaré) since 28; Nobel Prizeman for Physics 29; mem. Inst. de France, Acad. des Sciences 33-; Life Sec. Acad. des Sciences 42-; mem. Acad. Française 43-; mem. Scientific Cttee. Atomic Energy Comm. 57-; foreign mem. Royal Soc. 53; Hon. mem. Rumanian Acad. 65.
Publs. *La théorie de Quanta* 24, *Ondes et Mouvements* 36, *Introduction à l'étude de la mécanique ondulatoire* 20, *Conséquences de la rélativité dans le développement de la mécanique ondulatoire* 33, *Matière et Lumière, la Physique moderne et les quanta* 37, *Une nouvelle théorie de la lumière* 40, *Continue et Discontinue* 41, *Mécanique ondulatoire des corpuscules à spire* 42, *De la mécanique ondulatoire à la théorie du Noyau* 43, *Physique et Microphysique, Savants et Découvertes, Nouvelles perspectives en Microphysique, Sur le Sentiers de la Science,* etc.
94 rue Perronet, Neuilly-sur-Seine, France.
Telephone: Maillot 76-09.

Bröker, Leopold W.; German banker and chartered accountant; b. 5 June 1906.
President, Landeszentralbank in Hessen 58-; mem. Central Bank Council, Deutsche Bundesbank 58-; mem. Administrative Council, Hesse Radio 58-.
Office: c/o Landeszentralbank in Hessen, Neue Mainzer Strasse 47, Frankfurt a.M.; Home: Am Hang 42, 637 Oberursel (Taunus), German Federal Republic.

Bromberg, Adam Adolf, PH.D.; Polish publisher; b. 12 March 1912; ed. Warsaw Univ.
Editorial employee, Vienna 30-32; librarian Lwów 32-34; Editorial employee and bookseller Warsaw 36-39, Lwów 39-41; Military Service 41-45; Manager Ksiazka Publishing House 46, Prasa Wojskowa Publishing House 46-51; Vice-Pres. Central Editions Office 51-53; Man. Panstwowe Wydawnictwo Naukowe (State Scientific Publishing House) 53-65; Counsellor of Minister of Higher Educ. 65-; Pres. Polish Book Publishers Asscn. 48-50, Vice-Pres. 56-; mem. Editorial Cttee. *Great Universal Encyclopaedia, Library of Socialist Thought, Marxist Studies Library.*
Publs. include *Ksiazki i wydawcy* (Books and Publishers).
Flat 113, 36 Belwederska Street, Warsaw, Poland.
Telephone: 410995.

Bromberger, Merry Marie Louis (brother of Serge Paul Bromberger, *q.v.*); French journalist; b. 10 July 1906; ed. Lycée d'Aix-en-Provence, Aix-en-Provence and Strasbourg Univs.
Founded *Le Courrier de Provence* (daily) 26; Editor *Petit Marseillais*; legal corresp. *Le Matin* 30; Chief

Reporter *L'Intransigeant* 30-39, later with *Paris-Soir*, *Combat*, *Paris-Presse-L'Intransigeant*; with *Constellation* 49-; Chevalier Légion d'Honneur.
Publs. *Le Roman de l'Elysée, Comment ils ont fait Fortune, Le Destin secret de Georges Pompidou*; with Serge Paul Bromberger: *Le Comte de Paris et la Maison de France, Les Secrets de l'expédition d'Egypte, Les 13 complots du 13 mai, Barricades et Colonels*.
96 boulevard Maurice Barrès, Neuilly-sur-Seine (Seine), France.

Bromberger, Serge Paul (brother of Merry Marie Louis Bromberger, *q.v.*); French journalist; b. 29 Aug. 1912; ed. Lycée Mignet (Aix-en-Provence).
Journalist 34-; Reporter on *Figaro* 45-; mem. Asscn. des grands reporters français; Chevalier Légion d'Honneur, Croix du Combattant Volontaire.
Publs. *Retour de Corée* (co-author) 51, *Les Rebelles Algériens* 58, *En 1990* 64; with Merry Bromberger: *Les Secrets de l'expédition d'Egypte, Les 13 Complots du 13 mai* 59, *Barricades et Colonels* 60; *Les Coulisses de l'Europe* 68.
18 avenue Perrichont, Paris 16e, France.
Telephone: 525-47-64.

Bromley, Sir Thomas Eardley, K.C.M.G.; British diplomatist; b. 14 Dec. 1911; ed. Rugby, Magdalen Coll., Oxford.
Joined Consular Service 35; Vice-Consul, Japan 38; Asst. Private Sec. to the Perm. Under-Sec. of State 43, Private Sec. 45; attached to British Embassies, Washington 46, Baghdad 49; Head of African Dept. Foreign Office 54-55; Cabinet Office 57; Consul-Gen. in Mogadishu 60; Ambassador to Somali Republic 60, to Syrian Arab Republic 61-64, to Algeria 64-66; at Foreign Office 66; Amb. to Ethiopia 66-.
British Embassy, Addis Ababa, Ethiopia.

Bromley, Yulian Vladimirovich; Soviet historian; b. 1921; ed. Moscow Univ.; mem. C.P.S.U.
Junior Research Assoc. Inst. of Slav Studies, U.S.S.R. Acad. of Sciences; Scientific Sec. Dept. of History, U.S.S.R. Acad. of Sciences 52-66; Dir. Inst. of Ethnography, U.S.S.R. Acad. of Sciences; Corresp. mem. U.S.S.R. Acad. of Sciences 66-.
Publs. Works on history.
U.S.S.R. Academy of Sciences, 14 Lenin Prospekt, Moscow, U.S.S.R.

Bronfman, Edgar M.; American business executive; b. 20 June 1929; ed. Williams Coll., Williamstown, Mass., and McGill Univ., Montreal.
Distillers Corpn. Ltd., Canada 51-55; Chair. Admin. Cttee. Joseph E. Seagram and Sons Inc. (New York) 55-57, Pres. and Dir. 57-; Vice-Pres., Treas. and Dir. Distillers Corporation-Seagrams Ltd.; official of other firms and civic and philanthropic orgs.
Joseph E. Seagram and Sons Inc., 375 Park Avenue, New York City 22, N.Y., U.S.A.

Bronfman, Samuel; Canadian industrialist; b. 4 March 1891; ed. Brandon and Winnipeg Public and High Schools.
Organized Distillers Corpn. Ltd. 24; Pres. Distillers Corpn.-Seagrams Ltd. 28-, Distillers Corpn. Ltd., Thomas Adams Distillers Ltd., Seagrams Overseas Corpn. Ltd., Four Roses Distillers Ltd., Globe Bedding Co.; Dir. Joseph E. Seagrams and Sons Ltd., Calvert of Canada Ltd.; Pres. Canadian Jewish Cong. 38-62, Chair. Board of Govs. 62-; Hon. Pres. Zionist Org. of Canada, Fed. of Jewish Community Services of Montreal, Combined Jewish Appeal; Pres. United Jewish Relief Agencies, Canada-Israel Corpn., Canada-Israel Securities Ltd.; Chair. Nahum Goldman Inst. Cttee.; Vice-Pres. World Fed. of Young Men's Hebrew Asscns. and Jewish Community Centres, World Jewish Congress, Nat. Foundation for Jewish Culture; mem. Canada

Council 57-61, Nat. Council Boy Scouts of Canada, Board of Govs. of McGill Univ., of Canadian Council, Int. Chamber of Commerce, and of Canadian Welfare Council, Board of Exec. Cttee. of American Jewish Joint Distribution Cttee., etc.; Dir. Canadian Mental Health Asscn.; Assoc. Commdr. Order of St. John of Jerusalem; Hon. LL.D. Montreal Univ. and Univ. of Waterloo, Ont.
15 Belvedere Road, Westmount, Montreal, Que., Canada; 723 South Broadway, Tarrytown, N.Y., U.S.A.

Bronk, Detlev Wulf, A.B., M.S., PH.D., SC.D., ENG.D., D.MED.SC., D.LITT., M.D. (Hon.), L.H.D., LL.D., D.C.L.; American scientist and university president; b. 13 Aug. 1897; ed. Swarthmore Coll. and Univs. of Pa. and Mich.
Prof. Univs. of Pa., Mich. and Swarthmore Coll. 21-29; Dir. Eldridge Reeves Johnson Found., Univ. of Pa. 29-49; Pres. Johns Hopkins Univ. 49-53; Pres. Rockefeller Univ. 53-; Pres. Nat. Acad. of Sciences 50-62; Chair. Nat. Science Board, Nat. Science Foundation 56-64; Consultant, President's Science Advisory Cttee. Award for Exceptional Civilian Service 46; O.B.E. (Hon.); Longacre Award, Aero. Med. Asscn. 48; Priestley Award, Dickinson Coll. 56; Gold Medal Int. Benjamin Franklin Soc. 58; Franklin Medal, Franklin Inst. 61; Holland Soc. Gold Medal; John and Samuel Bard Award in Medicine and Science 61; George Washington Award, American Hungarian Studies Foundation 62; U.S. Presidential Medal of Freedom; foreign mem. Royal Soc., London, French Acad. of Sciences, Swedish Royal Acad. of Sciences, Acad. of Sciences, U.S.S.R., Brazilian Acad. of Sciences, and of the Royal Danish Soc. of Sciences and Letters; Hon. Fellow, Univ. Coll., London.
Publs. include numerous contributions to American and British scientific journals.
President's House, Rockefeller University, New York, N.Y. 10021, U.S.A.
Telephone: Lehigh 5-9000.

Bronowski, Jacob, M.A., PH.D., F.R.S.L.; British scientist; b. 18 Jan. 1908; ed. Central Foundation School and Jesus Coll., Cambridge.
Senior Lecturer, Univ. Coll., Hull 34-42; seconded to Govt. Service 42; Joint Target Group, Washington, and Chiefs of Staff Mission to Japan 45; statistical research into economics of building and other industries, Ministry of Works 46-50; seconded to UNESCO as Head of Projects 48; Carnegie Visiting Prof., Mass. Inst. of Technology 53; Dir. Coal Research Establishment, Nat. Coal Board 50-59, Dir.-Gen. Process Development Dept. 59-63; Senior Fellow and Trustee Salk Inst. for Biological Studies, San Diego, Calif. 63-; Hon. Fellow, Jesus Coll. Cambridge 67-; Foreign Hon. mem., American Acad. of Arts and Sciences 60; delivered inaugural *Man and Nature* lectures, American Museum of Natural History 65; numerous other lectures in the U.S.
Publs. *The Poet's Defence* 39, 66, *William Blake, a Man Without a Mask* 44, *The Common Sense of Science* 51, *The Face of Violence* 54, 67, *Science and Human Values* 58, *Selections from William Blake* 58, *The Western Intellectual Tradition* (with Bruce Mazlish) 60, *Insight* 64, *The Abacus and the Rose: A New Dialogue on Two World Systems* 63, *William Blake and the Age of Revolution, The Identity of Man* 65; also a number of radio plays, and an opera, *My Brother Died* 55.
The Salk Institute for Biological Studies, P.O.B. 1809, San Diego, Calif. 92112, U.S.A.

Bronston, Samuel; American film producer; ed. Université de Paris à la Sorbonne.
Former film distributor, Paris; fmr. unit production exec. with Columbia Studios Hollywood; founder Samuel Bronston Pictures Inc., now Pres.
Productions include: *King of Kings, El Cid* 60, *55 Days to Peking* 62, *Fall of the Roman Empire* 63.
505 Park Avenue, New York City 22, N.Y., U.S.A.

Brook, Alexander; American artist; b. 14 July 1898; ed. Art Students' League.
Logan Medal, Chicago Art Inst. 29, Beck Gold Medal, Pennsylvania Acad. 48; and several other awards.
Represented permanently in Metropolitan Museum New York City; Brooklyn (N.Y.) Museum; Art Inst. Chicago; Carnegie Inst. Pittsburgh; Nebraska Univ.; William Nelson Gallery, Kansas City, Mo.; Wadsworth Athenæum, Hartford, Conn.; Museum of Modern Art, New York City; Newark (N.J.) Museum; and many other U.S. museums, etc.
Sag Harbor, Long Island, N.Y., U.S.A.

Brook, Peter, C.B.E.; British theatre and film director; b. 21 March 1925; ed. Westminster and Gresham's Schools and Magdalen Coll., Oxford.
Producer and Co-Dir. Royal Shakespeare Theatre. Productions include *Dr. Faustus* 43, *Pygmalion, King John, Lady from the Sea* 45, *Romeo and Juliet* (at Stratford) 47, Dir. of Productions at Covent Garden Opera 49-50, *The Beggar's Opera* (film) 52, *Faust* (at Metropolitan Opera, N.Y.) 53, *The Dark is Light Enough* (in London) 54, *House of Flowers* (in N.Y.) 54, *Cat on a Hot Tin Roof* (in Paris) 56, *Eugen Onegin* (N.Y.) 58, *View from the Bridge* (Paris) 58, *The Fighting Cock* (N.Y.) 59, *Moderato Cantabile* (film) 60, *Irma la Douce* 60, *Lord of the Flies* (film) 62, *King Lear* 63, *The Physicists* (N.Y.) 64, *The Marat/Sade* (N.Y.) 65 (film 66), *US* 66, *Tell Me Lies* (film 68), *Oedipus* (Seneca) 68.
c/o Christopher Mann Ltd., 140 Park Lane, London, W.1, England.

Brooke, Edward William; American lawyer and politician; b. 26 Oct. 1919; ed. Howard Univ. and Boston Univ.
Admitted to Massachusetts Bar 48; Chair. Finance Comm., Boston 61-62; Attorney-Gen. of Massachusetts 63-67; Senator from Mass. 67-; Republican.
Office: Senate Office Building, Washington, D.C.; Home: 535 Beacon Street, Newton Centre, Mass., U.S.A.

Brooke, John; British tea merchant; b. 7 March 1912; ed. Bedales School.
Brooke Bond & Co. Ltd. 30-; fmr. apprentice salesman and trainee; Dir. Brooke Bond & Co. Ltd. 38; with Brooke Bond India 38-39; Royal Air Force, Second World War; Chair. Brooke Bond & Co. Ltd. 52-.
"Rowmore", Leigh Hill Road, Cobham, Surrey, England.
Telephone: Cobham 3361.

Brooke of Cumnor, Baron (Life Peer), cr. 66; **Rt. Hon. Henry Brooke,** P.C., C.H.; British politician; b. 9 April 1903; ed. Marlborough Coll. and Balliol Coll., Oxford.
Member of Parl. 38-45, 50-66; Deputy Chair. Southern Railway Co. 46-48; Minister of Housing and Local Govt., Minister for Welsh Affairs 57-61, Chief Sec. to Treasury and Paymaster-Gen. 61-62; Home Sec. 62-64; mem. Cen. Housing Advisory Cttee. 44-54, London County Council 45-55, Hampstead Borough Council 36-57; Conservative.
The Glebe House, Mildenhall, Marlborough, Wilts., England.
Telephone: Marlborough 2769.

Brookeborough, 1st Viscount, cr. 52, of Colebrooke; **Rt. Hon. Basil Brooke,** K.G., P.C., C.B.E., M.C., D.L.; British politician; b. 9 June 1888; ed. Winchester and Sandhurst.
Unionist M.P. Linsaskea Div. in Northern Ireland Parliament 29-68, Minister of Agriculture 33-41, of Commerce 41-43, of Commerce and Production 43-45; Prime Minister 43-63; Chair. Carreras Northern Ireland Ltd. 64-; Pres. Inst. of Dirs., Northern Ireland; H.M. Lieut. for Fermanagh; P.C. Northern Ireland 33.
Colebrooke, Brookeborough, Co. Fermanagh, Northern Ireland.
Telephone: 204.

Brooker, Robert Elton; American businessman; b. 18 July 1905; ed. Univ. of Southern California.
With Southern California Edison Co. 28-34, Firestone Tire and Rubber Co. 34-44, Sears, Roebuck & Co. 44-58; Pres. Whirlpool Corpn. 58-61; Pres. Montgomery Ward & Co. 61-66, Chair. 66-; Dir. Stein, Roe and Farnham, Stone Container Corpn.
Montgomery Ward & Co., 619 W. Chicago Avenue, Chicago, Illinois 60607; Home: 68 Locust Road, Winnetka, Illinois 60093, U.S.A.
Telephone: 467-3191 (Office); 446-7188 (Home).

Brookes, Edgar Harry, M.A., D.LITT.; South African journalist and writer; b. 4 Feb. 1897.
Prof. of Public Administration and Political Science, Univ. of Pretoria 20-33; Principal, Adams Coll., Natal 34-45; Senator representing Africans of Natal and Zululand in Union Parl. 37-52; mem. Permanent Native Affairs Comm. 45-50; Pres. S.A. Inst. of Race Relations 32-33, 46-48, 59-60; S.A. Del. to L.N. 27, and to UNESCO 47; Prof. of History and Political Science, Univ. of Natal 59-62; Nat. Chair. Liberal Party of South Africa 63-.
Publs. *History of Native Policy in South Africa* 24, *Native Education in South Africa* 29, *The Colour Problems of South Africa* 33, *The House of Bread* (poems) 44, *The Bantu in South African Life* 46, *South Africa in a Changing World* 53, *The Native Reserves of Natal* 56, *Civil Liberty in South Africa* 58, *The City of God and Politics of Crisis* 60, *Power, Law, Right and Love* 63, *A History of Natal* (with C. de B. Webb) 65, *A History of the University of Natal* 67.
12 Chamberlain Road, Pietermaritzburg, Natal, South Africa.

Brooks, Cleanth, A.B., A.M., B.A., B.LITT., D.LITT.; American university professor; b. 16 Oct. 1906; ed. The McTyeire School, Vanderbilt Univ., Tulane Univ. and Oxford Univ.
Professor of English, Louisiana State Univ. 32-47, Yale Univ. (now Gray Prof. of Rhetoric) 47-; Managing Editor, later Editor (with Robert Penn Warren) *Southern Review,* Baton Rouge, Louisiana 35-42; Hon. Consultant, Library of Congress 52-62; Cultural Attaché American Embassy, London 64-66.
Publs. *Modern Poetry and the Tradition* 39, *The Well Wrought Urn* 47; with Robert Penn Warren: *Understanding Poetry* 38, *Understanding Fiction* 43, *Modern Rhetoric* 50; *Literary Criticism: A short History* (with W. K. Wimsatt, Jr.) 57, *The Hidden God* 63, *William Faulkner: the Yoknapatawpha Country* 63; Gen. Editor (with David N. Smith) *The Percy Letters,* 10 vols. 42-; Editor: *The Correspondence of Thomas Percy and Richard Farmer* 46.
Forest Road, Northford, Conn., U.S.A.

Brooks, James; American painter; b. 18 Oct. 1906; ed. Southern Methodist Univ., Art Students League, N.Y.C., and with Wallace Harrison.
Federal Arts Mural Project 38-42; taught at Columbia, Yale and New Haven Univs. and at Queens Coll. 47-67; several one-man shows 49-64; represented in Museum of Modern Art, Metropolitan Museum, Guggenheim, Whitney, Brooklyn, New York; Tate Gallery, London, etc.; several shows abroad; retrospective exhbn. Whitney Museum of American Art 63-64; one-man show 68; Prof. Queens Coll. 68; Guggenheim Fellowship 67-68.
128 Neckpath, Springs, East Hampton, N.Y., U.S.A.
Telephone: 516-267-3453.

Brooks, John Wood, A.B.; American chemical executive; b. 9 Oct. 1917; ed. Groton School and Harvard Univ.
Sales positions in textile industry 39-53; Vice-Pres., Gen. Sales Man., Textile Div., Spring Mills, Inc. 53-54; Gen. Merchandise Man., Textile Div., Celanese Corpn. 55; Dir. Fibers Marketing 55-56, Vice-Pres., Gen. Man.

Fibers Div. 56-59, Exec. Vice-Pres. 60-65, Dir. 61, Pres. 65, Chief Exec. Officer 68.
Office: 522 Fifth Avenue, New York City, N.Y. 10036; Home: 363 Cantitoe Road, Bedford Hills, N.Y. 10507, U.S.A.

Brophy, Brigid (married to Michael Levey, *q.v.*); British novelist and critic; b. 12 June 1929; ed. St. Paul's Girls' School, London, and St. Hugh's Coll., Oxford.
Publs. *Hackenfeller's Ape* 53, *The King of a Rainy Country* 56, *Black Ship to Hell* (non-fiction) 62, *Flesh* 62, *The Finishing Touch* 63, *The Snow Ball* 64, *Mozart the Dramatist* (non-fiction) 64, *The Waste Disposal Unit* (play) 65, *Don't Never Forget* (non-fiction) 66; *The Burglar*, London 68.
Flat 3, 185 Old Brompton Road, London, S.W.5, England.

Brosio, Manlio, LL.D.; Italian lawyer and diplomatist; b. 17 July 1897; ed. Turin Univ.
Commenced practising law 20; joined political anti-Fascist movement "Rivoluzione Liberale"; collaborated in publications 19-26; political sec. of movement; mem. opposition cttee. against Fascism 24-26; mem. Cttee. of Nat. Liberation, Rome 43-44; Sec. Italian Liberal Party; Minister without Portfolio, Vice-Pres. of Council and Minister of War 45-46; Italian Ambassador to U.S.S.R. 47-52, to Great Britain 52-54, to U.S.A. 55-61, to France 61-64; Sec.-Gen. North Atlantic Treaty Organization (NATO) 64-.
North Atlantic Treaty Organization, Brussels 39; 43 Avenue Franklin-Roosevelt, Brussels, Belgium.

Brost, Erich Eduard; German publisher and journalist; b. 29 Oct. 1903; ed. St. Peter and St. Paul's High School, Danzig.
Ed. *Danziger Volksstimme* 24-36; journalist in Poland, Sweden, Finland and Great Britain 36-45, in Essen and Berlin 45-48; Publisher and Chief Ed. *Westdeutsche Allgemeine Zeitung*, Essen 48-.
36-38 Friedrichstr., 43 Essen, German Federal Republic.
Telephone: Essen 20641.

Broström, Dan-Axel; Swedish shipowner; b. 17 May 1915.
Managing Dir. Ångfartygs AB Tirfing, Ferm Steamship Co.; Chair. Swedish American Line, Swedish East Asia Co. Ltd., Eriksbergs Shipyard; Deputy Chair. Gothenburg Towing and Salvage Co., Neptun Salvage Co.; Dir. Skandinaviska Banken, Allmanna Svenska Elektriska AB (ASEA), Turitz and Co., Atlantica Insurance Co., Svea-Nornan Insurance Co., Swedish Shipowners Asscn., Swedish Shipowners Insurance Asscn., Lloyd's Register of Shipping, Swedish Cttee., Gen. Export Asscn. of Sweden.
Office: Broströmia, Box 2524, Gothenburg 2; Home: Viktor Rydbergsgatan 16, Gothenburg, Sweden.

Broström, Tor Erland J:son; Swedish shipowner; b. 6 June 1895.
Entered Axel Broström & Son 22; Man. Dir. Tirfing Steam Ship Co. Ltd. 34-49, Motortank Shipping Co. Ltd. 39-49 and Ferm Steam Ship Co. Ltd. 34-58; Pres. Tirfing Steam Ship Co. Ltd., The Swedish Orient Line, Ferm Steam Ship Co. Ltd., The Gothenburg Towage and Salvage Co. Ltd., The Maritime Museum of Gothenburg, etc.; Vice-Pres. The Swedish East Asia Co., etc.
Home: Lennart Torstensonsgatan 4, Gothenburg; Office: Axel Broström & Son, Gothenburg, Sweden.

Brouillet, René Alexis, K.C.V.O.; French diplomatist and civil servant; b. 9 May 1909; ed. Lycée St. Etienne, Lycée Louis-le-Grand, Ecole Normale Supérieure, Ecole des Sciences Politiques.
Asst., Inst. Scientifique de Recherches Economiques et Sociales 35; Sec.-Gen. Centre Polytechnicien d'Etudes Economiques 36; Auditeur, Cour des Comptes 37; Chef Adjoint du Cabinet of Pres. of Senate 39-40; Dir.

Juridical Service, Secretariat of State for Industrial Production 41-42; Conseiller Référendaire, Cour des Comptes 43; Dir. du Cabinet of Georges Bidault when Pres. Conseil Nat. de la Résistance 43-44; Dir. Adjoint du Cabinet, Gen. de Gaulle 44-46; mem. Council of Admin. Ecole Nat. d'Administration 45; Sec.-Gen. Tunisian Govt. 46-50; 1st. Counsellor French Embassy Berne 50-53; Dir. Adjoint du Cabinet, Ministry of Foreign Affairs (Bidault) 53; 1st. Counsellor French Embassy, Vatican 53-58; Sec.-Gen. à la Présidence du Conseil for Algerian Affairs June 58; Dir. du Cabinet, Gen. de Gaulle Jan 59-61; Ambassador to Austria 61-63, to Vatican 63-; Commdr. de la Légion d'Honneur, Grand Cross of the Order of Pius IX, Grand Cross Order of Merit of the Austrian Republic.
French Embassy to the Holy See, Villa Bonaparte, 23 Via Piave, Rome, Italy.

Brousse, Pierre; French politician; b. 26; ed. Lycée de Tulle, Corrèze, Institut d'Etudes Politiques, Paris and Univ. of Paris.
President, Radical Students Group 49; Ministry of Industry 54-56; Pres., Young Radicals Group 56-58; Joint Sec. Gen. Radical Party 58-61, Sec.-Gen. 61-; mem. and Delegué général, Fédération de la gauche démocratique et socialiste.
1 place de Valois, Paris 1e, France.
Telephone: GUTenberg 36-32.

Brouwenstyn, Gerarda; Netherlands opera singer.
Studied in Amsterdam; joined the Amsterdam opera and subsequently became First Soprano; has appeared in London, Berlin, Stuttgart, Brussels, Copenhagen, Paris, Vienna, Bayreuth, Barcelona, Buenos Aires, etc.; repertoire includes *Forza del Destino, Tosca, Aida, Othello, Un Ballo in Maschera, Tannhäuser, Walküre, Meistersinger, Le Nozze di Figaro, Jenufa, Troubadour, Cavalleria Rusticana, Don Carlos*, etc.; Order of Orange Nassau.
3 Bachplein, Amsterdam, Netherlands.

Brouwer, Luitzen Egbertus Jan; Netherlands mining engineer and business executive; b. 1 July 1910; ed. Technische Hogeschool te Delft.
Royal Dutch Shell Group 31-, assignments in Germany, Indonesia and Egypt; Mil. Service 40-46; assignments with Royal Dutch Shell Group in U.S.A. and Netherlands, Co-ordinator for Exploration and Production in Netherlands 51-; Gen. Man. Dir. Iranian Oil Consortium, Teheran 54-; Man. Dir. Royal Dutch Petroleum Co. and Shell Petroleum Co., and Principal Dir. Shell Petroleum N.V. 56; Chair. Board of Dirs. Shell Canada, Dir. Shell Oil Co. 65; Pres. Royal Dutch Petroleum Co. 65-; Knight Order of Netherlands Lion; Officer Order of Orange Nassau.
N.V. Koninklijke Nederlandsche Petroleum Maatschappij, Carel van Bylandtlaan 30, The Hague, Netherlands.

Brouwers, Gerard; Netherlands civil servant; b. 2 Aug. 1908; ed. Rotterdam School of Economics.
Assistant Sec. to Econ. Council in Netherlands 33-37; Head, Planning Dept., Ministry of Econ. Affairs 37-39; Head, Price Policy Dept., Ministry of Econ. Affairs, later Head of Secretariat, Ministry of Econ. Affairs; Dir.-Gen. of Prices 45-49; Sec.-Gen. Ministry of Econ. Affairs 49-; numerous decorations.
70 Bloemcamplaan, Wassenaar, Netherlands.

Brovka, Pyotr Ustinovich; Soviet poet; b. 1905; ed. Byelorussian State Univ.
Corresponding mem. Acad. of Sciences of Byelorussian S.S.R. 53-; mem. C.P.S.U. 40-; Deputy to Supreme Soviet of U.S.S.R.; Sec. Board of Byelorussian S.S.R. Union of Writers; mem. Board of U.S.S.R. Union of Writers; State prizewinner 47, 50; Lenin Prize 62.
Publs. *Hero's Arrival* 35, *Spring of the Homeland* 37,

Byelorus 43, *Bread* 46, *Road of Life* 50, *The Days Go By* 61, *Around Native Springs* 63, etc.
Writers' Union, Minsk, Byelorussia, U.S.S.R.

Brower, Charles Hendrickson; American advertising executive; b. 13 Nov. 1901; ed. Rutgers Univ.
Teacher, Bound Brook High School, New Jersey 25-26; Writer, Batten, Barton, Durstine and Osborn, New York 28-40, Vice-Pres. and Dir. 40-46, Exec. Vice-Pres. (Creative Services) 46, mem. Exec. Cttee. 51-, Gen. Man. and Vice-Chair. Exec. Cttee. 57, Pres. and Chair. Exec. Cttee. 57-64, Chair. of Board, Chief Exec. Officer and Chair. Exec. Cttee. 64-; official of educational orgs.
Batten, Barton, Durstine and Osborn, 383 Madison Avenue, New York City 17, N.Y., U.S.A.

Brown, Baron (Life Peer), cr. 64, of Machrihanish; **Wilfred Banks Duncan Brown,** M.B.E.; British business executive and politician; b. 29 Nov. 1908; ed. Rossall School.
With Glacier Metal Co. Ltd. 31-65, Sales Man. 35, Dir. 36, Joint Man. Dir. 37-39, Man. Dir. and Chair. 39-65; Dir. Associated Engineering Ltd. 64-65; Chair. Docks Modernization Cttee. 65-; mem. Govt. Advisory Cttee. on Technology; Minister of State, Board of Trade Oct. 65-; Fellow, British Inst. of Management; mem. Int. Acad. of Management; Pro-Chancellor, Brunel Univ.; Hon. D.Tech., Brunel Univ.; Hon. LL.D. Univ. of Southern Illinois, U.S.A.
Publs. *Managers, Men and Morale* (with Mrs. W. Raphael) 47, *Exploration in Management* 60, *Piecework Abandoned* 62, *Product Analysis Pricing* (with Dr. E. Jaques) 64.
20 Corfton Road, Ealing, London, W.5, England.
Telephone: Perivale 2914.

Brown, Aaron Switzer, A.B.; American diplomatist; b. 15 April 1915; ed. Princeton Univ.
Joined Foreign Service 37, served Mexico City, Dublin, Bogotá, Washington, Bangkok, Lisbon 37-56; Dep. Dir. of Personnel, Dept. of State 56-58, Dep. Asst. Sec. for Personnel 58-61; Ambassador to Nicaragua 61-.
American Embassy, Managua, Nicaragua.

Brown, Sir Allen Stanley, Kt., C.B.E., M.A., LL.M.; Australian diplomatist; b. 3 July 1911; ed. Wesley Coll., Melbourne, and Queen's Coll., Univ. of Melbourne.
Director-General of Post-War Reconstruction 48; Sec. Prime Minister's Dept. and Sec. to Cabinet 49-58; Deputy High Commr. for Australia in U.K. 58-65; Ambassador to Japan 65-; Vice-Pres. European Launcher Development Org. 64-65.
Australian Embassy, Tokyo, Japan.

Brown, Ben Hill, Jr.; American diplomatist; b. 8 Feb. 1914; ed. Wofford Coll., Spartanburg and George Washington Univ.
Law Practice 40-41; War Service in Army 41-46; Dept. of State 46-, Asst. Legal Adviser 46-49, Deputy Asst. Sec. 49-55, Nat. War Coll. 55-56, Dir. United States Operations Mission to Iraq 56-58, to Libya 59-60, Consul-Gen. Istanbul 60-64, Ambassador to Liberia 64-; U.S. Bronze Star 45, U.S. Legion of Merit.
Embassy of the U.S.A., Monrovia, Liberia; and 352 Twin Drive, Spartanburg, South Carolina, U.S.A.

Brown, Admiral Charles Randall; American naval officer; b. 13 Dec. 1899; ed. U.S. Naval Acad.
Served with the Atlantic Fleet, First World War; Commdr. escort carrier *Kalinin Bay* in South Pacific operations, for which he received the Bronze Star 43; Chief of Staff Fast Carrier Task Group West Pacific operations for which he received the Legion of Merit 44; Commdr. aircraft carrier *Hornet* 45; Chief of Staff, Naval War Coll. 49; Commdr. of Sixth Fleet 56; C.-in-C. Allied Forces, Southern Europe 59-62; Chief Rep. in Europe, McDonnell Aircraft Corpn., 62-; Distinguished Service Medal 60.
c/o Chase Manhattan Bank, 41 rue Cambon, Paris 1, France.

Brown, Chester M.; American chemical executive; b. 24 Nov. 1907; ed. South East Missouri State Coll. and Univ. of Missouri.
Allied Chemical Corpn. 29-, Plant Supt. 36, Asst. Production Man. 39, Plant Man. 42, Dir. of Sales Gen. Chemical Div. 48, Vice-Pres. (of Div.) 50-52, Exec. Vice-Pres. 52-55, Pres. 55-57, Pres. Nat. Aniline Div. 58-59, Vice-Pres. (of Co.) 57-59, Pres. and Dir. 59-66, Chief Operating Officer 59-62, Chief Exec. Officer 62-, Chair. of Board 66-; official of other business and civic orgs.
Allied Chemical Corporation, 61 Broadway, New York, City, N.Y. 10006; Home: 860 Gate Way, Hillside, N.J 07205, U.S.A.
Telephone: 212-HA-2-7300 (Office).

Brown, Sir David, Kt., M.I.A.E., M.I. MECH.E.; British engineer and business exec.; b. 1904; ed. Rossall School, private tuition, and Huddersfield Technical Coll.
David Brown and Sons (Huddersfield) Ltd. 21, Dir. 29-32, Managing Dir. 32; founder David Brown Tractors Ltd. 35; Chair. and Managing Dir. The David Brown Corporation (Aston Martin, Lagonda, etc.) 51-.
Chequers Manor, Cadmore End, nr. High Wycombe, Bucks., England.

Brown, Edmund Gerald (Pat), LL.B.; American lawyer and politician; b. 21 April 1905; ed. Lowell High School, San Francisco, Univ. of California Extension Division, San Francisco Coll. of Law.
Admitted to bar 27; asst. and successor to Milton L. Schmitt; District Attorney, San Francisco 43; Attorney General, California 50, re-elected on nomination of both Democratic and Republican parties 54; Gov. of California 59-66; Chair. Nat. Comm. on Reform of Criminal Laws 67-; Democrat.
San Francisco, Calif., U.S.A.

Brown, Ernest Henry Phelps, M.B.E., M.A., F.B.A.; British economist; b. 10 Feb. 1906; ed. Taunton School, Wadham Coll., Oxford.
Fellow of New Coll., Oxford 30-48; Rockefeller Travelling Fellow in U.S.A. 30-31; served with Royal Artillery 39-45; Prof. of Econs. of Labour, Univ. of London 47-; mem. Council on Prices, Productivity and Incomes 59, Nat. Econ. Devt. Council 62-66.
Publs. *The Framework of the Pricing System* 36, *A Course in Applied Economics* 51, *The Balloon* (novel) 53, *The Growth of British Industrial Relations* 59, *The Economics of Labour* 62.
73 Fitzjohn's Avenue, London, N.W.3, England.
Telephone: 01-435-7924.

Brown, Sir Frederick Herbert Stanley, Kt., C.B.E., B.SC., C.ENG., M.I.MECH.E., F.I.E.E.; British electrical engineer; b. 9 Dec. 1910; ed. King Edward School and Birmingham Univ.
Birmingham Electric Supply Dept. 32-46; W. Midlands Jt. Elec. Authy. 46-47; Liverpool Corpn. Elec. Supply Dept. 47-48; British Elec. Authy. 48-54; Generation Design Engineer, Central Elec. Authy. 54-57, Chief Engineer 57; mem. for Engineering, Central Elec. Generating Board 57-59, Deputy Chair. 59-64, Chair. Jan. 65-.
Central Electricity Generating Board, Sudbury House, 15 Newgate Street, London, E.C.1, England.

Brown, Rt. Hon. George Alfred, P.C., M.P.; British politician; b. 2 Sept. 1914.
Mem. of Parl. 45-; Parl. Private Sec. to Minister of Labour and Nat. Service 45-47, to Chancellor of Exchequer 47; Jt. Parl. Sec., Ministry of Agriculture and Fisheries 47-51; Minister of Works April-Oct. 51; Vice-Chair. and Deputy Leader, Parl. Labour Party 60-; First Sec. of State and Sec. of State for Econ. Affairs 64-66; Sec. of State for Foreign Affairs and Deputy Prime Minister 66-68; Productivity Counsellor (part-time), Courtaulds Ltd. 68-.
House of Commons, London, S.W.1, England.

Brown, George Rufus; American engineering executive; b. 12 May 1898; ed. Colo. School of Mines, Rice Univ., Houston.
Chair. Texas Eastern Transmission Corpn.; Chair. Board Brown Root, Inc.; Dir. Int. Telephone and Telegraph Corpn., Armco Steel Corpn., Southland Paper Mills, Trans World Airlines, First City Nat. Bank of Houston, Louisiana Land and Exploration Co.; Chair. Board of Trustees Rice Univ.
Office: P.O.B. 3, Houston, Texas 77001; Home: 3363 Inwood Drive, Houston, Texas 77019, U.S.A.

Brown, Harold, PH.D.; American physicist and government official; b. 19 Sept. 1927; ed. New York City public schools and Columbia Univ.
Lecturer in Physics, Columbia Univ. 47-50, Stevens Inst. of Technology 49-50; Univ. of California Radiation Laboratory, Berkeley 50-52; Livermore Radiation Laboratory 52-61, Group Leader 53, Div. Leader 55, Assoc. Dir. 58, Dep. Dir. 59, Dir. Lawrence Radiation Laboratory 60-61; mem. Polaris Steering Cttee., Dept. of Defense 56-58; Consultant to Air Force Scientific Advisory Board 56-57; mem. Scientific Advisory Cttee. on Ballistic Missiles to Sec. of Defense 58-61; mem. President's Science Advisory Cttee. 61-65; Dir. of Defense Research and Engineering 61-65; Sec. of the Air Force 65-; Hon. D.Eng., Stevens Inst. of Technology, Hon. LL.D., Long Island Univ.
416 Argyle Drive, Alexandria, Virginia, U.S.A.

Brown, (Harry) Leslie, B.A.; Canadian trade official; b. 31 Oct. 1903; ed. Univ. of British Columbia.
Officer, Dept. of Trade and Commerce 30-63, Trade Commr. Mexico City, London, Cape Town, Johannesburg, Buenos Aires, Caracas, and Minister (Commercial) London 31-50, 55-58, Asst. Deputy Minister (External Trade Promotion), Ottawa 58; Commr.-Gen. Canadian Govt. Participation Expo 67 Exhbn. (Montreal) 63-; Leader, Canadian Trade Del. to Latin America 50; Chief Exec. Officer, First Export Trade Promotion Conf. 60, and of subsequent Regional Confs. 61-62; Senior Officer in Charge of Operation World Markets 63.
The Chateau, Apartment C-90, 1321 Sherbrooke Street West, Montreal 25, Quebec, Canada.

Brown, Ivor John Carnegie, C.B.E.; British author and journalist; b. 25 April 1891; ed. Cheltenham Coll. and Balliol Coll., Oxford.
London drama critic for *Manchester Guardian* 19-35, *Saturday Review* 23-30, *Observer* 29-54, *Week End Review* 30-34; leader writing and special features for *Manchester Guardian* 20-42; Editor *Observer* 42-48, Assoc. Editor 48-54; Chair. British Drama League 55-65; Hon. LL.D. (St. Andrews and Aberdeen Univs.) 50.
Publs. *The Meaning of Democracy* 19, *Masques and Phases* 26, *Parties of the Play* 28, *Brown Studies* 30, *Master Sanguine* 34, *Heart of England* 35, *The Great and the Goods* 37, *Life Within Reason, Amazing Monument* (with George Fearon) 39, *A Word in Your Ear* 42, *Just Another Word* 43, *A Book of Words* 45, *I Give You My Word* 46, *Say the Word* 48, *Shakespeare* 49, *Having the Last Word* 51, *Winter in London* 51, *I Break My Word* 51, *Summer in Scotland* 52, *A Word in Edgeways* 53, *The Way of my World* 54, *Balmoral, Theatre, Chosen Words* 55, *Dark Ladies* 57, *Words in our Time, A Book of England* 58, *London* 60, *Shakespeare in his Time* 60, *Words in Season* 61, *How Shakespeare Spent the Day* 63, *Dickens in his Time* 63, *What is a Play?* 64, *Bernard Shaw in his Time, History of London* 65, *A Ring of Words* 66, *The Women in Shakespeare's Life* 67.
20 Christchurch Hill, London, N.W.3, England.

Brown, Sir (George) Lindor, Kt., C.B.E., M.SC., M.B., CH.B., LL.D., D. de l'Univ. de Liège, F.R.C.P., F.R.S.; British physiologist; b. 9 Feb. 1903; ed. Univ. of Manchester.

Lecturer in Physiology, Univ. of Leeds 28; mem. Scientific Staff Medical Research Council, Nat. Inst. for Medical Research 34-49; mem. Medical Research Council 51-55, Assessor 61-63; Hon. Sec. Physiological Soc. 41-49, Foreign Sec. 49-61; mem. Ed. Board *Journal of Physiology* 40-47, mem. Royal Danish Acad. of Sciences; Officer of Order of Southern Cross of Brazil; foreign mem. Brazilian Acad. of Sciences; Biological Sec. Royal Soc. 56-63; Vice-Pres. The Royal Soc. 56-63; Jodrell Prof. of Physiology, Univ. Coll., London 49-60; Waynflete Prof. of Physiology, Oxford Univ. 60-67; Pres. International Union of Physiological Sciences 62-68; Principal, Hertford Coll., Oxford 68-.
Hertford College, Oxford, England.
Telephone: Oxford 41434.

Brown, Peter McKenzie; South African politician; b. 24; ed. Michaelhouse, Cambridge Univ. and Univ. of Cape Town.
Natal Health Comm. 51; opened and organised first Natal Y.M.C.A., Pietermaritzburg 52; organised inter-racial discussion group which became South African Liberal Asscn.; mem. Liberal Party 53-64, Deputy Nat. Chair. 57-59, Nat. Chair. 59-64; detained under State of Emergency March-June 60; confined to Magisterial District of Pietermaritzburg for five years 64-.
268 Longmarket Street, Pietermaritzburg, Natal, S.A.

Brown, Sir Stephen, K.B.E.; British engineer; b. 15 Feb. 1906; ed. Taunton School and Bristol Univ.
Joined J. Stone & Co. Ltd. 32, Dir. 45-51; Man. Dir. J. Stone & Co. (Deptford) Ltd. 51, Chair. 56-59; Joint Man. Dir. J. Stone & Co. (Holdings) Ltd. 58, Chair. 59-66; Divisional Dir. Stone-Platt Industries Ltd. 58-59, Deputy Chair. 65, Chair. May 68-; Dir. Chloride Electrical Storage Co. Ltd. 55, Deputy Chair. 65; Pres. Engineering Employers Fed. 64-65; Deputy Pres. Confederation of British Industry Aug. 65, Pres. Sept. 66-May 68; Founder-mem. Export Council for Europe 60, Deputy Chair. Sept. 62-Dec. 63; Hon. D.Sc. Univ. of Aston.
Stone-Platt Industries Ltd., 25 St. James's Street, London, S.W.1; Coombe House, Bolney, Sussex, England.
Telephone: 01-839-9683 (Office); 0444-82-202 (Home).

Brown, W(illiam) Norman, A.B., PH.D.; American Sanskrit scholar; b. 24 June 1892; ed. Johns Hopkins Univ.
Harrison Research Fellow Univ. of Pa. 16-19; Johnston Scholar Johns Hopkins Univ. 19-22, also acting head Sanskrit Dept. 21-22; Prof. of English, Prince of Wales Coll. Jammu (India) 23-24; Dir. Half-Century Alumni Directory, Johns Hopkins Univ. 24-26, Assoc. in Sanskrit 25-26; Prof. of Sanskrit Univ. of Pa. 26-66, Emer. Prof. of Sanskrit 66-; Chair. S. Asia Regional Studies 48-66; Curator Oriental Section Univ. Museum 42-49; Pres. American Oriental Soc. 41-42; Curator of Indian Art Philadelphia Museum of Art 30-54; Fellow John S. Guggenheim Foundation 28-29; Fulbright Research Scholar in India 54-55; Pres. Asscn. for Asian Studies 60-61, American Inst. of Indian Studies 62-; Hon. D.Litt. (Madras, Jñāna-rātnākara, West Bengal Govt. Sanskrit Coll.), Litt.D. (Univs. of Pennsylvania and Michigan); Hon. Fellow Royal Asiatic Soc.
Publs. *The Indian and Christian Miracles of Walking on Water* 28, *The Story of Kalaka* 33, *Miniature Paintings of the Jaina Kalpasutra* 34, *Pillared Hall from Madura India in the Pennsylvania Museum of Art* 39, *Manuscript Illustrations of the Uttaradhyayana Sutra* 41, *India, Pakistan and Ceylon* (ed. and co-author) 51, 63, *The United States and India and Pakistan* 53, *The Saundaryalahari* 58, *The Vasanta Vilasa* 62, *The Mahimnastava* 65, *Man in the Universe* 66.
Box 17, Bennett Hall, University of Pennsylvania, Philadelphia, Pa. 19104, U.S.A.

Brown, Winthrop Gilman, B.A., LL.B.; American government official and diplomatist; b. 12 July 1907; ed. St. Paul's School, Concord, Yale Univ. and Yale Law School.

Private law practice 32-41; Lend Lease Admin. 41; Exec. Officer Harriman Mission, U.S. Embassy, London 41-45; State Dept. Trade Policy posts 45-52; Economic Affairs U.S. Embassy, London 52-57; Minister-Counsellor, New Delhi 57-60; Ambassador to Laos 60-62; Dep. Commdt. for Foreign Affairs, Nat. War Coll. 62-64; Amb. to Republic of Korea 64-67; Special Asst. to Sec. of State for Liaison with Governors 67-.
2435 Tracy Place, N.W., Washington, D.C., U.S.A.
Telephone: 483-2435.

Browne, Sir (Edward) Humphrey, Kt., C.B.E.; British business executive; b. 7 April 1911; ed. Repton School, Magdalene Coll., Cambridge, and Birmingham Univ.
Former Manager, Chanters Colliery; Dir. and Chief Mining Engineer Manchester Collieries Ltd. 43-46; Production Dir. North Western Div. Coal Board 47-48; Dir.-Gen. of Production, National Coal Board 48-55; Chair. W. Midlands Div., Nat. Coal Board 55-60; Dep. Chair. Nat. Coal Board 60-67; Chair. John Thompson 67-; Deputy Chair. Woodhall Duckham Ltd.; Pres. British Coal Utilisation Research Council 63-67; Dir. Nat. Industrial Fuel Efficiency Service.
Beckbury Hall, Shifnal, Shropshire; and 31 Dorset House, Gloucester Place, London, N.W.1, England.
Telephone: Ryton 207 and 01-935-8958.

Browne, H.E. Cardinal Michael David, O.P., S.T.M.; Irish ecclesiastic; b. 6 May 1887; ed. St. Thomas Coll. (Rome), Angelicum (Rome) and Fribourg Univ.
Entered Dominican Order 03; ordained priest 10; Master of Novices, Tallaght (Dublin) 15-19, Prof. of Philosophy 19-32, of Theology 32-51, Rector 32-41; Master Sacred Apostolic Palace 51-55; Master-General Dominican Order 55-62; Cardinal 62.
Publs. Numerous philosophical papers in the *Angelicum Review* and *Acts of the Roman Academy of St. Thomas.*
Palazzo del S. Offizio, Piazza del S. Offizio 11, Rome 47, Italy.
Telephone: 6982, Extension 3270.

Browne, William Herman; Canadian business executive; b. 25 March 1901; ed. Queen's Univ., Kingston, Ontario.
Cashier, British American Oil Co. Ltd. 23-25; Technical Service, Goodyear Tire and Rubber Co., Canada, Ltd. 25; Moore Corpn. Ltd., Toronto (business forms, etc.) 25-, Sec. 35-55, Exec. Vice-Pres. and Sec. 55-59, Exec. Vice-Pres. 59-62, Pres. 62-; Pres. and Dir. of subsidiary companies; mem. Canadian Council, Nat. Industrial Conf. Board.
Moore Corporation Ltd., 330 University Avenue, Toronto, Ontario, Canada.

Brownell, Herbert, A.B., LL.B.; American lawyer; b. 20 Feb. 1904; ed. Univ. of Nebraska and Yale Univ. School of Law.
Admitted to New York Bar 28; law practice, Root, Clark, Buckner, Howland and Ballantine 28-29; mem. New York State Assembly 32-37; practising attorney Lord, Day & Lord 29-53, 57-; Attorney-Gen. of United States 53-57; Pres. Asscn. of Bar of City of New York 62-64; Chubb Fellowship, Yale Univ. 59-; Assoc. Fellow Silliman Coll., Yale Univ. 55-; Chair. Comm. on Int. Rules of Judicial Procedure 58-59, American Bar Asscn. Cttee. on Constitutional Amendment relating to Presidential Disability; official of other legal orgs.
Lord, Day and Lord, 25 Broadway, New York 4, N.Y., U.S.A.

Brownell, Samuel Miller, A.B., M.A., PH.D.; American educationist; b. 3 April 1900; ed. Lincoln (Nebraska) High School, Univ. of Nebraska and Yale Univ.
Teacher Demonstration High School, State Teachers Coll., Peru 21-23; Asst. Prof. of Education, New York State Coll. for Teachers 26-27; Supt. of Schools, Grosse Pointe, Mich. 27-38; Prof. of Educational Admin., Yale Univ. 38-56; Pres. New Haven State Teachers' Coll. 47-53; U.S. Commr. of Education 53-56; Supt. of Schools, Detroit 56-66; Prof. Urban Educational Admin. Yale Univ. and Univ. of Conn. 66-; many hon. degrees.
Publs. *Progress in Educational Administration* 35, *Urban Education* 62.
Office: Graduate School, Yale University, New Haven, Connecticut; Home: Apartment A3, 311 St. Ronan Street, New Haven, Connecticut, U.S.A.

Brownstein, Philip N.; American government official; b. 14 Feb. 1917; ed. George Washington Univ. and Columbia Univ., Washington, D.C.
Federal Housing Admin. 34-44; U.S. Marine Corps 44-46; Veterans Admin. 46-63, Asst. Dir. for Loan Policy 54-58, Dir. of Loan Guaranty Service 58, later Chief Benefits Dir.; Head, Fed. Housing Admin. 63-66; Asst. Sec. for Mortgage Credit 66-.
Department of Urban Housing and Urban Development, Washington, D.C. 20411; Home: 560 N. Street, S.W., Apt. N-102, Washington, D.C. 20024, U.S.A.
Telephone: 202-554-5368.

Broz, Josip (*see* Tito).

Brubeck, David Warren, B.A.; American musician; b. 6 Dec. 1920; ed. Pacific and Mills Colls.
Formed his own trio 50, Dave Brubeck Quartet 51; numerous tours and recordings; many awards from trade magazines, *Metronome, Downbeat, Billboard, Melodymaker*; Hon. Ph.D. (Univ. of Pacific, Fairfield Univ.); composer of 250 songs; *Points of Jazz* (ballet), *Elementals* (orchestral), *The Light in the Wilderness* (oratorio).
c/o Associated Booking Corporation, 445 Park Avenue, New York, N.Y., U.S.A.

Brubeck, William H.; American government official; b. 19 Aug. 1920; ed. St. John's Coll., Maryland and Harvard Univ.
U.S. Army service 42-46; Teaching Fellow, St. John's Coll. 46-48, Harvard Univ. 50-52; Asst. Prof. Williams Coll. 52-56, Visiting Lecturer, Salzburg Seminary, Austria 55, Columbia Univ. 57; Legislative Asst. to mems. of Congress 56; Legal Consultant, private firm 57-60, to Development Loan Fund 61; Special Asst. to Under-Sec. of State 61, Dep. Exec. Sec., Exec. Secretariat Aug. 61-62, Special Asst. to Sec. of State and Exec. Sec. of Dept. of State 62-63; Political Counsellor, London Embassy 65-.
American Embassy, 1 Grosvenor Square, London, W.1, England.

Bruce, David K. E. (brother of James Bruce, *q.v.*); American diplomatist; b. 12 Feb. 1898; ed. Princeton Univ. and Univs. of Virginia and Maryland.
Served First World War; practised law in Baltimore 21-25; mem. Md. House of Dels. 24-26, Va. House of Dels. 39-42; foreign service of U.S. State Dept. 26-28; engaged in various banking and business enterprises 28-39; chief rep. American Red Cross, Great Britain 40; with Office of Strategic Services 41-45, Colonel in Army Air Forces 43-45; Asst. Sec. of Commerce 47; Chief French Mission for the E.C.A. 48; Ambassador to France 49-52; Under-Sec. of State 52-53; Special U.S. Observer, Interim Cttee., European Defence Community 53; Special rep. to European High Authority for Coal and Steel Mar. 53-54; Ambassador to German Federal Repub. 57-59, to United Kingdom 61-; awarded mil. decorations by U.S., Great Britain, France, Norway, Poland, Denmark, Czechoslovakia.
Publs. *Revolution to Reconstruction* 38, *16 American Presidents* 63.
1411 34th Street NW, Washington 7, D.C., U.S.A.; and American Embassy, Grosvenor Square, London W.1, England.
Telephone: 01-499-9000 (Embassy).

Bruce, James (brother of David Bruce, *q.v.*), LITT.B., LL.B.; American executive; b. 23 Dec. 1892; ed. Princeton Univ. and Univ. of Maryland.
Captain in U.S. Field Artillery, First World War; mil. aide to Pres. Wilson at Treaty of Versailles; Asst. Mil. Attaché, Italy, and Rep. of Versailles Peace Conf. in Montenegro and Albania 19; Vice-Pres. Atlantic Exchange Bank 21-26; Vice-Pres. Chase Nat. Bank 26-31; Pres. Baltimore Trust Co. 31-33; Financial Adviser Home Owners' Loan Corpn., Washington 33-34; Vice-Pres. and Dir. Nat. Dairy Products Corpn. 35-47; U.S. Amb. to Argentina 47-49; First Dir. Mutual Defence Assistance Programme 49-50; Dir. Avco Manufacturing Co., Loews Theatres Inc., Gen. American Investors, Fruehauf Trailer Corpns., Klein Dept. Stores Inc., Maryland State Fair, Technicolor Inc., U.S. Industries Inc., Revlon Inc., Ramco Enterprises, Lisco Inc.
Publs. *Those Perplexing Argentines, College Journalism.*
825 5th Avenue, New York 21, N.Y.; Office: 230 Park Avenue, New York City, N.Y. 10017, U.S.A.
Telephone: ORegon 9-6177.

Bruch, Walter; German development engineer; b. 2 March 1908; ed. Technische Hochschule.
Development Engineer in Denes V. Mihaly Physical Technical Research Lab. 33-35; at Lab. for Physical Research, Telefunken AG until 45; now Dir. of Advanced Devt., AEG - Telefunken; Geoffrey Parr Award, Royal Television Soc.; Grosses Bundesverdienstkreuz mit Stern; Goldener Ehrenring der Deutschen Gesellschaft für Film-und Fernsehforschung; **Dr. Ing. h.c.** Technische Hochscule, Hanover.
Publs. 27 technical articles in field of colour television; contributor *Fernsehempfänger* in *Fernsehtechnik* 63.
AEG - Telefunken, 3 Hanover, Göttinger Chaussee 76; Home: 3 Hanover, Menschingstrasse 13, German Federal Republic.
Telephone: 0511-4202265 (Office); 0511-817222 (Home).

Bruchési, Jean, B.A., LL.L., D.POL.SC.; Canadian university professor and civil servant; b. 01; ed. Univs. of Montreal and Paris, Ecole Libre des Sciences Politiques, Paris, and Ecole des Chartes, Paris.
Admitted to the Bar 24; Prof. of Gen. History, Univ. of Montreal 27-37, Prof. of Political Science and External Politics 29-58; Prof. of Canadian History, Marguerite-Bourgeoys Coll. Montreal 32-; Prof. of Economic History of Canada, Ecole Supérieure de Commerce, Laval Univ. 43-52; Under-Sec. of the Province of Quebec 37-; Editor of Foreign Politics, *Le Canada*, Montreal 28-31; Chief Editor *La Revue Moderne* 30-35, *L'Action Universitaire* 34-37; mem. (and founder) La Société des Ecrivains canadiens 37-, mem. Royal Society of Canada 40- (Pres. 53-54); Pres. Inst. Canadien de Québec 46-.
Publs. *Aux Marches de l'Europe* 31, *L'Épopée Canadienne* 34, *Histoire du Canada pour tous* 34-36, *Rappels* 41, *De Ville-Marie à Montréal* 42, *Le Chemin des Ecoliers* 44, *Evocations* 47, *Canada, réalités d'hier et d'aujourd'hui* 48, *Histoire du Canada* 51, *Le Canada* 52, *L'Université* 53, *Voyages . . . Mirages* 57.
185 avenue Laurier, Quebec, Canada.

Bruckner, Albert, PH.D.; Swiss historian; b. 13 July 1904; ed. Lausanne, Basle, Berlin, Florence, Münster, Cologne.
Chief Asst. Int. Press Exhibition Cologne 26-27; Pers. Asst. Prof. Kehr (Monumenta Germaniae) Berlin 29-30; 1st Asst. Basle Univ. Library 31-33; Chief Asst Archives, Basle 33-41, Privatdozent Basle Univ. 36-48; Extra. Prof. 48-66, Prof. 67-; State Archivist, Basle Town 61-66; mem. staff Schweiz. Herald. Gesellschaft 48-59; hon. mem. Öst. Inst. für Geschichtsforschung, Vienna; corresp. mem. Coimbra Acad.; corresp. Fellow Medieval Acad. of America, Cambridge, Mass.; corresp. Fellow Monumenta Germaniae, Munich; Editor-in-Chief

Neue Schweizer Biographie; Co-Editor *Umbrae Codicum Occidentalium* 60-; Pres. Curatorium *Helvetia Sacra.*
Publs. *Scriptoria medii aevi helvetica* I-XI 35-66, *Schweizer Fahnenbuch* 41-42; *Schweizer Stempelschneider und Schriftgiesser* 43; *Regesta Alsatiae, Merovingici et Karolini Aevi* 49; *Basel und die Eidgenossen* (with Bonjour) 51; *Das Notariatsformularbuch des Ulrich Manot (Schweizer Rechtsquellen)* 58; *Das Herkommen der Schwyzer und Oberbasler* 61; *Chartae Latinae Antiquiores* I-IV, 54-67, etc.
Schützenrainweg 44, Riehen BS, Switzerland.
Telephone: 061-513964.

Brugmans, Hendrik, D. ès L.; Netherlands literary critic and historian; b. 13 Dec. 1906; ed. Lycée Fontanes, Paris, Amsterdam Univ. and the Sorbonne.
Teacher at Arnhem, Terneuzen and Amersfoort; Pres. Workers' Educational Inst.; Socialist mem. of Parliament 39-40; teacher at Amersfoort and Amsterdam 40-42; arrested and imprisoned as hostage in St. Michielsgestel camp 42-44; released and joined "Je Maintiendrai" resistance movement 44; sent to report to Netherlands Govt. in Exile in London 45; Dir. of Information and Political Sec. of Prime Minister in first post-war Govt.; mission in Siam and Indonesia 46; has devoted himself to the European Federalist Movement since 46; first Pres. Union Européenne des Fédéralistes 46; Rector, Coll. of Europe, Bruges 50-; Gold Medal "Bene Meriti della Cultura" (Italy), Charlemagne Prize; Légion d'Honneur, Officer Order of Orange Nassau; Commandeur Order of Leopold III; Netherlands Labour Party (Partij van de Arbeid).
Publs. *Denis de Rougemont et le Personalisme français, La Littérature française contemporaine, Les Trésors littéraires de la France, Jean-Jacques Rousseau, Histoire de la Littérature Française Moderne, Crise et Vocation de l'Occident, Introduction à une Histoire Européenne* (Vol. I *Les Origines de la Civilisation Européenne* 58, Vol. II *L'Europe prend le Large* 61); also the federalist programme *La Cité Européenne, Panorama de la Pensée fédéraliste, Le Fédéralisme contemporain* (with P. Duclos), *L'Idée européenne, 1918-1966, Visages de l'Europe*; together with numerous articles on European problems in periodicals.
Collège d'Europe, 11 Dijver, Bruges, Belgium.

Bruhn, Erik Belton Evers; Danish ballet dancer; b. 3 Oct. 1928; ed. Royal Theatre, Copenhagen.
Début with Danish ballet 46, Leading Dancer 49, 58-61; Guest Artiste, Metropolitan Ballet, London 47-49, American Nat. Ballet Theatre 49, 51, 53, Perm. mem. 53-58, New York City Ballet 59, American Ballet 60; appeared with Bolshoi Ballet 61, Danish Ballet 61-, Royal Ballet (London) 62.
16 Violvej-Gent, Copenhagen, Denmark.

Bruller, Jean Marcel (*see* Vercors).

Brun, Alice A.; Danish financial official; b. 25 Feb. 1904; ed. Univ. of Copenhagen.
Ministry of Finance, Denmark 32-; Sec. to Minister of Finance 45-46; Principal, Secretariat and Budgetary Div., Ministry of Finance 46-62; mem. Govt. Cttee. for Technical Assistance to developing countries 51-; Exec. Dir. for Denmark, Finland, Iceland, Norway and Sweden of Int. Bank for Reconstruction and Development and affiliates 62-64; Head of Section, Ministry of Finance 64-
Finansministeriet, Christiansborg Slotsplads 1, Copenagen K., Denmark.
Telephone: 11-44-88.

Brun, Edmond Antoine Sylvestre; French space scientist; b. 31 Dec. 1898; ed. Lycée de Marseille and Univ. de Marseille.
Teacher, Nice 23-31, Paris 31-42; Prof., Faculty of Sciences, Paris 42; Dir. Laboratoire d'aérothermique, Centre nat. de la recherche scientifique 42-; Pres.

French Soc. of Astronautics 60-62, Int. Fed. of Astronautics 62-64; Vice-Pres. Int. Acad. of Astronautics 63-; Pres. Soc. française des thermiciens 64-; Chevalier Légion d'Honneur; mem. Nat. Acad. of Sciences (U.S.A.); Fellow Royal Aeronautical Soc., London; Hon. Fellow American Inst. of Aeronautics and Astronautics; Fellow American Astronautical Soc.; Lauréat, Acad. des Sciences.
Laboratoire d'aérothermique, 4 ter, route des Gardes, Meudon (Hauts-de-Seine), France.

Brun, Rudolf, M.D.; Swiss neurologist and psychobiologist; b. 15 March 1885; ed. Zürich, Geneva, Algiers Univs.; London, Paris, Zürich.
Neurologist, physician, biologist, asst. prof. of neuropathology Univ. Zürich 22-40, tit. prof. 42; Pres. Swiss Neurological Soc. 36-39, Hon. Pres. 54-; corr. mem. Soc. Neurologique, Paris 34; hon. mem. Belgian Psychiatric Soc.
Publs. include: *Die Raumorientierung der Ameisen* 14, *Die Bildungsfehler des Kleinhirns* 17-18, *Ein Fall von Hirntumor bei der Ameise* 25, *Das Kleinhirn, Anatomie, Physiologie und Entwicklungsgeschichte* 27, *Trauma und peripheres* 31, *Nervensystem* 31, *Die wissenschaftlichen Grundlagen der Ameisenpsychologie* 17, *Die psychischen Fähigkeiten der Insekten* 20, *Das Instinktproblem* 20, *Vergleichende Untersuchungen über Insektengehirne* 23, *Das Leben der Ameisen* 24, *Allgemeine Neurosenlehre* (3rd edn.) 54, *Psyche und Zwischenhirn* 45, *Die Innervationsvorgänge bei den Neurosen* 48, *Über biologische Psychologie* 49, *Der biologische Charakter der Freud'schen Psychoanalyse* 52, *3 Fälle von seltenem unterem Oblongatasyndrom* 52, *Gehirn, Anatomie, Physiologie und allgemeine Pathologie*, *Das Schädel-und Hirntrauma* 63, *Biologische Psychologie* 66.
Zürichbergstrasse 88, Zürich 7, Switzerland.

Brundage, Avery, B.S., M.P.E., LL.D.; American engineer and amateur sportsman; b. 28 Sept. 1887; ed. Univ. of Illinois.
Pres. Avery Brundage Co. (Builders) 15-47; Chair. Roanoke Real Estate Co. 32-, LaSalle Madison Hotel Co.; Pres. U.S. Olympic Asscn. 29-53, U.S. Olympic Cttee. 29-53; Pres. Int. Olympic Cttee.; Vice-Pres. Int. Amateur Athletic Fed. 30-52; Ex-Pres. Nat. Amateur Athletic Union (7 terms); Amateur All-round Champion of America 14, 16 and 18; numerous decorations.
10 North LaSalle Street, Chicago, Ill. 60602, U.S.A.
Telephone: State 2-6168.

Brundage, Howard Denton, B.A.; American publisher and advertising executive; b. 9 Nov. 1923; ed. Dartmouth Coll. and Harvard Graduate School of Business Admin.
With Morgan, Stanley and Co., New York 45-50; Asst. Sec. The Hanover Bank, New York 50-52; with J. H. Whitney and Co., New York 52-58, Partner 58-61; Pres. New York Herald Tribune Inc. 58; Vice-Pres. (Finance) and Dir. J. Walter Thompson Co. 62-; Dir. Faber, Coe and Gregg, Inc., G. W. Carnrick Co., and various insurance companies; Trustee Mountainside Hospital, Montclair, N.J.
120 Lloyd Road, Montclair, N.Y., U.S.A.

Brundage, Percival Flack, D.S.C.; American government official; b. 2 April 1892; ed. Harvard and New York Univs.
Partner, Price, Waterhouse & Co. 30-54, Consultant 58-; Dep. Dir. Bureau of the Budget 54-56, Dir. 56-58; Dir. Montclair Community Chest 50-54; Dir. Nat. Bureau of Economic Research 42-, Pres. 54; mem. Nat. Asscn. for Liberal Christianity and Religious Freedom, and Pres. 52-55; Dir. Fed. Union Inc. (Chair. 51-54), American Asscn. for U.N.; Chair. Unitarian Development Fund; Treas. Atlantic Council of the U.S. Inc.; Treas. People to People Health Foundation; mem. Unitarian Service Comm. (Dir. 49-54), American Unitarian Asscn. (Dir.

42-48), American Inst. of Accountants (Pres. 48-49), Council of Foreign Relations, Foreign Policy Asscn.
2601 Woodley Place N.W., Washington 8, D.C., U.S.A.

Brunei, Sultan of (*see* Bolkiah).

Brunel, Clovis; French philologist; b. 19 Feb. 1884.
Archivist for département de Lozère 08-13, for Vienne 13-16; teacher at Ecole des Chartes 16; Prof. of Romance Philology, Ecole des Chartes and Ecole des Hautes Etudes; Dir. Ecole des Chartes 30, Hon. Dir. 55; mem. of the Acad. des Inscriptions et Belles Lettres.
Publs. Numerous works on medieval history and literature, particularly in Provençal.
11 rue Cassette, Paris 6e, France.
Telephone: Lit 9726.

Brunet, Jacques, L. ès D.; French banker; b. 10 May 1901; ed. Paris Univ.
Secretary to Raymond Poincaré 28; Deputy Dir., later Dir. Ministry of Finance 35-46; Gen. Man. Banque d'Algérie et de Tunisie 46-48; Pres. and Gen. Man. Crédit Nat. 49-60; Gov. Banque de France 60-; Grand Croix de la Légion d'Honneur.
Banque de France, 3 rue de la Vrillière, Paris, France.

Brunet, Jean-Pierre; French diplomatist; b. 20 Jan. 1920; ed. Lycée Saint-Louis, Paris and Ecole Navale.
Sub-Lieut., French Navy 40; joined Free French Naval Forces 40, served in submarines 40-45; Diplomatic Service 45-; French Embassy, London 46-47; Ministry of Foreign Affairs 48-61; Deputy Rep. of France to EEC 61-64; Head of Econ. Co-operation Section, Ministry of Foreign Affairs 65-66, Dir. of Econ. and Financial Affairs 66-; Officier Légion d'Honneur.
4 rue Monsieur, Paris 7e, France.

Brunhes, Julien; French public servant; b. 25 Nov. 1900; ed. Lycée de Clermont-Ferrand, Lycée Saint-Louis, Paris, Ecole Navale, Ecole supérieure d'électricité.
Assistant Sec.-Gen. Etablissements d'Aviation Louis Breguet 45-46, Sec.-Gen. Cttee. of liaison between Transport and Management 49-; Counsellor of the Republic, Senator 46-48, 52-60; mem. European Parl. 60-, Vice-Pres. 64-65; mem. numerous asscns.; Chevalier Légion d'Honneur.
Office: 48 avenue de Villiers, Paris 17e; Home: 25 rue Galilée, Paris 16e, France.

Brüning, Heinrich, DR.PHIL., LL.D.; German politician and university professor; b. 26 Nov. 1885; ed. Munich, Strasbourg, Münster and Bonn Univs.
Officer on the Western Front 15-18; entered Prussian Min. of Welfare 19; Adviser to Deutscher Gewerkschaftsbund 21-29, resigned; founded and partly edited Union daily *Der Deutsche* 21; mem. of the Reichstag 24-33; succeeded Stegerwald as head of the parliamentary Centre Party 29; Reich Chancellor after Müller's resignation March 30; resigned and reconstructed his Cabinet Oct. 31 taking also portfolio of Foreign Affairs; resigned in May 32, when Von Papen took over the Govt.; Supernumerary Fellow and Lecturer in Political Theory, Queen's Coll. Oxford 37; Lecturer on Government and Tutor in Government and Economics, Harvard Univ. 37-39; Lucius N. Littauer Prof. of Public Admin., Harvard Graduate School of Public Admin. 39-52, Emeritus 52-; Prof. of Political Science, Cologne Univ. 51-55, Emeritus 55-.
University of Cologne, Albertus-Magnus-Platz, Cologne, German Federal Republic.

Brunner, Edmund de S., B.A., M.A., PH.D., L.H.D., LL.D.; American sociologist; b. 4 Nov. 1889.
Secretary Country Church Comm. of Moravian Church 12-17; Rural Sec. Cttee. on War Industrial Communities 17- 19; Dir. Rural Surveys Inst. of Social and Religious Research 20-33, Rural Social and Economic Studies in Asia 27-28; Associate in Rural Education Columbia Univ. 26-30 and Prof. 31-55, Emeritus 55-; mem. Pres.

Roosevelt's Advisory Cttee. on Education 37-38; Exec. Chair and Assoc. Dir. Bureau of Applied Social Research 51-63.
Publs. 38 vols., including *Immigrant Farmers and their Children* 29, *Village Communities* 27, *Rural Social Trends* 33, *A Study of Rural Society* (with J. H. Kolb) 35, Revision and new edns. 40, 46, 52, *Rural Trends in Depression Years* (with Irving Lorge) 37, *Rural Australia and New Zealand* 38, *Community Organisation and Adult Education* 42, *Rural America and the Extension Service* (with H. P. Yang) 49, *American Society: Urban and Rural Patterns* (with W. C. Hallenbeck) 55, *The Growth of a Science—A History of Rural Sociological Research in the United States* 57, *An Overview of Adult Education Research* 58, *The Educational Status of the American People* 59.
10 High Ridge Road, Wilton, Conn. 06897, U.S.A.

Brustad, Tor; Norwegian biophysicist; b. 20 Dec. 1926; ed. Univ. of Oslo and Univ. of California.
Research Fellow, Univ. of Oslo 53-54, Norwegian Cancer Soc. 54-57, U.S. Nat. Acad. of Sciences 57-59; Research Assoc. Univ. of California 59-60, Consultant in Biophysics 60-; Chair. Dept. of Biophysics, Norsk Hydro's Inst. for Cancer Research, Oslo 62-; Examiner, Univ. of Oslo 65-; Chair. Dept. of Medical Physics, The Norwegian Radium Hospital, Oslo 68-.
Publs. on radiation effects on enzymes and micro-organisms.
Norsk Hydro's Institute for Cancer Research, Montebello; and Nordveien 30, JAR, Norway.

Brutelle, Georges; French politician; b. 20 Nov. 1922; ed. Ecole Normale d'Instituteurs, Rouen, Ecole Supérieure de Commerce, Rouen and Univ. of Caen.
Resistance Movement 40-45; Chef du Cabinet, Ministry of Posts, Telegraphs and Telecommunications 45-46; Sec.-Gen., Fédération des Déportés de la Résistance 46; mem. Policy Cttee. Parti Socialiste, Section Française de l'International Ouvrière 46, Joint Sec.-Gen. 47-65; Army Service in Algeria 56-57; Pres. des Colloques Socialistes 64; Sec. Fed. of Democratic Left and Socialists 65-67, mem. Comité executif 65-; mem. Nat. Bureau S.F.I.O. 67-; contributor to *Paris Normandie de Rouen* and *L'Action de Tunis* 68-; Officier, Légion d'Honneur, Croix de Guerre.
Publs. *La Pensée Socialiste Contemporaine* 65.
8 rue Léon Vaudoyer, Paris 8e, France.

Brutyó, János; Hungarian trade union official; b. 1911.
Former carpenter; Building Workers' Union 33, mem. Central Board 37, Sec.-Gen. 55; Deputy Minister of Building Industry 56; mem. Central Cttee. Hungarian Socialist Workers' Party 57-66, Substitute mem. Political Cttee. 62-66; mem. Nat. Council, Patriotic People's Front 56, Presidential Council 61; Gen. Sec. Hungarian Nat. Council of Trade Unions 59, Pres. 65-66; Pres. Supervisory Cttee., Hungarian Socialist Workers' Party 66-.
c/o Hungarian Socialist Workers' Party, Budapest, Hungary.

Bruun, Egon, M.D.; Danish physician; b. 1 Feb. 1909; ed. Københavns Universitet.
Specialist in allergies; has trained at Univs. of Münster and Berlin 38, Forlanini Inst., Rome 40, Stockholm 43, Hopital Broussais and Institut Pasteur, Paris 50, London and Oxford 52; Head Physician, Danish Red Cross Asthma Sanatorium in Norway 46-52; Lecturer on Clinical Allergy, Univ. of Copenhagen 50-; Head Physician of Allergy Clinic, Univ. Hospital, Copenhagen 55-; Pres. Danish Soc. of Allergology 50-54, 58-60; Treas. Int. Asscn. of Allergology 54-64; Fellow, American Acad. of Allergy 52; Pres.-elect, European Acad. of Allergology 58-62, Pres. 62-65; Pres. Northern Soc. of Allergology 62-65; official of other medical orgs.;

Hon. mem. French, Argentine, Belgian and Finnish Allergy Socs.; Illum Prize of Honour and numerous awards.
8 Gersonsvej, Copenhagen-Hellerup, Denmark.
Telephone: HE 178.

Bruun-Rasmussen, Knud; Danish writer; b. 21 July 1898.
Novelist, poet and essayist.
Publs. *Digte* 20, *Kentaur* 26, *Novemberstorm* 27, *En Herre viser sig* 29, *Gaden og Mennesket* 30, *Dette ene Liv* 32, *Morgendrømme* 33, *Ansigtet i Spejlet* 47, *Hvordan skal jeg undervise?* 53, *Grundbog for talere* 54, *Bedömmelse af Mennesker* 54, *Kvinde og Mand i dagens lys* 55, *Talerkunst* 63.
Ved Stadsgraven 1, Copenhagen S, Denmark.
Telephone: SU: 546.

Bruyevich, Nikolai Grigorevich; Soviet mechanical engineer; b. 1896; ed. Moscow Univ. and Moscow Aviation Inst.
Teacher, Zhukovsky Air Force Engineering Acad. 29-; mem. U.S.S.R. Acad. of Sciences 42-; Assoc. Inst. of Machine Control, U.S.S.R. Acad. of Sciences 51-; mem. Communist Party 21-; three Orders of Lenin.
Publs. include: *Kinematics of very simple Spatial Mechanisms with Pairs of the Fifth Class* 37, *Kinestatics of Spatial Mechanisms* 37, *Foundations of the Theory of Calculation Systems* 64.
Institute of Machine Control of Academy of Sciences of U.S.S.R., 4 ulitsa Griboedova, Moscow, U.S.S.R.

Bryan, Wright, B.S.; American journalist; b. 6 Aug. 1905; ed. Clemson Coll. and Univ. of Missouri School of Journalism.
With *Atlanta Journal* 27-53, Editor 45-53; Editor *Cleveland Plain Dealer* 54-63; Vice-Pres. Devt. Clemson Univ. 64-.
100 Wyatt Avenue, Clemson, South Carolina, U.S.A.
Telephone: 803-654-5688 (Office); 803-654-3531 (Home).

Bryant, Sir Arthur, Kt., C.H., C.B.E., M.A., F.R.HIST.S., F.R.S.L.; British historian; b. 18 Feb. 1899; ed. Harrow and Queen's Coll., Oxford.
Principal Cambridge School of Arts, Crafts and Technology 23-25; Lecturer in History and English Literature Oxford Univ. Delegacy for Extra-Mural Studies 25-35; Producer Cambridge Pageant 24, Oxford Pageant 26, Fenland Pageant 31, Naval Pageant Greenwich 33; Editor *Ashridge Journal* 30-39; writer of "Our Note Book" in *Illustrated London News* 36-; a Gov. of Ashridge 36-49; Lecturer to H.M. Forces 40-46; Pres. English Asscn. 46; Chair. Soc. of Authors Management Cttee. 49-51; Chair. St. John and Red Cross Hospital Library 45-; Chesney Gold Medal 55; Hon. LL.D. (Edinburgh, St. Andrews, New Brunswick); Knight of Grace of St. John of Jerusalem.
Publs. *King Charles II* 31, *Macaulay* 32, *Samuel Pepys* 33, 35, 38, *The National Character* 33, *The England of Charles II* 34, *King George V* 36, *Letters and Speeches of Charles II* 36, *The American Ideal* 36, *Stanley Baldwin* 37, *Postman's Horn* 37, *Humanity in Politics* 38, *Unfinished Victory* 40, *English Saga 1840-1940* 40, *The Years of Endurance* 42, *Dunkirk* 43, *Years of Victory* 44, *Historian's Holiday* 47, *The Age of Elegance* 50 (*Sunday Times* Gold Medal and £1,000 Award), *The Turn of the Tide* 57, *Triumph in the West* 59, *Restoration England* 61, *The Story of England: Makers of the Realm* 53, *The Age of Chivalry* 63, *The Fire and the Rose* 65, *The Medieval Foundation* 66, *Protestant Island* 67.
Wotton Underwood, Bucks., England.

Bryant, Douglas Wallace, A.B., A.M.L.S.; American librarian; b. 20 June 1913; ed. Univs. of Munich, Stanford, Michigan.
Translator, Stanford Univ. 34-35; Asst. Curator of

Printed Books, Univ. of Michigan 36-38; Detroit Public Library 38-42; Lt.-Commdr., U.S. Naval Reserve 42-46; Asst. Librarian, Univ. of Calif. 46-49; Dir. of Libraries, American Embassy, London 49-52; Admin. Asst. Librarian, Harvard Coll. Library 52-56, Assoc. Dir., Harvard Univ. Library and Assoc. Librarian, Harvard Coll. 56-64; Univ. Librarian, Harvard Univ. 64-.
Widener Library, Harvard University, Cambridge, Mass., U.S.A.

Bryl, Ivan Antonovich; Soviet writer; b. 1917.
Began publishing 38; State Prize 52, Order of Red Banner of Labour 67.
Publs. *Dark-Browed Girl* 49, *Maria* 50, *The Righteous and the Wicked* 50, *Downing in Zabolotye* 50, *Galya* 53, *Inscription on a Wooden House* 56, *The Heart of a Communist* 57, *Confusion* 59, *My Native Land* 59, *Collected Works* (2 vols.) 60, *House of Orphan* 61, *Conversation is Continued* 62, *Green School* 63, *Lyrical Notes* 65, *Birds and Nests* 67.
Union of Writers of Byelorussian S.S.R., Minsk, U.S.S.R.

Brymer, Jack, O.B.E.; British clarinettist; b. 15; ed. Goldsmiths' Coll., London Univ.
Principal Clarinet, Royal Philharmonic Orchestra 47-63, B.B.C. Symphony Orchestra 63-; mem. Wigmore Ensemble, Prometheus Ensemble, London Baroque Ensemble and Dir./Founder London Wind Soloists; Prof. Royal Acad. of Music 50-56; Hon. R.A.M.; world-wide soloist recitals and numerous recordings; lecturer on musical topics on radio and television; two demonstration films on history, development and use of the clarinet as a solo and orchestral instrument.
Underwood, Ballards Farm Road, South Croydon, Surrey, England.

Brynielsson, Harry Anders Bertil; Swedish executive; b. 20 March 1914; ed. Royal Inst. of Technology, Stockholm.
With Kema-Bolagen, Stockholm 36-43; Man. Dir. LKB-Produkter Fabriks Aktiebolag, Stockholm 43-51; Man. Dir. Aktiebolaget Atomenergi (Swedish Atomic Energy Co.) 51-; Pres. European Atomic Energy Soc. 58-61; mem. Swedish Acad. of Engineering Sciences.
c/o Aktiebolaget Atomenergi, P.O. Box 43041, Stockholm 43, Sweden.
Telephone: Stockholm 18-80-20.

Bryzhin, Alexander Alexeyevich; Soviet politician; b. 1922; ed. Higher Party School of C.P.S.U. Central Cttee.
Soviet Army 40-46; Official, Young Communist League, and C.P., Volgograd Region 46-55; Party official, then Second Sec. Urals Regional Cttee. of C.P.S.U. 55-63; First Sec. Kokchetav Regional Cttee. of C.P. of Kazakhstan 63-; mem. Central C.P. of Kazakhstan; mem. C.P.S.U. 45-; Deputy to Supreme Soviet.
Kokchetav Regional Committee, Communist Party of Kazakhstan, Kokchetav, U.S.S.R.

Brzezinski, Zbigniew K., B.A., PH.D.; American (b. Polish) government official; b. 28 March 1928; ed. McGill and Harvard Univs.
Settled in N. America 38; Instructor in Govt. and Research Fellow, Russian Research Center, Harvard Univ. 53-56; Asst. Prof. of Govt., Research Assoc. of Russian Research Center and of Center for Int. Affairs, Harvard Univ. 56-60; Assoc. Prof. of Public Law and and Govt., Columbia Univ. 60-62, Prof. 62- (on leave 66-68) and Dir. Research Inst. on Communist Affairs 61- (on leave 66-68); mem. Policy Planning Council, Dept. of State 66-; mem. Joint Cttee. on Contemporary China (Social Science Research Council) 61-62; mem. Council on Foreign Relations, New York; Consultant to Rand Corpn.; mem. Advisory Council of Amnesty International; Guggenheim Fellowship 60.

Publs. include: *Political Controls in the Soviet Army* 54, *The Permanent Purge—Politics in Soviet Totalitarianism* 56, *Totalitarian Dictatorship and Autocracy* (co-author) 57, *The Soviet Bloc—Unity and Conflict* 60, *Ideology and Power in Soviet Politics* 62, *Africa and the Communist World* (Editor and contrib.) 63, *Political Power: U.S.A./U.S.S.R.* (co-author) 64, *Alternative to Partition: For a Broader Conception of America's Role in Europe* 65.
Office: Columbia University, Research Institute on Communist Affairs, 622 West 113th Street, New York, N.Y. 10025; Home: 40 Brayton Street, Englewood, New Jersey, U.S.A.
Telephone: 212-280-4638 (Office); 201-567-7223 (Home).

Bubenov, Mikhail Semenovich; Soviet writer; b. 1909.
Member Communist Party 51-; State Prize 47, Order of Red Banner of Labour 59, Order of Red Star.
Publs. Novels: *The Thundering Year* 32, *Immortality* 41, *The Silver Birch Tree* 47, *Orlinaya Steppe* 59; Stories: *At Flood Time* 40.
U.S.S.R. Union of Writers, 52 Vorovsky Street, Moscow, U.S.S.R.

Bubnovsky, Nikita Dmitrievich; Soviet politician; b. 1907; ed. Vinnitsa Inst. of Agriculture.
Agronomist, and Head of a district dept. of agriculture 30-44; exec. posts in Party and local govt. 44-50; Chair. Kiev Regional Soviet of Working People's Deputies 50-51; Vice-Chair. Ukrainian Council of Ministers 51-52; First Sec. Vinnitsa Regional Cttee. Ukrainian C.P. 52-54; Sec. Central Cttee. Ukrainian C.P. 52, 54-63; First Sec. Khmelnitsky Regional Cttee., Ukrainian C.P. 63-; mem. C.P.S.U. 39-; Alt. mem. C.P.S.U. Central Cttee. 56-; mem. Central Cttee. Ukrainian C.P.; Deputy to U.S.S.R. Supreme Soviet; Hero of Socialist Labour 51.
Khmelnitsky Regional Committee, Ukrainian Communist Party, Khmelnitsky, U.S.S.R.

Buburiza, Pascal; Burundi diplomatist; b. 32; ed. Groupe Scolaire of Astrida, Ruanda (now Rwanda).
Secretary of Service of Justice and Litigation of Ruanda-Urundi, Usumbura 55-57; Territorial Agent, Territory of Muchinga, Burundi 58-60; Asst. Provincial Administrator, Province of Bubanza 60-61, Dep. Public Prosecutor, Usumbura 61; Chef de Cabinet to Prime Minister of Burundi 61-62; Perm. Rep. to UN 62-63; Minister of Interior, Burundi 63-65; now Amb. to U.S.S.R.
Embassy of Burundi, Moscow, U.S.S.R.

Bucalossi, Pietro; Italian cancer specialist; b. 9 Aug. 1905; ed. Università degli Studi, Pisa.
Director-Gen. Nat. Cancer Inst., Milan; fmr. Pres. Fatebenefratelli Hospital, Milan; Mayor of Milan 64-; mem. Exec. Cttee. of the Int. Union Against Cancer (UICC), Vice-Pres. for Europe, Scientific Cttee. of the Int. Research Agency for Cancer and numerous medical socs.; Hon. Deputy Chamber of Deputies, attached to Work and Social Security Section; numerous articles on cancer and malignant tumours.
Palazzo Comunale, Piazza Scala 2, Milan; Istituto Nazionale per lo Studio e la Cura dei Tumori, P. le Gorini 22, Milan; Home: Via Bigli 15, Milan, Italy.
Telephone: 700510.

Bucciarelli Ducci, Brunetto; Italian politician; b. 18 June 1914; ed. Collegio Nazionale, Arezzo and Univ. degli Studi, Florence.
Judge, Tribunale di Arezzo; joined Christian Democrat Party immediately after the war; Deputy; Vice-Pres. Chamber of Deputies 58-63, Pres. 63-.
Publs. *Partiti, Gruppi e Parlamento, Introduzione allo Studio del Diritto Parlamentare, Cento Anni di Vita del Parlamento Italiano, Alcide de Gasperi e il suo Magistero Politico, La crisi dei partiti e la responsabilità dei cattolici, Siena e Dante, La figura e l'opera de Pio XI,*

Legislazione e Sport, Il Voto alle Donne, Il poeta Giosué Borsi a 50 anni dalla morte.
Camera dei Deputati, Rome, Italy.

Buch, Friedrich Wilhelm, D.IUR.; German diplomatist; b. 11 Jan. 1906; ed. Ludwigs-Georgs-Gymnasium, Darmstadt, and Univs. of Geneva and Frankfurt.
Lawyer, Frankfurt and Wetzlar 28-45; Mayor of Wetzlar 45-48; Head of Dept., Ministry of Interior, Hesse 48-52; Counsellor, Foreign Office, Bonn 52-57; Consul-Gen. Sydney and Marseilles 57-59; Head of Dept., Foreign Office 59-63; Amb. to Denmark 63-66, to Switzerland 66-.
German Embassy, Berne, Willadingweg 83, Switzerland.

Buchanan, Colin Douglas, C.B.E.; British town planner; b. 22 Aug. 1907; ed. Berkhamsted School and Imperial Coll. of Science and Technology, London.
With Public Works Dept., Sudan 30-32; Regional Planning Studies with F. Longstreth-Thompson, London 32-35; at Ministry of Transport 35-39; served with Royal Engineers 39-46; at Ministry of Town and Country Planning (later Ministry of Housing and Local Govt.) 46-61; Urban Planning Adviser, Ministry of Transport 61-63; Prof. of Transport, Imperial Coll., London 63-.
Publs. Numerous papers on town planning and related subjects and *Mixed Blessing, the Motor in England* 58.
32 Rectory Road, Wokingham, Berks., England.
Telephone: Wokingham 90.

Bucher, Ewald, D.IUR.; German lawyer and politician; b. 19 July 1914; ed. Univs. of Tübingen and Munich.
War service 40-45; fmr. lawyer; fmr. Organizing Man. Land Assen. of the Württemberg Gewerbe und Handelsverein; mem. Party Exec., Free Democrat Party; mem. Bundestag 53-; Fed. Minister of Justice 62-65, of Housing and Town Planning 65-Oct. 66.
Mutlangen, Beethovenstrasse, German Federal Republic.

Buchtal, Fritz, M.D.; Danish neurophysiologist; b. 19 Aug. 1907; ed. Albert-Ludwigs-Universität, Freiburg im Breisgau, Germany, Stanford Univ., California, U.S.A., and Humboldt-Universität zu Berlin.
Assistant in Physiology, Univ. of Berlin 30-32; Inst. for Theory of Gymnastics, Copenhagen Univ. 33-43; Physiological Inst., Lund Univ. 43-45; Dir. Inst. of Neurophysiology, Copenhagen Univ. 46-, Prof. of Neurophysiology 55-; Chief, Dept. of Neurophysiology, Univ. Hospital 45-; Consultant, Nat. Inst. of Health, U.S.A. 59; Visiting Prof. Univ. of California 62, Academia Sinica 64; mem. Royal Danish Acad. Sciences 46; Hon. mem. French Neurological Soc. and American Soc. for Electrodiagnosis and Electromyography; Corresp. mem. German Physiological and Neurological Socs.; Hon. M.D. (Münster, Zürich); numerous awards.
Publs. *Mechanical Properties of Muscle Fibre* 42, *Rheology of Muscle* 51, *An Introduction to Electromyography* 57, *Electrophysiological Aspects of Myopathy* 63, *Evoked action potential and conduction velocity in human sensory nerve* 66.
24 Søbredden, Copenhagen Gentofte, Denmark.
Telephone: Gentofte 6629.

Buchwald, (Arthur) Art; American journalist; b. 20 Oct. 1925; ed. Univ. of Southern Calif.
U.S. Marines 42-45; columnist *New York Herald Tribune* (European Edition) for twelve years; syndicated in 310 newspapers; reports from Washington, D.C.
Publs. *Paris After Dark, Art Buchwald's Paris, I Chose Caviar, More Caviar, A Gift from the Boys, Don't Forget to Write, How much is that in Dollars?* 61, *Is It Safe to Drink the Water?* 62, *I Chose Capitol Punishment* 63, *And Then I told the President* 65, *Son of the Great Society* 67.
1750 Penn Avenue, N.W., Washington, D.C., U.S.A.
Telephone: Washington 298-7990.

Buck, Pearl (Mrs. Richard J. Walsh), M.A.; American writer; b. 26 June 1892; ed. Randolph Macon Coll. for Women and Cornell Univ.
Advisory Editor The John Day Co.; awarded Nobel Prize for Literature 38.
Publs. *East Wind, West Wind* 30, *The Good Earth* 31, *Sons* 32, *The First Wife and Other Stories* 33, *Shui Hu Chuan* (trans.) 33, *The Mother* 34, *A House Divided* 35, *House of Earth* (trilogy: *Good Earth, Sons* and *A House Divided*) 35, *The Exile* 36, *Fighting Angel* 36, *This Proud Heart* 38, *The Patriot* 39, *Other Gods* 40, *To-day and Forever* 41, *Of Men and Women* 42, *Dragon Seed* 42, *American Unity and Asia* 42, *The Chinese Children Next Door* 42, *The Water-Buffalo Children* 43, *Asia and Democracy* 43, *The Promise* 44, *What America Means to Me* 44, *The Dragon Fish* 44, *Tell the People* 45, *Yu Lan: Flying Boy of China* 45, *Talk About Russia* 45, *Portrait of a Marriage* 45, *How It Happens* (with Erna von Pustau) 46, *Pavilion of Women* 46, *Far and Near* 47, *The Big Wave* 48, *Peony* 48, *Kinfolk* 49, *One Bright Day* 50, *God's Men* 51, *Lennie* 52, *The Hidden Flower* 52, *Come, My Beloved* 53, *My Several Worlds* 54, *The Beech Tre* 55, *Imperial Woman* 56, *Letter from Peking* 57, *Christmas Miniature* 57, *Command the Morning* 59, *The Christmas Ghost* 60, *With a Delicate Air* 62, *The Living Reed* 63, *Death in the Castle* 66, *The Time is Noon* 67, *To My Daughters with Love* 67.
Route 1, Box 164, Perkasie, Pa., U.S.A.

Buckle, (Christopher) Richard (Sandford); British writer, critic and exhibition designer; b. 6 Aug. 1916; ed. Marlborough Coll. and Balliol Coll., Oxford.
Founded *Ballet* 39; army service 40-46; Ballet Critic, *The Observer* 48-55, *Sunday Times* 59-; organiser The Diaghilev Exhibition, Edinburgh Festival and London 54, *The Observer* Film Exhibition, London 56, Telford Bicentenary Exhibition 57, Epstein Memorial Exhibition, Edinburgh, 61, The Shakespeare Exhibition (for Quatercentenary), Stratford-on-Avon and Edinburgh 64; designer, Exhibition Rooms, Harewood House, Yorks. and area in "Man in the Community" Pavilion, Expo 67 exhbn. Montreal; Plays: *Gossip Column*, Q Theatre 53 and *Family Tree*, Worthing 56.
Publs. *John Innocent at Oxford* (novel) 39, *The Adventures of a Ballet Critic* 53, *In Search of Diaghilev* 55, *Modern Ballet Design* 55, *The Prettiest Girl in England* 58, *Harewood* (a guide book) 59, *Dancing for Diaghilev* (the Memoirs of Lydia Sokolova) 60, introductions to *Epstein Drawings* 62, and *Epstein: An Autobiography* 63, *Jacob Epstein: Sculptor* 63.
34 Henrietta Street, Covent Garden, London, W.C.2, England.
Telephone: 01-240-2111.

Buckley, William Frank, Jr.; American editor and author; b. 24 Nov. 1925; ed. Univ. of Mexico and Yale Univ.
Formerly on staff *American Mercury*; Editor-in-Chief *National Review* 55-; syndicated columnist 62-; host of weekly television series *Firing Line* 66-; lecturer New School for Social Research 67; contributor to *Harper's, Esquire, Saturday Review, Atlantic*, etc.
Publs. *God and Man at Yale* 51, *Up from Liberalism* 59; co-author *McCarthy and His Enemies* 54; Editor *The Committee and Its Critics* 62, *Rumbles Left and Right* 63, *The Unmaking of a Mayor* 66, *The Jeweler's Eye* 68.
National Review, 150 East 35th Street, New York. N.Y. 10016, U.S.A.
Telephone: OR 9-7330.

Buckwitz, Harry; German theatre director and producer; b. 31 March 1904; ed. Realgymnasium and Univ. of Munich.
Hotel Man., Tanganyika 37-40; Dir. Münchner Kammerspiele 45-51; Gen. Man. Frankfurt/Main Municipal Theatres 51-; producer of opera, plays, TV; first pro-

duction several plays of Brecht, Thornton Wilder, Arthur Miller, Dürrenmatt, Max Frisch.
Schlosserstrasse 7, Frankfurt/Main, German Federal Republic.

Budakov, Arkady Vasilyevich; Soviet diplomatist; b. 1916; ed. Lenin Teachers' Training Inst., Kirov.
Diplomatic Service 45-; Second Sec., Paris 46-48; Second, later First Sec., First European Dept., U.S.S.R. Ministry of Foreign Affairs 49-50; Asst. to Deputy Minister of Foreign Affairs 51-54; Counsellor, Prague 54-56; Counsellor, Ministry of Foreign Affairs; Deputy Head of Dept. of African Countries, Ministry of Foreign Affairs 58-59; Amb. to Ethiopia 59-65; Counsellor, Third African Dept., Ministry of Foreign Affairs 65-.
U.S.S.R. Ministry of Foreign Affairs, Smolenskaya Sennaya ploshchad 32/34, Moscow, U.S.S.R.

Budashkin, Nikolai Pavlovich; Soviet composer; b. 10; ed. Moscow Conservatoire.
Honoured R.S.F.R. Art Worker; Order of Red Star 43. Compositions include 1st *Symphony* 37, *Sonatina for Piano* 37, *Holiday Overture* 37, *Russian Rhapsody, At the Fair*; State Prizes 47, 49, for *Russian Fantasia, Second Rhapsody* and *Thought*.
c/o Union of Composers, 8-10 Nezhdanova Street, Moscow, U.S.S.R.

Budd, Edward G., Jr.; American business executive; b. 23 March 1902; ed. Wesleyan Univ.
Edward G. Budd Manufacturing Co., Philadelphia 23-, Dir. 38-, Exec. Vice-Pres. 43-46, Pres. The Budd Co. 46-, Chair. 65-; official of other business and cultural orgs.
The Budd Co., 2450 Hunting Park Avenue, Philadelphia 32, Pa., U.S.A.

Budd, John Marshall, B.SC.; American railroad executive; b. 2 Nov. 1907; ed. St. Paul Acad., Phillips Exeter Acad., Yale Univ.
Minor positions in Engineering and Transport Depts., Great Northern Railway 30-42; military railway service, U.S. Army 42-45; Asst. Gen. Man., Great Northern Railway 45-47; Pres. Chicago & Eastern Illinois Railroad 47-49; Vice-Pres. Operations Great Northern Railway 49-51, Pres. 51-; Pres. Spokane Portland & Seattle Railway; mem. Board of Trustees, J. J. Hill Reference Library, St. Paul Acad.; Dir. New York Life Ins. Co., Int. Harvester Co., Marshall Field & Co., Chicago Burlington & Quincy R.R. Co.
175 East 4th Street, St. Paul, Minn. 55101, U.S.A.

Buddington, Arthur F., PH.B., M.S., PH.D.; American geologist; b. 29 Nov. 1890; ed. Brown and Princeton Univs.
Instructor Brown Univ. 17; Petrologist Geophysical Laboratory Carnegie Inst. Washington 19-20; Asst. Prof. of Geology Princeton Univ. 20-26, Assoc. Prof. 26-32 and Prof. 32-, Chair. Geology Dept. 36-50; Geologist U.S. Geological Survey, Summers 21-25, 30, 43-61; Geologist N.Y. State Museum, Summers 16-17, 26-29, 31-41; mem. Nat. Acad. of Sciences, American Philosophical Society, American Acad. of Arts and Sciences; Hon. mem. Mineralogical Soc., U.K.; Penrose Medal (American Geological Soc.) 54; Roebling Medal (American Mineralogical Soc.) 56; André Dumont Medal (Geological Soc., Belgium) 60; Hon. D.Sc. (Brown Coll.), Hon. LL.D. (Franklin and Marshall Colls.); Hon. Dr. of Applied Science (Liège Univ.).
Department of Geology, Princeton University, Princeton, N.J., U.S.A.

Budenny, Marshal Semyon Mikhailovich; Soviet army officer; b. 83.
Farm worker 92-03; military service 03, served wars 05, 14-18; mem. soldier Soviet 17; served in Revolution 17, created cavalry groups which later became 1st Cavalry Army, Commdr. 19; joined Communist Party 19; mem. R.S.F.S.R. Central Exec. Cttee. 20, U.S.S.R.

Central **Exec. Cttee.** 22; served Soviet-Polish War 20; studied Moscow Military Acad. 29; Marshal 35, Insp. of Cavalry 24-27; Commdr. Moscow Military District 37; People's Commissar of Defence 39, First Deputy 40; C.-in-C. S.W. Front, N. Caucasus 41-45; mem. Central Cttee. Communist Party 39-52, Cand. mem. 52-; mem. Presidium of Supreme Soviet 47-; Hero of the Soviet Union (twice); awarded Order of Lenin (seven times), Order of Suvorov 44; Order of the Red Banner (seven times), Hon. Revolutionary Sword (twice), Sword of Honour with Coat of Arms in Gold.
Publ. *Traversed Path* 58.
Ministry of Defence, 34 Maurice Thorez Embankment, Moscow, U.S.S.R.

Budinov, Ivan; Bulgarian economist and politician; b. 18; ed. Higher Inst. of Agriculture, Sofia.
Member Young Communist League 33-34, mem. Communist Party 43-; Head of Dept. and Deputy Chair. Export Dept., Ministry of Foreign Trade 49-53; Bulgarian Trade Rep. in Paris 53-59; Chair. Export Dept. 59-62; Minister of Foreign Trade 62-.
Ministry of Foreign Trade, Sofia, Bulgaria.

Budker, Gersh Itskovich; Soviet physicist; b. 1918; ed. Moscow Univ.
Associate Inst. of Atomic Energy, U.S.S.R. Acad. of Sciences 46-57; Prof., Moscow Eng. and Physics Inst. 56-57; Dir. Inst. of Nuclear Physics, Siberian Dept., U.S.S.R. Acad. of Sciences 57-, Presidium mem. Siberian Dept. U.S.S.R. Acad. of Sciences 58-, mem. U.S.S.R. Acad. of Sciences 64-.
Institute of Nuclear Physics, Siberian Department, U.S.S.R. Academy of Sciences, Novosibirsk, U.S.S.R.

Budo, Halim; Albanian diplomatist; b. 13.
Albanian Ministry of Justice and Ministry of Foreign Affairs; Dep. Minister of Foreign Affairs 58-61; Perm. Rep. of Albania to UN 61-.
Permanent Mission of the People's Republic of Albania to the United Nations, 446 East 86th Street, Tenth Floor, New York City, N.Y. 10028, U.S.A.

Bueno y Monreal, H.E. Cardinal José María, D.THEOL., D.PHIL., D.IUR.UTR.; Spanish ecclesiastic; b. 11 Sept. 1904; ed. Madrid Seminary, Gregorian Univ., Rome, and Madrid Univ.
Ordained priest 27; fmr. Prof. of Dogmatic Theology, Canon Law and Moral Theology, Madrid Seminary; fmr. Prof. Inst. Cen. de Cultura Religiosa Superior; Fiscal, Archbishopric of Madrid 29-45, Doctoral Canon 45; Bishop of Jaca 45-50, of Vitoria 50-54; Titular Archbishop of Antioch in Pisidia and Coadjutor Archbishop of Seville 54-57; Archbishop of Seville 57-; created Cardinal by Pope John XXIII 58; mem. Sacred Congregations of Religious, of Rites and of Ceremonies; Gran Oficial, Orden del Sol (Peru), Cruz Meritísima de San Raimundo de Peñafort, Gran Cruz, Orden de Isabel la Católica; Dr. h.c., Zaragoza Univ.
Publs. *Las Relaciones entre la Iglesia y el Estado en los modernos Concordatos* 31, *Principios fundamentales de Derecho público eclesiástico* 45.
Palacio Arzobispal, Seville, Spain.
Telephone: 22-56-57.

Buerger, Martin Julian, S.M., PH.D.; American mineralogist and crystallographer; b. 8 April 1903; ed. Mass. Inst. of Technology.
Research Asst., Dept. of Geology, Mass. Inst. of Technology 25, Instructor 27, Asst. Prof. of Mineralogy 29, Assoc. Prof. 35, Prof. of Mineralogy and Crystallography 44-, Faculty Chair. 54-56, Dir. School for Advanced Study 56-63, Inst. Prof. 56-; Pres. American Society of X-ray and Electron Diffraction 48, Crystallographic Soc. of America 39-46; Pres. Mineralogical Soc. of America 47; Co-Editor *International Tables for X-ray Crystallography* 46-; Councillor American Acad. of Arts and Sciences 50-54; Vice-Pres. Geological Soc. of

America 48; mem. Exec. Cttee. Int. Union of Crystallography 46; mem. Nat. Acad. of Sciences; foreign mem. Brazilian Acad. of Sciences and Turin Acad. of Sciences; Corresp. mem. Bavarian Acad. of Sciences 60-, Austrian Acad. of Sciences 62-; Hon. mem. German Mineralogical Soc. 57; Day Medallist, Geological Soc. of America 51; Roebling Medallist, Mineralogical Soc. of America 58; Dr. h.c. Berne 58; co-editor *Zeitschrift für Kristallographie.*
Publs. *Optical Crystallography* 35, *X-ray Crystallography* 42, *Elementary Crystallography* 56, *The Powder Method in X-ray Crystallography* (with L. V. Azaroff) 58, *Vector Space* 59, *Crystal-Structure Analysis* 60, *The Precession Method in X-ray Crystallography* 64, *Contemporary Crystallography* 68, about 190 scientific journal articles.
Department of Geology and Geophysics, Mass. Inst. of Technology 77, Massachusetts Avenue, Cambridge, Mass., U.S.A.; and Weston Road, Lincoln, Mass., U.S.A.

Buero Vallejo, Antonio; Spanish playwright; b. 29 Oct. 1916; ed. Instituto de Segunda Enseñanza de Guadalajara and Escuela de Bellas Artes de Madrid.
Visiting Lecturer numerous Univs. in U.S.A. 66; Hon. Fellow Circulo de Bellas Artes; Premio Lope de Vega 49; Premio Nacional de Teatro 57, 58, 59; Premio María Rolland 56, 58, 60; Premio March de Teatro 59; Premio de la Crítica de Barcelona 60; Premio Larra 62.
Plays: *Historia de Una Escalera* 49, *En la Ardiente Oscuridad* 50, *La Tejedora de Sueños* 52, *Madrugada* 53, *Irene, O el Tesoro* 54, *Hoy es Fiesta* 56, *Las Cartas boca Abajo* 57, *Un Soñador para un Pueblo* 58, *Las Meninas* 60, *El Concierto de San Ovidio* 62, *Aventura en lo Gris* 63, *El Tragaluz* 67.
Calle Hermanos Miralles 36, Madrid 1, Spain.
Telephone: 275-21-03.

Buetow, Herbert P., A.B.; American corporation executive; b. 25 Jan. 1898; ed. Univ. of Minnesota.
Office boy, Waldorf Paper Co., St. Paul, Minn. 13; accountant, St. Paul Athletic Club 16; staff accountant, Bishop-Brissman & Co. 18; Senior Accountant, City of St. Paul 20; Auditor, Minn. Mining and Mfg. Co. 26-35, Controller 35-39, Treas. 39-49, Dir. 40, Exec. Vice-Pres. 49, Pres. 53-64, Chair. Finance Cttee. 64-; Dir. and Vice-Pres. Nat. Synthetic Rubber Corpn.; Dir. American Lava Corpn., Big Rock Stone & Material Co., Insulation & Wires Inc., Minco Corpn. Ltd., Minn. Mining & Mfg. Int. Co., Nat. Advertising Co., Prehler Electrical Insulation Co., Samica Corpn., Zenith Plastics Co.; Chair. of Board, First Merchants State Bank, St. Paul 55-; Dir. First Nat. Bank of St. Paul, First Trust Co. of St. Paul; mem. Govt. Advisory Council on Unemployment.
1550 Edgcumbe Road, St. Paul 16, Minn., U.S.A.

Buffet, Bernard; French painter; b. 10 July 1928; ed. Lycée Carnot, Ecole Nationale Supérieure des Beaux-Arts.
Annual exhbns. 49-56 in Galerie Drouant-David, and in Galerie David & Garnier 57-; exhbns. in many foreign countries, including retrospective exhbns. Paris 58, Berlin 58, Belgium 59, Tokyo 63; illustrator of books, engraver, lithographer and stage designer; Grand Prix de la Critique 48.
Galerie Maurice Garnier, 6 avenue Matignon, Paris 8e, France.

Buganda, Kabaka of (*see* Mutesa).

Bugayev, Yevgeni Iosifovich; Soviet politician and journalist; b. 1912; ed. Chernyshevsky Inst. of History, Philosophy and Literature, Moscow, and Higher Party School Moscow.
Komsomol work 38-40; mem. C.P.S.U. 39-; party work 42-44; Sec. Gomel Regional Cttee., C.P. of Byelorussia 44-46; Sec. Central Cttee., C.P. of Byelorussia 46-47; Sec.

Minsk Regional Cttee. of C.P.S.U. 48-49, Omsk 49-54; Chief Editor *Partiinaya Zhizn* (Party Life) 54-56, 61-66; Apparatus of Central Cttee. of C.P.S.U. 56-58; Editorial Dept. Head *Problemy Mira i Sotsializma* (Problems of Peace and Socialism) 58-60; Chief Editor *Voprosy Istorii K.P.S.S.* (Questions of History of C.P.S.U.) 60-61, mem. Editorial Board *Kommunist* 66-; mem. Central Auditing Comm. of C.P.S.U. 61-66.
Kommunist, ul. Marx Engels 5, Moscow, U.S.S.R.

Bugnard, Louis; French biophysicist; b. 7 July 1901; ed. Ecole Polytechnique and Univ. of Toulouse.
Prof. Faculty of Medicine, Toulouse 30-46; Dir. Inst. Nat. d'Hygiène, Paris 46-64; Dir. of Biology and Health, Commissariat of Atomic Energy; Officier Légion d'Honneur; nat. corresp. mem. Acad. de Médecine; mem. Acad. de Chirurgie.
3 rue Léon Bonnat, Paris 16e, France.

Bühler, Hans, DR.RER.POL.; German business executive; b. 25 Nov. 1903; ed. Albert-Ludwigs Univ. Freiburg, Christian-Albrechts-Univ. Kiel, and Eberhard-Karls-Univ. Tübingen.
Chairman of Board of Management, Allgemeine Elektricitäts Gesellschaft, AEG-Telefunken; Verdienstkreuz des Verdienstordens der Bundesrepublik Deutschland, Bayerischer Verdienstorden.
Allgemeine Elektricitäts-Gesellschaft, AEG-Telefunken, 6 Frankfurt (Main) 70, AEG-Hochhaus; 85 Nuremberg, Steinplattenweg 95, German Federal Republic.

Buiter, Harm Geert, D.ECON.; Netherlands trade unionist; b. 8 Jan. 1922; ed. Univ. van Amsterdam.
Former mem. Socialist Youth Movement; Chair. Socialist Students Union of Amsterdam Univ.; active in Dutch resistance during Second World War; Research Officer Dutch Metalworkers Fed. 47; headed Joint Industrial Cttee. for metal industry in The Hague 48-51; Sec. to Workers Group of Metal Trades Cttee. of Int. Labour Org.; Pres. European Coal and Steel Community study mission sent to U.S. 54; headed Gen. Secretariat of ECSC Trade Union Cttee. in Luxembourg 56; Gen. Sec. European Trade Union Secretariat, Brussels 58-67; Gen. Sec. Int. Confederation of Free Trade Unions (ICFTU) 67-.
International Confederation of Free Trade Unions, 37-39 rue Montagne aux Herbes Potagères, Brussels 1, Belgium.

Bukharov, Alexandr Semyonovich; Soviet politician; b. 12; ed. Moscow Agricultural Inst. of Electrification and Mechanisation.
Member C.P.S.U. 42-; civil servant 38-48; Party work 48-57; Chief, Moscow Regional Board for Agriculture 57-58; First Deputy Chair. Moscow Regional Exec. Cttee. Council of Workers' Deputies, and Sec. Moscow Regional Cttee. C.P.S.U. 58-59; Deputy Chair. Council of Ministers R.S.F.S.R. 60-63; Bureau of Central Cttee. of C.P.S.U. for R.S.F.S.R. 63-; Cand. mem. Central Cttee. C.P.S.U. 61-66, mem. 66-.
Central Committee of the Communist Party of the Soviet Union, Moscow, U.S.S.R.

Bulanzhe, Yuri Dmitriyevich; Soviet geophysicist; b. 1911; ed. Moscow Geodesy Inst.
Research Assoc. Shmidt Inst. of Physics of Earth, U.S.S.R. Acad. of Sciences 34-; Corresp. mem. U.S.S.R. Acad. of Sciences 66; Vice-Pres. Int. Geodesy Asscn.
Publs. Works on experimental studies in gravimetry.
U.S.S.R. Academy of Sciences, 14 Lenin Prospekt, Moscow, U.S.S.R.

Bulatović, Miodrag; Yugoslav writer; b. 20 Feb. 1930; ed. Univ. of Belgrade.
Wrote his early works in hospitals and Red Cross Centres while leading a wandering life.
Publs. *Djavoli dolaze* (Devils Arrive) short stories 56, *Vuk i Zvono* (The Wolf and the Bell) novel-poem 58,

Crveni Petao leti prema nebu (The red cockerel) novel 60, *Hero on a Donkey* novel 65, *Godot Game* play 66. Ljubljana, Krekov trg 7, Yugoslavia.

Bulgakov, Alexandr Alexandrovich; Soviet politician; b. 1907; ed. Kharkov Electrotechnical Inst.
Member C.P.S.U. 37-; electrical engineer, factory party organizer, later Sec. Kharkov City Cttee., C.P. Ukraine 39-43; Chair. Exec. Cttee. Kharkov City Soviet of Workers' Deputies 53-54; Second Sec. Kharkov Regional Cttee. C.P. Ukraine 54-59; Sec. All-Union Central Council of Trade Unions 59-64; Chair. State Cttee. for Professional and Technical Education, U.S.S.R. Council of Ministers 64-; Cand. mem. Central Cttee. C.P.S.U. 61-; Deputy to U.S.S.R. Supreme Soviet.
State Committee for Professional and Technical Education in U.S.S.R. Council of Ministers, 16 Sadovo Sukharevskaya ul., Moscow, U.S.S.R.

Bulganin, Marshal Nikolai Alexandrovich; Soviet politician; b. 95.
Joined Communist Party 17; worked in Cheka 18-22; with Supreme Economic Council 22-27; Dir. Moscow Electrical Works 27-30; Chair. Moscow City Soviet 31-37; Chair. Council of People's Commissars of R.S.F.S.R. 37-38; Deputy Chair. Council of People's Commissars, U.S.S.R., and Head of State Bank 38-41; mem. Military Council, Western Front, 2nd Baltic Front and 1st Byelorussian Front 41-44; mem. State Defence Cttee. 44-45; Deputy People's Commissar of Defence 44-47; Minister of Defence 47-49 and 53-55; Deputy Chair. Council of Ministers 49-55, Chair. 55-58; Chair. State Bank 58; member of Supreme Soviet 37-58; Marshal of Soviet Union 47-; alt. mem. Central Cttee. Communist Party 34-39; fmr. mem. Politburo 48-52; mem. Praesidium Communist Party 52-58; Chair. Stavropol Econ. Region Aug. 58-Sept. 62; awards include Hero of Socialist Labour, Orders of Lenin, of the Red Banner, of Suvorov (1st and 2nd Class), of Kutuzov (1st Class twice) and of the Red Star, and medals.
Ministry of Social Security of R.S.F.S.R., 14 Shabolovka, Moscow, U.S.S.R.

Bulgaranov, Boyan; Bulgarian politician; b. 96; ed. Secondary School, Moscow Military Acad. and Int. Lenin School, Moscow.
Komsomo and Trade Union Official 19-22; political imprisonment 24-33; mem. Bulgarian Communist Party 20-, Central Cttee. 37-, Sec. 56-, mem. Politburo 57-; Bulgarian People's Army, Second World War; fmr. Head of Main Political Dept.; Deputy Nat. Assembly; Hero of Socialist Labour.
Central Committee of Bulgarian Communist Party, Sofia, Bulgaria.

Bulin, René Henri; French aeronautical engineer; b. 8 Aug. 1920; ed. Ecole Polytechnique Paris, Ecole Nationale Supérieure de l'Aéronautique.
Engineer responsible for setting up Centre d'Essais des Propulseurs 46-53; instructor, Ecole Nationale de l'Aviation Civile 55-63; Deputy Dir., then Dir. Air Navigation, Secrétariat Général de l'Aviation Civile, France 56-61; first Dir.-Gen. European Org. for the Safety of Air Navigation (EUROCONTROL) 61-, responsible for having set up the Air Traffic Services Agency, Brussels and the EUROCONTROL Experimental Centre, Bretigny-sur-Orge and for establishing the Upper Area Control Centre, Maastricht, Netherlands, and the EUROCONTROL Inst. of Air Navigation Services, Luxembourg; Officier de la Légion d'Honneur, Officier de l'Ordre de Léopold 1er, Officier de Lion du Juda, Médaille de l'Aeronautique, Chevalier des Palmes Académiques.
Publ. *Technique du Transport Aerien* 58.
EUROCONTROL, 72 rue de la Loi, Brussels 4, Belgium.
Telephone: 13-83-00.

Bull, Lt.-Gen. Odd; Norwegian air force officer and United Nations official; b. 28 June 1907; ed. Vestheim School, Oslo Univ. and Norwegian Army Acad.
Norwegian Army 28-31, Air Force 31-; Norwegian Air Force in U.K. and Canada 40-45, Norway 45-48; Dep. Chief of Air Staff, Royal Norwegian Air Force 48-51; Dep. Chief of Staff Operations, Allied Air Forces, N. Europe 51-53; Air Commdr., N. Norway 53-56; Commdr. Tactical Air Forces, Norway 56-58; Exec. mem. UN Observation Group, Lebanon 58; Commdr. Tactical Air Forces, Norway 59-60, Chief of Air Staff, Royal Norwegian Air Force 60-63; Chief of Staff, UN Truce Supervision Org. in Middle East June 63-; Commdr. Order of St. Olav and other foreign awards, UN Medal "In the Service of Peace" (twice).
United Nations Truce Supervision Organisation, Government House, Jerusalem (No Man's Land).
Telephone: 36225 (for Israel); 2285 (for Jordan).

Bull, William Frederick; Canadian administrator and diplomatist; b. 31 Dec. 1903; ed. Univ. of Toronto.
Joined Canadian Trade Commissioner Service and held, since 29, posts in New York, Port-of-Spain, Trinidad, Auckland (New Zealand); Commercial Attaché, Canadian Embassy, Washington 43; Dir. of Export Division and Chief of Export Permit Branch 45; Asst. Deputy Minister of Trade and Commerce 50; Deputy Minister of Trade and Commerce 51; Ambassador to Japan 57-62, to Netherlands 63-.
Canadian Embassy, Sophialaan 7, The Hague, Netherlands; and 520 Minto Place, Rockcliffe Park, Ottawa, Canada.

Bullard, Sir Edward C., SC.D., F.R.S.; British geophysicist; b. 21 Sept. 1907; ed. Repton and Clare Coll., Cambridge.
Demonstrator in Geodesy Cambridge 31-35; Smithson Research Fellow Royal Society 36-43; F.R.S. 41; research work for Admiralty 39-45; Fellow of Clare Coll., Cambridge 43-48 and 57-60, Churchill Coll., Cambridge 60-, Reader in Geophysics 45-48, 60-64; Head of Physics Dept., Univ. of Toronto 48-49; Dir. Nat. Physical Lab. 50-55; Fellow, Caius Coll., Cambridge 55-56, Prof. of Geophysics 64-; mem. Natural Environment Research Council 65-68; foreign assoc. U.S. Nat. Acad. of Sciences 59; foreign hon. mem. American Acad. of Arts and Sciences; foreign corresp. Geological Soc. of America; Hughes Medal of Royal Soc. 53, Chree Medal of Physical Soc. 57, Day Medal of Geological Soc. of America 59, Agassiz Medal of U.S. Nat. Acad. of Sciences 65, Gold Medal of Royal Astronomical Soc. 65, Wollaston Medal of Geological Soc. of London 67.
Department of Geodesy and Geophysics, Madingley Rise, Madingley Road, Cambridge, England.
Telephone: Cambridge 51686.

Bullard, Sir Reader (William), K.C.B., K.C.M.G., C.I.E.; British diplomatist; b. 5 Dec. 1885.
Acting Vice-Consul Beirut 09-10, Vice-Consul Bitlis 10-11; Acting Consul Trebizond 12, Erzerum 13, Basra 14; Civil Adviser to Principal Military Gov. Basra 14; Political Officer Kifri 18; Deputy Revenue Sec. Mesopotamia 19; Military Gov. Baghdad 20; Middle East Dept. Colonial Office 21; British Agent and Consul Jeddah 23-25; Consul Athens 25-28, Addis Ababa 28; Consul Gen. Moscow 30, Leningrad 31-34; Min. to Arabia 36-39, to Iran 39-44, Ambassador 44-46, retd. 46; Dir. Inst. of Colonial Studies, Oxford 51-56; mem. Governing Board of School of Oriental and African Studies, Univ. of London 53-65; mem. Buraimi Oasis Arbitration Tribunal 54-55.
Publs. *Britain and the Middle East* 52, *The Camels Must Go* (autobiog.) 61.
46 Plantation Road, Oxford, England.
Telephone: Oxford 59259.

Bullen, Keith Edward, M.A., B.SC., PH.D., SC.D., F.R.S.;
Australian university professor; b. 29 June 1906; ed.
Auckland Grammar School and Auckland Univ., New
Zealand, and St. John's Coll., Cambridge.
Master, Auckland Grammar School, New Zealand
26-27; Lecturer in Mathematics, Auckland Univ. 27-31,
34-40; Special Lectureship, Hull Univ. 33; Senior
Lecturer in Mathematics, Melbourne Univ. 40-45;
Prof. of Applied Mathematics, Univ. of Sydney 46-;
Pres. Int. Asscn. of Seismology and Physics of Earth's
Interior 54-57; Vice-Pres. Int. Union of Geodesy and
Geophysics 63-, Int. Scientific Cttee. for Antarctic
Research 58-62; Chair. Australian Nat. Cttee. for Int.
Geophysical Year 55-60; Convenor, Australian Nat.
Cttee. for Antarctic Research 58-62; Foreign Assoc.
U.S. Nat. Acad. of Sciences; Foreign Hon. mem.
American Acad. of Arts and Science, Hon. mem. Royal
Soc. of New Zealand; numerous medals.
Publs. *Introduction to the Theory of Seismology* 47 (3rd
edn. 63), *Introduction to the Theory of Mechanics* 49
(7th edn. 65), *Seismology* 54.
Department of Applied Mathematics, University of
Sydney, Sydney; and 132 Fuller's Road, Chatswood,
N.S.W., Australia.
Telephone: Sydney 41-7649 (Home).

Bullitt, John C.; American financial officer; b. 25;
ed. Harvard Coll. and Univ. of Pennsylvania Law
School.
Lawyer, Shearman and Sterling, New York 53-60; Dep.
Asst. Sec. for Int. Affairs, U.S. Treasury 61-62, Asst.
Sec. 62-65; Exec. Dir. Int. Bank for Reconstruction and
Devt. 62-65; Dir. New Jersey Office of Econ. Oppor-
tunity 65-; Alt. Gov. and Head, U.S. Del. to 4th
Annual Meeting Board of Govs. of Inter-American
Devt. Bank 63.
New Jersey Office of Economic Opportunity, Box 2748,
Trenton, N.J., U.S.A.

Bullock, Alan Louis Charles, F.B.A., M.A.; British
author and college principal; b. 13 Dec. 1914; ed.
Bradford Grammar School, Wadham and Merton Colls.,
Oxford.
B.B.C. European Service diplomatic and political
corresp. 40-45; Fellow, Dean and Tutor of New Coll.,
Oxford 45-52; Master of St. Catherine's Coll., Oxford 60;
mem. Hebdomadal Council, Univ. of Oxford, Vice-Chan-
cellor Designate (Oxford Univ.); Chair. Research Cttee.
and mem. Council, Royal Inst. of Int. Affairs (Chatham
House); fmr. Chair. Nat. Advisory Council on Training
and Supply of Teachers; mem. Advisory Council on
Public Records; Chair. The Schools Council; Joint
Editor *Oxford History of Modern Europe*, Int. Comm.
of Historians for publication of documents on German
Foreign Policy 1918-45; Hon. Dr. Aix-Marseille Univ.;
Hon. Fellow Merton Coll., Oxford, Wadham Coll.,
Oxford; Hon. D.Litt., Bradford Univ.
Publs. *Hitler, a Study in Tyranny* 52, 62, *The Liberal
Tradition* 56, *Schellenberg Memoirs* 56, *The Life and
Times of Ernest Bevin*, Vol. I 60, Vol. II 67, etc.
St. Catherine's College, Oxford, England.
Telephone: Oxford 49541.

Bullock, Sir Ernest, Kt., C.V.O., D.MUS., LL.D.,
F.R.C.M., F.R.C.O.; British musician; b. 15 Sept. 1890; ed.
Wigan Grammar School and privately; studied music
under Sir Edward C. Bairstow.
Asst. Organist, Leeds Parish Church; Organist, Mickle-
field Church and Adel Church; Sub-Organist, Man-
chester Cathedral 12; with H.M. Forces 15-19; Organist,
St. Michael's Coll., Tenbury 19, Exeter Cathedral 19-27;
Organist and Master of the Choristers, Westminster
Abbey 28-41, in charge of the music and conductor at
the Coronation of King George VI 37; Gardiner Prof.
of Music in the Univ. of Glasgow, and Principal of the
Royal Scottish Academy of Music 41-52; Dir. Royal
Coll. of Music 53-60; held office as Pres. of Incorporated

Society of Musicians, Royal Coll. of Organists, Incorpor-
ated Asscn. of Organists, etc.; Hon. R.A.M.
Works include songs, part-songs, organ music, church
music, choral, etc.
Welby Cottage, Long Crendon, Aylesbury, Bucks.,
England.

Bulman, Oliver Meredith Boone, PH.D., SC.D., F.R.S.;
British geologist; b. 20 May 1902; ed. Battersea
Grammar School, Chelsea Polytechnic, Imperial Coll.
of Science, and Sidney Sussex Coll., Cambridge.
Demonstrator in Zoology, later in Geology, Imperial
Coll. of Science, London 28-31; Univ. Demonstrator in
Geology, Cambridge 31-34; successively Lecturer and
Reader in Palaeozoology, Cambridge 34-55; Wood-
wardian Prof. of Geology, Univ. of Cambridge 55-66;
Editor *Geological Magazine* 34-; Vice-Pres. Geological
Soc. of London 53-57, 67-68, Pres. 62-64, Foreign Sec.
64-67; Pres. Section C, British Asscn. 59, Palaeonto-
logical Asscn. 60-62; Foreign mem. Geological Soc.,
Stockholm, Royal Physiographical Soc., Lund, etc.;
Lyell Medal (Geological Soc.) 53; Fellow, Imperial Coll.
61; Hon. Dr. phil. (Oslo) 65.
Publs. Numerous papers on graptolites and other
Lower Palaeozoic fossils.
The Sedgwick Museum, Cambridge, England.
Telephone: Cambridge 515851.

Bulmer-Thomas, Ivor (*see* Thomas, Ivor Bulmer-).

Bultmann, Rudolf Karl; German theologian; b.
20 Aug. 1884; ed. Univs. of Tübingen, Berlin and
Marburg.
Privatdozent for New Testament Exegesis, Univ. of
Marburg 12-16; Asst. Prof. Univ. of Breslau 16-20; Prof.
in Giessen 20-21; Prof. Univ. of Marburg 21-51, Emeritus
51-; hon. mem. Soc. of Biblical Literature and Exegesis;
D.Theol. (Marburg), D.D. (St. Andrews); D.S.Th.
(Syracuse, N.Y.), Dr. Phil. h. c. (Marburg).
Publs. *Die Geschichte der synoptischen Tradition* 6th edn.
64, *Jesus* 3rd edn. 51, *Das Evangelium des Johannes* 9th
edn. 68, *Das Urchristentum im Rahmen der antiken
Religionen* 3rd edn. 62, *Theologie des neuen Testaments*
5th edn. 65, *Geschichte und Eschatologie* 58, *Glauben und
Verstehen* Vols. I-IV 33-65, *Die 3 Johannesbriefe* 67.
Calvinstrasse 14, 355 Marburg/Lahn, German Federal
Republic.
Telephone: Marburg 2924.

Bultrikova, Mrs. Balzhan; Soviet politician; b. 1921;
ed. Kazakh Pedagogical Inst.
Member C.P.S.U. 43-; Head of a secondary school 41-49;
Chair. Central Cttee. Elementary and Secondary School
Workers' Union, Kazakh Repub. 49-55; Minister of
Social Maintenance, Kazakh S.S.R. 55-66; Vice-Chair.
Kazakh Council of Ministers and Minister of Foreign
Affairs, Kazakh S.S.R. 66-; Deputy to Supreme Soviet
of U.S.S.R.; Deputy to Supreme Soviet of Kazakh
S.S.R. 47-; mem. Central Cttee. C.P. of Kazakhstan.
Council of Ministers, Alma-Ata, U.S.S.R.

Bumbry, Grace; American opera singer; b. 4 Jan.
1937; ed. Boston, Chicago and Northwestern Univs.
Debut, Paris Opera as Amneris, *Aida* March 60; Basle
Opera 60-63; *Carmen* with Paris Opera, and toured
Japan; Royal Opera, Brussels; *Die Schwarze Venus*,
Tannhäuser, Bayreuth Festival 62; Vienna State Opera
63; Covent Garden 63; Salzburg Festival 64; Metro-
politan Opera 65; La Scala 66; Richard Wagner Medal
63.
Via Motta 42A, Lugano, Switzerland.
Telephone: 33255.

Bunaciu, Avram, D.IUR.; Romanian politician; b. 09;
ed. Law Faculty, Bucharest Univ.
Joined the Communist Party 39; active in the resistance
during the war; Sec.-Gen. Ministry of Internal Affairs
45; deputy of Grand Nat. Assembly 48-; Minister of
Justice 48-49; Pres. State Control Comm. 49; Asst.

Minister of Foreign Affairs 50; Sec. Presidium, Grand Nat. Assembly 54-57; Minister of Justice 57, of Foreign Affairs 58-61; Vice-Pres. of State Council 61-65; alt. mem. Central Cttee. Romanian C.P. 48-55, full mem. 55-; Rector, C.I. Parhon Univ. (now Bucharest Univ.) 52.
State Council, Bucharest, Romania.

Bunche, Ralph Johnson, A.M., PH.D.; American United Nations official; b. 7 Aug. 1904; ed. Univ. of Calif., Los Angeles, Harvard Univ., Northwestern Univ., London School of Economics, and Univ. of Cape Town.
Asst. in Political Science Univ. of Calif. 25-27; Instructor Howard Univ. 28-29, Asst. Prof. 29-33, Assoc. Prof. 33-38, Prof. 37-50; with Office of Strategic Services as social science analyst 41-44; Chief of Africa Section O.S.S. 43-44; Dept. of State 44-; U.S. Commr. Caribbean Comm. 45; Dir. Div. of Trusteeship UN 46-48, Acting Mediator in Palestine 48-49; Top ranking Dir. Dept. of Trusteeship 47-54, Under-Sec. 55-57, Under Sec. for Special Political Affairs 57-; UN Rep. in the Congo 60; Prof. of Govt. Harvard Univ. 50-52; Nobel Peace Prize 50; U.S. Presidential Freedom award 63.
115-24 Grosvenor Road, Kew Gardens, N.Y., U.S.A.

Bundvad, Kaj; Danish politician; b. 8 July 1904.
Engineering Apprentice 19-24, Mechanic 24-35; High School Teacher 35-45; M.P. 43-; Sec. to Information Centre of Labour Movement 45-56; Sec. to Social Democratic Federation 56-57; Minister of Labour and Housing 57-60, Labour 60-61, Labour and Social Affairs 61-63, Social Affairs 63-68; mem. Nordic Council 53-57, Cttee. of Foreign Affairs 56-57; Chair. Danish Section Scandinavian Parl. Cttee. for Freer Communication 53-57.
Vindingevej 63 C, Roskilde, Denmark.

Bundy, McGeorge; American professor and foundation official; b. 30 March 1919; ed. Yale Univ.
Political Analyst, Council of Foreign Relations 48-49; Visiting Lecturer, Harvard Univ. 49-51, Assoc. Prof. of Govt. 51-54, Dean, Faculty of Arts and Sciences 53-61, Prof. 54-61; Special Asst. for Nat. Security Affairs, The White House 61-66; Pres. Ford Foundation 66-.
Publs. *On Active Service in Peace and War* (with H. L. Stimson) 48, *Pattern of Responsibility* (Editor) 52.
Ford Foundation, 477 Madison Avenue, New York, N.Y. 10022; and 1040 Fifth Avenue, New York, N.Y. 10028, U.S.A.

Bundy, William Putnam; American lawyer and government official; b. 24 Sept. 1917; ed. Groton School, Yale Coll., Harvard Graduate School and Harvard Law School.
U.S. Army 41-46; Lawyer with Covington and Burling, Washington D.C. 47-51; Central Intelligence Agency 51-61; Dep. Asst. Sec. of Defense, International Security Affairs 61-63, Asst. Sec. of Defense, Int. Security Affairs Nov. 63-64; Asst. Sec. for Far Eastern Affairs, Dept. of State 64-; Legion of Merit, Hon. M.B.E.; Fellow, Yale Corpn. 61-; Trustee American Assembly 63-; Board of Dirs., Council on Foreign Relations 64-.
Department of State, Washington, D.C., U.S.A.

Büngeler, Walter, DR.MED.; German pathologist; b. 30 Dec. 1900; ed. Rostock, Frankfurt-a.-M., and Bonn. Lecturer in Pathology Frankfurt-a.-M. 29; Prof. of Pathology Danzig 34-36; Prof. of Pathology and Dir. of Pathological Section State Leprosy Research Inst., São Paulo, Brazil 36-42: Prof. of Pathology and Dir. of Pathological Inst. Kiel Univ. 42; Dean of Medical Faculty Kiel 46-47; Prof. of Pathology and Dir. of the Munich Institute of Pathology 56; Dean of Medical Faculty, Munich 57-58; Senator, German-Latin American Medical Acad.; hon. mem. and corresp. mem. of many medical societies.
Publs. *Die Gasbehandlung bösartiger Geschwülste* (with Fischer-Wasels) 29, *Patología Morfológica de las Enfermedades Tropicales* 44, *Molestias osseas na lepra* 42, *Krankheiten des Blutes und der blutbildenden Organe, Lehrbuch der Speziellen Pathologie von Kaufmann, Bösartige Geschwülste* in handbook *Das ärztliche Gutachten im Versicherungswesen* 54.
Thalkirchnerstrasse 36, 8 Munich 15, German Federal Republic.
Telephone: 5164835.

Bunker, Ellsworth, B.A.; American business executive and public servant; b. 11 May 1894; ed. Yale Univ.
Dir. Nat. Sugar Refining Co. 27-, Pres. 40, Chair. of Board 48; Dir. Curtis Publishing Co., Trustee Atlantic Mutual Insurance Co. and Centennial Insurance Co., New School for Social Research, Asia Foundation, Foreign Policy Asscn., Inst. for Int. Social Research, Hampton Inst.; Ambassador to Argentina 51-52, to Italy 52-53, to India 56-61 and Nepal 56-59, to Organization of American States 64-66, Chair. 65; Amb.-at-Large 66-67, to Repub. of Viet-Nam 67-; negotiation of agreement between Netherlands and Indonesia on transfer of Netherlands New Guinea (West Irian) 62; Pres. American Nat. Red Cross.
American Embassy, Saigon, Republic of Viet-Nam.

Bunker, George M.; American business executive; b. 2 Jan. 1908; ed. Massachusetts Inst. of Technology. Campbell Soup Co. 31-34; Wilson & Co. 34-36; Partner A. T. Kearney & Co. (Management Engineers) 36-42; Vice-Pres. The Kroger Co. 42-49; Pres., Gen. Manager and Dir. Trailmobile Inc. 49-52; Pres., Gen. Manager and Dir. The Martin Co., Baltimore 52-59, Chair. Board 59-61; Pres. Martin-Marietta Corpn., New York City 61-.
Martin-Marietta Corporation, 27 Park Avenue, New York City, N.Y.; and 4940 Indian Lane, N.W., Washington, D.C., U.S.A.

Bunker, John B. (son of Ellsworth Bunker, *q.v.*); American buisness executive; b. 8 March 1926; ed. Putney School, Vermont and Yale Univ.
U.S. Army 44-46; graduated from Yale 50; Asst. to Div. Chief of Staff, First Cavalry Div. in Korea 51; joined Nat. Sugar Refining Co. (NSR) 53, working in various capacities, Sales Dept. 54, Asst. Sec. 56; Gen. Man. NSR Godchaux Sugar Co. 59-61; Asst. Vice-Pres. in charge of Marketing with NSR 61; Asst. to Pres., Great Western Sugar Co. 62, Vice-Pres. and Dir. 64, then Exec. Vice-Pres., Exec. Cttee. 65, Pres. 66; Pres. Dir. and mem. Exec. Cttee. Holly Sugar Corpn. Feb. 67-.
Holly Sugar Corporation, P.O. Box 1052, Colorado Springs, Colorado, U.S.A.
Telephone: 303-471-0123.

Bunshaft, Gordon, B.ARCH., M.ARCH.; American architect; b. 9 May 1909; ed. Mass. Inst. of Technology. Chief Designer, Skidmore, Owings and Merrill 37-42, Partner 46-; mem. Comm. of Fine Arts, Int. Council of Museum of Modern Art, American Inst. of Architects, Nat. Acad. of Design, Nat. Inst. of Arts and Letters; Fellow American Inst. of Architects; Hon. mem. Buffalo Fine Arts Acad.; American Inst. of Arts and Letters Architectural Award 55; Hon. Dir. Fine Arts Univ. of Buffalo.
Projects include Lever House (New York), Manufacturers Trust Co. (Fifth Avenue, New York), Conn. Gen. Life Insurance Co. building (Hartford, Conn.), Beinecke Rare Book and Manuscript Library (Yale Univ.), Banque Lambert (Brussels), Albright-Knox Art Gallery, Buffalo, N.Y., Library-Museum of Performing Arts, Lincoln Center, N.Y., H. J. Heinz Co. Ltd., Middx., England, Joseph H. Hirshhorn Museum, Washington. Skidmore, Owings and Merrill, 400 Park Avenue, New York, N.Y. 10022; Home: 200 East 66th Street, New York City, N.Y., U.S.A.
Telephone: 212 PLaza 9-2121 (Office).

Buñuel, Luis; Mexican (b. Spanish) film director; b. 22 Feb. 1900.
Films include: *Un Chien Andalou* 29, *L'Age d'Or* 30, *Land without Bread* 36, *Los Olvidados* 50, *The Adventures of Robinson Crusoe* 53, *The Criminal Life of Archibald de la Cruz* 55, *La Mort en ce Jardin (Evil Eden)* 56, *Nazarin* 58, *La Fièvre monte à El Pao, The Young One* 60, *Viridiana* 61 (Prize, Cannes Festival), *El Angel Exterminador* 62, *Le Journal d'une femme de chambre* 64, *Simon of the Desert* 65 (Prize, Venice Festival), *Belle de Jour* 66 (Golden Lion of Saint Mark, Venice Film Festival 67).
Directores Cinematográficos, Chihuahua 167, Mexico D.F., Mexico.

Burbridge, Kenneth Joseph, M.A., B.C.L., PH.D.; Canadian lawyer and diplomatist; b. 11; ed. St. Thomas Univ., St. Francis Xavier Univ., Univ. of New Brunswick and Univ. of Ottawa.
Private legal practice, St. John. New Brunswick 39-41; Legal Counsel, Dept. of Munitions and Supply, Ottawa 41-43; Chief Legal Adviser to Nat. Selective Service, Ottawa 43-44; Legal Adviser to Unemployment Insurance Comm., Ottawa 45; Counsellor, Sec. of State, Ottawa 45-47; Legal Adviser, Dept. of External Affairs 47; Special Adviser to Canadian Dels. to UN 52-53; Canadian Dep. Perm. Rep. to North Atlantic Council (NATO) and Organisation for European Economic Co-operation (OEEC) 54-57; Consul-General, Seattle 57-63; High Commissioner for Canada in New Zealand 63-67.
c/o Ministry of External Affairs, Ottawa, Canada.

Burbury, Hon. Sir Stanley C., K.B.E., LL.B.; Australian judge; b. 2 Dec. 1909; ed. Univ. of Tasmania.
Barrister; Solicitor-Gen. Tasmania 52; Chief Justice of Tasmania 56-; Vice-Warden Univ. of Tasmania Senate 48-55, mem. Univ. Council 55.
Mary's, Hope Road, Rosetta, Tasmania, Australia. Telephone: 7-7984.

Burcham, Lester Arthur; American retailing executive; b. 26 April 1913; ed. Public Schools, Lancaster.
F. W. Woolworth Co., New York City 31-, Trainee, Manager, Superintendent, Sales Manager, District Manager 31-58, Vice-Pres. 58-62, Exec. Vice-Pres. 62-64, Pres. 64-; Dir. F. W. Woolworth Ltd. (Canada,) F. W. Woolworth Co. (Mexico), F. W. Woolworth Co. Ltd. (England).
F. W. Woolworth Co., 233 Broadway, New York City, N.Y., U.S.A.

Burckhardt, Charles J.; Swiss historian and diplomatist; b. 10 Sept. 1891; ed. Coll. Castle of Glarisegg, Thurgau Canton.
Attaché Swiss Legation, Vienna 18-22; Chief Del. of Int. Cttee. of Red Cross in Turkey; Prof. of Modern History, Univ. of Zürich 29; Prof. Post-Graduate School of Int. Studies, Geneva 32; High Commr. of L. of N. for Free City of Danzig 37-39; Pres. of Cttee. of Int. Red Cross; Pres. of Mixed Relief Comm. of Int. Red Cross; Swiss Minister to France 45-49; mem. Institut de France 49.
Publs. *Charles Chr. Burckhardt* 16, *Travel in Asia Minor* 24, *The Revolution in Bern, 1831,* 24, *Charles Neuhaus* 24, *Maria Theresia* 31, *Cardinal Richelieu: His Rise to Power* Vol. I 34, Vol. II 65, Vol. III 66, *Collection of Essays* 51, *Correspondence with Hofmannsthal* 56, *Missions in Danzig* 60, *La Bâtie*, and many other articles and publications.
1181 Vinzel, Switzerland.
Telephone: 021-74-11-45.

Burckhardt, Jakob Karl, DR. IUR.; Swiss public official; b. 25 June 1913; ed. schools and university, Basle.
Federal Political Dept., Berne 40-45, served Prague, Oslo, Stockholm, Rome 45-57; Pres. Swiss Atomic

Energy Comm. 57-60; Minister, Head of Div. of Int. Orgs. Fed. Political Dept. 61-March 66; Pres. of the Board, Eidgenössische Technische Hochschule, Zürich (Swiss Fed. Inst. of Technology) April 66-.
Eidgenössische Technische Hochschule, 8006 Zürich, Leonhardstrasse 33, Switzerland.

Burden, William Armistead Moale, A.B.; American financier and diplomatist; b. 8 April 1906; ed. Harvard Univ.
Vice-Pres. Nat. Aviation Corpn. 39-41, Defence Supplies Corpn. 41-42; Asst. Sec. of Commerce for Air 43-47; Aviation Consultant Smith Barney & Co. Inc. 47-49; Partner William A. M. Burden & Co. 49-; Special Asst. for Research & Development to Sec. of Air Force 50-52; mem. Nat. Aeronautics and Space Council 58; Ambassador to Belgium 59-61; Dir. of numerous companies; Trustee Museum of Modern Art; Chair. Board of Trustees Inst. of Defense Analyses; Pres. France America Soc.; mem. U.S. Citizens' Comm. for NATO 61-62; Commdr. Légion d'Honneur, Cruzeiro do Sul (Brazil), Bundesverdienstkreuz, Grand Cordon Ordre de Léopold II, Commdr. Order of Merit, Italy; Hon. D.Sc. (Clarkson Coll. of Technology), Hon. LL.D. (Fairleigh Dickinson Univ.).
Publ. *The Struggle for Airways in Latin America* 43.
820 Fifth Avenue, New York City, N.Y. 10021, U.S.A.

Burdick, Quentin Northrop, B.A., LL.B.; American lawyer and politician; b. 19 June 1908; ed. Univ. of Minnesota.
Admitted to N. Dakota Bar 32, practised Fargo 32-58; Candidate for Gov. 46, for U.S. Senator 56; Senator from N. Dakota 61-; Democrat.
U.S. Senate, Washington D.C.; and 310 10th Avenue South, Fargo, North Dakota, U.S.A.

Burelli Rivas, Miguel Angel, LL.B., DR.POL.SC.; Venezuelan lawyer and diplomatist; b. 8 July 1922; ed. Univ. of Los Andes, Bogotá, Central Univs., Venezuela and Ecuador, Nat. Univ. of Bogotá, and Univs. of Madrid and Florence.
Pre-Seminary Prof. of Political Sociology and Chief Prof. of Mining and Agrarian Legislation, Faculty of Law, Univ. of Los Andes, Bogotá, Chief Prof. of Humanities I and II, Faculty of Civil Eng., Dir. of Univ. Culture, Founder of School of Humanities, Founder-Dir. of Univ. reviews, *Bibliotheca* and *Universitas Emeritensis*; First Sec. Venezuelan Embassy, Colombia; Counsellor, U.S.; Chargé d'Affaires, Mexico; Political Dir. Ministry of the Interior; Dir.-Gen. Ministry of Foreign Affairs (nine times Acting Minister); Interim Minister of Foreign Affairs; returned to legal profession 61; mem. Venezuelan Supreme-Electoral Council 61; Minister of Justice 64-65; Amb. to Colombia 65-67, to U.K. 67-; Vice-Dir. Grand Colombian Merchant Fleet; Gen. Sec. Venezuelan Del. to Fourth Session UN Gen. Assembly; Asst. Sec.-Gen. Tenth Interamerican Conf.; Del. Perm. Coffee Comm. of Pan American Union; mem. Inquiry Comm. on British Guiana-Venezuela Boundary; mem. Editorial Cttee. *Meridanian Themes and Collection of Authors* 64-; Grand Cordon, Order of the Liberator, Grand Cross, Order of Merit (German Fed. Repub.), Grand Cross of Merit (U.A.R.), Grand Officer, Order of Merit and Grand Cross, Order of St. Gregory the Great (Italy), Grand Cross, Order of Boyacá and Medal of Postal Merit, First Class (Colombia).
Embassy of Venezuela, Flat 6, 3 Hans Crescent, London, S.W.1, England.

Burg, Josef, DR. PHIL.; Israeli politician; b. 31 Jan. 1909; ed. Univs. of Berlin and Leipzig; Pedagogical Inst., Leipzig; Rabbinical Seminary Berlin; and Hebrew Univ. of Jerusalem.
Directorate, Palestine Office, Berlin 36; Nat. Exec. Mizrachi; Zionist Gen. Council 39-51; mem. Exec. Hapoel Hamizrachi 44-; Deputy Speaker First Knesset (Israeli Parl.) 49-51; Minister of Health, Govt. of Israel

51-52; Minister of Posts and Telegraphs Dec. 52-58; Minister of Social Welfare 59-; Nat. Religious Party.
6 Ben Maymon Street, Jerusalem, Israel.

Burgbacher, Fritz, DR.RER.POL.; German businessman and university professor; b. 1 Sept. 1900; ed. Frankfurt/Main Univ.
Syndikus, Dresdner Bank, Mainz 23-25; auditor 25-29; Dir. Rhenag Rheinische Energie A.G., Cologne 29-; Chair. Elster & Co. A.G., Mainz; Dir. of various industrial and power-supplying companies; Deputy Chair. Verband der Deutschen Gas- und Wasserwerke; Chair. Board and Power Cttee. Landesplanungsgemeinschaft Rheinland; mem. Bundestag; mem. European Parliament, mem. Power Cttee.; Chair. Econ. Cttee., North Atlantic Assembly; Christian Democrat.
Publs. *Wesen und Gestaltungsformen der Gasverbundwirtschaft* 50, *Die Bedeutung sozialer, politischer und psychologischer Faktoren in der Entwicklung der Energiewirtschaft, Das Problem der oberen Führungskräfte* 53, *Der Bildungsauftrag des christlichen Unternehmers* 54, *Gedanken zu unserer Zeit* 57, *Politik auf drei Ebenen* 61, *Politik, Idee und Wirklichkeit* 65.
Bayenthalgürtel 9, 5 Cologne-Marienburg, German Federal Republic.
Telephone: 380281.

Burgers, Johannes Martinus, DR. PHIL.; Netherlands university professor; b. 13 Jan. 1895; ed. Univ. of Leiden.
Prof. Aero- and Hydro-dynamics Technical Univ. of Delft 18-55; Research Prof. Inst. for Fluid Dynamics and Applied Mathematics, Univ. of Maryland 55-; mem. Royal Neths. Acad. of Sciences 31-; Foreign mem. Accad. delle Scienze di Turino 64; Dr. h.c. Univ. Libre de Bruxelles 48, Univ. of Poitiers 50; mem. American Acad. of Arts and Sciences and of several societies; Knight Order of Netherlands Lion.
Publs. *Experience and Conceptual Activity* 65, and on hydro- and aero-dynamics, etc., since 20.
Home: 4622 Knox Road, Apt. 7, College Park, Md. 20740; Office: Institute for Fluid Dynamics and Applied Mathematics, Univ. of Maryland, Md. 20740, U.S.A.
Telephone: 301-454-2705 (Office); 301-277-6939 (Home).

Burgess, John Lawie, O.B.E. (Mil.), T.D., J.P.; British journalist; b. 17 Nov. 1912; ed. Trinity Coll., Glenalmond, Scotland.
Sec. Cumberland Newspapers Ltd. 34-45; war service abroad with Border Regt. 39-45; Editor-in-Chief and Man. Dir. Cumberland Newspapers Ltd. 45-; Dir. Press Asscn. 50-57, Chair. 57; Dir. Reuters 55-, Chair. 59-, Border T.V. Ltd. 60-; Hon. Col. 4th Battalion Border Regt. 56-; D.L. Cumberland 56.
The Old Hall, Rockcliffe, Carlisle, Cumberland, England.

Burghardt, Max; German actor; b. 27 Nov. 1893.
Actor at Stadttheater, Bremen after First World War; stage career until 35; Dir. Northwest German Radio, Cologne 46; Dir. Gen. City Theatres, Leipzig 50-54; Dir. German State Opera, Berlin 54-63; Pres.Deutscher Kulturbund 58-; Hon. Prof.; mem. Deutsche Akademie der Künste zu Berlin.
Deutscher Kulturbund, Otto-Nushcke-Str. 1, 108 Berlin, Germany.

Burhan, Shahidi (Pao-erh-han); Chinese politician; b. 94; ed. Berlin Univ.
Post in Sinkiang Govt. 16; Consul in Kazan 37; imprisoned, released 44; Asst. Gov. Sinkiang 46; Vice-Chair. Sinkiang 48; Chair. 49; North West Administrative Council 53; Vice-Chair. Nat. Cttee., 2nd C.P.P.C.C.; Vice-Chair. Nationalities Cttee., N.P.C. 55-, China Peace Cttee.; on Cttee of Uighur Autonomous Area 56; Pres. China-U.A.R. Friendship Asscn., Chair. China Islamic Asscn. 53-; mem. Asian Solidarity Cttee.; Dir. Inst. of Languages of Nat. Minorities, Chinese Acad. of Sciences.
Institute of Languages of National Minorities, Chinese Academy of Sciences, Peking, China.

Burian, Jiří; Czechoslovak agriculturalist and politician; b. 21; ed. agricultural college.
Apprenticed as bricklayer; agricultural work 42-48; Chair. Local Nat. Cttee., Dobříš, Bohemia 48-50; mem. Agricultural Dept., Regional Nat. Cttee., Prague 50-54; Head, Agricultural Dept., District Cttee. of Communist Party, Prague 54-58; Head of Div., Agricultural Dept., Central Cttee. of C.P. 62-63; Minister of Agriculture Sept. 63-67; mem. Agricultural Comm., Central Cttee. of C.P. of Czechoslovakia 63-; mem. Nat. Assembly 64-; Sec. Central Bohemian Regional Cttee. of C.P. of Czechoslovakia.
The National Assembly, Prague, Czechoslovakia.

Burin des Roziers, Etienne; French diplomatist; b. 11 Aug. 1913; ed. Ecole Libre des Sciences Politiques, Faculties of Law and Letters, Univ. of Paris, and Univ. of Oxford.
Head, French Del. to Int. Comm. of Enquiry on Former Italian Colonies 47-48; Sub-Dir. of the Saar, Ministry of Foreign Affairs 48-50; Atlantic Pact Del. 50-52; Technical Adviser to Prime Minister 53; Chargé d'Affaires, Yugoslavia 54-55; French Resident in Morocco 55-56; Consul-Gen. Milan 56-58; Ambassador to Poland 58-62; Sec.-Gen. of the Presidency of the Republic 62-67; Amb. to Italy 67-; Officier de la Légion d'Honneur, Croix de Guerre, Médaille de la Résistance, other decorations.
Ambassade de France, Piazza Farnese 67, Rome, Italy.

Burkatskaya, Galina Evgenievna; Soviet agronomist and politician; b. 1916; ed. Kharkov Artem Communist Univ.
Chairman, Radyanska Ukraine Collective Farm 49-; Deputy of the Supreme Soviet of the U.S.S.R. until 66; mem. C.P.S.U. 46-; Hero of Socialist Labour (twice).
Radyanska Ukraine Collective Farm, Geronimovka Village, Cherkass Region, Ukraine, U.S.S.R.

Burke, Admiral Arleigh A., American naval officer; b. 19 Oct. 1901; ed. U.S. Naval Acad. and Univ. of Michigan.
Commissioned 23, served all ranks to Rear-Admiral 50; served 1939-45 war; Head of Research and Development Div., Bureau of Ordnance, Washington 45; Chief of Staff to Commdr. Eighth Fleet in Atlantic 46, to C.-in-C. Atlantic Fleet 45-47; Dep. Chief of Staff to Commdr. Naval Forces, Far East; Commdr. Cruiser Div. Five; mem. Mil. Armistice Comm. under Commdr. Naval Forces, Far East 51; Dir. Strategic Plans Div., Navy Dep. 52; Commdr. Cruiser Div. Six 54; Commdr. Destroyer Atlantic Fleet 55; Chief of Naval Operations (with rank of Admiral) May 55-61, retd. 61; Director, Center for Strategic Studies, Georgetown Univ.; Dir. of numerous companies; Hon. D.Sc., Hon. LL.D., Hon. D.Eng.; Navy Cross; Legion of Merit (two gold stars with oak leaf cluster); Purple Heart; and others.
Office: Suite 600, 810 18th Street N.W., Washington, D.C. 20006; Home: 8624 Fenway Drive, Bethesda, Md. 20034, U.S.A.
Telephone: 783-6691 (Office); 365-0906 (Home).

Burke, Sir Aubrey Francis, Kt., O.B.E.; British businessman; b. 21 April 1904.
Chairman Hawker Siddeley Australia Pty. Ltd., Hawker de Havilland Australia Pty. Ltd., Hawker Siddeley Building Supplies Ltd., and other cos.; Deputy Chair. and Man. Dir. Hawker Siddeley Dynamics Ltd., Hawker Siddeley Holdings Ltd.; Deputy Chair. Hawker Siddeley Electric Ltd., R. A. Lister and Co. Ltd. (Chair. Oct. 67-); Exec. Vice-Pres. Dominion Steel and Coal Corpn. Ltd.; Dir. Hawker Siddeley Aviation Ltd. and numerous other cos.; Vice-Chair. Hawker-Siddeley Group 68-; Pres. Soc. of British Aircraft Constructors Ltd. 58-60; Council mem., Soc. of British Aerospace Companies Ltd.; High Sheriff of Herts. 66.
Rent Street Barns, Bovingdon, Herts.; and Ramster, Chiddingfold, Surrey, England.

Burke, Kenneth; American writer; b. 5 May 1897; ed. Ohio State and Columbia Univs.

Research worker Laura Spelman Rockefeller Memorial 26-27; music critic *The Dial* 27-29; mem. staff Bureau of Social Hygiene 28-29; Music Critic *Nation* 34-36; Lecturer in Practice and Theory of Literary Criticism New School for Social Research 37, Univ. of Chicago 38, 49-50, Kenyon Coll. 50, Ind. Univ. 52, 58, Drew Univ. 62, 64, Bennington Coll. 43-61, Pennsylvania State Univ. 63; Regents Professor, Univ. of California (Santa Barbara) 64-65, Central Washington State Coll. 66; Guggenheim Fellowship 35; mem. Nat. Inst. of Arts and Letters, American Acad. of Arts and Letters, American Acad. of Arts and Science; Fellow Center for Advanced Study in Behavioral Sciences 57-58; Hon. D.Litt., Bennington Coll., Rutgers Univ., Brandeis Univ.; Creative Arts Awards Comm. Award for Notable Achievements in the Arts 67.

Publs. *The White Oxen* 24, *Counter-Statement* 31, *Towards a Better Life* 32, 66, *Permanence and Change—Anatomy of Purpose* 35, *Attitudes Towards History—*Vol. I *Acceptance and Rejection, The Curve of History,* Vol. II *Analysis of Symbolic Structure* 37, *The Philosophy of Literary Form-Studies in Symbolic Action* 41, 67, *A Grammar of Motives* 45, *A Rhetoric of Motives* 50; *Book of Moments: Poems 15-54* 55, *The Rhetoric of Religion* 61, *Language as Symbolic Action, Essays on Life, Literature and Method* 66; translator Thomas Mann's *Death in Venice* 25, Emil Ludwig's *Genius and Character* 27, and Emil Baumann's *Saint Paul* 29.

R.D.2, Andover, New Jersey 07821, U.S.A.

Telephone: 201-347-3249.

Burke, Samuel Martin, B.A. (HONS.), M.A., F.R.S.A.; Pakistani diplomatist; b. 3 July 1906; ed. Govt. Coll., Lahore, and School of Oriental Studies, London.

Indian Civil Service 31-47; District Officer and District and Sessions Judge; Pres. Election Tribunal, Punjab 46; Pakistani Foreign Office 48-49; served as Sec. to Pakistani Del. to Inter-Dominion Confs. with India 48 and 49; Counsellor to Pakistani High Comm. in London 49-52; Minister in Washington 52-53; led Special Missions to Dominican Republic and Mexico 52; Chargé d'Affaires, Rio, Brazil 53; mem. U.N. Cttee. on Contributions 53-55; Deputy High Commr. for Pakistan in United Kingdom 53; Minister to Sweden (concurrently to Norway, Denmark and Finland) 53-56; Ambassador to Thailand and Minister to Cambodia and Laos 56-59; mem. Pakistani Del. to SEATO Council Meetings 57, 58, 59; High Commr. in Canada 59-61; led Special Mission to Argentina 60; Prof. and Consultant in South Asian Studies, Dept. of Int. Relations, Univ. of Minnesota 61-; Sitara-i-Pakistan.

Publ. *Zafrulla Khan: The Man and his career.*

University of Minnesota, Minn., U.S.A.

Burkov, Boris Sergeevich; Soviet journalist, publisher and social worker; ed. agricultural technical school and Moscow Pedagogic Inst.

Journalist 38-; Chief Editor *Komsomolskaya pravda* (Komsomol Truth) 42-48; Deputy Chief Editor *Ogonyek* (Little Light) 51-54; Chief Editor *Trud* (Labour), Trade Union Newspaper 54-61; Chair. of Board of Novosti Press Agency 61-; Sec. Union of Journalists of U.S.S.R. 57-; awarded numerous medals and orders.

Novosti Press Agency, M. Putinkovsky 2, Moscow, U.S.S.R.

Burleson, Omar, B.A., LL.B.; American lawyer and politician; b. 19 March 1906; ed. Abilene Christian Coll., Hardin-Simmons Univ., Cumberland Univ. Law School, and Univ. of Texas.

County Attorney, Jones County, Texas 31-34; County Judge, Jones County 40; Special Agent, Federal Bureau of Investigation 41-42; U.S. Navy 43-45; mem. U.S. House of Representatives 46-, Chair. House Admin. Cttee. 64; Democrat.

U.S. House of Representatives, Washington, D.C., U.S.A.

Burman, Stephen France, C.B.E., M.A.; British company director; b. 27 Dec. 1904; ed. Oundle School.

Chairman United Birmingham Hospitals 48-53; mem. Council of Birmingham Chamber of Commerce 47, Vice-Pres. 49, Pres. 50-51; Life Gov. and mem. of Council, Univ. of Birmingham 49-, Pro-Chancellor 55-66; mem. Royal Comm. on the Civil Service 53; also holds following posts: Chair./Man. Dir. Burman & Sons Ltd.; Dir. Burman, Cooper & Co. Ltd., Averys Ltd., Imperial Chemical Industries Ltd., Joseph Lucas (Industries) Ltd., Serck Ltd. (Chair.), W. Dowler & Sons Ltd., Duport Ltd., Henry Pooley & Sons Ltd., Midland Bank Ltd., Duport Iron & Steel Co. Ltd., Imperial Metal Industries Ltd., W. & T. Avery Ltd., Brown's Clipper Co., Birmingham Hospitals Centre; Chair. Birmingham branch of British Empire Cancer Campaign for Research.

Cooper's Hill House, Alvechurch, Worcestershire, England.

Telephone: Hillside 1703.

Burn, Joshua Harold, M.D., F.R.S.; British pharmacologist; b. 6 March 1892; ed. Barnard Castle School, Emmanuel Coll., Cambridge and Guy's Hospital.

Mem. staff Medical Research Council 20-25; fmr. Prof. of Pharmacology Univ. of London; Prof. of Pharmacology in Oxford Univ. 37-59; Visiting Prof. Washington Univ. St. Louis, Missouri 59-68; Hon. Fellow Nat. Inst. of Sciences of India; hon. mem. Pharmaceutical Society; hon. mem. Society of Pharmacology and Therapeutics of Argentine Medical Asscn., British Pharmacological Society, Deutsche Pharmakologische Gesellschaft; mem. Deutsche Akademie der Naturforscher (Leopoldina); Hon. D.Sc. Yale Univ.; Hon. M.D. Johannes Gutenberg Univ. Mainz; Dr. h.c. Paris Univ.; Gairdner Int. Award 59.

Publs. *Biological Standardisation* 37, *The Background of Therapeutics* 48, *Practical Pharmacology* 52, *Functions of Autonomic Transmitters* 56, *Drugs, Medicines and Man, Automatic Nervous System* 64, *Our Most Interesting Diseases* 64.

2 Capel Close, Oxford, England.

Telephone: Oxford 58209.

Burnet, Alastair (*see* Burnet, J. W. A.).

Burnet, Sir Frank Macfarlane, O.M., F.R.S., SC.D., F.R.C.P., F.R.A.C.P., F.A.C.P.; Australian scientist; b. 3 Sept. 1899; ed. Melbourne Univ.

Resident Pathologist, Melbourne Hospital 23-24; Beit Fellow for Medical Research at Lister Inst., London 26-27; Asst. Dir. Walter and Eliza Hall Inst. for Medical Research 28-31 and 34-44, Dir. 44-65; Dunham Lecturer, Harvard Medical School 44; Croonian Lecturer, Royal Society 50; Herter Lecturer, Johns Hopkins Univ. 50, Flexner Lecturer at Vanderbilt Univ. 58; Chair. Board of Trustees, Commonwealth Foundation; Foreign mem. Royal Swedish Acad. of Science 57; Foreign Assoc. Nat. Acad. of Sciences, U.S.A., Copley Medal Royal Society 59, Nobel Prize for Medicine 60; Pres. Australian Acad. of Sciences 65-.

Publs. *Biological Aspects of Infectious Disease* 40, *Production of Antibodies* 49, *Viruses and Man* 53, *Principles of Animal Virology* 55, *Enzyme, Antigen and Virus* 56, *Clonal Selection Theory of Immunity* 59, *Integrity of the Body* 62, *Auto-Immune Diseases* (with I. R. Mackay) 62.

13 Edward Street, Kew, Victoria, Australia.

Telephone: 34-0484.

Burnet, James William Alexander (Alastair); British journalist; b. 12 July 1928; ed. The Leys School, Cambridge, and Worcester Coll., Oxford.

Sub-Editor and Leader Writer *Glasgow Herald* 51-58, Leader Writer *The Economist* 58-62; Political Editor; Independent Television News 63-64; Editor *The Economist* 65-.

43 Hornton Court, Campden Hill Road, London, W.8, England; and 33 Westbourne Gardens, Glasgow, W.2, Scotland.

Telephone: Western (Glasgow) 8073; and 01-937-7563.

Burnett, Clinton Brown; American business executive; b. 29 July 1908; ed. Washington Univ., St. Louis and Kent Coll., Chicago.

Joined Johns-Manville Corpn. 31; Man. Kansas Ordnance Plant and Chair. Bomb and Shell Loading Cttee. U.S. Army 41-46; Vice-Pres Johns-Manville Products Corpn. 46-51; Dir. of Engineering Johns-Manville Corpn. 51-54; Gen. Man. Johns-Manville Celite Div. 54-57; Exec. Vice-Pres. and Dir. Johns-Manville Corpn. 57, Chair. Joint Operating Cttee. 58-60, Pres. 60-, Chief Exec. Officer and Dir. 60-.

Candlewood Isle, Conn., U.S.A.

Burnett, Leo, A.B.; American advertising executive; b. 21 Oct. 1891; ed. Univ. of Michigan.

Editor of House Magazine, later Advertising Man. Cadillac Motor Car Co., Detroit 15-20; Dir. of Advertising, LaFayette Motors, Indianapolis 20-23; Vice-Pres. (Creative) Homer-McKee Co., Indianapolis 23-30; in charge of creative work, Chicago Office, Erwin Wasey and Co. 30-35; Founder and Pres. Leo Burnett Co. Inc. (Advertising Agency) 35-, Chair. of Board 55-; Dir. (and fmr. Chair.) The Advertising Council Inc.; official of other social and welfare orgs.; numerous medals.

Publs. *Good Citizen* 48, *Communications of an Advertising Man* 61.

Leo Burnett Co. Inc., Prudential Plaza, Chicago, Ill. 60601; Home: Route 1, Box 1, Lake Zurich, Ill. 60047, U.S.A.

Burney, Leroy Edgar, M.D., M.P.H.; American physician; b. 31 Dec. 1906; ed. Indiana and Johns Hopkins Univs.

Joined U.S. Public Health Service 32, established first mobile venereal disease clinic in Brunswick, Georgia 37-39; Asst. Chief, Division of States Relations 43-44; detailed to U.S. Navy 44; Dir. U.S. Public Health Service, District IV, New Orleans 45; Sec. and State Health Commr., Indiana State Board of Health 45-54; Asst. Surgeon-Gen. and Deputy Chief, Bureau of State Service, U.S. Public Health Service 54-56; Surgeon-General, U.S. Public Health Service 56-61; Vice-Pres. Health Sciences, Temple Univ. 61-; Hon. D.Sc. (Jefferson, Woman's Medical Colls., Indiana Univ., De Pauw Univ.); Hon. LL.D. (Seton Hall Univ.).

Temple University, 3400 North Broad Street, Philadelphia, Pa. 19122, U.S.A.

Burnham, Donald Clemens, B.SC.; American business executive; b. 28 Jan. 1915; ed. Purdue Univ.

Former Asst. Chief Engineer, Oldsmobile Div., Gen. Motors; Westinghouse Electric 54-, Pres. July 63-; mem. American Soc. of Mechanical Engineers, The Business Council The President's Advisory Cttee. on Labor-Management Policy and other orgs.; several hon. degrees.

Westinghouse Electric Corporation, 3 Gateway Center, Pittsburgh 30; Home: 615 Osage Road, Mt. Lebanon, Pittsburgh, Pennsylvania, U.S.A.

Burnham, Lindon Forbes Sampson, Q.C.; Guyanese lawyer and politician; b. 20 Feb. 1923; ed. Kitty Methodist School, Central High School and Queen's Coll., British Guiana, and London Univ.

Called to Bar, Gray's Inn, London 48; Pres. W. Indian Students Union, London 47-48; Co-Founder People's Progressive Party 49, Chair. 49-55; mem. Legislature 53, 57-61, 61-64; Minister of Educ. 53; Founder, People's Nat. Congress 55, Leader 55-; Pres. British

Guiana Labour Union 52-56, 62-; Mayor of Georgetown 63-64; Prime Minister, British Guiana 64-66, Guyana 66-.

Prime Minister's Residence, Vlissengen Road, Georgetown, Guyana, West Indies.

Burniaux, Constant; Belgian writer and journalist; b. 1892.

Literary critic for *Eventail, Journal de Charleroi, Soir, Nouvelles Littéraires,* etc.; Vice-Pres. Belgian PEN Club; elected to the Belgian Académie Royale de Langue et de Littérature Française 45; Grand Prix triennal for novel 49; Grand Officier de l'Ordre de la Couronne; Grand Officier de l'Ordre de Léopold; Chevalier de la Légion d'Honneur.

Publs. *Poèmes en Prose* 32, *L'Aquarium* 33, Novels: *La Bêtise* 25, *Une Petite Vie* 29, *Crânes tondus* 30, *Un Pur* 32, *La Quinzaine du Plaisir* 33, *Rose et M. Sec* 37, *La Grotte* 39, *Clémence* 44, *Jeunesse* 45, *Route minée* 46, *Les Abandonnés* 48, *Ondes courtes* (poems) 51, *La Vérité est dans les coeurs* 52, *L'Autocar* 55, *Marines* 56, *Les soeurs de notre solitude* 58, *Les Ages de la Vie* 60, *Voyages* (poems) 62, *La Fille du Ciel* 63, *La Vie Plurielle* 65, *Poésie (1922-1963)* 65, *L'Odeur du matin* 67, *D'humour et d'amour* 68; and books for children.

43 rue Henri Werrie, Brussels 9, Belgium.

Telephone: 262902.

Burns, Lt.-Gen. Eedson Louis Millard, C.C., D.S.O., O.B.E., M.C.; Canadian army officer and public servant; b. 17 June 1897; ed. Royal Mil. Coll., Kingston, Ont., Imperial Defence Coll., London, and Staff Coll., Quetta, India.

Held various staff appointments in Canadian army; Officer-in-Charge Geographical Section, Nat. Defence Headquarters, Ottawa 30, directed experiments in air photo survey; Pres. Canadian Inst. of Survey 36-37; served 39-45 war; Dir.-Gen. of Rehabilitation, Dept. of Veteran Affairs 45-46, Asst. Deputy Minister 46-50, Deputy Minister 50-54; Pres. Ottawa Branch, UN Asscn. of Canada 47-48, Nat. Pres. 52 and 53; Alt. Del. to UN Gen. Assembly 49; Chief of Staff, UN Truce Supervision Organization in Palestine 54-56; Commdr. UN Emergency Force Nov. 56-Dec. 59; Adviser on Disarmament to Govt. of Canada 60-; Canadian Rep. on Ten-Nation Disarmament Conf. 60, and Eighteen-Nation Disarmament Conf. 62-.

Publs. *Manpower in the Canadian Army 39-45* 55, *Between Arab and Israeli* 62, *Megamurder* 66.

6 Park Road, Ottawa 2, Ont., Canada.

Burns, Hendry Stuart Mackenzie, B.SC., B.A.; Scottish-born American businessman; b. 29 April 1900; ed. Robert Gordon's Coll., Aberdeen and Cambridge Univs.

Settled in U.S.A. 26; with Shell Oil Co., Calif. 26-36; Gen. Man. Shell Co. of Colombia S.A. 36-46; Senior Vice-Pres. Shell Oil Co. Inc. 46-47, Pres. 47-60, Dir. 47-60; Dir. Ampex Corpn., Gen. Dynamics Corpn. 62-, American Petroleum Inst.; Hon. LL.D. Aberdeen Univ., Hon. D.Sc. St. Louis Univ.

484 Park Avenue, New York City, N.Y., U.S.A.

Telephone: Eldorado 5-0351.

Burns, John A.; American politician; b. 30 March 1909; ed. St. Louis High School, Honolulu.

Member Hawaiian House of Reps. 56-59; Gov. of Hawaii 62-; Hon. L.H.D. and LL.D.; Democrat.

State Capitol, Honolulu; Home: 147 Mookua Street, Kailua, Oahu, Hawaii, U.S.A.

Telephone: 583113 (Home).

Burns, John Howard, A.B.; American diplomatist; b. 12 Dec. 1913; ed. Univ. of Oklahoma.

Joined Foreign Service 41, served Ciudad Juarez and Pará; Third Sec. and Vice-Consul Rio de Janeiro 44, Second Sec. and Consul 47; First Sec. Port-au-Prince 49; Nat. War Coll. 54; Consul-Gen. Frankfurt 55; Exec. Dir. Bureau of European Affairs 57; Special Asst. to Dep. Asst. Under-Sec. of State for Admin. 58; First

Sec. Bonn 60, Counsellor, Political Affairs and Consul-Gen. 61; Ambassador to Central African Republic 61-63; Counsellor, Paris (SHAPE) 63-65; Ambassador to Tanzania 65-.
P.O.B. 9123, Dar-es-Salaam, Tanzania.

Burns, John Lawrence, D.SC.; American businessman and engineer; b. 16 Nov. 1908; ed. Northeastern Univ. and Harvard Univ.
Industrial Engineer, Western Electric Co. 27-30; Electrical Engineer, Dewey & Almy Chemical Co. 30-32; Asst. to Head of Dept. Harvard Engineering School 31-33; Prof. of Engineering, Lehigh Univ. 33-34; Dir. of Quality Control and of Process Engineering, Supt. of Large Ingot Manufacture and of Wire Division, and Man. of Grand Crossing Works, Republic Steel Corpn. 34-41; Dir. Metallurgical Laboratories; Co-ordinating Partner, Eastern Region, and Vice-Chair. Exec. Cttee., Booz, Allen & Hamilton 42-57; Pres. and Dir. Radio Corpn. of America 57-61; Chair. of Board, Rawlings Corpn.; Chair. Cities Service 63-68; Dir. several other companies.
Publs. include articles in scientific and business journals.
Fox Run Lane, Greenwich, Conn., U.S.A.

Burns, Norman, M.A.; American economist and university president; b. 14 Nov. 1905; ed. Wittenberg Univ., Ohio, Yale Univ. and Univ. of Montpellier, France.
Assistant Prof. of Econs., American Univ. of Beirut 29-32; U.S. Govt. Service as Foreign Trade Economist, U.S. Tariff Comm., Dir. Foreign Service Inst. of State Dept., Dep. Dir. for Near East and South Asia, Int. Co-operation Admin., Econ. Adviser, UN Relief and Works Agency, Beirut, Dir. United States Operations Missions, Amman 34-61. Pres. American Univ. of Beirut 61-65; Hon. LL.D. (Wittenberg Univ.).
Publs. *The Tariff of Syria* 33, *Government Budgets of Middle East Countries* 56, *Planning Economic Development in the Arab World* 59.
c/o American University of Beirut, Beirut, Lebanon.

Buron, Robert Gaston Albert, D. EN D.; French politician; b. 27 Feb. 1910; ed. Lycée Henri IV, Ecole Libre des Sciences Politiques and Faculté de Droit de Paris.
Engaged in professional organization 34-44; Gen. Admin. Radiodiffusion Française 44-45, co-Dir. weekly *Carrefour* 44-47; Dir.-Gen. of newsreel review *Gaumont-Actualités* 45-49; Deputy for Mayenne, Constituent Assembly 45, re-elected Nat. Assembly 46-; specialist on int. economic questions; alternate del. Council of Europe 49-50; Sec. of State for Economic Affairs Oct. 49-Aug. 51; Minister of Information Aug. 51; Minister of Economic Affairs Jan.-Feb. 52 and Jan.-May 53; Minister of Overseas Territories 54-55, of Finance Feb. 55; Minister of Public Works and Transport, de Gaulle Cabinet June 58-Jan. 59, Debré Cabinet Jan. 59-April 62, Pompidou Cabinet April-May 62; Mayor of Villaines-la-Juhel 59-; leader new political movement *Objectif 1972*; Chair. Nat. Cttee. for Productivity; fmr. Chair. OECD Devt. Centre; Médaille de la Résistance and many other awards.
Publs. *Malthus a-t-il menti?* (with others), *La notion de trustee en droit Anglo-Saxon, Dynamisme des Etats-Unis, Le plus beau des métiers, Les carnets politiques de la guerre d'Algérie, Les dernières années de la IV République.*
14 rue de Bellechasse, Paris 7e, France.

Burov, Ivan Mikhailovich; Soviet politician; ed Kuibyshev Aviation Inst. and Higher Party School of C.P.S.U. Central Committee.
Technician, design engineer, head of design group for aircraft eng. industry, Instructor at Kuibyshev Aviation Inst. 39-46; First Sec. Kuibyshev Regional Cttee. of Young Communist League 46-58; Second Sec. Kuibyshev Regional Cttee. of C.P.S.U. 58-61; Second Sec.

Tselinny Territory Cttee. of Kazakhstan C.P. 61-65; First Sec. Pavlodar Regional Cttee. of Kazakhstan C.P. 65-; mem. Central Cttee. Kazakhstan C.P.; Deputy to U.S.S.R. Supreme Soviet.
Pavlodar Regional Committee, Communist Party of Kazakh S.S.R., Pavlodar, U.S.S.R.

Burri, Alberto; Italian artist; b. 1915.
Qualified as surgeon; began painting while prisoner-of-war in U.S.A. 44; exhbns. throughout the world; winner of awards at Pittsburg, Venice, São Paulo; has pictures in many int. collections.
Via Nera 9, Rome, Italy.

Burrow, Harold; American gas executive; b. 1 Dec. 1914.
Tennessee Gas Transmission Co., Houston 43-, Vice-Pres. 50-54, Senior Vice-Pres. 54-58, First Vice-Pres., Asst. to Pres. 58-59, Exec. Vice-Pres., Dir. 59-61, Pres. and Dir. 61-; official of other companies.
Tennessee Gas Transmission Co., Commerce Building, Houston 1, Texas, U.S.A.

Burrows, Sir Bernard Alexander Brocas, K.C.M.G.; British diplomatist; b. 3 July 1910; ed. Eton and Oxford Univ.
Entered Foreign Service 34; served Cairo 38-45; Foreign Office 45-50; Counsellor, Washington 50-53; Political Resident in the Persian Gulf 53-58; Ambassador to Turkey 58-63; Dep. Under-Sec. at the Foreign Office 63-66; U.K. Perm. Rep., North Atlantic Council 66-.
U.K. Delegation to NATO, Brussels, Belgium.

Burt, Alfred LeRoy, M.A.; American historian; b. 28 Nov. 1888; ed. Univs. of Toronto and Oxford.
Rhodes Scholar 10; Lecturer in History, Univ. of Alberta 13-16, Asst. Prof. 16-20, Assoc. Prof. 20-21, Prof. and Head of Dept. 21-30; Prof. of History, Univ. of Minnesota 30-57, Emeritus Prof. 57-; awards include Tyrrell Gold Medal, Royal Society of Canada 46, Canada Centennial Medal for outstanding Literary Contributions to Canada 67; Pres. Canadian Historical Asscn. 49-50; fmr. mem. Canada-U.S. Cttee. on Education; Visiting Prof. of History, Carleton Univ., Ottawa 57-58, Univ. of Chicago 59-60, Univ. of Manitoba 60-61; F.R.Hist.S.; Hon. LL.D., Univ. of Alberta.
Publs. *Imperial Architects* 13, *A Short History of the League of Nations* 24, *High School Civics* 28, *The Romance of the Prairie Provinces* 30, *The Old Province of Quebec* 33, *The Romance of Canada* 37, *The United States, Great Britain and British North America* 40, *A Short History of Canada for Americans* 42, *The Evolution of the British Empire and Commonwealth from the American Revolution* 56.
316 Washington Street, Wellesley Hills 02181, Massachusetts, U.S.A.
Telephone: 617-237-9785.

Burt, Sir Cyril Lodowic, Kt., D.SC., M.A., F.B.A.; British psychologist and educationist; b. 3 March 1883; ed. Christ's Hospital, Jesus Coll., Oxford and Würzburg Univ.
Lecturer in Experimental Psychology and Asst. Lecturer in Physiology Liverpool Univ. 09-13; Lecturer in Psychology Cambridge Univ. 13-15; mem. Psychological Comm. on Industrial Fatigue of Medical Research Council; Psychologist to London County Council Education Dept. 13, and Prof. of Education in London Univ. 24-31; Prof. Psychology Univ. Coll. London 31-50, Emeritus 50-.
Publs. *The Distribution of Educational Abilities, Mental and Scholastic Tests, The Young Delinquent, The Subnormal Mind, How the Mind Works, The Backward Child, Factors of the Mind, The Causes and Treatment of Backwardness, The Psychological Study of Typography.*
9 Elsworthy Road, Hampstead, London, N.W.3, England.
Telephone: 01-722-0233.

Burton, Richard; British stage and film actor; b. 10 Nov. 1925; ed. Port Talbot Secondary School and Exeter Coll., Oxford Univ.

First appearance as Glan in *Druid's Rest*, Royal Court Theatre, Liverpool 43; St. Martin's Theatre, London 44; R.A.F. service 44-47.

Stage appearances include Richard in *The Lady's Not For Burning* 49, Cuthman in *The Boy With A Cart* 50, Hamlet, Sir Toby Belch, Henry V, Othello, Iago, Caliban with The Old Vic Company 53-54, 55-56; *Time Remembered* 57, *Camelot* 60, Hamlet 64; in *Doctor Faustus*, Oxford 66.

Films include *The Last Days of Dolwyn*, *The Desert Rats*, *The Robe*, *Look Back In Anger*, *Ice Palace*, *Cleopatra*, *Becket*, *The Night of the Iguana*, *The Sandpiper*, *The Spy who Came in from the Cold*, *Who's Afraid of Virginia Woolf*, *The Taming of the Shrew*, *Dr. Faustus*, *The Comedians*.

c/o Hugh French Agency Inc., 9348 Santa Monica Boulevard, Beverly Hills, California, U.S.A.

Bury, Hon. Leslie Harry Ernest, M.A.; Australian politician; b. 25 Feb. 1913; ed. Queens' Coll., Cambridge.

Bank of New South Wales 35-45; Econ. Relations, Dept. of External Affairs 45-48; Commonwealth Treasury 48-51; Alt. Dir. Int. Bank for Reconstruction and Devt., Int. Monetary Fund 51-53, Exec. Dir. 53-56; mem. Australian Parl. 56-; Minister for Air 61-62, for Housing 63-66, for Labour and Nat. Service 66-.

Parliament House, Canberra, A.C.T.; Home: Vaucluse Road, Vaucluse, N.S.W., Australia.

Telephone: 37-1431.

Busairi, Abdussalam; Libyan diplomat; b. 98; ed. Turin Univ., Italy.

Ministry of Foreign Affairs, Ankara 33-54; Minister of Foreign Affairs, Libya 54-55; Gov. Tripolitania 55; Head Royal Cabinet, Libya 55-58; Ambassador to United Kingdom 58-64, to the Netherlands 60-64, to Turkey 64-65, 66-; Minister of Industries 65-66; Libyan Order of Independence, Grade 1.

Publs. Translations into Arabic of the Italian Criminal Law; many newspaper articles.

Libyan Embassy, Ankara, Turkey.

Busch, August A., Jr.; American brewing executive; b. 28 March 1899; ed. Smith Acad.

General Supt. Anheuser-Busch Inc. 24-26, Sixth Vice-Pres. and Gen. Man. 26-31, Second Vice-Pres. and Gen. Man. 31-34, First Vice-Pres. and Gen. Man. 34-41, Pres. and Chair. 46-; official of numerous other companies.

Anheuser-Busch Inc., 721 Pestalozzi Street, St. Louis 18, Mo., U.S.A.

Busch, Eduard Axel Valdemar; Danish neurosurgeon; b. 9 Sept. 1899; ed. Østersogade Gymnasium and Københavns Universitet.

Studied surgery various clinics, neurosurgery in Sweden and U.S.A. 30-34; Dir. Dept. of Neurosurgery Univ. of Copenhagen 34-47, Prof. 47; Pres. Scandinavian Soc. of Neurosurgery 50-54 and World Federation of Neurosurgical Soc. 61; mem. numerous medical societies; Commdr. Order of Dannebrog and other awards; D.Med. h.c. Univ. of Iceland and Prof h.c. Univ. of Chile.

Publs. *Studies of Nerves of Blood-Vessels* 29, *Traumatology of the Nervous System* 42, and numerous papers on neurosurgery.

Rørmosehus, Hesselbjerg, Vejby, Denmark.

Busch, Ernst; German actor; b. 22 Jan. 1900.

Acted in *Kaufmann von Berlin* (Piscator), *Die Mutter* (Brecht-Eisler), *Dreigroschenoper* (Brecht), and in films, including *Kühle Wampe*; emigrated 33; joined Int. Brigade in Spain; returned to Germany and imprisoned by Nat. Socialists; resumed career as actor 45; joined Berliner Ensemble; Nat. Prize (twice); Vaterländischer Verdienstorden in Silber 60, Gold 65; Johannes-R-Becher-Medaille in Gold 65.

Berliner Ensemble, Am Schiffbauerdamm, Berlin N.4, Germany.

Bush, Alan; British composer, conductor and pianist; b. 22 Dec. 1900; ed. Highgate School, Royal Acad. of Music and Humboldt Univ., Berlin.

Prof. of Composition, Royal Acad. of Music 25-, Fellow 38-, Lecturer on History of Music 36-38; served army 41-45; Chair. Composers' Guild of G.B. 47-48; Pres. Workers' Music Asscn. 41-; has conducted leading orchestras in Europe and the U.S.S.R. and appeared frequently as pianist and lecturer; Carnegie Award for String Quartet 24; Arts Council Opera Prize 51; Corresp. mem. German Acad. of Arts 58; Handel Prize 62.

Works include: Choral: *Winter Journey* 46, *Ballad of Freedom's Soldier* 53; Orchestral: *Dance Overture* 35, *Piano Concerto* 37, *First Symphony* 40, *English Suite* 46, *Violin Concerto* 48, *Nottingham Symphony* 49, *Concert Suite for 'Cello* 52, *Dorian Passacaglia and Fugue* 59, *Byron Symphony* 60, *Variations, Nocturne and Finale for Piano and Orchestra* 62, *Partita Concertante* 64; Operatic: *Wat Tyler* 50, *Men of Blackmoor* 55, *The Sugar Reapers* 63, *The Man Who Never Died* 67.

Publ. *Strict Counterpoint in Palestrina Style*.

25 Christchurch Crescent, Radlett, Herts., England.

Telephone: Radlett 6422.

Bush, Admiral Sir John Fitzroy Duyland, K.C.B., D.S.C.; British naval officer; b. 1914.

Entered Royal Navy as Special Entry Cadet 33; served in H.M.S. *Nubian* in Second World War, subsequently commanding destroyers *Belvoir*, *Zephyr* and *Chevron*; joined Plans Div. at Admiralty 47; graduated from Armed Forces Staff Coll. U.S.A. 49; commanded destroyer *Cadiz* 50-51; promoted to Capt. and apptd. Deputy Sec. Chief of Staffs Cttee. at Ministry of Defence 52; Commodore of Royal Naval Barracks, Chatham 57-59; Dir. of Plans at Admiralty 59-60; Flag Officer Flotillas in Mediterranean 61-62; Naval Attaché, Washington 63; Vice-Chief of Naval Staff 65; Allied C.-in-C. Channel 67-.

North Atlantic Treaty Organisation, Brussels 39, Belgium.

Telephone: 41-00-40 and 41-44-00.

Bush, John Nash Douglas, M.A., PH.D.; American university professor; b. 21 March 1896; ed. Toronto and Harvard Univs.

Sheldon Fellow, Harvard 23-24; Instructor, Harvard 24-27; Asst. Prof. of English, Univ. of Minn. 27-28, Assoc. Prof. 28-31, Prof. 31-36; Guggenheim Fellow 34-35; Assoc. Prof., Harvard 36-37, Prof. of English 37-57, Gurney Prof., Harvard 57-66; mem. American Philosophical Society; Pres. Modern Humanities Research Asscn. 55; Fellow, British Acad; Hon. Litt.D. (Tufts Oberlin, Swarthmore Colls., Harvard, Princeton, Toronto Univs., Boston Coll.); L.H.D. (Southern Illinois Univ.) and Marlboro Coll.

Publs. *Mythology and the Renaissance Tradition in English Poetry* 32, 63, *Mythology and the Romantic Tradition in English Poetry* 37, *The Renaissance and English Humanism* 39, *Paradise Lost in Our Time* 45, *English Literature in the Earlier Seventeenth Century* (*Oxford History of English Literature*) 45, 62, *Science and English Poetry* 50, *Classical Influences in Renaissance Literature* 52, *English Poetry: the Main Currents from Chaucer to the Present* 52, *John Milton* 64, *Prefaces to Renaissance Literature* 65, *John Keats* 66, *Engaged and Disengaged* 66; Editor: *Keats Selected Poems and Letters* 59, *Shakespeare's Sonnets* (with A. Harbage) 61, *Complete Poetical Works of Milton* 65.

3 Clement Circle, Cambridge, Mass. 02138, U.S.A.

Bush, Vannevar, ENG.D., HON. SC.D.; American administrator and electrical engineer; b. 11 March 1890; ed. Tufts Coll., Mass. Inst. of Technology and Harvard.

With Inspection Dept. U.S. Navy 14; Instructor Mathematics Tufts Coll. 14-15, Asst. Prof. Electrical Engineering 16-17; research on Submarine Detection U.S. Navy 17-18; Associate Prof. Electrical Power Transmission Mass. Inst. of Technology 19-23, Prof. 23-32; Dean of Engineering School and Vice-Pres. Inst. 32-38; mem. (Chair. 39-41) Nat. Advisory Cttee. for Aeronautics; Chair. Nat. Defense Research Cttee. 40-41; Dir. Office of Scientific Research and Development 41-47; Chair. Joint Cttee. on New Weapons and Equipment of Joint U.S. Chiefs of Staff 42-46; Chair. Joint Research and Development Board, War and Navy Depts. 46-47; Chair. Research and Development Board, National Military Establishment 47-48; Chair. of Corpn., Mass. Inst. of Technology 55-59, Hon. Chair. 59-; Officier Légion d'Honneur; Hon. K.B.E., and many other awards.
Publs. *Operational Circuit Analysis* 29, *Endless Horizons* 46, *Principles of Electrical Engineering* (with William H. Timbie) 22, *Modern Arms and Free Men* 49, *Science is Not Enough* 68.
304 Marsh Street, Belmont, Mass. 02178, U.S.A.

Busia, Kofi Abrefa, M.A., D.PHIL.; Ghanaian university teacher and politician; b. 13; ed. Mfantsipim (Cape Coast), Achimota Coll., London and Oxford Univs.
Awarded Carnegie Research Fellowship, Oxford Univ. 45; Admin. Officer, Gold Coast Govt. 47-49; fmr. Prof. Sociology, Univ. Coll. of Ghana; fmr. Leader of the Opposition, Ghana Parl.; fmr. Leader of United Party; Visiting Prof. Northwestern Univ. 54, Wageningen Univ. (Netherlands) 56-57, Visiting Fellow Nuffield Coll., Oxford 55; Prof. of Sociology, Inst. of Social Studies, The Hague 59-61; Prof. of Sociology and Culture of Africa, Univ. of Leiden 60-61; Visiting Prof. Collège de Mexico, Mexico City 62; returned to Ghana 66; Chair. Nat. Liberation Advisory Council 66-; Exec. mem. Int. Sociological Asscn. 53-60; mem. Int. Social Science Council, Int. African Inst., Asscn. of Social Anthropologists.
Publs. include *Position of the Chief in the Political System of Ashanti* 51, *Self-Government, Education for Citizenship, Industrialisation in West Africa* 55, *Challenge of Africa* 62, *Purposeful Education for Africa* 64, *Africa in Search of Democracy* 67.
National Liberation Advisory Council, Accra, Ghana.

Buslenko, Nikolai Panteleymonovich; Soviet mathematician; b. 1922; ed. Dzerzhinsky Military Engineering Acad.
Service in the Army 41-; Corresp. mem. U.S.S.R. Acad. of Sciences 66-.
Publs. Works on machine mathematics and theory of large systems.
U.S.S.R. Academy of Sciences, 14 Lenin Prospekt, Moscow, U.S.S.R.

Bustamante, Rt. Hon. Sir William Alexander, P.C., G.B.E.; Jamaican politician; b. 84.
Fmr. soldier, policeman, and journalist; organised Bustamante Trade Union; Leader Jamaica Labour Party 43-; secured majority in Elections 44 and 49; mem. House of Representatives for Clarendon South; mem. Exec. Council as Minister for Communications 44-53; Chief Minister 53-55, Prime Minister 62-67; Commr. British Section Caribbean Comm. 50-55.
Kingston, Jamaica.

Bustamante y Rivero, José Luis; Peruvian judge; b. 15 Jan. 1894; ed. Univs. of Arequipa and Cuzco.
Member Bars of Arequipa 18, Cuzco 18, Puno 26; Legal practice 18-34; Substitute Judge and Deputy Public Prosecutor, Superior Court of Arequipa 20-34; mem. Bar of Lima 56, Legal Practice 56-60, Dean of Lima Bar 60, now Hon. mem.; Teacher of American Archaeology, Univ. of Arequipa 21, Peruvian Social Geography 21, Modern Philosophy (Asst. Prof.) 21, Asst. Prof. in

Legal Procedure 27, Prof. of Civil Law 30-34; mem. Arequipa City Council 21-24; Minister of Justice and Educ., Peru 30-31; Minister to Bolivia 34-38, to Uruguay 39-42; Amb. to Bolivia 42-45; Pres. of Repub. of Peru 45-48; mem. Consultative Comm. of Ministry of Foreign Affairs 60; Judge, Int. Court of Justice, The Hague 61-, Pres. Int. Court of Justice 67-; mem. Peruvian Soc. of Int. Law, Nat. Acad. of Law and Political Sciences, Peruvian Acad. of Language, Lima, Affil. Royal Spanish Acad. of Language, Madrid; Hon. mem. Inter-American Bar Asscn., Washington; mem. Francisco de Vitoria Inst. of Int. Law and Hispano-Luso-Americano-Filipino Inst. of Int. Law, Madrid; Corresp. mem. Colombian and Uruguayan Acads. of Language.
Publs. include: *Organización y procedimientos de la Justicia Militar en el Perú* 18, *Proyecto de ley de Juzgados de Paz, con exposición de motivos* 19, *El laudo arbitral sobre Tacna y Arica* 29, *La Teoría del abuso del Derecho* 32, *Las Transformaciones del Contrato Civil* 35, *Una visión del Perú* 41, *Ensayo histórico sobre Arequipa* 41, *El Tratado de Derecho Civil Internacional de 1940 de Montevideo* 42, *La O.N.U. en el Palacio de Chaillot* 52, *Panamericanismo e Ibero-americanismo* 53, *La subestimación del Derecho en el mundo moderno* 54, *Las nuevas Concepciones Jurídicas sobre el alcance del mar territorial* 55, *Las clases sociales en el Perú* 59.
International Court of Justice, The Hague, Netherlands.

Butement, William Alan Stewart, C.B.E., B.SC., D.SC., F.I.E.E., F.INST.P., F.A.I.P., F.I.R.E.,E. (Aust.), Australian scientist; b. 18 Aug. 1904; ed. Scots Coll., Sydney, Australia, Univ. Coll. School, Hampstead and London Univ.
Scientific Officer, War Office 28-39; Asst. Dir. Scientific Research, Ministry of Supply 39-47; First Chief Superintendent, Research Establishment and Rocket Range, Woomera, Australia 47-49; Chief Scientist, Australian Dept. of Supply 49-66; Dir. of Research, Plessey Pacific 67-.
Publ. *Precision Radar* 45-46.
Plessey Pacific, 70 Collins Street, Melbourne; and 5A Barry Street, Kew, Victoria, Australia.
Telephone: 638281 (Office); 868375 (Home).

Butenandt, Adolf Friedrich Johann, D.PHIL.; German physiological chemist; b. 24 March 1903; ed. Oberrealschule Bremerhaven, Univs. of Marburg and Göttingen.
Scientific Asst. Chemical Inst., Göttingen Univ. 27-30, Dozent in organic and biological chemistry 31, leader organic and biological chemistry laboratories 31-33; Prof. of Chemistry, Dir. Organic Chemistry Inst., Danzig School of Technology 33-36; Dir. Kaiser Wilhelm Inst. of Biochemistry, Berlin-Dahlem (later at Tübingen) (now Max Planck Inst. of Biochemistry, Munich) 36-; Prof. of Physiological Chemistry, Munich Univ. 56-; Pres. Max-Planck Soc. 64; Foreign mem. Royal Soc. (U.K.); Nobel Prize for Chemistry 39; Orden Pour le Mérite for Arts and Sciences 62, Österreichisches Ehrenzeichen für Wissenschaft und Kunst 64.
Publs. *Biochemie der Wirkstoffe* (*Sexualhormone, Genchemie, Insektenphysiologie*); numerous articles in *Hoppe-Seyler's Zeitschrift für Physiologische Chemie, Chemische Berichte, Zeitschrift für Naturforschung*, etc.
Office: 8 Munich 1, Postfach 647; Home: Marsopstrasse 5, 8 Munich 60, German Federal Republic.
Telephone: 885490 (Home); 225155 (Office).

Butler, Alan David; Rhodesian politician and business executive; b. 1927; ed. Eton Coll. and De Havilland Technical School.
Tobacco farmer 49-55; Head, commercial aircraft company 55-; mem. of Parliament 62-65; Chair. United Federal Party, later Rhodesia Party 63-; Leader of Opposition 65; represented Rhodesia in yachting classes, Olympic Games 60 and 64.
"Mufaro", Kent Road, Highlands, Salisbury, Rhodesia.

Butler, Frederick Guy, M.A.; South African university professor; b. 18; ed. Rhodes Univ., Grahamstown, and Brasenose Coll., Oxford.
War service Egypt, Lebanon, Italy, U.K. 40-45; Oxford 45-47; lecturer in English, Univ. of Witwatersrand 48-50; Prof. of English, Rhodes Univ. 52-; Editor *New Coin* (poetry quarterly); Pres. The English Acad. of Southern Africa.
Publs. *Stranger to Europe* (poems) 52, 60, *The Dam* (play) 53, *The Dove Returns* (play) 56, *A Book of South African Verse* 59, *South of the Zambesi* (poems) 66.
"High Corner", Somerset Street, Grahamstown, S. Africa.

Butler, Sir James Ramsay Montagu, Kt., M.V.O., O.B.E., M.A.; British historian; b. 89; ed. Harrow School and Trinity Coll., Cambridge.
Fellow of Trinity Coll., Cambridge 13-, Lecturer 19-47; Regius Prof. of Modern History, Cambridge 47-54, Vice-Master, Trinity Coll. 55-60; Chief Historian Official Mil. Histories of the War of 1939-45; M.P. Cambridge Univ. 22-23; Army Service 14-19 and 39-44; Chevalier de la Légion d'Honneur.
Publs. *The Passing of the Great Reform Bill* 14, *History of England 1815-1918* 28, *Grand Strategy, Sept. 1939-June 1941* 57, *Lord Lothian* 60, (with J. M. A. Gwyer) *Grand Strategy 1941-42* 64.
Trinity College, Cambridge, England.

Butler, Michael; American financier; b. 26 Nov. 1926; ed. Univ. of Colorado.
With Butler Company all working life; Vice-Pres. (Gen. Sales) Butler Co.; Dir. Butler Overseas Corpn., Overseas Bank Ltd., Butler Eastern Corpn., Intrafi (int. syndicate), Basic Investment Corpn.; Editor and Publisher Islands in the Sun Club.
673 Fifth Avenue, New York City, N.Y.; Oak Brook Road, Oak Brook, Ill., U.S.A.; P.O. Box 272, Nassau, Bahamas.

Butler, Sir Nevile Montagu, K.C.M.G., C.V.O.; British diplomatist; b. 20 Dec. 1893; ed. Harrow, Trinity Coll., Cambridge.
Served First World War 16-18; entered Foreign Office 20; Private Sec. to successive Parl. Under-Secs. of State for Foreign Affairs 24-27, to Viscount Cecil of Chelwood 27, and to Lord Cushendun 27-29; a Private Sec. to Prime Minister 30-35; Counsellor Legation, Teheran 35-40, Minister, Washington 40-41; Head North American Dept., Foreign Office 41-44; Asst. Under-Sec. 44-47; Ambassador to Brazil 47-51, to the Netherlands 52-54; Pres. Int. Inst. of Differing Civilisations 55-56.
North Lodge, Newick, Sussex, England.
Telephone: Newick 20.

Butler, Reg(inald Cotterell), A.R.I.B.A.; British sculptor; b. 1913; ed. Hertford Grammar School.
Lecturer, Architectural Asscn. School of Architecture, London 37-39; Technical Editor, Architectural Press 46-51; Gregory Fellow in Sculpture, Univ. of Leeds 51-53; First one-man show, London 49; Winner Int. Competition, The Unknown Political Prisoner 53; Retrospective exhbn. J. B. Speed Art Museum, Louisville, U.S. 63; Galleries: Hanover Gallery, London, Pierre Matisse Gallery, New York; Assoc., Acad. Royale des Sciences, des Lettres et des Beaux-Arts de Belgique.
Publ. *Creative Development* 62.
Studio: Ash, Berkhamsted Place, Berkhamsted, Hertfordshire, England.
Telephone: Berkhamsted 2933.

Butler, Thomas Clifton; American retail executive; b. 14 Nov. 1900; ed. Troy Conference Acad., Poultney, Vermont.
Grand Union Co. 18-, Asst. Sec. 28, Comptroller 30, Treas. 36, Dir. 48-, Vice-Pres.-Treas. 58-60, Pres. and Chief Exec. Officer 60-, Chair. of Board 66-; Dir. Eastern Shopping Centers Inc., Eastern Diversified Inc.; Sec., Dir. and mem. Exec. Cttee. Nat. Asscn. of Food Chains; Mayor of Glen Ridge, N.J. 54-58; official of other food and commercial orgs.; several awards; Hon. LL.D. St. Joseph's Coll., Philadelphia.
Grand Union Company, 100 Broadway, East Paterson, N.J. 07407; Home: 565 Ridgewood Avenue, Glen Ridge, N.J., U.S.A.

Butler of Saffron Walden, Baron (Life Peer), cr. 65, of Halstead; **Richard Austen Butler,** P.C., C.H., M.A., F.R.G.S.; British politician; b. 9 Dec. 1902; ed. Marlborough and Pembroke Coll., Cambridge.
Fellow Corpus Christi Coll., Cambridge 25-29; Conservative M.P. for Saffron Walden Div. of Essex 29-65; Parl. Private Sec. to the Sec. of State for India 31 and Under-Sec. of State for India 32-May 37; Parl. Sec. to Minister of Labour May 37-Feb. 38; Under-Sec. for Foreign Affairs Feb. 38-41, Pres. Board of Educ. 41-44, Minister of Educ. 44-45; Minister of Labour and Nat. Service May-July 45; Chancellor of the Exchequer 51-55; Lord Privy Seal and Leader of the House of Commons 55-57; Home Secretary, Lord Privy Seal and Leader of the House of Commons 57-59; Home Sec., Leader of the House of Commons and Chair. of the Conservative Party 59-61; Home Sec. 61-62; Cabinet Minister charged with the oversight of Common Market negotiations 61, Minister responsible for Central African Fed. 62-Oct. 63; Dep. Prime Minister and First Sec. of State July 62-Oct. 63; Sec. of State for Foreign Affairs Oct. 63-64; Master of Trinity Coll., Cambridge 65-; fmr. Chair. Conservative Party Research Dept.; Dir. Courtaulds Jan. 46-51, Dec. 65-; Pres. Royal Soc. of Literature; Rector Glasgow Univ. 56-59; High Steward Cambridge Univ. 58-66; High Steward of City of Cambridge 63-; Chancellor, Sheffield Univ. 60-, Univ. of Essex 62-; Hon. D.C.L. (Oxford), Hon. LL.D. (Cambridge, Nottingham, Bristol, Sheffield, St. Andrews, Manchester, Glasgow, Reading).
House of Lords, London, S.W.1; and The Master's Lodge, Trinity College, Cambridge, England.
Telephone: Cambridge 58201.

Butlin, Sir William Edmund, Kt., M.B.E.; British holiday camp proprietor; b. 29 Sept. 1899; ed. Canada and England.
Chairman and Man. Dir., Butlin's Ltd. 36-68; Pres. Vaudeville Golfing Soc.; Companion Grand Order of Water Rats; Elder Statesman, Variety Club of Great Britain.
Butlin Building, 439 Oxford Street, London, W.1, England.
Telephone: 01-629-6616.

Butoma, Boris Evstafievich; Soviet politician; b. 1907; ed. Leningrad Shipbuilding Inst.
Worked in various shipyards 37-48; Head of Board of Ministry of Shipbuilding Industry 48-52; U.S.S.R. Deputy Minister of Shipbuilding 52-57; Chair. State Cttee. for Shipbuilding 57-65; U.S.S.R. Minister of Shipbuilding 65-; Deputy to U.S.S.R. Supreme Soviet; State Prize 49; mem. Central Cttee. C.P.S.U.; Hero of Socialist Labour 59.
U.S.S.R. Ministry of Shipbuilding, 11/13 Sadovo-Kudrinskaya ulitsa, Moscow, U.S.S.R.

Butor, Michel; French lecturer and writer; b. 14 Sept. 1926; ed. Univ. of Paris.
Teacher at Sens (France) 50, Minieh (Egypt) 50-51, Manchester (England) 51-53, Salonica (Greece) 54-55, Geneva (Switzerland) 56-57; Visiting Prof. Bryn Mawr and Middlebury, U.S.A. 60, Buffalo, U.S.A. 62, Evanston, U.S.A. 65; reader at Editions Gallimard, Paris; Prix Felix Fénéon 57, Prix Renaudot 57, Grand prix de la critique littéraire 60.
Publs. Novels: *Passage de Milan* 54, *L'Emploi du Temps* 56, *La Modification* 57, *Degrés* 60; Essays: *Le*

Génie de Lieu 58, *Répertoire* 60, *Histoire Extraordinaire* 61, *Mobile* 62, *Réseau Aérien* 63, *Description de San Marco* 63, *Les Oeuvres d'art imaginaires chez Proust* 64, *Répertoire II* 64, *Portrait de l'artiste en jeune singe* 67, *Répertoire III* 68, *Essais sur les Essais* 68; Poetry: *Illustrations* 64, *6.810.000 litres d'eau par seconde* 65.
28 *bis* avenue de l'Eperon, 91-Ste. Geneviève des Bois, France.
Telephone: 921-06-39.

Butschkau, Fritz; German banker; b. 13 March 1901; ed. Berlin Univ.
Banking 22-; Head, Cologne German Control Clearing House 31, mem. management bd. 35; Man. Dir. Rhine Girozentrale und Provinzialbank (clearing house and bank), Düsseldorf 45; Pres. German Savings Bank and Clearing House Asscn., Bonn 61; Pres. Asscn. for Protection of the German Savers; Vice-Pres. Int. Savings Bank Inst.; Pres. Council Board of Asscn. Savings Banks of the EEC; Chair. Hüttenwerke Oberhausen A.G.; mem. Econ. and Social Cttee., EEC and Euratom; mem. Board of Dirs. Volkswagenwerk A.G., Bergwerksgesellschaft Hibernia A.G., Kreditanstalt für Wiederaufbau; Grosses Verdienstkreuz mit Stern des Verdienstordens der Bundesrepublik Deutschland; Dr. h.c. rer. pol., Univ. of Cologne.
Publs. *Saving between Fear and Hope* 51, *Saving—a Road to Freedom* 54, *Sparen in der vollbeschäftigten Wirtschaft* 56, *Unsere Aufgabe: Sicherung der Ersparnisse* 58, *Geldwert und Konjunktur* 60, *Die Sparkassen im Wandel von Wirtschaft und Gesellschaft, Thrift and International Progress* 66, etc.
Rheinische Girozentrale und Provinzialbank, Friedrichstrasse 56-60, Düsseldorf, German Federal Republic.

Butterfield, Sir Herbert, Kt., M.A., F.B.A.; British historian; b. 7 Oct. 1900; ed. Trade and Grammar School, Keighley and Peterhouse, Cambridge.
Fellow of Peterhouse 23-55, Master 55-68; Visiting Fellow, Univ. of Princeton 24-25; Lecturer in History, Cambridge 30-44; Editor *Cambridge Historical Journal* 38-52; Prof. of Modern History, Cambridge Univ. 44-63, Regius Prof. 63-68, Vice-Chancellor 59-Oct. 61; Foreign Hon. mem. American Acad. Arts and Sciences; Hon. mem. Royal Irish Acad.; Pres. Historical Asscn. 55-58; mem. Admin. Board Int. Asscn. of Univs. 60-65, Comm. on Higher Educ. in Ireland 60-68, Advisory Council on Public Records 62-; Historical Research Cttee. 63-; Gifford Lecturer, Glasgow Univ. 65-67; Hon. LL.D. (Aberdeen) 52, (Manchester) 66, Hon. D.Litt. (Dublin) 54, Hon. D.Lit. (Belfast) 55, Hon. Litt.D. (Harvard and Columbia) 56, (Hong Kong) 61, Hon. D.Litt. (Sheffield) 62, (Hull) 63, (Warwick) 67.
Publs. *The Historical Novel* 24, *The Peace Tactics of Napoleon, 1806-8,* 29, *The Whig Interpretation of History* 31, (ed.) *Select Documents of European History, Vol. III, 1715-1920,* 31, *Napoleon* (*Great Lives*) 39, *The Statecraft of Machiavelli* 40, *The Englishman and His History* 44, *Inaugural Lecture on the Study of Modern History* 44, *The Origins of Modern Science 1300-1800,* 49, *George III, Lord North, and The People 1779-1780* 49, *Christianity and History* 49, *History and Human Relations* 51, Riddell Memorial Lectures on *Christianity in European History* 51, *Liberty in the Modern World* 52; Beckly lecture *Christianity, Diplomacy and War* 53, *Man on His Past* 55, *George III and the Historians* 57, *International Conflict in the Twentieth Century* 60, *The Universities and Education Today* 62.
The Master's Lodge, Peterhouse, Cambridge, England.
Telephone: Cambridge 50256.

Butters, Lieut.-Col. Sir John H., Kt., C.M.G., M.B.E., V.D., M.I.C.E., F.A.S.C.E., F.I.E.E., M.I.E.AUST.; Australian industrialist and engineer; b. 23 Dec. 1885; ed. Univ. Coll., Southampton.

Gen. Man. Tasmanian Hydro-Electric Dept. 14-24; Chief Commr. Federal Capital 24-29; Chair. Assoc. Newspapers, Sydney 41-57; Hadfield Steel Works Ltd., North Shore Gas Co.; Dir. Gen. Motors Holdens Ltd., Bitumen and Oil Refineries Ltd., Petroleum and Chemical Corpn. Ltd.; Pres. Inst. of Engineers (Aust.) 27; Hon. Consulting Mil. Engineer, Headquarters Staff, Australian Mil. Forces 27-43.
Alverstoke, Wahroonga, N.S.W., Australia.
Telephone: 48-2656.

Butterworth, W. Walton, B.A.; American diplomatist; b. 7 Sept. 1903; ed. Lawrenceville School, Princeton and Oxford Univs.
Foreign Service Officer, Department of State 28-29, 31-32; Vice-Consul Singapore 29-31; Third Sec. Ottawa 32-34; Second Sec. and Special Treasury Rep. London 34-41; Special Asst. to Under Sec. of Commerce 41-42; mem. Advisory Cttee. Lend Lease Trade Policy; First Sec. Lisbon and Madrid, Dir. Gen. U.S. Commercial Co. in Iberian Peninsular 42-44; Counsellor Madrid 44-46, Nanking (with rank of Minister) 46-47; Dir. Far Eastern Affairs, Dept. of State 47-49; Asst. Sec. of State 49-50; Ambassador to Sweden 50-53; Minister, London 54-55; Rep. with rank of Ambassador to ECSC 56-62, to EEC and Euratom 58-62; Ambassador to Canada 63-.
100 Wellington Street, Ottawa, Ontario, Canada; and The Valley House, Brookeville, Maryland, U.S.A.

Butting, Max; German composer; b. 6 Oct. 1888.
Studied with Walter Courvoisier; Prof. German Society of Composers; Chair. Dir. of A.W.A.; radio lecturer; mem. German Acad. of Arts; Nat. Prize.
Compositions include 10 symphonies and other orchestral works, *Plautus im Nonnenkloster* (opera), 9 string quartets and other chamber music, piano music and children's pieces.
Waldstrasse 81, Berlin-Niederschönhausen, Germany.

Buwono, Hamengku, IX (*see* Jogjakarta, Sultan of, Hamengku Buwono IX).

Byam Shaw, Glen, C.B.E.; British theatrical director; b. 13 Dec. 1904; ed. Westminster School, London.
First stage appearance, Pavilion Theatre, Torquay 23; mem. J. B. Fagan Co., Oxford Repertory Theatre; played Trophimof (*The Cherry Orchard*), New York, Konstantin Treplev (*The Seagull*), Baron Tusenbach (*The Three Sisters*), London; played in Max Reinhardt's production of *The Miracle*; repertory tour of South Africa with Angela Baddeley (his wife); played Darnley in *Queen of Scots* and Laertes in John Gielgud's production of *Hamlet*; mem. Gielgud Co., Queen's Theatre, London; produced plays in London, New York and Stratford-upon-Avon; Dir. Old Vic Theatre Centre; Co.-Dir. Shakespeare Memorial Theatre 52-55, Dir. 56-59, Gov. 60; Dir. of Productions, Sadler's Wells Opera House 62-; Dir. Sadler's Wells 66-; Army Service 39-45; Hon. D.Litt. (Birmingham Univ.).
169 Ashley Gardens, London, S.W.1, England.

Bykhovsky, Bernard Emmanuilovich; Soviet philosopher; b. 1898; ed. Byelorussian Univ., Minsk.
Member C.P.S.U. 20-, Prof. 29-; mem. U.S.S.R. Acad. of Sciences 66-; State Prize 44.
Publs. Numerous philosophical works.
U.S.S.R. Academy of Sciences, 14 Leninsky Prospekt, Moscow, U.S.S.R.

Bykovsky, Col. Valery Fyodorovich; Soviet cosmonaut; b. 2 Aug. 1934; ed. secondary school and Zhukovsky Air Force Engng. Acad., Moscow.
Member C.P. 63-; Student Pilot, Moscow Aeroclub 52; Soviet Army 52-, Katcha Air Force School of Pilots 54, jet pilot 54-59, cosmonaut training 60-; Chief Asst. to Maj. Andrian Nikolayev in preparations for Nikolayev's Space Flight Aug. 62; made 81 orbits of the earth (48 orbits with Miss Valentina Tereshkova) June 14 to June 19, 1963; Order of Red Star, Order of

Lenin, Hero of Soviet Union; Pilot-Cosmonaut of U.S.S.R.

Zvezdny Gorodok, Moscow, U.S.S.R.

Bynum, William; American business executive; b. 1 Sept. 1902; ed. Univ. of Alabama and Auburn Univ. Athletic Director, Alabama Teachers Coll, Troy 25-27; Carrier Corporation, Syracuse 30-, Exec. Vice-Pres. 51-56, Dir. 52-, Pres. 56-, Pres. and Chief Exec. Officer 63-65, Chair. and Chief Exec. Officer 65-; Dir. Marine Midland Trust Co. of Central N.Y. and other companies; mem. Nat. Industrial Conf. Board; Hon. Sc.D. Univ. of Alabama.

Carrier Corporation, Carrier Parkway, Syracuse, N.Y. 13201; Home: Hunt Lane, Fayetteville, N.Y., U.S.A.

Byrd, Harry Flood, Jr. (son of late Harry Flood Byrd); American newspaperman and politician; b. 20 Dec. 1914; ed. Winchester public schools, John Marshall High School, Richmond, Virginia Military Inst. and Univ. of Virginia.

Editorial Writer Winchester *Evening Star* 33, Editor and Publisher 35-, Editor and Publisher Harrisonburg *Daily News-Record* 37-; also active in firm of H. F. Byrd, Inc., apple growers; mem. Virginia State Senate 47-65; mem. Democratic State Central Cttee. 40-; served U.S. Naval Reserve 41-46; Dir. Associated Press 50-; U.S. Senator from Virginia (succeeding his father, Harry Flood Byrd) 65-.

U.S. Senate, Washington, D.C., U.S.A.

Byrd, Robert C.; American politician; b. 15 Jan. 1918; ed. George Washington Univ. Law School and Washington Coll. of Law (American Univ.).

Member West Virginia House of Delegates 46-50, West Virginia Senate 50-52; mem. U.S. House of Representatives rep. 6th District of West Virginia 52-58; Senator from West Virginia 58-; mem. Senate Appropriations and Armed Services Cttees.; Democrat.

342 Senate Office Building, Washington 25, D.C., U.S.A

Byrnes, James Francis; American lawyer and politician; b. 1879.

Solicitor 09-11; mem. U.S. Congress 11-25; in law practice 25-30; U.S. Senator from South Carolina 30-41; Associate Justice U.S. Supreme Court 41-42; Dir. of Economic Stabilization 42-43; Dir. Office of War Mobilization 43-45; Sec. of State 45-Jan. 47; Gov. of S. Carolina 51-55; Democrat.

Publs. *Speaking Frankly* 47, *All in One Life Time* 58.

Heathwood Circle, Columbia, South Carolina, U.S.A.

Byrom, Fletcher Lauman; American business executive; b. 13 July 1918; ed. Pennsylvania State Univ.

Sales Engineer, American Steel and Wire Co., Cleveland 40-42; Naval Ordnance Laboratory and Bureau of Ordnance and Research Planning Board, Navy Dept. 42-47; Asst. to Gen. Man. Tar Products Div., Koppers Co. Inc., Pittsburgh 47-54, Asst. Vice-Pres. 54-55, Vice-Pres. 55-58, Vice-Pres. and Gen. Man. 58-60, Pres. and Chief Admin. Officer and Dir. 60-.

Koppers Co. Inc., Koppers Building, Pittsburgh 19, Pa., U.S.A.

C

Caballero Calderón, Eduardo; Colombian diplomatist and writer; b. 6 March 1910; ed. Gimnasio Moderna de Bogotá and Universidad Externado de Colombia.
Secretary, Embassy, Lima 37-40; Business Official, Madrid 46-48; Rep. in Congress, Bogotá 58-61; Amb. to UN Educational, Scientific and Cultural Org. (UNESCO), Paris 62-66; Editor *El Tiempo* 66-; mem. Colombian Acad.; Corresp. mem. Royal Spanish Acad.; Eugenio Nadal Prize for *El Buen Salvaje* 65.
Publs. *Tipacocque* (short stories) 39, *Suramérica, Tierra del Hombre* (essays) 41, *Brevario del Quijote* 47, *Ancha es Castilla* 47, *Siervo sin tierra* 48, *Diario de Tipacoque* 49, *Americanos y Europeos* 49, *Historia Privada de Los Colombianos* 49, *Cartas Colombianas* 51; novels: *El Cristo Espaldas* 50, *El Arte de Vivir sin soñar* 50, *La Penúltima Hora* 53, *Manuel Pacho* 65, *El Buen Salvaje* 65.
Calle 37, No. 19-07, Bogotá, Colombia.

Cabanis, José; French writer; b. 24 March 1922; ed. Univ. de Toulouse.
Works include: novels: *l'Age ingrat* 52, *Juliette Bonviolle* 54, *les Mariages de raison* 58, *le Bonheur du jour* (Prix des Critiques) 61, *les Cartes du temps* (Prix des Libraires) 62, *les Jeux de la Nuit* 64, *la Bataille de Toulouse* (Prix Théophraste Renaudot) 66; criticism: *un essai su Marcel Jouhandeau* 60, *Plaisir et lectures* 64.
5 rue Darquié, Toulouse (Haute-Garonne), France.

Cabot, John Moors, B.LITT.; American diplomatist; b. 11 Dec. 1901; ed. Harvard Univ. and Oxford Univ.
Entered U.S. Foreign Service 26; Vice-Consul Peru 27-28; Third Sec. Dominican Republic 29-31, Mexico 31-32; Third Sec., later Second Sec., Brazil 32-35; Second Sec. Netherlands 35-38; Sec. Sweden 38-39, Guatemala 39-41; assigned Dept. of State; Asst. Chief, Div. of American Republics 42; Chief, Div. of Caribbean and Central American Affairs 44; Counsellor of Embassy, Argentina 45-46, Yugoslavia 47; Consul-Gen. Shanghai 48; apptd. Career Minister 48; technical officer, U.S. dels., Dumbarton Oaks, Mexico City and San Francisco Confs.; Minister to Finland 50-52; Ambassador to Pakistan 52-53; Asst. Sec. of State 53; Del. to Tenth Int. Conf. American States, Caracas 54; Ambassador to Sweden 54-57, to Colombia 57-59, to Brazil 59-61, to Poland 61-65; Deputy Commdt. Nat. War Coll. 65-.
c/o Department of State, Washington 25, D.C., U.S.A.

Cabot, Paul Codman, A.B., M.B.A.; American banker; b. 21 Oct. 1898; ed. Harvard Univ.
With First Nat. Bank 23-24; Treas. State Street Investment Corpn. 24-34, Pres. 34-58, Chair. of Board 58-; partner State Street Research and Management Co. 28-; Dir. Morgan Guaranty Trust Co. of New York, Continental Can Co., Ford Motor Co. Inc., Nat. Dairy Products Corpn., B.F. Goodrich Co., The M. A. Hanna Co., mem. Business Council, Dept. of Commerce; Treas. Harvard Univ. 48-; Chair. Fed. Street Fund, Inc.; Hanna Diversified Investment Inc.
Home: 653 Chestnut Street, Needham, Mass.; Office: 225 Franklin Street, Boston, Mass. 02110, U.S.A.

Caccia, Baron (Life Peer), cr. 65, of Abernant; **Harold Anthony Caccia,** G.C.M.G., G.C.V.O.; British diplomatist; b. 21 Dec. 1905; ed. Eton, Trinity Coll., and Queen's Coll., Oxford.
Entered Foreign Service as Third Sec., Foreign Office 29, Legation, Peking 32; promoted to Second Sec. 34; transferred to Foreign Office 35; Asst. Private Sec. to Sec. of State 36; Legation, Athens 39; First Sec. 40; Foreign Office 41; seconded for service with Resident

Minister North Africa 43; Vice-Pres. Political Section Allied Control Comm., Italy 44; Political Adviser G.O.C.-in-C. Land Forces Greece 44; Minister, local rank, British Embassy Athens 45; Asst. Under-Sec. of State, Foreign Office 46, Deputy Under-Sec. of State 49; Minister, Vienna 49, Minister and High Commr. 50-51, Ambassador and High Commr. 51-54; Deputy Under Sec., Foreign Office 54-56; Ambassador to the U.S.A. 56-61; Perm. Under-Sec. Foreign Office 61-64; Head of Diplomatic Service 64-65; Provost of Eton 65-; Dir. Westminster Bank, Prudential Assurance Co., Standard Telephones and Cables 65-, Foreign and Colonial Telephones and Cables 65- (Chair. April 68-), Foreign and Colonial Investment Trust 65-; mem. Security Comm. 65-; Chancellor, Order of St. John 66.
The Provost's Lodge, Eton College, Windsor, Berks., England.
Telephone: Windsor 66304.

Cacoyannis, Michael; Barrister-at-law; Greek screen and stage director, writer and actor; b. 11 June 1922; ed. Greek Gymnasium, and in London at Gray's Inn, Central School of Dramatic Art and Old Vic School.
Called to the Bar 43; Producer for Overseas Service of B.B.C. 41-50; screen and stage producer 50-; Order of the Phoenix (Greece) 65.
Appeared as Herod in Wilde's *Salomé* 47, in Camus's *Caligula* 49, in *Two Dozen Red Roses* 49, etc.; directed and wrote script for *Windfall in Athens* 53-54, *Stella* 55, *A Girl in Black* 57, *A Matter of Dignity* 58, *Our Last Spring* (Eroica) 59-60, *The Wastrel* 60, *Electra* 61, *Zorba the Greek* 64, *The Day that the Fish Came Out*; also a number of stage productions in Athens, New York, etc., including *The Trojan Women* (Euripides) Paris 65, *The Devils* (Whiting), New York 66, also staged first world performance of M. Levy's opera *Mourning Becomes Electra*, Metropolitan Opera, New York 67; staged *Romeo and Juliet*, Paris 68.
6 Lykiou Street, Athens, Greece.
Telephone: 713-350.

Cadagua, Pedro Careaga Basabe, Conde del; Spanish banker and industrialist; b. 96; ed. Univ. of Deusto.
Pres. General Eléctrica Española, Sociedad Española de Construcciones Babcock & Wilcox, Firestone-Hispania, Hidroeléctrica Española, Iberduero and other industrial concerns; fmr. Pres. Bank of Vizcaya, Bilbao; Gran Cruz de Isabel la Católica.
Avenida del Ejército, 8 Neguri-Guecho (Vizcaya), Spain.

Cadbury, George Adrian Hayhurst, M.A. (son of Laurence John Cadbury, *q.v.*); British chocolate manufacturer; b. 15 April 1929; ed. Eton and King's Coll., Cambridge.
Director Cadbury Bros. Ltd. 58, Chair. 65-; Dir. British Cocoa and Chocolate Co. Ltd. 62, Chair. 65-; Dir. Daily News Ltd., Metal Box Co. Ltd. 68-.
Rising Sun House, nr. Knowle, Warwicks., England.

Cadbury, Laurence John, O.B.E., M.A. (father of George Adrian Cadbury, *q.v.*); British industrialist; b. 30 March 1889; ed. Leighton Park School and Trinity Coll., Cambridge.
Managing Dir. British Cocoa & Chocolate Co. Ltd., Cadbury Bros. Ltd. and Associated Companies 20-59; Chair. E.M.B. Co. Ltd. 26-, Daily News Ltd. 30-; Dir. Tyne Tees Television 59-67, Caps Ltd.; Chair. Bournville Village Trust 54-; Dir. Bank of England 36-61; Head Econ. Section, Mission to Moscow 41; High Sheriff, County of London 47-48, 60-61.
The Davids, Northfield, Birmingham 31, England.
Telephone: SEL 3654 (Office); PRI 1441 (Home).

Cadbury, Paul Strangman, C.B.E.: British business executive; b. 3 Nov. 1895; ed. Leighton Park School, Reading.
Friends' Ambulance Unit 15-18, Chair. Friends' Ambulance Unit 39-48; Vice-Chair. Cadbury Bros. Ltd. 49-59, Chair. 59-65; mem. Bournville Village Trust; fmr. Chair. J. S. Fry & Sons Ltd., British Cocoa & Chocolate Co. Ltd.
Publ. *Birmingham—Fifty Years On* 52.
Low Wood, 32 St. Mary's Road, Harborne, Birmingham 17, England.
Telephone: Harborne 0636.

Cadena Hernández, Ramón; Guatemalan lawyer and diplomatist; b. 28 July 1922; ed. Univ. de San Carlos, Guatemala, and Southern Methodist Univ., Dallas, Texas.
Former Pres. Guatemalan Law Asscn. and Guatemalan Bar Asscn.; fmr. Legal Counsellor, Ministry of Econs. and Labour; fmr. Under-Sec. Ministry of Econs. and Labour; fmr. mem. Monetary Board of Bank of Guatemala and Govt. Co-ordinator of Programme for Econ. Integration of Central America; Perm. Rep. of Guatemala to UN Sept. 66-.
Permanent Mission of Guatemala to the United Nations, 205 East 42nd Street, New York, N.Y. 10017, U.S.A.

Cadisch, Joos; Swiss geologist; b. 1 Sept. 1895; ed. Univ. of Berne.
Privat Dozent Fed. Inst. of Technology, Zürich 25; Prof. of Geology Basle Univ. 35; Prof. of Geology and Dir. Geological Inst. Berne Univ. 43-66, Prof. Emer. 66-, Rector of the Univ. 58; attached to Swiss Geological Comm. 20-30, mem. 45-; Hon. mem. Geologists' Asscn. (London); foreign mem. Geological Soc. of London and Accademia Nazionale dei Lincei.
Publs. *Der Bau der Schweizeralpen* 26, *Geologie der Insel Elba* 29, *Geologie der Schweizerischen Mineral- und Thermalquellen* 31, *Geologie der Schweizeralpen* (2nd edition) 53; co-editor Geological Map of Mittelbünden, Geological Map of Liechtenstein, Geological Atlas of Switzerland.
Gutenbergstrasse 26, Berne, Switzerland.
Telephone: (031) 253008.

Cadogan, Rt. Hon. Sir Alexander George Montagu, P.C., O.M., G.C.M.G., K.C.B.; British diplomatist; b. 25 Nov. 1884; ed. Eton and Oxford.
Attaché Constantinople 09; Foreign Office 12 and 14, and Vienna 13; First Sec. 19; Counsellor 28; has done special work in connection with the LN and in particular the Manchurian dispute; Minister to China 34 and Ambassador 35-36; Deputy Under-Sec. of State at Foreign Office 36-38, Permanent Under-Sec. of State Jan. 38-Feb. 46; Permanent Representative of U.K. on UN Security Council Feb. 46-50; retd. from Foreign Service 50; Chair. Board of Govs., B.B.C. 52-58; Dir. Nat. Provincial Bank 51-64, Phoenix Assurance Co.
2 Westminster Gardens, London, S.W.1, England.
Telephone: 01-834-2880.

Café Filho, José; Brazilian politician; b. 99; ed. American College in Natal, and Law and Commercial Coll. of Recife.
Journalist with *La Gazeta* 18; commanded revolutionary group in *coup d'état* 30; Social-Progressive Party Deputy 34, Pres. of Party 50; President of the Republic 54-55.
Av. Copacabana 1386, Apto. 202, Rio de Janeiro, Brazil.

Caggiano, H.E. Cardinal Antonio; Argentine ecclesiastic; b. 30 Jan. 1889; ed. Guadalupe Conciliar Seminary (Santa Fé) and Latin-American Coll., Rome.
Ordained priest 12; fmr. Prof. of Philosophy and Sciences, Santa Fé Seminary; Sec.-General 32nd Int. Eucharistic Congress, Buenos Aires 33-34; Bishop of Rosario 35-59; created Cardinal by Pope Pius XII 46;
Papal Legate, 3rd Inter-American Congress of Catholic Education, La Paz, 48; Archbishop of Buenos Aires and Primate of Argentina 59-67; Vicar-Gen. of Army; mem. Nat. Acad. of History; Grand Crosses, Order of Condor de Los Andes, Mil. Order of Malta, Order of Merit, Italy.
Publs. Numerous works on catholicism, the history of religion, catholic action, the fight against communism, pastoral work in urban parishes, etc.
c/o Palacio Arzobispal, Suipacha 1034, Buenos Aires, Argentina.

Çağlayangil, İhsan Sabri; Turkish politician; b. 1907; ed. School of Law, Istanbul.
Formerly with Ministry of Interior; Gov. of Antalya 48-53, of Çannakale 53-54, of Sivas 54, of Bursa 54-60; Senator for Bursa 61-; Minister of Labour Feb.-Oct. 65, of Foreign Affairs Oct. 65-; Justice Party.
Ministry of Foreign Affairs, Ankara, Turkey.

Caglioti, Vincenzo; Italian chemist and university professor; b. 26 May 1902; ed. Università di Napoli.
Professor Univ. of Florence 36; Prof. Univ. of Rome 38-; Pres. Consiglio Nazionale delle Ricerche 65-; mem. Accademia Nazionale dei Lincei; Nat. Prize for Chemistry Accademia Nazionale dei Lincei 55.
Consiglio Nazionale delle Ricerche, Piazzale delle Scienze 7, Rome; Istituto di Chimica Generale dell' Università di Roma, Piazzale delle Scienze 5, Rome, Italy.
Telephone: 4953635; 490324 (Univ.).

Caicedo Castillo, José Joaquín; Colombian lawyer and politician; b. 03; ed. National Univ. of Colombia.
Professor of Int. Law in the Nat. Univ. of Colombia; mem. House of Reps. 29-32, Senator 35-38; Minister of Labour 39-42; Minister to Italy 37, Ambassador to Cen. America (Costa Rica) 44-46, Rep. to Interamerican Juridical Cttee. 46-50, 54-61; *ad hoc* Judge at Int. Court of Justice 50-53; Minister of External Affairs 61-62.
Avenida 82 No. 10-57, Bogotá, Colombia.

Caillat, Claude, LL.D.; Swiss diplomatist; b. 1919; ed. Univ. de Genève.
Foreign Interests Div. of Political Dept. in Berne 42; various diplomatic posts in London, Athens and Washington; Trade Div. Fed. State Econ. Dept. 60-62; Counsellor of Embassy, First Asst. to Head of Mission, Paris then Chargé d'Affaires *ad interim* 62-67; Del. of Fed. Council and Amb. Extraordinary and Plenipotentiary 67; Head of Perm. Swiss Del. to Org. for Econ. Co-operation and Devt. 67-.
Organization for Economic Co-operation and Development (OECD), Château de la Muette, 2 rue André Pascal, Paris 16e, France.
Telephone: TRO-32-20.

Caillois, Roger, AGRÉGÉ DE L'UNIV.; French writer; b. 3 March 1913; ed. Lycée de Reims, Sorbonne, and Ecole Normale Supérieure.
Founder French Inst., Buenos Aires; Editor-Dir. *Lettres françaises* 41-45; Chief Editor *France libre* 45-47; mem. Board of literary reviews *Confluences* and *La Licorne* 45-48; Dir. *La Croix du Sud* (collection of Ibero-American authors), Gallimard; Chief Editor *Diogène* (int. review of philosophy and human sciences); Dir. of the Div. of Cultural Advancement, UNESCO; mem. of the jury of the Grand Prix National des Lettres, the Prix des Critiques and the Lecture de la Comédie Française; Officier Légion d'Honneur.
Publs. *Le Mythe et l'Homme* 38, *L'Homme et le Sacré* 39, *Puissance du Roman* 40, *Le Rocher de Sisyphe* 45, *Babel* 48, *Poétique de St. John Perse* 54, *L'Incertitude qui vient des Rêves* 56, *Les Jeux et les Hommes* 58, *Art poétique* 58, *Trésor de la Poésie universelle* (with Jean-Clarence Lambert) 58, *Méduse et Compagnie* 60, *Ponce-Pilate* 61, *Esthétique Généralisée* 62, *Bellone ou la Pente de la*

Guerre 63, *Instincts et société* 64, *Au Coeur du Fantastique* 65, *Pierres* 66, *Obliques* 67.
34 avenue Charles Floquet, Paris 7e, France.
Telephone: 306-50-60.

Cain, Julien; French librarian; b. 10 May 1887. Director-Gen. Bibliothèque Nationale 30-64, Hon. Dir.-Gen. Bibliothèques de France 64-; mem. Nat. Council of Museums, Higher Council of Archives, Comm. of Diplomatic Archives at Ministry of Foreign Affairs; mem. Exec. Council, UNESCO 58-, Vice-Pres. 60-; Pres. Int. Library Comm.; Pres. Centre Int. de Synthèse; Vice-Pres Int. Fed. Asscns. of Librarians, Programme Council, R.T.F. 58; mem. Inst. de France; Grand Croix Légion d'Honneur, Ordre des Arts et des Lettres; Palmes Academiques, Hon. K.B.E.
8 rue des Petits-Champs, Paris 2e, France.

Caine, Sir Sydney, K.C.M.G.; British civil servant and university administrator; b. 27 June 1902; ed. Harrow County School and London School of Economics.
Asst. Inspector of Taxes 23-26; Asst. Principal, Colonial Office 26-35, Principal 35-37; Financial Sec., Hong Kong 37-40; Asst. Sec., Colonial Office 40-44; Asst. Under-Sec. of State, Colonial Office 44-47, Deputy Under-Sec. of State 47-48; Third Sec., H.M. Treasury 48; Head of U.K. Treasury Delegation and British Supply Office, Washington, Jan. 49-51: head of Int. Bank Mission to Ceylon 51-52; Vice-Chancellor Univ. of Malaya 52-56; Chair. Caribbean Fed. Fiscal Comm. June-Sept. 55; Dir. London School of Economics 57-67; Chair. Int. Inst. of Educational Planning (UNESCO) 63; Gov. Reserve Bank of Rhodesia Dec. 65-67; Grand Officer Order of Orange-Nassau (Netherlands).
Soke Farm, Silchester, Berks, England.
Telephone: Silchester 346.

Cairncross, Sir Alexander Kirkland, K.C.M.G., M.A., PH.D.; British economist and civil servant; b. 11 Feb. 1911; ed. Hamilton Acad., Univ. of Glasgow and Trinity Coll., Cambridge.
Lecturer, Univ. of Glasgow 35-39; held various Civil Service posts 40-46; on staff of *The Economist* 46; Economic Adviser, Board of Trade 46-49; Dir. Economic Div. O.E.E.C. 50; Prof. of Applied Economics, Univ. of Glasgow 51-61; Dir., Economic Development Inst., Wash. 55-56; Economic Adviser to British Govt. 61-64; Head of British Govt. Economic Service 64-; Master Designate, St. Peter's Coll., Oxford; mem. Council, Royal Economic Soc. 55-, Council of Man., Nat. Inst. of Social and Economic Research, Advisory Cttee. Houblon-Norman Trustees, Council of British Academy, Council of Political and Economic Planning, Court of Governors London School of Economics; numerous cttees. (including Working of the Monetary System 57-59); Editor *Scottish Journal of Political Economy* 53-61; Dir., Scottish Amicable Life Assurance Soc. 58-61, Ailsa and Alva Investment Trusts 59-61; F.B.A., Hon. LL.D. Mount Allison Univ. 62, Glasgow Univ. 66.
Publs. *Introduction to Economics* 44, *Home and Foreign Investment 1870-1913* 53, *Monetary Policy in a Mixed Economy* 60, *Economic Development and the Atlantic Provinces* 61, *Factors in Economic Development* 62.
31 Carlton Drive, London, S.W.15, England.
Telephone: 01-788-9490.

Caldecote, 2nd Viscount, cr. 39, of Bristol, **Robert Andrew Inskip,** D.S.C., M.I.MECH., M.I.E.E., F.R.Ae.S.; British aeronautical engineer and business executive; b. 8 Oct. 1917; ed. Eton and King's Coll., Cambridge.
R.N.V.R. 39-45; Royal Naval Coll., Greenwich 46-47; Asst. Manager, Vickers-Armstrong Naval Yard, Walker-on-Tyne 47-48; Fellow, King's Coll., Cambridge, and Lecturer, Engineering Dept., Cambridge Univ. 48-55; Managing Dir. English Electric Aviation 60-63, British Aircraft Corpn. (G.W.) Ltd. 63-; Deputy Managing Dir. British Aircraft Corpn. 61-; Dir. English Electric Co.

53-, D. Napier and Son Ltd. 59-, English Electric, Leo Marconi 66-; Pres. Soc. of British Aircraft Constructors 65-66, Parl. and Scientific Cttee. 66; Pres. Asscn. Int. des Constructeurs de Matériel Aerospatial (AICMA); Chair. Ruston and Hornsby 66-;
Debden Manor, Saffron Walden, Essex, England.
Telephone: Saffron Walden 3231.

Calder, Alexander; American mechanical engineer and sculptor; b. 22 July 1898; ed. Stevens Inst. of Technology and Arts Student League, N.Y.
Worked as engineer until 23, when decided to take up painting as career; went to Paris 26; made wire sculptures 26-29, wood sculptures 28-30; "mobiles" first exhibited in Paris 32, "stabiles" 31, and also "constellations" and "towers"; designed Mercury Fountain, Spanish Pavilion, Paris 37; first prize for foreign sculptor, Biennale de Venezia 52; commissioned to do an outdoor "mobile" for UNESCO Building, Paris; 45-foot "mobile" at Idlewild Airport, New York; acoustic ceiling, Aréa Magna, Ciudad Universitaria, Caracas 53-54; large "mobile" in U.S. Pavilion, Brussels 58; first prize for sculpture Carnegie International 58; exhibition at Tate Gallery, London 62; retrospective exhibition, Guggenheim Museum, New York, Nov. 64; exhbn. at Museum of Modern Art, Paris 65; "stabile" *Le Guichet* 65; 67 foot high stainless steel stabile, Expo 67, Montreal 67.
Publs: *Fables d'Aesop* 31, *Three Young Rats* 44, *Autobiography with Pictures* 67.
Roxbury, Conn., U.S.A.

Caldeyro-Barcia, Roberto, M.D., F.A.C.S.; Uruguayan physiologist; b. 26 Sept. 1921; ed. Univ. of Uruguay.
Assistant Prof. of Physiology, Medical School Univ. of Uruguay 47-50, Prof. 50-, Prof. and Chair. Dept. of Physiopathology 65-; Chair. Service of Obstetrical Physiology 55-; Hon. mem. American Coll. of Surgeons, American Asscn. of Obstetricians and Gynæcologists.
Publs. articles on obstetrics, *Oxytocin* (with H.Heller) 61.
Servicio de Fisiología Obstétrica, Hospital de Clínicas, piso 16, Avda. Italia, Montevideo, Uruguay.
Telephone: 401151, Extension 216.

Caldicott, Sir John Moore, K.B.E., C.M.G.; British farmer and politician; b. 1900; ed. Shrewsbury School.
Pres. Rhodesia Tobacco Asscn. 43-45, Rhodesia Nat. Farmers' Union 46-48; mem. Southern Rhodesia Parl. 48; Minister of Agriculture, S. Rhodesian Govt. 51; Minister of Agriculture and Health, Fed. Govt. 53-58; Minister of Public Service 56-63; Minister of Economic Affairs 59-62; Minister for Defence 60-62, for Common Market Affairs 62, Finance 62-63.
Chigudu, P.B. 252A, Salisbury, Rhodesia.
Telephone: Umvukwes 01612.

Caldwell, Erskine; American writer; b. 17 Dec. 1903; ed. Erskine Coll., Univ. of Virginia, Univ. of Pennsylvania.
Former newspaper writer, cotton picker, stage hand, professional footballer, book reviewer, lecturer, editor; Motion Picture Screen Writer in Hollywood 30-34, 42-43; awarded Yale Review award for fiction 33; mem. Authors' League of America, Nat. Inst. of Arts and Letters, P.E.N. Club; Newspaper Corresp. in Mexico, Spain, Czechoslovakia 38-39; Newspaper and Radio Corresp. Russia 41; Editor of *American Folkways* 40-55.
Publs. *The Bastard* 29, *Poor Fool* 30, *American Earth* 31, *Tobacco Road* 32, *God's Little Acre*, *We Are the Living* 33, *Journeyman*, *Kneel to the Rising Sun*, *Some American People* 35, *Southways* 39, *Trouble in July* 40, *Jackpot* 40, *All Out on the Road to Smolensk* 42, *Moscow under Fire* 42, *All Night Long* 42, *Georgia Boy* 43, *Stories* 44, *Tragic Ground* 44, *A House in the Uplands* 46, *The Sure Hand of God* 47, *This Very Earth* 48, *Place Called Estherville* 49, *Episode in Palmetto* 50, *Call it Experience* 51, *The Courting of Susie Brown* 52, *A Lamp for Nightfall* 52, *The Complete*

Stories of Erskine Caldwell 53, *Love and Money* 54, *Gretta* 55, *Gulf Coast Stories* 56, *Certain Women* 57, *Molly Cottontail* (juvenile) 58, *Claudelle Inglish* 59, *When You Think of Me* 59, *Jenny by Nature* 61, *Close to Home* 62, *The Last Night of Summer* 63, *Around About America* 64, *In Search of Bisco* 65, *The Deer at Our House* (juvenile) 66, *In the Shadow of the Steeple* 66, *Miss Mamma Aimee* 67, *Deep South* 68; with Margaret Bourke-White: *You Have Seen Their Faces* 37, *North of the Danube* 39, *Is This the U.S.A.?* 41.

c/o McIntosh and Otis Inc., 18 East 41st Street, New York, N.Y. 10017; and P.O.B. 397, Rheem, Contra Costa County, Calif., U.S.A.

Telephone: MU9-1050 (New York).

Calhoun, John Archibald, M.A.; American diplomatist; b. 29 Oct. 1918; ed. Univ. of Calif. and Harvard Univ.

Foreign Service, Mexico, Teheran, Berlin 41-49; Dep. Dir. Office German Political Affairs, Dept. of State 49-52; 1st Sec. Seoul 53-55; Air War Coll., Maxwell AFB 55-56; 1st Sec. Paris 56-57; Dept. of State 57-60; Counsellor, Athens 60-61; Ambassador to Chad 61-63; Minister to Berlin 63-66; Minister Counsellor, Saigon 67-.

c/o Department of State, Washington, D.C. 20520, U.S.A.

Califano, Joseph Anthony, Jr., A.B., LL.B.; American lawyer and government official; b. 15 May 1931; ed. Holy Cross Coll. and Harvard Univ.

Admitted to New York Bar 55; U.S. Naval Reserve 55-58; with firm Dewey Ballantine, Bushby, Palmer and Wood, New York City 58-61; Special Asst. to Gen. Counsel, Dept. of Defense 61-62; Special Asst. to Sec. of Army 62-63; Gen. Counsel, Dept. of Army 63-64; Special Asst. to Sec. and Deputy Sec. of Defense 64-65; Special Asst. to Pres. 65-66; admitted to U.S. District Court; U.S. Court of Appeals for 2nd Circuit; U.S. Supreme Court Bar 66; mem. Fed. Bar Asscn.; Dept. of Army Distinguished Civilian Service Medal.

4704 Albemarle Street, N.W., Washington, D.C., U.S.A.

Calkins, Robert D., B.S., M.A., LL.D., PH.D.; American economist; b. 19 Jan. 1903; ed. Coll. of William and Mary, and Stanford Univ.

Research Assoc., Food Research Inst., Stanford 25-27, 30-32; Teaching Asst. and Instructor, Stanford 29-31; Asst. Prof. of Econs., Univ. of Calif. 32-36; Assoc. Prof. 36-40, Prof. 40-41; Chair. of Dept. of Econs. 35-41; Dean, Coll. of Commerce 37-41; Prof. and Dean, School of Business, Columbia Univ. 41-46; Vice-Pres. and Dir. Gen. Educ. Board, N.Y.C. 47-52; Pres. The Brookings Inst., Washington, D.C. 52-67; Vice-Chancellor, Social Sciences and Prof. of Econs., Univ. of Calif.-Santa Cruz 67-; Dir. N.Y. Fed. Reserve Bank 43-49; Mediator, War Labor Board 42-45; Consultant to Nat. Resources Planning Board 40-42, Office of Price Admin. 42, War Dept. 42, etc.

University of California-Santa Cruz, Santa Cruz, Calif., U.S.A.

Callaghan, Rt. Hon. (Leonard) James, P.C., M.P.; British politician; b. 27 March 1912; ed. Portsmouth Northern Secondary School.

Tax Officer 29; Asst. Sec. Inland Revenue Staff Asscn. 36-47; service in Royal Navy 39-45; M.P. 45-; Parl. Sec. Ministry of Transport 47-50; Parl. and Financial Sec., Admiralty 50-51; Chancellor of the Exchequer 64-Nov. 67; Home Secretary Nov. 67-; mem. Consultative Ass., Council of Europe 48-50, 54; Chair. Co-ordinating Advisory Cttee. on Oil Pollution of the Sea 53-64; Consultant to Police Fed. 55-64; mem. Nat. Exec. Cttee. Labour Party.

House of Commons, Westminster, London, S.W.1; and Home Office, London, S.W.1, England.

Callaghan, Morley (Edward); Canadian novelist; b. 1903; ed. St. Michael's Coll., Univ. of Toronto, and Osgoode Hall Law School.

Canada Council Medal Winner 66.

Publs: *Strange Fugitive* 28, *Native Argosy* 29, *It's Never Over* 30, *No Man's Meat* 31, *Broken Journey* 32, *Such is My Beloved* 34, *They Shall Inherit the Earth* 35, *My Joy in Heaven* 36, *Now that April's Here* 37, *Jake Baldwin's Vow* (for children) 48, *The Varsity Story* 48, *The Loved and the Lost* 55, *The Man with the Coat* 55, *A Many Coloured Coat* 60, *A Passion in Rome* 61, *That Summer in Paris* 63, *Morley Callaghan* Vols. I and II 64.

20 Dale Avenue, Toronto, Ontario, Canada.

Callard, Eric John, B.A., C.ENG., M.I.MECH.E.; British business executive; b. 15 March 1913; ed. Queen's Coll., Taunton, and St. John's Coll., Cambridge.

Deputy Chair. Imperial Chemical Industries Ltd. (I.C.I.), Paints Div. 51-55, Man. Dir. 55-59, Chair. 59-64; Dir. I.C.I. Ltd. April 64-, Deputy Chair. April 67-; Dir. Pension Funds Securities Ltd. 63-, Imperial Metal Industries 64-67, Imperial Chemical Insurance 66-; Chair. I.C.I. (Europa) Ltd. 65-67; mem. Council Univ. of Manchester, Manchester Business School 64-; mem. Council British Inst. of Management 64-, Fellow 66-; mem. Council Export Council for Europe 66-; Chair. Industrial Co-partnership Asscn. 67-; mem. Council of Industry for Management Education 67-; Co-opt. mem. Univ. of Cambridge Appointments Board 68-.

Imperial Chemical Industries Ltd., Imperial Chemical House, Millbank, London S.W.1; Home: Farthings, Jordans, nr. Beaconsfield, Bucks., England.

Callas, Maria Meneghini; Greek opera singer; b. 2 Dec 1923; ed. Athens Conservatoire.

Born New York; in Greece during 39-45 war; studied under Elvira de Hidalgo; sang with Athens Opera; sang in *Gioconda*, Verona 47, and many leading soprano roles, particularly Bellini's *Norma;* has sung in Rome, Florence, Naples, Milan, New York, San Francisco, London, Mexico, etc.; numerous recordings.

36 avenue George Mandel, Monte Carlo, France; and avenue Foch, Paris, France.

Callori di Vignale, H.E. Cardinal Federico; Vatican ecclesiastic.

Member Heraldic Commission for the Pontifical Court; Maggiordomo to the Pope; consecrated Archbishop 65; created Cardinal 65.

Vatican City, Rome, Italy.

Calmann-Lévy, Robert Paul Michel; French publisher; b. 20 Oct. 1899.

Director, Calmann-Lévy, publishers of French and foreign books.

3 rue Auber, Paris 9e, France.

Calmes, Christian, DR. EN DROIT.; Luxembourg lawyer and civil servant; b. 13; ed. Echternach Gymnasium, Strasbourg and Paris Univs.

Called to the bar 38; mem. Luxembourg del. at confs. setting up Benelux and E.C.S.C.; Sec.-Gen. Council of Ministers of European Communities (E.C.S.C., E.E.C., and EURATOM) 58-; Minister Plenipotentiary.

Publ. *Geôles sanglantes* 48, *1867 Affaire du Luxembourg.*

Ehnen, Luxembourg, Grand Duchy of Luxembourg; 103 rue Général Lotz, Brussels, Belgium.

Calmon Moniz de Bittencourt, Pedro; Brazilian literary historian and politician; ed. Bahia Univ.

Lecturer and Prof. Rio de Janeiro Univ. and Colégio Pedro II; Rector of Brazil Univ. (now Univ. Fed. do Rio de Janeiro) 48-67, now Prof. of Gen. Theory of the State; Minister of Educ. 50-51; Hon. Prof. of San Marcos de Lima and Mexico Univs.; mem. Acad. Brasileira de Letras and many other South American, Spanish and Portuguese Insts., Acads. and Scientific Societies; Merito Militar do Brasil, Légion d'Honneur,

Gran Croce San Silvestre di Roma and many other foreign decorations, Dr. h.c. Univ. of Coimbra, Mexico, Ecuador, etc.
Publs. More than 80 books, including *O Tesouro de Belchior* (1st Prize of Brazilian Academy, São Paulo 29), *História da Civilização Brasileira, O Brasil e America, História do Brasil* (seven vols.), *Vidas de D. Pedro I, D. Pedro II, Princesa Isabel, Castro Alves, História Social do Brasil, História da Ideias Politicas*, etc.
Universidade Federal do Rio de Janeiro, Avenida Pasteur 250, Rio de Janeiro, Brazil.

Calò, Giovanni, PH.D.; Italian philosopher and educationist; b. 24 Dec. 1882; ed. Florence Univ.
Prof. of Pedagogy Florence Univ. 11; Deputy 19-24; Sec. to Pres. of the Chamber 20; Under-Sec. of State for Fine Arts in Facta Cabinet 22; founder and fmr. Dir. Florence Nat. Didactic Centre; Pres. Italian Inst. of Philosophical Studies; Vice-Pres. Nat. Italian Comm. of UNESCO; Pres. of Cttee. of Co-ordination of the Nat. Didactic Centres; founder and Dir. of Florence Scuola Magistrale Ortofrenica; Dir. for Section of Psychology and Pedagogy of the Enciclopedia Filosofica (Venezia-Roma), Vols. I-IV 57; Pres. Italian Pedagogic Asscn. and of School of Social Service, Florence; Founder and Prof., Centre of Studies for Physical Educ. and Pres. of Higher Inst. for Physical Educ., Florence; mem. Accademia Nazionale dei Lincei (Rome) and other learned socs.
Publs. *Filippo Villani e il Liber de origine civitatis Florentiae* 04, *Il problema della libertà nel pensiero contemporaneo* 06, *L'individualismo etico nel secolo XIX* 07, *La Psicologia dell' attenzione in rapporto alla scienza educativa* 07, *Fatti e problemi del mondo educativo* 11, *Il problema della coeducazione* 14, *L'educazione degli educatori* 20, *Dalla guerra mondiale alla scuola nostra* 19, *Antologia pedagogica*, 3rd edn. 53, *Maestri e problemi di filosofia* (2 vols.) 24-25, *Dottrine e opere nella storia dell' educazione* 32, *Problemi vivi e orizzonti nuovi dell'educazione nazionale* 35, *Dall'Umanesimo alla Scuola del lavoro* 41, *L'anima del fanciullo* 43, *Elementi di Psicologia*, 9th edn. 58, *Educazione e Scuola*, 3rd edn. 50, *Corso di pedagogia*, 3 vols. 10th edn. 58, *Dall' Alfabeto a Dio Saggi di Didattica* 48, *Momenti di storia dell'educazione* 55, *Responsabilità d'educare* 55, *Per la riforma della scuola* (writings and speeches) 55, *Problemi attuali della Pedagogia e della Scuola* 58, *Pedagogia del Risorgimento* 65.
Via Scipione Ammirato 18, Florence, Italy.
Telephone: 676228.

Calogero, Guido; Italian philosopher and university professor; b. 4 Dec. 1904.
Former Prof., Florence and Pisa Univs.; one of the leaders of Liberal-Socialist Movement, arrested 42 as anti-Fascist; Editor for the section of philosophy of Italian Encyclopaedia; Visiting Prof. of Philosophy, McGill Univ., Montreal 48-49; Dir. Italian Inst., London 50-55; Visiting Prof. of Philosophy, Univ. of Calif., Berkeley 56-57; mem. Inst. for Advanced Study, Princeton 62-63; Pres. Institut International de Philosophie 63-66; Prof. of Philosophy, Rome Univ.
Publs. *I fondamenti della logica aristotelica* 27, *Studi sull' Eleatismo* 32, *La scuola dell' uomo* 39, *Lezioni di Filosofia* 46-48, *Logo e Dialogo* 50, *Scuola sotto inchiesta* 57, *Filosofia del Dialogo* 62.
Via S. Alberto Magno 5, Rome, Italy.

Cals, Joseph Maria Laurens Theo, DR. JUR., G.B.E.; Netherlands politician; b. 18 July 1914; ed. Univ. of Nijmegen.
Lawyer 40; Chair. Netherlands Mining Industry Council 48-50; M.P. 48-50, 63-65; Sec. of State for Education, Arts and Sciences 50-52; Minister of Education, Arts and Sciences 52-63; Prime Minister 65-67; Minister of State 66; Catholic People's Party.

20 Nieuwe Duinweg, The Hague, Netherlands.
Telephone: 55-05-24.

Calseyde, Paul J. J. Van de, M.D.; Belgian physician; b. 03; ed. Ghent Univ.
Medical Insp. Belgian Postal Admin. 30; Dir. Social Medicine, Ministry of Public Health 33; Principal Officer of Health. Eastern Flanders 39; Dir.-Gen. of Public Health, Ministry of Public Health 45-57, 68-; Sec. Council for Public Health 45-57; Regional Dir. WHO European Office 57-67; Hon. Fellow Society of Health, London, American Public Health Asscn. and Soc. Française d'Hygiène et de Médecine Préventive et Sociale; Commdr. Order of Leopold, Ordre de la Couronne, Order of Dannebrog, and other decorations.
Ministry of Health, Brussels, Home: 29 Avenue Brigmann, Brussels 6, Belgium.
Telephone: 64-11-17 (Ext. 18) (Office); 37-36-26 (Home).

Calvet, Pierre Louis, LL.L.; French civil servant; b. 27 June 1910; ed. Lycée Buffon, Law Faculty, Univ. of Paris, Ecole Libre des Sciences Politiques.
Financial Inspector 33; Financial Attaché, London 45; Gen. Dir. Office des Changes 47; Vice-Pres. European Payments Union 50-; Deputy Gov. Bank of France 52-; Vice-Pres. Banque Nationale de Paris 66-; mem. Council Nat. Museums; Commdr. Légion d'Honneur, Order of Orange Nassau; Officier Ordre de Léopold; Grand Officer, Order of Merit (Italian Repub.).
Banque Nationale de Paris S.A., 16 boulevard des Italiens, Paris, 9e; Home: 9 rue Newton, Paris 16e, France.
Telephone: LAF 55-00 (Office); KLE 97-68 (Home).

Calvet de Magalhaes, José; Portuguese diplomatist; b. 2 Oct. 1915; ed. Univ. of Lisbon.
Entered Foreign Service 41, served New York, Boston, Canton, Paris; mem. Del. to NATO 52-56; Minister and Head of Del. to OEEC 56-60, Ambassador to OEEC 60-61, to OECD 61-64; Head, Del. to ECSC 59-64; Ambassador to EEC and EURATOM 62-64; Dir.-Gen. Econ. Affairs 64-; Grand Cross, Cross of the South (Brazil), Grand Cross, Order of Merit (Spain), Grand Officer, Order of Merit (Germany).
Publs. *The Criminal Responsibility of Doctors in Case of the Patient's Death* 44, *Anthero de Quental and Socialism* 45, *José Accursio das Neves* (anthology and introduction) 45, *Anthero de Quental* (anthology and introduction) 46.
Rua do Brasil, 3-Estoril, Portugal.
Telephone: 260614.

Calvin, Melvin, B.S., PH.D.; American chemist; b. 8 April 1911; ed. Michigan Coll. of Mining and Technology and Univ. of Minnesota.
Instructor Dept. of Chemistry, Univ. of Calif., Berkeley 37-40, Asst. Prof. 41-45, Assoc. Prof. 45-47, Prof. 47-; Dir. Bio-Organic Chemistry Group, Radiation Laboratory 46-; nat. defence work 41-45; mem. Nat. Acad. of Sciences; Foreign mem., The Royal Society; recipient of several scientific awards; Nobel Prize for Chemistry 61; Davy Medal, Royal Society 64.
Publs. *The Theory of Organic Chemistry* (with G.E.K. Branch) 41, *Isotopic Carbon* (with Heidelberger, Reid, Tolbert and Yankwich) 49, *The Chemistry of the Metal Chelate Compounds* (with Martell) 52, *The Path of Carbon in Photosynthesis* (with Bassham) 57, *Chemical Evolution* 61, *Photosynthesis of Carbon Compounds* (with Bassham) 62.
Department of Chemistry, University of California, Berkeley 4, Calif.; Home: 2683 Buena Vista Way, Berkeley, Calif., U.S.A.
Telephone: 848-4036.

Calvino, Italo; Italian writer; b. 15 Oct. 1923.
Dir. of editorial staff Giulio Einaudi Editore.
Publs. *Il Sentiero dei Nidi di Ragno* 47, *Ultimo viene il Corvo* 49, *Il Visconte dimezzato* 52, *L'Entrata in Guerra* 54, *Fiabe Italiane* 56, *Il Barone Rampante* 57, *I Racconti*

58, *Il Cavaliere Inesistente* 59, *La Giornata di uno Scrutatore* 63, *Le Cosmicomiches* 66, *Ti con zero* (short stories) 67.
c/o Giulio Einaudi Editore, Via Umberto Biancamano 1, Turin, Italy.

Calwell, Rt. Hon. Arthur Augustus, P.C., M.H.R.; Australian politician; b. 28 Aug. 1896; ed. North Melbourne.
In Dept. of Agriculture, Victoria 13-23; Victoria Treasury 23-40; mem. Victoria Central Exec. Australian Labour Party 26-49, 64-; and Pres. Victoria Australian Labour Party 31; Victoria Del. to the Fed. Confs. of Australian Labour Party 30-51, 65-; mem. Melbourne City Council 39-45; Commr. Melbourne and Metropolitan Board of Works 39-45; mem. House of Representatives 40-; and Fed. Exec. of Australian Labour Party 31-50; mem. Joint Parl. Cttee. on Broadcasting 41-43; Chair. Aliens' Classification and Advisory Cttee. 42-43; mem. Central Medical Co-ordination Cttee. 42-43; Min. for Information 43-45; Min. for Immigration and Information 45-49; Deputy Leader of Labour Party and of Fed. Parl. Labour Opposition 51-60, Acting Leader at times 53 and 57, Leader 60-67; Chair. Melbourne Cricket Ground Trust 52-; Nat. Vice-Pres. Winston Churchill Memorial Trust; Knight Commdr. Order of St. Gregory the Great.
Publ: *Labour's Role in Modern Society* 63.
30 Baroda Street, Flemington, Melbourne; and Commonwealth Parliament Offices, 318 Post Office Place, Melbourne, Vic., Australia.

Camargo, Sergio de; Brazilian sculptor; b. 30; ed. Academia Altamira, Buenos Aires, and Univ. de Paris à la Sorbonne.
In France 48-50, 51-54, 61-; visited China 54; specialises in wood reliefs; Int. Sculpture Prize, Paris Biennale 63. Works are in permanent collections of Nat. Museum of Art, Rio de Janeiro, Museum of Art, São Paulo, Musée d'Art Moderne de la Ville de Paris, Tate Gallery, London, and in numerous private collections; represented in exhibitions in Paris and Brussels 63, Mannheim, Arras, London and Paris 64, New York 65, and Latin American exhibitions 54-.
23 avenue Pasteur, Vanves (Seine), France.

Cambanellis, Iakovos; Greek writer and film dir.; b. 22.
Publications, plays include: *Dance on the Sheaves* 50, *The Seventh Day of Creation* 56, *The Courtyard of Miracles* 57, *Story Without a Title* 59, *Neighbourhood of Angels* 63; Film Scripts for *Stella, The River, Snowdrop*; dir. of films including documentary *The Root*; regular contributor to Greek Radio and *Eleftheria*.
Dervenion 19, Athens, Greece.

Cambournac, Francisco José Carrasqueiro, M.D.; Portuguese medical scientist; b. 26 Dec. 1903; ed. Lisbon Univ., Lisbon, Hamburg and London Schools of Hygiene and Tropical Medicine.
Fellow and staff mem. Rockefeller Foundation, engaged mainly on malaria research and teaching 34-41; Assoc. Prof. of Hygiene, Public Health and Climatology, Lisbon Inst. of Tropical Medicine 42-44, Prof. 44-, Dir. 64-, also Dir. Portuguese Malaria Inst.; mem. del. to World Health Ass. 47-53; mem. WHO Expert Panel on Malaria 48-53; Head del. WHO Cttee. for S.E. Asia 49, Africa 51-53; WHO Consultant for Africa 49 to prepare first African Malaria Conf. 50; Chief Epidemiological Services Mission of Angola, Co-ordinator yellow fever survey of Angola, Mozambique and São Tomé and Príncipe 50-54; mem. CCTA, African Scientific Council (CSA), Admin. Inst. des Parcs Nat. du Congo et du Rwanda 59-67; Dir. WHO Regional Office for Africa 54-64; mem. WHO Expert Panel Public Health Admin. 64-; Pres. of the Direction of Liga Portuguesa de Educação Sanitaria 64-67, Sociedade Portuguesa de Medicina Tropical (Secção de Medicina Tropical) da Sociedade de Ciências Medicas 64-67; Dir. and Prof. Public Health in Tropical Regions, Escola National de Saúde Pública e de Medicina Tropical 67; hon. Fellow American Public Health Asscn.; hon. mem. Asscn. de Specialistas de Analises Clínicos (Spain); Comendador Orden Civil Sanidad (Spain); Hon. mem. Soc. Belge de Médecine Tropicale; Hon.-mem. Société de Pathologie Exotique 67.
Publs. More than 120 papers, particularly on epidemiology, parasitology, entomology, public health, nutrition, health education, malaria, sleeping sickness and relapsing fever.
Escola Nacional de Saúde Pública e de Medicina Tropical, Rua da Junqueira, Lisbon 3, Portugal.
Telephone: 632141.

Cameron, Donald Alastair, O.B.E., M.B., B.S.; Australian physician and politician; b. 17 March 1900; ed. Sydney Univ.
Former Hon. Medical Officer, Ipswich Hospital; served Second World War; mem. Fed. Parl. for Oxley, Queensland 49-61; Minister for Health 56-61; Minister in Charge Commonwealth Scientific and Industrial Research Organization; High Commr. in New Zealand 62-65; mem. Liberal Party of Australia.
43 Sefton Road, Clayfield, Brisbane, Queensland, Australia.
Telephone: 672021.

Cammann, Helmuth Carl, DR. RER. POL.; German economist; b. 8 Feb. 1927; ed. Technological Univ., Karlsruhe and Cologne Univ.
Foreign Trade and Balance of Payments Section, Econ. Research Inst., Essen 50-53; Econ. Adviser, Perm. German Del. to OEEC 53-56; Head of Div., Econ. Directorate, ECSC, Luxembourg 56-57; Econ. Sec. Del. in U.K. of ECSC 57-61; Head of Perm. Del. of EEC Comm. to OECD, Paris 61-66; Sec.-Gen. Bundesverband des privaten Bankgewerbes e.V., Cologne (German Bankers' Fed.) 66-.
Cologne, Mohrenstrasse 35, German Federal Republic.
Telephone: 21-99-02.

Campaigne, Jameson Gilbert, B.A.; American editor and writer; b. 16 Jan. 1914; ed. Montclair Acad., Williams Coll.
Salesman, Yardley & Co. 36-40; writer with Compton Advertising 40-44; U.S. Marine Corps 44-46; Chief Editorial Writer, *Indianapolis Star* 46-51, Editor, Editorial Page 51-60, Editor 60-; Lincoln Nat. Life Foundation Award for best editorial on Lincoln; Freedoms Foundation Award for editorial writing 51, 52, 57; Indiana Univ. World Affairs Award 60.
Publs. *American Might and Soviet Myth* 60, *Checkoff* 61.
22 West 54th Street, Indianapolis, Ind., U.S.A.

Campbell, Sir David, M.C., M.A., B.SC., M.D., LL.D., D.C.L., F.R.C.P., F.R.C.P.S., F.R.S.E.; British university professor; b. 6 May 1889; ed. Univ. of Glasgow and Johns Hopkins Univ.
Pollok Lecturer in Pharmacology, Univ. of Glasgow 20-30; Asst. Physician, Western Infirmary, Glasgow 20-30; Rockefeller Medical Fellow 25-26; Regius Prof. of Materia Medica, Univ. of Aberdeen 30-59, Dean, Faculty of Medicine 32-59; Physician, Aberdeen Royal Infirmary 30-59; mem. Gen. Medical Council 36-61, Pres. 49-61; Hon. LL.D. (Glasgow, Dublin, Liverpool and Aberdeen Univs.), Hon. D.C.L. (Durham).
Publ. *Handbook of Therapeutics* 30.
Carskeoch, Milltimber, Aberdeenshire, Scotland.
Telephone: Cutler 3335.

Campbell, Douglas Lloyd; Canadian farmer and politician; b. 27 May 1895; ed. Brandon Coll., Manitoba.
Mem. Manitoba Legislature 22-; mem. Exec. Council 36-; Min. of Agriculture and Immigration 36-48; Prime Minister of Manitoba 48-58; Leader of the Opposition 58-62; Liberal-Progressive.
326 Kelvin blvd., Winnipeg 29, Manitoba, Canada.
Telephone: WH6-7406 (Office); HU 9-2568.

Campbell, Evan Roy, C.B.E.; Rhodesian farmer and diplomatist; b. 2 Sept. 1908; ed. St. Andrews Coll., Grahamstown, Potchefstroom Agricultural Coll.
Farmer, Umvukwes, Southern Rhodesia 31-35, Inyazura 35-; Army service 40-45; mem. Rhodesia Tobacco Asscn. 46-50, Vice-Pres. 50-52, Pres. 52-58; Chair. Tobacco Export Promotion Council 58-63, Standard Bank Ltd., Albatros Fisons Fertlizers Ltd., Rhodesia Tea Estates Ltd., Export Sales (Pvt.) Ltd., Fisons Pest Control (C.A.) (Pvt.) Ltd., Central African Branch of Inst. of Dirs. 65-; High Commr. of Southern Rhodesia in U.K. Dec. 63-June 65; Dir. Rhodesian Nat. Insurance Co. Ltd., Metal Box Co. of C.A. Ltd. and other cos. 65-; Dir. Rhodesian Promotion Council 65-.
Zunidza, Private Bag 9, Inyazura, Rhodesia.
Telephone: Inyazura 0221.

Campbell, James H., B.S.M.E.; American business executive; b. 18 Oct. 1910; ed. Purdue Univ. and Massachusetts Inst. of Technology.
Asst. to Pres. Consumers Power Co. 49-51, Vice-Pres. 51-56, Senior Vice-Pres. 56-60, Pres. and Chief Operating Officer 60-, Dir. 51-; Dir. Tecumseh Products Co. 61-, Nat. Bank of Jackson 61-, Power Reactor Devt. Co. 58-, Hayes Albion Corp. 65-, American Gas Asscn. 65-; Vice-Pres. and Dir. Atomic Industrial Forum; Dir. Michigan Gas Storage Co. 60-; Hon. D.Eng. Purdue Univ.
Consumers Power Co., 212 Michigan Avenue, W., Jackson; Home: 3515 Stonewall Road, Jackson, Mich., U.S.A.

Campbell, John Garfield, C.A.; Canadian business executive; b. 13 March 1916; ed. public and high schools, Regina, Saskatchewan.
Audit Clerk, Rooke Thomas & Co., Regina 35-41; Gen. Auditor, Defense Industries Ltd., Montreal 41-46; Comptroller, Victory Mills Ltd. 46-51; Comptroller Canadian Breweries Ltd. 51; Pres. Victory Mills Ltd. 52; Vice-Pres. Canadian Breweries Ltd. 54-59, Exec. Vice-Pres. 59-65, Pres. 65-.
Office: Canadian Breweries Ltd., 297 Victoria Street, Toronto 2, Ontario; Home: 18 Saintfield Avenue, Don Mills, Ontario, Canada.

Campbell, Joseph, A.B.; American accountant, administrator and public servant; b. 25 March 1900; ed. Columbia Univ.
With Lingley Baird & Dixon 24-27, Valspar Corpn. 27-31; Gen. Partner, R. T. Lingley & Co. 31-33, Joseph Campbell & Co. 33-41; Asst. Treasurer, Columbia Univ. 41-49, Treasurer and Vice-Pres. 49-55; Comptroller-Gen. of U.S.A. 54-65; mem. U.S. Atomic Energy Comm. 53-54; Hon. LL.D. Colgate Univ., Columbia Univ.
3111 Woodland Drive, N.W., Washington, D.C., U.S.A.

Campbell, Nicholas Joseph, Jr., A.B., LL.B., LL.D.; American lawyer and oil executive; b. 22 April 1915; ed. St. Vincent Coll., Latrobe, Pennsylvania, and Harvard Law School.
Practising Attorney, Satterlee, Warfield & Stephens, New York 40-47; U.S. Air Force 42-46; Counsel, Creole Petroleum Corpn., New York 47-50; Man. Law Dept., Creole Petroleum Corpn., Caracas, Venezuela 51-56; Vice-Pres. and Dir. Creole Petroleum Corpn., New York 56; Assoc. Gen. Counsel Standard Oil Co. (N.J.), New York 56-62; Dir. Esso Int. Inc., New York 57-62; Dir. Esso Standard Sekiyu K.K., Tokyo, Japan 62-64, Pres. 63-64; Dir. Toa Nenryo Kogyo K.K., Tokyo 63-64; Exec. Asst. to L. W. Elliott (Exec. Vice-Pres. Standard Oil Co. (N.J.), New York) 64-65; mem. Board of Dirs. Standard Oil Co. (N.J.), New York 65-66; Dir. and Pres. Esso Europe Inc., London 66-.
Office: Esso Europe Inc., Stratton Street, London, W.1; Home: 5 Belgrave Place, London, S.W.1, England.

Campbell, Ross, D.S.C.; Canadian diplomatist; b. 4 Nov. 1918; ed. Univ. of Toronto Schools and Univ. of Toronto.

Royal Canadian Navy 40-45; Third Sec., Oslo 46-47; Second Sec., Copenhagen 47-50; European Div., Dept. of External Affairs, Ottawa 50-52; First Sec., Ankara 52-56; Head of Middle East Div. 57-59; Asst. Under-Sec. of State for External Affairs 62-64, Adviser to Canadian Dels. to UN Gen. Assemblies 58-63, Adviser to Canadian Dels. to North Atlantic Council 59-64; Amb. to Yugoslavia 64-67, concurrently accred. to Algeria 65-67; Perm. Rep. and Amb. to NATO, Paris May 67, Brussels Oct. 67-.
North Atlantic Treaty Organization, Brussels 39, Belgium.

Campbell, Hon. Thane Alexander, M.A., LL.D.; Canadian judge; b. 7 July 1895; ed. Prince of Wales Coll., Charlottetown, Dalhousie and Oxford Univs.
Attorney-Gen. of P.E.I. 30-31, 35-43; Chief Justice of P.E.I. 43-; mem. P.E.I. Legislative Assembly 31-43; Premier of P.E.I. 36-43; mem. Bar of P.E.I. 27-43; Man. P.E.I. Mutual Fire Insurance Co. 30-43; mem. Historic Sites and Monuments Board of Canada 48-59, Board of Govs. of Dalhousie Univ. and Saint Dunstan's Univ.; Chief War Claims Commr. for Canada 52-; Adviser on Claims by Canadians under Agreement with Bulgaria 67; mem. Nat. Library Advisory Council 48-59.
Box 1477, Summerside, Prince Edward Island, Canada.
Telephone: 894-3168 and 436-2722 (Office); 436-2556 (Home).

Campbell of Eskan, Baron (Life-Peer) cr. 66, of Camis Eskan; **John (Jock) Middleton Campbell,** Kt.; British business executive; b. 8 Aug. 1912; ed. Eton and Exeter Coll., Oxford.
Chairman, Booker Bros. McConnell & Co. Ltd., West India Merchants 52-June 67, Commonwealth Sugar Exporters 50-, *New Statesman* 63-; mem. Council Univ. of W. Indies 59-; Chair. Nat. Econ. Devt. Cttees. for Building and Civil Engineering 65-; Chair. of Board of Milton Keynes Devt. Corp.; mem. Exec. Cttee. Africa Bureau; Trustee Acton Soc.; mem. Court of Govs., London School of Econs.; Pres. W. India Cttee., W. Indian Club.
Office: Bucklersbury House, London, E.C.4; Homes: 15 Eaton Square, London, S.W.1; and Crocker End House, Nettlebed, Oxford, England.
Telephone: Nettlebed 202.

Campenhausen, Hans Erich, Freiherr von, D.THEOL.; German university professor; b. 16 Dec. 1903; ed. Marburg, Heidelberg, Berlin and Rome.
Lecturer in ecclesiastical history Marburg 28-30, Göttingen 30-35; Lecturer in Giessen, Kiel, Heidelberg and Vienna 35-45; Prof. of Ecclesiastical History Heidelberg 45-; Rector Univ. of Heidelberg 46-47; mem. Heidelberg Akademie der Wissenschaften 46, Göttingen Akad. der Wissenschaften, Brit. Academy; Hon. Dr. Theol. (Oslo Univ.) 56, Hon. D.D. (St. Andrews, Göttingen and Uppsala Univs.).
Publs. *Ambrosius v. Mailand als Kirchenpolitiker* 29, *Die Passionssarkophage* 30. *Die Idee des Martyriums in der alten Kirche* 36, 2nd ed. 64, *Luther: Die Hauptschriften, Karl Müller: Kirchengeschichte I (i)* 41, *Kirchliches Amt und Geistliche Vollmacht in den ersten drei Jahrhunderten* 53, *Die griechischen Kirchenväter* 55, *Lateinische Kirchenväter* 60, *Tradition und Leben* 60, *Die Jungfrauengeburt in der alten Kirche* 62, *Aus der Frühzeit des Christentums* 63.
Ladenburger Strasse 69, Heidelberg, Baden-Württemberg, German Federal Republic.

Campenhout, André Van; Belgian financial officer; b. 08; ed. Univ. of Brussels.
Private legal practice, Brussels 30-34, Court of Appeals, Brussels 34-36; Private Sec. to Prime Minister of Belgium 37-38, Counsellor, Prime Minister's Office 39-40, Chef de Cabinet, Acting Perm. Sec. Ministry of

Econ. Affairs 40-44, to Ministry of Communications 40-43; First Vice-Pres. Régie de la Marine 42-44; Dep. Head, then Head, Belgian Econ. Mission, London 44-46; Chair. Interdepartmental Cttee. on Control of Belgian Assets Outside Enemy Occupied Territory 42-44; Belgian Rep. and Mem. United Maritime Authority 41-46; Gen. Counsel, Int. Monetary Fund 46-54, Exec. Dir. 54-; Exec. Dir. for Belgium, Austria, Turkey, Korea and Luxembourg, Int. Bank for Reconstruction and Development, and Int. Finance Corpn. 60-.
International Bank for Reconstruction and Development, 1818 H Street, N.W., Washington, D.C., U.S.A.

Campigli, Massimo; Italian painter; b. 4 July 1895.
Journalist until 28; first one-man exhbn. Paris 29, also Rome, Milan, New York, Bucharest, Amsterdam; represented in about 30 Museums of Modern Art at home and abroad; mem. Accad. di S. Luca, Rome and Royal Flemish Acad., Brussels.
9 rue Delambre, Paris 14e, France; 34 Via Porta Pinciana, Rome, Italy; and St. Tropez, Var, France.

Campilli, Pietro; Italian politician; b. 30 Nov. 1891.
Helped found Italian Popular Party and *Il Popolo*; Councillor for Frascati, Rome district 20; in private business 29-45; member National Advisory Assembly 44-46; Deputy to Constituent Assembly 46; Minister of Foreign Commerce and Deputy Pres. Nat. Reconstruction Committee 46; Minister of Finance and Treasury 47; Minister without Portfolio 50-51; Minister of Transport 51, of Industry and Commerce 51; Minister for development of Southern Areas 53-57; Pres. Italian Catholic Bank Fed.; Chair. Italian Branch Int. Chamber of Commerce; Pres. European Investment Bank 58-59; Pres. National Council of Economy and Labour 59-.
Viale Bruno Buozzi 102, Rome, Italy.

Campion, Sir Harry, Kt., C.B., C.B.E., M.A., LL.D.; British civil servant; b. 20 May 1905; ed. Univ. of Manchester.
Robert Ottley Reader in Statistics, Univ. of Manchester 33-39; Dir. Central Statistical Office, Offices of Cabinet 41-67; Dir. Statistical Office, UN 46-47; mem. of Statistical Comm. UN and Pres. of Int. Statistical Inst. 63-67; Pres. Royal Statistical Society 57-59.
Publs. *Distribution of National Capital* 36, *Public and Private Property* 39.
Rima, Priory Close, Stanmore, Middlesex, England.

Campos, Milton Soares; Brazilian lawyer and politician; b. 1900.
Federal Dep.; Gov. of Minas Gerais 47-51, later Senator; Candidate for Vice-Pres. of Brazil 60; Minister of Justice and Interior, Brazil 64, of Justice 64-65; União Democrática Nacional (U.D.N.).
The Senate, Brasilia, Brazil.

Campos, Roberto de Oliveira, M.A.; Brazilian diplomatist; b. 17; ed. Junior Seminary, Guaxupe, Senior Seminary, Belo Horizonte, George Washington Univ. and Columbia Univ.
Diplomatic Service 39-; Third Sec., Washington 42-46; Brazilian Del. UN, New York 46-49; Head Econ. Dept. Ministry of Foreign Affairs, Rio de Janeiro 49-50; mem. Jt. Brazil-U.S. Comm. for Econ. Development 50-53; Econ. Dir. Brazilian Nat. Bank for Econ. Development 52-53; Consul, Los Angeles 53-54; Man. Dir. Brazilian Nat. Bank for Econ. Development 54-58, Pres.58-59; Del. to Int. Confs. including GATT 59-61; Ambassador-at-Large to Europe 61; Ambassador to U.S.A. 61-64; Minister of Planning and Econ. Devt. 64-67.
Publs. *Planning of the economic development of underdeveloped countries* 52, *As tres falácias do momento brasileiro* 56.
São Paulo, Brazil.

Campos Salos, Lic. Octaviano; Mexican economist and politician; b. 22 March 1916; ed. Escuela Nacional de Economía, Univ. Nacional Autónoma de Mexico, and Univ. of Chicago.
Former Man., Bank of Mexico; fmr. Exec. Sec. Mexican Cttee., Latin American Free Trade Area; fmr. Dir. School of Econs., Nat. Univ. of Mexico; fmr. Dir.-Gen., Inst. of Political, Econ. and Social Studies of Partido Revolucionario Institucional (PRI); fmr. Co-ordinator-Gen. of Planning, PRI; fmr. Dir.-Gen. of Commerce, Secr. of Industry and Commerce; later held posts with Secr. of Finance and Public Credit; fmr. Chief of Dept. of Econ. Studies, Bank of Mexico; fmr. Economist, UN Comm. for Latin America, Int. Monetary Fund; fmr. Visiting Prof., Univ. of Mexico; Sec.-Gen. of Teachers' Union of Mexico 38-40; Pres. Colegio de Economistas de México 56-58; mem. Exec. Council Int. Soc. of Econometrics 61-63; Sec. for Industry and Commerce 64-.
Publs. numerous articles on foreign trade, int. econs., Latin American econ. integration, balance of payments, central banking, public finance and nat. economy.
Secretaría de Industria y Comercio, Mexico, D.F., Mexico.

Camps, Francis Edward, M.D., M.R.C.P., F.C.PATH., D.M.J.; British professor of forensic medicine; b. 28 June 1905; ed. Marlborough Coll., Guy's Hospital Medical School, School of Tropical Medicine, Liverpool and Neuchâtel Univ., Switzerland.
Founder-mem. British Asscn. in Forensic Medicine, Hon. Sec. 50-59, Pres. 59-60; Founder-mem. and Hon. Sec.-Gen. British Acad. of Forensic Sciences, Past Pres. 63-64; Editor of Journal *Medicine, Science and the Law;* Organizer of Int. Meetings in Forensic Pathology and Medicine, Brussels 58, Sec.-Gen., New York 60, Pres., London 63; Reader in Forensic Medicine, London Hospital Medical Coll. 54-63, Prof. 63-; Hon. Consultant in Forensic Medicine to the Army 64-; Vice-Pres. Medico-Legal Soc.; Assoc. (hon. mem.) in Police Science, Harvard Univ.; mem. American Acad. of Forensic Sciences, New York Acad. of Sciences; Hon. mem. Asociación Española de Medicos Forenses, Soc. de Medicina Legal e Criminología, São Paulo; Pres. Soc. for Study of Addiction 66.
Publs. *Medical and Scientific Investigations of the Christie Case* 53, *Wounds of the Head and Body and their Interpretation* 54, *Practical Forensic Medicine* (with Sir Bentley Purchase) 56, *Poisoning* 59, *The Investigation of Murder* 66, Editor of *Legal Medicine* (Gradwohl) 2nd edition; numerous papers on pathological and medico-legal subjects.
37 Welbeck Street, London, W.1, England.
Telephone: 01-935-6373.

Campus, Ferdinand-Alexis-Auguste; Belgian univ. professor; b. 14 Feb. 1894; ed. Inst. Rachez, Ghent, Athénée Royal, Brussels, Univs. of Brussels and Liège.
Served in army, both World Wars; Civil Engineer, Ministry of Public Works, Liège and Nieuport 19-20; Technical Dir. of Public Works, Railways, Post, Telegraph and Telephone of Saar Territory 20-26; Prof. Univ. of Liège 26-64, Prof. Emer. 64-, Rector 50-53; Technical Dir. construction of new Insts. of Univ. of Liège, Val-Benoît 29-37; founder 30 and Dir. Civil Eng. Laboratories of Univ. of Liège; Provincial Commr. for Reconstruction, Liège 40-44; mem. State Comm. for protection of Liège region against floods 27, Pres. 47-; Pres. Belgian Society for Testing Materials; Hon. mem. of Int. Asscn. for Bridge and Structural Engineering; Hon. mem. R.I.L.E.M.; mem. many Belgian, foreign and int. asscns. in civil engineering and testing of materials; mem. Royal Overseas Acad., mem. Royal Acad. Belgium; Corresp. mem. Royal Acad. Sciences Madrid; mem. Polish Acad. Sciences; hon. degrees Univs. of Cambridge and Brussels and

Eidgenössische Technische Hochschule, Zürich; various medals and awards.

Publs. *Recherches, Études et Considérations sur les Constructions Soudées* 46; and many papers.

77 Avenue Armand Huysmans, Brussels 5, Belgium.

Telephone: 02-49-69-64.

Camrose, 2nd Viscount; **John Seymour Berry;** British officer, journalist and politician; b. 12 July 1909; ed. Eton and Christ Church, Oxford.

Conservative M.P. for Hitchin 41-45; Major, City of London Yeomanry; served N. Africa and Italian campaigns 44-45 (despatches); Deputy Chair. Daily Telegraph Ltd.; Vice-Chair. Amalgamated Press Ltd. 42-59.

Hackwood Park, Basingstoke, Hants., England.

Telephone: Basingstoke 630.

Camu, Louis; Belgian bank official; b. 05; ed. Univ. of Liège.

Former Lecturer, Univ. of Liège; Chef de Cabinet, Ministry of Public Information 34, Prime Minister's Office 38; Royal Comm. on Administrative Reform 35-39; Vice-Pres. Banque de Bruxelles 49, now Chair. Banque de Bruxelles, S.A., 2 rue de la Régence, Brussels, Belgium.

Camu, Pierre, PH.D.; Canadian public official; b. 19 March 1923; ed. Univ. of Montreal and Johns Hopkins Univ., Baltimore.

Professor, Econ. Geography and Dir. Research Center, Faculty of Commerce, Laval Univ. 56-60; Consultant to shipping orgs. in Eastern Canada and U.S.A. 56-60; Vice-Pres. St. Lawrence Seaway Authority 60-66, Pres. 66-.

The St. Lawrence Seaway Authority, Place de Ville, 112 Kent Street, Ottawa 4, Ontario, Canada.

Telephone: 992-0531.

Candau, Marcolino Gomes, M.D., M.P.H.; Brazilian physician; b. 30 May 1911; ed. Univ. of Brazil and Johns Hopkins Univ., U.S.A.

Held various positions in Health Service of State of Rio de Janeiro, Nat. Health Dept. and Ministry of Education and Public Health 34-50; Asst. Prof. of Hygiene, School of Medicine, Rio de Janeiro 38- (leave of absence 50-); Asst. Prof. of Epidemiology, Nat. Health Dept. 48-50; Dir. Div. of Organisation of Public Health Services, WHO 50-51, Asst. Dir.-Gen. Dept. of Advisory Services 51-52; Asst. Dir. Pan-American Sanitary Bureau and Deputy Regional Dir. for the Americas, WHO 52-53; Dir.-Gen. WHO 53-; mem. Brazilian Society of Hygiene, Rio de Janeiro State Society of Medicine and Surgery, Royal Society of Tropical Medicine and Hygiene, London; Hon. Fellow (Foreign) Argentine Medical Asscn., Nat. Acad. of Medicine, Peru, Royal Acad. of Medicine in Ireland, American Public Health Asscn., Royal Society for the Promotion of Health (U.K.), Peruvian Public Health Asscn., Royal Soc. of Medicine London, American Coll. of Dentists; hon. mem. Nat. Acad. of Medicine, Brazil, American Venereal Disease Asscn., Canadian Public Health Asscn., Inter-American Asscn. of Sanitary Eng., American Hospital Asscn., Geneva Medical Soc. and other societies; Fellow Royal Coll. of Physicians, London; Mary Kingsley Medal of Liverpool School of Tropical Medicine 66, Royal Soc. of Health Gold Medal (London) 66; numerous hon. degrees.

World Health Organization, Avenue Appia, Geneva, Switzerland.

Telephone: Geneva 34-60-61.

Candela (Outeriño), Félix; Spanish-born Mexican builder, engineer and architect; b. 27 Jan. 1910; ed. Instituto de Cardenal Cisneros, Madrid, and Escuela Superior de Arquitectura, Madrid.

Service in Spanish Civil War on Republican side 36-39; interned in France 39; emigrated to Mexico 39; supervision of architecture of La Colonia Santa Clara (Spanish Colony), Chihuahua 39-40; draftsman Mexico City 40; contractor Agapulco 41; assistant architect, Mexico City 42; partnership with his brother Antonio 45-; first Structure in thin-shell concrete 49; established Cubiertas Alá, S.A. with his brother 51; buildings include Cosmic Ray Pavilion, Mexico Univ. City 50, Mexico City Stock Exchange, Church of San Antonio de las Huertas, Church of La Virgen Milagrosa, Lederle Laboratories, and warehouses, Sports Palace for 1968 Olympic Games, Mexico City; major exhbn. of his work, Univ. of South Calif. 57; Prof., Escuela Nacional de Arquitectura, Mexico; Jefferson Memorial Prof., Univ. of Virginia 66; Charles E. Norton Prof. of Poetry Harvard Univ. 61-62; Hon. mem. Sociedad de Arquitectos Colombianos, Sociedad Venezolana de Arquitectos, and other societies; Gold Medal Inst. of Structural Engineers 61, Auguste Perret Prize of the Int. Union of Architects 61, Gold Medal, Soc. of Mexican Architects 63, and other awards; Hon. Fellow American Inst. of Architects 63, Hon. Corresp. mem. R.I.B.A. 63; Hon. D.F.A. (Univ. of New Mexico) 64.

P.O. Box 19149, Mexico 19, D.F.; Home: Juares 14, Tlacopac, Mexico 20, D.F., Mexico.

Canham, Erwin Dain, A.B., M.A., D.LITT., L.H.D., LL.D.; American newspaper editor; b. 13 Feb. 1904; ed. Bates Coll., and Oxford Univ.

Reporter *The Christian Science Monitor* 25; at League of Nations Assembly 26-28; chief corresp. for *The Christian Science Monitor* at London Naval Conf. 30; corresp. Geneva 30-32; head of Washington Bureau, *The Christian Science Monitor* 32-39; Gen. News Editor 39-41, Managing Editor 41-44, Editor 45-65, Editor-in-Chief 65-; covered London Economic Conf. 33; Radio commentator 38-39, 45-; Pres. American Society of Newspaper Editors 48-49; mem. U.S. Advisory Comm. on Information and of Corpn., Simmons College; Dir. Nat. Manpower Council; Trustee Bates and Wellesley Colls., Boston Public Library; Trustee of Twentieth Century Fund; Pres. U.S. Chamber of Commerce 59-60, Chair. of Board 60-61, Chair. of Exec. Comm. 61-62; Chair. Foreign Policy Cttee.; Dir. John Hancock Mutual Life Insurance Co.; Chair. Dirs. Fed. Reserve Bank of Boston; Dir. National Bureau of Economic Research, Resources for the Future Inc., Nat. Safety Council; Fellow American Acad. of Arts and Sciences; Officer Southern Cross of Brazil; Commdr. Order of Orange-Nassau; Order of George I (Greece); Officier Légion d'Honneur, Grosses Bundesverdienstkreuz (German Fed. Republic); Hon. C.B.E.

Home: 6 Acorn Street, Boston 8, Mass.; Office: 1 Norway Street, Boston, Mass., U.S.A.

Telephone: LA 3-2171 (Home).

Cannon, Howard W., B.S., LL.B.; American lawyer and politician; b. 12; ed. Arizona State Teachers' Coll. and Arizona Univ.

Admitted to Arizona Bar 37, to Utah Bar 38, to Nevada Bar 46; fmr. Reference Attorney, Utah State Senate and County Attorney, Washington County, Utah; City Attorney, Las Vegas 49-59; Senator from Nevada 59-; service with Air Force in Second World War, rising to rank of Maj. Gen. U.S.A.F. Reserve; D.F.C., Air Medal with two Oak Leaf Clusters, American Defense Citation, Presidential Unit Citation, Croix de Guerre with silver star; Democrat.

Senate Office Building, Washington 25, D.C., U.S.A.

Canterbury, Archbishop of (*see* Ramsey, Most Rev. Arthur Michael).

Canto, Jorge Del; Chilean economist; b. 16; ed. Univs. of Chile and Calif. (at Berkeley).

Officer, Chilean Foreign Office 37-38; Adviser, Central Bank of Chile 42-46; Prof. School of Econs. Univ. of Chile 42-; Int. Monetary Fund 46-, Dir. Western Hemisphere Dept. 57-.

5412 Christy Drive, Washington 16, D.C., U.S.A.

Cantril, (Albert) Hadley, PH.D.; American psychologist; b. 16 June 1906; ed. Dartmouth Coll., Univs. of Munich, Berlin and Harvard.

Instructor in Sociology, Dartmouth Coll. 31-32, Instructor in Psychology, Harvard 32-35; Asst. Prof. of Education, Columbia Univ. 35-36; Prof. of Psychology, Princeton Univ. 36-55; Research Assoc., Princeton Univ. 55-; Chair. of Board and Senior Counsellor, Inst. for Int. Social Research 55-; Dir. Office of Public Opinion Research, Princeton Univ.; Advisory Editor *Public Opinion Quarterly*; Past Pres. Society for the Psychological Study of Social Issues; Pres. Eastern Psychological Asscn. 49-50; Guggenheim Fellow 49; Hon. LL.D. Washington and Lee Univ.

Publs. *The Psychology of Radio* (with G. W. Allport) 25, *The Invasion from Mars* 40, *The Psychology of Social Movements* 41, *Gauging Public Opinion* (with research associates) 44, *The Psychology of Ego-Involvements* (with M. Sherif) 47, *Understanding Man's Social Behaviour: Preliminary Notes* 47, *The "Why" of Man's Experience* 50, *Public Opinion 1935-46* (Ed.) 50, *How Nations See Each Other* (jointly) 53, *Politics of Despair* 58, *Reflections on the Human Venture* 60, *Soviet Leaders and Mastery over Man* 60, *The Morning Notes of Adelbert Ames, Jr.* 60, *Human Nature and Political Systems* 61, *The Pattern of Human Concerns* 65.

124 Mercer Street, Princeton, N.J. 08540, U.S.A.

Caouette, Real; Canadian politician; b. 26 Sept. 1917; ed. Collège du Sacré-Coeur de Limbour, Collège de Victoriaville.

Former bank employee and commercial traveller; mem. of Parl. 46-49, 62, 63-65; founded Le Ralliement des Créditistes 58, Leader in House of Commons 63-65; Deputy Nat. Leader, Social Credit Asscn. of Canada 61-62.

321 Larrivière, Rouyn, Quebec, Canada.

Capanna, Alberto; Italian public official; b. 8 July 1910; ed. Univ. Commerciale Luigi Bocconi, Milan.

Free-lance 34-36; staff of Ministry for Africa 36; Dir. Commissariat-Gen. for Food and Econ. Co-ordination in Libya 40-42, for Food in Sicily 42-43; Technical Sec. Ministry for Industry and Commerce 43-49; joined Istituto per la Ricostruzione Industriale (I.R.I.) 50, successively First Dir. Finsider, Central Dir., Vice Dir.-Gen., now Dir.-Gen. Finsider; Dir. of numerous companies including Italsider, Dalmine, Breda Sid., Cosider, Cementir, Siderexport and Siderman; Asst. Dir. European Investment Bank; founder-mem. Consultative Cttee. ECSC; Grande Ufficiale della Repubblica Italiana.

Publs. include *Gli scambi dell'Italia con l'estero dalla fondazione del Regno ad oggi* 40, and books on economic subjects.

Via Isonzo 42, Rome, Italy.

Capdevila, Arturo, DR. LAWS and SOC. SC.; Argentine lawyer and writer; b. 18 March 1889; ed. Univ. of Córdoba.

Judge and Prof. of Philosophy in Córdoba 19-22; Prof. of Literature, Univ. Nacional de la Plata 22; Spanish and Argentine awards.

Publs. Over 100 works including (poetry): *Melpómene, El Poema de Nenúfar, Córdoba Azul*; (plays): *La Sulamita, El Amor de Scharazada*; (history): *Las Vísperas de Caseros, Las Invasiones Inglesas*; (miscellaneous): *La dulce patria, Córdoba del Recuerdo, Babel y el Castellano, El gitano y su leyenda, Loores Platenses, Tierra Mía, Abraces, Maestro de amor, Advenimiento, El gran Reidor Segovia*; also treatises on medicine.

Juncal 3575, Buenos Aires, Argentina.

Capehart, Homer Earl; American industrialist and politician; b. 6 June 1897.

With Baker-Capehart Co., Green Bay, Wisconsin 22-23; Sales Man. Sanford Bros., Chattanooga, Tenn. 23-24; Holcomb & Hoke Manufacturing Co., Indianapolis 25-27; Pres. Capehart Corpn., Fort Wayne 27-32; Vice-Pres. The Wurlitzer Co., Cincinnati 33-40; owner Capehart Farms, Indiana; Pres. Capehart Corpn. Indianapolis; Senator from Indiana 44-62; Republican.

Capehart Corpn., Indianapolis, Ind., U.S.A.

Capelle, Jean; French university professor; b. 16 March 1909; ed. Ecole Nat. Supérieure des Mines de Paris and Ecole Normale Supérieure, Université de Paris.

Professor (Faculty of Science) at Nancy Univ. 43-46, 65-, Rector 49-54; Dir. Ecole Nat. Supérieure d'Electricité et de Mécanique 46-47; Dir.-Gen. of Educ. in French West Africa 47-49; Dir.-Gen. of Educ. in French West Africa and Rector, Dakar Univ. 54-57; Dir.-Gen. Inst. Nat. des Sciences Appliquées, Lyon 57-61; Dir.-Gen. Ministry of Educ. 61-64.

Publs. *Génération des Engrenages par la Méthode des Roulettes* 38; *Théorie des Engrenages Hypoïdes* 48, *Cours de Résistance des Matériaux* 49; Editor *Bulletin de la Société d'Etudes de l'Industrie de l'Engrenage* 44, *Encylopédie Française*, Vol. 13 61, *Tomorrow's Education*, 67.

33 rue Croulebarbe, Paris 13e, France.

Capitant, René Alphonse Charles; French politician; b. 19 Aug. 1901; ed. Lycée Henri-IV and Faculty of Law, Univ. of Paris.

Professor Fac. of Law and Economic Science, Univ. of Paris; Minister of Nat. Educ. Paris 44-45; Deputy Nat. Assembly 45-51, 52-, Pres. Cttee. on Constitutional Laws, Legislation and Gen. Admin. of the Repub. 62-; Minister of Justice May 68-; Dir. Franco-Japanese Centre, Tokyo 57-60; mem. Union pour la Nouvelle-République–Union Démocratique du Travail (U.N.R.-U.D.T.); Chevalier Légion d'Honneur.

Publs. *L'Impératif juridique* 28, and books on law and political science.

National Assembly, Paris 7e; 8 Square Latour-Maubourg, Paris 7e, France.

Telephone: 468-28-46.

Capitini, Aldo, Dott. in Lettere; Italian author and professor; b. 23 Dec. 1899; ed. Scuola Normale Superiore di Pisa and Univ. of Pisa.

Promoter and organiser of Independent Liberal-Socialist Movement; Prof. of Pedagogy and History of Religious and Moral Philosophy, Univ. of Pisa 46-56; Prof. of Pedagogy and Moral Philosophy, Univ. of Cagliari 56-64; Prof. of Pedagogy and Sociology, Univ. of Perugia 65; Pres. Centre of Religious Orientation, Centre of Social Orientation, and Int. Co-ordination for Non-violence, Perugia; Dir. *Azione nonviolenta;* awarded the Salento Prize for poetry 56.

Publs. *Elementi di un'esperienza religiosa* 37, *Nuova socialità e riforma religiosa* 49, *Il fanciullo nella liberazione dell'uomo* 53, *Religione aperta* 55, *Colloquio corale* 56, *Discuto la religione di Pio XII* 57, *Batterzati non credenti* 61, *La Nonviolenza oggi* 62, *In cammino la pace* 62, *La compresenza dei morti e dei viventi* 66.

Casella postale 201, Perugia, Italy.

Caplin, Mortimer M., B.S., LL.B., J.S.D.; American lawyer, educator and government official; b. 11 July 1916; ed. Univ. of Virginia and New York Univ. Law School.

Law Clerk to U.S. Circuit Judge 40-41; legal practice with Paul, Weiss, Rifkind, Wharton & Garrison, New York City 41-50; U.S. Naval Reserve, Beachmaster in Normandy landings 42-45; Prof. of Law, Univ. of Virginia 50-61, Lecturer and Visiting Prof. 64-; Counsel to Perkins, Battle & Minor 52-61; U.S. Commr. of Internal Revenue 61-64; Partner, Caplin & Drysdale, Washington D.C. 64-; Chair. Exec. Cttee. Prentice-Hall Inc.; Pres. Nat. Civil Service League; Vice-Pres. People-to-People Sports Cttee; mem. American Bar Asscn., D.C., Va. and N.Y. State Bar Asscns., Nat. Tax Asscn., Fed. Bar Asscn., American Law Inst.; Raven Award, Alexander Hamilton Award, and other awards; Editor-in-Chief *Virginia Law Review* 39-40; mem. Board of Trustees George Washington Univ. and Coll. of the Virgin Islands; Hon. LL.D., St. Michael Coll. 64.

Publs. Numerous articles on tax and corporate matters.

Caplin & Drysdale, 1101 17th Street, N.W., Washington, D.C.; Home 4536 29th Street, N.W., Washington, D.C. 20008, U.S.A.

Telephone: 202-296-1900 (Office); 202-244-3040 (Home).

Capogrossi, Giuseppe, LL.L.; Italian painter; b. 7 March 1900.

Lived in Paris 27-32 where he founded the "Roman Group" with Cagli and Cavalli and the "Origine Group" with Burri and Colla in 49; has exhibited at the Venice Biennali, Brussels Exhibition 58, Museum of Modern Art, New York, Solomon Guggenheim Museum, New York, I.C.A., London, Musée des Beaux Arts, Brussels, etc.

Viale Marco Polo 80, Rome; Studio: Salita S. Nicolo da Tolentino 13, Rome, Italy.

Capote, Truman; American author; b. 30 Sept. 1924; ed. Greenwich High School, New York.

First published story *Miriam* in *Mademoiselle* magazine 44; *My Side of the Matter* (in *Story*) 45; *Other Voices, Other Rooms* (novel) 48; *Tree of Night* (short stories) 49; *Local Color* (travel essays) 50; *The Grass Harp* (novel, later dramatised by the author) 51; articles in *The New Yorker, Vogue, Theater Arts,* etc.; O. Henry Memorial Award for *Miriam* 46, *The House of Flowers* (musical) 54, *The Muses are Heard* (essay) 56, *Breakfast at Tiffany's* (short stories) 58, *Selected Writings* 63, *In Cold Blood* 64 (film 68).

c/o Random House Inc., 457 Madison Avenue, New York 22, N.Y., U.S.A.

Capp, Al(fred) Gerald; American author and artist; b. 28 Sept. 1909; ed. Philadelphia Acad. of Fine Arts, Boston Museum of Fine Arts.

Created comic strip " Li'l Abner" 34, appearing in over 1,000 newspapers throughout the world.

Publs. *Life and Times of the Shmoo, World of Li'l Abner,* and articles in *Atlantic Monthly, Life, Picture Post, Reader's Digest, Pageant.*

Capp Enterprises, 122 Beacon Street, Boston, Mass., U.S.A.

Cappelen, Andreas Zeier; Norwegian lawyer and politician; b. 31 Jan. 1915; ed. Univ. of Oslo.

Assistant, District Court 39-40, Barrister at Stavanger 41-45, District Attorney, County of Rogaland 45-47; Legal Lawyer and Asst. Chief of Wages to Municipal Authorities, Stavanger 47-57, Dep. Mayor of Stavanger 53, Sec. for Finance, Stavanger 57-58; Minister for Municipal and Labour Affairs 58-63, of Finance 63-65; Sec. for Finance, Stavanger 66-67; Judge, Stavanger 67-.

Øvre Strandgate 2, Stavanger, Norway.

Telephone: Stavanger 27060.

Cappello, Carmelo; Italian sculptor; b. 21 May 1912; ed. Istituto Superiore d'Arte di Monza.

Sculptor 37-; regular exhibitor at Venice Biennali, Milan Triennali and Rome Quadriennali since 47; represented in major collections and int. exhibitions throughout the world; mem. Nat. Cttee. of UNESCO Div. of Plastic Arts; mem. Accad. Nazionale di San Luca; numerous awards.

Major Works: *Freddoloso* 38, *Uomo nello spazio* 55, *Tempesta* 56, *Cristo e i due ladroni* 55, *Volo Stratosferico* 58, *Il Folle* 48, *Il Filosofo* 49, *Tuffatori* 58, *Gli Acrobati* 55, *Eclisse* 59, *Fughe ritmiche* 61, *Involuzione del cerchio* 62, *Fontana per curve d'acqua* 58, *Ala* 60, *Ritmi Chiusi* 63, *Superficie-Spazio: Itinerario Circolare* 64, *Traiettoria Dal Piano Dello Spazio* 65, *Occhio di Cielo* 66.

Via Melone 2, Milan, Italy.

Telephone: 854658.

Capra, Frank; American film producer; b. Italy 18 May 1897; ed. California Inst. of Technology.

Served U.S. Army both World Wars; fmr. Pres. Acad.

of Motion Picture Arts and Sciences and Screen Directors' Guild; has received Acad. Award for best direction three times and twice produced films which have won Acad. Award for best film of the year.

Productions include: *The Certain Thing, Submarine, Power of the Press, The Younger Generation, Ladies of Leisure, Dirigible, The Bitter Tea of General Yen, Lady for a Day, It Happened One Night, Mr. Deeds Goes to Town, Lost Horizon, You Can't Take It With You, Mr. Smith Goes to Washington, Meet John Doe, The Battle of Britain, Arsenic and Old Lace, It's a Wonderful Life, State of the Union, Riding High, Here Comes the Groom, A Hole in the Head, Pocketful of Miracles.*

Red Mountain Ranch, Fallbrook, Calif.; and Columbia Pictures Corpn., 1438 N. Gower Street, Hollywood, California, U.S.A.

Caradon, Baron (Life Peer), cr. 64, of St. Cleer in the County of Cornwall; **Hugh Mackintosh Foot** (brother of Sir Dingle Foot, *q.v.*, Lord Foot of Buckland Monachorum and Michael Foot, *q.v.*), P.C., G.C.M.G., K.C.V.O., O.B.E.; British overseas administrator; b. 8 Oct. 1907; ed. Leighton Park School, Reading and St. John's Coll., Cambridge.

President Cambridge Union 29; Admin. Officer Palestine Govt. 29-37; attached to Colonial Office 38-39; Asst. British Resident, Transjordan 39-42; British Military Admin., Cyrenaica 43; Colonial Sec. Cyprus 43-45; Colonial Sec. Jamaica 45-47; Chief Sec. Nigeria 47-50; Capt.-Gen. and Gov.-in-Chief of Jamaica 51-57; Gov. and Commdr.-in-Chief of Cyprus 57-60; U.K. Perm. Rep. UN Trusteeship Council 61-62; Consultant to UN Special Fund 63; Minister of State for Foreign Affairs and Perm. Rep. to UN Oct. 64-; mem. UN Expert group on S. Africa 64; Labour.

Publ. *A Start in Freedom* 64.

U.K. Mission to the UN, 845 Third Avenue, New York City, U.S.A.; Home; Trematon Castle, Saltash, Cornwall, England.

Telephone: PL2-8400 (New York); Saltash 3278.

Carafa d'Andria, Ettore; Italian industrial executive; b. 95; ed. Commercial Inst.

Secretary of Board AGIP, S.A. 26-35, Vice-Gen. Manager 28-35, Gen. Manager 35-44, Managing Dir. 48-51, Vice-Chair. 51-52; Vice-Chair. Finsider S.A. 53-, Condor S.A. 54-59; Dir. Iniziative Finanziarie S.A. 58-64, B.P. Italiana S.A. 60-; Chair. Raffineria Italiana B.P, S.A. 64-; several decorations.

Largo Elvezia 5, Rome, Italy.

Caragea, Boris; Romanian sculptor; b. 1906; ed. Bucharest School of Fine Arts.

Teacher of Sculpture, N. Grigorescu Fine Arts Inst., Bucharest; Chair. Plastic Arts Union 51-57; Chair. Plastic Arts Council of State Cttee. for Culture and Art; mem. Exec. Cttee. of Plastic Arts Union; Corresp. mem. Romanian Acad. 55; One-man exhbns. in Romania, Venice, Moscow, Belgrade, Prague, Berlin, Helsinki, Leningrad, Paris and Warsaw; represented at Venice Biennale 64; Merited Master of Arts 51, People's Artist 62, State prizewinner 51 and 53.

Major works: *The Meeting, The Mother, Liberation, V. I. Lenin, Fisher,* bas-relief on façade of Bucharest Opera, *Song,* and *G. Enescu.*

c/o Plastic Arts Council of State Committee for Culture and Art, Bucharest, Romania.

Carandini, Count Nicolo, LL.B.; Italian diplomatist and farmer; b. 6 Dec. 1895.

Served First World War and Libyan campaign 19; took part Nat. Ex-Servicemen's Asscn., expelled 25; retd. into private life and farmed on large scale in Roman Campagna; Pres. clandestine Exec. Cttee. of Liberal Party and Party rep. on Rome Cttee. of Nat. Liberation 43; founder and contrib. *Risorgimento Liberale;* Minister without Portfolio (Bonomi Cabinet)

Aug.-Nov. 44; mem. Consultative Assembly; elected mem. Constituent Assembly; resgnd. to become Italian rep. in London with rank of Ambassador 44-47; resumed political activity and farming in Italy after Peace Treaty; Chair. Italian Society for Int. Organisation 48; Pres. Alitalia (Italian Int. Airlines); Chair. Istituto Italiano di Credito Fondiario; resigned from Liberal Party and became founder of new Radical Party 55; joint editor *Il Mondo* 48-66.
Via XXIV Maggio 14, Rome Italy.

Caraway, Paul Wyatt; American army officer; b. 23 Dec. 1905; ed. U.S. Military Acad. and Georgetown Univ.
Commissioned 29, rose to Lieut.-Gen. 61; Senior Instructor (U.S.), Army Dept., NATO Defence Coll., Paris 51-53; Chief, Plans Div. Dept., Army Gen. Staff, Washington 53-55; Commanding Gen. 7th Infantry Div., Korea 55-56; Asst. Chief of Staff, H.Q. U.S. Forces, Japan 56-57, Chief of Staff 57-58, mem. Joint Strategic Survey Council, Office of Joint Chiefs of Staff, Washington 58-61; High Commr., Ryukyu Islands, Commdg. Gen. U.S. Army, Ryukyu Islands 61-65; mem. of firm, Reed and Caraway, Arkansas 65-; numerous mil. decorations.
9143 Santayana Drive, Fairfax, Virginia 22030, U.S.A. Telephone: 703-273-6747.

Carcopino, Jérôme, D.LITT.; French historian; b. 27 June 1881.
Professor Algiers Univ. 12-20; Prof. of Roman History, Univ. of Paris 20-37; Dir. French School in Rome 37-40, Hon. Dir. 51-; Minister of Educ. (Pétain Govt.) 41-42; mem. Acad. Française and Acad. des Inscriptions et Belles-Lettres; Corresp. mem. Accad. dei Lincei, Acad. royale de Belgique, Accad. delle Scienze, Turin, Junta americana de historia, Buenos Aires, Real Acad. de la Historia, Madrid, Acad. das Ciências de Lisboa, Pontifical Acad., Romanian Acad., Accad. di Milano, Accad. di Mantova; Dr. h.c. Oxford Univ.
Publs. *Le Forum Romain* 06, *Histoire de l'Ostracisme athénien* 09, *La loi de Hiéron et les Romains* 14, *Virgile et les origines d'Ostie* 19, *La louve du Capitole* 25, *La basilique pythagoricienne de la Porte Majeure* 27, *Autour des Gracques* 28, *Ostie* 29, *Virgile et le mystère de la IV-e Eglogue* 30, *Sylla ou la monarchie manquée* 31, *Histoire de la fin de la République romaine* 36-37, *La vie quotidienne à Rome* 39, *Aspects mystiques du Paganisme romain* 41, *Le Maroc Antique* 44, *Les secrets de la correspondance de Cicéron* 48, *Souvenirs de Sept Ans* and *Etudes d'Histoire Chrétienne* 53, *Le mystère d'un symbole chrétien* 55, *De Pythagore aux Apôtres* 56, *Promenades historiques aux pays de la Dâme de Vix* 57, *Passion et politique chez les Césars, Alésia et les ruses de César* 58, *Le Vatican* 59, *Les Etapes de l'Impérialisme romain, Profils de Conquérants* 61, *Rencontres de l'histoire et de la littérature romaines* 63, *Etudes d'histoire chrétienne II* 65.
35 rue de Babylone, Paris 7e, France.

Cardenas, José C., M.P.A.; Ecuadorean economist; b. 15; ed. Michigan and Harvard Univs.
Assistant Director, later Dir., Dept. of Economic Research, Central Bank of Ecuador 50-60; Inter-American Development Bank 60-63, Dir. Econ. Development Div. 61-63; Minister of Development, Ecuador 63-Oct. 64.
c/o Ministerio de Fomento, Guayaquil 1914 y Briceño, Quito, Ecuador.

Cárdenas, Gen. Lazaro; Mexican officer and politician; b. 95.
Fmr. Official Public Revenue Office; Captain 13 and Gen. Revolutionary Army; took part in many revolutionary campaigns 15-29; Gov. of Michoacan 28-32; leader Nat. Revolutionary Party 30; Minister Interior 31, of War and Marine 33; Pres. of Mexico for the term 34-40; Minister of Nat. Defence 43-45; C.-in-C. Mexican Army 45, retd.; exec. mem. Comisión del Rio Balsas 61-; awarded State Peace Prize 55.
Vocal Ejecutivo de la Comisión del Rio Balsas, Eguala, Gro., Mexico.

Cardin, Lucien; Canadian lawyer and politician; b. 1 March 1919; ed. Loyola Coll. and Montreal Univ.
Naval service 41-45; Barrister, Montreal; mem. House of Commons 52-, Assoc. Minister of Defence with seat in Cabinet 63-65; Minister of Public Works 65, of Justice July 65-67; Liberal.
House of Commons, Ottawa, Ontario; Home: Chemin du Chenal du Moine, Sorel, Quebec, Canada.
Telephone: R13-3159.

Cardinale, Most Rev. Hyginus Eugene; Vatican ecclesiastic and diplomatist; b. 14 Oct. 1916; ed. St. Agnes Acad. (U.S.A.), Pontifical Roman Major Seminary, Pontifical Lateran Univ., Pontifical Gregorian Univ. and Pontifical Ecclesiastical Acad., Rome.
Attaché of Nunciature 45, Sec. of Nunciature 46; Papal Representations Egypt, Palestine, Arabia, Cyprus 46-52; Domestic Prelate 58; Counsellor of Nunciature 58; Chief of Protocol, Papal Secretariat 61; Under-Sec. of Tech. Org. Comm., Second Vatican Ecumenical Council 62; Apostolic Del. to Great Britain, Malta, Gibraltar and Bermuda and Titular Archbishop of Nepte 63-; numerous decorations.
Publs. *La Représentation Pontificale* 48, *Church and State in the U.S.A.* 58, *Pontifical Diplomacy* 59, *Le Chiese Dissidenti d'Oriente dinanzi al Concilio* 61, *La Fedeltà del Patriarcato Greco-Melchita d'Antiochia alla Sede Apostolica* 61, *La Santa Sede e la Politica* 62, *Le Saint-Siège et la Diplomatie* 62.
Apostolic Delegation, 54 Parkside, Wimbledon, London, S.W.19, England.
Telephone: WIMbledon 1410.

Cardoso, Mario; Congolese diplomatist; b. 29 Sept. 1933; ed. Univ. de Louvain, Belgium, and Univ. Lovanium, Léopoldville.
Teacher 53-54; Applied Psychology and Educ. Studies, Univ. of Louvain 54-58; Teacher, Lovanium Univ. 58, Asst. Prof. 59; Technical Assistance Officer of UN, New York; Perm. Rep. of Congo to UN 60-62; Chargé d'Affairs, Washington 62-65; Amb. to U.K. 66-; Commdr. Ordre du Léopard.
Embassy of the Democratic Republic of the Congo (Kinshasa), 26 Chesham Place, London, S.W.1, England; and B.P. 3046, Kalina-Kinshasa, Democratic Republic of the Congo.
Telephone: 01-235-6137 (Ext. 9) (London).

Carey, James Baron; American trade unionist; b. 12 Aug. 1911; ed. Glassboro High School, Univ. Pennsylvania.
Philco Corpn. 29-34; Nat. Pres. Radio and Allied Trades 33-36; American Fed. of Labor Gen. Organiser for U.S. 34; Sec.-Treas. Congress Industrial Organisations 38-55; Gen. Pres. United Electrical, Radio and Machine Workers of America 36-41; mem. Production Planning Board, Office of Production Management 41; alternate mem. Nat. Defence Mediation Board; mem. Adv. Comm. European Recovery Programme; Chair. Cttee. to Abolish Discriminations, Health and Welfare Cttee.; Sec. C.I.O. Del. to World Fed. of Trade Unions, Paris, Oct. 45; Chair. C.I.O. Del. to Soviet Union Nov. 45; C.I.O. Del. W.F.T.U. Moscow May 46, Prague May 47, Paris 47-48, Rome May 48; Pres. Int. Union Electrical, Radio and Machine Workers 50; Vice-Pres. AFL-CIO and Sec.-Treas. Industrial Union Dept. AFL-CIO 55-; mem. Pres.'s Comm. on Civil Rights 47, and Public Advisory Cttee. ERP-ECA 47-52; Hon. LL.D. (Rollins Coll.).
1126 16th St. N.W., Washington 6, D.C., U.S.A.

Cargill, Ian Peter M.; British international bank official; ed. Oxford Univ.
Indian Civil Service 38-47; British Treasury, London and

Washington Office 48-52; World Bank, Desk Officer, Ethiopia, Sudan and Thailand 52-57; Asst. Dir., Dept. of Operations, Far East, World Bank 57-61, Dir. 61-. International Bank for Reconstruction and Development (World Bank), Washington, D.C. 20433, U.S.A.

Carleton, Alford, B.A., B.D., PH.D.; American foreign church missions executive; b. 26 March 1903; ed. Oberlin Coll. and Hartford Theological Seminary and Hartford Seminary.
Teacher in Turkey and Syria 24-27; Pres. of Aleppo Coll., Syria 30-53; Exec. Vice-Pres. United Church Board for World Ministries 54-; mem. Central and Exec. Cttees. World Council of Churches, American Friends of the Middle East (Pres. 63-).
475 Riverside Drive, New York, N.Y. 10027, U.S.A.
Telephone: 212-870-2815.

Carli, Guido, D. IUR.; Italian economist and banker; b. 14; ed. Padua Univ.
Dir. Ufficio Italiano dei Cambi 45; mem. Consulta Nazionale 45; mem. Man. Board Int. Monetary Fund 47; Gen. Adviser Ufficio Italiano dei Cambi 48; mem. European Payments Union Man. Board 50-58; Pres. 51-52; Pres. Mediocredito 52-, Consorzio Credito Opere Pubbliche 59-, Istituto Credito Imprese Pubblica Utilità 59-; Vice-Pres. Istituto Mobiliare Italiano 59-, Ufficio Italiano dei Cambi 59-; Gen. Man. Banca d'Italia 59-61, Gov. 61-; mem. Board Dirs. Bank of Int. Settlements 60-; Board European Monetary Agreement 59-; mem. EEC Monetary Cttee. 59-; Gov. for Italy Int. Bank for Reconstruction and Devt. 62-; Minister of Foreign Trade 57-58; Einaudi Prize 64.
Publs. *Verso il multilateralismo degli scambi e la convertibilità delle monete, Evoluzione della legislazione italiana sul controllo degli scambi e dei cambi, Commercio Estero-Maggio 1957-Giugno 1958.*
Piazza Borghese 3, Rome, Italy.

Carlson, Frank; American politician; b. 23 Jan. 1893; ed. Kansas State Coll.
Member Kansas Legislature 29 and 31; mem. House of Reps. 34-46; Gov. of Kansas 46-48; Republican Senator from Kansas 51-; Chair. Interstate Oil Compact Comm. 49; Chair. Council of State Govts. 50; Chair. Senate Post Office and Civil Service Cttee. 53-55.
Concordia, Kansas, U.S.A.

Carlson, Reynold Erland, PH.D.; American economist and diplomatist; b. 7 Sept. 1912; ed. Northwestern and Harvard Univs.
Assistant Prof. of Econs., Johns Hopkins Univ. 40-48; U.S. Army Air Corps 42-45; Econ. Consultant, United Nations, N.Y. 46-47; Econ. Comm. for Latin America (ECLA), Santiago, Chile 48; Assoc. Prof. of Econs. and Dir. Inst. for Brazilian Studies, Vanderbilt Univ. 50-53; Economist with Joint Brazil-U.S. Devt. Comm., Inst. of Inter-American Affairs, Rio de Janeiro 51-52; Senior Economist, W. Hemisphere Operations of World Bank 53-58; Prof. of Econs. and Dir. Graduate Program of Econ. Devt., Vanderbilt Univ. 58-63; Consultant to Ford Foundation 59-61; Ford Foundation Rep. in Rio de Janeiro 61-65; Assoc. Dir. Latin American Program, Ford Foundation 65-66; Amb. to Colombia Sept 66-.
Publs. *British Block Grants and Central Local Finance* 47; Co-author: *Development of Brazil* 54, *United States and Latin America* 63.
American Embassy, Bogotá, Colombia.

Carlsson, Eric Valfrid; Swedish newspaper publisher; b. 4 Nov. 1889.
Man. Dir. *Östgöten* at Linköping 22; mem. Council Liberal Party 25; Vice-Chair. Swedish Newspaper Publishers' Asscn. 33; Deputy Man. Dir. *Stockholms Tidningen* 30 and Dir. 31; Man. Dir. *Aftonbladet* 32, Newspapers' Telegraph News Agency 32, Swedish Press Agency Ltd. 32-55; Vice-Consul for Austria 34-38; Pres. Int. Shooting Union 47-60.
Karlbergsvägen 44, Stockholm, Sweden.

Carlu, Jacques; French architect; b. 7 April 1890.
Premier Grand Prix of Rome; Prof. of Architecture, Massachusetts Inst. of Technology 24-34; architect of many famous buildings including Palais de Chaillot and NATO headquarters in Paris; elected mem. Académie des Beaux-Arts, Paris 57; Commandeur de la Légion d'Honneur.
7 rue Michel-Ange, Paris 16e, France.
Telephone: 224-89-69; 224-88-93.

Carlyle, Joan Hildred; British soprano singer; b. 6 April 1931; ed. Howell's School, Denbigh, N. Wales.
Principal Lyric Soprano, Covent Garden 55-; major roles sung in U.K. include: Oscar, *Ballo in Maschera* 57-58, Sophie, *Der Rosenkavalier* 58-, Nedda, *Pagliacci* (Zeffirelli production) 59, Mimi, *La Bohème* 60, Titania, *Midsummer Night's Dream*, Britten (Gielgud production) 60, Pamina, *Magic Flute* 62, 66, Countess, *Marriage of Figaro* 63, Zdenka, *Arabella* (Hartman Production) 64, 67, Suor Angelica, *Suor Angelica* 65, Desdemona, *Otello* 65, Marschallin, *Der Rosenkavalier* 68; major roles sung abroad include Oscar, Nedda, Mimi, Pamina, Zdenka and Desdemona; debut at Salzburg, Metropolitan Opera, New York and Teatro Colón, Buenos Aires 68; several recordings including Von Karajan's production of *Pagliacci* as Nedda.
44 Abbey Road, St. John's Wood, London, N.W.8, England.

Carmel, Moshe; Israeli (b. Polish) politician; b. 1911; ed. Hebrew Univ., Jerusalem and Univ. de Paris.
Immigrated 24; mem. Kibbutz Na'an and a leader of Hakibbutz Hameuhad; mem. Haganah High Command; imprisoned for eighteen months for Haganah activities under British Mandatory Admin.; Area Commdr. Haifa and W. Galilee 48, later Commdr. Northern Front; Minister of Transport and Communications 55-59, 65-; a leader of Achdut Ha'avoda Poalei Zion Party.
Publs. *Bein Hachomot* (Within the Walls), *Ma'archot Tzafon* (The Campaign in the North).
Ministry of Transport and Communications, Jerusalem; and Kibbutz Na'an, Rehovoth, Israel.

Carmichael, Harry J., C.M.G.; Canadian industrialist; b. 29 Sept. 1891; ed. New Haven High School.
Joined McKinnon Industries, St. Catharines, Ont. 12, becoming Pres. and Gen. Man. on acquisition by Gen. Motors Corpn. 29; Vice-Pres. and Gen. Man. Gen. Motors of Canada Ltd. 36-41; Joint Dir.-Gen. of Munitions Production, Dept. of Munitions and Supply 41-42; Co-ordinator of Production and Chair. War Production Board; Canadian Chair. Joint U.S.-Canada W.P.B. 42-45; now Vice-Pres., Treasurer and Dir. Conroy Manufacturing Co. Ltd., St. Catharines, Ont.; Dir. Abitibi Power & Paper Co. Ltd., Argus Corpn. Ltd., Foster Wheeler Ltd., Massey-Harris Co. Ltd., Continental Can Co. of Canada Ltd., Hayes Steel Products Ltd., Canada Perm. Trust Co., Ventures Ltd.; Vice-Pres. and Dir. The Toronto-Dominion Bank; Dir. Hiram Walker, Gooderham & Worts Ltd., Ontario Jockey Club Ltd., Supervised Exec. Fund Ltd., T. G. Bright & Co. Ltd.
c/o Conroy Manufacturing Co. Ltd., St. Catharines, Ontario, Canada.

Carmichael, Leonard, PH.D., HON. LL.D., LITT.D., D.C.L., SC.D., L.H.D.; American psychologist; b. 9 Nov. 1898; ed. Tufts Coll., Harvard Univ. and Berlin Univ.
Instructor in Psychology, Princeton Univ. 24-26, Asst. Prof. 26-27; Assoc. Prof. Brown Univ. 27-28, Prof. 28-36; Dir. of Psychological Laboratory 27-36; Dir. Lab. of Sensory Physiology 34-36; Chair. Dept. of Psychology and Dean of Faculty of Arts and Science Univ. of Rochester 36-38; Pres. Tufts Coll. and Dir. Lab. of Sensory Psychology and Physiology 38-52; Dir. Nat. Roster of Scientific and Specialised Personnel, Washington, D.C. 40-44; Sec. Smithsonian Inst. 53-63; Vice-Pres. for Research and Exploration, Nat. Geographic Soc. 64-; mem. Nat. Acad. of Sciences, American Phil.

Soc., American Psychological Assen., American Physiol. Soc.; Pres. Int. Primatological Soc.; Fellow American Acad. of Arts and Sciences; foreign mem. Société Française de Psychologie; hon. mem. Ergonomics Research Society, England; Vice-Chair. Nat. Advisory Cttee. for Aeronautics 56-58; Pres. Section on Experimental Psychology and Animal Behaviour, Int. Union of Biological Sciences 61-; Trustee, Nat. Geographic Soc., and Vice-Pres. for Research and Exploration.
Publs. *Special Disabilities in Learning to Read and Write* (co-author) 25, *Elements of Human Psychology* (co-author) 30, *Reading and Visual Fatigue* (co-author) 47, *The Selection of Military Manpower* (co-editor) 52, *Basic Psychology* 57.
National Geographic Society, 17th and M Streets, N.W., Washington D.C. 20036, U.S.A.
Telephone: 202-296-7500.

Carmoy, Guy de, L. EN D., L. ÈS L.; French administrator and professor; b. 20 Feb. 1907.
Inspector of Finances 30-60; Gen. Information Commissariat 39; Head of Film Dept., Ministry of Information 40-41; Budgetary Controller 41-43; deported to Germany 43-45; Alternate Exec. Director Int. Bank for Reconstruction and Development 46-48; mem. French del. for European Economic Co-operation 48; Dir. of Admin. and Confs. Organisation for European Economic Co-operation 48-52; Prof. Inst. d'Etudes Politiques 50; Prof. Inst. Européen d'Administration des Affaires 61-; Officier Légion d'Honneur.
Publs. *Fortune de l'Europe* 53, *Les politiques étrangères de la France (1944-1966)* 67.
22 avenue de Suffren, Paris 15e, France.
Telephone: 783-12-73.

Carnap, Rudolf P., DR.PHIL.; American philosopher; b. Germany 18 May 1891; ed. Jena and Freiburg i.B. Univs.
Dozent 26, Extr. Prof. 30 Vienna Univ.; Prof. German Univ. Prague 31-36; Prof. of Philosophy Univ. of Chicago 36-54; Prof. of Philosophy, Univ. of Calif., Los Angeles 54-62, Research Philosopher 62-; Hon. Sc.D. (Harvard), Hon. LL.D. (California), Hon. H.L.D. (Michigan).
Publs. *Der logische Aufbau der Welt* 28 (English trans. 67), *Abriss der Logistik* 29, *Logische Syntax der Sprache* 34 (English trans. 37), *Philosophy and Logical Syntax* 35, *Foundations of Logic and Mathematics* 39, *Introduction to Semantics* 42, *Formalization of Logic* 43, *Meaning and Necessity* 47, *Logical Foundations of Probability* 50, *The Continuum of Inductive Methods* 52, *Einführung in die Symbolische Logik* 54, *Introduction to Symbolic Logic and its Applications* 58, *Induktive Logik und Wahrscheinlichkeit* (with W. Stegmüller) 59, *Intellectual Autobiography* and *Replies and Systematic Expositions* in *The Philosophy of Rudolf Carnap* (Editor P. A. Schilpp) 64.
University of California, Los Angeles, Calif. 90024, U.S.A.

Carné, Marcel; French film director; b. 18 Aug. 1906. Took course for film technicians; work interrupted by military service; on discharge entered insurance business; later returned to film work; assistant operator for *Les Nouveaux Messieurs* 28; asst. to Dir., Richard Oswald, for *Cagliostro* 29; won competition for film criticism organised by *Cinémagazine* and joined editorial staff of this publication; directed *Nogent, Eldorado du Dimanche* 29; assisted René Clair in direction of *Sous les Toits de Paris* 30; wrote criticisms for various journals; Asst. Dir. for *Le Grand Jeu, Pension Mimosa,* and *La Kermesse Héroïque;* scored first great success as dir. with *Jenny* 36; directed many films inc. *Drôle de Drame* 37, *Quai des Brumes* 38, *Le Jour se lève* 39, *Les Enfants du Paradis* 43, *Les Portes de la Nuit* 46, *Juliette ou la clé des songes, La Marié du Port, Thérèse Raquin, L'Air de Paris, Le Pays d'où je viens, Les Tricheurs, Terrain Vague, Du mouron pour les petits*

oiseaux, Trois chambres à Manhattan, Les Jeunes Loups.
57 boulevard Suchet, Paris 16e, France.
Telephone: 525-49-29.

Carneiro, Paulo de Berredo, D.SC.; Brazilian biochemist and diplomatist; b. 01; ed. Polytechnic School, Rio de Janeiro, and Université de Paris à la Sorbonne. Professor Agregé, Polytechnic School, Rio de Janeiro 31-; Sec. of State for Agriculture, Industry and Commerce, State of Pernambuco 35; founded Pernambuco Agronomical Inst. 35; research at Institut Pasteur, Paris 36-41; Del. to numerous General Confs. of UNESCO 45-; mem. Exec. Board UNESCO 46-, Chair. 51-54; Head Brazilian Perm. Del. to UNESCO 47-58, Ambassador to UNESCO 58-; Pres. Int. Comm. for a *History of the Scientific and Cultural Development of Mankind* 51-; Vice-Pres. Int. Children's Centre; Prix Nativelle, Paris Acad. of Medicine 51.
UNESCO, Place de Fontenoy, Paris 7e, France.

Carnot, Lazare; French businessman; b. 9 Nov. 1903; ed. Ecole Nationale Supérieure des Mines de Paris. Military service 26-27; mining engineer 27-28; Dir. Pricel; Dir. Rhône-Poulenc S.A., Rhodiaceta, Cellulose du Pin, Compagnie Financière de Suez et Union Parisienne, Compagnie d'activités associées; Chevalier Légion d'Honneur, Croix de Guerre.
77 avenue Henri Martin, Paris 16e, France.
Telephone: 870-27-07.

Caro, Anthony, M.A.; British sculptor; b. 8 March 1934; ed. Charterhouse School, Christs' Coll. Cambridge and Royal Acad. Schools, London.
Assistant to Henry Moore 51-53; Part-time Lecturer St. Martin's School of Art, London 53-; taught at Bennington Coll. Vermont 63-65; one-man show in Milan 56, others subsequently in London, Washington, Toronto, Zürich and in Holland; works in Tate Gallery and Arts Council (London), Brandeis Univ. (Boston), Ryksmuseum Kroller-Muller (Otterlo, Netherlands); Sculpture Prize Paris Biennale 59, David E. Bright Award Venice Biennale 67.
III Frognal, Hampstead, London N.W.3, England.

Caron, Giuseppe; Italian politician; b. 24 Feb. 1904; ed. Università degli Studi, Padua.
Senator 48-; Under-Sec. of State, Ministry of Public Works 55-57, Ministry of Civil Aviation 57-59; Vice-Pres. Comm. EEC 59-63; Under-Sec. of State for the Budget 63-; Sec. Interministerial Cttee. for the Plan (C.I.P.E.); mem. Nat. Council of Democrazia Cristiana 59-; Ordine al Merito della Repubblica; Commdr. dell'Ordine Piano; Grosses Verdienstkreuz (German Fed. Republic).
Publs. *Saggi e discorsi dell'integrazione europea, Economia e socialità, Saggi e discorsi sull'Aviazione civile.*
Via Cancani 5, Rome, Italy.
Telephone: 879990.

Caron, Leslie Claire Margaret; French ballet dancer and actress; b. 1 July 1931; ed. Convent of the Assumption, Paris, and Conservatoire de Danse.
With Ballet des Champs Elysées 47-50; with Ballet de Paris 54; has appeared in many films, incl.: *American in Paris, Man with a Cloak, Glory Alley, Story of Three Loves, Lili, Glass Slipper, Daddy Long Legs, Gaby, Gigi, The Doctor's Dilemma, The Man who Understood Women, The Subterraneans, Fanny, Guns of Darkness, The L-Shaped Room, Father Goose, A Very Special Favor, Promise Her Anything, Is Paris Burning?, Head of the Family;* has also appeared on stage in Paris and London.
c/o 31 Montpelier Square, London, S.W.7, England.

Carpeaux, Otto Maria, PH.D., LIT.D.; Brazilian journalist; b. 1900; ed. Vienna Univ.
Dir. Library, Nat. Faculty of Philosophy, Rio de Janeiro 41-45; Dir. Library, Getulio Vargas Founda-

tion, Rio de Janeiro 45-49; Editor *Correio da Manha*, Rio de Janeiro; Italian Order of Merit.
Publs. 12 vols. of essays, *Short Critical Bibliography of Brazilian Literature* 51, *History of the Occidental Literatures* (9 vols.) 59-, *A New History of Music* 58, *History of German Literature* 61.
101 Rua República do Peru, Rio de Janeiro, Brazil.

Carpenter, Sir Eric Ashton, O.B.E.; British company director; b. 12 Nov. 1896; ed. Cheadle Hulme School.
Chair. and Managing Dir. Greg Bros. & Co. Ltd. since 29; Chair. Lloyd's Packing Warehouses (Holdings) Ltd. 50-66, Williams Deacon's Bank 52-64, Dir. 49-; Dir. Yorkshire Bank 52-, Chair. 64-; Dir. Royal Bank of Scotland 52-, Industrial & Gen. Trust Ltd. 53-, Second Industrial Trust Ltd. 53-, Manchester Ship Canal Co. 56-, Royal Insurance Co. Ltd. 62-; mem. North-Western Gas Board 49-66; Pres. Manchester Chamber of Commerce 48-50, Asscn. of British Chambers of Commerce 54 and 55; mem. Dollar Exports Council 49-60; High Sheriff of Lancashire 59-60; Pres. The Inst. of Bankers 60-62.
Burrows Cross House, Gomshall, nr. Guildford, Surrey, England.
Telephone: Shere 2441.

Carpenter, Rt. Rev. Harry James, M.A.; British ecclesiastic; b. 20 Oct. 1901; ed. Churcher's Coll., Petersfield, Univ. Coll. of Southampton, and Queen's Coll., Oxford.
Fellow and Tutor, Keble Coll., Oxford 27-39, Warden 39-55; Bishop of Oxford 55-; Hon. D.D. (Oxford).
Cuddesdon, Oxford, England.
Telephone: Garsington 323.

Carpenter, Commdr. Malcom Scott; American naval officer and astronaut; b. 1 May 1925; ed. secondary school and Univ. of Colorado.
Aviation Cadet, U.S. Navy 43-45; Pilot, South Korea 49, later Navy Flight Officer, Electronics and Intelligence Officer; Project Mercury Astronaut 59-67, made triple orbit of the earth, May 24, 1962; spent 30 days beneath ocean in Sealab II, Aug.-Sept. 65; mem. U.S. Navy's Sealab Project 67.
c/o Department of the Navy, Washington 25, D.C., U.S.A.

Carpentier y Valmont, Alejo; Cuban writer; b. 26 Dec. 1904; ed. Universidad de Habana.
Former journalist, radio station dir. and musicologist; travelled in Mexico, France, Spain, Belgium, Holland, Haiti, U.S.A. and upper reaches of Orinoco River; fmr. columnist *El Nacional*, Caracas, Venezuela; now Cultural Attaché of Cuba in Paris; Prix du Meilleur Livre Etranger for *The Lost Steps* 56.
Publs. *Ecue-Yamba-O* (novel) 33, *A History of Cuban Music, El Reino de Este Mundo* (The Kingdom of this World) (novel) 49, *Los Pasos Perdidos* (The Lost Steps) (novel) 53, *El Acoso* (The Pursuit) (novel) 56, *Guerra de Tiempo* (The War of Time) (short stories) 58, *El Siglo de las Luces* (Explosion in a Cathedral) (novel) 63.
Embassy of Cuba, 3 rue Scribe, Paris, 4e, France; Apartado 6153, Havana, Cuba.

Carpino, H.E. Cardinal Francesco; Italian ecclesiastic, b. 18 May 1905.
Ordained Priest 27; Titular Archbishop of Nicomedia 51; Titular Archbishop of Sardica 61-; fmr. Archbishop of Palermo; also Assessor, Sacred Consistorial Congregation; created Cardinal by Pope Paul VI 67.
The Sacred Consistorial Congregation, Vatican City, Rome, Italy.

Carr, Edward Hallett, C.B.E.; British diplomatist; political scientist and historian; b. 28 June 1892; ed. Merchant Taylors School and Cambridge Univ.
Entered Foreign Office 16; mem. British Del. to Peace Conf. 19; attached to Ambassadors' Conf. Paris 20-21; First Sec. Legation Riga 25-29; Asst. Adviser on U.N.

Affairs, Foreign Office 30-33, First Sec. 33-36; Prof of Int. Politics, Univ. Coll. Wales 36-46; Dir. Foreign Div. Min. of Information 39-40; Asst. Editor *The Times* 41-45; Tutor in Politics, Balliol Coll. 53-55; Fellow Trinity Coll., Cambridge 55-.
Publs. *Dostoevsky: a new biography* 31, *The Romantic Exiles* 33, *Karl Marx* 34, *International Relations Since the Peace Treaties* 37, *Michael Bakunin* 37, *The Twenty Years' Crisis* 39, *Britain: A Study of Foreign Policy from Versailles to the Outbreak of War* 39, *Conditions of Peace* 42, *Nationalism and After* 45, *The Soviet Impact on the Western World* 46, *Studies in Revolution* 50, *The Bolshevik Revolution, 1917-1923*, Vol. I 50, Vol. II 52, Vol. III 53, *The New Society* 51, *German-Soviet Relations Between the Two World Wars* 51, *The Interregnum 1923-1924* (continuation of *The Bolshevik Revolution 1917-1923*) 54, *Socialism in One Country 1924-26* Vol. I 58, Vol. II 59, Vol. III 64, *What is History?* (The Trevelyan Lectures) 61.
Trinity College, Cambridge, England.

Carr, Rt. Hon. Robert, P.C., M.P.; British politician and business executive; b. 11 Nov. 1916; ed. Westminster School and Gonville and Caius Coll., Cambridge.
John Dale Ltd. 38-, Chief Metallurgist 45-48, Dir. of Research and Development 48-55; Dir. Carr, Day & Martin Ltd. 47-55; Isotope Developments Ltd. 50-55; M.P. 50-, Parl. Private Sec. to Sec. of State for Foreign Affairs 51-55, to Prime Minister April-Dec. 55, Parl. Sec. Ministry of Labour and Nat. Service 55-58, Sec. for Technical Co-operation May 63-Oct. 64; Dep. Chair. and Joint Man. Dir. Metal Closures Group Ltd. 60-63, Deputy Chair. 60-63; Chair. John Dale Ltd. 58-63; Dir. Scottish Union and Nat. Insurance Co. (London) 58-63; Dir. S. Hoffnung and Co. 65-, Securicor Ltd. 65-, (London) Norwich Union Insurance Group; Conservative.
Publs. Co-author *One Nation, Change is our Ally* 54, *The Responsible Society* 58, *One Europe* 65.
Monkenholt, Hadley Green, Barnet, Hertfordshire, England.

Carrelli, Antonio; Italian physicist; b. 1 July 1900; ed. Università degli Studi, Naples.
Professor of Experimental Physics, Naples Univ. 32-; Vice-Pres. Italian Radio and Television (R.T.I.) 46-55, Pres. 55-59; Pres. Microlamba Co. 48-52 and Filotecnica Salmoiraghi Co. 48-52; Chair. Nat. Cttee. for Physics of Nat. Research Council, Scientific Cttee. of Italian Nat. Comm. of UNESCO; Vice-Pres. Southern Finance Co.; Vice-Pres. European Atomic Energy Comm. (EURATOM) 64-67; mem. Accad. Lincei; several decorations; Pres Board of Dirs. of Post and Telecommunications Ministry.
c/o Instituto Fisica Sperimentale Università, Via Tari 3, Napoli; Home: Via Chiaia 149, Napoli, Italy.
Telephone: 392909.

Carrera Andrade, Jorgé; Ecuadorean diplomatist and writer; b. 18 Sept. 1903; ed. Colegio Mejía, Univ. Central del Ecuador and Univ. de Barcelona.
Consul, Paita, Peru 34, Le Havre 34-37; Consul-Gen., Yokohama 37-44; First Sec., Caracas 44-47, Chargé d'Affaires *a.i.*, Caracas 46; Minister, London 47-50; Foreign Office, Ecuador 50; Amb. to Venezuela 61-63, Nicaragua 63-64, France 64-66; Minister of Foreign Affairs, Ecuador Nov. 66-June 67; Amb. to Netherlands 67-; Pro-Sec. of Senate 33, Sec. of Congress 33; Vice-Pres. Casa de la Cultura Ecuatoriana 50-51; Dir. Spanish Edn. of *UNESCO Courier*, Paris 52-59; Del. to numerous UNESCO and UN Confs.; mem. Casa de la Cultura Ecuatoriana, Acad. Ecuatoriana de la Lengua; Corresp. mem. Real Acad. Española; several decorations.
Publs. Literary and historical works.
Embassy of Ecuador, Jan van Nassaustraat 99, The Hague, Netherlands.

Carrero Blanco, Luis; Spanish naval officer, politician and author; b. 1903; ed. Spanish Naval School and Paris Naval School.

Chief of Staff, Cruiser Div., Spanish Civil War; Second Vice-Pres. of Cortes 43; Under-Sec. of Presidency of Cabinet 51-65; Minister, Under-Sec. of Presidency of Cabinet 65-; Vice-Premier 67-; Grand Cross of St. Silvester 50.

Presidency of the Cabinet, Madrid, Spain.

Carrillo Flores, Antonio; Mexican lawyer, banker and politician; b. 09; ed. in New York and Nat. School of Jurisprudence, Mexico.

Prof. Faculty of Jurisprudence, Univ. of Mexico 32-; Joint Sec. Supreme Court of Justice 33; Head Law Dept. Attorney-Gen.'s Office 30-34 (except while with Supreme Court); Head, Law Dept., Ministry of Finance 35-36; mem. Admin. Council Bank of Mexico 38; Dir.-Gen. of Credit Ministry of Finance 41-45, of Nacional Financiera 45-52, Sec. of the Treasury 52-58; Ambassador to United States 59-64; Minister of Foreign Affairs 64-; mem. Admin. Council Fondo de Cultura Económica; Gov. Nat. Univ. 47-; decorations from Belgium, German Fed. Republic, Netherlands, France, Italy, Brazil, Paraguay, Argentina, Guatemala, El Salvador, Honduras, Nicaragua, Panama, Chile, Peru, United Arab Republic, Colombia, Japan and China; Dr. h.c. Lincoln Coll.

Publs. *Administrative Justice in Mexico* 39, *The Mexican Financial System* 46, *The Economy and Human Rights in the Mexican Constitution* 59, *The Ideas and the Economic Development in the Process of the Mexican Revolution* 60, *The Supreme Court in the United States and in Mexico* 64, *Some Aspects of International Economic Co-operation* 67, *Homages and Testimonies* 67.

Ministry of Foreign Affairs, Mexico D.F., Mexico.

Carrington, 6th Baron; **Peter Alexander Rupert Carington,** P.C., K.C.M.G., M.C.; British administrator; b. 6 June 1919; ed. Eton Coll. and Royal Military Coll., Sandhurst.

Grenadier Guards 39, and served N.W. Europe; Parl. Sec. Ministry of Agriculture 51-54, Ministry of Defence 54-56; High Commr. in Australia 56-59; First Lord of the Admiralty 59-63; Minister without Portfolio (at the Foreign Office), Leader of the House of Lords 63-64; Leader of the Opposition in the House of Lords 64-; Chair. Australia and New Zealand Bank Ltd.; Dir. British Metal Corpn. Ltd., Barclays Bank Ltd., and Hambros Bank Ltd.

House of Lords, London, S.W.1; Manor House, Bledlow, nr. Aylesbury, Buckinghamshire, England.

Telephone: Princes Risborough 499.

Carrington, Most Rev. Philip, M.A., LITT.D., D.D.; Canadian ecclesiastic; b. 6 July 1892; ed. Univs. of New Zealand and Cambridge.

Ordained deacon 18, priest 19; Curate St. Luke's Church Christchurch N.Z. 18; Vicar of Lincoln N.Z. 22; Warden of St. Barnabas Coll., Adelaide, South Australia 23; Dean of Divinity Bishop's Univ. Lennoxville, Quebec 27; Bishop of Quebec 35-43; Archbishop of Quebec 43-60.

Publs. *The Boy Scout's Camp Book* 18, *Christian Apologetics in the Second Century* 21, *The Soldier of the Cross* 30, *The Sign of Faith* 30, *The Meaning of the Revelation* 30, *The Road to Jerusalem* 33, *The Pilgrim's Way* 37, *The Primitive Christian Catechism* 40, *Church History for Canadians* 47, *The Primitive Christian Calendar* 51, *The Story of the Christ* 56, *The Early Christian Church* 57, *According to Mark* 60, *The Anglican Church in Canada* 63.

Quebec Lodge, Little Somerford, Chippenham, Wiltshire, England.

Carrión, Benjamín, LL.D.; Ecuadorean lawyer and writer; b. 97.

Former Consul, Le Havre; fmr. Minister of Education; fmr. Ambassador to Mexico, Colombia and Chile; Editor *El Sol* 52-; Pres. Casa de la Cultura Ecuatoriana, Radio Casa de la Cultura.

Publs. numerous literary and historical works.

Casa de la Cultura Ecuatoriana, Apdo. 67, Quito, Ecuador.

Carrobio di Carrobio, Renzo; Italian diplomatist; b. 1905; ed. Univ. degli Studi, Florence.

Diplomatic appointments Moscow, Toulon and Berne 27-48; Chargé d'Affaires, India 48-49; Political Rep. of Italian Govt., Trieste 52; Amb. to El Salvador 52-54; Deputy Dir.-Gen., Foreign Office, Rome 55-58; Dir.-Gen. of Econ. Affairs 58; Amb. to South Africa 59-62; Sec.-Gen. European Space Vehicle Launcher Devt. Org. (ELDO), Paris 62-; appointed full rank of Amb. 65; Gran Ufficiale del Ordine al Merito della Repubblica Italiana; Commdr. Légion d'Honneur.

European Space Vehicle Launcher Development Organization, 114 avenue de Neuilly, 92 Neuilly, France.

Carroll, Paul Vincent; Irish dramatist; b. 10 July 1900; ed. Dublin.

Schoolmaster in Scotland 21-37; Dir. Glasgow Citizens' Theatre.

Publs. *Things that are Caesar's, The Strings My Lord are False, The White Steed, Shadow and Substance, The Old Foolishness, Two Plays, Plays for My Children, The Wise have not Spoken* (play), *The Devil Came from Dublin* 52, *The Wayward Saint* (play), *Broadway* 55, *Irish Short Stories and Plays* 59.

22 Park Road, Bromley, Kent, England.

Carron, Baron (Life Peer), cr. 67, of the City and County of Kingston-upon-Hull; **William John Carron;** British trade union official; b. 19 Nov. 1902; ed. St. Mary's R.C. School, Hull, and Hull Technical Coll.

Branch Sec. Amalgamated Engineering Union 32, Full-time Organiser (12th Division) 45, mem. Exec. Council 50, Pres. 56-67; mem. Gen. Council of the T.U.C. 54-; Chair. Engineering Sub-Cttee., Confed. of Engineering and Shipbuilding Unions, British Section, Int. Metalworkers' Fed.; mem. British Productivity Council 59-, Nat. Econ. Development Council (N.E.D.C.) 62-; Dir. Bank of England; Dir. Co-operative Printing Soc. Ltd.; Trustee, Churchill Coll., Cambridge; Visiting Fellow, Nuffield Coll., Oxford; Knight of the Order of St. Gregory the Great; M.A. Oxford, Fellow Royal Soc. of Arts; Hon. D.Sc. (Loughborough); Labour.

174 Grierson Road, Honor Oak Park, London, S.E.23, England.

Carruthers, Robert, B.SC.(ENG.), C.ENG., A.C.G.I., F.I.E.E.; British electrical engineer; b. 21; ed. Harrow County School and London Univ., City and Guilds Coll.

Research at Telecommunications Research Establishment, Swanage and Great Malvern 41-46; Research engineer with Messrs. Standard Telecommunication Laboratories Ltd. development of R.F. equipment for microwave radio links 46-47; research and development of synchrotrons, Atomic Energy Research Establishment 47-51; research work on gas discharge phenomena and its application to the field of controlled thermonuclear reactors; Senior Principal Scientist, Atomic Energy Research Establishment, Harwell; Head, Technology Division, Culham Laboratory 61-.

Norman Cottage, 32 Norman Avenue, Abingdon, Berks., England.

Telephone: Abingdon 386.

Carry, Champ, M.E.; American business executive; b. 31 May 1898; ed. Cornell Univ.

With Haskell & Barker Car Co. 19, Pullman Car & Manufacturing Corpn. 22-32, Vice-Pres. 29-32; Vice-Pres. The Pullman Co. 32-41, Exec. Vice-Pres. 41-46; Pres. Pullman-Standard Car Mfg. Co. 46-50, Chair. of Bd. 50-; Pres. Pullman Inc. 50-61, Chair. of Bd. 61-.

200 South Michigan Avenue, Chicago 4, Ill., U.S.A.

Carstairs, George Morrison, M.A., M.D., F.R.C.P.E., D.P.M.; British psychiatrist; b. 18 June 1916; ed. George Watson's Coll., Edinburgh and Edinburgh Univ.
Medical Officer, Fighter Command, R.A.F. 42-46; Commonwealth Fund Fellow, U.S.A. 48-49, Rockefeller Research Fellow, India 50-51, Henderson Research Scholar, India 51-52; Registrar, Maudsley Hospital, London 53; Scientific Staff, Medical Research Council Social Psychiatry Research Unit 54-60, Hon Consultant, Maudsley Hospital 56-60; Dir. Medical Research Council Unit for Research on Epidemiology of Psychiatric Illness 60-; Prof. of Psychological Medicine, Univ. of Edinburgh 61-; B.B.C. Reith Lecturer 62.
Publs. *The Twice Born* 57, *This Island Now* (the 1962 Reith Lectures) 63.
18 Merchiston Avenue, Edinburgh 10, Scotland.

Carstens, Karl, DR. IUR.; German lawyer and diplomatist; b. 14 Dec. 1914; ed. Univs. of Frankfurt, Dijon, Munich, Königsberg, Hamburg and Yale.
War service 39-45; lawyer, Bremen 45-49; Rep. of Free Hanseatic City of Bremen to Fed. Govt., Bonn 49-54; Fed. German Del. to Council of Europe, Strasbourg 54-55; Dep. Head. Political Div., Fed. Foreign Office, Bonn 55-58, Head, European Div. 58-60, State Sec. 60-, Deputy of Fed. Minister of Foreign Affairs 61-66; Deputy of Fed. Minister of Defence 66-67; Head of the Fed. Chancellor's Office 68-; Prof. of Constitutional and Int. Law, Univ. of Cologne 60-.
Publs. *Basic Ideas of the American Constitution and their Realisation* 54, *The Law of the Council of Europe* 56.
Bundeskanzleramt, 53 Bonn, Adenauerallee 139-141, German Federal Republic.

Cartan, Henri Paul, D. ès sc.; b. 8 July 1904; ed. Lycée Buffon, Lycée Hoche, Versailles and Ecole normale supérieure.
Teacher, Lycée, Caen 28; Lecturer, Faculty of Science, Lille Univ. 29-31; Prof. Faculty of Science, Strasbourg Univ. 31-40, Univ. of Paris 40-; Pres. French Section, European Asscn. of Teachers 57-; Pres. Int. Mathematical Union 67-; Corresp. Acad. des Sciences 66; Officier de la Légion d'Honneur.
Institut Henri-Poincaré, 11 rue Pierre-Curie, Paris 5e; Home: 95 boulevard Jourdan, Paris 14e, France.

Carter, Edward Roger Erskine, B.C.L.; Canadian business executive; b. 20 Feb. 1923; ed. Univ. of New Brunswick, Osgoode Hall, Toronto, and Oxford Univ. (Rhodes Scholar).
Military Service 42-45; read law with McMillan, Binch, Wilkinson, Berry & Wright, Toronto; called to Bar of New Brunswick 47, Bar of Ontario 51; Assoc. with A. N. Carter, Q.C., law practice, Saint John, N.B. 49-53; Legal Officer, Abitibi Power & Paper Co. Ltd., Toronto 53-54; joined Fennell, McLean, Seed & Carter 54, Partner 55-58; now Pres. and Chief Exec. Officer The Patiño Mining Corpn.; Chair. and Dir. Consolidated Tin Smelters Ltd., British Tin Investments Corpn. Ltd., The Southern Maryland Agricultural Asscn. of Prince Georges' County, Maryland, Inc., C.D.R.H. Ltd.; Pres. and Dir. Advocate Mines Ltd.; Vice-Chair. and mem. Exec. Cttee. Rio Tinto Patiño S.A.; Deputy Chair. Amalgamated Metal Corpn. Ltd.; Dir. numerous other companies; mem. Law Soc. of Upper Canada, New Brunswick Barristers Soc.
The Patiño Mining Corporation, 7 King St. E., Toronto, Ontario, Canada; Consolidated Tin Smelters Ltd., 40 Basinghall Street, London E.C.4, England; Home: 331 Riverview Drive, Toronto 12, Ontario, Canada.
Telephone: 366-1685 (Toronto); 01-628-4571 (London).

Carter, Edward W.; American businessman; b. 29 June 1911; ed. Univ. of California, Harvard Univ.
President Broadway-Hale Stores, Inc., Los Angeles; Dir. American Telephone and Telegraph Co., Del Monte Corpn., Pacific Mutual Life Insurance Co., Southern Calif. Edison Co., United Calif. Bank, Western Bancor-poration; mem. Board of Regents, Univ. of Calif.; Chair. Los Angeles County Museum of Art; Trustee of Occidental Coll., The Brookings Inst., Washington,D.C., Stanford Research Inst.; Overseer's Visiting Comm., Harvard Business School; Dir. Southern Calif. Symphony-Hollywood Bowl Asscn., San Francisco Opera Asscn.
600 South Spring Street, Los Angeles, California, U.S.A.

Carter, Elliott Cook, Jr., A.B., A.M.; American composer; b. 11 Dec. 1908; ed. Harvard Univ., Ecole Normale de Musique, Paris.
Musical Dir. Ballet Caravan 37-39; critic *Modern Music* 37-42; tutor St. John's Coll., Annapolis 39-41; teacher of composition Peabody Conservatory 46-48, Columbia Univ. 48-50, Queen's Coll. (N.Y.) 55-56; Prof. of Music, Yale Univ. 60-; Andrew White Prof.-at-Large, Cornell Univ. 67-; mem. Board of Trustees, American Acad., Rome; American Composers' Alliance Prize for Quartet for Four Saxophones 43, First Prize Liège Int. Music Competition 53; mem. Int. Soc. for Contemporary Music, Dir. 46-52, Pres. American Section 52, Nat. Inst. of Arts and Letters, American Composers Alliance, Dir. 39-52, Treas. 49-50; awarded two Guggenheim Fellowships, Pulitzer Prize (for 2nd String Quartet), Sibelius Medal 60, New York Critics Circle Award (for Double Concerto) 61, Hon. degrees Swarthmore Coll. and Princeton Univ.
Works include: Symphony, Double Concerto, Variations for Orchestra, Piano Concerto, Woodwind Quintet, Sonatos for piano and cello and for flute, oboe, cello, and harpsichord, two String Quartets, the ballets *Pocahontas* and *The Minotaur*, choral and incidental music.
21 W. 12th Street, New York 11, N.Y., U.S.A.

Carter, Sir John, Kt., LL.B., Q.C.; Guyanan diplomatist; b. 27 Jan. 1919; ed. Queen's Coll., Georgetown, and London Univ.
Called to Bar, Middle Temple, London 42; Law practice British Guiana 45-66; mem. British Guiana Legislature 40-53, 61-64; Pro-Chancellor Univ. of Guyana 62-66; Amb. to U.S.A. June 66-; Perm. Rep. of Guyana to UN June-Dec. 66.
Embassy of Guyana, Washington, D.C., U.S.A.

Carter, Lieut.-Gen. Marshall Sylvester, B.S., M.S.; American army officer and government official; b. 16 Sept. 1909; ed. U.S. Military Acad., Mass. Inst. of Technology.
2nd Lieut., U.S. Army 31; service with artillery, Honolulu, Panama; Staff Officer, Washington 42-45; China Theater 45-46; Special Asst. to Sec. of State 47-49; Exec. to Sec. of Defense 50-52; Dep. Commdg. Gen., Alaska 52-55; Commdg. Gen. 5th Army Air Defence Region 55-56; Chief of Staff, North American Air Defense Command, Colorado Springs 57-59, Continental Air Defense Command 56-59; Chief of Staff, 8th Army, Korea 59-61; Commdg. Gen., Army Air Defense Center, Commdt. Army Air Defense School 61-62; Dep. Dir. Central Intelligence Agency 62-65; Dir. Nat. Security Agency 65-; Distinguished Service Medal with Oak Leaf Cluster, Legion of Merit with Oak Leaf Cluster, Bronze Star Medal, etc.
c/o The Adjutant General, Department of the Army, Washington, D.C., U.S.A.

Cartier-Bresson, Henri; French photographer; b. 22 Aug. 1908.
Studied painting in André Lhote's studio; took up photography 31; Asst. Dir. to Jean Renoir 37, 38; prisoner of war 40-43, escaped; founded Magnum-Photos with Capa, Chim, and Rodger 47; exhibitions New York Museum of Modern Art 46, The Louvre, Paris (later tour in Germany, Switzerland, London, Milan, Tokyo, U.S.A.) 55, Phillips Collection, Washington 64; Overseas Press Club awards.
Publs. *Images à la Sauvette* (U.S. edition *The Decisive*

Moment), *The Europeans, From One China to the Other, The People of Moscow, Danses à Bali.*

c/o Magnum-Photos, 125 Faubourg St. Honoré, Paris, France; 15 West 47th Street, New York, N.Y., U.S.A.

Cartwright, Rt. Hon. John Robert, P.C., M.C., LL.D.; Canadian judge; b. 23 March 1895; ed. Upper Canada Coll., Toronto, and Osgoode Hall, Toronto.
Served in First World War 14-19; awarded Military Cross 17; called to the Bar, Toronto 20; practised Toronto 20-49; K.C. 33; Judge Supreme Court of Canada 49-67, Chief Justice 67-; Bencher of the Law Society of Upper Canada 46-.
Chief Justice's Chambers, Supreme Court of Canada, Ottawa 4, Canada.
Telephone: 992-2757 (Office).

Cartwright, Mary Lucy, M.A., D.PHIL., SC.D., F.R.S.; British college principal; b. 17 Dec. 1900; ed. Godolphin School, Salisbury, and St. Hugh's Coll., Oxford Univ.
Asst. Mistress, Alice Ottley School, Worcester 23-24, Wycombe Abbey School, Bucks. 24-27; Yarrow Research Fellow, Girton Coll. 30-34; Faculty Asst. Lecturer in Mathematics. Cambridge 33-35; Fellow and Lecturer, Girton Coll. 34-49; Mistress of Girton Coll. 49-68, Univ. Lecturer in Mathematics, Cambridge 36-59, Reader in the Theory of Functions 59-; Consultant on U.S. Navy Mathematical Research Projects at Stanford and Princeton Univs. 49; Fellow, Cambridge Philosophical Society; Vice-Pres. London Mathematical Society 36-38; Pres. Mathematical Association 51-52, London Mathematical Soc. 61-63; Hon. LL.D. (Edinburgh Univ.), Hon. D.Sc. (Leeds Univ., Hull Univ., Univs. of Wales and Oxford).
Girton College, Cambridge, England.

Cartwright, William Frederick, D.L., M.I.MECH.E.; British engineer; b. 13 Nov. 1906; ed. Dragon School, Oxford, and Rugby.
Chief Mechanical Engineer's Dept., Great Western Railway 25-29; Guest, Keen and Nettlefolds Ltd., Dowlais 29-30; student, German and French steelworks 30-31; Asst. to Works Man. Guest, Keen, Baldwins Iron and Steel Co. Ltd., Port Talbot 31-35, Technical Asst. to Man. Dir. 35-40, Dir. and Chief Engineer, Guest, Keen, Baldwins Iron and Steel Co. Ltd. 40-43, Gen. Man. Margam and Port Talbot Works 43-47; Dir. Steel Co. of Wales 47-, Gen. Man. Steel Div. 47-62, Asst. Managing Dir. and Gen. Manager 54-62, Managing Dir. 62-67, Chair. Feb. 67-July 67; Man. Dir. S. Wales Group, British Steel Corpn. July 67-; Bessemer Gold Medal, Iron and Steel Inst. 58.
Castle-upon-Alun, St. Bride's Major, nr. Bridgend, Glamorgan, Wales.

Caruso, Casto, D.IUR. ET RER. POL.; Italian diplomatist; b. 10 Oct. 1904; ed. Istituto Orientale, Naples.
Italian Diplomatic Service 28-; Minister to Tangier 46-48; Minister and later Amb. to The Netherlands 51-54; Amb. to Greece 54-59; Dir.-Gen. of Econ. Affairs, Ministry of Foreign Affairs 59-61; Head of Italian Del. to Org. for Econ. Co-operation and Devt. (OECD) 61-65; Chief Insp. of Ministry of Foreign Affairs and Offices Abroad 65-.
Ministry of Foreign Affairs, Rome, Italy.
Telephone: N. 399-608.

Carvalho, Flavio de Rezende; Brazilian civil engineer, writer, architect and painter; b. 99; ed. Escola Americana (São Paulo, Brazil), Lycée Janson de Sailly, Paris, Durham Univ., and King Edward VII School of Fine Arts, Newcastle.
Civil engineer in São Paulo; innovator of modern architecture style in Brazil with design for new Government Palace 27; founder and Dir. Teatro da Experiencia 32-33; Pres. Club des Artistas Modernos 32; mem. New York Acad. of Sciences, Fellow Int. Inst. of Arts and Letters; mem. Inst. of Engineers, São Paulo, and

Inst of Architects of Brazil; hon. mem. Inst. of Psychotechnics of Prague; Chevalier Commdr. Order of Saint Hubert; prizes for sculpture and architecture 32, 39, 52, 59; Gold Medal, São Paulo Bienal and at Salaõ Paulista de Arte Moderna, São Paulo; special room at VII Bienal, São Paulo; Int. Prize at IX Bienal, São Paulo; has exhibited paintings in Brazil, London, Chile, Prague, Rome, Paris, and has paintings in Gallery of Modern Art, Rome, Museums of Modern Art of Paris, Rio, São Paulo, Bahia and New York, Museum of Art, São Paulo, Museum of Contemporary Art, São Paulo, Perm. room at Museum of Brazilian Art, São Paulo, Pushkin Museum of Fine Arts, Moscow, Museum of Manáus; designs clothes theatrical costumes and scenery.
Publs. *Experiencia No. 2, Os Ossos do Mundo, l'Aspect Psychologique et Morbide de l'Art Moderne* 37, *The City of Naked Man* 30, *The House of the XXth Century Man* 37, *Ballet of Dead God* (play 33), *Dialectics of Fashion* 56, *Notes for the Reconstruction of a Lost World* 57, 62.
Fazenda Capuava, Valinhos, E. de São Paulo, and Av. Ipiranga 81 ap. 1608, São Paulo 4, Brazil.

Carvalho, José Candido de Melo, M.SC., PH.D.; Brazilian zoologist and entomologist; b. 11 June 1914; ed. Escola Superior de Agricultura e Veterinaria, Viçosa, Univ. of Nebraska, and Iowa Univ. of Science and Technology.
Professor of Biology and Zoology, Viçosa 42-46; Zoologist, Museu Nacional, Rio de Janeiro 46-, Dir. of Museu Nacional 55-61; Dir. Museu Goeldi, Belém 54-55; Vice-Pres. Nat. Research Council, Brazil 62-63; mem. Exec. Board Int. Union for Conservation of Nature 63-; Pres. Asscn. for Tropical Biology 65-66; Prof. Nat. Coll. of Geology, Rio de Janeiro 60-; mem. Council, Univ. of Brazil 55-61, Nat. Council for Protection of Indians 55-58, Council for Nat. Culture 59-60; mem. Perm. Cttee. Int. Congress on Entomology 52-, Latin American Congresses on Zoology 62-; mem. Brazilian Acad. of Sciences, Vice-Pres. 55-56; John Simon Guggenheim Fellow 54-55; British Council Fellow 51; Corresp. mem. Zoological Soc. of London; carried out twelve expeditions to Hyléa (Amazonas); Pres. Brazilian Foundation for Nature Conservation 66-; Hon. mem. Mexican Inst. Nat. Research 67-; Fellow Agra Zoological Soc. 64-.
Publs. *Notas de Viagem ao Rio Negro* 52, *Notas de Viagem ao Javari-Itacoai-Jurua* 55, *Notas de Viagem ao Paru de Leste* 55, *Key to the Genera of Miridae of the World* 55, *Insects of Micronesia (Miridae)* 56, *Catalogue of the Miridae of the World* (5 vols.) 57-60, *The Miridae of Galapagos* 67.
Museu Nacional, Quinta da Boa Vista, Rio de Janeiro, Brazil.
Telephone: 48-6794.

Carver, David Dove, O.B.E. British secretary-general; b. 10 Aug. 1903; ed. Emanuel School, London.
Business exec. for short time; then studied singing (baritone) under Alfred Morelli, Carlotta da Feo, Rheinhold Von Warlich and John Goss; also studied composition; later gave recitals mainly of German lieder and English folk songs in U.K. and U.S.A.; R.A.F.V.R. 40-45; founded and directed Singers in Consort (male voice quintet specializing in 16th- and 17th-century music); Hon. Treas. English Centre P.E.N. and Int. P.E.N. 48-; Sec.-Gen. Int. P.E.N. 51-; Sec. P.E.N. Writers in Prison Cttee. 60; Dir. Int. Writers Fund 60; Chair. of Govs. Anglo-American Coll.; Registrar and mem. Council Royal Literary Fund.
International P.E.N., Glebe House, Chelsea, London, S.W.3; Homes: 2 Elsworthy Terrace, London N.W.3, and 2 The Knapp, Bishops Lydeard, Somerset, England.

Cary, William Lucius, A.B., LL.B., M.B.A.; American university professor, lawyer and government official; b. 27 Nov. 1910; ed. Yale and Harvard Univs.
Admitted Ohio Bar 34, law practice 34-36; Securities &

Exchange Comm. 38-40, Dept. of Justice 40-42, Office of Co-ordinator of Inter-American Affairs, Rio de Janeiro 42; Dir. Newark Telephone Co. 36-; Lecturer, Finance and Law, Harvard Graduate School of Business Admin. 46-47; Prof. Law Northwestern Univ. School of Law 47-55, Columbia Univ. 55-61, Dwight Prof. of Law, Columbia Univ. 64-; Chair. Securities and Exchange Comm. 61-64; Democrat.
Publs. *The Effect of Taxation on Corporate Mergers* 51, *Cases and Materials on Corporations* 59, *Politics and the Regulatory Agencies* 67.
Columbia University School of Law, New York City 10027, N.Y., U.S.A.

Casa-Debeljevic, Lisa Della; Swiss singer; ed. Berne Conservatoire.
Début at Zürich Opera House 43; mem. Vienna State Opera Co. 47-, New York Metropolitan Opera Co. 53-; has appeared at Festivals at Salzburg 47, 48, 50, 53-58, Glyndebourne 51, Bayreuth, Edinburgh 52, Zürich, Lucerne, Munich 51-58; has also appeared in London, Berlin, Paris, Milan, San Francisco and in South America, etc.; apptd. Austrian State Kammersängerin.
Schloss Gottlieben, Thurgau, Switzerland.

Casadesus, Robert; French concert pianist and composer; b. 7 April 1899; ed. Conservatoire, Paris.
Began concert career 20; has toured Europe, U.S.S.R., South America, U.S.A. and Canada; Dir.-Gen. Fontainebleau American Conservatory, Fontainebleau 55-; Commdr. Légion d'Honneur, Commdr. Order of Orange-Nassau, Officer Order of Leopold; Prix Diemer 20; Grand Prix du Disque 55.
Works include: 24 Preludes for Piano, 4 Piano Sonatas, 2 Piano and Violin Sonatas, 5 Symphonies, 7 Concertos for Piano and Orchestra, and *Danses Méditerranéennes*.
Lawrenceville Road, Princeton, N.J., U.S.A.

Casal, Jorje Emilio; Argentine architect and diplomatist; b. 5 May 1921; ed. Universidad de Buenos Aires.
Diplomatic Service 46-, served Spain, France, Switzerland, Nicaragua, Chile and Venezuela; Secr. of Deputy Minister and Minister of Foreign Affairs 57-60; Head, Admin. Secr. of Minister of Foreign Affairs 62-64; Counsellor-Minister, U.S.S.R. 64-66, Amb. Oct. 66-.
Embassy of Argentina, Ul. Lunacharskovo 8, Moscow, U.S.S.R.

Casals, Pablo; Spanish violoncellist; b. 29 Dec. 1876; ed. Municipal School of Music, Barcelona, and Madrid Conservatoire.
Composer and Conductor; made début in England 98; Conductor Pau Casals Symphony Orchestra, Barcelona; Dr. h.c. Edinburgh 34, Barcelona 39; Hon. Citizen Madrid, Barcelona; hon. mem. Spanish Acad. 35; corresp. mem. Hispanic Society, New York; Beethoven gold medal 12; hon. mem. Royal Philharmonic Society; F.R.C.M. 37; Gold Medal of Worshipful Co. of Musicians London 37; hon. mem. Gesellschaft der Musikfreunde, Vienna 30, and of Accad. de Sta. Cecilia, Rome, etc.; numerous decorations and hon. degrees; U.S. Presidential Medal of Freedom 63.
Publs. Symphonic and choral works, chamber music.
Route de Ria, Prades, Pyrénées Orientales, France.

Casardi, Alberico; Italian diplomatist; b. 03.
Diplomatic Service 27-, New York, Lima, London, Berlin, Buenos Aires, UN; fmr. Dep. Sec.-Gen. of NATO, Paris; Ambassador to Belgium 63-65; Ambassador to Japan 65-.
Italian Embassy, Tokyo, Japan.

Case, Clifford Philip, A.B., LL.B., HON. LL.D.; American lawyer and politician; b. 16 April 1904; ed. Rutgers and Columbia Univs.
Assoc. Simpson Thacher and Bartlett, New York 28-39, mem. firm 39-53; mem. Rahway (N.J.) Common Council 38-42; mem. House of Assembly of N.J. 43 and 44; mem. 79th-83rd U.S. Congresses, resigned 53; Pres.

and Dir. of the Fund for the Republic 53-54; Republican Senator from New Jersey 54-; mem. N.Y. Bar 28-; Liberty Magazine Award as outstanding mem. 82nd Congress; N.J. Society for Crippled Children and Adults (Board of Dirs.); mem. Advisory Board N.J. Chapter, Arthritis and Rheumatism Foundation, Rahway (N.J.) Red Cross (Trustee); mem. Council of Foreign Relations, Board of Trustees, Roper Public Opinion Research Center; mem. Bar Asscn., City of N.Y., N.Y. County, N.Y. State, and American Bar Asscns.; mem. American Judicature Soc.; Hon LL.D. from seven U.S. Colls. and Univs.
463 Senate Office Building, Washington, D.C.; Home: 191 West Milton Avenue, Rahway, N.J., U.S.A. Telephone: 202-225-3225 (Office).

Case, Everett Needham, B.A., M.A.; American foundation executive; b. 9 April 1901; ed. Princeton Univ., Corpus Christi Coll., Cambridge, and Harvard Univ.
Assistant in History, Harvard Univ. 26-27; Asst. to Owen D. Young 27-33; Exec. Sec. Central Banking and Industrial Cttee., Washington D.C. 32-33; Asst. Dean, Harvard Graduate School of Business Admin. 39-42; Pres. Colgate Univ. 42-62, Emer. 62-; Consultant on Far Eastern Affairs to Sec. of State 49; Chair. American Council on Educ. 51-52; Pres. Alfred P. Sloan Foundation 62-68; Dir. Fed. Reserve Bank of New York 61-, Chair. 66-; Dir. National Educational Television, 54-61; 62- (Chair. 63-); Trustee, Memorial Sloan-Kettering Cancer Center 63-68, Sloan-Kettering Inst. for Cancer Research 66-68, Millbrook School 44- (Chair. 60-68), Educational Broadcasting Corpn. 65-; mem. Council on Foreign Relations, UNA-U.S.A. China Panel 66-; several hon. degrees.
Van Hornesville, Herkimer County, N.Y. 13475, U.S.A. Telephone: 315-858-0036.

Casey, Baron (Life Peer, cr. 60) of Berwick (Victoria) and the City of Westminister; **Richard G. Casey,** P.C., G.C.M.G., C.H., D.S.O., M.C., K.ST.J.; Australian politician and diplomatist; b. 29 Aug. 1890; ed. Melbourne and Cambridge Univs.
Political Liaison Officer between British and Australian Govts. in London 24-30; mem. Federal Parliament 31-40, 49-60; Asst. Treas. to Commonwealth Govt. 33-35; Treas. of the Commonwealth 35-39, and Min. of Development 37-39; Privy Councillor 39; Min. for Supply and Development 39-40; resgnd. from Parl. and Cabinet on appointment as first Min. to U.S.A. 40-42; British Min. of State Resident in Middle East 42-44; Gov. of Bengal 44-46; Federal Pres. Liberal Party of Australia 47-49; Minister of Supply 49; Minister in Charge of C.S.I.R.O. 49-60; Minister of Nat. Development 50; Minister for External Affairs 51-60; mem. Exec. C.S.I.R.O. 60-65; Gov.-Gen. Australia 65-.
Publs. *An Australian in India* 46, *Double or Quit* 49, *Friends and Neighbours* 54, *Australian Foreign Policy* 54, *Personal Experience 39-46* 62, *The Future of the Commonwealth* 63, *Australian Father and Son* 66.
Government House, Canberra, A.C.T., Australia.

Caskey, John L., PH.D.; American classical archaeologist; b. 7 Dec. 1908; ed. Yale Univ. and Univ. of Cincinnati.
Teaching fellow, acting instructor, and mem. of staff of Univ. of Cincinnati Excavations at Troy 32-38; Instructor, Asst. Prof. Univ. of Cincinnati 39-48; U.S. Army 42-46; Asst. Dir. American School of Classical Studies, Athens 48-49, Dir. 49-59, Vice-Chair. Man. Cttee. 65-; Prof. of Classical Archaeology and Head, Dept. of Classics, Univ. of Cincinnati 59-, Fellow of Graduate School; Field Dir. Excavations at Lerna 52-58, in Ceos 60-; mem. Inst. for Advanced Study 60, 65; mem. American Philosophical Society 67-; Legion of Merit (U.S.A.); Commdr. Order of the Phoenix (Greece); Hon. Citizen of Athens.
Publs. *Troy* (co-editor and co-author) Vols. I-IV,

Preliminary Reports on Excavations at Lerna 54-59, *The Early Helladic Period in the Argolid* 60, *Preliminary Reports on Excavations in Ceos* 60-64; contrib. to *Cambridge Ancient History* vols. I and II, new edn. 64, 65.
Department of Classics, University of Cincinnati, Ohio 45221, U.S.A.
Telephone: Cincinnati 475-2571.

Caso y Andrade, Alfonso, PH.D.; Mexican archaeologist; b. 10 Feb. 1896; ed. Nat. Univ. of Mexico.
Prof. Faculty of Letters 18-40, School of Law 19-29; Dir. Nat. Preparatory School 28; Head of Dept. of Archæology Nat. Museum 30-33, Dir. Nat. Museum 33-34, Explorations, Monte Albán, Oax. 31-43; Dir.-Gen. of Higher Education and Scientific Research Mar.-Aug. 44; Rector of Nat. Autonomous Univ. of Mexico Aug. 44-Mar. 45; Sec. of State in the Office of Nat. Estates and Admin. Inspection Dec. 46-; Dir. Nat. Inst. for Indian Affairs 49-; Hon. mem. New York Acad. of Sciences, American Acad. of Arts and Sciences, Deutsche Gesellschaft für Völkerkunde, Academia Mexicana de la Historia; corresp. Academician Nat. Acad. of Arts and Letters, Cuba, etc.; Officier de la Légion d'Honneur (France), Commdr. Order of North Star (Sweden), etc.; Hon. Ph.D. (Albuquerque, N. Mexico).
Publs. *El Teocali de la Guerra Sagrada* 27, *Las Estelas Zapotecas* 28, *Las exploraciones de Monte Albán, Oaxaca* 32-34, *Exploraciones en Mitla* 34, *Urnas de Oaxaca* 52, *The Aztecs: People of the Sun* 58, *Interpretación del Códice Bodley* 2858 60, *Interpretación del Códice Selden* 3135 (A.2), *Interpretación Códice Colombino*, *La Cerámica de Monte Albán, Lys Calendaries Prehispánicos.*
Av. Central 234, Tlacopac, Villa Obregón, D.F., Zona 20, Mexico.

Cassels, Field Marshal Sir (Archibald) James (Halkett), G.C.B., K.B.E., D.S.O.; British army officer; b. 28 Feb. 1907; ed. Rugby School and Royal Military Coll., Sandhurst.
Commissioned 26; served Second World War, G.O.C. 51st Highland Div. 45, G.O.C. 6th Airborne 46; G.O.C. 1st British Commonwealth Div., Korea 51-52; Dir.-Gen. of Military Training, War Office 54-57; Dir. of Operations, Malaya 57-59; G.O.C.-in-C. Eastern Command 59; C.-in-C. British Army of the Rhine and Commr. NATO Northern Army Group 60-63; Adjutant-General to the Forces 63-65; Chief of General Staff 65-68.
c/o Lloyds Bank Ltd., 6 Pall Mall, London, S.W.1, England.

Cassin, René, LL.D.; French jurist; b. 5 Oct. 1887.
Member Constituent Council, Pres. European Court of Human Rights; fmr. Pres. Union Fédérale des Mutilés et Anciens Combattants; Founder Int. Confed. of Wounded (CIAMAC); Del. L.N. Assemblies 24-38; mem. L.N. Preparatory Cttee. for the Int. Relief Union; Del. to Gen. Conf. for limitation and reduction of armaments 32-33; Pres. French Cttee. of Action for the L.N.; Perm. Sec. Gen. de Gaulle's Council of Defence of the Empire 40-44; Nat. Commr. for Justice and Public Education, London 41-43; Pres. French Cttee. of Legal Questions (Algiers) 44; Vice Pres. Council of State 44-60; French Del. Comm. of Enquiry into War Crimes 43-45; mem. various educational (including UNESCO) Cttees. 42-45; Del UN 46, 48, 50, 51 and UNESCO Assemblies 45-46, 58-60; mem. and fmr. Pres. Human Rights Comm. of UN 46-68 (principal author of *Universal Declaration of the Rights of Man* 48); mem. and fmr. Pres. Acad. Moral and Political Sciences 49-; fmr. Pres. Superior Arbitration Court 50-60; fmr. Prof. Hague Acad. of Int. Law; Hon. mem. Council of State; Hon. Prof. of Law Paris Univ.; Pres. Soc. of Comparative Law 52-55; Pres. Int. Inst. of Administrative Sciences 53-56; Pres. Inst. for Int. Studies; Pres. of Universal Israelite Alliance; Hon. D.C.L. (Oxford, Mainz).

Publs. *Law on Contracts, Inheritance and Family, International Law and Relations, Domicile, Status of Companies in France, The Council of State, The League of Nations, The United Nations, Human Rights,* etc.
36 quai de Béthune, Paris 4e, France.

Cassirer, Henry R., B.A., PH.D.; American radio and television administrator; b. 2 Sept. 1911; ed. Univs. of Frankfurt, Paris, Cologne and London Univ.
Announcer/translator, B.B.C. European Service 38-40; Foreign News Editor, Columbia Broadcasting System (C.B.S.), New York 40-44; Television News Editor, C.B.S. 44-49; freelance producer of TV documentary programmes 49-52; teacher of TV Production and Public Affairs Programming, New School for Social Research, New York Univ. School of Radio Techniques Div., UNESCO 52-, Chief, Educational Uses of Mass Media; Adviser on Educational TV to Govt. of India 57-, Pakistan 60-, Israel 61-, Senegal 63-, Brazil 67-.
Publs. *Television, a World Survey* 54, *Television Teaching Today* 60; films: *Man of our Age—The Sculpture of Jo Davidson* 48, *Buma-African Sculpture Speaks* 52, *Television Comes to the Land* 58.
UNESCO, 7 and 9 place de Fontenoy, Paris 7e; Home: 6 rue de l'Abbaye, 92 Meudon, France.

Cassola, Carlo; Italian writer; b. 17 March 1917.
Strega Prize 60.
Publs. *La Visita* (short stories) 42, *Fausto e Anna* (novel) 52, *Il Taglio del Bosco* (short stories) 59, *La Ragazza di Bube* (novel) 60, *Un Cuore Arido* (novel) 61, *Il Cacciatore* (novel) 64, *Tempi Memorabili* (novel) 66, *Ferrovia Locale* (novel) 68.
Via Michelangelo 12, Grosseto, Italy.

Casson, Sir Hugh Maxwell, Kt., M.A., A.R.A., F.R.I.B.A., R.D.I., HON. DES. R.C.A.; British architect; b. 23 May 1910; ed. Eastbourne Coll., St. John's Coll., Cambridge, and Bartlett School of Architecture, Univ. Coll., London.
Private practice as architect 35-; Camouflage Officer in Air Ministry 40-44; Technical Officer Ministry of Town and Country Planning 44-46; Dir. of Architecture, Festival of Britain 51; mem. MARS Group 45-; Prof. of Interior Design, Royal Coll. of Art 53; mem. Royal Danish Acad. 54, Royal Fine Art Comm. 60.
Publs. *Houses: Permanence and Prefabrication* (with Anthony Chitty) 45, *Homes by the Million* 45, *Bombed Churches as War Memorials* 44, *An Introduction to Victorian Architecture* 48.
Office: 35 Thurloe Place, London, S.W.7; Home: 35 Victoria Road, London, W.8, England.

Casson, Sir Lewis, Kt., M.C.; British actor and theatrical producer; b. 26 Oct. 1875; ed. Ruthin Grammar School.
Began stage career 1900; acted in numerous theatres throughout Great Britain, often with his wife Dame Sybil Thorndike, q.v.; produced *Henry V, Henry VIII, Macbeth, King Lear,* etc.; many tours in British Commonwealth, Europe and Middle East; recent activities include tour of *The Chalk Garden* (Australia and New Zealand) 57-58, *Eighty in the Shade* (London) 59, *Waiting in the Wings* 60-61, *Teresa of Avila* 61, Chichester Festival Theatre 62, *Arsenic and Old Lace* 66; Pres. British Actors' Equity 41-45; Drama Dir. Council for the Encouragement of Music and the Arts 42-44; mem. Arts Council of Great Britain 45-47; Fellow Imperial Coll. of Science and Technology; Hon. LL.D. Univs. of Glasgow, Oxford and Wales.
98 Swan Court, London, S.W.3, England.

Cassou, Jean, L. ès L.; French writer; b. 9 July 1897; ed. Univ. de Paris à la Sorbonne.
Secretary, *Mercure de France* 20, later Editor at Ministry of Public Instruction; on personal staff of Minister of Nat. Educ. and Fine Arts 36; Asst. Keeper, Musée du Luxembourg 38; forced to retire and later imprisoned by Vichy régime 40, later fought in re-

sistance and seriously wounded 44; Head Keeper, Musée Nat. d'Art Moderne 45-65; now Dir. of Studies, Ecole Pratique des Hautes Etudes; mem. Acad. Royale de langue et littérature françaises de Belgique; Compagnon de la Libération, Commdr. Légion d'Honneur, Croix de Guerre 39-45.

Publs. Novels include: *Les Harmonies Viennoises* 25, *Les Massacres de Paris* 36; Essays include: *Grandeur et Infamie de Tolstoi* 32, *Parti pris* 53; Poetry includes: *Trente-trois sonnets composés au secret* 44; Art criticism includes: *Picasso* 39, *Ingres* 47, *Situation de l'Art Moderne* 51.

4 rue du Cardinal-Lemoine, Paris, 5e, France.

Castán Tobeñas, José; Spanish lawyer; b. 89; ed. Univs. of Saragossa and Madrid.

Sometime Prof. of Civil Law in Univs. of Murcia, Barcelona, Valencia and Saragossa; fmr. Dir. of the Escuela Social, Valencia, and fmr. Magistrate of the Supreme Court; Pres. of the Supreme Court 56-67; mem. Nat. Council of Spain; mem. of the Cortes; Pres. Gen. Comm. for the Codifying of Laws and Inst. of Procedural Law; Special Hon. Councillor, Council of Scientific Research (C.S.I.C.).

Publs. include: *La idea de equidad y su relación con otras ideas, morales y jurídicas, afines* 50, *La equidad y sus tipos históricos en la cultura occidental europea* 50, *Poder judicial e independencia judicial* 51, *Derechos de la personalidad* 53, *La formulación judicial del Derecho y el arbitrio de equidad* 53, *Juristas valencianos* 54.

Goya 46, Madrid, Spain.

Castberg, Frede, D.L.; Norwegian university professor; b. 4 July 1893; ed. Oslo Katedralskole and Oslo Univ.

Professor at Oslo Univ.; Rector 52-57; Legal Adviser to Min. of Foreign Affairs; Pres. Curatorium of the Acad. of Int. Law, Hague; mem. of the Inst. of Int. Law; hon. mem. Finnish Asscn. Lawyers; mem. of several scientific socs.; LL.D. St. Olafs Coll., Colgate Univ., U.S.A.; Dr. h.c. Univs. of Uppsala, Paris and Helsinki.

Publs. *Norges Statsforfatning* 35, *Folkerett* 37, *Innledning til Forvaltningsretten* 38, *Problems of Legal Philosophy* 39, *Norge under Okkupasjonen* 45, *Fra Norsk og Fremmed Statsliv* 46, *Studier i Folkerett* 52, *Freedom of Speech in the West* 60, *Forelesninger over rettsfilosofi* 65.

Holmenkollveien 16, Smestad pr. Oslo, Norway.

Telephone: 699551.

Castel Borja, Jacinto, LL.M., D.C.L.; Philippine lawyer and diplomatist; b. 05; ed. High School and Coll., Silliman Univ., Univ. of the Philippines, and Columbia Univ., New York.

Former Official, Dept. of Foreign Affairs; fmr. Gov. of Bohol; Professorial Law Lecturer; mem. Liberal Party 47-; mem. Exec. Cttee.; Perm. Rep. of Philippines to UN 62-64; Pres. UN Security Council Sept. 64; Pres. Foreign Affairs Asscn. of the Philippines 58-61; several medals.

c/o Ministry of Foreign Affairs, Manila, Philippines.

Castellani, Marchese Aldo, Conte di Chisimaio, D.S.C., M.D., F.R.C.P., F.A.C.P.; Italian physician; b. 77; ed. Florence and Bonn Univs., London School of Tropical Medicine.

Sent by British Foreign Office and Royal Soc. 02 to investigate Sleeping Sickness in Uganda, discovered causative organism; devised new serological methods (Castellani's absorption test, etc.); discovered the etiological agent of yaws (framboesia), several new fungi and bacteria; described new diseases (endemic funiculitis, broncho-pulmonary candiosis, tinea nigra, etc.); Prof. of Tropical Medicine Tulane Univ. of New Orleans and later Louisiana State Univ. Medical School; Dir. of Mycology, London School of Hygiene and Tropical Medicine; Prof. School of Tropical Medicine and Dir. Clinic for Tropical Diseases Univ. of Rome to July 46; Chief Consultant and Surgeon-Gen. Italian Forces in Ethiopia 35-36; Physician

to King George of Greece, to Prince Amedeo of Savoy; Medical Adviser to Italian High Command 42; Physician to King Umberto 39- (in exile 46-); Prof. Inst. of Tropical Diseases, Lisbon 47-; Senator 28-46; Fellow, Accademia dei Lincei and Pontifical Acad. of Sciences; Grand Cross, Sts. Maurice and Lazarus, Order of Crown of Italy and numerous foreign decorations.

Publs. *Manual of Tropical Medicine* (with A. J. Chalmers), *Fungi and Fungous Diseases, Climate and Acclimatization, Manuale di Clinica Tropicale* (with Jacono) 37, *Malattie dell' Africa* 46, *Little Known Tropical Diseases* 54, *Ulcérations de la Jambe* 58, *Microbes, Men and Monarchs* 60, 63, 65.

Instituto de Medicina Tropical, Junqueira, Lisbon; and Villa Azzurra, Rua Conde Ferreira, Cascais, Portugal.

Castellanos, Rosario; Mexican writer; b. 1915; ed. Universidad Nacional Autónoma de Mexico.

Spent childhood in Chiapas; made study of position of women in Mexico during scholarship year at Mexican Writing Centre; fmr. Dir. of Information at Nat. Univ. of Mexico.

Publs. include two plays, short stories and novels *Balún Canán* and *Oficio de Tinieblas*.

c/o Universidad Nacional Autónoma de México, University City, Villa Obregón, Mexico City, Mexico.

Castiella y Maíz, Fernando María; Spanish diplomatist and politician; b. 07; ed. Univs. of Madrid, Paris, Cambridge and Geneva, Acad. of Int. Law, The Hague.

Prof. of Int. Law, Univ. of Madrid 39, Dean, Faculty of Political and Economic Sciences 44-48; mem. Permanent Tribunal of Int. Arbitration, The Hague 39; Dir. Inst. of Political Studies, Madrid 43-48; mem. State Council and Pres. Int. Affairs Comm. of the Cortes 44-48; Ambassador to Peru 48-51, to the Holy See 51-57; Minister of Foreign Affairs 57-; Knight Grand Cross Carlos III, Isabel la Católica, Sol del Peru, Malta, Piana (Holy See) and other decorations.

Publs. *Reivindicaciones de España, El problema internacional en la mente del Papa.*

Ministry of Foreign Affairs, Madrid, Spain; and Palacio de Viana, Duque de Rivas, 1, Madrid, Spain.

Castillero-Pimentel, Ernesto, LL.B., M.A., D.POL.SC.; Panamanian lawyer and diplomatist; b. 18; ed. Univ. of Panama, Johns Hopkins Univ. and Universidad Nacional del Litoral, Argentina.

Professor of Int. Relations of Panama, School of Diplomatic and Consular Service, Univ. of Panama 50-; Vice-Minister of Foreign Affairs 56-58; Acting Minister of Foreign Affairs 57; Ambassador to U.K. 62-63; Grand Cross of Nat. Orders of Panama, Argentina, China, Lebanon, Netherlands, Cuba, Paraguay and Brazil.

Publs. *Panamá y los Estados Unidos* 53, *Política Exterior de Panamá* 61.

Edificio Atalaya, Avda. Balboa, Panama, Republic of Panama.

Castillero Reyes, Ernesto de Jesús; Panamanian educationist and historian; ed. Nat. Inst. of Panama.

Primary School Teacher 13-17; Provincial Inspector of Public Instruction 17-22; Sec.-Gen. Inspectorate of Education 22-27; Sec. Nat. Inst. 27-33; Prof. of History Colegio de Artes y Oficios, Escuela Normal de Institutoras 36-40; Nat. Inst. 29-35; Insp.-Gen. of Education 36-40; Dir. Nat. Library of Panama 42-45; special Ambassador for Rep. of Honduras 57; Pres. Panama Acad. of History; Hon. Pres. Bolivarian Society; corresp. mem. Spanish and ten Latin American Acads. of History; mem. Ateneo Dominicano, U.S. Int. Acad. etc.; Dir. Panamanian Inst. of Hispanic Culture; Pres. Nat. Comm. on Historical Monuments; numerous decorations.

Publs. *Documentos históricos sobre la independencia del istmo de Panamá* 30, *La causa inmediata de la emancipación de Panamá, Historia de los orígenes, la formación*

y el rechazo por el Senado colombiano del Tratado Herrán Hay 33, *Breve curso de Historia del Comercio* 35, *El Profeta de Panamá y su gran tradición* 36, *Panamá: Breve historia de la República* 39, *Galería de Presidentes de Panamá* 36, 53, *Historia de la Comunicación Interoceánica y de su influencia en el desarrollo de la entidad nacional panameña* 43, *La universidad interamericana: Historia de sus antecedentes y fundación* 43, *Historia de los Símbolos de la patria panameña* 47, *Leyendas e Historias de Panamá la Vieja* 50, *El General José Domingo Espinar* 51, *Historia de Panamá* 55, *Gonzalo Fernández de Oviedo* 57, *Episodios de la independencia de Panamá* 58, *Intimidades del Congreso de Panamá de 1826* 61, *La Isla que se transformó en Ciudad* 62, *El Canal de Panamá* 64, *Breve Historia de la Iglesia panameña* 65, *Lecciones de Historia Patria* 67.
Calle 31, 4-23 Panama City, Republic of Panama.

Castillo Yurrita, Alberto del, DR. HIST.; Spanish university professor; b. 99; ed. Univs. of Barcelona, Paris, London, Berlin, Munich and Bologna.
Prof. Medieval History, Univ. of Barcelona 31-; Art Critic 39; Cultural Attaché, Spanish Embassy, Paris 44-45; Curator, Archaeological Museum, Barcelona 31-65; Dir. Spanish Inst. of Mediterranean Studies 42-; Dir. Romantic Provincial Museum 49; Vice-Editor *Diario de Barcelona* 53-; Vice-Pres. Spanish Asscn. of Art Critics 62; Spanish Delegate at European Council for Modern Art 67; Hon. Archaeological Inspector, Barcelona province.
Publs. include: *La Cultura del Vaso Campaniforme* 29, *Historia General* (3 vols.) 41, *Barcelona a traves de los tiempos* 42, *De la Puerta del Angel a la Plaza de Lesseps* 43, *El Neolítico y el Eneolítico de la Península Ibérica* 43, *Cronología del Vaso Campaniforma en Europa* 44; *José María Sert: Su vida y su obra* 46, *Estética del Arte Paleolítico* 53, *La Maquinista Terrestre y Marítima, personaje histórico* 55, *La Barcelona de Menéndez y Pelayo (1871-1873)* 56, *Ramón Casas y su época* 58, *Lasar Segall* 58, (with M. Riu) *Historia del Transporte Colectivo en Barcelona (1872-1959)* 59, *Narciso Monturiol, inventor del Ictineo (1819-1885)* 63, *Historia de la Asociación de Ingenieros Industriales de Barcelona (1863-1963)* 63, *El manso medieval A de Vilosiu* 65.
Mallorca 305, Barcelona, Spain.
Telephone: 257-93-54.

Castle, Rt. Hon. Barbara Anne, P.C., B.A., M.P.; British politician; b. 6 Oct. 1911; ed. Bradford Girls' Grammar School, St. Hugh's Coll., Oxford Univ.
Admin. Officer, Ministry of Food 41-44; Corresp. for *Daily Mirror* 44-45; M.P. 45-; mem. St. Pancras Borough Council, London 37-45, Metropolitan Water Board 40-45, Nat. Exec. Cttee. of Labour Party 49-; Chair. of Labour Party 58-59; Minister of Overseas Development 64-65, Transport 65-68; First Sec. of State and Sec. of State for Employment and Productivity April 68-.
House of Commons, London, S.W.1; Home: 74 Woodlands, London, N.W.11, England.

Castle, William Bosworth, M.D.; American physician; b. 21 Oct. 1897; ed. Harvard.
Professor of Medicine, Harvard Univ. 37-57; George R. Minot Prof. of Medicine 57-63; Dir. Thorndike Laboratory Boston City Hospital 48-63, Hon. Dir. 63-68; Francis W. Peabody Faculty Prof. of Medicine, Harvard Univ. 63-68; John Phillips Memorial Prize 32, Proctor Award, Philadelphia Coll. of Pharmacy and Science 35, Walter Reed Medal, American Soc. of Tropical Medicine 39, and Mead, Johnson and Co. Award 50, for discovery of gastric intrinsic factor and its relation to vitamin B12 deficiency in pernicious anæmia, etc.; Hon. D.Sc. (Harvard), Hon. LL.D. (Jefferson), Hon. S.M. (Yale), Hon. M.D. (Utrecht), Hon. S.D. (Chicago), Kober Medal of the Asscn. of American Physicians 62, John M. Russell Award of the Markle Scholars 64; Hon.

L.H.D. Boston Coll. 66; Oscar B. Hunter Memorial Award of the American Therapeutic Soc.; Joseph Goldberger Award for Clinical Nutrition.
Boston City Hospital, Boston, 18, Mass, U.S.A.; and 22 Irving St., Brookline, Mass., U.S.A.
Telephone: Lo6-2676 (Home).

Castro, Almir de, M.D., M.SC.; Brazilian public administrator; b. 4 Dec. 1910; ed. Univ. do Brasil, Instituto Oswaldo Cruz and Johns Hopkins Univ.
Assistant Prof. Nat. Faculty of Medicine 32-36, 42-45; Health Officer, Civil Service 36-66; Federal Health Del. in N.E. Brazil 38-40; Public Health Teacher 38-46; Dir. Nat. Anti-Plague Service 42-54; Exec. Dir. C.A.P.E.S. (Nat. Campaign for Further Training of Upper-level Personnel) 54-64; acting Pres. Brazilian Centre for Physical Research 63-64; Vice-Rector Univ. of Brasilia 64-65; Assoc. Exec. Dir., Museum of Modern Art, Rio de Janeiro 66-67, Chief Consultant, Brazilian Soc. for Educ., Rio de Janeiro 67-.
Rua Assis Brasil 57, apto. 1002, Copacabana, Rio de Janeiro, Guanabara, Brazil.

Castro, Ferreira de; Portuguese writer; b. 98.
Publs. *Emigrantes* 28, *A Selva* (trans. into 18 languages) 30, *Eternidade* 33, *Terra Fria* 34, *Pequeños Mundos* 37, *A Tempestade* 40, *A Volta ao Mundo* 42, *Lã e Neve* 47 (trans. into 11 languages), *A curva da estrada* 49, *A missão* 54, *As Maravilhas Artisticas do Mundo* 58, *O Instinto Supremo* 68.
Rua da Misericordia 68, Lisbon, Portugal.

Castro, Josué de; Brazilian nutritionist; b. 5 Sept. 1908.
Professor of Human Geography, School of Sciences and Philosophy, Univ. Fed. do Rio de Janeiro 39-, Dir. Inst. of Nutrition; Head, Nat. Technical Bureau on Food 42-44; Chair. of Council, Food and Agriculture Org. of UN (FAO) 52-56; Pres. World Asscn. of Struggle Against Hunger; Chair. Govt. Cttee. of Freedom from Hunger Campaign, UN 60; Chair. Council of Intergovernmental Cttee. for European Migrations (ICEM) 63; mem. Brazilian Parl. 55-63; Vice-Chair. World Parl. Asscn.; Pres. Int. Centre for Devt., Paris; fmr. Ambassador to European Office of UN, Geneva; Officier Légion d'Honneur; Great Medal, City of Paris; Int. Peace Prize, World Peace Council; and other awards.
Publs. include *Geography of Hunger*.
Universidade Federal do Rio de Janeiro, Avenida Pasteur 250, Rio de Janeiro, Brazil.

Castro, Raul H., A.B., LL.B.; American (b. Mexican) lawyer and diplomatist; b. 12 June 1916; ed. Arizona State Coll., Flagstaff, and Univ. of Arizona, Tucson.
Former owner and operator Castro Pony Farm, Tucson, Arizona; in U.S. Foreign Service in Mexico 41-46; Spanish Instructor, Univ. of Arizona 46-49; Senior Partner law firm Castro and Wolfe 49-52; Deputy District Attorney, Pima County, Arizona 52-54, District Attorney 54-58; Judge of Superior Court, Arizona 59-61, Presiding Judge, Juvenile Court 63-64; Amb. to El Salvador 64-; Hon. S.J.D. N. Arizona Univ.
American Embassy, San Salvador. El Salvador.
Telephone: 25-17-70.

Castro Beeche, Ricardo; Costa Rican advocate and journalist; b. 94; ed. Escuela de Derecho, San José.
Consul-General, New York 15; mem. of Congress 24, 30-36; Private Sec. to Pres. of Republic 24; Pres. of Congress 35; Minister of Foreign Affairs 27; Dir. and Man. *Diario de Costa Rica* 28-34; Ambassador to U.S.A. and Mexico 36-40; Man. *La Nación* 46-50, Gen. Man. and Dir. 50-; Presiding Dir. Inst. Nacional de Seguros 50-52; Special Ambassador to Mexico and Panama 51-53; perm. mem. Consultative Council and Management Board, Soc. Inter-Americana de Prensa (Pres. 60-61).
La Nación, San José, Costa Rica.

Castro Jijón, Rear Admiral Ramón; Ecuadorean naval officer and politician; b. 15.
Studied naval engineering in United States; fmr. Naval Attaché, London; C. in C. of Navy, Ecuador; Pres. Military Junta July 63-66; in exile 66-.
Rio de Janeiro, Brazil.

Castro Ruz, Fidel, D.IUR.; Cuban lawyer and politician; b. 13 Aug. 1927; ed. Jesuit schools at Santiago and Havana, Havana Univ.
Law practice in Havana; began active opposition to Batista régime by attack on Moncada barracks at Santiago 26th July 53; sentenced to 15 years imprisonment 53; amnestied 56; went into exile in Mexico and began to organise armed rebellion; landed in Oriente Province with small force 2nd Dec. 56; carried on armed struggle against Batista régime until flight of Batista Jan. 59; Prime Minister of Cuba Feb. 59-; Chair. Agrarian Reform Inst. 65-; First Sec. Partido Unido de la Revolución Socialista (P.U.R.S.) 63-65, Partido Comunista 65-; Lenin Peace Prize 61; Hero of the Soviet Union 63.
Publ. *Ten Years of Revolution* 64.
Palacio del Gobierno, Havana, Cuba.

Castro Ruz, Raúl; Cuban politician; ed. Jesuit schools.
Younger brother of Fidel Castro; sentenced with him to fifteen years imprisonment for insurrection 53; amnestied 54; assisted his brother's movement in Mexico, and in Cuba after Dec. 56; Chief of the Armed Forces Feb. 59; Deputy Prime Minister and Minister of the Armed Forces 60-.
Ministry of the Armed Forces, Havana, Cuba.

Catalano, Nicola, D.IUR.; Italian lawyer; b. 17 Feb. 1910; ed. Rome Univ.
Attorney 32-39; Asst. Rome Univ. 39-50; agent of Italian Govt. to Conciliation Cttees. set up by peace treaty 48-50; Legal Adviser, Int. Zone of Tangier 51-53; Legal Adviser, ECSC High Authority 53-56; Deputy Advocate-Gen. 55; legal adviser to Italian del. drawing up Treaties of Rome setting up European Economic Community and Euratom; Judge, Court of Justice of the European Communities 58-62; now Barrister.
Publs. Numerous legal works, including *La Comunità economica europea e l'Euratom* 57 (trans. into French 59), *Manuale di diritto delle Comunità Europee* 62 (French edn. 65, Spanish 66).
Lungotevere Flaminio 76, Rome, Italy.
Telephone: 303297.

Catalano di Melilli, Felice; Italian diplomatist; b. 24 Jan. 1914; ed. Univ. degli Studi, Florence.
Joined Diplomatic Service 38; Vice-Consul Jerusalem 39, Leipzig 41-43; Sec. Washington 45-52; at Ministry of Foreign Affairs 52-55, 58-59; Counsellor Athens 55-58; Acting Sec.-Gen. Ministry of Foreign Affairs 65-66; Amb. to the United Arab Republic 66-; numerous honours including Ordine al Merito della Repubblica Italiana, Grosses Deutschesverdienstkreuz.
Italian Embassy, Sharia Salamlik, Garden City, Cairo, United Arab Republic.

Catargi, Henri; Rumanian painter; b. 1894; ed. Académie Julian, Paris and Académie Ranson.
Chairman of the Plastic Fund 57-59; One-man exhbns. in Rumania, Paris, Brussels, Dresden, Moscow, Tokyo; represented in Venice Biennale 58; Merited Master of Arts 62, State prizewinner 62, People's Artist 64.
Major works include: *Landscape in Pasárea, The Braila Shipbuilding Yards, Vase with Flowers, Gathering Apples, Relaxation, Landscape in Ciurel.*
c/o Ministry of Culture, Bucharest, Rumania.

Cater, Douglass; American writer, editor and government official; b. 24 Aug. 1923; ed. Harvard Univ.
Washington Editor *The Reporter* (magazine) 50-63, Nat. Affairs Editor 63-64; Special Asst. to Pres. of

United States 64-; Special Asst. to Sec. of Army 51; Consultant to Dir. of Mutual Security Agency 52.
Publs. *Ethics in a Business Society* (with Marquis Childs) 53, *The Fourth Branch of Government* 59, *Power in Washington* 63.
The White House, Washington, D.C., U.S.A.

Catherwood, Henry Frederick Ross; British public official; b. 30 Jan. 1925; ed. Shrewsbury and Clare Coll., Cambridge.
Chartered Accountant 51; Sec. Laws Stores Ltd., Gateshead 52-54; Sec. and Controller, Richard Costain Ltd. 54-55, Chief Exec. 55-60; Asst. Man. Dir. British Aluminium Co. Ltd. 60-62, Man. Dir. 62-64; Chief Industrial Adviser, Dept. of Econ. Affairs 64-66; mem. Nat. Econ. Devt. Council (N.E.D.C.) 64-; Dir. Gen. 66-; mem. British Nat. Export Council 65-.
Publs. *The Christian in Industrial Society* 64, *Britain with the Brakes Off* 66.
25 Woodville Gardens, London, W.5, England.
Telephone: 01-997-4117.

Catledge, Turner, B.S.; American newspaperman; b. 17 March 1901; ed. Mississippi State Coll.
Employed *Neshoba* (Miss.) *Democrat* 21; Res. Editor *Tunica* (Miss.) *Times* 22-23; Man. Editor *Tupelo* (Miss.) *Journal* 23; reporter *Memphis* (Tenn.) *Commercial Appeal* 23-27, *Baltimore* (Md.) *Sun* 27-29; City Staff *New York Times* 29, corresp. Washington Bureau 30-36, Chief Washington News Corresp. 36-41; Chief Corresp. *New York Times* 43-44, Exec. Man. Editor 50-51, Managing Editor 51-64, Exec. Editor 64-68, Vice-Pres. and Dir. 68-; Hon. D.Litt. (Washington and Lee Univ.), L.H.D. (South-western Univ.); Hon. D.Iur. (Kentucky Univ.) 57.
Publ. *The 168 Days* (with Joseph W. Alsop, Jnr.) 37.
Home: 120 East 81st Street, New York; Office: 229 West 43rd Street, New York, N.Y., U.S.A.

Catlin, George Edward Gordon, M.A., PH.D., F.R.S.L., F.R.S.A. (married to Vera Brittain, *q.v.*); British university professor, philosopher and political scientist; b. 29 July 1896; ed. New Coll., Oxford.
Professor of Politics, Cornell Univ. 24-35; candidate for Parl. 31 and 35; mem. of exec. of Fabian Society 35-37; mem. Int. Exec. Cttee., Int. Cttee. of Christian Socialist and Democratic Parties (Nouvelles Equipes Internationales) 48; Bronfman Prof. of Political Science and Chair. of Dept. of Econ. and Political Science. McGill Univ. 56-60, Emer. 60-; A pioneer of the idea of the Atlantic Community and draftsman of the Int. Declaration in support of Indian independence; Vice-Pres. World Acad. of Arts and Sciences (Israel); Tagore Centenary Lecturer (Royal Soc. Arts and Royal Soc. Literature) 61; Goethe Centenary Lecturer, Heidelberg Univ.; Lecturer, Bologna, Yale and Peking Univs.; Miembre de Honor, Instituto de Estudios Politicos, Spain 62; Grosses Verdienstkreuz, German Fed. Repub 64; Médaille de Vermeil, Société à l'Encouragement à Progrès (France).
Publs. *Thomas Hobbes* 21, *The Science and Method of Politics* 26, *Study of the Principles of Politics* 29, *Liquor Control* 31, *Preface to Action* 34, *New Trends in Socialism* (editor) 35, *Studies in War and Democracy* (editor) 37, *Durkheim's Rules of Sociological Method* (editor) 37, *The Anglo-Saxon Tradition* 39, *Story of the Political Philosophers* 39, *One Anglo-American Nation, The Foundation of Anglo-Saxony* 41, *Anglo-American Union as Nucleus of World Federation* 42, *The Unity of Europe* 44, *Above All Nations* (in collaboration) 45, *In the Path of Mahatma Gandhi* 48, *Political Goals* 57, *The Atlantic Community* 59, *Systematic Politics* 62, *Political and Sociological Theory and its Applications* 64, *The Grandeur of England and the Atlantic Community* 64, *Campaign* (autobiography) 68.
4 Whitehall Court, London, S.W.1; and Kingsgate Castle, Broadstairs, Kent, England.
Telephone: 01-839-5250.

Caton-Thompson, Gertrude, F.B.A.; British archaeologist; b. 88; ed. Miss Hawtrey's, Eastbourne, Paris and Newnham Coll. Cambridge (research).

Employed Ministry of Shipping 15-19; Paris Peace Conf. 19; Student British School of Archæology in Egypt 21-26; excavated at Abydos and Oxyrhynchos 21-22, Malta 21, 24, Qau and Badari 23-25, Northern Faiyum 24-26, 27-28, Zimbabwe and other Rhodesian sites 28-29, Kharga Oasis 30-33, Hadhramaut (Southern Arabia) 37-38; Pres. Prehistoric Society 39-46; fmr. Vice-Pres. Royal Anthropological Inst., fmr. Gov. Bedford Coll., Univ. of London, and School of Oriental and African Studies; mem. Governing Council, British School of East Africa; Fellow Newnham Coll., Cambridge 34-51; Cuthbert Peake Award, Royal Geographical Soc. 32; Rivers Medal, Royal Anthropological Inst. 34, Huxley Medal 46, Burton Medal, Royal Asiatic Soc. 54; Hon. Litt.D. (Cambridge).

Publs. *The Badarian Civilisation* (with Guy Brunton) 28, *The Zimbabwe Culture* 31, *The Desert Fayum* 35, *The Tombs and Moon Temple of Hureidha* 44, *Kharga Oasis in Prehistory* 52.

Court Farm, Broadway, Worcs., England.

Catroux, Gen. Georges; French army officer and diplomatist; b. 29 Jan. 1877; ed. St.-Cyr.

Entered Mounted Co. of Foreign Legion 99; A.D.C. to Gov. of Indo-China (Bau) 03-05; took part in Algerian-Moroccan operations under Col. Lyautey; served Morocco under Gen. d'Amade 11; A.D.C. to Gov. of Algeria (Gen. Lutaud) 11-14; served with Algerian Rifles Great War, wounded and taken prisoner 16; Military Attaché Constantinople with rank of Lt.-Col. 18; later Gov. of Damascus; Dir. "Deuxième Bureau" (Intelligence) during Riff campaign and Intelligence Bureau of Levantine Army 26; Col. Commanding 1st Regt. of Foreign Legion 27; took over Marshal Lyautey's fmr. Command Ain Sefra 28; Brig.-Gen. and Commdr. Marrakech 29, carried out pacification of Morocco; promoted Gen. of Div.; commanded 14th Infantry Div. Mulhouse 36, later 19th Corps Algiers; relieved of command by Gen. Gamelin 39; Gov.-Gen. Indo-China Aug. 39-July 40; declared adherence to Free French Forces; appointed Free French High Commr. and Gen. de Gaulle's Rep. in Near East 40; mem. French Council of Imperial Defence; Del.-Gen. Plen. and C.-in-C. French in Levant 41-43; Gov.-Gen. of Algeria and Commr. for Co-ordination of Moslem Affairs, French Cttee. of Nat. Liberation 43-44; Ambassador to U.S.S.R. 45-April 48; Adviser to French Govt. 48; Grand Chancellor Légion d'Honneur; G.C.B. (Hon.) 46; Médaille Militaire 52.

Publs. *Dans la Bataille de la Méditerranée* 50, *J'ai vu tomber le Rideau de Fer* 51, *Lyautey le Marocain* 52, *The French Union* 54, *Deux Missions en Moyen Orient* 59, *Deux Actes du Drame Indochinois.*

Palais de la Légion d'Honneur, 64 rue de Lille, Paris 7e, France.

Telephone: Solférino 99-89.

Catto, 2nd Baron, of Cairncatto; **Stephen Gordon Catto;** British company director; b. 14 Jan. 1923; ed. Eton Coll. and Cambridge Univ.

Air Force service 43-47; Man. Dir. Morgan Grenfell & Co. Ltd.; Dir. Australian United Corpn. Ltd., Australian Mutual Provident Soc. (London Board), The General Electric Co., Hongkong & Shanghai Banking Corpn. Ltd. (London Cttee.), Yule Catto & Co. Ltd. and other companies; mem. Advisory Council, Export Credits Guarantee Dept. 59-65; part-time mem. London Transport Board 62-.

Morgan Grenfell and Co. Ltd., 23 Great Winchester Street, London, E.C.2, England.

Catton, Bruce; American writer and civil servant; b. 9 Oct. 1899; ed. Oberlin Coll., Ohio.

Reporter, editorial writer and Washington correspondent 20-40; Dir. of Information, War Production Board 40-45; Dir. of Information, U.S. Dept. of Commerce, and Asst. Dir. of Information, U.S. Dept. of Interior; Senior Editor *American Heritage Magazine* 56-; Nat. Book Award, non-fiction 53; Pulitzer Prize for History 54.

Publs. *The War Lords of Washington* 48, *Mr. Lincoln's Army* 50, *Glory Road* 51, *A Stillness at Appomattox* 53, *U.S. Grant and the American Military Tradition* 54, *Banner at Shenandoah* 55, *This Hallowed Ground* 56, *America Goes to War* 58, *Grant Moves South* 60, *The Coming Fury* 61, *Terrible Swift Sword* 63, *Never Call Retreat* 65.

551 Fifth Avenue, New York City, N.Y., U.S.A.

Cau, Jean, LIC. PHIL.; French writer and journalist; b. 8 July 1925; ed. Lycée Carcassonne, Lycée Louis-le-Grand, and Univ. of Paris.

Former Sec. to Jean-Paul Sartre; travelled extensively in U.S.A., Brazil, Greece, Italy, Spain, North Africa; journalist on *L'Express, le Figaro littéraire, Candide,* etc., Paris; Prix Goncourt 61.

Publs. novels: *Le coup de barre, Les Paroissiens, La Pitié de Dieu;* stories: *Mon village;* chronicle: *Les oreilles et la queue, L'Incendie de Rome* 64; plays: *les Parachutistes, le Maître Monde, Dans un Nuage de Poussière* 67, *les Yeux Crevés* 68; translation of *Who's Afraid of Virginia Woolf, Numance; Lettre ouverte aux têtes de chiens occidentaux* 67.

13 rue de Seine, Paris 6e, France.

Causse, Jean-Pierre; French space scientist; b. 4 Oct. 1926; ed. Lycée de Montpellier and Ecole Normale Supérieure.

Pupil of Prof. Lallemand, Observatoire de Paris 52-55; industrial posts in U.S.A. 55-62; Dir. of Satellites Div., Centre Nat. d'Etudes Spatiales 62-66, Dir. of Programmes FR-1 and D-1, Dir. Brétigny Space Centre 66-; Chevalier Légion d'Honneur; Prix Galabert 66.

B.P. No. 4, 91 Brétigny-sur-Orge, France.

Telephone: 921-22-93.

Cauwenberg, Willy Van, DR. ECON.; Belgian diplomatist; b. 18 July 1914; ed. Rijksuniversiteit te Gent.

Joined Diplomatic Service 38; Vice-Consul New York 45, Consul, New York 46-52; Consul-Gen. Kansas City 52-54, San Francisco 54-58; Econ. Minister, Washington 58-63; Amb. to Australia 63-66, to Netherlands Dec. 66-; Commdr. Order of the Crown (Belgium), Grand Officer Order of Merit (Luxembourg), Grand Officer Order of Leopold (Belgium).

Royal Belgian Embassy, Andries Bickerweg 1c, The Hague, Netherlands.

Telephone: 392390.

Cavalcanti, José Costa; Brazilian army officer and politician; b. 6 Jan. 1918; ed. Cólegio dos Irmaõs Maristas and Escola Militar do Realengo.

Second Lieut. 38, rose to Col. 64; Instructor at Gen. Staff Coll. after Second World War; U.S. Infantry Training 52; Brazilian Mil. Attaché in U.S.A. 55-57; Sec. of Mixed Comm. on Brazilian-U.S. Defence 58; Sec. for Security, Pernambuco 59; mem. Fed. Chamber of Deputies 62-, Pres. Comm. on Nat. Security; Minister of Mines and Power 67-.

Ministry of Mines and Power, Brasilia, Brazil.

Cavalierato, Phedon Annino; Greek diplomatist; b. 1912; ed. Univ. of Athens.

Foreign Service Egypt, Ankara, and Moscow 36-; Econ. Affairs Dept. Foreign Ministry Athens 48; Greek Embassy, Washington 50; Head of Private Office of Ministry of Foreign Affairs 58; Dir. of Political Affairs for Western Europe at Foreign Ministry 59; Amb. to Australia and New Zealand 61; Dir.-Gen. Ministry of Foreign Affairs, Athens 63; Dir. of Econ. Affairs 64; Amb. to Bulgaria 64-66; Dir. of Political Affairs for Eastern Europe, Ministry of Foreign Affairs 66; Under-

Sec. of State, Ministry of Foreign Affairs 67, later Greek Perm. Rep. to NATO 67-; Grand Commdr. Order of Phoenix, Greece; Commdr. Order of George the First; numerous foreign decorations.
North Atlantic Treaty Organization, Brussels 39, Belgium.

Cavallier, Jean Albert; French industrialist; b. 27 Nov. 1898; ed. Ecole des Arts et Métiers.
Engineer with Soc. de Pont-à-Mousson 21, Man. Sens plant 23, Pont-à-Mousson plant 29, Gen. Man. 41, Dir. Gen. Man. 52; Vice-Pres. and Gen. Man. Soc. des Fonderies de Pont-à-Mousson 58, now Président d'Honneur Soc. des Fonderies de Pont-à-Mousson; Dir. Glamorgan Pipe and Foundry Co. (Lynchburg, Va.), Compagnie de Pont-à-Mousson, Union Sidérurgique Lorraine (SIDELOR), Halbergerhütte G.m.b.H.; Vice-Pres. Comité de l'Est des Conseillers du Commerce Extérieur de la France; mem. Comité Technique de la Fonderie; Officier Légion d'Honneur.
Office: 91 avenue de la Libération, Nancy; Home: 10 rue de Lota, Paris 16e and Route de Jezainville, Blénod-les-Pont-à-Mousson (Meurthe-et-Moselle), France.

Cavanagh, Jerome P.; American lawyer and politician; b. 16 June 1928; ed. St. Cecilia High School, Detroit, and Univ. of Detroit.
Private law practice (Sullivan, Romanoff, Cavanagh and Nelson) 55-61; Mayor of Detroit 62-66; Democrat.
c/o Office of the Mayor, City-County Building, Detroit, Michigan 48226, U.S.A.

Cavanaugh, Robert W., B.C.S.; American international banker; b. 27 Jan. 1914; ed. Univ. of Notre Dame.
With Fed. Deposit Corpn. 36; U.S. Office of Alien Property Custodian 42; U.S. Foreign Economic Admin. 44; State Dept. 46; Treasury Dept. 47; UN Int. Bank 47-59; Treasurer, Int. Bank, Int. Development Assoc. and Int. Finance Corpn.; Officer, Order of Leopold II.
1818 H Street, N.W., Washington, D.C., U.S.A.

Cavendish-Bentinck, Victor Frederick William, C.M.G.; British company director; b. 18 June 1897; ed. Wellington Coll., Berkshire.
Attaché, British Legation, Oslo 15; Army service 18; Diplomatic service 19-47; served in Paris, The Hague, Athens and Santiago, Asst. Under-Sec. of State 44, Ambassador to Poland 45-47; Chair. Cttee. of British Industrial Interests in Germany 48-, Bayer Dyestuffs Ltd. 64-, Baywood Chemicals Ltd. (England) 64-, F.B.A. Pharmaceuticals Ltd. (England), Rheinische Gerbstoff-Extrakt Fabrik Gebr. Müller AG (Germany), J. M. Steel & Co. Ltd. (England); Joint Vice-Chair. KERAMAG Keramische Werke A.G. (Germany); Dir. Austrian, British, Belgian and German companies.
21 Carlyle Square, Chelsea, London, S.W.3, England.
Telephone: 01-352-1258.

Cavert, Rev. Samuel McCrea, D.D., LL.D.; American ecclesiastic; b. 9 Sept. 1888; ed. Union Coll., Columbia Univ. and Union Theological Seminary.
Ordained Presbyterian ministry 15; Fellow of Union Theological Seminary 15-17; Chaplain U.S. Army 18-19; Assoc. Sec. Federal Council of Churches of Christ in America 20, Gen. Sec. 21-50; Gen. Sec. Nat. Council of the Churches of Christ in the U.S.A. 51-54; American Sec., World Council of Churches 54-57; Protestant liaison official between U.S. Mil. Govt. and German Churches, U.S. Zone 46; mem. Board of Dirs. Union Theological Seminary; Dir. The Interchurch Center, New York 63-64; mem. Advisory Cttee. Religious Book Club; mem. Editorial Board *Religion in Life* (quarterly); Senior Editor *The Pulpit Digest* 58-68; Hon. Chancellor, Union Coll.; Hon. D.Theol. (Göttingen), L.H.D., Litt.D.
Publs. *The Adventure of the Church, Christian Leaders for To-morrow, The Church Through Half a Century*

(with H. P. Van Dusen), *On the Road to Christian Unity, The American Churches in the Ecumenical Movement* 68.
161 Boulder Trail, Bronxville, N.Y., U.S.A.

Cayzer, Sir William Nicholas, Bt.; British shipowner; b. 21 Jan. 1910; ed. Eton and Corpus Christi Coll., Cambridge.
Joined Clan Line Steamers Ltd. 31, Chair. Brit. and Commonwealth Shipping Co. Ltd., Union-Castle Mail Steamship Co. Ltd., Clan Steamers Ltd., Cayzer Irvine & Co. Ltd., and various other companies; Chair. of Liverpool Steamship Owners Asscn. 44-45; Chair., Gen. Council of British Shipping 59; Pres., Chamber of Shipping of the United Kingdom 59, Inst. of Marine Engineers 63.
Cayzer House, 2-4 St. Mary Axe, London, E.C.3; and 95J Eaton Square, London, S.W.1, England.

Cazzaniga, Vicenzo; Italian oil executive; b. 3 Nov. 1907; ed. Bocconi Univ., Milan.
Executive, Società Italiana Lubrificanti Bedford (affiliate of Standard Oil Co.) 32, Man. Dir. 38; Head, N. Italy Mineral Oils Industrial Cttee. 45, N. Italy Mineral Oils Dept. 45-48, Head N. Italy Lubricants Dept., Italian Petroleum Cttee. 45-48; Pres. Esso Standard Italiana 51-; mem. Exec. Cttee. Confindustria (Italian Manufacturers' Asscn.) 57; Dir. Int. Chamber of Commerce 57, Pres. Unione Petrolifera 58, Sarpom 61, Rasiom 61, Esso Chimica 66, Milan Experimental Fuel Station; mem. Board Stanic 63; Cavaliere del Lavoro, etc.
Via Porta Latina 8, Rome, Italy.

Ceauşescu, Nicolae; Rumanian politician; b. 18.
Member, Union of Communist Youth 33-36, Communist Party of Rumania 36-44; Sec. Union of Communist Youth 44-45; acting mem. Central Cttee. Rumanian Workers' Party (now Communist Party) 45-48, mem. 48-, mem. Political Bureau 55-; Deputy Minister of Agriculture 48-50; Deputy Minister of Armed Forces 50-54; Sec. Central Cttee. of Rumanian Workers' Party (now Communist Party) 54-65, First Sec. 65, Sec.-Gen. 65-; Pres. State Council Dec. 67-; Hero of Socialist Labour 64.
Central Committee of Rumanian Communist Party, Bucharest, Rumania.

Cebollero, Pedro Angel, B.S., M.A., ED.D.; American university professor; b. 2 June 1898; ed. Univs. of Puerto Rico, Columbia and Chicago.
Elementary-School Principal 18; High-School Teacher 20; Superintendent of Schools 21; Instr. Univ. of Puerto Rico 26; Asst. Commr. of Educ. for Puerto Rico 31; Tech. Adviser Ministry of Educ. Venezuela 38; Minister of Educ. Panama 40; Visiting Prof. of Educ. Univ. of Texas 41; Perm. Sec. Higher Council of Educ. of Puerto Rico 42; Prof. of Educ. and Dean Coll. of Educ. Univ. of Puerto Rico 51; Dir. Dept. of Secondary Education, Educational Div., Pan American Union, Washington; Instituto Pedagógico, University of Chile 58; Universidad Católica, Santiago, Chile 60; Superintendency of Public Education, Chile 62-63; Consultant, Office of Co-ordinator of Educational Planning, Santiago, Chile 64-.
Publs. *The School Language Policy in Puerto Rico* 45, *Acquiring Spanish* 46, *Aritmética Social, grados III, IV, V, VI, Nuestro Mundo, grados II, III, IV, V, VI* 57, *La Enseñanza de las Ciencias Naturales en la Escuela Primaria* 53 (ed. Unión Panamericana), *Estado Actual de la Educación Secundaria en la América Latina* 57 (ed. Pan American Union), *La Evaluación del Trabajo Escolar* 57 (ed. Pan American Union), *Caminos* (poems) 66.
9004 Quintana Drive, Bethesda, Maryland, U.S.A.

Cecil, Lord (Edward Christian) David (Gascoyne), C.H.; British writer; b. 9 April 1902.
Trustee Nat. Portrait Gallery 37-51; Goldsmiths' Prof.

of English Literature, Oxford Univ. 48-; Fellow New Coll., Oxford 39-.

Publs. *The Stricken Deer* 29, *Sir Walter Scott* 33, *Early Victorian Novelists* 34, *Jane Austen* 35, *The Young Melbourne* 39, *The Oxford Book of Christian Verse* (Editor) 40, *Hardy, the Novelist* 43, *Two Quiet Lives* 48, *Poets and Story-Tellers* 49, *Lord M* 54, *The Fine Art of Reading* 57, *Max* 64.

28 Charlbury Road, Oxford, and Red Lion House, Cranborne, Wimborne, Dorset.

Cecil, Lester LeFevre; American judge; b. 21 Nov. 1893; ed. Univ. of Michigan.

Attorney, E. H. and W. B. Turner 17-21; City Prosecuting Attorney, Dayton 22-25, Judge, Municipal Court 26-29; Judge, Common Pleas Court, Montgomery County 29-53; Judge, U.S. District Court, Southern District, Ohio 53-59, Judge, U.S. Court of Appeals, Sixth Circuit 59-, Senior Circuit Judge 65-; Hon. LL.D. (Ohio Northern Univ.).

Federal Building, Dayton 1, Ohio; Home: 448 Red Haw Road, Dayton, Ohio 45405, U.S.A.

Telephone: 228-6062 (Office); 274-0713 (Home).

Cedergren, Hugo; Swedish Y.M.C.A. official; b. 26 July 1891; ed. Lund Univ.

Sec. Y.M.C.A. Stockholm 19-21; Gen. Sec. 21-24; Sec.-Gen. Swedish Y.M.C.A. 24-46; European Dir. War Prisoners' Aid Y.M.C.A. 41-47; Assoc. Gen.-Sec. World Cttee. of Y.M.C.A. 46-53; Pres. Swedish Y.M.C.A. 52-62, Hon. Pres. 62-; Vice-Pres. World Alliance of Y.M.C.A. 55-61, Hon. Life mem. 61-.

Skeppargatan 56, Stockholm, Sweden.

Telephone: 08-613322.

Cefis, Eugenio; Italian oil executive; b. 1921.

Vice-Pres. Ente Nazionale Idrocarburi (ENI) until 67, Pres. June 67-.

Ente Nazionale Idrocarburi, 72 Viale dell'Arte, Rome, Italy.

Cejka, Karl, D.IUR.; Austrian civil servant; b. 1 Dec. 1917; ed. Vienna Univ.

Began his career as journalist and lawyer; Asst. Man. Supervising Dept. Ministry of Food; Adviser to Ministry of Finance on financial management of Radio, Posts and Telegraph; mem. Radio Advisory Cttee.; Chair. Preparatory Cttee. for Radio Reorganisation 56-57; Dir.-Gen. Austrian Radio 57-60; Counsellor, Ministry of Finance; Head, Dept. for Development Aid; Head, Dept. for Public Debt and Export Promotion, Dept. for Credit Policy, Debt Administration and Int. Orgs.

Montecuccoliplatz 12, 1130 Vienna, Austria.

Telephone: 82-41-44.

Cela, Camilo José; Spanish writer; b. 11 May 1916; ed. Univ. de Madrid.

Director and Publisher of journal *Papeles de Son Armadans*; mem. Real Acad. Española 57; Premio de la critica 55.

Publs. include: *La Familia de Pascual Duarte* (novel) 42, *Pabellón de reposo* 43-57, *Nuevas andanzas y desventuras de Lazarillo de Tormes* (short stories) 44-55, *Pisando la dudosa luz del día* (poems) 45, *Mesa revuelta* 45 and 57, *Viaje a la Alcarria* 48, *La colmena* 51, *Del Miño al Bidasoa* 52, *Mrs. Caldwell habla con su hijo* 53, *La Catira* 55, *Judíos, moros y cristianos* 56, *El molino de viento* (short stories) 56, *Nuevo retablo de don Cristobita* 57, *Viaje al Pirineo de Lerida* 65.

La Bonanova, Palma de Mallorca, Spain.

Telephone: 233670.

Celan, Paul; German (b. Romanian) poet; b. 23 Nov. 1920.

Rudolf Alexander Schröder Prize, City of Bremen 57; Georg Büchner Prize, Deutsche Akad. für Sprache und Dichtung 60.

Publs. include: *Der Sand aus den Urnen* 48, *Mohn und*

Gedächtnis 52, *Von Schwelle zu Schwelle* 55, *Sprachgitter* 39, *Die Niemandsrose* 63, *Atemwende* 67.

78 rue de Longchamp, Paris 16e, France.

Celebrezze, Anthony J., LL.B.; American politician and lawyer; b. 4 Sept. 1910; ed. John Carroll and Ohio Northern Univs.

Admitted Ohio Bar 36; practised law in Cleveland; U.S. Navy Second World War; Senator, Ohio State 52-53; Mayor of Cleveland 53-62; U.S. Sec. of Health, Educ. and Welfare, July 62-65; Judge, U.S. Court of Appeals 65-; Order of Merit (Italy); Doctor of Humanity (Wilberforce Univ.) and many other hon. degrees; Democrat.

U.S. Court of Appeals, Sixth Circuit, Cincinnati, Ohio; Home 312 Federal Building, Cleveland, Ohio 44114, U.S.A.

Telephone: 522-4270 (Home).

Celibidache, Sergiu; Romanian-born German conductor; b. 28 June 1912; ed. Jassy and Berlin.

Conductor and Artistic Dir. Berlin Philharmonic Orchestra 46-51; now guest conductor to leading European orchestras; German Critics' Prize 53, Berlin City Art Prize 55; Grosses Verdienstkreuz (Fed. Germany).

c/o Camus, Via Boncompagni 12, Rome, Italy.

Celio, Nello, D.IUR.; Swiss lawyer and politician; b. 12 Feb. 1914; ed. Univs. of Basle and Berne.

Secretary Cantonal Interior Dept. 41-45; Public Procurator 45-46; State Councillor 46-49; Nat. Councillor 63-; Minister of Defence 66-67, of Finance 68-; Pres. Radical Democrat Party.

Ministry of Finance, Berne, Switzerland.

Celler, Emanuel; American politician; b. 6 May 1888; ed. Columbia Univ.

Legal practice, New York City 12-; mem. U.S. House of Reps. 23-, now Chair. Judiciary Cttee.; Author, Fed. Register Aøt, Foreign Trade Zone Act, Celler Anti-Merger Act, Celler Civil Rights Acts, 57-60; Dir. philanthropic and religious orgs.; Democrat.

1501 Broadway, New York City, New York, U.S.A.

Cento, H.E. Cardinal Fernando; Vatican ecclesiastic; b. 10 Aug. 1883.

Ordained priest 05; Bishop of Acireale 22; Titular Bishop of Seleucia Pieria 26; fmr. Apostolic Nuncio in Venezuela, Ecuador, Peru, Belgium and Luxembourg; Apostolic Nuncio in Portugal 53-58; created Cardinal by Pope John XXIII 58; Major Penitentiary 62-66; Titular Bishop of Velletri 65.

Palazzo della Cancelleria Apostolica, Piazza della Cancelleria, Rome, Italy.

Cépède, Michel; French agriculturalist; b. 20 Oct, 1908; ed. Lycées Louis-le-Grand and Saint Louis. Institut national agronomique and Univ. de Paris à la Sorbonne.

Assistant Prof. Rural Economy, Nat. Agronomic Inst. 31-47, Prof. 47-; with Ministry of Agriculture 44-59, Dir. of Studies and of the Plan 57-59; Pres. Agricultural Cttee. OECD 59-62; mem. French Del. to FAO 45-, Vice-Pres. 65; mem. Programme Cttee. 56-, Pres. 63-; numerous other posts with FAO; Sec.-Gen. Interministerial Cttee. for Food and Agriculture 46-57, Pres. 57-; Pres. Interministerial Cttee. of World Campaign against Hunger 60-; Corresp. mem. Acad. d'Agriculture de France, Foreign mem. Acad. of Agrarian Econ., Florence; numerous decorations and honours.

Publs. *Du Prix de Revient au Produit net en Agriculture* 46, *Economie alimentaire du Globe* 53, *Economía Mundial de la Alimentacion* 55, *L'Economie des Besoins* 56, *La Vie Rurale dans l'Arc Alpin* 60, *Agriculture et Alimentation en France durant la II Guerre Mondiale* 61, *Nourrir les Hommes* 63, *Population and Food* 65, *L'Agriculture en l'Administration française* 65, *La Faim* 67, and numerous articles on agricultural subjects.

135 rue Falguière, Paris 15e, France.

Telephone: 468-61-38 (Office); 783-28-08 (Home).

Čepek, Ladislav, D.SC., D.ENG.; Czechoslovak geologist; b. 10 Jan. 1899.
Former Dir. Central Inst. for Geology; Corresp. mem. Czechoslovak Acad. of Sciences 52-; Lecturer, Charles Univ., Prague; author of 90 scientific studies; Order of Labour 66.
Prague-Břevnov 1399, Bělohorská 32, Czechoslovakia.

Cerf, Bennett Alfred, A.B., LITT.B.; American publisher; b. 25 May 1898; ed. Columbia Univ.
Founder Pres. Modern Library Inc. 25-, Random House Inc. 27-65, Chair. 65-; Dir. Bantam Books; mem. Peabody Awards Cttee. 50-, Chair. 55-56.
Publs. *Bedside Book of Famous American Stories, Bedside Book of Famous British Stories, Pocketbook of War Humor, Try and Stop Me, Laughing Stock, Anything for a Laugh, Shake Well Before Using, Laughter Inc., Good for a Laugh, Encyclopaedia of American Humor, Life of the Party, Laugh Day.*
Home: 132 East 62nd Street, New York City; Office: 457 Madison Avenue, New York 22, N.Y., U.S.A.

Černík, Oldřich; Czechoslovak politician; b. 27 Oct. 1921; ed. Mining Coll., Ostrava.
Former machine fitter; at Vítkovice Iron Works 37-49; Sec. Regional Cttee. of Czech Communist Party, Ostrava 54-56; Sec. Central Cttee. of Czech Communist Party 56-60, mem. 58-, mem. Econ. Comm. Central Cttee. 63-; Minister of Fuel and Power 60-63, of Fuel 63; Deputy Prime Minister and Chair. State Planning Comm. 63-April 68; Prime Minister April 68-; Deputy to Nat. Assembly 60-; mem. Presidium Central Cttee. of Czechoslovak C.P. 66-.
Office of the Prime Minister, Prague, Czechoslovakia.

Černý, Jaroslav, PH.DR. (Prague), M.A., F.B.A.; Stateless (Czech-born) Egyptologist; b. 22 Aug. 1898; ed. Charles Univ., Prague.
Lecturer in Egyptology, Charles Univ., Prague 29-46; Edwards Prof. of Egyptology, Univ. Coll., London 46-51; Prof. Egyptology, Oxford Univ. 51-65, Emer. 65-; Fellow Emer. of Queen's Coll., Oxford; Corresp. mem. Fondation Egyptologique Reine Elisabeth, Brussels, American Oriental Soc., Archäol. Institut des Deutschen Reiches; Assoc. mem. Institut d'Egypte.
Publs. *Ostraca hiératiques* 35, *Catalogue des ostraca hiératiques non littéraires de Deir el Médineh* 35-51, *Late Ramesside Letters* 39, *Répertoire onomastique de Deir el Médineh* 49, *Ancient Egyptian Religion* 52, *Paper & Books in Ancient Egypt* 52, *The Inscriptions of Sinai,* 2nd edn. 52, *Part 2* 55, *Graffiti hiéroglyphiques et hiératiques de la nécropole thébaine* 56, *Hieratic Ostraca* 57, *Egyptian Stelae in the Bankes Collection* 58.
2 Linkside Avenue, Oxford, England.
Telephone: Oxford 59329.

Cerulli, Enrico, LL.D.; Italian diplomatist; b. 15 Feb. 1898; ed. Univ. of Naples.
Entered Civil Service 20; Sec. and later Dir. of Political Affairs, Italian Somaliland 20-25; First Sec. and later Counsellor, Italian Legation, Ethiopia 26-29; Italian rep. Anglo-Italian Boundary Comm., Somaliland 30-31; Head of Political Dept., later Sec.-Gen., Ministry for Italian Africa 32-35; mem. Italian del. to L.N. 35-37; Deputy Gov.-Gen. Italian East Africa 38-39; retd. 40-44; Counsellor of State and mem. of del. to Peace Conf. 44-47; Italian rep. Four-Power Confs., London, and later to U.N. re question of Italian African territories 47-49; Italian rep. UN Trusteeship Council 49-50; Ambassador to Iran 50-54; Counsellor of State 55; mem. Accad. dei Lincei, Real Acad. Española, Acad. Portuguesa de Historia, Société Asiatique, Royal Asiatic Soc., etc.; Hon. Litt.D. (Univs. of Brussels, Rome, Manchester).
Publs. *The Folk Literature of the Galla in Southern Ethiopia* 22, *Etiopia Occidentale* (2 vols.) 30-33; *Studi Etiopici* (4 vols.) 36-51, *The Book of the Staircase and the Spanish-Arabic Sources of Dante* 49, *History of Ethiopic Literature* 56, *Somalia* (3 vols.) 58-59, etc.
Council of State, Palazzo Spada, Rome; and 11, Via Lovanio, Rome, Italy.

Cerulli-Irelli, Giuseppe; Italian diplomatist; b. 7 July 1905; ed. Istituto Massimo and Università della Sapienza, Rome.
Diplomatic Service 34-; Attaché, Political Affairs Dept., Ministry of Foreign Affairs, Rome 35; Vice-Consul Buenos Aires, Sfax and Janina 36-40; Sec. of Political Affairs Dept., Ministry of Foreign Affairs 40-45; First Sec., Vatican 45-48; mem. Senate 48-63, Under Sec. of State for Budget Ministry 60; Head of Italian Del. to Economic and Social Council of UN (ECOSOC), Geneva 61-62; Ambassador to Portugal 64-.
Publs. *Il consiglio d'Europa* 49, *Discorsi Parlamentari* 53, *La politica di pace dell'Italia* 54, *La cittadinanza degli italiani all'estero* 59.
Embassy of Italy, Largo Conde Pombeiro 6, Lisbon, Portugal.

Césaire, Aimé Fernand, L. ès L.; French (Martiniquais) politician; b. 25 June 1913; ed. Fort-de-France (Martinique) and Lycée Louis-le-Grand (Paris), Ecole Normale Supérieure and the Sorbonne.
Teaching career until 45; mem. Constituent Assemblies 45 and 46; Dep. for Martinique 46-; Pres. Parti Progressiste Martiniquais; Mayor of Fort-de-France.
Publs. Verse: *Cahier d'un Retour au Pays Natal, Les Armes Miraculeuses, Soleil Coupé;* Essays: *Discours sur le Colonialisme;* Theatre: *la Tragédie du roi Christophe, Une saison au Congo.*
Assemblée Nationale, Paris 7e, France; La Mairie, Fort-de-France, Martinique, West Indies.

Chaban-Delmas, Jacques Michel Pierre; French politician; b. 7 March 1915; ed. Lycée Lakanal, Sceaux, Ecole Libre des Sciences Politiques, Paris.
Served army 39-40, Brig.-Gen. 40; nat. mil. del. responsible for co-ordination of mil. planning, Resistance 44; Inspector-Gen. of Army Nov. 44; Sec.-Gen. Ministry of Information 45; elected Radical deputy for Gironde 46; Mayor of Bordeaux 47-; leader of Gaullist group (Républicains Sociaux) in Nat. Assembly 53-56; mem. Consultative Assembly, Council of Europe; Inspecteur des Finances Feb. 56-May 57; Min. Nat. Defence, Gaillard Cabinet 57-58; Pres. of Nat. Assembly 58-; Pres. of Comm. for Regional Econ. Devt. of Aquitaine 64-; Pres. of European Ass. of Local Authorities; Commdr. Légion d'Honneur; Croix de Guerre.
4 avenue Raymond-Poincaré, Paris 16e, France.

Chabrol, Claude; French film director and producer; b. 24 June 1903; ed. Paris Univ., Ecole Libre des Sciences Politiques.
Formerly film critic and Public Relations Officer in Paris for 20th-Century Fox; director and producer 58-; wrote, directed and produced *Le Beau Serge, Les Cousins;* wrote and directed *A Double Tour, Les Bonnes Femmes, Les Godelureaux, Lamiel, Ophélia, l'Œil du Malin, Landru, les Plus Belles Escroqueries du Monde, Le tigre aime la chair fraîche, Le tigre se parfume à la dynamite, Marie-Chantal contre le Docteur Kha;* produced *Les Jeux de l'Amour, Le Signe du Lion, Le Scandale;* Locarno Festival Grand Prix (for *Le Beau Signe*) 58, Berlin Festival Golden Bear 59.
Publ. *Alfred Hitchcock* (with E. Rohmer).
6 rue des Marronniers, Paris 16e, France.

Chacón y Calvo, José María, LL.D., PH.D.; Cuban writer, lawyer and diplomatist; b. 92; ed. Univ. of Havana.
Consulting lawyer of Secretariat of Justice 15-18; Sec. of Cuban Legation in Madrid 18-26; Sec. of Cuban Embassy in Madrid 26-34; Dir. of Cultural Dept., Ministry of Education 34; Vice-Pres. Acad. of Arts and Letters and of Acad. of History of Cuba; Pres. of

Ateneo de la Habana; co-founder Society of Cuban Folklore; Dir. Cuban Acad. of Languages; Pres. of the Cuban Institute of Hispanic Culture; first Prof. and Head of Faculty of Philosophy and Letters, Catholic Univ. of Villanueva, Havana; Corresp. mem. of a number of Hispanic Academies; Corresp. mem. Hispanic Soc. of America 64.

Publs. *Cervantes y el Romancero, Tabla de Variantes en las poesías líricas de la Avellaneda, Ensayos sentimentales, Los comienzos literarios de Zenea, Ensayos de Literatura Cubana, Las cien mejores poesías cubanas, Colección de documentos inéditos, La poesía de Martí y lo popular hispánico 54, La iniciación literaria de Don Enrique José Varina 60.*

Calle 9, 454, Vedado, Havana, Cuba.

Chadenet, Bernard; French international banker; b. 16 Sept. 1915; ed. Univ. de Paris à la Sorbonne and Ecole Supérieure d'Electricité, Paris, and Harvard Business School.

Engineer and Chief, Public Utilities Div., Projects Dept., Int. Bank for Reconstruction and Devt. (World Bank) 54-56; Gen. Man., NEYRPIC, Grenoble 58-64; Assoc. Dir. Projects Dept., World Bank 64-67, Dir. 67-; Chevalier Légion d'Honneur.

International Bank for Reconstruction and Development, 1818 H Street, N.W., Washington, D.C. 20433, U.S.A.

Chadha, Manohar Singh, M.B., B.S., F.R.C.P.; Indian health administrator; b. 22 Oct. 1904; ed. Univs. of Lahore, London and Edinburgh.

Indian Medical Service 34-, Medical Officer and later Specialist in Pathology 34-45; served in Sudan and Egypt 40-42; Chief Health Officer, Delhi 47-48; Deputy Dir. of Health Services, Delhi 48-53, Dir. 53-58; Additional Deputy Dir.-Gen. and Deputy Dir.-Gen. of Health Services, Govt. of India 58-62, Dir.-Gen. 62-65; Dir. Nat. Inst. of Health Admin. and Educ. 65-.

National Institute of Health Administration and Education, Patiala House, New Delhi, India.

Telephone: 46408.

Chadourne, Marc; French novelist and essayist; b. 23 May 1895.

Professor Emeritus Connecticut Coll. for Women, New London, Conn., U.S.A., Grand prix de Littérature Acad. Française 50; Officier de la Légion d'Honneur.

Publs. Novels: *Vasco* 27 (Paul Flat Prize), *Libération* 28. *Cécile la Folie* 30 (Femina Prize), *Absence* 33, *Dieu créa d'abord Lilith* 38, *La Clé Perdue* 47, *Gladys ou les Artifices* 49; Essays: *Chine* 31 (Gringoire Prize), *L'U.R.S.S. sans passion* 32, *Anahuac, ou l'Indien sans plume* 34, *Extrême-Orient* 36, *Quand Dieu se fit américain* 50, *Le Mal de Colleen* 55, *Restif de la Bretonne, ou le Siècle Prophétique* 58, *Eblis ou l'enfer de William Beckford* 67. La Coustiera, Haut-de-Cagnes, Cagnes-sur-mer, A.M., France; and 173 Niles Hill Road, Waterford, Conn. 063851, U.S.A.

Telephone: 442-8190 (France); 31-32-35 (U.S.A.).

Chadwick, Sir James, M.SC., PH.D., F.R.S., F.R.S.E.; British physicist; b. 20 Oct. 1891; ed. Manchester and Cambridge Univs.

Fellow Gonville and Caius Coll. Cambridge 21-35, 59-; Asst. Dir. of Research Cavendish Laboratory Cambridge 23-35; Nobel Laureate in Physics 35; Lyon Jones Prof. of Physics, Liverpool Univ. 35-48; Master of Gonville and Caius Coll. Cambridge 48-59; Hon. Fellow Gonville and Caius Coll. 45-48; part-time mem. Atomic Energy Authority 57-62; Corresp. mem. Sächs. Akad. d. Wiss. (Leipzig); Assoc. Acad. Royal Belgium; foreign mem. K. Ned. Akad. Wet. Amsterdam; K. Danske Vid. Selskab; hon. mem. American Physical Society, American Philosophical Soc., Philadelphia; mem. Pontifical Acad. of Sciences; Orden Pour le Merite (German Fed. Repub.); U.S. Medal for Merit 46; Faraday Medal 50; Hughes Medal of the Royal Soc. 32; Copley Medal of

Royal Soc. 50; Franklin Medal 51; Hon. Sc.D. (Dublin), Hon; D.Sc. (Reading, Leeds, Oxford, Birmingham and McGill), Hon. LL.D. (Liverpool and Edinburgh).

Publs. *Radiations from Radioactive Substances* (co-author) 30, *Radioactivity and Radioactive Substances.* Wynne's Parc, Denbigh, N. Wales.

Telephone: Denbigh 2062.

Chadwick, John, M.A., F.B.A.; British classical scholar; b. 21 May 1920; ed. St. Paul's School, London, Corpus Christi Coll., Cambridge Univ.

War service in Royal Navy 40-45; Editorial Asst. *Oxford Latin Dictionary* 46-52; Lecturer in Classics, Cambridge Univ. 52-66; Reader in Greek Language, Cambridge Univ. 66-; Collins Fellow, Downing Coll., Cambridge 60-; Hon. Doctorate, Athens Univ. Philosophical School; Corresp. mem. German Archaeological Inst.; co-operated with Michael Ventris in the decipherment of the Minoan Linear B script.

Publs. *The Medical Works of Hippocrates* (with W. N. Mann) 50; *Documents in Mycenaean Greek* (with Michael Ventris) 56; *The Decipherment of Linear B* 58 (trans. into German and Italian 59, Swedish 60, Dutch 61, Danish, Spanish, Greek, Japanese 62, Polish 64); *The Pre-history of the Greek Language* (in Cambridge Ancient History, Vol. II) 63; Editor *The Mycenae Tablets III* 63; various articles in learned journals. Downing College, Cambridge, England.

Telephone: Cambridge 59491.

Chadwick, Lynn Russell, C.B.E.; British sculptor; b. 24 Nov. 1914; ed. Merchant Taylors School.

Works shown in London, New York, Paris, Brussels (Exposition 58) and Venice, where he won the International Sculpture Prize at the Biennale 56; 1st Prize Padua Int. Competition 59; Hors Concours, Bienal São Paulo 61.

Lypiatt Park, Stroud, Gloucestershire, England.

Chafee, John H., B.A., LL.B.; American lawyer and politician; b. 22 Oct. 1922; ed. Deerfield Acad., Yale Univ., and Harvard Law School.

U.S. Marine Corps 42-46, 51-52; admitted to Rhode Island Bar 51; State Rep. Rhode Island House 56-62; Gov. of Rhode Island 63-; Hon. LL.D. (Brown Univ., Providence Coll., Univ. of Rhode Island); Visiting Chubb Fellow, Yale Univ. 65; Chair. Compact for Educ. 65, Republican Governors' Assocn. 67-68; Republican.

The Governor's Office, State House, Providence 3, Rhode Island; and Ives Road, East Greenwich, Rhode Island, U.S.A.

Telephone: 401-UNI-3100.

Chagall, Marc; French artist; b. Russia 7 July 1887. Lived in France 10-14, Russia 14-22, France 22-41, U.S.A. 41-48, France 48-; works include paintings, engravings, murals, costumes and décor for ballet and theatre, and ceramics; stained glass windows for synagogue of Medical Centre near Jerusalem; ceiling for Paris Opera 64; murals for Metropolitan Opera House, Lincoln Center, New York 66; sets for *The Magic Flute* (Mozart), Metropolitan Opera 67; has exhibited in Tate Gallery, London, museums in Amsterdam, Paris, Chicago, New York, Venice, Jerusalem, Tel-Aviv, Berne, Zürich, Turin, Rome, Milan; exhbn. at Zürich Kunsthaus 67; Int. Prize for Engraving, Venice Biennale 48, Erasmus Prize 60; Commdr. des Arts et des Lettres, Commdr. Légion d'Honneur; Grand Cross Nat. Order of Merit (France).

Publ. *Ma Vie* 31, English trans. 65.

Les Collines, Vence, Alpes Maritimes, France.

Chagas, Carlos, M.D., SC.D., Brazilian biophysicist; b. 10; ed. Colegió Rezende, Univs. of Brazil and Paris. Began career as Asst. at Inst. Oswaldo Cruz and Medical School, Univ. of Brazil; Prof. Univ. of Brazil Medical School 37, Dir. Inst. of Biophysics 46-64; mem. Brazilian Nat. Research Council 50-55, U.N. Scientific Cttee. 56-,

WHO Scientific Advisory Cttee. 59-61, Pan American Health Org. Scientific Advisory Cttee. 62-; Chair. Exec. Cttee. Int. Brain Research Org.; Perm. Del. of Brazil to UNESCO; Adviser Puerto Rico Atomic Energy Comm.; mem. Brazilian Acads. of Science, Medicine and Pharmacy, Pontifical Acad. of Sciences, assoc. mem. Acad. de Médecine (Paris), Soc. de Biologie (Paris), London Physiological Soc.; Dr. h.c. Paris, Coimbra, Mexico, Recife Univs.; Premio Moinho Santista 60; Commdr. Order of Christ (Portugal), of Merit (Italy); Officer Legion of Honour (France), Order of Polar Star (Sweden), of Public Health (France).
Publs. include *Homens e Cousas de Ciencia* (essays) and a large number of medical and scientific papers 36-. Instituto de Biofisica, 458 Avenida Pasteur, Rio de Janeiro; Home: 38 Francisco Otaviano, Rio de Janeiro, Brazil.

Chagas, Paulo Pinheiro; Brazilian engineer, physician, journalist and politician.
Former Dep., Minas Gerais State Govt.; mem. State Constituent Assembly; Dir. *Diário Carioca* 49-51; mem. Fed. Chamber of Deputies; Minister of Health 63; Leader, Social Democrat Party.
Avda. Almirante Barroso 72, Rio de Janeiro, Brazil.

Chagla, Mahomedali Currim, B.A.; Indian barrister; b. 30 Sept. 1900; ed. St. Xavier's High School and Coll., Bombay, and Lincoln Coll., Oxford.
President Oxford Asiatic Soc. 21; Pres. Oxford Indian Majlis 22; called to Bar (Inner Temple) 22; Prof. of Constitutional Law, Govt. Law Coll., Bombay, 27-30; Hon. Sec. Bar Council of High Court of Judicature, Bombay 33-41; Puisne Judge Bombay High Court 41-47; Chair. Legal Education Cttee 48; Vice-Chancellor, Bombay Univ. 47; Chief Justice, High Court, Bombay 47-58; Del. to UN 46; Pres. Bombay Branch Royal Asiatic Soc. 47-58; Gov. of Bombay 56; Judge, Int. Court of Justice 57; mem. Law Commission 55-58; Ambassador to U.S., Mexico and Cuba 58-61; High Commissioner in the United Kingdom, Ambassador to Ireland 62-63; Minister of Educ., Govt. of India 63-66, of External Affairs 66-Sept. 67; mem. Rajya Sabha; Chair. Life Insurance Corpn. Inquiry Comm. 58; mem. Sikh Grievances Enquiry Comm. 61; Hon. Fellow, Lincoln Coll., Oxford 61; Hon. LL.D. Hartford, Temple, Boston, Leningrad and Punjab Univs., Dartmouth Coll.
Publs. *The Indian Constitution* 29, *Law, Liberty and Life* 50, *The Individual and the State, An Ambassador Speaks* 62, *Education and the Nation, Unity and Language.*
Pallonji Mansion, New Cuffe Parade, Bombay 5, India.

Chaikovsky, Boris Alexandrovich; Soviet composer; b. 1925; ed. Moscow Conservatoire.
Major works include: Sonatina for piano 44, suite for 'cello 46, First Symphony 47, *The Star* (opera) 49, Fantasia on Russian folk themes 50, *Slav Rhapsody* 51, Sonata for piano 52, *Symphonietta* for string orchestra 53, Trio for violin, 'cello and piano 53, *Cappriccio on English Themes* 54, First String Quartet 54, Trio for strings 55, Concertino for clarinet and orchestra 57, Sonata for cello and piano 57, Overture for 40th Anniversary of October Revolution 57, Sonata for violin and piano 59, Second String Quartet 61, Second Symphony 62, Piano Quintet 62; Exec. mem. Moscow Section, Composers' Union of R.S.F.S.R.
Composers' Union of R.S.F.S.R., 8-10 Ulitsa Nezhdanovoy, Moscow, U.S.S.R.

Chain, Ernst Boris, F.R.S., M.A., PH.D.; British biochemist; b. 19 June 1906; ed. Luisengymnasium and Friedrich-Wilhelm Univ., Berlin.
Research in Chemical Dept., Pathological Inst., Charité Hospital, Berlin 30-33; emigrated to England because of racial persecution 33; research in School of Biochemistry, Cambridge 33-35; Univ. Demonstrator and Lecturer in Chemical Pathology, Univ. of Oxford

35-49; Guest Prof. of Biochemistry, Istituto Superiore di Sanità, Rome 49; Prof. of Biochemistry and Scientific Dir. Int. Research Centre for Chemical Microbiology, Istituto Superiore di Sanità 50-61; Prof. of Biochemistry Imperial Coll. of Science and Technology, London 61-; awards include Nobel Prize for Physiology and Medicine 45, and Paul Ehrlich Prize 54; Commdr. Légion d'Honneur (France) 47; Grand Ufficiale al Mérito della Repubblica Italiana; several hon. degrees; mem. many foreign acads.
7th Floor Residence, Biochemistry Department, Imperial College of Science and Technology, Imperial Institute Road, London, S.W.7, England.

Chakovsky, Alexander Borisovich; Soviet writer; b. 1913.
Member C.P.S.U. 41-; Editor *Literaturnaya Gazeta.*
Publs. include: *It Was in Leningrad* (2 vols.) 46, *It's Already Morning With Us* (novel) 50, *Roads We Take* (novel) 60; stories: *Khvan Cher is on Guard* 52, *A Year of One Life* 57, *Star Light from Afar* 62.
Literaturnaya Gazeta, Moscow, U.S.S.R.

Chakravarty, Birendra Narayan, B.SC.; Indian diplomatist; b. 20 Dec. 1904; ed. Presidency Coll., Calcutta Univ., Univ. Coll., London, School of Oriental Studies, London.
Joined Indian Civil Service 29; held various appointments in Bengal districts and Bengal Secretariat; Finance Sec., Bengal Govt. 44; Sec. to Gov., West Bengal 47; Chargé d'Affaires, Embassy of India, Nanking Feb.-June 48; Head of Indian Liaison Mission, Tokyo, with personal rank of Minister 48-49; Joint Sec., Ministry of External Affairs 49-51; Sec. (Commonwealth Relations) 51-52; Ambassador to Netherlands 52-54; Senior Alt. Chair. Neutral Nations Repatriation Comm., Korea 53; Acting High Commr. to Great Britain 54; High Commr. to Ceylon 55-56; Special Sec. Ministry of External Affairs 56-60; High Commr. to Canada 60-62; Perm. Rep. to UN 62-65; Gov. of Haryana 67-.
Office of the Governor of Haryana, Chandigarh, India.

Chalandon, Albin Paul Henri, LIC. ès L.; French businessman and politician; b. 11 June 1920.
Inspecteur des Finances; Dir. Banque Nationale pour le Commerce et l'Industrie (Afrique) 49; Admin. and Dir-.Gen. Banque Commerciale de Paris until 64, Président-Directeur Général 64-68; Minister of Industry May 68-; Dir. Innofrance, Compagnie franco-africaine de recherches pétrolières, etc.; mem. Central Cttee. Union pour la Nouvelle République 58-, Sec.-Gen. 59; Officier Légion d'Honneur, Croix de Guerre.
Office: 11 rue de Tilsitt, Paris 17e; Home: 39 boulevard de Montmorency, Paris 16e, France.

Chałasiński, Josef, PH.D.; Polish sociologist; b. 17 Feb. 1904; ed. Poznań Univ.
Post doctorate fellowship in U.S.A. and U.K. 31-33; Prof. Free Univ. 36; Prof. and Rector Łódź Univ. 49-52; collaborated in *Yearbook of Education* 50-53; mem. Exec. Cttee. Int. Seminar for Family Research; Editor-in-Chief *Nauka Polska* 53-57, *Przeglad Socjologiczny* 57, *Kultura i Spoleczeństwo* 57-, *Młode Pokolenie Wsi Polski Ludowej* 64-; mem. Polish Acad. of Sciences (fmr. Deputy Scientific Sec.); mem. Int. Social Science Council 59-; Visiting Prof. California Univ. 58.
Publs. *Młode pokolenie chłopów* (The Young Generation of Peasants) 38, *Spoleczeństwo i wychowanie* (Society and Upbringing) 48, *Przeszłość i Przyszłość Intelligenczi Polskiej* (Past and Future of the Polish Intelligentsia) 58, *Kultura Amerykańska* (American Civilization) 62, *Bliżej Afryki* (Closer to Africa) with Krystyna Chałasińska 65.
Marszalkowska 16, Warsaw, Poland.

Chalfont, Baron (Life Peer), cr. 64; (**Arthur**) **Alun Gwynne-Jones,** P.C., O.B.E., M.C.; British politician; b. 5 Dec. 1919; ed. West Monmouth School.

Army service, commissioned as 2nd Lieut. 40; Military Service Burma and India 40-44, Cyprus, Malaya and East Africa 44-61; Defence Corresp. *The Times*, London 61-64; Minister of State for Foreign Affairs 64-, in charge of day-to-day negotiations for Britain's entry into Common Market 67-.
Publ. *The Sword and the Spirit* 63.
27 Ormonde Gate, London S.W.3, England.
Telephone: 01-352-8841.

Chaliha, Bimala Prasad; Indian politician; b. 26 March 1912; ed. Sibsagar Govt. High School and Calcutta Univ.
Joined National Movement 30; arrested and jailed for six months 32; patented mechanical automatic spinning wheel; Sec. Assam Branch, All India Spinners' Asscn; arrested in connection with "Quit India" Movement and imprisoned 42-44; Eastern Regional Organiser, All India Congress Cttee. 52; Chair. Reception Cttee., 63rd Session, Indian Nat. Congress; Chief Minister, Assam 57-; Leader, Assam Congress Parliamentary Party 62-; has taken a great interest in rural and cottage industries and founded the Silpanusthan Inst. at Sibsagar.
Publs. *The Philosophy of Khadi and Village Economy, Bee-Keeping*; numerous articles on Gandhi-ism, cottage industries and bee-keeping.
Chief Minister's Secretariat, Shillong, Assam, India.

Chalmers, Floyd Sherman; Canadian publisher; b. 14 Sept. 1898.
With Bank of Nova Scotia 14; Reporter on *Toronto News* and *Toronto World*; joined *Financial Post* 19, Montreal Editor 23, Editor 25-42; Exec. Vice-Pres. Maclean-Hunter Publishing Co. 42-52, Pres. 52-64, Chair. 64-; mem. Board of Govs. Stratford Shakespearean Festival of Canada, Vice-Pres. 63-65, Pres. 65-67; mem. Council, Commonwealth Press Union, London; Liveryman, Worshipful Co. of Stationers and Newspaper Makers, London; Hon. LL.D. (Univ. of Western Ontario, Waterloo Lutheran Univ.); Medal of Service, Order of Canada 67.
481 University Avenue, Toronto 2; Home: One Benvenuto Place, Toronto 7, Canada.
Telephone: 362-5311 (Office), 921-6168 (Home).

Chamant, Jean, L. en D.; French lawyer and politician; b. 23 Nov. 1913.
Advocate, Court of Appeal, Paris; Deputy for l'Yonne 46-; Sec. of State, Ministry of Foreign Affairs 55-56; Vice-Pres. Nat. Assembly 59-67; Minister of Transport 67-; Republican-Independent.
24 rue Boissière, Paris 16e, France.

Chamberlain, Owen, PH.D.; American physicist; b. 10 July 1920; ed. Germantown Friends School, Dartmouth Coll., and Univ. of Chicago.
Research physicist Manhattan Project, Berkeley 42-43, Los Alamos 43-46; graduate student (under Enrico Fermi) Univ. of Chicago 46-48; Instructor in Physics Univ. of Calif., Berkeley 48-50, Asst. Prof. 50-54, Assoc. Prof. 54-58, Prof. 58-: on leave at Univ. of Rome as Guggenheim Fellow 57-58; Loeb Lecturer, Harvard Univ. 59; mem. Nat. Acad. of Sciences; has specialised in research in spontaneous fission, proton scattering, discovery of antiproton, properties of antinucleons, etc.; shared Nobel Prize for Physics with Emilio Segre 59.
Department of Physics, University of California, Berkeley 4, Calif., U.S.A.

Chamberlin, William Henry, B.A.; American journalist; b. 17 Feb. 1897; ed. Haverford Coll., Pa.
Moscow Corresp. of *Christian Science Monitor* 22-34, Tokyo Corresp. 35-39, Paris 39-40; Visiting Lecturer, Haverford Coll., Yale Univ. Foreign Areas School and Harvard Civil Affairs Training School 40-; Contributing Editor *The New Leader* (New York) 42; Editorial contributor to *The Wall Street Journal* since 45.
Publs. *Soviet Russia* 30, *The Soviet Planned Economic*

Order 31, *Russia's Iron Age* 34, *The Russian Revolution 1917-1921* 35, *Collectivism: A False Utopia* 37, *Japan Over Asia* 38, *The Confessions of an Individualist* 40, *The World's Iron Age* 41, *Canada Today and Tomorrow* 42, *The Russian Enigma: An Interpretation* 43, *America. Partner in World Rule* 45, *World Order or Chaos* 46, *The European Cockpit* 47, *America's Second Crusade* 50, *Beyond Containment* 53, *The Evolution of a Conservative, The German Phoenix* 63, *What We Should Know About Communism* 65.
18 Francis Avenue, Cambridge, Mass., U.S.A.

Chambers, Maurice Ripley; American shoe manufacturer; b. 14 Feb. 1916.
Tweedie Footwear Corpn. 31-37; Montgomery Ward and Co. N.Y. 39-49; Int. Shoe Co. (now Interco Inc.) 49-, Sales Man. 49-56, Vice-Pres. (Sales) and Dir. 56-61, Pres. and Dir. 62-, Chair. 66-; Dir. other companies.
International Shoe Company, 1509 Washington Avenue, St. Louis 66, Mo., U.S.A.

Chambers, Richard H.; American judge; b. 7 Nov. 1906; ed. Arizona and Stanford Univs.
Private practice, Tucson, Arizona 32-42, 45-54; Army service 42-45; Chief Judge, U.S. Court of Appeals, Ninth Circuit 54-.
U.S. Courthouse, Tucson, Arizona, U.S.A.

Chambers, Sir (Stanley) Paul K.B.E., C.B., C.I.E., B.COM., M.SC.(ECON.); British businessman; b. 2 April 1904; ed. City of London Coll., and London School of Economics.
Mem. Indian Income Tax Enquiry Cttee. 35-36; Income Tax Adviser to the Govt. of India 37-40; Sec. and Commr. of Board of Inland Revenue 42-47; Chief of Finance Div. Control Comm. for Germany, British Element 45-47; Dir. I.C.I. Ltd. 47, Financial Dir. 48-52, Deputy Chair. 52-60, Chair. 60-68; mem. Cttee. appointed to review the organization of Customs and Excise 51-53; mem. Cttee. on Departmental Records 52-54; Chair. Cttee. of Inquiry into London Transport 53-55; Dir. Nat. Provincial Bank Ltd.; Deputy Chair. Royal Insurance Co. Ltd. (Chair. 68-), Liverpool, and London & Globe Insurance Co. Ltd., and London & Lancashire Insurance Co. Ltd.; Pres. Inst. of Dirs. 64-, British Shippers' Council 63-; Vice-Pres. The India, Pakistan, Burma Asscn.; Dir. Imperial Chemical Industries of Australia & New Zealand Ltd.; Deputy Chair. of African Explosives & Chemical Industries Ltd.; several Hon. degrees.
Home: Oak Lodge, The Bishop's Avenue, London, N.2, England.

Chambrun, Comte Charles de; French politician; b. 16 June 1930; ed. Lycée français New York, Univs. of New York, Harvard and Paris.
Member Chamber of Deputies 62-66; Sec. of State for Foreign Commerce 66-; Mayor of Montrodat, Lozère 54-.
41 Quai Branly, Paris 7e; and 11 rue de la Faisanderie, Paris 16e, France.

Chamoun, Camille, LL.D.; Lebanese lawyer and politician; b. 3 April 1900; ed. Coll. des Frères and Law School, Beirut.
Qualified as lawyer 24; mem. Parliament 34-; Minister of Finance 38; Minister of Interior 43-44; Minister to Allied Governments in London 44; Head of Del. to Int. Civil Aviation Conf., Chicago 44, UNESCO Conf. and U.N. Preparatory Comm. 45; Del. to U.N. Gen. Assembly, London and N.Y. 46; Lebanese rep. Interim Comm., U.N. 48; Pres. Lebanese Republic 52-58; leader Liberal Nationalist Party 58-.
Office of the Liberal Nationalist Party, Beirut, Lebanon.

Champetier, Georges, D. ès SC. PHY.; French scientist; b. 3 Feb. 1905.
Demonstrator, Ecole Pratique des Hautes Etudes, Paris 28-30; Asst. Inst. de Biologie Physico-chimique,

Paris 30-37; Head of Laboratory, Faculty of Sciences, Univ. of Paris 37-39; in charge of Research, Nat. Centre of Scientific Research 39-45; Deputy Prof. Faculty of Sciences, Univ. of Paris 45-47, Asst. Prof. 47; Dir. of Studies, Ecole Supérieure de Physique et de Chimie Industrielles Paris 47-; Prof. Faculty of Sciences Univ. of Paris 49-; Hon. Dir. Nat. Centre of Scientific Research 57; Pres. Société Chimique de France 62-64; Pres. Admin. Council, Institut Pasteur 66-; mem. Académie des Sciences 60-; Commdr. Légion d'Honneur.
Publs. *Traité de Chimie Générale, Notions et Principes fondamentaux* 39, *Les Eléments de la Chimie* 43, *La Chimie Générale* 45, *Dérivés cellulosiques* 47, *Les Molécules géantes* 48, *Chimie macromoléculaire* 57.
10 rue Vauquelin, Paris 5e, France.

Champin, Pierre Marcel Henri; French businessman; b. 26 Aug. 1903; ed. Ecole des Sciences Politiques, Paris. President and Gen. Man. Vallourec; Dir. Soc. Métal Déployé, Usinor, Denain-Nord-Est, Compagnie Industrielle de Matériel transport and of several other concerns; Pres. Dresser-Dujardin, Brossette S.A.; Officier Légion d'Honneur.
Home: 33 rue des Abonnances, 92-Boulogne Billancourt; Office: 7 rond-point Bugeaud, 75-Paris 16e, France.

Champion, George, B.SC.; American banker; b. 8 Feb. 1904; ed. San Diego High School and Dartmouth Coll. With Nat. Bank of Commerce, New York 26-29; joined Equitable Trust Co. 29, asst. sec. 30, on merger of Equitable and Chase Nat. became asst. cashier Chase Nat. 30; Vice-Pres. Canal Bank and Trust Co., New Orleans 31-33; returned to Chase National as second Vice-Pres. in South-eastern district 33, Vice-Pres. 39, head of South-eastern district 42, senior Vice-Pres. 49; exec. Vice-Pres. on merger of Chase Nat. Bank and Bank of Manhattan Co. 55; in charge of U.S. dept. 53-57; Dir. and Pres. Chase Manhattan Bank 57-60, Chair. 61-; Dir. American Smelting and Refining Co. and mem. Finance Cttee., Southern Railway Co. and Travelers Insurance Cos.; mem. Advisory Cttee. on special activities of American Bankers Asscn., Govt. Borrowing Cttee., etc.; mem. Assoc. of Reserve City Bankers; Nat. Treas. for Nat. Campaign of the United Negro Coll. Fund; mem. Advisory Board of the Business and Educ. Council of New York; Dir. of the Greater New York Fund.
1 Chase Manhattan Plaza, New York, N.Y. 10015, U.S.A.

Champion, Robert L., B.S., M.S.; American engineer; b. 13; ed. Univ. of Illinois and Stanford Univ. Engineering teacher at Univ. of Ill. 37-39, Mich. State Coll. 39-41, Northwestern Univ. 41-42; Research and Development Div., War Plans, Budocks 42-43; Project Engineer Amchitka Fido Installation 43; with Landing Aids Section BuAer, fog disposal liaison officer 43-44; BuAer Liaison Officer, R.A.F. Fido Project and Petroleum Warfare Dept., London 44; Commanding Officer U.S. Navy Landing Aids Experimental Station 44-45, Dir. 45-47; Pres. Int. Science Corp. 46-, Int. Science Foundation 54-; Technical Dir. Associação de Fomento da Aviação Ltda. 49-50; Dir. Cooperative Research Inst. 50-; Asst. Dir. Office of Int. Relations, Nat. Acad. of Sciences, San Francisco Bay Area Int. Science Center; Consultant to U.S. Army Ballistic Missile Agency, Johns Hopkins Univ. Operations Research Office and private cos.; mem. American Soc. of Civil Engineers, Calif. Acad. of Sciences, etc.
World Trade Center, Ferry Building, San Francisco, Calif., U.S.A.

Chamson, André Louis Jules; French writer and museum curator; b. 6 June 1900; ed. Ecole des Chartes. Curator Château de Versailles 33-39; Curator Petit Palais 45-; mem. Acad. Française 56-; Int. Pres. P.E.N. Club 56; Dir.-Gen. Archives de France 59, Grand Croix

de la Légion d'Honneur; Croix de Guerre; Médaille de la Résistance; many Foreign honours; Hon. Dr. Laval Univ. (Quebec).
Publs. *Roux le Bandit* 25, *Les Hommes de la route* 27, *Le Crime des Justes* 28, *Héritages* 30, *L'année des vaincus* 35, *Les quatre éléments* 36, *L'auberge de l'abîme* 36, *La Galère* 38, *Le Puits des Miracles* 45, *Le dernier village* 46, *L'homme qui marchait devant moi* 48, *La neige et la fleur* 51, *On ne voit pas le coeur* 52, *Le chiffre de nos jours* 54, *Languedoc* 56, *Adeline Venician* 56, *Nos Ancêtres, les Gaulois* 58, *Devenir ce qu'on est* 60, *Le rendez-vous des espérances* 61, *Comme une pierre qui tombe* 64, *La Petite Odyssée* 65, *La Superbe* 67.
Palais Soubise, 60 rue des Francs-Bourgeois, Paris 3e, France.
Telephone: ARC 70-72.

Chance, Britton, M.S., PH.D., D.SC.; American biophysicist; b. 24 July 1913; ed. Univ. of Pennsylvania and Cambridge Univ., England.
Acting Dir. Johnson Foundation 40-41; Investigator Office of Scientific Research and Development 41; staff mem. Radiation Laboratory, M.I.T.; Asst. Prof. of Biophysics, Univ. of Pennsylvania 41-46, Prof. and Dir. Johnson Foundation 49-, E. R. Johnson Prof. of Biophysics 49-; Guggenheim Fellow, Nobel and Molteno Insts. 46-48; scientific consultant, research attaché, U.S. Navy, London 48; consultant, Nat. Science Foundation 51-56; President's Scientific Advisory Cttee. 59-60; mem. Nat. Acad. of Sciences, American Acad. of Arts and Sciences, American Philosophical Soc., Royal Acad. of Science, Uppsala, Biochemical Soc., Biophysical Soc., Int. Soc. for Cell Biology; Fellow Inst. of Radio Engineers; Presidential Certificate of Merit 50; Paul Lewis award in enzyme chemistry, American Chemical Soc. 50; William J. Morlock award in biochemical electronics, Inst. of Radio Engineers 61.
Publs. *Waveforms* (with Williams, Hughes, McNichol, Sayre) 49, *Electronic Time Measurements* (with Hulsizer, McNichol, Williams) 49, *Enzyme-Substrate Compounds* 51, *Enzymes in Action in Living Cells* 55, *The Respiratory Chain and Oxidative Phosphorylation* 56, *Techniques for Assay of Respiratory Enzymes* 57, *Energy-Linked Functions of Mitochondria* 63, *Rapid Mixing and Sampling Techniques in Biochemistry* 64.
4014 Pine Street and 37th and Spruce Streets, Philadelphia, Pa., U.S.A.

Chancel, Ludovic; French diplomatist; b. 1 Jan. 1901; ed. Lycée Carnot and Faculty of Law, Univ. of Paris. Commercial Attaché, Brazil 29; Consul, Shanghai and Tallinn 39, later at Bucharest; Del., French Nat. Cttee. in East Africa 41; Counsellor to Arab Govt., later Dir. of Arabian Affairs 44; Consul Gen., New York 46-51; Minister 51-52; Ambassador to Iraq 52-54; Del. to French Residency General, Morocco 54-56; Ambassador to South Africa 56-58; Chief of Protocol, Ministry of Foreign Affairs 58; Ambassador to Czechoslovakia 61-64; Diplomatic Adviser to the Govt. 64-; Commandeur, Légion d'Honneur, Commandeur des Arts et des Lettres.
Ministère des Affaires Etrangères, 37 quai d'Orsay, Paris 7e, France.

Chancellor, Sir Christopher (John), Kt., C.M.G., M.A.; British business executive; b. 29 March 1904; ed. Eton Coll., and Trinity Coll., Cambridge.
Joined Reuters 30, Gen. Man. 44-59; Chair. Odhams Press Ltd. 60-61, Daily Herald (1929) Ltd. 60-61, Madame Tussaud's Ltd. 61-, The Bowater Paper Corpn. 62-; Dir. The Northern and Employers Assurance Co. Ltd., *The Observer* 61-.
Hunstrete House, Pensford, Somerset, England.

Chancellor, John; American newspaperman and TV compère; b. 14 July 1927; ed. Univ. of Illinois.
Chicago *Sun-Times*; NBC news staff 50-, compère NBC TV programme *To-day* 61-62; Producer of Special

Programmes 62-63; Head of N.B.C. Brussels Bureau to cover European Common Market July 63-64; White House Corresp. of N.B.C. 64-65; Dir. Voice of America 65-67, with N.B.C. 67-.
Home: 3126 Woodley Road, Washington, D.C., U.S.A.

Chand, Khub, B.A.; Indian diplomatist; b. 16 Dec. 1911; ed. Univ. of Delhi and Oriel Coll., Oxford.
Joined I.C.S. 35; Asst. and later Joint Magistrate, Shahjahanpur (U.P.) 35-37; Joint and later Additional District Magistrate, Kanpur (U.P.) 37-39; Under-Sec. to Govt. of India, Dept. of Defence and Sec. Indian Soldiers' Board, later Asst. Financial Adviser, Mil. Finance 39-43; District Magistrate, Azamgarh (U.P.) 43-45; Regional Food Controller, U.P. 45-47; Deputy Sec. Ministry of Defence 47-48; Head Indian Mil. Mission in Germany, with mil. rank of Major-Gen., Indian Army 48-50; Head of Indian Mission Allied High Comm. for Germany 49-50; Deputy High Commr. for India in Pakistan 50-52, Acting High Commr. 50-51; Minister to Iraq April 52-55, concurrently Minister to Jordan 54-55; Joint Sec. to Govt. of India, Ministry of External Affairs 55-57; Amb. to Italy 57-60, concurrently Minister to Albania; High Commr. for India in Ghana and Sierra Leone, Commr. in Nigeria and Amb. to Liberia, Guinea and Mali 60-62; Amb. to Sweden and Finland 62-66; Leader of Indian delegation to 41st session of Economic and Social Council of UN 66; Indian rep. on Ad Hoc Cttee. of Narcotics Comm. of UN; Amb. to Lebanon, Jordan, Kuwait and High Commr. in Cyprus 66-67, to German Fed. Repub. 67-.
Indian Embassy, Bonn, German Federal Republic.
Telephone: 21931.

Chand, Tara, M.A., D.PHIL.; Indian diplomatist; b. 88; ed. Meerut Coll., Meerut, Muir Central Coll., Allahabad, and Queen's Coll., Oxford.
Professor of History, Kayastha Pathshala Coll., Allahabad 13-18; Principal, K.P. Coll. 18-45; Prof. of Politics, Allahabad Univ. 45-47, Vice-Chancellor 47-48, now Prof. Emeritus; Pres. Secondary Educ. Conf.; Sec. Hindustani Acad. U.P.; Sec. and Educational Adviser to Govt. of India 48-51; Indian Amb. to Iran 51-56; Tagore Lecturer Allahabad Univ. 65, Nizam Lecturer Delhi Univ. 67; mem. Rajya Sahba 56.
Publs. *A Short History of the Indian People, Influence of Islam on Indian Culture, Hindustani, Dara Shukoh (Islamic Culture), Growth of Islamic Thought in India (History of Eastern and Western Philosophy), History of the Freedom Movement in India*, Vol. I, and *State and Society in the Mughal Age*, etc.
8 Tughlak Road, New Delhi, India.
Telephone: 40916 (Office); 617687 (Home).

Chanda, Asok Kumar, B.SC., O.B.E.; Indian financier and economist; b. 25 Oct. 1902; ed. Calcutta Univ. and London School of Economics.
Joined Indian Audit and Accounts Service 26; mem. Lend-Lease Del. to U.S.A. 46; Adviser, Punjab Partition Council 47; Financial Commr. for Railways 49-52; Sec. Ministry of Production 52-54; Chair. Board of Dirs., Sindri Fertilizers & Chemicals Ltd., Hindustan Machine Tools Ltd. and Hindustan Steel Ltd. 52-54; Comptroller and Auditor-General 54-60; Chair. Third Finance Comm. 61, Union Excise Reorganization Cttee. 63, Cttee. on Broadcasting and Information Media 67; Chair. Jessop and Co. Ltd., Delhi 60-.
Publs. *Indian Administration, Aspects of Audit Control, Federalism in India: A Study of Union-State Relations.*
76 Sundar Nagar, New Delhi, India.

Chanderli, Abdelkader; Algerian diplomatist; b. 15; ed. Univ. of Paris.
Former Foreign Correspondent and Editor; Chief, Public Relations Div. UNESCO 49-55; Rep. of Algerian Front de Libération Nationale (F.L.N.) in U.S.A. 56-62; Perm. Rep. of Algeria to UN 62-64; Vice-Pres. ECOSOC

64-65; Dir.-Gen. Center for Industrial Studies and Technology, Algiers.
c/o Ministry of Industry and Energy, Algiers, 11 rue Buffon, El-Biar, Algiers, Algeria.

Chandler, George, M.A., PH.D., F.L.A., F.R.HIST.S.; British librarian; b. 2 July 1915; ed. Central Grammar School, Birmingham, Birmingham and Midland Inst., Leeds Coll. of Commerce and Univ. of London.
With Leeds Public Libraries 36-46; Borough Librarian and Curator, Dudley 46-49; City Librarian, Liverpool 52-; established Int. Library 57, American Library 59, Commonwealth Library 59; organiser of int. literary and historical exhibitions of books, manuscripts and prints; External Examiner, Sheffield Univ.; Extra-Mural Lecturer, Univs. of Leeds, Birmingham and Liverpool; Pres. Soc. of Municipal and County Chief Librarians; Chair. Exec. Cttee. of the Library Asscn.; Dir. Ladsirlac Technical Information Centre; Editor, Int. Series of Monographs on Libraries and Information Science 64-; Pres. Int. Asscn. of Metropolitan City Libraries 67.
Publs. *Dudley* 49, *William Roscoe* 53, *Liverpool* 57, *Liverpool Shipping* 60, *Liverpool under James I* 60, *How to Find Out* 63, 67, *The Grasshopper and the Liver Bird* 64, *Liverpool under Charles I* 65, *Libraries in the Modern World* 65, *Four Centuries of Banking* 68; numerous papers and pamphlets.
23 Dowsefield Lane, Calderstones, Liverpool 18, England.
Telephone: GAT 2051.

Chandler, Norman (father of Otis Chandler, *q.v.*); American newspaper publisher and businessman; b. 14 Sept. 1899; ed. Stanford Univ.
Joined The Times-Mirror Co. 22; Dir. 38, Vice-Pres. and Gen. Man. 36-41, Pres. and Publisher Times-Mirror Co. 45-60, Pres. 60-61, Chair. and Pres. 61-66, Chair. and Chief Exec. Officer 66-, Corpn. Exec. 65-; Chair. Emett & Chandler; Dir. Chandis Securities Co., Pfaffinger Foundation; Vice.-Pres. and Dir. Chandler-Sherman Corpn., and Tejon Ranch Co.; Dir. Atchison, Topeka and Sante Fe Railway System, Kaiser Steel Corpn., Pan American Airways Inc., Security-First Nat. Bank of Los Angeles, etc.
Times Mirror Square, Los Angeles, Calif. 90053, U.S.A.

Chandler, Otis (son of Norman Chandler, *q.v.*); American newspaper executive; b. 23 Nov. 1927; ed. Andover Acad., Mass., and Stanford Univ.
Trainee, Times Mirror Co. 53, Asst. to President (assigned to *Mirror-News*) 57, Marketing Manager, *Los Angeles Times* 58-60, Publisher, *Los Angeles Times* 60-, Vice-Pres. Times Mirror Co. 61-, Snr. Vice-Pres. 66-, Dir. 62; Vice-Chair. Board Times Mirror Co. 68.
Times Mirror Square, Los Angeles, Calif. 90053; 1048 Oak Grove Place, San Marino, Calif., U.S.A.

Chandos, 1st Viscount, cr. 54, of Aldershot; **Oliver Lyttelton,** P.C., D.S.O., M.C.; British industrialist and politician; b. 15 March 1893; ed. Eton and Trinity Coll., Cambridge.
Grenadier Guards 14-18; fmr. Managing Dir. British Metal Corpn., Ltd.; Controller of Non-Ferrous Metals, Ministry of Supply 39-40; Cons. M.P. 41-54; Pres. Board of Trade 40; mem. War Cabinet 41-45, Minister of State in Middle East 41-42, Minister of Production 42-45; Pres. Board of Trade May-July 45; Chair. Associated Electrical Industries Ltd. 45-51; Sec. of State for Colonies 51-54; Chair. Associated Electrical Industries Ltd. 54-63, A.E.I.-John Thompson Nuclear Energy Co. Ltd. 56-63, Board of Partners The Nuclear Power Group 60-; Chair. N. Ireland Devt. Council 55-65; Dir. Alliance Assurance Co. Ltd., Imperial Chemical Industries Ltd. 54-, Sun Insurance Office Ltd., Strathmore Tin Pty. Ltd.; Chair. Nat. Theatre Board 62-;

Vice-Pres. Market Research Soc.; Trustee Churchill Coll.; Order of Suvorov, 1st Class 44.
Publ. *The Memoirs of Lord Chandos* 62.
20 Pelham Crescent, London, S.W.7, England.

Chandra, Avinash; Indian artist; b. 31; ed. Delhi Polytechnic, Delhi.
On staff of Delhi Polytechnic, Delhi 53-56; in London 56-; executed glass mural for Pilkington Brothers' Head Office, St. Helens, Lancs. and fibreglass mural for Indian Tea Centre, London, 64; Gold Medal, Prix Européenne, Ostend 62; John D. Rockefeller Third Fund Fellowship 65.
Works in following collections: National Gallery of Modern Art, New Delhi, Tate Gallery, London, Victoria and Albert Museum, London, Arts Council of Great Britain, London, Ashmolean Museum, Oxford, Ulster Museum, Belfast, City Art Gallery, Birmingham, Gulbenkian Museum, Durham, Musée National d'Art Moderne, Paris, Whitworth Art Gallery, Manchester, Museum of Modern Art, Haifa, Punjab Museum, Chandigarh, etc.; one-man exhbns. in Srinagar, New Delhi, Belfast, London, Oxford, Paris, Bristol, Arnhem, Amsterdam, Zürich, Copenhagen, Stockholm, etc.
24 Willoughby Road, Hampstead, London, N.W.3, England.

Chandra, Satish, M.A., B.SC.; Indian business exec. and politician; b. 17; ed. S.M. Coll., Chandausi, Govt. Agricultural Coll., Kanpur, and Bareilly Coll., Bareilly (Agra Univ.).
Indian Nat. Congress 36-; mem. Indian Constituent Ass. 48-50, Provisional Parl. 50-52, Lok Sabha 52-62; Parl. Sec. to Prime Minister 51-52; Union Dep. Minister for Defence 52-55, for Production 55-57, for Commerce and Industry 57-62; Chair. Indian Airlines Corpn. and Dir. Air-India 63, 64; Chair. British India Corpn. Ltd., The Elgin Mills Co. Ltd., Cawnpore Textiles Ltd., Cawnpore Sugar Works Ltd., Champarun Sugar Co. Ltd., Saran Engineering Co. Ltd. 62-; Dir. other cos.
Chitrakut, Parbati Bagla Road, Kanpur, U.P., India.

Chandrasekhar, Sripati, M.A., M.LITT., M.SC., PH.D., Indian economist and demographer; b. 22 Nov. 1918; ed. Univ. of Madras and Columbia, New York and Princeton Univs.
Visiting Lecturer, Univ. of Pa. and Asia Inst., New York 44-46; Prof. of Economics, Annamalai Univ. 47-50; Dir. Demographic Research, UNESCO, Paris 47-49; Prof. of Economics and Head of Dept., Baroda Univ. 50-53; Nuffield Fellow, London School of Economics 53-55; Dir. Indian Inst. for Population Studies 56-67; mem. Rajya Sabha 64-; Minister of State for Health and Family Planning 67-Nov. 67; Minister of State in Ministry of Health, Family Planning and Urban Development Nov. 67-; Research Prof. of Demography, Univ. of California; Editor *Population Review*.
Publs. *India's Population* 46, *Census and Statistics in India* 47, *Indian Emigration* 48, *Hungry People and Empty Lands* 52, *Population and Planned Parenthood in India* 55, *Infant Mortality in India* 59, *China's Population* 59, *Communist China Today* 61, *Red China: An Asian View* 62, *A Decade of Mao's China* (Editor) 63, *American Aid and India's Economic Development* 65, *Asia's Population Problems* 67.
Ministry of Health, New Delhi, India.

Chandrasekhar, Subrahmanyan, B.A., PH.D., SC.D., F.R.S.; American (b. Indian) university professor; b. 19 Oct. 1910; ed. Presidency Coll., Madras, and Cambridge Univ.
Fellow of Trinity Coll. Cambridge 33-37; Research Assoc. Univ. of Chicago 37-38, Asst. Prof. 38-41, Assoc. Prof. 42-43, Prof. 44-46; Distinguished Service Prof. of Theoretical Astrophysics 47-52, Morton D. Hull Distinguished Service Prof. of Theoretical Astrophysics 52-; Man. Editor *Astrophysical Journal* 52-; mem. American Philosophical Society, American Academy of Arts and Sciences, U.S. Nat. Acad. of Sciences; Bruce Gold Medal of Astronomical Soc. of the Pacific 52, Gold Medal, Royal Astronomical Soc. 53, Rumford Medal, American Acad. of Arts and Sciences 57, Royal Medal, Royal Soc., London 62, Nat. Medal of Science, U.S.A. 67.
Publs. *Introduction to the Study of Stellar Structure* 39, *Principles of Stellar Dynamics* 42, *Radiative Transfer* 50, *Hydrodynamic and Hydromagnetic Stability* 61.
Laboratory for Astrophysics and Space Research, 933 East 56th Street, Chicago, Illinois 60637, U.S.A.

Chandrasekharan, Komaravolu, M.A., M.SC., PH.D.; Indian mathematician; b. 21 Nov. 1920; ed. Presidency Coll., Madras, and Inst. for Advanced Study, Princeton, U.S.A.
Prof. Eidgenössische Technische Hochschule, Zürich; Sec. Int. Mathematical Union 61-66; Vice-Pres. Int. Council of Scientific Unions 62-66, Sec.-Gen. 66-; mem. Scientific Advisory Cttee. to Cabinet, Govt. of India 61-66; Fellow Nat. Inst. of Sciences of India, Indian Acad. of Sciences; Padma Shri 59; Shanti Swarup Bhatnagar Memorial Award for Scientific Research 63; Ramanujan medal 66.
Publs. *Fourier Transforms* (with S. Bochner) 49, *Typical Means* (with S. Minakshisundaram) 52, *Lectures on the Riemann Zeta-function* 53, *Analytic Number Theory* 68.
Eidgenössische Technische Hochschule, 8006 Zürich, Leonhardstrasse 33; Home: Hedwigstrasse 29, 8032 Zürich, Switzerland.
Telephone: 53-96-86.

Chang Chih-chung; Chinese soldier and politician; b. 91; ed. Paoting Mil. Acad.
Former General in the Kuomintang Army; formerly Governor of Hunan Province; Dir. North-West H.Q. and Governor of Sinkiang Province; Vice-Chair. Council of Nat. Defence 54-; Vice-Chair. Standing Cttee. Nat. People's Congress; Dir., Gen. Office for Culture and Educ., State Council; Vice-Chair. Revolutionary Cttee. of the Kuomintang.
National People's Congress, Peking, China.

Chang Chih-jang; Chinese jurist; b. 99; ed. Futan Univ., Columbia Univ. (U.S.A.).
Judge of Supreme Court under Nationalist Govt.; Dean of the Coll. of Law, Futan Univ.; imprisoned for anti-Japanese activities 36-37; Futan Univ. moved to Chungking in war; there he edited journal on international questions; Asst. High Judge of Central People's Courts 49; Vice-Pres. of Supreme People's Court 49.
c/o Supreme People's Court, Peking, China.

Chang Chih-yi; Chinese administrator.
Head of a brigade political dept. during Japanese War; Chair. Nationalities Cttee., Central and South Mil. and Administrative Council 51, Vice-Chair. Political and Legal Cttee. of same 52, Sec.-Gen. of same 53; Vice-Chair. Nationalities Cttee., N.P.C. 54-65.
c/o Nationalities Committee, National People's Congress, Peking, China.

Chang Chin-fu; Chinese economist.
Vice-Chair. Govt. Cttee. of Finance and Economy, Chekiang Province, and Dir. Board of Industry; Vice-Chair. Cttee. of Finance and Economy, East China Military Govt. Cttee. 52; Rep. for Anhwei to N.P.C. 54; fmr. Vice-Pres. Acad. of Sciences.
Academy of Sciences, Peking, China.

Chang Ching-wu; Chinese politician; b. 06.
In Shantung H.Q. of 8th Route Army 42, and, later, other high posts; Chinese Govt. Rep. in Tibet 51 and 55, fmr. Sec. of Tibet Work Cttee.; Chief of the Secretariat of the Chair. of the People's Republic 55-64; Central Govt. Rep. in Tibet 65-67; arrested in Peking Oct. 67; Sec. South-West Bureau, Chinese C.P.; Nat. People's Congress, mem. Standing Cttee. 65-.
c/o National People's Congress, Peking, China.

Chang Chung; Chinese soldier and administrator; b. 98; self-educated.
Leader of the Yi people of Yunnan Province; legendary figure in the '30s; set himself up as king in the mountains to avenge his father's murder; in the Japanese War led forces north and took part in operations; mem. of Nationalities Cttee. of People's Govt. 50; Asst. Gov. of Yunnan 55; Vice-Chair. Nationalities Cttee., N.P.C.; Dep. Dir. State Archives Bureau.
Nationalities Committee, National People's Congress, Peking, China.

Chang Dai-Chien; Chinese painter; b. 1 April 1899; ed. Chui-ch'ing School, Chungking and under Li Ch'ing, Shanghai.
Member Cttee. first Nat. Exhbn. of Fine Arts 29; Prof. Central Univ. Nanking 36; moved to Argentina 52; first one-man exhbn. Peking 34, then Shanghai 36, Chungking 39, 40, Chengtu 43, Shanghai 46, 47, Hong Kong 48, 62, New Delhi and Hyderabad 50, Buenos Aires 52, Tokyo 55, 56, Museum of Modern Art, Paris 56, Salon Nationale, Paris 60, Brussels 60, Athens 60, Madrid 60, Geneva 61, São Paulo 61, Singapore 63, Kuala Lumpur 63, New York 63, Cologne 64, Grosvenor Gallery, London 65; represented at Paris Exhbn. of Chinese Painting 33, London 35, UNESCO Exhbn., Paris 46; Gold Medal, Int. Council of Fine Arts, N.Y. 58.
Major works: *The Lotuses*, Jeu-de-Paume Museum, Paris 33, copied two hundred frescoes, caves of Tun-huang 40, *Giant Lotus* 45, twelve major works, Perm. Exhbn. Contemporary Chinese Art, Cernuschi Museum 59, Lotus painting, Museum of Modern Art, New York 61.
P.O. Box 249, Mogi das Cruzes, São Paulo, Brazil.

Chang Do Yung, General; Korean army officer; b. 23; ed. Tongyang University, Japan.
Fought in Japanese army in Second World War; further education in U.S.A. 53; Dep. C.-in-C. of Gen. Staff, S. Korean Army 56, later Cmmdr. Second Army; C.-in-C. of General Staff; Minister of Defence May-June 61, Chair. Supreme Council of Nat. Reconstruction and Prime Minister May-June 61; under house arrest July 61; sentenced to death Jan. 62, sentence commuted, later released 62.
Seoul, Republic of Korea.

Chang Hsi-jo; Chinese scholar and politician; b. 89; ed. Columbia Univ. (U.S.A.).
Took part in 1911 Revolution as mem. of the *Tung-menghui*; taught at Peking Univ. of Law and Politics, at the Univ. of China, and at Nanking Central Univ.; Prof. of Political Science in Tsinghua Univ. 29; after the outbreak of the Japanese War he taught at the South-West Combined Univ.; Minister of Education; Pres. Chinese People's Institute of Foreign Affairs; Peking Del. to First Nat. People's Congress 54; Chair. Comm. for Cultural Relations with Foreign Countries 58-.
Commission for Cultural Relations with Foreign Countries, Peking, China.

Chang Jen-hsia; Chinese artist, poet and art historian; b. 31 Jan. 1904.
Has lectured at the Int. Univ. of Santiniketan, India, at the Central Univ., Chungking, and at the Coll. of Oriental Studies, Kunming; Prof. of History of Art, Central Acad. of Fine Arts.
Central Academy of Fine Arts, Peking, China.

Chang Kuo-hua; Chinese politician.
Former 2nd Sec. Chinese C.P. Tibet Work Cttee.; fmr. Vice-Chair. Preparatory Cttee. for Tibet Autonomous Region; Commdr. Tibet Military Region; First Sec. Tibet Autonomous Region Sept. 65-.
Office of the First Secretary of Tibet Autonomous Region, Lhasa, Tibet, China.

Chang Lin-chih; Chinese administrator.
Sec. of the Chungking City Communist Party Cttee. 49; Asst. Chief of the Chungking Mil. Cttee.; on South-West Mil. Govt. Council 51; Vice-Minister of Second Ministry of Machine Building 52; post in Chungking City Govt. 54; Del. for Hopei at the First N.P.C.; reappointed Vice-Minister, Second Ministry for Machine Building; Minister of Electrical Equipment Industry 56-57, of Coal Industry 57-.
Ministry of Coal Industry, Peking, China.

Chang Tien-yi; Chinese writer; b. 06; ed. Hangchow Middle School.
Began writing in 29; mem. of Council of Chinese Writers' Union 54; his works include novels, short stories, and books for children; Vice-Gov. Shansi Province.
Publs. include *One Year, The Cogwheel, In the City, Three and a Half Days' Dream, The Bees, Hatred, The Story of Lo Wen-ying, They and We,* etc.
Taiyuan, Shansi Province, People's Republic of China.

Chang Ti-hsueh; Chinese administrator; b. 06.
First Dep. Sec. C.C.P., Hupeh Prov. Cttee. 54; Vice-Gov. Hupeh Prov. 55, Gov. 56-; Sec. C.C.P., Hupeh Prov. Cttee., 2nd Sec. Hupeh Prov. Cttee. Chinese C.P. 65-; Deputy for Hupeh, Nat. People's Congress 54-.
Governor's Residence, Wuhan, Hupeh, People's Republic of China.

Chang Ting-cheng; Chinese administrator; b. 97; ed. Kwangtung Peasants' School.
Formerly Chair. of West Fukien Soviet Govt.; led 21st Red Army in 31; commanded 7th Div. of New Fourth Army; mem. of Cttee. for Overseas Chinese Affairs; Chair. Fukien Provincial Govt. 52; transferred to duties in East China Mil. Region 53; Fukien Rep. at N.P.C. 54; mem. Central Cttee. of Eighth Congress of C.C.P. and on Supervisory Cttee. 56; Chief Procurator 54-.
Supreme People's Procuracy, Peking, China.

Chang Wen-tien; Chinese Marxist theoretician, novelist and politician; b. 1900; ed. Univ. of California.
Joined Communist Party of China in 25; studied in Moscow 27-29; held various official positions in the Communist Party; Ambassador to the U.S.S.R. 54-55; Alt. mem. Political Bureau, C.C.P. 56-.
Publs. Novels: *Chingchun te Meng, Changtu,* etc.; translations of works by D'Annunzio, Wilde, Tolstoy and Turgenev.
Political Bureau of Chinese Communist Party, Peking, People's Republic of China.

Chanlaine, Pierre; French writer; b. 27 July 1885; ed. Ecole Spéciale Militaire, Saint-Cyr.
Commissioned service in 155th Infantry Regt. 06-09; Pres. Assoc. des Ecrivains Combattants; fmr. Hon. Pres. Société des Gens de Lettres; fmr. Pres. Association des Auteurs de Films; Commdr. Légion d'Honneur, Croix de Guerre (France and Serbia) Cross for Merit in War (Italy), Commandeur Arts et Lettres, Officier de l'Ordre de Léopold (Belgium); Grand Officier de l'Etoile Noire.
Publs. *Les Concessionistes, Le grand bonhomme, Le poison intérieur, Les armes reposées, Napoléon vers Sainte Hélène, Ainsi va la Vie, Le comte d'Orsay, Mam'zelle Bonaparte* (with Gérard Bourgeois), *Vers les Marches du trône, L'Homme que j'étais pour toi, L'Homme d'un soir d'été, Karen, la Bienaimée, L'Enfer et le Paradis, Tournepête, Vedette ou Bourgeoise?, L'enfant de l'âme, La Vie brève et douloureuse du Roi de Rome, Edouard Detaille, Pasteur, La femme de personne, Ou est la Martyr? Espionage sous le Second Empire, Apprenez à parler,* etc.
83 avenue de la Grande Armée, Paris 16e, France.

Chao Po-ping; Chinese administrator.
Former Sec. Sian City Cttee., C.C.P.; Northwest China Military and Administrative Cttee. 50-53; Dir. Propaganda Dept. C.C.P. Northwest China Bureau; mem.

Northwest China Administrative Cttee. 53-54; Second Sec. C.C.P. Shensi Prov. Cttee. 54; Dep. Gov. Shensi 54-60, Gov. 60-63; Dep. from Sian City, Nat. People's Congress 54-, Deputy Sec.-Gen. N.P.C. 63-; mem. Bills Cttee.; Alternate mem. C.C.P. Central Cttee. 58-.
National People's Congress, Peking, People's Republic of China.

Chapelain-Midy, Roger; French painter; b. 24 Aug. 1904; ed. Lycée Louis le Grand, Paris.
Pictures hung in Musée d'Art Moderne and Musée des Beaux Arts, Paris, in museums in Boulogne, La Rochelle, Lyon, Saint-Etienne, Cambrai, Bordeaux, Dijon, Algiers, Tunis, etc.; also in Venice, Amsterdam, Brussels, Buenos Aires, Cairo, São Paulo and London; awards include Carnegie Prize 38, Prix de l'Ile de France 52, Prix de la Biennale de Menton 53; Grand Prix de la Ville de Paris 55; Prix du Costume de Théâtre at Int. Biennale São Paulo 61; Officier de la Légion d'Honneur; Officier des Arts et Lettres; mem. l'Académie Royale de Belgique.
Works include (in addition to pictures): murals in the theatre of the Palais de Chaillot, the Inst. Nat. Agronomique, and on the steamships *Provence, Bretagne, Jean Laborde, France*; and theatrical costumes and decors, in particular for *Les Indes Galantes* 52, *La Flûte Enchantée* (Mozart) 54 for the Théâtre National de l'Opéra and *La Répétition* (ballet) for Cologne Opera 63.
68 rue Lhomond, Paris 5e, France.
Telephone: PORt Royal 27-90.

Chapin, Roy Dikeman, Jr., A.B.; American automobile executive; b. 21 Sept. 1915; ed. Yale Univ.
Held various positions with Hudson Motor Car Co. and Hudson Sales Corpn. 38-54; Asst. Sales Man. Hudson Div. American Motors Corpn. 54-55; Asst. Treas. and Dir. American Motors Corpn. 54-55, Vice-Pres. and Treas. 55, Exec. Vice-Pres. 56-67, Chair. of Board 67-; Chair. and Dir. American Motors (Can.) Ltd.; Dir. Rambler Motors Ltd., Kelvinator (Canada) Ltd., Redisco Corpn.; Vice-Pres. and Trustee Roy D. Chapin Foundation 48-.
American Motors Corporation, Detroit, Michigan; Home: 411 Country Club Lane, Grosse Pointe Farms 30, Michigan, U.S.A.

Chaplin, Arthur Hugh, B.A., F.L.A.; British librarian; b. 17 April 1905; ed. University Coll., London.
Asst. Librarian, Reading Univ. 27-28, Queen's Univ. Belfast 28-29; Asst. Keeper, Dept. of Printed Books, British Museum 30-55, Deputy Keeper 55-59, Keeper 59-66, Principal Keeper 66-; Exec. Sec. I.F.L.A. Working Group on Cataloguing Principles 54-59, Exec. Sec. Organizing Cttee. Int. Conf. on Cataloguing Principles (1961) 59-66; Chair. I.F.L.A. Cttee. on Cataloguing Rules 66-; Pres. Microfilm Asscn. of Great Britain 67-68.
44 Russell Square, London, W.C.1, England.
Telephone: 01-636-7217.

Chaplin, Charles Spencer; British film actor and producer; b. 16 April 1889.
Formed own producing organisation and built Chaplin Studios, Hollywood 18; joint founder United Artists' Corpn. (with British affiliation Allied Artists); Officier de l'Instruction Publique (France); Officier Légion d'Honneur; Hon. D.Litt. (Oxford, Durham); Erasmus Prize 65.
Films include: *Shoulder Arms, The Kid, The Gold Rush, The Circus, City Lights, Modern Times, The Great Dictator, Monsieur Verdoux, Limelight, A King in New York, La Revue de Charlot, The Countess from Hong Kong.*
Publ. *My Autobiography* 64.
Vevey, Vaud, Switzerland.

Chaplin, Frederick Leslie; British company director; b. 6 Dec. 1905; ed. St. Osyth's School, Clacton.
Joined F. W. Woolworth & Co. Ltd. 28, Dir. 57, Man.

Dir. 60, Chair. 61-; Dir. F. W. Woolworth Co., U.S.A. 61-.
Links View, 5 Broad Walk, Winchmore Hill, London, N.21, England.

Chapman, Albert Kinkade, A.B., A.M., PH.D.; American businessman; b. 31 May 1890; ed. Ohio State and Princeton Univs.
Physiological optical research at Clark Univ. 16-17; served in U.S. Signal Corps and later in U.S. Air Corps (development of aerial photography) 17-19; with Eastman Kodak Co. 19-, Asst. to Vice-Pres. (Manufacturing) 22-29, Production Man. 30-41, Asst. Vice-Pres. 36-41, Vice-Pres. and Asst. Gen. Man. 41-43, Dir. 43-66, Vice-Pres. and Gen. Man. 43-52, Pres. 52-60, Vice-Chair. of the Board 60-62, Chair. 62-66, Chair. of Exec. Cttee. 61-66; Dir. Canadian Kodak Co. Ltd. 31-66, Kodak Ltd. 59-66; mem. of Advisory Cttee. to the Board Lincoln Rochester Trust Co.; Hon. Trustee Univ. of Rochester; Hon. Chair. Exec. Cttee., Rochester Inst. of Technology; Trustee George Eastman House Inc. (Exec. Cttee.); Chevalier Légion d'Honneur.
Eastman Kodak Co., 343 State Street, Rochester, New York 14650, U.S.A.

Chapman, Sydney, M.A., D.SC., F.R.S.; British mathematician; b. 29 Jan. 1888; ed. Manchester Univ. and Trinity Coll., Cambridge.
Chief Asst. Greenwich Royal Observatory 10-14; Fellow 13-19 and Lecturer 14-19 Trinity Coll., Cambridge; Prof. of Mathematics, Manchester Univ. 19-24; Chief Prof. Mathematics Imperial Coll. of Science 24-46; Research Assoc. Dept. of Terrestrial Magnetism, Carnegie Inst. of Washington 35-42; Deputy Scientific Adviser, War Office 43-45; Sedleian Prof. Natural Philosophy and Fellow, Queen's Coll., Oxford 46-53; Pres. London Mathematical Society 29-31, Royal Meteorological Society 32-34, Int. Meteorological Asscn. 36-48, Royal Astronomical Society 40-42, Int. Asscn. for Terrestrial Magnetism and Electricity 48-51, Physical Society 49-50, Int. Union of Geodesy and Geophysics 51-54; Foreign Assoc. Nat. Acad. of Sciences, U.S.A.; Hon. Fellow Indian Acad. of Sciences; foreign mem. Norwegian Royal Acad. of Sciences, Swedish Royal Acad. of Sciences, Finnish Acad. of Sciences, Leopoldina Acad., Royal Society of Sciences, Uppsala, Accad. Nazionale dei Lincei, Rome; corresp. mem. Göttingen Acad.; Research Assoc. Calif. Inst. of Technology 50-51; Advisory Scientific Dir. Geophysical Inst., Univ. of Alaska 51-; Hon. Fellow, Royal Society of Edinburgh, Queen's Coll., Oxford 54, Imperial Coll. 56, Trinity Coll., Cambridge 57; Hon. D.Sc. (Cambridge, Alaska, Michigan, Colorado, Paris, Exeter and Newcastle Univs.; Pres. Int. Comm. for the Int. Geophysical Year 53-59; Research Assoc. High Altitude Observatory, Boulder, Colo. 55; Senior Research Scientist, Inst. of Science and Technology, Univ. of Michigan 59-60; Copley Medal, Royal Soc. 64.
Publs. *The Earth's Magnetism, Mathematical Theory of Non-Uniform Gases* (with T. G. Cowling), *Geomagnetism* (with J. Bartels), *I.G.Y.: Year of Discovery, Solar Plasma, Geomagnetism and Aurora* 64.
High Altitude Observatory, Boulder, Colorado 80302, U.S.A.

Chapman-Andrews, Sir Edwin Arthur, K.C.M.G., O.B.E., B.A.; British diplomatist; b. 9 Sept. 1903; ed. Univ. Coll., London, Sorbonne, Paris, and St. John's Coll., Cambridge.
Appointed to the Levant Consular Service 26; studied Oriental languages, Cambridge 26-28; consular appts. Port Said, Cairo, Suez, Addis Ababa, Kirkuk, Harar 28-36; Asst. Oriental Sec. British Embassy, Cairo 37; commissioned Royal Sussex Regt. and apptd. Major on staff of C.-in-C., Middle East; liaison officer with H.I.M. Emperor Haile Selassie and entered Abyssinia with H.I.M. 41; Foreign Office 42; Counsellor and Head,

Personnel Dept. 44; one of H.M. Inspectors-Gen. of Overseas Establishments 46; Minister, British Embassy, Cairo 47; Minister to the Lebanon 51, Ambassador 52-56; Ambassador to the Sudan 56-61; London Rep. Massey-Ferguson (Export) Co. Ltd. 61-, Dir. Massey-Ferguson (Export) Co. Ltd. 64-, Mitchell Cotts (Exports) Ltd. 65-; Fellow, Univ. Coll. London 52; K.St.J. 52; mem. of Council of Lord Kitchener Nat. Memorial Fund; mem. Council for Middle East Trade 63, Chair. 65-; mem. Nat. Export Council 65; K.C.S.G. (Papal) 62.
2 The Leys, Brim Hill, London, N.2, England.

Chapman Nyaho, Daniel Ahmling, C.B.E., M.A., LL.D.; Ghanaian teacher, public servant and business executive; b. 5 July 1909; ed. Bremen Mission School (Keta), Achimota Coll., Univ. of Oxford, Columbia Univ. and New York Univ.
Teacher Govt. Senior Boys' School, Accra 30, Achimota Coll. 30-33, 37-46; Area Specialist, UN Secretariat Dept. of Trusteeship and Information from Non-Self-Governing Territories 47-54; Sec. to Prime Minister and Cabinet, Gold Coast 54-57; Head of Ghana Civil Service 57; Ambassador to U.S.A. and Perm. Rep. to UN 57-59; Headmaster Achimota School Nov. 59-63; Vice-Chair. Comm. on Higher Education in Ghana 60-61, mem. Interim National Council of Higher Education and Research, Ghana 61-62; mem. Ghana Acad. of Sciences; mem. UN Middle East/North Africa Technical Assistance Mission on Narcotics Control 63; First Vice-Chair. Governing Council UN Special Fund 59; Dir. UN Div. of Narcotic Drugs 63-66; Amb. Ministry of External Affairs 67; Exec. Dir. Pioneer Tobacco Co. Ltd. (British-American Tobacco Group); Chair. Arts Council of Ghana, Volta Union.
Publs. *Our Homeland* (Book I—*A Regional Geography of South-East Gold Coast*) 45, *The Human Geography of Eweland* 45.
Office: Pioneer Tobacco Co. Ltd., Liberty Avenue, P.O.B. 11, Accra; Home: 11 Ninth Avenue, Tesano, Accra, Ghana.
Telephone: 64151 (Office).

Chapsal, Jacques (Jean René); French political scientist; b. 11 May 1909; ed. Ecole des Sciences Politiques and Faculty of Law, Paris (Docteur en Droit).
Librarian of the Senate 36; Sec.-Gen. Ecole des Sciences Politiques 39; Dir. of Institut d'Etudes Politiques, Univ. of Paris 47-; Administrator Fondation Nationale des Sciences Politiques 50.
27 rue Saint-Guillaume, Paris 7e, France.

Char, René; French poet; b. 14 June 1907; ed. Lycée d'Avignon and Univ. d'Aix en Provence.
Chevalier Légion d'Honneur; Croix de Guerre; Corresp. mem. Bavarian Acad.; Hon. mem. Modern Language Asscn.; Prix des Critiques 66.
Publs. *Le Marteau sans Maître, Placard pour un chemin des écoliers, Dehors la nuit est gouvernée, Seuls demeurent, Feuillets d'Hypnos, Fureur et mystère, Les Matinaux, Le Soleil des eaux, A une Sérénité crispée, Poèmes et prose choisis, La Parole en archipel, Recherche de la base et du Sommet, Commune Présence, Poèmes des deux années, La Bibliothèque est en feu, L'âge cassant, Retour amont.*
c/o Editions Gallimard, 5 rue Sébastien-Bottin, Paris 7e; Home: Les Busclats, L'Isle-sur-Sorgue, Vaucluse, France.

Charbonnel, Jean; French politician; b. 22 April 1927; ed. Lycées Henri IV and Louis-le-Grand, Paris; Univ. de Paris à la Sorbonne, Ecole normale supérieure and Ecole nationale d'administration.
Research worker Centre National de Recherches Scientifiques; with Cour des Comptes 56; Asst. Prof. Inst. for Political Sciences, Sorbonne 57-59; Technical Counsellor Ministry of Public Health and later Ministry of Justice 59-62; Appeal Court Counsellor, Cour des Comptes 62; mem. Chamber of Deputies 62-66; Gen.

Counsellor Brive-Nord area 64-66; Mayor of Brive 66-; Sec. of State for Foreign Affairs (Co-operation) 66-; Nat. Sec. Union des Démocrates pour la V République 67-.
Publ. *Louis Veuillot et la deuxième république.*
14 rue Dupont-des-Loges, Paris 7e, France.

Chardonne, Jacques (*pseudonym* of Jacques Boutelleau); French novelist; b. 2 Jan. 1884.
Officier Légion d'Honneur.
Author of *L'Épithalame* 21, *Le Chant du Bienheureux* 28, *Les Varais* 29, *Eva ou le Journal Interrompu* 29, *Claire* 31, *L'Amour du prochain* 32, *Les destinées sentimentales* 34, *Romanesques* 35, *L'Amour c'est beaucoup plus que l'amour* 36, *Le Bonheur de Barbezieux* 38, *Journal pour 1940* 41, *Chimériques* 48, *Vivre à Madère, Matinales, Le ciel dans la fenêtre, Demi-jour, Propos comme ça.*
[*Died May* 1968.]

Charles-Roux, Edmonde; French writer; b. 1922; ed. Italy.
Served as nurse, then in Resistance Movement, during Second World War, in which she was twice wounded; Reporter, magazine *Elle*; Features Editor, French edn. of *Vogue* 47-54, Editor-in-Chief 54-66; awarded Prix Goncourt 66.
Publ. *Oublier Palerme* 66.
c/o Bernard Grasset, 61 rue des Saints-Pères, Paris 6e, France.

Charlesworth, James Clyde, A.M., PH.D.; American educator; b. 21 May 1900; ed. Carnegie Inst. of Technology and Pittsburgh and Harvard Univs.
Asst. Chief Engineer Miller Machinery Co., Pittsburgh 22-24; mem. teaching faculty Univ. of Pittsburgh 26-39 Univ. of Pennsylvania 39-, Prof. of Political Science 45-; Dir. Graduate Division Wharton School 42-43; served U.S. Army 43-46; supervisor educational programme, Inst. of Local and State Govt. 39-55; Sec. of Administration, Commonwealth of Pennsylvania 55-56; Exec. Dir. State Reorganisation Comm. 56-57; Pres. American Acad. of Political and Social Science 53-; mem. Nat. Advisory Board, Nat. Parks Asscn., Nat. Board of Trustees, United World Federalists; Legion of Merit.
Publs. *Governmental Administration, Governmental Reorganization of the Commonwealth of Pennsylvania;* Edited: *Contemporary Political Analysis, Design for Political Science, Leisure in America: Blessing or Curse?, Mathematics and the Social Sciences, Behavioralism in Political Science, Bureaucracy and Democratic Government, American Civilization and Its Leadership Needs, Ethics in America, Realignments in the Communist and Western Worlds,* and many vols. of *The Annals* dealing with international relations.
Home: 7125 Penarth Avenue, Upper Darby, Pa.; Office: 3937 Chestnut Street, Philadelphia 4, Pa., U.S.A.
Telephone: Evergreen (Philadelphia) 6-4397 (Home).

Charlotte, H.R.H., Grand-Duchess, of Luxembourg, Duchess of Nassau; b. 96.
Ascended throne Jan. 19; married to Felix, Prince of Bourbon and Parma, Prince of Luxembourg Nov. 19; abdicated Nov. 64 in favour of eldest son, now Grand-Duke Jean of Luxembourg.
Grand-Ducal Palace, Luxembourg.

Charlton, Alfred Evan; British journalist and writer; b. 9 June 1912; ed. St. Paul's School.
Sub-Editor *The Statesman*, New Delhi and Calcutta 36, Editor 64-67; Indian Army 40-46; Dep. Corresp. in India for *The Times*, London 54-62.
Publ. *Go and Order the Drums* 64.
c/o Lloyd's Bank Ltd., Cox's and King's Branch, 6 Pall Mall, London, S.W.1, England.

Charon, Jacques; French actor and producer; b. 27 Feb. 1920; ed. Lycée de Paris and Conservatoire National d'Art Dramatique.

Pensionnaire, later Sociétaire, Comédie Française; Vice-Doyen, Comédie Française.

Plays acted in incl.: *Un fil à la Patte, Le Misanthrope, Les Femmes Savantes, Feu la Mère de Madame, Le Mariage forcé, Le sexe faible, Dom Juan* (part of Sganarelle). *Le Médecin malgré lui, Le Bourgeois Gentilhomme.*

Plays produced incl.: *les Fourberies de Scapin, Un fil à la Patte, Piège pour un homme seul, Jéricho, Cyrano de Bergérac, Le Prince Travesti, Fleur de Cactus, La Dame de chez Maxim, Le Cheval Evanoui, A Flea in Her Ear* (London); also numerous film appearances; directing film *A Flea in Her Ear* 67.

34 rue Montpensier, Paris 1er, France.

Charry, René; French orthopaedic surgeon; b. 28 March 1898; ed. Univ. of Toulouse.

Career dedicated to orthopaedic surgery and pathology of the hip in Toulouse, then Paris 55-; mem. Soc. of Surgeons, Paris, Int. Soc. of Orthopaedic Surgeons, Int. Coll. of Surgeons, Socs. of German, Belgian and Italian Orthopaedic Surgeons, French League against Rheumatism; Chevalier Légion d'Honneur, Commdr. Nichan Iftikhar.

Publs. *La Chirurgie moderne de la hanche 48, Dix consultations d'orthopédie, La résection-angulation de la hanche en deux temps 64.*

Surgical films: *La reconstruction articulaire du coude, de la hanche, du genou, reconstruction plastique de la hanche au nylon, l'ostéotomie sous-trochantérienne avec synthèse permettant la marche précoce, La résection-angulation.*

16 rue Alphonse de Neuville, Paris 17e; and 167 avenue Wagram, Paris 17e, France.

Charteris, Leslie, F.R.S.A.; American author; b. 12 May 1907; ed. Rossall School and King's Coll., Cambridge.

Editor *The Saint Magazine*; producer of *The Saint* and other radio programmes; writer of the internationally syndicated *Saint* comic strip; originator of *The Saint* television programme; has written several film scripts.

Publs. *Meet the Tiger* 29, *Enter the Saint* 31, *The Last Hero* 31, *The Avenging Saint* 31, *Wanted for Murder* 31, *Angels of Doom* 32, *The Saint v. Scotland Yard* 32, *Getaway* 33, *The Saint and Mr. Teal* 33, *The Brighter Buccaneer* 33, *The Misfortunes of Mr. Teal* 34, *The Saint Intervenes* 34, *The Saint Goes On* 35, *The Saint in New York* 35, *Saint Overboard* 36, *The Ace of Knaves* 37, *Thieves' Picnic* 37, *Juan Belmonte: Killer of Bulls* (translated from Spanish) 37, *Follow the Saint* 38, *Prelude for War* 38, *The First Saint Omnibus* 39, *The Saint in Miami* 40, *The Saint Goes West* 42, *The Saint Steps In* 43, *The Saint at Large* 43, *The Saint on Guard* 44, *The Saint Sees It Through* 46, *Call for the Saint* 48, *Saint Errant* 48, *The Second Saint Omnibus* 51, *The Saint in Europe* 53, *The Saint on the Spanish Main* 55, *The Saint Around the World* 56, *Thanks to the Saint* 57, *Señor Saint* 58, *The Saint to the Rescue* 59, *Trust the Saint* 62, *Saint in the Sun* 63, *Vendetta for the Saint* 64, *The Saint on TV* 68, *The Saint Returns* 68.

8845 W. Olympic Boulevard, Beverly Hills, Calif., U.S.A.

Charue, André-Marie; Belgian ecclesiastic; b. 98; ed. Grand Séminaire de Namur, Catholic Univ. of Louvain. Prof. of Scriptures, Grand Séminaire de Namur 28-41; Bishop of Namur 41-; Vice-Pres. Theological Cttee. of Second Vatican Council; gave permission for the veneration of the shrine of Beaurang 43, declared that the authenticity of the apparitions should be admitted 49.

Publs. include *L'Incrédulité des Juifs dans le Nouveau Testament* 29, *L'Année sociale dans le diocèse de Namur* 50, *Les Epîtres Catholiques* (commentary on the collection *La Sainte Bible*) 51, *Le Clergé Diocésain tel qu'un Evêque le voit et le souhaite* 60.

Evêché de Namur, Namur, Belgium.

Charusathira, General Prapas; Thai army officer and politician; b. 12; ed. Chulachomklao Royal Military Acad. and National Defence Coll.

Army service 32-, rose to General 60; Minister of Interior 57-, Dep. Prime Minister 63-, Army Dep. Commdr. and Dep. Supreme Commdr. 63-64, Supreme Commdr. 64-; Vice-Pres. and Rector Chulalongkorn Univ. 61-; Crown of Thailand (Highest Class).

Publs. *The Rôle of the Ministry of Interior in the Development of National Security, The Rôle of the Ministry of Interior in Maintenance of National Peace and Order.*

132-5 Suan Puttan Residence, Bangkok, Thailand.

Charvát, Josef, M.D., D.SC.; Czechoslovak professor of medicine; b. 6 Aug. 1897; ed. Charles Univ., Prague.

Lecturer in Internal Medicine Univ. of Prague 28-33, Prof. 33-, Dir. Univ. Polyclinic 39-, Dir. 3rd Medical Dept., Faculty of Medicine 45-; Dir. Laboratory for Endocrinology and Metabolism 56-; mem. Scientific Council, Ministry of Health 52-; mem. Advisory Cttee. for Medical Research, W.H.O. 58-61, Pres. Endocrinological Soc. 37-; mem. UN Advisory Cttee. for Applications of Science and Technology; mem. Czechoslovak Acad. of Sciences 54-; Foreign mem. Polish Acad. of Sciences 66; Hon. degrees Cracow Univ. 64; Order of Labour 57, State Prize 62; Hero of Socialist Labour and Holder of the Gold Star 67.

Publs. *Internal Secretions* 35, *Avitaminoses* 38, *Metabolism of Carbohydrates* 42, *Steroid Hormones* 52, *Parathyroid* 54, *Growth Hormone* 55, *Neurohypophysis* 56.

Office: U nemocnice 1, Prague 2; Home: Ostrovní 5, Prague 1, Czechoslovakia.

Charyk, Joseph Vincent, PH.D., M.S., B.SC.; American scientist and administrator; b. 9 Sept. 1920; ed. Univ. of Alberta, Calif. Inst. of Technology.

Instructor of Aeronautics, Calif. Inst. of Technology 45; Asst. (later Assoc.) Prof. of Aeronautics, Princeton Univ. 46; Dir. of Aerophysics and Chemistry Lab., Lockheed Aircraft Corpn. 55-; Dir. of Missile Technology Lab., Gen. Man. Space Technology Div. Aeronutronic Systems Inc. (Subsidiary of Ford Motor Co.) 56-59; Chief Scientist U.S. Air Force 59, Asst. Sec. of Air Force for Research and Development 59; Under-Sec. U.S. Air Force 60-63; Pres. and Dir. Communications Satellite Corpn. Mar. 63-; mem. Int. Acad. of Astronautics; Fellow in American Inst. of Aeronautics and Astronautics; mem. Nat. Space Club, Armed Forces Communications and Electronics Asscn.; Hon. LL.D.

5126 Tilden Street, N.W., Washington, D.C. 20016, U.S.A.

Telephone: 244-3761.

Chase, Mary Ellen, PH.D., LITT.D., L.H.D., LL.D.; American philologist; b. 24 Feb. 1887; ed. Univs. of Maine and Minnesota and in Germany.

Instructor in English Literature Univ. of Minnesota 17-22; Asst. Prof. Univ. of Minnesota 22-26; Assoc. Prof. English Language and Literature Smith Coll. 26-29, Prof. 29-55, Prof. Em. 55-; author and lecturer.

Publs. *A Goodly Heritage* 32, *Mary Peters* 34, *Silas Crockett* 35, *This England* 36, *Dawn in Lyonesse* 38, *A Goodly Fellowship* 39, *Windswept* 41, *The Bible and The Common Reader* 44, *Jonathan Fisher: Maine Parson* 48, *The Plum Tree* 49, *Abby Aldrich Rockefeller* 50, *Readings from the Bible* 52, *The White Gate* 54, *Life and Language in the Old Testament* 55, *The Edge of Darkness* 57, *The Lovely Ambition* 60, *The Psalms for the Common Reader* 62, *The Prophets for the Common Reader* 63, *A Journey to Boston* 65, *Recipe for a Magic Childhood* 66.

16 Paradise Road, Northampton, Mass., U.S.A.

Chase, Stuart, S.B.; American social scientist; b. 8 March 1888; ed. Mass. Inst. Technology and Harvard Univ.

Certified Public Accountant 16; Staff U.S. Federal Trade Comm. 17 and U.S. Food Administration 18-19;

Consulting Economist for Nat. Resources Board, Resettlement Administration, and Securities Exchange Comm., Tennessee Valley Authority; mem. Nat. Inst. of Arts and Letters; Hon. Lit.D. (American Univ., Washington) 50.
Publs. *The Tragedy of Waste* 25, *Your Money's Worth* 27, *Men and Machines* 29, *Mexico: a Study of Two Americas* 31, *A New Deal* 32, *The Economy of Abundance* 34, *Government in Business* 35, *Rich Land, Poor Land* 36, *The Tyranny of Words* 38, *The New Western Front* 39, *Idle Money, Idle Men* 40, *A Primer of Economics* 41, *The Road We are Travelling* 42, *Goals for America* 42, *Where's the Money Coming From?* 43, *Democracy under Pressure* 45, *Men at Work* 45, *To-morrow's Trade* 46, *For This We Fought* 47, *The Proper Study of Mankind* 48, *Roads to Agreement* 51, *Power of Words* 54, *Guides to Straight Thinking* 56, *Some Things Worth Knowing* 58, *Live and Let Live* 60, *American Credos* 62, *Money to Grow On* 64, *The Most Probable World* 67.
Georgetown, Conn., U.S.A.

Chastel, André (Adrien), DR. ès LETTRES; French art historian; b. 15 Nov. 1912; ed. Sorbonne, Paris.
Asst. in Art History, Sorbonne 45-48; Focillon Fellowship, Yale 49; Dir. of Studies for the History of the Renaissance, Ecole Pratique des Hautes Etudes 51-; lecturer on History of Modern Art, Sorbonne, Prof. 55-; art critic, *Le Monde* 50-; Sec. Comité International d'Histoire de l'Art 61-; Croix de Guerre 39-40; Chevalier Légion d' Honneur.
Publs. *Vuillard* 46, *L'art italien* (2 vols.) 57, *Botticelli* 58, *Art et Humanisme à Florence au temps de Laurent le Magnifique* 59, *L'Age de l'Humanisme* (with R. Klein) 63, *Italie 1460-1500* (2 vols.) 65.
30 rue de Lubeck, Paris 16e, France.

Chastenet de Castaing, Jacques, LL.D., C.B.E.; French journalist and historian; b. 20 April 1893.
Former Editor *Le Temps*; mem. Acad. des Sciences Morales et Politiques 47- and Académie Française 56-; Commdr. Légion d'Honneur.
Publs. *William Pitt, Godoy Prince de la Paix, Wellington, Vingt ans d'histoire diplomatique, Le Parlement d'Angleterre, Le Siècle de Victoria, R. Poincaré, La France de M. Fallières, Histoire de la Troisième République* (7 vols.), *Winston Churchill et l'Angleterre du XX Siècle, La vie privée en Angleterre au début du Règne de Victoria, Jours Sanglants 1914-1918, L'Angleterre d'aujourd'hui, En avant vers l'Ouest.*
71 rue du Faubourg St. Honoré, Paris 8e, France.

Chataigneau, Yves; French diplomatist; b. 22 Sept. 1891; ed. Paris Univ.
Liaison officer with American Army 18; Chief of a Section, Ministry of Foreign Affairs 24-37; Minister Plenipotentiary 39; Dir. Archives, Ministry of Foreign Affairs 39; served with French Army, Great War and 39-46; Sec.-Gen. to Presidency of Council 37-39; Minister to Afghanistan to 42, resgnd. to join de Gaulle; Del.-Gen. to Levant 43, Gov.-Gen. Algiers 44-47; Ambassador to U.S.S.R. 48-52; Adviser to Ministry of Foreign Affairs 52-58; Pres. Asscn. for the Devt. of Islamic Studies; Vice-Pres. Inst. of Slavic Studies, Univ. of Paris 52-; Man. Bureau pour le Développement de la Production Agricole (B.D.P.A.) 58-61; mem. Board of Dirs. Havas Agency 61-; mem. and officer of many socs.; D.S.C. 18, M.V.O. 38; Grand Officier Légion d'Honneur; Ambassadeur de France; mem. Institut de France (Académie des Sciences Morales et Politiques) 67.
Publs. many articles in learned journals, etc.
18 rue Durét, Paris 16e, France.
Telephone: 727-14-77.

Chatenet, Pierre, LIC. en DR.; French politician; b. 6 March 1917; ed. Lycée Buffon and Ecole des Sciences Politiques.
Auditor Conseil d'Etat 41; Chargé de Mission, Provi-

sional Govt. 44, Labour Office 44-45; mem. French Del. UN Conf. San Francisco 45; Maître des Requêtes, Conseil d'Etat 46; Counsellor French Del. to UN 46-47; Political Dir. Residence Gen. Tunis 47-50; Counsellor French Perm. Del. to NATO 50-54; Dir. of Civil Service (Présidence du Conseil) 54; mem. UN Rights of Man Comm., Consultative Cttee. Fonction Publique Int.; Sec. of State (Prime Minister's Office) Jan.-May 59; Minister of the Interior May 59-61; Pres. of EURATOM 62-67; Conseiller d'Etat 63-; Pres. Comm. des Opérations de Bourse 67; mem. Conseil Constitutionnel 68; Chevalier Légion d'Honneur; Grand Croix de l'Ordre de la Couronne de Belgique.
3 avenue d'Orsay, Paris 7e, France.

Chatin, Lucien Emile Louis Marie; French businessman; b. 29 Sept. 1896; ed. Ecole Centrale, Lyon.
President and Gen. Man. Soc. de Moulinage et Retorderies de Chavanoz; Pres. Soc. des Verre textile; Pres. Lyon Int. Fair; Commdr. Légion d'Honneur, du Mérite Commercial, Croix de Guerre.
Home: 12 avenue Verguin, Lyon; Office: 23 place Tolozan, Lyon (Rhône), France.

Chatin, Marc; French businessman; b. 5 Oct. 1894.
President Soc. Textile; Vice-Pres. Syndicat Gén. de l'Industrie Cotonnière; Officier Légion d'Honneur, Croix de Guerre.
Home: 2 rue d'Andigné, Paris 16e; Office: 23 rue de Marignan, Paris 8e, France.

Chatterjee, Dwarka Nath, B.A.; Indian diplomatist; b. 2 Nov. 1914; ed. Calcutta Univ., King's Coll., London, London School of Economics and School of Oriental Studies, London.
Army Service 40-47; Indian Foreign Service 47-; First Sec., Paris 48-49, London 49-54; Deputy Sec., Ministry of External Affairs 54-55; Deputy High Commr. in Pakistan 56-58; Consul-Gen., Geneva 58-59; Minister, Washington 59-62; Ambassador to Congo (Léopoldville) 62-64; High Commr. in Australia 65-67; Deputy High Commr. in U.K. 67-.
Indian High Commission, India House, Aldwych, London, W.C.2, England; and 9 Lovelock Place, Ballygune, Calcutta, India.

Chatterji, Suniti Kumar, M.A., D.LIT. (London); Indian educationist, philologist and writer; b. 26 Nov. 1890; ed. Calcutta, School of Oriental Studies, London, and Univ. of Paris.
Khaira Prof. of Indian Linguistics and Phonetics, Calcutta Univ. 22-52, Emeritus Prof. of Comparative Philology 52-; Visiting Prof., Univ. of Pa., U.S.A. 51-52; Chair., Upper House, West Bengal State Legislature 52-65; Nat. Prof. of India in Humanities 65-; fmr. Pres. Bangiya Sahitya Parishad, Asiatic Soc. of Bengal, Linguistic Soc. of India; hon. mem. Société Asiatique, Paris, American Oriental Soc., Norwegian Acad. of Sciences, Royal Siam Soc., Ecole Française de l'Extrême Orient, Linguistic Soc. of America; Fellow, Indian Council for Cultural Relations 61-, etc.; awarded Padma-Vibushan (Order of the Republic of India); Hon. F.A.S., D.Litt. (Univs. of Rome and Delhi and Visva Bharati Univ.).
Publs. *Origin and Development of the Bengali Language* 26, *Dvipamaya Bharat* 40, 2nd edn. 64, *Indo-Aryan and Hindi* 42, 2nd edition 60, *Kirata-jana-Krti or the Indo-Mongoloids* 51, *Africanism* 60, *Indianism and the Indian Synthesis* 62, *Languages and Literatures of Modern India* 63, *Dravidian* 66, *People, Language and Culture of Orissa* 66, *Balts and Aryans* 68, and other works in English, Bengali and Hindi.
"Sudharma", 16 Hindusthan Park, Calcutta 29, India.
Telephone: 46-1121 (Home); 45-5319 (Office).

Chattopadhyaya, Harindranath; Indian poet, dramatist, musician and actor; b. 98; ed. U.K., Germany, U.S.A. and U.S.S.R.
Studied theatrecraft under Stanislavsky and Meyer-

boldt; pioneer modern Indian Theatre; leader progressive movt. in literature; produced a film, *Azadi* (Freedom); has written screen script for *Legend of Gautam Buddha*, 1942, and *Abul Hassan* (musical comedy); Mem. of Lok Sabha (Parliament) 52.

Publs. *The Coffin, Feast of Youth, Ancient Wings, Grey Clouds and White Showers, Poems and Plays, Five Plays in Verse, Five Plays in Prose, Dark Well, The Divine Vagabond, Horizon—Ends, Edgeways and the Saint, Lyrics, Blood of Stones, Perfume of Earth, Magic Tree, Crossroads, Life and Myself* (Vol. I: Autobiography), *Hunter of Kalahasti* (play), *Treasury of Poems, Land of the New Man, The Toy-Maker of Kondapalli* (play), *Spring in Winter* (lyrics), etc.

3 Krishna Iyer Street, Nungumbakam, Madras, India.

Chatty, Habib; Tunisian diplomatist; b. 16; ed. Sadiki Coll., Tunis.

Journalist 37-52, Editor *Ez-Zohra* 43-50, *Es-Sabah* 50-52; imprisoned 52, 53; Head, Press Cabinet of Pres. of Council 54-55, Head, Information Service 55; mem. Nat. Council, Neo-Destour Party 55; Dir. *Al Amal* 56; Vice-Pres. Constituent Nat. Assembly 56; Amb. to Lebanon and Iraq 57-59, to Turkey and Iran 59-62, to U.K. 62-64, to Morocco 64-; several decorations.

Tunisian Embassy, 5 rue Montaigne, Rabat, Morocco. Telephone: 306-37 and 592-47.

Chatzidakis, Manos; Greek composer; b. 25.

Composer of ballet music, incidental music for theatre and films, piano and orchestral music, and popular songs; numerous national and int. awards, including Oscar 61; composed music for *Lysistrata, Birds, Plautos* (Aristophanes), and for films *Stella* 56, *Never on Sunday* 60, *Topkapi* 64, etc.

Leoforos Vas. Konstantinou 46, Athens, Greece.

Chau, Hon. Sir Sik-Nin, Kt., C.B.E., LL.D., M.B., B.S.; Hong Kong business executive; b. 1903; ed. St. Stephen's Coll., Hong Kong, Univs. of Hong Kong, London and Vienna.

Chairman, Hong Kong Trade Devt. Council, Hong Kong Management Asscn., Assoc. Dairies Int. Ltd., Hong Kong Model Housing Soc., Wellcome Co. Ltd., Hong Kong Marine Food Co. Ltd., The Hong Kong Chinese Bank Ltd., The Dairy Farm, Ice & Cold Storage Co. Ltd., Dairy Lane Ltd., Kowloon Motor Bus Co., Man. Lee Cheung Co. Ltd., Pioneer Trade Devt. Co. Ltd., Repulse Bay Enterprises Ltd., Far East Insurance Co. Ltd., Nin Fung Hong, Oriental Express Ltd., Sik Yuen Co. Ltd.; Vice-Pres. Hong Kong Anti-Tuberculosis Asscn.; dir. numerous companies; official, educational and philanthropic orgs.

3547 Hatton Road, Hong Kong.

Chaudet, Paul; Swiss vine-grower and politician; b. 17 Nov. 1904.

Treas. Rivaz Commune; mem. Council of States; Nat. Councillor; Head, Dept. of Justice and Police 46-47, of Agriculture, Industry and Commerce 48-55; Federal Councillor 55-; Chief Defence Dept. 55-66; Vice-Pres. Fed. Council 58, 61, Pres. 59 and 62; Radical Liberal.

Clos du Rocher, Chexbres, Switzerland.

Chaudhuri, Gen. Joyanto Nath, O.B.E.; Indian army officer; b. 10 June 1908; ed. Highgate School and Royal Military Coll., Sandhurst.

Served North Staffordshire Regt., Indian 7th Cavalry, Middle East and Burma 39-45; Military Gov. Hyderabad 48-49; fmr. G.O.C.-in-C. Indian Southern Command; Commdr. Goa Operation 62; Chief of Indian Army Staff Nov. 62-June 66; High Commr. in Canada 66-; awarded Padma-Vibhushan.

Publs. *Operation Polo, Arms, Aims and Aspects.*

Indian High Commission, 200 MacLaren Street, Ottawa, Canada.

Telephone: 232-3549; 749-8553.

Chaudhuri, Naranarain (Sankho), B.A.; Indian sculptor; b. 25 Feb. 1916; ed. Armanitoba High School,

Dacca and Bishwa Bharti Santiniketan, West Bengal. Freelance artist 47-; Chief, Dept. of Sculpture, Maharaja Sayajirao Univ. of Baroda 51-, Prof. 57-; mem. Lalit Kala Akademi 56-; Pres. Indian Sculptors' Asscn. 64-65; mem. Indian Cttee. Int. Asscn. of Plastic Arts; Exhibited São Paulo Bienal 61, One-Man Exhibitions Bombay and Delhi; numerous Indian awards.

Major works: Sculptures, All India Radio, Delhi 55, Statue of Mahatma Gandhi, Rio de Janeiro, and works in collections in India, U.K. and U.S.A.

Adhyapak Nivas, Bardoa 2, India.

Chaudhuri, Nirad Chandra, B.A.; Indian writer; b. 23 Nov. 1897; ed. Calcutta Univ.

Former Asst. Editor *The Modern Review* (Calcutta); fmr. Sec. to Sarat Bose (Leader of Congress Party, Bengal); fmr. Commentator, All India Radio; has contributed to *The Times, Encounter, New English Review, The Atlantic Monthly, Pacific Affairs;* also contributed to Indian papers *The Statesman, The Illustrated Weekly, The Hindustan Standard, The Times of India;* Duff Cooper Memorial Prize for *The Continent of Circe* 67.

Publs. *The Autobiography of an Unknown Indian* 51 (published as *Jaico*, India 64), *A Passage to England* 59, *The Continent of Circe* 65, *Woman in Bengali Life* (in Bengali) 68.

P. and O. Buildings, Nicholson Road, Delhi-6, India.

Chaudhuri, Sachindra; Indian lawyer and politician; b. 24 Feb. 1903; ed. Presidency Coll., Calcutta, Cambridge Univ., and Lincoln's Inn, London.

Member Lok Sabha; mem. Indian Law Comm.; fmr. mem. Indian Del. to UN Gen. Assembly; Minister of Finance Dec. 65-67; High Commr. in U.K. 67.

New Delhi, India.

Chauvel, Jean Michel Henri, D. en D.; French diplomatist; b. 16 April 1897.

Sec. at French Embassy Peking 24; Sec.-Gen. of High Commissariat in Syria and the Lebanon; Consul-Gen. in Vienna 38; Sub-Dir. Asia-Oceania 38; Del. in France of the Commr. for Foreign Affairs of French Cttee. of Nat. Liberation 43; Sec.-Gen. Commissariat of Foreign Affairs 44; Amb. of France and Sec.-Gen. of Ministry of Foreign Affairs 44-49; Perm. Rep. on Security Council and Perm. Head of French del. to UN 49-52; Amb. to Switzerland 52-54; High Commr. and Amb. to Austria 54; Amb. to U.K. 55-62; Conseiller Diplomatique du Gouvernement 62-63; Grand Cross Legion of Honour; D.C.L. h.c. Oxon.; Hon. G.C.M.G., G.C.V.O.

Publs. *Préludes, Labyrinthe, D'une Eau Profonde, Infidèle, Imaginaires, Clepsydre, Sables.*

123 rue de la Tour, Paris 16e, France.

Chauviré, Yvette; French ballerina; b. 22 April 1917; ed. Paris Opera Ballet School.

Joined Paris Opera Ballet 30, Danseuse Etoile 42; with Monte Carlo Opera Ballet 46-47; Artistic and Technical Adviser to Admin. of Paris Opera 63-; Chevalier Légion d'Honneur; Officier des Arts et des Lettres; ballets in which she has performed leading roles include *Istar, Les Deux Pigeons, La Vie Triomphante, Giselle, Les Créateurs de Prométhée, Roméo et Juliette, L'Ecuyère, Les Suites Romantiques, Lac des Cygnes, l'Oiseau de Feu, Petrouchka, Sylvia, La Belle Hélène, Casse-Noisette, Les Mitrages, Le Cygne.*

Publ. *Je suis Ballerine.*

21 Place du Commerce, Paris 15e, France.

Chavan, Yeshwantrao Balwantrao, B.A., LL.B.; Indian politician; b. 12 March 1913; ed. Rajaram Coll., Kolhapur, and Law Coll., Poona.

Practised law at Karad; directed underground movement in Satara District 42-43; arrested 43-44; Pres. District Congress Cttee. 42; Sec. Maharashtra Provincial Congree Cttee. 48-50; mem. Bombay Legislative Assembly and Parlty. Sec. 46; started a Marathi daily, *Prakash*, at Satara; Minister for Civil Supplies

52, later Minister of Local Self-Govt. and Forests; Chief Minister, Bombay State 56-60, Maharashtra State 60-62; mem. Bombay Legislative Assembly 57-60; Treas. Working Cttee. All-India Congress 58; Minister of Defence, India Nov. 62-Nov. 66, of Home Affairs Nov. 66-; mem. Indian Nat. Congress Party.
1 Race Course Road, New Delhi, India.

Chavanon, Christian, D. en D.; French lawyer and radio administrator; b. 12 March 1913.
Law practice in Bordeaux; Auditeur 41, later Maître des Requêtes, Conseil d'Etat 46, Conseiller d'Etat 63-; Dir. du Cabinet, Ministry of Reconstruction 51-53; Prof. Inst. d'Etudes Politiques; Prés.-Dir. Gén. Soc. Nat. des Entreprises de Presse 53-55, Hon. Prés. Dir.-Gén. 55-; Sec.-Gén. of Information June 58, Dir.-Gén. Radiodiffusion-Télévision Française July 58-60; Prés.-Dir. Gén. l'Agence Havas 60-; Officier Légion d'Honneur.
18 Boulevard Maillot, Neuilly-sur-Seine, France.

Chaves Batista, Augusto; Brazilian mycologist and university professor; b. 15 June 1916; ed. Ginásio Santamarense and Escola Agronômica, Bahia and Agricultural and Mechanical Coll., Texas.
Professor of Phytopathology and Microbiology, Escola Agronômica da Bahia 40-45, Univ. Rural de Pernambuco 46-60, Full Prof. 60-; Founder and Dir. Inst. of Mycology, Univ. of Pernambuco 50-; mem. numerous scientific socs., and representative at many national and international scientific conferences; several honours; Dr. h.c. Univ. of Pernambuco.
Publs. include: *Monografia dos fungos Micropeltaceae* 56, *Sistemática dos Fungos Imperfeitos de Picnostromas com Himénio invertido* 59, *The Chaetothyriales* (with R. Ciferri) 62, *Capnodiales* (with R. Ciferri) 63; over 600 scientific works published and over 40 on fungi.
[*Died 30 Nov. 1967*].

Chávez, Carlos; Mexican composer; b. 99.
Studied the piano with Manuel Ponce 09-14, with Pedro Luis Ogazón 15-20, harmony with Juan B. Fuentes 17-18; first public concert of own compositions Mexico City 21; organised and conducted "Conciertos de Música Nueva" Mexico City 23-25; Founder Conductor Orquesta Sinfónica de México 28-48; Dir. Nat. Conservatoire 28-29, 34, founded Coro del Conservatorio 29; Chief Dept. of Fine Arts 33-34; Founder Dir. Nat. Inst. of Fine Arts 47-52; Founder Orquesta Sinfónica Nacional; conducted orchestras in North and South America 35-; Charles Eliot Norton Prof. Harvard 58-59; numerous commissions including Guggenheim Memorial Foundation, Museum of Modern Art (New York), Library of Congress, Mexican Ministry of Education; Caro de Boesi Prize, Caracas 54; Officier de la Légion d'Honneur, Commdr. Order of the Crown of Belgium, Order of the Polar Star (Sweden), Cross of the Star of Italian Solidarity.
Publ. *Toward a New Music* 37.
Works include: Stage works: *El Fuego Nuevo* 21, *Los Cuatro Soles* 26, *Caballos de Vapor* 27, *La Hija de Cólquide* 44 (ballets), *Pánfilo and Lauretta* (opera) 56; Orchestral works: *Sinfonía de Antígona* 33, *Sinfonía India* 36, Concerto for Four Horns 38, Piano Concerto 40, Violin Concerto 48, Third Symphony 54, Fourth Symphony 53, Fifth Symphony (for strings), Sixth Sympathy, Seventh Symphony; Chamber works: three String Quartets, Violin and Cello Sonatinas, Sonata for Four Horns, Toccata for Percussion; three Piano Sonatas, piano pieces, choral and vocal works.
Av. Pirincos 775, Lomas de Chapultepec, Mexico City, D.F., Mexico.

Chávez, Ignacio, M.D.; Mexican physician; b. 31 Jan. 1897; ed. National Univ. of Mexico.
Clinical Prof. Nat. Univ. of Mexico 23-50, Dir. Nat. School of Medicine 33-34; Prof. of Cardiology, School of Graduates 46-61, Rector of Nat. Univ. 61-66; Founder

and Dir. Nat. Inst. of Cardiology of Mexico 44-66, Hon. Dir. 66-; Founder Mexican Cardiological Soc. 35; founder-mem. Colegio Nacional 43; Hon. Rector Univ. of Michoacán; Hon. Prof. Univs. of Guadalajara, Guatemala, San Salvador, Rio de Janeiro, etc.; Hon. Pres. Interamerican Soc. of Cardiology; Pres. Int. Soc. of Cardiology 58-62, Hon. Pres. 62-; mem. Acads. of Medicine of Mexico, N.Y., Buenos Aires, etc.; Scientific Prize of Mexico; hon. degrees from Univs. of Paris, Montpellier, Lyons, Mexico, São Paulo, Oxford, Bologna, Prague, Cracow, etc.; Commdr. Légion d'Honneur (France), Commdr. Order of Finlay (Cuba), Order of Quetzal (Guatemala), Order of Public Health (France), Order of Cruzeiro do Sul (Brazil); Medal of Civil Merit (Mexico).
Publs. *Enfermedades del Corazón, Cirugía y Embarazo* 45, *México en la Cultura Médica* 47, *La Digitalina a pequeñas dosis en el tratamiento de las Cardiopatias* 20, *Lecciones de Clínica Cardiológica* 31, *Exploración Funcional de los Riñones y Clasificación de la Nefropatias* 31, *Diego Rivera, Sus Frescos en el Instituto Nacional de Cardiología* 46, *México en la Cultura Médica* 47, *El Instituto Nacional de Cardiología a los diez años de su fundación* 54.
Paseo de la Reforma 211, Mexico City, D.F., Mexico.

Chayefsky, Paddy; American writer; b. 29 Jan. 1923; ed. New York.
Author of television plays 52-; Writer and Assoc. Producer of the films: *Marty* 55, *Bachelor Party* 57; Writer of films: *The Goddess* 58, *Middle of the Night* 59, *The Americanization of Emily* 64; *Paint Your Wagon* 68; Writer of the plays: *Middle of the Night* 56, *The Tenth Man* 59, *Gideon* 61, *The Passion of Josef D* 64, *The Latent Heterosexual* 67; Pres. Sudan Corpn. 56-; Carnegie Productions 57, S.P.D. Inc. 59; mem. Dramatists Guild, Screenwriters Guild, etc.
Publs. *Television Plays* 55, *The Goddess* 58, *Middle of the Night* 59, *The Tenth Man* 60, *Gideon* 61, *The Passion of Josef D* 64, *The Latent Heterosexual* 67.
850 7th Avenue, New York, N.Y., U.S.A.

Chayes, Abram J.; American lawyer and government official; b. 18 July 1922; ed. Harvard Univ.
U.S. Army service 43-46; Legal Adviser to Gov. of Connecticut 49-50; Assoc.-Gen. Counsel President's Materials Policy Comm. 51; Law Clerk to Justice Felix Frankfurter 51-52; private legal practice 52; Asst. Prof. of Law, Harvard Univ. 55-60, Prof. of Law 65-; The Legal Adviser, Dept. of State 61-64.
c/o Harvard Law School, Cambridge, Mass.; Home: 3 Hubbard Park, Cambridge 38, Mass., U.S.A.
Telephone: 491-0072.

Cheatham, Owen Robertson; American business executive; b. 9 July 1903; ed. Hargrave Military Acad., Presbyterian Coll., and Clemson Coll.
Porter Brothers 22-24; Treas. Dolan Lumber Co. 24-27; Founder-Pres. Georgia-Pacific Corpn. 27-57, Chair. 57-; Dir. other companies.
Georgia-Pacific Corporation, 375 Park Avenue, New York 22, N.Y., U.S.A.

Chebotarev, Dmitry Fedorovich; Soviet gerontologist; b. 1908; ed. Kiev Medical Inst.
Intern Physiotherapeutical Inst., hospital, Chernigov 33-36; Postgraduate 2nd Moscow Medical Inst. 33-36; Army Surgeon 41-44; Postgraduate, Senior Research Assoc. 45-53; Deputy Dir. Inst. of Clinical Medicine, Kiev 53-54, Prof. 54; Head of Chair, Inst. of Postgraduate Medical Training, Kiev 53-61; Dir., Head of Dept., Inst of Gerontology, U.S.S.R. Acad. of Medical Sciences 61-; Corresp. mem. U.S.S.R. Acad. of Medical Sciences 61, mem. 66-; Chair. U.S.S.R. Soc. of Gerontologists and Germoatrists; Deputy Chair. U.S.S.R. and Ukrainian Socs. of Internists; mem. Presidium U.S.S.R. Soc. of Cardiologists; Chair. "Gerontology and Geriatrics" Comm., U.S.S.R. Ministry of Public Health;

Order of Red Banner of Labour, Merited Scientist Ukrainian S.S.R.
Publs: Over 90 works; monographs *Hypertensive Syndrome of Pregnancy, Internal Pathology in Clinic of Obstetrics and Gynecology, Cardio-vascular System of Ageing Organism.*
Institute of Gerontology and Experimental Pathology, 53 Melnikov Street, Kiev, U.S.S.R.

Cheesman, Lucy Evelyn, o.b.e., f.r.e.s.; British entomologist; b. 1881.
Curator of Insects London Zoological Society 20-26; Entomologist St. George Pacific Expedition 24-25; expedition to New Hebrides to collect insects for British Museum 29-31; Expedition to Papua 33-34, to Dutch New Guinea 36, to Waigeu, Japen and Torricelli Mountains 38-39, to New Caledonia 49-50, to Aneityum Island, New Hebrides 54-55.
Publs. *Everyday Doings of Insects* 24, *Islands Near the Sun* 27, *Hunting Insects in the South Seas* 32, *Backwaters of the Savage South Seas* 33, *The Two Roads of Papua* 35, *The Land of the Red Bird, Camping Adventures in New Guinea* 47, *Marooned in Du-bu Cove* 48, *Six-legged Snakes in New Guinea* 49, *Sealskins for Silk* (Italian edn. 53, U.S. edn. 56), *Insects Indomitable* (also U.S., French and Swedish edns.), *Charles Darwin and his Problems* 53 (U.S. edn. 55), *Things Worth While* (autobiography) 57, *Time well Spent* 60, *Look at Insects* 60, *Who Stand Alone* 65.
Royal Entomological Society, 41 Queen's Gate, London, S.W.7, England.

Cheetham, Sir Nicolas John Alexander, k.c.m.g.; British diplomatist; b. 8 Oct. 1910; ed. Eton Coll., and Christ Church, Oxford.
Diplomatic Service 34-, Foreign Office, Athens, Buenos Aires, Mexico City and Vienna 34-54; U.K. Dep. Rep. to NATO 54-58; Minister to Hungary 59-61; Asst.Under-Sec. of State, Foreign Office 61-63; Ambassador to Mexico 64-68.
c/o Foreign Office, London S.W.1, England.

Chehab, Gen. Fuad; Lebanese officer and politician; b. 03; ed. Damascus Military School and St. Cyr.
Served as officer in French Army; General 43; C.-in-C. Lebanese Army 45-58; Prime Minister, Minister of Interior and Defence, interim Govt. Sept. 52; Minister of Defence 56; Pres. of Lebanon 58-64; Commdr., Légion d'Honneur, Grand Cordon, Ordre National du Cèdre and many other decorations.
Beirut, Lebanon.

Chéhab, Emir Maurice; Lebanese archæologist and historian; b. 04; ed. Univ. St. Joseph, Beirut, Ecole du Louvre, and Ecole des Hautes Etudes Historiques, Paris.
Conservator Lebanese Nat. Museum 28; Chief of Antiquities Service 37, Dir. 44; Prof. Lebanese History Ecole Normale and Gen. History Ecole des Sciences Politiques 45; Prof. of Oriental Archaeology Inst. of Oriental Literature 46; Prof. of Ancient History, Univ. of the Lebanon; Curator of Lebanese Antiquities 53-59, Gen. Dir. 59-.
Musée National, Beirut, Lebanon.

Chehou, Mehmet; Albanian politician; b. 13; ed. Tirana Technical Coll., higher studies in France.
Fought in Spanish Civil War; Chief of Staff Albanian Nat. Army 46; mem. Political Bureau Albanian Workers' Party 48-; Vice-Pres. Council of Ministers and Minister of the Interior 48-54; Pres. Council of Ministers 54-.
Office of the Council of Ministers, Tirana, Albania.

Chelomey, Vladimir Nikolaevich; Soviet applied mathematician; b. 14; ed. Kiev Aviation Inst.
Instructor, Kiev Aviation Inst. 36-41; mem. C.P.S.U. 41-; research work, Central Inst. Aircraft Engines and other research orgs. 41-44; Prof. at Moscow Higher Technical School 52-; Corresp. mem. U.S.S.R. Acad. of Sciences 58-62, mem. 62-.
Publs. *Spring Theory* 38, *The Dynamic Stability of Air-craft Structural Elements* 39, *Pneumatic Servomechanisms* 54, *Stability Increasing Possibility of Elastic Systems by Vibrations* 56.
U.S.S.R. Academy of Sciences, 14 Lenin Prospekt, Moscow, U.S.S.R.

Chen Cheng-jen; Chinese politician; b. 05.
Sec., C.C.P. Kiangsi Prov. Cttee., and mem. Central-South China Mil. and Admin. Cttee. 50-53; Dir. of Mil. Construction, HQ People's Liberation Army and Minister of Building Construction, Govt. Admin. Council 52-54; Dep. Dir. Rural Works Dept., C.C.P. Central Cttee. 55-; Dep. Dir. 7th Office, State Council 55-59; Minister of Agricultural Machinery Building Industry 59-65; Eighth Minister of Machine Building 65-; Deputy Dir. Office of Agriculture and Forestry, State Council 55-; Alternate mem. C.C.P. Central Cttee. 56-; Chair. Water and Soil Conservation Cttee., State Council; mem. Standing Cttee., Nat. Cttee. of People's Political Consultative Conf. 54-.
Eighth Ministry of Machine Building, Peking, People's Republic of China.

Chen Chia-kang; Chinese diplomatist; ed. Wuhan Univ.
Active in int. youth activities; Asst. Head of Asian Dept. of Ministry of Foreign Affairs 49; Head of same Dept. 52; mem. of Council of Institute of Foreign Affairs 55; Ambassador to the United Arab Republic 56-.
Embassy of the People's Republic of China, Cairo, United Arab Republic.

Chen Feng-tung; Chinese agronomist.
Vice-Chair. All-China Asscn. for the Dissemination of Scientific and Technical Knowledge 53; Deputy Dir. Dept. of Biology, Geology and Geography, Academia Sinica 54; Del. for Honan to the First N.P.C.; Vice-Pres., Acad. of Agricultural Sciences 57-.
Academy of Agricultural Sciences, Peking, People's Republic of China.

Chen Han-seng; Chinese economist; b. 1897; ed. Germany and U.S.A.
Former History Prof., Peking Univ.; Head of the Institute of Social Sciences of Academia Sinica; after the war he was a prof. in Washington State Univ. until he returned to China in 51; Vice-Pres. Chinese People's Institute of Foreign Affairs 51-; Vice-Pres. Sino-Indian Friendship Asscn. 52; Del. for Hopeh Province to the Nat. People's Congress 54, 58 and 64; Deputy Dir. of Research Inst. of Int. Relations 56-; Vice-Chair. of Editorial Board, *China Reconstructs* 52-.
Publs. *The Agrarian Regions of India and Pakistan* 59, articles on agrarian problems in various periodicals, Chinese and foreign.
China Reconstructs, Peking 37, China.

Chen Kang-pai; Chinese scientist.
On Standing Cttee. of North China State Planning Commissions and mem. of the Cultural Cttee. 49-54; Vice-Chair. All-China Fed. of Scientific Societies; Dir. of Harbin Technical Univ. 51-54; Del. to the Second Session of the C.P.P.C.C. 54; Sec.-Gen. Chinese Acad. of Sciences 55-.
Chinese Acad. of Sciences, Peking, China.

Chen Po-ta; Chinese Marxist theoretician and historian; b. 04; ed. Shanghai Workers' Univ.
Member C.P. 27-; fmr. Political Sec. to Mao Tse-tung; Vice-Pres. Marx-Lenin Institute; Vice-Chair. All-China Asscn. of Social Science Workers; Vice-Pres. Academia Sinica; Vice-Dir. Board of Propaganda of the Communist Party of China 49-, Dep. Chair. State Planning Comm. 62-; Alt. mem. Politburo of Chinese C.P.; Leader, Group in Charge of Cultural Revolution; later

mem. Standing Cttee. of Politburo; Rector Peking Univ. 67-; Editor *Red Flag*.
Publs. include *The Thought of Mao Tse-tung, The Pursuit of Truth, On the Cultural Front*, a work on Yuan Shih-kai, another on the "Four Great Families", etc.
Peking University, Peking, China.

Chen, Reignson C.; Chinese financial officer; b. 96; ed. Tsinghua Coll., Peking, Colorado Coll. and New York Univ.
Manager, Wah Chang, Trading Corpn., Shanghai 23-26; Prof. Coll. of Commerce, Southeastern Univ., Shanghai 23-25, Peiyang Univ., Tientsin 26-27; Chief Rep., China Defence Supplies Inc. for China-Burma-India (U.S.A. Lend-Lease Supplies) 40-45; Sec.-Gen. Export-Import Board, Shanghai 46-48; Chair. Foreign Exchange Bankers Asscn., Shanghai 46-49; Man. Dir. and Gen. Man. Bank of China (Taipei), Gen. Man. China Insurance Co. (Taipei); Chair. China Products Trading Corpn. (Taipei) 52-60; Exec. Dir. for China (Taiwan), Int. Bank for Reconstruction and Development and Int. Devt. Asscn. 60-; U.S. Medal of Freedom.
International Bank for Reconstruction and Development, 1818 H Street, N.W., Washington, D.C., U.S.A.

Chen Wei-tsie (Chen Wei-chi); Chinese textile engineer; ed. England.
Chief engineer, printing and dyeing, in Nat. Cotton Mill, Shanghai; Vice-Minister of Textile Industry 49; mem. China Cttee. for Promotion of International Trade 52; Vice-Minister of Textile Industry 49-; del. to Second C.P.P.C.C. 54; Chair. China Asscn. of Textile Engineers; on Exec. Cttee. All-China Fed. of Industry and Commerce.
Ministry of Textile Industry, Peking, China.

Chen Yi, Marshal; Chinese soldier and politician; b. 1905; ed. Univ. of Communications, Shanghai.
Founded the Chungking newspaper *Hsin Shu Pao* in 21; joined the Communist Party of China in 23; after the break between the Kuomintang and the Communist Party in 27 he went to the Soviet Area in Kiangsi; mem. Central Executive Cttee. of the Chinese Soviet Provisional Govt. 31; commanded first detachment of the New Fourth Army 38; commanded People's Liberation Army of Eastern China; captured Tsinan 48; commanded Third Field Army 49; occupied Shanghai 49; Mayor of Shanghai 49; Vice-Chair. Council of Nat. Defence; mem. Political Bureau of C.P. of China; Pres. Nat. Asscn. for Eliminating Illiteracy 56-; Minister of Foreign Affairs 58-; a Vice-Premier 59-; Pres. Inst. of Int. Relations 61-.
Ministry of Foreign Affairs, Peking, China.

Chen Ying-Ning; Chinese philosopher.
Acting Chairman, Chinese Taoist Asscn. 59-.
China Taoist Association, Peking, People's Republic of China.

Chen Yü; Chinese trade union leader and administrator; b. 07.
Formerly led the Fed. of Seamen's Unions; Head of Dept. of Industry under N.E. Administration Council 49; Del. from All-China Fed. of Trade Unions to Political Consultative Conference 49; Minister of Fuel Industry 49-55; Minister of Coal Industry 55-58; Gov. of Kwangtung 57; Sec. Central-South Bureau 65, 3rd Sec. 65-.
Canton, Kwangtung, People's Republic of China.

Chen Yun; Chinese politician; b. 05.
Joined Communist Party 25; took part in workers' movement in Shanghai 26 and 27; mem. Kiangsu Provincial Cttee. and helped lead peasants in revolutionary struggle; alternate mem. Central Cttee. Communist Party 30, Vice-Chair. 60; Leader, Party Group, All-China Fed. of Trade Unions 32; mem. Political Bureau of Party's Central Cttee. 33, also Dir. Dept. of Party Work for White Areas 33, Dir. Admin. Dept. 37-44, mem. Standing Cttee. of Politburo until 67; Deputy Dir.

Financial and Economic Affairs, North-West 44; after establishment of Peoples Republic 49, elected mem. Central People's Govt. Council and Vice-Chair. Govt. Admin. Council, also Chair. its Cttee. on Financial and Economic Affairs, mem. Secretariat 50-; Vice-Pres. State Council 54-; a Vice-Premier 58-; Chair. State Capital Construction Comm. 58.
State Council, Peking, China.

Chenery, Hollis Burnley, B.S., PH.D.; American economist; b. 6 Jan. 1918; ed. Arizona, Oklahoma and Harvard Univs.
Officer, U.S. Army Air Corps 42-46; Economist, U.S. Econ. Co-operation Admin., Paris 49-50; Head, Programme Div., U.S. Mutual Security Agency, Rome 50-52; Econ. Consultant to Pakistan Govt. 55, Japanese Govt. 56, UN 57-61, Bank of Israel 59-61, Bank of Sicily 61; Prof. of Econs., Stanford Univ. 52-61; Asst. Administrator for Program, Agency for Int. Devt., Dept. of State 61-65; Prof. of Econs. and mem. Center for Int. Affairs, Harvard Univ. 65-; Dir. Southern Natural Gas Co., Alabama; mem. Council of Econometric Soc., American Economic Asscn., American Acad. of Arts and Sciences; Guggenheim Fellowship.
Publs. with others *Arabian Oil* 49, *Interindustry Economics* 59.
1010 Memorial Drive, Cambridge, Mass. 02138, U.S.A. Telephone: 617-864-4457.

Chenevière, Jacques, L. ès L.; Swiss writer; b. 17 April 1886; ed. Paris Univ.
Hon. Vice-Pres. Int. Red Cross Cttee.; Hon. D. ès L. (Geneva); Grand Prix de Littérature Française hors de France (Acad. Royale Belge) 66.
Publs. *Les Beaux Jours* (crowned by French Acad.), *La Chambre et le Jardin* (poems), *l'Ile déserte, Jouvence ou la Chimère, Les Messagers inutiles, La Jeune fille de neige, Innocences, Les Aveux Complets, Connais ton Coeur, Valet, dames, roi, Les Captives, Le Bouquet de la Mariée,* (novels and short stories); *La Comtesse de Ségur, née Rostopchine* (a biography), *Campagne Genevoise, Retours et images.*
Bellevue, near Geneva, Switzerland.

Chenevix-Trench, Anthony; British headmaster; b. 10 May 1919; ed. Shrewsbury School and Christ Church, Oxford.
Army service 39-45; Asst. Master, Shrewsbury School 48-51; Tutor in Classics, Christ Church, Oxford 51-52; House Master, Shrewsbury School 52-55; Headmaster, Bradfield Coll. 55-63, Headmaster, Eton Coll. 64-.
The Cloisters, Eton College, Windsor, Berkshire, England.

Cheng Tzu-hua; Chinese soldier and administrator; b. 07; ed. National Normal School, Taiyüan.
Joined Communist Party of China 26; commanded 41st Div. of the Red Army 32; Commissar during the Japanese War; Chair. Shansi Provincial People's Govt. 49; commanded 59th, 61st and 62nd Armies in the Korean War; mem. Standing Cttee. First Nat. People's Congress 54; Vice-Chair. Budget Cttee. Nat. People's Congress; Minister of Commerce 58-60; Dep. Chair. State Planning Comm. 61-; mem. Nat. Defence Council.
State Planning Commission, Peking, China.

Chenot, Bernard, L. en DR.; French politician; b. 20 May 1909; ed. Lycée Montaigne, Lycée Louis-le-Grand, Ecole libre des Sciences Politiques, Faculté de Droit, Paris.
Chef de Cabinet in numerous Ministries 32-39, including Public Health 35, Public Works 38 and 39; Del. Gen. of Tourism 38-42; Sec. Gen. Houillères Nat. du Nord et du Pas de Calais 44-46; Sec. Gen. Conseil Economique 51-58; Minister of Public Health and Population July 58-Jan. 59 (de Gaulle Cabinet), Jan. 59-Aug. 61 (Debré Cabinet), Minister of Justice Aug. 61-April 62 (Debré Cabinet); mem. Conseil Constitutionnel 62; Président de la Cité

internationale de l'Université de Paris; Pres. of Groupe des Assurances Générales de France 64-; fmr. Prof. Ecole Libre des Sciences Politiques, Inst. d'Etudes Politiques; Pres. French Section, Centre Européen de l'Entreprise Publique; mem. Admin. Council, Fondation des Sciences Politiques; Officier Légion d'Honneur, Grand Croix Ordre de St.-Charles, Grand Croix Ordre du Cèdre (Lebanon); Gold Medal, Education Physique et des Sports.

Publs. *Organisation Economique de l'Etat* 51, *Les Entreprises Nationalisées* (Collection *Que sais-je?*) 56; various published lectures, including *Les Institutions administratives de la France* and *Histoire des Doctrines Politiques, Etre Ministre* 67.

87 rue de Richelieu, Paris 2e, France.

Telephone: 742-70-10.

Cherednichenko, Evgeny Trofimovich; Soviet trade union official; b. 12; ed. Leningrad Inst. of Railway Transport Engineers and Higher Party School.

Departmental Head, Railway Line Section 38-40, 42-43; Party work 44-48; Asst. Head Div., Ministry of Railways 48-51; Chair. Central Cttee. Railwaymen's Trade Union 51-; mem. Central Auditing Cttee. of C.P.S.U.; mem. Presidium of All-Union Central Cttee. of Trade Unions; Order of Red Banner of Labour (three times); Badge of Honour (twice), etc.

Central Committee of the Railway Transport Workers' Union, 21 Sadovo-Spasskaya, Moscow, U.S.S.R.

Cherenkov, Pavel Alexeevich; Soviet physicist; b. 1904; ed. Voronezh Univ.

Discoverer of the Cherenkov Effect; mem. Inst. of Physics, U.S.S.R. Acad. of Sciences; State Prize 46, Nobel Prize for Physics (with Tamm and Frank) 58; Corresp. mem. Acad. of Sciences 64; Order of Red Banner of Labour (twice).

Lebedev Physics Institute of U.S.S.R. Academy of Sciences, Lenin Prospekt, Moscow, U.S.S.R.

Cherkaoui, Mohammed; Moroccan politician.

Ambassador of Morocco to France 61-64; Minister of Nat. Economy and Finance Aug. 64-65, of Development 65-66, of Foreign Affairs 66-67, of Nat. Defence 67; Pres. Comité Permanent Consultatif du Maghreb 64-; Pres. Org. for Afro-Asian Econ. Co-operation; Democratic Constitutional.

c/o Ministry of National Defence, Rabat, Morocco.

Cherkassky, Shura; Russian-born American pianist; b. 7 Oct. 1911; ed. Curtis Inst. of Music, Philadelphia. Studied under his mother and then Josef Hofmann; début Baltimore 23; numerous world tours since that date; regular contributor to Salzburg Festival concerts; many records.

c/o Ibbs and Tillett, Ltd., 124 Wigmore Street, London, W.1, England.

Telephone: 01-486-4021 (Agency).

Cherkes, Alexander Ilyich; Soviet pharmacologist; b. 1894; ed. Kharkov Univ.

Physician 17-21; Research Assoc., Asst. Prof. Kharkov Medical Inst. 21-29; Head of Laboratory, Ukrainian Inst. of Labour Hygiene 24-36; Head of Dept. Ukrainian Inst. of Experimental Medicine 33-41; Prof., Head of Chair, Kharkov Medical Inst. 29-44; Head of Chair, Kiev Medical Inst. 44-; Corresp. mem. U.S.S.R. Acad. of Medical Sciences 45; mem. U.S.S.R. Acad. of Medical Sciences 60-; mem. Board U.S.S.R. Soc. of Pharmacologists 65-; Chair. Board Ukrainian Soc. of Pharmacologists 61-; Deputy Chair. Kiev Branch Soc. of Pharmacologists 64-; Order of Red Banner of Labour (twice), Badge of Honour, Merited Scientist of Ukrainian S.S.R.

Medical Institute, 22 Pushkin Street, Kiev, U.S.S.R.

Cherkezia, Otari Evtikhievich; Soviet politician; b. 1933; ed. Georgian Polytechnic Inst.

Member C.P.S.U. 55-; Chief of Section, Central Cttee.

of Young Communist League, Georgia, then Deputy Chief of Section, Central Cttee. of Y.C.L. 57-61; First Sec. Central Cttee. of Y.C.L., Georgian S.S.R. 61-68; First Sec. Ordjonikidze District Cttee. of Tbilisi 68-; mem. Central Cttee. of C.P., Georgian S.S.R.; Deputy to U.S.S.R. Supreme Soviet; mem. Budget Cttee. Union Soviet.

Ordjonikidze District Cttee., Tbilisi, U.S.S.R.

Chermont, Jayme Sloan, LL.B.; Brazilian (b. London) diplomatist; b. April 1903; ed. Rio de Janeiro Law School.

At Brazilian Embassy, Washington 30-32; Second Sec. Foreign Office, Brazil 32-37; at London Embassy 37-38; First Sec., Brazil 41-43, Buenos Aires 43-45; Minister, London 50, Minister Counsellor and Chargé d'Affaires, London 53; various posts at Foreign Office, Brazil 53-57; Consul-Gen., New York 57; Amb. Haiti 60-61; Head of Political and Cultural Depts., Brazil 61; Sec.-Gen. Foreign Office 61-63; Amb. to Netherlands 63-67, to United Kingdom 67-68; Head of Del. to UN Gen. Assembly 62.

c/o Brazilian Embassy, 54 Mount Street, London, W.1, England.

Chernigovsky, Vladimir Nicolaievich; Soviet physiologist and neurophysiologist; b. 1907; ed. Perm State Univ.

Began physiological investigations of circulation, hæmatology and neurophysiology 33; Prof. of Physiology, Naval Medical Acad., Leningrad 43-52; Dir. of Inst. of Normal and Pathological Physiology, Moscow 52-59; Vice-Pres. Acad. of Medical Sciences 53-56; Head of Pavlov Inst. 59-; mem. U.S.S.R. Acad. of Medical Sciences, mem. and Sec. Dept. of Physiology, U.S.S.R. Acad. of Sciences; Corresp. mem. Rumanian Acad. of Sciences; Deputy to U.S.S.R. Supreme Soviet; Pavlov Prize 43 and Pavlov Gold Medal 64, U.S.S.R. Acad. of Sciences; Order of Red Banner of Labour (twice), Order of Red Star.

Publs. include: *The Afferent Systems of the Internal Organs* 43, *Problems of the Nervous Regulation of Blood Compositions* 53, *Morpho-physiological Structure of Interoceptive Analyser and Some Details of its Function* 59, *The Interceptors* 60, *Participation of Some Structures of Limbic System in Conducting Visceral and Somatic Signals* 64, *Morpho-physiological Architecture of Subcortical and Cortical Projections of Afferent Fibres of Vagus* 64.

I. P. Pavlov Institute of Physiology, Makarov Embankment, Leningrad, U.S.S.R.

Chernuschenko, Guerodot Gavrilovich; Soviet (Byelorussian) diplomatist; b. 1928; ed. Moscow State Inst. of International Relations.

Ministry of Foreign Affairs, Byelorussian S.S.R. 52-64; Perm. Rep. of Byelorussian S.S.R. to the UN 64-.

Permanent Mission of the Byelorussian Soviet Socialist Republic to the United Nations, 136 East 67th Street, New York, N.Y. 10021, U.S.A.

Chernyshev, Vasili Yefimovich; Soviet politician; b. 08; ed. Workers' Educational Inst. and Aviation Inst.

Member C.P.S.U. 28-; Komsomol work 28-30, 33-37; party work in Byelorussia 37-; Partisan 41-44; Second Sec. Baranovichi Regional Cttee., C.P. of Byelorussia, the First Sec. Brest and Minsk Regional Cttees., then Sec. Central Cttee. C.P. of Byelorussia 44-51; First Sec. Kaliningrad Regional Cttee., C.P.S.U. 51-59, Primorye Territorial Cttee. 59-; mem. Central Cttee. C.P.S.U. 52-; Deputy to U.S.S.R. Supreme Soviet; Hero of the Soviet Union; Order of Lenin.

Territorial Committee of C.P.S.U., Vladivostok, U.S.S.R.

Chernyshev, Vyacheslav Ivanovich; Soviet journalist and politician; b. 14; ed. Communist Inst. of Journalism, Leningrad.

Compositor 30-33; Deputy Editor-in-Chief *Tikhoo-*

keansky Komsomolyets (Pacific Komsomol Member), Khabarovsk 35-37; Corresp., later Head of Dept. *Komsomolskaya Pravda* (Komsomol Truth) 38-43; Press Attaché, Soviet Embassy, Mexico 43-46, Chile 46-47; Head of Dept. *Literaturnaya Gazeta* (Literary Paper) 47-48; Chief Editor Moscow Radio, later Deputy Head Supreme Broadcasting Board, U.S.S.R. Ministry of Culture 48-56; Head of Dept. *Sovietskaya Rossia* (Soviet Russia) 56-58; Deputy Head of Dept. of Int. Problems *Problemy mira i sotsialisma* (Problems of Peace and Socialism) 58-60; Head of U.S.S.R. Supreme Broadcasting Board and Deputy Chair. U.S.S.R. State Cttee. for Radio and Television 60-65; Sec., Union of Journalists of U.S.S.R. 65-; mem. C.P.S.U. 37; Order of Red Banner of Labour.
Union of Journalists of U.S.S.R., Moscow, U.S.S.R.

Chervonenko, Stepan Vasilievich, M.SC.; Soviet diplomatist; b. 1915; ed. Kiev State Univ.
Headmaster, secondary school 37-41; mem. C.P.S.U. 40-; Soviet Army service 41-44; teacher of Marxism-Leninism, Dep. Dir. Cherkass Pedagogical Inst. 44-48; on staff of Central Cttee. C.P. Ukraine 49-56; Sec. Central Cttee. C.P. Ukraine 56-59; Ambassador to Chinese People's Republic 59-65, to Czechoslovakia 65-; mem. Central Cttee. C.P.S.U.
Soviet Embassy, Prague, Czechoslovakia.

Cheshire, Geoffrey Chevalier, D.C.L., F.B.A.; British barrister-at-law; b. 27 June 1886; ed. Denstone Coll., and Merton Coll., Oxford.
Lecturer Univ. Coll. of Wales, Aberystwyth 09-10; Fellow of Exeter Coll. Oxford 12-45; All Souls' Lecturer in Private Int. Law 22-33; All Souls' Reader in English Law 33-44; Vinerian Prof. of English Law, Univ. of Oxford 44-49, Fellow of All Souls 44-49; Reader in Private Int. Law to Council of Legal Education 45-60; Hon. Bencher Lincoln's Inn; mem. of Inst. of Int. Law 50-65; Fellow of British Acad.
Publs. *Modern Real Property* 25, *Private International Law* 35; joint author of *Cheshire and Fifoot on Contracts* 45, *International Contracts* 48.
Laundry Cottage, Empshott, Liss, Hants., England.
Telephone: Blackmoor (Hampshire) 202.

Cheshire, Group Captain Geoffrey Leonard, V.C., D.S.O., D.F.C., B.A.; British Air Force officer (retd.); b. 7 Sept. 1917; ed. Stowe School, Merton Coll., Oxford Univ.
Commissioned 39; Flying Officer 40; Wing Commdr. commanding 76 Squadron 42, 617 Squadron 43; attached Eastern Air Command H.Q., South-East Asia 44, British Joint Staff Mission, Washington 45; observer at dropping of atomic bomb on Nagasaki 45; Founder, Cheshire Foundation Homes for the Sick and co-founder Ryder Cheshire Mission for the Relief of Suffering.
Publs. *Bomber Pilot* 43, *Pilgrimage to the Shroud* 56, *Face of Victory* 61.
Cavendish, Suffolk, England.
Telephone: 01-499-2267.

Chesser, Eustace, L.R.C.P., L.R.C.S.; British surgeon and psychologist; b. 22 March 1902; ed. George Watson's Acad., Edinburgh, Royal Coll. of Physicians and Royal Coll. of Surgeons.
Formerly Hon. Sec. Soc. for Sex Education and Guidance; Research Dir. Research Council into Marriage and Human Relationships; Clinical Asst. Tavistock Clinic; Hon. Surgeon Dilke Memorial Hospital; Chair. Advisory Council, Married Women's Asscn.; mem. Council, Int. Cttee. for Sex Equality; mem. Medico-Legal Council, Marriage Law Reform Soc., Royal Medico-Psychological Soc., Asscn. for Advancement of Psychotherapy, etc.; mem. Royal Inst.; mem. British Social Biology Council; Pres. Progressive League 60-.
Publs. *Love without Fear* 41, *Marriage and Freedom* 43, *Unwanted Children* 45, *Grow up—and Live* 49, *Successful Living* 50, *Cruelty to Children* 51, *Unquiet Minds, How to make a Success of your Marriage* 52, *Humanly Speaking*

54, *The Sexual, Marital and Family Relationships of the English Woman* 56, *Live and Let Live* 58, *Outline of Human Relationships* 59, *Women* 59, *Is Chastity Outmoded?* 60, *You've Got to Have Love* 60, *Life is for the Living* 62, *Woman and Love* 62, *The Cost of Loving* 64, *Shelley and Zastrozzi—Self-Revelation of a Neurotic* 65, *Unmarried Love* 65, *Living with Suicide* 67.
17 Wimpole Street, London, W.1, England.
Telephone: 01-580-4707.

Chester, Daniel Norman, C.B.E., M.A.; British political scientist; b. 27 Oct. 1907; ed. Manchester Univ.
Rockefeller Fellow 35-36; Lecturer in Public Admin., Manchester Univ. 36-45; mem. Economic Section, War Cabinet Secretariat 40-45; Official Fellow, Nuffield Coll., Oxford 45-54, Warden 54-; mem. Oxford City Council 52-; fmr. Chair. and now Vice-Pres. Royal Inst. of Public Admin.; fmr. Pres. Int. Political Science Asscn.; Chair. Oxford Centre for Management Studies; mem. South-East Regional Economic Planning Council; fmr. Editor *Public Administration*.
Publs. *Public Control of Road Passenger Transport* 36, *Central and Local Government, Financial and Administrative Relations* 51, *The Nationalised Industries* 51; Edited *Lessons of the British War Economy* 51, *Organisation of British Central Government 1914-1956* (Edited) 57, *Questions in Parliament* (with Mrs. Bowring) 62.
Nuffield College, Oxford; Home: 136 Woodstock Road, Oxford, England.
Telephone: Oxford 48014 (Office), Oxford 55323 (Home).

Chevalier, Louis; French university professor and political scientist; b. 29 May 1911; ed. Ecole Normale Supérieure.
Prof. Coll. de France; Prof. Institut d'Etudes Politiques de Paris; mem. Inst. Nat. d'Etudes Démographiques, Conseil supérieur de la Recherche Scientifique; Technical Adviser Préfecture de la Seine; Prés. du Conseil Scientifique du Centre Int. d'Etude des Problèmes Humains de Monaco; mem. Conseil Economique et Social du District de Paris; Hon. degree Columbia Univ.
Publs. *Les Paysans, Le Probème démographique nord-africain, La Formation de la population parisienne, Madagascar, Démographie générale;* contributor to *Population, Le choléra de 1832, Classes laborieuses et classes dangereuses, Les Parisiens.*
Institut National d'Etudes Démographiques, 23 avenue Franklin D. Roosevelt, Paris 8e, France.

Chevalier, Maurice; French actor and music hall star; b. 12 Sept. 1888.
Embarked on career through medium of amateur concert stage; star of Eden Music Hall Paris 04; on tour in France 04-06, at Eldorado Music Hall Paris 07; at Folies Bergères with Mistinguett 09; served French Army First World War; season in London 18; many successful seasons in Paris and a tour of Argentina 19-29; made a number of musical films, including *The Love Parade* 29, *The Big Pond* 30, *Playboy of Paris* 31, *La Veuve Joyeuse* and *L'Homme du Jour* 35, etc.; appeared before Their Majesties, The King and Queen, London 39; remained in Paris during occupation; tour U.S. and Canada 47-48; series of recitals at Théâtre des Champs-Elysées, Paris 48, 63; recent films *Le Roi* 49, *Ma Pomme* 50, *Gigi* 58, *Count Your Blessings* and *Can-Can* 59, *Jessica* 62; Chevalier Légion d'Honneur, Croix de Guerre, etc.
Publs. *Ma Route et Mes Chansons* (autobiography), *With Love* 60.
Villa La Louque, Parc de Marnes la Coquette, S. et O., France.

Chevalier, Roger; French aeronautical engineer; b. 3 May 1922; ed. Ecole Polytechnique and Ecole nationale supérieure de l'aéronautique.
Head of Dept., Aeronautical Arsenal 48-53; Chief

Engineer, Nord-Aviation 54-60; Technical Dir. Soc. pour l'Etude et la Réalisation d'Engins Balistiques (SEREB) 60-, Dir.-Gen. 67; mem. Int. Acad. of Astronautics; Officier Légion d'Honneur; Médaille de l'Aéronautique; Prix Galabert 66.
Telephone: CAR 59 28.
4 rue Edouard Detaille, Paris 17e, France.

Chevallier, Gabriel Régis Marie Emile; French writer; b. 3 May 1895; ed. Ecole des beaux-arts, Lyon.
Chevalier Légion d'Honneur, Croix de Guerre 14-18.
Publs. *Durand, voyageur de Commerce, La Peur, Clarisse Vernon, Clochemerle, Propre à rien, Sainte-Colline, Ma petite amie Pomme, les Héritiers Euffe, Mascarade, Le Petit Général, Le Ravageur* (play), *Clochemerle-Babylone, Chemins de Solitude, Carrefours des Hasards, Lyon 2000, Olympe, Les filles sont libres, Miss taxi, Clochemerle-les-Bains, L'Envers de Clochemerle, Brume Rives,* etc.
41 rue Duguesclin, Lyon, Rhône, France.

Chevallier, Jacques-George-Marie-François; French industrialist and politician; b. 15 Nov. 1911; ed. Ferrel Military Institute (New Orléans), St. François-Regis (Montpellier), Coll. de St. Elme (Arcachon), and Notre Dame d'Afrique (Algiers).
Mayor of El Biar and mem. Financial Cttee. for Algeria 41-43; participated Italian campaign, later led mil. mission to U.S.A. 43-45; Deputy for Algiers 46; del. to Algerian Assembly 51; Mayor of Algiers 53-58; Pres. Caisse Interprofessionelle d'Allocations Familiales du Département d'Alger 52; Sec. of State for War 54; Minister of Nat. Defence 55; Vice-Pres. Chamber of Commerce of Algiers 63-66, Port of Algiers 63-64; Independent; Chevalier Légion d'Honneur, Croix de Guerre, many foreign decorations.
Publ. *Nous Algériens* 58.
Le Bordj, El Biar, Algiers, Algeria.

Chevrier, Hon. Lionel, Q.C., P.C.; Canadian lawyer; b. 2 April 1903; ed. Cornwall, Ont., High School, Cornwall Collegiate Inst., Univ. of Ottawa, Osgoode Hall (Law School) Toronto, Ont.
Called to Bar 28; appointed K.C. 38; mem. of Dominion Parl. 35-54, 57-63; Deputy Chief Govt. Whip 40; Chair. Sub-Cttee. on Production and Munitions Contracts (Parl. War Expenditure Cttee.) 42; Parl. Asst. to Minister of Munitions and Supply 43; Minister of Transport April 45-54; Pres. The St. Lawrence Seaway Authority 54-57; Minister of Justice 63; High Commr. for Canada in U.K. 64-67; Commr.-Gen. for Overseas Visits, *Expo 67*, Montreal; Del. Bretton Woods Conf. 45; Chair. Canadian del. to UN Gen. Assembly, Paris 48; Pres. of Privy Council 57; Hon. LL.D. (Univ. of Ottawa, Queen's Univ., Laval Univ.); Hon. D.C.L. (Bishop's Univ.); Liberal.
Publ. *The St. Lawrence Seaway* 59.
1321 Sherbrooke Street W., Montreal, Canada.

Cheysson, Claude; French public servant; b. 13 April 1920; ed. Ecole Polytechnique and Ecole d'Administration, Paris.
Escaped from occupied France to Spanish prison 43; Officer in the Free French Forces 43-45; entered French Diplomatic Service 48; attached to U.N. Mission in Palestine 48; Head of French liaison office with Fed. German Govt., Bonn 49-52; adviser to Prime Minister of Vietnam, Saigon 52-54; Chef de Cabinet to French Prime Minister (Mendès-France) 54-55; technical adviser to Minister for Moroccan and Tunisian Affairs 55-56; Sec.-Gen. Comm. for Technical Co-operation in Africa (C.C.T.A.), Lagos 57-62; Dir.-Gen. Sahara Authority (Organisme Saharien), Algiers 62-65; Dir.-Gen. Organisme coopération industrielle, Algiers 66; Amb. to Indonesia 66-; Officier, Légion d'Honneur; Croix de Guerre (five citations).
The French Embassy, 11 Imam Bondjol, Djakarta, Indonesia.

Chia Ch'i-Yun; Chinese politician and administrator. Dir. State Statistical Bureau, Peking; mem. Chinese C.P., Peking; Sec. of Kweichow Province Cttee. of Chinese C.P. 65-.
Regional Committee of the Chinese Communist Party, Kweiyang, Kweichow Province, People's Republic of China.

Chiang Ching (wife of Mao Tse-tung, *q.v.*); Chinese politician; b. *c.* 1915; ed. Junior Middle School, Shantung, Shantung Practical Theatrical Coll. and Lu Hsun Art Coll., Chiao Erh Kou.
Former stage and film actress, Shanghai; stage debut as Nora in *A Doll's House* (Ibsen); appeared in films under name of Lan Pin (Blue Apple); joined China Alliance Film Enterprise, Shanghai 36, then Shanghai Practical Amateur Dramatic Theatre; later, with Central Film Studio of the Propaganda Bureau of Kuomintang Govt.; married Mao Tse-tung 39; Co-Dir. Northeast Film Producers of C.C.P. Central Cttee. 46; First Deputy Leader, Cultural Revolution Sub-Cttee. 66-; Adviser on Cultural Work to People's Liberation Army Dec. 66-; mem. C.P. 33-, Film Studies Cttee., Ministry of Culture, Peking 50.
c/o Central Committee of Chinese Communist Party, Peking, China.

Chiang Ching-kuo; Chinese politician; b. 18 March 1910; ed. Sun Yat-Sen Univ., Moscow, and U.S.S.R. Military and Political Inst.
Eldest son of Generalissimo Chiang Kai-shek; Admin. Commdr. for South Kiangsi 39-45; Foreign Affairs Commdr. of Mil. and Political Admin. for N.E. China 45-47; Deputy Econ. Control Supervisor for Shanghai 48; Chair. Kuomintang Taiwan Province H.Q. 49-50; Dir., Gen. Political Dept., Ministry of Nat. Defence 50-54; mem. Central Revision Cttee. of Kuomintang 50-52; Minister without Portfolio 63; Deputy Minister of Nat. Defence 64-65; Minister of Nat. Defence 65-; Deputy Sec.-Gen. Nat. Defence Council 54-67; Chair. Nat. Gen. Mobilization Cttee.; mem. Standing Cttee. of Kuomintang.
18 Chang An East Road, 1st Section, Taipei, Taiwan, Republic of China.

Chiang Kai-shek (Chiang Chung-cheng), Generalissimo; Chinese politician; b. 31 Oct. 1887; ed. Paoting and Tokyo Military Acad.
Founder and Commdt. Whampoa Mil. Acad. 24; took part in the first and second revolutions under Sun Yat-Sen; Commdr.-in-Chief Revolutionary Armies 26-28; Chair. of Nat. Govt. 28; married Mayling Soong 27; President of National Military Council 32-46; President of Executive Yuan, Chair. of Supreme National Council, Chair. of National Govt. and Governor of Szechwan 32-47; mem. Central Exec. Comm., Kuomintang 26-50, Dir.-Gen. of Kuomintang 38-; Supreme Commdr. of Allied Forces China Theatre 42-45; elected Pres. of Republic at China's First Nat. Assembly 48, retd. 49; Head of Supreme Policy Council Canton 49; resumed Presidency (in Taiwan) 50, re-elected 54, re-elected 60, re-elected 66, also Chair. Nat. Security Council 67-; Hon. G.C.B., Hon. D.C.L.; Croix de Guerre.
Publs. *China's Destiny* 43, *The Collected Wartime Messages of Generalissimo Chiang Kai-shek 1937-1945, Soviet Russia in China* 57.
Office of the President, Taipei, Republic of China (Taiwan).

Chiang Kai-shek, Madame (Soong, Mayling), LL.D., L.H.D.; Chinese sociologist; ed. Wellesley Coll., U.S.A.
Married (Pres.) Chiang Kai-shek 27; first Chinese woman appointed mem. of Child Labour Comm.; inaugurated Moral Endeavour Asscn.; established schools in Nanking for orphans of revolutionary soldiers; fmr. mem. Legislative Yuan; served as Sec.-Gen. of Chinese Comm. on Aeronautical Affairs; Dir.-Gen. New Life Movement; founded and directed Nat. Chinese Women's Asscn. for

War Relief and Nat. Asscn. for Refugee Children; accompanied husband on mil. campaigns; Hon. Pres. American Bureau for Medical Aid to China and Cttee. for the promotion of the Welfare of the Blind; Patroness Int. Red Cross Cttee.; Hon. Chair. British United Aid to China Fund and United China Relief; First Hon. Mem. Bill of Rights Commemorative Society; first Chinese woman to be decorated by Nat. Govt. of China, awards include Gold Medal of Nat. Inst. of Social Sciences; L.D.H. John B. Stetson Univ., Bryant Coll., Hobart and William Smith Colls.; LL.D. Rutgers Univ., Goucher Coll., Wellesley Coll., Loyola Univ., Russell Sage Coll., Hahnemann Medical Coll., Univs. of Michigan and Hawaii, and Wesleyan Coll., Maçon; Hon. F.R.C.S. (Eng.).
Publs. *China in Peace and War* 39, *China Shall Rise Again* 39, *This Is Our China* 40, *We Chinese Women* 41, *Little Sister Su* 43, *The Sure Victory* 55, *Madame Chiang Kai-shek: Selected Speeches* 58-59.
Taipei, Republic of China (Taiwan).

Chiang Kuang-nai; Chinese soldier and politician; b. 89; ed. Paoting Mil. Acad.
C.-in-C. 19th Route Army 32; Minister of Textile Industry 52-67; mem. Standing Cttee. of the Revolutionary Cttee. of the Kuomintang; mem. Peking Urban Council.
Peking, China.

Chiao Kuan-hua; Chinese administrator in international affairs; b. 03; ed. Tsinghua Univ. and in Germany.
Vice-Chair. Policy Cttee. of Ministry of Foreign Affairs 49; Head of Int. News Dept. of Central News Office 49; Vice-Pres. Inst. of Foreign Affairs 49-; Asst. to Minister of Foreign Affairs 54-64; Vice-Foreign Minister 64-.
Ministry of Foreign Affairs, Peking, China.

Chiari, Hermann; Austrian medical doctor; b. 97; ed. Medical Faculty, Univ. of Vienna.
Asst., Medical Institutes, Vienna 22-36; Dir. Inst. of Pathological Anatomy, Univ. of Vienna 36-; Vice-Pres. Austrian Acad. of Sciences.
Publs. many monographs on the pathological anatomy of rheumatic diseases and of metabolic, infectious, heart and joint diseases.
Pathological Anatomy Institute, Vienna University, Spitalgasse 4, Vienna IX, Austria.

Chiari, Roberto; Panamanian businessman and politician; b. 2 March 1905.
Sugar maufacturer; President of Panama 60-64; Conservative.
Panama City, Panama.

Chiba, Saburo; Japanese industrialist and politician; b. 94; ed. Tokyo Imperial and Princeton Univs.
Entered Royal Oil Co., U.S.A. 21; Dir. Japanese Business Joint Organisation 22; mem. House of Reps. 25-; Dir. South American Development Co. 28; Dir. and Chief of Sales Dept., Jijishimpo Newspaper Co. Ltd. 32; Man. Dir. Sozan Petroleum Co. Ltd. 35; Pres. Japan Petro-chemical Industry Co. Ltd. 38; Vice-Pres. Technical Authority 45; Gov. Miyagi Prefecture 45; Sec.-Gen. Democratic Party 49, People's Democratic Party 50; Dir. Tokyo Agricultural Univ. 51, Pres. and Chair. Board of Dirs. 55-; Chair. Finance Cttee. House of Reps. 53; mem. Gen. Affairs Cttee. 63-; Minister of Labour 54-55.
31 Maruyama-cho, Bunkyo-ku, Tokyo, Japan.

Chiba, Yujiro; Japanese journalist and radio administrator; b. 98; ed. Tokyo Univ.
Asahi Shimbun 22-, London Corresp., later Editor-in-Chief; Dir. of Journalism, Research Inst. of Tokyo Univ. 50-; fmr. Chair. Board of Govs. Japan Broadcasting Corpn.; Radio Cultural Prize 58.
c/o Japan Broadcasting Corporation, No. 2, 2-chome, Uchisaiwai-cho, Chiyoda-ku, Tokyo, Japan.

Chichester, Sir Francis, K.B.E.; British map publisher, air navigator and pilot, and yachtsman; b. 17 Sept. 1901; ed. Marlborough Coll.
In New Zealand 19-29; flew solo to Australia 29; made first solo flight across Tasman Sea 31; flew solo from New Zealand to Japan in seaplane 31; Chief Navigation Instructor, Empire Central Flying School 40-45; writer of navigation instruction, Air Ministry 40-45; Francis Chichester Ltd. (map and guide business) 45-; Warden of Court of Guild of Air Pilots and Air Navigators 45-59; winner First Solo Transatlantic Race (yacht) 60, broke his own record 62, second in Second Transatlantic Solo Race 64; sailed solo Plymouth (England) to Sydney non-stop in 107 days 66; sailed solo Sydney to Plymouth via Cape Horn 67; Johnston Memorial Trophy 31, *Observer* Trophy 60, Yachtsman of the Year Trophy 60, Gold Medal, Inst. of Navigation 61, Blue Water Medal by C.C.A. (twice); Gold Medal, Australian Inst. of Navigation; Yacht Club of France Special Centenary Award; San Remo Figurehead of Courage.
Publs. *Solo to Sydney* 30, *Alone over the Tasman Sea* 32, 46, *Ride on the Wind* 37, *Astro-Navigation* 40, *Pinpoint the Bomber* 41, *Alone Across the Atlantic* 61, *Atlantic Adventure* 62, *The Lonely Sea and the Sky* (autobiography) 64, *Along the Clipper Way* 66, *Gipsy Moth Circles the World* 67.
9 St. James's Place, London, S.W.1, England.
Telephone: 01-493-0931.

Chikovani, Mikhail Gerasimovich; Soviet politician; b. 1911; ed. Higher Party School.
Worker, then foreman 29-34; Sec. District Cttee. of C.P., Uzbekistan; later, Sec. Central Cttee. of Young Communist League of Uzbekistan; then Sec., Tashkent and Samarkand Regional Cttees. of C.P., Uzbekistan 34-41; Soviet Army 41-45; Sec. Tashkent City Cttee. of C.P., Uzbekistan 46-50; First Sec. Sukhumi City Cttee. of C.P., Georgia 54-58; Chair. Council of Ministers, Abkhazian A.S.S.R. 58-; mem. C.P.S.U. 32-, Central Cttee. of C.P., Georgia; Deputy to Supreme Soviet.
Council of Ministers of Abkhazian A.S.S.R., Sukhumi, U.S.S.R.

Childers, Erskine Hamilton; Irish politician; b. 11 Dec. 1905; ed. Gresham's School, Holt, and Trinity Coll., Cambridge.
Advertisement Man. Irish Press Ltd. 32-35; Sec. Fed. of Irish Manufacturers 36-44; mem. Dáil 38-; Parl. Sec. to Minister for Local Govt. 47-48; Minister for Posts and Telegraphs 51-54, for Lands 57-59, for Transport and Power 59-66, for Transport and Power and Posts and Telegraphs 66-.
68 Highfield Road, Rathgar, Dublin, Ireland.

Childs, Marquis William, A.B., A.M.; American journalist; b. 17 March 1903; ed. Wisconsin and Iowa Univs.
With United Press 23 and 25-26; Corresp. *St. Louis Post Dispatch* 26-44, Special Corresp. 54-62, Washington Corresp. 62-; United Feature Syndicate Columnist 44-54; Hon. LL.D. Upsala Coll.
Publs. *Sweden: The Middle Way, They Hate Roosevelt* 36, *Washington Calling* 37, *This is Democracy* 38, *This is Your War, I Write from Washington* 42, *The Cabin* 44, *The Farmer Takes a Hand* 52, *Ethics in Business Society* (with D. Cater) 54, *The Ragged Edge* 55, *Eisenhower: Captive Hero* 59, *The Peacemakers* 61.
Home: 3554 Edmunds Street, N.W., Washington 7, D.C.; Office: 1028 Connecticut Avenue, Washington 6, D.C., U.S.A.

Chillida Juantegui, Eduardo; Spanish sculptor; b. 10 Jan. 1924; ed. Colegio Marianistas San Sebastian and Univ. de Madrid.
Started executing sculptures 47; first one-man exhbn., Madrid 54; one-man exhbns. at Duisburg and Houston, Texas 66, and at New York 67; has exhibited in numerous group exhbns. in America, France, Germany, Italy,

Spain, Switzerland, and U.K. since 49 including Venice Biennali 58, 62; Premio del Comune di Venezia per la Scultura, Venice Biennale 58, Prix Kandinsky 60, Carnegie Prize, Pittsburgh Int. 64, North Rhine West-phalian Prize for Sculpture 65, Wilhelm Lehmbruck Prize, Duisburg.
Villa Paz, Alto de Maracruz, San Sebastian, Spain.
Telephone: 51587.

Chin Chung-hua; Chinese politician.
On editorial staff of Kaiming Book Co.; in war edited *Hsing-tao jih-pao* in Singapore; after war edited *Hsin-wen jih-pao* in Shanghai; Chair. C.P.P.C.C. and mem. Nat. Cttee.; Dir. Cultural Dept. East China Mil. Govt. Council 50; Vice-Mayor, Shanghai 52-53; Head of Chinese News Asscn., East China Admin. Council; Vice-Chair. Shanghai Consultative Cttee. 54; Shanghai Del. to First N.P.C.; Vice-Mayor, Shanghai 55; Vice-Pres. All-China Journalists' Asscn. 56; re-elected Vice-Mayor of Shanghai 57.
Shanghai Town Council, Shanghai, China.

Chirac, Jacques; French politician; b. 29 Nov. 1932; ed. Lycée Carnot, Lycée Louis-le-Grand and Ecole nationale d'Administration.
Military Service in Algeria; Auditor, Cour des Comptes 59-62; Head of Dept., Secr.-Gen. of Govt. 62; Head of Dept., Private Office of M. Pompidou 62-65; Counsellor, Cour des Comptes 65-67; State Sec. for Employment Problems 67-.
57 rue Boissière, Paris 16e, France.

Chirkov, Boris Petrovich; Soviet actor; b. 13 Aug. 1901; ed. Leningrad Inst. of State Art.
Acted at Leningrad Theatre of the Young Spectator 25-30, Leningrad Red Theatre 30-32, Leningrad New Theatre of the Young Spectator 36-38, Theatre Studio of the Film Actor, Moscow 45, Moscow Pushkin Drama Theatre 50; People's Artist of the U.S.S.R. 50; State prizewinner 41, 47, 49, 52; awarded Order of Lenin; First prize in the All-Union Film Festival for the best male part (film *Kievlanka*) 60. Principal roles: Maxim (*Youth of Maxim* 35, *Return of Maxim* 37, *Vyborg Side* 39), Makhno (*Alexander Parkhomenko* 42), Udivitelno (*Front* 43), Dr. Chizhov (*True Friends* 54), Biryukov (*The Living and the Dead* 63), The Little Man (*Extra-ordinary Mission* 65).
Publs. *Actor and his Role,* from *Thirty Years of the Soviet Cinematograph Industry* 50, 4 books of essays, *About Us, The Actors, On the Screen and Behind the Screen* 61, *Experience and Reflections* 64.
Moscow Pushkin Drama Theatre, Moscow, U.S.S.R.
Telephone: 62-79-36.

Chiryaev, Gavriil Iosifovich; Soviet politician; b. 1925; ed. Yakutsk Pedagogical Inst.
Teacher 42-43; Soviet Army 43-50; educational work 51-53; Instructor, Schools Sector, Yakutsk Regional Cttee. of C.P., later, Second Sec., Verkhny Vilyui District Cttee. of C.P. 53-58; Deputy Chief, later Chief, of Section, Yakutsk Regional Cttee. of C.P. 58-61; Sec. Yakutsk Regional Cttee. of C.P. 61-65, First Sec. 65-; Candidate mem. Central Cttee. C.P.S.U. 66-; mem. C.P.S.U. 44-; Deputy to U.S.S.R. Supreme Soviet.
Yakutsk Regional Committee of Communist Party, Yakutsk, U.S.S.R.

Chisholm, George Brock, C.C., C.B.E., M.C., E.D. MD.; Canadian psychiatrist; b. 18 May 1896; ed. Univ. of Toronto.
General medical practice 25-31; on staff Inst. of Human Relations at Yale Univ., and Queen Square Hospital and Maudsley Hospital, London 31-34; practised psychological medicine, Toronto 34-40; Commdr. Northern Area M.D.2 then Gen. Staff Officer Mil. Training (Canadian Army), Dir. of Personnel Selection, Deputy Adjutant-Gen. 40-42; Dir.-Gen. Medical Services (with rank of Major-Gen.) 42-44; Deputy Minister of Health

in Dept. of Nat. Health and Welfare 44-46; Exec. Sec. of W.H.O. Interim Comm. 46-48; Dir.-Gen. W.H.O. 48-53; Chair. Canadian Medical Procurement and Assignment Board 42-44; Pres. Canadian Nat. Cttee. for Mental Hygiene and Chair. Health Cttee. Canadian Youth Comm. 43-46; Vice-Pres. World Fed. for Mental Health 56-57, Pres. 57-58; Vice-Pres. World Asscn. of World Federalists; Hon. Pres. World Federalists of Canada; Lasker and Lewin Memorial awards, American Unitarian Asscn. Award, Medal of the Pasteur Inst., World Govt. News Award; Hon. Fellow Royal Soc. of Medicine, American Psychiatric Asscn., and American Public Health Asscn.; Fellow World Acad. of Art and Science; Dr. h.c. (Univs. of Nancy and B.C.); Hon. D.Sc. (Univ. of North Carolina, Dartmouth Coll.); Hon. D. Humane Letters (Brandeis Univ.); Order of Merit of Syria, Lebanon, and Cuba, Golden Anniversary Mental Health Award, Connecticut Asscn. for Mental Health, Humanist of the Year Award 59, American Humanist Asscn.
Publs. *Morale* 40, *William Alanson White Memorial Lectures* 45, *Prescription for Survival* 57, *Can People Learn to Learn?* 58.
Hampshire House, Apartment 301-1159 Beach Drive, Victoria, B.C., Canada.
Telephone: 384-7241.

Chittenden, María del Carmen Gutiérrez Chamberlain de; Costa Rican teacher and diplomatist; b. 19; ed. San José, Costa Rica.
Teacher, Centro Cultural Costarricense-Norteamericano, San José 56-62; Amb. to U.K. 62-66, concurrently accredited Amb. to Norway 64-66.
c/o Ministry of Foreign Affairs, San José, Costa Rica.

Chiu Chuang-Cheng; Chinese army officer and politician.
Former artillery officer; Major-Gen 55; Fifth Minister of Machine-Building Sept. 63-; mem. Nat. Defence Council 65-.
Fifth Ministry of Machine-Building, Peking, People's Republic of China.

Choi Doo Sun; Korean business executive and politician; b. 1894; ed. Waseda Univ., Japan, and Marburg Univ., Germany.
Former President, Seoul Textile Co.; Pres. *Dong A Ilbo* (newspaper) 47-63; Pres. Korean Red Cross 60-; Prime Minister of Republic of Korea Dec. 63-64.
Seoul, Republic of Korea.

Chongchareon, Pramote; Thai police officer, diploma-tist and Barrister-at-Law; b. 08; ed. Assumption Coll., Bangkok, and Univ. of Hong Kong.
Entered Police Dept. 29, Brig.-Gen. 52; Vice-Consul, Penang 40-42; Military Gov., S. Province of Thailand 43; Ambassador to Republic of Viet-Nam 56-61; Dir.-Gen. of Economic Dept., Ministry of Foreign Affairs 61-63; Ambassador to U.S.S.R. June 63-; Special Grand Cordon Most Noble Order of the Crown of Thailand.
Royal Thai Embassy, 3 Eropinsky pereulok, Moscow, U.S.S.R.; Home: 56/1 Lang Suan Lane, Bangkok, Thailand.

Chopra, Lt.-Col. Inder Sen, O.B.E.; Indian diplomatist; b. 09; ed. Govt. Coll. and Punjab Univ., Lahore, and Royal Military Coll., Sandhurst, England.
Commissioned Indian Army 30; joined Indian Political Service 36, and served as Asst. Political Agent, Loralai, Asst. Political Agent and Colonisation Officer, Nasira-bad, Dir. of Food and Civil Supplies, and Sec. of Revenue, Baluchistan Govt., Sec. to Agent to Gov.-Gen. and Resident in Baluchistan 36-46; Sec. Indian Embassy, Washington, 46, Counsellor 48-49; served Ministry of External Affairs as Deputy Sec. 49, Joint Sec. and concurrently Chief of Protocol 50-55; Minister to Sweden (concurrently to Denmark and Finland) 55-56; Ambassador to Sweden 56-58, Denmark 58, Iraq

and Jordan 58-60, Jordan 60, Lebanon 62, Kuwait 63, and High Commr. to Cyprus 62-64, to Argentina, Uruguay and Paraguay 64-.
Embassy of India, Buenos Aires, Argentina.

Chopra, Mulk Raj, B.ENG.; Indian civil engineer and university vice-chancellor; b. 18 Aug. 1906; ed. Govt. Coll., Lahore and Thomason Coll. (now Roorkee Univ.). Joined Irrigation Branch, Punjab 30, rising to position of Under-Sec. to Govt., Punjab Irrigation Branch; promoted to Superintending Engineer 48; in charge of Harrike Barrage construction 49; Sec. Vhakra Control Board 50; Joint Dir., Directorate of Construction and Plant Design, Bhakra Dam and Power Plant 57, promoted to Chief Engineer, then Gen. Man. 58; in charge of Beas Project Admin. 60; Chair. Central Water and Power Comm., Govt. of India 62-66; Vice-Chancellor Roorkee Univ. Sept. 66-; Padma Bhushan Award 67. Vice-Chancellor's Lodge, University of Roorkee, Roorkee, U.P., India.

Chorley, 1st Baron, cr. 45, of Kendal; **Robert Samuel Theodore Chorley,** M.A.; British jurist; b. 29 May 1895; ed. Kendal Grammar School and Queen's Coll., Oxford. Formerly in Foreign Office and Ministry of Labour; Barrister 20; Pres. Hardwicke Soc. 21-22; Tutor Law Society's School of Law 20-24, Lecturer in Commercial Law 24-30; Sir Ernest Cassel Prof. of Commercial and Industrial Law, London Univ. 30-47; Hon. Sec. Council for Preservation of Rural England 38-67; Vice-Chair. Nat. Trust; mem. staff Ministry Home Security 41-42; Nat. Parks Cttee.; Deputy Regional Commr. for Civil Defence, N.W. Region 42-45; Chair. Westmorland Court of Quarter Sessions 45; mem. Parl. del. to India 46; Royal Comm. on Justices of the Peace 46; Chair. Cttee. on Civil Service Salaries 48; a Lord-in-Waiting to the King 46-49; mem. Mocatta Cttee. on Cheque Endorsements 55; Pres. Commons and Footpaths Preservation Soc. 61-; Gen. Editor *Modern Law Review.* Publs. *Law of Banking, Leading Cases in Commercial Law* (in collaboration), *Shipping Law* (in collaboration), *Arnould's Law of Marine Insurance* (ed. 13th, 14th and 15th edns.), *Leading Cases in the Law of Banking* (in collaboration).
The Rookery, Stanmore, Middlesex, England.

Chou Chien-jen; Chinese administrator; b. 12 Nov. 1888.
Fmr. Prof. of Biology; Education Dept., N. China People's Govt. 48; Vice-Chair. Chekiang Prov. People's Govt. 49-54; Vice-Minister of Higher Education 54-58; Gov. Chekiang Prov. 58-67; Deputy from Chekiang, Nat. People's Congress 54-, mem. Standing Cttee. 54-, Vice-Chair. 65-; mem. Nat. Cttee. People's Political Consultative Conf. 54-; Dir. Sino-Soviet Friendship Asscn. 49-; Vice-Chair. Chinese Asscn. for Promoting Democracy 50-; Pres. China-Nepal Friendship Asscn. 56-.
National People's Congress, Peking, People's Republic of China.

Chou En-lai, Gen.; Chinese politician; b. 98; ed. Nankai High School, Tientsin.
Active as a student in Chinese political movement; Chair. student asscn. during anti-Yuanshihkai movement; editor-in-chief of daily newspaper of Tientsin Student Asscn. during May 4th revolutionary movement 19; arrested and imprisoned by govt. authorities for six months; went to France 20; founded in Paris Chinese Communist Youth Group 22; Instructor and later Head of political training dept. of Whampoa Mil. Acad. Canton 24-26; organizer of second and third armed Labour uprising in Shanghai 27; one of leaders of Nanchang Uprising, Kiangsi Province Aug. 27; helped found Chinese Red Army after failure of Great Revolution; underground activities in Shanghai until 31; political commissar in Chinese Red Army in Kiangsi Soviet Region 31-34; with Red Army in its Long March 34-35; chief communist negotiator with Chiang Kai-shek

36; deputy head of political training dept. of Mil. Affairs Council of Nat. Govt. 37-40; communist del. in Political Consultative Council 46; communist rep. on Cttee. of Three, with Gen. Marshall as chair., in peace negotiations between Communists and Kuomintang 46; mem. Central Cttee. Chinese Communist Party 26-, mem. Political Bureau and Secretariat of Central Cttee; mem. Standing Cttee. of Political Bureau; Premier of Govt. Admin. Council, Minister for Foreign Affairs and Vice-Chair. of People's Revolutionary Cttee. 49-58; Premier of State Council of People's Republic of China 58-; Chair. Chinese People's Political Consultative Conf. (C.P.P.C.C.).
Office of the Prime Minister, Peking, China.

Chou Hsin-fang; Chinese actor; b. 95.
Became famous in aged male character parts, *Iao sheng;* like Mei Lan-fang reformed and renewed Peking Opera; organised troupe in Shanghai 37; produced patriotic plays in Japanese War; invited to First C.P.P.C.C.; Dir. East China Inst. for Research in Peking Drama 53; on Standing Cttee. Chinese Dramatic Asscn.; Shanghai del. to first N.P.C. 54; on Shanghai City Council 55.
Publs. Acting versions of operas in which he has played.
Chinese Dramatists' Association, Shanghai, China.

Chou Hsing; Chinese politician.
Former Sec. Cttee. of Communist Party, Shantung Province; fmr. First Political Commissar of Shantung Military District; now Sec. of Cttee. of Chinese C.P. of Yunnan Province; Gov. of Yunnan 65-.
Office of the Governor of Yunnan, Kunming, People's Republic of China.

Chou Jung-hsin; Chinese politician.
Former Deputy Sec.-Gen. State Council, Acting Sec.-Gen. 63-65, Sec.-Gen. 65-.
Office of the Secretary-General of State Council, Peking, People's Republic of China.

Chou Yang; Chinese literary critic; b. 08; ed. Ta Hsia Univ. and Japan.
During the war he guided cultural activities as Head of Yenan Univ. and Prof. in the Lu Hsün Acad. of Art; Vice-Chair. All-China Fed. of Literary and Art Circles 49-; Dir. of the literary periodical *Wen Yi Pao* 49-; Vice-Chair. of Council of Chinese Writers' Asscn. 53; mem. of Council of Chinese People's Asscn. for Cultural Relations with Foreign Countries 54-; Vice-Dir. Propaganda Dept. of Central Cttee. of Communist Party of China 55-.
Publs. *Marxism and Literature and Art* 44, etc.
Chinese Writers' Association, Peking, China.

Chouard, Pierre; French botanist; b. 29 Oct. 1903; ed. Ecole Saint-Aspais, Melun, Univ. de Paris, Inst. catholique, Paris, and Ecole normale supérieure.
At Ecole normale supérieure 28-32; Teacher, Ecole nationale d'horticulture 32-35; Editor-in-Chief *Revue Horticole* 32-50; Dir. of Studies in Botany, Univ. of Bordeaux 35-37; Prof. of Pure and Applied Botany, Univ. of Rennes 37-38; Prof. of Agriculture, Conservatoire nat. des arts et métiers 38-54; Prof. of Plant Physiology, Univ. of Paris 53-; Sec.-Gen. 8th Int. Congress of Botany 54; Pres. Botany Section, Int. Union of Biological Sciences 53-; Vice-Pres. Int. Union of Biological Sciences 55-64; mem. Acad. d'Agriculture 53-; Pres. Botanical Soc. of France 49-50; Officier Légion d'Honneur; Commdr. des Palmes Académiques; Dr. h.c. (Montreal and Louvain).
11 rue du Val-de-Grâce, Paris 5e, France.

Christenberry, Herbert William; American judge; b. 97; ed. Soule Coll., New Orleans and Loyola Univ.
Private practice 24-33; Asst. Attorney, Board of Commrs. of Port of New Orleans 33-35; Dep. Commr. Louisiana Debt Moratorium Comm. 35; Asst. District Attorney, Parish of Orleans 35-37; Asst. U.S. Attorney, Eastern District, Louisiana 37-42, U.S. Attorney 42-47,

Chief Judge, U.S. District Court, Eastern Circuit, Louisiana 47-; mem. several legal asscns.
U.S. Courthouse, New Orleans 12, Louisiana, U.S.A.

Christensen, Christian Arthur Richardt; Norwegian journalist and author; b. 17 Dec. 1906; ed. Oslo Univ. Reporter *Dagbladet* (Oslo daily) 26-34; with Aschehoug Publishing Co. 34-45; Editor-in-Chief *Verdens Gang* 45-; active in resistance 40-45, twice arrested; mem. U.N. Sub-Comm. on Freedom of Information and the Press 47-49; Chair. Oslo Editors' Asscn. 47-49; Pres. Norwegian Press Asscn. 58-62; edited *Familieboka* (encyclopaedia); Independent Liberal.
Publs. *Det hendte igår* (It Happened Yesterday) 33, *Verden igår og idag* (The World Yesterday and Today) 3 vols. 35-36, 2nd edn. in 5 vols. 53-54, last vol. of Grimberg's *History of the World* 58, last 2 vols. of *Vårt folks historie* (History of Norway) 61, *Norge under okkupasjonen* (Occupied Norway) 64, *A History of the Norwegian Life Insurance Companies' Association, Dåd* (on heroes of the resistance in Norway 40-45) 65, *Life of Fridtjof Nansen* 66.
Hagan terrasse 5, Oslo 3, Norway.

Christensen, Kai; Danish architect; b. 28 Dec. 1916; ed. Kongelige Akademi for de Skonne Kunster, Copenhagen.
Director, Technical Dept. of Fed. of Danish Architects 47-52; Managing Dir. Danish Building Centre 52-61; Attached to Danish Ministry of Housing 61-; Chief, Scandinavian Design Cavalcade 62-; mem. Danish Soc. of Arts and Crafts and Industrial Design, Swedish Soc. for Industrial Design, Fed. of Danish Architects, The Architectural Asscn., London; mem. Danish Cttee. for Building Documentation 50-; Sec. Scandinavian Building Conf. 50-; Pres. Int. Conf. of Building Centres 60; mem. Scandinavian Liaison Cttee. concerning Govt. Building 63-; awards and prizes in public competition. Major works: furniture for the Copenhagen Cabinet Makers' Exhibitions 42-46, and articles and treatises in technical magazines.
100 Vester Voldgade, Copenhagen V, Denmark.
Telephone: 121337.

Christiansen, Ernst; Danish journalist and politician; b. 28 March 1891.
Chair. and Manager, Union of Social Democratic Youth 13-19; mem. Council and Exec. Cttee. Social Democratic Party 15-19; Chair. Left Socialist (later Communist) Party and Co-editor of its periodicals 19-27; on the staff of the Social Democratic daily newspaper, Copenhagen 31; mem. Exec. Cttee. Workers Radio Union 30-, Chair. 50-51 and 53-66; mem. Council, Danish Broadcasting Service 40-55 and 57-63; mem. *Landsting* 47-53, Danish Del. to UN 47, 53 and 54; Chair. for UN Delegation 55, 56, 57, 58, 59 and 60; Consultative Assembly of the Council of Europe 50-55, Danish Board of Foreign Policy 50-53; Minister without Portfolio 55-57; mem. Social Democratic Party.
Publs. *Statskapitalismen* 33, *Fra Lenin til Stalin* 36, *Amerika* 39, *Radioen under Krigen* (with P. Nørgaard) 45, *Danske Smede 1888-1948* 48, *Hvorfor er Socialdemokratiet forsvarsvenligt?* 49, *Statsradiofonien 1925-50* (co-author) 50, *En Stjernevogn kørte ud* (with J. Christensen) 52, *Arbejderne og socialismen* 52, *En bygning vi rejser* (co-author) 54, *— men det gik anderledes* 60; *Smede för og nu* 63; translation of More's *Utopia*.
31 Tagensvej, Copenhagen, Denmark.
Telephone: NORA 711.

Christiansen, Jens Anton, D.SC.; Danish professor of chemistry; b. 6 Sept. 1888; ed. Technical Univ. of Denmark, and Copenhagen Univ.
Assistant in Carlsberg Laboratory 11-15; Asst. Chemistry Laboratory Univ. of Copenhagen 15-31; Lecturer Inorganic Chemistry 21-31; Assoc. Prof. 31, Prof. 31-59, Pro-Rector 55-56; Head Chemical Laboratory A, Danish Technical Univ. 31-48; Pres. Danish Chemical Soc. 31-

34, and 43-46; Head Institute for Physical Chemistry, Univ. of Copenhagen 48-59; Pres. Comm. on Physics and Chemistry Symbols (U.P.A.C.) 51-59; Hon. mem. Polish Chemical Soc., Warsaw 47, Chemical Soc., London 54, N.Y. Acad. of Sciences 55, Royal Soc. of Science & Arts, Gothenburg 53, Danish Chemical Soc. 61; foreign mem. Royal Swedish Acad. of Science 59, Finnish Acad. of Sciences; H.C. Ørsted Medal 59; mem. Norwegian Acad. of Science 60; mem. Finnish Acad. Science 65; Commdr. and Silver Cross of Dannebrog.
Publs. *On the Reaction between Hydrogen and Bromine* 19, *Reaktionskinetiske Studier* 21, *Note on negative catalysis* 24, *On the kinetics of enzymatic reactions* 49, *Fysisk Kemi, Hefte I* (textbook) 50, *On the periodicity of chemical reactions* 57, etc., *Functions of Hyaluronate in the Inner Ear* 60.
Sundvaenget 9, Hellerup, Denmark.
Telephone: HE 3329.

Christidis, Theodore; Greek economist; b. 24 Oct. 1900; ed. English High School, Constantinople and Ecole Supérieure de Commerce de Marseille.
Director of Athens Chamber of Commerce and Industry 24-45; Gen. Sec. Ministry of Nat. Economy 46; Counsellor to Greek Perm. Del. to OEEC (now OECD) 48-50, Gen. Counsellor 50-53, Deputy Head of Delegation 53-55, Head 56-; concurrently Ambassador to European Econ. Community, Brussels 59-62; decorations include: Officier Légion d'Honneur, Grand Officer Order of Phoenix (Greece), Grand Officer Order of King George (Greece) and Grand Officer Order of Merit of Italian Republic, Grand Cross of Fed. Repub. of Germany.
Délégation Hellénique auprès de l'O.C.D.E., 15 Villa Saïd, Paris 16e; (Home): 64 rue Pergolèse, Paris 16e, France.
Telephone: KLE 68-27 (Office) PAS 40-66 (Home).

Christie, Agatha, C.B.E., F.R.S.L. (wife of Prof. Sir Max Mallowan, *q.v.*); British novelist and playwright.
Writer of detective stories, which include *Poirot Investigates, The Murder of Roger Ackroyd, The Mystery of the Blue Train, The Mysterious Mr. Quin, Death in the Clouds, The A.B.C. Murders, Murder in Mesopotamia, Cards on the Table, Murder in the Mews, Death on the Nile, Dumb Witness, Appointment with Death, Hercule Poirot's Christmas, Ten Little Niggers, Sad Cypress, Evil Under the Sun, The Moving Finger, Towards Zero, Death Comes as the End, Sparkling Cyanide, They Came to Baghdad, Mrs. McGinty's Dead, Hickory-Dickory Dock, After the Funeral, A Pocketful of Rye, Destination Unknown, Dead Man's Folly, 4.50 from Paddington, Cat among the Pigeons, The Pale Horse, The Mirror Crack'd from Side to Side*; plays include: *The Mousetrap* (sixteenth year of continuous performance at London's Ambassadors Theatre 68), *Witness for the Prosecution, Spiders Web, The Unexpected Guest, Go back for Murder, Rule of Three, Endless Night*.
Winterbrook House, Wallingford, Berkshire, England.

Christie, John Traill; British educationalist; b. 19 Oct. 1899; ed. Winchester and Trinity Coll., Oxford.
Sixth Form Master Rugby 22-28; Fellow and Tutor of Magdalen Coll. Oxford 28-32; Head Master of Repton 32-37, of Westminster School 37-49; Principal of Jesus Coll. Oxford 50-67.
Jesus College, Oxford, England.

Christie, Ronald Victor, M.D., D.SC., F.R.C.P., F.A.C.P.; British physician; b. 1902; ed. George Watson's Coll., Edinburgh and Edinburgh Univ.
Asst. Rockefeller Inst. for Medical Research, New York City 26-28; Asst. Dept. of Pathology, Freiburg Univ. 29-30; Associate McGill Univ. Clinic, Royal Victoria Hospital, Montreal 30-35; Asst. Dir. and Asst. Physician Medical Unit, London Hospital 35-38; Dir. Medical Professorial Unit and Physician St. Bartholomew's Hospital 38-55; Prof. of Medicine, London Univ. 38-55, McGill Univ. 55-; Physician-in-Chief, Royal Victoria

Hospital, Montreal 55-64; Dean Faculty of Medicine, McGill Univ. 64-; Hon. Sc.D. (Dublin).
Faculty of Medicine, McGill University, Montreal, Quebec, Canada.

Christoff, Boris, D.JUR.; Bulgarian singer; b. 18 May 1919; ed. Sofia Univ. and Italy.
Began career as a lawyer; studied singing in Rome; interned in Austria in World War II; professional debut in Italy 45; has appeared at principal European opera houses, including La Scala, Milan, Rome, Naples, Venice, Palermo, Paris, London and Vienna and in America; Dr. (h.c.) Paris Opera.
Complete recordings of *Boris Godunov*, Gounod's *Faust*, *Don Carlos* and Mussorgsky's Songs.
Via Bertolini 1, Rome, Italy.

Christy, Robert Frederick, B.A., M.A., PH.D.; American physicist; b. 14 May 1916; ed. Univs. of British Columbia, and California (Berkeley).
On U.S. Atomic Energy Project, Chicago and Los Alamos (Calif.) 42-46; Prof. of Physics, Calif. Inst. of Technology, Pasadena 46-; mem. U.S. Nat. Acad. of Sciences 65; Eddington Medal, Royal Astronomical Soc. (U.K.) 67.
Publs. *Cosmic Ray Bursts* 41, *The μ Meson Spin* 41, *Determination of the Fine Structure Constant* 42, *Angular Distribution of γ Rays* 49, *The Coupling of Angular Momenta in Nuclear Reactions* 53, *Low Excited States of F^{19}* 54, *Analysis of Nuclear Scattering Data* 56, *Corrections to Nuclear Q Values* 61, *Direct Capture Nuclear γ Rays* 61, *The Calculation of Stellar Pulsation* 64, *A Study of Pulsation in RR Lyrae Models* 66, *Review of Pulsation Theory* 66.
1330 South Euclid Avenue, Pasadena, Calif., U.S.A.

Chrysler, Walter P., Jr.; American art collector; ed. Dartmouth Coll.
Organiser, York Publishing House 26; Pres. and Chair. Cheshire House, Inc., Publications, N.Y.C. 30; Pres. Chrysler Building, N.Y.C. 37; Pres. Chrysler Art Museum, Provincetown, Mass.; collection of paintings and sculpture.
Room 444, Chrysler Building, New York City, N.Y., U.S.A.

Chrysostomos; Greek ecclesiastic; b. 80; ed. Halki Theological Coll., Lausanne Univ.
Bishop of Philippi, Neapolis and Thasos 24-62; Archbishop of Athens and All Greece 62-May 67.
[*Died* 9 *June* 1968].

Chu Hsüeh-fan; Chinese politician and trade union leader; b. 06; ed. Shanghai Legal Univ. and Harvard.
Chair. General All-China Labour Asscn. 35; five times Chinese Del. to World Labour Union; Vice-Chair. All-China Fed. of Trade Unions 48; Minister of Posts and Telecommunications 49-; mem. Standing Cttee. of Revolutionary Cttee. of the Kuomintang.
Ministry of Posts and Telecommunications, Peking, China.

Chu Ko-chen (Coching Chu), PH.D.; Chinese meteorologist; b. 90; ed. Harvard.
Dir. Institute of Meteorology of Academia Sinica 27-46; Pres. Chekiang Univ. 46-49; Vice-Pres. Academia Sinica; Chair. Cttee. on Exploration of Natural Resources, Academia Sinica (now Chinese Acad. of Sciences); Pres. Geographical Soc. of China.
Chinese Academy of Sciences, Peking, China.

Chu, Peter, D. ès LETTRES; Chinese professor and businessman; b. 02; ed. Univ. of Paris.
Man. Dir. The Agricultural & Industrial Bank of China 41-49; Publisher of *Life Today*; Prof. of Kwang Hsia Univ.; Dean of the Great China Univ.; Dir. South-Eastern Asia Development Corpn. Ltd.
Publs. *L'Emigration Japonaise depuis 1918*, *A Study of Scientific Management* 45.
26 Homantin Street, Hong Kong.

Chu Teh, Marshal; Chinese officer and politician; b. 86; ed. Yunnan Military Acad., Berlin and Göttingen.
Former Commr. of Finance, Yunnan; mem. Tung-Meng-hui, later mem. Kuomintang; joined Chinese Communists in Germany 22, expelled from Germany 25; went to France and U.S.S.R., to Nanchang 27; organised Nanchang Communist Uprising with Ho Lung and formed Chinese Red Army; Commander-in-Chief Communist Forces 30; served Kiangsi 30-34; led Communists to N.W. 35-36; apptd. Commander-in-Chief Chinese 8th Route Army 37; Commander-in-Chief 18th Group Army 46-49; Vice-Chair. Central People's Govt., Vice-Chair. People's Revolutionary Mil. Council, and C.-in-C. Chinese People's Liberation Army 49-54; Vice-Chair. Central Cttee. C.P. of China, mem. Standing Cttee. of Politburo; Vice-Chair. of the Republic 54-59; Chair. Nat. People's Congress 59-.
National People's Congress, Peking, China.

Chu Tu-nan; Chinese educationist; b. 99; ed. Peking Higher Normal School.
Joined the *Laotung Hsüehhui* (organisation for studying Marxist theory); taught in Harbin in 28; imprisoned for three years; taught in various univs. and schools; Prof. at Peking Normal Coll. 48; Chair. Cttee. for Elimination of Illiteracy 53-54; Pres. of Chinese People's Asscn. for Cultural Relations with Foreign Countries 54-; mem. World Peace Council 55; Dir. of Classical Opera Company on visit to Northern Europe 55; mem. China Olympic Cttee. 56; mem. Central Cttee. of Democratic League.
Chinese People's Association for Cultural Relations with Foreign Countries, Peking, China.

Chudakov, Alexander Evgenievich; Soviet physicist; b. 1921; ed. Moscow Univ.
Research Assoc. Lebedev Inst. of Physics, U.S.S.R. Acad. of Sciences 46-; Corresp. mem. U.S.S.R. Acad. of Sciences 66-.
Publs: Works on nuclear physics.
U.S.S.R. Academy of Sciences, 14 Lenin Prospekt, Moscow, U.S.S.R.

Chudik, Michal; Czechoslovak politician; b. 29 Sept. 1914.
Commissioner for Nutrition, Slovak Nat. Council 48-49; Chair. Regional Nat. Cttee., Košice 48-55; First Deputy Chair. Board of Commrs. and Comm. for Agriculture, Slovak Nat. Council 55; Chair. Slovak Nat. Council 63-68; Deputy Chair. Nat. Assembly 65-68; mem. Central Cttee. of C.P. of Czechoslovakia 58-68; mem. Agricultural Comm. of Central Cttee. of C.P. of Slovakia 63-66; mem. Presidium of Central Cttee. 64-68; Order of 25th Feb. 48, 49; Order of the Republic 64.
c/o Slovak National Council, Bratislava, Czechoslovakia.

Chugunov, Ivan Ivanovich; Soviet politician; b. 1907; ed. Gorky State Univ.
In Soviet Army 29-32; Chief of Section, later Sec., Krasnodar Territorial Soviet of Working People's Deputies 37-51; First Vice-Chair. Council of Ministers, Mari A.S.S.R. 51-55; Chair. Exec. Cttee., Gorky Regional Soviet of Working People's Deputies 55-63; First Sec. Gorky Regional Agricultural Cttee. of C.P. 63-64; Chair. Exec. Cttee., Gorky Regional Soviet of Working People's Deputies 64-; mem. C.P.S.U. 32-; Deputy to U.S.S.R. Supreme Soviet; mem. Budget Cttee. Soviet of Union.
Gorky Regional Soviet of Working People's Deputies, Gorky, U.S.S.R.

Chuikov, Marshal Vasili Ivanovich; Soviet army officer; b. 1900; ed. Frunze Mil. Acad.
Joined army 18, fought in Civil War 18-21, Commdr. of 62nd Army 42-45; Deputy C.-in-C. 46-49, C.-in-C. of Soviet Army of Occupation and Chair. of Soviet Control Comm. in Germany 49-53, Alternative mem. of Central Cttee. of C.P.S.U. 52; Commdr. of Kiev Mil. District

53-60; Supreme Commdr. U.S.S.R. Land Forces 60-64; Head of U.S.S.R. Civil Defence 64-; mem. Central Cttee. of C.P.S.U. 61-; mem. Central Cttee. of the C.P. of the Ukraine; Deputy to U.S.S.R. Supreme Soviet; Marshal of the Soviet Union; twice Hero of the Soviet Union, awarded Orders of Lenin (four times), Order of the Red Banner (four times); Red Star and other decorations.
Publ. *The Beginning of the Road* (memoirs) 63, *Immortal Heroic Deed* 65.
Council of Ministers, Moscow, U.S.S.R.

Chukhrai, Grigori Naumovich; Soviet film director; b. 1921; ed. All-Union State Inst. of Cinematography.
Soviet Army 39-45; mem. C.P.S.U. 44-; Dir. Mosfilm 55-64; Dir. Experimental Film Studio 65-; Honoured Art Worker of R.S.F.S.R., Lenin Prize 61, Order of Red Star, Order of Patriotic War.
Films: *The 41st* 56, *Ballad of a Soldier* 59, *The Clear Sky* 61, *There Lived an Old Man and Old Woman* 64.
Mosfilm Studio, 1 Mosfilmovskaya ulitsa, Moscow, U.S.S.R.

Chukovsky, Kornei Ivanovich; Soviet writer and literary student; b. 1882.
Awarded Order of Lenin, Lenin Prize, Order of Red Banner of Labour (twice); Hon. D.Litt. (Oxford Univ.).
Publs. *From Chekhov to our Days* 08, *Poetry of the Dawning Democracy: Walt Whitman* 14, *Faces and Masks* 14, *From Two to Five* 28 (19th edn. 66), *Men and Books of the Sixties* 34, *Contemporaries (Repin, Gorky, Mayakovsky, Chekhov, Kritko, Brusyov, Blok, Koni)* 63, *The Noble Art* (Art of Translation) 64, *Chekhov the Man* 59, *Nekrasov's Mastery* 66 (5th edn.), *Alive as Life* 66 (3rd edn.), *The Silver Insignia* 66; poems for children *Moidodyr, Crocodile, Barmalay* (68th edn. 65), etc.; translations of many English language classics.
Union of Writers, 52 Vorovsky Street, Moscow, U.S.S.R.

Chulaki, Mikhail Ivanovich; Soviet composer; b. 19 Nov. 1908; ed. Leningrad Conservatoire.
Taught at the Leningrad Conservatoire 33, Moscow Conservatoire 48-; Sec. of the Union of Soviet Composers of the U.S.S.R. 48-57; Vice-Chair. of Cttee. for Arts Affairs under the U.S.S.R. Council of Ministers 51-53; Deputy Chief of Dept. for Arts Affairs of the U.S.S.R. Ministry of Culture 53-55; Dir. of the Bolshoi Theatre 55-59, 63-; Sec. of Union of Composers of R.S.F.S.R. 59-; mem. Supreme Soviet R.S.F.S.R. 63-; State prize-winner 47, 48, 50; awarded Badge of Honour and title of Honoured Art Worker of R.S.F.S.R.
Works. Three symphonies 34, 45, 59; ballets: *The Story of the Priest and his Servant Balda* 39, *The Imaginary Bridegroom* (based on the Goldoni comedy *Servant of Two Masters*) 46, *Youth* (based on the novel by N. Ostrovsky *How the Steel was Tempered*) 47, Cantata *On the Banks of the Volhov River* 43, *A Symphony Cycle of Songs and Dances of Old France* 59, nine choruses (a capella), *Lenin is with us* 60, *Russian Festival* (for violin ensemble), *Romances on Whitman's verses* 62.
State Academic Bolshoi Theatre, 1 Ploshchad Svezdlova, Moscow, U.S.S.R.

Chumakov, Mikhail Petrovich; Soviet virologist; b. 1909; ed. First Moscow Medical Inst.
Physician, Postgraduate, Senior Research Assoc. Inst. of Microbiology, U.S.S.R. Acad. of Medical Sciences 31-38; Senior Research Assoc., Head of Lab., U.S.S.R. Inst. of Experimental Medicine 38-44; Head of Dept. Inst of Neurology, U.S.S.R. Acad. of Medical Sciences 44-50; Corresp. mem. U.S.S.R. Acad. of Medical Sciences 48; mem. U.S.S.R. Acad. of Medical Sciences 60; Dir., Head of Lab. Inst. of Virology, U.S.S.R. Acad. of Medical Sciences 50-55; Organizer, Dir. Inst. of Poliomyelitis and Virus Encephalitis U.S.S.R. Acad of Medical Sciences 55-; mem. C.P.S.U. 40; mem. Purkinyě Medical Soc., Czechoslovakia; Order Badge of Honour,

Red Banner of Labour, State Prize 41, Ivanovsky Prize, Lenin Prize 63.
Publs. Over 170 works on epidemiology of virus infections (tick encephalitis, trachoma, poliomyelitis, tick fever); monographs *Poliomyelitis—Epidemic Infantile Paralysis, Antibioticotherapy of Trachoma* and many others.
Institute of Poliomyelitis and Virus Encephalitis, 27th Kilometre, Kiev Highway, Moscow Region, U.S.S.R.

Chung Il Kwon, Gen.; Korean army officer (retd.), diplomatist and politician; b. 1917; ed. Military Acad. of Japan, U.S.A. Command and General Staff Coll., Harvard and Oxford Univs.
Former Army Chief of Staff, Chair. Joint Chiefs of Staff; Amb. to Turkey, France, U.S.A., concurrently to Brazil, Colombia, Argentina, Paraguay and Ecuador; Prime Minister 64-, concurrently Minister of Foreign Affairs 66-67.
Office of the Prime Minister, Seoul, Republic of Korea.

Chung Yul Kim; Korean diplomatist and former air force officer; b. 17; ed. Japanese Military Acad.
Commandant, Republic of Korea Air Acad. 49, Chief of Staff, Korea Air Force 49-52, 54-56; Chief, Korean Liaison Group to United Nations Command, Tokyo 52; Special Asst. to Minister of Nat. Defence 54-57, Minister of Nat. Defence 57-60; Ambassador to U.S.A. 63-; Chief Commdr. Legion of Merit, Order of Military Merit Taeguk.
2838 McGill Terrace, N.W., Washington D.C., U.S.A.

Churayev, Victor Mikhailovich; Soviet politician; b. 04; ed. Engineering and Economics Inst., Kharkov.
Member C.P.S.U. 29-; Engineer, Workshop Foreman, Chief Mechanic, Machine Tool Factory 35-38; Perm. staff, Kharkov Regional Cttee., Ukraine C.P. 39-40; Second Sec. Kharkov City Cttee., Ukraine, C.P. 40-41, 43-44; Soviet Army 41-43; First Sec. Kharkov Regional and City Cttees. 44-48, 48-50; Perm. staff of Central Cttee. of C.P.S.U. 48, 51-56, mem. Bureau of Central Cttee., C.P.S.U. for R.S.F.S.R. 56-61, Staff of Party State Control C.P.S.U., Central Cttee. Bureau for R.S.F.S.R. and R.S.F.S.R. Council of Ministers 62-65, First Deputy Chair. R.S.F.S.R. People's Control Cttee. 65-; Cand. mem. Central Cttee. of C.P.S.U. 56-61, mem. 61-66.
R.S.F.S.R. People's Control Committee, 8 Sadovaya-Cheznogryazskaya ulitsa, Moscow, U.S.S.R.

Church, Alonzo, A.B., PH.D.; American professor of mathematics and philosophy; b. 14 June 1903; ed. Ridgefield School, Conn. and Princeton Univ.
National Research Fellow in Mathematics, Harvard, Göttingen and Amsterdam Univs. 27-29; Asst. Prof. of Maths. Princeton Univ. 29-39, Assoc. Prof. 39-47, Prof. 47-61, Prof. of Maths. and Philosophy 61-67; Editor *The Journal of Symbolic* 36-; Prof. of Philosophy and Maths. Univ. of Calif. at Los Angeles July 67-; mem. American Acad. of Arts and Sciences, Acad. Internationale de Philosophie des Sciences; Corresp. mem. British Acad.
Publs. *The Calculi of Lambda-Conversion* 41, *Introduction to Mathematical Logic* vol. I 56.
c/o Department of Philosophy, University of California at Los Angeles, Los Angeles, Calif. 90024, U.S.A.
Telephone: 213-478-9711, Ext. 7468.

Church, Frank, A.B., LL.B.; American politician; b. 25 July 1924; ed. Stanford and Harvard Univs.
Commissioned Infantry Officer 44; Military Intelligence in China, India and Burma; law practice in Boise, Idaho 50-56; Senator from Idaho 56-; del. O.A.S. Economic Conf., Buenos Aires 57; del. to Interparliamentary Union Conf., Warsaw 59; del. to Canadian-American Parliamentary Conferences, Ottawa, Montreal and Washington 59-60; Keynoter, Democratic Nat. Convention 60; mem. Senate Foreign Relations Cttee.;

Senatorial mem. U.S. Mission to the U.N. 66; Democrat.
405 Senate Office Building, Washington, D.C., U.S.A.
Telephone: 225-6142.

Church, Richard, C.B.E., F.R.S.L.; British writer; b.
26 March 1893; ed. London.
Civil Service 09-33, retd.; Pres. P.E.N. 58-59; Pres.
English Asscn.; Vice-Pres. Royal Soc. Literature.
Publs. 19 vols. poetry, *Collected Poems* 48; many prose
books; novels: *Apple of Concord* 35, *The Porch* 37
(Femina Vie Heureuse Prize 38), *The Stronghold, Calling
for a Spade* 39, *The Room Within* 40, *The Solitary Man*
42, *The Sampler* 42, *Green Tide* 44, *The Lamp* 46, *Kent*
48, *The Cave, A Window on a Hill* 51, *The Nightingale* 52,
Portrait of Canterbury 53, *Dog Toby* 53, *Small Moments*
55, *Over the Bridge* (autobiog. vol. I) 55, (*Sunday Times
£1,000 Prize and Gold Medal*), *The Dangerous Years* 56,
Down River 57, *The Golden Sovereign* (autobiog. vol. II)
57, *The Inheritors* (Foyle £250 Prize), *A Country
Window* 58, *The Crabapple Tree* 59, *North of Rome* 60,
The Bells of Rye 60, *Calm October* (essays) 61, *Prince
Albert* 63, *The Little Kingdom* 64, *The Voyage Home*
(autobiog. vol. III) 64, *A Stroll Before Dark* 65,
Speaking Aloud 68, *The White Doe* 68.
Sissinghurst Castle, Cranbrook, Kent, England.
Telephone: Sissinghurst 397.

Churchill, Hon. Gordon, D.S.O., M.A., LL.B.; Canadian
barrister and politician; b. 8 Nov. 1898; ed. Public and
High School, Port Arthur, Ontario, and Winnipeg,
Manitoba, and United Coll., and Univ. of Manitoba.
Former school principal; served in both world wars;
M.P. for Winnipeg South Centre 51-; Minister of Trade
57-60; Minister of Veterans' Affairs 60-63, of Defence
63; Progressive Conservative.
Savoy Apartments, Ottawa, Ontario, Canada.

Churchill, Odette Marie Celine (see Hallowes.)

Chursin, Admiral Serafin Evgenevich; Soviet naval
officer; b. 1905; ed. Frunze Higher Naval School and
General Staff Acad., Leningrad.
Joiner 21-27; Naval Service 27; Commdr. of Ships and
higher formations 31-41; Commdr. Submarine Brigade
41-45; Commdr. Danube and Caspian Flotillas, Chief
of Staff, First Deputy Fleet Commdr. 54-62; Commdr.
Black Sea Fleet 62-; mem. C.P.S.U. 29-; Deputy to
U.S.S.R. Supreme Soviet; mem. Mandate Comm.,
Soviet of the Union; mem. Central Cttee. C.P. of
Ukraine.
Ministry of Defence, 34 Maurice Thorez Embankment,
Moscow, U.S.S.R.

Chyorny, Alexei Klementyevich; Soviet politician;
b. 1921; ed. Moscow Inst. of Chemical Engineering.
Shop Supt., then Deputy Dir. of plant in Komsomolsk-
on-Amur 42-49; Chief of Section, later, Second Sec.,
Komsomolsk-on-Amur City Cttee. of C.P., then First
Sec., District Cttee. of C.P. 49-56; Sec., later Second
Sec., Regional Cttee. of C.P., Jewish Autonomous
Region 56-62; Chair. Exec. Cttee., Khabarovsk Terri-
torial Soviet of Working People's Deputies 62-; mem.
C.P.S.U. 46-; Deputy to U.S.S.R. Supreme Soviet.
Khabarovsk Territorial Soviet of Working People's
Deputies, Khabarovsk, U.S.S.R.

Chyorny, Vassily Ilyich; Soviet politician; b. 1913;
ed. Belgorod Agricultural School and Higher Party
School.
Agronomist, Crimea 32-35, 39-41; in Soviet Army
35-37; Leader, Komsomol 37-39; Sec., District Cttee.
of C. P. 39-41; Commissar, Bakhchisarai Partisan
Regt. 41-42; in machine and tractor station, Kirghiz
S.S.R. 42-43; Party and Soviet worker 44-50; Official,
Central Cttee., C.P.S.U. 50-54, 60-61; First Vice-Chair.
Council of Ministers, North Ossetian A.S.S.R. 54-55;
Second Sec., North Ossetian Regional Cttee. of C.P.
55-60; First Sec. of Tambov Regional Cttee. of C.P. 66-;
mem. Central Auditing Comm. of C.P.S.U. 66-; mem.
C.P.S.U. 39-.
Tambov Regional Committee of Communist Party of
U.S.S.R., Tambov, U.S.S.R.

Cibulka, Josef, DR. PHIL., DR. THEOL.; Czechoslovak
archæologist and art historian; b. 1 July 1886; ed.
Rome, Vienna, Paris.
Hon. Lecturer, Inst. of Theology, Hradec Králové 10;
External Lecturer in Archæology and History of Art,
Catholic Theological Faculty, Bratislava 19; ditto at
Charles Univ. Prague 22-26; Prof. of Christian Archaeo-
logy and History of Art, Charles Univ. 26-50; Dir. Nat.
Gallery, Prague 39-45; Vice-Pres. of Int. Cttee. of
History of Art 58-; Chevalier Légion d'Honneur 36;
Silver Plaque, Czechoslovak Acad. of Sciences, etc.
Publs. *Ancient Christian Iconography* 24, *Crowned
Assumption on the Cresent Moon* 28, *Wenceslas Rotunda
of St. Guy in Prague* 32, *Bohemian Coronation Procedure
and its Origin* 35, *St. George's Church in Prague Castle* 36,
Greco 41, *Albrecht Dürer* 44, *The St. Wenceslas Crown
of the Bohemian Kingdom* 48, *The Irish Church of Modrá*
and *The Beginning of Moravian Christianity* 58, *Christian Missions of the Slavs in Pannonia, Moravia and
Slovakia after the Period of the Avars* 59, *The Origin of
the Kentish Group of Churches* 62, *Bohemian Polyptychs
1350-1450* 63, *Great Moravian Churches of the 9th Century* 63, *The Date 864 of the arrival of Constantine and
Methode in Moravia* 65, *Bohemian Gothic Triptych
Recently Found* 65.
Valentinská I, Prague I, Czechoslovakia.

Cicogna, Furio; Italian businessman; b. 91; ed.
Bocconi Commercial Univ.
Joined Bombrini Parodi Co. 13, Gen. Man. 20-21; Gen.
Man. Cotonerie Meridionali 21-25; Co-founder Chatillon
Co. 18, Gen. Man. and Man. Dir. 25-27, Chair. 57-;
Founder of Star Co. 50 and Meyercord Italiano Co. 54;
Dir. Società Edison and Cartiere Burgo; Vice-Pres.
Banco Lariano; Pres. of the Lombardy Region Indus-
trial Asscn. 55-61; Pres. Confindustria 61-66, Manage-
ment del. to the Nat. Econ. and Labour Council; Chair.
Governing Body, Luigi Bocconi Univ., Milan; Pres.
Ospizio Sacra Famiglia.
Via Conservatorio 7, Milan, Italy.

Cicognani, H.E. Cardinal Amleto Giovanni, S.T.D.,
PH.D., J.U.D.; Vatican ecclesiastic; b. 24 Feb. 1883; ed.
Rome Pontifical Univ.
Advocate of the Sacred Roman Rota 22; fmr. Assessor
to the Congregation of the Oriental Church; Sec. of
Holy See Cttee. for Codification of Oriental Canon Law
29; Titular Archbishop of Laodicea in Phrygia 33;
Apostolic Del. to U.S.A. 33-58; created Cardinal by
Pope John XXIII 58; Sec. Sacred Congregation for the
Oriental Church 59-61; Sec. of State of Holy See 61-;
Pres. of Pontifical Comm. Aug. 61-; mem. Sacred
Congregations of the Consistory, de Propaganda Fide,
of Extraordinary Ecclesiastical Affairs, of the Holy
Office and of Sacraments.
Vatican City, Rome, Italy.

Cikker, Ján; Czechoslovak (Slovak) composer; b.
29 July 1911; ed. Banská Bystrica Conservatoire and
Master School of Composition, Prague, and conducting
under Felix Weingartner in Vienna.
Professor of Theory of Music Bratislava Conservatoire
39-51; Dramaturgist, Opera House 45-48; Prof. of
Composition, High School of Musical Arts 51-; Czecho-
slovak Prize for Peace 51, State Prize 55, 63, Nat.
Artist 66, Herder Prize of Vienna Univ. 66, Madach
Prize, Hungary 66.
Works include *Sonatina for Piano* 33, *Symphonic
Prologue* 34, Two string quartets 35, 37, *Capriccio* 36,
Cantus Filiorum (cantata) 40, *About Life* (trilogy of
symphonic poems) 41, 43, 46, *Concertino for Piano and
Orchestra* 42, *Bucolic Poem* (ballet music) 44, Scenic
music for *Hamlet* 47, and *The Taming of the Shrew* 50,

The Tatra Streams (three studies for piano) 54, *What the Children Told Me* 57; meditation on the H. Schütz theme *Glorified are the Dead* 64; Orchestral studies 65; and operas: *Juro Jánošík* 54, *Beg Bajazid* 57, *Resurrection* 62, *Mr. Scrooge* 63, a play about *Love and Death*, after Romain Rolland 67.
Fialkové údolie č. 1042, Bratislava, Czechoslovakia.
Telephone: 533-14.

Cilento, Sir Raphael West, Kt., M.D., B.S., D.T.M. and H. Eng., F.R. SAN. I. London; Australian barrister; b. 2 Dec. 1893; ed. Prince Alfred Coll., Adelaide Univ. and School of Tropical Medicine, London.
Dir. Australian Inst. of Tropical Medicine; dir. Public Health and Quarantine Mandated Territory of New Guinea for four years; dir. Div. Tropical Hygiene and Chief Quarantine Officer N.E. Div. of Commonwealth 28-33; Senior Admin. Health officer Commonwealth Dept. of Health 34; Dir.-Gen. Health and Medical Services, Queensland 34-45; Hon. Prof. Social and Tropical Medicine Queensland Univ. 37-46; Pres. Medical Board Queensland 39-45; Barrister, Supreme Court, Queensland 39-; Assessor, Medical Assessment Tribunal Queensland 39-45; apptd. head of U.N.R.R.A. work in British zone of occupation in Germany 45-46; Dir. Div. of Refugees and Displaced Persons U.N. 46, Div. of Social Activities, Economic and Social Council U.N. 46-47.
Publs. *Malaria* 23, *Filariasis* 23, *Diagnosis of Bowel Diseases in North Australia* 24, *White Man in the Tropics* 25, *Health Conditions in the Pacific* 29, *Tropical Diseases in Australasia* 40, *Blue Print for the Health of a Nation* 44.
Altaville, 268 Vulture Street, South Brisbane, Queensland, Australia.

Cimpaye, Joseph; Burundian politician.
Prime Minister and Minister of Justice, Kingdom of Urundi, Belgian administered UN Trusteeship Territory of Ruanda-Urundi Jan. 61-Sept. 61; Pres. Nat. Union of Burundi (UNB) in independent State of Burundi 62, fmr. Pres. Popular Gathering of Burundi (RPB); Dir. External Relations, SABENA—Belgian World Air Lines (Burundi) 64-.
Sabena, 10 Chaussée Prince Louis Rwagasore, Bujumbura, Burundi.

Cintra do Prado, Luiz; Brazilian professor and physicist; ed. Escola Politécnica, Univ. de São Paulo, Univ. de Paris à la Sorbonne and Collège de France.
Laboratory Asst. Polytechnic Univ. of São Paulo 28-30, Asst. Lecturer Physics 29-33, Prof. 38-64, Prof. Emer. 64-; Lecturer Physics, Faculty of Medicine and Faculty of Sciences, Univ. of São Paulo 33-37; Dir. Escola Politécnica, Univ. of São Paulo 40-42, Vice-Rector 53-54; Prof. Pontificia Univ. Catolica, São Paulo 38-54; Chief, Nuclear Engineering Dept. Inst. of Atomic Energy 60-63, Dir. 61-63; Pres. Nat. Comm. for Nuclear Energy 64-66; mem. Del. to Int. Atomic Energy Agency (IAEA) 57-67; mem. Nat. Research Council 51-64; Vice-Pres. Brazilian Acad. of Sciences 59-64; mem. Scientific Advisory Cttee. of UN and of IAEA 60-; mem. Int. Cttee. on Weights and Measures 67-; over 120 publs.
Escola Politécnica, Universidade de São Paulo; Home: 840 rua Altino Arantes, Ribeirao Preto, Est São Paulo, Brazil.

Ciolkosz, Adam; Polish politician, writer and journalist; b. 01; ed. Cracow Univ. and Cracow School Political Science.
Served and wounded Polish Wars 18-20; participated in Silesian Uprising 21; Socialist mem. Diet 28 and 30 and Sec. Polish Parlty. Socialist Party; imprisoned in fortress of Brest Litovsk as one of opposition leaders 30 and 33-34; mem. Central Exec. Cttee., Polish Socialist Party 31-; mem. Nat. Council in Great Britain 40-45; fmr. Editor *Robotnik* London; mem. in charge external

relations, Exec. of Polish Political Council 49-54; Vice-Chair. Polish Council of Nat. Unity Exec. Cttee. 54-56, Chair. 56-59 and 63-67; Chair. Polish Socialist Party in Great Britain 47-57; Chair. Central Council, Polish Socialist Party in Exile 57-59; Chair. London Del. Assembly of Captive European Nations 57-59, 64-65
Publs. *Trzy wspomnienia* 45, *The Curtain Falls* (with others) 51, *Rocznik spraw krajowych* (with others) 60, *Róza Luksemburg a rewolucja rosyjska* 61, *Od Marksa do Chruszczowa* 62, *Karol Marks a Powstanie Styczniowe* 63, *Koniec monolitu* 64, *Zarys dziejów socjalizmu polskiego* (with Dr. Lidia Ciolkosz) vol. I 66, *Granice odwagi myslenia* 66, *Ludzie P.P.S.* 67, *Socjalizm na zachodzie Europy* 68.
9 Balmuir Gardens, London, S.W.15, England.
Telephone: 01-788-5231.

Ciry, Michel; French painter, etcher and graphic artist; b. 31 Aug. 1919; ed. Ecole des Arts Appliqués, Paris.
Religious and secular paintings and etchings; Prof. School of Fine Arts Fontainebleau 57-58, Académie Julian 60; fmr. mem. Conseil Supérieur de l'Enseignement des Beaux-Arts; Vice-Pres. Comité National de la Gravure; numerous exhbns. in Europe and America including Paris, London, New York, Boston, Amsterdam, Rome and Berlin; works in Museums of Europe and America; has illustrated numerous books including books by Montherlant, Green, Claudel and Mauriac; Prix National des Arts 45, Grande médaille de vermeil de la Ville de Paris 62, Prix de l'Ile de France 64, Prix Eugène Carrière 64.
Major works: *Chemin de Croix* 60-64, *Stabat Mater* 60, 61, 63, 65, *Fièvres* 65, *Christ's Passion* 55, 57, 60, 64, *Marie-Madeleine* 61, 63, 65, *Saint François* 50, 54, 59, 60, 64, 65.
La Bergerie, Varengeville-sur-Mer, Seine-Maritime, France.

Cisař, Čestmir; Czechoslovak politician; b. 2 Jan. 1920; ed. Grammar School, Duchcov and Charles Univ., Prague.
Department of Propaganda and Agitation, Regional Cttee. of C.P., Prague, later Central Cttee. of C.P. 47-51; Head of Dept. for Propaganda and Agitation, Central Cttee. of C.P. 51-52; Sec. of C.P. Regional Cttee., Plzen 52-57, later Dep. Chief Editor *Rudé právo;* Chief Editor *Nová mysl* 61-63; Sec. Central Cttee. of C.P. April-Sept. 63; Minister of Education and Culture Sept. 63-65; Amb. to Romania 65-68; Sec. Central Cttee. of Czechoslovak C.P. 68-; Deputy to Nat. Assembly 64-66.
Central Committee of Czechoslovak C.P., Prague, Czechoslovakia.

Cisler, Walker Lee; American engineer; b. 8 Oct. 1897; ed. Cornell Univ.
Joined Public Service Electric & Gas Co., Newark 22, rose to Asst. Chief Engineer Electric Dept. by 41; Chief, Equipment Production Branch, Office War Utilities, War Planning Board, Washington 41-43; Chief Engineer power plants, Detroit Edison Co. 45-47, Exec. Vice-Pres. 48-51, Pres. 51-64, Chair. and Chief Exec. Officer 64-; Chair. Fruehauf Corpn.; Pres. Power Reactor Development Co., Atomic Power Development Associates Inc.; Dir. numerous other companies; Pres. Fund for Peaceful Atomic Development, Thomas Alva Edison Foundation; Official Adviser U.S. Del. Int. Conf. on Peaceful Uses Atomic Energy 55; official of numerous other scientific and educational institutions; Chief, Public Utilities Section, SHAEF, later Chief, Public Utilities Section, Office Military Govt. for Germany 43-45.
Home: 1071 Devonshire Road, Grosse Pointe Park, Mich. 48230; Office: 2000 2nd Avenue, Detroit 26, Mich., U.S.A.

Citrine, 1st Baron, cr. 46, of Wembley; **Walter McLennan Citrine,** P.C., G.B.E., COMP.I.E.E.; British trade unionist and administrator; b. 22 Aug. 1887.
Mersey District Sec. Electrical Trades Union 14-20; Pres. 17-18 and Sec. 18-20 Mersey Fed. of Engineering and Shipbuilding Trades; Asst. Gen. Sec. Electrical Trades Union 20-23; Asst. Sec. Trades Union Congress 24-26 and Gen. Sec. 26-46; mem. Nat. Coal Board 46-47; Chair. Central Electricity Authority 47-57; part-time mem. Electricity Council, Atomic Energy Authority 58-62; Chair.Miners' Welfare Comm. 46-47; Pres. Int. Fed. of Trade Unions 28-45; mem. H.M. Economic Advisory Council 30-33; Dir. Daily Herald Ltd. 29-46; mem. Gen. Advisory Council B.B.C. 34; Gov. London School of Economics 32-36; Trustee Imperial Relations Trust 37-49; mem. Cinematograph Council 38-48; mem. Royal Comm. on West Indies 38; mem. Consultative Council to Treasury 40-46; Chair. Production Cttee. on Regional Boards (Munitions) 42; Hon. LL.D. (Manchester).
Publs. *The British Trade Union Movement* 26, *Labour and the Community, I Search for Truth in Russia* 36, 38, *A B C of Chairmanship, My Finnish Diary* 40, *My American Diary* 41, *In Russia Now* 42, *Men and Work* (autobiography) 64, *Two Careers* 67.
"Dorislade", 59 Royston Park Road, Hatch End, Middlesex, England.
Telephone: 01-428-2732.

Civil, Alan; British horn player and composer; b. 13 June 1929; ed. studied under Aubrey Brain, London, and Willy von Stemm, Hamburg.
Principal Horn, Royal Philharmonic Orchestra 52-55; Co-Principal Horn with late Dennis Brain, Philharmonia Orchestra 55-57, Principal 57-; Prof. of the Horn Royal College of Music; Solo Horn B.B.C. Symphony Orchestra 66-; Guest Principal Horn with Berlin Philharmonic Orchestra; mem. several Chamber Music Ensembles including London Wind Quintet, London Wind Soloists, Wigmore Ensemble, Prometheus Ensemble, Alan Civil Horn Trio, Music Group of London; has performed horn concertos as soloist in the U.S.A., South America, the Caribbean and Europe; records for Columbia.
Compositions: *Symphony* (for Brass and Percussion) 50, *Wind Octet* 51, *Wind Quintet* 51, *Horn Trio in E Flat* 52, *Divertimento for Trombone Quartet, Suite for Two Horns*; Songs, Music for Brass Ensemble, Horn Studies.
Downe Hall, Downe, Kent, England.

Clair, René; French film producer and writer; b. 11 Nov. 1898.
Began life as a journalist and writer; later became film producer; worked in France, England and America; mem. Acad. Française 60-; Légion d'Honneur and other nat. and foreign decorations; Dr. h.c. (Cambridge Univ., Royal Coll. of Art (U.K.)).
His films include *The Italian Straw Hat, Sous les Toits de Paris, Le Million, A nous la Liberté, 14 Juillet, The Ghost Goes West, I Married a Witch, It Happened Tomorrow, Le Silence est d'or, La Beauté du Diable, Les Belles-de-Nuit, Les Grandes Manoeuvres, Porte des Lilas, Tout l'or du Monde, Les Fêtes Galantes.*
Publs. *Reflections on the Cinema, Star Turn, La Princesse de Chine, Comédies et Commentaires, La Serrure* (play) 67.
c/o Seca, 44 Champs Elysées, Paris 8e, France.

Clairmont Dueñas, Ramón de; Salvadorean diplomatist; b. 27; ed. Colegio Externado de San José, El Salvador, Southwestern Louisiana Univ. and Universidad Nacional de El Salvador.
Foreign Service, Belgium and U.K. 50-52; Asst. Chief of Regional Office for Central America of U.N. Technical Assistance Board 58-61; Gen. Manager of Salvadorean Inst. for Production Development 61; Asst. Sec. for Foreign Affairs 62; Pres. Salvadorean Inst. for Industrial Development 62-64; Rep. of El Salvador to Org. of American States Jan. 65-, concurrently Ambassador to U.S.A. and Canada.
Representation of El Salvador to Organization of American States, 2308 California Street, N.W., Washington, D.C. 20008, U.S.A.

Clapp, Margaret, PH.D.; American educationist; b. 11 April 1910; ed. Wellesley Coll., and Columbia Univ.
Teacher, Todhunter and Dalton Schools 30-41; Instructor Coll. of City of N.Y. 42-44; Research Asst. B.B.C. 42-43; Instructor, N.J. Coll. for Women 45-46, Columbia Univ. Gen. Sessions 46-47; Asst. Prof. Brooklyn Coll. 47-49; Pres. Wellesley Coll. 49-66; Principal Lady Doak Coll., India 66-67.
Publ. *Forgotten First Citizen: John Bigelow* 48 (Pulitzer Prize).
Lady Doak College, Madurai, South India; and Tyringham, Mass., U.S.A.

Clapp, Norton; American businessman; b. 15 April 1906; ed. Occidental Coll., and Univ. of Chicago.
Admitted to Calif. and Wash. bars 29, private practice 29-42; U.S. Navy 42-46; Chair. Metropolitan Building Corpn., Seattle 54-; Pres. Pelican (Alaska) Cold Storage Co. 47-60; Boise (Ida.) Payette Lumber Co. 49-55, Laird, Norton Co. 50-60; Vice-Pres. Weyerhaeuser Timber Co. 56-57, Chair. 57-60, 66-, Pres. 60-66; dir. numerous other companies; Vice-Pres. Nat. Council Boy Scouts of America; Trustee, Coll. Puget Sound, Tacoma, The Menninger Foundation, Univ. of Chicago.
Tacoma Building, Tacoma, Washington, U.S.A.

Clapp, Verner Warren, A.B.; American librarian; b. 3 June 1901; ed. Trinity Coll., and Harvard Univ.
Library of Congress Washington 23-56, Dir. Admin. Dept. 40-43, Dir. Acquisitions Dept. 43-47, Chief Asst. Librarian 47-56; Pres. Council on Library Resources, Inc., 56-; mem. American Library Asscn., Special Libraries Asscn., D.C. Library Asscn., Bibliographical Soc. of America.
Publ. *The Future of the Research Library* 64.
1028 Connecticut Avenue, Washington 6, D.C., U.S.A.

Clappier, Bernard; French economist; b. 9 Nov. 1913; ed. Ecole Polytechnique, Ecole Libre des Sciences Politiques.
Deputy Sec.-Gen. Office of Industrial Production 43; Dir. of the Cabinet of R. Schuman (Minister of Finance) 47, (Minister of Foreign Affairs) 48-50; Dir. External Econ. Relations, Ministry of Econ. Affairs 51-61; Chair. Conf. between Member States of the European Communities and other states which applied for membership of the Communities 62; Deputy Gov. Banque de France 63-; Inspector-Gen. of Finances 64-; Vice-Pres. of Monetary Cttee. E.E.C.
3 rue de la Vrillière, Paris 1er, France.

Claret, Lucien Armand Joseph; French industrialist; b. 8 Jan. 1903; ed. Ecole Spéciale des Travaux Publics, Paris.
Founded Etablissements A. L. Claret, Colombes 26, Société Industrielle de Travaux Electro-Mécaniques, Asnières 41, Société Industrielle de Découpage et d'Emboutissage, Paris 44, Société d'Exploitation des Procédés Leland & Claret 45, Fonderies de Carrières 47, Société Immobilière Claret, Colombes 48, Société Starlec, Paris 49, L'Unité Hermétique S.A., La Verpillière (Isère) 54, Société S.E.I.R.A.R., Paris 56, Claret-Normandie, St. Pierre-de-Varengeville (Seine-Maritime) 57, Claret-Ouest, Barentin (Seine-Maritime) 59; Pres./Dir.-Gen. Société d'Exploitation des Procédés Leland & Claret, Société L'Unité Hermétique S.A.; Man. Etablissements A. L. Claret, Fonderies de Carrières, Société de Distribution de Matériel, Claret-Normandie, Claret-Ouest; Adviser, French Foreign Trade; Vice-Pres. Constructeurs de Matériel Frigorifique

Français; officer of several other companies; Officier, Légion d'Honneur; Commdr. Mérite Commercial.
312 rue Gabriel-Péri, 92-Colombes, France.
Telephone: CHA 32-81.

Clark, Col. Charles Willoughby, D.S.O., O.B.E., M.C.; British engineering executive; b. 6 April 1888; ed. Atherstone Grammar School.
Apprentice, Alfred Herbert Ltd., Coventry 04, Dir. 34-, Chair. and Joint Man. Dir. 58-66, Pres. 66-; Pres. of all subsidiaries; Army service 14-18; Pres. Coventry Chamber of Commerce 51-53; Chair., Mfrs. Section, Cttee. of Machine Tool Trades Asscn. 46-55; mem. Board of Trade Machine Tool Advisory Council 57-; Deputy Lieut. of Warwickshire; Fellow, Royal Commonwealth Soc.
Alfred Herbert Ltd., Edgwick, Coventry, Warwickshire, England.

Clark, Colin Grant, M.A.; British economist; b. 2 Nov. 1905; ed. Dragon School, Oxford, Winchester Coll., and Brasenose Coll., Oxford.
Asst. Social Surveys of London 28-29, of Merseyside 29-30; Economic Advisory Council 30-31; Lecturer, Cambridge Univ. 31-37; Visiting Lecturer, Univs. of Sydney, Melbourne and Western Australia 37-38; Under-Sec. of State for Labour and Industry, Dir. Bureau of Industry, Financial Adviser to Treasury, Queensland 38-52; Dir. Inst. for Research in Agricultural Economics, Oxford 53-.
Publs. *The National Income, The Conditions of Economic Progress, The Economics of 1960, Welfare and Taxation, British Trade in the Common Market, Economics of Irrigation, Population Growth and Land Use,* etc.
Institute for Research in Agricultural Economics, Parks Road, Oxford, England.

Clark, Sir George Norman, M.A., D.LITT., F.B.A.; British historian; b. 27 Feb. 1890; ed. Balliol Coll., Oxford.
Fellow of All Souls Coll. Oxford 12 and 61; served in Army 14-18; Fellow of Oriel Coll. 19-31; Editor *English Historical Review* 20-26, 38-39; Chichele Prof. of Econ. History, Oxford 31-43; Regius Prof. of Modern History, Cambridge 43-47; work for Govt. Depts. 39-45; Provost of Oriel Coll., Oxford 47-57; Pres. British Acad. 54-58; Commdr. Order of Orange-Nassau (Neths.); Hon. LL.D. (Aberdeen); Hon. Litt.D. (Dublin, Cambridge); Hon. D.Litt. (Durham, Sheffield, Columbia, Hull); Hon. Fellow Balliol and Oriel Colls. Oxford, Trinity Coll., Cambridge, Trinity Coll., Dublin, and Royal Coll. of Physicians; Dr. h.c. (Utrecht).
Publs. *The Dutch Alliance and the War against French Trade* 23, *The Seventeenth Century* 29, *The Later Stuarts* 34, *Science and Social Welfare in the Age of Newton* 37; edited *The Campden Wonder* 59, *History of the Royal College of Physicians,* 2 vols. 64-66.
20 Horwood Close, Headington, Oxford, England.
Telephone: Oxford 64527.

Clark, Most Rev. Howard Hewlett, D.D., D.C.L.; Canadian ecclesiastic; b. 23 April 1903; ed. Thorold High School, St. Catherine's Collegiate, Trinity Coll., Toronto, and Univ. of Toronto.
Asst. Curate St. John's Church, Norway, Toronto 30; Curate Christ Church Cathedral, Ottawa 32-39, Rector 39-41, Canon 41-45, Dean 45-54; Bishop of Edmonton 54-59; Archbishop of Edmonton and Primate of the Anglican Church of Canada 59-61; Archbishop and Metropolitan of Rupert's Land and Primate of the Anglican Church of Canada 61-; D.D. Trinity Coll. 45; D.C.L. Bishop's Univ. 60, etc.
Publ. *The Christian Life, according to the Prayer Book* 57.
Church House, 600 Jarvis Street, Toronto 5, Ontario, Canada.

Clark, Howard Longstreth; American business exec.; b. 14 March 1916; ed. Stanford Univ., Harvard Law School and Columbia Univ. Graduate Business School.

Price Waterhouse and Co. 37-39; admitted to New York Bar 42; War Service, Navy 42-45; American Express Co. 45-, Vice-Pres. 48, Senior Vice-Pres. 52-56, Exec. Vice-Pres. 56-60, Pres. and Chief Exec. Officer 60-; Dir. of numerous companies.
American Express Company, 65 Broadway, New York, N.Y. 10006, U.S.A.

Clark, John A.; British business exec.; b. 26; ed. Harrow.
Royal Naval Volunteer Reserve, Second World War; formerly with Metropolitan Vickers and Ford Motor Co.; studied American electronics industry in U.S.A.; Asst. to Gen. Man., Plessey Int. Ltd. 49; Dir. and Gen. Man. Plessey (Ireland) Ltd. and Wireless Telephone Co. Ltd. 50; mem. Board of Dirs. Plessey Co. Ltd. 53; Gen. Man. Components Group 57, Man. Dir. and Chief Exec. 62-, Deputy Chair. 67-; Past Pres. Telecommunication Engineering and Mfg. Asscn; Vice-Pres. Inst. of Works Mans.
The Plessey Co. Ltd., Vicarage Lane, Ilford, Essex.
Telephone: 01-478-3040.

Clark, J(ohn) Desmond, C.B.E., F.B.A., F.S.A., PH.D.; British anthropologist; b. 10 April 1916; ed. Monkton Combe School and Christ's Coll., Cambridge.
Director Rhodes-Livingstone Museum, Livingstone, N. Rhodesia 38-61; Prof. of Anthropology, Univ. of Calif. (Berkeley) 61-; Mil. Service in E. Africa, Abyssinia, the Somalilands and Madagascar 41-46; Founder mem. and Sec. N. Rhodesia Nat. Monuments Comm. 48; Corresp. mem. Scientific Council for Africa South of the Sahara 56-; Fellow, American Acad. of Arts and Sciences 65.
Publs. *The Prehistoric Cultures of the Horn of Africa* 54, *The Prehistory of Southern Africa* 59, *The Stone Age Cultures of Northern Rhodesia* 60, *Prehistoric Cultures of Northeast Angola and their Significance in Tropical Africa* 63, *Atlas of African Prehistory* 67.
1941 Yosemite Road, Berkeley, Calif. 94707, U.S.A.

Clark, John Grahame Douglas, M.A., PH.D., SC.D., F.B.A.; British archaeologist; b. 28 July 1907; ed. Marlborough Coll., and Peterhouse, Cambridge.
Research student Peterhouse, Cambridge 30-32, By-Fellow 32-35; Faculty Asst. Lecturer in Archæology, Cambridge 35-46; Squadron Leader, R.A.F.V.R. 41-45; Univ. Lecturer in Archæology, Cambridge 46-52; Disney Prof. 52-; Head Dept. of Archæology and Anthropology 56-61, 68, Pres. Prehistoric Society 59-62, also its Editor 35-; Vice-Pres. Society of Antiquaries of London 60-62; mem. Royal Comm. on Ancient Monuments; mem. Ancient Monuments Board; Hodgkins Medal Smithsonian Inst. 67; Order of Dannebrog.
Publs. *The Mesolithic Settlement of Northern Europe* 36, *Archæology and Society* 39, 58, *Prehistoric England* 40, *Prehistoric Europe: the Economic Basis* 52, *Excavations at Star Carr* 54, *World Prehistory—an Outline* 61, (with Stuart Piggott) *Prehistoric Societies* 65.
19 Wilberforce Road, and Peterhouse, Cambridge, England.
Telephone: Cambridge 59376.

Clark, Joseph Sill, LL.B.; American politician; b. 21 Oct. 1901; ed. Harvard Univ., and Univ. of Pa. Law School.
Practised law in Philadelphia 26-50; Col. U.S. Air Force in World War II; Mayor of Philadelphia 52-56; U.S. Senator from Pennsylvania 56-; mem. Foreign Relations Cttee., Labor and Public Welfare Cttee.; mem. American, Pennsylvania and Philadelphia Bar Asscns.; D.Iur. h.c. Harvard and Temple Univs.; Philadelphia (Bok) Award 56, Drexel Inst; numerous other hon. degrees; Democrat.
Publs. *The Senate Establishment, Congress, The Sapless Branch.*
Room 361, Senate Office Building, Washington 25, D.C., U.S.A.

Clark, Sir Kenneth Mackenzie, C.H., K.C.B.; British art historian; b. 13 July 1903; ed. Winchester and Trinity Coll., Oxford.
Worked with Bernard Berenson in Florence 26-28; mem. Cttee. Exhibition of Italian Art at Burlington House 30; Keeper Dept. of Fine Art, Ashmolean Museum, Oxford 31-33; Dir. Nat. Gallery, London 34-45; Surveyor of the King's Pictures 34-45; Ryerson Lecturer, Yale Univ. 36; Dir. Film Dept., Ministry of Information 39-41; Chair. War Artists Advisory Cttee. 39-45; Slade Prof. of Fine Art, Oxford Univ. 46-50 and 61-62; Chair. Arts Council of Great Britain 53-60; Chair. Independent Television Authority 54-57; Trustee British Museum; mem. of the Cttee. of the Art Collection Fund, Conseil Artistique des Musées Nationaux, Nat. Theatre Board; hon. mem. Royal Scottish Acad., Swedish Acad., Spanish Acad.; Commendatore della Corona d'Italia and Commendatore al Ordine di Merito; Commdr. Légion d'Honneur, Knight of the Lion of Finland, Austrian Silver Medal of Honour; Fellow British Acad. and Royal Coll. of Arts; Hon. D.Lit. (Columbia), Hon. LL.D. (Glasgow), Hon. D.Lit. (Oxford, London and Liverpool Univs.).
Publs. The Gothic Revival 30, *Catalogue of Drawings by Leonardo da Vinci at Windsor* 35, *Leonardo da Vinci* 39, *One Hundred Details from the National Gallery* (two vols.), *Florentine painting of the Quattrocento, Hay Wain, Landscape into Art, Piero della Francesca, The Nude, Looking, Ruskin Today, Dark Ghetto, Rembrandt and the Italian Renaissance,* etc.
Saltwood Castle, Hythe, Kent, England.

Clark, Ligia; Brazilian sculptress; b. 23 Oct. 1920; ed. Sacré Coeur de Marie, Belo Horizonte, Minas Gerais, and in Paris under Fernand Léger, Dobrinsky and Arpad Szénes.
Co-founder Brazilian Neo-concrete Group 59; first exhbn. of transformable sculptures *Bichos* 60; One-man exhbns., Paris, Rio de Janeiro, New York, São Paulo, Stuttgart and London; Group exhbns. in France, Argentina, Germany, U.S.A., Italy, U.K., Israel, Czechoslovakia; numerous prizes and special exhbn., São Paulo Biennal 63.
Avenida Prado Junior 16, Apdo. 801, Copacabana, Rio de Janeiro, Brazil.

Clark, Gen. Mark W., D.S.C.; American army officer; b. 1 May 1896; ed. U.S. Military Acad.
2nd Lieut. 17, promoted through grades to Brig.-Gen. 41, Major-Gen. 42, Lieut.-Gen. 42, Gen. 45; served as an infantry officer in France in First World War; mem. Gen. Staff Corps 35-36, 37-40, March-June 42; apptd. Chief of Staff for Ground Forces in Europe July 42; led secret mission by submarine to obtain information in N. Africa preparatory to Allied invasion 42; Commanded Fifth Army in invasion of Italy 43, capture of Rome 44; Gen. in Command 15th Army Group Dec. 44, U.S. forces in Austria 45-47, 6th U.S. Army 47-49; Deputy U.S. Sec. of State 47; Chief of Army Field Forces, Fort Monroe, Va. 49-52; C.-in-C. UN Command and U.S. Far East Command 52-53; Pres. The Citadel (Mil. Coll.) 54-65, Pres. Emeritus 65-; Chair. Govt. Cttee. to investigate Central Intelligence Agency 54; numerous hon. degrees; decorations include Hon. K.B.E. 44, Grand Officier Légion d'Honneur, Mil. Order of Suvorov 1st Degree (U.S.S.R.), D.S.M. with three oak leaf clusters (U.S. Army).
Publs. Calculated Risk 50, *From the Danube to the Yalu* 54.
Francis Marion Hotel, Charleston, South Carolina 29402, U.S.A.

Clark, Ramsey, B.A., A.M., J.D. (son of Thomas Campbell Clark, *q.v.*); American lawyer and government official; b. 18 Dec. 1927; ed. Univs. of Texas and Chicago.
Marine Corps 45-46; admitted to Texas Bar 51, U.S.

Supreme Court 56; with Clark, Reed and Clark, Dallas 51-61; Asst. Attorney-Gen., Dept. of Justice 61-65, Deputy Attorney-Gen. 65-67, Attorney-Gen. 67-.
Department of Justice, Washington 25, D.C., U.S.A.

Clark, Thomas Campbell, A.B., LL.B. (father of Ramsey Clark, *q.v.*); American lawyer; b. 23 Sept. 1899; ed. Virginia Military Inst. and Univ. of Texas.
Admitted to Texas Bar 22; practised in Dallas 22-37; civil district attorney for Dallas County, Texas 27-32; Partner in firm McCraw and Clark of Dallas 33-35; U.S. Dept. of Justice 37-43; Asst. Attorney-Gen. of U.S. 43-45; Attorney-Gen. of U.S. 45-49; Assoc. Justice Supreme Court of U.S. 49-67; Chair. Joint Cttee. for Effective Admin. of Justice 61-64, Chair. Board of Dirs. Nat. Coll. of State Trial Judges; Fellow, Inst. of Judicial Admin., Pres. 66; Chair. Board of Dirs. American Judicature Soc. 67-; Chair. Advisory Board Nat. Comm. on Reform of Fed. Criminal Laws 67-; Dir. Fed. Judicial Center 68-; mem. American, Texas, Federal Bar Asscns. and other socs.; holds hon. degrees from various American Univs. and colleges.
Supreme Court of United States, Washington D.C. 20543; Home: 2101 Connecticut Avenue, N.W., Washington, D.C., U.S.A.

Clark, Sir Thomas Fife, Kt., C.B.E.; British civil servant; b. 29 May 1907; ed. Middlesbrough High School.
Political and diplomatic corresp. Westminster Press provincial newspapers 36-39; P.R.O. Ministry of Health 39-49; Controller, Central Office of Information (C.O.I.) 49-52; Adviser on Govt. Public Relations and to the Prime Minister 52-55; Dir.-Gen. C.O.I. 54-; First Pres. Int. Public Relations Asscn. 55-57; Fellow and founder mem. of Council, British Inst. of Public Relations, Pres. 58-59.
Wave Hill, Nevill Road, Rottingdean, Sussex, England. Telephone: Brighton 33020.

Clark, Sir Wilfrid Edward Le Gros, M.A., M.D., D.SC.; LL.D., F.R.C.S., F.R.S.; British anatomist; b. 5 June 1895; ed. London Univ.
Principal Medical Officer of Sarawak 20-23; Prof. of Anatomy, London Univ. 23-34, Oxford Univ. 34-62; mem. Norwegian Acad. of Art and Science; Pres. Int. Anatomical Congress 50, British Asscn. for the Advancement of Science 61; Foreign Assoc. U.S. Nat. Acad. of Sciences 63.
Publs. The Antecedents of Man 62, *The Fossil Evidence of Human Evolution* 64, *The Tissues of the Body* 65.
Fawler's End, Fawler, Charlbury, Oxford, England. Telephone: Stonesfield 267.

Clark, William Donaldson, M.A.; British author and civil servant; b. 28 July 1916; ed. Oriel Coll., Oxford.
Commonwealth Fellowship, Univ. of Chicago 38; served Ministry of Information Services, Chicago, and British Embassy, Washington, D.C. 39-45; London Editor *Encyclopaedia Britannica* 46-49; Diplomatic Correspondent *The Observer* 49-55; Adviser on Public Relations to the Prime Minister 55-56; Corresp. of *The Observer* at New Delhi Mar.-Dec. 57; Ed. of *The Week* section of *The Observer* 58-60; Consultant on current affairs to Associated Television 58-; Dir. of Overseas Development Inst. 60-68; Dir. of Information, World Bank 68-; mem. Nat. Cttee. UNESCO, Exec. Cttee. British Council.
Publs. Less than Kin 57, *Number 10* (novel and play) 66.
1818 H. Street N.W., Washington, D.C.; Overseas Development Institute, 160 Piccadilly, London W.I. Telephone: 01-493-2654.

Clarke, Arthur Charles, B.SC.; British science writer and underwater explorer; b. 16 Dec. 1917; ed. Huish's Grammar School, Taunton, and King's Coll., London. H.M. Exchequer and Audit Dept. 36-41; R.A.F. 41-46;

Inst. of Electrical Engineers 49-50; Technical Officer on first G.C.A. radar 43; originated communications satellites 45; Chair. British Interplanetary Soc. 46-47, 50-53; Asst. Editor *Science Abstracts* 49-50; engaged (with Mike Wilson) on underwater exploration on Great Barrier Reef of Australia and coast of Ceylon 54-; extensive lecturing, radio and TV, U.K. and U.S.; UNESCO Kalinga Prize 61; Stuart Ballantine Medal, Franklin Inst.
Publs. Non-fiction: *Interplanetary Flight* 50, *The Exploration of Space* 51, *The Young Traveller in Space* 54 (publ. in U.S.A. as *Going into Space*), *The Coast of Coral* 56, *The Making of a Moon* 57, *The Reefs of Tabropane* 57, *Voice across the Sea* 58, *The Challenge of the Spaceship* 60, *The Challenge of the Sea* 60, *Profiles of the Future* 62, *Voices from the Sky* 65, *The Promise of Space* 68; with Mike Wilson: *Boy Beneath the Sea* 58, *The First Five Fathoms* 60, *Indian Ocean Adventure* 61, *The Treasure of the Great Reef* 64, *Indian Ocean Treasure* 64; with R. A. Smith: *The Exploration of the Moon* 54; with Editor of *Life: Man and Space* 64; Fiction: *Prelude to Space* 51, *The Sands of Mars* 51, *Islands in the Sky* 52, *Against the Fall of Night* 53, *Childhood's End* 53, *Expedition to Earth* 53, *Earthlight* 55, *Reach for Tomorrow* 56, *The City and the Stars* 56, *Tales from the White Hart* 57, *The Deep Range* 57, *The Other Side of the Sky* 50, *Across the Sea of Stars* 59, *A Fall of Moondust* 61, *From the Ocean, From the Stars* 62, *Tales of Ten Worlds* 62, *Dolphin Island* 63, *Glide Path* 63, *Prelude to Mars* 65; with Stanley Kubrick: *2001: A Space Odyssey* (novel and screenplay) 66.
47/4 Gregory's Road, Colombo 7, Ceylon.
Telephone: Colombo 94255.

Clarke, Sir (Henry) Ashley, G.C.M.G., G.C.V.O.; British diplomatist; b. 26 June 1903; ed. Repton and Pembroke Coll., Cambridge.
Served with diplomatic missions in Hungary 25, Poland 27, Turkey 28-31; mem. British Del. to League of Nations and Disarmament Conf. 32-34; mission to Japan 34-38; at Foreign Office 39-44, latterly as Head, Far-Eastern Dept.; Minister at Lisbon 44-46; Minister in Paris 46-49; Deputy Under-Sec. of State, Foreign Office 50-53; Ambassador to Italy 53-62; Gov. of B.B.C. 62-67, of Nat. Theatre 62-66, of British Inst. of Recorded Sound 64-67; Chair. Royal Acad. of Dancing 64-; mem. Cttee. of Man., Royal Acad. of Music 67-; London Adviser Banca Commerciale Italiana 62-, and Assicurazioni Generali, Trieste 64-; Hon. Fellow, Pembroke Coll., Cambridge; Hon. Dr. Pol.Sc. of Genoa Univ.; Grand Cross of the Order of Merit of the Italian Republic.
16 Walton Street, London, S.W.3, England.
Telephone: 01-584-7874.

Clarke, Denzil Robert Noble; British chartered accountant and business executive; b. 9 July 1908; ed. Stonyhurst Coll.
Joined British-American Tobacco Co. Ltd. (accounting), travelling in U.S.A., India, Burma, Ceylon, Europe and Caribbean 32; Army Service 42-45; Asst. to Finance Dir., British-American Tobacco Co. Ltd. 45, Finance Dir. 54-60, Deputy Chair. 60-62, Vice-Chair. 62-66, Chair. July 66-; Dir. Sun Life Assurance Soc., Tobacco Securities Trust Co., Mardon Packaging Int. Ltd.
British-American Tobacco Co. Ltd., Westminster House, Millbank, London, S.W.1; Home: Puffins, South Drive, Wokingham, Berks., England.
Telephone: 01-222-1222 (Office).

Clarke, Sir Ellis Emmanuel Innocent, Kt., C.M.G., LL.B.; Trinidadian lawyer and diplomatist; b. 28 Dec. 1917; ed. St. Mary's Coll., Port of Spain, Trinidad, London Univ. and Gray's Inn, London.
Private law practice, Trinidad 41-54; Solicitor-Gen. Trinidad and Tobago 54-56; Dep. Colonial Sec. 56-57; Attorney-Gen. 57-61; Constitutional Adviser to the Cabinet 61-62; Ambassador to the United States and Perm. Rep. to UN 62-.
7530 17th Street, N.W., Washington, D.C., U.S.A.

Clarke, Mrs. Irene Fortune Irwin, B.A., M.A.; Canadian publisher; b. 1903; ed. Parkdale Collegiate Inst., Victoria Univ., and Univ. of Toronto.
Associated with her husband, the late William Henry Clarke, founder and Pres. of Clarke, Irwin & Co. Ltd., Book Publishers, until his death 55, Pres. and Chair. of Board 55-; official of several civic and educational orgs.
Office: Clarke, Irwin & Co. Ltd., 791 St. Clair Avenue West, Toronto 10, Ontario; Home: 43 The Kingsway, Toronto 18, Ontario, Canada.

Clasen, Andrew Joseph, B.SC., A.R.S.M., DR. ING.; Luxembourg diplomatist; b. 06; ed. Beaumont Coll., Windsor, Univs. of Oxford, London and Aix-la-Chapelle.
Consul-Gen. and Chargé d'Affaires a.i., Acting Sec.-Gen., Luxembourg Ministry of Foreign Affairs 41-44; Luxembourg Minister to Great Britain 44-55, Ambassador 55-; NATO Council Deputy 49-52; Grand Officier Order of Adolph of Nassau, Commandeur Ordre Couronne de Chêne; Grand Cross, Order of Orange Nassau.
The Luxembourg Embassy, 27 Wilton Crescent, London, S.W.1, England.
Telephone: 01-235-6961.

Clausetti, Eugenio, D.IUR.; Italian music publisher; b. 7 Jan. 1905.
Managing Dir. G. Ricordi & Co., Milan 44-; Pres. Soc. of Italian Music Publishers; Pres. SEDRIM, Italian Society for Collection of Mechanical Rights of Authors and Composers; Vice-Pres. BIEM, International Bureau of Mechanical Editions; Vice-Pres. International Union of Publishers, Music Section; Pres. Arti Grafiche Ricordi.
G. Ricordi & Co., s.p.a., Via Berchet 2, Milan, Italy.
Telephone: 89-82-42.

Clausse, Gilbert-Roger; Belgian professor; b. 1 Dec. 1902; ed. Univ. of Liège.
Prof. Athénée de St. Gilles 28-37; Dir. French broadcasts, Institut National Belge de Radiodiffusion 37-46, Asst. Dir. of the Institut 47-53, Dir.-Gen. 53-57; Prof. Université Libre de Bruxelles 45-; Dir. of Centre d'Etude des Techniques de diffusion collective 58-.
Publs. *Critique matérialiste de l'Education* 34, *L'Education de base pour un Humanisme social* 35, *Mesure des Humanités anciennes* 37, *La Radio, Huitième Art* 45, *La Radio scolaire* 49, *L'Information à la Recherche d'un Statut* 51, *L'Information d'Actualité: Critique de la Relation* 53, *Synopsis de l'information d'actualité* 61, *Les Nouvelles: Synthèse critique* 63, *Turquie: développement du Journalisme* 64, *Le Journal et l'Actualité* 67.
116 avenue Winston Churchill, Brussels 18, Belgium.
Telephone: 43-77-86.

Clavé, Antoni; Spanish painter; b. 5 April 1913; ed. evening classes at Escuela Superior de Bellas Artes de San Jorge, Barcelona.
Magazine and book illustrator 30-49; First Studio 45 rue Boissonade, Paris 41; influenced by Picasso's blue period 40, and by Vuillard and Bonnard 42; designed sets for theatre 46-55, starting with *Los Caprichos*, for Ballets des Champs-Elysées 46; full-time painter since 55; commenced carpet painting 57 and metal work 60; first one-man exhbn., Perpignan, France 39, later in Paris, London, Oran, Gothenburg, Buenos Aires, Rome, Milan, Barcelona, Bilbao, Los Angeles and Geneva; Matarasso Prize, Bienal São Paulo 57.
Major works: Illustrations for *La Dame de Pique*, Pushkin 46, black lithographs *Candide*, Voltaire 48, *Gargantua*, Rabelais 50.
c/o Galerie Creuzevault, 9 avenue Matignon, Paris 8e, France.

Clay, Gen. Lucius DuB., B.S.; American business executive and retired army officer; b. 23 April 1897; ed. U.S. Military Acad.

Commissioned as Second Lieut. 18; advanced through grades to General 47; instructor Officers' Training School (Engineers) 18; with Engineer troops 18-24; instructor in civil and military engineering, U.S. Military Acad. 24-28; river and harbour assignments; rep. U.S. at Permanent Int. Navigation Conf., Brussels 34; on Gen. MacArthur's staff in Philippines 37; in charge of construction of Red River Dam, Denison, Texas 38-40; in charge of defence airport programme, Civil Aeronautics Administration 40-41; Dir. of Material, U.S. Army 42-44; Deputy Dir. for War Mobilization and Reconversion 44-45; Deputy Mil. Gov. Germany (U.S.) 45-47; C.-in-C. European Command and Military Gov. of Germany (U.S.) Mar. 47-49; Pres. Kennedy's Personal Rep. in Berlin 61-62; Dir. Lehman Corpn., Chase Int. Investment Corpn., Allied Chemical Corpn., American Express Co., Continental Co. Inc., Standard Brands Inc.; Senior Partner, Lehman Brothers 63-; mem. American Soc. of Civil Engineers, Soc. of American Mil. Engineers, Perm. Int. Navigation Congress, American Red Cross, American Acad. Arts and Sciences; Trustee Sloan Foundation; Aerospace Corpn.

Publs. *Decision in Germany* 50, *Germany and the Fight for Freedom.*

Office: One William Street, New York, N.Y. 10004; Home: 200 East 66th Street, New York City, N.Y. 10021, U.S.A.

Telephone: B 09-3700 (Office), TE 8-2887 (Home).

Clayden, Rt. Hon. Sir (Henry) John, P.C.; lawyer; b. 26 April 1904; ed. Capetown, Charterhouse and Brasenose Coll., Oxford.

Barrister Inner Temple 26; Advocate Transvaal 27; war service 40-45, S.A. Engineer Corps, S.A. Staff Corps; K.C. 45; Judge of Supreme Court of S. Africa, Transvaal Provincial Division 46-55, 64-65; Judge of Federal Supreme Court, Federation of Rhodesia and Nyasaland 55-60; Chief Justice of Federal Supreme Court, Federation of Rhodesia and Nyasaland 60-64, Acting Gov.-Gen. of Fed. May-June 61; Chair. Hammarskjöld Accident Comm. 62, Industrial Tribunals, London.

8 Walton Street, London, S.W.3, England.

Telephone: 01-589-1300.

Clayton, Jack; British film director; b. 1921.

Entered film industry 35; served in R.A.F. Film Unit 39-45; Production Man. for *An Ideal Husband;* Assoc. Producer *Queen of Spades, Flesh and Blood, Moulin Rouge, Beat the Devil, The Good Die Young, I am a Camera;* Producer and Dir. *The Bespoke Overcoat* 55; Dir. *Room at the Top* 58; Producer and Dir. *The Innocents* 61; Dir. *The Pumpkin Eater* 64; Producer and Dir. *Our Mother's House* 67.

c/o Romulus Films Ltd., Brook House, Park Lane, London, W.1, England.

Clegg, Sir Cuthbert Barwick, Kt., T.D.; British cotton manufacturer; b. 9 Aug. 1904; ed. Charterhouse and Trinity Coll., Oxford.

Cotton Industry Working Party 46; Cotton Manufacturing Comm. 47-49; Anglo-American Council on Productivity 48-52; Pres. British Employers' Confederation 50-52; mem. Economic Planning Board 49-53, British Productivity Council 52-54; Pres. U.K. Textile Manufacturers Asscn. 61-, Cotton, Silk and Man-made Fibres Research Asscn. 62-67; Chair. Martins Bank Ltd. 64-; Dir. Halifax Building Soc., Stone-Platt Industries Ltd., Viyella Int. Ltd.

Barn Close, Beetham, Milnthorpe, Westmorland, England.

Cleland, Brig. Sir Donald Mackinnon, Kt., C.B.E., C.ST.J., Australian administrator; b. 28 June 1901; ed. Guildford Grammar School, Western Australia.

Lawyer, W. Australia 25-39; Second World War, Middle East, Chief of Staff, Military Admin., Papua and New Guinea 43-45; Chair. Australian-New Guinea Production Control Board 43-45; Dir. Federal Secretariat Australian Liberal Party 45-51; Asst. Admin. Papua and New Guinea 51, Acting Admin. 52-53, Admin. 53-66; Pres. Exec. and Legislative Councils, Papua and New Guinea 51-64; Hon. Colonel, Pacific Islands Regiment 53-66.

Chester Street, Box 358, P.O. Port Moresby, Papua, South Pacific.

Clemen, Wolfgang; German university professor; b. 29 March 1909; ed. Univs. of Heidelberg, Freiburg, Bonn, Berlin, Munich and Cambridge.

Lecturer, Cologne Univ. 38, Kiel Univ. 39; Prof. of English, Kiel Univ. 40-46, Munich Univ. 46-; mem. Bavarian Acad. of Sciences 48; Vice-Pres. German Shakespeare Soc. 49; Visiting Prof. Columbia Univ., New York 53; Pres. Modern Humanities Research Asscn. 64; Corresp. mem. British Acad. 64; Churchill Fund Visiting Prof. Bristol 64; Hon. mem. American Modern Language Asscn. and Modern Humanities Research Asscn. 65; Hon. D.Litt. (Birmingham) 64; Hon. D.Phil. (Rouen) 67.

Publs. *Shakespeares Bilder* 36, *Der junge Chaucer* 38, *Shelleys Geisterwelt* 48, *The Development of Shakespeare's Imagery* 51, 59, *English Tragedy before Shakespeare* 61, *Chaucer's Early Poetry* 63, *Kommentar zu Shakespeares Richard III* 57, *Shakespeare's Soliloquies* 64, *Spenser's Epithalamion* 64, *Shakespeare's Midsummer Night's Dream* (ed.) 63, *Past and Future in Shakespeare's Drama* 66, *A Commentary on Shakespeare's Richard III* 68, *Das Problem des Stilwandels in der engl. Dichtung* 68.

Endorf, Upper Bavaria, German Federal Republic.

Clemence, Gerald Maurice, PH.B.; American astronomer; b. 16 Aug. 1908; ed. Brown Univ.

Junior Astronomer U.S. Naval Observatory 30, Asst. Astronomer 37, Astronomer 40, Senior Astronomer 42, Head Astronomer and Dir. Nautical Almanac 45-58; Visiting Prof. of Astronomy, Columbia Univ. 58; Scientific Dir. Naval Observatory 58-63; Senior Research Assoc. and Lecturer in Astronomy, Yale Univ. 63-66, Prof. of Astronomy 66-; Editor *American Ephemeris* and *Nautical Almanac, American Nautical Almanac, American Air Almanac* 45-58; Assoc. Editor *Astronomical Journal* 49-63, Co-Editor 64-66, Editor 66-67; Councillor American Astronomical Soc. 50-52, Vice-Pres. 52-54, Pres. 58-60; Chair. Comm. 7, Int. Astronomical Union 48-55, Comm. 4 64-67; mem. Nat. Acad. of Sciences; Hon. D.Sc. (Case Inst. of Technology, Univ. of Cuyo, Argentina); Gold Medal Royal Astronomical Soc.

Publs. *The Motion of Mercury 1765-1937*, 43, *On the Elements of Jupiter* 46, *The Relativity Effect in Planetary Motions* 47, *First-order Theory of Mars* 49, *Standards of Time and Frequency* 56, and (with others) *Methods of Celestial Mechanics* 61.

Yale University Observatory, Box 2023, Yale Station, New Haven, Conn. 06520; Home: 475 Greenville Avenue, Johnston, Rhode Island 02919, U.S.A.

Clement, Frank G(oad), LL.B.; American lawyer and politician; b. 2 June 1920; ed. Cumberland Univ., Tenn., and Vanderbilt Univ., Tenn.

Served U.S. Army 43-46; Gen. Counsel, Tenn. Railroad and Public Utilities Comm. 46; Tenn. State Chair. Young Democrats Club 46-48; Gov. of Tenn. 52-58, 62-; Chair. Comm. on Mental Health Training and Research of the Southern Region Education Board; Chair. Southern Governors Conf.; Keynote speaker, Democratic Nat. Convention 56.

State Capitol, Nashville, Tenn., U.S.A.

Clément, René; French film director; b. 18 March 1913; ed. School of Architecture, Paris.

Films include *Bataille du rail* 46, *Les Maudits* 47, *Walls*

of Malapaga 48, *Château de verre* 50, *Jeux interdits* 52, *Lion d'or* 52, *Monsieur Ripois* 54, *Gervaise* 56, *Sea Wall* 58, *Demain est un autre jour* 62, *Quelle joie de vivre*, *Purple Noon (Plein Soleil)* 60, *The Love Cage (Les Félins)* 64, *Paris brûle-t-il?* 65, *A la Recherche du Temps Perdu* 66.
Publs. *Bataille du rail* (with C. Audry) 47.
91 Avenue Henri Martin, Paris 16, France.

Clemente Maurer, H.E. Cardinal José; Bolivian (b. Germany) ecclesiastic; b. 13 March 1900.
Ordained Priest 25; Archbishop of Sucre 50-; created Cardinal by Pope Paul VI 67.
Arzopispado, Casilla 205, Sucre, Bolivia.

Clements, George L.; American businessman; b. 24 Feb. 1909; ed. Univ. of Illinois.
Joined Jewel Tea Co. Inc. Chicago 29, Dir. 48-51, Pres. 51-64, Chair. Board of Dirs. 65-; Dir. Supermarches G.B., Belgium, Super Bazars, S.A., Belgium, Northern Illinois Gas Co., Universal Oil Products Co.; Dir. Chicago Asscn. of Commerce; Dir. and mem. exec. cttee. Nat. Asscn. of Food Chains.
1955 W. North Avenue, Melrose Park, Illinois, 60160, U.S.A.

Clemmensen, Carl Johan; Danish administrator; b. 26 Dec. 1916; ed. Rungsted Statsskole and Københavns Universitet.
Secretary, Danish Employers' Confederation 46-49, Principal 49-55, Chief of Statistical-Econ. Dept. 55-60, Vice-Dir. 60-62, Dir. and mem. Board of Dirs. 62-; mem. numerous Govt. and other Cttees.; Editor *Statistiken*.
Office: Dansk Arbejdsgiverforening, Vester Voldgade 113, Copenhagen V; Home: Hummeltoften 13a, Virum, Denmark.
Telephone: 84-57-57 (Home).

Clemmesen, Johannes, D.M.SC.; Danish pathologist; b. 14 Nov. 1908; ed. Metropolitan School and Univ. of Copenhagen.
Pathologist, Old People's Town 50-55; Assoc. Prof. of Pathology, Royal Dental Coll. 50-56; Chief Pathologist, Finsen Inst., Copenhagen 55-; Dir. Danish Cancer Registry 42-; mem. WHO Sub-cttee. on Cancer Registration and other cttees. on statistics and endemiology of cancer 50-; mem. Exec. Cttee. Int. Union against Cancer 54-62; mem. Secr., Cttee. on Geographical Pathology of Cancer 50-62, Cttees. on Tumour Nomenclature 50-65.
Publs. *X-radiation and Immunity to Heterotransplantation* 38, *Statistical Studies in the Aetiology of Malignant Neoplasms* 65.
Finsen Institute, Strandboulevard 49, Copenhagen O; Home: Ax. Møllers Have 22, Copenhagen F, Denmark.
Telephone: Tria 6850 (Office).

Clercq, Willy De, LL.D.; Belgian barrister and politician; b. 8 July 1927.
Former Barrister, Court of Appeal, Ghent; with Gen. Secretariat of UN, New York 52; mem. Chamber of Representatives for Ghent-Eklo 58-; Deputy Prime Minister, in charge of Budget 66-68; Parti pour la liberté et le progrès (P.L.P.); Head of P.L.P. Group.
Chamber of Representatives, Brussels, Belgium.

Clerides, Glavkos John, B.A., LL.B; Cypriot lawyer and politician; b. 24 April 1919; ed. Pancyprian Gymnasium, Nicosia, University Tutorial Coll., London, King's Coll., London Univ., Gray's Inn, London.
Served with R.A.F. 39-45; shot down and taken prisoner 42-45 (mentioned in despatches); practised law in Cyprus 51-60; Head of Greek Cypriot Del., Constitutional Comm. 59-60; Minister of Justice 59-60; mem. House of Representatives 60-, Pres. of House Aug. 60-; Gold Medal, Order of the Holy Sepulchre.
56 Metochio Street, Nicosia, Cyprus.

Cleve, Nils Joachim Otto, PH.D.; Finnish archaeologist; b. 1905; ed. Univ. of Helsinki and Åbo Acad.
Director, Municipal Museum of Turku 34-45; Dir., Historical Dept., Nat. Museum (Kansallismuseo) 45-59; Lecturer Åbo Acad. 44-59, Univ. of Helsinki 48-63; State Archaeologist (Nat. Museum) 59-.
Kansallismuseo, Helsinki 10; Home: Grävlingsvägen 6. B, Helsinki 80, Finland.
Telephone: 789918.

Cleveland, Harlan, A.B.; American administrator, educationist and government official; b. 19 Jan. 1918; ed. Princeton Univ. and Oxford Univ.
Served Allied Control Commission, Rome 44-45; served UNRRA, Rome and Shanghai 46-48; Economic Co-operation Admin., Washington 48-51; Asst. Dir. for Europe, Mutual Security Agency 52-53; Exec. Editor *The Reporter*, New York City 53-55, Publisher 55-56; Dean, Maxwell Graduate School of Citizenship and Public Affairs, Syracuse Univ. 56-61; Asst. Sec. for International Organization Affairs, State Dept. 61-65; Ambassador to NATO 65-; Democrat.
c/o NATO, Brussels 39, Belgium.

Cliburn, Van (Harvey Lavan, Jr.); American pianist; b. 12 July 1934; studied with mother and at Juilliard School of Music.
Public appearances, Shreveport 40; début, Houston Symphony Orchestra 52, N.Y. Philharmonic Orchestra 54, 58; concert pianist on tour U.S. 55-, U.S.S.R. 58; appearances in Brussels, London, Amsterdam, Paris, etc.; Hon. H.H.D. (Baylor), numerous prizes.
c/o Hurok Attractions Inc., 730 Fifth Avenue, New York 19, N.Y., U.S.A.

Clifford, Clark McAdams; American lawyer and government official; b. 25 Dec. 1906; ed. Washington Univ.
Holland, Lashly and Donnell, St. Louis, Missouri 28-33, Holland, Lashly and Lashly 33-37, Partner, Lashly, Lashly, Miller and Clifford 38-68, Senior Partner, Clifford & Miller, Washington 50-68; Special Counsel, President of U.S.A. 46-50; Chair. Foreign Intelligence Advisory Board 63-68; Sec. for Defense 68-; Dir. Nat. Bank of Washington, Washington-Sheraton Corpn.
Office: The Pentagon, Washington, D.C.; Home: 9421 Rockville Pike, Bethesda, Maryland 20014, U.S.A.
Telephone: OLiver 2-2842 (Home).

Clifford, John McLean; American publisher; b. 9 Dec. 1904; ed. Univ. of Utah, and Southwestern Univ.
Admitted to Californian Bar 30, D.C. Bar 39; Vice-Pres. Nat. Broadcasting Co. Inc. New York 53-54, Admin. Vice-Pres. 54-56, Exec. Vice-Pres. 56-61; Staff Vice-Pres. Radio Corpn. of America 61-62; Exec. Vice-Pres. and Dir. Curtis Publishing Co. Philadelphia 62-64, Pres. 64-; Chair. Board New York and Pennsylvania Co. Inc., Dir. Curtis Circulation Co., etc.
965 Via Fruteria, Hope Ranch Park, Santa Barbara, California 93105, U.S.A.

Clift, David Horace, B.S., B.S. in L.S.; American librarian; b. 16 June 1907; ed. Kentucky, Columbia Univs.
Kentucky Univ. Library 27-30; Columbia Univ. Libraries 30-31; New York Public Library 31-37; Asst. to Dir. Libraries, Columbia Univ. 37-42; U.S. Army 42-45; Library of Congress Mission to Germany 45-46; Assoc. Librarian Yale 45-51; Exec. Sec. American Library Asscn. 51-58, Exec. Dir. 58-; Head, Exchange delegation of U.S. librarians to U.S.S.R. 61; mem., Advisory Cttee., U.S. Commr. of Educ. on the Library Services Program of the U.S. Office of Educ.
American Library Association, 50 East Huron Street, Chicago, Illinois 60611, U.S.A.

Clinchy, Everett Ross, B.S., M.A., PH.D.; American educationist; b. 16 Dec. 1896; ed. Lafayette Coll., Columbia Univ., and Drew Univ.

Chaplain, Wesleyan Univ. 24-28; Pres. Nat. Conf. of Christians and Jews Inc. 28-58; Pres. The Council of World Tensions 50-; fmr. Dir. Williamstown Inst. of Human Relations; Pres. Inst. on Man and Science 63-. Publs. *All in the Name of God* 31, *Centers in Human Relations* 40, *Handbook on Human Relations* 50.
304 East 42nd Street, New York 17, N.Y., U.S.A.

Clinchy, Russell James, B.D., B.S.T.; American clergyman; b. 26 Dec. 1893; ed. Columbia Univ., Drew Theological Seminary, Yale Divinity School.
Army Y.M.C.A. 18; First Church, Cornwall, Conn. 22; Assoc. Minister, Broadway Tabernacle, New York 27; Minister, Mount Pleasant Congregational Church, Washington 31; Minister, First Church of Christ in Hartford 38-51; senior staff mem. Foundation for Economic Education, Irvington, N.Y. 51-53; Sec. League to uphold Congregational Principles 53; Minister, Church in the Gardens, Forest Hills, New York 54-63; Minister Emeritus 63-; Pres. Washington Council of Social Agencies 36, Del. Int. Congregational Council 30; Del. World Christian Conf. Oxford 37; Commr. of American Congregational Churches to Churches in Britain 43; mem. Exec. Cttee. Congregational Churches 36-42; Exchange pastorate, Edinburgh 47; mem. Chapel Advisory Council, Princeton Univ.; Hon. Litt.D. (Marietta Coll.), Hon. D.D. (Elon Coll.).
Publs. *A Reasonable Faith* 36, *Faith and Freedom* 47, *An Answer for Agnostics* 66.
131 Patton Avenue, Princeton, New Jersey, U.S.A.

Clitheroe, 1st Baron, cr. 55, of Downham; **Ralph Assheton,** Bt., P.C., D.L., M.A., F.S.A.; British businessman; b. 24 Feb. 1901; ed. Eton Coll., and Christ Church, Oxford.
Barrister, Inner Temple 25; mem. London Stock Exchange 27-39; Nat. Conservative M.P. Rushcliffe Div. of Notts. 34-45, City of London Nov. 45-50, Blackburn West 50-55; Parl. Sec. to Ministry of Labour and Nat. Service Sept. 39-Feb. 42, to Ministry of Supply 42-43; Financial Sec. to Treasury 43-44; Chair. Conservative Party 44-46; Chair. Public Accounts Cttee. 48-50, Select Cttee. on Nationalized Industries 51; Chair. Mercantile Investment Trust Co. Ltd., Borax (Holdings) Ltd.; Deputy Chair. Nat. Provincial Bank Ltd., John Brown & Co. Ltd., Tube Investments Ltd.; Dir. Coutts & Co., Rio Tinto Zinc Corpn. Ltd., and other companies; Vice-Lieut. County of Lancs.; High Steward of Westminster.
17 Chelsea Park Gardens, London, S.W.3, England.
Telephone: 01-352-4020.

Cloete, (Edward Fairley) Stuart (Graham); South African soldier, farmer and author; b. 23 July 1897; ed. Lancing Coll., England.
Army officer 14-25, Coldstream Guards, retd.; farming and ranching in South Africa 23-35.
Publs. *Turning Wheels* 37, *Watch for the Dawn* 39, *Yesterday is Dead* 40, *Hill of Doves* 41, *The Young Men and the Old* (poems) 41, *Congo Song* 43, *The Third Way* 46, *African Portraits, The Curve and the Tusk* 53, *The African Giant* 55, *Mamba* 56, *The Mask* 57, *Gazella* 58, *The Soldier's Peaches* (short stories) 59, *The Fiercest Heart* 60, *The Silver Trumpet* 60 and *The Looking Glass* 63 (short stories), *Rags of Glory* 63, *The Honey Bird* 64, *The 1001 Nights of Jean Macacque* 65, *The Abductors* 66.
P.O.B. 37 Hermanus, South Africa.

Clore, Charles; British businessman; b. 26 Dec. 1904; ed. London.
Chairman, Sears Holdings Ltd., Sears Engineering Ltd., British Shoe Corpn., Scottish Motor Traction Ltd., European Shipping Co. Ltd., Princes Investments Ltd., Taylor & Lodge Ltd., Garrard & Co. Ltd., Mappin & Webb Ltd., Selfridge's Ltd.; Deputy Chair. City Centre Properties Ltd.; Dir. Anglo Norness Shipping Co. Ltd., Consolidated Laundries Corpn. (U.S.A.), Transatlantic Real Estate Corpn. (U.S.A.).
22 Park Street, London, W.1, England.

Close, Frederick J., B.A.; American business executive; b. 21 June 1905; ed. Pittsburgh public schools and Pennsylvania State Univ.
Joined Aluminum Co. of America (ALCOA) 29, Man. of Architectural Sales 45-55, Man. of Market Dept. 55-58, Gen. Man. of Sales Dept. and Commercial Research Divs. 58, Vice-Pres. 58-60, Vice-Pres. and Gen. Sales Man. 60-63, Exec. Vice-Pres. 63-65, Chair. of Board 65-; mem. Housing Industry Council, Industrial and Professional Advisory Board, Pa. State Univ.
Aluminum Co. of America, 401 Alcoa Building, Pittsburgh, Pa. 15219, U.S.A.

Clouzot, Henri-Georges, L. en D.; French film director; b. 20 Nov. 1907; ed. Lycée de Brest, Lycée Sainte-Barbe and Paris Univ.
Int. Prize Venice Film Festival 47 and 49, Cannes Grand Prix 53, Prix Louis-Delluc for *Les Diaboliques* 54, Cannes Special Prize for *Le Mystère Picasso* 56, Grand Prix du Cinéma français for *La Vérité* 60; Officier des Arts et des Lettres.
Films include *L'Assassin Habite au 21, Le Corbeau, Quai des Orfèvres, Manon, Le Salaire de la Peur, Les Diaboliques, Le Mystère Picasso, Les Espions, La Verité, L'Enfer.*
"La Colombe d'Or", Saint-Paul-de-Vence (Alpes-Maritimes), France.

Clunes, Alexander Sherriff de Moro; British actor, manager and producer; b. 17 May 1912; ed. Cliftonville and Margate.
First acted with Ben Greet Players; founder Arts Theatre Group of Actors, Arts Theatre Club, Theatre Dir. 42-53.
Acted at Old Vic. 34, 35, 36; in *Hell for Leather* 36, *George and Margaret* 37, *Road to Ruin* 37, *Taming of the Shrew, Yes, My Darling Daughter, I Killed the Count* 37, at Malvern Festival 38, *In Good King Charles's Golden Days* 39, *Coriolanus, Othello, Taming of the Shrew, Much Ado About Nothing* Stratford 38-39; *Pygmalion* 47, *The Lady's Not for Burning* 48, *The Barretts of Wimpole Street* 48, *Gog and Magog* 48, *Diary of a Scoundrel* 49, *Macbeth* 50, *Carrington V.C.* 53, *Facts of Life* 54, *Richard III, Hamlet, Who Cares* 56, *King John, Julius Caesar, The Tempest,* Stratford 56-57, *My Fair Lady* 59-61, *The Affair* 62, *Getting Married* 67.
Films include *Melba* 52, *The Brighton Story* 55.
Publ. *The British Theatre* 64.
c/o London Management, 8 Upper Brook Street, London, W.1, England.

Clurman, Harold; American theatrical director and critic; b. 18 Sept. 1901; ed. New York public schools, Columbia Univ. and the Sorbonne, Paris.
Actor and stage manager 24-29; playreader for Theatre Guild, New York 29-31; co-founder Group Theatre, New York 31; Man. Dir. 37-41; Art Columnist *To-Morrow* magazine 46-53; Drama Critic *New Republic* 48-53, *The Nation* 53-; Exec. Consultant Repertory Theatre Lincoln Center 63-; productions directed include *Awake and Sing* 35, *Golden Boy* (Odets) 37, *Montserrat* (Robles) (Habimah Theatre, Tel Aviv) 41, *Member of the Wedding* (Carson McCullers) 49, *Desire Under the Elms* (O'Neill) 52, *The Autumn Garden* (Hellman) 53, *Tiger at the Gates* (Giraudoux) (London and N.Y.), in television 60, *Waltz of the Toreadors* (Anouilh) 56, *Orpheus Descending* (Tennessee Williams), *A Touch of the Poet* (O'Neill) 58, *Heartbreak House* (Shaw) 59, *A Shot in the Dark* (Achard-Kurnitz) 61; Chevalier, Légion d'Honneur; Hon. D. Litt. (Bard Coll.).
Publs. *The Fervent Years* 45, *Lies like Truth* 58.
334 East 69th Street, New York City, N.Y., U.S.A.

Clutton-Brock, (Arthur) Guy; British and Rhodesian (dual nationality) agriculturist and social worker; b. 5 April 1906; ed. Rugby School and Magdalene Coll., Cambridge Univ.

Cambridge House University Settlement 27-29; Rugby House Settlement 29-33; Borstal Service 33-36; Principal Probation Officer, Metropolitan Area of London 36-40; Head Oxford House University Settlement 40-45; Youth and Religious Affairs Officer, British Military Govt., Berlin 45; with Christian Reconstruction in Europe 46; farm labourer in U.K. 47-48; Diocesan Agricultural Officer, Mashonaland (Southern Rhodesia) and Dir. of Farm Activities, St. Faith's Mission, Rusape (Southern Rhodesia) 49-59; briefly detained by Fed. Rhodesian Govt. on declaration of emergency March 59; Hon. Dir. Bamangwato Development Asscn., Bechuanaland Protectorate 61-62; Field Officer of the African Development Trust 62-65; retired 66.
Publ. *Dawn in Nyasaland* 59.
Box 2097, Salisbury, Rhodesia.

Cluver, Eustace H., K.ST.J., E.D., M.A., M.D., B.CH., D.PH., F.R.S.H.; South African physician; b. 28 Aug. 1894; ed. Victoria Coll., Stellenbosch, and Oxford Univ.
Rhodes Scholar to Oxford 13; fmr. Prof. of Physiology Witwatersrand Univ. Medical School, Sec. for Public Health and Dir. S. African Inst. for Medical Research Johannesburg; Prof. of Medical Education and Dean Faculty of Medicine, Univ. of Witwatersrand.
Publs. *Medical and Health Legislation in the Union of South Africa* 49 (2 edn. 61), *Social Medicine* 51, *Recent Medical and Health Legislation* 55, *Public Health in South Africa* (6th edn.) 59.
Mornhill Farm, Walkerville, Transvaal, South Africa.
Telephone: Walkerville 1212.

Clyne, Hon. John Valentine; Canadian business executive; b. 14 Feb. 1902; ed. Florence Nightingale School and King Edward High School, Vancouver, Univ. of British Columbia, London School of Economics and King's Coll., London.
Various business firms 23-29; Partner, McRae, Duncan and Clyne, Vancouver 29-46, Campney, Owen, Clyne and Murphy 47-50; Judge of Supreme Court of British Columbia 50-57; Chair. of Board MacMillan and Bloedel Ltd., Vancouver 58-59; Chair. of Board and Chief Exec. Officer, MacMillan, Bloedel and Powell River Ltd. (name changed to MacMillan Bloedel Ltd. April 66), Vancouver 60-; Dir. Canadian Imperial Bank of Commerce, Canadian Pacific Railway Co., Canada Trust Co.
MacMillan Bloedel Ltd., 1199 W. Pender Street, Vancouver 1; Home: 3738 Angus Drive, Vancouver 9, B.C., Canada.
Telephone: 733-6120 (Home).

Cobbold, 1st Baron, cr. 60, of Knebworth; **Cameron Fromanteel Cobbold**, P.C., G.C.V.O.; British banker and Palace official; b. 14 Sept. 1904; ed. Eton and King's Coll., Cambridge.
Deputy Governor, Bank of England until 49, Gov. 49-61; Lord Chamberlain Jan. 63-; H.M. Lt. for City of London; High Sheriff County of London 46-47; mem. H.M. Privy Council 59; Dir. British Petroleum Co. Ltd., Hudson's Bay Co.; mem. Court of Royal Exchange.
Knebworth House, Knebworth, Herts.; and St. James's Palace, London, S.W.1, England.

Cochran, Jacqueline (Mrs. Floyd B. Odlum); American airwoman and business executive.
Pilot since 32; winner Bendix Transcontinental Air Race 38; headed U.S. Women's Airforce Service Pilots in Second World War (Lieut.-Col. U.S.A.F.R.); special consultant, U.S.A.F. Chief of Staff 50; holds numerous world air speed records; first woman to break sonic barrier 53; Dir. Northeast Airlines; Pres. Nat. Aeronautic Asscn. 60; Pres. Int. Aeronautic Fed. 58-; Consultant to Nat. Aeronautics and Space Admin., Dir. George Washington Univ; D.S.M.; Légion d'Honneur; Gold Medal Int. Aeronautic Fed. 54, etc.
Publ. *The Stars at Noon* 54.
Cochran Odlum Ranch, Indio, Calif., U.S.A.

Cockburn, Sir Robert, K.B.E., C.B., PH.D., M.SC.; British civil servant; b. 31 March 1909; ed. Municipal Coll., Portsmouth, and London Univ.
Taught science at West Ham Municipal Coll. 30-37; research in communications at Royal Aircraft Establishment, Farnborough 37-39; radar research at Telecommunications Research Establishment, Malvern 39-45; atomic energy research at A.E.R.E., Harwell 45-48; scientific adviser to Air Ministry 48-53; Principal Dir. of Scientific Research (Guided Weapons and Electronics), Ministry of Supply 54-55, Deputy Controller of Electronics 55-56, Controller of Guided Weapons and Electronics 56-59; Chief Scientist, Ministry of Aviation 59-64; Dir. Royal Aircraft Establishment, Farnborough 64-; U.S. Congressional Medal for Merit.
21 Fitzroy Road, Fleet, Hampshire, England.

Cockerell, Christopher Sydney, C.B.E., M.A., F.R.S.; British engineer; b. 4 June 1910; ed. Gresham's, Holt and Peterhouse, Cambridge.
Joined Marconi's 35, in charge Airborne Division and Navigational Research 46-48, research 48-50; started boat-building business later known as Ripplecraft Co. Ltd. 48-; inventor of Hovercraft, formed Hovercraft Ltd. 57; consultant to Ministry of Supply on Hovercraft Project 57-58; consultant Hovercraft Development Ltd. 58-; Chair. Ripplecraft Co. Ltd. 50-, Hovercraft Ltd. 58-; Dir. Hovercraft Development Ltd. 58-66; Fellow Royal Soc. of Arts 60; Hon. Fellow Soc. of Engineers, Manchester Univ. of Science and Technology, Swedish Soc. of Aeronautics; D.Sc., Leicester Univ.; Hon. D.Sc. Royal Coll. of Art 68; awarded numerous medals by various learned socs.
13 Ardnave Crescent, Bassett, Southampton, Hants., England.
Telephone: Southampton 69418.

Cockfield, Francis Arthur, LL.B., B.SC. (ECON.); British business executive; b. 28 Sept. 1916; ed. Dover County School, London School of Economics.
Called to Bar, Inner Temple 42; Inland Revenue Dept. of Civil Service 38; Asst. Sec. Bd. of Inland Revenue 45, Commr. 51-52, also Dir. of Statistics and Intelligence to Bd. of Inland Revenue 45-52; Finance Dir. Boots Pure Drug Co. Ltd. 53-61, Man. Dir. and Chair. Exec. Man. Cttee. 61-; mem. Nat. Econ. Development Council (N.E.D.C.) 62-64.
11 Queensmead, St. John's Wood Park, London N.W.8., England.

Code, James Arthur, Jr., B.S., M.S., E.E.; American business executive; b. 17 Jan. 1893; ed. U.S. Military Acad., Yale Univ., Ohio State Univ., and Univ. of California.
Commissioned U.S. Army 17; staff service in U.S., Philippines, Panama; Asst. Prof. Ohio State Univ. 18-22; Prof. of Communications Engineering Univ. of Calif. 34-38; Major Signal Corps 32, Lt.-Col. 40, Col. 41, Brig.-Gen. Deputy, Chief Signal Officer 42, Major-Gen. 42; Asst. Chief Signal Officer 42-45; Chief Signal Officer European Theatre 45; retd. 46; Chief Exec. Gary Group; Chair. Telephone Services Inc., U.S.; Vice-Pres. and Dir. Assoc. Tel. and Tel. Co., U.S., Pan-American Tel. and Tel. Co., U.S., Anglo-Canadian Tel. Co., Canada, Linwood Investment Co., U.S. Automatic Electric Co. (1946), U.S., Int. Automatic Electric Corpn., U.S., Continental Tel. Co., U.S., Tel. Bond and Share Co., U.S. and numerous other companies; Decorations include Bronze Star (U.S.A.), D.S.M. (U.S.A.), Officer Legion of Honour (France), Commander Order of the Crown (Belgium); author of articles and papers on electrical engineering and military subjects.
1386 Dana Avenue, Palo Alto, Calif., U.S.A.
Telephone: 325-5985.

Cody, H.E. Cardinal John Patrick; American ecclesiastic; b. 24 Dec. 1907; ed. N. American Coll., Rome. Ordained 31; Auxiliary Bishop, Diocese of St. Louis 47-54; Coadjutor with right of succession to the Bishop of St. Joseph, Missouri 54, Apostolic Admin. 55; Coadjutor to Archbishop-Bishop of Kansas City, St. Joseph Aug. 56, Bishop 56-61; Coadjutor with right of succession to Archdiocese of New Orleans 61, Apostolic Admin. 62-64; Archbishop of New Orleans 64-65; Archbishop of Chicago 65-; cr. Cardinal 67; mem. Pontifical Comms. for seminars and studies; Pres. Nat. Catholic Educ. Asscn.
P.O. Box 1979, Chicago, Illinois 60690, U.S.A.

Cœdès, George; French orientalist; b. 10 Aug. 1886; ed. Sorbonne and Ecole Pratique des Hautes Etudes. Pensionnaire, Ecole Française d'Extrême-Orient (Hanoi) 11, Prof. 14; Curator, Nat. Library of Siam (Bangkok) 18; Sec.-Gen. Royal Inst. of Siam 27; Dir. Ecole Française d'Extrême-Orient 29; Curator, Musée d'Ennery (Paris) 46; Pres. Société Asiatique de Paris 65; Corresp. Fellow British Acad.; mem. Institut de France; foreign mem. Akad. v. Wetenschappen; Hon. LL.D. (Hong Kong).
Publs. include: *Recueil des inscriptions du Siam* 24, 29, *Bronzes Khmers* 23, *Les Collections archéologiques du Musée National de Bangkok* 28, *Inscriptions du Cambodge* 37, 43, 51, 52, 53, 54, 64, 66, *Pour mieux comprendre Angkor* 47 (English trans. *Angkor, an introduction* 63), *Les Etats hindouisés d'Indochine et d'Indonésie* 48, 2nd edn. 64 (English trans. *The Indianized States of Southeast Asia* 68), *Etudes cambodgiennes* 11-56, *Les Peuples de la Péninsule indochinoise: histoire, civilisations* 62 (English trans. *The Making of Southeast Asia* 66).
59 avenue Foch, Paris 16e, France.
Telephone: 553-57-96.

Coelho, Vincent H.; Indian diplomatist; b. 20 July 1917; ed. Madras Univ.
Indian Audit and Accounts Service 42, later Indian Foreign Service; Asst. Financial Adviser (Supply Dept.) 44; Under-Sec. Ministry of Finance 45-46; Under-Sec. Cabinet Secr. 46-47; Private Sec. to Prime Minister 47-48; Foreign Service 48-; First Sec. Berne 48-49; Trade Commr., Alexandria 49-50; Consul-Gen., Goa 51-54; Deputy Sec. Ministry of External Affairs 54-57; Chargé d'Affaires, Ankara 57-59; Joint Sec. Ministry of External Affairs 59-61; Ambassador to Brazil 63-65; Indian Political Officer in Sikkim 66-.
Office of the Indian Political Officer, The Residency, Gangtok, Sikkim.

Coerr, Wymberley DeR., B.A.; American diplomatist; b. 2 Oct. 1913; ed. Yale Univ.
Joined Foreign Service 39, served Montreal, La Ceiba, Mexico City, Suva and Djakarta; Officer in Charge, Indonesian Affairs 51; First Sec. Tegucigalpa 54, Guatemala City 55, Counsellor 56; Nat. War Coll. 56; Counsellor, La Paz 57; Dir. Office of West Coast Affairs 59; Dep. Asst. Sec. for Inter-American Affairs 60; with Agency for Int. Development 62; Ambassador to Uruguay 62-65, to Ecuador 65-67.
American Embassy, Avda. Patria 120, Quito, Ecuador.

Coffin, Frank Morey; American lawyer and government official; b. 11 July 1919; ed. Bates Coll., and Harvard Univ.
Admitted to Maine Bar 47, legal practice 47-56; mem. U.S. House of Reps. 57-61; Man. Dir. Development Loan Fund, Dept. of State 61; Dep. Administrator, Agency for Int. Development 61-62, Dep. Administrator for Operations 62-64; U.S. Rep. to Development Assistance Cttee., Organisation for European Co-operation and Development (OECD), Paris 64-; U.S. Circuit Judge, Court of Appeals for First Circuit 65-.
1 Ocean Road, South Portland, Maine, U.S.A.

Coggan, Most Rev. Frederick Donald, D.D.; British ecclesiastic; b. 9 Oct. 1909; ed. Merchant Taylors' School, St. John's Coll., Cambridge and Wycliffe Hall, Oxford.
Asst. Lecturer in Semitic Languages and Literature, Manchester Univ. 31-34; Curate, St. Mary, Islington 34-37; Prof. at Wycliffe Coll. Toronto 37-44; Principal, London Coll. of Divinity 44-56; Bishop of Bradford 56-61, Archbishop of York, July 61-; Hon. Fellow, St. John's Coll., Cambridge 61; Prelate Order of St. John of Jerusalem 67-; Pro-Chancellor Univ. of York 62-; Univ. of Hull 68-.
Publs. *The Ministry of the Word* 45, revised edn. 64, *The Glory of God* 50, *Stewards of Grace* 58, *Five Makers of the New Testament* 62, *Christian Priorities* 63, *The Prayers of the New Testament* 67.
Bishopthorpe, York, England.
Telephone: 67021.

Coghill, Nevill Henry Kendal Aylmer, M.A.; British university teacher; b. 19 April 1899; ed. Haileybury Coll. and Oxford Univ.
Research Fellow, Exeter Coll., Oxford 24; Fellow and Tutor in English Literature 25; Fellow Royal Soc. of English Literature 54; Merton Prof. of English Literature, Oxford 57-66; produced *A Midsummer Night's Dream* (Haymarket Theatre, London) 45, *Pilgrim's Progress* (Covent Garden, London) 51; Gov. Shakespeare Memorial Theatre, Stratford 56; has broadcast on Shakespeare, Chaucer, Langland, etc.; F.R.S.L. 50; Pres. of the Poetry Soc. 64-68.
Publs. *Visions from Piers Plowman*, *The Poet Chaucer* 49, *The Canterbury Tales* (in modern English) 51, *Geoffrey Chaucer* 56, *Shakespeare's Professional Skills* 64, Co-author (with Martin Starkie) *Canterbury Tales* (theatre) 68.
Savran House, Aylburton, nr. Lydney, Glos., England.
Telephone: Lydney 2240.

Cogny, Gen. René, D. en D.; French army officer; b. 25 April 1904; ed. Ecole Polytechnique.
Army service with artillery; commanded mobile battery 39; attached Third Army Headquarters 40, taken prisoner 40, escaped from Oflag XIIIA 41; joined resistance movement and later arrested and deported to Buchenwald; Col. commanding Infantry Brigade 45; Chief Mil. Adviser to Ministry of Nat. Defence 47-48; Liaison Officer between Marshals Montgomery and de Lattre de Tassigny 49; served Indo-China 50, becoming Commdr. of French Forces in Tonkin and Gen. of Division 53; Mil. Gov., Metz, commanding sixth mil. region April 56-, C.-in-C. French Forces in Morocco 56-58, C.-in-C., Central Africa 59-64; Légion d'Honneur (Grand Officer), Croix de Guerre and many other French and foreign decorations.
20 rue Louis-Besquel, Vincennes, (Val de Marne), France.
Telephone: 328-12-13.

Cohen, Sir Andrew (Benjamin), K.C.M.G., K.C.V.O., O.B.E.; British civil servant; b. 1909; ed. Malvern and Trinity Coll., Cambridge.
Entered Inland Revenue Dept. 32; transferred to Colonial Office 33, Asst. Sec. 43, Asst. Under-Sec. of State 47-51; Gov. and C.-in-C., Uganda 52-57; Permanent Rep. to U.N. Trusteeship Council 57-61; Dir.-Gen. British Dept. of Technical Co-operation 61-64; Perm. Sec., Ministry of Overseas Development 64-.
Publ. *British Policy in Changing Africa* 59.
[*Died 17 June 1968.*]

Cohen, Sir Edgar Abraham, K.C.M.G.; British government official; b. 5 Dec. 1908; ed. Manchester Grammar School and Balliol Coll., Oxford.
Asst. Edinburgh Univ. Dept. of Moral Philosophy 31 joined Board of Trade 32, Second Sec. 52-60; Perm

U.K. Rep. to European Free Trade Asscn. (EFTA) and GATT, Geneva 60-65, to Org. for Economic Co-operation and Devt. (OECD) 65-.
69 avenue Victor Hugo, Paris 16e, France.

Cohen, Manuel Frederick; American government official; b. 9 Oct. 1912; ed. Brooklyn Coll. of City of New York, and Brooklyn Law School of St. Lawrence Univ.
Research Assoc., Twentieth Century Fund studies of securities markets 33-34; private corporate and real estate practice, New York 37-42; Securities and Exchange Comm. 42-, Chief Counsel, Div. of Corpn. Finance 52-59, Adviser 59-60, Dir. Div. of Corpn. Finance 60-61, Commr. 61-64, Chair. Securities and Exchange Comm. 64-; Professorial Lecturer in Law, George Washington Univ. 58-.
Securities and Exchange Commission, 500 North Capitol Street, Washington, D.C. 20549; Home: 6403 Marjory Lane, Bethesda, Md. 20034, U.S.A.

Cohen, Ruth Louisa, M.A.; British university official; b. 10 Nov. 1906; ed. Newnham Coll., Cambridge.
Commonwealth Fund Fellow, Stanford and Cornell Univs., U.S.A. 30-32; Research Officer, Agricultural Research Inst., Oxford 33-39; with Ministry of Food 39-42, Board of Trade 42-45; Fellow, Newnham Coll., Cambridge 39-54, Principal 54-, University Lecturer in Econs. 45-.
Publs. *History of Milk Prices* 36, *Economics of Agriculture* 39.
Newnham College, Cambridge, England.
Telephone: Cambridge 62273.

Cohen, Wilbur Joseph, PH.B., L.H.D.; American government official; b. 10 June 1913; ed. Univ. of Wisconsin, Adelphi Coll.
With Cttee. Econ. Security 34-35; Social Security Admin. 36-56; Prof. Public Welfare Admin., Univ. of Michigan 56; Asst. Sec. Dept. of Health, Educ. and Welfare 61-65, Under-Sec. 65-68, Sec. 68-; Chair. Presidents' Task Force on Health and Social Security 60; mem. Royal Health Soc., Nat. Social Welfare Assembly and numerous cttees.; Distinguished Service Award of Dept. of Health, Educ. and Welfare 56, Group Health Asscn. 56; Florina Lasker Award 61; Blanche Ittleson Award 62; mem. Nat. Conf. Social Welfare, Distinguished Service Award 57.
Publs. *Retirement Policies in Social Security* 57, *Social Security: Programs, Problems and Policies* (with W. Haber) 60, Co-author *Income and Welfare in the United States* 62, numerous articles.
Office: Department of Health, Education and Welfare, Washington 25; Home: 9819 Capital View Avenue, Silver Spring, Maryland, U.S.A.

Cohen of Birkenhead, 1st Baron, cr. 56; Rt. Hon. **Henry Cohen,** Kt., M.D., F.R.C.P., F.S.A., F.R.S.A., J.P.; British physician; b. 1900; ed. St. John's School, Birkenhead, Birkenhead Inst., Liverpool, London and Paris Univs.
Senior Physician, Royal Infirmary, Liverpool 34-65; Prof. of Medicine, Liverpool Univ. 34-65; Bradshaw Lecturer, R.C.P. 40; Skinner Lecturer, Faculty of Radiologists 42; Lettsomian Lecturer, Medical Soc. of London 44; Moynihan Lecturer, Royal Coll. of Surgeons 48; Newsholme Lecturer, Univ. of London 50; Croonian Lecturer, Royal Coll. of Physicians 63, etc.; Pres. Royal Soc. of Medicine, Royal Soc. of Health, Gen. Medical Council, Nat. Soc. of Clean Air, Asscn. of Physicians, Great Britain and Ireland; fmr. Chair. Central Health Services Council, Standing Medical Advisory Cttee., Ministry of Health; Governing Trustee, Nuffield Provincial Hospitals Trust; mem. Asscn. British Neurologists, Physiological Soc., Société Internationale de Gastro-entérologie; Crown rep. on Gen. Medical Council; Pres. B.M.A. 50; Assoc. K.St.J.; several hon. degrees; medals include Gold Medal of B.M.A.,

Nuffield Gold Medal of Royal Soc. of Medicine; Hon. F.A.C.P., F.R.C.P.Ed., F.R.C.P.I., F.R.C.P.S., F.R.I.C., F.F.R., F.F.A.R.C.S.Eng., F.D.S.R.C.S.Eng., F.R.S.M., F.A.P.H.A., F.R.S.H., F.R.C.O.G., F.C.G.P., F.B.Ps.S., F.P.S.; Hon. Freeman of Birkenhead 56; Hon. Freeman of Soc. of Apothecaries 68.
Publs. *New Pathways in Medicine* 35, *The Nature, Method and Purpose of Diagnosis* 43, *Sherrington* 58, articles in *Surgery of Modern Warfare* 41, contributed to *Lancet* volume on *Prognosis, Modern Methods of Treatment, Pye's Surgical Handicraft,* also *British Encyclopaedia of Medical Practice* (Editor).
31 Rodney Street, Liverpool 1, England.
Telephone: 051-709-2233.

Cohn, Haim; Israeli lawyer; b. 11 March 1911; ed. Univs. of Munich, Hamburg and Frankfurt-on-Main, Germany, Hebrew Univ. of Jerusalem and Govt. Law School, Jerusalem.
Admitted to Bar of Palestine 37; Sec. Legal Council, Jewish Agency for Palestine, Jerusalem 47; State Attorney, Ministry of Justice, Hakirya 48, Dir.-Gen. 49; Attorney-Gen., Govt. of Israel 50; Minister of Justice and Acting Attorney-Gen. 52; Attorney-Gen. (later) Justice, Supreme Court of Israel 60-; mem. Perm. Court of Arbitration, The Hague 62-, UN Comm. on Human Rights 65-; Deputy Chair. Council of Higher Educ., Israel; Chair. Exec. Council Hebrew Univ. of Jerusalem.
Publ. *The Foreign Laws of Marriage and Divorce* (English) 37.
36 Tchernihovsky Street, Jerusalem, Israel.
Telephone: (02) 3-9973.

Cohu, LaMotte Turck, B.A.; American aircraft executive; b. 23 Sept. 1895; ed. Princeton Univ.
Security salesman 18-21; partner Myron S. Hall Co. and Hall, Cohu Bros. Co. 21-33; Pres. Air Investors Inc. 30-39, Aviation Corpn. 31-32, American Airways (now American Airlines) 31-32; Dir. North American Aviation Inc. 33-34, Transcontinental Air Transport 33-34; Chair. of Board, Dir., and Gen. Man. Northrop Aircraft Inc. 39-47; Pres. and Dir. Northrop Hendy Co. 45-46, Transcontinental & Western Air Inc. 47-48; Pres. and Gen. Man. Consolidated Vultee Aircraft Corpn. 48-52, Vice-Chair. of Board 52-53; Chair. Kay Laboratories (now Cohu Electronics Inc.) 54-.
La Madrina, P.O. Box 752, Rancho Santa Fé, Calif., U.S.A.

Coing, Helmut, DR. JUR.; German jurist; b. 28 Feb. 1912; ed. Hanover, Lille, Kiel, Munich and Göttingen.
Professor of Jurisprudence, Goethe Univ. Frankfurt (Main) 40, Ord. Prof. 48, Faculty Dean 50-51, Univ. Rector 55-57; Pres. West German Conf. of Rectors 56-57, Wissenschaftsrat 58-61; Chair. Wissenschaftlicher Beirat, F. Thyssen-Stiftung 61-; Dir. Max Planck Inst. for History of European Law 64-; mem. Accademia delle Scienze dell'Istituto di Bologna 65; Commendatore Ordine al Merito (Italy); Grosses Verdienstkreuz des Verdienstordens der Bundesrepublik Deutschland, etc.; Dr. Iur. h.c. Lyons, Montpellier and Vienna.
Publs. *Die Rezeption des Römischen Rechts in Frankfurt am Main* 39, *Die obersten Grundsätze des Rechts* 47, *Grundzüge der Rechtsphilosophie* 50, *Lehrbuch des Erbrechts* 53, *Staudinger-Kommentar zum Allgemeinen Teil des BGB* 57, *Römisches Recht in Deutschland* (contribution to *Ius Romanum Medii Aevi*) 64.
Kennedyallee 96, 6 Frankfurt (Main)-S10, German Federal Republic.

Coke, Gerald Edward, C.B.E.; British merchant banker; b. 25 Oct. 1907; ed. Eton and New Coll., Oxford.
Lieutenant-Colonel, Second World War; Chair. Rio Tinto Co. Ltd. 56-62; Dep. Chair. Rio Tinto-Zinc Corpn. 62-66, now Dir.; Dep. Chair. Mercury Securities Ltd. 64-; Dir. S. G. Warburg and Co. Ltd., United

Kingdom Provident Inst. and other companies; Treas. Bridewell Royal Hospital (King Edward's School), Witley 46-; Chair. Glyndebourne Arts Trust 55-; Dir. Royal Acad. of Music 57-, Royal Opera House, Covent Garden 59-64; Governor of B.B.C. 61-66. Rio Tinto-Zinc Corporation, 6 St. James's Square, London, S.W.1, England.

Colbert, Edwin Harris, A.B., A.M., PH.D.; American vertebrate palaeontologist; b. 25 Sept. 1905; ed. Univ. of Nebraska and Columbia Univ.
Student Asst. Univ. of Nebraska 26-29; Univ. Fellow Columbia Univ. 29-30; Research Asst. American Museum of Natural History 30-32, Asst. Curator 33-42, Curator and Chair. Dept. of Amphibians and Reptiles 44-45, Chair. Dept. of Geology and Palaeontology 58-60; Dept. of Vertebrate Palaeontology 60-66, Curator 66-; Prof. of Vertebrate Palaeontology, Columbia Univ. 45-; Assoc. Curator, Acad. of Natural Sciences of Philadelphia 37-48; Research Assoc., Museum of Northern Arizona 54-; mem. Nat. Acad. of Sciences; Pres. Society of Vertebrate Palaeontology 46-47, Society for Study of Evolution 58; Vice-Pres. Palaeontological Soc. 63-; Daniel Giraud Elliot Medal (N.A.S.). Publs. *The Dinosaur Book* 51, *Evolution of the Vertebrates* 58, *Millions of Years Ago: Prehistoric Life in North America* 58, *Dinosaurs* 61, *Stratigraphy and Life History* (with Marshall Kay) 65, *The Age of Reptiles* 65, *Men and Dinosaurs* 68, and over 200 papers, etc.
The American Museum of Natural History, Central Park West at 79th Street, New York 24, N.Y.; Home: 497 Park Avenue, Leonia, N.J., U.S.A.

Colbert, Lester Lum, B.B.A., LL.B.; American automobile manufacturer; b. 13 June 1905; ed. Texas and Harvard Univs.
Cotton buyer, Texas 21-29; Law practice with Larkin, Rathbone and Perry (New York City) 29-33; joined Chrysler Corpn. 33; Resident Attorney 33-36; Vice-Pres. Dodge Division 36-46; Gen. Man. Dodge Chicago plant (aircraft engines) 43-46; Pres. Dodge Div. 46-51; Vice-Pres. Chrysler Corpn. 49-50, Dir. 49-61, Pres. 50-61, Chair. of Board 60-61; Trustee Hanover Bank and Automotive Safety Foundation 55-61; mem. Automobile Manufacturers' Asscn.; mem. American Bar Asscn.; mem. National Industrial Conf. Board; Hon. LL.D. Bethany Coll.; Chevalier de la Légion d'Honneur.
Office: Fisher Building, Detroit 31, Mich.; Home: 491 Martell Drive, Bloomfield Hills, Mich., U.S.A.

Coldwell, M. J., P.C., C.C., LL.D.; Canadian politician; b. 2 Dec. 1888; ed. Hele's School, Royal Albert Memorial, and Univ. Coll., Exeter (England).
Born in England; emigrated to Canada 10; schoolteacher and principal 10-34; Alderman for Regina 22-32; Pres. Canadian Teachers' Fed. 27-28, Sec.-Treas. 28-34; Chair. Royal Comm. of Inquiry into Public Services of Saskatchewan 29-30; Vice-Chair. Saskatchewan Farmers' Political Asscn. 29-32, and Pres. Independent Labour Party, Saskatchewan 30-32; Nat. Sec. Co-operative Commonwealth Fed. (C.C.F.) 34-37, Nat. Chair. 38-42; elected to House of Commons 35, re-elected 40, 45, 49, 53 and 57; House Leader of Co-operative Commonwealth Fed. 40, 45, 49, 53 and 57; Del. Commonwealth Parly. Conf. in London 41, 48, Ottawa 52; Nat. Pres. and Parly. Leader Co-operative Commonwealth Fed. 42-60, Hon. Pres. 60-61; Hon. Life Pres. New Democratic Party; mem. Canadian Del. to San Francisco Conf. 45 and UN, N.Y. 46, 50, 53 and 54; Vice-Pres. U.S. League for Industrial Democracy 46; Chair. UN Evaluation Mission to India 58-59; Resident Fellow Carleton Univ., Ottawa 63-64; mem. Queen's Privy Council of Canada 64-, Advisory Cttee. on Election Expenses 64-66, Royal Comm. on Security 66-68; Fellow Royal Canadian Geographical Soc.
Publs. *Left Turn, Canada*.

Apartment 1010, 330 Metcalfe Street, Ottawa 4, Canada.
Telephone: 233-6006.

Cole, Baron (Life Peer) cr. 65, of Blackfriars; **George James Cole;** British businessman; b. 3 Feb. 1906; ed. Raffles School, Singapore.
Joined Niger Co. Ltd. (subsidiary of Lever Bros. Ltd. later merged into United Africa Co. Ltd.) 23; various posts in London and Africa, Controller for British West Africa 39; Dir. United Africa Co. Ltd. 45-63, Joint Man. Dir. 52-55; Dir. Taylor Woodrow (West Africa) Ltd. 47-55; Dir. Palm Line Ltd. 49-55, Chair. 52-55; Dir. Unilever Ltd. 48-, Vice-Chair. 56-60, Chair. 60-; Dir. Unilever N.V. 48-, Vice-Chair. 60-; Dir. Finance Corpn. for Industry Ltd. 57-; Trustee of The Leverhulme Trust Fund, of the Civic Trust; Deputy Chair. Board of Governors, London Graduate School of Business Studies; Chair. Govt. Advisory Cttee. on the Appointment of Advertising Agents; Dir. Commonwealth Devt. Finance Co. Ltd.
50 Victoria Road, London, W.8, England.
Telephone: 01-937-9085.

Cole, Charles Woolsey, M.A., PH.D., L.H.D., LL.D., LITT.D., SC.D.; American ex-college president, diplomatist, consultant and author; b. 8 Feb. 1906; ed. Amherst Coll., and Columbia Univ.
Instructor in History, Columbia Univ. 29-35; Travelling Fellow, Social Science Research Council (Paris) 32-33; Assoc. Prof. Econs., Amherst Coll. 35-37, George D. Olds Prof. of Econs. 37-40; Prof. of History, Columbia Univ. 40-46; Pres. Amherst Coll. 46-60; Vice-Pres. Rockefeller Foundation 60-61; U.S. Ambassador to Chile 61-64; mem. Council on Foreign Relations.
Publs. *French Mercantilist Doctrines Before Colbert* 31, *Colbert and a Century of French Mercantilism* (2 vols.) 39, *Economic History of Europe* (with S. B. Clough) 41, *French Mercantilism 1638-1700* 43, *History of Europe* (with C. J. H. Hayes and M. Baldwin) 49, *History of Western Civilization* (with C. J. H. Hayes and M. Baldwin) 62, 67.
Box 66, Amherst, Massachusetts, U.S.A.
Telephone: 413-253-2211.

Cole, David Lee, C.M.G., M.C.; British diplomatist; b. 31 Aug. 1920; ed. Cheltenham Coll., and Sidney Sussex Coll., Cambridge.
Royal Inniskilling Fusiliers, Second World War; Dominions Office 47; U.K. Del. to United Nations, New York 48-51; First Sec., British High Comm., New Delhi 53-56; Private Sec. to Sec.of State for Commonwealth Relations 56-60; Head, Personnel Dept., Commonwealth Relations Office 61-63; Dep. High Commr. in Ghana 63-64, Acting High Commr. 63; High Commr. in Malawi 64-67; Minister (Political), British High Comm., New Delhi, 67-.
British High Commission, New Delhi, India.

Cole, Edward N.; American automobile executive; b. 17 Sept. 1909; ed. Grand Rapids Junior Coll., and General Motors Inst., Flint, Michigan.
Joined Gen. Motors Corpn. as Lab. Asst. 33; successively lab. technician, technician and designer, engineer, Chief Design Engineer, Asst. Chief Engineer, Chief Engineer, Works Man., Plant Man. Cadillac—Cleveland Tank Plant, Chief Engineer and Gen. Man. Chevrolet Motors Div. Detroit, Group Vice-Pres. of Car and Truck Divs. Gen. Motors; Pres. Gen. Motors Oct. 67-; designed new engine for G.M. Tank used in World War II, the *Corvan* rear-engine car; mem. Soc. Automotive Engineers, American Ordance Asscn., Nat. Automobile Manufacturers Asscn.
Office: General Motors Building, Detroit 2; Home: 1371 Kirkway Drive, Bloomfield Hills, Michigan, U.S.A.

Cole, Margaret Isabel (widow of late G. D. H. Cole); British historian and writer; b. 6 May 1893; ed. Roedean School and Girton Coll., Cambridge.

Classical Mistress St. Paul's Girls' School London 14-17; Asst. Sec. Labour Research Dept. 17-26; Tutorial Class Tutor Univ. of London 25-46; Hon. Sec. New Fabian Research Bureau 35-39; Hon. Sec. Fabian Society 39-53; Vice-Chair. 54-55, Chair. 55-56, Pres. 62-; Alderman, London County Council 52-65, Chair. Further Educ. Cttee. 50-59, 60-65, Vice-Chair. 59-60, 64-67; Chair. Battersea Coll. of Educ. 62-67; mem. Inner London Educ. Authority 64-67; Chair. Geffrye Museum 52-67; Chair. Sidney Webb Coll. 61-.

Publs. *The New Economic Revolution, Books and the People, Women of To-Day, Marriage, Past and Present, Education for Democracy, Evacuation Survey* (with R. Padley), *Beatrice Webb, Makers of the Labour Movement, Growing up into Revolution, Robert Owen, Servant of the County, Story of Fabian Socialism*; Editor: *Democratic Sweden, Our Soviet Ally, Twelve Studies in Soviet Russia, The Road to Success, The Webbs and their Work, Our Partnership, Beatrice Webb's Diaries 1912-24* and *1924-32*; wrote many detective novels and books on social subjects jointly with the late G. D. H. Cole.
74 Addison Way, London, N.W.11, England.
Telephone: 01-455-0245.

Cole, Sterling, B.A., LL.B.; American lawyer and public servant; b. 18 April 1904; ed. Colgate Univ. and Albany Law School.
Practised law in Bath, N.Y. 29-34; mem. U.S. House of Representatives 34-57, Chair. Joint Cttee. on Atomic Energy 53-54, and mem. of several other House Cttees.; Dir.-Gen. Int. Atomic Energy Agency, Vienna 57-61; mem. Washington Inst. of Foreign Affairs; private legal practice, Washington 61-; Hon. LL.D. (Colgate Univ.), Hon. D.Sc. (Union Coll.); Hon. LL.D. (Elmira Coll.); Order of Merit (Italy); Republican.
Cole & Norris, 1737 H Street, N.W., Washington, D.C., U.S.A.
Telephone: 333-0166.

Coleman, S. Othello; Liberian international bank official; b. 12 Feb. 1928; ed. Liberia Coll. and American Int. Coll., Springfield, Mass.
Self-employed 54-60; Asst. Research Officer, Bureau of Econ. Research, then Research Officer 60-61; Asst. Dir. of Econ. Research and Planning in charge of Bureau of Plans, Preparation and Co-ordination, Nat. Planning Agency 62-63; Dir. of Projects Preparation, Review, Evaluation and Aid Co-ordination, Nat. Planning Agency 64; Alternate Dir., Int. Bank for Reconstruction and Devt., Int. Finance Corpn., and Int. Devt. Assn. 64-66, Exec. Dir. Nov. 66-.
International Bank for Reconstruction and Development, Washington D.C. 20433, U.S.A.

Coleman, William Frank Kobena, M.B.E., B.SC., C.ENG., F.I.E.E.; Ghanaian engineer and radio administrator; b. 21 March 1922; ed. Achimota Coll., Accra, Univs. of Southampton and London.
Lecturer, Electrical Engineering, Achimota 47-48; Dep. Chief Engineer Ghana Broadcasting System 55-58, Chief Engineer and Dep. Dir. 58-60; Dir.-Gen., Ghana Broadcasting Corpn. 60-; Dir. Ghana News Agency 60-; Chair. Board of Dirs. State Electronic Products Corpn. 65-67; Pres. Union of Nat. Radio and TV Orgs. of Africa 64-66.
Broadcasting House, P.O.B. 1633, Accra; Home: 153 North La Bone, Accra, Ghana.
Telephone: 76434.

Colin, André, D. en D.; French politician; b. 19 Jan. 1910; ed. Collège de Brest and Paris Univ.
After military service, Sec. French Assn. Catholic Youth; elected Pres. Gen. 36; Prof. of Faculty of Law Lille; naval officer for Maritime Law in Levant 39; opposed Armistice and appealed to all Frenchmen to support De Gaulle; returned to France and active in Resistance; called to Algiers to Consultative Assembly

43; worked secretly to found Mouvement Républicain de Libération which became Mouvement Républicain Populaire (Christian Party) of which he was appointed Sec. Gen.; mem. Nat. Council of Resistance and Consultative Assembly Paris elected Sec. of its Youth Comm.; Deputy for Finistère 45-; Sec. of State in Prime Minister's Office 46-48; Minister for Merchant Navy 48-50; Sec. of State for Interior 50 and 51; Minister of the Interior 53; Minister, France d'Outre-Mer May 58; del. European Parl. 58; Senator 59; National Pres. Mouvement Républicain Populaire 59-63, Pres. M.R.P. in Senate; Pres. Conseil général du Finistère; Chevalier Légion d'Honneur, Croix de Guerre, Médaille de la Résistance.
Sénat, Palais du Luxembourg, Paris 6e, France.

Colina Riquelme, Rafael de la; Mexican diplomatist; b. 20 Sept. 1898.
Chancellor, Consular Service of Mexico, Philadelphia, Pa. 18-22; Vice-Consul, St. Louis 22, Eagle Pass, Tex. 22-23; Chief Admin. Section, Consular Dept. of Mexico 23-24; Consul, Boston 24-25, New Orleans 25-28, Laredo, Tex. 28-30, Los Angeles 30-32; Chief Consular Dept., Mexico City 32-33; Chief Bureau of Licences, Govt. of Fed. District, Mexico City 33; Consul-Gen., San Antonio, Tex. 34-35, New York 36-43; Minister Counsellor, Mexican Embassy, Washington, D.C. 44-48; Ambassador to U.S.A. 49-53; Permanent Representative to UN 53-59; Mexican Ambassador to Canada 59-62, to Japan 62-64; Perm. Rep. to Org. of American States (OAS) 65-; Deputy Sec.-Gen. Inter-American Conf. on Problems of War and Peace, Mexico City 45; Mexican del. UN Gen. Assembly, N.Y. 46 and 48, 53-58, Japanese Peace Conf., San Francisco 51, and to several other Int. Confs.; Order of Merit (Chile); Order of Honour and Merit (Haiti); Juan Pablo Duarte Order of Merit (Dominican Republic), Grand Cross Vasco Núñez de Balboa (Panama); Imperial Order of Rising Sun (Japan).
Delegation of Mexico to O.A.S., 2440 Massachusetts Avenue, N.W., Washington, D.C. 20008, U.S.A.

Collado, Emilio Gabriel, S.B., A.M., PH.D.; American economist; b. 20 Dec. 1910; ed. Phillips Acad., Andover, Massachusetts Inst. of Technology, and Harvard.
U.S. Treasury Dept. 34-36; Fed. Reserve Bank of N.Y. 36-38; U.S. State Dept. 38-46; Associate Economic Adviser, Special Asst. to Under-Sec., Dir. of Office of Financial and Development Policy, Deputy on Financial Affairs; Alternate, Inter-American Financial and Economic Advisory Cttee. 39-45; Alternate, Inter-American Economic and Social Council 45-46; mem. Inter-American Statistical Inst. 43-46; Chair. Inter-American Coffee Board 43-44; Trustee Export-Import Bank of Washington 44-45; U.S. Exec. Dir. Int. Bank of Reconstruction and Development 46-47; Standard Oil Co. (New Jersey) 47-, Treas. 54-60, Dir. 60, Vice-Pres. 62-66, Exec. Vice-Pres. 66-; mem. U.S.A./B.I.A.C. for Organization for European Co-operation and Development (OECD), Discount Corpn. of New York; mem. Council on Foreign Relations; mem. Int. Council of Morgan Guaranty Trust Co.; mem. and Dir. Nat. Bureau of Econ. Research; mem. Council for Latin America on Board of Dirs. of The Atlantic Council of U.S.; Trustee Cttee. for Econ. Devt. and Chair. of its Research and Policy Cttee.; Trustee American Econ. Assn.; mem. American Acad. of Arts and Sciences, U.S. Council of Int. Chamber of Commerce.
Standard Oil Company (New Jersey), 30 Rockefeller Plaza, New York, N.Y. 10020, U.S.A.
Telephone: 212-974-2345.

Collard, Léo, DR. EN DROIT; Belgian politician; b. 02.
Former prof. of International Law at Institut supérieur de Commerce, Hainault; Burgomaster of Mons 52-; mem. of Walloon Economic Council; Minister of Educa-

tion 46 and 54-58; Minister of State 63-; Pres. Socialist Party 59-.
Parti Socialiste Belge, 13 Boulevard de l'Empereur, Brussels, Belgium.

Colley, George Joseph; Irish solicitor and politician; b. 18 Oct. 1925; ed. Scoil Mhuire, Marino, St. Joseph's Christian Brothers' School, Fairview, and Univ. Coll., Dublin.
Member of Dáil Éireann for Dublin N.E. 61-; mem. Legal Cttee. and Political Cttee., Council of Europe (Irish Parl. Del.) 62-64; Leader, Irish Del. to Council of Europe 64-65; Parl. Sec. to Minister for Lands and Fisheries 64-65; Minister for Educ. 65-66, for Industry and Commerce 66-; Fianna Fáil.
10 Palmerston Gardens, Rathmines, Dublin 6, Ireland.

Collier, Gershon Beresford Onesimus, M.A., B.C.L.; Sierra Leonean politician and diplomatist; b. 27; ed. Fourah Bay Coll., Durham Univ., Middle Temple, London.
Practising barrister 56-61; Solicitor for Municipality of Freetown 61; Perm. Rep. to UN 61-63, 64-67, concurrently Amb. to the U.S.A. 63-67; Chief Justice of Sierra Leone Jan. 67-; mem. numerous Sierra Leone dels. to Int. Conferences; People's Nat. Party.
Office of the Chief Justice, Freetown, Sierra Leone.

Collin, Fernand (Jozef Maria Fanny), LL.D.; Belgian company director and university professor; b. 18 Dec. 1897; ed. Univ. of Louvain.
Lawyer, Antwerp 23-38; Lecturer, Univ. of Louvain 25, Prof. 27-, Dean Faculty of Law and mem. Rectorial Council 45-48; Chair. Board of Dirs. Kredietbank 38-; Chair. Imperial Products Co. 59-66; Dir. Gevaert Photo-Products 52; Chair. Banque Diamantaire Anversoise 64-; mem. Higher Council for Physical Education and Sports 30-40; Royal Commissary to middle classes 37; Chair. Central Section, Belgian Banking Asscn. 39-45; Chair. Supreme Family Council 52-59, Utrecht-Allerlei Risico's 59-; mem. Man. Cttee. Inst. de Réescompte et de Garantie 40-63; Chair. Benelux Cttee. 59-; Chair. Belgian Assoc. Investment Funds 58-62; Chair. Cardiolog. Foundation Princess Liliane 61; Commdr. Order of the Crown and Commdr. Order of Léopold, Grand Officer Order Léopold II (Belgium); Commdr. Order of Orange-Nassau (Neths.), Commdr. Italian Order of Merit, Commander Order St. Gregory the Great and other decorations.
Publs. *Enrico Ferri et l'Avant-Projet du Code penal italien de 1921* 25, *Rapport sur les Classes Moyennes* 37, *Strafrecht* 48, *Code d'instruction criminelle et Lois complémentaires* (with M. H. Bekaert) 49.
Mechelsesteenweg 196, Antwerp, Belgium.
Telephone: 03/37-31-43.

Collingwood, Charles; American radio and television broadcaster; b. 4 June 1917; ed. Cornell Univ. and New Coll., Oxford.
Foreign Corresp. United Press, London 39, Amsterdam 40; Foreign Corresp. Columbia Broadcasting System, North Africa 42-43, France and Germany 44-45; CBS U.N. Corresp. 46-47; CBS White House Corresp. 48-51; Special Asst. Dir. for Mutual Security (U.S. Govt.) 51-52; Chief, London Bureau CBS 57-59; corresp. New York 59-64, Chief European Corresp. CBS News 64-; Chevalier, Légion d'Honneur.
CBS News, 26 Hallam Street, London, W.1, England.

Collins, Vice-Admiral Sir John Augustine, K.B.E., C.B.; Australian naval officer and diplomatist; b. 7 Jan. 1899; ed. Royal Australian Naval Coll.
Joined Royal Australian Navy as Cadet Midshipman 13; served in British Fleet during First World War and since then in various H.M. and H.M.A. ships in Australia and abroad; Asst. Chief of Naval Staff, Melbourne 38-39; Captain H.M.A.S. *Sydney* 39-41; Commodore Commdg. China Force Java 42, H.M.A.S.

Shropshire 43-44, H.M.A. Squadron 44-46; Rear-Admiral 47; Imperial Defence Coll. 47; First Naval Member and Chief of Naval Staff, Australian Naval Board 48-55; Australian High Commr. in New Zealand 56-62; Vice-Admiral 50; Commdr. Cross of Order of Orange-Nassau, and U.S. Legion of Merit (Officer).
13 Dumaresq Road, Rose Bay, Sydney, N.S.W., Australia.
Telephone: Sydney 37-8171.

Collins, Gen. Joseph Lawton; American army officer; b. 1 May 1896; ed. Louisiana State Univ., and U.S. Mil. Acad.
Graduated Mil. Acad. 17, instructor U.S. Mil. Acad. 21-25, Infantry School 27-31; student Command & Gen-Staff School 31-35, Army Industrial Coll. 36-37, Army War Coll. 37-38; advanced through grades to Brig.-Gen. 42, Major-Gen. 42, Lieut.-Gen. 45, Gen. 48; Instructor Army War Coll. 38-40; Asst. Sec. War Dept. Gen. Staff 40-41; Chief of Staff, VII Army Corps 41, Hawaiian Dept. 41-42; Commdr. 25th Div. 42-44, VII Corps 44-45; Deputy Commdg.-Gen. and Chief of Staff Army Ground Forces 45; Chief of Public Information War Dept. 45-47; Deputy Chief of Staff, then Vice-Chief of Staff, U.S. Army 47-49, Chief of Staff Aug. 49-53; U.S. Representative to Military Cttee. and Standing Group, N.A.T.O. 53-56; spec. representative of U.S. in Viet Nam with rank of Ambassador 54-55; retd. from active service 56; Dir. and Vice-Chair. of the President's Cttee. for Hungarian Refugee Relief 56-57; elected to Bd. of Dirs., Chas. Pfizer & Co. Inc., New York City; Vice-Chair. of the Bd., Pfizer International Inc., N.Y. City 57-; Chair. Board of Dirs., Foreign Student Service Council of Greater Washington 57-58, Hon. Chair. 58-; Board of Trustees of Inst. of Int. Education Inc., New York 57-65; mem. USO Corpn. 59-60, USO Nat. Council 60-; Chair. Greater Washington Council of Organisations Serving Int. Visitors 62-64.
1700 Pennsylvania Avenue, N.W., Washington 5, D.C., U.S.A.

Collins, Norman Richard; British writer; b. 3 Oct. 1907; ed. William Ellis School, Hampstead.
With Oxford Univ. Press 26-29; Asst. Literary Editor *News Chronicle* 29-33; Deputy Chair. Victor Gollancz 34-41; Empire Talks Man., B.B.C. 41-44, Dir.-Gen. Overseas Service 44-46, Head of Light Programme 46-47, Controller of Television 47-50; Chair. High Definition Films Ltd., Hyde Park Films and Watergate Productions Ltd.; Gov. British Film Inst. 49-51; Pres. Radio Industries Club 50; Dep. Chair. Assoc. Television Ltd.; Dir. Orchestral Concerts Soc.; Councillor English Stage Co.; Gov. Sadler's Wells, Atlantic Inst.; Pres. Lifeline, and Nat. Appeals Cttee. of Nat. Playing Fields Asscn.
Publs. *The Facts of Fiction* 32, *Penang Appointment* 34, *The Three Friends* 35, *Trinity Town* 36, *Flames Coming Out of the Top* 37, *Love in Our Time* 38, *I Shall Not Want* 40, *Anna* 42, *London Belongs to Me* 45, *Black Ivory* 48, *Children of the Archbishop* 51, *The Bat that Flits* 53, *The Captain's Lamp* (play) 38, *The Bond Street Story* 59, *The Governor's Lady* 68.
ATV House, 17 Great Cumberland Place, London, W.1, England.

Collins, Thomas LeRoy, LL.B.; American lawyer and politician; b. 3 Oct. 1909; ed. Eastman Business Coll., N.Y., and Cumberland Univ.
Practised law in Florida 31-54; mem. U.S. House of Representatives 38-50; Senator of Florida 40-54; Gov. of Florida 55-60; Pres. Nat. Asscn. of Broadcasters 61-64; Perm. Chair. Democratic Nat. Convention 60; Dir. Community Relations Service, U.S. Dept. of Commerce 64-65; Under Sec. of State for Commerce 65-66.
Fowler, White, Collins, Gillen, Humkey and Trenham, P.O.B. 1438, Tampa, Florida, U.S.A.

Colombani, Ignace Jean Aristide; French overseas administrator; b. 08; ed. Ecole Pascal-Paoli, Morosaglia, Bastia Lycée and Ecole Nat. de la France d'Outre-Mer.

Admin., French West Africa 33-49; Gov. Niger 49-50, Oubangui-Chari (now Central African Republic) 50-51, Chad 51-56; Officier de la Légion d'Honneur, Commandeur de l'Etoile Noire, Chevalier du Mérite Agricole, Croix du Mérite de 1ère Classe de l'Ordre Souverain de Malte; Pres. "Lingua Corsa".

15 rue César Campinchi, Bastia, Corsica.

Colombo, Emilio; Italian politician; b. 11 April 1920; ed. Rome Univ.

Took active part in Catholic youth organisations; former Vice-Pres. Italian Catholic Youth Asscn.; Deputy, Constituent Assembly 46-48, Parl. 48-; Under-Sec. of Agriculture 48-51, of Public Works 53-55; Minister of Agriculture 55-58, of Foreign Trade 58-59, of Industry and Commerce 59-60, March-Apr. 60, July 60-63, of the Treasury 63-; Pres. Nat. Cttee. for Nuclear Research 61; mem. Cen. Cttee. Christian Dem. Party 52 and 53.

Palazzo Montecitorio, Rome, Italy.

Colombo, H.E. Cardinal Giovanni; Italian ecclesiastic; b. 6 Dec. 1902.

Ordained priest 26; consecrated Titular Bishop of Philippopolis in Arabia 60; Archbishop of Milan 63-; mem. Cttee. of the Ecumenical Council on Catholic Seminaries and Educ.; created Cardinal 65.

Archbishop's Palace, Piazza Fontana 2, Milan, Italy.

Colombo, Ricardo M.; Argentine lawyer and diplomatist; b. 14 Jan. 1922; ed. Nat. Coll. of San Juan "Monseñor Pablo Cabrera" and Nat. Univ. of Cordoba.

Provincial Deputy 50-57; mem. Nat. Assembly 57; fmr. Sec.-Gen. of Exec. Board of Unión Cívica Radical del Pueblo; Rep. of Argentina to Org. of American States 64-66.

Mitre 1369, San Juan, Argentina.

Colonna di Paliano, Don Guido; Italian diplomatist; b. 16 April 1908; ed. Università degli Studi, Naples.

Foreign Service 33-, served New York, Toronto, Cairo, Stockholm, London, OEEC, Paris; Dep. Dir. of Political Affairs, Ministry of Foreign Affairs 56-58; Ambassador to Norway 58-62; Dep. Sec.-Gen. North Atlantic Treaty Org. (NATO) 62-64; mem. Comm. of European Economic Community, Brussels 64-67; mem. Combined Comm. of EEC, ECSC and Euratom 67-.

Commission of EEC, Brussels, Belgium.

Colotka, Peter, LL.D., C.SC.; Czechoslovak lawyer and politician; b. 10 Jan. 1925; ed. Comenius Univ., Bratislava.

Assistant Lecturer, Faculty of Law, Comenius Univ., Bratislava 50-56, Asst. Prof. 56-64, Prof. 64-, Vice-Dean 56-57, Dean 57-58, Pro-Rector of Univ. 58-61; Commr. for Justice, Slovak Nat. Council 63-; Deputy Premier 68-; Deputy to Slovak Nat. Council 63-; mem. Presidium Slovak Nat. Council 63-; mem. Central Cttee. of C.P. of Czechoslovakia and Central Cttee. of C.P. of Slovakia 66-; mem. Int. Court of Arbitration, The Hague 62-; Distinction for Merit in Construction 65.

Publs. *Personal Property* 56, *Our Socialist Constitution* 61; scientific studies and articles in collaboration with Dr. Matoušek.

Presidium of the Government, Prague 1, nábř. kpt. Jaroše 4, Czechoslovakia.

Colquhoun, (Cecil) Brian (Hugh), B.SC. (ENG.), M.I.C.E., M.I.STRUCT.E., M.CONS.E., M.A.S.C.E., M.E.I.C.; M.SOC.C.E. (France); British consulting engineer; b. 13 Nov. 1902; ed. King's Coll., London Univ.

Served with Dr. C. H. Lobban on design and construction of various buildings in London 25-26; with Eagle Oil Company Ltd. in Mexico 26-30; apptd. Resident Engineer on construction of Mersey Tunnel 30; later became Resident Engineer-in-Charge; Engineer-in-Chief Royal Ordnance Factories at Chorley, Risley and Kirkby 36-39, also Adviser on Maas (Rotterdam) Tunnel, Tamar (Plymouth) Tunnel, and Rossall sea wall 35-39; Rehabilitation of war-production factories in main industrial centres 40; with Ministry of Aircraft Production as Dir.-Gen. of Aircraft Production Factories 41-44; seconded as Engineering Adviser to Int. Bank for Reconstruction and Devt., Washington 54-56; Senior Partner, Brian Colquhoun and Partners, Consulting Engineers.

3 Fountain House, Park Lane, London, W.1; Home: North Munstead, Godalming, Surrey, England.

Colum, Padraic; Irish poet and dramatist; b. 8 Dec. 1881.

On invitation of Legislature visited Hawaii 23 to write stories for Hawaiian children based on native folklore and mythology; Pres. Poetry Society of America 38-39; mem. Acad. of Irish Letters, American Inst. Arts and Letters.

Publs. include poems and plays: *Castle Conquer, The Big Tree of Bunlahy, The Road Round Ireland, The King of Ireland's Son, The Legend of St. Columba, The Story of Lowry Maen, Flower Pieces, Where the Winds Never Blew and the Cocks Never Crew* 40, *The Frenzied Prince* 43, *Anthology of Irish Verse* 48, *Ten Poems* 58, *Our Friend James Joyce* (with Mary Colum) 59, *Arthur Griffith* 60, *The Poets Circuit* 60, *The Flying Swans* (novel); many children's books.

415 Central Park West, New York 25, N.Y., U.S.A.; and 11 Edenvale Road, Ranelagh, Dublin, Ireland.

Colwell, Ernest Cadman, PH.B., B.D., PH.D.; American educationalist; b. 19 Jan. 1901; ed. Emory Univ., Candler School of Theology, Univ. of Chicago.

Instructor Emory Univ. 24-28; Univ. of Chicago since 30, Prof. 30-, Dean of Divinity School 39-45, Dean of Faculties 43-45, Vice-Pres. 44-45, Pres. 45-51; Dean of Faculties, Emory Univ. 51-57, and Vice-Pres. 54-57; Pres. S. Calif. School of Theology, Claremont, Calif. 57-68; Dist. Prof. of New Testament, Claremont Graduate School, and Chair. Research Council, Inst. for Antiquity and Christianity 68-; Hon. Litt.D. (Emory Univ.) 44; Hon. S.T.D. (Harvard Univ.) 47; Hon. LL.D. (Colby Coll.) 47; Hon. S.T.D. (Ripon Coll.) 62; Hon. L.H.D. (Claremont Grad. School) 66.

Publs. *The Greek of the Fourth Gospel* 31, *Studies in The Lectionary Text of The Greek New Testament, Prolegomena to The Study of the Lectionary Text of The Gospels* (with Donald W. Riddle) 33, *A Greek Papyrus Reader* (with E. J. Goodspeed) 35, *John Defends the Gospel* 36, *The Study of the Bible* 37, 64, *The Four Gospels of Karahissar*, Vol. I, 36, *Elizabeth Day McCormick Apocalypse*, Vol. II 39, *A Hellenistic Greek Reader* (with J. R. Mantey) 39, *An Approach to the Teaching of Jesus* 47, *What Is The Best New Testament* 52, *The Gospel of the Spirit* (with E. Titus) 53, *Jesus and the Gospel* 63, *A Beginner's Reader-Grammar for New Testament Greek* (with Ernest W. Tune) 65.

Institute for Antiquity and Christianity, Claremont Graduate School, 880 N. College Avenue, Claremont, Calif. 91711; Home: 613 Marion Court, DeLand, Fla. 32720, U.S.A.

Comas Camps, Juan, D.SC.; Mexican anthropologist; b. 22 Jan. 1900; ed. Madrid and Univ. of Geneva.

Inspector of Primary Education Spain 21-39; Adviser, Council of Cultural Relations, Ministry of Foreign Affairs, Madrid 33-39; Sec.-Gen. Ministry of Public Instruction 38; Sec. *Revista de Pedagogía* Madrid 33-36; Anthropologist Nat. Anthropological Inst. of Mexico 40-43; Prof. Nat. School of Anthropology of Mexico 41-59; Sec. Inter-American Indian Inst. 42-55; Research Prof. Univ. of Mexico 55-, Head Dept. of Anthropology 63-; Dir. *Boletín Bibliográfico de Antropología Americana* 45-52; Editor-in-Chief *América Indígena* and *Boletín Indigenista* 42-55; Editor *Anales de Antropología* 63-.

Publs. *El sistema de Winnetka en la práctica* 30, *Las prácticas de las pruebas mentales y de instrucción* 34, *Manual del Inspector de primera enseñanza* 35, *Aportaciones al estudio de la prehistoria de Menorca* 36, *Como se comprueba el trabajo escolar* 40, *Existe una raza judía?* 41, *Contribucion à l'étude du Metopisme* 42, *La Antropología física en México y Centroamérica* 43, *La discriminación racial en América* 44, *Osteometria Olmeca* 44, *Bosquejo histórico de la Antropología en México* 50, *Les Mythes Raciaux* 51, *Cultural Anthropology and Fundamental Education in Latin America* 52, *Ensayos sobre Indigenismo* 53, *Bibliografía Selectiva de las Culturas Indígenas de América* 53, *Los Congresos Internacionales de Americanistas* 54, *Influencia indígena en la Medicina hipocrática en la Nueva España del siglo XVI* 54, *Ensayo sobre "raza" y Economía* 55, *Las lenguas vernáculas y el bilinguismo en Educación* 56, *Contribuciones indígenas Precolombinas a la Cultura Universal* 56, *Historia y Bibliografía de los Congresos Internacionales de Ciencias Antropológicas* 56, *Manual de Antropología Física* 57, *Buffon, precursor de la Antropología* 58, *La educación ante la discriminación racial* 58, *La deformación cefálica intencional en la región del Ucayali, Perú* 58, *L'Anthropologie américaine et le diffusionisme de P. Laviosa Zambotti* 58, *Manual of Physical Anthropology* (Eng. ed.) 60, *Pigmeos en América* 60, *La Antropología Física en México: 1943-59* 60, *La heterogeneidad cultural y el planeamiento integral de la educación en América Latina* 60, *Datos para la historia de la deformación craneal en México* 60, *Las culturas agrícolas de América y sus relaciones con el Viejo Mundo* 61, *Race Relations—in Latin America* 61, *Scientific Racism Again?* 61, *El origen del hombre americano y la Antropología física* 61, *Primeras Instrucciones para la investigación antropológica: 1862* 62, *Combatir el racismo es defender la paz* 64, *Trayectoria de la Antropología social en México* 64, *Una decada de Congresos Internacionales de Americanistas: 1952-62* 64, *El antigeno Diego entre los amerindios* 65, *Cranes mexicaines scaphocephals* 65, *Somatometría de los indios Triques, México* 65, *Manual de Antropología Física* 2nd edn. 66, *Características físicas de la familia linguistica Maya* 66, *Unidad y variedad de la especie humane* 67, *Medicina y antropologia* 68, *Dos microcefalos aztecas* 68.

Alberto Zamora 69, Coyoacán, D.F., Mexico.

Comay, Michael, B.A., LL.B.; Israeli diplomatist; b. 8 Oct. 1908; ed. Cape Town Univ., South Africa. Major, South African Army 40-45; Special Rep. South African Zionist Fed., attached to Political Dept. Jewish Agency, Jerusalem 46-48; mem. Israel del. to UN 47-48; Dir. British Commonwealth Div., Israel Foreign Ministry 48-51, Asst. Dir.-Gen. Ministry for Foreign Affairs 57-59; Perm. Rep. to UN 59-67; Political Adviser to Foreign Minister 67-.
Ministry of Foreign Affairs, Jerusalem, Israel.

Comfort, Alexander, M.A., M.B., D.SC., M.R.C.S., L.R.C.P., D.C.H.; British medical biologist and writer; b. 10 Feb. 1920; ed. Highgate School, Trinity Coll., Cambridge, and The London Hospital.
Medical and hospital practice 44-48; Lecturer in Physiology The London Hospital 48-51; Nuffield Research Asst. Univ. Coll., London 51-54, Nuffield Research Fellow in Biology of Senescence 54-63; Dir. Medical Research Council Research Group in Ageing, Univ. Coll., London 63-.
Publs. Novels: *No Such Liberty* 41, *The Almond Tree* 43, *The Powerhouse* 45, *On This Side of Nothing* 48, *A Giant's Strength* 52, *Come out to Play* 61; Verse: *A Wreath for the Living* 42, *Elegies* 44, *The Signal to Engage* 46, *And All but he Departed* 52, *Haste to the Wedding* 62; stories: *Letters from an Outpost* 47; Essays: *Art and Social Responsibility* 46, *The Novel and Our Time* 48,

The Pattern of the Future 51, *Darwin and the Naked Lady* 61; Other: *Barbarism and Sexual Freedom* 48, *Sexual Behaviour in Society* 49, *First-Year Physiological Technique* 49, *Authority and Delinquency in the Modern State* 50, *The Biology of Senescence* 56, *Sex in Society* 63, *Ageing* 64, *The Koka Shastra* (translation) 64, *The Process of Ageing* 64, *Nature and Human Nature* (essays) 66, *The Anxiety Makers* 67.
44 The Avenue, Loughton, Essex, England.

Comfort, Harold Wesley; American businessman; b. 7 Nov. 1896; ed. Yale and Williams Coll.
Joined Reid Ice Cream Co. 19-; with the Borden Co. since 28 as Vice-Pres. Reid Ice Cream, Pres. 31-33, Vice-Pres. of Pioneer Ice Cream Div., Borden Co. 33-35, Chair. Metropolitan Fluid Milk Div. 37-, Dir. 38-, Exec. Vice-Pres. 44-56, Pres. Borden Co. 56-67; Dir. Cayuga Rock Salt Co. (Myers, N.Y.); Dir. Chemical Bank New York Trust Co.; Trustee, other orgs.
Home: Lake Avenue, Greenwich, Conn., U.S.A.

Comisso, Giovanni, DR. IN LEGGE; Italian journalist, author and painter; b. 3 Oct. 1895; ed. Univ. of Siena. Corresp. for *Corriere della Sera* in Japan, China and Russia 30; Corresp. in North Africa for *Gazzetta del Popolo* and *La Stampa* 53-56; Corresp. of *Il Mondo*.
Publs. *Gente di Mare* (Bagutta Prize 28), *Giorni di Guerra, Agenti Segreti Veneziani nel 700, La Favorita, Amori d'Oriente, La mia casa di campagna, Capricci Italiani* (Viareggio Prize 52); *Un gatto attraversa la strada* (Strega Prize 55), *Satire italiane, La donna del Lago, Le relazioni degli ambasciatori veneti,* also paintings at Galleria Obelisco, Rome.
S.M. del Rovere 38, Treviso, Italy.

Commager, Henry Steele, PH.B., M.A., PH.D., M.A. (Cantab.), M.A. (Oxon.); American historian; b. 25 Oct. 1902; ed. Chicago and Copenhagen Univ.
Prof. New York Univ. 25-39, Columbia 39-, Cambridge 42-43; Pitt Prof. American History, Cambridge Univ. 47-48; Harmsworth Prof. of American History, Oxford Univ. 52-53; Gottesman Prof. Uppsala 53; Prof. History, Amherst Coll. 56-; Hon. Fellow, Peterhouse, Cambridge; Visiting Prof. Univ. of Copenhagen 56; Commonwealth Lecturer, Univ. of London 65; consultant U.S. War Dept. Historical Branch, 19-, Office War Information, State Dept., U.S. Army I. & E. Div.; Trustee American Scandinavian Foundation; mem. U.S. War Dept. Comm. on History of War, UNESCO Nat. Comm., Exec. Cttee., U.S. Del. to UNESCO, American Acad. of Arts and Letters; Hon. LL.D. Brandeis Univ. and Washington Coll., Michigan State, Franklin and Marshall Coll., Hon. D.H.L. Hartford Univ. and Marietta Coll., etc., Hon. D.E.D. Rhode Island; Hon. D.Litt. Ohio Wesleyan, Monmouth, Cambridge, Carleton, Hon. D.C.L. Alfred Univ., Univ. of Puget Sound; Knight Order of Dannebrog.
Publs. *The American Republic* (2 vols., with S. E. Morison) 30, *Documents of American History* 34, *Theodore Parker* 36, *America: Story of a Free People* (with A. Nevins) 42, *Majority Rule and Minority Rights* 43, *History of the Second World War* 45, *The American Mind* 50, *The Great Declaration* 59, *The Great Proclamation* 60, *The Great Constitution* 61, *The Story of Human Rights* 61, *Living Ideas in America* 51, *America's Robert E. Lee* 51, *The Blue and the Gray* (2 vols.) 51, *Freedom, Loyalty and Dissent* 54, *Joseph Story* 54, *The Spirit of Seventy-Six* (with R. B. Morris), *Europe and America* (with G. Bruun), *Writings of Theodore Parker* 61, *The Era of Reform* 61, *Studies in Immigration* 61, *Crusaders for Freedom* 61, Editor *Tocqueville's Democracy in America* 47, *America in Perspective* 48, *St. Nicholas Anthology* 48, *The Rise of the American Nation* (50 vols. in progress), *Documents of American History* 50, *Chester Bowles: An American Purpose* 61, *Lester Ward and the Welfare State, Defeat of the Confederacy, The Nature and Study of History* 65, *Freedom*

and Order 66, *The Struggle for Racial Equality* 67, *Search for a Usable Past* 67, *Was America a Mistake* (with E. Giordanetti) 67, *Our Schools Have Kept Us Free* 67.

405 S. Pleasant Street, Amherst, Mass., U.S.A.; and Linton, Cambridgeshire, England.

Commins, Thomas Vincent; Irish diplomatist; b. 3 Oct. 1913; ed. Rockwell Coll., and Univ. Coll., Dublin.

Irish Govt. Service 33-46; Diplomatic Service 46-; Commercial Sec., Washington, D.C. 46-48; Counsellor, Dept. of External Affairs 48-54; Counsellor, Paris 54-55; Chargé d'Affaires *en titre*, Lisbon 55-59; Minister to Argentina 59-60; Ambassador to Italy 60-62, to Holy See 62-66, to France 66-, also Perm. Rep. of Ireland to OECD; Knight Grand Cross Order of Pius IX.

Embassy of Ireland, 4 rue Rudé, Paris 16e, France.

Compton, Sir Edmund Gerald, K.C.B., K.B.E., M.A.; British Ombudsman; b. 30 June 1906; ed. Rugby School and New Coll., Oxford Univ.

Joined Civil Service 29; attached to Colonial Office 30; joined Treasury 31; Private Sec. to Financial Sec. to Treasury 34-36; Private Sec. to Minister of Aircraft Production 40; with Ministry of Supply 41; Asst. Sec., Treasury 42-47, Under Sec. 47-49, Third Sec. 49-58; Comptroller and Auditor Gen. 58-66, Parl. Commr. for Administration (Ombudsman) 67-.

53 Evelyn Gardens, London, S.W.7, England.

Telephone: 01-370-3220.

Compton-Burnett, Dame Ivy, D.B.E.; British novelist. James Tait Black Memorial Prize 56; Hon. D.Litt. (Leeds) 60.

Publs. *Pastors and Masters, Brothers and Sisters, Men and Wives, More Women than Men, A House and its Head, Daughters and Sons, A Family and a Fortune, Parents and Children, Elders and Betters, Manservant and Maidservant, Two Worlds and their Ways, Darkness and Day, The Present and the Past, Mother and Son, A Father and his Fate, A Heritage and its History, The Mighty and their Fall, A God and His Gifts.*

5 Braemar Mansions, Cornwall Gardens, London, S.W.7.

Conant, James Bryant, A.B., PH.D., L.H.D., LITT.D., S.D., LL.D., D.C.L.; American educationist; b. 26 March 1893; ed. Harvard Univ.

Chemistry Dept. Harvard Univ. 16-33, Prof. of Organic Chemistry 29-33, Pres. Harvard Univ. 33-53, Emeritus Pres. 53-; U.S. High Commr. in Germany 53-55; Ambassador to Fed. Republic of Germany 55-57; Dir. Study of the American High School 57-61; Study of the Educ. of American Teachers 63-, and of American Educ.; Lieut. Sanitary Corps, U.S. Army 17, Maj. Chemical Warfare Service 18; mem. Nat. Acad. of Sciences, Royal Societies London and Edinburgh (foreign mem.), Royal Inst. of Chemistry and Chemical Society of England, Educational Policies Commission 41-46 and 47-; Chair. National Defense Research Cttee. and Deputy Dir. of Office of Scientific Research and Development 41-46, Steering Cttee. for Manhattan District 42-45, Gen. Advisory Cttee. of Atomic Energy Commission 47-52; Commdr. Légion d'Honneur; C.B.E., Medal for Merit with Oak Leaf Clusters, Freedom House Award 53; Hon. Sc.D. (Cambridge, London, Lyon Univs. and Free University of Berlin and American universities); LL.D. (Princeton, Yale, California, Pennsylvania, Bristol, Queens, Toronto, Michigan, Yeshiva, Birmingham, Harvard, Edinburgh, Leeds Univs. and other American universities and colleges); L.H.D. (Boston); Litt.D. (Hamilton Coll.); Honoris causa (Melbourne, Canterbury, U. Coll. New Zealand); F.E.I.S. (Educ. Inst. Scotland); admitted to U. of Adelaide *ad eundem gradum*; Dr. (U. of Algiers).

Publs. *Our Fighting Faith* 43, *On Understanding Science* 47, *Education in a Divided World* 48, *Science and Commonsense* 51, *Modern Science and Modern Man* 52, *Education and Liberty* 53, *The Citadel of Learning* 56, *Germany and Freedom* 58, *The American High School Today* 59, *The Child, The Parent, and the State* 59, *Education in the Junior High School Years* 60, *Slums and Suburbs* 61, *Thomas Jefferson and the Development of American Public Education* 62, *The Education of American Teachers* 63, *Two Modes of Thought* 64, *Shaping Educational Policy* 64, *The Comprehensive High School* 67; Editor Vols. 2 and 9 *Harvard Case Histories in Experimental Science;* chemistry textbooks.

Office: c/o T.I.A.A., 730 Third Avenue, New York, N.Y.; Home: 200 East 66th Street, New York, N.Y., U.S.A.

Conant, Kenneth John, A.B., M.ARCH., PH.D., LITT.D. (h.c.); American archaeologist; b. 28 June 1894; ed. Harvard Univ.

Apptd. to Harvard Univ. staff 20, Asst. Prof. 25, Prof. of Architecture 36-55, Prof. Emeritus 56-; Harvard Exchange Prof. Sorbonne 35-36 and 50, Nat. Univ. of Mexico 42; Guggenheim Fellowships 27-29 (for expeditions to Cluny) and 55; excavations at Cluny 28-50; expeds. to cathedrals of Santiago de Compostela 20, 24 and 50, expeditions to Middle America 26, Kiev 35 and 36, to Abbey of Montecassino 35, Holy Sepulchre 38, 55, St. Sophia, Constantinople 35 and 38; hon. mem. Faculty of Architecture, Univ. of Buenos Aires, Acad. de Mâcon, France, American Inst. of Architects; Hon. F.S.A. London Royal Soc. of Arts, Benjamin Franklin Fellow 60; corresp. Fellow of Société des Antiquaires de France; non-resident mem. Acad. de Dijon; Fellow American Philosophical Soc., Mediaeval Acad. of America; Hon. Pres. Archaeological Inst. of America, Soc. of Architectural Historians; Hon. Corresp. Compagnie des Architectes en Chef des Monuments Historiques; Medallist of the Soc. of Architectural Historians, and of the Signet 60; Officier de la Légion d'Honneur, and other decorations; Dr. (h.c.) Lawrence Univ., Univs. of Dijon (France) and Illinois.

Publs. *The Early Architectural History of the Cathedral of Santiago de Compostela* 26, *Brief Commentary on Early Mediaeval Church Architecture* 42, *Benedictine Contributions to Church Architecture* 49, *Arquitectura Moderna en los Estados Unidos* 49, *Carolingian and Romanesque Architecture* 59, *Cluny-Les Eglises et la Maison du Chef d'Ordre* 68, etc.

274 Grove Street, Wellesley, Mass. 02181, U.S.A.

Telephone: 617-235-4502.

Concha, H.E. Cardinal Luis; Colombian ecclesiastic b. 7 Nov. 1891; ed. Bogotá Seminary and Biblical Inst. Rome.

Editor *El Catolicismo* 18-19; fmr. Archbishop of Manizales; Archbishop of Bogotá and Primate of Colombia 59-; created Cardinal 61.

Palacio Arzobispal, Bogotá, Colombia.

Conchon, Georges; French writer and journalist; b. 9 May 1925; ed. Lycée Henri IV, Paris, and Univ. de Paris à la Sorbonne.

Secretary of Debates, Assemblée de l'Union française 47-52, Divisional Head 52-58; Sec.-Gen. Parl. Central African Repub. 59; Sec. of Debates at the Senate 60-; Prix des Libraires de France 60, Prix Goncourt 64.

Publs. *Les Grandes Lessives* 53, *Les Honneurs de la Guerre* 55, *La Corrida de la Victoire* 59, *L'Etat Sauvage* 64, *Pourquoi pas Vamos* (play) 65, *L'Apprenti gaucher* 67.

159 rue de Rome, Paris 17e, France.

Telephone: 924-99-50.

Condliffe, John Bell, M.A., D.SC., LL.D., LITT.D.; American economist; b. 23 Dec. 1891; ed. Canterbury Coll. of New Zealand, Gonville and Caius Coll., Cambridge.

Prof. of Economics Canterbury Coll. 20-26; Research Sec. Inst. of Pacific Relations, Hawaii 27-31; Visiting Prof. of Economics Univ. of Michigan 30-31; mem. Economic Intelligence Service L.N. 31-37; Prof. of

Commerce London Univ. 37-39; Prof. of Economics Univ. of California 40-58; Adviser Indian Nat. Council of Applied Economic Research 59-60; Sen. Economist Stanford Research Inst. 61-; Associate Dir. Div. Economics and History, Carnegie Endowment for Int. Peace 43-47; mem. Royal Economic Society, American Economic Asscn., Economic Society of Australia and N.Z.; Fellow A.A.A.S. 53; Howland Memorial Prize Yale Univ. 39; Wendell Wilkie Prize 50; Gold Cross, Royal Order of Phoenix (Greece).
Publs. *Nrw Zealand in the Making* 30 (revised 58), *Problems of the Pacific* 27, 29, *China Today—Economic* 32, *World Economic Survey* 31-37, *Reconstruction of World Trade* 40, *Agenda for a Post-War World* 42, *Commerce of Nations* 50, *The Welfare State in New Zealand* 59, *The Development of Australia* 63, *Foresight and Enterprise* 65.
257 Stanford Avenue, Berkeley 94708, Calif., U.S.A.

Condon, Edward U., A.B., PH.D.; American physicist; b. 2 March 1902; ed. Univ. of California.
International Education Board Fellow at Göttingen and Munich 26-27; Lecturer in Physics Columbia Univ. 27-28; Asst. Prof. of Physics Princeton Univ. 28-29; Prof. of Theoretical Physics Univ. of Minnesota 29-30; Assoc. Prof. of Physics Princeton Univ. 30-37; Assoc. Dir. of Research Westinghouse Electric Corporation 37-45; Adviser, U.S. Senate Cttee on Atomic Energy 45-46; Dir. (U.S.) National Bureau of Standards 45-51; Dir. of Research, Corning Glass Works 51-54; Prof. of Physics, Washington Univ., St. Louis, Mo. 56-63; Prof. of Physics, Univ. of Colorado 63-; Chair. Editorial Boards Int. Science and Technology 61-; Pres. American Asscn. for the Advancement of Science 53, American Physical Soc. 46, American Asscn. of Physics Teachers 64; D.Sc. (Hon.) 50.
Publs. *Quantum Mechanics* (with P. M. Morse) 29, *The Theory of Atomic Spectra* (with G. H. Shortley) 35, *Handbook of Physics* (joint author) 58, Editor *Reviews of Modern Physics* 57-.
761 Cascade Avenue, Boulder, Colo. 80302, U.S.A.

Cone, Fairfax Mastick; American business executive; b. 21 Feb. 1903; ed. Univ. of California.
San Francisco Examiner 26-29; copywriter and account exec. Lord and Thomas advertising agency 29-38, Vice-Pres. and Man. 38-40, Vice-Pres. New York 41, Chicago 42; organizer of Foote, Cone & Belding 42, Chair., Exec. Cttee. 42-48, Chair. of Board 48-51, Pres. 51-57, Chair. Exec. Cttee. 57-67, Dir. 67-.
401 North Michigan Avenue, Chicago, Ill. 60611, U.S.A.

Confalonieri, H.E. Cardinal Carlo; Vatican ecclesiastic; b. 25 July 1893.
Ordained priest 16; fmr. Private Sec. to Pope Pius XI; Archbishop of Aquila 41-50; Titular Archbishop of Nicopolis al Nesto and Sec. Sacred Congregation of Seminaries and Universities 50-58; created Cardinal 58; Archpriest of Liberian Patriarchal Basilica; Prefect Sacred Consistorial Congregation 61; mem. Sacred Congregations for the Doctrine of Faith, Oriental Church, Council, De Propaganda Fide, Rites, Ceremonies, Extraordinary Ecclesiastical Affairs, Seminaries and Universities.
Via Rusticucci 13, Rome, Italy.

Connally, Ben C.; American judge; b. 28 Dec. 1909; ed. Univ. of Texas and Harvard Univ.
Admitted to Texas Bar 33; private legal practice 34-49; U.S. District Judge, Southern District, Texas 49-, now Chief Judge; U.S. Army 42-45.
Post Office Building, Houston, Texas, U.S.A.

Connally, John Bowden, Jr., LL.B.; American lawyer and politician; b. 28 Feb. 1917; ed. Univ. of Texas.
Served in U.S. Navy 41-46; fmr. executive in oil, oilfield services, radio and television, carbon, ranches,

insurance, New York Central Railroad; Sec. of the Navy Jan.-Nov. 61; Gov. of Texas 63-; Democrat.
State Capitol, Austin, Texas, U.S.A.

Connell, James Charles; American judge; b. 20 Sept. 1897; ed. Cleveland-Marshall Law School and John Carrol Univ., Cleveland.
Admitted to Ohio Bar 18; Asst. Police Prosecutor, City of Cleveland 22-23; Asst. County Prosecutor, Cuyahoga County, Cleveland 23-27, Chief Asst. County Prosecutor 28; private legal practice 28-41; Judge, Court of Common Pleas, Cuyahoga County 41-54; Judge, U.S. District Court, Cleveland 54-, now Chief Judge.
Federal Building, Cleveland, Ohio, U.S.A.

Connelly, Marc; American dramatist; b. 13 Dec. 1890; ed. Trinity Hall, Washington.
Fmr. Pres. Authors' League of America, Nat. Inst. of Arts and Letters; fmr. Prof. of Playwriting, Yale Univ.; Pulitzer Prize, O. Henry award 30; Hon. Litt.D. Bowdoin.
Publs. *The Green Pastures, The Wisdom Tooth, A Souvenir from Qam* 65; co-author *Beggar on Horseback, Dulcy, Merton of the Movies, To the Ladies, The Farmer Takes a Wife, Hunter's Moon* 58 (plays); *Helen of Troy N.Y.* (musical comedy).
25 Central Park West, New York City; and Players' Club, New York City, N.Y., U.S.A.

Connolly, Cyril Vernon; British writer; b. 10 Sept. 1903; ed. Eton and Balliol Coll., Oxford.
Contrib. to *New Statesman* 27-, *Life and Letters, Sunday Times* 51-, *Architectural Review*; founded *Horizon* 39, Editor 39-50; Literary Editor *The Observer* 42-43; Chevalier Légion d'Honneur.
Publs. *The Rock Pool* 35, *Enemies of Promise* 38, *The Unquiet Grave* 44, *The Condemned Playground* 45, *The Missing Diplomats* 53, *Ideas and Places* 53, *Les Pavillons* (with Jerome Zerbe) 62, *Previous Convictions* 63, *The Modern Movement 1880-1920* 66; Editor *The Golden Horizon* 53, *Great English Short Novels* 53.
Bushey Lodge, Firle, Lewes, Sussex, England.

Connolly, Hon. John Joseph, P.C., O.B.E., Q.C., PH.D., LL.D.; Canadian lawyer and politician; b. 06; ed. Ottawa Separate Schools, Univ. of Ottawa, Queen's Univ., Kingston, Ontario, Univ. of Notre Dame, South Bend, Indiana, U.S.A., and Univ. of Montreal.
Member of Bar of Province of Ontario and Province of Quebec; Exec. Asst. to Minister of Nat. Defence for Naval Services 41-45; fmr. partner Clark, Macdonald, Connolly, Affleck, Brocklesby, Gorman and McLaughlin; Pres. Nat. Liberal Fed. 61-64; Senator from Ontario 53-; Minister without Portfolio and Leader of Govt. in Senate 64-65; Liberal.
The Senate, Ottawa, Ontario, Canada.

Connor, John Thomas, LL.B., A.B.; American business executive and government official; b. 3 Nov. 1914; ed. Holy Rosary High School, Syracuse, N.Y., Holy Rosary Grammar School, Harvard Law School and Syracuse Univ.
Formerly assoc. with law firm Cravath, de Gersdorff, Swaine and Wood; General Counsel, Office of Scientific Research and Development 42-44; U.S. Marine Corps 44-45; Counsel, Office of Naval Research, later Special Asst. to U.S. Sec. of Navy 45-47; General Attorney, Merck & Co. (pharmaceuticals) 47, Pres. 55-65; U.S. Sec. of Commerce 65-66; Pres. Allied Chemical Corpn. 67-; Hon. D.Sc. (Philadelphia Coll. of Pharmacy and Science, Hahnemann Medical Coll.); Hon. LL.D. (Rutgers).
2429 Kalorama Road, N.W., Washington D.C., U.S.A.

Connor, Ralph, B.S., PH.D.; American chemist; b. 12 July 1907; ed. Univs. of Illinois and Wisconsin.
Assistant Professor, Assoc. Professor and Prof. of Chemistry, Univ. of Pennsylvania 35-41; Technical Aide, Section Chief, and Chief of Div. 8, Nat. Defense

Research Cttee. of Office of Scientific Research and Development 41-45; Assoc. Dir. of Research, Rohm & Haas Co. 45-48, Vice-Pres. (Research) and Dir. 48-. Chair. of Board 60-; mem. Board of Dirs. American Chemical Soc. 54-65, Chair. 56-58; Hon. D.Sc. (Philadelphia Coll. of Pharmacy and Science, Univ. of Pennsylvania, Polytechnic Inst. of Brooklyn), Hon. LL.D. (Lehigh Univ.); several medals.
234 N. Bent Road, Wyncote, Pa. 19095, U.S.A.

Conrad, Hermann, DR. JUR.; German university professor; b. 21 Oct. 1904; ed. Univ. of Cologne.
Dozent Cologne Univ. 36; Lecturer Univs. of Lausanne and Geneva 38-40; Prof. of Law, Univ. of Marburg/Lahn 42-48, Univ. of Bonn 48-; Dr. h.c., Dr. rer. pol. h.c.
Publs. *Liegenschaftsübereignung und Grundbucheintragung in Köln während des Mittelalters* 35, *Die Amtleutebücher der Kölnischen Sondergemeinden* (with Dr. Thea Buyken) 36, *Dantes Staatslehre im Spiegel der scholastischen Philosophie seiner Zeit* 46, *Geschichte der deutschen Wehrverfassung* 39, *Deutsche Rechtsgeschichte Frühzeit und Mittelalter* 54, 2nd edn. 62, *Grundprobleme einer Reform des Familienrechtes* 54, *Individuum und Gemeinschaft in der Privat-Rechtsordnung des 18. und beginnenden* 19. *Jahrhunderts* 56, *Das Gottesurteil in den Konstitutionen von Melfi, Friedrich II. von Hohenstaufen (1237) (Festschrift für Schmidt-Rimpler)* 57, *Freiherr von Stein als Staatsmann im Übergang vom Absolutismus zum Verfassungsstaat* 58, *Der Deutsche Juristentag 1860-1960, Festschr. z 100. Dt. Juristentag* 60; Ed. (with G. Kleinheyer) *C. G. Suarez, Vorträge über Recht und Staat* 60, *Rechtsstaatliche Bestrebungen im Absolutismus Preussens und Österreichs am Ende des 18. Jahrhdts.* 61, *Religionsbann, Toleranz und Parität am Ende des alten Reiches, Röm. Quartalschr.* (with Kleinheyer and others) 62, *Recht und Verfassung des Reiches in der Zeit Maria Theresia* 64, *Zu den geistigen Grundlagen der Strafrechtsreform Josephs II* 64, *Das Allgemeine Landrecht von 1794 als Grundgesetz des friderizianischen Staates* 65, *Deutsche Rechtsgeschichte Neuzeit bis 1806* 66.
Oberstrasse 31, 532 Bad Godesberg-Mehlem, German Federal Republic.
Telephone: Bad Godesberg 12141.

Conroy, Sir Diarmaid William, Kt., C.M.G., O.B.E., T.D., Q.C.; British jurist; b. 22 Dec. 1913; ed. Gray's Inn, London.
Practised at English Bar 35-39; served in army 39-46; Crown Counsel, N. Rhodesia 46-50, Legal Draftsman 50-52; Attorney-Gen. Gibraltar 52-55; Solicitor-Gen. and Dep. Speaker, Kenya 55-61; Chief Justice, N. Rhodesia 61-65; Pres. Industrial Tribunals (England and Wales) 65-.
39 Sun Hill, Cowes, Isle of Wight, England.

Consagra, Pietro; Italian sculptor; b. 4 Oct. 1920; ed. Acad. of Fine Arts, Palermo.
One-man shows: Rome 47, 49, 51, 59, 61; Milan 58, 61; Venice 48; Brussels 58; Paris 59; Zürich 61; São Paulo Bienal 55, 59; Venice Biennale 56, 60, New York 62, Buenos Aires 62, Boston 62; Works in following museums: Tate Gallery, London; Nat. Museum and Middleheim Park, Antwerp; Museums of Modern Art, São Paulo, Paris, Rome, New York, Buenos Aires, Caracas, Zagreb, Helsinki; Guggenheim Museum, New York; Art Inst., Chicago; Carnegie Inst., Pittsburgh; Inst. of Fine Arts, Minneapolis and Houston; Grand Prize for Sculpture, Venice Biennale 60.
Via Archimede 201, Rome, Italy.

Consolo, Federico; Italian international bank official; b. 18 March 1906; ed. in Milan and London, and Univs. of Cambridge and Rome.
With Montecatini S.p.A. and Pirelli S.p.A. 28-43; liaison between Italian Govt. and Allied Comm. and subsequently UNRRA, Rome 45-47; with Int. Bank for Reconstruction and Devt., rising to Asst. Dir., W.

Hemisphere Dept. 47-58; Dir.-Gen. Special Adviser to Comm., EURATOM, Brussels 58-64; Special Rep. for UN Orgs., Int. Bank for Reconstruction and Devt. 64-. IBRD, Washington, D.C. 20433, U.S.A.

Constable, W. G., M.A., F.S.A.; British art historian; b. 28 Oct. 1887; ed. St. John's Coll., Cambridge and Slade School.
Specialist in Italian and English art; Asst. Dir. Nat. Gallery 24-31; fmr. Prof. History of Art, Univ. of London and Dir. of the Courtauld Inst., Univ. of London; Slade Prof. of Fine Art, Cambridge Univ.; Curator of Paintings, Boston Museum of Fine Arts 38-58; Adviser to Nat. Gallery of Canada 58-60; Hon. D.C.L. (Durham), Hon. D.Litt. (Nottingham), and LL.D. (New Brunswick); Hon. Fellow, St. John's Coll., Cambridge.
Publs. *John Flaxman* 27, *16th and 17th Century Painting in England* 31, *Art History and Connoisseurship* 38, *Richard Wilson* 53, *The Painter's Workshop* 54, *Canaletto* 62, *Art Collecting in the United States* 63; contributor *Cambridge Medieval History*.
23 Craigie Street, Cambridge, Mass., U.S.A.

Constantine, King of the Hellenes; b. 2 June 1940; ed. Anavryta School and Law School, Athens Univ.
Military Training 56-58; visited United States 58, 59; succeeded to throne March 64; married Princess Anne-Marie of Denmark Sept. 64; daughter, Princess Alexia b. 1965, son, prince Paul b. 1967; left Greece 14 Dec. 67; Gold Medal, Yachting, Olympic Games, Rome 60.
c/o Greek Embassy, Viale Gioacchino Rossini 4, Rome, Italy.

Constantine, Sir Learie Nicholas, Kt., M.B.E.; Trinidadian diplomatist, cricketer and barrister; b. 21 Sept. 1901.
Has played cricket for Trinidad and West Indies; Welfare Officer, U.K., Second World War; called to Bar 54; returned to Trinidad 54; mem. Legislative Council 56-61; Minister of Works and Transport 56-61; High Commr. of Trinidad and Tobago in U.K. 62-64; mem. Race Relations Board (U.K.) 66-; Rector St. Andrews Univ. 68-.
Publs. *Cricket and I, Cricket in the Sun, Cricketers' Carnival, Cricketer's Cricket, Cricket Crackers, Colour Bar, Young Cricketer's Pocket Companion.*
11 Kendall Court, Shoot-up-Hill, Hampstead, N.W.2, London, England.

Constantinople, Patriarch of; (*see* Athenagoras).

Conté, Sadiou, DR. MED.; Guinean surgeon and diplomatist; b. 25; ed. Ecole William Ponty and Lycée, Dakar, Paris Univ. Medical Faculty.
Asst. Surgeon Dakar hospitals 57-58; Chief Surgeon, Ballay Hospital, Conakry 59; Ambassador to U.S.S.R. 59-61, to U.S.A. 61-63; Minister of Educ. 63, of Justice 67; now Prof. of Surgery and Chief Surgeon, Ignace Deen Hospital, Conakry.
Publs. Surgical papers in French and African journals; *Le Noir et les Cultures indo européennes* 56.
Hôpital Ignace Deen, Conakry, Guinea.

Conway, H.E. Cardinal William John, D.D., D.C.L.; Irish ecclesiastic; b. 22 Jan. 1913; ed. Queen's Univ., Belfast, St. Patrick's Coll., Maynooth and Gregorian Univ., Rome.
Professor of Moral Theology and Canon Law, St. Patrick's Coll., Maynooth 42-57, Vice-Pres. 57-58; Titular Bishop of Neve, Auxiliary to His Eminence Cardinal D'Alton 58-63; Archbishop of Armagh and Primate of all Ireland Sept. 63-; created Cardinal 65.
Publs. *The Church and State Control* 52, *Problems in Canon Law* 55, *The new law on the Eucharistic Fast* 55, *The Child and the Catechism* 59, *Youth Problems* 60.
Ara Coeli, Armagh, Ireland.
Telephone: Armagh 2045.

Coobar, Abdulmegid; Libyan politician; b. 09; ed. Arabic and Italian schools in Tripoli, and privately.
With Birth Registration Section, Tripoli Municipal Council and later its Section Head, Adviser on Arab Affairs for the Council 43-44; resigned from Govt. Service 44; mem. Nat. Constitutional Assembly 50, and mem. its Cttee. to draft the Libyan Constitution; mem. of Parl. for Eastern Gharian 52-55, Pres. of Parl. Assembly 52-55; Deputy Prime Minister and Minister of Communications 55-56; again elected for Eastern Gharian to the new Chamber of Deputies 55-, Pres. 56; mem. of Council of Viceroy 56; Deputy Prime Minister and Minister of Foreign Affairs 57; Prime Minister 57-60; concurrently Minister for Foreign Affairs 58; Independence Award (First Class).
Asadu el-Furat Street 29, Garden City, Tripoli, Libya.

Cook, Chauncey William Wallace; American food company executive; b. 22 June 1909; ed. Univ. of Texas, Columbia Univ. Graduate School of Business Admin.
Proctor and Gamble Co. 31-42; Gen. Foods Corpn. 42-, Chief Engineer 42-44, Div. Manager (Manufacturing and Engineering) 44-46, Production Manager Maxwell House Div. 46-51, Product Manager, Maxwell House 51-52, Sales and Advertising Manager, Maxwell House Div. 52-53, Asst. Gen. Manager, Maxwell House Div. 53-55, Gen. Manager Maxwell House Div. and Vice-Pres. Gen. Foods 55-59, Exec. Vice-Pres. (Operations) 59-62, Pres. 62-66, Chief Exec. 65-, Chair. 66-; Dir. Gen. Foods Corpn. 60-, Whirlpool Corpn. 62-, Chase Manhattan Bank 63-.
General Foods Corporation, 250 North Street, White Plains, N.Y. 10602, U.S.A.
Telephone: 914-694-2315.

Cook, Donald C., A.B., M.B.A., J.D., L.L.M.; American public utility executive; b. 14 April 1909; ed. Univ. of Michigan and George Washington Univ. Law School.
Securities and Exchange Commission 35-45; Exec. Asst. to Attorney-Gen. of U.S. 45-46; Dir. Office of Alien Property, U.S. Dept. of Justice 46-47; Partner, Cook & Berger (attorneys) 47-49; Commr., Securities and Exchange Comm. 49-50, Vice-Chair. 50-52, Chair. 52-53; Vice-Pres. American Electric Power Service Corpn. 53-54, Exec. Vice-Pres. and Dir. 54-61; Pres. and Dir. American Electric Power Service Corpn., American Electric Power Co. and subsidiaries 61-.
American Electric Power Co., 2 Broadway, New York, N.Y. 10004, U.S.A.
Telephone: 212-422-4800.

Cook, Sir James Wilfred, Kt., D.SC., PH.D., F.R.I.C., F.R.S.; British chemist; b. 10 Dec. 1900; ed. Sloane School and Univ. Coll., London.
Demonstrator in Chemistry Univ. Coll. London 20; Lecturer in Organic Chemistry Sir John Cass Technical Inst. London 20-28; Research Chemist Dept. of Scientific and Industrial Research 28-29; Reader in Pathological Chemistry Univ. of London 32-35; Prof. of Chemistry Univ. of London 35-39; Research Chemist Royal Cancer Hospital London 29-39; Hon. Sec. Chemical Society 36-39; Pres. Royal Inst. of Chemistry 49-51; Regius Prof. of Chemistry Glasgow Univ. 39-54; Principal, Univ. Coll. of the South West, Exeter 54-55; Vice-Chancellor, Univ. of Exeter 55-66, Univ. of East Africa 66-; mem. Council for Nat. Academic Awards 64-66; Chair. Chemical Council 59-63; mem. Council for Scientific and Industrial Research 60-65; Chair. Advisory Cttee. on Pesticides and other Toxic Chemicals 62-66, Advisory Cttee. on Scientific and Technical Information 65-66.
University of E. Africa, P.O.B. 7110, Kampala, Uganda.
Telephone: Kampala 3835.

Cook, Mercer, A.B., A.M., PH.D.; American university professor and diplomatist; b. 30 March 1903; ed. Amherst Coll., Univ. of Paris and Brown Univ.

Assistant Professor of French, Howard Univ. 27-36; Prof. of French, Atlanta Univ. 36-43; Supervisor, English-Teaching, Haitian Schools 43-45; Prof. of French, Howard Univ. 45-58; Foreign Rep. American Soc. of African Culture 58-60; Dir. African Programme, Congress for Cultural Freedom 60-61; Ambassador to Republic of Niger 61-64, to Senegal 64-.
Publs. *Le Noir* 34, *Five French Negro Authors* 44, *Education in Haiti* 49; trans. Senghor's *African Socialism* 59, Mamadou Dia's *African Nations and World Solidarity* 61.
American Embassy, Dakar, Senegal, West Africa.

Cook, Ransom M.; American banker; b. 23 Sept. 1899; ed. Oregon State Coll.
American Trust Co. 21-60, Vice-Pres. 26-51, Senior Vice-Pres. 51-59, Dir. 56-60, Pres. 59-64, Chair. of Board, Chief Exec. Officer and Dir. Wells Fargo Bank 64-; Chair. Western American Bank (Europe), London 67-, Wells Fargo Bank Int. Corpn., New York 67-.
Wells Fargo Bank, 464 California Street, San Francisco, California 94120, U.S.A.

Cook, William Harrison, O.B.E., M.SC., PH.D., LL.D., D.SC., F.R.S.C., F.A.I.C., F.C.I.C., F.A.A.A.S.; Canadian scientist; b. 2 Sept. 1903; ed. Univ. of Alberta and Leland Stanford Univ.
Research Asst., Univ. of Alberta 24-30; Biologist, Div. of Applied Biology, Nat. Research Laboratories, Ottawa 30-41, Dir. Div. of Biosciences 41-; Editor *Canadian Journal of Research* 43-47; mem. Royal Soc. of Canada (Hon. Sec. 50-53, Pres. Sect. V 56-57, Pres. 62-63); mem. UN Technical Assistance Administration Mission to Central America 53; Vice-Pres. Exec. Cttee. Int. Inst. of Refrigeration 55-63; fmr. Vice-Pres. First Int. Congress of Food Science and Technology, London 62; Trustee *Biological Abstracts* 55-60; mem. Board of Govs., Univ. of Guelph 65-; Exec. Dir. Nat. Research Council 67-.
Division of Biosciences, National Research Council, 100 Sussex Drive, Ottawa, Ont.; Home: 201 Maple Lane, Rockcliffe Park, Ont., Canada.

Cook, Sir William Richard Joseph, Kt., C.B., F.R.S., M.SC.; British physical research scientist; b. 10 April 1905; ed. Bristol Univ.
Various scientific posts in Research Establishments of War Office and Ministry of Supply 28-47; Dir. of Physical Research, Admiralty 47-50; Chief of the Royal Scientific Service 50-54; Deputy Dir. Atomic Weapons Research Establishment, Aldermaston 54-58; mem. for Engineering and Production of the U.K. Atomic Energy Authority 58-59, for Development and Engineering 59-61, for Reactors 61-64; Deputy Chief Scientific Adviser, Ministry of Defence 64-67; Chief Adviser (Projects and Research) to Minister of Defence (Equipment) 68-.
Ministry of Defence, Whitehall, London, S.W.1; Home: Adbury Springs, Newbury, Berks., England.
Telephone: Newbury 409 (Home).

Cooke, (Alfred) Alistair; American journalist; b. 20 Nov. 1908 in England; ed. Jesus Coll., Cambridge, Yale and Harvard Univs.
Film Critic, B.B.C. 34-37; London Corresp. Nat. Broadcasting Co. 36-37; Special Corresp. on American Affairs, *The Times* 38-41; Special Corresp. B.B.C. 38-; American feature writer, *Daily Herald* 41-44; U.N. Corresp. *The Manchester Guardian* 45-48 (now *The Guardian*), Chief Corresp. in U.S.A. 48-; Peabody Award 52.
Publs. *Garbo and the Night Watchmen* (edited) 37, *Douglas Fairbanks* 40, *A Generation on Trial: U.S.A. v. Alger Hiss* 50, *One Man's America* (English title *Letters from America*) 52, *Christmas Eve* 52, *A Commencement Address* 54, *The Vintage Mencken* (edited) 55, *Around the World in Fifty Years* 66.
Nassau Point, Cutchogue, Long Island, N.Y., U.S.A.

Cooke, James, B.S.; American retail executive; b. 1 Nov. 1909; ed. Wharton School, Univ. of Pennsylvania. Store Clerk, The Penn Fruit Co., Philadelphia 27, rose to Vice-Pres. and Gen. Manager 27-59, Pres. and Chief Exec. Officer 64-; Pres. and Chief Exec. Officer Allied Supermarkets Inc. 59-65; Dir. and Sec.-Treas. of Topco Assocs. Inc.; Dir. Nat. Asscn. of Food Chains (Chair. 63-64), Dir. Supermarket Inst.; Chair. Rolling Hill Hospital.
1355 Washington Lane, Rydal, Pa., U.S.A.

Cooke, Samuel; American businessman; b. 29 Dec. 1898; ed. schools in Philadelphia.
Ship chandler, trucker, taxi-cab operator 16-20; produce speculator 20-27; assisted estab. of Topco Assoc. (Nat. Buying Group) 42, Pres. 42-50, Chair. 50-; Pres. Hanna Realty Co. 27-; Dir. Camden Cold Storage Co., Albert Einstein Medical Center; mem. Nat. Deciduous Fruit Cttee., U.S. Dept. of Agriculture; Trustee, Nat. Agric. Coll.; mem. Nat. Asscn. Food Chains, Super Market Inst.; pioneer of Supermarkets, Philadelphia area.
Home: Skipper Pike and Sheaff Lane, Ambler, Pa.; Office: Grant Avenue, Philadelphia, Pa., U.S.A.

Cooke, Most Rev. Terence James, M.A.; American Roman Catholic Archbishop; b. 1 Mar. 1921.
Ordained to the Priesthood 45; Sec. to Cardinal Spellman 57; Vicar-Gen. Archdiocese of New York 65; Archbishop of New York March 68-.
452 Madison Avenue, New York 22, N.Y., U.S.A.

Cool, Pierre Auguste; Belgian trade unionist; b. 28 Aug. 1903; ed. Technical High School St. Antonius, St. Niklaas-Waas, High School for Workers, Louvain.
Engineer, St. Nicolas-Waas 19-20, Eisden 20-21; studied High School for Workers, Louvain 21-24; Sec. Regional Union, Beringen 24-25, Free Miners Union for Limburg 25-28, for Flemish Region of Belgium 28-32; Sec.-Gen. Fed. of Christian Trade Unions of Belgium 32-46, Pres. 46-; Vice-Pres. Int. Fed. of Christian Trade Unions, Regent Nat. Bank of Belgium, Nat. Labour Council of Belgium, Belgian Productivity Centre, European Organization of ICFTU; mem. Econ. and Social Cttee. of Common Market-Euratom, Nat. Board for Scientific Policy; Christian Social Party; Commdr. Order of Crown (Belgium); Commdr. Order of St. Gregory the Great, Chevalier Légion d'Honneur (France); Grosses Verdienstkreuz (German Federal Republic); Commdr. Order of Orange-Nassau (Netherlands).
Franciskanenlaan 46, St. Pieters-Woluwe, Brussels 15, Belgium.

Coolbaugh, Frank; American mining executive; b. 21 Dec. 1908; ed. Colorado School of Mines.
U.S. Fuel Co., Mohrland, Utah 28-30; Climax Molybdenum Co., Climax, Colorado 33-42, Planning Dir., Asst. Gen. Supt., Resident Man., Gen. Man., Vice-Pres. 46-59, Dir. 55-, Pres. 59-; Pres. and Dir. Climax Uranium Co.; Vice-Pres. and Dir. American Metal Climax Inc. 58-60, Pres. 60-, Chair. of Board 66-; Dir. of several other companies; U.S. Army 42-46.
American Metal Climax Inc., 1270 Avenue of the Americas, New York City 20, N.Y.; Home: Calhoun Drive, Greenwich, Conn., U.S.A.
Telephone: 203-869-0622 (Home).

Cooley, Harold Dunbar; American politician, lawyer and farmer; b. 26 July 1897; ed. Univ. of North Carolina and Law School of Yale Univ.
President, Nash Co. N. Carolina; mem. U.S. House of Reps. 34-; Chair. House Cttee. on Agriculture, 81st, 82nd, 84th, 85th, 86th and 87th Congress; mem. Council Inter-Parliamentary Union (IPU) and Vice-Pres. American Group IPU; mem. and officer of several professional organizations; Democrat.
Nashville, North Carolina, U.S.A.

Cools, Hyppolyte G. A. E., D. en D., LIC. COMM.CONS. FIN.; Belgian diplomatist; b. 15 June 1902.
Joined Foreign Service 34; Attaché, Consulate-Gen., Bombay 35, Dir. 37, Vice-Consul 38; Sec., Lima 38, Chargé d'Affaires a.i. 39-41; Chargé d'Affaires a.i., Quito 41, Consul 42, Counsellor 44; Chargé d'Affaires a.i., Buenos Aires 45-46; Commercial Counsellor London 47-59; Amb. to U.S.S.R. 59-67; Commdr. Ordre de la Couronne, Grand Officier Ordre de Léopold; British, Peruvian and other decorations.
c/o Ministry of Foreign Affairs, Brussels, Belgium.

Coombs, Herbert Cole, M.A., PH.D.; Australian banker; b. 24 Feb. 1906; ed. Univ. of Western Australia and London School of Economics and Political Science.
Assistant Economist, Commonwealth Bank of Australia 35; Economist to Commonwealth Treasury 39; mem. Commonwealth Bank Board 42; Dir. of Rationing 42; Dir.-Gen. of Post-War Reconstruction 43; Gov. Commonwealth Bank of Australia 49-60; Chair. Commonwealth Bank Board 51-60; Gov. Reserve Bank of Australia 60-68, Chair. Reserve Bank Board 60-68; Chair. Australian Council for Aboriginal Affairs 68-; Chair. Australian Council for the Arts 68-; Chancellor Australian Nat. Univ.; Hon. LL.D. (Melbourne), Hon. D.Litt. (Western Australia), Hon. Fellow London School of Economics.
119 Milson Road, Cremorne, N.S.W. 2090, Australia.

Coombs, Philip H.; American economist and educator; b. 15 Aug. 1915; ed. Holyoke Public Schools, Amherst Coll., Univ. of Chicago and Brookings Inst.
Instructor in Economics, Williams Coll., Mass. 40-41; Economist, Office of Price Admin. 41-42; Econ. Adviser, Office of Strategic Services 42-45; Econ. Adviser to Dir. of Office of Econ. Stabilization 45-46; Dep. Dir. Veterans Emergency Housing Program 46-47; Prof. of Economics, Amherst Coll. 47-49; Exec. Dir. President's Materials Policy Comm. (Paley Comm.) 51-52; Sec. and Dir. of Research, Fund for Advancement of Education (Ford Foundation) 52-61, Program Dir., Education Div., Ford Foundation 57-61; Asst. Sec. of State for Educational and Cultural Affairs, Dept. of State 61-62; Fellow Council on Foreign Relations 62-63; Dir. Int. Inst. for Educational Planning (UNESCO), Paris 63-; official numerous educational orgs.; Hon. L.H.D., Amherst Coll., LL.D., Brandeis Univ. and Monmouth Coll.
Publs. *The Fourth Dimension of Foreign Policy* 64, *Education and Foreign Aid* 65, *The World Educational Œrisis—A Systems Analysis* 68.
International Institute for Educational Planning, 7 rue Eugène Delacroix, Paris 16e; Home: 94 quai Louis Blériot, Paris 16e, France.

Coon, Carleton Stevens, B.A., M.A., PH.D.; American anthropologist; b. 23 June 1904; ed. Phillips Acad., Andover, Harvard Coll., and Harvard Univ.
Instructor and later Assoc. Prof. Harvard 34-41; Assoc. Prof. and later Prof. Harvard 45-48; Prof. and Curator, Univ. of Pennsylvania 48-63, Research Curator 63-; expeditions to Morocco 24-28, 62, Albania 29-30, Ethiopia, Yemen and Aden Protectorate 33-34, Iraq 48-49, Iran 48-49, 51, Afghanistan 54, Syria 55, Japan and India 56-57, S. Chile (Alakaluf Indians) 59, Sierra Leone 65, Chad, Cameroon and Libya 66-67; mem. Nat. Acad. of Sciences 55; served in Second World War in diplomatic and military posts 42-45; Legion of Merit; hon. mem. Asscn. de la Libération Française; Wenner-Gren Foundation Medallist 51; Gold Medal of Philadelphia Athenæum for book *The Origin of Races* 63.
Publs. include: *Measuring Ethiopia* 35, *The Races of Europe* 39, *Southern Arabia* 43, *Principles of Anthropology* (with E. D. Chapple) 42, *A Reader in General Anthropology* 48, *Races* (with S. M. Garn and J. B. Birdsell) 49, *The Mountains of Giants* 50, *Caravan* 51, 58, *Cave Explorations in Iran* 51, *The Story of Man* 54, 62,

The Seven Caves 57, *The Origin of Races* 62, *The Living Races of Man* 65.
207 Concord Street, Gloucester, Mass. 01930, U.S.A.
Telephone: 617-283-1612.

Cooper, James Lees; British journalist; b. 6 March 1907; ed. Darwen Grammar School, Lancs.
Articled journalist, *Darwen News*, later reporter Ashton-under-Lyne, Allied Newspapers, Manchester, *Daily Express*, London; War Correspondent 41-45; *Daily Express* Staff Correspondent, Canada 47-55, Head, New York Bureau 55-57; Organizer, Overseas Edition, *The Globe and Mail*, Toronto 58, Asst. to Editor and Publisher, Canada 59-63, Vice-Pres., Editor-in-Chief 63-, Publisher 65-; Dir. The Globe and Mail Ltd., Imperial Trust, Montreal; Dir. Canadian Daily Newspapers Asscn.; Vice-Chair. Canadian Section Commonwealth Press Union; Trustee Toronto Gen. Hospital.
Office: 140 King Street West, Toronto 1, Ontario, Canada.
Telephone: 368-7851.

Cooper, John Sherman, A.B., LL.D.; American lawyer and politician; b. 23 Aug. 1901; ed. Yale and Harvard Univs. and Univ. of Kentucky.
Mem. Lower House Kentucky State Legislature 28-30; Judge Pulaski County, Kentucky 30-38; served army 42-46; Circuit Judge 28th Judicial District, Kentucky 45-51; Senator from Kentucky 46-48 and 52-54; U.S.A. Del. to 4th Session U.N. 49; alternate Del. to 5th and 6th Sessions U.N. 50 and 51; Adviser to Sec. of State London and Brussels meetings, N.A.T.O. Council of Ministers 50; Del. to U.N. 49, alternate Del. 50 and 51; Ambassador to India and Nepal 55-56; Republican Senator from Kentucky 56-; mem. Cttee. on Rules and Administration, Cttee. on Labor and Public Welfare, law firm Gardner, Morrison and Rogers, Washington, D.C. 49-51, Board of Trustees Univ. of Kentucky 35-46; mem. American Bar Asscn., Cttee. on Agriculture and Forestry; Bronze Star Medal for Services in Second World War; Hon. degrees from many American Univs.
2900 N Street, N.W., Washington, D.C.; and 125 Senate Office Building, Washington 25, D.C., U.S.A.
Telephone: 202-225-2542.

Cooper, Major Leroy Gordon, Jr.; American astronaut; b. 27; ed. Univ. of Hawaii.
U.S. Marine Corps, Second World War, Presidential Honor Guard, Washington; U.S. Air Force 49-; Project Mercury 59-63; completed flight of 22 orbits of the earth May 16, 63; completed Gemini V Flight of 8 days, 120 orbits of the earth May 21-28, 65.
National Aeronautics and Space Administration, Washington, D.C., U.S.A.

Cooper, Martin Du Pré, B.A.; British music critic and writer; b. 17 Jan. 1910; ed. Winchester Coll., Hertford Coll., St. Edmund Hall, Oxford, studied music in Vienna with Egon Wellesz 32-34, Hon. Fellow Trinity Coll. Music, London.
Asst. Editor *Royal Geographical Society Journal* 35-36; Music Critic, *London Mercury* 35-39, *Daily Herald* 46-50, *The Spectator* 46-54; joined music staff *Daily Telegraph* 50 and since 54 music editor; Editor *The Musical Times* 53-56; Pres. Critics' Circle 59-60; mem. Editorial Board *New Oxford History of Music* 61-.
Publs. *Gluck* 35, *Bizet* 38, *Opéra Comique* 49, *French Music from the Death of Berlioz to the Death of Fauré* 51, *Russian Opera* 51, *Les Musiciens anglais d'aujourd'hui* 52, *Ideas and Music* 66.
35 Ossington Street, London, W.2, England.
Telephone: 01-229-5229.

Cooper, Sisson; South African director; b. Canada 88; ed. S. Wales.
Dir. Argus Printing and Publishing Co. Ltd. (*Star, Johannesburg, Cape Argus, Natal Daily News*) and Rhodesian Printing and Publishing Co. (*Bulawayo Chronicle, Rhodesia Herald*); Pres. Newspaper Press Union 33-35; Chair. S.A. Press Asscn. 39-48; Gen. Man. Argus Co. Ltd. 39-49.
c/o Argus South African Newspapers Ltd., 85 Fleet Street, London, E.C.4, England.

Cooray, H.E. Cardinal Thomas B.; Ceylonese ecclesiastic; b. 28 Dec. 1901.
Ordained priest 29; Titular Archbishop of Preslavo and Co-adjutor Archbishop of Colombo 45; Archbishop of Colombo 47-; mem. Pontifical Comm. for Canon Law; created Cardinal 65.
Archbishop's House, Colombo 8, Ceylon.
Telephone: 95471.

Cooremans, Lucien, D. en D.; Belgian administrator; b. 99; ed. Univ. Libre de Bruxelles.
Secretary to Paul Hymans 28-34; Sec. of the Cabinet and Minister of Justice 40; fmr. mem. Chamber of Reps.; Pres. Brussels Exhibition 58; Pres. Brussels Int. Fair; fmr. Pres. Union of Int. Fairs; Mayor of Brussels 56-; Hon. Pres. and founder of the Union of Capitals of the European Community; many Belgian and foreign orders.
Hôtel de Ville, Brussels, Belgium.

Coote, Sir Colin Reith, Kt., D.S.O.; British journalist; b. 19 Oct. 1893; ed. Rugby School and Balliol Coll., Oxford.
Served Gloucestershire Regiment 14-18; M.P. for Isle of Ely 17-22; Rome corresp. of *The Times* 22-25, Parliamentary Sketch-writer 25-30, Leader writer 30-42; Deputy Editor *The Daily Telegraph* 42-50, Managing Editor 50-64; Légion d'Honneur.
Publs. include *In and About Rome* and *Italian Town and Country Life* 21, *Maxims and Reflections of Winston Churchill* 50, *Sir Winston Churchill: a Self-Portrait* 54 (with P. D. Bunyan), *History of the Butterley Company* (with R. A. Mottram) 49, *Companion of Honour* 65, *Editorial* 65.
16 Bigwood Road, London, N.W.11, England.

Cope, S. Raymond, B.SC.(ECON.), PH.D.; British financial administrator (World Bank); b. 14 May 1907; ed. London School of Economics and Political Science.
Mem. of Guinness, Mahon and Co., merchant bankers 23-41, 46-47; Private Sec., Air Ministry Controller of Communications, Sec. Airborne Forces Cttee. 41-45; Finance Division, Control Comm. for Germany 45-46; Sec. and Treas. Esso Transportation Co. Ltd. 47; Int. Bank for Reconstruction and Devt. 47-, Loans Dept. 47-52, Asst. Dir., Dept. of Operations, Europe, Africa and Australasia 52-55, Dir. Dept. of Operations, Europe, Africa and Australasia 55-62, Dir. Dept. of Operations, Europe 62-65, Dir. Europe and Middle East Dept. 65-67, Dir. Europe Dept. 67-.
IBRD, Washington, D.C. 20433; Home: 3413 R Street, N.W., Washington, D.C. 20007, U.S.A.
Telephone: 338-1972 (Home).

Cope, Sir Zachary Vincent, Kt., B.A., M.D., M.S., F.R.C.S.; British surgeon; b. 14 Feb. 1881; ed. Westminster City School and St. Mary's Hospital Medical School.
Served Great War, Capt. and temp. Major Royal Army Medical Corps; 3rd London Gen. Hospital and Mesopotamia; Hunterian Prof. Royal Coll. of Surgeons 16, 20, 25, 27, Arris and Gale Lecturer 22, Bradshaw Lecturer 49, Vicary Lecturer and Tomes Lecturer 52; Consulting Surgeon to St. Mary's Hospital, Paddington, and to the Bolingbroke Hospital, Wandsworth; fmr. Group Officer, Sector 6, London Emergency Medical Service; mem. Council Royal Coll. of Surgeons 40-49, Vice-Pres. 48; Fellow, fmr. Hon. Librarian, Royal Society of Medicine, Hon. Fellow 51; Chair. Nat. Medical Manpower Cttee. 55-61.
Publs. *The Surgical Aspect of Dysentery* 21, *The Early Diagnosis of the Acute Abdomen* 22 (13th ed. 68), *Human Actinomycosis* 38, *The Versatile Victorian* (life of Sir

Henry Thompson) 51, *Life of William Cheselden* 53, *Florence Nightingale and the Doctors* 58, *The History of the Royal College of Surgeons of England* 59, *The History of the Acute Abdomen* 65, *Almroth Wright* 66, etc.
170 Chiltern Court, Baker Street, London, N.W.1, England.
Telephone: 01-486-1946.

Copeland, Lammot du Pont; American business executive; b. 5 May 1905; ed. Harvard Univ.
E. I. du Pont de Nemours & Co. Inc. 29-, Dir. 42-, mem. Finance Cttee. 43-59, Sec. 47-54, Vice-Pres. 54-62, Pres. 62-67, Chair. of Board 67-; mem. Exec. Cttee. 59-; Dir. Chemical Bank of New York Trust Co.; Dir. and Trustee of numerous financial orgs.
Du Pont Building, Wilmington 98, Delaware, U.S.A.

Copic, Branko; Yugoslav writer; b. 15; ed. Belgrade Univ.
Recipient of several Yugoslav literary awards; Order of Meritorious Service to the People, First and Second Class, Order of Brotherhood and Unity, First Class, 1941 Partisan Commemoration Medal.
Publs. include *A Warrior's Spring, Fighters and Fugitives, Dew on the Bayonets, Partisan Stories,* and volumes of verse.
c/o Yugoslav Academy of Sciences and Arts, Zrinski trg. 11, Zagreb 1, Yugoslavia.

Copland, Aaron; American composer; b. 14 Nov. 1900. Enrolled Fontainebleau School of Music 21; studied with Nadia Boulanger in Paris 21-24; returned to U.S. 24; Guggenheim Fellowship 25-27; with Roger Sessions organised Copland-Sessions Concerts 28-31; Dir. American Festival of Contemporary Music, Yaddo; toured South America 41 and 47; Lecturer on Music, New School for Social Research, N.Y. 27-37; has taught composition at Harvard and Berkshire Music Center; Charles Eliot Norton Prof. 51-52; Dir. League of Composers, Edward MacDowell Asscn., Koussevitzky Music Foundation, Walter W. Naumberg Music Foundation and American Music Center; numerous awards.
Works include: *First Symphony* 25, *Concerto for Piano and Orchestra* 26, *Two Pieces for String Quartet* 28, *Lincoln Portrait* 42, *Billy the Kid* 38, *Violin Sonata* 43, *Appalachian Spring* 44, *Clarinet Concerto* 48, *Twelve Poems by Emily Dickinson* 50, *John Henry* (revised 57), *The Tender Land* 54, *Symphonic Ode* 55, *Piano Fantasy* 57, *Orchestral Variations* 58, *Nonet* 60, *Connotations for Orchestra* 62, *Music for a Great City* 63, *Emblems for Band* 64, *Inscape for Orchestra* 67.
Publs. *What to Listen for in Music* 39, *Our New Music* 41, *Music and Imagination* 52, *Copland on Music* 60.
c/o Boosey & Hawkes Inc., 30 West 57th Street, New York 19, N.Y., U.S.A.

Copland, Sir Douglas Berry, K.B.E., C.M.G., M.A., D.SC., LITT.D., D.C.L.; Australian economist and diplomatist; b. 24 Feb. 1894; ed. Waimate District High School and Canterbury Coll., New Zealand.
Lecturer in History and Economics and Dir. of Tutorial Classes in Univ. of Tasmania 17; Prof. of Economics, Univ. of Tasmania 20-24; Sidney Myer Prof. of Commerce and Dean of Faculty of Commerce, Univ. of Melbourne 24-44; Truby Williams Prof. of Economics, Univ. of Melbourne 44-45; Commonwealth Prices Commr. 39-45; Economic Consultant to Prime Minister 41-45; Editor *Economic Record* 25-45; Commr. Victorian State Savings Bank 40-45; Chair. State Economic Cttee. of Victoria 38-45; Australian Minister to China 46-48; Prof. Emeritus Univ. of Melbourne 46; First Vice-Chancellor Australian Nat. Univ. 48-53; Australian Admin. Staff Coll. 56-60; High Commr. Canada 53-56; Econ. Consultant and Company Dir. 61-; Dir. Ansett Transport Industries; Pres. Nat. Council for Balanced Development; Founder, Cttee. for Econ. Development of Australia 61; mem. American Philoso-

phical Soc. 48; Hon. Litt.D. (Queensland and Harvard); Hon. LL.D. (McGill, Clark, Carleton, British Columbia, Adelaide, Tasmania, Melbourne Univs.); D.C.L. (Bishop's Univ.).
Publs. *Monetary Policy and its Application to Australia* 26, *Australia in the World Crisis 1929-33* 34, *The Australian Economy* (6th edn.) 47, *Towards Total War* 42, *The Road to High Employment* 45, *Report to Prime Minister on Economic Conditions in United Kingdom, United States and Canada* 45; (with E. O. G. Shann), *The Crisis in Australian Finance* 31, *The Battle of the Plans* 31, *The Australian Price Structure* 33; (with C. V. Janes) *Cross Currents in Australian Finance* 37, *Australian Marketing Problems* 38, *Australian Trade Problems* 38, *Back to Earth in Economics* 48, *Inflation and Expansion* 51; (with R. H. Barback) *The Conflict of Expansion and Stability* 57, *Adventure of Growth* 60, *The Changing Structure of the Western Economy* 63.
Darjeeling, Mount Macedon, Victoria, Australia.
Telephone: Mount Macedon 61-555.

Coppé, Albert; Belgian politician; b. 26 Nov. 1911; ed. Catholic Univ. of Louvain.
Mem. (Christian-Social Party) Chamber of Representatives 46-52; Minister of Public Works 50, of Economic Affairs and the Middle Classes 50-51, of Reconstruction 52; Vice-Pres. High Authority of the European Coal and Steel Community 52-67, Acting Pres. 67; mem. Combined Comm. of EEC, ECSC, and Euratom July 67-; Prof. Extraordinary Univ. of Louvain; Commdr. Ordre de Léopold, Grand Cordon, Ordre du Chêne (Luxembourg), etc.; Dr. h.c., Univs. of Montreal and San Antonio, Texas.
Commission of the European Communities, 23 Avenue de la Joyeuse Entrée, Brussels, Belgium.

Coppieters de ter Zaele, Emmanuel, DR. ECON., DR. IUR., M.SC. (ECON.); Belgian economist and jurist; b. 1925; ed. Louvain and London Univs.
Professor Int. Econ. Organizations, Nat. Univ. Faculty of Econs., Antwerp 54-, Royal Military Col., 63-66; Dir.-Gen. Institut Royal des Relations Internationales, Brussels 54-; Editor *Chronique de Politique Etrangère;* Co-Editor *Internationale Spectator, Tijdschrift voor Internationale Politiek:* Consul Gen. of Honduras in Belgium 61-; mem. Belg. Nat. Council of Statistics; Assoc. mem. Royal Acad. of Overseas Sciences; mem. Belgian Nat. Comm. UNESCO, Gov. Asscn. pour l'Etude des Problèmes de l'Europe, Paris; Sec.-Gen. of the Belgian Comm. for the European Cultural Foundation and of the Cultural Fund of the Council of Europe; Barrister; Reserve Capt.-Commdr.; Officier Ordre de Léopold, Commdr. Order of the Holy Sepulchre, Résistance and Volontaire de Guerre Medals.
Publ. *English Bank Note Circulation 1694-1954* 55, *L'Accord Monétaire Européen et le Progrès de la Convertibilité des Monnaies* 59, *Internationale Organisaties en Belgische Economie* 60, etc.
88 avenue de la Couronne, Brussels, Belgium.

Corbin, Edmond Emile; French engineer and international civil servant; b. 11 April 1908; ed. Ecole Polytechnique and Ecole Nationale des Ponts et Chaussées.
Bridges and Highways Engineer, Lorient 32-34, Cherbourg 34-41, Nancy 41-45; Chief Engineer of Bridges and Highways, Asst. to Dir.-Gen. of Railways and Transport, Ministry of Public Works and Transport, later Head of Dept. of Int. Affairs 45-61; Engineer-Gen. of Bridges and Highways in charge of Int. Relations 61-66; Sec.-Gen. of European Conf. of Ministers of Transport Jan. 66-; Officier Légion d'Honneur, Commdr. Ordre National du Mérite; Knight Order of Isabel the Catholic (Spain), Officer Order of Vasa (Sweden).
Office: 3 rue André Pascal, Paris 16e; Home: 18 avenue Charles Floquet, Paris 7e, France.

Cordeiro de Farias, General Oswaldo; Brazilian army officer and politician; b. 01; ed. Colégio Militar, Rio de Janeiro and other higher military schools.
Army service 19-; Organiser and Commdr. Artillery Div. of the Brazilian Expeditionary Force in Italy 44-45; Military Attaché to Argentina 45-46; Commdt. 5th Mil. Region (Paraná) 46-49; Organiser and First Commdt. Staff Coll. 49-52; Commdt. North Region 53-54, Chief of Del. and Pres. Mixed Mil. Comm. to U.S.A. 58-61; Chief of Staff of the Armed Forces 61; Minister Extraordinary for the Co-ordination of Regional Orgs. 64-65, Minister of Interior 65-67; numerous articles and pamphlets on mil. matters, and numerous nat. and int. awards.
Praça Eugênio Jardim 42, 502°, Copacabana, Guanabara, Brazil.

Cordier, Andrew Wellington, M.A., PH.D.; American university official; b. 3 March 1901; ed. Manchester Coll., Ind., and Univ. of Chicago.
Chair. Dept of History and Political Science, Manchester Coll., Ind. 27-44; Lecturer in Social Sciences, Ind. Univ., Extension Div. 29-44; U.S. Dept. of State, Expert on Int. Security 44-46; Technical Expert, U.S. Delegation, U.N. Conference, San Francisco, 45; U.N. Preparatory Commission, London 45; Exec. Asst. to the Sec.-Gen., U.N. (rank of Under-Sec.) 46-61; Under-Sec. in charge of Gen. Assembly and Related Affairs 61-62; Dean of Graduate School of International Affairs, Columbia Univ. 62-; Editor *The Dean's Papers* 66.
6 Merrivale Road, Great Neck, L.I., N.Y., U.S.A.

Cordier, Ernest André Gabriel; French engineer; b. 29 July 1899; ed. Ecole Centrale des Arts et Manufactures.
President Société Centrale de Dynamite, Compagnie Française Thomson Houston-Hotchkiss Brandt; Vice-Pres. Péchiney, Compagnie Universelle d'Acétylène et d'Electro-Métallurgie, Crédit Commercial de France, Alsthom; Administrator, Compagnie Financière de Suez et de l'Union Parisienne, Crédit National; Commandeur, Légion d'Honneur.
Cie. Française Thomson Houston-Hotchkiss Brandt, 173 Boulevard Haussmann, Paris 8e, France.
Telephone: Alma 96-00.

Cordova, Roberto; Mexican lawyer and public official; b. 99; ed. Nat. Prep. School, Nat. Univ. of Mexico, Univ. of Texas.
Del. Sec. to Inter-American Conf., Havana 28; Legal Rep. Claims and Arbitration Comm. between Mexico and U.S. 28-33, 37-40; Prof. Int. Law, Escuela Libre de Derecho 26-37; Counsellor, Foreign Service 41; Ambassador to Costa Rica 42; mem. Cttee. preparing Statute for Int. Court of Justice, Washington 45; Adviser to U.N. Conf. on Int. Organisation, San Francisco 45; Del. to Int. Labour Conf. (Paris) 46, to Int. Conf. on Petroleum (Los Angeles) 47, to Inter-American Conf. on Peace and Security, Quintandinna 47; Adviser to Sec. of State for Foreign Affairs 47-51; led Del. to Inter-American Conf., Bogotá 48, Caracas 54; mem. U.N. Comm. on Int. Law 48-53; Gen. *Rapporteur* (51) and Special *Rapporteur* on Nationality and Statelessness 52; Rep. U.N. Gen. Assembly, Paris 51; Del. to Inter-American Council of Jurists, Buenos Aires 53; Judge, Int. Court of Justice 54-64; mem. Nat. Acad. of History and Geography of Mexico.
12 Colonia Valle, Mexico City, Mexico.

Cordova Moscoso, Wilson; Ecuadorean politician; b. 13 May 1917; ed. Univ. Nacional de Santiago de Chile and Univ. of Michigan.
Professor of History Instituto Nacional "Mejia", Quito 38-40; Sec. Presidency of the Republic 40-42; First Sec., Washington 48, UN, New York 49-52; mem. Council Quito 55-57, Vice-Pres. 56-57; Ambassador to Argentina August 56; Judicial Dept. Banco Popular Quito 54-58;

Lawyer Inter-American Devt. Bank 60-64; Minister of Foreign Affairs 65; Ecuadorean Spokesman Inter-American Lawyers Confederation 59-65; mem. several UN and legal Cttees.; Order Libertador San Martín.
c/o Ministerio de Relaciones Exteriores, Quito, Ecuador.

Corea, Gamani, M.A., D.PHIL.; Ceylonese civil servant; b. 4 Nov. 1925; ed. Royal Coll., Colombo, Corpus Christi Coll., Cambridge, and Nuffield Coll., Oxford.
Director, Planning Secr. and Sec. Nat. Planning Council 56-60; Dir. of Econ. Research and Asst. to Gov. of Central Bank of Ceylon 60-65; Perm. Sec. to Ministry of Planning and Econ. Affairs and Econ. Sec. to Cabinet 65-; Consultant to Sec.-Gen., UN Conf. on Trade and Devt.; fmr. Chief, UN Econ. Mission to British Honduras; fmr. Chair. UNCTAD Expert Group on Int. Monetary Issues; mem. UN Cttee. on Devt. Planning; fmr. Pres. Section F, Ceylon Asscn. for Advancement of Science; mem. Nat. Science Council of Ceylon, Consultative Cttee. Asian Agricultural Survey, Asian Devt. Bank.
Horton Lodge, 21 Horton Place, Colombo 7, Ceylon.

Cori, Carl Ferdinand, M.D.; American university professor; b. 5 Dec. 1896; ed. German Univ., Prague.
Asst. in Pharmacology Univ. of Graz 20-21; went to U.S.A. 22, naturalised U.S. citizen 28; Biochemist, State Inst. for Study Malignant Disease, Buffalo, N.Y. 22-31; Prof. of Pharmacology and Biochemistry, Wash. Univ. School of Medicine 31-; Visiting Lecturer, Harvard Univ.; mem. Nat. Acad. of Sciences, American Asscn. for Advancement of Science, American Philosophical Soc., American Chemical Soc., American Soc. of Biological Chemists (Pres. 49-50); Pres. Fourth Int. Congress of Biochemistry Vienna 58; foreign mem. Royal Soc.; Lasker Award 46, Mid-West Award (American Chemical Soc.) 46, Sugar Research Foundation Award 47, 50, Squibb Award 47; Nobel Prize in Medicine and Physiology 47; Willard Gibbs Medal (American Chemical Soc.) 48; numerous hon. degrees.
167 Brattle Street, Cambridge, Mass. 02138, U.S.A.

Corish, Brendan; Irish politician; b. 1918.
Mem. of Parl. 45-; Vice-Chair. Labour Party 46, Chair. 49-53, Parl. Leader 60-, mem. Council of State 64-; Parl. Party Whip 45-54; Parl. Sec. to Minister of Local Govt. and Minister of Defence 48; Minister of Social Welfare 54-57; Del. to Council of Europe 55-59; Del. to Int. Affairs Asscn. Conf. 49; Del. to Inter-Parl. Union Conf., Istanbul 51; assoc. mem. Del. to Commonwealth Relations Conf., Ottawa 52.
Belvedere Road, Wexford, Ireland.

Corneille (*see* Beverloo, Cornelis Van).

Cornelis, Henri Arthur Adolf Antoon Marie Christophe; Belgian administrator; b. 18 Sept. 1910; ed. Univ. of Ghent and Geneva School of International Studies.
Belgian Congo 34-60, Territorial Administrator 34-38, Head, Finance and Customs Office 38-42, Principal Territorial Administrator 42-46, Sub.-Dir. Econ. Affairs 46-48, Dir. Econ. Affairs 48-50, Dir.-Gen. Econ. Affairs 50-51, Commr. Ten Year Plan 51-53, Vice-Gov-Gen. of Belgian Congo 53-58, Gov.-Gen. 58-60; Adviser Banque de Paris et des Pays-Bas, Brussels 61-64; Dir., Adviser to the Chair. Cominière, Brussels 65-.
2 rue de la Sarte, Dion le Mont, Belgium.

Cornelius, Alvin Robert, B.SC.; Pakistani judge; ed. Holkar Coll., Indore, Muir Central Coll., Allahabad and Selwyn Coll., Cambridge.
Entered Indian Civil Service 24; District Judge, Punjab 32-42; Legal Remembrancer 44-46; Judge, High Court 46-50; appointed to Supreme Court (fmrly. Fed. Court) 56, Chief Justice 60-67.
Supreme Court, Lahore, Pakistan.

Cornell, Katharine; American actress-manager, producer and actress; b. 16 Feb. 1893; ed. in New York.
Made stage debut 16; has appeared in numerous plays,

including *A Bill of Divorcement, The Way Things Happen, Candida, The Green Hat*; became actress-manager 31 with *The Barretts of Wimpole Street* as her first production; later productions include *Romeo and Juliet* 34-35, *The Doctor's Dilemma* 41, *The Three Sisters* 42-43, *Anthony and Cleopatra* 47-48, *The Dark is Light Enough* 54-55, *The Firstborn* 58, *Dear Liar* 59-60; many hon. degrees.
Publs. *I Wanted to be an Actress* 38, *Curtain Going Up* 41.
Palisades, New York 10964, U.S.A.

Corner, Frank Henry, M.A.; New Zealand diplomatist; b. 17 May 1920; ed. Victoria Univ. of Wellington.
First Sec. Washington 48-51; Senior Counsellor, London 52-58; Dep. Sec. of External Affairs 58-62; Perm. Rep. to UN 62-67.
c/o Ministry of External Affairs, Wellington, New Zealand.

Corner, George Washington, A.B., M.A., M.D., SC.D., LITT.D., LL.D.; American physician and scientist; b. 12 Dec. 1889; ed. Johns Hopkins Univ.
Asst. in Anatomy, Johns Hopkins Univ. 13-14, Resident House Officer, Johns Hopkins Hospital 14-15; Asst. Prof. Univ. of Calif. 15-19; Assoc. Prof. Johns Hopkins Univ. 19-23; Prof. Univ. of Rochester 23-40; Dir. Dept. of Embryology, Carnegie Inst. of Washington, Baltimore 40-55; Eastman Prof. Oxford 52-53; Historian, The Rockefeller Inst. N.Y. 56-60, Visiting Prof. 61-; mem. U.S. Acad. of Sciences (Vice-Pres. 53-57), Amer. Philosophical Soc. (Vice-Pres. 53-56, Exec. Officer 60-); Hon. Fellow, Zoological Society (London), Hon. F.R.C.O.G.; foreign mem. Royal Soc. of London; Fellow, Royal Soc. of Edinburgh.
Publs. *Anatomical Texts of the Earlier Middle Ages* 27, *The Hormones in Human Reproduction* 42, *Ourselves Unborn* 45, *Anatomist at Large* 58, *George Hoyt Whipple and his Friends* 63, *Two Centuries of Medicine* 65, *History of the Rockefeller Institute* 65.
American Philosophical Society, 104 S. 5th Street, Philadelphia, Pa. 19106, U.S.A.
Telephone: WALnut 5-3606 (Office).

Cornforth, John Warcup, M.SC., D.PHIL., F.R.S.; Australian research scientist; b. 7 Sept. 1917; ed. Univs. of Sydney and Oxford.
Scientific Staff, Medical Research Council 46-62; Dir. Milstead Laboratory of Chemical Enzymology, "Shell" Research Ltd. 62-; Assoc. Prof. Univ. of Warwick 65-; Corday-Morgan Medal, Chem. Soc. 53, Flintoff Medal, Chem. Soc.; Pedler Lecturer, Chem. Soc. 68-69; Ciba Medal, Biochem. Soc. 66; Stouffer Prize 67.
Publs. *The Chemistry of Penicillin* (part author) 49, and numerous papers on chemical and biochemical topics.
Milstead Laboratory of Chemical Enzymology, "Shell" Research Ltd., Broad Oak Road, Sittingbourne, Kent, England.
Telephone: Sittingbourne 4444.

Cornut-Gentille, Bernard; French diplomatist and politician; b. 26 July 1909; ed. Ecole Libre des Sciences Politiques.
Fmr. prefect of Rennes, Amiens and Strasbourg 44-45; **High Commr. and Gov-Gen. French Equatorial Africa, then French West Africa; Permanent Del. to U.N. 56;** Ambassador to Argentina 57-58; Sec. of State, de Gaulle Cabinet 58; Minister of Posts, Telegraphs and Telephones (Debré Cabinet) Jan. 59-Feb. 60; Mayor of Cannes 59-61; Conseiller-Général, Canton of Cannes 63-; Dir. of numerous companies.
76 Avenue Marceau, Paris 8e, France.

Cornwell, David John Moore (*pseudonym* John Le Carré); British writer; b. 19 Oct. 1931; ed. St. Andrew's Preparatory School, Pangbourne, Sherborne School, Berne Univ., and Lincoln Coll., Oxford.
Teacher, Eton Coll. 56-58; in Foreign Service 60-64; Somerset Maugham Award 63.

Publs. *Call For the Dead* 61, *Murder of Quality* 62, *The Spy Who Came in From the Cold* 63, *The Looking Glass War* 65, film *The Deadly Affair* 67, *A Small Town in Germany* 68.
c/o A. P. Watt and Son, 10 Norfolk Street, London, W.C.2, England.

Corona, Achille; Italian lawyer, journalist and politician; b. 30 July 1914; ed. Scuola Normale, Pisa, and Germany and France.
Former Partisan, took part in publishing secret *Avanti*, later arrested; mem. Chamber of Deputies 48-; mem. Directorate, Italian Socialist Party (P.S.I.) 49-; Minister of Tourism and Entertainment Dec. 63-.
Publ. *Problema dello Stato dal Giusnaturalismo a Rousseau* 38.
Via Venanzio Fortunato 58, Rome, Italy.

Corona del Rosal, General Alfonso, LIC. EN DER.; Mexican army officer and politician.
Lieutenant of Cavalry in various regts., Presidential Guard and at Colegio Militar; rose to Div. Gen., took part in campaigns of 24, 27 and 29; Man. Banco Nacional del Ejército y la Armada; Prof. of Mil. Ethics, Colegio Militar; Prof. of Political Economy, Univ. Nacional Autónoma de México; Dir. of Labour and Social Welfare and other admin. posts in Fed. District; Deputy, later Senator for 5th District of Hidalgo State, then Constitutional Gov.; Pres. Exec. Cttee. Partido Revolucionario Institucional, also Asst. Sec., Acción Militar (then called Partido de la Revolución Mexicana), Pres. Regional Cttee. Fed. District; Pres. Nat. Exec. Cttee., Partido Revolucionario Institucional; Sec. of State for Nat. Heritage in Ordaz Govt.; Mayor of Fed. District 66-; Cruz de Guerra, Cruz de Mérito Técnico Militar.
Publ. *Textbook on military ethics*.
Departamento del Distrito Federal, Zócalo, Mexico 1, D.F., Mexico.

Corona Martín, Ramón; Mexican architect; b. 06; ed. Xaverian Coll. Brighton, Oxford Univ., Escuela Nacional Preparatoria, Escuela Nacional de Arquitectos de México, and Universidad Nacional de México.
Architectural Practice 29-; Vice-Pres. Int. Union of Architects; mem. Board of Dirs. Universidad Autónoma de Guadalajara; mem. Board of Honour, Colegio de Arquitectos de México and Sociedad de Arquitectos de México; mem. numerous int. architectural societies.
Monte Libano 670, Mexico 10, D.F., Mexico.

Corre, Max, L. ès L.; French journalist; b. 25 Feb. 1912; ed. Paris Univ.
Former Editor-in-Chief *Samedi-Soir*; Dir. of *Paris-Match;* Dir.-Gen. of *Paris Presse, France-Dimanche;* now Dir.-Gen. of *Télé-7-jours*; Officier Légion d'Honneur, Croix de Guerre.
19 rue Octave-Feuillet, Paris 16e, France.

Correa, José Antonio, IUR.D.; Ecuadorean diplomatist and banker; b. 1915; ed. Universidad Central de Quito.
Assistant Chief, Diplomatic Section, Ministry of Foreign Affairs 35-38, Chief 38-40; Second Sec., Ecuadorean Embassy, Washington 40-44, First Sec. 44; Dir. Diplomatic Dept., Ministry of Foreign Affairs 45; Sec.-Gen. Perm. Del. of Ecuador to UN 46-48, Alt. Rep. of Ecuador to UN. 48-50; Senior Officer, Exec. Office of Sec.-Gen. of UN 51-56; Dep. Dir., Div. of Trusteeship, Dept. of Trusteeship and Non-self-governing Territories of UN 56-57; Perm. Rep. of Ecuador to UN 58-60; Dir. Bureau of Relations with Member States, UNESCO 61-63; Ambassador of Ecuador to U.S.A. 63-64; Pres. José Antonio Correa y Compañía (law firm) 65-; Pres. Ecuatoriana de Desarrollo S.A. (COFIEC) (Devt. finance company) 66-.
Office: Avenida 10 de Agosto 1564, P.O.B. 411, Quito, Ecuador.
Telephone: 239-129.

Corrêa do Lago, Antonio, M.A., LL.B.; Brazilian diplomatist; b. 28 Aug. 1918; ed. Colégio Santo Ignácio, Rio de Janeiro, Univ. of Brazil, Rio de Janeiro, and Univ. of S. California, Los Angeles.
Foreign Service 39-, Buenos Aires 44, Montevideo 45-47; Consul, Los Angeles 51-53; Head, Econ. Div., Ministry of External Relations 54-58; Consul-Gen. Paris 59-61; Head of Brazilian Del. to Conf. of Latin American Free Trade Asscn. 61; Ambassador to Venezuela 61-64; Perm. Rep. to European Office of UN, Geneva, and Del. to Disarmament Cttee. 64-66; Dir. Instituto Rio Branco (Foreign Service Inst.) 66-.
Ministério das Relações Exteriores, Palácio Itamaraty, Rio de Janeiro, Brazil.

Corrêa d'Oliveira (*see* da Cunha Sottomayor Corrêa d'Oliveira).

Correns, Erich, DR. h.c.; German chemist and politician; b. 12 May 1896; ed. Univs. of Berlin and Tübingen.
Chemist in rayon industry; works dir. cellulose and paper factory, Blankenstein, and rayon factory, Schwarza; Dir. Fibre Research Inst., German Acad. of Sciences, Berlin 51; mem. German Acad. of Sciences; mem. Volkskammer; Pres. of Nat. Council of Nat. Front of Democratic Germany 54-; mem. Council of State 61-; Vaterländischer Verdienstorden in Gold and other awards.
Staatsrat, Berlin, Germany.

Corrigan, Leo F(rancis); American real estate and hotel executive; b. 30 Aug. 1894.
Began his career as real estate advertisement salesman 12; since 17 has specialised in ownership and development of real estate; Pres. and Dir. Corrigan Properties Inc., Corrigan-Houston Inc., Los Angeles Biltmore Hotel Co. and numerous other property companies.
211 N Ervay, Dallas 1, Texas. U.S.A.

Corson, Bishop Fred Pierce, M.A., LL.D.; American ecclesiastic; b. 11 April 1896; ed. Dickinson Coll., and Drew Univ.
Ordained 20, successively Pastor, Jackson Heights (N.Y.), New Haven (Conn.), Pt. Washington (N.Y.), Simpson Church, Brooklyn (N.Y.) until 29; Superintendent, N.Y. East Methodist Conf. 30-34; Pres. Dickinson Coll. (Carlisle, Pa.) 34-44; Methodist Bishop of Philadelphia 44-68; Pres. Methodist Gen. Board of Educ. 48-60; Pres. Council of Methodist Bishops 52-53; Pres. World Methodist Council 61-66; Vice-Pres. Methodist Council on World Service and Finance 60-; Protestant Observer to the Vatican Council 62, 63, 64, 65; Trustee, numerous Colls.; Hon. Chancellor, Union Coll., Schenectady, N.Y.; mem. numerous socs.; Hon. D.D., L.H.D., Litt.D., S.T.D., Sc.D., J.U.D., D.C.L., D.S.L., Pd.D., D.R.E., Arts D., Ecu.D., E.J.D.; Order of St. Olav of Norway 64, Peace Medal Award of Third Order of St. Francis of Assisi 67.
Publs. include *Dickinson College, A Christian Philosophy of Education for the Postwar World, The Minister and Christian Higher Education, The Education we have and the Education we need, Free Masonry and the Framing of the Constitution, Your Church and You, American Methodism's Magna Charta, How Good is Communism? Pattern for Successful Living, The Christian Imprint.*
Office: 1701 Arch Street, Philadelphia, Pennsylvania 19103, U.S.A.
Telephone: 567-4902 (Office).

Cort, Stewart Shaw; American steel executive; b. 9 May 1911; ed. Yale Univ. and Harvard Business School.
Bethlehem Steel Corpn. 37-, Clerk, Commercial Research Div. 37-39, Sales Dept., Pacific Coast Div. 39, later Manager, Commercial Research and Sheet and Tinplate Sales; Asst. Gen. Manager, Sales, Pacific Coast Div. 50-52, Gen. Man. 52-54, Vice-Pres. Sales (Pacific Coast Div.) 54-60, Asst. Gen. Man. Sales 60-61, Vice-Pres.

61-63, Pres. and Dir. 63-; Dir. Continental Ill. Nat. Bank and Trust Co. of Chicago; Trustee, Blair Acad., Cttee. for Econ. Devt., Princeton Theological Seminary; mem. many insts. and cttees.
Bethlehem Steel Corporation, 701 E. 3rd Street, Bethlehem, Pennsylvania 18016, U.S.A.

Cortázar, Julio; Argentine writer; b. 1914.
Shorter works have appeared in *New World Writing* (New York), *La Table Ronde* (Paris), *Akzente* (Germany); on staff of UNESCO, Paris; mem. Jury, Casa de las Américas Award.
Publs. *Bestiario* (short stories) 51, *Final del juego* (short stories) 56, *Las armas secretas* (short stories) 59, *Rayuela* (novel) 63, *Los premios* (novel) 64, *Hopscotch* (novel) 66, *Story of Cronopios and Famas* (stories), *All the Fires, Fire* (stories), *Devil's Drool*; anthology of short stories.
place Général Beuret, Paris 15e, France.

Corthésy, Jean; Swiss business executive; b. 11 April 1907.
Vice-Chair. and Man. Dir. Nestlé Alimentana Co. S.A.; Pres. Unilac Inc., Panama; Dr. h.c. (Univ. of Lausanne); mem. Board of Trustees of IMEDE, Management Development Inst., Lausanne.
Nestlé Alimentana S.A., Vevey, Switzerland.

Cortina Mauri, Pedro; Spanish politician and diplomatist; b. 1909; ed. Acad. of Int. Law, The Hague.
Former Prof. of Public Law, Univ. of Seville; entered Diplomatic Service 33; Minister Plenipotentiary 52; Dir. int. orgs. for Ministry of Foreign Affairs 52-55; Consul-Gen., Paris 55-58; Under-Sec. for Foreign Affairs 58-66; Amb. to France 66-; Perm. mem. Int. Court of Justice, The Hague.
Spanish Embassy, avenue George V, Paris 8e, France.

Cortlandt, Lyn, B.A., F.I.A.L., F.R.S.A.; American artist; ed. Chouinard Art Inst., Jepson Art Inst., Los Angeles; Art School of Pratt Inst., Columbia Univ. School of Painting and Sculpture, Hans Hofmann School of Fine Arts and China Inst. in America (all in New York City), and private instruction.
Works in Metropolitan Museum of Art, New York, Museum of Fine Arts, Boston, Fogg Museum of Art, Art Inst. of Chicago, Brooklyn Museum, Baltimore Museum of Art, Cincinnati Art Museum, Musée National d'Art Moderne, Paris, Stedelijk Museum, Amsterdam, Springfield Museum of Fine Arts, Mass., New York Public Library, Boston Public Library, etc.
Represented in Group Exhibitions in U.S.A., Belgium, Switzerland, Greece, Holland, Japan, Italy, Portugal and France; One-man Exhibitions in U.S., Brazil, Argentina, Curaçao, Puerto Rico, Jamaica, and Trinidad; mem. many socs.; many awards for oils, watercolours, graphics.
1070 Park Avenue, New York City, N.Y. 10028, U.S.A.
Telephone: Atwater 9-6370.

Corwin, Norman; American writer-producer-director of radio, television, stage and cinema; b. 3 May 1910.
Newspaperman 29-38; writer, director, producer for Columbia Broadcasting System 38-48; Chief, Special Projects, UN Radio 49-53; Chair. Documentary Awards Cttee. of Motion Picture Arts and Sciences; recipient of Peabody Medal, Edward Bok Medal; Award of American Acad. of Arts and Sciences 42; American Newspaper Guild Page One Award 44, 45; Wendell Wilkie One-World Award 46; entered in Radio Hall of Fame 62; Chair. Documentary Awards Cttee. of Acad. of Motion Picture Arts and Sciences 64-; other awards.
Publs. *They Fly through the Air* 39, *Thirteen by Corwin* 42, *More by Corwin* 44, *On a Note of Triumph* (both as a book and album of recordings) 45, *Untitled, and Other Dramas* 47, *Dog in the Sky* 52, *Overkill and Megalove* 62; Films: *The Blue Veil, The Grand Design,*

Lust for Life, The Story of Ruth; Cantatas: *The Golden Door, Now Therefore It is Proclaimed* (commissioned by UN 68); Stage plays: *The Rivalry, The World of Carl Sandburg, The Hyphen.*
Office: 10401 Wellworth Avenue, Los Angeles, Calif. 90028; Home: 14145 Greenleaf Street, Sherman Oaks, Calif. 91043, U.S.A.
Telephone: Crestview 4-8601 (Writers' Guild of America, West).

Cosgrave, Liam, LL.B.; Irish politician; b. 20; ed. St. Vincent's Coll. Castleknock and King's Inns.
Fine Gael mem. Dail 43-, Leader of Opposition 65-; Chair. Cttee. of Public Accounts 45; Parl. Sec. to Prime Minister and Minister for Commerce and Industry 48-54; Minister for External Affairs 54-57.
Beechpark, Templeogue, Co. Dublin, Ireland.

Cosic, Dobrica; Yugoslav novelist and politician; b. 21.
Joined national liberation movement 41; Deputy to Yugoslav parliament; Order of Bravery, Order of Meritorious Service to the People, Second Class, Order of Brotherhood and Unity, Second Class.
Publs. include *The Sun is Far Away, Roots, Divisions* 61.
National Assembly, Belgrade, Yugoslavia.

Costa, Angelo; Italian industrialist; b. 18 April 1901; ed. Scuola Superiore di Commercio, Genoa.
President Confederazione Generale dell'Industria Italiana 45-55, Life mem. of Admin. and Exec. Cttee. 55-, Pres. 66-; Vice-Pres. Pirelli 64-; Pres. Asscn. of Shipowners of Tirreno 46-; Pres. Confed. of Independent Shipowners (now Nat. Confed. of Independent Shipowners) 46-, Nat. Asscn. for the Oil Industry.
Publs. numerous books and articles on economic and social subjects.
Centro Pirelli, Piazza Duca d'Aosta 3, Milan, Italy.

Costa, Lucio; Brazilian architect; b. 02; ed. England, France and Escola National de Belas Artes, Rio de Janeiro.
With Le Corbusier and others designed Brazilian Govt. buildings 36, with Niemeyer designed Brazilian Pavilion at New York World Fair 39, won int. competition for design of city of Brasilia 57.
Brasilia, Brazil.

Costa e Silva, Gen. Arthur; Brazilian army officer and politician; b. 3 Oct. 1902; ed. Brazilian Military Acads. and Army Armor School, Fort Knox, Kentucky, U.S.A.
Commissioned 21, Gen. 52, Lieut.-Gen. 58, Corps Commdr. 61, Marshal 66; Commdr. of 9th Infantry Regt.; Chief of Staff 3rd Mil. Command; Mil. Attaché, Brazilian Embassy in the Argentine; Commdr. Armoured Div., 2nd Infantry Div., 4th Army; Adjutant-Gen.; Dir. of Ordnance; mem. Supreme Command of Revolution 64; Minister of War 64-66; Pres. of Brazil 67-; Grand-Officer of the Brazilian Mil. Orders for Merit in the Naval, Mil. and Air divs.; War Medal; Mil. Medal for Distinguished Services; Marshal Hermes Medal; Medal for Industrial Merit, Mil. Justice Medal; orders from Belgium, Luxembourg, Argentina, Portugal, Italy, France, U.S.A., Italy, German Fed. Repub. and Lebanon.
Office of the President, Brasilia, Brazil.

Costa Méndez, Nicanor, D IUR.; Argentine lawyer and politician; b. 1922.
Former Lecturer in Law and Politics; later Adviser, Ministry of Interior; Amb. to Chile 62-64; Minister of Foreign Affairs and Religion 66-.
Ministerio de Asuntos Exteriores, Buenos Aires, Argentina.

Costar, Sir Norman, K.C.M.G.; British diplomatist; b. 18 May 1909; ed. Battersea Grammar School and Jesus Coll., Cambridge.
Assistant Principal, Colonial Office 32-35; Private Sec.

to Perm. Under-Sec., Dominions Office 35; U.K. High Commr.'s Office, Australia 37-39, New Zealand 45-47; Dep. High Commr. for U.K. in Ceylon 53-57; Asst. Under-Sec. Commonwealth Relations Office 58-60; Dep. High Commr. in Australia 60-62; British High Commr., Trinidad and Tobago Aug. 62-66, Cyprus 67-.
British High Commission, Nicosia, Cyprus.

Coste-Floret, Paul, D. en D.; French lawyer and politician; b. 9 April 1911; ed. Coll. Saint-François-Régis and Grand Lycée Montpellier, Univs. of Montpellier and Paris.
Asst. Prof. Faculty of Law Paris 35-37; Prof. Faculty of Law Algiers 38; Prof. of Law Montpellier Univ. 46; after Armistice one of founders of Resistance Movement organ *Combat* and mem. of Liberation Asscn.; Sec. to Minister of Justice in Provisional Govt. Algiers 43, and later technical adviser to Comm. for Interior; Joint Sec. at Ministry of Justice 44-45; Sec.-Gen. of Comm. for Reform of Civil Code and then Joint Procurator-General for France at Trials of War Criminals Nuremberg 45; Extraordinary Counsellor of State 45-46; Deputy for L'Hérault 45-58, 62-; Minister of War 47; Minister for Overseas Territories 47-49; Minister of Information Jan.-Feb. 52, of State Jan.-June 53, of Public Health and Population June 53-June 54; mem. of Finance Comm. of Nat. Assembly 49; Pres. Comm. Universal Suffrage and Constitutional Laws 52; del. to UN 52, 53, 54-55; associated with newspaper *L'Aube* and several legal publications; Mayor of Lodève; Chevalier de la Légion d'Honneur, Médaille de la Résistance.
Assemblée Nationale, Paris 7e, France.

Costello, John Aloysius, S.C., B.A., LL.B.; Irish politician; b. 91; ed. Univ. Coll. Dublin.
Called to the Bar 14; called to Inner Bar 25; Bencher of the Honourable Society of King's Inns 26; Asst. to Law Officer, Provisional Govt. 22; Asst. to Attorney-Gen., Irish Free State 22-26; Attorney-Gen. 26-32; T.D. for Co. Dublin 33-37, Dublin Townships 37-43 and 44-48, Dublin South (East) 48-; Taoiseach (head of the Govt. of Eire) 48-51 and 54-57; Leader of the Opposition 51-54, 57-59; Hon. LL.D. (Montreal, Ottawa, and Fordham Univs.) 48.
20 Herbert Park, Ballsbridge, Dublin, Ireland.

Costopoulos, Stavros; Greek lawyer and politician; b. 14 Sept. 1900; ed. Univs. of Athens and Paris.
Lawyer, Athens 26; fmr. Liberal M.P., Centre Union M.P. 61-; Minister of National Economy 32, 47, of Supply 48, of Merchant Marine 50, of Co-ordination 50, of Finance 50; Gov. of Nat. Bank of Greece 51-53; Chair. of Board of Commercial Credit Bank 53; Minister of Interior Nov. 63-Feb. 64, of Foreign Affairs Feb. 64-65, of National Defence 65-66.
Publs. *L'Empire de l'Orient* 25, *Inter-Allied Debts* 28, *A General Introduction to the Budget* 32, *The Policy of Bank Mergers* 53, *Chinese Earth* 60.
Antheon 5, P. Psychico, Athens, Greece.
Telephone: 672-739.

Cot, Pierre-Donatien; French engineer and airline executive; b. 10 Sept. 1911; ed. Lycée Louis-le-Grand, Paris, and Ecole Polytechnique, Paris.
Engineer, Paris 36; Chief Exec. of Port of Le Havre 45; Technical Man., Paris Airport Authority 51-55, Pres. 55-67; Pres. of Air France 67-; Commdr. Légion d'Honneur, Croix de Guerre (39-45), mem. Victorian Order (U.K.), Médaille de l'Aéronautique.
2 avenue Emile-Bergerat, Paris 16e, France.

Cottesloe, 4th Baron, cr. 74; **John Walgrave Halford Fremantle,** Bt., G.B.E., T.D., D.L., M.A.; British businessman; b. 2 March 1900; ed. Eton Coll. and Trinity Coll., Cambridge.
Chairman, Thomas Tapling & Co., Humphries & Taplings Ltd., Yiewsley Engineering Co., Arts Council

of Great Britain 60-65, Reviewing Cttee. on Export of Works of Art, Hammersmith Hospital, British Postgraduate Medical Fed., Nat. Rifle Asscn., South Bank Theatre Board; fmr. Vice-Chair. Port of London Authority.
South Heath, Hampstead, London, N.W.3, England.
Telephone: 01-435-6626.

Cottier, Jean; French international civil servant; b. 2 Sept. 1912; ed. Ecole Normale Supérieure and Paris Univ.
Insp. of Finances 41-51; Financial Counsellor, Latin America 51-53; Dep. Dir. Foreign Finance Dept., Ministry of Finance 53-57; Financial Counsellor, French Embassy, Washington 57-61; Alt. Exec. Dir. Int. Bank for Reconstruction and Development 58-61; Dep. Sec.-Gen., Org. for Econ. Co-operation and Development (OECD) 61-; Chevalier, Légion d'Honneur, Croix de Guerre.
2 Place de Bagatelle, Neuilly sur Seine, France.

Cotton, Sir Charles Andrew, K.B.E., D.SC., F.R.S.N.Z.; New Zealand geologist; b. 24 Feb. 1885; ed. Univ. of Otago.
Lecturer in Victoria Univ. Coll. 09; Prof. of Geology in Univ. of New Zealand 21-54, Emeritus 54-; Foreign and Commonwealth mem., Geological Soc. of London; Hon. Fellow Geological Society of America; Dumont Medallist and hon. mem. Geological Society of Belgium; Victoria Medallist, Royal Geographical Society; Corresp. Fellow, Edinburgh Geological Society; Hon. LL.D.
Publs. *Geomorphology of New Zealand* 22, *Landscape* 41, *Geomorphology* 42, *Climatic Accidents* 42, *Volcanoes as Landscape Forms* 44, *Earth Beneath* 45, *New Zealand Geomorphology* 55.
2 Manuka Avenue, Lower Hutt, New Zealand.
Telephone: 60-815.

Cotton, Norris; American lawyer and politician; b. 11 May 1900; ed. Wesleyan and George Washington Univs.
Mem. New Hampshire Legislature 23; Editor *Granite Monthly*, Concord 23-24; Sec. to Senator George H. Moses 24-28; admitted to N.H. Bar 28; with firm Demond, Woodworth, Sulloway and Rogers, Concord 28-33; with firm Cotton, Tesreau and Stebbins since 45; District Attorney Grafton County 33-39; Justice Municipal Court of Lebanon, N.H. 39-44; mem. N.H. House of Reps. 43, Speaker 45; mem. House of Reps. 47-54; Senator from New Hampshire 54-; Republican.
15 Kimball Street, Lebanon, N.H., U.S.A.

Cottrell, Donald Peery, M.A., PH.D.; American university teacher and administrator; b. 17 Feb. 1902; ed. The Ohio State Univ. and Columbia Univ.
Public School Teaching and Admin. in Ohio 23-26; Tutor, Hunter Coll. of the City of New York 27-29; Asst. and Assoc. in Coll. Admin., Teachers' Coll., Columbia Univ. 27-29; Asst. Prof. 29-31, Assoc. Prof. 31-41, Prof. 41-46 (Education); Asst. Dir., Div. of Instruction 41-44, Exec. Dir. Horace Mann-Lincoln School 43-46, Exec. Officer, Division of Instruction 46 (all at Teachers' Coll., Columbia Univ.); Dean, Coll. of Education, The Ohio State Univ. 46-67, Prof. of Educ. 67-; Expert Consultant, U.S. War Dept. to advise Military Govt. (U.S.) in the field of University Education in Germany 47; Chair. of Comm. to survey the educational institutions of the Foreign Missions Conf. of N. America in the Philippines 48; Chief U.N. Educational Planning Mission to Korea 52-53; Pres. The American Asscn. of Colleges for Teacher Education 57; Chair. The Nat. Comm. on Teacher Education and Professional Standards of the Nat. Education Asscn. 62; Exec. Consultant in Secondary and Teacher Education to Ministry of Education, Govt. of India, and U.S. A.I.D. Mission, India, 58, 61, 64; Chair. Comm. on Education for the Teaching Profession 66.

Office: College of Education, The Ohio State University, 29 West Woodruff Avenue, Columbus, Ohio 43210; Home: 6671 Olentangy River Road, Worthington, Ohio 43085, U.S.A.
Telephone: 885-6065 (Home).

Cottrell, Leonard; British author; b. 21 May 1913; ed. King Edward's Grammar School, Birmingham.
B.B.C. Writer and Producer (Features) 42-51, War Correspondent 44-45, Senior Producer 46-51; UNESCO 51-53; B.B.C. Television (Drama) Writer and Producer 56-60; free-lance radio and television writer 60-.
Publs. *All Men are Neighbours* 47, *The Lost Pharaohs* 50, *The Bull of Minos* 53, *Madame Tussaud* 54, *Life Under The Pharaohs* 55, *Seeing Roman Britain* 56, *The Mountains of Pharaoh* 56, *Lost Cities* 57, *The Great Invasion* 58, *Anvil of Civilisation* 58, *Enemy of Rome* 60, *Concise Encyclopaedia of Archaeology* 61, *The Tiger of Ch'in* 62, *Lost Worlds* 62, *The Lion Gate* 63, *Guide to Egypt, Digs and Diggers, Tutankhamun* 64, *Land of Shinar* 65, *Queens of the Pharoahs* 66.
Sevenhampton Manor, Andoversford, nr. Cheltenham, Glos., England.

Couch, John Nathaniel, A.M., PH.D.; American teacher and research worker; b. 12 Oct. 1896; ed. Univ. of North Carolina, Duke Univ., Univ. of Wis., Univ. of Nancy, France.
Instructor in Botany 17-18 and 22-25, Asst. Prof. 25-28, Assoc. Prof. 28-32, Prof. 32-, all of North Carolina Univ.; Chair., Botanical Dept., Univ. of North Carolina 44-60, Kenan Prof. of Botany 45-; Visiting Assoc. Prof. Johns Hopkins Univ. 33 and Prof. 35; Hopkins Tropical Experimental Station, Jamaica 26; awarded Jefferson Medal, N. Carolina Acad. of Sciences 37; Walker Grand Prize in Nat. History 38; Certificate of Merit 56; Pres. of North Carolina Acad. of Sciences 46; mem. Nat. Acad. of Sciences 43; Pres. Mycological Society of America 43, Chair. South-Eastern Section Botanical Society of America; Assoc. Editor *Mycologia* 37; Editor *Journal Elisha Mitchell Scientific Society* 46-60; Hon. Sc.D. (Catawba Coll.); discovered sporangia and motile cells in actinomycetales 49.
Publs. *The Gasteromycetes of the Eastern United States and Canada* (W. C. Coker and J. N. Couch) 28, *The Genus Septobasidium* 38.
University of North Carolina, Chapel Hill, N.C., U.S.A.

Couch, Virgil Lee, B.S.; American government official; b. 12 Nov. 1907; ed. Univ. of Kentucky.
Agent for the Texas Co., Lexington, Kentucky 30-35; Personnel Adviser and Consultant, Resettlement Admin., Raleigh, N.C. 35-37; Regional Personnel Officer, Farm Security Admin., Dept. of Agriculture, Raleigh, N.C. 37-43; Chief Personnel Officer and Dir. of Labor Relations, Farm Security Admin., Washington 43-46; Chief Personnel Officer and Dir. of Labor Relations, Farmers Home Admin., Washington 46-48; Dir. of Personnel, Econ. Cooperation Admin. (Marshall Plan) 48-51; Dep. Asst. Admin., Dir. of Personnel, Dir. Nat. Civil Defense Staff Coll. and Training Center, Exec. Officer for Training and Educ., Dir. Field Exercises Atomic Test Operations, Dir. Warden Div., Dir. Industry Office, Fed. Defense Admin., Office of Civil and Defense Mobilization, and Dept. of Defense, Washington, D.C., and Battle Creek, Michigan 51-62; Asst. Nat. Dir. of Civil Defense (Industrial Participation), Washington, D.C. 62-; U.S. Rep. to NATO to develop civil defence plans for industry 55-; Consultant to Venezuelan Govt. on public admin. and org. 53-; Editor many technical and professional articles and booklets; official of numerous personnel and management orgs.
Office of Civil Defense, Department of Defense, Washington, D.C.; Home: 4906 North 28th Street, Arlington, Virginia 22207, U.S.A.
Telephone: 202-695-5282 (Office); 703-536-9319 (Home).

Couder, André, DR. ès SCIENCES PHYSIQUES; French astronomer; b. 27 Nov. 1897; ed. Univs. of Paris and Strasbourg.

Began astronomical career at Strasbourg Observatory; moved to Paris Observatory 25, Asst. Astronomer 30, Deputy 37, Astronomer 43, Dir. Optics Laboratory. Vice-Pres. Admin. Council 53-; mem. Nat. Cttee. of Scientific Research 45-66; mem. and Pres. Bureau des Longitudes 51-53; mem. of the Inst. de France (Acad. des Sciences) 54-; Vice-Pres. Int. Astronomical Union 52-58; Pres. Société Astronomique de France 55-57; Pres. Comité de direction de l'Observatoire de Haute-Provence 64-; Assoc. Royal Astronomical Soc. 46-, Royal Acad. of Belgium 61-; Grand-Prix Scientifique de la Ville de Paris 61; Officier Légion d'Honneur, and other decorations.

Publs. *Lunettes et Télescopes* (with A. Danjon) 35, and numerous papers.

11 rue Bobierre de Vallière, 92 Bourg-la-Reine, Seine, France.

Telephone: 702-0981.

Couderc, Paul; French astronomer; b. 15 July 1899; ed. Faculté des Sciences, Paris, and Ecole Normale Supérieure.

Teacher of Mathematics, Lycée, Chartres 26-29, then at Lycées Montaigne, Charlemagne and Janson-de-Sailly, Paris 30-44; Astronomer, Paris Observatory 44-; fmr. Sec.-Gen. French Nat. Cttee. for Astronomy; fmr. Vice-Pres. Astronomical Soc. of France; Officier de la Légion d'Honneur; Officier des Palmes Académiques; UNESCO Kalinga Prize for 1966-67.

Publs. include: *L'Architecture de l'Univers* 30, *Parmi les étoiles* 38, *La Relativité* 42, *L'Expansion de l'Univers* 52.

61 avenue de l'Observatoire, Paris 14e, France.

Coulet, François, L. ès L., L. en D., HON. C.B.E.; French diplomatist; b. 16 Jan. 1906; ed. Univs. of Montpellier and Paris.

Entered Diplomatic Service 35; Third Sec. Moscow 36-37, Second Sec. Helsinki 37-40; served Free French Forces 40-44; Sec.-Gen. of Corsica 43; Commr. of the Republic for the Liberated Territories of the Normandy Beachhead 44; in charge of inter-allied relations 45; Dir. European Dept. (with rank of Minister) Ministry of Foreign Affairs 46-47; Minister to Finland 47-50; Ambassador to Iran 50-55, to Yugoslavia 55-56; granted leave on personal request 56; volunteered for service in Algeria; Lieut.-Col. C.O. Parachute Regt., French Air Force 56-60; Minister and Dir. of Political Affairs to Delegation General, Algiers 60; Pres. Société Financière de Radio-diffusion 62-65; Commdr. de la Légion d'Honneur, Croix Val. Mil. with 3 palms and gold star, etc.

Publ. *Vertu des Temps Difficiles* 67.

81 boulevard de Port-Royal, 75-Paris 13e; and Juvanzé par Vendeuvre, Aube, France.

Coulibaly, Sori; Malian diplomatist; b. *c.* 1925.

Served French Foreign Ministry, Paris; fmr. Sec.-Gen. Ministry of Foreign Affairs, Mali; Perm. Rep. to UN 62-66; Amb. to U.S.S.R. 67-.

Embassy of Mali, Novokuznetskaya ul. 11, Moscow, U.S.S.R.

Coulomb, Jean; French physicist; b. 7 Nov. 1904; ed. Ecole Normale Supérieure.

Dir. Institut de Physique du Globe Algiers 37; Dir. Institut de Physique du Globe Paris 41-56; Prof. at the Sorbonne 41-; Visiting Prof. Istanbul Univ. 54-55; Pres. Int. Asscn. of Terrestrial Magnetism and Electricity 51-54; Dir.-Gen. Centre National de la Recherche Scientifique 56-62; mem. of Cttee. for the Int. Geophysical Year 57-59; Pres. of the Centre National d'Etudes Spatiales 62-67; Vice-Pres. Int. Union of Geodesy and Geophysics 63-67, Pres. 67-; Pres. Bureau des Longitudes 66-; mem. Acad. of Sciences 60, Int. Acad. of Astronautics 66.

Publs. *La Physique des Nuages* (in collaboration) 40, *La*

Constitution Physique de la Terre 52, *Physical Constitution of the Earth* (in collaboration) 63.

102 quai de la Rapée, Paris 12e; Faculté des Sciences, 9 quai St. Bernard, Paris 5e, France.

Telephone: 343-13-36; 336-25-25 (Faculté des Sciences).

Coulson, Charles Alfred, M.A., PH.D., D.SC., F.INST.P., F.I.M.A., F.R.S.E., F.R.S.; British mathematician; b. 13 Dec. 1910; ed. Clifton Coll., and Trinity Coll., Cambridge.

Former Fellow, Trinity Coll. Cambridge; fmr. Lecturer in Mathematics, Univ. Coll. Dundee; Mathematician and Chemist, Oxford Univ. 45-47; Wheatstone Prof. of Physics, King's Coll. London 47-52; Rouse Ball Prof. of Mathematics, Oxford Univ. 52-; Fellow, Wadham Coll. Oxford 52-; Lay Preacher, Methodist Church; Vice-Pres. British Methodist Conf. 59-60; Chair. Oxfam 66-; mem. Central Cttee. World Council of Churches 62-; Pierre Lecomte de Nouy Prize 55.

Publs. Four scientific textbooks, three general books, about 300 research papers, numerous articles on the relations between science and religion.

Mathematical Inst., 24-29 St. Giles, Oxford; Home: 64 Old Road, Headington, Oxford, England.

Coulson, Sir John Eltringham, K.C.M.G.; British diplomatist; b. 13 Sept. 1909; ed. Cambridge Univ.

Entered Foreign Service 32; served Rumania 34-37, Foreign Office, Ministry of Economic Warfare and War Cabinet 37-46; Counsellor, Paris 46-48; Deputy U.K. Rep. O.E.E.C. Paris 48-50; Deputy Permanent Rep. to U.N. 50-52; Asst. Under-Sec. of State, Foreign Office 52-55; Minister in Washington 55-57; Adviser to the Paymaster-Gen. 57-59; Ambassador to Sweden 60-63; Deputy Under-Sec. of State, Foreign Office 63-64; Chief of Admin., Diplomatic Service 65; Sec.-Gen. European Free Trade Asscn. (EFTA) 65-.

32 chemin des Colombettes, Geneva, Switzerland; Home: The Old Mill, Selborne, Hants., England.

Telephone: 34-90-00 (Office).

Courant, Richard; German-born American mathematician; b. 8 Jan. 1888; ed. Breslau, Zürich and Göttingen Univs.

Instructor of Mathematics, Münster Univ. 19-20; Prof. of Mathematics, Göttingen Univ. 20-33; Dir. Inst. of Mathematical Sciences, New York Univ. 34-58, Dir. Emer. and Science Adviser 58-; mem. Nat. Acad. of Sciences, Royal Danish Acad. of Sciences and Letters. Accademia Nazionale dei Lincei, Göttingen Akad. der Wissenschaften, Calcutta Mathematical Soc., Acad. of Sciences of U.S.S.R., etc.; Dr. (h.c.) Darmstadt and Aachen Technical High Schools.

Publs. include: *Funktionentheorie* (with A. Hurwitz) 22, *Methoden der mathematischen Physik*, Vol. I (with D. Hilbert) 23, *Differential and Integral Calculus*, Vol. I 34, Vol. II 36, *Supersonic Flow and Shock Waves* (with K. O. Friedrichs) 48, *Dirichlet's Principle, Conformal Mapping and Minimal Surfaces* 50, *Methods of Mathematical Physics* (Interscience) (with D. Hilbert) 53, *Introduction to Calculus and Analysis*, Vol. I (with F. John).

142 Calton Road, New Rochelle, N.Y., U.S.A.

Telephone: 914-NE6-5312.

Courcel, Geoffroy Chodron de, D. en DR., L. ès L., DIP. ECOLE DES SC. POL.; French diplomatist; b. 11 Sept. 1912; ed. Coll. Stanislas and Paris Univ.

Attaché Warsaw 37; Sec. Athens 38-39; joined Free French forces June 40; Chef de Cabinet, Gen. de Gaulle 40-41; military service in Egypt, Libya and Tunisia 41-43; Dep. Dir. du Cabinet, Gen. de Gaulle 43-44; Regional Comm. for Liberated Territories 44; Deputy Dir. Central and Northern European Sections, Ministry of Foreign Affairs 45-47; First Counsellor Rome 47-50; Dir. Bilateral Trade Agreements' Section, Ministry of Foreign Affairs 50-53; Dir. African and Middle East Section, Ministry of Foreign Affairs 53-54; Dir.-Gen. Political and Economic Affairs, Ministry of Moroccan

and Tunisian Affairs 54-55; Permanent Sec. of Nat. Defence 55-58; Permanent Rep. to N.A.T.O. 58-59; Sec. Gen. Présidence de la République 59-62; Ambassador to U.K. 62-, Ambassadeur de France 65; Commdr. Légion d'Honneur, Compagnon de la Libération, Croix de Guerre, Military Cross, Hon. G.C.V.O., etc.
Publ. *L'influence de la Conférence de Berlin de 1885 sur le droit Colonial International* 36.
French Embassy, 58 Knightsbridge, London, S.W.1, England; and 7 rue de Medicis, Paris, France.

Cournand, André; American (b. France) physician; b. 24 Sept. 1895; ed. Paris Univ.
Resident U.S. since 30; held teaching appointments with Coll. of Physicians and Surgeons, Columbia Univ. 35-, Prof. of Medicine same Coll. 51-60, Emer. 64-; Chair. cardiovascular study section of Nat. Heart Inst. of Washington; mem. several medical and research societies, including American Physiological Society, Asscn. of American Physicians, American Clinical and Climatological Asscn., Nat. Acad. of Sciences; Foreign mem. Académie Nationale de Médecine, Académie des Sciences, Institut de France; hon. mem. British Cardiac Society, Royal Society of Medicine, Swedish Cardiac Society, Sté. Médicale des Hôpitaux de Paris, and Columbia Univ. Chapter of Alpha Omega Alpha; on editorial board of *Circulation* (journal of American Heart Asscn.), *Journal de Physiologie* (Paris), *Revue Française d'Etudes Cliniques et Biologiques* (Paris), and *American Journal of Physiology*; Andreas Retzius Silver Medal of the Swedish Society of Internal Medicine 46; Lasker Award of U.S. Public Health Asscn. 49; John Phillips Memorial Award of American Coll. of Physicians 52; Gold Medal of Royal Academy of Medicine, Brussels 56; served in French Army 15-18, awarded Croix de Guerre with three stars; joint winner Nobel Prize for Medicine 56; Hon. Dr. Univ. of Strasbourg; Hon. Dr. (Univ. of Lyon, Univ. of Brussels, and other univs.); Officier de la Légion d'Honneur.
1361 Madison Avenue, New York City 28, N.Y., U.S.A.

Courrier, Robert, D.SC., D.MÉD.; French professor; b. 6 Oct. 1895; ed. Coll. de France, Paris.
Prof. of Experimental Morphology and Endocrinology at Coll. de France; mem. Scientific Council, Atomic Energy Comm. 57-; mem. Inst. de France and Académie Nationale de Médecine; foreign mem. Royal Soc. 53; Dr. h.c. (Univs. of Brazil, Brussels, Istanbul, Louvain, Athens, Quebec and Geneva); Perm. Sec., Acad. des Sciences; Commdr. Légion d'Honneur.
Publs. include *Endocrinologie de la Gestation, Gabriel Bertrand* 64, *Paul Portier* 66.
3 rue Mazarine, Paris 6e, France.

Courtemanche, Henri, P.C., B.A., LL.B.; Canadian politician and business man; b. 16; ed Acad. de Mont Laurier, Séminaire St. Joseph, Mont Laurier, Coll. St. Laurent, Montreal, and Univ. of Montreal.
Hon. Vice-Pres. of the Rural Bar Asscn. of the Province of Quebec; Dir. and Treas. Hôpital Jean Talon, Montreal; mem. House of Commons 49-53 and 57-60, Deputy Speaker 57; Sec. of State 58-60; Senator 60-; mem. Knights of Columbus; Progressive Conservative. 226 St. James Street, W., Montreal, Canada.

Courthion, Pierre-Barthélemy; French art historian; b. 14 Jan. 1902; ed. Univ. de Genève, Ecole des Beaux-Arts, Paris and Ecole du Louvre.
Former Asst. Dir. Arts section at Int. Inst. of Intellectual Co-operation of Soc. des Nations and Dir. Archaeological Museum, Valère; fmr. Dir. fondation Suisse dans la Cité universitaire de Paris; fmr. Vice-Pres. Union of French Artistic Press; Vice-Pres. Int. Asscn. of Art Critics; mem. Jury of Int. Guggenheim Prize 60-; Cultural Mission to Brazil and Venezuela 63, to American Univs. 65, 67; Silver Medal Reconnaissance française.
Publs. *Gabriele d'Annunzio* 25, *Panorama de la peinture*

contemporaine 27, *Vie d'Eugène Delacroix* 27, *Nicolas Poussin* 29, *Claude Lorrain* 32, *Courbet* (2 vols.), *Henri Matisse* 34, *Genève ou le Portrait des Töpffer* 36, *Delacroix* 40, *Henri Rousseau le Douanier* 44, *Le Visage de Matisse* 45, *Bonnard, Peintre du merveilleux* 45, *Géricault* 47, *Utrillo* 48, *Peintres d'aujourd'hui, Raoul Dufy* 51, *La Montagne, L'Art indépendant, Montmartre* 55, *Paris d'autrefois* 57, *Paris des temps nouveaux* 57, *Le Romantisme* 61, *Manet* 62, *Georges Rouault* 62, *Autour de l'impressionnisme* 65, *Paris de sa naissance à nos jours* 66, *L'Ecole de Paris de Picasso à nos jours* 68, *Seurat* 68; Dir. of art films: *Ingres peintre du nu* 68, *Georges Rouault*, etc.
11 rue des Marronniers, Paris 16e, France.
Telephone: 647-58-03.

Cousins, Rt. Hon. Frank, P.C.; British trade unionist; b. 8 Sept. 1904; ed. King Edward School, Doncaster.
Service with Transport and General Workers Union; appointed successively Organiser (38), Nat. Officer (44), Nat. Sec. (48) of Road Transport Section; Asst. Gen.-Sec. T. & G.W.U. 55, Gen. Sec. 56-64, 66-; mem. British Transport Joint Consultative Council 55-63, Ministry of Labour Nat. Joint Advisory Council 56-, Exec. Council Int. Transport Workers Fed. 56-64, Pres. 58-60, 62-64; elected mem. Gen. Council TUC 56-64, 66-; mem. Dept. Scientific and Industrial Research 60-66, Export Credits Guarantee Dept., Advisory Cttee. 62, Nat. Econ. Development Council (N.E.D.C.) 62-, British Nat. Export Council 67-, Central Advisory Council for Science and Technology 67-; Minister of Technology 64-66; M.P. 65-66; Labour.
Office: Transport and General Workers Union, Transport House, Smith Square, London, S.W.1; Home: 7 Pine Walk, Carshalton Beeches, Surrey, England.
Telephone: 01-828-7788 (Office).

Cousins, Norman, LITT.D., L.D.H., LL.D., D.E.; American editor and author; b. 24 June 1915; ed. Columbia Univ.
Education writer with *New York Evening Post* 35-36; Man. Editor *Current History* 36-40; Editor *Saturday Review* 40-; mem. Board of Dirs. McCall Corpn. and Chair. Editorial Cttee. 61-; Editor *U.S.A.* during Second World War; Pres. United World Federalists 54-56, Hon. Pres. 56-; Pres. World Asscn. of World Federalists 65-; mem. Board of Dirs. UN Asscn. of U.S.A.; officer of many organizations; Service to Educ. Awards 51, 57, 58, 64, 65, 66; Eleanor Roosevelt Peace Award 63.
Publs. *The Good Inheritance, A Treasury of Democracy* 41, *The Poetry of Freedom* (with William Rose Benet) 43, *Modern Man is Obsolete* 45, *Talks with Nehru* 51, *Who Speaks for Man* 53, *In God We Trust* 58, Ed. *March's Dictionary Thesaurus* 58, *Dr. Schweitzer of Lambaréné* 60, *In Place of Folly* 61, *Present Tense* 66.
380 Madison Avenue, New York 17, N.Y., U.S.A.

Cousseran, Paul; French civil administrator; b. 30 July 1922; ed. Ecole nationale de la France d'outre-mer, Ecole Nationale d'Administration.
French Admin., Far East 47-54; Office of Sec. of State for Algeria 56-57; Technical Counsellor, later Dir. of Office of Sec. of State for the French Community 60, Minister of Co-operation 61-62; Amb. to Gabon 63-64; Dir. Secr.-Gen. of Nat. Defence 64-65; Mayor of Limours 65; Pres. Comm. on Nat. Service 66-; Officier Légion d'Honneur.
193, rue de l'Université, Paris 7e, France.

Cousteau, Jacques-Yves; French naval officer and ocean explorer; b. 11 June 1910; ed. Naval School, Brest.
Enseigne de Vaisseau 32, Lieut. 40, Capitaine de Corvette 48; Pres. Compagnies Océanographiques Françaises and Commdr. of the ship *Calypso* 50-; inventor of the Aqualung diving apparatus and of a process to use television under water; founder of the Groupe de Recherches Sous-Marines at Toulon and of the Office Français des Recherches Sous-Marines at

Marseille; Dir. Musée Océanographique de Monaco 57-; Head, Calypso Research Ship Expedition on which 5 divers lived for 4 weeks under Red Sea, July 63; promoted Conshelf saturation dive programme 65; produced the film Le Poisson d'Or; author of films Le Monde du silence 56, Le Monde sans soleil 64; Légion d'Honneur and Croix de Guerre, etc.

Publs. Par 18 Mètres de Fond 46, La Plongée en Scaphandre 48, The Silent World 53, The Living Sea 63, Le Monde du silence et Le Voyage de la Calypso.

Villa Richard, Monaco; Villa Baobab, Sanary-sur-Mer (Var), France.

Coutts, Frederick, C.B.E.; British Salvation Army officer; b. 21 Sept. 1899; ed. Leith Acad. and The Salvation Army Training Coll.

Salvation Army Officer 20-; Literary Dept., Salvation Army Headquarters 35-53; Principal, William Booth Training Coll., London 53-58; Territorial Commdr. Australia East 58-63; General of the Salvation Army Nov. 63-.

Publs. Half Hours with Heroes, The Call to Holiness, The Timeless Prophets, Short Measure, Well Played, In the Dinner Hour, The Battle and the Breeze, Our Father, The Kingdom of God, He had no Revolver, The Salvationist and his Leisure, Portrait of a Salvationist, Jesus and our Need.

The Salvation Army, 101 Queen Victoria Street, London, E.C.4, England.
Telephone: 01-236-5222.

Couture, Pierre Julien; French mining executive; b. 25 Feb. 1909; ed. Lycée St. Louis and Ecole Polytechnique.

Engineer, Chief Engineer and Engineer-Gen. of Mines 33-60; Asst. Dir.-Gen., Houillères de Lorraine 46-60; Dir.-Gen. Mines de la Sarre 50-57; Govt. Admin.-Gen., Commissariat of Atomic Energy 58-63; Adviser, Charbonnages de France 59-63; mem. Board of Admins., Electricité de France 59-63; mem. Council, Ecole Nat. des Mines de Paris; Pres. Devt. Cttee., Ecole Polytechnique 58-63; Pres. of Board of Dirs., Les Mines Domaniales de Potasse d'Alsace 64-67; Pres. Supervisory Board Soc. Commerciale des Potasses d'Alsace 64-68; Pres. Soc. Potasses et Engrais Chimiques 64-67; Pres. Board of Dirs. Entreprise minière et chimique 67-, Mines de Potasses d'Alsace S.A. 68-; Commandeur Légion d'Honneur; Officier du Mérite Saharien; Officier des Palmes Académiques.

22 rue Beaujon, Paris 8e, France.
Telephone: 924-37-95.

Couve de Murville, (Jacques) Maurice; French politician; b. 24 Jan. 1907; ed. Paris Univ.

Principal Personal Sec. to Gen. Giraud, Algiers; mem. French Cttee. for Nat. Liberation June-Nov. 43; Commr. for Finance to 44; Italian Advisory Council 44; Ambassador to Italy 45; Dir.-Gen. Political Affairs, Foreign Office 45-50; Ambassador to Egypt 50, and later to U.S.A.; Amb. to German Fed. Repub. 56-58; Minister of Foreign Affairs 58-68, of Finance May 68-; Pres. North Atlantic Council 67-68.

44 rue du Bac, Paris 7e, France.

Coward, Noel; British playwright, actor and composer; b. 16 Dec. 1899; ed. privately.

First stage appearance 10, later in Present Laughter 48, The Apple Cart 53, etc. Plays: The Rat Trap, Easy Virtue, Fallen Angels, The Vortex, Hay Fever, Private Lives, Point Valaine, Tonight at Eight-thirty, Blithe Spirit, Present Laughter, This Happy Breed, Peace in our Time, Ace of Clubs, Relative Values, Quadrille, After the Ball, South Sea Bubble, Nude with Violin, Look After Lulu, Waiting in the Wings; A Song at Twilight, Shadows of the Evening, Come into the Garden Maud (Suite in Three Keys) 66; Composed music for and wrote revues This Year of Grace 29, Words and Music 32, Sigh No More 45, Ace of Clubs 50; for operettas Bitter Sweet 29, Conversation Piece 34, Operette 38, Pacific 1860 46, Cavalcade 31, Sail Away (musical play), Paris When it Sizzles, Bunny Lake is Missing.

Films: Brief Encounter, In which we Serve, This Happy Breed, The Astonished Heart, Our Man in Havana, Suprise Package, Bunny Lake is Missing 65, Goforth 67.

Publs. To Step Aside 39, Middle East Diary 44, Star Quality 51, Present Indicative 37, Future Indefinite 54 (autobiographies), Pomp and Circumstance (novel) 60, The Collected Short Stories of Noel Coward 62, Pretty Polly Barlow 64, Lyrics of Noel Coward 65, Not Yet the Dodo (poetry) 67, Bon Voyage and Other Stories 67.

Les Avants, sur Montreux, Switzerland.

Cowles, Gardner, A.B.; American publisher; b. 31 Jan. 1903; ed. Phillips Exeter Acad., and Harvard Univ.

City Editor Des Moines Register 25, News Editor 26-27; Assoc. Man. Editor Des Moines Register and Tribune 27, Man. Editor 27-31, Exec. Editor 31-39, Assoc. Publisher 39-43, Pres. 43-; Pres. Register and Tribune Co.; Dir. United Air Lines, R. H. Macy & Co., Bankers Life Co., Gen. Development Corpn.; Chair. of Board and Editor-in-Chief Cowles Communications Inc.; Vice-Pres. and Trustee Museum of Modern Art, New York; Hon. LL.D. Drake Univ. 42, Coe Coll. 48, Long Island Univ. 55, Grinnell Coll. 57; Litt.D. Iowa Wesleyan Coll. 55, Morningside Coll. 58; L.H.D. Bard Coll. 50, Cornell Coll. 51.

Cowles Communications Inc., 488 Madison Avenue, N.Y. 10022, U.S.A.

Cowles, John, A.B.; American newspaperman; b. 14 Dec. 1898; ed. Phillips Exeter Acad., and Harvard Univ.

President, Minneapolis Star and Tribune, Chair. Des Moines Register and Tribune; Dir. Associated Press 34-43, First Nat. Bank of Minneapolis; mem. Hoover Comm. Nat. Defense Establishment Cttee. 48; mem. Business Council; Consultant Nat. Security Council 53; mem. White House Educ. Conf. Cttee. 55; mem. Gen. Advisory Cttee. U.S. Arms Control and Disarmament Agency 62-; Trustee Phillips Exeter Acad. 36-54, American Assembly, Ford Foundation 56-; Carnegie Endowment for Int. Peace; mem. Board of Overseers, Harvard Univ. 44-50, 60-66, Pres. Alumni Asscn. 53-54; Presidential Certificate of Merit (Lease-Lend Admin.), Centennial Award Northwestern Univ., Award for Distinguished Service in Journalism Univ. of Minnesota; Hon. LL.D. (Harvard, Grinnell Coll., Boston Univ., Macalester Coll., Allegheny Coll., Rochester Univ., Carleton), Hon. L.H.D. (Simpson Coll., Drake Univ., Coe Coll.), Hon. Litt.D. (Jamestown Coll.).

Minneapolis Star and Tribune, 425 Portland Avenue, Minneapolis, Minnesota 55415, U.S.A.
Telephone: 612-372-4141.

Cowley, Malcolm, A.B.; American writer; b. 24 Aug. 1898; ed. Harvard and Montpellier Univs.

Copy writer Sweet's Architectural Catalogue 20 and 23-25; free-lance writer 25-29; Literary Editor The New Republic 29-40; staff critic 40-53; literary adviser to the Viking Press 48-; mem. Harvard and Century Clubs, N.Y., American Acad. of Arts and Letters, American Acad. of Arts and Sciences, Nat. Inst. of Arts and Letters (Pres. 56-59, 62-65); Hon. D. Litt.

Publs. Blue Juniata 29, Exile's Return 34 (revised 51), The Dry Season 41, The Literary Situation 54, Black Cargoes 62 (with Daniel P. Mannix), The Faulkner-Cowley File 66, Think Back on Us 67, Blue Juniata: Collected Poems 68; trans. Valéry's Variety 26, Princess Bibesco's Catherine-Paris 27, Gide's Imaginary Interviews 44, etc.; Editor: Adventures of an African Slaver 27, After the Genteel Tradition 37, Books that Changed our Minds 39, The Portable Hemingway 44, The Portable Faulkner 46, The Portable Hawthorne 48, The

Complete Whitman 48, *The Stories of F. Scott Fitz-gerald* 51, *Writers at Work* 58, etc.
Sherman, Conn. 06784, U.S.A.
Telephone: 203-354-6636.

Cox, Archibald, A.B., LL.B.; American lawyer; b. 17 May 1912; ed. St. Paul's School, Concord, and Harvard Univ.
Admitted to Mass. Bar 37; in practice with Ropes, Gray, Best, Coolidge and Rugg, Boston 38-41; Attorney, Office of Solicitor-Gen., U.S. Dept. of Justice 41-43; Assoc. Solicitor, Dept. of Labor 43-45; Lecturer on Law, Harvard Univ. 45-46, Prof. of Law 46-61; Solicitor-Gen. of U.S. 61-65; mem. Board of Overseers, Harvard Univ. 62-.
Publs. *Cases on Labor Law* (5th edn.) 62, and articles in legal periodicals.
4201 Forest Lane, McLean, Virginia, U.S.A.

Cox, Sir Christopher William Machell, K.C.M.G., M.A.; British educationist; b. 17 Nov. 1899; ed. Clifton and Balliol Coll., Oxford.
Fellow New Coll., Oxford 26, Sub-Warden 31, Dean 34-36; Dir. of Education, Anglo-Egyptian Sudan, and Principal Gordon Coll., Khartoum 37-39; Educational Adviser to Colonial Sec. 40-61; Educational Adviser to the Sec. for Technical Co-operation 61-64, to Ministry of Overseas Development 64-; Hon. D.Lit. (Belfast), Hon. LL.D. (Hong Kong, Leeds), Hon. D.C.L. (Oxford). Athenaeum Club, Pall Mall, London, S.W.1; and Ministry of Overseas Development, Eland House, Stag Place, London, S.W.1, England.

Cox, Garfield V., A.B., LL.D., PH.D.; American economist; b. 4 May 1893; ed. Earlham Coll., Richmond, Ind., Beloit Coll., Wis., and Univ. of Chicago.
Professor of Speech, Wabash College Ind. 17; Instr. in Business Admin. Univ. of Chicago 20-25, Asst. Prof. 25-29, Assoc. Prof. of Business Economics 29-30; Prof. of Finance 30-36, Robert Law Prof. of Finance 36-58, Emeritus 58-; Act. Dean, School of Business 42-45, Dean 45-52; Chair. Board South East Nat. Bank 35-60; Trustee Earlham Coll. 54-59; served under American Friends Service Cttee. in War Relief and Reconstruction France 18-19; Chair. Exec. Cttee. Midwest Branch, American Friends Service Cttee. 46-55; Pres. American Finance Asscn. 53-54; Ex. Pres. Chicago Chapter, American Statistical Asscn.; mem. Exec. Cttee. American Asscn. of Collegiate Schools of Business 49-52; Clerk, Claremont Meeting of Friends (Quakers) 62-64; Special Lecturer, Southern Calif. School of Theology 61-65; Lecturer, Claremont Graduate School 62-63, Chicago Theological Seminary 64.
Publs. *Forecasting Business Conditions* (with C. O. Hardy) 27, *An Appraisal of American Business Forecasts* 30; contributions to *Encyclopedia of Social Sciences*, and others.
660 W. Bonita Ave., Apt. 24E, Claremont, Calif. 91711, U.S.A.
Telephone: 714-626-7480.

Cox, Sir (Ernest) Gordon, K.B.E., T.D., F.R.I.C., F.INST.P., D.SC., F.R.S.; British scientist; b. 24 April 1906; ed. City of Bath Boys' School and Univ. of Bristol.
Research Asst. Davy-Faraday Laboratory, Royal Inst. 27; Asst. Lecturer in Chemistry, Univ. of Birmingham 29, Lecturer 32, Senior Lecturer 39, Reader in Chemical Crystallography 40; Prof. of Inorganic and Structural Chemistry, Univ. of Leeds 45-60; mem. Agricultural Research Council 57-60, Sec. 60-; Vice-Pres. Inst. of Physics 50-53.
Publs. papers, chiefly on the crystal structures of chemical compounds.
117 Hampstead Way, London, N.W.11, England.
Telephone: 01-455-2618.

Cox, Oscar Sydney, PH.B., LL.B.; American lawyer; b. 3 Dec. 1905; ed. Massachusetts Inst. of Technology, Yale Coll., and Law School.
Law Firm Cadwalader, Wickersham & Taft 29-34; Asst. Corpn. Counsel of Taxes, New York City 34-38; Asst. to Gen. Counsel of U.S. Treasury 38-41; Gen. Counsel Lend-Lease Admin. and Office for Emergency Management 41-43; Asst. Solicitor-Gen. of U.S. 42-43; Gen. Counsel of Foreign Econ. Admin. 43-45; Dep. Admin., Foreign Econ. Admin. 45; mem. Law Firm Cox, Langford & Brown, Washington D.C.; Chair. U.S. Comm. on Int. Rules of Judicial Procedure; several decorations.
1521 New Hampshire Avenue, N.W., Washington, D.C. 20036, U.S.A.

Cox, Sir Trenchard, Kt., C.B.E., D.LITT., M.A., F.S.A., F.M.A.; British museum official; b. 31 July 1905; ed. Eton Coll., and King's Coll., Cambridge.
Asst. to Keeper, Wallace Collection 32-39; served 39-45 war in Home Office; Dir. City Museum and Art Gallery, Birmingham 44-55; Dir. and Sec. Victoria and Albert Museum 56-66; Chevalier Légion d'Honneur 67.
Publs. *Jehan Foucquet* 31, *David Cox* 47, *Peter Bruegel* 51, *Pictures: A Handbook for Collectors* 56.
33 Queens Gate Gardens, London, S.W.7, England.

Coyne, James E(lliott), B.A., B.C.L.; Canadian banker; b. 17 July 1910; ed. Univ. of Manitoba and Oxford Univ.
Barrister and solicitor, Manitoba 34-38; with research staff, Bank of Canada 38; Sec. Canadian Foreign Exchange Control Board 39-41; Asst. to Chair. War-Time Prices and Trade Board 41, apptd. Deputy Chair. 42; Exec. Asst. to Gov. Bank of Canada 44, Deputy Gov. 49-55, Gov. 55-61; Pres. Industrial Development Bank 55-61, Bank of Western Canada Dec. 66-July 67; Chair. York Trust Savings Co. 63-.
2 Willingdon Road, Rockcliffe, Ottawa 2, Ont., Canada.

Cozzens, James Gould; American writer; b. 19 Aug. 1903; ed. Harvard Univ.
Mem. Nat. Inst. Arts and Letters; Howells Medal, American Acad. of Arts and Letters 60.
Publs. *Confusion* 24, *Michael Scarlett* 25, *Cockpit* 28, *The Son of Perdition* 29, *S.S. San Pedro* 31, *The Last Adam* 33, *Castaway* 34, *Men and Brethren* 36, *Ask Me Tomorrow* 40, *The Just and the Unjust* 42, *Guard of Honor* 48, *By Love Possessed* 57, *Children and Others* 64.
Shadowbrook, Williamstown, Mass., U.S.A.

Crăciun, Constanza; Romanian politician.
Member Central Cttee. Romanian Communist Party 48-; fmr. Pres. of Union of Democratic Romanian Women; Minister of Culture 53-57, Vice-Minister of Culture 57-62; Pres. of State Cttee. for Culture and Arts 62-65; Vice-Pres. of State Council 65-.
State Council, Bucharest, Romania.

Craig, Thomas Rae, O.B.E., T.D.; British steel executive; b. 11 July 1906; ed. Glasgow Acad., and Lycée Malherbe, Caen.
Entire career with Colvilles Ltd., Chair. 65-67; Man. Dir. Scottish and Northwest Group, British Steel Corpn. July 67-; Dir. Bank of Scotland; Army Service 39-45.
Invergare, Rhu, Dunbartonshire, Scotland.

Craig, Walter Early, A.B., LL.B.; American lawyer and judge; b. 26 May 1909; ed. Stanford Univ.
Law practice 34-; Assoc. Fennemore, Craig, Allen and Bledsoe 36-45, Partner 45-55; Partner Fennemore, Craig, Allen and McClennen 55-64; Pres. Maricopa County Bar Asscn. 41, Board of Govs. 49-53, Pres. 51-52; Vice-Pres. Western States Bar Council 55-56, Pres. 56-57; House of Delegates 47-, Board of Govs. 58-65, Pres. American Bar Asscn. 63-64; Council Inter-American Bar Asscn. 64-, and Int. Bar Asscn. 64-; U.S. District Judge Arizona 63-; mem. numerous judicial bodies, several hon. degrees, and numerous awards.
Suite 7012, U.S. Court House, Phoenix, Arizona 85025, U.S.A.
Telephone: 602-261-3547.

Cramér, Harald, PH.D.; Swedish university professor, b. 25 Sept. 1893; ed. Stockholm Univ.
Membership of Govt. Cttees. on Insurance Questions 17-; Prof. of Mathematical Statistics and Actuarial Mathematics, Univ. of Stockholm 29-58, Pres. 50-58; Chancellor of Univs. 58-61; Visiting Prof. Princeton, Yale and Berkeley Univs. 46-47, Columbia Univ. 63, Moscow and Leningrad 63, Berkeley 66; mem. Royal Swedish Acad. of Science, Norwegian Acad. of Science, mem. American Acad. of Arts and Sciences; Hon. mem. Int. Statistical Inst.; Hon. Pres. Swedish Soc. of Actuaries; Hon. D.Sc. Princeton, Stockholm and Copenhagen Univs.
Publs. *Random Variables and Probability Distributions* 37, *Mathematical Methods of Statistics* 45, *Elements of Probability Theory* 54, *Collective Risk Theory* 55, *Stationary and Related Stochastic Processes* (with M. R. Leadbetter) 67.
Skärviksvägen 33, Djursholm, Sweden.
Telephone: 08-755 23 19.

Cramer, Morgan J.; American business executive; b. 6 Oct. 1906; ed. Lehigh Univ., Bethlehem, Pennsylvania.
P. Lorillard Company 31-66, Sales Dept. 31-60, Dir. 58-65, Vice-Pres. 60-61, Asst. to Pres. 61, Pres. 61-62, Pres. and Chief Exec. Officer 62-65; Pres. and Chief Exec. Officer Royal Crown Cola Int. Ltd. 66-; U.S. Army 43-46.
35 Sutton Place, New York City 10022, N.Y., U.S.A.

Cramois, André; French engineer; b. 9 Oct. 1900; ed. Ecole Supérieure d'Electricité and Ecole des Sciences Politiques.
Président, Confédération internationale du Crédit agricole; admin. of Nat. Bank for Commerce and Industry; mem. Acad. d'Agriculture; Commdr. Légion d'Honneur; Commdr. du Mérite agricole.
Publs. *Co-opératives agricoles* 47; (with others): *Mémento du chimiste* 27, *La Science et ses applications* 30.
1 rue Oudinot, Paris 7e, France.

Crane, Jacob Leslie; American engineer, administrator, town planning consultant; b. 14 Sept. 1892; ed. Univs. of Harvard and Michigan.
Engineer on municipal works and housing 13-21; consulting engineer and city planner since 21; worked on development plans for 60 towns and cities in U.S., China, Russia and Latin America; U.S. Housing Authority 38-40; Asst. Co-ordinator Defense Housing 40-42; Dir. Div. of Urban Development Nat. Housing 32-39; Special Asst. to Administrator 45-48; Asst. to Administrator, Housing and Home Finance Agency 48-54, Consultant 54-; lecturer at several Univs.; consultation on housing and urban reconstruction in Britain, France, Italy 44-45, in South America 45-46; Consultant to UN 46-; Senior Consultant Doxiadis Associates 55-; Chair. Special UN Housing Mission to S. Asia 50-51; Past Pres. American City Planning Inst.; mem. American Soc. of Civil Engineers and Int. Fed. for Housing and Planning.
Cosmos Club, Washington, D.C.; and 1224 Boucher Avenue, Annapolis, Maryland 21403, U.S.A.

Cranko, John; British choreographer; b. 15 Aug. 1927; ed. Univ. of Cape Town.
Worked with Cape Town Univ. Ballet for which he choreographed and produced *The Soldier's Tale, Primavera, Tritsch-Tratsch,* etc.; joined Sadler's Wells Ballet School 46; resident choreographer at Sadler's Wells Theatre 50; freelance with The Royal Ballet, La Scala, The English Opera Group, the Edinburgh Festival, the Paris Opera; Dir. of Württemberg State Opera Ballet, Stuttgart, Germany 61-.
Productions include, for the Sadler's Wells Ballet, *Sea Change* 49, *Beauty and the Beast* 50, *Pastorale, Pineapple Poll* 51, *Harlequin in April, Bonne Bouche* 53, *The Shadow* 53, *The Lady and the Fool* 54, *The Prince of the Pagodas* 57, *Antigone* 59; also for the New York City Ballet at Covent Garden, *The Witch,* and a revue for the New Watergate Theatre Club (in conjunction with John Addison) *Cranks,* and *Keep Your Hair On* (a musical); *Sweeney Todd* 59, *New Cranks* (revue) 60, *The Catalyst* 61, *Scènes de Ballet* 61, *Daphnis and Chloe* 62, *Romeo and Juliet* 63, *L'Estero Harmonico* 63; for Württemberg State Opera Ballet, *Swan Lake, Fire Bird* 64, *Onegin* 65, *The Nutcracker* 67.
7 Stuttgart Sud, Neue Weinsteige 73B, German Federal Republic; and 19 Alderney Street, London, W.1, England.

Craw, Charles; New Zealand diplomatist; b. 1919.
Served Fleet Air Arm and R.A.F., Second World War; joined N.Z. Dept. of External Affairs 46; Second Sec., Perm. Mission of New Zealand to UN 48-50; Asst. Sec. Dept. of External Affairs 56-58, 62-64; N.Z. Rep. on SEATO Council and Chargé d'Affaires, Bangkok 58-61, Amb. to France 64, later Deputy High Commr. in U.K.; Perm. Rep. to UN 67-.
Permanent Mission of New Zealand to the United Nations, 733 Third Avenue, New York, N.Y. 10017, U.S.A.

Crawford and Balcarres, Earl of; Lord David Lindsay Balniel, K.T.; British public official; b. 20 Nov. 1900; ed. Eton and Magdalen Coll., Oxford.
Conservative M.P. for Lonsdale Div. of Lancashire 24-40; succeeded to Earldom 40; Parl. Private Sec. to Min. of Agriculture 24-29; fmr. Pres. Library Asscn.; Trustee Nat. Gallery, Tate Gallery and British Museum; Chair. Royal Fine Arts Comm. 43-57; Chair. Board of Trustees Nat. Library of Scotland 44-; Deputy Gov. Royal Bank of Scotland 62-; Chair. Nat. Trust 45-65; mem. Standing Comm. on Museums and Galleries 37-; Rector St. Andrews Univ. 52; Hon. LL.D. (Cambridge).
Balcarres, Colinsburgh, Fife, Scotland.

Crawford, Sir Frederick, G.C.M.G., O.B.E.; British colonial administrator; b. 9 March 1906; ed. Hymers Coll., Hull, and Balliol Coll., Oxford.
Cadet, Tanganyika 29, Asst. District Officer 31, District Officer 41; seconded to East Africa Governors' Conf. 42-43 and 45-46; Economic Sec. N. Rhodesia 47, Dir. of Development 48-50; Gov. and C.-in-C. Seychelles 51-53; Dep. Gov., Kenya 53-57; Gov. of Uganda 57-61; Dir. (Rhodesia) Anglo-American Corpn. of South Africa Ltd., and other companies.
Anglo-American Corpn. Rhodesia Ltd., 70 Jameson Avenue, Salisbury, Rhodesia.

Crawford, Joan; American film actress and business executive; b. 23 March 1908; ed. Stevens Coll., Columbia, Missouri.
Appeared in more than seventy films 25-; Dir. Pepsi Cola Bottling Co. 59-; in silent films 25-29.
Talking films include: *Hollywood Revue* 29, *Untamed* 29, *Montana Moon* 30, *Paid* 30, *Dance, Fools, Dance, Laughing Sinners* 31, *This Modern Age* 31, *Possessed* 32, *Letty Lynton* 32, *Grand Hotel* 32, *Rain* 32, *Today We Live* 33, *Dancing Lady* 33, *Sadie McKee* 34, *Chained* 34, *Forsaking All Others* 34, *No More Ladies* 35, *I Live My Life* 35, *The Gorgeous Hussy* 36, *Love on the Run* 36, *The Last of Mrs. Cheyney* 37, *The Bride Wore Red* 37, *Mannequin* 38, *The Shining Hour* 39, *The Ice Follies of 1939* 39, *The Women* 39, *Strange Cargo* 39, *The Gay Mrs. Trexel* 40, *A Woman's Face* 41, *When Ladies Meet* 42, *They All Kissed the Bride* 42, *Reunion in France* 43, *Above Suspicion* 43, *Mildred Pierce* 46, *Humoresque, Daisy Kenyon* 48, *Flamingo Road, The Damned Don't Cry* 50, *Harriet Craig* 50, *Goodbye My Fancy* 51, *This Woman is Dangerous* 52, *Sudden Fear* 52, *Torch Song* 53, *Johnny Guitar* 54, *Female on the Beach* 55, *Queen Bee* 56, *Autumn Leaves* 56, *Story of Esther Costello* 57, *The Best of Everything* 59, *The Caretakers* 62, *What Ever Happened*

to Baby Jane 62, *Strait-Jacket* 63, *I Saw What You Did* 65, *Berserk* 68.
Publ. *A Portrait of Joan* (autobiog.).
8008 W. Norton Avenue, Hollywood, California 90046, U.S.A.

Crawford, Sir John Grenfell, Kt., C.B.E., M.EC.; Australian administrator; b. 4 April 1910; ed. Univ. of Sydney.
Lecturer in Rural Economics, Univ. of Sydney 34-42; Economic Adviser, Rural Bank of N.S.W. 35-46; Adviser, Dept. of War Organisation of Industry 42-43; Dir. of Research, Commonwealth Ministry of Post-War Reconstruction 43-46; Dir. Commonwealth Bureau of Agricultural Economics 45-50; Commonwealth Wool Adviser 49-55; Sec. Dept. of Commerce and Agriculture, Canberra 50-56, Dept. of Trade 56-60; Consultant to Int. Bank for Reconstruction and Devt.; Dir. School of Pacific Studies, Australian Nat. Univ. 60-67, Vice-Chancellor of Australian Nat. Univ. 68-, and Fiscal Adviser to Univ.; Vice-Chair. Commonwealth Econ. Enquiry 63-64; Walter and Eliza Hall Fellow 33-35; Commonwealth Fund Fellow, U.S.A. 38-40; Farrer Medallist (and Orator) 57; Fellow Australian Inst. of Agricultural Science 58.
Publs. *National Income of Australia* (with Colin Clark) 38; Editor and author *Australian War-Time Agriculture* 54; *Australian Trade Policy 1942-1949: A Documentary History* 68.
Australian National University, Canberra, A.C.T. 2600, Australia.

Crawford, Sir (Robert) Stewart, B.A., K.C.M.G., C.V.O.; British diplomatist; b. 27 Aug. 1913; ed. Gresham's School, Holt, and Oriel Coll., Oxford.
Air Ministry 36; Private Sec. to Chief of Air Staff 40-46; Asst. Sec. Control Office for Germany and Austria 46-47; Foreign Office 47-52; Counsellor, Oslo 54-56; Counsellor, later Minister, Baghdad 57-59; Deputy U.K. Del. to OEEC, Paris 59-60; Asst. Under-Sec., Foreign Office 61-66; Political Resident in Persian Gulf, Bahrain 66-.
c/o D.S.A.O., King Charles St., London S.W.1, England.

Crawford, William Avery; American diplomatist; b. 14 Jan. 1915; ed. Haverford Coll., Haverford, Pa., Centro de Estudios Historicos, Madrid, Ecole Libre des Sciences Politiques, Paris, Harvard Coll., Columbia Univ. and Nat. War Coll., Washington, D.C.
Foreign Service 41-, Havana 41-44, Dept. of State 44-45, Moscow 45-47, Dept. of State 47-50, Paris 50-54, Dept. of State 54-57, Prague 57-59; Dir. Office of Research and Analysis for Sino-Soviet Bloc, Dept. of State 59-61; Minister to Rumania 61-64, Ambassador 64-65; Special Asst. for Int. Affairs to Supreme Allied Commdr., Europe, NATO 65-.
Supreme Headquarters, Allied Powers in Europe, Casteau-Masière, nr. Mons, Belgium.

Crean, Gordon Gale, B.A., F.R.S.A.; Canadian diplomatist; b. 14; ed. Upper Canada Coll., Toronto, Trinity Coll., Univ. of Toronto and New Coll., Oxford Univ.
British Army 40-45; Second Sec.. Dept. of External Affairs, Canada 45-, First Sec., Canadian Embassy, Belgrade, Counsellor, Office of High Commr., London 52; Head of Division, Dept. of External Affairs, Ottawa 53-58; Minister, Canadian Embassy, France 58-61; Ambassador to Yugoslavia 61-64, to Italy 64-, and High Commr. to Malta 65-.
27 Via G.B. de Rossi, Rome, Italy.

Creighton, Donald Grant, C.C., B.A., M.A., D.LITT.' LL.D.; Canadian univ. professor; b. 15 July 1902; ed· Victoria Coll., Univ. of Toronto and Balliol Coll., Oxford·
Lecturer in History, Univ. of Toronto 27-32, Asst. Prof. 32-39, Assoc. Prof. 39-45, Prof. 45-; Chair. Dept. of History 55-59; Research Asst. Royal Comm. on Dominion-Provincial Relations 38-39; John Simon Guggen-

heim Memorial Fellowship 40-41; Rockefeller Fellow 44-45; Nuffield Fellow 51-52; Pres. Canadian Historical Assoc. 56-57; mem. Historic Sites and Monuments Board of Canada; Chair. Canadian Board of Editors, *Encyclopaedia Americana;* Fellow, Royal Soc. of Canada; mem. Monckton Comm. 60, Ontario Advisory Cttee. on Confed. 65; Sir John A. Macdonald Prof. of History, Univ. of Toronto 65, Univ. Prof. 67; Tyrrell Medal for History 51, Gov.-General's Medal for Academic Non-Fiction 52 and 55, Univ. of British Columbia Medal for Popular Biography 55, Univ. of Alberta Nat. Award in Letters 57, Molson Prize of Canada Council 64; D.Litt. (Univ. of Manitoba 57, McGill Univ. 59), Hon. LL.D. (Univ. of New Brunswick 49, Queen's Univ., Kingston, Ontario 56, Univ. of Saskatchewan 57, Univ. of British Columbia 59, St. Francis Xavier 67, Victoria (B.C.) 67).
Publs. *The Commercial Empire of the St. Lawrence* 37, *Dominion of the North: a History of Canada* 44, *John A. Macdonald: The Young Politician* 52, *John A. Macdonald: The Old Chieftain* 55, *Harold Adams Innis: Portrait of a Scholar* 57, *The Story of Canada* 59, *The Road to Confederation: The Emergence of Canada 1863-1867* 64.
Dept. of History, Univ. of Toronto, Toronto 5, Canada.

Cremer, Fritz; German sculptor; b. 22 Oct. 1906; ed. Hochschule für bildende Künste, Berlin-Charlottenburg.
Studied in France, England and Italy; master's studio, Prussian Acad. of Arts, Berlin 38; Prof. of Sculpture, Akad. für angewandte Kunst, Vienna; mem. Deutsche Akad. der Künste, Berlin 50-; Nat. Prize; Art Prize of Freier Deutscher Gewerkschaftsbund 61; Vaterländischer Verdienstorden in Gold 65.
Deutsche Akademie der Künste, Robert-Koch-Platz 7, Berlin, N.4, Germany.

Cremer, Herbert William, C.B.E., M.SC., C.ENG., F.R.I.C., M.I.CHEM.E., F.INST.F., M.CONS.E.; British consulting chemical engineer; b. 22 Jan. 1893; ed. King's School, Canterbury, and King's Coll., Univ. of London.
Technical Staff Dept. of Explosives Supply 15-18; Dir. of Chemical Warfare Supplies Dept. of Mil. Requirements 18; H.Q. Staff Dept. of Scientific and Industrial Research 19-20; Lecturer in Chemistry King's Coll. 20, inaugurated study of chemical engineering, becoming Dir. of Chemical Engineering Studies King's Coll. 28-39; Chief Chemical Engineer to Sir Alexander Gibb & Partners, Consulting Engineers 39-46; Pres. Royal Inst. of Chemistry 51-53; Pres. Inst. of Chemical Engineers 47-49; Vice-Pres. Society of Chemical Industry 47-50; mem. Gen. Board and Exec. Cttee. of Nat. Physical Laboratory; Chair. Water Pollution Research Board 46-51; Thames Survey Cttee. 48-63; and Chemical Engineering Research Cttee. 49-52, of Dept. of Scientific and Industrial Research; Chair. Standing Technical Cttee. on Synthetic Detergents 56-; mem. Nat. Advisory Council for Education in Industry and Commerce 52-58; mem. of Governing Body of Loughborough Univ. of Technology and of Imperial Coll., Univ. of London.
Publs. Joint compiler of *Technical Records of Explosives Supply* 15-19; Gen. Ed. *Encyclopaedia of Chemical Engineering Practice* (12 vols.) 56-65.
Bickley Court, Chislehurst Road, Bromley, Kent, England.
Telephone: 01-467-5260.

Cremin, Cornelius Christopher, M.A., B.COMM.; Irish diplomatist; b. 6 Dec. 1908; ed. Nat. Univ. of Ireland, British Schools at Athens and Rome, Oxford Univ.
Served Paris 37-43, Berlin 43-45, Lisbon 45-46; Asst. Sec. Dept. of External Affairs 48-50; Irish Del. to O.E.E.C. Conf. 48; Ambassador to France and Head of Irish Del. to O.E.E.C. 50-54; Ambassador to Holy See 54-56, to the U.K. 56-58, 63-64; Perm. Rep. of Ireland to United

Nations 64-; Sec. Dept. of External Affairs, Dublin 58-62; Grand Officier Légion d'Honneur; Knight Grand Cross Order of Pius, Grosses Bundesverdienstkreuz.
Permanent Mission of Ireland to United Nations, 866 United Nations Plaza Suite 520, New York, N.Y. 10017, U.S.A.

Crepin, Général d'Armée Jean-Albert-Emile; French army officer; b. 1 Sept. 1908; ed. Ecole Polytechnique.
Served China, Cameroun 33-39; with Free French Army 40-44, served Chad, Fezzan, Tunisia, France, Germany; served Indo-China 45; attached to 8th Infantry Div., Paris 51; Inspector-General of Works and Planning for the Armed Forces 54-60; Général de Corps d'Armée, Algeria 59; Cmmdr. Forces in Algeria 60-61; Général d'Armée, C-in-C. French Forces in Germany 61-63; C.-in-C. Allied Forces, Central Europe 63-66; Pres. Nord-Aviation 67-; Grand Officier, Légion d'Honneur, Compagnon de la Libération, Croix de Guerre (39-45), Croix de la Valeur Militaire.
6 rue Francisque-Sarcey, Paris 16e, France.

Crespin, Régine; French soprano; ed. Lycée de Nîmes and Conservatoire National d'Art Dramatique.
Singer, Opéra, Paris 51-; has sung in principal concert houses, Europe and United States; Officier des Arts et Lettres 61, Officier Légion d'Honneur 65.
3 avenue Frochot, Paris 9e, France.

Creswell, Keppel Archibald Cameron, C.B.E., F.B.A., F.S.A.; British archaeologist; b. 13 Sept. 1879; ed. Westminster School.
Served First World War; Inspector of Monuments, Occupied Enemy Territory (Syria, Palestine) 19-20; lived in Cairo 20-; mem. Cttee. Persian Exhibition, London 31; Prof. of Muslim Architecture, Fouad I Univ. 31-51, American Univ., Cairo 56-; Trustee, Palestine Museum of Antiquities 49-; mem. of Cttee. for the Conservation of Muslim Monuments, Cairo; Syrian Order of Merit (First Class); Order of Ismali, Third Class; Hon. D.Litt. (Oxford), Hon. Lit.D. (Princeton), Hon. A.R.I.B.A.
Publs. *Brief Chronology of the Muslim Monuments of Egypt* 19, *Origin of the Cruciform Plan of Cairene Madrasas* 22, *Archæological Researches at the Citadel of Cairo* 24, *The Works of Sultan Bibars in Egypt* 26, *Early Muslim Architecture,* 2 vols., folio, 32-40, *The Muslim Architecture of Egypt,* 2 vols., folio, 52-59, *A Short Account of Early Muslim Architecture* 58, *A Bibliography of the Architecture, Arts and Crafts of Islam* 61.
American University, Cairo; 2 rue Baehler, Qasr en-Nil, Cairo, United Arab Republic; The Athenaeum, Pall Mall, London, S.W.1 England.

Creswell, Sir Michael Justin, K.C.M.G.; British diplomatist; b. 21 Sept. 1909; ed. Rugby School, New Coll., Oxford, and Queen's Coll., Oxford.
Entered foreign service 33; served Berlin 35-38, Madrid 39-44, Athens 44, Foreign Office 45-47, Teheran 47-49, Singapore 49-51; Minister in Cairo 51-54; Minister to Helsinki 54, Ambassador Sept. 54-58; Senior Civilian Instructor, Imperial Defence Coll. 58-60; Ambassador to Yugoslavia 60-64, to Argentina 64-.
British Embassy, Buenos Aires, Argentina.

Crew, Francis Albert Eley, T.D., M.D., D.SC., PH.D., LL.D., F.R.S., F.R.C.P.ED., F.R.S.ED.; British biologist; b. 88; ed. King Edward's School, Birmingham and Edinburgh Univ.
Dir. Inst. of Animal Genetics, Edinburgh Univ. 19-28; Prof. of Animal Genetics, Edinburgh Univ. 28-44; Prof. of Public Health and Social Medicine, Edinburgh Univ. 44-55; Dir. of Medical Research, Army Medical Directorate, War Office 42-45; Prof. of Preventive and Social Medicine, Ein Shams Univ., Cairo 56; WHO Visiting Prof. of Preventive and Social Medicine, Rangoon Univ. 57-58, Bombay 59-61; Hon. D.Sc.
Publs. *Animal Genetics* 25, *The Genetics of Sexuality*

in Animals 27, *Organic Inheritance in Man* 27, *Sex-determination* 65, *Genetics in Relation to Clinical Medicine* 47, *Measurements of the Public Health, Essays in Social Medicine, Official Medical History of War Vol. I* 53, *Vol. II* 54, *Vol. III* 56, *Vol. IV* 57, *Vol. V* 59, *Vol. VI* 62, *Vol. VII* 66, *Health, its Nature and Conservation* 65, *The Foundation of Genetics* 66.
22 Lansdowne Road, Tunbridge Wells, Kent, England.

Crick, Francis Harry Compton, PH.D., F.R.S.; British biologist; b. 8 June 1916; ed. Univ. Coll., London, and Cambridge Univ.
Scientist, Admiralty, Second World War; Medical Research Council (M.R.C.) Student, Strangeways Laboratory, Cambridge 47-49; M.R.C. Laboratory of Molecular Biology, Cambridge 49-; Protein Structure Project, Brooklyn Polytechnic, New York 53-54; Fellow, Churchill Coll., Cambridge 60-61; Univ. Coll., London 62; Nobel Prize for Medicine (with J. D. Watson and M. H. F. Wilkins) 62.
Publs. Over 30 papers on the structure of deoxyribonucleic acid (DNA) polynucleotides, polypeptides, proteins, viruses; *Of Molecules and Men* 67, etc.
Laboratory of Molecular Biology, Hills Road, and The Golden Helix, 19 Portugal Place, Cambridge, England.

Critchfield, Charles Louis, B.S., M.A., PH.D.; American physicist; b. 7 June 1910; ed. Eastern High School, George Washington Univ.
With Nat. Bureau of Standards 30-37; Instructor Univ. of Rochester 39-40; Nat. Research Fellow Princeton Univ. and Inst. for Advanced Study 40-41; Instructor Harvard Univ. 41-42; physicist, Geophysical Laboratory 42-43; group leader Los Alamos 43-46; Assoc. Prof. George Washington Univ. 46; physicist, Monsanto Chemical Co., Oak Ridge, Tenn. 46-47; Assoc. Prof. Univ. of Minnesota 47-49, Prof. of Physics 49-55; Dir. of Scientific Research, Convair Div. of Gen. Dynamics Corpn. 55-60; Vice-Pres. Research Telecomputing Corpn. 60-61; assoc. division leader Theoretical Physics Division, Los Alamos Scientific Laboratory 61-; mem. Editorial Board *Annual Review of Nuclear Science* 57-61; Assoc. Editor *Journal of the Franklin Inst.* 56-62; Assoc. Editor *Physical Review* 51-54; Fellow American Physical Soc.; Nat. Research Fellowship 40.
Publs. *Theory of Atomic Nucleus and Nuclear Energy Sources* (with G. Gamow) 49, and many papers.
Home: 391 El Conejo, Los Alamos, New Mexico; Office: Theoretical Division, Los Alamos Scientific Laboratory, Los Alamos, N.M., U.S.A.

Critchley, Thomas Kingston, C.B.E., B.EC.; Australian diplomatist; b. 16; ed. North Sydney Boys' High School and Sydney Univ.
Asst. Econ. Adviser, Dept. of War Organization of Industry 43-44; Head, Research Section, Far Eastern Bureau, New Delhi, British Ministry of Information 44-46; Head, Economic Relations Section, Dept. of External Affairs, Canberra 46-47; Australian Rep. UN Cttee. of Good Offices on Indonesian Question 48-49; Rep. UN Comm. for Indonesia 49-50; Acting Australian Commr. Malaya 51-52; Rep. UN Comm. for Unification and Rehabilitation of Korea (UNCURK) 52-54; Head, Pacific and Americas Branch, Dept. of External Affairs, Canberra 54-55; Commr. Fed. of Malaya 55-57, High Commr. 57-63, High Commr. in Malaysia 63-65; Senior External Affairs Rep., Australian High Comm., London 66-.
Australia House, Strand, London, W.C.2, England.

Crocker, Walter Russell, C.B.E.; Australian diplomatist; b. 25 March 1902; ed. Balliol Coll., Oxford, Univ. of Adelaide, Australia, and Stanford Univ., California.
With British Colonial Service 30-34, L.N. and I.L.O. 34-40; served army 40-46; with U.N. 46-49; Prof. of Int. Relations, Australian Nat. Univ. 49-52, Acting Vice-

Chancellor 51; High Commr. for Australia in India 52-55; Ambassador to Indonesia 55-57; High Commr. in Canada 57-59; High Commr. in India 59-62 and Ambassador to Nepal 60-62; Ambassador to the Netherlands and Belgium 62-65; Ambassador to Ethiopia and High Commr. to Kenya and to Uganda 65-67, to Italy 68-; Croix de Guerre, Order of the Lion (Belgium).
Publs. *The Japanese Population Problem* 31, *Nigeria: Critique of Colonial Administration* 36, *On Governing Colonies* 46, *Self-Government for Colonies* 49, *Can the U.N. Succeed?* 51, *The Racial Factor in International Relations* 55, *Nehru* 66.
Australian Embassy, Rome, Italy.

Crockett, William J., B.S.; American government official; b. 22 July 1914; ed. Univ. of Nebraska.
Served City National Bank, Hastings, Neb. 33-51; in Dept. of State, served Beirut, Karachi, Rome 51-58, Washington 58-61, Asst. Sec. for Admin. 61-63; Deputy Under Sec. for Admin. 63-.
Department of State, Washington 25, D.C., U.S.A.

Croft-Cooke, Rupert, B.E.M. (Military); British writer and poet; b. 20 June 1903; ed. Tonbridge School and Wellington Coll., Shropshire.
Publs. *Some Poems* 29; novels: *Troubadour* 30, *Give Him the Earth* 30, *Night Out* 32, *Cosmopolis* 32, *Release the Lions* 33, *Picaro* 34, *Shoulder the Sky* 34, *Blind Gunner* 35, *Crusade* 36, *Kingdom Come* 37, *Rule, Britannia* 38, *Same Way Home* 39, *Glorious* 41, *Octopus* 46, *Ladies Gay* 46, *Wilkie* 48, *Brass Farthing* 50, *Three Names for Nicholas* 51, *Nine Days with Edward* 52, *Harvest Moon* 53, *Fall of Man* 55, *Seven Thunders* 56, *Barbary Night* 58, *Thief* 60, *Clash by Night* 61, *Paper Albatross* 65; general: *Madeira* 61; play: *Banquo's Chair*; autobiography: *The World is Young* 37, *The Man in Europe Street* 38, *The Circus Has No Home* 40, *The Moon in my Pocket* 48, *The Life for Me* 53, *The Blood Red Island* 53, *The Verdict of You All* 55, *The Tangerine House* 56, *The Gardens of Camelot* 58, *The Circus Book* (anthology) 47, *The Quest of Quixote* 59, *The Altar in the Loft* 60, *English Cooking* 60, *The Glittering Pastures* 62, *The Numbers Came* 63, *The Last of Spring* 64; *Bosie: The Life of Lord Alfred Douglas* 63 (biography), *The Wintry Sea* 64, *The Gorgeous East* 65, *The Purple Streak* 66, *The Wild Hills* 66, *The Happy Highways* 67, *Feasting with Panthers* 68.
Box 2044, Tanger-Socco, Tangier, Morocco.

Cromer, The Earl of; **George Rowland Stanley Baring**, P.C.; British merchant banker and financial administrator; b. 28 July 1918; ed. Eton Coll., and Trinity Coll., Cambridge.
Served with Grenadier Guards, rising to rank of Lt. Col. 39-46; Man. Dir. Baring Brothers and Co. Ltd. 47-58; Economic Minister and Head of U.K. Treasury Del., Washington, U.K. Exec. Dir. Int. Monetary Fund, Int. Bank for Reconstruction and Development, Int. Finance Corpn. 59-61; Gov. Bank of England 61-66; U.K. Gov., Int. Bank for Reconstruction and Devt., Int. Finance Corpn., Int. Devt. Asscn. 63-66; Partner Baring Brothers and Co. Ltd.; Dir. Union Carbide Corpn. 67-; Chair. IBM (U.K.) Ltd. 67-; Hon. D.LL. Univ. of New York 66.
Baring Brothers and Co. Ltd., 8 Bishopsgate, London, E.C.2, England.
Telephone: 01-588-2830.

Cronin, Archibald Joseph, M.D., M.R.C.P., D.PH.; British physician and writer; b. 19 July 1896; ed. Glasgow Univ.
Practised medicine until 30; Hon. D.Litt. Bowdoin Coll. and Lafayette Coll.
Publs. *Hatter's Castle*, *Three Loves*, *Grand Canary*, *The Stars Look Down*, *The Citadel*, *Jupiter Laughs* (play), *The Keys of the Kingdom*, *The Green Years*, *Shannon's Way*, *The Spanish Gardener*, *Adventures in Two Worlds*, *Beyond this Place*, *Crusaders' Tomb*, *The Northern Light*,

The Judas Tree, *A Song of Sixpence;* creator *Dr. Finlay's Casebook.*
Villa Allwinden, Kastanienbaum, Lucerne, Switzerland.

Cronkite, Walter Leland, Jr.; American television correspondent; b. 4 Nov. 1916; ed. Univ. of Texas.
News writer and Editor, Scripps-Howard & United Press, Houston, Kansas City, Dallas, Austin, El Paso and New York City; United Press War Corresp. 42-45, later Foreign Corresp., Chief Corresp. Nuremberg War Crimes Trials, Bureau Manager, Moscow 46-48; Lecturer 48-49; Columbia Broadcasting System, television commentator 50-, News Analyst, CBS T.V. News 50-, Managing Editor CBS *Evening News with Walter Cronkite*; Narrator for *Twentieth Century.*
Columbia Broadcasting System Inc., 524 West 57th Street, New York City, New York, U.S.A.

Crooker, John Henry, Jr., A.B., LL.B.; American lawyer and government official; b. 26 Oct. 1914; ed. Rice Univ. and Univ. of Texas.
Member law firm Fulbright, Crooker, Freeman, Bates and Jaworski, Houston, Texas and Washington, D.C. 37-68; Chair. U.S. Civil Aeronautics Board 68-; mem. Council of Corpn., Banking and Business Law Section of State Bar of Texas, Section Chair. 58-59; U.S. Naval Reserve 41-45; mem. Rice Univ. Board of Assocs., Board of Regents, State Senior Colls. of Texas; Pres. Episcopal Churchmen's Asscn., Houston, etc.
Civil Aeronautics Board, 1825 Connecticut Avenue, N.W., Washington, D.C. 20428, U.S.A.
Telephone: 202-393-3111.

Crosby, Bing (Harry Lillis); American actor and singer; b. 2 May 1904; ed. Gonzaga Univ., Spokane.
Singer with dance bands 25-30; has broadcast since 31; has appeared in numerous films, including *Pennies from Heaven, Holiday Inn, Going My Way, Blue Skies, Mr. Music, Little Boy Lost, White Christmas, Country Girl, Anything Goes, High Society, Say One For Me, The Jimmy Durante Story, The Bells of St. Mary's, Road to Hong Kong;* Pres. Bing Crosby Productions Ltd.; Hon. Ph.D. Gonzaga Univ.
780 North Gower, Los Angeles, Calif. 90038, U.S.A.

Crosby, John Campbell; American journalist; b. 18 May 1912; ed. Exeter, Yale Univ.
Reporter *Milwaukee Sentinel* 33, *New York Herald Tribune* 35-41, syndicated columnist 46-65; U.S. Army 41-46; columnist *Observer*, London 65-; John Crosby TV Programme (New York); Peabody Award, Newspaper Guild Award.
Publs. *Out of the Blue* 52, *With Love and Loathing.*
3 Ormonde Gate, London, S.W.3, England.
Telephone: 01-352-5550.

Crosland, Rt. Hon. (Charles) Anthony Raven, P.C., M.A., M.P.; British politician; b. 29 Aug. 1918; ed. Highgate School and Trinity Coll., Oxford.
War service 40-45; Fellow and Lecturer in Economics Trinity Coll., Oxford 47-50; M.P. (Lab.) South Gloucestershire 50-55, Grimsby 59-; Sec. Independent Comm. of Enquiry into Co-operative Movement 56-58; Econ. Sec. to the Treasury Oct. 64-Jan. 65; Sec. of State for Education and Science 65-67; Pres of the Board of Trade 67-.
Publs. *New Fabian Essays* (contrib.) 52, *Britain's Economic Problem* 53, *The Future of Socialism* 56, *The Conservative Enemy* 62.
37 Lansdowne Road, London, W.11, England.

Cross, Bert S.; American business executive; b. 16 Oct. 1905; ed. Univ. of Minnesota.
Laboratory Technician, Minnesota Mining and Manufacturing Co. 26-31, Factory Manager, Abrasives Div. 31-42, New Products Manager 42-45, Gen. Manager Scotchlite Div. 45-48, Vice-Pres. Scotchlite Div. 48-52, Vice-Pres. Graphic Products Group 52-57, Dir., mem. Management and Exec. Cttees. 57-, Pres., Chief Exec.

Officer and mem. Finance Cttee. 63-66, Chair. and Chief Exec. Officer 66-; Dir. Ferrania S.p.A., Milan, 3M Research Ltd., Harlow, England, Business Products Sales Inc.

Office: Minnesota Mining and Manufacturing Co., 3M Center, St. Paul 1, Minn. 55101; Home: 45 Evergreen Road, Pine Tree Hills, Dellwood, Minn. 55115, U.S.A.

Cross, Rev. Canon Frank Leslie, B.SC., M.A., D.PHIL., D.D.; British ecclesiastic; b. 22 Jan. 1900; ed. Bournemouth School, Balliol Coll., Oxford, Marburg and Freiburg Univs.

Ordained deacon 25; priest 26; Librarian of Pusey House, Oxford 27-44; Univ. Lecturer at Oxford in Philosophy of Religion 34-44; Wilde Lecturer in Natural and Comparative Religion 35-38; Editor of the *Lexicon of Patristic Greek* 41-48; Sec. Int. Conf. on Patristic Studies at Oxford 51, 55, 59, 63, 67; Sec. New Testament Conf. at Oxford 57, 61, 65; Lady Margaret Prof. of Divinity and Canon of Christ Church Oxford 44-; Hon. D.D. (Aberdeen 59, Bonn 60); F.B.A. 67.

Publs. *Religion and the Reign of Science* 30, *John Henry Newman* 33, *Anglicanism* (with P. E. More) 35, *St. Athanasius' De Incarnatione* 39, *Darwell Stone* 43, *St. Cyril of Jerusalem's Lectures on the Sacraments* 51, *I Peter* 54, *The Jung Codex* 55, *Studia Patristica I-II* (ed. with K. Aland) 57, *Oxford Dictionary of the Christian Church* 57, *Baumstark's Comparative Liturgy* 58, *Studia Evangelica* I 59, II-III 64, *Early Christian Fathers* 60, *Studia Patristica* III-VI 61-62, VII-IX 66.

Christ Church, Oxford, England.

Telephone: Oxford 43588.

Cross, G(eorge) L(ynn), M.S., PH.D.; American university president and professor; b. 12 May 1905; ed. South Dakota Coll., and Univ. of Chicago.

Instructor Bacteriology, South Dakota State Coll. 27-28; Head Botany Dept. Univ. of South Dakota 30-34. Prof. of Botany Univ. of Oklahoma 34-38, Head of Botany Dept. 38-42. Act. Dean Graduate Coll. 42-44, Act. Dir. Research Inst. 42-44, Pres. of the Univ. 44-; mem. Board Dirs. Midwest Research Inst. Kansas City; mem. of Univ. Pres.'s Board of William Rockhill Nelson Trust Kansas City; mem. of many learned socs.

407 West Boyd Street, Norman, Okla., U.S.A.

Cross, Ira B., A.M., PH.D.; American economist; b. 1 Dec. 1880; ed. Wisconsin and Stanford Univs.

Instructor and Asst. Prof. Stanford Univ. 09-14; Asst. and Associate Prof. California Univ. 14-19 and Prof. of Economics 19-51, Emeritus 51-; Vice-Pres. American Economic Asscn. 26; Pres. Pacific Coast Economic Asscn. 29; Hon. LL.D. (Univ. of Wisconsin) 51, (Univ. of California) 57; Fellow American Genealogical Soc., Univ. of Calif.; Highest Award, Nat. Chrysanthemum Soc. 63.

Publs. *Economics, Money and Banking, Domestic and Foreign Exchange, History of Banking in California, History of the Labour Movement in California, Frank Roney: Irish Rebel and California Labour Leader, Essentials of Socialism, Collective Bargaining in San Francisco.*

1454 Le Roy Avenue, Berkeley 8, Calif. 94708, U.S.A.

Cross, Richard Eugene; American lawyer and automobile executive; b. 20 Sept. 1910; ed. St. Thomas Military Acad., Assumption Coll., Univ. of Wisconsin and Univ. of Michigan.

Fmr. Chair. Board of Dirs. American Motors Corpn. now Chair. Exec. Cttee. and Dir.; Partner Cross, Wrock, Miller, Vieson & Kelley (lawyers); Dir. Hiram Walker-Gooderham & Worts Ltd., Great Lakes Tractor & Equipment Co., Ohio Tractor & Implement Co., The Packer Corpn., Automobile Mfg. Asscn.

20008 Lichfield Road, Detroit 21, Michigan, U.S.A.

Crossland, Leonard; British motor executive; b. 2 March 1914; ed. Penistone Grammar School.

Purchase Dept., Ford Motor Co. Ltd. 37-39; Royal Army Service Corps 39-45; Purchase Dept., Ford Motor Co. Ltd. 45-50, Chief Buyer, Tractor and Implement Dept. 50-57, Chief Buyer, Car and Truck Dept. 57-59, Asst. Purchase Man. 59-60, Purchase Man. 60-62, Exec. Dir., Supply and Services 62-66, Dir. Mfg. Staff and Services 66, Asst. Man Dir. 66-67, Man. Dir. 67-.

Ford Motor Co. Ltd., Eagle Way, Warley, Brentwood, Essex; Home: Rivenhall Old Rectory, Witham, Essex.

Crossman, Rt. Hon. Richard Howard Stafford, P.C., O.B.E., M.P., M.A.; British politician and journalist; b. 15 Dec. 1907; ed. Winchester and New Coll., Oxford.

Fellow and Tutor of New Coll. Oxford 30-37; Lecturer for Oxford Univ. Delegacy for Extra-Mural Studies and for Workers Educational Asscn. 38-40; leader of Labour group on Oxford City Council 34-40; Deputy-Dir. Psychological Warfare A.F.H.Q. Algiers 43 and SHAEF 44-45; mem. Anglo-American Palestine Comm. 46; mem. Malta Round Table Conf. 55; Labour M.P. for Coventry East 45-; Asst. Editor *New Statesman & Nation* 43-55; Chair. Labour Party Working Party on Superannuation 56-64, on Science 63-64; mem. Labour Party Exec. 52-67; Minister of Housing and Local Government 64-66; Lord Pres. of the Council and Leader of the House of Commons 66-.

Publs. *Plato To-day* 37, *Socrates* 38, *Government and the Governed* 39, *How we are Governed* 39, *Palestine Mission* 47; Edited *The God that Failed* 50 and *New Fabian Essays* 52, *The Charm of Politics* 58, *A Nation Reborn* 60, *Planning for Freedom* 65.

9 Vincent Square, London, S.W.1, England.

Crosti, Luigi; Italian industrialist; b. 10 Jan. 1895; ed. Politecnico di Milano.

As Dir. Snia Viscosa plant at Pavia 19-30, and Cesano Maderno 30-45, researched into and developed short cellulose fibres and casein; also supervised the construction of the production assembly line of Torviscosa for the production of rayon fibres; Vice-Dir.-Gen. Snia Viscosa 46-, then Dir.-Gen. for Technical Affairs; mem. Admin. Council 49-55, Admin. Del. 55-65, worked on the construction of factories for the production of polyamide, acrilic and polyester fibres; Vice-Pres. Snia Viscosa 65-67, Pres., Dir.-Gen. and Council Del. 67-; Grand'Ufficiale della Repubblica, Maestro del Lavoro, Stella al Merito, Medaglia d'Oro al Merito.

Via Fatebenefratelli 19, Milan, Italy.

Crouy-Chanel, Etienne Marie René de, C.M.G.; French diplomatist; b. 27 March 1905; ed. Univ. of Paris.

Served Ministry of Foreign Affairs 31, French Del. to L.N.; 31-32 Private Sec. to Sec.-Gen. of Foreign Affairs 32-39; Liaison Officer to G.O.C.-in-C. of French Armies 39-40; with French Resistance Forces 44-45; Counsellor, Brazil 45-48, Belgium 48-50 (Minister Sept. 50); Minister-Counsellor in London 50-55; Asst. Dir.-Gen. for Political Affairs, Ministry of Foreign Affairs, Paris 55; French Rep. to NATO Council 57-58; Amb. to Austria 58-61; Amb. to the Netherlands 61-65; Amb. to Belgium 65-; Commdr. Légion d'Honneur; Croix de Guerre.

French Embassy, Brussels, Belgium; Home: 4 rue Saint-Florentin, Paris 1er, France.

Crowe, Sir Colin Tradescant, K.C.M.G.; British diplomatist; b. 7 Sept. 1913; ed. Stowe School and Oriel Coll., Oxford.

Served Embassy Peking 36-38, 50-53, Shanghai 39-40, Washington 40-45; mem. U.K. Del. to OEEC Paris 48; served Tel-Aviv Legation 49, Imperial Defence Coll. 57; Chargé d'Affaires Cairo Dec. 59-61; Dep. Perm. Rep. to UN 61-63; Ambassador to Saudi Arabia 63-64; Fellow, St. Antony's College, Oxford 64-65; Chief of Admin., Diplomatic Service 65-.

c/o D.S.A.O., King Charles Street, London, S.W.1; Home: Pigeon House, Bibury, Glos., England.

Crowe, Colonel Philip Kingsland; American journalist and diplomatist; b. 7 Jan. 1908; ed. Univ. of Virginia. Reporter, and Asst. Financial Editor, *New York Evening Post* 30-34; explorer and big game hunter in French Indo-China 35-36; on advertising staff of *Life* and later *Fortune* 37-41, 45-48; Lieut.-Col. U.S. Army Air Force 41-45; Special Rep. of E.C.A. Mission to China 48-49; farmer and writer 49-53; Ambassador to Ceylon 53-57; U.S. Del. to ECAFE Conf. 54; Special Asst. to Sec. of State 57-58; Ambassador to the Union of South Africa 59-61, to the Republic of South Africa 61; Dir. World Wildlife Fund; Bronze Star Medal, Officier Légion d'Honneur, Cloud Banner of the Republic of China, Military Order of Christ, Portugal.

Publs. *Sport is Where You Find It* 54, *Diversions of a Diplomat* 58, *Sporting Journeys* 66, *The Empty Ark* 67. "Third Haven", Easton, Maryland, U.S.A.

Telephone: 301-457-2252.

Crowley, Leo T.; American businessman; ed. schools in Madison, Wisconsin.

Pres. Gen. Paper & Supply Co. 17-; Chair. Chicago, Milwaukee, St. Paul and Pacific Railroad Co. 45; Wis. Public Service Corpn. 48-, Standard Gas & Electric Co. 39-47, mem. Pres. Roosevelt's Cabinet 42-43; Head, Office Econ. Warfare 43; Foreign Econ. Admin. 43-45.

Home: 1110 Edgewood Avenue, Madison, Wis.; Office: Union State Building, Chicago 6, Ill., U.S.A.

Crown, Henry; American businessman; b. 13 June 1896; ed. Chicago public schools.

Clerk Chicago Firebrick Co. 10-12; Traffic Man. Union Drop Forge Co. 12-16; Partner S.R. Crown & Co. 16-19; Treas. Material Service Corpn. 19-21, Pres. 21-41, Chair. 41-59; Chair. Material Service Div. of Gen. Dynamics Corpn., Chair. Exec. Cttee. and Dir. 59-66; Chair. Board Henry Crown and Co.; Vice-Pres., Dir., Exec. Cttee., Hilton Int. Co.; Chair. Finance Cttee. and Dir. Chicago, Rock Island and Pacific Railroad; Vice-Pres. and Dir. 208 South La Salle Street Building Corpn.; Dir. and mem. Exec. Cttee. City Products Corpn., Waldorf Astoria; Trustee Univ. of Chicago Cancer Research Foundation and Syracuse Univ., New York; Colonel of Engineers in Second World War; Legion of Merit; Chevalier Légion d'Honneur, Gold Cross, Royal Order of the Phoenix (Greece); Horatio Alger Award (American Schools and Colls. Asscn.) 53; Hon. Dr. Eng. (Tri-State Coll., Angola, Ind.) 55, Hon. LL.D. (Barat Coll., Lake Forest, Ill. 55, Syracuse Univ. 57, De Pauw Univ. 64).

Home: 900 Edgemere Court, Evanston, Ill.; Office: 300 W. Washington, Chicago, Ill., U.S.A.

Crowther, Sir Geoffrey, Kt., M.A., LL.D., D.SC. (cr. Life Peer June 68); British economist; b. 13 May 1907; ed. Clare Coll., Cambridge, Yale Univ., and Columbia Univ. Commonwealth Fund Fellow 29-31; Economic Adviser to Irish Banks' Standing Cttee. 32; mem. staff *The Economist* 32-35, Asst. Editor 35-38, Associate Editor 38, Editor 38-56, Man. Dir. 56-63, Chair. 63-; Chair. Cen. Advisory Council of Education 56-60; Dir. and Editor Europa Publications Ltd. until 40, Dir. 45-50; with Ministries of Information, Supply and Production 40-43; Chair. Trust Houses Ltd., Trafalgar House Ltd., and Dir. other companies.

Publs. *Ways and Means, An Introduction to the Study of Prices* (with Sir Walter Layton), *The New Deal: An Analysis and Appraisal* (with the Editors of *The Economist*), *Economics for Democrats, Ways and Means of War, An Outline of Money.*

29 Dover Park Drive, Roehampton, London, S.W.15, England.

Crump, Norris Roy, M.E., D.ENG., LL.D., D.SC.; Canadian railway executive; b. 30 July 1904; ed. Purdue Univ., Lafayette, Ind.

Machinist apprentice with Canadian Pacific Railway 20;

posts of increasing importance 20-40; Asst. Supt. of Motive Power and Car Dept. Winnipeg 41; Asst. to Vice-Pres. Montreal 42; Gen. Supt. Ontario District 43; Gen. Man. Eastern Lines, Toronto 46; Vice-Pres. and Gen. Man. 47; Vice-Pres. Eastern Region 47; Vice-Pres. in charge of all rail services and communications 48; Dir. Canadian Pacific Railway 49-, mem. Exec. Cttee. 49-, Vice-Pres. 49-55, Pres. 55-61, Chair. and Pres. 61-64, Chair. and Chief Exec. Officer 64-; Chair. and Dir. Canadian Pacific Investments Ltd.; Gov. Exec. Cttee. Board, McGill Univ., Royal Victoria and Gen. Hospitals, Montreal; numerous other companies and mem. commercial orgs.; Hon. LL.D. (Queens' Univ., Kingston, Ont.); Dr. Eng. (Purdue Univ.); D.Sc. (Clarkson Coll. of Technology, Potsdam, N.Y., Laval Univ.); D.C.L. (Bishop's Univ.); Hon. LL.D. (Univ. of Montreal) 58.

c/o Canadian Pacific Railway Company, Windsor Station, Montreal, Que., Canada.

Telephone: 861-6811, Ext. 601.

Cruz, Ivo; Portuguese composer and conductor; b. 01; ed. Univs. of Lisbon and Munich.

Has conducted in Austria, France, Germany, Switzerland, Spain, Holland, Belgium, Eire, Rumania, Brazil and Portugal; his compositions have been played in Europe, North America, Brazil, New Zealand, North Africa and the Republic of South Africa; founder and Pres. Nat. Union of Musicians; Dir. Conservatoire National de Lisbonne; Head of the Lisbon Philharmonic Orchestra, of the Duarte Lobo Choral Soc., Pres. Pro Arte; Commdr. Order of St. Jacques; Knight Order of Alfonso el Sabio (Spain).

Compositions include two concertos for piano and orchestra, a violin sonata and many pieces for orchestra (e.g. *Sinfonia de Amadis, Sinfonia de Queluz* and *Pastoral* (ballet)), piano (e.g. *Aquarelas, Homenagens,* Suite and Caleidoscopio), and guitar; songs include *Triptico* (with Orchestra), *Les Amours du Poète, Ballades Lunatiques, Chansons Perdues, Chansons Profanes.*

Rua do Salitre, 166-2 E, Lisbon, Portugal.

Cruz-Diez, Carlos; Venezuelan painter; b. 17 Aug. 1923; ed. School of Plastic and Applied Arts, Caracas. Director of Art, Venezuelan subsidiary of McCann-Erickson Advertising Agency 46-51; Teacher, History of Applied Arts, School of Arts, Caracas 53-55; in Barcelona and Paris working on physical qualities of colour now named *Physichromies* 55-56; opened studio of visual arts and industrial design, Caracas 57; Prof. and Asst. Dir. School of Arts, Caracas 59-60; moved to Paris 60; First one-man exhbn., Caracas 47, later in Madrid, Genoa, Turin, London, Paris and Essen; Retrospective exhbns. at Signals, London and Galerie Kerchache, Paris 65; represented at numerous Group exhbns.; works in Museum of Fine Arts, Caracas, Victoria and Albert Museum, London, Casa de la Cultura, Havana, Stadtisches Museum, Leverkusen, Germany, Museum of Modern Arts, New York, Museum of Contemporary Art, Montreal; Grand Prix at 3rd Biennale, Cordoba, Argentina.

24 rue Pierre Semard, Paris 9e, France.

Telephone: TRU 9816.

Csanádi, György; Hungarian engineer, economist and politician; b. 28 July 1905; ed. Univ. of Technical Sciences.

Track maintenance and Building Engineer, Directorate of Hungarian State Railways, Pecs 29-45, Head of Directorate 45-47; Head of Technical Dept. (Railways), Ministry of Transport and Communications 47-48; Dir.-Gen. Hungarian State Railways 49-59; First Dep. Minister of Transport and Communications 57-63, Minister of Transport and Communications 63-; Prof. Budapest Technical Univ. of Construction and Com-

munications 51-; corresp. mem. Hungarian Acad. of Sciences.
Ministry of Transport and Communications, Budapest; Home: Budapest VII, Dob u. 75, Hungary.

Csatorday, Károly; Hungarian diplomatist; b. 26; ed. Faculty of Law, Budapest Univ.
Diplomatic Service 48-; Attaché, The Hague 49-51; Second Sec. (later First), Peking 51-55; Chargé d'Affaires, Hanoi 55; Chief of Protocol Dept., Ministry of Foreign Affairs, Budapest 56-60; Minister, Japan 60-62; Perm. Rep. to UN 62-; Rep. of Hungary to the Security Council 68-69.
Permanent Mission of Hungary to the United Nations, 10 East 75th Street, New York 10021 N.Y., U.S.A.
Telephone: LES 8660.

Cseterki, Lajos; Hungarian trade unionist and politician; b. 1921; ed. teachers' training college and Soviet political school.
Lecturer, Soviet Forces until 47; Lecturer, Trades Union Council, Budapest 47-50; Tutor, Party Acad. of Hungarian Working People's Party 50-51; Sec.-Gen., later Pres. Teachers' Union 51-53; Sec. Trades Union Council 54-56; Liaison Duties, Revolutionary Worker-Peasant Govt., County Fejér 56-57, First Sec., County Fejér Cttee. 57-61, County Borsod Cttee. 61-62; mem. Cen. Cttee. Hungarian Socialist Workers' Party 59-, Substitute mem. Political Cttee. Nov. 62-66, Sec. Central Cttee. 63-; Presidential Council 67-.
Hungarian Socialist Workers' Party, Budapest V, Szécheny Rakpart 19, Hungary.

Csokor, Franz Theodor; Austrian writer, art critic, playwright and theatrical producer; b. 6 Sept. 1885; ed. Vienna Univ.
Poet and art historian; Pres. Austrian PEN Club 47-; Vice-Pres. Int. PEN Club, London; Prof. h.c.
Publs. *Die Gewalten, Dolch und Wunde, Ewiger Aufbruch, Das Schwarze Schiff, Immer ist Anfang* (poems); *Die Sünde wider den Geist, Die rote Strasse, Das Gesetz, Ballade von der Stadt, Gesellschaft der Menschenrechte, Besetztes Gebiet, Die Weibermühle, Gewesene Menschen, Der tausendjährige Traum, Die Herren von Svjet, Die ungöttliche Komödie, 3 November 1918, Jadwiga, Gottes General, Satans Arche, Kalypso, Der verlorene Sohn, Pilatus, Medea Postbellica, Wenn sie zurückkommen, Caesar's Witwe, Hebt den Stein ab!, Treibholz, Die Erweckung des Zosimir, Das Zeichen an der Wand, Die Kaiser zwischen den Zeiten, Grenzzwischenfall* (plays); *Als Zivilist im Polenkrieg, Als Zivilist im Balkankrieg, Über die Schwelle, Der Schlüssel zum Abgrund, Auf fremden Strassen, Der zweite Hahnenschrei, Zeuge einer Zeit* (novels), *Ein paar Schaufeln Erde* (stories) 65.
A1030 Vienna, Neulinggasse 11, Austria.
Telephone: Vienna 7353-87.

Cudlipp, Hugh, O.B.E.; British journalist; b. 28 Aug. 1913; ed. in Wales.
With various provincial newspapers in Cardiff and Manchester 27-32; Features Editor *Sunday Chronicle* 32-35, *Daily Mirror* 35-37; Editor *Sunday Pictorial* 37-40; served army 40-46; Editor *Sunday Pictorial* 46-49; Man. Editor *Sunday Express* 50-52; Editorial Dir. *Daily Mirror* and *Sunday Pictorial* (now *Sunday Mirror*) 52-63; Jt.-Man. Dir. Daily Mirror Newspapers Ltd., Sunday Pictorial Newspapers Ltd. 60-63; Chair. Daily Mirror Newspapers Ltd. 63-; Chair. Odhams Press Ltd. 61-63, Daily Herald (1929) Ltd. 61-64; Dir. Associated Television Ltd., Reuters Ltd.; Editorial Dir. Int. Publishing Corpn. 63-May 68, Deputy Chair. 64-May 68, Chair. May 68-.
Publs. *Publish and be Damned!* 53, *At Your Peril* 62.
Daily Mirror Newspapers Ltd., Holborn Circus, London, E.C.1, England.

Cuevas Cancino, Francisco; Mexican diplomatist; b. 7 May 1921; ed. Free School of Law, Mexico City, McGill Univ., Montreal, Ottawa Univ., Univ. of London and Columbia Univ.
Former Guggenheim and Rockefeller Foundation Scholar; Mexican Diplomatic Service 45-; Third Sec., London 46-49; Adviser and Sub Dir.-Gen. for Int. Orgs., Ministry of Foreign Affairs, Mexico City; UN Secretariat 50-53; Legal Counsel to Mexican Mission to UN 59-62; Alt. Del. to UN 62-65, Perm. Rep. to UN 65-; Simon Bolivar Literary Prize, Bolivar Soc. of Venezuela 51.
Publs. include *Bolivar and the Pan American Ideal of the Liberator.*
Permanent Mission of Mexico to the United Nations, 8 East 41st Street, New York 17, N.Y., U.S.A.

Cuevas, José Luis; Mexican painter; b. 26 Feb. 1934; ed. Univ. de Mexico, School of Painting and Sculpture "La Esmeralda", Mexico.
Over forty one-man exhbns. in New York, Paris, Milan, Mexico, Buenos Aires, Toronto, Los Angeles, Washington, etc.; Group Exhbns. all over N. and S. America, Europe, India and Japan; works are in Museum of Modern Art, Solomon R. Guggenheim Museum, Brooklyn Museum (New York), Art Inst. Chicago, Phillips Collection, Washington, D.C., Museums of Albi and Lyons, France, etc.; First Int. Award for Drawing, São Paulo Bienal 59; First Int. Award, Mostra Internazionale di Bianco e Nero de Lugano, Zürich 62; First Prize, Bienal de Grabado, Santiago, Chile 64; has illustrated following books: *The World of Kafka and Cuevas* 59, *Recollections of Childhood* 62, *Cuevas por Cuevas* (autobiog.) 64, *Cuevas Charenton* 65, *Visions Without LSD* 68.
Providencia 1028, Colonia Del Valle, México, D.F., Mexico; c/o Grace Borgenicht Gallery, 1018 Madison Avenue, New York City, U.S.A.
Telephone: 43-80-05; 43-22-96 (both Mexico D.F.).

Culligan, Matthew Joseph; American broadcasting and publishing executive; b. 25 June 1918; ed. Columbia Univ.
Advertisement Salesman, Hearst Magazines 45-50; Advertising Dir. Ziff-Davis Publications 51-52; Sales Man. N.B.C. TV 52-53; Nat. Sales Man. TV Network 54-55, Vice-Pres. and Dir. Sales 55-56; Exec. Vice-Pres., N.B.C. Radio Network 56-62; Pres. Curtis Publishing 62-64, Chair. 64-65; Pres. Mutual Broadcasting System 66-.
Polly Park Road, Rye, N.Y., U.S.A.

Cullman, Joseph Frederick, 3rd; American business executive; b. 9 April 1912; ed. Hotchkiss School, Yale Univ.
Sales Man. Eastern area, Webster Tobacco Co. 36-41; Vice-Pres. Benson & Hedges 46-53, Exec. Vice-Pres. 53, Pres. 55-61; Vice-Pres. Philip Morris 54, Exec. Vice-Pres. 55-57, Pres. 57-66, Chair. of the Board and Chief Financial Officer 67-; Dir. IBM World Trade Corpn., Philip Morris Inc., Cullman Bros. Inc., Bankers Trust Co., State-Planters Bank of Commerce and Trusts.
100 Park Avenue, New York 17, N.Y., U.S.A.
Telephone: 212-679-1800.

Culmann, Herbert Ernst, DR. IUR.; German airline executive; b. 15 Feb. 1921; ed. Gymnasium Neustadt and Ruprecht-Karl Universität, Heidelberg.
German Air Force 39-45; legal studies and legal practice 45-53; Deutsche Lufthansa A.G. 53-, Dir. of Central Office (Law, Personnel, Org., Admin.) 57-64, mem. Management Board 64-; official of other companies; mem. Int. Law Asscn. 54-.
Deutsche Lufthansa A.G., 5 Cologne, Claudiusstrasse 1; Home: 506 Bensberg-Refrath, Neuertrassweg 30, German Federal Republic.
Telephone: 2068221 (Office).

Cumberlege, Geoffrey Fenwick Jocelyn, D.S.O., M.C., M.A.; British publisher; b. 18 April 1891; ed. Charterhouse and Worcester Coll., Oxford.
Man. Oxford Univ. Press in India 19-27; Man. and Vice-Pres. Oxford Univ. Press N.Y. Inc. 28-34; Asst. to the Publisher to the Univ. 34-45, Publisher to the Univ. of Oxford 45-56; Vice-Chair. Oxford Univ. Press Inc. (N.Y.) 58; Hon. D.C.L. (Durham) and Hon. Fellow, Worcester Coll., Oxford.
Idlehurst, Birch Grove, Haywards Heath, Sussex, England.
Telephone: Chelwood Gate 224.

Cumming, Sir Ronald Stuart, Kt.; British distiller; b. 10 April 1900; ed. Uppingham and Aberdeen Univ.
Director, John Walker and Sons Ltd. 31-39; Dir. The Distillers Company Ltd. 46-, mem. Management Cttee. 51-, Chair. 63-67; Chair. John Walker and Sons Ltd. 57-63, The Scotch Whisky Asscn. 61-67; Army service 18-19, 39-46.
Sourden Brae, Rothes, Morayshire, Scotland.

Cumming-Bruce, Hon. Sir Francis, K.C.M.G.; British diplomatist; b. 9 March 1912; ed. Shrewsbury School and Trinity Coll., Cambridge.
Assistant Principal, Dept. of Agriculture for Scotland 35-37, Dominions Office 37; Asst. Sec. Office of U.K. High Commr. in New Zealand 39-44, in Canada 44-46; Principal Private Sec. to Sec. of State 46-48; Asst. Sec. Commonwealth Relations Office (C.R.O.) 48; Head of Political Div., Office of U.K. High Commr. in India 49-52; Establishment Officer, C.R.O. 52-54, Head of Commodities Dept. 54-55; Adviser on External Affairs to Gov. of Gold Coast 55-57, Dep. High Commr. for U.K. in Ghana 57-58; Asst. Under-Sec. of State, C.R.O. 58; Deputy High Commr. for U.K. in Canada 58-59, High Commr. 59-63, High Commr. in Nigeria 64-66.
c/o Diplomatic Service Administration Office, Great George Street, London, S.W.1, England.

Cummings, Nathan; American business executive; b. 14 Oct. 1896; ed. Economist Training School, New York.
Retail shoe business 14-17; wholesale shoe business 17-24; shoe manufacturing 24-30; importing gen. merchandise 30-34; manufacturing biscuits and candy 34-38 (all in Canada); took up residence in U.S.A. 39; Pres. C. D. Kenny Co. (wholesale food), Baltimore 39; acquired this and other firms to form Consolidated Foods Corpn., of which he is Chair. of Board; Chair. Board Associated Products Inc.; Patron and benefactor several art socs.; Chevalier Légion d'Honneur, Commendatore Al Merito della Repubblica Italiana and other awards, including hon. degrees from American and Canadian Univs.
Home: 179 Lake Shore Drive, Chicago 11; Office: 135 South La Salle Street, Chicago 3, Ill., U.S.A.

Cummings, Tilden, B.S., M.B.A.; American banker; b. 18 Sept. 1907; ed. Princeton Univ. and Harvard Graduate School of Business Administration.
Dir. Continental Illinois Nat. Bank and Trust Co. of Chicago, Pres. 60-; Dir. Northern Natural Gas Co., Omaha, American Brake Shoe Co., New York, Consolidated Foods Corpn., Chicago, Consolidation Coal Corpn., Pittsburgh; Vice-Pres. Board of Trustees, Northwestern Univ.; official of many civic and philanthropic orgs.
Continental Illinois National Bank and Trust Co. of Chicago, 231 South La Salle Street, Chicago 4, Illinois, U.S.A.

Cumont, Lieut.-Gen. Charles P. Baron de, O.B.E.; Belgian army officer; b. 02; ed. Ecole Royale Militaire and Ecole de Guerre.
Asst. Mil. Attaché, London 39; Commdr. 1st Battalion Belgian Fusiliers 40; Chief Instructor Western Command, Company Command School 42; Adviser to High Commr. State Security 44; Commdr. Infantry School 45; Commdr. Senior Officer School, Brussels 47; Chief Instructor Staff Coll. 48; Belgian Del. Brussels Pact, London 49; Head of Operations, Belgium G.H.Q. 53; Deputy Chief of Staff, Northern Army Group 53; CCRA Belgian Corps 55; Chief of Staff, Land Forces, Central Europe, Chair. Chief of Staff Cttee., Brussels 60-62; Chair. Military Cttee., North Atlantic Treaty Org. (NATO), Washington 64-.
30 Av. Hamoir, Brussels 18, Belgium.

Cunha, Paulo A. V., LL.D.; Portuguese university professor and politician; b. 08; ed. Univ. of Lisbon.
Lecturer in Law, Univ. of Lisbon 30, Extra. Prof. of Juridical Science 35, Prof. of Civil Law 38, Vice-Rector 47-62, Rector 62-65; mem. Portuguese Upper Chamber 42, Vice-Pres. 46; Minister of Foreign Affairs 50-58; Grand Cross Order of Isabel la Católica (Spain), of the Order of Leopold (Belgium), of the Order of the North Star (Sweden), of the Sovereign Order of Malta, etc.
Publs. include: *Do Patrimonio* 34, *Da Simulação* 35.
R. Pinheiro Chagas 25, Lisbon, Portugal.

Cunha, Vasco da; Portuguese diplomatist; b. 17 May 1900; ed. Universidade de Lisboa.
Ministry of Foreign Affairs 21-, served Mexico, London, Tangier 30-47; Asst. Dir.-Gen. for Political Affairs, Ministry for Foreign Affairs 47-51, Dir.-Gen. for Political Affairs 51-54; Sec.-Gen., Ministry for Foreign Affairs 54-58; Ambassador to the Holy See 58-61; Perm. Rep. of Portugal on North Atlantic Council (NATO) 61-; Grand Officer Military Order of Christ, Hon. G.C.V.O., Grand Cross Order of Pius IX, Grand Cross Order of Isabel la Católica, and other awards.
147 Rua da Escola Politécnica, Lisbon, Portugal.

Cunningham, Sir Graham, K.B.E., LL.B.; British company director; b. 19 May 1892; ed. Bancroft's School.
Solicitor 14; served Royal Fusiliers 15-19; with Parson, Lee & Co., solicitors 19-33; Man. Dir. Tuck & Co. Ltd. 24-30; Man. Dir. Triplex Safety Glass Co. Ltd. 29-60; Chair. 35-61; Chair. Triplex Holdings Ltd., Stern & Bell Ltd., Weldall and Assembly Ltd. 61; Dep. Dir.-Gen. Children's Overseas Reception Board 40; Dir. of Claims, War Damage Comm. 41; Chief Exec. and Controller-Gen. of Munitions Production, Ministry of Supply 41-46; Gov. Bancroft's School; Gov. and Dep. Chair. and Hon. Fellow Imperial Coll. of Science and Technology; Chair. Shipbuilding Advisory Cttee. 46-60; Dir. Disabled Persons Employment Corpn. Ltd. 46-49; mem. Econ. Planning Board 47-61, Royal Comm. on Press 61-62; Chair. Dollar Exports Board 49; Fellow and Past Pres. Soc. of Glass Technology.
Woolmers, Mannings Heath, near Horsham, Sussex, England.
Telephone: Horsham 3809.

Cunningham, Harry Blair; American retail executive; b. 23 July 1907; ed. Miami Univ. and Oxford, Ohio.
Newspaper Reporter *Harrisburg Patriot* 27-28; S. S. Kresge Co., Lynchburg, Va. 28-29, Washington 30, Brooklyn 31-32, Detroit 33-35, Wheeling 36, Lafayette (Ind.) 36-38, Muncie (Ind.) 39-40, Grosse Pointe (Mich.) 40-41, Highland Park (Mich.) 42-46, Superintendent, Stores 47-50, Asst. Sales Dir. 51-52, Sales Dir. 53-57, Gen. Vice-Pres. 57-59, Pres. 59-; official of other companies.
S. S. Kresge Co., 2727 2nd Avenue, Detroit 32, Mich. 48232, U.S.A.

Cunningham, John Philip; American advertising executive; b. 17 Sept. 1897; ed. Harvard Coll.
Vice-President and Partner, Newell-Emmett Company 30-50; Exec. Vice-Pres. Cunningham & Walsh Inc. (successor to Newell-Emmett Co.) 50-54, Pres. 54-58, Chair. Board 58-61, Chair. Exec. Cttee. 61-.
5225 Sycamore Avenue, Riverdale 71, New York, U.S.A.

Cupp, Paul J.; American businessman; b. 7 Dec. 1902; ed. Wharton School of Commerce, Univ. of Pennsylvania.
Chief Exec. Officer, Acme Markets Inc.; Dir. Philadelphia Nat. Bank, Provident Mutual Life Insurance Co., Y.M.C.A.; John Wanamaker Phila.; Alan Wood Steel Co.; Chem. Leaman Tank Lines Inc.; Greater Phila. Movement; Man. Western Savings Fund Soc.; Trustee, Univ. of Pennsylvania; mem. Philadelphia Chamber of Commerce; Hon. LL.D.
Home: 933 Muirfield Road, Bryn Mawr, Pa.; Office: 124 N. 15th Street, Philadelphia, Pa. 19102, U.S.A.

Curie, Eve Denise (see Labouisse, Eve Denise).

Curti, Merle, A.B., PH.D.; American historian; b. 15 Sept. 1897; ed. Harvard.
Dwight Morrow Prof. of History Smith Coll. 36-37; visiting Prof. Chicago and Calif. Univs. and Inst. of Technology Calif.; Prof. Columbia Univ. 37-42, Wisconsin 42-; Frederick Jackson Turner Prof. of History, Univ. of Wis. 47-; Visiting Prof. Univ. of Tokyo 59-60; mem. Board of Advisers American Council Learned Socs., mem. Social Science Research Princeton Univ. Advisory Council 18; awarded Pulitzer Prize 44; Pres. Miss. Valley Historical Asscn. 51-52; and American Historical Asscn. 53-54; Fellow, Inst. for Behavioral Sciences 55-56; A.C.L.S. Prize for "extraordinary scholarly achievement" $10,000 60; Knight Order of Northern Star (Sweden); Hon. L.H.D.
Publs. *Austria and the United States 1848-1852* 26, *Bryan and World Peace* 27, *American Peace Crusade 1815-1861* 29, *War or Peace: The American Struggle 1636-1936* 36, *The Social Ideas of American Educators* 35, *American Issues* 41, *Growth of American Thought* 44 (Pulitzer Prize), *The Roots of American Loyalty* 46, *American Scholarship in the Twentieth Century* (jointly), *Prelude to Point Four* (jointly) 54, *Probing Our Past* 55, *An American Paradox* 56, *The Making of an American Community* 59, *Rise of the American Nation* (with Paul Todd) 60, *American Philanthropy Overseas: a History* 63, *Philanthropy in the Shaping of American Higher Education* (with Roderick Nash) 65, etc.
Department of History, University of Wisconsin, Madison, Wis.; Home: 3516 Tally Ho Lane, Madison, Wis., U.S.A.
Telephone: 233-0671 (Home).

Curtis, Carl Thomas; American lawyer and politician; b. 15 March 1905; ed. Wesleyan Univ.
Began career as teacher; admitted to Nebraska Bar 30; practised law, Minden; County Attorney 31-34; mem. U.S. House of Reps. 39-55; Senator from Nebraska 55-; mem. Nebraska State Bar Asscn.; Republican.
Minden, Nebraska, U.S.A.

Curtis, Ellwood F., B.A., C.P.A.; American accountant and business executive; b. 14 May 1914; ed. Dartmouth Coll.
With Haskins & Sells, Certified Public Accountants 35-39; with Deere & Company (manufacturers of agricultural and industrial equipment) 39-, Comptroller 44, Dir. 51-, Vice-Pres. 56-59, Pres. April 64-.
Deere & Company, John Deere Road, Moline, Ill., 61265, U.S.A.

Curtis, Kenneth M.; American politician; b. 8 Feb. 1931; ed. Cony High School, Maine Maritime Acad., and Portland Univ. Law School.
Attorney; Asst. to U.S. Rep. James C. Oliver 58-60; Co-ordinator, U.S. Area Redevt. Admin. 60-63; Maine Sec. of State 64-66; Gov. of Maine 67-; Lt.-Commdr. U.S. Naval Reserve; Democrat.
State House, Augusta, Maine, U.S.A.

Curtis, Dame Myra, M.A., D.B.E.; British educationist and administrator; b. 2 Oct. 1886; ed. Newnham Coll., Cambridge.
Mem. staff War Trade Intelligence Dept. 15-17. Min.

of Food 17-22, of Pensions 23-24, Post Office Savings Bank 24-34, Post Office Headquarters 35-37; Asst. Sec. and Dir. Women's Establishments, Treasury 38-41; Principal Asst. Sec. War Damage Comm. April-Dec. 41, Commissioner 43-59; Principal Newnham Coll. Cambridge 42-54; Chair. Dept. Cttee. on Children deprived of a normal home life 45-46; mem. Central Land Board 47-49; mem. Gen. Medical Council 55-60.
Publ. *Modern Money* (with Hugh Townshend) 37.
5A Northgate, Chichester, Sussex, England.
Telephone: Chichester 86892.

Curtis, Air Marshal Wilfred Austin, S.M., C.B., C.B.E., D.S.C., LL.D., E.D.; Canadian officer (retd.) and businessman; b. 21 Aug. 1893; ed. Toronto.
Entered Canadian Army 15; R.N.A.S. 16; served in France 17-18; directed own insurance firm, Toronto 19-39; joined R.C.A.F. on active service, apptd. Dir. of Postings and Careers 40-41; Commanded Uplands Air Station 41; Dep. C.-in-C. R.C.A.F. overseas 41-44; air mem. for Air Plans 45-47; Chief of Air Staff 47-53; Dir. Empire Life Insurance Co., W. A. Curtis & Co. Ltd., Toromont Industrial Holdings Ltd.; Chair. of Board Clare Bros. Ltd., W. H. Curtis and Co. Ltd., W. E. Dillion and Co., Lloyd Truax Co. Ltd., Viking Pump Co. Ltd.; Chancellor of York Univ., Toronto; Pres. Canadian Opera Co.; Hon. F.C.A.S.I.; D.Mil.Sc.
619 Avenue Road, Apt. 1403, Toronto, Canada.

Curzon, Clifford, C.B.E., F.R.A.M.; British concert pianist; b. 18 May 1907; ed. Royal Acad. of Music, London, and studied in Berlin under Schnabel and in Paris under Wanda Landowska and Nadia Boulanger.
Toured Europe for the British Council 36-37; recent tours throughout the world; coast-to-coast tours U.S.A. 37-67, including engagements with the N.Y. Philharmonic Orchestra, the Philadelphia Orchestra, etc.
The White House, Millfield Place, London, N.6, England.

Cushing, H.E. Cardinal Richard James; American ecclesiastic; b. 24 Aug. 1895; ed. Boston Coll., and St. John's Seminary, Boston.
Ordained priest 21; Auxiliary Bishop of Boston, Titular Bishop of Mela 39; Archbishop of Boston 44-; created Cardinal by Pope John XXIII 58; Prior, Knights of the Holy Sepulchre; Grand Officier Légion d'Honneur, Grosses Verdienstkreuz; Hon. L.H.D. (Brandeis Univ.).
2101 Commonwealth Avenue, Brighton 35, Boston, Mass., U.S.A.

Cushman, Austin Thomas; American retailing executive; b. 01; ed. Univ. of California.
Sears Roebuck & Co. 31, Vice-Pres. (Pacific Coast) 49-62, Dir. 50-, Chair. Board and Chief Exec. Officer 62-.
Sears Roebuck & Co., 925 S. Homan Avenue, Chicago 7, Illinois, U.S.A.

Cushman, Robert Eugene, B.A., PH.D., LITT.D.; American political scientist; b. 27 March 1889; ed. Oberlin and Columbia Univs.
Instructor in Political Science Illinois Univ. 15-19; Assoc. Prof. and Prof. of Political Science Minnesota Univ. 19-23; Prof. of Government and Head of Dept. Cornell Univ. 23-57; Pres. American Political Science Asscn. 43; mem. Board of Editors *American Political Science Review* 23-48; Editor-in-Chief, Documentary History of Ratification of Constitution of U.S. 58-.
Publs. *Excess Condemnation* 17, *Leading Constitutional Decisions* 25, *American National Government* 31, *The Independent Regulatory Commissions* 41, *Civil Liberties in U.S.* 56.
National Archives, Washington, D.C., U.S.A.

Cutler, Sir (Arthur) Roden, V.C., K.C.M.G., C.B.E., K.ST.J., B.EC.; Australian public servant and diplomatist; b. 24 May 1916; ed. Sydney High School and Univ. of Sydney.
Justice Dept. N.S.W. (Public Trust Office) 35-42;

State Sec. Retd. Servicemen's League N.S.W. 42-43; mem. of Aliens' Classification and Advisory Cttee. to advise Commonwealth Govt. 42-43; Asst. Dep. Dir. of Security Service N.S.W. 43; Commonwealth Asst. Commr. of Repatriation 43-46; High Commr. in New Zealand 46-52; High Commr. in Ceylon 52-55; Minister to Egypt 55-56; Sec.-Gen. SEATO 57; Chief of Protocol, Dept. of External Affairs, Canberra 57; State Pres. Retd. Servicemen's League, Australian Capital Territory; Australian High Commr. in Pakistan 59-61; Australian Consul-Gen., New York 61-65; Australian Amb. to the Netherlands 65-66; Gov. New South Wales 66-; 2/5th Field Regiment, A.I.F., Middle East 40-42; Hon. LL.D. Sydney Univ., Hon. D.Sc. Univ. of N.S.W.; Hon. Col. Royal N.S.W. Regt., Sydney Univ. Regt.; Hon. Air Commodore No. 22 Sqdn. R.A.A.F.
Government House, Sydney, N.S.W., Australia.

Cutts, Trevett Wakeham, LL.B.; Australian diplomatist; b. 28 May 1914; ed. Melbourne High School and Melbourne Univ.
Naval war service; joined Dept. of External Affairs 46; mem. Mission Singapore and Indonesia 46-50; Official Sec. High Comm. in Canada 52-54; Counsellor UN 54-57; Chargé d'Affaires Moscow 59-60; Consul-Gen. San Francisco 60-62; Ambassador to the Philippines 63-65; High Commr. to Pakistan 66-.
Australian High Commission, Rawalpindi, Pakistan.

Cybis, Jan; Polish painter; b. 16 Feb. 1897; ed. Wrocław, Cracow and Paris.
Prof. Warsaw Acad. of Fine Arts 45-; works exhibited at Venice Biennali 36 and 48, Galerie Zak (Paris), Galerie Moos (Geneva), Carnegie Inst. (Pittsburgh), Museum of Modern Art and Finch Coll. Museum of Art, New York; Berlin, Rome, Warsaw, Cracow, Poznań, etc.; easel paintings and murals include *Paris Suburban Landscape, Motel Landscape, Flowers in a Glass, Skoki Mill,* etc.; State Prize 55, 66, Guggenheim Foundation Prize, Paris 56.
14/16 Karowa, Warsaw, Poland.
Telephone: 26-80-99.

Cyrankiewicz, Josef; Polish politician; b. 23 April 1911; ed. Jagiellonian Univ., Cracow.
Sec. Cracow Socialist Party 35-; served in the artillery from the outbreak of war, captured by the Germans, escaped and organized resistance in the Cracow district; arrested and imprisoned in Auschwitz and Mauthausen concentration camps 41-45; Sec.-Gen. Socialist Party 45-48; Mem. of Parl. and Prime Minister 47; mem. Political Bureau of Central Cttee. of Polish United Workers' Party 48-; Chair. Council of Ministers 54-.
1/3 Al. Ujazdowskie, Warsaw, Poland.

Czerny-Stefańska, Halina; Polish pianist; b. 22; studied in Cracow and Warsaw.
Numerous concerts in Poland and abroad (U.S.A., South America, Canada, China, Japan, Turkey and all European countries) 49-; State Prizes, 1st and 2nd Class; Banner of Labour, 1st Class; 1st Prize IV Int. Chopin Competition 49.
3/8 Garncarska, Cracow, Poland.

Cziffra, Gyorgy; French (b. Hungarian) pianist; b. 5 Nov. 1921; ed. Conservatoire of Music, Budapest.
Recitals and concerts in U.S.A., U.K., Canada, France, Israel, Belgium, Netherlands, Italy and Switzerland; plays Liszt, Grieg, Tchaikovsky, Beethoven, Schumann, etc.
Grande Rue 28, Montigny les Corneilles, Seine et Oise, France.

Czinege, Lajos; Hungarian politician; b. 24.
Agricultural labourer; official Communist Party 47-51; Lieut.-Col. 51-54; Lieut.-Gen. 60; Col.-Gen. 62; mem. Central Cttee., Hungarian Socialist Workers Party 59-, Substitute mem. Pol. Cttee. 61-; Minister of Defence 60-.
Ministry of Defence, Budapest, Hungary.

Czottner, Sándor; Hungarian politician; b. 03; ed. Technical Univ.
Engine fitter; Minister of Mining and Power 51, of Heavy Industry 61-63.
Bimbó utca 168, Budapest II, Hungary.

D

Daane, James Dewey; American financial official; b. 6 July 1918; ed. Duke Univ. and Harvard Univ.
Federal Reserve Bank of Richmond 39-60, Monetary Economist 47, Asst. Vice-Pres. 53, Vice-Pres., Dir., Research Dept., 57; Chief, Int. Monetary Fund Mission to Paraguay 50-51; Vice-Pres., Econ. Adviser, Federal Reserve Bank of Minneapolis May-July 60; Asst. to Sec. of U.S. Treasury, Principal Adviser to Under-Sec. for Monetary Affairs 60-61; Dep. Under-Sec. of Treasury for Monetary Affairs and Gen. Dep. to Under-Sec. for Monetary Affairs 61-63; mem. Board of Govs., Federal Reserve System 63-.
1137 North Ivanhoe Street, Arlington, Virginia 22205, U.S.A.

Dabrowski, Konstantin, Magister Econ. Sci.; Polish politician and economist; b. 06; ed. Faculty of Finance, High School of Commerce, Warsaw.
Held various financial posts 25-39; compelled to go into hiding during German occupation; after liberation joined Nat. Economy and Finance Dept. of Polish Nat. Liberation Cttee.; mem. Nat. Assembly and Seym 45-56; Chair. Supreme Board Control 58-; mem. Central Cttee. Polish United Workers' Party.
Najwyzsej Izby Kontroli, AL I Armii, W.P.25, Warsaw, Poland.

Dacko, David; Central African Republic politician; b. 30; ed. Ecole Normale, Brazzaville.
Minister of Agriculture, Stockbreeding, Water and Forests, Central African Govt. Council 57-58; Minister of Interior, Economy and Trade, Central African Provisional Govt. 58-59; Premier, Central African Republic 59-66, Minister of Nat. Defence, Guardian of the Seals 60-66; Pres. of Central African Republic 60-66; mem. Mouvement pour l'Evolution Sociale de l'Afrique Noire (MESAN).
Bangui, Central African Republic, Equatorial Africa.

da Cunha Sottomayor Corrêa d'Oliveira, José Gonçalo; Portuguese lawyer and politician; b. 16 March 1921; ed. Colégio de Belinho and Lisbon Univ.
Vice-President Conselho Técnico Corporativo 49; Pres. Econ. Co-ordination Comm. 50, Export Development Fund and Supplies Fund 50, Technical Comm. for External Econ. Co-operation 61; Head, Portuguese Del. to OEEC and OECD (mem. Trade Directing Cttee. and Pres. Exchange and Payments Cttee. 55); Sec. of State for the Budget 55-58; Minister of State, Asst. to Prime Minister 61-65; Minister of Economy 65-; Rep. EFTA Council of Ministers 60-67, Chair. 63; Chair. OECD Council 67; Grand Cross Military Order of Christ (Portugal), Order of the Southern Cross (Brazil), Etoile Noire du Bénin (France); Order of Merit (Germany).
Publs. *A Revisão ao 1° Plano de Fomento, A Produção e Comércio das Conservas de Peixe, A Livre circulação de mercadorias e o sistema de pagamentos inter-regionais no espaço Português, Hora certa de Portugal: A integração económica de espaço Português.*
Rua das Amoreiras 128-1°, Lisbon, Portugal.

Daddah, Abdallahi Ould; Mauritanian diplomatist; b. 25 April 1935; ed. Lycée Wan Wollenhoven and Université de Paris.
Former Directeur de Cabinet, Ministry of Foreign Affairs; Sec.-Gen. Ministry of Foreign Affairs 62-64; Amb. to France, concurrently accred. to U.K., Italy and Switzerland 64-66; Amb. to U.S.A. and Perm.

Rep. to UN 66-; Commandeur du Mérite Nat. Mauritanien.
Permanent Mission of Mauritania, 150 East 52nd Street, New York 10022, U.S.A.

Daddah, Moktar Ould; Mauritanian politician; b. 20 Dec. 1924; ed. secondary school, Senegal and Paris.
Interpreter; studied law; with firm Boissier Palun, Dakar; territorial councillor 57; Premier, Islamic Republic of Mauritania 58-; Pres. of the Republic 61-, also Minister of Nat. Defence and Foreign Affairs; Pres. Org. Commune Africaine et Malgache 65; Leader Parti du Peuple.
Office of the President, Nouakchott, Islamic Republic of Mauritania, West Africa.

Daehli, Sverre; Norwegian lawyer; b. 96; ed. Univ. of Oslo; studied in Austria, England, France and U.S.A.
Deputy Judge 18; practising lawyer Court of Appeals 19; with Ministry of Justice 20; Barrister Supreme Court of Appeals 25; Judge Mixed Courts of Egypt 31, The Court of Appeals, Oslo, Norway 47, Supreme Court of Appeals 49; Pres. The Court of Arbitration and Mixed Comm. for the London Agreement on German External Debts 54-; Orders of St. Olav and of the Nile.
Schloss, Koblenz, German Federal Republic.

D'Aguiar, Peter; Guyanese politician and business executive; b. 1912; ed. Stonyhurst Coll., England.
Former Man. Dir. D'Aguiar Bros. Ltd. 32; fmr. Man. Dir. Bank Breweries Ltd. 55; Chair. Daily Chronicle Ltd. 61-; Leader United Force 60-; Minister of Finance 64-Sept. 67.
Byways, Kitty, East Coast, Demerara, Guyana.
Telephone: 4444.

Dahanayake, W.; Ceylonese politician; ed. Richmond Coll. Galle and St. Thomas' Coll. Mount Lavinia.
Trained teacher; elected to Galle Municipal Council 35, Mayor of Galle 39, 40 and 41; elected to the State Council for Bibile 44; M.P. 48-; Minister of Education 56-59; Prime Minister, Sept. 59-March 60; Minister of Home Affairs 65-; founded Ceylon Dem. Party 59.
Ministry of Home Affairs, Colombo, Ceylon.

Dahl, Odd; Norwegian research engineer; b. 3 Nov. 1898.
Air pilot and photographer, Roald Amundsen Arctic *Maud* Expedition 22-25; photograph travel, Amazon Basin 26; Research Asst. Carnegie Inst., Washington 27, Asst. Physicist 28-36; magnetic field work, Asia 28; Research Engineer, Chr. Michelsens Inst., Norway 37-, mem. of the Institute 43-; in charge design and construction, Norwegian-Dutch Nuclear Reactor, Kjeller, Norway 48; Group Dir. European Council for Nuclear Research (C.E.R.N.) 52-55; in charge design and construction Norwegian boiling heavy water reactor project (H.B.W.R.) 55-; mem. Norwegian Academy of Science; awarded prize, American Asscn. for the Advancement of Science (jointly with Tuve and Hafstad) 31; awarded prize, Norwegian Engineering Soc. 51; Commdr. St. Olav (Norway) and Commdr. of Orange-Nassau; Hon. D.Phil. (Univ. of Bergen).
Chr. Michelsens Institut, Nygårdsgaten 114, Bergen, Norway.
Telephone: Bergen 17633.

Dahl, Major-General Ørnulf; Norwegian army officer; b. 15 Feb. 1900; ed. Norwegian Cadet Acad., and Staff Coll.
First-Lieut. 21, Captain 34, Major 42, Colonel 46, Major-

Gen. 55; comm. Norw. Independent Brigade Gp. 481 Germany 48; Commdr. 1st Div. 56; Deputy C.-in-C. Norwegian Army, Commdr. Allied Land Forces in Norway 57-61; Commandant Akershus Fortress 61-68; fought in Norwegian campaign 40; Asst. Mil. Attaché to Finland 40, Sweden 41-44; Norwegian Army Command London 44-45; numerous Norwegian and foreign decorations.

Akershus Fortress, Oslo, Norway.

Dahl, Torsten; Danish scholar; b. 29 Aug. 1897; ed. Copenhagen Univ., and London, Oxford and Cambridge.

Prof. Aarhus Univ. until 67; collaborator in *Annual Bibliography of English Language and Literature*, Cambridge 25-67, Emeritus 67-; co-editor of the series *Anglistica*, Copenhagen 53-; mem. Philological Soc., London.

Publs. *Form and Function, i.e., Studies in Old and Middle English Syntax, Conflicting Comments on the Union of England and Scotland, Linguistic Studies in Some Elizabethan Writings: I. An Inquiry into Aspects of the Language of Thomas Deloney. II. The Auxiliary "Do"*; annotated translation into Danish of selections from the Anglo-Saxon Chronicle, papers on modern English syntax and English words in the Danish language.

Ejgaards Tvaervej 2, 2920 Charlottenlund, Denmark. Telephone: Ordrup 9447.

Dahlbeck, Eva; Swedish actress; b. 8 March 1920; ed. Royal Dramatic Theatre School, Stockholm.

Films acted in include: *The Counterfeit Traitor* 61, *Biljett till Paradiset* 61, *För att inte tala om alla dessa Kvinnor* 64, *Älskande par* 64, *Kattorna* 65, *Les Créatures* 65, *Den Röda Kappan* 66.

Plays acted in include: *Candida* 61, *Ändå älskar vi varavdra* 63, *Tchin-Tchin* 63, *The Balcony* 64, *Doctors of Philosophy* 64.

Publs. *Dessa mina minsta* (play) 55, *Hem till Kaos* (novel) 64, *S'is'ta Spegeln* (novel) 65, *Den S'junde Natten* (novel) 66, *Domen* (novel) 67.

c/o Svenska Filminstitutet, Kungsgatan 48, Stockholm C, Sweden.

Dahlgaard, Bertel; Danish politician; b. 7 Nov. 1887; ed. Salling High School, Dalum Agricultural School, Askov High School, Copenhagen Univ.

Dir. Copenhagen Statistical Office 14, Senior Dir. 18, Chief Dir. 22-29; Dir. Danish Nat. Bank 41-57; Minister of Interior 29-40; Minister of Economics and Nordic Affairs 57-61; mem. of Parl. 20-60, of Nordic Council 53-57; Social-Liberal (Radikale Venstre).

Gentoftegade 55, Gentofte, Denmark. Telephone: Gentofte 960.

Dahlgaard, Tyge; Danish economist and politician; b. 8 April 1921; ed. Københavns Universitet.

Junior Economist, Ministry of Agriculture 47-49; Perm. Rep. to UN, Geneva 49-50; Asst. Head of Section (Multilateral Econ. Problems), Ministry for Foreign Affairs 50-54; Danish Sec.-Gen. Nordic Cttee. for Econ. Co-operation 54-57; Counsellor, Danish Perm. Del. to OEEC, Paris 57-59; Counsellor (Econ. Affairs), Danish Embassy, Washington, D.C. 59-64; Amb. and Perm. Rep. to EEC, ECSC and Euratom, Brussels 64-66; Minister of Commerce and European Market Relations 66-Oct. 67.

c/o Ministry of Commerce, Slotholmsgade 12, Copenhagen K, Denmark.

Dahlgrün, Dr. Rolf; German lawyer, business executive and politician; b. 19 May 1908; ed. Realgymnasium, Hanover, and Univ. of Göttingen.

Legal Dept., Phoenix Rubber Co., Hamburg-Harburg 36, Dir. 38-62; mem. Hamburg Corpn. 53-57, Bundestag 57-; Fed. Minister of Finance 62-66; Free Democrat.

Office: 53 Bonn, Blücherstrasse 18; Home: 2 Hamburg 90 Harburg, Haakerstrasse 63, German Federal Republic.

Telephone: 7907429.

Dahl-Iversen, Erling, M.D., D.M.SC.; Danish surgeon; b. 30 Nov. 1892; ed. Univ. of Copenhagen and Copenhagen hospitals.

Professor of Surgery, Univ. of Copenhagen 35-63, Emeritus 63-; Surgeon-in-Chief, Univ. Clinic C, Rigshospitalet, Copenhagen 35-63; Hon. Fellow American Coll. of Surgeons, Royal Coll. of Surgeons (U.K. and Ireland); Hon. mem. Soc. int. de chirurgie; Foreign Assoc. Académie de Chirurgie, Paris.

Publs. *Etude expérimentale de l'influence de la cholécystectomie sur les voies biliaires et la sécrétion gastrique* 24, *Operative Surgery* 39, *Special Urological Diagnostics* 42, *Physical Signs in Surgery* 44, *Clinical Surgery I* 52, *II* 55, *The Importance of Sex-Hormones in the Physiological and Pathological Conditions of the Breast* 35, *The Influences of Endocrines in the Post-operative Period* 55, *Surgery in Denmark in the 19th Century* 60, *Surgery in Denmark in the 18th Century* 65, and numerous surgical papers.

Tranegaardsvej 24, Copenhagen-Hellerup, Denmark. Telephone: 7820.

Dahrendorf, Ralf Gustav, DR. PHIL., PH.D.; German sociologist; b. 1 May 1929; ed. Hamburg Univ., and London School of Economics.

Imprisoned in concentration camp 44-45; Privatdozent Univ. des Saarlandes, Saarbrücken 57; Fellow, Center for Advanced Study in the Behavioral Sciences 57-58; Prof. of Sociology, Hamburg Acad. of Econs. and Politics 58-60; Prof. of Sociology and Dir. of Sociological Seminar, Tübingen Univ. 60-65; Vice-Chair. Founding Cttee. of University of Constance 64-, Prof. of Sociology 66-; mem. Fed. Exec. Cttee. of Free Democratic Party (F.D.P.) 68-; Journal Fund Award 59.

Publs. *Marx in Perspektive* 53, *Der Mensch das Mass aller Dinge* (editor) 55, *Industrie- und Betriebssoziologie* 56, *Soziale Klassen und Klassenkonflikt* 57, *Sozialstruktur des Betriebes* 59, *Homo Sociologicus* 59, *Der Zweite Bildungsweg* (editor) 59, *Über den Ursprung der Ungleichheit* 61, *Gesellschaft und Freiheit* 61, *Das Mitbestimmungsproblem in der deutschen Sozialforschung* 63, *Die angewandte Aufklärung* 63, *Gesellschaft und Demokratie in Deutschland* 65, *Bildung ist Bürgerrecht* 65, *Pfade aus Utopia* 67, *Essays in the Theory of Society* 67, *Für eine Erneuerung des Demokratie in der Bundesrepublik* 68.

Zur Torkel 10, Constance, German Federal Republic. Telephone: Constance 63814.

Dakin, Allin Winston, M.A., M.B.A.; American educational administrator; b. 2 June 1905; ed. State Univ. of Iowa and Harvard Univ.

Instructor in Commerce, State Univ. of Iowa 26-29; J. & W. Seligman & Co. and Tri-Continental Corpn. (investment bankers and investment trust), New York 31-34; Bursar and Commerce Dept., Robert Coll., Istanbul 34-39; Bursar, American Coll. for Girls, Istanbul 35-39; Controller, Pomona, Scripps and Claremont Colls. 40-44; Admin. Dean and Asst. to the Pres., State Univ. of Iowa 44-; Fellow Archæological Inst. of America; Nat. Geographical Society; American Geographic Society; Inst. Int. de Ideales Americanistas (Mexican Section), Nat. Council, Boy Scouts; District Gov., Vice-Pres. and Dir. Rotary Int.; Chair. Rotary Convention Cttee. 60; Chair. Rotary Int. Finance Cttee. 63, Program Planning 66, Public Relations 67; Pres. UN Asscn., Iowa, Dir. 62-70; Dir. Partners for the Alliance 65-; Hon. LL.D., Westmar.

Publs. *Foreign Securities in the American Money Market* 32, *Adventuring Around Africa*.

Home: 329 Ellis Avenue, Iowa City, Iowa; Office: Old Capitol, Iowa City, Iowa, U.S.A. Telephone: 319-338-8487.

Daladier, Edouard, G.C.M.G.; French politician; b. 18 June 1884.

Fmr. teacher; Radical-Socialist Deputy for Vaucluse 19-58; Minister for Colonies (Herriot Cabinet) 24-26, of Public Works (Chautemps and Steeg Cabinets) 30-31;. Minister of Public Works (Herriot Cabinet) June-Dec. 32; Minister of War (Paul-Boncour Cabinet) Dec.-Feb. 32, Prime Minister and Minister of War Jan-Oct. 33; Minister of War (Chautemps Cabinet) Nov. 33-Jan. 34; Prime Minister and Minister of Foreign Affairs Jan.-Feb. 34; Hon. Pres. Radical-Socialist Party, and Chair. 36; Minister of Nat. Defence and Deputy Prime Minister 36-37; Minister of Nat. Defence 37; Prime Minister and Minister of Nat. Defence 38-40, also of War and Foreign Affairs 39-40; fmr. Pres. Supreme Air Council; arrested September 40, detained at Fort Portalet after condemnation without trial, deported to Germany, liberated by Allies 45; mem. Constituent Assembly 46, Nat. Assembly 46-58; fmr. Mayor of Avignon; Chevalier Légion d'Honneur; Croix de Guerre.

Publ. *The Defence of France* 39.

6 place de la Porte-de-Passy, Paris 16e, France.

Dalai Lama, The; Tibetan ruler and religious leader; Fourteenth Incarnation; b. 35.

Born of Tibetan peasant family in Amdo district of Chhija Nangso Province; enthroned at Lhasa 40; rights exercised by regency 34-50; assumed power 50; left Tibet for India after abortive resistance to Chinese 59; Dr. of Buddhist Philosophy 59; Supreme Head of all Buddhist sects in Tibet.

Publs. *My Land and People* 62, *Losar Migje* 63.

Swarg Ashram, Upper Dharmsala, Kangra/Punjab, India.

Dale, Sir Henry Hallett, O.M., G.B.E., F.R.S., M.A., M.D., D.SC., LL.D., F.R.C.P.; British scientist; b. 9 June 1875; ed. Trinity Coll., Cambridge.

Staff of Nat. Inst. for Medical Research 14, Dir. 28-42; Sec. Royal Society 25-35; mem. Gen. Medical Council 27-37; mem. L.N. Cttee. on Standardisation of Sera and Biological Products; shared Nobel prize for Medicine 36; mem. Court, Univ. of London 39-50; Hon. Fellow Trinity Coll. Cambridge; Pres. Royal Society 40-45; Fullerian Prof. of Chemistry and Dir. Davy-Faraday Laboratory, Royal Inst. 42-46; Pres. British Asscn. 47; Pres. Royal Society of Medicine 48-50; Chair. of the Wellcome Trust 38-60; Pres. British Council 50; Grand Cross Ordre de la Couronne (Belgium) 49; Orden Pour le Mérite (German Federal Republic) 55.

Publs. *Adventures in Physiology* 53, *An Autumn Gleaning* 54.

The Evelyn Nursing Home, Trumpington Road, Cambridge; Office: Wellcome Trust, 52 Queen Anne Street, London, W.1, England.

Dale, William B.; American financial official; b. 24 March 1924; ed. Wayne High School, Michigan, Univ. of Michigan and Fletcher School of Law and Diplomacy.

Assistant U.S. Treasury Rep., Brussels 48-50, Acting U.S. Rep. 51-52; Deputy Chief, British Commonwealth and Middle East Div., U.S. Treasury Dept. 52-53; U.S. Treasury Rep. in Middle East 53-55; Program Man., Int. Research, Stanford Research Inst., Washington 56-61; Dir. Bureau of Int. Programs, U.S. Dept. of Commerce 61-62; Deputy Asst. Sec. for Int. Affairs, U.S. Dept. of Commerce 62; U.S. Exec. Dir. Int. Monetary Fund 62-.

International Monetary Fund, Washington, D.C. 20431, U.S.A.

Daley, Richard J.; American lawyer and politician; b. 02; ed. Nativity of Our Lord Grammar School, De La Salle High School and De Paul Univ.

Member, Illinois House of Representatives 36-38; mem. Illinois Senate 39-43, Floor Leader 42; Tax Dir. of Illinois 49-52; Clerk of Cook County 53-55; Mayor of Chicago 55-; several decorations; Democrat.

Room 507, City Hall, Chicago, Illinois, U.S.A.

Daley, Sir (William) Allen, Kt., M.D., CH.B., B.SC., F.R.C.P., D.P.H., F.A.P.H.A.; British physician; b. 19 Feb. 1887; ed. Merchant Taylors School, Crosby, and Liverpool Univ.

Resident hospital appointments 09-11; Medical Officer of Health, Bootle 11-20, Blackburn 20-25, City of Hull 25-29; Port Medical Officer of Health Hull and Goole Port Sanitary Authority 25-29; Principal Medical Officer London County Council 29-39, Medical Officer of Health and School Medical Officer, County of London 39-52; Assoc. Health Officer, City of Baltimore, Md., U.S.A. 52; Board of Govs. Hammersmith Hospital and Bethlem Royal Maudsley Hospitals 48-63; Chair. Inst. of Psychiatry, Univ. of London 48-62; Gov. Body British Post-graduate Medical Fed., Royal Postgraduate Medical School (London), Pres. Soc. of Medical Officers of Health 47; Hon. Physician to the King 47-50; Pres. Nat. Asscn. for Maternal and Child Welfare and Chair. Chadwick Trust; Past Pres. Central Council for Health Educ. and Pres. U.K. Cttee. for WHO; Hon. LL.D. (Univ. of Liverpool).

24 Edith Road, London, W.14, England.

Telephone: 01-603-6204.

Dalhousie, 16th Earl of; **Simon Ramsay,** G.B.E., M.C., D.L., LL.D.; British politician and Governor-General; b. 17 Oct. 1914; ed. Eton Coll., and Oxford Univ.

Served in Black Watch 36-45; Mem. of Parl. 45-50; Conservative Whip 46-48; Gov.-Gen. Fed. of Rhodesia and Nyasaland 57-63; Lord Lieut. County of Angus 67-; Hon. LL.D. (Dundee Univ.) 67.

Brechin Castle, Brechin, Scotland.

Dali, Salvador; Spanish painter; b. 11 May 1904; ed. Acad. of Fine Arts, Madrid and Paris.

Impressionist, Futurist, Constructivist and Surrealist; designer of film scenarios, scenery and costumes for ballet and opera; lecturer in Museum of Modern Art, New York 35; Exhbn. of Jewels, London 60.

Publs. *Babaoua, Secret Life of Salvador Dali, Hidden Faces, Fifty Secrets of Magic Craftmanship, Dali on Modern Art, The World of Salvador Dali, Le Mythe Tragique de l'Angélus de Millet, Diary of A Genius.*

Hotel St. Regis, Fifth Avenue and 55th Street, New York 22, New York, U.S.A.; Port-Lligat, Cadaqués, Spain.

Dallapiccola, Luigi; Italian professor of music; b. 3 Feb. 1904; ed. Liceo, Pisino and Conservatorio di Musica Cherubini, Florence.

Professor of Piano, Conservatorio Cherubini Florence 34-68; engaged twice by Berkshire Music Center, Mass., U.S.A. 51-52; engaged by Queen's Coll., Flushing, New York 56-57, 59, Univ. of California (Berkeley) 62-63; mem. Acad. Philharmonique de Rome, Accad. Santa Cecilia, Rome, Gli Agiati, Rovereto, Akad. der schönen Künste, Munich, and Akad. der Künste, Berlin, Royal Acad., Stockholm, American Acad. of Arts and Letters, Nat. Inst. of Arts and Letters, New York, Acad. Nacional de Bellas Artes, Buenos Aires, Musik Verein, Graz, Inst. de France (Acad. des Beaux-Arts).

Principal works: Theatre: *Vol de Nuit* 40, *Marsyas* 43, *Le Prisonnier* 48, *Job* 50; Choral works: *Six Choeurs de Michelangelo le Jeune* 33-36, *Canti di prigionia* 38-41, *Canti di Liberazione* 55, *An Mathilde* 55, *Requiescant* 58; Orch. works: *Partita* 30-32, *Due Pezzi* 48, *Variazioni* 54, *Piccola Musica Notturna* 54; Voice and instruments: *Divertimento* 34, *Tre Laudi* 37, *Liriche Greche* 42-45, *Tre Poemi* 49, *Goethe-Lieder* 53, *Five Songs* 56, *Prayers* 62; *Parole di San Paolo* 64; Chamber Music: *Rencesvals* 46, *Machado-Songs* 48, *Musique pour Trois Pianos* 36, *Due Studi* 47, *Sonatina Canonica* 43, *Quaderno Musicale di Annalibera* 53, *Tartiniana Seconda* 55;

Others: *Piccolo Concerto per Muriel Couvreux 41, Tartiniana 52, Christmas Concerto 57, Dialoghi 59-60.* Via Romana 34, 50125 Florence, Italy.
Telephone: 22-76-98.

Dalrymple, Ian Murray, B.A., F.R.S.A.; British writer, film producer and director; b. 26 Aug. 1903; ed. Rugby School and Trinity Coll., Cambridge.
Film Editor 27-35; writer of screen plays 35-40; Exec. Producer, Crown Film Unit, Ministry of Information 40-43; Assoc. Exec. Producer, M.G.M.-London Films 43-46; Producer and Man. Dir. Wessex Film Productions Ltd. 46-; Advisory Producer, British Lion Film Corpn. Ltd. 52-54; Chair. British Film Academy 57-58; mem. British Film Producers' Asscn.
Principal productions: *A Cry from the Streets, The Admirable Crichton, A Hill in Korea, Raising a Riot, The Heart of the Matter, Bank of England, The Changing Face of Europe* (a series of six short films in colour on European recovery), *The Wooden Horse, All over the Town, Once a Jolly Swagman, Dear Mr. Prohack, Esther Waters, The Woman in the Hall, Western Approaches, Target for To-night, London Can Take It*; as writer of screen plays: *South Riding, The Citadel, Storm in a Teacup, Pygmalion,* etc.
Horseshoes, Beaumont, Thorpe-le-Soken, Essex, England.

Dalton, Jack; American librarian; b. 21 March 1908; ed. Virginia and Michigan Univs.
Instructor in English, Virginia Polytechnic Inst. 30-34; Reference Librarian, Univ. of Virginia 34-42, Assoc. Librarian 42-50, Librarian 50-56; Dir. Int. Relations Office, American Library Asscn. 56-59; Dean, School of Library Service, Columbia Univ. 59-.
School of Library Service, Columbia Univ., New York 27, N.Y.; Home: 445 Riverside Drive, New York, N.Y. 10027, U.S.A.
Telephone: MO3-3359.

Daly, Ivan de Burgh, C.B.E., M.D., F.R.C.P., F.R.S.; British physiologist; b. 14 April 1893; ed. Rossall, Gonville and Caius Coll., Cambridge and St. Bartholomew's Hospital, London.
Served 14-18 war; Asst. Physiologist Univ. Coll. London; Beit Research Fellow 20; Lecturer in Experimental Physiology, Welsh Nat. School of Medicine 23; Prof. of Physiology, Birmingham Univ. 27-33, Edinburgh Univ. 33-47; Dir. Medical Research Council Physiological Laboratory, Armoured Fighting Vehicle Training School 42-45; Dir. Inst. of Animal Physiology of Agricultural Research Council, Babraham, Cambridge 48-58; Wellcome Research Fellow 58-63; Research, Univ. Laboratory of Physiology, Oxford 63-; mem. Agricultural Research Council 45-47; contrib. to physiological journals; co-editor *Quarterly Journal of Experimental Physiology,* co-author *The Bronchial and Pulmonary Vascular Systems.*
25 High Street, Long Crendon, Aylesbury, Buckinghamshire, England.
Telephone: Long Crendon 298.

Daly, John (Charles), Jr.; American (b. South Africa) broadcaster; b. 20 Feb. 1914; ed. Boston Coll.
Schedule Engineer, Capital Transit Co., Washington 35-37; Corresp. and News Analyst, Columbia Broadcasting System 37-49; Special Events Reporter and White House Corresp. 37-41, service in U.S.A., Europe and South America for C.B.S. 45-49; Corresp.-Analyst, American Broadcasting Co., also Moderator, television programmes on all networks; Vice-Pres. American Broadcasting Co., in charge of News, Special Events and Public Affairs 53-60; mem. Water Pollution Advisory Board 60-67; Dir. Voice of America broadcasts, Nat. Broadcasting Co. 67-June 68.
33 W. 56th Street, New York City 10019, U.S.A.

Dam, (Carl Peter) Henrik, DR. PHIL.; Danish biochemist; b. 21 Feb. 1895; ed. Polytechnic Inst., Copenhagen and Univ. of Copenhagen.
Instructor in Chemistry, School of Agriculture and Veterinary Medicine, Copenhagen 20, Physiological Laboratory, Univ. of Copenhagen 23; Assoc. Prof. Inst. of Biochemistry, Univ. of Copenhagen 29-41; Prof. of Biochemistry and Nutrition, Polytechnic Inst. Copenhagen 41-65, Prof. emeritus Polytechnic Inst. Copenhagen 65-; Dir. Biochemical Div. of Danish Fat Research Inst. 56-63; mem. Royal Danish Acad. of Sciences and Letters, Danish Acad. of Tech. Sciences; Pres. Danish Nutrition Soc. 67-; Fellow of American Inst. of Nutrition; mem. of several other scientific socs.; studied Microchemistry with F. Pregl Graz 25, Metabolism of Sterols in Rudolf Schönheimer's Laboratory, Freiburg 32-33 (Rockefeller Fellow), worked with P. Karrer, Zürich 35, and later; lectured in U.S. and Canada 40-41 and 49; research work, Woods Hole Marine Biological Laboratories 41; Senior Research Assoc. Univ. of Rochester, N.Y. 42-45; Assoc. mem. Rockefeller Inst. for Medical Research 45-48; Joint Hon. Pres. Int. Union of Nutritional Sciences; awarded Nobel Prize 43 (for discovery of Vitamin K); Hon. F.R.S. (Edinburgh), Hon. D.Sc. (St. Louis Univ.).
Office: Østervoldgade 10 III, Copenhagen K; Home: Jagtvej 229, Copenhagen Ø, Denmark.

Damon, Roger Conant, B.A.; American banker; b. 4 Aug. 1906; ed. Hotchkiss School, Yale Coll., and Stonier Graduate School of Banking.
Joined First Nat. Bank of Boston 29, Asst. Cashier 36-41, Asst. Vice-Pres. 41-43, Vice-Pres. 43-52, Senior Vice-Pres. 52-59, Dir. 56-, Pres. and Chair. of Exec. Cttee. 59-, Chair. of Board and Chief Exec. Officer 66-; Dir. Boston Overseas Financial Corpn.; Pres. and Dir. First Small Business Investment Corpn. of New England, Corporacion Financiera de Boston; Dir. Massnat Corpn., Bank of Boston International, Boston Edison Co., New England Mutual Life Insurance Co., Old Colony Trust Co., Raytheon Co., United Fund of Greater Boston, Firstbank Financial Corpn., Eastern Air Lines, Inc., and other companies; official of other financial and educational orgs.
First National Bank of Boston, 67 Milk Street, Boston, Mass. 02106, U.S.A.

Damongo Dadet, Emmanuel; Congolese diplomatist; b. 18 Aug. 1914; ed. primary school.
Former teacher; Rep. Councillor of Middle Congo 46-52; Councillor of French Union 47-53; Asst. Dir. Radio-AEF 54-57; Principal Private Sec. Ministry of Budget and Financial Affairs, Middle Congo 57-58; Minister of Works and Transport 58-60; Del. of Congo to Secretariat of French Community 60; Ambassador of Congo (Brazzaville) to U.S.A. and Perm. Rep. to UN 61-64; Prefect of Letili District 64-; Officer of Congolese Merit.
Publs. *Congolela* (novel) 45, *Préludes* (poetry) 46, *Louise Oumba* (novel) 56.
Zanaga (Letili), Congo, (Brazzaville).

Dana, Charles Anderson; American business executive; b. 25 April 1881; ed. Columbia Univ.
Chairman of Board and Dir., Dana Corpn.; Pres. and Trustee, Coralitos Co.; Dir., Manufacturers Trust Co., Kelsey-Hayes Co., Curtiss-Wright Corpn.
The Homestead, Wilton, Connecticut, U.S.A.

Danahar, John Anthony, A.B.; American jurist; b. 9 Jan. 1899; ed. Yale Univ.
Law clerk White & Case N.Y. 21-22; admitted to Conn. Bar 22, in practice Hartford and Washington; Asst. U.S. Attorney 22-34; Sec. State of Conn. 33-35; U.S. Senator from Conn. 39-45; Judge, U.S. Court of Appeals, Washington, D.C. 53-; mem. Conn., Hartford County and American Bar Asscns.; Republican.
5836 U.S. Court House, Washington, D.C., U.S.A.

Danckwerts, Rt. Hon. Sir Harold Otto, Kt., P.C., M.A.; British lawyer; b. 23 Feb. 1888; ed. Winchester Coll., Balliol Coll., Oxford, and Harvard Law School, U.S.A. Called to Bar Lincoln's Inn 13; served in First World War 14-19; practised as Barrister until May 49, also Tutor and Reader to the Law Society 14-41; Junior Counsel to the Treasury and Board of Trade in Chancery Matters and Counsel to the Attorney-Gen. in Charity Matters 41-49; apptd. Judge of the High Court of Justice (attached to the Chancery Div.) May 49-; knighted July 49, Lord Justice, Court of Appeal 61-.
4 Stone Buildings, Lincoln's Inn, London, W.C.2; and Royal Courts of Justice, Strand, London, W.C.2, England.

Dange, S. A.; Indian trade union leader; b. 10 Oct. 1899.
Took a prominent part in organising Textile Workers' Unions in Bombay; arrested on many occasions for trade union and political activity; sentenced to twelve years' transportation in the Meerut conspiracy trial; released 36; imprisoned 39-43; Pres. Girni Kamgar Union; Pres. All-India T.U.C. 43-45; Del. to W.F.T.U. Paris 45, Moscow 46; Vice-Pres. W.F.T.U. 48; Editor and Founder of *Socialist* 22, first Marxist paper in India; Editor and Founder of *Kranti*, first working-class paper in Marathi language; mem. Legislative Assembly, Bombay 46; imprisoned 48-50; Gen. Sec. All-India Trade Union Congress 56; mem. Legislative Assembly, New Delhi; Chair. Indian Communist Party 62-.
Publs. *Gandhi versus Lenin, Hell Found, Literature and the People, India from Primitive Communism to Slavery.*
9 Kohinoor Road, Dadar, Bombay, India.

Danialov, Abdurakhman Danialovich; Soviet politician; b. 1908; ed. Moscow Inst. of Water Economy and Higher Party School.
Member C.P.S.U. 28-; State and party work 37-40; Chair. Council of Ministers, Dagestan Autonomous Republic 40-48, First Sec. Dagestan Regional Cttee. C.P.S.U. 48-; Cand. mem. Central Cttee. C.P.S.U. 52-56, mem. 56-; Deputy Supreme Soviet U.S.S.R.; mem. Presidium Supreme Soviet 66-.
Regional Committee of C.P.S.U., Makhachkala, Dagestan A.S.S.R., U.S.S.R.

Daniel, (Elbert) Clifton, Jr.; American newspaperman; b. 19 Sept. 1912; ed. Univ. of North Carolina.
Associate Editor *Daily Bulletin,* Dunn, N.C. 33-34; Reporter *News and Observer,* Raleigh, N.C. 33-37; Associated Press, New York City, Washington, Berne, London 37-43; *New York Times* 44-, London SHAEF Headquarters, Paris, Middle East, Germany, U.S.S.R. 44-55, New York City 55-, Asst. to Managing Editor 57-59, Asst. Managing Editor 59-64, Managing Editor 64-.
New York Times, 229 W. 43rd Street, New York City 36, N.Y., U.S.A.

Daniel-Lesur, J. Y.; French composer; b. 19 Nov. 1908; ed. Paris Conservatoire.
Musical Adviser to Radiodiffusion-Télévision Française; contrib. to *Arts, La Gazette des Lettres Polyphonie, La Revue Musicale* and other publs.; teaches, and writes film music; Dir. hon. Schola Cantorum, mem. Conseil Supérieur de l'Enseignement musical, French Comm. UNESCO; Chevalier Légion d'Honneur, Officier Ordre des Arts et des Lettres.
Works include: *Suite Française pour Orchestre* 35, *Passacaille* 37, *Pastorale pour Petit Orchestre* 38, *Ricercare pour Orchestre* 39, *Quatre Lieder pour Chant et Orchestre* 33-39, *Trio d'Anches* 39, *Trois Poèmes de Cécile Sauvage* 39, *Quatuor à Cordes* 41, *L'Enfance de l'Art* 42, *Variations pour piano et orchestre à Cordes* 43, *Clair comme le Jour* 45, *Suite pour Trio à Cordes et Piano* 43, *Suite Médiévale pour Flûte, Harpe et Trio à Cordes* 44, *Chansons Cambodgiennes* 46, *Berceuses à tenir éveillé* (chant) 47, *Pastorale variée pour piano* 47, *Ballade pour*

piano 48, *Andrea del Sarto* (symphonic poem) 49, *Dix chansons populaires à trois voix égales* 50, *Ouverture pour un festival* 51, *Chansons françaises à quatre voix mixtes* 51, *L'Annonciation* (cantata) 52, *Cantique des Cantiques, pour 12 voix mixts* 53, *Concerto da Camera pour piano et Orchestre de Chambre* 53, *Cantique des Colonnes pour ensemble vocal féminin et orchestre* 54, *Sérénade pour orchestre à cordes* 54, *Le Bal du Destin* (ballet), *Elégie pour deux guitares* 56, *Symphonie de Danses* 58, *Messe du Jubilé pour choeur mixte, orchestre et orgue* 60, *Fantasie pour deux pianos, Trois études pour piano* 62, *Chanson de mariage pour choeur de voix de femmes* 64, *Deux Chansons de Marins pour choeur d'Hommes* 64, *Deux Chansons de bord pour choeur mixte* 64.
82 Boulevard Flandrin, Paris 16e, France.
Telephone: 727-49-86.

Daniels, Farrington, PH.D.; American physical chemist; b. 8 March 1889; ed. Univ. of Minnesota and Harvard Univ.
Instructor and Asst. Prof. Worcester Polytechnic Inst. 14-17; First Lieut. Chemical Warfare Service 18; Asst. Prof., Assoc. Prof., Prof., Univ. of Wisconsin 20-59, Emer. 59-, research in solar energy applications, Engineering Experiment Station, Univ. of Wisconsin; also research in chemical kinetics, photochemistry, electrochemistry, nitrogen oxides, atomic energy, thermoluminescence of crystals; Visiting Prof. Stanford Univ. 30, Cornell Univ. 35; Dir. Metallurgical Laboratory (Atomic Energy), Chicago 45-46; Chair. Board of Govs. Argonne Nat. Laboratory 46-48; Chair. Dept. of Chemistry, Univ. of Wisconsin 53-59; Pres. American Chem. Soc. 53, Geochem. Soc. 58; Vice-Pres. Nat. Acad. of Sciences 57-61; Pres. Solar Energy Soc. 64-67; Fellow American Asscn. for Advancement of Science, American Nuclear Soc.; mem. American Philosophical Soc., American Acad. of Arts and Sciences; Priestly Medal; Willard Gibbs Medal; Norris Award, American Chem. Soc.; Dr. h.c. Univs. of Rhode Island, Minnesota, Louisville and Wisconsin, and Dakar Univ.
Publs. *Mathematical Preparation for Physical Chemistry, Chemical Kinetics, Direct Use of the Sun's Energy;* Co-author: *Physical Chemistry, Experimental Physical Chemistry, Solar Energy Research, Challenge of Our Times, Photochemistry of Solid and Liquid States.*
Solar Energy Laboratory, Univ. of Wisconsin, Madison, Wisconsin 53706, U.S.A.

Daniels, John Hancock; American business executive; b. 28 Oct. 1921; ed. St. Paul Acad., Phillips Exeter Acad., Yale Univ., and Harvard Univ.
Archer Daniels Midland Co. 46, Flax Buyer, and Sales Management, Linseed Oil Div., Asst. Vice-Pres. 55-57, Dir. of Production and Procurement, Dehydrated Alfalfa Div. 56-57, Vice-Pres., Dir. and Manager Formula Feed Div. 57-58, Pres. and Chief Exec. Officer 58-68, Chair. of Board 68-; Dir. SOO Line Railroad, Northwestern Nat. Bank of Minneapolis, Warwick Electronics, Inc.; Trustee of Cttee. for Econ. Devt.; mem. Business Council.
Worsted Skeynes, Gem Lake, White Bear Lake, Minnesota, U.S.A.

Daniels, Thomas Leonard; American business executive; b. 4 July 1892; ed. St. Paul Acad., Hill School and Yale Univ.
Archer-Daniels Co. 14-17; U.S. Army 17-19; U.S. Diplomatic Service 21-29, served Brussels, Rio de Janeiro, Rome; Archer Daniels Midland Co. 29-, Pres. until 58, Chair. of Board 58-64, Dir. Emer. 64-.
Archer Daniels Midland Company, Minneapolis 2, Minnesota, U.S.A.

Daniels, Troy C(ook), B.S., PH.D.; American pharmacist and organic chemist; b. 27 Aug. 1899; ed. Univ. of Michigan and Indiana Univ.
Instructor in Pharmacy, State Coll. of Washington 23-24; Asst. Prof. 24-27; Asst. in Organic Chemistry,

Indiana Univ. 28-29; Asst. Prof. of Pharmacy, Coll. of Pharmacy, Univ. of Calif. 29-33; Prof. of Pharmaceutical Chemistry 33-; Asst. Dean 37-44; Dean of School of Pharmacy 44-67; Chair. Calif. Section of American Chemical Society 44; mem. American Chemical Society, American Pharmaceutical Asscn.; mem. Exec. Cttee. American Asscn. of Colls. of Pharmacy 45-47 and 51-54, Pres. 52-53; mem. Cttee. on World Congress for Pharmaceutical Education 49-50, Revision Cttee. of U.S. Pharmacopeia 50-60; Pres. American Asscn. of Colls. of Pharmacy 52-53; Chair. House of Delegates, American Pharmaceutical Asscn. 56-57; mem. Council of American Pharmaceutical Asscn. 58-64; Fellow N.Y. Academy of Sciences; Faculty Fellow, American Coll. of Apothecaries; Hon. mem. Japanese Pharmaceutical Asscn. and Pharmaceutical Soc. of Japan.
University of California School of Pharmacy, S.F. Medical Center, San Francisco 22, Calif.; Home: 67 Parkwood Drive, Daly City, Calif. 94015, U.S.A.
Telephone: 755-6229.

Danielsson, Bengt Emmerik, PH.D.; Swedish anthropologist and writer; b. 6 July 1921; ed. Univ. of Uppsala, Sweden and Univ. of Washington, Seattle.
Field research among Jibaro Indians, Upper Amazonas 46-47, in Tuamotu Archipelago, French Polynesia 49-51, Australia 55-56; mem. Kon-Tiki Expedition 47; Assoc. Anthropologist, Bernice P. Bishop Museum, Honolulu 52-; mem. Pacific Science Board expedition to Tuamotu Archipelago 52; Leader George Vanderbilt expedition to Society Islands 57, Swedish TV expedition to South Seas 62; technical adviser for film *Mutiny on the Bounty* 61; Producer series *Terry's South Sea Adventures*; Swedish Consul French Polynesia 60-67; Dir. Nat. Museum of Ethnography, Stockholm 67-.
Publs. *The Happy Island* 51, *The Forgotten Islands of the South Seas* 52, *Love in the South Seas* 54, *Work and Life on Raroia* 55, *From Raft to Raft* 59, *What Happened on the Bounty* 62, *Gauguin in the South Seas* 65; Children's Books: *Terry in the South Seas* 57, *Terry in Australia* 58, *Terry's Kon-Tiki Adventure* 63.
Etnografiska Muséet, Stockholm, Sweden.
Telephone: Stockholm 60-31-22.

Daninos, Pierre, French writer; b. 26 May 1913; ed. Lycée Janson de Sailly.
Began as journalist 31; liaison agent to the British Army, Flanders 40; Columnist for *Le Figaro*.
Publs. *Les Carnets du Bon Dieu* (Prix Interallié) 47, *Sonia, les autres et moi* (Prix Courteline) 52, *Les Carnets du Major Thompson* 54, *Le Secret du Major Thompson* 56, *Vacances à Tous Prix* 58, *Un Certain Monsieur Blot* 60, *Le Jacassin* 62, *Snobissimo* 64, *Le 36e Dessous* 66.
20 rue Parmentier, Neuilly, Paris, France.

Dankevich, Konstantin Fyodorovich; Soviet composer; b. 1905; ed. Odessa Conservatoire.
Professor, Kiev Conservatoire 48; Chair. Ukrainian Composers' Union; Honoured Worker of the Arts of the Ukrainian S.S.R. 41, People's Artist of the U.S.S.R.; Orders of Red Banner of Labour 51, of Lenin 60.
Principal compositions: Festival Overture 28, *Night of the Tragedy* (opera) 33, *No Pasarán* (suite for symphony orchestra) 36, *Othello* (symphonic poem) 37, First Symphony (for 20th Anniversary of October Revolution) 37, *Taras Shevchenko* (symphonic poem) 38, *Lily* (ballet) 40, Second Symphony (dedicated to heroic mothers of First World War) 45, *Bogdan Khmelnitsky* 53, *1917* (symphonic poem) 56, *Youth Greets Moscow* 56, *October* (oratorio).
Composers' Union of the Ukrainian S.S.R., Ulitsa Chekistov 3, Kiev, U.S.S.R.

Dankovtsev, Alexander Georgievich; Soviet agronomist and politician; b. 1913; ed. Voronezh Inst. of Agriculture.
Senior Agronomist at a machine and tractor station,

Chief Agronomist for Krasnoyarsk Territory Land Dept. 36-40; Dir. of a machine and tractor station, Chair. of a district Soviet, First Sec. of a district cttee. of the C.P.S.U., Head of Khakass Regional Dept. of Agriculture 40-56; Vice-Chair. Krasnoyarsk Territory Soviet, Head of the Territory Dept. of Agriculture 56-61; First Sec. Khakass Regional Cttee. of C.P.S.U. 61-; Deputy to U.S.S.R. Supreme Soviet; mem. C.P.S.U. 39-.
Khakass Regional Committee of the Communist Party of the Soviet Union, Abakan, U.S.S.R.

Dannay, Frederic (co-writer with Manfred B. Lee under pseudonym **Ellery Queen**); American writer and editor; b. 20 Oct. 1905; ed. Boys High School, Brooklyn.
Editor *Ellery Queen's Mystery Magazine* 41-, 25th Anniversary 66; Editor 51 anthologies; Visiting Prof. Univ. of Texas 58-59; owner of Ellery Queen Collection of First Editions of mystery short stories and Sherlock Holmes in Library of Univ. of Texas; several awards.
Publs. include 56 crime and mystery novels (32 about Ellery Queen), 6 books of short stories, 3 books of criticism, history and bibliography, 4 novels under pseudonym Barnaby Ross.
29 Byron Lane, Larchmont, New York 10538, U.S.A.

Danton, J. Periam, B.A., B.L.S., M.A., PH.D.; American professor and librarian; b. 5 July 1908; ed. Leipzig, Columbia and Chicago Univs., and Oberlin and Williams Colls.
Served in N.Y. Public Library 28-29; Williams Coll. Library 29-30, American Library Asscn. 30-33; Librarian & Assoc. Prof. Colby Coll. Library 35-36; Librarian and Assoc. Prof. Temple Univ. 36-46; Visiting prof. Univs. of Chicago 42 and Columbia 46; Prof. Librarianship 46-, and Dean, School of Librarianship, Calif. Univ. 46-60; Pres. Asscn. American Library Schools 49-50; Fulbright Research Scholar, (Univ. Göttingen), 60-61, (Vienna) 64-65; U.S. Dept. of State, American Specialist, Ethiopia 61; Ford Foundation Consultant on University Libraries in Southeast Asia 63; Surveyor and Consultant, numerous libraries; Dir. U.S. Dept. of State-American Library Asscn. Multi-Area Group Librarian Program 63-64; Guest Lecturer, The Hague 61, Univ. Toronto 63, Hebrew Univ, Jerusalem 65, Univ. Belgrade, Ljubljana and Zagreb 65, Univ. of British Columbia 68.
Publs. *Library Literature, 1921-32* 34, *Education for Librarianship* 49, *United States Influence on Norwegian Librarianship 1890-1940* 57, *The Climate of Book Selection: Social Influences on School and Public Libraries* 59, *Book Selection and Collections: A Comparison of German and American University Libraries* 63; mem. Board of Editors Asscn. of Coll. and Research Libraries *Monographs* 66-, *Library Quarterly* 68-.
School of Librarianship, University of California, Berkeley 4, Calif., U.S.A.
Telephone: TH-5-6000, Extension 1464.

Daoud Khan, H.R.H. Sardar Mohammad; Afghan army officer and politician; ed. Habibia Coll. Kabul, Prelcadet School Kabul, and in France.
Gov. of Kandahar 32; Gov. and C.-in-C. Eastern Provinces 34; C.-in-C. Central Forces and Mil. Schools 37-; suppressed revolt of 45; Prime Minister 53-63, concurrently Minister of Defence and of the Interior.
Shehr-e-Nan, Kabul, Afghanistan.

Daphtary, Chandra Kisan; Indian lawyer; b. 1 April 1893; ed. St. Paul's School, London, and Magdalene Coll., Cambridge.
Advocate-General, Bombay State 45-51; Solicitor-Gen. of India 51-63; Attorney-Gen. 63-; Chair., Bar Council of India.
3 Hastings Road, New Delhi, India.
Telephone: 34936.

Darby, Harry, B.S., M.E.; American manufacturer, shipbuilder and farmer; b. 23 Jan. 1895; ed. local public schools Kansas, and Univ. of Illinois.

With Missouri Boiler Works Co. 11-15; Shop Supt. 15-17; Vice-Pres. 17-19; with The Darby Corpn. since 20; Pres. 23-45; at present Chair. of Board and owner; Dir. Commercial Nat. Bank, Kansas Heart Asscn. Inc., Navy League of U.S., Washington, D.C., Univ. of Kansas Research Foundation; mem. Advisory Cttee. Nat. Rivers and Harbours Congress, Washington; Chair. State Highway Comm., Kan. 33-37, *Kansas City Post;* Soc. of American Mil. Engineers; Chair. of Board American Royal Live Stock and Horse Show; Dir. and mem. several other livestock asscns.; Nat. Conventions 40, 44 and 48; mem. Republican Del. to Republican Nat. Cttee. for Kansas 40-64, Exec. Cttee. of 15 of Republican Nat. Convention since June 44; U.S. Senator from Kansas 49-51; U.S. Army First World War; Hon. LL.B. (Kansas and Missouri).

Office: 1st Street and Walker Avenue, Kansas City 15, Kan.; Home: 1220 Hoel Parkway, Kansas City 2, Kan., U.S.A.

D'Arcy, Very Rev. Martin Cyril, S.J., M.A.; British Roman Catholic priest; b. 15 June 1888; ed. Stonyhurst Coll., and Oxford.

Lecturer in Philosophy Oxford Univ. 27-45; Master of Campion Hall Oxford 33-45; English Provincial of the Society of Jesus 45-50; Hon. D.Litt. (Nat. Univ. of Ireland, Fordham Univ.), Hon. LL.D. (Georgetown Univ.).

Publs. *Thomas Aquinas* 30, *Mirage and Truth* 35, *Nature of Belief* 37, *Death and Life* 42, *The Mind and Heart of Love* 45, *Communism and Christianity* 56, *The Meeting of Love and Knowledge* 57, *The Sense of History* 59, *No Absent God* 63.

31 Farm Street, London, W.1, England.

Daridan, Jean-Henri; French diplomatist; b. 15 Aug. 1906; ed. Collège de Juilly, Ecole des Chartes and Univ. de Paris à la Sorbonne.

Entered French Ministry of Foreign Affairs 32; Third Sec. Rome, Prague 33-38; war and resistance services 42-44; Counsellor Chungking 45-46; Chargé d'Affaires Bangkok 47; Minister-Counsellor Washington 48-54; Deputy High Commr. French Indochina 54; Deputy Dir.-Gen. Political and Econ. Affairs, Paris 55, Dir.-Gen. 56; Ambassador to Japan 59-62; Diplomatic Adviser to French Govt. 63-65; Ambassador to India and Nepal 65-; two prizes from Académie Française; Officier Légion d'Honneur, Croix de Guerre, Hon. K.B.E. (U.K.).

Publs. *John Law, Père de l'Inflation* 38, *Abraham Lincoln* 62, *Noirs et Blancs, de Lincoln à Johnson* 65.

Embassy of France, 2 Aurengzeb Road, New Delhi, India.

Dark, Eleanor; Australian author; b. 26 Aug. 1901; ed. Sydney.

Publs. *Prelude to Christopher* 34, *Return to Coolami* 36, *Sun across the Sky* 37, *Waterway* 38, *The Timeless Land* 41, *The Little Company* 45, *Storm of Time* 48, *No Barrier* 53, *Lantana Lane* 59.

Varuna, Katoomba, New South Wales, Australia.
Telephone: Katoomba 378.

Darling, Sir James Ralph, Kt., C.M.G., O.B.E.; British teacher and broadcasting official; b. 18 June 1899; ed. Repton School and Oriel Coll., Oxford.

Served in First World War; Schoolmaster, Liverpool 21-24, Charterhouse, Godalming 24-29; Headmaster, Geelong Church of England Grammar School, Australia 30-61; mem. Commonwealth Universities Comm. 42-51, Australian Broadcasting Control Board 55-61; Chair. Australian Broadcasting Comm. 61-67; Pres. Australian Coll. of Educ. 59-63; Chair. Australian Road Safety Council 61-; Chair. Australian Frontier Commission 62-;

mem. Commonwealth Immigration Advisory Council. 11 Maple Grove, Toorak, Melbourne, Australia.
Telephone: Melbourne 20-6262.

Darlington, Charles Francis, A.B.; American diplomatist; b. 13 Sept. 1904; ed. Harvard Univ., New Coll., Oxford and Inst. des Hautes Etudes Int., Geneva.

Worked in the Secr., LN, Geneva 29-31; with Bank of Int. Settlements, Basle 31-34; Asst. Chief, Div. of Trade Agreements, Washington 35-39; Foreign Exchange Man., Gen. Motors Overseas Operations 39-42; Lt. Commdr. U.S.N.R. 43-44; Sec. Exec., Steering and Co-ordination Cttees. UN, San Francisco 45; with Socony Mobil Oil Co., Iraq Petroleum Co., Near East Devt. Co. 46-61; Ambassador to Gabon 61-66.

Publ. (with Alice B. Darlington) *African Betrayal* 68.
Charles Road, Mount Kisco, N.Y. 10549, U.S.A.
Telephone: 914-Mo6-5924.

Darlington, Cyril Dean, D.SC., F.R.S.; British scientist; b. 19 Dec. 1903; ed. St. Paul's School and Wye Coll.

Director John Innes Institute 39-53; Sherardian Prof. of Botany, Oxford Univ. 53-; Keeper of the Oxford Botanic Garden 53-; Fellow of Magdalen Coll.; foreign mem. Royal Danish Acad. and Accad. Nazionale dei Lincei; awarded Royal Medal of Royal Society for research in Cytology and Genetics 46; founder (with Sir Ronald Fisher) of *Heredity* 47.

Publs. *Chromosomes and Plant Breeding* 32, *Recent Advances in Cytology,* 3rd edn. 65, *The Handling of Chromosomes* (with L. F. La Cour) 5th edn. 68, *The Conflict of Science and Society* 48, *The Dead Hand on Discovery* 49, *Elements of Genetics* 49, *Genes, Plants and People* (with K. Mather) 50, *The Facts of Life* 53, (transl. French, German, Italian, Japanese), *Chromosome Botany and the Origins of Cultivated Plants* 2nd edn. 63, *Chromosome Atlas of Flowering Plants* (with A. P. Wylie) 2nd edn. 56, *Evolution of Genetic Systems* 2nd edn. 58, *Darwin's Place in History* 59, *Genetics and Man* 64, *Teaching Genetics* (co-editor) 63, *Chromosomes Today* (editor) 66, *Evolution of Man and Society* 68.

Botany School, Oxford, England.
Telephone: Oxford 57857.

Darlington, William Aubrey, C.B.E., M.A.; British dramatic critic, dramatist and writer; b. 20 Feb. 1890; ed. Shrewsbury School and St. John's Coll. Cambridge.

Served with Northumberland Fusiliers Great War 14-19; contrib. to *Punch* and other publs.; Editor *The World* 19; joined *Daily Telegraph* 20, Dramatic Editor 25-; London Drama Corresp. *N.Y. Times* 39-60.

Publs. Plays: *Alf's Button, Carpet Slippers, The Key of the House, The Streets of London* (burlesque version); Novels: *Alf's Button, Wishes Limited, Egbert, Alf's Carpet, Mr. Cronk's Cases, Alf's New Button;* Criticism: *Through the Fourth Wall, Literature in the Theatre, Sheridan, J. M. Barrie, The Actor and his Audience, The World of Gilbert and Sullivan, Six Thousand and One Nights, Olivier;* also *I Do What I Like* (autobiography) and *A Knight Passed By* (translation of play by Jan Fabricius).

Monksdown, Bishopstone, Sussex, England.
Telephone: 01-589-4918 (Office); Seaford 2657 (Home).

Darmojuwono, H.E. Cardinal Justine; Indonesian ecclesiastic; b. 2 Nov. 1914.

Ordained Priest 47; Archbishop of Semarang 63-; created Cardinal by Pope Paul VI 67.
Djl. Pandanaran 13, Semarang, Java, Indonesia.

Darrieux, Danièle; French actress; b. 1 May 1917; ed Paris Univ.

Chevalier Légion d'Honneur.

Has played important roles in the following films: *Le Bal, Mayerling, Un mauvais garçon, Battement de coeur, Premier rendez-vous, Ruy Blas, Le Plaisir, Madame*

de . . . , *Le Rouge et le Noir, Bonnes à tuer, Le Salaire du péché, L'Amant de Lady Chatterley, Typhon sur Nagasaki, Adorable Julia, La Ronde, Alexander the Great, La Vie à Deux, Marie Octobre, L'Homme à femmes, Les lions sont lâchés, Vive Henri IV, vive l'amour, Le Crime ne paie pas, le Diable et les Dix Commandements, Landru, Méfiez-vous, Mesdames, Du grabuge chez les veuves, le Coup de grâce, Patate, l'Or du duc.*
Has acted in the following plays: *la Robe mauve de Valentine* 63, *Gillian* 65, *Comme un oiseau* 65, *Secretissimo* 65, *Laurette* 66.
Villa Christabelle, Fourcherolles, par Dampierre (Seine-et-Oise), France.

Dart, Justin; American business executive; b. 17 Aug. 1907; ed. Northwestern Univ.
Walgreen Co. 29-41, rose to Gen. Manager and Dir.; United Drug Co. (now Rexall Drug and Chemical Co.) 41-, Pres. 42-; Dir. United Air Lines 42-; Trustee, Univ. of Southern California 61-; Chair. Board of Trustees Univ. of Southern California; mem. Los Angeles and Bel Air Chamber of Commerce.
8480 Beverly Boulevard, Los Angeles, Calif. 90048, U.S.A.

Dart, Raymond Arthur, M.SC., M.D., CH.M.; Australian anatomist; b. 4 Feb. 1893; ed. Queensland and Sydney Univs.
House Surgeon, Royal Prince Alfred Hospital, Sydney 17-18; Capt. Australian Army Medical Corps 18-19; Senior Demonstrator in Anatomy, Univ. Coll., London 19-20; Fellow Rockefeller Foundation 20-21; Senior Demonstrator in Anatomy and Lecturer in Histology, Univ. Coll., London 21-22; Prof. of Anatomy 23-59, Dean Faculty of Medicine 25-43, Univ. of the Witwatersrand, Johannesburg; mem. Int. Comm. on Fossil Man 29-; Fellow Royal Society of South Africa 30-, mem. Council 38; mem. Board South African Inst. for Medical Research 34-46; mem. South African Medical Council 34-48; mem. S. African Nursing Council 44-50; Pres. S. African Soc. of Physiotherapy 59-, Anthropological Section, Pan-African Congress of Prehistory 47-51, Vice-Pres. 59-63; Pres. S. African Asscn. for the Advancement of Science 52-53, Pres. Anthropological Section 25, Gold Medallist 39; Guest Lecturer, Viking Fund Seminar, N.Y. 49; Lowell Lecturer, Boston Oct. 49; John Hunter Memorial Lecturer, Sydney 50; Senior Captain Scott Medal, South African Biological Soc. 55; Hon. D.Sc. (Natal and Witwatersrand Univs.); Viking Medal and Award for Physical Anthropology (New York) 57; Woodward Lecturer (Yale) 58; Simon Biesheuvel Medal 63; Pres. Ass001. Scientific and Technical Socs. of S. Africa 63-64; Drennan Memorial Lecturer (Cape Town) 66; United Steelworkers Prof. of Anthropology in The Inst. of Man, in The Insts. for the Achievement of Human Potential 66-.
Publs. include: *Australopithecus Africanus: the Man-Ape of South Africa* 25, *Racial Origins in the Bantu speaking Tribes of South Africa* 37, *African Serological Patterns and Human Migrations* 51, *The Osteodontokeratic Culture of Australopithecus Prometheus* 57, *Adventures with the Missing Link* 59, *Africa's Place in the Emergence of Civilisation* 60, *Beyond Antiquity* 65.
Walmer, 26 Park Street, Oaklands, Johannesburg, South Africa.

Dart, Thurston; British musician; b. 3 Sept. 1921; ed. Hampton Grammar School, Royal Coll. of Music and Univ. Coll., Exeter.
War Service, Operational Research for R.A.F. 42-45; Asst. Lecturer in Music, Cambridge Univ. 47-52, Lecturer 52-62, Prof. 62-64; King Edward Prof. of Music, Univ. of London King's Coll. 64-; Artistic Dir. Philomusica of London 55-59; Editor *Galpin Society Journal* 47-55; Sec. *Musica Britannica* 50-64; Fellow, Jesus Coll., Cambridge 54-64; Cobbett Medal 57.
Publs. include: *The Interpretation of Music* 54; Co-

editor *Dowland's Ayres for Four Voices* 53, *Jacobean Consort Music* 55; Editor *Bull's Keyboard Music II* 63; Reviser *The English Madrigalists, The English Lute-Songs, Works of William Byrd, Louis Couperin,* etc.; Editor Purcell's *Fantazias and other Instrumental Music* 59; numerous articles and reviews.
King's College, The Strand, London, W.C.2, England. Telephone: 01-836-5454.

Darvall, Frank Ongley, C.B.E., M.A., PH.D.; British writer, lecturer and administrator; b. 16 April 1906; ed. Dover Coll., Reading, London and Columbia Univs.
Commonwealth Fund Fellow U.S.A. 29-31; Assoc. Sec., Dept. of Int. Studies and Cultural Co-operation, Int. Student's Service 31-32; Dir. Students' Int. Union Geneva 33; Lecturer in Economics and History, Queen's Coll., London 33-36; Dir. of Research and Discussion and Public Relations Officer, English-Speaking Union of the British Commonwealth 36-39; Deputy or Acting Dir. American Div. Ministry of Information 39-45; British Consul Denver U.S.A. 45-46; First Sec. British Embassy Washington 46-49; Dir.-Gen. English-Speaking Union of the Commonwealth 49-57; Vice-Pres. Congress of European-American Asscns. 51-54, Chair. 54-57, Chair. Emeritus 57-; Hon. Dir., U.K. Nat. Cttee. Atlantic Congress 58-59; Chair. Channel Islands Television Ltd. 59-60; Attaché office of the U.K. High Commr., Cyprus 60-62; Dir. British Information Services, British High Comm., Port of Spain, Trinidad 62-66; British Consul, Boston, U.S.A. 66-.
Publs. *Popular Disturbances and Public Order in Regency England* 34, *The Price of European Peace* 37, *The American Political Scene* 39.
301 Berkeley Street, Boston, Massachusetts, U.S.A. Telephone: Boston 262-5782.

Darvas, József; Hungarian writer and politician; b. 10 Feb. 1912.
An early mem. of the progressive peasant movement; former Vice-Pres. People's Patriotic Front; Vice-Pres. Nat. Peasant Party 45; mem. of Parl. 45-; Editor-in-Chief of the Party's daily paper *Szabad Szó*; Minister of Construction and Public Works 47-53, of Education 53, of Popular Culture 53-56; Dir. Hunnia Film Studios 56-59; Pres. Hungarian Writer's Union; Kossuth Prize 56, 60.
Publs. *Látástól vakulásig, Vizkereszttól Szilveszterig, Egy parasztcsalád története, A törökverö, Harangos kút, Város az ingoványon,* etc.
c/o Hungarian Writers' Union, Bajza-u. 18, Budapest VI; and Gyarmat utca 39, Budapest XIV, Hungary. Telephone: 229-073.

Darwin, Sir Robin, Kt., C.B.E., A.R.A.; British painter; b. 7 May 1910; ed. Eton Coll., and Slade School of Fine Art, Univ. of London.
Assistant Master, Eton Coll. 33-38; Camouflage Directorate, Ministry of Home Security 39-44; Council of Industrial Design 45-46; Prof. of Fine Art, Univ. of Durham 46-47; Principal, Royal Coll. of Art, London 48-67, Rector and Vice-Provost, Royal Coll. of Art 68-; mem. Nat. Advisory Council for Art Educ., Council for the Award of Diplomas in Art and Design, Council of Industrial Design 47-55, 62-67, Royal Mint Advisory Cttee.; Fellow, Univ. Coll., London; Bicentenary Medal, Royal Soc. of Arts 62; Hon. D.Litt. (Newcastle and Birmingham).
Works: one-man shows, London 33-; pictures purchased by Queen Elizabeth II, Contemporary Arts Soc., and by Manchester, Leeds and other galleries.
Royal College of Art, London, S.W.7, England.

Das, Sudhi Ranjan, B.A., LL.B.; Indian judge; b. 1 Oct. 1894; ed. Tagere's School, Santiniketan, Bangabasi Coll., Calcutta and Univ. Coll., London.
Called to Bar, Gray's Inn 18, to Calcutta Bar 19; Lecturer Univ. Law Coll. Calcutta; Additional Judge, High Court, Calcutta 42, Puisne Judge 44; Chief Justice East

Punjab High Court (Simla) 49-50; Judge Fed. Court of India 50; Judge Supreme Court of India 50-55; Chief Justice of India 56-59; Vice-Chancellor, Visva-Bharati Univ. 59-66; Vice-Pres. Indian Council for Cultural Relations 64-65; edited *Mulla's Transfer of Property Act.*
Office: Swapanpuri, Kalimpong, West Bengal; Home: 118 Netaji S. C. Bose Road, P.O. Regent Park, Calcutta 40, India.
Telephone: Calcutta 46-3103.

Das Gupta, Bimal; Indian artist; b. 27 Dec. 1917; ed. Krishnalth Collegiate School, Berhampore, W. Bengal, and Govt. Coll. of Arts and Crafts, Calcutta.
Originally painted landscapes in water colours; is now avant-garde painter in oils; Senior Lecturer in Painting, Coll. of Art, Delhi 63-; paintings in Nat. Gallery of Modern Art, New Delhi, Nat. Gallery of Poland, Warsaw, Berlin Museum, Pilnitz Gallery, Dresden, Hermitage Gallery, Leningrad; one-man exhbns. in Delhi, Calcutta, Bombay, Madras, Amritsar, Mysore, Berlin, Poland, London, New York, Cairo, Moscow, Belgrade and Paris; exhibited at São Paulo Bienal, and int. exhbns. in Japan, New York and U.S.S.R.
E. 13 Motibag II E Block, New Delhi, India.

Das Gupta, Prodosh Kusum, B.A.; Indian sculptor and art gallery director; b. 10 Jan. 1912; ed. Univ. of Calcutta, Government Schools of Arts and Crafts, Lucknow and Madras, Royal Acad. of Arts, London and Ecole de Grand Schaumère, Paris.
Founder, Calcutta Group (pioneer org. of modern art in India) 43, Sec. 43-51; Reader and Head, Dept. of Sculpture, Baroda Univ. 50; Prof. of Sculpture, Govt. Coll. of Arts and Crafts, Calcutta 51-57; Dir. Nat. Gallery of Modern Art, New Delhi 57-; Pres. Third Congress, Int. Asscn. of Arts, Vienna 60; mem. Indian Artists' Dels. to U.S. and U.S.S.R.; represented India in int. sculpture competition *The Unknown Political Prisoner*, Tate Gallery, London; works in Nat. Gallery of Modern Art, New Delhi, New Delhi, Madras Museum, Acad. of Fine Arts Gallery, Calcutta and in private collections in India and abroad.
Publs. *My Sculpture*, and numerous articles on art.
National Gallery of Modern Art, Jaipur House, New Delhi 11; Home: 5 Jatin Das Road, Calcutta 29, India.

Dashkevich, Vladimir Pavlovich; Soviet foreign trade official; b. 1909; ed. Moscow Inst. of Chem. Engineering.
Member C.P.S.U. 31-; Chief Engineer *Tekhnopromimport* Rep. in France (import and export of instruments, etc.) 36-41; Soviet Army 41-43; Vice-Chair. *Tekhnopromimport* 43-45; Deputy Commercial Rep. of U.S.S.R. in Czechoslovakia 45-48, Commercial Rep. 48-50; Chair. *Tekhnopromimport* 50-54, 64-; U.S.S.R. Commercial Rep. in France 54-62; Vice-Chair. *Mashinoimport* 62-64; Order of Red Banner of Labour (thrice), Order of Red Star.
Tekhnopromimport, Ministry of Foreign Trade, 32-34 Smolenskaya-Sennaya Ploshchad, Moscow, U.S.S.R.

Dashti, Ali; Iranian writer, politician and diplomatist; b. 95; ed. Iraq.
Former mem. *Majlis*, fmr. mem. Senate; fmr. Editor *Shafaq Soekh* (Red Dawn); Ambassador to Egypt 50, Ambassador to Lebanon 60-63; Senator 63-.
Publs. *Prison Days* (novel); psychological novels, short stories, essays, analytical works on poetry of Hafez, Saadi, Rumi, Omar Khayam and Khaghani.
The Senate, Teheran, Iran.

Daskalakis, Apostolos; Greek university professor; b. 03; ed. Athens Univ. and Univ. de Paris à la Sorbonne.
Began career as journalist 21; Foreign Corresp. of various Athens newspapers 27-32; Prof. of Medieval and Modern History, Athens Univ. 39-, of Ancient Greek History 50-54, and of Modern Greek History

55-; Vice-Chancellor, Athens Univ. 53-55; Cultural Counsellor, Ministry of Foreign Affairs 50-; Hon. Prof. of many European univs.
Publs. *The Causes of the Greek War of Independence* 27, *Chypre hellénique à travers quarante siècles d'histoire* 32, *History of Modern Greece* 52, *The Hellenism of the Ancient Macedonians* 60, *La Bataille des Thermopyles* 62, *Alexander the Great* 63, *Rhigas Velestinlis* 64, and many other books and articles.
Evrou 3, Athens, Greece.

Dassin, Jules (husband of Melina Mercouri, *q.v.*); American film director; b. 12 Dec. 1911; ed. Morris High School.
Attended drama school in Europe 36; Asst. Dir. to Alfred Hitchcock 40; films directed in U.S. include *Brute Force, Naked City, Night and the City*; settled in France 54 and directed *Rififi, Celui qui doit mourir, La Loi, Never on Sunday* 60, *Phaedra* 61, *Topkapi* 63, *10.30 p.m. Summer* 66, etc.; Director's Prize, Cannes Film Festival 55 for *Rififi.*
c/o Alain Bernheim, 16 avenue Hoche, Paris 8e, France.

Dato, Abdul Hamid Bin Haji Jumat; Singapore businessman and politician; b. 17; ed. Raffles Institution.
Leader, United Malay Nat. Org.; Opposition Leader Legislative Assembly; Minister, Local Govt. Lands and Housing 55-59; Dep. Chief Minister 56-59; knighted by H.M. The Yang di-Pertuan Agong 58.
3 Lorong M. Telok Kurau Road, Singapore 15.

Daubeny, Peter Lauderdale, C.B.E.; British impresario; b. 14 April 1921; ed. Marlborough Coll.
After he left coll., joined Liverpool Playhouse Company; served through war in Coldstream Guards; formed theatrical company and produced many shows including Frederick Lonsdale's *But for the Grace of God*, Ivor Novello's *We Proudly Present* and *The Gay Invalid* (with Elisabeth Bergner); presentations include Sacha Guitry, Edwige Feuillère, Maurice Chevalier, Jean-Louis Barrault-Madeleine Renaud Company, Bertolt Brecht Berliner Ensemble, Roland Petit and De Cuevas ballets, Indian Ballet, Moscow Arts Theatre, Antonio, Carmen Amaya, Katherine Dunham, The Chinese Classical Theatre, Red Army Choir, Martha Graham, the Russian Moiseyev, Obrastzov and Beryoshka cos., Ingmar Bergman's Malmö Theatre, Jerome Robbin's "Ballets: U.S.A."; World Theatre Seasons, Aldwych Theatre, London 64, 65, 66, 67, 68; Chevalier de la Légion d'Honneur; Gold Cross, Royal Order of George I (Greece); Cavaliere dell'Ordine al Merito della Repubblica Italiana.
Publ. *Stage by Stage*, a biography 52.
26 Chester Square, London, S.W.1, England.
Telephone: 01-730-3939.

Daubner, Vojtech; Czechoslovak politician and trade union official; b. 23 April 1912.
Trained locksmith-mechanic; Deputy, Slovak Nat. Council 54-, mem. Presidium Slovak Nat. Council 54-; Chair. Slovak Trade Union Council 55-; Sec. Central Council of Trade Unions 52-55, mem. Presidium Central Council of Trade Unions 49-, mem. Secr. Central Council of Trade Unions 52-, Deputy Chair. Central Council of Trade Unions 67-; Czechoslovak Del., Gen. Council of World Fed. of Trade Unions (WFTU) 65-; mem. Central Cttee. Communist Party of Slovakia 53-, mem. Presidium Central Cttee. Communist Party of Slovakia 62-; Order of Labour 62, and other decorations.
Slovak Trade Union Council, Odborárske nám. 3, Bratislava, Czechoslovakia.

Daum, Earl Charles, A.B., M.C.S.; American automobile executive; b. 24 Sept. 1903; ed. Dartmouth Coll., Hanover and Amos Tuck School of Business Administration.
Overseas Operations Div., Gen. Motors Corpn. 25-;

Regional Group Exec. in New York City Gen. Motors 59-60; Asst. Gen. Manager. 60-61, Gen. Manager 61-, Vice-Pres. U.S.A. Gen. Motors Corpn. and mem. Admin. Cttee. 61-; mem. Board Dirs. subsidiaries abroad; Commdr. of the Order of Leopold II.
1775 Broadway, New York, N.Y. 10019, U.S.A.

Daux, Georges; French Hellenist; b. 21 Sept. 1899; ed. Univ. of Paris.
Worked at French Archæological School, Athens 20-24; Cultural Counsellor, French Embassy, Istanbul 24-26; fmr. Prof., Dean of the Faculty of Letters and Pres. of Dijon Univ.; now Prof. of Greek History, Sorbonne and Dir. of French Archæological School at Athens 50-; mem. of Security Council's Comm. of Inquiry in the Balkans 47; mem. Inst. for Advanced Studies, Princeton 47-48; visiting Prof. Harvard 49-50; Sather Prof. Berkeley 56-57; mem. Deutsches Archäologisches Inst., Berlin, Accademia Pontificale, Rome, Yugoslav Acad., Zagreb, Deutsche Akademie der Wissenschaften, Berlin, and American Philosophical Society and hon. life mem. Society for Promotion of Hellenic Studies, London; Dr. h.c. (Brussels).
6 Avenue Paul Appell, Paris 14e, France; and P.O. Box 208, Athens, Greece.
Telephone: Paris 402-2192.

Davachi, Abbas, ING.AGRIC., DR.SC.NAT.; Iranian agriculturalist; b. 06; ed. Teheran, Paris and Montpellier Univs.
Entomologist, Ministry of Agriculture 36; Dir.-Gen. Dept. of Plant Protection 44-47; Pres. Teheran Int. Locust Cttee. 44-46; Prof. of Plant Pests and Disease Control, Faculty of Agriculture, Teheran Univ. 46-, Dean of Faculty 47-49, mem. Agricultural Academy of France 57; Chair. F.A.O. Nat. Cttee. 58; Légion d'Honneur (France); mem. Agricultural Council.
Publs. *Applied Entomology and Phytopathology, Insects Harmful to Plants Cultivated in Iran,* etc.
Faculty of Agriculture, University of Teheran, Teheran, Iran.

Dávalos-Hurtado, Eusebio, M.SC.; Mexican anthropologist; b. 09; ed. Nat. School of Homeopathic Medicine, Nat. School of Anthropology and History, Mexico, and Univ. of Paris.
Asst. in Anthropology, Nat. Anthropological Museum 41; Prof. Nat. School of Anthropology and History 45-; Ethnologist, Dept. of Indian Affairs 47; fmr. Sec. Mexican Anthropological Soc.; Consultant, Mexican Congress of History 48; Sec. *Revista Mexicana de Estudios Antropológicos* 48-; Adviser, Historical Comm. of Pan-American Inst. of Geography and History 49; Dir. Nat. School of Homeopathic Medicine 50; Prof. Summer School, Nat. Univ. of Mexico 51; Dir. Nat. Anthropological Museum 52-56; Dir. *Bibliographical Bulletin of American Anthropology* 53; Dir. Gen. Inst. Nacional de Antropología e Historia 56-; Pres. Comité de Antropología del Inst. Panamericano de Geografía e Historia 59; mem. Consejo Nacional Técnico de la Educación 59; mem. Nat. Acad. of Sciences, Mexico; life mem. Société des Américanistes, Paris and American Asscns. of Physical Anthropologists; Hon. LL.D. (Nat. Coll., Ont.).
Publs. *Contribución al estudio del Pyrogenium* 37, *El Hallazgo de Ichcateopan* (with Javier Romero) 50, *Los restos atribuidos a Hernán Cortés* 53, *La deformación craneana entre los Tlatelolcas* 51.
[*Died January* 1968.]

Davico, Oskar; Yugoslav poet and novelist; b. 09; ed. Belgrade Univ.
Imprisoned for working with Resistance 41; escaped and joined partisans 43; mem. Fed. Cttee. on Film Censorship 58-; recipient of several literary awards.
Publs. *With the Partisans of Markos, Poetry and Resist-*

ance, *The Poem* (novel), *A Man's Man* (poetic drama), *Gedichte* 65.
c/o Serbian Writers' Association, Belgrade, Yugoslavia.

David, Donald Kirk, A.B., M.B.A.; American former foundation executive; b. 15 Feb. 1896; ed. Idaho and Harvard Univs.
Instructor Harvard Univ. Business School 19-21, Asst. Dean 20-27, Asst. Prof. of Marketing 21-26, Assoc. Prof. of Marketing 26-27; Vice-Pres. and Pres. of Royal Baking Powder Co. 27-30; Vice-Pres. Great Island Holding Corpn. 30-41; Pres. American Maize Products Co. 32-41; William Ziegler Prof. of Business Admin. Harvard Univ. Graduate School of Business Admin., and Assoc. Dean 42, Dean 42-55; Vice-Chair. of the Ford Foundation 56-66; Dir. of Aluminium Ltd., Ford Motor Co., Pan American World Airways, Inc., R. H. Macy & Co., Ind.; Trustee, The Rockefeller University; Dir. The Great Atlantic and Pacific Tea Co., Sinclair Oil Corp., City Investing Co.; Chair. Board of Cttee. for Econ. Devt. 57-62; Orders of Orange-Nassau and St. Olaf; Hon. LL.D. (Idaho Univ. 41, St. Lawrence Univ. 46, Harvard 48, Washington and Lee Univ. 49, Northeastern Univ. 51, Carleton Coll. 52, Colgate Univ. 54, Univ. of California 64); Hon. Litt.D. (Univ. of Western Ontario 51, Ohio Univ. 62).
Publs. *Retail Store Management Problems* 22, *Problems in Retailing* (with M. P. McNair) 26.
c/o The Ford Foundation, 477 Madison Avenue, New York 22, N.Y.; Home: Osterville, Mass., U.S.A.

David, Václav; Czechoslovak politician; b. 23 Sept. 1910; ed. Commercial Coll., Prague.
Worked for ČKD Libeň 29-32; mem. of the illegal Central Cttee. of the Communist Party of Czechoslovakia 44-45; Mem. of the National Assembly 45-; Minister of Foreign Affairs 53-68; mem. of the Central Cttee. of the Communist Party of Czechoslovakia 45-; several decorations for part in Resistance Movement during World War II; Order of the Republic 55; Klement Gottwald Order 60.
National Assembly, Prague, Czechoslovakia.

David, Wilmot Adolphus, C.B.E.; Liberian diplomatist; b. 4 Feb. 1911; ed. St. John's Academic and Industrial School, Cape Mount, and Univ. of Liberia.
State Dept. 34-; Consul-Gen. Liverpool 45-48, First Sec. London 48-52; Counsellor U.S.A. 52-56; Minister to Italy 56-57; Ambassador to Haiti 57-58, to Ghana 58-60; Under-Sec. of State 60-64; Ambassador to France 64-; numerous decorations and special missions.
Liberian Embassy, 12 place Malesherbes, Paris 17e, France.
Telephone: (Paris) WAGram 58-55.

Davidson, George F., PH.D., LL.D., L.H.D.; Canadian public official; b. 18 April 1909; ed. Univs. of British Columbia and Harvard.
Superintendent of Welfare and Neglected Children for British Columbia 34; Exec. Dir. Vancouver Welfare Fed. and Council of Social Agencies 35; Dir. of Social Welfare, British Columbia 39; Exec. Dir. of Canadian Welfare Council 42; Deputy Minister of Nat. Welfare 44-60, of Citizenship and Immigration 60-63; Dir. Bureau of Government Organization 63, Sec. of Treasury Board 64-67; Pres. Canadian Broadcasting Corpn. 68-; has served since 46 as Canadian Rep. or mem. Canadian dels. to various sessions of UN Gen. Assembly, Economic and Social Council and Social Comm. and Chair. of the Social, Humanitarian and Cultural Cttee. 53; Pres. Inst. of Public Admin. of Canada 51; Pres. of the UN Economic and Social Council 58; Pres. Int. Conf. of Social Work 56-60; Chair. Nat. Joint Council of Public Service 54-60.
Home: 435 Island Park Drive, Ottawa 3, Ont., Canada.

Davidson, James Norman, M.D., D.SC., F.R.S., F.R.I.C.; British biochemist; b. 5 March 1911; ed. George Watson's Boys' Coll., Edinburgh, and Edinburgh Univ. Carnegie Research Fellow 37-38; Lecturer in Biochemistry, Univ. Coll., Dundee (Univ. of St. Andrews) 38-40, Univ. of Aberdeen 40-45; mem. of Scientific Staff of Medical Research Council, Nat. Inst. for Medical Research, London 45-46; Prof. of Biochemistry, St. Thomas's Hospital Medical School (Univ. of London) 46-47; Gardiner Prof. of Biochemistry, Univ. of Glasgow 48-.
Publs. *The Biochemistry of the Nucleic Acids* 50, 5th edn. 65, *Textbook of Physiology and Biochemistry* (with others) 50, 6th edn. 65.
Biochemistry Department, The University of Glasgow, Glasgow, W.2, Scotland.
Telephone: 041-339-8855.

Davie, Alan; British painter; b. 20; ed. Edinburgh School of Art.
Jazz musician and maker of jewellery; Gregory Fellowship, Leeds Univ. 56-59; first one-man exhbn. Edinburgh 46; one-man exhbns. in Europe and U.S.A. 49-; rep. at Dunn Int. Exhbn., London 63; Prize for the best foreign painter at his one-man exhbn. at the 7th Bienal de São Paulo, Brazil 63; Gulbenkian Painting and Sculpture of a Decade Exhbn., Tate Gallery, London 64; several exhbns. at the Salon de Mai.
Gamels Studio, Rushgreen, near Hertford, Hertfordshire, England.
Telephone: Ware 3684.

Davies, David Arthur, M.SC., F.INST.P.; British meteorologist; b. 11 Nov. 1913; ed. Univ. of Wales.
Meteorological Office, Air Ministry 35-39, R.A.F. 39-47; Principal Scientific Officer, Meteorological Office, Air Ministry 47-49; Dir. East African Meteorological Dept., Nairobi 49-55; Pres. W.M.O. Regional Asscn. for Africa 51-55; mem. Royal Inst. of Public Admin. 50-; Sec.-Gen. World Meteorological Organisation 55-.
Publs. include meteorological papers, mainly on experiments on artificial stimulation of rain in East Africa.
World Meteorological Organisation, 41 Avenue Giuseppe Motta, Geneva; Home: 34 Avenue Krieg, Geneva, Switzerland.
Telephone: Geneva 35-07-79.

Davies, John Emerson Harding, M.B.E., F.C.A.; British oil executive; b. 8 Jan. 1916; ed. St. Edward's School, Oxford.
Trained as an accountant; Combined Operations experimental establishment Second World War; joined Anglo-Iranian Oil Co. 46; Svenska B.P. Stockholm 47-48, Paris 53-55 and London; Dir. S.F.B.P., Paris 51-60; Dir. B.P. Trading Ltd. 60-61; Vice-Chair. and Man. Dir. Shell-Mex and B.P. Ltd. 61-65; mem. Nat. Econ. Devt. Council (N.E.D.C.) 64-, Council of Industrial Design 65-, British Productivity Council 65-, British Nat. Export Council 65-; Dir.-Gen. Confederation of British Industry 65-.
Office: 21 Tothill Street, London, S.W.1; Home: Tall Oaks, Wineham, nr. Henfield, Sussex, England.
Telephone: 01-930-6711 (Office).

Davies, Martin, C.B.E., F.B.A., F.S.A.; British museum curator; b. 22 Mar. 1908; ed. Rugby Coll. and King's Coll., Cambridge.
Assistant Keeper, Nat. Gallery, London 32-60, Keeper 60-, Dir. 68-.
16 Rupert House, Nevern Square, London, S.W.5, England.

Davies, Paul Lewis, B.S.; American manufacturer; b. 27 July 1899; ed. Univ. of California and Graduate School of Business Harvard Univ.
Clerk Nat. Bank of Commerce N.Y. 22; Asst. Cashier, Asst. Vice-Pres., Vice-Pres. Wells Fargo Bank, San Francisco 29-33, now Dir.; Vice-Pres. and Treas. Food Machinery Corpn. 29-33, Exec. Vice-Pres. 33-40, Pres. FMC Corpn. (fmrly. Food, Machinery and Chemical Corpn.) 40-, Chair. of Board 56-66; Dir. Wells Fargo Bank, Chase Manhattan Bank, S. Pacific Co., Caterpillar Tractor Co., American Ordnance Asscn., The Lehman Corpn., Pacific Gas and Electric Co., Stanford Research Inst., etc.; mem. Business Council; Trustee Cttee. for Economic Development; mem. Advisory Council, School of Business Admin., Univ. of Calif.; Visiting Comm. Harvard Business School; mem. Advisory Board of Dirs. Asscn. of the U.S. Army; Dir. Nat. Industrial Conf. Board, Int. Business Machines Corpn.
1598 University Avenue, San José, Calif., U.S.A.

Davies, Peter Maxwell, B.MUS.; British composer; b. 8 Sept. 1934; ed. Leigh Grammar School, Manchester Univ., Royal Manchester Coll. of Music, and Princeton Univ. (Harkness Fellowship).
Director of Music, Cirencester Grammar School 59-62; Olivetti Prize 59, Koussevitsky Award 64, Koussevitsky Recording Award 66.
Compositions: *St. Michael* sonata for 13 wind instruments 57, *Prolation* for orchestra 58, *O Magnum Mysterium* for chorus, instruments and organ 60, *String Quartet* 61, *Leopardi Fragments* for soprano, contralto and chamber ensemble 61, *First Fantasia on John Taverner's In Nomine* 62, *Veni Sancte Spiritus* for chorus and orchestra 63, *Second Fantasia on John Taverner's In Nomine* 64, *Revelation and Fall* for Soprano and Instrumental Ensemble 66, *L'homme armé* 68.
c/o Boosey and Hawkes, 295 Regent Street, London, W.1, England.

Davies, Ralph Kenneth; American business executive; b. 9 Sept. 1897; ed. Univ. of Calif., Berkeley and San Francisco.
With Standard Oil Co. of California 12-46; with Anglo-American Oil Co., England 28-29; organiser and Exec. Vice-Pres. Int. Bitumen Emulsions Co. 29, Pres. 38-41; Exec. Vice-Pres. Standard Stations Inc. 30-38, Pres. 38-40; Dir. Standard Oil Co. of Calif. 30-42, Senior Vice-Pres. 35-46; Exec. Vice-Pres. Standard Oil Co. of British Columbia Ltd. 35-38, Vice-Pres. and Dir. Pacific Public Service Co. 40-42; Dir. Coast Counties Gas Co. 40-42, Calif. State Chamber of Commerce 35-41; Consulting Prof. Stanford Univ. 37-61; Pres. Fair Practices Asscn. (Petroleum Products) 37-39; Deputy Petroleum Admin., Petroleum Admin. for War, Washington, D.C. 42-46; President's mission to London to negotiate Anglo-American oil treaty; special consultant to Sec. of Interior 46-47; organised and first Dir. Oil and Gas Div., Interior Dept. 46; Pres. Trunkline Gas Co. 47-49, Dir. 47-52; Pres. and Dir. American Independent Oil Co. 47-58; Chair. Board and Dir. Independent Tankships Inc. 48-57; Pres. and Dir. American Independent Oil Co. 48-58, Chair. and Dir. 58-; Dir. and Chair. Exec. Cttee. Golden State Co. Ltd. 48-54; Dir. Foremost Dairies 54; Dir. American President Lines Ltd. 48-, Chair. of Board 52-56; Pres. and Dir. APL Assocs. Inc. 52-56; Chair. of Board and Dir. Natomas Co. 56-; Dir. Bank of Calif. 56-; mem. Nat. Petroleum Council 50; awarded Presidential Medal of Merit for distinguished War service 45.
Home: Woodside, Calif.; Office: International Bldg., St. Mary's Square, San Francisco, Calif., U.S.A.

Davies, Rt. Hon. Sir (William) Arthian, Kt., P.C., M.A.; British judge; b. 10 May 1901; ed. Dulwich Coll., and Trinity Coll., Oxford.
Called to the Bar (Inner Temple) 25; Junior Counsel to Ministry of Labour and Nat. Service 34-47; Recorder of Merthyr Tydfil 46-49; K.C. 47; Recorder of Chester 49-52; J.P. (Buckinghamshire) 48; Deputy Chair. Quarter Sessions 51-61, Chair. 61-; Dep. Chair. Cardiganshire Quarter Sessions 49-52; Judge, High Court of Justice

52-61; Dep. Chair. Parl. Boundary Commission for Wales 59-61; Lord Justice of Appeal 61-; Privy Councillor 61.
Publ. *The Arbitration Acts* 34.
Royal Courts of Justice, London, W.C.2; and Ballinger Lodge, Great Missenden, Bucks., England.

Davis, Artemus Darius; American business executive; b. 22 Nov. 1905; ed. Univ. of Idaho.
Manager, Table Supply Store, Little River, Florida 25-29, Vice-Pres. Table Supply Stores Inc. 29-34, Pres. 34-39; Pres. and Dir. Winn-Dixie Stores Inc., Jacksonville, Florida 39-65, Vice-Chair. and Chair. Exec. Cttee. 65-.
5050 Edgewood Court, Jacksonville, Florida, U.S.A.

Davis, Bette; American actress; b. 5 April 1908; ed. Cushing Acad., Ashburnham, Mass.
Motion Picture Acad. Award as best actress of year, in *Dangerous* 35, *Jezebel* 38.
Films acted in include: *Of Human Bondage, Bordertown, Dangerous, The Petrified Forest, Jezebel, Dark Victory, Juarez, The Old Maid, The Private Lives of Elizabeth and Essex, The Great Lie, The Bride Came C.O.D., All About Eve, Payment on Demand, Phone Call from a Stranger, The Star, The Virgin Queen, Storm Center, The Catered Affair, John Paul Jones, The Scapegoat, What Ever Happened to Baby Jane, Hush... Hush, Sweet Charlotte, The Nanny, The Anniversary.*
Publ. *The Lonely Life* 62.
Laguna Beach, California, U.S.A.

Davis, Chester Charles, A.B.; American executive; b. 17 Nov. 1887; ed. Grinnell Coll., Iowa.
Newspaper work in S. Dakota and Montana 11-17; Editor and Man. *Montana Farmer* 17-21; Commr. for Agriculture and Labour, State of Montana 21-25; Dir. of Grain Marketing for Ill. Agricultural Asscn., Chicago 25-26; Agricultural Service for farm organisations 26-28; Exec. Vice-Pres. Maizewood Products Corpn. 29-33; Dir. of Production Div., Agricultural Adjustment Admin., U.S. Dept. of Agriculture 33, Administrator A.A.A. 33-36; mem. Board of Govs. Fed. Reserve System 36-41; Pres. Fed. Reserve Bank of St. Louis 41-51; Associate Dir. The Ford Foundation 51-54; mem. Nat. Defence Advisory Comm. 40-41; Trustee Grinnell Coll., Ia.; Cttee. for Economic Development; mem. Business Advisory Council, Dept. of Commerce; Chair. Public Policy Cttee., The Advertising Council Inc., etc.; Regents Prof. Agricultural Economics, Univ. of Calif., Berkeley 55; awarded medal "for distinguished service to agriculture" by American Farm Bureau Fed. 39; Hon. LL.D. (Grinnell Coll. 35, Univ. of Arkansas 48, Washington Univ., St. Louis 51, Montana State Univ. 51), Hon. D.Sc. (Clemson Coll. 37).
254D Calle Aragon, Laguna Hills, Calif., U.S.A.

Davis, Colin Rex, C.B.E.; British musician; b. 25 Sept. 1927; ed. Christ's Hospital and Royal Coll. of Music.
Assistant Conductor, B.B.C. Scottish Orchestra 57-59; Conductor, Sadler's Wells Opera House 60, Musical Dir. 61-65; Chief Conductor, B.B.C. Symphony Orchestra 67-.
Office: c/o Harold Holt Ltd., 122 Wigmore Street, London, W.1; Home: 25 Arlington Avenue, London, N.1, England.

Davis, Jacob E.; American business executive; b. 31 Oct. 1905; ed. Ohio State Univ., and Harvard Univ. Admitted to Ohio Bar 30; legal practice 30-37; mem. Ohio Gen. Assembly 35-37; Judge, Court of Common Pleas, Pike County, Ohio 37-40; mem. U.S. House of Reps. 41-43; Special Asst. Sec. Navy, Asst. Gen. Counsel, Navy Dept. 43-44; Vice-Pres. Kroger Co. 45, Dir. 49-, Exec. Vice-Pres. 61-62, Pres. 62-.
Office: Kroger Co., 1014 Vine Street, Cincinnati, Ohio; Home: 1122 Rookwood Drive, Cincinnati, Ohio, U.S.A.

Davis, James Elsworth; American business executive; b. 31 July 1907; ed. High School, Burley, Idaho and Univ. of Idaho.
President, Economy Wholesale Grocery Co. 30-42; U.S. Army service 43-45; Vice-Pres. Winn-Dixie Stores, Inc. 45-50, Chair. Board of Dirs. 50-; Chair. Board of Dirs. American Heritage Life Insurance Co.; Dir. Barnett Nat. Bank, Jacksonville, St. Luke's Hospital Asscn.; Hon. D. Humanities.
3960 Ortega Bvd., Jacksonville 10, Florida, U.S.A.

Davis, Jerome, PH.D.; American sociologist; b. 2 Dec. 1891; ed. Oberlin Coll., Union Theological Seminary and Columbia Univ.
Lecturer, extension courses, N.Y. City 14; Sec. to Sir Wilfred Grenfell, Labrador 15; Russian war work 16-18; Asst. Prof. of Sociology, Dartmouth Coll. 21-24; Gilbert L. Stark Prof. of Practical Philanthropy, Yale Univ. 24-37; mem. Board of Trustees, Oberlin Coll.; Dir. Promoting Enduring Peace Inc.; Pres. American Fed. of Teachers 36-39, Eastern Sociological Society 36-37; Chair. Conn. Legislative Comm. on Jails 31-39; Dir. of work in P.O.W. camps for all Canada for World's Cttee., Y.M.C.A. 40-43; made survey on Arab-Israel situation 53; Visiting Prof. Univ. of Colorado 50, Fisk Univ. 54, Japanese Univs. 55, 65; Hon. D.D. (Oberlin), LL.D. (Hillsdale Coll.), D.Litt. (Fla. Southern); Directed American-European Seminars to Russia and other European countries 57, 59-64, 66, Around the World Seminar 67; Winner of the Gandhi Peace Award 67.
Publs. *The Russians and Ruthenians in America* 21, *The Russian Immigrant* 22, *Christian Fellowship among the Nations* (with R. B. Chamberlin) 25, *Adventuring in World Co-operation* 25, *Business and the Church* 26, *Introduction to Sociology* (with H. E. Barnes) 27, *Readings in Sociology, Christianity and Social Adventuring* 27, *Labor Speaks for Itself on Religion* 29, *Contemporary Social Movements* 30, *The New Russia* 33, *The Jail Population of Connecticut, Capitalism and its Culture* 35, *Labor Problems in America* (with E. Stein) 40, *Behind Soviet Power* 46, *Character Assassination* 51, *Peace, War and You* 52, *Religion in Action* 55, *On the Brink* 59, *Citizens of One World* 61, *World Leaders I Have Known* 63, *Disarmament—a World View* 64, *A Life Adventure for Peace* 67, *Peace or World War III* 68.
Promoting Enduring Peace Inc., P.O. Box 103, Woodmont, Conn., U.S.A.

Davis, John Henry; British industrialist; b. 10 Nov. 1906; ed. City of London School.
Chairman and Chief Exec. Rank Org. Ltd. 62-; Chair. of principal subsidiary cos. in U.K. and abroad principally concerned with films, leisure activities, television, manufacturing, technology and xerography; Dir. Southern Television Ltd., Eagle Star Insurance Co. Ltd., Xerox Corpn. (U.S.A.); Gov. British Film Inst., Central School of Speech and Drama; Trustee British Commonwealth Int. Newsfilm Agency.
Office: 38 South Street, London, W.1; Home: Monk's Horton Manor, Monk's Horton, nr. Ashford, Kent, England.

Davis, John Herbert, B.S., M.A., PH.D.; American agriculturalist and international administrator; b. 9 Oct. 1904; ed. Iowa State Univ. of Sciences and Technology and Univ. of Minnesota.
Principal and Agricultural Teacher, Douds-Leando, Iowa, Agricultural School 28-30, Superintendent 30-35; Agricultural Economist, Department of Agriculture, Washington 36-38; Superintendent of Schools, Story City (Iowa) 38-40; research, Minnesota Univ. 40-41; Agricultural Economist, Farm Credit Admin., Washington 41-42; Chief of Wheat Section, Commodity Credit Corpn., Washington 42-44; Exec. Vice-Pres., Nat. Council of Farmer Co-ops. 44-52; Gen. Man., Nat. Wool Marketing Corpn., Boston 52-53; Chair. U.S. del. F.A.O. Conf., Rome, Int. Cotton Conf., Washington 53; Asst.

Sec. of Agriculture, Pres. Commodity Credit Corpn., Fed. Crop Insurance Corpn. 53-54; Chair. U.S. del. Int. Cotton Conf., São Paulo 54; Dir. of Program (Agriculture and Business), Harvard Graduate School of Business Admin. 54-59; Dir. U.S. Department of Agriculture Economic Survey Mission to Brazil 57; mem. Food and Nutrition Board, Nat. Res. Council, American Acad. Sciences 56-59; Consultant to Under-Sec. of State for Economic Affairs Jan.-July 58; Commr.-Gen. UN Relief and Works Agency for Palestine Refugees (UNRWA) 59-63; Vice-Chair. Board of Trustees and Dir. New York Office of American Univ. of Beirut 64-66; Consultant, FAO on Admin. Structure and Organization 67; Adviser on Middle East Affairs to U.S. Sec. of State 66-; Exec. Dir. Americans for Middle East Understanding 68-; numerous American and foreign awards and honours.
Publs. *Economic Analysis of the Tax Status of Farmer Co-operatives* 50; co-author *A Concept of Agribusiness* and *Farmer in a Business Suit* 57.
Home: 1192 Park Avenue, New York City, New York 10028, U.S.A.
Telephone: ATwater 9-9089.

Davis, John King, C.B.E., F.R.G.S.; Australian master mariner and polar navigator; b. 84; ed. Burford Grammar School, Oxfordshire.
Chief Officer *Nimrod*, Sir Ernest Shackleton's Antarctic Expedition 07-09; Master *Aurora* and Second-in-Command Sir Douglas Mawson's Australian Expedition 11-14; commanded Ross Sea Relief Expedition which rescued survivors of Shackleton Antarctic Expedition; marooned Cape Evans 16; Dir. Navigation in Australia 20-49; Master *Discovery* and Second-in-Command Mawson Antarctic Research Expedition 29-30.
Publs. *With the Aurora in the Antarctic* 20, *Willis Island, a Storm-warning Station in the Coral Sea* 23, *High Latitude—The Recollections of an Antarctic Navigator* 62.
Melbourne Club, Collins Street, Melbourne, C.1, Victoria, Australia.

Davis, Joseph Stancliffe, A.B., PH.D., L.H.D.; American economist; b. 5 Nov. 1885; ed. Harvard Univ.
Instructor in Economics, Harvard Univ. 13-17; Tutor 15-20 and Asst. Prof. 17-21; statistician Allied Maritime Transport Council London 18-19; contrib. Editor *Review of Economic Statistics* 19-25 and *Wheat Studies* of Food Research Inst. 24-44; Chief Economist Federal Farm Board 29-31; Dir. Food Research Inst., Stanford Univ. 21-52, Prof. of Economic Research 38-52, Emeritus 52-; mem. President's Council of Economic Advisers 55-58.
Publs. *Essays in the Earlier History of American Corporations* 17, *Wheat and the A.A.A.* 35, *On Agricultural Policy 1926-1938* 39, *International Commodity Agreements: Hope, Illusion or Menace* 47, *The Population Upsurge in the United States* 49.
691 Mirada Avenue, Stanford, Calif. 94305, U.S.A.
Telephone: 415-323-4791.

Davis, Kingsley, PH.D., M.A., A.B., A.M.; American sociologist; b. 20 Aug. 1908; ed. Univ. of Texas and Harvard Univ.
Instructor in Sociology, Smith Coll., 34-36; Asst. Prof. Clark Univ. 36-37; Assoc. Prof. Pennsylvania State Univ. 37-42, Prof. 42-44, Head, Sociology Div. 37-42; Research Assoc. Office of Population Research, Princeton Univ. 42-48; Assoc. Prof. Princeton 44-48; Prof. of Sociology, Graduate Faculty of Political Science, Columbia 48-55; Assoc. Dir. Bureau of Applied Social Research 48-49, Dir. 49-52; Prof. of Sociology, Univ. of California at Berkeley 55-; Pres. American Sociological Asscn., Population Asscn. of America.
Publs. *Modern American Society* (with Bredemeier and Levy) 49, *Human Society* 49, *The Population of India*

and Pakistan 51, *World's Metropolitan Areas* (with others) 59.
199 Hillcrest Road, Berkeley, California, U.S.A.

Davis, Gen. Leighton Ira; American air force officer; b. 20 Feb. 1910; ed. U.S. Military Acad., Massachusetts Inst. of Technology and Air War Coll.
Technical Exec., Chief Armament Lab., Air Material Command 43-46; Commandant, U.S. Air Force Inst. of Technology 51; Dir. Armament H.Q., Air Research and Devt. Command 51-54; Commdr. Air Force Missile Devt. Center 54-58; Dep. Commdr. for Research, H.Q. Air Research and Devt. Command, Andrews A.F.B., Md. 58-59; Asst. D.C.S./Devt., H.Q. U.S.A.F., Washington 59-60; Commdr. Air Force Missile Test Center, Patrick Air Force Base, Florida 60-64; Commdr. Nat. Range Div., A.F.S.C., Andrews A.F.B. May 64-; Commandant Ind. Coll. of the Armed Forces 67-; numerous awards including N.A.S.A. Outstanding Leadership Award.
National Range Division, A.F.S.C., Andrews A.F.B., Md., U.S.A.

Davis, Nathanael Vining; Canadian businessman; b. 26 June 1915; ed. Harvard Univ., London School of Economics and Political Science, and Grenoble Univ.
Joined Alcan Aluminium Ltd. Group 39; Pres. and Dir. Alcan Aluminium Ltd. 47-; Dir. Canada Life Assurance Co., Bank of Montreal and Aluminium Co. of Canada Ltd.; Trustee American School of Classical Studies, Athens.
Box 6090, Montreal 3, Quebec, Canada.

Davis, Owen Lennox, B.A., LL.B.; Australian diplomatist; b. 12 April 1912; ed. King's School, Sydney and Sydney Univ.
Barrister-at-Law 38-40; Australian Forces (Capt.) 40-45; joined Australian Dept. of External Affairs 46; First Sec. Washington 48-51, Karachi 52-53; Acting High Commr., Wellington N.Z. 54-55; Senior External Affairs Rep. London 57-59; Australian High Commr. to S. Africa 59-61, Ambassador 61-62; Australian Ambassador to Brazil 62-64; Asst. Sec. Ministry of External Affairs 65-66, First Asst. Sec. 67-.
c/o Department of External Affairs, Canberra, Australia.

Davis, Richard Hallock, A.B., M.B.A.; American diplomatist; b. 7 Feb. 1913; ed. Phillips Exeter Acad., Harvard and Princeton Univs., and Russian Inst., Columbia Univ.
Foreign Service Officer 38-; Vice-Consul, Hamburg 38-39, Tsingtao 40-42; Third Sec. Chungking 42-43, New Delhi 42; Second Sec. Moscow 43-46, First Sec. 48-49; Asst. Chief Eastern European Div., Dept. of State 46-48; Officer in Charge, U.S.S.R. Affairs, Office Eastern European Affairs 50-53; Counsellor, Vienna, and Asst. Deputy High Commr. for Austria 53-55; mem. Policy Planning Staff, Dept. of State 55-57; Minister-Counsellor, Moscow 57-59; Dir. Office of Soviet Union Affairs 59-60; Deputy Asst. Sec. of State for European Affairs 60-65; Ambassador to Romania 65-.
American Embassy, Bucharest, Romania; Home: 3410 Que Street, N.W., Washington, D.C. 20007, U.S.A.

Davitadze, Levan Mikhailovich; Soviet politician; b. 1916; ed. Shota Rustaveli State Pedagogical Inst., Batumy and Higher Party School of C.P.S.U. Central Committee.
Teacher, School Dir., Insp., then Head of a district dept. of educ. 37-42; Sec. Khulo District Cttee. of the Party, Chair. Khulo District Soviet, Official of Communist Party of Georgia 42-53; Sec. Adzhar Regional Cttee. C.P. of Georgia 53-61; Chair. Council of Ministers, Adzhar Autonomous S.S.R. 61-; mem. Central Cttee. C.P. of Georgia; Deputy to U.S.S.R. Supreme Soviet; mem. C.P.S.U. 39-; Hero of Socialist Labour.
Council of Ministers, Adzhar Autonomous S.S.R., Batumi, U.S.S.R.

Davy, Georges Ambroise, D. ès L.; French university professor; b. 31 Dec. 1883; ed. Ecole Normale Supérieure and Univ. de Paris.
Professor of Literature and Dean, Dijon 19-30; Rector, Rennes Univ. 31-38; Insp.-Gen. Public Instruction 39-44; Prof. Faculty of Letters, Paris 44-55, Dean 50-56; mem. Inst. of Acad. of Political and Moral Sciences 52, Pres. 65; Pres. Int. Inst. of Political Science; Pres. Cttee. Sociological Study Centre; mem. Dir. C.N.R.S. until 63, Nat. Cttee. C.N.R.S. 63-; fmr. Vice-Pres. Int. Sociological Asscn., Int. Council of Social Sciences of UNESCO; Hon. Dean, Faculty of Letters, Paris; Dir. Thiers Foundation; Prof. h.c. Univ. of Brazil; Dr. h.c. Brussels Univ.; Assoc. mem. Royal Acad. of Belgium; mem. French Inst.; Hon. K.B.E. (England), Grand Officier Légion d'Honneur; Commdr. numerous foreign orders.
Publs. include: *La Foi jurée* 22, *Le Droit, l'idéalisme et l'Expérience* 23, *Sociologie politique* 25, *Sociologiques d'Hier et d'Aujourd'hui* 35.
Fondation Thiers, 5 rond-point Bugeaud, Paris 16e, France.

Davydov, Alexander Nikolayevich; Soviet trade corporation official; b. 05.
Teacher, later Principal, Secondary School 23-31; Communist Party and Trade Union official, Moscow 31-39; Soviet Army 41-46; mem. staff, Presidium Supreme Soviet 46-53; Ministry of Cinematography 48-53, Ministry of Culture 53-55; Chair. *Sovexportfilm* (cinema films) 55-; numerous decorations.
Vsesojuznoje Objedinenije Sovexportfilm, Kalashny Pereulok 14, Moscow, K-9, U.S.S.R.

Davydovsky, Ippolit Vasilyevich; Soviet pathologist; b. 1887; ed. Moscow Univ.
Sanitary Insp. in Yaroslovl region 11-12; Asst. at Moscow Univ. 12-14; Army Physician 14-18; Prosector and Asst., Moscow Univ. 18-30; Head of Dept., Second Moscow Medical Inst. 30-; mem. U.S.S.R. Acad. of Medical Sciences 44-, Presidium mem. 44-46, 53-57, Vice-Pres. 46-50, 57-60; Head of Laboratory, Inst. of Morphology of Man 62-; Founder of Mil. Pathology Museum; Chair. Board All-Union Soc. of Pathologists; Hon. mem. Purkyně Medical Soc. (Czechoslovakia); Order of Lenin 47, 57, Order of Red Banner of Labour 43; Honoured Scientist of R.S.F.S.R.; Hero of Socialist Labour 57.
Publs. *Bullet Wound*, and over 80 works on morbid anatomy.
Department of Morbid Anatomy, Second Moscow Medical Institute, Internatsionalnaya 11, Moscow, U.S.S.R.

Dawnay, Lt.-Col. Christopher Payan, C.B.E., M.V.O.; British business executive; ed. Winchester and Magdalen Coll., Oxford.
Dawnay Day & Co. Ltd., Merchant Bankers 33-39, 46-50; Army service 39-45; Partner, Edward de Stein & Co., Merchant Bankers 51-60; Managing Dir., Lazard Bros. & Co. 60-; Chair. Dalgety & New Zealand Loan Ltd., Philblack Ltd., and Dir. other companies.
Longparish House, Andover, Hampshire, England.

Dawson, William L.; American lawyer and politician; b. 26 April 1886; ed. Fisk Univ., Chicago, Kent Coll. of Law and Northwestern Univ. School of Law.
Army service, First World War; Sec. Democratic Congressional Cttee.; mem. U.S. House of Representatives 42-, Chair. House Cttee. for Exec. Expenditures 49-64.
U.S. House of Representatives, Washington, D.C., U.S.A.

Day, J. Edward, A.B., LL.B.; American lawyer and politician; b. 11 Oct. 1914; ed. Univ. of Chicago and Harvard Univ.
Admitted Illinois Bar 38, in private law practice 39-40, 45-49; served U.S. Navy 40-45; Legal and Legislative

Asst. to Gov. Adlai Stevenson 49-50; Commr. of Insurance, Illinois 50-53; with Prudential Insurance Co., America 53-61, Vice-Pres. Western Operations, Los Angeles 57-61; Postmaster Gen. of U.S. 61-63; Democrat.
Publs. *Bartholf Street, Descendants of Christopher Day of Bucks County, Pennsylvania, My Appointed Round—929 Days as Postmaster General, Speeches Don't Have to be Dull, Humor in Public Speaking.*
Chevy Chase, Maryland, U.S.A.

Day, William Lang, B.S. in M.E.; American banker; b. 5 Dec. 1907; ed. Germantown Friends School and Univ. of Pennsylvania.
Junior engineer, Day and Zimmermann, Inc., Philadelphia 31-36; statistician and syndicate officer, Morgan Stanley & Co., New York 36-41; partner, Drexel & Co., Philadelphia 41-48; Vice-Pres. First Pennsylvania Banking and Trust Co. 49, Dir. 49, Exec. Vice-Pres. 50, Pres. 52, Chair. 55-; official of other companies.
15th and Chestnut Streets, Philadelphia 1, Pa.; Home: Beaumont Road, Devon, Pa. 19333, U.S.A.
Telephone: LOcust 8-1700.

Dayal, Rajeshwar, M.A.; Indian diplomatist; b. 12 Aug. 1909; ed. P.S. Coll., Nainital, U.P. Allahabad Univ., and New Coll., Oxford.
Entered Indian Civil Service 32; Deputy Secretary, Civil Supplies Dept., U.P. Govt. 43-46, Home Sec. 46-48; Minister-Counsellor and Chargé d'Affaires Moscow 48-50; Special Commr. to Indian Govt. and Joint Sec. to Govt. External Affairs Dept. 50; Alternate Rep. Security Council 50-51, Permanent Rep. to U.N. 52-54, mem. U.N. Peace Observation Comm., U.N. Comm. of Twelve on Disarmament, U.N. Comm. for Relief and Rehabilitation of Korea, U.N. Trusteeship Council, U.N. Human Rights Comm.; Amb. to Yugoslavia 55-58, concurrently Minister to Bulgaria and Rumania; High Commr. to Pakistan 58-60, May 61-63; Personal Rep. of Sec.-Gen. of UN in the Congo Sept. 60-May 61; Special Sec. Ministry of External Affairs 63-65; Commonwealth Sec. Ministry of External Affairs 65; Amb. to France 65-67; Sec.-Gen. Ministry of Foreign Affairs 67-.
Ministry of Foreign Affairs, New Delhi, India.

Dayan, Moshe; Israeli soldier; b. 20 May 1915; ed. agricultural high school, Nahalal, and Staff Coll., Camberley, U.K.
Trained in Haganah (Jewish militia) 29; second in command to Capt. Orde Wingate 37; imprisoned by British when Haganah declared illegal 39; released for training as intelligence scout in Syria 41; Colonel after 45; took leading part in war with Arabs 48-49; Chief of Staff 53-58; Minister of Agriculture 59-64, of Defence June 67-; Mapai Party; mem. of Knesset 59-.
Publ. *Diary of the Sinai Campaign* 66.
11 Yoav Street, Zahala, Israel.
Telephone: 427-318.

Day-Lewis, Cecil, C.B.E., D.LIT., C.LIT., M.A., F.R.S.L., F.R.S.A.; British writer; b. 27 April 1904; ed. Sherborne School, Wadham Coll., Oxford.
Asst. Master, Summerfields School, Oxford 27-28, Larchfield, Helensburgh 28-30, Cheltenham Coll. 30-35; with Publications Div. Ministry of Information 41-46; Clark Lecturer, Cambridge Univ. 46; Prof. of Poetry, Oxford Univ. 51-56; Gresham Prof. of Rhetoric 63; Charles Eliot Norton Prof. of Poetry, Harvard Univ. 64-65; Dir. Chatto & Windus Ltd. 54-; Vice-Pres. Royal Soc. of Literature 58-; mem. Arts Council of Great Britain 62-67; Poet Laureate 68-; Hon. Fellow Wadham Coll., Oxford 68; Compton Lecturer, Univ. of Hull 68.
Publs. *A Hope for Poetry* 34, *The Friendly Tree* 36, *Starting Point* 37, *Overtures to Death, Anatomy of Oxford* (with Charles Fenby) 38, *Child of Misfortune* 39, *The Georgics of Virgil* 40, *Word Over All* 43, *Poetry for You* 44, *The Poetic Image* 47, *Poems 1943-1947, The Aeneid*

of Virgil 52, *An Italian Visit* 53, *Collected Poems* 54, *Pegasus and other poems* 57, *The Buried Day* (autobiography) 60, *The Gate and other Poems* 62, *The Eclogues of Virgil* 63, *The Lyric Impulse* 65, *The Room* 65; also detective novels under pseudonym Nicholas Blake.
6 Groom's Hill, Greenwich, London, S.E. 10, England.
Telephone: 01-858-4000.

Deakin, Frederick William Dampier, D.S.O., M.A.; British university official; b. 3 July 1913; ed. Westminster School and Christ Church, Oxford.
Fellow and Tutor, Wadham Coll., Oxford 36-49, Research Fellow 49; with Queen's Own Oxfordshire Hussars 39-41; seconded to Special Operations, War Office 41; led first British Mil. Mission to Marshal Tito 43; First Sec. Embassy, Belgrade 45-46; Warden of St. Antony's Coll., Oxford 50-; Russian Order of Valour 44, Chevalier Légion d'Honneur 53, Bundes Ehrenkreuz (German Federal Republic) 58.
70 Woodstock Road, Oxford, England.
Telephone: Oxford 57421.

Dean, Arthur Hobson, A.B., LL.B., LL.D.; American lawyer; b. 16 Oct. 1898; ed. Cornell Univ.
Admitted to New York Bar 23, practised with Sullivan & Cromwell, N.Y., partner of firm since 29; general counsel to various corporations and investment banking firms; Dir. and Trustee numerous companies including American Bank Note Co., American Metal Climax, Inc., Bank of New York; Chair. Board Trustees, Cornell Univ.; Trustee Carnegie Foundation for the Advancement of Teaching, and of other organisations and foundations; mem. American Bar Asscn.; Dir. Council on Foreign Relations, Japan Soc. Inc., Netherland-America Foundation, Fund for Peaceful Atomic Devt., United Nations Asscn., etc.; Rep. for U.S. and 16 nations contributing troops at Panmunjom negotiations; special U.S. Amb. to Korea 53-54; Amb. to UN Conf. on Law of the Sea, Geneva 58, 60, to Nuclear Test Ban Negotiations, Geneva 61-62, to Disarmament Conf., Geneva 62; Consultant to advise Dir., U.S. Arms Control and Disarmament Agency 63-; Chair. Consultative Cttee., American Soc. of Int. Law 56-59, Pres. 61-62, Hon. Vice-Pres. 62-; mem. Acad. of Political Science, and Political and Social Science, American Econ. Asscn., American Law Inst., American Judicature Soc., Int. Law Asscn., etc.; Hon. LL.D. (Hamilton, Allegheny, Rutgers, Washington, Brown, Dartmouth, Bowdoin and C.W. Post Colls. and Adelphi Univ.); Hon. D.C.L. (Hofstra Coll.); Hon. D.Hum. (Washington Coll.); Officier Légion d'Honneur.
Publs. include: *Investment Banking in a Changing World* 51, *Can Conventional Accounting Cope with Inflation?* 51, *The Relation of Law and Economics to the Measurement of Income* 52, *Investment Banking and the Antitrust Laws* 52, *Test Ban and Disarmament: The Path of Negotiation* 66.
Office: 48 Wall Street, New York, N.Y. 10005; Home: Mill River Road, Oyster Bay, L.I., N.Y. 11771, U.S.A.

Dean, Basil, C.B.E.; British theatre and film manager and producer; b. 27 Sept. 1888.
Member Horniman Repertory Co. 07-10; first Dir. Liverpool Repertory Theatre 11-13; Man. Dir. Reandean Productions 19-25; Joint Man. Dir. Theatre Royal, Drury Lane 24-25; Gov. Dir. Basil Dean Productions 26-; Chair. and Man. Dir. Radio Keith Orpheum Ltd. 30-32; Shute Lecturer Liverpool Univ. 32-33; Chair. and Man. Dir. Associated Talking Pictures Ltd., A.T.P. Studios Ltd. 28-38; Founder and Dir.-Gen. Entertainment Nat. Service Asscn. (ENSA) 39-46; Dir. Nat. Service Entertainment 41-46.
Productions include: *Bill of Divorcement* 21, *Loyalties* 23, *Hassan* 23, *A Midsummer Night's Dream* 24, *Constant Nymph* 26, *Autumn Crocus* 28, *Call it a Day* 30, *When we are married* 38, *An Inspector Calls* 46, *The*

Diary of a Nobody 54, *Touch it Light* 58; films: *Sally in our Alley, Constant Nymph, Escape, Sing As We Go.*
Publ. *Theatre at War* 56.
18 Norfolk Road, London, N.W.8, England.

Dean, Sir Patrick Henry, G.C.M.G.; British diplomatist; b. 16 March 1909; ed. Rugby School and Gonville and Caius Coll., Cambridge.
Called to Bar at Lincoln's Inn 34; legal practice 34-39; Asst. Legal Adviser, Foreign Office 39-45, Head, German Political Dept. 45-50, Minister in Rome 50-51; Senior Civilian Instructor Imperial Defence Coll. 52; Asst. Under-Sec. Foreign Office 53-56, Deputy Under-Sec. 56-60; Perm. Rep. to U.N. 60-64; Ambassador to U.S.A. 65-; Hon. LL.D. (Columbia, Lincoln Wesleyan Univ., Chattanooga, Hofstra), Hon. Bencher Lincoln's Inn, Hon. Fellow Clare Coll. and Gonville and Caius Coll., Cambridge.
British Embassy, Washington, D.C., U.S.A.
Telephone: Washington HO2-1340.

Dean, Robert Hall, B.A.; American food executive; b. 27 June 1916; ed. Grinnell Coll.
Manager, Checkerboard Elevator Co., Buffalo 41-43; Man. Ralston Purina Co., Ohio 43-45, Grain Div., St. Louis 45-48, Pres. Int. Div., St. Louis 58-, Vice-Pres., Asst. to Pres. 58-61, Exec. Vice-Pres., Dir. 61-63, Chief Operating Officer 63-66, Pres. 66-.
Office: 835 South 8th Street, St. Louis, Mo.; Home: 4 Devon Road, Glendale 22, Mo., U.S.A.

De Bakey, Michael Ellis, B.S., M.D., M.S.; American surgeon; b. 7 Sept. 1908; ed. Tulane Univ., New Orleans.
Instructor Tulane Univ. 37-40, Asst. Prof. of Surgery 40-46; War Service, Colonel, ultimately Dir. Surgical Consultant Div., Office of the Surgeon Gen. 42-46; U.S. Army Surgical Consultant to Surgeon-General 46-; Assoc. Prof. Tulane Univ. 46-48; Prof. and Chair. Dept. of Surgery, Baylor Univ. Coll. of Medicine, Houston 48-; Dir. Cardiovascular Research Center, Houston Methodist Hospital; Surgeon-in-Chief, Ben Taub Gen. Hospital; Senior Attending Surgeon, Methodist Hospital and Consultant in Surgery, Veterans Admin. Hospital, Houston; consultant surgeon to many hospitals in Texas; mem. Nat. Advisory Heart Council 57-61, Program Planning Cttee. and Cttee. on Training 61-, Nat. Advisory Council on Regional Medical Programs 65-; Chair. Pres. Comm. on Heart Disease, Cancer and Stroke 64-; implanted first artificial heart in man April 66; editorial staff of numerous medical journals and editor of *General Surgery: Vol. II, History of World War II,* and *Year Book of General Surgery,* co-editor *American Lectures in Surgery;* mem. numerous medical societies and asscns.; over 700 articles published; many awards and honorary degrees.
1200 Moursund Avenue, Houston, Texas 77025, U.S.A.
Telephone: JA 9-4951.

de Beer, Sir Gavin, M.A., D.SC., F.R.S., F.S.A., F.L.S., F.Z.S.; British zoologist and man of letters; b. 1 Nov. 1899; ed. Ecole Pascal, Paris, Harrow School and Oxford Univ.
Fellow of Merton Coll. 23-38; Senior Demonstrator in Zoology, Univ. of Oxford 26-38, Jenkinson Memorial Lecturer in Embryology 27-38, Reader 38; served army 14-18 and 39-45 wars; Prof. of Embryology, Univ. Coll., London 45-50; Gen. Editor Methuen's *Biological Monographs* 30-45; Editor Notes and Records of the Royal Society 45-52; Science Editor, Home University Library 45-52; Pres. Linnean Society 46-49; Pres. Ray Society 47-50; Dir. British Museum (Natural History), 50-60; corresp. mem. Acad. des Sciences, Paris; mem. Int. Inst. of Embryology; hon. mem. Société Zoologique de France, Société Royale Zoologique de Belgique, Zoological Society of India; Hon. D. ès L. (Lausanne); Hon. Sc.D. (Cantab.); Hon. D. de l'Univ. (Bordeaux); Pres. Int. Congress of Zoology 58, Chevalier Légion d'Honneur.

Publs. *Growth* 24, *Introduction to the Study of Genetics* 24, *Comparative Anatomy, Histology and Development of the Pituitary Body* 26, *Introduction to Experimental Embryology* 26, *Vertebrate Zoology* 28, *Embryology and Evolution* 30, *Early Travellers in the Alps* 30, *Alps and Men* 32, *The Elements of Experimental Embryology* (with J. S. Huxley) 33, *A German Reader for Biology Students* (with H. G. Fiedler) 34, *Le Voyage en Suisse de Mme. Roland* 37, *Development of the Vertebrate Skull* 37, *On Shelley* (with E. Blunden and S. Norman) 38, *Embryos and Ancestors* 40, *Escape to Switzerland* 45, *Thomas Pennant's Tour on the Continent* 48, *Travellers in Switzerland* 49, *A Journey to Florence in 1817* 51, *Speaking of Switzerland* 52, *Journal du Voyage de Gibbon en Suisse* 52, *Sir Hans Sloane* 53, *Archaeopteryx* 54, *Alps and Elephants* 55, *The First Ascent of Mont Blanc* (with T. Graham Brown) 57, *The Sciences Were Never at War* 60, *Reflections of a Darwinian* 62, *Darwin* 63, *Atlas of Evolution* 64, *Voltaire's British Visitors* (with A. Rousseau) 67, *Gibbon* 68, *Hannibal's March* 67.
La Colline, 1880 Bex, Switzerland.
Telephone: 025-5-20-52.

De Benedetti, Giulio; Italian journalist; b. 1890.
Foreign Corresp. of *La Stampa*, Turin 15-18; Special Corresp. in Germany 19-30; Chief Editor and Dir. of the *Gazzetta del Popolo*, Turin; Dir. of *L'Opinione* (Liberal Party), Turin 45; Chief Editor and Dir. of *La Stampa* and *Stampa Sera*, Turin 48-; Grande Ufficiale della Repubblica.
La Stampa, Via Roma 80, Turin; and 94 corso Giovanni Lanza, Turin, Italy.

de Besche, Hubert W. A.; Swedish diplomatist; b. 7 July 1911; ed. Univ. of Stockholm and Grenoble and Heidelberg.
Ministry of Foreign Affairs 36-, served in London and Stockholm 36-47, Head Comm. of Trade and Commerce 47-49, Economic Counsellor, Washington; Head, Trade Dept., Ministry of Foreign Affairs 53-56, Deputy Sec.-Gen. Ministry of Foreign Affairs 56-63; Ambassador to U.S.A. 64-; mem. Steering Board for Trade, OEEC 56-60; Vice-Chair. Trade Cttee., OECD 60-63; Chair. EFTA Negotiations 59; del. to numerous trade negotiations; Grand Cross Homayoun, Iran, Grand Cross Order of Christ; Hon. K.B.E., etc.
Office: Royal Swedish Embassy, 2249 R Street, N.W., Washington 8, D.C.; Home: 3900 Nebraska Avenue, N.W., Washington, D.C. 20016, U.S.A.
Telephone: EM2-3270 (Home).

Debeyre, Guy Edouard Pierre Albert; French university professor; b. 6 Nov. 1911; ed. Lille Univ.
Prof. Faculty of Law and Economic Sciences, Univ. of Lille 45-55, Dean 50-55, now Rector; Président-Général, Cttee. for Econ. Expansion of the North and Pas de Calais 56-; mem. Conseil Supérieur du Plan 62- and other official Comms.; Officier, Légion d'Honneur, Croix de Guerre (39-45).
Publs. *La Responsabilité de la puissance publique en France et en Belgique* 36, *Le Conseil d'Etat Belge* 47, *Traité de Droit Administratif* 54, *Le Droit public des Français* 56.
Hotel Académique, 22 rue St. Jacques, Lille, France.

De Biasi, Vittorio; Italian engineer and industrialist; b. 8 Feb. 1895; ed. Turin Engineering High School.
Engineer on staff of Ferrovie Calabro-Lucane 21-24; Società Edison, Milan 24-26; Asst. Gen. Manager Società Emiliana di Esercizi Elettrici, Parma 27-28; Man. Dir. Società Ovesticino, Novara 28-38 and 39-42; Technical Man. Compañia Italo-Argentina de Electricidad, Buenos Aires 38-39; Pres. CISE 46-64; Gen. Man. Società Edison, Milan 43, Dir. and Gen. Man. 47, Man. Dir. 52; Dir. of Board CESI, Milan 56-64; Vice-Pres. and Man. Dir. Società Edison 65-66; Vice-Pres. Montecatini Edison S.p.A.; also holds several other offices, among which: Pres. MITTEL (Soc. Italiana Strade

Ferrate del Mediterraneo) Milan, SINCAT (Soc. Industriale Catanese) Palermo, SALCI Milan, STECAV Como, Ferrovie Umbro Aretine, Rome, Vetrocoke-Cokapuania; Vice-Pres. ITALPI.
Foro Bonaparte 31, Milan, Italy.
Telephone: Milan 8835.

De Boor, Helmut, DR. PHIL.; German literary scholar; b. 24 March 1891; ed. Univs. of Freiburg, Marburg, Leipzig.
Lector in Gothenburg 19-22; lecturer Greifswald 21-26; Extra. Prof. Leipzig 26-30; Prof. in Berne 30-45; Prof. Free Univ. of Berlin 49-59, Emer. 59-; Corresp. mem. Bavarian Academy of Sciences 63-.
Publs. *Das Nibelungenlied* 40, *Geschichte der deutschen Literatur von den Anfängen bis zur Gegenwart* Vols. I and II 57, Vol. III 62, *Kleine Schriften* Vol. I 64, Vol. II 66, *Die deutsche Literatur Texte und Zeugnisse* Vol. I, 1-2 65, *Die Textgeschichte der lateinischen Osterfeiern* 67.
Bachstelzenweg 11, Berlin-Dahlem, Germany.
Telephone: Berlin 761813.

Debré, Michel, D. en D.; French politician; b. 15 Jan. 1912; ed. Ecole des Sciences Politiques, Paris.
Auditeur, Conseil d'Etat 34; Commr. de la République, Angers region 44; mem. Comm. for Reform of the Civil Service 45; attached to Saar Economic Mission 47; Sec. Gen. German and Austrian Affairs, Ministry of Foreign Affairs 48; elected Senator from Indre et Loire 48, re-elected 55, Deputy from St. Denis, Réunion 63-, re-elected 67; Garde des Sceaux June 58-59; Prime Minister Jan. 59-April 62; Minister of Economic Affairs and Finance 66-68, of Foreign Affairs May 68-; Officier Légion d'Honneur, Croix de Guerre, Union pour la Nouvelle République (UNR).
Publs. *Refaire la France, Demain la Paix, La République et son Pouvoir, La République et ses Problèmes, La Mort de l'Etat Républicain, Ces Princes qui nous gouvernent, Au Service de la Nation, Jeunesse, quelle France te faut-il?*.
18 rue Spontini, Paris 16e, France.

Debrot, Nicolaas, LL.D., M.D.; Netherlands physician, writer and Governor; b. 4 May 1902; ed. primary and secondary schools in Curaçao and Nijmegen and Univs. of Utrecht and Amsterdam.
Lived in France and U.S.A. 28-32; practised medicine, Amsterdam and Curaçao 42-50; official and governmental posts 50-; successively mem. Exec. Council Netherlands Antilles, Gen. Rep. of Netherlands Antilles in The Hague, Dir. of Cabinet of Minister of Netherlands Antilles, mem. Council of State; Gov. of Netherlands Antilles Sept. 62-; Knight Order of Netherlands Lion; Grand Cross in the Order of Vasco Nuñez de Balboa.
Publs. (Prose): *My Sister the Negro* 35, *Pray for Camille Willocq* 46, *Clouded Existence* 48, *Pages from a Diary in Geneva* 62; (Poetry): *Confession in Toledo* 44, *Poignant Summer* 45, *Those Absent* 52.
Gouvernementhuis, Willemstad, Curaçao, Netherlands Antilles.
Telephone: 13916-22.

Debu-Bridel, Jacques, L. en D.; French writer and politician; b. 22 Aug. 1902; ed. Colleges of Lausanne and Dreux, Faculty of Law, Sorbonne, Paris, and Ecole Libre des Sciences Politiques.
Journalist with *l'Eclair* 22; then with various publs., notably *l'Avenir* and *Comédia*; co-founder of Federalist review *Latinité*; wrote for *l'Ordre* for six years; mem. of Ligue des Patriotes and l'Union pour la Nation; Chief Sec. to Minister for Merchant Marine 39; French Army 40; Leader of Resistance in Occupied Zone; mem. of l'Organisation Civile et Militaire and of Front National; rep. of Nat. Republicans to Council of Resistance 43-45; Provisional Sec.-Gen. for Navy 45; mem. of Provisional Consultative Assembly and of Comms. for National Defence, Propaganda and Information; Dir. of journal

Front National; resgnd. because of Communist domination 45; mem. of R.P.F. (Gaulliste); Vice-Pres. Organising Cttee. R.P.F. for the Seine; Paris Municipal Councillor 47-48; Senator for the Seine 48, re-elected 52-58; mem. Paris Municipal Council 53; founder Union Démocratique du Travail 58; Chair. of Budget Cttee. for Fine Arts, Council of the Republic; Dir. of Paris Services, Radio Monte Carlo 60-66, Dir. of Information 66-; Dir. of weekly *Notre République* 66-; Médaille de la Résistance, Croix de Guerre, Officier de la Légion d'Honneur.

Publs. Novels: *Jeunes Ménages* 35 (Prix Interallié), *Exil au Grand Palais* 48, *Déroute* 45, *Sous la Cendre* 51, *Frère esclave* (new ed. 57); Essays: *Alphonse Daudet et la Famille* 29, *Alger* 30, *La Grande tragédie du Monde animal* 55; Biographies: *La Fayette* 45, *Emily Brontë* 50, *Journées Révolutionnaires de Paris, Vol. I* 60, *Vol. II* 61, *Conjuration d'Amboise* 63.

26 rue Beaujon, Paris 8e, France.

de Bunsen, Sir Bernard, Kt., C.M.G., M.A.; British university administrator; b. 07; ed. Leighton Park School and Balliol Coll., Oxford.

Schoolmaster, Liverpool Public Elementary Schools 31-34; Asst. Dir. of Education, Wiltshire County Council 34-38; H.M. Inspector of Schools, Ministry of Education 38-46; Dir. of Education, Palestine 46-48; Prof. of Education, Makerere Univ. Coll. 48, Act. Principal Aug. 49, Principal 50-63; Vice-Chancellor, Univ. of East Africa 63-65; Principal, Chester Coll., England 66-; Hon. LL.D. Univ. of St. Andrews.

Chester College, Chester, England.
Telephone: Chester 28401.

Debus, Kurt Heinrich, PH.D., M.S.; American (b. German) engineer; b. 29 Nov. 1908; ed. Technische Hochschule, Darmstadt.

Assistant Prof. Technische Hochschule, Darmstadt 39-42; Test Engineer, Flight Test Dir., Peenemuende Rocket Centre, Germany 42-45; Deputy Dir. Guidance and Control Div., and Staff Asst. to Wernher von Braun, Army Ballistic Missile Agency, Huntsville, Ala. 45-52; U.S. citizen 50-; Dir. Missile Firing Lab., Army Ballistic Missile Agency, Cape Canaveral (later Cape Kennedy), Florida 60-62; Dir. Launch Operations Center, Nat. Aeronautics and Space Admin. (N.A.S.A.), Cape Canaveral 62-63; Dir. John F. Kennedy Space Center, N.A.S.A. Kennedy Space Center 63-; mem. Advisory Board, British Interplanetary Soc.; Hon. mem. Hermann Oberth Gesellschaft; Fellow American Inst. of Aeronautics and Astronautics; Life mem. American Ordnance Asscn.; Hon. mem. German Soc. for Rocket Technology and Space Flight; Exceptional Civilian Service Award, U.S. Army 59; Frank A. Scott Gold Medal, American Ordnance Asscn. 64; N.A.S.A. Outstanding Leadership Award 64; Pioneer of Windrose Award, Order of Diamond 65; Hon. LL.D. (Rollins Coll.) 67.

Publs. Numerous works, designs, etc. on launch of ballistic missiles and space vehicles 39-.

John F. Kennedy Space Center, N.A.S.A. Kennedy Space Center, Florida 32899, U.S.A.
Telephone: 305-867-3333.

Decaris, Albert Marius Hippolyte; French artist; b. 6 May 1901; ed. Ecole Estienne, Ecole Nationale Supérieure des Beaux-Arts.

Frescoes, Int. Exhibition, Paris 37, New York 38, Town Hall, Vesoul; engravings and book illustrations; design of French and French Overseas postage stamps; Premier Grand Prix de Rome 19; mem. Acad. des Beaux. Arts, Prés. 60; Prés. Inst. de France 60; Officier, Légion d'Honneur; Croix de Guerre (1939-45).

3 quai Malaquais, Paris 6e, France.
Telephone: 0338261.

de Chirico, Giorgio; Italian painter; b. 10 July 1888; ed. Acad. of Fine Arts, Munich.

Went to Paris 11; creator of Metaphysical School of painting 14; first exhibited in Rome 19; visited U.S. 36-38; executed numerous designs for the theatre.

Works include: *The Enigma of an Autumn Afternoon, Nostalgia of the Infinite, Joys and Enigmas of a Strange Hour, Departure of a Poet, Mystery of a Street, The Departure of the Knight Errant, Mysterious Bathing.*

Publs. include: *Hebdomeros* (novel) 29, *Gustave Courbet* 25, *Piccolo trattato di technica pittorica* 28, *Commedia dell'arte moderna* (jointly) 45, *Memorie della mia vita* (autobiography) 45.

31 Piazza di Spagna, Rome, Italy.

Decker, William Conway, B.S., M.B.A.; American business executive; b. 26 Dec. 1900; ed. Pennsylvania State Coll., Columbia Univ., and Harvard Business School.

Engineering Dept. Western Electric Co. N.Y. 22; Sales Dept. Brown Co. Portland, Maine 27; Sales Manager Corning Glass Works, Corning, N.Y. 30, Chief Cost Accountant 34, Treas. 36, Controller and Asst. to Pres. 39, Vice-Pres. 41, Pres. and Dir. 46-61, Chief Exec. Officer 57-60, Chair. of Board and Chief Exec. Officer 61-64, Chair. of Exec. Cttee. 64-65, Hon. Vice-Chair. 64-; Chair. of Board, Signetics Corp. 66-; Trustee Corning Glass Works Foundation; Dir. Dow Corning Corpn., Pittsburgh Corning Corpn.; Hon. LL.D. (Alfred Univ.); Hon. D.Eng. (Clarkson Coll.).

5 East Fifth Street, Corning, N.Y., U.S.A.

Dédéyan, Charles, D. ès L.; French university professor; b. 4 April 1910; ed. Coll. Notre Dame de Ste. Croix, Neuilly and Sorbonne.

Reader in French Literature, Univ. of Rennes 42; Prof. of French and Comparative Literature, Univ. of Lyons 45; Prof. of Comparative Literature at the Sorbonne 49-; Sec.-Gen. Int. Fed. of Modern Languages and Literature 46-54; Dir. Inst. of Comparative Modern Literature, Sorbonne 55-; Editor of *Encyclopédie permanente Clartés* 61-.

Publs. *La Sophonisme de Mairet* 45, *Montaigne chez ses amis anglo-saxons* 46, *Essai sur le Journal de Voyage de Montaigne* 46, *Le Journal de Voyage de Montaigne* 47, *Argile* 47, *Studies in Marivaux, Stendhal, Du Fail, Balzac, V. Hugo* 50-53, *Le Thème de Faust dans la Littérature Européenne* 54-67, *Madame de Lafayette, La Nouvelle Héloïse, Stendhal et les Chroniques italiennes* 55, *Voltaire et la Pensée anglaise* 56, *Le "Gil Blas" de La Sage* 56, 65, *Gérard de Nerval et l'Allemagne* 57-59, *L'Angleterre dans la pensée de Diderot* 59, *Dante en Angleterre* 58-66, *"Le Roman Comique" de Scarron* 59, *Rilke et la France* 61, *L'Influence de Rousseau sur la sensibilité européenne à la fin du XVIIIe. siècle* 61, *Stendhal Chroniqueur* 62, *Victor Hugo et l'Allemagne* 63, 65, *L'Italie dans l'oeuvre romanesque de Stendhal* 63, *Le Cosmopolitisme littéraire de Charles Du Bos* 68, *Racine et sa "Phèdre"* 68, *Le Nouveau Mal du Siècle de Baudelaire à Nos Jours.*

27 rue de la Ferme, Neuilly-sur-Seine, France.

Dedijer, Vladimir, DR. IURIS, M.A.; Yugoslav writer; b. 4 Feb. 1914; ed. Belgrade Univ.

Lieut.-Col. in Tito's army, Second World War; Yugoslav Del. to U.N. Gen. Assemblies 45, 46, 48, 49, 51, 52; mem. Yugoslav Del. to Peace Conf., Paris 46; mem. Central Cttee. League of Communists of Yugoslavia 52-54; Prof. of Modern History, Belgrade Univ. 54-55; defended right of M. Djilas to free speech 54; expelled from Central Cttee. of League of Communists 54; sentenced to 6 months on probation 55; Simon Senior Fellow, Manchester Univ. 60-62 now Hon. Fellow; Fellow of St. Antony's Coll., Oxford 62-63; Research Assoc., Harvard Univ. 63-64; Visiting Prof. Cornell Univ. 64-65; Full mem. Historical Inst. Serbian Acad. of Sciences July 64-; Order of Liberation of Yugoslavia.

Publs. *Partisan Diary* 45, *Notes from the United States* 45, *Paris Peace Conference* 48, *Yugoslav-Albanian Relations* 49, *Tito* 52, *The Beloved Land* 62, *Sarajevo* 63.
Gorkičeva 16/V, Ljubljana, Yugoslavia.

Dedushkin, Pyotr Semyonovich; Soviet diplomatist; b. 1915; ed. Novozybkov Teachers' Training Inst. and Chelyabinsk Pedagogic Inst.
Member of C.P. of Soviet Union 39-; Counsellor, Soviet Embassy, Bucharest 53-55; Deputy Head, Head of Fifth European Dept., Ministry of Foreign Affairs 57-60; Counsellor-Minister, Belgrade 60-63; Amb. to Lebanon 66-.
Soviet Embassy, Beirut, Lebanon.

Dee, Philip Ivor, C.B.E., M.A., F.R.S.; British physicist; b. 8 April 1904; ed. Sidney Sussex and Pembroke Colls., Cambridge.
Univ. Lecturer in Physics, Cambridge 35; Fellow, Sidney Sussex Coll., Cambridge; Prof. of Natural Philosophy, Glasgow Univ. Oct. 43-; Superintendent, Telecommunications Research Establishment 39-45; mem. Advisory Council for Scientific and Industrial Research 47-52.
11 The University, Glasgow, Scotland.

Deedes, Rt. Hon. William Francis, P.C., M.C., M.P.; British politician; b. 1 June 1913; ed. Harrow School.
Member of Parliament for Ashford (Kent) 50-; Parl. Sec., Ministry of Housing and Local Govt. 54-55; Parl. Under-Sec. Home Dept. 55-57; Minister without Portfolio (Information) July 62-64.
New Hayters, Aldington, Kent, England.

de Ferranti, Basil Reginald Vincent Ziani, M.A., A.M.I.E.E.; British business executive; b. 2 July 1930; ed. Eton and Trinity Coll., Cambridge.
Graduate Apprenticeship Course, D. Napier & Sons, Acton 53-54; Manager of Domestic Appliances, Ferranti Ltd. 54-57; Dir. of Overseas Operations, Ferranti Ltd. 57-62; Dep. Managing Dir., Int. Computers & Tabulators Ltd. 63-64, Managing Dir. ICT 64-; M.P. 58-64; Parl. Sec. Ministry of Aviation July-Oct. 62; Conservative.
ICT House, Putney, London, S.W.15, England.

de Ferranti, Sebastian Basil Joseph; British electrical engineer; b. 5 Oct. 1927; ed. Ampleforth Coll.
Commissioned in 4th/7th Royal Dragoon Guards; practical training with Brown Boveri, Switzerland and Alsthom, France; Transformer Dept., Ferranti Ltd. 50, Dir. 54-, Man. Dir. 58-, Chair. Feb. 63-.
Ferranti Ltd., Hollinwood, Lancashire; Home: Kerfield House, Knutsford, Cheshire, England.

de Ferranti, Sir Vincent Ziani, Kt., M.C., LL.D., D.ENG., M.I.E.E., F.R.A.E.S.; British electrical engineer; b. 16 Feb. 1893; ed. Repton School.
Served First World War 14-19; Man. Transformer Dept., Ferranti Ltd. 21-30, Chair. Ferranti Ltd. 30-63; Chair. British Electrical and Allied Manufacturers' Asscn. 38-39, Vice-Pres. 46-57, Pres. 57-59; served Second World War 39-40; Hon. Col. 123 Field Engineer Regt., R.E., T.A. 48-57; Pres. Inst. of Electrical Engineers 46-47; Chair. British Nat. Cttee. and Chair. Int. Exec. Council of World Power Conf. 50-62; Pres. British Electrical Power Convention 49-50; Pres. Television Society 54-57.
Henbury Hall, Macclesfield, Cheshire, England.
Telephone: Macclesfield 2400.

De Ferrariis Salzano, Carlo; Italian diplomatist; b. 20 Aug. 1905; ed. Università degli Studi, Naples and Perugia.
Entered diplomatic service 32; early posts in Geneva 33, Cannes 34, Paris 35-36, Ministry of Foreign Affairs 37-42; First Sec. Budapest 42-44; Head American and Far East Division Ministry of Foreign Affairs 45-46; Counsellor Mexico City 46-49, Brussels 49-51; Consul-Gen. Chicago 52, New York 52-58; Head Personnel,

Minister Plenipotentiary and Sec.-Gen. Ministry of Foreign Affairs 58-59; Amb. to Canada 59-65, to Switzerland 65-67; perm. rep. of Italy to the North Atlantic Council, Brussels 67-; Grande Ufficiale al Merito della Repubblica Italiana; several foreign decorations.
Brussels: OTAN-NATO, Brussels 39, Belgium; Ministry of Foreign Affairs, Rome, Italy.

Defferre, Gaston, LIC. en D.; French lawyer, politician and journalist; b. 14 Sept. 1910; ed. Coll. de Nîmes, Aix-en-Provence Univ.
Legal practice in Marseille before the second World War, resistance activity in the "Brutus" organisation 40-44; Dir. *Le Provençal* 44-; Pres. Municipal Resistance Del., Marseille 44; Mayor of Marseille April-Oct. 45, May 53-; Dep. from Bouches du Rhône to Constituent Assemblies 45-46, Nat. Assembly 46-58; Sec. of State, Présidence du Conseil Jan.-June 46; Under-Sec. of State for Overseas France Dec. 45-Jan. 46; Minister of the Merchant Marine July 50-August 51; Minister of Overseas France Jan. 56-May 57; Senator 59-62; Dep. Nat. Assembly 62-; Socialist Candidate for President of the Republic 64-65; Officier, Légion d'Honneur, Croix de Guerre, Rosette de la Résistance, King's Medal for Courage in the Cause of Freedom; fmr. mem. Dir. Cttee. Parti Socialiste (S.F.I.O.).
Publ. *Un nouvel horizon.*
Le Provençal, 1 rue Caumartin, Paris 9e, France.

De Filippo, Eduardo (brother of Peppino De Filippo, *q.v.*); Italian playwright, actor and producer; b. 1900.
Worked as actor, producer and writer with Compagnia Vincenzo Scarpetta and Compagnia Teatro Nuovo; Co-founder Il Teatro Umoristico I De Filippo 31-44; Dir. and Owner Teatro San Ferdinando, Naples 53-; many prizes as playwright, actor and producer.
Publs. *Natale in Casa Cupiello, Non ti Pago, Napoli Milionaria, Filumena Marturano, Questi Fantasmi, Le Voci di Dentro, Le Bugie con le gambe lunghe,* and many other one-act plays, operas and films.
Via Ximenes 8, Rome, Italy.

De Filippo, Giuseppe (Peppino De Filippo) (brother of Eduardo De Filippo, *q.v.*); Italian playwright, actor and producer; b. 24 Aug. 1903.
Debut 09; with brother Edward founded variety company 31; Founder and Dir. Italian Theatre Co. of Peppino de Filippo 44-, Company toured Russia May 65; writer of over sixty farces, musical *Le metamorfosi di un suonatore ambulante,* and numerous poems and songs; also appears in films and on television.
Viale Parioli 96, Rome, Italy.

de Fischer Reichenbach, Henry-Béat, DR. JUR.; Swiss diplomatist; b. 22 July 1901; ed. Stella Matutina, Feldkirch, Univs. of Berne, Fribourg, Munich and Paris.
Entered Swiss Diplomatic Service 29, The Hague, Buenos Aires, Warsaw, Riga and Helsinki; Counsellor, Bucharest 42-47; Asst. to Head of Mission, Cairo 47-49, Minister, Cairo 49-54, Addis Ababa 52-54, Lisbon 54-59; Ambassador to Austria 59-64; Ambassador to United Kingdom 64-66; mem. Council of Patrons, C. G. Jung-Inst. Zürich; Pres. Centre d'étude des Suisses à l'étranger, Société des amis suisses de Versailles; Camões prize 61.
Publs. *Contributions à la connaissance des relations suisses-égyptiennes* 56, *Dialogue luso-suisse* 60.
Le Pavillon, Thunplatz 52, Berne, Switzerland.
Telephone: 031-44-15-09.

DeFrance, Smith J.; American aeronautics research engineer; b. 19 Jan. 1896; ed. Univ. of Michigan.
Research Engineer, N.A.C.A. (Nat. Advisory Cttee. for Aeronautics) 22-40, Dir. Ames Aeronautical Lab. 40-58, Dir. Ames Research Center, N.A.S.A. (Nat. Aeronautics and Space Admin.) 58-65; Aero-Space Consultant.
12220 Fairway Drive, Los Altos, California, U.S.A.

de Freitas, Rt. Hon. Sir Geoffrey Stanley, K.C.M.G., M.P.; British barrister, politician and diplomatist; b. 7 April 1913; ed. Haileybury, Clare Coll., Cambridge, and Yale Univ.
Borough Councillor in Shoreditch 36-39; mem. General Council of the Bar 39; served Royal Air Force 40-45; Labour M.P. for Central Nottingham 45-50, for Lincoln 50-61, for Kettering 64-; Parl. Private Sec. to Prime Minister 45-46; Under Sec. of State for Air 46-50; Del. to UN Assembly 49, 64; Under-Sec. of State Home Office 50-51; Del. to Council of Europe 51-54 (Leader of Del. 65-66), to NATO Parl. Conf. 55-60 (Treas. 58-60), 65-66; Chair. Soc. Labour Lawyers 56-58, Labour Party Housing Cttee. 51-55; Air Cttee. 55-60, Agriculture Cttee. 60-61, Defence Cttee. 64-; High Commr. in Ghana 61-63, in Kenya 63-64; Pres. Assembly of Council of Europe 66-.
Office: House of Commons, London, S.W.1; Home: 11 Trumpington Road, Cambridge, England.
Telephone: 01-930-6240 Extension 734 (Office).

de Gaulle, Gen. (*see* Gaulle, Gen. de).

De Geer, Jan Gustaf Gérard; Swedish international official; b. 7 Sept. 1918.
Swedish Red Cross Liaison Officer with British Red Cross in Germany 46, with British Red Cross Comm. for N.W. Europe and Control Comm. for Germany 47; A.D.C. to Count Bernadotte, Palestine 48; Chief, Swedish Red Cross Mission to Berlin 48-49; Chief, Foreign Relations Dept., Swedish Red Cross 49-56, Acting Sec.-Gen. (ex officio) 56-57; Sec.-Gen., World Fed. of United Nations Asscns. 63, now Vice-Pres.; several foreign decorations.
World Federation of United Nations Associations, 65 rue de Lausanne, Geneva; 14 avenue de Budé, 1202 Geneva, Switzerland.

Degerbøl, Magnus, DR. PHIL.; Danish zoologist; b. 8 July 1895; ed. Københavns Universitet.
Curator of Mammals, Zoological Museum, Univ. of Copenhagen 24-43, Keeper of Vertebrate Dept. 43-50, Dir. Quaternary-Zoological Laboratory 56-66; Univ. of Copenhagen Lecturer Quaternary-Zoology 50-56, Prof. 56-66; Pres. Danish Natural History Soc. 44-49, and Zootopografical Investigations of Denmark 46-62; Editor *Videnskabelige Meddelelser Dansk Naturhistorisk Forening* 31-44, *Danmarks Fauna* 40-46, and *Acta Arctica* 43-60; mem. Royal Danish Acad. of Sciences and Letters; Hon. mem. American Soc. of Mammalogists; Corresp. Fellow Arctic Inst. N. America 67; Knight Order of Dannebrog.
Expeditions: Blossevilles Coast, East Greenland 32, Equatoria, Central Africa Expedition 47, Subantarctic Seas, Galathea Expedition 52, Andes Mountains 54, Pres. Danish Thule-Ellesmere Island Expedition 39-41. Publs. *The Prehistoric Mammals of Denmark compared with Recent Forms* 33, *Mammals, Fifth Thule Expedition Arctic North America* 35, *Mammals of Denmark* 35, *Mammalia Zoology of the Faroes* 40, and works on evolution, domestication, Norse culture and Eskimo habitation in Greenland.
Fuglevadsvej 4, Kgs. Lyngby, Denmark.
Telephone: 870529.

Degtyar, Dmitry Danilovich; Soviet diplomatist and politician; b. 1904; ed. Moscow Planning Inst.
Trade Union activity 35-38; State Exec. 38-39; Chair. State Planning Cttee. of the R.S.F.S.R. 39-47; Vice-Chair. U.S.S.R. State Planning Comm. 49-53; Vice-Chair. Council of Ministers of the R.S.F.S.R. 39-47; mem. later Deputy Chair. State Cttee. for Foreign Econ. Affairs 57-62; Ambassador to Guinea 62-64; Dep. Chair. State Cttee. for Foreign Econ. Affairs 65-.
State Cttee. for Foreign Economic Affairs, Moscow, U.S.S.R.

Degtyar, Mikhail Vasilyevich; Soviet diplomatist; b. 1906; ed. Moscow Inst. of Planning.
Party official 33-35; Soviet Army 35-36; Head of Cultural Dept., then Vice-Chair. State Planning Cttee. of U.S.S.R. 38-43; Vice-Chair. Cttee. for Cinematography of U.S.S.R. Council of Ministers 43-45; Diplomatic Service 45-; Counsellor, Ottawa 45-51; at U.S.S.R. Ministry of Foreign Affairs (consultant) 51-53; Amb. to Afghanistan 53-60; Deputy Sec.-Gen. U.S.S.R. Ministry of Foreign Affairs 60-65; Amb. to Pakistan 65-.
U.S.S.R. Embassy, Flench Street, Karachi, Pakistan.

Degtyarev, Vladimir Ivanovich; Soviet politician; b. 1920; ed. Moscow Inst. of Mining.
Executive work in mining industry 42-57; Sec. Donetsk Regional Cttee. C.P. of the Ukraine 57-62; Chair. Donetsk Council of Nat. Economy 62-63; Second Sec. Donetsk Regional Cttee. of the C.P. of the Ukraine Jan. 63-July 63, First Sec. July 63-; Alt. mem. Politburo, Central Cttee. C.P. of the Ukraine; mem. Central Cttee. C.P.S.U.; Deputy to U.S.S.R. Supreme Soviet; mem. C.P.S.U. 45-; Hero of Socialist Labour 57.
Donetsk Regional Committee of the Communist Party of the Ukraine, Donetsk, U.S.S.R.

de Guingand, Major-General Sir Francis W., K.B.E., C.B., D.S.O.; b. 28 Feb. 1900; ed. Ampleforth Coll., Royal Military Coll., Sandhurst.
Joined Army 20, served in King's African Rifles 26-31; Military Asst. to Sec. of State for War 39-40; Dir. Military Intelligence, Middle East 42; Chief of Staff 8th Army 42-44, 21st Army Group 44-45, retd. 47; Chair. Rothmans of Pall Mall Ltd., London 61-, Rothmans in S. Africa 61-; Pres. South Africa Foundation; Chair. T.I. South Africa (Pty.) Ltd.
Publs. *Operation Victory* 47, *African Assignment* 53, *Generals at War* 64.
P.O.B. 7035, Johannesburg, Republic of South Africa. Telephone: Johannesburg 834-8429.

Dehejia, Venilal, B.SC.; Indian civil servant; b. 23 July 1908; ed. Wilson Coll., Bombay Univ. and Imperial Coll. of Science, London.
Indian Civil Service 31-; Asst. Collector, Collector and District Magistrate, Commr.; Sec. to Govt. for Home Affairs and Finance, Bombay; Chief Sec. Govt. of Sind, Karachi; Chief Sec. Govt. of Saurashtra, Rajkot; Sec. Govt. of India, Ministry of Finance; now Chair. State Bank of India, also Chair. State Banks of Bikaner and Jaipur, Hyderabad, Indore, Mysore, Patiala, Saurashtra and Travancore; Vice-Pres. Indian Inst. of Bankers.
5 Harkness Road, Bombay 6, India.

Dehlavi, S. K.; Pakistani diplomatist; b. 14 Sept. 1913; ed. Univs. of Bombay and Oxford.
Joined Indian Civil Service 38, served in Province of Bengal, later District Magistrate, Tipperah and Chittagong, E. Pakistan; later in Pakistani Foreign Office; Deputy Sec. Ministry of Foreign Affairs and Commonwealth Relations 50; Chargé d'Affaires *a.i.*, Paris 50-53; Joint Sec. Ministry of Foreign Affairs and Commonwealth Relations 53-57; Amb. to Italy, concurrently to Tunisia 57-61; Foreign Sec. 61-63; Amb. to U.A.R., also to Libya and Yemen 63-65, to Switzerland, concurrently to Malta and Albania 65-66; High Commr. in U.K. 66-; Sitara-i-Pakistan; Grand Cross of Merit of Italian Repub.
Pakistani High Commission, 35 Lowndes Square, London, S.W.1, England.

Dehnkamp, Willy; German politician; b. 22 July 1903; ed. elementary school.
Apprenticeship as locksmith 18-22; mem. Social Democrat Party 20-; mem. Blumenthal County Council 25-33; persecuted by Nazis 33-45; Army Service 42-45; Prisoner-of-War in U.S.S.R. 45-48; Municipal Official Bremen-Blumenthal 49-51; Senator for Educ., Bremen 51-65, Pres. of Senate 65-67; Deputy mem. Bundesrat 52-63, mem. 63-67; Mayor of Bremen 63-67; Pres.

Standing Conf. of Ministers for Cultural Affairs of German Federal Republic 54-55, 62-63; mem. German Scientific Council 57-65.
Bremen, Rathaus, German Federal Republic.

Dehousse, Fernand; Belgian university professor and politician; b. 06; ed. Athénée Royal de Liège, Univ. de l'Etat à Liège.
Asst. Prof. Univ. de Liège 35-40, Prof. 40- (except during occupation 40-44); Senator (Parti Socialiste Belge) 50-; Belgian Rep. E.C.S.C. 52-60; mem. Consultative Assembly, Council of Europe 54-61, Western European Union Assembly 55-; mem. European Parliament 58-; Pres. European Comm. for the Saar Referendum 55, of the Saar Comm. of Western European Union 55-56; Pres. Consultative Assembly of the Council of Europe 56-59; Co-Pres. Franco-German Arbitration Tribunal for the Saar; mem. Perm. Arbitration Court; Minister of Nat. Educ. 65-66.
17 rue Saint-Pierre, Liège, Belgium.

de Icaza y León, Francisco A.; Mexican diplomatist; b. 1905; ed. Univ. of Madrid.
Entered Foreign Service 25; served Foreign Office 25-29, Costa Rica 29-30, El Salvador 30, Cuba 31, Costa Rica 32, Foreign Office 32, Berlin 33, Denmark 34, Netherlands 34, Berlin 35-40, Argentina 40-42, Guatemala 42-43, Foreign Office 43-47; Minister to the Lebanon 47-49; Minister to Belgium and Luxembourg 49-52; Ambassador to London 52-55, to Guatemala 55-58, to Argentina 59-65; Kt. Commdr. Order of Quetzal (Guatemala); Grand Cross Order of the Crown of Cedar (Luxembourg) and of the Order of the Crown (Belgium).
c/o Ministry of Foreign Affairs, Mexico D.F., Mexico.

Deineka, Alexandr Alexandrovich; Soviet artist; b. 99; ed. Moscow Higher School of Art.
Rep. at numerous important exhibitions in the U.S.S.R. and in Germany, Hungary, Austria, Czechoslovakia, Yugoslavia, Universal Exhibition, Paris 37, XV, XVII, XVIII and XIX Venice Biennali, Brussels Int. Exhibition 58; mem. Acad. of Arts of the U.S.S.R., Vice-Pres. 62-; Hon. Art Worker of the R.S.F.S.R.; People's Artist, U.S.S.R.; Lenin Prize 64.
Academy of Arts of the U.S.S.R., 21 Kropotkinskaya Street, Moscow, U.S.S.R.

Deininger, Walter Thilo; Salvadorean plantation owner; b. 91; ed. privately and in Dresden, Germany.
Apprentice, Import and Export Firm, Hamburg 10-12; Commercial School, Boston, Mass. 12; administered plantations, El Salvador 12-; Dir. Banco Hipotecario 35-; deported to U.S.A. 42-46; José Matias Delgado Decoration, Order of San Silvestre (Vatican), Order of Hermano Pedro (Guatemala).
Puerta de la Laguna, El Salvador, Central America.

Dejean, Maurice; French diplomatist; b. 30 Sept. 1899; ed. Sorbonne.
Served Ministry of Foreign Affairs 26, Berlin 29-39; Chef de Cabinet (for Foreign Affairs) to Daladier and Reynaud 39-40; collaborated with Coulondre in editing French *Yellow Book* 40; Nat. Commr. for Foreign Affairs French Nat. Cttee. 41-42; Diplomatic Adviser to French Cttee. of Nat. Liberation 42-43; Min. Plenipotentiary to Allied Governments in London 43-44; Gen. Dir. for Political Affairs Foreign Office 44-45; Del. San Francisco Conf. 45, U.N. Gen. Assembly N.Y. 46; French Ambassador to Czechoslovakia Dec. 45-Dec. 49; French Del. Int. Ruhr Authority May 49-Feb. 50; Head of French Mission, SCAP, Tokyo (rank of Ambassador) 50-52, Ambassador to Japan 52-54; Commr.-Gen. in Indo-China 54-55; Amb. to U.S.S.R. 55-64; Ambassadeur de France 64-; Dir. Shell française 65-, Soc. des bains de mer et du Cercle des étrangers de Monaco 66-; Pres. Soc. franco-soviétique de co-opération industrielle (SOFRACOP) 66-; Commdr. Légion d'Honneur.
110 boulevard de Courcelles, Paris 17e, France.

Dejmek, Kazimierz; Polish actor and theatre director; b. 17 May 1924; ed. State Theatrical Acad., Łódź.
Actor, Rzeszów, Jelenia Góra Companies 45; Actor, Teatr Wojska Polskiego 46-49; Founder and Gen. Dir. Teatr Nowy, Łódź 49-61; Head, State Theatrical Acad., Łódź 52-55; Gen. Manager and Artistic Dir., Teatr Narodowy, Warsaw 61-; numerous decorations.
Principal productions: *Winkleried's Day* (Andrzejewski and Zagórski) 56, *Measure for Measure, Julius Caesar* (Shakespeare) 56, 60, *The Inquisitors* (Andrzejewski) 57, *Agamemnon* (Aeschylus), *Electra* (Euripides), *The Frogs* (Aristophanes) 61, 63, *The Story of the Glorious Resurrection of Our Lord* (Nicolai of Wilkowieck) 61, 62, *Word about Jacob Szela* (Bruno Jasieński) 62, *The Life of Joseph* 65, *Kordian* (Slowacki) 65, *Darkness Covers the Earth* (Andrzewski) 67.
Krasińskiego 26 m. 23, Warsaw, Poland.

Dekeyser, Willy Clément, D.SC.; Belgian university professor; b. 16 Feb. 1910; ed. Albert School and Athénée Royal, Ostend, Ghent Univ.
Teacher, Athénée Royal, Ghent 31; Asst. Ghent Univ. 38, Lecturer 44, Prof. of Crystallography 48-; mem. Scientific and Technical Cttee. Euratom, Advisory Panel NATO, Flemish Acad. of Sciences; Croix de Guerre, Commdr. Ordre de Léopold.
Publs. *Les dislocations et la croissance des cristaux* (with S. Amelinckx) 55, *The structure and properties of grain boundaries* (with S. Amelinckx) in *Solid State Physics* Vol. 8.
Laboratorium voor Kristallografie en Studie van de Vaste Stof, Krijgslaan 105, Ghent, Belgium.
Telephone: 09-22-57-15.

de Kiewiet, Cornelis Willem, M.A., PH.D., LL.D., L.H.D., LITT.D.; American (b. Netherlands) historian; b. 21 May 1902; ed. Jeppe High School, Johannesburg, and Univs. of Witwatersrand, London, Paris and Berlin.
Teaching Asst. in History, Univ. of Witwatersrand 23; Teacher of Afrikaans and History, Prince Edward High School, Salisbury, S. Rhodesia 23-25; Asst. Prof. of History, State Univ. of Iowa 29-35; Assoc. Prof. 35-37; Prof. 37-41; Prof. of Modern European History, Cornell Univ. 41-48; Dean of Coll. of Arts and Sciences, Cornell Univ. 45-48, Provost 48-49; acting Pres. 49-51; Pres. Rochester Univ. June 51-61, Emer. 61-; Special Consultant to Navy Dept. and Dir. of Army Specialized Training Programmes in Area and Language, Cornell Univ. 43-45; Sec.-Treas. Asscn. American Univs. 51-54, Vice-Pres. 54-56, Pres. 56-58; Council Higher Educ., N.Y. State 58-; Nat. Acad. of Sciences Advisory Comm. for Africa 58-; Comm. for Education Liaison between U.S. and Sub-Sahara Africa 59-; Special Cttee. on Sponsored Research A.E.E. 58-.
Publs. *British Colonial Policy and the South African Republics* 29, *The Imperial Factor* 37, *A History of South Africa* 41, *The Anatomy of South African Misery* 56; collaborator in many works, including *Cambridge History of the British Empire*.
22 Berkeley Street, Rochester, N.Y., U.S.A.

de Klerk, Albert; Netherlands organist and composer; b. 4 Oct. 1917; ed. Amsterdamsch Conservatorium under Dr. Anthon van der Horst.
Organist St. Joseph's Church, Haarlem 33-; City Organist Haarlem 56-; Prof. of Organ and Improvization, Amsterdamsch Conservatorium 64-; Dir. of Catholic Choir, Haarlem 46-; numerous gramophone records for Telefunken; Prix d'Excellence, Amsterdam 41, Prix du Disque, Edison (for *Die Kleinorgel*) 62.
Compositions: several works for organ including two Concertos for Organ and Orchestra, chamber-music, and liturgical music (seven masses).
Crayenesterlaan 22, Haarlem, Netherlands.
Telephone: 80654.

de Klerk, Jan; South African politician; b. 22 July 1903; ed. Potchefstroom Univ. for Christian Higher Educ.

Started teaching 27; Principal of Primrose Afrikaans School, Germiston 37-45; Sec. of Witwatersrand section of National Party 47-48, of Transvaal section 48-; mem. Transvaal Provincial Council 49-54, Executive Cttee. 49-54; Minister of Labour and Public Works 54-58; Minister of Labour and Mines 58-61, of Interior and Mines Jan.-Aug. 61, of Interior, Labour and Immigration Aug.-Nov. 61, of Interior, Education, Arts and Science Nov. 61-66, of Educ., Arts and Science, and Information 66-.

Ministry of Education, Pretoria, South Africa.

De Kooning, Willem; American (b. Netherlands) artist; b. 04; ed. Rotterdam Acad. of Fine Arts.

Display work, dept. stores in the Netherlands 20-24; worked in Belgium 24-25, America 26, housepainter, muralist, New York 26, Mural, Hall of Pharmacy, New York World's Fair 39; Teacher, Black Mountain Coll. 48, Yale 50-51; One-man shows Egan Gallery 48, 50, Sidney Janis Gallery 53; Knoedler & Co., Manhattan 67; retrospective exhbn. at Tate Gallery, London 68; pictures in Museum of Modern Art, New York, St. Louis Museum, Chicago Art Inst. and in private collections.

Sidney Janis Gallery, 15 E. 57th Street, New York City, N.Y., U.S.A.

De la Bedoyere, Count Michael; British writer and editor; b. 16 May 1900; ed. Stonyhurst, Oxford Univ.

Asst. Master Beaumont Coll. 28-29; Lecturer in Philosophy Univ. of Minnesota 30-31; Asst. Editor *Dublin Review* 32-34; Editor *New Catholic Herald* 34-62; Founder and Editor *Search* 62-.

Publs. *The Drift of Democracy* 31, *Lafayette, a Revolutionary Gentleman* 33, *George Washington, an English Judgment* 35, *Sociology* (Vol. 5 of *European Civilisation, Its Origin and Development*) 36, *Christian Crisis* 40: *Christianity in the Market Place* 43, *No Dreamers Weak* 44, *Catherine, Saint of Siena* 46, *Life of Baron von Hügel* 51, *Living Christianity* 54, *The Layman in the Church* 54, *Cardinal Griffin* 55, *The Archbishop and the Lady* 55, *The Meddlesome Friar* 58, *The Cardijn Story* 58, *François de Sales* 60, *Francis: A biography of the Saint of Assisi* 62, Editor *Objections to Roman Catholicism* 64, *The Future of Catholic Christianity* 66.

Elylands, Edenbridge, Kent, England.

Delage, Emile Jean-Baptiste, D. ès L.; French university professor; b. 23 July 1890; ed. Univ. of Paris.

Lecturer Faculty of Letters Bordeaux 29-31, Prof. 31-32, Prof. of Greek Language and Literature 32-46, Dean of Faculty of Letters 41-46; Rector Académie de Clermont-Ferrand 46-50; Rector Acad. de Bordeaux 50-60, Hon. Rector 60-; served in First and Second World Wars; Croix de Guerre, Officier de la Légion d'Honneur, Commdr. des Palmes Académiques.

Pubs. *Biographie d'Apollonios de Rhodes* 30, *La Géographie dans les "Argonautiques" d'Apollonios de Rhodes* 30.

100 rue Chevalier, Bordeaux, France.

Telephone: 48-75-82.

de la Mare, Richard Herbert Ingpen, M.A.; British publisher; b. 4 June 1901; ed. Oxford Univ.

Faber and Gwyer Ltd. 25-, Dir. 26; Dir. Faber & Faber Ltd. 29, Vice-Chair. 46, Chair. 60-; Chair. Fine Art Engravers Ltd.

Much Hadham Hall, Much Hadham, Hertfordshire, England.

Delaney, James J.; American politician; b. 19 March 1901.

Former mem. Danahy & Delaney Law Firm, Brooklyn; fmr. Asst. District Attorney, District Attorney's Office, Queen's County, New York; mem. U.S. House of Reps. 45-46, 49-; Democrat.

Suite 2267, Rayburn House Office Building, Washington, D.C. 20515, U.S.A.

Telephone: 202-225-3965.

Delano, William A., B.A., LL.B.; American lawyer and government official; b. 25 May 1924; ed. Yale Coll. and Yale Law School.

American Friends' Service Cttee. in Germany 48-50; Law Practice, Winthrop, Stimsom, Putman and Roberts, New York City 53-61; mem. American Bar Asscn.; Chair. Cttee. on Bill of Rights Asscn. of Bar of City of New York City; mem. Special Cttee. to Study Commitment Procedures, Special Cttee. on Passport Procedures; Nat. Dir. American Civil Liberties Union; Legal Adviser during formation of U.S. Peace Corps 61, first Gen. Counsel, U.S. Peace Corps 61-63, Special Asst. to Dir., U.S. Peace Corps 63-64; Sec.-Gen. Int. Secretariat for Volunteer Service 64-.

Publs. *Freedom to Travel* 58, *Mental Illness and Due Process*.

3411 O Street, N.W., Washington, D.C., U.S.A.

De Laurentiis, Dino; Italian film producer; b. 8 Aug. 1919.

Founded Real Ciné, Turin 41; Exec. Producer Lux Film 42; acquired Safir Studios and founded Teatri della Farnesina 48; co-founder Ponti-De Laurentiis S.p.A. 50; numerous awards and prizes include Oscars for *La Strada* 57, *Le Notti di Cabiria* 58, Golden David Awards for *Le Notti di Cabiria* 58, *The Tempest* 59, Silver Ribbon (Italian Film Critics) for *La Strada* 54, Venice Silver Lion for *Europa 51* 52.

Films produced include: *La Figlia del Capitano, Il Bandito, Molti Sogni per la Strada, Anna, Bitter Rice, La Strada, Le Notti di Cabiria, Ulysses, War and Peace, The Tempest, This Angry Age, Europa 51, The Gold of Naples, The Great War, Five Branded Women, I Love, You Love, The Best of Enemies, Barabbas, To Bed or not to Bed, The Bible, The Three Faces of a Woman.*

Casella Postale 10060, Rome, EUR, Italy.

Delavignette, Robert; French civil servant; b. 29 March 1897.

Served French Army 16-19; Commr. for Native Affairs de l'Afrique Occidentale française 19-22; Asst. Admin. for Colonies 22-31, Admin. 31-36; Asst. Head of Secr. of Minister for French Overseas Territories 36; Head of Nat. School of French Overseas Territories 37-46; later took up post in Colonies (rank of Gov. 3rd Class) 42; High Commr. of Republic in Cameroons 46-47; Gov.-Gen. 47; Dir. of Political Affairs, Ministry of French Overseas Territories 47-51; mem. Economic Council and Prof. Nat. School of French Overseas Territories 51-; mem. Acad. des Sciences d'outre-mer and Int. African Inst.; Commdr. de la Légion d'Honneur.

Publs. *Paysans Noirs* (novel), filmed 48, *Service Africain* (English trans.: *Freedom and Authority in West Africa*), *Birama, l'Afrique Noire Française et son Destin, Christianisme et Colonialisme*, etc.

26 rue de Babylone, Paris 7e, France.

De La Warr, Earl; Herbrand Edward Dundonald Brassey Sackville, P.C., G.B.E., J.P.; British politician; b. 12 June 1900; succeeded to title 15; ed. Eton and Magdalen Coll., Oxford.

Mayor of Bexhill 32-33, 33-34 and 34-35; Lord-in-Waiting 24 and 29-31; Under-Sec. of State for War in Labour Govt. 29-31; Parl. Sec. to Min. of Agriculture in Nat. Govt. 31-35 and to Board of Education 35-36; Parl. Under-Sec. for Colonies 36-37; Lord Privy Seal 37-38; Pres. Board of Education 38-40; First Commr. of Works 40; Chair. Agricultural Research Council 43-; Dir. Home Flax Production, Min. of Supply 43; joined Conservative Party 45; Postmaster-General 51-55; Chair. Comm. on Higher Education 37, Joint East and Central African Board; Chair. Royal Empire Society 57-58, Royal Commonwealth Society 58-60.

Fisher's Gate, Withyham, Hartfield, Sussex, England.

Delay, Jean, DR. en MED., DR. ès L.; French psychologist; b. 14 Nov. 1907; ed. Paris Univ.
Prof. of Mental Diseases and Encephalography, Dir. Inst. of Psychology, Sorbonne; Pres. 1st World Congress of Psychiatry 50; mem. Acad. de Médecine 55-, Acad. Française 59-; Commandeur, Légion d'Honneur; Dr. h.c. Zürich and Montreal Univs.
Publs. *Les Dissolutions de la Mémoire, Les Dérèglements de l'Humeur, La Psychophysiologie humaine, Aspects de la Psychiatrie Moderne*; novels: *La Cité Grise* 46, *Hommes sans Nom* 48; *La Jeunesse d'André Gide.*
53 avenue Montaigne, Paris 8e, France.

Del Balzo di Presenzano, Giulio, LL.D., D.ECON.; Italian diplomatist; b. 28 Nov. 1903.
Entered diplomatic service 27; served London 29, subsequently Budapest and Paris; Ministry of Foreign Affairs 44; Counsellor Holy See 46; Minister to Australia 48; Dir.-Gen. Political Affairs 52; Ambassador to Spain 55-58; Ambassador to Venezuela 58-59; Dir.-Gen. Cultural Relations 59-; Ambassador to Holy See 64-.
Via Flaminia 166, Rome, Italy.

Delbarre, Florian François, D. en MED.; French professor of medicine; b. 7 Sept. 1918; ed. Lycée Michelet, and Faculties of Science and Medicine, Paris.
Served as intern in Paris Hospitals 43-49; Head of Clinic of Faculty of Medicine, Paris 49-55; Fellow of the Faculty of Medicine, doctor, Paris Hospitals 55-60, Prof. of Rheumatology at the Faculty of Medicine 60-, Prof. Clinic of Rheumatology 67-; Dir. Research Centre on Osteo-Articular Diseases at L'Hôpital Cochin; Hon. Prof. of Medical and Social Rheumatology, Faculty of Medicine, Paris; mem. Scientific Cttee. of the Nat. Centre of Scientific Research; Consultant to the World Health Organization; Sec.-Gen. Int. League against Rheumatism; Pres. French League against Rheumatism; Chevalier de la Légion d'Honneur, Chevalier de la Santé Publique, Officier du Mérite de la Répubblique Italienne, Medaille d'Or des Hôpitaux, Lauréat de l'Académie Nationale de Médecine.
Publs. *L'insuffisance alimentaire* (with Prof. C. Richet) 50, *Les Stimulines hypophysaires* (with Profs. Lemaire and Michard) 50, *Cortisone et cortico-stimuline en Rheumatologie* (with Profs. F. Coste and J. Cayla) 52.
15 rue Gay-Lussac, Paris 5e, France.

Delbart, Georges, D. ès SC.; French engineer; b. 11 April 1899; ed. Lycée de Valenciennes, Faculty of Science, Lille Univ.
Laboratory Chief Société Escaut et Meuse 22-27; entered Anciens Etablissements Cail and was successively Laboratory Service Chief, Head of the steelworks and Chief Metallurgist; engaged in manufacture of armaments, especially of tanks; Scientific Adviser to the "Armoured Vehicles" service Ministry of Armaments 39-40; missions to England 40, Germany 46, Western Europe 51, U.S.A. and Canada 52, Brazil 54, 58, Argentina, Chile 59, Peru, Brazil 60, India 64, Brazil 66, Mexico 66, Australia 67, Japan 67; Admin. Scientific Dir. of the French Iron and Steel Research Inst.; Pres. Dir.-Gen. of *Revue de Métallurgie*, Dir. standardization office, French Steel Industry; Officier Légion d'Honneur.
185 rue President Roosevelt, Saint Germain en Laye (S.-et-O.), France.
Telephone: 963-2401.

Del Bo, Rinaldo; Italian politician and lawyer; b. 19 Nov. 1916; ed. Inst. Leo XIII, Milan, Law School, Univ. of Milan (Doctor of Laws), and Univ. of Pavia.
Member Camera dei Deputati 48; Under-Sec. of State, Ministry of Labour 51-56, Foreign Office 56-57; Minister for Relations between Govt. and Parl. 57-Jan. 59, of Foreign Trade Feb. 59-60; Pres., High Authority of European Coal and Steel Community 63-67; Chair. Italian Del. at the Int. Conf. of Labour at Geneva; Commdr. de la Légion d'Honneur; Viareggio Prize for a Literary Essay 57.

Publs. *Problema dell'egualianza nello Stato contemporaneo* 48, *Nuovi aspetti della sovranità degli Stati* 50, *La Volontà dello Stato* 57.
Via Eleonora Duse 53, Rome, Italy.

Delbrück, Max; American (b. German) biologist; b. 4 Sept. 1906; ed. Univs. of Tübingen, Berlin, Bonn and Göttingen.
Went to U.S. 37, naturalized 45; Prof. of Biology, Calif. Inst. of Technology 47-; mem. Nat. Acad. of Sciences; Fellow Leopoldina Acad., Halle, Royal Danish Acad., Foreign mem. Royal Soc. (U.K.); Kimber Gold Medal (Genetics), U.S. Nat. Acad. of Sciences; Hon. Ph.D. (Copenhagen, Chicago).
1510 Oakdale Street, Pasadena, California, U.S.A.

Delden, Pieter van; Netherlands chemical engineer; b. 29 April 1899; ed. Delft Univ.
Koninklijke Nederlandsche Hoogovens en Staalfabrieken N.V. (Royal Netherlands Blast Furnaces and Steelworks) 27-, Manager, Cement Factory IJmuiden (CEMIJ) 31-36, Head, Sales Dept. Mekog 36, Technical Manager 38, Managing Dir. CEMIJ and Mekog 45, Managing Dir. Kon. Ned. Hoogovens en Staalfabrieken N.V. 52-64, Co-ordinator of Management policy 59-; Dir. Gen. Bank of the Netherlands, Kon. Ned. Stoomboot-Maatschappij N.V. (Royal Netherlands Steamship Co.), and numerous other companies; Netherlands honours.
Drift 22, Laren (N.H.), Netherlands.

De Leeuw, Ton; Netherlands composer; b. 16 Nov. 1926; ed. musical colls. in Netherlands and France and under Jaap Kunst, Amsterdam.
With Radio Hilversum 54-, responsible for annual radio programmes of Contemporary Music 56-; Prof. Composition Conservatoires of Amsterdam and Utrecht 59-; Lecturer Univ. of Amsterdam 62-; Study of Indian classical music and dance 61; numerous prizes including Prix Italia 56 and Prix des Jeunesses Musicales 61.
Compositions: *Hiob* (Radiophonic Oratorio) 56, *Mouvements Rétrogrades* 57, *First String Quartet* 58, *Antiphonie* (chamber music with 4 electronic sound-tracks) 60, Symphonies for Wind Instruments 63, *The Dream* (Opera) 63, *Men go their ways* (piano) 64, *Second String Quartet* 65.
Publ. *The Music of the 20th Century* 64,
Costeruslaan 4, Hilversum, Netherlands.

Delfim Neto, Antonio; Brazilian economist and politician; b. 1 May 1929; ed. Univ. of São Paulo.
Professor of Econs., São Paulo Univ. until 66; fmr. mem. Nat. Economic Council and Advisory Council on Planning; Finance Minister of São Paulo June 66-67; Minister of the Treasury, Govt. of Brazil March 67-.
The Treasury, Brasilia, Brazil.

Delforge, Marc, DOC. EN DROIT; Belgian journalist; b. 09; ed. Coll. Notre Dame de la Paix, Namur and Univ. of Louvain.
Barrister Namur 32-34 and 40-42; Asst. Editor *Vers l'Avenir* 32-34, Editor-in-Chief 34-; Chef de Cabinet to Belgian Minister of Information, London 42-44; lecturer Univ. of Louvain 46; Pres. Int. Fed. of Catholic Journalists 50; mem. Christian Social Party; Officer, Order of the Crown and of Leopold II, Commdr., Order of St. Gregory the Great, Resistance Medal, etc.
22 Rue de la Falise, Namur, Belgium.
Telephone: 21064.

Delgado, Pedro Abelardo; Salvadorean economist; b. 3 Nov. 1919; ed. Univ. de San Carlos, Guatemala and American Univ., Washington, D.C.
Vice-Dir. Commerce, Industry and Mining 51; Technical Asst. Min. of Economics 50, 52-53, Dir. Economic Studies Dept. 53-55; Prof. Economic Theory and Economic Problems Univ. of El Salvador 54-55, 59-60; Commercial Attaché, Bonn 57-59; Sec. Central American Economic Co-operation Cttee. (UN Economic

Commission for Latin America,) 57-59, 60-61; Deputy and Acting Minister of Economy 59-60; Sec.-Gen. Permanent Secretariat of the General Treaty on Central American Economic Integration 61-66; Gov. Inter-American Bank for Development, Washington, D.C. 59-60; del. at Punta del Este Meeting 61 and UN Conference on Trade and Development, Geneva, 64.
c/o Permanent Secretariat of the General Treaty on Central American Economic Integration, 4A Avenida 10-25, Zona 14, Guatemala City, Guatemala, Central America.

De L'Isle, 1st Viscount, cr. 56, 6th Baron De L'Isle and Dudley; **William Philip Sidney,** V.C., P.C., K.G., G.C.M.G., G.C.V.O., K.ST.J., M.A., D.L.; British Peer of the Realm; b. 23 May 1909; ed. Eton and Magdalene Coll., Cambridge.
Fellow of Inst. of Chartered Accountants 34; commissioned Grenadier Guards (Reserve) 29; served France and Belgium 39-40, Italy 43-44; Conservative M.P. for Chelsea 44-45; Parl. Sec. to Ministry of Pensions 45; Joint Treas. Conservative Party 48; Sec. of State for Air 51-55; Gov.-Gen. of Australia 61-65; Chair. Phoenix Assurance Co.; First Dir. Schweppes; Dir. Cape Town and District Gas Light and Coke Co., IBM United Kingdom Holdings, Finance Corpn. Ltd.
Penshurst Place, near Tonbridge, Kent, England.

Delius, Anthony Ronald St. Martin, B.A.; South African journalist; b. 11 June 1916; ed. St. Aidans Coll., Grahamstown, Rhodes Univ., Grahamstown.
Served with S.A. Military Intelligence; helped found *Saturday* (now *Evening*) *Post*, Port Elizabeth 47; *Cape Times*, Cape Town 50-; South African Poetry Prize 59.
Publs. *Young Traveller in South Africa* 47, *Unknown Border* (poems) 54, *The Long Way Round* (travel) 56, *The Last Division* (satire) 59, *The Fall* (play) 60, *A Corner of the World* (poems) 61, *The Day Natal Took Off* 62.
Midway, Bertram Crescent, Rondebosch, Cape, S.A.

Delivanis, Dr. Dimitrios J.; Greek university teacher; b. 3 April 1909; ed. Univs. of Athens, Paris, Berlin, and London School of Economics.
Assistant Prof. Econs., Univ. of Athens 38-44; Sec.-Gen. Ministry of Welfare 39-41; Greek Co-ordinator, Joint Relief Cttee. for Greece 43-45; Assoc. Prof. of Econs. Salonika Univ. 44-47, Prof. 48-; mem. Exec. Cttee. Centre of Econ. Research, Athens 61-64, Centre of Social Sciences, Athens 60-67; Vice-Pres. Greek Econ. Asscn. 61-; mem. Exec. Cttee. Int. Econ. Asscn. 65-; mem. Board of Mediterranean Social Sciences Research Centre 61, Pres. 65-; mem. Board Inst. of Balkan Studies 60-; Vice-Rector, Univ. of Salonika 64-65, Rector 65-66, Pro-rector 66-67; Orders of Phoenix (First Class) and George I (Second Class), Greece; Officier Légion d'Honneur.
Publs. *La politique des banques allemandes en matière de crédit à court terme* 34, *Greek Monetary Developments 1939-48* 49, *L'économie sous-développée* 63, *Die internationale Liquidität* 65, *Economics* (in Greek), five edns. 52-67, numerous articles in Greek, French, German and English.
Jan Smuts 50, Salonika; Morgenthaou I, Athens, Greece.

Delivanis, Miltiades; Greek diplomatist; b. 17 April 1912; ed. Univ. of Athens.
Attaché, Ministry of Foreign Affairs 38, served Ankara, Antwerp, Paris 46-56; Dep. Dir., Second Political Dept., Ministry of Foreign Affairs 56; Dir. of Foreign Minister's Private Office 56; Counsellor, London 58-61, Bonn 61-62; Ambassador to Cyprus 62-64; Ambassador to Iran 64-66, to Turkey 66-; numerous decorations.
Royal Greek Embassy, Ankara, Turkey.
Telephone: 128-007.

Della Casa-Debeljevic, Lisa; *see* Casa-Debeljevic.

Dell'Acqua, H. E. Cardinal Angelo; Italian ecclesiastic; b. 9 Dec. 1903.
Ordained Priest 26; Titular Archbishop of Calcedonia 58-; Vicar-Gen. for Rome 68-; also Deputy for Ordinary Affairs, Secretariat of State, Vatican; created Cardinal by Pope Paul VI 67.
Secretariat of State, Palazzo Apostolico Vaticano, Vatican City, Rome, Italy.

Delle Fave, Umberto; Italian politician; b. 13 Dec. 1912; ed. San Severo, Naples, Milan and Ancona.
Branch Dir., Fed. of Catholic Graduates; mem. Christian Democrat Party, Political Sec., Jesi 44, Provincial Sec. for Ancona 45, Dir. Labour Problems Dept. 52-53, 59-60; mem. Chamber of Deputies 48-, Under-Sec. to Ministry of Labour 53-58, Under-Sec. to Ministry of Posts and Telecommunications 58, later Under-Sec. to Presidency of Council of Ministers; Minister-Sec. of State 63, Minister without Portfolio 63; Minister of Labour and Social Security 64.
Chamber of Deputies, Rome, Italy.

Delmer, (Denis) Sefton, O.B.E.; British journalist; b. 24 May 1904; ed. St. Paul's School, London and Lincoln Coll., Oxford.
Joined *Daily Express* 27, Berlin Corresp. 28-33, Paris Corresp. 33-36, War Corresp., Spanish Civil War 36-38, Chief European Reporter from 37, War Corresp. Poland 39, and with French Army 39-40; with Foreign Office 41-45; rejoined *Daily Express* 45-59; Editorial Adviser to *Der Spiegel*, Hamburg 63-64.
Publs. *Trail Sinister* 61, *Black Boomerang* 62, *Die Deutschen und ich* 62.
Valley Farm, Lamarsh, Near Bures, Suffolk, England.

Del Monaco, Mario; Italian singer; b. 1919; ed. Scuola d'Arte, Pesaro.
Début in *Madame Butterfly* (Teatro Puccini, Milan) 40; La Scala début in *La Bohème* 43; foreign début Royal Opera House, Covent Garden (London) 45; American début in *Manon Lescaut* (New York Metropolitan Opera House) 50; South American début in *Otello* (Teatro Colon, Buenos Aires) 50; has appeared in numerous films; Arena d'Oro 55, Orfeo d'Oro 57, Maschera d'Oro 58.
c/o Metropolitan Opera Association, 147 West 39th Street, New York City 18, N.Y., U.S.A.

de Loës, Charles, LL.D.; Swiss businessman and banker; b. 30 Aug. 1895; ed. Mulhouse Coll., and Univs. of Geneva and Berne.
Partner, Hentsch and Co., Bankers, Geneva 30-; Vice-Chair. Helvetia-Vie, Life Insurance Co., Geneva 32; Vice-Chair Société Générale pour l'Industrie, Geneva 43; Dir. Helvetia Accident Insurance Co., Zürich 47; Dir. Crédit Foncier Suisse, Zürich 49; Chair. of Board Swiss Bankers' Asscn., Basle 50; Dir. Int. Chamber of Commerce, Paris 51; Chair. Soc. Int. pour Participations Industrielles et Commerciales S.A., Basle 58.
Ch. Belle-Fontaine 10, Cologny, Geneva, Switzerland.

Deloffre, Paul Claude Marie; French executive; b. 20 Aug. 1902; ed. Lycée de Nogent, Ecole Nat. Supérieure des Arts Décoratifs.
President and Dir.-Gen., Entreprise Deloffre, S.A.; Pres. and Dir.-Gen., Compagnie Industrielle des Matériaux de Construction; Admin., Banque de l'Entreprise, Forges de Clairvaux, Perforations Pinchard Deny, Soc. La Vermiculite et Perlite, Plâtrières de l'Ouest Parisien (plaster works), Immobilière d'Etudes et de Gestion; Vice-Pres. Union Int. des Entrepreneurs de Plâtrerie; Admin. Chambre Syndicale de Maçonnerie (Masonry); Croix de Guerre (39-45).
Office: 201 rue des Voies-du-Bois, Colombes (Hauts-de-Seine); Home: 2 rond-point Saint-James, Neuilly-sur Seine (Hauts-de-Seine), France.

Delon, Alain; French actor; b. 8 Nov. 1935.
With French Marine Corps 52-55; independent actor-producer under Delbeau (Delon-Beaume) Productions 64-.
Films include: *Christine* 58, *Faibles Femmes* 59, *Le Chemin des Ecoliers* 59, *Purple Noon* 59, *Rocco and His Brothers* 60, *Eclipse* 61, *The Leopard* 62, *Any Number Can Win* 62, *The Black Tulip* 63, *The Love Cage* 63, *L'Insoumis* 64, *The Yellow Rolls Royce* 64, *Once a Thief* 64, *Les Centurions* 65, *Paris Brûle-t-il?* 65, *Texas Across the River* 66, *Les Aventuriers* 66, *Le Samourai* 67; Stage performance: *Tis Pity She's a Whore* 61 and 62.
51 rue de la Bienfaisance, Paris 8e, France.
Telephone: Laborde 00-64 and 17-75.

Delorme, Jean; French engineer and businessman; b. 25 Oct. 1902; ed. Ecole Nat. Supérieure des Mines, Paris.
Pres. and Dir.-Gen. Air Liquide 45-; Pres. and Dir.-Gen. Soc. d'Oxygène et d'Acétylène d'Extrême Orient, American Air Liquid Inc.; Chair. Canadian Liquid Air; Vice-Pres., La Soudure Autogène Française, Società per l'Industria dell'Ossigeno e di Altri Gas (Milan), La Oxigena S.A. (Buenos Aires), Comité Parlementaire Français du Commerce; Dir. Crédit Lyonnais, Compagnie Générale des Eaux, Soc. des Produits Azotes, etc.; Pres. Soc. d'Oxygène et d'Acétylène de Madagascar, Eurospace, etc.; mem. Board French Nat. Cttee. Int. Chamber of Commerce, Inst. France-Canada, Asscn. Française d'Action Artistique, etc.; Croix de Guerre, Médaille de la Résistance, Commdr. Légion d'Honneur.
Publ. *La Mer et l'Espace*.
Office: 75 quai d'Orsay, Paris 7e; Home: 1 Avenue du Maréchal Manoury, Paris 16e, France.

De Los Angeles, Victoria; Spanish singer; b. 1 Nov. 1923; ed. Univ. and Conservatoire of Barcelona.
Barcelona début 45, Paris Opera and La Scala, Milan 49, Royal Opera House, Covent Garden, London 50, Metropolitan Opera House, New York 51, Vienna State Opera 57; numerous appearances at other opera houses, concert tours and recordings; 1st Prize, Geneva Int. Competition 47; Cross of the Order of Isabel the Catholic and numerous other orders and decorations.
c/o Señor E. Magriña, Paseo de Gracia, 87-7-D, Barcelona, Spain.

Delouvrier, Paul; French civil servant; b. 25 June 1914; ed. Collège Saint-Etienne, Strasbourg, Faculté de Droit and Inst. d'Etudes Politiques, Paris.
Inspector, Ministry of Finance 41; Dir. Finance Division, Monnet Plan Commissariat General 46-47; Dir. du Cabinet, Ministry of Finance 47-48, Dir.-Gen. of Taxes 48-53; Sec.-Gen. Interministerial Cttee. on European Economic Co-operation; Dir. of Finance, European Iron and Steel Community 55-58; Delegate Gen. in Algeria Dec. 58-60; Prof. Inst. of Political Studies, Paris; Del.-Gen. Paris Region 61-; Prefect of Paris Region 66-; Prof. Inst. of Housing and Town Planning, Paris Region 62-; Croix de Guerre, Commdr. de la Légion d'Honneur.
7 avenue de Ségur, Paris 7e, France.

Delprat, Daniel Apollonius, DR. JUR.; Netherlands shipowner; b. 10 Jan. 1890; ed. Amsterdam High School and Univ. of Amsterdam.
Joined Nederland Line Royal Dutch Mail 15, apptd. rep. in Neths. East Indies 20, Man. Dir. 27-, Chair. 57, Dir. 58; Chair. Royal Netherlands Navigation Co.; Hon. Chair. Amsterdam Chamber of Commerce; first Vice-Pres. and mem. First Chamber, States-Gen.; Knight, Order of Neths. Lion; Grand Officer Order of Orange-Nassau; Commdr. Légion d'Honneur; Commdr. 1st Class Order of Vasa, 1st Class Order of Merit, Austria.

Publs. *Treatise on Through Bills of Lading* 15, *Treatise on Flag Discrimination* 52.
Museumplein 7, Amsterdam, Netherlands.
Telephone: 73-66-90.

De Lullo, Giorgio; Italian actor and theatre producer; b. 24 April 1921; ed. Accad. Nazionale d'Arte Drammatica, Rome.
Joined Compagnia Ninchi-Pagnani 45; founder-mem. Piccolo Teatro, Milan and Rome; founded Compagnia dei Giovani with R. Falk, R. Valli and A. M. Guarnieri 55; numerous tours in Europe including World Theatre Season, London 65, 66; produces open-air theatre seasons in Florence, Capri and Verona; St. Vincent Prize 58 for production *D'amore si muore* (Patroni-Griffi); Gold Medal 60.
Via Appia Antica 140, Rome, Italy.

Delvaux, Louis, D.IUR.; Belgian lawyer; b. 21 Oct. 1895.
Law practice at Jodoigne; Catholic Deputy 36-46; Min. of Agriculture 45; Judge, Court of the ECSC 52-58; Judge, Court of the European Communities 58-67; legal adviser, Banque Nat. de Belgique 48-.
Home: 30 Boulevard d'Avranches, Luxembourg, Grand Duchy of Luxembourg; and 11 avenue des Commandants, Borlée, Jodoigne, Belgium.
Telephone: 264-36 (Luxembourg); 811-22 (Jodoigne).

Delvaux, Paul; Belgian artist; b. 97; ed. Brussels Acad. of Fine Arts.
Began as a painter of portraits, land- and sea-scapes; after travel in France and Italy adopted the surrealistic style; has executed murals in the Kursaal, Ostend, Institut de Zoologie, Liège, and in private houses in Brussels; Prof. Inst. Nat. Supérieur d'Architecture et des Arts Décoratifs, Brussels; exhbn. at Piccadilly Gallery, London 66.
Institut National Supérieur d'Architecture et des Arts Décoratifs, Brussels, Belgium.

Del Vecchio, Gustavo, DR.IUR.; Italian economist; b. 22 June 1883.
Professor of Political Economy and Finance, Univ. of Trieste 20-26, Univ. of Bologna 26-49, Univ. of Geneva 43-45, Univ. of Rome 49-; Pres. of Statistical Comm. for War Damage at Ministry of Reconstruction 45; Ministry of the Treasury 47-48; Gov. Int. Monetary Fund 48-49; mem. of Nat. Council of Econs. and Work 58-; co-editor of *G. d. Economisti*; editor of Econ. and Statistical sections of *Enciclopedia Italiana*; Assoc. of Acad. of Science Bologna and Accademia dei Lincei, Rome; Fellow Econometric Soc. of Chicago; Pres. Società Italiana di Statistica, Demografia ed Economia.
Publs. *Prodotto netto e monopolio* 05, *Ricchezze immateriali e capitali immateriali* 08, *Cronache della lira in pace e in guerra* 32, *Vecchie e nuove teorie economiche* 32, *Ricerche sulla teoria generale della moneta* 33, *Progressi della teoria economica* 36, *Politica economica* 37, *Dinamica economica* 37, *Economia pura* 39, *La sintesi economica e la teoria del reddito* 50, *Introduzione alla Finanza* 57, *Capitale e interesse* 56, *Economia Generale* 60, *Scritti di Teoria Economica e di Statistica* 66.
Via Acherusio 36, Rome (140), Italy.
Telephone: 8310653.

de Maizière, General Ulrich; German army officer; b. 1912; ed. Humanistisches Gymnasium, Hanover.
Army service 30, commissioned 33; Battalion and Regimental Adjutant, 5th Prussian Infantry Regt.; Gen. Staff Coll., Dresden 39; during Second World War Gen. Staff Duties with 14th Motorized Infantry Div., G3 of 10th Infantry Div., wounded 44, at end of war G3 in Operations Div. Gen. Army Staff; Prisoner-of-war 45-47; dealer in books, sheet music and musical instruments 47-51; Office of Fed. Commr. for Nat. Security Affairs 51; Col. and Chief of Ops. Branch, Fed.

Armed Forces Staff 55; Commdr. of Combat Team A1 and Commdr. 1st Brigade 58; Deputy Commdr. 1st Armoured Infantry Div. 59; Commandant, Fed. Armed Forces School for Leadership and Character Guidance 60-62, Fed. Armed Forces Command and Staff Coll. 62-64; Chief of Army Staff 64-66; Chief of Fed. Armed Forces Staff 66-; Commandeur Légion d'Honneur 62, Frieherr vom Stein-Preis 65; Commdr. Legion of Merit 65.
c/o Bundesministerium der Verteidigung, 53 Bonn, Ermekeilstrasse 27, German Federal Republic.

Demant, Rev. Vigo Auguste, B.SC. (Eng.), D.LITT.; British theologian; b. 8 Nov. 1893; ed. Univs. of Durham and Oxford and Ely Theological Coll.
Assistant Curate St. Thomas's, Oxford 19-23, St. Silas, Kentish Town, London 29-33; Dir. of Research, The Christian Social Council, London 29-33; Vicar of St. John the Divine, Richmond, Surrey 33-42, Canon of St. Paul's, London 42-49; Gifford Lecturer (St. Andrews) 56-58; Prof. of Moral and Pastoral Theology and Canon of Christ Church, Oxford.
Publs. *God, Man and Society* 33, *Christian Polity* 36, *The Religious Prospect* 39, *Theology of Society* 47, *What is Happening to Us* (Broadcast Talks) 49, *Religion and the Decline of Capitalism* 52, *A Two-Way Religion* 57, *Christian Sex Ethics* 63.
Christ Church, Oxford, England.
Telephone: Oxford 43887.

Demarteau, Joseph, DOC. en DROIT; Belgian journalist; b. 19; ed. Coll. Saint Servais, Liège, and Univ. of Liège.
Asst., Univ. of Liège 42; barrister 42; Sec. *Gazette de Liège* 44, Dir. and Editor-in-Chief 59-; mem. Christian Social Party; medal *Pro Ecclesia et Pontifice*, Officier Ordre Mérite Civil Espagnol, Chevalier Ordre de la Couronne, and other foreign orders.
23 rue de Waroux, Liège; Home: 5 place Emile Dupont, Liège, Belgium.
Telephone: 23-70-03.

de Martino, Ciro; Italian banker; b. 12 Dec. 1903; ed. Università degli Studi, Rome.
Former Prof. of Econs. and Finance; joined Banca d'Italia 27, Sec. to Vice Gen. Man. 32-34, Head of Accounting and Admin. Div. 52-57, Gen. Inspector and Head of Banks Control Div. 60-65; Pres. Board of Dirs. Banco di Sicilia, Palermo 65-; Pres. Regional Cttee. Econ. Planning of Molise 65; Adviser for Econ. and Banking Affairs Montenegro 41; Rep. of Banca d'Italia in exchange Cttee. of the currency 47; Chair. Interbanks Cttee. Eastern Africa 48; Banking Adviser to Admin. of Somalia 50; Grande Ufficiale al Merito della Repubblica, Gold Medal al Merito Direttivo.
Via Generale Magliocco, Palermo, Sicily, Italy.

De Martino, Francesco; Italian university professor and politician; b. 31 May 1907; ed. Liceo Gianbattista Vico, Naples, and Univ. degli Studi, Naples.
Professor of History of Roman Law, Univ. of Naples 34-38, Univ. of Messina 38-40, Univ. of Bari 40-50, Univ. of Naples 50-; mem. Chamber of Deputies 48-; Sec. Partito Socialista Italiano 64-66; Joint Sec. Unified Italian Socialist Party 66-.
Publs. *Storia della Costituzione Romano*, Vol. 5, and numerous legal, historical and political articles.
Direzione del P.I.S.U., Via del Corso 476, Rome; and Via Aniello Falcone 258, Naples, Italy.

De Mel, Most Rev. Hiyanirindu Lakdasa, D.D.; Ceylonese ecclesiastic; b. 24 March 1902; ed. The Royal Coll., Colombo, Keble Coll., Oxford, and Cuddesdon Theological Coll.
Curate, Kennington, London 26, Kandy, Ceylon 27-29; Incumbent, Baddegama 29-40; Vicar of St. Paul's, Kandy 40; Officiating Chaplain, 34th Indian Div. 42-45; Asst. Bishop of Colombo 45-50; Bishop of Kurunagala 50-62; Bishop of Calcutta and Metropolitan

of Church of India, Pakistan, Burma and Ceylon 62-. Bishop's House, 51 Chowringhee Road, Calcutta 16, India.

De Menil, John, B.A., LL.B.; American (b. French) business executive; b. 4 Jan. 1904; ed. Univ. of Paris. Vice-President Banque Nat. pour le Commerce et l'Industrie, Paris 32-38; Pres. Schlumberger Overseas and Schlumberger Surenco, Houston 41-57; Chair. Exec. Cttee., Dir. Schlumberger Ltd., Houston 58-, Chair. of the Board 68-; Dir. Bank of Southwest, Houston; Dir. Istel Fund Inc.; Trustee Museum Fine Arts, Houston, Amon Carter Museum of Western Art, Fort Worth, Museum of Primitive Art New York, Museum of Modern Art, Inst. of Int. Educ.
Home: 3363 San Felipe Road, Houston 19, Texas; Office: 277 Park Avenue, New York, N.Y., U.S.A.

Dementyev, Pyotr Vasilevich; Soviet government official; b. 1907; ed. Zhukovsky Air Force Engineering Acad.
With Aircraft Industry 31-53; Minister Aviation Industry 53-57; Chair. State Cttee. Aircraft Industry 57-65; Minister of Aircraft Industry 65-; mem. Central Cttee. Soviet Communist Party 56-; Deputy to U.S.S.R. Supreme Soviet; Order of Lenin (five times), Order of Red Banner, Order of Red Banner of Labour, etc.; Hero of Socialist Labour, Gold Medal *Hammer and Sickle*.
Ministry of Aircraft Industry, Moscow, U.S.S.R.

Demetriadis, Phokion; Greek journalist and cartoonist; b. 18 Nov. 1894; ed. National School of Languages and Commerce, Istanbul.
Journalist 22-; regular contributor to Athens *Vima, Ta Nea* and to *Makedonia* of Thessaloniki; European and World first prizes in World Political Cartoonists' Competition, Los Angeles 61.
Publs. *Shadow over Athens* 45, *The Spotted Goat* 50, *With the Cartoonist's Eye* 59.
3rd September Street 174, Athens, Greece.
Telephone: 871381.

Demichev, Pyotr Nilovich; Soviet politician; b. 1918; ed. Moscow Mendeleev Chemical and Technological Inst.
Soviet Army 37-44; Instructor, Moscow Mendeleev Chemical and Technological Inst. 44-45; Party Work 45-56; Sec. Moscow Regional Cttee. C.P.S.U. 56-58; Business-Man. U.S.S.R. Council of Ministers 58-59; First Sec. Moscow Regional Cttee., C.P.S.U. 59-60; First Sec. Moscow City Cttee., C.P.S.U. 60-61; Sec. C.P.S.U. Central Cttee. 62-, mem. 61-; mem. C.P.S.U. Central Cttee. Bureau for R.S.F.S.R.; Alt. mem. Politburo C.P.S.U. Central Cttee. 64-; Deputy to U.S.S.R. Supreme Soviet; Order of Lenin 68.
C.P.S.U. Central Committee, 4 Staraya Ploshchad, Moscow, U.S.S.R.

Demidova, Alexandra Ivanovna; Soviet politician; b. 1916; ed. Kaluga Agricultural School and Higher Party School.
Laboratory worker 35-38; Agronomist 38-50; Sec. Dzerzhinsky District Cttee. of C.P. 50-61; Chair. "Svetly Put" Collective Farm 51-52; First Sec. Lev-Tolstovsky District Cttee. of C.P., Chief of Section of Regional Cttee. of C.P., First Sec. Tartussky District Cttee. of C.P. 52-61; Sec. Kaluga Regional Cttee. of C.P. 61-66; Chair. Exec. Cttee. Kaluga Regional Soviet of Workers' Deputies 66-; Deputy to R.S.F.S.R. Supreme Soviet; mem. C.P.S.U. 44-.
Kaluga Regional Soviet of Workers' Deputies, Kaluga, U.S.S.R.

Demiéville, Paul; French orientalist; b. 13 Sept. 1894. Mem. Ecole française d'Extrême-Orient, Hanoi 19-24; Prof. Univ. of Amoy, China 24-26; mem. Maison Franco-Japonaise, Tokyo 26-30; Prof. School of Oriental Languages, Paris 31-45; Dir. of Studies, Ecole des Hautes Etudes, Paris 45; Prof. of Chinese

Language and Literature, Coll. de France 46-64; mem. Inst. de France (Acad. des Inscriptions et Belles-Lettres).
234 boulevard Raspail, Paris 14e, France.
Telephone: 033-41-84.

Deming, Frederick Lewis, A.B., A.M., PH.D.; American banker and government official; b. 12 Sept. 1912; ed. Woodward Grammar School, Cleveland High School, and Washington Univ., St. Louis, Missouri.
Federal Reserve Bank of St. Louis 41-57, Asst. Man. Research Dept. 41-47, Man. 47-48, Asst. Vice-Pres. 48-50, Vice-Pres. 51-52, First Vice-Pres. 53-57; Pres. Federal Reserve Bank of Minneapolis 57-65; Under-Sec. of Treasury for Monetary Affairs 65-.
1510 Dumbarton Rock Court, Washington, D.C. 20007, U.S.A.

Deming, Olcott Hawthorne, B.A.; American diplomatist; b. 28 Feb. 1909; ed. Rollins Coll., and Univ. of Tennessee.
Research Asst., Tennessee Valley Authority 35-37; school teacher 37-41; Office of Co-ordination of Inter-American Affairs 41-43; joined Dept. of State as Div. Asst. 43; Act. Exec. Sec. Interdepartmental Comm. on Scientific and Cultural Co-operation 46, Exec. Sec. 47; First Sec. Bangkok 48, Tokyo 51; Department of State 53-57; Special Asst. Office of Asst. Sec. for Int. Organisation Affairs 56; Counsellor and Consul-Gen. Tokyo 57; Public Affairs Adviser, Bureau of African Affairs 59; Dir. Office of East and South African Affairs 60; Amb. to Uganda 63-66.
c/o Department of State, Washington, D.C., U.S.A.

Demirel, Suleiman; Turkish engineer and politician; b. 1924; ed. Istanbul Technical Univ.
Qualified engineer; worked in U.S.A. 49-51, 54-55; with Dir.-Gen. of Electrical Studies, Ankara 50-52; in charge of building various hydro-electric schemes 52-54; Head of Dept. of Dams; Dir.-Gen. of Water Control 54-55; first Eisenhower Fellow for Study in U.S.A. 55; Dir. State Hydraulics Admin. 55-60; Teacher of Engineering, Middle East Technical Univ. 60-64; in private practice 61-65 (consultant to Morrison-Knudsen); Pres. Justice Party 64-; Deputy Prime Minister Feb.-Oct. 65; Prime Minister Oct. 65-.
Office of the Prime Minister, Ankara, Turkey.

Dempsey, John N.; American politician; b. 3 Jan. 1915; ed. Putnam High School and Providence Coll., Rhode Island.
Mayor of Putnam, Connecticut 48-60; Connecticut State Rep. from Putnam 49-53; Lieut.-Gov. of Connecticut 58-61; Gov. of Connecticut Jan. 61-; Chair. New England Governors' Conf. 63, 64; Democrat.
State Capitol, Hartford, Connecticut, U.S.A.

Demus, Otto, DR. PHIL.; Austrian art historian; b. 4 Nov. 1902; ed. Univ. of Vienna.
Asst. Inst. for History of Art, Univ. of Vienna 28-29; keeper of monuments in Carinthia 29-36; monuments officer in Federal Monuments Office 36-39; voluntary emigration to England 39; returned to Austria 46; Pres. Federal Monuments Office 46-; lecturer on history of Art, Univ. of Vienna 37-39, 46-51, Prof. 51-; mem. Vienna Acad. of Science and Inst. of Archaeology; Austrian Cross of Honour for Science and Art (1st class) 59, Fellow, Soc. of Antiquaries 60; Commendatore Dell'Ordine di Merito Della Repubblica Italiana 65.
Publs. *Byzantine Mosaics in Greece* (with E. Diez) 31, *Die Mosaiken von San Marco in Venedig 1100-1300* 35, *Byzantine Mosaic Decoration* 47, *Sicilian Mosaics of the Norman Period* 49, *The Church of San Marco in Venice* 60.
Prinz Eugenstrasse 27, 1030 Vienna III, Austria.

Demuth, Richard H., A.B., LL.B.; American lawyer and financier; b. 11 Sept. 1910; ed. Princeton Univ. and Harvard Law School.

Law Clerk to Fed. Circuit Judge 34-35; practised law in New York with firm of Simpson, Thacher and Bartlett 35-39; Special Asst. to U.S. Attorney-Gen., Office of Solicitor-Gen. 39-42; Asst. to Chief of Procurement Div., Air Technical Service Command 42-45; Legal Adviser, Industry Division, U.S. Mil. Govt. in Germany, mem. Central German Admin. Departments (Economic) Cttee Allied Control Council 45-46; Asst. to Pres., Int. Bank for Reconstruction and Development 46-47, Asst. to Vice-Pres. 47-51, Dir. Technical Assistance and Liaison 51-61, Dir. Development Services Dept. 61-; Asst. to Pres. Int. Finance Corpn. 56-57; led Bank missions to Brazil 49, Surinam 51, Burma 53, Spain 58, Turkey 65.
International Bank for Reconstruction and Development, Washington, D.C.; Home: 5404 Bradley Boulevard, Bethesda, Maryland 20014, U.S.A.

Demy, Jacques; French film director; b. 5 June 1931; ed. Collège de Nantes and Ecole Nationale de Photographie et Cinématographie, Paris.
Prix Louis Delluc 64, Palme d'Or Festival de Cannes 64.
Short films: *Le sabotier du Val de Loire* 57, *Le Bel Indifférent* 58, *Ars* 59; full-length films: *Lola* 60, *La Baie des Anges* 62, *Les Parapluies de Cherbourg* 63, *Les Demoiselles de Rochefort* 66.
86 rue Daguerre, Paris 14e, France.
Telephone: SEG. 57-17.

den Hollander, Franciscus Querien; Netherlands mechanical engineer; b. 1893; ed. Technical Univ. of Delft.
Trained with Holland Railway Co. 16-17; employed by Netherlands Indies State Railways 18-37; Asst. Man. Govt. Artillery Establishments, Hembrug 38-40, Gen. Man. 40; Perm. Under-Sec., Min. of Econ. Affairs 45; Man. Dir. of Traffic, Ministry of Transport 45-46; Gen. Man. and Acting Pres. of Netherlands Railway 46-47, Pres. 47-59; Hon. Life Fellow Perm. Way Inst.; F.R.S.A.; hon. mem. Inst. of Transport, Inst. of Railway Signal Engineers, Inst. of Mechanical Engineers London, Royal Inst. of Engineers The Hague; Knight Order of Netherlands Lion; Grand Officer Order of Orange-Nassau; Officier Légion d'Honneur (France); Hon. Dr. Tech. Sc. (Delft Technological Univ.).
9A Amersfoortseweg, Maarn, The Netherlands.
Telephone: 03432-1355.

Deniau, Jean Francois, D. en D., L. ès L.; French economist and diplomatist; b. 31 Oct. 1928; ed. Univ. of Paris.
Ecole Nationale d'Administration 50-52; Finance Insp. 52-55; Sec.-Gen. Inter-Ministerial Cttee. on European Econ. Co-operation 55-56; Del. to OEEC. 55-56; Del. to Inter-Govt. Conf. on the Common Market and Euratom 56; Head of Mission, Cabinet of Pres. of Counsel 57-58; Technical Adviser, Ministry of Industry and Commerce 58-59; Dir. Comm. on countries seeking association with EEC 59-61; Head of Del., Conf. with States seeking membership of EEC 61-63; Dir. External Econ. Relations, Ministry of Finance and Econ. Affairs (France) 63; Amb. to Mauritania 63-66; Pres. Comm. Franco-Soviétique pour la télévision en couleur; mem. Combined Comm. of EEC, ECSC, and Euratom July 67-.
Publ. *Le Marché Commun* 58, 60.
135 boulevard du Général Koenig, Neuilly sur Seine, France.
Telephone: MAI 10-16.

Denise, Auguste; Ivory Coast politician; b. 3 Feb. 1906.
Secretary-General P.D.C.I. 46; Pres. Conseil-Gen. 47-50; First Vice-Pres. Territorial Assembly 52-57; Pres. Council of Govt. 58-59; Minister of State 59-; mem. Rassemblement Démocratique Africain (R.D.A.).
Office of the Minister of State, Abidjan, Ivory Coast.

Denisov, Georgy Apolinaryevich; Soviet diplomatist; b. 09.
Member of Communist Party 28-; mem. Central Cttee. C.P.S.U. 52-; Sec. Saratov Regional Party Cttee. 55-60; Amb. to Bulgaria 60-63, to Hungary 63-65; Pres. Danube Comm. 63-; Ministry of Foreign Affairs 65-66. c/o Ministry of Foreign Affairs, Moscow, U.S.S.R.

Denisse, Jean-François; French astronomer; b. 16 May 1915; ed. Ecole Normale Supérieure.
Teacher at Lycée, Dakar 42-45; at Centre Nat. de la Recherche Scientifique (C.N.R.S.) 46-47; Guest Worker, Nat. Bureau of Standards, U.S.A. 48-49; Head of Research of C.N.R.S. at Ecole Normale Supérieure 50-51, Dir. of Studies, Inst. des Hautes Etudes, Dakar 52-53; Asst. Astronomer, Paris Observatory 54-56, Astronomer 56-63, Dir. 63-68; Chair. of Board of Nat. Space Research Centre 68-; mem. Acad. des Sciences 67-; Chevalier Légion d'Honneur.
Centre National d'Etudes Spatiales, 129 rue de l'Université, Paris 7e, France.

Denjoy, Arnaud, D.SC.; French mathematician; b. 5 Jan. 1884.
Lecturer in Mathematics Montpellier Univ. 09; Prof. of Mathematics Utrecht Univ. 17 and Strasbourg Univ. 19; Lecturer Paris Univ. 22; Prof. of Differential Calculus Paris Univ. 31; Prof. of Higher Geometry 41; Prof. of Functional Theory 46-56, Prof. Emeritus 55-; Pres. Société Mathématique de France 31-55; Conseiller général du Gers 25-45; First Vice-Pres. Int. Math. Union. 54-58; mem. French Inst. Acad. des Sciences, Section de Géométrie, Royal Acad. of Amsterdam, American Acad. of Arts and Sciences, Boston, Acad. of Belgium, Acad. Nacional de Ciencias, Lima, Polish Acad. of Sciences, and Mathematical Socs. of Moscow, Brussels and Warsaw; awarded Albert I of Monaco Prize of Acad. of Sciences, Paris 38; Hon. Pres. Analysis Conf. of the Int. Congress of Mathematicians, Cambridge (U.S.A.) 50; Hon. mem. Rumanian Acad.; Hon. Prof. Univ. of Moscow 56; Dr. h.c. (Univs. of Warsaw, Utrecht and Bucharest).
Publs. on the theory of sets and functions.
Institut Henri Poincaré, 11 rue Pierre Curie, Paris 5e; Castel Lina, Cap D'Ail (A.M.), France.
Telephone: Paris 805-32-34 (Office); Cap d'Ail 82-23-17 (Home).

Denkstein, Vladimir, PH.D., D.SC.; Czechoslovak National Museum director; b. Feb. 1906; ed. Charles Univ., Prague.
Assistant, Inst. of Art History, Charles Univ., Prague 30-32; Asst. Curator, Regional Museum, České Budějovice 32-40; Asst. Curator, Dept. of Historical Archaeology, Nat. Museum, Prague 40-45, Head Curator 45-56, Dir. of the Nat. Museum, Prague 56-; Editor *Acta Musei Nationalis Pragae*; Chair., Czechoslovak Nat. Cttee. of Int. Council of Museums 58-; Chair., Central Museums Council; dist. for Merits in Construction 66. Publs. *Jihočeská gotika* (South Bohemian Gothic Art) 53, *Lapidarium Národního muzea* (Lapidary of the National Museum) 58, *Pavises of the Bohemian Type* 1, 62, 11, 64, 111, 65.
Lomená 52, Prague 6, Czechoslovakia.

Dennery, Etienne Roland; French diplomatist; b. 20 March 1903; ed. Ecole Normale Supérieure, Univ. of Paris.
Economic expert L.N. Study Comm., Manchuria 32; Prof. Ecole Libre des Sciences Politiques, Paris 32-39; Sec.-Gen. Centre d'Etudes de Politique Etrangère, Paris 35-39; Dir. of Information, Fighting French H.Q., London 41-42; Capt. Artillery, Fighting French Forces Libya and Italy 43-44; Dir. American Section, Ministry of Foreign Affairs, Paris 45-50; Amb. to Poland 50-54, to Switzerland 54-61, to Japan 61-64; Gen. Admin. of Nat. Library and Dir. French Libraries and Public Reading 64-; mem. UNESCO Exec. Council 66-.

Publ. *Foules d'Asie* 30.
8 rue des Petits Champs, Paris 2e, France; and Bibliothèque Nationale, 58 rue de Richelieu, Paris 2e, France. Telephone: Richelieu 32-03.

Denning, Lord Alfred Thompson, P.C., M.A.; British lawyer; b. 23 Jan. 1899; ed. Magdalen Coll., Oxford.
Called to the Bar, Lincoln's Inn 23; K.C. 38; High Court Judge 44; Lord Justice of Appeal 48-57; Nominated Judge for War Pensions Appeals 45-48; Chair. Cttee. on Procedure in Matrimonial Causes 46-47; Lord of Appeal in Ordinary 57-62; Master of the Rolls 62-; Chair. Cttee. on Legal Educ. for Students from Africa 62-; Pres. Birkbeck Coll.; Treas. Lincoln's Inn 64; Head of Security Enquiry 63; Hon. D.C.L. (Oxford) 65.
Publs. *Freedom under the Law* 49, *The Changing Law* 53, *The Road to Justice* 55.
The Lawn, Whitchurch, Hants., England.

Dennison, Admiral Robert Lee, B.S., M.S., D.ENG.; American naval officer; b. 13 April 1901; ed. U.S. Naval Acad., Pennsylvania State Coll., Johns Hopkins Univ.
Ensign 23, promoted through grades to Admiral 59; commanded U.S.S. *Ortolan* 35-37, *Cuttlefish* 37-38, *John D. Ford* 40-41, *Missouri* 47-48; Chief of Staff, Pacific Fleet Amphibious Forces 42-43, 9th Amphibious Fleet 43; mem. Joint War Plans Cttee. (Joint Chiefs of Staff) 44-45; Asst. Chief of Naval Operations (Politico-Mil. Affairs) 45-47; Naval Aide to Pres. of U.S. 48-53; Commdr. 4th Cruiser Div. Atlantic Fleet 53-54; Dir. Strategic Plans Div., Asst. Chief of Naval Operations, mem. Joint Strategic Plans Cttee. 54-56; Commdr. 1st Pacific Fleet 56-58; Dep. Chief of Naval Operations (Plans and Policy) 58-59; C.-in-C. U.S. Naval Forces, Eastern Atlantic and Mediterranean 59-60; C.-in-C. Atlantic Command, Atlantic Fleet and N.A.T.O. Supreme Allied Commdr. Atlantic 60-63; Vice-Pres. and mem. Board Copley Press Inc. 63-; Dir. Atlantic Council 66-; numerous American and overseas decorations.
5040 Westpath Terrace, Washington, D.C. 20016, U.S.A.

Denny, Charles R., A.B., LL.B.; American lawyer; b. 11 April 1912; ed. Amherst Coll., and Harvard Law School.
Served with Dept. of Justice 38-42; as Attorney, Asst. Chief and Chief of the Appellate Section in Lands Division; apptd. Special Asst. to the Attorney General; General Counsel of Federal Communications Comm. 42-45, Commr. 45-46, Chair. of F.C.C. 46-47; Chair. Int. Telecommunications Conf. 47; Exec. Vice-Pres. Nat. Broadcasting Co. 48-58; Vice-Pres. Radio Corpn. of America 58-67; Hon. LL.D. (Amherst Coll.) 48.
Pine Island, Rye, N.Y., U.S.A.

Denny, Ludwell; American journalist; b. 18 Nov. 1894; ed. Chicago Univ., and Meadville Theological School.
Fmr. Diplomatic Correspondent United Press Asscn., News Editor Federated Press and European Correspondent of *The Nation*; Associate Editor Scripps-Howard Newspaper Alliance; Editor *Indianapolis Times* 35-39; Columnist and Foreign Editor Scripps-Howard Newspaper Alliance 51-59, Emeritus 60-.
Publs. *We Fight for Oil* 28, *America Conquers Britain* 30.
1661 Crescent Place, Washington, D.C. 20009, U.S.A.

Denson, John; American journalist; b. 25 July 1903; ed. Briarley Hall Military Acad.
Newspaperman Washington and Midwest 21-27; Washington Corresp. *New York Herald Tribune* 27-29; reporter, *New York World, New York World Telegram* 30-33; Asst. Man. Ed. *Washington Post* 34-35; *Chicago Times* 36-37; Wash. Ed. Int. News Service 37-39; Publicity News Ed. C.B.S. 39-41; Asst. Chief, Wash. Bureau, *Time* magazine 41-44; Asst. Exec. Ed. *Chicago Herald-American* 45; Assoc. Ed. *Fortune* magazine 46; Man. Ed. *Kiplinger* magazine 47-48; Man. Ed., Foreign Ed. and War Corresp. *Colliers* magazine 49-52; Ed.

Newsweek 53-61; Ed. *New York Herald Tribune* 61-62; Special Editorial Adviser *New York Journal-American* 62-65, Exec. Editor 65-66; Editor *Los Angeles Herald-Examiner* 63-65.
570 N. Rossmore St., Apartment 311, Los Angeles, California, U.S.A.

de Oriol y Urquijo, Antonio Maria; Spanish lawyer and politician; b. 15 Sept. 1913; ed. Stonyhurst Coll., England, and Universidad Central de Madrid.
Captain in civil war; later in private business; Dir.-Gen. of Charities and Social Works 57-65; fmr. Pres. Supreme Assembly of Spanish Red Cross; Minister of Justice July 65-; Gran Cruz del Mérito Civil and other decorations.
Ministerio de Justicia, Montabán 14, Madrid; Home: Finca Valgrande, El Plantío (Madrid), Spain.

De Peyer, Gervase, A.R.C.M.; British clarinettist; b. 11 April 1926; ed. King Alfred's School, London, Bedales School and Royal Coll. of Music, London.
Studied in Paris 49; Int. soloist 49-; Founder-mem. Melos Ensemble; Principal Clarinet, London Symphony Orchestra 55-65; Prof. Royal Acad. of Music 59-; recording artist with all major companies; Charles Gros Grand Prix du Disque 61, 62.
70 Wood Vale, Highgate, London, N.10, England.
Telephone: 01-883-4688.

Depoid, Pierre; French statistician; b. 15 Dec. 1909; ed. Ecole Polytechnique, Paris.
Statistician, Statistique générale de France 32-40; Dir. Service commun de Statistique des Sociétés d'Assurances 41-45; Dir. Compagnie d'Assurances générales contre les Accidents 45-51; Dir.-Gen. Compagnies d'Assurances La Prévoyance 52-63; Asst. Dir.-Gen. Compagnie d'Assurances Paternelle-Prévoyance-M.A.C.L. Minerve 64-; Prof. Institut de Statistique, Univ. of Paris 43-; Hon. Pres. Société de Statistique de Paris 63-; Officier de la Légion d'Honneur; Croix de Guerre (39-45).
26 boulevard Haussmann, Paris 9e, France.

De Pous, Jan Willem; Netherlands politician; b. 23 Jan. 1920; ed. Amsterdam Univ.
On staff of *Trouw* 43-46; Fellow Northwestern Univ. Evanston, U.S.A. 47-48; Sec. Christian Employers' Organization in the Netherlands 49-53, Econ. Adviser 53-59; Lecturer, Free Univ. of Amsterdam 53-59; mem. Council of State 58-59; Minister of Econ. Affairs May 59-63; Christian-Historical Union; Pres. Social-Econ. Council.
c/o Social-Economic Council, Bezuidenhoutseweg 60, The Hague; Home: Van Zaeckstraat 65, The Hague, Netherlands.
Telephone: 814341 (Office); 241575 (Home).

Depreux, Edouard Gustave; French lawyer and politician; b. 31 Oct. 1898; ed. Faculty of Law, Paris.
Delegate to Provincial Consultative Assembly 44; Mayor of Sceaux 44-59; Deputy to Constituent Assembly 46-58, Minister of the Interior 46-47, of Nat. Educ. Feb.-April 48, Pres. Socialist Party, Nat. Assembly 46-56; formerly Pres. of High Court of Justice; Nat. Sec. Parti Socialiste Unifié 60-67, Hon. Nat. Sec. 67-; Croix de Guerre (14-18 and 39-45); médaille de la Résistance avec rosette.
Publ. *Renouvellement du socialisme, La Chine Nouvelle et son héritage.*
34 boulevard Desgranges, Sceaux, Seine, France.

Dequae, André, L. ès SC.ECON.; Belgian politician; b. 3 Nov. 1915; ed. Louvain Univ.
Member Chamber of Representatives 46-, Vice-Pres. 58-60, First Vice-Pres. 65-; Minister of Reconstruction 50, of Colonies 50-54, of External Trade 58, of Econ. Co-ordination 60-61, of Finance 61-65; mem. of The Council of Europe and UEO; Christian Social Party; Commdr. de l'Ordre de Léopold, Médaille de la Résistance, Médaille du Souvenir.
St. Elooidreef 36, Kortryk, Belgium.

De Quay, Jan Eduard, D.LITT.; Netherlands politician; b. 01; ed. Utrecht Univ.
Lecturer and later Prof. Tilburg Roman Catholic Univ. 34-46; Labour Organisation Commr. 40; leader Netherlands Union 40-41; Prov. Governor North Brabant 46-59; Minister for War in second Gerbrandy cabinet; Prime Minister and Minister of General Affairs 59-63; Dir. K.L.M. 64-.
c/o K.L.M., The Hague, The Netherlands.

Dereli, Cevat; Turkish artist; b. 1900; ed. Ecole des Beaux Arts, Paris.
Lived in Paris 24-28; Prof. of Painting, Istanbul Acad. of Fine Arts; rep. at numerous exhibitions, including the Venice Biennale 56 and the Brussels Int. Exhibition 58.
Academy of Fine Arts, Istanbul, Turkey.

Deressa, Yilma, B.SC.; Ethiopian politician; b. 21 Sept. 1907; ed. Menelik School, Addis Ababa, Victoria Coll., Alexandria, Egypt, London School of Economics and Georgetown Univ., U.S.A.
Director-General, Ministry of Finance 40, Vice-Minister, Ministry of Finance 42-48; Minister of Commerce and Industry and Pres. Planning Board 48-52; Ambassador to U.S.A. 52-58; Minister of Foreign Affairs 58-60; Minister of Finance 60-; Acting Minister of Mines and State Domain 61-63; Chair. Board of Governors, Haile Selassie I Univ., Addis Ababa 62; Gov. Int. Bank for Reconstruction and Development and assoc. orgs. 65-; Ethiopian and foreign decorations.
Ministry of Finance, P.O. Box 1905, Addis Ababa, Ethiopia.
Telephone: 45559.

De Robertis, Eduardo Diego Patricio, M.D.; Argentine histologist; b. 11 Dec. 1913; ed. Univ. of Buenos Aires.
Rockefeller Fellow, Chicago and Johns Hopkins Univs. 40; at Biophysical Laboratory, Rio de Janeiro 43; Dir. Dept. of Cellular Ultrastructure, Inst. de Investigaciones de Ciencias Biológicas 46; Walker-Ames Prof. Univ. of Washington (Seattle) 53; Prof. Histology, Univ. of Buenos Aires 57-; Dir. Inst. de Anatomía Gen. y Embriología 57-; mem. Argentine Acad. of Sciences, Argentine Research Council; Fellow New York Acad. of Sciences; Mitre Inst. Award, Van Meeter Award; Argentine Nat. Prize; Buenos Aires Gold Medal.
Publs. *Citología General* 46, 52, 55, 65 (English trans. 48, 54 and 65, Japanese trans. 55, Russian trans. 62); *Histophysiology of synapses and Neurosecretion* 64 (French trans.), *Biologia Celular* 6th edn. 65 (English trans. *Cell Biology* 65, Italian trans. 66); more than 200 papers on cytology, thyroid gland, electromicroscopy, neurology and neurochemistry.
Paraguay 2155, Buenos Aires, Argentina.

Deroy, Henri, L. ès L., D. en D.; French banker and company director; b. 12 June 1900; ed. Faculty of Law, Paris, and Ecole Libre des Sciences Politiques.
Entered General Inspectorate of Finance 23; became deputy Dir. of Budget 26, Asst. Dir. 29; Head of various depts. in same organisation 30-35; Dir.-Gen. Caisse des Dépôts et Consignations 35-45, Gov. of Crédit Foncier de France 45-55, mem. Council of Admin. La Banque de France 36-55; Hon. Gov. Crédit Foncier de France; Hon. Pres. Banque de Paris et des Pays-Bas; Pres. Compagnie Int. des Wagon-Lits; Dir. Bank for Int. Settlements, Banque Ottomane, Crédit Foncier de France, Banque Française et Italienne pour l'Amérique du Sud, Crédit foncier franco-canadien, Wendel et Cie., Invest, Electrobel, Hachette, Soc. des Raffineries de Sucre de Saint-Louis, Paribas Corpn., New York, Esso-Standard, Banque de Paris Ltd., London; Prof. of Budgetary Legislation, Ecole des Sciences Politiques 26-47; Grand Officier de la Légion d'Honneur.
Publ. *Œuvres du Moulin-Vert.*
56 avenue Foch, Paris 16e, France.
Telephone: PAS 27-61.

Derthick, Lawrence Gridley, B.A., M.A., LL.D.; American administrator and educationist; b. 23 Dec. 1906; ed. Univs. of Tennessee, Columbia and Chattanooga.
Has held many educational appointments since 27; United States Commr. of Education, Dept. of Health, Education and Welfare 56-61; Asst. Exec. Sec. for Educational Services, Nat. Educ. Asscn. of U.S. 61-.
Publ. *Be Safe and Live* (co-author); numerous educ. and other works.
National Education Association, 1201 16th Street, N.W., Washington 6, D.C., U.S.A.

Déry, Tibor; Hungarian author; b. 18 Oct. 1894; ed. Grammar school and Commercial Acad., Budapest.
As a young office clerk early joined the revolutionary movements, organized strikes; took part in 18-19 revolution; spent several years in exile; in prison 57-60; Kossuth Prize 48.
Publs. Poetry: *Ló Buza Ember, Énekelnek és meghalnak;* Novels: *Országuton, Szemtöl-szembe, A Tengerparti Gyár, A Befejezetlen Mondat, Felelet, Niki, Pesti felhöjáték, G.A. ur X-ben, A Kiközösitö;* Short Stories: *Alvilági Játékok, Jókedv és Buzgalom, Simon Menyhért születése, Hazáról emberekröl, A ló meg az öregasszony, Utkaparo, Szerelem, Theokritosz Ujpesten* I, II; Theatre: *Tanuk, Tükör, Itthon, A csodacsecsemö,* etc.
Krecsànyi-u. 10, Budapest II, Hungary.

de Sá, Mem; Brazilian journalist and politician; b. 10 May 1905; ed. Ginásio Anchieta and Univ. do Rio Grande do Sul.
Member of Nat. Directorate Liberation Party 29-65; Journalist 30-54; Dir. State Statistical Dept. of Rio Grande do Sul 39-45; mem. Legislative Assembly Rio Grande do Sul 51-54; Supplementary Senator 54, Senator 56-; Minister of Justice and Internal Affairs 66-67; Observer of Brazilian Senate at UN 65.
Rua Gago Coutinho 85, Ap. 703, Rio de Janeiro, G.B.; and SQS 105, Bl. 1-Ap. 601, Brasilia, D.F., Brazil.

Desai, Chandulal Chunilal; Indian diplomatist; b. 27 April 1900; ed. Elphinstone Coll., Bombay, Cambridge Univ.
Entered Indian civil service 23; subsequently Asst. Commr. Central Provinces and Berar, Under-Sec. Govt. Central Provinces; Deputy Commr. Buldana District; Deputy Dir.-Gen. of Supply, Govt. of India 42; Controller-Gen. Civil Supplies 43-45; Sec. Indian Tariff Board, Chair. 45-47; Sec. Ministry of States 47-48; visited Australia as leader ECAFE, and Geneva as leader of GATT 48; Sec. Ministry of Commerce 48-51, Ministry of Works, Housing and Supply and Ministry of Production 51-53; leader Indian Del. negotiating trade treaties with Pakistan, Afghanistan, Switzerland, Hungary, Czechoslovakia, Australia and Ceylon 48-51; leader Indian Steel Del. to U.K. and U.S.A.; High Commr. in Ceylon 53-54, in Pakistan 55-59 (retd.); Dir. and Chair. numerous Indian companies; mem. of Lok Sabha (House of the People) 67-.
6 Akbar Road, New Delhi-11, India.
Telephone: 33733.

Desai, Khandubhai K.; Indian politician; b. 23 Oct. 1898; ed. High School, Bulsar and Wilson Coll.
Joined Non-co-operation Movement under Gandhi 20; taught at Gujerat Vidyapith Nat. Inst.; with Labour Union, Ahmedabad 21; elected to Bombay Assembly 37 and to Constituent Assembly 46; served with many Cttees. in the Ministries of Commerce, Industries, Railways and Labour; mem. of Congress Working Cttee., Industrial Finance Corpn. and Employers' State Insurance Corpn.; Minister of Labour 54-57; founded Indian Nat. Trade Union Congress 47, Pres. for three years, and fmr. Gen.-Sec.
Gandhi Majdoor Sevalaya, Bhadra, Ahmedabad, Gujerat, India.

Desai, Shri Morarji Ranchhodji; Indian politician; b. 29 Feb. 1896; ed. Bulsar and Wilson Coll., Bombay.
Served in the Provincial Civil Service in the Bombay Presidency 18-30; joined Civil Disobedience Movement led by Mahatma Gandhi 30, and was convicted for it; mem. of All-India Congress Cttee. since 31; Sec. Gujerat Provincial Congress Cttee. 31-37, 39-46; Min. for Revenue and Forests 37-39; imprisoned in the Quit India Movement for about five years; Home and Revenue Minister, Bombay 46-52; Chief Minister of Bombay 52-56; Union Minister for Commerce and Industry 56-58, Finance Minister 58-63; Deputy Prime Minister and Minister of Finance 67-; mem. Congress Party Parliamentary Board 63; Treas. of Congress 50-58; mem. All India Congress Cttee.; Hon. Fellow, Coll. of Physicians and Surgeons, Bombay; Hon. LL.D. Karnatak Univ.
Ministry of Finance, New Delhi, India.

Desailly, Jean; French actor; b. 24 Aug. 1920; ed. Paris Ecole des Beaux Arts.
Pensionnaire, Comédie Française 42-46; mem. Renaud-Barrault Company 57-; plays include: *La Nuit du Diable, Le Bossu, Malatesta, Le Procès, On ne badine pas avec l'Amour, Le Château, Madame Sans-Gêne, Tête d'Or, La Cerisaie, Le Marchand de Venise, Comme il vous plaira, Hamlet, Andromaque, le Soulier de Satin, Il faut passer par les nuages, le Mariage de Figaro;* films include *Le Père Goriot, La Symphonie Pastorale, Le Point du Jour, Occupe-toi d'Amélie, Si Versailles m'était Conté, Les Grandes Manoeuvres, Maigret tend un Piège, Les Grandes Familles, Le Baron de l'Ecluse, Plein Soleil, la Mort de Belle, Un soir sur la plage, les Sept Péchés capitaux, les Amours célèbres, l'Année du bac, la Peau douce, le Doulos, les Deux Orphelines.*
53 quai des Grands Augustins, Paris 6e, France.

Desbordes, Joseph-Noël; French steel executive; b. 23 Dec. 1898; ed. Ecole Polytechnique.
President-Director-General Havre Drawing and Rolling Mills until 62; Vice-Pres. Dir.-Gen. Tréfimétaux (merger of Havre Drawing and Rolling Mills and French Metal Co.) 62-; Officier, Légion d'Honneur.
Tréfimétaux, 28 rue de Madrid, Paris 8e; Home: 17 Avenue Paul Doumer, Chatou (Seine-et-Oise), France.

Desbrière, Georges; French business executive; b. 25 Nov. 1901; ed. Ecole Centrale des Arts et Manufactures and Ecole Supérieure d'Electricité.
Engineer, Compagnie Française des Métaux 25-32, Sec.-Gen. 32-38, Dir. Gen. 38-47, Administrator Dir.-Gen. 47-52, Vice-Pres. Dir.-Gen. 52-56, Pres. Dir-Gen. 56-62, Pres. of Société Tréfimétaux (merger of Tréfileries et Laminoirs du Havre and Compagnie Française des Métaux) 62-, now Vice-Pres. of Péchiney; Administrator of Crédit Industriel et Commercial, Sidelor, Comptoir Lyon-Alemand, Fonderie de Précision, Trafilerie E Laminatori Di Metalli, Pres. Chamber of Commerce and Industry, Paris 60-63; mem. Conseil Economique et Social; Commdr. Légion d'Honneur, Commdr. du Mérite Commercial et du Mérite Touristique.
28 rue de Madrid, Paris 8e, France.

Descamps, Albert Louis; Belgian theologian and university official; b. 27 June 1916; ed. Collège St.-Léon, Bruges, Petit Séminaire de Bonne-Espérance, Catholic Univ., Louvain and Institut Biblique Pontifical, Rome.
Professor, Great Seminary of Tournai 47-55; Lecturer, Catholic Univ., Louvain 52; Prof., Faculty of Theology, Catholic Univ., Louvain 53-60; Pres., Holy Ghost Coll. 56-60; Pres., Institut Supérieur des Sciences Religieuses 54-60; Rector, Catholic Univ. of Louvain 62-; Titular Bishop of Tunis 60-; mem. Studiorum Novi Testamenti Societas, Cambridge 57-, mem. Société des Sciences, des Arts et des Lettres du Hainaut, Société scientifique de Bruxelles; Officier Ordre de Léopold.

Publs. *Le Peuple de Dieu* 56, and numerous articles.
13 Oude Markt, Louvain, Belgium.
Telephone: 016-20431.

Descamps, Eugène; French metallurgist and trade unionist; b. 17 March 1922.
Secretary-Gen. Union Métaux de la Sidérurgie de l'Est 50-54; Sec.-Gen. Metallurgical Fed., French Democratic Confed. of Labour (C.F.T.C.) 54-61, Sec.-Gen. of C.F.T.C. re-named French Confed. of Labour (C.F.D.T.) 64-; Vice-Pres. Int. Metallurgy (C.I.S.C.) 57, mem. of Staff (C.I.S.C.) 57-64; mem. Econ. Advisory Council 58-59, mem. Econ. and Social Council 59-65.
26 rue Montholon, Paris 9e, France.

Desch, Kurt; German publisher; b. 2 June 1903; ed. Oberrealschule.
Formerly in advertising and journalism, including *Frankfurter Zeitung* and *Dortmunder General-Anzeiger*; expelled from Reichsschrifttumskammer 36; with Zinnen-Verlag, Vienna and Munich 41-44; escaped to Tirol 44; took over Zinnen-Verlag and founded his own firm, Kurt Desch, Munich, and Theaterverlag Kurt Desch Nov. 45 (branches in Basle and Vienna 53); founded Deutscher Laienspielverlag, Weinheim 47, Welt im Buch 53, Kurt Desch Film G.m.b.H., Munich 57.
Desch-Insel an der Romanstrasse 7-9, Munich 19, German Federal Republic.

Deschamps, Hubert; French colonial governor and university professor; b. 22 July 1900; ed. Univ. de Paris à la Sorbonne, Ecole Nationale de la France d'Outre-Mer and Ecole Nationale des Langues Orientales Vivantes.
Professor, Casablanca 21-22; Colonial Administrator, Madagascar 26-36; Asst. to Léon Blum 36-38; Prof. Ecole Nat. des Langues Orientales Vivantes 36-38, Gov. 38-50; Asst. to Sec. of State for France Overseas 54-55; Research Posts 50-62; Prof. of Modern African History, Univ. of Paris 62-.
Publs. *Madagascar, Les Religions de l'Afrique noire, Les Institutions politiques africaines, Les Méthodes et les doctrines coloniales de la France, Histoire de Madagascar, Afrique noire Précoloniale, L'Afrique au XXe siècle* and others.
30 rue Jacob, Paris 6e, France.

Deschamps, Paul; French art critic; b. 19 Sept. 1888; ed. Ecole nationale des Chartes.
Honorary Keeper of the Musée National des Monuments Français (Palais de Chaillot); Hon. Dir. Office de Documentation sur les Monuments Historiques; Hon. Prof. Ecole nationale des Chartes; Hon. Prof. Ecole du Louvre, Hon. Dir. of Studies 55; mem. Institut de France (Acad. des Inscriptions et Belles-Lettres); Commdr. Légion d'Honneur.
Publs. *French Sculpture of the Romanesque Period* 30, *Les châteaux des Croisés en Terre Sainte* (2 vols.), Vol. I 34, Vol. II 39; *La Peinture Murale en France; Le Haut Moyen Age et l'Epoque Romane* (with Marc Thibout) 51, *La Peinture Murale en France au début de l'époque Gothique 1180-1380* with Marc Thibout) 63, *Terre Sainte Romane* 64.
37 rue Vaneau, Paris 7e, France.

Deschatelets, Jean-Paul; Canadian lawyer and politician; b. 13; ed. St. Mary's Coll., Montreal.
Lawyer, Montreal; fmr. Counsel, Prices and Trade Board; M.P.; Minister of Public Works 63-65; mem. Senate 66-; Liberal.
The Senate, Ottawa, Canada.

de Seversky, Major Alexander P., H.S.; American aeronautical engineer and consultant, airplane designer, pilot and author; b. 7 June 1894; ed. Imperial Naval Acad. of Russia, Military and Naval Schools Aeronautics, Russia.
Served with Russian Naval Air Service First World War; Vice-Chair. Russian Naval Aviation Mission U.S. and Asst. to Naval Attaché Washington 18; remained in U.S. becoming Inspector Battle Planes, Buffalo District 18-19; Consulting Engineer to U.S. Air Service 21; Founder, Pres., Gen. Manager and Dir. Seversky Aero Corpn. 22-35, Seversky Aircraft Corpn. (now Republic Aviation Corpn.) 31-39; Dir. Republic Aviation Corpn. 39-40; Consultant Chrysler Corpn. 33; Founder Aircraft Ordnance Corpn. 40; special consultant to Sec. of War 45, and his personal rep. atom bomb tests Bikini 46; Lecturer, U.S. Air Univ. 47-; Founder and Pres. Seversky Aviation Corpn. 48-, Electronatom Corpn. 52-; Vice-Pres. and Trustee, Air Force Historical Foundation 54-; Consultant to Chief of Staff U.S. Air Force 57-; invented and designed bombsight 15, universal landing gear for seaplanes 16, first in-flight refuelling system, trailing-edge wing flap, ion propelled aircraft 59, ionic air pollution control system 55; established many speed records including world's record for amphibians Detroit 35; Fellow, New York Acad. of Sciences, Soc. of Experimental Test Pilots, American Inst. of Aeronautics and Astronautics; Royal Soc. of Arts; decorations include Knight of St. George (Russia); U.S. Medal for Merit; Officier de la Légion d'Honneur (France); Hon. D.Sc. (Rollins Coll.) 44, (Southern Univ.) 57.
Publs. *Victory Through Air Power* 42 (also Walt Disney-Seversky adaptation for screen 43); *Air Power: Key to Survival* 50, *America: Too Young to Die* 61.
30 Rockefeller Plaza, New York 20, N.Y., U.S.A.
Telephone: CI 6-3046.

Desguin, Georges Maurice; Belgian journalist; b. 1913; ed. in France.
With *Aero*, Paris, before 39; imprisoned during Second World War; Sec. to Editor *Le Matin*, Antwerp 44-50, Chief Editor 50-53, Man. Dir. 53-; Order of Merit (Italy).
Home: Beau Soleil, 6-8 Eikendreef, Kapellen, near Antwerp; Office: *Le Matin*, 29 Vieille Bourse, Antwerp, Belgium.

de Shalit, Amos, DR.SC.NAT.; Israeli physicist; b. 29 Sept. 1926; ed. Hebrew Univ., Jerusalem and Eidgenössische Technische Hochschule, Zürich.
With Israel Defence Forces 47-49; Research Asst., Princeton Univ. 52; Research Assoc. Massachusetts Inst. of Technology (M.I.T.) 52-53, Saclay, France 53-54; Head, Nuclear Physics Dept., Weizmann Inst. of Science 54-64, Scientific Dir. 61-63, Dir.-Gen. 66-; Visiting Prof. Hebrew Univ., Jerusalem 56-61; mem. Israel Atomic Energy Comm. 56-57; Scientific Consultant to Ministry of Defence 56-58; Pres. Israel Physical Soc. 58; Chair. Cttee. for Promotion of Natural Science Teaching in Secondary Schools 64-; Visiting Prof. Stanford Univ. 60, M.I.T. 60-61; mem. Israel Acad. of Sciences and Humanities 63; Israel Prize 65.
Publs. *Nuclear Shell Theory* 63, and papers in experimental nuclear physics, theoretical nuclear structure, and theory of nuclear reaction.
Weizmann Institute of Science, Rehovoth, Israel.

Deshmukh, Sir Chintaman Dwarkanath, Kt., C.I.E., B.A.; Indian administrator and banker; b. 14 Jan. 1896; ed. Elphinstone Coll., Bombay, and Jesus Coll., Cambridge.
Served in Central Province and Berar as Asst. Commr. Under-Sec. to Govt.; Deputy Commr. and Settlement Officer 19-30; Sec. to second Round Table Conf. 31; Revenue and Financial Sec. Govt. of Central Province and Berar 32-39; Joint Sec. Dept. of Education; Health and Lands Officer on Special Duty, Finance Dept.; Custodian Enemy Property April-Oct. 39; Sec. Central Board of the Reserve Bank of India 39-41; Deputy Gov. Reserve Bank of India 41-43; del. World Monetary Conf. 44; Gov. Reserve Bank of India 43-49; Gov. for India on Int. Monetary Fund and Int. Bank for Re-

construction and Development 46-49; Pres. Indian Statistical Inst. 45-64; Financial Rep. of Govt. of India in Europe and America 49-50; mem. Planning Comm.; Minister of Finance Govt. of India 50-56; Chair. Int. Monetary Fund and Int. Bank for Reconstruction and Development 50; Chair. Univ. Grants Comm. 56-61; Chair. Nat. Book Trust 57-60; Hon. Fellow Jesus College, Cambridge 52; Chair. Admin. Staff Coll. of India, Hyderabad 60-; Pres. India Int. Centre, New Delhi 59-; Vice-Chancellor, Univ. of Delhi 62-67; mem. Board of Trustees, UN Inst. for Training and Research 65-, Vice-Chair. 66-; Chair. Central Sanskrit Board 67-; Ramon Magsaysay Award 59.
Rachana, nr. Engineering College, University Road, Hyderabad 7, A.P., India.

De Sica, Vittorio; French (b. Italian) actor and director; b. 7 July 1901.
Began his career in revue; first appeared on legitimate stage 23; formed his own company with Rissone and Tofano 33; has appeared in films since 17.
Films under his own direction or production in some of which he has acted include: *The Little Martyr, Tomorrow is too Late, Shoe Shine, Bicycle Thieves, Miracle in Milan, Umberto D, Bread, Love and Dreams, Bread, Love and Jealousy, The Sign of Venus, Scandal in Sorrento, Like Father, Like Son, Il Tetto, L'Oro di Napoli, Anna of Brooklyn, La Ciociara, The Last Judgment, Bocaccio 70, Yesterday, Today and Tomorrow, Un mondo nuovo, Matrimonio al Italiana, After the Fox, Woman Times Seven.*
c/o Joseph Burstyn Inc., 113 West 42nd Street, New York 18, N.Y., U.S.A.

de Silva, Charles Percival; Ceylonese politician; b. 12; ed. St. Thomas Coll. Colombo, Univ. of London.
With Ceylon Civil Service 35-50; entered politics 50; elected to Parl. 52; Minister for Lands and Land Development, and Leader of the House 56-59, Minister of Agriculture 59, of Agriculture, Lands, Irrigation and Power 60-63, of Finance 62; of Lands, Irrigation and Power 63-; Leader Sri Lanka Freedom Party 59-60.
Ministry of Lands, Colombo, Ceylon.

Desio, Ardito, F.D.S., F.R.G.S., F.M.G.S.; Italian geologist and explorer; b. 18 April 1897; ed. Dept. of Natural Science, Univ. of Florence (Dr. Geology).
Lecturer of Geology, Univ. of Milan 27-31; Prof. of Geology, Univ. of Milan 31; Dir. Inst. of Geology, Univ. of Milan; led fifteen overseas exploratory expeditions and scientific missions in Libya, Sahara, Ethiopia, Jordan, Iran, Afghanistan, Pakistan (Karakoram), India, Antarctica; leader of the successful expedition to K2 (28,250 feet), second highest peak in the world 54; Patron's Medal.
Publs. include a number of volumes about the geology and geography of Libya, Aegean Islands, Eastern Alps, Karakoram Range (Himalaya), Hindu Kush Range, etc.
Istituto di Geologia, Piazza Gorini 15, 20133 Milan, Italy.
Telephone: 292813.

De Siqueira Freire, Antonio, LL.D.; Portuguese diplomatist; b. 17 April 1918; ed. Univ. de Lisboa.
Entered Ministry of Foreign Affairs 43; served successively in consular and diplomatic posts in Tangier, Ankara, Havana, Santiago, Buenos Aires, Paris, Leopoldville, Beirut and Geneva; Head of Portuguese Del. to EFTA and GATT 67-; Order of Dannebrog (Denmark), Al Merito (Chile), Légion d'Honneur (France).
16 Chemin de Crêts de Champel, Geneva, Switzerland. Telephone: 463113; 357920; 357929.

de Sitter, Lamoraal Ulbo, D.SC.; Netherlands geologist; b. 6 March 1902; ed. Universität Zürich, Univ. de Lausanne and Rijksuniversiteit te Leiden.

Military service 25-26; field geologist, Bataafse Petroleum Mij. (Royal Dutch Shell), Borneo 26-29; field geologist Shell Oil Co., Venezuela 29-31; in Hague Office, Shell 32; Chief Geologist, Java, Bataafse Petroleum 33-34; Univ. of Leiden 34-, Prof. of Structural and Applied Geology 48-; mem. Royal Netherlands Acad. of Science; Hon. mem. Royal Irish Acad. (Science Section); Foreign mem. Geol. Soc. of London; Hon. mem. Soc. Belge de Géologie, de Paléontologie et d'Hydrologie, Geol. Soc. of America.
Publs. *Structural Geology* (2nd edn.) 64, *Geology of the Bergamasc Alps* 49, *Geologic Maps of Central Pyrenees* (1 : 50,000, sheets 1, 2, 3, 4, 5, 6), *Geologic Maps of the Paleozoic of the Cantabrian Mountains* (1 : 50,000, 3 sheets), *Variation in Tectonic Style* 63, *Hercynian and Alpine Orogenies in N. Spain* 65.
Geological Institute, University of Leiden, Garenmarkt 1B, Leiden, Netherlands.

Deslandes, General Venancio; Portuguese air force officer and government official; ed. Military School.
Second Lieut. 28, Cavalry 28-35; Air Force 35-, Officer Commanding Air Base No. 2 51-53, Gen. 58-; fmr. Prof., Inst. of Higher Mil. Studies; Dep. Nat. Assembly; Ambassador to Spain 59-61; Gov.-Gen. and Supreme Commdr. Angola 61-62; decorations from Portugal, Brazil and Spain.
c/o Foreign Office, Lisbon, Portugal.

Desnuelle, Pierre Antoine Edouard; French biochemist; b. 8 Aug. 1911; ed. Lycée Ampère, Lyons, and Univs. of Lyons, Heidelberg and Cambridge.
Professor of Biochemistry, Univ. of Marseilles 46-, Dir. Inst. of Biochemistry, Faculty of Sciences, Marseilles 61-; mem. Nat. Cttee. on Scientific Research 48-; Pres. of Soc. of Biochemistry 60-; Sec. Gen. Int. Union of Biochemistry; Chevalier de la Légion d'Honneur, Officier de l'Ordre Nat. du Mérite, Chevalier des Palmes Académiques.
17 avenue du Colonel-Sérot, Marseilles 8, Bouches-de-Rhône, France.

De Souza, Tori; Ceylonese journalist; b. 11; ed. St. Joseph's Coll., Colombo.
Joined editorial staff, *The Times of Ceylon* 29, Editor 52; Editor-in-Chief of English language publications of The Times of Ceylon Ltd. 54-.
The Times of Ceylon Ltd., P.O. Box 159, Colombo 1, Ceylon.

Dessau, Einar; Danish industrialist and mechanical engineer; b. 17 July 1892; ed. Copenhagen Royal Technical Univ.
With firm of Melchior, Armstrong and Dessau Inc., New York City 16-17; own export business, New York 18-20; Dir. United Breweries and Tuborg Breweries, Copenhagen 20-63; Dir. Tuborg Harbour Crane Co., Crystal Icework Ltd., Danish Brewers' Asscn.; Chair. Vitamon A-S; Pres. Danish Mineral Water Manufacturers' Asscn.; Vice-Chair. Royal Danish Aero Club; Dir. Danish Refrigeration Research Inst.; mem. Cttee. Danish Technical Museum; Vice-Chair. Danish Coll.; Dir. Cité Universitaire, Paris, etc.; on Cttee. of Denmark-America Foundation and of Dano-Belgian Soc.; mem. New York Acad. of Science.
Baunegårdsvej 50, Hellerup, Denmark.

Dessau, Paul; German composer; b. 19 Dec. 1894; ed. High School and Music School Klindworth-Scharwenka.
Conductor in Hamburg, Bremen, Cologne, Mainz and Berlin; three Nat. Prizes; Vaterländischer Verdienstorden in Gold.
Works include: *Lilo Hermann, Thälmann-Kolonne, Lukullus* (opera), *Puntila* (opera), two symphonies, *In Memoriam Bertold Brecht, Six Vietnam Choruses, Three Vietnam Melodramas.*
Zeuthen-Berlin, Karl Marx Strasse 20, Germany.

Dessureault, Jean-Marie; Canadian senator and lumber merchant; b. 30 Dec. 1888; ed. Coll. of the Sacred Heart, Victoriaville, Quebec.
Lumber merchant in Quebec 17-; Pres. Province of Quebec Retail Lumber Dealers' Asscn. 27-28; Vice-Pres. Quebec Forest Products Comm. 31-36; Gov. Province of Quebec, rep. to Imperial Conf. in Ottawa 32; Vice-Pres. Quebec Board of Trade 33-34; mem. E. Canadian Timber Advisory Cttee. to Timber Controller; Pres. J. M. Dessureault Inc.; Proprietor J. M. Dessureault Lumber Co., Quebec; Dir. Windsor Hotel, Montreal; Vice-Pres. Cie. de Courtage Immobilier de Québec Ltée; Dir.-Gen. Trust of Canada, Montreal; Vice-Pres. Quebec Land Co.; mem. Board of Govs. School of Commerce, Laval Univ.; mem. Canadian Senate 45-.
1270 Holland Avenue, Quebec, Canada.

De Staercke, Roger; Belgian industrial official; b. 1902.
President, Fed. of Belgian Industries 62-; fmr. Vice-Pres. Gen. Council of Econs., Nat. Council of Labour; Regent Nat. Bank of Belgium; Pres. Board of Dirs., Belgian Office of Foreign Trade; Administrator Office of Nat. Export Credits Guarantee; Chair. Econ. and Social Cttee., European Econ. Community and Euratom 58-60, Vice-Chair. 60-62.
Fédération des Industries Belges, 4 rue Ravenstein, Brussels 1, Belgium.

Destrée, Jacques (*pseudonym* of Marcel Renet), D. en M.; French doctor, journalist and politician; b. 16 Jan. 1905; ed. Lycée Français, Mayence, the Sorbonne, l'Ecole des Hautes Etudes Historiques and Faculty of Medicine, Paris.
Worked in Paris hospitals and then practised medicine in Montrouge and Paris 33-43; research on stammering 34; active in Resistance Movement from 40; Founder and Dir. of clandestine journal *Résistance*; founded Clandestine Press Federation which later became French Press Federation 43; in German concentration camps 43-45; on return became Gen. Man. of *Résistance*, later of *Ce Matin* and finally Pol. Dir. of *Aurore* 45-67; Senator (R.P.F., Gaulliste) for the Seine 46-52; mem. of Foreign Affairs Comm. and Vice-Pres. of Press Comm.; Commdr. de la Légion d'Honneur; Croix de Guerre (39-45); Rosette de la Résistance; Officier de la Santé publique; Croix du Combattant volontaire.
30 rue de Miromesnil, Paris 8e, France.
Telephone: 265-75-58.

Deswarte, Willem; Belgian lawyer and public servant; b. 6 Sept. 1906; ed. Univs. of Brussels and Geneva.
Practising lawyer, assoc. with Bâtonnier Soudan till 33; then entered S.A. Grands Magasins "A l'Innovation," became Sec.-Gen., Dir., and Admin.-Dir. Gen.; Pres. Tribunal Maritime Belge à Londres 45; Counsellor Ministère des Finances 46; Private Sec. to Prime Minister and later to Minister of Interior 47; Dir.-Gen. Soc. Anonyme Belge d'Exploitation de la Navigation Aérienne (SABENA) 49-; Officier Ordre de la Couronne.
Publs. *La Limitation des Dividendes* 42, *L'Impôt sur le Capital Appliqué aux Sociétés par Actions* 46.
35 rue Cardinal Mercier, Brussels, Belgium.
Telephone: 11-90-60.

de Terra, Helmut, PH.D.; American (b. German) anthropologist; b. 11 July 1900; ed. public school, Marburg (Hesse) and Univ. of Munich.
Assistant, Inst. of Geology, Univ. of Munich 25-27; Instructor and Asst. Prof. Yale Univ. 30-36; Research Assoc. Carnegie Inst. of Washington, D.C. 36-50; Geographer, U.S. Dept. of Interior 42-44; Research Assoc. Wenner-Gren Foundation for Anthropological Research 45-50; Research Assoc. and Adjunct Prof., Columbia Univ. 52-61; Guest Prof. Univ. of Munich 62-63; Dir. Werner Reimers Foundation for Anthropogenetic Research, Frankfurt (Main) 63-66; Silliman Fellow, Yale Univ.; Fellow, Geological Soc. of America;

special research: pleistocene geology of early man in Asia and Mexico and biographical studies of leaders in natural science.
Publs. *Geologische Forschungen in K'un-lun und Karakorum Himalaya* 30, *Geological Studies in the Northwest Himalayas* 35, *Studies on the Ice Age in India and Associated Human Cultures* 39, *Durch Urwelten am Indus* 40, *The Pleistocene of Burma and Java* 44, *Tepexpan Man (Mexico)* 49, *The Life and Times of Alexander von Humboldt* 55, *Man and Mammoth in Mexico* 56, *Studies of the Documentation of Alexander von Humboldt* 58-60, *Memoirs of P. Teilhard de Chardin* 64.
Chalet Montclair, Château d'Oex, Vaud, Switzerland.

Detweiler, Frederick O.; American businessman; b. 6 Aug. 1911; ed. Denison Univ.
Joined Pratt & Whitney Aircraft Div., United Aircraft Corpn. 33, Divisional Accountant and Asst. Sec. 43-46, Man. Mo. plant 45; Div. Controller, Sikorsky Aircraft Div., United Aircraft Corpn. 46-48; Asst. Gen. Man. Chance Vought Aircraft Div. 48-50, Gen. Man. 50-54, Pres. Chance Vought Corporation 54, Chair. 61; Pres. Crown Machine and Tool Co. 61-63; Dir. Texas Bank & Trust Co., Dallas Power & Light Co., Nat. Industrial Conf. Board; Vice-Pres. Dallas Chamber of Commerce.
1001 N. Grand Avenue, Sherman, Texas, U.S.A.

Deulofeu, Venancio, DR. CHEM.; Argentine chemist; b. 1 April 1902; ed. Univ. of Buenos Aires.
Asst., Instituto Bacteriológico, Buenos Aires; Head, Organotherapeutic Section 32-44; Asst. Prof. of Biochemistry, Rosario Univ. 25; Asst. Prof. of Organic Chemistry, Buenos Aires 29, Prof. 39-, Head of Dept. 63-; Asst. Prof. of Biochemistry 31-48; Pres. Argentine Asscn. for the Advancement of Science, 52-57; mem. Bureau IUPAC 47-51, 63-68, Council for Scientific and Technological Research (Argentina) 58-67; Vice-Pres. 64; Vice-Pres. Nat. Inst. for Technological Research 58-65, and mem. of many scientific societies, including Nat. Acad. of Sciences, and Nat. Acad. of Medicine, Buenos Aires; Dr. h.c. Paris, Santiago.
Publs. *Enseñanza e Investigación Científicas* 47, *Curso de Química Biológica* with A. D. Marenzi) (8th edn.) 57.
Parera 77, Buenos Aires, Argentina.
Telephone: 44-1422.

Deupree, Richard R.; American executive; b. 7 May 1885; ed. public schools, Covington, Ky.
Began career as clerk in office of Cincinnati & Covington Street Railway Co. 01-05; associated with Procter & Gamble 05-, beginning as clerk in treasury dept., later various positions in sales dept., Man. Western Sales Div. 12, Gen. Sales Man. 17, Dir. 24-, Gen. Man. 27, Vice-Pres. and Gen. Man. 28, Pres. 30, Chair. 48-59, Hon. Chair. 59-; mem. Directors Advisory Council, Morgan Guaranty Trust Co.; Dir. Cincinnati and Suburban Bell Telephone Co.; Trustee, Equitable Life Insurance Co. of Iowa; during Second World War served as Chief of Agricultural and Forest Products' Division of W.P.B.; apptd. Exec. Chair. Army-Navy Munitions Board; Trustee Emeritus, Cincinnati Inst. for Fine Arts; hon. mem. Business Council; mem. Citizens Advisory Cttee. to President 57; Hon. Trustee, Cincinnati Children's Hospital.
Procter and Gamble, Cincinnati, Ohio 45201; Home: 6305 Park Road, Indian Hill, Cincinnati, Ohio 45243, U.S.A.
Telephone: 562-1100 (Office); 831-2240 (Home).

Deuss, Hanns, DR. RER. POL.; German banker; b. 18 Feb. 1901; ed. Univ. of Cologne.
Trained with Barmer Bank-Verein and Dresdner Bank; with Commerzbank, Berlin 42; after 45 with Bankverein Westdeutschland, Düsseldorf, Dir. 55-; Chair. Buderus'sche Eisenwerke, Deutsche Hypotheken-Bank, Gerling-Konzern Lebensversicherungs A.G., Gerling-

Konzern Speziale Kreditversicherungs A.G., Rudolf Karstadt A.G., Commerzbank A.G.; Dep. Chair. Ausfuhrkredit-A.G., Gerling-Konzern Globale Versicherungs-A.G., Hotelbetriebs-A.G., Schnellpressenfabrik A.G., Phrix-Werke A.G.; Dir. Brown, Boveri & Cie. A.G., Deutsche Centralbodenkredit-A.G., Daimler-Benz A.G., Farbwerke Hoechst A.G. (formerly Meister Lucius & Brüning), and many other companies.
Beckbuchstrasse 28, Düsseldorf-Lohausen, German Federal Republic.

Deutsch, Babette; American writer; b. 22 Sept. 1895; ed. Barnard Coll.
Lecturer Columbia Univ.; Hon. Litt.D. (Columbia Univ.); mem. Nat. Inst. of Arts and Letters, P.E.N.
Publs. *Banners* 19, *Honey Out of the Rock* 25, *A Brittle Heaven* 25, *In Such a Night* 27, *Fire for the Night* 30, *Epistle to Prometheus* 31, *Mask of Silenus* 33, *This Modern Poetry* 35, *One Part Love* 39, *Heroes of the Kalevala* 40, *Walt Whitman: Builder for America* 41, *It's a Secret* 41, *Rogue's Legacy* 42, *The Welcome* 42, *Take Them, Stranger* 44, *The Reader's Shakespeare* 46, *Poetry in Our Time* 52, 56, 63, *Tales of Faraway Folk* (with A. Yarmolinsky) 52, *Animal, Vegetable, Mineral* 54, *Poetry Handbook* 57, 62, *Coming of Age: New and Selected Poems* 59, *Collected Poems 1919-62*, 63, *More Tales of Faraway Folk* (with A. Yarmolinsky) 64, *The Steel Flea* (with A. Yarmolinsky) 64, *Poetry in Our Time* 64, *Poetry Handbook* 64, *Eugene Onegin* (with A. Yarmolinsky) 65; trans. poems from *The Book of Hours*, by Rilke 41, *Two Centuries of Russian Verse* (with A. Yarmolinsky) 66, *I Often Wish* 66, *Poems of Samuel Taylor Coleridge* 67.
300 West 108th Street, New York 25, N.Y. 10025, U.S.A.

De Valéra, Éamon, B.A., B.SC., H. DIP. in EDUC., LL.D., PH.D.; Irish politician; b. New York 14 Oct. 1882; ed. National School, Bruree, Christian Brothers' School, Rathluire, Blackrock Coll., Dublin, Nat. Univ. of Ireland, and Trinity Coll., Dublin.
For many years a student of Irish and active mem. of Gaelic League; joined Irish Volunteers at foundation 13; Adjutant, Dublin Brigade 15-16, and Commdt. in Irish Nat. Insurrection, Easter 16; sentenced to death, commuted to penal servitude for life; released Gen. Amnesty 17; elected Sinn Féin M.P., East Clare 17; Pres. Sinn Féin 17-26, when Fianna Fáil was founded; Pres. Irish Volunteers 17-22; re-imprisoned 18; escaped 19; visited U.S.A. 19-20 and raised loan of six million dollars for Irish Republican Govt.; Pres. Irish Republic 19-22; rejected Anglo-Irish Treaty in Dáil Eireann Dec. 21-Jan. 22; Parl. rep. for East Mayo 18-21; M.P. for Down (N. Ireland) 21-29, for S. Down 33-37; Leader of Opposition in Irish Free State Parl. 27-32; Pres. Exec. Council, Irish Free State and Minister for External Affairs 32-37; introduced new Constitution in Dáil Eireann 37; Taoiseach (Prime Minister) and Minister for External Affairs, Govt. of Ireland 37-48 and Minister of Education 39-40; Leader of Opposition in Dáil Eireann 48-51 and 54-57; Taoiseach (Prime Minister) 51-54, 57-59; Pres. Fianna Fáil 26-59; Pres. Republic 59-; Pres. Council of LN at its 68th and Special Sessions, Sept. and Oct. 32; Pres. Assembly of LN 38; Chancellor Nat. Univ. of Ireland 21-; Grand Cross Order of Pius IX 33, Grand Cross of the Order of Charles 61, Supreme Order of Christ 62; Hon. Bencher of King's Inns; Hon. M.R.I.A., Hon. F.R.C.S.I.; Hon. Ph.D. (Nat. Univ. of Ireland), Hon. D.Sc. (Dublin Univ.), LL.D. h.c.
Aras an Uachtaráin, Phoenix Park, Dublin, Ireland.
Telephone: 72815.

de Valois, Dame Ninette, D.B.E.; British choreographer; b. 6 June 1898.
Prima Ballerina, Royal Opera Season, Covent Garden 19 and 28; British Nat. Opera Company 18; mem. The Diaghileff Russian Ballet 23-26; Choreographic Dir.
to the Old Vic, Festival Theatre, Cambridge, and the Abbey Theatre 26-30; Dir. The Royal Ballet and the Royal Ballet School from its foundation in 31 until 63; Hon. Mus. Doc. (London) 47; Hon. D.Mus. (London, Sheffield, Trinity Coll. Dublin); Chevalier de la Légion d'Honneur 50; Hon. D.Litt. (Reading, Oxford); D.F.A. Smith Coll. Mass. 57; Hon. LL.D. Aberdeen 58.
Choreographic works include: *Job, The Rake's Progress, Checkmate, The Prospect Before Us, Don Quixote.*
Publs. *Invitation to the Ballet* 37, *Come Dance with Me* 57.
c/o Royal Ballet School, 153 Talgarth Road, London, W.14, England.

De Vaucouleurs, Gerard Henri, DR. de L'UNIV. (Paris), D.SC.; American (b. French) astronomer; b. 25 April 1918; ed. Univ. of Paris.
Assistant astronomer, Peridier Observatory 39, 41-42; C.N.R.S. research student, Physics Research Laboratory, Sorbonne 43-45; Research Fellow, Astrophysical Inst. C.N.R.S., Paris 45-49; Science programme, B.B.C. London 50-51; Research Fellow Australian Nat. Univ. at Commonwealth Observatory, Mt. Stromlo 51-54; Observer-in-charge, Yale-Columbia Southern Station, Mt. Stromlo 54-57; Astronomer Lowell Observatory, Flagstaff, Ariz. 57-58; Research Assoc. Harvard Coll. Observatory, Cambridge, Mass. 58-60; Assoc. Prof. Astronomy Univ. of Texas 60-64; Prof. Univ. of Texas 65-; mem. Int. Astronomical Union, Cttee. of (American) Nat. Acad. of Sciences for Exploration of the Moon and Planets, etc.
Publs. *Astronomie* (with L. Rudaux) 48, English, Spanish and Italian trans. 59-67, *Physique de la planète Mars* 51, English trans. 54, Russian trans. 56, *Discovery of the Universe* 56, *Manuel de Photographie Scientifique* 56, *L'exploration des galaxies voisines* 58, *Astronomical Photography* 61, *Reference Catalogue of Bright Galaxies* 64, *A Survey of the Universe* (with D. Menzel and F. Whipple) 68, and about 200 papers.
Department of Astronomy, University of Texas, Austin, Texas 78712, U.S.A.
Telephone: GR1-1426.

Devaux, Louis Armand; French oil executive; b. 5 April 1907; ed. Lycée Louis-le-Grand and Univ. de Paris à la Sorbonne.
With Banque de Paris et des Pays-Bas 27-29; Cartier S.A. 29-46, Pres. 44-46, Chair. Board Cartier Inc., New York 46-49; Pres. Pétroles Toneline S.A. 49-51; Asst. Dir.-Gen. Compagnie des Produits Chimiques et Raffineries de Berre 49-51; Asst. Dir.-Gen. Shell Française 52-60, Pres. Dir.-Gen. 60-67; Pres. Soc. des Pétroles Shell Berre 60-67; Pres. Dir.-Gen. Soc. Le Nickel 67; Dir. Shell Française, Soc. Minière et Métallurgique de Penarroya, The Rio Tinto Zinc Corpn., Cartier Jewellers; Officier Légion d'Honneur, Croix de Guerre.
14 rue Jean-Richepin, Paris 16e, France.

Devitt, Edward James; American judge; b. 5 May 1911; ed. Univ. of North Dakota.
Private legal practice, East Grand Forks, Minnesota 35-39, Municipal Judge 35-39, Asst. Attorney-Gen., Minnesota 39-42, Instructor in Law, Univ. of North Dakota 35-39; St. Paul Coll. 45-; mem. U.S. House of Reps. 47-48; Probate Judge, Ramsey County, St. Paul 50-54, Judge, U.S. District Courts, Minnesota 54-, Chief Judge 58-.
Federal Courts Building, St. Paul, Minnesota 55101, U.S.A.

Devkota, Rajeshwar Prasad; Nepalese poet, journalist and politician; b. 1930; ed. Sanskrit Coll., Varanasi.
Member Nat. Panchayet (legis. chamber of Nepal) 63-, Chair. 64-67; Asst. Minister of Educ. 63-64; Asst. Minister of Agriculture, Forestry and Land Reform 64, Minister 67-.
National Panchayet, Katmandu, Nepal.

Devlin, Baron (Life Peer, cr. 61), of West Wick in the County of Wiltshire, **Patrick Devlin,** Kt., P.C., F.B.A.; British lawyer; b. 25 Nov. 1905; ed. Stonyhurst Coll., and Christ's Coll., Cambridge.

Called to the Bar 29; K.C. 45; Attorney-Gen. to the Duchy of Cornwall 47-48; Justice of the High Court 48-60; Master of the Bench of Gray's Inn 47-; Pres. of Restrictive Practices Court 57-60, British Maritime Law Asscn. 62-; Chair. Cttee. Inquiry into Dock Labour Scheme 56, into decasualisation of Dock Labour 64, Nyasaland Inquiry Comm. 59; Lord Justice of Appeal 60-61; Lord of Appeal in Ordinary 61-63; Chair. the Press Council 64-; Hon. LL.D. (Glasgow) 62, (Toronto) 62, (Cambridge) 66; Hon. D.C.L. (Oxford) 65.

Publs. *Trial by Jury* 56, *Criminal Prosecution in England* 58, *Samples of Lawmaking* 62, *The Enforcement of Morals* 65, *Inside Journalism* 67.

West Wick House, Pewsey, Wilts., England.

Devoto, Giacomo, D.L.; Italian university professor; b. 19 July 1897; ed. Univs. of Pavia, Berlin, Basle, Paris.

Prof. Univ. of Florence 24; Prof. of Linguistics, Univ. of Cagliari 27, Univ. of Padua 30, Univ. of Florence 35; Visiting Prof. Univ. of California 60; mem. Accad. dei Lincei, Accad. della Crusca, German Archæological Inst. at Rome, Lombardy Inst. of Science and Letters, Venice Inst. of Science and Letters, Inst. of Etruscan Studies; Pres. Tuscan Acad. of Science and Letters; mem. of the Institut de France, Acads. of Science of Denmark, Norway, Sweden, Finland, Rumania and Bavaria; Hon. mem. American Soc. of Linguistics; Chevalier de la Légion d'Honneur; Dr. h.c. Univs. of Paris, Strasbourg, Basle, Cracow, Lima, Berlin.

Publs. *Storia della lingua di Roma* (2nd edn.) 44, *Tabulae Iguvinae* (2nd edn.) 40, *Gli antichi Italici* (2nd edn.) 52, *Introduzione alla Grammatica* (3rd edn.) 48, *La lingua omerica* (3rd edn.) 48, *Studi di Stilistica* 50, *Fondamenti della Storia Linguistica* 51, *Profilo della Storia Linguistica Italiana* 53, *Scritti minori I* 58, *II* 67, *Origini Indoeuropee* 62, *Nuovi Studi di Stilistica* 62, *Civiltà di Parole* 65, *Avviamento all'etimologia* 67.

Via di Camerata 25, Florence, Italy.

Telephone: 51403.

Devreesse, Mgr. Robert, D. ès L.; French ecclesiastic; b. 1894; ed. Inst. Catholique de Paris and Ecole des Hautes Etudes, Paris Univ.

French Army 14-19; Chaplain of St. Louis-des-Français 22-26; Greek Scriptor of Vatican Library 26-50; Curator Dept. of Manuscripts, Nat. Library Paris 42-44; Vice-Prefect of Vatican Library 46-50, Emeritus 50-; Chevalier de la Légion d'Honneur, Médaille Militaire, Croix de Guerre.

Publs. *Chaînes Exégétiques Grecques* 28, *Pelagii in Def. Trium Capitulorum* 32, *Catalogue des Manuscrits Grecs du Vatican* 37, 50, *Catalogue des Manuscrits Grecs de la Bibliothèque Nationale (Fonds Coislin)* 45, *Le Patriarcat d'Antioche depuis la Paix de l'Eglise jusqu'à la Conquête Arabe* 45, *Le Commentaire de Théodore de Mopsueste sur les Psaumes* 40, *Essai sur Théodore de Mopsueste* 48, *Les Homélies catéchétiques de Théodore de Mopsueste* (with R. Tonneau) 49, *Introduction à l'Etude des manuscrits Grecs* 54, *Les Manuscrits Grecs de l'Italie méridionale* 55, *Les anciens commentateurs grecs de l'Octateuque et des Rois* 59, *Les Evangiles et L'Evangile* 63.

2 rue Diderot, Asnières (Seine), France.

De Vries, Peter, A.B.; American writer; b. 27 Feb. 1910; ed. Calvin Coll., Michigan, and Northwestern Univ.

Free-lance writer 31-; Assoc. Editor *Poetry* 38, co-Editor 42; joined editorial staff of *New Yorker* 44.

Publs. *No but I saw the Movie* 52, *The Tunnel of Love* 54, *Comfort me with Apples* 56, *The Mackerel Plaza* 58; dramatization of *The Tunnel of Love* (with Joseph Fields) 57, *The Tents of Wickedness* 59, *Through the Fields of Clover* 61, *The Blood of the Lamb* 62, *Reuben, Reuben* 64, *Let Me Count the Ways* 65, *The Vale of Laughter* 67.

170 Cross Highway, Westport, Conn., U.S.A.

Dewall, Hans Werner von, DIPL.ING., DR.ING.; German mining executive; b. 14 Sept. 1901; ed. Berlin Technical High School and Bonn Univ.

Mines official in Prussian Ministry for Trade and Commerce 28-32; with Bergwerksgesellschaft Hibernia (Herne) 32-33; with Bergrevier (Duisburg) 34; Mining Dir. Saargruben A.G. 35-40; Head and Technical Dir. Oberschlesien Mining Admin. 40-45; Mining Dir. and mem. Board Hibernia 48-; Deputy Chair. Unternehmensverband Ruhrbergbau; posts in other mining, chemical, shipping and business concerns.

Unterer Pustenberg 60, 43 Essen-Werden, German Federal Republic.

Telephone: Essen 493422.

De Wet, Carel, B.SC., M.B., B.CH.; South African physician, politician and diplomatist; b. 25 May 1924; ed. Vrede High School, Orange Free State, Pretoria Univ., and Univ. of Witwatersrand.

Medical practice, Boksburg, Transvaal, Winburg, Orange Free State, and Vanderbijlpark, Transvaal; Mayor of Vanderbijlpark 50-52; mem. Parl. 53-63; Amb. to U.K. 63-67; Minister of Planning and Mines 67-.

Ministry of Planning, Pretoria, South Africa.

Dewey, Thomas Edmund, A.B., LL.M.; American lawyer and politician; b. 24 March 1902; ed. Michigan and Columbia Univs.

Admitted to New York Bar 26; with law firm Larkin, Rathbone and Perry 25-27; with McNamara and Seymour 27-31; Chief Asst. U.S. Attorney, Southern District of New York 31-33, U.S. Attorney 33; in private practice 34-35; Counsel to Asscn. of the Bar of the City of N.Y. in Removal of Municipal Justice Harold L. Kunstler 34; Special Asst. to U.S. Attorney-Gen. 34-35; Special Prosecutor, Investigation of Organised Crime in New York 35-37; District Attorney, New York County 37-41; Republican candidate for Gov. State of N.Y. 38, elected 42, 46 and 50-54; Republican, Nominal Candidate for Pres. of U.S. 44 and 48; mem. Dewey, Ballantine, Bushby, Palmer and Wood, N.Y. 55-; awarded medal for excellence, Columbia Univ., in recognition of public service 36; Cardinal Newman Distinguished Service Award, Univ. of Illinois 39; LL.D. (Tufts Coll., Brown Univ., Dartmouth, St. Lawrence Univ., New York Univ., Union Coll., Alfred Univ., Fordham, Colgate, Hamilton Coll., Univ. of Mich., Williams Coll., Columbia Univ., St. Bonaventure Univ., Yeshiva Univ., Rochester Univ.).

Publ. *The Case Against the New Deal* 40, *Journey to the Far Pacific* 52, *Thomas E. Dewey on the Two Party System* 66.

114 E. 72nd Street, New York, N.Y., U.S.A.

Dewitt, J. Doyle; American insurance executive; b. 25 June 1902; ed. Colfax High School and Drake Univ.

Navy service in First World War; joined Travelers Insurance Co., Des Moines, as claim investigator 25, held various managerial positions 33-43, sec. in charge of all Claim Depts. of The Travelers Cos. 43-45, asst. to the Pres. 45-52, Vice-Pres. 50-52, Pres. Travelers Insurance Co., Travelers Indemnity Co. and Charter Oak Fire Insurance Co. 52-64, Chair. of Board 64-; Dir. Hartford Nat. Bank and Trust Co., Veeder Industries Inc., Broadcast-Plaza Inc., Chase Manhattan Bank, United Aircraft Corpn., and many other orgs.; Chair. Exec. Cttee. Int. Claim Asscn. 42-43, Pres. 43-44; a founder Univ. of Hartford; hon. Dr. of Laws, Drake Univ.

Office: 1 Tower Square, Hartford, Conn. 06115; Home: 111 Stoner Drive, West Hartford, Conn., U.S.A.

Dey, Bishnu; Bengali poet; b. 18 July 1909; ed. Calcutta Univ.
Prof. of English, Central Calcutta Coll.
Publs. *Urbasi-o-Artemis* 32, *Chorabali* 36, *Purbolekh* 41, *22nd June* 42, *Shāt Bhai Champā* 45, *Roochi-o-Pragatee* (essays) 46, *Sandipér Char* 47, *The Art of Jamini Roy* (with John Irwin) 45, *Samudrér Mauno* 45, *Caramel Doll* (English trans. of *Abanindranath Tagore's Story*) 46, *Introducing Nirode Mazumdar* 46, *Bengal Painters' Testimony* 46, *Anwista* 50, *Sahityér Bhabisyat* (essays) 52; *Eliotér Kabita* (translations of T. S. Eliot's poems) 53, *Nām Rékhéchhi Komal Gāndhār* 53, *An Introduction to Jamini Roy* 53, *Hé Bidéshi Phul* 57, *Paintings of Rabindranath Tagore, India and Modern Art*; *Alekhya* 58, *Tumi Shudhu Panchisé Baisakh* 58, *Mao Tse-tung* (translations in verse) 58, *Prodosh Das Gupta—His Sculpture* 61, *Élo-mélo-jiban o Silpa-sahitya* (essays) 58, *Sāhityer Désh Bidésh* (essays) 63, *Smriti Sattā Bhabisyat* (poems) 63, *Ékalér Kabita* 63, *Satyendranath Bose, A Legend in His Lifetime* 63, *Sei Andhakār chai* (poems) 66, *Rabindranath-o-Adhunikatar Samasya* (essays) 66, *Michael, Rabindranath-o-anyānya-jigansa* (critical essays) 67, *Rushati Panchāsati* (poems) 67.
9/17 Fern Road, Calcutta 19, West Bengal, India.

Dey, Mukul C., M.C.S.E. (U.S.A.), F.R.S.A., A.R.C.A. (London), F.I.A.L. (Germany), I.E.S. and B.S.E.S.; Indian artist; b. 23 July 1895; ed. Santiniketan School (Bengal). Studied art with Dr. Abanindranath Tagore (Calcutta), and in Japan, Chicago and London; exhibited Indian Soc. of Oriental Art, Calcutta 13, Tokyo 16, Art Int., Chicago 16; studied Slade School of Art, London 20; scholarship Royal Coll. of Art, London 20-22; Art Teacher King Alfred School, Hampstead 20-21; Lecturer Indian Art, L.C.C. London 25-27; Royal Acad. 22-23; 1st one-man show, London 27; executed murals Wembley Exhbn., London 25; exhibited Philharmonic Hall, Berlin 26, Indian Soc. of Oriental Art, Calcutta 28; Principal Govt. School of Art, Calcutta; Officer-in-Charge Art Section and Keeper Govt. Art Gallery, Indian Museum, Calcutta; Trustee Indian Museum 28-43; Founder Mukul Dey Art Gallery at Kalika 44; Fulbright Visiting Prof. of Art in U.S.A. 53-54; Curator Nat. Gallery of Modern Art, Govt. of India, New Delhi 55-57; exhbn., Commonwealth Inst., London 60.
Works include paintings, portraits, drypoint-etchings, engravings, copies of frescoes in Ajanta and Bagh Caves, Pollonaruwa temples, Ceylon, Sittanavasal caves, S. India, British Museum, London, etc.
Publs. *12 Portraits* 17, *My Pilgrimages to Ajanta and Bagh* 25 and 51, *My Reminiscences* 38, *15 Drypoints* 39, *20 Portraits* 43, *Portraits of Mahatma Gandhi* 48, *Birbhum Terracottas* 60, *Indian Life and Legends* 67.
"Chitralekha", P.O. Santiniketan, West Bengal, India.

Dey, Surendra Kumar, M.SC.; Indian electrical engineer and politician; b. 15 Sept. 1906; ed. Zilla School, Rangpur, Bengal Engineering Coll., Purdue and Michigan Univs., U.S.A.
Rose from position of Sales Engineer to Divisional Man. for India, Burma and Ceylon with Victor X-ray Corpn. (India) Ltd. 32-47; Hon. Technical Adviser, Ministry of Rehabilitation 47-52; built township of Nilokheri, a pilot experiment in agro-industrial development; mem. of Exec., United Council for Relief and Welfare 49-53; Admin., Community Projects Admin., mem. Central Board. Bharat Sewak Semaj 52-56; Minister for Community Development 56-58 and Co-operation 59-62; Minister of State for Community Devt. 63-65, of Mines and Metals 65-67; mem. Akhil Bharatya Congress Rachanatmak Karya Samiti, Youth Advisory Cttee. (All-India Congress Cttee.); awarded Padma Bhushan 55; Congress Party.
Publs. *The Quest, Fragments Across, Missing Link,*

Planning for Life, Random Thoughts I, II and III, Community Development, Panchayati Raj, Nilokheri, Community Development: A Chronicle.
1 Tin Murti Marg, New Delhi, India.

DeYoung, Russell; American businessman; b. 3 April 1909; ed. Akron Univ., and Mass. Inst. of Technology, Joined Goodyear Tire & Rubber Co. 30-, Vice-Pres. (Production) 47-; Exec. Vice-Pres. 56-58, Pres. 58-63. Chair. and Chief Exec. Officer 63-; Dir. Youngstown Sheet and Tube Co.; Dir. Kennecott Copper Corpn.
Home: 910 Eaton Avenue, Akron, Ohio 44303; Office: 1144 E. Market Street, Akron, Ohio 44316, U.S.A.

Dhani Nivat, Prince, B.A., LL.D., D.LITT.; Thai government official; b. 7 Nov. 1885; ed. Rugby School, and Oxford Univ.
Joined Govt. Service in Ministry of Interior 08; Private Sec. to King Rama VI and Sec. of Cabinet Council 17; Minister of Public Instruction 26; Pres. Privy Council; mem. Supreme Council of State which acted as Council of Regency; Regent 51 till King's return; since then Pres. Privy Council; Hon. Pres. Siam Society; Corresp. mem. Hist. Comm., UNESCO; created Kromamun Bidyalabh and Knight of the Royal Family Order of Chakri.
Publs. In English: *The Coronation of His Majesty King Prajadhipok, The Inscriptions of Wat Phra Jetubon, The Rama Jataka, The Old Siamese Conception of the Monarchy, SEATO lectures* 60, *Monarchical Protection of the Buddhist Church of Siam* 64, etc.; and works in Siamese.
Chamber of the Privy Council, Grand Palace, Bangkok, Thailand.

Dhavan, Shanti Sarup; Indian judge and diplomatist; b. 2 July 1905; ed. Government Coll., Lahore, Forman Christian Coll., Lahore, Emmanuel Coll., Cambridge, Inner Temple, London, and Univs. of Bonn and Heidelberg.
Former Pres. Cambridge Union; Advocate, Allahabad High Court; Senior Standing Counsel, Govt. of Uttar Pradesh 56-58; Puisne Judge, Allahabad High Court 58-67; High Commr. of India in U.K. 68-; Lecturer in Law, Univ. of Allahabad 40-54; Pres. Uttar Pradesh Section, Indo-Soviet Cultural Soc. 65-67.
Indian High Commission, India House, Aldwych, London, W.C.2, England.

Dhebar, Uchhrangrai Navalshankar; Indian politician; b. 21 Sept. 1905; ed. Bombay.
Lawyer, Western India States Agency Court 29-36; Indian Nat. Congress 36; Pres. Viramgam Taluka Congress Cttee. 36; Sec. Kathiawar Political Conf. 37-48; Chief Minister, Saurashtra 48-54; Pres. Indian Nat. Congress 54-59; mem. Lok Sabha 62-63; Head, Khadi and Village Industries Comm. 63-.
Irla Road, Bombay 56, India.

Dia, Mamadou; Senegalese politician; b. 10.
Councillor, Senegal 46-52; Grand Councillor, French West Africa 52-57; Senator for Senegal 49-55; Dep. to Nat. Assembly, Paris 56-59; Dep. to Legislative Assembly, Senegal 59; Vice-Pres., Council of Ministers Senegal 57-58, Pres. 58-59; Vice-Pres., Mali Fed. 59-60; Pres. Council of Ministers, Senegal 60-62, concurrently Minister of Defence and Security 62; Govt. overthrown Dec. 62, sentenced to life detention May 63; Chevalier, Palmes Académiques.
Publs. *Réflexions sur l'économie de l'Afrique Noire* 53, *Contributions à l'étude du mouvement coopératif en Afrique Noire* 57, *L'économie africaine* 57, *Nations Africaines et solidarité mondiale* 60.
Dakar, Senegal, West Africa.

Diaconescu, Gheorghe; Romanian lawyer and diplomatist; b. 12 March 1915; ed. School of Law, Iaşi Univ. In Supreme Court and Gen. State Prosecuting Magistracy until 54; Minister of Justice 51-61; Amb. to

Poland 61-66; Perm. Rep. of Romania to UN 66-; Prof. of Law, Bucharest Univ.

Publs. several works and studies in field of law.

Permanent Mission of Socialist Republic of Romania to the United Nations, 60 East 93rd Street, New York, N.Y. 10028, U.S.A.

Diah, Burhanudin Mohamad (husband of Herawati Diah, q.v.); Indonesian journalist and diplomatist; b. 1917; ed. Taman Siswa High School, Medan, Sumatra and Ksatrian School for Journalism, Bandung, Java.

Asst. Editor daily *Sinar Deli*, Medan 37-38; free-lance journalist 38-39; Chief of Indonesian Information Desk, British Consulate-Gen. 39-41; Editor-in-chief Indonesian monthly *Pertjaturan Dunia dan Film* 39-41; radio commentator and editorial writer daily *Asia Raya* 42-45; Editor-in-chief daily *Merdeka* 45-59; Pres. Merdeka Press Ltd., Masa Merdeka Printing Presses; active in political movement, especially during Japanese occupation; Chair. New Youth (underground) movement and jailed by Japanese in 42 and again in 45; active in forcing proclamation of Indonesian Independence Aug. 45; mem. Provisional Nat. Cttee., Republic of Indonesia 45-49; mem. Provisional Indonesian Parl. 54-56; mem. Nat. Council 57-59; Ambassador to Czechoslovakia 59-62, to U.K. 62-64, to Thailand 64-66; Minister of Information 66-.

Ministry of Information, Djakarta, Indonesia.

Diah, Herawati, B.A. (wife of Burhanudin Mohamad Diah, q.v.); Indonesian journalist; b. 1917; ed. Barnard Coll. (Columbia Univ.).

Announcer and feature writer, Indonesian Radio 42; Sec. to Minister of Foreign Affairs, Republic of Indonesia Sept.-Dec. 45; reporter daily *Merdeka* 46; Editor Indonesian Sunday paper *Minggu Merdeka* Jan.-July 47 (when it was banned by Dutch authorities); reporter *Merdeka* Aug. 47-Jan. 48; Editor illustrated weekly *Madjalah Merdeka* 48-51, of *Minggu Merdeka* May 51; Editor of women's monthly magazine, *Keluarga* (Family) 53-59, of daily, *Indonesian Observer* 55-59.

c/o Ministry of Information, Djakarta, Indonesia.

Diakité, Moussa; Guinean government official; b. 27; ed. Ecole Primaire Supérieure, Ecole Technique Supérieure.

Treasury 54; Dep. Mayor of Kankan 56; Vice-Pres. Grand Council of West Africa 58; Sec. of State, Grand Council of West Africa 58; Gov. Central Bank of Guinea and Minister of Finance 60-63; Minister of Foreign Trade and Banking 63-; Compagnon de l'Indépendance.

Ministry of Foreign Trade and Banking, Conakry, Republic of Guinea.

Diamand, Peter; Netherlands (b. German) musical administrator; b. 8 June 1913; ed. Schiller-Real-gymnasium, Berlin and Friedrich Wilhelm Univ., Berlin.

Studied in Berlin until Nazi laws made this impossible; emigrated to Holland 33; Private Sec. to Artur Schnabel 34-39; Asst. Dir. Netherlands Opera 46-48; Gen. Man. Holland Festival 48, Artistic Adviser 65-; co-founder Netherlands Chamber Orchestra and mem. of Board 55-; Dir. Edinburgh Festival 65-; Knight Order of Orange-Nassau, Grand Cross of Merit Austria.

Edinburgh Festival Society, 29 St. James's Street, London, S.W.1, England.

Diarra, Oumar Baba; Mali politician; b. 30 Dec. 1929; ed. Ecole normale, Bamako, and Univ. de Montpellier.

Formerly worked in Office of Overseas Scientific Research, Paris; later Directeur du Cabinet to Minister of Public Works, Mali, concurrently Prof. of Political Econ. and Public Law, Nat. School of Admin., Mali; Sec. of State for Labour and Social Affairs 59, then Sec. of State for Public Works and Labour, Minister of Labour 66-; Pres. Fourth Session UN Econ. Comm. for Africa 62; mem. Mali Del. Int. Labour Conf., Int.

Labour Office (ILO) 59, Pres. Comm. on Apartheid 64; Vice-Pres. African Regional Conf. of ILO, Addis Ababa 64; Pres. of Council of Admin., ILO 65-66.

Ministry of Labour, Bamako, Mali.

Dias, Felix (Bandaranaike); Ceylonese politician; b. 31.

Minister of Finance and Parl. Sec. to Minister of Defence and of External Affairs July 60-62; Minister without Portfolio Nov. 62-May 63, of Agriculture, Food and Co-operatives May 63-65.

Colombo, Ceylon.

Diaz Ambrona, Adolfo; Spanish politician; b. 26 July 1908; ed. Universidad de Madrid.

State lawyer 31; Provincial Counsellor, Province of Badajoz 37, Pres. 49-; Court Lawyer 52-, Pres. Finance Comm. Cortes Españolas; mem. Council of Inst. of Fiscal Studies; Pres. Irrigation Transformation Comm., Econ. Devt. Plan 64-67; Minister of Agriculture 65-; numerous decorations.

Ministerio de Agricultura, Madrid, Spain.

Díaz de Guijarro, Enrique; Argentine lawyer and journalist; b. 10 Oct. 1902; ed. Univ. of Buenos Aires.

Mem. editorial board *La Acción* 22-25, *La Argentina* 26, *Jurisprudencia Argentina* 26-; Dir. *Antología Jurídica* 30-44; Prof. of Spanish Nat. Coll. 28-52; Prof. Civil Law, Faculty of Economic Sciences, Univ. of Buenos Aires 32-46 and 55-65, Vice-Dean 45-46; Dir. of Dept. of Legislation 56-65; Pres. Pedagogic Council 58-59; Prof. Civil Law, Faculty of Law and Social Sciences, Univ. of Buenos Aires 55-65; Sec.-Gen. Argentine Congress on Oral Procedure in Courts 42; Sec.-Gen. First Conf. of Buenos Aires Advocates 43; Sec. of Board, Coll. of Lawyers, Buenos Aires 48-49; Vice-Pres. Argentine Eugenics Society 44-49; Dir. *Revista del Colegio de Abogados de Buenos Aires* 52; Treas. Fed. Argentina de Colegios de Abogados 53-55; Pres. Comm. for Reform of Civil Judicial Organisation and Procedure Law 55-57; Head of the Court of Nat. Appeal 55-58.

Publs. *El contrato de pasaje* 28 and 36, *Transformaciones modernas del derecho civil* 34 and 36, *La prescripción de los créditos y el concurso civil* 37, *La reforma del matri-monio civil por las leyes eugénicas* 38, *Estudios sobre el proyecto de reformas del código civil* 41, *Régimen económi-co del proyecto de reforma del código civil*, *Problemas de eugenesia* 43, *El impedimento matrimonial de enfermedad* 44, *Tratado de Derecho de Familia* 53, *El acto jurídico familiar* 61.

Rodríguez Peña 556, Buenos Aires, Argentina.

Díaz de Molina, Afredo Hugo Florencio, D.JUR. AND SOCIAL SC.; Argentine writer; b. 27 Oct. 1901; ed. Nat. Univ. of Buenos Aires.

Minister of Government, Justice and Education, Jujuy 43; Head of Monopolies Department, Ministry of Industry and Commerce 43-49; Legal Adviser 50-52; Lawyer Vialidad 55-63; mem. Nat. Comm. on Anni-versary of Sovereign Assembly of 13, 63; Teacher at Reconquista Nat. Coll.; hon. mem. Co-operative Asscn. 50-64; Santiago Derquix and José Figueroa Alcorta Colls.; Prof. Civil Law, Univ. of La Plata 55-62; Prof. History of Argentine Insts., Univ. of Buenos Aires 58-63; Founder and Dean of Faculty of Economics at the Free Univ. of Morón 61-63, Rector 63; Vice-Pres. Argentine Inst. of Genealogical Science; Founder and Editor first Argentine *Heraldic Review* 40; Pres. Argentine-Cuban Cultural Inst.; Vice-Pres. Bolivar Soc. of Argentina; mem. chief historical and genea-logical institutes of Europe and America; Chevalier Légion d'Honneur.

Publs. include: *El Poema del Olimpo* 19, *Ja, ja, ja*, 23, *El genio epónimo del Libertador José de San Martín* 50, *Los orígenes constitucionales argentinos* 55; *La constitu-ción cordobesa de 1821 y su influencia institucional* 58, *El sindicato y los derechos sindicales en la reforma*

constitucional de 1957 60, *La oligarquia argentina Córdoba* 65.
3931 Juan Maria Gutiérrez, Buenos Aires, Argentina.

Díaz Ordaz, Gustavo; Mexican lawyer and politician; b. 11; ed. Instituto de Ciencias y Artes Oaxaca and Colegio del Estado de Puebla.
Legal and judicial posts, Puebla, Tlatlangui and Tehuacán 37; Dep. to Fed. Legis. Assembly and Senator 46-52; fmr. Prof. of Admin. and Labour Law, Puebla Univ.; Chief Officer, Secretariat of the Govt. 52-58; Sec. of the Govt. 58, later Minister of the Interior; Pres. of Mexico July 64-; Partido Revolucionario Institucional.
Palacio Presidencial, Mexico D.F., Mexico.

Diba, Dr. Fereidun; Iranian diplomatist; b. 20; ed. Univs. of Teheran and Rome.
Ministry of Foreign Affairs, successively Library Dept., Dept. of Ministerial Work, First Political Dept.; Iranian Consulate, Nanking and Shanghai; First Sec. Rome; Dep. Dir. Third Political Dept., Dir. Passport Dept. and Head Nationality Dept., Ministry of Foreign Affairs; Dir. Information and Publications Dept., Ministry of Foreign Affairs; Amb. to Syria 64-65, to Belgium 65-67; Dir.-Gen. (for Asian and African Affairs), Foreign Ministry, Teheran 67-.
Foreign Ministry, Teheran, Iran.

di Belgiojoso, Lodovico Barbiano; Italian architect; b. 1 Dec. 1909; ed. School of Architecture, Milan.
Architect 32; Prof. of Architecture 49; Prof. Venice Univ. Inst. of Architecture 56-63; Prof. of Architectural Composition, School of Architecture, Milan Polytechnic 63-; private practice with Peressutti and Rogers in town planning, architecture, interior decoration and industrial design; mem. Nat. Council of the Italian Town Planning Inst.; mem. Accademia di S. Luca, Rome.
Works include houses, factories, pavilions; Italian Merchant Navy Pavilion, Paris Int. Exhbn. 37; health resort for children, Legnano 39; Post Office, Rome 39; monument to the dead in German concentration camps, Milan cemetery 46; U.S. Pavilion at Triennale 51; Olivetti Showroom, Fifth Avenue, New York, and Labyrinth at the Tenth Triennale 54; restoration and re-arrangement of Castello Sforzesco Museums 56; skyscraper Torre Velasca, Milan 57; Canadian Pavilion, Venice Biennale; collaborator Italian Pavilion, Brussels Exhbn. 58; Hispano Olivetti Building, Barcelona 65.
Publs. (in collaboration with Banfi, Peressutti and Rogers): *Piano regolatore della val d'Aosta* 37, *Piano A.R.* 46, *Stile* 36, etc.
Studio Architetti B.B.P.R., 2 via dei Chiostri, Milan, Italy.

di Cagno, Vito Antonio; Italian lawyer and public administrator; b. 30 March 1897; ed. Bari.
Infantry Officer, two world wars; Pres. Soc. Meridionale di Elettricità 57; Pres. Ente Nazionale per l'Energia Elettrica (Enel); Mayor of Bari 46-.
Ente Nazionale per l'Energia Elettrica, Via del Tritone 181, Rome, Italy.

Dichter, Ernest, PH.D.; American psychologist; b. 14 Aug. 1907; ed. Univs. of Paris and Vienna.
Consultant Psychologist on Programs, Columbia Broadcasting System 42-46; developed application of social science to advertising, public service, politics (motivational research); Pres. Inst. for Motivational Research Inc. 46-.
Publs. *Successful Living* 47, *Strategy of Desire* 60, *Handbook of Consumer Motivations* 64.
Albany Post Road, Croton-on-Hudson, N.Y., U.S.A.
Telephone: Croton 1-4721.

Dicke, Robert H(enry), A.B., PH.D.; American physicist; b. 6 May 1916; ed. Princeton Univ. and Univ. of Rochester.
Microwave Radar Devt., Mass. Inst. of Technology

41-46; Physics Faculty, Princeton Univ. 46-, Cyrus Fogg Brackett Prof. of Physics 57-, Chair. Physics Dept., Princeton Univ. 67-; mem. Advisory Panel for Physics, Nat. Science Foundation 59-61; Chair. Advisory Cttee. on Atomic Physics, Nat. Bureau of Standards 61-63; mem. N.A.S.A. Cttee. on Physics 63-, Chair. 63-66; Chair. Physics Panel, Advisory to Cttee. on Int. Exchange of Persons (Fulbright-Hays Act) 64-66; Nat. Lecturer, Sigma Xi 67; Fellow American Physical Soc., American Geophysical Union, American Acad. of Arts and Sciences; mem. American Astronomical Soc.; Rumford Medal, American Acad. of Arts and Sciences 67.
Publs. (with Montgomery and Purcell) *Principles of Microwave Circuits* 48, (with J. P. Wittke) *An Introduction to Quantum Mechanics* 60, *The Theoretical Significance of Experimental Relativity* 64.
Palmer Physical Laboratory, Princeton Univ., Princeton, N.J. 08540, U.S.A.

Dickel, Maj.-Gen. Friedrich; German army officer and politician; b. 9 Dec. 1913; ed. elementary school.
Former moulder; mem. Kommunistische Partei Deutschlands until 45, Sozialistische Einheits Partei (S.E.D.) 45-; in Saar, France, Netherlands 33-36; fought in Spanish Civil War 36-37; in U.S.S.R. 37-46; Maj. Gen. Regular People's Police 53-56, Maj.-Gen. People's Army 56-63; Minister of Interior and Chief of People's Police (Volkspolizei) 63-.
Innenministerium, Berlin; Home: Mauerstrasse 29/31, 108 Berlin, Germany.

Dickens, Frank, M.A., D.SC., PH.D., F.INST.BIOL., F.R.S.; British biochemist; b. 1899; ed. Northampton Grammar School and Magdalene Coll., Cambridge.
Lecturer in Biochemistry, Middlesex Hospital Medical School, at same time working for Medical Research Council 29-31; mem. Scientific Staff, Medical Research Council 31-33; Research Dir. North of England Council of British Empire Cancer Campaign 33-46; Research for Naval Personnel Cttee. of Medical Research Council, Nat. Inst. for Medical Research 43-44; mem. Scientific Advisory Cttee. of British Empire Cancer Campaign 34-; an Editor of *Biochemical Journal* 37-47; Philip Hill Prof. of Experimental Biochemistry, Middlesex Hospital Medical School, Univ. of London; Chair. British Nat. Cttee. for Biochemistry 64-66; now Dir. Tobacco Research Council's Laboratories; Hon. Fellow Univ. of Leeds 67-.
Publs. *Chemical and Physical Properties of the Internal Secretions* (with E. C. Dodds), translation of *The Metabolism of Tumours* (by O. Warburg), Editor *Oxygen in the Animal Organism* (with E. Neil), *Carbohydrate Metabolism and its Disorders* (with P. Randle and W. J. Whelan).
Home: 48 Rutland Close, Harrogate, Yorks.; Office: Tobacco Research Council's Laboratories, Otley Road, Harlow Hill, Harrogate, Yorks., England.
Telephone: 3799 (Home); 67265 (Office).

Dickey, James, B.A., M.A.; American poet; b. 2 Feb. 1923; ed. Clemson Coll. and Vanderbilt Univ.
Served Second World War with U.S. Army Air Force and U.S. Air Force in Korea; Consultant in Poetry, Library of Congress, Washington 66-; *Sewanee Review* Fellow 54-55, Guggenheim Fellow 62-63; Vachel Lindsay Award and Longview Award 59.
Publs. Poems: *Into the Stone* 60, *Drowning with Others* 62, *Helmets* 64, *Two Poems of the Air* 64, *Poems 1959-1967* 67; Criticism: *The Suspect in Poetry* 64.
8950 Balboa Boulevard, Northridge, Calif. 91324, U.S.A.

Dickey, John Sloan, A.B., LL.B.; American college president and lawyer; b. 4 Nov. 1907; ed. Dartmouth Coll., and Harvard Law School.
Began practice in Boston 32; Asst. to Asst. Sec. of

State and Asst. to legal adviser, U.S. Dept. of State 34-36; law practice with Gaston, Snow, Hunt, Rice & Boyd, Boston 36-40; Special asst. to Sec. of State 40; Special Asst. to Co-ordinator of Inter-American Affairs 40-44, and detailed to U.S. Dept. of State as Chief, Div. of World Trade Intelligence; Dir. Office of Public Affairs, Dept. of State 44-45, and served as public liaison officer U.S. del., UN Conf. on Int. Organization, San Francisco 45; Pres. of Dartmouth Coll. 45-.
Publs. Contributor to *The Secretary of State* 60, Editor *The United States and Canada* 64.
Dartmouth College, Hanover, New Hampshire, U.S.A. Telephone: 603-646-2222.

Didricksen, Jan, LL.M.; Norwegian lawyer and business executive; b. 15 May 1917; ed. Universitetet i Oslo and Harvard Business School.
District Commdr. Underground Mil. Forces 41-42; Judge 46-54; Chief, Law Dept., Norwegian Employers' Fed. 54-62, Del. to Int. Labour Org. (ILO) 56-62; Dir. Fed. of Norwegian Industries 63-65, Dir.-Gen. 65-.
Norges Industriforbund, Drammensveien 40, P.O.B. 2435 Solli, Oslo 2; Home: Sörkedalsveien 94, Oslo 3, Norway.

Diebold, John; American management consultant; b. 8 June 1926; ed. Swarthmore Coll. and Harvard Business School.
With Griffenhagen & Assocs., management consultants, New York City, also Chicago 51-57, owner 57-, merged with Louis J. Kroeger and Assocs. to become Griffen-hagen-Kroeger Inc. 60; established Diebold Group Inc., New York City 54, Pres., Chair. Board, Los Angeles, San Francisco, Washington, Chicago 54-; established Urwick Diebold Ltd., England 58, Co-Chair. 58-; established Raadgevend Bur. Berenschot-Diebold, N.V. 58, Diebold Europe, S.A., Pres. 60-; Chair. Diebold Computer Leasing Inc. 67-; coiner of word *automation*.
Publs. *Automation—The Advent of the Automatic Factory* 52, *Beyond Automation* 64.
John Diebold and Assoc., 430 Park Avenue, N.Y., U.S.A.

Dieckmann, Johannes; German politician and professor; b. 19 Jan. 1893; ed. Univs. of Berlin, Giessen, Göttingen and Freiburg.
General Secretary German People's Party 19-33; mem. Saxon Diet 30-33; worked in coal industry 33-45; co-founder of Liberal-Democratic Party in Dresden July 45; elected to Saxon Diet Oct. 46; Minister of Justice in Seydewitz Cabinet April 48-50; Pres. of People's Chamber of the German Democratic Republic Oct. 49-; Deputy Pres. State-Council of the German Democratic Republic 60-; Dr. jur. h.c. (Leipzig).
Publs. *The (Postwar-) Constitutions of the German Länder* 48, *In memoriam Robert Schumann* 56, *In the decisive time of Germany* 58, *In Memoriam Chopin* 60, *Where Goes the Way?* 63, *Fifty Years since the October Revolution—Fifty Years of German-Soviet Relations* 67.
Luisenstrasse 58, 104 Berlin, Germany.
Telephone: Berlin 42008321.

Diederichs, Georg, DR.RER.POL; German politician; b. 1900; ed. Univs. of Göttingen and Rostock.
Soldier 18-19; mem. German Democratic Party 26-30, Social Democratic Party 30-; in pharmaceutical industry 30-45; concentration camp and prison for illegal resistance work 35, 36; soldier 39-45; Mayor, Northeim 45-46; M.P. Council 48-49; mem. Landtag, Lower Saxony 47-; Vice-Pres. Lower Saxony Landtag 55-57, Minister for Social Affairs 57-61, Prime Minister 61-; mem. (Federal) Bundesrat 62-, Dep. Pres. 62-63, Pres. 63-64.
Leinerandstrasse 23, Laatzen near Hanover, German Federal Republic.

Diederichs, Nicolaas, M.A., D.LITT. et PHIL.; South African economist and politician; b. 25 Dec. 1903; ed.

Boshof High School, Grey Univ. Coll., Univs. of Munich, Cologne and Leiden.
Former Chair. Economic Inst., Decimal Coinage Comm.; fmr. Prof. Free State Univ.; M.P. for Losberg; Minister for Econ. Affairs, also Minister of Mines 61-64; Minister for Econ. Affairs 66-67, of Finance 67-; Chancellor Randse Afrikaanse Universiteit 68.
Union Buildings, Pretoria, Republic of South Africa.

Diefenbaker, Rt. Hon. John George, P.C., Q.C., M.A., LL.B., F.R.S.C., M.P.; Canadian lawyer and politician; b. 18 Sept. 1895; ed. Saskatchewan Univ.
Served overseas with Canadian Army 16-17; called to Bar of Saskatchewan 19; King's Counsel 29; Vice-Pres. Canadian Bar Asscn. 39-42; mem. Canadian Parl. 40-; Leader Progressive Cons. Party Dec. 56-Sept. 67; Prime Minister of Canada June 57-April 63; Fellow Royal Soc. of Arts, Fellow Royal Soc. of Canada; Fellow Royal Architectural Inst. of Canada; Hon. Bencher, Gray's Inn, London; numerous hon. degrees; Hon. Fellow (Bar-Ilan Univ., Israel); Hon. Freeman of City of London 63.
House of Commons, Ottawa, Ont.; Prince Albert, Sask.; 541 Acacia Avenue, Rockcliffe Park, Ottawa, Ont., Canada.

Diehl, Günter; German diplomatist; b. 8 Feb. 1916; ed. Albertus-Magnus-Platz Univ., Cologne, and Université de Bordeaux.
Entered Diplomatic Service 39; Foreign Office 45; Foreign Editor *Hamburger Abendblatt* 48; Foreign Dept. Press Office 50; Foreign Office Spokesman 52; Counsellor German Embassy Santiago 56; Head of Foreign Dept. Press and Information Service 60; Head Planning Div. Foreign Office 66; Chief, Press and Information Office of German Federal Republic 67-.
Presse und Informationsamt der Bundesregierung, 53 Bonn, Welckerstrasse 11, German Federal Republic.
Telephone: Bonn 2081.

Diehl, Harold Sheely, M.A., M.D., SC.D.; American physician; b. 4 Aug. 1891.
Assistant Principal and Teacher of Mathematics, Fulton High School, New York 12-14; part-time Instructor in Chemistry Augsburg Seminary Minneapolis 14-16; Asst. in Bacteriology and Pathology Univ. of Minnesota 16-18; Pathologist Univ. Hospital 20-21; Dir. Students' Health Service 21-35; Asst. Prof. of Preventive Medicine and Public Health 21-24, Assoc. Prof. 24-29, Prof. and Head Dept. of Preventive Medicine and Public Health 29-36, Dean Medical Sciences 35-58; mem. American Medical Asscn. Council on Nat. Defense 47-54, Chair. 54-59; Fellow American Public Health Asscn., mem. Governing Council 46-49; mem. Exec. Council Asscn. American Medical Colls. 39-42, Vice-Pres. 55 and 56; Chair. Cttee. on Allocation of Medical Personnel during War; mem. Medical Advisory Cttee., American Red Cross 45-50; mem. Nat. Advisory Health Council, U.S. Public Health Service 40-44, consultant on cancer control 60-; mem. Office Defense Mobilization Advisory Cttee. on Health Resources 50-57, U.S. Nat. Advisory Food and Drug Council 64-67; U.S. Del. to World Health Assembly 54, 55, 58 and to Int. Cancer Congress 58, 62; Hon. Consultant Surgeon-Gen. U.S. Navy 52-56; Deputy Exec. Vice-Pres. for Research and Medical Affairs of American Cancer Soc. 58-68, Special Consultant 68-; Vice-Chair. Nat. Interagency Council on Smoking and Health 64-.
Publs. *Healthful Living* 35, *Albuminuria in Young Men* (in *Kidney in Health and Disease*) 35, *Periodic Health Examinations* (in *Practitioners Library*, Vol. XII) 37, *Text-book of Healthful Living* 8th edn. 68; *The Health of American College Students* (with C. E. Shepard) 39, *Elements of Healthful Living* 3rd edn. 55, *Healthful Living for Nurses* (with R. E. Boynton) 44, *Personal and Community Health* (with R. E. Boynton) 51, *Health*

and Safety for You (with Anita Laton and Franklin C. Vaughn) 54, 61, 64.
11 Riverside Drive, New York, N.Y. 10023, U.S.A.
Telephone: SU7-2254.

Dieng, Diakha; Senegalese international official; b. 16 Aug. 1933; ed. Lycée Faidherbe, St. Louis, Université de Paris à la Sorbonne, and Ecole des Impôts, Paris.
Registry Officer, France 60, Dakar 61; Sec., later First Sec., Embassy of Senegal, Brussels 62-63; First Sec. Embassy of Senegal, Paris 63-64; Sec.-Gen. Union Africaine et Malgache de Coopération Economique (U.A.M.C.E.), Yaoundé 64-65, Organisation Commune Africaine et Malgache, Yaoundé (O.C.A.M.) 64-, Chevalier, Ordre National Sénégalais.
Organisation Commune Africaine et Malgache, B.P. 437, Yaoundé, Cameroon.

Dietrich, Helmut; German banker; b. 23 March 1922; ed. Hochschule für Ökonomie, Berlin.
Former Branch Dir., Deutsche Notenbank, fmr. Area Dir., Pres. Deutsche Notenbank 64-; now Vice-Pres. Staatsbank der Deutschen Demokratischen Republik; Pres. Deutsche Investitionsbank; Vaterländischer Verdienstorden, Verdienstmedaille der Deutschen Demokratischen Republik, etc.
108 Berlin, Charlottenstrasse 33, German Democratic Republic.

Dietrich, Marlene; German-born American actress and singer; b. 27 Dec. 1904; ed. Augusta Victoria School, Berlin.
Début in Berlin; worked with Max Reinhardt; emigrated to U.S. 30; has appeared in numerous films including *Golden Earrings, Foreign Affair, Stage Fright, Rancho Notorious, The Blue Angel, Witness for the Prosecution*, etc.; also numerous stage and cabaret appearances, including solo show, New York Oct. 67.
Paramount Studios, Hollywood, Calif., U.S.A.

Dietz, David (Henry), A.B., LITT.D., LL.D.; American newspaper editor and author; b. 6 Oct. 1897; ed. Western Reserve Univ.
Mem. Editorial staff of The Cleveland Press 15-; Science Editor of the Scripps-Howard Newspapers 21-; Lecturer in General Science, Western Reserve Univ. 27-; Visiting Lecturer on the Science of Modern War at Yale Univ. 42; Science Commentator, Nat. Broadcasting Co. 45-50; Winner Pulitzer Prize in Journalism 37; Westinghouse Award for Distinguished Science Writing 45; Lasker Medical Journalism Award 54; James T. Grady Award 60; was Consultant to the Surgeon-General of the U.S. Army during Second World War, newspaper corresp. and radio commentator, atomic bomb tests, Bikini 46; Hon. Litt.D. (Western Reserve Univ.) 48; Hon. LL.D. (Bowling Green State Univ.) 54.
Publs. *The Story of Science* 31, *Medical Magic* 37, *Atomic Energy in the Coming Era* 45; article on "The Atomic Bomb" in the 1946 edition of the *Encyclopædia Britannica, Atomic Science, Bombs and Power* 54, *All about Satellites and Space Ships* 58, *All About Great Medical Discoveries* 60, *All About the Universe* 65.
2891 Winthrop Road, Shaker Heights, Ohio 44120, U.S.A.
Telephone: 991-3834.

Dietzfelbinger, Hermann; German ecclesiastic; b. 14 July 1908; ed. Friedrich-Alexander-Univ. zu Erlangen-Nürnberg, Eberhard-Karls Univ., Tübingen, and Ernst Moritz Arndt-Univ., Greifswald.
Protestant Bishop of Bavaria 55-; Pres. Council of German Evangelical Church 67-.
8 Munich 37, Meiserstrasse 13, German Federal Republic.

Diez de Medina, Raúl; Bolivian diplomatist; b. 11; ed. Colegio Nacional Ayacucho, La Paz, and School of Foreign Service, Georgetown Univ., Washington, D.C.

Diplomatic Service, Washington 28, Cuba 29, Washington 30; Latin American Editor *Sunday Star*, Washington 30-37; Counsellor, Mexico and Washington 37-46; Del. of Bolivia to UN Relief and Rehabilitation Admin. 46; Ambassador of Bolivia to UN Palestine Comm. 48; Dir. Dept. of Public Information, Pan American Union 48; Pres. COPESA, La Paz 55-58; Dir. Pan American Union Office, Bolivia 58-64; Ambassador of Bolivia to Council of Org. of American States 64-, Vice-Chair. Council of OAS 66-67.
Publs. *Autopsy of the Monroe Doctrine* 34, *The U.S. versus Europe in Latin America* 37.
Pan American Union, Washington D.C. 20006, U.S.A.

Dikambayev, Kazy Dikambaevich; Soviet politician; b. 1913; ed. Tashkent Inst. of National Economy.
State activity 39-40; Deputy Chair. Council of People's Commissars and People's Commissar of State Control 40-44; Minister of Foreign Affairs 44-48; Vice-Chair. Council of Ministers, Kirghiz S.S.R. 48-49; Sec. Cen. Cttee. Communist Party of the Kirghiz S.S.R. 49-51; First Sec. Frunze Regional Cttee. 51-58; Chair. Council of Ministers, Kirghiz S.S.R. 58-61; Deputy Chair. Kirghiz *Gosplan* 63-; mem. C.P.S.U. 40-.
Frunze, Council of Ministers of Kirghiz S.S.R., U.S.S.R.

Dike, Kenneth Onwuka, M.A., PH.D.; Nigerian historian; b. 17 Dec. 1917; ed. Dennis Memorial Grammar School (Onitsha), Achimota Coll. (Ghana), Fourah Bay Coll. (Sierra Leone), Univs. of Durham, Aberdeen and London.
Lecturer in History, Univ. Coll. Ibadan 50-52, Senior Lecturer 54-56, Prof. History 56-60, Principal 58-60; Vice-Chancellor, Univ. of Ibadan 60-Dec. 66; Senior Research Fellow, West African Inst. of Social and Econ. Research 52-54; Founder-Dir. Nigerian Nat. Archives 51-64; Chair. Nigerian Antiquities Comm. 54-; Pres. Historical Soc. of Nigeria 55-; Dir. Inst. of African Studies, Univ. of Ibadan 62-67; Chair. Planning Cttee., Univ. of Port Harcourt 67-; Fellow Royal Historical Soc.; Hon. LL.D. (Aberdeen, Leeds, Northwestern, London, Columbia, Princeton, Ahmadu Bello Univs.); Hon. D.Litt. (Boston and Birmingham), Hon. D.Sc. (Moscow).
Publs. *Report on the Preservation and Administration of Historical Records in Nigeria* 53, *Trade and Politics in the Niger Delta 1830-1895* 56, *A Hundred Years of British Rule in Nigeria* 57, *The Origins of the Niger Mission* 58; numerous articles in learned journals on Nigerian and West African history.
P.O.B. 59, Awka, Via Enugu, Eastern Region, Nigeria.

Dikushin, Vladimir Ivanovich; Soviet scientist; b. 02; ed. Moscow Higher Technical School.
Experimental Scientific Research Inst. of Metal Cutting Lathes 32-; Chief engineer of plan of first automatic factory in U.S.S.R.; specialist in field of machine-tool engineering; mem. Acad. of Sciences of the U.S.S.R.; State prizewinner 41, 51.
Publs. include *Ultrasonic Erosion and its Dependence on Vibration Characteristics of Tool* 58.
Experimental Scientific Research Institute of Metal Cutting Lathes, 21b Donskoi Projezd, Moscow B-71, U.S.S.R.

Dilhorne, 1st Viscount, cr. 65, 1st Baron, cr. 62; Reginald Edward Manningham-Buller, Bt., Kt., P.C., Q.C., B.A.; b. 1 Aug. 1905; ed. Eton Coll. and Magdalen Coll., Oxford.
Called to Inner Temple Bar 27; M.P. 43-62; Solicitor-Gen. 51-54; Attorney-Gen. 54-62; Lord Chancellor 62-64; Conservative.
6 King's Bench Walk, Temple, London, E.C.4; Green's Norton Court, Towcester, Northants, England.

Diller, Hans, PH.D.; German professor of classics; b. 8 Sept. 1905; ed. Univs. of Frankfurt/Main, Hamburg, Munich and Florence.

Lecturer, Leipzig Univ. 32; Lecturer, Hamburg Univ. 33; Prof. at the Univ. of Rostock 37; Prof., Univ. of Kiel 41-; mem. Akademie der Wissenschaften und der Literatur, Mainz, 52; Editor *Hermes* and *Zetemata;* Dr. Phil. h.c. Athens; Dr. Med. h.c. Kiel.
Publs. *Die Überlieferung der hippokratischen Schrift,* etc. 32, *Wanderarzt und Aitiologe* 34, *Göttliches und menschliches Wissen bei Sophokles* 50, *Die Bakchen und ihre Stellung im Spätwerk des Euripides* 55, *Hippokrates, Schriften: Die Anfänge der abendländischen Medizin* 62, *Die dichterische Form von Hesiods Erga* 62, *Tophosen-Wege der Forschung* 67.
Sternwartenweg 18, Kiel 23, German Federal Republic.
Telephone: Kiel 46194.

Dillon, C. Douglas, A.B.; American investment banker and diplomatist; b. 21 Aug. 1909; ed. Groton School and Harvard Coll.
Mem. N.Y. Stock Exchange 31-36; with U.S. and Foreign Securities Corpn. and U.S. and Int. Securities Corpn. 37-53, Pres. 46-53, 67-, Dir. 38-53, 67-; Dir. Dillon, Read & Co. Inc. 38-53, Chair. of Board 46-53; served as Ensign, advancing to Lieut.-Commdr. U.S.N.R. 41-45; awarded Air Medal, Legion of Merit with Combat Device; American Amb. to France Jan. 53-57; Under-Sec. of State for Economic Affairs 57-59; Under-Sec. of State 59-61; Sec. of the Treasury 61-65; Chair. Pres. Cttee. to study Int. Monetary Problems 65-; LL.D. (Harvard, Columbia, New York, Hartford, Rutgers, Pennsylvania and Princeton Univs., Lafayette, Williams and Middlebury Colls.); Republican.
757 Third Avenue, New York City, N.Y. 10017, U.S.A.

Dillon, James; Irish farmer and merchant; b. 02; ed. Mount of St. Benedict and Nat. Univ. of Ireland.
Studied business organisation in London and Chicago; barrister, King's Inns 31; mem. Dail for Co. Donegal 32-37, for Co. Monaghan 37-; Min. of Agriculture 48-51 and 54-57; Leader of Fine Gael and of Opposition 59-65. Ballaghaderreen, Co. Mayo, Ireland.

Dilworth, Richardson; American lawyer and politician; b. 29 Aug. 1898; ed. St. Marks School, Southboro, Yale Univ., and Yale Law School.
Admitted to Philadelphia Bar 27, Partner, Dilworth, Paxson, Kalish & Green 38-55; District Attorney, Philadelphia 52-55; Democratic Candidate Mayor, Philadelphia 47, Gov. of Pennsylvania 50; Mayor of Philadelphia 55-62; Partner Dilworth, Paxson, Kalish, Kohn & Dilks 63-; Pres. U.S. Conf. of Mayors 60; Pres. Philadelphia Board of Educ. 65-.
225 E. Washington Square, Philadelphia 6, Pennsylvania, U.S.A.

Dimechkié, Nadim; Lebanese diplomatist; b. 1919; ed. American Univ. of Beirut.
Entered Ministry of Supply 43, Dir. Econ. Affairs 44; entered Foreign Service 44; served London 47-49, Ottawa 49-51; Dir. Econ. and Social Dept., Ministry of Foreign Affairs 51-52; Chargé d'Affaires, Cairo 52, Minister and Chargé d'Affaires 53-55; Minister to Switzerland 55-58; Amb. to U.S.A. 58-62; Dir. Econ. Affairs, Ministry of Foreign Affairs 62-66; Amb. to U.K. 66-; awards include Ordre du Cèdre, Egyptian Order of Ismail.
Lebanese Embassy, 21 Kensington Palace Gardens, London, W.8, England.

Dimény, Imre; Hungarian agronomist and politician; b. 1922.
Candidate in Agricultural Sciences; agronomist 45-55; Deputy Chair. Nat. Planning Bureau 60-62; Alt. mem. Central Cttee. Hungarian Socialist Workers' Party 62-66, mem. 66-; Minister of Agriculture and Food 67-. Ministry of Agriculture, Budapest; Kossuth Lajos tér II, Budapest V, Hungary.

Dinçer, Hasan; Turkish lawyer and politician; b. 1910; ed. Law Faculty, Istanbul Univ.
Lawyer and Public Prosecutor until 46; fmr. Deputy Prime Minister, Minister of Defence; mem. Nat. Assembly 61-; Minister of Justice 65-; Justice Party. Ministry of Justice, Ankara; Home: Olgunlar Sok. No 2/10, Yenişehir-Ankara, Turkey.

Dinesen, Erling; Danish trade unionist and politician; b. 25 Feb. 1910; ed. Public School, Naestved, and Commercial School, Naestved.
President Roskilde Branch, Commercial and Office Employees' Union 37; Sec. Danish Commercial and Office Employees' Union 43-45, Business Manager 45-49, Pres. 49-63; mem. Exec. Board Danish Fed. of Trade Unions 50-63, mem. Apprentice Council 50-63; mem. Industrial Council of Labour Movement 50-63, Cttee. of Productivity of Ministry of Commerce 53-63, Labour Council 54-63, Nat. Assessment Cttee. 57-63, Cttee. of Social-Democratic Press in Denmark 58-63, Exec. Cttee. of Int. Fed. of Commercial, Clerical and Technical Employees, Amsterdam 52-63; Minister of Labour 63-68; mem. Exec. Board Social-Democratic Party 65-.
Ullasvej 3, Bagsvaerd, Denmark.
Telephone: 98-22-78.

Dingle, Herbert, D.I.C., A.R.C.S., D.SC., F.R.A.S.; British physicist; b. 2 Aug. 1890; ed. Plymouth Technical School and Royal Coll. of Science.
Emeritus Prof. of History and Philosophy of Science, University College, London.
Publs. *Relativity for All* 22, *Modern Astrophysics* 24, Portions of *Life and Work of Sir Norman Lockyer* 28, *Science and Human Experience* 31, *Through Science to Philosophy* 37, *The Special Theory of Relativity* 40, *Mechanical Physics* 41, *Sub-atomic Physics* 42, *Science and Literary Criticism* 49, *Practical Applications of Spectrum Analysis* 50, *The Scientific Adventure* 52, *The Sources of Eddington's Philosophy* 54, (with Viscount Samuel) *A Threefold Cord* 61.
104 Downs Court Road, Purley, Surrey CR2 IBD, England.
Telephone: 01-660-3581.

Dinsdale, Walter Gilbert, D.F.C., P.C., M.A.; Canadian politician; b. 3 April 1916; ed. Brandon Coll., McMaster, Toronto and Chicago Univs.
C.P.R. Express 37-39; social work in Salvation Army 39; R.C.A.F. 41-45 (with 410 Mosquito Night Fighter Squadron); Dir. Adult Education and Asst. Prof. Social Science Brandon Coll. 46; M.P. 51-; Parl. Asst. Min. of Veterans Affairs 57, Parl. Sec. 59; Minister of Northern Affairs and Nat. Resources 60-63; Progressive-Conservative.
House of Commons, Ottawa, 461 11th Street, Brandon, Manitoba, Canada.
Telephone: 613-992-2503.

Dinur, Benzion; Israeli historian; b. 2 Jan. 1884; ed. Berlin and Berne Univs.
Went to Palestine 21; Mapai del. to Zionist Congress 33; elected to Knesset 49; fmr. Principal Teachers' Seminary, Jerusalem; Lecturer, Prof. and Head Faculty of Humanities Hebrew Univ.; Chair. Literary Council Bialik Institute; Minister of Education and Culture 51-55.
Publs. *Eretz Yisrael Bishnat Tarpag* 24, *Yisrael ba Gola* 26; *Hibat Zion* 34, *Ha Rambam* 35, *Bemifne Hadorot* 55, *Arakhim u-Dereakhim* 57, *Baolam she-Shaka* 58, *Zakhor* 58.
Histadrut Quarter, Kiriat Moshe, Jerusalem, Israel.

Diop, Alioune; Senegalese politician and writer.
Teacher of literature 37; Chef de Cabinet to High Commr., Dakar 46; Senator of French Republic 46-48; Organiser of Int. World Congress of Black Writers and Artists 56; Sec.-Gen. Société Africaine de Culture 57;

Leader of Senegalese Cultural Delegation to Nigeria March 65; Founder and Dir. Présence Africaine.
42 rue Descartes, Paris 5e, France.

Diop, Ousmane Socé; Senegalese diplomatist; b. 31 Oct. 1911.
Former veterinary surgeon; fmr. mem. of the Legislative Assembly of Senegal and Rep. to the Senate of the French Community; Ambassador to U.S.A. 61-, to Haiti 61-; Perm. Rep. to UN 61-, also accred. to Canada 64-, to Mexico 65-, to Trinidad and Tobago 65-.
Embassy of Senegal, 2112 Wyoming Avenue, Washington, D.C., U.S.A.

Diorditsa, Aleksandr Filipovich; Soviet government official; b. 11; ed. Leningrad Finance Acad. and Higher Party School.
Minister of Finance, Moldavia 46-55; Deputy Chair. Moldavian Council of Ministers 55-58, Chair. and Minister for Foreign Relations, Moldavian S.S.R. 58-; Alt. mem. Central Cttee. C.P.S.U. 61-; Deputy to U.S.S.R. and Moldavian S.S.R. Supreme Soviets.
Council of Ministers, Kishinev, Moldavian S.S.R., U.S.S.R.

Diori, Hamani; Niger politician; b. 16 June 1916; ed. Victor Ballot School, Dahomey, and Ecole William Ponty, Senegal.
Deputy, Niger Territory, French Nat. Assembly 46-51, 56-58; Vice-Pres. Nat. Assembly 57; Prime Minister, Republic of the Niger 58-60; Pres. of the Republic of Niger 60-, Council of Ministers 60-, also Minister of Foreign Affairs; mem. Rassemblement Démocratique Africain (R.D.A.); Chair. O.C.A.M. 67-.
Bureau du Président, Niamey, Niger, West Africa.

Dipcharina, Zanna Bukar; Nigerian politician; b. 17; ed. Elementary School, Dikwa, Middle School, Maiduguri, and Higher Training Coll., Katsina.
Teacher 38-46; Man. John Holt 48-54; Northern Area Councillor (Police and Prison) 54-56; Northern People's Congress, mem. Legislative Assembly 54-59; Parl. Sec. Ministry of Transport 56-57; Minister of State 57-58; Fed. Minister of Commerce and Industry 58-65, of Transport 65-66; District Head of Yerwa, in Maiduguri, N. Nigeria.
Maiduguri, N. Nigeria.

Dirac, Paul Adrien Maurice, F.R.S., B.SC., PH.D.; British physicist; b. 8 Aug. 1902; ed. Bristol, Cambridge Univ.
Fellow St. John's Coll., Cambridge; Lucasian Prof. of Mathematics, Cambridge Univ. 32-; Nobel Prizeman for Physics 33; awarded Royal Medal of Royal Society for development of new quantum mechanics 39; Copley Medal of Royal Society; Dr. h.c. (Moscow Univ.).
Publs. *Principles of Quantum Mechanics.*
St. John's College, Cambridge, England.

Diringer, David, D.LITT., M.A.; British university professor; b. 1900; ed. Univ. of Florence.
Univ. Lecturer Florence 31, Prof. 34-; Univ. lecturer in Semitic Epigraphy, Cambridge 48-66; Reader in Semitic Epigraphy, Cambridge 66-68; Sec. Permanent Cttee. for Etruscan Studies 29; Sec. Congress of Coll. Studies 31, 34, 37; Epigraphical rep., excavations at Lachish 39; Editor *Il Corriere del Sabato* 45; Pres. Soc. for Near East Studies, Univ. of Cambridge; founder Alphabet Museum and Seminar, Cambridge, and Alphabet Museum, Tel Aviv; mem. Exec. Cttee., Palestine Exploration Fund, Anglo-Israeli Archaeological Soc., etc.; Fellow Royal Anthropological Soc., Univ. Coll., Cambridge; has lectured in Great Britain, Italy, U.S.A., Spain, France, Israel, U.S.S.R., Turkey.
Publs. *Early Hebrew Inscriptions* 34, *The Alphabet in the History of Civilization* 37, *The Alphabet, a Key to the History of Mankind* 48, *The Hand-produced Book* 53, *The Illuminated Book* 58, *The Story of the Aleph-Beth*

58, *Writing* 62, *Skrift* (in Swedish) 62, (in Danish) 64, *Alphabet* (in Russian) 63.
50 St. Barnabas Road, Cambridge, England.
Telephone: Cambridge 55924.

Dirkse-van-Schalkwyk, Willem, B.A.; South African diplomatist; b. 19 Nov. 1907; ed. Potgietersrust High School and Univ. of South Africa.
Attaché Berlin 34-37; Sec. Del. to L.N. 35-36; Attaché Washington 37-38, Ottawa 38-44; Diplomatic Div. Dept. of External Affairs 44-46; First Sec. Washington 46-51; Alt. Del. U.N. 47; Consul Gen. Léopoldville 51-54, Hamburg 54-56; Minister London 56-60; High Commr. in Canada 60-61, Ambassador 61-64; Amb. to France 64-.
South African Embassy, Avenue Hoche 51, Paris 8e, France.

Dirksen, Everett Mckinley; American lawyer and politician; b. 4 Jan. 1896; ed. Univ. of Minnesota.
Member Illinois State Congress 33-49; Senator from Illinois 50-; Minority whip 57-59, leader of Minority 59-; Republican.
U.S. Senate, Washington, D.C., U.S.A.

Dirzhinskaite-Pilyushenko, Leokadia Yuozovna; Soviet politician; b. 1921; ed. Higher Party School.
Komsomol worker 40-51; Party worker 51-53; Sec., later First Sec. Shyaulyaiskay City Cttee. of C.P. of Lithuania 53-61; Deputy Chair. Council of Ministers and Minister of Foreign Affairs of Lithuanian S.S.R. 61-; mem. Central Cttee. of C.P. of Lithuania; mem. C.P.S.U. 50-.
Council of Ministers of Lithuanian S.S.R., Vilnius, U.S.S.R.

DiSalle, Michael Vincent, LL.B.; American government official; b. 6 Jan. 1908; ed. Georgetown Univ.
Assistant District Counsel, Home Owners' Loan Corpn. 33-35; mem. Ohio Legislature 37-38; Asst. City Law Dir. Toledo 39-41; Councilman Toledo 42-50, Vice-Mayor 44-48, Mayor 48-50; Founder and first Chair. Labour-Management-Citizens Cttee., Toledo; Dir. Office of Price Stabilisation, Washington, D.C. 50-52; nominated Democratic candidate for U.S. Senate from Ohio 52; Dir. Economic Stabilisation Agency Dec. 52-Jan. 53; Gov. of Ohio 58-62; Partner Chapman, DiSalle and Friedman; law practice, Columbus, Ohio 63-.
Office: 1620 E. Broad Street, Columbus, Ohio 43203; Home: 266 McNaughten Road, Columbus, Ohio 43213, U.S.A.

Di Stefano, Giuseppe; Italian opera singer; b. 21.
Debut in *Manon* 46; has sung in national opera houses throughout the world; recordings for Columbia, H.M.V., Decca, Deutsche Grammophon, Ricordi.
Via Palatino 10, Milan, Italy.

Diwakar, Ranganath, LL.B., M.A.; Indian author and politician; b. 94; ed. Bombay Univ.
Teacher and Prof. of English 16-20; founded *Karmaveer* (Kannada weekly paper) 21, editor until 30, now sole trustee of People's Education Trust, Hubli, controlling *Karmaveer* and *Samyukta Karnatak* (Kannada daily paper) and *Kasturi* (monthly Kannada paper); Pres. Karnatak Provincial Congress Cttee. 30-34; mem. Constituent Assembly 46; Min. of Information and Broadcasting 48-52; Gov. of Bihar 52-57; Chair. Gandhi Smarak Nidhi 57-, and Peace Foundation, New Delhi 59-; imprisoned for sedition (during freedom movement) 21-23, 24-26 and took part in civil disobedience 41; mem. of Rajya Sabha (Parl.) 62-.
Publs. In English: *Satyagraha—Its History and Technique* 46, *Glimpses of Gandhiji* 49, *Satyagraha in Action* 49, *Upanishads in Story and Dialogue* 50, *Satyagraha—Pathway to Peace* 50, *Mahayogi* (biography of Aurobindo Ghose); and many books in Kannada and Hindi on religion, philosophy, and other subjects.
2 Residency Road, Bangalore 25, Mysore State, India.

Dix, Otto; German painter; b. 2 Dec. 1891; ed. art school.
Professor, State Acad. of Art, Dresden 27-33; Home Guard, Second World War, Prisoner of War, Colmar 45-46; Exhibitions: Degenerate Art Exhbn. 37, Stuttgart Exhibition 63; paintings in U.S., German and French museums and art galleries; mem. Acad. of Arts, W. Berlin 55; Cornelius Prize, Düsseldorf 59, Grosses Bundesverdienstkreuz 59; Hon. Fellow Medizinischen Akad. "Carl Gustav Carus," Dresden; Hon. mem. Accad. delle Arti del Disegno, Florence.
Works: war drawings and paintings, biblical subjects.
7761 Hemmenhofen, Bodensee, German Federal Republic.

Dixey, Frank, C.M.G., O.B.E., D.SC., F.R.S., F.G.S., F.R.G.S.; British geologist; b. 7 April 1892; ed. Univ. of Wales.
Lecturer in Geology, Univ. of Wales 14-15; mil. service, R.G.A., Western Front 15-18; Govt. Geologist, Sierra Leone 18-21; Dir. Geological Survey of Nyasaland 21-39; Dir. Water Development Dept. Northern Rhodesia 39-44; Dir. Geological Survey, Nigeria 44-47; Geological Adviser to Colonial Sec. and Dir. of Overseas Geological Surveys 47-59; Murchison Medal, Geological Society, London; Draper Medal, Geological Society, S. Africa; Hon. mem. Geological Society, Belgium and Geological Soc. South Africa; Hon. M.I.M.M.
Publ. *Practical Handbook of Water Supply, London.*
Woodpecker Cottage, Bramber, Sussex, England.
Telephone: Steyning 2313.

Dixon, Rt. Hon. Sir Owen, P.C., O.M., G.C.M.G., M.A., LL.B.; Australian lawyer; b. 28 April 1886; ed. Melbourne Univ.
Called to Victoria Bar 10; K.C. 22; Acting Justice Victoria Supreme Court 26; Justice High Court of Australia 29-52; Chair. Central Wool Cttee., Shipping Control Board, etc. 41-42; Minister to U.S.A. 42-44; UN mediator for Kashmir 50; Chief Justice, Australian High Court 52-64; Howland Prize, Yale Univ. 55; Hon. LL.D. Harvard 58, Hon. D.C.L. Oxford 58.
4 Higham Road, Auburn, Melbourne, Australia.

Dixon, Paul Rand; American government official; b. 29 Sept. 1913; ed. Vanderbilt Univ. and Univ. of Florida.
Assistant Football Coach, Florida Univ. 36-38; Trial Attorney, Fed. Trade Comm. 38-57, Chair. 61-; U.S. Naval Service 42-45, Chief Counsel, Staff Dir., Sub-Cttee. on Antitrust and Monopoly, U.S. Senate 57-61. Federal Trade Commission, Washington 25, D.C.; Home: 5911 Carlton Lane, Washington, D.C. 20016, U.S.A.

Dixon, Shirley Greenshields, Q.C., B.A., B.C.L.; Canadian industrialist; b. 1891; ed. McGill Univ.
Advocate 14; served First World War; partner Laverty, Hale & Dixon, Montreal 21-28; K.C. 28; partner Stairs, Dixon & Claxton, Montreal 28-39; now partner Dixon, Claxton, Senecal, Turnbull & Mitchell; mem. Canadian Bar Asscn.; Dir. Gypsum Lime and Alabastine; Pres. Courtaulds (Canada) Ltd., Dir. American Viscose Corpn., Cockshutt Plow Co. Ltd.; Administrator Rayon Products Wartime Prices and Trade Board; Liberal.
3236 The Boulevard, Westmount, P.Q., Canada.

Dixon, Thomas F., B.S.ENG., B.S. and M.S. CHEM.ENG., M.S.AERO.ENG.; American executive and aerospace engineer; b.15 March 1916; ed. Vanderbilt and Michigan Univs., and California Inst. of Technology.
Research Engineer, N. American Aviation 46-54, Dir. Propulsion Center, Rocketdyne Div. N. American Aviation 54-55, Chief Engineer 55-60, Vice-Pres. Research and Engineering 60-63, Vice-Pres. 63-; Dep. Assoc. Administrator Nat. Aeronautics and Space Admin. 61-63; Robert M. Goddard Memorial Award 57;

shared Louis W. Hill Space Transportation Award 61; Fellow, American Rocket Soc.
434 Chautauqua Boulevard, Pacific Palisades, Calif., U.S.A.

Diz, Adolfo Cesar, C.P.A., D.ECON., M.A., D.PHIL.; Argentine economist; b. 12 May 1931; ed. Univ. de Buenos Aires and Univ. of Chicago.
Instructor of Statistics, Univ. of Buenos Aires 51-55, 58-59; Prof. of Statistics, Univ. of Tucumán 59-60, Dir. Inst. of Econ. Research 59-65, Prof. of Statistics and Econometrics 60-61, 64, Prof. of Monetary Theory 62, 65-66; Exec. Dir. Int. Monetary Fund (IMF) 66-; mem. of Argentine socs. and of Directive Cttee., Argentine Branch, Inst. of Applied Econ. Science, Paris, American Econ. Asscn. and Econometric Soc.
Publs. Numerous economic articles.
International Monetary Fund, 19th and H. Streets, N.W., Washington D.C. 20431, U.S.A.
Telephone: DUI-2901/4.

Djerassi, Carl, A.B., PH.D.; American chemist; b. 29 Oct. 1923; ed. Kenyon Coll. and Univ. of Wisconsin. Research Chemist, Ciba Pharmaceutical Co., Summit, N.J. 42-43, 45-49; Assoc. Dir. of Research, Syntex, S.A., Mexico City 49-51, Research Vice-Pres. 57-60; Assoc. Prof. of Chemistry Wayne State Univ., Detroit 52-54, Prof. 54-59, Stanford Univ. 59-; Dir. Syntex Corpn. 60-; Chair. of the Board Synvar Associates 66-; British Chemical Soc. Centenary Lecturer 64; mem. Editorial Board *Journal of Organic Chemistry* 55-58, *Tetrahedron* 58-, *Steroids* 63-, *Proceedings* of Nat. Acad. of Sciences 64-; mem. Latin-American Science Board of Nat. Acad. of Sciences 65, Chair. 66-; American Chemical Soc. awards: Award in Pure Chemistry 58, Baekeland Medal 59, Fritzsche Medal 60; mem. Nat. Acad. of Sciences, Brazilian Acad. of Sciences; Hon. D.Sc., Nat. Univ. of Mexico and Kenyon Coll., Ohio; Hon. Fellow British Chemical Soc. 68.
Publs. (author or co-author) over 600 articles and *Optical Rotatory Dispersion* 60, *Steroid Reactions* 63, *Interpretation of Mass Spectra of Organic Compounds* 64, *Structure Elucidation of Natural Products by Mass Spectrometry* (2 vols.) 64, *Mass Spectrometry of Organic Compounds* 67.
Department of Chemistry, Stanford University, Calif. 94305, U.S.A.

Djermakoye, Issoufou Saidou; Niger politician; b. 10 July 1920; ed. Niger and France.
Counsellor, French Union 47-57; Senator to French Senate 57; Vice-Pres. Council of Ministers of Niger 58; Minister of Justice 59; Perm. Rep. of the Republic of Niger to UN 61-62; Minister of Justice 63-65; Under-Sec. in charge of Trusteeship Affairs, UN 67-68, Under Sec.-Gen. 68-.
United Nations Secretariat, New York City, N.Y.; and 118 East 76th Street, New York, N.Y. 10021, U.S.A.

Djilas, Milovan; Yugoslav writer and politician; b. 11; ed. Belgrade Univ.
Member Communist Party 32, imprisoned 32-35; mem. Central Cttee. Communist Party 38, Politburo 40; successively Minister, Head of Parliament, Vice-Pres. of Yugoslavia until 54; expelled from Communist Party 54; imprisoned 56-61, May 62-Dec. 66.
Publs. *Essays 1941-46* 47, *Struggle of the Communist Party of Yugoslavia* 48, *On National History as an Educational Subject* 49, *Lenin and the Relations Between Socialist States* 50, *On New Roads to Socialism* 50, *Reflections on Various Questions* 51, *On the Aggressive Pressure of the Soviet Bloc against Yugoslavia* 51, *The Legend of Njegoš* 52, *The New Class* 57; in English: *Land without Justice* 58, *Montenegro* 64, *The Leper* 65.
Belgrade, Yugoslavia.

Djioyev, Kosta Kargoyevich; Soviet politician; b. 1916; ed. Tskhinvali State Pedagogic Inst. and Higher Party School of C.P.S.U. Central Committee.
Accountant, Party Official 34-41; Soviet Army 41-46; Party Official, Sec. for South Ossetian Regional Cttee. of the Party, First Vice-Chair. South Ossetian Regional Soviet 46-65; Chair. South Ossetian Autonomous Regional Soviet 65-; mem. Central Cttee. C.P. of Georgia; Deputy to U.S.S.R. Supreme Soviet; mem. C.P.S.U. 39-.
South Ossetian Regional Soviet of Working People's Deputies, Tskhinvali, U.S.S.R.

Djussoyev, Georgi Nikolayevich; Soviet politician; b. 1926; ed. Tskhinvali State Pedagogical Inst. and Higher Party School of C.P.S.U. Central Committee.
Member C.P.S.U. 50-; Official at Regional Cttee. of Young Communist League, Official, South Ossetian Regional Cttee. of C.P. of Georgia, Chair. Tskhinvali District Soviet, Chair. South Ossetian Regional Soviet of Working People's Deputies 50-65; First Sec. South Ossetian Regional Cttee. of C.P. of Georgia 65-; mem. Central Cttee. of C.P. of Georgia; Deputy to U.S.S.R. Supreme Soviet.
South Ossetian Regional Committee, Communist Party of Georgia, Tskhinvali, U.S.S.R.

Doan, Charles Austin, B.S., M.D.; American physician; b. 5 June 1896; ed. Hiram Coll., Johns Hopkins Medical School, Univ. of Cincinnati and Harvard Medical School.
Asst. Dept. of Anatomy, Johns Hopkins Medical School 24; Asst., Dept. of Medicine, Harvard Medical School; Asst. Physician, Boston City Hospital and Asst., Thorndike Memorial Laboratory 25; Assoc. in Medical Research, Rockefeller Inst. for Medical Research 25-30; Prof. of Medicine and Dir., Dept. of Medical and Surgical Research, Ohio State Univ. 30-36; Chair. and Prof. Dept. of Medicine and Dir. of Medical Research 36-44; Dean, Coll. of Medicine, Dir. Univ. Health Centre, Ohio State Univ. 44-61, Prof. of Medicine and Dir. Medical Research 44-61, Dir. Division of Hematology, Dept. of Medicine, Coll. of Medicine; Pres. American Soc. of Hematology 62-63; Pres. Ohio Public Health Asscn. 38-40; Dir.-at-large, Nat. Tuberculosis Asscn., Medical Dir. Columbus Cancer Clinic 47; mem. Asscn. American Physicians, American Society for Experimental Pathology, American Asscn. for Advancement of Science; Gov. for Ohio of F.A.C.P.; Chair. Board of Govs., Vice-Pres. M.A.C.P. 57-59; A.M.A. Dist. Service Citation, Gold Medal Award 60.
Home: 4935 Olentangy Boulevard; Office: 3600 Olentangy River Road, Columbus, Ohio, U.S.A.

Doan, Herbert D., B.CH.E. (son of Leland I. Doan, q.v.); American chemical executive; b. 5 Sept. 1922; ed. Cornell Univ.
Manager, Chemicals Dept., Dow Chemical Co. 56-60, Exec. Vice-Pres. Dow Chemical Co. 60-62, Pres. 62-; Dir. Chemical State Savings Bank; mem. Planning Comm., City of Midland; Trustee Dow Foundation; mem. American Inst. of Chemical Engineers, Cornell Univ. Engineering Coll. Council, American Chem. Soc., Board of Fellows Saginaw Valley Coll.
The Dow Chemical Company, Midland, Michigan, U.S.A.

Doan, Leland Ira (father of Herbert D. Doan, q.v.); American executive; b. 9 Nov. 1894; ed. Univ. of Michigan.
Started with Dow Chemical Co. 17, Sales Dept. 18, Gen. Sales Man. 29, Dir. of Sales 35-49, Dir. of Dow Chemical Co. 35-, Vice-Pres. 38-49, Pres. 49-62, Chair. Exec. Cttee. 62-; Dir. of Dowell Inc., Michigan Bell Telephone Co., Nat. Bank of Detroit, Bendix Corpn.; Board Chair. Dow Corning Corpn..
Home: 3701 Valley Drive, Midland, Michigan; Office:

The Dow Chemical Company, Midland, Michigan 48640, U.S.A.
Telephone: 517-TE2-2000.

Doane, Richard Congdon; American businessman; b. 26 Feb. 1898; ed. Yale Univ.
North African rep. Lamborn & Co. of N.Y., Algiers 22-23; joined Sales Dept., Int. Paper Co., N.Y.C. 24, Manager Newsprint Sales 23-38, Dir. 48-, Vice-Pres. 48-54, Pres. 54-59, Chief Exec. Officer 59-67, also Chair. until 67; Dir. Canadian Int. Paper Co. 38-, Gen. Man. 47-48, Chair. Board 61-, Dir. Int. Envelope Corpn., Commerce and Industry Asscn., N.Y.
Home: 127 E. 64th Street; Office: 220 E. 42nd Street, New York City, N.Y., U.S.A.

Dobb, Maurice Herbert, M.A., PH.D.; British economist; b. 1900; ed. Charterhouse and Pembroke Coll. Cambridge.
Research Student London School of Economics 22-24; Lecturer in Economics in Cambridge Univ. 26 and Lecturer and Fellow of Trinity Coll. 48; Visiting Lecturer (Russian Economic and Social History) Univ. of London School of Slavonic Studies 43-46; Visiting Prof. Univ. of Delhi School of Economics 51; Reader in Economics, Cambridge Univ. 59-67; Hon. Dr. Econ. Sc. Charles Univ., Prague.
Publs. *Wages* 28, *Political Economy and Capitalism* 37, 40, *Studies in the Development of Capitalism* 46, *Soviet Economic Development since 1917* 47, 67, *Economic Theory and Socialism, Collected Papers* 55, *An Essay on Economic Growth and Planning* 60, *Papers on Capitalism, Development and Planning* 67; collaborated in editing Royal Econ. Soc.'s edn. *Works and Correspondence of David Ricardo* 48-54.
Trinity College, Cambridge, and College Farmhouse, Fulbourn, Cambridgeshire, England.

Dobbs, Mattiwilda; American singer; ed. Spelman Coll., Atlanta ,and Columbia Univ.
Studied with Lotte Leonard 46-50; Marian Anderson scholarship, soloist at Mexico Univ. Festival 47; studied at Mannes Music School and Berkshire Music Center 48, with Pierre Bernac, Paris 50-52; 1st Voice Prize, Geneva Int. Competition 51; concert tour Netherlands, France and Sweden 52; debut La Scala (Milan) in *L'Italiana in Algeri* 53; sang at Glyndebourne 53, 54, 56, 61, Royal Opera House, Covent Garden (London) 54, 55, 56, 59, San Francisco Opera 55, Metropolitan Opera (New York) 56-; Stockholm Royal Opera 57-; Hamburg State Opera 61-63; concert appearances in Europe, U.S.A., Mexico, Israel, Australia, New Zealand and U.S.S.R.; Order of the North Star (Sweden).
Vastmannagatan 50, Stockholm, Sweden.
Telephone: 34-83-00.

Dobell, Sir William, Kt., O.B.E.; Australian artist; b. 24 Sept. 1899; ed. Julia Ashton School, Sydney, and Slade School of Fine Arts, London.
Part-time Art Master, East Sydney Technical Coll.; Loan Exhbn. with Margaret Preston, Art Gallery of New South Wales 41; Twelve Australian Artists Exhbn., London 53; Venice Biennale 54; Australian Painting Exhbn., Tate Gallery, London 62; one-man exhbn., London 65.
c/o Hal Missingham, National Art Gallery, Sydney, Australia.

Dobi, István; Hungarian politician; b. 31 Dec. 1898.
Active in labour movement from youth, and in organizing agricultural labourers during 'twenties; also active Social Democrat in early 'thirties, but joined Smallholders' Party 37; resistance movement during 39-45 war; returned to Hungary 45; rep. Smallholders' Party to provisional Nat. Assembly, became Vice-Pres. of the party; mem. of the govt. from 45, first as Minister without Portfolio, later as Minister of Agriculture; Pres.

Smallholders' Party 47-49; Prime Minister 48-52; Pres. Presidential Council 52-67, mem. 67-; Pres. Nat. Council of Agricultural Production Co-op. 51-66; Pres. Nat. Fed. of Co-operatives 67; Vice-Pres. People's Patriotic Front; Order of Merit 55; mem. Central Cttee. Socialist Workers' Party 59-; Lenin Peace Prize 62.
National Co-op. Council, Budapest V, Szabadság tér 14, Hungary.
Telephone: 124-016.

Dobiáš, Václav; Czechoslovak composer; b. 22 Sept. 1909.
Professor of Composition, Acad. of Music and Dramatic Art, Prague 50; Sec. Union of Czechoslovak Composers 51-63; awarded Golden Medal of the Int. Congress of the Defenders of Peace 50; Laureate of the Czechoslovak State Prize 52, 56 and 58; mem. Cultural Board 57; mem. Central Cttee. Communist Party of Czechoslovakia 58-; Deputy to Nat. Assembly 60-; Order of Labour 59.
Compositions include cantatas *Stalingrad* 45, *Command No. 368 for the Liberation of Prague* 46, *To my Country and to Peace* 50; also instrumental and chamber music and three symphonies.
Slavíčkova 13, Bubeneč, Prague 6, Czechoslovakia.

Dobozy, Imre; Hungarian writer; b. 30 Oct. 1917.
General Sec., Asscn. of Hungarian Writers; Kossuth Prize.
Publs. *New Seed in Cumenia* (novel), *Spring Wind* (short story), *Storm* (play and film), *Continuation To-morrow* (play), films: *Yesterday, Dawn, The Song of the Swain, Corporal and the Others*.
Hungarian Writers' Asscn., Budapest VI, Bajza u. 18, Hungary.
Telephone: 229-073.

Dobrée, Lieut-Col. Bonamy, O.B.E., M.A.; British literary critic; b. 2 Feb. 1891; ed. Haileybury and Cambridge Univ.
Entered Royal Military Acad. Woolwich 09, Royal Field Artillery 10; served First World War France and Palestine; Lecturer, London Univ. 25-26; Prof. of English, Egyptian Univ. Cairo 26-29; Prof. of English Literature Leeds Univ. 36-55; served Second World War 39-45.
Publs. *Restoration Comedy, Restoration Tragedy, Sarah Churchill, The Lamp and the Lute, Variety of Ways, John Wesley, Giacomo Casanova, As their Friends Saw Them, Modern Prose Style, The Floating Republic* (with G. E. Manwaring), *The Letters of King George III, From Anne to Victoria* (Editor), *English Revolts* 37, *The Victorians and After* (with Edith Batho) 38, *The Unacknowledged Legislator* 42, *English Essayists* (*Britain in Pictures*) 47, *The London Book of English Verse* (with Herbert Read) 32, *The London Book of English Prose* 49, *Alexander Pope* 51, *The Broken Cistern* 54, *William Penn, The Early Eighteenth Century* (Oxford History of English Literature, Vol. VII), *Three Eighteenth Century Figures* 62, *Rudyard Kipling: Realist and Fatalist* 67.
15 Pond Road, Blackheath, London, S.E.3, England.

Dobrovolsky, Nikolai Nikolayevich; Soviet politician; b. 1916; ed. Moscow Machine Tool Inst.
Head of Dept., S. M. Kirov Machine Tool Factory, Kishinev, Moldavia 41; Soviet Army 41-45; Deputy Perm. Rep. of Council of Ministers of Moldavian S.S.R. to U.S.S.R. Council of Ministers 46-65, 67-; Acting Perm. Rep. 66-67; Order of Red Star, Badge of Honour and other awards.
Permanent Representation of Moldavian Council of Ministers to U.S.S.R. Council of Ministers, 18 Kuznetsky Most, Moscow, U.S.S.R.

Dobrynin, Anatoly Fedorovich, M.SC.; Soviet diplomatist; b. 1919; ed. technical coll.
Engineer at aircraft plant, Second World War; joined diplomatic service 44; Counsellor, later Minister-

Counsellor, Soviet Embassy, Washington 52-55; Asst. Deputy Minister of Foreign Affairs 55-57; Under-Sec.-Gen. for Political and Security Council Affairs UN 57-60, Head American Dept., U.S.S.R. Ministry of Foreign Affairs 60-61; Ambassador to U.S.A. 61-.
Embassy of the Union of Soviet Socialist Republics, Washington 6, D.C., U.S.A.

Dobson, Sir Roy Hardy, Kt., C.B.E., J.P.; British aeronautical engineer; b. 27 Sept. 1891.
Served apprenticeship with T. & R. Lees, Engineers, Manchester; joined engineering staff of A. V. Roe & Co. Ltd. 14, appointed Works Man. 19, Gen. Man. 34, Dir. 36, Man. Dir. 41; Chair. of Board A. V. Roe, Canada, Ltd. 51; Dir. Hawker Siddeley Aircraft Co. Ltd. (now Hawker Siddeley Group Ltd.) 44, Man. Dir. and Vice-Chair. 58-63; Chair. Hawker Siddeley Group 63-July 67, Hawker Siddeley Canada Ltd., Kelvin Construction Co. Ltd.; Dir. Hawker Siddeley Aviation Ltd., High Duty Alloys Ltd., Dominion Steel & Coal Corpn. Ltd., Dominion Coal Co. Ltd., Pres. of S.B.A.C. 63-64; Pres. Locomotive and Allied Manufacturers Asscn. 62; Hon. F.R.Ae.S.; Founders Medal, Air League 66.
18 St. James's Square, London, S.W.1; Medstead Grange, Medstead, nr. Alton, Hants., England.
Telephone: 01-930 2064 (Office).

Dobson, William Arthur Charles Harvey, M.A., D.LITT., F.R.S.C.; Canadian sinologist; b. 8 Aug. 1913; ed. Christ Church, Oxford.
Service with Argyll and Sutherland Highlanders, rising to rank of Lieut.-Col. 40-45; lecturer in Chinese, Oxford Univ. 48-52; Prof. of Chinese, Toronto Univ. 52-, Head, Dept. of East Asian Studies 52-64; Senior Fellow Massey Coll., Toronto Univ. 64; Order of Cloud and Banner, Fifth Class (China).
Publs. *Civilisations of the Orient* 55, *Late Archaic Chinese* (grammar) 59, *Early Archaic Chinese* 62, *Mencius* 63, *Late Han Chinese* 64, *The Language of the Book of Songs* 67.
Massey College, University of Toronto, Toronto 5, Ontario, Canada.
Telephone: 928-2902.

Dobzhansky, Theodosius; American (b. Russian) zoologist and biologist; b. 25 Jan. 1900; ed. Univ. of Kiev.
Asst. Prof. of Zoology, Polytechnic Inst., Kiev 21-24; Lecturer in Genetics, Univ. of Leningrad 24-27; went to U.S. 27; Fellow Int. Editorial Board, Rockefeller Foundation 27-29; Asst. Prof. of Genetics, Calif. Inst. of Technology 29-36, Prof. 36-40; Prof. of Zoology, Columbia Univ. 40-62, Prof. of Population Genetics, Rockefeller Univ. 62-; mem. numerous American socs.; Foreign mem. Royal Soc. (U.K.); Hon. D.Sc. (São Paulo, Münster, Montreal, Chicago, Sydney, Oxford, Columbia, Syracuse, Michigan Univs., Wooster Coll., Coll. of Agriculture, Louvain, Clarkson Coll. of Technology, N.Y., Kalamazoo Coll.); Daniel Giraud Elliott Medal (Nat. Acad. of Sciences) 41, Kimber Genetics Award 58, Darwin Medal (German Leopoldina Acad.) 59, Pierre Lecomte du Nouy Award 63, Nat. Medal of Science 64.
Publs. *Genetics and the Origin of Species* 37, *Evolution, Genetics, and Man* 55, *Biological Basis of Human Freedom* 56, *Mankind Evolving* 62, *Heredity and the Nature of Man* 64.
The Rockefeller University, York Avenue at 66 Street, New York, N.Y. 10021; and 425 East 63rd Street, New York, N.Y. 10021, U.S.A.

Dodd, Rev. Charles Harold, C.H., M.A.; British theologian; b. 7 April 1884; ed. Wrexham and Univ., Magdalen and Mansfield Colls., Oxford, and Berlin.
Ordained 12; Min. of Independent or Congregational Church Warwick 12-15, 18-19; Yates Lecturer in New Testament Greek and Exegesis Mansfield Coll. 15-30; Univ. Lecturer in New Testament Studies Oxford 27-30;

Grinfield Lecturer on the Septuagint Oxford 27-31; Rylands Prof. of Biblical Criticism and Exegesis Manchester Univ. 30-35; Speaker's Lecturer in Biblical Studies Oxford 33-36; Norris-Hulse Prof. of Divinity Cambridge Univ. 35-49; Fellow Jesus Coll. Cambridge 36-49, Hon. Fellow 49-; Hon. Fellow Univ. Coll. Oxford 51-; Fellow of British Acad. 46-; Gen. Dir. New Translation of the Bible (*New Testament* published 61) 50-65, Joint Dir. 66-; Hon. D.D.

Publs. *The Meaning of Paul for To-day* 20, *The Gospel in the New Testament* 26, *The Authority of the Bible* 28, *The Bible and its Background* 31, *The Epistle to the Romans* 32, *There and Back Again* 32, *The Bible and the Greeks* 35, *Parables of the Kingdom* 35, *The Apostolic Preaching and its Developments* 36, *History and the Gospel* 38, *The Johannine Epistles* 46, *The Bible To-day* 46, *Benefits of His Passion* 47, *About the Gospels* 50, *Gospel and Law* 51, *The Coming of Christ* 51, *According to the Scriptures* 53, *The Interpretation of the Fourth Gospel* 53, *New Testament Studies* 53, *Historical Tradition in the Fourth Gospel* 63, *More New Testament Studies* 68.

1 Wellington Place, Oxford, England.

Dodd, Thomas J., PH.B., LL.B., LL.D.; American politician; b. 15 May 1907; ed. Providence Coll., Yale Univ., Rollins Coll.

Assistant Chief, Civil Rights Section, Dept. of Justice 38-45; Chief Trial Counsel Nuremberg Trials 45-46; private law practice, Hartford 47-; mem. of Congress for Conn. 53-57; Senator from Conn. 59-; numerous national and foreign awards; Democrat.

Senate Office Building, Washington 25, D.C., U.S.A.

Dodds, Sir Edward Charles 1st Bt., cr. 64, M.V.O., D.SC., PH.D., F.R.S., F.R.C.P., F.R.I.C., F.R.S.E., M.D.; British biochemist; b. 89; ed. Harrow County School and London Univ.

Courtauld Prof. of Biochemistry, Univ. of London, and Dir. Courtauld Inst. of Biochemistry at Middlesex Hospital 27-65; Hon. Dir. Rheumatology Research Dept. Arthur Stanley House, Middlesex Hosp. 65-68; late Pathologist to Royal Nat. Orthopaedic Hospital; Cameron Prizeman 40; William Julius Mickle Fellowship, London 43; Charles L. Meyer Prize and Walker Prize, Royal Coll. of Surgeons 46; Garton Prize and Medal, British Empire Cancer Campaign 48; Berzelius Medal, Swedish Medical Soc.; Medals of Univs. of Ghent and Brussels; Pasteur Medal of VIIIth Congrès de Chimie Biologique de la Société de Chimie Biologique Française; Gold Medal in Therapeutics, Soc. of Apothecaries 51; Gold Medal Soc. of Chemical Industry 51; Harben Medal Royal Inst. of Public Health; Chair. Scientific Advisory Cttee. British Empire Cancer Campaign; mem. Royal Inst.; Vice-Pres. Eugenics Soc.; Past Master of Worshipful Society of Apothecaries; Vice-Pres. Royal Soc. 57-59, and Empire Rheumatism Council; Pres. Royal Coll. of Physicians 62. Publs. *Recent Advances in Medicine* (with G. E. Beaumont), *Chemical and Physiological Properties of Internal Secretions* (with F. Dickens), *The Laboratory in Surgical Practice* (with L. E. H. Whitby), and articles on biochemical subjects.

49 Sussex Square, London, W.2, England.

Dodds, Eric Robertson, M.A., F.B.A.; British classical scholar; b. 26 July 1893; ed. Campbell Coll., Belfast, and Univ. Coll., Oxford.

Lecturer in Classics Univ. Coll. Reading 19-24; Prof. of Greek, Birmingham Univ. 24-36; Regius Prof. of Greek, Oxford Univ. 36-60; Sather Visiting Prof. Univ. of Calif. 49; Pres. Classical Asscn. 63; corresp. mem. Bavarian Acad.; Hon. mem. American Acad. of Arts and Sciences; Hon. D.Litt. (Manchester, Belfast and Edinburgh); Hon. Litt.D. (Dublin Univ.); Hon. Fellow, Univ. Coll., Oxford; Hon. Student, Christ Church, Oxford.

Publs. *Select Passages Illustrative of Neoplatonism* 23 and 24, *Thirty-two Poems* 29, *Proclus' Elements of Theology* 33, *Journal and Letters of Stephen MacKenna* 36, *Euripides' Bacchae* 44, *The Greeks and the Irrational* 51, *Plato's Gorgias* 59, *Pagan and Christian in an age of Anxiety* 65.

Cromwell's House, Old Marston, Oxford, England. Telephone: Oxford 41024.

Dodds, Harold Willis, A.M., PH.D., LL.D., LITT.D.; American educationist; b. 28 June 1889; ed. Princeton and Pennsylvania Univs.

Instructor Purdue Univ. 14-16; Asst. Prof. Western Reserve Univ. 19-20; Prof. of Politics Princeton Univ. 27-34 and Pres. 33-57; Electoral Adviser to Nicaraguan Govt. 22-24; Trustee, Union Theological Seminary, Danforth Foundation; mem. American Philosophical Soc., Technical Adviser to Pres. Tacna-Arica Plebiscitary Comm. 25-26; Chief Adviser to Pres. Nat. Board of Elections of Nicaragua 28; Consultant in Election Law and Procedure, Cuban Govt. 35; Chair. American Delegation, Anglo-American Conf. on Refugee Problem, Bermuda 43; Chair. President's Comm. on Integration of Govt. Medical Services 45; mem. President's Advisory Comm. on Universal Training 47; Chair. Task Force on Personnel, 2nd Hoover Comm. 54-55.

Publs. *Out of this Nettle ... Danger* 43, *The Academic President—Educator or Caretaker?* 62.

87 College Road West, Princeton, N.J., U.S.A.

Dodge, Cleveland E., A.B., LL.D.; American company director and executive; b. 5 Feb. 1888; ed. Princeton, New York and Columbia Univs.

Phelps Dodge Corpn. 10-, Vice-Pres. 24-61; Officer First World War 17-19; Pres. Y.M.C.A. New York City 25-35, Mining and Metallurgical Society of America 37, and Woodrow Wilson Foundation 50; Alumni Trustee, Princeton Univ. 41-45; Dir. Emeritus Int. House, New York City; Chair. Exec. Cttee. Int. Cttee. Y.M.C.A.; Board of Trustees, Teacher's Coll., Columbia Univ.; Dir. Near East Foundation, Protestant Council, New York; Hon. Trustee, American Museum of Natural History; Trustee, Grant Foundation; Dir. Merchants Refrigerating Co., Atlantic Mutual Insurance Co.; Dir. Phelps Dodge Corpn.; Grand Commdr. Order of George I of Greece; Order of Homayoun (Iran).

Dodgewood Road, Riverdale, New York City 71, N.Y.; Office: 300 Park Avenue, New York City 22, U.S.A.

Dodge, John Vilas; American editor; b. 25 Sept. 1909; ed. Northwestern Univ., Illinois and Univ. of Bordeaux. Freelance writer 31-32; Editor *Northwestern University Alumni News*, and Official Publications of Northwestern Univ. 32-35, Exec. Sec. Northwestern Univ. Alumni Asscn. 37-38; Asst. Editor *Encyclopaedia Britannica*, and Assoc. Editor *Britannica Book of the Year* 38-43, Assoc. Editor *Ten Eventful Years* (4 vol. History 37-46) 47; Asst. Editor *Encyclopaedia Britannica* 46-50, Managing Editor 50-60, Exec. Editor 60-64, Senior Vice-Pres. Editorial 64-65, Senior Editorial Consultant 65-; Editor *Britannica World Language Dictionary* 54.

Office: 425 N. Michigan Avenue, Chicago, Illinois 60611; Home: 1043 Briarwood Lane, Northbrook, Illinois 60062, U.S.A.

Doe, G. E. K.; Ghanaian diplomatist; b. 27; ed. Presbyterian Primary School, Keta, Methodist Middle School, Cape Coast, Adisadel Coll., Cape Coast and Gray's Inn, London.

Clerk in Political Admin., Ashanti; with United Africa Co. of Ghana; Officer, Colonial Secretary's Office, Ministry of Local Govt.; called to Bar, Gray's Inn, London 56; private legal practice, Ghana 56-62; Sec. and Dir. of various companies, Ghana; High Commr. to Nigeria 62-63; Ambassador to German Fed. Rep. 63-. Embassy of Ghana, Bonn, German Federal Republic.

Doğramaci, Ihsan, M.D., LL.D.; Turkish pediatrician; b. 3 April 1915; ed. Istanbul and Wash. Univs.
Assistant Prof. of Pediatrics, Ankara Univ. 49-54, Prof. and Head of Dept. 54-63; Dir. Research Inst. of Child Health, Ankara 58-; Prof. of Pediatrics and Head of Dept., Hacettepe Faculty of Medicine 63-, Dean of Faculty June 63-Nov. 63; Pres. Ankara Univ. 63-65; Pres. Hacettepe Medical Centre, Ankara 65-; Chancellor, Hacettepe Univ. 67-; mem. of UNICEF Exec. Board 60-; Hon. Fellow American Acad. Pediatrics 59; mem. Deutsche Gesellschaft für Kinderheilkunde 50, Soc. de Pédiatrie de Paris 58, British Paed. Asscn. 64; Hon. LL.D. Nebraksa Univ.
Publs. include 3 books, 6 monographs and articles on child health and pediatric topics.
Hacettepe University, Ankara, Turkey.
Telephone: 11-94-42.

Doi, Masaharu; Japanese chemical executive; b. 1 May 1894; ed. Tokyo Univ.
Sumitomo Chemical Co. 20-, Gen. Man. 42, Dir. 44-, Pres. 47-63, Chsir. 63-; Dir. Japan Atomic Industrial Forum; Vice-Chair. Fed. of Econ. Orgs.; Exec. Consultant Japan Chem. Soc.; Chair. Japan-Italy and Italy-Japan Econ. Cttees., Kansai Nikkan Kyokai.
Sumitomo Chemical Co., 15 5-chome, Kitahama, Hihashiku, Osaka; No. 9, 2-chome, Kuise Minamishinmachi, Amagasaki City, Hyogo Pref., Japan.
Telephone: Osaka 203-1231.

Doi, H.E. Cardinal Peter Tatsuo; Japanese ecclesiastic; b. 22 Dec. 1892; ed. Sendai Seminary and College De Propaganda Fide, Rome.
Ordained Priest 21; Parish Priest at Wakamatsu 22-33; Private Sec. Tokyo Apostolic Del. 33-37; Archbishop of Tokyo 38-; created Cardinal by Pope John XXIII 60.
Archbishop's House, 16-15 Sekiguchi 3 chome, Bunkyo-ku, Tokyo, Japan.
Telephone: 943-2301.

Doisy, Edward Adelbert, A.B., M.S., PH.D.; American university professor; b. 13 Nov. 1893; ed. Univ. of Illinois and Harvard Univ.
Asst. in Biochemistry, Harvard Medical School 15-17; Army service 17-19; Instructor, Assoc. and Assoc. Prof. in Biochemistry, Washington Univ. School of Medicine 19-23; Prof. of Biochemistry, and Dir. of Dept., St. Louis Univ. School of Medicine 23-65; Distinguished Service Prof. Emeritus of Biochemistry and Dir. Emer. of Edward A. Doisy Dept. of Biochemistry 65-; awarded gold medal, St. Louis Medical Soc. 35; Willard Gibbs Medal 41; Squibb award 44; shared the Nobel Prize in Physiology and Medicine for 43 with Dr. Henrik Dam; Hon. Sc.D. Washington Univ., Yale, Chicago, Central Coll., Illinois Univ., Gustavus Adolphus Coll.; Dr. h.c. Paris; LL.D. (Hon.) St. Louis Univ.; mem. Pontifical Acad. of Science 48, American Acad. of Arts and Sciences, Nat. Acad. Sciences, American Philosophical Soc.
Office: 1402 South Grand Boulevard, St. Louis, Missouri 63104, U.S.A.
Telephone: TOwnsend 5-2288.

Doke, Clement Martyn, M.A., D.LITT.; British philologist; b. 16 May 1893; ed. Transvaal Univ. Coll., Pretoria, and London Univ.
Missionary S. African Baptist Missionary Society 14-21; Lecturer in Bantu Languages, Univ. of Witwatersrand, Johannesburg 23; Prof. and Head of Dept. of Bantu Studies 31-53; Editor *South African Baptist* 22-47; Joint Editor *Bantu Studies* 31-41 and *African Studies* 42-53; has conducted research trips to Lamba, Ila, Shona, the Bushman tribes, etc.; Pres. Baptist Union of S. Africa 49-50; Acting Principal, Baptist Theological Coll. of Southern Africa 51 and 55.
Publs. *Ukulayana Kwawukumo* (translation of New Testament in Lamba) 21, *Lamba Folklore* 27, *Text Book*

of Zulu Grammar 27, *Unification of the Shona Dialects* 31, *The Lambas of Northern Rhodesia* 31, *Comparative Study in Shona Phonetics* 31, *Bantu Linguistic Terminology, Text Book of Lamba Grammar* 38, (with the late Dr. B. W. Vilakazi) *Zulu-English Dictionary* 48, *The Southern Bantu Languages* 54, *Textbook of Southern Sotho Grammar* 57 (with the late Dr. S. M. Mofokeng), *English-Zulu Dictionary* 58 (with the late Dr. D. McK. Malcolm and J. M. A. Sikakana), *Amasiwi Awalesa* (trans. of Bible in Lamba) 59, *Contributions to the History of Bantu Linguistics* 61 (with D. T. Cole), *English-Lamba Vocabulary* 63.
5 Recreation Road, Alice, Cape Province, South Africa.
Telephone: Alice 92.

Doko, Toshiwo; Japanese business executive; b. 15 Sept. 1896; ed. Tokyo Inst. of Technology.
Former Pres., Ishikawajima-Harima Heavy Industries; also Tokyo Shibaura Electric.
Ishikawajima-Harima Heavy Industries, New Ohtemachi Building, 2-4 Ohtemachi, Chiyodaku, Tokyo, Japan.

Dolanský, Jaromír, LL.D.; Czechoslovak politician; b. 25 Feb. 1895; ed. Charles Univ., Prague.
Imprisoned by the Nazis 39-45; Minister of Finance 46-49; Minister-Chair. State Planning Comm. 49-51; Deputy Prime Minister 51-63; mem. of Presidium of Central Cttee. of C.P. of Czechoslovakia 46-68; Chair. State Wages Comm. 55-65; Chair. Comm. of Central Cttee. of C.P. of Czechoslovakia for questions of Living Standards 63-66, mem. 67-68; mem. State Comm. for Finance, Prices and Wages 65-66; Klement Gottwald Order 55, 65; Korean and Indonesian decorations.
National Assembly, Prague, Czechoslovakia.

Dolci, Danilo; Italian writer and social worker; b. 28 June 1924; ed. Faculty of Architecture, Milan Polytechnic.
Collaborated with Saltini, founder of Christian community Nomadelfia; social work in Sicily 52-; opened five centres for study of problem of providing full employment for a traditionally under-employed population 58; Premio della Bontà, Milan 54, Lenin Peace Prize 58.
Publs. *Banditi a Partinico* 55 (English trans. 60), *Inchiesta a Palermo* 56, *Processo all' articolo 4* 58, *To Feed the Hungary* 59, *Spreco* 60 (English trans. 63), *Conversazioni* 62, *Verso un mondo nuovo* 64 (English trans. 65), *Chi Gioca Solo* 66, *Ai piu giovani* 67.
Centro Studi e Iniziative, Largo Scalia 5, Partinico (Palermo), Sicily, Italy.

Dölger, Franz, DR. PHIL.; German byzantinist; b. 4 Oct. 1891; ed. Aschaffenburg Gymnasium and Univ. of Munich.
Director of Byzantine Inst., Univ. of Munich 31-59, Prof. Emeritus 59-; mem. Bavarian Acad. of Sciences 35-, Sec. Philology and History Section 46-64; Pres. Asscn. Int. des Etudes Byzantines 61-; Publisher *Byzantinische Zeitschrift* 24-63; Orden Pour le Mérite; numerous honorary degrees.
Publs. *Regesten der Oströmischen Kaiser I-V* 24-64, *Facsimiles byzant. Kaiserurkunden* 31, *Aus den Schatzkammern des Heiligen Berges* 48, *Byzanz. und die europäische Staatenwelt* 53, *Byzantinische Diplomatik* (essays) 56, *Paraspora* (essays) 61, *Einführung in die byz. Diplomatik*, Vol. 1 (with J. Karagiannopulos) 68.
Agnesstrasse 38, Munich 13, German Federal Republic.

Dolgoplosk, Boris Alexandrovich; Soviet organic chemist; b. 1905; ed. Moscow Univ.
At synthetic rubber plants 32-46; Instructor, later Prof. Yaroslavl Technical Inst. 44-46; Assoc. All-Union Research Inst. of Synthetic Rubber 46-; Assoc., Inst. of High Molecular Compounds, U.S.S.R. Acad. of Sciences; mem. C.P.S.U. 45-; Corresp. mem. U.S.S.R

Acad. of Sciences 58-64, mem. 64-; State Prize (twice). U.S.S.R. Academy of Sciences, 14 Lenin Prospekt, Moscow, U.S.S.R.

Dolin, Anton (Patrick Healey-Kay); British ballet dancer and choreographer; b. 27 July 1904; ed. privately.

Actor and dancer 16-23; Diaghilev's Russian Ballet Co. 23-27, 29-31, created roles in *Le Train Bleu, Le Bal, Zepher and Flore, Le Facheaux, Fils Prodigue, Les Biches;* associated with Camargo Soc.; Guest Dancer, Vic-Wells Ballet Co. 31-35, Markova-Dolin Ballet Co. 35-37; founded as Artistic Dir. and Premier Dancer London Festival Ballet 50-59; Rome Opera Dir. of Ballet 60, now artistic adviser to Les Grands Ballets Canadiens; choreographic works: *David, Job, Nightingale and the Rose, Rhapsody in Blue, Quintet, Capriccioso, Pas de Quatre, Hymn to the Sun, Espagnol, Giselle, Variations for Four, The Swan of Tuonela.*
Publs. *Divertissement* 30, *Ballet Go Round* 39, *Pas de Deux* 50, *Markova* 53, *Autobiography* 59, *The Sleeping Ballerina* 66.
c/o Martins Bank, 5 Hanover Square, London, W.1, England.

Doll, William Richard Shaboe, O.B.E., F.R.S., M.D., D.SC., F.R.C.P.; British epidemiologist and medical researcher; b. 28 Oct. 1912; ed. Westminster School and St. Thomas's Hospital Medical School, Univ. of London.
Military Service 39-45; with Medical Research Council's Statistical Research Unit 48-, Dir. 61-; mem. Advisory Cttee. on Medical Research WHO 63, Council of Int. Epidemiological Asscn. 61, Scientific Cttee. Int. Agency for Cancer Research 65-; Hon. Assoc. Physician Central Middlesex Hospital 49-; Bisset Hawkins Medal, Royal Coll. of Physicians, London 62, UN Award for Cancer Research 62.
Publs. Articles on aetiology of lung cancer, leukaemia, epidemiology, etc., including *Medical Treatment of Gastric Ulcer* 64, *Mortality in Relation to Smoking* 64.
24 Lansdowne Road, Holland Park, London, W.11, England.

Dölle, Hans, Dr. Jur., Dr. h.c.; German lawyer; b. 25 Aug. 1893; ed. Berlin, Freiburg and Lausanne Univs. Professor of Law, Hamburg; Vice-Pres. Max Planck Soc. 61-.
Publs. *Kernprobleme des internationalen Rechts der freiwilligen Gerichtsbarkeit* 61, *Familienrecht, mit rechtsvergleichenden Hinweisen* 2 vols. 64-65, *Der Beitrag der Rechtsvergleichung zum deutschen Recht, Hundert Jahre deutsches Rechtsleben 1860-1960* 62.
2 Hamburg 22, Schöne Aussicht 16, German Federal Republic.
Telephone: 220-60-19.

Dollezhal, Nikolay Antonovich; Soviet combustion engineer; b. 99; ed. Moscow Higher Technical School.
Instructor, Inst. of Nat. Economy, and Moscow Higher Technical School 23-32; Technical Dir. Leningrad Inst. of Nitrogen Mfg. Equipments 32-34; Chief Engineer Kiev "Bolshevik" plant 35-38; Dir. Moscow Research Inst. of Chemical Machinery 42-53; mem. Bureau of Dept. of Physico—Technical Problems of Energy of U.S.S.R. Acad. of Sciences 63-; Corresp. mem. U.S.S.R. Acad. of Sciences 53-62, mem. 62-; Bureau mem. Dept. Technical Science, U.S.S.R. Acad. of Sciences 60-; State Prize thrice, Lenin Prize 57, Hero of Socialist Labour, etc.
Publs. *The Principles of Designing Steam Operated Power Units* 33, *Theory of Compressor Valves* 41; *Reactor of Atomic Power Station of U.S.S.R. Academy of Sciences* 56; *Uranium-graphite reactors in power stations with steam heating* 57.
U.S.S.R. Academy of Sciences, 14 Lenin Prospekt, Moscow, U.S.S.R.

Dollinger, Werner, DR. RER. POL.; German politician and industrialist; b. 10 Oct. 1918; ed. School of Commerce, Nuremberg and Frankfurt Univ.
Military service 43-45; Chair. Neustadt Chamber of Commerce and Industry 48; founder mem. of CSU and Neustadt Town Councillor 46-; Dist. Chair. CSU 51; Dist. Councillor 52-; mem. Bundestag and CDU/CSU Parl. group 53-; mem. ECSC Common Assembly 56-58; Dep. Chair. CSU Land chapter in Bundestag 57-62; Chair. CDU/CSU working cttee. on budget, finance and taxes 57-62; Minister of Fed. Property 62-66; Minister of Posts and Telecommunications 66-.
Office: Adenauerallee 81, 53 Bonn; Home: 30 Hampfergrundweg, 853 Neustadt/Aisch, German Federal Republic.

Dolmatovsky, Evgeny Aronovich; Soviet poet; b. 1915; ed. Moscow Literature Inst.
State Prizewinner 49; Orders of Great Patriotic War (1st Class), of Red Star, Badge of Honour, and other decorations.
Publs. Anthologies: *Lyrics* 34, *Songs of the Dnieper* 42, *Notes on the Steppes* 45, *A Word about the Future* 59, *African Poems* 62; Novel in verse *Volunteers* 56, *Selected Works* 59, *Years and Songs* 63, *Poems about Us* 64, *Life of Lyrics* 65, *Selected Works* 65, *The Last Kiss.*
Writers' Union, 52 Vorovsky Street, Moscow, U.S.S.R.

Dolmetsch, Carl Frederick, C.B.E., HON. D.LITT., HON. F.T.C.L., HON. F.L.C.M.; British musician; b. 23 Aug. 1911; ed. privately.
First public concert performance at age of 7 and first concert tour aged 8; toured North and South America, Australia, Austria, Belgium, France, Germany, Holland, Italy, New Zealand, Sweden and Switzerland; Dir. Soc. of Recorder Players 37-; Dir. Haslemere Festival of Early Music and Instruments 40-; Man. Dir. Arnold Dolmetsch Ltd. (musical instrument makers); mem. Art Workers' Guild, I.S.M.; Hon. D.Litt. (Univ. of Exeter).
Publs. Many editions of recorder music; books on recorder playing 57 and 62.
Jesses, Haslemere, Surrey, England.
Telephone: Haslemere 3818.

Dombrovskaya, Yulia Fominichna; Soviet pediatrician; b. 1891; ed. Medical Institute for Women, St. Petersburg (Leningrad).
Pediatrician at a hospital 13-16; Intern, Asst., Lecturer, Prof., Head of Dept. First Moscow Medical Inst. 16-; Corresp. mem. U.S.S.R. Acad. of Medical Sciences 45-53, mem. 53-; Chair. of Boards of All-Union and Moscow Pediatric Socs.; mem. Purkyně Medical Soc. (Czechoslovakia) and Bulgarian Pediatric Soc.; Order of Lenin 53, 61, 65; Red Banner of Labour 45.
Publs. Over 160 works on child pathology, classification of pneumonia and role of vitamins in child physiology and pathology.
First Moscow Medical Institute, Bolshaya Pirogorskaya 19, Moscow, U.S.S.R.

Dombrowski, Erich Franz Otto; German journalist; b. 23 Dec. 1882; ed. Kiel and Berlin.
Political Editor, later Chief Editor *Geraer Tageblatt* 07-13; Corresp. *Berliner Tageblatt* 13-16, Chief Political Editor, Leader Writer and Deputy Chief Editor 16-26; Chief Editor *Frankfurter General-Anzeiger* 26-36; dismissed by Nazi Régime 36; academic work 36-45; founded *Allgemeine Zeitung* (Mainz) 45; Jt. Publisher *Frankfurter Allgemeine Zeitung* 49-; Hon. Chair. Rhineland Palatinate Press Asscn.; Frankfurt City Medal; Goethe Medal (Hesse); Grosses Verdienstkreuz der Bundesrepublik; Officier, Ordre des Palmes Académiques, Freeman, Johannes Gutenberg Univ. (Mainz); Dr. h.c. Mainz Univ.
Publs. *Das alte und das neue System* (political portraits) (German, English and American editions); numerous

articles, including *Blitzlichter aus Amerika* 56, *Wie es war: Mainzer Schicksalsjahre 1945-1948*.
6 Eichenwald Strasse, 62 Wiesbaden, German Federal Republic.
Telephone: 377470.

Dominick, Peter Hoyt, A.B., LL.B.; American lawyer and politician; b. 7 July 1915; ed. Yale Univ. and Yale Law School.
U.S. Army Air Corps 42-45; Partner, law firm Holland and Hart, Denver, Colorado 46-61; mem. Colorado House of Reps. 57-61; mem. U.S. Congress 61-63; U.S. Senator from Colorado 63-; Republican.
5050 East Quincy Street, Englewood, Colorado, U.S.A.

Domoto, Hisao; Japanese painter; b. 28; ed. Kyoto Acad. of Fine Arts.
First Prize, Acad. of Japan 51 and 53; studied in France, Italy and Spain 52; settled in Paris 55; abandoned traditional Japanese style and exhibited abstract paintings Salon des Indépendants, Salon de Mai, Paris 56, 57; rep. at Rome/New-York Art Foundation first exhbn. Rome, "Otro Arte" Exhbn. Madrid, Facchetti and Stadler Galleries, Paris 57; First Prize of Musée d'Art Moderne for foreign painters in Paris 58; One-man exhbn. Martha Jackson Gallery, New York 59.
9 rue St. Didier, Paris 16e, France.

Donald, Maxwell Bruce, A.R.C.S., S.M.; British chemical engineer; b. 20 July 1897; ed. Felsted School, Royal Coll. of Science, and Mass. Inst. of Technology.
Served First World War; Research Dept. Chilean Nitrate Producers' Asscn. 25-28; Royal Dutch Shell Group 29-31; Univ. Coll., London 31-65, now Prof. Emeritus of Chemical Engineering; Chair. Chemical Engineering Group, Society of Chemical Industry 45-47; Joint Hon. Sec. Inst. of Chemical Engineers 36-49, and 52-56, Vice-Pres. 49-51.
Publs. *Rubber in Chemical Engineering* (with H. P. Stevens) 33, *Elizabethan Copper* 55, *Elizabethan Monopolies* 61.
University College, Gower Street, London, W.C.1; Home: Rabbit Shaw, Stagbury Avenue, Chipstead, Surrey, England.
Telephone: Downland 53365.

Donini, Ambrogio, PH.D.; Italian historian, politician and diplomatist; b. 8 Aug. 1903; ed. Univ. of Rome and Harvard Univ.
Reader in History of Christianity, Univ. of Rome 26; obliged to emigrate to U.S.A. in 28 because of opposition to Fascist régime; research for Th.D. at Harvard Univ. Theological School 28-30; Lecturer in Italian Literature, Brown Univ., Providence 29; Asst. Prof. of Italian, Smith Coll., Northampton, Mass. 30; anti-fascist political activity in Europe 32-39; Editor of anti-fascist daily *La Voce degli Italiani*, Paris; in U.S.A. as Editor of Italian anti-fascist weekly *L'Unità del Popolo* 39-45; Lecturer of History of Religion, Jefferson School, New York 43-45; returned to liberated Italy after 17 years' exile 45; Free Prof. of History of Christianity, Univ. of Rome; Dir. of Gramsci Cultural Institute, Rome 49; joint editor of Rome review *Ricerche Religiose;* elected to Rome City Council Nov. 46; Ambassador to Poland 47-48; mem. World Peace Council 50; elected to the Senate 53, 58; mem. Communist Party of Italy since 27; elected to Central Cttee. 48, to Central Control Cttee. 56; Prof. History of Christianity, Univ. of Bari 60.
Publs. *Ippolito di Roma, Polemiche teologiche e controversie disciplinari nella Chiesa di Roma agli inizi del III secolo* 25, *Manuale introduttivo alla Storia del Cristianesimo* (joint author) 26, *Per una storia del pensiero di Dante in rapporto al movimento gioachimita* (Dante Prize, Harvard Univ.) 30, *Le basi sociali del Cristianesimo primitivo* 46, *L'Italia al bivio* 55, *I Manoscritti ebraici del Mar Morto e le origini del Cristianesimo* 57, *Chiesa e Stato nell'Italia d'oggi* 58, *Lineamenti*

di Storia delle Religioni 59, *Lezioni di Storia del Cristianesimo*, vol. I, *Le Origini* 64.
Via Asmara 34, Rome, Italy.
Telephone: Rome 831-95-98.

Donleavy, James Patrick; American author; b. 23 April 1926; ed. Preparatory School, New York, and Trinity Coll., Dublin.
Served in the U.S.N. during the Second World War; Brandeis Univ. Creative Arts Award.
Publs. *The Ginger Man* (novel) 55, (play) 59, *Fairy Tales of New York* (play) 60, *A Singular Man* (novel) 63, (play) 64, *Meet My Maker the Mad Molecule* (short stories and sketches) 64, *The Saddest Summer of Samuel S* (novella) 66, (play) 68, *The Beastly Beatitudes of Balthazar B* (novel) 68.
40A Broughton Road, London, S.W.6, England.
Telephone: 01-736 6933.

Donnay, J(oseph) D(ésiré) H(ubert), E.M., PH.D.; American university professor; b. 6 June 1902; ed. Liège and Stanford Univs.
Engineer and geologist, Société financière franco-belge de colonisation, French Morocco 29-30; Research Assoc. and Teaching Fellow, Stanford Univ. 30-31; Assoc. in Mineralogy and Petrography, Johns Hopkins Univ. 31-39; Prof. Laval Univ. Quebec 39-45; Research Chemist, Hercules Powder Co. 42-45; Visiting Prof., Johns Hopkins Univ. 45; Prof., Univ. of Liège 46-47; Prof. of Crystallography and Mineralogy, Johns Hopkins Univ. 46; Sec.-Treas. American Soc. for X-ray and Electron Diffraction 44-46; Vice-Pres. Société géologique Belgique 46-47; Vice-Pres. Mineralogical Society of America 49 and 52, Pres. 53; Vice-Pres. Crystallographic Society of America 46 and 48, Pres. 49; corresp. mem. Société Royale des Sciences de Liège; Vice-Pres. Société française de Minéralogie 49; Vice-Pres. Geological Society of America 54; Hon. Prof. Univ. of Liège 48-; Pres. American Crystallographic Asscn. 56; Fulbright Lecturer, Sorbonne 58-59; Vice-Pres. Assoc. française de Cristallographie 59-60, Visiting Prof. Univ. Marburg 66, 68; Corresp. mem. Soc. géologique, Belgium 66.
Publs. *Spherical Trigonometry* 45, *Crystal Data* 54, 63.
8204 Stone Trail Drive, Bethesda, Md. 20034; Office: Johns Hopkins University, Baltimore, Md. 21218, U.S.A.
Telephone: HO7-3300, Extension 264.

Donnell, James C., II, A.B., LL.D., D.S., L.H.D.; American business executive; b. 30 June 1910; ed. Princeton Univ.
Director Marathon Oil Co. 36-, Vice-Pres. 37-48, Pres. 48-; Dir. Mountain Fuel Supply Co. 35-; Dir. Nat. City Bank of Cleveland, First Nat. Bank of Findlay, Armco Steel Corpn., Phelps Dodge Corpn., American Petroleum Inst., New York Life Insurance Co..; Trustee Princeton Univ.; Chair. Nat. Petroleum Council; mem. Nat. Industrial Conf. Board; Pres. World Alliance of Y.M.C.A's; mem. Nat. Board Y.M.C.A.
539 South Main Street, Findlay, Ohio, U.S.A.
Telephone: 419-422-2121.

Donner, Andreas Matthias, D. IUR.; Netherlands jurist; b. 18; ed. Amsterdam Free Univ.
Legal Adviser Assoc. of Christian Schools in the Netherlands 41-45; Prof. of Constitutional Law Free Univ. of Amsterdam 45-58; Pres. Court of Justice of the European Communities 58-64, Judge 64-, now Pres. of First Chamber; Hon. Dr. Iur. (Univ. of Louvain), Fellow, Royal Netherlands Acad. of Sciences and Art.
Publs. *Nederlands Bestuursrecht* (Netherlands Administrative Law) 53, 2nd edn. 63, *Handboek van het Nederlandse Staatsrecht* 62.
Cour de Justice des Communautés Européennes, rue de la Côte d'Eich 12, Luxembourg; and Route de Thionville 235, Luxembourg.
Telephone: 21521.

Donner, Frederic G., B.A.; American businessman; b. 1902; ed. Michigan Univ.
Joined General Motors Corpn. 26, Asst. Treas. 34-37, Gen. Asst. Treas. 37-41, Vice-Pres. 41-56, Exec. Vice-Pres. 56-58, Chair. and Chief Exec. Officer 58-Oct. 67, remains mem. Board and mem. Finance Cttee.
1775 Broadway, New York City 19, N.Y., U.S.A.

Donner, Jan, DR. JUR., DR. RER. POL.; Netherlands jurist; b. 91; ed. Univs. of Utrecht and Leiden.
Adviser of the Min. of Justice 20-26; Min. of Justice 26-33; mem. of Supreme Court 33-46, Pres. 46-61.
Scheveningseweg 86c, The Hague, Netherlands.

Donner, Otto R.; German financial officer; b. 22 April 1902; ed. Univ. of Berlin.
Institute for Business Cycle Research, Berlin 25-33; Inst. of Int. Econs., Kiel Univ. 33-35; German Statistical Office 35-37; Reich Banking Supervisory Office 37-39; German Ministry of Econs. 39-41; Prof. of Econs., Hamburg Univ. 41-47, at Georgetown Univ., U.S.A. 47-52; Alternate Dir. Int. Monetary Fund 52-54; Exec. Dir. for Germany, Int. Bank for Reconstruction and Development 54-, Dir. Int. Finance Corpn. 56-, Dir. Int. Development Asscn. 60-.
Publs. *Factors Affecting Cotton Prices* 29, *Factors Affecting Stock Market Prices* 34, *Money and Credit* 34, *Economic Statistics* 36, *Zum Unbehagen über die Entwicklungshilfe* 62.
International Bank for Reconstruction and Development, 1818 H Street, N.W., Washington, D.C.; Home: 10011 Connecticut Avenue, Kensington, Maryland 20795, U.S.A.
Telephone: WH2-4164 (Home).

Donoso, José, A.B.; Chilean writer; b. 5 Oct. 1924; ed. The Grange School, Santiago, Instituto Pedagógico (Universidad de Chile), and Princeton Univ., U.S.A.
Worked as shepherd in Patagonia before going to Univ.; later lived in Buenos Aires; Prof. of English Conversation, Catholic Univ. of Chile 52, later Teacher of Techniques of Expression, School of Journalism, Univ. of Chile; journalist on *Revista Ercilla*, Santiago 59-64; Visiting Lecturer, Writers' Workshop, English Dept., Univ. of Iowa, U.S.A. 66-67; Premio Municipal de Santiago 55; Chile-Italia Prize for Journalism 60; William Faulkner Foundation Prize (for *Coronación*) 62.
Publs. *Veraneo y otras Cuentos* 55, *Coronación* 58, *El Charleston* (short stories) 60, *Este Domingo* (novel) 66, *El Lugar sin Limites* (novel) 66.
c/o Embassy of Chile, Lisbon, Portugal.

Donovan, Hedley Williams; American journalist; b. 24 May 1914; ed. Univ. of Minnesota and Hertford Coll., Oxford.
Reporter, *Washington Post* 37-42, U.S. Naval Reserve 42-45; Writer and Editor *Fortune* 45-53, Managing Editor 53-59; Editorial Dir. Time Inc. 59-64, Editor-in-Chief 64-; Trustee New York Univ., Carnegie Endowment for Int. Peace.
Time Inc., Time and Life Building, Rockefeller Center, New York, N.Y. 10020, U.S.A.

Donskoi, Mark Semyonovich; Soviet film producer and scenario writer; b. 8 March 1901.
Member C.P.S.U. 45-; State Prizwinner (for *Gorky's Childhood* 41, *Rainbow* 46, *Village School* 48); Richard Winnington Award 55, Honoured Art Worker of Turkmen S.S.R.
Principal productions: *Gorky's Childhood* 38, *My Apprenticeship* 39, *My Universities* 40 (Trilogy); *The Rainbow* 46, *Village School* 47, *At A High Price*, *Mother* 55, *Foma Gordeev* 60, *Good Day, Children* 61, *Mother's Heart* 65, *Mother's Fidelity* 66.
Association of Film Makers of the U.S.S.R., 14 Vassilievskaya, Moscow, U.S.S.R.

Doob, Leonard W., PH.D.; American psychologist; b. 3 March 1909; ed. Dartmouth Coll., Duke Univ., Univ. of Frankfurt, and Harvard Univ.
Department of Psychology, Yale University 34-, Prof. of Psychology 50-; Psychologist, War Dept., 42-43; Policy Co-ordinator, Overseas Branch, Office of War Information 44-45; Chair. Council of African Studies, Yale Univ. 61-; Dir. of Social Sciences, Yale 63-66; Fellow John Simon Guggenheim Foundation 60-61.
Publs. *Propaganda* 35, *Frustration and Aggression* 39, *The Plans of Men* 40, *Public Opinion and Propaganda* 48, *Social Psychology* 52, *Becoming More Civilised* 60, *Communication in Africa* 61, *Patriotism and Nationalism* 64, *Ants will not Eat Your Fingers* 66.
Yale University, 333 Cedar Street, New Haven, Connecticut, U.S.A.

Doolittle, Lieut.-Gen. James H., B.A., D.SC.; American aviator and business executive; b. 14 Dec. 1896; ed. Univ. of Calif., and Mass. Inst. of Technology.
Enlisted in U.S. Army Signal Corps as aviation cadet 17; commissioned as Second Lieut.; flight and gunnery instructor; served in Army as Second and First Lieut. 17-30; established a number of air records, including the following: (1) first flight across U.S. in less than 24 hours; (2) won Schneider Cup Race 25; (3) first man to do outside loop; (4) first man to fly over 300 m.p.h. in a land plane; retd. from Army with a reserve commission to become Manager of Aviation for Shell Oil Co. 30; awarded Harmon trophy of Ligue Internationale des Aviateurs for pioneering work in blind flying 31; established new transcontinental flight record 31; new world speed record for land planes 32; recalled to active duty with U.S. Army 40; as Lieut.-Col. led famous Tokyo raid April 42; later commanded 12th and 15th Air Forces, and, in Jan. 44, 8th Air Force, ret'd Air Force Feb. 59; Vice-Pres. of Shell Oil Co. 46-58, Dir. of Corpn. April 46-67; Chair. Exec. Cttee.; Vice-Chair. Board of Trustees Aerospace Corpn. 65-; Chair. Board, Space Technology Laboratories 59-62, Consultant 62-66, Dir. 62-; Dir. Mutual of Omaha Insurance Co. 61-, United Benefit Life Insurance Co. 64-, Tele-Trip Co., Inc. 66-; adviser to govt. boards; decorations include Congressional Medal of Honor, D.F.C., and D.S.M. with Oak-Leaf Clusters, Air Medal with three Oak-Leaf Clusters, Silver Star, Bronze Star, and many foreign awards, including Hon. K.C.B. (U.K.).
Office: 5225 Wilshire Boulevard, Los Angeles, Calif.; Home: 233 Marguerita, Santa Monica, Calif., U.S.A.
Telephone: 213-936-8109.

Dooyeweerd, Herman, LL.D.; Netherlands lawyer and philosopher; b. 94; ed. Reformed Gymnasium and Free Univ., Amsterdam.
Chief Juridical Officer, Dept. of Labour 19; Dir. Dr. A. Kuyper Foundation, The Hague 22; Senior Prof. of Legal Theory, Philosophy and History of Law, Free Univ. of Amsterdam 26-67; Fellow and fmr. Sec. Royal Dutch Acad. of Sciences and Humanities (Humanities Section); Pres. Dutch Asscn. for Philosophy of Law; fmr. Vice-Pres. Board of Trustees, Inst. of Social Studies, The Hague; Vice-Pres. of the Int. Asscn. for Reformed Philosophy; Editor-in-Chief *Philosophia Reformata*; Knight of the Order of the Lion of the Netherlands and of the Order of Orange-Nassau.
Publs. *De Ministerraad in het Ned. Staatsrecht* 17, *De Crisis in de Humanistische Staatsleer* 31, *De Wysbegeerte der Wetsidee* (three vols.) 35-36, *Recht en Historie* 38, *Reformatie en Scholastiek in de Wysbegeerte* (Vol. I) 49, *Transcendental Problems of Philosophical Thought* 48, *De Stryd om het Souvereiniteitsbegrip in de Moderne Rechts- en Staatsleer* 50, *A New Critique of Theoretical Thought* (four vols.) 53-58, *Conférences Parisiennes* (Revue Réformée) Vol. X 59, *Encyclopedie der Rechtswetenschap* 60, *In the Twilight of Western Thought* 61 (2nd edn. 65), *Verkenningen* 62, *Vernieuwing*

en Beztnning 64 (2nd edn.), *Die Bedeutung der Philosophie der Gesetres—idee für die Rechts—und Soziolphilosophie* 67.
Oranje Nassaulaan 13, Amsterdam O.Z, Netherlands.

Döpfner, H.E. Cardinal Julius; German ecclesiastic; b. 26 Aug. 1913.
Ordained priest 39; Bishop of Würzburg 48-57, of Berlin 57-61, Archbishop of Munich 61-; created Cardinal by Pope John XXIII 58; mem. of the Sacred Congregations of the Oriental Church, of the Discipline of the Sacraments, of Catholic Instruction, and of the Propagation of the Faith among the peoples; Chair. German Bishops Conf.
Archbishop's Palace, Kardinal-Faulhaberst 7, 8,000 Munich 2, German Federal Republic.
Telephone: 224081.

Dorati, Antal; American (b. Hungarian) conductor and composer; b. 9 April 1906; ed. Franz Liszt Acad. of Music, Budapest, and Univ. of Vienna.
Asst. conductor Royal Opera, Budapest 24-28; First conductor Opera House, Münster 29-32; Musical Dir. de Ballet Russe de Monte Carlo 33-39, Ballet Theatre of N.Y. 39-41, New Opera Co., N.Y. 42-43, Dallas Symphony Orchestra 45-49, Minneapolis Symphony Orchestra 49-60; Chief Conductor B.B.C. Symphony Orchestra 62-66, Stockholm Philharmonic Orchestra 66-; Hon. Pres. Philharmonia Hungarica; mem. Royal Acad. Sweden; guest conductor of several American and European Orchestras and at numerous festivals; has made over 200 symphonic recordings; 2 Grand Prix de Disque, Bruckner Medal, Mahler Medal, etc.; Hon. Dr. Macalester Coll., Minn.
Compositions: *Concerto for cello and orchestra, The Way of the Cross* (Dramatic Cantata), *Missa Brevis* (for chorus and percussion), *The Two Enchantments of Li-Tai-Pe* (Chamber Cantata), *Nocturne and Capriccio* (for Oboe and String Quartet), *Magdalena* (Ballet), *Symphony, Octet for Strings, Largo Concertato* (for string orchestra), *Chamber Music* (song cycle), *Madrigal Suite* (chorus and small orchestra), *Seven Pieces for Orchestra*, violin and piano pieces, ballet arrangements.
c/o Ibbs & Tillett, 124 Wigmore Street, London, W.1., England; c/o S. Hurok, 730 Fifth Ave., New York, U.S.A.; Via dei Foraggi 74, Rome, Italy (Home).

Dorfman, Ben, M.A., PH.D.; American economist and government official; b. 16 Feb. 1902; ed. Reed Coll., Portland and Univ. of California.
Teaching Fellow, Economics, Univ. of California 25-27; Instructor in Economics, Univ. of Hawaii 27-28; Head, Foreign Trade Laboratory, Univ. of California 28-30; Asst. Prof. of Economics, Univ. of North Dakota 30-37; Principal Economist, U.S. Tariff Comm. 37-42, Adviser on Far Eastern Trade Problems 42-43, Chief Economist 43-50, Chief Economist and Chief of Economics Div. 50-61, Chair. 61-.
4719 39th Street, N.W., Washington 8, D.C. ,U.S.A.

Dorgelès, Roland; French novelist; b. 15 June 1886. Member Acad. Goncourt 29-, Pres. 55-.
Publs. *Les Croix de bois* 19, *Le Cabaret de la Belle Femme* 21, *La Boule de gui* 21, *Saint-Magloire* 21, *Le Réveil des Morts* 23, *Sur la Route Mandarine* 25, *Partir* 25, *La Caravane sans Chameaux* 28, *Le Château des Brouillards* 32, *Si c'était vrai?* 34, *Quand j'étais Montmartrois* 36, *Vive la liberté?* 37, *Retour au front* 40, *Sous le casque blanc* 41, *Route des Tropiques* 44, *Carte d'identité* 45, *Bouquet de Bohème* 48, *Bleu horizon* 49, *Portraits sans retouche* 52, *Tout est à vendre* 56, *La Drôle de guerre* 58, *Au beau Temps de la Butte* 64, *A bas l'argent* 65, *Lettre ouverte à un millionaire* 67.
2 rue Mabillon, Paris 6e, France.

Dori, Major-Gen. Yaakov; Israeli civil engineer; b. 8 Oct. 1899; ed. Reali High School, Haifa, Univ. of Ghent.
Deputy Chief Engineer. Technical Dept.. Jewish Agency,

Jerusalem 26-31; Officer Commanding Haganah Forces, Haifa area 31-39; Chief of Staff, Haganah Forces of Palestine 39-47; Chief of Staff, Israel Defence Army 48-50; Head of Science Dept., Prime Minister's Office 50-52; Pres. Israel Inst. of Technology, Haifa 51-65.
103 Hatishbi, Haifa, Israel.

Doriot, Georges Frederic, B.S.; American educator and business executive; b. 24 Sept. 1899; ed. Lynton Coll., Kent, England, Paris Univ., Harvard Graduate School of Business Admin.
Prof. of Industrial Management, Harvard Graduate School of Business Admin. 29-; Brigadier Gen., U.S. Army 41-47, serving as Dir. of Military Planning (Office of the Quartermaster-Gen.), Deputy Dir. for Research and Development (War Dept. Gen. Staff) and Deputy Admin., War Assets Admin. (Office of Asst. Chief of Staff G-4); Pres. American Research and Development Corpn. 46-, European Enterprises Development Co. (E.E.D.) S.A.; Dir. John Hancock Mutual Life Insurance Co., Nat. Shawmut Bank of Boston, Molybdenum Corpn. of America, The Kendall Co., High Voltage Engineering Corpn., Ionics Inc.; Dir., Technical Studies, Inc. (channel tunnel study group), Textron, Inc.; Conseiller, Institut Européen d'Administration des Affaires, Paris; Distinguished Service Medal (U.S.), Commdr. Légion d'Honneur (France), C.B.E. (U.K.), G.O. du Mérite, Recherche et Invention (France).
Room 2308, 200 Berkeley Street, Boston, Mass., U.S.A.

Dorival, Bernard; French museum curator and writer; b. 14 Sept. 1914; ed. Lycées Carnot and Condorcet, Paris and Ecole normale supérieure.
Professor Ecole du Louvre 41-; Curator Musée Nationale de l'Art Moderne, Paris 41-65, Chief Curator 65-; Curator Musée Nat. des Granges de Port-Royal 55-; Chevalier Légion d'Honneur, Officier des Arts et des Lettres.
Publs. *La Peinture française* 42, *Les Etapes de la peinture française contemporaine* 43-46, *Du Côté de Port-Royal* 46, *Les Peintres du XXe siècle* 55, *L'Ecole de Paris au Musée nationale d'art moderne* 61; monographs on Cezanne and Rouault.
78 rue Notre-Dame-des-Champs, Paris 6e, France.

Dorling, Capt. Henry Taprell, R.N. (retired), D.S.O., F.R.HIST.S.; British naval officer and writer; b. 8 Sept. 1883; ed. H.M.S. *Britannia*.
Entered Royal Navy 97; Midshipman H.M.S. *Terrible* Boer War; served with Naval Brigade China 1900; commanded destroyer Great War; retired from Navy 29; Naval Corresp. *The Observer* 36-39; served R.N. 39-46; Staff C.-in-C. Med. (N. Africa, Italy) 42-45; Legion of Merit (Officer) U.S.A.; mem. Navy Records Society and Society for Nautical Research; writer and journalist under pseudonym "Taffrail"; has written many nautical and naval programmes for B.B.C.
Publs. Over 40 books, novels and naval and nautical history, some of which have been trans. into French, German, Norwegian, etc., the most recent being *Chenies* 43, *The Battle of the Atlantic* 46, *Blue Star Line* 48, *Toby Shad* 49, *The Jade Lizard* 51, *The New Moon* 52, *Salt Water Quiz* 52, *Eurydice* 53, *Arctic Convoy* 56.
4A Station Road, Bexhill-on-Sea, Sussex, England.

Dorman, Sir Maurice Henry, G.C.M.G., G.C.V.O., M.A.; Governor-General of Malta; b. 7 Aug. 1912; ed. Sedbergh School, Magdalene Coll., Cambridge.
Admin. Officer, Tanganyika Territory 35, Clerk of Council 40-45; Asst. to Lieut.-Gov., Malta 45; Principal Asst. Sec., Palestine 47; seconded to Colonial Office as Asst. Sec., Social Services Dept. 48; Dir. Social Welfare, Gold Coast 50; Colonial Sec., Trinidad and Tobago 52, Acting Gov., Trinidad 54, 55; Gov., C.-in-C. and Vice-Admiral of Colony and Protectorate of Sierra Leone 56-61, Gov.-Gen. Independent State of Sierra Leone 61-62; Gov. and Commdr.-in-Chief State of Malta 62-64, Gov.-Gen. of Malta 64-; Hon. D.C.L. (Durham), Hon.

LL.D. (Royal Univ. of Malta), K.St.J. 57; Gran Croce al Merito Melitense (Sov. Ordine Militare di Malta) 66.
The Palace, Valletta, Malta.
Telephone: C.21221.

Dornier, Claudius, DR.ING.; German aeronautical engineer and professor; b. 14 May 1884; ed. Munich Technical Univ.
Proprietor Dornier-Werke G.m.b.H. Friedrichshafen; Hon. Senator Munich Technical Univ.; Senator Lilienthal Asscn. for Aeronautical Research; mem. German Acad. for Aeronautical Research; corresp. mem. Real Acad. Hispano-Americana de Ciencias y Artes, Cadiz.
Brueschrain 20, Zug, Switzerland.

Dorodnitsyin, Anatoliy Alekseevich; Soviet geophysicist; b. 10; ed. Grozny Petroleum Inst.
Instructor, higher educational and research establishments, Moscow, Leningrad 36-41; Central Aerodynamics Inst. Moscow 41-55; Mathematics Inst. U.S.S.R. Acad. of Sciences 45-55; Prof. Moscow Physics-Technical Inst. 47-; mem. U.S.S.R. Acad. of Sciences 53-; Dir. Computing Centre, U.S.S.R. Acad. of Sciences 55-; State Prizes 46, 47, 51.
Publs. *The Boundary Layer in Compressible Gas* 42, *The Effects of the Earth's Surface Topography on Air Currents* 50, *Asymptotic Laws of Distribution of Proper Meanings for Some Special Types of Second Order* 52, *Solution of Mathematical and Logical Problems with Help of Fast Electronic Computers* 56, *Laminar Border Layer in Compressible Gas* 57, *Some Cases of Axial Symmetric Supersonic Currents of Gas* 57, *A Contribution to Solution of Mixed Problems of Transonic Aerodynamics* 59, *A Method of Solution of Equation of Laminar and Border Layer* 60.
Computing Centre, U.S.S.R. Academy of Sciences, 28 Ul. Vavilova, Moscow, U.S.S.R.

Dorofeyev, Boris Yakovlevich; Soviet diplomatist; b. 1920; ed. Moscow State Inst. of International Relations.
Member C.P. of Soviet Union 48-; First Sec. Soviet Embassy, Canberra 61-63; at Ministry of Foreign Affairs 63-65; Soviet Minister to New Zealand 65-.
U.S.S.R. Mission, Wellington, New Zealand.

Dorolle, Pierre-Marie; French international health official; b. 14 Nov. 1899; ed. Univs. of Marseilles, Paris and Bordeaux and Post-Graduate School of Tropical Medicine, Marseilles.
Overseas Army Medical Corps, later with Govt. Medical Service, French Indochina 25-37; Rapporteur, League of Nations Intergovernmental Conf. of Rural Hygiene, Far East 37; Chief Medical Expert, Rep. of Sec.-Gen. of League of Nations Technical Co-operation with China 37-40; successively Dir., Health Services Saigon-Cholon, Dir., Health Services, Annam Protectorate, Dir. Health Services, Office of High Commr. 40-50; Dep. Dir.-Gen., World Health Organization 50-; Légion d'Honneur.
Publs. Articles and books on tropical medicine, preventive and social medicine, public health.
World Health Organization, Avenue Appia, 1211 Geneva, Switzerland.

Doronina, Tatiana Vasilyevna; Soviet actress; b. 1933; ed. Studio School of Moscow Art Theatre.
At Leningrad Lenin Komsomol State Theatre 56-59; at Leningrad Maxim Gorky State Bolshoi Drama Theatre 59-66; Moscow Art Theatre 66-; Honoured Artist of R.S.F.S.R.
Main roles include: Zhenka Shulzhenko (*Factory Girl* by Volodin), Lenochka (*In Search of Happiness* by Rozov), Sophia (*Wit Works Woe* by Griboyedov), Nadya Rozoyeva (*My Elder Sister* by Volodin), Nadezhda Polikarpovna (*The Barbarians* by Gorky), Lashka (*Virgin Soil Upturned* by Sholokov), Nastasya Filippovna (*The Idiot* by Dostoyevsky), Valka (*Irkutsk*

Story by Arbuzov), Oxana (*Loss of the Squadron* by Korneichuk).
Moscow Art Theatre, 3 Proyezd Khudozhestvennogo Teatra, Moscow, U.S.S.R.

Doroshenko, Pyotr Emelyanovich; Soviet politician; b. 1907; ed. Azovo-Chernomorsk Agricultural Inst.
Member C.P.S.U. 39-; agronomist 27-34; teacher, Head of Technical School, Chief Regional Dept. of Agriculture 34-42; Soviet Army 42-46; Chief of Section, Central Cttee. of C.P. of Ukraine, First Sec. Vinnitsa Regional Cttee. of C.P. of Ukraine, Chief of Section, Central Cttee. of C.P.S.U. 46-59; First Sec. Chernigov, Odessa Agricultural, and Kirovograd Regional Cttees., C.P. of Ukraine 59-65; Minister of Agriculture of Ukrainian S.S.R. 65-; mem. Central Cttee. C.P. of Ukraine; Deputy to U.S.S.R. Supreme Soviet.
Council of Ministers of Ukrainian S.S.R., Kiev, U.S.S.R.

Dorrance, John Thompson Jr.; American business executive; b. 7 Feb. 1919; ed. St. George's School and Princeton Univ.
Assistant Treasurer, Campbell Soup Co. 50-55, Asst. to the Pres. 55-62, Chair. of Board 62-; mem. Board of Dirs. Campbell Soup Co. 47-, Morgan Guaranty Trust Co. 55-, Pennsylvania New York Central Transportation Co. 68-, Penn. Mutual Ins. Co.
Campbell Soup Co., 375 Memorial Avenue, Camden, New Jersey 08101, U.S.A.

Dorsey, Bob Rawls; American oil executive; b. 27 Aug. 1912; ed. Univ. of Texas.
With Gulf Oil Corpn., Port Arthur Refinery 34-38; Univ. of Texas 38-40; Port Arthur Refinery, Gulf Oil Corpn. 40-48; Man. Venezuela Gulf Refining Co., Puerto la Cruz, Venezuela 48-55; Gen. Office, Gulf Oil Corpn. 55-58, Admin. Vice-Pres. 58-61, Senior Vice-Pres. 61, Exec. Vice-Pres. 61-65, Pres. 65-, Dir. 64-; mem. Board of Dirs. Nat. Petroleum Refiners Asscn.; Dir. American Petroleum Inst.
Gulf Oil Corporation, Gulf Building, Pittsburgh 30; Home: 102 Pheasant Drive, Fox Chapel, Pa., U.S.A.
Telephone: AC 412-781-0178.

Dorticos Torrado, Osvaldo; Cuban lawyer and politician; b. 19; ed. Havana Univ.
Leader of Castro revolutionary movement in Cienfuegos 57-58; arrested and imprisoned Dec. 58; escaped and fled to Mexico; returned upon success of revolution; Minister of Revolutionary Laws Jan.-July 59; Pres. of Cuba July 59-; Minister of Economy and Chair. Central Board of Planning 64-; Vice-Pres. Cuban Nat. Bar Asscn.
Palacio Presidencial, Havana, Cuba.

Dos Passos, John; American novelist; b. 14 Jan. 1896; ed. Harvard Univ.
Feltrinelli Int. Prize 67.
Publs. *A Pushcart at the Curb* (verse); *One Man's Initiation, Three Soldiers, Streets of Night, Manhattan Transfer, The 42nd Parallel, Nineteen Nineteen, The Big Money, U.S.A., Adventures of a Young Man, Number One, The Grand Design, Chosen Country, District of Columbia, The Most Likely to Succeed, The Great Days* (novels); *The Garbage Man, Airways Inc., Fortune Heights* (plays); *Rosinante to the Road Again, Orient Express, Journeys Between Wars, The Ground We Stand On* (essays); *State of the Nation, Tour of Duty, The Prospect Before Us* (reporting); *The Head and Heart of Thomas Jefferson, The Theme is Freedom* (essays); *The Men Who Made the Nation* 57, *Prospects of a Golden Age* 59, *A Contemporary Chronicle* 60, *Midcentury* 61, *Mr. Wilson's War* 63, *Brazil on the Move* 63, *The Shackles of Power* 66, *World in a Glass* 66, *The Best Times* 67.
Westmoreland, Virginia, U.S.A.

Doty, Paul Mead, B.S., M.A., PH.D.; American chemist; b. 1 June 1920; ed. Pennsylvania State Coll., and Columbia Univ.

Instructor and Research Associate, Polytechnic Inst., Brooklyn 43-45, Asst. Prof. Chemistry 45-46; Asst. Prof. Chemistry, Univ. of Notre Dame 46-48; Asst. Prof. Harvard 48-50, Assoc. Prof. Chemistry 50-56, Prof. 56-; Pres. Science Advisory Cttee. 61-65; Fellow, Nat. Acad. of Sciences.
Harvard University, Cambridge 38, Massachusetts, U.S.A.

Dougan, Robert Ormes, M.A., F.L.A.; American (b. British) librarian; b. 21 Aug. 1904; ed. Univ. Coll., London.
Librarian, Royal Historical Soc. London 25-35; Cataloguer and Bibliographical Research Worker, E. P. Goldschmidt & Co. (London antiquarian booksellers) 26-40; service with R.A.F. 41-45; Librarian, Sandeman Public Library, Perth 45-52; Organiser, Scottish Books Exhibitions (Edinburgh and Glasgow), Festival of Britain 50-51; Dep. Librarian, Trinity Coll. Dublin 52-58; Lecturer on Book of Kells for Forás Eireann 56-58; Keeper, Archbishop Marsh's Library, Dublin 57-58; Librarian, Henry E. Huntington Library, San Marino (Calif.) 58-.
Publ. *Scottish Tradition in Photography* 49.
1275 Hillcrest Ave., Pasadena, Calif. 91106, U.S.A. Telephone: SY6-6425.

Douglas, David Charles, M.A., F.B.A., D.LITT.; British historian; b. 5 Jan. 1898; ed. Sedbergh and Keble Coll., Oxford.
Lecturer in Medieval History Glasgow Univ. 24-34; Prof. of History Univ. Coll. of the South-West 34-39; mem. Council Royal Historical Society 35-38, Vice-Pres. 49-54; Prof. of Medieval History, Leeds Univ. 39-45; Prof. of History Bristol Univ. 45-63; Dean Faculty of Arts 58-60; Ford's Lecturer, Oxford Univ. 62-63; Trustee London Museum 45-; Hon. Fellow Keble Coll., Oxford 59-.
Publs. *The Norman Conquest* 26, *The Social Structure of Medieval East Anglia* 27, *The Age of the Normans* 28, *Feudal Documents from the Abbey of Bury St. Edmunds* 32, *The Development of Medieval Europe* 35, *English Scholars* (awarded James Tait Black Memorial Prize) 39, *Domesday Monachorum* 45, *William the Conqueror* 64; Gen. Editor *English Historical Documents* 53- (in progress).
4 Henleaze Gardens, Bristol, England.

Douglas, Donald W., B.SC.; American engineer; b. 6 April 1892; ed. U.S. Naval Acad., and Mass. Inst. of Technology.
Chief Engineer Glenn L. Martin Co. 15-16 and 17-20; Chief Civilian Engineer U.S. Signal Corps for Aviation 16-17; Pres. Douglas Co., Santa Monica, Calif. 20-28; Pres. Douglas Aircraft Co. Inc. 28-57, Chair. Board, Chief Exec. Officer 57-67; Hon. Chair. McDonnell Douglas Corpn. 67-.
McDonnell Douglas Corporation, Santa Monica, Calif., U.S.A.

Douglas, Donald Wills, Jr.; American businessman; b. 3 July 1917; ed. Stanford Univ.
Joined Douglas Aircraft Co., Inc., Santa Monica, Calif. 39, Chief, Flight Test Group in charge testing models 43-, Dir. Contract Admin. 48, in charge, Research Laboratories, Santa Monica Div. 49, Vice-Pres. Mil. Sales 51-57, Dir. 53-, Pres. 57-67; Pres. Douglas Aircraft Div. of McDonnell Douglas Corpn. 67-; Dir. Gen. Aniline & Film Corpn., Stanford Research Inst.
3000 Ocean Park Boulevard, Santa Monica, Calif., U.S.A.

Douglas, Kirk, A.B.; American actor; b. 9 Dec. 1918; ed. St. Lawrence Univ., and American Acad. of Dramatic Arts.
Pres. Bryna Productions 55-; Dir. Los Angeles Chapter, UN Asscn.; Acad. Awards 48, 52, 56; New York Film Critics Award, Hollywood Foreign Press Award etc.; Hon. Dr. of Fine Arts (St. Lawrence Univ.) 58.
Appeared on Broadway in *Spring Again, Three Sisters, Kiss and Tell, The Wind is Ninety, Alice in Arms, Man Bites Dog*; films include *The Strange Love of Martha Ivers, Letter to Three Wives, Ace in the Hole, The Bad and the Beautiful, 20,000 Leagues under the Sea, Ulysses, Lust for Life, Gunfight at O.K. Corral, Paths of Glory, The Vikings, Last Train from Gun Hill, The Devil's Disciple, Spartacus, Strangers When We Meet, Seven Days in May, Town without Pity, The List of Adrian Messenger, In Harms Way, Cast a Giant Shadow, The Way West, War Waggon.*
Home: 707 North Canon Drive, Beverly Hills, Calif.; Office: Bryne Prods. Inc., 5451 Marathon Street, Hollywood 38, Calif., U.S.A.

Douglas, Lewis Williams, B.A., LL.D., D.C.L.; American business executive and diplomatist; b. 2 July 1894; ed. Amherst Coll., and Mass. Inst. of Technology.
Fmr. Lecturer Amherst Coll.; mem. Arizona State Legislature 23-25; mem. U.S. House of Reps. 27-33; Dir. of the Budget 33-34; Vice-Pres. and mem. Board American Cyanamid 34-38; Principal McGill Univ. 38-39; Pres. Mutual Life Insurance Co. of New York 40-47, Chair. Board of Trustees 47-59, Dir. 59-; Chair. of Board Southern Arizona Bank & Trust Co., Tucson, Ariz. 51-; Chair. Western Bancorporation, Int. Bank 62-; Deputy War Shipping Administrator 42-45; Ambassador to Great Britain 47-50; Dir. Union Corpn. Int. Nickel Co., Council on Foreign Relations, Harshaw Chemical Co., Empire Trust, Nichols Engineering and Research Corpn., Western Bancorporation, Gen. Motors Corpn., American Investment Comm., Employers Liability Assurance Corpn. Ltd., Newmont Mining; Grand Croix de la Légion d'Honneur (France); Grand Cross Order of Crown (Belgium); Hon. LL.D. (Bristol, St. Andrews, London, Glasgow, Edinburgh, Birmingham, Columbia, Calif., Dalhousie, Leeds, Arizona, Wesleyan, New York, Brown, Princeton, Queens, Harvard, Amherst, McGill); Hon. D.C.L. (Oxford Univ.).
c/o Southern Arizona Bank & Trust Co., Tucson, Arizona, U.S.A.

Douglas, Paul Howard, A.M., PH.D.; American politician and university professor; b. 26 March 1892; ed. Bowdoin Coll., Columbia and Harvard Univs.
Instructor in Economics, Univ. of Ill. 16-17; Instructor and Asst. Prof. Reed Coll., Portland, Oregon 17-18; Asst. Prof. of Economics, Univ. of Washington 19-20; Asst. Prof. of Industrial Relations, Univ. of Chicago 20-23, Assoc. Prof. 23-25, Prof. 25; Acting Dir. Swarthmore Unemployment Study 30; Sec. Pa. Comm. on Unemployment, and Adviser to the N.Y. Comm. 30; mem. Consumers' Advisory Board Nat. Recovery Admin. 33-35; mem. Advisory Cttee. to U.S. Senate and Social Security Board 37; U.S. Senator from Illinois 48-66; served in U.S. Marine Corps, Second World War; Fellow Econometric Soc., American Acad. Arts and Sciences; mem. American Philosophical Soc., American Econ. Asscn. (Pres. 47), American Statistical Asscn.; hon. degrees from William and Mary, Bates, De Paul, Oberlin, Tulane, Rollins, Bowdoin, Rochester, etc.; Democrat.
Publs. *American Apprenticeship and Industrial Education* 21, *Worker in Modern Economic Society* (with others) 23, *Wages and the Family* 25, *Adam Smith, 1776-1926* (with others) 28, *Real Wages in the United States, 1890-1926* 30, *Movement of Real Wages 1926-1928* (co-author) 30, *The Problem of Unemployment* (co-author) 31, *Standards of Unemployment Insurance* 33, *The Theory of Wages* 34, *Controlling Depressions* 35, *Social Security in the United States* 36, *Economy in the National Government* 52, *Ethics in Government* 52.
5658 Blackstone Avenue, Chicago, Illinois, U.S.A.

Douglas, Thomas Clement, M.A.; Canadian politician; b. 20 Oct. 1904; ed. Brandon Coll., McMaster and Chicago Univs.

Nat. Pres. Co-operative Commonwealth Youth Movement 36-40; Provincial Pres. Co-operative Commonwealth Fed. 41-43; Provincial Political Leader 43-; mem. House of Commons 35-44; resgnd.; elected Saskatchewan Legislature 44-61, Premier and Pres. Exec. Council 44-61, concurrently Minister of Public Health 44-49; Leader New Democratic Party of Canada 61-. 217 Angus Crescent, Regina, Saskatchewan, Canada.

Douglas, William Orville, A.B., LL.B.; American jurist; b. 16 Oct. 1898; ed. Whitman Coll., Columbia Univ., New York.

Instructor, Yakima High School, Washington 20-22; with law firm Cravath, de Gersdorff, Swaine and Wood, New York 25-27; Lecturer in Law, Columbia Univ. Law School 24-28; collaborated with U.S. Dept. of Commerce, bankruptcy studies 29-32; Dir. Bankruptcy Studies, Inst. of Human Relations, Yale Univ. 29-32; Sec. to Cttee. on Study of Business of Federal Courts (Nat. Comm. on Law Observance and Enforcement) 30-32; Prof. of Law, Yale Law School 28-32, Sterling Prof. of Law 32-39; Dir. Protective Cttee. Study, Securities and Exchange Comm., Washington, D.C. 34-36, Commr. Securities and Exchange Comm. 36-39, Chair. 37-39; mem. Temporary Nat. Economic Cttee. 38-39; Associate Justice, Supreme Court of U.S. 39-. Publs. *Democracy and Finance* 40, *Being an American* 48, *Of Men and Mountains* 50, *Strange Lands and Friendly People* 51, *Beyond the High Himalayas* 52, *North from Malaya* 53, *An Almanac of Liberty* 54, *We the Judges* 56, *Russian Journey* 56, *The Right of the People* 58, *West of the Indus* 58, *Exploring the Himalaya* (*Landmark*) 58, *My Wilderness: East to Kathadin* 61, *A Living Bill of Rights* 61, *America Challenged* 60, *Muir of the Mountains* 61, *Democracy's Manifesto* 62, *Anatomy of Liberty* 63, *Mr. Lincoln and the Negroes* 63, *Freedom of the Mind* 63, *A Wilderness Bill of Rights* 65, *The Bible and the Schools* 66.

U.S. Supreme Court, Washington, D.C., U.S.A.

Douglas of Kirtleside, 1st Baron, cr. 48, of Dornock, **Marshal of the R.A.F. William Sholto Douglas,** G.C.B., M.C., D.F.C.; British officer; b. 23 Dec. 1893; ed. Tonbridge School, and Lincoln Coll., Oxford (hon. fellow).

Served Great War 14-18, Commanded Nos. 43 and 84 (Fighter) Squadrons 17-18; Commanded R.A.F. in Sudan 29-32; Instr. Imperial Defence Coll. 32-35; Dir. of Staff Duties Air Min. 36-37; Asst. Chief of Air Staff 38-40; Deputy Chief 40; Air Officer Commanding-in-Chief Fighter Command 40-42, Middle East Command 43-44, Coastal Command R.A.F. 44-45; Air C.-in-C. British Air Forces of Occupation, Germany 45-46; C.-in C. and Mil. Gov. British Zone of Germany 46-47; Dir. B.O.A.C. 48-49; Chair. B.E.A. 49-64; Pres. Int. Air Transport Asscn. 56-57; Chair. Horizon Holidays Ltd. 64-; awarded Legion of Merit (degree of Chief Commander) by Gen. Eisenhower and U.S. Navy's Distinguished Service Medal Nov. 44.

Publs. *Years of Combat* 63, *Years of Command* 66. Shepherd's Holt, Denham, Bucks., England. Telephone: Denham 2136.

Douglas-Home, Rt. Hon. Sir Alexander Frederick, K.T., P.C., M.P.; British politician; b. 2 July 1903; ed. Eton Coll., and Christ Church, Oxford.

Member, House of Commons 31-45, 50-51, 63-, House of Lords 51-63; Parl. Private Sec. to Sec. of State for Scotland 31-35, to Chancellor of Exchequer 35, to Prime Minister 38-39; Joint Parl. Under-Sec. to Foreign Office 45; Minister of State, Scottish Office 51-55; Sec. of State for Commonwealth Relations 55-60, for Foreign Affairs 60-Oct. 63; Prime Minister Oct. 63-64; Leader of Conservative Party 63-65; Leader of Opposition 64-65; Lord Pres. of the Council 57, 59-60; renounced title of

14th Earl of Home Oct 63; Chancellor Heriot-Watt Univ., Edinburgh 66-; Hon. D.C.L. (Oxford); Hon. LL.D. (Harvard, Edinburgh, Aberdeen and Liverpool Univs.); Conservative.

Publ. *Peaceful Change* 64.

The Hirsel, Coldstream, Berwickshire, Scotland and Castlemains, Douglas, Lanarkshire, Scotland; Office: 24 Roebuck House, Palace Street, London, S.W.1. Telephone: Coldstream 1 (Home).

Doulatram, Jairamdas, B.A., LL.B.; Indian politician; b. 21 July 1891.

Joined Indian Home Rule Movement 16; took part in Gandhi's Satyagraha Movement 19; mem. All-India Congress Cttee. 27-40; Editor *The Bharatvasi* 19-20; participated in Gandhi's Non-Co-operation Movement 20-21; imprisoned for sedition 21-23; Editor *The Hindustan Times* Delhi 25-26, Gandhi's *Young India* 30; mem. Bombay Legislative Council 27-29; joined Satyagraha Movement for Indian Freedom 30; imprisoned twice during Civil Disobedience Movement 30-32, released 34; Gen. Sec. Indian Nat. Congress 31, Acting Pres. I. N. Congress 34, mem. Congress Working Cttee. 29-40; Chair. Textile Labour Wage Enquiry Cttee. 38; detained in prison during "Quit India" movement 42-45; mem. All-India Village Industries Board 41-46; Indian Constituent Assembly 46-50; Gov. of Bihar 47; Minister of Food and Agriculture Govt. of India 48-50; Gov. of Assam 50-56; Chief Editor *Collected Works of Mahatma Gandhi* 57-59; mem. Governing Body Gandhi Peace Foundation 58-; mem. Indian Parliament 59-.

Rajya Sabha, Parliament House, New Delhi 1; Home: 14 Tughlak Road, New Delhi 11, India.

Doumbia, Ya; Mali diplomatist; b. 14; ed. Ecole Normale William Ponty.

Chief, Financial and Accounting Services of Afrique Centrale Française (A.C.F.) 46-47; Counsellor of French Union 47-59; First Vice-Pres. of Assembly of French Union 56-57; Federal Deputy 59-60; Dir.-Gen. Banque Populaire du Mali 60-61; Ambassador to Morocco and Tunisia 61-64; Municipal Counsellor of Bamako; Ambassador to France, Italy, Switzerland and U.K. 64-66, to Yugoslavia 66-; Chevalier Etoile Noire du Benin, Grand Cordon du Ouissan Alouite, Grand Cordon Ordre du Trône (Morocco).

Embassy of Mali, Vojislava Vuckoviça 25, Belgrade, Yugoslavia.

Dours, Jean, L. ès D.; French administrator; b. 14 Jan. 1913; ed. Lycée d'Auch, Coll. de Saint-Gaudens and Faculté de Droit, Paris.

Adviser, Council of Prefecture of Rouen 39; Asst. Prefect, Albertville 43; Asst. Chief, Office of Central Admin. 45; Asst. Dir. Private Office, Prefect of Seine 47-57; Technical Adviser, Private Office of René Billères, Minister of Educ.; Adviser, Head Office of Nat. Defence 58, Dir. 59; Prefect, Bône Dec. 61-May 62; Dir. Private Office of Christian Fouchet, High Commr. of France in Algeria April 62-June 62, Private Office of Christian Fouchet, Minister of Information 62, then of Nat. Educ. 62-66; Dir.-Gen. Sûreté Nationale 67-; Officier Légion d'Honneur, Croix de Guerre, Commdr. des Palmes Académiques, and other awards.

81 boulevard Suchet, Paris 16e, France.

Dow, John Christopher Roderick, B.SC. (Econ.); British economist; b. 1916; ed. Bootham School, York, Brighton, Hove and Sussex Grammar School, and Univ. Coll., London.

Drummond-Fraser Research Fellow, Dept. of Economics Univ. of Manchester 38-39; R.A.F. 40-43; Ministry of Aircraft Production 43-45; Econ. Section, Cabinet Office, later Treasury successively Econ. Asst., Econ. Adviser, Senior Econ. Adviser 45-54, 62-63; Research in Management of British Economy, Cambridge Univ. 54-55; Nat. Inst. of Econ. and Social Research, London

55-62, Dep. Dir. 57-62; Asst. Sec.-Gen. (Econ. and Statistics) OECD 63-.
Organisation for Economic Co-operation and Development, 2 rue André-Pascal, Paris 16e, France.

Dowell, Dudley, LL.D.; American insurance executive; b. 24 Aug. 1903; ed. Little Rock High School, and Univ. of Arkansas.
New York Life Insurance Co. 21-, Clerk, Little Rock 21-25, Cashier, Jackson, Mississippi 25-27, Asst. Manager Little Rock 27-29, Manager Butte, Montana 29-36, Seattle 36-39, Supervisor Allegheny Dept. Pittsburg 39-41, Inspector of Agencies 41, Superintendent, Home Office 41, Asst. Vice-Pres. 42, Vice-Pres. 43-45, Vice-Pres. in charge Agencies New York City 45-54, Exec. Vice-Pres. 54-62, Dir. 58-, Chair. Exec. Cttee. 59, Pres. and Chief Admin. Officer 62-; Dir. J. Henry Schroder Banking Corpn. and Schroder Trust Co.; Pres. of numerous Insurance Asscns.
New York Life Insurance Co., 51 Madison Avenue, New York, N.Y.; and 200 East 66th Street, New York, N.Y., U.S.A.

Dowie, Ian R.; Canadian business executive; b. 07; ed. George Heriot's School, Edinburgh, and Edinburgh Univ., Scotland.
President and Dir. Canadian Breweries Ltd. 58-; Chair. of Board Carling Brewing Co. Inc., Cleveland, Ohio, Western Canada Breweries Ltd.
Canadian Breweries Ltd., 297 Victoria Street, Toronto, Ontario, Canada.

Dowling, Robert Whittle; American property executive; b. 9 Sept. 1895; ed. Cutler School, New York.
Real estate and building 18-; Pres. and Dir., City Investing Co. 43-; Dir. United Artists Corpn., Knickerbocker Investing Co., French & Co., Hotel Waldorf-Astoria Corpn., Chemway Corpn., City Bank Farmers Trust Co., Home Insurance Co., Inc., Hilton Hotels Inc.; Chair., Borough of Manhattan Planning Board; official of many nat. cttees.; Chevalier, Légion d'Honneur, Brazilian Order of the Southern Cross.
980 Madison Ave., New York 21, N.Y., U.S.A.

Dowling, Walter, B.A., LL.D.; American diplomatist; b. 4 Aug. 1905; ed. Mercer Univ. (Ga.).
Foreign Service Officer 32; Vice-Consul Oslo 32-36, Lisbon 36-38; 3rd Sec. Rome 38-41; 2nd Sec. Rio de Janeiro 42-44, Rome 44-45; State Dept. 45-59; Counsellor Vienna 49-53, also Deputy High Commr. for Austria 50-53; Deputy High Commr. for Germany 53-55; Minister, Bonn 55-56; Ambassador to Korea 56-59, to German Federal Republic 59-63; Dir.-Gen. Atlantic Inst., Paris; LL.D. Seoul Nat. Univ. 59, Mercer Univ. 61, Maryland Univ. 62.
9 rue Bonaparte, Paris 6e, France.
Telephone: MED 78-50.

Down, Alastair Frederick, O.B.E., M.C., T.D., C.A.; British oil executive; b. 23 July 1914; ed. Marlborough Coll.
British Petroleum (then Anglo-Iranian Oil Co.) 38-; Army Service 40-45; with BP in Iran 45-47, London 47-54; Chief Rep. of BP, Canada 54, later Pres. The British Petroleum Co. of Canada Ltd., BP Canada Ltd., BP Refinery Canada Ltd., BP Exploration Co. of Canada Ltd.; Managing Dir. The British Petroleum Co. Ltd. March 62-.
The British Petroleum Co. Ltd., Britannic House, Moor Lane, London, E.C.2, England.

Downer, Hon. Sir Alexander Russell, K.B.E., M.A., F.R.S.A., Barr.-at-Law; Australian diplomatist; b. 7 April 1910; ed. Geelong Grammar School, Victoria, Brasenose Coll., Oxford, and Inner Temple, London.
Served with Australian Imperial Forces 40-45; prisoner of war of Japanese 42-45; Liberal Mem. Australian House of Representatives 49-64; mem. Parlty. Foreign Affairs Cttee. 52-58; mem. of Constitutional Review Cttee. 56-59; Rep. of the Australian Parl. at the Coronation of H.M. Queen Elizabeth II 53; Minister of State for Immigration 58-63; High Commr. for Australia in the United Kingdom 64-; Freeman of City of London 65.
45 Hyde Park Gate, London, S.W.7, and Oare House, Oare, Wilts., England; 10 Mugga Way, Canberra, A.C.T., Australia.

Downes, Ralph (William), M.A., B.MUS., A.R.C.M.; British organist; b. 16 Aug. 1904; ed. Royal Coll. of Music, Keble Coll., Oxford, and Pius X School of Liturgical Music, New York.
Director of Music, Univ. Chapel, Princeton Univ. 28-35; Concert organist and Organist, the London Oratory 36-; Organ Consultant to L.C.C., Royal Festival Hall 49-53, Govt. of Malta 60-62, Corpn. of Croydon 61-64; Curator of Organs, Royal Festival Hall 54-, and Fairfield Hall, Croydon; Prof. of Organ, Royal Coll. of Music 54-; Jury-mem. Int. Organ Festivals, Haarlem, Munich, St. Albans; designer of organs; Organ, Choral and Piano compositions and articles on organ design and its musical significance; Hon. R.A.M., Hon. R.C.O.
c/o The Oratory, Brompton Road, London, S.W.7, England.

Downs, Brian Westerdale, M.A., D.LITT.; British university professor; b. 4 July 1893; ed. Abbotsholme School and Christ's Coll., Cambridge.
Fellow of Christ's Coll. 19-50, 63-; Lecturer in English, Cambridge Univ. 26-50; British Council Rep. in the Netherlands 45-46; Master of Christ's Coll. 50-63 and Prof. of Scandinavian Studies 50-60; Vice-Chancellor, Cambridge Univ. 55-57; Commdr. of the Royal Swedish Order of the North Star; Officier Légion d'Honneur.
Publs. *Richardson* 28, *Ibsen, the intellectual Background* 46, *Six Plays by Ibsen* 50, *Strindberg* (in collaboration with Miss Mortensen) 49, *Norwegian Literature 1860-1918* 66.
Christ's College, Cambridge, England.
Telephone: Cambridge 59601.

Dowouna-Hammond, Alfred Jonas; Ghanaian politician; b. 20; ed. Accra Government Boys School and O'Reilly Educational Inst., Accra.
Probationer Man. United Africa Co. 42-52; mem. Legislative Assembly 54-66; Minister of Educ. 60-64, of Communications 64-66.
P.O.B. 39, Winneba, Ghana.

Dowty, Sir George, Kt., D.SC., M.I.MECH.E.; British business executive; b. 27 April 1901; ed. Worcester Royal Grammar School.
Chairman and Managing Dir., Dowty Group Ltd.; Pres. Royal Aeronautical Soc. 52-53, Soc. of British Aircraft Constructors 60-61; Chair. Industrial Development Board for Malta 60-63; Gold Medal for Advancement of Aeronautical Science, Royal Aeronautical Soc. 55; Hon. F.R.Ae.S.
Dowty Group Ltd., Arle Court, Cheltenham, Glos., England.

Doxiadis, Constantinos A., D.ENG., LL.D.; Greek architect; b. 13; ed. Athens Technical Univ. School of Architecture and Berlin-Charlottenburg Univ.
Chief Town Planning Officer Athens 37-38; Head Dept. of Regional and Town Planning, Ministry of Public Works 39-44; Lecturer and Acting Prof. of Town Planning, Athens Technical Univ. 39-43; Minister of Housing and Perm. Sec. of Reconstruction 45-48; Co-ordinator Greek Recovery Programme 48-51; Chair. Board of Dirs. Athens Technological Org. 58-; Pres. Doxiadis Associates Int. Co. Ltd., Consultants on Development and Ekistics, Athens 53-; mem. Del. UN Conf., San Francisco 45, Head Del. Int. Conf. on Housing, Planning and Reconstruction 47, Head Del. to Greco-Italian War Reparations Conf. 49-50, Del.

Housing, Building and Planning Cttee. of Econ. and Social Council of UN 63, 64; Chair. Session on Urban Problems, UN Conf. on Application of Science and Technology for the Benefit of Less Developed Areas 63; Consultant to UN, IBRD, ICA, Ford Foundation, Redevelopment Land Agency (Washington) and Govts. of Cyprus, Ethiopia, France, Ghana, Greece, India, Iraq, Jordan, Lebanon, Libya, Pakistan, Saudi Arabia, Spain, Sudan, Syria, U.S.A., Zambia; Hon. LL.D. (Swarthmore and Mills Coll. and Univ. of Mich.), D.H. (Wayne State Univ.), L.H.D. (North Mich. Univ.), D.S. (Detroit Inst. Technology), D.F.A. (Univ. of Rhode Island); Sir Patrick Abercrombie Prize, Int. Union of Architects; Cali de Oro award, Soc. of Mexican Architects, Industrial Designers Soc. of America Award of Excellence, Aspen Award 66.

Major projects include: nat. ekistic and housing programmes for Iraq, Lebanon and Libya; plans and devt. programmes for Islamabad, Pakistan, Greater Rio de Janeiro, Accra-Tema region, Ghana, Greater Khartoum, Baghdad; urban renewal and devt. plans for several U.S. cities; new campus of Univ. of Panjab; Agricultural Univ. of Lyallpur, Pakistan; new buildings for Agricultural Univ. of Athens; survey for Int. Asian Highway; design of highways in Greece; design and supervision of construction of airports in Libya; housing projects in Iraq, Pakistan, Libya, Greece, etc. Publs. *Raumordnung im Griechischen Städtebau* 37, *Ekistic Analysis* 46, *Destruction of Towns and Villages in Greece* 47, *A Plan for the Survival of the Greek People* (with others, 2 vols.) 47, *Our Capital and its Future* 60, *Architecture in Transition* 63, *The New World of Urban Man* (with T. B. Douglass) 65, *Urban Renewal and the Future of the American City* 66, *Between Dystopia and Utopia* 66.

Doxiadis Associates, Athens; Stratiotikou Syndesmou 24, Athens 136, Greece.

Doyenin, Vasily Nicolaevich; Soviet politician; b. 1909; ed. Far Eastern Polytechnical Inst.
Director of a works making light motor vehicles 48-50; later Chair. Econ. Council of R.S.F.S.R.; Minister of Machine-Building for Light and Food Industry and Household Articles 65-, mem. C.P.S.U. 40-, Alt. mem. Central Cttee. C.P.S.U. 66-; Deputy to U.S.S.R. Supreme Soviet 66-.
Ministry of Machine-Building for Light and Food Industry and Household Articles, Moscow, U.S.S.R.

Dozza, Giuseppe; Italian politician; b. 29 Nov. 1901. Member, Central Cttee. of Italian C.P. 31-, of Directorate 51-; fmr. Partisan; Mayor of Bologna 45-66.
Bologna, Italy.

Dracos, George; Greek business executive; b. 16; ed. Economic Univ. of Athens.
Managing Dir. Isola Manufacturing Co. 38-, Pres. 63-; Dir. P. Dracos S.A. Trading Co., 37-; Pres. VES Trading Co. 62-; Pres. Federation of Greek Industries 58-; mem. Board, Athens Technological Inst.; High Order of Phoenix.
22 Homer Street, Athens, Greece.

Dragan, Dr. Joseph Constantin; Romanian industrialist (lives in Italy); b. 17; ed. Univs. of Bucharest and Rome.
Founder-Manager Dacia Co. 40, Dacia Inc. 47, Banca Gallia & Co. and Butane-Gas 48, Dragochimica Co. 52, Traschimici Shipping Co. 52; and various companies in Europe and Africa, all controlled by Dragofina Petroleum Investment Trust Reg. Lugano, Switzerland and Vaduz, Liechtenstein; founded *Romanian Catholic Monitor* and *European Bulletin* 49 and *Eastern Europe Monitor* 54; Chair. N. Italy Marketing Asscn., Spanish Marketing Asscn.; mem. Int. Chamber of Commerce; Vice-Chair. for Europe of Int. Marketing Fed.
9 via Larga, Milan, Italy.

Draghici, Alexandru; Romanian politician; b. 26 Sept. 1913.
Member, Communist Part of Romania 34-48, Central Ctee. of Romanian Workers' Party (now Communist Party) 48-68; Political Bureau 55-65, Perm. Presidium 65-68, Sec. of Central Cttee. 65-68; Deputy Minister of Home Affairs 51-52, Minister 52-65; Deputy Chair. Council of Ministers 61-65.
Bucharest, Romania.

Drago, Mariano José; Argentine lawyer, writer and diplomatist; b. 3 May 1896; ed. Col. Lacordaire, Col. Nacional Buenos Aires, Inst. Sainte Marie, Paris, and Univ. of Buenos Aires.
Prof. Int. Law, Buenos Aires Univ.; mem. Soc. Argentina de Criminología, Soc. de Historia Argentina, Inst. of Paris Univ. in Buenos Aires and Institución Mitre; mem. Juridical Comm. for reorganisation of the Judicial Power in Argentina 55; fmr. Permanent Del. to UN Vice-Pres. Acad. Nac. de Derecho y Ciencias Sociales de Buenos Aires; Minister of Foreign Affairs 62; mem. Asoc. Argentina de Cultura Inglesa; Grand Cross Order of Orange-Nassau, Grand Cross Order of Vasco Núñez de Balboa, Commdr. de la Légion d'Honneur. Publ. a great number of juridical and political works including *El derecho al nombre, Introducción a los Discursos y Escritos de Luis María Drago, Los Presidentes de la IIIa. República (setenta años de historia francesa), El bloqueo francés de 1838 en el Río de la Plata, Actualidad de Monroe,* etc.
Carlos Pellegrini 1521, Buenos Aires, Argentina.

Drake, Arthur Eric Courtney, C.B.E., M.A., F.C.A.; British business executive; b. 29 Nov. 1910; ed. Shrewsbury School and Pembroke Coll., Cambridge.
Anglo-Persian Oil Co. Ltd. (now The British Petroleum Co. Ltd.) 35-, Gen. Man. Iran and Iraq 50-51, Rep. in U.S.A. 52-54; Man. Dir. The British Petroleum Co. Ltd. 58-, Dep. Chair. 62-; Pres. Chamber of Shipping of U.K. 64; mem. Gen. Cttee. of Lloyd's Register of Shipping; Gov. Pangbourne Nautical Coll.; mem. Board of Govs. of London School of Econs.
The Old Rectory, Cheriton, Alresford, Hants., England. Telephone: 01-920 1200 (London Office).

Drapeau, Jean, Q.C., LL.B.; Canadian lawyer and politician; b. 18 Feb. 1916; ed. Jean-de-Brébeuf and Le Plateau Schools, Montreal, and Univ. of Montreal.
Admitted to Montreal Bar 43; practised law in Criminal and Civil Courts, specializing in commercial and corporation law; Mayor of Montreal 54-57, 60-; founded Montreal Civic Party 60; Hon. degrees from Univ. of Moncton 56, Univ. of Montreal 64, McGill Univ. 65, Boswell Inst., Loyola Univ. 66, Sir George Williams Univ. and Laval Univ. 67; Hon. mem. American Bar Asscn.
Cabinet du Maire, Ville de Montréal, Montreal, Canada.

Draper, Charles Stark, B.A., B.S., M.S., PH.D.; American aeronautical engineer; b. 2 Oct. 1901; ed. Univ. of Missouri, Stanford Univ., and Mass. Inst. of Technology.
Asst. Prof. of Aeronautical Engineering, M.I.T. 35-38, Assoc. Prof. 38-39, Prof. 39-, Dir. Instrumentation Laboratory 40-, Head of Dept. of Aeronautics and Astronautics 51-66; research and development on fire control, flight control and inertial guidance systems for U.S. Air Force and Navy, consulting engineer to many aeronautical companies and instrument manufacturers; mem. several advisory groups connected with military services; Pres. Int. Acad. of Aeronautics; Medal of Merit (presidential citation) 46, Exceptional Civilian Service Award (Dept. of Air Force) 51, Navy Distinguished Public Service Award 56, 60, Holley Medal (American Soc. of Mech. Engrs.) 57, American Hon. Fellowship for 1958 of Inst. of Aeronautical Sciences

59, Potts Medal Award, Franklin Inst. 60, Nat. Medal of Science 65; Hon. degree Eidgenossische Technische Hochschule, Switzerland; Guggenheim Award 67; N.A.S.A. Distinguished Public Service Medal 67.

Publs. *Instrument Engineering* (with W. McKay and S. Lees) Vol. I 52, Vol. II 53, Vol. III 55, and numerous papers in the fields of instrumentation and control.

Office: Massachusetts Institute of Technology, 68 Albany Street, Cambridge, Mass.; Home: 62 Bellevue Street, Newton, Mass., U.S.A.

Telephone: 464-0670.

Draper, William H., Jnr., M.A.; American investment banker and diplomatist; b. 10 Aug. 1894; ed. New York Univ.

Major, Inf., U.S. Army, during First World War; with Nat. City Bank N.Y. City 19-21; Asst. Treas. Bankers' Trust Co. N.Y. City 23-27; with Dillon, Read & Co. 27-51; Chief of Staff 77th Reserve Div. 36-40; active duty as Col. Inf. with Gen. Staff, U.S. Army, Washington 40-41; commd. 136th Inf. Regt., 33rd Inf. Div. 42-44, including service in Pacific Theatre; Brigadier Gen. 45; Chief, Economic Div., Control Council for Germany 45-46, Economic Adviser to C-in-C. European Theatre with rank of Major-Gen. 47; Mil. Govt. Adviser to Sec. of State at Moscow Conf. of Foreign Ministers 47; Under-Sec. of War (later Under-Sec. of Army) 47-49; fmr. U.S. Special Rep. in Europe, with rank of Ambassador; permanent rep. NATO 52 and 53; fmr. Chair. Long Island Transit Authority and Trustee Long Island Rail Road Co.; Chair. Board of Mexican Light and Power Co. Ltd., Mexico 53-59; Chair. Board of Combustion Engineering 63-65; Chair. Pension Corpn. of America 65-67; Dir. Western Bancorporation, Insurance Securities Inc., U.S. Leading Corpn.; Legion of Merit (Army 43, Navy 45); D.S.M. 48; Order of Orange Nassau (Neths.) 49; Great Cross Order of Merit (Italy) 54; Hon. LL.D. (New York Univ., Univ. of Louisville and Duke Univ.).

2202 Foxboro Place N.W., Washington D.C., U.S.A.

Drda, Jan; Czechoslovak novelist and playwright; b. 4 April 1915.

State Prize 53, Order of the Republic 55, Order of 25 February 48, Honoured Artist 65.

Publs. *The Town of Rukapán, Silent Barricade, Plays with the Devil, The Fair Tortiza, The Hot Soil.*

c/o Union of Czechoslovak Writers, Národní 11, Prague I, Czechoslovakia.

Drees, W.; Netherlands politician; b. 5 July 1886; ed. Commercial School.

Joined Twentsche Bank; stenographer to States-Gen. 07; Chair. Hague Federation of the S.D.A.P. (Social Democratic Workers' Party) 11-31; mem. Hague Municipal Council 13; mem. Provincial States of Zuid Holland 19, and in 33 mem. Second Chamber; mem. S.D.A.P. party executive since 27; filled many other Social posts; during the occupation Chair. of Convention of Political Parties and Central Cttee. Resistance Movement; mem. Gov. Advisory Council; Min. Social Affairs in Schermerhorn's Govt. June 45-46, and Beel's Govt. June 46-48; introduced Old Age Pensions Act 47; Prime Minister Aug. 48-Dec. 58; awards include, Hon. G.C.M.G., Grand Cross of Order of Léopold (Belgium), of Order of Crown of Oak (Luxembourg), Grand Croix Légion d'Honneur and Order of Dannebrog, Grand Cross Order of the Netherlands Lion, Hon. Minister of State., etc.; Hon. D.Econ.; Hon. Dr.Jur.

Beeklaan 502, The Hague, Netherlands.

Telephone: 070-335424.

Dreier, John Caspar, A.B.; American public servant; b. 27 Dec. 1906; ed. Harvard Univ.

Began career in Dept. of State 41; Asst. Exec. Sec. San Francisco Conf. 45; del. to Inter-American Confs. Rio de Janeiro 47, Bogotá 48, Caracas 54, Buenos Aires Economic Conf. 57, Santiago 59; U.S. rep. Council of Organization of American States (O.A.S.) 51-60; Chair. 51-52; mem. O.A.S. Investigating Cttee. on hostilities between Costa Rica and Nicaragua, chosen by these two Governments as Pres. Permanent Cttee. of Investigation and Conciliation 55; mem. O.A.S. peace mission on hostilities between Honduras and Nicaragua 57; five times U.S. del. to U.N. Gen. Ass.; Acting Dir. Office of Inter-American Regional Political Affairs 59-60; Dir. Inter-American Center, School of Advanced Int. Studies, Johns Hopkins Univ. 60-; U.S. mem. and Chair. Inter-American Peace Cttee.

4717 Fulton Street N.W., Washington, D.C. 20007, U.S.A.

Drew, Hon. George Alexander, P.C., C.C., Q.C., LL.D.; Canadian lawyer and diplomatist; b. 7 May 1894; ed. Upper Canada Coll., and Toronto Univ.

Served First World War; called Ontario Bar 20, law practice Guelph to 25; Asst. Master Ontario Supreme Court 26, Master 29; K.C 33; Chair. Ontario Securities Comm. 31-34; elected Ontario Legislature 39; Prime Minister, Pres. of Council and Min. of Education, Ontario 45-48; Nat. leader Progressive Conservative Party of Canada 48-56; High Commr. in U.K. 57-64; Chair. Board Lake Ontario Cement Ltd.; Gov. Univ. of Toronto; Chancellor, Univ. of Guelph; M.P. for Carleton, Ont., and Leader of the Opposition, House of Commons 49-57.

Publs. *Canada's Fighting Airmen, The Truth about the War, Salesmen of Death, Tell Britain, The Truth about War Debts.*

Office: Suite 2111, 44 Victoria Street, Toronto 1, Ontario; Home: 60 Old Forest Hill Road, Toronto 7, Ontario, Canada.

Telephone: 366-3452 (Office); 489-3340 (Home).

Drewes, Alfred H(erman); American metals executive; b. 24 Oct. 1913; ed. Columbia Univ., N.Y.

National Lead Co., New York City 35-, Asst. to Pres. 47-50, Dir., mem. Exec. Cttee. 50-, Vice-Pres. 51-63, Exec. Vice-Pres. 63-65, Pres. 65-; Dir. Titanium Metals Corpn. of America, Barker Castor Oil Co., The Chas. Taylor's Sons Co., Master Metals Inc., Pioneer Aluminum, Barber Die Casting Co. Ltd., Mineral Deposits Pty. Ltd., American Re-insurance Co., Nat. Starch & Chemical Corpn.

National Lead Company, 111 Broadway, New York 6, N.Y.; Home: 191 S. Woodland Street, Englewood, N.J., U.S.A.

Dreyfus, Pierre; French business executive; b. 18 Nov. 1907.

Inspector-Gen. of Industry and Commerce, Chief of Gen. Inspectorate, and Dir. of Cabinet to Minister of Industry and Commerce 47-49; Pres. Houillères de Lorraine 50, Charbonnages de France 54; Pres. of Energy Comm. of the Plan, and Dir. of Cabinet to Minister of Industry and Commerce 54; Vice-Pres. Régie nationale des usines Renault 48-55, Pres. Dir. Gen. 55-; Pres. Société des Aciers fins de l'Est; Commdr. Légion d'Honneur.

Régie Nationale des Usines Renault, 8 avenue Emile-Zola, Boulogne-Billancourt (Seine); Home: 51 avenue des Champs-Elysées, Paris 8e, France.

Dreyfus, Pierre; French industrialist; b. 2 Nov. 1907; ed. Lycée de Mulhouse, Ecole de Filature et Tissage, Mulhouse.

Joined Etablissement Dreyfus Frères, Mulhouse 29, Admin. Dir. 33, Man. Dir. 49-65; Président-directeur-général, P. Dreyfus et Cie, Mulhouse 65-; Président du Directoire de Schaeffer-Impression, Vieux-Thann; Chevalier Légion d'Honneur.

Schaefer-Impression S.A., 68 Vieux-Thann, France.

Dreyfuss, Henry; American industrial designer; b. 2 March 1904; ed. Ethical Culture Fine Arts High School, New York.

DRI INTERNATIONAL WHO'S WHO DRO

Began his career in theatrical design, and in 29 opened his first office; the Henry Dreyfuss and Associates org. has since worked on almost every kind of industrial product and on mil. problems for the U.S. Armed Forces; Chair. of Board Industrial Designers Soc. of America; Prof.-in-Residence, Univ. of California (Los Angeles); mem. Board of Trustees and Faculty California Inst. of Technology, Board of Dirs. Educ. Facilities Lab. of Ford Foundation, Board of Govs. Performing Arts Council of Los Angeles Music Center; Benjamin Franklin Fellow, Royal Soc. of Arts; awarded Architectural League Gold Medal 51; Order of Orange-Nassau 52; Hon. D.Sc. (Occidental Coll.) 53, Ambassador Award for Achievement (England) 65, and other awards.
Publs. *Ten Years of Industrial Design* 39, *A Record of Industrial Designs* 47, *Industrial Design—A Progress Report* 52, *Designing for People* 55, *Industrial Design—A Pictorial Accounting* 57, *The Measure of Man* 60, *Industrial Design*, vol. 5, 64.
4 West 58th Street, New York, N.Y. 10019; and 500 Columbia Street, South Pasadena, Calif. 91030, U.S.A. Telephone: Plaza 3-8030.

Driberg, Thomas Edward Neil, M.P.; British journalist and politician; b. 22 May 1905; ed. Lancing and Christ Church, Oxford.
Mem. Editorial Staff *Daily Express* 28-43; Ind. M.P. for Maldon Div. of Essex 42-45, Lab. 45-55; M.P. for Barking 59-; mem. Nat. Exec. Cttee., Labour Party 49-, Chair. 57-58; contributor *Sunday Citizen* (formerly *Reynolds News*) 43-66; television and radio critic for *New Statesman* 55-61; war corresp. 44-45 and in Korea 50; mem. Parl. Delegation, Buchenwald Camp 45; Chair. Commonwealth and Colonies Group, Parliamentary Labour Party 64-; Chair. Select Cttee. on Broadcasting etc. of Proceedings in Parl. 66-67; mem. Historic Buildings Council for England 66-.
Publs. *Colonnade* 49, *The Best of Both Worlds* 53, *Beaverbrook, a Study in Power and Frustration* 56, *Guy Burgess: A Portrait with Background* 56, *The Mystery of Moral Re-Armament: A Study of Frank Buchman and His Movement* 64.
House of Commons, London, S.W.1, England.

Drijver, Alexander, M.MECH.ENG.; Netherlands mechanical engineer; b. 17 Nov. 1904; ed. Technische Hogeschool te Delft.
Mechanical Engineer, N.V. Koninklijke Nederlandsche Hoogovens en Staalfabrieken, IJmuiden 28, Chief, Engineering Dept. 45-50, Dir. of Engineering 50-59, Asst. Man. Dir. 59-61, Man. Dir. 61-67, Chair. of Board of Man. Dirs. 67-; Vice-Pres. Centre Nat. de Recherche Métallurgiques, Liège 60-; Dir. Int. Iron and Steel Inst. 67-; mem. State Council of Min. of Waterworks 67-; mem. Royal Soc. of Engineers (Holland), Iron and Steel Inst. (U.K.), Verein Deutscher Eisenhüttenleute; Hon. mem. Iron and Steel Inst. of Japan; Gold Medal of Honour of Mech. Eng. and Shipbuilding Section of Royal Netherlands Soc. of Engineers; Knight Order of Netherlands Lion.
Publs. Articles and papers on technical and econ. devt. in iron and steel industry in nat. and int. magazines.
Koninklijke Nederlandsche Hoogovens en Staalfabrieken N.V., IJmuiden; Home: Akerendamlaan 15, Beverwijk, Netherlands.
Telephone: Beverwijk 23634.

Driscoll, Alfred E.; American lawyer and pharmaceutical executive; b. 25 Oct. 1902; ed. Williams Coll., and Harvard Univ.
Admitted to New Jersey Bar 29; State Senator, New Jersey 38-41; Gov. of New Jersey 47-54; Pres. and Dir. Warner-Lambert Pharmaceutical Co. 54-67. Hon. Chair. of Board and Dir. 67-; Dir. other companies; Vice-Chair. President's Comm. on Inter-Governmental Relations 54-55; Pres. Nat. Municipal League; mem.

Board of Fellows, Fairleigh Dickinson Univ.; Dir Curtis Publishing Co., Chemical Fund, Pharmaceutical Manufacturers Asscn.; Republican.
Warner-Lambert Pharmaceutical Co., 201 Tabor Road, Morris Plains, New Jersey, U.S.A.

Driss, Rachid; Tunisian journalist and diplomatist; b. 27 Jan. 1917; ed. Sadiki Coll. Tunis.
Joined Neo-Destour party 34; journalist exiled in Cairo, and with Pres. Bourguiba founder mem. Bureau du Maghreb Arabe; returned to Tunisia 55; Editor *El Amal*; Deputy, Constitutional Assembly 56; Sec. of State Post Office and Communications 57-58, mem. National Assembly 58; Ambassador to the U.S.A. and Mexico 64-; Grand Cordon de l'Ordre de l'Indépendance de la République Tunisienne and many foreign decorations.
Embassy of Tunisia, 2408 Massachusetts Avenue, Washington, D.C.; Home: 5131 Broad Branch Road, N.W., Washington, D.C., U.S.A.

Driver, Sir Godfrey Rolles, Kt., C.B.E., M.C., M.A., F.B.A.; British university professor (rtd.); b. 20 Aug. 1892; ed. Winchester Coll., and New Coll., Oxford.
Mil. and Nat. service 15-19, 40-44; Fellow and Classical Tutor Magdalen Coll. Oxford 19-28, Librarian 23-42, Fellow by Special Election 28; Reader in Comparative Semitic Philology Univ. of Oxford 28, Prof. of Semitic Philology 38-62; Grinfield Lecturer on the Septuagint 35-38, Curator of Bodleian Library 34-53; Visiting Prof. Chicago Univ. 25, Louvain Univ. 50; Joint Ed. *Journal of Theological Studies* 33-47; assoc. mem. Royal Flemish Acad. of Science, Letters and Arts 54; mem. of Cttee. revising English Bible 47; Pres. Int. Organisation of Old Testament Scholars; Hon. D.D. (Aberdeen, Manchester), Hon. Litt.D. (Durham and Cambridge); Joint Dir. New English Bible 65.
Publs. *Letters of the First Babylonian Dynasty* 25, *Grammar of the Colloquial Arabic of Syria and Palestine* 25, *Nestorius, the Bazaar of Heracleides* (with Rev. L. Hodgson) 25, *Assyrian Laws* (with Sir John Miles) 35, *Problems of the Hebrew Verbal System* 36, *Semitic Writing* 48, *Babylonian Laws I-II* (with Sir John Miles) 52-55, *Aramaic Documents of the 5th Century* B.C. 54, 57, *Canaanite Myths and Legends* 56, *The Problem of the Judaean Scrolls* 65.
41 Park Town, Oxford, England.
Telephone: Oxford 55165.

Driver, William J., B.B.A., LL.B.; American government official; b. 9 May 1918; ed. Niagara Univ., Rochester, N.Y., and George Washington Univ., Washington, D.C.
Executive and Admin. Officer, H.Q., Adjutant-Gen., European Theatre of Operations, U.S. Army 42-46; Office of Asst. Chief of Staff, U.S. Army 51-53; Chief Benefits Dir., Veterans Administration 59-61; Deputy Admin., Veterans Admin. 61-65, Admin. of Veterans Affairs 65-; numerous awards.
215 W. Columbia Street, Falls Church, Virginia, U.S.A.

Drobnis, Alexandras Antonovich; Soviet politician; b. 1912; ed. Vilnius State Univ.
Chief of State Bank office 40-42; Deputy People's Commissar of Finance, Lithuanian S.S.R., later People's Commissar 42-47; Vice-Chair. Council of Ministers and Chair. State Planning Cttee. of Lithuanian S.S.R. 57-; mem. Central Cttee. of C.P. of Lithuania; mem. C.P.S.U. 44-.
Lithuanian Council of Ministers, Vilnius, U.S.S.R.

Drobyazko, Alexander Ivanovich; Soviet engineer and economist; b. 16; ed. Moscow Aviation Inst., Acad. of Foreign Trade.
Soviet Army, Kalinin Front 41-42; Soviet Trade Mission, U.K. 42-48; Dir. *Raznoimport* (rubber, etc.) Office 48-52, Deputy Chair. *Raznoimport* 52-56, Chair.

56-66; Export, Ministry of Foreign Trade 66-; mem. C.P. 39-; Order of the Red Banner of Labour.
Ministry of Foreign Trade, Smolenskaya-Sennaya Ploshchad 32-34, Moscow, U.S.S.R.

Drogheda, 11th Earl of Drogheda; **Charles Garrett Ponsonby,** K.B.E.; b. 23 April 1910; British newspaper executive and arts administrator; ed. Eton and Trinity Coll., Cambridge.
Joined staff of *Financial News* 32; worked for Ministry of Production 42-45; Man. Dir. *Financial Times* 45-; Chair. Industrial & Trade Fairs Ltd.; Dir. Economist Newspaper Ltd.; Chair. Royal Opera House, Covent Garden Ltd., City (of London) Arts Trust Ltd., Newspaper Publishers Asscn. Ltd.; Gov. The Royal Ballet.
Parkside House, Wick Lane, Englefield Green, Surrey; and 8 Lord North Street, London, S.W.1, England.
Telephone: Egham 2800.

Droit, Michel; French journalist and writer; b. 23 Jan. 1923; ed. Lycée Louis le Grand, Paris, Univ. of Paris, and Ecole Libre des Sciences Politiques.
Resistance Movement 42-44; War Correspondent and Reporter for press, radio and TV 44-56; Foreign Affairs Commentator, French TV 56-60; Editor-in Chief *Tribunes et Débats*, French TV 60-61; Editor-in-Chief *Le Figaro Littéraire* 61-; Producer TV Programme *A propos* 61-; Prix Max Barthou 55; Prix Carlos de Lazerme 61, Grand Prix du Roman de l'Académie Française 64; Chevalier Légion d'Honneur; Médaille Militaire.
Publs. novels: *Plus rien au monde, Pueblo, Le Retour, Les Compagnons de la Forêt-Noire;* travel: *Jours et nuits d'Amérique, Visas pour l'Amérique du Sud, J'ai vu vivre le Japon, Panoramas mexicains;* essays: *André Maurois, La Camargue;* biography: *De Lattre Maréchal de France;* short stories: *A propos.*
29 avenue d'Eylau, Paris 16e, France.
Telephone: Kleber 23-10.

Droogleever Fortuyn, Jan, M.D., M.SC.; Netherlands neurologist; b. 12 April 1906; ed. Univs. of Utrecht, Amsterdam.
Department of Neurology, Amsterdam 39-51; Prof. of Neurology, Groningen 51-; Montreal Neurological Inst. 46-47; Dutch Central Inst. for Brain Research 47-51.
Publs. *Experimental Study on Cortico-Thalamic Relationships* 38, *Studies in Epilepsy* 47, *Studies on Topographical Relationships in the Brain* 56, *Petit Mal* 57, *Geometrical properties of the neurons in general and of the lateral geniculate body of the rabbit in particular* 64.
Department of Neurology, University Hospital, Oostersingel 59, Groningen, Netherlands.
Telephone: 05900-39123, Extension 430.

Dropsy, Henri; French engraver; b. 21 Jan. 1885; ed. Ecole Nationale Supérieure des Beaux-Arts.
Prof. at Ecole Nationale Supérieure des Beaux-Arts 30-; mem. Académie des Beaux-Arts, Inst. de France 42-; Officier de la Légion d'Honneur.
Works include medals of Clémenceau, Aristide Briand, Albert Lebrun, Commemoration medals for the 150th anniversary of the Inst. de France, 3rd centenary of the Académie Royale de Peinture et de Sculpture, 150th anniversary of Prefecture of Police, Council of Europe, visits of H.M. Queen Elizabeth to Paris 53 and 57, Inauguration of Orly Airport, Millennium of Mt. Athos Monastery 963-1963, 8th centenary of Notre Dame, etc.
20 rue Simon-Dereure, Paris 18e, France.
Telephone: 606-85-68.

Drucker, Peter F., DR. IUR.; American (b. Austrian) writer and business consultant; b. 19 Nov. 1909; ed. Gymnasium, Vienna, and Univs. of Hamburg and Frankfurt.
Newspaperman, Europe 29-33; Economist in banks London 34-37; in U.S.A. 37-; Management Consultant

(own firm) 40-; Prof. of Political Philosophy, Bennington Coll., Vermont 42-49; Prof. of Management, New York Univ. Graduate School 50-, Chair. of Dept. 56-62; Pres. Soc. History of Technology 65-66.
Publs. *The End of Economic Man* 39, *The Future of Industrial Man* 42, *Concept of the Corporation* 46, *The New Society* 50, *The Practice of Management* 54, *America's Next Twenty Years* 57, *Gedanken für die Zukunft* 59, *Landmarks of Tomorrow* 60, *Managing for Results* 64, *The Effective Executive.*
138 North Mountain Avenue, Montclair, N.J., U.S.A.
Telephone: 201-746-8123.

Drumalbyn, 1st Baron, cr. 63, of Whitesands; **Niall Malcolm Stewart Macpherson,** P.C.; British politician; b. 3 Aug. 1908; ed. Edinburgh Acad., Fettes Coll., and Trinity Coll., Oxford.
Manager, Turkish Branch, J. & J. Colman Ltd. 33-35, Export Branch, London 36-39; Major, Queen's Own Cameron Highlanders 39-45; M.P. 45-63; Jt. Under-Sec. of State for Scotland 55-60; Parl. Sec. Board of Trade 60-62; Minister of Pensions and Nat. Insurance 62-63; Minister of State, Board of Trade 63-64; Chair. Advertising Standards Authority 65-; Hon. Treas. Nat. Lib. Org. 66-; Nat. Liberal and Unionist.
High Larch, Iver Heath, Bucks, England.

Drummond, Roscoe, B.S.J.; American writer; ed. Syracuse Univ.
Reporter with *Christian Science Monitor*, Boston 24, later editorial writer, Chief, Washington News Bureau; on leave as Dir. of Information, E.C.A. (Paris) 49-51; Chief, Washington Bureau *New York Herald Tribune* 53-55; Washington columnist for Publishers Newspaper Syndicate 55-; Hon. Litt.D. Dartmouth Coll. 47, Hon. D.D.L. Principia Coll. 54.
Publ. *Duel at the Brink: John Foster Dulles' Command of American Power* (with Gaston Coblenz) 60.
Suite 1320, 1750 Pennsylvania Avenue N.W., Washington, D.C. 20006, U.S.A.

Drummond de Andrade, Carlos; Brazilian writer; b. 30 Oct. 1902.
Head of Private Office of Minister of Educ. and Culture 34-45; Head of History Section, Office of Nat. and Artistic Heritage 45-62; Historian of *Correio da Manhã* (Rio de Janeiro) 54-.
Publs. Poetry includes: *Alguma Poesia* 30, *Brejo das Almas* 34, *Sentimento do Mundo* 40, *A Rosa do Povo* 45, *Claro Enigma* 51, *Fazendeiro do Ar* 53, *Lição de Coisas* 62; prose: *Contos de Aprendiz* 51, and four vols. of history.
Rua Conselheiro Lafaiete 60, Ap. 701, Rio de Janeiro, Estado da Guanabara, Brazil.

Druon, Maurice Samuel Roger Charles; French author; b. 23 April 1918; ed. Lycée Michelet and Ecole des Sciences Politiques, Paris.
War Corresp. Allied Armies 44-45; mem. Académie Française 66-; Prix Goncourt for novel *Les Grandes Familles* 48; Prix de Monaco 66; Prés. de l'Association des Lauréats du Concours général 58.
Publs. *Lettres d'un Européen* 46, *La Dernière Brigade* 46, *La Fin des Hommes* (3 vols. *Les Grandes Familles* 48, *La Chute des Corps* 50, *Rendez-vous aux Enfers* 51), *La Volupté d'être* 54, *Les Rois Maudits* 55-60 (6 vols. *Le Roi de Fer, La Reine Etranglée, Les Poisons de la Couronne, La Loi des Mâles, La Louve de France, Le Lis et le Lion), Tiston les paices verts* 57, *Alexandre le Dieu* 58, *Des Seigneurs de la plaine à l'hôtel de Mondez* 62, *Les Mémoires de Zeus, L'aube des dieux* 63, *Bernard Buffet* 64, *Paris, de César à Saint Louis* 64, *Le Pouvoir* 65, *Les Tambours de la Mémoire* 65, *Le Bonheur des uns ... 67, Les Mémoires de Zeus* Vol. II—*les jours des hommes* 67, *Discours de Réception à l'Academie française* 68; plays: *Mégarée* 42, *Un Voyageur* 53, *La Contessa* 62.
c/o Institut de France, 23 quai de Conti, Paris, France.

Drury, Allen Stuart, B.A.; American writer; b. 2 Sept. 1918; ed. Stanford Univ.
Editor *Tulare Bee* 40-41; County Editor *Bakersfeld Californian* 42; army service 42-43; Senate Staff, United Press 43-45; freelance corresp. Washington 46-47; Nat. Editor *Pathfinder Magazine* 47-52; Nat. Staff, *Washington Evening Star* 52-54; Senate Staff, *New York Times* 54-59; Washington contrib. *Readers' Digest* 60-67; Pulitzer Prize for novel *Advise and Consent* 60.
Publs. *Advise and Consent* 59, *A Shade of Difference* 62, *A Senate Journal* 63, *That Summer* 65, *Three Kids in a Car* 65, *Capable of Honour* 66, "*A Very Strange Society*" 67.
Box 927, Maitland, Florida, U.S.A.

Drury, Charles Mills, C.B.E., D.S.O.; Canadian politician; b. 17 May 1912; ed. McGill Univ., Royal Military Coll., Kingston, Ontario, and Univ. of Paris.
Chief, UNRRA Mission, Poland 45-47; Dep. Minister, Dept. of Nat. Defence 49-55; Pres. Provincial Transport Co. 56-60; Pres. Avis Transport of Canada Ltd. 58-63, Needco Frigistors Ltd. 60-63; Dir. Livingstone Range Syndicate Ltd. 61-63; Minister of Defence Production and Industry May 63-; Liberal.
400 Kensington Avenue, Westmount, Quebec, Canada.

Druto, Jan; Polish diplomatist; b. 28 April 1909; ed. St. Batory's Univ., Vilnius (Wilno).
Asst. teacher, Univ. of Vilnius 34-36; Vice-Pres. Central Planning Office 46-47; Chief, Econ. Dept. Ministry of Agriculture 47-48; Ambassador to Turkey 48-52, Italy 52-59; Head of Dept., Ministry of Foreign Affairs 59-61; Ambassador to France 61-.
Ambassade de Pologne, 1 rue de Talleyrand, Paris 7e, France.

Druzhinin, Nicolai Mikhailovich; Soviet (Russian) historian; b. 86; ed. Moscow Univ.
Officer in World War I 16-18; Educ. Officer, Red Army 19-21; gen. educ. work 19-29; Prof. Moscow Univ. 34-48; mem. Historical Inst. of U.S.S.R. Acad. of Sciences 38-; mem. U.S.S.R. Acad. of Sciences 53-; State Prize, Order of Lenin, Order of Red Banner of Labour.
Publs. include: *Decembrist Nikita Muravjev* 33, *On Periods of History of Capitalist Economic System in Russia* 49, *State Peasantry and P. D. Kiselev's Reform,* Vols. 1-2 46-58, *Conflict Between Productive Forces and Feudal Economic System Before 1861 Reform* 57.
U.S.S.R. Academy of Sciences, Department of History, 19 Ul. Dmitry Ulyanov, Moscow, U.S.S.R.

Drygin, Anatoli Semyonovich; Soviet politician; b.14; ed. Michurin Inst., Michurinsky.
Member C.P.S.U. 40-; Soviet army service 41-46; party and govt. work, Leningrad 46-57; First Deputy Chair. Exec. Cttee. Leningrad Regional Soviet of Working People's Deputies 57-60; Sec. Leningrad Regional Cttee. C.P.S.U. 60-61; First Sec. Vologda Regional Cttee. C.P.S.U. 61-; Candidate mem. Central Cttee. C.P.S.U. 61-; deputy to Supreme Soviet U.S.S.R.
Vologda District Committee of the Communist Party of the Soviet Union, Vologda, U.S.S.R.

Drysdale, (George) Russell; British-born Australian artist; b. 7 Feb. 1912; ed. Geelong Grammar School, Victoria, Australia.
Art studies in Melbourne, London and Paris; works in New York Metropolitan Museum of Art, Nat. Gallery, London, Tate Gallery, London, Nat. Galleries of New South Wales, Victoria, South Australia, etc.; mem. Australian Soc. of Artists; mem. Commonwealth Art Advisory Board 62-; Dir. Pioneer Sugar Mills Ltd.
Publ. (with Jock Marshall) *Journey Among Men* 62.
Bouddi Farm, Kilcare Heights, Hardy's Bay, N.S.W., Australia.

Dualeh, Ahmad Yusuf; Somali politician; b. 35; ed. Bakht er Ruda Teachers' Institute, Sudan, and Cairo Univ.
Teacher 53-56; Cairo Univ. 56-58; staff of Arabic weekly journal *Hargeisa* 58-62; Deputy, Nat. Assembly 64-; Minister of Foreign Affairs, June 64-67.
The National Assembly, Mogadishu, Somalia.

Duarte, Paulo; Brazilian writer, journalist, and anthropologist; b. 99; ed. Institut Champagnat, France and Faculty of Law, São Paulo, Institut d'Ethnologie and Musée de l'Homme, Paris.
Former Deputy 34-37; Editor of *Diario Nacional, O Estado de São Paulo,* and Dir. of Editora Anhambi; during the 1932 revolution commanded the Frente de Bianor and Trem Blindado which fought and took part in the retreat of Cruzeiros; exiled, returned to Brazil 34; elected State Legislature; exiled again 37, returned 46; Pres. Cttee. for Prehistory, São Paulo Inst. of Prehistory and Ethnology; worked at Musée de l'Homme, Paris, and Museum of Modern Art, New York; founded the periodical *Anhembi;* Pres. Sociedade de Escritores and Sec.-Gen. Institut Français des Hautes Etudes Brésiliennes, Paris; Dir. Inst. of Prehistory, Univ. of São Paulo.
Publs. *Sob as Arcadas* 27, *Agora Nos* 27, *Versos de Trilussa* 28, *Que e que há* 31, *Contra o Vandalismo e o Exterminio* 36, *Variações sobre a gastronomia* 42, *Lingua Brasileira* 42, *Prisão, Exilio e Luta* 45, *Palmares pelo Avesso* 47, *Trilussa* 55, *O Espirito das Catedrais* 58, *Paul Rivet, por ele mesmo* 60, *O resto não é silencio* 66, *O Sambaqui Visto atraves de alguns Sambaquis* 68.
Cuidade Universitaria, caixa Postal 11.133, São Paulo, Brazil.

Dubček, Alexander, D.SC.S.; Czechoslovak politician; b. 27 Nov. 1921; ed. Communist Party Coll., Moscow, and Law Faculty, Comenius Univ., Bratislava.
Chief Sec. of Regional Cttee. of C.P. of Slovakia in Banská Bystrica 53-55; Chief Sec. Regional Cttee. of C.P. of Slovakia, Bratislava 58-60; mem. Presidium and Sec. of Central Cttee. of C.P. of Slovakia 62; mem. Presidium Central Cttee. of C.P. of Czechoslovakia 63-; First Sec. Central Cttee. of C.P. of Slovakia 63-68; First Sec. Central Cttee. C.P. of Czechoslovakia 68-; Chair. Central Cttee. of Slovak Nat. Front; mem. Presidium of Central Cttee. of Nat. Front; Deputy to Nat. Assembly 48, 60, 64-, and to Slovak Nat. Council 64-; Order of 25 Feb. 1948, 49; Award for Merits in Construction 58.
Central Committee, C.P. of Czechoslovakia, Prague 1, náb. Kyjevskébrigady 12, Czechoslovakia.

Dubilier, William; American engineer; b. 25 July 1888; ed. Technical Inst., and Cooper Inst., New York.
Inventor of various electrical devices for the radio industry; obtained over 600 patents on various electrical devices; organised Dubilier Condenser Co. Ltd., London 11; Pres. Dubilier Condenser Co., Radio Patents Corpn. and other companies; Consultant Cornell-Dubilier Electric Co., Siemens and Halske, U.S., etc.; Vice-Pres. and Technical Dir. Cornell Dubilier Electric Corpn.; Fellow American Inst. of Electrical Engineers, Inst. of Radio Engineers; mem. Franklin Soc., etc.; Hon. Medal Asscn. des Ingénieurs-Docteurs de France; Légion d'Honneur 50; Officer French Acad. 50; awarded Dunn Medal (Cooper Union) 55; 12 hon. degrees and Citation, Cooper Union for Advancement of Science and Art.
c/o Dubilier Condenser Co., Victoria Road, North Acton, London, W.3, England; Home: 339 Garden Road, Palm Beach, Florida, U.S.A.

Dubinin, Mikhail Mikhailovich; Soviet physical chemist; b. 1 Jan. 1901; ed. Moscow Higher Technical School.
In Moscow Higher Technical School 21-32, Prof. 33-; Head of Laboratory of Sorbtion Processes, Inst. of Physical Chemistry, U.S.S.R. Acad. of Sciences 46-; mem. U.S.S.R. Acad. of Sciences 43-; Pres. Mendeleyev Chemical Soc. 46-50; Head Chemical Section U.S.S.R. Acad. of Sciences 48-57; Editor-in-Chief *Bulletin of*

U.S.S.R. Academy of Sciences, Chemical Series; Hon. mem. Hungarian Acad. of Sciences; State Prize 42, 50; Order of Lenin; Order of the Patriotic War; Order of the Red Star (twice), etc.

Publs. *Fiziko-khimicheskie osnovy sortsionnoi tekhniki* 35, 39, *V. Sorbtsiya i struktura aktivnykh uglei I-II* 47, *III-IV* 49, *VIII-IX* 50, *Modern State of the Theory of Gas and Vapour Absorption by Microporous Adsorbents* 65, *Porous Structure and Adsorption Properties of Active Carbons* 66, *Adsorption in Micropores* 67, *Porous Structure of Adsorbents and Catalysts* 67, *Sorbtion Properties of and Secondary Structure of Synthetic Zeolotes VII* 62, *VIII-X* 64, *XI* 65, *XII-XIII* 66.

c/o U.S.S.R. Institute of Physical Chemistry, Academy of Sciences, Leninsky Prospekt 31, Moscow, U.S.S.R.

Dubinin, Nikolai Petrovich; Soviet biologist; b. 1906; ed. Moscow Univ.

At Moscow Zootechnical Inst. 28-32; at Inst. of Cytology, Histology and Embryology, U.S.S.R. Acad. of Sciences 32-48; at Inst. of Forestry 49-55, Inst. of Biophysics 55-58; Dir. Inst. of Cytology and Genetics, Siberian Dept., U.S.S.R. Acad. of Sciences 58-60; Presidium mem. Siberian Dept., U.S.S.R. Acad. of Sciences 58; Corresp. mem. U.S.S.R. Acad. of Sciences 46-66, mem. 66-; Darwin Medal 59.

U.S.S.R. Academy of Sciences, Novosibirsk, U.S.S.R.

Dubinsky, David; Polish-born American trade unionist; b. 22 Feb. 1892.

Emigrated to U.S.A. 11, naturalised 16; Man. Sec. Local Branch Int. Ladies' Garment Workers' Union 21-29; Vice-Pres. Int. Ladies' Garment Workers' Union 22-29, Gen. Sec. and Treas. 29-32, Pres., Gen. Sec. and Treas. 32-59, Pres. 59-66; Vice-Pres. and mem. Exec. Council A.F.L. 34-36 (resigned) 45-55, A.F.L.-C.I.O. 55-; a founder of the American Labor Party 36; founder Vice-Chair. Liberal Party 44; founder Americans for Democratic Action 47.

Home: 24 5th Avenue, New York City, N.Y., U.S.A.

Dubois, Jacques-Emile, D.SC.; French university professor; b. 13 April 1920; ed. Univs. de Lille et Grenoble.

Mem. Liberation Cttee., Isère 43-47; Ramsay Fellow, Univ. Coll., London 48-50; Scientific Adviser to French Cultural Counsellor, London 48-50; Prof. of Physical Chemistry and Petrochemistry, and Dir. of Chemistry Inst., Univ. of Saar 49-57, Dean of Science Faculty 53-57; Prof. of Physical Organic Chemistry, Univ. of Paris 57-; Research Fellow, Columbia Univ., New York 56; Guest Prof. of Physical Chemistry, Univ. of Saar 58; Scientific Adviser to French Minister of Educ. 62-63; Joint Dir. of Higher Educ. 63-65; Dir. of Research for Ministry of Defence 65-; mem. Directorate Nat. Research Council 63-; mem. Council French Chemical Soc. 65-; Chevalier Légion d'Honneur, Médaille de la Résistance, Commdr. des Palmes Académiques; Jecker Prize and Berthelot Medal (Acad. of Sciences); Le Bel and Ancel Prizes (French Chemical Soc.); Stas Medal (Belgian Chemical Soc.).

Publs. works in field of kinetics, fast reaction rates, electro-chemistry, automation applied to chemistry and coding of organic compounds by use of matrixes, and a systematic approach by these methods to correlations between structure and reactivity of organic compounds; the whole comprising the topological system D.A.R.C.

100 rue de Rennes, Paris 6e, France.

Telephone: 222-45-16.

Dubos, René Jules, PH.D.; American (b. French) bacteriologist; b. 20 Feb. 1901; ed. Coll. Chaptal and Inst. Nat. Agronomique (Paris).

Asst. Editor Int. Inst. of Agronomy, Rome 22-24; settled in U.S.A. 24 (naturalised U.S. citizen 38-); Research Asst. Rutgers Univ. N.J. Experimental Station 24-27; Fellow Rockefeller Univ. for Medical Research 27-28, Asst. 28-30, Assoc. 30-38, Assoc.

mem. 38-41, mem. 41-42; Fabyan Prof. of Comparative Pathology and Tropical Medicine Harvard Univ. Medical School 42-44; mem. Rockefeller Univ. for Medical Research 44-56, mem. and Prof. 56-; mem. Nat. Acad. of Sciences, American Philosophical Soc., Nat. Research Council; numerous awards include John Phillips Memorial Award (American Coll. of Physicians) 40, George Wilson Medal (American Clinical and Climatological Asscn.) 46, Lasker Award (American Public Health Asscn.) 48, Hitchcock Award (Univ. of Calif.) 54; Scientific Achievement Award (American Medical Asscn.); Arches of Science Award 66; numerous hon. degrees.

Publs. include: *The Bacterial Cell* 45, *Bacterial and Mycotic Infections of Man* 48, *Louis Pasteur* 50, *The White Plague—Tuberculosis, Man and Society* 52, *Biochemical Determinants of Microbial Disease* 54, *Mirage of Health* 59, *The Unseen World* 63, *Health and Disease* 65, *Man Adapting* 65, *Man, Medicine & Environment* 68, *So Human an Animal* 68.

Office: Rockefeller University, 66th Street and York Avenue, New York 10021; Home: Old Albany Post Road Garrison, New York City, N.Y., U.S.A.

DuBridge, Lee Alvin, M.A., PH.D.; American physicist and educator; b. 21 Sept. 1901; ed. Cornell Coll., and Univ. of Wisconsin.

Instructor in Physics, Univ. of Wisconsin 25-26; Fellow Nat. Research Council at Calif. Inst. of Technology 26-28; Asst. Prof. of Physics, Washington Univ. St. Louis, Missouri 28-33; Assoc. Prof. 33-34; Prof. of Physics and Chair. of Dept., Univ. of Rochester 34-46; Dean of Faculty of Arts and Science 38-42; on leave of absence, Univ. of Rochester, for war service as Dir. of Radiation Lab. at M.I.T., under the Nat. Defense Research Cttee. 40-45; Pres. of Calif. Institute of Technology 46-; mem. Gen. Advisory Cttee. U.S. Atomic Energy Comm. 46-52; Chair. Science Advisory Cttee., Office of Defense Mobilisation 52-56; mem. Nat. Acad. of Sciences, American Philosophical Society; Pres. American Physical Society 47; mem. Governing Board, American Inst. of Physics 41-46; Fellow, American Asscn. for Advancement of Science; mem. Board of Trustees, Carnegie Endowment for Int. Peace 51-57, Nat. Science Foundation Board 50-54, 58-64; mem. Board of Trustees, Rockefeller Foundation 56-67; mem. Board of Trustees Mellon Inst. 58-67; Trustee, U.S. Churchill Foundation 60-; Thomas Alva Edison Foundation, Inc. 60-, Henry E. Huntington Library and Art Gallery, San Marino, Calif.; various directorships; Benjamin Franklin Fellow, Royal Soc. of Arts, London, England 62-; Research Corpn. award 47; Medal for Merit 48; King's Medal for Service in Cause of Freedom 46; Hon. Fellow and Gold Medal award American Coll. of Cardiology 66; Hon. Sc.D. (Cornell Coll., Brooklyn Polytechnic Inst., Wesleyan Univ., Univ. of B.C., Washington Univ., Occidental Coll., Indiana Univ., Columbia Univ., Univ. of Md., Pennsylvania Military Coll., De Pauw Univ., Pomona Coll., Univ. of Wisconsin, Rockefeller Inst., Carnegie Inst. of Technology), Hon. LL.D. (Univs. of Calif., Southern Calif., Rochester, Northwestern Univ., Loyola Univ., Univ. of Notre Dame, Indiana), Hon. L.H.D. (Univ. of Redlands, Univ. of Judaism), Hon. D.C.L. (Union Coll.).

Publs. *Photoelectric Phenomena* (with A. L. Hughes) 32, *New Theories of the Photoelectric Effect* 35, *Introduction to Space* 60.

Home: 415 South Hill Avenue, Pasadena, Calif. 91106; Office: California Institute of Technology, 1201 E. California Boulevard, Pasadena, Calif. 91109, U.S.A.

Dubs, Homer H., M.A., B.D., PH.D., D.LITT. (Oxon); American sinologist and philosopher; b. 28 March 1892; ed. Yale, Columbia, and Chicago Univs., and Union Theological Seminary, New York City.

Missionary in China 18-24; Instructor in Philosophy,

Univ. of Minnesota 25-27; Prof. of Philosophy, Marshall Coll., Huntington, W. Va. 27-34; Dir. Translation of Chinese Histories Project of American Council of Learned Societies 34-37; Acting Prof. of Philosophy, Duke Univ. 37-43; Visiting Prof. of Chinese, Columbia Univ. 44-45; Prof. of Chinese Studies, Kennedy School of Missions, Hartford Seminary Foundation, Conn. 45-47; Prof. of Chinese, Oxford Univ. England 47-59, Emeritus Prof. 59-.
Publs. *Hsüntze, the Moulder of Ancient Confucianism* 27, *The Works of Hsüntze* (trans. from Chinese) 28, *Rational Induction, An Analysis of the Method of Philosophy and Science* 30, *The History of the Former Han Dynasty*, by Pan Ku (a critical trans. with annotations) Vol. I 38, II 44, III 55, *A Roman City in Ancient China* 57.
133A Banbury Road, Oxford, England.

Dubuffet, Jean; French artist; b. 31 July 1901; ed. Paris art schools.
Worked alternatively as painter and commercial traveller 24-42; free-lance artist 42-; travels in the Sahara 47-49; settled at Vence 55; has made extensive study of "Art Brut"—the work of criminals, mental defectives, etc.; has experimented widely in the production of works from unusual materials such as sand, sponges, nails, tar and glass; retrospective exhbn., Tate Gallery, London 66, Guggenheim Museum, N.Y. 67.
114 *bis* rue de Vaugirard, Paris 6e, France.

Dubuisson, Marcel Georges V. C.; Belgian university professor; b. 03; ed. Liège Univ.
Dir. Dept. of Zoology, Ecole des Hautes Etudes 25-31; Dir. Dept. of Anatomy, Ghent Univ. 28-31; Dir. Biology, Liège Univ., Prof. Faculty of Science 36-, Rector and Pres. 53-; Pres. Royal Acad. of Sciences 60-61.
Publs. 130 papers on Physiology, Biochemistry and Biophysics of muscular contraction.
University of Liège, Liège, Belgium; Place du 20 Août 7, Liège, Belgium.

du Cann, Rt. Hon. Edward Dillon Lott, P.C., M.A., M.P.; British politician; b. 28 May 1924; ed. Woodbridge School, Suffolk, and St. John's Coll., Oxford.
M.P. 56-; Managing Dir. Unicorn Group of Unit Trusts 57-62, 64-; Econ. Sec. to the Treasury 62-63; Minister of State, Board of Trade 63-64; Chair. of Conservative Party 65-Sept. 67; Dir. Capital & Counties Property Co. 68-, Keyser Ullmann 68-, Keyser Ullmann Industries 68-.
Publ. *Investing Simplified* 59.
19 Lord North Street, London, S.W.1. England.

Ducat, David, M.A., A.C.I.S.; British business executive; b. 1 June 1904; ed. Merchant Taylors' School, Gonville and Caius Coll. Cambridge.
Ministry of Production 42-45; British Tin Box Manufacturers Fed., Chair. 52-61, Vice-Chair. 61-; mem. Court of Assts., Merchant Taylors' Co., 56-, Master 64; mem. Council, British Inst. of Management 65, Chair. 66-; Man. Dir. Metal Box Co. Ltd. 49-66, Vice-Chair. 52-66, Deputy Chair. 66-67, Chair. 67-.
The Metal Box Co. Ltd., 37 Baker Street, London, W.1; Morar, 32 Ducks Hill Road, Northwood, Middlesex, England.

Ducaux, Annie; French actress; b. 10 Sept. 1908; ed. Lycée de Bordeaux and Conservatoire National d'Art Dramatique.
Pensionnaire, later Sociétaire, Comédie Française; has also acted in films; Chevalier, Légion d'Honneur.
67 *bis* quai Branly, Paris 7e, France.

Ducci, Roberto, LL.D.; Italian diplomatist; b. 8 Feb. 1914; ed. Rome Univ.
Entered Foreign Service 37; served Ottawa 38, Newark N.J. 40; Italian del. to Peace Conf. 46, Warsaw 47, Rio 49, Italian del. to N.A.T.O. and O.E.E.C. 50-55; mem. del. Brussels Six-Power Conf. 55-57; Chair. Drafting Cttee. Rome Treaties 56-57; Asst. Dir.-Gen. Economic Affairs, Ministry of Foreign Affairs 55-58; Ambassador to Finland 58-62; mem. of Board, European Investment Bank 58-; Head, Italian Del. to Brussels U.K.-EEC Conf. 61-63; Deputy Dir.-Gen. for Political Affairs 63-64; Amb. to Yugoslavia 64-67, to Austria 67-; Grand Officer Italian Order of Merit.
Publs. *Prima Età di Napoleone* 33, *Questa Italia* 48, and numerous political essays and articles.
Italian Embassy, 27 Rennweg, 1030 Vienna, Austria. Telephone: 125121.

Duchamp, Marcel; French-born American artist; b. 28 July 1887; ed. Acad. Julian, Paris.
Younger brother of Jacques Villon and Raymond Duchamp-Villon; paintings include *Nude Descending Staircase* shown in New York Armory Show 13; mem. Paris Dadaist and Surrealist movements; settled in New York 44; retrospective exhbn. at Tate Gallery, London 66.
28 West 10th Street, New York City, N.Y., U.S.A.

Duchesne, Lucien R.; French international officer; b. 08.
Member Staff, Int. Chamber of Commerce 32-, now Asst. Sec.-Gen. and Admin. Dir.; Sec. Int. Congresses 33-; Sec. of Council, Exec. Cttee. and Budget Comm.; Sec. Int. Bureau of Information Chambers of Commerce 50-56; mem. Soc. for Accountancy and French Inst. of Expert-Accountants 36-; mem. Ecole Nouvelle d'Organisation Economique et Sociale 45-; Mayor of La Celle-Saint-Cloud 59-.
15 Allée Corot, La Celle-Saint-Cloud (S.-et-O.), France.

Duchet, Roger; French landowner, wine producer and politician; b. 4 July 1904.
Mayor of Beaune 34-65; Councillor of the Republic for Côte d'Or 46-; Founder and Sec.-Gen. Centre Nat. des Republicains Indépendants et Paysans 46-61; Political Dir. *France Indépendante*; Pres. Asscn. Nouvellistes Parisiens; Under-Sec. for Public Works, Transport and Tourism in Pleven Govt. 51; Minister of Posts in Pleven, Faure, Pinay and Mayer Govts. 51-53; Minister of Reconstruction and Housing 55-56; mem. Senate 48-; Founder and Pres. Union pour le progrès 65.
Publ. *Pour le Salut Public.*
Palais du Luxembourg, Paris 6e; and la Maison Rose, Gambais (Yvelines), France.

Duckmanton, Talbot Sydney; Australian broadcasting executive; b. 26 Oct. 1921; ed. Newington Coll., Stanmore, New South Wales, Sydney Univ., and Australian Administrative Staff Coll.
Australian Army and Air Force Service; Australian Broadcasting Comm. 39-, Man. for Tasmania 53-57, Controller of Admin. 57-59, Asst. Gen. Man. (Admin.) 59-64, Deputy Gen. Man. 64-65, Gen. Man. 65-.
Australian Broadcasting Commission. Broadcast House, 145 Elizabeth Street, Sydney, New South Wales, Australia.
Telephone: 310211.

Duckwitz, Georg Ferdinand; German diplomatist; b. 29 Sept. 1904; ed. Univs. of Freiburg and Bonn.
Served German Legation, Copenhagen 39-45; represented German Chambers of Commerce in Copenhagen 46-50; Commercial Counsellor, Copenhagen 50-53; Counsellor, German Commercial Office, Helsinki 53-55; Amb. to Denmark 55-58; Asst. Under-Sec. of State German Fed. Foreign Office 58-61; Amb. to India 61-65; Head of German del. German-American-British trilateral talks Jan.-Apr. 67; State Sec. Foreign Office 67-; Commdr. Order of Dannebrog.
c/o Ministerium für Auswärtige Angelegenheiten, Bonn, German Federal Republic.

Duclos, Jacques; French politician; b. 2 Oct. 1896.
Served in French Army in First World War; wounded at Verdun; taken prisoner at Chemin-des-Dames; on

return to France joined Asscn. Républicaine des Anciens Combattants (A.R.A.C.); mem. of its Central Cttee. 25, Vice-Pres. 32; mem. of Communist Party since its foundation; mem. of Central Cttee. 26, Pol. Bureau and Party Sec. 31-; Dep. for Paris 26-32, for Seine 36-40; Vice-Pres. Chamber of Deputies and Finance Comm. 36; helped organise resistance movement during German occupation; one of the principal organisers of the Paris rising Aug. 44; Dep. to and fmr. Vice-Pres. of the Constituent and Nat. Assemblies; fmr. Vice-Pres. Finance Comm.; fmr. rapporteur of Foreign Affairs budget; Senator 59-; fmr. Pres. Communist Party Group; contrib. to *Cahiers du Communisme*, *L'Humanité*; Dir. *Démocratie Nouvelle*, *La Voix de l'Est*.
Publs. *A l'assaut du ciel* 61, *L'avenir de la démocratie* 62, *Gaullisme, Technocratie, Corporatisme* 63, *De Napoléon III à de Gaulle, La Première Internationale* 64, *Octobre 17 vu de France* 67.
22 avenue du Président Wilson, Montreuil-sous-Bois (Seine), France.

Ducreux, Louis Raymond; French theatrical and operatic manager; b. 22 Sept. 1911.
Artistic Man. Theatrical Company *Le Rideau Gris* 31-35, Co.-Dir. with André Roussin 35-40; Stage Dir. *Compagnie Claude Dauphin*, Cannes 40-42; Actor-Man. *La Comédie de Lyon* 42-43; playwright, actor, composer and stage dir. in Paris 44-61; Man. Opéra de Marseille 61-65; Man. Opéra de Monte Carlo 65-; Officier Légion d'Honneur, Officier des Arts et Lettres.
Publs. Plays: *La Part du Feu, Un Souvenir d'Italie*, French versions of *The Heiress* and *Bell, Book and Candle*; Musical Plays: *L'Amour en papier, Le Square du Pérou*.
Opéra de Monte Carlo, Monte Carlo; and 2 rue Ballu, Paris 9e, France.
Telephone: Trinité 83-73.

Duda, Karel, LL.D.; Czechoslovak diplomatist; b. 26; ed. Charles Univ., Prague.
Ministry of Finance 49-54, of Foreign Affairs 54-; First Sec., Washington 56-59; Ambassador to the United States 63-.
Embassy of the Czechoslovak Socialist Republic, 2349 Massachusetts Avenue, N.W., Washington, D.C., U.S.A.
Telephone: NO7-3301.

Dudin, Yury Ivanovich; Soviet politician; b. 1 Sept. 1906; ed. Kiev Agricultural Economics Inst.
Turner at machine-tool factory 19-25; mem. C.P.S.U. 25-; Young Communist League, C.P. and Govt. posts 25-45; Minister of Food Industry, Ukraine, later First Deputy Minister of U.S.S.R. Meat and Dairy Industry 46-53; Perm. Rep. of Ukrainian Council of Ministers to U.S.S.R. Council of Ministers 53-; Deputy to U.S.S.R. Supreme Soviet; Cttee. mem. of the Soviet Parl. Group; mem. Mandate Cttee. Soviet of the Union.
Permanent Representation of Ukrainian Council of Ministers to U.S.S.R. Council of Ministers, 18 Stanislavsky Street, Moscow, U.S.S.R.
Telephone: B-1-28-04.

Dudinskaya, Natalya Mikhailovna; Soviet ballerina; b. 1912; ed. Leningrad School of Choreography.
Prima Ballerina Kirov Academic Opera and Ballet Theatre, Leningrad; theatre coach in the Kirov Theatre 51-; principal parts include all ballets by Tchaikovsky, *Raimonda* by Glazunov, *Giselle, Les Sylphides, Don Quixote* and *The Bayadere* by Mincous; has created leading roles in *Laurencia* by Krein, *Gayane* by Khachaturyan, *Cinderella* by Prokofiev, *The Bronze Horseman* by Gliere, *Shuralé* by Yarullin, the Polish Maiden in *Taras Bulba* by Soloviev-Sedoy 56, Sarie in *The Path of Thunder* by Kara Karayev 58, Baroness Strahl in *The Masquerade* by Laputin 60, Titania in *A Midsummer Night's Dream* 63, The Wicked Fairy in the film *The Sleeping Beauty* 64, *The Spanish*

Suite by Viana López Gerardo 66, *Miniature* by Krein 67; guest artist in many foreign countries; People's Artist of U.S.S.R.; State Prizewinner 41, 47, 49, 51.
Kirov Opera and Ballet Theatre, Leningrad, U.S.S.R.

Dudintsev, Vladimir Dmitrievich; Soviet writer; b. 29 June 1918; ed. Moscow Legal Inst.
Soviet Army 41-45; Feature Writer of *Komsomolskaya Pravda* 46-51; mem. Union of Soviet Writers.
Publs. *With Seven Brothers* (collected stories) 52, *In His Place* 54, *Not By Bread Alone* 56, *Tales and Stories* 59, *A New Year's Tale* 60, *Stories* 63.
U.S.S.R. Union of Writers, 52 Vorovsky Street, Moscow, U.S.S.R.

Duesenberry, James Stembel, B.A., M.A., PH.D.; American economist; b. 18 July 1918; ed. Univ. of Michigan.
Teaching Fellow in Econs., Univ. of Michigan 39-41; in U.S. Air Force 42-45; Instructor, Mass. Inst. of Technology 46; Teaching Fellow in Econs., Harvard Univ. 46-48, Asst. Prof. of Econs. 48-53, Assoc. Prof. 53-57, Prof. 57-; Fulbright Research Prof. Cambridge Univ. 54-55; Ford Foundation Research Prof. 58-59; Consultant, Cttee. of Econ. Devt. 56; mem. President's Council of Econ. Advisers 66-.
Publs. *Income, Saving and the Theory of Consumer Behavior* 49, *Business Cycles and Economic Growth* (with Lee Preston) 58, *Cases and Problems in Economics* 59, *Money and Credit: Impact and Control* 64.
4521 Cumberland Avenue, Chevy Chase, Maryland 20015; and 25 Fairmont Street, Belmont, Mass., U.S.A.

Dufek, Rear-Admiral George J.; American naval officer and polar explorer; b. 10 Feb. 1903; ed. U.S. Naval Acad.
Served with U.S. Navy 25-59; commanded destroyers and naval air stations in Japan, Kwajalein and the State of Washington during Second World War; commanded aircraft carrier *Antietam* during Korean War; accompanied two arctic and six antarctic expeditions; Chief Staff Officer, Arctic Task Force 46; Commdr. of a group of ships in Antarctic Operation *Highjump* 46-47; headed Task Force 80 in the Arctic 47-48; Commdr. U.S. Naval Support Force, Antarctica 54-59 (retd.); Commdr. Task Force 43 for Operation *Deep Freeze*, U.S.N. Antarctic Expedition 55-59; U.S. Antarctic Projects Officer; Director Mariners Museum, Newport News, Va. 60-; Distinguished Service Medal 57, and Gold Star 59, Legion of Merit (with two gold stars), Antarctic Expedition Medal, Croix de Guerre, Chevalier of the Legion of Honour, André Medal of the Swedish Geographical Society, Hubbard Medal 59; Hon. Comp. Most Hon. Order of the Bath 59, Commr. de L'Ordre de la Couronne, Belgium 59; several honorary degrees.
Publs. *Operation Deep Freeze, Through The Frozen Frontiers*.
Mariners Museum, Newport News, Va., U.S.A.

Duff, Charles St. Lawrence; Irish writer; b. 7 April 1894; ed. Portora Royal School, Ireland, and Gray's Inn, London.
Barrister-at-law; merchant service 10-14; war service 14-18; mem. staff Foreign Office 19-36; Lecturer Inst. of Education London Univ. 37-38; Prof. of Occidental Languages, Nanyang Univ., Singapore 54-55.
Publs. *A Handbook on Hanging* 28, *This Human Nature* 30, *Truth About Columbus* 36, *No Angel's Wing, How to Learn a Language* 47, *Ordinary Cats* 51, *Ireland and the Irish* 52, *French for Adults* 52, *England and The English* 54, *English for Adults* 56, *Spanish for Adults* 56, *German for Adults* 57, *Italian for Adults* 58, *First, Second Stage Russian* 60-61, *Russian for Adults* 62, *Russian Reader* 62, *A Mysterious People* 65; Gen. Editor of series *Basis and Essentials* 33-65, *Six days to Shake an Empire* 66; text-books in French, German, Spanish, Russian, Italian, Portuguese, Welsh.
Levally, Monea, Enniskillen, Northern Ireland.

Duff, Sir James Fitzjames, M.A., M.ED.; British educationist; b. 1 Feb. 1898; ed. Winchester and Trinity Coll., Cambridge.
Served Royal Flying Corps 16-17; Asst. Lecturer in Classics Manchester Univ. 21; Lecturer in Education Armstrong Coll. Newcastle-upon-Tyne 22; Educational Supt. Northumberland County Council 25; Senior Lecturer in Education, Manchester Univ. 27; Sarah Fielden Prof. of Education and Dir. Dept. of Education 32-37; Vice-Chancellor Durham Univ. and Warden Durham Colls. 37-60; Gov. B.B.C. 59-, Vice-Chair. 60 65, Chair. 64-65; Hon. LL.D., Hon. D.C.L.; Lord Lieutenant, County Durham 64.
Publ. (with Dr. R. O. Berdahl) *University Government in Canada* 66.
Low Middleton Hall, Middleton-One-Row, Darlington, Durham, England.
Telephone: Dinsdale 245.

Dufhues, Josef Hermann; German politician and lawyer; b. 11 April 1908; ed. Gymnasium Herne and Univs. of Tübingen and Berlin.
Lawyer 35-; Artillery, Second World War; mem. Council of North Rhine-Westphalia 47-50, 50-, Minister of the Interior 58-62; Dir. Emscher-Lippe Bergbau A.G., Gebrüder Eickhess Maschinenfabrik und Eisengiesserei G.m.b.H.; mem. Cttee. Westdeutscher Rundfunk; fmr. Man. Chair. Christian Democratic Union Party.
Baumhofstrasse 42, Bochum, German Federal Republic.

Dufourcq, Norbert, D. ès L.; French musicologist and organist; b. 21 Sept. 1904; ed. Collège Stanislas and Lycée Henri IV, Paris, Sorbonne and Ecole Nationale des Chartes.
Teacher of History Coll. Stanislas Paris 35-45; Prof. of History of Music and Musicology at Paris Conservatoire 41-; Organist Eglise Saint-Merry 23-; Sec.-Gen. of Soc. of Friends of Organ 27-; mem. of Comm. for Historic Organs 32-; Editor-in-Chief review *L'Orgue* 29-; Prof. Sweet Briar Coll. (Paris) 49; Pres. Société Française de Musicologie 56-58; Prof. Ecole Normale de Musique de Paris 58-63; Dir. *Orgue et Liturgie, les Grands Heures de l'Orgue;* Lecturer Jeunesses Musicales de France 42-61.
Publs. *Documents Inédits Relatifs à l'Orgue Français, XIVe-XVIIIe siècles* 34-35, *Esquisse d'une histoire de l'Orgue en France du XIIIe au XVIIIe siècles* 35, *La musique d'orgue française de J. Titelouze à J. Alain, Orgues comtadines et provençales, Les Clicquot, César Franck, Le Clavecin, L'Orgue, Petite Histoire de la Musique en Europe, Bach, Génie allemand, Génie latin?, Bach, Le Maître de l'Orgue* 48, *La musique française, Autour de Coquard, Nicolas Lebègue* 54, *Notes et références . . . sur Michel R. Delalande* 57, *Jean de Joyeuse et la pénétration de la facture parisienne dans le Midi de la France au XVIIe siècle* 58, *Pièces de Clavecin de N. Lebègue* 57, *J. B. de Boesset* 62, *Le Grand Orgue du Prytan Militaire de la Flèche* 64, preface to organ compositions of G. Jullien, N. de Grigny, A. Raison, Clérembault, G. G. Nivers, F. Couperin, A. Dornel; *L'orgue parisien sous le règne de Louis XIV* 57; edited *La Musique, des origines à nos jours* 48, *Histoire de France,* Vol. I, *Larousse de la Musique* 57-58 (2 vols.), *La Vie Musicale en France sous les Rois Bourbons, Recherches sur la Musique Classique Française,* 8 vols. 60-68, musical section of *Que Sais-Je?, La Musique, les Hommes, les Instruments, les Oeuvres* 65 (2 vols.); Gen. Editor *Le lys d'or, Les Neuf Muses.*
37 avenue Lowendal, Paris 15e, France.
Telephone: SUF-43-30.

Dufournier, Bernard Alfred Eusèbe; French diplomatist; b. 23 March 1911; ed. Lycée Janson de Sailly, Sorbonne, Ecole des Sciences Politiques, Paris.
Counsellor in Brussels 54-56; Amb. to Pakistan 57-60, 57-60, to Chile 60-63, to Libya 63-66, to Finland 66-.
Embassy of France, Helsinki, Finland; 4 rue Marietta Martin, Paris 16e, France.

Dugardin, Hervé; French opera director; b. 10; ed. Schola Cantorum, Paris.
Director, French Branch, Ricordi (music publishers); Artistic Dir. Théâtre des Champs-Elysées 48-52; Dir. Théâtre National de l'Opéra Comique 62-65.
Théâtre National de l'Opéra Comique, Place Boïeldieu, Paris 2e, France.

Duke, Angier Biddle; American diplomatist; b. 30 Nov. 1915; ed St. Paul's School, Concord, N.H., and Yale Univ.
U.S. Army Air Force, Second World War; entered American Foreign Service 49, Sec. and Consul, Buenos Aires 49-51; Special Asst. to Stanton Griffis, Ambassador in Madrid 51-52; Ambassador to El Salvador 52-53; Pres. Int. Rescue Cttee. 54-61; Vice-Pres. CARE 55-58; Chair. Exec. Cttee. American Friends of Viet-Nam 57-60; Chief of Protocol, Dept. of State, Washington, D.C. 61-65, and Chief of Protocol for White House with rank of Amb. 61-65, 68-; Amb. to Spain 65-68; Pres. American Immigration and Citizenship Conf. 59-64; Trustee Inst. for American Univs., Aix-en-Provence, France, Iona Coll.; Commdr. Nat. Order of Viet-Nam, Grand Cross of Merit of Order of Malta (Austria), Order of Honour and Merit (Haiti); Hon. LL.D. (Iona Coll.).
c/o The White House, Washington D.C., U.S.A.

Duke-Elder, Sir William Stewart, G.C.V.O., M.A., D.SC., M.D., CH.B., PH.D., LL.D., F.R.C.S. (Eng.), F.A.C.S., F.R.A.C.S., F.R.C.P., F.R.S., K.G.ST.J.; Scottish ophthalmic surgeon; b. 98; ed. St. Andrews, Edinburgh and London Univs.
Practised Ophthalmic Surgery London 27-; Ophthalmic Surgeon Moorfields Eye Hospital 28, St. George's Hospital 29; Howe Lecturer Harvard 30; Brig. R.A.M.C. 40-46; Surgeon-Oculist to Their Majesties King Edward VIII, George V and Queen Elizabeth until 65, Extra Surgeon-Oculist to Queen Elizabeth 65-; Hon. Consulting Surgeon to the R.A.F.; Pres. Inst. of Ophthalmology, Univ. of London; Fellow Univ. Coll.; Con. Surgeon Moorfields Eye Hospital and St. George's Hospital; Pres. Int. Council of Ophthalmology 50-62 and 16th Int. Congress, Life Pres. 62-; Examiner in Ophthalmology, Royal Coll. of Surgeons 47-; Editor *British Journal of Ophthalmology* and *Ophthalmic Literature;* numerous awards, including British Asscn. Medal 15, B.M.A. Middlemore Prize 28, Mackenzie Medal (Glasgow) 32, Nettleship Medal 33, Howe Medal (U.S.A.) 46, Research Medal, American Medical Asscn. 47, Donders Medal (Netherlands) 47, Doyne Medal (Oxford) 48, Gullstrand Medal (Stockholm) 52, Craig Prize (Belfast) 52, Gonin Medal 54, Lister Medal 56, Bowman Medal 57; Fothergillian Gold Medal 62; Star of Jordan (1st Class); Bronze Star (U.S.A.); Proctor Medal (U.S.A.) 60; Lang Medal 65, Commdr. Royal Order of the Phoenix (Greece) 65; numerous hon. degrees.
Publs. *Textbook of Ophthalmology,* Vols. I-VII 32-54, *Recent Advances in Ophthalmology,* 4th edn. 51, *Diseases of the Eye,* 14th edn. 64, *System of Ophthalmology* (10 vols.) 58-68, *The Practice of Refraction,* 7th edn. 63.
63 Harley Street, London, W.1; 28 Elm Tree Road, London, N.W.8, England.
Telephone: 01-580-1264.

Dulbecco, Renato; American (b. Italian) virologist; b. 22 Feb. 1914; ed. Università degli Studi, Turin.
Assistant Prof. of Pathology, Univ. of Turin 40-46, of Experimental Embryology 47; Research Assoc. Dept. of Bacteriology, Indiana Univ. 47-49; Senior Research Fellow California Inst. of Technology 49-52, Assoc. Prof. 52-53, Prof. 54-63; Senior Fellow, Salk Inst. for Biological Studies 63-; mem. Genetics Society of America, American Asscn. for Cancer Research, American Asscn. for the Advancement of Science; mem. Nat. Acad. of Sciences, American Acad. of Arts and

Sciences: several awards, including Ehrlich Prize. The Salk Institute, P.O.B. 1809, San Diego, Calif. 92112, U.S.A.
Telephone: 714-453-4100.

Dullea, James Atwood; Canadian business executive; b. 17 March 1898; ed. St. Lawrence Univ.
Aluminum Co. of America 19-28, Aluminum Ltd. 28-, Senior Vice-Pres., Sec. and Dir. 43-64, Dir. 64-; Dir. Aluminum Co. of Canada, Sagueney Power Co. Ltd.
Aluminum Ltd., 1155 Metcalfe Street, Montreal 2, Quebec, Canada.

Dulles, Allen Welsh, M.A., LL.B., LL.D.; American lawyer, author and government official; b. 7 April 1893; ed. Princeton and George Washington Univs.
Entered diplomatic service 16, served Vienna, Berne, Paris, Berlin, Constantinople 16-22; Chief, Division Near East Affairs, Dept. of State, Washington 22-26; resigned to practise law with Sullivan and Cromwell, New York City 26-; Deputy Dir. Central Intelligence Agency 51-53, Dir. 53-62; mem. of American dels. Arms Traffic, Disarmament and Naval Confs., Geneva 25-33; mem. President's Comm. to investigate assassination of Pres. Kennedy 63-64; Medal for Merit, for Freedom; Officer Legion of Honour, Order of Leopold (Belgium), Ordine di S.S. Maurizio e Lazzaro (Italy); Hon. LL.D. Publs. *Can We Be Neutral?* (with H. F. Armstrong) 35, *Can America Stay Neutral?* (with H. F. Armstrong) 39, *Germany's Underground* 47, *The Craft of Intelligence* 63, *The Secret Surrender* 66, *Great True Spy Stories* 68.
2723 Q Street, N.W., Washington, D.C. 22207, U.S.A.

Dumarçay, Jacques; French diplomatist; b. 29 April 1901.
Entered diplomatic service 25; with High Commissariat Syria 25-29; in charge of Chancelleries Jedda and Baghdad 29-33; at disposal of Residency General Morocco 33-43; dismissed by Vichy for supporting Free French; Algiers Govt. placed him on staff of Gen. Del. to Levant; Consul 44; Counsellor at Damascus 46-48; Minister to Jordan 48-52, Ambassador 52; Minister to Libya 52-57, Ambassador 57-58; Ambassador to Sudan 59-63, to Iraq 63-; Commdr. Légion d'Honneur; Commdr. de l'Etoile Noire du Bénin.
French Embassy, Baghdad, Iraq.

Dumas, Sir F. Lloyd, K.T., Australian journalist; b. 15 July 1891; ed Adelaide Teache7s, Traing Coll.
Joined staff Adelaide *Advertiser* 07, mem. Parl. Gallery staff 08; mem. staff Melbourne *Argus* 15, Chief of Staff 21-24; Editor Melbourne *Sun News Pictorial* 24-27; Manager and Editor Australian Newspapers Cable Service 27-29; Managing Editor *The Advertiser* and Dir. Advertiser Newspapers Ltd. 29-38, Managing Dir. 38-60, Chair. 42-67; Dir. Australian Newsprint Mills Ltd. 38-66, Australian Associated Press 41-61, Chair. 49-61; fmr. Fed. Vice-Pres. Australian Journalists' Asscn.; Fellow Inst. of Journalists and Royal Geographical Soc.; Pres. Australian Newspapers Conf. 38-39; Dir. Elder Smith & Co. Ltd. 41-67, Elder Smith Goldsbrough-Mort Ltd. 62-67; mem. Nat. Gallery Board 54-63, Chair. 56-63; Dir. Herald and Weekly Times Ltd., Melbourne 46-67; Dir. Reuters (Eng.) 50-53; Chair. Television Broadcasters Ltd. 58-67.
53 Dutton Terrace, Medindie, South Australia.

Dumas, Pierre, L. ES D.; French politician; b. 15 Nov. 1924; ed. Ecole Libre des Sciences Politiques.
Sales Man. Box Co., La Rochette; Mayor of Chambéry 59-; Dep. 58-; Sec. of State for Public Works April-Oct. 62, Sec. of State for Relations with Parl., responsible for Tourism 62-; Sec. of State to Prime Minister, in charge of Tourism 67-; Union pour la Nouvelle République.
80 rue de Lille, Paris 7e; Home: 17 rue de Boigne, 73 Chambéry, France.

du Maurier, Daphne (Lady Browning); British writer; b. 1907; ed. privately, Paris.
Publs. *The Loving Spirit* 31, *I'll Never be Young Again* 32, *The Progress of Julius* 33, *Gerald, a Portrait* 34, *Jamaica Inn* 36, *The du Mauriers* 37, *Rebecca* 38, *Frenchman's Creek* 41, *Hungry Hill* 43, *The Years Between* (play) 45, *The King's General* 46, *September Tide* (play) 48, *The Parasites* 49, *My Cousin Rachel* 51, *The Apple Tree* 52, *Mary Anne* 54, *The Scapegoat* 57, *The Breaking Point* 59, *The Infernal World of Branwell Brontë* 60, *Castle Dor* 62 (continuation of MS. left by late Sir A. Quiller-Couch), *The Glass-Blowers* 63, *Flight of the Falcon* 64, *Vanishing Cornwall* 67.
Menabilly, Par, Cornwall, England.

Duminy, Jacobus Petrus; South African university professor and administrator; b. 16 Dec. 1897; ed. Cape Town Univ., Oxford Univ., and Univ. of Paris.
Lecturer, Mathematics and Astronomy, Transvaal Univ. Coll. 23-30; Prof. of Mathematics, Univ. of Pretoria 30-42; Principal, Pretoria Technical Coll 42-58; Principal and Vice-Chancellor, Univ. of Cape Town 58-67.
c/o University of Cape Town, Rondebosch, Cape Town, South Africa.
Telephone: 69-4351.

Dumitriu, Petru; Romanian novelist and essayist; b. 8 May 24; ed. Ludwig-Maximilians-Universität, Munich.
Chief Editor *Viata Romaneasca* (literary monthly), Bucharest 53-55; Man. State Publishing House for Literature and Art, Bucharest 55-58; Chair. Council of Publishing Houses, Ministry of Culture, Bucharest 58-60; in W. Europe 60-; Editor, S. Fischer Verlag, Frankfurt am Main, German Federal Republic 63-; Romanian State Prize for Literature 50, 52, 54; Star of the Republic; Order of Labour, etc. (Romania).
Publs. Novels: *The Boyars* (3 vols., Romanian) 56, *Meeting at the Last Judgement* 61, *Incognito* 62, *L' Extrême Occident* 64, *Die Transmoderne* (essay, German) 65, *Les Initiés* 65, *Le Sourire Sarde* (French) 67.
Seilerstrasse 12, Frankfurt am Main, German Federal Republic.

Dummett, R. B.; British oil executive; b. 1912; ed. Rugby School and Univs. of Cambridge and Göttingen.
With British Petroleum Co. (B.P.) (then Anglo-Iranian Oil Co.) 36-, Area Man. (Switzerland, Italy and Malta), Distribution Dept. 48-53; Man. Dir. Commonwealth Oil Refineries Ltd. (now B.P. Australia Ltd.) 53; Man. Dir. B.P. 57-67, Deputy Chair. 67-.
British Petroleum Co., Moor Lane, London, E.C.2, England.

Dumont, Donald, B.S., M.A.; American diplomatist; b. 6 Dec. 1911; ed. Oberlin Coll., Trinity Coll., and Yale Univ. School of International Relations.
History and Science Master, Brent School, Philippines 35-37; Instructor in English, Trinity Coll. 37-39; Clerk and Vice-Consul, American Foreign Service 40, Dakar 41-42, Rabat 43-46, Tunis 46-50; Consul, Istanbul 50-51, Stuttgart 51-54; Officer in Charge Sub-Saharan Affairs, Dept. of State 54-57; Consul-Gen., Dakar 58-60, Chargé d'Affaires, Fed. of Mali 60; UN Adviser, Bureau of African Affairs, Dept. of State 61, Dep. Dir. of African and Malagasy Union Affairs 61-62; U.S. Minister to Burundi 62-63, Amb. 63-66; Visiting Prof. and Diplomat-in-Residence, Univ. of Tenn. 66-67; Foreign Affairs Research Council, Dept. of State 67-.
Publ. *Brief History of Philippines* 40.
c/o Department of State, Washington, D.C. 20520; Home: 1661 Crescent Place, N.W., Washington, D.C. 20009, U.S.A.
Telephone: 383-2875 (Office); 232-3270 (Home).

Dunbar, Carl Owen, B.A., PH.D.; American palaeontologist and stratigrapher; b. 1 Jan. 1891; ed. Univ. of Kansas and Yale Univ.

Instructor in Geology, Univ. of Minnesota 18-20; Asst. Prof. Historical Geology, Yale Univ. 20-27; Assoc. Prof. 27-30; Prof. Palaeontology and Stratigraphy 30-59; Asst. Curator, Invertebrate Palaeontology, Peabody Museum of Natural History, Yale Univ. 20-26; Curator 26-; Dir. 42-59; mem. Nat. Acad. of Sciences, American Philosophical Society, American Acad. of Arts and Sciences, Geological Society of America, Geological Societies London and Mexico; Hayden Medal of the Philadelphia Acad. of Sciences 59, Citation for Distinguished Service Univ. Kansas 61.

Publs. *Brachiopoda of the Pennsylvanian System in Nebraska* (with G. E. Condra) 32, *Historical Geology* 49, *Permian Fusulinidae of Texas* (with J. W. Skinner) 37, *Pennsylvanian Fusulinidae of Illinois* (with L. G. Henbest) 43, *Permian Brachiopod Faunas of Central East Greenland* 55, *Principles of Stratigraphy* (with John Rodgers) 57, *Historical Geology* 60, *The Earth* 66.

1615 Santa Barbara Drive, Dunedin, Florida 33528, U.S.A.

Telephone: 813-733-7027.

Duncan, Ronald, M.A.; British poet and playwright; b. 6 Aug. 1914; ed. Switzerland and Cambridge Univ. Founded English Stage Company 56.

Publs. *The Dull Ass's Hoof* 41, *Postcards to Pulcenella* 42, *Journal of a Husbandman* 44, *This Way to the Tomb* (play) 46, *The Rape of Lucretia* (libretto) 46, *Home Made Home* 47, *Ben Jonson* 47, *Songs and Satires of the Earl of Rochester* 48, *Stratton* (play) 48, *Jan's Journal* 48, *Tobacco Cultivation in England* 48, *The Typewriter* (play) 48, *Beauty and the Beast* 48, *Pope's Letters* 48 *The Cardinal* 49, *The Mongrel and Other Poems* 50, *Tobacco Growing in England* 50, *Our Lady's Tumbler* 51, *Selected Writings of Mahatma Gandhi* 51, *The Blue Fox* 51, *Jan at the Blue Fox* 52, *The Last Adam* 52, *Where I Live* 53, *Don Juan* (play) 54, *The Death of Satan* (play) 55, *The Catalyst* (play) 57, *Christopher Sly* (opera) 59, *The Solitudes* (poems) 60, *Blind Man's Buff* (play) *Saint Spiv* (novel) 60, *Judas* (poem) 60, *Abelard and Helöise* (play) 60, *The Rabbit Race* 63, *O-B-A-F-G* (play) 65, *The Rebel* (opera) 65, *The Trojan Women* (play) 66, *How to Make Enemies* (Autobiography Vol. II) 67.

Mead Farm, Welcombe, Nr. Bideford, N. Devonshire, England.

Duncan, Sir Val (John Norman Valette), Kt., O.B.E.; British business executive; b. 18 July 1913; ed. Harrow and Brasenose Coll., Oxford.

Called to Bar 38; Royal Engineers 39-45; Asst. Sec. Control Office, Germany and Austria 46-47; Asst. Dir. (Marketing) National Coal Board 47-48; Commercial Manager, The Rio Tinto Co. Ltd. 48-50, Managing Dir. 51-62, Man. Dir. and Chief Exec., The Rio Tinto-Zinc Corpn. 62-64, Chair. and Chief Exec. April 64-; American Legion of Merit (twice), Commdr., Order of Orange-Nassau (Netherlands).

The Rio Tinto-Zinc Corpn. Ltd., 6 St. James's Square, London, S.W.1; Edenbridge House, Edenbridge, Kent, England.

Duncanson, Thomas Sherriff; Canadian (b. Scotland) business executive; b. 15 Nov. 1896; ed. Toronto Technical School.

With Moore Corpn. Ltd., Toronto 13-, Sec. 29-48, Dir. 48-, Exec. Vice-Pres. 53-55, Pres. 55-62, Chair. Board 62-, also Chair. of subsidiary companies; Gen. Man. F. N. Burt Co. Inc., Buffalo 35, Vice-Pres., Gen. Man. 46-55, Pres. 52-62, Chair. of Board 62-; official of other companies.

Moore Corporation Ltd., 330 University Avenue, Toronto, Ontario, Canada.

Dunckel, Wallis Bleecker, B.A.; American banker; b. 9 May 1901; ed. Trinity School, New York City, and Yale Univ.

Joined Bankers Trust Co. 23, Head, Pension Div. 38-57,

mem. Senior Management 57-60, Pres. and Dir. 60-66; Pres. and Dir. BT New York Corpn. (now Bankers Trust New York Corpn.) 66-; Dir. American Bank Note Co., Crown Zellerbach Corpn., Lincoln Nat. Life Insurance Co.; Trustee and Treas. Tax Foundation, Inc. Easton, Conn.; Office: 280 Park Avenue, New York, N.Y. 10017, U.S.A.

Dundee, 11th Earl, cr. 1660 (Scot), Henry James Scrymgeour-Wedderburn, P.C., J.P., D.L., LL.D.; British politician; b. 3 May 1902; ed. Winchester and Balliol Coll., Oxford.

President, Oxford Union 24; M.P. 31-45; Parl. Under-Sec. of State for Scotland 36-39; Additional Parl. Under-Sec. of State, Scottish Office 41-42; Minister without Portfolio 58-61; Minister of State for Foreign Affairs 61-64; Deputy Leader House of Lords 62-64; Hereditary Royal Standard bearer for Scotland; Hon. LL.D. St. Andrews Univ.; Conservative.

Birkhill, Cupar, Fife, Scotland.

Dungan, Ralph Anthony, M.S.; American government official and diplomatist; b. 22 April 1923; ed. Princeton Univ.

Lieutenant U.S. Navy (Air) 42-45; Bureau of the Budget 51-56; Legislative Asst. Senator John F. Kennedy 56-57; Staff, U.S. Senate Cttee. on Labor and Public Welfare 57-60; Special Asst. to the President 61-64; Amb. to Chile 64-67.

c/o Department of State, Washington D.C., U.S.A.

Dunham, Katherine; American dancer and choreographer; ed. Chicago and Northwestern Univs.

Debut, Chicago World's Fair 34; with Chicago Opera Co. 35-36; Julius Rosenwald Travel Fellowship 36-37; Dance Dir. Labor Stage 39-40; has appeared in numerous films 41-; founded Katherine Dunham School of Cultural Arts and Katherine Dunham Dance Co. 45; numerous tours and personal appearances in North and South America and Europe.

Publs. *Journey to Accompong, Form and Function in Primitive Dance, Form and Function in Educational Dance,* etc.

c/o Lee Mosell, 608 Fifth Avenue, New York City, N.Y., U.S.A.

Dunham, Kingsley C., F.R.S., PH.D., D.SC., M.S., S.D.; British geologist; b. 2 Jan. 1910; ed. Johnston School, Durham, Univ. of Durham and Harvard Univ.

Temporary Geologist, New Mexico Bureau Mines 35; Geologist, Geological Survey of Great Britain 35-45; Head of Petrographical Dept. 46-50; Prof. of Geology and Head of Dept. Univ. of Durham 50-66, Sub-Warden 59-61; Consulting Geologist, Laporte Industries Ltd. 53-66, Consolidated Gold Fields Ltd. 54-66; Geological Adviser Imperial Chemical Industries Ltd. 61-66; Dir. Inst. of Geological Sciences (Natural Environment Research Council) 66-; Pres. Yorks. Geological Soc. 58-60, Section C of British Asscn. for the Advancement of Science 61, Inst. of Mining and Metallurgy 63-64, Geological Soc. of London 66-68; mem. Council, Royal Soc. 64-66, Council for Scientific Policy, Dept. of Educ. and Science 64-66; Bigsby Medal of Geological Soc. 54; Murchison Medal 66; D.Sc. h.c. (Durham and Liverpool).

Publs. *Geology of the Organ Mountains of New Mexico* 36, *Geology of the Northern Pennine Orefield* 49, *Fluorspar* 52, *Geology of North Skye* (with F. W. Anderson) 66; Editor *Symposium on the Paragenesis and Reserves of the Ores of Lead and Zinc* 48.

Institute of Geological Sciences, Exhibition Road, London, S.W.7; Home: 29 Bolton Gardens, London, S.W.5, England.

Telephone: 01-589-9441 (Office); 01-370-2279 (Home).

Dunlop, John Wallace; British business executive; b. 10; ed. Geelong Grammar School (Australia).

Chair. The Colonial Sugar Refining Co. Ltd., Edwards

Dunlop and Co. Ltd., The United Insurance Co. Ltd.; Dir. Bank of New South Wales, Perpetual Trustee Co. Ltd., Darling and Co. Ltd.
1 O'Connell Street, Sydney, N.S.W., Australia.

Dunlop, Robert Galbraith, B.S. (ECON.); American petroleum executive; b. 2 July 1909; ed. Wharton School of Finance and Commerce, Univ. of Pennsylvania.
Accountant Barrow, Wade, Guthrie & Co. 31-33; Certified Public Accountant State of Pa. 34; Accountant Sun Oil Co. 33-41, Asst. Comptroller 41-44, Comptroller 44-47, Pres. 47-.
1608 Walnut Street, Philadelphia 3, Pa., U.S.A.

Dunlop, Ronald O., R.A.; British artist; b. 94; ed. Friends' School, Saffron Walden; studied Manchester and Wimbledon Schools of Art.
One of founders Emotionist Group of Painters and Writers; mem. London Group; 1st one-man show Redfern Galleries 28, exhbn. Reid and Lefevre Galleries 40; several exhibitions Leger Galleries, London, Edinburgh, Liverpool, etc.; works purchased by Contemporary Art Soc., Leeds, Bradford, Hull, New South Wales, Australia, Preston, Southport, Glasgow and Newcastle Art Galleries; pictures purchased by Chantrey Bequest for Tate Gallery.
Publs. *Painting for Pleasure, Sketching for Pleasure, Landscape Painting, Understanding Pictures, Struggling with Paint.*
Old Mill Cottage, Barnham, Sussex, England.
Telephone: Eastergate 2084.

Dunn, Halbert Louis, M.D., M.A., PH.D.; American statistician; b. 17 May 1896; ed. Univ. of Minnesota.
Instructor of Anatomy, Univ. of Minnesota 22-23; Asst. in Medicine, Presbyterian Hospital, N.Y. 23-24; Fellow in Medicine, Mayo Clinic, Rochester, Minn. 24-25; Assoc. Prof., Johns Hopkins Univ. 25-29; Head, Dept. of Statistics, Mayo Clinic 29-32; Dir., Univ. Hospital and Prof. of Medical Statistics, Univ. of Minn. 32-35; Chief Statistician and Chief of Vital Statistics Div., Bureau of the Census, Dept. of Commerce, Washington 35-46; Chief of Nat. Office of Vital Statistics, Dept. of Health, Education and Welfare 46-60, Special Asst. on Ageing, U.S. Public Health Service 60-61; Sec.-Treas. Public Health Conf. on Records and Statistics 49-58, Chair. 58-60; Charter mem. Inter-American Statistical Inst. 40-, Sec.-Gen. 42-52, Consultant to its Exec. Cttee. 52-54, Hon. Pres. 55-; Consultant and Lect. High-Level Wellness and Consultant on Ageing, U.S. Office of Educ. 62-66; Fellow, American Public Health Asscn., American Statistical Asscn., American Asscn. for the Advancement of Science.
Publs. *Creative Destiny, Your World and Mine, High-Level Wellness,* and numerous articles.
9130 Riverside Drive, Washington, D.C. 20022, U.S.A.
Telephone: 248-7036.

Dunn, Leslie C., A.B., D.SC.; American geneticist; b. 2 Nov. 1893; ed. Dartmouth Coll., and Harvard Univ.
Asst. in Zoology Harvard Univ. 15-17, 19; geneticist Storrs Agricultural Experiment Station 20-28; Prof. of Zoology Columbia Univ. 28-62, Prof. Emeritus 62-; Dir. Inst. for the Study of Human Variation, Columbia Univ. 52-58; Visiting Lecturer on Biology Harvard Univ.; Managing Editor *Genetics* 36-41; Editor-in Chief Columbia *Biological Series* 36-62; Managing Editor *The American Naturalist* 50-59; Senior Research Scientist, Columbia Univ. 62-; mem. Nat. Acad. of Sciences, American Acad. of Arts and Sciences, American Philosophical Soc., Acad. Patavina, Italy, Norwegian Acad. of Sciences; Hon. D.Sc. (Dartmouth).
Publs. *Principles of Genetics* (with E. W. Sinnott and Th. Dobzhansky) 58, *Heredity and Variation* 32, *Heredity, Race and Society* (with Th. Dobzhansky) 52, *Biology and Race* 51, *Heredity and Evolution in Human*

Populations 67, *A Short History of Genetics* 65.
Nevis Biological Station, Irvington-on-Hudson, N.Y.; 635 West 247th Street, New York, N.Y. 10471, U.S.A.
Telephone: 212-546-8228.

Dunnett, Alastair MacTavish; British journalist; b. 26 Dec. 1908; ed. Overnewton School and Hillhead High School, Glasgow.
Entered Commercial Bank of Scotland Ltd. 25; co-founder, The Claymore Press 33-34; with *Glasgow Weekly Herald* 35-36, *The Bulletin* 36-37, *Daily Record* 37-40; Chief, Press Office, Sec. of State for Scotland 40-46; Editor *Daily Record* 46-55, *The Scotsman* 56-; Managing Dir. The Scotsman Publications Ltd. 62-; Dir. Thos. Nelson and Son 62-; Gov. Pitlochry Festival Theatre; mem. Press Council 59-62; Dir. Thomson Regional Newspapers Ltd., and Highland Printers Ltd.
Publs. *Treasure at Sonnach* 35, *Heard Tell* 46, *Quest by Canoe* 50, *Highlands and Islands of Scotland* 51; Plays: *The Original John Mackay* 56, *Fit to Print* 62.
Office: The Scotsman Publications Ltd., North Bridge, Edinburgh 10; 87 Colinton Road, Edinburgh 10, Scotland.
Telephone: 225-2468 (Office); 337-2107 (Home).

Dunning, John Ray, A.B., PH.D.; American physicist; b. 24 Sept. 1907; ed. Shelby High School, Nebraska, Wesleyan Univ., and Columbia Univ.
Asst. in Physics Columbia Univ. 29-32; Univ. Fellow 32-33; Instr. in Physics 33-35; Cutting Travelling Fellow 35-36; Asst. Prof. of Physics 35-38; Ernest Kempton Adams Fellow 40-41; Assoc. Prof. 38-46; Dir. Research 42-46; Scientific Dir. 46-; Prof. of Physics 46-, Chair. Science and Engineering Research 49-, Dir. Scientific Research 50-, Dean, Faculty of Eng. 50-; mem. Bd. of Dirs. American Asscn. for the Advancement of Science, Oak Ridge Inst. of Nuclear Studies, Vitro Corpn.; Board of Visitors, West Point; Chair. New York City Board of Education Advisory Cttee. on Science Manpower 56-; mem. Scientific Advisory Panel, Dept. of Army, N.Y. Acad. Science, Nat. Acad. of Sciences, American Society Mech. Engineers, American Asscn. Physics Teachers, Society Engineering Education, Engineering Index Inc. 56-; Nat. Science Foundation, Cttee. for Mathematical, Physical and Engineering Sciences 58-, for Institutional Programs 61-, etc.; developed U-235 separation methods and atomic energy systems; Industrial Consultant; President's Medal for Merit 46; mem. Congressional Panel of Joint Cttee. on Peaceful Uses of Atomic Energy 55; Chair. Nuclear Energy Policy Board; Chair. American Soc. of Mechanical Engineers, New York State Science, Advisory Council to the Legislature 63-, President's Cttee. on Super-sonic Transport-Sonic Boom, Nat. Acad. of Sciences 64-; Dir. City Investing Corpn., Armstrong Memorial Research Foundation; Dir. Science Service 58-; Chair. New York City Advisory Council on Science and Technology 65-.
Publ. *Matter, Energy and Radiation* 40.
Spring Lake Road, Sherman, Conn., U.S.A.

Dunoyer de Segonzac, André; French painter; b. 6 July 1884; ed. Lycée Henri IV and Ecole des Beaux Arts (Merson studios), Paris.
Sergeant, later sub-lieut. in French Army 14-18; works include illustrations for Virgil's *Georgics*, Ronsard's *Sonnets*, Colette's *La Treille Muscate*, etc.; many paintings exhibited in museums; Chevalier Légion d'Honneur; Carnegie Prize 33; Grand Prix Biennale, Venice 34; Grande Médaille d'or de la Ville de Paris 64; hon. mem. Royal Academies, London and Belgium and Inst. of Arts and Letters, U.S.A.
13 rue Bonaparte, Paris 6e, France.

Dunphie, Major Gen. Sir Charles Anderson Lane, C.B., C.B.E., D.S.O.; British company director; b. 20 April 1902; ed. Royal Naval Colls., Osborne and Dartmouth, Royal Military Acad., Woolwich.

Commissioned into Royal Artillery 21; G.S.O. 1st Armoured Division 40; Brigadier, Gen. Staff, Royal Armoured Corps 41; Commdr. 20th Armoured Brigade, U.K. 42, 26th Armoured Brigade, North Africa 42-43; British Asst. Chief of Staff, U.S. 7th Corps, North Africa 43; Deputy Dir. Royal Armoured Corps 43-44; Dir. Gen. Armoured Fighting Vehicles 45-48; joined Vickers Group 48, Dir. all Vickers Ltd., Royal Exchange Assurance, Westminster Bank Ltd.; mem. Her Majesty's Corps of Gentlemen-at-Arms 52-62; mem. Board of Govs. Welbeck Coll.; Commdr. Legion of Merit (U.S.), Silver Star (U.S.).
Elliscombe House, Wincanton, Somerset, England.

Dunsheath, Percy, C.B.E., M.A., D.SC.(ENG.), D.ENG., LL.D., M.I.E.E.; British engineer; b. 16 Aug. 1886; ed. Sheffield, Cambridge and London Univs.
General Post Office Engineer 08-19; served in First World War 15-18; Dir. of Research W. T. Henley's Telegraph Works Co. Ltd. 19-29, Chief Engineer 29-34, Dir. 36-60; Chair. Cambridge Instrument Co. 56-64; mem. Senate Univ. of London; Chair. of Convocation London Univ. 49-61; Pres. Electrical Development Asscn. 52-53 Pres. Inst. of Electrical Engineers 46, Hon. mem. 64-; Pres. ASLIB 49-50; Leader Univs./Industry Team visiting U.S.A. 51; Chair. Special F.B.I. Cttee. on shortage of Science Teachers; Pres. Int. Electro-technical Comm. 55-58; LL.D. h.c. London Univ.; Hon. Fellow, Univ. Coll., London 67.
Publs. *Industrial Research* (Advisory Editor) 47, *The Graduate in Industry* 48, *Century of Technology* (editor) 51, *The Electrical Current* 51, *Convocation in the University of London* 58, *Electricity, How it Works* 60, *A History of Electrical Engineering* 61, *Giants of Electricity* 67.
Sutton Place, Abinger Hammer, Dorking, Surrey, England.
Telephone: Abinger 309.

Dunsmore, Robert Lionel, M.C., B.SC., D.C.S.; Canadian executive; b. 2 Sept. 1893; ed. Queen's Univ., Kingston, Ont.
Assistant Engineer Imperial Oil Co., Sarnia, Ont. 19-25; Asst. Supt. Calgary Refinery, Imperial Oil Co. 22-25; Gen. Supt. Talara (Peru) Refinery, Int. Petroleum Co.; Ltd. 26-30; Supt. Halifax Imperial Oil Co. 30-43; Man. Montreal Refinery 44-46; Co-ordinator Manufacturing Int. Petroleum Co. Ltd.; Pres. Champlain Oil Products Ltd. 49-58, Dir. 58-; Pres. Montreal Board of Trade 56-57; Chair. of Board, Canadian Broadcasting Corpn. 58-63; mem. Board of Trustees, Queen's Univ., Kingston, Ont.; Vice-Pres. Commercial and Industrial Finance Co. Ltd., Montreal; Fellow E.I.C.
Home: 4305 Montrose Avenue, Montreal 6, P.Q., Canada.
Telephone: We3-8810.

Dunstan, Donald Allan, Q.C., LL.B., M.P.; Australian solicitor and politician; b. 21 Sept. 1926; ed. Collegiate School of St. Peter, Adelaide, and Univ. of Adelaide.
Labour mem. of Parl. 53-; Attorney-Gen. of South Australia 65, Treas. 66, Minister of Housing; Premier of South Australia May 67-.
Premiers' Department, Angas Street, Adelaide; Home: 104 George Street, Norwood, Adelaide, South Australia.
Telephone: 312442 (Home); 282400 (Office).

Dunton, Arnold Davidson, D.SC., LL.D.; Canadian university president; b. 4 July 1912; ed. Lower Canada Coll., Montreal, McGill Univ., Univ. of Grenoble, Cambridge Univ., Univ. of Munich.
Reporter *Montreal Star* 34; Assoc. Ed. 37; Ed. *Montreal Standard* 38; Wartime Information Board 42, Gen. Man. 44; Chair. Board of Govs. Canadian Broadcasting Corpn. 45; Pres. and Vice-Chancellor Carleton Univ. 58-.
410 Maple Lane, Ottawa, Ont., Canada.

Duong Van Minh, Lt.-Gen.; Viet-Namese army officer and politician; b. 16; ed. French Lycée, Army General Staff School, Paris, and U.S. Army Command School.
French Colonial Army 40-52, Prisoner-of-War; Major, Viet-Namese Army 52; Campaign against Binh Xuyen bandits 55, Viet Cong guerillas 58-62; Military Adviser to Pres. Diem 62-63; Chair. of Revolutionary Council Oct. 63-Jan. 64; Chief of State Jan.-Aug. 64.
Saigon, Republic of Viet-Nam.

Du Plessis, Wentzel Christoffel; South African diplomatist; b. 5 March 1906; ed. Transvaal Univ. Coll.
In Dept. of Lands 24-27, Dept. of External Affairs 27-45; Admin. Sec. S.A. Del. to Imperial Conf., London 30; Private Sec. to Prime Minister 31-34; Sec. The Hague 34-38; Chief Diplomatic and Consular Div. and Sec. to Prisoners of War Cttee. 38-45; entered commerce 45, politics 48; M.P. 48-54; High Commr. in Canada and Permanent Rep. to UN 54-56; Ambassador to U.S.A. 56-60; Dir. Africa Inst. Univ. of S. Africa 60-61; Sec. for Information Rep. of S. Africa 61-63; Administrator of S.W. Africa 63-.
Administrator's Office, Windhoek, S.W. Africa.

Dupont, Clifford Walter, M.A.; Rhodesian solicitor, farmer and politician; b. 6 Dec. 1905; ed. Bishops Stortford Coll., and Clare Coll., Cambridge.
Solicitor, London 29-39, 45-48; Royal Artillery, rose to Major 40-45; emigrated to Rhodesia 48; M.P. in Fed. Assembly 58-62; mem. S. Rhodesian Parl. 62-; Minister of Justice and Minister of Law and Order, S. Rhodesia 62-64; Minister without Portfolio June-Aug. 64; Deputy Prime Minister and Minister of External Affairs 64-65; Deputy Prime Minister and Minister of External Affairs and of Defence 65; appointed Head of State (with title of "Officer Administering the Govt.") by Prime Minister of Rhodesia, Mr. Ian Smith Nov. 65.
P.O.B. 2078, Salisbury, Rhodesia.

Du Pont, Edmond; American businessman; b. 23 Aug. 1906; ed. Andover Acad., Princeton Univ., and Oxford Univ.
Senior Partner, Francis I. duPont & Co.; Pres. Francis I. duPont Co. S.A.; Dir. Continental American Life Insurance Co.; Dir. Winterthur Corpn.; Dir. Episcopal Church Foundation.
2106 Grant Avenue, Wilmington 6, Del., U.S.A.

DuPont, Henry B.; American businessman; b. 23 July 1898; ed. Yale Univ., and Mass. Inst. of Technology.
In engineering dept. Gen. Motors Corpn. 24-27; with E. I. du Pont de Nemours and Co. 27-, Vice Pres. and Dir. 39-, mem. Finance Cttee. 63-; Dir. North American Aviation Corpn., Wilmington Trust Co.; Pres. and Dir. Christiana Securities Co.
Home: Greenville, Del.; Office: du Pont Building, Wilmington, Del., U.S.A.

du Pont, Henry Francis, B.A.; American executive and horticulturist; b. 27 May 1880; ed. Harvard Univ.
Dir. E. I. du Pont de Nemours & Co. 15-, Wilmington Trust Co. 19-, Owner Winterthur Farms, Delaware; Founder, Henry Francis du Pont Winterthur Museum 51; Vice-Pres. New York Horticultural Soc.; mem. and fmr. Chair. Fine Arts Cttee. for the White House; Trustee Fairchild Tropical Garden, Archives of American Art, Univ. of Delaware; Vice-Pres. The Royal Horticultural Soc.; Hon. L.H.D. (Yale Univ., Williams Coll., Univ. of Penn.), Hon. LL.D. (Delaware Univ.), Hon. D.F.A. (Pratt Inst.); many awards and citations.
Winterthur, Delaware 19735, U.S.A.
Telephone: 302-656-4446.

duPont, Irénée, Jr.; American engineer; b. 8 Jan. 1920; ed. Dartmouth Coll., Massachusetts Inst. of Technology.
Fairchild Engine & Airplane Corpn. 43-46; E. I. du Pont de Nemours & Co. 46-, Supervisor Parkersburg,

W. Va., 48-51, Charleston, W. Va. 51-53, Wilmington, Del. 53-; mem. Cttee. on Audit 64-, Dir. and Laboratory Dir., polychemicals technical services; Dir. Wilmington Trust Co.
Box 38, Montchanin, Delaware 19710, U.S.A.

Dupont, Jacques-Bernard; French inspector of finances and diplomatist; b. 5 April 1922; ed. Univ. of Toulouse and Ecole Nationale d'Administration, Paris. Lecturer, Tübingen Univ. 46-49; French High Comm., Germany 49-52; Ecole Nationale d'Administration 52-54; Insp. of Finances 54-; with Financial Counsellor, Saarbrücken 57, Technical Adviser, Ministry of Foreign Affairs 58, Head Office, Insp.-Gen. of Finances 61; Ambassador to Dahomey 61-64; Dir.-Gen. O.R.T.F. 64-; Vice-Pres. European Broadcasting Union 66-.
Office de la Radiodiffusion-Télévision française (O.R.T.F.), Maison de la Radio-Télévision, 116 avenue du Président-Kennedy, Paris 16e, France.

DuPont, Jessie Ball (Mrs. Alfred Irénée DuPont); American philanthropist and business executive; ed. Longwood Coll., Farmville, Va.
Director Florida Nat. Bank, Jacksonville; Pres. Nemours Foundation, Alfred I. duPont Radio Awards Foundation; Vice-Pres. Alfred I. duPont Foundation, Virginia Museum of Fine Arts; many hon. degrees.
Barnett Bank Building, Jacksonville, Fla.; Epping Forest, Jacksonville, Fla., U.S.A.

Dupont, Pierre, L. ès D.; Swiss diplomatist; b. 1912; ed. legal studies in Geneva.
Swiss Political Dept., Berne; legations in Paris and Brussels; fmr. mem. Swiss Del. to OECD; fmr. Head Finance Dept. of Swiss Political Dept.; fmr. Head Swiss del. to Perm. Franco-Swiss Comm. on Haute-Savoie and Pays de Gesc; fmr. Amb. to Poland; Amb. to Netherlands 65-67, to France 67-.
Ambassade de Suisse, 142 rue de Grenelle, Paris 7e, France.
Telephone: INValides 62-92.

du Pont, Pierre Samuel, III; American business executive; b. 1 Jan. 1911; ed. Tower Hill School, Phillips Exeter Acad., Massachusetts Inst. of Technology.
E. I. du Pont de Nemours & Co. 34-, Development Dept. 40-41, Nylon Div. 42-45, Trade Analysis Div. 45-47, Dir. 48, Sec. 54-, mem. Finance Cttee. 59-63, Vice-Pres. and mem. Exec. Cttee. 63-65; Dir. Wilmington Trust Co. 51-66; mem. American Chemical Soc.
E. I. du Pont de Nemours & Co., Wilmington, Del., U.S.A.

Dupont-Sommer, André Louis; French university professor; b. 23 Dec. 1900; ed. Univ. de Paris à la Sorbonne.
Secretary, Collège de France 34-40; Dir. of Studies, School of Higher Studies 38-; Prof. Univ. of Paris 45-63; Pres. of Inst. of Semitic Studies, Univ. of Paris 52-; Prof. Collège de France 63-; mem. Institut de France (Secrétaire Perpétual de l'Académie des Inscriptions et Belles-Lettres) 61-; Chevalier Légion d'Honneur, Commdr. dans l'Ordre des Palmes académiques.
Publs. *La Doctrine gnostique de la lettre wâw* ... 46, *Les Araméens* 49, *Les inscriptions araméennes de Sfiré* 48, *Aperçus préliminaires sur les manuscrits de la mer Morte* 53, *Les Ecrits esséniens découverts près de la mer Morte* 59, 60, 64, etc.
9 rue du Val-de-Grace, Paris 5e, France.
Telephone: Paris 033-08-48.

Dupouy, Gaston, D. ès sc.; French scientist; b. 7 Aug. 1900.
Research at Sorbonne Laboratory 22; taught at Ecole Normale Supérieure de Jeunes Filles, Sèvres; in charge of research, Caisse Nationale des Sciences; joint Dir. of Ecole Pratique des Hautes Etudes 33; research at electro-magnetic laboratory Bellevue; Dir. of Lectures,

Faculty of Science, Rennes Univ. 35; Sec. Société Française de Physique; Prof. of Faculty of Science Toulouse Univ. 37, Dean; mem. New York Acad. of Sciences 51; Dir. Laboratoire d'Optique Electronique C.N.R.S., Toulouse; Hon. Dir.-Gen. Nat. Centre for Scientific Research 57; Mem. of Nat. Comm. of UNESCO; mem. of Consultative Cttee. of Universities; mem. Inst. de France (Acad. des Sciences) 50; mem. Atomic Energy Cttee., Cttee. of Scientific Action for Nat. Defence 54; research work in fields of magnetism, electron-optics and high voltage electron microscopy; Hon. Fellow several Socs.; Pres. Int. Fed. of Socs. for Electron Microscopy 68; Commdr. de la Légion d'Honneur, Ordre de Léopold I, Order of Orange-Nassau, Grand Officier de l'Ordre Nat. du Mérite.
Laboratoire d'Optique Electronique, rue Jeanne-Marvig, Toulouse (Haute-Garonne), France.
Telephone: 52-65-96.

du Pré, Jacqueline; British violoncellist; b. 1945; ed. London 'Cello School, Guildhall School of Music under William Pleeth, under Paul Tortelier in Paris and Rostropovich in Moscow.
Debut at Wigmore Hall at sixteen; soloist with principal English orchestras and conductors at Royal Festival Hall, Royal Albert Hall and Bath and Edinburgh Festivals; concerts in Berlin, Paris, Rotterdam, Stavanger, U.S.A. and U.S.S.R.
c/o Ibbs and Tillett Ltd., 124 Wigmore Street, London, W.I, England.

Dupré, Marcel; French organist and composer; b. 3 May 1886; ed. Lycée de Rouen, Nat. Conservatoire de Musique, Paris.
First public appearance at Elbeuf Church 94; apptd. organist at Church of St. Vivien, Rouen 98 (aged 12); student Nat. Conservatoire 01-14; temporary organist Notre Dame 16-20; asst. at St. Sulpice 20; began career as concert organist 21; organist at St. Sulpice 34-; Prof. of Organ and Improvisation, Nat. Conservatoire 26-54, Dir. of the Conservatoire 54-56; mem. Acad. des Beaux-Arts, Pres. 61; Commdr. Légion d'Honneur; Hon. Dr. Pontifical Inst. Rome; Commdr. Arts et Lettres, Grand Croix Ordre National du Mérite.
Works include two organ symphonies and many other organ works, two symphonies and a concerto for organ and orchestra, works for piano and organ, *De Profundis* for voices, organ and orchestra; *La France au Calvaire* for voices, organ and orchestra.
40 boulevard Anatole France, Meudon (Seine-et-Oise), France.
Telephone: 027-14-45.

Dupuis, Raymond, Q.C.; Canadian lawyer and company director; b. 2 Aug. 1907; ed. Univ. of Montreal.
Called to Province of Quebec Bar 30; Dir. Dupuis Frères 33, Pres. 45-61; Dir. Royal Bank of Canada, Canadian Broadcasting Corpn., Dominion Tar and Chemical Co. Ltd., Burns & Co. Ltd., Canada Life Assurance Co., Globe Indemnity Co. of Canada, Hudson Bay Insurance Co., Western Assurance Co., British America Assurance Co., Compagnie d'Assurance du Quebec, Soc. Nationale de Fiducie; Nat. Pres. Canadian Chamber of Commerce 56-57; official of numerous civic and philanthropic orgs.
Office: 612 St. James Street, West Montreal, Quebec; Home: 21 Messier Street, Sainte-Hilaire, Quebec, Canada.

Dupuis, Yvon; Canadian politician; b. 26; ed. Collège de Varennes, Quebec, Collège de Longueil, Quebec, and Ecole Normale Jacques-Cartier, Montreal.
Minister without Portfolio, Canadian Federal Cabinet Feb. 64- Jan. 65; Liberal.
523 Morais, St.-Jean, P.Q., Canada.

Dupuy, Pierre, C.M.G., LL.L., L.LITT.; Canadian diplomatist; b. 9 July 1896; ed. St. Mary's Coll., Montreal, Univs. of Montreal and Paris.

Diplomatic Service 22-, Chargé d'Affaires, Belgian and Netherlands Govts., London 40, French Govt., Vichy 40, Norwegian, Polish, Belgian, Dutch, Yugoslav and Czechoslovak Govts., London 43; Ambassador to Netherlands 45, to Italy 52-58, to France 58-63; Commr.-Gen. of World Exhbn., Montreal 1967; Hon. Dr. Laval Univ.
Publ. *André Laurence* 27.
Canadian Corporation for Expo 67, Administration Building, Cité du Havre, Montreal, Canada.
Telephone: 397-7700.

Durant, Will, A.M., PH.D.; American writer; b. 5 Nov. 1885; ed. St. Peter's Coll., and Columbia Univ.
Publs. *The Story of Philosophy* 26, *Transition* 27, *The Mansions of Philosophy* 29, *Adventures in Genius* 31, *The Story of Civilisation:* Vol. I *Our Oriental Heritage* 35, Vol. II *The Life of Greece* 39, Vol. III *Caesar and Christ* 44, Vol. IV *The Age of Faith* 50, Vol. V *The Renaissance* 53, Vol. VI *The Reformation* 57, Vol. VII *The Age of Reason Begins* (with Ariel Durant) 61, Vol. VIII *The Age of Louis XIV* (with Ariel Durant) 63, *The Age of Voltaire* (with Ariel Durant) 65, *Rousseau and Revolution* (with Ariel Durant) 67.
5608 Briarcliff Road, Los Angeles 28, Calif., U.S.A.

Duras, Marguerite; French writer; b. 4 April 1914; ed. Sorbonne.
Graduated in law; Sec. Ministry of Colonies 35-41; writer 43-.
Publs. *Les Impudents* 43, *La Vie Tranquille* 44, *Un Barrage contre le Pacifique* 50, *Le Marin de Gibraltar* 52, *Les Petits Chevaux de Tarquinia* 53, *Des Journées entières dans les Arbres* 54 (short stories), *Le Square* 55, *Moderato Cantabile* 58, *Les Viaducs de la Seine-et-Oise* 60, *Hiroshima Mon Amour* (film), *Dix Heures et demie du Soir en Eté* 60 (film 67), *L'Apres-Midi de Monsieur Andesmas* 62, *Le Ravissement de Lol. V. Stein, Des Journées Entières dans les Arbres* (play) 64, *La Música* (play) 65 (film) 67, *Les Eaux et les Forêts* (play) 65, *Le Vice-Consul* (novel) 66, *L'Amante Anglaise* (novel) 67, *Yes, peut-être* and *Le Shaga* (two plays) 68.
5 rue Saint-Benoit, Paris 6e, France.

Durbet, Marius Léon; French pharmacist and politician; b. 28 Feb. 1904; ed. Institution Notre-Dame-de-la-Villette, La Ravoiré and Catholic Univ. of Lille.
Mayor of Nevers 47-53; Dep. to Nat. Assembly 51-; mem. Central Cttee. Union pour la Nouvelle République (U.N.R.); Pres. of Nat. Assembly Cttee. for Cultural, Family and Social Affairs 59-63; Chevalier, Légion d'Honneur.
National Assembly, Paris 7e, France; and 4 rue de la Basilique, Nevers, Nièvre, France.

Düren, Albrecht, DR. SOC. POL.; German trade association official; b. 25 June 1910; ed. Univs. of Berlin and Halle/Saale.
Trade Asscn. official 37-; Military service 42-45; Sec. Bremen and Hamburg Cereal and Seed Import and Wholesale Asscns. 48-60; Exec. Sec. Deutscher Industrie- und Handelstag 60-; mem. Bremen Chamber of Commerce 55-, Exec. Sec. 56-.
Adenauerallee 148, 53 Bonn; Home: 534 Bad Honnef, Finkenpfad 4, German Federal Republic.

Durgadas, Lala; Indian journalist; b. 23 Nov. 1900; ed. D.A.V. Coll., Lahore.
Parliamentary Corresp. and Editor, Associated Press of India, New Delhi and Simla 19-38; Special Rep. for *Statesman,* United Provinces 38-42, New Delhi 42-44; Co-Editor *Hindustan Times* 44-58, Chief Editor 57-60; Chief Editor India News and Feature Alliance 61-; War Corresp. 45; Pres. All-India Newspaper Editors' Conf. 59-61; Founder Pres. Press Club of India, New Delhi 59-63; mem. Indo-Pakistan Press Consultative Cttee. 49-51; Chair. Press Gallery Cttee., Indian Parl. 51-63; mem. Press Council of India.

Publs. *Report on America, India and the World.*
2 Tolstoy Lane, New Delhi 1, India.
Telephone: 48044.

Ďuriš, Július; Czechoslovak politician; b. 9 March 1904.
Studied law in Prague; joined Communist Party, became its organiser and editor in Czechoslovakia and France; elected Communist deputy Slovak Provincial Diet 35; with underground 39-41; was Leader Slovak Communist Party; arrested and sentenced to 15 years' imprisonment 41; escaped and joined partisans 45; Minister of Agriculture 45-51; Chair. Board of Commrs., Slovakia 51-53; Minister for Forests Mar.-Sept. 53; Minister of Finance 53-63.
c/o Communist Party of Slovakia, Bratislava, Hlboká 2, Czechoslovakia.

Durrell, Gerald Malcolm; British zoologist and writer; b. 7 Jan. 1925.
Student keeper, Whipsnade Park 45-46; finances, organizes and leads zoological collecting expeditions 46-, expeditions have been led to the Cameroons, British Guiana, Argentina, Paraguay, New Zealand, Australia, Malaysia and Sierra Leone; established own zoo in Jersey 59-, renamed Jersey Wildlife Preservation Trust 64; contributes to many magazines and dailies including *Daily Telegraph* and *Daily Mail;* numerous lectures, B.B.C. broadcasts and 3 major T.V. series on animals.
Publs. *The Overloaded Ark* 52, *Three Singles to Adventure* 53, *The Bafut Beagles* 53, *The Drunken Forest* 55, *My Family and Other Animals* 56, *Encounters with Animals* 59, *Zoo in My Luggage* 60, *Whispering Land* 62, *Menagerie Manor* 64, *Rosy is My Relative* (novel) 68; Childrens' Books: *The New Noah* 56, *Island Zoo* 61, *My Favourite Animal Stories* 63, *Two in the Bush* 66.
Jersey Zoo Park, Les Augres Manor, Trinity, Jersey, Channel Islands.
Telephone: North 949-172.

Durrell, Lawrence George, F.R.S.L.; British author and official; b. 27 Feb. 1912; ed. Coll. of St. Joseph, Darjeeling, India, and St. Edmund's Coll., Canterbury, England.
Formerly Foreign Service Press Officer (Athens and Cairo), Press Attaché (Alexandria and Belgrade), Dir. of Public Relations (Dodecanese Islands), Dir. of British Council Institutes (Kalamata, Greece, and Cordoba, Argentina), and Dir. of Public Relations (Govt. of Cyprus).
Publs. *A Private Country, Cities, Plains and People, On Seeming to Presume, The Tree of Idleness, Selected Poems, Collected Poems* 60, *Sappho: A Verse Play, Acte: A Verse Play* 61, *An Irish Faustus: A Verse Play* 62, *The Ikons* 66; Prose, Novels and Travel: *Panic Spring, Cefalu (The Dark Labyrinth), The Black Book, Justine, Balthazar* (Prix Du Meilleur Libre Etranger, Paris 59), *Mountolive, Clea, Reflections on a Marine Venus, Prospero's Cell, Bitter Lemons* (Duff Cooper Memorial Award 58), *Tunc* 68; Trans.: *Pope Joan, Four Greek Poets;* Humour: *Esprit de Corps, Stiff Upper Lip, Sauve Qui Peut* 66; Juvenile: *White Eagles Over Serbia;* Letters: *A Private Correspondence* (exchanged with Henry Miller) 62.
c/o The National and Grindlay's Bank Ltd., 13 St. James's Square, London, S.W.1, England.

Dürrenmatt, Friedrich; Swiss writer; b. 5 Jan. 1921; ed. Univs. of Berne and Zürich.
Publs. Comedies: *Der Blinde, Die Ehe des Herrn Mississippi, Romulus der Grosse, Ein Engel kommt nach Babylon, Der Besuch der alten Dame, Es steht geschrieben, Die Physiker, Der Meteor;* radio plays: *Stranitzky und der Nationalheld, Nächtliches Gespräch mit einem verachteten Menschen, Herkules und der Stall des Augias, Das Unternehmen der Wega, Abendstunde im Spätherbst;* novels: *Der Richter und sein Henker, Der Verdacht; Griechе sucht*

Griechin, Komödien I (omnibus edn. incl. *Die Ehe, Alte Dame, Ein Engel, Romulus*), *Das Versprechen*; short stories: *Die Stadt, Die Panne*; essay: *Theaterprobleme, Theaterschriften und Reden* 65.
Pertuis du Sault 34, Neuchâtel, Switzerland.

Dürrenmatt, Peter Ulrich; Swiss journalist; b. 29 Aug. 1904; ed. Univs. of Berne and Geneva.
Began career as teacher; mem. staff *Schweizer Mittelpresse* 34; Editor Swiss Section *Basler Nachrichten* 43-49, Chief Editor 49-; mem. Nat. Council 59.
Publs. *Die Bundesverfassung, ihr Wert und ihre Bewährung* 48, *Kleine Geschichte der Schweiz im zweiten Weltkrieg* 49, *Zerfall und Wiederaufbau der Politik* 51, *Schweizergeschichte* 57, *Die Welt zwischen Krieg und Frieden* 59, *Europa will leben* 60, *50 Jahre Weltgeschichte* 62, *In die Zeit gesprochen* 65.
Basler Nachrichten, Dufourstrasse 40, Basle, Switzerland.

Duruflé, Maurice; French organist and composer; b. 11 Jan. 1902; ed. Paris Conservatoire.
Prize for organ (Conservatoire) 22; prize for harmony 24; prize for accompaniment 26; prizes for fugue and for composition 28; Prix des "Amis de l'Orgue" 30; Organist of Saint-Etienne-du-Mont; Asst. Prof. at Conservatoire Paris 42; Prof. d'harmonie, Conservatoire de Paris 43-.
Works include: Organ: *Prélude, Adagio et Choral Varié sur le Veni Creator* 29; *Prélude et Fugue* 42; Chamber Music: *Trio pour Flûte, Alto et Piano*; Orchestra: *Trois Danses* 35, *Andante et Scherzo* 40, *Requiem pour Soli, Choeurs, Orchestre et Orgue* 47.
6 Place du Panthéon, Paris, 5e, France.

Dushkin, Alexei Nikolaevich; Soviet architect; b. 03; ed. Architectural Dept. of Kharkov Building Inst.
Builder 14-28; Architect in Moscow; Chief Architect, Metropolitan Designing Inst. 33-43, 59-; Chief Architect, Ministry of Railways 43-59; State prizewinner (three times); awarded Order of Lenin (twice), Order of Red Banner of Labour.
Works include: help with design of 'Kropotkinskaya', Square of the Revolution, Mayakovsky, Avtozavodskaya, Novoslobodskaya (Moscow underground stations), one of designers of building at Lermontov Square (former Red Gates), department stores, Moscow, and several railway stations.
Architects' Union, Ul. Shchusseva 3, Moscow, U.S.S.R.

Dusseaulx, Roger; French engineer and politician; b. 18 July 1913; ed. agricultural coll.
Mem. First Constitutional Ass. 45, Second Constitutional Ass. 46; mem. Paris City Council 45-49; M.P. for Rouen 46-51, 58-; mem. Ass. of French Union and Pres. Econ. Comm. 52-58; mem. Rouen City Council and Dep. Mayor of Rouen 59; mem. Central Cttee. of Union pour la Nouvelle République (U.N.R.), Sec.-Gen. of U.N.R. 61-62, Parl. Leader Dec. 62-63, Leader, U.N.R.—U.D.T. (amal. of U.N.R. and Union Démocratique de Travail, and now called Union Démocratique pour la Ve République) 63-; Minister of Transport 62; Resistance Medal.
31 rue Jeanne-d'Arc, Rouen (Seine-Maritime), France.

Dutilleux, Henri; French composer; b. 22 Jan. 1916; ed. Conservatoire national de Musique, Paris.
Career devoted to music 45-; Dir. Musical Services Radiodiffusion française 45-63; Prof. of Composition Ecole Normale de Musique, Paris 61-; fmr. mem. UNESCO Music Council; 1st Grand Prix de Rome 38, Grands Prix du Disque 57 and 58, Grand Prix du Conseil Général de la Seine 59.
Compositions: *Sonata for Piano* 48, *First Symphony* 51, *Le Loup* (Ballet) 53, *Second Symphony* 59, *Cinq Métaboles* 64.
12 rue Saint-Louis en L'Ile, Paris 4e, France.

Dutra, Tarso; Brazilian politician; b. 15 May 1914; ed. Ginásio Santa Maria, Porto Alegre, and Univ. do Rio Grande do Sul.
Federal Insp. of Educ.; Legal Adviser to Caixa Economica of Rio Grande do Sul; Sec. to State Gov. of Rio Grande do Sul; Deputy to State Legislature Assembly, Rio Grande do Sul 47-51; Minister of Educ. 67-.
Ministry of Education, Brasilia, Brazil.

Dutt, Rajani Palme; British journalist and politician; b. 96; ed. Balliol Coll. Oxford.
Sec. Int. Section Labour Research Dept. 19-22; Editor *Labour Monthly* 21-; Editor *Workers' Weekly* 22-24; Editor *Daily Worker* 36-38; mem. Exec. Cttee. Communist Party 22-65; Hon. Dr. Historical Science, Moscow Univ. 62.
Publs. *Labour International Handbook, Socialism and the Living Wage, Lenin, Fascism and Social Revolution, World Politics 1918-1936, Political and Social Doctrine of Communism, India To-day* 40, *Britain and the World Front* 42, *Crisis of Britain and the British Empire* 53 (new, enlarged edn. 57), *India Today and Tomorrow* 56, *Problems of Contemporary History* 63, *The Rise and Fall of the Daily Herald* 64, *The Internationale* 64, *Whither China?* 67.
8 Highfield Court, Highfield Road, London, N.W.11, England.

Dutt, Subimal, B.SC.; Indian diplomatist; b. 05; ed. Presidency Coll. Calcutta and Univ. Coll. London.
Asst. Magistrate, Joint Magistrate and Collector, Additional District and Session Judge, Magistrate Collector, Province of Bengal 28-38; in Dept. of Education, Health and Lands, Govt. of India 38-41; Agent, Govt. of India in Malaya 41; served Govt. of Bengal 41-47; Sec. in Ministry of Commonwealth Relations, also External Affairs 47-52; Ambassador to German Federal Republic 52-54; Commonwealth Sec. Ministry of External Affairs 54-55, Foreign Sec. 55-61; Ambassador to U.S.S.R. 61-62; Sec. to the President of India 62-65.
c/o President's Secretariat, New Delhi, India.

Duval, H.E. Cardinal Léon-Etienne; Algerian (b. French) ecclesiastic; b. 9 Nov. 1903; ed. Petit Séminaire, Roche-sur-Foron, Grand Séminaire Annecy, Séminaire français Rome, and Pontificia Universitas Gregoriana.
Ordained priest 26; Prof. Grand Séminaire Annecy 30-42; Vicar-Gen. and Dir. of works, Diocese of Annecy 42-46; consecrated Bishop of Constantine and Hippo 46; Archbishop of Algiers 54-; created Cardinal 65; Officier Légion d'Honneur.
Publs. *Paroles de Paix* 55, *Messages de Paix 1955-1962* 62.
Archbishop's House, 13 rue Khelifa-Boukhalfa, Algiers, Algeria.

Duvalier, François, M.D.; Haitian physician and politician; b. 14 April 1907; ed. Lycée Alexandre Pétion and Faculty of Medicine, Port-au-Prince.
Began his career as physician St. François-Xavier Hospital, Port-au-Prince; later consultant, Séguineau Clinic, Dir. Gressier Rural Clinic and School; attached to U.S. Medical Mission as Dir. of Malaria Control; Under-Sec. of State for Labour; Sec. of State for Labour and Public Health; mem. Govt. Mil. Council 56-57; Pres. of Haiti 57-; mem. Int. Society of Afro-Cuban Studies, Int. Inst. of Anthropology (Paris), Paris Demographic Society, Haitian Medical Asscn., Royal Society of Tropical Medicine (London).
Publs. *Les Tendances d'une Génération, Mémoire sur la Mortalité Haitienne, Psychologie ethnique et historique, La Contribution des Nègres à la Civilisation de l'Humanité, La Civilisation Négro-africaine et le Problème haitien.*
Palais du Gouvernement, Port-au-Prince, Haiti.

Duverger, Maurice; French political scientist; b. 5 June 1917; ed. Bordeaux Univ.
Prof. of Political Sociology, Paris Univ.; Dir. of Study and Research, Fondation Nat. des Sciences Politiques; contributor to *Le Monde.*
Publs. *Les Partis Politiques* 51, *Institutions Politiques* 55, *La Participation des Femmes à la Vie Politique* 55, *Les Finances publiques* 56, *Demain, la République . . .* 58, *Méthodes de la Science Politique* 59, *De la Dictature* 61, *La VIème République et le Régime Présidentiel* 61, *Introduction to the Social Sciences* 64, *Introduction à la Politique* 64, *Sociologie politique* 66, *La démocratie sans le peuple.*
24 rue des Fossés Saint-Jacques, Paris 5e, France.

Duvieusart, Jean Pierre, D.EN.D.; Belgian lawyer and politician; b. 1900; ed. Collège des Pères Jésuites, Charleroi, and Univ. of Louvain.
Mayor of Frasnes lez Gosselies 27-47; Provincial Judge, Hainault 33-36; mem. House of Reps. 44-49, Senator 49-; Minister of Econ. Affairs and of the Middle Classes 47-50, 52-54, Prime Minister 50; Del. to UN Gen. Assembly 50; Pres. European Parl. 64-65; lawyer, Charleroi; Commdr. Ordre de Léopold, numerous other decorations.
12 rue de l'Athénée, Charleroi, Belgium.

du Vigneaud, Vincent, PH.D.; American university professor; b. 18 May 1901; ed. Univs. of Illinois and Rochester.
Asst. Prof. Univ. of Ill. 30-32; Prof. and Head Dept. of Biochemistry George Washington Univ. 32-38; same at Cornell Univ. Medical Coll. 38-67, Emeritus 67-; Prof. of Chemistry, Cornell Univ. 67-; awarded Hillebrand Prize of Chemical Society of Washington 36; mem. Nat. Acad. of Sciences; Foster Lecturer Univ. of Buffalo 39; Mead-Johnson Vitamin B Complex Award, American Inst. of Nutrition 43; Hitchcock Prof. Univ. of California 44; Nichols Medal, New York Section of the American Chemical Society 45; Julius Stieglitz Memorial Lecturer 48; Lasker Award 48; Eastman Lecturer 49; Lecturer, Univ. of London 49, Messenger Lecturer Cornell 50, Harvey Society Lecturer 42 and 54, Dakin Memorial Lecturer 56, etc.; Osborne and Mendel Award 53, Passano Award 55, American Coll. of Physicians Award 65, etc.; Nobel Prize for Chemistry 55; Hon. Sc.D. (Yale and New York Univs.) 55; Hon. Sc.D. (Univ. of Illinois) 60; Hon. Sc.D. (Univs. St. Louis and Rochester) 65.
Home: 100 Fairview Square, Ithaca, New York; Office: Dept. of Chemistry, Cornell University, Ithaca, New York, U.S.A.

Duvillard, Henri; French politician; b. 3 Nov. 1910.
Journalist, Dir. *La Dépêche du Loiret* 47-52; on staff of Gen. Koenig (Minister of Nat. Defence) 54, 55; on staff of H. Ulvet (Minister of Industry and Commerce) 54-55; on staff of Maurice Lemaire (Sec. of State for Industry and Commerce) 56-57; Deputy for Loiret, Vice-Pres. U.N.R. Group in Nat. Assembly; fmr. Public Relations Officer, Papéteries de France; Minister for Ex-Servicemen 67-; Médaille Militaire, Croix de Guerre (39-45), Médaille de la Résistance.
12 rue du Grenier-à-sel, Orléans (Loiret), France.

Duwaerts, Leon-Louis; Belgian journalist; b. 13 Jan. 1905; ed. Athénée de Saint-Gilles-lez-Bruxelles.
Sec.-Gen. Union professionelle de la presse belge 28-35, Association générale de la presse belge 35-58, Pres. 58-60; Pres. Association professionelle de la presse cinématographique belge 35-37, 40-50, now Hon. Pres.; Editor-in-Chief Agence Belga; Hon. Pres. Fédération Int. de la presse cinématographique; Prof. Belgian Journalists' Inst.; Commdr. Ordre de II Leopold, etc.
Publs. *Le Statut du Journaliste professionnel de la presse filmée* 35, *Droits et Devoirs du Journaliste* 52.
120 avenue Henri Jaspar, Brussels 6, Belgium.
Telephone: 02/37-57-27.

Dvořák, Richard; Czechoslovak politician; b. 28 Dec. 1913; ed. Commercial Coll., Teplice.
Imprisoned by Gestapo 39-45; mem. Nat. Assembly 48; Minister, Foreign Trade 53-59; Ambassador, U.S.S.R. 59-63; Head, Central Board for Dev. of Local Economy 63; Minister of Finance Sept. 63-67; Amb. to India 67-; mem. of Comm. of Central Cttee. of C.P. of Czechoslovakia for questions of Living Standards 63-66; Deputy to Nat. Assembly; Alternate mem. Central Cttee. of C.P. of Czechoslovakia 58-62, mem. 62-; Order of Labour 63.
Embassy of Czechoslovakia, New Delhi, India.

Dvornik, Francis, D.D., D. ès L.; Czech-born American Byzantinist; b. 14 Aug. 1893; ed. Faculty of Divinity, Olomouc, Charles IV Univ., Prague, Sorbonne, Paris, and School of Political Sciences, Paris.
Priest 16; Lecturer Charles IV Univ. 26; Prof. Church History 28, 32; Dean of Faculty of Divinity 35; Schlumberger Lecturer Coll. de France 40; Birkbeck Lecturer Trinity Coll. Cambridge 46; Prof. at Harvard Univ. 49-; Corresp. Fellow British Acad., Royal Historical Society (London); mem. Amer. Medieval Acad.; Fellow American Acad. of Arts and Sciences; Assoc. Royal Acad. (Belgium); Chevalier de la Légion d'Honneur; Hon. D.Lit. (London, Lisle, Farleigh Dickinson Univs.).
Publs. *Les Slaves, Byzance et Rome au IX siècle, La vie de S. Grégoire le Décapolite* 26, *St. Wenceslas, Duke of Bohemia* 28, *Les Légendes de Constantin* 33, *National Churches* 44, *The Photian Schism: History and Legend* 48 (French edn. 50); *The Making of Central and East Europe* 49, *The Slavs, Their Early History and Civilisation* 56, *The Idea of Apostolicity in Byzantium* 58, *The Ecumenical Councils* 61, *The Slavs in European History and Civilisation* 62, *Byzance et la Primauté Romaine* 64, *Early Christian and Byzantine Political Philosophy* 66.
1703 32nd Street, Washington, D.C., U.S.A.
Telephone: 232-3101.

Dworak, Franz Gustav; Austrian businessman; b. 02. Joined Rudolph Kirner furnace and metallurgical firm 30, now owner; Pres. Austrian Fed. Chamber of Commerce 53-60; mem. Austrian Nat. Council (Nationalrat) 50-; mem. Central Cttee. Austrian People's Party (Ö.V.P.); Pres. Austrian Nat. Cttee. Int. Chamber of Trade; Grand Officer Order of Orange Nassau (Netherlands), Ordre de l'Etoile Noire (France); Grosses Verdienstkreuz mit Stern (German Fed. Republic), Grosses Silbernes Ehrenzeichen mit Stern für Verdienste um die Republik (Austria), Grand Officier de l'Ordre de la Couronne (Belgium), Grande Ufficiale dell'Ordine "Al Merito della Repubblica Italiana" (Italy).
Gloriettegasse 15, Vienna XIII, Austria.

Dy, Francisco Justiniano, M.D., M.P.H.; Philippine public health administrator; b. 17 Sept. 1912; ed. Univ. of Philippines and School of Hygiene and Public Health, Johns Hopkins Univ., U.S.A.
Research Asst. and Instructor, Inst. of Hygiene, Univ. of Philippines 38-41; U.S. Army 42-45; Senior Surgeon, U.S. Public Health Service 45-46; Consultant and Chief of Malaria Division, U.S. Public Health Service Rehabilitation Programme in Philippines 46-50; Prof. of Malariology and Chair. Dept. of Parasitology, Inst. of Hygiene, Univ. of Philippines 50-52; Deputy Chief, Malaria Section, World Health Org. (WHO), Geneva 50-51; Regional Malaria Adviser, WHO, for W. Pacific Region 51-57; Dir. of Health Services, WHO Regional Office for W. Pacific 58-66, Regional Dir. of WHO for W. Pacific July 66-; mem. Nat. Research Council of Philippines; Distinguished Service Star (Philippines); Legion of Merit, with Oak Leaf Cluster (U.S.A.).
Regional Office for the Western Pacific, World Health Organization, P.O.B. 2932, Manila, Philippines.
Telephone: 5-20-41.

Dyhrenfurth, Günter Oskar; Swiss geologist, mountaineer and explorer; b. 12 Nov. 1886; ed. Freiburg i. Br., Vienna and Breslau Univs.

Professor of Geology, Breslau Univ. 19-33; leader Int. Himalayan Expeditions 30 and 34; awarded Olympic Golden Medal 36, Prix d'Alpinisme; retired univ. prof.-in-ordinary and chronicler of the Himalayas; Grosses Verdienstkreuz des Verdienstordens der Bundesrupublik Deutschland 56; Hon. mem. The Alpine Club.

Publs. *Monographie der Fusulinen* 09, *Ducangruppe*, *Plessur-Gebirge und die Rhätischen Bogen* 13, *Monographie der Engadiner Dolomiten* 15, *Alpine Geologie* 31, *Himalaya* 31, *Bericht der Internationalen Karakoram-Expedition* 35, *Baltoro* 39, *Himalaya-Fahrt* 42, *Chronicles of the Himalayas since 1950*, *Zum dritten Pol* 52, *Das Buch vom Nanga Parbat* 54, *Das Buch vom Kantsch* 55, *Mount Everest* 59, *Die Achttausender und ihre Trabanten* 60, *Winke für Himalaya-Aspiranten* 63, *Die Höchsten Gebirge der Erde* 65; over 200 articles on scientific and Alpine subjects.

Chalet Irene, 3852 Ringgenberg, Bernese Oberland, Switzerland.

Telephone: (036) 2-15-00.

Dykes Bower, Sir John, Kt., c.v.o.; British organist; b. 13 Aug. 1905; ed. Cheltenham Coll., and Corpus Christi Coll., Cambridge.

Organist and Master of the Choir, Truro Cathedral 26-29, Succentor 29; Organist, New Coll., Oxford 29-33, Durham Cathedral 33-36; Fellow, Corpus Christi Coll., Cambridge 34-37; Organist, St. Paul's Cathedral, London 36-67; Pres. Inc. Asscn. of Organists 49-50, Royal Coll. of Organists 60-62, Hon. Sec. 68-; Hon. D.Mus. (Oxford), and several hon. Diplomas.

42 Artillery Mansions, Westminster, London, S.W.1, England.

Telephone: 01-222-647.

Dykstra, John; American (b. Netherlands) automobile executive; b. 16 April 1898; ed. Day School, Technical High School (night classes).

Emigrated to U.S.A. as a boy; U.S. Army First World War; Clayton and Lambert Mfg. Co. 19; General Motors (Oldsmobile) 34; Ford Motor Co. 47-63 (Production Asst., Vice-Pres. for Manufacturing, and Dir.), Pres. 61-63; Dir. Tecumseh Products.

1147 Glengarry Road, Birmingham, Mich., U.S.A.

Dymshyts, Veniamin Emmanuilovich; Soviet engineer and politician; b. 1910; ed. Higher Technical School, Moscow.

Member C.P.S.U. 37-; in metallurgical construction 31-50; Deputy Minister construction enterprises in metallurgical and chemical industries 50-57; Chief Engineer (Construction), Bhilai Steel Plant, India 57-59; Chief of Dept., State Planning Cttee. 59-61, First Dep. Chair. 61-62, Chair. 62; Chair. Econ. Council U.S.S.R. 62-65; Chair. U.S.S.R. State Cttee. for Material and Technical Supplies 65-; Deputy Chair. U.S.S.R. Council of Ministers 62-; mem. Central Cttee. C.P.S.U. 61-; Deputy to Supreme Soviet; State Prize 46, 50; Order of Lenin; Order of the Red Banner of Labour (twice).

State Committee for Material and Technical Supplies, Moscow, U.S.S.R.

Dyson, Freeman John, F.R.S.; American (b. British) physicist; b. 15 Dec. 1923; ed. Cambridge and Cornell Univs.

Fellow of Trinity Coll. Cambridge 46; Warren Research Fellow, Birmingham Univ. 49; Prof. of Physics, Cornell Univ. 51-53; Prof., Inst. for Advanced Study, Princeton 53-; Chair. Fed. of American Scientists 62; mem. U.S. Nat. Acad. of Sciences 64-; Heineman Prize, American Inst. of Physics 65; Lorentz Medal, Royal Netherlands Acad. 66.

Publs. Papers in *The Physical Review, Journal of Mathematical Physics*, etc.

Institute for Advanced Study, Princeton, N.J. 08540, U.S.A.

Telephone: 609-924-4400.

Dyukarev, Semyon Petrovich; Soviet diplomatist; b. 1 May 1914; ed. North Caucasus Teachers' Training Inst. and Moscow Univ.

Diplomatic Service 39-; Consul-Gen., Milan 46-49; Counsellor, Rangoon 51-55, Bangkok 58-61; Deputy Head of S.E. Asian Countries Dept., U.S.S.R. Ministry of Foreign Affairs 63-64; Ambassador to Somalia 64-.

U.S.S.R. Embassy, Corso Repubblica, Mogadishu, Somalia.

Dzerzhinsky, Ivan Ivanovich; Soviet composer; b. 09; ed. Gnesin Inst., Moscow and Leningrad Conservatoire.

Studied piano under Prof. B. L. Yavorsky, and composition under Profs. M. G. Gnesin, P. B. Ryazanov, B. Asafyevch; composer of operas; mem. Board of Union of Soviet Composers 36-48; State Prize 50; Order of Lenin 39.

Works include, operas: *Quiet Don* 35, *Virgin Soil Upturned* 37, *Days of Volochaevsk* 39, *Thunderstorm* 40, *Blood of the People* 41, *Nadezhda Svetlova* 42, *Prince Lake* 47, *The Snow Storm* 46, *Far from Moscow* 54; symphonic poem *Ermak;* three piano concertos; piano cycles: *Spring Suite* and *Russian Painters;* song cycles: *First Love* 43, *The Flying Bird* 45, *Earth* 49, *To a Woman Friend* 50, *The New Village* 50, *The Northern Bojan* 55, *Leningrad* 57, *Destiny of a Man* (opera) 61, *The Whirlwind* (opera) 65-66, *Grigory Melexov* (opera, cont. *Quiet Don*) 66-67, *Native Rivers* (song cycles) 66.

Union of Soviet Composers, R.S.F.S.R., 8/10 Ul. Nezhdanovoi, Moscow, U.S.S.R.

Dzhavakhishvili, Givi Dmitrievich; Soviet politician; b. 1912; ed. Tbilisi Polytechnic Inst. and High School.

Party and advisory work 44-53; mem. C.P.S.U. 40; Chair. Council of Ministers, Georgian S.S.R. 53-; mem. Central Cttee. of C.P.S.U. 56-; mem. Central Cttee. Georgian S.S.R. C.P.; Deputy to Supreme Soviet U.S.S.R. and Georgian S.S.R.

Council of Ministers of Georgian S.S.R., Tbilisi, Georgian S.S.R., U.S.S.R.

Dzotsenidze, Georgi Samsonovich, D.SC.; Soviet scholar and politician; b. 1910; ed. Tbilisi Univ.

Dozent, then Prof. of Geology, State Pedagogical Inst., Kutaisi 33-34; mem. C.P.S.U. 40-; Dozent, Prof., later Dean, Tbilisi Univ. 34-59; Deputy Sec. Acad. of Sciences, Georgia 51-55, Vice-Pres. 55-58; Rector, Tbilisi Univ. 58-59; Chair. Presidium Supreme Soviet Georgia 59-; Dep. Chair. Presidium Supreme Soviet U.S.S.R. 60-; mem. Cen. Auditing Comm. C.P.S.U. 61-; mem. Cen. Cttee. of Georgian C.P.

Presidium of the Supreme Soviet of the Georgian S.S.R., Tbilisi, U.S.S.R.

Telephone: 97225.

Dzúr, Col-Gen. Martin; Czechoslovak army officer and politician; b. 12 July 1919; ed. School of Wood Processing, V. M. Molotov Military Acad. of Rear Echelon Services, Kalinin, U.S.S.R., and Military Staff Acad. of Armed Forces, U.S.S.R.

Technical clerk, Slovak Paper Mills, Ruzomberok 39-41; Army service 41-43; joined 1st Czechoslovak Independent Brigade, Soviet Army, U.S.S.R.; served in U.S.S.R. 43-45; Div. Gen. Staff Officer, State Sec.'s A.D.C., A.D.C. to Chief of Mil. Office of Pres. of Czechoslovakia 45-49; various important posts in Army and Ministry of Nat. Defence 53-58; Deputy Minister of Nat. Defence 56-68, Minister 68-; Soviet, Czechoslovak and Polish medals.

Ministry of National Defence, Prague, Czechoslovakia.

Dzuverovic, Nikola; Yugoslav politician; b. 17; ed. Secondary School of General Education.

Former Sec. Regional Cttee. of Communist Party for Prokuplje, Dir.-Gen. of Machine Building Directorate, Serbia, mem. Exec. Council, Serbia, Pres. Board of Management, Fed. Chamber of Industry; Fed. Sec. for Foreign Trade 62-67.

c/o Secretariat for Foreign Trade, Belgrade, Yugoslavia.

Dzyubenko, Grigori Nikiforovich; Soviet diplomatist; b. 1914; ed. Ukrainian Inst. of Journalism.

Member C.P. of Soviet Union 40-; Journalistic work 31-36; Party work 40-42; at Ministry of Foreign Affairs 44-45; Senior Asst. Deputy Political Counsellor to Soviet Section, Allied Comm. on Austria 45-50; Asst. Head, Third European Dept., Ministry of Foreign Affairs 50-56; Counsellor, Soviet Embassy, Vienna 56-59; Counsellor, Ministry of Foreign Affairs, Moscow 59-65; Amb. to Nepal 65-; Red Banner of Labour, etc.

U.S.S.R. Embassy, Katmandu, Nepal.

E

Eames, Charles; American designer.
Independent designer of furniture, toys, films, exhibits, etc.; in partnership with wife, Ray Eames.
Office: 901 Washington Boulevard, Venice, Calif.; Home: 203 Chautauqua Boulevard, Pacific Palisades, Calif., U.S.A.

Earle, Arthur Frederick, PH.D.; Canadian economist and business executive; b. 13 Sept. 1921; ed. Univ. of Toronto and London Business School.
Royal Canadian Navy 39-46; Canada Packers Ltd. 46-48; Aluminium Ltd. in British Guiana, West Indies and Canada 48-53; Treas. Alumina Jamaica Ltd. 53-55; Sales Exec., Aluminium Union, London 55-58; Vice-Pres. Aluminium Ltd. Sales, Inc., New York; Dep. Chair. Hoover Ltd. 61-65, Managing Dir. 63-65; Principal, London Graduate School of Business Studies 65-; Dir. Hoover Ltd., and The British Aluminium Co. Ltd.; mem. The Consumer Council, Nat. Econ. Devt. Council for the Electrical Eng. Industry, N.E.D.C. Cttee. on Management Educ., Training and Devt.; Gov., London School of Econs.; Fellow, British Inst. of Management.
The London Business School, 28 Northumberland Avenue, London, W.C.2; "Rotherfield", The Ridgeway, Gerrards Cross, Bucks., England.
Telephone: 01-930 2180 (Office); 498-2110 (Home).

Earle, Ion, B.A., T.D.; British commercial official; b. 12 April 1916; ed. Stowe School, Univ. Coll., Oxford and Univ. of Grenoble.
Head of Regional Org., Fed. of British Industries 52-60; Chief Exec., Export Council for Europe 60-64; Dir. British Nat. Export Council 64-66, Deputy Dir.-Gen. 66-.
British National Export Council, 6-14 Dean Farrar Street, London, S.W.1; Home: 5 McKay Road, London, S.W.20, England.

Eason, Henry, C.B.E., J.P., B.COM., F.I.B.; British banking administrator; b. 12 April 1910; ed. Yarm and King's Coll., Univ. of Durham.
Barrister; Lloyds Bank Ltd. until 39; Royal Air Force (Wing Commdr.), Second World War; Sec.-Gen. Inst. of Bankers 59-.
Institute of Bankers, 10 Lombard Street, London, E.C.3, England.

Eastland, James O.; American politician; b. 28 Nov. 1904; ed. Univs. of Mississippi and Alabama and Vanderbilt Univ.
Admitted to Mississippi Bar 27; Practised law; mem. Mississippi House of Reps. 28-32; Senator from Miss. 43-; Democrat.
Ruleville, Miss., U.S.A.

Eastman, Max, A.B.; American writer; b. 4 Jan. 1883; ed. Williams Coll. and Columbia Univ.
Assistant in Philosophy Columbia Univ. 07-10 and Assoc. in Philosophy 11-; Editor *The Masses* 13-17 and *The Liberator* 18-22; Roving Editor *The Reader's Digest* 42-; organised Men's League for Woman Suffrage in U.S. 10.
Publs. *Enjoyment of Poetry* 13, *Journalism Versus Art* 16, *Colours of Life* (poems) 18, *The Sense of Humour* 21, *Since Lenin Died* 25, *Marx and Lenin, the Science of Revolution* 26, *Venture* (novel) 27, *Kinds of Love* (poems) 31, *The Literary Mind* 32, *Artists in Uniform, Art and the Life of Action* 34, *Enjoyment of Laughter* 36, *The End of Socialism in Russia* 37, *From Czar to Lenin* (motion picture history) 37, *Stalin's Russia and the Crisis in Socialism* 39, *Marxism: Is it Science?* 40, *Heroes I Have Known* 42, *Lot's Wife* (dramatic poem) 42, *Enjoyment of Living* (autobiographical) 48; co-author with Jacob Rosin of *The Road to Abundance* 53,

Poems of Five Decades 54, *Reflections on the Failure of Socialism* 55, *Great Companions, Critical Memoirs of Some Famous Friends* 59, *Love and Revolution: My Journey through an Epoch* 65, *Seven Kinds of Goodness* 67; translated: Pushkin's *Gabriel* 29, Leon Trotsky's *The History of the Russian Revolution* 32; edited *Capital and Other Writings* by Karl Marx 32.
Chilmark, Mass., U.S.A.

Eaton, Cyrus Stephen, A.B., D.C.L., LL.D.; American industrialist and railroad executive; b. 27 Dec. 1883; ed. McMaster Univ., Toronto.
Co-founder Cliffs Corpn.; founder Republic Steel Corpn.; former Dir. Cleveland Trust Co., Republic Steel Corpn., Youngstown Sheet and Tube Co., Inland Steel, Nat. Acme; Chair. and Dir. Chesapeake and Ohio Rly., Steep Rock Iron Mines Ltd., West Kentucky Coal Co.; Chair. Pres. and Dir. Portsmouth Steel Corpn.; fmr. Dir. Sherwin-Williams Co., Cleveland Electric Illumination Co., Kansas City Power and Light Co.; Trustee, Denison Univ., Univ .of Chicago, Cleveland Museum of Natural History; mem. American Council of Learned Socs., American Historical Asscn., American Philosophical Asscn.; Dir. Harry S. Truman Library Inst. of Nat. and Int. Affairs; mem. Atlantic Province Econ. Council, Royal Norwegian Acad. of Sciences, American Acad. of Arts and Sciences.
Publs. *The Third Term "Tradition"* 40, *Financial Democracy* 41, *The Professor Talks to Himself* 42, *Investment Banking—Competition or Decadence?* 44, *A New Plan to Re-open the U.S. Capital Market* 45, *A Capitalist Looks At Labor* 47, *Is the Globe Big Enough for Capitalism and Communism?* 58, *Canada's Choice* 59, *The Engineer as Philosopher* 61.
Terminal Tower, Cleveland 44101; Home: Acadia Farms, Northfield, Ohio 44067, U.S.A.
Telephone: 216-861-2200 (office); 216-467-7125 (home).

Eban, Abba; Israeli diplomatist and politician; b. 2 Feb. 1915; ed. Univ. of Cambridge.
Apptd. Liaison Officer of Allied H.Q. with the Jewish population in Jerusalem 40; Chief Instructor at the Middle East Arab Centre in Jerusalem; entered service of Jewish Agency 46; apptd. Liaison Officer with U.N. Special Comm. on Palestine 47; apptd. by the Provisional Govt. of Israel as its rep. in the U.N. 48, permanent rep. with rank of Minister 49-59; Ambassador to U.S.A. 50-59; Minister without Portfolio 59-60; Minister of Educ. 60-63; Deputy Prime Minister 63-66; Minister of Foreign Affairs 66-; Pres. Weizmann Inst. of Science 58-66; M.A. (Cambridge); Hon. Dr. (Univs. of New York, Boston, Maryland, Cincinnati, Temple, etc.); Fellow World Acad. of Arts and Sciences, Fellow American Acad. of Arts and Sciences.
Publs. *The Modern Literary Movement in Egypt* 44, *Maze of Justice* 46, *Voice of Israel* 57, *Tide of Nationalism* 59, *Israel in the World* 66.
Ministry of Foreign Affairs, Jerusalem, Israel.
Telephone: 57211.

Ebdon, Hubert George; American engineer; b. 98; ed. Cooper Union and Brooklyn Polytechnic Inst.
Joined Combustion Eng. Inc., N.Y.C. 17, Sales Rep. 29-38, Asst. Sales Man. 38-40, Gen. Sales Man. 40-50, Vice-Pres. (Sales) 50-56, Exec. Vice-Pres. 56-57, Pres. 57-63, Vice-Chair. Board 63-; mem. various professional orgs.
277 Park Avenue, New York, N.Y. 10017, U.S.A.

Eberhard, Harmon Sewell; American manufacturer; b. 1900.
Joined Caterpillar Tractor Co. 16, successively Draftsman, Chief Engineer, Vice-Pres. Research, Eng. and

Mfg., Exec. Vice-Pres. 16-54, Pres. 54-, Chair. of Board 62-66; Dir. Central Illinois Light Co., Commercial Nat. Bank, Illinois Central Industries, Caterpillar Tractor Co., Whirlpool Corpn., Del Monte Corpn.
7618 North Edgewild Drive, Peoria, Ill., U.S.A.

Eberhart, Richard, M.A., LITT.D.; American poet; b. 5 April 1904; ed. Univ. of Minnesota, Dartmouth Coll., St. John's Coll., Cambridge and Harvard Univ.
Master of English, St. Mark's School, Southborough, Mass. 33-41, Cambridge School, Kendal Green, Mass, 41-42; Visiting Prof. of English and Poet in residence, Univ. of Washington 52-53; Prof. of English, Univ of Connecticut 53-54; inaugural Visiting Prof. of English, Poet in residence, Wheaton Coll., Norton, Mass. 54-55; Resident Fellow in Creative Writing, Christian Gauss Lecturer, Princeton 55-56; Prof. of English, Poet in residence, Dartmouth 56-; Consultant in Poetry, Library of Congress 59-61; mem. Nat. Inst. Arts and Letters 60, American Acad. Arts and Sciences 67; Founder and Pres. Poets' Theatre Inc., Cambridge, Mass. 51; Harriet Monroe Memorial Prize 50; Shelley Memorial Prize 51, Bollingen Prize 62; Pulitzer Prize 66; Hon. Consultant in American Letters, Library of Congress 1963-1966, 1966-1969.
Publs. *A Bravery of Earth* 30, *Reading the Spirit* 37, *Song and Idea* 42, *Poems New and Selected* 44, *Burr Oaks* 47, *Brotherhood of Men* 49, *An Herb Basket* 50, *Selected Poems* 51, *Undercliff* 53, *Great Praises* 57, *Collected Poems 1930-60* 60, *Collected Verse Plays* 62, *The Quarry* 64, *Selected Poems 1930-65* 65, *New Directions* 65, *Thirty One Sonnets* 67, *Shifts of Being* 68.
5 Webster Terrace, Hanover, New Hampshire, U.S.A.

Eberle, Josef; German newspaper publisher; b. 01; ed. Grammar School, Rottenburg.
Fmr. bookseller; with Radio Stuttgart until 33; served American consulate, Stuttgart until 42; publisher and ed. *Stuttgarter Zeitung* 45-; Pres. Württemberger Bibliotheksgesellschaft and Galerie-Verein, Stuttgart; Vice-Pres. Deutsche Schillergesellschaft, Stuttgart-Marbach; mem. Deutsche Akad. Darmstadt, Pen Club; Prof. Dr. phil. h.c. Tübingen.
Publs. *Interview mit Cicero, Laudes, Stunden mit Ovid, Ovid, Heilmittel* (translation), *Amores* (Latin poetry), *Sal Niger* (100 Epigrams, Latin and German). *Lateinische Nächte* (essays).
Rosengartenstrasse 9, Stuttgart-Frauenkopf, German Federal Republic.
Telephone: 299-171.

Ebert, Carl (Anton Charles), C.B.E. American (b. German) opera director; b. 20 Feb. 1887; ed. Max Reinhardt's School of Dramatic Art, Berlin.
Began career as actor at Max Reinhardts Deutsches Theater, Berlin 09-14; Schauspielhaus, Frankfurt a.M. 15-22, Staatstheater, Berlin 22-27; Founder, Dir., teacher in Schools of Dramatic Art in Frankfurt 19, and Berlin (Prof.) 25; acted in silent films, recited European Literature; parts included Faust, Egmont, Lear, Brutus, Petruchio, Peer Gynt, etc.; Gen. Dir. and Producer, Hess. Landestheater 27-31, Städtische Oper, Berlin, 31-33; left Germany because of Nazi régime March 33, acted Zürich and Basle, Guest Producer Basle, Salzburg Festival, State Opera and Burgtheater Vienna, Arena Verona 32-38; Maggio Musicale Florence 33-37, Teatro Colon Buenos Aires 33-36; Artistic Dir. and Producer Glyndebourne Opera 34-59, of Glyndebourne productions at Edinburgh Festivals 47-55; Adviser to Turkish Ministry of Educ., Founder Dir. (and teacher) Turkish State School of Opera and Drama, Ankara 36- and Turkish Nat. Theatre, Ankara 39-47; Prof. and Head Opera Dept., Univ. of Southern Calif., Los Angeles 48-54; Artistic Dir. and Producer Guild Opera Co., Los Angeles 50-; Gen. Dir. and Producer Städtische Oper, Berlin 54-61; Pres. German section of Int. Theatre Inst., Berlin 56-61; Guest Producer London,

Milan, Ankara, Venice, Paris, New York, Copenhagen 47-59; Biennale world première Stravinsky's *The Rake's Progress*; Producer Metropolitan Opera New York, Glyndebourne Opera England, also Zürich, Ireland, Copenhagen, Deutsche Oper, Berlin 61-67; Master Class in Opera, B.B.C. T.V. London 65; Hon. mem. Deutsche Oper Berlin, Staatstheater Darmstadt; Board of Dirs. Opera Guild of S. California, Int. Theatre Inst.; Hon. Mus.D., Edinburgh Univ. 54; Hon. D. Fine Arts, Univ. of Southern Calif. 55; Ernst Reuter Plakette, Berlin 57; Knight of Dannebrog, Denmark 59; Grosses Verdienstkreuz mit Stern, Germany 59; Grosses Ehrenzeichen, Austria 59; Hon. C.B.E. 60; Commendatore Ordine Al Merito, Italy 66.
809 Enchanted Way, Pacific Palisades (Los Angeles), Calif.; and c/o Huttenback Artist Bureau, Philharmonic Auditorium, Los Angeles 13, Calif., U.S.A.

Ebert, Friedrich; German politician; b. 18 Sept. 1894; ed. elementary and secondary schools.
Book printer by trade; war service in First World War; Editor of *Brandenburger Zeitung* 25-33; mem. of Reichstag 28-33; imprisoned in concentration camps; official of Social Democratic Party 45; elected to Brandenburg Diet as mem. of Socialist Unity Party (SED) 46, mem. Politburo 50-; mem. German-Soviet Friendship Soc. 50-58; mem. State Council 60-; Pres. of Diet 64; elected to German People's Council March 48; Lord Mayor of Berlin (Eastern Sector) Nov. 48-July 67; mem. of the Volkskammer 50-.
Wahnschaffestrasse 11, Berlin-Pankow, Germany.

Eberts, Christopher Campbell, B.A.; Canadian diplomatist; b. 13; ed. Bishop's and Oxford Univs.
Assistant Sec., Canadian Inst. of Int. Affairs, Toronto 38-40; Dept. of External Affairs 40-, Third Sec. 40, Vice-Consul, St. Pierre et Miquelon 41, Dept. of External Affairs, Ottawa 42, Second Sec. Legation to Allied Govts., London 43, to Mexico 44-48; Jt. Board of Defence 48-50; Sec. Cabinet Defence Cttee. 50-52; Consul-Gen., San Francisco 53; High Commr. in Pakistan 60-63; Acting Under-Sec. of State, Dept. for External Affairs 63-64; Chief of Protocol 64-.
Department for External Affairs, Ottawa, Canada.

Eble, Charles E.; American business executive; b. 23 Nov. 1900; ed. Alexander Hamilton School of Business Administration.
Consolidated Gas Co. (from 36 called Consolidated Edison Co. of N.Y.) 16-, Asst. Controller 35-46, Controller 46-53, Vice-Pres. 53-57, Pres. and Trustee 57-; Dir. East River Savings Bank, Empire State Atomic Development Associates, Inc.; Trustee New York City Museum of Science and Technology, etc.
Consolidated Edison Company of New York, 4 Irving Place, New York 3; 1161 York Avenue, New York, N.Y., U.S.A.

Eboo Pirbhai, Sir, Kt., O.B.E.; Kenyan company director; b. 25 July 1905; ed. Duke of Gloucester School, Nairobi.
Representative of Aga Khan in Africa; mem. Nairobi City Council 38-43; mem. Legislative Council, Kenya 52-60; Pres. Muslim Asscn.; Pres. Aga Khan Supreme Council, Africa; mem. other official bodies; Brilliant Star of Zanzibar 56.
P.O.B. 898, Nairobi; and 12 Naivasha Avenue, Muthaiga, Nairobi, Kenya.

Ebtehaj, Abol Hassan; Iranian banker and administrator; b. 29 Nov. 1899; ed. Paris and Beirut.
Joined Imperial Bank of Iran 20; Govt. Inspector Agricultural Bank and Controller of State-owned Cos. 36; Vice-Gov. Bank Melli Iran 38; Chair. and Man. Dir. Mortgage Bank 40; Gov. Bank Melli Iran (National Bank of Persia) 42-50; Chair. Persian Del. Middle East Financial and Monetary Conf., Cairo 44; Chair. Persian Del. Bretton Woods Conf. 44; Am-

bassador to France 50-52: Adviser to Man. Dir. Int. Monetary Fund 52; Dir. Middle East Dept., Int. Monetary Fund 53; Man. Dir. Plan Organisation (Development Board), Teheran 54-59; Chair. and Pres. Iranians' Bank (private bank) 59-.
Iranians' Bank, Khiaban, Hafez, Teheran, Iran.
Telephone: 851299, 46786.

Eccles, 1st Viscount (cr. 64), of Chute, 1st Baron (cr. 62); **David McAdam Eccles,** K.C.V.O., P.C., M.A.; British politician; b. 18 Sept. 1904; ed. Winchester and New Coll., Oxford.
Mem. staff Central Mining and Investment Corpn. 23-39; joined Min. of Economic Warfare Sept. 39; Economic Adviser to H.M. Ambassadors in Madrid and Lisbon 39-42; Ministry of Production 42-43; Conservative M.P. for Chippenham Div. of Wilts. Aug. 43-62; Minister of Works 51-54, of Education 54-57; Pres. Board of Trade 57-59; Minister of Education 59-62; Dir. Courtaulds Ltd. 62-; Chair. West Cumberland Silk Mills Ltd. 64-, Trustees of the British Museum.
Publs. *Wages on the Farm* 45, *Half-Way to Faith* 66, *Life and Politics* 67.
Dean Farm, Chute, nr. Andover, Hampshire, England.
Telephone: 01-930-1387 (Office); Chute Standen 210 (Home).

Eccles, Sir John Carew, Kt., M.B., B.S., D.PHIL., F.R.A.C.P., F.R.S.N.Z., F.A.A., F.R.S.; Australian research physiologist; b. 27 Jan. 1903; ed. Melbourne Univ., Magdalen Coll., Oxford.
Rhodes Scholar 25; Junior Research Fellow, Exeter Coll., Oxford 27-32, Staines Medical Fellow 32-34; Fellow and Tutor, Magdalen Coll., Oxford, lecturer in physiology 34-37; Dir. Kanematsu Memorial Inst. of Pathology, Sydney, Australia 37-43; Prof. of Physiology, Otago Univ., New Zealand 44-51, Australian Nat. Univ., Canberra 51-66; at AMA/ERF Inst. for Biomedical Research, Chicago 66-; Waynflete lecturer, Oxford 52; Herter lecturer, Johns Hopkins Univ., Baltimore 55; Foreign Hon. mem. American Acad. of Arts and Sciences, Accademia Nazionale dei Lincei, Deutsche Akad. der Naturforscher Leopoldina; mem. Pontifical Acad. of Sciences, American Philosophical Soc.; Ferrier Lecturer, Royal Soc. 60; Pres. Australian Acad. of Science 57-61; Cothenius Medal; Hon. Fellow Exeter Coll. and Magdalen Coll., Oxford, Hon. Fellow New York Acad. of Sciences; Hon. Sc.D. (Cambridge, Tasmania, Univ. British Columbia, Gustavus Adolphus Coll.), Hon. LL.D. (Melbourne); Royal Medal, Royal Soc. 62, Nobel Prize for Medicine 63.
Publs. *Reflex Activity of the Spinal Cord* (in collaboration) 32, *Neurophysiological Basis of Mind* 53, *Physiology of Nerve Cells* 57, *Physiology of Synapses* 64, *The Cerebellum as a Neuronal Machine* 67.
Institute for Biomedical Research, 535 N. Dearborn Street, Chicago, Ill. 60610, U.S.A.
Telephone: 312-527-1500, extension 282.

Eccles, Marriner Stoddard; American financier and business executive; b. 9 Sept. 1890; ed. in district schools and at Brigham Young Coll.
Organized Eccles Investment Co. 16, Vice-Pres. and Gen. Man. 16-29, Pres. 29-; Pres. First Nat. Bank of Ogden and Ogden Savings Bank and Successor Banks 20-34, Utah Bankers' Asscn. 24-25; organised First Security Corpn., a bank holding co., Pres. 28-34, Chair. 51-; Chair. Amalgamated Sugar Co., First Security Bank of Utah, N.A., Utah Construction Mining Co.; Pres., Eccles Investment Co. 29-; Dir. First Security Investment Co., Marcona Mining Co., Cía. San Juan, S.A., Utah Home Fire Insurance Co., and many other companies; Asst. to Sec. of Treasury 34; Gov. Fed. Reserve Board 34-36; mem. Board of Govs. Fed. Reserve System 34-51, Chair. 36-48; U.S. Del. Bretton Woods 44; mem. Board of Econ. Stabilisation 42-46, Nat. Advisory Council on Int. Monetary and Finan-

cial Problems 45-48, Advisory Board of Export-Import Bank 45-48; mem. of Comm. on Money and Credit 58-61, Advisory Comm. on Econ. Policy of Democratic Advisory Council 57-60; Dir. Planned Parenthood-World Population 60-; sponsor, The Atlantic Council 62-; Hon. LL.D. (Univ. of Utah) 43, Hon. LL.D. (Utah State Univ.) 63; Elector of Hall of Fame 45-; Trustee the American Assembly of Columbia Univ. 59-.
Publ. *Beckoning Frontiers.*
Office: First Security Bank of Utah, N.A., Main at First South, Salt Lake City, Utah, and Utah Construction and Mining Co., 550 California Street, San Francisco, Calif.; Home: Hotel Utah, Salt Lake City, Utah and 290 Lombard Street, San Francisco, Calif., U.S.A.

Ecevit, Bülent, B.A.; Turkish journalist and politician; b. 25; ed. Robert Coll., Istanbul, and Harvard Univ.
Govt. official 44-50, Turkish Press Attaché's Office 46-50; Foreign News Ed., Man. Ed., later Political Dir. *Ulus* (Ankara) 50-62, Political Columnist, *Ulus* 56-62; M.P. (Republican People's Party) 57-60, Oct. 61-; mem. Constituent Assembly 61; Minister of Labour 61-65; Political Columnist *Milliyet* 65-; Sec.-Gen. Republican People's Party Oct. 66-.
6 Sokak 37, Bahçelievler, Ankara, Turkey.

Echandi Jiménez, Mario, LL.D.; Costa Rican diplomatist and politician; b. 1915; ed. Univ. of Costa Rica.
Legal career 38-47; Sec.-Gen. Partido Unión Nacional 47; Ambassador to U.S.A. 50-51, 66-68; Minister for Foreign Affairs 51-53; Presidential candidate 53; mem. Nat. Assembly 53-58; President of Costa Rica 58-62.
San José, Costa Rica.

Echeverria, Lic. Luis; Mexican lawyer and politician; b. 17 Jan. 1922; ed. Univ. Nacional Autónoma de México.
Private Sec. to Pres. of Exec. Cttee. of Partido Revolucionario Institucional (PRI) 40-52, also Dir. of Press and Propaganda, PRI 49-52; Dir. of Accounts and Admin., Sec. of Marine 52-54; Senior Official, Sec. of Public Educ. 54-57; Senior Official, Central Exec. Cttee. of PRI 57; Under-Sec. of Interior 58-63, Sec. of Interior 63-; Asst. Prof. of Law, Univ. Nac. de México.
Secretaría de Gobernación, Mexico, D.F., Mexico.

Echeverria G., Rafael; Venezuelan diplomatist; b. 14 Dec. 1903.
President of Municipal Council of District of Maracaibo 45-47; several diplomatic posts; Vice-Pres. Fed. of Chambers of Commerce and Production 59-60, Pres. 60-61; Ambassador to Trinidad and Tobago 63-, and also to Jamaica 65-.
Embassy of Venezuela, 18 Victoria Avenue, Port-of-Spain, Trinidad; Home: 1-3 Wainwright Street, St. Clair, Port-of-Spain, Trinidad, W.I.
Telephone: 22215.

Eck, Hendrik Johannes van, M.SC., DR.ING., M.I.CHEM.E.; South African business executive; b. 27 April 1902; ed. Boys' High School, Wellington, Cape Province, and Univs. of Stellenbosch, Leipzig and Charlottenburg.
Chairman: Industrial & Agricultural Requirements Comm. 40-44, Social and Econ. Planning Council 42-52, Social Security Cttee. 43, Nat. Feeds Ltd. 43-51, Industrial Devt. Corpn. of South Africa Ltd. 44-, Fine Wool Products of South Africa Ltd. 45-56, Good Hope Textile Corpn. (Pty.) Ltd. 46-, Consolidated African Industries Ltd. 47-51, Comm. on Conditions of Employment in the Gold Mining Industry 48, Ubombo Ranches Ltd. 49-, South African Industrial Cellulose Corpn. (Pty.) 52-, Advisory and Co-ordinating Cttee. of Council for Scientific and Industrial Research and S.A. Bureau of Standards 54, Nat. Cancer Fund 54, Comm. of Inquiry into Oil Pipeline Project 55-58, Research Advisory

Cttee. of Atomic Energy Board 56-, Board of Trustees of Nat. Cancer Asscn. of S.A. 56-, Industrial Finance Corpn. of S.A. Ltd. 57-, Swaziland Sugar Milling Co. Ltd. 58-, Accepting Bank for Industry Ltd. 58-, Phosphate Devt. Corpn. Ltd. 61-, Industrial Selections Ltd. 62-, Nuclear Power Cttee. of Atomic Energy Board 63-, Safbulk (Proprietary) Ltd. 63-65, South African Financial Gazette Ltd. 64-, Munitions Production Board 64-, Resabi Investments Ltd. 64-, S.A.W. Water-en Elektrisiteitskorporasie (Eiendoms) Beperk 65-, Van Eck Beleggings (Eiendoms) Beperk 65-, Fund Advisers Ltd. 65-, South African Iron & Steel Industrial Corpn. Ltd. 66-, African Metals Corpn. Ltd. 66-, Vanderbijl Eng. Corpn. Ltd. 66-, Elektrode Maatskappy van Suid-Afrika (Eiendoms) Beperk 66-.
37 First Avenue, Houghton, Johannesburg, South Africa.

Eckardt, Felix von; German journalist; b. 18 June 1903.
With *Hamburger Fremdenblatt* and *Münchener neueste Nachrichten* 24-26; foreign correspondent of *Verlag Ullstein* 26-29; Press Attaché, German Embassy in Brussels 29-32; employed in film industry 33-45; f. *Weser-Kurier* in Bremen 45 and became Editor-in-Chief; Head of Press and Information Dept., German Federal Govt. 52-55; Perm. Observer to UN 55-56; Head of Press and Information Dept., German Fed. Govt. 56-62; Fed. German Representative in Berlin 62-65; mem. Bundestag 65-; Christian Democrat.
532 Bad Godesberg, Am Steubenring 4, German Federal Republic.

Eckerberg, Per, B.A.; Swedish civil servant; b. 17 Aug. 1913; ed. Univ. of Lund.
Secretary, Public Comm. on Population 44-46; Ministry of Social Affairs 48-50, Under-Sec. of State 50-56; Gov., Province of Ostergötland 56-; Pres. of Bd., Swedish Broadcasting Corpn. 56-; Rep. to ILO Confs. 51-57; Pres. Bank of Sweden 56-57; Pres. of Bd., Göta Canal 57; Pres. Swedish Savings Bank Asscn. 61, Nat. Supplementary Pensions Fund 60, Cttee. for Labour Market Policy 61; Editor *Tiden* 47-49.
Castle of Linköping, Linköping, Sweden.

Eckert, J. Presper, Jr., M.A.; American engineer; b. 9 April 1919; ed. William Penn Charter School and Univ. of Pennsylvania.
Research Assoc., Moore School of Electrical Eng., Univ. of Pa. 41-46; co-designer, co-inventor Electronic Numerical Integrator and Calculator—ENIAC (with Dr. J. W. Mauchly) 42-46; Co-designer, co-inventor automatic computers BINAC 46-49, UNIVAC 48-51; Partner, Electronic Control Co. 46-47; Vice-Pres. Eckert-Mauchly Computer Corpn. 47-50; Dir. of Eng., Eckert-Mauchly Div. Remington Rand Inc. 50-54; Vice-Pres. (Eng.) Remington Rand Inc. 54-55; now Vice-Pres. UNIVAC Div., Sperry Rand Corpn.
Sperry Rand Building, 1290 Avenue of the Americas, New York City, N.Y. 10019, U.S.A.

Eckhardt, Alexander (Sándor), DR. PHIL.; Hungarian literary historian; b. 23 Dec. 1890; ed. Grammar school, Arad, and Budapest Univ.
Prof. at Eötvös Coll. 14-23; Prof. of French Language and Literature Budapest Univ. 23-58, Emer. 58-.
Publs. *Remy Belleau, A francia forradalom eszméi Magyarországon, De Sicambria à Sans-Souci, Histoires et légendes Franco-Hongroises, Balassi Bálint, Az ismeretlen Balassi, Attila a mondában, Dictionnaire Français-Hongrois, Oeuvres Complètes de V. Balassi, Le génie français, Dictionnaire Hongrois-Français, Rimay János összes müvei, Bornemisza Péter: Ördögi kisértetek, Ujabb fejezetek Balassi B. viharos életéböl, Le cercueil flottant de Mahomet, La préface primitive des Essais, Balassi Bálint Szép Magyar Komédiája, Torony i Tamás.*
Maros utca 36, Budapest XII, Hungary.
Telephone: 359-327.

Eckhardt, Felix, D.IUR.; German businessman; b. 13 Nov. 1896; ed. Jena and Munich Univs.
Law practice in Cologne 30-; mem. of Board, Dortmunder Union-Brauerei Aktiengesellschaft 38-42, Chair. 42-; Pres. Deutscher Brauer-Bund 49-51, Dir. 51-; mem. of Board, Bundesverband der Deutschen Industrie 52-58; Chair. Kurfürsten-Bräu Aktiengesellschaft, Bonn, Apollinaris Brunnen Aktiengesellschaft, Bad-Neuenahr, Apollinaris Overseas Ltd., London, Dortmunder Hotelgesellschaft, Presta Overseas Ltd., Grubenvorstand der Gewerkschaft Philippine, Dortmund 50-; mem. of Board, Dortmund-Hörder Hüttenunion A.G., Markenverband 52-, Siepmann-Werke A.G., Belecke-Möhne 58-.
Rote Beckerstrasse 31, Dortmund, German Federal Republic.

Eckman, Samuel, Jr.; former American motion picture and television consultant; ed. New York Public Schools and Coll. of City of New York.
Entered film industry as exhibitor in N.Y.; later elected Vice-Pres. Goldwyn Distributing Corpn.; with formation Metro-Goldwyn-Mayer, in charge New England, New Jersey and New York Districts; Man. Dir. Metro-Goldwyn-Mayer, London 27-54, Chair. until 57; fmr. Pres. Cinema Veterans, London; mem. Advisory Cttee. Royal Naval Film Corpn., mem. Motion Pictures Pioneers, New York; Hon. C.B.E. (U.K.) 47.
London, England.

Eckstein, Otto, PH.D.; American economist; b. 1 Aug. 1927; ed. Princeton and Harvard Univs.
U.S. Army 46-47; Instructor, Harvard Univ. 55-57, Asst. Prof. 57-60, Assoc. Prof. 60-63, Prof. of Econs. 63-; Technical Dir., Study of Employment, Growth and Price Levels, Joint Econ. Cttee., U.S. Congress 59-60; mem. Council of Econ. Advisers, Exec. Office of the Pres. 64-66.
Publs. *Water Resource Development: The Economics of Project Evaluation* 58, *Multiple Purpose River Development* (with J. V. Krutilla) 58, *Staff Report on Employment, Growth, and Price Levels* (with others) 59, *Economic Policy in Our Time: An International Comparison* (with others) 64, *Public Finance: Budgets, Taxes, Fiscal Policy* 64.
Department of Economics, Littauer Center, Harvard University, Cambridge 38, Massachusetts, U.S.A.

Eco, Umberto; Italian publisher; b. 5 Jan. 1932; ed. Univ. degli Studi, Turin.
With Italian Television 54-59; Asst. Lecturer in Aesthetics, Univ. of Turin 56-63, Lecturer 63-64; Lecturer Faculty of Architecture, Univ. of Milan 64-65; Prof. of Aesthetics, Univ. of Florence 66-67; Dir. Non-Fiction Dept. Casa Editrice Bompiani 59-67; Columnist on *L'Espresso* 65-.
Publs. *Il Problema Estetico in San Tommaso* 56, *Sviluppo dell'Estetica Medievale* 59, *Opera Aperta* 62, *Diario Minimo* 63, *Apocalittici e Integrati* 64, *L'Oeuvre Ouverte* 65.
Via Pisacane 12, Milan, Italy.
Telephone: 73-83-460.

Economides, Constantine; Greek journalist; b. 95; ed. Athens University.
Journalist 13-; Theatre Critic, *Ethnos* 15-, Editor 37-; mem. Artistic Cttee. Nat. Theatre 46-50; translator of numerous plays.
2 Zaimi Street, Athens, Greece.

Economou-Gouras, Paul; Greek diplomatist; b. 98; ed. Athens Univ.
Entered Foreign Service 21, served Belgrade, Paris, Lyon, London, Moscow, Bucharest, Ankara, Iran, Portugal, Rome, Washington 22-49, Minister to Brazil 50-52, to Union of South Africa 52-55; Dir. 3rd Political Div. Royal Ministry of Foreign Affairs 55-56; Chair. Cttee. of Treaty of Ankara 56; Dir. Gen. Ministry of Foreign Affairs 58-60; Perm. Rep. to UN 60-61;

Amb. to Belgium 62-63; Minister of Foreign Affairs Sept. 63-Nov. 63, 66-67, 67-Oct. 67; Leader of Del. which concluded Greek-Bulgarian Agreements 64; Grand Officer of the Royal Order of George I, Grand Officer of the Royal Order of the Phoenix, foreign decorations.

Publ. *The Truman Doctrine and the Agony of Greece* 57.
Patesion 235, Athens, Greece.

Edberg, Rolf; Swedish journalist, diplomatist and administrator; b. 14 March 1912.
Chief Editor *Oskarshamns Nyheter* 34-37; Asst. Editor *Östgöten*, Linköping 38-40, Chief Editor 41-45; Chief Editor *Ny Tid*, Gothenburg 45-56; mem. Parl. 41-44 and 49-56; Del. to U.N. 52-61; Ambassador to Norway 56-67; Gov. Province of Värmland 67-; Rep. to Council of Europe 49-52, to Scandinavian Council 53-56; Pres. Swedish Press Club 51-53; Del. Disarmament Conf. 62-65.
Publs. Author of several works on political and philosophical matters.
Länsstyrelsen, Karlstad, Sweden.
Telephone: 15070.

Edel, (Joseph) Leon, M.A., D. ès L.; American writer and teacher; b. 9 Sept. 1907; ed. Yorkton Collegiate Inst., Saskatchewan, McGill Univ. and Univ. of Paris.
Graduate Asst. in English, McGill Univ. 27-28; Asst. Prof. Sir George Williams Univ., Montreal 32-34; journalism and broadcasting 34-43; U.S. Army 43-47; Adjunct Prof., New York Univ. 50-53, Assoc. Prof. 53-55, Prof. of English 55-66; Henry James Prof. of English and American Letters 66-; Fellow American Acad. of Arts and Sciences, Sec. Nat. Inst. of Arts and Letters 65-67, Pres. U.S. P.E.N. 57-59, Council Authors Guild 66-68; mem. Advisory Board Guggenheim Foundation 67-68; Hon. mem. William Alanson White Psychoanalytic Soc. 67-; Fellow American Studies Asscn.; Hon. D.Litt. (Union Coll., Schenectady, N.Y., and McGill Univ.); Pulitzer Prize (biography) 63, Nat. Book Award (non-fiction) 63.
Publs. *The Life of Henry James (I The Untried Years* 53, *II The Conquest of London* 62, *III The Middle Years* 62), *Willa Cather* (with E. K. Brown) 53, *The Psychological Novel* 55, *Literary Biography* 57; Editor: *The Complete Plays of Henry James* 49, *Selected Letters of Henry James* 55, *The Complete Tales of Henry James* (12 vols.) 62-65, *The Diary of Alice James* 64, *Literary History and Literary Criticism* 64, *The American Scene* 68.
19 University Place, New York University, New York, N.Y. 10003, U.S.A.
Telephone: 598-1212.

Edelmann, Otto Karl; Austrian opera singer; b. 5 Feb. 1917; ed. Realgymnasium and State Acad. of Music, Vienna.
First opera appearances 38; P.O.W. in U.S.S.R. two years during Second World War; mem. Vienna State Opera 48-; with Salzburg Festival 48-; perm. mem. Metropolitan Opera New York 54-; took part in first Bayreuth Festival 51; world-famous as *Sachs* in Meistersinger; Knight Order of Dannebrog.
Vienna 23, Breitenfurterstrasse 547, Austria.

Edenman, Ragnar H. L., PH.D.; Swedish politician; b. 1 April 1914.
Mem. Municipal Council of Uppsala 43-50; Mem. Parl. 49-; Pres. of Cttees. on wider access to higher education 46-48, support to good literature 48-52, secondary schools 54-55, development of the univs. 55-57, comprehensive schools 57-61; Minister of Church Affairs and Education 57-67.
Home: Väderkvarnsgatan 22, B Uppsala, Sweden.
Telephone: 018-133451 (Home).

Edgar-Bonnet, George; D. en D.; French company director; b. 9 Nov. 1881; ed. Lycée Janson-de-Sailly, the Sorbonne, and Ecole des Sciences Politiques.

Sec.-Gen. Suez Canal Co. 20, Dir. 26, Dir.-Gen. 34, Administrator 46-; Vice-Pres. Air France 33; Commdr. de la Légion d'Honneur; Croix de Guerre.
Publs. *Les Expériences Monétaires Contemporaines, Ferdinand de Lesseps* (Grand Prix d'Histoire de l'Académie Française) 51.
33 Avenue Georges-Mandel, Paris 16e, France.

Edgerton, William Franklin, A.B., PH.D.; American egyptologist; b. 30 Sept. 1893; ed. Cornell Univ., Univs. of Chicago, Pennsylvania, Columbia and Munich.
Sergeant Medical Dept. U.S. Army 18-19; mem. Archeological Survey Mesopotamia and Syria, Oriental Inst., Univ. of Chicago 20; Asst. Oriental Inst. 22-23; Asst. Prof. Ancient History Univ. of Louisville 24-25; Associate Prof. of History Vassar Coll. 25-26; epigrapher Epigraphic and Architectural Survey, Oriental Inst., Univ. of Chicago, Luxor 26-29; Associate Prof. of Egyptology Univ. of Chicago 29-37, Prof. 37-59, Emeritus 59-; Chair. Dept. Oriental Languages and Literatures, Univ. of Chicago 48-54; Visiting Prof. Univ. of Calif. 65-67; served Signal Corps, U.S. Army, 42-45; mem. Council, American Asscn. of Univ. Profs. 53-56.
Publs. *Earlier Historical Records of Rameses III* (with H. H. Nelson, J. A. Wilson and others) 30, *Notes on Egyptian Marriage, Chiefly in the Ptolemaic Period* 31, *The Thutmosid Succession* 33, *Medinet Habu Graffiti Facsimiles* 37, etc.
Home: 1321 East Hyde Park Blvd., Chicago 60415; Oriental Institute, University of Chicago, Chicago 37, Ill., U.S.A.
Telephone: 212-FA4-333.

Edinburgh, H.R.H. The Prince Philip, Duke of, Earl of Merioneth and Baron Greenwich of Greenwich in the County of London (all titles cr. 47), created Prince of the United Kingdom of Great Britain and Northern Ireland 57, K.G., K.T., O.M.; b. 10 June 1921; ed. Cheam School, Salem (Baden), Gordonstoun School and Royal Naval Coll., Dartmouth.
Served 39-45 war with Mediterranean Fleet in Home Waters and with British Pacific Fleet in S.E. Asia and Pacific; renounced right of succession to the Thrones of Greece and Denmark and was naturalised a British subject 47, adopting the surname of Mountbatten; married Nov. 20th 47 H.R.H. Princess Elizabeth (now H.M. Queen Elizabeth II), elder daughter of H.M. King George VI; Personal A.D.C. to H.M. King George VI 48-52; Privy Councillor 51; Chancellor, Univ. of Wales 48-, Univ. of Edinburgh 52-; Visitor, Royal Coll. of Art 67-; Admiral of the Fleet, F.M. and Marshal of the R.A.F. Jan. 53; received Freedom of City of London and of the Borough of Greenwich 48, of Edinburgh 48, of Belfast 49, of Cardiff 52, of Glasgow 55, of Melbourne (Australia) 56, of Dar es Salaam (Tanzania) 61, of Nairobi (Kenya) 63, of Guadalajara and Acapulco (Mexico) 64, Bridgetown (Barbados) 64; Lord High Steward of Plymouth 60-; Freeman and Liveryman of the Worshipful Company of Fishmongers 47, of Worshipful Company of Shipwrights 48 (Perm. Master 55); Grand Master of the Guild of Air Pilots and Air Navigators 52-; Freeman, Company of Mercers 53, Liveryman 59; Admiral, Hon. Company of Master Mariners 57; Greek War Cross; 1939-45 Atlantic, Africa, Italy and Burma (with Pacific Rosette) Stars; 1939-45 War Medal (with Oak Leaf); Croix de Guerre (with Palm Leaf) 48, Grand Master, O.B.E. 53; Grand Cross Orders of St. Charles of Monaco 51, St. Olaf of Norway 52, Manuel Amador Guerrero (Panama) 53, Tower and Sword (civil) (Portugal) 55, King Faisal I (Iraq) 56, Légion d'Honneur (France) 57, Netherlands Lion 58, Merit (1st Class) (German Fed. Repub.) 58, San Martin (Argentina) 62, Condor of Bolivia 62, Boyaca (Colombia) 62, Merit (Ecuador) 62, Sun (with Brilliantes) (Peru) 62, Icelandic Falcon 64; Knight Grand Cross Order of Merit (Italy) 58; Knight Grand

Band Star of Africa (Liberia) 61; Knight Order of the Elephant of Denmark 47, Orders of the Redeemer, St. George and St. Constantine (Greek Royal Household) Fourth Class (with Swords), Phoenix of Greece; mem. Order of the Seraphim of Sweden 54; Chain of the Most Exalted Order of the Queen of Sheba (Ethiopia) 54; Order of Ojaswae Rajanya of Nepal 60; Order of Merit (1st Class) (Brazil) 62; Chain of Chilean Order of Merit 62; Nat. Order of Merit (Paraguay) 62; Grand Cordon of Order of Leopold of Belgium 63; Order of Brilliant Star of Zanzibar (1st Class) 63; Decoration of the Repub. of Sudan (1st Class) 64; Collar of the Aztec Eagle of Mexico 64; Order of Al Nahda Jordan 66; Hon. LL.D. (Univs. of Wales, London, Edinburgh, Cambridge, Karachi and Malta); Hon. D.C.L. (Univs. of Durham and Oxford); Hon. D.Sc. (Univs. of Delhi and Reading); Hon. Degree (Eng. Univ., Lima, Peru); Pres. British Medical Asscn. 59.

Publs. *Birds from Britannia* 62.

Buckingham Palace, London, S.W.1, England.

Edison, Charles; American industrialist; b. 3 Aug. 1890; ed. Carteret Acad., N.J., Hotchkiss School, Lakeville, Conn. and Massachusetts Inst. of Technology. Joined Thomas A. Edison, Inc. 13, Pres. 26-50, Chair. Board 50-57; Chair. Board McGraw-Edison 57-61; Fmr. Dir. Jones and Laughlin Steel Co.; Reg. Dir. Fed. Housing Admin. 34-36; Asst. Sec. to Navy 37-39; Sec. to Navy Dec. 39-June 40; Gov. of New Jersey 41-44; Hon. LL.D. (John Marshall Coll., Jersey City 40, Newark Univ. and Rutgers Univ. 41, Upsala Coll., East Orange 43, Hobart and William Smith Coll., Geneva, N.Y. 44, Lafayette Coll., Easton 45); Hon. Dr.Eng. (Stevens Inst. of Technology, N.J. 49); Hon. Dr. Comm. Sc. (New York Univ. 50); Hon. Dr. of Humanities (Indiana Technical Coll. 56).

Apt. 36A, The Waldorf-Astoria Towers, Park Avenue and 50th Street, New York, N.Y. 10022, U.S.A.

Edlén, Bengt, DR.PHIL.; Swedish university professor; b. 2 Nov. 1906; ed. Uppsala Univ.

Asst. Physics Dept., Uppsala Univ. 28, Asst. Prof. 34; Prof. of Physics, Lund Univ. 44-; mem. Swedish, Danish, Norwegian Acads. of Sciences, American Acad. of Arts and Sciences, etc.; Commandeur de l'Ordre des Palmes Académiques; Hon. D.Sc.(Kiel); awards in recognition of research on atomic spectra with applications to astrophysical problems, including the solar corona, include: Arrhenius Gold Medal of Swedish Acad. of Sciences, Gold Medal of Royal Astronomical Soc., London, H. N. Potts Medal of Franklin Inst., Philadelphia, Mees Medal of Optical Soc. of America, Henry Draper Medal of Nat. Acad. of Sciences, Washington.

Physics Department, University of Lund, Lund, Sweden. Telephone: 046-111037.

Edusei, Krobo; Ghanaian politician; b. 15; ed. Govt. Boys' School, Kumasi.

Fmr. reporter and debt collector on *Ashanti Pioneer*; appointed Regional Propaganda Sec. of Ashanti Convention People's Party and Chair. Boycott Cttee. in Ashanti during anti-inflation campaign; imprisoned 50 during "Positive Action"; elected M.P. for Kumasi North-West 51; subsequently Govt. Chief Whip and Ministerial Sec., Ministry of Justice; C.P.P. Nat. Propaganda Sec. 54; Minister Without Portfolio 56-57; Minister of the Interior 57-58, of Transport and Communications 58-61, for Ceremonies 60-61, of Light and Heavy Industry 61-62, of Agriculture 62-65; Chief of State Protocol 65-66.

c/o Office of State Protocol, Accra, Ghana.

Edwards, Corwin D.; American politician and university professor; b. 1 Nov. 1901; ed. Univ. of Missouri, Oxford (England) and Cornell Univs.

Assistant Prof. of Econs., New York Univ. 26-33; Economist and Technical Dir. Consumers Advisory Board, Nat. Recovery Administration 33-35, Coordinator, Trade Practice Studies 35; Economist President's Cttee. on Industrial Analysis 36; Asst. Chief Economist, Fed. Trade Comm. 37-39; Chief of Staff, American Technical Mission to Brazil 42-43; Economist, Chair. Policy Board, Anti-Trust Div., Dept. of Justice 39-44; Consultant on Cartels, Dept. of State 43-48; Head Mission on Japanese Combines 46; Dir. Bureau of Econs., Fed. Trade Comm. U.S.A. 48-53; U.S. Rep. ad hoc Cttee. on Restrictive Practices of ECOSOC 51-52; Pitt Prof. Univ. of Cambridge 53-54, Prof. of Econs., Univ. of Virginia 54-55, Prof. of Business and Govt., Graduate School of Business, Univ. of Chicago 55-63, Prof. of Econs., Univ. of Oregon 64-.

Publs. Co-author *Economic Behavior* 31, *Economic Problems in a Changing World* 39, *A Cartel Policy for the United Nations* 45; author *Maintaining Competition* 49, *Big Business and the Policy of Competition* 56, *The Price Discrimination Law: A Review of Experience* 59, *Cartelization in Western Europe* 64, *Trade Regulation Overseas: The National Laws* 66, *Control of Cartels and Monopolies: An International Comparison* 67.

2355 Van Ness Street, Eugene, Oregon, U.S.A.

Edwards, Sir George Robert, C.B.E., D.SC.; British aeronautical designer and executive; b. 9 July 1908; ed. London Univ.

Design Staff, Vickers Armstrong, Weybridge 35, Experimental Manager 40, Chief Designer 45, Gen. Manager and Chief Engineer 53; mem. of Bd., Vickers Ltd. 55-; fmr. Chair. Vickers-Armstrongs (Aircraft), Bristol Aircraft, English Electric Aviation, Hunting Aircraft, British Aircraft Corpn. (Guided Weapons) Ltd.; Chair. British Aircraft Corpn. (Operating) Ltd. 64-; Managing Dir. British Aircraft Corpn. Ltd. 60-; Pro-Chancellor Univ. of Surrey 64-; Daniel Guggenheim Medal 59; Taylor Gold Medal; Hon. F.R.Ae.S., Hon. F.A.I.A.A.

British Aircraft Corporation, Brooklands Road, Weybridge, Surrey, England.

Edwards, Gordon; American food products executive; b. 29 May 1907; ed. Virginia Polytechnic Inst., Benjamin Franklin Univ. and George Washington Univ.

National Dairy Products Corpn., Washington 27-35, New York City 35-36, Zone Controller, Chicago 36-49, with Kraft Foods Div., Chicago, finally becoming Pres. 49-65; Pres. Nat. Dairy Products Corpn. Nov. 65-.

National Dairy Products Corporation, 260 Madison Ave., New York 16, N.Y., U.S.A.

Edwards, Leverett, LL.B.; American lawyer and government official; b. 21 Jan. 1902; ed. Univ. of Oklahoma.

Law Practice, Oklahoma City 26-50; mem. or Chair. Presidential Emergency Boards 46-50; Democratic member Nat. Mediation Board 50-, now Chair.

5300 Westbard Avenue, Apartment 16, Washington, D.C., U.S.A.

Edwards, Robert John; British journalist; b. 26 Oct. 1925; ed. Ranelagh School.

Editor *Tribune* 51-55; Deputy Editor *Sunday Express* 57-59; Man. Editor *Daily Express* 63-65; Editor *The People* 66-.

Old Thatch, Altwood Road, Maidenhead, Berks., England.

Edwards, Sir Ronald Stanley, K.B.E., B.COM., D.SC.; British economist and accountant; b. 1 May 1910; ed. Southgate County School.

Professional Accountancy 26-35; Asst. Lecturer, later Lecturer in Business Admin. (with special reference to Accounting), London School of Econs. 35-40; Dep. Dir. of Labour and Asst. Sec. Ministry of Aircraft Production 40-45; Sir Ernest Cassel Reader in Commerce (with special ref. to Industrial Admin.), Univ. of London 46-49; Prof. of Economics (with special ref. to Industrial Organisation 49-); Chair. The Electricity

Council 62-68; to be Chair. Beecham Group Nov. 68-; mem. Univ. Grants Cttee. 55-64; Gov. Admin. Staff Coll., Henley and London Graduate School of Business Studies; Pres. Market Research Soc. 65-; Chair. Cttee. of Enquiry into Civil Air Transport 67-.
Publs. *Co-operative Industrial Research* 50, *Industrial Research in Switzerland* 51, *Business Enterprise* 58, *Studies in Business Organisation* (with H. Townsend) 61, many other articles on economic, industrial and accounting questions.
Home: 49 Lowndes Square, London, S.W.1; Nothe House, Weymouth, Dorset, England.
Telephone: 01-235-4253; Weymouth 4923.

Edwards, William Philip Neville, C.B.E., M.A.; British industrialist; b. 5 Aug. 1904; ed. Rugby, Corpus Christi Coll., Cambridge, and Princeton Univ. (Davison Scholar).
Public Relations Officer, London Passenger Transport Board 39-41; Asst. to Chair. of Supply Council, Ministry of Supply 41-43; Head of Industrial Information Div., Ministry of Production, and alternate Dir. of Information, British Supply Council, Washington 43-45; Dir. Overseas Information Div., Board of Trade, London 45-46; Counsellor, British Embassy, Washington, D.C., in charge of British Information Services 46-49; Deputy Overseas Dir. Federation of British Industries (F.B.I.) 49-51; Dir. Promotion and Information, F.B.I. 51-65, Confederation of British Industry (C.B.I.) 65-66; Dir. of British Overseas Fairs Ltd. 53-66, Chair. 66-.
Baddiley House, Church Hill, Merstham, Surrey; Office: British Overseas Fairs Ltd., Commonwealth House, 1-19 New Oxford Street, W.C.1, England.
Telephone: 01-242-9011.

Eeg-Henriksen, Haakon; Norwegian company director and civil engineer; b. 17 March 1892; ed. Norwegian Univ. of Technology.
Began engineering career abroad 15-17; with Christiania Cementstöperi 17-19, with Solbergfossen Hydro-Electric Power Plant 19-22; managed own contracting firm 22-29; Partner, Eeg-Henriksen & Diderich Lund Ltd. 30-52, Dir. and Owner 52-; Dir. Construction Directorate, Ministry of Defence 52-54; Dir. H. Eeg-Henriksen Ltd. 54-; mem. Board Sigyn Life Insurance Co.; mem. Cttee. Norwegian Life Insurance Co.; fmr. Pres. Norwegian Defence Asscn.; Chair. Hausmannsgatens Industribygg; Commdr. Order of St. Olav.
Havna Allé 11, Oslo 3, Norway.

Efanov, Vasili Prokofievich; Soviet painter; b. 1900; ed. Samara Industrial Arts Technicum.
Known mainly for his portraits of Lenin, Gorky, Zhdanov, Ordzhonidze and Molotov; works include: *In a New Home, Stalingrad, Tank Manoeuvres, Zhukovsky Military Aviation Academy Students Meet Stanislavsky Theatre Company* 38, *Meeting of Presidium of U.S.S.R. Academy of Sciences* 51; paintings exhibited in the Moscow Tretiakov Gallery, Leningrad Russian Museum; mem. C.P.S.U. 54-; mem. U.S.S.R. Acad. of Arts 57-; People's Artist of R.S.F.S.R. 51, State prizewinner 41, 46, 48, 50, 52; Order of Lenin, etc.; mem. editorial collegium *Iskusstvo.*
Academy of Arts of the U.S.S.R., Moscow, U.S.S.R.

Efholm, Mogens; Danish business executive; b. 20 May 1910; ed. univ., and commercial studies in England, Germany and France.
Copenhagen trade agencies 30-45; Managing Dir. Emil Warthoe & Soenner A/S 45-50, Nordisk Andelsforbund (Scandinavian Co-operative Wholesale Soc.) 51-64, "National" Co. 53-57, Nordisk Andels-Eksport (Scandinavian Co-operative Export) 54-64; mem. Central Cttee. Int. Co-operative Alliance, London 61-64; mem. the "Maritime and Commercial Court" 61-; Chair. Nordisk Andelsforbund, Calif., Inc., San Francisco 62-64; Sec.-Gen. European Co-operative Wholesale Cttee. for Developments in Production and Marketing

Fields 63-64; Commercial Adviser 64-; Knight Order of Dannebrog.
33 Parkovsvej, Gentofte, Copenhagen, Denmark.
Telephone: Gentofte 8548.

Efimov, Alexander Pavlovich; Soviet foreign trade official; b. 1905; ed. Moscow Inst. of Steel.
Member C.P.S.U. 27-; engineer, Party worker until 54; later First Deputy Minister of Forestry Industry; U.S.S.R. Commercial Rep. in Czechoslovakia 58-; Order of Red Banner of Labour; Order of Red Star.
U.S.S.R. Trade Representation, Prague, Czechoslovakia.

Efimov, Boris Yefimovich; Soviet artist and caricaturist; b. 1900.
Began contributing to Red Army papers 19; contributed to *Izvestia, Pravda, Literaturnaya Gazeta, Red Star, Krokodil;* corresp. mem. of Acad. of Arts 55-; State Prize 50, 51; People's Artist of R.S.F.S.R. 59; Order of the Red Banner of Labour 60, 62; People's Artist of the U.S.S.R. 67.
Publs. *Cartoons* 24, *Fascism—Enemy of the Peoples* 37, *Hitler and his Gang* 43, *For a Lasting Peace, Against the Incendiaries of War* 50; Autobiography: *Forty Years* 61, *Work, Memoirs, Meetings* 63.
U.S.S.R. Academy of Arts, 21 Kropotkinskaya, Moscow, U.S.S.R.

Efremov, Leonid Nikolayevich; Soviet politician; b. 12; ed. Agricultural Mechanisation Inst., Voronezh.
Member C.P.S.U. 41-; party work 45-49; Second Sec. Kuibyshev City Cttee. 46-49, District Cttee. 49-51; First Sec. Kursk and Gorkov District Cttees. 52-62; mem. Central Cttee. C.P.S.U. 52-; mem. Bureau, Central Cttee. of C.P.S.U. for R.S.F.S.R. 59-64 and First Deputy Chair. Bureau Central Cttee. C.P.S.U. for agricultural management; First Sec. Stavropol Territorial Cttee. C.P.S.U. 64-; Deputy to U.S.S.R. Supreme Soviet.
Office of the First Secretary, Stavropol Territorial Committee, Stavropol, U.S.S.R.

Efremov, Mikhail Timofeyevich; Soviet politician; b. 11; ed. Industrial Inst., Kuibyshev.
Member C.P.S.U. 32-; party work 42-; Sec. Kuibyshev District Cttee. C.P.S.U. 51-59; Perm. Staff, Central Cttee. of C.P.S.U. 59-61; mem. Central Cttee. C.P.S.U. 56-; First Sec. Cheliabinsk District Cttee., C.P.S.U. 61-63; First Sec. Gorky District Cttee., C.P.S.U. 63-65; Deputy Chair. U.S.S.R. Council of Ministers 65-; mem. Mandate Cttee. Soviet of Union; Deputy to U.S.S.R. Supreme Soviet.
Council of Ministers of the U.S.S.R., The Kremlin, Moscow, U.S.S.R.

Efremov, Oleg Nikolaevich; Soviet actor and director; b. 1927; Studio School of Moscow Art Theatres 45-49. Actor and producer at Central Children's Theatre 49-56; Dir. Sovremennik Theatre 56-; has produced many plays at Sovremennik Theatre; film work 55-; Hon. Art Worker of R.S.F.S.R. 57.
Ploshchad V. Mayakovskogo 1/29, Moscow, U.S.S.R.

Efremov, Stepan Andrianovich; Soviet agriculturalist and politician; b. 1907; ed. Moscow Land Inst.
Chief Engineer, Head of Land Org. Dept. of Udmurt Autonomous S.S.R. 32-39; mem. C.P.S.U. 39-; research student, Lecturer, Land Inst., Chief Engineer for *Sovkhozmeliostroi* (org. for promoting construction of State Farms), Kazakh S.S.R. 39-43; Soviet Army 43-46; Exec. posts in agriculture in Udmurtia 46-51; First Vice-Chair. Council of Ministers and Minister of Agriculture of Udmurt A.S.S.R. 51-59; Chair. of Council of Ministers of Udmurt A.S.S.R. 59-; Deputy to U.S.S.R. Supreme Soviet.
Council of Ministers of the Udmurt A.S.S.R., Izhevsk, U.S.S.R.

Egal, Mohamed Ibrahim; Somali politician; b. 15 Aug. 1928; ed. secondary education in Somali Republic and private studies in U.K.
Secretary, Berbera Branch, Somali Nat. League Party 56; Sec.-Gen. Somali Nat. League Party 58-60; Prime Minister of Somaliland 60; Minister of Defence, Somali Repub. 61-62, of Educ. 62-63; re-elected to Parl. March 64; mem. Somali Youth League Party 66-; Prime Minister and Minister of Foreign Affairs, Somali Repub. July 67-.
Government Headquarters, Mogadishu, Somali Republic.
Telephone: 3389 (Office); 3662 (Residence).

Egala, Imoru; Ghanaian politician; b. 16; ed. Achimota Coll., Univ. Coll. of Ghana.
Primary School Headmaster 45-54; Minister of Health 54-56, 59-60; Chair. Cocoa Marketing Bd. 56-59; Chair. Ghana Housing Corpn. July-Sept. 60; Minister of State for Foreign Affairs Oct. 60-May 61; Minister of Information May-Sept. 61; Exec. Dir. (Cocoa) Div., Agric. Produce Marketing Board Oct. 61-April 62; Minister of Industries May 62-66; Convention People's Party.
c/o Ministry of Industries, P.O.B. M.39, Accra, Ghana.

Egan, William A.; American merchant and politician; b. 8 Oct. 1914; ed. Valdez (Alaska) High School.
Mem. Alaska House of Reps. 41, 43, 47, 49, 51, Alaska Senate 53 and 55; Del. and Pres. Alaska Constitutional Convention 55-56; "Tennessee Plan" Senator to Washington to promote Statehood for Alaska; First Gov., State of Alaska 58-; elected Chair. Western Governors' Conf. 61, re-elected 62; served in Infantry and Air Corps 43-46; Mayor of Valdez 46; Democrat.
P.O. Box 1571, Juneau, Alaska, U.S.A.

Egeland, Leif, M.A., B.C.L.; South African diplomatist and businessman; b. 19 Jan. 1903; ed. Durban High School, Natal Univ. Coll., and Trinity Coll., Oxford.
Rhodes Scholar for Natal 24, Harmsworth Scholar Middle Temple 27; Barrister 30; Fellow Brasenose Coll. 27-30; Advocate Supreme Court S. Africa 31; M.P. Durban 33-38, Zululand 40-43; with 6th S. African Armoured Div., Middle East 43; Union Minister to Sweden 43-46, to Neths. and Belgium 46-48; High Commr. for Union of South Africa in London 48-50; S. African Del. to San Francisco Conf. 45; leader of S. African Del. to Final Assembly L.N., Geneva 46; S. African Del. to First and Third Gen. Assemblies of U.N., Paris, to Paris Peace Conf. 46 and Pres. Comm. for the political and territorial questions in the draft Peace Treaty with Italy at that Conf.; Chair. Cape Asbestos Insulations Pty. Ltd., African Chartering (Pty.) Ltd.; Dir. Johannesburg Consolidated Investment Co., S. African Breweries Ltd., Rhodesian Breweries Ltd., English Electric (S.A.) Pty. Ltd., Goodyear Tyre & Rubber Co. (S.A.) Ltd., Johannesburg Local Board of Natal Building Soc., Babcock & Wilcox of S. Africa Ltd., Standard Gen. Insurance Co. Ltd.; Chair. Smuts Memorial Trust; Dir. Standard Bank of South Africa; Hon. Bencher Middle Temple; Hon. LL.D. (Cambridge Univ.).
Home: 97 Fourth Road, Hyde Park, Johannesburg; Office: c/o P.O.B. 590, Johannesburg, South Africa.
Telephone: 421642 (Home); 838-5981 (Office).

Egger, Walter, DR. JURIS.; Swiss newspaper editor; b. 95; ed. Univ. of Berne.
Economic Editor *Der Bund*, Berne 21-32, political editor 32-41, Editor-in-Chief 41-67; mem. Berne Cantonal Parl. 34-48; mem. Swiss Fed. Parl. 51-55; mem. Council Agence Télégraphique Suisse; Liberal.
Muristrasse 16, Berne, Switzerland.

Eggers, Henry Howard, C.M.G., O.B.E.; British telecommunications executive; b. 13 Nov. 1903; ed. Dulwich Coll. and Magdalen Coll., Oxford.
Central and South American merchant 24-39; Ministry

of Economic Warfare 40-45; Treasury 45-54; Dir. Cable and Wireless Ltd. and subsid. companies 54-, Managing Dir. 55-; Dir. Nigerian External Telecommunications Ltd., Lagos, Nigeria 62-, East African External Telecommunications Co. Ltd., Nairobi, Kenya 63-, Sierra Leone External Telecommunications Ltd., Freetown, Sierra Leone 64-.
The Barn, Ockenden Lane, Cuckfield, Sussex, England.

Eghbal, Manouchehr, M.D.; Iranian physician and politician; b. 09; ed. Persia and Univs. of Montpellier and Paris.
Prof. of Infectious Diseases, Medical Faculty, Univ. of Teheran 39-53; from 42-50 successively apptd. Under-Sec. of State for Public Health, Minister for Public Health, Minister of Posts, Telegraph and Telephones, Minister of Nat. Educ., of Roads and Communications, of Interior; Gov.-Gen. Azerbaidjan (Northern Region of Iran) 50-51; Rector, Univ. of Tabriz; Senator 53; Dean of Faculty of Medicine of Teheran Univ. 55-57, also Rector, Teheran Univ. 55-57; Minister to the Imperial Court 56; Prime Minister 57-60; Prof. Teheran Univ. 60-61; mem. of Parl. 61-; Perm. Iranian Rep. to UNESCO 61-; Chair. of Board and Gen. Managing Dir. Nat. Iranian Oil Co. Oct. 63-; corresp. mem. Acad. of Medicine, Paris; Hon. Dr. (Lafayette Coll., U.S.A., Paris Univ., Bordeaux Univ., Univ. of Punjab); 33 decorations.
Office: National Iranian Oil Co., Ave. Takhte Jamshid, P.O. Box 1863; Home: Elahieh, Tehran, Iran.
Telephone: 6151 (Office); 81080 (Home).

Egk, Werner; German composer; b. 17 May 1901; ed. Univ. of Munich.
Conductor, Prussian State Opera, Berlin 36-40; Dir. Hochschule für Musik, Berlin (West) 50-53; Hon. Pres. of *Cisac* (Confédération Internationale des Sociétés d'Auteurs et Compositeurs); mem., Music Section of the Bayerische Akademie der Schönen Künste, Akademie der Künste Berlin; Pres. of *Deutscher Komponistenverband*.
Publs. Operas: *Zaubergeige* 35, *Peer Gynt* 38, *Columbus* 41, *Irische Legende* 55, *Revisor* 57, *Die Verlobung in San Domingo* 63, *17 Tage und 4 Minuten* 66; ballets: *Joan von Zarissa* 40, *Abraxas* 48, *Sommertag* 49, *Chinesische Nachtigall* 53, *Danza* 60; concert works: *Furchtlosigkeit und Wohlwollen* (oratorio) 31, *La Tentation de Saint Antoine* 47, *Orchestersonate* 48, *Französische Suite* 50, *Chanson et Romance* 53, etc.
8032 Lochham bei München, Lindenstrasse 1, German Federal Republic.
Telephone: Munich 851024.

Eglevsky, André; American (b. Russian) ballet dancer and producer; b. 17 Dec. 1917; ed. Nice, Paris and London.
With René Blum's Ballet de Monte Carlo 36; went to United States 37; Grand Ballet du Marquis de Cuevas 47; New York City Ballet Co. 50-58; with wife founded André Eglevsky School of Ballet 55; Teacher and Artistic Dir. André Eglevsky Ballet Co. 60-.
126 Rumson Road, Massapequa, Long Island, N.Y., U.S.A.

Egorov, Anatoli Grigorievich; Soviet journalist; b. 20; ed. Liebknecht Inst., Moscow.
Soviet army service 41-46; mem. C.P.S.U. 41-; Teacher, Pedagogical Inst., Vladivostok 46-48; Dep. Editor, then Editor, *Kommunist* 52-56, Chief Editor, *V Pomoshch Politicheskomu Samoobrazovaniu* (Political Self-Education Guide) 56-60; Perm. staff Central Cttee. C.P.S.U. 61-; mem. Central Auditing Comm. C.P.S.U. 61-66; Corresp. mem. Soviet Acad. of Sciences.
Central Committee of the Communist Party of the Soviet Union, Staraya ploshchad 4, Moscow, U.S.S.R.

Egorov, Boris Borisovich, M.SC.(MED); Soviet cosmonaut; b. 37; ed. Moscow Medical Inst.
Scientist in field of aviation and cosmic medicine;

doctor in team of spacecraft *Voskhod I* in flight Oct. 64; Hero of Soviet Union; Order of Lenin, Golden Star Medal; Pilot-Cosmonaut of U.S.S.R.
c/o Presidium of Academy of Sciences of U.S.S.R., 14, Lenin Prospekt Moscow, U.S.S.R.

Egorov, Boris Grigorievich; Soviet neurosurgeon; b. 1892; ed. Moscow Univ.
Intern, Asst., Moscow Univ. 15-23; Surgeon, Sklifosovsky First Aid Inst. 26-28; Asst., Head of Dept., Dir. Inst. of Neurosurgery, U.S.S.R. Acad. of Medical Sciences 28-64; Consulting Prof. 64-; mem. C.P.S.U. 52-; Corresp. mem., U.S.S.R. Acad. of Medical Sciences 48-53, mem. 53-; mem. Int. Soc. of Surgeons, Swedish Medical Soc., American Soc. of Neurosurgeons; Order of Lenin 51, 63; Red Banner of Labour 43; Red Star 43 Badge of Honour 60; Honoured Scientist of R.S.F.S.R. 58.
Publ. Over 130 works on surgical treatment of nervous diseases, neurosurgery for major affection of central and peripheral nervous systems, and complex methods all treating neuroectodermal tumours and vascular affections.
Institute of Neurosurgery, 1st Tverskoy-Yamskoy per. 13/5, Moscow, U.S.S.R.

Egorychev, Nikolai Grigorievich; Soviet politician; b. 20; ed. Moscow Higher Technical Inst.
Member C.P.S.U. 42-; army service 41-46; Sec. Bauman Regional Cttee. (Moscow) C.P.S.U. 54-60; Perm. staff Central Cttee. 60-61; First Sec. Moscow City Cttee. C.P.S.U. 61-67; Deputy Minister of Tractor and Agricultural Machinery Building Oct. 67; mem. Central Cttee. of C.P.S.U. 61-; mem. Bureau for R.S.F.F.R.; Deputy to U.S.S.R. Supreme Soviet; mem. Presidium Supreme Soviet of U.S.S.R. 66-67.
Ministry of Tractor and Agricultural Machinery Building, Moscow, U.S.S.R.

Egtvedt, Clairmont Leroy; American aircraft manufacturer; b. 18 Oct. 1892; ed. Univ. of Washington.
Joined Boeing Airplane Co., designer and stress engineer 17, Chief Engineer 18, Sec. 22, Vice-Pres. 26, Gen. Man. 26, Pres. and Gen. Manager 33-39, now Chair. The Boeing Co.; Fellow American Inst. of Aeronautics and Astronautics; mem. Royal Aeronautical Soc.; Dir. Washington Mutual Savings Bank, Pacific Nat. Bank. 3146 Lakewood Avenue, Seattle, Wash., U.S.A.

Ehard, Hans, DR. JUR.; German lawyer and politician; b. 10 Nov. 1887; ed. Univs. of Munich and Würzburg.
Served in Bavarian Min. of Justice, rising to rank of Ministerial Counsellor 19-33; Asst. State Prosecutor in Hitler trial, Munich 24; seconded to Reich Min. of Justice 25-28; owing to non-membership of Nat. Socialist Party was transferred to Oberlandesgericht, Munich, as Senate Pres. 33; State Counsellor in Bavarian Min. of Justice Oct. 45; as State Sec. became mem. of Bavarian State Govt.; Minister-Pres. of Bavaria 46-54, 60-62, Minister of Justice 62-66; Pres. Bavarian Parl. 54-60; mem. Christian Social Union; Pres. Bavarian Red Cross 55-; numerous decorations.
8 Munich 90, Am Schilcherweg 4A, German Federal Republic.
Telephone: 476554.

Ehrgott, John D.; American food retailing executive; b. 96.
Great Atlantic and Pacific Tea Co. Inc. 23-, Vice-Pres. and Treas. until 63, Pres. 63, now Chair.
Great Atlantic and Pacific Tea Co. Inc., 420 Lexington Avenue, New York 17, N.Y., U.S.A.

Ehrlich, Julius; German-born American conductor; b. 3 Feb. 1894; ed. Staatliche Hochschule für Musik, Frankfurt-am-Main, Germany.
Dir. "Stadthallen" Concerts and Radio Station, Hanover 23-28; Prof. Leningrad Conservatory, Conductor Leningrad Opera 30-33; Conductor, Royal Flemish

Opera, Antwerp 34-36; emigrated to U.S.A. 37; Conductor Milwaukee Symphony Orchestra, Milwaukee Sinfonietta 39-47; Dir. Milwaukee Annual Brotherhood Week Concerts; Grand Prix de Disque 34; regular guest conducting tours to Europe 47-.
Garten Strasse 8, 8 Munich 13, German Federal Republic.

Ehrlich, Ludwik, DR.JUR., D.LITT., D.J.S.; Polish jurist; b. 11 April 1889; ed. Lwów, Halle, Berlin and Oxford Univs.
Literary Sec. to Sir Paul Vinogradoff 14-16; Lecturer Calif. Univ. 17-20, Lwów Univ. 20-24; Judge Permanent Court of Int. Justice, The Hague 27-28; mem. Permanent Court of Arbitration 48-53; Prof. of Int. Law and Gen. Political Theory, Lwów Univ. 24-39; Lectured Univ. of Oxford 16, Acad. de Droit Int., The Hague 28, 62, School of Politics, Prague 29, Univ. of Jassy, Rumania 34, Faculty of Law, Univ. of London 37, Institut Universitaire d'Etudes Européennes, Turin 63; Pres. Central Cttee. of Polish Insts. of Political Science 34-37; Prof. of Int. Law, Jagiellonian Univ., Cracow 45-; Dir. of School of Politics 46-49.
Publs. *Year Books of Michaelmas, 6 Edward II* (with Sir Paul Vinogradoff), *Proceedings Against the Crown, 1216-1377, Petitions of Right, The Regal Regulation of the Seas and of the Continental Shelf, Interprétations des Traités, Guillaume de Rennes et les origines de la Science du Droit de la Guerre, The development of international law as a science*; books in Polish include: *The Law of Nations, Charter of the United Nations, A XV Century Polish Lecture on the Law of War, Genealogy of the Science of International Law, Sovereignty and the Sea in International Law.*
Al. Slowackiego 15, Cracow, Poland.
Telephone: Cracow 34594.

Eich, Günter (husband of Ilse Aichinger, *q.v.*); German author; b. 1 Feb. 1907; ed. in Berlin, Leipzig and Paris.
Freelance writer 32-; mem. Bavarian Acad. of Fine Arts, Acad. of Sciences and Literature, Mainz, German Acad. of Language and Literature, PEN Club; Prize for Literature, Bavarian Acad. 52, Georg Büchner Prize 59.
Publs. *Abgelegene Gehöfte* 48, *Träume* 53, *Botschaften des Regens* 55, *Stimmen* 58, *Zu den Akten* 64, *In anderen Sprachen* 64, *Unter Wasser* 64, *Anlässe und Steingärten* 66.
D-8232 Bayerisch Gmain, Obb., German Federal Republic.

Eichfeld, Johan Hansovich; Soviet (Estonian) botanist and government official; b. 93; ed. Leningrad Agricultural Inst.
Asst. at polar research station Kola Peninsular until 40; Dir. All Union Research Inst. Plant Growing, Leningrad 40-46; Pres. Estonian Acad. of Sciences 50-; Chair. Presidium Estonian Supreme Soviet 58-61; State Prize for agricultural experimental work in the Polar regions and four Orders of Lenin.
Estonian Academy of Sciences, Kochta Street, Tallinn 2, Estonian S.S.R., U.S.S.R.

Eickhoff, Gottfred; Danish sculptor and professor; b. 11 April 1902; ed. Københavns Universitet, and Paris under Charles Despiau.
Professor of Sculpture, Acad. of Fine Arts, Copenhagen, Pro-rector 56-66; mem. Council of Art 56-; exhibitions and works in museums in Europe and U.S.A.; Knight, Order of Dannebrog; Henri Nathansens Prize 51, Eckersberg Medal 44, Viggo Jarls Prize 62.
Frederiksholms Kanal 28A, Copenhagen, Denmark.
Telephone: BY-1418.

Eiermann, Egon, DR.ING. E.H.; German architect; b. 29 Sept. 1904; ed. Althoff-Realgymnasium, Nowawes bei Berlin, and architectural studies under Prof. Hans Poelzig, Technische Hochschule zu Berlin.

In architectural office of Rudolf Karstadt A.G., Hamburg 27-28, Berliner Elektrizitätswerke A.G. 28-29; freelance architect in Berlin, working on residential devt., redevt. and country houses 30-, industrial buildings 38-; Prof. Faculty of Architecture, Technische Hochschule, Karlsruhe 47-; mem. Acad. of Arts, Berlin 55-; Hon. mem. Central Council of Austrian Architects 60-; Hon. corresp. mem. Royal Inst. of British Architects 63-; Prix d'architecture, Cercle d'Etudes Architecturales, Paris 59; Berliner Kunstpreis 62, Architectural Award of Excellence, American Inst. of Steel Construction, New York 65; Architectural Prize of Board of Trade, Washington 65; Provincial Prize for Architecture, North Rhine-Westphalia 65; Dr.-Ing. e.h. (Technical Univ., Berlin).
Principal works: Textile Mill, Blumberg 49-51; German Pavilion, Brussels Exhibition (with Prof. Sep Ruf) 56-58; Admin. Buildings, Essener Steinkohlenbergwerke A.G. 56-60; Despatch centre and warehouse for Neckermann-Versand K.G., Frankfurt/Main 58-61; Kaiser-Wilhelm Memorial Church, Berlin 57-63; German Embassy, Washington 58-64; also designs furniture (Good Design Award, Museum of Modern Art, Washington 53).
Technische Hochschule, Karlsruhe, Englerstrasse 7, German Federal Republic.

Eigen, Manfred, DR. RER. NAT.; German physical chemist; b. 9 May 1927; ed. Georg-August-Univ. zu Göttingen.
Max-Planck Inst. of Physical Chemistry, Göttingen, as Asst., later as Prof. and Head of Dept. 53-; Otto Hahn Prize 62; Nobel Prize for Chemistry (with Norrish and Porter) for investigation of extremely rapid chemical reactions by means of disturbing the (molecular) equilibrium by the action of very short energy pulses 67; Hon. Dr. Univ. of Washington, St. Louis Univ., Harvard Univ. and Cambridge Univ.
Max-Planck-Institut für Physikalische Chemie, 3400 Göttingen, Bunsenstrasse 10, German Federal Republic.

Eilers, Louis Kenneth, PH.D.; American business executive; b. 4 Nov. 1907; ed. Blackburn Coll. and Univs. of Illinois and Virginia, and Northwestern Univ.
Superintendent Roll Coating Finishing Dept. Eastman-Kodak Co. 46-50; Asst. to Man. Film Mfg. 50-52, Asst. Man. 52-53; Admin. Asst. to Gen. Man. Kodak Park 53, Asst. Gen. Man. 54-56; Vice-Pres. and Asst. Gen. Man. Eastman Kodak Co. 56-59; Pres. Eastman Chemical Products Inc. 59-61; First Vice-Pres. Tennessee Eastman Co. and Texas Eastman Co. 59-61, Pres. 61-63; Pres. Carolina Eastman Co. 61-63; Exec. Vice-Pres. Eastman Kodak Co. 63-67, Dir. and mem. Exec. Cttee. 63-; Pres. 67-; Hon. Sc.D. (Blackburn Coll.); Assoc. Fellow Soc. of Photographic Scientists and Engineers.
Eastman Kodak Co., 343 State Street, Rochester, N.Y. 14650; 57 Knollwood Drive, Rochester, N.Y. 14610, U.S.A. (Home).

Einarson, Lárus; Danish anatomist and neuropathologist; b. 5 June 1902; ed. Univ. of Iceland, Copenhagen, Munich, Harvard and Johns Hopkins Univs.
Lecturer, Univ. of Iceland and consulting neuropathologist, Reykjavík Mental Hospital 33-35; Asst. Neuropathologist, Psychiatric Laboratory, Copenhagen 35; Prof. of Anatomy Aarhus Univ. 36-; Consulting Neuropathologist State Mental Hospital, Aarhus 45-; Visiting Prof. George Washington Univ., Washington, D.C. 57-58; Fellow, Iceland Soc. of Sciences, Denmark Asscn. of Natural Sciences, British Neuropathological Soc., Royal Danish Acad. of Sciences and Letters, Royal Physiographic Soc. Lund; Augustinus Science Prize 56.
Universitetsparken, Norrebrogade 47, Aarhus C, Denmark.

Einaudi, Giulio; Italian publisher; b. 2 Jan. 1912; ed. Liceo Massimo d'Azeglio and Univ. of Turin.
Founder Publishing House, Giulio Einaudi Editore 33, Gen. Manager 54-; Libro d'Oro (Italy) 63.
Via Umberto Biancamano 1, 10121 Turin, Italy.
Telephone: 553761.

Einem, Gottfried von; Austrian professor and composer; b. 24 Jan. 1918; ed. Gymnasium at Ratzeburg and musical studies with Boris Blacher.
Coach, State Opera in Berlin 39-44; Musical Adviser to Dir. of Dresden State Opera, Coach Bayreuth Festival 38-39; mem. board of Salzburg Festival 48-; mem. board of Vienna Festival 59-, and Vienna Konzerthaus Gesellschaft 63-; Prof. Acad. of Music, Vienna 59-; numerous awards and prizes including Austrian State Prize 65.
Compositions: Operas *Death of Danton* (Büchner), *The Trial* (Kafka), *Der Zerrissene* (Nestroy), five Ballets and various other works.
Vienna III, Dannebergplatz 14, Austria.

Einem, Herbert Günter von, DR. PHIL.; German art historian; b. 16 Feb. 1905; ed. High Schools in Erfurt and Göttingen, and Univs. of Göttingen, Berlin and Munich.
Assistant at Landesmuseum, Hanover 29-36; Art History studies, Göttingen 36; Prof. of Art History, Greifswald Univ. 43-46, Univ. of Frankfurt 46-47, Univ. of Bonn 47-; Chair. Asscn. of German Art Historians; Pres. Int. Cttee. on History of Art; mem. Research Council of North Rhine-Westphalia, Acad. of Science and Literature, Mainz; Corresp. mem. Acad. of Sciences, Göttingen, Acad. of Sciences, Munich; Foreign mem. Royal Swedish Acad.; Commendatore al Merito della Repubblica Italiana.
Publs. *Karl Ludwig Fernow* 35, *Caspar David Friedrich* 38, 3rd. edn. 50, *Beiträge zu Goethes Kunstauffassung* 56.
Kunsthistorisches Institut, 53 Bonn, Liebfrauenweg 1; Home: 53 Bonn-Ippendorf, Quellenweg 7, German Federal Republic.
Telephone: 282960 (Home).

Einzig, Paul, D.SC. (Pol. and Econ.); British financial journalist; b. in Hungary 25 Aug. 1897; ed. Oriental Acad. Budapest and Univ. of Paris.
Paris corresp. *Financial News* 21, Foreign Editor 23, Political corresp. 39; Political corresp. *Financial Times* 45-56; London corresp. *Commercial and Financial Chronicle*, New York 45-.
Publs. *International Gold Movements* 29, *Exchange Control* 34, *The Exchange Clearing System* 35, *The Theory of Forward Exchange* 37, *Primitive Money in its Ethnological, Historical and Economic Aspects* 49, *The Economic Consequences of Automation* 56, *The Control of the Purse: Progress and Decline of Parliament's Financial Control* 59, *In the Centre of Things: An Autobiography* 60, *A Dynamic Theory of Forward Exchange* 61, *The History of Foreign Exchange* 62, *The Euro-Dollar System* 64, *Monetary Policy—Ends and Means* 64, *Foreign Dollar Loans in Europe* 65, *A Textbook on Foreign Exchange* 66, *Foreign Exchange Crises* 68, *Leads and Lags—The Main Cause of Devaluation* 68.
120 Clifford's Inn, London, E.C.4, England.
Telephone: 01-405-1444.

Eisenhower, Dwight David (brother of Dr. Milton Eisenhower, *q.v.*); American army officer and politician; b. 14 Oct. 1890; ed. Abilene High School and U.S. Mil. Acad.
Commissioned 2nd-Lieut. infantry, United States Army 15, and advanced through grades to Gen. of Army Dec. 44; graduated from Army War Coll. June 28; Asst. Exec., Office of Asst. Sec. of War 29-33; served in office of Chief of Staff 33-35; Asst. to the Mil. Adviser in the Philippines 35-40; Chief of Staff of 3rd Div. 40; Chief of

Staff IX Army Corps March 41; Chief of Staff Third Army June 41; Chief of War Plans Div., War Dept. Gen. Staff Feb. 42; Asst. Chief of Staff in charge of Operations Div., Office of Chief of Staff April 42; Commanding Gen., European Theatre June 42; C.-in-C. Allied Forces, N. Africa Nov. 42; Supreme Commander, Allied Expeditionary Forces Dec. 43-45; Mil. Gov. of U.S. Occupied Zone in Germany May-Nov. 45; Chief of Staff U.S. Army Nov. 45-48; Pres. of Columbia Univ. 48-53; Supreme Allied Commdr. Europe 50-52; resigned from Army July 52; President of the U.S.A. 53-61; Chair. Editorial Board *Encyclopedia Americana* 61-; holds over forty decorations including D.S.M. with four Oak Leaf Clusters, U.S. Navy D.S.M., Legion of Merit (all U.S.A.), Hon. G.C.B. and O.M. (both British), Grand Cordon, Légion d'Honneur and Médaille Militaire (France), and Order of Suvorov, First Degree (U.S.S.R.), numerous Hon. Degrees and City Freedoms.

Publs. *Crusade in Europe* 48, *Mandate for Change, the White House Years* 63, *Waging Peace, the White House Years 1956-61* 65, *At Ease* 68.

Gettysburg, Penn., U.S.A.

Eisenhower, Dr. Milton Stover (brother of Dwight D. Eisenhower, *q.v.*); American public official and educationist; b. 15 Sept. 1899; ed. Kansas State Univ. and Univ. of Edinburgh, Scotland.

Vice-Consul, Edinburgh 24-26; Dir. of Information U.S. Dept. of Agriculture 28-41; Land Use Co-ordinator 37-42; Pres. Kansas State Univ. 43-50; Pres. Pa. State Univ. 50-56; Pres. The Johns Hopkins Univ. 56-67; Special Amb. and Personal Rep. of Pres. of U.S. on Latin American Affairs 53, 57, 59, 60; Chair. President's Comm. to Examine Violence June 68-; hon. degrees many univs. U.S. and abroad; decorations from Colombia, Bolivia, Venezuela, Korea, Ecuador, Mexico and Chile.

Publ. *The Wine is Bitter* 63.

The Johns Hopkins University, Baltimore 18, Md., U.S.A.

Eissfeldt, Otto Hermann W. L., D.D., PH.D.; German theologian; b. 1 Sept. 1887; ed. Göttingen and Berlin Univs.

Preacher at a Berlin Church 12; Lecturer in Theology 13-22; Prof. of Biblical Science Halle Univ. 22-; hon. mem. British Society for Old Testament Study and American Society for Biblical Literature and Exegesis; mem. Sächsische Akad. der Wissenschaften Leipzig, Deutsche Akad. der Wissenschaften Berlin, Akad. der Wissenschaften und der Literatur Mainz, Akad. des Inscriptions et Belles-Lettres, Paris, British Acad., London, Deutsches Archäologisches Institut, Berlin.

Publs. *Der Maschal im Alten Testament* 13, *Israels Geschichte* 14, *Krieg und Bibel* 15, *Erstlinge und Zehnten im Alten Testament* 17, *Hexateuch-Synopse* 22, *Die Quellen des Richterbuches* 25, *Die Komposition der Samuelisbücher* 31, *Baal Zaphon* 32, *Einleitung in das Alte Testament* 34, *Molk als Opferbegriff und das Ende des Gottes Moloch* 35, *Philister und Phönizier* 36, *Ras Schamra und Sanchunjaton* 39, *Tempel und Kulte syrischer Städte in hellenistisch-römischer Zeit* 41, *Geschichtliches und Übergeschichtliches im Alten Testament* 47, *Geschichtsschreibung im Alten Testament* 48, *Von den Anfängen der phönizischen Epigraphik* 48, *Die ältesten Traditionen Israels* 50, *El im ugaritischen Pantheon* 51, *Sanchunjaton von Berut und Ilimilku von Ugarit* 52, *Taautos und Sanchunjaton* 52, *Der Gott Karmel* 53, *Einleitung in das Alte Testament* (2nd edn.) 56, *Die Genesis der Genesis* 58, *Enno Littmann gestorben am 4. Mai 58* 58, *Das Lied Moses Deuteronomium 32: 1-43* 58, *Der Beutel der Lebendigen* 60, *Die Genesis der Genesis* (2nd edn.) 61, *Einleitung in das Alte Testament* (3rd edn.) 64, *Hexateuch-Synopse* (2nd edn.) 62, *Kleine Schriften* I 62, II 63, III 66, IIII 68, *The Old Testament: An Introduction* (English trans.) 65, *Stammessage und*

Menscheitserzählung in der Genesis 65, *Neue keilalphabetische Texte aus Ras Schamra-Ugarit* 65, *Franz Delitzsch und Wolf Graf Bandissin* 66, *Die Komposition der Sinai-Erzählung Exodus 19-34*, 66.

Steffens-Strasse 7, 402 Halle a.S., Germany.

Telephone: Halle 29566.

Ejbye-Ernst, Arne; Danish journalist and editor; b. 16 Dec. 1927; ed. Marselisborg Gymnasium, and Danish Coll. of Journalism.

Journalist Danish Labour Press 49-56; Editor *Ny Tid*, Aalborg 56-59; Editor-in-Chief *Aktuelt*, Copenhagen 59-64, Editor-in-Chief *Politiken*, Copenhagen 66-; Lecturer and Leader, Danish Coll. of Journalism, Aarhus 64-66; Adviser to Danish Newspaper Asscn. 64-66; Chair. Copenhagen Editors' Soc. 67-.

Office: Politikens Hus, Raadhusplads, Copenhagen V, Denmark.

Telephone: 11-85-11.

Ekeberg, Birger, LL.D., PH.D.; Swedish jurist; b· 10 Aug. 1880; ed. Uppsala Univ.

Prof. Stockholm Univ. 07-25; Min. of Justice 20-21; 23-24; Judge Swedish Supreme Court of Justice 25-27; Pres. Svea Court of Appeal 31-46; Marshal of the Realm 47-59; Pres. Nobel Foundation 47-60; Pres. Board of Stockholm Univ. 28-58, and of Stockholm School of Economics 40-57; Swedish del. 6th Hague Conf. 28, Geneva Conf. 30, 31; mem. Permanent Arbitration Court in The Hague 37-55; Pres. Cttee. for Civil Law 27-31, Criminal Law 37-53; Copyright Cttee. 38-56. Family Law Cttee. 41-54; Pres. Swedish Cttee. for Int. Relief Work 44-50; Air Law Cttee. 45-53; mem. Swedish Acad., Acad. of Sciences, Acad. of History, Acad. of Agriculture; Hon. LL.D. (Heidelberg, Copenhagen, Helsinki), Ph.D. (Stockholm).

Sturegatan 14, Stockholm, Sweden.

Eker, Bjarne Reidar, DR. MED.; Norwegian doctor; b. 26 Nov. 1903; ed. Universitet i Oslo.

Scientific Asst., Anatomy Inst., Oslo Univ. 32-36; Pathologist, Univ. Hospital 36-39; Chief Pathologist, Norwegian Radium Hospital 39-, Dir. 47-; Dir. Norsk Hydros Inst. of Cancer Research; Pres. Norwegian Cancer Soc. 50-; Chair. Radiation Hygiene Advisory Council 56-.

Publs. about 50 scientific publications in the field of genetics, radiobiology and tumour pathology.

The Norwegian Radium Hospital, Montebello, Oslo 3, Norway.

Ekloh, Herbert H.; German retail executive; b. 3 March 1905; ed. High School.

Retailer 28-; opened first self-service store in Europe 38; opened first European Supermarket—Rheinlandhalle, Cologne 57; Pres. Rudolph Hussel A.G., Hagen, Westphalia; mem. Board of Dirs. Choco-Candy A.G., Horgen (Switzerland), Intercandy Holdings A.G. (Zürich), Aviation Schools, North Rhine-Westphalia; owner Herbert Ekloh Flymobil K.G.; Pres. German Aero Club Section for North Rhine-Westphalia.

P.O. Box 1609, 58 Hagen/Westf., German Federal Republic.

Telephone: Hagen 28445.

Eklund (Arne) Sigvard; Swedish nuclear physicist; b. 19 June 1911; ed. Univ. of Uppsala.

Secretary-General Second U.N. Conf. on Peaceful Uses of Atomic Energy 58; Chair. Int. Board of Management, OECD High Temperature Reactor Project *Dragon*, Winfrith Heath; Dir.-Gen. Int. Atomic Energy Agency (IAEA) Dec. 61-.

International Atomic Energy Agency, Kaerntnerring, A-1010, Vienna I, Austria.

Telephone: 52-45-25.

Ekman, Wilhelm; Swedish steel executive; b. 13 Nov. 1912; ed. Royal Inst. of Technology, Stockholm.

Blast Furnace and Open Hearth Engineer, Fagersta

Bruks AB 37-43, Manager 43-51; Technical Dir. Steelworks of Uddeholms AB 52-56, Managing Dir. 56-; Pres. Tuollovaara Gruv AB, and School of Mines Filipstad; mem. Board of Swedish Employers' Confederation, Fed. of Swedish Industries (Pres. 65-66), Gen. Export Asscn. of Sweden, Swedish Ironmasters' Asscn., Scandinaviska Banken, and Asscn. of Logfloating of the River Klarälven; Commdr. Royal Order of Vasa.
Bruksdisponent Wilhelm Ekman, Uddeholm, Sweden.
Telephone: 0563-11400.

Elath, Eliahu, B.A., M.A.; Israeli university president; b. 30 July 1903; ed. Hebrew Univ. of Jerusalem and American Univ. of Beirut.
Jewish Agency 34; Jewish Agency Observer to San Francisco Conf. 45; Head of Jewish Agency's Political Office in Washington, D.C. and Special Representative of Provisional Council of Govt. of Israel 47; Israel Ambassador to U.S.A. 48-50; Minister to Great Britain 50-52, Ambassador 52-59; Adviser, Ministry of Foreign Affairs 59-; Pres. Hebrew Univ., Jerusalem; Hon. Ph.D. Publs. *Bedouin, their Life and Manners* 34, *Trans-Jordan* 35, *Israel and her Neighbours* 59.
17 Bialik Street, Beth Hakerem, Jerusalem, Israel.

Elbrick, Charles Burke, A.B.; American diplomatist; b. 25 March 1908; ed. Williams Coll.
Entered Foreign Service 31, served in Warsaw 37, Prague 38, Lisbon 40, Tangier 43, Dept. of State 44, Warsaw 45, Asst. Chief E. European Div. 46-48, Nat. War Coll. 48, Havana 49, Del. to NATO, London 51, Paris 52, Dep. Asst. Sec. of State for European Affairs 53, Asst. Sec. of State 57; Ambassador to Portugal 58-64, to Yugoslavia 64-.
American Embassy, Belgrade, Yugoslavia.

Eley, Sir Geoffrey Cecil Ryves, Kt., C.B.E.; British company director; b. 18 July 1904; ed. Eton, Trinity Coll., Cambridge, and Harvard Univ.
On editorial staff of *Financial News* 26-28; int. banking and finance in England, France, Switzerland and U.S.A. 28-32; London Man. of Post and Flagg N.Y. 32-39; Naval Intelligence Div. Admiralty 39-40; Capital Issues Cttee. 40-41; Dir. of Contracts Min. of Supply 41-46; Dir. of Overseas Disposals 46-47; Chair. British Drug Houses Ltd. 48-65, Brush Group Ltd. 56-58, Richard Thomas and Baldwins Ltd. 59-64; mem. London Electricity Board 48-58; Dir. Bank of England 49-66; Chair. Thomas Tilling & Co. Ltd., Richard Crittall & Co.; Vice-Chair. British Oxygen Ltd.; Deputy Chair. British Bank of the Middle East; Dir. Equity and Law Assurance Soc.; mem. Council Royal U.K. Benevolent Asscn., Vice-Pres. Middle East Asscn.
13 Holland Villas Road, London, W.14, England.
Telephone: 01-603-6265.

Elfving, Gösta; Swedish journalist and politician; b. 2 Sept. 1908.
On staff of *Värmlands Folkblad* 25; Ed. of same 34-40; Ed.-in-Chief *Västgöta-Demokraten* Borås 40-44; Ed.-in-Chief *Morgon-Tidningen* Stockholm (leading Swedish Labour daily) 44-57; mem. Exec. Social Democratic Party 44-, State Youth Cttee. 39-51, State Tourist Cttee. 48-51, of Parl. 54-57; Chairman or member of several Royal Commissions; Gov. Kopparbergs (Län) 57-.
Residenset, Falun, Sweden.

Elias, Hadji Muhammad; Indonesian politician; b. 11; ed. State school, Islamic centre, Tebu-Ireng, Mecca.
Head, Educational Dept., Religious Movement, Nahdlatul-Ulama 35-42; mem. Advisory Council, Residency of Pekalongan 42-45, Dep. Chief for Religious Affairs 43-48; mem. Exec. Council and Defence Cttee. 45-48; mem. Provincial Council, Central Java 49; mem.

House of Reps. 50-55, Minister of Religion 55-59, Minister, later Amb. to Saudi Arabia 60-65.
c/o Ministry of Foreign Affairs, Djakarta, Indonesia.

Elias, Taslim Olawale, Q.C., B.A., LL.M., PH.D., LL.D.; Nigerian lawyer and politician; b. 11 Nov. 1914; ed. C.M.S. Grammar School, Lagos, Igboli Coll., Lagos, Univ. Coll., London, and Inst. of Advanced Legal Studies, London.
Yarborough Anderson Scholar of Inner Temple 46-49; called to the Bar 47; Simon Research Fellow, Univ. of Manchester 51-53; Oppenheim Research Fellow, Inst. of Commonwealth Studies, Nuffield Coll. and Queen Elizabeth House, Oxford 54-60; Visiting Prof. in Political Science, Delhi Univ. 56; mem. Del. to Nigerian Constitutional Conf., London 58; Fed. Attorney-Gen. and Minister of Justice, Nigeria 60-66, Attorney-Gen. Oct. 66-, Commr. for Justice June 67-; mem UN Int. Law Comm. 61-; mem. Governing Council, Univ. of Nigeria 59-66; Gov. School of Oriental and African Studies, London Univ. 58-61; Chair. UN Cttee. of Constitutional Experts to draft Congo Constitution 61, 62; Prof. of Law and Dean of Faculty of Law, Univ. of Lagos, Nigeria April 66-; Hon. LL.D. (Dakar).
Publs. *Nigerian Land Law and Custom* 51, *Nigerian Legal System* 54, *Ghana and Sierra Leone: Development of their Laws and Constitutions* 62, *British Colonial Law: A Comparative Study* 62, *Government and Politics in Africa* 2nd. ed. 63, *Nature of African Customary Law* 2nd edn. 62, *Nigeria: Development of its Laws and Constitution* 65; Co-author of *British Legal Papers* 58, *International Law in a Changing World* 63, *Sovereignty Within the Law* 65, *African Law: Adaptation and Development* 65, *Law, Justice and Equity* 67, many articles.
20 Ozumba Mbadiwe, Victoria Island, Lagos, Nigeria.
Telephone: 27549.

Eliot, George Fielding, B.A.; American writer; b. 22 June 1894; ed. Melbourne Univ.
Served with A.I.F. 14-18, with Military Intelligence, U.S. Army (Reserve) 22-30; writer on military and int. affairs 26-; radio commentator; Military and Naval corresp. *New York Herald Tribune* 39-47; Military Analyst Columbia Broadcasting System 39-47; Columnist *New York Post* 47-49; Mil. Analyst, Mutual Broadcasting System 50-52, *The Military Scene* (Gen. Features Syndicate) 50-; Pres. Asscn. of Radio News Analysts 43 and 51; Pres. Cttee. for Nat. Morale 42-45; Dir. Australian Society of New York 42-43.
Publs. *If War Comes* (with Col. R. E. Dupuy) 37, *The Ramparts We Watch* 38, *Bombs Bursting in the Air* 39, *Hour of Triumph* 44, *The Strength We Need* 46, *Hate, Hope and High Explosives* 48, *If Russia Strikes* 49, *Caleb Pettengill, U.S.N.* 56, *Victory without War* 58, *Sylvanus Thayer of West Point* 59, *Reserve Forces and the Kennedy Strategy* 62, *Franklin Buchanan* 62.
1175 York Avenue, New York 21, N.Y., U.S.A.

Eliot, Martha May, A.B., M.D.; American pediatrician; b. 7 April 1891; ed. Radcliffe Coll. and Johns Hopkins School of Medicine.
Instr. in Pediatrics Yale Univ. School of Medicine 21-27, Asst. Clinical Prof. 27-32, Associate Clinical Prof. 32-35, Lecturer 35-49; attending pediatrician New Haven Hospital and Dispensary 23-34; Dir. Div. Child and Maternal Health, U.S. Children's Bureau 24-34, Asst. Chief 34-41, Assoc. Chief 41-49; Asst. Dir.-Gen. WHO 49-51; Chief U.S. Children's Bureau, Washington, D.C. 51-56; Prof. of Maternal and Child Health, Harvard School of Public Health 57-60, Emer. 60-; U.S. Rep. Exec. Board UN Children's Fund 52-57; Consultant in Maternal and Child Health to WHO 60-61.
21 Francis Avenue, Cambridge 38, Massachusetts, U.S.A.

Eliseev, Georgy Ivanovich; Soviet sports administrator; b. 1913; ed. Leningrad Builders' School and Leningrad Inst. of Physical Culture.
Technician, then building engineer 35-37; Chief Training Sports Dept., then Asst. Chair. Regional Council Sporting Soc. *Burevestnik*, Leningrad 37-39; mem. C.P.S.U. 44; engineer for sporting constructions, Regional Council Sporting Soc. *Burevestnik*, Leningrad 47-49; Chair. Central Council Sporting Soc. *Burevestnik* 49-53, 55-56, 62-; Section Chief of Physical Culture and Sports Dept. of U.S.S.R. Central Council of Trade Unions 53-55, Chief 56-61; Pres. U.S.S.R. Council Voluntary Sporting Socs. of Trade Unions 61-; Deputy Pres. Central Council U.S.S.R. Union of Sporting Socs. and Orgs. 65-; Orders Red Banner (twice), Alexander Nevsky, Great Patriotic War, Red Star, Red Banner of Labour.
Central Council U.S.S.R. Union of Sporting Societies and Organisations, 4 Skatertniy pereulok, Moscow, U.S.S.R.

Elistratov, Pyotr Matveyevich; Soviet politician; b. 17; ed. Higher Party School of the Central Cttee., C.P. Ukraine.
Komsomol and party work 37-41; mem. C.P.S.U. 39-; Sec., then First Sec. Vladivostok City Cttee., Komsomol 41-42; Third Sec. Vladivostok City Cttee. C.P.S.U. 42-43; Soviet army service 43-46; Second Sec. Odessa, then First Sec. Kherson Regional Cttee., Komsomol Ukraine 46-49; First Sec. Kakhovka City Cttee. C.P. Ukraine 52-54; Sec., Second Sec., then First Sec. Kherson Regional Cttee. C.P. Ukraine 54-61; Second Sec. Central Cttee. C.P. Azerbaijan 61-; mem. Central Auditing Comm. C.P.S.U. 61-66; Candidate mem. C.P.S.U. Central Cttee. 66-; Deputy to U.S.S.R. Supreme Soviet.
Central Committee of the Communist Party of Azerbaijan, Baku, Azerbaijan S.S.R., U.S.S.R.

Elizabeth II; Queen of Great Britain and Northern Ireland and of her other Realms and Territories (*see under Reigning Royal Families at front of book for full titles*); b. 21 April 1926.
Succeeded to the Throne following death of her father, George VI, 6th Feb. 52; married, Nov. 47, H.R.H. the Duke of Edinburgh, b. 10th June 21; children: Prince Charles Philip Arthur George, Prince of Wales (heir apparent), b. 14th Nov. 48; Princess Anne Elizabeth Alice Louise, b. 15th Aug. 50; Prince Andrew Albert Christian Edward, b. 19th Feb. 60; Prince Edward Antony Richard Louis, b. 10th March 64.
Buckingham Palace, London; Windsor Castle, Berkshire, England; Balmoral Castle, Aberdeenshire, Scotland; Sandringham, Norfolk, England.

Elizabeth Angela Marguerite; H.M. Queen Elizabeth the Queen Mother, Lady of the Order of the Garter, Lady of the Order of the Thistle, C.I., G.C.V.O., G.B.E.; member of the British Royal Family; b. 4 Aug. 1900; m. 23 H.R.H. The Duke of York, later H.M. King George VI (died 52); reigned as Queen 36-52.
Clarence House, London, S.W.1; Royal Lodge, Windsor Great Park, Berks., England; Castle of Mey, Caithness, Scotland.

Elizalde, Felix Gilberto María, DR. ECON.; Argentine banker; b. 17 Sept. 1924; ed. Nat. Univ. of Buenos Aires and Columbia Univ.
Professional practice 50-56, 58-63; mem. Board of Dirs. Central Bank of Argentina; Under-Sec. of Treasury 56-57; Pres. of Board of Dirs., Central Bank of Argentina 63-.
Central Bank of Argentina, Reconquista 274, 2° Piso, Buenos Aires, Argentina.

Elkes, Joel, M.B., CH.B., M.D.; American physician; b. 12 Nov. 1913; ed. Univ. of Birmingham Medical School, England.

Sir Halley Stuart Research Fellow in Pharmacology, Univ. of Birmingham 42-45, Lecturer in Pharmacology 45-48, Senior Lecturer and Act. Dir. Dept. of Pharmacology 48-50, Prof. and Chair. Dept. of Experimental Psychiatry 51-57; Consultant Psychiatrist, Birmingham Hospitals and Scientific Dir. Birmingham Regional Psychiatric Early Treatment Centre 53-57; Chief, Clinical Neuropharmacology Research Centre, Nat. Inst. of Mental Health (U.S. Nat. Insts. of Health) 57-63; Dir. of Behavior and Clinical Studies Center, St. Elizabeth's Hospital 57-63, Clinical Prof. of Psychiatry, George Washington Univ. School of Medicine 57-63; Henry Phipps Professor and Dir. Dept. of Psychiatry, The Johns Hopkins Univ. School of Medicine, Psychiatrist-in-Chief, The Johns Hopkins Hospital, Baltimore, Md. 63-; Ed. *Psychopharmacologia*, Assoc. Ed. *Journal of Psychiatric Research*; Org. Sec. 1st Int. Neurochemical Symposium; mem. Central Council Int. Brain Research Org. Research Cttee; Mental Health Research Fund, Fellow American Academy of Arts and Sciences Harvey Lecturer 62, Salmon Lecturer 64, etc.
Publs. *Effects of Psychosomimetic Drugs in Animals and Man* 56, *Drug Effects in Relation to Reactor Specificity within the Brain* 58, *Ataractic and Hallucinogenic Drugs in Psychiatry* 58, *Psychopharmacology: The Need for some Points of Reference* 59, *Schizophrenic Disorder in Relation to Levels of Neural Organisation: The Need for Some Conceptual Points of Reference* 61, *Subjective and Objective Observation in Psychiatry* 62.
3925 Canterbury Road, Baltimore, Md., U.S.A.

Elkins, Sir Anthony Joseph, C.B.E.; British business executive; b. 30 May 1904; ed. Haileybury Coll.
Honorary Presidency Magistrate, Bombay 28; mem. Advisory Cttee. E. India and E. Bengal Railways 38-40; Controller of Supplies, Bengal Circle, Dept. of Supply, India 41-45; Chair. Darjeeling Himalayan Railway 45-47; Chair. Gillanders Arbuthnot & Co. Ltd., Calcutta 45-54; Chair. Bryant and May Ltd. 55-64; Dep. Chair. British Match Corpn. 55-64, Chair. 64-; Chair. Airscrew-Weyroc Ltd. 59-64; Chair. Gestetner Ltd. 64-; Vice-Chair. and Dir. Army and Navy Stores 65-; Pres. Inst. of Export 67-68.
Lynchets, Upper Lambourn, Berks, England.

Ell, Carl Stephens, A.B., S.B., M.S., ED.M.; American engineer and educator; b. 14 Nov. 1887; ed. DePauw Acad., DePauw Univ., Massachusetts Inst. of Technology, Harvard Univ.
Professional practice and mem. of Faculty, Northeastern Univ. 10-17, Dean of Coll. of Engineering 17-40, Vice-Pres. 25-40; Trustee and Corpn. mem. Northeastern Univ. 36-, Pres. 40-59, Pres. Emeritus, Hon. Chancellor and Trustee 59-; mem. Boston Soc. of Civil Engineers, Eng. Soc. of New England; New England Asscn. of Colls. and Secondary Schools, Soc. for the Advancement of Educ.; Fellow Emeritus American Acad. of Arts and Sciences; Dir. Arkwright Boston Insurance Co.; Hon. LL.D. (Tufts, Rhode Island and Emerson Coll.), Hon. Sc.D. (DePauw), Hon. L.H.D. (Boston Univ.), Hon. D.S. in Educ. (Northeastern Univ.), M.S. and S.B. (Mass. Inst. of Technology), Ed.M. (Harvard Univ.).
Northeastern University, 360 Huntington Avenue, Boston, Mass. 02115, U.S.A.

Ellender, Allen Joseph, M.A., LL.B.; American lawyer and politician; b. 24 Sept. 1890; ed. St. Aloysius Coll., New Orleans, and Tulane Univ. of Louisiana.
Farmer; City Attorney Houma 13-15; District Attorney Terrebonne Parish 15-16; served in First World War; Del. to Constitutional Convention Louisiana 21; mem. Louisiana House of Reps. 24-36; Floor Leader, Louisiana State Legislature 28-32; Speaker, House of Reps. 32-36; U.S. Senator from Louisiana 37-; mem. Democratic Nat. Cttee. from Louisiana 39.
Senate Office Building, Washington, D.C.; Home: 235 East Park Avenue, Houma, La., U.S.A.

Ellery Queen (*see* Dannay, Frederic and Lee, Manfred).

Elling, Christian, M.A., PH.D.; Danish art historian; b. 14 Nov. 1901; ed. Sorø Acad. and Copenhagen Univ. Lecturer, Copenhagen Univ. 32-39, Provost, Dept. of Art History 39-, Prof. of History of Art 39-, Dean, Faculty of Letters 44-45; mem. Board, Nat. Museum, Frederiksborg 51-, Danish Acad. in Rome 54-57; Fellow, Royal Danish Acad. of Sciences and Letters 48-, Royal Danish Historical Soc. 48-, Danish Acad. 60-; Kt. Commdr. Swedish Order of Polar Star; Italian Order of Merit; Officer Order of Dannebrog; Italian Gold Medal of Merit.
Publs. *Projets de J. A. Gabriel et N. H. Jardin* 31, *Holmens Bygnings Historie 1680-1770* 32, *Studien und Quellen zur Geschichte der spätbarocken Baukunst in Dänemark* 37-39, *Operahus og Casino* 42, *Den italienske Nat* 47, *Villa Pia in Vaticano* 47, *Man loser Dickens* 49, *Function and Form of the Roman Belvedere* 50, *Rom fra Bernini til Thorvaldsen* 56, *Paraden I* 58, *Shakespeare I* 59, *Monumenta Architecturae Danicae* 61, *København i Fortrolighed* 61, *Et yndigt Land* 61, *Mellemakter-Essays i Udvalg ved Paul V. Rubow* 61, *Motiver-Prosa i Udvalg ved Aage Marcus* 63, *Min Yndlingslæsning* 64, *Kransen om Rom-Barokkens Værker i Compagnen og Bjergene* 66.
22 Kristianiagade, Copenhagen, Denmark.

Ellington, Buford; American politician; b. 27 June 1907; ed. Goodman Agricultural High School and Millsaps Coll.
Elected to Tennessee Gen. Assembly for Marshall County 48; Dir. sales force of Tennessee Farm Bureau Insurance Service; campaign man. for Gov. Frank Clement 52; Agriculture Commr., Tennessee 52-58; Chair. Southern Regional Educational Board 59-; Chair. National Governor's Conf. Cttee. on Road and Highway Safety 60; Gov. of Tennessee 59-62; Chair. Southern Governor's Conf. 61; Dir. Office of Emergency Planning, Nat. Security Council; Chair. Civil Defense Advisory Council; Democrat.
Curtiswood Lane, Nashville, Tennessee, U.S.A.

Ellington, Edward Kennedy ("Duke"); American bandleader and composer; b. 29 April 1899; ed. Armstrong High School.
Studied piano 06-; first professional appearance 16; New York 22, Cotton Club, Harlem 27-32; first tour in Europe 33; concerts at Carnegie Hall and Metropolitan Opera House; numerous recordings and radio and television appearances; compositions include suites *Blue, Black and Beige, Such Sweet Thunder* (settings of Shakespeare's sonnets), *Concert of Sacred Music* 66, and numerous songs; Hon. D.H. (Milton Coll.); Hon. D.Mus. (Yale).
333 Riverside Drive, New York, N.Y., U.S.A.

Elliot, Francis R., LL.B.; American business executive; b. 10 July 1903; ed. Coll. of William and Mary, Virginia.
Legal practice, Norfolk, Virginia 26-29; lawyer, The Border Co. 29, Head of Milk Operations, New York metropolitan area 46-55; Gen. Man. of Nat. Milk Operations, Milk and Ice Cream Co. Div., The Borden Co. 55-57, Pres. 57-; Vice-Pres. The Borden Co. 57-60, Dir. 59-, Exec. Vice-Pres. 60-64, Pres. and Chief Exec. Officer 64-67, Chair. and Chief Exec. Officer 67-; mem. Nat. Industrial Conf. Board Inc., American Inst. of Management, The Nutrition Foundation Inc., and New York Chamber of Commerce.
The Borden Company, 350 Madison Avenue, New York, N.Y. 10017, U.S.A.

Elliot, Sir John; British business executive; b. 98; ed. Marlborough and Sandhurst.
Served 3rd Hussars 17-20; journalist 20-24; joined Southern Railway (public relations and advertising) 25, Traffic Development Officer 30, Asst. Traffic Man. 33; many visits to U.S.A. and Canada to study rail, road

and air services; Deputy Gen. Man., Southern Railway 37, Acting Gen. Man. 47; Chief Regional Officer, Southern Region, British Railways 48-49, London Midland Region 50-51; visited Australia by invitation of Govt. of Victoria to report on transport services in that State 49; Chair., Railway Exec. 51-53; Chair. London Transport Exec. 53-59; Chair. Thos. Cook and Son Ltd. 59-67, Pullman Car Co. Ltd. 59-62, Willing and Co. Ltd. 59-; Dir. Commonwealth Devt. Corpn. 59-66, Thos. Tilling and Co. Ltd. 59-, British Airports Authority 65-; Vice-Pres. Union Internationale des Chemins de Fer 47 and 51-53; Pres. Inst. of Transport 53-54; Officier Légion d'Honneur, American Medal of Freedom.
Publs. *The Way of the Tumbrils* 58, *Early Days of the Southern Railway* 60, *Where Our Fathers Died* 64, *Speaking of That* 64.
356 Gray's Inn Road, London, W.C.1, England.

Elliott, Byron Kauffman, A.B., LL.B.; American lawyer and business executive; b. 5 May 1899; ed. Indiana Univ., Harvard Univ.
Chief Dep. County Prosecutor, Marion County, Ind. 23-25; Asst. Attorney-Gen., Ind. 25; Judge, Superior Court, Ind. 26-29; Man. and Gen. Counsel, American Life Convention 29-34; Pres. American Service Bureau 29-33, Chair. 33-34; Ed. *Monthly Legal Bulletin* 29-34; Dir. American Research and Development Corpn., Arthur D. Little Inc., Boston Edison Co., etc.; Trustee American Heritage Foundation, Northeastern Univ., etc.; Gen. Solicitor, John Hancock Mutual Life Insurance Co. 34-37, Vice-Pres. and Gen. Counsel 37-45, Dir. 45-, Exec. Vice-Pres. and Gen. Counsel 48-57, Pres. 57-63, Chair. Finance Cttee. 61-, Pres. and Chair. of the Board 63-65, Chair. of the Board 65-.
200 Berkeley Street, Boston, Mass. 02117, U.S.A.

Elliott, Osborn, A.B.; American journalist; b. 25 Oct. 1924; ed. The Browning School (N.Y.), St. Paul's School (Concord) and Harvard Univ.
Reporter N.Y. *Journal of Commerce* 46-49, Metals Editor, Tax-Exempt Bond Editor 47-49; Contributing Editor *Time* 49-52, Assoc. Editor 52-55; Senior Business Editor *Newsweek* 55-59, Managing Editor 59-61, Editor 61-; Dir. Washington Post. Co. 61-; Trustee American Museum of Natural History, Asia Soc., New York Public Library; served with U.S. Naval Reserve 44-46.
Publ. *Men at the Top* 59; Editor *The Negro Revolution in America* 64.
Home: 40 East 62nd Street; *Newsweek,* 444 Madison Avenue, New York 22, N.Y., U.S.A.

Ellis, Sir Charles Drummond, Kt., B.A., PH.D., F.R.S.; British physicist; b. 11 Aug. 1895; ed. Harrow, Royal Military Acad. Woolwich, Trinity Coll., Cambridge.
Fmrly. Fellow and Lecturer Trinity Coll. Cambridge, Lecturer Physics Dept. Cambridge Univ.; Wheatstone Prof. of Physics King's Coll. London Univ. 36-46; External Prof. of Physics at all Canadian universities 38-39; Scientific Adviser to Army Council 43-46; Dir. Finance Corpn. for Industry 45-; Gov. Harrow School; mem. Nat. Coal Board 46-55; Pres. British Coal Utilisation Research Asscn. 46-55; Scientific Adviser to Gas Council, to Battelle Inst., and to British American Tobacco Co. Ltd.
Publ. *Radiations from Radioactive Substances* 30.
Seawards, Cookham Dean, Berkshire, England.
Telephone: Marlow 3166.

Ellis, Elmer, B.A., A.M., PH.D.; American historian b. 27 July 1901; ed. Univ. of N. Dakota and State Univ. of Iowa.
Instructor N. Dakota State Teachers' Coll. 25-28; Lecturer in History, State Univ. of Iowa 28-30; Asst. Prof., Assoc. Prof. and Prof. of History, Univ. of Missouri 30-67; Acting Dean of Graduate School, Univ. of Mo., summers 36, 39, 41, Vice-Pres. in charge of Extra

Divisional Educational Activities 45-46, Dean of Faculty Coll. of Arts and Science 46-55, Acting Pres. 54-55, Pres. 55-66; Pres. Nat. Council for Social Studies 37; U.S. Army Hist. Branch, War Dept. Gen. Staff 43-45; mem. Hist. Advisory Cttee., U.S. Army, and Chair. 57-59; Pres. Miss. Valley Hist. Asscn. 50; mem. Board of Editors *Mississippi Valley Historical Review* 47-50, Board of Dirs. Social Science Research Council 46-51; Fulbright Visiting Lecturer, Univ. of Amsterdam 51-52; Pres. Board of Dirs. Harry S. Truman Inst. for Nat. and Int. Affairs 57-; mem. Board of Foreign Scholarships, U.S. Dept. of State 58-61, Civil Rights Advisory Cttee. U.S. Dept. of Agriculture 65-; Pres. Nat. Comm. on Accrediting 62-64; Pres. Nat. Asscn. State Univs. and Land-Grant Colls. 64-65; Consultant Educ. Cttee. of States 67-, Rockefeller Foundation 67-; Hon. LL.D. (Univ. of N. Dakota, Central Coll., Fayette, Missouri 55, Drury Coll., Springfield, Missouri 56, Washington Univ. 60); Hon. Litt.D. (Culver-Stockton Coll., Canton, Mo. 61); D.Litt. (St. Louis Univ. 65). Publs. *Education Against Propaganda* 37, *Mr. Dooley at his Best* 38, *Henry Moore Teller, Defender of the West* 41, *Mr. Dooley's America, a Life of Finley Peter Dunne* 41, *Towards Better Teaching in College.* Office: 323 Jesse Hall, University of Missouri, Columbia, Missouri; Home: 107 W. Brandon Road, Columbia, Missouri, U.S.A. Telephone: 449-9232 (Office).

Ellis, Frank Burton; American lawyer and government official; b. 07; ed. Gulf Coast Military Acad., Univ. of Virginia and Louisiana State Univ. Admitted to Louisiana Bar 30, legal practice 30-61; mem. Louisiana Senate 40-44; mem. Democratic Nat. Cttee. 52-54; Democratic State Chair., Louisiana 60-61; National Dir. Office of Civil Defense and Mobilisation, National Dir. Office of Emergency Planning, mem. National Security Council 61-62; U.S. District Judge, New Orleans, Louisiana 62-. Suite 314, 400 Royal Street, New Orleans 70130, La., U.S.A.

Ellis, Howard S., B.A., M.A., PH.D., LL.D.; American economist; b. 2 July 1898; ed. Univs. of Iowa, Michigan, Harvard, Heidelberg and Vienna. Instructor and later Prof. Univ. of Michigan 20-22, 24-38, of Calif. 38-43, 46-50 and 51-65; visiting Prof. Columbia 44-45, 49-50, Tokyo 51; economic analyst, Fed. Reserve Board, Washington 43-44; Asst. Dir. of Research and Statistics 44-45; Economic Policy Cttee., U.S. Chamber of Commerce 45-46; Dir. Marshall Aid Research Project Council on Foreign Relations 49-50; Pres. American Economic Asscn. 49; Pres. Int. Economic Asscn. 53-56, mem. Exec. Cttee. 56-62; Visiting Prof. Univ. of Bombay 58-59; Head, UNESCO Mission on Econs. in Latin America 60, Economic Research Center, Athens 63; U.S. Aid Mission, Rio de Janeiro 65-. Publs. *German Monetary Theory 1905-1933* 34, *Exchange Control in Central Europe* 41, *The Economics of Freedom: The Progress and Future of Aid to Europe* 50, *Approaches to Economic Development* 55. 936 Cragmont Avenue, Berkeley, California, U.S.A.

Ellison, Rt. Rev. Gerald Alexander, M.A., D.D.; British ecclesiastic; b. 19 Aug. 1910; ed. Westminster School, New Coll., Oxford and Westcott House, Cambridge. Curate Sherborne Abbey 35-37; Domestic Chaplain to Bishop of Winchester 37-39, to Archbishop of York 43-46; Chaplain to R.N.V.R. 40-43; Vicar St. Mark's Portsea and Hon. Chaplain to Archbishop of York 46-50; Canon of Portsmouth 50; Bishop of Willesden 50-55, of Chester 55-. Bishop's House, Chester, England.

Ellscheid, Robert, D.IUR.; German lawyer and business executive; b. 19 Feb. 1900; ed. Cologne and Bonn Univs.

Served First World War; lawyer 24-; Chair. Advisory Econ. Council, British Zone 46-47; Lecturer on Industrial Rights, Cologne Univ. 47-52, Prof. 52; Chair. Bd. of Dirs. Thyssen Röhrenwerke A.G., Düsseldorf, Heinr. Auer Mühlenwerke K.G.a.A., Cologne, Herbol-Werke Herbig-Haarhaus A.G., Cologne, Troponwerke Dinklage & Co., Cologne, Gerdsteiner Sprudel K.G., Gerdstein; mem. Board of Dirs. August Thyssen-Hütte A.G., Duisburg-Hamborn, Kaufhof A.G., Cologne, Schwäbische Zellstoff A.G., Ehingen, Deutsche Atlas Copco G.m.b.H., Essen, Rheinischer Erz und Metallhandel, Cologne, official of four other companies; Pres. German Asscn. for Industrial Patents and Copyright, Berlin. 9 Habsburgerring, Cologne, German Federal Republic.

Ellsworth, Ralph E., A.B., B.S. in L.S., PH.D., LL.D.; American librarian and professor; b. 22 Sept. 1907; ed. Oberlin Coll., Western Reserve Univ., Chicago Univ. Librarian, Adams State Coll. 31-34; Dir. Libraries, Colorado Univ. 37-43; Dir. Libraries, Iowa State Univ. 44-58; Dir. Libraries and Prof. of Library Science, Colorado Univ. 58-. Publs. (with D. E. Bean) *Modular Planning for College and Small University Libraries* 48, *Library Buildings* 60, *The American Right Wing* 60, *Planning College and University Buildings* 60, *The School Library: Facilities for Independent Study* 64, *The School Library* 65. 860 Willowbrook Road, Boulder, Colo., U.S.A.

Elmandjra, Mahdi, PH.D.; Moroccan international official; b. 13 March 1933; ed. Lycée Lyautey, Casablanca, Putney School, Vermont, U.S.A., Cornell Univ., London School of Economics and Univ. de Paris, Faculté de droit à la Sorbonne. Head of Confs., Law Faculty, Univ. of Rabat 57-58; Adviser, Ministry of Foreign Affairs, and to Moroccan Del. to UN 58-59; Dir.-Gen., Radiodiffusion Télévision Marocaine 59-60; Chief of African Div., Office of Relations with Mem. States, UNESCO 61-63; Dir. Exec. Office of Dir.-Gen. of UNESCO 63-66; Asst. Dir.-Gen. of UNESCO for Social Sciences, Human Sciences and Culture July 66-. Office: UNESCO, place de Fontenoy, Paris 7e; Home: 9 *bis* rue Michel Ange, Paris 16e, France, and 6 rue Chenier, Casablanca, Morocco.

Elmendorff, Wilhelm, DR. RER. POL.; German accountant; b. 3 Sept. 1903; ed. Univs. of Freiburg (Breisgau), Berlin and Cologne, and London School of Economics. With Economic Statistical Insts. and commercial press 27-34; Chartered Accountant 34-; Chair. Supervisory Board Preussische Bergwerks- und Hütten A.G., VTG (Vereinigte Tanklager und Transportmittel G.m.b.H.), Hamburg, Schachtbau Thyssen G.m.b.H., Mülheim-Ruhr; fmr. Pres. German Inst. of Certified Public Accountants, Düsseldorf; fmr. Pres. Union Européenne des Experts Comptables Economiques et Financiers. Düsseldorf, Goldsteinstrasse 29, German Federal Republic.

Elmhirst, Leonard Knight, M.A., B.SC.; British agriculturalist; b. 6 June 1893; ed. Repton School, Trinity Coll., Cambridge and Cornell Univ. Director Institute of Rural Reconstruction, Visva-Bharati (Bengal) 21-24; purchased Dartington Hall (Devon, England) for experiments in Rural Industry, Research and Education 25, Chair. Dartington Hall Trust; Pres. Int. Conf. of Agricultural Economists 30-58, Hon. Founder Pres. 58-; Chair. Political and Economic Planning 39-53; Pres. Int. Asscn. of Comm. on Nat. Parks 45-47; Pres. Royal Forestry Soc. of England and Wales 46-48; Development Commr. 49-65; mem. Indian Govt. Comm. on Higher Education for Rural Areas 54-55; mem. Council, Exeter Univ. 55-; Hon. D.Pol.Sci. (Freiburg), Hon. D.Litt. (Visva-Bharati Univ., India), Hon. D.C.L. (Durham).

Publs. *Robbery of the Soil* 22, *Rural Reconstruction* 23, *The Application of Economic Research to a Village in Bengal* 30, *Trip to Russia* 33, *Social Trends in Rural Areas* 38, *Collected Notes on Agricultural Problems in Bengal* 45, *Rabindranath Tagore and Santiniketan* 58, *Rabindranath Tagore, Pioneer in Education* 61.
Dartington Hall, Totnes, Devon, England.

Elmi, Hassan Nur; Somali diplomatist; b. 26; ed. Univs. of Mogadishu, Florence and Rome.
Governor of Mijerteein, Hiran and Banadir Regions 56-59; Chief of Cabinet to Minister of Foreign Affairs 60-61; Perm. Rep. to UN 61-65; Amb. to Belgium, also accred. to Luxembourg and Netherlands 66-.
Embassy of Somalia, 29 Avenue Brugmann, Brussels, Belgium.

Elslande, Renaat van; Belgian lawyer, university professor and politician; b. 21 Jan. 1916.
Professor, Inst. for Physical Educ., Univ. of Louvain; mem. Chamber of Reps. 49-; Minister, Under-Sec. of State for Cultural Affairs 60, later Minister for Culture and Educ.; Minister for European Affairs and Flemish Culture 66-68; Christian Social Party.
39 Kerkstraat, Lot, Belgium.
Telephone: 76-32-39.

Elst, Baron Joseph Marie Ghislain van der; Belgian diplomatist; b. 96; ed. Louvain Univ.
Entered diplomatic service 21, served Brussels, Washington, Athens, Vienna and Budapest; Counsellor U.S.A. 40-45; Minister to Portugal 46-51; Ambassador to Italy 51-62.
Publs. *The Last Flowering of the Middle Ages* (New York) 47; *The Picture Frame* (London) 48; *Les Trois Madones et autres Contes Flamands* (Paris) 50; *Le Portugal* (Paris) 51; *L'Age d'Or Flamand* (Paris) 52; *Florence* (Paris) 53.
Bastide Saint Julien, Biot (A.M.), France.

Eltester, Walther, D. THEOL.; German theologian; b. 18 April 1899; studied theology in Jena and Berlin.
Scientific Asst. Prussian Acad. of Science 31-40; Scientific Officer and Prof. 40-45; Reader in Ecclesiastical History, Univ. of Berlin 40-45; Extraordinary Prof. of Ecclesiastical History and Dean of Theological Faculty, Univ. of Berlin 45-49, Ordinary Prof. 47-49; Ordinary Prof. of New Testament and Old Church History, Univ. of Marburg 49-55; Prof. of Church History, Univ. of Tübingen 55-; mem. of Comm. for History of Religion, German Acad. of Sciences, Comm. for Patristic Studies in the German Federal Republic, Soc. Novi Testamenti Studiorum.
Joint Editor *Zeitschrift für neutestamentliche Wissenschaft* and *Arbeiten zur Kirchengeschichte.*
Waldeckstrasse 23, 74 Tübingen-Lustnau, German Federal Republic.
Telephone: Tübingen 23717.

Elton, 1st Baron, cr. 34, of Headington; **Godfrey Elton,** M.A.; British writer and politician; b. 29 March 1892; ed. Balliol Coll., Oxford.
Fellow Queen's Coll. Oxford, Lecturer in Modern History 19-39, Dean 21-23, Tutor 27-34; Hon. Political Sec. Nat. Labour Cttee. 32; Hon. Editor Nat. Labour *News Letter* 32-38; created Baron 34; mem. Ullswater Cttee. on Broadcasting 35; Chair. Exec. Cttee. Road Accidents Emergency Council 36-40; Sec. to Rhodes Trust 39-59; Pres. Christian Service Union; Pres. Metropolitan Asscn. of Building Societies 43-61.
Publs. *Schoolboys and Exiles* (verse) 20, *The Revolutionary Idea in France* 23, *Years of Peace* (verse) 25, *The Testament of Dominic Burleigh* 26, *Against the Sun* 28, *The Stranger* 30, *England, Arise!* 31. *Towards the New Labour Party* 32, *Among Others* 38, *The Life of James Ramsay MacDonald* (Vol. I, *1866-1919*) 39, *It Occurs to Me* 39, *Notebook in Wartime* 41, *St. George or the Dragon* 42, *Imperial Commonwealth* 45, *Such is the Kingdom* 47, *The Two Villages* 49, *General Gordon* 5 4 *Edward King and Our Times* 58, *General Gordon's Khartoum Journal* (Editor) 61, *Simon Peter: a study of discipleship* 64, *The Unarmed Invasion* 65.
Adderbury, nr. Banbury, Oxfordshire, England.

Elvin, Herbert Lionel, M.A.; British educationist; b. 7 Aug. 1905; ed. Trinity Hall, Cambridge, and Yale Univ.
Fellow of Trinity Hall, Cambridge, and mem. of Faculty of English, Cambridge, 30-45; temporary civil servant, Air Ministry 40-42, Ministry of Information (American Div.) 42-45; Principal, Ruskin Coll., mem. Faculty of English, Oxford 45-50; mem. Univ. Grants Cttee. 46-50; Dir. Dept. of Education, UNESCO 50-56; Prof. Education (Tropical Areas). London Univ., Inst. of Education 56-58; Dir. Inst. of Education, London Univ. 58-; Chair. Commonwealth Educ. Liaison Cttee. 65-; mem. Govt. of India Educ. Comm. 65-66.
Publs. *Men of America* 41, *An Introduction to the Study of Poetry* 49, *Education and Contemporary Society* 65.
Dundridge Cottage, St. Leonards, near Tring, Hertfordshire, England.

Elvin, Violetta (Violetta Prokhorova—Mrs. Fernando Savarese); American (born Russian) ballerina; b. 3 Nov. 1925; ed. Bolshoi Theatre School, Moscow.
Mem. Bolshoi Theatre Ballet 42; evacuated to Tashkent 43; ballerina, Tashkent State Theatre; rejoined Bolshoi Theatre as soloist 44; joined Sadler's Wells Ballet, Royal Opera House, Covent Garden (now The Royal Ballet) as guest soloist 46, and later as regular mem., prima ballerina 51-56; guest artist, Stanislavsky Theatre, Moscow 44, Sadler's Wells Theatre 47; guest prima ballerina, La Scala 52-53; guest artist, Cannes 54, Copenhagen 54, Teatro Municipal, Rio de Janeiro 55, Festival Hall 55; guest prima ballerina, Royal Opera House, Stockholm 56; Royal Opera House, Covent Garden 56 (concluded her stage career); film appearances: *The Queen of Spades, Twice Upon a Time, Melba.*
c/o British Consulate-General, Via Crispi, Naples, Italy.

Elworthy, Marshal of the Royal Air Force Sir Charles, G.C.B., C.B.E., D.S.O., M.V.O., D.F.C., A.F.C.; British air force officer; b. 23 March 1911; ed. Marlborough Coll. and Trinity Coll., Cambridge.
Reserve of Air Force Officers 33; Called to Bar (Lincoln's Inn) 35; R.A.F. 36-, Bomber Command 39-45, Commandant R.A.F. Staff Coll. 57-59; Dep. Chief of Air Staff 59-60; C.-in-C. Middle East 60-63; Chief of Air Staff Sept. 63-67; Chief of Defence Staff 67-.
Ministry of Defence, Whitehall, London, S.W.1; Home: Perseverence Cottage, Harpsden, Henley on Thames, Berks., England.
Telephone: Henley 2241.

Ely, General Paul Henry Romuald, G.B.E.; French army officer; b. 17 Dec. 1897; ed. Lycée de Brest, Ecole Spéciale Militaire de Saint-Cyr, Ecole Supérieure de Guerre.
C.O. 10th Chasseurs 41-42; Rep. of Allied High Command with Résistance 44; Commdr. of Infantry 45; Mil. Dir. Min. of Nat. Defence 46; Commdr. 7th Region 47-48; Chief of Staff to Inspector-Gen. of Armed Forces 48; French Rep. to Western Union 48-49 and to NATO 50-53; Chief of the Gen. Staff 53-54; High-Commdr. and C.-in-C. in Indo-China 54-55; Chief Gen. Staff Mar. 56-May 58, June 58-Jan. 59; Chief Staff Officer of Defence Jan. 59-Feb. 61; Grand Croix de la Légion d'Honneur, Médaille Militaire.
Publs. *L'Armée dans la Nation* 61, *L'Indochine dans la Tourmente* 64.
4 rue Puvis de Chavannes, Paris 17e, France.

Elytis, Odysseus; Greek poet and essayist; b. 11; ed. Univs. of Athens and Paris.
Contributed first to review *Nea Grammata* 35; became

expounder of surrealism; art critic for newspaper *Kathimerini* 46-48; Broadcasting and Programme Dir. Hellenic Nat. Broadcasting Inst. 45-46 and 53-54; represented Greece at Rencontres Int. de Genève 48 and Congrès de l'Association des Critiques d'Art 49; Councillor of the Arts Theatre.

Publs. *Orientations* 36, *Clepsydras of the Unknown* 37, *Sporades* 38, *Sun the First* 43, *Heroic and Funeral Song for the Lost Sub-lieutenant in Albania* 45, *Six and One, Regrets for Heaven* 60, *Axion Esti* 59, *Open Papers*. 23 Skoufa Street, Athens, Greece.

Elyutin, Vyacheslav Petrovich, DR.TECH.SC.; Soviet scientist and politician; b. 07; ed. Moscow Steel Inst. Instructor, Moscow Steel Inst. 30-35; Dean, Deputy Dir. All-Union Industrial Acad., Moscow 35-41; Soviet Army 41-45; Dir. Moscow Steel Inst. 45-51; mem. C.P.S.U. 29; Deputy Minister of Higher Educ. of the U.S.S.R. 51-54, Minister of Higher Educ. 54-59; Minister of Higher and Middle Special Educ. 59-; corresp. mem. Soviet Acad. of Sciences; Alternate mem., Cen. Cttee., Communist Party of the Soviet Union 56-61, mem. 61-; Deputy to U.S.S.R. Supreme Soviet; State Prize 52; Order of Lenin (twice); Order of the Red Banner of Labour, Badge of Honour (twice).
Ministry of Higher and Secondary Education, 11 Ulitsa Zhdanova, Moscow, U.S.S.R.

Emanuel, Nikolai Markovich; Soviet physical chemist; b. 1 Oct. 1915; ed. Leningrad Industrial (Polytechnical) Inst.
Scientific worker at Inst. of Chemical Physics, U.S.S.R. Acad. of Sciences 38-; Instructor, Moscow Univ. 44-50, Prof. 50-; mem. C.P.S.U. 48-; Corresp. mem. U.S.S.R. Acad. of Sciences 58-66, mem. U.S.S.R. Acad. of Sciences 66-; Deputy Chief Scientific Sec. to Presidium of U.S.S.R. Acad. of Sciences, Vice-Chair. Chemical-Technological and Biological Sciences Section, U.S.S.R. Acad. of Sciences 63-; Lenin Prize for research into properties and particular features of chain reactions 58; Order of Red Banner of Labour 65.
U.S.S.R. Academy of Sciences, 14 Leninsky Prospekt, Moscow, U.S.S.R.

Emanuels, Severinus D.; Netherlands Surinam lawyer and politician; b. 10; ed. Univs. of Leyden and Utrecht, Ecole de Droit, Paris.
District Attorney's Office, Magelang, Indonesia 37-38; Acting Judge, Court of Justice, Makassar 38-42; Royal Netherlands Army Service 42-45; Chief, Bureaux of Law, Dean of Law School, Celebes 46-48; Sec.-Gen. Dept. of Justice, Celebes 48-51; District Attorney, Paramaribo 51-52; Minister of Finance, Surinam 52-55; Counsellor, Netherlands Embassy, U.S.A. 56-58; Prime Minister of Surinam, Minister of General Affairs and Interior Affairs 58-63; Minister Plenipotentiary at The Hague 63-64; Counsellor for Press and Cultural Affairs, Netherlands Embassy in Mexico.
Calle de Londres 40, 4° piso, Mexico D.F., Mexico.

Emary, Abdel Galeel El-; United Arab Republic (Egyptian) banker; b. 07; ed. Cairo Univ. and Leeds Univ., England.
Civil Service, Ministries of Finance and Commerce, Egypt 32-47; Under-Sec. of Finance 47-50; Minister of Finance 52-54; Gov. of Central Bank of Egypt 57-60; Dir. Development Bank Services, Int. Finance Corpn., Washington, D.C. 62-63; Dir. of Investments, Africa, Asia and Middle East, Int. Finance Corpn. 63-65; Dir. Africa Dept., Int. Bank for Reconstruction and Development, Washington D.C. 65-.
International Bank for Reconstruction and Development, Washington, D.C. 20433, U.S.A.

Emelyanov, Vasily Simonovich; Soviet physicist; b. 01; ed. Moscow Mining Acad.
Director Standards Cttee. 40-46; metallurgist in tank factory in Urals during Second World War, designed

gun turret for T-34 tank, Dir. Admin. for Peaceful Uses of Atomic Energy 58-60; Chair. State Cttee. for Atomic Energy 60-62, Deputy Chair. 62-; Editor-in-Chief *Atomic Energy* 58; Corresp. mem. Soviet Acad. of Sciences; Alt. mem. C.P.S.U. Central Cttee. until 66; Chair. Comm. on Scientific Problems of Disarmament under Presidium of U.S.S.R. Acad. of Sciences; State prizewinner; Hero of Socialist Labour; Order of Lenin. Publs. include: *On Production of Manganese Steel* 34, *Influence of Nitrogen on Properties of Steel* 35, *Mechanical Properties of Dual and Triplet Alloys of Zirconium with Tantalum and Niobium at Normal and High Temperatures* 58.
State Committee for Atomic Energy, Moscow, U.S.S.R.

Emeneau, Murray Barnson, M.A., PH.D.; Canadian-born American university professor; b. 28 Feb. 1904; ed. Dalhousie, Oxford and Yale Univs.
Instructor in Latin, Yale Univ. 26-31; Fellowships, Yale Univ. and American Council of Learned Societies 31-40; research in India 35-38; Asst. Prof. of Sanskrit and Gen. Linguistics, Univ. of Calif. 40-43, Assoc. Prof. 43-46, Prof. 46-; Guggenheim Fellowship 49, 56-57, 58; Vice-Pres. Linguistic Society of America 49, Pres. 50; Assoc. Editor American Oriental Society 40-47, Editor 47-52, Pres. 54-55, Western Branch 64-65; Hermann Collitz Prof. of Indo-European Comparative Linguistics, Indiana Univ. 53; Faculty Research Lecturer, Berkeley, Univ. of Calif. 55-56, Chair. Dept. of Linguistics 53-58, Chair. Dept. of Classics 59-62; mem. American Philosophical Soc. 52; hon. mem. Nat. Inst. of Humanistic Sciences, Vietnam 57, Linguistic Soc. of India 64; Vice-Pres. Int. Asscn. for Tamil Research 66; Presented with *Studies in Indian Linguistics* by Centres of Advanced Study in Linguistics, Deccan Coll. and Annamalai Univ., and Linguistic Soc. of India 68.
Publs. *Jambhaladatta's Version of the Vetālapañcaviṇśati* 34, *A Union List of Printed Indic Texts and Translations in American Libraries* 35, *Kota Texts* 44-46, *Studies in Vietnamese (Annamese) Grammar* 51, *Kolami, a Dravidian Language* 55; *Vedic Variants* Vol. III (with M. Bloomfield & F. Edgerton) 34; *A Dravidian Etymological Dictionary* (with T. Burrow) 61, *Dravidian Borrowings from Indo-Aryan* (with T. Burrow) 62, *Brahui and Dravidian Grammar* 62, *Kālidāsa's Sakuntalā* translated from the Bengali Recension 62, *A Dravidian Etymological Dictionary: Supplement* (with T. Burrow) 68.
Department of Linguistics, University of California, Berkeley 4, Calif., U.S.A.

Emery, Walter Bryan, M.B.E., M.A., D.LIT., F.B.A., F.S.A.; British egyptologist; b. 2 July 1903; ed. St. Francis Xavier's Coll., Liverpool, and Inst. of Archaeology, Univ. of Liverpool.
Dir. Mond Expedition of Univ. of Liverpool to Egypt 24-29; Dir. Archæological Survey of Nubia of Egyptian Govt. 29-34; Dir. of Excavations at N. Sakkara, Antiquities Service of Egyptian Govt. 34-39; war service in British Army 39-45; Attaché and 1st Sec. British Embassy, Cairo 46-51; Edwards Prof. of Egyptology, Univ. of London 51-; Field Dir. Egypt Exploration Society.
Publs. *Excavations and Survey between Wadi es Sebua and Adindan* 35, *The Royal Tombs of Ballena and Qustol* 37, *The Tomb of Hemaka* 38, *Hor-aha* 39, *Nubian Treasure* 45, *Great Tombs of the First Dynasty* Vol. I 46, Vol. II 54, Vol. III 58, *Archaic Egypt* 60, *Egypt in Nubia* 65.
University College, Gower Street, London, W.C.1, England.

Emilio (*see* Pucci di Barsento, Marchese Emilio).

Emmanuel, Pierre; French writer; b. 3 May 1916. Director of the English Service 45-47, North-American Service 47-59, Radiodiffusion Française; Visiting Prof.

Harvard, Johns Hopkins, Brandeis, Buffalo, Queen's Univs.; Dir. Int. Asscn. for Cultural Freedom; Officier de la Légion d'Honneur, Grand Officier de l'Ordre Nat. du Mérite, Commandeur des Arts et Lettres, Commdr. of Yugoslav Flag, Grand Prix de Poésie de l'Académie Française.

Publs. Poetry: *Tombeau d'Orphée* 41, *Combats avec tes Défenseurs* 42, *Sodome* 44, *Le poète fou* 44, *Babel* 51, *Visage Nuage* 56, *Versant de l'âge* 58, *Evangéliaire* 61; *La Nouvelle Naissance* 63, novel: *Car enfin je vous aime* 49; autobiography: *Qui est cet homme* 48, *L'ouvrier de la onzième heure* 54; essay: *Le Goût de l'Un* 63, *La face humaine* 65, *Baudelaire devant Dieu* 67, *Le Monde est intérieur* 67.

61 rue de Varenne, Paris 7e, and Le Mas des Fidèles, 13 Eygalières, France.
Telephone: 468 91-06.

Emmet, Dorothy Mary, M.A.; British university professor; b. 29 Sept. 1904; ed. Lady Margaret Hall, Oxford.

Adult education work Maesyrhaf Settlement 27-28, 31-32; Commonwealth Fellowship in U.S. 28-30; Research Fellow, Somerville Coll., Oxford 30-31; Lecturer in Philosophy, King's Coll., Newcastle-on-Tyne 32-38; Lecturer in Philosophy of Religion, Univ. of Manchester 38-45; Reader in Philosophy 45-46; Sir Samuel Hall Prof. of Philosophy, Univ. of Manchester 46-66; Hon. Fellow Lady Margaret Hall, Oxford; Fellow Lucy Cavendish Coll., Cambridge.

Publs. *Whitehead's Philosophy of Organism* 32, *Philosophy and Faith* 36, *The Nature of Metaphysical Thinking* 45, *Function, Purpose and Powers* 58, *Rules, Roles and Relations* 66.

11 Millington Road, Cambridge, England.

Emminger, Otmar; DR.OEC.PUBL.; German bank director; b. 2 March 1911; ed. Berlin, Munich, Edinburgh and London Univs.

Mem. and Division Chief German Inst. for Business Research 35-39; at Bavarian Ministry of Economic Affairs 47-49; mem. German del. to O.E.E.C. Paris 49-50; Dir. Research and Statistics Dept. Bank Deutscher Länder 51-53; mem. Board of Managers Bank Deutscher Länder (now Deutsche Bundesbank) 53-, mem. Board of Dirs. Deutsche Bundesbank 57-; Exec. Dir. Int. Monetary Fund 53-59; Vice-Pres. EEC Monetary Cttee. 58-; Chair. of Deputies of "Group of Ten" (important mems. of Int. Monetary Fund) 63-67.

Publs. *Die englischen Währungsexperimente der Nachkriegszeit* 34, *Die Bayerische Industrie* 47, *Deutschlands Stellung in der Weltwirtschaft* 53, *Währungspolitik im Wandel der Zeit* 66.

Hasselhorstweg 36, Frankfurt/Main, S. 10, German Federal Republic.
Telephone: 268219 (Office).

Empson, William, M.A.; British university professor; b. 27 Sept. 1906; ed. Winchester Coll. and Magdalene Coll., Cambridge.

Prof. of English Literature at Bunrika Daigaku, Tokyo 31-34; Prof. of English Literature, Peking Nat. Univ., then part of Combined South-Western Univs. 37-39, and, after its return, at Peking 47-52; Chinese Editor, B.B.C. 41-47; Prof. of English Literature, Sheffield Univ. 53-.

Publs. *Seven Types of Ambiguity* 33, 62, *Some Versions of Pastoral* 35, *Poems* 35, *The Gathering Storm* (verse) 40, *The Structure of Complex Words* 51, *Collected Poems* 55, *Milton's God* 61.

Studio House, Hampstead Hill Gardens, London, N.W.3, England.

Enckell, (Carl Fredrik) Ralph (Alexander), M.A.; Finnish diplomatist; b. 13 May 1913.

Second Secretary, Finnish Legation, Stockholm 44-45; First Sec., Paris 45-50, Moscow 50-55; Head, Political Dept., Foreign Office, Helsinki 55-59; Permanent Rep. to UN, New York 59-65, Ambassador to Sweden 65-.

Embassy of Finland, Västra Trädgårdsgatan 13, Stockholm, Sweden.
Telephone: Stockholm 23-58-15.

Endacott, Paul; American petroleum executive; b. 13 July 1902; ed. Kansas Univ.

Joined Phillips Petroleum Co. as engineer 23, worked in Philgas Div., Detroit 27-34, Dir. Sales Research, Bartlesville 34-38, Asst. to Exec. Vice-Pres. 38-43 also Vice-Chair. Operating Cttee. (later Chair.), Vice-Pres. 43-49, and Dir., mem. Exec. Cttee. 43-, Exec. Vice-Pres. and Asst. to Pres. 49-51, Pres. 51-63, Vice-Chair. 63-67; Dir. American Independent Oil Co., American Petroleum Inst., Independent Petroleum Asscn. of America and official of many civic and industrial bodies.

c/o Phillips Petroleum Company, Phillips Building, Bartlesville, Okla., U.S.A.

Ende, Konrad, DR. ING.; German engineer and executive; b. 1 July 1895; ed. Oberrealschule St. Peter und Paul, Danzig, Mining Acad., Clausthal and Technische Hochschule, Breslau.

Man. Vereinigte Untertage u. Schachtbau GmbH., Essen 33-39; military service 39-40; Reichswerke AG für Berg-u. Hüttenbetriebe, Berlin 41-45, Dir. 43-; Dir. AG für Berg-u. Hüttenbetriebe, Salzgitter, 50-52, Chair. 52-; Chair. Advisory Board Salzgitter A.G., Chair. of Advisory and Supervisory Councils of allied companies; mem. Supervisory Council, Deutsche Bank A.G., Fritz Werner Verwaltungs-G.m.b.H., Berlin; Saarbergwerke A.G.; Hon. Dr. Ing. (Mining Acad., Clausthal); Grosses Verdienstkreuz mit Stern.

Gutshaus, 3322 Saltzgitter-Steterburg, German Federal Republic.

Endeley, E. M. L., O.B.E.; Nigerian medical doctor and politician; b. 16; ed. Buea Govt. School, Catholic Mission, Bojongo, Govt. Coll. Umuahia, Higher Coll., Yaba.

Qualified as doctor 42; entered Govt. service 43; served Lagos, Port Harcourt, etc.; in charge of Cottage Hospital, Buea; trade union leader 47; formed Cameroons Nat. Fed. (afterwards Kamerun Nat. Congress) 49; Pres. Bakweri Co-op. Marketing Union 55; led South Cameroons Del. to Constitutional Conf., London 57; first Premier of South Cameroons 58-59; Leader of the Opposition 59-61; Leader Nat. Convention Party (now Cameroon Peoples' National Convention Party), West Cameroon 61-.

Cameroon Peoples' National Convention Party, Buea, West Cameroon, Federal Republic of Cameroon.

Ender, Rudolf, LL.D. (son of Dr. Otto Ender, fmr. Austrian Federal Chancellor); Austrian diplomatist; b. 11 June 1911; ed. Coll. Stella Matutina, Feldkirch, and Univs. of Innsbruck, Vienna, London and Paris.

Foreign Office, Vienna 47-48; Sec., Austrian Legation, Rio de Janeiro 48-52; Foreign Office, Vienna 52-55; attached to Austrian Observer at Council of Europe 55-56; Foreign Office, Vienna 56-58; Minister, Prague 58-60; Amb. to Portugal 60-64; Chief of Protocol, Foreign Office, Vienna 64-66; Amb. to German Fed. Repub. 66-; numerous decorations.

Österreichische Botschaft, Poppelsdorfer Allee, Bonn, German Federal Republic.

Enders, John Franklin, PH.D., D.SC., LL.D., L.H.D.; American bacteriologist; b. 10 Feb. 1897; ed. Yale and Harvard Univs.

Assistant Dept. of Bacteriology and Immunology, Harvard Medical School 29-30, Instructor 30-32, Faculty Instructor 32-35, Asst. Prof. 35-42, Assoc. Prof. 42-56, Prof. 56-62, Univ. Prof. (Harvard) 62-67, Emeritus 68; Chief Research Div., Infectious Diseases, Children's Hospital Medical Center 47-; mem. Nat. Acad. of

Sciences; Foreign mem. Royal Soc. (U.K.); Passano Award 53; Lasker Award 54; Nobel Prize in Physiology and Medicine 54, Cameron Prize in Practical Therapeutics 60, Robert Koch Medal 63, Presidential Freedom Medal 63.
The Children's Hospital Medical Center, 300 Longwood Avenue, Boston 15, Mass., Home: 64 Colbourne Crescent, Brookline, Mass., U.S.A.

Endicott, Kenneth Milo, M.D.; American physician; b. 6 June 1916; ed. Univ. of Colorado.
Intern, U.S. Marine Hospital 39-40; U.S. Public Health Service 40-, Medical Dir. 51; Experimental Pathology, Nat. Insts. of Health 42-51, Scientific Dir. Div. of Research Grants 51-55, Chief, Cancer Chemotherapy Nat. Service Center 55-58, Assoc. Dir. (Training) NIH 58-60, Dir. Nat. Cancer Inst. 60-, Assoc. Dir. Nat. Insts. of Health 58-; mem. American Medical Asscn., American Asscn. of Pathologists and Bacteriologists, American Soc. for Experimental Pathology, American Asscn. for Advancement of Science, Soc. for Experimental Biology and Medicine, American Asscn. for Cancer Research, Washington Acad. of Sciences.
National Institutes of Health, Bethesda 14, Maryland; Home: Beall Mount, River Road, Potomac, Maryland, U.S.A.

Engel, Ir. Antonie Jacobus; Netherlands industrialist; b. 96; ed. Elementary School, Hillegom, Secondary School, Leiden, Univ. of Delft.
State Mines, Limburg; Algemene Kunstzijde Unie N.V. (rayon and synthetic yarns and fibres) 24-, Mechanical Engineer, Plant Manager, Chief. Gen. Engineering Dept., Manager Staple Fibre Plant, Vice-Pres. 52-54, Pres. 54-62, Deputy Chair. Supervisory Council 62-67; Chair. Machinefabriek Te Strake, De Waerdye; Dir. Van Hattum en Blankevoort, Tebodin N.V.; mem. Royal Inst. of Engineers; Knight in the Order of the Netherlands Lion; Officer Order of Orange-Nassau and other orders; Peter Stuyvesant Award (U.S.A.).
Home: Rozenhagelaan 4, Velp (Gld.), Netherlands.
Telephone: 08302-3118.

Engelhardt, Vladimir Aleksandrovitch; Soviet biochemist; b. 4 Dec. 1894; ed. Moscow Univ.
Public Health Biochemical Inst. 21-29; Prof. Kazan Univ. 29-34, Leningrad Univ. 34-40, Moscow Univ. 39-59; Head of Laboratory, Inst. of Biochemistry, Moscow 35-59; Academic Sec. Biological Dept., Acad. of Sciences 55-59; Dir. Inst. of Molecular Biology, Moscow 58-; mem. Bureau, Vice-Pres. I.C.S.U. 55-63; mem. U.S.S.R. Acad. of Sciences, Hon. Foreign Mem. Royal Inst., London, American Acad. of Arts and Sciences, Nat. Inst. of Sciences, India, Leopoldina Acad. of Nat. Sciences, German Acad. of Sciences, Berlin; Fellow Royal Soc., Edinburgh; Editor *Biochimia* 36-; State Prize; Order of Lenin (twice); Order of the Red Banner of Labour, etc.
U.S.S.R. Academy of Sciences, 14 Lenin Prospekt, Moscow, U.S.S.R.

Engellau, Gunnar Ludvig; Swedish civil engineer; b. 11 Nov. 1907; ed. Kung. Tekniska Högskolan, Stockholm.
Dept. Head, Motala Verkstad 35-37, Purchase and Sales Manager 37-39; Technical Sales Manager Electrolux, Stockholm and Motala 39-43; Pres. Svenska Flygmotor, A.B. Trollhättan 43-56; Managing Dir. A. B. Volvo, Gothenburg 56-; Head of the Volvo Group of companies.
A.B. Volvo, Box 382, Gothenburg 1, Sweden.
Telephone: 54-00-00.

Engone, Jean; Gabonese politician; b. 1 Jan. 1932; ed. Lycée Léon Mba, Libreville, Lycée de Châteroux, Indre (France) and Inst. des Hautes Etudes d'Outremer, Paris.
Civil Admin., Libreville Prefecture, Gabon 60; Asst.

Dir., then Dir., of Civil Service 60-62; attached to the Presidency, and Sec.-Gen. of Nat. Assembly 62-63; Dir. of Public Health Sept. 63; Minister of Finance 64-65; Minister of Foreign Affairs March 65-; decorations from China, Ivory Coast, Central African Repub. and Spain.
Ministère des Affaires Etrangères, B.P. 389, Libreville, Gabon.

Engstrom, Elmer W.; American electronics executive; b. 25 Aug. 1901; ed. elementary schools, St. Paul, Minn. and Univ. of Minnesota.
Joined Radio Engineering Dept., Gen. Electric Co. 23; G.E.C. radio engineering activities transferred to Radio Corpn. of America (R.C.A.) 30, Div. Engineer in charge of Photophone 30, research into television and colour television; Dir. of Gen. Research R.C.A. 42-43, Dir. of Research of R.C.A. Laboratories 43-45, Vice-Pres. (Research, R.C.A. Labs. Div.) 45-51, Vice-Pres. (R.C.A. Labs. Div.) 54-55, Exec. Vice-Pres. (Research and Engineering) 54-55, Senior Exec. Vice-Pres. R.C.A. 55-61, Pres. R.C.A. 61-65, Chief Exec. Officer and Chair. Exec. Cttee. 66-Dec. 67; holds Hon. Degrees from 14 U.S. Colls. and Univs.; official of numerous scientific, cultural and civic orgs.; several foreign decorations.
Radio Corporation of America, R.C.A. Building, 30 Rockefeller Plaza, New York, N.Y. 10020, U.S.A.

Engur, Yokosafate Atoke; Ugandan diplomatist; b. 19; ed. secondary and higher schools, Uganda.
Hospital pharmacist, Kampala 45-47; local govt. posts 47-52; mem. Uganda Nat. Congress 52-; Head of Lango District 60; mem. Uganda People's Congress 60-; Ambassador to U.S.S.R. 64-.
Embassy of Uganda, Lomonosovsky per. 83, Moscow, U.S.S.R.

Enikopolov, Nikolai Sergeyevich; Soviet chemist; b. 1924; ed. Erevan Polytechnical Inst.
Research Assoc., Chemistry Inst., Acad. of Sciences Armenian S.S.R. 45-46, Inst. of Chemical Physics U.S.S.R. Acad. of Sciences 46-; Lecturer Moscow Physico-Chemical Inst. 53-, Prof.; Corresp. mem. U.S.S.R. Acad. of Sciences 66-.
U.S.S.R. Academy of Sciences, 14 Lenin Prospekt Moscow, U.S.S.R.

Enright, Dennis Joseph, M.A., D.LITT.; British teacher and writer; b. 11 March 1920; ed. Leamington Coll., and Downing Coll., Cambridge.
Lecturer in English, Farouk I Univ. Alexandria 47-50; Org. Tutor, Birmingham Univ. Extra-Mural Dept. 50-53; Visiting Prof. Konan Univ. (Japan) 53-56; Gastdozent, English Seminar, Berlin Free Univ. 56-57; British Council Prof. Chulalongkorn Univ. Bangkok 57-59; Johore Prof. of English, Univ. of Singapore 60-; contributor to *Scrutiny, Essays in Criticism, New York Review of Books, New Statesman, Encounter, Listener.*
Publs. *The Laughing Hyena and Other Poems* 53, *Academic Year* 55, *The World of Dew: Aspects of Living Japan* 56, *Bread rather than Blossoms: Poems* 56, *The Poetry of Living Japan: An Anthology* 57, *The Apothecary's Shop: Essays on Literature* 57, *Insufficient Poppy* 60, *Some Men are Brothers: Poems* 60, *Addictions: Poems* 62, *Figures of Speech* 65, *The Old Adam* (poetry) 65, *Conspirators and Poets: literary criticism* 66, *Unlawful Assembly* (poetry) 68, *Selected Poems* 68.
c/o University of Singapore, Singapore 10.

Enters, Angna; American mime, painter and sculptor; b. 28 April 1907; ed. privately.
Presented *Composition in Dance Form* (later called *Theatre of Angna Enters*), which combined mime, dance, music, etc., in solo performance, in N.Y. 24; London debut 28; Paris debut 29, rep. U.S.A. in Berlin Arts Festival 51; 10th London season 56; presented mime *Pagan Greece* under auspices N.Y. Metropolitan Museum of Art 43; Guggenheim Foundation Fellowships for research in Mime and Art in Greece, Egypt 34-35;

Painting: N.Y. debut 33; various exhibitions Newhouse Galleries N.Y.; London debut 34; exhibition Brook Street Galleries 50; 3rd London exhibition at Foyle Gallery 56; Sculpture: N.Y. debut 45; work exhibited in N.Y. Metropolitan Museum of Art and other museums and private collections; composed scores for own play and mimes; play-within-play for Commedia dell'Arte sequence, choreography and dance for *Scaramouche* (film) 52; author of *Lost Angel* (film) 44, *10th Avenue Angel* (film) 46, and *You Belong to Me* (film) 48-49; first work in ceramics exhibited 52; exhibition in New York 58; 32nd annual Lecture Tour of U.S. and Canada in her one-woman theatre 60; directed and designed sets and costumes for *Yerma* 58; 22nd Broadway season solo theatre 60; Fellow Center for Advanced Studies, Wesleyan Univ., Middletown, Conn. 62-.
Publs. *First Person Plural* (own illustrations) 37; *Love Possessed Juana* (play) 39; *Silly Girl* (autobiography) 44; *A Thing of Beauty* (novel) 48; and stories for screen; *Among the Daughters* 55, *Artist's Life* (sequel to *First Person Plural*) 57; author of article on *Pantomime* for *Encyclopaedia Britannica*, adaptor-translator of Edmond Rostand's *Chantecler* 60, *The Loved and the Unloved* 61; *Angna Enters on Mime* 65.
35 West 57th Street, New York City 19, N.Y., U.S.A.

Enwonu, Benedict Chuka, M.B.E.; Nigerian sculptor; b. 21; ed. Holy Trinity School, Onitsha, Govt. Colls. Umu-Ahia and Ibadan, Univ. Coll., London.
First One-Man Show, Lagos 42; on the strength of this he was given a special scholarship by Shell-Mex to study in England; rep. UNESCO Exhibition, Paris 46; first One-Man Exhibition, London 48, subsequent exhibitions 50, 52, 55; exhibition U.S. 50; commissioned to execute statue of H.M. Queen Elizabeth, Doors, Panels and Speaker's Chair, Lagos House of Representatives, and the group *The Risen Christ* for the Chapel, Univ. Coll., Ibadan; Art Adviser to the Federal Govt. of Nigeria; his works have been purchased by H.M. Queen Elizabeth, the late Sir Jacob Epstein and others; R. B. Bennett Empire Art Prize 57.
Federal Government Information Services Department, Lagos, Nigeria; and 31A Redington Road, London, N.W.3, England.

Enzensberger, Hans Magnus, DR. PHIL.; German poet and writer; b. 11 Nov. 1929; ed. Univs. of Erlangen, Freiburg im Breisgau, Hamburg and Paris.
Third Programme Editor, Stuttgart Radio 55-57; Lecturer, Hochschule für Gestaltung, Ulm 56-57; Literary Consultant to Suhrkamp's (publishers), Frankfurt 60-61; mem. "Group 47"; Editor *Korsbuch* (review) 65-; Hugo Jacobi Prize 56; Kritiker Prize 62; Georg Büchner Prize 63.
Publs. *Verteidigung der Wölfe* (poems) 57, *Landessprache* (poems) 60, *Museum der Modernen Poesie* 60, *Allerleirauh* 61, *Clemens Brentanos Poetik* 61, *Einzelheiten* (essays) 62, *Blindenschrift* (poems) 64, *Politik und Verbrechen* (essays) 64, *Deutschland, Deutschland unter Anderen* 67, English edition of Poems: *Poems for People Who don't Read Poems* 68.
c/o Suhrkamp Verlag, Fach 2446, Frankfurt/Main, German Federal Republic.

Ephrussi, Boris; French (b. Russian) geneticist; b. 9 May 1901; ed. Univ. de Paris à la Sorbonne.
Associate Prof. of Biology, Johns Hopkins Univ., U.S.A. 41-44; Prof. of Genetics, Univ. of Paris 46-; Dir. Laboratory of Physiological Genetics, Centre Nat. de la Recherche Scientifique (France) 46-; Exchange Prof. Harvard Univ. 54, Calif. Inst. of Technology 59; F. H. Herrick Distinguished Prof. of Biology, Western Reserve Univ., U.S.A. 61-; mem. Royal Danish Acad.; Foreign Assoc. Nat. Acad. of Sciences (U.S.A.); Légion d'Honneur.

Publs. *La Culture des Tissus* 32, *Nudeo-cytoplasmic Relations in Micro-organisms* 53.
Laboratoire de Génétique Physiologique, 91 Gif-sur-Yvette, France.

Epishev, Gen. Alexei Alexeyevich; Soviet politician and Army Officer; b. 08; ed. Red Army Acad. of Mechanisation.
Member C.P.S.U. 29-; First Sec. Kharkov Regional and City Cttees. C.P. Ukraine, Plenipotentiary Rep. Military Council, Stalingrad Front, Dep. People's Commissar for Medium Machine Building U.S.S.R. 38-43; Soviet army service 43-46; Sec. Central Cttee. C.P. Ukraine 46-51; Dep. Minister of State Security U.S.S.R. 51-53; First Sec. Odessa Regional Cttee. C.P. Ukraine 53-55; Ambassador to Rumania 55-61, to Yugoslavia 61-62; Head, Political Dept., Soviet Army and Navy 62-; Cand. mem. Central Cttee. C.P.S.U. 52-64, mem. of the Central Cttee. of C.P.S.U. 64-; Gen. of the Army 62-; Deputy to U.S.S.R. Supreme Soviet; Awarded Order of Lenin (twice), Order of the Red Banner (thrice), Red Star, Bogdan Khmelnitsky (first class) and others.
Ministry of Defence, 37 Maurice Thorez Embankment, Moscow, U.S.S.R.

Epley, Marion Jay, Jr., LL.B.; American oil executive; b. 17 June 1907; ed. Tulane Univ. and Tulane Law School, New Orleans, Louisiana.
Private law practice, New Orleans 30-42, 45-47; U.S. Navy 42-45; Gen. Attorney, Texaco Inc. Louisiana and New York 48-57, Asst. to Chair. of Board of Dirs. 58-60, Vice-Pres. 58-60, Senior Vice-Pres. 60-61, Exec. Vice-Pres. 61-65, Pres. 65-; Board of Dirs. Texaco Inc. and American Petroleum Inst.; Vice-Chair. Supervisory Board Deutsche Erdol-Aktiengesellschaft, Hamburg.
Texaco Inc., 135 E. 42nd Street, New York, N.Y.; and Smithfield Farm, Amenia, N.Y., U.S.A.
Telephone: 212-697-8000.

Eppelsheimer, Hanns W., DR. PHIL.; German librarian and literary historian; b. 17 Oct. 1890; ed. Univs. of Freiburg, Munich and Marburg.
Director, Hesse Land Library 29-33, 45; Dir. Univ. Library, Frankfurt 46-58; Founder and Dir. Deutsche Bibliothek 47-59; Prof. of Univ. Frankfurt for Library Science 47-; mem. German UNESCO Comm. 51-66; mem. German Acad. of Languages and Poetry, Darmstadt 53, Vice-Pres. 58-62, Pres. 63-66, Hon. mem. 66-; Grosses Bundesverdienstkreuz mit Stern.
Publs. *Petrarca* 27, *Handbuch der Weltliteratur* 37, 47-50, 60, *Schild des Aeneas* 55, *Bibliographie der Deutschen Literaturwissenschaft* 45- (5 vols. 64).
Untermainkai 15, Frankfurt am Main, German Federal Republic.
Telephone: 281607.

Eppert, Ray R.; American business executive; b. 5 July 1902.
Joined Burroughs Corpn. as shipping clerk 21, Vice-Pres. (Marketing) 46-51, Exec. Vice-Pres. 51-58, Pres. 58-66, Chair. and Chief Exec. Officer 66-, Dir. 48-; Dir. Michigan Bell Telephone Co., Michigan Consolidated Gas Co., Nat. Bank of Detroit; official of many business and public bodies; mem. Advisory Group, Inst. for Social Research, Univ. of Michigan, etc.
Burroughs Corporation, Detroit, Mich. 48232, U.S.A.

Epron, Pierre; French industrialist; b. 31 March 1897; ed. Ecole des Arts et Manufactures, Paris.
Administrator, Houillères du Bassin de Lorraine 46-, Carbonisation, Entreprise Céramique 56-, Hon. Dir.-Gen. Soc. Lorraine-Escaut 62-; fmr. Pres. Ingénieurs Civils de France; fmr. Pres. Conseil Nat. des Ingénieurs Français; Dir. Soc. Métallurgique de Jorcy; Vice-Pres. Soc. Générale de Fonderie; Commandeur de la Légion d'Honneur, Croix de Guerre 14-18.
Home: 62 boulevard Flandrin, Paris 16e, France.
Telephone: 647-0047.

Eralp, Orhan, B.A., LL.B., PH.D.; Turkish diplomatist; b. 28 Jan. 1915; ed. Robert Coll., Istanbul, Univ. Coll., London, and London School of Economics.
Ministry of Foreign Affairs 39-; Sec. Washington 42-48; Adviser to Turkish Del., UN Conciliation Comm. for Palestine 49-51; Perm. Rep. to European Office of UN, Geneva 51; Counsellor, London 52; Dir.-Gen. Second Dept., Ministry of Foreign Affairs 52-56; Ambassador to Sweden 57-59, to Yugoslavia 59-64; Perm. Rep. of Turkey to UN, New York 64-.
Permanent Mission of Turkey to the United Nations, 866 United Nations Plaza, New York 10017, N.Y., U.S.A.

Erdei, Ferenc; Hungarian economist and academician; b. 24 Dec. 1910; ed. Szeged Univ.
Worker in an onion growers' co-operative at Mako, later started horticultural work near Budapest; active in the March Front Political movement; joined Peasant Party, staff member *Szabad Szó* (Free Word) (then its only legal organ) during 39-45 war; published essays on sociology and history; twice jailed for political and literary activities; during German occupation (March 44) took part in resistance and in illegal reorganisation of the Nat. Peasant Party; Minister of the Interior in provisional Nat. Govt. 44-45; Vice-Pres. Nat. Peasant Party 45-47; took part in development of agricultural co-operative movement; Sec.-Gen. Nat. Peasant Party 47; Minister of State 48; Minister of Agriculture 49-53; Minister of Justice 54; Deputy Premier 55-56; Dir. Inst. of Agricultural Econs., Budapest; Sec.-Gen. Hungarian Acad. of Sciences 58-64, Vice-Pres. 64-; Sec.-Gen. Hungarian Patriotic People's Front 64-; Kossuth Prize (twice); mem Presidential Council.
Publs. *Futóhomok, Parasztok, Magyar Város, Magyar Falu, Magyar Tanyák, Mezőgazdaság és Szövetkezet, A Termelési Körzetek és a Specializáció a Mezőgazdaságban, Üzemszervezési Kérdések a Szocialista Mezőgazdasági Nagyüzemben, A Mezőgazdasági Üzemszervezés Néhány Elméleti és Gyakorlati Kérdése, Üzemi Szervezet és Üzemvezetés a Szocialista Mezőgazdaságban.*
Benczúr u. 44, Budapest VI, Hungary.
Telephone: 428-198.

Erdey-Gruz, Tibor, PH.D.; Hungarian physico-chemist; b. 1902; ed. Péter Pázmány Univ., Budapest.
Professor of Physical Chemistry R. Eötvös Univ., Budapest; Sec. of Chemistry Section Hungarian Acad. of Sciences 48-50, 59-64, Gen. Sec. 50-53, 56-57, 64-; Minister of Educ. 52-56; Pres. of the Council for Science and Higher Educ. 62-64; mem. Hungarian Acad. of Sciences 43, mem. German Acad. of Sciences, Berlin 62; Hon. mem. Romanian Acad. of Sciences 65; Foreign mem. of the Soviet Acad. of Sciences 66; Kossuth Prize 50, 65.
Publs. *The Practice of Physical Chemistry* 34, 62, 65, 67-68 (with János Proszt), *Atoms and Molecules* 45, 66, *Theoretical Physical Chemistry* 52-54, 62-64 (with Géza Schay), *The Foundations of Physical Chemistry* 58, 63, *The Foundations of the Structure of Matter* 61, 67, *The Knowledge of Chemicals* 43, 64, *Matter and Motion* 62, *Philosophical Gleaning in the Natural Sciences* 65, *The Material Structure of the World* 66, *The Chemical Sources of Energy* 67.
Roosevelt tér 9, Budapest V, and Lékai J. tér 2, Budapest XII, Hungary.
Telephone: 355-452.

Eremenko, Marshal Andrei Ivanovich; Soviet army officer; b. 92; ed. Frunze Military Acad.
Member C.P.S.U. 18-; Soviet army service 18-, Cavalry Company Commdr., later Div. Commdr. 19-40; Commdr. Mechanised Corps. 40-41; during Second World War Commdr. on Briansk, Western, South-Eastern, Stalingrad, Southern, Kalinin, Baltic and Ukrainian Fronts; Commdr. military areas 45-58; Insp.-Gen. U.S.S.R. Ministry of Defence 58-; Marshal of the Soviet Union 55-; Cand. mem. Central Cttee. C.P.S.U. 56-; Deputy to U.S.S.R. Supreme Soviet; Hero of the Soviet Union 44; Awarded Order of Lenin (four times), Order of the Red Banner (four times), Suvorov (first class) (thrice), Golden Star Medal, October Revolution, Kutuzov first class Sword of Honour with Coat of Arms in gold and other decorations.
Publs. *Against Falsification of the 2nd World War History* 60, *At the Outbreak of the War* 67.
Ministry of Defence, 37 Maurice Thorez Embankment, Moscow, U.S.S.R.

Erhard, Ludwig; German economist and politician; b. 4 Feb. 1897; ed. Handelshochschule, Nuremberg, and Univ. of Frankfurt.
War service 16-19; on staff of Handelshochschule, Nuremberg, rising to be Head of Institut für Wirtschaftsbeobachtung 28-42; Head of Institut für Industrieforschung, Nuremberg 43-45; Bavarian State Minister of Economics 45-46; Chair. Sonderstelle Geld und Kredit (Special Agency entrusted with task of preparing plan for currency reform) Oct. 47; Dir. of Dept. of Economics in United Economic Territory, Frankfurt-Höchst March 48-Sept. 49; Federal Minister of Economic Affairs 49-63; Dep. Fed. Chancellor 57-63, Fed. Chancellor 63-66; Chair. of Christian Democrat Party 66-67; Hon. Prof. Univ. of Munich 47, Univ. of Bonn 49; mem. Council of Ministers of the European Econ. Community (EEC) 58-63; Hon. LL.D. (Harvard, Columbia and others).
Publs. *Prosperity Through Competition* 58, *The Economics of Success* 63.
Bonn, 143 Koblenzerstrasse, German Federal Republic.

Ericson, Admiral Stig H:son; Swedish naval officer; b. 12 July 1897; ed. Stockholm.
Joined Navy 15, Commodore 43, Rear-Admiral 45; Commanding Active Fleet 50-53; Vice-Admiral 53; Commdr. in Chief 53-61, Admiral 61; Grand Marshal of the Royal Court 62-; A.D.C. to King of Sweden; Pres. and mem. of Board *Svenska Dagbladet* newspaper, Carnegie Foundation of Sweden, AB Turitz & Co., AB Marabou.
Publs. books on naval affairs and memoirs.
Royal Palace, Stockholm C, Sweden.
Telephone: 10-09-87.

Ericsson, John August; Swedish politician; b. 6 April 1907; ed. privately.
Member of Parl. 37-; Head of Div. and Vice-Chair. State Labour Comm. 43; Minister without Portfolio 45-48; Minister of Commerce 48-55, of Social Affairs, Labour and Housing 55-57; Managing-Dir. AB Vin-and Spritcentralen 57-; Social Democrat.
Reimersholmsgatan 5, Stockholm, Sweden.

Eriksen, Erik; Danish politician; b. 20 Nov. 1902; ed. Agricultural Coll.
Man. ancestral farm 28; proprietor 39; Chair. Liberal party's Youth Organisation 29-32; mem. Folketing 35; Counsellor Danish Broadcasting 40; Min. of Agriculture and Fishing 45-47; Prime Minister 50-53; Liberal Party.
Brangstrup pr. Ringe, Denmark.

Erikson, Erik H.; American psychoanalyst; b. 15 June 1902; ed. Vienna Psychoanalytic Inst. and Harvard Univ.
Training psychoanalyst, Insts. of American Psychoanalytic Asscn. 42-; Prof. of Psychology, Univ. of California 50-51; Senior Staff, Austen Riggs Center 51-60; Prof. of Human Development and Lecturer on Psychiatry, Harvard Univ. 60-; Fellow, American Acad. of Arts and Sciences.
Publs. *Childhood and Society* 50, *Young Man Luther* 58, *Insight and Responsibility* 64.
746 Widener Library, Harvard University, Cambridge, Mass. 02138, U.S.A.

Erkelenz, Hans; German banker; b. 14 April 1894. Trained with Barmer Bank-Verein, returned to them after war service 14-18; Man. Commerzbank, Berlin 32-45, Dir. 45; with Bankverein Westdeutschland after 45, Dir. 52; Deputy Chair. Advisory Board Vereinigte Deutsche Nickel-Werke A.G., Schwerte/Ruhr; Order of Merit.
Leuchtenberger Kirchweg 47C, Düsseldorf-Kaiserswerth, German Federal Republic.

Erkin, Feridun Cemal; Turkish diplomatist; b. 99; ed. Galatasaray Lyceum and Univ. of Paris (Law Faculty), First Sec. Turkish Embassy London 28-29; Counsellor in Berlin 34-35; Consul-Gen. Beirut 35-37; Head of Commercial Dept. of Min. of Foreign Affairs 37-38; Head of Political Dept. Ministry of Foreign Affairs 39-42; Asst. Sec.-Gen. with rank of Minister 42-45; Sec.-Gen. with rank of Ambassador 45; Turkish del. at U.N. Conf. San Francisco 45; Head of Turkish del. final meeting of League of Nations 46; Ambassador to Italy 47-48, to U.S.A. June 48-55, to Spain 55-57, to France 57-60, to U.K. 60; Minister of Foreign Affairs March 62-65; mem. Turkish Nat. Assembly; mem. Int. Diplomatic Acad., Geneva; mem. Acad. of Political Sciences, New York; mem. Inst. de France (Academy of Moral and Political Sciences).
Hariciye, Köskü, Ankara, Turkey.

Erlander, Tage Fritiof, B.A.; Swedish politician; b. 13 June 1901; ed. elementary school, public high school of Karlstad, and Univ. of Lund.
Graduated 28; on the Editorial Staff of *Svensk Upplagsbok* (Swedish Encyclopaedia) 28-38; mem. of Parl. Second Chamber 33-44, 49-; Under-Sec. of State of Min. of Social Affairs 38; Minister without Portfolio Aug. 44-July 45; Min. of Education July 45-Oct. 46; mem. of Parl. First Chamber 45-48; Prime Minister Oct. 46-; Social Democratic Labour Party.
Fyrverkarbacken 21, Stockholm K, Sweden.

Erlanger, Philippe (son of late Camille Erlanger); French writer and international art organizer; b. 11 July 1903; ed. Lycée Janson de Sailly, Université de Paris à la Sorbonne and Ecole libre des sciences politiques.
Organizer of about 500 exhbns. and over 1,000 theatrical and musical presentations; Dir. French Asscn. for Artistic Affairs 38-; Head of Artistic Exchange Dept., Ministry of Foreign Affairs 46-; Inspector-Gen. Ministry of Nat. Educ. 60-; Founder and Hon. Pres. Cannes Int. Film Festival 46; Grand Prix du Rayonnement Français 62, Grand Prix Littéraire du Départment de la Seine 63, Prix des Ambassadeurs 66; numerous French and foreign decorations.
Publs. include *Henri III* 35, *Le Régent* 38, *Monsieur, Frère de Louis XIV* 53, *Diane de Poitiers* 55, *L'étrange mort de Henri IV* 57, *Le Massacre de la Saint-Barthélemy* 60, *Cinq Mars* 62, *Louis XIV* 65.
23 rue Lapérouse 8e; Home: 3 rue de Castiglione, Paris 1er, France.

Ermilov, Viktor Vasilievich; Soviet politician; b. 21 Oct. 1909; ed. State Secondary School.
Fitter 29-30; Fitter "Krasny Proletary" Machine Tool Building Factory, Moscow 30-; mem. C.P.S.U. 46, mem. Central Cttee. of C.P.S.U. 61-66; Deputy to U.S.S.R. Supreme Soviet 66-; Hero of Socialist Labour 57.
"Krasny Proletary" Factory, 15 Malaya Kaluzhskaya ul., Moscow, U.S.S.R.

Ermin, Lev Borisovich; Soviet politician; b. 1923; ed. Azov-Black Sea Inst. of Agriculture.
Soviet Army 41-47; Chief Agronomist, Manych-Veselovskoye Machine and Tractor Station, Rostov Region 52; Sec. Veselovskoye District Cttee. C.P.S.U., then First Sec. Razdorskaya District Cttee. C.P.S.U. Rostov Region 52-59; Official, Central Cttee. C.P.S.U.

59-61; Second Sec., then First Sec., Penza Regional Cttee. C.P.S.U. 61-; Alt. mem. C.P.S.U. Central Cttee. 61-; Deputy to U.S.S.R. Supreme Soviet; mem. C.P.S.U. 43-.
Penza Regional Committee, C.P.S.U., Penza, U.S.S.R.

Ermini, Giuseppe, DR.JUR.; Italian lawyer and politician; b. 20 July 1900.
Prof. of History of Italian Law, Urbino Univ., Fellow 26; Prof. of Univ. of Cagliari 27, subsequently of Perugia Univ.; Rector of Perugia Univ. 45-; Christian Democrat deputy 46-; Pres. of Comm. for Educ. and Fine Arts; Under-Sec. Entertainments Office 54; Minister of Educ. 54-55.
Università degli Studi, Perugia, Italy.

Ermolyeva, Zinaida Vissarionovna; Soviet biologist; b. 98; ed. Rostov Univ.
Dir. and Lecturer, Bacteriology Dept., Inst. of Bacteriology, Rostov Univ. 21-25; Dir. Microbial Biochemistry Dept., All-Union Inst. for Experimental Medicine, Moscow 25-44; Dir. Inst. for Biological Prevention of Infections, Moscow 45-47; Dir. Dept. of Experimental Chemotherapy, Antibiotics Research Inst., Moscow 47-; Dir. Dept. of Microbiology, Central Postgraduate Med. Inst., Moscow 52-; Pres. Cttee. for Antibiotics, Soviet Acad. of Sciences 54-; Ed. journal *Antibiotiki* 56-; mem. U.S.S.R. Acad. Medical Sciences; Order of Lenin 43, State Prize 43.
Publs. *Cholera* 43, *Penicillin* 46, *Antibiotics and their Applications* 54, *Streptomycin Therapy* 58, *Antibiotics, Experimental and Clinical Investigations* Vol. I 56, Vol. II 59, *Biological Active Substances of Natural Origin* 64, *Antibiotics, Interferous and Microbial Polysaccharides* 65.
Department of Microbiology, Central Postgraduate Medical Institute, 1/2 Vosstanya Square, Moscow, U.S.S.R.

Ermoshin, Pavel Konstantinovich; Soviet diplomatist; b. 29 Sept. 1907; ed. Kazan Teachers' Training Inst.
Diplomatic Service 41-; Counsellor, Stockholm 52-54; Envoy to Iceland 54-55, Ambassador to Iceland 55-58; Counsellor, Second European Dept., U.S.S.R. Ministry of Foreign Affairs 58-59, Deputy Head of Second European Dept. 59-60; Ambassador to Cyprus 60-.
U.S.S.R. Embassy, 6 Gladstone Street, Nicosia, Cyprus.
Telephone: 75314.

Ernesaks, Gustav Gustavovich; Soviet composer; b. 1908; ed. Tallin Conservatoire.
Executive mem. Estonian Composers' Union, U.S.S.R. Composers' Union; Honoured Worker of Arts of Estonian S.S.R. 42, People's Artist of Estonian S.S.R. 47, State Prize 47, 51, People's Artist of the U.S.S.R. 56; Orders of Lenin (twice) 50, 67; Badge of Honour 65; Principal compositions: *War Bugle* (cantata for unaccompanied mixed choir) 43, *Puhajarv* (opera) 45, *Coast of Storms* (opera) 48, *Sing Out, Free People* (cantata) 50, *Fisherman's Life* (suite for unaccompanied choir) 53, *From a Thousand Hearts* (cantata for unaccompanied choir) 54, *Hand in Hand* (opera) 54, *Baptism of Fire* (opera) 57, *Suitors from Mulgimaa* (opera) 60.
Estonian Composers' Union, Estonia Boulevard No. 4, Tallin, U.S.S.R.

Erni, Hans; Swiss painter; b. 21 Feb. 1909; ed. Académie Julien, Paris and Vereinigte Staatsschulen für freie und angewandte Kunst, Berlin.
Mem. Groupe Abstraction-Création, Paris; mem. S.W.B.; Exhibitions Lucerne, Paris, Basle, Oxford, Liverpool, London, Cambridge, Leicester, Zürich, Milan, Rotterdam, Prague, Stockholm, Chicago, New York, Rome, Copenhagen, Tokyo, San Francisco, Los Angeles, Washington, Mannheim, Cologne; abstract mural picture Swiss section Triennale Milan, frescoes Lucerne; great

mural *Switzerland* for Swiss Nat. Exhibition Zürich 39; Great Murals Exposition internationale de l'Urbanisme et de l'Habitation Paris 47, Mural in Bernese hospital Montana; mem. Alliance Graphique Int.; Int. Prize at the Biennale del Mare 53; great mural at the Musée Ethnographique, Neuchâtel 54; has illustrated bibliophile edns. of classics by Plato, Pindar, Sophocles, Virgil, Buffon, Renard, Valéry, Homer (*Odyssey*), Albert Schweitzer (*La Paix*), Paul Eluard, etc.; murals for Internat. Exhibition in Brussels 58; mosaics for the Abbey of St. Maurice 61, for Swiss TV and Radio Building, Berne 64; Engraved glass panels "Day and Night" and "Towards a Humanistic Future" for the Société des Banques Suisses, Geneva, 63; exhibitions in Japan and Australia 63, 64.
Publ. *Wo steht der Maler in der Gegenwart?* 47.
Meggen, Lucerne, Switzerland.

Ernst, Max; French painter and sculptor; b. Rhineland 2 April 1891; ed. Bonn.
Taught himself to paint; founded the Dadaist movement with Arp and Baargeld; lived in Paris 22-, exhibited at first surrealist exhibition 25; lived in U.S. 41-49; Grand Prize, Venice Biennale 54, rep. at Dunn Int. Exhbn., London 63.
c/o Musée d'Art Moderne, Paris; and Le Pin Perdu, Huismes, France.

Erofeyev, Vladimir Ivanovich; Soviet diplomatist; b. 1920; ed. First Moscow State Inst. of Foreign Languages.
Diplomatic Service 42-; Asst. to Minister of Foreign Affairs 55; Counsellor, Paris 55-59; Deputy Head, First European Dept., U.S.S.R. Ministry of Foreign Affairs 59-62; Amb. to Senegal 62-66; on staff Ministry of Foreign Affairs 66-.
Ministry of Foreign Affairs, 32-34 Smolenskaya-Sennaya ploshchad, Moscow, U.S.S.R.

Erofeyev, Vladimir Yakovlevich; Soviet diplomatist; b. 09; ed. Moscow Machine Tool Inst.
Diplomatic Service 39-; Deputy Dir. and Chief of Consular Dept., State Cttee. for Foreign Affairs 39-40; Counsellor to Turkey 40-42; Deputy Chief, Second European Dept., Ministry of Foreign Affairs 42-48, Head of Dept. for Latin American Countries 48-49; Counsellor, London 49-52; Counsellor Ministry of Foreign Affairs 52-54; Minister Counsellor, Paris 54-55; Chief of Second European Dept., Ministry of Foreign Affairs 55-58, of Near East Dept. 58-59; Amb. to the U.A.R. 59-65; on staff Ministry of Foreign Affair 65-68; Amb. to Iran 68-.
U.S.S.R. Embassy, Teheran, Iran.

Errera, Jacques, U.L.B.; Belgian scientific adviser.
Counsel on nuclear matters to the Ministry of Foreign Affairs, of Foreign Commerce and Economic Affairs; Commr., Atomic Energy Comm.; Commdr. Ordre de Léopold.
Publs. *Polarisation Diélectrique* 28, *Moment électrique et structure moléculaire* 35, *Chimie physique nucléaire appliquée* 55.
Belgian Atomic Energy Commission, Ministry of Foreign Affairs, 2 rue Quatre Bras, Brussels, Belgium.

Erroll of Hale, 1st Baron (cr. 64) of Kilmun in the County of Argyll; **Frederick James Erroll,** P.C., M.A., C.ENG., F.I.E.E., M.I.MECH.E.; British politician; b. 27 May 1914; ed. Oundle School and Trinity Coll., Cambridge.
Served in engineering industry 37-39; war service, Tank Div., reached rank of Col. 39-45; M.P. for Altrincham and Sale 45-64; Parl. Sec. Ministry of Supply 55-56, Board of Trade 56-58; Econ. Sec. Treasury 58-59; Minister of State, Board of Trade 59-60; Privy Counsellor 60-; Pres. Board of Trade 61-63; Minister of Power 63-64; mem. Nat. Econ. Development Council 62-63; Chair. or Dir. of several companies 65-; Pres. London

Chamber of Commerce 66-; Deputy Cha . Decimal Currency Board 66-; Conservative.
21 Ilchester Place, London, W.14, England.
Telephone: 01-937 2707.

Ershov, Pavel Ivanovitch; Soviet diplomatist; b. 1914; ed. Leningrad Inst. of Education.
Diplomatic Service 41-; Counsellor, Turkey 44-48; Minister to Israel 48-53; Deputy Chief, then Chief, First European Section, Ministry of Foreign Affairs 53-55; Amb. to Switzerland 55-57; Consultant, Ministry of Foreign Affairs 57-60; Asst. Dir.-Gen. UNESCO 61-64; with Ministry of Foreign Affairs 65-.
Ministry of Foreign Affairs, 32-34 Smolenskaya-Sennaya ploshchad, Moscow, U.S.S.R.

Erskine Ralph, A.R.I.B.A., A.M.T.P.I., S.A.R.; British architect; b. 24 Feb. 1914; ed. Friends' School, Saffron Walden, Essex, Regent Street Polytechnic, London, and Konst. Akad., Stockholm.
Own practice in Sweden since 39, engaged in city renewal plans, town planning, designs for flats, private houses, housing estates, industrial buildings, churches, shopping centres, and homes for the elderly; designed Hall of Residence, Clare Coll., Cambridge, England; studies and research in architectural problems on building in sub-arctic regions; Guest Prof. at Technical School, Zürich; lectures in Holland, Japan, Canada, Sweden, Finland, Poland, Denmark, Switzerland, England and America; has participated in exhbns. in Sweden, Canada, Holland, Denmark and Switzerland; Hon. A.I.A.
Gustav III's väg, Drottningholm, Sweden.
Telephone: 7720352.

Erskine, Sir (Robert) George, Kt., C.B.E., B.L.; British merchant banker; b. 5 Nov. 1896; ed. Kirkcudbright Acad. and Edinburgh Univ.
On staff of Nat. Bank of Scotland 13-29; served First World War 14-18; joined Morgan Grenfell & Co. Ltd. 29, Dir. 45-68, now mem. Advisory Cttee.; Dir. Investment Trust Corpn. Ltd., London & Clydesdale Trust Ltd. (Chair.), London & Provincial Trust Ltd. (Chair.) London & Thames Haven Oil Wharves Ltd., London Maritime Investment Co. Ltd., The Metropolitan Trust Co. Ltd., Union Castle Mail Steamship Co. Ltd.; Master of Glaziers Co. 60-61; High Sheriff of Surrey 63-64; Pres. Inst. of Bankers 54-56; Deputy Chair. Navy, Army and Air Force Inst. 41-52; mem. Jenkins Cttee. on Company Law 59-62, Council and Finance and Gen. Purposes Cttee. R.A.F. Benevolent Fund.
Busbridge Wood, Godalming, Surrey, England.
Telephone: Hascombe 378.

Erskine of Rerrick, 1st Baron (cr. 64), **John Maxwell Erskine,** Bart., G.B.E., Kt., K.ST.J., D.L., J.P., F.R.S.E.; British public servant; b. 14 Dec. 1893; ed. Kirkcudbright Acad. and Edinburgh Univ.
Governor of Northern Ireland 64-68; Gen. Man. Commercial Bank of Scotland Ltd. (now Nat. Commercial Bank of Scotland), Edinburgh 32-53, Dir. 51-; Dir. Caledonian Insurance Co., Guardian Assurance Co. Ltd.; official of numerous commercial and civic orgs.; Hon. LL.D. (Glasgow).
c/o Government House, Hillsborough, Co. Down, Northern Ireland.

Ertuğruloğlu, Mehmet, D.en.D.; Cypriot diplomatist; ed. Ankara and Paris.
Civil servant, Cyprus; Turkish Govt. service, Turkish Treasury; Turkish Rep. to Int. Confs.; Rep. to London Conf. on Cyprus 60; Cypriot Ambassador to Turkey 60-64.
c/o Ministry of Foreign Affairs, Nicosia, Cyprus.

Ervin, Samuel James, Jr., A.B., LL.D.; American lawyer and politician; b. 27 July 1896; ed. Univ. of North Carolina and Harvard Univ.

Admitted to North Carolina Bar 19; has practised law in Morgantown, N.C. since 22; mem. N.C. Gen. Assembly 23; 25 and 31; Judge, Burke County Criminal Court 35-37, N.C. Superior Court 37-43, resigned to resume law practice; Assoc. Justice N.C. Superior Court 48-54; Senator from North Carolina 54-; mem. American Bar Asscn.; awards include Silver Star, Distinguished Service Cross; Democrat.
Morgantown, N.C., U.S.A.

Ervine, St. John Greer, LL.D. (St. Andrews), D.LITT. (Queen's Univ. Belfast), F.R.S.L.; British novelist, dramatist and dramatic critic; b. 28 Dec. 1883.
Man. Abbey Theatre Dublin 15; served Great War; Prof. of Dramatic Literature Royal Society of Literature 32-36; former Dramatic Critic *The Observer*; mem. Irish Acad.; Fellow Royal Society of Literature; Pres. League of British Dramatists.
Publs. Novels: *Mrs. Martin's Man, Alice and a Family, Changing Winds, The Foolish Lovers, The Wayward Man, The First Mrs. Fraser, Sophia*; plays: *The Magnanimous Lover, Mixed Marriage, Jane Clegg, John Ferguson, The Ship, Mary Mary Quite Contrary, The Lady of Belmont* (a sequel to *The Merchant of Venice*), *Anthony and Anna, The Wonderful Visit* (with H. G. Wells), *The First Mrs. Fraser, People of Our Class, Boyd's Shop, Robert's Wife, Friends and Relations, Private Enterprise, The Christies, My Brother Tom, Ballyfarland's Festival, Martha, Esperanza, Charles and Mary*; various works: *Some Impressions of My Elders, Parnell, If I were Dictator, The Organised Theatre, How to Write a Play, The Theatre in My Time, God's Soldier* (Life of Gen. Booth), *A Journey to Jerusalem, Craigavon: Ulsterman* (Life of Viscount Craigavon, first Prime Minister of Northern Ireland), *Oscar Wilde: a Present-time Appraisal, Bernard Shaw: his Life, Work, and Friends* 56.
Honey Ditches, Seaton, Devon, England.

Escande, Leopold, D. ès SC. PHYS.; French university professor; b. 1 June 1902; ed. Inst. Electrotechnique et de Mécanique Appliquée Toulouse and Toulouse Univ.
Professor of Hydraulics Toulouse Univ.; Head of L'Ecole Nationale Supérieure d'Electrotechnique et d'Hydraulique; Dir. of Institut de Mécanique des Fluides, Toulouse; consulting engineer to Société Nationale de l'Electricité de France, to Schneider works, Entreprises Métropolitaines et Coloniales, Entreprise Industrielle, Empresa Nacional Ribagorzana (Spain); Scientific Adviser to Délégation Générale à la Recherche Scientifique; mem. Acad. des Sciences (Paris) and corresp. mem. Acad. de Coimbra (Portugal), of Rio de Janiero, of Bologna, Bogotá, Madrid, Barcelona, Lima, etc.; Commdr. Légion d'Honneur; Dr. h.c. Univs. of Recife, São Paulo, Lisbon, Liège, Portô Alegre, Lima, Rio de Janeiro, Vienna Grand, Buenos Aires, Berlin, Cracow, Salonica, Sherbrooke, Genes.
Publs. *Etude Théorique et Expérimentale sur la Similitude des Fluides Incompressibles Pesants* 29, *Barrages* 37, *Etudes des Veines de Courant* 40, *Hydraulique Générale* 41-43, *Recherches Théoriques et Experimentales sur les Oscillations de l'Eau dans les Chambres d'Equilibre* 43, *Compléments d'Hydraulique* Vol. I 47, Vol. II 51, *Méthodes Nouvelles pour le Calcul des Chambres d'Equilibre* 49, *Nouveaux Compléments d'Hydraulique* Vol. I 53, Vol. II 55, Vol. III 58, Vol. IV 63.
"Enseeht", 2 rue Camichel, Toulouse, France.

Escande, Maurice; French actor and administrator; b. 14 Nov. 1892; ed. Paris Conservatoire d'Art Dramatique.
Doyen, Comédie Française; Administrator, Comédie Française since May 60; has appeared in numerous plays including *Le Burlador, La Reine Morte, Maman Colibri, Jeunesse, Polydora* and in a large number of films including *Les Trois Mousquetaires, Lucrèce Borgia, Le Père Goriot, Le Diable Boiteux, La Dame aux*

Camélias, Napoléon; Commandeur Légion d'Honneur, Croix de Guerre, Médaille Militaire, Commandeur des Palmes Académiques, Commandeur des Arts et des Lettres.
190 rue de Rivoli, Paris 1er, France.

Escher, Alfred Martin, DR. JUR.; Swiss diplomatist; b. 23 March 1906; ed. Univs. of Zürich, Berlin and Kiel, Acad. for Int. Law, The Hague.
Entered service of Fed. Political Dept. 31; Attaché, Bangkok 32; Sec. of Legation, Warsaw 35, Berlin 39; First Sec., Berlin 41, Ankara 41; Consul, Baghdad 42, Athens 44; Counsellor, London 45; Commr. Int. Cttee. of the Red Cross for Refugees in Palestine 48; Minister to Iran 51-54, concurrently to Afghanistan 53-54; mem. Neutral Nations Supervisory Comm. for Armistice Korea 54; Minister to Italy 55-57, Ambassador to Italy 57-59; Ambassador to German Federal Republic, May 59-64, to Austria 64-.
Swiss Embassy, Prinz Eugenstrasse 7, Vienna III, Austria.

Escholier, Raymond; French writer; b. 25 Dec. 1882.
Novelist, essayist and critic; awarded Grand Prix for Literature of Acad. Française 31; fmr. Sec. Dir. of Fine Arts; Keeper Victor Hugo Museum 13-33; Chef de Cabinet to Briand 21-22; Keeper Petit Palais 33, Hon. Keeper 43; Conseiller Culturel de la Ville de Paris 57; Grand Officier Légion d'Honneur, Médaille Militaire, Croix de Guerre.
Publs. Novels: *Cantegril* 21, *La Nuit* 23, *Le Sel de la Terre* 24, *Mahmadou Fofana* 29, *L'Herbe d'amour* 31; essays: *Daumier* 23, *Delacroix* 26, *Greco* 37, *La peinture française au XIX siècle* 40, *Marquis de Gascogne* 46, *Victor Hugo, cet inconnu* 51, *Le Secret de Mont-Segur* 52, *Un Amant de Génie: Victor Hugo* 53, *Matisse, ce vivant* 56, *La Neige qui brûle: Marie Noël* 57, *Mes Pyrénées* 58, *Eugène Delacroix* 63, *Delacroix et les Femmes* 63, *Daumier et son Monde* 65, *Briand Secret* 65.
1 rue Bonaparte, Paris 6e, France.

Escobar, María Luisa; Venezuelan composer; b. 08; ed. Paris.
Founder and Pres. until 43 Ateneo de Caracas; founder and Dir.-Gen. Asociación Venezolana de Autores y Compositores (A.V.A.C.) 47; founder and Artistic Dir. the Ballet-Theatre of Caracas; rep. Venezuela at Int. Congress on Musical Education, Paris 37, Int. Conf. of Society Authors and Composers, Buenos Aires 48, 25th Biennial Convention of Fed. of Music Clubs, U.S.A. 49, First Inter-American Music Conf., U.S.A. 51; awarded medals and diplomas of honour by Venezuela, France, Cuba, Mexico, U.S.A., and India.
Works include *Orquídeas azules* (symphony and ballet), *La Princesa Girasol* (operetta), *Guaicaipuro* (ballet), *Vals Sentimental* (piano and orchestra), *El Rey Guaicaipuro* (opera) and many folksongs, etc.
P.O. Box 10233, Sabana Grande, Caracas, Venezuela.

Escobar Cerda, Luis; Chilean economist and politician; b. 27; ed. Univ. of Chile and Harvard Univ.
Director of School of Economics, Univ. of Chile 51-55, Dean of Faculty of Econs. 55-64; Financial Adviser to Univ. of Chile 54-60; Minister of Econ. Development and Reconstruction 61-63; mem. Inter-American Cttee. for Alliance for Progress 64-; Exec. Dir. Int. Monetary Fund 64-66, of World Bank 66-.
Publs. *The Stock Market* 59, *Organization for Economic Development* 61, *A Stage of the National Economic Development* 62, *Considerations on the Tasks of the University* 63, *Organizational Requirements for Growth and Stability* 64, *The Role of the Social Sciences in Latin America* 65.
Los Tulipanes 2979, Santiago, Chile.

Escrivá de Balaguer, Mgr. Josemaría, D.IUR., S.T.D.; Spanish ecclesiastic; b. 9 Jan. 1902; ed. Saragossa, Madrid and Lateran Pontifical Univs.

Ordained 25; founded *Opus Dei* 28; former Superior, Saragossa Seminary, Rector, Real Patronato de Santa Isabel, Prof. of Philosophy, Madrid School of Journalism, Prof. of Roman Law, Univ. of Madrid and Saragossa, Doctor, h.c. of Univ. of Saragossa, mem. Colegio de Aragon, Grand Chancellor Univ. of Navarra; mem. Accademia Theologica Romana, Consultor (Adviser) of the S.C. of Seminaries and Univs., of the Pontifical Comm. for the Authentic Interpretation of the Code of Canon Law, Holy See; Pres. Gen. *Opus Dei*.
Publs. *The Way, Holy Rosary, The Abbess of Cas Huelgas, Spiritual Considerations, The Apostolic Constitution Provida Mater Ecclesia and Opus Dei*, and works of ascetic literature, law and history.
Viale Bruno Buozzi 73, Rome, Italy.

Escudero, Gonzalo, D.IUR.; Ecuadorean lawyer and diplomatist; b. 03; ed. Central Univ., Quito.
Former Prof. of Logic and Theory of Knowledge, Public Int. Law, Central Univ., Quito; fmr. Chargé d'Affaires *a.i.*, France and Panama; fmr. Chargé d'Affaires, Buenos Aires; fmr. Minister in Mexico, Chile and Uruguay; fmr. Amb. to Peru and to France; Ambassador to Org. of American States (OAS); fmr. Minister of Foreign Affairs.
c/o Ministry of Foreign Affairs, Quito, Ecuador.

Esenov, Shakhmardan Esenovich; Soviet geologist; b. 1927; ed. Kazakh Mining and Metallurgical Inst.
Member C.P.S.U. 56-; on geological expedition 57-60; Deputy Minister of Geology of Kazakh S.S.R. 60-64; Chair. Kazakh State Geological Cttee. 64-65; Vice-Chair. Kazakh Council of Ministers 65-67; Pres. Kazakh Acad. of Sciences 67-; Lenin Prize 66.
Presidium of Kazakh Academy of Sciences, Shevchenko Street 28, Alma-Ata, U.S.S.R.

Eshkol (Shkolnik), Levi; Israeli politician; b. 25 Oct. 1895; ed. Hebrew Gymnasium, Vilna, Poland.
Emigrated to Palestine 13; agricultural worker at various settlements; served in Jewish Legion 18-20; returned to agricultural work 20; helped found Degania B settlement; elected Rep. of Assembly of Palestine Jewry (Sessions 1-3) and del. to all Zionist Congresses from 12th onwards; Chair. Settlement Cttee. at several congresses; Sec. Tel-Aviv-Jaffa Workers' Council and Sec. Mapai (Workers' Party) 44-48; mem. Exec. Nat. Workers Fed. (Histadrut); emissary of Histadrut to Lithuania and other countries and to Socialist Int., Dir. Agricultural Settlement Section, Palestine Office, Berlin, for three years during Nazi régime; with Hehalutz movement in Germany and Lithuania for some years; participated in admin. of transfer of German-Jewish property to Palestine and in founding and directing Nir and Mekoroth Shikun and Amidar companies; Hehalutz and Ihud Olami Confs., U.S.A.; fmr. mem. Exec. Jewish Agency, Treas. 50-52; fmr. Head of Agric. Settlement Dept.; active in Haganah since its foundation; fmr. Dir. Ministry of Defence of State of Israel; Minister of Agriculture 51-52; Minister of Finance June 52-63; Prime Minister and Minister of Defence 63-67, Prime Minister 67-; Pres. Israeli Atomic Energy Agency 66-; Hon. LL.D. (Roosevelt Univ.).
Publ. *Bechavley Hitnachalut* (In the Areas of Settlement) 58.
Office of the Prime Minister, Jerusalem, Israel.

Eshpai, Andrei Yakovlevich; Soviet composer; b. 1925; ed. Moscow Conservatoire.
Secretary R.S.F.S.R. Composers' Union; Honoured Worker of Arts of Mari Autonomous S.S.R. 61, Honoured Worker of Arts of Yakutsk Autonomous S.S.R. 64, Order of Red Star 46, Badge of Honour 67.
Principal compositions: *Symphonic Dances on Mari Themes* 52, *Hungarian Melodies* (for violin and orchestra) 52, Concerto for Piano and Orchestra 54, Concerto for Violin and Orchestra 56, Symphony 59;

Piano Pieces, Sonatina, Six Preludes, suite romances, folk song arrangements, film music.
R.S.F.S.R. Composers' Union, 8-10 Ulitsa Nezhdanovoi, Moscow, U.S.S.R.

Eshtokin, Afanasy Fyodorovich; Soviet politician; b. 1913; ed. Donetsk Industrial Inst.
Worked in coal mines, Donets, Lugansk and Chelyabinsk Regions (rising to mine dir.), Party Organizer for C.P.S.U. Central Cttee. 37-48; Exec. industrial posts in Chelyabinsk and Sverdlovsk Regions 48-58; Second Sec. Sverdlovsk Regional Cttee. C.P.S.U. 58-62; Chair. Sverdlovsk Regional Soviet 62-63; First Sec. Kemerovo Regional Cttee. C.P.S.U. 63-; mem. C.P.S.U. 43-, C.P.S.U. Central Cttee.; Deputy to Supreme Soviet of the U.S.S.R.; State Prize 48.
Kemerovo Regional Committee of the C.P.S.U., Kemerovo, U.S.S.R.

Eshun, Isaac; Ghanaian journalist; b. 24; ed. Wesley Coll., Kumasi.
Teacher 47-49; *Ashanti Times* 50-51; *Daily Graphic* 51-64, Ed. 59-63; Dir. Ghana News Agency 60-63, 67-; Exec. Dir. Ghana Graphic Co. Ltd. 60-64; Public Relations Man., Pioneer Tobacco Co. 64-; Chair. of Board Cadco (Ghana) Ltd. (State-owned advertising agency) 67-.
Pioneer Tobacco Company, P.O.B. 11, Accra, Ghana.

Esin, Seyfullah; Turkish diplomatist; b. 02; ed. School of Political Sciences, Berlin, and George Washington Univ.
Entered foreign service and served Athens 25, Palermo 26, Berlin 27, Washington, D.C. 33, Buenos Aires 39, Tokyo 39, Stockholm 42; Dir.-Gen. of Int. Organizations Dept., Foreign Ministry, Ankara 45, of Political Affairs Dept. 46; Minister to Israel 49, to Austria 52; Ambassador to U.S.S.R. 54, to Germany 56; Perm. Rep. to U.N. 57-60 with rank of ambassador; Ambassador to United Arab Republic 60-61; Ambassador to India 62-65; Ambassador to Spain 65-67.
c/o Ministry of Foreign Affairs, Ankara, Turkey.

Eskildsen, Clarence Raymond; American government official; b. 27 Oct. 1913; ed. Minnesota State Coll., Univs. of Minnesota and Harvard.
Newspaper reporter 36-38; Research Asst., Reference Bureau 38-39; Clerk, Dept. of Agriculture 39-40; U.S. Army service 41-45; Admin. Officer, Dept. of Agriculture 45-47, Analyst 47-49; Asst. Econ. Commr., Econ. Co-operation Admin., Korea, Tokyo, Philippines 49-53; Budget Officer, Dept. of Agriculture 54; Admin. Officer, Foreign Agriculture Service 54; Dir. Foreign Trade Program Div. 56; Agricultural Attaché, New Delhi 57-58, Bonn 60-62; Assoc. Administrator, Foreign Agriculture Service 62-66; Deputy Asst. Sec. of Agriculture for Int. Affairs 66-.
U.S. Department of Agriculture, Washington, D.C. 20250; Home: 326 Grove Avenue, Falls Church, Virginia 22046, U.S.A.
Telephone: 534-8161 (Home).

Esmer, Ahmed Sükrü, LL.B., M.A., PH.D.; Turkish journalist; b. 93; ed. Columbia Univ.
Prof. of English, Galatasaray Lyceum, Istanbul 21-23; Prof. of Political History, School of Political Science 30-41; mem. Grand Nat. Assembly 41-46; Dir. Turkish Information Office, New York 47-49; Dir.-Gen. Turkish Press, Broadcasting and Tourist Dept. Ankara 49-50; Prof. of Political History, Ankara Univ. 50-; Dir. Inst. of Int. Affairs, Ankara 55-; Visiting Prof. Univ. of Idaho 58-59, Visiting Prof. Univ. of Chattanooga 60; has held editorial and admin. posts on many newspapers.
Publs. *Political History, Diplomatic History, 1919-1939.*
2-3 Etemefendi Sokak, Erenköy, Istanbul, Turkey.

Espinosa-San Martín, Juan José; Spanish politician; b. 30 June 1918; ed. Colegio de Nuestra Señora del Pilar, Madrid and Universidad de Madrid.

Head Technical Council Ministry of Finance 57-59; Dir.-Gen. of Treasury 59-65; Vice-Pres. Industrial Credit Bank 62-65; Minister of Finance 65-; Commdr. Order Alfonso X, Officier Légion d'Honneur.
Publs. Works dealing with fiscal and financial affairs.
Joaquín Costa 47, Madrid 6, Spain.

Esplá Triay, Oscar; Spanish composer; b. 5 Aug. 1886; ed. Univ. of Barcelona and Escuela de Ingenieros, Barcelona.
Former Dir. Scientific Musical Laboratory, Brussels; Dir. Instituto Musical Oscar Esplá, Alicante, named in his honour; mem. Real Acad. de Bellas Artes de San Fernando, Madrid; Foreign mem. Inst. de France; Hon. mem. Int. Soc. of Contemporary Music and Hispanic Soc. of America; Pres. Spanish Section SIMC, Pres. Spanish Cttee. of Int. Musical Section UNESCO; Gran Cruz Alfonso el Sabio; Officier Ordre de la Couronne de Belgique.
Compositions include: *Nochebuena del Diablo* (dramatic cantata) 24, *Don Quijote, velando las armas* (symphonic overture) 26, *Canciones Playeras* (Soprano and orchestra) 28, *Sonata del Sur* (piano concerto) 45, *El Contrabandista* (ballet) 30, *Aitana* (symphony) 65, *La Balteira* (opera); and numerous compositions for piano and chamber works.
Publs. *Función musical y Música Comtemporánea, Misterio de Elche* (Editor), numerous articles in musical magazines.
Paseo de las Acacias 1, Apdo. 3, Madrid 5, Spain.

Espy, R. H. Edwin, B.A., PH.D., L.H.D.; American church executive; b. 30 Dec. 1908; ed. Univ. of Redlands, California, Union Theological Seminary, Univs. of Tübingen and Heidelberg and Yale Univ.
Youth Secretary, Universal Christian Council for Life and Work, and World Alliance for Int. Friendship through the Churches, Geneva 36-39; Sec. First World Conf. of Christian Youth Amsterdam 39; Sec. European Student Relief Fund, New York 40; Gen.-Sec. Student Volunteer Movement for Foreign Missions 40-43; Exec. Sec. Nat. Student Council, Y.M.C.A., New York 43-55; Assoc. Exec. Sec. Div. of Christian Life and Work, Nat. Council of Churches, New York 55-57; Assoc. Gen. Sec. Nat. Council of Churches 58-63, Gen. Sec. 63-; Dir. World University Service 43-57; del. to numerous Int. Religious Confs.; mem. Joint Working Group World Council of Churches and Roman Catholic Church 65-; Hon. D.D. (Univ. of Redlands).
Publ. *The Religion of College Teachers* 51.
375 Riverside Drive, New York, N.Y. 10025, U.S.A.

Essaafi, M'hamed; Tunisian diplomatist; b. 26 May 1930; ed. Collège Sadiki and Univ. of Paris.
Secretariat of State for Foreign Affairs, Tunis 56; Tunisian Embassy, London 56-57; First Sec., Washington 57-60; Dir. of American Dept., Secr. of Foreign Affairs, Tunis 60-62, American Dept. and Int. Conf. Dept. 62-64; Ambassador to U.K. 64-; Commandeur de l'Ordre de la République Tunisienne.
Tunisian Embassy, 29 Princes Gate, London, S.W.7; 42 Winnington Road, London, N.2., England.
Telephone: 01-584-5167 (Office); 01-455-3040 (Home).

Estang, Luc; French writer; b. 12 Nov. 1911; ed. Artois and in Belgium.
Journalist and Literary and Dramatic Critic, *La Croix* (Paris) 34-55; Editorial Sec. of *Editions du Seuil*, Paris, weekly collaboration in *Figaro Littéraire*, and on radio; Chevalier de la Légion d'Honneur, Grand Prix de Littérature, de l'Académie Française 62.
Publs. Novels: *Les Stigmates, Cherchant qui dévorer, Les Fontaines du grand abîme, L'Interrogatoire, L'Horloger du Cherche-Midi, Le Bonheur et le Salut, Que ces mots répondent l'Apostat*; poetry: *Les Quatre Eléments, Les Béatitudes, D'une Nuit Noire et Blanche*; essays: *Le Passage du Seigneur, Présence de Bernanos, Saint-*

Exupéry par lui-même, Ce que je crois, Invitation à la poésie; play: *Le Jour de Cain*.
28 rue de l'Université, Paris 7e; and Les Playes, Six-Fours-La-Plage, Var, France.
Telephone: LIT.29-91.

Esterquest, Ralph Theodore, A.B., B.S. in L.S., M.A.; American librarian; b. 6 May 1912; ed. Northwestern, Columbia and Illinois Univs.
Reference Librarian, Northwestern Univ. 36-37; Order Asst. Illinois Univ. 37-40; Asst. Librarian Inst. of Advanced Study, Princeton 40-42; Sales Man. American Library Asscn., Chicago 42-43; Dir., Pacific Northwest Bibliographic Centre, Seattle 43-46; Prof. Denver Univ. 46-49; Dir. Midwest Inter-Library Center, Chicago 49-58; Librarian, Francis A. Countway Library of Medicine, Harvard Medical School 58-; Dir. Int. Relations Office, American Library Asscn. 67-68; Consultant to various universities; mem. Asscn. American medical colls.; Fulbright Senior Research Fellow 53-54.
Harvard Medical School, 10 Shattuck Street, Boston 15, Mass., U.S.A.

Estes, Joe Ewing; American judge; b. 24 Oct. 1903; ed. East Texas State Teachers Coll. and Univ. of Texas.
Admitted to Texas Bar 27, partner Crosby and Estes 28-30, Phillips, Trammell, Estes, Edwards & Orn 30-45, Sanford, King, Estes & Cantwell 46-52, Estes & Cantwell 52-55; U.S.N.R. 42-45; U.S. District Judge, Dallas 55-60, Chief Judge, U.S. District Court, Texas, Northern District 60-; mem. Advisory Cttee. on Rules of Evidence of Jud. Conf. of U.S., Co-ordinating Comm. for Multiple Litigation of Jud. Conf. of U.S., Fed. American Dallas Bar Asscns., State Bar of Texas, American Judicature Soc., Nat. Lawyers Club, Philosophical Soc. of Texas, Newcomen Soc., American Legion; Trustee mem. Exec. Comm. S.W. Legal Foundation, American Law Inst., Cttee. on Trial Practice and Technique of the Judicial Conf. of the United States; Fellow and Chair. Judicial Section, American Bar Asscn. 61-62; now Research Fellow.
Publs. co-author of *Handbook for Effective Pre-Trial Procedure, Handbook for Newly Appointed U.S. Dist. Judges*.
U.S. Court House, Dallas; 5846 Desco Drive, Dallas, Texas 75225, U.S.A.

Estes, Thomas Stuart; American diplomatist; b. 23 Jan. 1913; ed. American Univ. and Harvard Graduate School of Business Administration.
U.S. Marines 34-37; Foreign Service Bangkok, Vienna, Quebec, Athens; Allied Force HQ (Mediterranean) 42-44; Dep. Asst. Sec. Dept. of State 54-60; Ambassador to Upper Volta 61-.
American Embassy, Ouagadougou, Upper Volta, West Africa.

Estreicher, Karol, PH.D.; Polish art historian; b. 06; ed. Cracow Univ.
Asst. Lecturer, Jagiellonian Univ., Cracow 31-39; with Bureau for Recovery of Works of Art, London 40-44; Docent, Jagiellonian Univ. 45-50, Prof. 52-; Prof. Cracow Acad. of Fine Arts 47; Dir. Bureau for Reissue of Polish 19th Century Bibliography (Polish Acad. of Sciences) 59.
Publs. *Tryptyk swietej Trjócy* (The Triptych of the Holy Trinity) 36, *Katalog strat kultury polskiej pod okupacja niemiecka* (Catalogue of Polish cultural losses under German occupation 39-44), *Kristianna* (novel) 57.
Wola Justowska 243, Cracow, Poland.

Ete, Muhlis, M.A., PH.D.; Turkish economist; b. 23 Oct. 1904.
Asst. Instructor 30, later Asst. Prof. Faculty of Law and Economics Istanbul Univ.; Teacher of Statistics School of Political Science, Istanbul, and of Money and Exchange, Higher School of Commerce and

Economics Istanbul; Prof. of Business Economics, later at Gen. Principles of Economics, Ankara School of Political Science 40-50; Minister of State Enterprises 50-51; Minister of Economy and Commerce 51-52; Vice-Pres. of the Council of Europe 53; Pres. Prime Minister's High Control Board 58-61; Minister of Commerce 62-63; mem. of Parl.; fmr. Chief Ed. *Türk Ekonomisi*; Pres. Turkish Econ. Asscn.; Dir. School of Econs. and Commerce, Istanbul 67-.

Publs. *Transportation, Money and Exchange, Lessons in Business Economics, Administration of Temporary and Permanent Exhibits, Commerce, Banking and Exchanges, Probleme der Assozierung der Türkei mit der Europäischen Wirtschaftsgemeinschaft*, and numerous translations.

Istanbul, Göztepe, Yeşil Çeşme Sok. 30/8, Turkey.
Telephone: 554832.

Etemadi, Nour Ahmad; Afghan diplomatist; b. 1920; ed. Istiqlal Lyceum and Kabul Univ.

Former diplomatic posts in London and Washington; Econ. Section, Ministry of Foreign Affairs 53-64, Deputy Minister of Foreign Affairs 63, Minister 65-, now also Prime Minister; Ambassador to Pakistan 64.
Office of the Prime Minister, Kabul, Afghanistan.

Etherington, Edwin Deacon, B.A., LL.B.; American attorney and executive; b. 25 Dec. 1924; ed. Lawrenceville School, New Jersey, Wesleyan Univ. and Yale Law School.

Instructor and Asst. to Dean, Wesleyan Univ. 48-49; Law Clerk, Hon. Henry W. Edgerton, U.S. Court of Appeal, Washington, D.C. 52-53; Attorney, Wilmer and Broun, Washington, D.C. 53-54, Milbank, Tweed, Hope and Hadley, New York City 54-56; Sec. New York Stock Exchange 56-58, Vice-Pres. 58-61; Partner, Pershing Co., New York City 61-62; Pres. American Stock Exchange 62-66; Pres. Wesleyan Univ. 66-.
Wesleyan University, Middletown, Conn., U.S.A.
Telephone: 203-347-4421.

Ethridge, Mark Foster; American newspaper publisher; b. 22 April 1896; ed. Univ. of Mississippi, and Mercer Univ., Georgia.

Began career as reporter; with N.Y. Sun and Consolidated Press 23-24, Associated Press 33; Asst. Gen. Man. *Washington Post* 33-34; Pres. and publisher *Richmond (Va.) Times Dispatch* 34-36; Vice-Pres. and Gen. Man. *Courier Journal and Louisville Times* 36-42; Publisher 42-62, Chair. Board 62-63; Vice-Pres., Editor *Newsday*, Long Island, N.Y. 63-65, Consultant to Editor and Dir. 65-; mem. of President's Farm Tenancy Comm. 36; elected Pres. of Nat. Asscn. of Broadcasters 38; Chair. Fair Employment Practices Comm. 41-43; U.S. mem. of U.N. Comm. of Inquiry in the Balkans 47; Chair. U.S. Advisory Comm. on Information 48, mem. until 51; Trustee Ford Foundation.
365 Steward Avenue, Long Island, New York, U.S.A.

Etoungou, Simon Nko'o; Cameroonian diplomatist and politician; b. 14 Feb. 1932; ed. secondary and post-secondary schools, and diplomatic training in France.

Head of Office in Ministry of Econ. Planning 56-57; Cabinet Attaché, Ministry of Finance 58-59; First Sec., Cameroon Embassy, Paris 60; Minister-Counsellor 60-61; Amb. to Tunisia 61-64; led numerous Cameroon dels. 63-64; concurrently Amb. to Algeria July-Nov. 64; Amb. to U.S.S.R. 64-65; Minister of Foreign Affairs 65-66, 68-; Minister of Finance 66-68; Knight of Nat. Order of Merit (Cameroon), and decorations from Senegal, Tunisia, German Fed. Repub. and Gabon.
Ministry of Foreign Affairs, Yaoundé, Cameroon.
Telephone: 20-30 (Yaoundé).

Etter, Philipp; Swiss lawyer and politician; b. 21 Dec. 1891; ed. Einsiedeln Gymnasium and Zürich Univ.

Examining Judge, Zug canton 17; mem. Zug cantonal Govt. 23; Deputy to Council of States 30; mem. Fed. Council 34-59; Pres. Swiss Confederation 39, 42, 47, 53; fmr. Dir. Fed. Department of the Interior; Dr. h.c. Neuchâtel Univ. and Zürich Fed. Inst. of Technology; Hon. Senator Freiburg Univ.; Conservative.
Publs. *Reden an das Schweizervolk* 39, *Sens et Mission de la Suisse* 42, *Stimmrecht der Geschichte* 53.
Dalmazirain 6, Berne, Switzerland.

Ettinghausen, Richard, PH.D.; American art writer and curator; b. 5 Feb. 1906; ed. Univs. of Munich, Cambridge and Frankfurt a.M.

Asst. Islamic Dept., State Museum, Berlin 31-33; Asst. to Editor *A Survey of Persian Art* 33-34; Research Assoc., American Inst. for Persian Art and Archæology, N.Y. 34-37; Lecturer on Islamic Art, Inst. of Fine Arts, N.Y. Univ. 37-38; mem. Inst. of Advanced Study, Princeton, N.J. 37-38; Assoc. Prof. of Islamic Art, Univ. of Mich., Ann Arbor 38-44; Assoc. in Near Eastern Art, Freer Gallery of Art, Smithsonian Inst., Washington, D.C. 44-58; Research Prof. of Islamic Art, Mich. Univ. 48-, Curator of Near Eastern Art, Freer Gallery of Art 58-61, Head Curator 61-66; Adjunct Prof. of Fine Arts, New York Univ. 60-67, Prof. 67-; Editor *Ars Islamica* 38-54; Near Eastern Editor *Ars Orientalis* 51-57; mem. Consultative Cttee. *Ars Orientalis* 58-; Editorial Board *The Art Bulletin* 40-, *Kairos* 59-.
Publs. *The Unicorn (Studies in Muslim Iconography I)* 50, *Paintings of the Sultans and Emperors of India in American Collections* 61, *Persian Miniatures in the Bernard Berenson Collection* 61, Preface to *Turkey*, *Ancient Miniatures* 61, *Arab Painting* 62, *Turkish Miniatures* 65; Editor and Contributor: *A Selected and Annotated Bibliography of Books and Periodicals in Western Languages dealing with the Near and Middle East, with special emphasis on Medieval and Modern Times* 52, *Aus der Welt der islamischen Kunst* 59.
Institute of Fine Arts, New York University, 1 East 78th Street, New York, N.Y. 10021, U.S.A.

Etzdorf, Hasso von, LL.D.; German diplomatist; b. 2 March 1900; ed. Univs. of Berlin, Göttingen and Halle.

Held various posts at Foreign Office and diplomatic appointments in Tokyo, Rome, Genoa, etc.; Chief of German Del. to Interim Cttee. for European Defence Community (E.D.C.), Paris 53; Dep. Sec.-Gen. Western European Union (W.E.U.), London 55; Ambassador to Canada 56-58; Dep. Under Sec. of State, Foreign Office 58-61, Ambassador to U.K. 61-65; Hon. G.C.V.O.
8019 Eichtling, Post Moosach bei Grafing, Obb., German Federal Republic.
Telephone: GLONN-08107-402.

Etzel, Franz; German politician; b. 12 Aug. 1902; ed Univs. of Frankfurt, Munich and Münster.

Barrister, Duisburg District and Municipal Court 30-52; fought in German Army 39-45; Chair. Duisburg District Group of the Christian Democratic Union 45-48; mem. Exec. Cttee. C.D.U. Rhineland Section 46-53; Chair. C.D.U. Economic Policy Cttee. for the British Zone 47-49, and for the whole of Germany 48-; mem. Bundestag and Chair. of the Bundestag Economic Policy Cttee. 49-53; Vice-Pres. High Authority European Coal and Steel Community 52-57; appointed by the Govts. of Belgium, France, Italy, Luxemburg and the Netherlands to help prepare a report on *Objects and Tasks for Euratom* (Report of the Three Wise Men); mem. Bundestag 57-65; Fed. Minister of Finance 57-61; mem. Christian Democratic Union; partner Bankhaus Friedrich Simon KGaA, Düsseldorf; Grand Croix de l'Ordre Grand Ducal de la Couronne de Chêne, Grosskreuz des Verdienstordens der Bundesrepublik, Grand Cross Order of Aztec Eagle, Grand Cross Order of Orange-Nassau.
Publ. *Gutes Geld durch Gute Politik* 59.
Am Töllershof 10, Wittlaer, nr. Düsseldorf, German Federal Republic.

Evang, Karl, M.D.; Norwegian health official; b. 19 Oct. 1902; ed. Universitetet i Oslo.
General practitioner for many years; on staff of Municipal Hospital, Oslo 32-34; Norwegian Govt. Service 37-, Dir.-Gen. Norwegian Health Services 39-; Léon Bernard Medal and Prize, World Health Org. 66.
Norwegian Health Services, Oslo, Norway.

Evans, Sir Charles Lovatt, Kt., F.R.S., F.R.C.P., D.SC.; British physiologist; ed. Birmingham and Univ. Coll. Hosp. and Univ. of London.
Served R.A.M.C. (Major) 16-18; Prof. of Physiology Leeds 18-19; Research for Medical Research Council 19-22; Prof. of St. Bartholomew's Medical Coll. 22-26; Jodrell Prof. of Physiology and Dean Faculty of Medical Sciences, Univ. Coll., London 26-49; Pres. Physiology Section British Asscn. 28; Consultant to Ministry of Supply 49-59, Ministry of Defence 59-; Nat. Service 39-44; mem. Council and Vice-Pres. Royal Soc. 46-48; mem. Medical Research Council 46-50; Chair. Council, Royal Veterinary Coll. 49-63; Fellow, Univ. Coll., London, and Royal Veterinary Coll.; mem. Royal Physiographical Soc., Sweden, Italian Soc. Exp. Biol., and Soc. Argentina de Biología; Hon. LL.D. (Birmingham, London).
Publs. *Recent Advances in Physiology* 30, *Principles of Human Physiology* (12th edn.) 56.
Hedgemoor Cottage, Winterslow, Wilts., England.
Telephone: Winterslow 225.

Evans, Earl Alison, Jr., PH.D.; American biochemist; b. 11 March 1910; ed. Baltimore Polytechnic Inst., Johns Hopkins and Columbia Univs.
Assistant in Pharmacology, School of Medicine, Johns Hopkins Univ. 31-32, Asst. endocrine research 32-34; Univ. Fellow in Biochemistry, Columbia Univ. 34-36; Instructor in Biochemistry, Chicago Univ. 37-39, Asst. Prof. 39-41, Assoc. Prof. and Acting Chair. of Dept. 41-42, Prof. and Chair. of Dept. 42-; Reserve Officer, U.S. Foreign Service, Chief Scientific Officer, American Embassy, London 47-48; Consultant to Sec. of State 51-53; mem. Board of Scientific Counselors, Nat. Inst. of Arthritis and Metabolic Diseases, Nat. Insts. of Health 60-63; mem. Div. Cttee. for Biological and Medical Sciences, Nat. Science Foundation 63-66; Chair. Postdoctoral Fellowship Cttee., Div. of Biology and Agriculture, Nat. Acad. of Sciences, Nat. Research Council 63-65; mem. Air Force Office of Scientific Research Fellowship Board 66-, Advisory Board American Foundation for Continuing Educ. 62-; Rockefeller Fellow, Univ. of Sheffield, England 40-41; Eli Lilly Medal of American Chemical Soc. 41; mem. American Chemical Soc., American Asscn. for Advancement of Science (Fellow), Soc. for Experimental Biology and Medicine, British Biochemical Soc., American Soc. of Biological Chemists, American Soc. of Bacteriologists.
Publs. *Biochemical Studies of Bacterial Viruses* 52; co-author: *Biological Symposia V* 41, *Symposium of Respiratory Enzymes* 42; Editor: *Biological Action of the Vitamins* 42.
12 East Scott Street, Chicago, Illinois 60610, U.S.A.

Evans, Dame Edith (Mary), D.B.E.; British actress; b. 8 Feb. 1888; ed. St. Michael's School, Chester Square, London.
First appearance as Cressida in *Troilus and Cressida* at King's Hall, Covent Garden 12; later roles include Agatha Payne in *The Old Ladies* New Theatre 35, Arcadina in *The Seagull* New Theatre 36, Kit Markham in *Old Acquaintance* Apollo Theatre 42, Hesione Hushabye in *Heartbreak House* Cambridge Theatre 43; Lady Pitts in *Daphne Laureola* Wyndham's 49, Helen in *Waters of the Moon* Haymarket Theatre 51-53; The Countess in *The Dark is Light Enough* 54; Mrs. St. Maugham in *The Chalk Garden* 56, Queen Katherine in *Henry VIII* 58; Stratford-upon-Avon: Countess of

Rousillion in *All's Well that Ends Well*, Volumnia in *Coriolanus* 59, Margaret in *Richard III*, Nurse in *Romeo and Juliet* 61; Violet in *Gentle Jack* 64, Judith in *Hay Fever* 64, Mrs. Forrest in *The Chinese Prime Minister* 65; gave dramatic reading of Shaw's *The Black Girl in Search of God*, Mermaid Theatre 68; films: *The Queen of Spades* 48, *The Last Days of Dolwyn* 48, *The Importance of Being Earnest* 52, *The Nun's Story, Look Back in Anger* 59, *Tom Jones* 63, *Chalk Garden* 64, *Young Cassidy* 65, *The Whisperers* 66, *Fitzwilly* 66, *Prudence and the Pill* 67; Hon. D.Lit. (London Univ.) 50; Hon. Litt.D. (Cambridge Univ.), Hon. D.Litt. (Oxford Univ.).
L4, Albany, Piccadilly, London, W.1, England.

Evans, Sir Francis Edward, G.B.E., K.C.M.G., D.L.; British diplomatist; b. 4 April 1897; ed. Belfast Royal Acad. and London School of Economics.
Service, First World War; Consular Service 20, New York 20-26, Boston 26-29, Panama 29-32, Boston 32-34. Los Angeles 34-39; Foreign Office 39-43; Consul, New York 43, Consul Gen. 44-50; Under-Sec. of State 51; Minister to Israel 51; Ambassador to Israel 52-54, to Argentina 54-57; Dep. Chair. N. Ireland Development Council 57-63; Agent, Govt. of N. Ireland in Great Britain 62-66.
Home: Helen's Bay, Co. Down, N. Ireland.
Telephone: Helen's Bay 3244.

Evans, Geraint Llewellyn, C.B.E.; British opera singer; b. 16 Feb. 1922; ed. Guildhall School of Music.
Principal baritone, Royal Opera House, Covent Garden 48-, Glyndebourne Festival Opera 50-; mem. Vienna State Opera; has sung at La Scala (Milan), San Francisco, Chicago, Metropolitan Opera House, New York, Salzburg, Teatro Colon, Buenos Aires, Mexico, etc.; sang Don Pasquale with Welsh Nat. Opera, Cardiff 66; Fellow, Guildhall School of Music and Drama 60; Hon. D.Mus. (Univ. of Wales) 63.
Lone Pool, 34 Birchwood Road, Petts Wood, Kent, England.

Evans, Herbert McLean, B.S., M.D.; American university professor; b. 23 Sept. 1882; ed. Univ. of California, Johns Hopkins Univ.
Asst., Instructor, Assoc. and Assoc. Prof. of Anatomy, Johns Hopkins Univ. 08-15; Research Assoc. Carnegie Inst., Washington 13-15; Prof. of Anatomy, Univ. of California 15-52; Prof. Emeritus 52-; Herzstein Prof. of Biology and Dir. Inst. of Experimental Biology, Univ. of California 30-52, Prof. Emeritus and Dir. Emeritus 52-; Hon. Prof. Facultad de Biología y Ciencias Médicas, Univ. de Chile, and Facultad de Ciencias Médicas, Univ. Central del Ecuador 41; Fellow, American Acad. of Arts and Sciences; mem. Nat. Acad. of Sciences, and mem. of many other scientific societies; Visiting Lecturer Several Univs. and many scientific institutes, etc.; Gold Medal American Medical Asscn., San Francisco 46; Banting Medal 49; Charles Mickle Fellow, Univ. of Toronto 49, etc., Dr. ès Sciences h.c. Geneva.
Publs. include over 700 scientific papers.
Institute of Experimental Biology, Berkeley, Calif. 94122, U.S.A.

Evans, Joan, D.LITT., D.LIT., F.S.A., F.R.HIST.S.; British archaeologist; ed. Berkhamsted Girls' School, Oxford and London Univs.
Librarian, St. Hugh's Coll., Oxford 17-22; Travelling Fellow, Anglo-Swedish Society 22; Suzette Taylor Fellow, Lady Margaret Hall, Oxford 37-39; Hon. Fellow, St. Hugh's Coll. 36-, Supernumerary Fellow 51-58; Fellow, Univ. Coll., London 50; Pres. Royal Archaeological Inst. 48-57, Treas. 59-63; Dir. Soc. of Antiquaries 54-59, Pres. 59-64; Trustee, London Museum 51-66, British Museum 63-67; mem. Advisory Cttee. Victoria and Albert Museum 53-; Hon. LL.D. Edinburgh Univ., Hon. D.Litt., Cambridge Univ., Hon. A.R.I.B.A.,

Hon. Vice-Pres. Soc. of Antiquaries; Chevalier of the Legion of Honour.

Publs. *Magical Jewels of the Middle Ages and Renaissance* 22, *Life in Medieval France* 25, 58, *Pattern: a Study of Decorative Art*, *Monastic Life at Cluny* 31, *Romanesque Architecture of the Order of Cluny* 38, *Taste and Temperament* 39, *Time and Chance—the story of Arthur Evans and his Forbears* 43, *Art in Medieval France* 48, *English Art 1307-1461* (Oxford History of English Art, Vol. V) 49, *Cluniac Art of the Romanesque Period* 50, *A History of Jewellery* 53, *John Ruskin* 54, *A History of the Society of Antiquaries* 56, *Diaries of John Ruskin* 56-59, *The Lamp of Beauty* 59, *Madame Royale* 59, *Monastic Architecture in France from the Renaissance to the Revolution* 64, *Prelude and Fugue* (autobiography) 64, *The Victorians* 66, *The Conways* 67, *Later Monastic Architecture in France* 67.

72 Campden Hill Court, London, W.8, England.

Evans, John William, M.A., SC.D., D.SC., F.I.BIOL.; British entomologist; b. 16 Jan. 1906; ed. Wellington Coll. and Jesus Coll., Cambridge.

Entomologist C.S.I.R. (Australia) 27-35; Chief Biologist, Tasmanian Dept. of Agriculture 35-43; Senior Entomologist, Imperial (Commonwealth) Inst. of Entomology, London 44-49; Deputy Chief Scientific Officer, U.K. Ministry of Agriculture 49-54; Dir. Australian Museum, Sydney 54-65; mem. Permanent Cttee. Int. Entomological Congresses.

Publs. *Tasmanian Insect Pests* 43, *The Injurious Insects of the British Commonwealth* 52, and numerous articles on entomological topics.

47 Bundarra Road, Bellevue Hill, Sydney, N.S.W., Australia.

Evans, Sir Lincoln, Kt., C.B.E.; British trade unionist; b. 18 Sept. 1889; ed. Swansea elementary school.

Gen. Sec. The Iron and Steel Trades Confed. until 53; mem. Iron and Steel Board 46-48; mem. Economic Planning Board 49-; mem. B.B.C. Advisory Council 52; Vice-Chair. Iron and Steel Board 53-.

16 East Meads, Onslow Village, Guildford, Surrey, England.

Telephone: Guildford 67176.

Evans, Llewellyn Johnson, LL.B.; American aircraft executive; b. 2 Aug. 1920; ed. Univ. of Calif. (Berkeley) and Harvard Univ.

U.S. Army Air Force 43-45; admitted to D.C. Bar 47, N.Y. Bar 52; with Grumman Aircraft Eng. Corpn. 51-, Vice-Pres. 60-63, Senior Vice-Pres. 63-66, Pres. 66-; D.F.C. and Air Medal.

Grumman Aircraft Engineering Corporation, Bethpage, N.Y. 11714; Home: 211 Richard Court, Massapequa Park, N.Y., U.S.A.

Evans, Luther Harris, M.A., PH.D.; American political scientist and librarian; b. 13 Oct. 1902; ed. Univ. of Texas and Stanford Univ.

Instructor in citizenship Stanford Univ. 24-27, in government New York Univ. 27-28, and in political science Dartmouth Coll. 28-30; Asst. Prof. of Politics Princeton Univ. 30-35; Dir. Historical Records Survey, Work Projects Administration 35-39; Dir. Legislative Reference Service, Library of Congress 39-40; Chief Asst. Librarian of Congress 40-45, Librarian June 45-53; Adviser UNESCO London 45; mem. U.S. Nat. Comm. for UNESCO 46-52 (Chair. 52), 59-63; Adviser or Del. to UNESCO Gen. Confs. 47-53 (mem. Exec. Board 49-53); Dir.-Gen. of UNESCO 53-58; Senior Staff mem. Brookings Inst., Washington D.C. 59-61; Dir. Project on Educ. Implications of Automation, Nat. Educ. Asscn., Washington D.C. 61-62; Dir. Int. and Legal Collections Columbia Univ., N.Y. 62-; Democrat.

Publs. *The Virgin Islands from Naval Base to New Deal* 45, *Automation and the Challenge to Education* 62,

Federal Department Libraries 63, *The Decade of Development: Problems and Issues* 66.

25 Claremont Ave., New York City, N.Y. 10027, U.S.A.

Telephone: 212-666-4289.

Evans, Maurice; American (b. British) actor-manager; b. 3 June 1901; ed. Grocers' Company School, London. In America 36-; U.S. Army 42-45; Artistic Supervisor, New York City Center Theatre 49-51; Pulitzer and Critics Prizes for production of *Teahouse of the August Moon* 53.

Plays acted in include: *Richard II*, *Hamlet* 38-39, *Henry IV, Part I* 39, *Twelfth Night* 40-41, *Macbeth* 41-42, *Hamlet* 45-47; produced and acted in *Man and Superman* 47-49, *The Browning Version* 49, *The Devil's Disciple* 50, *Richard II* 51, *Dial "M" for Murder* 52-54, *The Apple Cart* 56-57, *Heartbreak House* 59-60, *Tenderloin* (musical) 60-61, *The Aspern Papers* 61-62.

Films include *Kind Lady* 50, *Androcles and the Lion*, *Gilbert and Sullivan*, *Macbeth* 60, *Warlord* 65, *Jack of Diamonds*, *Planet of the Apes* 67, *Rosemary's Baby* 68.

c/o L. V. Almirall, 1 Chase Manhattan Plaza, New York 5, N.Y., U.S.A.

Evans, Robert Beverley; American business executive and financier; b. 19 March 1906; ed. Virginia Episcopal School, Univ. of Michigan and Univ. of Lausanne, Switzerland.

Former Dir. and Vice-Pres. Evans Products Co.; fmr. Pres. Precision Science Co.; fmr. Dir. Detroit-Windsor Freedom Festival; fmr. Vice-Commodore Yachtsmen's Asscn. of America and Commodore and Chair. Finance Cttee. Detroit Int. Regatta Asscn.; Chair. Board American Motors Corpn., until 67, Staudacher Marine Industries; mem. Board of Dirs. M.B. Corpn., Automobile Manufacturers Asscn.; Pres. Ready Power Co., La Coquille Real Estate Corpn.; Patron, Detroit Symphony; mem. Founders Soc. Detroit Inst. of Arts; Dir. Detroit City Center Comm.; inventor of industrial and marine equipment.

American Motors Corporation, 14250 Plymouth Road, Detroit, Michigan 48232, U.S.A.

Evans, Thomas Mellon, B.A.; American business executive; b. 8 Sept. 1910; ed. Shadyside Acad. and Yale Univ.

Pres. H. K. Porter Co. Inc. 39-56, Chair. 56-; Chair. Crane Co. 59-; Dir. H. K. Porter France Usines de Marpent (France), H. K. Porter (Nederland) N.V. H. K. Porter Co. (Great Britain) Ltd., Fed. Wire and Cable Co. Ltd. (Canada), Société d'Applications Hydrauliques et Electriques (France); Chair. and Dir. Crane Canada Ltd., Dir. Crane Ltd. (England), Crane S.A. France, N.V. Nederlands-Amerikaanse Fittingfabriek (Holland), Orion Petro-Chimica S.p.A.

Round Hill Road, Greenwich, Conn., U.S.A.

Evans of Hungershall, Baron (Life-Peer) cr. 67, of the Borough of Royal Tunbridge Wells; **(B.) Ifor Evans,** M.A., D.LIT., HON. D. ès L. (Paris), F.R.S.L.; British writer and educationist; b. 19 Aug. 1899; ed. Stationers' Co. School and Univ. Coll., London.

Lecturer in English Literature Manchester Univ. 21-24; Prof. of English Language and Literature Univ. Coll. Southampton 25-26; Prof. of English Literature Sheffield Univ. 26-33; Albert Kahn Travelling Fellowship 24; Univ. Prof. of English Language and Literature Queen Mary Coll. Univ. of London 33-44; Principal 44-51; Provost of Univ. Coll. London 51-66; Fellow Univ. Coll. London; Vice-Chair. A.C.G.B. 46-51; with Ministry of Information 39-41; Educational Dir. to British Council 41-44; Public Orator, Univ. of London 47-52; mem. of Exec. British Council 50-54; Chair. *Observer* Trustees 57-66, Nat. Insurance Advisory Cttee. 57; Trustee of the British Museum; Consultant Wates Foundation; Chair. Rediffusion Educational Council;

Officer Legion of Honour (France); Knight of the Order of the Crown (Belgium); Commdr. of the Order of Royal Nassau.

Publs. *William Morris and his Poetry* 24, *Encounters* 26, *Keats and the Chapman Sonnet* 30, *English Poetry in the Later Nineteenth Century* 33, *The Limits of Literary Criticism* 33, *Keats* 34, *Romanticism and Tradition* 39, *A Short History of English Literature* 40, *In Search of Stephen Vane* 46, *The Shop in the King's Road* 47, *Literature Between the Wars* 47, *Short History of British Drama* 48, *The Church in the Markets* 48, *The Arts in England* (with Mary Glasgow) 48, *The Use of English* 49, *A Victorian Anthology* (with Marjorie R. Evans) 49, *The Language of Shakespeare's Plays* 51, *Literature and Science* 54, *English Literature: Values and Traditions* 62.

317 Minster House, St. James's Court, Buckingham Gate, London, S.W.1, England.

Evans-Pritchard, Edward Evan, M.A., PH.D.; British social anthropologist; b. 21 Sept. 1902; ed. Winchester Coll. and Exeter Coll., Oxford.

Expeditions to Central, East and North Africa 26-39; Prof. of Sociology Egyptian Univ. Cairo 30-33; Leverhulme Fellow 34-35; Research Lecturer Oxford 35-40; Active Service 40-45; Reader, Cambridge 45-46; Prof. of Social Anthropology Univ. of Oxford 46-; Pres. Royal Anthropological Inst. 49-51; Fellow, British Acad. 56; Hon. mem. American Acad. Arts and Sciences 58; Hon. Fellow School of Oriental and African Studies, London 63; Hon. D.Sc. Univ. of Chicago 67.

Publs. *Witchcraft, Oracles and Magic among the Azande* 37, *The Nuer* 40, *The Sanusi of Cyrenaica* 49, *Kinship and Marriage among the Nuer* 51, *Social Anthropology* 51, *Nuer Religion* 56, *Essays in Social Anthropology* 62, *The Position of Women in Primitive Societies and other Essays in Social Anthropology* 65.

All Souls College, Oxford, England.
Telephone: Oxford 49641.

Everton, John Scott, B.A., B.D., PH.D., D.D.; American educationist and diplomatist; b. 7 March 1908; ed. Colgate-Rochester Divinity School, Yale Univ. and Cambridge Univ.

Minister, Central Baptist Church, Pennsylvania 37-41; Dean of Chapel and Prof. Philosophy and Religion, Grinnell Coll. 41-49; Pres. Kalamazoo (Mich.) Coll. 49-53; rep. Ford Foundation, Burma 53-56, Exec. Assoc., New York City 56-59, Assoc. Dir. Int. Training and Research Program 59-61; former Lecturer, External Examiner in Philosophy, Univ. of Rangoon; Ambassador to Burma 61-63; Vice-Pres. Educ. and World Affairs 63-; Exec. Dir. of the Overseas Educational Service 63-; Chair. Burma Council Exec. Cttee. of the Asia Soc. 63-; mem. of numerous cttees.; Hon. D.D. (Grinnell Coll.) 49; Hon. LL.D. (Univ. of Redlands) 63; Hon. Dr. of Humane Letters (Univ. of Chattanooga) 64.

73 Old Post Road, Rye, New York, 10580, U.S.A.
Telephone: 914-WO-7-1304.

Evtushenko, Evgeny Alexandrovich; Soviet poet; b. 1933; ed. Moscow Literary Inst.

Geological expeditions with father to Kazakhstan 48, the Altai 50; literary work 49-; visits to France, Africa, U.S.A., Cuba, U.K., Germany 60-63; mem. Editorial Board of *Yunost* magazine; U.S.S.R. Cttee. for Defence of Peace Award 65.

Publs. verse: *Scouts of the Future* (collected verse) 52, *The Third Snow* (lyric verse) 55, *The Highway of Enthusiasts* 56, *Zima Junction* 56, *The Promise* (collected verse) 59, *Conversation with a Count, Moscow Goods Station, At the Skorokhod Plant, The Nihilist, The Apple* 60-61, *A Sweep of the Arm* 62, *Tenderness* 62, *A Precocious Autobiography* 63, *Cashier, Woman, Mother, On the Banks of the Dniepr River, A Woman and a Girl,*

Do the Russians Want War? Bratskaya Hydro-Electric Power Station 65.

Union of Soviet Writers, ul. Vorovskogo 52, Moscow, U.S.S.R.

Ewald, Georg; German politician; b. 30 Oct. 1926; ed. Agricultural Coll., Stralsund, and Karl Marx Party School.

Deputy Chair. Stralsund District Council 50-53; First Sec. Bad Doberan District Cttee., Socialist Unity Party of D.D.R. (S.E.D.) 54-55, Rügen 55-60, Neu Brandenburg Area Cttee. 60-63; mem. Central Cttee. S.E.D. and Cand. mem. Politburo 63-; Minister and Chair. Agricultural Council 63-; mem. Volkskammer 63-; several decorations.

Majakowski-Ring, Berlin-Pankow, Germany.

Ewert, Alfred, M.A.; British university professor; b. 14 July 1891; ed. Univs. of Manitoba and Oxford.

Rhodes Scholar for Manitoba 12; served in Western Ontario Regt., First World War 14-18; Lecturer in French, Univ. of Oxford 21-30; Prof. of the Romance Languages and Fellow of Trinity Coll. Oxford 30-58; Senior Proctor 43-44; Pres. of Modern Humanities Research Asscn. 59; Pres. Anglo-Norman Text Soc. 58-62; Pres. Medieval Soc. 58-63; Fellow of the British Acad.; Corresp. Fellow of Medieval Acad. of America; Officier de la Légion d'Honneur; Hon. Litt. D. (Leeds).

Publs. *Gui de Warewic, roman du XIIIe siècle* (2 vols.) 32, *The French Language* 33, *Béroul, Romance of Tristan* 39, *Marie de France, Lais* 44, *Of the Precellence of the French Tongue* 58; Gen. Editor *French Studies Quarterly* 47-65.

15 Blandford Avenue, Oxford, England.
Telephone: Oxford 55276.

Ewertsen, Harald Wind; Danish ear, nose and throat specialist; b. 17 April 1913; ed. Københavns Universitet.

Assistant, Salmonella Dept. State Serum Inst. 42-44; Dir. State Hearing Rehabilitation Centre of Copenhagen 51-; Lecturer, teachers treating speech and hearing disorders 55-; Vice-Pres. Int. Soc. of Audiology 62-66; Co-editor *International Audiology* 62-66; many specialist publs.

208 Virum Stationsvej, Virum, Denmark.

Ewing, Alfred Cyril, M.A., D.PHIL., LITT.D., F.B.A.; British philosopher; b. 11 May 1899; ed. Univ. Coll., Oxford.

Assistant Lecturer in Philosophy, Swansea Univ. Coll. 27-31; Univ. Lecturer in Moral Science, Cambridge 31-54, Reader in Philosophy 54-66; Fellow, British Acad. 41-; Visiting Prof. at Princeton and Northwestern Univs., U.S.A. 49, in India 50-51, and Univ. of S. Calif. 61-62, Univ. of Colorado 63, San Francisco State Coll. 67; Treas. of Int. Fed. of Philosophical Socs. 53-; Chair. Philosophy Section of British Acad. 53-61; Fellow Jesus Coll., Cambridge 62-66, Hon Fellow 66-; Chair. Faculty Board of Moral Science, Cambridge 57-59, 64-66.

Publs. *Kant's Treatment of Causality* 24, *The Morality of Punishment* 29, *Idealism: a Critical Survey* 34, *A Short Commentary on Kant's Critique of Pure Reason* 38, *Reason and Intuition* (annual philosophical lecture to British Acad.) 41, *The Individual, the State, and World Government* 47, *The Definition of Good* 47, *The Fundamental Questions of Philosophy* 51, *Ethics* 53, *The Idealist Tradition in Philosophy* (selections) 57, *Second Thoughts in Moral Philosophy* 59, *Non-Linguistic Philosophy* 68.

10 Lyndhurst Road, Manchester 20, and Matterdale End, Penrith, Cumberland, England.

Telephone: Did. 5121 (Manchester); Glenridding 282 (Cumberland).

Exeter, 6th Marquess of; **David George Brownlow Cecil,** K.C.M.G., LL.D., D.L., J.P.; British politician, businessman and sportsman; b. 9 Feb. 1905; ed. Eton and Cambridge.
Winner Olympic 400 metres hurdles 28, three British Empire and eight British championships, etc.; Conservative M.P. 31-43; Parl. Private Sec. to Parl. Sec. Minister of Supply 39-41; Lt.-Col., Asst. Dir. Tank Supply 41; Controller Repairs and Overseas Supplies of Aircraft, Ministry of Aircraft Production 41-43; Gov. and Commdr.-in-Chief Bermuda 43-45; Chair. Organizing and Exec. Cttee. of 1948 Olympic Games, London; Rector, St. Andrews Univ. 49-52; Pres. Radio Industry Council 52; Mayor of Stamford 61; Pres. Int. Amateur Athletic Fed., Amateur Athletic Asscn.; Chair. British Olympic Asscn.; Vice-Pres. Int. Olympic Cttee.; Chair. Birmid Industries, Midland Motor Cylinder Co., Birmingham Aluminium Castings Co., Sterling Metals, Deputy Chair. London Board of the Royal Insurance Co.; Dir. Nat. Provincial Bank, Firestone Tyre & Rubber Co., Lands Improvement, Grosvenor House; Pres. Empire Chambers of Commerce; Hereditary Grand Almoner; Hon. LL.D., Hon. F.R.C.S.
Burghley House, Stamford, Lincolnshire, England.
Telephone: Stamford 3131.

Eyadema, Colonel Etienne Guessingbe; Togolese army officer and politician; b. 1937.
Served with French Army 53-61, especially in Indo-China, Dahomey, Niger and Algeria; commissioned 63; Army Chief-of-Staff (Togo) 65-; seized power Jan. 67; Pres. of Togo and Minister of Defence April 67-.
Office of the President, Lomé, Togo.

Eyre, Dean Jack; New Zealand politician; b. 8 May 1914; ed. Hamilton High School and Auckland Univ.
Founder, D. J. Eyre & Co. 36; naval service, World War II; M.P. 49-, Minister of Industries, Commerce and Customs 54, of Social Security, and of Tourist and Health Resorts 56-57, of Housing and State Advances 57, of Defence 57, of Police 60-63, Minister of Defence 60-66, of Tourism and Publicity 61-66; National Party.
Parliament Buildings, Wellington, New Zealand.

Eyring, Henry, M.S., PH.D.; American professor of chemistry; b. 20 Feb. 1901; ed. Univ. of Arizona, Univ. of California.
Instructor in Chemistry, Univs. of Arizona and Wisconsin 24-28; Research Assoc. Univ. of Wisconsin 28-29; Nat. Research Fellow, Kaiser Wilhelm Inst., Berlin 29-30; Lecturer in Chemistry Univ. of Calif. 30-31; Asst. and Assoc. Prof. in Chemistry, Princeton Univ. 31-38, Prof. 38-46; Prof. of Chemistry 46-; Dean of Graduate School, Univ. of Utah 46-66; research work for the Army, Navy and OSRD on the theory of smokes and of high explosives, during Second World War; Dir. of the fundamental research programme of the Textile Foundation, Princeton 44-46; Editor *Annual Reviews of Physical Chemistry*; mem. of U.S. Acad. of Arts and Sciences, Utah Acad. of Science, Arts and Letters, American Philosophical Soc.; Pres. American Chemical Soc. 63; Pres. Board of Dirs. American Asscn. Adv. of Science; award from Research Corpn. for outstanding contribution to science 49, Bingham Medal (American Chemical Soc.) 51; Hon. D.Sc. (Northwestern Univ., Univ. of Utah and Princeton Univ.); Nat. Medal of Science 66.
Publs. with others: *The Theory of Rate Processes* 41, *Quantum Chemistry* 44, *The Kinetic Basis of Molecular Biology* 54, *Modern Chemical Kinetics* 63, *Statistical Mechanics and Dynamics* 64.
Institute for the Study of Rate Processes, University of Utah, Salt Lake City 12, Utah; Home: 1922 East 9th South, Salt Lake City, Utah, U.S.A.
Telephone: 322-7708.

Eysenck, Hans Jurgen, PH.D.; British psychologist; b. 4 March 1916; ed. Univs. of Dijon, Exeter and London.
Research Psychologist, Mill Hill Emergency Hospital 42-45; Psychologist, Maudsley Hospital, London 45; Reader and Dir., Psychological Dept., Inst. of Psychiatry, Univ. of London 50-55; Prof. of Psychology 55-.
Publs. *Dimensions of Personality* 47, *The Scientific Study of Personality* 52, *The Structure of Human Personality* 53, *Uses and Abuses of Psychology* 53, *The Psychology of Politics* 54, *Sense and Nonsense in Psychology* 56, *The Dynamics of Anxiety and Hysteria* 57, *Perceptional Processes and Mental Illness* 57, *Manual for the Maudsley Personality Inventory* 59, *Experiments in Personality* (2 vols.) 60, *Behaviour Therapy and the Neuroses* 60, *Handbook of Abnormal Psychology* 60, *Manual for the Eysenck Personality Inventory* 63, *Experiments with Drugs* 63, *Crime and Personality* 64, *Experiments in Motivation* 64, *Causes and Cures of Neuroses* 65, *Experiments in Behaviour Therapy* 65, *Fact and Fiction in Psychology* 65, *Smoking, Health and Personality* 65, *The Biological Basis o- Personality* 67, *Structure and Measurement of Personf ality* 68.
Department of Psychology, Institute of Psychiatry, Maudsley Hospital, Denmark Hill, London, S.E.5; Home: 10 Dorchester Drive, London, S.E.24, England.

Eyskens, Gaston, M.S., DR. RER. POL., DR. SC.COM., LIC. SC.ECON.; Belgian economist and politician; b. 1 April 1905; ed. Univ. of Louvain and Columbia Univ.
Professor Univ. of Louvain 31; Cabinet Dir., Ministry of Labour 34-35; mem. of Parl. 39; Minister of Finance 45 and 47; Gov. Int. Bank for Reconstruction and Devt. 47; Prime Minister 49; Minister of Econ. Affairs 50; Vice-Pres. Econ. and Social Council U.N. 51; Prime Minister 58-61, June 68-; Minister of State; Minister of Finance 65-66; Hon. Dr. Econ. (Cologne), Hon. Dr. of Laws (Columbia); mem. Christian Social Party.
Publs. *Le Port de New York dans son rôle économique* 29, *De Arbeider en de Bedrijfsleiding in Amerika* 31, *La conjoncture économique du Congo Belge* 34, etc.
60 rue de Namur, Louvain, Belgium.
Telephone: 224-43.

Eytan, Walter, M.A.; Israeli civil servant; b. 24 July 1910; ed. St. Paul's School, London, and Queen's Coll., Oxford.
Lecturer in German, Queen's Coll., Oxford 34-46; Principal, Public Service Coll., Jerusalem 46-48; Dir.-Gen., Ministry for Foreign Affairs, Israel 48-59; Ambassador to France 59-.
Publ. *The First Ten Years* 58.
41 avenue Foch, Paris 16e, France.
Telephone: 553-25-96.

Eyuboğlu, Bedri Rahmi; Turkish painter and poet; b. 13; ed. Académie des Beaux Arts, Constantinople, and André Lhote Atelier, Paris.
Exhibited in Turkey with advanced painters' *Group D* 33-37; influenced by Anatolian handicraft designs 41-45; worked on block printing, serigraphy, engraving and textile printing 45-50; mosaic work since 57; Ford Foundation Grant for travel in Europe and U.S.A. 61-63; Prof. Acad. of Fine Arts, Istanbul; has also written poems, essays and travel notes in books, magazines and newspapers; Prize at São Paulo Bienal 56, Gold Medal, Brussels Fair 58; exhbns. in several cities of Europe and U.S.A.
Major works: Panel at Brussels Fair 58, Mosaic panel for NATO Building in Paris 59, Christmas Card for UNICEF 61, mosaic murals in Ankara, Izmir and Istanbul 63-65.
29/3 Manolya Sokak, Kalamis, Kızıltoprak, Istanbul, Turkey.

Ezekiel, Mordecai J. B., M.S., PH.D., DR.SCI.; American economist; b. 10 May 1899; ed. Maryland and Minnesota Univs. and Robert Brookings Graduate School.

Statistical Asst. U.S. Census Bureau 19-22; with Div. of Farm Management U.S. Dept. of Agriculture 22-30; Asst. Chief Economist Federal Farm Board 30-33; Economic Adviser to Sec. of Agriculture 33-46; Economist F.A.O. 47-50, Dep. Dir. Economics Div. 51-58, in charge of Economics Dept. 59-60, Asst. Dir.-Gen. 61, Special Asst. to Dir.-Gen. 62; Chief UN Section U.S. Admin. for Industrial Development 62-68; Consultant to A.I.D. 68-; Visiting Lecturer or Prof. Univs. of Arizona, Missouri and Maine.

Publs. *Methods of Correlation Analysis* 30, 41, 59, *$2,500 a Year—from Scarcity to Abundance* 36, *Jobs for All* 39; Editor *Towards World Prosperity* 47, *Uses of Agricultural Surpluses to Finance Economic Development in Underdeveloped Countries, A Pilot Study in India* (FAO) 55.

5312 Allandale Road, Washington 16, D.C. 20016, U.S.A.

Ezhevsky, Alexander Alexandrovich; Soviet politician; b. 15; ed. Irkutsk Agricultural Inst.

Metal craftsman, Irkutsk 30-39; student Irkutsk Agricultural Inst. 39-43; Chief Engineer car repair factory 43-51; Dir. tractor factory 51-53, Rostov Agricultural Machine Building Factory 53-54; Deputy Minister of Tractor and Agricultural Machine Building, U.S.S.R. 54-57; Deputy and later Head of Dept., U.S.S.R. Gosplan 57-62; Chair. All-Union Farm Machinery Supply Agency "Sojuzselknostechnika", Council of Ministers of U.S.S.R. 62-; mem. U.S.S.R. Council of Ministers 65-; Candidate mem. Central Cttee. C.P.S.U.; mem. C.P.S.U. 45-; Deputy to U.S.S.R. Supreme Soviet.

All-Union Farm Machinery Supply Agency of the Council of Ministers, 1-11 Orlikov pereulok, Moscow, U.S.S.R.

Ezhov, Igor Matveevich; Soviet diplomatist; b. 1921; ed. Moscow Univ.

Diplomatic Service 45-; First Sec. U.S.S.R. Embassy, Switzerland 55-57; Counsellor, U.S.S.R. Embassy, Paris 59-61; Deputy Chief of Press Affairs, Ministry of Foreign Affairs 61-62; Ambassador to Luxembourg 63-67; Deputy Head of First European Dept., U.S.S.R. Ministry of Foreign Affairs 67-.

Ministry of Foreign Affairs, 32-34 Smolenskaya-Sennaya ploshchad, Moscow, U.S.S.R.

Ezhov, Leonid Savvich; Soviet foreign trade official; b. 1916; ed. Moscow Inst. of Mechanical Engineering and Acad. of Foreign Trade.

Member C.P.S.U. 44-; U.S.S.R. Trade Rep., Italy 49-51; Commercial Attaché, later, U.S.S.R. Commercial Rep. in Lebanon 51-56; Official, Ministry of Foreign Trade 56-62; Commercial Rep. in Belgium 62-66; Chief of Dept., Ministry of Foreign Trade 66-; Badge of Honour.

Ministry of Foreign Trade, 32-34 Smolenskaya-Sennaya ploshchad, Moscow, U.S.S.R.

Ezhov, Valentin Ivanovich; Soviet screen-play writer; b. 1921; ed. All-Union State Inst. of Cinematography.

Member C.P.S.U. 51-; Lenin Prize for script of *Ballad of a Soldier*; co-author scripts for *Our Champions* 54, *World Champion* 55, *Liana* 56, *A Man from the Planet Earth* 58, *The House of Gold* 59, *The Volga Flows* 62, *Story of a Woman Flier* 64.

Mosfilm Studios, 1 Mosfilmovskaya ulitsa, Moscow, U.S.S.R.

Ezpeleta, Mariano; Philippine diplomatist; b. 05; ed. Philippine Lyceum and Law School.

Called to Bar and practised 26; Del. Philippine Constitutional Convention 35; Congressional Sec. and Political Adviser to Pres. Manuel Roxas 46-47; Consul-Gen. Shanghai 47-49, San Francisco 50, First Sec. and Consul-Gen. London 50-53; Minister to Mexico 53-55; Ambassador to Vietnam, and Chief of Mission to Cambodia and Laos 55-58; Ambassador to Thailand and Chief of Mission to Malaya 58-60; Ambassador to Australia and Chief of Mission to New Zealand 60-; Mexican decoration El Aguila Azteca.

Publ. *Rules of Court, Annotated.*

Philippine Embassy, 1 Moonah Place, Yarralumla, Canberra, A.C.T., Australia.

F

Fabbri, Diego; Italian playwright; b. 2 July 1911.
Former lawyer; Nat. Theatre Prize for *Inquisizione* 50;
Marzotto Int. Prize for *Portrait of a Young Man*.
Plays include: *Orbite* 41, *Paludi* 42, *La Libreria del Sole*
43, *Inquisizione* 50, *Rancore* 50, *Il Seduttore* 51, *Processo
di famiglia* 54, *Processo a Gesù* 55, *La Bugiarda* 56,
Veglia d'armia 57, *Delirio* 58, *Figli d'arte* 59, *Processo
Karamazov* 61, *Portrait of a Young Man* 62, *The
Confidant* 64, libretto for *L'Avventuriero* 68.
Santa Prisca 15, Rome, Italy.

Faber, Paul L., LL.D., D.ECON.; Guinean lawyer and
economist; b. 18 Dec. 1924; ed. Facultés de Droit et de
Sciences Economiques de Lyon et de Bordeaux.
Attorney-Gen. Guinea 58; Vice-Pres. Asscn. of Demo-
cratic Jurists, Sofia 60; Minister of Justice, Guinea 61;
Acting Sec.-Gen., later Joint Pres., Org. of Afro-Asian
Jurists 62; Resident Minister of Guinea in Ghana 63;
Exec. Dir. Int. Monetary Fund (IMF) 66-; Companion
of the Independence 60.
International Monetary Fund, Washington, D.C.
20431, U.S.A.

Fabiani, Dante Carl; American industrialist; b. 13
Aug. 1917; ed. Tri-State Coll. and Purdue Univ.
Auburn Rubber Corpn., Indiana 38-42; Gen. Electric
Co., Ind. 42-45; Continental Can Co., Ohio 45-47; Con-
troller, Asst. Man. Standard Products Co. Ohio, 48-51;
Dir., Sec.-Treas. Townsend Co., Pa. 51-59; Vice-Pres.
Finance, H. K. Porter Co. Inc. 59-60; Dir., Vice-Pres.
Finance, McDonnell Aircraft Corpn., Missouri 60;
Pres. and Dir. Crane Co., New York 60-; Dir. Sawhill
Tubular Products 67-.
300 Park Avenue, New York City 22, N.Y., U.S.A.

Fabiani, Simonetta; Duchessa Colonna di Cesarò;
Italian fashion designer; b. 10 April 1932.
Opened her own studio 46, and, under the name
"Simonetta", has since become one of the leading
Italian designers; opened Paris House 62.
Publ. *Snob in the Kitchen* 67.
Office: 40 rue François Premier, Paris 8e, France.
Telephone: OPE 6268 (Home); ELY 5671 (Office).

Fabinyi, Andrew, D.PHIL., O.B.E.; Australian pub-
lisher; b. 27 Dec. 1908; ed. Minta Gymnasium and
Pazmany Univ., Budapest, Hungary.
British Publishers Rep. in Hungary 33-39; Publishing
Manager, F. W. Cheshire Pty. Ltd. 39-54; Australian
Army Educ. Service 42-46; Publishing Dir. F. W.
Cheshire Pty. Ltd. 54-; Pres. Australian Book Fair
Council 55-60, Victorian Branch of Library Asscn. of
Australia 55, 59, 65, 66, Public Libraries Div. of Library
Asscn. of Australia 62, Dir. Lansdowne Press Pty. Ltd.
62-; Pres. Australian Book Publishers' Asscn. 65, 66;
mem. Exec. Cttee. for Econ. Development of Australia
65-; mem. of the General Council (Fed.) Library Asscn.
of Australia 67; Chair. of Australian Inst. of Int.
Affairs Victorian Branch 68-, Australian Book Trade
Advisory Cttee. 67-, Australian UNESCO Nat. Cttee.
Sub-Cttee., Book Production and Distribution 68-;
Deputy Chair. Cheshire Group Publishers and Book-
sellers 67-; Man. Dir. F. W. Cheshire Publishing Pty.
Ltd. 67; Dir. Jacaranda Press Pty. Ltd. 67, Bellbird
Books Pty. Ltd. 67-.
17 Scott Grove, Glen Iris 3146, Victoria, Australia.
Telephone: 25-3096.

Fábri, Zoltán; Hungarian film director; b. 1917; ed.
grammar school, Acad. of Fine Arts, Budapest, and
Acad. of Dramatic Art, Budapest.
Former painter, later actor at Nat. Theatre 41; Army

Service, Second World War; joined Artists' Theatre,
Budapest, after Second World War; later Head of
Youth Theatre; joined State Film Production Org. 50,
film dir. 52-; Chair. Union of Hungarian Film Artists;
Grand Prix, Carlovy-Vary Film Festival for *Professor
Hannibal* 56; Grand Prix, Moscow Film Festival for
Twenty Hours 65, Kossuth Prize 53, 55.
Films: *The Storm* 52, *Fourteen Lives Saved* 54, *Merry-
Go-Round* 55, *Professor Hannibal* 56, *April Fool* 57,
Anna 58, *The Beast* 59, *Two Half-Times in Hell* 61,
Darkness in Daytime 63, *Twenty Hours* 64, *Late
Season* 67.
c/o Hungarofilm, Budapest 5/5, Hungary.
Telephone: 116-650.

Fabricius, Johan; Netherlands writer; b. 99; ed.
Batavia, Leyden, and The Hague.
Former war corresp. on Austro-Italian front; B.B.C.
and *The Times* corresp. in Indonesia 45-46.
Publs. include: *De scheepsjongens van Bontekoe* 24, *Hans
de klokkeluider* (play) 25, *Het meisje met de blauwe hoed*
27, *Charlotte's grote reis* 28, *Mario Ferraro's ijdele
liefde* 29, *Komedianten trokken voorbij* 31 (awarded Van
der Hoogt Prize 32), *Melodie der verten* 32, *Leeuwen
hongeren in Napels* 34, *De dans om de galg* 34, *Flipje* 36,
Kasteel in Carinthië 38, *Eiland der Demonen* 40, *Nacht
over Java* 42, *De kraton* 45, *Halfbloed* 46, *Hoe ik Indie
terugvond, Hotel Vesuvius* 47, *De Grote Geus* 48, *De
Grote Beproeving* 50, *Mijn Huis staat achter de Kim*
(memoirs) 51, *De Ontvoering van Europa* 52, *Langs de
Leie* 52, *Een Wereld in Beroering* (memoirs) 52, *Gordel
van Smaragd* 53, *De Nertsmantel* 53, *Het Duistere Bloed*
(play) 53, *Idylle 1871* (play) 53, *Toernooi met de Dood*
54, *Nacht zonder Zegen* 55, *Setoewo de Tijger* 56, *Nuit
Maudite, Die heiligen Pferde, Ma Rosalie, Hopheisa in
regen en wind* (memoirs) 64, *Wat u nodig hebt, mevrouw,
is een vriend* 64, *Dag Leidse Plein* 65, *Dromen is ook
leven* 65, *Weet je nog, Yoshi?* 66, *Wij Tz'e Hsi, Keizerin
van China* 67, *Het Water Weet van niets* 68.
H. P. Leopold's Uitgeversmij., P.O. Box 149, The
Hague; 15 Meentweg 7, Glimmen (gem. Haren, Gron.),
Netherlands.
Telephone: Glimmen 606.

Facio, Gonzalo J.; Costa Rican lawyer and diplo-
matist; b. 28 March 1918; ed. National Univ. of Costa
Rica, New York Univ. School of Law, and Inst. of
Inter-American Law, New York.
Founder Law Firm of Facio, Fournier and Cañas; Prof.
Philosophy of Law, Nat. Univ. of Costa Rica 44-47,
Prof. Admin. Law 47-51, Prof. Econ. and Social Org.
59-61, Prof. Admin. Law 59-62; founder-mem. Nat.
Liberation Party 48, mem. Exec. Cttee. 48-56, Chair.
Planning Board 59-62; Ambassador, Rep. to the Org.
of American States (OAS) 56-58, 62-, Vice-Chair.
Council 57-58, Chair. Council OAS 62-63; Ambassador
to U.S.A. 62-; Editor magazine *Surco* 42-45, weekly
Democratic Action 45-48, daily *La República* 55-56.
Embassy of Costa Rica, Washington, D.C., U.S.A.

Fadahunsi, Sir Odeleye, K.C.M.G., G.C.O.N.; Nigerian
politician; b. 01; ed. Oshu Methodist School, Oshu-
Ilesha, and Wesley Coll., Ibadan, Nigeria.
Teacher, Methodist Schools, Ikorodu and Lagos 25-26;
Produce Buyer, Storekeeper, Salesman 27-48; Man.
Dir. Ijesha United Trading and Transport Co. Ltd. 48;
mem. Nigeria Cocoa Marketing Board 48-53, Western
Region Production Devt. Board 48-53, Eastern
Nigeria Produce Marketing Board 54-57; Dir. Nigeria
Produce Marketing Co. 52-53; Chair. Ijesha Div.
Council 55-60, Nigeria Airways Corpn. 61-62; mem.

Western Nigeria House of Assembly and Dep. Leader of Opposition 51-61; Gov. of Western Nigeria 63-66; Adviser to Military Governor, W. Provinces, Nigeria 66-; Queen's Coronation Medal 53, knighted 63; Grand Commander of the Niger 63.

c/o Government House, Ibadan, Western Nigeria, Nigeria.

Fadden, Rt. Hon. Sir Arthur William, P.C., G.C.M.G.; Australian politician; b. 13 April 1895.

Mem. House of Assembly for Kennedy, Queensland 32-35; mem. House of Reps. for Darling Downs, Queensland 36-49, Macpherson, Queensland 49-58; temporary Chair. of Cttees. 37-40; Minister assisting Treas. and Minister for Supply and Development March-Aug. 40; Minister for Air and Civil Aviation Aug.-Oct. 40; Treas. Oct. 40-Aug. 41; Prime Minister and Treas. Aug.-Oct. 41; mem. Australian Advisory War Council 40-45; Leader of Opposition 41-43; Deputy Leader and Acting Leader Australian Country Party 40-41, Leader 41-58; mem. War Cabinet and Economic Cabinet 40-41; Deputy Prime Minister and Treas. Dec. 49-58; Acting Prime Minister July-Aug. 50, Dec. 50-Feb. 51, May-June and Nov.-Dec. 52, May-July 53, June 54, Jan.-Mar. 55, May-Sept. 56, April and May-Aug. 57.

Box 575J, G.P.O., Brisbane, Queensland, Australia.

Fadeyechev, Nikolai Borisovich; Soviet ballet dancer; b. 27 Jan. 1933; ed. Bolshoi Theatre Ballet School.

Bolshoi Ballet Company 52-; People's Artist of R.S.F.S.R.

Chief roles: Siegfried (*Swan Lake*), Albert (*Giselle*), Jean de Brien (*Raimonde*), Harmodius (*Spartacus*), Frondoso (*Laurensia*), Danila (*Stone Flower*), Romeo (*Romeo and Juliet*), Prince Desire (*Sleeping Beauty*).

State Academic Bolshoi Theatre of U.S.S.R., 1 ploshchad Sverdlova, Moscow, U.S.S.R.

Faesi, Robert, PH.D.; Swiss literary historian and writer; b. 10 April 1883; ed. Zürich, Lausanne and Berlin Univs.

Prof. of German Literature Zürich Univ. 22-53; poet, dramatist, film writer, novelist and essayist; G. Keller-Preis 43; Zürcher Literaturpreis 45.

Publs. *Zürcher Idylle, Odysseus und Nausikaa, Aus der Brandung, Die Fassade, Der König von Ste. Pélagie, Opferspiel, Der brennende Busch, Vom Menuett zur Marseillaise, Das Antlitz der Erde, Füsilier Wipf, Der Magier, Die Stadt der Väter, Die Stadt der Freiheit, Die Stadt des Friedens, Ungereimte Welt gereimt, Alles Korn meinet Weizen, Die Gedichte, Die schwarze Spinne, Erlebnisse, Ergebnisse-Paul Ernst, C. F. Meyer, Gestalten und Wandlungen schweizerischer Dichtung, R. M. Rilke, Spittelers Weg und Werk, Heimat und Genius, G. Keller, Dichtung und Geschichte, Thomas Mann, Thomas Mann-Robert Faesi Briefwechsel.*

Goldhaldenstr. 16, Zollikon-Zürich, Switzerland.

Telephone: 65-50-68.

Fagerholm, Karl-August; Finnish politician; b. 1901; ed. Helsinki.

Barber 17-23; Chair. Finnish Barbers T.U. 20-23; Mem. of Parl. 30-66; mem. Presidential electorate 31; Minister of Social Affairs 37-43; mem. of Castren Govt. 44; Speaker of the Diet 45-48, 50-56, 59-61, 65-66; Prime Minister July 48-Mar. 50, Mar. 56-May 57, Aug. 58-Jan. 59; Chair. Shopworkers' Union 30-42, Hon. Chair. 43-; Workers' Rep. at Labour Conf. Geneva 30, Govt. Rep. 38 and 39; Dir.-Gen. State Alcohol Monopoly 52-; Spokesman for several professional workers' unions; mem. Exec. Cttee. Social Democratic Party.

Temppelik 15, Helsinki, Finland.

Fagley, Rev. Richard Martin, B.A., B.D., D.D.; American Congregational clergyman; b. 24 Dec. 1910; ed. Yale Coll., Yale Divinity School and London School of Economics and Political Science.

Ordained 39; Research Asst. Council for Social Action,

Congregational Christian Churches 36-37; Education Sec. Church Peace Union and American Council of World Alliance for Int. Friendship through the Churches 38-45; Editor *World Alliance News Letter* 38-45; Sec. Comm. on a Just and Durable Peace, Fed. Council of Churches of Christ in America 45-47, Co-Sec. Dept. of Int. Justice and Goodwill, Fed. Council 48-50; Dir. Dept. of Int. Justice and Goodwill, Nat. Council of Churches of Christ in U.S.A. 50-51; Exec. Sec. Comm. of Churches on Int. Affairs, World Council of Churches 51-.

Publs. *Proposed Roads to Peace* 34, *Population Explosion and Christian Responsibility* 60.

24 Commodore Road, Chappaqua, New York, U.S.A.

Fahlström, Öyvind Axel Christian, Swedish artist and writer; b. 28 Dec. 1928.

Former critic for periodicals and *Expressen* Stockholm; manifesto for *Concrete poetry* 52, increasingly active as painter since mid-'fifties; One-man exhbns. Galerie Daniel Cordier, Paris 59 and 62, New York 63 and 65, Stockholm 62 and 64; Rep. of Sweden, Venice Biennale 66.

Publs. *Minneslista till Dr. Schweitzer's sista uppdrag* (poetry) 64, *Den Helige Torsten Nilsson* (novel for tape) 65, *Bord* (poetry) 66.

128 Front Street, New York, N.Y. 5, U.S.A.; and Köpmangatan 8, Stockholm C, Sweden.

Faina, Conte Carlo, D.IUR., D.ECON.; Italian industrialist; b. 12 Oct. 1894; ed. Bocconi Univ., Milan, and Perugia Univ.

Branch Man. Banco Nazionale d'Agricoltura 22-26; with Montecatini Co. 26-, Sec. to Pres. 26-46, Man. Dir. 46-, Vice-Pres. 52-56, Pres. and Managing Dir. 56-; Vice-Pres. Assicurazioni Generali; Cavaliere del Lavoro, Légion d'Honneur.

Largo Donegani, 1/2, Milan, Italy.

Fairbairn, Hon. David Eric, D.F.C.; Australian grazier and politician; b. 17; ed Geelong Grammar School and Jesus Coll., Cambridge.

Farmer and grazier, Woomargama, nr. Albury, New South Wales; R.A.A.F., Second World War; M.P. 49-; Minister for Air 62-64; Acting Minister for Supply 63; Minister for Nat. Development 64-, and Leader in House 66-; Liberal.

"Dunraven", Woomargama, via Albury, New South Wales, Australia.

Fairchild, Sherman M.; American aircraft manufacturer; b. 7 April 1896; ed. Arizona, Harvard and Columbia Univs.

Inventor Fairchild Aerial Camera; Chair. Fairchild Camera and Instrument Corpn.; Dir. Pan-American Airways, Int. Business Machines Corpn., G. M. Giannini & Co. Inc., Fairchild Engine and Airplane Corpn., Fine Sound Inc., Perspecta Sound Inc.; Pres. Sherman Fairchild and Assocs. Inc. 61-, Chair 61-; Fairchild Recording Equipment Co.

Huntington, Long Island, N.Y., U.S.A.

Fairfax, Warwick Oswald, M.A.; Australian journalist; b. 01; ed. Geelong Grammar School and Sydney and Oxford Univs.

Chair. of Dirs. John Fairfax Ltd. (*Sydney Morning Herald, The Sun, The Sun-Herald,* etc.).

Publs. *A Century of Journalism, The Sydney Morning Herald and Its Record of Australian Life* (Editor); *Men, Parties, and Policies, Metaphysics of the Mystic*; plays: *A Victorian Marriage, Vintage for Heroes, The Bishop's Wife.*

Barford, Bellevue Hill, Sydney, N.S.W., Australia.

Fairfield, Ronald McLeod, C.B.E., B.SC.(ENG.), F.I.E.E., M.I.MECH.E.; British electrical engineer and company director; b. 1911; ed. Llandaff Cathedral School, King Edward's School, Bath, Erith Technical Coll., and London Univ.

With British Insulated Callender's Cables Ltd. (B.I.C.C.) 45-, Chief Engineer, Designs and Processes 45; Dir. and Gen. Manager, St. Helen's Cable and Rubber Co. Ltd. and Chair. Veedip Ltd. 48; Dir. and Gen. Manager, W. T. Glover & Co. Ltd. 52; Dir. of Production and Engineering, B.I.C.C. 54, Dir. Home Operations 58, now Deputy Chair. and Man. Dir.; Chair. European Cables Ltd.; Chair. British Insulated Callender's Construction Co., British Insulated Callender's (Submarine Cables) Ltd.; Pres. British Electrical and Allied Manufacturers' Asscn.; F.R.S.A.
Publ. Paper entitled *British Columbia-Vancouver Island 138 kV Submarine Power Cable.*
66 Whitehall Court, London, S.W.1; Owlswood, Tennyson's Lane, Haslemere, Surrey, England.
Telephone: 01-636-1600 (Office); 01-930-3160; Haslemere 3465.

Fairhall, Allen; Australian company director and politician; b. 24 Nov. 1909; ed. Newcastle Technical Coll.
Engaged in commercial broadcasting 31-47; Supervising Engineer, Radio and Signals Supply Div., Ministry of Munitions 42-45; mem. Federal Parl. for Paterson Div. 49-; Minister for the Interior and Minister for Works 56-58; Chair. Parl. Works Cttee. 59-61; Minister for Supply 61-66, Defence 66-; Liberal.
7 Parkway Avenue, Newcastle, N.S.W., Australia.
Telephone: Newcastle 22295; 23271.

Faisal, H.M. King Malik Faisal ibn Abdel Aziz; Saudi Arabian monarch; b. 05.
Brother of former King Ibn Sa'ud; Viceroy of the Hejaz 26-64; Prime Minister and Minister of Foreign Affairs 53-60; Minister of Foreign Affairs 61; Deputy Prime Minister 61-62; Prime Minister 63-64; Regent 63-64; King 64-, also Prime Minister and Minister of Foreign Affairs; rep. Saudi Arabia at San Francisco Conf. 45; Hon. G.B.E., K.C.M.G. and other honours.
The Royal Palace, Riyadh, Saudi Arabia.

Faizi, Djaudat Kharisovich; Soviet composer; b. 1910; ed. Kazan Univ., and Tatar Opera Studio of Moscow Conservatoire.
Executive mem. Composer's Union of Tatar Autonomous S.S.R.; Honoured Worker of Arts of the Tatar Autonomous S.S.R. 44, and of the R.S.F.S.R. 57, People's Artist of the Tatar Autonomous S.S.R. 64.
Principal works: *Bashmachki* (Slippers) 42, *Seagulls* 44, *On the Banks of the Volga* 49 (all musical comedies); *Undispatched Letters* (opera) 59; over 150 songs and romances, instrumental music and theatre music.
Composers' Union of the Tatar A.S.S.R., Kazan, U.S.S.R.

Fajans, Kasimir, PH.D.; Polish chemist; b. 27 May 1887; ed. Leipzig, Heidelberg and Manchester Univs.
Assistant 11 and Lecturer 13-17, Karlsruhe Institute of Technology; Extraordinary Prof. Munich Univ. 17 and Prof. 25-35; Baker Lecturer, Cornell Univ. 30; Prof. Univ. of Michigan 36-57; Prof. Emeritus 57-; mem. Academies of Science of Munich, Leningrad and Cracow; hon. mem. Spanish Society for Physics and Chemistry, Societas physico-medica Erlangensis, Polish Chemical Society, Mexican Chemical Society and Society of Nuclear Medicine, and London Royal Institution; Victor Meyer Prize, Heidelberg 09; Medal of Univ. of Liège 48; Kasimir Fajans Award in Chemistry estab. at Univ. of Michigan 56.
Publs. *Radioaktivität und neueste Entwicklung der Lehre von den chemischen Elementen* 19, *Physikalisch-chemisches Praktikum* (with J. Wüst) 30, *Radioelements and Isotopes, Chemical Forces and Optical Properties of Substances* 31, *Adsorptionsindikatoren für Fällungstitrationen* 35, *Refractometry* (with N. Bauer) 45, *Polarization* 57, *Quanticule Theory* (in Polish) 61.

1016 Lincoln Avenue, Ann Arbor, Michigan 48104, U.S.A.
Telephone: 313-66-88468.

Fajon, Etienne; French politician and journalist; b. 11 Sept. 1906.
Member of the Central Cttee., French C.P. 32; Dep. for Courbevoie 36-40; Del. to Provisional Ass. 44-45; mem. Constituent Ass. 45-46; Dep. for Seine 46-58 and 62-; Dep. for Seine-Saint-Denis 67; mem. of Party Political Bureau 45, Party Sec. 54-56, Dir. *L'Humanité* 58-.
L'Humanité, 6 Boulevard Poissonnière, Paris 9, France.
Telephone: 770-15-01.

Fakhreddine, Mohamed; Sudanese diplomatist; b. 12 Oct. 1924; ed. Gordon Memorial Coll., Khartoum, and Univ. of Durham.
Chief of Protocol, Head of UN Section, Ministry of Foreign Affairs, Khartoum 56-58; Counsellor, London 58-60; Amb. to Pakistan and Afghanistan 60-64; Amb. to Pakistan, Afghanistan and People's Republic of China 64-65; Perm. Rep. to UN 65-.
Permanent Mission of Sudan to the United Nations, 757 Third Avenue, New York, N.Y., U.S.A.

Falaize, Pierre-Louis; French diplomatist; b. 18 Aug. 1905; ed. Lycée Henri IV and Univ. of Paris.
Political Commentator *l'Aube* 32-39, *Paris-Soir* 37-39; Dir. of Cabinet to Georges Bidault 44-48, to the Pres. of the Council 49-50, to Minister of National Defence 51-52; Dir. of UN Centre in the Middle East, Dir. of Cabinet to Minister of Foreign Affairs 53; Ambassador to Jordan 54-57, Libya 58-59, Laos 59-64, Lebanon 64-67.
37 Quai d'Orsay, Paris 7e, France.

Falck, Giovanni; Italian industrialist; b. 16 Sept. 1900; ed. Politecnico of Milan (Doctorate of Engineering).
Pres. Acciaierie e Ferriere Lombarde Falck.
Corso Matteotti 4, Milan, Italy.

Falck, Thomas Scheen, Jr.; Norwegian shipowner; b. 19 Feb. 1892; ed. Bergen Commercial School and Commercial Univ. of Cologne.
Held appts. in England, France and Russia 11-19; Foreign Man. Bergen S/S Co. Ltd. 19-, Asst. Dir. 29, Dir. 33, Man. Dir. 43-60, Chair. 43-63; fmr. Pres. Norwegian Shipowners Asscn., The Baltic and Int. Maritime Conf.; fmr. Chair. Norwegian Tourist Asscn., etc.
Home: Nubbebakken 6, Bergen, Norway.

Falcón-Briceño, Marcos; Venezuelan lawyer, diplomatist and politician; b. 4 April 1907.
Government Service 36-; Commercial Agent in Germany, Holland, Denmark 38-42, Washington 42-43; First Sec. Washington 43-44, Commercial Counsellor 44-45, Counsellor and Minister Counsellor 45-48 (Chargé d'Affaires 46-47); resigned 48; Economics Division, Pan-American Union, U.S.A. 49-51; lawyer in Venezuela 51, Attorney, Banco Comercio, Caracas; Pres., Caracas Municipal Council 51-58; Ambassador to U.S.A. 58-60; Minister of Foreign Affairs 61-63; Ambassador to U.K. 63-65.
Publs. *Maritime Politics of Latin America, Latin America on the High Seas, The Coffee Policy of Latin American Countries.*
c/o Ministry of Foreign Affairs, Caracas, Venezuela.

Falk, Isidore Sydney, PH.D.; American medical economist, social security expert; b. 30 Sept. 1899; ed. Yale Univ.
Assistant Dept. of Public Health 15-20; Instructor Yale Univ. 20-23; Asst. Prof. of Hygiene and Bacteriology 23-26, Associate Prof. 26-29 and Prof. 29 Univ. of Chicago; Associate Dir. Cttee. on Costs of Medical Care 29-33; Research Associate Milbank Memorial Fund 33-36; Statistical Consultant U.S. Public Health Service 36;

Chief of Health Studies Social Security Board 36-38, Asst. Dir. Bureau (later Division) of Research and Statistics 38-40, Dir. 40-54; mem. Int. Bank Mission to Malaya 54; Consultant on Public Health and Social Security to Govt. of Panama 55 and 56; Consultant on Health to Panama Canal Zone Govt. 57; Consultant on Health Services to United Steelworkers of America 58-; Prof. of Public Health (Medical Care), Yale Univ. 61-.
Publs. *Laboratory Outlines in Bacteriology and Immunology* (with J. F. Norton) 26; co-Editor *The Newer Knowledge of Bacteriology and Immunology* 28, *The Costs of Medical Care* (with C. R. Rorem and M. D. Ring) 33, *Security Against Sickness* 36, *Disability Among Gainfully Occupied Persons* (with Barkev S. Sanders and David Federman) 45, *Medical Care Insurance, A Social Insurance Program for Personal Health Services* (with staff) 46, *Social Insurance Program for Haiti* 52, *The Social Services* (in *Economic Development of Malaya*) 55, *A Review of the Social Security Program of Panama* (English and Spanish texts) 56, *Health in Panama: A Survey and a Program* (English and Spanish texts) 57, *A Survey of Health Services and Facilities in the (Panama) Canal Zone* 58, *Medical Care Program for Steelworkers and their Families* (with others) 60; numerous papers.
R.F.D. 1, Stonington, Conn., U.S.A.; Yale School of Medicine, 60 College Street, New Haven, Conn., U.S.A. Telephone: 562-1151 (Office).

Falk, Rosella (Falzacappa, Antonia); Italian actress; b. 10 Nov. 1928; ed. Accad. Nazionale d'Arte Drammatica, Rome.
Joined Piccolo Teatro, Rome 49, with Compagnia Stoppa-Morelli (L. Visconti) 52-53; Piccolo Teatre, Milan 54; founded Compagnia dei Giovani with G. De Lullo, R. Valli and A. M. Guarnieri 55, numerous tours in Europe including World Theatre Season, London 65, 66, 68; St. Vincent Prize for *D'amore si muore* (Patroni-Griffi) 58, Gold Medal 59.
Plays acted in include: *Sei personaggi in cerca d'autore* (Pirandello), *Oreste* (Alfieri), *Invito al castello* (Anouilh), *La Locandiere* (Goldoni), *Lorenzaccio* (Musset), *D'amore si muore* (Patroni-Griffi), *La Bugiarda* (Fabbri).
Compagnia dei Giovani, Rome, Italy.

Falkenhausen, Gotthard Freiherr von, DR. IUR.; German banker; b. 20 Jan. 1899; ed. Humboldt-Universität zu Berlin, Georg-August-Universität zu Göttingen and Martin Luther-Universität Halle-Wittenberg.
Attorney, Königsberg 26-28; Legal Adviser, Disconto Gesellschaft (later Deutsche Bank) 38-; Partner, Burkhardt & Co., Essen (bankers) 38-; mem. Essen City Council 48-; Chair. Supervisory Board, Kundenkreditbank (Consumer Credit Bank), Düsseldorf; mem. Supervisory Board Klöckner-Werke, Duisburg (iron and steel), Porzellanfabrik Kahla, Schönwald (china); Pres. German Bankers' Asscn., Chamber of Commerce for Cities of Essen, Mülheim and Oberhausen; Hon. Pres. German-French Chamber of Commerce, Paris; Chair. Atlantic Bridge Org., Hamburg; mem. Board of Dirs. Reconstruction Loan Corpn., Frankfurt, Union Investment Co., Frankfurt; Hon. Pres. German Bankers Asscn.; mem. Board of Management German Council, European Movement, Bonn, Centre d'Etudes de Politique Etrangère, Paris, Rheinisch-Westfalische Börse, Düsseldorf.
Office: Essen, Lindenallee 7/9; Home: Essen-Bredeney, Brachtstrasse 21, German Federal Republic.
Telephone: 22-14-01.

Falkenheim, Ernst, G.P.; German business man; b. 7 May 1898; ed. Univ. of Munich.
Served in First World War; worked for Hugo Stinnes Concern; joined Deutsche Shell 36; mem. of the Board of Deutsche Shell until 1963; Chair. of the Board of Fichtel und Sachs, A.G., Schweinfurt, and other com-

panies; Hon. Senator Tübingen Univ.; Grosses Bundesverdienstkreuz Deutschland; Bayerischer Verdienstorden.
Hagrainerstrasse 15, 8183 Rottach-Egern Obb., Postfach 20, German Federal Republic.
Telephone: 08022-6238.

Falkner, Sir (Donald) Keith, Kt., F.R.C.M.; British musician; b. 1 March 1900; ed. New Coll. School, Oxford, Perse School, Cambridge and Royal Coll. of Music, London.
Professional Singer 23-46; Music Officer, British Council in Italy 46-50; Assoc. Prof. Cornell Univ. 52, Prof. 56-60; Dir. Royal Coll. of Music 60-67; Hon. R.A.M., Hon G.S.M. (Guildhall School of Music), Hon. F.T.C.L. (Trinity Coll. of Music, London).
Royal College of Music, Prince Consort Road, London, S.W.7, England.
Telephone: 01-589-3643.

Falls, Cyril Bentham, M.A.; British military historian, professor and journalist; b. 88; ed. Bradfield Coll., Portora Royal School, London Univ. and abroad.
Late Royal Inniskilling Fusiliers; served First World War with regt. and on Gen. Staff (French Croix-de-Guerre with two citations); Historian in Historical Section (Military Branch) Cttee. of Imperial Defence 23-39; Mil. Corresp. of *The Times* 39-53; Prof. History of War and Fellow of All Souls Coll. Oxford 46-53.
Publs. *Rudyard Kipling* 15, *The Birth of Ulster* 36, *Marshal Foch* 39, *The Nature of Modern Warfare* 41, *Ordeal by Battle* 43, *The Man for the Job* 47, *The Second World War* 48, *Elizabeth's Irish Wars* 50, *A Hundred Years of War* 53, *Mountjoy-Elizabethan General* 55, Vols. of the Official History of the First World War 30-40, *The Gordon Highlanders in the First World War* 58, *The First World War* 60 (in U.S.A. as *The Great War* 59), *The Art of War* 61, *Armageddon: 1918* 64, *Caporetto 1917* 66.
16 Archery Close, Hyde Park, London, W.2, England.

Fan Wen-lan; Chinese historian; b. 91; ed. Peking Univ. Prof. at Nankai Univ., etc.; arrested for political reasons 35; on East China Governing Council 48; Dir. Third institute of History (Modern History), Academia Sinica; Honan Del. to N.P.C. 54; on Cttee. Dept. of Philosophy and Social Sciences, Academia Sinica, and on Standing Cttee. 55.
Publs. Work on Wen-hsin tiao-lung, introduction to classics, history; directed compilation of standard histories of China and Modern China, etc.
Third Institute of History, Academia Sinica, Peking, China.

Fanfani, Amintore; Italian economist and politician; b. 16 Feb. 1908.
Fellow, Catholic Univ. of Milan 32, Titular Prof. in Economic History 36, later Prof. Univ. of Rome 54; mem. Constituent Assembly for XVI District 46, M.P. for same district 48-68; Minister of Labour and Social Security in 4th, 5th and 6th De Gasperi Cabinets 47-50; Minister of Agriculture and Forestry, 8th De Gasperi Cabinet July 51, Minister of the Interior 53 and Prime Minister Jan. 54; Sec. Christian Democrat Party July 54-59; Prime Minister July 58-Jan. 59, July 60-April 63; Minister of Foreign Affairs 65, 66-68; Pres. of Senate 68-; Pres. UN Gen. Assembly 65-66.
Publs. *Le origini dello spirito capitalistico* 32, *Cattolicesimo e protestantesimo nella formazione storica del capitalismo* 34, *Storia delle dottrine economiche*, 3 vols. 38-46, *Indagini sulla rivoluzione dei prezzi* 39, *Storia economica* 40-65, *Storia del lavoro* 43, *Colloqui sui poveri* 41, *Persona, beni, società* 45, *Le tre città* 46, *Poemi Omerici ed Economia Antica* 60.
The Senate, Rome, Italy.

Fang, Roland Chung, B.A., M.A.; Chinese scholar; b. 02; ed. Tsing Hua Coll., Peking, Calif. and Stanford Univs.

Prof. of English Literature, Central Univ. Nanking 28-30; Prof. of English Literature and Head of English Dept., Wuhan Univ. 31-44; Visiting Prof. Trinity Coll. Cambridge Univ. 44-46; Prof. of English and Head of Dept. of Foreign Languages, Chekiang Univ. 47-51, Chekiang Teachers' Coll. 51-52; Prof. Anhwei Univ., Wuhu 52-53, East China Teachers' Univ. Shanghai 53-54, Futan Univ., Shanghai 54-56; Head, English Dept., Shanghai Inst. of Foreign Languages 57-.
Publs. *Book of Modern English Prose* (2 vols.) 34, *Studies in English Prose and Poetry* 39, *A Chinese Verse Translation of Shakespeare's Richard III* 59, *Complete Works of Chaucer translated into Chinese* 62, *Chaucer's Canterbury Tales* (revised edn.) 63.
Shanghai Institute of Foreign Languages, Shanghai, China.

Fang Chiang; Chinese naval officer and politician.
Vice-Admiral, Chinese Navy 55; Vice-Minister, First Ministry of Machine-Building 60-63; Sixth Minister of Machine-Building 63-.
Sixth Ministry of Machine-Building, Peking, People's Republic of China.

Fang Yi; Chinese government official.
Vice-Mayor of Shanghai 52; Vice-Chair. Cttee. of Financial and Econ. Affairs, State Admin. Cttee. 52-54; Vice-Minister of Finance 53-54; Ministry of Foreign Trade, Hanoi 54; Dir., Office for Economic Relations with Foreign Countries 61-; alt. mem. Central Cttee. of Chinese Communist Party.
Office for Economic Relations with Foreign Countries, Peking, People's Republic of China.

Fannin, Paul Jones, B.A.; American politician; b. 29 Jan. 1907; ed. Arizona and Stanford Univs.
Partner Fannin Brothers (Industrial Developments); fmr. Pres. Maricopa County Better Business Bureau; Gov. of Arizona 58-65; Chair. Western Govs. Conf. 63; mem. President's Civil Defense Advisory Council 63-64; Senator from Arizona 64-; del. to Mexico-U.S. Interparl. Conf. 65, 66, 67; del. to Int. Labor Org., Geneva 66; mem. several Senate Cttees.
U.S. Senate, Washington, D.C., U.S.A.

Faraco, Daniel Agostinho; Brazilian bank official, economist and politician; b. 11.
Federal Dep. Rio Grande do Sul 46-, mem. Constituent Assembly; fmr. Chair. Economic Cttee., Chamber of Deputies; State Sec. of Finance, Rio Grande do Sul 63-64; Minister of Industry and Commerce, Brazil 64-66; Partido Social Democrático (P.S.D.).
Ministry of Industry and Commerce, Brasilia, Brazil.

Farah, Abdulrahim Abby; Somali diplomat; b. 1919; ed. Univ. of Exeter and Balliol Coll., Oxford.
Ambassador to Ethiopia 61-65; Perm. Rep. of Somalia to the United Nations 65-.
Permanent Mission of Somalia to the United Nations, 236 East 46th Street, New York 17, N.Y., U.S.A.

Faricy, William Thomas, LL.B.; American railroad executive; b. 7 March 1893; ed. St. Paul Coll. of Law.
Attorney, C., St. P. M. & O. Railway Co. 14; gen. practice St. Paul 16-17, 19-20; gen. attorney C., St. P. M. & O. Railroad Co., St. Paul 20-24; commerce attorney, C. & N. W. Railway Co., Chicago 24-25; Vice-Pres. Hauser Securities Co. and Asst. to Pres. Hauser Construction Co., Portland, Oregon, and Long Beach, Calif. 25-27; Minn. attorney, C. & N. W. Railway Co., St. Paul 27-29; gen. solicitor C. St. P. M. & O. Railway Co., St. Paul 29-33, C. & N. W. Railway System, Chicago 33-42; Gen. Counsel C. & N. W. Railway Co. 42-44; Vice-Pres. and Gen. Counsel C. St. P. M. & O. Railway Co. 42-47, C. & N. W. Railway Co. 44-47; Chair. Western Conf. of Railway Counsel 44-46; Pres. Asscn. of American Railroads 47-57, Chair. of Board 57-58; Dir. Riggs Nat. Bank, Washington, D.C.; Chair. Civilian Components Policy Board, Dept. of Defense

49-50; Chair. U.S. Nat. Comm. Pan American Railway Congress Asscn. 49-58, mem. 59-; fmr. Pres. Hauser Securities Co. of Portland, Oregon, Grant Smith & Co. & McDonnell Ltd., Vancouver, B.C. 60-; Life Trustee, Northwestern Univ.
Home: 4914 Glenbrook Road, N.W., Washington 16; Transportation Building, Washington 6 D.C., U.S.A.

Farland, Joseph S., A.B., LL.B.; American diplomatist; b. 11 Aug. 1914; ed. West Virginia Univ. and Coll. of Law.
Attorney and counsellor to private cos. 38-42; Govt. service 42-44; U.S. Navy 44-45; Pres. of coal cos. 46-; Consultant to Special Asst. to Under-Sec. of State for Mutual Security Affairs 56; Ambassador to Dominican Republic 57-60, to Panama 60-63; Consultant on Latin American Affairs, *Readers Digest*.
2539 Massachusetts Avenue, N.W., Washington, D.C., U.S.A.

Farley, James A., HON. D.C.L., LL.D.; American politician; b. 30 May 1888; ed. Stony Point High School and Packard Commercial School, N.Y. City.
Book-keeper 06; for many years Sales Man. for Universal Gypsum Co., N.Y. City; founded James A. Farley & Company Inc. 26; President and Director General Builders' Supply Corporation 29-33, 49-, Chairman 57; Chairman Coca-Cola Export Corporation September 40; Dir. Coca-Cola Co. of Canada Ltd.; Town Clerk Stony Point 12-19; Port Warden, N.Y. City 18-19; Chair. N.Y. State Athletic Comm. 25-33; Postmaster-Gen. in Roosevelt's Cabinet Mar. 33-Aug. 40; Sec. N.Y. Dem. State Cttee. 28-30, Chair. 30-July 44; Chair. Dem. Nat. Cttee. 32-40; Dir. Nat. Foreign Trade Council; mem. American Acad. of Political and Social Science, New York State Banking Board; holds many Hon. Degrees of American Colls. and Univs.
Publs. *Behind the Ballots* 38, *Jim Farley's Story* 49.
301 Park Avenue, New York City, N.Y., U.S.A.

Farmer, James Leonard; American Civil Rights leader; b. 20; ed. Wiley Coll. and Howard Univ.
Former Program Director, National Association for the Advancement of Colored People (NAACP); fmr. Int. Rep. State, County and Municipal Employees Union; Dir. Congress of Racial Equality 61-March 66; Pres. Center for Community Action Educ. Inc. 66-.
Publ. *Freedom—When?* 66.
165 Park Row, New York, N.Y. 10038, U.S.A.

Farmer, Sir (Lovedin) George (Thomas), Kt., M.A., F.C.A., J.DIP.M.A.; British motor executive; b. 13 May 1908; ed. Oxford High School.
Chair. Rover Co. Ltd.; Dir. Leyland Motor Corpn. Ltd., Standard-Triumph Int. Ltd., Empresa Nacional de Autocamiones S.A., Madrid; Second Vice-Chair. and mem. Exec. Cttee., Metalurgica de Santa Ana S.A., Madrid; Pres. Birmingham Chamber of Commerce 60-61, Soc. of Motor Manufacturers and Traders 62-64, Deputy Pres. 64-65, Chair. of its Exec. Cttee.; mem. Export Council for Europe, Management Board of W. Midlands Engineering Employers' Asscn.; Gov. Chair. of Exec. Council and Finance Cttee. of Royal Shakespeare Theatre; Pres. Loft Theatre, Leamington Spa; Pro-Chancellor Univ. of Birmingham.
The Rover Company Ltd., Meteor Works, Solihull, Warwicks.; Home: Park House, 17 Park Road, Leamington Spa, Warwicks., England.
Telephone: 01-743-4242.

Farner, Donald S., PH.D., D.SC.; American zoophysiologist; b. 2 May 1915; ed. Hamline Univ. and Univ. of Wisconsin.
Instructor in Zoology, Univ. of Wisconsin 41-43; Asst. Prof. of Zoology, Univ. of Kansas 46-47; Assoc. Prof. of Zoophysiology, Washington State Univ. 47-52, Prof. of Zoophysiology 52-65, Dean of Graduate School 60-64; Prof. of Zoophysiology, Univ. of Washington

65-, Chair. Dept. of Zoology 66-; Fulbright Research Fellow and Hon. Lecturer Univ. of Otago 53-54; Guggenheim Fellow and Hon. Lecturer in Zoology, Univ. of W. Australia 58-59; Pres. Int. Union of Biological Sciences 67-; Nat. Sigma Xi Lecturer 63; Brewster Medal, American Ornithologists Union 62; mem. American Soc. of Zoologists, American Physiol. Soc., American Chem. Soc., Ecological Soc. of America, American Soc. of Naturalists, American Ornithologists Union, Soc. for Endocrinology, Soc. for Experimental Biology and Medicine, American Asscn. for Advancement of Science.

Publs. Approx. 150 research and review publs. 41-.

Department of Zoology, University of Washington, Seattle, Washington 98105, U.S.A.

Telephone: 206-543-1620; 206-543-6441.

Farra, Jamal E.-D., M.SC.; Syrian diplomatist; b. 11; ed. Univ. of Paris.

Employed in Ministry of Education, in various posts including Sec.-Gen. 34-39; Chargé d'Affaires, Brussels 49-50; Sec.-Gen., Ministry of Foreign Affairs 50; Minister to Sweden 52, to Norway, Denmark and Finland 53, to Germany 54-56; Ambassador to U.S.S.R. 56-58; United Arab Republic Ambassador to Brazil 58-61; Syrian Arab Republic Ambassador to Fed. Germany 61-62; Minister of Foreign Affairs 62; Ambassador to Italy 63-64; Order of Syrian Merit, Officer Order of Cedar (Lebanon), Order of the Star (Jordan), Order of Civil Merit (Spain), Order of the Phoenix (Greece), Order of Merit (Germany), Order of the Iftikhan (Tunisia), Order of Pole Star (Sweden), Order of the Southern Cross (Brazil), Queen Elizabeth II Coronation Medal, Order of St. Peter and St. Paul of Greek Orthodox Patriarch of Antioch and the Orient, Order of St. Silvestro, Order of Grande Croce del Merito (Italy).

24 Boulevard Adnan, Malky, Damascus, Syrian Arab Republic.

Farra, Muhammad H. El-; Jordanian diplomatist; b. 20 April 1921; ed. Boston Univ. and Univ. of Pennsylvania.

Director for Arab Affairs, Ministry of Foreign Affairs, Amman 59-60, Dir. Palestine Div. 60-61; Jordan Rep. Econ. and Social Council, UN 60-61, Vice-Chair. ECOSOC 62; Minister, Cairo 63; Pres. Arab Council for Econ. Unity 64-65; Perm. Rep. of Jordan to UN 65-. Permanent Mission of Hashemite Kingdom of Jordan to the United Nations, 866 United Nations Plaza, New York, N.Y. 10017, U.S.A.

Farrell, Eileen; American opera singer; b. 13 Feb. 1920.

Debut with Columbia Broadcasting Co. 41, own programme for six years; opera debut with San Francisco Opera; toured throughout the U.S.A. and in other parts of the world.

c/o Columbia Artists Management, 113 W. 57th Street, New York City, N.Y., U.S.A.

Farrell, James Augustine, Jr.; American shipping executive; b. 13 Jan. 1901; ed. Yale Univ.

Shipping business 24-; Chair. of the Board and Dir. Farrell Lines Inc.; Dir. American Merchant Marine Inst., Nat. Foreign Trade Council Inc., Maritime Asscn. of Port of New York, New York Shipping Asscn., Canterbury School, Maritime Exchange; mem. American Soc. of Mechanical Engineers, American Soc. of Naval Architects; U.S. Naval Reserve 41-44; Fellow Royal Soc. of Arts and Design; Hon. Dr. Commercial Science (Duquesne Univ.); Commdr. Star of Africa; Grand Cross Humane Order of Africa Redeemed; Naval Order of the U.S..

Farrell Lines Inc., 1 Whitehall Street, New York, N.Y. 10004; 25 Old Farm Road, Darien, Conn., U.S.A.

Farrell, James Thomas; American writer and columnist; b. 27 Feb. 1904; ed. Chicago Univ.

Cigar store clerk, filling-station attendant, part-time journalist; Guggenheim Fellow 36-37; mem. Nat. Inst. of Arts and Letters; Hon. degrees Oxford and Ohio Univs.

Publs. *Young Lonigan—a boyhood in Chicago Streets* 32, *Gas House McGinty* 33, *The Young Manhood of Studs Lonigan* 34, *Calico Shoes* 34, *Judgement Day* 35, *Guillotine Party and Other Stories* 35, *A Note on Literary Criticism* 36, *A World I Never Made* 36, *Can All This Grandeur Perish* 37, *Collected Short Stories* 37, *No Star is Lost* 38, *Tommy Gallagher's Crusade* 39, *Father and Son* 40, *Ellen Rogers* 41, *$1,000 a week and other stories* 42, *My Days of Anger* 43, *To Whom It May Concern* 44, *The League of Frightened Philistines* 45, *Bernard Clare* 46, *When Boyhood Dreams Come True* 46, *Literature and Morality* 47, *The Life Adventurous* 47, *The Road Between* 49, *An American Dream Girl and Other Stories* 50, *This Man and this Woman, Yet Other Waters* 52, *The Face of Time* 53, *Reflections At Fifty* 54, *French Girls are Vicious* 55, *A Farrell Omnibus* 56, *A Dangerous Woman and Other Stories* 57, *My Baseball Diary* 57, *It Has Come to Pass* 58, *Side Street and Other Stories* 61, *Boarding House Blues* 61, *Sound of the City* 62, *The Silence of History* 63, *What Time Collects* 64, *Lonely for the Future* 65, *The Collected Poems of James T. Farrell* 65, *When Time was Born* 66, *New York's Eve 1929* 67, *A Brave New Life* 68.

c/o Doubleday & Co., 277 Park Avenue, New York City, N.Y., U.S.A.

Farren, Sir William Scott, C.B., M.B.E., M.A., F.R.S., M.I.MECH.E.; British aero engineer; b. 3 April 1892; ed. Perse School and Trinity Coll., Cambridge.

In charge aerodynamic experiment and design, Royal Aircraft Establishment, Farnborough 15-18; on technical staff Armstrong Whitworth Aircraft 18-20; Univ. Lecturer in Engineering and Aeronautics, Cambridge 20-37, and Lecturer on Aircraft Structure, Royal Coll. of Science 22-31; Fellow Trinity Coll. Cambridge 34-37; Deputy Dir. of Scientific Research, Air Ministry 37-39; Deputy Dir. Research and Development (Aircraft) Air Ministry and subsequently Ministry of Aircraft Production 39-40; Dir. of Technical Development, Ministry of Aircraft Production 40-41; mem. Aeronautical Research Council 57-60; Dir. Royal Aircraft Estab., Farnborough 41-46; Dir. Hawker Siddeley Nuclear Power Co. Ltd. 56-61; Consultant, Hawker Siddeley Aviation Ltd. 61-; Chair. Aircraft Research Asscn. 62-; Pres. Royal Aeronautical Society 53-54; Technical Dir. A. V. Roe & Co. Ltd. 47-61; Hon. F.R.Ae.S., Hon. F.I.Ae.S. (U.S.A.), Hon. Dr. Sc.

Crossways Cottage, Kingston, Cambs., England.

Farrer-Brown, Leslie, C.B.E., J.P.; British public servant; b. 2 April 1904; ed. London School of Economics.

Assistant Registrar, London School of Econs. 27-28; Admin. Staff, Univ. of London 28-36; Sec. Cen. Midwives Board 36-44; Ministry of Health 41-44; Dir. The Nuffield Foundation 44-64; Chair. Overseas Visual Aid Centre 58-, Centre for Educational Television Overseas 64-, Inst. of Race Relations 64-, Cttee. for Research and Development in Modern Languages 65-; Nat. Council of Social Service; Voluntary Cttee. on Overseas Aid and Devt. 66-, Inst. of Child Health (Univ. of London) 66-; Trustee, Commonwealth Foundation, Nuffield Provincial Hospitals Trust 55-57; Gov. London School of Econs., Vice-Chair. of Council, Univ. of Sussex; Hon. LL.D. (Birmingham and Witwatersrand); Hon. D.Sc. (Keele); Hon. F.D.S., R.C.S.

Dale House, Keere Street, Lewes, Sussex, England.

Telephone: Lewes 2007.

Farrow, Leslie William, C.B.E., F.C.A.; British chartered accountant; b. 7 Oct. 1888; ed. Alleyn's School, Dulwich, and London School of Economics.

Senior Partner Farrow, Bersey, Gain, Vincent & Co. 13-; Dir. of Finance, Ministry of Munitions 17-19; Chair. Wiggins, Teape and Co. Ltd. 18-66, Hon. Pres. 66-

Assoc. Paper Mills 26-; Sub-Gov., Royal Exchange Assurance 30-; mem. Bacon Devt. Board 37-45; Deputy Controller of Paper, Ministry of Supply 39-40, Dir. for Commercial Relations 40-42; Deputy Chair. Rubber Control Board 42-43; Deputy Dir.-Gen. (Raw Materials) Ministry of Supply 42-43; Chair. Nat. Brick Advisory Council, Ministry of Works and Planning 42-45, Paper Economy Cttee., Ministry of Production 42-45; Chair. Castrol Ltd. 43, now Dir.
Dengie Manor, nr. Southminster, Essex, England.

Fasi, Mohammed El; Moroccan university rector; b. 2 Sept. 1908; ed. Al Qarawiyin Univ., Fez, Univ. de Paris à la Sorbonne and Ecole des langues orientales, Paris.
Teacher, Inst. des Hautes Etudes Marocaines 35-40; Head Arab manuscript section, Bibliothèque Gén., Rabat 40; Tutor to Prince Moulay Hassan 41-44, 47-52; Rector Al Qarawiyin Univ. 42-44, 47-; Vice-Pres. Conseil des Uléma 42-; Founder-mem. Istiqlal Party 44; under restriction 44-47, 52-54; Minister of Nat. Educ. 55; Rector of the Univs. of Morocco 58-; Pres. Moroccan Del. to Gen. Conf. of UNESCO 56, 58, 60, 64, Vice-Pres. 62, leader of numerous UNESCO Confs. in the Arab World, Pres. Exec. Council of UNESCO 64-; Pres. Admin. Council of the Asscn. of partially or entirely French-speaking Univs. (AUPELF) 66; Pres. Asscn. of African Univs. 67; mem. Acad. of Arabic Language, Cairo 58, Acad. of Iraq; Dr. h.c. Univ. of Bridgeport 65, Univ. of Lagos 68.
Publs. Numerous works in Arabic and French including *L'évolution politique et culturelle au Maroc* 58, *La Formation des Cadres au Maroc* 60, *Chants anciens des Femmes de Fes* 67.
University Mohammed V, avenue Moulay Cherif, Rabat, Morocco.

Fasolino, H.E. Cardinal Nicolas; Argentine ecclesiastic; b. 1887.
Ordained Priest 09; Archbishop of Santa Fé 32-; created Cardinal by Pope Paul VI 67.
Palacio Arzobispal, Avenida General Lopez 2720, Santa Fé, Argentina.

Fast, Howard; American writer; b. 11 Nov. 1914; ed. Nat. Acad. of Design.
Began writing 31; translated into 82 languages; film has been made of *Spartacus* (with Kirk Douglas); Bread Loaf Literary Award 34, Schomburg Award for Race Relations 44, Newspaper Guild Award 47, Int. Peace Prize 54, Screenwriters Award 60, Secondary School Book Award 62.
Publs. Novels: *The Children* 35, *Place in the City* 37, *Conceived in Liberty* 39, *The Last Frontier* 41, *The Unvanquished* 42, *Citizen Tom Paine* 43, *Freedom Road* 44, *The American* 46, *Clarkton* 47, *My Glorious Brothers* 48, *The Proud and the Free* 50, *Spartacus* 51, *The Passion of Sacco and Vanzetti* 53, *Silas Timberman* 54, *Moses, Prince of Egypt* 58, *The Winston Affair* 59, *April Morning* 61, *Power* 62, *Agrippa's Daughter* 64, *Torquemada* 66, *The Hunter and the Trap* 67; Short stories: *Patrick Henry and the Frigate's Keel, Departure and Other Stories, The Last Supper*; History: *Romance of a People, Peekskill: U.S.A., The Naked God*; Plays: *The Crossing, The Hill*; Screen plays: *Spartacus* 59, *The Hill* 63, *Martian Shop* 64, *Torquemada* 66, *Time Forgot* 67.
c/o Paul Reynolds Inc., 599 Fifth Avenue, New York City 17, N.Y., U.S.A.

Faubus, Orval Eugene; American administrator; b. 7 Jan. 1910.
Schoolteacher 28-38; Circuit Clerk and Recorder, Madison County, Ark. 39-42; acting Postmaster, Ark. 46-47, Postmaster 53-54; Owner-Editor *Madison County Record* 47-; Highway Comm. for Arkansas 49-53;

Gov. of Arkansas 55-67; Owner *Arkansas Statesman* 60-, also *Advance Reporter*; Democrat.
Box 87a, Huntsville, Ark. 72740, U.S.A.
Telephone: RE8-2515.

Faulkner, James Morison, A.B., M.D.; American physician; b. 16 Dec. 1898; ed. Harvard.
Asst. Resident Physician, Hospital of Rockefeller Inst. 26; Johns Hopkins Hospital 26-27; Junior Visiting Physician and Asst. Visiting Physician, Boston City Hospital 28-47; Physician and Cardiologist, Mass. Memorial Hospital 40-43; Dir. 1st and 3rd Medical Services, Boston City Hospital 45-47; Asst. in Medicine Johns Hopkins Medical School 26-27; Asst. in Medicine Harvard Medical School 28-37; Instructor 37-40; Asst. Prof. in Medicine, Boston Univ. Medical School 40-43; Prof. Tufts Coll. Medical School 43-47; Prof. of Clinical Medicine Boston Univ. School of Medicine 47-58, Dean 47-55; Medical Dir. Mass. Inst. of Technology 55-60; Trustee, Phillips Exeter Acad. 54-59; mem. American Acad. Arts and Sciences, New England Board of Higher Education 54-56, Nat. Board of Medical Examiners; Dir. BU-MMH Medical Center 61; mem. Bd. United Health Foundations, United Community Funds and Councils of America; mem. Board of Overseers, Harvard Coll. 58-; Capt. (M.C.), U.S.N.R.
535 Boylston Street, Boston, Mass. 02116, U.S.A.

Faure, Edgar, D. en D.; French lawyer and politician; b. 18 Aug. 1908; ed. Ecole des Langues Orientales Paris.
Advocate at Paris Court of Appeal; Dir. of Legislative Services to the Presidency of the Council of the French Cttee. of National Liberation 43-44; took part, as asst. del., in War Crimes Trials Nuremberg 45; Deputy for the Jura (Radical-Socialist) 46-58; Vice-Pres. of Comm. of Enquiry into Events in France between 33-45; Vice-Pres. of High Court of Justice; Sec. of Finance Comm. of National Assembly; Sec. of State for Finance 49-50; Minister of Budget in Queuille Cabinet July 50, Pleven Cabinet 50-51 and Queuille Cabinet Mar.-July 51; Minister of Justice in Pleven Cabinet 51-52; Prime Minister Jan-Feb. 52; Minister of Finance and Economic Affairs 53-54, of Foreign Affairs Feb. 55; Prime Minister Feb. 55-Jan. 56; Minister of Finance, May-June 58; Senator 59-; Prof. of Law, Univ. of Dijon 62-66; Minister of Agriculture 66-.
Publs. *La Politique française du pétrole, M. Langois n'est pas toujours égal à lui-même* (novel), *Le Serpent et la Tortue* (study of China) 57, *La Disgrâce de Turgot* 61, *Etude sur la capitation de Dioclétien d'après le panégyrique VIII, Prévoir le présent* 66.
83 avenue Foch, Paris 16e, France.

Faure, Maurice Henri, D. en D.; French politician; b. 2 Jan. 1922; ed. Lycée de Periguen, Faculty of Law and Letters, Bordeaux and Toulouse Univs.
Deputy to Nat. Assembly (Lot) 51-; Sec. of State for Foreign Affairs (Mollet Cabinet) Jan. 56-June 57, (Bourgès-Manoury Cabinet) June-Nov. 57, (Gaillard Cabinet) Nov. 57-May 58; Minister for European Institutions May-June 58; Pres. French del. Common Market and Euratom Conf., Brussels 56; mem. del. 11th Session U.N. Gen. Assembly, New York 56; Special Asst. Minister for Foreign Affairs on Morocco and Tunisia Nov. 56-June 57; mem. European Coal and Steel Community Assembly; Mayor of Prayssac (Lot) 53-; Conseiller Général, Salviac canton (Lot) 57-58; Pres. Departmental Asscn. of Mayors of Lot, Mouvement Européen; Pres. Entente Démocratique of the Nat. Ass. 60-62; Pres., later Leader, Parti Republicain Radical et Radical-Socialiste 61-; Pres. Rassemblement Démocratique Group, Nat. Assembly 62-; Pres. Econ. Devt. Comm. for Midi-Pyrénées 64; Mayor of Cahors 65-.
Assemblée Nationale, Paris 7e, France.

Fauser, Giacomo; Italian industrial executive; b. 11 Jan. 1892; ed. Politecnico of Milan.
Manager Montecatini-Edison Co.; Dir. and Technical

Adviser of other companies; Hon. Dr. Chem. Eng. (Zürich), Hon. Dr. Industrial Chem. (Milan, Louvain, Veszprem).
5 Via Marconi, Novara, Italy.
Telephone: 27047.

Faust, Clarence H., B.D., M.A., PH.D., LL.D.; American educator; b. 11 March 1901; ed. North Central Coll., Evangelical Theological Seminary and Univ. of Chicago. Instructor in English, Univs. of Arkansas and Chicago 29-35; Dean of Students in Div. of Humanities, Univ. of Chicago 35-41; Prof. of English and Dean of the Coll. 41-46; Prof. of English and Humanities and Dean of Graduate Library School 46-47; Dir. of Univ. Libraries, Stanford Univ. 47-48, Dean of Faculty of Humanities and Sciences 48-51; Acting Pres., Stanford Univ. 49; Pres. Fund for the Advancement of Education April 51-66; Vice-Pres. Ford Foundation 57-66.
Publs. include *Jonathan Edwards* (with Clarence Johnson) 35.
520 Baughman Avenue, Claremont, California 91711, U.S.A.
Telephone: 714-626-2863.

Fauvet, Jacques, L. en D.; French editor; b. 9 June 1914; ed. Lycée St. Louis, Paris, and Faculté de Droit, Univ. de Paris.
An editor, *l'Est Républicain*, Nancy 37-39; joined *Le Monde* 45, Head of Domestic Politics Dept. 48-58, Asst. Editor-in-Chief 58-63, Editor-in-Chief of *Le Monde* 63-; Officier Légion d'Honneur, Croix de Guerre (39-45).
Publs. *Les partis politiques dans la France actuelle* 47, *Les Forces politiques en France* 50, *La France déchirée* 57, *La politique et les paysans* 58, *La IVe République* 59, *La fronde des généraux* 61, *Histoire du parti communiste français*, Vol. I 64, Vol. II 66.
Le Monde, 5 rue des Italiens, Paris 9e, France.

Favre, Alexandre Jean Auguste; French scientist; b. 23 Feb. 1911; ed. Univs. de Aix-Marseille et de Paris.
Assistant Lecturer, Faculty of Science, Univ. of Marseilles 32-38, Lecturer 38-41, Asst. Prof. 41-45, Assoc. Prof. 45-51, Prof. 51-; Dir. Inst. of Mechanical Statistics of Turbulence 60-; Scientific Asst. Ministry of Air 32; Scientific Counsellor, Nat. Office of Aerospacial Studies and Research 47, Atomic Energy Commissariat 58; mem. Nat. Cttee. for Scientific Research 63; mem. Mathematical Soc. of France, Physical Soc. of France and American Physical Soc.; Chevalier Légion d'Honneur, Officier des Palmes Académiques; Prix Marquet of Académie des Sciences, mem. Académie des Sciences, Lettres Arts de Marseille.
Major Research includes: hypersustentation 34, hyperconvection 51; inventor of centrifugal sub-transsupersonic compressor 40; inventor of apparatus for statistical measurement of time correlation 42, and of appliance for detection of random noise 52; research on turbulence of fluids and space-time correlations 42-69, and on statistical equations of turbulent compressible gas 48-68.
Institut de Mécanique Statistique de la Turbulence, 12 avenue Général Leclerc, 13 Marseilles; Home: La Cadenelle, 122 Rue Ct. Rolland, Marseilles (8), France.
Telephone: 641650 (Office); 532460 (Home).

Fawzi, Mahmoud; United Arab Republic (Egyptian) politician; b. 1900; ed. Univs. of Cairo, Rome, Liverpool and Columbia.
Vice-Consul, N.Y. and New Orleans 26-29; Consul, Kobe, Japan 29-36; 2nd Sec. Athens 36-37; Consul then Consul-Gen. Liverpool 37-40; Dir. Dept. of Nationalities, Ministry of Foreign Affairs 40-41; Consul-Gen., Jerusalem 41-44; Egyptian rep. Security Council, UN 46; alternate rep. UN Gen. Assembly, N.Y. 46; later perm. rep. of Egypt to U.N.; Ambassador to Great Britain 52; Minister of Foreign Affairs Dec. 52-58; Minister of Foreign Affairs, United Arab Republic 58-64; mem. Presidency Council 62-64; Dep. Prime Minister for Foreign Affairs 64-67; Vice-Pres. and President's Asst. for Foreign Affairs 67-68.
c/o Ministry of Foreign Affairs, Cairo, U.A.R.

Fay, General Pierre; French air force officer; b. 22 March 1899; ed. St. Cyr Military Acad.
Pilot 21-, Gen. Staff Graduate 30, mem. French Military Mission in Brazil 32-35, Commdr. Bombardment Group 42-43, Commdr. French Air Forces in Far East 45-46, Chief of Staff, Air Forces Europe Centre 51-53, Chief of Staff, French Air Forces 53-55; Feugères par Saint-Lô (Manche), France.
Telephone: 1-Feugères.

Fay, William Patrick, B.A., LL.B.; Irish diplomatist; b. 09; ed. Clongowes Wood Coll., Univ. Coll. Dublin and Kings Inns Dublin.
Practising barrister 31-37; entered Attorney-General's Dept. 37; First Sec. Dept. of External Affairs 41-46; Sec. Irish High Commissioner's Office, London 46-47; Chargé d'Affaires in Brussels 47-50; Minister to Sweden and Norway 50-51; Asst. Sec. and Legal Adviser, Dept. of External Affairs 51-54; Ambassador to France 54-60; Head Perm. Irish Del. to O.E.E.C. 54-60; Ambassador to Canada 60-64, to U.S.A. 64-.
Irish Embassy, 2234 Massachusetts Avenue, N.W., Washington, D.C. 20008, U.S.A.
Telephone: HU3-7639.

Fayat, Henri, D.LL.; Belgian lawyer and politician; b. 28 June 1908; ed. Royal Athenaeum, Brussels and Univ. of Brussels.
Advocate, Brussels 35-; Legal Attaché, Belgian Foreign Office, London 42-43; Chief Assistant to the Belgian Ministry of the Interior, London 43, and in Brussels 44; Chief Asst. to Deputy Prime Minister 44-45; mem. House of Reps. 46-; Prof. Faculty of Law, Univ. of Brussels 48-; mem. Consultative Assembly of the Council of Europe 49-50, Common Assembly of the European Coal and Steel Community 54-57; Minister of Foreign Trade 57-58, June 68-; Deputy Foreign Minister 61-66; Chair. Brussels Conf. on British application for membership of European Econ. Community 63.
51A Aarlenstraat, Brussels, Belgium.

Faye, Jean Pierre; French writer; b. 19 July 1925; ed. Univ. de Paris à la Sorbonne.
Teacher, Lycée de Reims 51-54; Exchange Fellow Univ. of Chicago 54-55; Asst. Prof. Univ. de Lille 55-56, Univ. de Paris à la Sorbonne 56-60; Research, Centre Nat. de la Recherche Scientifique 60-64; Prix Renaudot 64.
Publs. Novels: *Entre les Rues* 58, *La Cassure* 61, *Battement* 62, *Analogues* 64, *L'Ecluse* 64; Poems: *Fleuve Renversé* 59; *Théâtre* 64, produced in Odéon Théâtre de France by Roger Blin 65; *Couleurs Pliées* 65, *Le Récit Hunique* 67.
1B rue Vaneau, Paris 7e, France.
Telephone: 468-1803.

Fayer, Yury Fyodorovich; Soviet conductor; b. 90; ed. Moscow Conservatoire.
Violinist 15-19, Assistant Conductor 19-23, Ballet Conductor of the Bolshoi Theatre 23-; mem. C.P.S.U. 41; State prizewinner 41, 46, 47, 50; awarded Order of Lenin and People's Artist of the U.S.S.R. 51, Order of the Red Banner of Labour 51 and 59.
State Academic Bolshoi Theatre, 1 ploshchad Sverdlova, Moscow, U.S.S.R.

Fayez, Akef Mithqal Al-; Jordanian politician; b. 24; ed. Aleh Univ., Lebanon.
President Jordanian Agricultural Asscn. 45; Chief of Protocol for Tribes, Royal Palace 46; Co-founder Jordanian People's Party; mem. House of Reps. 47-, Speaker 62-, successively Minister of Agriculture

Development and Construction, Defence, Communications, and Public Works 57-62; Chair. Nat. Group, Inter. Parl. Union 64-.
House of Parliament, P.O. Box 72, Amman, Jordan.

Fearing, Lamar Munroe; American paper industry executive; b. 19 Jan. 1903; ed. Princeton Univ.
International Paper Co., New York City 24-, Div. Sales Man. 51-54, Asst. Gen. Sales Man. 54-57, Vice-Pres. 57-59, Exec. Vice-Pres. 59-61, Dir. 59-, Pres. 61-66, Vice-Chair. of Board 66-68, Senior Vice-Pres. 68-; Dir. McKesson and Robbins Inc. 64-.
International Paper Co., 220 E. 42nd Street, New York City 17, N.Y.; Home: 266 Old Colony Road, Hartsdale, N.Y., U.S.A.
Telephone: 914-SC3-1487.

Feber, G. A. H.; Netherlands judge; b. 21 Sept. 1900; ed. Univs. of Leiden and Amsterdam.
Deputy Recorder, The Hague 29-35; Dep. Judge, The Hague 35-36; Judge, Almelo Law Court 36-45; mem. Court for war criminals 45; mem. Supreme Court of Netherlands 46; Prof. of Criminology, Univ. of Amsterdam 47-55; fmr. Vice-Pres., now Pres. Supreme Court of the Netherlands.
Supreme Court of the Netherlands, The Hague, Netherlands.
Telephone: 241961.

Federbush, Rabbi Simeon, PH.D.; American Zionist leader and writer; b. 1892.
One of leaders of Mizrachi Movement since 18, mem. Seym 22-27; Editor *Jüdische Blätter* 28 and of Hebrew monthly *Mizracha* since 30, *Jewish Horizon*; N.Y.; fmr. Chief Rabbi of Finland; now Exec. World Jewish Congress, New York; mem. World Zionist Organisation Action Cttee.; Chair. Exec. Council of World Union for Hebrew Culture; Pres. of Moriah Publishing Society; Pres. of Hebrew Organization of America; Pres. Soc. of Jewish Religious Writers of America; Editor, *World Jewry—Today, Maimonides Volume, Rashi Volume,* Three Vols. *Hochmath Israel, Hason Tora Vezion, Tora Umlucha, Federbush Jubilee Book, Hasiduth Vezion.*
Publs. *Ijjunim* 29, *Zion's Wisest Protocol in Saningens Ijus* 35, *Shlemuth Hayaduth* 27, *Hikre Talmud* 38, *Hamusar Vehamishpat* 48, *Mishpat Hamlucha* 51, *Jewish Concept of Labor* 56, *Benthivoth Hatalmud* 57, *Hikre Hayaduth* 65, *History of the Hebrew Language* 68.
2105 Ryer Avenue, Bronx 57, New York, N.Y., U.S.A.
Telephone: SE3-9852.

Federspiel, Per T., C.B.E.; Danish barrister; b. 9 April 1905; ed. Harrow School and Copenhagen Univ.
London corresp. to Danish newspapers 31-32; Secretary to Danish Counsel in the East Greenland sovereignty case at the Int. Court at The Hague 32-33; Counsel at the Danish Courts of Appeal 37; Legal Adviser to the British Embassy Copenhagen; Min. of Special Affairs 45-47; mem. Danish Parl.; Del. to the UN Ass. 46-49; mem. UN Palestine Comm. 47-48; mem. Consultative Ass., Council of Europe 49-, Chair. 60-63; Chair. Econ. Cttee. 53-60; Vice-Pres. Int. Comm. of Jurists 59-62, mem. Exec. Cttee. 63-; mem. Board of Govs. Atlantic Inst. 63-; Liberal.
Frennehus, Hørsholm, Denmark.

Fedin, Konstantin Alexandrovich; Soviet novelist; b. 1892; ed. Moscow Commercial Inst.
Interned in Germany 14-18; returned to U.S.S.R. 18; with Commissariat of Educ.; later journalist and war corresp.; mem. Secretariat, Union of Soviet Writers 53-; Chair. Moscow Union of Soviet Writers 55-59; mem. Acad. of Sciences, U.S.S.R. 58-; corresp. mem. Deutsche Akad. der Künste 54-; Chair. Soviet-German Cultural and Friendship Society 58-; First Sec. Writers' Union of U.S.S.R. 59-; Deputy to U.S.S.R. Supreme Soviet; Order of Lenin (twice), Order of Red Banner of

Labour (twice), Hero of Socialist Labour 67; Dr. h.c. Humbolt Univ.; awarded Silver Medal of World Peace Council.
Publs. *Anna Timofsevna* 22, *The Waste Land* 23, *Cities and Years* 24, *Transvaal* 26, *Brothers* 28, *I Was an Actor* 37, *Rape of Europe* 34, *Bakunin in Dresden* (play) 22, *Sanatorium Arktur* 40, *Gorky among Us* 43-44 (enlarged ed. 67), *Return to Leningrad* 45, *Early Joys* 45, *No Ordinary Summer* 48, *Die Flamme* 62; collected works in 6 vols. 52-54, in 9 vols. 59-62, *Dichter, Kunst, Zeit* 57.
U.S.S.R. Writers' Union, Ul. Vorovskogo 52, Moscow; and Lawrushensky 17, ap. 38, Moscow J-17, U.S.S.R.

Fedorenko, Nikolai Trofimovich, D.PHIL.; Soviet sinologist and diplomatist; b. 9 Nov. 1912; ed. Moscow Inst. of Oriental Studies.
Diplomatic service 39-, Counsellor, Soviet Embassy, Chungking 46; Chargé d'Affaires, Nanking 48, Peking 52; Head, First Far East Dept. (China); mem. Policy Planning Board, Ministry of Foreign Affairs 50-55; Dep. Foreign Minister 55; Ambassador to Japan 58-July 62; Perm. Rep. to UN Dec. 62-67; on staff of Ministry of Foreign Affairs 67-; mem. Central Auditing Cttee. of C.P.S.U.; Corresp. mem. U.S.S.R. Acad. of of Sciences 58-.
Publs. twelve books and over 80 articles on Chinese literature.
Ministry of Foreign Affairs, 32-34 Smolenskaya-Sennaya ploshchad, Moscow, U.S.S.R.

Fedorov, Evgeny Konstantinovich; Soviet geophysicist; b. 1910; ed. Leningrad Univ.
Polar station, Franz Joseph Land 32-33, Cape Chelyuskin 34-35; Geophysicist and Astronomer, Soviet Drifting Station *North Pole 1* 37-38; Chief of Board Hydrometeorological Service, U.S.S.R. Council of Ministers 39-47; Geophysical Inst., U.S.S.R. Acad. of Sciences 47-55; Dir. Inst. of Applied Geophysics, U.S.S.R. Acad. of Sciences 55-; Chief Scientific Sec. Presidium of U.S.S.R. Acad. of Sciences 60-62; Head of Chief Board Hydrometeorological Service of the Council of Ministers 63-; mem. C.P.S.U.; Academician 60-; State Prize 46; Order of Lenin (four times), Hero of the Soviet Union, Order of the Red Banner of Labour, etc.
Publs. *Astronomical Measurements* 40, *Meteorological Instruments and Observations* 41-45, *Principal Problems of Hydrometeorological Service* 46, *Influence of Atomic Blasts on Meteorological Processes* 56, *Physical Methods of Influence on Weather* 59, *Some Problems of Developments of Sciences of Earth* 62, *Active Influence on Meteorological Processes* 62, etc.
Chief Board of the Hydrometeorological Service, per. Pavlika Morozova 12, Moscow, U.S.S.R.

Fedorov, Nikolai Alexandrovich; Soviet haemotologist; b. 1904; ed. Voronezh Univ.
Senior Research Assoc. Central Inst. of Haemotology and Blood Transfusion 29-33; Head of Laboratory 33, Head of Dept., Moscow Stomatology Inst. 43-; Corresp. mem. U.S.S.R. Acad. of Medical Sciences 57-, mem. 63-; mem. Board Int. Soc. of Haemotologists; Order of Red Banner of Labour.
Publs. Over 100 works on blood transfusion and conservation, new blood and plasma substitutes, especially heteroproteoseones; established existence and duration of burn putoantigens thus creating a new trend in haemotology (immunchemotherapy).
Central Institute of Blood Transfusion, U.S.S.R. Ministry of Public Health, 4 Novosykovsky By-Street, Moscow, U.S.S.R.

Fedorov, Sergei Filippovich; Soviet geologist; b. 1896; ed. Moscow Mining Acad.
Professor, Moscow Oil Inst. 34-54; U.S.S.R. Acad of Sciences 34-; Corresp. mem. 39-; mem. C.P.S.U. 20-; State Prize 50, 52; Gubkin Prize 52; Order of Lenin, etc.

Publs. *Mud Volcanoes in the U.S.S.R. and their Relation with Oil Content* 37, *Oil Deposits of the Soviet Union* 39, *Methods of Compiling Charts for Oil Content Forecasts* 40, *Geological Structure of the Southern Part of Siberian Plateau* 53, *New Data on the Origin of Oil Bearing Areas* 53, *Essays on History of Oil Geology* 53, *Conditions of Formations of Oil and Gas Deposits in Some Oil-Bearing Regions of U.S.S.R.* 58, *Relative Estimation of Prospects of Oil and Gas Deposits in Siberia and Far East* 58, *On Formation of Oil and Gas Deposits* 59, *Stepped Migration of Oil and Gas* 62.

Geology and Combustible Minerals Processing Institute, 29 Leninski Prospekt, Moscow, U.S.S.R.

Fedorov, Victor Stepanovich; Soviet politician; b. 12; ed. Grozny Oil Inst.
Member C.P.S.U. 39-; Dir. Grozny Oil Inst. 37-40; in oil industry 40-46; First Deputy Minister of Oil Industry U.S.S.R. 46-57; Chair. of Council for Nat. Economy of Bashkir Econ. Region 57-58; Chair. of State Cttee. for Oil Refining and Petro-Chemicals for Gosplan U.S.S.R. 58-64; Minister of Oil Refining and Petro-Chemicals 65-; Deputy Supreme Soviet, U.S.S.R.; Hero of Socialist Labour; State Prize U.S.S.R.; candidate mem. Central Cttee. C.P.S.U.
Ministry of Oil Refining and Petro-Chemicals, 1 Ulitsa Marx-Engels, Moscow, U.S.S.R.

Fedoseyev, Petr Nikolayevich; Soviet philosopher; b. 08; ed. Gorky Teachers' Inst. and Moscow Inst. of History, Philosophy and Literature.
Director U.S.S.R. Acad. Inst. of Philosophy 55-62; mem. U.S.S.R. Acad. of Sciences 60-, Vice-Pres. and Chair. section of Social Sciences, U.S.S.R. Acad. of Sciences 62-; mem. Int. Social Sciences Council; Deputy to U.S.S.R. Supreme Soviet; mem. C.P.S.U. 39-; mem. C.P.S.U. Central Cttee.; Deputy to U.S.S.R. Supreme Soviet; Hon. mem. Hungarian Acad. of Sciences; Chair. U.S.S.R.-Hungarian Friendship Soc.; Order of Patriotic War, Order of Red Banner of Labour (twice).
Publs. *How Did Human Society Appear?* 34, *Historical Materialism as a Science About the Laws of Society Development* 54, *Productive Forces and Relations of Production of Socialist Society* 55, *Socialism and Humanism* 58, *Communism and Philosophy* 62, *Dialectics of the Contemporary Epoch* 66.
U.S.S.R. Academy of Sciences, Moscow, U.S.S.R.

Fehér, Lajos; Hungarian politician; b. 17; ed. Univ. of Debrecen.
Secondary school teacher; Deputy Chief, Political Police; Man. Editor *Szabad Föld*; mem. Editorial Board *Szabad Nép*; mem. Central Cttee. Hungarian Socialist Workers' Party 57-, Sec. 59-62, mem. Political Cttee. 57-; Deputy Prime Minister 62-; Pres. Hungarian Fed. of Partisans.
Akadémia u. 17, Budapest V, Hungary.

Feichtinger, Arne Ferdinand, M.S. in ENG.; Swedish electrical executive; b. 29 Oct. 1906.
Electrical Engineer, Siemens & Halske A.G., Berlin-Siemensstadt 28-29; Sales Manager, Svenska Siemens AB, Stockholm 30-38, Dir. 39-51, Vice-Pres. 52-54, Pres. 55-; mem. Board of Dirs. Dansk Siemens A/S, Copenhagen; mem. of many asscns.; Del. to numerous int. confs.
Office: Svenska Siemens AB, Fack, Stockholm 23; Home: 27 Villavagen, Stocksund, Sweden.

Feiffer, Jules; American cartoonist and writer; b. 26 Jan 1929; ed. Art Students League, Pratt Inst.
Assistant to syndicated cartoonist Will Eisner 46-51; cartoonist, author, syndicated Sunday page, Clifford, engaged in various art jobs 53-56; contributing cartoonist *Village Voice*, New York City 56-; cartoons published weekly in *The Observer* (London), monthly in *Playboy* (magazine); cartoons nationally syndicated in U.S. 59-; sponsor Nat. Cttee. for Sane Nuclear Policy;

U.S. Army 51-53; Acad. Award for Animated Cartoon, Munro 61; Special George Polk Memorial Award 62.
Publs. *Sick, Sick, Sick* 59, *Passionella and other stories* 60, *The Explainers* 61, *Crawling Arnold* (one act play) 61, *Boy, Girl, Boy, Girl* 62, *Hold Me!* 62, *Harry, The Rat With Women* (novel) 63, *Feiffer's Album* 63, *The Unexpurgated Memoirs of Bernard Mergendeiler* 65, *Little Murders* (play) 66, *The Great Comic Book Heroes* 67, *Feiffer's Marriage Manual* 67.
c/o Hall Syndicate, 30 East 42nd Street, New York City, N.Y., U.S.A.

Feiling, Sir Keith Grahame, Kt., O.B.E., D.LITT., M.A.; British writer and historian; b. 84; ed. Marlborough and Balliol Coll. Oxford.
Fellow All Souls Coll. 06; Lecturer Toronto Univ. 07-09, Lecturer 09, Student and Tutor 11-36; Research Student Christ Church Oxford 36-46; served with Black Watch 15, Sec. Central Recruiting Board India 17; Lecturer in Modern History 28-36, Ford Lecturer in English History 31-32, Chichele Prof. of Modern History, Oxford 46-50, Emeritus 50-; Hon. Student, Christ Church; Hon. Mem. Massachusetts Historical Society; founded Oxford Univ. Conservative Asscn. 24; contributor to *The Observer, The Times* and *English Historical Review.*
Publs. *History of the Tory Party 1640-1714* 24, *England under the Tudors and Stuarts* 26, *British Foreign Policy 1660-1672, Sketches in Nineteenth Century Biography* 30, *The Second Tory Party 1714-1832* 38, *Life of Neville Chamberlain* 46, *A History of England* 50, *Warren Hastings* 54, *In Christ Church Hall* 60.
Little London, Hingham, Norfolk, England.

Feinberg, Nathan, DR.JUR.UTR.; Prof. Emer. The Hebrew Univ., Jerusalem; b. 6 June 1895; ed. Univ. of Zürich and Graduate Inst. of Int. Studies, Geneva.
Head of Dept., Ministry of Jewish Affairs, Lithuania 19-21; Sec. Cttee. of Jewish Dels., Paris 22-24; law practice in Palestine 24-27 and 34-45; Lecturer, Univ. of Geneva 31-33; Lecturer, Hebrew Univ., Jerusalem 45-49, Assoc. Prof. 49-52, Prof. of Int. Law and Relations 52-66, Dean of Faculty of Law 49-51; mem. Perm. Court of Arbitration; mem. Inst. Int. Law; Chair. Int. Law Asscn., Israel Branch; Fellow Int. Inst. of Arts and Letters.
Publs. *La Question des Minorités à la Conférence de la paix de 1919-1920 et l'action juive en faveur de la Protection Internationale des Minorités* 29, *La Juridiction de la Cour Permanente de Justice Internationale dans le Système des Mandats* 30, *La Juridiction de la Cour Permanente de Justice dans le Système de la Protection Internationale des Minorités* 31, *La Pétition en Droit International* 33, *Some Problems of the Palestine Mandate* 36, *L'Admission de Nouveaux Membres à la Société des Nations et à L'Organisation des Nations Unies* 52, *The Jewish Struggle against Hitler in the League of Nations—the Bernheim Petition* (in Hebrew) 57, *The Legality of a 'State of War' after the Cessation of Hostilities* 61, *Palestine under the Mandate and the State of Israel—Problems in International Law* (in Hebrew) 63, *The Jewish League of Nations Societies* (in Hebrew) 67; co-editor *The Jewish Year Book of International Law* 49; editor *Studies in Public International Law in Memory of Sir Hersch Lauterpacht* (in Hebrew) 62.
6 Ben Labrat Street, Jerusalem, Israel.
Telephone: 33345.

Feis, Herbert, A.B., PH.D.; American historian; b. 7 June 1893; ed. Harvard Univ.
Head Dept. of Economics Univ. of Cincinnati 26-29; mem. Staff Council on Foreign Relations 30-31; Economic Adviser to Dept. of State Washington 31-37; Adviser on Int. Economic Affairs 37-43; Special Consultant to Sec. of War 44-48; Chief Technical Adviser American Del. to World Economic Conf. London 33, Conf. of American Republics, Buenos Aires 36-37;

Adviser 8th Int. Conf. of American States. Lima 38. Special Asst. to Sec. of War 44-46; Policy Planning Staff State Dept. 50-51; mem. Inst. for Advanced Study, Princeton 51-53, 57-; Visiting Prof. Harvard Univ. 58-60, Columbia Univ. 61, Univ. of Tokyo 64; Pulitzer Prize for History 61; Hon. D.Litt. (Princeton Univ., and Univ. of Michigan); Hon. LL.D. (Univ. of Cincinnati) 68.

Publs. *Settlement of Wage Disputes, Principles of Wage Settlement, Europe: the World's Banker* 30, *The Changing Pattern of International Economic Affairs* 40, *Petroleum and American Foreign Policy* 44, *The Sinews of Peace* 45, *Seen from E.A.* 47, *The Spanish Story* 48, *The Road to Pearl Harbor* 50, *Diplomacy of the Dollar* 51, *The China Tangle* 53, *Churchill-Roosevelt-Stalin* 57, *Between War and Peace* 60, *Japan Subdued: The Atomic Bomb and the End of the Pacific War* 61, *Foreign Aid and Foreign Policy* 64, *1933: Characters in Crisis* 65, *Contest Over Japan* 67.

York, Maine, U.S.A.

Telephone: 207-363-3806.

Fejic, Salko; Yugoslav lawyer and diplomatist; b.14. War of Liberation 41-45; Public Prosecutor for Bosnia and Hercegovina 45-46; Secretariat of State for Foreign Affairs 46-, Counsellor, Moscow 46-49, Perm. Del. at Geneva 50-53, Minister to the Netherlands 55-57; Ambassador to Argentina 57-60, to United Arab Republic 63-; numerous decorations.

Yugoslav Embassy, Cairo, United Arab Republic.

Feki, Ahmed Hassan el-; United Arab Republic (Egyptian) soldier and diplomatist; b. 11; ed. Cairo Mil. Acad. and Staff Coll., Gunnery Staff Coll. (U.K.). Army service, reaching rank of Maj.-Gen. 30-54; fmr. Instructor Mil. Acad. and Staff Coll., Mil. Attaché Rome; Ambassador to Libya of Egypt and subsequently of U.A.R. 54-59; Ambassador of U.A.R. to India 59-64, to Canada 64-65; Under-Sec. of State, Ministry of Foreign Affairs 65-68; Amb. to U.K. 68-.

Embassy of United Arab Republic, South Audley Street, London, W.1, England.

Fekini, Mohieddine, DR.IUR.; Libyan diplomatist; ed. Univ. of Paris.

Former Head of Executive Council in Tripoli; fmr. Ambassador to U.A.R., Cairo; fmr. Minister of Justice; Ambassador to U.S. and Perm. Rep. to the UN 60-63; Prime Minister of Libya 63-64.

c/o Office of the Prime Minister, Tripoli, Libya.

Feldman, Myer, B.S.(ECON.), LL.B.; American lawyer and politician; b. 22 June 1917; ed. Univ. of Pennsylvania.

Gowen Fellow, Univ. of Pennsylvania 38-39, Assoc. in Law, 40-42; Special Counsel, S.E.C., Exec. Asst. to Chair., S.E.C. 49-53; Counsel, Senate Banking and Currency Cttee. 55-57; Prof. of Law, American Univ. 56-59; Legislative Asst., Senator John F. Kennedy 58-61; Dir. of Research, Democratic Nat. Cttee. 60; Deputy Special Counsel to Pres. of the United States 61-64, Counsel 64-65; Gov. Weizmann Inst., Israel 62-; Overseer Coll. of the Virgin Islands 63-; Trustee Eleanor Roosevelt Foundation 63-; Contributor to *The Saturday Review* 65-; partner Ginsburg and Feldman 65-; Dir. Flying Tiger Line 66-; Dir. Imperial-American Corpn. 67-, Royal Resources Corpn. 67-, Flame of Hope, Inc. 67-; Democrat.

Publ. *Standard Pennsylvania Practice* (4 vols.).

1700 Pennsylvania Avenue, N.W., Washington, D.C. 20006, U.S.A.

Felek, Burhan, L. en D.; Turkish journalist; b. 89; ed· Scutari Lycée and Istanbul Univ.

Civil servant 08; served in Army Reserve First World War; sports journalist and photographer 19; Editor *Cumhuriyet* (Istanbul daily) 25-; Pres. Asscn. of Turkish Journalists; Pres. Turkish Olympic Cttee.;

Hon. O.B.E. (U.K.); mem. People's Republican Party, IPI.

Publs. Works on photography, sport and travel; two collections of humorous stories and one play; translations of novels into Turkish, including *Il Piccolo Mondo di Don Camillo, Il Compagno Don Camillo.*

Home: Dost apt. 8/9 Eytam ed, Nişantaş, Istanbul (winter), Santral sok. Ömerpaşa caddesi Erenköy, Istanbul (summer); Office: *Cumhuriyet*, Istanbul, Turkey.

Telephone: 481436-552476.

Felici, H.E. Cardinal Pericle; Italian ecclesiastic; b. 1 Aug. 1911.

Ordained Priest 33; Titular Archbishop of Samosata 60-; also Co-Chair. Commission on Revision of Canon Law; created Cardinal by Pope Paul VI 67.

Via Serristori 10, Rome, Italy.

Fellini, Federico; Italian film director; b. 20 Jan. 1920. Assistant Director: *Quarta pagina* 42, *Roma città aperta* 44-45, *Paisà* 46, *Il delitto di Giovanni Episcopo* 47, *In nome della legge* 48-49, *La città si difende* 51, *Il brigante di Tacca di Lupo* 53, etc.; Director *Lo sceicco bianco* 52, *I vitelloni* 53, *La strada* 54, *Il bidone* 55, *Cabiria* 57, *Fortunella* 58, *La Dolce Vita* (Cannes Festival 1st Prize) 60, *The Temptation of Dr. Antonio* (from *Boccaccio* 70 Triptych) 62, $8\frac{1}{2}$ 63, *Giulietto degli spiriti* (Golden Globe, Hollywood) 64; musical *Sweet Charity* (from *Le notti de Cabiria*) 65; has frequently written scripts for his films.

141a Via Archimede, Rome, Italy.

Fellman Velarde, José; Bolivian politician and diplomatist; b. 22; ed. Univ. of Santiago.

Former Head of President's Secretariat; fmr. Under-Sec. of Press and Propaganda; Counsellor, Bolivian Embassy, London 56-58; Minister of Education 60-62; Minister for Foreign Affairs 62-64; many awards and decorations.

Publs. *El Pensiamento de Murillo a través de Nuestra Historia* 47, *El Sentido de lo Nacional en la Teoría y en la Práctica* 48, *Una Bala en el Viento* 52, *Víctor Paz Estenssoro, el Hombre y la Revolución* 54, *Trabajos Teóricos* 55, *La Montaña de los Angeles* 58, *Imperios Andinos* 61.

Ministry of Foreign Affairs, La Paz, Bolivia.

Fellner, William John; Hungarian-born American economist; b. 31 May 1905; ed. Budapest Univ., Fed. Inst. of Technology, Zürich and Berlin Univ.

Industrial management 29-38; mem. Dept. of Economics Univ. of Cal., Berkeley 39-52; Prof. of Economics Yale Univ. 52, Chair. Dept. of Econs. 62-64; Consultant U.S. Treas. Dept. 45; mem. Cttee. of Independent Experts OEEC 59-60; Fellow, American Acad. of Arts and Sciences.

Publs. *Monetary Policies and Full Employment* 46, *Competition Among the Few* 49, *Trend and Cycles in Economic Activity* 56, *Emergence and Content of Modern Economic Analysis* 60, *Probability and Profit* 65.

Home: 131 Edgehill Road, New Haven, Conn.; Office: Department of Economics, Yale University, New Haven, Conn., U.S.A.

Telephone: 787-3131, Extension 2609 (Office); 777-4186 (Home).

Felsenstein, Walter; Austrian actor and producer; b. 01; ed. Graz Technical High School.

Student at Vienna Burgtheater 21-23; acted in Lübeck 23-24, Mannheim 24-25; actor and director Beuthen-Gleiwitz-Hindenburg 25-27; Dir. of Productions, Stadttheater Basel 27-29, Freiburg-im-Breisgau 29-32; Opera Dir. Cologne 32-34, Frankfurt-am-Main 34-36; Dir. of Productions, Stadttheater Zürich 38-40, Schiller-Theater, Berlin 40-44, Hebbel-Theater, Berlin 45-47; Intendant and Dir. Berlin Comic Opera 47-; numerous guest productions at Theater im Admiralspalast,

Berlin, Salzburg Festival, Vienna Burgtheater, Hamburg State Opera, etc.; productions include *Die Fledermaus, Kaiserin Katharina, Der Zigeunerbaron, John Gabriel Borkmann, Achill unter den Weibern, Clavigo, Falstaff, Tannhäuser, Figaros Hochzeit, Pariser Leben, Die Kluge, Zauberflöte, Eine Nacht in Venedig, Die Irre von Chaillot, Torquato Tasso, Das Schlaue Füchslein, Hoffmanns Erzählungen, Othello, La Traviata, A Midsummer Night's Dream, Orpheus in der Unterwelt, Die Verkaufte Braut, Der Freischutz, Die Schweigsame Frau,* etc., and the films *Ein Windstoss, La Pathétique* and *Fidelio*.
Miquelstrasse 42a, Berlin-Dahlem, Germany.

Feltin, H.E. Cardinal Maurice; French ecclesiastic; b. 15 May 1883.
Ordained Priest 09; Curate at Sainte-Madeleine Besançon; French Army 14-18; Vicar-Dean of Giromagnay 20; Rector, Sainte-Madeleine, Besançon 25; hon. Canon 27; consecrated Bishop of Troyes 28; Archbishop of Sens 32; Archbishop of Bordeaux 35; Archbishop of Paris 49-66; created Cardinal by Pope Pius XII 53; Commdr. de la Légion d'Honneur, Médaille Militaire, Croix de Guerre; mem. Sacred Congregations of the Consistory, of the Council and of Rites.
32 rue Barbet de Jouy, Paris 7e, France.

Feltrinelli, Giangiacomo; Italian publisher; b. 19 June 1926.
Owner and Pres. of Giangiacomo Feltrinelli Editore, Milan; Pres. Feltrinelli Inst. for research in political, social and econ. history.
Via Andegari 6, Milan, Italy.

Feng Hsuan; Chinese politician.
Former Ambassador to Switzerland; Deputy Sec.-Gen. State Council; Vice-Pres. China-Latin America Friendship Asscn.; Deputy Sec.-Gen. Standing Cttee. Chinese C.P. 65-.
Office of the Standing Committee of the Chinese Communist Party, Peking, People's Republic of China.

Feng Yu-lan, PH.D., LL.D.; Chinese historian of philosophy; b. 94; ed. Nat. Univ., Peking, and Columbia Univ.
Taught at Sun Yat-sen Univ., Yenching Univ. and Tsinghua Univ.; lectured in Kunming during the Japanese War; returned to Peking as Prof. at Tsinghua Univ. and Dean of Arts Faculty; LL.D. Princeton Univ. 46; Head of Dept. of Philosophy, Peking Univ. 54-; mem. of Cttee. of the Democratic League.
Publ. *A History of Chinese Philosophy*.
Department of Philosophy, Peking University, Peking, China.

Fenn, Ingemund; Norwegian newspaper editor; b. 18 Sept. 1907; univ. education.
Journalist 28-; on staff of *Bergens Tidende* 36-, editor Oslo office and parl. corresp. 46-56, Chief Editor 56-; Pres. Parl. Corresp. Asscn. 51-56; Chair. Norwegian Liberal Press Asscn. 59-; mem. board Norwegian Editors' Asscn., Norwegian Press Asscn., Norwegian News Bureau; mem. Town Council; Liberal.
Bergens Tidende, Bergen, Norway.

Fenn, Wallace Osgood, A.M., PH.D., D.SC.; American physiologist; b. 27 Aug. 1893; ed. Harvard Univ.
Instructor in Physiology Harvard Medical School 19-23; Travelling Fellow Rockefeller Inst. 23-25; Prof. of Physiology School of Medicine and Dentistry, Rochester Univ. 25-, Chair. 25-59; Asst. Dean 49-53; Assoc. Dean for Graduate Studies 57-59; Dist. Univ. Prof. of Physiology 61-; Dir. of Space Science Center 64-66; mem. Cttee. on Sensory Devices Nat. Research Council; mem. Cttee. Medical Sciences Research and Devt. Board of Nat. Mil. Estab.; Chair. Physiology Study Section Nat. Inst. of Health 47-51; mem. Nat. Acad. of Sciences;

American Philosophical Society; American Acad. Arts and Sciences; Pres. American Physiological Society 46-48; mem. Nat. Science Foundation 50-52, Chair. Biology Division 52; Pres. American Inst. Biological Sciences 57-58; Pres. Experimental Biology Medicine 57-59; Chair. Panel on Underwater Swimmer Technology, Nat. Research Council 57-59; Vice-Pres. *Biological Abstracts* 56-59, Pres. 60-61; Sec.-Gen. Int. Union of Physiological Science 59-65; Pres. XXIV Int. Congress of Physiological Sciences, Washington 68; Hon. mem. Canadian Physiological Soc., British Physiological Soc.; mem. Int. Acad. of Astronautics, Accad. Nazionale dei Lincei; Hon. Dr. (Chicago, Paris, Rochester, Brussels); Guggenheim Award, Int. Acad. of Astronautics 64, Antonio Feltrinelli Int. Prize for Experimental Medicine, Accad. Nazionale dei Lincei, Rome 64; Distinguished Achievement Award of *Modern Medicine* 67, Research Achievement Award, American Heart Asscn. 67.
1394 Highland Avenue, Rochester, N.Y. 14620, U.S.A. Telephone: 716-271-2626.

Fenner, Frank John, M.B.E., M.D., F.A.A., F.R.S., Australian research biologist; b. 21 Dec. 1914; ed. Thebarton Technical High School, Adelaide High School, Adelaide Univ.
Medical Officer, Hospital Pathologist, Australian Forces 40-43, Malariologist 43-46; Francis Haley Research Fellow, Walter and Eliza Hall Inst. for Medical Research, Melbourne 46-48; Travelling Fellow, Rockefeller Inst. for Medical Research 48-49; Prof. of Microbiology, Australian Nat. Univ. 49-; Dir. John Curtin School of Medical Research, Australian Nat. Univ. 67-; David Syme Prize, Melbourne Univ. 49; Harvey Lecturer, Harvey Soc. of N.Y. 58; Overseas Fellow, Churchill Coll., Cambridge 61-62; Mueller Medal 64; Britannica Australia Award 67.
Publs. about 100 scientific papers, mainly on acidfast bacilli and pox viruses, *The Production of Antibodies* (with F. M. Burnet) 49, *Myxomatosis* (with F. N. Ratcliffe) 65.
John Curtin School of Medical Research, Australian National University, Canberra, Australia.
Telephone: 49-2597.

Fenoaltea, Sergio; Italian diplomatist; b. 9 June 1908.
Under-Sec. Council of the Presidency 44; mem. Nat. Assembly 45-46; Amb. to China 46-50; joint Sec.-Gen. NATO, Paris 52-55; Amb. to Canada 55-58; Amb. to Belgium 59-61, to U.S.A. 61-May 67; Gran Croce Ordine al Merito Repubblica Italiana.
Via Bruxelles 34, Rome, Italy.

Fenton, Beatrice; American sculptor; b. 12 July 1887; ed. School of Industrial Art and Pennsylvania Acad. of Fine Arts.
Works include: Seaweed Fountain, Fairmount Park, Philadelphia 22, Schmitz Memorial Tablet, Acad. of Music 26, Gate Post Figures at Children's Hospital, Philadelphia 32, Garden Figure Danby Park, Wilmington, Del. 31, Bust of Wm. Penn for Penn Club, Philadelphia 32, Fountain, Brookgreen Gardens, S.C. 32, Bust of Felix E. Schelling, Furness Library, Univ. of Pa. 35, Bust of Thomas H. Fenton, M.D., Art Club of Philadelphia 37, Ariel Sun-Dial, Shakespeare Garden, Univ. of Pa. 38, Drinking Fountain, Hahnemann Medical Coll., Philadelphia 42, Lizette Woodworth Reese Memorial, Pratt Library, Baltimore, Md. 43, Evelyn Taylor Price Memorial Sun-Dial, Rittenhouse Square Philadelphia 48; winning design for Vice-Pres. Barkley Congressional Medal 50; bust of Joseph Moore for Moore Inst., Philadelphia 54; Two Fountain groups *Fish on Coral Reef*, Fairmount Park, Pa. 64.
Home: 621 Westview Street, Philadelphia 19, Pa., U.S.A.; Studio: 311 West Duval Street. Philadelphia 44, Pa., U.S.A.

Fenton, Roy Pentelow, C.M.G.; British banker; b. 1 July 1918; ed. Salford Grammar School.
War Service 39-46; Bank of England 46-58; Governor, Central Bank of Nigeria 58-63; Dep. Chief, Central Banking Information Dept., Bank of England 63-65, Chief Overseas Dept. 65-; U.K. mem. Man. Board of European Monetary Fund 67-.
Bank of England, London, E.C.2, England.

Feoktistov, Konstantin Petrovich, D.SC.; Soviet cosmonaut; b. 1926; ed. Moscow Higher Technical School.
Injured in World War II; group instructor for cosmonauts; the scientific mem. of the team aboard the first-ever multi-seater space ship "Voskhod I" (12 Oct. 64); Hero of the Soviet Union; Pilot-Cosmonaut of U.S.S.R.
Presidium of Academy of Sciences of U.S.S.R., 14 Leninsky Prospekt, Moscow, U.S.S.R.

Feoktistov, Lev Petrovich; Soviet physicist; b. 1928; ed. Moscow Univ.
Postgraduate, Asst. Prof., Prof. Moscow Univ. 50-; mem. C.P.S.U. 56; Corresp. mem. U.S.S.R. Acad. of Sciences 66-; Hero of Socialist Labour.
Publs. Works on various problems of nuclear physics.
U.S.S.R. Academy of Sciences, 14 Leninsky Prospekt, Moscow, U.S.S.R.

Fere, Vladimir Georgievich; Soviet composer; b. 1902; ed. Moscow Univ., and Moscow Conservatoire.
Professor Moscow Conservatoire 62; Sec. R.S.F.S.R. Composers' Union: Honoured Worker of Arts of Kirghiz S.S.R. 39, People's Artist of Kirghizia 44, Honoured Worker of Arts of Bashkirian Autonomous S.S.R. 55, of Tadjik S.S.R. 57, of R.S.F.S.R. 63, of Buryat Autonomous S.S.R. 63; Orders: Red Banner of Labour 39, 58, Badge of Honour 46, 66.
Principal compositions: *May* (symphonic poem) 28, *Beloved Land* (symphonietta) 28, *On Guard* (symphonic poem) 32, *Snows of Mount Elbrus* (suite) 35, *The Patriots* (overture) 41, *Kirgizstan* (symphony) 46, *Forest Tale* 62; Ballets: *Anar* 41, *Selkinchep* 43, *Spring in Alatoo* 57; Operas: *Altyn Kyz* 37, *Adjal Orduna* 38, *Aichurek* 39, *For the Happiness of the People* 41, *Patriots* 41, *Manas* 46, *Son of the People* 47, *On the Shores of Issyk Kul* 52, *Toktogul, People's Bard* 58, *The Sorcerer* 60, *Batyr Manas* (opera) 65; over 150 settings of Russian and Soviet poems, and much other instrumental, choral and folk music.
R.S.F.S.R. Composers' Union, 4-6 Miusskaya ulitsa, Moscow, U.S.S.R.

Ferencsik, János; Hungarian musician; b. 18 Jan. 1907; ed. Conservatoire, Budapest.
Musical Dir. Hungarian State Opera House; Musical Dir. Hungarian State Concert Orchestra; Chief Conductor Budapest Philharmonic Orchestra; Asst. Bayreuth Festival 30-31; guest conductor Vienna Opera House 48-50; has given concerts in Austria, Belgium, Czechoslovakia, Finland, Germany, Romania, U.K., U.S.A., and U.S.S.R.; Kossuth Prize 51, 61.
Hungarian State Opera House, Népköztársaság utja 22, Budapest VI, Hungary.
Telephone: 312-550.

Ferguson, C. Vaughan, Jr., A.B.; American diplomatist; b. 12 Jan. 1915; ed. Harvard Univ. School of Business Administration.
Joined Foreign Service 40, served Winnipeg, Teheran, Bucharest; Officer in Charge Iranian Affairs 51; at Naval War Coll. 52; Consul, Dakar 53, Consul-Gen. 54, Tangier 55; Dir. Office of South African Affairs 57, of West African Affairs 60, of West African and Malagasy Affairs 61; Ambassador to Malagasy Republic 63-.
American Embassy, Tananarive, Malagasy Republic (Madagascar).

Ferguson, Glenn Walker, B.A., M.B.A., LL.B.; American government official; b. 28 Jan. 1929; ed. Cornell Univ.,

Georgetown Univ., Univ. of Santo Tomas (Manila), George Washington Univ., Univ. of Chicago and Univ. of Pittsburgh.
Staff Associate, Governmental Affairs Inst., Washington, D.C. 54-55; Asst. Editor and Asst. Sec.-Treas., American Judicature Soc., Chicago 55-56; successively Admin. Asst. to Chancellor, Asst. Dean and Asst. Prof. Graduate School of Public and Int. Affairs, Assoc. Dir., Coordinated Educ. Center, Univ. of Pittsburgh 56-60; Management Consultant 60-61; Special Asst. to Dir., U.S. Peace Corps 61, Peace Corps Dir. in Thailand 61-63, Assoc. Dir. 63-64; Dir. Vista Volunteers, Office of Econ. Opportunity, Washington, D.C. 64-66; U.S. Air Force 51-53; mem. Pres. Task Force on Poverty 64, Conf. on the Public Service 65-, Fed. Bar Asscn.; U.S. Amb. to Kenya 66-.
Office: American Embassy, Nairobi, Kenya; Home: 7610 Fairfax Road, Bethesda, Maryland 20014, U.S.A.

Ferguson, Harry S., A.B., LL.B.; American lawyer and businessman; b. 2 Oct. 1902; ed. Amherst Coll. and Columbia Law School.
Assoc., Cravath, Swaine and Moore 26-33; Head, Legal Dept. Allied Chemical Corpn., Vice-Pres. 51-57, Dir. 55-, mem. Exec. Cttee. 57-59, Exec. Vice-Pres. 57-59, Chair. Exec. Cttee. and Chief Admin. Officer 59-.
Allied Chemical Corporation, 61 Broadway, New York 10006, N.Y., U.S.A.

Ferguson, Homer, LL.B.; American lawyer and politician; b. 25 Feb. 1889; ed. Pittsburgh Univ., Michigan Univ. Law School.
Law practice Detroit 13-29; Circuit Judge Wayne County, Mich. 29-41; One-man grand jury, Wayne County, Mich. 39-42; U.S. Senator from Mich. 43-55; Chair. Republican Policy Cttee. 83rd Congress; mem. Foreign Relations Cttee. and Appropriation Cttee. 83rd Congress; mem. 2nd Hoover Comm.; Amb. to the Philippines 55-56; resigned 56 to accept presidential appointment; Judge, U.S. Court of Military Appeals 56-; mem. Michigan and American Bar Asscns.; mem. American Judicature Soc., Washington Inst. of Foreign Affairs, Metropolitan Club, World Peace Thru Law Center; Hon. mem. Interparliamentary Union; Republican.
Home: 5054 Millwood Lane, N.W., Washington 16, D.C.; Office: U.S. Court of Military Appeals, Washington, D.C. 20442, U.S.A.
Telephone: OX6-6125 (Office).

Ferguson, John Haven, A.B., LL.B.; American lawyer and diplomatist; b. 4 Feb. 1915; ed. Yale Univ. and Harvard Law School.
Lawyer, Root, Clark, Buckner and Ballantine 40-42; Office of Sec. of Navy 42-43; Asst. to Under-Sec. of State 44-46; Asst. to Pres. Int. Bank for Reconstruction and Devt. (World Bank) 46-47; Lawyer, Root, Ballantine, Harlan Bushby and Palmer 47-51; Dep. Dir. Policy Planning Staff, Dept. of State 51-53; Partner, Cleary, Gottlieb, Friendly and Ball 54-62; Ambassador to Morocco 62-65; Special Asst. to Under-Sec. of State 65-.
U.S. Department of State, Washington, D.C., U.S.A.

Ferguson, Roy King; American businessman; b. 7 Dec. 1893; ed. Central High School, Paterson, N.J.
Asst. Man. Lake Placid Club, N.Y. 12-17; Vice-Pres. Northern N.Y. Securities Co. 17-21; Vice-Pres. F. L. Carlisle and Co., N.Y. 21-32; Vice-Pres. and Treas. United Corpn., N.Y. 32-34; Pres. St. Regis Paper Co., N.Y. 34-57, Chair. and Chief Exec. Officer 57-; Pres. St. Regis Paper Co. (Canada) Ltd., Eastern States Corpn.
150 E. 42nd Street, New York City, N.Y., U.S.A.

Ferguson, Wallace Klippert, PH.D., LITT.D., F.R.S.C.; Canadian historian; b. 23 May 1902; ed. Univ. of Western Ontario and Cornell Univ.
Instructor, New York Univ. 28-30, Asst. Prof. 30-40,

Assoc. Prof. 40-45, Prof. 45; Chair. History Dept., Univ. of W. Ontario 56, Senior Prof. 65-; Pres. Canadian Historical Asscn. 60-61, Renaissance Soc. of America 65-67, Council of American Historical Asscn. 64-68; Social Science Research Council Fellowship 27-28; Guggenheim Fellowship 39-40; Canada Council Medal 67.
Publs. *Opuscula Erasmi* (*A Supplement to the Omnia Opera*) 33, *A Survey of European Civilization* (with G. Bruun) 36, *The Renaissance* 40, *The Renaissance in Historical Thought* 48, *Europe in Transition 1300-1520* 62, *Renaissance Studies* 63.
1061 Waterloo Street, London, Ontario, Canada.
Telephone: 519-432-4751.

Fergusson, Sir Bernard Edward, G.C.M.G., G.C.V.O., D.S.O., O.B.E.; formerly Governor-General of New Zealand, British army officer and author; b. 6 May 1911; ed. Eton Coll., Royal Military Coll., Sandhurst.
Joined the Black Watch 31; served in Palestine 37-38, in Middle East and Burma Second World War, including Wingate Expeditions into Burma 43-44; Palestine Police 46-47; Commanded the Black Watch 48-51; Col. Intelligence SHAPE 51-53; Commdr. 29 Infantry Brigade 57-58; retd. from army 58; Gov-Gen. of New Zealand 62-67.
Publs. *Eton Portrait* 37, *Beyond the Chindwin* 45, *Lowland Soldier* (verse) 45, *The Wild Green Earth* 46, *The Black Watch and the King's Enemies* 50, *Rupert of the Rhine* 52, *The Rare Adventure* 54, *The Watery Maze* 61, *Wavell: Portrait of a Soldier* 61, *Return to Burma* 63.
Auchairne, Ballantrae, Ayrshire, Scotland.
Telephone: Ballantrae 344.

Fernandel (*pseudonym* of Fernand-Joseph-Désiré Contandin); French actor; b. 8 May 1903.
Began career as bank employee; embarked upon a career in cinema, making a large number of films, among which are: *Topaze* and 6 others by Marcel Pagnol; *Carnet de Bal, Le Petit Monde de Don Camillo* (for which 11 Oscars were awarded 53), *Le Retour de Don Camillo* (all directed by Julien Duvivier); *L'Auberge Rouge, Coiffeur pour Dames, Le Fruit défendu, Le Boulanger de Valorgues, La Table aux Crevés, L'Ennemi Public No. 1, Le Mouton à 5 Pattes, Ali Baba et les 40 voleurs, La Loi, c'est la Loi, L'Armoire volante, Le Diable et les Dix Commandements, Crésus, Le Voyage à Biarritz, l'Age Ingrat, La Vache et le prisonnier, Le Caïd, Don Camillo Monseigneur, Dynamite Jack, Blague dans le coin, La Cuisine au beurre, Don Camillo en Russie, Le Voyage du père,* etc.; Operettas: *Ignace et le Rosier de Madame Husson,* etc.; star in Sacha Guitry comedy *Tu m'as sauvé la Vie*; Officier d'Académie; Légion d'Honneur, Croix de Dévouement, etc.; at A.B.C. Théâtre, Paris 35-44, 45-50, Oscar Européen 60; Grand-Prix Mondial du Rire, Prix Courteline 63, 64.
44 avenue Foch, Paris 16e, France.

Fernández, Carlos Alberto; Argentine lawyer and diplomatist; b. 2 Dec. 1907; ed. Colegio de la Salle and Universidad Nacional de Buenos Aires.
Lawyer, Buenos Aires City Council 32-45; with Provincial Govt. of La Rioja 45-47; joined Ministry of Foreign Affairs 47, early service in Rome and Costa Rica; Sub-Dir. Legal Council, Ministry of Foreign Affairs 55, Sub-Dir.-Gen. Political Dept. 58-59, Dir.-Gen. Political Dept. 62-65; Minister Dublin 59-61; Ambassador to United Arab Republic 62; Ambassador to Brazil 63-; Grand Cross Orden Nacional al Mérito (Paraguay) and Orden del Cruzeiro do Sul (Brazil).
Argentine Embassy, Rua Farani 29, Rio de Janeiro, Brazil.

Fernández-Muro, José Antonio; Argentine painter; b. 1 March 1920.
Director, Nat. School of Fine Arts, Buenos Aires 57-58; travelled and studied in Europe and America on UNESCO Fellowship of Museology 57-58; lives in New York 62-; one-man exhbns. in Buenos Aires, Madrid, Washington, New York, Rome and Detroit; represented in numerous Group Shows including *50 ans de Peinture Abstraite*, Paris and *The Emergent Decade*, Guggenheim Museum 65; prizes include Gold Medal, Brussels World Fair 58, Guggenheim Int. and Di Tella Int. awards.
Major works: *Superimposed circles* 58, *In Reds*, Di Tella Foundation, Buenos Aires 59, *Horizonte terroso*, Museum of Modern Art, Caracas 61, *Circulo azogado*, Museum of Modern Art, New York 62, *Lacerated Tablet*, Rockefeller, New York 63, *Elemental Forms*, Massachussetts Inst. of Technology 64, *Silver Field*, Guggenheim Museum 65, *Summit*, Bonino Gallery, N.Y.
353 East 50th Street, New York, N.Y., U.S.A.

Fernández Retamar, Roberto, DR. en FIL.; Cuban writer; b. 9 June 1930; ed. Univ. de la Habana, Univ. de Paris à la Sorbonne and Univ. of London.
Professor, Univ. of Havana 55-; Visiting Prof. Yale Univ. 57-58; Dir. *Nueva Revista Cubana* 59-60; Cultural Counsellor of Cuba in France 60; Sec. Union of Writers and Artists of Cuba 61-65; Dir. of Review *Casa de las Américas* 65-; Visiting Lecturer Columbia Univ., New York 57, Univ. of Prague 65; Nat. Prize for Poetry, Cuba 52.
Publs. Poetry: *Elegía como un Himno* 50, *Patrias* 52, *Alabanzas, Conversaciones* 55, *Vuelta de la Antigua Esperanza* 59, *Con las Mismas Mános* 62, *Poésia Reunida 1948-1965* 66, *Buena Suerte Viviendo* 67; studies: *La Poésia Contemporánea en Cuba* 54, *Idea de la Estilistica* 58, *Papeleria* 62.
Calle H 508, Vedado, Havana, Cuba.

Fernando, Hugh Norman Gregory, O.B.E., B.A., B.C.L.; Ceylonese judge; b. 17 Nov. 1910; ed. St. Joseph's Coll., Colombo, Trinity Coll., Kandy, and Balliol Coll., Oxford.
Barrister of Gray's Inn (London); Legal Draftsman, Ceylon 50-54; Commr. of Assizes and Puisne Justice, Supreme Court 54-66; Chief Justice of Ceylon 66-; Leader, Ceylon Del. to Afro-Asian Legal Consultative Cttee. 62; Chair. Cheshire Homes Foundation, Ceylon; Chair. Appeal for Children Fund, Ceylon.
Chief Justice's House, Colombo, Ceylon.

Fernando, Thusew Samuel, C.B.E., Q.C., LL.B.; Ceylonese judge; b. 5 Aug. 1906; ed. Royal College, Colombo, Univ. Coll., Colombo, Univ. Coll., London, and Lincoln's Inn, London.
Crown Counsel 36-52; Solicitor-Gen., Ceylon 52-54; Attorney-Gen. 54-56; Justice of Supreme Court of Ceylon 56-; mem. Judicial Service Comm. 62-; Pres. Int. Comm. of Jurists, Geneva 66-; mem. Int. Cttee. of Inst. on Man & Science, New York; Co-Chair. Space Law Cttee. of World Peace Through Law Centre, Geneva.
3 Cosmas Avenue, Barnes Place, Colombo 7, Ceylon.

Ferniot, Jean; French journalist; b. 10 Oct. 1918; ed. Lycée Louis-le-Grand.
Head, Political Dept., *France-Tireur* 45-47; Political Columnist, *L'Express* 57-58; Chief Political Correspondent *France-Soir* 59-63; Editor *L'Express* 63-66; on staff Radio Luxembourg and Political Commentator *France-Soir* Dec. 66-; Prix Interallié 61; Croix de Guerre.
Publs. *Les Ides de Mai* 58, *L'Ombre Porté* 61, *Pour le Pire* 62, *Derrière la Fenêtre* 64, *De Gaulle et le 13 Mai* 65.
4 rue Gustave-Flaubert, Paris 17e, France.

Ferrari, Alberto, LL.D., M.A.; Italian banker; b. 16 Dec. 1914; ed. Univ. di Pisa, Yale Univ., and Univ. Bocconi Milan.
With Banca Commerciale Italiana 38-51, with Presidency of Cabinet as Financial Expert 47, Italian Del. to European Co-operation Cttee., Paris 47, Italian Perm. Rep. to European Payments Cttee., Paris 48-50;

Gen. Sec. Bank for Int. Settlements, Basle 51-61; Man. Dir. Consorzio di Credito per le Opere Pubbliche 61-67; Man. Dir. Banca Nazionale del Lavoro, Rome Nov. 67-.
Publs. *La Gestione del Credito* 47, *Politica Monetaria* 59, *Politica monetaria en su perspectiva historica* 61.
Banca Nazionale del Lavoro, Direzione Generale, Via Vittorio Veneto, 00187 Rome, Italy.

Ferrari, Enzo; Italian racing car executive; b. 20 Feb. 1898.
Entered motor racing 20-, driver with Alfa Romeo 20-31; founder Ferrari Ltd. 29-, began building own cars 40-; cars have won numerous Grand Prix and Championship Races.
Publ. *Le mie gioie terribili* (autobiog.).
Ferrari Works, Maranello, Modena, Italy.

Ferrari Aggradi, Mario; Italian economist and politician; b. 13 March 1916; ed. Univ. of Rome.
Assistant Prof. of Political Economy and Finance, Univ. of Rome 39; mem. Central Econ. Cttee. of Cttee. of Liberation of N. Italy 44-45; Vice-Pres. Industrial Council for N. Italy 45; Gen. Sec. Interministerial Cttee. for Reconstruction 46; mem. Chamber of Deputies 53-; Under-Sec. for Budget 53-58; Minister of Agriculture 58-59, of State Participations 59-60, of Agriculture and Forests 63-65; mem. Nat. Council Christian Democratic Party.
Publs. *I cicli economici, La finanza italiana dal 1923 al 1938.*
c/o Ministry of Agriculture and Forests, Rome, Italy.

Ferras, Gabriel, D. en D.; French banker and international civil servant; b. 14 Aug. 1913; ed. Law Faculty, Paris Univ., and School of Political Science, Paris.
Fmr. Insp. Bank of France; Alt. Rep. for France, European Payments Union 50-53; Alt. Exec. Dir., Man. Bd., Int. Monetary Fund 53, Dep. Dir. Exchange Restrictions Dept. IMF 53-56, Dir. European Dept., IMF 56-63; Gen. Man. Bank for Int. Settlements 63-. Bank for International Settlements, 7 Zentralbahnstrasse, Basle, Switzerland.

Ferrazzi, Ferruccio; Italian painter; b. 15 March 1891.
Titular Prof. of Decoration, Inst. of Fine Arts, Rome 29-; Instructor, American Acad., Rome 35-36; mem. Accad. dei Lincei 35-, Accad. Naz. S. Luca 25, First Int. Prize Carnegie Inst.
Works include: *Focolare* (Rome Modern Art Gallery) 10, *Genitrice* (Rome) 12, *Presagio* (Bologna Municipal Gallery) 14, *Vita gaia* (Galleria Capitolina, Rome) 21, *Festa notturna, Adolescente* 22, *Horitia* (Florence Modern Art Gallery) 23, *Caratteri della famiglia* (New York) 23, *Viaggio tragico* (Pittsburgh), *Idolo* (Coll., Wedekind) 25, *Tempesta* (Jeu de Paume, Paris) 25, *La Monta* 29, *Il toro romano* (Rome Modern Art Gallery) 30, Seven tapestries (Palace of Corpns., Rome) 32, *Sabaudia* (mosaic) 35, *Clemenza di Traiano* (Palace of Justice, Milan) 38, *Fabiola e Ninetta che pariano* (Art Gallery, Bucharest) 33; frescoes for churches: S. Eugenio, Rome, S. Rita, Cascia 51, Univ. of Padua, etc.; encaustic paintings for S. Benedetto Church, Rome 49; mosaic *Dell' Apocalisse* 27-54, Acqui; frescoes: *Risurrezione,* Amatrice 53-55; *l'Ultima Cena di Cristo,* Assisi 56, *Le Opere e i Giorni,* Mausoleo Acqui 54-60; four sculptures *Nella Villa di S. Liberata* 59-65; mosaic, Propaganda Fide Coll., Rome 65-66; Dir. Scuola Vaticana del Mosaico 67.
Studio: Strada del Pianone, Santa Liberata, Grosseto 58010; and Piazza delle Muse, Via G. G. Porro 27, Rome 00197, Italy.
Telephone: Santa Liberata 74-327; Rome 87-87-36.

Ferrero, Romulo A.; Peruvian economist and agricultural engineer; b. 07; ed. Nat. School of Agriculture, Lima.
Agricultural Experimental Station, Cañete 28-29; Farming 29-31; Staff of Agricultural Bank of Peru 33-45;

Prof. (Money and Banking) Catholic Univ. of Peru 40-, Dean, Faculty of Economic Sciences 42-48; Pres. Peruvian Asscn. of Agricultural Engineers 42 and 47; mem. Advisory Comm. to Min. of Foreign Affairs 45-48; Pres. Peruvian Del. Trade and Employment Conf., Havana 47-48; Min. of Finance and Commerce 45 and 48; Min. of Agriculture 48; Pres. Agricultural Comm. of I.L.O. 53; Adviser Chamber of Commerce and Cotton Chamber of Peru; Orden del Sol (Peru), Orden del Mérito Agrícola (Peru), Ordre du Mérite Agricole (France).
Publs. *Tierra y Población en el Perú* 38, *Política Agraria Nacional* 40, *La Realidad Económica Nacional* 42, *El Comercio Exterior del Perú* 44, *Perspectivas Económicas de la Post-Guerra* 43, *La Política Fiscal y la Economía Nacional* 45, *Historia Monetaria del Perú en el Presente Siglo* 53, *La Inflación y sus peligros* 54, *El Desarrollo Económico y el Comercio Exterior* 55, *El Desarrollo Económico y la Estabilidad Monetaria* 56, *Estudio Comparado de los Impuestos a la Renta en el Perú y otros países de América* 52, *Estudio Económico de la Legislación Social peruana* 57, etc.
Avenida Petit Thouars 3943, San Isidro, Lima, Peru.

Ferrero Rebagliatti, Dr. Raul; Peruvian politician.
Prime Minister of Peru and Minister of Foreign Affairs *ad interim* Nov. 67-, concurrently Minister of Finance Jan.-April 68.
Office of the Prime Minister, Lima, Peru.

Ferretto, H.E. Cardinal Giuseppe; Vatican ecclesiastic; b. 9 March 1899.
Ordained priest 23; Assessor of the Sacred Consistorial Congregation 50; Archbishop of Sardica 58; created Cardinal titular priest of S. Croce in Jerusalem 61; Bishop of Sabina and Poggio Mirteto 62; mem. Sacred Consistorial Congregation, Sacred Congregations de Propaganda Fide, of the Council and of Extraordinary Ecclesiastical Affairs, Tribunal of the Apostolic Signatura, Comm. of the Vatican City State; Penitentiarus Major of Sacred Apostolic Penitentiary 67-.
Piazza S. Calisto 16, Rome, Italy.
Telephone: Vatican City 500001.

Ferronnière, Jacques J.; French banker; b. 2 Dec. 1906; ed. Ecole Libre des Sciences Politiques and Univ. de Paris à la Sorbonne.
Inspector of Finances 29-35; Pres. Board of Dirs. of Soc. Générale pour favoriser le développement du Commerce et de l'Industrie en France; Pres. Soc. anonyme de crédit à l'industrie française (CALIF), Soc. Générale Marocaine de Banques; Vice-Pres. Soc. Générale Alsacienne de Banque; Dir. Compagnie Bancaire, Etablissements J. J. Carnaud et Forges de Basse-Indre, Soc. Française de Banque et de Dépôts, Soc. Générale de Banque; Officier Légion d'Honneur.
Publ. *Les Opérations de Banque.*
1 avenue Camoëns, Paris 16e, France.

Fesenkov, Vasily Grigoryevich; Soviet astronomer; b. 89; ed. Kharkov Univ.
From 23 Prof. Moscow Univ.; Dir. Astrophysical Inst. of Acad. of Sciences of Kazakh S.S.R. 42-; Chair. of Cttee. for Meteorites, Acad. of Sciences, U.S.S.R. 45-; Academician 35; mem. Acad. of Sciences Kazakh S.S.R. 46-; mem. of some Cttees. Int. Astronomical Union; Order of Lenin (twice); Order of Banner of Labour.
Publs. include *On the Origins of the Solar System* 60, *On the Density of Meteoric Material in Interplanetary Space* 61, *On the Nature and Origins of Comets* 62, *On the Optic Characteristics of the Dust Cloud around the Earth* 64.
U.S.S.R. Academy of Sciences, 14 Leninsky Prospekt, Moscow; and Ulitsa M. Ulianova 3, Moscow, U.S.S.R.

Fessard, Alfred Eugene, D.SC.; French neurophysiologist; b. 28 April 1900; ed. Paris Univ.
Prof. of Gen. Neurophysiology, Coll. de France 49-;

Dir. Inst. Marey (now Cen. d'Etudes de Physiologie Nerveuse, Cen. Nat. de Recherches Scientifiques) 47-; Pres. Nat. Sciences Section, Ecole Pratique des Hautes Etudes 51-; mem. Acad. des Sciences, Acad. de Médecine and of numerous foreign acads. and socs.; Prix Lallemand 35, Prix Roy-Vaucouloux 54; Officier Légion d'Honneur, Chevalier Ordre de Léopold II, Commandeur Palmes Académiques, Commandeur Ordre National du Mérite.

Publs. A large number of scientific works on neurology, electro-encephalography, electric fish, etc.

Office: 4 avenue Gordon Bennett, Paris 16e; Home: 51 rue Moliter, Paris 16e, France.

Telephone: 527-2837.

Fessler, Ernst; German banker; b. 23 Aug. 1908; ed. Univs. of Freiburg and Cologne.

Ministry of Justice 34; Supervisory Office for Banking 35-45; mem. Board of Management, Landeszentral-bank of Lower Saxony 48-51, Vice-Pres. 51-53; Vice-Pres. Landeszentralbank, North-Rhine Westphalia 53-56, Pres. 56-; mem. Central Bank Council Deutsche Bundesbank 56-; mem. Supervisory Board Stahlwerke Bochum, 66-; mem. Energy-Council of North-Rhine Westphalia 67-.

Poststrasse 56, 4005 Büderich b/Düsseldorf, German Federal Republic.

Fetscher, Iring, DR. PHIL.; German political scientist; b. 4 March 1922; ed. König-Georg-Gymnasium, Dresden, Eberhard-Karls-Universität, Tübingen, Université de Paris, and Johann Wolfgang Goethe-Universität, Frankfurt.

Editor *Marxismusstudien* 56-; radio commentator on political, philosophical and sociological questions; Prof. of Political Science, Johann Wolfgang Goethe-Universität, Frankfurt 63-, Dir. of Inst. of Political Science.

Publs. include *Comte, Rede über den Geist des Positivismus* 56, *Von Marx zur Sowjetideologie* 56, 63, *Über dialektischen und historischen Materialismus* (Commentary of Stalin) 56, 62, *Rousseaus politische Philosophie* 60, *Der Marxismus, seine Geschichte in Dokumenten* Vol I 62, Vol. II 64, Vol. III 65, *Marx-Engels Studienausgabe* 4 vols. 66, *Introduction to Hobbes' Leviathan* 66, *Karl Marx und der Marxismus* 67, *Der Rechtsradikalismus der Gegenwert* 67.

Institut für Politikwissenschaft, Gräfstrasse 39, 6 Frankfurt am Main, German Federal Republic.

Telephone: 52-15-42.

Feuillère, Edwige; French actress; b. 29 Oct. 1910; ed. Conservatoire National de Paris.

Appeared for two years at the Comédie Française, at Théâtre National Populaire 65; has played leading parts in *La dame aux camélias, Sodome et Gomorrhe, L'Aigle à deux têtes, Partage de Midi, La Parisienne, Phèdre, Constance, Rodogune, La Liberté est un dimanche, Pour Lucrèce, Lucy Crown, Eve et Line, La Folle de Chaillot;* films include *Sans Lendemain, De Mayerling à Sarajevo, J'étais une aventurière, L'Idiot, Olivia, Cap de l'Espérance, Adorables créatures, Le Blé en herbe, Les Fruits de L'été, En Cas de Malheur, La Vie à Deux, Les Amours Célèbres, Le Crime ne paie pas;* Chevalier de la Légion d'Honneur, Commandeur des Arts et Lettres.

19 rue Eugène Manuel, Paris 16e, France.

Feynman, Richard Phillips, PH.D.; American physicist; b. 11 May 1918; ed. Massachussetts Inst. of Technology and Princeton Univ.

Member staff atomic bomb project, Princeton 42-43, Los Alamos 43-45; Assoc. Prof. of Theoretical Physics, Cornell Univ. 45-50; Prof. of Theoretical Physics, Calif. Inst. of Technology 50-; mem. American Physical Soc., American Asscn. for Advancement of Science; Foreign mem. Royal Soc. (U.K.); Einstein Award 54; Nobel Prize for Physics 65.

Physics Department, California Institute of Technology, Pasadena, California 91109, U.S.A.

Feyzioğlu, Turhan, LL.D.; Turkish university professor and politician; b. 19 Jan. 1922; ed. Galatasaray Lycée, Istanbul Univ., and Ecole Nationale d'Administration, Paris.

Assistant Prof. Ankara Political Science School 45-47, Assoc. Prof. 47-54; Research, Nuffield Coll., Oxford 54; Co-editor *Forum* 54-58; Prof. Ankara Univ. 55; Dean, Political Science School, Ankara 56; M.P. 57, 61, 65-; mem. Nat. Exec. Cttee. Republican People's Party 57-61, Vice-Pres. 65, 66; Pres. Middle East Technical Univ. 60; mem. Constituent Assembly 60; Minister of Education 60; Minister of State 61; Deputy Prime Minister 62-63; mem. Turkish High Planning Council 61-63; Turkish Rep. Consultative Assembly Council of Europe 64, 65, 66; leader Reliance Party 67-.

Publs. *Administrative Law* 47, *Judicial Review of Unconstitutional Laws* 51, *Les Parties Politiques en Turquie* 53, *The Reforms of the French Higher Civil Service* 55, *Democracy and Dictatorship* 57.

Office: T.B.M.M., Ankara; Home: 6 Sokak 41, Bahçelievler, Ankara, Turkey.

Telephone: 131226 (Home).

fforde, Sir Arthur Frederic Brownlow, Kt., G.B.E., M.A., LL.D.; British solicitor and educationist; b. 23 Aug. 1900; ed. Rugby School, and Trinity Coll., Oxford.

Admitted as solicitor 25; partner Linklaters and Paines, London 28-48; mem. Council of Law Society 37-48; Deputy Dir.-Gen. Ministry of Supply 40-41; Under-Sec. Ministry of Supply 43; Under-Sec. Treasury 44-45; Headmaster Rugby School 48-57; Chair. Board of Governors, B.B.C. 57-64, Central Board of Finance, Church of England 60-65; Dir. Equity and Law Life Assurance, Westminster Bank.

Wall's End, Wonersh, Surrey, England.

Fidel Durón, Jorge; Honduran diplomatist and politician; b. 02; ed. Instituto Nacional de Honduras, and Loyola Univ. New Orleans.

Chancellor New Orleans 28-30; Sec., Managua 37-41, Port-au-Prince 41-42, Rio de Janeiro 42-45, San Francisco 45, UN 45-48; Head, Office of Strategic Materials 42; Del. to UN 46, 48, 54; Rector Universidad de Honduras 48-54; Minister of Foreign Affairs 64-65; Pres. Honduras Press Asscn. 56-57; journalist and writer; numerous decorations; Nat. Party.

749 La Leona, Tegucigalpa, Honduras.

Fieandt, Berndt Rainer v.; Dr. h.c.; Finnish banker; b. 26 Dec. 1890.

Gen. Man. Nordiska Föreningsbanken, Helsinki 24, Asst. Chief Gen. Man. 31, Chief Gen. Man. 45-55; Gov. Bank of Finland 55-57; Gov. for Finland Int. Monetary Fund 55-58; Del. for Finland to World Economic Conf., London 33; Minister of Supply 39-40; Prime Minister 57-58; Gov. for Finland Int. Bank for Reconstruction and Development 58-65.

Merikatu 7, Helsinki, Finland.

Field, Henry, B.A., M.A., D.SC.; American anthropologist; b. 15 Dec. 1902; ed. Eton Coll. and New Coll., Oxford.

Asst. Curator of Physical Anthropology, Field Museum of Natural History (Chicago) 26-34, Curator 34-41; engaged in Govt. research work in Washington 41-45; Research on Anthropology of S.W. Asia 46-47; Univ. of Calif. African Expedn. 47-48; Peabody Museum-Harvard Expedn. to Near East 50 and West Pakistan 55; Research Fellow, Peabody Museum, Harvard 50-; Adjunct Prof. of Anthropology, Univ. of Miami 66-.

Publs. *Arabs of Central Iraq, their History, Ethnology and Physical Characters* 35, *Contributions to the Anthropology of Iran* 39, *The Anthropology of Iraq, Part I:* No. 1 40, Nos. 2-3 49, *Part II,* No. 1 51, Nos. 2, 3 52, *Contributions to the Anthropology of the Faiyum, Sinai, Sudan and Kenya* 52, *The Track of Man* 53, *Contributions to the Anthropology of the Caucasus* 53, *Biblio-*

graphy on S.W. Asia, I-VII 53-64, *Ancient and Modern Man in S.W. Asia* (vol. I) 56, (vol. II) 61, *Anthropological Reconnaissance in W. Pakistan* 59, *North Arabian Desert Archaeological Survey* 25-50, 60, "M" Project for F.D.R.: *Studies on Migration and Settlement* 62.
Office: Peabody Museum, Cambridge 38, Mass.; Home: 3551 Main Highway, Coconut Grove, Miami 33, Fla., U.S.A.
Telephone: Highland 3-8306.

Field, Winston Joseph, C.M.G., M.B.E.; Rhodesian farmer and politician; b. 6 June 1904; ed. Bromsgrove School, England.
Went to Rhodesia 21; Pres. Rhodesia Tobacco Asscn. 38-40; Military Service, rose to rank of Major 40-45; mem. Fed. Parl. and Leader of the Opposition 58-62; M.P., S. Rhodesia Legislative Assembly; Prime Minister and Minister of the Public Service, Southern Rhodesia Dec. 62-April 64.
Karimba Farm, Box 51, Marandellas, Rhodesia.

Fierlinger, Zdeněk; Czechoslovak diplomatist and politician; b. 11 July 1891; ed. Commercial Coll., Olomouc, Moravia.
Joined Ministry of Foreign Affairs after First World War; later Minister Plenipotentiary in the Hague, Bucharest, Washington, Geneva, Berne, Vienna and Moscow; Prime Minister 45-46; Deputy to Nat. Assembly 45-; Deputy Prime Minister 46-47, 48-53; Dir. of Administration of State Office for Ecclesiastical Affairs 50-53; Pres. of the Nat. Assembly 53-64; Chair. Central Cttee. of Czechoslovak-Soviet Friendship Union 64-; mem. of the Presidium of the Central Cttee. of the C.P. of Czechoslovakia until 66; Klement Gottwald Order 51, 61; Order of 25th February 1948 49.
c/o Central Committee Czechoslovak-Soviet Friendship Union, Smetanovo nábr. 18, Staré Město, Prague 1, Czechoslovakia.

Fieser, Louis Frederick, A.B., PH.D.; American chemist; b. 7 April 1899; ed. Williams College and Harvard University.
Travelling Fellow to Univs. of Frankfurt-on-Main and Oxford 25; Assoc. and Assoc. Prof. at Bryn Mawr 25-30; Asst. Prof. Harvard 30-34; Assoc. Prof. 34-37; Prof. 37-39; Sheldon Emery Prof. of Organic Chemistry 39-; mem. Nat. Acad.; received K. Berkham Judd prize 41; Hon. D. Pharm. (Paris); Hon. D.Sc. (Williams Coll.).
Publs. *Experiments in Organic Chemistry* 35, *Natural Products Related to Phenanthrene*, 3rd edn. (with Mary Fieser) 49, *Organic Chemistry* (with Mary Fieser) 44.
27 Pinehurst Road, Belmont, Massachusetts, U.S.A.

Figgures, Frank Edward, C.B., C.M.G.; British civil servant; b. 5 March 1910; ed. Oxford and Yale Univs.
Called to Bar 36; Mil. Service (R.A.) 40-46; Treasury 46-; Dir. Trade and Finance, O.E.E.C. 48-51; Under-Sec. Treasury 55-60; Sec.-Gen. European Free Trade Asscn. (EFTA) 60-65; Third Sec. Treasury 65-.
Treasury, Great George Street, London, S,W.1. England.

Figini, Luigi; Italian architect; b. 27 Jan. 1903; ed. Politecnico di Milano.
Active collaborator with *Gruppo 7* of Milan, later with *Architetti di Quadrante;* collaborates mainly with Gino Pollini; mem. Accad. de S. Luca; numerous prizes.
Major works: numerous offices, villas, artists' studios and factories including Offices for De Angeli Frua, Milan 31; Ina Casa quarter Via Harrar, Milan 51, drawings for Borgo Porto Conte 51, House in Via Circo, Milan 56, working on church SS. Giovanni e Paolo 66.
Publs. *L'elemento verde e l'abitazione* 50, and numerous articles in architectural magazines.
Studio: Via Manin 3, Milan; Home: Via Perrone di S. Martino 8, Milan, Italy.

Figueiredo, Fidelino de; Portuguese writer and university professor; b. 89.
Dir. Bibliotheca Nacional 18 and 27; Deputy 18; exiled

for political reasons 27; Prof. successively at Univs. of Madrid 27, California 31, Columbia 31, Santiago 32, California 37, São Paulo 38-54, and Rio de Janeiro 40; Pres. P.E.N. Club 44; mem. Madrid Acad. de Historia, Acad. Brasileira de Letras, Acad. de Historia de Buenos Aires, Acad. Argentina de Letras, Hispanic Society of America, Bavarian Acad. of Sciences; Hon. D. ès L. (São Paulo); awarded several decorations.
Publs. include: *A critica litteraria como sciencia* 12, *Historia da Litteratura romantica* 13, *Historia da Litteratura Realista* 14, *Historia da Litt. Classica* 17-22, *Estudos de Litteratura* 15-51, *Sob a cinza do tedio* 25, *As duas Hespanhas* 32, *Pyrene* 35, *Aristarchos* 39, *Ultimas aventuras* 41, *Anthero* 42, *Cultura intervallar* 45, *Um colleccionador de angustias* 51, *Musica e Pensamento* 54, *Um Homem na sua humanidade* 56, *O Mêdo da Historia* 57, *Dialogo ao Espelho* 57, *Entre dois Universos* 59, *Ideario Critico de Fidelino de Figueiredo* (anthology) 62, *Symbolos y Mythos* 64.
Rua Duarte Lobo 32, Lisbon 5, Portugal.

Figueres Ferrer, José; Costa Rican politician; b. 25 Sept. 1906; ed. Costa Rica, Mexico Univs., Massachusetts Inst. of Technology.
Coffee planter and rope maker in Costa Rica until 42; exiled to Mexico 42-44; became Junta Pres. of the Repub. after 48, resigned 49; worked on economic problems 49-52; Pres. 53-58; Visiting Prof., Harvard Univ. 63-64; Pres. Nat. Liberation Party.
Publ. *Cartas a un Ciudadano*, and numerous articles.
Apdo. 4484, San José, Costa Rica.

Figueroa, Ana; Chilean educationalist and international civil servant; b. 07; ed. Public High School, Santiago, State Univ., Santiago, and Columbia Univ., New York.
Teacher of English and Philosophy, High Schools, Chile 29-38, Principal 38-45; Gen. Supervisor for Secondary Educ. in Chile 47-49; Head of Dept. for Women, Ministry of External Relations 49-50; Perm. Alt. Del. of Chile to UN 50-52; Chief, Women's and Young Workers' Div., Int. Labour Office 54-59, Asst. Dir.-Gen. ILO Feb. 60-67.
Publs. *Educación Sexual en los Colegios Secundarios, Características de la Educación Secundaria en los Estados Unidos, Educación para la Ciudadanía.*
Home: 50 Résidence Moillebeau, Geneva, Switzerland.

Filatov, Antonin Nikolayevich; Soviet surgeon and haemotologist; b. 1902; ed. Moscow Univ.
Intern, Research Assoc. Inst. of Medicine 25-36; Asst. Prof. 36-39; Asst. Prof. Inst. of Postgraduate Medical Training, Leningrad 39-42; Deputy Dir. and Head of Research Inst. of Blood Transfusion, Leningrad 42-; Corresp. mem. U.S.S.R. Acad. of Medical Sciences 53-; mem. Int. Asscn. of Surgeons, Int. Soc. of Haemotologists; mem. Board U.S.S.R. and R.S.F.S.R. Socs. of Surgeons; Hon. mem. Pirogov Surgical Soc.; Order of Red Star; Badge of Honour; Red Banner of Labour; State Prize 53; Merited Scientist R.S.F.S.R.
Publs. About 200 works on surgical treatment of vascular derangements, transplantation and substitution of tissues and organs, application of biological haennostatic methods.
Institute of Blood Transfusion, R.S.F.S.R. Ministry of Public Health, 2nd Sovietskaya Street, Leningrad, U.S.S.R.

Filbinger, Hans Karl, D. IUR.; German lawyer and politician; b. 15 Sept. 1913; ed. Albert-Ludwigs-Univ., Freiburg im Breisgau, Ludwig-Maximilians-Univ., Munich, and Univ. de Paris à la Sorbonne.
Teacher, Univ. of Freiburg 37-40; War Service and Prisoner-of-War 40-46; lawyer, Freiburg 46-60; mem. Landtag of Baden-Württemberg 60-; Minister of Interior, Baden-Württemberg 60-66; Minister-Pres. of Baden-Württemberg Dec. 66-; mem. Comm. on Decartelisation Questions 47; Founder mem. German-

French Soc., Freiburg, Soc. for Supra-national Co-operation; mem. NATO Parl. Conf.; Chair. South Baden Christian Democrat (C.D.U.) Federation; Grosses Verdienstkreuz and other awards.
Freiburg-Günterstal (Breisgau), Riedbergstrasse 26, German Federal Republic.

Filip, Jan, PH.D., D.SC.; Czechoslovak historian; b. 25 Dec. 1900; ed. Charles Univ., Prague.
Professor of Pre-History and of Early History, Charles Univ.; corresp. mem. of the Czechoslovak Acad. of Sciences 52, Academician 55; Chair. History Section of the Czechoslovak Acad. of Sciences 55-57; Vice-Pres. Acad. of Sciences 57-61, mem. Presidium 62-; Dir. Archaeological Inst., Acad. of Sciences 63-; Pres. Int. Union of Prehistoric and Protohistoric Sciences 63-; Laureate of the State Prize 57; Order of Labour 61; foreign mem. Royal Danish Acad. of Sciences and Art 65; Polish Order of the Gold Cross 65.
Publs. *Historic Beginnings of the Český ráj, an area in North-Eastern Bohemia, Pre-history of Czechoslovakia, The Beginnings of Slav Settlements in Czechoslovakia, The Celts in Central Europe, The Urnfields in Bohemia, Celtic Civilization and its Heritage.*
Archaeological Institute, Letenská 4, Prague 1, Czechoslovakia.

Filippov, Ivan Filippovich; Soviet diplomatist; b. 1907; ed. Moscow Inst. of History and Philosophy.
Journalist, Chief Tass office in Berlin 39-41; Diplomatic Service 47-; Deputy Head Press Dept. Foreign Ministry; Counsellor at Soviet Embassies in Hungary and Finland; Amb. to Luxembourg 68-.
U.S.S.R. Embassy, Luxembourg.

Filippov, Vasily Rodionovich; Soviet politician; b. 13; ed. Buryat-Mongolian Zoo-Veterinary Inst. and Kharkov Veterinary Inst.
Assistant Dir., later Dir. Buryat-Mongolian Zoo-Veterinary Inst. 47-58; Chair. of Council of Ministers of Buryat A.S.S.R. 58-60; First Sec. Buryat Regional Cttee. of C.P.S.U. 60-62; Alt. mem. Central Cttee. of C.P.S.U.; Deputy to U.S.S.R. Supreme Soviet; Rector Buryat Agricultural Inst. 62-.
Buryat Agricultural Institute, 16 Pushkin Street, Ulan-Ude, Buryat A.S.S.R., U.S.S.R.

Filliozat, Jean, D. en MED., D. ès L.; French professor; b. 4 Nov. 1906; ed. Univ. of Paris.
Dept. of Manuscripts, Nat. Library, Paris 36-41; Lecturer in Modern Indian Languages, Ecole Nat. des Langues Orientales 37-39; temporary Lecturer, Ecole Pratique des Hautes Etudes 37-39, and 41; Dir. of Studies, Indian Philology 41-; Prof. Coll. de France 52-; Dir. Institut français d'Indologie, Pondicherry 55-, Ecole française d'Extrême-Orient, Paris 56-; mem. Académie des Inscriptions et Belles Lettres 66-; Sec. Société Asiatique de Paris.
Publs. *Etude de démonologie indienne, Le Kumaratantra de Ravana* 37, *Catalogue du fonds sanskrit de la Bibliothèque nationale* 41, *Magie et médecine* 43, *Fragments de textes koutchéens de médecine et de magie* 48, *La doctrine classique de la médecine indienne, ses origines et ses parallèles grecs* 49, *L'Inde classique, Manuel des Etudes indiennes* (in collaboration) 47-53, *Inde, nation et traditions* 61.
35 rue François Rolland, 94-Nogent s/Marne, France.

Finch, William G. H.; American radio engineer; b. 28 June 1895; ed. Woodward High School, Cincinnati, Marconi Inst. N.Y., and Columbia Univ.
With Cleveland Illuminating Co. 16-17; Nat. District Telegraph Co. (N.Y.) 17-19 and Royal Indemnity Co. 19-21; Radio Engineering Editor *Int. News Service* 21-; established first radiotypewriter press circuit between New York and Chicago 32, between New York and Havana 33; Chief Radio Consulting Engineer and Technical Dir. Hearst Newspapers; Chief Engineering

Sec. Amer. Radio News Corp. 29-34; Asst. Chief Fed. Communications Comm. 34-35; Founder and Pres. Finch Telecommunications Inc. 35-41; Chief Engineer 74th Congress Investigation Cttee.; served U.S. Navy 41-44 and 49, now Special Asst. Electronics to Asst. Chief Bureau of Shipping for Electronics; inventor automatic highspeed radio printing system, radio relay and recorder, and high fidelity transmission system; holds 160 patents; mem. Int. Radio Consulting Cttee., Tech. Commission on radio and cable communications to Amer. Publishers Asscn. 24-; Fellow A.I.E.E., etc. Legion of Merit, etc.
Home: "Elfin", Newtown, Conn., U.S.A.; Office; Office of Naval Research, Department of the Navy, Washington D.C., U.S.A.

Fineberg, Evgeny Lvovich; Soviet physicist; b. 1912; ed. Moscow Univ.
Postgraduate, Moscow Univ. 35-38; Research Assoc., Lebedev Inst. of Physics U.S.S.R. Acad. of Sciences 38-, Head of Sector 52-; Lecturer, Asst. Prof. Moscow Power Inst. 35-39; Prof. Gorky Univ. 44-45; Prof. Moscow Engineering Physics Inst. 46-54; Corresp. mem. U.S.S.R. Acad. of Sciences 66-.
Publs. Works on radiophysics, nuclear physics, cosmic rays, statistical acoustics.
U.S.S.R. Academy of Sciences, 14 Leninsky Prospekt, Moscow, U.S.S.R.

Fini, Leonor; Italian painter; b. 30 Aug. 1918; ed. Trieste.
Attached to Iolas Gallery, Paris and New York; numerous one-man exhbns. in Paris, Rome, London, New York, retrospective exhbn. Knokke-le-Zoute, Belgium 65; created numerous décors for La Scala, Milan, Paris Opera, Comédie française, Compagnie Madeleine Renaud, Jean-Louis Barrault etc.; has participated in numerous group exhbns. including Venice Biennale and Salon de Mai, Paris; has illustrated numerous books; Dott. h.c. Free Univ. of Trieste.
8 rue de la Vrillière, Paris 1er, France.

Finlay, Allan Martyn, PH.D., LL.M.; New Zealand lawyer and politician; b. 1 Jan. 1912; ed. Otago Boys High School, Otago Univ., London School of Economics and Harvard Law School.
Research Asst., League of Nations 38; Private Sec. to various N.Z. Govt. Ministers 39-43; M.P. 46-49, 63-; Dir. Tasman Empire Airways Ltd. 58-61; Vice-Pres. N.Z. Labour Party 56-59, Pres. 60-.
Publs. *Third Party Contract* 39, *Social Security in New Zealand* 40.
6, Beckham Place, Auckland, C.3., New Zealand.
Telephone: 20-510.

Finletter, Thomas K(night), B.A., LL.B., LL.D.; American lawyer; b. 11 Nov. 1893; ed. Episcopal Acad., Philadelphia, and Univ. of Pennsylvania.
Special Asst. to U.S. Sec. of State, Washington 41-44; Consultant U.S. del. to U.N. Conf. San Francisco 45; Chair. President's Air Policy Comm. 47; Min.-in-Charge Economic Co-operation Admin. Mission to U.K. 48-49; Sec. of the Air Force 50-53; partner, Coudert Bros. (lawyers), New York 26-41, 44-48, 49-50, 53-; U.S. Perm. Rep. to NATO 61-July 65.
Publs. *Principles of Corporate Reorganisation* 37, *Cases on Corporate Reorganisation* 38, *Law of Bankruptcy Reorganisation* 39, *Can Representative Government do the Job?* 45, *Power and Policy* 54, *Foreign Policy: The Next Phase* 58, *Foreign Policy: The Next Phase, the 1960s* 61.
151 East 79 Street, New York City, U.S.A.

Finley, David Edward, A.B., LL.B.; American museum director (retired); b. 13 Sept. 1890; ed. Univ. of South Carolina and George Washington Law School.
U.S. Army 17-18; Asst. Counsel, War Finance Corpn. 21-22; mem. War Loan Staff, U.S. Treasury 22-27;

Special Asst. to Sec. of Treasury 27-32; Dir. Nat. Gallery of Art 38-56; Vice-Chair. American Comm. for Protection and Salvage of Artistic and Historic Monuments in War Areas 43-46; Pres. American Asscn. of Museums 45-49; mem. The Comm. of Fine Arts 43-63, Chair. 50-63; Chair. Nat. Trust for Historic Preservation 47-62, Chair. Emeritus 62, Hon. Trustee 64-; Trustee, Corcoran Gallery of Art 57-; mem. Smithsonian Art Comm.; mem. National Portrait Gallery Comm. 63-; hon. mem. American Inst. of Architects; Theodore Roosevelt Distinguished Service Medal 57; Hon. D. Litt. (Univ. of South Carolina), Hon. LL.D. (George Washington Univ.), Hon. L.H.D. (Georgetown Univ.), Hon. D.F.A. (Yale).
Office: Transportation Building, 17th and H Streets, Washington, D.C.; Home: 3318 "O" Street, Washington, D.C. 20007, U.S.A.
Telephone: Fed. 8-1093.

Finley, James Danielly, B.S.; American textile exec.; b. 14 July 1916; ed. Georgia Inst. of Technology and Harvard Business School.
Military Service, Second World War; Textile Engineer, Firestone Tyre and Rubber Co.; joined J. P. Stevens and Co., Inc. 45, Dept. Man., Woollen and Worsted Div. 51-56, Asst. to Vice-Pres. for Sales and Merchandising, Cotton Div. 56-58, Vice-Pres. (of Company) 58-61, Vice-Pres. in Charge of Cotton Div. Sales and Merchandising 61, mem. Exec. Cttee. 59, Exec. Vice-Pres. and mem. Mfg. Advisory Cttee. 64-65, Chair. of the Board July 65-.
Office: J. P. Stevens and Co., Inc., 1460 Broadway, New York, N.Y. 10036; Home: 12 Blossom Cove Road, Red Bank, N.J., U.S.A.

Finney, Albert; British actor; b. 9 May 1936; ed. Salford Grammar School and Royal Academy of Dramatic Art.
Birmingham Repertory Co. 56-58; Shakespeare Memorial Theatre Co. 59; Nat. Theatre 65.
Plays acted in include: *Julius Caesar, Macbeth, Henry V, The Beaux Stratagem, The Alchemist, The Lizard on the Rock, The Party, King Lear, Othello, A Midsummer Night's Dream, The Lily-White Boys, Billy Liar, Luther, Much Ado About Nothing, Armstrong's Last Goodnight, Miss Julie, Black Comedy, Love for Love, A Flea in her Ear.*
Films acted in include: *The Entertainer, Saturday Night and Sunday Morning, Tom Jones, Night Must Fall, Two for the Road;* Directed and acted in *Charlie Bubbles.*
c/o London International, Park House, Park Street, London, W.1, England.

Finniss, Guillaume Max, D.C.L.; French civil servant; b. 4 Oct. 1909; ed. Lycée Buffon, and Faculté de Droit, Paris, Ecole des Hautes Etudes Commerciales.
Inspector of Industry and Commerce 47; Technical Adviser to Sec. of State for Commerce 48-49; Dir. Inst. of Industrial Property 50-65; Pres. Cttee. of Co-ordination for the harmonization of legislative procedures in Industrial Property in the countries of European Econ. Community 59-; Pres., Dir.-Gen. Int. Patent Inst. 56-; Pres. Council of Europe 60-; Officier de la Légion d'Honneur, Commandeur du Mérite commercial, du Mérite artisanal, Grand Officier de l'ordre du Nichan Iftikhar, Commandeur de Saint Charles, du Mérite de la République Italienne, d'Orange-Nassau, de la Couronne de chêne, du Ouissan Alaouite, de la Couronne de Belgique.
97 Nieuwe Parklaan, The Hague, Netherlands; 40 blvd. des Invalides, Paris 7e, France.

Finniston, Harold Montague, PH.D.; British metallurgist; b. 15 Aug. 1912; ed. Allen Glen's School, Glasgow, Glasgow Univ. and Royal Coll. of Science and Technology, Glasgow.
Joined Stewarts & Lloyds 34; Chief Research Officer, Scottish Coke Research Cttee. 37; metallurgist, Atomic

Energy of Canada, Chalk River 45-46; U.K. Atomic Energy Authority, Harwell 48-58; Research Dir. C. A. Parsons & Co. and Man. Dir. Int. Research and Devt. Co. Ltd. 59-67; Deputy Chair.-Technical, British Steel Corpn. 67-; mem. Board Nat. Research Devt. Corpn.; Dir. Int. Research Devt. Co. Ltd.; Assoc. of Royal Coll. of Science and Technology; Fellow Inst. of Metallurgists; Hon. D.Sc. (Strathclyde) 68.
British Steel Corporation, 22 Kingsway, London, W.C.2; Home: Flat 11, Imperial Court, Prince Albert Road, St. John's Wood, London, N.W.8, England.
Telephone: 01-242-1616 (Office).

Firestone, Harvey Samuel, Jr. (brother of Raymond C. Firestone, *q.v.*): American businessman; b. 20 April 1898; ed. Asheville School (Asheville, N.C.), Princeton Univ.
With Firestone Tire and Rubber Co. 20-, Vice-Pres. and Man. Firestone Steel Products Co. 22-26, Pres. Firestone Plantations Co. 32-55, Dir. and Chair. 55-, Vice-Pres. Firestone Tire and Rubber Co. 29-41, Pres. 41-48, Chair. 48-66, Hon. Chair. and Dir. 66-; Vice-Pres. and Dir. Fabrik für Firestone Produkte, A.G. (Switzerland); Dir. Firestone Hispania, S.A., Firestone International Co., Ravenna Arsenal Inc.; Chair. United Service Organizations Inc.; mem. Int. Devt. Advisory Board 50-59; Trustee U.S. Council of Int. Chamber of Commerce; Chair. Ohio Sesquicentennial Comm. 53; Sponsor Cttee. for Int. Economic Growth; Officier Légion d'Honneur; Commdr. Star of Africa (Liberia), White Rose of Finland, Isabel la Católica (Spain), Commdr. Cross of Merit of the Fed. Repub. of Germany, etc.
Publs. *The Romance and Drama of the Rubber Industry* 33, *The Story of Transportation* 33, *Man on the Move* 67.
Firestone Tire and Rubber Co., 1200 Firestone Parkway, Akron, Ohio 44317, U.S.A.
Telephone: 216-379-6312.

Firestone, Raymond Christy, B.A. (brother of Harvey S. Firestone, *q.v.*); American businessman; b. 6 Sept. 1908; ed. Princeton Univ.
Joined Sales Div., The Firestone Tire and Rubber Co. 33; Gen. Man. Memphis, Tenn. plant 36-37; Pres. Firestone Tire and Rubber Co. of Tennessee 37-49; Dir. The Firestone Tire and Rubber Co. 42-, Vice-Pres. (Research and Development) 49-54, Exec. Vice-Pres. 54-57, Pres. 57-64, Chair. Exec. Cttee. and Chief Exec. Officer 64-66, Chair of the Board 66-; Dir. The Firestone Bank; Vice-Pres. Board of Dirs. Nat. 4-H Service Cttee. 58-; mem. numerous civic and business orgs. and recipient of several awards including: Hon. LL.D. (Akron), Hon. D. Hum. (Univ. of Liberia).
Office: The Firestone Tire and Rubber Co., 1200 Firestone Parkway, Akron, Ohio 44317; Home: Lauray Farms, Bath, Ohio 44210, U.S.A.

Firkusny, Rudolf; American (b. Czechoslovak) pianist; b. 11 Feb. 1912; ed. Conservatoires of Music, Brno and Prague.
First appeared with Czechoslovak Philharmonic Orchestra 22; world-wide concert tours including tours of Europe 30-39, South America 43-, annual tours of Europe 50-.
Staatsburg, New York, U.S.A.

Firth, Raymond William, M.A., PH.D., F.B.A.; British social anthropologist; b. 25 March 1901; ed. Auckland Univ. Coll. and London School of Economics.
Field Research in Anthropology, Tikopia, British Solomon Islands Protectorate 28-29; Lecturer in Anthropology Univ. of Sydney 30-31, Acting Prof. 31-32; Lecturer in Anthropology London School of Economics 32-35, Reader 35-44, Prof. 44-68; Hon. Sec. Royal Anthropological Inst. 36-39, Pres. 53-55; research in peasant economics and anthropology in Malaya as Leverhulme Research Fellow 39-40; served with Naval Intelligence Div. Admiralty 41-44; Sec. of

Colonial Social Science Research Council Colonial Office 44-45; research surveys in West Africa 45, Malaya 47, New Guinea 51; field research in Tikopia 52, 63, 66; Visiting Prof. Univ. of Chicago 55; Fellow Center for Advanced Study in the Behavioral Sciences, Stanford, Calif. 59; Foreign Hon. mem. American Acad. of Arts and Sciences, American Philosophical Soc., Royal Soc. of New South Wales, Royal Soc. of New Zealand, Royal Danish Acad. of Sciences and Letters; Viking Fund Medal 59; Huxley Memorial Medal 59; Hon. Ph.D. Oslo 65, Hon. LL.D. Michigan 67.
Publs. *The Kauri Gum Industry* 24, *Primitive Economics of the New Zealand Maori* 29, *Art and Life in New Guinea* 36, *We, The Tikopia: A Sociological Study of Kinship in Primitive Polynesia* 36, *Human Types* 38, *Primitive Polynesian Economy* 39, *The Work of the Gods in Tikopia* 40, *Malay Fishermen: Their Peasant Economy* 46, *Elements of Social Organization* 51; Ed. *Two Studies of Kinship in London* 56, Ed. *Man and Culture: An Evaluation of the Work of Malinowski* 57, *Social Change in Tikopia* 59, *History and Traditions of Tikopia* 61, *Essays on Social Organisation and Values* 64, *Tikopia Ritual and Belief* 67.
London School of Economics and Political Science, Houghton Street, Aldwych, London, W.C.2, England. Telephone: 01-405-7686.

Firyubin, Nikolai Pavlovich; Soviet diplomatist; b. 1908; ed. Ordzhonikidze Aviation Inst., Moscow.
Member C.P.S.U. 29-; engineer, aircraft industry 35-38; party and Soviet work 38-53; Sec. Moscow Regional Cttee. C.P.S.U. 40-49; Diplomatic Service 53-, Minister-Counsellor, U.S.S.R. Embassy, Czechoslovakia 53, Ambassador 54-55, to Yugoslavia 55-57; Dep. Minister of Foreign Affairs U.S.S.R. 57-; Cand. mem. Central Cttee. C.P.S.U. 56-66; Orders of Lenin, Red Banner of Labour, Great Patriotic War (1st Class), Red Star, etc.
Ministry of Foreign Affairs, 32-34 Smolenskaya-Sennaya ploshchad, Moscow, U.S.S.R.

Fischer, Annie (wife of Aladár Tóth, *q.v.*); Hungarian pianist; b. 14; ed. Budapest Acad. of Music.
Studies with Arnold Székely and Ernő von Dohnányi; concert début in Beethoven's C Major Concerto 22; numerous concerts, tours and recordings 26-; 1st Prize, Int. Liszt Competition, Budapest 33; Kossuth Prizes 49, 55 and 65; Hon. Prof. of Acad. of Music, Budapest 65.
Szent Istvan Park 14, Budapest XIII, Hungary.

Fischer, Gottfried Bermann, DR. MED.; American (b. German) publisher; b. 31 July 1897; ed. Univs. of Breslau, Freiburg and Munich.
Assistant Surgeon in Berlin hospital 23-25; with S. Fischer Verlag 25-, Owner and Pres. 34, firm moved to Vienna 36, to Stockholm 38; emigrated to U.S.A. 40, founded L. B. Fischer Corpn., New York (now S. Fischer Corpn.); re-established S. Fischer Verlag in Frankfurt/Main 50, now Chair. of Board S. Fischer Verlag GmbH; founded Fischer Bücherei, Frankfurt (paperback publishers) 52; Autobiography *Fischer Verlag* 67; Editor *Neue Rundschau* (literary periodical); Goethe Plakette (Frankfurt) 57, Grosses Bundesverdienstkreuz 58.
6 Frankfurt/Main, Mainzer Landstrasse 10-12, German Federal Republic, and Casa Fischer, Camaiore (Lucca), Italy.
Telephone: Camaiore 68088.

Fischer, John; American editor; b. 27 April 1910; ed. Oklahoma Univ. and Oxford Univ.
Reporter, *Daily Oklahoma* 32-33; U.S. Dept. of Agriculture 36; Washington Corresp. for Associated Press 37; Board of Econ. Warfare, Intelligence Div. 39; Chief of Econ. Intelligence, Lend-Lease for Foreign Econ. Admin., India 43; Assoc. Editor, *Harper's Magazine* 44-47, Editor-in-Chief Gen. Book Dept., Harper's 46; Editor-in-Chief *Harper's Magazine* 53-67,

Contrib. Editor July 67-, Vice-Pres. Harper & Row Inc., Dir. Harper Atlantic Sales Co.; Trustee, Univ. of Denver Social Science Foundation; mem. Exec. Cttee., American Soc. of Magazine Editors; Dir. h.c. Kenyon Coll. 53, Massachusetts Univ. 50, Bucknell Univ. 59.
Publs. *Why they Behave like Russians* (English title *Scared Men in the Kremlin*) 47, *Master Plan U.S.A.* 51, *The Stupidity Problem* 64.
Two, Park Avenue, New York, N.Y., U.S.A.

Fischer, Josef Ludvík, PH.D.; Czechoslovak university professor; b. 6 Nov. 1894; ed. Charles Univ., Prague.
Reader in Sociology and Philosophy, Masaryk Univ., Brno 27, Prof. of Philosophy 35 (removed from post by the Germans 41-45); Dean of Faculty of Philosophy 45; Rector of Palacký Univ., Olomouc 46-49; Prof. Masaryk Univ. 57-60, Prof. Palacký Univ. 68; mem. Int. Inst. of Sociology, Geneva, Royal Czech Soc. of Sciences, Czech Acad. of Sciences and Arts, Int. Soc. for Comparative Study of Civilizations, Salzburg, Leipzig Soc. Hannover, Editorial Board Indian Journal of Sociological Research.
Publs. Several books on various aspects of philosophy and sociology.
Olomouc, Dukelská 19, Czechoslovakia.
Telephone: 59454.

Fischer, Louis; American writer; b. 29 Feb. 1896; ed· Philadelphia School of Pedagogy.
School teacher to 17; served with British Army Canada, England, Egypt, Palestine and Syria 17-19; journalist 21-, free-lance corresp. in various countries for American and British periodicals; Research Assoc. Inst. for Advanced Study, Princeton, New Jersey 59-61, Princeton Univ. 61-.
Publs. *Oil Imperialism* 26, *The Soviets in World Affairs* (2 vols.) 30, *Why Recognise Russia?* 32, *Machines and Men in Russia* 33, *Soviet Journey* 35, *Why Spain Fights On* 37, *Men and Politics* (autobiography) 41, *Stalin and Hitler* 41, *Dawn of Victory* 42, *A Week with Gandhi* 43, *Empire* 43, *The Great Challenge* 46, *Gandhi and Stalin* 47, Editor *Thirteen Who Fled* 49, *The God that Failed* (one of 6 authors) 50, *The Life of Mahatma Gandhi* 50, *The Life and Death of Stalin* 52, *This is Our World* 56, *Russia Revisited* 57, *The Story of Indonesia* 59, *Russia. America and the World* 61, *The Life of Lenin* 65, *Fifty Years of Soviet Communism, an Appraisal.*
Woodrow Wilson School, Princeton Univ., Princeton, N.J.; Home: 42 South Stanworth Drive, Princeton, N.J., U.S.A.
Telephone: 609-921-6990.

Fischer, Paul; Danish diplomatist; b. 24 March 1919; ed. Lyceum Alpinum, Zurs, Switzerland and Univ. of Copenhagen.
Foreign Service 44-, Stockholm, The Hague, Ministry of Foreign Affairs 44-60; Ambassador to Poland 60-61; Perm. Under-Sec. of State for Foreign Affairs 61-; Commdr. Order of Dannebrog (1st Class).
Publ. *The European Coal and Steel Community* 51.
Ministry of Foreign Affairs, Christiansborg, Slot; Copenhagen K, Denmark.
Telephone: 150825.

Fischer-Dieskau, Dietrich; German singer; b. 28 May 1925; ed. high school in Berlin, singing studies with Prof. Georg Walter and Prof. Hermann Weissenborn.
Military service 43-45; prisoner of war in Italy until 47 First Lyric and Character Baritone, Berlin State Opera 48-; mem. Vienna State Opera Co. 57-; numerous concert tours in Europe and U.S.A.; has appeared at a number of festivals: Bayreuth, Salzburg, Lucerne, Montreux, Edinburgh, Vienna, Holland, Munich, Berlin, Coventry, etc.; mem. Akad. der Künste, Int. Mahler-Gesellschaft (Vienna) and German Section, Int. Music Council, Hon. mem. Wiener Konzerthausgesellschaft 63; Int. Recording Prizes 55, 57, 58, 60, 63, 64 and 65; Berlin

Kunstpreis 50, Mantua Golden Orpheus Prize 55; Bundesverdienstkreuz, 1st Class 58; Edison Prize 60, 62, 64 and 65; Mozart Medal 62; Golden Orpheus 67. Lindenallee 22, 1 Berlin 19, Germany.

Fish, Sir (Eric) Wilfred, C.B.E., M.D., CH.B., L.D.S.(Man.), D.D.SC. (Melbourne), D.D.SC. (Durham), D.SC. (London), F.D.S.R.C.S. (Eng.), F.R.C.S. (Eng.), F.D.S.R.C.P. and S., and H.D.D. (Glasgow), SC.D. (Dublin); British consulting dental surgeon; b. 30 Jan. 1894; ed. Kingswood, Owen's Coll., Manchester, Univ. Coll., London.
Fmr. Capt. R.A.M.C. and temporary Surgical Specialist Bombay Brigade; fmr. Hon. Civilian Consultant Royal Army Dental Corps, Hon. Consulting Dental Surgeon Royal Dental Hospital, London, and St. Mary's Hospital, London; Visiting Post-Graduate Lecturer, Dental Board of Victoria and S. Australia 35; John Tomes Prizeman, Royal Coll. of Surgeons 33; 1st Howard Mummery Prizeman 33; Dumville Surgical Prizeman, Manchester Univ. 16; Pres. XIth Int. Dental Congress, London 52; Colyer Gold Medal, Royal Coll. of Surgeons 62; Pres. Gen. Dental Council until 64; Hon. Fellow Royal Soc. of Medicine; hon. mem. British Dental Assen., Asociación Española de Odontologia, Zahnärztliche Gesellschaft, Vienna, Vereeniging van Nederlandsche Tandartsen, Svenska Tandlakaresellskapet, Danish Dental Assen.
Publs. *Parodontal Disease, Principles of Full Denture Prosthesis, Surgical Pathology of the Mouth.*
Hurst Lodge, Sandgate Lane, Storrington, Sussex, England.
Telephone: Storrington 2070.

Fishbein, Morris, M.D., B.S.; American physician; b. 22 July 1889; ed. Univ. of Chicago and Rush Medical Coll.
House Physician Durand Hospital of McCormick Inst. for Infectious Diseases 12-13; Asst. Editor *Journal of American Medical Assen.* 13-24, Editor 24-49; Prof. Emeritus, School of Medicine, Univ. of Chicago; Prof. Emeritus, Medical Coll., Univ. of Illinois; Consultant Medical Editor, Doubleday & Co., New York City; Medical Editor *Britannica Book of the Year*; Editor *Medical World News, World Wide Abstracts of General Medicine, Excerpta Medica*; Fellow, American Medical Assen., etc.
Publs. *Medical Writing: Its Art and Technic, Tonics and Sedatives, Handbook of Therapy, Your Weight and How to Control it, Why Men Fail* (with Dr. William A. White), *The Medical Follies, The New Medical Follies, Shattering Health Superstitions, The Human Body and its Care, An Hour on Health, Doctors and Specialists, Fads and Quackery in Healing, Modern Home Medical Adviser, Syphilis, Your Diet and Your Health, Do You Want to Become a Doctor? The National Nutrition, First Aid Training* (co-author), *Successful Marriage, Medical Uses of Soap, Doctors at War, Health and First Aid* (co-author), *Common Ailments of Man, Popular Medical Encyclopædia, A History of the American Medical Association, Handy Home Medical Adviser, Crusading Obstetrician* (with S. T. DeLee), *Medical Progress, Children for the Childless, New Advances in Medicine, Illustrated Medical and Health Encyclopaedia, Modern Marriage and Family Living, Modern Family Health Guide, Heart Care.*
5454 South Shore, Chicago 15, Ill., U.S.A.

Fisher, Adrian Sanford; American government official; b. 21 Jan. 1914; ed. Univs. of Princeton and Harvard.
U.S. Army service 42-46; Law Secretary to Associate Justices of U.S. Supreme Court 38-39; Attorney, Bonneville Power Admin. 39, Securities and Exchange Comm. 39-40, Tennessee Valley Authority 40-41; Asst. to Legal Adviser Dept. of State 41, Asst. Chief, Foreign Funds Control Div. 41-42; Solicitor, Dept. of Commerce 46-48; Gen. Counsel, Atomic Energy Comm. 48-49; Legal Adviser, Dept. of State 49-53; private legal

practice 53-54; Prof. of Int. Law and Trade, Georgetown Univ. 53-58; mem. U.S. Panel on Perm. Court of Arbitration 53-59; Vice-Pres. and Counsel, The Washington Post Co. 55-61; Dep. Dir. U.S. Arms Control and Disarmament Agency 61-.
U.S. Arms Control and Disarmament Agency, Washington 25, D.C., U.S.A.

Fisher, Ernest M(cKinley), A.M., PH.D., LL.D.; American economist; b. 15 May 1893; ed. Coe Coll. and Northwestern and Wisconsin Univs.
Instructor American Univ. Beirut 14-17, Wisconsin Univ. 19-22; dir. of Research Nat. Assen. of Real Estate Boards 23-26; Prof. of real estate management, Univ. of Michigan 26-34; economic adviser Federal Housing Admin. 34-40; Chair. Housing Census Advisory Cttee., Bureau of the Census 39-42, 59-; dir. of mortgage and real estate finance and dep. man. American Bankers Assen. 40-45; Prof. of Urban Land Economics, Columbia Univ. 45-61, Emer. 61-; Special Lecturer, School of Architecture 61-64; Special Lecturer in Planning, Yale Univ. 62-; Chair. Admin. Board and Dir. of the Institute for Urban Land Use and Housing Studies, Columbia Univ. 47-55; Consultant Board of Govs. Fed. Reserve System 50-53; Dir. First Fed. Savings and Loan Assen. of New York 54-; Consultant to Ford Foundation 61, 64-; and to Fed. Deposit Insurance Corpn. 65-; Consultant to Worcester County Inst. for Savings 55-, to Small Business Adminstration 66-67, to First Nat. Mortgage Bank Ltd., Nassau 66-67; mem. American Econ. Assen.; Fellow American Statistical Assen.; one-time Fellow American Geographical Soc. and American Assen. for the Advancement of Science.
Publs. *Advanced Principles of Real Estate Practice* 30; *European Housing Policy and Practice* (with Richard U. Ratcliff) 36, *Urban Real Estate Markets: Characteristics and Financing* 51, *Urban Real Estate* (with Robert Moore Fisher) 54, *The Mutual Mortgage Insurance Fund* (with Chester Rapkin) 56; Editor *Home Mortgage Lending, Home Mortgage Loan Manual*, etc.
199 Hillcrest Avenue, Leonia, New Jersey 07605, U.S.A.
Telephone: 201-944-3302.

Fisher, Harold Henry, A.B., L.H.D.; American historian; b. 15 Feb. 1890; ed. People's Acad., Vermont and Columbia Univs.
1st Lieut. 17, Capt. Field Artillery, American Expeditionary Force 18-19; Editorial writer *Washington Herald*, D.C., 19-20; Officer American Relief Admin. in U.S.A., Europe and Russia 20-24; Lecturer in History Stanford Univ. 24-33, Associate Prof. 33-36, Prof. 36-55; Dir. Hoover Library 24-55; Dir. Russian Research Inst. 30-52; Prof. San Francisco State Coll. 55-60, Univ. of California, Berkeley 60-61, Mills Coll. 61-64; Chair. Hoover Inst. 43-55; Dir. Civil Affairs Training School 43-45; Dir. Civil Communications Intelligence School 45-54; Dir. School of Naval Admin. 46-48; Chair. Pacific Council, Inst. of Pacific Relations 53-61; Editor *Far Eastern Survey.*
Publs. *Famine in Soviet Russia* 27, *America and the New Poland* 28, *Public Relations of the Commission for Relief in Belgium* 29, *The Bolshevik Revolution* 34, *The Bolsheviks and the World War* 40; *Tower to Peace* 45; *America and Russia in the World Community* 46; Editor *Out of My Past* (Count Kokovtsov's Memoirs) 35, *Testimony of Kolchak* 35, *Features and Figures of the Past* (V. I. Gurko) 39, *The Life of a Chemist* (V. N. Ipatieff) 46, *Communist Revolution* 55, *Soviet Russia and the West 1920-27* 57, Ed. and contributor *American Research on Russia* 59.
1331 Martin Avenue, Palo Alto, Calif., U.S.A.

Fisher, James Maxwell McConnell, M.A.; British ornithologist and writer; b. 3 Sept. 1912; ed. Eton Coll. and Magdalen Coll., Oxford.
Assistant Master, Bishop's Stortford Coll. 35-36;

Asst. Curator, Zoological Soc. of London 36-39; Research Zoologist, Oxford Univ. Bureau of Animal Population 40-43, Research Ornithologist, Edward Grey Inst. of Field Ornithology 44-46; an Ed. Collins' *New Naturalist* books 42-; Ed. Dir. Rathbone Books Ltd. 56-61, Aldus Books Ltd. 60-64; Deputy Chair. The National Parks Comm. 66-; mem. and fmr. Pres. Asscn. for Study of Animal Behaviour, British Ornithologists' Union, British Trust for Ornithology, Linnean Soc. of London, Royal Soc. for the Protection of Birds, Wildfowl Trust, Fauna Preservation Soc.; Corresp. Fellow, American Ornithologists' Union; Hon. mem. Danish Ornithological Soc.; Chair. Northamptonshire Naturalists' Trust; mem. of The Survival Service Comm. of the Int. Union for Conservation of Nature and Natural Resources; commentator and writer (over 1,000 radio and television programmes for B.B.C.).
Publs. *Birds as Animals* 39, *Watching Birds* 42, *Birds of the Village* 43, *Bird Recognition* 47-61, *The Fulmar* 52, *Nature Parliament* (with others) 52, *Birds of the Field* 53, *A Thousand Geese* (with Peter Scott) 53, *Fine Bird Books* (with others) 53, *Sea-Birds* (with R. M. Lockley) 54, *A History of Birds* 54, *Adventure of the World* 54, *Rockall* 56, *Wild America* (with R. T. Peterson) 55, *Adventure of the Sea* 56, *Shackleton* (with M. Fisher) 57, *Adventure of the Air* 58, *Nature* (ed.) 60, *The World of Birds* (with R. T. Peterson) 64; *The Migration of Birds* (with Crispen Fisher) 66, *Shell Nature Lovers' Atlas* 66, *The Shell Bird Book* 66, *Zoos of the World* 66, *Thorburns' Birds* 67, *The Red Book* 68; numerous scientific papers.
Ashton Manor, Northampton, England.
Telephone: Roade 277.

Fisher, William Bayne, B.A., DR. DE L'UNIV. (Paris); British university professor; b. 24 Sept. 1916; ed. Univs. of Manchester, Louvain, Caen and Paris.
Research Fellow 37-40; served in Royal Air Force 40-46, commissioned 41, O.C. R.A.F. Liaison Unit, Syria and Lebanon 44-45; Lecturer, Univ. of Manchester 46; Senior Lecturer, Dept. of Geography, Aberdeen Univ. 47-53; Reader and Head of Dept. of Geography, Univ. of Durham 54-56, Prof. 56-; Principal, Graduate Soc. 65-; Consultant, H.M. Govt., Govt. of Libya and Harvard Univ., U.S.A.; Leader Univ. Expedition to Libya 51. Editor Vol. I *The Cambridge History of Iran* 68.
Publs. *The Middle East—a Physical, Social and Regional Geography* 50, *Spain* (with H. Bowen-Jones) 58, *Malta* (with H. Bowen-Jones and J. C. Dewdney.)
Home: 42 South Street, Durham; Office: Science Labs., South Road, Durham and 38 Old Elvet, Durham, England.
Telephone: 4291 (Home); 4971 and 4350 (Office).

Fisher of Lambeth, Baron, cr. 61 (Life Peer); **Most Rev. and Rt. Hon. Geoffrey Francis Fisher,** P.C., D.D.; British ecclesiastic; b. 5 May 1887; ed. Marlborough Coll., Oxford Univ.
Assistant Master Marlborough Coll. 11-14; Headmaster Repton School 14-32; Bishop of Chester 32-39; Bishop of London 39-45; Dean of the Chapels Royal 39-45; Prelate of the Order of the British Empire 39-45; Archbishop of Canterbury, Primate of all England 45-61; Pres. World Council of Churches 48-54; Prelate of the Order of S. John of Jerusalem 46; Grand Cross of the Order of the Redeemer (Greece), of the Order of St. Olav (Norway) 47; Czechoslovak Order of the White Lion (2nd Class) 48; Royal Victorian Chain 49, Knight Grand Cross of the Royal Victorian Order 53; Hon. D.D. (Oxford, Cambridge, Edinburgh and Princeton Univs., Trinity Coll. Dublin, LL.D. (London, Pennsylvania, Columbia, British Columbia, Rikkyo, Yonsei, Yale and Manchester Univs.); D.Theol. (Theological Seminary of New York City) 57; LL.D. Assumption Univ. of Windsor, Canada.
Trent Rectory, Sherborne, Dorset, England.

Fisk, James Brown, B.S., PH.D.; American physicist; b. 30 Aug. 1910; ed. Mass. Inst. of Technology and Trinity Coll. Cambridge.
Jnr. Fellow of Society of Fellows, Harvard Univ. 36-38; Associate Prof. of Physics, Univ. of N. Carolina 38-39; electronics research engineer and later Asst. Dir Physical Research, Bell Telephone Laboratories 39-47; Dir. other cos.; Gordon McKay Prof. of Applied Physics, Harvard Univ. (resigned 49), Dir. Physical Research 49-52, Dir. of Research, Physical Sciences 52-54, Vice-Pres. Research 54-55, Exec. Vice-Pres. 55-59, Pres. 59-, Bell Telephone Laboratories, Dir. 55-; Fellow American Acad. of Arts and Sciences; mem. American Philosophical Soc.; mem. Nat. Acad. of Sciences; Fellow American Physical Soc.; Fellow Inst. of Electrical and Electronics Engineers; Dir. of Research Div., U.S. Atomic Energy Comm. (resigned 48); mem. Pres. Science Advisory Cttee. 52-60, Consultant 60-; mem. Gen. Advisory Cttee. to U.S. Atomic Energy Comm. 52-58; Dir. Sandia Corp., The Equitable Life Assurance, Soc. of the U.S., American Cyanamid Co., Trust Co. Nat. Bank; Hon. Sc.D. Carnegie Inst. of Technology 56, Williams Coll. 58, Newark Coll. of Engineering 59; Hon. M.A. Harvard Univ. 47; Hon. Sc.D. Columbia Univ. 60, Colby Coll. 62, New York Univ. 63; Hon. Dr. of Engineering Univ. of Michigan 63, Univ. of Akron 63; Life mem. Mass. Inst. of Technical Corp.; mem. Board of Overseers of Harvard Coll. 61-67; Trustee John Simon Guggenheim Memorial Foundation, Alfred P. Sloan Foundation; Dir. Cummins Engine Co.
Publs. Articles in *Proceedings of Royal Society* 33-34, *Physical Review* 34-40, *Bell System Technical Journal* 46.
Lees Hill Road, Basking Ridge, N.J., U.S.A.; Office: Bell Telephone Laboratories, Inc., Murray Hill, New Jersey 07974, U.S.A.
Telephone: 201-582-4471.

Fison, Rt. Rev. Joseph Edward, M.A., B.D.; British ecclesiastic; b. 18 March 1906; ed. Shrewsbury School, Queen's Coll. and Wycliffe Hall, Oxford.
Teacher, English Mission Coll., Cairo 30-33; Tutor-Chaplain, Wycliffe Hall, Oxford 34-37; Curate, St. Aldate's Church, Oxford 37-40; Chaplain to the Forces 40-45; Canon Residentiary, Rochester Cathedral 45-52, Canon Residentiary and Sub-Dean, Truro Cathedral, Rector of St. Mary, Truro 52-59, Vicar of St. Mary the Great with St. Michael, Cambridge 59-63, Hon. Canon of Ely Cathedral 60-63, Bishop of Salisbury 63-; Hon. D.D. (Aberdeen).
Publs. *The Blessing of The Holy Spirit* 50, *The Christian Hope* 54, *The Faith of the Bible* 57, *Fire Upon The Earth* 58.
South Canonry, The Close, Salisbury, Wilts., England.
Telephone: Salisbury 4031.

Fistoulari, Anatole; British conductor; b. 20 Aug. 1907; ed. Kiev, Berlin and Paris.
First Symphony Concert, Kiev 14, later conducted all over Russia; concerts in Western Europe 20; conducted Grand Opera Russe, Paris, with Chaliapin 31; conducted Ballet de Monte Carlo with Massine in England, France, Italy and U.S.A.; first symphony concert with London Symphony Orchestra 42, Principal Conductor, London Philharmonic Orchestra 43-44; founded London International Orchestra 46; numerous engagements in Europe, Israel, South Africa and the Americas; numerous recordings.
65 Redington Road, London, N.W.3, England.

Fitts, Dudley, A.B., LITT.D.; American writer and educator; b. 28 April 1903; ed. Harvard Univ.
English master and organist Choate School (Conn.) 26-41; Prof. of English, Phillips Acad., Andover, Mass. 41-; Visiting Lecturer in Comparative Literature, Harvard Univ. 63-; Fellow Jonathan Edwards Coll., Yale Univ. 64-; visiting Cttee. to Dept. of English, Harvard Univ. 66-; has frequently lectured, chiefly on classical literature, at Yale, Princeton, Bennington, New York Univs.,

etc., Exec. Cttee. Nat. Translation Centre 66-; Fellow American Acad. of Arts and Sciences; mem. Nat. Inst. of Arts and Letters; Editor *Yale Series of Younger Poets* 59-; mem. juries Nat. Book Award and Bollingen Foundation; Nat. Inst. of Arts and Letters Award 48; Democrat.
Publs. *Poems 1929-1936, Poems from the Greek Anthology, Sixty Poems of Martial* 67; translations: with Robert Fitzgerald *Oedipus Rex* and *Antigone* (Sophocles), *Alcestis* (Euripides); alone: *Lysistrata, Frogs, Birds, Thesmophoriazusae* (Aristophanes); Edited: *Antologia de la poesia americana contemporanea.*
23 Porter Road, Andover, Mass., U.S.A.

FitzGerald, Dennis A., B.S.A., M.S., PH.D.; American economist; b. 1 Jan. 1903; ed. Univ. of Saskatchewan, Iowa State Coll. and Harvard Univ.
Research economist, Brookings Inst. 33-35; U.S. Dept. of Agriculture, Principal Agricultural Economist 35-41, Head Admin. Officer, Production Div., Office of Agricultural Defence Relations 41-42, Chief Agricultural Economist, Bureau of Agricultural Economics 42, Asst. Dir., Office for Agricultural War Relations, Sec. of Food Requirements Cttee. 42-43, Deputy Dir., Food Production Admin. 43-45, Dir. Office of Requirements and Allocations 45-46, Sec. of Policy and Programme Cttee. of Dept. of Agriculture 46; Sec.-Gen. Int. Emergency Food Council 46-48; Dir. Office of Foreign Agricultural Relations U.S. Dept. of Agriculture 48-49; Dir. Food and Agriculture Div., Economic Co-operation Admin. 48-51; Asst. Administrator for Supply E.C.A. 51-52; Assoc. Deputy Dir. M.S.A. 52-53; Deputy Dir. Operations, Foreign Operations Admin. 53; Int. Co-operation Admin. (now Agency for Int. Devt.) 55-63; Senior Consultant to Managing Dir. UN Special Fund 65-.
Publ. *Livestock under the A.A.A.* 35.
1775 Massachusetts Ave., Washington 6, D.C., U.S.A.

Fitzgerald, Ella; American singer; b. 25 April 1918.
Sang with Chick Webb Band 34-39; toured with Jazz at the Philharmonic troupe in United States, Japan, and Europe 48-; appeared in film *Pete Kelly's Blues* 55; numerous night club and television appearances 56-; toured with An Evening of Jazz troupe in Sweden, Norway, Denmark, France, Belgium, Germany, Italy, Switzerland 57; many awards from musicians polls and *Downbeat* and *Metronome* magazines; recordings for Decca 36-55, Verve 56-.
c/o Salle Productions Inc., 451 North Canon Drive, Beverly Hills, Calif., U.S.A.

Fitzhugh, Gilbert Wright; American insurance executive; b. 8 July 1909; ed. Princeton Univ.
Metropolitan Life Insurance Co. 30-, Asst. Gen. Man. Canadian Head Office 46, 47, Vice-Pres. in charge of Planning and Development, New York City 58-60, Vice-Pres., Gen. Man. for Canada 60-61, Exec. Vice-Pres. New York City 62, Pres. 63-66; Chair. of Board and Chief Exec. Officer 66-.
1 Madison Avenue, New York City 10, New York, U.S.A.

Fitzmaurice, Sir Gerald (Gray), G.C.M.G., Q.C., B.A., LL.B.; British lawyer; b. 24 Oct. 1901; ed. Malvern and Gonville and Caius Coll., Cambridge.
Called to Bar, Gray's Inn 25, Bencher 61; legal practice 25-29; Third Legal Adviser, Foreign Office 29; Legal Adviser, Ministry of Econ. Warfare 39-43; Second Legal Adviser, Foreign Office 45-53, Legal Adviser 53-60; Legal Adviser to U.K. Dels., San Francisco UN Charter Conf. 45, Paris Peace Conf. 46, UN Assembly 46, 48-59, Japanese Peace Conf., San Francisco 51, Berlin and Manila Confs. 54, Law of the Sea Confs. 58, 60; Judge, Int. Court of Justice 60-; mem. UN Int. Law Comm. 55-60, Pres. 59; mem. Inst. Int. Law; Pres. Grotius Soc. 56-60.

76 Riouwstraat, The Hague, Netherlands; 3 Gray's Inn Square, London, W.C.1, England.
Telephone: 54-38-68 (The Hague); 01-242-4339 (London).

Fitzpatrick, Daniel Robert; American cartoonist; b. 5 March 1891; ed. Superior, Wis. High School and Chicago Art Inst.
Cartoonist *Chicago Daily News* 11, *St. Louis Post-Dispatch* 13-58; now doing series for Nat. Educational Television; first show of paintings, St. Louis 68; winner F. J. F. Lewis prize for caricature 24, Pulitzer cartoon prize 26 and 55; Sidney Hillman Foundation Award 55; Hon. Dr. Letters Washington Univ., St. Louis 49.
Publ. *As I Saw It* 53.
501 Clara Avenue, St. Louis, Mo., U.S.A.

Fjeldstad, Öivin; Norwegian violinist and conductor; b. 2 May 1903; ed. Oslo Conservatoire under Gustav Fr. Lange, Leipzig Conservatoire under Walther Davisson, and Berlin Conservatoire under Clemens Kraus.
Debut as violinist 21; violinist, Oslo Philharmonic Orchestra 23-45; debut as conductor with Oslo Philharmonic Orchestra 31; Chief Conductor, Norwegian State Broadcasting 45-62, Norwegian State Opera Orchestra 58-59; Musical Dir. and Chief Conductor Oslo Philharmonic Orchestra 62-; has appeared as guest conductor in Austria, Belgium, British Columbia, Czechoslovakia, Denmark, Finland, France, German Federal Republic, Great Britain, Greece, Israel, Italy, Netherlands, Poland, Sweden, Turkey, U.S.A., U.S.S.R. and Yugoslavia; Knight, Order of St. Olav, Order of Finland's Lion, Ordre de la Couronne, Order Orange-Nassau; Golden Honour Medal of Norwegian King, Honour Medal of Norwegian Musicians, Arnold Schoenberg Diploma (Salzburg) 52.
Damfaret 59, Bryn-Oslo 6, Norway.

Flamand, Paul; French publisher; b. 25 Jan. 1909; ed. Collège Saint-Paul, Angoulême.
Founder and Dir. of Editions du Seuil, Paris.
Editions du Seuil, 27 rue Jacob, Paris 6e, France.

Flanders, Michael, O.B.E.; British actor and writer; b. 1 March 1922; ed. Westminster School, Oxford Univ.
Royal Navy; hospital (polio) 43-46; in wheelchair 46-; Radio 48-; TV 53-; revue writer 48-; with Donald Swann (*q.v.*) in two-man revues *At the Drop of a Hat* and *At the Drop of Another Hat* 56- (New York 67); with Royal Shakespeare Co. 62.
Publ. *Creatures Great and Small* 64.
c/o Robert Fenn Assoc. Ltd., 15 Berkeley Street, London, W.1, England.
Telephone: 01-584-7747.

Flanders, Ralph E., M.E., A.M., D.SC., LL.D.; American politician and businessman; b. 28 Sept. 1880; ed. Central Falls High School, R.I.; Int. Correspondence School.
Designer Int. Paper Box Machinery Co. Nashua N.H. 03; Associate Editor *Machinery*, New York 05-10; Pres. Jones and Lamson Machine Co., Springfield, Vt., and Bryant Chucking Grinder Co. to 46; mem. Industrial Advisory Board of Nat. Recovery Administration 33-35; Dir. Nat. Life Insurance Co. 35-; fmr. Pres. American Society of Mechanical Engineers and of Nat. Machine Tool Builders' Asscn.; mem. Corpn. Massachusetts Inst. of Technology; fmr. mem. War Production Board Advisory Cttee. for Machine Tool Industry; Chair. Research Cttee., Cttee. for Econ. Development 43-46; Pres. Fed. Reserve Bank of Boston 44-46; Senator from Vermont 46-59; Dir. American Research and Development Corpn. 59-, Jones & Lamson Machine Co. 59-64; Republican.
Publs. *Gear Cutting Machinery* 09, *Taming Our Machines* 31, *Platform for America* 36, *The American Century* 51, *Letter to a Generation* 56, *Senator from Vermont* 61.
Box 479, Springfield, Vt., 05156, U.S.A.
Telephone: 802-885-2000.

Fléchet, Max; French businessman and politician; b. 10 May 1901.
President Comité Nat. des Conseillers du Commerce Extérieur, Union des Fabricants de Chapeaux de Feutre, Laine et Poil de France; Senator (Loire) 48-58, 63-65; fmr. Vice-Pres. Finance Comm. Conseil de la République; High Commr. for Nat. Economy and Foreign Trade July 58; Sec. of State for Economic Affairs, Industry and Trade (Debré Cabinet) Jan. 59-Jan. 60; fmr. Mayor of Chazelles-sur-Lyon.
La Montiliette, Chazelles-sur-Lyon (Loire); 139 rue de Longchamp, 92 Neuilly-sur-Seine, France.

Fleck, 1st Baron (cr. 61), of Saltcoats in the County of Ayr; **Alexander Fleck,** K.B.E., D.SC., LL.D., F.R.S.; British chemist; b. 11 Nov. 1889; ed. Saltcoats School, Technical Coll., Glasgow and Glasgow Univ.
Joined Castner-Kellner Alkali Co. Ltd. (subsequently merged into I.C.I.) 17; Man.-Dir. I.C.I. (Gen. Chemicals) Ltd. 31; Chair. I.C.I. (Fertilizer & Synthetic Products) Ltd. 37; Dir. of I.C.I. responsible for Billingham Div. and Central Agricultural Control 44; Chair. Scottish Agricultural Industries Ltd. 47-51; Deputy Chair. Imperial Chemical Industries Ltd. 51, Chair. 53-60; Deputy Chair. African Explosives and Chemical Industries Ltd. 53-60; Dir. of Imperial Chemical Industries of Australia and New Zealand Ltd. 53-60; Dir. Midland Bank Ltd. 55-; Pres. British Association 58, Soc. of Chemical Industry 60-62; Chair. Nuclear Safety Advisory Cttee. 60-65; Radio Astronomy Planning Cttee. 61-64; Advisory Council on Research and Development 58-65; Treas. and Vice-Pres. Royal Soc. 60-; Chair. Int. Research and Development Co. Ltd. 63-; Pres. Royal Institution 63-.
Aberleven, Crathorne, Yarm, Yorkshire, England.

Fleckenstein, Günther; German theatre director; b. 13 Jan. 1925; ed. Realgymnasium, Mainz, and Univ. Mainz.
Producer of plays and operas, Theater Ulm 54-55, theatre in Essen/Gelsenkirchen 55-57; Chief Producer of Plays, theatre in Münster 57-59; Producer and Dir. Landestheater, Hanover 59-65; Dir. Deutsches Theater, Göttingen 66-; Guest Dir. for theatres in Berlin, Hamburg and Stuttgart; Guest Dir. TV in Munich and Stuttgart; has dramatized for stage and TV *Der Grosstyrann und das Gericht* (Bergengruens); stage production in German of *Les jeux sont faits* (Sartre).
Deutsches Theater in Göttingen, 34 Göttingen, Theaterwall; Home: Göttingen-Geismar, Jenaer Strasse 17, German Federal Republic.
Telephone: 5-94-71.

Fledderus, Mary L.; Netherlands industrial sociologist; b. 4 June 1886.
Factory Administrator 08-18; Dir. Industrial Relations, Leerdam Glassworks, Netherlands 18-25; Dir. Int. Industrial Relations Inst. The Hague 25-48 and Editor *Fundamental Relationships in the Industrial Community, Rational Organisation and Industrial Relations, World Social Economic Planning*, etc.; Research Assoc. Russell Sage Foundation, New York 38-48; mem. American Asscn. for the Advancement of Science.
Publs. *Technology and Livelihood* (in collaboration), and *The Technological Basis for National Development*.
150 Byrdcliffe Road, Woodstock, N.Y. 12498, U.S.A.
Telephone: Oreole 9-2035.

Fleischman, Théo; Belgian writer; b. 93.
On editorial staff of *La Gazette*, Brussels 20; Dir. of Talks, Radio-Belgique 24; Dir. of Talks in French, Belgian Nat. Broadcasting Inst. (I.N.R.) 30-37; Dir.-Gen. 37; Dir.-Gen. of Belgian Nat. Broadcasting in London 42; Director-General of Broadcasting (French), I.N.R. 45-53; Administrative Director of the Musical Chapel of Queen Elizabeth of Belgium; Président Universal Radiophonic Inst., Télévisuelle Internationale d'Honneur; Commdr. Order of the Crown,

Chevalier Order of Léopold, Croix de Guerre with Palm, Commdr. Légion d'Honneur; Commdr. Order of Polonia Restituta, etc.
Publs. *Ce vieil enfant* (poems) 22, *Archipel* (poems) 23, *L'Aventure (1914-18)* 24, *Anthologie des Poètes de l'Yser* 25, *Ici Londres—le Message du Jour* 45, *Un curieux récit de Waterloo* 46, *Icare* 47, *Le Roi de Gand, Napoléon au bivouac, Un qui revient de loin, Bruxelles pendant la bataille de Waterloo, Tapin tambour de Bonaparte en Egypte, Le Peuple aux Yeux Clairs, En écoutant parler Napoléon, En écoutant parler les grognards de Napoléon, Napoléon et la Musique, L'Epopée impériale racontée par la Grande Armée, L'Evadé de Sainte-Hélène*; has written many radio features.
43 Avenue Hamoir, Brussels (Uccle), Belgium.
Telephone: 74-09-72.

Fleischmann, Rudolf, DR. RER. NAT.; German physicist; b. 1 May 1903; ed. Univs. of Erlangen, Munich.
Inst. of Physics, Göttingen 30-32, Heidelberg 32-34; Kaiser Wilhelm Physical Inst. Heidelberg 34-41; Extraordinary Prof. of Physics, Univ. of Strasbourg 41-44; Prof. of Physics, Univ. of Hamburg, and Dir. of State Physical Inst. 47-53; Prof. of Physics, Head of Physics Dept., Univ. of Erlangen 53-.
Office: 6 Gluckstrasse, 852 Erlangen; Home: 9 Langemarickpl., 852 Erlangen, German Federal Republic.
Telephone: 87071 (Office); 26221 (Home).

Fleming, Hon. Donald Methuen, P.C., Q.C., B.A., LL.B., D.C.L.; Canadian barrister; b. 23 May 1905; ed. Univ. of Toronto and Osgoode Hall Law School.
Called to Bar 28; created King's Counsel 44; Mem. of Parl. for Toronto-Eglinton 45-63; mem. Board of Governors Univ. of Toronto and Toronto Western Hospital; Minister of Finance 57-62; Gov. Int. Bank, Monetary Fund, Int. Finance Corpn., Int. Development Agency 57-63; Minister of Justice and Attorney-Gen. of Canada 62-63; Dir. Mutual Life Assurance Co. of Canada, Gore Mutual Insurance Co., British Commercial Property Investments (Canada) Ltd., and many other companies; Gen. Counsel to Bank of Nova Scotia in Bahamas and Caribbean; Man. Dir. of many banks; mem. Progressive Conservative Party.
P.O. Box 1355, Nassau, Bahamas.
Telephone: 21269 (Office); 34616 (Home).

Fleming, Peter, O.B.E. (husband of Celia Johnson, *q.v.*); British author and journalist; b. 31 May 1907; ed. Eton and Christ Church Oxford.
As Special Corresp. of *The Times* has travelled in China, Russia, Japan, Brazil, Manchuria; served in Grenadier Guards in Norway 40, Greece 41, S.E.A.C. 42-45; High Sheriff of Oxfordshire 52.
Publs. *Brazilian Adventure, One's Company, News from Tartary, The Flying Visit, A Story to Tell, The Sixth Column, Invasion 1940, A Forgotten Journey, My Aunt's Rhinoceros, The Gower Street Poltergeist, With the Guards to Mexico, The Siege at Peking, Bayonets to Lhasa, Goodbye to the Bombay Bowler, The Fate of Admiral Kolchak*; trans. *Tibetan Marches*.
Merrimoles House, Nettlebed, Oxon., England.

Fleming, Maj-Gen. Robert John, Jr.; American army officer, government official and business exec.; b. 13 Jan. 1907; ed. Phillips Exeter Acad., U.S. Military Acad., Massachusetts Inst. of Technology, and Army Engineer School.
Special Asst. to Commanding Gen., Hawaiian Dept. 42-43; Army Service, Europe 44-47; Army Engineer appointments, U.S. 47-57; Commander, Theater Army Support Command, Europe, Verdun 57-60; Southwestern Div. Engineer, Dallas 60-62; Gov. Panama Canal Zone and Pres. Panama Canal Co. 62-67; D.S.M., Legion of Honor and other awards.
99 Bay View Drive, Swampscott, Mass. 01907.

Fleming, Rt. Rev. William Launcelot Scott, M.A., M.S., D.D.; British ecclesiastic and explorer; b. 7 Aug. 1906; ed. Rugby School, Trinity Hall and Westcott House, Cambridge, and Yale Univ.

Ordained deacon 33, priest 34; Fellow of Trinity Hall from 33, Dean and Chaplain 37-49; expeditions to Iceland and Spitzbergen 32-33; Chaplain and Geologist, British Graham Land Expedition 34-37; Examining Chaplain to Bishop of Southwark 37-49, St. Albans 39-45, Hereford 45-49; Chaplain, R.N.V.R. 40-44; Dir. Service Ordination Candidates 44-46; Dir. Scott Polar Research Inst. Cambridge 46-49; Bishop of Portsmouth 49-59; Bishop of Norwich 59-; Chair. Church of England Youth Council 50-61; Hon. Chaplain R.N.V.R. 50; Hon. Fellow, Trinity Hall, Cambridge 56; Hon. Vice-Pres. Royal Geographical Soc. 61.

Bishop's House, Norwich, NOR 10A, Norfolk, England. Telephone: Norwich 29001.

Flemming, Arthur Sherwood, A.M., LL.B.; American educator and government official; b. 12 June 1905; ed. Ohio Wesleyan, American and George Washington Univs.

Instructor, American Univ. 27-30, Dir. School of Public Affairs 34-39, Exec. Officer 38-39; mem. U.S. Civil Service Comm. 39-48, Int. Civil Service Advisory Board 50-64, Nat. Advisory Cttee. of Peace Corps 61-; Pres. Ohio Wesleyan Univ. 48-58 (on leave 51-57); Asst. to Dir. Office of Defense Mobilisation 51-53, Dir. 53-57; statutory mem. Nat. Security Council, participating by invitation of the Pres. of the U.S. in Cabinet meetings 53-57; Sec. of Health, Educ. and Welfare 58-61; Pres. Univ. of Oregon 61-; Chair. Board of Trustees, Citizenship Clearing House 59-62; Pres. Nat. Council of Churches in America 67-; numerous hon. degrees; Republican.

University of Oregon, Eugene, Oregon, U.S.A.; 2315 McMorran Drive, Eugene, Oregon, 97403, U.S.A. Telephone: 345-5731-503.

Flemming, Hon. Hugh John, LL.D., D.C.L.; Canadian politician; b. 5 Jan. 1900; ed. Woodstock High School. Carleton County Municipal Councillor 21-35; defeated candidate federal election 35; New Brunswick Legislature 44-, Ldr. Progressive Conservative Party 51-, Premier 52-56, 56-60; Minister of Forestry, Fed. Govt. 60-63, and Nat. Revenue 62-63.

252 Waterloo Row, Fredericton, New Brunswick, Canada.

Flerov, Georgy Nikolayevich; Soviet (Russian) physicist; b. 13; ed. Leningrad Industrial Inst.

Scientific Work, Leningrad Inst. of Physics and Technology 38, later Chief Laboratory of Multicharged Ions, Kurchatov Inst. of Atomic Energy, Moscow; Dir. Nuclear Reaction Laboratory, Joint Inst. for Nuclear Research, Dubna; Hero of Socialist Labour, State Prize, etc.

Publs. *The Absorption of Slow Neutrons by Cadmium and Mercury* 39, *The Spontaneous Fission of Uranium* (with K. A. Petrzhak) 40, *Experiments on the Fission of Uranium* (with L. I. Russinov) 40, *On the Proton Decay of Radioactive Nuclei* (with others) 64, *Synthesis of Transuranium Elements* (with others) 57, 64.

Laboratory of Nuclear Reactions, Joint Institute for Nuclear Research, Dubna, Moscow Region, U.S.S.R.

Fletcher, Harvey, B.S., PH.D.; American physicist; b. 11 Sept. 1884; ed. Brigham Young Univ. and Univ. of Chicago.

Head of Dept. of Physics, Brigham Young Univ. 11-16; on engineering staff of Research Dept. of Bell Telephone Laboratories 16-49, Dir. Physical Research 33-49; Prof. of Electrical Engineering Columbia 49-52; Dir. Research, Brigham Young Univ. 52-, Dean Coll. Physics and Engineering Sciences 53-60; Pres. Utah Acad. of Science 15-16, Fellow American Physical Soc. (Pres. 45) and Acoustical Society of America, co-organiser and

First Pres. 29; mem. Nat. Acad. of Sciences 33; Fellow American Asscn. for the Advancement of Science (Chair. Section B. 37); Pres. American Fed. of Organisations for the Hard of Hearing 29-30; Hon. Sc.D. (Columbia and Utah Univs., Kenyon Coll., Stevens Inst. of Technology, Brigham Young Univ. and Case School of Applied Science).

Publs. *Speech and Hearing* 29, *Speech and Hearing in Communications* 53.

272 Eyring Science Center, Brigham Young University, Provo, Utah 84601, U.S.A.

Fletcher-Cooke, Sir John, Kt., C.M.G., M.A.; British colonial official (retd.); b. 8 Aug. 1911; ed. Malvern Coll., Paris and Oxford Univs.

Colonial Office, Private Sec. to Perm. Under-Sec. 34-37; Malayan Civil Service 37-42; Served in R.A.F. and taken P.O.W. by Japanese 42-46; Sec. to Constitutional Comm. Malta 46; Under-Sec. to Palestine Govt. 46-48; Counsellor, U.K. Del. to U.N. 49-51; Colonial Sec. Cyprus 51-55; Minister for Constitutional Affairs, Tanganyika 56-59; Chief Sec. to Govt. 59-60; Dep. Gov. of Tanganyika 60-61; M.P. (Southampton Test) Oct. 64-66; Commonwealth Parliamentary Asscn. Del. to Nigeria 65; Visiting Prof. Colorado Univ. 61-62, 66; mem. Kenya Constituencies Delimitation Comm. 62; Adviser to Ottoman Bank 62-64; mem. Exec. Cttee. Overseas Employers' Fed. 63-65; Vice-Chair. Int. team to review structure and org. of FAO, Rome 67; Dir. Programmes in Diplomacy, Carnegie Endowment, New York 67.

Publ. *Parliament as an Export* (co-author).

"Salterns", Old Bursledon, Southampton, Hants., England; Carnegie Endowment, 345 East 46th Street, New York, N.Y. 10017, U.S.A.

Telephone: Bursledon 202; Oxford 7-3131.

Fleure, Herbert John, D.SC., M.A., LL.D., F.R.S.; British geographer and anthropologist; b. 6 June 1877; ed. Guernsey, Univ. Coll. of Wales, Aberystwyth, and Zürich Univ.

Lecturer in Zoology and Geography Univ. Coll. Aberystwyth 07-10, Prof. of Zoology and Lecturer in Geography 10-17 and Prof. of Geography and Anthropology 17-30; Prof. of Geography Manchester Univ. 30-44; Hon. Sec. Geographical Asscn. and Hon. Editor *Geography* 17-47; Fellow of Royal Soc. of London 36; awarded Huxley Medal of Royal Anthropological Inst. 37; Charles P. Daly Medal of American Geographical Soc. 39; Research Medal and Gold Medal Royal Scottish Geographical Soc. 39 and 46, Victoria Medal Royal Geographical Soc. London 47; Pres. Royal Anthropological Inst. 45-47, Folklore Soc. 47-48, Conf. of Corresp. Socs. of British Asscn. Adv. Sci. 48, Geographical Asscn. 48; Commdr. of Order of Leopold (Belgium); Hon. LL.D. (Edinburgh and Wales), Hon. Sc.D. (Bowdoin Coll. U.S.A.).

Publs. include *Peoples of Europe, Races of England and Wales, The Corridors of Time* (with H. J. Peake), *Human Geography in Western Europe, French Life and its Problems, A Natural History of Man in Britain.* Corner House, West Drive, Cheam, Surrey, England. Telephone: 01-642-8873.

Flexa Ribeiro, Carlos Octavio; Brazilian UNESCO official; b. 1914.

Secretary of State for Educ. and Culture, State of Guanabara 60-65; Prof. of Art and Aesthetics, Nat. Faculty of Architecture, Univ. of Brazil, Rio de Janeiro 65-67; Fed. Deputy for Guanabara; Asst. Dir.-Gen. for Educ., UNESCO 67-.

UNESCO, 7/9 place de Fontenoy, Paris 7e, France.

Flick, Friedrich; German business executive; b. 10 July 1883; ed. Realgymnasium and Commercial Coll. Cologne.

Head Clerk, Bremen Foundry 07; mem. Management Board Charlottenhütte 15-19, Gen. Dir. 19; founded

Vereinigte Stahlwerke A.G., Vereinigte Oberschlesische Hüttenwerke and Mitteldeutsche Stahlwerke 26; took over Maximilianshütte, Bavaria 29; annexed Harpener Bergbau A.G. 32, Essener Steinkohlen A.G. 36; rebuilt Flick Group (comprising Feldmühle (Düsseldorf), Dynamit Nobel (Troisdorf), Daimler-Benz (Stuttgart), Buderus (Wetzlar), Krauss-Maffei (Munich), Maximilianshütte (Sulzbach-Rosenberg), Stahlwerke Sudwestfalen (Geisweid)) 50-60; numerous hon. degrees and medals.
Friedrich Flick K.G., 4 Düsseldorf, Postfach 3209, Friedrichstrasse 62/68, German Federal Republic.

Flindt, Flemming Ole; Danish ballet dancer; b. 30 Sept. 1936; ed. Royal Danish Ballet School.
Ballet dancer 55-; solo dancer Royal Theatre, Copenhagen 57-60; Danseur Etoile Théâtre Nat. de l'Opéra, Paris 60-; Dir. Royal Danish Ballet 65-; guest artist Royal Ballet Covent Garden 63; guest choreographer Metropolitan Opera House, New York and La Scala, Milan 65; Grand Prix Italia (*La Leçon*) 63.
Choreography: *La Leçon*, Ionesco 63, *Jeune Homme à Marier*, Ionesco 64, *The Three Musketeers* 66, *The Miraculous Mandarin* 66.
Bülowsvej 26, Copenhagen, Denmark.
Telephone: 144665.

Flint, Sir William Russell, Kt., R.A.; British artist; b. 4 April 1880.
On staff *Illustrated London News* 03-07; Silver Medallist Paris Salon 13; Pres. Royal Society Painters in Water Colours 36-56; Fellow Royal Society of Painters-Etchers 33; R.A. 33; Trustee Royal Acad. 43; Vice-Pres. Artists Gen. Benevolent Instn. 43; Knighted 47; exhibitor Royal Acad., and other art exhibitions; works appear in many permanent exhibitions including the British and Victoria and Albert Museums, London, the Fitzwilliam, Cambridge, and over a hundred other galleries in Great Britain, the Commonwealth and U.S.A., etc.; has illustrated editions of Chaucer, Homer, Malory, etc.
Publs. *Drawings* 50, *Models of Propriety* 51, *Herrick's Poems* 55, *Minxes Admonished* 56, *Shadows in Arcady* 65, *The Lisping Goddess, Breakfast in Périgord* 67.
Peel Cottage, 80 Peel Street, London, W.8, England.

Flitner, Andreas, DR. PHIL., M.A.; German educationist; b. 28 Sept. 1922; ed. "Christianeum" Gymnasium, Hamburg, and Univs. of Hamburg, Heidelberg, Basle and Oxford.
Lecturer in German, Univ. of Cambridge 50-51; Tutor, Leibniz-Kolleg, Tübingen and High School Teacher 51-54; Dozent in Educ., Tübingen 55; Extraordinary Prof. of Education, Erlangen 56-58; Prof. of Education, Univ. of Tübingen 58-; Visiting Prof. Evanston, Ill. 67.
Publs. *Erasmus im Urteil seiner Nachwelt* 52, *Die politische Erziehung in Deutschland—Geschichte und Probleme* 57, *Die Kirche vor den Aufgaben der Erziehung* 58, *Glaubensfragen im Jugendalter – Die neueren Erhebungen zur religiösen Lage der Jugend* 61, *Wege zur pädagogischen Anthropologie* 63, *Die Jugend und die überlieferten Erziehungsmächte* (with G. Bittner) 65, *Soziologische Jugendforschung – Darstellung und Kritik aus pädagogischer Sicht* 63, *Goethe an W. von Humboldt, Goethe Jb.* 65, *Einführung in pädagogisches Sehen und Denken* (with H. Scheuerl) 67; Editor *Erasmus, Briefe* (3rd edn.) 56, *J. A. Comenius, Grosse Didaktik* 54, *Wilhelm v. Humboldt, Works* in 5 vols. (with K. Giel) 60-, *Deutsches Geistesleben und Nationalsozialismus* 65, *Erziehung in Wissenschaft und Praxis* 67-; Co-Editor *Anthropologie und Erziehung* 59-, *Zeitschrift für Pädagogik* 62-.
Im Rotbad 43, 74 Tübingen, German Federal Republic.

Florentyev, Leonid Yakovlevich; Soviet agriculturalist and politician; b. 1911; ed. Gorki Agricultural Institute.
Teacher 31-39; mem. C.P.S.U. 39-; Deputy People's Commissar, People's Commissar of Mari A.S.S.R.,

Sec. Regional Cttee. of C.P. 39-49; scientific worker 49-54; Chief Territorial Dept. of Agriculture, Sec. Altai Territorial Cttee. of C.P. 54-56; First Sec. Kostroma Regional Cttee. of C.P. 56-65; Minister of Agriculture of R.S.F.S.R. 65-; mem. Central Cttee. of C.P.S.U. 66-; Deputy to U.S.S.R. Supreme Soviet
Council of Ministers of R.S.F.S.R., 3 Delegatskaya ulitsa, Moscow, U.S.S.R.

Flores-Avendaño, Guillermo; Guatemalan politician and diplomatist.
President of Guatemala 57-58; Ambassador to Costa Rica, Mexico and Italy 58-61; Perm. Rep. of Guatemala to UN 61-63.
c/o Ministry of Foreign Affairs, Guatemala City, Guatemala.

Florit, H.E. Cardinal Ermenegildo; Italian ecclesiastic; b. 01; ed. Seminario Diocesano di Udine, Pontificia Univ. Lateranense and Univ. Gregoriana.
Ordained Priest 25; Chaplain at Palmanova 27-29; Canon of San Marco 33; Prof. of Theology, Pontificia Univ. Lateranense 29-51, Pro-Rector 51-54; Pro-Rector Pontificium Institutum Utriusque Juris 51-54; Domestic Prelate to His Holiness 50-; Coadjutor Archbishop of Florence 54-62, Archbishop 62-; created Cardinal 65; mem. Pontifical Comm. on Bishops and Diocesan Org. for Ecumenical Council 60-, for Revision of Code of Canon Law 65-; mem. Catholic Biblical Asscn. of America.
Founded magazine *Lateranum* and published various books on biblical culture, in particular *Il Metodo della Storia delle Forme*.
Arcivescovado, Piazza S. Giovanni 3, Florence, Italy.
Telephone: 29-88-13.

Florkin, Marcel, M.D.; Belgian biochemist; b. 15 Aug. 1900; ed. Univ. de Liège.
Prof. of Biochemistry, Univ. of Liège 34; Pres. Int. Union of Biochemistry 58; Pres. Biochemical Section, Int. Union of Biological Sciences; mem. Exec. Cttee. Int. Council of Scientific Unions 59-; Pres. Council for Int. Orgs. of Medical Sciences 64-; Pres. Int. Acad. of History of Medicine 62-; Pres. of Biology Working Group, Cttee. on Space Research (COSPAR) 63-; mem. Exec. Cttee. Int. Biological Programme 63-, Int. Cell Research Org. 62-; mem. Belgian Del. to Gen. Confs. of UNESCO 46-66; Visiting Prof. of Physiology, Duke Univ., U.S.A. 59-60; Walker-Ames Prof., Univ. of Washington 63; Visiting Prof. Univ. of Oregon 66; mem. Acad. Royale de Belgique, Acad. Royale de Médecine de Belgique; Hon. mem. Royal Inst. (U.K.); Hon. Fellow Royal Soc. of Edinburgh; mem. Leopoldina Acad., Halle; Prix Francqui 46, Prix K. Jonckheere 60, Prix Henri de Parville 66; Dr. h.c. (Montpellier, Bordeaux, Rio de Janeiro, Gembloux).
Publs. *Biochemie générale* 43, *L'évolution biochimique* 44, *Introduction biochimique à la Médecine* 59, *Comparative Biochemistry* (Editor) 60-64, *Comprehensive Biochemistry* (Editor) 62-, *Aspects moleculaires de l'adaptation et de la phylogénie* 66, *A molecular approach to phylogeny* 66; history: *Médecine et Médecins au Pays de Liège* 54, *Un Prince, Deux Préfects* 57, *Naissance et Déviation de la Théorie cellulaire dans l'oeuvre de Théodore Schwann* 60, *Lettres de Théodore Schwann* 61, *Médecins, Libertins et Pasquins* 64.
6 rue Naimette, Liège, Belgium.

Flowers, Brian Hilton, M.A., D.SC., F.INST.P., F.R.S.; British physicist; b. 13 Sept. 1924; ed. Gonville and Caius Coll., Cambridge, and Univ. of Birmingham.
Anglo-Canadian Atomic Energy Mission (Tube Alloys) at Montreal and Chalk River, Canada 44; Scientific Officer, Nuclear Physics Div., Atomic Energy Research Establishment, Harwell 46; transferred to Theoretical Physics Div. 48; Head of Theoretical Physics Div. 52; Deputy Chief Scientist 54; Chief Research Scientist 58; Prof. Theoretical Physics, Manchester Univ. 58-60,

Langworthy Prof. of Physics 60-; Fellow, Cambridge Philosophical Society 51 and of Physical Society 56; mem. Council Physical Society 60; mem. Council Inst. of Physics and the Physial Soc. 61, Vice-Pres. 62-66; mem. Advisory Council on Scientific Policy 62-64, Council on Scientific Policy 65-67; Del. Pugwash Conf. Cambridge 62, Dubrovnik 63, Karlovy Vary 64, Venice 65; Chair. Steering Cttee. of the Nat. Physical Laboratory 65-68; Chair. Computer Board for Univs. and Research Councils 66-; Chair. Science Research Council 67-.
Publs. Editor *Advances in Physics* 59, 63, *Cambridge Monographs in Physics* 61 and numerous scientific papers in the journals of learned societies on nuclear reactions and the structure of atomic nuclei.
Science Research Council, State House, High Holborn, London, W.C.1, England.
Telephone: 01-242-1262.

Fobes, John Edwin; American diplomatist and international official; b. 16 March 1918; ed. Northwestern Univ., Fletcher School of Law and Diplomacy and School for Advanced International Studies, Johns Hopkins Univ.
U.S. Army Air Force 42-45; UN Secretariat, London and New York 45-46; Admin. Analyst, U.S. Bureau of the Budget 47-48; Asst. Dir. Technical Assistance, U.S. Marshall Plan, Washington 48-51; Dep. Dir. Organization and Planning, Mutual Security Agency, Washington 51-52; Adviser, U.S. Del. to NATO and European Regional Orgs., Paris 52-55; Dir. Office of Int. Admin., Dept. of State 55-59; (elected) mem. UN Advisory Cttee. on Admin. and Budgetary Questions 55-60; Senior Adviser, U.S. Del. to the 10th ,11th, 12th, 13th, 14th sessions of UN Gen. Assembly; Special Adviser to Asst. Sec. of State, Washington 59-60; Program Officer and Dep. Dir. U.S. Agency for Int. Devt. Mission to India 60-64; Asst. Dir.-Gen. (Admin.), UNESCO, Paris 64-.
UNESCO, 7/9 place de Fontenoy, Paris 7e; 50 rue Fabert, Paris 7e, France.

Focaccia, Basilio; Italian scientist; b. 14 Dec. 1889; ed. Univ. of Naples.
Assistant, Naples University 22-34; Prof. of Electrotechnics, Naples Univ. 34-38; mem. Board of Dirs. Italian State Railways 38-41; Prof. of Electrotechnics, Univ. of Rome 38-62; Senator of the Republic 48-; fmr. Under-Sec. of State for Merchant Marine, and for Trade and Industry; fmr. Vice-Pres. Nat. Cttee. for Nuclear Energy (C.N.E.N.); Gold Medal of Merit of the Scuola di Scienze ed Arti.
Publs. *Applicazioni elettriche*, Vols. I, II 40; papers on physics, mathematics, general electrotechnics, electrical equipment, electrical measurements, electrical machines, radio engineering, nuclear energy.
Via Belisario 15, Rome, Italy.

Foccart, Jacques; French civil servant; b. 31 Aug. 1913; ed. Collège de l'Immaculée Conception, Laval.
Exporter; Adviser, Rassemblement du Peuple Français (R.P.F.) Group, Council of the Republic 52-58; Sec.-Gen. R.P.F. 54; Technical Adviser, Gen. de Gaulle's office (Pres. of the Council) 58-59; Technical Adviser in Secretariat-Gen. of Presidency of Republic 59; Sec.-Gen. Presidency for French Community and African and Madagascan Affairs 61-; Officier, Légion d'Honneur, Croix de Guerre 39-45, Rosette de la Résistance.
Secretariat-Général pour la Communauté et les Affaires Africaines et Malgaches, 138 rue de Grenelle, Paris 7e, France.

Fock, Cornelis L. W., LL.D.; Netherlands administrator; b. 05; ed. Leiden Univ.
Agent Holland-Africa Line 28-40; served in the war, rising to Colonel Royal Netherlands Army 40-45; Councillor, Ministry of Gen. Affairs 46-49, Sec.-Gen. 49-62; Commr. of the Queen in the Province of Groningen 62-; Chevalier Order Netherlands Lion, Grand-Officier Ordre de la Couronne (Belgium), Grand Silver Star (Austria), Commdr. Légion d'Honneur (France), Hon. O.B.E. (United Kingdom).
17 Marktstraat, Groningen, Netherlands.

Fock, Jenö; Hungarian politician; b. 16.
Mechanic; Nat. Youth Cttee. Communist Party 37; Dep. Minister, Metallurgy and Engineering 52-54; Sec. Nat. Council of Trade Unions 55-57; Sec. Central Cttee. Hungarian Socialist Workers' Party 57-61, mem. Political Cttee. 57-; Dep. Prime Minister 61-67, Prime Minister 67-.
Akadémia u. 17, Budapest V, Hungary.

Fock, Vladimir Alexandrovitch; Soviet physicist; b. 22 Dec. 1898; ed. Univ. of Leningrad.
Professor Univ. of Leningrad 32-; mem. Acad. of Sciences of the U.S.S.R. 39-; scientific worker, Leningrad Physicotechnical Inst. 34-41, Physics Inst., Acad. of Sciences 44-53; awarded Mendeleyev Prize 36; State Prize 46; Leningrad Univ. Prize 56, Lenin Prize 60; Leningrad Defence Medal 44; Order of Lenin 45, 53 and 58; Red Banner of Labour 53, mem. Norwegian (Trondheim) Acad. of Sciences 58-; mem. Royal Danish Acad. 65.
Publs. *Monographs and Collections: Works on Quantum Theory of Fields* 28-37; Editor *Leningrad University Press* 57; *The Theory of Space Time and Gravitation* 59, 64, *Electromagnetic Diffraction and Propagation Problems* 65; other works on Quantum Mechanics, Electrodynamics, Theory of Gravitation, Theory of Diffraction, Mathematical Physics, etc.
Physical Institute of University of Leningrad, Leningrad 164, U.S.S.R.

Foerder, Yeshayahu Herbert, PH.D.; Israeli banker; b. 25 March 1901; ed. Heidelberg, Königsberg and Freiburg Univs.
Law practice, Berlin 26-32; Man. Dir. RASSCO Rural and Suburban Settlement Co., Tel-Aviv 32-57; mem. (Liberal Party) Knesset 48-57; mem. B'Nai Brith; Chair. Board of Dirs., Bank Leumi Le-Israel B.M., Tel-Aviv 57-; Chair. and Dir. of numerous industrial companies.
Office: Bank Leumi Le-Israel B.M., 26-28 Yehuda Halevi Street, Tel-Aviv; Home: 18 McDonald Street, Tel-Benjamin, Ramat Gan, Israel.

Fog, Mogens, M.D.; Danish professor of neurology; b. 9 June 1904; ed. Københavns Universitet.
Chief Prof. of Neurology, Univ. of Copenhagen 38-, Rector of Copenhagen Univ.; mem. Danish Freedom Council during German occupation 43-45, Minister for Repatriation and Compensation 45, mem. of Folketing 45-50; Klein's Prize 62; Dr. h.c. Oslo Univ., Hon. mem. Royal Soc. of Medicine and Asscn. British Neurologists.
Publs. *Aphasia* (with Knud Hermann) 41, *Neurology for Psychologists* 55 and numerous other articles on scientific and political themes.
Neuromedicinsk Afdeling Rigshospitalet, Tagensvej 18, Copenhagen N, Denmark.

Fogarty, Thomas Cyril; American businessman; b. 13 Dec. 1903; ed. Harvard Univ.
Vice-Pres. (Sales), Continental Can Co., New York City 46-50, Exec. Vice-Pres. 50-56, Pres. 56-63, Chair. 63-, Chief Exec. Officer 61-; Dir. Continental Can Co. Inc. (parent company) 51-; Dir. Irving Trust Co., American Sugar Co.; Trustee of Consolidated Edison Co.
19 East 72nd Street, New York, N.Y. 10021, U.S.A.
Telephone: TR9-7494.

Fogh-Andersen, Poul, M.D., DR. MED.; Danish plastic surgeon; b. 7 Dec. 1913; ed. St. Jörgen's High School and Copenhagen Univ.
Scientific Asst., Univ. Inst. of Human Genetics, Copenhagen 39-40; Asst., various Copenhagen hospitals

41-45; Asst. Surgeon Copenhagen Municipal Hospital 46-49; First Asst. Surgeon, Univ. Hospital 50-53, Deaconess Hospital 54-55; Chief Surgeon, Dept. of Surgery A (Plastic Surgery), Deaconess Hospital, Copenhagen 56-; Consultant Plastic Surgeon, Univ. Hospital 56-62; Plastic Surgeon Dronning Louise's Children's Hospital, Copenhagen 59-; Consultant Surgeon, State Inst. for Defective Speech 56-; Co-founder and Pres. Danish Soc. of Plastic and Reconstructive Surgery 64-; Pres. Org. Danish Plastic Surgeons 66-; Pres. Scandinavian Asscn. of Plastic Surgeons 66-; Corresp. mem. American Soc. of Plastic and Reconstructive Surgery 55-.
Dronningensvej 12, Copenhagen F., Denmark.

Fohrmann, Jean; Luxembourg trade unionist, journalist and international official; b. 5 June 1904; ed. Ecole Technique Arbed-Dudelange and Ecole Ouvrière Supérieure, Brussels.
Skilled workman 19-25; Trade Union Sec. 26-32; Dir. of Workman's Co-operative 32-40; deportation and concentration camps 42-45; Sec. Trade Union Congress 45-54; Dir. of newspaper *Tageblatt* 54-65; Deputy 35-65; Mayor of Dudelange 46-65; mem. High Authority of European Coal and Steel Community (ECSC) 65-67; numerous decorations.
Luxembourg.

Folchi, Alberto Enrico; Italian lawyer and politician; b. 17 June 1897; ed. Nazarene Coll. of the Scolopi Order and Univ. of Rome.
Served in 14-18 and 39-45 wars; active mem. Christian Democratic Party of Rome, Sec. 48-49; mem. Nat. Council Christian Democratic Party 48-50, 60; mem. Chamber of Deputies 53-; Under-Sec. for Foreign Affairs 55-60; Minister of Sports and Tourism 60-63; Prof. of Law, Univ. of Rome and fmr. Pres. Nat. Inst. for Welfare of Employees of Local Boards (INADEL); Knight Order of Malta.
Publs. *I Mandati Coloniali* 36, *Sull' Ordinamento Giuridico della Tunisia* 40, *Democrazia Politica e Democrazia Economica* 46, *L'Occidente di Fronte al Comunismo* 55, *Europa unita: i trattati per l'Euratom e il mercato comune* 57, *Politica Europea ed energia atomica* 57, *Le Nazioni Unite nella presente situazione internazionale* 58, *Incontro al Vertice* 59, *Somalia Indipendente* 60.
Via Nizza 36, Rome, Italy.

Foldes, Andor; American (b. Hungarian) concert pianist; b. 21 Dec. 1913; ed. Classical Gymnasium, Budapest, and under Dohnanyi, Liszt Acad. of Music, Budapest.
Debut with Budapest Philharmonic Orchestra 21; First Prize, Int. Franz Liszt Piano Competition, Budapest 33; numerous world tours; resident in U.S. 39-61, Switzerland 61-; Grosses Bundesverdienstkreuz (German Fed. Repub.), Ordre du Mérite Culturel et Artistique (France).
Publs. *Keys to the Keyboard* 50, *Gibt es einen zeitgenössischen Beethoven-stil?* 63.
Herrliberg, near Zürich, Switzerland.

Földes, Pál; Hungarian textile expert and diplomatist; b. 01; ed. Brno Univ.
Head of Hungarian woollen industry 48; Dir. of the first Hungarian Scientific Textile Research Inst. 50-57; Minister to Great Britain 57-58; Kossuth Prize 54.
Publs. include several books in the field of textile theory and on the development and introduction of textile research methods.
c/o Scientific Textile Research Institute, Budapest, Hungary.

Foley, James Walling; American oil executive; b. 11 Sept. 1911; ed. Agricultural and Mechanical Coll. of Texas.
Joined Texaco Inc., New York City 32, Production Dept., Vice-Pres. 53-55, Exec. Vice-Pres. 55-56, Pres.

56-63, Vice-Chair. 64-66; Hartford Fire Insurance Co.; Trustee, Columbia Presbyterian Hospital.
135 E. 42nd Street, New York, N.Y. 10017, U.S.A.

Foley, Milton Joseph, B.A.; Canadian business executive; b. 10; ed. Duval and Robert E. Lee High Schools, Florida, Notre Dame Univ.
Vice-Pres. Brooks-Scanlon Corpn. 38-41, Pres. 41-46; Vice-Pres. Brooks-Scanlon Inc. 46-48; Exec. Vice-Pres. Powell River Co. Ltd., Vancouver 48-55, Pres. 55-60; Pres. MacMillan, Bloedel & Powell River, Vancouver 60-61; Vice-Pres. and Dir. Anglo-Canadian Pulp and Paper Mills Ltd., Quebec 61-; Dir. Hudson's Bay Oil & Gas Co., Brooks-Scanlon, Inc., Ittesco Canada, Suwanne Lumber Co.
1060 Raymond-Casgrain Street, Quebec 6, Canada.

Folger, John Clifford, B.S., M.S.; American investment banker and diplomatist; b. 28 May 1896; ed. State Coll. of Washington.
Chairman Bd. of Folger, Nolan, Fleming (Investment Bankers) 41-; Pres. Cumberland Trust Co. 41; Pres. Investment Bankers Asscn. of America 43-45; Chair. Bd. Universal Ball Co., Bingham & Taylor Corpn., Piedmont Mortgage Co.; Dir. Chesapeake & Potomac Telephone Co., Hiram-Walker-Gooderham & Worts Ltd., Int. Business Machines, Hilton Hotels Corpn., World Banking Corpn. Ltd.; Ambassador to Belgium 57-59; Gov. N.Y. Stock Exchange; Chair. Republican Nat. Finance Cttee. 55-57, 60-61; mem. Exec. Cttee. for Int. Econ. Reconstruction, Nat. Inst. of Social Science, The Pilgrims; Hon. Chair. District Chapter American Red Cross; Washington Cathedral Chapter; Trustee, Nat. Trust for Historical Preservation; Republican.
Home: 2991 Woodland Drive, N.W., Washington 8; Office: 725 15th Street, N.W., Washington 5, D.C., U.S.A.

Follett, Sir David Henry, Kt., M.A., PH.D.; British scientist and civil servant; b. 5 Sept. 1907; ed. Rutlish School, Brasenose Coll., Oxford and Birkbeck Coll., London.
With Adam Hilger Ltd. (optical instrument manufacturers) 29-37; Asst. Keeper Dept. of Physics, Science Museum, London 37-39, 45-49; with Meteorological Branch, R.A.F. Volunteer Reserve 39-45; Dep. Keeper Dept. of Physics, Science Museum 49-57, Keeper Dept. of Electrical Engineering and Communications 57-60, Dir. and Sec. 60-; Vice-Pres. Inst. of Physics and Physical Soc. 65-.
3 Elm Bank Gardens, Barnes, London, S.W.13, England. Telephone: 01-876-8302.

Folsom, Frank M., LL.D.; American business executive; b. 14 May 1894; ed. Univs. of San Francisco, Fordham and Notre Dame; St. Joseph's, Manhattan and Providence Colls.
Montgomery Ward & Co. 32-39, Goldblatt Bros. (Chicago) 40-41; Office of Production Management, Washington 41-42; Special Asst. to Under-Sec. of Navy, Washington 42-43; Exec. Vice-Pres. and Dir. Radio Corpn. of America 44-49, Pres. 49-57, Chair. Exec. Cttee. 57-67; Dir. of numerous companies.
Radio Corporation of America, R.C.A. Building, 30 Rockefeller Plaza, New York City 20, N.Y., U.S.A.

Folsom, Marion Bayard; American business executive; b. 23 Nov. 1893; ed. Georgia and Harvard Univs.
Joined Eastman Kodak Co. 14, Treasurer 35-53, Dir. 47-53, 58-; served U.S. Army, First World War; helped draft Social Security Act 34; helped to organise Cttee. for Economic Development 42; Staff Dir. House Cttee. on Postwar Economic Policy and Planning 44-46; Under-Sec., Treasury 53-55; Sec. of Health, Education and Welfare July 55-58; Vice-Chair. White House Conf. on Health; Chair. Governor's Cttee. on Hospital Cost.
106 Oak Lane, Rochester, N.Y. 14610, U.S.A.

Fomin, Andrei Andronovich; Soviet diplomatist; b. 18; ed. Nicolayevsk Shipbuilding Inst.
Soviet Foreign Ministry 46-; Adviser to Soviet Del. UN 54-59; Chargé d'Affaires (a.c.) Congo (Léopoldville) 60; Counsellor for American Countries, U.S.S.R. Ministry of Foreign Affairs 60-61; Minister-Counsellor, Rio de Janeiro 61-62; Amb. to Brazil 62-65; Deputy Sec.-Gen. Ministry of Foreign Affairs 65-67; Head, Dept. for S. Asia, Ministry of Foreign Affairs 67-.
Ministry of Foreign Affairs, 32-34 Smolenskaya-Sennaya ploshchad, Moscow, U.S.S.R.

Fomin, Gennadiy Ivanovich; Soviet diplomatist; b. 1914; ed. Moscow Municipal Inst.
Diplomatic Service 39-; Deputy Head, Protocol Dept., U.S.S.R. Ministry of Foreign Affairs 41-45; First Sec. Soviet Mission to Venezuela 45-48; Counsellor, U.S.S.R. Mission to Cuba 48-52, to Israel 53-55; Head, Protocol Dept. Presidium of U.S.S.R. Supreme Soviet 55-56; on staff of U.S.S.R. Ministry of Foreign Affairs 56-57; Minister-Counsellor, Rome 58-60; Amb. to Somalia 60-64; Dir. Third African Dept., U.S.S.R. Ministry of Foreign Affairs 65-67; Amb. to Mexico 67-.
U.S.S.R. Embassy, Mexico City, Mexico.

Foncha, John Ngu; Cameroonian politician; b. 21 June 1916.
Member House of Assembly 51-65; Prime Minister and Minister of Local Govt., Southern Cameroons 59-61; Prime Minister, Western Cameroon 61-65; Vice-Pres., Fed. Republic of Cameroon 61-; Leader, Kamerun Nat. Democratic Party (KNDP) 55-66; Vice-Pres. Cameroon Nat. Union (CNU) 66-.
Cameroon National Union, Buea, Western Cameroon, Federal Republic of Cameroon.

Fonda, Henry; American actor; b. 16 May 1905; ed. Univ. of Minnesota.
Debut at Omaha 25; mem. of touring companies; first appearance in New York 34; in films 35-; has appeared in the plays: *The Farmer takes a Wife, Blow, Ye Winds, Mr. Roberts, Point of No Return, The Caine Mutiny Court Martial*; films include: *Trail of the Lonesome Pine, Jesse James, Young Mr. Lincoln, Grapes of Wrath, Oxbow Incident, My Darling Clementine, The Fugitive, Twelve Angry Men, Warlock, The Longest Day, How the West Was Won, Fail Safe, The Best Man, Sex and the Single Girl, In Harm's Way, Madigan, The Beardsley Story*, etc.
c/o John Springer, 667 Madison Avenue, New York City, N.Y., U.S.A.

Fong, Hiram, LL.B., LL.D.; American attorney and politician; b. 1 Oct. 1907; ed. Kalihi Waena Grammar School, St. Louis Coll. and McKinley High School, Univ. of Hawaii and Harvard Law School.
Former Deputy City Attorney, Honolulu, and Speaker Hawaii Territorial House of Representatives; Founder of law firm of Fong, Miho, Choy and Robinson; Pres. Finance Factors, Grand Pacific Life Insurance Co., Finance Realty, Finance Investment Co., and Market City, Ltd.; U.S. Senator from Hawaii 59-; Republican; Hon. LL.D. (Tufts and Hawaii Univs., Lafayette Coll.).; 1107 New Senate Office Building, Washington, D.C., U.S.A.; 1102 Alewa Drive, Honolulu 17, Hawaii, U.S.A.

Fonseca, Gen. Arthur Duarte Candal; Brazilian army officer and oil executive; b. 5 April 1909; ed. Escola Militar do Realengo, Army General Staff Coll., Fort Leavenworth, U.S.A., and Escola Superior de Guerra.
Second Lieut. 29, rose to Gen. of Div. 65; has been Chief Instructor in Engineering and Communications, Gen. Staff Coll.; Chief of Gen. Staff Section of Army; Commdr. of Mil. Coll., Rio de Janeiro; Commdr. of 5th Mil. Region and 5th Infantry Div.; Chief of Educ. Dept. at Coll. for Warfare; Pres. of Petrobrás (state petroleum company) 67-; numerous decorations.
Petrobrás, Praca Pio X, 119, Rio de Janeiro, Brazil.

Fontaine, Athanas Paul; American aircraft exec.; b. 1 Aug. 1905; ed. New York Univ.
Aircraft designer, Fairchild Aircraft Corpn., Hagerstown, Maryland 35-36; Project Engineer, Republic Aircraft Corpn., Farmingdale, N.Y. 36-39; Chief Engineer, Convair's Stinson Div., Vultee Aircraft Corpn. 39-40, Convair's Vultee Field Div. 40-42; Asst. Dir. of Engineering, Consolidated Vultee Aircraft Corpn. 42-44, Exec. Vice-Pres. 51-52; Dir. Experimental Aircraft Div., Bendix Aviation Corpn., Detroit 44-45, Vice-Pres. (Engineering) 55-60; Exec. Vice-Pres. Bendix Corpn. 60-65, Chair. and Chief Exec. Officer 65-; Dir. Aero Research Center, Univ. of Mich. 45-51.
Bendix Corporation, Fisher Building, Detroit 2, Mich., U.S.A.

Fontaine, Georges (Jean Paul); French administrator; b. 8 Aug. 1900; ed. Faculty of Letters, Paris, and Ecole du Louvre.
On staff of Nat. Museum of Fontainebleau 29, Dep. Keeper 34-41, Head Keeper, Dept. of Objets d'Art, Musée du Louvre 41-44; Man. Dir. of the Mobilier National and of the Manufactures nationales des Gobelins et de Beauvais 44-; Inspector-Gen. Enseignement des Beaux-Arts 50, Honorary 68; Officier Légion d'Honneur; Officier Arts et Lettres; Commdr. Palmes Académiques.
Publs. *Pontigny, Abbaye cistercienne* 28, *Les Gobelins* 42, *La Céramique française* 47, new ed. in English 65.
62 boulevard de Courcelles, Paris 17e, France.
Telephone: 227-02-56.

Fontanet, Joseph, D. en D.; French politician; b. 9 Feb. 1921.
In Secret Army, Second World War, joined French forces in N. Africa 43; on staff of Sec. of State for Public Health and Population 50-51; Conseiller Général, Moutiers (Savoy) 51-, Vice-Pres. Conseil Général 61; Counsellor, French Union 56-; Deputy for Savoy 56-58, 62-; Sec. of State for Industry and Commerce 59; Sec. of State for Internal Commerce 59-61; Minister of Public Health and Population 61-62; Sec.-Gen. Mouvement Républicain Populaire (M.R.P.) 63-66; Croix de Guerre (39-45).
Mouvement Republicain Populaire, 7 rue de Poissy, Paris 7e, France.

Fontanne, Lynn (Mrs. Alfred Lunt); British actress.
Began as child in pantomime, Drury Lane; small parts, various London companies with Lewis Waller, Beerbohm Tree, Lena Ashwell; played in touring companies with Weedon Grossmith for few seasons, playing name part in *Young Lady of 17*, and other small parts in various curtain-raisers; on tour in *Milestones*, then revival in London; small parts in *My Lady's Dress*; U.S.A.: many plays with Laurette Taylor; name part in *Dulcy*, followed by many leads, including *Goat Song, Strange Interlude, Arms and the Man, Second Man, Caprice, At Mrs. Beams, Pygmalion, In Love with Love, The Guardsman, Meteor, Reunion in Vienna, Design for Living, Point Valaine, Taming of the Shrew, Idiots' Delight, The Seagull, Amphytrion 38, There Shall Be No Night* by Robert Sherwood, *Love in Idleness* by Terence Rattigan, *I Know My Love* (adapted from Achard's *Auprès de ma Blonde*); played in *Quadrille* 52-53, *The Great Sebastian, The Visit*; many hon. degrees.
c/o Theatre Guild, 245 West 52nd Street, New York City, N.Y., U.S.A.

Fonteyn, Margot (*see* Arias, Señora doña Margot Fonteyn de).

Foot, Rt. Hon. Sir Dingle Mackintosh, P.C., Kt., M.P., Q.C. (brother of Lord Caradon, *q.v.*, and Michael Foot, *q.v.*); British politician; b. 24 Aug. 1905; ed. Balliol Coll., Oxford.
Queen's Counsel; fmr. Pres. Oxford Union; Liberal M.P. for Dundee 31-45; Parl. Sec. to Min. of Economic Warfare 40-45; mem. British Delegation San Francisco

Conf. 45; mem. Royal Comm. on Justices of the Peace 46, Cttee. on Intermediaries 49; Bencher of Gray's Inn 52; Chair. of *Observer* Trustees Board 53-55; joined Labour Party 56; M.P. 57-; Solicitor-Gen. Oct. 64-Aug. 67.
2 Paper Buildings, Temple, London, E.C.4, England. Telephone: 01-236-9119.

Foot, Michael, M.P., (brother of Lord Caradon, *q.v.*, and Sir Dingle Foot, *q.v.*); British journalist and politician; b. 13 July 1913; ed. Forres School, Swanage, Leighton Park School, Reading, and Wadham Coll. Oxford Univ.
Pres. Oxford Union 33; contested Monmouth 35; Asst. Editor *Tribune* 37-38, Joint Editor 48-52, Editor 52-59, Managing Dir. 52-; mem. staff *Evening Standard* 38, acting Editor 42-44; political columnist *Daily Herald* 44-64; Labour M.P. 45-55, 60-.
Publs. *Armistice 1918-1939* 40, *Trial of Mussolini* 43, *Brendan and Beverley* 44, *Still At Large* 50, part author *Guilty Men* 40 and *Who Are the Patriots?* 49, *Full Speed Ahead* 50, *The Pen and the Sword* 57, *Parliament in Danger* 59, *Aneurin Bevan* Vol. I 62, Vol. II 64, *Harold Wilson: A Pictorial Biography* 64.
House of Commons, London, S.W.1; *Tribune*, 24 St. John Street, London, E.C.1, England.

Foot, Robert William, O.B.E., M.C.; British company director; b. 7 June 1889; ed. Winchester Coll.
Served with Royal Field Artillery in France, First World War 14-18; Gen. Man. Gas Light and Coke Co. 29-42; Joint Dir.-Gen. B.B.C. 42-43, Dir.-Gen. 43-44; Chair. Mining Asscn. of Great Britain 44-47, Pres. 47-52; Pres. British Coal Utilisation Research Asscn. 44-47, Coal Utilisation Joint Council 45-47; Deputy Chair. Powell Duffryn Ltd., Chair. Powell Duffryn Technical Services Ltd. 47-52; Dir. Australia & New Zealand Bank 49-52, Barclays Bank D.C.O. 49-53; Chair. Wankie Colliery Co. Ltd. 49-53.
Publ. *A Plan for Coal.*
2 Queensberry House, Friars Lane, Richmond, Surrey, England.
Telephone: 01-940-8238.

Foote, Emerson; American advertising executive; b. 13 Dec. 1906; ed. public schools.
Clerk 23-31; Leon Livingston Advertising, San Francisco 31-35; Yeomans and Foote (own advertising business) 35-36; with J. Stirling Getchell Inc., New York 36-38; Vice-Pres., Dir. and Exec. Vice-Pres. Lord & Thomas 38-42; Pres. and Dir. Foote, Colne & Belding 42-50; Vice-Pres. and Dir. McCann-Erickson Inc. 51, Exec. Vice-Pres. 52-57, Senior Vice-Pres. 58-60, Pres. 60-63, Chair. of Board 62-64; official of philanthropic orgs.
Gipsy Trail Road, Carmel, N.Y., U.S.A.

Foote, Paul D., M.A., PH.D., D.SC.; American physicist; b. 27 March 1888; ed. Western Reserve, Nebraska and Minnesota Univs. and Carnegie Inst. of Technology.
Physicist U.S. Bureau of Standards 11-27; Dir. of Research Gulf Research Laboratory 27-53; Exec. Vice-Pres. Gulf Research & Development Co. 33-53; Vice-Pres. Gulf Oil Corpn., Gulf Refining Co. 45-53; Fellow American Physical Society and Pres. 33; Asst. Sec. Defense (Research and Engineering), Washington, D.C. 57-58; Chair. Nat. Acad. of Sciences Panels advising Bureau of Standards 60-65; mem. American Philosophical Soc. (Sec. 56-59), Optical Soc. of America, Washington Acad. Sciences (Vice-Pres. 36), Nat. Acad. of Sciences.
5144 Macomb Street, N.W., Washington, D.C. 20016, U.S.A.

Forbes, Sir Archibald Finlayson, G.B.E., Kt.; British chartered accountant and business executive; b. 6 March 1903; ed. Paisley and Glasgow Univ.
Chartered accountant 27; fmr. mem. firm of Thomson McLintock & Co.; Exec. Dir. Spillers Ltd. 35-; Dir. of Capital Finance, Air Ministry 40; Deputy Sec. Ministry of Aircraft Production 40-43; Controller of Repair, Equipment and Overseas Supplies 43-45; mem. Aircraft Supply Council 43-45; Chair. Iron and Steel Board 46-49; Chair. The Debenture Corpn. 49-; Pres. Fed. of British Industries 51-53; Chair. Iron and Steel Board 53-59; Chair. Central Mining and Investment Corpn. 59-64; Chair. Midland Bank 64-; Chair. Spillers Ltd. 65-.
26 Orchard Court, Portman Square, London, W.1. England.
Telephone: 01-935-9304.

Forbes, Bryan; British film director and screenwriter; b. July 1926; ed. West Ham Secondary School.
Studied at Royal Acad. Dramatic Art, first stage appearance 42; served in Intelligence Corps 44-48; entered films as actor 48; wrote and co-produced *The Angry Silence* 59; Dir. *Whistle Down the Wind* 61; Writer and Dir. *The L-Shaped Room* 62, *Seance on a Wet Afternoon* 63, *King Rat* 64; Producer and Dir. *The Wrong Box* 65; Writer, Producer and Dir. *The Whisperers* 66, *Deadfall* 67, *The Madwoman of Chaillot* 68; British Film Acad. Award for *The Angry Silence*; Best Screenplay Awards for *Only Two Can Play*, *Seance on a Wet Afternoon*; United Nations Award for *The L-Shaped Room*; many Film Festival prizes.
Publ. *Truth Lies Sleeping* (short stories) 51.
Pinewood Studios, Iver Heath, Bucks., England.
Telephone: Iver 700.

Forbes, Harland C., B.S., M.S.; American engineer and executive; b. 21 Feb. 1898; ed. Univ. of New Hampshire and Mass. Inst. of Technology.
With New York Edison Co. and its successor Consolidated Edison Co. of New York Inc. 24-, successively Research Engineer, System Engineer, Vice-Pres., Exec. Vice-Pres. and Pres., Chair. 57-; Dir. Commerce and Industry Asscn., Erie Lackawanna Railroad; Trustee Consolidated Edison Co. of New York, New York Bank for Savings; Fellow American Inst. of Electrical Engineers.
4 Irving Place, New York City 3, N.Y., U.S.A.

Ford, Benson; American executive; b. 20 July 1919; ed. Detroit Univ. School, Hotchkiss School, Princeton Univ.
Joined Ford Co. 40; currently Vice-Pres., Chair. Dealer Policy Board; Dir. Seaboard Properties Co.; Trustee The Edison Inst., Ford Foundation; Pres. Henry Ford Hospital, Detroit; Dir. Ford Motor Co.; Pres. Ford Motor Co. Fund.
Home: 635 Lake Shore Road, Grosse Pointe Shores 36, Mich. 48236; Office: The American Road, Dearborn, Mich. 48121, U.S.A.

Ford, Gerald R.; American politician; b. 14 July 1913; ed. Univ. of Michigan and Yale Univ. Law School.
Partner, law firm Ford and Buchen 41-42; U.S. Navy service 42-47; mem. law firm Butterfield, Keeney and Amberg 47-49; mem. U.S. House of Reps. 49-; House Minority Leader 65-; mem. Interparliamentary Union, Warsaw 59, Brussels 61, Belgrade 63; mem. U.S.-Canadian Interparliamentary Group; American Political Science Distinguished Congressional Service Award; Republican.
1624 Sherman Street S.E., Grand Rapids, Mich., U.S.A.

Ford, Henry, II; American industrialist; b. 4 Sept. 1917; ed. Yale Univ.
Spent one year at Ford Motor Co. 40; joined Navy 41; released because of his father's death and rejoined Ford Motor Co. 43, Vice-Pres. 43-44; Exec. Vice-Pres. 44; succeeded his grandfather as Pres. Sept. 45-60, Chair. 60-; Alt. Del. to UN 53; Chair. Trustees, Ford Foundation 43-56, Trustee 56-.
Ford Motor Co., The American Road, Dearborn, Mich. 48121, U.S.A.

Ford, John; American film director; b. 1 Feb. 1895. Fmr. Dir. Universal City Films Calif.; directed films for Universal-Fox, Metro-Goldwyn-Mayer, United Artists, Radio-RKO; Rear-Admiral (retd.) U.S. Naval Reserve; mem. Motion Picture Dirs. Asscn. (fmr. Pres.), Screen Directors Guild (fmr. Treas.); films include *The Grapes of Wrath, How Green Was My Valley, They Were Expendable, The Informer, The Fugitive, She Wore a Yellow Ribbon, Rio Grande, Command, The Quiet Man, The Sun Shines Bright, Mogambo, The Horse Soldiers, Sergeant Rutledge, Cheyenne Autumn, Seven Women, Mary of Scotland, The Plough and the Stars, The Adventures of Marco Polo, Stagecoach, Young Mr. Lincoln, The Long Voyage Home, Tobacco Road, Fort Apache, Mister Roberts, The Searchers, The Last Hurrah, The Man Who Shot Liberty Valance.*
6860 Odin St., Hollywood, Calif., U.S.A.

Ford, Robert Arthur Douglass, M.A.; Canadian diplomatist; b. 8 Jan. 1915; ed. Univ. of Western Ontario and Cornell Univ.
Instructor, History Dept., Cornell Univ. 39-40; Dept. of External Affairs 40-, served Rio de Janeiro, Moscow, London 40-51; Chargé d'Affaires, Moscow 51-54; Head of European Div., Dept. of External Affairs 54-57; Amb. to Colombia 57-58, to Yugoslavia 59-61, to United Arab Republic 61-63, to U.S.S.R. 63-; Gov.-General's Award for Poetry 56; Hon. D.Litt., Univ. Western Ontario 65.
Publ. *A Window on the North* (poetry) 56.
c/o Department of External Affairs, Ottawa, Canada.

Ford, William Clay, B.S.(ECON.); American businessman; b. 14 March 1925; ed. Univ. of Mich. and Yale Univ.
Dir. Ford Motor Co. 48; mem. of Sales and Advertising Staff 48 and of the Industrial Relations Staff 49; quality control Man. Lincoln-Mercury Div. Jet Engine Defence Project 51; Man. Special Product Operations 52; Vice-Pres. Ford Motor Co. and Gen. Man. Continental Div. 53; Group Dir. Continental Div. 55; Vice-Pres. Product Planning and Styling 57-; Chair. Planning and Styling Cttees.
Ford Motor Co., Dearborn, Michigan, U.S.A.

Forde, Daryll, PH.D.; British professor of anthropology; b. 16 March 1902; ed. Univ. Coll. London.
Lecturer Dept. of Geography, University Coll. London 23-28; Commonwealth Fellow in Anthropology, Univ. of Calif. U.S.A. 28-30; Gregynog Prof. of Geography and Anthropology, Univ. of Wales 30-45; Prof. of Anthropology, London Univ. 45-; Fellow, Univ. Coll., London; Dir. of Int. African Inst. 44-; Anthropological Field Expeditions Arizona and Northern Mexico 28-29; New Mexico 29, Nigeria 35 and 39; Pres. Royal Anthropological Inst. 48-50; Editor *Africa, African Abstracts and Ethnographic Survey of Africa.*
Publs. *Ethnography of the Yuma* 31, *Habitat, Economy and Society* 34, *Marriage and the Family among the Yakö of S.E. Nigeria* 41, *Native Economies of Nigeria* 46, *The Yoruba of S.W. Nigeria* 51, *The Context of Belief* 58, *Yakö Studies* 64; Editor and Contributor: *African Systems of Kinship and Marriage* 50, *African Worlds* 54, *Peoples of the Niger-Benue Confluence* 55, *Social Effects of Industrialisation and Urbanisation in Africa* 56, *The Efik of Old Calabar* 56.
8 The Boltons, Kensington, London, S.W.10, England.

Forde, Rt. Hon. Francis Michael, P.C.; Australian schoolteacher, electrical engineer, politician and diplomatist; b. 1890; ed. Christian Brothers Coll., Toowoomba.
Member Queensland Legislature 17-22; Fed. M.P. 22-46; mem. Royal Comm. on Motion Picture Industry 27-28; Minister for Trade and Customs 30-31 and 32; Act. Minister for Markets and Transport 30-31; Dep.-leader Fed. Labour Party and of Opposition 31-41; Dep.

Prime Minister, Deputy Leader Federal Labour Party and Minister for the Army 41-46; Minister for Defence 46; Act. Prime Minister 44-45; Prime Minister July 45; Leader, Australian Del. to San Francisco Conf. April 45; Australian High Commr. in Canada Nov. 46-53; mem. for Flinders, Queensland Legislature 55-57; Hon. LL.D. (Ottawa, Montreal and Laval Univs.).
44 Highland Terrace, St. Lucia, Brisbane, Queensland, Australia.
Telephone: Brisbane 75447.

Foreman, Carl; American cinema writer, producer and director; b. 14; ed. Crane Coll., Univ. of Illinois and Northwestern Univ.
Managing Dir., Exec. Producer, Open Road Films Ltd.; Commdr. Order of the Phoenix (Greece); mem. Board of Govs. British Film Inst. 66-; mem. Exec. Council, British Production Asscn. 67-; Writers' Guild of America Award; Best American Drama: *High Noon* 52; Writers' Guild of Great Britain Laurel Award for Distinguished Service to Writers 68.
Film Scripts: *So This is New York* 48, *Champion* 49, *Home of the Brave* 49, *The Men* 50, *Cyrano de Bergerac* 50, *The Bridge on the River Kwai* 57; Film Writer-Producer: *High Noon* 52, *The Key* 57, *The Guns of Navarone* 61; Film Writer-Producer-Director: *The Victors* 63; Exec. Producer: *Born Free* 65, Writer-Producer *Mackenna's Gold* 67; Exec. Producer *Otley* 68.
25 Jermyn Street, London, S.W.1, England.
Telephone: 01-437-4534.

Forman, Miloš; Czechoslovak film director; b. 18 Feb. 1932; ed. Film Faculty, Acad. of Music and Dramatic Art, Prague.
Director of Film Presentations, Czechoslovak Television 54-56; of Laterna Magika, Prague 58-62; mem. Artistic Cttee., Sebor-Bor Film Producing Group; Czechoslovak Film Critics' Award for *Peter and Pavla* 63; Grand Prix 17th Int. Film Festival, Locarno, for *Peter and Pavla* 64, Prize Venice Festival 65; Grand Prix of French Film Acad. for *A Blonde in Love* 66.
Films include: *Talent Competition, Peter and Pavla, The Knave of Spades, A Blonde in Love, Episode in Zruč, Fire and Firemen.*
Mjr. Schramma 31, Prague 6, Czechoslovakia.
Telephone: 34-14-47.

Formentini, Paride, DR.ECON. and COMM.SC.; Italian businessman; b. 12 June 1899; ed. Genoa Univ.
Held diplomatic posts 21-24; Personal Sec. to Dr. Alberto Pirelli of Società Italiana Pirelli (Milan) 24-25; Dep. Man., Sec. Board of Dirs. and Exec. Cttee. Central Management, Banco di Roma 26-31; Dep. Gen. Man. Istituto Mobiliare Italiano (IMI) 32-33; Gen. Man. Società Torinese Esercizi Telefonici (S.T.E.T.) 34-36; Gen. Man. Società Finanziaria Marittima Finmare 37-; Dep. Gen. Man. Banca d'Italia 47-48, Gen. Man. 48-59; Pres. European Investment Bank 59-.
European Investment Bank, 85 Boulevard de Waterloo, Brussels 1, Belgium.
Telephone: 13-40-00.

Fornari, Giovanni, DR. JUR.; Italian diplomatist; b. 21 May 1903; ed. Univ. of Rome.
Vice-Consul, France 26-30; Ministry of Foreign Affairs 30-34; Del. to League of Nations 32; First Sec., Madrid, Morocco, Athens 34-40; Missions to Turkey 33, Yugoslavia 40; Min. Foreign Affairs 41-42, 44-45; Chargé d'Affaires, Netherlands 43, Argentina 46-47; Ambassador to Chile 48-49; Gov. of Italian Somaliland 50-53 (with rank of Ambassador); Ambassador to Brazil 53-55, to U.A.R. 55-61; Dir.-Gen. of Political Affairs, Ministry of Foreign Affairs, Rome 61-64; Ambassador to France 64-.
Italian Embassy, 47 rue de Varenne, Paris 7e, France.
Telephone: LITtré 67-32.

Fornasetti, Piero; Italian painter, designer, manufacturer of large line of household articles and decorative arts consultant; b. 1913; ed. Brera Acad. of Arts.
Designer of textiles, mosaics, furniture, decorations and porcelain; Editor of books in limited editions, etc.; Perm. Exhbn., Milan; Sarfatti Scholarship, Neiman Marcus Award.
Principal works: screens, furniture, panels, porcelain and ceramic items, decorating accessories, etc.; Interior decoration: Padua Univ., Hilton Hotel, Istanbul; Hotel Duomo (Milan); interior decoration for ships: *Giulio Cesare, Conte Grande, Andrea Doria, Australia, Oceania,* and for hotels, etc.
Via Antonio Bazzini 14, Milan, Italy.

Forni, Giuseppe Gherardo, DR. MED.; Italian doctor and university administrator; b. 6 Feb. 1885.
Former Head, Civil Hospital, Venice, Dir. of Surgery, Cagliari Hospital; Prof. of General Surgery, Clinics and General Therapy, Bologna Univ. 38-56, Rector 56-64; mem. Nat. Council of Research 47-55; mem. Acad. of Science, Bologna.
Publ. *Manuale di Patologia Chirurgica Generale e Speciale.*
5 Via S. Giorgio, Bologna, Italy.

Foroughi, Mahmoud; Iranian diplomatist; b. 8 Aug. 1915; ed. Teheran Univ.
Iranian Foreign Service 39-, London 43-48, Ministry of Foreign Affairs 48-50; Consul-Gen. in New York, Del. to UN Gen. Assembly 50-56; Ambassador to Brazil 57-62; Under-Sec. for Political Affairs, Ministry of Foreign Affairs 62; Ambassador to Switzerland 62-63, to U.S.A. 63-65, to Afghanistan 66-.
Imperial Iranian Embassy, Kabul, Afghanistan.

Forssmann, Werner, M.D.; German surgeon; b. 29 Aug. 1904; ed. Univ. of Berlin.
Asst. at Eberswalde, where he undertook a dangerous experiment on himself, thus finding process of heart-catheterization angio-cardiography; Nobel Prize 56; Charité Clinics and Robert Koch Hospital, Berlin 39; Army physician until 45; practised in Black Forest 45-50; urologist in Bad Kreuznach 50-57; Chief Doctor Surgical Clinic, Düsseldorf Evangelical Hospital 58-; Hon. Prof. of Surgery and Urology, Joh. Gutenberg Univ., Mainz 56; Hon. Prof. Univ. Nacional de Córdoba 61, Univ. of Düsseldorf 64; mem. Deutsche Gesellschaft für Chirurgie, Deutsche Gesellschaft für Unfallheilkunde, American Coll. of Chest Physicians; Hon. mem. Royal Swedish Soc. for Cardiology, Deutsche Gesellschaft für Urologie; Foreign Corresp. mem. British Medical Asscn. 66; Hon. Fellow Indian Acad. of Sciences 67; Leibniz-Medaille of German Acad. of Sciences 54.
Office: Evangelisches Krankenhaus, Fürstenwall 91, Düsseldorf; Home: 4041 Holzbüttgen, Feldstrasse 11, German Federal Republic.
Telephone: Düsseldorf 8-44-44 (Office); Neuss 6-58-40 (Home).

Forster, Edward Morgan, C.H., C.LIT.; British writer; b. 79; ed. Tonbridge and King's Coll., Cambridge.
Hon. Corresp. mem. American Society of Arts and Letters; Hon. Fellow King's Coll. Cambridge 46; Hon. Litt.D. (Liverpool, Hamilton Coll. U.S.A., Cambridge, Nottingham, Manchester and Leiden), LL.D. (Aberdeen).
Publs. include *Where Angels Fear to Tread, Howard's End, Collected Stories, Goldsworthy Lowes Dickinson, Aspects of the Novel, Abinger Harvest, Alexandria: a History and Guide, The Longest Journey, A Passage to India, Two Cheers for Democracy, The Hill of Devi, Marianne Thornton, England's Pleasant Land* (Play Pageant), *Nordic Twilight, Diary for Timothy* (film script); co-librettist, with Eric Crozier, for Benjamin Britten's opera *Billy Budd.*
Reform Club, 104/5 Pall Mall, London, S.W.1, England.

Forster, Isaac; Senegalese international judge; b. 14 Aug. 1903; ed. Lycée Hoche, Versailles, and Univ. of Paris.
General State Counsel's Dept. for French West Africa 30; Dep. Judge, Dakar 33, Dep. to Prosecutor, Conakry, Guinea 33; Judge, St. Denis, Réunion, then Madagascar 41; Judge of Court, Guadeloupe 45, French West Africa 47; Pres. of Chamber, Dakar 57; Sec.-Gen. of Govt., Senegal 58-60; Prosecutor-Gen., Dakar 59; First Pres. Supreme Court of Senegal 60-64; Judge, Int. Court of Justice, The Hague 64-; assoc. mem. Inst. of Int. Law; numerous decorations.
International Court of Justice, The Hague, Netherlands.

Forster, James Franklin, B.S., M.B.A.; American business exec.; b. 20 May 1908; ed. U.S. Naval Acad. and Harvard Univ.
Staff Accountant, Arthur Anderson & Co. 36-39; with Sperry Rand Corpn. 39-; Treasurer, Exec. Vice-Pres., Pres. Vickers Inc., Detroit 41-64; Pres. Dir. Univac Div., New York City 64-66; Pres. and mem. Exec. Cttee. Sperry Rand Corpn. 65-67, Chair. and Chief Exec. Officer 67-; mem. Soc. of Automotive Engineers, Naval Engineers.
Office: Sperry Rand Corporation, 1290 Avenue of the Americas, N.Y. 10019; Home: 200 E. 66th Street, New York City 10021, U.S.A.

Forster of Harraby, 1st Baron (cr. 59), of Beckenham; **John Forster,** K.B.E., Q.C.; British jurist; ed. Sedbergh.
Served with Royal Artillery First World War; called to Bar, Gray's Inn 19; Pres. Trinidad Labour Riots Comm. 37, Court of Inquiry into London Bus Dispute; Deputy Umpire under Unemployment Insurance Act 35; Chair. Nat. Arbitration Tribunal 44-; Chair. Railway Staff Nat. Tribunal 40-60; Pres. of Industrial Court 46-60; Judge Int. Labour Org. Admin. Tribunal 57-60.
84 Albemarle Road, Beckenham, Kent, England.

Forsyth, William Douglass, O.B.E., M.A., B.LITT., DIP.ED.; Australian diplomatist; b. 5 Jan. 1909; ed. Ballarat High School, Melbourne Univ. and Balliol Coll., Oxford.
Teacher of history, Victorian High Schools 30-35; Rockefeller Fellow, Europe 36-37 and 39; Research Fellow, Melbourne Univ. 38 and 40; Research Sec. Australian Inst. of Int. Affairs 40-41; Ed. *Australasiatic Bulletin* 40; Dept. of Information 41-42; Dept. of External Affairs 42-; Counsellor to Washington 47; Rep. to Far East Advisory Comm., Tokyo 46, to UN Trusteeship Council, New York 47-48 and 52-55; Sec.-Gen. South Pacific Comm. 48-51, 63-66; Minister to UN 51-56; del UN Gen. Assembly 51-58; Asst. Sec. Dept. of External Affairs, Canberra 56-59; Amb. to Viet-Nam 59-61, Minister to Laos 59-60; Asst. Sec., Dept. of External Affairs 61-63; Amb. to Lebanon 67-.
Publs. *Governor Arthur's Convict System—Van Diemen's Land 1824-36* 35, *The Myth of Open Spaces—Australian, British and World Trends of Population and Migration* 42.
Department of External Affairs, Canberra, A.C.T., Australia.

Fortas, Abe; American lawyer, government official and judge; b. 19 June 1910; ed. Southwestern Coll., Memphis, and Yale Univ.
Assistant Prof. of Law, Yale 33-37; Asst. Chief, Legal Div., Agricultural Adjustment Admin. 33-34; Asst. Dir. Corporate Reorganization Study, Securities and Exchange Comm. 34-37; Consultant 37-38; Asst. Dir. Public Utilities Div. 38-39; Gen. Counsel, Public Works Admin. 39-40, Bituminous Coal Div. 39-41; Dir. Div. of Power, Dept. of Interior 41-42; mem. law firm Arnold, Fortas and Porter, Washington, D.C. 46-65; Judge, U.S. Supreme Court 65-, nominated as Chief Justice June 68.
3210 R Street, N.W., Washington, D.C., U.S.A.

Forte, Charles, F.H.C.I.; British caterer; b. 26 Nov. 1908; ed. Alloa Acad., Dumfries Coll., and Mamiani, Rome.
Came to London and opened first milk bar 35; acquired Criterion Restaurant 53, Monico Restaurant, Café Royal, Slater and Bodega chain 54, Hungaria Restaurant 56, Waldorf Hotel 58, Fuller's Ltd. 59; Chair. Forte's (Holdings) Ltd.; Dir. Forte's and Co. Ltd., C. Kunzle Ltd., Flav-R Straws Ltd., Nat. Sporting Club, Theatre Restaurants Ltd., etc.; Consul-Gen. in London of San Marino; Pres. Italian Chamber of Commerce for Great Britain 52-; Board mem. British Travel Asscn.; Grand Officer of the Order of the Italian Republic.
Office: Café Royal, 68 Regent Street, London, W.1; Home: 7 Greenaway Gardens, London, N.W.3, England. Telephone: 01-930-2373 (Office).

Fortner, Wolfgang; German composer; b. 12 Oct. 1907; ed. Univ. of Leipzig and Leipzig Conservatory of Music.
Lecturer Evangelical Church Music Inst., Heidelberg 31-53; Prof. of Composition N.W. German State Acad. of Music, Detmold 54-57, State High School for Music, Freiburg 57-; Founder and Dir. Heidelberg Chamber Orchestra 35-41; Founder and Dir. *Musica Viva* Heidelberg 46, Freiburg 58, Munich 64; Pres. German Section Int. Soc. for Contemporary Music; several awards.
Compositions: Opera: *Bluthochzeit* 57, *In seinem Garten liebt Don Perlimphin Belisa* 62; Ballet: *Die weisse Rose* 53; Cantata: *Die Pfingstgeschichte* 63; Orchestral works: *Capriccio* 38, *Sinfonie* 47, *Phantasie über B-A-C-H* 50, *Impromptus* 57, *Triplum*, etc.; and many other works.
Mühltalstrasse 122D, Heidelberg, German Federal Republic.

Fosdick, Harry E., A.B., B.D., A.M., D.D., S.T.D., LL.D.; American ecclesiastic; b. 24 May 1878; ed. Colgate Univ., Union Theological Seminary and Columbia Univ.
Minister of Baptist Church 04; Instructor in Homiletics Union Theological Seminary 08-15 and Prof. 15-46; Pastor Riverside Church, New York 26-46.
Publs. *The Second Mile* 08, *The Manhood of the Master* 13, *The Assurance of Immortality* 13, *The Meaning of Prayer* 15, *The Meaning of Faith* 17, *Twelve Tests of Character* 23, *Modern Use of the Bible* 24, *Adventurous Religion* 26, *A Pilgrimage to Palestine* 27, *As I See Religion* 32, *The Hope of the World* 33, *The Secret of Victorious Living* 34, *The Power to See It Through* 35, *Successful Christian Living* 37, *A Guide to Understanding the Bible* 38, *Living under Tension* 41, *On Being a Real Person* 43, *A Great Time to be Alive* 44, *On Being Fit to Live With* 46, *The Man from Nazareth* 49, *Rufus Jones Speaks to our Time* 51, *Great Voices of the Reformation* 52, *A Faith for Tough Times* 52, *What is Vital in Religion?* 55, *Martin Luther* 56, *The Living of These Days* 56, *Riverside Sermons* 58, *A Book of Public Prayers* 59, *Jesus of Nazareth* 59, *Dear Mr. Brown* 61, *The Life of St. Paul* 62.
Rivermere Apartments, Alger Court, Bronxville, New York City, N.Y., U.S.A.

Fosdick, Raymond B., M.A., LL.D.; American lawyer; b. 9 June 1883; ed. Princeton Univ. and New York Law School.
Asst. Corpn. Counsel New York 08-10; Commr. of Accounts N.Y.C. 10-13; Comptroller Finance Cttee. of Democratic Nat. Comm. 12; mem. New York City Board of Education 15-16; Under-Sec.-Gen. L.N. 19-20; Pres. Rockefeller Foundation July 36-48; Emeritus Pres. Rockefeller Foundation; Pres. Gen. Education Board 36-48; mem. Curtis, Fosdick and Belknap, New York 20-36; Grand Officier Légion d'Honneur, Woodrow Wilson Award, Princeton Univ.
Publs. *European Police Systems* 15, *Keeping Our Fighters Fit* 18, *American Police Systems* 20, *The Old Savage in the New Civilisation* 28, *Toward Liquor Control* 33, *The Story of the Rockefeller Foundation* 51, *Within our Power* 52, *John D. Rockefeller, Jr.: A Portrait* 56, *Chronicle of a Generation: An Autobiography* 58, *Adventure in Giving: The Story of the General Education Board* 62, *Letters on the League of Nations* 66.
Boggs Hill Road, Newtown, Conn., U.S.A.

Foster, Clyde Tanner, A.B., LL.B.; American business executive; b. 9 Feb. 1893; ed. Western Reserve Univ. and John Marshall Law School Cleveland.
First Lieut. U.S. Army 17-19; employed Trust Dept. Garfield Bank and Cleveland Trust Co. 19-22; Asst. Man. Credit Dept. The Higbee Co. 22-23; admitted Ohio Bar 22; practised law 23-29; various managerial posts with Standard Oil Co. Ohio 29-42, Asst. to Pres. 42, Asst. to Pres. and Man. Industrial Relations 43-46, Vice-Pres. Finance and Accounting 46-48, Dir. 46-63, Exec. Vice-Pres. 48, Pres. 49-57, Chair. 57-60; Pres. United Appeal, Greater Cleveland 59; Chair. Board of Trustees, Western Reserve Univ. (Cleveland) 61-; Hon. Dir. American Petroleum Inst. 60-; Dir. Ferro Corpn.; mem. Nat. Petroleum Council for 52-60; Hon. Chair. of the Board Standard Oil Co. 63-; Hon. LL.D. (Western Reserve Univ. 50, Fenn Coll. 58).
17873 Lake Road, Lakewood 7, Ohio, U.S.A.

Foster, John Frederick, C.M.G., M.A., LL.M.; British (Australian) barrister and administrator; b. 28 March 1903; ed. Wesley Coll., Melbourne, Queen's Coll., Univ. of Melbourne and London School of Economics.
Admitted to Bar, Victoria 28; Vice-Master Queen's Coll. 29-34; Registrar Univ. of Melbourne 37-47; Sec.-Gen. Asscn. of Commonwealth Univs. 47-; Sec. U.K. Cttee. of Vice-Chancellors 47-64; Sec. Marshall Aid Commemoration Comm. 53-, Kennedy Memorial Trust 65-; Sec. Commonwealth Scholarship Comm., in the U.K. 60-; Sec. U.K. Del. to Council of Europe Cttee. on Higher Educ. and Research 60-; Editor *Commonwealth Universities Yearbook* 47-62, Joint Editor 63-68; mem. Courts of Govs. Univs. of Hull and Exeter; Hon. M.A. (Oxford), Hon. LL.D. (Laval).
Association of Commonwealth Universities, 36 Gordon Square, London, W.C.1, England.
Telephone: 01-387-8572.

Foster, Sir Robert Sidney, K.C.M.G.; British official; b. 11 Aug. 1913; ed. Eastbourne Coll. and Peterhouse, Cambridge.
Cadet, Northern Rhodesia Administrative Service 36-38, Dist. Officer 38-40; Military Service 40-43; Dist. Officer, N. Rhodesia 43-53, Senior Dist. Officer 53-57, Provincial Commr. 57-60, Sec., Native Affairs 60-61; Chief Sec., Nyasaland 61-63, Dep. Gov. 63-64; High Commr., Western Pacific June 64-.
Government House, Honiara, British Solomon Islands, Western Pacific.

Foster, William Chapman; American government official; b. 27 April 1897; ed. Massachusetts Inst. of Technology.
With Pressed and Welded Steel Products Co. 22-46, Pres. 46; resigned to become Under Sec. of Commerce 46-48; Deputy U.S. Representative abroad to E.C.A. 48-49, Deputy Administrator 49-50, Administrator 50-51; Deputy Sec. of Defense 51-53; Pres. Manufacturing Chemists Asscn. 53-55, Exec. Vice-Pres. and Dir. Olin Mathieson Chemical Corpn., Chair. and mem. Board of Dirs. Reaction Motors Inc. 55-58; Vice-Pres. and Senior Adviser, Olin Mathieson 58-61; Chair. of Board and Pres. United Nuclear Corpn. 61; Dir. U.S. Arms Control and Disarmament Agency 61-; served U.S. Army World War I and War Dept. World War II; U.S. Medal for Merit.
3304 R Street, N.W., Washington, D.C. 20007, U.S.A.

Foster-Sutton, Sir Stafford William Powell, K.B.E., Kt., C.M.G., Q.C.; British lawyer; b. 24 Dec. 1898; ed. St. Mary Magdalen School and private tutor.
Served in army 14-26; active service, R.F.C. and R.A.F. First World War 14-18; called to the Bar (Gray's Inn) 26; private practice 26-36; Solicitor-Gen. Jamaica 36; Attorney-Gen. Cyprus 40; Col. Commdg. Cyprus Volunteer Force and Inspector Cyprus Forces 41-44; mem. for Law and Order and Attorney-Gen. Kenya 44-48, Acting Gov. Aug.-Sept. 47; Attorney-Gen. Malaya 48-50; Chief Justice Fed. of Malaya 50; Officer Administering the Govt., Fed. of Malaya Sept.-Dec. 50; Pres. West African Court of Appeal 51-56; Chief Justice, Fed. of Nigeria 56-58; Acting Gov.-Gen. May-June 57; Pres. Pensions Appeal Tribunals for England and Wales 58-, Chair. Regional Boundaries and Constituencies Delimitation Commissions, Kenya 62.
7 London Road, Saffron Walden, Essex, England.
Telephone: 01-636-6877 (Office); Saffron Walden 2246 (Home).

Fou Ts'ong; Chinese pianist; b. 10 March 1934; ed. Shanghai and Warsaw.
First performance, Shanghai 53, concerts in Eastern Europe and U.S.S.R. 53-58; London debut 59, concerts in Europe, North and South America, Australia and Far East.
118 Cheyne Walk, London, S.W.3, England.

Fouché, Jacobus Johannes; State President of the Republic of South Africa; b. 6 June 1898; ed. Victoria Coll., Stellenbosch.
M.P. for Smithfield 41-59, for Bloemfontein West 60-68; Administrator, Orange Free State 51-59; Minister of Defence 59-66, of Agricultural Technical Services and Water Affairs 66-68; State Pres. of South Africa 68-; National Party.
Office of the State President, Pretoria, Transvaal, Republic of South Africa.

Fouché, Dr. Jacobus Johannes, B.A., LL.D. (son of Hon. Jacobus Johannes Fouché, *q.v.*); South African company director and diplomatist; b. 4 Sept. 1921; ed. Rouxville High School and Univ. of Stellenbosch.
Member of Parl. 50-64; Leader Nasionale Jeugbond 46-56; mem. Provincial Head Cttee. Nationalist Party, mem. Fed. Council Nationalist Party until 64; Ambassador to Netherlands 64-67.
c/o Department of Foreign Affairs, Pretoria, South Africa.

Fouchet, Christian, L. en D.; French diplomatist and politician; b. 17 Nov. 1911; ed. Faculté de Droit de Paris and Ecole des Sciences Politiques.
Free French paratrooper and liaison officer; First Sec., Moscow 44; Del., Poland 44; Consul-Gen., India 45-47; M.P. 51-55, Minister of Moroccan and Tunisian Affairs 54-55; Ambassador to Denmark 58-62; Pres. Fouchet Political Comm., EEC 61-62; High Commr., Algerian Repub. March 62-July 62; Minister of Information Sept.-Dec. 62, of Educ. Dec. 62-67, Minister of Interior 67-May 68; Pres. French Del. 13th UNESCO Session 64; Commdr. Légion d'Honneur; Croix de Guerre, Médaille de la Résistance; Grand Cross, Order of Dannebrog.
4 place de Bagatelle, Neuilly-sur-Seine (Hauts-de-Seine), France.

Fouchet, Paul Jacques; French diplomatist; b. 25 Jan. 1913; ed. Lycée Condorcet and Faculty of Law, Paris.
French Consulate, Addis Ababa 38-39, Third Sec. Ankara 41, French Consulate, Baghdad 41-42, resigned 42; recalled by Vichy Govt. 43, Civil and Military Command, Algeria 43; Allied Military Govt., Italy 43-44, mem. French Del. to Consultative Council on Italian Affairs 44-45, Consul, Milan 45-46; Office of Foreign Affairs, Paris 46-47; First Sec. New Delhi 47-49; mem. French Del. to UN Special Comm. on Balkans 49-50;

First Sec. Athens 50-52, Second Counsellor, Vienna 54-59; Head of Dept. for Technical Co-operation 59-62; Amb. to Niger 62-64, to Dominican Repub. 64-66, to Libya 66-; Officier Légion d'Honneur.
French Embassy, Sharia Almalika, Tripoli, Libya.

Fourest, Henry-Pierre; French ceramist; b. 22 Dec. 1911; ed. Ecole du Louvre and Institut d'Art et Archéologie.
Asst. in Dept. of Paintings, Musée du Louvre; Asst. in Musée Céramique de Sèvres; Curator of Musée Céramique de Sèvres 46-; Curator of Musée Nat. Céramique de Sèvres, Musée Nat. Adrien Debouché; Lecturer Ecole Nationale Supérieure Céramique de Sèvres; fmr. Prof. Ecole du Louvre, Chevalier Légion d'Honneur, Chevalier des Arts et des Lettres.
16 rue de Liège, Paris 9e, France.

Fourie, Bernardus Gerhardus, M.A., B.COM.; South African diplomatist; b. 16; ed. Pretoria and New York Univs.
On staff of Berlin Embassy 39, Brussels 40, London High Comm. 39, 40-45; Del. to San Francisco Conf. 45, U.N. Prep. Comm. and 1st Gen. Ass. 46; with Dept. of External Affairs Int. Orgs. Div. 52-57, Asst. Sec. African Div. 57-58; Perm. Rep. to U.N. 58-62; Under Sec. African Div., Dept. of Foreign Affairs 62-63; Sec. for Information 63-66; Sec. for Foreign Affairs 66-.
Department of Foreign Affairs, Private Bag 141, Union Buildings, Pretoria, Republic of South Africa.
Telephone: Pretoria 2-5431.

Fournier, Pierre Eugène; French company director; b. 25 Aug. 1892; ed. Lycée Montaigne and Lycée Louis-le-Grand, Paris, Univ. of Paris and Ecole Libre des Sciences Politiques.
Entered Inspectorate-Gen. of Finances 19, Inspector of Finances 22; transferred to Secretariat of Minister of Finance 23; Deputy Dir. of Budget Jan. 25; Dir. of Budget Aug. 25; Deputy Gov. Banque de France 29, Gov. 37, now Hon. Gov.; Pres. Soc. Nat. des Chemins de fer français 40; Pres. Soc. Nat. d'Investissement 49-; Dir. Suez Canal Co. and of many French and foreign cos.; Grand Officier Légion d'Honneur; Croix de Guerre.
250 *bis* boulevard Saint-Germain, Paris 7e, France.
Telephone: 548-34-58.

Fournier, Pierre Léon Marie; French concert artist—violoncello, international soloist; b. 24 June 1906.
Former Prof. Paris Nat. Conservatory of Music; Officier Légion d'Honneur.
14 Parc Château Banquet, Geneva, Switzerland.

Fourquet, Jean, DR. ès L.; French university professor; b. 23 June 1899; ed. Ecole Normale Supérieure, Paris. School teacher 25-33; Univ. of Strasbourg 33-55; Prof. of Philology of Germanic Languages Univ. of Paris 55-; Dir. Linguistic Atlas of Alsace, Strasbourg; Chevalier Légion d'Honneur.
Publs. *L'ordre des éléments de la phrase en germanique ancien* 38, *Wolfram d'Eschenbach et le Conte del Graal* 38, *Les mutations consonantiques du germanique* 48, 56, *Grammaire de l'allemand* 52.
95 boulevard Pasteur, Fresnes (Val-de-Marne), France.

Fourquet, Gen. Michel Martin Léon; French air force officer; b. 9 June 1914; ed. Lycée Louis-le-Grand and Ecole Polytechnique, Paris.
Air Force Officer 44-; Commdt. First Tactical Air Group 60-61, 5th Air Region, Algiers 61-62; Chief Commdt. Forces in Algeria 62; Sec.-Gen. of Nat. Defence 62-66; Perm. Under-Sec. for Armaments 66-68; Chief of Staff of Armed Forces 68-; mem. Higher Air Council 62-; Grand Officier Légion d'Honneur, Compagnon de la Libération, Croix de Guerre, Croix de la valeur Militaire, Médaille de l'Aéronautique, D.F.C. (U.K.), etc.
Home: 12 avenue de Verzy, Paris 17e, France.

Fowler, Henry Hamill, A.B., LL.B., J.S.D.; American lawyer and government official; b. 5 Sept. 1908; ed. Roanoke Coll. and Yale Univ.
Admitted to Virginia Bar 33, D.C. Bar; Counsel, Tennessee Valley Authority 34-38, Asst. Gen. Counsel 39; Asst. Gen. Counsel, War Production Bd. 42-44; served Foreign Econ. Admin. 45; Production Authority 51-52; Administrator Defense Production Admin., mem. Nat. Security Council 52-53; law practice 46-51, 53-61; Under-Sec., Treasury 61-64, Sec. 65-; Democrat.
209 S. Fairfax Street, Alexandria, Va., U.S.A.

Fowler, Sir Robert William Doughty, K.C.M.G.; British diplomatist; b. 6 March 1914; ed. Queen Elizabeth's Grammar School, Mansfield and Emmanuel Coll., Cambridge.
Burma Civil Service 37-48, Military Admin., Burma Army 44-46; Additional Sec. to Gov. of Burma 47; Commonwealth Relations Office (C.R.O.) 48-; mem. U.K. Delegation to UN 50-53; Head of Fed. of Rhodesia and Nyasaland and High Comm. Territories Dept., C.R.O. 54-56; Deputy High Commr. Pakistan 56-58, Canada 60-62, Nigeria 63-64; High Commr. in Tanzania 64-66; Amb. to Sudan 66-; Under-Sec. (African Affairs) Commonwealth Office 66; Amb. to Sudan Oct. 66-.
British Embassy, P.O. Box 801, Khartoum, Sudan.

Fox, Rev. Adam, M.A., D.D.; British ecclesiastic and educationist; b. 15 July 1883; ed. Winchester Coll. and Univ. Coll. Oxford.
Asst. Master Lancing Coll. 06-18, Diocesan Coll. Rondebosch, Cape Province 25-29; Warden of Radley Coll. 18-24; Fellow and Dean of Divinity Magdalen Coll. 29-42; Canon of Chichester 36-42; Prof. of Poetry Oxford 38-43; Canon of Westminster 42-63, Archdeacon of Westminster 51-59, Sub-Dean 59-63, Treas. 46-59, retired 63.
Publs. *Old King Coel* 33, *Dominus Virtutum* 36, *Plato for Pleasure* 46, *English Hymns and Hymn Writers* 47, *Meet the Greek Testament* 52, *John Mill and Richard Bentley* 54, *Plato and the Christians* 57, *God is an Artist* 57, *Dean Inge* 60.
4 Little Cloister, Westminster Abbey, London, S.W.1. Telephone: ABBey 5821 (or 01-222-5821).

Fox, Bertrand, PH.D.; American economist; b. 28 Feb. 1908; ed. Northwestern Univ. and Harvard Univ.
Instructor and Tutor in Economics, Harvard Univ. 31-35; Asst. Prof. of Economics, Williams Coll. 35-40, Assoc. Prof. 40-45; Dir. Military Div., War Production Board 41-44; Prof. of Economics, Williams College 45-49; Admin., Merrill Foundation 47-62; Edsel Bryant Ford Prof. of Business Admin. Harvard Business School 49-, Dir. of Research 53-68; Research Dir. and Chief of Staff, Comm. on Money and Credit 58-62.
Publ. *Monetary and Fiscal Policy 1919-1939.*
Harvard Business School, Soldiers Field, Boston, Massachusetts 02163, U.S.A.

Fox, Uffa; British yachtsman; b. 15 Jan. 1898.
Served with Royal Naval Air Service 14-18; American paddling and sailing championship, New York Int. Canoe Trophy 33; during Second World War designed and built craft for the armed forces; owner and Man. Dir. Uffa Fox Ltd., designers of small-class racing yachts.
Publs. *Sailing, Seamanship and Yacht-construction, Sail and Power, Thoughts on Yachts and Yachting, Beauty of Sail, Racing, Cruising and Design, Crest of the Wave, Sailing Boats, Joys of Life,* etc.
Uffa Fox Ltd., Cowes, Isle of Wight, England.

Foy, Frederick Calvert, A.B.; American business executive; b. 28 Jan. 1905; ed. Univ. of California.
Assistant Public Relations Manager, San Joaquin Light and Power Corpn., Fresno, Calif. 28-30; J. Walter Thompson Co. 30-31; Asst. Gen. Manager, Seattle Gas Co. 31-32; Manager, Los Angeles Office, J. Walter

Thompson Co. 32-33; Advertising Manager, Shell Oil Co. 33-38; Vice-Pres. Wilding Pictures 38-39; Young and Rubicam 39-42; Vice-Pres. J. Walter Thompson Co., Detroit 45-48; Vice-Pres. and Sales Manager, Koppers Co. Inc. 48, Chair. and Pres. 58-60, Chair. of Board 60-.
Koppers Company Inc., Koppers Building, Pittsburgh 19, Pennsylvania, U.S.A.
Telephone: 412-391-3300.

Foyer, Jean, D.en D.; French civil servant; b. 27 April 1921.
Former Prof. Lille Univ., Dep. for Maine-et-Loire, Mayor of Contigné; Sec. of State for Relations with Member States of the French Community (Debré Cabinet) 60; Minister of Co-operation 61-62, of Justice 62-67; Chevalier du Mérite Agricole.
Contigné (Maine-et-Loire), France.

Foyle, Christina; British bookseller; b. 1911; ed. Parliament Hill School and Aux Villas Unspunnen, Switzerland.
Entered book trade 28; Man. Dir. W. & G. Foyle Ltd., Foyle's Libraries Ltd. 63-, Dir. John Gifford Ltd., Foyle's Gallery, The Book Club, Foyle's Literary Luncheons.
121 Charing Cross Road, London, W.C.2; and Norton Park House, Cold Norton, Essex, England.

Frachon, Benoit; French politician and trade union leader; b. 13 May 1893.
Factory worker and militant trade union leader at early age; served French Army 14-18; joined Socialist Party 19; worked for adhesion of party to Communist International; Sec. of Syndicat des Métaux du Chambon 22-24; Sec. of Union Départementale des Syndicats de la Loire 24-26; Sec. of regional organisation of Communist Party and mem. of Central Cttee. 26-; Nat. Sec. of party 28-33; Sec. of Confédération Générale du Travail Unitaire 33-36; Sec. of Confédération Générale du Travail 36-39, Gen. Sec. 45-67; Pres. Confédération Générale du Travail 67-; clandestine activity 39-44.
213 rue Lafayette, Paris 10e, France.

Fradkin, Mark Grigoryevich; Soviet composer; b. 1914; ed. Leningrad Theatre Inst. and Byelorussian Conservatoire, Minsk.
Order of the Red Star 43.
Principal compositions: Music for the films: *They Were the First, Good Luck!, Volunteers, First Day of Peace, Foes, Farewell, Doves!, An Ordinary Incident, On a Business Mission, The Volga Flows, Last Harvest, In Performance of his Duties, If You are Right,* and over 100 songs.
Composers' Union of the R.S.F.S.R., 8-10 Nezhdanovoi ulitsa, Moscow, U.S.S.R.

Fraenkel, Eduard, M.A., D.PHIL.; German-born British classical scholar; b. 17 March 1888; ed. Askanisches Gymnasium, Berlin, and Berlin, Rome and Göttingen Univs.
Asst. *Thesaurus Linguae Latinae* 13; Privatdozent, Berlin Univ. 17-20, Extraordinary Prof. 20-23; Prof. Kiel Univ. 23-28, Göttingen Univ. 28-31, Freiburg im Breisgau Univ. 31-33; Fellow, Trinity Coll., Cambridge Univ. 34; Corpus Christi Prof. of Latin, Oxford Univ. 35-53, Prof. Emeritus 53-; Hon. Fellow, Corpus Christi Coll., Oxford; mem. Bologna, Göttingen, Lund, Munich, and Stockholm Acads.; mem. Istituto Lombardo, Milan; hon. mem. Linguistic Soc. of America; Hon. D.Phil. (Freie Univ., West Berlin, Urbino, St. Andrews, Florence, Fribourg, Switzerland).
Publs. *De media et nova comoedia quaestiones selectae* 12, *Plautinisches im Plautus* 22, *Iktus und Akzent im lateinischen Sprechvers* 28, *Das Pindar Gedicht des Horaz* 33, *Aeschylus' Agamemnon* 50, *Horace* 57, *Beobachtungen zu Aristophanes* 62, *Zu den Phoenissen des Euripides* 63, *Kleine Beiträge zur Klassischen Philologie* 64, *Noch*

einmal Kolon und Satz 65; numerous articles in learned periodicals.

Corpus Christi College, Oxford, England.

Fraga Iribarne, Manuel; Spanish writer and politician; b. 23 Nov. 1922; ed. Santiago and Madrid Univs.

Professor of Political Law, Valencia Univ. 45-; Diplomatic Service 45-; Prof. Political Law and Constitutional Law, Madrid Univ. 48; Gen. Sec. Inst. of Hispanic Culture 51; Gen. Sec. Nat. Educ. Ministry 55; Dir. Inst. of Political Studies 61; Minister of Information and Tourism 62-, also Sec.-Gen. of Cabinet Oct 67-; mem. Cttee. for Defence of Christian Civilization, Union of Family Orgs.

Publs. Thirty books on press, art, constitutional and social subjects.

Ministry of Information, Madrid, Spain.

Fragoso, Aguinaldo Boulitreau; Brazilian diplomatist; b. 3 March 1907.

Foreign Service 30-, Berne 36-37, Lima 37-38, Washington 38-41; Sec.-Gen. Brazilian Del., Bretton Woods 44; Sec. of Del., Inter-American Conf., Mexico City 45, U.N. Conf., San Francisco 45, UNESCO, London 45; First Sec. Montevideo 46; Ambassador to Panama 57-58, to Argentina 58-63; Sec.-Gen. Ministry of Foreign Affairs 63-64; Ambassador to Portugal 64-.

Embassy of Brazil, Praça Marques de Pombal, Lisbon, Portugal.

Fragoso, José Manuel; Portuguese diplomatist; b. 20; ed. Universidade Tecnica de Lisboa.

Attaché, Secr. of State 46; Third Sec., London 47-49, Second Sec. 49-50; Perm. Del. to Secr. of Comm. for Technical Co-operation in Africa South of the Sahara 50-54; First Sec., Secr. of State 54-59; Consul-Gen., New York 59-61; Dir. Overseas Political Service 61-62; Dir.-Gen. of Political Affairs and Internal Admin., Secr. of Foreign Affairs 62-64; Head of Portuguese Del. to Org. for Econ. Co-operation and Development (OECD) 64-67, Amb. to Brazil 67-.

Embassy of Portugal, Praia do Flamengo 382, Rio de Janeiro, Brazil.

Frame Clutha, Janet Paterson; New Zealand writer; b. 24; ed. Oamaru North School, Waitaki Girls' High School, Dunedin Training Coll. and Otago Univ.

Hubert Church Award for New Zealand Prose; New Zealand Scholarship in Letters 64, Burns Fellow Otago Univ. Dunedin.

Publs. *Lagoon* 51, *Owls do Cry* 57, *Faces in the Water* 61, *The Edge of the Alphabet* 62, *Scented Gardens for the Blind* 63, *The Reservoir* (stories), *Snowman, Snowman* (fables), *The Adaptable Man* 65, *A State of Siege* 67, *The Pocket Mirror* (poetry).

c/o Bank of New South Wales, Berkeley Square, London, W.1, England.

Franca, José-Augusto, D.HIST., M.A.; Portuguese writer; b. 16 Nov. 1922; ed. Lisbon Univ., Ecole des Hautes Etudes and Univ. of Paris.

Travels in Africa, Europe and Americas 45-; Editor Lisbon literary review *Unicornio* 51-56, Co-Editor *Cadernos de Poesia* 51-53; Founder-Dir. Galeria de Marco, Lisbon 52-54; art critic 46-; film critic 48-; lexicographical publisher 48-58; settled in Paris 59; Prof. History and Sociology of Art, Lisbon 64-.

Publs. *Natureza Morta* (novel) 49, *Charles Chaplin—the Self-Made Myth* (essay) 52, *Azazel* (play) 57, *Amadeo de Souza-Cardoso* (essay) 57, *Despedida Breve* (short stories) 58, *Situação da Pintura Ocidental* (essay) 59, *Da Pintura Portuguesa* (essays) 60, *Dez Anos de Cinema* (essays) 60, *Une Ville des Lumières: La Lisbonne de Pombal* (essay) 63, *A Arte em Portugal no Seculo XIX* (essay) 67, *Oito Ensaios sobre Arte Contemporanea* (essays) 67, *Edgard Pillet: L'Artiste et L'Oeuvre* (essay) 67.

3 rue Desrenaudes, Paris 17e, France; Mailing address: Rua Escola Politecnica 49/4, Lisbon 2, Portugal. Telephone: CAR 5693 (Paris); 362028 (Lisbon).

Francescatti, Zino; French concert violinist; b. 9 Aug. 1902; ed. privately.

Has played with most of the world's leading orchestras; frequently mem. of jury in int. musical contests; Hon. mem. Paris Conservatoire Orchestra, Philadelphia Orchestra, etc.; Officier, Légion d'Honneur; Commdr. de l'Ordre de Léopold de Belgique 67.

Salle Pleyel, 252 rue du Faubourg-Saint-Honoré, Paris 8e, France; and 3 East 85th Street, New York City, N.Y., U.S.A.

Francfort, Pierre Jean; French diplomatist; b. 28 Oct. 1908; ed. Lycée Carnot and Ecole des Sciences politiques. Third Sec., Peking 35, Madrid 38-39; with Free French Govt. in London 42-45, Counsellor, London 45-48, Moscow 48-50, Washington 51-53; Minister Rumania 54-57; Private Sec. to Sec. of State 57-58; at Ministry of Foreign Affairs 60-62; Ambassador to Hungary 62-65, to Yugoslavia 65-; Officier Légion d'Honneur.

French Embassy, Belgrade, Yugoslavia; and 44 avenue de la Bourdonnais, Paris 7e, France.

Franchy, Franz Karl; Austrian journalist and author; b. 21 Sept. 1896; ed. Univs. of Klausenburg and Debreczin.

President Austrian Authors' Society; mem. P.E.N.; Hon. Prof. (Presidential title).

Plays: *Nero, Der Junge Wolf, Vroni Mareiter, Anna Gorth, Summa cum laude, Zwischen den Geleisen* (for which he was awarded the State Prize for Drama 55), *Einbruch der Wirklichkeit, Gesicherte Existenz*; novels: *Maurus und sein Turm, Spiesser und Spielmann, Abel schlägt Kain, Ankläger Mitmann, Berufene und Verstossene, Die vielen Tage der Ehe, Die Brandgasse* (German Novelist's Prize).

1090 Vienna IX, Porzellangasse 4, Austria.

Francis, Sir Frank Chalton, K.C.B., M.A., F.S.A., F.M.A.; British librarian; b. 5 Oct. 1901; ed. Liverpool Inst., Liverpool and Cambridge Univs.

Classical Master, Holyhead County School 25-26; Asst. Keeper, British Museum 26-46; Sec. of British Museum 46-48; Keeper Dept. of Printed Books 48-59; Dir. and Principal Librarian, British Museum 59-Oct. 68; Hon. Fellow, Emmanuel Coll., Cambridge; Hon. Sec. Bibliographical Society; Lecturer in Bibliography, Univ. Coll., London; Chair. Council of British Nat. Bibliography, Int. Relations Cttee., ASLIB (Asscn. Special Libraries and Information Bureaux), Executive Cttee., Library Asscn., Univ. and Research Section, Library Asscn., Nat. Cttee. for ICOM (Int. Council of Museums); mem. Library Advisory Council, England; Editor of *The Library* 36-53; Joint Editor *Journal of Documentation* 47-; Advisory Editor *Library Quarterly*; Assoc. Editor *Libri*; Vice-Pres. Int. Advisory Cttee. on Bibliography, UNESCO; Pres. ASLIB 57-59, Int. Fed. of Library Asscns. 63-, Bibliographical Soc. 64-65, Library Asscn. 65; Pres. Museums Asscn. 65-66; Chair. Int. Conf. on Cataloguing Principles, Paris 61, Anglo-Swedish Soc.; Hon. F.L.A.; Hon. D.Litt. (Dublin, Liverpool, Exeter, British Columbia, Leeds, New Brunswick, Oxford, Cambridge Univs.); Corresp. mem. Massachusetts Historical Soc., Acad. des Beaux-Arts, Paris; Foreign Hon. mem. American Acad. Arts and Sciences; Hon. mem. Gustav Adolfs Akademien, Sweden.

The Director's House, British Museum, London, W.C.1, England.

Telephone: 01-580-5759.

Francis, Sam, M.A.; American artist; b. 1923; ed. Univ. of California at Berkeley.

First exhibition 47; subsequent exhibitions San

Francisco 48, Paris 51, 55, 56, New York 56, London, Berne, Tokyo, Osaka 57, Brussels 58, Dunn Int. Exhbn., London 63, Tokyo Prize for American Artists in Japan; rep. in permanent collections of Museum of Modern Art and Guggenheim Foundation, New York, Tate Gallery, London; three mural panels, Kunsthalle, Basle, Switzerland 56-57, mural, Söfu School Tokyo 57.
222 West 23rd Street, New York City, N.Y., U.S.A.

Francis-Williams, Baron (Life Peer), cr. 62, of Abinger; **(Edward) Francis Williams,** C.B.E.; British author, journalist and broadcaster; b. 10 March 1903; ed. Queen Elizabeth's Grammar School, Middleton.
Formerly on staff various newspapers; Financial Editor *Daily Herald* 29-36, Editor 36-40; Controller of Press and Censorship, Ministry of Information 41-45; Adviser on Public Relations to the Prime Minister 45-47; Special American corresp. of London *Observer* 49; British rep. UN Sub-Comm. on Freedom of Information and the Press 48-51; a Gov. of the B.B.C. 51-52; Regent's Prof. Univ. of California, Berkeley 61; Kemper Knapp Prof. Univ. of Wisconsin 67; U.S. Medal of Freedom with Silver Leaves for War Services.
Publs. *Plan for Peace* 36, *War by Revolution* 40, *Democracy's Last Battle* 41, *Ten Angels Swearing* 42, *No Man is an Island* (novel) 45, *Press, Parliament and People* 46, *The Triple Challenge: The future of Socialist Britain* 48 (in U.S.A. as *Socialist Britain*), *Fifty Years' March: The Rise of the Labour Party* 49, *A Provincial Affair* (novel) 49, *The Richardson Story* (novel) 51 (in U.S.A.: *It Happened Tomorrow*), *Ernest Bevin: Portrait of a Great Englishman* 52, *Transmitting News: A Study of Telecommunications and the Press* (UNESCO) 53, *Magnificent Journey, The Rise of Trade Unions* 54, *Dangerous Estate: The Anatomy of Newspapers* 57, *A Prime Minister Remembers* (with Earl Attlee) 61, *The American Invasion* 62, *A Pattern of Rulers* 65.
Office: House of Lords, Westminster, London, S.W.1; Home: Griffins, Abinger Hammer, Surrey, England.
Telephone: Abinger 444.

Franck, Hans; German writer; b. 79.
Novelist, dramatist, short-story writer and critic.
Publs. *Das Pentagramm der Liebe* 18, *Meta Koggenpoord* 25, *Septakkord* 26, *Der Regenbogen* 27, *Recht ist Unrecht* 28, *Zeitenprisma* 31, *Die richtige Mutter* 32, *Um Liebe* 33, *Reise in die Ewigkeit* 34, *Jakob Johannes* 35, *Der Kreis* 35, *Die Geschichte von den beiden gleichen Brüdern* 36, *Annette, ein Droste-Roman* 37, *Die Stadt des Elias Holl* 38, *Wort der Worte* 39, *Der Wald ohne Ende* 41, *Das letzte Lied* 41, *Die Schicksalsuhr* 43, *Zwiegesang von Leben, Tod und Liebe* 48, *Die Pilgerfahrt nach Lübeck* 49, *Sebastian* 49, *Der Tribun* 52, *Marianne* 53, *Gedichte* 54, *Die Frauenbarke* 54, *Tidemann Butthoff* 54, *Die vier grossen B* 54, *Herbstliches Herz* 55, *Lux und Lukas* 55, *Lass Dich trösten* 57, *Wiedersehen* 58, *Letzte Liebe* 58, *Das Kaleidoskop* 59, *Predigt des Holzes* 59, *Cantate* (Bach novel) 60, *Ernst Barlach—Leben und Werk* 61, *Ein Dichterleben in 111 Anekdoten* 61, *Frühe Glocken* 62, *Friedemann—Der Sohn Johann Sebastian Bachs* 63, *Der Scheideweg—Roman einer tapferen Frau* 64.
[*Died,* 11 *April* 1964.]

Franco Bahamonde, Generalísimo Francisco; Spanish officer and politician; b. 4 Dec. 1892; ed. Infantry Academy.
Took part in campaign in Morocco 12-17; Captain 13; Major 16; with Oviedo garrison 17-20; Deputy Commdr. Foreign Legion Morocco 20-23; Commdr. 23-27; Lieut.-Col. 23; Brigadier 26; Dir.-Gen. Military Acad. Saragossa 27-31; Captain-Gen. Balearic Islands 33; C.-in-C. Moroccan Army 34; Chief of Gen. Staff 35; C.-in-C. Canary Islands 36; Generalissimo of Nat. Armies 36-, Head of State 39-; Pres. Political Junta of Falange

42-; Medalla Militar, Commandeur de la Légion d'Honneur, Croix de Mérite Militaire et Naval (France).
El Pardo Palace, Madrid, Spain.

Franco Guachalla, Alfredo; Bolivian politician; b. 1925; ed. Colegio Nacional "Ayacucho" and Universidad Mayor de San Andrés, La Paz.
Chief of Cabinet to Under-Sec. to Minister of Foreign Affairs 52; Oil Executive 52-54; Economic Counsellor, Bolivian Embassy, Argentina 54-55; Dir. Yacimientos Petrolíferos Fiscales Bolivianos 56-57; Minister of Labour and Social Security 60-63; Minister of Mines and Petroleum 63; Movimiento Nacionalista Revolucionario.
Publs. *En torno a la Cuestión Social, Acotaciones para la Doctrina del Partido, Pobreza y Atraso son los Términos Simples de la Ecuación Latinoamericana, Lo que dije a los Universitarios Nortamericanos, Ejército y Política, Política Petrolera Inmediata, Por qué nos reorganizamos?*
c/o Ministry of Mines and Petroleum, La Paz, Bolivia.

François-Poncet, André, LL.D.; French politician and diplomatist; b. 13 June 1887; ed. Ecole Normale Supérieure.
Dir. Société des Etudes et Informations Economiques; mem. Cttee. Republican Party; Deputy 24-31; Under-Sec. of State for Fine Arts 28-29; Under-Sec. for Nat. Economy in Tardieu Cabinet 30; Under-Sec. of State to the Prime Minister's office in Laval Cabinet 31; Ambassador to Germany 31-38, to Italy 38-40; mem. Nat. Council 41; arrested by Gestapo 43; liberated by Allies May 45; Special diplomatic counsellor to Ministry of Foreign Affairs Dec. 48; French High Commr. in Germany 49-55; Pres. French Red Cross 55-; Grand Croix de la Légion d'Honneur; mem. Acad. Française 52-; Chancellor Institut de France 61-64.
Publs. *Les Affinités électives de Goethe, Ce que pense la Jeunesse allemande, La France et le problème des réparations, Discours français, Réflexions d'un républicain moderne, De Versailles à Potsdam. Souvenirs d'une Ambassade à Berlin, Carnets d'un Captif, Au Fil des Jours, Propos d'un Libéral—Au Palais Farnèse.*
92 rue du Ranelagh, Paris 16e, France.

Frandsen, Johannes; Danish doctor; b. 13 June 1891; ed. Roskilde Cathedralskole and Københavns Univ.
Director-General Nat. Health Service 27-61; mem. of Folketing 47-50; Chief Danish del. to World Health Org. (WHO) 48-61, Pres. European Cttee. WHO Regional Org. for Europe 53-54, 57-58, 60-61; Pres. Danish Red Cross 61-; Leon Bernard Medal and Prize 53; hon. mem. numerous medical assocns. and socs.; Grand Cross Order of Dannebrog, hon. C.B.E.
Espérance Allé 16, 2920 Charlottenlund, Denmark.
Telephone: HE-2014.

Frangulis, A. F.; Greek diplomatist; b. 8 Nov. 1888; ed. Univs. of Athens, Geneva, Lausanne, Berlin and Paris.
Mem. of Greek Del. to Supreme Council, London, to negotiate peace with Turkey 20-21; subsequently del. to League of Nations 20-46; co-founder of Académie Diplomatique Internationale 26, now its Permanent Sec.-Gen. (with rank of Ambassador).
Publs. *Dictionnaire Diplomatique,* Vols. I-VII, *La Conception Nouvelle de la Neutralité, Une ligue des Nations comme garantie d'une Paix durable, Wilson, sa vie, son oeuvre, Les Précurseurs de la S.d.N., La Norvège et le droit des gens, Le principe des nationalités et le droit de libre disposition, Les Sanctions contre les responsables de la Guerre, L'Albanie et l'Empire du Nord, La question du proche Orient, La Grèce et la crise mondiale* (2 vols.), *Théorie et Pratique des Traités Internationaux,* etc.
4 *bis* avenue Hoche, Paris 8e, France.

Franju, Georges; French film director; b. 12 April 1912.
Stage Designer; then Co-Founder, Cinémathèque française 37, and of journal *Cinématographe* 38; Exec. Sec. Int. Fed. of Film Archives 38-45; Gen. Sec. Inst. of Scientific Cinematography 45-52; Dir. of short films 49-, full-length films 58-; Gen. Sec. Acad. du Cinéma; Chevalier des Arts et des Lettres.
Short films include: *Le Sang des bêtes, En passant par la Lorraine, Hôtel des Invalides, Le Grand Méliès, M. et Mme Curie, A propos d'une rivière, Mon chien, Les Poussières, La Première nuit, Le Théâtre nationale populaire, Notre-Dame, Cathédrale de Paris*; Full-length films: *La Tête contre les murs* 58, *Les Yeux sans visage* 59, *Pleins feux sur l'assassin* 60, *Thérèse Desqueyroux* 62, *Judex* 63, *Thomas l'Imposteur* 65, *Les Rideaux Blancs* 66.
Office: 9 rue du Cirque, Paris 8e; Home: 13 quai des Grands-Augustins, Paris 6e, France.

Frank, Gleb Mikhailovich; Soviet biophysicist; b. 1904; ed. Simferopol Univ.
Associate Leningrad Physico-technical Inst., later All-Union Inst of Experimental Medicine 29-43; laboratories of U.S.S.R. Acad. of Sciences 43-52; Head, Lab. of the Biophysics of Animate Structures and Dep. Scientific Dir., Inst. of Biophysics of Acad. of Sciences of U.S.S.R. 52-60, Dir. Inst. of Biophysics 60-; Prof. of Biophysics, Moscow Univ.; Corresp. mem. U.S.S.R. Acad of Sciences until 66, mem. 66-; mem. C.P.S.U. 47-; State Prize.
U.S.S.R. Academy of Sciences, 14 Lenin Prospekt, Moscow, U.S.S.R.

Frank, Ilya Mikhailovich, Soviet physicist; b. 23 Oct. 1908; ed. Moscow Univ.
Fmr. Asst. to Prof. S. I. Vavilov 28; worked at Leningrad Optical Inst. (Laboratory of Prof. A. N. Terenin) 30-34; at Lebedev Inst. of Physics (U.S.S.R. Acad. of Sciences) 34-; Prof. of Physics, Moscow Univ. 44-; Corresp. mem. U.S.S.R. Acad. of Sciences 46-; Nobel Prize for Physics (with Tamm and Cherenkov) 58, State Prize 46, Order of Lenin (twice), Order of the Red Banner of Labour, etc.
Publs. *Function of Excitement and Curve of Absorption in Optic Dissociation of Tallium Ioclate* 33, *Coherent Radiation of Fast Electron in a Medium* 37, *Pare Formation in Gripton under Y Rays* 38, *Doppler Effect in Refracting Medium* 42, *Neutron Multiplication in Uhran-Graphit Systems* 55, *On Group Velocity of Light in Radiation in Refracting Medium* 58, *Vavilov-Cherenkov Radiation* 60, *Optics of Light Sources* 60, *On Some Peculiarities of Elastic Deceleration of Neutrons* 64.
P.N. Lebedev Institute of Physics, Academy of Sciences of the U.S.S.R., 53 Lenin Prospekt, Moscow, U.S.S.R.

Franke, Herbert, PH.D., LL.D.; German university professor; b. 27 Sept. 1914; ed. Univs. of Cologne, Bonn and Berlin.
Reader Cologne Univ. 49; British Council Fellow, Cambridge 51; Prof. of Far Eastern Studies Univ. of Munich 52-, Dean Faculty of Letters 58-59; Sec.-Gen. XXIVth Int. Congress of Orientalists 57; Sec. 53, Pres. 65, Deutsche Morgenländische Gesellschaft, Editor of its *Zeitschrift* 60-65; Visiting Prof. Univ. of Washington, 64-65; Prix Stanislas Julien (Acad. des Inscriptions et Belles-Lettres, Paris) 53.
Publs. *Beiträge zur Wirtschaftsgeschichte Chinas unter der Mongolenherrschaft* 49, *Sinologie* 53, *Beiträge zur Kulturgeschichte Chinas unter der Mongolenherrschaft* 56, etc.
Ostasiatisches Seminar, Universität München, Munich, Home: Fliederstrasse 23, 8035 Gauting, German Federal Republic.
Telephone: Munich 86-29-07.

Fränkel, Jonas, PH.D.; Swiss literary critic and essayist; b. 12 Aug. 1879; ed. Vienna, Berne Univs.
Prof. German literature, Univ. Berne 21-49; Editor *Goethes Briefwechsel mit einem Kinde* 06; *Aus der Frühzeit der Romantik* 07; *Goethes Briefe an Charlotte von Stein* (3 vols.) 08 (new edn., 60-62), *Heines Gedichte* (3 vols.) 11-13, *Conrad Ferdinand Meyers Gedichte und Hutten* 24, *In Memoriam Carl Spitteler* 25, *Gottfried Kellers sämtliche Werke* 26-39 (17 vols., uncompleted), *Gottfried Kellers Briefe an Vieweg* 38, *Das Gottfried Keller-Büchlein* 40, *Gottfried Kellers Liebesspiegel* 50, *J. V. Widmanns Feuilletons* 64.
Publs. *Zacharias Werners Weihe der Kraft, Wandlungen des Prometheus, J. V. Widmann, Gottfried Kellers politische Sendung, Spitteler—Huldigungen und Begegnungen, Spittelers Recht, Goethes Erlebnis der Schweiz* 49, *Dichtung und Wissenschaft* 54, *Heinrich Heine* 60.
Riedegg bei Thun, Switzerland.

Frankel, Sir Otto Herzberg, Kt., D.SC., D.AGR., F.R.S., F.A.A., F.R.S.N.Z., F.W.A.; Australian geneticist; b. 4 Nov. 1900; ed. Agricultural Univ. of Berlin.
Chief, Div. of Plant Industry, Commonwealth Scientific and Industrial Research Organization 51-62, mem. of Exec. 62-66, Senior Research Fellow Div. 66-.
C.S.I.R.O., P.O. Box 109, Canberra City, A.C.T.; Home: 40 Nicholson Crescent, Acton, A.C.T. 2601, Australia.

Frankel, Sally Herbert, M.A., PH.D., D.SC.; British economist; b. 22 Nov. 1903; ed. St. John's Coll. Johannesburg, Univ. of Witwatersrand and London School of Economics.
Prof. of Economics and Head of Dept. of Economics and Economic History, Univ. of Witwatersrand 31-46; Chair. Comm. to report on Rhodesia Railways Ltd. 42-43; Chair. Comm. of Enquiry into Mining Industry of S. Rhodesia 45; mem. Royal Comm. on East Africa 53-55; Prof. in Economics of Underdeveloped Countries, Oxford; Prof. Fellow Nuffield Coll. 46-.
Publs. *Co-operation and Competition in the Marketing of Maize in South Africa* 26, *The Railway Policy of South Africa* 28, *Coming of Age: Studies in South African Citizenship and Politics* 38, *Capital Investment in Africa: Its Course and Effects* 38, *The Concept of Colonisation* 49, *The Economic Impact on Under-Developed Societies* 53.
The Knoll House, Hinksey Hill, Oxford, England.

Frankfurt, Stephen Owen, B.A.; American advertising executive; b. 17 Dec. 1931; ed. New York Univ. and Pratt Inst.
Joined Young & Rubicam 55, Art and Copy Supervisor 57, Vice-Pres. and Dir. of Special Projects 60, Senior Vice-Pres. and Co-Creative Dir. of Agency 64, Creative Dir. Jan. 67-, Pres. Jan. 68-; Gold Medal, N.Y. Art Dirs. Club 58, 59, 61, 62, 63; Special Gold Medal Outstanding TV Advertising 61, Winner TV Category Venice Film Festival 64, Achievement Award, N.Y. Art Dirs. Club April 68.
Young & Rubicam U.S.A., 285 Madison Avenue, New York City, N.Y., U.S.A.
Telephone: 576-8608.

Franklin, Sir Eric Alexander, Kt., C.B.E., B.A.; British civil servant; b. 3 July 1910; ed. English School, Maymyo, Burma, and Cambridge Univ.
Joined Indian Civil Service 35; Deputy Registrar, Rangoon High Court of Judicature 39; District and Sessions Judge, Arakan 41; Deputy Sec. Govt. of Burma 42; Registrar, Rangoon High Court of Judicature 46, retd. on transfer of power 48; Deputy Sec. Govt. of Pakistan, Establishment Division 49, Joint Sec. 52, Establishment Officer 53, Establishment Sec 56-57; Chair. Terms of Service Comm., Govt. of the Sudan 58-59; Adviser and Acting Resident Rep. of UN Technical Assistance Board (TAB) in Jordan 60-61;

Civil Service Adviser to Jordan Govt. 62-63; UN Senior Public Admin. Adviser to Nepal Govt. 64-66.
c/o National and Grindlays Bank Ltd., 13 St. James' Square, London, S.W.1, England.

Franklin, John M.; American shipping executive; b. 18 June 1895; ed. Harvard Univ.
Pres. and Dir. U.S. Lines Co. 46-60, Chair. 60-; Pres. Roosevelt Steamship Co., Inc., U.S. Lines Operations Inc., Number One Broadway Corpn., U.S. Lines Co. (Canada) Ltd.; Dir. Manufacturers' Trust Co., Worthington Corpn., Atlantic Transport Co. Ltd., American Bureau of Shipping, American Steamship Owners' Mutual P. & I. Asscn. Inc., American Merchant Marine Inst., Home Insurance Co., Continental Can Co. Inc., Baltimore and Eastern R.R. Co.
1 Broadway, New York, N.Y., U.S.A.

Franklin, William Henry; American agricultural machinery exec.; b. 30 Jan. 1909; ed. Phillips Exeter Acad. and Princeton Univ.
Auditor, Price Waterhouse & Co., Chicago 34-41; Asst. Controller Caterpillar Tractor Co. 41-44, Controller 44-52, Vice-Pres. 52-62, Exec. Vice-Pres. 62-66, Pres. 66-; mem. Nat. Asscn. Accountants, American Inst. of Accountants and other orgs.
Caterpillar Tractor Company, 600 W. Washington Street, Peoria, Illinois; Home: 500 Miller Road, Peoria, Illinois, U.S.A.

Franks, Baron (Life Peer) cr. 62, of Headington in the County of Oxford; **Oliver Shewell Franks,** P.C., G.C.M.G., K.C.B., C.B.E., M.A.; British college principal; b. 16 Feb. 1905; ed. Bristol Grammar School and Queen's Coll., Oxford.
Fellow and Praelector in Philosophy, Queen's Coll. Oxford 27-37; Prof. of Moral Philosophy Univ. of Glasgow 37-45; Civil Servant (temporary) Ministry of Supply 39-46; Perm. Sec. Ministry of Supply 45-46; Provost Queen's Coll. Oxford 46-48; Hon. Fellow of Queen's Coll., Oxford 48; British Ambassador to U.S.A. 48-52; Chair. Lloyds Bank 54-62; Provost, Worcester Coll., Oxford 62-; Chancellor, Univ. of E. Anglia 65-; Chair. Friends' Provident and Century Life Office 55-62; Chair. Cttee. of London Clearing Bankers 60-62; mem. Nat. Econ. Devt. Council (NEDC) 62-64; Hon. D.C.L. Oxford and other hon. degrees.
The Provost's Lodgings, Worcester College, Oxford, England.

Frantsov, Georgi Pavlovich; Soviet journalist and historian; b. 1903; ed. Leningrad Univ.
Lecturer, Leningrad Univ. 24-31; Dir. Museum of History of Religion 31-45; mem. C.P.S.U. 40-; Dir. Inst. of Int. Relations 45-48; Supervisor, Press Dept., Ministry of Foreign Affairs 48-52; editorial staff *Pravda* 52-57, Dep. Chief Editor 57-58; Rector, C.P.S.U. Acad. of Social Science 58-65; Editor-in-Chief *Problems of Peace and Socialism* (Prague) 65-; Cand. mem. Central Cttee. C.P.S.U. 61-; mem. U.S.S.R. Acad. of Sciences 67-; Order of Lenin (twice), etc.
Publs. *On the History of Ancient Egyptian Autobiographies* 30, *Ancient Egypt* 38, *Fetishism and the Problem of the Origin of Religion* 40, *Sources of Religions and Free-thinking* 59, and others
Sadova 3, Prague B, Czechoslovakia.

Franz Joseph, Prince of Liechtenstein; b. 16 Aug. 1906; ed. Schotten gymnasium and Forestry and Agricultural Univ., Vienna.
Ruler Principality of Liechtenstein, succeeded July 38.
Schloss Vaduz, Principality of Liechtenstein, Europe.

Franzen, Ulrich J., B.A., B.ARCH.; American architect; b. 15 Jan. 1921; ed. Williams Coll., and Harvard Univ.
Head of Ulrich Franzen and Assocs., New York City; Lecturer Yale and Cornell Univs., Univs. of Cincinnati and Illinois, etc.; Visiting Prof. Yale, Harvard and Washington Univs. and Carnegie Inst. of Technology;

Chair. Architectural Board of Review, City of Rye 58-63, Urban Design Review Board, City of Cincinnati 64-65, Nat. Council on Schoolhouse Construction and U.S. Navy Review and Advisory Panel on Architecture 65-; Pres. Architectural League of New York 66-; mem. American Inst. of Architects; numerous awards for design and construction 56-66.
Works include: Barkin Levin Co., Long Island City 58, Philip Morris Research Center, Richmond, Va. 59, Plans for Helen Whiting Inc., Pleasantville, N.Y. 62, Philip Morris Operations Center 63, Agronomy Building for Cornell Univ. and New Alley Theatre, Houston, Texas.
Office: 41 East 57th Street, New York City 22; Home: 975 Park Avenue, New York City 28, N.Y., U.S.A.

Fraser, Sir Bruce Donald, I.C.B.; British Auditor Gen.; b. 18 Nov. 1910; ed. Bedford School and Trinity Coll., Cambridge.
Civil Servant 33-66, serving in Scottish Office, Treasury (Third Sec. 56-60), Ministry of Aviation (Deputy Sec. 60), Ministry of Health (Perm. Sec. 60-64), Dept. of Education and Science (Joint Perm. Under-Sec. of State) 64-65, Ministry of Land and Natural Resources (Perm. Sec. 65-66); Comptroller and Auditor Gen. 66-.
72 Queen's Gate, London S.W.7, England.

Fraser, Sir Hugh, 2nd Bt.; British business executive; b. 18 Dec. 1936; ed. St. Mary's, Melrose, and Kelvinside Acad.
Director, House of Fraser Ltd. 58-65, Deputy Chair. 65-66, Chair. 66-; Chair. Harrods Ltd., John Barker & Co. Ltd., Binns Ltd., Scottish and Universal Investments Ltd., George Outram & Co. Ltd.; Chair. House of Fraser (Northern Management) Ltd. 62-; Dir. Highland Tourist (Cairngorm Devt.) Ltd.; succeeded to father's Baronetcy (Lord Fraser of Allander, Bt.) 66, and disclaimed Barony.
Dineiddwg, Mugdock, nr. Milngavie, Stirlingshire, Scotland.

Fraser, Rt. Hon. Hugh Charles Patrick Joseph, P.C., M.P., M.B.E.; British politician; b. 23 Jan. 1918; ed. Ampleforth Coll., Balliol Coll., Oxford, and Univ. of Paris.
With Lovat Scouts, Phantom and Special Air Service, Second World War; Cons. M.P. 45-; Parl. Private Sec. to Sec. of State for the Colonies 51-54; Parl. Under Sec. of State and Financial Sec., War Office 58-60; Parl. Under-Sec. of State for Colonies 60-62; Sec. of State for Air 62-64; Minister of Defence for the Royal Air Force 64; Dir. Ionian Bank 64-.
52 Campden Hill Square, London, W.8, England.

Fraser, Sir (Richard) Michael, Kt., C.B.E.; British politician; b. 28 Oct. 1915; ed. Aberdeen Grammar School, Fettes Coll., Edinburgh, and King's Coll., Cambridge.
Royal Artillery 39-46; Conservative Research Dept. 46-64, Head of Home Affairs Section 50-51, Joint Dir. 51-59, Dir. 59-64; Sec. Conservative Party's Advisory Cttee. on Policy 51-64, Deputy Chair. Conservative Party Oct. 64-; Sec. to Conservative Leader's Consultative Cttee. 64-; Smith-Mundt Fellowship, U.S.A. 52.
18 Drayton Court, London, S.W.10, England.
Telephone: 01-370-1543.

Fraser, Sir Robert Brown, Kt., O.B.E., B.A., B.SC.; British television administrator; b. 26 Sept. 1904; ed. St. Peter's School, Adelaide, Univs. of Melbourne and London.
Leader Writer, *Daily Herald* 30-39; Empire Div., Min. of Information, London 39-41; Dir. Publications Div., M.O.I. 41-45; Controller of Production M.O.I. 45-46; Dir.-Gen. Central Office of Information 46-54; Dir.-Gen. Independent Television Authority 54-; Hon. Fellow London School of Econs. 65.
Flat 5M, Portman Mansions, Chiltern Street, London, W.1, England.

Fraser, Rt. Hon. Tom, P.C.; British public official; b. 18 Feb. 1911; ed. Blackwood School and Lesmahagow Higher Grade School.
Underground mine worker 25-43; Miners' Union Branch official 38-43; Sec. and Pres. Coalburn Miners' Lodge 39-43; Sec. Lanark Constituency Labour Party 39-43; M.P. 43-67; Parl. Private Sec. to Pres. of Board of Trade 44; Joint Parl. Under-Sec. of State Scottish Office 45-51; Minister of Transport Oct. 64-65; Chair. North of Scotland Hydro-Electric Board 67-.
Office: 16 Rothesay Terrace, Edinburgh; Home: 15 Broompark Drive, Lesmahagow, Lanarkshire, Scotland.
Telephone: Caledonian 1361 (Office); Lesmahagow 3223 (Home).

Fraser, Hon. William, O.B.E., T.D.; British oil executive; b. 8 May 1916; ed. Loretto and Clare Coll., Cambridge.
Served in army 39-45; Barrister-at-Law, in private practice 46-50; joined The British Petroleum Co. Ltd. 50, rep. in New York 56-58; Man. Dir. Kuwait Oil Co. 59-62; Man. Dir. British Petroleum Co. Ltd. 62-.
19 Cumberland Terrace, Regent's Park, London, N.W.1, England.

Fraser of Lonsdale, Baron (Life Peer), cr. 58; **Lieut.-Col. (William Jocelyn) Ian Fraser,** C.H., C.B.E.; British politician; b. 30 Aug. 1897; ed. Marlborough and R.M.C. Sandhurst.
Conservative M.P. for N. St. Pancras 24-29 and 31-36; for Lonsdale Div. of Lancs. 40-50, for Morecambe and Lonsdale 50-58; mem. London County Council 22-25; mem. Govt. Comm. of Enquiry on Broadcasting 25-26; Barrister, Inner Temple 32; blinded in First World War, active in education and welfare work for the blind; Chair. St. Dunstan's Council 21-; Pres. British Legion 47-58; Chair. Frasers Ltd., S. Africa, Sun, Alliance and London Insurance Ltd. (West End), Bass Charrington Vintners Ltd.; Dir. Aspro-Nicholas Ltd., Bass Charrington Ltd., Thomson Newspapers, S. Africa (Pty.) Ltd., and many other companies; Gov. B.B.C. 37-39 and 41-46.
Publs. *Whereas I Was Blind* 42, *My Story of St. Dunstan's* 61.
St. John's Lodge, Inner Circle, Regent's Park, London, N.W.1, England.
Telephone: 01-935-8232.

Frauwallner, Erich, PH.D.; Austrian indologist; b. 28 Dec. 1898; ed. Vienna Univ.
Lecturer Vienna Univ. 28, Prof. of Indology 38-, emeritus 63-; Editor *Wiener Zeitschrift für die Kunde Süd- und Ostasiens;* mem. Austrian Acad. of Sciences.
Publs. *On the date of the Buddhist Master of the Law Vasubandhu* 51, *Geschichte der indischen Philosophie* 53-56, *The earliest Vinaya and the beginnings of Buddhist literature* 56, *Die Philosophie des Buddhismus* 56, *Aus der Philosophie der Sivaitischen Systeme* 62, *Abhidarma-Studien I-II* 63, *Raghunatha Siromani* 66-67.
Sieveringerstrasse 16, 1190 Vienna XIX, Austria.

Frazer, Alastair, C.B.E., F.R.C.P., M.D., PH.D., D.SC.; British medical scientist; b. 26 July 1909; ed. Lancing Coll., St. Mary's Hospital Medical School, Univ. of London.
Lecturer in Physiology, St. Mary's Hospital Medical School 31-41, Acting Prof. 34-35; Independent Reader in Pharmacology, Univ. of Birmingham 42, Prof. of Medical Biochemistry and Pharmacology 43-67; mem. East African Council for Medical Research 52-55, Cttee. for Medical Research in Caribbean Region 56-61; Pres. British Industrial Biological Research Assen. 60; Vice-Chair. Tropical Medical Research Board 60; Chair. Research Cttee. on Toxic Chemicals 63, Toxicology Cttee. of Safety of Drugs Cttee. 64; mem. Agricultural Research Council 61; First Dir.-Gen. British Nutrition

Foundation 67-; mem. Royal Flemish Acad. of Sciences, Soc. Philomathique de Paris, New York Acad. of Sciences; Buckstone Browne Medal of Harveian Soc.
28 Montpelier Street, London, S.W.7, England.

Frazer, Sir Thomas, Kt., O.B.E.; British businessman; b. 19 Jan. 1884; ed. Daniel Stewart's Coll., Edinburgh.
Member Capital Issues Cttee. 36-, Chair. 59-; mem. Council of Foreign Bondholders; Fellow, Faculty of Actuaries in Scotland.
Flat 98, Grosvenor House, London, W.1, England.

Freccia, Massimo; American (b. Italian) conductor; b. 19 Sept. 1906; ed. Cherubini Royal Conservatoire, Florence.
Guest conductor New York Philharmonic Orchestra 38, 39, 40; Musical Dir. and Conductor, Havana Philharmonic Orchestra 39-43, New Orleans Symphony Orchestra 44-52, Baltimore Symphony Orchestra 52-59; Chief Conductor Rome (R.A.I.) Orchestra 59-; frequent appearances as Guest Conductor of famous orchestras in Europe and U.S.; Australian tour 63; appeared at various int. Festivals, including Vienna, Prague, Berlin, Lisbon; Hon. D.Mus., Tulane Univ., New Orleans; Order of the Star of Italian Solidarity.
230 Via Appia Antica, Rome, Italy.

Fréchet, Maurice René, D. ès Sciences Mathématiques; French university professor (Emeritus); b. 2 Sept. 1878; ed. Ecole Normale Supérieure, Paris.
Teacher at Besançon 06-07, Nantes 07-08; Prof. in Faculty of Science, Univ. of Rennes 08-09, of Poitiers 09-19; served in First World War 14-18; Prof. Faculty of Science, Univ. of Strasbourg 20-27; Prof. Faculty of Science, Univ. of Paris 27-49; fmr. Pres. Société Mathématique de France, Société de Statistique de Paris and Société française de Biométrie; Hon. Pres. Conféd. des Sociétés Scientifiques françaises; Pres. Internacia Scienca Esperantista Asocio 49-51; mem. Polish Acad. of Sciences and Letters 29-, Netherlands Acad. of Sciences 50-; Spanish Acad. of Sciences; mem. of Int. Inst. of Statistics 33-, hon. mem. 59-, Vice-Pres. 60; mem. Acad. Int. de Philosophie des Sciences 49-, Pres. 59-61; Fellow, Econometric Soc. 51-, etc.; mem. Acad. des Sciences 56; Dr. h.c. Freie Univ., Berlin; Officier de la Légion d'Honneur.
Publs. include *Les Espaces Abstraits* 29, *Les Probabilités Associées à un Système d'Evénements Compatibles et Dépendants* 39-43, *Recherches Théoriques Modernes sur le Calcul des Probabilités* 52, *Pages choisies d'analyse générale* 53, *Les Mathématiques et le concret* 55, *La Vie et L'Oeuvre d'Emile Borel* 63.
2 rue Emile Faguet, Paris 14e, France.
Telephone: GOB 9614.

Fred, Edwin Broun, M.S., PH.D.; American university president (Emeritus) and bacteriologist; b. 22 March 1887; ed. Virginia Polytechnic Inst. and Univ. of Göttingen.
Asst. in Bacteriology, Virginia Polytechnic Inst. 07-08; Asst. Prof. 12-13; Asst. Prof. in Bacteriology Univ. of Wisconsin 13-14, Associate Prof. 14-18, Prof. 18-58; Prof. Emer. 58-, Dean of the Graduate School 34-43, Dean Coll. of Agriculture and Dir. of Agricultural Experiment Station 43-45, Pres. of the Univ. 45-58, Pres. Emeritus 58-; Hon. LL.D. (Lawrence and Michigan State Colls. and Northwestern Univ.); Hon. D.Sc. (Marquette Univ., Beloit Coll., Univ. of N.C., Northland Coll. and Univ. of Wisconsin).
Publs. *Textbook of Agricultural Bacteriology* (with F. Löhnis) 23, *Laboratory Manual of Microbiology* (with S. A. Waksman) 28, *Root Nodule Bacteria and Leguminous Plants* (with Baldwin and McCoy) 32.
Home: 10 Babcock Drive, Madison, Wisconsin 53706; Office: Van Hise Hall, The University of Wisconsin, Madison, Wisconsin, U.S.A.
Telephone: 255-1244.

Frédéricq, (Baron) Louis Paul Simon; Belgian lawyer and university professor; b. 25 Nov. 1892; ed. Univ. of Ghent.
Lecturer, Univ. of Ghent 24, Prof. 29, and Rector 36-38; Gov. of Eastern Flanders 38; Chef de Cabinet to the King June 39; returned to Univ. of Ghent and to practise at the Bar 45-; Prof. Univ. of Brussels 46-; mem. Royal Flemish Acad. of Science, Letters and Fine Arts of Belgium; Past Pres. International Acad. of Comparative Law; Hon. Dr. Univs. of Rennes, Lille, Paris and Utrecht.
Publ. *Traité de Droit Commercial belge* (10 vols.).
112 Gonhode Reinweg, Merelbek, Belgium.
Telephone: 526412.

Frederik IX, King of Denmark; b. 11 March 1899.
Son of King Christian X; married Princess Ingrid, daughter of King Gustaf VI Adolf of Sweden 35; succeeded his father as King, April 47.
Amalienborg Palace, Copenhagen, Denmark.

Frederiksen, Emil; Danish literary critic; b. 2 June 1902; ed. St. Andreas Kollegium (Charlottenlund), Univs. of Copenhagen, Uppsala, Lund, Berlin and Paris.
Lecturer in Danish Language and Literature, Univ. of Paris 29, Univs. of Stockholm, Gothenburg, and Lund 30-36; Literary critic, *Kristeligt Dagblad,* Copenhagen 36-44, *Berlingske Tidende* Copenhagen 44-; Editor *Gads Danske Magasin* 42-55.
Publs. *Modern Dansk Literatur* (in Swedish) 31, *Fra Saxo til Hjalmar Gullberg* 44, *Ung Dansk Literatur* 45, 52, *Johannes Jørgensens Ungdom* 46, *Den unge Grundtvig og andre Essays* 48, *Dante* 65, *Jacob Palulau* 66, *H. C. Branner* 67.
Berlingske Tidende, Copenhagen, Denmark.
Telephone: 01-15-75-75.

Frédérix, Pierre; French author and journalist; b. 26 May 1897; ed. Lycée Condorcet and Univ. of Paris.
French Army 15-18; writer 26-, journalist 32-; contributor to *La Revue de Paris* 30-64; Lecturer, Coll. and Univ., U.S.A. 37-39; French Army 39-40; War Corresp. 44-45; contrib. to Agence France-Presse, *Le Monde,* etc. 45-; Chevalier Légion d'Honneur, Grand Prix de la Critique.
Publs. novels: *L'Ange et la Couronne* 26, *Ta Main Gauche* 28, *Souvenirs du Tir aux Hommes* 38, *Le Bal des Saintes Maries* 46, *Mort à Berlin* 48; essays, biography, travel: *Irlande Extreme-Occident* 31, *Machines en Asia* 34, *Washington ou Moscou* 48, *Herman Melville* 50, *Une Porte s'ouvre sur la Chine* 55, *Un siècle de Chasse aux Nouvelles (De Havas à l'AFP)* 54, *Monsieur René Descartes* 59, *Swift, le véritable Gulliver* 64, *La Millième Année* 65.
7 rue de Villersexel, Paris 7e, France.

Fredga, Arne, DR. CHEM.; Swedish professor of organic chemistry; b. 18 July 1902; ed. Univ. of Uppsala.
Asst. at the Chemical Inst. Uppsala Univ. 30-35; Asst. Prof. of Chemistry 35-39; Prof. of Organic Chemistry 39-; mem. of the Swedish Royal Acad. of Sciences 43-; mem. various other scientific societies; Hon. mem. Société Chimique Belge, Finska Kemistsamfundet; mem. of the Nobel Cttee. of Chemistry 44-, Nat. Science Research Council 52-54, Nat. Cttee. for Chemistry 56-62.
Börjegatan 3 A, Uppsala, Sweden.
Telephone: 018-13-57-34.

Fredriksson, Karl Hjalmar; Swedish journalist; b. 95; ed. elementary school.
Farmhand, wood-cutter and metal worker 08-22; began journalistic career 22; Editor *Frihet,* fortnightly review of Socialist Youth movement 30-37; on staff of Socialist Party Information Office 37-40; Political corresp. *Morgon-Tidningen* 40-57, Chief Editor 57-58; on staff of *Stockholms-Tidningen* 58-; frequently writes under the name Nordens Karlsson.
Stockholms-Tidningen, Vattugatan 12, Stockholm, Sweden.

Freed, Louis Franklin, M.A., D.PHIL., M.B., C.H.B., M.D., D.P.M., D.P.H., D.T.M. and H., D.PHIL., D.LITT. ET PHIL., D.I.H., F.R.S.S.A.F., F.S.S., F.R.A.I., F.R.G.S.; South African medical psychologist; b. 1903; ed. Univs. of St. Andrews, Pretoria, Witwatersrand, Stellenbosch, and Orange Free State and South Africa.
Former South African Ed. of *International Journal of Sexology;* former Medical Officer, Tara Neuro-Psychiatric Hospital, Johannesburg 57; Medical Officer, Sterkfontein Mental Hospital, Krugersdorp 56-57; Lecturer on Social Medicine 49-; Lecturer in Dept. of Psychiatry and in Dept. of Sociology, Univ. of Witwatersrand, Johannesburg 53-; Guest Lecturer, Inst. of Criminology, Cambridge, Inst. of Criminology, Hebrew Univ. of Jerusalem, Oxford Univ. Mental Health Soc. 65; D.Phil. Univ. of Orange Free State 58; fmr. mem. New York Acad. of Sciences, S. African Asscn. for the Advancement of Science, Exec. Cttee. of Convocation, Univ. of Witwatersrand; mem. Exec. Cttee. Mental Health Soc., Witwatersrand, Exec. Cttee. South African P.E.N., Exec. Cttee. of Inst. for the study of Man in Africa, Exec. Cttee. Inst of Adult Education, Exec. Cttee. Johannesburg Youth Council, Exec. Cttee. S. African Nat. Epilepsy League.
Publs. *The Problem of European Prostitution in Johannesburg* 49, *Sex Education in Transvaal Schools* 38, *The Philosophy of Sociological Medicine* 48, *Findings of an Investigation into a Group of Patients presenting the Symptoms of Schizophrenia* 53, *The Social Aspect of Venereal Disease* 51, *The Psychosociology of Neoplasia* 58, *A Methodological Approach to the Problem of Mental Disorder* 56, *The Use of Methodological Principles in the Investigation of a Case of Trichomoniasis* 57, *The Problem of Crime in the Union of South Africa: An Integralistic Approach, An Enquiry into the Causality of Cancer* (with G. Giannopoulos), *Cancer-Killer No. 1* 60, *The Problem of Alcoholism: An Integralist Approach* 61, *A Critical Analysis of R. F. A. Hoernle's Contributions to Philosophy with Special Reference to his Synoptic Treatment of Diverse Dimensions of Reality* 65, *The Problem of Suicide in Johannesburg Examined from the standpoint of Incidence, Causality and Control* 67, *The Psychopath: A Social Challenge, A Case of Temporal Lobe Epilepsy.*
15 Lystanwold Road, Saxonwold, Johannesburg, South Africa.
Telephone: 23-0009 (Office); 41-8877 (Home).

Freehafer, Edward Geier, A.B., B.S.; American librarian; b. 11 Feb. 1909; ed. Brown Univ., Columbia School of Library Service, Columbia Univ.
Columbia Univ. School of Business Library 31-32; New York Public Library 32-44: Asst. Librarian, Brown Univ. 44-45; Exec. Asst., New York Public Library 45-47, Chief, Personnel Office 47-53, Reference Dept. 54, Dir. 54-; Hon. L.H.D.
The New York Public Library, Fifth Avenue and 42nd Street, New York 18, N.Y., U.S.A.

Freeman, Fulton, A.B.; American diplomatist; b. 7 May 1915; ed. Pomona Coll. and Princeton Univ.
Joined Foreign Service 39; Mexico, Washington, China 39-48; Washington, Rome, Norfolk (Va.) 48-57; Senior Foreign Service Inspector 57-58; Dep. Chief Mission, Brussels 59-61; Amb. to Colombia 61-64, to Mexico 64-.
American Embassy, Mexico D.F., Mexico.

Freeman, Gaylord Augustus, Jr., B.A., LL.B.; American banker; b. 19 Jan. 1910; ed. Morgan Park High School, Dartmouth Coll., Harvard Law School.
Attorney, First Nat. Bank of Chicago 40-50, Vice-Pres. 50-59, Pres. 60-62, Vice-Chair. of the Bd. 62-; Dir. Borg-Warner Corpn., Central Coal & Coke Co., Chicago

& North Western Railway Co., Clearing Industrial District, Container Corpn., Caterpillar Tractor Co., Time Inc.; Trustee, Northwestern Univ.
White Thorn Road, Wayne, Illinois, U.S.A.

Freeman, Rt. Hon. John, P.C., M.B.E.; British journalist and diplomatist; b. 19 Feb. 1915; ed. Westminster School and Brasenose Coll., Oxford.
Advertising Consultant 37-40; active service in North Africa, Italy and North-West Europe 40-45; M.P. (Lab.) Watford 45-55; Financial Sec. to the War Office 46-47; Under-Sec. of State for War 47-48; Parl. Sec. to the Ministry of Supply 48-51 (resgnd.); retd. from politics 55; Deputy Editor *New Statesman* 58-61, Editor 61-65; British High Commr. in India 65-68; Amb. Designate to U.S.A. 68.
D.S.A.O., King Charles Street, London, S.W.1, England.

Freeman, Nelson Wright; American business executive; b. 6 Aug. 1908; ed. Univ. of Illinois.
Branch Man. Universal Credit Corpn., Detroit 29-34; Pres. and Gen. Man. Freeman & Riesen Motors Co. Milwaukee 34-38; Man. Assocs. Investment Co., Houston 38-42; Personnel and Safety Dir. Lummus Co. Houston 42-43; with Tenneco Inc. Houston (then named Tennessee Gas Transmission Co.) 43-59, as Man. Personnel Dept., Asst. to Pres. 47, Vice-Pres. 50, Senior Vice-Pres. 54; Pres. Midwestern Gas Transmission Co. Houston 54-61; natural gas consultant, banker and rancher 62-64; Pres. Houston Nat. Bank 64-66; Pres. and Dir. Tenneco Inc. 66-; Chair. of the Board J. I. Case Co., Racine; Dir. Tenneco Chemicals Inc., New York, Packaging Corpn. of America, Kern County Land Co. and others; Vice-Pres. and Dir. Houston Fat Stock & Rodeo; Trustee United Fund of Houston and Harris County; mem. Natural Gas Industry Council 56.
Tenneco Inc., P.O. Box 2511, Houston, Texas; Homes: Route 5, Box 31, Brenham, Texas, and 1233 Post Oak Park, Houston, Texas, U.S.A.

Freeman, Orville Lothrop, B.A., LL.B.; American lawyer and politician; b. 9 May 1918; ed. Central High School, Minneapolis, Minnesota Univ. Law School.
Worked his way through college as janitor, harvest hand, etc.; served with U.S. Marine Corps 41-45; Asst. to Mayor of Minneapolis 45-49; Sec. State Cen. Cttee. 46-48, Chair. Exec. Cttee. 48-50; in private law practice 50-54; candidate Attorney General 50, Gov. 52; Gov. of Minnesota 54-61; U.S. Sec. of Agriculture 61-; Hon. LL.D. Univ. of Seoul, Korea, St. Joseph's Coll., Philadelphia, U.S.A.; Democratic-Farmer-Labor.
2805 Daniel Road, Chevy Chase, Md., U.S.A.

Freeth, Hon. Gordon, M.P., LL.B.; Australian politician; b. 6 Aug. 1914; ed. Univ. of Western Australia.
Barrister and solicitor of Supreme Court of W. Australia; Solicitor, Katanning, W. Australia 39-49; Royal Australian Air Force 42-45; mem. Parl. 49-; Minister for Interior and Works 58-63; Minister assisting the Attorney-Gen. 61-63; Minister for Shipping and Transport 63-68; Minister for Air and Minister assisting the Treas. 68-; Liberal.
Commonwealth Parliament Offices, Perth; Home: 142 Victoria Avenue, Dalkeith 6009, Western Australia.
Telephone: 21-2280 (Office).

Frei Montalva, Eduardo, LL.D.; Chilean lawyer and politician; b. 16 Jan. 1911; ed. Public School, Lentue, Inst. of Humanities, Santiago and Catholic Univ. of Chile.
Former mem. Chamber of Deputies, now mem. Senate; fmr. Minister of Public Works; founder-mem. Nat. Falange later Christian Democrat Party 35, Pres. of Party on three occasions, and fmr. Chair.; Pres. of Chile 64; Editor *El Tarapacá* (daily) 35-37.
Publs. *The Regime of Fixed Salaries and its Possible Abolition, Unknown Chile, Now is the Time, Politics and the Spirit, The History of Chilean Political Parties, Truth Has Its Hour, Political Meaning and Form, Thought and Action.*
El Palacio de la Moneda, Santiago, Chile.

Freitas-Valle, Cyro de, C.B.E.; Brazilian diplomatist; b. 96; ed. Sao Paulo.
Second Sec. Buenos Aires, Washington, Vienna, Paris, 18-26; First Sec. Lima, Montevideo, The Hague 26-32; Counsellor of Embassy and Chief Boundary Div. Foreign Office 32; Minister to Bolivia, Cuba, Rumania, 34-38; Gen. Sec. Foreign Office 39; Ambassador to Germany 39-42; Dir. Gen. Fed. Council Foreign Trade 43; Ambassador to Canada 44-45; Brazilian Del. to the San Francisco Conf.; Head of the Brazilian Del. to the U.N. Preparatory Comm.; Del. to U.N. Gen. Assembly in London; mem. of Security Council 46; Del. to Paris Peace Conf.; Ambassador to Argentina 47; Sec.-Gen. Foreign Office 49; Acting Minister for External Relations 49; Head of Del. to UN Gen. Assemblies; Amb. to Chile 52-54; Perm. Del. to UN 55-61.
532 Avenida Ruy Barbosa, Rio de Janeiro, Brazil.

Frère, Jean; Belgian diplomatist and banker; b. 19; ed. Germany, Austria, Brussels Univ.
With Solvay & Cie. (Chemical Industries), Brussels 41-46; entered diplomatic service 46, Attaché (Commercial and Econ.), Belgian Legation, Prague 48-51; Political Div., Ministry of Foreign Affairs 51-52; First Sec. (Econ.), Belgian Embassy, Rome 52-58; Gen. Sec. European Investment Bank 58-; mem. Belgian del. Conf. between EEC mem. countries and Britain 62; Conseiller Banque Lambert 62-, Man. Partner Banque Lambert 67-; mem. of the Board, Banco di Roma (Belgique) S.A., Generalfin Milano; many Belgian and foreign Orders.
Banque Lambert S.C.S., 24 avenue Marnix, Brussels 5, Belgium.
Telephone: 13-81-81.

Frère, Maurice; Belgian banker and economist; b. 8 Aug. 1890; ed. Brussels.
Asst. Brussels Univ. 12-14; Dir. Min. of Economic Affairs and Lecturer Brussels Univ. 18; Dir. Economic Service of Reparations Comm. 20-24; Economic Counsellor Berlin Transfer Cttee. under Dawes Plan 24-30; Financial Counsellor Belgian Govt. attached to Legation Berlin 30-32; L.N. Counsellor at Austrian Nat. Bank 32-37; Head of Prime Min.'s Economic Mission and Dir. at Min. of Foreign Affairs 37-38; Chair. Bank Comm. for control of Banks and public issues 38-44; Gov. Belgian Nat. Bank 44-57; mem. Board B.I.S. since 44, Chair. and Pres. 46-58, Vice-Chair. 65-; Permanent mem. Board, Brussels Univ. 46; Gov. Int. Monetary Fund and Alternate Gov. Int. Bank for Reconstruction and Development (for Belgium) 46-57; Chair. Board of Sofina 57.
Office: 38 rue de Naples, Brussels 5; Home: 341 avenue Louise, Brussels 5, Belgium.
Telephone: 12-66-10 (Office); 47-15-51 (Home).

Fresnay, Pierre (*pseudonym* of Pierre Laudenbach); French actor; b. 4 April 1897.
Made his cinema debut 22; has also directed numerous plays in the theatre; his films include: *Le Petit Jacques, Le Diamant Noir, Marius, La Dame aux Camélias, César, Koenigsmark, Le Puritain, Trois Valses, Le Corbeau, Monsieur Vincent, La Grande Illusion, La Valse de Paris, Dieu à besoin des hommes, Les Aristocrates, L'homme aux clefs d'or,* etc.; Prix de la Biennale 47; Prix féminin du Cinéma 49.
8 *bis* rue St. James, Neuilly-sur-Seine, France.

Freud, Anna, C.B.E., LL.D., SC.D. (daughter of late Sigmund Freud); British (naturalized) psychoanalyst; b. 3 Dec. 1895.
Member Vienna Psycho-Analytic Soc.; Chair. Training Inst. of the Vienna Psycho-Analytic Society; Chair. of

the Vienna Psycho-Analytic Society 25-38; Organiser of a Residential War Nursery for Homeless Children, London 40-45; mem. of the British Psycho-Analytic Society and Inst. of Psycho-Analysis 38-; Dir. of the Hampstead Child-Therapy Course and Clinic 38-; Vice-Pres. Int. Psycho-Analytic Asscn. 38-.
Publs. *Introduction to Psycho-Analysis for Teachers* 31, *The Ego and the Mechanisms of Defence* 37, *The Psycho-Analytical Treatment of Children* 46, *Normality and Pathology in Childhood* 65, and, with Dorothy Burlingham, *Young Children in War-time* 42, *Infants Without Families* 43.
20 Maresfield Gardens, London, N.W.3, England.

Freud, Lucien; British painter; b. 8 Dec. 1922; ed. Central School of Art, Goldsmiths' Coll., London.
Teacher at Slade School of Art, London; first one-man exhibition 44, subsequently 46, 50, 52, 58, 63; works have been acquired by New York Museum of Modern Art, Melbourne Nat. Gallery, Tate Gallery, London, etc.; rep. at Dunn Int. Exhibition, London 63.
Slade School of Fine Art, Gower Street, London, W.C.1, England.

Freudenberg, Karl Johann, DR.PHIL.; German chemist; b. 29 Jan. 1886; ed. Realprogymnasium Weinheim, Goethe-Gymnasium Frankfurt, Rheinische Friedrich-Wilhelms-Universität, Bonn, and Univ. of Berlin.
Worked with Emil Fischer, Berlin 08-13; Privatdozent, Univ. of Kiel 14; First World War (Iron Crosses) 14-18; Privatdozent, Univ. of Munich 20; Extraordinary Prof. Univ. of Freiburg 21; Full Prof. and Dir. Chemical Laboratory, Technical Univ. Karlsruhe 22-26; Full Prof. and Dir. Chemical Laboratory, Univ. of Heidelberg 26-56, Rector of Univ. of Heidelberg 49; Dir. of Research Inst. for Chemistry of Wood and Poly-saccharides, Chemical Inst., Heidelberg 56-; Carl Schurz Memorial Prof., Univ. of Wisconsin 31; Dohme Lecturer, Univ. of Baltimore 31; Cooch Behar Prof. Lecturer, Indian Asscn. for Cultivation of Science, Jadavpur, Calcutta 58; mem. Acads. of Heidelberg, Göttingen, Munich, Uppsala, Stockholm, Lund, Helsinki; Foreign mem. Royal Soc., London; Hon. mem. Acad. Leopoldina, Halle, Swiss Chemical Soc., Japanese Chemical Soc., Japanese Agricultural Chemical Soc., Spanish Soc. of Physics and Chemistry, Soc. of Austrian Chemists, Chemical Soc. London, Societas Scientiarum Fennica, etc.; Dr. h.c. Technical Univs. of Graz and Darmstadt, Univs. Basle and Berlin, Humboldt Univ.
Publs. *Chemie der natürlichen Gerbstoffe* 20, *Stereochemistry* 33, *Tannin, Cellulose, Lignin* 33, *Organische Chemie* (with Plieninger—11th edition) 67; papers on stereochemistry, natural organic high molecular substances: tannins, cellulose, starch, proteins, lignin.
6900 Heidelberg, Wilckenstrasse 34, German Federal Republic.

Freund, Mrs. Miriam Kottler, M.A., PH.D.; American Zionist organizer; b. 17 Feb. 1906; ed. Hunter Coll., New York Univ.
Teacher high schools, N.Y.C. to 44; Nat. Board Hadassah, Women's Zionist Organisation 40-, Vice-Pres. 53-56, Pres. 56-60; Chair. Nat. Youth Aliyah 53-56; mem. Actions Cttee., World Zionist Organisation 56-; Chair. Exec. American Zionist Council 60-; mem. Nat. Board Jewish Nat. Fund and Keren Hayesod 47-; Del. 21st Orientalist Congress, Moscow 60; mem. American Asscn. Univ. Women, Jewish History Soc.; mem. Exec. World Council of Synagogues; Editor Hadassah Magazine.
Publs. *Jewish Merchants in Colonial America* 36, *Jewels for a Crown* 63.
200 East 71st Street, New York City 21, N.Y., U.S.A.
Telephone: RHinelander 4-2763.

Frewen, Admiral Sir John Byng, K.C.B.; British naval officer; b. 28 March 1911; ed. Royal Naval Coll., Dartmouth.

Flag Officer Second-in-Command (U.K.), Far East Fleet 61-62; Vice-Chief of Naval Staff (U.K.) Feb. 63-April 65; C.-in-C. British Home Fleet and C.-in-C. (NATO), Allied Forces in E. Atlantic July 65-67, additionally C.-in-C., Channel (NATO) 66-67; C.-in-C. Portsmouth 67-.
Clench Green, Northiam, Rye, Sussex, England.

Frey, Roger; French politician; b. 11 June 1913.
Counsellor of the French Union 52; Sec. Gen. Parti Républicain Social 54, U.N.R. 58; Minister of Information 59-Feb. 60; Minister attached to Prime Minister's Office 60-62; Minister of the Interior 62-67; Minister of State responsible for relations with Parl. 67-; Croix de Guerre, Légion d'Honneur; Union pour la Nouvelle République (U.N.R.).
56 boulevard Flandrin, Paris 16e, France.

Freymond, Jacques, D. ès L.; Swiss professor of history; b. 5 Aug. 1911; ed. Univs. of Lausanne, Munich and Paris.
Teacher in various secondary schools 35-42; Prof. of Modern and Contemporary History, Univ. of Lausanne 43-55; Prof. of Diplomatic History, Ecole des Sciences sociales et politiques, Univ. of Lausanne 46-55; Diplomatic Chronicler, *Gazette de Lausanne* 46-55; Rockefeller Fellow in U.S. for studies, especially Yale and Columbia Univs. 49-50; Prof. of History at Graduate Inst. of Int. Studies, Geneva 51-, Dir. Graduate Inst. of Int. Studies 55-; Prof. History of Int. Relations, Univ. of Geneva 58-; corresp. mem. Académie des Sciences Morales et Politiques 61; mem. Int. Red Cross Cttee.; Pres. Int. Political Science Asscn. 64-67.
Publs. *La politique de François Ier à l'égard de la Savoie* 39, *Lénine et l'Impérialisme* 51, *De Roosevelt à Eisenhower: la politique étrangère américaine* 53, *Le conflit Sarrois* 59, *La Première Internationale, recueil de documents* 62, *Etudes et documents sur la Première Internationale en Suisse* 64, *Western Europe since the War* 64, *Contributions à l'étude du Comintern* 65.
Office: 132 rue de Lausanne, c/o Institut Universitaire de Hautes Etudes Internationales, 1211 Geneva; Home: 1294 Genthod, Geneva, Switzerland.
Telephone: 311730.

Freyre, Gilberto de Mello, B.A., M.A., D.LITT.; Brazilian writer and social anthropologist; b. 1900; ed. Colegio Americano, Recife, Baylor and Columbia Univs., U.S.A. Research in England, France, Germany and U.S. 22, 31, 36, 37; Prof. of Sociology, Pernambuco State Normal School 28-30; Prof. of Sociology and Founding Prof. of Social Anthropology, Rio de Janeiro Univ. 35-38; Supervisor North East Brazil Social and Educational Research Centre 57-; M.P. 46-50; del. U.N. Gen. Assembly 49, 64; Technical Adviser, Dept. for Protection of Historical and Artistic Monuments, U.N. Cttee. on Race Relations in South Africa 54; founded Recife Inst. for Research in Social Sciences 49; Visiting Prof. and Lecturer at many univs.; hon. mem. American Sociological Soc., Brazilian Historical and Geographical Inst., American Acad. of Arts and Sciences, World Acad. or Arts and Sciences, French Acad. of Sciences; Hon. Prof. Columbia, Recife and Bahia Univs.; mem. Portuguese, Ecuadorean and Colombian Historical Acads., American Anthropological Asscn., Lisbon Geog. Soc., American Philosophical Soc.; Hon. Aggregatus of Sociology, Buenos Aires Univ.; Dr. h.c. (Columbia, Sussex, Coimbra, Sorbonne Univs.); Dir. *Diogène* and *Cahiers Internationaux de Sociologie* (Paris), Inst. Int. de Civilisations Différentes (Belgium); Filipe d'Oliveira Award 34, Amsfield-Wolf Award (Princeton) 57, Brazilian Acad. of Letters Award for high literary merit 59, 60; Great Cross of Military Merit 60, Great Cross of the Brazilian Order of Baron of Rio Branco (Diplomacy) 66.
Publs. *Casa-Grande e Senzala* (in English as *The Masters and the Slaves*) 34, *Sobrados e Mucambos* (in English as

The Mansions and the Shanties) 36, *Sociologia, Problemas brasileiros de Antropologia* (Brazil: An Interpretation) 45, *Ingleses no Brazil* 48, *Aventura e Rotina* 53, *Vida Social no Brasil nos Meades do Seculo XIX* 64, *Dona Sinká e o Filho Padre* (in English as *Mother and Son*), *Talvey Poesia*.

Apipucos, Recife, Brazil.

Frey-Wyssling, Prof. Albert, DR. SC. NAT.; Swiss university professor; b. 8 Nov. 1900; ed. Swiss Federal Inst. of Technology (E.T.H.), and Univs. of Geneva, Jena and Paris.

Rockefeller Fellow, Univ. of Jena 25, at Paris 26; Teacher of Gen. Botany at E.T.H. 27; Plant Physiologist, Experimental Station AVROS, Sumatra, Indonesia 28-32; Asst. and Lecturer, Gen. Botany, E.T.H., Zürich 32-38, Prof. Gen. Botany and Plant Physiology, E.T.H. 38-, Rector, E.T.H. (Eidgenössische Technische Hochschule) 57-61; Dr. h.c. (Utrecht, Münster, Rennes, Vancouver); Foreign mem. Royal Society, London 57. Publs. *Stoffausscheidung der höheren Pflanzen* 35, *Submikroskopische Morphologie des Protoplasmas* 38, *Submicroscopic Morphology of Protoplasm* 48 and 53, *Submikroskopische Struktur des Cytoplasmas* 55, *Macromolecules in Cell Structure* 57, *Die pflanzliche Zellwand* 59, *Ultrastructural Plant Cytology* (with K. Mühlethaler) 65.

Department of General Botany, E.T.H., Universitätsstrasse 2, Zürich 6; Home: Schiltrai, 8706 Meilen, Zürich, Switzerland.

Friberg, Sten Axel, M.D.; Swedish orthopaedic surgeon; b. 5 Sept. 1902; ed. Karolinska Institutet, Stockholm.

Professor 43-, Head of Univ. Clinic of Orthopaedic Surgery 43-, Rector of Karolinska Institutet 53-; mem. Board of Nobel Foundation 53-; Chair. Nobel Cttee. 60-; mem. Scientific Council at Nat. Swedish Social Welfare Board; mem. Nat. Swedish Industrial Injuries Insurance Court; Editor *Acta Orthopaedica Scandinavica* 47-; Pres. Soc. Int. de Chirurgie Orthopédique et de Traumatologie; mem. Acad. de Chirurgie, France; Hon. or Corresp. mem. Orthopaedic Asscns. in Argentina, Austria, France, Germany, Great Britain, Italy, U.S.A.; Corresp. mem. Soviet Acad. of Medical Sciences. Publs. Approx. 60 works, mainly on orthopaedics.

Karolinska Institutet, Solnavägen 1, S-104 01 Stockholm, Sweden.

Telephone: (Stockholm) 23-54-80; 60-70-50.

Frič, Martin; Czechoslovak film director; b. 29 March 1902; ed. School of Fine and Applied Arts, Prague. Made his first silent film 22, first sound film 31; also stage and screen actor, cameraman, scriptwriter, Barrandov Film Studio; Chair. Czechoslovak Union of Film and TV Artists 66-; Czechoslovak Prize 39; Order of Republic 55; Hon. Artist 62, Nat. Artist 65.

Films include: *Zocelení* (The Steel Town, Nat. and State Prize) 51, *Císařův pekař* and *Pekařův císař* (The Emperor's Baker *and* The Baker's Emperor, Czechoslovak Art Award, and shown at int. film festivals in Edinburgh, Karlovy Vary, Locarno and Mar del Plata) 51, *Bylo to v máji* (It Happened in May, State Prize) 51, *Tajemství krve* (The Secret of Blood, State Prize) 53. Czechoslovak Film, Jindřišska 34, Prague 1, Czechoslovakia.

Frick, Alexander; Liechtenstein politician; b. 10; ed. Training Coll. for Teachers.

Began career as teacher 29; official in Tax Dept. 30-36, Chief of Dept. 36; Head of Govt. 45-62; now Pres. of the Diet; awarded Grand Cross of Liechtenstein Order of Merit, Great Silver Insignia of Honour (Bande der Republik Österreich); mem. Bürgerpartei.

Schaan, Principality of Liechtenstein, Europe.

Frick, Gottlob; German bass opera singer; b. 1906; ed. Stuttgart Opera Chorus and under Neudörfer-Opitz. First small part in Bayreuth Festival 30; with Coburg

Opera 34, then Freiburg-im-Breisgau and Königsberg Opera; with Dresden Opera 40-50; joined West Berlin City Opera 50; regular committments with Vienna State Opera, Bavarian State Opera and guest artist at Covent Garden and Metropolitan, New York; chiefly known for Wagnerian roles including Daland, Hermann, King Heinrich, King Mark, Pogner, Gurnemann and bass parts in *The Ring* especially Fasolt, Hunding and Hagen; also sings in Oratorio.

c/o Royal Opera House, Covent Garden, London, W.C.2, England.

Fricker, Peter Racine, F.R.C.O., A.R.C.M.; British musician; b. 5 Sept. 1920; ed. St. Paul's School and Royal Coll. of Music.

Served R.A.F. 39-45; worked in London as composer, conductor and music administrator 46-64; Dir. of Music; Morley Coll. 52-64; Prof. of Music, Univ. of Calif. 64-, Hon. D.Mus. (Leeds) 58; W. German Order of Merit 65; Hon. mem. Royal Acad. of Music.

Works: *First String Quartet* 48, *First Symphony* 49, *First Violin Concerto* 50, *Violin Sonata* 50, *Second Symphony* 51, *Viola Concerto* 53, *Second String Quartet* 53, *Second Violin Concerto* 53, *Piano Concerto* 54, *Dance Scene for Orchestra* 54, *Horn Sonata* 55, *Litany for Double String Orchestra* 55, *Musick's Empire* (Chorus and Orchestra) 55, *'Cello Sonata* 56, *The Vision of Judgement* (Oratorio) 57, *Octet* 58, *Comedy Overture* 58, *Toccata for Piano and Orchestra* 59, *Serenade No. 1 for Six Instruments* 59, *Serenade No. 2 for Flute, Oboe and Piano* 59, *Third Symphony* 60, *12 Studies for Piano* 61, *Cantata for Tenor and Chamber Ensemble* 62, *O Longs Désirs* (song cycle for soprano and orchestra) 63, *Ricercare for Organ* 65, *Four Dialogues for Oboe and Piano* 65, *Four Songs, Voice and Piano, Texts by Andreas Gryphius* (also with Orchestra) 65, *Fourth Symphony* 66, *Fantasy for Viola and Piano* 66, *Three Scenes for Orchestra, The Day and the Spirits* (soprano and harp) 67, *Seven Counterpoints for Orchestra* 67, *Ave Maris Stella* (male voices and piano) 67, *Refrains for Solo Oboe* 68, *Magnificat for Soloists, Chorus and Orchestra* 68, *Episodes for Piano* 68, *Concertante No. 4 for Flute, Oboe, Violin and Strings* 68.

Office: Department of Music, University of California, Santa Barbara, California 93106; Home: 6155 Verdura Avenue, Goleta, California 93017, U.S.A.

Telephone: 805-964-3737.

Friday, William Clyde, B.S., LL.B., LL.D.; American educator; b. 13 July 1920; ed. Wake Forest Coll., North Carolina State Coll. and Univ. of N. Carolina Law School.

Assistant Dean of Students, Univ. of N. Carolina at Chapel Hill 48-51, Acting Dean of Students 50-51, Admin. Asst. to Pres. Univ. of N. Carolina 51-54, Sec. of Univ. of N. Carolina 54-55, Acting Pres. of Univ. of N. Carolina 56, Pres. Oct. 56-; Hon. LL.D. (Wake Forest Coll., Belmont Abbey, Duke Univ., Princeton Univ., Elon Coll. and Davidson Coll.).

402 East Franklin Street, Chapel Hill, North Carolina 27514, U.S.A.

Fridh, Gertrude; Swedish actress; b. 26 Nov. 1921; ed. Gothenburg School of Dramatic Art.

Gothenburg Theatre 44-49; Intima Theatre, Stockholm 50; Allé Theatre, Stockholm 55-57; Royal Dramatic Theatre, Stockholm 58-.

Plays acted in include: *Ett Dockhem* 53, *Som ni behagar* 54, *Le Misanthrope* 57, *Anna Karenina* 58, *Hedda Gabler* 64 (London 68).

Films acted in include: *Skepp till indialand* 47, *Två trappor över gården* 49-50, *Hjärter Knekt* 50, *Smultrunstället* (Wild Strawberries) 57, *Ansiktet* (The Face) 58, *Djävulens Öga* 60.

c/o Svenska Filminstitutet, Kungsgatan 48, Stockholm C, Sweden.

Friedensburg, Ferdinand, DR. PHIL.; German scientist and administrator; b. 17 Nov. 1886; ed. Mining Acad. of Berlin and Univs. of Marburg, Berlin and Breslau. Landrat at Rosenberg/Westpr. 21-25; Police Vice-Pres., Berlin 25-27; Regierungspräsident at Kassel 27 till dismissed by Hitler 33; scientific research in Mining Economics 33-45; Pres. Central Admin. of Fuel and Power, Berlin 45-46; Deputy Lord Mayor of Berlin 46-51; until 68 Pres. Deutsches Inst für Wirtschaftsforschung; Pres. Arbeitsgemeinschaft deutscher wirtschaftswissenschaftlicher Forschungsinstitute; Prof. Technical Univ., Berlin; until 64 mem. Bundesrat, Bonn and mem. European Parl.; one of founders and leaders of Christian Democratic Union; Hon. LL.D. (Wayne State Univ.) 59, Hon. LL.D. (Columbia Univ., New York).
Publs. *Kohle und Eisen im Weltkrieg und in den Friedensschlüssen* 34, *Die mineralischen Bodenschätze als weltpolitische und militärische Machtfaktoren* 36, *Die Bergwirtschaft der Erde* 38 (6th edn. 65), *Das Erdöl im Weltkrieg* 39, *Rohstoffe und Energiequellen im neuen Europa* 43, *Die Weimarer Republik* 46 (2nd edn. 57), *Das Erzproblem der amerikanischen Eisenindustrie* 53, *Berlin-Schicksal und Aufgabe* 53, *Gold* 53, *Das Erzproblem der Deutschen Eisenindustrie* 57.
1/Berlin 33, Königin-Luise Strasse 5, Germany.
Telephone: 76-1033.

Friedenthal, Richard, DR. PHIL.; British (b. German) writer; b. 9 June 1896; ed. Gymnasium, Berlin, Humboldt-Universität zu Berlin, Friedrich-Schiller-Universität, Jena, and Ludwig-Maximilians-Universität, Munich.
Former Reader and Editor, Knaur Verlag, Berlin; writer and editor in England 38-; mem. German Acad., Darmstadt; Grosses Bundesverdienstkreuz (German Fed. Republic).
Publs. include poetry, novels, short stories; biographies: *Der Eroberer* 32, *Leonardo da Vinci* 59, *G. F. Handel* 59, *Goethe—His Life and Times* 65; travel books: *Die Party bei Herrn Tokaido* 58, *London zwischen gestern und morgen* 60; Editor *Knaurs Lexikon* 31, *Facts* (4 vols.) 34, *Letters of the Great Artist* (2 vols.) 64.
15 Burgess Hill, London, N.W.2, England.

Friedland, Samuel; American businessman; b. 23 Nov. 1896.
Co-founder, Chair. Food Fair Stores Inc.; Chair. Lefcourt Realty Corpn. 59-.
2223 E. Alleghany Avenue, Philadelphia 34, Pa., U.S.A.

Friedman, Irving S., A.B., M.A., PH.D.; American financial economist; b. 31 Jan. 1915; ed. City Coll., N.Y., and Columbia Univ., N.Y.
Member Office of Sec. of Treasury, U.S. 41-46; Chief of U.S.-Canada Div., Research Dept., Int. Monetary Fund (IMF) 46-48; Asst. for Policy Matters to Deputy Managing Dir. IMF 48-50; Dir. Exchange Restrictions Dept., IMF 50-64; Econ. Adviser to Pres. of Int. Bank for Reconstruction and Development (World Bank) 64-; Chair. Econ. Cttee., U.S.; mem. President's Council, U.S.
Publs. include numerous books and articles on international economics.
Office: International Bank for Reconstruction and Development, 1818 H Street, N.W., Washington, D.C.; Home: 6620 Fernwood Court, Bethesda, Maryland, U.S.A.
Telephone: EM-5-5023 (Home).

Friedman, Milton, B.A., M.A., PH.D.; American economist; b. 31 July 1912; ed. Rutgers Univ., Chicago and Columbia Univs.
Associate Economist, Nat. Resources Cttee. 35-37, Nat. Bureau of Economic Research 37-45 (on leave 40-45), 48-; Principal Economist, Div. of Tax Research, U.S.

Treasury Dept. 41-43; Assoc. Dir. Statistical Research Group, Div. of War Research, Columbia Univ. 43-45; Prof. of Economics, Univ. of Chicago 48-; Board of Editors *Econometrica*; Pres. American Econ. Asscn. 67; Hon. LL.D. (Tokyo, Kalamazoo Coll., Rutgers Univ.).
Publs. *Income from Independent Professional Practice* (with Simon Kuznets) 46, *Sampling Inspection* (with others) 48, *Essays in Positive Economics* 53, *A Theory of the Consumption Function* 57, *A Program for Monetary Stability* 59, *Capitalism and Freedom* 62, *Price Theory: a provisional text* 62, *A Monetary History of the United States 1867-1960* (with Anna J. Schwartz) 63, *Inflation: Causes and Consequences* 63, *Dollars and Deficits* 68; econ. columnist with *Newsweek*.
1126 East 59th Street, Chicago, Ill. 60637, U.S.A.
Telephone: MI 3-0800, Extension 4523.

Friedmann, Georges Philippe; French university professor and sociologist; b. 13 May 1902; ed. Ecole Normale Supérieure and Univ. of Paris.
Inspector-Gen. of Technical Education 45; Prof. Conservatoire Nat. des Arts et Métiers 46-62; Dir. d'Etudes, Ecole Pratique des Hautes Etudes (Sorbonne) 48-62; Dir. du Centre d'Etudes Sociologiques 49-51; Pres. Int. Sociological Asscn.; Pres. Latin-American Faculty of Social Science, Santiago 58-64; Joint Editor of the revue *Annales* 47-; Officier Légion d'Honneur, Médaille de la Resistance.
Publs. *La Crise du Progrès* 36, *De la Sainte Russie à l'U.R.S.S.* 38, *Leibniz et Spinoza* 46, *Problèmes Humains du Machinisme Industriel* 46, *Où va le travail humain?* 50, *Villes et Campagnes* (edited) 53, *Le Travail en miettes* 56, *Problèmes d'Amérique Latine* (2 vols.) 59, 61, *Traité de Sociologie du Travail* (2 vols.) 61, 62, *Fin du Peuple Juif?* 65, *Sept Etudes sur l'homme et la technique* 66.
11 rue François Ponsard, Paris 16e, France.

Friedmann, Werner; German newspaper editor; b. 09; ed. Wilhelmsgymnasium, Munich, and Univ. of Munich.
Editorial staff *Süddeutsche Sonntagspost* and *Münchener Illustrierte* 29-33; arrested and forbidden to practise journalism 33; army service 40-45; editorial staff *Süddeutsche Zeitung* 45-, Chief Editor 51-60; founded Werner Friedmann-Institut zur Ausbildung des journalistischen Nachwuchses.
Harthauserstrasse 58, Munich 9, German Federal Republic.

Friedrich, Carl Joachim; American (born German) professor of political science; b. 5 June 1901; ed. Marburg, Frankfurt, Vienna and Heidelberg Univs.
Emigrated to U.S.A. 22; Lecturer in Govt. Harvard 26-27, Asst. Prof. 27-31, Assoc. Prof. 31-36, Prof. of Govt. 36-; Eaton Prof. Science of Govt. 55-; Prof. of Political Science Heidelberg 56-68.
Publs. *Studies in Federalism* 54, *The Philosophy of Law in Historical Perspective* 56, 58, *Die Demokratie als Staats-und Lebensform* 59, *The Age of the Baroque* 62, *Man and His Government* 63, *Transcendent Justice* 64, *Totalitarian Dictatorship and Autocracy* 65, *Introduction to Political Theory* 67, *Federalism* 68, *Constitutional Government and Democracy* 68.
14 Hawthorn Street, Cambridge 02138, Mass., U.S.A.

Friedrich, Johannes, DR.PHIL.; German orientalist; b. 27 Aug. 1893; ed. Leipzig Univ.
Privat Dozent Leipzig Univ. 24, Extra. Prof. 29, Prof. of Oriental Philology 35, Rector 48-49; Prof. Ancient Oriental Philology, Berlin Free Univ. 50, Emer. 61; Ord. mem. Saxon Acad. of Sciences; hon. mem. Linguistic Society of America; corresp. mem. Oriental Inst., Prague, German Archaeological Inst. (Istanbul Section), Ex Oriente Lux Asscn., Leiden, and Societas Orientalis Fennica, Helsinki; Co-Editor *Zeitschrift für Assyriologie*, *Zeitschrift der Deutschen Morgenländischen Gesellschaft*.

Publs. *Staatsverträge des Hatti-Reiches in hethitischer Sprache* (Vol. I 26, Vol. II 30), *Kleinasiatische Sprachdenkmäler* 32, *Einführung ins Urartäische, Ras Schamra* 33, *Kleine Beiträge zur churritischen Grammatik* 39, *Entzifferungsgeschichte der hethitischen Hieroglyphenschrift* 39, *Hethitisches Elementarbuch* (Vol. I 40, 2nd edn. 60, Vol II 46, 2nd edn. 67), *Phönizisch-punische Grammatik* 51, *Hethitisches Wörterbuch* 52, 57, 61, 66, *Entzifferung verschollener Schriften und Sprachen* 54 (2nd edn. 66), *Kurze Grammatik der alten Quiché-Sprache im Popol Vuh* 55, *Hethitische Gesetze* 59, *Zwei russische Novellen in neusyrischer Übersetzung* 60, *Hethitisches Keilschrift-Lesebuch* 60, *Geschichte der Schrift* 66.
Schloss-Strasse 49, Berlin 41, Germany.

Friedrich, Otto Andreas; German industrialist; b. 3 July 1902; ed. Univs. of Marburg, Königsberg, Frankfurt, Heidelberg, Berlin and Vienna.
Emigrated to U.S.A. and employed by B. F. Goodrich Co., Akron, Ohio; Man. Phoenix Gummiwerke A.G. (rubber works), Hamburg-Harburg 39-49 and Pres. 49-65; Man.-Partner Friedrich Flick KG, Düsseldorf 65-; Vice-Pres. and Treas. Fed. Asscn. of German Industry, Cologne, mem. Exec. Cttee., Cultural Council; mem. Fed. Comm. on Space Research; Dir. Siemens AG, Munich; Dir. Phoenix Gummiwerke AG; Chair. Advisory Board Allianz Versicherungs-AG, Munich-Berlin.
Office: Mönchenwerther Str. 15, 4 Düsseldorf-Oberkassel; Home: Anton-Fahne-Weg 8, 4 Düsseldorf 1, German Federal Republic.
Telephone: Düsseldorf 580250 (Home).

Friedrich, Walter, D.PHIL.; German medical physicist; b. 25 Dec. 1883; ed. Geneva and Munich Univs.
Asst. Munich Univ. 12-14; Lecturer, Freiburg Univ. 14-21, Extraordinary Prof. 21-22; Prof. of Medical Physics, Berlin Univ. 22, Dir. Inst. of X-ray research 23, Dean, Faculty of Medicine 29, currently Prof. Emeritus; Pres. Deutsche Röntgengesellschaft 28, Deutsche Gesellschaft für Lichtforschung 30, Third Int. Congress for Light Research, Wiesbaden 36; mem. Deutsche Akad. der Wissenschaften 49-, Pres. 51-56, Vice-Pres. 56-58, Dir. Inst. Med. and Biology 48, Pres. 55-56; Rector Humboldt Univ. 49-52; Hon. Pres. Int. Cttee. on Light, Deutsche Biophysikalische Gesellschaft; Hon. mem. Research Council of the German Democratic Republic; Pres. German Peace Council; mem. of the Presidium World Peace Council; fmr. mem. Bulgarian and Hungarian Acads. Science; Nat. Prize 50, Vaterländischen Verdienstorden, etc.; Dr. Med. h.c.
Lindenberger Weg 70, Berlin-Buch, Germany.
Telephone: 56-98-51.

Friendly, Alfred, A.B.; American journalist; b. 30 Dec. 1911; ed. Amherst Coll.
Reporter, *Washington Daily News* 36-38; Reporter, *Washington Post* 39-51, Asst. Managing Editor 52-55, Managing Editor 55-65, Assoc. Editor 66-, Vice-Pres. and Dir. 63-; Asst. to Trustee, Associated Gas and Electric Corpn. 40; served in Air Force Intelligence 42-45; Chief European Information Branch, Econ. Co-operation Admin. 48-49; Dir. American Soc. of Newspaper Editors 61-65; Trustee Amherst Coll. 61-; hon. mention Heywood Broun Award 48; hon. mention Raymond Clapper Award 48; Hon. L.H.D. (Amherst Coll.) 58.
Publ. *The Guys on the Ground* 44.
1645 31st Street N.W., Washington, D.C. 20007, U.S.A.

Friendly, Fred W., H.L.D.; American broadcaster and journalist; b. 30 Oct. 1915; ed. Cheshire Acad., Connecticut, and Nichols Coll., Dudley, Massachusetts.
Began broadcasting career writing, producing and narrating series *Footprints in the Sands of Time* on local radio station 38; U.S. Army 41-45 as lecturer in Educ.

section and corresp. for China, Burma and India on Army newspaper *Roundup*; commenced long professional partnership with Edward R. Murrow with historical gramophone record *I Can Hear It Now*; then Columbia Broadcasting System (C.B.S.) Radio Series *Hear It Now* and TV Series *See It Now* 51; Exec. Producer C.B.S. Reports 59-66; Pres. C.B.S. News 64-66; Edward R. Murrow Prof. of Journalism, Columbia Univ. 66-; Adviser on Television to Ford Foundation 66-; Head Public Broadcast Lab.; Soldiers Medal of Heroism; Legion of Merit with four battle stars; ten George Foster Peabody Awards.
Publs. *See It Now* (co-author) 55, *Due to Circumstances Beyond Our Control* 67.
Ford Foundation, 320 East 43rd Street, New York, N.Y. 10017; 4614 Fieldston Road, Riverdale, N.Y. 10471, U.S.A.
Telephone: 202-573-4848 (Office).

Friis, Finn Tage Blichfeldt; Danish civil servant and writer; b. 20 March 1897; ed. Københavns Universitet, Berkeley Univ., Univ. of Minnesota and Columbia Univ.
Member Secr. League of Nations 23-40; Adviser to Foreign Office (UN Affairs) 46-57; mem. Danish Del. to UN 46-48, 50-55, to ECOSOC 48-50; mem. Advisory cttee. High Cmmr. for Refugees 51-56; Rep. Quaker Int. Affairs, Vienna 57-60.
Publs. *Schweiz. Enhed i Mangfoldighed* 44, *H. C. Andersen og Schweiz* 49 (German ed. 65), *De Forenede Nationer* 48, *De Forenede Nationer, Mål, midler og virke* 63 (also editions in Norwegian, Swedish and Finnish).
Opnaesgård 79, 2970 Hørsholm, Denmark.
Telephone: 01-86-53-56.

Friis, Henning Kristian; Danish social research officer; b. 11 Oct. 1911; ed. Københavns Universitet.
Social Science Adviser, Ministry of Social Affairs 41-58; Sec.-Gen. Danish Govt. Youth Comm. 45-52, Cttee. on Scientific and Technical Personnel 56-59; Chair. OECD Cttee. for Scientific and Technical Personnel 58-65; Exec. Dir. Danish Nat. Inst. of Social Research 58; Chair. Board of Trustees, Danish Schools of Social Work 66; Chair. European Social Research Cttee.; Int. Gerontological Asscn. 54-60; mem. Exec. Cttee. Int. Sociological Asscn. 59-65; mem. Board of Trustees, UN Inst. on Training and Research; mem. Int. Social Science Council; Editor *Scandinavia between East and West* 50, and *Family and Society* 64.
Publs. *Social Policy and Social Trends* 58, *Longstanding Public Assistance Clients* 60, *Old People in a low-income Area in Copenhagen* 61, *Institutional Means of Collaboration between the Social Sciences* 62, *Development of Social Research in Ireland* 65, *Social Policy and Social Research in India* 68.
Borgergade 28, Copenhagen, Denmark.
Telephone: Minerva 9811.

Friis, Torben; Danish banker; b. 1 Dec. 1904.
With Aarhus Privatbank 21-26; Banque des Pays du Nord, Paris 26-27; Sec. Danish Consulate-Gen., Paris 27-28, 31-33; with Danish company 29-31; Danmarks Nationalbank 34-54, special foreign responsibilities, later Man. 58-66; Perm. Del., Payments Cttee., Org. for European Econ. Co-operation (OEEC); with Int. Monetary Fund (IMF) 54-, Alt. Exec. Dir. 56-58, Exec. Dir. 66-; mem. Nordic Financial and Currency Cttee. 60-65, Chair. 65-66; Knight, Legion of Honour and Order of Dannebrog.
International Monetary Fund, Washington, D.C. 20431, U.S.A.

Friis Johansen, Knud, PH.D.; Danish archaeologist; b. 1 Nov. 1887; ed. Copenhagen Univ.
Assistant Keeper Copenhagen Nat. Museum 11 and Keeper 22; Prof. of Archæology Copenhagen Univ. 27-56.
Publs. *Les Vases Sicyoniens* 23, *Hoby-Fundet* 23, *De*

forhistoriske Tider i Europa 27, *Corpus Vasorum Anti-quorum, Copenhague, Musée National, Iliaden i tidlig graesk Kunst* 34, *Thésée et la danse à Délos* 45, *The Attic Grave Reliefs* 51, *Exochi* 58, *Eine Dithyrambos-Aufführung* 59, *Ajas und Hector* 61, *The Iliad in Early Greek Art* 67.
Egernvej 27, Copenhagen F, Denmark.

Frings, H.E. Cardinal Joseph, DR. THEOL.; German ecclesiastic; b. 6 Feb. 1887; ed. Gymnasium, Neuss, and Univs. of Innsbruck, Bonn and Freiburg im Breisgau, and Priests' Seminary of Cologne.
Ordained 10; Auxiliary Priest in Köln-Zollstock; went to Papal Biblical Inst., Rome 13-14; Rector in Köln-Fühlingen and Neuss; Parish Priest in Köln-Braunsfeld; Regent of Priests' Seminary of Bensberg; Archbishop of Cologne 42-; created Cardinal by Pope Pius XII 46; mem. Praesidium, 2nd Vatican Council 62; mem. Sacred Congregations of the Council, of Religious Orders, of Rites, for the Eastern Church, of Seminaries and Univs. of Study, for the Propagation of the Faith; Dr. Phil. h.c.
Eintrachstrasse 164, 5 Cologne, German Federal Republic.

Frisch, Karl von; German zoologist and university professor; b. 20 Nov. 1886; ed. Univs. of Vienna and Munich.
Privatdozent, Munich Univ. 12; Prof. and Dir. Zoological Inst., Rostock Univ. 21, Breslau 23, Munich 25, Graz 46, Munich 50-58; mem. Acad. of Science (Munich, Vienna, Göttingen, Washington, Uppsala, Boston, Stockholm, etc.); foreign mem. Royal Society, London; hon. mem. Royal Entomological Society, London, and American Physiological Soc.; Hon. Ph.D. (Univs. of Berne, Graz, Harvard and Tübingen); Hon. D.Sc. (Fed. Tech. Inst., Zürich); Magellan Prize of American Philosophical Soc., Kalinga Prize 59, Orden pour le mérite.
Publs. *Aus dem Leben der Bienen* 27 (*The Dancing Bees* 54), *Du und das Leben* 36 (*Man and the Living World* 63), *Bees* 50, *Biologie* 52-53 (*Biology* 64), *Erinnerungen eines Biologen* 57 (*A Biologist Remembers* 67), *Tanzsprache und Orientierung der Bienen* 65 (*The Dance Language and Orientation of Bees*).
Zoologisches Institut, Luisenstrasse 14; and Über der Klause 10, 8000 Munich 90, German Federal Republic.
Telephone: 692938.

Frisch, Max; Swiss writer and architect; b. 15 May 1911; ed. Zürich Univ. and Technical High School.
Worked as foreign corresp. for newspapers throughout Europe and the Near East; diploma in architecture 41; designs executed include the Zürich Recreation Park; first play published 45; abandoned architecture for full-time writing 55; Rockefeller Grant for Drama 51, Prize of the German Academy 58, Jerusalem Prize, Ehrenpreis des Schillergedächtnispreises des Landes Baden-Württemberg 65.
Publs. Plays: *Nun singen sie wieder* 45, *Die chinesische Mauer* 46, *Graf Oederland* 50, *Don Juan, oder die Liebe zur Geometrie* 52, *Biedermann und die Brandstifter* 58, *Andorra* (translated into eleven languages) 61, *Biografie* 67; novels: *Tagebuch 1945-1949* 50, *Stiller* 54 (translated into ten languages), *Homo Faber* (translated into seven languages) 57, *Mein Name sei Gantenbein* 64.
c/o Suhrkamp-Verlag, Frankfurt/Main, German Federal Republic.

Frisch, Otto Robert, O.B.E., DR. PHIL., F.R.S.; British experimental physicist; b. 1 Oct. 1904; ed. Vienna Univ.
Engaged in Physics Research at Berlin 27-30, Hamburg 30-33, London 33-34, Copenhagen 34-39, Birmingham and Liverpool 39-43, Los Alamos, N.M., U.S.A. 43-46, Atomic Energy Establishment Harwell 46-47; Jacksonian Prof. of Natural Philosophy Cambridge 47-; in

charge Nuclear Physics Section of Cavendish Laboratory; Fellow of Trinity Coll., Cambridge.
Publs. *Meet the Atoms* 47, *Atomic Physics Today* 61, *Working with Atoms* 65.
Trinity College, Cambridge, England.

Frisch, Ragnar, DR. PHIL.; Norwegian economist; b. 3 March 1895; ed. Univ. of Oslo.
Visiting Prof. Yale Univ. 30, Sorbonne 33; Prof. of Economics Oslo Univ. 31-; Dir. of Research, Economic Inst., Oslo Univ.; Fellow and one of Founders of Econometric Society 31; Chief Editor of *Econometrica* 33-55; elected Chair. of first session of Economic and Employment Comm. of U.N.; mem. Det Norske Videnskapsakademi Oslo, Kungl. Humanistiska Vetenskapssamfundet Lund, Kungl. Svenska Vetenskapsakademien, Accad. Nazionale dei Lincei, Int. Statistical Inst. 37-; hon. mem. American Economic Asscn., American Acad. of Arts and Sciences; corresp. Royal Economic Society, London; Fellow Inst. of Mathematical Statistics; Hon. Fellow Royal Statistical Society 56; advising mem. Acad. of Human Rights; Antonio Feltrinelli Prize, Rome 61; Hon. Dr. (Handelshögskolan, Stockholm 59, Copenhagen Univ. 59, Stockholms Universitet 66, Univ. of Cambridge 67), Prof. Emer. of Econ. and Statistics, Univ. of Oslo; Corresp. Fellow of the British Acad. 66.
University Institute of Economics, Oslo; Home: Slemdalsveien 98, Vinderen, Oslo-3, Norway.
Telephone: 69-97-36.

Frische, Carl Alfred, PH.D.; American scientist and business executive; b. 13 Aug. 1906; ed. Miami Univ., Ohio, and Univ. of Iowa.
Physicist, Research Fellow, Columbia Univ. 32-33; Sperry Gyroscope Co. 33-; Chief Research Div. 43-45, Vice-Pres. (Engineering) 45-54, Vice-Pres. (Operations) 54-57; Exec. Vice-Pres. Sperry Gyroscope Div., Sperry-Rand Corpn. 57-58, Pres. 58-; Dir. other companies.
c/o Sperry Gyroscope Co., Great Neck, Long Island, N.Y., U.S.A.

Fröhlich, Paul; German politician; b. 21 March 1913; ed. elementary school.
Former cook; mem. Sozialistische Einheitspartei Deutschlands (S.E.D.) 45-; Sec. for Propaganda and Culture, S.E.D., Dresden 46-49; First Sec. S.E.D., Bautzen 49-50; First Sec. S.E.D., Leipzig City 50-52, Leipzig District 52-; mem. Volkskammer 54-58; mem. Central Cttee. and Sec. S.E.D. 60-, mem. Politburo 63-; Vaterländischer Verdienstorden in Silber.
Sozialistische Einheitspartei Deutschlands, Am Werderschen Markt, Berlin C.2, Germany.

Frølund, Hakon; Danish forester; b. 10 Sept. 1916; ed. Kgl. Veterinaer- og Landbohøjskole, Copenhagen.
Assistant Forest Officer Danish State Forest Service 42-53, Chief Commercial Div. 53-58; Inspector, Price Directorate 44-53; Chair. Danish Soc. of Forest Engineers 55-59; Dir. Danish State Forest Service 58-; mem. Danish FAO Cttee. 54-; Chair. FAO/ECE/ILO Study Group on Forest Workers' Training, Health, Safety 54; mem. Nordic Forest Union 55-59, Chair. Danish Cttee. 59-; Pres. Nordic Forest Union 62; Chair. Danish Forest Research Comm. 58; Vice-Chair. Danish Forestry Soc. 58-, FAO European Forestry Comm. 63-; mem. Danish Council Nature Conservation 59-, mem. Danish F.F.H.C. Cttee. 64-; Danish Order Knight of Dannebrog, French Order Commandeur de Mérite Agricole.
Enghavevej 4, Klampenborg, Denmark.

Fromm, Erich, PH.D.; American (b. German) psychoanalyst; b. 23 March 1900; ed. Univs. of Frankfurt, Heidelberg and Munich, and Berlin Inst. of Psychoanalysis.
Guest Lecturer, Columbia Univ. 35-39; Lecturer, New School for Social Research 38-54; mem. Faculty

Bennington Coll. 42-50; Prof. Michigan State Univ. 58-62; Dir. Mexican Inst. of Psychoanalysis, affiliated with Nat. Univ. of Mexico 55-67; Adj. Prof. of Psychology, New York Univ. 62-; Diplomate of American Psychological Asscn.

Publs. *Man for Himself* 47, *Escape from Freedom* (Fear of Freedom) 41, *Psychoanalysis and Religion* 50, *The Forgotten Language* 51, *The Sane Society* 55, *The Art of Loving* 56, *Sigmund Freud's Mission* 59, *Zen Buddhism and Psychoanalysis* (with D. T. Suzuki and R. de Martino) 60, *Marx's Concept of Man* 61, *May Man Prevail?* 61, *Beyond the Chains of Illusion* 62, *The Dogma of Christ and other Essays* 63, *The Heart of Man* 64, *You shall be as Gods* 66.

180 Riverside Drive, New York 24, N.Y., U.S.A.; Patricio Sanz 748-5, Mexico 12, D.F., Mexico.

Frommel, Gerhard; German composer and music teacher; b. 7 Aug. 1906; ed. Leipzig Musikhochschule and Prussian Acad. of Arts, Berlin.

Teacher of music since 29, Prof. of Composition, Frankfurt Hochschule für Musik 60-.

Compositions: Two symphonies, *Sinfonietta* for string orchestra, *Symphonisches Vorspiel*, piano concerto (with string orchestra and clarinet), *Suite* and *Variationen* for orchestra, *36 Lieder nach St. George*, seven piano sonatas, two violin sonatas, two operas, ballet and chamber music.

Werderplatz 10, Heidelberg, German Federal Republic. Telephone: 40102.

Frondel, Clifford, PH.D., M.A.; American mineralogist; b. 8 Jan. 1907; ed. Mass. Inst. of Technology, Columbia Univ. and Colorado School of Mines.

Teaching Fellow, M.I.T. 37-39; Research Assoc. Harvard Univ. 39-42; Senior Physicist, U.S. War Dept. 42-43; Dir. of Research, Reeves Sound Laboratories 43-45; Assoc. Prof. of Mineralogy, Harvard Univ. 46-54, Prof. 54-, Chair. Dept. of Geological Sciences 65-; Pres. Mineralogical Soc. of America 56; Fellow A.A.A.S., Geological Soc. America and American Acad. of Arts and Sciences; Foreign mem. Austrian Acad. of Sciences, Accademia Nazionale dei Lincei, Deutsche Akademie der Naturforscher; Chair. Dept. of Geological Sciences; Becke Medal, Mineralogical Soc. of Austria; Roebling Medal, Mineralogical Soc. of America.

Publs. *Dana's System of Mineralogy* (co-editor), 3 vols., 43, 51, 62, *Systematic Mineralogy of Uranium and Thorium* 58.

Department of Mineralogy, 12 Geological Museum, Oxford Street, Cambridge, Mass., U.S.A.

Frondistis, Athanassios; Greek army officer and politician; b. 26 Sept. 1900; ed. Univ. of Athens, Military School and Higher School of War.

Held various military positions and fought in wars of 22, 40-41 and in guerilla warfare; Chief of Defence Gen. Staff 59-62; in Reserves 62-; Deputy for Nat. Radical Union 63, 64-; Minister for Communications 67.

Athens, Greece.

Frondizi, Arturo, D.IUR.; Argentine lawyer and politician; b. 08; ed. Buenos Aires Univ.

Formed a resistance movement as a student and imprisoned 30; in law practice 32-; mem. Metropolitan Convention Radical Party, Prof. Buenos Aires Univ. 32; Radical deputy 46; Pres. Parliamentary Radical Party 46-50; candidate for Vice-Presidency 52; Pres. Nat. Cttee. Radical Party 54; Pres. of Argentina 58-62; now leader of Movimiento de Integración y Desarrollo.

Publs. *Petroleum and Politics* 55, *Los intereses de los trabajadores y el destino de la nacionalidad* 57, *Política económica nacional* 63, *Politica exterior argentina* 63, *Petroleo y Nacion* 64, *Estrategia y Táctica del Movimiento Nacional* 65, *El problema Agrario Argentino* 65.

Luis Maris Campos 665, Buenos Aires, Argentina.

Frondizi, Risieri; Argentine professor of philosophy; b. 20 Nov. 1910; ed. Instituto Nacional, Buenos Aires and Harvard, Michigan and Mexico Univs.

Prof. Philosophy, Tucuman Univ. 38-46; Visiting Prof. Venezuela 47-48, Pennsylvania 48-49, Yale 49-50, Puerto Rico 50-52, Columbia 55, Texas 65, California (Los Angeles) 66-68; mem. Inst. for Advanced Study, Princeton 64; Prof. Ethics, Buenos Aires Univ. 56-66; Rector, Buenos Aires Univ. 57-62; Pres. Inter-American Union of Latin American Univs. 59-62; mem. Admin. Board Int. Asscn. of Univs. 60-; mem. Inst. International de Philosophie (Paris); Comité Directeur International Federation Philosophical Societies (Brussels).

Publs. *Philosophy's Point of Departure* 45, *The Nature of the Self* 52, *What is Value?* 58.

Junin 1925, Buenos Aires, Argentina.

Fronius, Hans; Austrian artist; b. 12 Sept. 1903; ed. Mittelschule, Graz, and Akad. der Bildenden Künste, Vienna.

Professor of Fine Arts, Fürstenfeld 29-60, Mödling 60-64; over fifty one-man exhibitions, including Prague 37, Vienna 52, Paris 55, Mexico City 57, Venice Biennale 58, Madrid (Biblioteca Nacional) 67, Mainz 68, and in many German and Austrian cities; Army Service, Russia and Italy 43-45; has illustrated 60 books; Staatspreismedaille 37, Meisterpreis für Malerei und Graphik 50; Grosser Österreichischer Staatspreis für Malerei und Graphik 66.

A.2380 Perchtoldsdorf bei Wien, Guggenberggasse 18, Austria.

Telephone: 86-29-872.

Fruh, Eugen; Swiss painter and illustrator; b. 22 Jan. 1914; ed. Zürich School of Art and in Paris and Rome.

C. F. Meyer Foundation Fine Arts Prize 43, Fine Arts Prize, Kanton Zürich 67.

Works include: *Die kleine Stadt* 41, *Pastorale d'été* 46, *La comédie et la musique* 47, *Capricci* 48, *Spanisches Gespräch* 51, *Notturno* 57, *Château d'Artiste* 62, *Gartenfest* 64; also murals and book illustrations.

Römergasse 9, Zürich, Switzerland. Telephone: 051-478863.

Fruhauf, Hans, DR. ING., DR. ING. E.h.; German scientist; b. 4 Jan. 1904; ed. Eberhard-Ludwigs-Gymnasium, Stuttgart, and Technische Hochschule, Stuttgart.

Professor, Technical Univ. of Dresden 50-, Prorector Technical Univ. Dresden; Dir. of Inst. of High Frequency Technology and Electronics, Technical Univ. of Dresden 50-; Vice-Pres. German Acad. of Sciences 57-63, mem. German Acad. of Sciences, mem. of the Forschungsrat (Vice-Pres. until 62) (D.D.R.); Editor *Hochfrequenztechnik und Elektroakustik*, Leipzig, Editor *Bücherei der Hochfrequenztechnik*, Leipzig, Editor *Über Wissenschaftliche Grundlagen der modernen Technik*, Berlin, Editor *Elektronisches Rechnen und Regeln*, Berlin; Nat. Prize, Second Class 51, First Class 61.

Zeunerstrasse 91, 8027 Dresden 27, German Democratic Republic.

Telephone: 42-6-92 (Home), 483-5072 (Office).

Frumkin, Alexander Naumovich; Soviet scientist; b. 24 Oct. 1895; ed. Univ. of Odessa.

Prof. at Inst. of Education, Odessa 22; Prof. at Karpov Inst. of Physical Chemistry 22-46; read course of lectures on Colloidal Chemistry at Inst. of Wisconsin, U.S.A. 28-29; Academician 32; Dir. Inst. of Physical Chemistry of U.S.S.R. Acad. of Sciences 39-49; concurrently Head of the Chair. of Electrochemistry at the Univ. of Moscow 30-; Dir. Inst. of Electrochemistry, U.S.S.R. Acad. of Sciences 58-; awarded Lenin Prize 31; 1st State Prize 41; Lenin Order 45, etc.; mem. U.S.S.R. Acad. of Sciences 32, Polish Acad. of Sciences 45, Akad.

Deutscher Naturforscher Leopoldina 56, Bulgarian Acad. of Sciences, Royal Acad. of Sciences of the Netherlands 65; Hon. F.N.I. Delhi 65; Corresp. mem. Deutscher Akad. Wiss., Berlin 56; Hon. mem. All-Union Mendeleev Chemical Soc. 65, Yugoslav Acad. of Sciences and Arts 65; Dr. rer. nat. h.c. Tech. Univ. Dresden 58; Palladium Medal Electrochemical Soc., U.S.A. 59; Hero of Socalist Labour 65, Corresp. mem. Saxon Acad. of Sciences, Leipzig 66.
Institute of Electrochemistry, Academy of Sciences of the U.S.S.R., Leninsky Prospekt 31, Moscow v-71, U.S.S.R.

Frutkin, Arnold Wolfe, A.B.; American public administrator and economist; b. 18; ed. Harvard Univ. and Columbia Univ.
U.S. Naval Reserve 42-; Dir. Office of Public Affairs, U.S. Nat. Cttee. for Int. Geophysical Year, Dep. for Int. Affairs to Exec. Dir. of U.S. Nat. Cttee. for Int. Geophysical Year 57-59; Sec. Int. Relations Cttee., Nat. Acad. of Sciences, Space Science Board 58-59; Adviser to Nat. Acad. of Sciences Del. to COSPAR 58-; Managing Editor and Dir. The Bureau of Nat. Affairs, Inc. 50-57; Dir. Office of Int. Programs, Nat. Aeronautics and Space Admin. (NASA) 59-63, Asst. Admin. (Int. Affairs) 63-; mem. U.S. Del. to UN Cttee. on Peaceful Uses of Outer Space 62-; Alt. Del. to Scientific and Technical Sub-cttee., UN Cttee. on Peaceful Uses of Outer Space 62-; Adviser, bilateral negotiations on co-operation in outer space matters with U.S.S.R. 62-.
3702 Ingomar Street, N.W., Washington, D.C., U.S.A.

Fry, Christopher; British dramatist; b. 18 Dec. 1907; ed. Bedford Modern School.
Actor, Citizen House, Bath 27; Teacher, Hazelwood Preparatory School 28-31; Dir. Tunbridge Wells Repertory Players 32-35; Dir. Oxford Repertory Players 40 and 44-46; at Arts Theatre, London, 45; Fellow of the Royal Soc. of Literature 62; Awarded The Queen's Gold Medal for Poetry.
Publs. *The Boy with the Cart* 39, *The Firstborn* 46, *A Phoenix too Frequent* 46, *The Lady's Not for Burning* 49, *Thor, with Angels* 49, *Venus Observed* 50, *A Sleep of Prisoners* 51, *The Dark is Light Enough* 54, *Curtmantle* (R. S. L. Heinemann Award) 62; Trans. *Ring Round the Moon, The Lark* (Anouilh), *Tiger at the Gates, Duel of Angels, Judith* (Giraudoux) 62; Film Scripts: *The Beggars' Opera, The Queen is Crowned, Ben Hur, Barabbas, The Bible*.
37 Blomfield Road, London, W.9, England.

Fry, Donald William, M.SC.; British physicist; b. 30 Nov. 1910; ed. King's Coll., London Univ.
Research Physicist, G.E.C. Research Laboratories 32-40; with Air Ministry Research Establishment at Swanage and Malvern 40-49; on staff of Atomic Energy Research Establishment 46-49; Head, Gen. Physics Div. 50-54, Chief Physicist 54-, Deputy Dir. 58, A.E.R.E., Harwell; Dir. Atomic Energy Establishment, Winfrith 59-; awarded Duddell Medal of the Physical Soc. 50; Fellow of the Physical Soc., Inst. of Physics, Inst. of Electrical Engineers, Inst. of Electrical and Electronic Engineers.
Office: U.K.A.E.E., A.E.E. Winfrith, Dorchester, Dorset; Home: Coveway Lodge, Overcombe, Weymouth, Dorset, England.
Telephone: Dorchester 1700 (Office); Preston 3276 (Home).

Fry, E. Maxwell, C.B.E., LL.D., B.ARCH., A.R.A., F.R.I.B.A., M.T.P.I.; British architect; b. 2 Aug. 1899; ed. Liverpool Inst., and Liverpool Univ. School of Architecture.
Studied in Europe and New York; partner Adams, Thompson & Fry 27-34; with Prof. Walter Gropius 34-36;

served R.E.'s 39-45; Town Planning Adviser to Resident Minister W. Africa 43-45; in partnership with Jane Drew (wife) since 45; a Senior Architect to Chandigarh, Punjab Govt. Capital Project 51-54; now partner in Fry, Drew, and Partners; work includes Impington Village Coll., Ibadan Univ. in Nigeria, Govt. Centre, Mauritius, Schools and Colls. for Gold Coast Govt., Flats and Houses at Harlow New Town, Engineering and Veterinary Buildings, Liverpool Univ. Headquarters, Rolls-Royce Ltd. and Pilkington Brothers Ltd.; Prof. of Architecture, Royal Acad.; Royal Gold Medal for Architecture 64.
Publs. *Fine Building* (with Jane B. Drew) 45, *Architecture for Children, Architecture in Humid Tropics, Tropical Architecture* (with Jane B. Drew) 64.
63 Gloucester Place, London, W.1, England.

Fry, Rev. Franklin C., A.B., D.D.; American ecclesiastic; b. 30 Aug. 1900; ed. Hamilton Coll., Philadelphia Lutheran Seminary.
Ordained 25; Sec. United Lutheran Church of America Comm. on Evangelism 30-38; mem. Board of American Missions 34-42; mem. Exec. Board, United Lutheran Church 42-44, Pres. 45-62; Pres. Lutheran Church in America 62-; Pres. Lutheran World Relief, Inc.; mem. Exec. Cttee., Lutheran World Fed. 47-, Treas. 48-52, First Vice-Pres. 52-57, Pres. 57-63; Dir. Wittenberg Coll. 34-38; Chair. Central and Exec. Cttees. World Council of Churches 54; Hon. D.D., L.H.D., S.T.D., Th.D., Litt.D., LL.D., D.C.L., S.J.D., H.H.D., J.C.D., D.I.R.; Hon. Citizen of Korea 53, Hon. mem. Theological Acad., Moscow; Grosses Verdienstkreuz mit Stern, Germany 53; Silbernes Ehrenzeichen mit Stern, Austria 55, Grosskreuz des Verdienstordens der Bundesrepublik 63.
[*Died, 6 June 1968.*]

Fry, Thornton Carl, A.M., PH.D.; American mathematician; b. 7 Jan. 1892; ed. Findlay Coll. and Wisconsin Univ.
Mathematics Instructor, Wisconsin Univ. 12-16; with Western Electric Co. 16-24; on staff of Bell Telephone Laboratories 24-56, Dir. mathematical research 40-44, switching research 44-47 and engineering 47-49, Asst. to Exec. Vice-Pres. 49-51, to Pres. 51-56; Vice-Pres. and Dir. Univac Engineering Division, Remington Rand 57-60; Vice-Pres. Research and Engineering Remington Rand Division of Sperry Rand Corpn. 60; Consultant to Dir., Nat. Center for Atmospheric Research 61-; Consultant and mem. board of directors, Granville-Phillips Co. 63-; Consultant, The Boeing Co. 64-; Fellow, American Physical Society, American Asscn. for Advancement of Science, American Inst. of Electrical Engineers, etc.; mem. Amer. Math. Society, Amer. Astronomical Society, etc.; Hon. D.Sc. Findlay Coll. 58.
Publs. *Elementary Differential Equations, Probability and its Engineering Uses*: numerous articles.
P.O. Box 5966, Carmel, Calif. 93921, U.S.A.

Frye, Rev. Herman Northrop, M.A.; Canadian university professor; b. 14 July 1912; ed. Univ. of Toronto, Emmanuel Coll., and Univ. of Oxford.
Department of English, Victoria Coll., Univ. of Toronto 39-, Chair. of Dept. 52, Principal of Victoria Coll. 59, Univ. Prof. and Prof. of English in Victoria Coll. 67-; Lorne Pierce Medal, Royal Soc. of Canada 58; Canada Council Medal 67.
Publs. *Fearful Symmetry: A Study of William Blake* 47, *Anatomy of Criticism* 57, *The Well-Tempered Critic* 63, *The Educated Imagination* 63, *T. S. Eliot* 63, *A Natural Perspective* 65, *The Return of Eden* 65, *Fools of Time* 67, *The Modern Century* 67.
Massey College, 4 Devonshire Place, Toronto 5, Ontario, Canada.
Telephone: 928-2631.

15

Frye, Richard Nelson, PH.D.; American orientalist; b. 10 Jan. 1920; ed. Univ. of Ill., Harvard Univ., and School of Oriental and African Studies, London.
Junior Fellow, Harvard 46-49; Visiting Scholar, Univ. of Teheran 51-52; Aga Khan Prof. of Iranian, Harvard 57-; Visiting Prof., Oriental Seminary, Frankfurt Univ. 58-59; Assoc. Editor *Central Asian Journal, Indo-Iranica* (Calcutta).
Publs. *Notes on the early coinage of Transoxiana* 49, *History of the Nation of the Archers* 52, *Narshakhi, The History of Bukhara* 54, *Iran* 56, *Heritage of Persia* 62, *Bukhara, The Medieval Achievement* 65, *The Histories of Nishapur* 65.
546 Widener Library, Cambridge 38, Mass., U.S.A.

Fu Lien-chang; Chinese physician and surgeon; b. 95; ed. Tingchow Christian Institute of Medicine.
Joined Red Army as doctor 27; founded Central Hospital at Juichin and Central Red Medical Coll. 33; Dir. Medical Bureau at Yenan 40; Vice-Minister of Health 49-; Pres. Chinese Medical Assen. 50-; mem. of Council of Assen. for Cultural Relations with Foreign Countries 54; Vice-Chair. Chinese People's Nat. Cttee. in Defence of Children.
Ministry of Public Health, Peking, China.

Fu Pao-shih; Chinese artist; b. 04; ed. Imperial Coll. of Fine Arts, Japan.
Prof. of Art in the Central University 35; formerly Prof. of Fine Arts and Head of Teaching Section in the Dept. of Chinese Painting, Nanking Normal Coll.; mem. Nat. Cttee. of Political Consultative Conference; mem. of Classical Arts Cttee. of Union of Chinese Artists; council mem. of Kiangsu Province Assen. of Writers and Artists.
Publs. *A Chronology of Chinese Art, Chinese Artists on the Art of Painting, Chinese Portrait and Landscape Painting*, etc.
Union of Chinese Artists, Peking, China.

Fuchs, Sir Vivian Ernest, M.A., PH.D.; British geologist and explorer; b. 11 Feb. 1908; ed. St. John's Coll., Cambridge.
With Cambridge East Greenland Expedition 29, Cambridge Expedition to East African Lakes 30-32; Leader, Lake Rudolf Rift Valley Expedition 33-34; Leader, Lake Rukwa Expedition 37-38; served Second World War; Commdr. Falkland Islands Dependencies Survey (Antarctica) 47-50; Dir. Falkland Islands Dependencies Scientific Bureau 51-60; Dir. British Antarctic Survey 59-; Leader, Trans-Antarctic Expedition 55-58; Founder's Gold Medal 51, Polar Medal 53, Clasp and Bar, Special Gold Medal 58 (Royal Geog. Soc.); Silver Medal (R.S.A.), Gold Medal (Royal Scottish Geog. Soc.); Richthofen Gold Medal (Berlin Geog. Soc.), Kirchenpauer Gold Medal (Hamburg Geog. Soc.), Gold Medal (Paris Geog. Soc.) 58, Hubbard Gold Medal (American Nat. Geog. Soc.), Gold Medal (Royal Netherlands Geog. Soc.) 59, Hans Egede Medal (Royal Danish Geog. Soc.) 61, Prestwick Medal (Geological Soc., London) 60; Hon. LL.D. (Edinburgh Univ.), Hon. D.Sc. (Durham Univ.) 58; Hon. D.Sc. (Cambridge Univ.) 59.
Publs. *The Crossing of Antarctica* (with Sir Edmund Hillary) 60, various geological and geographical papers.
78 Barton Road, Cambridge; and British Antarctic Survey, 30 Gillingham Street, London, S.W.1, England. Telephone: 01-834-3687 (Office).

Fuentes, Carlos; Mexican author; b. 28; ed. Univ. of Mexico and Institut des Hautes Etudes Internationales, Geneva.
Member, Mexican Del. to Int. Labour Organization (ILO), Geneva 50-52; Asst. Head, Press Section, Ministry of Foreign Affairs, Mexico 54; Asst. Dir. Cultural Dissemination, Univ. of Mexico 55-56; Head, Dept. of Cultural Relations, Ministry of Foreign Affairs 57-59; Editor *Revista Mexicana de Literatura*

54-58, Co-Editor *El Espectador* 59-61, Editor *Siempre* and *Política* 60-.
Publs. *Los días enmascarados* 54, *La región más transparente* 58, *Las buenas conciencias* 59, *Aura* 62, *La muerte de Artemio Cruz* 62, *Cantar de ciegos* 65.
2a Cerrada de Frontera 14, San Angel, Mexico D.F., Mexico.

Fuentes Irvrozqui, Manuel; Spanish lawyer and economist; b. 10.
Head of Acad. de Ciencias Económicas de Barcelona; Counsellor of Nat. Econ. Council 64-65; Under-Sec. Econ. Planning; Procurator of Cortes; State commercial official.
Publs. inc. *Síntesis de la Economía Española, Geografía Iberoamericana, Historia Económica de la Segunda Guerra Mundial, Política Comercial y Arancelaria*, etc.
Delegación Nacional de Sindicatos, Paseo del Prado 18-20, Madrid, Spain.

Fugisang-Damgaard, Hans, D.D.; Danish ecclesiastic; b. 29 July 1890; ed. Copenhagen Univ.
Prof. of Theology 25; Dean of Copenhagen Cathedral 33; Bishop of Copenhagen and Primate of Denmark 34; mem. Cttee. of Fourteen, preparing World Council of Churches 38; Vice-Pres. World Council of Christian Education 47; mem. Publ. Board *Lutheran World Review* 48; mem. Central Cttee. World Council of Churches 48; Vice-Pres. The Mission to Lepers 49; Pres. Internationale Gesellschaft für Religionspsychologie 52; Chair. Church of Denmark Council of Inter-Church Relations 54; Pres. Danish Church abroad 61-; Hon. D.D. Sopron Univ.; Knight Grand Cross of the Order of Dannebrog.
Publs. *Videnskabelig og Kristelig Livstydning* 25, *Pariserskolens Teologi* 30, *Religionspsykologi* 33, *Privatskriftemaalets Fornyelse* 33, *Oxford Gruppen* 36, *Land, Land, hør Herrens Ord* 40, *Gud er vor Tilflugt og Styrke* 41, *Taler ved Bispevielser* 42, *Fest og Alvor i Danmarks Kirke* 46, *Kirken og Tiden* 46, *The Problem of South Schleswig and the Christian Church* 46, *Gudsordet i Atomalderen* 47, *Der stander et Hus* 47, *Kirken og de Sociale Problemer* 56, *Kirken og Diakonien* 57, *Menighedsraadene og Folkekirken* 58.
Österbrogade 114, Copenhagen Ø, Denmark.
Telephone: Öbro 8723.

Fujii, Shinzo, LL.B.; Japanese business executive; b. 13 Dec. 1893; ed. Tokyo Imperial Univ.
Mitsubishi Shipbuilding and Engineering Co. Ltd. 18-45; Gen. Manager Kobe Shipyard and Engine Works, Mitsubishi Heavy Industries Ltd. 45-46, Dir. and Gen. Manager Kobe Shipyard 46-49, Managing Dir. 49-50; Pres. Shin Mitsubishi Heavy Industries Ltd. 50-59, Chair. Board of Dirs. 59-62, Pres. 62-64; Pres. Mitsubishi Heavy Industries Ltd. 64-65, Chair. Board of Dirs. 65-; Blue Ribbon Medal; Second Order of Merit with the Order of the Sacred Treasure.
Mitsubishi Heavy Industries Ltd., 10, 2-chome, Marunouchi, Chiyoda-Ku, Tokyo, Japan.
Telephone: 03-212-3111.

Fujimoto, Ichiroz, B.ENG.; Japanese iron and steel executive; b. 21 Jan. 1909; ed. Tokyo Univ.
Joined Kawasaki Dockyard Co., Ltd. 32, Man. Rolling Dept. No. 1, Fukiai Works 45; Dir. Kawasaki Steel Corpn. (a breakaway company of Kawasaki Dockyard) and Asst. Gen. Man. of Fukiai Works 53-55, Gen. Man. of Fukiai Works 55-57, Man. Dir. Kawasaki Steel Corpn. 57-62, Senior Man. Dir. 62-64, Exec. Vice-Pres. 64-66, Pres. July 66-; Hattori Award for contribution to devt. of Japanese iron and steel industry 64.
33 Shimizu-cho, Ashiya, Hyogo-ken, Japan.
Telephone: Ashiya (2)4765.

Fujioka, Shingo; Japanese oil executive; b. 27 June 1901; ed. Keio Univ. Tokyo.
Director and Gen. Man. Kawasaki Refinery, Mitsubishi

Oil Co. Ltd. 50-55, Managing Dir. Mitsubishi Oil Co. Ltd. 55-61, Pres. 61-; mem. Cttee. World Petroleum Conf. 61-, Petroleum Deliberative Council 63-; Chair. Japan Petroleum Asscn.; Blue Ribbon Award 63.
35-12, 3 chome, Wakamiya Nakano-ku, Tokyo, Japan.

Fujisawa, Tokusaburo; Japanese banker; b. 13 Sept. 1907; ed. Tokyo Univ. of Commerce.
Bank of Japan 30-62, Chief of Admin. Dept. 52-54, of Foreign Exchange Dept. 54-56, Bank of Japan Rep., New York 56-58, Chief of Bank Relations and Supervision Dept. 58-59, Dir. Bank of Japan, concurrently Man. Osaka Branch 59-62; Vice-Pres. The Export-Import Bank of Japan 62-.
Office: The Export-Import Bank of Japan, Ohte-Machi, Chiyoda-ku, Tokyo; Home: 13-10, No. 3 Nake-ochiai, Shinzyuku-ku, Tokyo, Japan.
Telephone: 952-0760.

Fujiyama, Aiichiro; Japanese businessman and politician; b. 97; ed. Keio Univ.
Pres. Dai Nippon Sugar Manufacturing Co. 34 and Nitto Chemical Industry 37; Pres. Japan Air Lines 51, Adviser 53-; Pres. Japan and Tokyo Chambers of Commerce 51-57; Foreign Minister 57-60; mem. Council, Int. Chamber of Commerce 54-; Dir. Int. Telegraph and Telephone Co. 53-; Pres. Japan Fed. UNESCO Asscns. 51-; Pres. Advertising Fed. 53-; Pres. Society for Economic Co-operation in Asia 54-61; State Minister in charge of Econ. Planning Board 61-62, June 65-Nov. 66.
Publs. *Shacho gurashi Sanju-nen* 52, *Okyaku-shobai,* 53 *Kuchibeni-kara kikansha-made* 53.
60 1-chome, Shiba Shirokane-Daimachi, Minato-ku, Tokyo, Japan.

Fukakusa, Katsumi, LL.B.; Japanese government official; b. 1918; ed. Tokyo Univ.
Ministry of Railways (now Transportation) 41-; Chief, Section for Rolling Stock Industry, Railway Supervision Bureau 52-54; Chief, Finance Section, Nat. Railways Div., Railway Supervision Bureau 54-59; Chief, Planning Section, Secretariat to Minister 59-60; Dir. Kukuoka District Land Transport Bureau 60-62; Dir. Tokyo District Land Transport Bureau 62; Councillor, Secretariat to Minister 63; Dir. Nat. Railways Div., Railway Supervision Bureau 64; Sec.-Gen. Secretariat to Minister 65; Dir. Bureau of Tourism 66-.
Tourist Industry Bureau, Ministry of Transportation, 2-1-3 Kasumigaseki, Chiyoda-ku, Tokyo, Japan.
Telephone: 580-4488.

Fukuda, Chisato; Japanese business executive; b. 20 Oct. 1896; ed. Kyoto Imperial Univ.
Fujitomo Bill-Broker Bank (later The Fujimoto Securities Co. Ltd.) 21-43; Dir. Daiwa Securities Co. Ltd. 43, Exec. Vice-Pres. 54-57, Pres. 57-63, Chair. 63-; Gov. Fed. of Econ. Organisations 58-, Tokyo Stock Exchange 60-; Tokyo Securities Dealers' Asscn.
4-13-1, Denenchofu, Ota-ku, Tokyo, Japan.

Fukuda, Hajime; Japanese politician; b. 01; ed. Tokyo Univ.
Rengo News Agency 27; Domei News Agency 36, Man. Domei Bureaux, Nanking and Singapore 40-45; mem. House of Reps. 49; Vice-Minister of Labour 52-53; Dir. of Public Information and Publicity, Bureau of Liberal Democratic Party; Chair., Cabinet Cttee., Steering Cttee., House of Reps.; Minister of Int. Trade and Industry 62-July 64.
22-5, Inokuchi, Ono-Shi, Fukui-Ken, Japan.

Fukuda, Takeo; Japanese politician; b. 14 Jan. 1905; ed. Tokyo Imperial Univ.
With Ministry of Finance 29-50, Deputy Vice-Minister 45-46, Dir. of Banking Bureau 46-47, Dir. Budget Bureau 47-50; mem. House of Reps. 52-; Chair. Policy Board Liberal-Democratic Party, later Sec.-Gen.; fmr. Minister of Agriculture and Forestry; Minister of

Finance 65-Dec. 66; Sec.-Gen. Liberal Democratic Party Dec. 66-.
1-247 Nozawa-machi, Setagaya-ku, Tokyo, Japan.

Fukuda, Tokuyasu; Japanese politician; b. 06; ed. Tokyo Univ.
Ministry of Foreign Affairs, rising to become Chief of Section, Information Bureau; Foreign Service, Europe, America, China; fmr. Chief Private Sec. to Prime Minister Yoshida; mem. House of Reps. 49-; fmr. Vice-Minister for Econ. Affairs; Head Gen. Affairs Section, Prime Ministers' Office 59; Head of Defence Agency July 63-July 64; Minister of State, Dir. of Admin. Management Agency and Hokkaido Development Agency June 65-66; Liberal Democratic Party.
3 Kioi-cho, Chiyoda-ku, Tokyo, Japan.

Fukushima, Shintaro; Japanese diplomatist and newspaper executive; b. 07; ed. Tokyo Univ.
Joined Foreign Service, served U.S.A., Australia and the Philippines 30-41; Private Sec. to fmr. Prime Minister Shidehara 45-48; Deputy Sec.-Gen. of Cabinet 48; Dir.-Gen. Procurement Agency 53-55; Pres. Kyodo News Service, Tokyo; Pres. *The Japan Times.*
7-3, 6-chome, Hatanodai, Shinagana, Tokyo, Japan.

Fukushima, Toshiyuki; Japanese business executive; b. 95; ed. Hosei Univ.
President, Nippon Express Co. Ltd.; resigned, and later arrested 68.
12-9, 3-chome, Soto-Kanda, Chiyoda-ku, Tokyo, Japan.

Fulbright, James William, LL.B., M.A.; American politician; b. 9 April 1905; ed. Univ. of Arkansas, Oxford Univ. and George Washington Univ.
Special Attorney Anti-Trust Div., U.S. Dept. of Justice 34-35; Instructor in Law, George Washington Univ. 35-36; Lecturer in Law Univ. of Arkansas 36-39, Pres. 39-41; mem. 78th Congress (43-45), 3rd District, Arkansas; U.S. Senator from Arkansas 45-; Chair. Senate Cttee. Foreign Relations 59; Democrat.
Publ. *Old Myths and New Realities* 65, *The Arrogance of Power* 67.
Senate Office Building, Washington 25, D.C.; and Fayetteville, Ark., U.S.A.

Fuleihan, Anis; American composer, pianist and conductor; b. 2 April 1900; ed. English School, Cyprus, Polytechnic, Brooklyn, N.Y., and Von Ende School of Music, New York.
Concert pianist 19; Prof. of Piano and Composition, Indiana Univ. 47-52; Dir. Nat. Conservatoire of Music, Beirut, Lebanon 53-60; Musical Adviser, Baalbek Festival 56-60, Int. Cultural Centre, Tunis 62-63; Conductor Orchestre Classique de Tunis 63; Visiting Lecturer, Univ. of Illinois 67-68; Guest Conductor N.Y. Philharmonic Orchestra 67.
Compositions: orchestral, operatic and chamber music, concerti with orchestra, sonatas for piano and various instruments, suites for strings, choral and vocal music, short works for piano and other instruments, etc.
438 West 116th Street, New York, N.Y., U.S.A.

Fulla, Ludovít; Czechoslovak painter; b. 27 Feb. 1902; ed. School of Fine and Applied Arts, Prague.
Professor at School of Arts and Crafts, Bratislava 29-38, Dir. 38-39; schoolteacher, Bratislava 49-52, Asst. Prof. Art Coll., Bratislava 49-52; over 800 works, including stage designs, paintings, designs for tapestries, graphic works and book illustrations; exhibited at Venice Biennials 34, 42, 54, 56, 62, Brussels Int. Exhbn. 35, 58, Milan Triennial 36, Paris World Fair 37, São Paulo Biennial 57, Moscow 58-59, Second Int. Tapestry Biennial, Lausanne 56; Grand Prix and Silver Medal, Paris 37; Gold Medal and Diploma, Int. Brussels Exhbn. 58; Order of Labour 62, Nat. Artist 63, State Prize 66.
Union of Slovak Artists, Ružomberok, Galeria Fulla, Czechoslovakia.

Fuller, Richard Buckminster; American professor and engineer; b. 12 July 1895; ed. Milton Acad., Harvard Univ., Annapolis Naval Acad.

Asst. Export Man. Armour & Co. 19-21; Nat. Accounts Sales Man. Kelly-Springfield Truck Co. 22; Pres. Stockade Building System 22-27; Founder Pres. 4-D Co., Chicago 27-32; Founder, Dir. and Chief Engineer Dymaxion Corpn. 32-35; Asst. to Dir. of Research and Development, Phelps Dodge Corpn. 36-38; Technical Consultant *Fortune* magazine 38-40; Vice-Pres. and Chief Engineer, Dymaxion Co. Inc. 41-42; Chief, Mechanical Engineering Section, Board of Economic Warfare, Special Asst. to Dir. Foreign Economic Admin. 42-44; Chair. Dymaxion Dwelling Machines 44-46; Pres. Geodesics Inc. 54-, Synergetics Inc. 54-59, Plydomes Inc. 57-; Prof. of Generalised Design Science Exploration, Southern Ill. Univ. 59-; The Charles Eliot Norton Prof. of Poetry, Harvard Univ. 61-62; Fellow and life mem. A.A.A.S.; hon. life mem. American Inst. of Architects; inventor-discoverer of energetic-synergetic geometry and of geodesic and tensegrity structures; built domes for U.S. Marine Corps and U.S. Navy (in all over 2,000 geodesic domes in 30 countries, including geodesic dome for Expo 67, Montreal 67); Hon. Dr. Arts, Michigan Univ. 55, S. Illinois Univ. 59; Hon. D.Sc. Washington Univ. 57, Colorado Univ. 64; Hon. Dr. Design N. Carolina Univ. 54; Hon. Dr. Hum., Rollins Coll. 60, Monmouth Coll. 65, etc.; awarded Royal Gold Medal for Architecture, Royal Inst. of British Architects 68.

Publs. *Nine Chains to the Moon* 38, *No More Second-Hand God* 62, *Unfinished Epic of Industrialization* (poetry) 63, *Education Automation* 63, *Ideas and Integrities* 63.

Office: P.O. Box 909, Carbondale, Ill. 62901; Home: 407 South Forest Street, Carbondale, Ill. 62901, U.S.A. Telephone: 618-457-8064 (Office); 618-457-6636 (Home).

Fuller, Roy Broadbent; British solicitor and author; b. 11 Feb. 1912.

Asst. Solicitor, Woolwich Equitable Building Soc. 38, Solicitor 58; war service in Royal Navy 41-46; mem. Arts Council Poetry Panel 55-59; Chair. Building Societies Asscn. Legal Advisory Panel 58; mem. board Poetry Book Soc. 60; Fellow, Royal Soc. of Literature.

Publs. Verse: *The Middle of a War* 42, *A Lost Season* 44, *Epitaphs and Occasions* 49, *Counterparts* 54, *Brutus's Orchard* 57, *Collected Poems* 62, *Buff* 65, *New Poems* 68; Novels: *The Second Curtain* 53, *Fantasy and Fugue* 54, *Image of a Society* 56, *The Ruined Boys* 59, *The Father's Comedy* 61, *The Perfect Fool* 63, *My Child, My Sister* 65; Edited: *The Building Societies Acts.*

37 Langton Way, London, S.E.3, England. Telephone: 01-858-2334.

Fulton, Baron, Life-Peer (cr. 66), of Fulmer; **John Scott Fulton,** Kt.; British university administrator; b. 27 May 1902; ed. Dundee High School, St. Andrews Univ. and Balliol Coll., Oxford.

Assistant in Logic and Scientific Method, London School of Econs. 26-28; Fellow, Balliol Coll., Oxford 28-47, Tutor in Philosophy 28-35, in Politics 35-47; Jowett Lecturer 35-38, Jowett Fellow 45-47; Faculty Fellow, Nuffield Coll. 39-47; Principal Asst. Ministry of Fuel and Power 42-44; Principal, Univ. Coll. of Swansea 47-59; Vice-Chancellor, Univ. of Wales 52-54, 58-59; Vice-Chancellor, Univ. of Sussex 59-67; Chair. Board for Mining Qualifications 50-62, Univs. Council for Adult Education 52-55, Univs. Central Council on Admissions 61-64, B.B.C. Liaison Advisory Cttee. on Adult Educ. 62-, I.T.A. Adult Educ. Advisory Cttee; Gov. and Vice-Chair. B.B.C. 65-67; Chair. of Cttee. to Examine Structure, Recruitment, Training and Management of Home Civil Service 66-; Chair. British Council 68-.

Publ. *In Defence of Democracy* (with C. R. Morris) 35.

Brook House, Priestman's Lane, Thornton-le-Dale, Pickering, Yorkshire, England. Telephone: Thornton-le-Dale 221.

Fulton, Hon. Edmund Davie, P.C., Q.C., M.P.; Canadian lawyer and politician; b. 10 March 1916; ed. Univ. of British Columbia and St. John's Coll., Oxford (Rhodes Scholar).

Called to Bar and admitted as solicitor 40; served in Europe with Seaforth Highlanders of Canada 40-45; mem. House of Commons 45-64; Pres. Young Progressive Conservatives of Canada 46-49, Minister of Justice and Attorney-Gen. 57-62; Acting Minister of Citizenship and Immigration 57-58; Minister of Public Works 62-63; Leader Progressive Conservative Party, British Columbia 63-; Hon. LL.D. (Ottawa, Queens Univ.).

157 Battle Street, Kamloops, British Columbia, Canada.

Fumagalli, Guido; Italian businessman; b. 12 Oct. 1902; ed. Istituto Tecnico C. Cattaneo, Milan.

Commission Agent Stock Exchange, Milan 46-56; Stockbroker, Milan 56-; mem. Stock Exchange Cttee. 63-64, Pres. 65-; Pres. Union of Italian Stock Exchange Cttees. 65-; Cavaliere Ufficiale della Corona d'Italia.

Via Meravigli 16, Milan; and Viale Romagna 5, Milan, Italy.

Funcke, Friedrich, D.IUR.; German business exec.; b. 27 Sept. 1903; ed. Univs. of Freiburg, Berlin and Erlangen.

Joined Gelsenkirchener Bergwerks-Aktien-Gesellschaft (coal mining) 31, mem. Man. Board 45-67, Chair. Jan. 67-; Chair. Advisory Board Gelsenberg Benzin AG, Gelsenkirchen Wasserwerks für das nördliche westfalische Kohlenrevier, Gelsenkirchen, Münsterischer Schiffahrts-und Lagerhaus AG, Dortmund; Chair. Advisory Cttee. Raab Karcher GmbH, Karlsruhe, "Pres." Ruhrkohlen-Verkaufs GmbH, Essen; Deputy Chair. Unternehmensverband Ruhrbergbau, Westdeutsche, Wohnhäuser AG, Essen; mem. Advisory Board ARAL AG, Bochum, Rütgerswerke u. Teerverwertung AG, Frankfurt, Steinkohlen-Elektrizität AG, Essen.

Gelsenkirchener Bergwerks-Aktien-Gesellschaft, 43 Essen, Rosastrasse 2, German Federal Republic. Telephone: Essen 79981.

Funès, Louis de; French actor; b. 31 July 1914.

Plays include *Winterset, Un Tramway Nommé Désir, Ornifle, Les Belles Bacchantes*; films include *Le Blé en Herbe, Mam'zelle Nitouche, Papa, Maman, la Bonne et Moi, L'Impossible Monsieur Pipelet, Courte Tête, La Traversée de Paris, Un Cheveu sur la Soupe, Ni Vu ni Connu, La Vie à Deux, Certains l'Aiment Froide, Mon Pote le Gitan, Chair à Poisson, Candide, Les Dix Commandements, Le Gendarme de Saint-Tropez, Le Corniaud, les Bons Vivants, le Gendarme à New York, Fantomas se déchaine, le Grand Restaurant, la Grande Vadrouille.*

45 rue de Monceau, Paris 8e, France.

Fung Yu-Lan; Chinese philosopher; b. 95; ed. Chung-chou Inst., Kaifeng, China Academy, Shanghai and National Peking Univ.

Editor *Mind's Echo*, Kaifeng 18; Post-graduate studies, Columbia Univ., New York 19-23; Prof. of Philosophy, Tsinghua Univ. 27-52, Head, Dept. of Philosophy, Dean of College of Arts 33-52; Prof. of Philosophy, Peking Univ. 52-; Fellow, Academia Sinica (now Chinese Acad. of Sciences) 48-, mem. Research Inst. of Philosophy, Acad. of Sciences 57-; mem. Chinese People's Political Consultative Conf. 56-; Prix Stanislas Julien, Académie des Inscriptions et Belles-Lettres, Institut de France 50.

Publs. *Jen-sheng Che-hsueh* (Philosophy of Life) 26, *Chung-kuo Che-hsueh Shih* (History of Chinese Philosophy) (2 Vols.) 31, 34, Supplement 36, *Hsin Li-hsueh* 39, *Hsin Shih Lun* 40, *Hsin Shih-hsun* 40, *Hsin Yuan Jen* 43, *Hsin Yuan Tao* 44, *Hsin Chih Yen* 46, *A Short*

History of Chinese Philosophy (in English) 48, *The Development of Chinese Philosophy* (in Great Soviet Encyclopaedia) 50.

Department of Philosophy, Peking University, Peking, People's Republic of China.

Funston, George Keith; American executive; b. 12 Oct. 1910; ed. Sioux Falls High School, Trinity Coll., Hartford, Conn., and Harvard School of Business Admin.

Asst. to Vice-Pres. in Charge of Sales, American Radiator and Standard Sanitary Corpn. 35-38, Asst. to Treas. 38-40; Sales-Planning Dir., later Dir. of Purchases, Sylvania Electric Products, Inc. 40; War Production Board 41-44; Lieut.-Commdr. U.S. Navy 44-45; Pres. Trinity Coll., Hartford, Conn. 44-51; Pres. New York Stock Exchange 51-Sept. 67; Chair. Olin Mathieson Chemical Corpn. 67-; Dir. Metropolitan Life Insurance Co., and several other companies; has 22 Hon. degrees from American univs.

Olin Mathieson Chemical Corpn., 460 Park Ave., New York, N.Y. 10022, U.S.A.

Telephone: 212-572-2291.

Fuoss, Robert; American editor; b. 16 Dec. 1912; ed. Michigan Univ.

Editor Saline *Observer* 33; salesman Vick Chemical Co.; Batten, Barton, Durstine and Osborn, Inc., advertising; Promotion Manager *Country Gentleman* 37-39; Promotion Manager *Saturday Evening Post* 39-42, Man. Editor 42-55, Exec. Editor 55-62, Vice-Pres., Public Relations 62-64; Senior Editor *Reader's Digest* 64-65, Exec. Vice-Pres. 65-, mem. Man. Cttee. 65-; Trustee Dickenson Coll., Pennsylvania 66-; Board of Dirs. Presbyterian Life, Philadelphia 65-; Dir.-at-Large, Nat. Retail Merchants Asscn. 67-; Distinguished Service Award, Overseas Press Club 61.

Office: 22 West 7th Street, Cincinnati 45202; Home: 6700 Shawnee Ridge Lane, Cincinnati, U.S.A.

Telephone: 513-721-7600 (Office); 513-831-7802 (Home).

Furler, Hans; German politician and lawyer; b. 5 June 1904; ed. Univs. of Freiburg, Berlin and Heidelberg.

Lecturer at Technical High School, Karlsruhe 30-40; Prof. of Law Univ. of Freiburg 40-49, Extraordinary 49-; member Bundestag 53-, and Chairman of Foreign Relations Cttee.; President Parliamentary Cttee. for the Common Market and Euratom 56-57; specialist on problems of European integration; mem. E.C.S.C. Common Assembly 55-58, Pres. 56-58; mem. Consultative Assembly, Council of Europe 57-; Vice-Pres. European Parliament 58-60, Pres. 60-62, Vice-Pres. 62-; Pres. German Council of European Movement 58; Grand Cross of Order of Merit, of the Italian Republic, of the German Fed. Republic, and of Greece.

Publs. include various legal works.

Hauptstrasse 6, 7602 Oberkirch, Baden, German Federal Republic.

Telephone: 07802-2231.

Furnas, Clifford Cook, B.S., PH.D.; American scientist and author; b. 24 Oct. 1900; ed. Purdue Univ. and Univ. of Michigan.

With U.S. Bureau of Mines 26-31; Assoc. Prof. Yale Univ. 31-42; Technical Aide, Nat. Defense Research Cttee. 41-43; Dir. of Research, Curtiss-Wright Corpn. Research Laboratory 42-46; Dir. Cornell Aeronautical Laboratory 46-54; Chancellor, Univ. of Buffalo 54-62, granted leave of absence to assume post of Asst. Sec. of Defense for Research and Development 55-57; Chair. Air Naval Development Board 56, Army Scientific Advisory Panel; mem. Nat. Advisory Cttee. on Aeronautics 56-57; mem. Defense Science Board 57-64; Pres. State Univ. at Buffalo 62-66, Pres. Emeritus 66; Pres. West, N.Y. Nuclear Research Center 66-; Board of Trustees, Aerospace Corpn.; mem. Navy Research Advisory Cttee. 60-; mem. Nat. Acad. of Engineering

67-; Vice-Chair. Nat. Research Council 68-; D.Eng. h.c. Purdue Univ. 46, Univ. of Mich. 57; D.Iur. Alfred Univ. 58; Golden Cross, Order of the Phoenix, Hon. Degree Univ. de Asuncion 63.

Publs. *America's Tomorrow* 32, *The Next Hundred Years* 36, *The Storehouse of Civilisation* 39; Editor: *Roger's Manual of Industrial Chemistry* 42, *Industrial Research—Its Organisation and Management* 48, *The Engineer* 66.

651 Le Brun Road, Buffalo 26, N.Y., U.S.A.

Telephone: TF2-5982.

Furstenberg, H.E. Cardinal Maximilian van; Netherlands ecclesiastic; b. 23 Oct. 1904.

Ordained Priest 31; Titular Archbishop of Palto 49-; also Apostolic Nuncio in Portugal until 68; Head of Sacred Congregation for the Eastern Churches 68-; created Cardinal by Pope Paul VI 67.

Sacred Congregation for the Eastern Churches, Vatican City, Rome, Italy.

Furtado, Celso, M.A.; Brazilian economist; b. 20; ed. Univs. of Brazil, Paris and Cambridge.

Head, Development Div., UN Econ. Comm. for Latin America 50-53; Brazilian Nat. Development Bank, Dir. 58-61; Del. to Econ. Conf. of Punta del Este 61; Gov., Latin American Inst. for Econ. and Social Planning 62; Superintendent of the Development of the Brazilian Northeast 59-64; State Minister for Econ. Development 62-63; mem. Brazilian Nat. Acad.; Editor *Economica Brasileira*; Pres. Economists Club, Rio de Janeiro.

Publs. *The Brazilian Economy* 54, *A Dependent Economy* 56, *Prospects for the Brazilian Economy* 58, *Brazilian Economic Formation* 59, *Development and Underdevelopment* 61, *Reflexions upon the Brazilian Pre-revolution* 62, *The Economic Growth of Brazil* 63, *Diagnosis of the Brazilian Crisis* 66.

Av. Atlantica, 4066, Apt. 508, Rio de Janeiro, Brazil.

Furtseva, Ekaterina Alexeyevna; Soviet politician; b. 1910; ed. Moscow Inst. of Chemical Technology and Higher Party School.

Joined Communist Party 30; exec. work in Young Communist League 30-37; Sec. Frunze District Cttee. of C.P. 42-50; Second Sec., Moscow City Cttee. of C.P.S.U. 50-54, 1st Sec. 54-57; alt. mem. Cen. Cttee. C.P.S.U. 52-56, mem. 56-, Sec. 57-60; alt. mem. Presidium of Cen. Cttee. C.P.S.U. 56-57, mem. 57-61; Minister of Culture 60-; Dep. to Supreme Soviet; awarded Order of Lenin, Order of the Red Banner of Labour, Badge of Honour, and other decorations.

Ministry of Culture, 10 Ulitsa Kuibysheva, Moscow, U.S.S.R.

Furukaki, Pierre Tetsuro, LL.D.; Japanese journalist and broadcasting official; b. 1900; ed. Lyon Univ.

With L.N., Geneva 24-29; Chief European and American Section *Asahi* Newspapers 37, Editorial Writer 39, Dir. 43; mem. House of Peers 46; Gen. Man. Dir. Nippon Hoso Kyokai (Japanese Broadcasting Corpn.) 46-49, Pres. 49-56; Ambassador to France 56-61; Adviser to Foreign Minister 61-.

Publs. *Mandate System of the League of Nations* (in French) 23, *League of Nations and World Peace* (in Japanese) 25, *On International Arbitration* (in French) 28, *London Melancholy* (in Japanese) 37, *La Fenêtre de Tokio* (in English and Japanese), 54, *Pink Handkerchief* (Poems in English and Japanese) 54, *Vol de Nuit* (Poems in English, French and Japanese) 55, *Rosa . . . Rosae* (Poems in French and English) 58, *Paris qui Vit* (Poems in French and Japanese) 59, *Paris de Mon Coeur* (Poems in French) 61.

316 3-chome, Kamiosaki 3, Shinagawa-ku, Tokyo, Japan.

Fuson, Reynold Clayton, M.A., D.SC., PH.D.; American chemist; b. 1 June 1895; ed. Univ. of Montana, Univ. of Calif., Univ. of Minnesota.

Nat. Research Fellow, Harvard Univ. 24-26, Instructor 26-27; Assoc. in Chemistry, Univ. of Illinois 27-28, Asst. Prof. 28-30, Assoc. Prof. 30-32, Prof. of Organic Chemistry 32-63, Prof. Emer. 63-; Prof. of Chemistry, the Rice Inst. 47-48; Visiting Prof. Univ. of Nevada 63-66, Prof. Emer. 66-; mem. Nat. Acad. of Sciences, Center for Advanced Study; awarded William H. Nichols Medal 53, College Chemistry Teacher Award, Manufacturing Chemists' Asscn. 60, John R. Kuebler Award 64, Distinguished Achievement Award, Univ. of Minnesota 51.

Publs. *A Brief Course in Organic Chemistry* (with others) 41, 59, *Advanced Organic Chemistry* 50, *Organic Chemistry* (with H. R. Snyder) 55, *The Systematic Identification of Organic Compounds* (with others) 56, *Reactions of Organic Compounds* 62.

1442 Hillside Drive, Reno, Nevada 89503, U.S.A. Telephone: 786-6974.

Fysh, Sir Wilmot Hudson, K.B.E., D.F.C., F.R.G.S. (Austr.), F.R.AE.S., M.INST.T.; Australian air transport executive; b. 7 Jan. 1895; ed. Geelong Grammar School. Lieut. No. 1 Squadron, Australian Flying Corps in First World War; surveyed original trans-Australia air route from Longreach to Darwin (with Lieut. P. J. McGuinness) 19; one of the founders of Qantas Ltd. 20; pilot of first official air-mail service in Queensland and Eastern Australia 22; Man. Dir. Qantas Ltd. (later Qantas Empire Airways Ltd.) 23-47; Chair. and Man. Dir. Qantas Empire Airways Ltd. 47-55; Chair. Qantas Empire Airways Ltd. 55-66; fmr. Chair. Qantas Wentworth Holdings Ltd.; Pres. Int. Air Transport Asscn. 61; fmr. mem. Exec. Cttee. Int. Air Transport Asscn.; Deputy Chair Australian Nat. Travel Asscn.

Publs. *Taming the North* 33, *Qantas Rising* 65.

c/o Qantas Empire Airways Ltd., Qantas House, 70 Hunter Street, Sydney, Australia.

G

Gaay Fortman, Wilhelm Friedrich de, DR.JUR.; Netherlands university professor and politician; b. 8 May 1911; ed. Free (Protestant) Univ. of Amsterdam. Served in Ministry of Economic Affairs 34-38, of Social Affairs 38-47; Prof. of Civil and Labour Law, Free (Protestant) Univ. of Amsterdam 47-, Vice-Chancellor 65-; mem. of the First Chamber of Parl.; Chamberlain of H.M. the Queen; mem. Netherlands Del. to UN Gen. Assembly 54-57, to the Econ. and Social Council 59-60; mem. European Comm. of Human Rights 65; Knight Order of the Netherlands Lion.
Zuidwerfplein 7, The Hague, Netherlands.

Gabaldón, Arnoldo; Venezuelan malariologist; b. 09; ed. Universidad Central de Venezuela, Hamburg Inst. of Tropical Diseases and Johns Hopkins Univ.
Hospital Intern, Caracas 28-30; Laboratory Asst. Bacteriological and Parasitological Lab., Caracas 30-32; Sanitary Officer 32-33; Rockefeller Fellow, Johns Hopkins Univ. 34-36; Chief, Div. of Malariology, Ministry of Health 36-50; Technical Consultant, WHO Anti-Malaria Operations, India 50; Dir. Inst. of Aphtous Fever, Ministry of Agriculture, Venezuela 50; Consultant Div. of Malariology, Ministry of Health and Social Assistance 51-59; Technical Consultant, Panamerican Sanitary Org. 54, Panamerican Sanitary Office Anti-Malaria Campaign, Trinidad 57; Minister of Health and Social Assistance, Venezuela 59-64; mem. Venezuelan Nat. Acad. of Medicine; Consultant, Bureau of Malariology and Environmental Health, Ministry of Health and Social Assistance, Venezuela 64-.
Publs. Numerous studies on malaria, public health and parasitology.
Ministry of Health, Caracas, Venezuela.

Gabel, Father Emile, Licencié en Théologie; French priest and journalist; b. 1 Sept. 1908; ed. Catholic Univ., Louvain, and Faculty of Catholic Theology, Strasbourg Univ.
Took vows 31; ordained Priest 34; Prof. of Theology Lormoy 34-43; Editorial Dir. of La Maison de la Bonne Presse 43-49; Editor-in-Chief of La Croix 49-57; Pres. of Permanent Comm. of Editors of Catholic Journals 50-; Chief of Religious Broadcasting, Radio Luxembourg 66-; mem. Bureau of Int. Union of Catholic Press; mem. Perm. Comm. of the Semaines Sociales; mem. Vatican Secr. for Press and Entertainment, Union Int. d'Etudes Sociales.
43 rue Saint-Augustin, Paris 2e, France.

Gabin, Jean (*pseudonym* of Jean-Alexis Moncorgé); French actor; b. 17 May 1904.
Fmr. labourer and delivery boy; began stage career at Folies Bergères; film debut in *Chacun sa Chance* 30.
Films include *Gloria, Coeur de Lilas* 31, *Adieu les Beaux Jours, Le Tunnel* 33, *Maria Chapdelaine* 34, *La Bandera* 35, *Pépé le Moko, La Grande Illusion, Le Messager* 37, *Quai des Brumes, La Bête Humaine* 38, *Le Jour se lève* 39, *Moontide* 42, *Martin Roumagnac* 46, *Au-delà des Grilles* 48, *La Marie du Port* 50, *La Traversée de Paris, French Can Can, Le sang et la tête, Crime et Châtiment, Sans douleur, The Possessors, Ne Touchez Pas Au Grisbi, Le Rouge est Mis, Les Grandes Familles, Le Président, The Big Snatch, Le cave se rebiffe, Un singe en hiver, le Gentleman d'Epsom, Mélodie en sous-sol, Monsieur, le Deuxième Souffle, le Tonnerre de Dieu, Du rififi à Paname, le Jardinier d'Argenteuil*; Co-Producer (with Fernandel) *L'Age Ingrat* 64.
Office: c/o Bernheim, 55 avenue George V, Paris 8e; Home: "la Pichonnière", Bonnefoi (Orne), France.

Gabo, Naum; American (b. Russian) sculptor; b. 5 Aug. 1890; ed. Munich, Paris, and Oslo.
Lived in Berlin 21-32, Paris 32-36, England 36-46, U.S.A. 46-; rep. at numerous exhbns., including the Brussels Int. Exhbn. 58, and Coolsingel, Rotterdam, Tate Gallery, London 66; mem. American Inst. of Arts and Letters; Dr. h.c. Royal Coll. of Art (U.K.).
Publs. *Gabo* 57, *Of Divers Arts* 62.
Breakneck Hill Road, Middlebury, Conn., U.S.A.
Telephone: 203-758-9487.

Gabor, Dennis, D.SC.DR.ING, F.INST.P., M.I.E.E., F.R.S.; British electrical engineer; b. 5 June 1900; ed. Technical Univ., Budapest, and Technische Hochschule, Charlottenburg.
Research engineer in German Research Asscn. of High Voltage Plants 26-27; Siemens and Halske, Berlin-Siemensstadt 27-33; British Thomson Houston Co. Research Lab., Rugby 34-48; Reader in Electronics, Imperial Coll. of Science and Technology, Dept. of Electrical Engineering 49-58; Prof. Applied Electron Physics at Imperial Coll., Univ. of London 58-; Hon. mem. Hungarian Acad. of Sciences; inventor of holography.
Publs. *Inventing the Future* 63; about eighty papers on high-speed oscillography of transients, gas discharges and plasmas, electron optics and electron microscopy, physical optics (diffraction and interference microscopes), communication theory and communication techniques (television).
78 Queens Gate, London, S.W.7, England.
Telephone: 01-370-1410.

Gabriel, Ralph Henry, PH.D.; American historian; b. 29 April 1890; ed. Yale Univ.
Mem. staff Yale Univ. 15 and Prof. 28-58; mem. staff U.S. War Dept. School of Military Government 43-46; mem. American Historical Asscn.; mem. Newcomen Society; Visiting Prof. Sydney Univ., Australia 46; Prof. American History Cambridge Univ. 51-52, Prof. of American Civilisation, American Univ. 58-64; Visiting Prof. Tokyo Univ. 64, George Washington Univ. 65; U.S. Del. at Tenth Session of UNESCO 58; mem. of U.S. Nat. Comm. for UNESCO; Editor *Pageant of America* (15 vols.) 24-29; Joint-Editor *The American Mind* 37; Editor Library of Congress Series in American Civilisation.
Publs. *Evolution of Long Island* 22, *Toilers of Land and Sea* 26, *Lure of the Frontier* 29, *The Course of American Democratic Thought* 40, 59, *Religion and Learning at Yale* 58, *Traditional Values in American Life* 60.
484 Whitney Avenue, New Haven, Conn. 06511, U.S.A.

Gabriel-Robinet, Louis, L. EN D., L. ès L.; French journalist; b. 17 Dec. 1909.
Advocate at Court of Appeal, Paris 32; Reporter *Echo de Paris* 34; Editor *Figaro*, Deputy Dir. 65-; Vice-Pres. Société des Gens de Lettres de France; Officier de la Légion d'Honneur.
Publs. *Le Blocus à travers les âges* 43, *Le Diable, sa vie, son oeuvre* 44, *Bras de Fer* 45, *Aranga, Histoire de la Presse, Je suis Journaliste, Journaux et journalistes d'hier et d'aujourd'hui* 61, *La censure* 65.
26 rue Guynemer, Paris 6e, France.
Telephone: 256-80-00.

Gabrielli, Francisco José Marcelino; Argentine industrial engineer and politician; b. 1902; ed. National Univ. of Buenos Aires.
Private building work 25-30; Public Works Dept., Mendoza 30-34; Director-President, Provincial Directorate, Vialidad 34-41; Superintendent-Gen. of Irriga-

tion, Vialidad 41-46; founder and Pres. Construcciones Gabrielli, Willmott y Cía. S.R.L. 46-61; Dir. Bodegas y Viñedos Gabrielli y Baldini S.A. Ltd. 46-61, Gabrielli Hnos. S.R.L. 46-61; Gov. of Mendoza 61-62, Oct. 63-June 66.

Godoy Cruz 310, Ciudad de Mendoza, Argentina.

Gadd, Cyril John; British antiquarian; b. 2 July 1893; ed. King Edward VI School, Bath, and Brasenose Coll., Oxford.

British Museum excavations, Ur 23-24, Alalakh 46, Nimrud 52; Keeper Dept. of Egyptian and Assyrian Antiquities, British Museum 48-55; Prof. of Ancient Semitic Languages and Civilizations, Univ. of London 55-60; Hon. D.Litt. (Oxford).

Publs. *The Early Dynasties of Sumer and Akkad* 21, *Cuneiform Texts* 36, 39-41, *The Fall of Nineveh* 23, *A Sumerian Reading Book* 24, *History and Monuments of Ur* 29, *Stones of Assyria* 36, *Ideas of Divine Rule* 48, *Ur: Royal Inscriptions* and *Literary and Religious Texts* (with L. Legrain and S. N. Kramer) 28, 63, 66.

221 Rosendale Road, London, S.E.21, England. Telephone: 01-670-4069.

Gadda, Carlo Emilio; Italian writer; b. 14 Nov. 1893; ed. Liceo Parini, Milan, Politecnico, Milan, and Univ. degli Studi, Milan.

Engineer in Argentina, Italy, France, Belgium, and Germany 22-30; with Italian Radiocultural programmes 50-56; Premio Viareggio 53, Prix international de Littérature 63.

Publs. *L'Adalgisa* (short stories) 43, *Quer Pasticciaccio Brutto de Via Merulana* (novel) 57, English translation 65, *La cognizione del dolore* 63, *Da Eros a Priapo* 67.

c/o Einaudi Editore, Via Umberto Biancamano 1, Turin, Italy.

Gadda Conti, Piero, LL.D.; Italian writer; b. 13 Feb. 1902; ed. Pavia Univ.

Novelist and journalist; Italian Literary Prize-winner 30.

Publs. *L'Entusiastica Estate* 24, *Liuba* 26, *Verdemare* 27, *Mozzo* 30, *A Gonfie Vele* 31, *Gagliarda* 32, *Orchidea* 34, *Festa da Ballo* 37, *Nuvola* 38, *Moti del Cuore* 40, *Vocazione Mediterranea* 40, *Incomparabile Italia* 47, *Beati Regni* 54, *Vita e melodie di Giacomo Puccini* 55, *Adamira* 56, *Vanterie Adolescenti* 60, *Cinema e civiltà* 60, *Cinema e Giustizia* 61, *Cinema e Sesso* 62, *Cinema e Libertà* 63, *La Milano dei Navigli* 65, *Cinema e Società* 65, *La Brianza* 66; plays: *La Veste d'Oro* 24, *Dulcinea* 27.

Piazza Castello 20, Milan, Italy. Telephone: 873-771.

Gaddafi, Wanis; Libyan politician.

Head of Exec. Council in Cyrenaican Provincial Govt. 52-62; Fed. Minister of Foreign Affairs Jan. 62-63, of Interior 63-64, of Labour 64; Ambassador to the Fed. German Repub. 64-65; now Minister of Planning and Devt.

Ministry of Planning and Development, Tripoli, Libya.

Gadgil, Dhananjay Ramchandra, M.A., D.LITT.; Indian economist; b. 1901; ed. Patwardhan High School, Nagpur, and Queen's Coll., Cambridge.

Additional Asst. Sec., Finance Dept., Bombay 24-25; Principal, M.T.B. Coll., Surat 25-30; Dir. Gokhale Inst. of Politics and Econs. 30-; mem. numerous Boards and Comms.; Vice-Chancellor Univ. of Poona 66-67; Deputy Chair. Indian Planning Comm. Sept. 67-.

Indian Planning Commission, New Delhi, India.

Gadgil, Narhar Vishnu, B.A., LL.B., M.L.A.; Indian politician; b. 96; ed. Neemuch, Bombay, Baroda, and Poona.

Called to Bar, Poona 20; Sec. Poona District Congress Cttee. 21-32, All-India Congress Cttee. 26-32; Pres. Maharashtra Provincial Congress Cttee. 31; Vice-Pres. Bombay Presidency Youth League 28-32; Pres. Poona

Youth League 28-32; mem. Poona Municipality 28-32; Pres. G.I.P. Workers' Union, Poona 30-; returned to Legislative Assembly from Central Division, Bombay Presidency, as Congress candidate 35; fmr. Whip and Sec. of Congress Party; imprisoned several times in connection with Satyagraha; Minister of Works, Mines, and Power Aug. 47-Dec. 50; Minister of Works, Production and Supply 50-52; mem. Parl. 52-57; Vice-Chair. State Bank of India 57-58; Governor of Punjab 58-62.

419 Shanwar Peth, Poona-2, India.

Gadjibekov, Sultan Ismail Ogly; Soviet composer; b. 1919; ed. Baku Conservatoire.

Vice-Chair. Azerbaijan Composers' Union 52; Prof. Baku Conservatoire 65-; State Prize 52, Honoured Worker of Arts of Azerbaijan S.S.R. 58, Red Banner of Labour 59, People's Artist of Azerbaijan S.S.R. 60.

Principal compositions: *Gyzyl-Gyul* (musical comedy) 40, Sonata for Piano 40, Six Preludes for Piano, *Motherland* (cantata) 41, First Symphony 44, *Caravan* (symphonic picture) 45, Second Symphony 46, Concerto for Violin and Orchestra 47, *Gyulshen* (ballet) 50, Overture for Symphony Orchestra 56; music for theatre and other works.

Azerbaijan Composers' Union, 58 Ulitsa Nizami, Baku, U.S.S.R.

Gadsby, Edward N., B.A., J.D.; American lawyer; b. 11 April 1900; ed. Amherst Coll., and New York Univ. Law School.

With law firm of Mudge, Stern, Williams and Tucker, New York 29-37; law practice in North Adams, Mass. 37-47; Commr. Mass. Dept. of Public Utilities 47-52, Chair. 47-49, Gen. Counsel 52-56; mem. law firm Sullivan & Worcester, Boston 56-57; Chair. Securities and Exchange Comm. 57-61; Partner, Gadsby, Hannah, Colson and Morin, Washington 61-; Hon. M.A. (Amherst Coll.); Dr. Pub. Admin. (Suffolk Univ.); Republican.

Offices: 19 Congress Street, Boston, Mass., 729 15th Street, Washington D.C.; Home: Green River Road, Williamstown, Mass., U.S.A.

Gaganova, Valentina Ivanovna; Soviet textile spinner and politician; b. 32; ed. technical textile inst.

Turner, factory at Kovrov 47-48; Apprentice Spinner, Vyshny Volochok 48-49, Spinner 49-50, Foreman Planner 50-; mem. Central Cttee. of C.P.S.U. 61-; Hero of Socialist Labour 59.

Cotton Plant, Vyshny Volochok, Kalinin Region, U.S.S.R.

Gaggero, Sir George, Kt., O.B.E., J.P.; British industrialist; b. 5 April 1897; ed. Gibraltar, Germany and England.

Chair. M. H. Bland & Co. Ltd. (Bland Line), Rock Hotel Ltd., Bland (Morocco), S.A., Thomas Mosley & Co. Ltd., M. H. Bland & Co. (U.K.) Ltd., Bland Aerial Ropeway Ltd.; Swedish Consul-Gen. at Gibraltar 39-66; public positions held include Dir. Gibraltar Chamber of Commerce 18-22 and Pres. Employers' Fed. 25-40; unofficial mem. Executive Council 24-30, 36-43; Fellow R.S.A., Chevalier (First Class) Royal Swedish Order of Vasa.

75 Prince Edward's Road, Gibraltar.

Gagnebin, Albert P., B.S., M.S.; American mining executive; b. 23 Jan. 1909; ed. Yale Univ.

Research Engineer, Int. Nickel Co. Inc. 32-49, Ductile Iron Group Leader 49-54, Asst. Man. of Nickel Sales 54-56, Man. 56-57, Asst. Vice-Pres. 57-58, Vice-Pres. 58-64, Vice-Pres. Int. Nickel Co. of Canada Ltd. 60-64, Exec. Vice-Pres. Int. Nickel Co. of Canada Ltd. and Int. Nickel Co. Inc. 64-67, Pres., Dir. and mem. of Exec. Cttee. Int. Nickel Co. of Canada Ltd. and Int. Nickel Co. Inc. 67-; Dir. Abex Corpn., Sterling Forest (N.Y.) Board of Design, Centennial Insurance Co., Toronto-Dominion Bank, Int. Copper Research Asscn.;

Pres., Dir. Int. Nickel Services Ltd., Int. Nickel Benelux S.A., Int. Nickel France S.A., Int. Nickel (Italia) S.p.A.; Dir. American Cttee. for Inst. for Advanced Study-Europe Inc., Yale Eng. Asscn., Albert Gallatin Assocs. of New York Univ.; Councillor French Chamber of Commerce in U.S.; mem. Board of Dirs. Canadian Export Asscn.; co-inventor of Ductile Iron; Hon. Life mem. American Foundrymen's Soc.; Awards 52, 65 and 67.
Publs. *Fundamentals of Iron and Steel Castings* 57, and numerous articles.
143 Grange Avenue, Fair Haven, N.J. 07702, U.S.A. Telephone: 212-944-1000.

Gagnon, Wilfred; Canadian industrialist; b. 15 Sept. 1898; ed. Notre Dame Collegiate Inst., and Coll. St. Marie, Montreal.
Min. of Commerce and Industry Quebec Govt. June-Aug. 36; Dir. Canadian Nat. Railways 36; Pres. Wilfrid Gagnon Ltd., Shoe Manufacturers; Pres. Aird and Sons Ltd., Dir. Dominion Commercial Travellers' Asscn. 36; Pres. Shoe Manufacturers' Asscn. of Canada 35; mem. Canadian Manufacturers' Asscn., Chamber of Commerce and Board of Trade.
286 Outremont Avenue, Outremont, Quebec, Canada.

Gaillard, Félix, D.IUR.; French politician; b. 5 Nov. 1919; ed. Ecole Libre des Sciences Politiques.
Inspector of Finances 43; Personal Asst. to Jean Monnet 44-45; Deputy to National Assembly from La Charente 46-; Under-Sec. for Economic Affairs 46-47; Sec. d'Etat à la Présidence du Conseil 51 and 53; Sec. d'Etat aux Finances 52; del. to European Assembly 49, Pres. del. Brussels Conf. 55; mem. Council for Scientific and Technical Research 55; Pres. Comm. de l'Economie Générale et du Financement du Plan 56; Minister of Finance and Econs. 57; Prime Minister 57-58; mem. Senate of the French Community 58-61.
National Assembly, Palais Bourbon, Paris; and 22 ave. Foch, Paris 16e, France.

Gainza Paz, Alberto; Argentine journalist; b. 16 March 1899; ed. Nat. Univ. of Buenos Aires (graduated from its Law School).
Editor *La Prensa*, Buenos Aires, which he joined in 33; Dr. h.c. of Columbia Univ. New York and Northwestern Univ. Ill.
La Prensa, Avenida de Mayo 567, Buenos Aires, Argentina.

Gairbekov, Muslim Gairbekovich; Soviet politician; ed. Kabardino-Balkar State Univ.
Member C.P.S.U. 32; Teacher 32-35; Exec. Party and Local Govt. posts 36-40; People's Commissar for Educ. and Vice-Chair. Council of People's Commissars of the Chechen-Ingush Autonomous S.S.R. 40-57; Chair. Council of Ministers of the Chechen-Ingush Autonomous S.S.R., Deputy to U.S.S.R. Supreme Soviet 57-; mem. Educ., Science and Cultural Cttee., Soviet of Union.
Council of Ministers, Chechen-Ingush Autonomous S.S.R., Grozny, U.S.S.R.

Gairdner, Lieut.-General Sir Charles Henry, K.C.M.G., K.C.V.O., K.B.E., C.B., K.G.ST.J.; British administrator; b. 20 March 1898; ed. Repton and Royal Military Acad., Woolwich.
Gazetted 2nd Lieut., Royal Artillery 16; served in France and Flanders; transferred to 10th Royal Hussars 26, Major 31, Lieut.-Col. 37, Col. 40, Major-Gen. 42, Lieut.-Gen. 44; commnd. 10th Royal Hussars 37-40; Col. 49-52; Gen. Staff Officer, 1st Grade, 7th Armoured Div. 40-41; Deputy Dir. of Plans, Middle East 41; G.O.C. 6th Armoured Div. 42; Chief of Gen. Staff, N. Africa 43; Major-Gen. Armoured Fighting Vehicles, India 44; Personal Rep. of Prime Minister of U.K. in Far East 45-48; retd. 48; Gov. of Western Australia 51-63, Tasmania 63-; Medal of Freedom with Silver

Palm (U.S.A.); Hon. D.Litt. (W. Australia); Hon. LL.D. (Tasmania).
Government House, Hobart, Tasmania; and 24 The Esplanade, Perth, Western Australia.

Gaiser, Gerd, DR. PHIL.; German writer; b. 15 Sept. 1908; ed. Art Academies at Stuttgart and Königsberg, and Univ. of Tübingen.
Studied painting and the history of art; served German Air Force in Second World War; Fontane Prize of City of Berlin 51, Literature Prize of Bavarian Fine Arts Acad. 55 etc.; mem. Acad of Arts, Berlin.
Publs. *Zwischenland* (short stories) 49, *Eine Stimme hebt an* 50, *Das Schiff im Berg* 53, *Die Sterbende Jagd* 54, *Einmal und Oft* 56, *Schlussball* 57, *Sizilianische Notizen* 59, *Gib acht in Domokosch* 59, *Am Pass Nascondo* 60, *Klassiker der Modernen Malerei* 62, *Alte Meister der Moderne* 62, *Aktuelle Malerei* 63, *Gazelle Grün* 65.
Robert-Koch-Str. 39, Reutlingen, Württemberg, German Federal Republic.
Telephone: 41637.

Gaitonde, Vasudeo; Indian artist; b. 24; ed. Sir J. J. School of Art, Bombay.
Exhibited in London, New York, Paris, Sao Paulo, Tokyo; one man shows in New Delhi and Bombay; John D. Rockefeller Third Fund Grant 64; First Prize, Young Asian Artists' Exhibition, Tokyo 57.
Works in: Nat. Gallery of Modern Art and Lalit Kala Akademi, New Delhi, Tata Inst. of Fundamental Research and Atomic Energy Establishment, Bombay, Museum of Modern Art, New York.
89 Bhulabhai Desai Road, Bombay 26, India.

Gaivorontsev, Ivan Petrovich; Soviet politician; b. 1928; ed. Azov-Black Sea Inst. of Agriculture.
Agronomist 49-58; Party Official, Sec. of Chelyabinsk Regional Cttee. of C.P.S.U. 58-65; Chair. Chelyabinsk Regional Soviet 65-; Deputy to U.S.S.R. Supreme Soviet; mem. Educ., Science and Cultural Cttee., Soviet of Union; mem. C.P.S.U. 55-.
Chelyabinsk Regional Soviet of Working People's Deputies, Chelyabinsk, U.S.S.R.

Gajendragadkar, Pralhad Balacharya, M.A., LL.B.; Indian judge; b. 16 March 1901; ed. Karnatak Coll., Dharwar, Deccan Coll., Poona, Law Coll., Poona, and Univ. of Bombay.
Joined the Appellate Side Bar 26; Editor *Hindu Law Quarterly*; Sir Lallubhai Shah Lecturer, Bombay Univ., on Hindu Law of Adoption 50; Chair. Bank Award Comm. 55; Judge of the Bombay High Court 45-57; Judge, Supreme Court of India 57-63, Chief Justice 64-66; Vice-Chancellor, Bombay Univ. March 66-; Pres. S. P. Mandali, Poona; Pres. Swastik League, Bombay; Pres. Gen. Educ. Soc., Bombay; Visiting Lecturer, U.S. univs. 65; leader dels. Indian Jurists to U.S.S.R. and Australia 65; Hon. LL.D. (Karnatak).
Publs. Sanskrit Text of Nanda Pandit's *Dattaka Mimamsa* and its English translation, *Law, Liberty and Social Justice*.
Bombay University, Bombay 32, India.

Gajewski, Stanislaw; Polish lawyer and diplomatist; b. 12; ed. Univ. of Warsaw.
Entered diplomatic service 45; served Prague 45-48; Chief of Dept., Ministry of Foreign Affairs 48-53; Del. to Neutral Nations Repatriation Comm., Korea 53-54; Ambassador to France 54-61; Counsellor for External Relations in Seym (Parliament) 62-; Commdr. Polonia Restituta, Grand Officier de la Légion d'Honneur.
Plac Na Rozdrozij 3/30, Warsaw, Poland.

Galanis, Demetrius N.; Greek banker; b. 1900; ed. Athens Univ. and Univ. of Berlin.
Studied org. of banks in Germany; joined Commercial Bank of Greece 16; Minister of Nat. Econ. 45; Man., Econ. Research and Insp. of branches abroad, Commer-

cial Bank of Greece 46; mem. Board, High Board for Reconstruction 48; Prof., Graduate School of Industrial Management 48; Vice-Chair. Public Power Corpn. 50; Under-Sec. of State for Commerce 52; Gen. Administrator of American Aid Rehabilitation Loans 54; Gen. Man. Econ. Devt. Financing Org. 54; Deputy Gov., Bank of Greece 55-67, Gov. 67-; Chair. Board Post Office Savings Inst.; mem. Council of Europe 54, Econ. Comm. for Europe 55; Grand Cross Royal Order of Phoenix, Knight Commdr. Royal Order of George I; Grosses Verdienstkreuz mit Stern (German Federal Republic).
Publs. *Banks as Private and State Institutions, Monetary Policy and Credit Control, Prospects and Problems of the Greek Capital Market, Bank Share Capital and the Capital Market, Sources and Methods of Financing Investment in Greek Industry.*
Bank of Greece, P.O.B. 105, Athens, Greece.

Galanshin, Konstantin Ivanovich; Soviet politician; b. 1912; ed. Urals Industrial Inst.
Electrical Fitter 30-37; Engineer, Central Relay Service of "Uralenergo" Power System, Deputy Chief, then Chief of Relay Service of "Permenergo" Power System, Dir. of Perm Region Hydro-electric Power Station 37-50; First Sec. Berezniki Town Cttee. of C.P.S.U. 50-54; Party Official 54-60; First Sec. Perm Regional Cttee. of C.P.S.U. 60-; Deputy to U.S.S.R. Supreme Soviet; mem. C.P.S.U. 44-.
Perm Regional Committee, C.P.S.U., Perm, U.S.S.R.

Galbraith, J. Kenneth, B.S., M.S., PH.D.; American economist, diplomatist and writer; b. 15 Oct. 1908; ed. Toronto, California and Cambridge (England) Univs.
Research fellow, Calif. Univ. 31-34; Instructor, Harvard Univ. 34-39; Lecturer 48-49, Prof. of Econs. 49-; Amb. to India 61-63; B.B.C. Reith Lecturer 66; Asst. Prof. Princeton Univ. 39-42; Dep. Administrator, Office of Price Admin. 41-43; mem. Board of Editors *Fortune* magazine 43-48; Dir. Office of Economic Security Policy, State Dept. 45; Fellow, American Acad. of Arts and Sciences; Freedom Medal 46.
Publs. *Theory of Price Control, American Capitalism 52, The Great Crash, Economics and the Art of Controversy 55, The Affluent Society 58, Journey to Poland and Yugoslavia 59, The Liberal Hour 60, Made to Last 64, The Economic Discipline 67, The New Industrial State 67, The Triumph* (novel) 68.
30 Francis Avenue, Cambridge, Mass., U.S.A.

Galbraith, Vivian Hunter, M.A., F.B.A.; British historian; b. 15 Dec. 1889; ed. Highgate School, Manchester Univ., and Balliol Coll., Oxford.
Asst. Lecturer Manchester Univ. 20-21; Asst. Keeper Public Records 21-28; Fellow and Tutor in Modern History Balliol Coll. and Univ. Reader in Diplomatic History 28-37; Prof. History, Edinburgh Univ. 37-44, London Univ. 44-47, Dir. Inst. Hist. Research 44-47; Regius Prof. of Modern History Oxford Univ. 47-57; mem. Royal Comm. Ancient and Hist. Monuments England and Scotland; Hon. D. Litt. (Belfast, Edinburgh and Manchester).
Publs. *Anonimalle Chronicle of St. Mary's Abbey York 27, Intro. to use of the Public Records 34, Literacy of Medieval English Kings 35, St. Albans Chronicle 1406-1420 37, Roger Wendover and Matthew Paris 44, Studies in the Public Records 48, Herefordshire Domesday 50, Historical Research in Medieval England 51, The Making of Domesday Book 61, The Historian at Work 62, An Introduction to the Study of History 64.*
20A Bradmore Road, Oxford, England.

Gale, General Sir Richard, G.C.B., K.B.E., D.S.O., M.C.; British army officer; b. 25 July 1896; ed. Merchant Taylors School, Aldenham and Royal Military Coll.
Commissioned Worcestershire Regt. 15; served through all ranks to Major-Gen. 44; Commdr. 6th Airborne Div.

42-44, 1st British Airborne Corps 44-45; G.O.C. 1st Infantry Division, Palestine 46-47, British Troops Mediterranean 48-49; Lieut.-Gen. 47; Dir.-Gen. Military Training 49; General 52; Commdr. Northern Army Group and C.-in-C. British Army of the Rhine 52-56; Dep. Supreme Allied Commdr. Europe 58-60; Chair. Army League 61; Commdr. Legion of Merit and Légion d'Honneur, Croix de Guerre.
Publ. *Battles of the Bible* 63, *Call to Arms* (autobiography) 68.
3 Sydney Place, London, S.W.7, England.

Galea, Joseph, M.B.E., M.D., D.P.H.; British doctor and writer; b. 02; ed. St. Aloysius Coll., Univs. of Malta and Edinburgh.
Port Health Officer, Malta 30-37; M.O.H. Valletta 37-48; Senior Health Officer, Ministry of Health 48-51; Chief Govt. M.O. and Superintendent of Public Health of Malta 51-61; Prof. and Examiner, Royal Univ. Malta; Pres. Acad. of Maltese Writers, Soc. Welfare of Mentally Handicapped, Royal Soc. of Health (Malta Branch), Asscn. Maltese Writers 45-; mem. Public Service Comm. of Malta; holds Medal and Prizes for Maltese literary work; Officer of the Order of St. John of Jerusalem; Knight of Grace of the Sovereign Order of Malta, Grand Officer of Merit Order of Malta.
Publs. include: *First Aid to War Casualties, Health and Design of Dwelling Houses, The Sources of Maltese Literature, Ragel Bil Ghaqal, Grajja Tal Gwerra, San Guan, Id-Dinja Rota, History of Malta since 1530, The Health Conditions of the Maltese Islands, Short History of the Sovereign Order of Malta.*
34 Strait Street, Valletta, Malta; and St. John Club, 50 Eaton Place, London, S.W.1, England.
Telephone: 24311 (Malta).

Galichon, Georges, L.EN.D.; French administrator and airline executive; b. 3 Nov. 1915; ed. Lycée Janson-de-Sailly and Ecole des Sciences Politiques.
Auditeur au concours, Conseil d'Etat 41, Maître des Requêtes 47; Dir. at the Presidency of the Council 49-55; Gen. Sec. High Cttee. of the Youth of France and Overseas Territories at the Presidency of the Council 55-58; Dir. du Cabinet, to Pierre Chatenet, Minister of the Interior 59, to the Pres. of the Repub. 61-67; Councillor of State 63-; Pres. Air France Jan. 67-; Officier Légion d'Honneur, Croix de Guerre.
Air France, 1 Square Max-Hymans, Paris 15e; Home: 176 boulevard Saint-Germain, Paris 6e, France.

Galindo Pohl, Reinaldo; El Salvador diplomatist; b. 18 Oct. 1918; ed. Univ. of El Salvador.
President Nat. Constitutional Assembly 50; Minister of Educ. 50-56; Amb. in special mission to Chile 52; Prof. of Int. and Admin. Law, Univ. of El Salvador 59-; Dir. Bureau of Relations with Mem. States, UNESCO 57-59; mem. Inter-American Comm. on Educ., Science and Culture 62-63, Inter-American Comm. on Human Rights 60-64; Perm. Rep. of Ecuador to UN 67-.
Permanent Mission of Ecuador to the United Nations, 820 Second Avenue, New York, N.Y. 10017, U.S.A.

Galinos, Michael; Greek newspaper executive and politician; b. 1911; ed. Athens Univ. Law School.
Former law practice, Athens; Deputy for Nat. Progressive Union of Centre 50, 51, Deputy for Democratic Party 56, Independent Deputy 58, Centre Union 61, 63, 64-; Minister of Labour 65, of Social Welfare Oct. 65-66; Second Deputy Speaker of Parl. 51; Mayor of Mytilene 55; Publisher and Dir. of newspaper *Progressive Mytilene* 50-60; several decorations.
c/o Ministry of Social Welfare, Athens, Greece.

Gallegos, Rómulo; Venezuelan politician and author; b. 84.
Minister of Education 36; Co-Founder, Democratic Action Party 44; Pres. of Venezuela Feb.-April 48; now Chair. Inter-American Comm. on Human Rights

(Organization of American States); Dr. h.c. Columbia Univ. (U.S.A.).
Publs. *Doña Bárbara, Canaima, Cantaclararo, Pobre Negro, La Doncella.*
Avenida Avila 36, Altamira, Caracas, Venezuela.

Gallico, Paul William, B.S.; American writer; b. 26 July 1897; ed. Clinton High School, and Columbia Univ.
Seaman Gunner in U.S. Naval Reserve during First World War; Sports Editor *New York Daily News* 22-36; freelance writer 36-; War Corresp. *Cosmopolitan* magazine during Second World War; contributor to *Saturday Evening Post, Cosmopolitan, Vanity Fair, Red Book, Esquire,* etc.
Publs. *The Snow Goose* 41, *The Lonely* 47, *Confessions of a Story Writer* 48, *Jennie* 50, *The Small Miracle* 51, *Snowflake, Trial by Terror* 52, *The Foolish Immortals* 53, *Love of Seven Dolls* 54, *Ludmilla* 55, *Thomasina* 57, *The Steadfast Man, Flowers for Mrs. Harris, The Hurricane Story* 59, *Mrs. Harris Goes to New York* 60, *Too Many Ghosts* 61, *Further Confessions of a Story-Teller* 61, *Scruffy* 62, *Coronation* 62, *The Day the Guinea Pig Talked, Love, Let Me Not Hunger* 63, *The Hand of Mary Constable* 64, *The Silent Miaow* 64, *Mrs. Harris M.P.* 65, *The Day Jean-Pierre went round the World* 65, *The Man who was Magic* 66, *The Story of a Silent Night* 67.
c/o Hughes Massie and Co. Ltd., 18 Southampton Place, London, W.C.1, England; Apt. 7, Le Ruscino, Quai Antoine Premier, Monaco.

Gallien, Louis; French embryologist and university professor; b. 2 Jan. 1908; ed. Lycée de Cherbourg, Univ. de Caen and Univ. de Paris à la Sorbonne.
Assistant Prof. Univ. of Paris 32-37; Prof. Fac. Sc. Univ. of Rennes-Caen 38-44; Prof. Univ. of Paris 45; Dir. Laboratoire Embryologie 54; mem. Institut de France; assoc. mem. Académie Royale de Belgique; Grand Prix des Sciences Physiques de l'Académie des Sciences; Dr. h.c. Univ. de Louvain.
Publs. *La Sexualité* 41, *Le Parasitisme* 43, *La Sélection animale* 46, *L'insémination artificielle chez les animaux domestiques* 48, *Problèmes et Concepts de l'Embryologie expérimentale* 58, *Sex détermination* 59, *L'Embryologie* 65.
31, rue Gazan, Paris 14e, France.

Gallimard, Gaston; French publisher; b. 18 Jan. 1881.
Dir. Librairie Gallimard (publishing firm); publisher *La Nouvelle Revue Française;* and of works of Proust, Gide, Claudel, Martin du Gard, etc.
Office: 5 rue Sébastien-Bottin, Paris 7e; Home: 17 rue de l'Université, Paris 7e, France.

Gallin-Douathe, Michel; Central African Republic diplomatist; b. 4 June 1920.
Ambassador to the U.S. 60; Perm. Rep. to the UN 60-.
Permanent Mission of the Central African Republic to the United Nations, 386 Park Avenue South, Room 1614, New York, N.Y., U.S.A.
Telephone: MU5-2717.

Gallopin, Roger Edouard, D.IUR.; Swiss lawyer; b. 14 Dec. 1909; ed. Munich and Geneva Univs., London School of Economics.
Barrister, Geneva 35-37; Head of P.O.W. section, Int. Red Cross Cttee., Second World War; Dep. Sec.-Gen. Int. Cttee. of the Red Cross 43-50, missions in Europe, Asia, America, Exec. Dir. 50-; Del. to Int. Red Cross Confs., Stockholm, Toronto, Delhi, Vienna; mem. and Dir.-Gen. Int. Cttee. of the Red Cross.
Publ. *Le Conflit anglo-irlandais considéré spécialement depuis les articles d'accord de 1921* 35.
50 Quai Gustave Ador, Geneva, Switzerland.
Telephone: 35-65-25.

Galloway, Alexander Henderson, A.B.; American tobacco executive; b. 27 Dec. 1907; ed. Woodberry Forest School, Orange, Virginia, and Univ. of North Carolina.

R. J. Reynolds Tobacco Co. 29-, Asst. Treasurer 37-51, Treas. and Dir. 51-55, Vice-Pres. and Treas. 55-59, Exec. Vice-Pres. and Chief Financial Officer 59-60, Pres. 60-62, Pres. and Chair. Exec. Cttee. 62-.
1048 Arbor Road, Winston-Salem, North Carolina, U.S.A.

Gallup, George Horace, M.A., PH.D., LL.D.; American statistician; b. 18 Nov. 1901; ed. Univ. of Iowa.
Lecturer Univ. of Iowa 23-29; Head, Dept. of Journalism, Drake Univ. 29-31; Prof. of Journalism, Northwestern Univ. 31-32; Dir. of Research, Young and Rubicam Advertising Agency 32-47, Vice-Pres. 37-47; Prof. Pulitzer School of Journalism, Columbia Univ. 35-37; founded American Inst. of Public Opinion 35, Dir. 35-; founded British Inst. of Public Opinion 36; Ed. *Gallup Political Almanac;* Pres. Nat. Municipal League 52-56; Chair. of Council, Chair. All-America Cities Award Cttee; Board of the Gallup Org. Inc.; Pres. of the Int. Asscn. of Public Opinion Insts.; Hon. D.Sc. (Tufts Univ.), Hon. LL.D. (Drake, Boston, Chattanooga, Northwestern, Colgate, Rider Univs.); numerous awards.
Publs. include: *Public Opinion in a Democracy* 39, *Guide to Public Opinion Polls* 44 and 48, *The Miracle Ahead* 64.
The Great Road, Princeton, New Jersey, U.S.A.

Galuška, Miroslav; Czechoslovak journalist and diplomatist; b. 9 Oct. 1922.
Foreign Editor *Rudé Právo* 45; Editor *Tvorba* 48; Head, Press Dept., Foreign Ministry 52-58; Amb. to U.K. 58-61; Deputy Editor-in-Chief *Rudé Právo* 61; Editor-in-Chief *Kulturní Tvorba* 63; Amb. and Commr.-Gen., Czechoslovak participation at World Exhbn., Montreal 64-67; Minister of Culture and Information 68-; Chair. British Cttee. of Czechoslovak Soc. for Int. Relations, Prague.
Na Ostrohu 17, Prague 6, Czechoslovakia.
Telephone: 32-30-96.

Galvão, Captain Henrique Carlos Malta; Portuguese soldier and politician; b. 96; ed. for Army.
Army service in Africa; Gov. Huila Province, Angola; Senior Insp. Overseas Territories; Dep. (for Angola) Nat. Assembly; reported on economic conditions in Angola 47; arrested 51, sentenced to three years in gaol for subversion 53; in detention 56-58; sentenced to sixteen years in gaol 58; escaped 59; seized *Santa Maria* on the High Seas 61; fmr. leader Movimento Nacional Independente, expelled May 62; Librarian *O Estado* (newspaper), São Paulo.
Publs. *Santa Maria: My Crusade for Portugal* 61, *My Struggle Against Salazarism and Communism in Portugal* 65.
c/o *O Estado,* São Paulo, Brazil.

Galvin, Robert W.; American executive; b. 9 Oct. 1922; ed. Univs. of Notre Dame and Chicago.
Motorola, Inc. Chicago 40-, Chair. of Board; Dir. Harris Trust and Savings Bank, Chicago; Trustee Illinois Inst. of Technology; official of other public bodies.
9401 West Grand Ave, Franklin Park, Illinois 60131, U.S.A.

Gam, Mikael; Danish educationist and politician; b. 14 Feb. 1901; ed. Silkeborg Seminarium and Danmarks Laererhøjskole.
School teacher, Godthåb Seminarium, Greenland 25-28; Headmaster, Boarding School, Egedesminde, Greenland 28-48; Schools' Inspector, North Greenland 31-48; mem. Comm. of Greenland Affairs 48-50; Dir. Schools in Greenland 50-61; mem. Danish Parl. 60-64; Minister for Greenland 60-64; Chair. Greenland Soc. 65.
Publs. Text books for schools 28-43, *The History of Schools in Greenland* 52, *The Woman's Position in Greenland* 54.
Niels Bohr's Allé 18, Søborg, Copenhagen, Denmark.
Telephone: 01-691599.

Gamage, Sir Leslie Carr, Kt., M.C., C.ST.J., M.A., F.C.I.S.; British company director; b. 5 May 1887; ed. Marlborough and Exeter Coll., Oxford.

Asst. Sec., Sec., Sec.-Dir., Joint Gen. Man., General Electric Co. Ltd. 19-42, Vice-Chair. and Joint Man. Dir. 42-57, Chair. and Man. Dir. 57-60; Pres. of Chartered Inst. of Secs. 41; Pres. Inst. of Export 42-57; mem. Council of Industrial Design 45-56; mem. of Council, Fed. of British Industries 29-65; Master, Worshipful Company of Glaziers 45; Pres. Royal Commercial Travellers Schools 51-; Chief Business Adviser, Ministry of Civil Aviation 47-60; Pres. British Electrical and Allied Manufacturers Asscn. 59-60.

Springmead, Ascot, Berks., England.

Telephone: Ascot 23619.

Gamba, Pierino; Italian conductor; b. 16 Sept. 1936. First concert Opera House, Rome 45; has conducted concerts in numerous towns in 30 countries in Europe, America and Africa; guest conductor with Philharmonia Orchestra, Accademia di Santa Cecilia, Rome, Danish State Radio Orchestra, Belgian Nat. Orchestra and numerous other orchestras; Hon. Dir. eight symphony orchestras; Arnold Bax Medal 62.

La Scala, Monte-Carlo, Monaco.

Gamble, Clark Robinson; American shoe manufacturer; b. 16 Sept. 1893; ed. High School, St. Louis.

United Railways St. Louis 12-15; Reinholdt & Gardner (brokers) St Louis 15-17; Brown Shoe Co. 19-, Vice-Pres. 37-48, Pres. 48-61, Chair. of Board and Pres. 61-63, Chair. of Board 63-; Chair. Wohl Shoe Co.; Vice-Pres. Nulsen Investment Co.; dir. of many business and public bodies.

8300 Maryland Avenue, St. Louis 5, Missouri, U.S.A.

Gamow, George; PH.D.; American physicist; b. 4 Mar. 1904; ed. Univs. of Leningrad, Copenhagen and Cambridge.

Carlsberg Fellow, Univ. of Copenhagen 28-29, Rockefeller Fellow, Cambridge Univ. 29-30; Master in Research, U.S.S.R. Acad. of Sciences, Leningrad 31-33; Prof. of Physics, The George Washington Univ., Wash., D.C. 34-56; Prof. of Physics, Univ. of Colo. 56-; mem. Royal Danish Acad. of Sciences, Nat. Acad. of Sciences (U.S.A.); Oversea Fellow, Churchill Coll., Cambridge 65-; UNESCO Kalinga Prize 56.

Publs. include: *The Constitution of Atomic Nuclei and Radioactivity* 31, *Structure of Atomic Nuclei and Nuclear Transformations* 37, *Mr. Tompkins in Wonderland* 39, *The Birth and Death of the Sun* 40, *Biography of the Earth* 41, *Mr. Tompkins Explores the Atom* 44, *Atomic Energy in Cosmic and Human Life* 47, *One, Two, Three . . . Infinity* 47, *Theory of Atomic Nucleus and Nuclear Energy Sources* 49, *The Creation of the Universe* 52, *Mr. Tompkins Learns the Facts of Life* 53, *The Moon* 53, *Puzzle-Math* (with M. Stern) 58, *Matter, Earth and Sky* 58 (revised) 63, *Physics: Foundations & Frontiers* (with J. M. Cleveland) 60, *The Atom and its Nucleus* 61, *Biography of Physics* 61, *Gravity* 62, *A Planet Called Earth* 63, *A Star Called the Sun* 64, *Mr. Tompkins in Paperback* 65, *Thirty Years that Shook Physics* 66, *Mr. Tompkins Inside Himself* (with M. Ycas) 67.

Department of Physics and Astrophysics, University of Colorado, Boulder 80302, Colorado; Home: 785 6th Street, Boulder 80302, Colorado, U.S.A.

Telephone: 303-442-3525.

Gamzatov, Rasul Gamzatovich; Soviet poet and politician; b. 23; ed. Moscow A.M. Gorky Literary Institute.

National poet of Dagestan; mem. Communist Party of Soviet Union 44-; Chair. of Board of Union of Dagestan Writers 51-; Deputy of Supreme Soviet of U.S.S.R.; mem. Parl. Cttee. of U.S.S.R. Group of Inter-Parliamentary Union; State Prize 52, Lenin Prize 63, Orders of Lenin 60, of Red Banner of Labour 66.

Publs. *High Stellars* 62, *Mountains and Valleys* 63, *And*

Stars are Talking 64, *Selected Lyrics* 65, *Sick Teeth* (poetry) 67.

Supreme Soviet of U.S.S.R., Moscow, U.S.S.R.

Ganao, David-Charles; Congolese (Brazzaville) politician; b. 20 July 1928; ed. Teachers Training Coll.

Teacher, then Headmaster; Diplomatic training in France 60; Head of Political Affairs, Congolese Foreign Ministry 60-63; Minister of Foreign Affairs 63-, of Co-operation, Tourism and Civil Aviation 66-.

Ministry of Foreign Affairs, Brazzaville, Republic of the Congo.

Gance, Abel; French film director and writer; b. 25 Oct. 1889; ed. Collège Chaptal, Paris.

President Television Cttee. Radiodiffusion-Télévision française 58-; Théâtre de l'Empire renamed Théâtre Abel Gance 61; Officier Légion d'Honneur, Commdr. des Arts et Lettres, etc.

Invented triple screen 26, sound perspective 32, picto-scope 33.

Director of numerous films including: *La Folie du Docteur Tube* 12, *Barberouse* 16, *Les Gaz Mortels* 16, *J'accuse* 18, *La Roue* 22, *Napoléon* 26, *La Fin du Monde* 30, *Mater Dolorsa* 32, *Le Maître de forges* 33, *La Dame aux camélias* 34, *Lucrece Borgia* 35, *Un Grand Amour de Beethoven* 36, *Paradis Perdu* 39, *Vénus aveugle* 40, *La Capitaine Fracasse* 42, *La Tour de Nesle* 54, *Austerlitz* 60, *Cyrano contre d'Artagnan* 62.

Publs. *Un Doigt sur le clavier* (poetry), *La Victoire de Samothrace* (play), *J'accuse* 22.

2 avenue de Lamballe, Paris 16e, France.

Gandhi, Shrimati Indira; Indian politician and social worker; b. 19 Nov. 1917; ed. in India, Switzerland and at Oxford Univ.

Daughter of late Pandit Jawaharlal Nehru; founded Vanar Sena, a children's organisation to aid Congress non-cooperation movement 29; joined Congress 38; imprisoned for thirteen months 42; hostess for her father 46-64; worked in riot areas under Mahatma Gandhi 47; Minister for Information and Broadcasting, New Delhi 64-66, Prime Minister 66-, also in charge of Planning Ministry 67-; mem. Rajya Sabha 64-67, Leader of Lok Sabha 67-; Founder-Pres. Bal Sahayog, New Delhi; Pres. Training Centre for Vagrant Boys, Allahabad; Vice-Pres. Indian Council of Child Welfare; Chair. Standing Cttee. Children's Film Soc.; mem. Standing Cttee. Cen. Social Welfare Board, Children's Book Trust; mem. Working Cttee., All-India Congress Cttee., Pres. Women's Dept., mem. Cen. Electoral Board, Youth Advisory Board; Pres. All-India Congress Party 59-60; mem. UNESCO Exec. Board 60; Deputy Pres. Int. Union of Child Welfare.

Office of the Prime Minister, New Delhi, India.

Gandhi, Manmohan Purushottam, M.A., F.R.ECON.S., F.S.S.; Indian businessman; b. 5 Nov. 1901; ed. Bahauddin Coll., Junagad, Gujerat Coll., Ahmedabad, Hindu Univ., Benares, Bombay Univ.

Statistical Asst. Govt. of Bombay Labour Office 26; Asst. Sec. Indian Currency League Bombay 26; Sec. Indian Chamber of Commerce 26-36; Officer-in-Charge Credit Dept., Nat. City Bank of New York, Calcutta 36-37; Chief Commercial Man. Rohtas Industries Ltd., Dalmia Cement Ltd., Kharkhari Coal Co. Ltd., Indian Cement and Paper Marketing Co. Ltd.; Calcutta Manager Aluminium Corpn. of India Ltd.; Editor *Major Industries of India* and *Indian Textile Industry* (annuals) 37-; Dir. Indian Sugar Syndicate Ltd., Indian Link Chain Manufacturers Ltd., E. India Cotton Asscn. Ltd., Saru Eng. Corpn. Ltd. 59-; mem. All India Council Technical Educ., Gujarat State Advisory Council of Industries, All India Handloom Board, Central Silk Board, Small Scale Industries Board 66-, Senate and Syndicate Bombay Univ. 65-, Fed. of Indian Chambers of Commerce and Industry 29-30; Sec. Indian Nat. Cttee. Int. Chamber of Commerce,

Calcutta 29-31; mem. E. Indian Railway Advisory Cttee. 39-41; Controller of Supplies for Bengal 41-44; Hon. Prof. Sydenham Coll. of Commerce and Econs. 43-49.

Publs. *A Mercantile Marine for India* 25, *Foreign Capital in India* 26, *Economic Planning in India* 35, *A Revised Tariff Policy for India* 37, *Unemployment in India* 38, *Problems of the Indian Sugar Industry* 45, *Handloom Weaving Industry Annual* 52-53, *Some Impressions of Japan* 55.

Nanabhay Mansion, Pherozeshah Mehta Road, Fort, Bombay, India.

Telephone: 261047 (Office), 353326 (Home).

Ganger, Robert Mondell; American advertising executive; b. 20 June 1903; ed. Ohio State Univ.
Vice-President, Geyer, Cornell, Newell Inc., New York City 33-45; Partner, Geyer, Newell and Ganger Inc. 45-50; Exec. Vice-Pres. Lorillard and Co. 50-52, Pres. 52-53, Dir., mem. Exec. Cttee. 50-58; Chair. Board and Exec. Cttee. D'Arcy Advertisement Co. Inc. 53-; official of other advertising orgs.
D'Arcy Advertisement Co. Inc., 430 Park Avenue, New York City, U.S.A.

Gannon, Rev. Robert Ignatius, S.J., A.B., LITT.D., A.M., S.T.D., L.H.D., LL.D.; American ecclesiastic and educationist; b. 20 April 1893; ed. Georgetown and Gregorian Univs., and Christ's Coll., Cambridge.
Entered Society of Jesus 13; Ordained Priest 26; Instructor in English and Philosophy Fordham Univ. 19-22, in English 22-23; Dean St. Peter's Coll. Jersey City 30-36, Hudson Coll. of Commerce and Finance 32-35; Pres. Fordham Univ. 36-49; Dir. Mt. Manresa House of Retreats 49-52; Rector, St. Ignatius Loyola Church of New York 52-58; Superior Jesuit Missions House 58-64; Pres. Emeritus Fordham Univ. 64-; Hon. Life Mem. Newcomen Soc.; F.R.S.A.; Hon. Vice-Pres. Pan-American Soc.; Trustee Free Europe Univ. in Exile; Trustee Netherlands America Foundation; Knight Order of Orange-Nassau (Netherlands), Knight Commdr. with Star, Order of Polonia Restituta, Knight of Sovereign Military Order of Malta.
Publ. *The Technique of the One-Act Play* 25, *After Black Coffee* 47, *The Poor Old Liberal Arts* 61, *Cardinal Spellman: a Biography* 62, *After More Black Coffee* 64, *The Story of Fordham* 66.
Fordham University, New York 58, N.Y., U.S.A.

Telephone: 212-933-2233.

Ganshof, François Louis, LL.D., D.LIT.; Belgian professor of history and law; b. 14 March 1895; ed. Royal Athenaeum, Bruges, and Univs. of Ghent and Paris.
Served at the Bar in Brussels 22-23; Lecturer 23-29, and Prof. 29-61, of Medieval History and Legal History, Univ. of Ghent; served in Belgian Army in both World Wars; mem. Royal Flemish Acad. of Sciences of Belgium; corresp. F.B.A. and F.R.H.S.; Dr. h.c. Edinburgh, London, Cambridge.
Publs. *Etudes sur les Ministériales* 26, *Recherches sur les tribunaux de châtellenie* 32, *Etude sur le développement des villes entre Loire et Rhin* 43, *Feudalism* 64, *La Belgique Carolingienne, Recherches sur les capitulaires* 58, *Charlemagne et les institutions de la monarchie francque* 65, *Histoire des relations internationales*, vol. I, *Le moyen âge* 65.
12 rue Jacques Jordaens, Brussels 5, Belgium.

Ganshof van der Meersch, Walter, LL.D.; Belgian jurist; b. 1900; ed. Royal Athenaeum, Bruges, and Univ. of Brussels.
Professor of Constitutional Law and Political Science 38, European Law 58, Univ. of Brussels; Pres. Inst. of European Studies, Brussels, and Inter-university Centre of Public Law; First Vice-Pres. Inter-Univ. Centre of Comparative Law; Judge Advocate-Gen. 40; Served in Belgian Army in both World Wars; Lieut.-Gen. High Commr. for Security of the Realm 43; mem.

Supreme Court of Justice 47-, now Attorney-Gen.; Minister of Gen. Affairs in Africa 60; Assoc. mem. Académie Internationale de Droit comparé, Académie Royale des Sciences d'Outremer; Hon. C.B. (U.K.); Grand Cross Order of Crown (Belgium); Grand Cross Order of Leopold (Belgium); Commdr. Legion of Merit (U.S.A.); Commdr. Légion d'Honneur; Grand Officier Order Crown of Oak (Luxembourg); Belgian and French Croix de Guerre and other war medals.
Publs. *Pouvoir de fait et règle de droit dans le fonctionnement des institutions politiques* 56, *Fin de la souveraineté belge au Congo* 63, *Le droit des Organisations européennes* 64.
33 avenue Jeanne, Brussels 5, Belgium.
Telephone: 02-47-29-14.

Gapurov, Mukhamednazar; Soviet politician; b. 22; ed. Chardzhou Pedagogic Inst.
Soviet Army 41-43; Young Communist League and Party work 43-57; mem. C.P.S.U. 44-; First Sec. Chardzhou District C.P. Turkmenian S.S.R. 57-61; Chair. of Council of Ministers and Minister of Foreign Affairs of Turkmenian S.S.R. 63-; mem. Presidium Cen. Cttee. C.P. Turkmenian S.S.R.; Deputy to Supreme Soviet of the U.S.S.R.; Alternate mem. Cen. Cttee. C.P.S.U. 66-.
Council of Ministers, Ashkhabad, Turkmenian S.S.R., U.S.S.R.

Garba, John Mamman; Nigerian civil servant and banking official; b. 18; ed. Igbobi Coll., Yaba, Agricultural School, Zaria and London School of Economics.
Department of Agriculture, Nigeria 37-56; Asst. Sec. Office of Nigerian Commissioner, London 57-58; Second Sec. Office of U.K. High Commr., Ottawa 58; Acting Senior Asst. Sec., Office of Nigerian Commr., London 58-59; Asst. Pilgrim Officer, Nigerian Pilgrim Office, Khartoum 59-60; Chargé d'Affaires, later Minister, Washington, D.C. 60-61; Acting Deputy Perm. Sec., Ministry of Finance, Nigeria 61, Deputy Perm. Sec. 62; Deputy Sec. to Council of Ministers 63; Exec. Dir. Int. Bank for Reconstruction and Development, Int. Development Asscn., and Int. Finance Corpn. 63-66; Amb. to Italy 66-.
Embassy of Nigeria, 11 Via di Villa Sacchetti, Rome, Italy.

Garbo, Greta Lovisa; American (b. Swedish) film actress; b. 18 Nov. 1905.
National Theatre 24; star of first film *Gösta Berlings Saga* in Sweden 24; went to U.S.A. 25.
Films include *Joyless Streets*, *The Torrent*, *The Temptress*, *Flesh and the Devil*, *Love*, *The Divine Woman*, *The Mysterious Lady*, *The Woman of Affairs*, *Wild Orchids*, *The Single Standard*, *The Kiss*, *Romance*, *Inspiration*, *Mata Hari*, *Grand Hotel*, *Queen Christina*, *The Painted Veil*, *Anna Karenina*, *Camille*, *Conquest*, *Ninotchka*, *Two Faced Woman*.
450 East 52nd Street, New York, N.Y., U.S.A.

Garbuzov, Vassili Fyodorovich; Soviet politician; b. 11; ed. Finance and Economics Inst., Kharkov.
Dozent, Finance and Econs. Inst., Kharkov 33-42; Commissariat for Finance, Kirghizia, later All-Union Commissariat for Finance 42-44; Dir. Finance and Econs. Inst., Kiev 44-50; Chair. Ukraine State Plan 50-52; Dep. then First Dep. Minister of Finance, U.S.S.R. 52-60, Minister of Finance 60-; mem. C.P.S.U. 39-, mem. Central Cttee., C.P.S.U. 61-; Deputy to Supreme Soviet U.S.S.R.; Order of Lenin, Order of the Red Banner of Labour.
Ministry of Finance, 9 Kuibyshev Street, Moscow, U.S.S.R.

Garcia, Carlos P.; Philippine politician; b. 4 Nov. 1896; ed. Philippine Law School.
Fmr. teacher (for 2½ years), Rep. for Bohol (for 6 years) and Governor of Bohol (for 9 years); resisted Japanese

forces of occupation in underground movement 41-43; Minority Floor Leader of the Senate 46-53; Minister for Foreign Affairs 54-57 and Vice-Pres. 53-57, President 57-61; poet in Visayan Vernacular.
41 Bobol Avenue, Quezon City, Philippines.
Telephone: 93684.

García, Eduardo Augusto, D.IUR.; Argentine lawyer and diplomatist; b. 25 May 1898; ed. Univ. of Buenos Aires.
Former Under-Sec. for Foreign Affairs; fmr. Ambassador to Organization of American States; Asst. Prof. of Trial Law, La Plata Nat. Univ. 53-; editor *La Prensa* 28-32; Pres. of various Argentine Bar Asscns.
Publs. include: *Lo que vendrá* 29, *Juicio Oral* (5 vols.) 36-38, *Administración nacional de los derechos de autor* 44, *Anteproyecto del Tratado Internacional sobre Protección de los Derechos Humanos* 51.
c/o Universidad Nacional de la Plata, La Plata, Argentina.

García, Francisco Javier Conde; Spanish lawyer and diplomatist; b. 3 Dec. 1908; ed. Madrid Univ.
Professor Faculty of Law, Univ. of Madrid 41; Prof. Political Law, Univ. of Santiago de Compostela 43; Prof. Political Law, Univ. of Madrid 49; Prof. of Sociology; entered Diplomatic Corps 47; Dir. Inst. Political Studies 48; Nat. Adviser for Educ. 52; Pres. Spanish Cttee. of Labour and Social Sciences at UNESCO 55; fmr. Amb. to Philippines, later to Uruguay, now to Canada; Visiting Prof. Univ. of Ottawa; mem. Real Academia de Ciencias Morales y Políticas de Madrid; Gran Cruz de la Orden de Cisneros, Cruz de Isabel la Católica, Cruz de Caballero de la Real y muy distinguida Orden de Carlos III, etc.
Publs. *El Pensamiento Político de Bodino* 35, *Introducción al Derecho Político Actual* 42, *Teoría y sistema de las formas políticas* 44, *Representación política y régimen español* 45, *El saber político en Maquiavelo* 48, *Sobre los modos actuales de historiar el pensamiento político* 48, *Misión política de la inteligencia* 50, *Los supuestos históricos de la Sociología* 51, *La Revolución* 52, *El teorema político de la concurrencia en Rousseau* 53, *Introducción a la antropología de Xavier Zubiri* 53, *El Hombre–animal político* 57.
Office: 124 Springfield Road, Ottawa 2, Ont.; Home: 11 Crescent Road, Rockliffe Park, Ottawa, Ont., Canada.
Telephone: 745-7064 (Office); 749-9782 (Home).

García Barragan, General Marcelino; Mexican army officer; ed. Colegio Militar.
Fought in Mexican Revolution in Ojinaga, Chihuahua, Lerdo, Gómez Palacio y Torréon, San Pedro de las Colonias, Paredón and Zacatecas; visited Panama, Argentina and Uruguay 22; Adjutant-Gen., Colegio Militar 26-29; Dir. of Colegio Militar 41-43; Gov. of Jalisco and Commdr. 11th Cavalry Regt. 43-53; later Commdr. 17th, 22nd and 11th Mil. Areas; Sec. for Defence 64-.
Secretaría de la Defensa Nacional, Mexico, D.F., Mexico.

García Bauer, Carlos, LL.D.; Guatemalan diplomatist, professor, writer and lawyer; b. 1916.
Minister Foreign Affairs, Guatemala 58; Perm. Rep. of Guatemala to UN 48-50; Judge Ad-Hoc Int. Court of Justice 55; Ambassador to U.S.A., Canada and OAS 63-66; Rep. of Guatemala numerous int. confs.
Publs. several books and essays on international law and philosophy of law.
c/o Ministry of Foreign Affairs, Guatemala.

García Godoy, Hector; Dominican lawyer, diplomatist and politician; b. 11 Jan. 1921; ed. Law Dept. of Univ. of Santo Domingo.
Diplomatic Service 44-48, served Costa Rica and Nicaragua 45-46; Head of Consular Section, Ministry of Foreign Affairs 47-48; Sec. to Board of Dirs. of Reserve

Bank 48-55; Vice-Gov. Dominican Central Bank 55-56; Minister, Dominican Embassy, London, and Perm. Rep. to Int. Sugar Council 56-58; Amb. to Belgium and Luxembourg 58, later to U.K., Netherlands, Turkey and Lebanon; Minister of Foreign Affairs 63; Vice-Pres. Tabacalera Anónima (tobacco firm) 63-65; Provisional Pres. of Dominican Repub. Sept. 65-66; Amb. to U.S.A. and the Org. of American States 66-; Reformist Party.
Embassy of the Dominican Republic, Washington, D.C., U.S.A.

García Mata, Rafael; Argentine agronomist and politician; b. 12 Mar. 1912; ed. Colegio del Salvador, Buenos Aires, and Faculty of Agronomy and Veterinary Science, Univ. de Buenos Aires.
On staff of *Revista de Economía Argentina* 29-30; First Sec. Ministry of Finance and Public Works, Province of Santa Fe 30-31; Editorial Sec. *Revista de Economía Argentina* 31-35, mem. Board of Dirs. 36-53; Technical Sec., Office of Econ. Studies of Argentine Industrial Fed. 32-35; Head of Econ. Service of Nat. Cotton Council 35-36, Dir.-Gen. 36-43; Dir.-Gen. of Agriculture, Ministry of Agriculture 43-45, Dir.-Gen. of Agric. Research 45-52; Titular Prof. of Econs. and Agrarian Org., Univ. of Buenos Aires 47-56; Dir. and Vice-Pres. Nat. Bank of Argentina 49-50; Under-Sec. for Agric. and Livestock 58-62; Minister to Spain 66-67; Sec. of State for Agric. and Livestock July 67-; mem. numerous dels. and missions.
Publs. include: *Geografía Económica Argentina* 36, *Argentina Económica* 39, 42, 43, *El Problema Agrario Argentino* 50.
Secretaría de Estado de Agricultura y Ganadería, Buenos Aires, Argentina.

García Moncó, Faustino; Spanish politician; b. 13 Oct. 1916; ed. Academia de Infanteria, Granada and Univ. de Oviedo.
State Lawyer on Financial Del. in Soria, Santander and Vizcaya 42-57; Asst. Dir.-Gen. Banco de Balbao 57; Under-Sec. for Commerce 57-60; Dir.-Gen. Banco de Bilbao 61-65; Minister of Commerce 65-; Counsellor Nat. Inst. of Industry 57-; Court Lawyer 60-; Spokesman Plan for Social Econ. Devt. 62; Gran Cruz Orden del Mérito Civil, Grosses Bundesverdienstkreuz.
Ministerio de Comercio, Paseo Castellana 14, Madrid, Spain.
Telephone: 2-25-79-80.

García Peláez, Raúl, LL.D.; Cuban lawyer, politician and diplomatist; b. 15 Jan. 1922; ed. Univ. de Habana.
Former mem. July 26th Revolutionary Cttee.; later Prosecutor at Camaguey Court of Appeal, then Chair. Camaguey Municipal Council for Co-ordination and Inspection; then Gen. Treas. Revolutionary Forces in Camaguey Province, Rep. of Nat. Inst. of Agrarian Reform in Nuevitas, and Gen. Sec. Matanzas Provincial Cttee. of United Party of Cuban Socialist Revolution; mem. Cen. Cttee. of Cuban C.P. 65-, Head of Revolutionary Orientation Comm. of Cen. Cttee. of Cuban C.P. until 67; Amb. to U.S.S.R. 67-.
Embassy of Cuba, Pomerantsev per. 6, Moscow, U.S.S.R.

García-Peña, Roberto; Colombian journalist; b. 10; ed. Externado de Colombia, Bogotá, and Univ. of Chile.
Reporter *El Tiempo* 29; Private Sec. to Minister of Govt. 30; Sec. Colombian Embassy, Peru 34, Chile 35, Chargé d'Affaires 37; Sec.-Gen. Ministry of Foreign Affairs 38; Editor *El Tiempo* 39-; mem. Council of Dirs., Inter-American Press Soc.
Avenida Jimenez 6-77, Bogotá, Colombia.

García Robles, Alfonso, LL.D.; Mexican diplomatist; b. 20 March 1911; ed. Universidad Nacional Autónoma de México, Univ. of Paris, and Acad. of International Law, The Hague.

Foreign Service 39-, Sweden 39-41; Head, Dept. of Int. Orgs., later Dir.-Gen. of Political Affairs and Diplomatic Service 41-46; Dir. of Div. of Political Affairs, UN Secretariat 46-57; Head of Dept. for Europe, Asia and Africa, Mexican Ministry of Foreign Affairs 57-61; Amb. to Brazil 62-64; Under-Sec. for Foreign Affairs 64-; several decorations from various countries.
Publs. *Pan-Americanism and the Good Neighbour Policy* 40, *The Sorbonne Yesterday and Today* 43, *Post-War Mexico* 44, *Mexican International Policy* 46, *Echoes of the Old World* 46, *The Post-War World: From the Atlantic Charter to the San Francisco Conference* (2 vols.) 49, *The Geneva Conference and the Extent of Territorial Waters* 59, *The Denuclearization of Latin America* 67.
Sierra Vertientes 691, Mexico 10, D.F., Mexico.

Gardent, Paul; French mining executive; b. 10 July 1921; ed. Ecole Polytechnique.
Mining Engineer, Valenciennes 44-48; Asst. Chief Mining Engineer, Lille 48-49, Chief Mining Engineer 50; Technical Adviser to J. M. Louvel (Minister of Industry and Commerce) 50-52; Dir. of Gen. Studies, Charbonnages de France 52-58; Dir. of Gen. Studies and Financial Services, Houillères du bassin de Lorraine 58-63; Asst. Dir., then Dir.-Gen. Houillères du bassin du Nord et du Pas-de-Calais 63-68; Dir.-Gen. Charbonnages de France 68-.
Charbonnages de France, 9 avenue Percier, Paris 8e, France.

Gardiner, Baron (Life Peer cr. 63), of Kittisford, in the county of Somerset; **Gerald Gardiner,** P.C., Q.C., M.A.; British barrister; b. 30 May 1900; ed. Harrow School and Magdalen Coll., Oxford.
President Oxford Union and Oxford Univ. Dramatic Soc. 24; called to Bar 25; mem. Cttee. on Supreme Court Practice and Procedure 47-53; Q.C. 48; mem. Lord Chancellor's Law Reform Cttee. 52-63; Master of Bench of Inner Temple 55; Chair. General Council of the Bar 58, 59; Lord Chancellor 64-.
Publs. *Capital Punishment as a Deterrent and the Alternative* 56, *Law Reform Now* (Jt. Editor) 63.
House of Lords, London, S.W.1, England.

Gardiner, Robert Kweku Atta, M.A., B.SC.; Ghanaian civil servant and international administrator; b. 29 Sept. 1914; ed. Fourah Bay Coll., Sierra Leone, Selwyn Coll., Cambridge, and New Coll., Oxford.
Lecturer in Econs. Fourah Bay Coll. 43-46; Area Specialist UN Trusteeship Dept. 47-49; Dir. Dept. of Extra-Mural Studies, Univ. Coll. Ibadan Nigeria 49-53; Dir. Dept. of Social Welfare and Community Development, Ghana 53-55; Chair. Kumasi Coll. of Technology Council Ghana 54-58; Perm. Sec. Ministry of Housing Ghana 55-57; Establishment Sec. and Head of Civil Service 57-59; Dep. Exec. Sec. UN Economic Comm. for Africa, Addis Ababa 59-61, Exec. Sec. June 63-; Special Envoy of UN Sec.-Gen. to the Congo 61; Dir. UN Div. for Public Admin. 61; UN Special Rep. to the Congo 62-63; B.B.C. Reith Lecturer 65.
Publ. *Development of Social Administration* 54 (jointly).
Economic Commission for Africa, P.O.B. 3001, Addis Ababa, Ethiopia.

Gardner, Bertie Charles, M.C.; Canadian banker; b. 31 May 1884; ed. Bristol Grammar School, England.
Entered Bank of British North America, Montreal after 5 years with Stuckey's Banking Co. Ltd. in England 06; Man. Bank of British North America, Trail, B.C. 10, Rossland 11, Asst. Man. Vancouver 13, Asst. Inspector Winnipeg 14; overseas service in First World War; several years at Head Office of Bank of Montreal and as Asst. Man. at St. John's Newfoundland, Man. 28, Man. St. John, N.B. 30, Supt. Foreign Dept., Head Office, Montreal 31, Second Agent 32, First Agent 34, New York, Asst. Gen. Man., Head Office 35, Gen. Man. 42, Dir., Vice-Pres. and Gen. Man. 44, Exec. Vice-Pres.

47, Pres. and Chief Exec. Officer 48-52, Chair. of Board 52-54, Dir. and mem. Exec. Cttee. 54-59; Dir. British Newfoundland Corpn. Ltd.; Hon. Dir. Royal Trust Co.; Dir. Canadian Scudder Investments Fund Ltd., Scudder International Investment Ltd.; Pres. and Dir. Canafund Co. Ltd.; Chancellor, McGill Univ. 52-57; Pres. Canadian Bankers' Asscn. 46-47; Hon. D.C.L. (Bishop's Univ.); Hon. LL.D. (McGill Univ.).
Mountain Place, 3468 Drummond Street, Montreal, Quebec, Canada.
Telephone: 845-8944.

Gardner, Erle Stanley; American author and lawyer; b. 17 July 1889; ed. Palo Alto High School and with legal firms.
President, Consolidated Sales Co., San Francisco 18-20; private legal practice, Ventura, California 21-45; an organiser of *Argosy Magazine's Court of Last Resort;* mem. American Acad. of Forensic Sciences, American Judicature Soc.; Hon. D.Iur., McGeorge Coll. of Law, Sacramento 56.
Publs. Over 100 detective novels (under own name and pen-name A. A. Fair) and the following travel books: *Neighbourhood Frontiers* 54, *Hunting the Desert Whale* 60, *Hovering over Baja* 61, *The Hidden Heart of Baja* 62, *The Desert is Yours* 63, *The World of Water* 64, *Hunting Lost Mines by Helicopter* 65, *Off the Beaten Track in Baja* 67, *Gypsy Days on the Delta* 67.
Rancho del Paisano, Temecula, California, U.S.A.

Gardner, George Peabody; American businessman; b. 28 Jan. 1888; ed. Harvard Univ.
Secretary Harvard Corpn. 11-14; Hon. Chair. Board Gardner Assocs. Inc., Chair. Board of Trustees, Chase Fund of Boston; Chair. Board of Trustees, Shareholders Trust of Boston; mem. Advisory Cttee. Boston Fund; Pres. Boston and Providence R.R.; Dir. Mass. Hospital Life Insurance Co., American Tel. and Tel. Co. (retd.), Gen. Electric Co. (retd.), First Nat. Bank of Boston (retd.), Income & Capital Shares Inc.; official of numerous educational and charitable bodies.
Home: 135 Warren Street, Brookline, Mass.; Office: 225 Franklin Street, Boston, Mass., U.S.A.

Gardner, Dame Helen Louise, D.B.E., M.A., D.LITT., F.B.A., F.R.S.L.; British teacher and author; b. 13 Feb. 1908; ed. North London Collegiate School, and St. Hilda's Coll., Oxford.
Lecturer, Royal Holloway Coll. 31-34, Univ. of Birmingham 34-41; Tutor, St. Hilda's Coll. Oxford 41-54, Fellow 42-66, Hon. Fellow 66-; Reader in Renaissance English Literature, Oxford Univ. 54-66; Merton Prof. of English Literature, Oxford Univ. 66-; Fellow, Lady Margaret Hall, Oxford 66-; Del. Oxford Univ. Press 59-; Visiting Prof. Univ. of Calif. 54; Riddell Lecturer, Univ. of Durham 56; Alexander Lecturer, Univ. of Toronto 62; Ewing Lecturer, Univ. of Calif. 66; Messenger Lecturer Cornell Univ. 67; mem. Cttee. for Higher Educ. 61, Council for Nat. Academic Awards 64-; Trustee Nat. Portrait Gallery 67-.
Publs. *The Art of T. S. Eliot* 49, *The Divine Poems of John Donne* (ed.) 52, *The Metaphysical Poets* (ed.) 57, *The Business of Criticism* 59, *The Elegies and the Songs and Sonnets of John Donne* 65, *A Reading of 'Paradise Lost'* 65.
Myrtle House, Eynsham, Oxford, England.

Gardner, John William, PH.D., LL.D.; American government official; b. 8 Oct. 1912; ed. Stanford Univ., and Univ. of Calif.
Teaching Asst. in Psychology, Univ. of Calif. 36-38; Instructor in Psychology, Conn. Coll. 38-40; Asst. Prof. Mount Holyoke Coll. 40-42; Head Latin-American Section, Foreign Broadcasting Intelligence Service, Fed. Communications Comm. 42-43; served U.S. Marine Corps 43-46; staff mem. Carnegie Corpn. of New York 46-47, Exec. Assoc. 47-49, Vice-Pres. 49-55, Pres. 55-65; Pres. Carnegie Foundation 55-65, Consultant 68-;

U.S. Sec. of Health and Educ. and Welfare 65-68; Head of Urban Coalition (Campaign to transform cities of America) 68-; Dir. Time Inc. 68-; Fellow, American Psychological Asscn., American Acad. of Arts and Sciences; Chair. Soc. Sciences Panel, Scientific Advisory Board, U.S. Air Force 51-55; Trustee, New York School of Social Work 49-55, Metropolitan Museum of Art, Educational Testing Service; Dir. Shell Oil Co., American Asscn. for the Advancement of Science, N.Y. Telephone Co.; mem. Div. Cttee. for Social Sciences, Nat. Science Foundation; mem. Council on Foreign Relations, Pres. Kennedy's Task Force on Educ. 60; Chair. U.S. Advisory Comm. on Int. Educational and Cultural Affairs 62-64, Pres. Johnson's Task Force on Educ. 64, White House Conf. on Educ. 65; Hon. LL.D. (Brown Univ., Univ. of Calif., Univ. of Maryland, Univ. of British Columbia, Middlebury Coll., Oberlin Coll., Univ. of Notre Dame, Hamilton Coll., Univ. of Rochester, Columbia Univ., Brandeis Univ., Michigan State Univ., Princeton Univ., Harvard Univ., Villanova Univ., Washington Univ.); Hon. Fellow (Stanford Univ.); Hon. Litt.D. (New York Univ.); U.S.A.F. Exceptional Services Award 56, Presidential Medal of Freedom 64, Family of Man Educ. Award 66.
Publs. *Excellence: Can We be Equal and Excellent too?* 61, *Self-Renewal: The Individual and the Innovative Society* 64; Editor *To Turn the Tide* (by John F. Kennedy).
5325 Kenwood Avenue, Chevy Chase, Maryland, U.S.A.

Gardner, Kenneth Burslam, B.A., A.L.A.; British orientalist and librarian; b. 5 June 1924; ed. Alleyn's Grammar School, Stevenage, Univ. Coll., London, and School of Oriental and African Studies, Univ. of London.
Asst. Librarian, School of Oriental and African Studies, Univ. of London 50-54; Asst. Keeper, Dept. of Oriental Printed Books and Manuscripts, British Museum 55-57, Keeper 57-.
1 Duncombe Road, Bengeo, Hertford, England. Telephone: Hertford 3591.

Garibi y Rivera, H. E. Cardinal José; Mexican ecclesiastic; b. 89.
Ordained 13; Elected to the Titular Church of Roso 29; Bishop 30; Titular Archbishop of Bizia 34; Archbishop of Guadalajara 36-; elected Cardinal 58.
Palacio Arzobispal, Apartado 331, Guadalajara, Mexico.

Garin, Vasco Vieira; Portuguese diplomatist; b. 07; ed. Univ. of Lisbon.
Third Sec., Ministry of External Affairs, Lisbon 31; Consular Attaché London 34; Second Sec. Portuguese Embassy, London 35; First Sec. Ministry of External Affairs; First Sec. Washington 40, Counsellor 43, Chargé d'Affaires Oct.-Dec. 44; Chief of Political Bureau, Ministry of External Affairs 46; Consul-Gen. Montreal 47; Minister to India 49-55, concurrently Minister to Ceylon and Thailand 52-55; Ambassador to Canada 55-60; Perm. Rep. to UN 55-63, Ambassador to United States 63-; Knight Commdr. Order of Dannebrog (Denmark); Hon. M.V.O. (U.K.); Knight Order of Southern Cross (Brazil); Order of Polonia Restituta (Poland), and decorations from Spain and Portugal.
Embassy of Portugal, 2125 Kalorama Road, N.W., Washington, D.C., U.S.A.

Garland, George David, PH.D., F.R.S.C.; Canadian geophysicist; b. 29 June 1926; ed. Univ. of Toronto and St. Louis Univ.
Geophysicist, Dominion Observatory, Ottawa 50-54; Prof. of Geophysics, Univ. of Alberta, Edmonton 54-63; Prof. of Geophysics, Univ. of Toronto 63-; Deputy Sec.-Gen. Int. Union of Geodesy and Geophysics 60-63, Sec.-Gen. 63-.
Publs. *The Earth's Shape and Gravity* 65, and papers in scientific journals dealing with gravity, terrestrial magnetism, structure of the earth's crust, electrical conductivity of the crust, heat flow from the earth.

Department of Physics, University of Toronto, Toronto 5; Home: 1 Forest Glen Crescent, Toronto 12, Canada. Telephone: 928-3159 (Office); 488-5127 (Home).

Garner, Robert Livingston, B.S.; American international banker; b. 7 Aug. 1894; ed. Vanderbilt Univ., and Columbia Univ. School of Journalism.
Reporter with *St. Louis Star* 16; served in U.S. Infantry attaining rank of Capt. 17-19; Guaranty Trust Co. New York 19-25; Analyst Financial Dept. Continental Insurance Co. 26; Asst. Treas., Treas., Vice-Pres. and Treas. Guaranty Trust Co. 26-43; Treas. and Vice-Pres., Financial Vice-Pres. and Dir. General Foods Corpn. New York 43-47; Vice-Pres. Int. Bank for Reconstruction and Development Mar. 47-July 56; Pres. Int. Finance Corpn. July 56-61; Dir. and Consultant, American Security Trust, Washington, D.C.; Pres. and Dir. Japan Fund Inc. 62-; Dir. Hewlett-Packard Co.; mem. Banking Board, State of N.Y. 44-47.
Suite 514, 730 Fifteenth Street, N.W., Washington 5, D.C., U.S.A.

Garner, Sir (Joseph John) Saville, G.C.M.G.; British civil servant; b. 14 Feb. 1908; ed. Jesus Coll., Cambridge.
Apptd. Dominions Office 30; Private Sec. to successive Secs. of State 40-43; Senior Sec. Office of High Commr. Ottawa 43-46, Deputy High Commr. 46-48; Asst. Under-Sec. Commonwealth Relations Office 48-51; Deputy High Commr. in India 51-53; Deputy Under-Sec. Commonwealth Relations Office 53; High Commr. in Canada 56-61; Perm. Under-Sec. of State, Commonwealth Relations Office (C.R.O.) 62-66, Commonwealth Office 66-68; Head of Diplomatic Service 65-68.
Publs. Translated from German: *The Books of the Emperor Wu Ti* 30.
11 Chapel Street, London, S.W.1, England.

Garnett, David, C.B.E.; British novelist; b. 9 March 1892; ed. Imperial Coll. of Science, South Kensington.
Educated as biologist; Fellow, Imperial Coll. of Science and Technology.
Publs. *Lady into Fox* (Hawthornden and Tait-Black Prizes) 22, *A Man in the Zoo* 24, *The Sailor's Return* 25, *Go She Must* 27, *The Old Dove-cote* 28, *No Love* 29, *The Grasshoppers Come* 31, *A Rabbit in the Air* 32, *Pocahontas* 33, *Beany-Eye* 35, *The War in the Air* 41, *The Golden Echo* 53, *Flowers of the Forest, Aspects of Love* 55, *A Shot in the Dark* 58, *A Net for Venus* 59, *The Familiar Faces* 62, *Two by Two* 63, *Ulterior Motives* 66; Editor: *The Letters of T. E. Lawrence, The Novels of Thomas Love Peacock, The Essential T. E. Lawrence.*
Hilton Hall, Huntingdon, England.
Telephone: 048088-223.

Garnier, Jean-Paul, D. en D., L. ès L.; French diplomatist; b. 3 Oct. 1904; ed. Lycée Carnot, Univ. of Paris and Ecole des Sciences Politiques, Paris.
Attaché, Warsaw 28; Ministry for Foreign Affairs 30; Deputy Head Secretariat of Foreign Minister 32-33; Second Sec., Rome 34, First Sec. 38, Counsellor 39; Ministry of Foreign Affairs 40; in charge of re-establishment of Ministry services 44, Deputy Dir. in charge of Southern Section, European Div. 44; First Counsellor, Berne 45, Prague (with rank of Minister) 45; Minister Plenipotentiary, Inspector-Gen. Diplomatic and Consular Posts 46; Asst. Sec.-Gen., Paris Peace Conf. 46; Dir. Personnel and Accounts Dept. 47; mem. Civil Service Supreme Council 48; Ambassador to the Netherlands 49-55, to Turkey 55-57; mem. Central Administration Commission 57; Diplomatic Counsellor 58; Pres. Commission du Titre XIII (Asscn.) de la Constitution 59; Ambassador to Czechoslovakia 59-61, India 61-65, concurrently to Nepal; Paris Diplomatic Counsellor 67; Commdr. de la Légion d'Honneur; Croix de Guerre; Médaille de la Résistance; Lauréat de l'Académie française et des Sciences morales et politiques 36, 60.

Publs. *Le Sacre de Charles X* 27, *La Tragédie de Dantzig* (Drouin de Lluys Prize) 36, *Naszeddin Hodjah et ses histoires Turques* 58, *Murat, roi de Naples* 59 (Therouanne Prize, Acad. Française), *Le dernier roi de Naples* 61 (Drouin de Lluys Prize, Acad. des Sciences morales et politiques), *Excellences et Plumes blanches* 61, *Charles X-Le Roi-Le Proscrit* 67 (Grand Prix d'histoire Broquette-Jonin, Acad. Française 67 and Prix du cercle de l'Union 68).
1 rue de Franqueville, Paris 16e, France.

Garnier-Coignet, Jean Paul, L. en D.; French jurist; b. 7 Nov. 1895; ed. Ecole des Sciences Politiques, Paris. Sec. to the Presidency of the Perm. Court of Int. Justice 22-40; Head of French (Interministerial) Service of Prize, Foreign Maritime Captures and Requisitions 41-44; Rep. of French Govt. for restitution of certain property in Germany 45; Dep.-Registrar Int. Court of Justice 46-60, Registrar 60-66.
The International Court of Justice, The Hague, Netherlands.

Garofalides, Theodore; Greek doctor and airline executive; b. 17 Nov. 1898; ed. Univs. of Athens and Paris.
Assistant, First Surgery Clinic, Athens Univ. 24-29; Resident Surgeon "Evangelismos" Clinic 33-40; Asst. Prof. of Orthopaedics, Athens Univ. 35-48, Special Prof. 48-59, Perm. Prof. 56-; Dir. Voula "Asclipeion" Hospital 38-; Dir. Konialidian Orthopaedic Clinic 50-; Prof. of Orthopaedics, Physiotherapeutic School 56-; Pres. Greek Soc. of Surgeons 60; Publisher *Orthopaedic Chronicle* 50-; Chair. of Board of Olympic Airways and Olympic Cruises; numerous decorations.
37 King George II Avenue, Glyfada, Athens; Office: 24 Hòmere Street, Athens, Greece.
Telephone: Glyfada 04101 (Home); 611340 (Office).

Garran, Sir (Isham) Peter, K.C.M.G.; British diplomatist; b. 15 Jan. 1910; ed. Melbourne Grammar School, and Trinity Coll., Melbourne Univ., Australia.
British Diplomatic Service 34-; Belgrade 37-41, Lisbon 41-44, Berlin 47-50, The Hague 50-52; Insp. of Foreign Service Establishments 52-54; Commercial Minister, Washington 55-60, Ambassador to Mexico 60-64, to Netherlands 64-.
British Embassy, The Hague, Netherlands.
Telephone: 18-26-60.

Garrett, Johnson; American government official; b. 26 Oct. 1912; ed. Princeton Univ.
Rose to Lieut.-Colonel, U.S. Army 39-45; Station Man., Damascus, Pan American Airways 46-49; First Nat. City Bank of New York 49-60, Manager, Paris Branch 52-60; Asst. Sec.-Gen. (for Production, Logistics and Infrastructure) NATO 60-65; Rep. for Industrial Devt. of U.S. Dept. of Commerce in Europe 66-.
c/o Department of Commerce, Washington, D.C., U.S.A.

Garrett, Lieut.-Gen. Sir Ragnar, P.S.C., K.B.E., C.B.; Australian officer; b. 12 Feb. 1900; ed. Guildford Grammar School, Perth, and Duntroon Royal Military Coll.
Lieut. Australian Staff Corps 21; served in Middle East and South West Pacific in Second World War; mentioned in despatches; Lieut. Col. 40, Brigadier 43; Commandant Australian Staff Coll. 50-51; Maj. Gen. 51; G.O.C. Western Command Australia 51-53; Deputy Chief of Gen. Staff 53-54; Lieut. Gen. 54; G.O.C. Southern Command 54-58; Chief Australian Gen. Staff 58-60; Principal Australian Admin. Staff Coll. 60-64; Chair. West Australian Shipping Service 65-.
129 Forest Street, Peppermint Grove, Perth, Western Australia.

Garrido Diaz, Luis, LL.D., D.ECON.; Mexican lawyer and educationist; b. 98; ed. Univ. Nacional Autónoma de México.

Lawyer, Prof. Col. de San Nicolás de Hidalgo, Pres. of Supreme Tribunal of Michoacán State and Rector Univ. of Michoacán 24-28; Prof. Schools of Law and Economics, Univ. Nacional Autónoma de México 29-, Rector 48-50; mem. Comm. for drafting new Penal Code; fmr. Head Diplomatic Dept., Ministry of Foreign Affairs; co-founder Mexican Asscn. of Univs. and Insts. of Higher Education; Hon. Pres. Nat. Acad. of History and Geography; Vice-Pres. Nat. Athenæum of Science and Art; Pres. Latin American Univ. Union; mem. Exec. Council, Int. Asscn. of Univs., Int. Asscn. for Penal Law; Treas. Mexican Acad. of Languages; many Mexican and foreign hon. degrees and decorations.
Publs. *Los Apólogos de mi Breviario* 22, *El Amor Inglosable* (novel) 26, *Meditaciones de un Idealista* 28, *La Reforma de Nuestra Constitución Política* 32, *El Plan Sexenal ante la Doctrina Administrativa* 33, *La Ley Penal Mexicana* 34, *La Delincuencia Infantil de México* (with J. Angel Ceniceros) 36, *En Torno a la Paradoja* (short stories) 37, *La Doctrina Mexicana de Nuestro Derecho Penal* 41, *El Valor Doctrinario de la Revolución Mexicana* 46, *Notas de un Penalista* 46, *El Espíritu de Francia* 46, *Ensayos Penales, Discursos y Mensajes.*
Patricio Sanz 725, Mexico D.F., Mexico.

Garrigues y Diaz Canabate, Antonio; Spanish lawyer and diplomatist; b. 4 Feb. 1904; ed. Univ. of Madrid.
Assistant Attorney-Gen. Ministry of Justice 31-; Legal practice 31-62; Gen. practice; specialised in corporation and international law; Ambassador to the U.S. 62-64, to the Vatican 64-; Pres. and Dir. of numerous commercial and industrial companies.
Publs. many books and articles on legal, political, economic and financial topics.
Embassy of Spain to the Holy See, Palazzo di Spagna, Rome, Italy; 8 Acalá Galiano, Madrid, Spain.

Garrone, H.E. Cardinal Gabriel Marie, D.PHIL., D.THEOL.; French ecclesiastic; b. 12 Oct. 1901; ed. Inst. Notre-Dame de la Villette, Univ. de Grenoble and Pontificia Universitas Gregoriana, Rome.
Professor, Grand Seminary, Chambéry 45; Archbishop Coadjutor, Toulouse 47; Archbishop, Toulouse and Narbonne, Primate of Narbonne 56-66; Vice-Pres. Perm. Council of Plenary Assembly of French episcopate 64-66; Pro-Prefect, Congregation of Seminaries and of Univs., Rome 66-; created Cardinal by Pope Paul VI 67; Chevalier Légion d'Honneur; Croix de Guerre (39-45).
Publs. *Psaumes et Prières, Invitation à la prière, Leçons sur la foi, La Morale du Credo, La Porte rama du Credo, Voilà ta mère, L'Action catholique, Foi et Pédagogie, L'Euchariste, Pourquoi Prier?, La Religieuse, Signe de Dieu dans la Monde, Les Psaumes, prière pour aujourd'hui.*
The Sacred Congregation of Seminaries and of Universities, Vatican City, Rome, Italy.

Garroway, Dave; American broadcaster; b. 13 July 1913; ed. Washington Univ.
Radio announcer KDKA, Pittsburg 38-40, WAMQ, Chicago 40-42, 45-47; served U.S. Navy 42-45; *Dave Garroway Show*, NBC 47-49, *Garroway at Large* (TV) 49-51; Communicator *Today* (TV) 52-61; Narrator, *Wide Wide World* 55-59; star *Exploring the Universe*, Nat. Educational TV 61-62, *Garroway AM and PM*, C.B.S. 64-.
37 W. 12th Street, New York City, N.Y., U.S.A.

Garson, Stuart Sinclair, P.C.(CAN.), Q.C., LL.B., LL.D.; Canadian lawyer and politician; b. 1 Dec. 1898; ed. Manitoba Univ.
Called to Manitoba Bar 19; law practice Ashern, Man. 19-28; mem. law firm Johnston, Garson Co. Winnipeg 28; partner Johnston, Garson, Forrester Davison and Taylor 57-65; mem. of Manitoba Legislature 27, 32, 36, 41, 45; Provincial Treas. 36; Treasury Rep. Ottawa

Conf. of Nat. Finance Cttee. 36, and before Rowell-Sirois Comm.; Premier, Provincial Treas. and Minister Dominion-Provincial Relations 43-48; Fed. Minister of Justice and Attorney-Gen. of Canada 48-57; Lieut.-Gov. of Manitoba 65-; Chair. Continuing Cttee. on Constitutional Amendment 50; Chair. Canadian del. Sixth Gen. Assembly UN, Paris 52; mem. Parl. from Marquette 48, 49 and 53; Liberal-Progressive.
Government House, Winnipeg, Manitoba, Canada.

Gary, Romain; French writer and diplomatist; b. 8 May 1914; ed. Lycée de Nice and Paris Univ.
Served as pilot with Free French Air Force squadron "Lorraine" in Africa, Palestine and Russia 40-45; attached to Foreign Ministry 45-56; Consul-Gen. in Los Angeles (U.S.) 56-60; attached to Ministry of Information 67-; Officier de la Légion d'Honneur; Compagnon de la Libération; Croix de Guerre; Prix des Critiques 45, Prix Goncourt 56.
Publs. many works including *Education Européenne* 43, *Tulipe* 46, *Le Grand Vestiaire* 49, *Les Couleurs du Jour* 52, *Les Racines du Ciel* (Prix Goncourt 56), *Promesses de l'Aube* 59, *Madame L* 59, *The Ski Bum* 65, *Frère Océan* 65, *Pour Sganarelle* 65, *Le Mangeur d'étoiles* 66, *La danse de Gengis Cohn* 67; for the theatre: *Johnie Coeur, Gloire à nos illustres pionniers*; film: *Les Oiseaux vont mourir au Pérou* 68.
c/o Editions Gallimard, 5 rue Sébastien-Bottin, Paris 7e, France.

Gascar, Pierre; French writer; b. 13 March 1916.
Army service in France and Scotland 39-40; captured, twice escaped, recaptured and sent to Rawa-Ruska concentration camp (Ukraine); journalist for *France-Soir*, journeys in Europe, China, S.E. Asia and Africa; film-maker; Prix des Critiques and Prix Goncourt 53.
Publs. *Les Meubles* 49, *Les Bêtes, Le Temps des Morts* 53, *Les Femmes* 55, *La Graine, Chine Ouverte* 56, *L'Herbe des Rues, Voyage chez les Vivants* 58, *La Barre de Corail, Soleils, Les Pas Perdus* 59, *Le Fugitif* 61, *Vertiges du Présent, Les Moutons de Feu* 63, *Le Meilleur de la Vie* 64, *Les Charmes* 65, *Auto* 68.
21 rue Gay-Lussac, Paris 5e, France.
Telephone: MED 02-81.

Gaskill, William; British theatre director; b. 24 June 1930; ed. Salt High School, Shipley, and Hertford Coll., Oxford.
Director, Granada Television 56-57; Asst. Artistic Dir. Royal Court Theatre, London 58-60; Dir. Royal Shakespeare Company 61-62; Assoc. Dir. Nat. Theatre, London 63-65; Artistic Dir. English Stage Company, Royal Court Theatre 65-.
Stage productions include: (Royal Court Theatre) *Epitaph for George Dillon, One Way Pendulum, Saved, A Chaste Maid in Cheapside;* (National Theatre) *The Recruiting Officer, Mother Courage, Philoctetes, Armstrong's Last Goodnight;* (Royal Shakespeare Co.) *The Caucasian Chalk Circle, Richard III, Cymbeline;* (Phoenix Theatre) *Baal.*
74 Northside, Clapham Common, London, S.W.4, England.

Gáspár, Sándor; Hungarian politician; b. 17.
Motor mechanic; mem. Communist Party 36-, several posts in C.P. 45-; formerly high posts in Iron and Metal Workers Trade Union; Asst. Gen. Sec. Central Council of Trade Unions 52, Gen. Sec. 56-59, 65-; Gen. Sec. Budapest Cttee. of Hungarian Socialist Workers' Party 59-60, 62-65; Sec. Central Cttee. Hungarian Socialist Workers' Party 61-; mem. Political Cttee. 62-; Deputy Pres. Hungarian Presidential Council 63-.
Central Council of Trade Unions, Budapest, Hungary.

Gaspard, Roger Germain Charles; French business executive; b. 27 April 1902; ed. Lycée Henri-IV, Paris, and Ecole Polytechnique.
Director-Gen. Electricité de France 46-62, Pres. 62-63,

Hon. Pres. 64-; Vice-Pres. Compagnie Nat. du Rhône 46-62; Vice-Pres. Conseil Général des Ponts et Chaussées 63, Assoc. Partner Schneider S.A. 63, Vice-Pres. 64, Pres.-Dir. Gen. 66-; Pres.-Dir. Gen. Forges et Ateliers du Creusot (Usines Schneider) 64; Dir. Union européenne industrielle et financière, Soc. Le Nickel; Commdr. de la Légion d'Honneur, Médaille de la Résistance.
Schneider S.A., 42 rue d'Anjou, Paris 8e, France.

Gassman, Vittorio; Italian actor and director; b. 1 Sept. 1922; ed. Law Univ. of Rome and Dramatic Acad. of Rome.
Plays acted in include: *Hamlet, Othello, As You Like It, Troilus and Cressida, Oedipus Rex, Prometheus Bound, Ghosts, Peer Gynt, Orestes, Rosencrantz and Guildenstern are Dead, Richard III,* etc.; has directed his own group since 51; Films acted in include: *Bitter Rice, Anna, Rhapsody, War and Peace, The Miracle, I Soliti Ignoti,* etc.; Dir. *Kean* 56 and *The Great War,* Venice Festival winner; Dir. musical-play *Irma la Douce;* four awards for the best Italian theatre actor of the year, four for the best film actor; created Teatro Popolare Italiano (mobile theatre, 3,000 seats); dir. and played Agamemnon in production of Aeschylus' *Oresteia,* Syracuse 60.
Piazza S. Alessio 32, Rome, Italy.

Gastaut, Henri Jean; French biologist; b. 5 April 1915; ed. Monaco and Nice Lycées, Marseilles Univ.
Head Nervous Anatomy Laboratory 39, Nervous Diseases Clinic 44, Tit. Prof. Pathological Anatomy 52-, Marseilles Univ. Medical Faculty; Head Marseilles Hospitals Neurobiological Laboratory 53-, Marseilles region Centre for Epileptic Children 60-; Dir. Neurobiological Research Unit, Inst. Nat. de la Santé Marseilles 61-; Marseilles Hospitals Biologist 63-; Dean of the Medical Faculty, Marseilles 67; Sec., later Pres., Int. Fed. of Socs. for Electroencephalography and Clinical Neurophysiology, Int. League against Epilepsy; Hon. mem. or corresp. Soc. de Neurologie Française, American Acad. of Neurology, Royal Medico Psychological Asscn. (U.K.), Royal Soc. of Medicine (U.K.), etc.; Prix Monthyon (French Acad. des Sciences) 57.
Publs. Twenty books and monographs on applied neuro-physiology.
87 boulevard Périer, Marseilles 8, France.
Telephone: 33-44-82.

Gates, Sylvester Govett, C.B.E.; British lawyer and banker; b. 2 Sept. 1901; ed. Winchester, New Coll., Oxford, and Harvard Univ.
Legal practice, London and Western Circuit 28-39; Controller of Home Publicity, Ministry of Information 41-44, attached to Office of Minister of Reconstruction 44; Chair., British Film Inst. 56-64; mem. Port of London Authority 58-64; now Deputy Chair. Westminster Bank Ltd.; Chair. Tecalemit Ltd.; Chair. Int. Commercial Bank 67-; Deputy Chair. Standard Bank Ltd.; mem. Royal Comm. on Taxation 53.
29 Eaton Square, London S.W.1, England.
Telephone: 01-235-5503.

Gates, Thomas Sovereign, Jr.; American politician; b. 10 April 1906; ed. Univ. of Pennsylvania.
Associated with Drexel and Co. 28-, partner 40-53; Under-Sec. for Navy 53-57; Sec. for Navy 57-59; Sec. of Defense 59-61; Naval Reserve Officer 42-45; Chief Exec. Cttee. Morgan Guaranty Trust Co., Pres. Aug. 62-65, Chair. of Board and Chief Exec. Officer 65-; Trustee Univ. of Pa.; Bronze Star, Yale; Hon. LL.D., Coumbia and Yale Univs., and Univ. of Pa.
Mill Race Farm, Devon, Pennsylvania, U.S.A.

Gaud, William Steen, B.A., LL.B.; American lawyer and government official; b. 9 Aug. 1907; ed. Yale Univ., and Law School.
Instructor Yale Law School 31-33; law practice, N.Y. 35-41; Special Asst. to Sec. of War 45-46; mem. Carter,

Ledyard and Milburn law firm 46-61; Asst. Administrator (in charge of the Middle East and South Asia Region) Agency for Int. Development 61-64; Dep. Administrator, Agency for International Development 64-66, Administrator 66-.

Agency for International Development, Washington, D.C., U.S.A.

Gaulle, Gen. Charles André Joseph Marie de; French army officer and politician; b. 22 Nov. 1890; ed. Saint-Cyr Acad.

Served as Captain 14-18 war; Gen. of Brigade and Commdr. 4th Armoured Div. 40; Under-Sec. Nat. Defence June 40; Chief of Free French and later Pres. of French Nat. Cttee., London and Brazzaville 40-42; Pres. of French Cttee. of Nat. Liberation, Algiers 43; Pres. of Provisional French Govt. of French Republic, C.-in-C. French Armies 44-46; founder Rassemblement du Peuple Française 47; retired 47-58; Prime Minister June 58-Jan. 59; President of France Jan. 59-.

Publs. *La Discorde chez l'Ennemi, Le Fil de l'Epée, Vers l'Armée de Métier, La France et son Armée, Discours et Messages, Mémoires de Guerre* 54, 56, 59.

Palais de l'Elysée, Paris; and "La Boisserie", Colombey-les-Deux-Eglises (Haute Marne), France.

Gautier, Georges Armand Léon; French overseas administrator; b. 11 April 1901; ed. Univ. de Paris, Ecole Nationale de la France d'Outre-Mer.

Administrator in the Civil Service in Indo-China 25; Sec.-Gen. Indo-China Government 41; Governor of the Colonies 42; Sec.-Gen. of Madagascar 50; Gov.-Gen. of France Overseas 51; Sec.-Gen. of the High Comm. of France in Indo-China 51; High Comm. of the French Republic of Vietnam 53; Pres. Conseil d'Administration de l'Institut d'Emission de l'A.E.F. et du Cameroun 55; Pres. of the Administrative Council of Central Bank of the States of Equatorial Africa and of the Cameroun 59-; Commdr. Légion d'Honneur.

Office: 29 rue du Colisée, Paris 8e; Home: 96 rue de Longchamp, Neuilly-sur-Seine (Seine), France.

Gautier, Jean-Jacques; French dramatic critic; b. 4 Nov. 1908; ed. Collège de Dieppe, Lycée de Laon, and Univ. of Paris.

Journalist *L'Echo de Paris* 35; Editorial Staff *L'Epoque* until 39; Dramatic Critic *Figaro* 44-; Sec.-General Comédie Française until 46; Officier Légion d'Honneur; Croix de Guerre; Prix Goncourt 46, Grand Prix de la Nouvelle 57.

Publs. *Histoire d'un fait divers* 46, *Vous aurez de mes nouvelles* 57, *Deux fauteuils d'orchestre* 62, *Raisons d'aimer La Comédie Française* 64, and thirteen novels.

25 quai d'Anjou, Paris 4e, France.

Telephone: Odéon 05-89.

Gavin, Ltd.-Gen. James M.; American army officer. diplomatist and business executive; b. 22 March 1907; ed. U.S. Military Acad.

Enlisted as Private 24, Lieut. 29, Lt.-Gen. 44; Commanded 505th Paratroop Combat Team, landing in Sicily and Salerno 43; Asst. Div. Commdr. 82nd Airborne Div. landing in Normandy and Nijmegen 44; Ardennes 45; Deputy Chief of Staff for Plans and Research 55; Chief of Research and Devt. 55-59; Amb. to France 61-62; mem. American Acad. Sciences; Pres. Arthur D. Little, Inc. 60-61, 63-64, Chair. of the Board 64-; Dir. American Electric Power Co. Inc., John Hancock Life Insurance Co.

Publs. *Airborne Warfare* 47, *War and Peace in the Space Age* 58, *France and the Civil War in America* 64, *Crisis Now* 68.

c/o Arthur D. Little Inc., 25 Acorn Park, Cambridge, Mass. 02140, U.S.A.

Telephone: 617-864-5770 (Office).

Gavrilov, Mikhail Alexandrovich; Soviet politician; b. 1910; ed. Higher Party School, Moscow.

Member C.P.S.U. 31-; party work 39; First Sec. Nizhne-Amur Regional Cttee. of C.P.S.U. 39-41; Sec. Khabarovsk Territorial Cttee. of C.P.S.U. 41-45; Sec. Kursk Regional Cttee. of C.P.S.U. 45-49; Apparatus of Central Cttee. of C.P.S.U. 52-61; Second Sec. and mem. Presidium Central Cttee. of Kirghiz C.P. 61-66; Dep. Minister of R.S.F.S.R. Local Industry 66-; Cand. mem. Central Cttee. of C.P.S.U. 61-66.

R.S.F.S.R. Ministry of Local Industry, 15 Bolshoi Cherkassky pereulok, Moscow, U.S.S.R.

Gaxotte, Pierre; French writer; b. 19 Nov. 1895; ed. Ecole Normale Supérieure.

Taught history 20-22; Editor-in-chief of *Candide* 24-40; now writes for *Figaro*; mem. Acad. Française 53-.

Publs. *La Révolution Française* 28, *Le Siècle de Louis XV* 33, *Frédéric II* 38, *La France de Louis XIV* 46, *Histoire des Français*, 2 vols. 51, *Thèmes et variations* 57, *Histoire de France* 61, *Histoire de L'Allemagne*, 2 vols. (Prix des Ambassadeurs 63) 63, *Aujourd'hui* 65, *L'Académie française* 65.

23 rue Froidevaux, Paris 14e; and Musée Condé, Chantilly (Oise), France.

Gazenko, Oleg Georgievich; Soviet physiologist; b. 1918; ed. Moscow Medical Inst.

Service in the Army 41-46; Research Assoc. Kirov Mil. Medical Acad. 46-47; U.S.S.R. Inst. of Experimental Medicine 47; mem. C.P.S.U. 53; Corresp. mem. U.S.S.R. Acad. of Sciences 66-.

Publs. Works on experimental physiology.

U.S.S.R. Academy of Sciences, 14 Lenin Prospekt, Moscow, U.S.S.R.

Gazier, Albert, L. en D.; French politician; b. 16 May 1908.

Employed by Presses Universitaires de France, Paris; joined Socialist Party; Sec.-Gen. of Chambre des Employés de la Région Parisienne; active in Resistance during Occupation; came to England and later returned to France; mem. of Bureau of Confédération Générale du Travail (C.G.T.); C.G.T. delegate to Provisional Constituent Assemblies Algiers 43-44, Paris 44-45; later Sec. of C.G.T. Bureau; Deputy for Seine; Under-Sec. for Nat. Economy in Gouin Govt.; Under-Sec. for Public Works and Transport in Bidault Govt.; Sec. to Presidency of Council in Blum Govt.; Minister of Information in Pleven and Queuille Govts. 50-51; Minister of Social Affairs 56-57; Minister of Information May 58; mem. of Exec. French Socialist Party.

12 avenue du Parc, 92 Vanves (Seine), France.

Gazzar, Abdel Hadi el; United Arab Republic (Egyptian) artist; b. 25; ed. Cairo and Rome Acad. of Fine Arts.

Professor of Painting, Cairo Faculty of Fine Arts; rep. at numerous exhibitions, including the 28th and 30th Venice Biennali, Brussels Int. Exhibition 58 and São Paulo Bienal 61; Exhibitions in Cairo, Alexandria and Rome; First Prize "10 Years of the Revolution" Exhibition 62.

Faculty of Fine Arts, Cairo University, Cairo, United Arab Republic.

Gbedemah, Komla Agbeli; Ghanaian politician; b. 13; ed. Adisadel Coll., Cape Coast and Achimota Coll.

First Vice-Chair. Convention People's Party, was responsible for organising general elections 51; Minister of Health and Labour 51-52; Minister of Commerce and Industry 52-54; Minister of Finance 54-61, of Health 61; Minister of State for Presidential Affairs 60-61; fmr. Gov. for Ghana, Int. Bank Reconstruction and Development; fmr. Pres. World Asscn. of World Federalists.

Accra, Ghana.

Gebre-Egzy, Dr. Tesfaye; Ethiopian diplomatist.

Permanent Rep. to the UN 61-66; Sec.-Gen. Org. of African Unity (O.A.U.) 63-64.

c/o Ethiopian Mission to the UN, New York, N.Y., U.S.A.

Gedda, Nicolai; Swedish operatic tenor; b. 11 July 1925; ed. Musical Acad., Stockholm.
Debut, Stockholm 52; Concert appearances Rome 52, Paris 53, 55, Vienna 55, Aix-en-Provence 54, 55; first operatic performances in Munich, Lucerne, Milan and Rome 53, Paris, London and Vienna 54; Salzburg Festival 57-59, Edinburgh Festival 58-59; with Metropolitan Opera, N.Y. 57-.
Falks Väg 8, Danderyd, Sweden.

Geddes, 2nd Baron; **Ross Campbell Geddes,** C.B.E., M.A.; British shipowner and business executive; b. 20 July 1907; ed. Rugby School and Gonville and Caius Coll., Cambridge.
Shell Group of Oil Companies 31-46; British Merchant Shipping Mission, Washington 42-44; Deputy Dir. Tanker Div., Ministry of War Transport 44-45; Partner, Chr. Salvesen and Co., Leith 46-50; Chair. Admiralty Fuels and Lubricants Advisory Cttee. 51-57; Pres. Inst. of Petroleum 56-58; Pres. Chamber of Shipping of the U.K. 68, British Travel Asscn. 64-; Dir. Peninsular and Oriental Steam Navigation Co. 57-; Chair. Trident Tankers Ltd. 63-; Chair. Limmer and Trinidad Co. 64-; Chair. Clerical, Medical and Gen. Life Assurance Soc., Gen. Reversionary and Investment Co.; Chair. Monks Investment Trust Ltd.; Dir. Minerals Separation Ltd., London Scottish Investment Trust Ltd., Electronics Trust Ltd., Technology Investment Ltd., Geddes and Co. Ltd.; Chair. Ministry of Transport Cttee. on Carriers Licensing 63.
40 Wimpole Street, London, W.1; and Nagshead Field, Lymington, Hampshire, England.

Geddes, Sir (Anthony) Reay (Mackay), K.B.E.; British business executive; b. 7 May 1912; ed. Rugby and Cambridge Univ.
Chairman The Dunlop Co. Ltd. 68-; Dir. "Shell" Transport & Trading Co. Ltd. 68-, Midland Bank Ltd. 67-; Chair. Shipbuilding Inquiry Cttee. 65-66.
Dunlop House, 25 Ryder Street, St. James's, London, S.W.1, England.

Geddes, Ford Irvine, M.B.E.; British shipping executive; b. 17 Jan. 1913; ed. Loretto School and Gonville and Caius Coll., Cambridge.
Anderson Green and Co. Ltd., London 34, Dir. 47-; Army Service 39-45; Man. Dir. P. and O. Steam Navigation Co. 63-, Deputy Chair. 68-; Man. Dir. P. and O. Orient Management Ltd., and Orient Steam Navigation Co. Ltd. 60-; Pres. Equitable Life Assurance Soc. 63-; Dir. Bank of New South Wales (London Advisory Board), Scottish Australian Co. Ltd., Hall-Thermotank Ltd., R. and H. Green and Silley Weir Ltd., British United Turkeys Ltd., British India Steam Navigation Co. Ltd.; Chair. Technical Cttee., Chamber of Shipping of U.K. 60-65; Vice-Chair. British Shipping Fed. 61, Chair. 65-.
Havensfields, Great Missenden, Bucks., England.

Geddes of Epsom, Baron (Life Peer), cr. 58, of Epsom, **Charles John Geddes,** C.B.E.; British trade unionist; b. 2 March 1897; ed. Blackheath School.
Mem. Exec. Council Union of Post Office Workers 28, Asst. Gen. Sec. 41, Gen. Sec. 45-57; Chair. Post Office Departmental Whitley Council, Staff Side; mem. Civil Service Nat. Whitley Council; mem. Gen. Council, Trades Union Congress 46-58, Chair. 54-55; mem. Exec. Board I.C.F.T.U.; Pres. European Regional Org. of I.C.F.T.U.; Pres. Postal, Telegraph and Telephone Int. 56-58; Part-time mem. London Transport Exec., Central Electricity Generating Board 58-; mem. Inst. Int. Affairs; mem. Labour Party.
112 Chapel Way, Epsom, Surrey, England.

Gedye, George Eric Rowe, M.B.E.; British journalist and author; b. 27 May 1890; ed. Queen's Coll., Taunton.
Served First World War 14-18 (France 15) in infantry, later Intelligence Corps; on Mil. Govt. Staff (subsequently Rhineland High Comm.) 18-22; *The Times* Special Corresp., Rhine and Ruhr 23-24, Central and S.E. Europe 25-26; *Daily Express* Corresp. Central and S.E. Europe 27-29; *Daily Telegraph* and *New York Times* Corresp. Central and S.E. Europe 29-Mar. 38 (stationed Vienna 25-38); expelled from Austria on Nazi invasion Mar. 38; *Daily Telegraph* and *New York Times* Corresp., Prague Mar. 38-Mar. 39; *New York Times* Corresp., Moscow 40, Istanbul 41; employed under War Office on special duties in Near and Middle East 41-45; *Daily Herald* Corresp. for Central and S.E. Europe (stationed Vienna) 45-60, *The Observer* Corresp. 50-52, *Manchester Guardian* 53; Chief Evaluation Section, Radio Free Europe 54, Vienna Corresp. 55-60; Lecturer on Central and Eastern European countries.
Publs. *Wayfarer in Austria* 29, *Revolver Republic* 30, *Heirs to the Habsburgs* 32, *Fallen Bastions* 39, *We Saw it Happen* (part author, published U.S.A.) 39, part author *Fodor's Modern Guide to Austria* 53, *Introducing Austria* 55.
"Crownhill", Granville Road, Lansdown, Bath, England.
Telephone: Bath 21961.

Gegesi Kiss, Pal, M.D.; Hungarian pediatrician; b. 1900.
Rector of Budapest Medical Univ. 55-61; Dir. Budapest Clinic of Pediatrics No. 1; mem. Hungarian Acad. of Sciences; Pres. Hungarian Nat. Red Cross; Hon. mem. Soviet Soc. of Pediatrics 57, Purkinje Medical Soc. of Czechoslovakia 63; Kossuth Prize 57; subjects of study include circulation disorders in the newborn and infant; childhood diabetes.
Publs. *Diabetes Mellitus in Newborns and Infants* 56; (co-author) *Cardiac and Circulatory Diseases in Infancy and Childhood* 53.
No. 1 Clinic of Pediatrics, University Medical School, Bókay János-u. 53, Budapest VIII, Hungary.
Telephone: 343-186.

Geijer, Karl Arne; Swedish trade union executive; b. 7 May 1910; ed. Trade Union Coll.
Metal worker until 38; Educational Sec., Swedish Metal Workers' Union 38-45, Sec. 45-49, Pres. 49-50; Pres. Confederation of Swedish Trade Unions 56-; fmr. Pres. Int. Confederation of Free Trade Unions (ICFTU); M.P., Social Democratic Party 55-.
Barnhusgatan 18, Stockholm C, Sweden.

Geijer, Per Adolf, PH.D.; Swedish geologist; b. 7 May 1886; ed. Universitet i Uppsala.
Lecturer, Stockholm Univ. 10-25; Geologist, Geological Survey of Sweden 14-31; Prof. of Mineralogy and Geology, Royal Inst. of Technology, Stockholm 31-41; Dir. Geological Survey of Sweden 42-51; Foreign Assoc. U.S. Acad. of Sciences; Rinman Medal, Jernkontoret (Asscn. of Ironworks), Sweden 45; Brinell Medal, Acad. of Eng. Sciences, Sweden 61.
Publs. include monographs and papers in geology and mineralogy, mainly on ore deposits.
Agnevaegen 5, Djursholm, Sweden.

Geill, Torben, M.D.; Danish physician; b. 14 Aug. 1896; ed. Københavns Universitet.
Medical Asst., Univ. Medical Clinic, Copenhagen 26-28; Medical Asst., Bispebjerg Hospital, Copenhagen 30-36; Medical Dir. De Gamles By (Geriatric Unit), Copenhagen 36-; mem. State Disablement Court 43-; Pres. Danish Gerontological Soc. 50-62, Int. Asscn. of Gerontology 63-66; Hon. mem. Italian Gerontological Soc., Argentine Gerontological Soc., Danish Gerontological Soc.; Knight Order of Dannebrog, 1st degree.
Publs. *Studies on Albumin and Globolin in Serum and Urine* 28, *Textbook on Geriatrics* (with S. Eckerstrom).
18 Barsehøj, Copenhagen-Hellerup, Denmark.
Telephone: GE 2717.

Gelber, Jack, B.S.; American playwright; b. 12 April 1932; ed. Univ. of Illinois School of Journalism.
Guggenheim Fellow for Creative Writing for the Theatre 63-64.
Publs. Plays: *The Connection* 60, *The Apple* 61, *Let's Face It, Square in the Eye* 65; Novel: *On Ice* 64.
250 Riverside Drive, New York 25, N.Y., U.S.A.

Gélin, Daniel Jean French actor; b. 19 May 1921; ed. Lycée de St. Malo, Paris Conservatoire.
Mem. Théâtre Nat. Populaire Company 60-; films include *La Ronde, Dieu a Besoin des Hommes, Les Mains Sales, Paris-Canaille, Les Amants du Tage, En Effeuillant la Marguerite, Mort en Fraude, Charmants Garçons, Suivez-moi Jeune Homme, Ce Corps Tant Désiré, Austerlitz, Monsieur Masure, La Morte Saison des Amours, La Proie pour l'Ombre, Le Testament d'Orphée, Carthage en flammes, Peur panique, Le Jour le plus long, Règlements de compte, La Bonne Soupe, Vacances Portugaises, Le Soleil Noir.*
Publ. *Fatras* (verse).
Boutigny-sur-Opton (E.-et-L.), France.

Gell-Mann, Murray, PH.D.; American physicist; b. 15 Sept. 1929; ed. Yale Univ. and Massachusetts Inst. of Technology.
Member Inst. for Advanced Study, Princeton 51, 55; Instructor, Asst. Prof., and Assoc. Prof., Univ. of Chicago 52-55; Assoc. Prof., Calif. Inst. of Technology 55-56, Prof. 56-66, R. A. Millikan Prof. of Theoretical Physics 67-; Research Assoc. Univ. of Illinois 51, 53; Visiting Assoc. Prof. Columbia Univ. 54; Visiting Prof. Collège de France and Univ. of Paris 59-60, Mass. Inst. of Technology 63; mem. Nat. Acad. of Sciences, American Physical Soc., American Acad. of Arts and Sciences; Consultant, Inst. for Defense Analyses, Arlington, Va. 61-, Rand Corpn., Santa Monica, Calif. 56-; mem. N.A.S.A. Physics Panel 64-; Consultant to Los Alamos Scientific Laboratory, Los Alamos, N.M. 56-; Dannie Heinemann Prize, American Physical Soc. 59; Ernest O. Lawrence Award 66; Hon. Sc.D. (Yale) 59.
Major works: Developed strangeness theory, theory of neutral K mesons, eightfold way theory of approximate symmetry, current algebra; contributed to theory of dispersion relations, and knowledge of structure of weak interaction.
Publ. (with Yuval Ne'eman) *The Eightfold Way* 64.
California Institute of Technology, Pasadena, California, U.S.A.

Gellhorn, Martha; American writer; ed. John Burroughs School and Bryn Mawr Coll.
War Corresp., covering Spanish Civil War, Finnish-Russian War, Sino-Japanese War, Second World War, Java, Vietnam and Arab-Israeli War; now occasional journalism in Europe and Africa.
Publs. *The Trouble I've Seen* 36, *A Stricken Field* 39, *The Heart of Another* 40, *Liana* 43, *The Wine of Astonishment* 48, *The Honeyed Peace* 53, *Two by Two* 58, *The Face of War* 59, *His Own Man* 61, *Pretty Tales for Tired People* 65, *The Lowest Trees Have Tops* 67.
c/o Morgan Guaranty Trust Co., 31 Berkeley Square, London, W.1, England.

Gelsted, Otto; Danish writer; b. 4 Nov. 1888; ed. secondary school.
Literary Editor *Land og Folk*; mem. of the Danish Acad. 61; Hon. mem. Norwegian Soc. of Authors; Danish Union of Translators Prize of Honour 58; Emil Aarestrup-Medal and Drachman Foundation 58; Danish Soc. of Authors, Poetry Prize 61; Henri Nathansen Foundation 62; Holberg Medal 63.
Publs. *Johs. V. Jensen* 13, *De evige Ting* 20, *Dansens Almagt* 21, *Enetaler* 22, *Jomfru Gloriant* 23, *Lazarus Opvækkelse* 24, *Gunnar Gunnarson* 26, *Rejsen til Astrid* 27, *Enehøje Digte* 29, *Henimod Klarhed* 31, *Danmark-Rusland i Literaturen* 37, *Udvalgte Digte* 38, *De danske Strande* 40, *Arnulf Øverland* 46, *Frihedens Aar* 47, *Std op og taend lys* 48, *Guder og Helte* 56, *Graesk drama* 57, *Aldrig var dagen saa lys* 59, *Oluf Høst* 60, *Digte fra en solkyst* 61.
Land og Folk, Dronningens Tvaergade 3, Copenhagen, Denmark.
Telephone: 140114.

Geneen, Harold Sydney, B.S.; American business executive; b. 22 Jan. 1910; ed. New York Univ., Harvard Business School.
Worked for Wall Street brokers 26-32; Accountant, Mayflower Associates Inc. 32-34, Lybrand, Ross Bros. & Montgomery 34-42; American Can Co. 42-46; Bell & Howell Co., Chicago 46-50; Jones & Laughlin Steel Corp., Pittsburgh (Vice-Pres. and Controller) 50-56; Exec. Vice-Pres. and Dir. Raytheon Manufacturing Co., Waltham 56-59; Chair. and Pres., Dir. and Mem. Exec. Cttee. Int. Telephone and Telegraph Corpn. 59-, Chair. 64-; mem. Board Int. Rescue Cttee.; Grand Officer, Order of Merit for Distinguished Service, Peru; Commdr. of Belgian Order of the Crown; Doctor of Laws, PMC Colls.
320 Park Avenue, New York, N.Y. 10022, U.S.A.

Genet, Jean; French playwright; b. 07.
Publs. *Haute Surveillance, Les Bonnes, Le Balcon, Les Nègres, Les Paravents* (plays); *Notre Dame des Fleurs* (novel); *Adam-Miroir* (ballet); *Journal d'un Voleur; Lettres à Roger Blin* 67.
c/o Librairie Gallimard, 5 rue Sébastien-Bottin, Paris 7e, France.

Genevoix, Maurice; French novelist; b. 29 Nov. 1890; ed. Ecole Normale Supérieure.
Prix Goncourt winner 25; mem. Acad. Française 46-, Perpetual Sec. 58-; mem., Conseil de la Radiodiffusion Française 58-; Hon. Pres. of the Librairie Académique Perrin 60-; mem. Conseil Supérieur des Gens de Lettres; Grand Croix de la Légion d'Honneur, Croix de Guerre, Commdr. des Arts et des Lettres.
Publs. *Sous Verdun* 14, *Nuits de guerre* 17, *Au seuil des guitounes* 18, *Jeanne Robelin* 20, *La boue* 21, *Rémi des Rauches* 22, *Les Eparges* 23, *La joie* 24, *Euthymos, vainqueur olympique* 24, *Raboliot* 25, *La boîte à pêche* 26, *Les mains vides* 28, *Cyrille* 28, *L'assassin* 30, *Rroû* 31, *H.O.E.* 31, *Forêt voisine* 33, *Gai l'amour* 32, *Marcheloup* 34, *Tête baissée* 37, *La dernière harde* 38, *Les compagnons de l'Aubepin* 38, *L'hirondelle qui fit le printemps* 41, *La framboise et Belhumeur* 42, *Canada* 45, *Eva Charlebois* 44, *Sanglar* 46, *L'écureuil du bois bourru* 47, *Afrique blanche, Afrique noire* 49, *Ceux de 14* 50, *L'Aventure est en nous, Fatou Cissé, Routes de L'Aventure, Au Cadran de mon clocher, Vaincre à Olympie, Jeux de Glaces* 61, *La Loire, Agnès et les Garçons* 62, *Derrière les Collines* 64, *Beau-François* 65, *La Fôret Perdue* 67.
1 rue de Seine, Paris 6e, France.

Genovese, Sebastiano; Italian hydrobiologist; b. 1926; ed. Univ. of Messina.
Assistant Inst. of Hydrobiology, Univ. of Messina 51-57, lecturer 57-58; Prof. of Hydrobiology Univ. of Messina 58-; Dir. Inst. of Hydrobiology 62-; Pres. Società Peloritana; mem. Int. Comm. for Scientific Exploration of the Mediterranean, Societas Internationalis Limnologiae, American Soc. for Microbiology, Unione Zoologica Italiana.
Publs. Numerous papers on marine biology.
Office: Istituto Idrobiologia, Universitá di Messina; Home: Via N. Bixio 89, Messina, Italy.
Telephone: 42995 (Office); 30145 (Home).

Gentil Nuñes, Lt. Col. Janary; Brazilian officer; b. 12; ed. Inst. Nossa Senhora de Nazaré and Ginásio Paraense Paes de Carvalho (Belem), Escola Militar do Realengo.
Sec. Inter-Ministerial Comm. on Brazilian Nat. Symbols 39; Staff courses 42, 49; Commandant 1st Machine Gun Company 43; Gov. Fed. Territory of Amapá 43-49, 49-

56; Pres. Petroleo Brasileiro S.A. (PETROBRAS) 56-58; Fellow Santa Catarina Inst. Histórico e Geográfico, Acad. Amapaense de Letras; Medalha de Guerra, Medalha de Prata Comemorativa do Cinquentenário da Proclamação da República, Legion of Merit (U.S.A.), Officier de l'Etoile Noire du Bénin (France).

Publs. *Bandeira do Brasil* 38, *Relátorio sôbre o Territário Federal do Ampará referente ao ano de 1944*; reports, plans, articles.

Avenida Rui Barbosa 830, apto. 502, Flamengo, Rio de Janeiro, Brazil.

Gentner, Wolfgang; German physicist; b. 23 July 1906; ed. Univs. of Erlangen and Frankfurt.

Lecturer, Univ. of Frankfurt 37-41; mem. Inst. for Physics of Kaiser Wilhelm Inst. for Medical Research, Heidelberg; engaged in atomic research 39-45; lecturer, Univ. of Heidelberg 41-45; Prof. of Physics Univ. of Freiburg 46-58; Dir. Synchro-Cyclotron Div., Org. for European Nuclear Research (CERN), Geneva 55-59; Dir. Max Planck Institute for Nuclear Physics, Heidelberg 58-; Prof. of Physics, Univ. of Heidelberg 58-; mem. Heidelberger Akademie der Wissenschaften, Bayerische Akademie der Wissenschaften, Akademie, Leopoldina, Halle; mem. Comité des directives scientifiques, CERN, and Ausschuss für Wissenschaft und Technik, EURATOM; Officier de la Légion d'Honneur 65.

Max Planck Institute for Nuclear Physics, 6900 Heidelberg 1, Saupfercheckweg, German Federal Republic.
Telephone: 516201.

Georgadze, Mikhail Porfizyevich; Soviet government official; b. 1912; ed. Moscow Inst. of Mechanisation of Agriculture.

Worked as tractor driver 29-34; Engineer and subsequently Chief Engineer and Dept. Chief at U.S.S.R. Ministry of Agriculture 41-51; Chief Transcaucasian Motor Tractor Stations Admin. 51-53; Minister of Agriculture, Georgia, and Deputy Chair. Georgia Council of Ministers 53-54; and Sec. Central Cttee. Georgian C.P. 54-56; First Deputy Chair. Georgian Council of Ministers 56-57; Alt. mem. C.P.S.U. Central Cttee. 66-; Sec. Presidium U.S.S.R. Supreme Soviet 57-.

Presidium of Supreme Soviet of U.S.S.R., The Kremlin, Moscow, U.S.S.R.

George, André, D.L.; French critic, essayist and physicist; b. 31 July 1890; ed. Paris Univ.

Mem. Comité du Langage Scientifique (founded by Acad. des Sciences); mem. Editorial Cttee. *Nouvelles Littéraires*; Dir. series *Sciences d'aujourd'hui* and *Les Savants et le Monde*; Science corresp. for *Figaro*; Pres. Société Scientifique de Bruxelles 51-53; Air Commandant 40; Awarded Métais-Larivière Prize of Acad. Française for *Pasteur*; Grand Prix Acad. Française for Collected Works 62; Officier de la Légion d'Honneur, Croix de Guerre, Officier des Arts et des Lettres.

Publs. *Henri Poincaré* (critical essay), *Arthur Honegger* 26, *Tristan et Isolde de Wagner* 27, *L'oratoire* 28, *L'œuvre de Louis de Broglie et la Physique d'aujourd'hui* 31, *Mécanique quantique et Causalité* 32, *Les Conséquences générales de la Physique contemporaine* 33, *Pierre Termier* (awarded Bordin Prize of Acad. Française) 33, *Les Nébuleuses spirales et l'Univers en expansion* 34, *Paris* (essay) 37, *Le Véritable Humanisme* 42, *Dimensions du Temps* 43, *Les Grands Appels de l'Homme Contemporain* (ouvrage collectif) 46, *Pasteur* 58, trans. and complementary chapter of *Einstein, his Life and Time* (by Ph. Frank) 52-68, trans. and introduction of *Scientific Autobiography and Last Papers* (Max Planck) 60, *Science et Foi* 62, *Napoléon et les Sciences* (in *Napoléon*, ouvrage collectif) 68.

256 boulevard St. Germain, Paris 7e, France.
Telephone: 548-45-00.

George-Day (Mme. L. Debeauvais); French writer; secondary education.

Secretary-Gen. of Société des Gens de Lettres de France

46-66, Hon. Pres. 67-; Pres. La Maison de Poésie (7 mems.); Vice-Pres. Académie Ronsard; Vice-Pres. Mérite Civique; Prix d'ensemble, Grand Prix de la Pensée Française, Prix Montyon, Grand Prix de Poésie (Acad. Française) 60, etc.; Officier Légion d'Honneur; Commdr. de l'Ordre des Palmes Académiques, Officier des Arts et Lettres, Officier de l'Ordre de la Couronne Belge.

Publs. Novels: *La Griffe du Diable* 28, *Le Crépuscule de l'amour* 30, *L'anneau de Gygès* 32, *La Porte Close* 32, *La Colombe noire* 38, *L'Eau Ardente* 51, *Le Visage Obstiné* 54; Verse: *Rapsodies en mauve* 32, *Clavier de Cristal* 34, *Miroir de Narcisse* 36, *Grappes* 38, *L'Arche d'Amour* 42, *Spirales* 46, *Visite de l'ombre* 49, *La Lampe d'Héro* 50, *Suite à Moi-Même* 53, *L'oiseau d'Hermes* 56; Essays: *Dumont d'Urville* 47, *Les Transports dans l'Histoire de Paris* 47, *Marie Laurencin* 47, *Propos sur l'Homme I* 51, *II* 66, *III* 67, *Nouveaux propos* 57, *Variations, Les noces de Ste. Cécile* 59, *L'Adieu et la Voix* 61, *Contes et Nouvelles* 63, *Carnets d'une Assistante Sociale Gloulège* 66, *Florilège* 66.

63 boulevard St. Michel, 75 Paris 5e, France.
Telephone: 633-48-07.

Georges-Picot, Guillaume, L. en D.; French diplomatist and business executive; b. 10 Aug. 1898.

Served French Army First World War; entered diplomatic service as Embassy Attaché 24, Ministry of Foreign Affairs Paris, placed on reserve list at his own request 26, rejoined service 28; Sec. Moscow 28-30; Ministry of Foreign Affairs Paris 30; took part in Int. Conf. Lausanne 32; successively Sec. Sofia, Sec. Bangkok, Sec. Peking, Sec. Mexico City; at disposal of Residency-Gen. Tunisia 40-41; sent to Washington 41; joined Free French and became Dir of Civil Services French Mission to Washington 42; served Free French Forces 43-44; later at Commissariat of Foreign Affairs; after Liberation at Ministry of Foreign Affairs, Paris; sent on mission to China; Minister to Albania 46; Ambassador to Venezuela 46-48; Ambassador to Argentina 48-51; Asst. Sec.-Gen. of U.N. 51-54; Ambassador to Mexico 54-57; Permanent Rep. to U.N. and to Security Council 57-59; Dir., then Pres. Compagnie industrielle maritime 62-; Pres. Compagnie française des phosphates de l'Océanie 62-; Vice-Pres. Soc. d'investissements métropolitains et d'outre-mer (SIMER) 59-, Soc. des plantations réunies de Mimot 59-; Dir. of other companies; Commdr. de la Légion d'Honneur; Croix de Guerre.

66 avenue Foch, Paris 16e, France.
Telephone: 704-23-07.

Georges-Picot, Jacques Marie Charles; French company director; b. 16 Dec. 1900; ed. Lycée Janson-de-Sailly, Ecole Libre des Sciences Politiques and the Sorbonne.

Inspector of Finance 25; Deputy Head of Secretariat, Ministry of Air 28; Head of Secretariat, Ministry of Budget 30; Deputy Dir. of Budget 31; Dir. of Taxes 35; an Asst. Manager, Suez Canal Co. 37, Pres.-Dir. Gen. 57-, (renamed Suez Finance Co. 58); Pres. Crédit Industriel de l'Ouest 57-; Vice-Pres. Compagnie de Pont-à-Mousson 66-, Compagnies d'assurances La Providence; Dir. Saint-Gobain, Compagnie française des pétroles etc.; Dir. Fondation Nationale des Sciences Politiques 61, Institut Catholique de Paris; Commdr. de la Légion d'Honneur, Hon. K.B.E.

2 Square Mignot, Paris 16e, France.

Georgiades, Lefkos, B.SC. (ECON.), F.I.S.; Cypriot economist and diplomatist; b. 19; ed. Univ. of London.

Former statistician, United Nations; fmr. mem. UN. Expanded Technical Assistance Admin. for Libya; fmr. Development Officer, Republic of Cyprus; fmr. Chair. Electricity Authority of Cyprus; fmr. Special Adviser on Economic Affairs to Cyprus Ministry of Foreign

Affairs; Amb. to U.S.S.R. 63-; concurrently Amb. to Finland 64, Czechoslovakia 65, Sweden 65.
Embassy of Cyprus, Moscow, U.S.S.R.; Evagoral Avenue 23, Nicosia, Cyprus.

Georgiev, Alexandr Vasilievich; Soviet politician; b. 1913; ed. All-Union Agricultural Extra-Mural Inst.
Agronomist 32-43; mem. C.P.S.U. 43-; Chair. Regional District Exec. Cttee. of the Workers' Soviet, Kluchev, Altai 43-44; party work 44-61; First Sec. Altai Regional Rural Cttee. C.P.S.U. 60-61, First Sec. Altai Regional Cttee. 61-; mem. Central Cttee. of C.P.S.U. 61-; Deputy to Supreme Soviet U.S.S.R.
Altai Regional Committee of the Communist Party of the Soviet Union, Barnaul, U.S.S.R.

Georgiev, Vladimir Ivanov; Bulgarian university professor; b. 1908; ed. Univs. of Sofia, Vienna, Paris, Berlin and Florence.
Professor Univ. of Sofia since 31; Dean Faculty of Letters 47-48; Rector 51-56; Dir. Inst. for Linguistics Acad. of Science; Vice-Pres. Bulgarian Acad. of Science. Publs. many works, including *Vorgriechische Sprachwissenschaft* 41, *Issledovanija po sravniteljno-istoricheskomu jezykoznaniyu* 58, *Les deux langues des inscriptions crétoises* 63, *Vokalnata sistema v riazvoja na slavjanskite ezici* 64, *Introduzione alla storia delle lingue indeuropee* 66, etc.
Sofia, ul. Oborishte 11, Bulgaria.

Georgy, Guy-Noël; French diplomatist; b. 17 Nov. 1918; ed. Faculty of Law, Bordeaux and Paris.
Chief of Cabinet and Head of Information Dept., Cameroun 45-49; Attaché, Ministry for French Overseas Territories 50; Head of North-Cameroun District, Maroua 51-55; Chief of Cabinet, Ministry for French Overseas Territories 55; Gen. Sec. to Gabon 56; Gen. Manager of Econ. Affairs and Plan, Equatorial Africa 57, West Africa 58; High Commr. in Congo 59; High Commr. Congo (Brazzaville) 60; Ambassador to Bolivia 61-64, to Dahomey 64-.
French Embassy, Cotonou, Dahomey, West Africa.

Géraldy, Paul (*pseudonym* of Paul Lefèvre-Géraldy); French writer; b. 6 March 1885; ed. Lycée Henri IV, Lycée Buffon, Paris.
Commdr. Légion d'Honneur.
Publs. include *Toi et Moi, Vous et Moi* (verse), *Les Noces d'Argent, Les Grands Garçons, Aimer, Duo* (adapted from Colette), *Christine, Robert et Marianne* (plays), *Clindindin* (for children), *L'Homme et l'Amour, Trois Comédies Sentimentales, Vous qui passez* (play).
3 rue de Martignac, Paris 7e, France; and Beauvallon, Var, France.

Gerasimov, Innokentii Petrovich, D.GEOG.; Soviet geographer; b. 9 Dec. 1905; ed. Univ. of Leningrad.
Dokuchaev Inst. of Soil Science 46-56, Chief, Div. of Geography and Cartography of Soils 50-56; Inst. of Geography, Acad. of Sciences of U.S.S.R. 46-, now Dir.; Prof., Geographical Faculty, Lomonosov State Univ. of Moscow 46-; Editor-in-Chief *News of the U.S.S.R. Academy of Sciences, Geography Series;* mem. of Geog. Soc. of U.S.S.R.; Pres. All-Union Soc. of Soil Science; mem. U.S.S.R. Acad. of Sciences; mem. Acad. of Sciences of Bulgaria, Acad. Leopoldina; Hon. mem. Geog. Socs. of Poland, Finland, Serbia, Austria, Italy, Colombia, France, Hungary, Royal Geog. Soc. England, Royal Geog. Soc. Scotland; Vice-Pres. Int. Geog. Union; mem. C.P.S.U. 45-; Order of Lenin, Order of Red Star, Badge of Honour, etc.
Publs. *Lednikovyi period na teritorii S.S.S.R.* (Glacial Period of the Territory of the U.S.S.R.) 39, *Ocherki po fizicheskoi geografii zarubezhnykh stran* (Essays on the Physical Geography of Foreign Countries) 59, *Osnovy pochvovedenia i geografii pochv* (Principles of Soil Science and Geography of Soils) 60, *Pochvite v Bolgaria*

(Soils of Bulgaria) 60, *Strukturnye cherty reliefa SSSR* (Structural Features of the Relief of the U.S.S.R.) 58, *Pochvy tsentralnoi Yevropy* (Soils of Central Europe) 60.
Institute of Geography, Academy of Sciences of the U.S.S.R., Staromonetny pereulok 29, Moscow, U.S.S.R.

Gerasimov, Konstantin Mikhailovich; Soviet politician; b. 10; ed. Moscow Higher Technical Inst.
Member C.P.S.U. 39-; Head of Supreme Board of Ministry of Armaments 41-51, Dir. of Research Inst. 51-57; Deputy Minister of Armaments 54-57; First Deputy Chair., later Chair. Gorki Regional Econ. Cttee. 58-60; Chair. *Gosplan,* R.S.F.S.R., Deputy Chair. Council of Ministers, R.S.F.S.R. 60-; Cand. mem. Central Cttee. of C.P.S.U. 61-; Deputy to Supreme Soviet U.S.S.R. and R.S.F.S.R.; State Prize 51.
Council of Ministers of R.S.F.S.R., 3 Delegatskaya ulitsa, Moscow, U.S.S.R.

Gerasimov, Pavel Ivanovich; Soviet diplomatist; b. 1915; ed. Leningrad Polytechnic Inst.
Ministry of Foreign Affairs 45-; Deputy Head, Dept. for Near and Middle Eastern countries 53-54, 60-61; counsellor to U.S.S.R. Embassy in U.A.R. 54-59; Amb. to Guinea 59-60; Amb. to Luxembourg 61-62; Amb. to Belgium 62-67, Deputy Head of Dept., Ministry of Foreign Affairs 67-.
Ministry of Foreign Affairs, 32-34 Smolenskaya-Sennaya ploshchad, Moscow, U.S.S.R.

Gerasimov, Sergei Appolinarievich; Soviet film director and dramatist; b. 21 May 1906.
Began work in films as an actor 24; acted in films *The Overcoat* 26, *S.V.D.* 27, *One* 30, *The Border* 35, *Masquerade* 41; organized Leningrad Actor's Workshop and directed films *Seven Brave People* 35, *Komsomolsk* 37, *The Teacher* 39; other films *The Unvanquished* 42, *Great Land* 44, *The Young Guard* 48, *Liberated China* 50, *Country Doctor* 52, *Quiet Flows the Don* 58, *The Sputnik Speaks* 59, *Men and Beasts* 62, *The Journalist* (First Prize, Moscow Film Festival 67); mem. Praesidium Soviet Peace Cttee., Praesidium Union of Soviet Socs. of Friendship and Cultural Relations with Foreign Countries, Editorial Board of *Foreign Literature;* People's Artist of U.S.S.R.; State prizes for films *The New Teacher* 41, *The Young Guard* 49, *Liberated China* 51; Prof. and Head of the Directors' and Actors' Studios of the All-Union State Inst. of Cinematography; Sec. Asscn of Film Makers of the U.S.S.R.; mem. C.P.S.U.; Deputy of the Supreme Soviet of the R.S.F.S.R.; numerous decorations.
Publs. screenplays *The Teacher* 39, *Our Days* 40, articles on cinema.
Association of Film Makers of the U.S.S.R., 14 Vasilevskaya, Moscow, U.S.S.R.

Gerdes, Robert H.; American utility executive; b. 4 July 1904; ed. Univ. of California.
Associate Attorney, Pacific Gas and Electric Co. 29-35; private legal practice 35-44; Asst. General Counsel Pacific Gas and Electric Co. 44-46, General Counsel 46-53, Vice-Pres., General Counsel and Dir. 53-55, Exec. Vice-Pres. 55-63, Pres. 63-65, Chair. and Chief Exec. Officer 65-; Chair. and Dir. Pacific Gas Transmission Co., Alberta Natural Gas Co., Alberta & Southern Gas Co. Ltd., S. & M. Pipeline Ltd.; Pres. and Dir. Natural Gas Corpn. of Calif., Pacific Gas Communications Co., Gas Lines Inc.; Vice-Pres. Edison Electric Inst.
Pacific Gas and Electric Company, 245 Market Street, San Francisco, California 94106, U.S.A.
Telephone: 415-781-4211.

Gere, Mihai; Romanian politician; b. 2 Sept. 1919.
Member C.P. 40-; Alt. mem. Exec. Cttee. of Central Cttee. of Romanian C.P. 65-; Vice-Pres. State Council 65-; Sec. Central Cttee. 66-.
Central Committee of the Romanian Communist Party, Bucharest, Romania.

Gerhardie, William Alexander, O.B.E., M.A., B.LITT.; British writer; b. 21 Nov. 1895 in St. Petersburg of English parents; ed. St. Petersburg schools and Worcester Coll., Oxford.

Fought in the First World War as trooper, cadet and capt.; with European Div. B.B.C. 42-45; First Editor of *English by Radio.*

Publs. *Futility* 22, *The Polyglots* 25, *My Sinful Earth* 28, *Pending Heaven* 30, *Resurrection* 34, *Of Mortal Love* 36, *My Wife's the Least of It* 38 (novels); *Pretty Creatures* (short novels) 27; a critical study of Chekhov 23, and an autobiography *Memoirs of a Polyglot* 31; *The Romanovs* (a biography of the dynasty) 39; *My Literary Credo: an Introduction to the Collected Revised Uniform Edition of the Works* 47, *Highlights of Russian History* 50; *Donna Quixote* 27, *I Was A King In Babylon* 46, *Rasputin* 60, *The Fool of the Family* (with C. P. Snow) 66 (plays); *The Life and Times of Lord Beaverbrook* 68.

19 Rossetti House, 106 Hallam Street, London, W.1, England.

Telephone: 01-580-4878.

Gerhardsen, Einar; Norwegian politician; b. 10 May 1897.

Road worker 14-22; Chair. Road Repairers' Union 19; Sec. Norwegian Municipal Asscn. 22-23; Sec. Oslo Labour Party 25-35; Sec. Norwegian Labour Party 35-45; mem. Oslo Town Council 32-45; Mayor of Oslo 40, dismissed by Germans; worked as road repairer; mem. Secret Central Cttee.; arrested 41; deported to Germany 42; held in Gestapo Headquarters in Oslo as hostage against British Mosquito raids 44; again Mayor of Oslo 45; Chair. Labour Party 45-65; Prime Minister 45-51; Leader Labour Party in Parl. 51-55; Pres. of Parl. 54-55; Prime Minister 55-Aug. 63 and Sept. 63-Oct. 65; mem. Parl. 65-.

Stortinget, Oslo, Norway.

Gerkan, Armin von, DR. ING., DR. PHIL., DR. THEOL., H.C.; Russian-born German archaeologist and architect; b. 30 Nov. 1884; ed. Technical Univs., and Univ. of Greifswald.

Excavations at Miletus and Didyma 08-13; second Dir. German Inst. of Archæology at Rome 24-38, first Dir. 38-45; Visiting Prof. Greifswald, Göttingen, Bonn; Grosses Bundesverdienstkreuz and 12 other decorations; mem. Naples and Göttingen Acads. of Science.

Publs. *Publications of Miletus* (5 vols.) 15-35, *Das Theater von Priene* 21, *Griechische Städteanlagen* 24, *Gesammelte Aufsätze* 59, *Das Theater von Epidauros* 61, and other works.

Gleiwitzer Kehre 4/vii, 2 Garstedt Bez. Hamburg, German Federal Republic.

Telephone: Hamburg 527-95-22.

Gerlach, Manfred, DR. JUR.; German politician; b. 8 May 1928.

Joined Liberal-Democratic Party 45; co-founder F.D.J. (Free German Youth), Leipzig; mem. of Central Cttee. of F.D.J.; First Mayor of Leipzig 50; Editor *Liberal-Demokratische Zeitung,* Halle; Gen. Sec. Central Cttee. Liberal-Demokratische Partei Deutschlands (L.D.P.D.) 54-; mem. Volkskammer 49-, Nat. Council of Nat. Front 54-; Deputy Chair. of the State Council (Straatsrat) 60-; Vice-Pres. German-British Soc. 63-; Chair. L.D.P.D. 67-.

L.D.P.D., Taubenstrasse 48/49, 108 Berlin, German Democratic Republic.

Gerlach, Walther, DR. RER. NAT.; German physicist; b. 1 Aug. 1889; ed. Univ. of Tübingen.

Lecturer at Tübingen 16, Göttingen 17, Frankfurt 20; Extraordinary Prof. Univ. of Frankfurt 21-25; Prof. of Physics, Tübingen Univ. 25 and Munich Univ. 29-57; mem. Bavarian Acad. of Science, Göttingen Acad. of Science, Acad. Leopoldina Halle; Dr. Med. h.c.; Dr. Rer. h.c.

Publs. *Grundlagen der Quantentheorie* 21, *Atombau und Atomabbau* 23, *Materie, Elektrizität, Energie* 23, *Die chemische Spektralanalyse* 30, Part II 33, Part III 36, *Magnetismus* 31, *Foundations and Methods of Chemical Analysis by the Emission Spectrum* 34, *Methoden der naturwissenschaftlichen Erkenntnis* 36, *Max Planck-Werk und Wirkung* 48, *Akademische Provinz* 49, *Humaniora und Natur* 50, *Physik des täglichen Lebens* 56, *Physik (Fischer Lexikon)* 60, 67, *Humanität und Naturwissenschaftliche Forschung* 62, *Die Sprache der Physik* 62, *Physik in Geistesgeschichte und Pädagogik* 64, *Johannes Kepler* 66.

15 Franz Joseph Strasse, 8000 Munich 13, German Federal Republic.

Gerling, Hans, DR.RER.POL.; German insurance executive; b. 6 June 1915; ed. Universität zu Köln.

With Gerling-Konzern Versicherungsgesellschaft (insurance companies) 37-; Army Service 40-45; Pres. all Gerling-Konzern Insurance Companies 45-; Chair. Board, Global Group Insurance Companies, Toronto, Canada (Global Gen. Insurance Co., Global Life Insurance Co., Global Reinsurance Co.), Gerling Global Offices Inc., New York, Gerling Global Reinsurance Co. Ltd., London, Gerling Global Reinsurance Co. of South Africa Ltd., Johannesburg, I. D. Herstatt K.G. a A. (Bank), Cologne; Vice-Chair. Board, Frankona Reinsurance Co., Munich; Partner, Global Bank, Gerling & Co. K.G., Hamburg/Düsseldorf; Dir. Deutsche Hypothekenbank, Bremen, Commerzbank-Bankverein A.G., Düsseldorf; mem. Insurance Advisory Council Fed. Insurance Control Office, Berlin; mem. Exec. Cttee. German Insurance Asscn., Cologne; mem. Chamber of Commerce, Cologne; Royal Swedish Consul-Gen.

Office: Cologne, Gereonshof; Home: Cologne, von-Werth-Strasse 14, German Federal Republic.

Germán Otero, Dr. Andrés; Venezuelan engineer, business executive and politician; b. 09; ed. Stevens Inst. of Technology, U.S.A., Harvard Univ., and Central Univ. of Venezuela.

Engineer, Gorki, U.S.S.R. 32-33, Tennessee Valley Authority, U.S.A. 33-36; Dir. of Nat. Laboratory, Ministry of Fuel, Venezuela 36-44; Dir. of Industry, Ministry of Fuel 42-44; Dir. Venezuelan Fuel Corpn., 47-48; Pres., Mezeladora Mixta Listo Consolidada C.A., C.A. La Mezeladora, C.A. Agregados Hormigón, C.A. Productos Hormigón 44-61; Vice-Pres. and Dir. other companies 44-61; Minister of Finance, Venezuela 61-65; two Venezuelan decorations.

c/o Ministry of Finance, Caracas, Venezuela.

Germani, Gino; Argentine (b. Italian) sociologist; b. 4 Feb. 1911; ed. Univs. of Rome and Buenos Aires.

Research Assoc., Inst. of Sociology, Univ. of Buenos Aires 41-45; Prof. of Sociology, Colegio Libre de Estudios Superiores, Buenos Aires and Rosario (Argentina) 46-55; Prof., Dept. of Sociology, Univ. of Buenos Aires 55-66, Head of Dept. 57-62, Dir. Inst. of Sociology 55-66; Research Program Dir., Centro de Sociología Comparada, Inst. Torcuato Di Tella, Buenos Aires 64-66; Visiting Prof. of Sociology, Univ. of Chicago 59, Columbia Univ., N.Y. 64-65; First Monroe Gutman Prof. of Latin American Affairs, Harvard Univ. 66-; Vice-Pres. Int. Sociological Asscn. 62-66; mem. Int. Social Science Council 61-68; Pres. Asociación Sociológica Argentina 60-66; Fellow American Acad. of Arts and Sciences; mem. Latin American Social Science Council 67-.

Publs. *La Sociología Científica* 56, 62, *Estudios de Psicología Social* 56, *Estructura Social de la Argentina* 55, *Política y Massa* 61, *Política y Sociedad en una Epoca de Transición* 62, 64, 66, *La Sociología en la*

América Latina 64, 65, *Estudios de Sociología y de Psicología Social* 66.
Office: William James Hall 568, Harvard University, Cambridge, Mass. 02138; Home: 201 Highland Street, West Newton, Mass. 02160, U.S.A.
Telephone: 868-7600 (Office); 332-5989 (Home).

Germani, Fernando; Italian musician; b. 5 April 1906; ed. Rome Conservatoire and Pontifical Inst. of Sacred Music.
Professor of Organ Music at the Rome Conservatoire, Chigiana Music Acad. (Siena); recitals in the Americas, Australasia, South Africa, South America, Europe; Commdr. Order of St. Gregorius Magno; Commdr. Order of St. Sylvester; Knight Crown of Italy.
Publs. Revision of works of Girolamo Frescobaldi 36, *A Method of Organ Playing* 42.
Via delle Terme Deciane 11, Rome, Italy.

Germann, Frank E. E., A.B., DR. ès SC.; American chemist; b. 6 Dec. 1887; ed. Indiana, Wisconsin, Geneva, Berlin, Neuchâtel and Lausanne Univs.
Instructor at Geneva, Indiana and Cornell Univs. 12-18; Prof. Colorado School of Mines 18-19; Prof. of Chemistry Univ. of Colorado 19-56, Dir. Div. Physical Chemistry 19-56, Prof. of Chemistry Emeritus 56-; Pres. Colorado-Wyoming Acad. of Science 30-31 and Editor its journal 28-31; Vice-Pres. Colorado Section of American Chemical Society 33-35, mem. Council 36-38, Pres. 35-37; Vice-Pres. Southwestern and Rocky Mountain Div. American Asscn. for Advancement of Science 32-34, Pres. 36-38, Exec. Sec. 40-57; Consulting Chemist, Nat. Bureau of Standards Cryogenic Engineering Laboratories, Boulder, Colo. 56-; Fellow, American Asscn. for Advancement of Science (mem. Council 30-); Fellow, American Physical Society; Société Française de Physique (Life); mem. Geneva Chemical Society, Swiss Chemical Society; mem. Council American Asscn. Univ. Profs. 43-46; Société de Chimie-Physique; mem. Board of Govs. Int. Science Foundation.
Publs. *Boiling-Point Charts for Organic Compounds* 33, *Experimental Physical Chemistry* 50 (2nd edn. 53).
Home: 1800 Sunset Boulevard, Boulder, Colorado 80302; Office: University of Colorado, and National Bureau of Standards, Boulder, Colo., U.S.A.
Telephone: 442-5913.

Germanus, Gyula (Julius); Hungarian orientalist; b. 1884; ed. Univs. of Budapest, Istanbul, Vienna and Leipzig.
Lecturer at Oriental Acad. of Commerce 12, Univ. of Political Economy, Dept. of Oriental Sciences 29, Univ. of Santiniketan, Bengal 29-32; Sec. Hungarian P.E.N. Club 26-44; Prof. of Arab Language, Budapest Univ. 48-65; numerous journeys in Near and Far East; pilgrimage to Mecca 34; Visiting Lecturer Syrian, Egyptian, Moroccan and Indian Univs.; Corresp. mem. Arab Acad. of Cairo, Arab Acad. of Baghdad, Arab Acad. of Damascus; mem. Accad. del Mediterraneo (Italy).
Publs. *Evliya Celebi on 17th Century Guilds in Turkey* 07, *The Role of the Turks in Islam* 33-34, *Allah Akhbar* 36, *Sulle orme di Maometto* 38, *Az arab szellemiség megujhodása* (The Rebirth of Arab Mentality) 44, *Dichtkunst Ibn Rúmis* 57, Autobiography: *A félhold fakó fényében* (The Half-Moon's Dim Light) 58.
V. Petöfi tér 3, Budapest V, Hungary.

Germer, Lester Halbert, M.A., PH.D.; American physicist; b. 10 Oct. 1896; ed. Cornell and Columbia Univs.
Served U.S. Air Service 14-18 war; research physicist, Cornell Univ.; awarded Elliott Cresson Medal of Franklin Inst. 31; Fellow American Physical Soc., N.Y. Acad. of Sciences, and American Soc. for X-rays and Electron Diffraction; Vice-Pres. 43, Pres. 44, American Asscn. for the Advancement of Science;

research in electron diffraction, order-disorder phenomena, surface chemistry, contact physics, etc.
968 Long Hill Road, Millington, New Jersey, U.S.A.

Germi, Pietro; Italian film director; b. 14 Sept. 1914.
Gave up early studies in Acad. for Marine Captains, Genoa; took up acting in Rome, later became film dir.
Films include: *Il Testimone* (The Witness), *In Nome della Legge* (In the Name of the Law), *Il Cammino della Speranza* (The Road of Hope), *Il Ferroviere* (The Railroader), *L'Uomo di Paglia* (The Straw Man), *Divorzio all'Italiana* (Divorce Italian Style), *Sedotta e Abbandonata* (Seduced and Abandoned), *Signore e Signori* (Ladies and Gentlemen), *The Birds, the Bees and the Italians* 67.
Via Scipione Gaetano, Rome, Italy.

Gerot, Paul Sylvester; American businessman; b. 30 Oct. 1902; ed. Iowa Wesleyan Acad., and Coll. (Mt. Pleasant) and Northwestern Univ.
Vice-Pres. Pillsbury Co. 50, Exec. Vice-Pres. 51, Pres. 52-, Chair. 65-; Dir. Northwestern Nat. Bank, Northwest Bancorporation, Northwestern Bell Telephone Co., Minneapolis-Honeywell Regulator Co., J. F. Anderson Lumber Co., Abbot Hospital, Minneapolis; Trustee Cttee. for Econ. Development.
Office: Pillsbury Building, Minneapolis 2, Minn.; Home: Route 5, Box 556, Wayzata, Minn., U.S.A.

Gerstacker, Carl A.; American chemical executive; b. 6 Aug. 1916; ed. Univ. of Michigan.
Accounting Dept., Dowell Inc. 38-40; Chemical Engineer, Dow Chemical Co. 46-48, Dir. 48-, Treas. 49-59, Vice-Pres. 55-, mem. Exec. Cttee. 57-, Chair. Finance Cttee. 59-, Chair. Board of Dirs. 60-; official of other companies; Chair. Manufacturing Chemists' Asscn., Research Foundation of Nat. Asscn. for Mental Health, Export Expansion Council of U.S. Commerce Dept.; mem. U.S. Comm. UNESCO.
Dow Chemical Co., Midland, Michigan, U.S.A.
Telephone: 517-6360010.

Gerstenmaier, Eugen Karl Albrecht; German politician; b. 25 Aug. 1906; ed. Univs. of Tübingen, Zürich and Rostock.
Priv. dozent Berlin Univ. 37; Prof. staff Foreign Section, Evangelical Church; took part 20th July Plot 44, imprisoned, released by Allies 45; organised relief work of the Evangelische Kirche Deutschlands 45; mem. Synod 48-; mem. Bundestag 49-, Pres. 54-; mem. Council of Europe 50; Vice-Pres. C.D.U.; Pres. Deutsche-Afrika Gesellschaft.
Publs. *Die Kirche und die Schöpfung* 37, *Hilfe für Deutschland* 46, *Die Evangelische Kirche und ihre Sozialpolitik* 52, *Reden und Aufsätze* vol. 1 56, vol. 2 61, *Neuer Nationalismus?* 65.
Bundeshaus, Bonn, German Federal Republic.
Telephone: 02221-206-2900-01.

Gesing, Franciszek, LL.M., M.ECON.; Polish politician; b. 18 Jan. 1904; ed. Joannes Casimir Univ., Lvov.
Member Council of *Spolem* co-operative branch during Nazi occupation, and of the Underground authorities of the S.L. (Peasant Party) 43-44; worked in various banks after the liberation; mem. Voivodship People's Council in Cracow 45-; Chair. Z.S.L. (United Peasant Party) Voivodship Cttee. 57-62; Chair. Cen. Union of Agricultural Circles 62-; mem. of S.L. 31-39, P.S.L. 45-49, Z.S.L. 49-, Praesidium of Z.S.L. Cen. Cttee. 62-; mem. Seym 61-; mem. Council of State 65-; Order of the Banner of Labour, First Class 64, etc.
Zjednoizone Stronnictwo Ludowe, 4/8 Grzybowska, Warsaw, Poland.

Gesing, Roman; Polish politician; b. 23 Dec. 1903; ed. Lwów Polytechnic School.
Former forestry worker; mem. Gen. Council of People's Party and mem. Supreme Council of Peasants' Party until 39; mem. Resistance, Second World War; prisoner

in Auschwitz 42; Forestry and Wood Industry Dept., Head of Dept. 50-57; Vice-Minister of Forestry and Wood Industry 57-61, Minister 61-; mem. Seym; mem. Cen. Cttee. of United Peasants' Party.
Wawelska Street, 52/54 Warsaw, Poland.
Telephone: 214361.

Getman, General Andrei Lavrentievich; Soviet army officer; b. 03; ed. Military Acad. of Mechanisation.
Soviet Army 24-; mem. C.P.S.U. 27-; rose to Dep. Commdr. Tank Army, Second World War; Area Military Commdr. Mechanised Forces 45-48; Chief of Staff, Armoured Forces 48-54; Dep. Chief, Armoured Forces 54-56; Army Commdr. 56-58; Area Military Commdr. 58-64; Chair. DOSAAF (Voluntary Soc. for Helping Armed Forces) 64-; Deputy to Supreme Soviet U.S.S.R.; Cand. mem. Central Cttee. of C.P.S.U. 61-; Hero of the Soviet Union; awarded Order of Lenin (thrice), Order of Suvorov, Order of Bogdon Khmelnitsky, Order of the Red Banner (five times); Weapon of Honour with a Coat-of-Arms in Gold; Hon. K.B.E.
DOSAAF Central Committee, 88 Volokolamskoe Shosse, Moscow, U.S.S.R.

Getty, George Franklin, II; American businessman; b. 9 July 1924; ed. Princeton Univ.
Ind. oil operator, Calif., Texas 47-48; discovered South Crane oilfield, Texas 48; Man. Saudi Arabian Div., Pacific Western Oil Corpn. 49-50, Man. Mid-Continent Div. 51-52; Vice-Pres. Spartan Aircraft Co. 52-56; Pres. Minnehoma Insurance Co., Minnehoma Financial Co. 52-56; Exec. Vice-Pres. Pacific Western Oil Corpn. (the Getty Oil Co.) 55-56; Vice-Pres., Gen. Man., Eastern Div. Tidewater Oil Co. 56-58, Pres. 58-; Pres. Tulsa Boosters Inc. 54-55; Trustee, J. Paul Getty Museum.
4201 Wilshire Boulevard, Los Angeles, Calif. 90005, U.S.A.

Getty, Jean Paul; American oil executive; b. 15 Dec. 1892; ed. California and Oxford Univs.
President and Gen. Man. George F. Getty Inc. 30-33; Pres. Mission Corpn. 56-, Getty Oil Co. 48-; Officier Légion d'Honneur, Grande Médaille City of Paris (Silver), Benjamin Franklin Fellow R.S.A.
Publs. *A History of the Oil Business of George F. and J. Paul Getty* 40, *Europe in the Eighteenth Century* 41, *Collector's Choice* (with Ethel Levane) 55, *My Life and Fortunes* 63, *The Joys of Collecting* 65, *How to be Rich* 66.
17985 Pacific Coast Highway, Malibu, Calif., U.S.A.; Sutton Place, nr. Guildford, Surrey, England; Castello di Palo, Ladispoli, Rome, Italy.

Geyer, Albertus Lourens, M.A., PH.D.; South African diplomatist; b. 11 Aug. 1894; ed. Univs. of South Africa, Stellenbosch, and Berlin.
Teacher 14; Acting Prof. of History, Univ. of Stellenbosch 20; Asst. Editor *Die Burger* (Cape Town) 23, Editor 24; Editor-in-Chief, newspapers of Die Nasionale Pers Co., Cape Town 45; High Commr. for Union of South Africa in Great Britain 50-54; Hon. Ph.D. (Stellenbosch Univ.); Hon. Life Pres. S. African Bureau for Racial Affairs.
Publ. *Das wirtschaftliche System der niederländischen ostindischen Kompanie am Kap der Guten Hoffnung, 1785-1795*; co-editor *Die Geskiedenis van Suid-Afrika.*
P.O. Box 14, Barrydale, Cape Province, South Africa.

Geyer, Gerhard; German businessman; b. 5 Sept. 1897.
Chairman, Supervisory Board Esso A.G., Esso Tankschiff Reederei G.m.b.H., Gewerkschaft Brigitta, Gesellschaft für Kernenergieverwertung in Schiffbau und Schiffahrt m.b.H.; Deputy Chair. Supervisory Board Ruhrgas A.G.
Neuer Jungfernstieg 21, Hamburg 36, German Federal Republic.

Ghaffari, Abolghassem, D.SC., PH.D.; Iranian mathematician; b. 09; ed. Darolfonoun School, Teheran, and Univs. of Nancy, Paris, London, and Oxford.
Assoc. Prof. Teheran Univ. 37-42, Prof. of Mathematics 42-; Mathematics Research Asst. King's Coll. London 47-48; Research Fellow, Harvard 50-51, Research Assoc. Princeton 51-52; mem. Inst. for Advanced Study, Princeton 51-52; Senior mathematician, Nat. Bureau of Standards, Washington, D.C. 56-57; Aeronautical research scientist 57-64; Aerospace scientist NASA, Goddard Space Flight Center, Maryland 64-; Professional Lecturer in Mathematics and Statistics, American Univ. Wash., D.C. 58-62, and other American Univs.; mem. American, French and London Mathematical Socs.; American Astronomical Soc., Philosophical Soc. of Washington; Soc. of Engineering Science; Fellow N.Y. Acad. of Sciences 61 and Wash. Acad. of Sciences 63; American Asscn. for Advancement of Science 65; Orders of Homayoun, Danesh (1st class) and Sepass (1st class).
Publs. *Sur l'Equation Fonctionnelle de Chapman-Kolmogoroff* 36, *The Hodograph Method in Gas Dynamics* 50.
National Aeronautics and Space Administration, Goddard Space Flight Center, Greenbelt, Md., U.S.A.; and Shah Reza Avenue, 31 Ladan Street, Teheran, Iran.

Ghalen, Mohamed Mourad; United Arab Republic (Egyptian) diplomatist.
Ambassador to Congo Republic (Léopoldville) 61-62, to U.S.S.R. 63-.
Embassy of the United Arab Republic, 56 ulitsa Guerizena, Moscow, U.S.S.R.

Ghika, Nicolas; Greek painter and designer; b. 06; ed. Athens and Acad. Ranson, Paris.
Has designed décors, costumes and masks for plays and ballets; rep. at numerous exhibitions in Europe and N. America.
c/o Academy of Fine Arts, Athens, Greece.

Ghirshman, Roman; French archaeologist; b. 3 Oct. 1895; ed. Sorbonne, Paris and Ecole du Louvre.
Mem. French Archæological Mission in Iraq 30; Dir. similar mission in Iran 31; exploration of Seistan desert, Afghanistan 36; Head of French Archæological Del. in Afghanistan 41-43; mem. Inst. français d'archéologie orientale, Cairo 44-45; Dir. Suse Mission, Iran 46-67; Hon. Dir. French Archaeological Del. in Iran; Prof. Univ. of Aix-en-Provence; mem. Acad. des Inscriptions et Belles Lettres (three times prizeman); Officier Légion d'Honneur, Grand Officer Commdr. of the Iranian Orders; hon. degrees (Sorbonne and Univ. of Teheran).
Publs. *Fouille de Tepe Giyan* 36, *Fouilles de Sialk* (2 vols.) 38, 39, *Bégram-Histoire des Kouchans* 46, *Les Chionites-Hephtalites* 48, *Iran, des origines à l'Islam* 50, *Iran—La Perse ancienne* 2 vols., Collection "Univers des Formes" 62-64, and other works.
96 rue La Fontaine, Paris 16e, France.

Ghosh, Amalananda, M.A.; Indian archaeologist; b. 3 March 1910; ed. A.B. High School, Banaras, Queen's Coll., Banaras, and Univ. of Allahabad.
Asst. Superintendent, Archaeological Survey of India 37-44, Superintendent 44-50; Deputy Dir.-Gen. for Exploration, Archaeological Survey of India 50-52; Joint Dir.-Gen. of Archaeology in India, Archaeological Survey of India 52-53, Dir.-Gen. 53-68; mem. Perm. Council of Int. Congress for Prehistoric and Proto-historic Sciences; Corresp. mem. Int. Cttee. on Museums, Int. Cttee. on Monuments, Artistic and Historical Sites and Archaeological Excavation; mem. Int. Cttee. for Study of Megaliths; Hon. Fellow Soc. of Antiquaries of London; Fellow, Deutsches Archäologisches Inst.
c/o Office of Director-General of Archaeology in India, Janpath, New Delhi 11, India.
Telephone: 381228.

Ghosh, Devaprasad, M.A., B.L.; Indian lawyer, professor and politician; b. 15 March 1894; ed. City Coll., Calcutta, Presidency Coll., Calcutta and Ripon Law Coll., Calcutta.

Prof. of Mathematics, Ripon Coll., Calcutta 14-41; Advocate, Calcutta High Court 19; Principal Carmichael Coll., Rangpur, Bengal 41-50; Pres. All-Bengal Coll. and Univ. Teachers' Asscn. 43-44; Pres. All-Bengal Teachers' Asscn. 50-52; Fellow Calcutta Univ. 46-51 and 53-57; mem. Indian Parl. (Council of States) 52-54; Pres. West Bengal Jana Sangha 55-63; Vice-Pres. Bharatiya Jana Sangha 55, 60-63, Pres. 56-59.

Publs. include mathematical schoolbooks and a number of works in Bengali (some translated into English).

59B Upper Circular Road, Calcutta, 9, India.

Ghosh, Parimal, M.A.; Indian business executive and politician; b. 15 March 1917; ed. St. Paul's Coll., Univ. of Calcutta.

Dir. Himalay Paper & Board Mills Private Ltd., Himalay Paper (Machinery) Ltd., P. Ghosh & Co., Card Board and Printing & Processing Industries Ltd. until 67; mem. Lok Sabha 67-; Minister of State for Railways 67-.

20 Seven Tanks Lane, Calcutta 30, India.

Ghosh, Tushar Kanti, B.A.; Indian journalist; b. 4 Oct. 1899; ed. Calcutta Univ.

Editor *Amrita Bazar Patrika*; former Pres. Indian Journalists' Asscn.; Pres. Andhra Journalists' Conf., Guntur 37; All-India Printers' Conf., Poona 39; former Pres. Indian and Eastern Newspaper Society, All-India Newspaper Editors' Conf., United Press of India; Chair. Press Trust of India; founder *Jugantar*, Calcutta; Chair. Commonwealth Press Union, Indian Section; mem. Exec. Cttee., Int. Press Inst.; Padma Bhusan 64.

Patrika House, 14 Ananda Chatterjee Lane, Calcutta, India.

Ghoussein, Talat Al-; Kuwaiti diplomatist; b. 16 May 1924; ed. American Univ. of Cairo.

Foreign News Editor *As-Shaab* (Jaffa, Palestine) 46-47; Controller, Arab Bank Ltd., Jaffa, Palestine 47-48; Editor Foreign News and Dir. of English Section, Broadcasting Station of Jordan 48-49; Dir. Press and Public Information, Ministry of Foreign Affairs, Yemen 49-53; Sec. Gen., Development Board, Kuwait 53-60; Dep. Private Sec. to Emir of Kuwait 60-61; Minister-Counsellor, Kuwait Embassy, Washington 62-63, Ambassador of Kuwait to U.S.A. 63-.

2940 Tilden Street, N.W., Washington, D.C. 20008, U.S.A.

Ghulam Faruque, Khan Bahadur, C.I.E., O.B.E.; Pakistani official; b. 99; ed. M.A.O. Coll. Aligarh, India.

Asst. Traffic Superintendent, Eastern Railway (India) 21-29, District Superintendent 29-37; promoted to junior administrative post 37; Transport Advisory Officer, Railway Board, India 40-42; Controller of Coal Distribution 42-46; Transport Man., Superintendent and finally Gen. Man. East India Railway 46-48; Sec. Ministry of Industries, Govt. of Pakistan 48-49; Chair. Cotton Board and Jute Board 49-52; Chair. Pakistan Industrial Devt. Corpn. 52-58, Chair. of W. Pakistan Water and Power Devt. Authority 58-61; Gov. of E. Pakistan 62; Minister of Commerce 65-67; Hilal-e-Pakistan.

49 Clifton, Karachi 6, Pakistan.

Telephone: 53361; 50504.

Giacchero, Enzo, D.ENG.; Italian politician and administrator; b. 25 Feb. 1912; ed. Turin Polytechnic.

Prefect, Asti Province 45-46; Deputy to Constituent Assembly 46-48, to Chamber of Deputies 48-52; Pres. Federalist Group in Italian Parliament 47-52; Vice-Pres. European Parliament Union 47-51; Sec. External Affairs Comm., Chamber of Deputies and Vice-Pres. Christian Democrat Parliamentary Group 48-52; mem. Consultative Assembly, Council of Europe 49-52; Pres. Scientific and Cultural Affairs Comm. 52; mem.

High Authority of European Coal and Steel Community 52-59; Hon. Pres. European Federal Union 55; Gen. Sec. Nat. Cttee. for Celebration of Italian Unity 60-61; Vice-Pres. Alitalia; Knight Grand Cross, Italian Order of Merit, Silver Medal for Military Valour, Grand Officier de l'Ordre Granducal de la Couronne de Chêne (Luxembourg); Christian Democrat.

Publs. *Mezzogiorno nel mercato italiano* 58, *The Sources of Energy,* V.T.E.T. 62.

Via Ripalta 16, Pecetto, Turin, Italy.

Giacopini Zarraga, José Antonio; Venezuelan lawyer and oil executive; b. 4 Sept. 1915; ed. Colegio de la Salle and Universidad Central de Venezuela (Caracas).

Law practice 40-; Legal Adviser Ministry of Health 45-46, Office Dir. 46; Deputy, Constituent Nat. Assembly 46-; Sec. Revolutionary Govt. Military Junta 47-48; Gov. Amazonas Fed. Territory 48-49; Public Relations Dir. Royal Dutch/Shell Venezuela 49-57, mem. Board of Dirs. Compañia Shell de Venezuela and Asst. to Pres. 58-; Pres. Liga Naval de Venezuela; Founder and Prof. Public Relations Central Univ., Venezuela; mem. numerous legal and commercial socs. and numerous honours.

Cuartel Viejo a Pineda 33, Caracas; and Apartado 809, Caracas, Venezuela.

Giap, General Vo Nguyen: Viet-Namese army officer; b. 1912; ed. French lycée in Hué, and law studies at Univ. of Hanoi.

History teacher, Thang Long School, Hanoi; joined Viet-Nam C.P. in early 1930s; fled to China 39; helped organize Vietminh Front, Viet-Nam 41; Minister of Interior 45, became Commdr.-in-Chief of Vietminh Army 46; defeated French at Dien Bien Phu 54; now Deputy Prime Minister, Minister of Defence and Commdr.-in-Chief, North Viet-Nam; mem. Politburo Lao-Dong Party.

Publs. *People's War, People's Army, Big Victory, Great Task* 68.

Ministry of Defence, Hanoi, Democratic Republic of Viet-Nam.

Giauque, William Francis, B.S., PH.D.; American chemist; b. 12 May 1895; ed. Univ. of California.

Instructor in Chemistry Univ. of California 22-27, Asst. Prof. 27-30, Assoc. Prof. 30-34, Prof. of Chemistry 34-; mem. Nat. Acad. of Sciences 36-, American Acad. of Arts and Sciences 50-; mem. American Philosophical Society 40; awarded Chandler Medal of Columbia Univ. 36 for invention and first application of adiabatic demagnetization method of producing temperatures below 1° absolute, Elliott Cresson Medal of Franklin Inst. 37; discovered with H. L. Johnston, oxygen isotopes 17 and 18 by means of absorption of sunlight in earth's atmosphere; Nobel Prize for Chemistry 49; Willard Gibbs Medal 51; Gilbert N. Lewis Medal 55; Hon. D.Sc. (Columbia), Hon. LL.D. (Calif.).

2643 Benvenue Avenue, Berkeley 4, Calif., U.S.A.

Gibb, Sir Hamilton Alexander Rosskeen, Kt., M.A., LL.D., F.B.A.; British university professor; b. 2 Jan. 1895; ed. Royal High School, Edinburgh, Edinburgh and London Univs.

Lecturer, School of Oriental Studies, Univ. of London 21; Prof. of Arabic, Univ. of London 30-37; Laudian Prof. of Arabic, Univ. of Oxford 37-55; Univ. Prof. Harvard Univ. 55-64; Hon. Litt.D.

Publs. *The Arab Conquests in Central Asia* 23, *Arabic Literature* 26, *Travels of Ibn Battuta* 29, *Studies in Contemporary Arabic Literature* 28-33; Editor *Whither Islam?* 32; *Modern Trends in Islam* 47, *Mohammedanism* 49, *Islamic Society and the West* (with Harold Bowen) 50, 57, *Studies on the Civilisation of Islam* 62.

86 Norreys Road, Cumnor, Oxford, England.

Gibberd, Sir Frederick, Kt., C.B.E.; British architect; b. 7 Jan. 1908; ed. King Henry VIII School, Coventry. Architectural town-planning and landscape design

practice in London 30-, Harlow New Town 56-; fmr. Principal, Architectural Asscn. School of Architecture; Assoc. Royal Acad.; Fellow, Royal Inst. of British Architects, Soc. of Industrial Artists; mem. Town Planning Inst., Inst. Landscape Architects, Royal Fine Art Comm.; Architect-Planner Harlow New Town 47-; Planning Consultant Nuneaton 48-, Doncaster and Hull 54-, Leamington Spa 57-, Swindon 57-, Santa Teresa, Venezuela 59-.
Works include: Somerford Estate (Hackney), Scunthorpe steel works, technical colls. at Hull, Huddersfield and numerous schools, London Airport, Belfast Hospital, Nat. Dock Labour Board offices (London), civic centres for Doncaster, Edmonton, Harlow, Hull and St. Albans, nuclear power stations at Hinkley Point and Sizewell; landscape design includes Queen's Gardens, Hull, and reservoirs at Derwent and Tryweryn; winner of open competitions for Metropolitan Roman Catholic Cathedral, Liverpool 60 (opened 67) and new monastery, Douai Abbey 61.
Publ. *The Architecture of England, Town Design* 53.
Office: 8 Percy Street, London, W.1; Home: 49 Downshire Hill, London, N.W.3, England.

Gibbons, Stella Dorothea (Mrs. Allan B. Webb), F.R.S.L.; British poet and novelist; b. 5 Jan. 1902; ed. North London Collegiate School and Univ. Coll., London.
Journalist 22-33, British United Press, *Evening Standard, The Lady.*
Publs. *The Mountain Beast* (poems) 30, *Cold Comfort Farm* (Femina Vie Heureuse Prize 33) 32, *Bassett* 34, *The Priestess* (poems) 34, *Enbury Heath* 35, *The Untidy Gnome* 35, *Miss Linsey and Pa* 36, *Roaring Tower* (short stories) 37, *Nightingale Wood* 38, *The Lowland Venus* (poems) 38, *My American* 39, *Christmas at Cold Comfort Farm* (short stories) 40, *The Rich House* 41, *Ticky* 43, *The Bachelor* 44, *Westwood* 46, *The Matchmaker* 49, *Conference at Cold Comfort Farm* 49, *Collected Poems* 50, *The Swiss Summer* 51, *Fort of the Bear* 53, *Beside the Pearly Water* (short stories) 54, *The Shadow of a Sorcerer* 55, *Here Be Dragons* 56, *White Sand and Grey Sand* 58, *A Pink Front Door* 59, *The Weather at Tregulla* 62, *The Wolves were in the Sledge* 64, *The Charmers* 65, *Starlight* 67.
19 Oakeshott Avenue, Highgate, London, N.6, England.
Telephone: 01-340-2566.

Gibbs, Hon. Sir Geoffrey Cokayne, K.C.M.G.; British banker; b. 20 July 1901; ed. Eton Coll., and Christ Church, Oxford.
With Ministry of Econ. Warfare 39-45; Dir. Antony Gibbs & Sons Ltd., Chair. 66-; Chair. Australia and New Zealand Bank Ltd. and Barclays Overseas Devt. Corpn.; Fmr. Chair. Advisory Council Export Credits Guarantee Dept., Chair. Managing Trust, Nuffield Foundation, Imperial Relations Trust, Nat. Corpn. for Care of the Aged; mem. Court of Grocers' Company (Master 38-39); Hon. D.C.L. (Oxford).
The Manor House, Clifton Hampden, Abingdon-on-Thames, England.

Gibbs, Sir Humphrey Vicary, K.C.M.G., K.C.V.O., O.B.E.; British Crown Governor; b. 22 Nov. 1902; ed. Eton Coll., and Trinity Coll., Cambridge.
Farmer, Bulawayo 28-; Gov. Southern Rhodesia 60-; Acting Gov.-Gen. Fed. of Rhodesia and Nyasaland 63-64.
Government House, Salisbury; P/Bag 52L, Bonisa Farm, Bulawayo, Rhodesia.

Gibbs, R. Darnley, M.SC., PH.D.; Canadian botanist; b. 30 June 1904; ed. Univ. Coll., Southampton, and McGill Univ.
Mem. McGill Univ. staff, Demonstrator to Assoc. Prof. of Botany 25-55, Prof. of Botany 55-65, Macdonald

Prof. of Botany 65-; fmr. Pres. Fraser-Hickson Inst. Montreal; Fellow, Royal Society of Canada (Pres. Section V 53-54); Fellow, Linnean Society of London.
Publs. *A Modern Biology* (with E. J. Holmes) 37, *Botany, An Evolutionary Approach* 50.
Apartment 1007, 1400 Pine Avenue W., Montreal 25, Quebec, Canada.
Telephone: 845-0592.

Gibrat, Robert Pierre Louis, LIC. ès SC., DR. en DROIT; French engineer; b. 23 March 1904; ed. Ecole Polytechnique, Ecole Nat. Supérieure des Mines and the Sorbonne.
Dir. of Electricity, Ministry of Public Works 40-42; Sec. of State for Communications March-Sept. 42; Consulting Engineer Electricité de France (Tidal Energy Plants) 42-; Dir.-Gen. Groupement pour l'Industrie Atomique 55-; Chair. Société pour l'Industrie Atomique, SOCIA; Consulting Engineer Centrales Thermiques 42-; fmr. Pres. Soc. Française des Electriciens; mem. Int. Inst. of Statistics; Fellow Int. Econometric Soc.; fmr. mem. Scientific Cttee., Commissariat Energie Atomique; fmr. Pres. Soc. des Ingénieurs Civils; fmr. Pres. Asscn. technique pour l'Energie nucléaire; fmr. Pres. Scientific and Technical Cttee. Euratom; Pres. Soc. de Statistique de Paris.
Publ. *Les Inégalités Economiques.*
105 rue du Ranelagh, Paris 16e, France.
Telephone: BAL 83-40 (Office); JAS 13-47 (Home).

Gibson, Alexander Drummond, C.B.E., L.R.A.M., A.R.C.M., A.R.C.O.; British conductor; b. 11 Feb. 1926; ed. Dalziel School, Glasgow Univ., Royal Scottish Acad. of Music, Royal Coll. of Music, London, Mozarteum, Salzburg, and Accademia Chigiano, Siena.
Royal Corps of Signals 44-48; studied Royal Coll. of Music 48-51; Asst. Conductor B.B.C. Scottish Orchestra 52-54; Staff Conductor Sadler's Wells Opera 54-56, Musical Dir. 57-59; Guest Conductor Royal Opera House, Covent Garden 57-58; Musical Dir. and Principal Conductor Scottish Nat. Orchestra 59-; Founder, Artistic Dir. and Principal Conductor of Scottish Opera 62-; Guest Conductor all major symphony orchestras of Great Britain and many in Europe and America; Hon. LL.D. (Aberdeen).
14 Westbourne Gardens, Glasgow, W.2, Scotland.
Telephone: Glasgow Western 6668.

Gibson, Col. the Hon. Colin William George, P.C. (Can.), Q.C., M.C., V.D.; Canadian jurist; b. 16 Feb. 1891; ed. Royal Military Coll., Kingston, Osgoode Hall, Toronto.
Served Royal Fusiliers 14-19; awarded Ordre de Léopold and Croix de Guerre; practised Law in Hamilton, Ontario; commanded Royal Hamilton Light Inf. 29-34; 4th Inf. Brigade 35-38, Hamilton Garrison 39-40; six times mem. of Canadian rifle team to Bisley; Hon. A.D.C. to Lords Bessborough and Tweedsmuir when Govs.-Gen. of Canada; elected M.P. 40, 45 and 49; Min. of Nat. Revenue 40-45; Min. of Nat. Defence for Air 45-46; Sec. of State of Canada 46-49; Minister of Mines and Resources 49-50; Judge of Court of Appeal, Ont. 50-65; Commdr. Order of Polonia Restituta 46; Chair. of Council, Dominion of Canada Rifle Asscn. 28-48, Pres. 52-54; Pres. Canadian Citizenship Council 52-54; Vice-Pres. Nat. Rifle Asscn. (G.B.) 51-; Hon. LL.D. (Royal Mil. Coll.) 65.
"Oxley", Ancaster, Ontario, Canada.

Gibson, Joe; American business executive; b. 11 June 1901; ed. Gates Business Coll.
Rath Packaging Co., Waterloo, Iowa 21-, successively clerk, book-keeper, Chief Accountant, Controller, Sec., Exec. Vice-Pres. 56-60, Pres. 60-63, Pres. and Chief Exec. Officer 63-65, Chair. 65-.
221 Byrnes Drive, Waterloo, Iowa, U.S.A.

Gichuru, James Samuel; Kenyan teacher and politician; b. 14; ed. Kikuyu High School and Makerere Coll. Uganda.

Teacher Kikuyu High School 35-40; Headmaster Church of Scotland Mission School, Kikuyu 40-50; Pres. Kenya African Union 44-47; Chief, Dagoretti location 50-52; under restriction order during state of emergency 55-60; teacher Roman Catholic secondary school, Githunguri 58-60; Pres. Kenya African Nat. Union (KANU) 60-61, Vice-Pres. 66-; M.P. 61-; Minister of Finance, April 62-63, of Finance and Econ. Planning 63, and Dec. 64-.

Ministry of Finance, Nairobi; Thogoto, Kiambu, Kenya.

Gideonse, Harry David, B.S., M.A., LL.D.; American economist; b. 17 May 1901; ed. Columbia and Geneva Univs.

Lecturer in Economics Columbia Univ. 24-26; Dir. of int. student work Geneva 26-28; Asst. Prof. of Economics Rutgers Univ. 28-30; Assoc. Prof. of Economics Univ. of Chicago 30-38; Prof. of Economics Columbia Univ. 38-39; Pres. Brooklyn Coll. New York City 39-66; Chancellor, New School for Social Research, New York City 66-; Pres. Wilkie Memorial Building of Freedom House, Pres. Freedom House; American Editor *Revue Economique Internationale*, Brussels.

Publs. *Transfert des Réparations et Plan Dawes* 28, *The International Bank* 30, *War Debts* 33, *The Higher Learning in a Democracy* 37, *The Commodity Dollar* 37, *Organised Scarcity and Public Policy* 39; joint author: *United States Foreign Policy—Its Organisation and Control* 52, *Against the Running Tide* 67.

New School for Social Research, 66 West 12 Street, N.Y., N.Y.10011, U.S.A.

Gielen, Michael Andreas; Austrian conductor and composer; b. 20 July 1927; ed. Univ. of Buenos Aires; studied composition under E. Leuchter and J. Polnauer.

Pianist in Buenos Aires; on music staff of Teatro Colón 47-51; with Vienna State Opera 51-60, perm. conductor 54-60; First Conductor, Royal Swedish Opera, Stockholm 60-65.

Kirchweg 36, 5022 Junkersdorf bei Köln, German Federal Republic.

Gielgud, Sir (Arthur) John, Kt., D.LITT., LL.D. (brother of Val Gielgud, *q.v.*); British actor and theatrical producer; b. 14 April 1904; ed. Westminster. First stage appearance at Old Vic 21; Plays acted in include: Shakespeare's plays, Restoration comedies, *The Constant Nymph, The Good Companions, Richard of Bordeaux, The Potting Shed, Ivanov*; Productions include: Shakespeare's plays, Restoration drama, *The Importance of Being Earnest, The School for Scandal, The Three Sisters, Dear Brutus, The Circle, The Heiress, The Lady's not for Burning, Ivanov*; Plays directed include: *A Day by the Sea, The Chalk Garden, Nude with Violin, Five Finger Exercise, The Last Joke, Big Fish, Little Fish, The School for Scandal, Halfway Up the Tree*; Films played in include: *The Barretts of Wimpole Street, St. Joan, Julius Caesar, Richard III, Becket, The Loved One, Chimes at Midnight, Mister Sebastian, The Charge of the Light Brigade*; Operas directed: *The Trojans* (Berlioz), *A Midsummer Night's Dream* (Britten); Shakespeare recital: *Ages of Man* in Europe, America and Australasia.

Publs. *Early Stages* 38, *Stage Directions* 63, 64. 16 Cowley Street, London, S.W.1, England.

Gielgud, Val Henry, C.B.E. (brother of Sir John Gielgud, *q.v.*); British writer; b. 28 April 1900; ed. Rugby and Oxford Univ.

Actor, free-lance journalist, private sec. 21-28; joined staff of *Radio Times* 28; Head of Drama B.B.C. 29-52, of Sound Drama 52-63.

Publs. *Black Gallantry* 28, *Chinese White* (a play) 28,

Gathering of Eagles 29, *Imperial Treasure* 30, *Under London* 30, *The Broken Men* 31, *How to Write Broadcast Plays* 32, *Death at Broadcasting House* 33 (with Eric Maschwitz), *Gravelhanger* 34, *Death as an Extra* 35 (with Eric Maschwitz), *Outrage in Manchukuo* 37, *Death in Budapest* 37 (with Eric Maschwitz), *The Red Account* 38, *Punch and Judy* (a play) 38, *The First Television Murder* 40, *Beyond Dover* 41, *Confident Morning* 43, *Radio Theatre* 46, *Years of the Locust* 47, *The Right Way to Radio Playwriting* 48, *Fall of a Sparrow* 49, *Special Delivery* 50, *One Year of Grace* 50, *Party Manners* (play) 50, *Iron Curtain* (play) 51, *Poison in Jest* (play), *The High Jump* 53, *The Bombshell* (play) 53, *Cat* 55, *Mediterranean Blue* (play) 56, *British Radio Drama, 1952-1956* 57, *Gallows' Foot* 58, *To Bed at Noon* 60, *And Died So?* 61, *The Goggle-Box Affair* 63, *Years in a Mirror* 65, *Prinvest-London* 65, *Cats, A Personal Anthology* 66, *Conduct of a Member* 67.

Wychwood, Barcombe, Sussex, England.
Telephone: Barcombe 268.

Gierek, Edward; Polish politician; b. 13; ed. Cracow Acad. of Mining and Metallurgy.

Lived in Belgium and France before Second World War; organiser of Polish resistance groups in Belgium during German occupation; after the war Chair. Nat. Council of Poles in Belgium and one of the organisers of the Polish Workers' Party and Union of Polish Patriots in Belgium; returned to Poland 48; First Sec. Katowice Voivodship Cttee., Polish United Worker's Party; Dep. to Seym (Parl.) 57-; Sec. Central Cttee. Politburo, Polish United Workers' Party 59-.

The Seym, Warsaw, Poland.

Gierster, Hans; German musical director; b. 12 Jan. 1925; ed. Musikhochschule, Munich, and Mozarteum, Salzburg.

Formerly Musical Dir. Freiburg-im-Breisgau Municipal Theatres; Gen. Musical Dir. City of Nuremberg Oct. 65-, concurrently Perm. Dir. Munich State Opera; Regular Dir. Munich Opera Festival 64-, Schwetzinger Festival 64; Guest appearance with Bavarian State Opera with *Cosi Fan Tutte*, Edinburgh Festival 65; presented *The Magic Flute*, Glyndebourne 66; has conducted Berlin Philharmonic Orchestra, Bavarian State Orchestra, London Philharmonic Orchestra, Vienna Symphony Orchestra and Bamberg Symphony Orchestra.

Stadtische Bühnen Nürnberg-Fürth, 8500 Nuremberg, Lessingstrasse 1, German Federal Republic.

Gieysztor, Aleksander; Polish historian; b. 17 July 1916; ed. Warsaw Univ.

Adjunct and Docent Warsaw Univ. 45-49, Prof. 49-, Dir. of Research into origins of Polish State 49-53, Pro-Rector 56-59, Dir. Historical Inst. 55-; Pres. Univ. Comm. of State Educ. Council 60-; mem. Bureau Int. Cttee. of Historical Sciences 65-.

Publs. Works on medieval history.
Wilcza 8/20, Warsaw, Poland.
Telephone: 28-41-38.

Giffen, Albert Egges van, DR.SS.; Netherlands archæologist; b. 84; ed. State Univ. of Groningen.

Asst., State Univ. of Groningen 11; Keeper State Museum of Antiquities, Leyden 12-14; Keeper Zoological Laboratory, State Univ. of Groningen, Provincial Museum of Drenthe and Municipal and Provincial Museum, Groningen 17; Dir. Biological-Archæological Inst., State Univ. of Groningen 20, Lecturer in Prehistory and Germanic Archæology 30, Extra. Prof. 39, Ord. Prof. 43-45, Extra. Prof. Univ. of Amsterdam 41-43 and 46-54; Govt. Adviser 55-; Gold Medal, Society of Antiquaries, London 51; Knight of Netherlands Lion; Chevalier de la Légion d'Honneur.

Publs. *De hunebedden in Nederland,* I 25, II 27, *Atlas,* I and II 25, *Die Bauart der Einzelgräber: Beitrag zur Kenntnis der älteren individuellen Grabhügelstrukturen*

in den Niederlanden 30, *Jaarverslagen van de Vereniging voor Terpenonderzoek 1-37*, 17-53, *Oudheidkundige aantekeningen over Drentse vondsten, Nieuwe Drentse Volksalmanak* 18-54, *Opgravingen in Drentse, een handboek voor het kennen van het Drentse leven in voorbije eeuwen* (pp. 393-628) 44.
Zwolle, Weteringpark 7, Zalnéflat 62, Netherlands.
Telephone: 0-5200-13943.

Gil Preciado, Prof. Juan; Mexican agriculturist; b. 26 June 1909; ed. Colegio Internacional, Guadalajara.
Director Primary School, Octolán 27-28; Army Major; Dir. Primary School of Mascota; Sec. and Prof. of Mathematics, Polytechnic School, Univ. of Guadalajara; Sec. in Govt. of Baja California Sur, later, Govt. official; Head of Extension and founder of Peasant Faculty, Univ. of Guadalajara; Organizing Sec. CNOP; Deputy of Congress 40; Dir. of Planning, Dept. of Agriculture 43-47; Chief of Information for Mexican-North American Comm. for the eradication of foot and mouth disease 47, Sec. of Comm. 48; Deputy of Congress for Jalisco 53; Pres. Regional Cttee. of Partido Revolucionario Institucional (PRI) 53-56; Municipal Pres. of Guadalajara 56-59; Gov. State of Jalisco 59-66; Sec. for Agriculture and Cattle 66-.
Secretaría de Agricultura y Ganadería, Mexico D.F., Mexico.

Gil Robles, José Maria; Spanish lawyer and politician; b. 99.
Leader, Spanish Christian Democrat Party; mem. Privy Council of Don Juan, Pretender to Spanish Throne; exiled 62.
Living abroad.

Gilbert, Carl Joyce; American lawyer and business executive; b. 3 April 1906; ed. Univ. of Virginia and Harvard Univ.
Admitted to Massachusetts Bar 31, with Ropes, Gray, Boyden and Perkins 31-48; U.S. Army 41-46; Vice-Pres. The Gillette Co., Boston 48-56, Pres. 56-58, Chair. of Board 58-66, Chair. Exec. Cttee. 66-; Dir. of other companies.
The Gillette Co., 3900 Prudential Tower, Boston 02199, Massachusetts, U.S.A.

Gilbert, Ian H. G.; British business executive; b. 25 Nov. 1910; ed. Bradfield Coll., Berkshire.
Deloitte, Plender, Griffiths & Co. (Chartered Accountants) 30-38; Accountant and later Sec. The Leopoldina Railway Co. Ltd., London 38-51; Dir. Bryant & May Ltd. 51-55, Managing Dir. 55-64, Chairman 64-; Dir. British Match Corpn. Ltd. 53-64, Deputy Chair. 64-; Chair. Bryant & May (Latin America) Ltd. 64-; Airscrew-Weyroc Ltd. 65-; Chair. British Moulded Fibre Ltd. 63.
45 Belgrave Mews North, London, S.W.1, England.

Gilbert, Milton, M.A., PH.D.; American economist; b. 8 April 1909; ed. Temple Univ., and Univ. of Pennsylvania.
Editor *Survey of Current Business*, U.S. Dept. of Commerce 38-41; Chief Nat. Income Div., U.S. Dept. of Commerce 41-51; Dir. of Statistics and Nat. Accounts, OEEC 51-55, Dir. of Economics and Statistics 55-60; Bank for International Settlements, Econ. Adviser 60-; Fellow American Statistical Asscn.
Publs. *Currency Depreciation and Monetary Policy* 39, *An International Comparison of National Products and the Purchasing Power of Currencies* (with Irving B. Kravis) 54.
Bank for International Settlements, Centralbahnstr. 7, Basle, Switzerland.

Gilbert, Pierre-Eugène, L. ès L., L. en D.; French diplomatist; b. 12 Jan. 1907; ed. Univ. de Paris à la Sorbonne and Ecole des Langues Orientales.
Ministry of Foreign Affairs Paris 32-33; Sec. Interpreter

Far East, successively at Foochow, Yünnanfu, Peking and Nanking 33-37; mem. of French Del. Brussels Conf. 37; Embassy Shanghai 37-39; Ministry of Foreign Affairs Paris 39; later at Vancouver and Helsinki; joined Free French 40, Lieut.-Commdr. R.N. 40-44; dismissed and deprived of nationality by Vichy; Commissariat of Foreign Affairs Algiers 44; after Liberation mem. Purge Comm. Ministry of Foreign Affairs, Paris; Govt. Commr. at sessions of Council of State 45-47; Minister to Thailand 47-49, Ambassador to Peru 49-52; Ambassador to Israel 53-59; Diplomatic counsellor 59-61; Président-Directeur Général Soc. de Gestion et d'Expansion Electronique (Gexelec) 61-; Commandeur de la Légion d'Honneur, Croix de Guerre, Médaille de la Résistance.
48 rue Boissière, Paris 16e, France.

Gilchrist, Sir Andrew Graham, K.C.M.G.; British diplomatist; b. 19 April 1910; ed. Edinburgh Acad., and Exeter Coll., Oxford.
Siam Branch, British Consular Service 33-36, 38-41, also served Paris, Marseilles, Morocco; Army service, S.E. Asia 44-46; Foreign Office 46-51; Consul-Gen., Stuttgart 51-54; Foreign Office Counsellor, Staff of U.K. Commr.-Gen. for S.E. Asia, Singapore 54-56; Ambassador to Iceland 56-59; Consul-Gen., Chicago 60-63; Amb. to Indonesia 63-66; Asst. Under-Sec. Commonwealth Office 66-67; Amb. to Ireland 67-.
British Embassy, Dublin, Ireland.

Gilchrist, Huntington, A.M., PH.D.; American business executive and diplomatist; b. 16 Nov. 1891; ed. Williams Coll., Harvard and Columbia Univs.
Instructor, Anglo-Chinese Coll., Foochow 13-14; Peking Univ. 14-15; research in govt., China and Japan 13-15; served U.S. Army 18-19; attached to American Comm. to Negotiate Peace, Paris 19-20; Personal Asst. to Under-Sec.-Gen. of L.N. 19-20, L.N. Secretariat 19-28, Mandates Section 25-28; Exec. in chemical industry in U.S. and Europe 28-49; Man. Dir. Cyanamid Products Ltd., London 35-40; Exec. American Cyanamid Co. 40-49; Dir. Industry Div., European H.Q., Marshall Plan 49-50; ECA (later MSA and FOA) chief for Belgium and Luxembourg 50-55; Resident Rep. UN Technical Assistance Board, Karachi 55-57; Sec.-Gen. UNRRA Council, Montreal 44; on staff San Francisco Conf. 45, UN Prep. Comm. and 1st Gen. Ass. London and N.Y. 45 and 46; mem. Board of Trustees, Brookings Inst. 46-, Vice-Chair. 49-55; Dir. Inst. of Pacific Relations 45-47, Int. Chair. 47-50; Trustee, Woodrow Wilson Foundation 48-53, and Belgian-American Educational Foundation 53-; Chair. Advisory Council Columbia Univ. Graduate School of Social Work 59-62; Vice-Chair. and Chair. Exec. Cttee. Int. Schools Foundation 59-60, Chair. 60-63; mem. Board of Trustees, Lingnan Univ. 47-; Chair. Exec. Cttee. 67-; Trustee, Storm King School 59-62, 66-; mem. Council on Foreign Relations N.Y.C. 29-.
Publ. *The Governor's Budget in Maine* 17.
Ridgebury Road, Ridgefield, Conn., U.S.A.

Gilels, Emil Grigorevich; Soviet pianist; b. 19 Oct. 1916; ed. Odessa Musical and Dramatic Inst., and Moscow Conservatoire.
First Prize, All-Russia Music Competition 33; Prof. Moscow Conservatoire before Second World War and 54-; European concert tours 45-, U.S. and Mexico 55, U.S. 60; People's Artist of the U.S.S.R.; State Prize 46, Lenin Prize 62.
Moscow State Conservatoire 13, Ul. Herzena, Moscow, U.S.S.R.

Giliarov, Merkury Sergeyevich; Soviet entomologist; b. 1912; ed. Kiev Univ.
Research Assoc., U.S.S.R. Inst. of Sugar Industry 33-34, Ukrainian Research Station *Kauchukonos* 34-36, Inst. of Rubber-bearing Plants 36-44, Inst. of Morphology of

Animals, U.S.S.R. Acad. of Sciences 44-; Prof. 49; Corresp. mem. U.S.S.R. Acad. of Sciences 66-; State Prize 51.
Publs. Works on harmful insects living in soil, agrotechnical methods of fighting them.
U.S.S.R. Academy of Sciences, 14 Lenin Prospekt, Moscow, U.S.S.R.

Gill, Evan William Thistle, B.SC.; Canadian diplomatist; b. 2 Nov. 1902; ed. McGill Univ.
Engaged in mining and business 25-40; served army 40-45; Sec. of Cabinet Defence Cttee. and various other Cabinet cttees. 45-50; Counsellor to Canadian High Commr. in United Kingdom and Alternative Rep. on NATO Defence Production Board 50-51; Chief of Personnel, Dept. of External Affairs 52-53; High Commr. for Canada in Union of South Africa 54-57, Ghana 57-59; Asst. Under-Sec. of State for External Affairs 59-62; High Commr. for Canada in Australia 62-65; Ambassador to Ireland 65-.
Canadian Embassy, 10 Clyde Road, Ballsbridge, Dublin, Ireland.

Gill, Naranjan Singh; Indian diplomatist; b. 15 Jan. 1906; ed. Prince of Wales Royal Indian Military Coll. at Dehra Dun, and Royal Military Coll., Sandhurst.
Commissioned Indian Army 25, Major 40, acting Lieut.-Col. 42; Malayan Campaign 40-42; Indian Nat. Army, imprisoned, Singapore 42-45, retd. 46; Pres. Sikh Community 46; worked for Indian Nat. Congress and farmers' movement 47-54; Ambassador to Ethiopia 55-60, to Thailand 60-64, to Mexico, Cuba and Panama 64-.
Indian Embassy, Mexico City, Mexico; Majitha, District Amritsar, Punjab, India.

Gillard, (Frank) Francis George, C.B.E., B.SC.; b. 1 Dec. 1908; British radio administrator; ed. St. Luke's Coll., Exeter.
Schoolmaster 31-41; B.B.C. War Corresp. 41-45; B.B.C. W. Region Programme Dir. 45-55; Chief Asst. Dir. of Sound Broadcasting 55-56; Controller W. Region 56-63; Dir. of Sound Broadcasting Aug. 63-.
Office: B.B.C., Broadcasting House, London, W.1; Home: Flat 57, 49 Hallam Street, London, W.1, and Poole Farm, Wellington, Somerset, England.
Telephone: 01-580-4468 (Office); 01-580-3960 and Wellington 2442 (Home).

Gillemot, László; Hungarian mechanical engineer; b. 1912.
Rector of Budapest Technical Univ. 54-57; Dir. of Metal Industry Research Inst.; Prof. Technical Univ. of Budapest; mem. Hungarian Acad. of Sciences; Kossuth Prizes 49, 57; Commdrs. Degree of Medal of Merit for Scientific Research, Acad. Française 66.
Major subjects of study: the material structure of metals with reference to fracture energy and to welding technology; discovered new features relating to reaction kinetics in Titan production.
Technical Univ. of Budapest and Research Institute of the Metal Industry, Fehérvári Str. 144, Budapest, Hungary.
Telephone: 268-272 and 258-608.

Gillen, John Stewart; American newspaper editor; b. 29 Jan. 1914.
Worked for *Philadelphia Inquirer* 37-, Man. Ed. 54-.
930 Remington Road, Wynnewood, Pa., U.S.A.

Gillen, Stanley James, B.B.A.; American motor executive; b. 10 Aug. 1911; ed. St. Fredrick's High School, Pontiac, Michigan, U.S.A., and Univ. of Detroit.
Financial Analyst, Fisher Body Division, Gen. Motors Corpn. 33-47; Contract Administrator, Defense Products, Ford Motor Co., U.S.A. 47-48, Controller, Steel Div. 48-55, Controller, Tractor and Implement Div. 55-56, Asst. Gen. Man. Steel Div. 56-60, Gen. Man. Steel Div. 60-61, Gen. Man. Gen. Parts Div. 61-65; Chair. Autolite Motor Products Ltd. 62-65; Man. Dir. and

Chief Exec. Officer, Ford of Britain 65-67; Vice-Pres. (Manufacturing) Ford of Europe 67-; Dir. Ford Credit Co. Ltd., Henry Ford and Son Ltd., Cork, Ireland; mem. British Manufacturers Section Cttee. of Soc. of Motor Manufacturers and Traders, Soc. of Automotive Engineers.
St. Leonards, Ingatestone, Essex, England.

Gillés, Daniel; Belgian writer; b. 1917; ed. law studies.
Prix Rossel (Belgium); Grand prix de la critique littéraire (France) 67.
Publs. include: *Jeton de présence, le Coupon 44, les Brouillards de Bruges, l'Etat de grâce, la Termitière, Mort-la-Douce* (stories); biographies: *Tolstoi, D. H. Lawrence ou le puritain scandaleux.*
c/o René Julliard, 30 rue de la Université, Paris 7e, France.

Gillet, Guillaume; French architect; b. 20 Nov. 1912; ed. Ecole Nat. Supérieure des Beaux Arts, Paris.
Premier Grand Prix de Rome 46; Chief Architect, Bâtiments Civils et Palais Nationaux 54-; Prof., Ecole nationale supérieure des beaux-arts 53-; Consulting Architect to Ministry of Building; Head Architect, French Section, Brussels Int. Exhibition 58; Head of UNESCO Town-Planning Mission to Israel; mem. Acad. des Beaux Arts 68; Commdr. Ordre des Arts et Lettres 66, Ordre de la Couronne (Belgium) 58, Chevalier Légion d'Honneur 59, etc.
17 rue Bonaparte, Paris 6e, and 10 rue des Nonnains-d'Hyère, Paris 4e, France.
Telephone: ARC 44-17 and ARC 85-36.

Gillet, Jean-François; French lawyer and administrator; b. 23; ed. Secondary School, Limoges, and Univ. of Poitiers.
Barrister, Limoges Appeal Court 45-49; Gen. Sec. Grand Council of French Equatorial Africa 49-59; Gen. Sec. Chief of State's Conf., Equatorial Africa 59; mem. Board of Dirs. of the Equatorial Transport Agency 59-; Admin., Central African Higher Educ. Foundation 62-; Auditor Central Bank of Equatorial countries and Cameroon 63-; Technical Adviser to the Gen. Sec. of Central African Econ. and Customs Union 66; several decorations.
Conférence des Chefs d'Etat de L'Afrique Equatoriale, P.O.B. 970, Bangui, Central African Republic.

Gillet, Robert, L. ès L., L. en D.; French diplomatist; b. 17 April 1912; ed. Ecole Libre des Sciences Politiques, and Oxford Univ.
Attaché, Ankara 41-43; Deputy Dir. at Ministry of Foreign Affairs (Econ. and Finance Section) 45-51; Counsellor, Madrid 51-53, Cairo 53-55; Minister Tunis 55-57; Technical Counsellor Minister of Foreign Affairs 57-58; Dir. Office of M. Couve de Murville, Ministry of Foreign Affairs 58-64, Deputy Dir. Political Affairs, Ministry of Foreign Affairs 64; Ambassador to Morocco 65-; Officier Légion d'Honneur, Hon. K.C.M.G., and other honours.
Embassy of France, Boulevard Mohammed V, Rabat, Morocco; 21 bis avenue d'Iena, Paris 16e, France.
Telephone: PAS 61-93.

Gilliéron, Charles, D.IUR.; Swiss lawyer and radio administrator; b. 28 March 1912; ed. Lausanne, Paris, Vienna Univs.
Pres. Société Romande de Radiodiffusion 39; Privatdozent Lausanne Univ. 45; Vice-Pres. Société Suisse de Radiodiffusion 47-58; Pres. des Tribunaux 55-58; Dir. Admin. Office European Broadcasting Union 58-65.
Publs. *Droits Radiodiffusion* 36, *Concurrence Déloyale, Code Fédéral: Propriété Intellectuelle* 43, etc.
Avenue Dapples 15, Lausanne, Switzerland.

Gillon, Etienne, L. ès L., L. en D., C.P.A.; French editor; b. 21 March 1911; ed. Ecole Libre des Sciences Politiques.

Librairie Larousse 32-, Man. Dir. 52-; Vice-Pres. Syndicat National des Editeurs; Vice-Pres. Asscn. for Graphic and Plastic Arts; Croix de Guerre; Chevalier, Légion d'Honneur.
17 rue du Montparnasse, Paris 6e, France; 23 avenue Emile-Deschanel, Paris 7e, France.

Gillon, Mgr. Luc-Pierre-A., D.SC.; Belgian ecclesiastic and scientist; b. 15 Sept. 1920.
Research physicist, Inst. Interuniversitaire des Sciences Nucléaires 48; guest staff mem. Brookhaven Nat. Laboratory, New York 53; Extraordinary Prof. Louvain Univ.; now Pres. Lovanium Univ., Kinshasa; Perm. Sec. Nuclear Sciences Commissariat, Republic of the Congo.
Université Lovanium, Kinshasa XI, Republic of the Congo.
Telephone: 78-83.

Gilmore, Voit; American government official; b. 13 Oct. 1918; ed. Univ. of N. Carolina.
With Senator Josiah Bailey; Pan American World Airways; Navy Air Transport Service, Second World War; took over family lumber business, Southern Pines 48; Pres. North Carolina Travel Council 57-59; observer on four polar expeditions; Dir. U.S. Travel Service 62-64; Pres. Holly Corpn. 64-; mem. North Carolina State Senate 65, 67.
Southern Pines, North Carolina, U.S.A.
Telephone: 692-2811.

Gilpatric, Roswell Leavitt, A.B., LL.B.; American lawyer and government official; b. 4 Nov. 1906; ed. Yale Univ.
Admitted to New York Bar 32, U.S. Supreme Court 35, Fed. Court 36; Partner, Cravath, de Gersdorff, Swaine and Wood (now Cravath, Swaine and Moore), New York City 31-51, 53-61; Under-Sec. of Air Force 51-53; Deputy Sec. of Defense 61-64; Partner, Cravath, Swaine and Moore 64-; Democrat.
124 E. 62nd Street, New York City 21, N.Y., U.S.A.

Gilroy, His Eminence Cardinal Norman Thomas; Australian ecclesiastic; b. 22 Jan. 1896; ed. St. Columba's Coll., Springwood, and Urban Coll., Rome. Ordained priest 23; Bishop of Port Augusta 34-37; Coadjutor Archbishop of Sydney 37-40; Archbishop of Sydney, Metropolitan 40-; created Cardinal Feb. 46.
St. Mary's Cathedral, Sydney, N.S.W., Australia.

Gilruth, Robert Rowe, B.S., M.S.; American engineer; b. 8 Oct. 1913; ed. Univ. of Minnesota.
With Nat. Advisory Cttee. for Aeronautics (later Nat. Aeronautics and Space Admin.—N.A.S.A.) 37-, Dir. Space Task Group (Project Mercury) 58; Dir. N.A.S.A. Manned Spacecraft Center (Projects Mercury, Gemini and Apollo) 61-; Fellow, American Rocket Soc., Institute of Aerospace Sciences, American Astronautical Soc.; Gov. Nat. Rocket Club; Sylvanus Albert Reed Award 50, Outstanding Achievement Award (Univ. of Minn.) 54, Louis W. Hill Space Transportation Award 62, N.A.S.A. Distinguished Service Medal 62, Goddard Memorial Trophy 62, U.S. Chamber of Commerce Great Living American Award 62, Dr. Robert H. Goddard Memorial Award of American Rocket Society 62; Hon. Fellow, Inst. of Aerospace Sciences 63; Spirit of St. Louis Medal by American Soc. of Mechanical Engineers 65; Americanism Award by China-Burma-India Veterans Asscn. 65; mem. Int. Acad. of Astronauts 65-; mem. Houston Philosophical Soc. 66-; Daniel Florence Guggenheim Award, Int. Acad. of Astronautics 66, four hon. degrees.
Office: National Aeronautics and Space Administration, Manned Spacecraft Center, Houston, Texas 77058; Home: 5128 Park Avenue, Dickinson, Texas 77539, U.S.A.

Gilson, Arthur, D. en DROIT; Belgian lawyer and politician; b. 15; ed. Univ. Catholique de Louvain. Dep. 46-; Sec. European Parl. Union 47-; Pres. NATO Parl. Military Cttee.; Minister of Nat. Defence 58-61, of the Interior and Civil Service 61-66; mem. of numerous parl. commissions; Christian Socialist; several decorations.
11 avenue de la Folle Chanson, Brussels, Belgium.

Gilson, Etienne, D.LITT., PH.D., LL.D.; French historian and philosopher; b. 13 June 1884; ed. Sorbonne. Prof. Lille Univ. 13 and Strasbourg Univ. 19; Prof. of Medieval Philosophy in Sorbonne 21-32; Prof. Coll. de France 32-50; Dir. Inst. of Medieval Studies at Toronto 29; Prof. Harvard Univ.; mem. Acad. Française 46-; corresp. mem. British Acad., Royal Acad. of Netherlands; Conseiller de la République; Commdr. Légion d'Honneur, Croix de Guerre; Dr. h.c. Oxford, Aberdeen, St. Andrews, Glasgow.
Publs. *La philosophie au Moyen-Age* 22, *Le Thomisme* 22, *La philosophie de St. Bonaventure* 24, *Introduction à l'étude de St. Augustin* 29, *L'esprit de la philosophie médiévale* 32, *La théologie mystique de St. Bernard* 34, *Le réalisme méthodique* 35, *Christianisme et philosophie* 36, *The Unity of Philosophical Experience* 37, *Héloïse et Abélard, Reason and Revelation in the Middle Ages* 38, *Dante et la Philosophie* 39, *God and Philosophy* 41, *L'être et l'essence* 48, *L'école des muses* 50, *La Philosophie de St. Augustin, Jean Duns Scot, Le Philosophe et le Théologien, Peinture et réalité, Introduction aux arts du beau.*
6 rue Collet, Vermenton (Yonne), France.

Gimbel, Bruce A.; American businessman; b. 28 July 1913; ed. Choate School and Yale Univ.
Joined Gimbel Bros. Inc. 35, Pres. 53-; joined Saks Fifth Avenue 36, Vice-Pres. 46-53.
Home: 435 East 52nd Street, New York City, N.Y.; Office: 33rd Street and Broadway, New York City, U.S.A.
Telephone: PL2-3917 (Home); LO4-3300 (Office).

Ginastera, Alberto; Argentine composer; b. 11 April 1916; ed. Conservatorio Nac. de Música y Arte Escénico. Director Instituto Torcuato di Tella, Centro Latinoamericano de Altos Estudios Musicales.
Works include: *Ollantay* (symphonic poem) 48, Music for film *Cabailito Criollo* 54, *Variaciones concertantes* 57, *Obertura para el Fausto Criollo* (orchestra), two symphonies, *Panambí* (ballet), *Estancia* (ballet), *Don Rodrigo* (opera), *Bomarzo* (opera) 67.
Instituto Torcuato di Tella, Centro Latinoamericano de Altos Estudios Musicales, Florida 936, Buenos Aires, Argentina.

Gingrich, Arnold, A.B.; American editor and author; b. 5 Dec. 1903; ed. Michigan Univ.
Advertising copy writer 25; Editor *Apparel Arts*, Vice-Pres. Apparel Arts Publications Inc. 31-45; Editor *Esquire*, Vice-Pres. Esquire Inc. 33-45; Editor *Coronet* 36-45, *Ken* 38-39; European Editor *Esquire* and *Coronet* 45-49; Gen. Man. *Flair*, Vice-Pres. Cowles Magazines Inc. 49-51; Senior Vice-Pres. and Publisher, *Esquire* 52-. Publs. *Cast Down the Laurel* 35, *The Well-Tempered Angler* 65, *Toys of a Lifetime* 66.
Office: 488 Madison Avenue, New York 22; Home: 605 East Saddle River Road, Ridgewood, New Jersey, 07450, U.S.A.
Telephone: PLaza 9-3232.

Ginsberg, Morris, D.LIT., LL.D.; British philosopher and sociologist; b. 14 May 1889; ed. University Coll., London.
Lecturer in Philosophy Univ. Coll. 14-23, Lecturer in Sociology London School of Economics 23-29, and Martin White Prof. of Sociology 29-54, Prof. Emeritus 54-; Fellow, British Acad.

Publs. *The Psychology of Society, The Material Culture and Social Institutions of the Simpler Peoples* (joint-author), *Studies in Sociology, L. T. Hobhouse: Life and Work, Sociology, The Idea of Progress: a Revaluation, Essays in Sociology and Social Philosophy: Vol. I, On the Diversity of Morals, Vol. II, Reason and Unreason in Society, Vol. III, Evolution and Progress, Reason and Experience in Ethics, Law and Opinion in England in the XXth Century* (Editor), *Nationalism: a Reappraisal, On Justice in Society.*
5 Millfield Lane, London, N.6, England.

Ginsburg, Marcel; Belgian diamond merchant; b. 91. President, Belgian Diamond Exchange; Treas. of Diamond Office; Vice-Pres. of the Fed. of Belgian Diamond Exchanges; Officer of the Order of Leopold; Officer Order of the Crown.
65 Avenue de Belgique, Antwerp, Belgium.
Telephone: 39-63-25.

Ginsburg, Semen Zacharovich; Soviet politician; b. 97; ed. Moscow Higher Technical School.
Member Communist Party of Soviet Union 17-; People's Commissariat of Heavy Industry 30-38; People's Commissar for Construction 39-46; U.S.S.R. Minister of Building Materials 47-50; Deputy Minister of Machine Building 50-51; First Deputy Minister of Building Enterprises of Oil Industry 51-57; Deputy Chair. State Cttee. for Construction, U.S.S.R. Council of Ministers 57-63; Chair. Stroibank 63-.
Tverskoy boulevard 13, Moscow, U.S.S.R.

Ginsburg, Vitaly Lazarevich; Soviet physicist; b. 1916; ed. Moscow Univ.
At Inst. of Physics, U.S.S.R. Acad. of Sciences 40-45; Prof., Gorky Univ. 45-; mem. C.P.S.U. 44-; Corresp. mem. U.S.S.R. Acad. of Sciences 53-66, mem. 66-; Lomonosov Prize 62.
U.S.S.R. Academy of Sciences, 14 Lenin Prospekt, Moscow, U.S.S.R.

Giobbe, H.E. Cardinal Paolo; Italian ecclesiastic; b. 10 Jan. 1880.
Ordained priest 04; Titular Archbishop of Tolemais 25; fmr. Apostolic Nuncio in Colombia; Apostolic Internuncio in the Netherlands 35-58; created Cardinal by Pope John XXIII 58; mem. Sacred Congregations of the Consistory, De Propaganda Fide, of Rites and of Extraordinary Ecclesiastical Affairs; Apostolic Datary 58-.
Largo del Colonnato 3, Rome, Italy.

Giolitti, Antonio; Italian politician; b. 12 Feb. 1915; ed. Univ. of Rome.
Member Constituent Assembly 46; Under-Sec. of Foreign Affairs June-Oct. 46; mem. Chamber of Deputies 48-, Pres. Commission for Industry and Trade, Chamber of Deputies June-Dec. 63, Dec. 64-; Minister of the Budget Dec. 63-July 64.
Publs. *Riforme e rivoluzione* 57, *Il Comunismo in Europa* 60, *Un socialismo possibile* 67.
Camera dei Deputati, Rome, Italy.

Giono, Jean; French novelist; b. 30 March 1895. Chevalier Légion d'Honneur and Order of Orange-Nassau; mem. Acad. Goncourt; Commdr. Arts et Lettres de Monaco.
Publs. *Colline* (Brentano Prize) 29, *Un de Baumugnes, Naissance de l'Odyssée* 30, *Le Grand Troupeau* 31, *Le serpent d'étoiles, Regain* (Northcliffe Prize), *Jean le Bleu, Le Chant du Monde, Solitude de la Pitié, Que ma joie demeure, Les vraies richesses, Lanceurs de graines, Bataille dans la Montagne, Le poids du ciel, Refus d'obéissance, Lettre aux Paysans sur la pauvreté et la paix* 38, translation of Melville's *Moby Dick* 40, *Le Bout de la Route* 40, *L'eau vive* 40, *Triomphe de la vie* 40, *Pour saluer Melville* 40, *Deux cavaliers de l'orage, La Femme du Boulanger* (play), *Le voyage en calèche* (play), *Un roi sans divertissement, Manosque des Plateaux, Les Ames Fortes* 49, *Mort d'un Personnage* 49, *Les grands chemins* 51, *Le Hussard sur le toit* 51, *L'Iris de Suse* 51, *Le Moulin de Pologne* 53, *Le voyage en Italie, Le bonheur fou, Angelo, Deux Cavaliers de l'orage*; trans. of the complete works of Machiavelli; *Crésus* (film), *La Bataille de Pavie.*
Le Parais, Manosque 04, Basses-Alpes, France.
Telephone: Manosque 132.

Girard de Charbonnières, Guy de, L. en D.; French diplomatist; b. 7 Jan. 1907; ed. Lycée Janson de Sailly, Ecole des Sciences politiques.
Attaché French Embassy Brussels 30; Third Sec. London 33, Second Sec. 38, First Sec. 41; joined Gen. de Gaulle's Comité National 43, Second Counsellor 43, Dir. du Cabinet, Commissariat, later Ministry of Foreign Affairs 43; First Counsellor 44; Minister to Copenhagen 45, Amb. 47-51, to Argentina 51-55, to Greece 57-64, to Switzerland 64-65; Diplomatic Counsellor to the French Govt. 66; Commdr. Légion d'Honneur; Grand Cross Order of Dannebrog (Denmark), etc.
55 Avenue Foch, Paris 16e, France.
Telephone: Passy 66-04.

Giri, Dr. Tulsi; Nepalese politician; b. Sept. 1926. Deputy Minister of Foreign Affairs 59; Minister of Village Development 60; Minister without Portfolio 60; Minister of Foreign Affairs, the Interior, Public Works and Communications 61; Vice-Chair. Council of Ministers and Minister of Palace Affairs 62; Chair. Council of Ministers and Minister of Foreign Affairs 62-65.
Jawakpurdham, Dist. Dhanuka, Nepal.

Giri, Varahgiri Venkata; Indian barrister-at-law and diplomatist; b. 10 Aug. 1894; ed. Nat. Univ. of Ireland.
Trade Union leader for many years; fmr. Gen. Sec. and Pres. All-India Railwaymen's Fed.; twice Pres. All-India Trade Union Congress; Indian workers' del. to Int. Labour Conference Geneva 26; workers' rep. Second Round Table Conf., London 31; mem. Central Legislative Assembly for several years; Minister of Labour, Industries, Commerce and Co-operation, Madras 37-39; Minister in Madras Govt. again 46-47; High Commr. for India in Ceylon 47-51; Minister of Labour, Govt. of India 54 (resigned Sept. 54); Gov. Uttar Pradesh 57-60, Kerala 60-65, Mysore 65-67; Vice-Pres. of India 67-; Pres. Indian Conf. of Social Work 58-60.
Office of the Vice-President, New Delhi, India.

Girodias, Maurice; French publisher; b. 19; ed. Lycée Pasteur, Neuilly-sur-Seine.
Founder "Les Editions de Chêne" (art books), Paris 40, Galerie Vendôme, Paris 45, Olympia Press 53, which published in Paris original English versions of works by V. Nabokov, H. Miller, L. Durrell, S. Beckett, J. P. Donleavy, W. Burroughs, G. Corso, and first English trans. of J. Genet, R. Queneau; founded "La Grande Séverine" restaurant and club 59.
Publ. *The Black Diaries: An Account of Roger Casement's Life and Times, with a collection of his Diaries and Public Writings* (with Peter Singleton-Gates) 59.
7 rue Saint Séverin, Paris 5e, France.

Giroud, Françoise; French journalist; b. 21 Sept. 1916; ed. Lycée Molière, Coll. de Groslay.
Editor *Elle* 45-52, *L'Express* 53-; Médaille de la Résistance.
Publs. *Le Tout Paris* 52, *Nouveaux Portraits* 53, *La Nouvelle Vague: portrait de la jeunesse* 58; film: *Antoine et Antoinette* 47.
25 rue de Berri, Paris 8e, France.

Giroul, Paul Jules Victor Marie, LL.D.; Belgian lawyer; b. 88; ed. Univ. of Liège.
Barrister, Huy 11; Judge, Court of First Instance, Huy 30; Judge, Court of Appeal, Liège 37; Pres. Chamber of the Court-Martial 45; Judge, Supreme Court 46-64, Pres. 61-64; mem. House of Representatives; Commdr. Ordre de Léopold, Grand Officier, Ordre de la Couronne.
42 rue Breydel, Brussels, Belgium.

Giscard d'Estaing, Edmond, L. ès L., D. en D. (father of Valéry Giscard d'Estaing, *q.v.*); French financier; b. 29 March 1894; ed. Univs. de Clermont-Ferrand and Paris.
Served French Army 14-19; Inspector of Finances 19-30; numerous financial missions abroad; Dir. of Finances to French High Commissariat Rhineland 21-26; Pres. Société Financière pour la France et les Pays d'Outre-Mer; Pres. Société du Tunnel du Mont-Blanc; Dir. Thomson-Houston, Air France, Sucrière Marocaine, Bergougnan, Carbone Lorraine, Crédit Foncier Immobilier, Cie. Industrielle Maritime, etc.; Hon. Pres. Secours Catholique; mem. Institut de France; Grand Officier de la Légion d'Honneur; Chevalier de l'Ordre de Malte; Commdr. de l'Ordre de Saint Grégoire le Grand; Commdr. de la Couronne de Belgique; Commdr. Grosses Verdienstkreuz (Austria); Commdr. Order of Dannebrog; Officier de Saint-Maurice et Saint-Lazare (Italy), Croix de Guerre (14-18).
Publs. *Misère et Splendeur des Finances Allemandes* 24, *Capitalisme* 30, *La Maladie du Monde* 33, *Le Chemin de la Pauvreté* 47, *La France et l'Unification Economique de l'Europe* 53, *Les Finances: Terre inconnue* 59.
Home: 101 avenue Henri-Martin, Paris 16e; Office: 23 rue de l'Amiral d'Estaing, Paris 16e, France.

Giscard d'Estaing, François, L. en DR.; French civil servant; b. 17 Sept. 1926; ed. Ecole Nat. d'Administration, Inst. d'Etudes Politiques.
Dep. Inspector of Finance 52, Inspector 54; Technical Adviser to Minister of Agriculture 55-56, 58-59, to Sec. of State for the Budget 56-57; Head of Cen. Admin. Ministry of Agriculture 57; Dir. Banque Cen. des Etats d'Afrique Equatoriale et du Cameroun 59-; Mayor of Saint-Amant-Tallende 65-; Croix de Guerre.
6 rue Adolphe Yvon, Paris 16e, France.

Giscard d'Estaing, Valéry (son of Edmond Giscard d'Estaing, *q.v.*); French civil servant and politician; b. 2 Feb. 1926; ed. Ecole Polytechnique, Ecole Nat. d'Administration.
Official, Inspection des Finances 52, Inspecteur 54; Deputy Dir. du Cabinet de Prés. du Conseil June-Dec. 54; Deputy for Puy de Dôme 56-58, re-elected for Clermont 58, for Puy de Dôme 62, 67; Sec. of State for Finance 59, Minister for Finance and Econ. Affairs 62-66; Pres. Comm. des Finances, de l'Economie générale et du plan 67; Founder-Pres. Fed. Nat. des Républicains Indépendants; Del. to UN Gen. Assembly 56, 57, 58; Croix de Guerre, etc.
11 rue Bénouville, Paris 16e, France.

Gish, Lillian Diana; American actress; b. 14 Oct. 1899.
Began acting at the age of five, in the theatre, and has appeared in many plays and films.
Plays include *Camille, Dear Octopus, Hamlet* (when she played Ophelia), *Crime and Punishment, Life with Father, The Curious Savage, The Trip to Bountiful, The Chalk Garden, The Family Reunion, All the Way Home, A Passage To India, Too True to be Good, Romeo and Juliet* (nurse) 65, *Anya* (musical) 65; films include *Birth of a Nation, Hearts of the World, True Heart Susie, Orphans of the Storm, The Scarlet Letter, Annie Laurie, The Swan, Duel in the Sun, The Night of the Hunter, The Cobweb, The Unforgiven,* Walt Disney's *Follow Me Boys* 66, *Warning Shot* 66, *The Comedians* 67.
430 East 57th Street, New York, 22, N.Y., U.S.A.

Gislason, Gylfi Th., DR. RER. POL.; Icelandic economist and politician; b. 7 Feb. 1917; ed. Reykjavik Coll., Univs. of Frankfurt am Main and Vienna.
Lecturer of Econs., Univ. of Iceland 41-46, Prof. 46-56; mem. of Parl. 46-; Minister of Educ. and Industries 56-58, of Educ. and Commerce 58-; mem. Central Cttee. Social-Democratic Party 42-, Sec. 46-65, Vice-Chair. 65-; Gov. for Iceland, Int. Monetary Fund 56-65; Gov.

for Iceland Int. Bank for Reconstruction and Devt. 65-; Dir. Iceland Bank of Devt. 53-66; Dir. Devt. Fund of Iceland 66-, Nat. Theatre 54-; Chair. State Research Council 65-; mem. Icelandic Science Soc.
Publs. *General Business Theory* 41, *Bookkeeping* 42, *Finance of Private Business Enterprises* 45, *Management of Industrial Enterprises* 53, *Accountancy* 55, *The Marshall Plan* 48, *Socialism* 49, *Capitalism, Socialism and the Co-operative Movement* 50, *The Foreign Policy of Iceland* 53.
Aragata 11, Reykjavík, Iceland.

Gislason, Vilhjalmur, M.A.; Icelandic educationist and writer; b. 97; ed. Reykjavík Univ.
Dir. Gen. State Broadcasting Corpn.; mem. Board of Culture; Chair. Nat. Theatre, etc.
Publs. *Islensk endurreisn* 23, *Islensk Thjothfraethi* 24, *Eggert Olafsson* 26, *Snorri Sturluson og godafraedin* 42, *Jon Sigurdsson i raedu og riti* 44, *Sjómannasaga* 45, *Eiríkur a Brunum* 46, *Bessastadir* 47, *Reyjavík fyrrum og nú* 48, *Reyjavík í myndum* 48, *Brautryojendur* 50, *Allingisrímur* 51, *Mannfundir* 54, *Gamlar myndir* 55, *Islenzk verzlun* 55; translated Victor Hugo, Dostoievsky and others into Icelandic.
Starhagi 2, Reykjavík, Iceland.

Giulini, Carlo Maria; Italian conductor; b. 9 May 1914; ed. Accademia S. Cecilia, Rome.
Debut as conductor, Rome 44; fmr. Dir., Italian Radio Orchestra; Principal Conductor, La Scala, Milan 53-55; Conductor, Philharmonia Orchestra, London (renamed New Philharmonia Orchestra); Edinburgh Festival 65.
Via Giovanni da Procida 29, Milan, Italy.

Giuranna, Bruno; Italian viola player; b. 6 April 1933; ed. Coll. S. Giuseppe and Conservatorio di Musica Santa Cecilia, Rome, and Conservatorio di Musica S. Pietro a Maiella, Naples.
Founder, I Musici 51; Prof. Conservatorio G. Verdi, Milan 61-65, Conservatorio S. Cecilia, Rome 65-67; Prof. Accad. Chigiana 66-67; mem. Int. Music Competition jury, Munich 61-62, 67; soloist at concerts in festivals including Edinburgh Festival, Holland Festival and with orchestras including Berlin Philharmonic Orchestra, Amsterdam Concertgebouw Orchestra and Teatro alla Scala, Milan.
Via Misurina 71, Rome, Italy.
Telephone: 325575.

Giustiniani, Pier Candiano; Italian industrialist; b. 1900; ed. Univ. of Naples.
Sec. of the Presidency of the Montecatini Co. 30; Gen. Man. of A.C.N.A. Co. (company for the manufacturing of dyestuffs and similar products) 35, and of Farmaceutici Italia Co. (Italian Pharmaceuticals Co.) 40, both belonging to the Montecatini Group; Gen. Man. of the Montecatini Co. (now Montecatini-Edison) 42, Dir. 49-, Man. Dir. 49-63; Pres. Econ. and Social Cttee., EEC.
Via Filippo Turati 18, Milan, Italy.

Gizenga, Antoine; Congolese politician; b. 25; ed. Congolese Seminary.
President, Parti de la Solidarité Africaine (P.S.A.); del. Brussels Round Table Conf. on Congolese independence, Dec. 59; Dep.-Premier, Lumumba cabinet June 60; dismissed by Pres. Kasavubu, Sept. 60; Pres. Orientale Province 60-62; Pres. P.S.A. 59-62; Dep. Premier, Congolese Republic, Aug. 61-Jan. 62; arrested Feb. 62; on Bolabemba Island at mouth of River Congo Feb. 63-June 64; founded United Lumumbist Party 64; mem. Senate; later went to Moscow 66.
Kinshasa (Léopoldville), Congo Republic.

Gjesdal, Tor; Norwegian journalist; b. 24 Oct. 1909; ed. Univ. of Oslo.
Reporter and later foreign corresp. in Norway, Western and Eastern Europe and Middle and Far East for Nor-

wegian Labour Press 29-40 and 45-46; Press Attaché, Washington, D.C. 40; Head of Norwegian Govt. Information Services, London 41-45; Principal Dir. U.N. Dept. of Public Information, New York 46-, Dep. Under-Sec. 55; Principal Dir. Dept. of Mass Communication, UNESCO 55; Asst. Dir.-Gen. of UNESCO in Charge of Communication 66-; mem. Exec. Norwegian T.U.C. 41-45; Vice-Pres. Int. Fed. of Journalists 42-44 and of Int. Org. of Journalists 46-47; U.S. Medal of Freedom with Bronze Palms and Danish Medal of Freedom, Norwegian Military Medal with Star, Knight, Order of St. Olav.
154 rue de Lourmel, Paris 15e, France.
Telephone: LECourbe 97-42.

Gladwyn, 1st Baron (cr. 60), of Bramfield; **Hubert Miles Gladwyn Jebb**, G.C.M.G., G.C.V.O., C.B.; British diplomatist; b. 25 April 1900; ed. Eton and Magdalen Coll., Oxford.
Entered Diplomatic Service 24; served in Teheran and Rome; Private Sec. to Parl. Under-Sec. of State 29-31; Private Sec. to Permanent Under-Sec. of State 37-40; appointed to Ministry of Economic Warfare 40; Acting Counsellor in Foreign Office 41; Head Reconstruction Dept., Foreign Office 42-45; Counsellor 43; appointed Exec. Sec. of Preparatory Comm. of U.N. Aug. 45; Acting Sec.-Gen. of U.N. Feb. 46; Asst. Under-Sec. of State in Foreign Office, May 46-49; Deputy Under-Sec. of State 49-50; U.K. Rep. on Permanent Comm. of Treaty of Brussels, April 48; Permanent Rep. of U.K. to U.N. 50-54; Ambassador to France 54-60; Dir. S. G. Warburg & Co.; Pres. Atlantic Treaty Asscn., Britain in Europe; Vice-Pres. Atlantic Inst.; Grand Croix de la Légion d'Honneur 57; Hon. D.C.L. (Univ. of Oxford) 54; Liberal.
Publs. *The European Idea* 66, *Half-Way to 1984* 67.
62 Whitehall Court, London, S.W.1; Bramfield Hall, Halesworth, Suffolk, England.
Telephone: 01-839-3800 (Office).

Glaister, John, M.D., D.SC., J.P., F.R.S.E., F.R.C.P. (GLAS.); British professor of forensic medicine; b. 31 May 1892; ed. Glasgow High School, and Univ. of Glasgow.
Barrister-at-Law Inner Temple; Medico-Legal Consultant to Egyptian Govt. and Prof. of Forensic Medicine Univ. of Egypt 28-32; Emeritus Prof. of Forensic Medicine Univ. of Glasgow; Medico-Legal Examiner in Crown Cases Glasgow and West of Scotland; Swiney Prizeman 39 and 49.
Publs. *Medico-Legal Aspects of the Ruxton Case* (with Prof. J. C. Brash), *Recent Advances in Forensic Medicine* (with Prof. Sydney Smith) (2nd edn.) 38, *Hairs and Wools of Mammalia Considered from the Medico-Legal Aspect*; Textbook: *Medical Jurisprudence and Toxicology* (12th edn.) 66; *The Power of Poison* 54, *Final Diagnosis* (Autobiography) 64.
"Cluan", Buchanan, Drymen, Stirlingshire, Scotland.
Telephone: Drymen 291.

Glasbergen, Willem; Netherlands prehistorian; b. 24 July 1923; ed. State Univ. of Groningen.
Asst. Inst. for Biological Archæology, State Univ. of Groningen 43-47, Conservator 50-60; Asst. State Service for Archæological Investigations in the Netherlands 47-50; Curator Archæological Dept., Groningen Museum of Antiquities 55-56; Curator Archæological Dept., Provinciaal Museum van Drenthe, Assen 55-56; Extra. Prof. Univ. of Amsterdam and Dir. Inst. of Præ- and Protohistory 56-60, Ordinarius 60-; mem. Royal Netherlands Acad. of Sciences and Letters 59.
Publs. *Barrow Excavations in the Eight Beatitudes* 54, *De Voorgeschiedenis der Lage Landen* 59.
Instituut voor Prae- en Protohistorie, Nieuwe Prinsengracht 41, Amsterdam-C; Home: Abraham Kuyperlaan 25, Amersfoort, Netherlands.

Glaser, Donald Arthur, B.S., PH.D.; American physicist; b. 21 Sept. 1926; ed. Case Inst. of Technology, Calif. Inst. of Technology.
Univ. of Michigan 49-59; Univ. of California 59-; Henry Russell Award 55, Charles Vernon Boys Prize (The Physical Soc.) 58, Nobel Prize 60; Nat. Science Foundation Fellow 61; Guggenheim Fellow 61-62; mem. U.S. Acad. of Sciences; Hon. Sc.D.
Publs. *Some Effects of Ionizing Radiation on the Formation of Bubbles in Liquids* 52, *A Possible Bubble Chamber for the Study of Ionizing Events* 53, *Bubble Chamber Tracks of Penetrating Cosmic-Ray Particles* 53, *Progress Report on the Development of Bubble Chambers* 55, *Strange Particle Production by Fast Pions in Propane Bubble Chamber* 57, *Weak Interactions: Other Modes, Experimental Results* 58, *The Bubble Chamber* 58, *Development of Bubble Chamber and Some Recent Bubble Chamber Results in Elementary Particle Physics* 58, *Decays of Strange Particles* 59; many papers written jointly with other physicists.
Molecular Biology Department, University of California, Berkeley, Calif. 94720, U.S.A.

Glasser, Georges Charles; French industrialist; b. 24 Aug. 1907.
President and Man. Dir. Soc. Alsthom 59-; Pres. Syndicat Générale de la Construction Electrique; Hon. Pres. Soc. Nat. Sud-Aviation, Union Syndicale des Industries Aéronautiques, Soc. d'Etude de Propulsion par Réaction; Officier Légion d'Honneur, Chevalier du Mérite Agricole, Grand Officer, Order of Orange Nassau, Médaille de l'Aéronautique, Commdr. Order of the Lion (Finland).
38 avenue Kléber, Paris 16e, France.
Telephone: 727-00-90.

Glavanis, Ioannis; Greek politician; b. 1892; ed. Commercial School, Manchester.
Managing Dir. Glavanis Farm Machinery Manufacturing Co. until 40; M.P. 46-55, 61-; Minister of Nat. Econ. 44-45, Reconstruction 47, Welfare, Health and Reconstruction 49, Industry and Commerce 50-51, Commerce 65, of Public Works Sept. 65-66; Pres. Thessalian Asscn. of History and Folklore; formerly mem. Liberal Party, now Centre Union Party.
3 Paparrigopolou Street, Athens, Greece.

Glazunov, Mikhail Fedorovich; Soviet oncologist; b. 1896; ed. Military Medical Academy.
Red Army physician 19-23; physician at Mil. Medical Acad. 23-25; Asst., Instructor, Senior Instructor at Mil. Medical Acad. 25-41; Soviet Army physician 41-44; Prof. 38; Senior Instructor at Mil. Medical Acad. 44-45; Corresp. mem., U.S.S.R. Acad. of Medical Sciences 44-60, mem. 60-; Head of Dept., Leningrad Inst. for Postgraduate Medical Training 45-50; Head of Laboratory, Consultant at Inst. of Experimental and Clinical Oncology, U.S.S.R. Acad. of Medical Sciences 50-; Hon. mem. All-Russia Soc. of Oncologists; Order of Lenin 45; Red Star 43; Red Banner 44; Badge of Honour 61.
Publ. Over 70 works on classification and structure of malignant tumours and tumour-like processes; Monograph *Ovarian Tumours* 61.
Institute of Experimental and Clinical Oncology, U.S.S.R. Academy of Medical Sciences, Kashirskoye Shosse 30, Moscow, U.S.S.R.

Glemser, Oskar Max, DR.-ING., German chemist; b. 12 Nov. 1911; ed. Gymnasium Bad-Canstatt and Technische Hochschule, Stuttgart.
Senior Engineer, Inst. for Inorganic Chemistry and Electro Chemistry, Technische Hochschule, Aachen 39-41, Dozent 41-48, Extra-Mural Prof. 48-52; Prof. and Dir. of the Inst. of Inorganic Chemistry, Univ. of Göttingen 52-; Pres. of Acad. of Sciences, Göttingen; mem. Leopoldina German Acad. for Scientific Research, Halle.

Office: Anorganisch Chemisches Institut der Universität, Hospitalstrasse 8-10, Göttingen; Home: Richard-Zsigmondy-Weg 10, 34 Göttingen, German Federal Republic.
Telephone: 05-51-59722 (Office); 05-51-58181 (Home).

Glen, Sir Alexander Richard, K.B.E., D.S.C.; British business executive; b. 18 April 1912; ed. Fettes Coll., and Balliol Coll., Oxford.
Organiser and Leader, Oxford Univ. Arctic Expedition 33, 35-36; Banking, New York and London 36-39; R.N.V.R. 39-59; Chair. H. Clarkson & Co. Ltd.; Deputy Chair. Export Council for Europe 60-64, Chair. 64-66; mem. Council Royal Geographical Soc. 45-47, 54-57, 61-62; mem. Council, Mount Everest Foundation 55-57; numerous medals and decorations.
Publs. *Young Men in the Arctic* 35, *Under the Pole Star* 37.
46 Wilton Crescent, London, S.W.1, England.

Glen, Robert, B.SC., M.SC., PH.D.; Canadian entomologist and research administrator; b. 20 June 1905; ed. Univs. of Saskatchewan and Minnesota.
Junior and Asst. Entomologist, Dominion Entomological Laboratory, Saskatoon, Saskatchewan 28-35, in charge wireworm investigations, Dominion Entomological Laboratory 35-45; Research Co-ordinator, Entomology Div., Canada Dept. of Agriculture, Ottawa 45-50, Chief, Entomology Div. 50-57; Assoc. Dir. Science Service, Canada Dept. of Agriculture 57-59; Dir.-Gen. Research Branch, Canada Dept. of Agriculture 59-62, Asst. Deputy Minister (Research) 62-; Fellow, Agricultural Inst. of Canada, Royal Soc. of Canada; Pres. E. Ontario Branch, Agricultural Inst. of Canada 50-51, Entomological Soc. of Canada 57, Entomological Soc. of America 62; Caleb Dorr Fellowship, Univ. of Minnesota 31-32; Shevlin Fellowship, Univ. of Minnesota 32-33; mem. Science Council of Canada 66; Foreign Assoc. Nat. Acad. of Sciences (U.S.A.) 67; Outstanding Achievement Award, Univ. of Minnesota 60.
Publs. include: *Elaterid larvae of the tribe Lepturoidini* 50, and reports on Canadian entomology 54-56.
832 Riddell Avenue, Ottawa 13, Ontario, Canada.

Glenn, Lt.-Col. John Herschel, Jr.; D.F.C. (8 times) and Air Medal with 18 clusters; American aviator and astronaut; b. 18 July 1921; ed. Muskingum Coll., Univ. of Maryland.
Naval aviation cadet 42; commissioned Marine Corps 43; Marine Fighter Squadron 155 in Marshall Islands 44 (59 combat missions); mem. Fighter Sq. 218 North China Patrol; Instructor Corpus Christi, Texas 48-50; Marine Fighter Sq. Korea (63 missions); Fighter Design Branch, Navy Bureau of Aeronautics, Washington 56; speed record Los Angeles–New York (3 hr. 23 min.) 57; training for space flight 60-61, completed 3 orbits of the earth in Spaceship *Friendship VII,* 20th February 62; resigned from U.S. Marine Corps 65; Dir. Royal Crown Cola Co. 65-; Consultant to N.A.S.A.; N.A.S.A. Distinguished Service Medal 62.
Publ. (co-author) *We Seven* 62.
203 Sleepy Hollow Court, Timbercove, Seabrook, Texas, U.S.A.

Glennan, T. Keith, B.S.; American engineer and administrator; b. 8 Sept. 1905; ed. Eau Claire (Wis.) High School, Eau Claire State Teachers' Coll., and Yale Univ. Sheffield Scientific School.
Western Electric Co. Ltd. 28-30; Electrical Research Products Co. 30-35; Paramount Pictures Inc. 35-41; Studio Man. Samuel Goldwyn Studios 41-42; Admin., later Dir. U.S. Navy Underwater Sound Laboratories (Columbia Univ. Div. of War Research), New London, Conn. 42-45; exec. with Ansco, Binghamton (New York) 45-47; Pres. Case Inst. of Technology, Cleveland 47-66; mem. Atomic Energy Comm. 50-52; First Admin. Nat. Aeronautics and Space Admin. (N.A.S.A.) 58-61;

Pres. Associated Universities Inc. 65-68; Dir. Republic Steel Corpn., and other companies; Fellow, American Acad. of Arts and Science; Medal for Merit; Hon. LL.D. (Tulane Univ., Miami Univ., Western Reserve Univ., Columbia Univ.); Hon. D.Sc. (Oberlin Coll., Clarkson Coll. of Technology, John Carroll Univ., Akron Univ., Univ. of Toledo, Muhlenberg Coll., Cleveland State Univ.); Hon. D.Eng. (Stevens Inst. of Technology, Case Institute of Technology, Fenn Coll.); Hon. M.A. (Yale Univ.), Univ. Medal of Honor (Rice Univ.), N.A.S.A. Distinguished Service Medal 66.
11483 Waterview Cluster, Reston, Va. 22070, U.S.A.

Gligorov, Kiro; Yugoslav politician; b. 17; ed. Univ. of Belgrade.
Member Antifascist Cttee. of People's Liberation of Yugoslavia 44; Commr. for Finance of Antifascist Cttee. of People's Liberation of Macedonia 45; Asst. to Sec.- Gen. of Govt. of Yugoslavia 47-52; Asst. to Pres. of Economic Council of Yugoslavia, Deputy Dir.-Gen. Federal Inst. for Economic Planning 52-55; Sec. for Gen. Econ. Affairs of Federal Exec. Council 55-62; Federal Sec. for Finance 62-; a Vice-Pres. Fed. Exec. Council; mem. Cen. Cttee. of League of Communists of Yugoslavia 62-; mem. Federal Council of Soc. Alliance of Working People of Yugoslavia 62-; numerous decorations.
Bulevar Oktobarske revolucije 14, Belgrade, Yugoslavia.

Glob, Peter Vilhelm, DR.PHIL.; Danish archaeologist and museum curator; b. 20 Feb. 1911; ed. Univ. of Copenhagen.
Archaeological expedition, Greenland 32-33, 53; Chief of Danish Archaeological Expeditions, Bahrein 53-65, Qatar 57-64, Kuwait 58-62; Prof. of Archaeology and Prehistory of Europe, Aarhus Univ. 49-60; Danish Rigsantikvar (Dir.-Gen. of Central Office and of Museum of National Antiquities in Denmark) 60-.
Publs. *Eskimo Settlements in Kempe Fjord and King Oscar Fjord* 35, *Études sur la civilisation des sépultures individuelles de Jutland* 45, *Danske Oldtidsminder* 42 (new edn. 67), *Eskimo Settlements in North East Greenland* 46, *Ard and Plough* 51, *Danske Oldsager II* 52, *Grauballemanden* 59, *Hommes des tourbières* 65.
Nationalmuseet, Copenhagen, Denmark.

Globke, Hans; German politician; b. 10 Sept. 1898; ed. Grammar School and Univ.
Assessor at Court 24; Assessor in Govt. Police Praesidium, Aachen 26, Govt. Counsellor, Ministry of the Interior, Berlin 30; Dept. Dir. 38; Alderman, City of Aachen 46; Vice-Pres. Court of Audit, Land Nordrhein-Westfalen 49; Gen. Dir. Office of the Fed. Chancellor 49-53; Sec. of State 53-63; German and foreign decorations.
Diezstrasse 10, Bonn, German Federal Republic.
Telephone: 23724.

Glock, William Frederick, C.B.E.; British musician; b. 3 May 1908; ed. Christ's Hospital, West Horsham, Gonville and Caius Coll., Cambridge and under Artur Schnabel, Berlin.
Music Critic, *Daily Telegraph* 34, *The Observer* 34-45, *New Statesman* 58-59; served with Royal Air Force 41-46; Dir. Summer School of Music, Bryanston 48-52, Dartington Hall, Devon 53-; Founder and Editor *The Score* 49-; Chair. British Section, Int. Soc. of Contemporary Music 54-58; Controller of Music, B.B.C. 59-; Hon. D.Mus. (Nottingham Univ.).
30 Connaught Square, London, W.2, England.
Telephone: 01-262-2943.

Glocker, Richard, PH.D.; German physicist; b. 21 Sept. 1890; ed. Munich Univ.
Lecturer, Stuttgart Technical Univ. 19, and Extra. Prof. 23; Prof. for Röntgen-Technique 25; Head of X-Ray Laboratory and mem. Council of Max Planck

Inst. for Metal Research (retd. 61); Hon. mem. Deutsche Röntgen-Gesellschaft, Deutsche Gesellschaft für Metallkunde, Gesellschaft für Biophysik; Co-Editor *Fortschritte auf dem Gebiet der Röntgenstrahlen und der Nuklearmedizin*; Dr. Med. h.c.
Publs. *Materialprüfung mit Röntgenstrahlen* 27 (4th edn. 58), *Röntgen- und Kernphysik für Mediziner und Biophysiker* 65.
Robert Boschstrasse 10, Stuttgart-N., German Federal Republic.

Glossbrenner, Alfred S.; American businessman; b. 6 June 1901; ed. Univ. of Wisconsin.
With tin plate plant, American Sheet and Tin Plate Co. 30-31; Foreman, South Chicago plant, Ill. Steel 32-35; Asst. Supt. Campbell hot strip mill, Youngstown Sheet and Tube Co. 35-36, Supt. 36-42, Supt. Brier Hill Works 42-43, Gen. Supt. Youngstown Dist. 43-47, Asst. Vice-Pres. 47-50, Vice-Pres. (Operations) 50-56, Pres. 56-65, Dir 53-, Chief Exec. Officer 60-66, Chair. Exec. Cttee. 63-, Chair. of Board 65-; Dir. Carbon Limestone Co., Youngstown Steel Door Co., Dollar Savings and Trust Co., Nat. City Bank of Cleveland, Ohio Bell Telephone Co., Pickards Mather & Co.; mem. Board Y.M.C.A., Youngstown Community Chest; official of other business and educational orgs.
Office: Box 900, Youngstown, Ohio 44501; Home: 2782 Logan Road, Youngstown, Ohio, U.S.A.

Glossop, Peter; British opera singer (baritone); b. 6 July 1928; ed. High Storrs Grammar School, Sheffield.
Joined Sadler's Wells Opera 52; with Covent Garden Opera Co. 62-66; freelance singer 66-; First Prize Bulgarian First Competition for Young Opera Singers 61; debut at La Scala, Milan as Rigoletto 65.
50 Aylmer Road, London, N.2, England.
Telephone: 01-340-7357.

Gloucester, Duke of; **Prince Henry William Frederick Albert,** K.G., K.T., K.P., G.C.M.G., G.C.V.O.; b. 31 March 1900.
Son of King George V; brother of the late King George VI of the United Kingdom; married 35 Lady Alice Montagu-Douglas-Scott, b. 01, daughter of 7th Duke of Buccleuch; Col. Scots Guards; Col.-in-Chief 10th Hussars, Royal Inniskilling Fusiliers, Gloucestershire Regt., Gordon Highlanders, Deputy Col.-in-Chief the Royal Greenjackets Regiment Royal, Corps of Transport; Chief Liaison Officer British Field Forces 39-40; Hon. Commodore R.N.R.; Field Marshal; Marshal of the Royal Air Force; Gt. Master of the Bath; Grand Prior of the Order of St. John; Gov.-Gen. of Australia 45-47.
York House, St. James's Palace, London, S.W.1; and Barnwell Manor, nr. Peterborough, Northants, England.

Glubb, Lieut.-Gen. Sir John Bagot, K.C.B., C.M.G., D.S.O., O.B.E., M.C.; British officer; b. 16 April 1897; ed. Cheltenham and Royal Military Acad., Woolwich.
2nd Lieut. Royal Engineers 15, served France; served Iraq 20; Admin. Insp. Iraq Govt. 26; Officer Commdg. Desert Area (Colonial Service, Transjordan) 30; Officer Commdg. Arab Legion, Transjordan (now Jordan) 38-56.
Publs. *Story of the Arab Legion* 48, *A Soldier with the Arabs* 57, *Britain and the Arabs* 59, *War in the Desert* 60, *The Great Arab Conquests* 63, *The Empire of the Arabs* 63, *The Course of Empire* 65, *The Lost Centuries* 67, *Syria, Lebanon and Jordan* 67, *A Short History of the Arab Peoples* 68.
West Wood St. Dunstan, Mayfield, Sussex, England.
Telephone: Mayfield 3136.

Glueck, Nelson, PH.D., LL.D., D.H.L., LIT.D.; American archaeologist and teacher of biblical archaeology; b. 4 June 1900; ed. Hebrew Union Coll., Univ. of Cincinnati, and Univs. of Jena, Berlin and Heidelberg, Germany.

Instructor, Hebrew Union Coll. 29-31, Assoc. Prof. 32-33, Prof. of Bible and Biblical Archaeology 36-, Pres. 47-50; Pres. Jewish Inst. of Religion, Cincinnati, Ohio 49-50; Pres. Combined Hebrew Union Coll.-Jewish Inst. of Religion 50-; Dir. American School of Oriental Research, Palestine 32-33, 36-40, 42-47; Field Dir. American Schools of Oriental Research, Jerusalem and Baghdad 42-47; Archæological explorations in the Negev 52-65.
Publs. *Explorations in Eastern Palestine*, Vol. I 34, Vol. II 35, Vol. III 39, Vol. IV 52, *The Other Side of the Jordan* 40, *The River Jordan* 46, *Rivers in the Desert: A History of the Negev* 59, *Deities and Dolphins: The Story of the Nabataeans* 66.
Home: 162 Glenmary Avenue, Cincinnati 20; Office: Hebrew Union College, Clifton Avenue, Cincinnati 20, Ohio, U.S.A.
Telephone: UN1-3316.

Glueck, Sheldon, LL.M., PH.D.; American criminologist; b. 15 Aug. 1896; ed. George Washington Univ., Nat. Univ. Law School and Harvard Univ.
Instructor, Dept. of Social Ethics, Harvard Univ. 25-29; Asst. Prof. of Criminology, Harvard Univ. Law School 29-31, Prof. 31-50, Roscoe Pound Prof. of Law 50-63, Emer. 63-; Dir. Basic Researches in Causes, Management and Prevention of Juvenile Delinquency, Harvard Law School 25-; fmr. mem. U.S. Supreme Court Advisory Cttee. on Revision of Rules of Criminal Procedure; fmr. mem. American Law Inst., Cttee. on Youth Correction Authority and Model Penal Code; mem. American Bar Asscn. Cttee. on Juvenile Delinquency, Nat. Council on Crime and Delinquency, Int. Acad. of Law and Science, Int. Soc. of Criminology, American Soc. of Criminology, German Soc. of Criminology; Fellow American Acad. of Arts and Sciences, American Psychiatric Asscn.; Hon. LL.D. (Univ. of Salonika) 48, Hon. S.D. (Harvard Univ.) 58, S.S.D. (George Washington Univ.) 68; numerous awards.
Publs. *Mental Disorder and the Criminal Law* 25, *War Criminals: their Prosecution and Punishment* 44, *The Nuremberg Trial and Aggressive War* 46, *The Problem of Delinquency* (Editor) 59, *Law and Psychiatry: Cold War or Entente Cordiale?* 62, *Roscoe Pound and Criminal Justice* (Editor) 65; and books on delinquency and crime with Eleanor T. Glueck.
Austin Hall, Harvard Law School, Cambridge, Mass. 02138, U.S.A.

Glushko, Valentin Petrovich; Soviet combustion engineer; b. 1908; ed. Leningrad Univ.
Corresponding mem. U.S.S.R. Acad. of Sciences 53-58, mem. 58-; Bureau mem. Dept. of Physical-Technical Problems of Energetics, U.S.S.R. Acad. of Sciences 60-; mem. C.P.S.U. 56-; Deputy to U.S.S.R. Supreme Soviet; Hero of Socialist Labour (twice); Lenin Prize.
U.S.S.R. Academy of Sciences, 14 Lenin Prospekt, Moscow, U.S.S.R.

Glushkov, Viktor Mikhailovich; Soviet mathematician; b. 1923; ed. Rostov on Don Univ.
At Urals Timber Inst. 48-56; at Inst. of Mathematics, Ukrainian Acad. of Sciences 56-57; Dir. Computer Centre, Ukrainian Acad. of Sciences 57; Corresp. mem. Ukrainian Acad. of Sciences 48-57, mem. 57-, Vice-Pres. 61-; Dir. Inst. of Cybernetics, Ukrainian Acad. of Sciences 62-; mem. U.S.S.R. Acad. of Sciences 66-.
Institute of Cybernetics, Ukrainian Academy of Sciences, Kiev, U.S.S.R.

Glyn, Sir Francis Maurice Grosvenor, K.C.M.G.; British bank executive; b. Aug. 1901; ed. Eton Coll.
Former Deputy Chair., now Dir. Bank of London & South America Ltd.; Dir. Glyn, Mills & Co., Liebig's Extract of Meat Co. Ltd. and other companies; fmr. Deputy Chair. of Advisory Council of Exports Credits Guarantee Dept., Board of Trade.
Hole Farm, Albury, Much Hadham, Herts., England.

Gmyrya, Boris Romanovich; Soviet singer; b. 03; ed. Kharkov Building Engineering Inst. and Kharkov Conservatoire.
Sings for Kiev Shevchenko Opera House; played Trofim in film-opera *The Servant-Woman* 63; People's Artist of the U.S.S.R.; State prizewinner 52, Order of Lenin 60.
Opera House, Kiev, Ukraine, U.S.S.R.

Gnägi, Rudolf; Swiss lawyer and politician; b. 3 Aug. 1917; ed. Progymnasium and Gymnasium, Bienne, and Universität Bern.
Lawyer 43-46; Sec. Farmers', Tradesmen' and Burghers' Party of Berne 46, also Peasants' Fed. of Berne 46; Sec. of Farmers', Tradesmen' and Burghers' Party of Switzerland 47; Govt. Councillor for Canton of Berne 52; Nat. Councillor 53; Swiss Fed. Councillor, Head of Ministry of Transport, Communications and Power Dec. 65-Dec. 67, Minister of Defence 68-.
Spiegel-Berne, Steingrubenweg 8, Switzerland.

Gnatt, Poul Rudolph; New Zealand (b. Danish) dancer, choreographer and producer; b. 24 March 1923; ed. Royal Danish Ballet School.
Joined Royal Danish Ballet 29, Principal Dancer 49; Principal Dancer, Ballettes des Champs Elysées 46-47, Metropolitan Ballet 47-49, Ballet Russe 50-51, Borovansky Ballet 51-53; Founder and Artistic Dir. New Zealand Ballet 53-63; guest performances and short return to Royal Danish Ballet 63-64; Resident Teacher, Australian Ballet School and Producer/Ballet-master, The Australian Ballet 64-.
Choreography: *Satan's Wedding* 55, *Sonata* (Beethoven) 55, *Valse Triste* 55, *Peer Gynt* 56, *Prismatic Variations* (with Russell Kerr) 58.
18 Spencer Road, Camberwell, Victoria, Australia.

Gnedov, Alexi Trofimovich; Soviet politician; b. 1912; ed. Teacher-training courses and Higher Party School.
Teacher 30-32; School Insp., later Dir. of a school, Smolensk Region 32-38; Chief, Dneprovsk Regional Section of People's Educ. 38-41; Party Worker 41-44; First Sec., Yershich Regional Cttee. of C.P. 44-47, Yartsevo City Cttee. of C.P. 47-48; Section Chief, Smolensk Regional Cttee. of C.P. 51-52; First Sec. Smolensk City Cttee. of C.P. 52-54; Second Sec. Smolensk Regional Cttee. of C.P. 54-56; Chair. Exec. Cttee. of Smolensk Regional Soviet of Workers' Deputies 56-; Deputy to R.S.F.S.R. Supreme Soviet; mem. C.P.S.U. 39-.
Smolensk Regional Soviet of Workers' Deputies, Smolensk, U.S.S.R.

Gnesina, Elena Fabianovna; Soviet musician and teacher; b. 1874; ed. Moscow Conservatoire of Music.
With sisters Eugenia and Maria founded school of music in Moscow 95, given name of Gnesin School 25, name of Gnesin Music Teachers' Training Inst. 44, Dir. of School 95-53, Art Dir. 53-; Honoured Art Worker of R.S.F.S.R.; Order of Lenin (twice), Order of Red Banner of Labour (twice).
Compositions include: piano works for children *The Alphabet*, *Little Studies for Beginners*; *Violin Duets*.
The Gnesin State Music Teachers' Training Institute, ulitsa Vorovskogo, Moscow, U.S.S.R.

Goad, Edward Colin Viner; British international civil servant; b. 21 Dec. 1914; ed. Cirencester Grammar School and Cambridge Univ.
Ministry of Transport 37-63, Asst. Sec. 48, Under-Sec. 63; Deputy Sec.-Gen. (and Sec. Maritime Safety Cttee.) UN Inter-Governmental Maritime Consultative Organization 63-67, Sec.-Gen. 68-.
Office: 22 Berners Street, London, W.1; Home: 23A Burgh Heath Road, Epsom, Surrey, England.
Telephone: Epsom 20020.

Gobbi, Tito; Italian baritone opera singer; b. 24 Oct. 1915; ed. Padua Univ.
Opera début in *La Traviata*, Rome 38; has sung in numerous operas in major theatres throughout the world; also in a number of films; also produces operas including *Simon Boccanegra*, Covent Garden 65.
Via Asmara 10, Rome, Italy.

Gočár, Jiří; Czechoslovak architect; b. 12 June 1913; ed. Faculty of Civil and Structural Engineering, Czech Technical Univ.
Own practice until 48; *Stavoprojekt*, Prague 49-54; Union of Architects affil. to Union of Czechoslovak Artists 54-56; Union of Architects of Czechoslovakia 56-, Chair. 59-; Head of Architects' *atelier* 65-; mem. Council for Adaption of Prague Castle 59-; mem. Exec. Cttee. Union Int. des Architectes; work on housing, public and industrial buildings; mem. Cen. Cttee. C.P. of Czechoslovakia 66-; Order of Labour 63.
Union of Architects of Czechoslovakia, Prague 1, Letenská 5, Czechoslovakia.

Godard, Jean-Luc; French film director; b. 3 Dec. 1930; ed. Lycée Buffon.
Journalist and film critic; film director 58-; Prix Jean Vigo for *A Bout de Souffle* 60, Jury's Special Prize and Prix Pasinetti, Venice Festival 62.
Films: *Charlotte et son Jules, Tous les garçons s'appellent Patrick, A Bout de Souffle, Le Petit Soldat, Une femme est une femme, Vivre sa vie, Les Sept Péchés capitaux, Les Plus Belles Escroqueries du monde, Les Carabiniers, Une Femme Mariée, Bande à Part, Le Démon de Onze Heures, Une nouvelle Histoire de Lemmy Caution, Alphaville, Pierrot le Fou, Masculin, Féminin, Made in U.S.A., Deux ou Trois Choses que Je Sais d'Elle, La Chinoise, Week-end.*
Cahiers du Cinéma, 5 rue Clément-Marot, Paris 8e, France.

Godber, 1st Baron, cr. 56, of Mayfield in the County of Sussex; **Frederick Godber,** Kt.; British director of oil companies; b. 6 Nov. 1888.
In U.S.A. 19-29; Dir. Shell Union 22, Chair. 37-46; Chair. Shell Transport and Trading Co. Ltd. 46-61; fmr. Chair. Anglo-Saxon Petroleum Co. Ltd., Shell Petroleum Co. Ltd. and of associated companies; Chair. Commonwealth Development Finance Co. Ltd. 53-; Trustee Churchill Coll. Trust Fund, Cambridge 58-.
50 Kingston House, Princes Gate, London, S.W.7, England.
Telephone: 01-589-4722.

Godber, Rt. Hon. Joseph Bradshaw, P.C., M.P.; British politician; b. 17 March 1914; ed. Bedford School.
Family Business 32; Beds. County Councillor 46-52; M.P. 51-; Parl. Private Sec. to Parl. Sec. to Ministry of Labour 52-55; Asst. Govt. Whip 55-57; Joint Parl. Sec., Ministry of Agriculture, Fisheries and Food 57-60; Joint Parl. Under-Sec. of State, Foreign Office 60-61; Minister of State, Foreign Office 61-63; led British delegation to Geneva Disarmament Conference 62-63; Minister of War 63; Minister of Labour 63-64; Conservative.
Willington Manor, nr. Bedford, England.

Goddard, Baron (Life Peer), cr. 44, of Aldbourne, **Rayner Goddard,** G.C.B., P.C.; British judge; b. 77; ed. Marlborough and Trinity Coll. Oxford.
Called to Bar (Inner Temple) 99; took silk 23; Recorder of Poole 17-25, of Bath 25-28, and of Plymouth 28-32; Judge King's Bench Div. of High Court of Justice 32-38; a Lord Justice of Appeal 38-44; Lord of Appeal in Ordinary 44-46; Lord Chief Justice of England 46-58, retd.
Queen Elizabeth Building, Temple, London, E.C.4, England.

Goddard, Samuel Pearson, A.B., LL.B.; American lawyer and politician; b. 8 Aug. 1919; ed. Harvard Coll., and Univ. of Arizona Law School.

U.S. Army Air Corps 41-46; law firm Terry and Wright 46; fmr. senior partner, law firm Goddard, Gin, Hanshaw & Gianas; Exec. Vice-Pres. Niles Radio Corpn.; Pres. of United Fund 60-62, Pres. Western Conference of United Funds 61-63; mem. Nat. Board Dirs. United Community Funds and Councils of America 63-; Gov. of Arizona 65-; Democrat.

Office: State House, Phoenix, Arizona 85007; Home: 4813 Calle Jabeli, Tucson, Arizona 85711, U.S.A.

Godden, Rumer (Mrs. Margaret Rumer Haynes Dixon); British author; b. 10 Dec. 1907; ed. privately.

Publs. *Chinese Puzzle* 35, *The Lady and the Unicorn* 37, *Black Narcissus* 39, *Breakfast with the Nikolides* 41, *Fugue in Time* 44, *The River* 46, *A Candle for St. Jude* 48, *Kingfishers Catch Fire* 52, *An Episode of Sparrows* 55, *The Greengage Summer* 59, *China Court* 61, *The Battle of the Villa Fiorita* 63; trans. *Prayers from the Ark* 62, *Two Under the Indian Sun* (autobiography) 65; *The Kitchen Madonna* 67; poems, children's books, films.

Lamb House, Rye, East Sussex, England.

Gödel, Kurt, PH.D.; American logician; b. 28 April 1906; ed. Universität Wien.

Dozent, Univ. of Vienna 33-38; mem. Inst. for Advanced Study, Princeton, N.J. 33, 35, 38-53, Prof. 53-; mem. Nat. Acad. of Sciences, American Philosophical Soc.; Foreign mem. Royal Soc. (U.K.); Einstein Award (co-recipient) 51; Hon. Litt.D., Yale Univ., Hon. Sc.D. Harvard Univ., Amherst Coll.

Publs. *Ueber formal unentscheidbare Saetze* 31, *The Consistency of the Continuum Hypothesis* 40, *Rotating Universes in General Relativity Theory* 50.

Institute for Advanced Study, Princeton, N.J., U.S.A. Telephone: 609-WA4-4400.

Godley, George McMurtrie; American diplomatist; b. 23 Aug. 1917; ed. Yale and Chicago Univs.

U.S. Naval Reserve 39-41, U.S. Marine Corps 45-46; Foreign Service Officer 41-, served Marseilles, Berne, Paris, Pnom Penh 41-55; Foreign Affairs Officer, Dept. of State 57-60; Staff Co-ordinator, Dept. of State 60; Counselor, Consul, Léopoldville 61-62; Dir., Office of Central African Affairs, Dept. of State 62-64; Amb. to Republic of Congo (Kinshasa) 64-.

American Embassy, Kinshasa, Republic of Congo.

Godwin, Francis Wood, Jr., A.B., M.S., PH.D.; American research director; b. 10; ed. State Univ. of Iowa.

Dir. of Coal Research, Armour Research Foundation 37-38, Dir of Chemical Engineering Research 38-41, Asst. Dir. Armour Research Foundation 41-45, Assoc. Dir. 45-46; Dir. Inter-American Research Service 46-47; Dir. Int. Div., Armour Research Foundation 47-50; Adviser on Int. Development 50-52; Consultant on Industrial Development, Int. Bank for Reconstruction and Development 50-52, Chief Technical Research Inst. Programme 52-60; Adviser, Laboratorios Nacionales de Fomento Industrial, Mexico 50; Dir. and Vice-Chair. Governing Board, Ceylon Inst. of Scientific and Industrial Research 55-59; mem. Board of Dirs. Development Finance Corpn. of Ceylon 56-59; Industrial Development Consultant, governments and international bodies 60-; Dir. and Project Man. Sudan Industrial Research Inst. 64-; Planning Consultant U.S. Peace Corps 62-63.

Publs. ed. and co-author: *Technological and Economic Survey of Argentine Industries* 43, *Technological Audit of Selected Mexican Industries* 46; co-author: *Report on Cuba* 51, *The Economic Development of Ceylon* 53, *The Economic Development of Nigeria* 55; ed.: *The Economic Development of Guatemala* 51, *Human Skills in the Decade of Development* 63.

Sudan Industrial Research Institute, Khartoum, Sudan.

Godwin, Harry, M.A., PH.D., SC.D., F.G.S., F.L.S., F.R.S.; British botanist; b. 9 May 1901; ed. Long Eaton County Secondary School and Clare Coll., Cambridge.

Fellow of Clare Coll., Cambridge 25-; Univ. Demonstrator in Botany 23-, Univ. Lecturer 34-48, Reader 48-60; Head of Univ. Sub-Dept. of Quaternary Research 48-66; Prof. of Botany 60-68; Pres. British Ecological Soc. 43; Pres. 10th Int. Botanical Congress, Edin. 64; Pres. Botanical Section, British Asscn. 56; mem. Nature Conservancy 49-54, 65-; co-Editor *New Phytologist* 31-61; Editor *Journal of Ecology* 58-65; mem. Svenska Växtgeografiska Salskapet 37-; Corresp. mem. Botanical Soc., Gothenburg 53; Hon. Fellow Botanical Soc. of Edinburgh 61; Corresp. mem. Botanical Soc. of America 66; Foreign mem. Royal Scientific Soc., Uppsala 61; Foreign mem. German Acad. of Sciences, Leopoldina 62; Foreign mem. Royal Danish Acad. of Science and Letters 62; Prestwich Medal, Geological Soc. of London 51; Croonian Lecturer Royal Soc., London 60; Gold Medal, Linnean Soc., London 66; Medal of Univ. of Helsinki 66; Hon. Sc.D. (Trinity Coll., Dublin) 60.

Publs. *Plant Biology* 30, *History of the British Flora* 56; also scientific papers on ecology of bogs and fens 29-41; on vegetational history, pollen-analysis, radiocarbon dating in context of Quaternary history 35-; pollen-grain ontogeny 66-.

30 Barton Road, Cambridge, England. Telephone: 50883.

Goehr, Alexander (son of conductor Walter Goehr); British composer; b. 1932; ed. Berkhamsted School, Royal Manchester Coll. of Music, Paris Conservatoire (with Olivier Messiaen), and privately with Yvonne Loriod.

Composer, teacher, conductor 56-; held classes at Morley Coll., London; part-time post with B.B.C., being responsible for production of orchestral concerts 60-; works performed in Darmstadt, Prague, Venice, Zagreb, Warsaw, Cologne, Donaueschingen, Lucerne and other cities in Europe and America; Hon. Fellow Royal Manchester Coll. of Music; awarded Churchill Fellowship 68.

Works include: *Songs of Babel* 51, *Sonata* 52, *Fantasias* 54, *String Quartet* 56-57, *Cappriccio* 57, *The Deluge* 57-58, *La Belle Dame Sans Merci* 58, *Variations* 59, *Four Songs from the Japanese* 59, *Sutter's Gold* 59-60, *Suite* 61, *Hecuba's Lament* 59-61, *A Little Cantata of Proverbs* 62, *Concerto for Violin and Orchestra* 61-62, *Two Choruses* 62, *Virtutes* 63, *Little Symphony* 63, *Little Music for Strings* 63, *Five Poems and an Epigram of William Blake* 64, *Three Pieces for Piano* 64, *Pastorals* 65, *Piano Trio* 66, *Arden muss sterben* (Arden Must Die—opera) 66, *Quartet* 67, *Romanzer* 68.

3 Meredyth Road, Barnes, London, S.W.13, England.

Goenka, Ramanath; Indian newspaper director; b. 11 May 1902; ed. Dharbhanga, Bihar.

Managing Dir. *Indian Express* Group of Newspapers; Del. to Empire Press Union Conf. 51.

Express Estates, Mount Road, Madras 2, India. Telephone: 83151 (Madras).

Goethem, Fernand Van; Belgian lawyer; b. 95; ed. Univs. of Louvain, Paris, Vienna and Geneva.

Prof. of Law, Univ. of Louvain (Dean 51-52); Assessor, Legal Section, Conseil d'Etat; Pres. Inst. Interuniversitaire de Droit Social; mem. Brussels Conf. for the Revision of the Berne Convention on Copyright 48; Del. to UN, New York 52; Vatican City del. to Universal Postal Union Conf. 52; mem. Royal Flemish Acad. of Science, Pres. 58; Pres. 2nd Int. Congress for Social Law, Brussels 58; Emeritus Prof. 62.

Publs. include: *Précis de législation sociale belge* 39, *Droit du Travail* (with Geysen) 50, *Droit de la Sécurité Sociale* (with Leen and Geysen) 55, *Beginselen van het*

Volkenrecht 55, *Nieuwe Vormen vaan Internationale Gemeenschapsorganisatie* 55, *Rechtsfilosophie* 58, *Internationale Orde Nieuwe Wegen* 62, *Volkenrecht* (with Suy) 65.
2 Parkplein, Royal Park Residence 4e, Ghent, Belgium.
Telephone: 09-22-37-27.

Goett, Harry Joseph; American aeronautical engineer; b. 14 Nov. 1910; ed. Holy Cross Coll.
Aeronautical Engineer, New York Univ. 33; Chief, Full Scale and Flight Research Div., Ames Aero Lab., Nat. Advisory Cttee. for Aeronautics, Moffett Field, California 48-60; Dir. Goddard Space Flight Center, Nat. Aeronautics and Space Admin. (N.A.S.A.) 60-.
Goddard Space Flight Center, Greenbelt, Maryland, U.S.A.

Goetz, Wolfgang; German writer; b. 85.
Novelist and playwright; fmr. Counsellor to Board of Official Film Examiners.
Publs. *Die Wiederkehr* 13, *Das Wunder* 19, *Die Reise ins Blaue* 20, *Das wilde Säuseln* 21, *Gneisenau* 25, *Robert Emmet* 27, *Muspilli* 27, *Eine deutsche Geschichte* 31, *Der Mönch von Heisterbach* 35, *Der Ministerpräsident* 36, *Ergötzliches* 37, *Das Wiegenlied* 46, *Du und die Literatur, Werner Krauss* 54, *Das Glück sitzt an der nächsten Ecke* 58, *Begegnungen und Bekentnisse*.
Konstanzerstrasse 64, Berlin W.15, Germany.
Telephone: 8811544.

Goetze, Albrecht; American assyriologist; b. Germany 11 Jan. 1897; ed. Munich, Leipzig, Berlin and Heidelberg Univs.
Privatdozent, Heidelberg Univ. 23-30; Prof. Marburg Univ. 30-33; Visiting Prof. Yale Univ. 34, William M. Laffan Prof. of Assyriology and Babylonian Literature, Yale Univ. 36-56; Sterling Prof. Yale Univ. 56-65; Emer. 65-; mem. Royal Danish Acad.; corresp. mem. Inst. for Comparative Research in Human Culture; mem. American Philosophical Soc.; Dir. American School of Oriental Research Baghdad 47-54; Editor *Journal of Cuneiform Studies*; hon. mem. Société Asiatique de Paris; corresp. mem. Acad. des Inscriptions et Belles Lettres; mem. Deutsches Arch. Inst.
Publs. *Kulturgeschichte Kleinasiens* 33, *Hethiter, Churriter und Assyrer* 36, *The Hittite Ritual of Tunnawi* 38, *Kizzuwatna* 40, *Old Babylonian Omen Texts* 47, *Laws of Eshnunna* 56; various other books.
2 Maplewood Road, New Haven, Conn., U.S.A.

Goff, Abe McGregor, LL.B.; American lawyer and government official; b. 21 Dec. 1899; ed. Univ. of Idaho.
Army Service, First World War; Law Practice, Idaho 24, Prosecuting Attorney 26-34; State Senator, Idaho 40-41; Pres. Idaho State Bar 40-41; army service, Africa, Europe, Pacific, Japan, Second World War; mem. U.S. Congress 47-48; Law Practice 48-54; Gen. Counsel, U.S. Post Office Dept. 54-58; U.S. Interstate Commerce Comm. 58-67, Chair. 64-67; Legion of Merit and other awards; Republican.
503 East C Street, Moscow, Idaho 83843, U.S.A.
Telephone: 208-882-2627.

Gogoleva, Elena Nikolaevna; Soviet actress; b. 1900; ed. Moscow Philharmonic Soc. School of Music and Drama.
Acted at Maly Theatre 18-; People's Artist of the U.S.S.R.; State prizewinner (thrice).
Principal roles: plays by Ostrovsky, Gorky and contemporary playwrights.
Maly Theatre, 1/6 Ploshchad Sverdlova, Moscow, U.S.S.R.

Goheen, Robert Francis, B.A., M.A., PH.D., LITT.D., LL.D.; American classics professor; b. 15 Aug. 1919; ed. Lawrenceville School and Princeton Univ.
Instructor, Princeton Univ. 48-50, Asst. Prof. 50-57, Prof. 57-; Senior Fellow in Classics, American Acad. in Rome 52-53; Dir. Nat. Woodrow Wilson Fellowship

Programme 53-56; Pres. Princeton Univ. July 57-; Hon. Law Degree (Madras, Harvard, Yale, Rutgers, Temple, Columbia and Pa. Univs., State Univ. of New York, Hamilton Coll., Univ. of North Carolina, St. Mary's Coll., Moraga, New York Univ.); Hon. D.Litt. (Brown Univ. and Trinity Coll.); Trustee, Robert Coll., Istanbul, Carnegie Foundation for the Advancement of Teaching; mem. of the Board Carnegie Foundation for Advancement of Teaching, Rockefeller Foundation, mem. American Council on Education, Chair. 61; Defense Advisory Cttee. on Education in the Armed Forces, Council on Foreign Affairs, Woodrow Wilson Foundation, Equitable Life Assurance Soc. of U.S.
Publ. *The Imagery of Sophocles' Antigone.*
1 Nassau Hall, Princeton University, Princeton, N.J., U.S.A.

Goka, F. K. D.; Ghanaian politician; b. 19; ed. Presbyterian Training Coll., Akropong.
Commissioner, Volta Region 60; Minister of Finance and Trade 61-64; now Chair. Sugar Products Corpn.
Sugar Products Corporation, Accra, Ghana.

Gökmen, Oğuz; Turkish diplomatist; b. 4 May 1916; ed. Ankara Üniversitesi and Univ. de Paris à la Sorbonne.
Entered Ministry of Foreign Affairs, Ankara 40; Second Sec. Turkish Embassy, Paris 44-47, First Sec. 47-49; Chief of Section, Dept. of Trade, Ministry of Foreign Affairs 49-50; Chargé d'Affaires, Buenos Aires 50-53; Counsellor, Sofia 53-54; Asst. Chief, Dept. of Trade and Trade Agreements 56; Gen. Dir. Econ. Dept. of Ministry 58; Amb. to Argentina (concurrently to Uruguay and Paraguay) 62-64; Perm. Rep. of Turkey to European Econ. Community (EEC) 64-66; Amb. to German Fed. Repub. Dec. 66-.
Türkischer Botschafter, 532 Bad Godesberg-Mehlem, Utestrasse, German Federal Republic.
Telephone: Bad Godesberg 15061.

Golanski, Henryk; Polish politician; b. 1 Jan. 1908; ed. Electricity Faculty, Warsaw Polytechnic.
Under-Secretary of State, Ministry of Industries 45-49; Minister of Light Industries 49-50; Under-Sec. of State, Ministry of Higher Education and Science 50-59, Minister of Higher Educ. 59-65; Chair. Main Council for Higher Education 47-65; mem. Liaison Cttee. of Polish Acad. of Sciences, State Council for Peaceful Uses of Nuclear Energy, Praesidium Cttee. for State Awards; Amb. to Greece 66-.
Polish Embassy, Athens, Greece.

Gold, Thomas, F.R.S., M.A.; American (fmrly. British, b. Austrian) astronomer; b. 22 May 1920; ed. Zuoz Coll., Switzerland, and Trinity Coll., Cambridge.
Experimental Officer, British Admiralty (radar research) 43-46; Fellow, Trinity Coll., Cambridge 47; Chief Asst. to Astronomer Royal, Royal Greenwich Observatory 52-56; Prof. of Astronomy, Harvard Univ. 57-59; Prof. of Astronomy, Chair. Dept. of Astronomy, Cornell Univ. 59-; Dir. Cornell Univ. Centre for Radio, physics and Space Research 59-; Fellow A.A.A.S.
Publs. *The Steady State Theory of the Expanding Universe* 48, *The Alignment of Galactic Dust* 52, *The Field of a Uniformly Accelerated Charge* 54, *Instability of the Earth's Axis of Rotation* 55, *The Lunar Surface* 56, *Cosmic Rays from the Sun* 57, *Plasma and Magnetic Fields in the Solar System* 59, *The Origin of Solar Flares* 60, etc.
410 Space Sciences, Cornell University, Ithaca, N.Y. 14850, U.S.A.
Telephone: 607-275-5284.

Goldberg, Arthur Joseph, B.S. in L., DR. JUR.; American lawyer and politician; b. 8 Aug. 1908; ed. City Coll., Chicago and Northwestern Univ.
Private Law Practice 29-48; Gen. Counsel, Congress of Industrial Workers 48-55; Gen. Counsel, United Steelworkers 48-61; Special Counsel, American Federa-

tion of Labor-Congress of Industrial Organisations 55-61; Gen. Counsel, Industrial Union Dept., A.F.L.-C.I.O. 55-61; Sec. of Labor 61-62; Judge of U.S. Supreme Court 62-65; Perm. Rep. of U.S. to U.N. 65-68; Democrat.
Publs. *Civil Rights in Labor-Management Relations: a Labor Viewpoint* 51, *A.F.L.-C.I.O.—Labor United* 56, *Unions and the Anti-Trust Laws* 56, *Management's Reserved Rights* 56, *Ethical Practices* 58, *A Trade Union Point of View* 59, *Suggestions for a New Labor Policy* 60, *The Role of the Labor Union in an Age of Bigness* 60, *The Annals of The American Academy of Political and Social Science* (Vol. 339) 62, *The Defenses of Freedom: The Public Papers of Arthur J. Goldberg* 66.
c/o United States Mission to the United Nations, 799 United Nations Plaza, New York 17, N.Y., U.S.A. Telephone: YUkon 6-2424.

Goldblatt, Harry, B.A., M.D., C.M.; American pathologist; b. 14 March 1891; ed. McGill Univ., Montreal. Assistant Dept. of Pathology, Royal Victoria Hospital, Montreal 16-17; Medical Corps. U.S. Army 17-19; Pathologist-in-Charge, Lakeside Hospital, Cleveland, Ohio 19-21; Beit Memorial Fellow; Research in Experimental Pathology, Lister Inst. of Preventive Medicine, London 21-23; Research in Experimental Physiology, London Univ. 23-24; Asst. Prof. of Pathology, Western Reserve Univ., Cleveland 24-27, Assoc. Prof. 27-35, Assoc. Dir. of Pathology 29-46, Prof. of Experimental Pathology 35-46, 54-61, Emeritus 61-; Dir. Inst. of Medical Research, Cedars of Lebanon Hospital, Los Angeles 46-53, Laboratories of Mount Sinai Hospital 53-61, Louis D. Beaumont Memorial Research Laboratories, Mount Sinai Hospital 61-; mem. numerous U.S. medical asscns. and socs. including American Asscn. of Pathologists and Bacteriologists, American Soc. of Clinical Pathologists and American Medical Asscn.; mem. Physiological Soc. (Great Britain); Hon. Fellow American Coll. of Cardiology; Hon. mem. Brazilian Soc. of Cardiology; many awards including John Phillips Award of the American Coll. of Physicians 36, Gold-headed Cane Award March 66, Stouffer Award and American Heart Asscn. Research Achievement Award Oct. 66; Distinguished mem. Acad. of Medicine, Cleveland 66; D.Sc. h.c., Western Reserve Univ. 66.
Publs. Over 100 scientific articles for various journals and learned socs.
c/o Mount Sinai Hospital, Cleveland, Ohio 44106, U.S.A.

Goldby, Frank, M.D., F.R.C.P.; British anatomist; b. 25 May 1903; ed. Mercers' School, London, and Gonville and Caius Coll., Cambridge.
Asst. Pathologist, King's Coll. Hospital, London 29; Senior Demonstrator in Anatomy, Univ. Coll., London 31; Lecturer in charge Anatomy Dept., Hong Kong 33; Lecturer in Anatomy, Cambridge Univ., and Fellow Queens' Coll. 34-37; Prof. of Anatomy and Histology, Adelaide Univ., South Australia 37-45; Prof. of Anatomy, St. Mary's Hospital Medical School, London Univ. 45-.
Publs. papers on Embryology and on the Pathology and Comparative Anatomy of the Nervous System.
St. Mary's Hospital Medical School, London, W.2.

Goldenbaum, Ernst; German politician; b. 15 Dec. 1898; ed. elementary school.
Mem. of Communist Party since 20; mem. of Diet of Mecklenburg-Schwerin 24-26 and 29-32; Editor of *Volkswacht*, Schwerin 27-32; farmer in Parchim 35; in concentration camp during Second World War; elected to Mecklenburg Diet 46; mem. German People's Council March 48; Chair. Exec. Cttee. of German Peasants' Party (D.B.D.); mem. German Economic Comm.; fmr. Minister of Agriculture in Govt. of German Democratic Republic; Vice-Pres. Volkskammer.
Volkskammer, Berlin, Germany.

Golding, William (Gerald), C.B.E.; British writer; b. 19 Sept. 1911; ed. Marlborough Grammar School, and Brasenose Coll., Oxford.
Publs. *Lord of the Flies* 54 (film 63), *The Inheritors* 55, *Pincher Martin* 56, *Free Fall* 59, *The Spire* 64, *The Hot Gates* 65, *The Pyramid* 67; play *Brass Butterfly* 58.
Ebble Thatch, Bowerchalke, Wiltshire, England.

Goldman, Eric F., M.A., PH.D., LITT.D., LL.D., L.H.D.; American historian and writer; b. 17 June 1915; ed. Baltimore City Coll., and Johns Hopkins Univ.
Professor, Princeton Univ. 40-, Rollins Prof. of History 62-; Special Consultant to Pres. Johnson Feb. 64-66; Pres. Soc. of American Historians 62-; Moderator N.B.C. TV Discussion Panel 59-67; Bancroft Prize 52, Library of Congress Fellow 47, Guggenheim Fellow 56; McCosh Fellow 62.
Publs. incl. *Rendezvous with Destiny: A History of Modern American Reform, The Crucial Decade, America 1945-55, The Crucial Decade—and After, America 1945-60.*
Princeton University, Princeton, New Jersey, U.S.A. Telephone: 609-452-4174.

Goldmann, Nahum; Israeli (fmrly. American, b. Polish) Zionist leader; b. 10 July 1895; ed. Heidelberg, Berlin and Marburg Univs.
Editor and Publisher German Hebrew Encyclopedia 22-34; mem. Zionist Political Comm. 27; Act. Chair. Zionist Action Cttee. 33; escaped from Germany 34; Rep. of Jewish Agency to L. of N.; in U.S. 40-46; Dir. Jewish intelligence service, New York during Second World War; fmr. personal rep. of Weizmann; Pres. World Jewish Congress, World Zionist Organisation, Conf. on Jewish Claims against Germany; Chair. Cttee. on Jewish Claims against Austria.
16 rue Crespin, Geneva, Switzerland.

Goldmark, Peter Carl, PH.D.; American (b. Hungary) scientist; b. 2 Dec. 1906; ed. Univs. of Vienna and Berlin.
Went to U.S. 33; joined Columbia Broadcasting System as Chief Engineer, Television Research Dept. 36, Vice-Pres. (Engineering) 50, Pres. and Dir. of Research, C.B.S. Laboratories (Div. of Columbia Broadcasting System) 54-; Visiting Prof. of Medical Electronics, Univ. of Pennsylvania Medical School; mem. Nat. Acad. of Engineering 66-; Morris Liebmann Memorial Prize for Electronic Research 46; Television Broadcasters Asscn. Medal (for work on colour television) 54; Vladimir K. Zworykin Television Prize 61.
Major works: developed first practical colour television system (field-sequential system) 40; developed long-playing record 48; transmission of Lunar Orbiter's photographs of the lunar surface; contributed to development of special electron tubes, audio and acoustical systems, magnetic recording, and data storage and display; supervised development of Linotron (computer-tape-driven, ultra high speed photocomposing system); supervised development of Electronic Video Recording (E.V.R.).
C.B.S. Laboratories, High Ridge Road, Stamford, Conn., U.S.A.

Goldschmidt, Bertrand, DR. ès SC.; French scientist; b. 2 Nov. 1912; ed. Ecole de Physique et de Chimie, Univ. of Paris.
Asst. Curie Laboratory, Paris 35-40; Section Leader Anglo-Canadian Atomic Project 42-45, Head, Chemistry Div. 46; Head Chemistry Div. Commissariat à l'Energie Atomique 46-59, Head, External Relations Div. 53-59, Head, External Relations and Planning 59-; Gov. for France Int. Atomic Energy 57; Prof. Inst. d'Etudes Politiques 60-65; Exec. Vice-Pres. European Atomic Energy Soc. 55-58; Pres. Soc. Industrielle des Minerais de l'Ouest 55-61; Commdr. Légion d'Honneur; Atoms for Peace Award 67.

Publs. *L'Aventure atomique* 62, *Les Rivalités atomiques* 67.
Commissariat à l'Energie Atomique, 29-33 rue de la Fédération, Paris 15e, France.

Goldstein, Rabbi Israel, M.A., D.D., D.H.L., LITT.H.D., LL.D.; American Rabbi; b. 18 June 1896; ed. Univ. of Pennsylvania, Jewish Theological Seminary of America, and Columbia Univ.
Rabbi Congregation B'nai Jeshurun N.Y. City 18-60, Rabbi Emeritus 61-; Pres. Jewish Conciliation Board of America 29-, Jewish Nat. Fund of America 33-43 (now Hon. Pres.); Pres. Synagogue Council of America 42-44, Zionist Organisation of America 44-46; Assoc. Consultant to U.S. Del. U.N. Conf. San Francisco 45; Chair. World Confed. of Gen. Zionists 46-, United Palestine Appeal 47-49; Co-Chair. United Jewish Appeal 47-49; Treas. Jewish Agency 47-49; Pres. Amidar Israel Nat. Housing Co. for Immigrants 48-49; mem. World Jewish Congress Exec. 48- and Chair. of its Western Hemisphere Exec. 50-60, Hon. Vice-Pres. 59-; Pres. American Jewish Congress 51-58, now Hon. Pres.; Pres. World Hebrew Union; mem. Jewish Agency for Israel Exec. 48-; World Chair. Keren Hayesod-United Israel Appeal; mem. Board of Govs. Hebrew Univ. of Jerusalem; mem. Board of Govs. Weizmann Inst. of Science; Vice-Pres. Conf. Jewish Organizations on Material Claims *vs.* Germany 51-; mem. Joint Exec. Board Jewish Claims on Austria 52-; Pres. Jewish Restitution Successor Organisation 50-61; Chair. American Cttee. for Israel's Tenth Anniversary Celebration; Hon. Vice-Chair. Liberal Party 50-; Founder Brandeis Univ. 46; Hon. degrees from New York Univ., Brandeis Univ.; Israel Goldstein Chair. in Zionism at Hebrew Univ. of Jerusalem; Israel Goldstein Chair. in Practical Theology, Jewish Theological Seminary of America.
Publs. *A Century of Judaism in New York* 30, *Towards a Solution* 40, *Mourner's Devotions* 41, *Brandeis University* 51, *American Jewry Comes of Age* 55, *Transition Years* 62.
270 West 89th Street, New York, N.Y., U.S.A.; Keren Hayesod, Jerusalem, Israel.

Goldstein, Sydney, PH.D., M.A., F.R.S., F.R.Ae.S.; British university professor; b. 3 Dec. 1903; ed. Bede Collegiate School, Sunderland, and Univs. of Leeds and Cambridge.
Rockefeller Research Fellow Univ. of Göttingen 28-29; Lecturer in Applied Mathematics, Univ. of Manchester 29-31, Univ. of Cambridge 31-45; Fellow, St. John's Coll., Cambridge 29-32, 33-45, Hon. Fellow 65-; Leverhulme Research Fellow, Calif. Inst. of Technology 38-39; Aerodynamics Div., Nat. Physical Laboratory 39-45; Beyer Prof. of Applied Mathematics, Univ. of Manchester 45-50; Chair. Aeronautical Research Council of Great Britain 46-49; Prof. of Applied Mathematics, Inst. of Technology, Haifa 50-55, Chair. Aeronautical Engineering 50-54, Vice-Pres. 51-54; Gordon-McKay Prof. of Applied Mathematics, Harvard Univ. 55-; foreign mem. Royal Netherlands Acad. of Sciences; Dr. h.c. of Engineering (Purdue Univ. 67), of Science (Case Inst. of Technology 67); Timoshenko Medal (American Soc. Mech. Eng.) 65.
Publs. *Lectures on Fluid Mechanics* 60; Editor: *Modern Developments in Fluid Dynamics* 38 (Dover edn. 65); papers on mathematics, mathematical physics, hydrodynamics and aerodynamics.
Division of Engineering and Applied Physics, Pierce Hall, Harvard University, Cambridge, Mass. 02138, U.S.A.

Goldstücker, Eduard, PH.D.; Czechoslovak university professor; b. 30 May 1913; ed. Charles Univ., Prague, and Oxford Univ., England.
Secretary of League for Human Rights, Prague 36-38; secondary school teacher 38-39; in U.K. 39-45, worked at Czechoslovak Ministry of Foreign Affairs in London 43-44; Ambassadorial Sec., Paris 44-45; Deputy Amb. in London 47-49; Envoy to Tel-Aviv 50-51; political imprisonment 51-55; Dept. of German Literature, Faculty of Philosophy, Charles Univ., Prague 56-, Prof. 63-, Pro-Rector of Charles Univ. 66-; Chair. Union of Czechoslovak Writers 67-; several awards including Goethe Gold Medal of Goethe Inst., Munich 67.
Publs. History of German literature, especially German literature in Prague; *Rainer Maria Rilke und Franz Werfel* 60, *Franz Kafka* 64 (Prize of Publishing House of Czechoslovak Writers).
Philosophy Faculty, Charles University, Prague 1, nám. Krasnoarmějcu 2, Czechoslovakia.

Goldwater, Barry; American politician; b. 1 Jan. 1909; ed. Staunton Military Acad., Univ. of Arizona.
Republican Senator from Arizona 52-64; nominated as Republican candidate for Pres. of United States, July 64; Goldwater's Inc. 29-, President 37-53, Chair. Board 53-; U.S. Army Air Force 41-45.
Publs. *Arizona Portraits* 40, *Journey Down the River of Canyons* 40, *Speeches of Henry Ashurst: The Conscience of a Conservative* 60, *Why Not Victory?* 60, *Where I Stand* 64.
Phoenix, Arizona, U.S.A.

Goldwyn, Samuel; American film producer; b. Poland 27 Aug. 1882.
Organiser Jesse Lasky Feature Play Co. 13, Goldwyn Pictures Corpn. 16, Eminent Authors Pictures Inc. 19; independent producer 23-; Chair. Samuel Goldwyn Productions; Motion Picture Academy award 47 for *The Best Years of Our Lives*, Irving Thalberg Award.
1041 N. Formosa Avenue, Los Angeles 46, Calif., U.S.A.

Golikov, Marshal Filipp Ivanovich; Soviet army officer and politician; b. 1900; ed. Frunze Military Acad.
Soviet Army 18-; mem. C.P.S.U. 18-; Dep. Chief of Gen. Staff 40-41; commanded forces Bryansk and Voronezh Fronts, Dep. Commdr. Stalingrad Front 41-43; Chief of Gen. Board of Cadres of the Soviet Army 43-50; Military Command Posts 50-56; Head, Military Acad. of Armoured Tank Forces 56-58; Head, Chief Political Board of Soviet Army and Navy 58-62; Insp.-Gen. Ministry of Defence 62-; Marshal of the Soviet Union 61; mem. Central Cttee. of C.P.S.U. 61-66; Deputy to Supreme Soviet U.S.S.R. 61-66; Awarded Order of Lenin (four times), October Revolution, Suvorov, Kutuzov, Order of the Red Banner (four times), Red Star, Weapon of Honour with Coat-of-Arms in Gold, and other awards.
Ministry of Defence, 34 Maurice Thorez Embankment, Moscow, U.S.S.R.

Golovchenko, Fyodor Petrovich; Soviet politician; b. 1918; ed. Moscow Aviation Engineering Inst.
Engineer 44-47; at Kharkov S. Orjonikidze Tractor Works, becoming Sec. of Party Cttee. 47-58; Exec. posts, Central Cttee. of C.P. of the Ukraine 58-65; Second Sec. Kiev Regional Cttee. of C.P. of the Ukraine 65-66, First Sec. March 66-; also mem. Central Cttee. of C.P. Ukraine, Alt. mem. Central Cttee. C.P.S.U. and Deputy to U.S.S.R. Supreme Soviet; mem. C.P.S.U. 49-; mem. Legislative Proposals Cttee., Soviet of Union.
Kiev Regional Committee of the Communist Party of the Ukraine, Kiev, U.S.S.R.

Golovin, Vasili Vasilievich; Soviet trade corporation official; b. 07; ed. Leningrad Engineering and Economics Inst.
Economic work, Moscow 32-37; People's Commissariat of Foreign Trade 37-41; Soviet Army 41-45; Ministry of Foreign Trade 45-52; Chair. *Raznoexport* (non-ferrous metals, etc.) 52-55, *Sojuzkhimexport* (medical and cosmetic goods), *Medexport* (medicines) 61-; mem.

C.P.S.U. 21-; Order of Lenin, Red Banner of Labour (twice); numerous decorations.
Vsesojuznoje Objedinenije Medexport, 31 Ul. Kakhovka, Moscow, U.S.S.R.

Golovkin, Alexandr Ivanovich; Soviet engineer and social worker; ed. Moscow Machine Building Inst.
Compositor and then engineer in the publishing industry 25-43; Party work 43-57; mem. Presidium and Gen. Sec. U.S.S.R. Chamber of Commerce 57-; Vice-Pres. U.S.S.R. Chamber of Commerce 68-; Order of Red Banner of Labour; several decorations.
U.S.S.R. Chamber of Commerce, 6 ulitsa Kuibysheva, Moscow, U.S.S.R.

Golschmann, Vladimir, American conductor; b. 16 Dec. 1893; ed. in Paris.
Conducted Golschmann concerts in Paris 19-24; and also all major symphony orchestras of France; conducted Scottish Orchestra 28-30; also conducted throughout Europe and the Americas; conductor of the Saint Louis Symphony Orchestra 31-57; now Conductor, Denver Symphony Orchestra; toured in more than 250 cities; Officer of the Legion of Honour.
1615 California Street, Denver, Colorado, U.S.A.

Gołubiew, Antoni; Polish novelist; b. 07.
Publs. Cycle of historical novels *Bolesław Chrobry*, *Puszcza* (The Forest), *Szło nowe* (The Coming of the New), *Złe dni* (Bad Days), *Rozdroża* (Crossroads), *Listy do Przyjaciela* (Letters to a Friend), *Poszukiwania* (Searches).
Jaskółcza 4, Cracow, Poland.

Golzio, Silvio; Italian statistician and business executive; b. 2 Feb. 1909; ed. Università degli Studi, Turin.
University lecturer, Florence and Turin Univs.; deported to Germany 43-45; Head, Research Office Comitato Interministriale per la Ricostruzione 47-50; Dir. Istituto Nazionale delle Assicurazioni; Gen. Manager then Pres. Società Idroelettrica Piemonte; Pres. and Managing Dir. Società Finanziaria Telefonica (STET) 61-; Dir.-Gen. Istituto Ricostruzione Industriale 64-; Pres. Italian Business Press Association; two war decorations.
Piazza Solferino 11, Turin, Italy.

Gombault, Charles Henri; French journalist; b. 25 Aug. 1907; ed. Lycée Condorcet, Paris.
Journalist *Le Soir*, later *Le Populaire* 27; Soc. and Political Journalist, *Paris-Midi*, *Paris-Soir* 28-32; Asst. Editor-in-Chief *Match* 39; Ed. and co-founder, *France London* 40-45; Sec.-Gen., later Editor-in-Chief, *France-Soir* 45; Man. Dir. 60-; Officier, Légion d'Honneur.
France-Soir, 100 rue Réaumur, Paris 2e, France.

Gombrich, Ernst (Hans Josef), C.B.E., PH.D., M.A., F.B.A., F.S.A.; British art historian; b. 30 March 1909; ed. Theresianum, Vienna, and Vienna Univ.
Research Asst., Warburg Inst., Univ. of London 36-39; B.B.C. Monitoring Service, Second World War; Senior Research Fellow, Warburg Inst. 46-48, Lecturer 48-54, Reader 54-56, Special Lecturer 56-59, Dir. 59-; Prof. of History of the Classical Tradition, Univ. of London 59-; Slade Prof. of Fine Art, Univ. of Oxford 50-53; Durning-Lawrence Prof. of History of Art, Univ. Coll., London 56-59; Visiting Prof. Harvard Univ. 59; Slade Prof. of Fine Art, Univ. of Cambridge 61-63; Corresp. mem. Turin Acad.; Hon. mem. American Acad. of Arts and Sciences; Hon. D. Lit. (Queen's Univ., Belfast), Hon. LL.D. (St. Andrews), Hon. D.Litt. (Leeds); W. H. Smith and Son Annual Literary Award 64.
Publs. *Caricature* (with E. Kris) 40, *The Story of Art* 50, *Art and Illusion* 60, *Meditations on a Hobby Horse* 63, *Norm and Form* 66.
19 Briardale Gardens, London, N.W.3, England.

Gombrowicz, Witold, L. en D.; Polish writer; b. 4 Aug. 1904.
Lived in Argentina 40-63, Germany 64, France 65-; Prix int. de Littérature 67.
Publs. *Yvonne* (play) 35, *Ferdydurke* (novel) 37, *Le Mariage* (play) 47, *La Pornografie* (novel) 50, *Le Trans-atlantique* (novel) 50, *Journal* (3 vols.) 53-68, *Cosmos* (novel) 64, *Opérette* (play) 66.
36 Place du Grand-Jardin, Vence (A.M.), France.
Telephone: 32-13-96.

Gomes, Orlando; Brazilian university professor; b. 7 Dec. 1909; ed. Faculty of Law, Bahia.
Lecturer in Law, Bahia 30-31, Prof. Social Law, Faculty of Econ. Sciences 32-36, Civil Law, Faculty of Law 37-; fmr. Pres. Inst. of Advocates and Inst. of Labour Law, Bahia; fmr. Dir. Faculty of Law, fmr. Vice-Rector, Univ. of Bahia; Pres. Commercial Asscn. and Banking Syndicate of Bahia; Montezema Prize, Prize of the Inst. of Advocates; Pres. Banco Comercial do Nordeste S.A.
Publs. *Direitos Reais, Memoria Justificativa do Ante-projeto de Código Civil, A Reforma do Código Civil, Transformações Gerais do Direito das Obricações.*
Avenida dos Estados Unidos 18, Salvador, Bahia, Brazil.
Telephone: 2-2092.

Gómez, Mario; Costa Rican lawyer; b. 1 Nov. 1914; ed. Liceo de Costa Rica, Univ. of Costa Rica, and Univ. of Delaware.
Criminal and Fiscal Attorney 48-55; Magistrate Appeals Court, Supreme Court of Justice 61-62; Prof. of Introduction to Study of Law, Univ. of Costa Rica; Ambassador to Ecuador 55-57; Minister of Foreign Affairs and Culture 57-58, Vice-Minister, Dir.-Gen. 62-64; Minister of Foreign Affairs and Culture 65-66; Del. to numerous UN and Latin-American Confs.; numerous decorations.
Santa Eduviges, Colima de Tibás, San José, Costa Rica.

Gómez, Marte R.; Mexican hydro-agricultural engineer; b. 96; ed. Mexican National School of Agriculture.
Dir. of Nat. Agrarian Comm. until 22; Dir. Nat. Agricultural School 23-24; Pres. Tamaulipas Local Agrarian Comm. 25; Vice-Dir. Nat. Agricultural Credit Bank 26-27; mem. Federal Congress 28-30; Sec. of Agriculture 29; Senator 30-34; Under-Sec. of Treasury 33; Sec. of Treasury and Pres. Nat. Railways 34; Minister to France and Austria and Ambassador to LN 35; Gov. of Tamaulipas 37-40; Sec. of Agriculture 40-46; Pres. Nat. Credit Bank (Ejidal) and Nat. Agricultural Credit Bank 40-46; Pres. Nat. Irrigation Comm. 40-46; Pres. Worthington de México, S.A. 50-; Pres. Council of Promotion and Co-ordination of Nat. Production 54-58; decorations from Venezuela, Panama, Cuba, Finland, Ethiopia, etc.
Publs. *Convenciones de la Liga Comunidades Agrarias de Tamaulipas* (3 vols.) 27, 28, 29, *Iturbide* 39, *La Región Lagunera* 41, *Problemas Económico-Agrícolas de Campeche* 41, *Tendencias, Medios y Fines de la Política Agrícola de México* 45, *Bibliografía Agrícola y Agraria de México* (2 vols.) 46, *La Verdad sobre los Cebús* 47, *Luces y Sombras de la Reforma Agraria Mexicana* 53, *La Cuestión Agraria en los Primeros Congresos del México independiente* 55, *Anecdotario de San Jacinto* 58.
Paseo de la Reforma 540, Lomas de Chapultepec, Mexico, D.F., Mexico.

Gómez, Rodrigo; Mexican banker.
Banco de Mexico, S.A. 33-, Dir.-Gen. 52-; fmr. Senator Nuevo León State, Mexico; fmr. Exec. Dir. Int. Monetary Fund; fmr. mem. Inter-American Cttee. on Alliance for Progress.
Banco de Mexico S.A., Avenida 5 de Mayo 2, Mexico, D.F., Mexico.
Telephone: 12-66-14; 12-66-03.

Gómez Martínez, Fernando; Colombian politician; b. 97; ed. Universidad de Antioquia.
Former Deputy to Dept. Assembly, Antioquia; Senator,

Nat. Assembly; fmr. Mayor of Medellín and twice Gov. of Antioquia; fmr. Minister to the Netherlands; Minister of Foreign Affairs 63-66; Prof. Universidad Pontificia Bolivariana; several decorations.
Publs. *Fuegos Fatuos, Contra centralismo descentraliza-ción, Favor pasar a bordo, Biografía económica de las industrias de Antioquia* (with others), *Mordaza.*
c/o Ministry of Foreign Affairs, Bogotá, Colombia.

Gómez Millas, Juan; Chilean university professor and politician; b. 1900.
Former Minister of Education; Prof. of History and Geography; fmr. Rector of Univ. of Chile; Minister of Education Nov. 64-; Independent.
Ministry of Education, Santiago, Chile.

Gomułka, Władysław (Wiesław); Polish politician; b. 6 Feb. 1905.
Was Sec. of several Trade Union Organizations 27, and leader of Polish working class for many years; imprison-ed twice by the Sanacja regime for his anti-Fascist activities; took active part in Defence of Warsaw 39; joined ranks of Polish Workers' Party immediately it was formed; organized detachments and groups People's Army in Sub-Carpathian district; Sec. Warsaw group Polish Workers' Party 42; Sec. Central Cttee. 43-48; an initiator of armed opposition against Germans and an organiser of Nat. Council of Poland; arranged first meeting of Nat. Council of Poland; first Deputy Prime Min. Polish Gov. of Nat. Unity June 45; Vice-Premier and Minister for Regained Territories 45-Jan. 49; Vice-Pres. Supreme Nat. Control Chamber Jan.-Sept. 49; expelled from United Workers Party Nov. 49; arrested 51, released Dec. 54; First Sec. Central Cttee. Polish United Worker's Party Oct. 56, re-elected 59 and 64; mem. Council of State.
6 Nowy Świat, Warsaw, Poland.

Gonard, Samuel Alexandre, LL.D.; Swiss jurist and soldier; b. 8 June 1896; ed. Neuchâtel Univ., and Ecole Supérieure de Guerre, Paris.
Chief of Staff of C.-in-C. Swiss Army 39, later Corps Commdr. and Lecturer, Fed. Polytechnical High School, Zürich; fmr. mem. Nat. Defence Comm.; retired from Army 61; Prof. of War and Politics, Graduate Inst. of Int. Studies, Geneva 61-66; mem. Int. Cttee. of Red Cross and mem. Presidential Council 61-64, Pres. 64-; missions in Asia, Africa, the Americas, Europe and the Middle East.
Publ. *La recherche opérationelle et la Décision.*
Office: International Committee of the Red Cross, 7 avenue de la Paix, 1211 Geneva 1; Home: "Les Gonelles", Corseaux sur Vevey, Vaud, Switzerland.

Gonçalves Cerejeira, H.E. Cardinal Manuel; Portuguese ecclesiastic; b. 29 Nov. 1888; ed. Braga Seminary and Univ. of Coimbra.
Student of Braga Seminary 06-09; Univ of Coimbra 09-12; ordained Priest 11; Prof. Univ. of Coimbra 19; Archbishop of Mitylene 28; Patriarch of Lisbon 29-; created Cardinal by Pope Pius XI 29; mem. Sacred Congregations de Propaganda Fide, of Rites and of Seminaries and Univs. of Study; Dr. h.c. Rio de Janeiro, Brazilian Fed. and Montpellier Univs.
Publs. *O Renascimento em Portugal* (2 vols.) 18; *Do Valor Histórico de Fernão Lopes* 25, *Notas Históricas sôbre os Ordenados dos Lentes da Universidade* 27, *A Alma de S. Francisco de Assis* (2nd edn.) 43, *Cartas aos Novos* (2nd edn.) 43, *Vinte Anos de Coimbra* 43; *Obras Pastorais,* 1st vol. 36, 2nd vol. 43, 3rd vol. 47, 4th vol. 53, 5th vol. 60, 6th vol. 64; *A Idade Media* (2nd edn.) 44, *A Igreja e o Pensamento Contemporaneo* (5th edn.) 53, *Clenardo e a Sociedade Portuguesa do seu tempo* (3rd edn.) 49, *Cartas de Roma* 66, *Na Hora do Diálogo* 67.
Palácio de Sant'Anna, Campo dos Mártires da Pátria 45, Lisbon, Portugal.
Telephone: 43181.

Gonda, Jan, PH.D.; Netherlands Sanskrit scholar; b. 14 April 1905; ed. State Univ. Utrecht and Leyden.
Extra. Prof. Sanskrit State Univ. Utrecht 32-41, Prof. Sanskrit and Indo-European Linguistics 41-; mem. Royal Dutch Acad. of Sciences; Hon. Fellow Royal Asiatic Society.
Publs. *Oud-Javaans Brahmanda Purana* (2 vols.) 32, *Similes in Sanskrit Literature* 39, *Ursprung und Wesen des indischen Dramas* 40, *Sanskrit in Indonesia* 52, *Repetition in the Veda* 59, *Die Religionen Indiens* (Vol. I) 60 (Vol. II) 63, *The Vision of the Vedic Poets* 63, *The Savayajñas* 65, and many other works on Sanskrit and Indo-European linguistics.
Office: Institute of Oriental Languages, Nobelstraat, 2B, Utrecht; Home: 13 van Hogendorpstraat, Utrecht, Netherlands.
Telephone: 031-20132 (Office); 030-14531 (Home).

Gonella, Guido; Italian lawyer, journalist and politi-cian; b. 18 Sept. 1905; ed. Univs. of Milan, Rome, Paris, London and Berlin.
Asst. in Faculty of Philosophy of Law, Univ. of Rome 25; Prof. of Philosophy of Law, Bari and Pavia; Editor *Osservatore Romano* 32; founder of clandestine news-paper *Popolo* 43; Dir. of *Popolo* (official organ of Chris-tian Dem. Party) 44-46; mem. of Constituent Assembly; Minister of Education 46-51; Minister without Port-folio 51-53; Min. of Justice 53-54, 57-58, July 58-Jan. 59, Feb. 59-Feb. 60, March 60-62; Mem. of Parl. 48-; Vice-Pres. Chamber of Deputies 66-; fmr. Sec.-Gen. Christian Democratic Party.
Publs. *La valutazione del machiavellismo nell' etica di B. Croce* 30, *I dualismi nella dottrina eticogiuridica di Hegel* 32, *Al di qua del bene e del male* 32, *La filosofia del diritto secondo Antonio Rosmini* 34, *La dottrina della personalità ed alcuni suoi riflessi sociali* 34, *Etudes critiques* 36, *Schopenhauer—Studien in Rom* 37, *La persona nella filosofia del diritto* 38, *La crisi del con-trattualismo* 38, *La nozione di bene comune* 38, *Principi di un ordine sociale* 42, *Presupposti di un ordine inter-nazionale* 43, *Pace romana e pace cartaginese* 47.
Camera dei Deputati, Rome, Italy.

Gonseth, Ferdinand; Swiss professor of higher mathematics; b. 90; ed. Swiss Fed. Inst. of Technology, Zürich.
Lecturer at the Swiss Fed. Inst. of Technology 15-17 and at Univ. of Zürich 17-19; extraordinary Prof. Univ. of Zürich 19-20; ordinary Prof. Univ. of Berne 20-30; ordinary Prof. Swiss Fed. Inst. of Technology, Zürich 30-60, Hon. Prof. 61-; Dir. Int. Review of Philosophy of Knowledge *Dialectica;* organiser of the *Entretiens de Zürich;* Vice-Pres. of the Int. Acad. of Philosophy of Science; Corresp. mem. Inst. de France, Officier Légion d'Honneur.
Publs. *Qu'est-ce que la logique?* 37, *Les mathématiques et la réalité* 36, *La géométrie et le problème de l'espace* 45-55, *Philosophie scolastique et philosophie ouverte* 54, *Chron-iques de philosophie des sciences de l'Institut international de philosophie* 58, *Le problème du Temps, essai sur la méthodologie de la recherche* 64.
Chemin du Muveran 12, Lausanne, Switzerland.

González Blanco, Salomón; Mexican lawyer and politician; b. 03; ed. Escuela Nacional Preparatoria de Mexico, Escuela Libre de Derecho and Universidad Nacional Autónoma de Mexico.
Assistant Sec. Higher Tribunal of Justice of Mexico D.F. 27-30; Judge, Court of First Instance, Villaher-mosa 30; Magistrate of Higher Tribunal of Justice, Tabasco 31; Dir. Instituto Juarez, Tabasco 31-32; Senator 34; Minister of Supreme Court of Justice 35-40; Magistrate of Higher Tribunal of Justice, Mexico D.F. 47; Dir. of Conciliation Board, Ministry of Labour 47, Senior Official 47-52, Under-Sec. 53-57, Minister of Labour 58-; Under-Sec. State Dept. 57-58.

Publ. *El Sindicalismo y la Evolución Social.*
Paseo de la Reforma 1320, Lomas de Chapultepec, Mexico 10, D.F., Mexico.

Gonzi, Most Rev. Michael, K.B.E., D.D., I.C.D., B.LITT.; Maltese ecclesiastic; b. 13 May 1885; ed. Seminary and Royal Univ., Malta, and Beda Coll., Rome.
Ordained priest 08, Prof. Holy Scripture and Hebrew, Malta Univ. 15; Senator Malta Legislature 21; Canon Theologian Malta Cathedral Chapter 23; Bishop of Gozo 24, of Malta 43, Archbishop and Metropolitan of Malta 44-; Asst. at the Pontifical Throne 49.
Archbishop's Palace, Valletta, Malta.

Gooch, George Peabody, O.M., C.H., D.LITT., F.B.A.; British historian; b. 73; ed. King's Coll. London and Trinity Coll. Cambridge.
Joint-Ed. *The Contemporary Review* 11-60, the *Cambridge History of British Foreign Policy,* and *British Documents on the Origins of the War 1898-1914*; contrib. to the *Cambridge Modern History*; Pres. Nat. Peace Council 33-36 and English Goethe Society; Liberal M.P. Bath 06-10.
Publs. *English Democratic Ideas in the 17th Century, History and Historians in the 19th Century, History of Modern Europe 1878-1919, Annals of Politics and Culture, History of Our Time, Life of Charles, Third Earl Stanhope, Political Ideas from Bacon to Halifax, Germany and the French Revolution, Life of Lord Courtney, Nationalism, Franco-German Relations 1871-1914, Germany, The Later Correspondence of Lord John Russell, Recent Revelations of European Diplomacy, Studies in Modern History, Before the War* (2 vols.), *Studies in Diplomacy and Statecraft, Courts and Cabinets, Frederick the Great, Studies in German History, Maria Theresa and other Studies, Catherine the Great and other Studies, Louis XV, Under Six Reigns, The Second Empire, French Profiles, Historical Surveys and Portraits* 66.
Upway Corner, Chalfont St. Peter, Bucks., England.

Goodale, Sir Ernest William, Kt., C.B.E., M.C.; British solicitor; b. 6 Dec. 1896; ed. Richmond Secondary School.
Partner in firm Minet Pering Smith & Co., Solicitors 28-; Sec. and Dir. Warner & Sons Ltd. 28-30, Man. Dir. 30-61, Chair. 49-; Vice-Pres. Royal Soc. of Arts; Vice-Pres. Int. Silk Asscn. 42-68; Pres. Silk and Man-Made Fibre Users Asscn.; Vice-Pres. British Man-Made Fibres Fed.; Pres. Textile Inst. 39-40, 57-59; Vice-Pres. Inst. of Exports; Chair. Furnishing Fabric Fed., Furnishing Fabric Export Group 42-67; Pres. Furnishing Fabric Manufacturers' Asscn., etc.; Pres. British Colour Council 53-; mem. Nat. Advisory Council on Art Educ. 59-66; mem. Board Nat. Film Finance Corpn.; Hon. Fellow Soc. Industrial Artists.
Office: Mappin House, Winsley Street, Oxford Street, London, W.1; Home: Stonecroft, Chichester Close, Dorking, Surrey, England.
Telephone: 01-580-1927 (Office); 0306-2718 (Home).

Goodall, Rev. Norman, M.A., D.PHIL; British ecclesiastic; b. 30 Aug. 1896; ed. Oxford Univ.
Former Private Sec. to Parl. Sec. to Minister of Nat. Service; Congregational Minister, Walthamstow 22-28, New Barnet 28-36; Foreign Sec. London Missionary Soc. for India, South Seas and New Guinea 36-44; Editor *International Review of Missions* 44-52; Sec. Int. Missionary Council 44-55; Sec. Joint Cttee. World Council of Churches and Int. Missionary Council 55-62, Asst. Gen. Sec. World Council of Churches 62-; Moderator, Int. Congregational Council 62-.
Publs. *With All Thy Mind, Pacific Pilgrimage, One Man's Testimony, Congregationalism-Plus, History of the London Missionary Society 1895-1945, The Ecumenical Movement.*
Route de Malagnou 17, Geneva, Switzerland; Greensleeves, Benson, Oxford, England.

Goodarzi, Dr. Manuchehr; Iranian administrator; b. 1925; ed. American Univ. of Beirut, Princeton Univ., and Univ. of California.
Former Lecturer Princeton Univ. and Univ. of Teheran; Founder of Org. Management Bureau, Plan Org.; Dir. Dept. of Social and Municipal Devt., Deputy Man. Dir. Plan Org.; Deputy Prime Minister and Sec.-Gen. of High Admin. Council 63-64; Minister in charge of Admin. Reform and Sec.-Gen. of State Org. for Admin. and Employment Affairs, Chair. of Exec. Council of Eastern Regional Org. for Public Admin.; decorations from Iran, Republic of Korea and Philippines.
High Administrative Council, Teheran, Iran.

Goodhart, Arthur Lehman, K.B.E., Q.C., LL.D., D.C.L., F.B.A.; American jurist; b. 1 March 1891; ed. Yale, Cambridge and Oxford Univs.
Barrister 15; Asst. Corpn. Counsel New York 15-17; Counsel to American Mission to Poland 19; Fellow and Lecturer Corpus Christi Coll., Cambridge Univ. 19 and Sec. to Vice-Chancellor of Univ. 21; Editor *Cambridge Law Journal* 21; Chair. Cambridge Law Examiners 23; Prof. of Jurisprudence Oxford Univ. 31-51, Emeritus 51-; Master of Univ. Coll. 51-63, Hon. Fellow 63-; Fellow Nuffield Coll. Oxford and Hon. Fellow Corpus Christi Coll. and Trinity Coll., Cambridge; Editor *Law Quarterly Review*; Chair. S. Region Local Price Regulation Cttee.; mem. Law Revision Cttee., Supreme Court Procedure Cttee., Company Law Revision Cttee., Royal Commission on the Police, etc.; Curator Bodleian Library; Pres. Int. Asscn. of Univ. Profs. 48; Vice-Pres. Int. Law Asscn.; hon. mem. American Acad. of Arts and Sciences; Hon. LL.D. (Edinburgh, Yale, Calif., Harvard, Princeton, Columbia, London, Pennsylvania, Belfast, Melbourne, Williams and Wesleyan Univs.).
Publs. *Poland and the Minority Races* 20, *Law and the Needs of Society* 25, *The General Strike* 27, *Essays in Jurisprudence and the Common Law* 31, *Precedent in English and Continental Law* 34, *The Government of Great Britain* 46, *English Contributions to the Philosophy of Law* 49, *Five Jewish Lawyers on Common Law* 50, *English Law and the Moral Law* 53, *Law of the Land* 66.
c/o University College, Oxford; and Whitebarn, Boars Hill, Oxford, England.

Goodman, Baron (Life Peer, cr. 65) of the City of Westminster; **Arnold Abraham Goodman,** M.A., LL.M.; British solicitor and public official; b. 21 Aug. 1913; ed. Univ. Coll., London, and Downing Coll., Cambridge.
Partner, Goodman Derrick & Co., Solicitors; Chair. Arts Council of Great Britain 65-; Chair. British Lion Films (Holdings) 65-; Fellow, Univ. Coll., London; Chair. Board of Trustees of newspaper *The Observer*; mem. Exec. Cttee. The British Council; Chair. Cultural Cttee. British UNESCO; Dir. South Bank Theatre Board.
Goodman Derrick & Co., 30 Bouverie Street, London, E.C.4, England.

Goodman, Benny; American musician; b. 30 May 1909.
With the Ben Pollack Band, Los Angeles 25-29; radio and recording work, New York 29-34; formed Benny Goodman Orchestra 35; also formed smaller groups for "chamber jazz"; recorded commissioned works by Bartok, Copland and Hindemith 40; European tour 50; new orchestra formed 57, toured American Univs. 56-57, the Far East, Europe 59, South America 61, U.S.S.R. 62; guest soloist with various symphony orchestras; numerous recordings; has appeared in the films *Hollywood Hotel, Sweet and Low Down, Stage Door Canteen,* etc.; recorded the soundtrack of *The Benny Goodman Story.*
Publ. *Kingdom of Swing* (with Irving Kolodin).
200 East 66th Street, New York City, N.Y., U.S.A.

Goodman, Paul, PH.D.; American writer; b. 9 Sept. 1911; ed. Coll. of City of New York and Univ. of Chicago.

Has taught at Univ. of Chicago, Univ. of Wisconsin, San Francisco State Coll., Sarah Lawrence Coll., N.Y. Univ., Black Mt. Coll., New School for Social Research; Editor *Liberation* (magazine); Fellow Cleveland Inst. for Gestalt Therapy, Inst. for Policy Studies, Washington, D.C.

Publs. *Communitas* 47, *Gestalt Therapy* 50, *The Break-up of Our Camp* 53, *The Structure of Literature* 55, *The Empire City* 58, *Growing Up Absurd* 60, *Our Visit to Niagara* 61, *The Lordly Hudson* 61, *Making Do* 62, *The Community of Scholars* 63, *People or Personnel* 65, *Five Years* 66, *Hawkweed* 67, *Like a Conquered Province* 67.

402 W. 20 Street, New York City, N.Y., U.S.A.

Goodrich, Carter, PH.D.; American economic historian; b. 10 May 1897; ed. Amherst Coll., and Chicago Univ. Scholar and Fellow, Amherst Coll. 19, research on British labour problems; research on American Coal Industry 21-22, 23-24; Instructor in Economics, Amherst Coll. 22-23; Asst. Prof. of Economics at Michigan Univ. 24-27, Assoc. Prof. 27-29, Prof. 29-31; Fellow, Social Science Research Council 27; Dir. Study of Population Redistribution (Wharton School, Univ. of Pennsylvania) 34-36; United States Labour Commr., Geneva 36-37 and 38-40; mem. Governing Body Int. Labour Office 36-45, Chair. 39-45; Prof. Economics, Columbia Univ. 31-63, Prof. Emeritus 63-; Exec. Officer Dept. of Economics 46-49; Programme Dir. UN Scientific Conf. on Resources 49; Consultant UN 47-52; UN Special Rep. to Bolivia 52-53 (awarded Order of the Condor of the Andes); Chief UN Economic Survey Mission, Viet-Nam 55-56; Pres. Econ. History Asscn. 54-56; Rep., Columbia Graduate School of Business, Univ. of Buenos Aires 61-62; Andrew Mellon Prof. History and Econs., Univ. of Pittsburgh 63-; mem. American Philosophical Soc.; Fellow American Acad. of Arts and Sciences; L.H.D. Amherst Coll. 58.

Publs. *The Frontier of Control* 21, *The Miner's Freedom* 25, *Migration and Planes of Living* (with others) 35, *Migration and Economic Opportunity* (senior author) 36, *Govt. Promotion of American Canals and Railroads* 60, *Canals and American Economic Development* (senior author) 61, *The Government and the Economy, 1783-1861* (editor) 67.

Department of History, University of Pittsburgh, Pittsburgh 13, Pa., U.S.A.

Telephone: 621-3500, extension 585.

Goodwin, Richard N.; American lawyer and government official; b. 7 Dec. 1931; ed. Brookline High School, Tufts Univ., and Harvard Law School.

Law Clerk for Justice Felix Frankfurter, U.S. Supreme Court 58-59; Special Counsel for House Sub-cttee's Legislative Oversight Cttee. 59; worked for Senator Kennedy during Pres. election campaign 59-60; mem. President's Task Force on Latin American Affairs 60-61; Asst. Special Counsel to Pres. 61; Dep. Asst. Sec. of State for Inter-American Affairs 61-63; Sec.-Gen. Int. Peace Corps Secr. 63-64; Special Asst. to Pres. 64-65; Fellow, Center for Advanced Studies, Wesleyan Univ. 65-67.

Publs. *The Sower's Seed* 65, *Triumph or Tragedy: Reflections on Viet-Nam* 66.

35 Home Avenue, Middletown, Conn., U.S.A.

Gooneratne, Tilak Eranga, B.A.; Ceylonese civil servant and lawyer; b. 27 March 1919; ed. St. John's Coll., Panadura, Ceylon, Ceylon Univ., and Ceylon Law Coll.

Joined Ceylon Civil Service 43; Asst. Sec. Ministry of External Affairs 47-51; Govt. Agent, Trincomalee 51-54, Matra 54-56; Registrar Gen. Marriages, Births and Deaths 56-58; Dir.-Gen. of Broadcasting and Dir. of Information, Ceylon 58-60; Commr. Co-operative Devt. 60-63; Acting Perm. Sec. Ministry of Commerce and Trade 63; Dir. of Econ. Affairs 63; Deputy Sec. to Treasury 63-65; Pres. Colombo Plan Council for Technical Co-operation in South and South East Asia 64-65; Ceylon Del. to UN Gen. Assembly 64-65; Deputy Sec.-Gen. Commonwealth Secr., London, Nov. 65-.

Publs. *An Historical Outline of the Development of the Marriage and Divorce Laws of Ceylon, An Historical Outline of the Development of the Marriage and Divorce Laws Applicable to Muslims in Ceylon, Fifty Years of Co-operative Development in Ceylon.*

Commonwealth Secretariat, Marlborough House, Pall Mall, London, S.W.1; Home: 29 The Water Gardens, Burwood Place, London, W.2, England.

Telephone: 01-723-0757 (Home).

Goonetilleke, Sir Oliver Ernest, G.C.M.G., K.C.V.O., K.B.E., K.ST.J., B.A., LL.D., F.R.S.A., F.R.E.S.; Ceylonese politician; b. 20 Oct. 1892; ed. London Univ.

Asst. Auditor for Railways, Ceylon 21; Asst. Colonial Auditor 24-31; Colonial Auditor 31; Auditor-Gen. July 31; Ceylon Govt. Del. to Int. Railway Congress, Cairo 33; Chair. Retrenchment Comm. Ceylon 38; Civil Defence and Food Commr. 42; mem. Ceylon War Council 42; Financial Sec. Govt. of Ceylon 45-47; Home Minister 47; High Commr. in U.K. 48-51; Minister of Home Affairs 51-52, of Agriculture and Food 52-53, of Civil Defence 53, also Leader of the Senate; Minister of Finance 54; Gov.-Gen. of Ceylon 54-62; Vice-Pres. Royal Inst. of Int. Affairs; Dir. Bentola Holdings Ltd., Kepitigala Rubber Estates Ltd., South Wanarajah Co. Ltd.; Dir. and Chair. Bandarapola Co. Ltd., Rangalla Consolidated Ltd.; Underwriting mem. Lloyd's, London.

c/o National Liberal Club, Whitehall Place, London, S.W.1, England.

Goormaghtigh, John Victor, D. en DROIT; Belgian lawyer and public servant; b. 15 March 1919; ed. Brussels Univ.

Admitted to the Bar 42; Advocate, Court of Appeal 45; Dir. Belgian Inst. of Int. Affairs 47-52, then mem. Board and Hon. Sec.; Joint Sec. Int. Academic Union 49; Consultant to UNESCO 50; Sec. Preparatory Cttee. Int. Political Science Asscn. 49, Sec.-Gen. 55-60; Dir. European Centre, Carnegie Endowment for Int. Peace 50-; Prof. of Political Science, Univ. of Geneva 61-62; Chair. Board Int. School of Geneva 61-66; Chair. Int. Schools Exam. Syndicate 65-; Editor *Chronique de Politique Etrangère* 48-52; Chevalier Order of the Crown; Croix de Guerre (Belgium and France), Médaille de la Résistance.

Office: 58 rue de Moillebeau, 1211 Geneva 19; Home: La Ferme, 77 avenue d'Aïre, 1203 Geneva, Switzerland.

Telephone: 34-23-50 (Office); 44-49-78 (Home).

Goossens, Léon Jean, C.B.E., F.R.C.M.; British oboist; b. 12 June 1897; ed. Christian Brothers Catholic Inst., Liverpool, Liverpool Coll. of Music and Royal Coll. of Music.

Principal Oboist Queen's Hall Orchestra 13-15; war service; Principal Oboist Royal Philharmonic Orchestra; world-wide oboe recitals since 27; Prof. Royal Coll. of Music and Royal Acad. of Music; numerous lecture recitals; encouraged a new school of oboe-playing with oboe as solo instrument; Cobbett Medal for Chamber Music 54.

7A Ravenscourt Square, London, W.6, England.

Gopal-Ayengar, Anekal Ramaswamiengar, M.SC., M.A., PH.D.; Indian biologist; b. 1 Jan. 1909; ed. Univs. of Mysore and Toronto.

Lecturer in Botany, Mysore Univ. 33-38; Vincent Massey Fellow, Univ. of Toronto 38-39; Senior Instructor, Barnard Skin and Cancer Hospital 41-45; Kettering Research Fellow 45-47; Research Assoc., Washington Univ., St. Louis, Mo. 45-47; Chief Research

Cytologist, Tata Memorial Hospital, Bombay 47-51; Head, A.E.C. Unit on Cell Biology 48-51; Senior Int. Research Fellow, Lady Tata Trust, Chester Beatty Research Inst., London and Inst. for Cell Research, Karolinska Inst., Stockholm 51-53; Chief Scientific Officer and Head, Biological and Medical Divs., Atomic Energy Establishment, Tromblay 60-61, Dir. Biology Group 62-; Expert, Radiation Cttee. of World Health Org. (WHO) 58-68; mem. of Council, Advisory Cttee. on Radiobiology of Int. Comm. on Radiobiological Protection 58-66 and Int. Org. for Pure and Applied Biophysics 61-67; Rep. for South East Asia on Genetics Section of Int. Union of Biological Sciences (IUBS) and Int. Cell Research Org. 63-66; Chair. Nat. Cttee. for Biophysics 63-64; Pres. Indian Soc. of Genetics and Plant Breeding 63-64 and Comm. on Radiation Biophysics of Int. Org. for Pure and Applied Physics (IOPAB); Associated with Int. Soc. for Cell Biology, New York Acad. of Sciences and American Asscn. for Cancer Research; mem. Editorial Board *Radiation Botany* and *Biophysik*; Fellow, Indian Acad. of Sciences; J. H. Bhabha Prize 48.
Framroz Court, Marine Drive, Bombay 1, India.

Gopalan, A. K., M.P.; Indian politician; b. 1 Oct. 1904; ed. Tellicherry, Malabar and Kerala.
Deputy Leader Communist Group in Parl. until 67, Leader 67-; Sec. Nat. Council C.P. of India; Pres. All India Kisan (Peasants) Sabha; Editor *New Kerala*.
2 Windsor Place, New Delhi, India.

Gopalkrishnan, P. A., O.B.E.; Indian business executive; b. 20 Dec. 1909; ed. Presidency Coll., Madras, and Univ. College. London.
Indian Civil Service 32-; fmr. Joint Sec. Ministry of Food and Agriculture; Chair. Life Insurance Corporation of India 58-62; Chair. Indian Oil Corpn. Ltd. 62-.
Indian Oil Corporation, Clarke Road, Bombay 34, India.

Gopallawa, William, M.B.E.; Ceylonese diplomatist; b. 16 Sept. 1897; ed. Dharmarajah Coll., St. Anthony's Coll., Kandy and Law Coll., Colombo.
Enrolled as Proctor of Supreme Court 24; mem. and later Chair. Matale Urban Council 27-39; Municipal Comm. Kandy 39-52, Colombo 52-57; Ambassador to People's Repub. of China 58-61, to U.S.A., Cuba and Mexico 61-62; Gov.-Gen. of Ceylon, March 62-; Chancellor, Univ. of Ceylon, Vidyodaya Univ., and Vidyalankara Univ.; LL.D. (Univs. of Ceylon and Vidyalankara) 62; D.Litt. (Vidyodaye Univ.) 62.
Queen's House, Colombo, Ceylon.
Telephone: Colombo 5321.

Goppel, Alfons; German lawyer and politician; b. 1 Oct. 1905; ed. Humanistisches Gymnasium, Regensburg, and Ludwig Maximilians Univ., Munich.
State Attorney 34, Judge 38; Vice-Mayor of Aschaffenburg 52; State Sec. of Justice (Bavaria) 57; Minister of Interior (Bavaria) 58-62; Minister-Pres. of Bavaria 62-; mem. Bavarian Land Diet 54-; numerous decorations; Dr. h.c.
Sommerweg 2, Krailling; Home: 8 Munich 22, Prinzregentenstrasse 7, German Federal Republic.
Telephone: 228951 (Home).

Goray, Narayan Ganesh, B.A., LL.B.; Indian politician; b. 15 June 1907; ed. Fergusson Coll., Poona.
Congress Socialist Party 30, mem. Nat. Exec. 34, Poona Municipal Corpn.; Joint Sec. Socialist Party 48; Gen. Sec. Praja Socialist Party 49-54, 54-65, Chair. 65-; mem. Lok Sabha 57-62.
Publs. *History of the United States of America*, etc.
1813 Sadashivpeth, Poona 2, India.

Gorbach, Alfons, LL.D.; Austrian politician; b. 98; ed. Graz Univ.
War service 14-16; municipal school supervisor, Graz; mem. Styrian Diet and provincial govt.; Styrian leader

of the Fatherland Front; forced labour and concentration camps 38-45; Chair., Austrian Cttee. for the repatriation of Austrian Detainees, Dachau 45; People's Party mem. of Nat. Assembly 45; Pres. 45; Chair. Nat. Defence Board 55; Chair. People's Party, Styrian Province; mem. Defence Cttee. People's Party; Fed. Chancellor 61-64; Grand Cross in Gold, Austrian Order of Merit and several foreign decorations.
Vienna I, Austria.

Gorchakov, Andrei Ivanovich; Soviet diplomatist; b. 1914; ed. Teachers' Training Inst., Moscow.
Diplomatic Service 56-; Head of European Dept. 56-59; Minister-Counsellor, Berlin 59-63; Amb. to Korean People's Democratic Repub. 65-67; on staff of Ministry of Foreign Affairs 67-; mem. C.P.S.U. Cen. Auditing Comm. 66-.
Ministry of Foreign Affairs, 32-34 Smolenskaya-Sennaya ploshchad, Moscow, U.S.S.R.

Gordey, Michel; French journalist and writer; b. 17 Feb. 1913; ed. Lycée Janson de Sailly, Law Faculty and Sorbonne and Ecole des Sciences Politiques, Paris.
Lawyer, Paris 33-37; French Army 37-40; U.S. Office of War Information, French Editor, Voice of America 41-45, Chief Editor 44-45; U.S. Corresp. *Paris-Presse* 45; U.S. and UN Corresp., Agence-France-Presse, New York and Washington 45-46; Roving Foreign and Diplomatic Corresp. *France-Soir*, Paris 46-56, Chief Foreign Corresp. 56-; articles have been published in magazines and newspapers in U.K., U.S.A., German Federal Republic, Japan, Italy and Switzerland; TV and radio broadcasts in U.K., U.S.A., Canada and German Federal Republic; several journalistic awards.
Publ. *Visa pour Moscou* 51.
16 rue de Savoie, Paris 6e, France.
Telephone: 033-7982.

Gordeyev, Boris Stepanovich; Soviet foreign trade official; b. 1920; ed. Moscow Bauman Higher Technical Coll. and Acad. of Foreign Trade.
Member C.P.S.U. 45-; Chief Economist, Section Chief, then Deputy Commercial Rep. of U.S.S.R. in England 50-53; Official, Ministry of Foreign Trade 53-63; U.S.S.R. Commercial Rep. in Brazil 63-65; Chief of Head Dept., Ministry of Foreign Trade 65-66; U.S.S.R. Commercial Rep. in England 66-; Order of Red Banner of Labour, Honour Badge.
U.S.S.R. Trade Legation, London, England.

Gordimer, Nadine; South African writer; b. 20 Nov. 1923; ed. convent school.
Recipient of W. H. Smith Literary Award 61.
Publs. *The Soft Voice of the Serpent* (stories), *The Lying Days* (novel) 53, *Six Feet of the Country* (stories) 56, *A World of Strangers* (novel) 58, *Friday's Footprint* (stories) 60, *Occasion for Loving* (novel) 63, *Not For Publication* (stories) 65, *The Late Bourgeois World* (novel) 66; co-Editor *South African Writing Today* 67.
7 Frere Road, Parktown, Johannesburg, South Africa.
Telephone: 31-4369.

Gordis, Robert, B.A., PH.D.; American rabbi and biblical scholar; b. 6 Feb. 1908; ed. Coll. of City of New York, The Dropsie Coll., Philadelphia and Jewish Theological Seminary.
Mayer Sulzberger Fellow in Biblical Philology, Dropsie Coll. 26-29; Instructor in Bible and Jewish History, Hebrew Teachers' Training School for Girls 28-30; Instructor, Teachers' Inst. of Jewish Theological Seminary 30-31; Rabbi, Temple Beth-El, Rockaway Park, Long Island 31-; Seminary Prof. of Bible, Jewish Theological Seminary 37-; Pres. Rabbinical Assembly of America 44-46; Vice-Pres. Synagogue Council of America 46-48, Pres. 48-49; Adjunct Prof. in Religion, Columbia Univ. 49-57; Lecturer in Old Testament, Union Theological Seminary 53-54; Prof. of Bible,

Jewish Theological Seminary of America 61-; Consultant to Center for Study of Democratic Insts. of Fund for Repub. 60-; Prof. of Religion, Temple Univ. 67-; Assoc. Editor Dept. of the Bible and contrib. to *Universal Jewish Encyclopaedia*; Chair. Board of Editors *Judaism*; Hon. D.D. (Jewish Theological Seminary) 50. Publs. *Biblical Text in the Making* 37, *The Jew Faces a New World* 41, *The Wisdom of Ecclesiastes* 45, *Conservative Judaism—An American Philosophy* 45, *Koheleth—The Man and His World* 51, *Song of Songs* 54, *Judaism and the Modern Age* 55, *A Faith for Moderns* 60, *The Root and the Branch—Judaism and the Free Society* 62, *The Book of God and Man: A Study of Job* 65, *Sex and the Family in Jewish Tradition, Leave a Little to God* 66.
Office: 445B 135 Street, Rockaway Park 94, New York City, N.Y. 11694; Home: 153B 133 Street, Rockaway Park, N.Y. 11694, U.S.A.
Telephone: 212-NE4-8100 (Office); 212-NE4-1269 (Home).

Gordon, Donald, C.M.G., LL.D., D.C.L., D.C.SC.; Canadian railway executive; b. 11 Dec. 1901; ed. public schools, Scotland and Canada.
Went to Canada 14; on staff of Bank of Nova Scotia 16-35; Sec. Bank of Canada Feb. 35-38; Deputy Gov. 38-49; Chair. Wartime Prices and Trade Board 41-47; Dir. Industrial Devt. Bank Nov. 44-49; Exec. Dir. Int. Bank for Reconstruction and Devt. 48-49; Chair. of Board and Pres. Canadian Nat. Railways 50-66; Dir. Air Canada 50-66; Hon. LL.D. (Queen's Univ. 47 and Univ. of Western Ontario 52), Hon. D.C.L. (Bishop's Univ. 58); Knight of Grace, Order of St. John of Jerusalem 58.
172 Edgehill Road, Montreal, P.Q. 6, Canada.

Gordon, James Roycroft, B.SC.; American mining executive; b. 26 May 1898; ed. Queen's Univ.
Served in Canadian Army 14-18; Research Metallurgist, M. J. O'Brien Ltd., 20-29, Ontario Research Foundation 29-36; Joined Int. Nickel Co. of Canada at Copper Cliff 36, Dir. of Research 36-41, Asst. to Vice-Pres. 47-52; Asst. Gen. Man. 52-53, Vice-Pres., Dir. and Gen. Man. Canadian Operations 53, transferred to N.Y. 55, Exec. Vice-Pres. 57-60, Pres. Int. Nickel Co. of Canada Ltd., Int. Nickel Co., Inc. 60-67, Chair. Exec. Cttee. 67-; Dir. Canada Life Assurance Co., Toronto-Dominion Bank, British-American Oil Co. Ltd., The Steel Co. of Canada Ltd., Babcock and Wilcox Co., Borden Co.; Trustee, Bank of New York; mem. Board of Govs. Ontario Research Foundation; mem. Board of Trustees, Queen's Univ.; Medal, Canadian Inst. of Mining and Metallurgy 48, James Douglas Gold Medal, American Inst. of Mining, Metallurgical and Petroleum Engineers 57; Medal for the Advancement of Research of the American Soc. for Metals 67.
179 East 70th Street, New York, N.Y. 10021, U.S.A.
Telephone: 212-944-1000.

Gordon, John F., M.SC.; American executive; b. 15 May 1900; ed. Naval Acad. and Michigan Univ.
Design engineer, Cadillac Div., Gen. Motors 23-40; Engineering Exec., Allison Div., General Motors 40-43; Gen. Man. Cadillac and Vice-Pres. in charge of Gen. Motors Engineering Staff 46-50; Vice-Pres., Gen. Motors 51-58, Pres. and Chief Operating Officer 58-65.
Rathmor Road, Bloomfield Hills, Mich., U.S.A.

Gordon, John Rutherford, LL.D., F.J.I.; British journalist; b. 8 Dec. 1890; ed. Morgan Acad., Dundee.
Chief Sub-Editor London *Evening News* 22; Chief Sub-Editor *Daily Express* 24; Editor *Sunday Express* 28-52, Editor-in-Chief 52-; Chair. London District Inst. of Journalists 47-48; Pres. Inst. of Journalists 48-49; Dir. Beaverbrook Newspapers Ltd., Sunday Express Ltd.; Trustee of the Beaverbrook Foundation; Doctor of Laws, Univ. New Brunswick 66.
78 Addiscombe Road, Croydon, Surrey, England.

Gordon, Kermit; American economist; b. 3 July 1916; ed. Swarthmore Coll., Univ. Coll., Oxford, and Harvard Univ.
Research Asst. Econs., Swarthmore Coll. 39-40; Admin. Fellow, Harvard 40-41, Teacher of Econs. 50, 54; Office of Price Admin. 41-43; Special Asst. to Sec. for Econ. Affairs, State Dept. 45-46; Consultant 46-53; Econs. Faculty, Williams Coll. 46-, Prof. of Econs. 55-62, David A. Wells Prof. of Political Econ. 61-62; mem. Council of Econ. Advisers 61-62; Dir. of Budget 62-65; Vice-Pres. Brookings Inst. 65-67, Pres. 67-; mem. several econ. orgs; mem. Board of Trustees Ford Foundation 67-.
The Brookings Institution, 1775 Massachussetts Avenue, N.W., Washington, D.C. 20036, U.S.A.
Telephone: 202-483-8919.

Gordon, Lincoln, B.A., D.PHIL.; American political economist and diplomatist; b. 10 Sept. 1913; ed. Harvard Univ. and Balliol Coll., Oxford.
Instructor in Govt., Harvard Univ. 36-40; Prof. of Govt. and Admin., Harvard Business School and Graduate School of Public Admin. 46-50; Govt. service with Nat. Resources Planning Board 39-40; Nat. Defense Advisory Cttee. 40-41; W.P.B. 42-45; Deputy Programme Vice-Chair., W.P.B. 44, Programme Vice-Chair. 45; Consultant, Dept. of State in development of European Recovery Programme 47-48; Dir. Programme Div. ECA in Office of Special Rep. in Europe 49-50; Economic Adviser to Special Asst. to the Pres. (W. A. Harriman) 50-51; Asst. Dir. for Programme, Office of Dir. for Mutual Security 51-52; Minister for Economic Affairs and Chief of MSA Mission to U.K. Oct. 52-55; William Ziegler Prof. of Int. Economic Relations, Harvard Univ. Graduate School of Business Administration July 55-61; Ambassador to Brazil 61-66; Asst. Sec. of State for Inter-American Affairs 66-67; Pres. The Johns Hopkins Univ. 67-.
Publs. *The Public Corporation in Great Britain* 38, *Government and the American Economy* (with M. Fainsod) 41; Editor *International Stability and Progress: United States Interests and Instruments* 57; *United States Manufacturing Investment in Brazil* (with E. L. Grommers) 61, *O Progresso Pela Aliança* 62, *A New Deal for Latin America* 63.
Office and Home: The Johns Hopkins University, Baltimore, Maryland 21218, U.S.A.
Telephone: 301-467-3300.

Gordon, Hon. Walter Lockhart, P.C., F.C.A.; Canadian politician; b. 27 Jan. 1906; ed. Upper Canada Coll., Toronto, and Royal Military Coll., Kingston.
Partner, Clarkson, Gordon & Co., Toronto, Chartered Accountants 35-63; Partner, Woods, Gordon & Co., Management Consultants, Toronto 40-63; Special Asst. to Dep. Minister of Finance, Canada 40-42; M.P. 62-, Minister of Finance and Receiver Gen. of Canada 63-65; Minister without Portfolio Jan. 67-April 67; Pres. of Privy Council April 67-68; Chair. Canadian Corporate Management Co. Ltd. 68-; Chair several Royal Comms.; Liberal.
22 Chestnut Park Road, Toronto 5, Ontario, Canada.

Gordon-Lazareff, Hélène; French journalist; b. 21 Sept. 1909.
Director and Editor-in-Chief *Elle* (weekly) 45-; mem. Television Programme Cttee. of O.R.T.F. 65-.
Publ. *L'U.R.S.S. à l'heure Malenkov* (with P. Lazareff).
Office: 100 rue Réaumur, Paris 2e; Home: Château de la Grille Royale, Louveciennes (Yvelines), France.

Gordon-Smith, Ralph; British business executive; b. 22 May 1905; ed. Bradfield Coll.
Smiths Industries Ltd. 27-, Dir. 33, Group Man. Dir. 47-, Chair. 51-; Dir. E.M.I. Ltd. 51-.
Office: Smiths Industries Ltd., Cricklewood Works,

London, N.W.2; Home: "The Old Ship", Bosham, Sussex, England.
Telephone: 01-452-3333 (Office).

Gordon Walker, Rt. Hon. Patrick Chrestien, P.C., C.H., M.P., M.A., B.LITT.; British politician; b. 7 April 1907; ed. Wellington Coll., and Christ Church, Oxford.
Student and History Tutor, Christ Church 31-40; B.B.C. European Service 40-44; Chief Editor Radio Luxembourg 44; Asst. German Service Dir., B.B.C. 45; M.P. (Labour) for Smethwick 45-64, for Leyton 66-; P.P.S. to Mr. Morrison 46; Parl. Under Sec. of State for Commonwealth Relations 50-51; Foreign Sec. Oct. 64-Jan. 65; Minister without Portfolio Jan. 67-Aug. 67; Sec. of State for Educ. and Science Aug. 67-April 68; Chair. British Film Inst. 46; Adviser to Initial Teaching Alphabet Foundation 65-67.
Publs. *History of Europe in the Sixteenth and Seventeenth Centuries* 35, *Outline of Man's History* 39, *The Lid Lifts* 45, *Re-statement of Liberty* 51, *The Commonwealth* 62.
22 South Square, London, N.W.11, England.

Gore, Albert, B.S., LL.B.; American teacher, lawyer and politician; b. 26 Dec. 1907; ed. Middle Tennessee State Teachers' Coll., and Nashville Y.M.C.A. Night School.
Taught in rural schools in Tennessee 26-36; admitted to the Bar 36 and began practice; Commr. of Labor, Tenn. 36-37; Senator from Tennessee 53-; Democrat.
Carthage, Tenn., U.S.A.

Gore-Booth, Sir Paul Henry, G.C.M.G., K.C.V.O.; British diplomatist; b. 3 Feb. 1909; ed. Eton and Balliol Coll., Oxford.
Third Sec. Foreign Office 33, Vienna 36, Tokyo 37; Second Sec. Tokyo 38, Shanghai Oct.-Nov. 41, Washington Dec. 42, acting First Sec. Nov. 43; mem. U.K. Del. to Int. Food Conf. Hot Springs 43, UNRRA Conf. Atlantic City 43, Civil Aviation Conf., Chicago 44, U.N. Preparatory Confs., Dumbarton Oaks 44, San Francisco 45; transferred to Foreign Office 45; Sec. to U.K. Del. to first meeting of U.N. Gen. Assembly, London Jan. 46; promoted to Foreign Service Officer, Grade 6, as Head of Refugee and U.N. Economic and Social Depts. July 47; Head of European Recovery Dept., Foreign Office 48; Dir.-Gen. British Information Services, Washington 49-53; Ambassador to Burma 53-56; Deputy Under-Sec. of State, Foreign Office 56-60; High Commr. in India 60-65; Perm. Under-Sec. of State Foreign Office 65-; Head of Diplomatic Service Feb. 68-.
c/o The Foreign Office, London, S.W.1; 29 The Vale, Chelsea, London, S.W.3, England.

Goret, Pierre; French veterinary researcher; b. 27 Aug. 1907; ed. Coll. Providence, Amiens, Ecole de Médecine, Amiens, and Ecole Vétérinaire, Alfort.
Professor, Ecole Vétérinaire Lyon 46-55, Ecole Vétérinaire Alfort 55-; Asst. Lecturer, Univ. de Paris à la Sorbonne, l'Institut Pasteur, l'Institut Agronomique, etc.; mem. Académie de Médecine and Académie Vétérinaire; Fellow Ecoles Vétérinaires 45; Officier Légion d'Honneur; Foreign Corresp. mem. Royal Soc. of Medicine, London; Expert, WHO Zoonoses Cttee.
Publs. on various subjects dealing with comparative pathology and bacteriology especially with reference to virus ailments in animals and zoonoses.
31 rue Faidherbe, 94 Saint-Mandé (Val-de-Marne), France.
Telephone: 328-26-70.

Gorev, Nikolai Nikolaevich; Soviet pathologist; b. 1900; ed. Irkutsk Univ.
Junior Research Assoc. Irkutsk Univ. 26-39; Head of Dept. Inst. of Experimental Biology and Pathology 34-53; Corresp. mem. U.S.S.R. Acad. of Medical Sciences 45-, mem. 53-; Head of Chair. Kiev Stomatological Inst. 45-55; Head of Laboratory, Kiev Inst. of Tuberculosis 55-58; Dir. Inst. of Gerontology and Experimental Pathology 58-61, Head of Lab. 61-; Vice-Chair. Board U.S.S.R. Soc. of Pathophysiologists, mem. of Board, U.S.S.R. Soc. of Pathophysiologists; has participated in gerontology symposiums in Norway, Britain, Czechoslovakia, Hungary; Order of Lenin, Badge of Honour, Merited Scientist of Ukranian S.S.R. Publs. About 90 works on pathology of cardiovascular system, shock, hypertension, gerontology.
Institute of Gerontology and Experimental Pathology, 53 Melnikov Street, Kiev, U.S.S.R.

Gorham, Maurice Anthony Coneys; Irish journalist and author; b. 19 Aug. 1902; ed. Stonyhurst Coll., and Balliol Coll., Oxford.
Member editorial staffs *Weekly Westminster* and *Westminster Gazette* 23-26; Asst. Editor *Radio Times* 26, Art Editor 28, Editor 33-41; Dir. North American Service, B.B.C. 41-44, Allied Expeditionary Forces Programme 44-45, Light Programme 45, Television Service 46-47; resigned 47, worked as author and journalist; Broadcasting and Television Critic, *Sunday Times* 49-50, *Star* 51-52; mem. UNESCO's first Expert Conf. on Television 52; Dir. of Broadcasting, Repub. of Ireland 53-60.
Publs. *The Local* 39, *Sound and Fury* 48, *Back to the Local* 49, *Television, Medium of the Future* 49, *Professional Training for Radio* (study for UNESCO) 50, *Inside the Pub* (part author) 50, *Showmen and Suckers* 51, *Londoners* 51, *Broadcasting and Television* 52, *Forty Years of Irish Broadcasting* 67.
33 Sydney Parade Avenue, Dublin, Ireland.
Telephone: Dublin 692587.

Gori, His Beatitude Albert; Latin Patriarch of Jerusalem; b. 89; ed. in Franciscan Order.
Ordained priest 14; served First World War; service of the Custody of the Holy Land Palestine 19; Prof. and Dep. Dir., Coll. of Aleppo, Syria, Dir. 22-37; Custodian of the Holy Land 37-49; Latin Patriarch of Jerusalem 49-; consecrated Bishop Dec. 49; Grand Prior of the Equestrian Order of St. Sepulchre (Jerusalem).
Latin Patriarchate of Jerusalem, P.O. Box 1154, Jerusalem Old City, via Amman, Jordan.

Goriachev, Fyodor Stepanovich; Soviet politician; b. 1905; ed. Higher Party School.
Komsomol, Soviet and party work, Bashkirian Autonomous Republic 34-51; mem. C.P.S.U. 27-; First Sec. Tiumen District Cttee., C.P.S.U. 51-55, Kalinin District Cttee. 55-59, Novosibirsk 59-; mem. Central Cttee. of C.P.S.U. 52-; Deputy to Supreme Soviet U.S.S.R.; mem. Mandate Cttee. Union Soviet, U.S.S.R. Supreme Soviet.
Novosibirsk District Committee of the Communist Party of the Soviet Union, Novosibirsk, U.S.S.R.

Gorinov, Trofim Iosifovich; Soviet politician; b. 1926; ed. Higher Party School of C.P.S.U. Central Cttee.
Accountant 41-44; Local Govt. Official 44-55, Party Official 55-63; Chair. of the Party and of State Control Cttee. of Mary Regional Cttee. of C.P.S.U. and Council of Ministers of Mary Autonomous S.S.R., Sec. Mary Regional Cttee. of C.P.S.U., Vice-Chair. Council of Ministers of Mary Autonomous S.S.R. 63-64; Chair. Council of Ministers of Mary Autonomous S.S.R. 64-; Deputy to U.S.S.R. Supreme Soviet 64-; mem. C.P.S.U. 46-.
Council of Ministers, Mary Autonomous S.S.R., Yoshkar-Ola, U.S.S.R.

Gorizontov, Petr Dmitrievich; Soviet pathophysiologist; b. 1902; ed. Omsk Medical Inst.
Junior Research Assoc., Head of Lab., Senior Research Assoc., Lenin Acad. of Agricultural Sciences 27-32; Head of Laboratory, Deputy Dir. Inst. of Socialist Health Protection 32-34; Junior Research Assoc., Asst. Prof., Head of Chair First Moscow Medical Inst. 34-52; Head of Chair Cen. Inst. of Postgraduate Medical

Training 53-60; Head of Laboratory, Deputy Dir., Dir. Inst. of Biophysics, U.S.S.R. Ministry of Public Health 50-; mem. C.P.S.U. 57-; Corresp. mem. U.S.S.R. Acad. of Medical Sciences 52-62, mem. 62-; Chair. Board U.S.S.R. Soc. of Röntgenologists and Radiologists, mem. Board U.S.S.R. Soc. of Pathophysiologists; Order of Lenin (twice), Badge of Honour, Red Banner of Labour, Lenin Prize 63.

Publs. Over 100 works, including monograph *Pathological physiology of acute radiation sickness resulting from external ionizing radiation.*

Institute of Biophysics, U.S.S.R. Ministry of Public Health, 7 Profsoyuznaya Street, Moscow, U.S.S.R.

Gorkin, Alexandr Fyodorovich; Soviet politician and lawyer; b. 1897; ed. Tver High School.

Held Party and Soviet Exec. posts 17-37; mem. C.P.S.U. 16-; mem. Presidium and Sec. to Cen. Exec. Cttee. of the U.S.S.R. 37; Sec. of Presidium of Supreme Soviet of the U.S.S.R. 38-53, Deputy Sec. 53-56, Sec. 56; Pres. of the Supreme Court of the U.S.S.R. 57-; Deputy to the Supreme Soviet of the U.S.S.R. 37-; mem. Auditing Comm. C.P.S.U.; awarded Order of Lenin (twice).

Supreme Court of the U.S.S.R., Moscow, U.S.S.R.

Gorkov, Lev Petrovich; Soviet physicist; b. 1929; ed. Moscow Physico-Technical Inst.

Postgraduate work, Moscow Physico-Technical Inst. 53-55; Junior Research Assoc., Inst. of Physical Problems, U.S.S.R. Acad. of Sciences, Head of Section, Inst. of Chemical Physics, U.S.S.R. Acad. of Sciences 57-66; Head of Dept. Inst. of Theoretical Physics, U.S.S.R. Acad. of Sciences 66-; Corresp. mem. U.S.S.R. Acad. of Sciences 66-; Lenin Prize 66.

Publs. Works on theory of solid body, including superconductivity.

U.S.S.R. Academy of Sciences, 14 Lenin Prospekt, Moscow, U.S.S.R.

Gorman, Paul A.; American business executive; b. 16 Dec. 1907; ed. Univ. of Missouri.

Western Electric Co. 29-53, 54-58, 64-; Asst. Vice-Pres. American Telephone and Telegraph Co. (Personnel) 53-54, Exec. Vice-Pres. 59-64; Vice-Pres. and Dir. New Jersey Bell Telephone 58, Pres. 58-59; Pres., Dir. and mem. of Exec. Comm. Western Electric Co. Jan. 64-.

Western Electric Co. Inc., 195 Broadway, New York 7, N.Y. 10007, U.S.A.

Gorodovikov, Basan Badminovich; Soviet politician; b. 1910; ed. Frunze Military Acad.

Soviet Army, attaining rank of Deputy Commdr. of a mil. district 27-61; Second Sec., First Sec., Kalmyk Regional Cttee. of C.P.S.U. 61-; Alt. mem. C.P.S.U. Central Cttee., Deputy to U.S.S.R. Supreme Soviet; mem. C.P.S.U. 39-; Hero of the Soviet Union 44.

Kalmyk Regional Committee of the C.P.S.U., Elista, U.S.S.R.

Gorresio, Vittorio, D.IUR.; Italian writer; b. 18 July 1910; ed. Rome Univ.

Rome correspondent of *La Stampa* (Turin) 48-; Liberal.

Publs. *Un Anno di Libertà* 45, *I Moribondi di Montecitorio* 47, *I Carissimi Nemici* 49, *I Bracci Secolari* 51, *Risorgimento Scomunicato* 58, *L'Italia a Sinistra* 63, *Il Papato di Giovanni XXIII* 68.

Piazza Navona 106, Rome, Italy.
Telephone: 561468.

Gorse, Georges; French diplomatist; b. 15 Feb. 1915; ed. Lycée Louis-le-Grand and Ecole Normale Supérieure (Agrégé de Lettres).

Prof. French Lycée at Cairo 39-40; Prof. Fouad I Univ. 40; joined Gen. de Gaulle 40; Dep.-Chief Cabinet of Gen. de Gaulle at Algiers 44 and at Paris 45; Mem. of the Consultative and Constituent Assemblies; Dep. of la Vendée 46; Under Sec. of State for Moslem Affairs 47;

Under Sec. of State for French territories overseas 49; Mem. of the Assembly of the Union Française 51-; Del. UN sessions at San Francisco and New York; Ambassador to Tunisia 57-61; Sec. of State for Foreign Affairs (relations with African States of *Expression Française*) 61-62; Minister of Co-operation May-Nov. 62; Amb. to Algeria 63-67; Minister of Information April 67-May 68.

11 rue de Magellan, Paris, France.

Gorshkov, Georgy Stepanovich; Soviet geochemist; b. 1921; ed. Moscow Univ.

Postgraduate Moscow Univ. 43-47; Chief Klyuchevskaya Vulcanological Station, Kamchatka, 48-50, 54-57; Research Assoc., Vulcanology Laboratory U.S.S.R. Acad. of Sciences 50-54, 57-62, Inst. of Vulcanology, U.S.S.R. Acad. of Sciences 62-; Dir. Inst. of Vulcanology 66-; Corresp. mem. U.S.S.R. Acad. of Sciences 66-.

Publs. Works on problems of modern vulcanism.

U.S.S.R. Academy of Sciences, 14 Lenin Prospekt, Moscow, U.S.S.R.

Gorshkov, Admiral Sergei Georgievich; Soviet naval officer; b. 26 Feb. 1910; ed. Naval School, Frunze.

Flotilla Commdr. Black Sea, Sea of Azov, and Danube 41-44; Squadron Commdr. Black Sea Fleet 44-48, Chief of Staff 48-51, Commdr. Black Sea Fleet 51-55; First Deputy C.-in-C. U.S.S.R. Fleet 55-56; Deputy Minister of Defence of U.S.S.R. 56-; Commdr.-in-Chief U.S.S.R. Fleet 56-; Admiral of the Fleet 62-; Admiral of the Fleet of the Soviet Union 67-; mem. C.P.S.U. 42-; Deputy to Supreme Soviet U.S.S.R.; Candidate mem. Central Cttee., C.P.S.U. 56-61, mem. 61-; Hero of the Soviet Union; awarded Order of Lenin (thrice), October Revolution, "Golden Star" Medal, Kutuzov (1st class), Ushakov (1st and 2nd class), Red Banner (twice), Red Star, Sword of Honour with a Coat-of-Arms in Gold, and other awards.

Ministry of Defence, 34 Maurice Thorez Embankment, Moscow, U.S.S.R.

Gorter, Cornelis Jacobus, PH.D., D.SC., LL.D.; Netherlands physicist; b. 14 Aug. 1907; ed. Univ. of Leiden.

Lecturer, Univ. of Groningen 36-40; Prof. Univ. of Amsterdam and Dir. of Zeeman Laboratory 40-46; Prof. Univ. of Leiden and Dir. Kamerlingh Onnes Laboratory 46; Vice-Pres. Int. Union of Pure and Applied Physics 46-51 and 60-66; mem. Royal Neths. Acad. of Sciences 46-, Vice-Pres. 50-60, Pres. 60-66; Foreign Assoc. Nat. Acad. of Sciences (U.S.A.) 67-; discovered paramagnetic relaxation 36.

Publs. *Paramagnetische Eigenschaften von Salzen* 32, *Paramagnetic Relaxation* 47, *Progress in Low Temperature Physics*, Vol. I 55, Vol. II 57, Vol. III 61, Vol. IV 64, Vol. V 67.

Office: Kamerlingh Onnes Laboratorium, Leiden; Home: Burggravenlaan 3, Leiden, Netherlands.
Telephone: 01710-24705.

Gorton, Rt. Hon. John Grey, P.C., M.P., M.A.; Australian politician; b. 9 Sept. 1911; ed. Geelong Grammar School and Brasenose Coll., Oxford.

Served Royal Australian Air Force during Second World War, severely wounded; Councillor Kerang Shire 47-52, and Pres. of Shire; Senator for State of Victoria 49-68, Govt. Leader in Senate 67-68; Minister for Navy 58-63; Minister Assisting Minister for External Affairs 60-63; Minister-in-Charge of Commonwealth Scientific and Industrial Research Org. (C.S.I.R.O.) 62-68; Minister for Works and under-Prime Minister, Minister-in-Charge of Commonwealth Activities in Educ. and Research 63-66; Minister for Interior 63-64, for Works 66-67; Minister for Educ. and Science 66-68; Prime Minister of Australia Jan. 68-; mem. House of Reps. Feb. 68-; Liberal.

Parliament House, Canberra, A.C.T. 2600, Australia.

Goryachkin, Alexander Vasilyevich; Soviet politician; b. 1910; ed. Moscow Engineering and Economics Inst. Director, later Chief Engineer of textile mill in Kostroma 30-39; mem. C.P.S.U. 39-; Deputy People's Commissar of Textile Industry of Byelorussian S.S.R. 40-45; Minister of Textile Industry of Byelorussian S.S.R. 45-52; Chair. Council of Producers' Co-operatives of Byelorussian S.S.R. 52-54; Deputy Minister of Light Industry of U.S.S.R. 55-56; Perm. Rep. of Byelorussian S.S.R. Council of Ministers to U.S.S.R. Council of Ministers 56-; mem. Central Cttee. of C.P. of Byelorussia 56-; Deputy to Supreme Soviet of Byelorussian S.S.R.

Permanent Representation of Byelorussian S.S.R. Council of Ministers to U.S.S.R. Council of Ministers, ulitsa Bogdana Khmelnitskogo, Moscow, U.S.S.R.

Goryunov, Dmitry Petrovich; Soviet journalist and diplomatist; b. 1915; ed. Higher Party School. Worked as lathe-turner in Kovrov and Ivanovo 30-40; mem. C.P.S.U. 40-, mem. Central Auditing Comm.; Editor youth paper *Leninetz* 34; Leader, Ivanovo District Komsomol Cttee. (youth organization) 40-42; in charge of propaganda, Central Cttee. H.Q. of Komsomol, Moscow 42-45; training at Party school 46-49; Editor *Komsomolskaya Pravda* 49-57; Asst. Editor *Pravda* 57-60; Dir.-Gen. *Tass* Agency 60-67; Amb. to Kenya 67-; Deputy to Supreme Soviet U.S.S.R.; Alt. mem. of C.P.S.U. Central Cttee.; Order of Red Banner of Labour.

U.S.S.R. Embassy, Nairobi, Kenya.

Gös, Albrecht; German writer; b. 22 March 1908; ed. Tübingen Univ. Evangelical pastor, Württemberg 30-52; writer 53-; Lessing Prize, Hamburg 53; mem. Berliner Akad. für Künste, Deutsche Akad. für Sprache und Dichtung. Publs. *Unruhige Nacht, Von Mensch zu Mensch* 49, *Gedichte* 50, *Das Brandopfer* 53, *Freude am Gedicht* 54, *Vertrauen in das Wort* 55, *Ruf und Echo* 56, *Genesis* 57, *Hagar am Brunnen* 58, *Rede auf Goethes Mutter* 58, *Ravenna* 59, *Aber im Winde das Wort* 63, *Das Löffelchen* 65.

Im langen Hau 5, Stuttgart-Rohr, German Federal Republic.

Gošnjak, Ivan, Gen. of the Army; Yugoslav soldier and politician; b. 09; ed. Grammar School in Pakrac. Sometime carpenter and local trade union leader in Sisak; joined (illegal) Communist Party 33; in U.S.S.R. 35-37; fought with Spanish Republican Army 37-39; imprisoned in concentration camp in France 39-41; fought with Nat. Liberation Army in Yugoslavia 42-45, commanded 1st Croation Corps; Commdr. Gen. Headquarters of Croatia; Commdr. Zagreb Army after 45; Mem. of Parl. 45-63; Deputy Minister of Defence 48-53; mem. of Fed. Exec. Council of Yugoslavia and Sec. of State for Defence 53-67; mem. Praesidium of Cen. Cttee. of the Communist League of Yugoslavia; mem. Council of the Fed.; decorations include Orders of Freedom, of the National Hero, and Spanish (Republican), French, Greek, Soviet, Czechoslovak, Romanian, Polish, Albanian, Egyptian, Ethiopian and other honours.

Kneza Miloša 33, Belgrade, Yugoslavia.

Gosztonyi, János; Hungarian politician and editor; b. 1925; ed. Univ. of Economic Sciences, Budapest. Member of Parl. 47-; mem. Presidential Council of People's Republic of Hungary 54-63; Head of Cultural Cttee. of Parl. 63-; Head of Editorial Board *Népszabadság* 65-; mem. Central Cttee. Hungarian Socialist Workers' Party.

Népszabadság, Budapest VIII, Blaha Lujza tér 3, Hungary.

Telephone: 343-100.

Gotsche, Otto; German writer and politician; b. 3 July 1904; ed. elementary school, Klempner. Member German Communist Party 18-; anti-fascist activities 33-45; Private Sec. to First Dep. Chair. of Council of Ministers 49-60; Sec. Council of State of German Democratic Republic 60-; several decorations. Publs. novels: *Tiefe Furchen* 49, *Märzstürme* 53, *Zwischen Nacht und Morgen* 55, *Die Fahne von Kriwoj Rog* 59, *Unser kleiner Trompeter* 61.

Council of State, Berlin, Germany.

Gott, Edwin Hays; American steel executive; b. 22 Feb. 1908; ed. Lehigh Univ. With U.S. Steel Corpn. 37-; beginning as Industrial Engineer, Ohio Works; Vice-Pres. (Operations-Steel) 56-58, Vice-Pres. (Production-Steel Producing Divs.) 58-59, Admin. Vice-Pres. (Cen. Operations) 59, Exec. Vice-Pres. (Production) 59-67, Pres. and Chief Admin. Officer, U.S. Steel Corpn. 67-; official and mem. of civic and business orgs.

U.S. Steel Corporation, 525 William Penn Place, Pittsburgh, Pa. 15230, U.S.A.

Gott, Rodney Cleveland; American business executive; b. 11 Sept. 1911; ed. U.S. Military Acad. American Radiator and Standard Sanitary Corpn. 35-41; American Machine & Foundry Co., New York City 46-, Vice-Pres. 46-54, Exec. Vice-Pres. 54-62, Pres. 62-, also Chair. and Chief Exec. Officer 68-.

American Machine and Foundry Co., 261 Madison Avenue, New York City 16, N.Y., U.S.A.

Gotta, Salvatore; Italian novelist and dramatist; b. 18 May 1887. Publs. *Pia* 12, *Il figlio inquieto* 17, *La più bella donna del mondo* 19, *L'amante provinciale* 19, *Tre mondi* 21, *Il primo re* 22, *La donna mia* 24, *Lula—misticismo e sensualità* 25, *Ombra la moglie bella* 26, *Il nome tuo* 27, *La sagra delle virgini* 28, *Il peccato originale* 29, *Tu, la mia ricchezza* 30, *L'amica dell'ombra* 32, *Il gioco dei colori* 32, *I figli degli amanti* 33, *Lilith* 34, *Il paradiso terrestre* 35, *L'angelo ferito* 36, *Portofino* 37, *I giganti innamorati* 38, *Amina* 39, *La sposa giovane* 40, *I sensitivi* 46, *Piccolo alpino* 26, *Il diavolo in provincia* 29, *Serenata alle vergini* 30, *Bella figlia dell'amore* 34, *La signora di tutti* 35, *A bocca nuda* 37, *Tre donne innamorate* 39. *Un fiore sull'autostrada* 40, *Ottocento* 43, *Di là dal fiume c'è una donna* 44, *Il volto dell'umano amore* 44, *Ingrid, l'amica delle nuvole* 44, *Quartetto in paradiso* 45, *Macerie a Portofino* 46, *Signore salvaci, ci perdiamo* 47, *Lo specchio dei sensi* 48, *Domani a Te* 50, *Tempo della Regina Margherita* 51, *La Saga dei Vela* (3 vols.) 55, *Ilaria* 56, *L'Almandco di Gotta* 58, *Orgasmo* 60, *Due Donne a Sirmione* 61, *Le Signore della Villa Antica* 62, *I Diavoli del Gran Paradiso* 62, *Zaira ragazza del Cirro* 63, *Aria del mio Paese* 64, *L'ultimo dei Vela* 65, *Il progresso si diverte* 67.

Villa Aranci, Portofino (Genoa), Italy.

Götting, Gerald; German politician; b. 9 June 1923; ed. August-Hermann-Francke-Stiftung, Halle, and Martin Luther Univ., Halle. Secretary-General Christian Democratic Union 49-66; Vice-Pres. People's Chamber of D.D.R. 49-58; mem. Presidium German Peace Council 55-; Deputy Chair. Defence Cttee. People's Chamber of D.D.R. 58-, Deputy Chair. State Council of D.D.R. 60-; Vice-Pres. German African Soc. 61-; Chair. Cttee. of Foreign Affairs of People's Chamber of D.D.R. 63-; Pres. Christian Democratic Union 66-; Patriotic Order of Merit in Gold and Silver, Banner of Labour. Publs. *The Christian says Yes to Socialism* 60, *My Dear Friend* 61, *Meeting with Albert Schweitzer* 61, *Star Hour of Africa* 61, *The Christian in the Construction of Socialism* 63, *Land under Kilimanjaro* 64, *Visiting Lambaréné* 64, *Christian Co-responsibility in the Socialist*

Society 65, *Albert Schweitzer, Contributions on Life and Work.*
Otto-Nuschke-Strasse 59/60, 108 Berlin, German Democratic Republic.
Telephone: 225061.

Gottlieb, Adolph; American artist; b. 14 March 1903. First one-man exhbn. 30, then Paris 59, London 59, Milan 61, Basle 61; 10-year retrospective exhbn., Bennington and Williams Colls. 54, retrospective exhbn. Jewish Museum 57; represented in numerous galleries including Metropolitan Museum of Art and Museum of Modern Art, New York, Whitney Museum of American Art, Solomon R. Guggenheim Museum, Detroit Inst. of Art, Art Inst. of Chicago, Albright-Knox Art Gallery, Walker Art Center, Tel Aviv Museum; rep. in Tokyo Int. Exhbn., New Delhi Contemporary Art Exhbn.; Grande Premio VII São Paulo Bienal 63.
27 West 96th Street, New York 25, N.Y., U.S.A.

Gotz, Sir Léon Aroha, K.C.V.O.; New Zealand diplomatist; b. 12 Sept. 1892; ed. Ecole de L'Ile de France, Liancourt, King's Coll., Auckland, Wanganui Coll., and Univ. of Otago, New Zealand.
Planter Malaya 13-25; war service, Malay States, Volunteer Rifles and R.A.F.; Gen. Man. New Zealand Reparation Estate, Western Samoa 30-35; mem. of Parliament 49-63; Minister of Internal Affairs, Civil Defence and Island Territories 61-63; High Commr. in Canada 65-68.
New Zealand High Commission, 77 Metcalfe Street, Ottawa, Canada; Home: 337 Fenton Street, Rotorua, New Zealand.

Götze, Heinz, DR. PHIL.; German publisher; b. 8 Aug. 1912; ed. Univs. of Leipzig, Munich and Naples.
Partner (Co-Proprietor) Springer-Verlag, Berlin, Heidelberg, New York 57-, J. F. Bergmann Verlagsbuchhandlung, Munich 57-; Lange & Springer, Scientific Bookshop, Berlin 57-; Pres. of Springer-Verlag New York Inc. 64-66; Chair. Board of Dirs. Universitäts-druckerei H. Stürtz A.G., Würzburg 65-; Corresp. mem. German Archaeological Inst. 56-.
Ludolf Krehl-Strasse 41, Heidelberg, German Federal Republic.
Telephone: 41177.

Goudsmit, Samuel Abraham, O.B.E., PH.D.; American physicist; b. 11 July 1902; ed. Univs. of Leyden and Amsterdam.
Published theory of electron spin (with George Uhlenbeck) 25; Rockefeller Fellowship 26; Lecturer in Physics, Univ. of Michigan 27-32, Prof. 32-46; Guggenheim Fellowship 38; Visiting Prof. Harvard Univ. 41; mem. radar research team at Mass. Institute of Technology and in England 42-46; Head of Scientific Intelligence Mission in Europe 44-45; Prof. of Physics, Northwestern Univ. 46-48; joined Brookhaven Nat. Laboratory 48, Head of Physics Dept. 52-60; corresp. mem. Royal Netherlands Acad. of Sciences; mem. American Acad. of Sciences, American Philosophical Soc.; Editor-in-Chief American Physical Soc.; Editor *Physical Review Letters*; Medal of Freedom; Research Corpn. Award 55, Hon. D.Sc. Case Inst.; Max Planck Medal, German Physical Soc. 64.
Publs. *Alsos* 47 and numerous articles on the structure of atoms.
Brookhaven National Laboratory, Upton, N.Y. 11973, U.S.A.
Telephone: 516-924-6262, ext. 2333.

Gough, Rt. Rev. Hugh Rowlands, C.M.G., O.B.E., T.D., M.A., D.L.; British ecclesiastic; b. 19 Sept. 1905; ed. Cambridge Univ., London Coll. of Divinity.
Deacon 28, Priest 29; Curate St. Mary Islington 28-31; Perpetual Curate St. Paul, Walcot, Bath 31-34; Vicar St. James Carlisle 34-39, St. Matthew Bayswater 39-46, of Islington and Rural Dean 46-48; Prebendary St.

Paul's Cathedral 48; Archdeacon West Ham 48-58; Suffragan Bishop of Barking 48-59; Archbishop of Sydney May 59-66, Primate of Australia and Tasmania Oct. 59-66; mem. Council London Coll. of Divinity, Clifton Theological Coll., Haileybury Coll., Monkton Combe School, St. Lawrence Coll., Chigwell School, Stowe School, Kingham Hill Trust; war service 39-45. O.B.E. (Mil.), mentioned in despatches; Hon. C.F. 2nd Class; Hon. D.D. Wycliffe, Toronto; Hon. Th.D. Australia.
Freshford Rectory, nr. Bath, Somerset, England.
Telephone: Limpley Stoke 3135.

Gouhier, Henri Gaston; French university professor and writer; b. 5 Dec. 1898; ed. Ecole normale supérieure and Faculté des lettres de Paris.
Professor, Faculty of Literature, Lille Univ. 29-41, Univ. of Paris 41-; mem. Acad. des Sciences morales et politiques 61-; Officier Légion d'Honneur; Grand Prix de littérature de l'Acad. Française 65.
Publs. *la Pensée religieuse de Descartes* 24, *la Vocation de Malebranche* 26, *la Philosophie de Malebranche et son expérience religieuse* 26, *Notre ami Maurice Barrès* 28, *la Vie d'Auguste Comte* 31, *l'Essence du théâtre* 43, *la jeunesse d'Auguste Comte et la formation du positivisme* (3 vols.) 33, 36, 41, *les Conversions de Maine de Biran* 47, *la Philosophie et son histoire* 44, *l'Histoire et sa philosophie* 52, *le Théâtre et l'existence* 52, *les Premières Pensées de Descartes* 58, *l'Oeuvre théâtrale* 58, *Bergson et le Christ des Evangiles* 61 (Prix Lecomte de Nouy 62), *la Pensée métaphysique de Descartes* 62, *Pascal, Commentaires* 66, *Benjamin Constant* 67.
21 boulevard Flandrin, Paris 16e, France.
Telephone: TRO-16-09.

Goulart, Dr. João Belchior Marques; Brazilian politician; b. 1 March 1918; ed. Rio Grande do Sul Univ.
Joined Partido Trabalhista 45, National Party Dir. 51; Minister of Labour, Industry and Commerce 53-54; elected Vice-Pres. of Brazil 56, re-elected 61; Pres. of Brazil 61-64.
Montevideo, Uruguay.

Gould, Beatrice Blackmar (wife of Charles Bruce Gould, *q.v.*), B.A., M.S.; American magazine editor and writer; ed. State Univ. of Iowa and Columbia Univ.
Newspaper reporter and woman's editor *N.Y. Sunday World* 26-29; writer for magazines 29-35; Editor (with husband) *Ladies' Home Journal* 35-62; various journalistic awards (with husband).
Publs. *Man's Estate* 27, *The Terrible Turk* 34, *American Story* 68 (two plays and autobiography, with husband).
Hopewell, New Jersey, U.S.A.
Telephone: 609-466-0170

Gould, Charles Bruce (husband of Beatrice Blackmar Gould, *q.v.*), A.B.; American magazine editor and writer; b. 1898; ed. Grinnell Coll., State Univ. of Iowa, and Columbia Univ.
Reporter *Des Moines Tribune* 22, *New York Sun* 23-24, *New York Evening Post* 24-27; literary editor *N.Y. Evening Post* 27-28, aviation editor 28-31; dramatic critic *Wall Street News* 27-30; assoc. editor *Saturday Evening Post* 34-35; Ed. (with wife) *Ladies' Home Journal* 35-62.
Publs. *Skylarking* 29, *Flying Dutchman* 31, and two plays with wife; also *Reunion* (film) 36, *Conversations on the Edge of Eternity* 65, *American Story* 68 (autobiography, with wife).
Hopewell, New Jersey, U.S.A.
Telephone: 609-466-0170.

Gould, Laurence McKinley, LL.D., SC.D., L.H.D., LITT.D., B.S., M.A.; American geologist; b. 22 Aug. 1896; ed. Univ. of Michigan.
Prof. of Geology Univ. of Michigan 21-32; Prof. of Geology Carleton Coll. Northfield 32-45; Chief Arctic

Section U.S. Army Air Force 42-44; Pres. Carleton Coll. 45-62; Prof. of Geology, Univ. of Arizona 63-; Dir. U.S. Antarctic Programme for Int. Geophysical Year; Trustee Ford Foundation; mem. Nat. Science Board; Trustee Carnegie Foundation for the Advancement of Teaching; Sc.D. h.c.
Publs. *Geological and Geographical Results of Putnam Baffin Island Expedition, Geographical Results of Byrd Antarctic Expedition* 31, *The Geology of La Sal Mountains, Utah* 36, *Glaciers of Antarctica, Structure of Queen Maud Mountains, Antarctica, Cold—The Record of an Antarctic Sledge Journey.*
Route 8, Box 131, Tucson, Arizona, U.S.A.

Gould, Samuel Brookner, A.B., A.M.; American university Chancellor; b. 11 Aug. 1910; ed. Bates Coll., New York Univ., Oxford, Cambridge and Harvard Univs.
Instructor, William Hall High School, W. Hartford, Conn. 32-38; Head, Dept. of Speech, Brookline, Mass. Schools 38-47; Prof. of Radio, Speech, Dir. of Div. of Radio, Speech and Theatre, Boston Univ. 47-50; Asst. to Pres., Boston Univ. 50-53; Senior Assoc., Cresap, McCormick & Paget 53-54; Pres. Antioch Coll. 54-59; Chancellor, Univ. of Calif. at Santa Barbara 59-62; Pres. Educational Broadcasting Corpn. 62-64; Chancellor, State Univ. of New York 64-; mem. numerous educational and civic cttees.; Hon. LL.D. (Bates Coll., Wilberforce Univ., Union Coll., New York Univ., Alfred Univ.).
Publs. *Knowledge is Not Enough* 59, *Training the Local Announcer* (with S. A. Diamond) 50.
State University of New York, 8 Thurlow Terrace, Albany, N.Y. 12201; Home: 40 Marion Avenue, Albany, N.Y. 12203, U.S.A.
Telephone: 518-474-4060 (Office); 518-538-7595 (Home).

Goulden, Mark; British journalist and publisher; b. 28 Feb. 1898; ed. Clifton, Bristol.
Reporter on *Cambridge Daily News* 13; Managing Editor and Dir. *Eastern Morning News* and *Hull Evening News* 23-30; Managing Editor *Yorkshire Evening News*, Leeds 30-32; Managing Editor *Sunday Referee* 32-36; fmr. Managing Editor *Cavalcade*, etc.; Chief Editor Argus Press Ltd.; Dir. Illustrated Publications Ltd. and Macfadden's Magazines Ltd. 36-41; Chair. W. H. Allen & Co. (now a division of Doubleday and Co. Inc., N.Y.) 42-.
St. James's Chambers, Ryder Street, London, S.W.1, England.

Goulian, Mehran, A. B., M.D.; American (Armenian) doctor; b. 31 Dec. 1929; ed. Columbia Coll. and Columbia Coll. of Physicians and Surgeons.
Fellow in Medicine (Hematology), Yale Univ. School of Medicine 59-60; Research Fellow in Medicine (Hematology), Harvard Univ. July-Dec. 60, 62-63, Instructor in Medicine 63-65; Clinical Research Fellow in Medicine (Hematology), Mass. Gen. Hospital July-Dec. 60, 62-63, Asst. in Medicine 63-65; Fellow in Biochemistry, Stanford Univ. School of Medicine 65-67; Assoc. Prof. in Medicine, Argonne Cancer Research Hospital, and Research Assoc. in Biochemistry, Univ. of Chicago 67-.
950 East 59th Street, Chicago, Illinois 60637, U.S.A.
Telephone: MU4-6100, Ext. 5012.

Gourley, Wallace S.; American judge; b. 4 Aug. 1904; ed. Ohio State Univ.
Admitted to Bar 29, Asst. District Attorney, Washington County, Pennsylvania 36-44; mem. Pennsylvania Senate 41-45; Judge, U.S. District Court for Western District, Pa. 45-, Chief Judge 51-.
U.S. Court House, Pittsburgh 19, Pa., U.S.A.

Gouveia de Bulhões, Otávio; Brazilian lawyer, economist and politician; b. 06; ed. Univs. of Brazil and Washington.
Former civil servant, Ministry of Finance; fmr. Vice-Governor, Int. Monetary Fund; Minister of Finance 54,

64-; Exec. Dir. Finance and Credit Advisory Board (SUMOC) 54, 61-63.
Ministry of Finance, Brasilia, Brazil.

Govrin, Akiva; Israeli politician; b. 12 Aug. 1902.
Came to Palestine 22; mem. Exec. Cttee. Histadrut 42; mem. Knesset, Chair. Knesset Labour Cttee., Chair. Mapai Parl. Party 53-; Minister without Portfolio 64, of Tourism 64-66.
28 Mapu Street, Tel Aviv, Israel.

Gowon, Maj.-Gen. Yakubu; Nigerian army officer and head of state; b. 19 Oct. 1934; ed. Govt. Coll., Zaria, Regular Officers' Special Training School, Teshie, Ghana, Eaton Hall and Sandhurst Military Acad., England.
Second Lieut., 4th Battalion, Nigerian Army 57, Adjutant 60; Platoon Commdr. Southern Cameroons 60; with UN Forces, Congo 60-61, 63; Staff Officer, Army H.Q., Nigeria 61, promoted Lt.-Col. and appointed Adjutant-Gen. Nigerian Army; Commdr. 2nd Battalion 66; Head of Fed. Mil. Govt. and Supreme Commdr. of the Armed Forces 66-.
Office of the Supreme Commander, Lagos, Nigeria.

Graaff, Sir de Villiers, Bart., M.B.E., M.P.; South African politician; b. 8 Dec. 1913; ed. Univs. of Cape Town, Oxford and Leyden (Holland).
Served Second World War; M.P. 48-April 58, June 58-; Chair. United Party, Cape Province 56-58; Leader of the Opposition (United South African Nat. Party) 56-.
De Grendel, Pte. Bag G.P.O. Capetown, Cape Province, South Africa.

Grabar, André, D. ès L.; French (b. Russian) archaeologist; b. 26 July 1896.
Former Prof. of History of Art, Strasbourg Univ., Ecole des Hautes Etudes 37; Prof. of Early Christian and Byzantine Archaeology, Coll. de France 46-66; mem. Acad. des Inscriptions et Belles Lettres 55-, Dumbarton Oaks Inst., Deutsches Archaologisches Inst. and of other Acads. in U.K., U.S.A., Austria, Denmark, Norway, Serbia; founded *Cahiers Archéologiques*; Dr. h.c. Princeton and Uppsala Univs.
Publs. *La Peinture Réligieuse Bulgare* 28, *L'Empereur dans l'Art Byzantin* 36, *Martyrium* 46, *La Peinture Byzantine* 54, *Le Haut Moyen-Age* 57, *La Peinture Romane* 58, *L'Iconoclasme Byzantin* 58, *Sculptures Byzantines* 63, *Byzance* 63, *Le Premier Art Crétien* 66, *Le Siècle d'Or de Justinien* 66.
Collège de France, 11 place Marcelin Berthelot, Paris, France.

Grabar, Pierre; French immunologist; b. 10 Sept. 1898; ed. Lycée Kief and Univs. of Strasbourg and Paris.
Lecturer, Univ. of Strasbourg 28-38; Chief of Laboratory, Institut Pasteur 38-45, Chief of Service 45-; Dir. Cancer Research Inst., Nat. Centre for Scientific Research 61-; mem. Nat. Cttee. for Scientific Research; mem. numerous int. learned socs.; Officier Légion d'Honneur, Commdr. des Palmes académiques; Behring Int. Prize; Gairdner Award, Univ. of Toronto; Grande Médaille de la Ville de Lille; Prizes of the French Acad. of Science.
Institut Pasteur, 28 rue du Dr. Roux, Paris 15e; and Institut du Cancer, Villejuif, 94 Val de Marne; Home: 6 avenue Marcel Doret, Paris 16e, France.
Telephone: AUT-82-52 (Home).

Grabowski, Franz; German business executive; b. 25 Dec. 1897.
President, Buderus'sche Eisenwerke, Wetzlar 53-; Chair. Supervisory Board Krauss Maffei A.G., Munich, Edelstahlwerke Buderus A.G., Wetzlar, Burger Eisenwerke A.G., Burg, Hessische Berg- und Hüttenwerke A.G., Wetzlar; mem. Supervisory Board Commerzbank A.G., Düsseldorf, Metallhüttenwerke Lübeck G.m.b.H.;

Hon. Dr. Ing.; mem. Grand Order of Merit, German Federal Republic.
Buderus'sche Eisenwerke, Wetzlar, German Federal Republic.

Grace, Her Serene Highness Princess; American-born Princess of Monaco; b. 12 Nov. 1929; ed. Philadelphia and American Acad. of Dramatic Arts, New York.
Began stage career in Philadelphia; appeared on Broadway in the play *The Father* 49; films 51-55 include *Fourteen Hours, High Noon, Dial M For Murder, Rear Window, The Country Girl* (Oscar), *The Bridges at Toko-Ri, To Catch a Thief, The Swan, High Society, Mogambo, Green Fire*; married His Serene Highness Prince Rainier III of Monaco 56; Pres. of Monégasque Red Cross 58-; Grand Croix Order of St. Charles, Grand Cordon Order of Greece, Grand Croix of the Equestrian Order of the Holy Sepulchre of Jerusalem, Lady of the Sovereign Order of Malta, Gold Medals of French, Italian and Austrian Red Cross.
Palais Princier, Monte Carlo, Principality of Monaco. Telephone: 30-18-31.

Grace, J. Peter; American business executive; b. 25 May 1913; ed. Yale Univ.
Joined W. R. Grace & Co. 36, Sec. 42-43, Dir. 43-, Vice-Pres. 45, Pres. 45-; Dir. Kennecott Copper Corpn., The First Nat. City Bank of N.Y., Ingersoll-Rand Co., The Magnavox Co., Marine Midland Corpn., Miller Brewing Co., Deering Milliken Inc., Brazilian Traction, Light & Power Co. Ltd., Stone & Webster Inc., Assurance Co. of America, Northern Insurance Co. of N.Y., and many other cos.; Trustee Atlantic Mutual Insurance Co., Emigrant Industrial Savings Bank; mem. Nat. Advisory Council of Peace Corps; Trustee U.S. Council for Int. Chamber of Commerce; active in many fields of public service; Hon. LL.D. from several colls. and univs.; many foreign decorations.
Office: W.R. Grace & Co., 7 Hanover Square, New York City, N.Y. 10005; Home: 41 Shelter Rock Road, Manhasset, L.I., N.Y., U.S.A.

Grace, William Edwin; American trailer manufacturer; b. 27 April 1908; ed. public schools.
Bookkeeper, Hobbs Manufacturing Co., Fort Worth 30, Office Manager 31-33, Credit Manager 33-35, Sales Manager 35-37, Vice-Pres. and Gen. Manager 37-41, Exec. Vice-Pres. (Operations) 41-55; Vice-Pres. (Hobbs Trailer Div. and Southwestern Div.) Fruehauf Trailer Co. (now named Fruehauf Corpn.) 55-58, Pres. 58, Chief Exec. Officer 59-; Pres. W. E. Grace Finance Co. 34-; official of numerous other corps.
Fruehauf Corporation, 10940 Harper Avenue, Detroit 32, Michigan, U.S.A.

Gracias, H.E. Cardinal Valerian, D.D., M. AGG.; Indian ecclesiastic; b. 23 Oct. 1900; ed. St. Patrick's High School, Karachi, St. Joseph's Seminary, Mangalore, Papal Seminary, Kandy, and Gregorian Univ., Rome.
Sec. to the Archbishop 29-36; Chancellor of the Archdiocese 29; Editor *Messenger of the Sacred Heart* 35; Co-editor *The Examiner* 38; Rector of the Pro-Cathedral, Bombay 41; Titular Bishop of Tannis and Auxiliary to the Archbishop of Bombay 46-50; Archbishop of Bombay 50-; created Cardinal by Pope Pius XII 53; mem. Sacred Congregations for the Oriental Church, of Sacraments and De Propaganda Fide; Pres. Catholic Bishops' Conf. of India; mem. Council for Implementation of the Constitution on the Sacred Liturgy, and Comm. for Revision of Code of Canon Law; awarded "Padma Vibhushan" by Pres. of India 66.
Publs. *Features of Christian Life, Heaven and Home, The Vatican and International Policy, The Decline of Public Morals; The Chief Duties of Christians as Citizens.*
Archbishop's House, Wodehouse Road, Bombay 1, India. Telephone: 213131.

Gracq, Julien; French professor and writer; b. 27 July 1910; ed. Ecole Normale Supérieure and Ecole des Sciences Politiques, Paris (Prof. agrégé d'histoire).
Prof. d'histoire 35-47; Prof. d'histoire Lycée Claude Bernard, Paris 47-.
Publs. *Au château d'Argol* 39, *Un Beau Ténébreux* 45, *Le Roi Pêcheur* 47, *Liberté Grande* 47, *André Breton* 47, *La littérature à l'estomac* 50, *Le Rivage des Syrtes* 51, *Un Balcon en Forêt* 58, *Préférences* 61, *Lettrines* 67.
61 rue de Grenelle, Paris 7e, France.

Gradl, Johann Baptist, DR. RER. POL.; German newspaper publisher and politician; b. 25 March 1904; ed. Kaiser-Wilhelm-Realgymnasium, Berlin, Humboldt-Universität zu Berlin, and Martin Luther-Universität, Halle-Wittenberg.
On staff of *Germania*, Berlin 26-30; mem. Exec. Board Deutsche Sparkassen-und Giroverband (Union of German Savings and Deposit Banks) 31-38; mem. Reichsgruppe Banken 38-45; newspaper publisher, W. Berlin 48-65; mem. Centre Party until 33; mem. Christian Democratic Union (C.D.U.) 45-, mem. Fed. Board of Dirs. of C.D.U. 53-; mem. Bundestag 57-; Fed. Minister for Expellees, Refugees and War Victims 65-66; Grosses Bundesverdienstkreuz.
Publ. *The History of Reparation Payments.*
Office: Bonn, Bundeshaus; Home: Zerbster Strasse 28, 1 Berlin 45-Lichterfelde, Germany.
Telephone: 73-28-87.

Graf, Ferdinand; Austrian politician; b. 07; ed. Klagenfurt Coll.
Secretary Carinthian Farmers' League 29-35, Dir. 35-; Dir. Austrian Farmers' League 45-; Org. Exec. Austrian People's Party 45-; Under-Sec. Ministry of Interior 45-56; Minister of Defence 56-61; Pres. Creditanstalt-Bankverein 61-; Grand Honour Medal; Austrian People's Party.
Creditanstalt-Bankverein, Vienna 1, Schottengasse 6, Austria.

Graf, Herbert, D.PHIL., D.MUS.; Austrian-born American operatic producer; b. 10 April 1903; ed. Vienna Univ., and State Conservatoire of Music.
Operatic work in Germany 26-33; in U.S.A. 34-, Stage Dir. Metropolitan Opera House, N.Y. 36-60; Gen. Manager Municipal Opera House, Zürich 60-62; Gen. Manager Opera House, Geneva 65-; Dir. Opera Dept. Curtis Inst. of Music, Philadelphia 50; has directed opera productions with Toscanini, Walter, Furtwängler, Beecham and other leading conductors; productions at Milan, Munich, Salzburg, Vienna, Florence, Verona, London, etc.
Publs. *The Opera and its Future in America* 41, *Opera for the People* 51, *Producing Opera for America* 61.
Office: Grand Théâtre, 11 boulevard du Théâtre, Geneva; Home: 5 chemin du Presbytère, 1294 Genthod, Switzerland.
Telephone: Geneva 264360 (Office); 8-46-14 (Home).

Graffman, Gary; American pianist; b. 14 Oct. 1928; ed. Curtis Inst. of Music, Philadelphia under Mme. Isabelle Vengerova.
Professional debut with Philadelphia Orchestra 47; concert tours all over the world; appears annually in America with major orchestras; gramophone recordings for Columbia Masterworks and RCA Victor including concertos of Tchaikovsky, Rachmaninoff, Brahms, Beethoven, Chopin and Prokofieff.
c/o Judson, O'Neill, Beall and Steinway, 119 West 57th Street, New York City, N.Y. 10019, U.S.A.

Graham, Clarence Henry, B.A., A.M., PH.D.; American psychologist; b. 6 Jan. 1906; ed. Clark Univ.
Instructor, Temple Univ. 30-31; Nat. Research Council Fellow, Johnson Foundation, Univ. of Pennsylvania 31-32; Asst. Prof. Clark Univ. 32-36; Asst. Prof. to Prof. Brown Univ. 36-45; Prof. Columbia Univ. 45-; on leave

as Scientific Liaison Officer, Office Naval Research, London 52-53; Guggenheim Fellow, Imperial Coll., London 59; mem. Applied Psychology Panel, Nat. Defence Research Cttee. 42-46; Pres. Eastern (U.S.) Psychological Asscn. 55-56; Warren Medal (Soc. Experimental Psychologists) 41; Presidential Certificate of Merit 48, Tillyer Medal (Optical Soc.) 63; Distinguished Scientific Contribution Award (American Psychological Asscn.) 66; mem. Nat. Acad. of Sciences; Sc.D. h.c.
70 Haven Avenue, New York, N.Y. 10032, U.S.A.

Graham, Gerald Sandford, M.A., PH.D., F.R.HIST.S.; Canadian university professor; b. 27 April 1903; ed. Queen's Univ. (Ontario) and Harvard, Cambridge, Berlin and Freiburg Univs.
Instructor in History and Tutor Harvard Univ. 30-36; Lecturer, Asst., Assoc. and later Prof. Queen's Univ. 36-46; Guggenheim Fellowship to U.S.A. 41-42; served R.C.N.V.R. 42-44; Reader in History, Birkbeck Coll., Univ. of London 46-48, Rhodes Prof. of Imperial History, King's Coll. 49-.
Publs. *British Policy and Canada 1774-91* 30, *Sea Power and British North America 1783-1820* 41, *Canada, A Short History* 50, *Empire of the North Atlantic* 50, 58, *The Walker Expedition to Quebec, 1711* 54, *The Navy and South America 1807-1823* (with R. A. Humphreys) 62, *The Poltiics of Naval Supremacy* 65, *A Concise History of Canada* 68; Editor *Imperial Studies Series* (auspices Royal Commonwealth) 58-, *West Africa History Series* 56-; contributor to *Newfoundland, Economic, Diplomatic and Strategic Studies* 46, *Cambridge History of the British Empire* (Vol. III) 59; Advisory Editor *The British Commonwealth* 56, *Britain in the Indian Ocean 1810-1850* 67.
Office: King's College, Strand, London, W.C.2; Home: 49 Norland Square, London, W.11, England.
Telephone: 01-836-5454 (Office); 01-229-8372 (Home).

Graham, Katharine (née Meyer); American newspaper executive; b. 16 June 1917; ed. Madeira School, Vassar Coll., and Univ. of Chicago.
Reporter *San Francisco News* 38-39; editorial staff *The Washington Post* 39-45; married late Philip L. Graham, late Pres. of *The Washington Post* Co. 40 (deceased 63); Pres. The Washington Post Company (owns *The Washington Post*, Washington, *Newsweek* magazine, *Art News* magazine, and several radio and TV stations) Sept. 63-; Dir. Bowaters Mersey Paper Co. Ltd.; Trustee, George Washington Univ., Cttee. for Econ. Devt., John F. Kennedy Library; official of other civic orgs.
Office: 1515 L Street, N.W., Washington, D.C. 20005; Home: 2920 R Street, N.W., Washington, D.C. 20007, U.S.A.

Graham, Martha, LL.D.; American dancer; ed. Bard Coll.
Founded Dance Repertory Theatre, N.Y. 30; solo performances with leading orchestras of the U.S.; Head, Martha Graham School of Contemporary Dance, New York City; teacher, Neighborhood School of Theatre, Juilliard School of Music; Guggenheim Fellow 32, 39; Capegio Award 59; Aspen Award 65.
Martha Graham School of Contemporary Dance, 316 East 63rd Street, New York City 21, N.Y., U.S.A.

Graham, William Franklin (Billy), B.S., D.D., D.HUM., LL.D., D.LITT.; American evangelist; b. 7 Nov. 1918; ed. Florida Bible Seminary, Tampa and Wheaton Coll.
Ordained to Baptist Ministry 39; Broadcaster on *Songs in the Night* 43-45; Founder, Suburban Professional Men's Club, Chicago 43; Vice-Pres. Youth for Christ International 46-; Pres. Northwestern Schools, Minneapolis 47-51; evangelistic campaigns 46-: weekly broadcast *Hour of Decision* 50-; *My Answer* (syndicated column in 250 U.S. daily newspapers); founder and editor-in-chief *Decision* magazine; Pres. Billy Graham Evangelistic Asscn.
Publs. *Calling Youth to Christ* 47, *Revival in our Time* 50, *Hour of Decision* 52, *I saw your Sons at War* 53, *Peace with God* 53, *The Secret of Happiness* 55, *My Answer* 60, *World Aflame* 65.
Office: 1300 Harmon Place, Minneapolis, Minn.; Home: Montreat, N. Carolina 28757, U.S.A.
Telephone: 332-8081 (Office).

Grainger, Isaac B.; American banker; b. 15 Jan. 1895; ed. Woodberry Forest School (Orange, Va.), and Princeton Univ.
Formerly Vice-Pres. Murchison Nat. Bank, Wilmington, North Carolina; Exec. Vice-Pres. North Carolina Bank and Trust Co. 29-34; Pres. Montclair Trust Co. 34-43; Vice-Pres. Chemical Bank (New York) Trust Co. 43-50, Exec. Vice-Pres. 50-56, Pres. 56-60; Dir. Fort Myers Southern Railroad Co., Hartford Fire Insurance Co., Hartford Accident and Indemnity Co., Pa. Central Company, Nichols Engineering and Research Corp., American Manufacturing Co., Shearson Capital Fund Inc.; Trustee, Inst. for Crippled and Disabled, Nat. Realty Investors; mem. New York Chamber of Commerce; Adviser Dir. Union Electric Co., Hon. Dir. Montclair Chapter; mem. Advisory Ctee., Board of Chemical Bank, New York Trust Co., North Carolina Soc., Soc. of Colonial Wars in State of New Jersey, Pilgrims of U.S., Newcomen Soc. (England); Infantry Capt. in First World War.
Chemical Bank New York Trust Co., 11 West 51st Street, New York, N.Y.; Home: 200 East 66th Street, New York, N.Y., U.S.A.
Telephone: Templeton 8-2121.

Gram, Victor Bernhard; Danish politician; b. 30 Jan. 1910.
Factory worker 24-37; mem. Exec. Cttee., Social Democratic Party 35-46, Sec.-Gen. 37-42, Chair. Social Democratic Youth Movement 42-46; Mem. of Parl. 43-; Chief, Information and Welfare Services, Danish Armed Forces 51-62; Minister of Defence 62-68.
Skriverengen 16, Dragør, Denmark.

Granado, Donald Casimir; Trinidad trade unionist, politician and diplomatist; b. 4 Mar. 1915.
Former School Teacher; Sec. Union of Commercial and Industrial Workers 50-54; Sec./Treas. Trinidad and Tobago Fed. of Trade Unions 53-54; Pres. C.G.A. Credit Union 54-56; Sec./Treas. People's Nat. Movement 55-56; Minister of Labour and Social Services 56-61; Minister of Health and Housing and Dep. Leader of House of Reps. 61-63; Trinidad and Tobago Ambassador to Venezuela 63-64; High Commr. in Canada 64-; Amb. to Brazil and Argentina 64-.
Office: Room 508, 75 Albert Street, Ottawa 4, Ontario; Home: 359 Buena Vista Road, Rockliffe Park, Ottawa, Ontario, Canada.
Telephone: 232-2418 (Office).

Granatkin, Valentin Alexandrovich; Soviet sports administrator; b. 08; ed. Moscow technical school.
Electrical engineer until 42; on staff of Central Cttee. of Communist Party of Soviet Union 42-50; Chair. Moscow Regional Cttee. of Physical Culture and Sport 51-53; Deputy Chair. of Cttee. for Physical Culture and Sport, R.S.F.S.R. Council of Ministers 54-59; mem. Central Presidium of Soviet Union Sports Socs. and Orgs. 59-64; Pres. Football Federation of U.S.S.R. 50-64; Vice-Pres. Int. Football Federation 46-.
Skatertny pereulok 4, Moscow, U.S.S.R.

Grand, Gordon, Jr.; B.A., LL.D.; American chemical executive; b. 14 March 1917; ed. The Hill School, and Yale and Harvard Univs.
Teacher at Millbrook School, New York 38-39; admitted to N.Y. Bar 43, to practise before U.S. Supreme Court; lawyer, Spence, Hotchkiss, Parker & Duryee, New York

City 46-48; Counsel, Republican mems. Ways & Means Cttee., U.S. Congress 48-52, Clerk to Ways & Means Comm., U.S. Congress 53; Sec. Olin Mathieson Chemical Corpn., New York City 54-55, Corporate Vice-Pres. 55-63, Vice-Chair. Board, Exec. Vice-Pres. 64-65, Pres. and Chief Exec. Officer 65-, also Chair. 66-67; Dir. Nat. Starch & Chemical Co., United Nuclear Corpn.; Major, U.S. Army Reserve; Croix de Guerre (twice), France.
Publs. *Federal Legislative Process* 51, *Proposals for Revising the Tax System* 54.
Olin Mathieson Chemical Corporation, 460 Park Avenue, New York City 10022; Home: Knollwood Drive, Greenwich, Conn., U.S.A.

Grandgeorge, René Jean; French engineer and businessman; b. 27 Feb. 1899; ed. Ecole Centrale de Paris.
Honorary Gen. Man. Compagnie de Saint-Gobain; Pres. Placements Internationaux et France Investissements; Dir. Banco di Roma; Commdr. Légion d'Honneur, Commdr. Ordine al Merito (Italy).
Home: 8 rue de l'Abbaye, Paris 6e; and La Mougine, Mougins (A.M.); Office: Compagnie de Saint-Gobain, 62 Bd. Victor Hugo, Neuilly-sur-Seine (Seine), France.

Grandi, Dino, Count (di Mordano); Italian lawyer, politician and diplomatist; b. 4 June 1895; ed. Bologna Univ.
Served Italian Army First World War (decorated); led Fascist movement in Northern Italy and took part in March on Rome as Chief of Gen. Staff of the Quadrumvirate; mem. Gen. Council of Fascist Party; mem. Gen. Council of Italian Nat. Trade Unions 20-23; elected to Chamber of Deputies 21; Vice-Pres. 24; Under-Sec. of State for Home Affairs 24; for Foreign Affairs 25-29; Ministry of Foreign Affairs 29-32; Ambassador to Great Britain 32-39; Head of Italian Del. to Locarno Conf. 25; to Confs. for Settlement of War Debt 25, 26, and 29; to Financial Conf., Paris and London 31; to Naval Conf. in London 30 and 36; to Reparations Conf. Lausanne 32; to Disarmament Conf. Geneva 32; Permanent Italian Del. to L.N. Council and Assembly 25-32; Italian Representative on Non-Intervention Cttee. 36-39; Ministry of Justice 39-43; Pres. of the Chamber of the Fasci and Corporations 39-43; Prof. of Law in Rome Univ. during Second World War; involved in overthrow of Mussolini 43; now in retirement.
Publs. *Origins of Fascism* 29, *Italian Foreign Policy* 31, *The Spanish War in the London Committee* 39, *The Frontiers of the Law* 39, *Humanity and Law* 41, and other legal works.
Albareto Di Modena, Italy.

Grandpierre, André Marie Eugène; French industrialist; b. 4 Oct. 1894; ed. Ecole Polytechnique and Ecole Libre des Sciences Politiques.
Engineer with Société de Pont-à-Mousson 18, Sec. 24, Gen. Man. 41, Dir. and Gen. Man. 44, Pres. and Chair. 46-59, Vice-Pres. 59; Pres. and Chair. Compagnie de Pont-à-Mousson and Société des Fonderies de Pont-à-Mousson 46-59, Vice-Pres. 59-64, Hon. Chair. 64-; Chair. Centre Nat. du Commerce Extérieur (C.N.C.E.); Pres. Société Industrielle de l'Est; Vice-Pres. Nancy Chamber of Commerce, Chambre Syndicale de la Sidérurgie de l'Est; Dir. Union Sidérurgique Lorraine (SIDELOR), Charbonnages de Beeringen (Belgium); Grand Officier Légion d'Honneur, Croix de Guerre.
39 rue de Beauregard, Nancy, France.

Grandval, Gilbert Yves Edmond; French government official and politician; b. 12 Feb. 1904; ed. Lycée Condorcet.
Chemical Industry 27-40, Military Gov. Saar 45-48. French High Commr. Saar 48-52, Ambassador 52-55; Resident-Gen. in Morocco 55; Sec. Gen. Merchant Marine 58; Sec. of State for External Trade April-May 62; Minister of Labour 62-66; mem. Directing Cttee.

Notre République 66-; Pres. Compagnie des Messageries maritimes 66-; Commdr. Légion d'Honneur.
Publ. *Ma Mission au Maroc.*
9 rue Armengaud, Saint-Cloud (Hauts-de-Seine), France.

Grandy, Air Chief Marshal Sir John, G.C.B., K.B.E., D.S.O.; British air force officer; b. 8 Feb. 1913; ed. Univ. Coll. School, London.
Pilot Officer 31; served Second World War; Air Marshal 61; Commdr.-in-Chief, R.A.F., Germany (Second Tactical Air Force) and Commdr. Second Allied Tactical Air Force 61-63; C.-in-C. Bomber Command 63-65; Air Chief Marshal 65-; C.in-C. Far East Command 65-67; Chief of Air Staff 67-.
Room 6211, Ministry of Defence (Air), Main Building, Whitehall, London, S.W.1, England.

Granit, Ragnar Arthur, MAG. PHIL., M.D.; Swedish neurophysiologist; b. 30 Oct. 1900; ed. Swedish Normallyceum, Helsinki, and Helsinki Univ.
Docent Helsinki Univ. 29-37, Prof. of Physiology 37-40; Fellow Univ. of Pennsylvania 29-31; Invited Royal 46-67; Dir. Nobel Inst. for Neurophysiology 45-67; visiting Prof. Rockefeller Inst. 56-66; Pres. Royal Swedish Acad. of Science 63-65, Vice-Pres. 65-; foreign mem. Royal Soc., London, and several other Acads.; several prizes and hon. degrees; Nobel Prize for Physiology or Medicine 67.
Publs. *Ung Mans Väg till Minerva* 41, *Sensory Mechanisms of the Retina* 47, *Receptors and Sensory Perception* 55, *Charles Scott Sherrington, An Appraisal* 66.
14 Eriksbergsgatan, Stockholm Ö, Sweden.

Granli, Leif; Norwegian farmer and politician; b. 25 Sept. 1909.
Member of Parl. 45-; mem. Board Norges Kommunalbank 51-; Minister of Agriculture Sept. 63-65; Labour Party.
c/o Ministry of Agriculture, Akersgt. 42, Oslo, Norway.

Grano, H.E. Cardinal Carlo; Italian ecclesiastic; b. 14 Oct. 1887.
Ordained Priest 12; Titular Archbishop of Salonica 58-; Apostolic Nuncio in Italy; created Cardinal by Pope Paul VI 67.
Apostolic Nunciature, Via Po 27-29, Rome, Italy.

Grant, Cary; British-born American actor; b. 18 Jan. 1904; ed. Fairfield Acad., Somerset.
Has lived in U.S. 21-; naturalised American citizen 42; films include *Arsenic and Old Lace, None but the Lonely Heart, The Bishop's Wife, The Bachelor and the Bobby Soxer, Mr. Blandings Builds His Dream House, Philadelphia Story, His Favourite Wife, To Catch a Thief, The Pride and the Passion, An Affair to Remember, Indiscreet, North By North-West, But Not For Me, Operation Petticoat, A Touch of Mink, Charade, Father Goose, Walk, Don't Run.*
Universal-International Pictures, Universal City, Calif.; West Pico Blvd., Los Angeles 64, Calif., U.S.A.

Grant, Duncan James Corrowr; British artist; b. 85; ed. St. Paul's School; studied painting in Paris, Italy and London.
Member of Camden Town Group, London Group, etc.; exhibited at Exhibition of British Art, Tokyo 31; pictures in the Tate Gallery, London, The Walker Art Gallery, Liverpool, Bucharest.
Charleston, Firle, Sussex, England.

Grant, William T.; American retail executive b. 27; June 1876; ed. High School, Malden, Mass.
Founded W. T. Grant Co. 06, now Hon. Chair.; founded The Grant Foundation Inc. 36, now Hon. Chair.
Field Point Park, Greenwich, Conn., U.S.A.

Grantham, Vincent Alpe; British banker; b. 17 April 1889; ed. Elizabeth Coll., Guernsey.
Served 14-18 war; mem. Legislative Council of Gov. of Bombay 23-24, Board of Trustees, Port of Bombay 24-25; Deputy Chair. East India Cotton Asscn. Ltd. 23-25;

Vice-Pres. Indian Central Cotton Cttee. 23-25, Associated Chambers of Commerce of India, Burma and Ceylon 25; Pres. Bombay Chamber of Commerce 25; Chair. Chartered Bank 40-67.
St. Clere's Hall, St. Osyth, Essex, England.
Telephone: St. Osyth 264.

Grass, Günter; German artist and writer; b. 16 Oct. 1927; ed. art school.
Lyric Prize, Süddeutscher Rundfunk 55, Group 47 Prize 59, Literary Prize, Asscn. of German Critics 60, Georg-Büchner Prize 65.
Publs. *Die Vorzüge der Windhühner* (poems and drawings) 55, *Die Blechtrommel* 59, *Gleisdreieck* (poems and drawings) 60, *Katz und Maus* 61 (film 67), *Hundejahre* 63, *Ausgefragt* (poems), *Über das Selbstverständliche* 68; plays: *Hochwasser* 56, *Noch 10 Minuten bis Buffalo* 58, *Onkel, Onkel* 58, *Die bösen Köche* 61, *Die Plebejer proben den Aufstand* 65.
Niedstrasse 13, Berlin 41, Germany.

Grassberger, Roland, LL.D.; Austrian criminologist; b. 05; ed. High School and Univ. of Vienna.
Practice at Criminal Court 29-30, at Police Office 31-32; Asst. Lecturer in Criminology, Univ. of Vienna 30, Lecturer 31-46, Director, Inst. of Criminology, Univ. of Vienna 46-, Prof. of Criminal Law and Criminology 48-, Dean, Faculty of Law 54-55, 60-61, Rector of Univ. of Vienna 62-63; Sworn Expert for Criminology at Austrian Courts 31-.
Publs. *Die Brandlegungskriminalität* 28, *Die Strafzumessung* 32, *Gewerbs-und Berufsverbrechertum in den U.S.A.* 33, *Die Lösung kriminalpolitischer Probleme durch die mechanische Statistik* 46, *Psychologie des Strafverfahrens* 50.
Tendlergasse 17, 1090 Vienna, Austria.

Grassé, Pierre, D. ès sc.; French biologist; b. 27 Nov. 1895; ed. Paris Univ.
Specialised in research on cellular structure, cytology, animal sociology, etc.; Prof. Faculty of Science Paris; Dir. Laboratoire d'Evolution des Etres Organisés; mem. scientific council, Nat. Council for Scientific Research; corresp. mem. Belgian Royal Acad. of Arts and Sciences; mem. Acad. of Sciences (Anatomy and Zoology) 48-, Vice-Pres. 66, Pres. 67; Dr. h.c. (Brussels Univ. 46, Basle Univ. 60, Univ. of Ghent 65).
Publs. *Parasites et Parasitisme, La Reproduction Sexuée et L'Analyse Expérimentale de la Fécondation, L'Evolution: faits, expériences, théories, Précis de Biologie animale* (8th edn.); *Précis de Zoologie* (2 vols.); Dir. and Editor *Traité de Zoologie* (24 vols.).
Laboratoire d'évolution, Faculté des Sciences, 105 boulevard Raspail, Paris 6e, France.

Graur, Alexandru; Romanian philologist; b. 9 July 1900; ed. Bucharest Univ., and the Sorbonne, Paris.
Prof. of Philology, Univ., Bucharest (Dean of Philological Faculty 54-56); mem. Acad. of Romanian People's Repub.; Gen. Manager Publishing House of the R.P.R. Acad.; State Prize 53; Star of the Romanian People's Republic, Fourth Class, Order of Labour, First Class.
Publs. include *Les consonnes géminées en latin* 29, *I et V en latin* 29, *Nom d'agent et adjectif en roumain* 29, *Incercare asupra fondului principal lexical al limbii române* 54, *Studii de lingvistică generală* 60, *Etimologii românesti* 63, *The Romance Character of Romanian* 67; contributions to *Gramatica Limbii române* (Vols. I-II) 63; numerous articles in newspapers and learned periodicals in Romania, U.S.S.R., Great Britain, China, etc.
Office: Institutul de Lingvistică al Academiei R.S.R., Str. I. C. Frimu 22, Bucharest; Home: Boul. A. Ipătescu 12, Bucharest (22), Romania.

Grave, Walter Wyatt, M.A., PH.D.; British educationist; b. 16 Oct. 1901; ed. Emmanuel Coll., Cambridge.
Fellow of Emmanuel Coll., Cambridge 26-66, Tutor 36-40; Lecturer in Spanish, Cambridge Univ. 36-40, Senior Proctor 38-39, Admin. Officer, Ministry of Labour and Nat. Service 40-43; University Registrary 43-52; Principal, Univ. Coll. of West Indies 53-58; Censor, Fitzwilliam House, Cambridge, Jan. 59-66; Master, Fitzwilliam Coll., Cambridge 66-; Hon. LL.D. (Cambridge and McMaster Univs.).
18 Luard Road, Cambridge, England.
Telephone: 47415.

Graves, Harold N., Jr., A.B., M.S.; American journalist; b. 20 Jan. 1915; ed. Princeton and Columbia (School of Journalism) Univs.
Editorial Research Asst. for *Literary Digest* 36; Assoc. Ed. *Pathfinder* 36-39; Dir. Princeton Listening Center 39-41; Asst. to Dir. Foreign Broadcast Intelligence Service, Fed. Communications Comm., Washington 41-43; attached to U.S. Navy, Office of Strategic Services, Washington, Ceylon and Thailand 43-45; Washington correspondent Providence (Rhode Island) *Evening Bulletin* 46-50; Dir. of Information, Int. Bank for Reconstruction and Devt. 50-67, Int. Devt. Asscn. 59-67, Int. Finance Corpn. 60-67; Assoc. Dir. Devt. Services Dept., Int. Bank for Reconstruction and Devt. 67-.
International Bank for Reconstruction and Development, Washington, D.C. 20433; Home: 4816 Grantham Avenue, Chevy Chase, Maryland 20015, U.S.A.
Telephone: OLiver 4-1694 (Home); DUdley 1-3592 (Office).

Graves, Robert Ranke, F.R.A.I.; British writer; b. 95; ed. Charterhouse and St. John's Coll. Oxford.
Served France with Royal Welch Fusiliers; Prof. of English Literature Egyptian Univ. 26; Prof. of Poetry, Oxford Univ. 61-66; now residing in the Balearic Islands.
Publs. include *Goodbye to All That* 29, *But It Still Goes On* 30, *No Decency Left* (with Laura Riding) 32, *The Real David Copperfield* 33, *I, Claudius* 34 (awarded Hawthornden Prize), *Claudius the God* (awarded James Tait Black Prize) 34, *Antigua, Penny Puce* 36, *Count Belisarius* 38 (awarded Femina-Vie-Heureuse Stock Prize 39), *Collected Poems* 38, *T. E. Lawrence to his Biographers* (with Liddell Hart) 39, *Sergeant Lamb of the Ninth* 40, *Proceed, Sergeant Lamb* 41, *The Long Week End* (with Alan Hodge) 41, *Wife to Mr. Milton* 43, *The Reader Over Your Shoulder* (with Alan Hodge) 43, *The Golden Fleece* 44, *King Jesus* 47, *Poems 1938-1947* 47, *The White Goddess* 48, *Watch the North Wind Rise* 49, *The Common Asphodel* 49, Translation of *Golden Ass* 49, *The Islands of Unwisdom* 49, *Poems and Satires* 51, *The Nazarene Gospel Restored* (with Joshua Podro) 54, *Poems* 53, *The Greek Myths* 54, *Homer's Daughter* 55, *Adam's Rib* 55, *The Infant with the Globe* (translation) 55, *Winter in Majorca* 55, *The Cross and the Sword* 55, *The Crowning Privilege* 55, *Catacrok!* 56, Lucan's *Civil Wars* (translation) 56, Suetonius' *Twelve Cæsars* (translation) 56, *Jesus in Rome* (with Joshua Podro) 56, *They Hanged My Saintly Billy* 57, *Steps: A Miscellany* 58, *Collected Poems. The Anger of Achilles* (adapted translation of *The Iliad*) 59 (awarded Alexander Droutzkoy Gold Medal of the Nat. Poetry Society of America and the William Foyle Award for Poetry, London 60), *Food for Centaurs* 60, *The Penny Fiddle* 61, *More Poems* 61, *Six Oxford Addresses* 62, *Comedies of Terence* (translation) 62, *New Poems* 62, *Hebrew Myths* (with Dr. Raphael Patai) 63, *Man Does, Woman Is* (poetry) 64, *Love Re-spelt* (poetry) 65, *Collected Poems* 65, *Majorca Observed* 65, *Mammon and the Black Goddess* 65, *Poetic Craft and Principle* 67, *Arrive at Highwood Hall* 67, *The Rubaiyyat of Omar Khayaam* (with Omar Ali-Shah) 68,

The Poor Boy Who Followed His Star 68, *Poems about Love* 68, *Poems 1965-68* 68.
c/o A. P. Watt & Son, 10 Norfolk Street, Strand, London, W.C.2, England; Deya, Mallorca, Balearic Islands, Spain.

Gray, Bowman, A.B.; American industrialist; b. 15 Jan. 1907; ed. Woodberry Forest (Va.) School, and Univ. of North Carolina.
Salesman R. J. Reynolds Tobacco Co., Winston-Salem, N.C. 30-39, Asst. Sales Man. 39-49, Vice-Pres. 49-52, Sales Man. 52-55, Exec. Vice-Pres. 55-57, Pres. 57-59, Chair. of Board 59-, Dir. 47-; Dir. Wachovia Bank and Trust Co.; U.S.N.R. 42-45; mem. board of Nat. Industrial Conf. Board 50- (later senior mem.); Dir. Piedmont Aviation; Trustee Univ. of N. Carolina.
Brookberry Farm, Route 8, Winston-Salem, N.C., U.S.A.

Gray, Elisha, II; American businessman; b. 7 Sept. 1906; ed. Mass. Inst. of Technology.
With Sears, Roebuck & Co. 28-33; Vice-Pres., Gen. Operating Man. Cutler Shoe Co., Chicago 33-38; joined Whirlpool Corpn., St. Joseph, Mich. 38, Vice-Pres. 40, Dir. 43, Exec. Vice-Pres. 47, Pres. 49-58, Chair. 58-; Dir. Gen. Foods Corpn., Sears Bank and Trust Co., Dir. 43, Exec. Vice-Pres. 47, Pres. 49-58, Chair. 58-; Chair. and Dir. Warwick Electronics Inc. 67-; Dir. Gen. Foods Corpn., Sears Bank and Trust Co., Chicago; mem. Business Council, Mass. Inst. of Technology.
Home: 400 Nickerson Avenue, Benton Harbor; Office: Whirlpool Corpn., Benton Harbour, Mich., U.S.A.

Gray, Gordon, A.B., LL.D.; American politician; b. 30 May 1909; ed. Univ. of North Carolina and Yale Law School.
Admitted to N.Y. Bar 34; with Carter, Ledyard & Milburn 33-35; admitted N.C. Bar 36; with Manly, Hendren & Womble 35-37; Pres. Piedmont Publishing Co., Winston-Salem, N.C. 37-47, Chair. Board 61-; mem. N.C. Senate 38-42, 46-47; Asst. Sec. of Army 47-49, Under-Sec. 49, Sec. 49-50; Special Asst. to Pres. April-Nov. 50; Pres. Univ. of N. Carolina 50-55; Asst. Sec. of Defense for Int. Security Affairs 55-57; Dir. Psychological Strategy Bd. 51-52; Chair. Nat. Comm. in Financing of Hospital Care 51-54; Dir. Office of Defense Mobilisation 57-58; mem. Presidential Cttee. on U.S. overseas information policy 60; Special Asst. to Pres. for Nat. Security Affairs 58-61; mem. President's Foreign Intelligence Adv. Board 61; Chair. Piedmont Publishing Co., Winston-Salem, N. Carolina 61-; Chair. Nat. Trust for Historic Preservation; mem. Boards American Security and Trust Co., R. J. Reynolds Tobacco Co.; Trustee Corcoran Gallery of Art, Brookings Inst.; Democrat.
1224 30th Street, N.W., Washington 7, D.C., U.S.A.

Gray, Harold E.; American airline executive; b. 15 April 1906; ed. State Univ. of Iowa and Univ. of Detroit.
Pilot, Ford Motor Co. 28; Pilot, Pan American World Airways 29-39, Chief Pilot, Atlantic Div. 39-44, Operations Man. 44-47, Div. Man. Pacific-Alaska Div. 47-49, Vice-Pres. 49-52, Vice-Pres. (Atlantic Div.) 52-53, Exec. Vice-Pres. (Atlantic Div.) 53-60, Exec. Vice-Pres. (Overseas Div.) 60-64, Pres. 64-68, Chair. 68-.
Pan American World Airways, Pan Am Building, New York City, N.Y. 10017, U.S.A.

Gray, Sir James, C.B.E., M.C., M.A., SC.D., LL.D., D.SC., F.R.S.; British zoologist; b. 14 Oct. 1891; ed. Merchant Taylors' School, and King's Coll., Cambridge.
Fellow of King's Coll., Cambridge 14-; Dean 20-23; Dir. of Studies 26-31; Prof. of Zoology, Cambridge Univ. 37-59; Pres. British Asscn. 59.
King's Field, West Road, Cambridge, England.
Telephone: Cambridge 50439.

Gray, Robert F.; American businessman; b. 05.
Vice-Pres. George A. Hormel & Co., Austin, Minn. 42-55, Pres. 55-, Chief Exec. Officer 62-.
Home: 203 Southwood Road; Office: George A. Hormel & Co., Austin, Minn., U.S.A.

Graylin, John Cranmer, C.M.G.; British (Rhodesian) lawyer and politician; b. 12 Jan. 1921; ed. Mid-Essex Technical Coll., Chelmsford, England, and Law Society School of Law, London.
Royal Air Force, Second World War; Solicitor 49; settled in Rhodesia 50; law practice, Livingstone 51-; Livingstone Municipal Councillor 52; mem. Fed. House of Parl. 53-63; Dep. Chair. of Cttees. 54; Minister of Agriculture 59-August 63 (resigned); Chair. Tobacco Export Promotion Council of Rhodesia 64-.
Drew Road, Glen Lorne, Salisbury, Rhodesia.

Grazier, Joseph Albert; American businessman; b. 10 Sept. 1903; ed. Lafayette Coll., Easton, Pa., and Univ. of Pa.
With Sullivan & Cromwell, New York City 28-37, joined American Standard Inc. 37, Asst. Sec. 39-47, Sec. 47-51, Vice-Pres. 51-52, Dir. 52-, Exec. Vice-Pres. 52-53, Pres. 53-, Chair. and Pres. 65-66, Chair. 66-; Dir. Nat. Cash Register Co., First Nat. City Bank, Johns-Manville Corpn., Bristol-Myers Co., Sinclair Oil Co.; Chair. Nat. Industrial Conf. Board; Hon. L.H.D. Lafayette Coll.; Grand Officer of the Order of Merit of the Italian Repub.
Home: 435 E. 52nd Street, New York City; Office: 40 W. 40th Street, New York City, N.Y., U.S.A.
Telephone: PL5-2291.

Grechko, Marshal Andrei Antonovich; Soviet army officer; b. 17 Oct. 1903; ed. Frunze Military Acad., Moscow, and General Staff Military Acad.
In First Cavalry Army 19; Officers' School 22, later Platoon Commdr. and Squadron Commdr.; at Frunze Mil. Acad. until 36, later Regimental Commdr. and Chief-of-Staff of Cavalry Div.; graduated from Gen. Staff Mil. Acad. 41; Commdr. 34th Cavalry Div., Southwest Front 41, later Commdr. of Cavalry Corps, Army, and Second-in-Command of Front; took part in liberation of N. Caucasus and Ukraine, Poland and Czechoslovakia; Commdr. Kiev Mil. Area 45-53; Commdr.-in-Chief Soviet Army Group in Germany 53-57; C.-in-C., Land Forces 57-60; First Deputy Minister of Defence and C.-in-C. Warsaw Pact Forces 60-67; Minister of Defence 67-; mem. C.P.S.U. 28-; mem. Central Cttee. C.P.S.U.; Deputy to U.S.S.R. Supreme Soviet 46-; Hero of Soviet Union; Order of Lenin (five times), and numerous other decorations.
Ministry of Defence, 34 Maurice Thorez Embankment, Moscow, U.S.S.R.

Greco, Emilio; Italian sculptor; b. 11 Oct. 1913; ed. Accad. di Belle Arti, Palermo.
Professor of Sculpture Accad. di Belle Arti, Rome; mem. Accad. Nazionale di San Luca; first sculpture exhbn., Catania 33; one-man exhbns. in Rome, Milan, Naples, London, San Francisco, Rhode Island; represented in numerous group exhbns. in Italy and abroad including 4th Rome Quadriennale, 28th Venice Biennale, Bienal São Paulo 57, Palazzo Barberini 58, Zwerge Garden Salzburg 59; works in public and private collections in Rome, Milan, Venice, Florence, Trieste, Città del Capo, London, Leeds, Monaco, Hamburg, Cologne, St. Louis and Pinacoteca Vaticana; engaged on monument to Pope John XXIII 65-67; Medaglia d'Oro of Italian Pres. 61, Comune di Venezia prize, Venice Biennale 56.
Major works: *Monumento a Pinocchio in Collodi* 53-56, *Grande Bagnante I* (Tate Gallery, London) 56, *Grande Bagnante 3* (Musée National d'Art Moderne, Paris) 57, *Testa di Donna* (Pinacoteca Vaticana) 57, *Grande Figura Accoccolata* (Museum of Modern Art, Kyoto,

Japan) 61, three bronze doors, Cathedral of Orvieto 61-64, Monument to Pope John XXIII 65-67.
Viale Cortina d'Ampezzo 132, Rome, Italy.
Telephone: 32-41-48.

Green, Howard C.; Canadian former politician; b. 5 Nov. 1895.
M.P. for Vancouver Quadra; represented Vancouver constituencies 35-63; served overseas in First World War; Minister of Public Works 57-59; Sec. of State for External Affairs 59-63; Progressive Conservative.
4160 N. 8th Avenue, Vancouver, British Columbia, Canada.

Green, (James) Maurice Spurgeon, M.B.E., M.A.; British newspaper editor; b. 8 Dec. 1906; ed. Rugby School and Univ. Coll., Oxford.
Editor *The Financial News* 34-38; Financial and Industrial Editor, *The Times* 38-39, 44-53, Asst. Editor 53-61; Dep. Editor *The Daily Telegraph* 61-64, Editor 64-; Royal Artillery 39-44.
Daily Telegraph, 135 Fleet Street, London, E.C.4, England.

Green, Julien; American novelist; b. 6 Sept. 1900; ed France and Univ. of Virginia.
Prix National des Lettres (France) 66.
Publs. *Adrienne Mesurat* (crowned by Acad. Française) 27, *Leviathan* 29, *Le voyageur sur la terre, Les clefs de la mort, Épaves* 32, *Le Visionnaire* 34, *Minuit* 36, *Journal* 38, *Varouna* 40, *Memories of Happy Days* 42, *Journal* 46, *Si j'étais vous . . .* 47, *Journal* 49, *Moira* 50, *Journal* 51, *Sud* 53, *L'Ennemi* 54, *Journal* 55, *Le Malfaiteur* 56, *L'ombre* 56, *Le Bel Aujourd'hui* 58, *Chaque Homme dans sa Nuit* 60, *Partir avant le Jour* 63, *Mille Chemins ouverts* 64, *Journal* 28-58, *Terre Lointaine* 66, *Vers l'invisible* 67.
52 bis rue de Varenne, Paris 7e, France.

Green, Leon, M.A., LL.B., LL.D.; American jurist; b. 31 March 1888; ed. Ouachita Coll., and Univ. of Texas.
Admitted to Texas Bar 12; in law practice 12-15 and 18-20; Adjunct Prof. of Law, Texas Univ. 15-18 and Prof. 21-26; Prof. of Law and Dean, North Carolina Univ. 26-27; Visiting Prof. Yale Univ. 26, Prof. 27-29; Prof. of Law and Dean Northwestern Univ. Law School 29-47; Distinguished Prof. of Law, Univ. of Texas 47-. Visiting Prof. of Law, Univ. of California, Hastings Coll. of Law 58-59, Univ. of California, Los Angeles 62, Miami 63; Nat. Sec.-Treas. The Order of the Coif.
Publs. *Rationale of Proximate Cause* 27, *Judge and Jury* 30, *The Judicial Process in Tort Cases* 31, 39, *My Philosophy of Law* 41, *Cases on Injuries to Relations* 40, 53, 58; co-author *Cases on Torts* 57-68, *Traffic Victims: Tort Law and Insurance* 58, *The Litigation Process in Tort Law* 65, *Encyclopaedia Britannica, Negligence* 67.
207 Yaupon Road, Austin 4, Texas 78746, U.S.A.
Telephone: GR7-5673.

Green, Marshall, B.A.; American diplomatist; b. 27 Jan. 1916; ed. Groton School, and Yale Univ.
Private Sec. to American Ambassador to Japan 39-41; Lieut. U.S. Navy 42-45; U.S. Foreign Service 45-; Third Sec., Wellington, N.Z. 46-47; Japanese Desk Officer, State Dept., Washington 47-50; Second, later First Sec., Stockholm 50-55; Nat. War Coll. 55-56; Policy Planning Adviser, Far East, State Dept. 56-59; Minister-Counsellor, Seoul 60-61; Consul-Gen., Hong Kong 61-63; Deputy Asst. Sec. of State, Far East 63-65; Amb. to Indonesia 65-; Meritorious Service Award.
American Embassy, Djakarta, Indonesia.

Green, Maurice, *see* **Green, James Maurice S.**

Green, Paul, A.B., LITT.D.; American playwright; b. 17 March 1894; ed. Univ. of North Carolina and Cornel Univ.
2nd Lieut. American Expeditionary Force 18-19; Instructor in and Prof. of Philosophy, Univ. of North Carolina 23-32; Pulitzer Prizewinner 27, Guggenheim Fellow 28-30; Prof. of Dramatic Art, Univ. of North Carolina 35-50; Pres. National Folk Festival 34-45, National Theatre Conference 40-42; Lecturer in Asia on American Theatre for Rockefeller Foundation and U.N.E.S.C.O. 51; mem. Nat. Inst. of Arts and Letters.
Publs. *The Lord's Will* 25, *In Abraham's Bosom and The Field God* 27, *Lonesome Road* 26, *Wide Fields* 28, *In the Valley and Other Plays* 28, *The House of Connelly and Other Plays* 31, *The Laughing Pioneer* 32, *Roll Sweet Chariot* 34, *Shroud My Body Down* 35, *This Body the Earth* 35, *Hymn to the Rising Sun* 36, *Johnny Johnson* 37, *The Lost Colony* 37, *The Enchanted Maze* 39, *Out of the South* 39, *The Highland Call* 41, *Native Son* (with Richard Wright) 41, *The Hawthorn Tree* 43, *Forever Growing* 45, *Salvation on a String and Other Stories* 46, *The Common Glory* 48, *Dog on the Sun* 49, *Peer Gynt* (adaptation) 51, *Dramatic Heritage* 53, *Wilderness Road* 56, *The Founders* 57, *Drama and the Weather* 58, *Wings for to Fly, The Confederacy* 59, *The Stephen Foster Story* 60, *Five Plays of the South* 63, *Plough and Furrow* 63, *Cross and Sword* 66, *The Sheltering Plaid* 65, *Texas* 67, *Sing All a Green Willow* 68; also numerous screen plays.
Windy Oaks Farm, Old Lystra Road, Chapel Hill, North Carolina, U.S.A.
Telephone: 942-3858.

Greene, Graham (brother of Sir Hugh Greene, *q.v.*), C.H.; British writer; b. 2 Oct. 1904; ed. Balliol Coll., Oxford.
Sub-Editor *The Times* 26-30; Lit. Editor *Spectator* 40-41; Foreign Office 41-44; Dir. Eyre and Spottiswoode (Publishers) Ltd. 44-48; Dir. of Bodley Head 58-; Hon. Assoc. American Inst. of Arts and Letters 61; Hon. Litt.D. (Cambridge) 62, (Edinburgh) 67; Hon. Fellow, Balliol Coll., Oxford 63.
Publs. *Babbling April* 25, *The Man Within* 29, *The Name of Action* 30, *Rumour at Nightfall* 31, *Stamboul Train* 32, *It's a Battlefield* 34, *England made me* 35, *Journey without Maps, A Gun for Sale* 36, *Brighton Rock* 38, *The Lawless Roads* 39, *The Confidential Agent* 39, *The Power and the Glory* 40 (Hawthornden Prize), *British Dramatists* 42, *The Ministry of Fear* 43, *Nineteen Stories* 47, *The Heart of the Matter* 48, *The Lost Childhood and Other Essays* 51, *The End of the Affair* 51, *Essais Catholiques* 53, *Twenty-one Stories* 54, *Loser Takes All* 55, *The Quiet American* 55, *Our Man in Havana* 58, *A Burnt-Out Case* 61, *In Search of a Character: Two African Journals* 61, *A Sense of Reality* 63, *A Man of Extremes* 64, *The Comedians* 65, *May We Borrow Your Husband?* 67.
Plays: *The Living Room* 53, *The Potting Shed* 57, *The Complaisant Lover* 59, *Carving a Statue* 64.
Screen plays: *Brighton Rock* 48, *The Fallen Idol* 48, *The Third Man* 49, *Our Man in Havana* 60, *The Comedians* 67.
Childrens Books (with Dorothy Craigie): *The Little Train* 47, *The Little Fire Engine* 50, *The Little Horse Bus* 52, *The Little Steamroller* 53.
c/o The Bodley Head, 9 Bow Street, London, W.C.2, England.

Greene, Sir Hugh (Carleton) (brother of Graham Greene, *q.v.*), K.C.M.G., O.B.E.; British broadcasting official; b. 15 Nov. 1910; ed. Berkhamsted School and Merton Coll., Oxford.
Newspaper correspondent in Germany 34-39; expelled from Germany 39; correspondent in Poland 39; R.A.F. 40; Head of German Service, B.B.C. 40-46; Controller of Broadcasting, British Zone, Germany 46-48; Head of East European Service, B.B.C. 49-50; Head of Emergency Information Service, Malaya 50-51; Asst. Controller Overseas Service, B.B.C. 52-55; Controller 55-56; Dir. of Admin., B.B.C. 56-58; Dir. of News and

Current Affairs 58-59; Director-General, B.B.C. Jan. 60-; Vice-Pres. European Broadcasting Union 63-.
Broadcasting House, Portland Place, London, W.1, England.
Telephone: 01-580-4468.

Greene, John James, B.A., LL.D.; Canadian politician; b. 24 June 1920; ed. Univ. of Toronto and Osgoode Hall Law School.
Served Canadian Air Force 41-45; mem. Parl. 63-; Minister of Agriculture 65-; Chair. World Food Programme (WFP) Pledging Conf., New York 66; Vice-Chair. Meeting of Ministers of Agriculture of OECD countries, Paris 66; D.F.C.; Liberal.
30 John Street, Arnprior, Ontario, Canada.

Greene, General Wallace M., Jr., D.S.M.; American marine officer; b. 27 Dec. 1907; ed. U.S. Naval Acad., Marine Corps Schools, British School of Combined Operations and National War Coll.
U.S. Marine Corps 30-; Joint Staff, Joint Chiefs of Staff 53-55; Asst. Div. Commdr., 2nd Marine Div. 55-56; Commanding Gen. Recruit Training Command, Parris Island, South Carolina 56-57, Marine Corps Base, Camp Lejeune, N. Carolina 57; Asst. Chief of Staff, Headquarters, U.S. Marine Corps 58, Deputy Chief of Staff 59, Chief of Staff 60-64; Commandant, U.S. Marine Corps Jan. 64-; Legion of Merit with Gold Star.
Headquarters U.S. Marine Corps, Washington, D.C. 20380, U.S.A.

Greenewalt, Crawford Hallock, B.S.; American executive; b. 16 Aug. 1902; ed. William Penn Charter School, Philadelphia and Massachusetts Inst. of Technology.
Joined E.I. du Pont de Nemours and Co. 22; Pres. du Pont de Nemours 48-62, Chair. of Board 62-67, Chair. of Finance Cttee. 67-; Fellow American Acad. of Arts and Sciences; mem. Nat. Acad. of Sciences, American Philosophical Soc., U.S. Chamber of Commerce Business Advisory Council, Mass. Inst. of Technology Corpn.; Trustee, American Museum of Nat. History, Carnegie Wash. Inst., Kenyon Coll.; Regent, Smithsonian Inst.; Chemical Industry Award 52, William Proctor Prize (American Asscn. for the Advancement of Science) 57, Medal for Advancement of Research (American Soc. of Metals) 58, Poor Richard's Club Gold Medal of Achievement 59.
Publs. *The Uncommon Man* 59, *Hummingbirds* 60.
Home: Greenville, nr. Wilmington, Del.; Office: Du Pont Building, Wilmington, Del. 19898, U.S.A.

Greenfield, James Lloyd; American government official; b. 16 July 1924; ed. Harvard Univ.
Cleveland Press 39-41; Voice of America 49-50; Corresp. for *Time* Magazine, Korea and Japan 51-55, Bureau Chief, New Delhi 56-57, Deputy Bureau Chief London 58-61; Chief Diplomatic Corresp. *Time-Life*, Washington, D.C. 61-62; Deputy Asst. Sec. of State, Public Affairs 62-64; Asst. Sec. of State, Public Affairs 64-66; Asst. Vice-Pres. Continental Air Lines, L.A., Calif. 66-.
Home: 8555 Hedges Pl., Los Angeles, Calif.; Office: 7300 World Way West, Los Angeles, Calif. 90009, U.S.A.
Telephone: 657-1793 (Home); 646-6654 (Office).

Greenfield, Julius Macdonald, C.M.G., Q.C., LL.B., B.C.L.; British (Rhodesian) lawyer and politician; b. 13 July 1907; ed. Milton School, Bulawayo, and Univs. of Cape Town and Oxford.
Rhodesian Rhodes Scholar 29; admitted to practise as advocate of High Court of S. Rhodesia 33, practised at Bulawayo till 50; elected to S. Rhodesia Parl. (United Party) 48; Minister of Justice and Internal Affairs 50-53; elected to Parl. of Fed. of Rhodesia and Nyasaland (Fed. Party) 53; Minister of Home Affairs and Education 53-55; Minister of Education and Law 55-58; Minister of Law 58-62, of Law and Home Affairs

62-63; returned to law practice 64; Puisne Judge of High Court of Rhodesia 68-.
P.O.B. 535, Bulawayo, Rhodesia.
Telephone: 88060.

Greenough, Allen J.; American railway executive; b. 20 Sept. 1905; ed. Union Coll., Schenectady, New York.
Engineer, Pennsylvania Railroad 28-33, Track Supervisor 33-39, Div. Engineer 39-45, Div. Supt. 45-48, Gen. Supt. 48-52, Gen. Man. 52-53, Vice-Pres. 53-55, Vice-Pres. (Transportation and Maintenance) 55-59, Pres. 59-; official of subsid. and other companies.
c/o Pennsylvania Railroad, 1836 Transportation Center, Philadelphia 4, Pennsylvania, U.S.A.

Greenstein, Jesse Leonard, PH.D.; American astronomer; b. 15 Oct. 1909; ed. Horace Mann School for Boys and Harvard Univ.
Engaged in real estate and investments 30-34; Nat. Research Fellow 37-39; Assoc. Prof., Yerkes Observatory, Univ. of Chicago 39-48; Research Assoc. McDonald Observatory, Univ. of Texas 39-48; Mil. Researcher under Office of Scientific Research and Devt. (optical design), Yerkes 42-45; Prof. and Head, Dept. of Astronomy, Calif. Inst. of Technology and staff mem. Mount Wilson and Palomar Observatories 48-, Chair. Faculty of Inst. 65-67; Visiting Prof. Inst. for Advanced Studies, Princeton 64; mem. Nat. Acad. of Sciences, American Acad. of Arts and Sciences, Int. Astronomical Union, Consultant to Nat. Science Foundation, Nat. Aeronautics and Space Admin.
Publ. *Stellar Atmospheres* (Editor), many technical papers.
California Institute of Technology, Pasadena, California, U.S.A.
Telephone: 213-795-6841.

Greenwood, Rt. Hon. Anthony, P.C., J.P., M.P.; British politician; b. 14 Sept. 1911; ed. Kingston Grammar School, Merchant Taylors' School, and Balliol Coll., Oxford.
Member of Parliament 46-; Vice-Chair. Parl. Labour Party 50-51; mem. Nat. Exec. Cttee. Labour Party 54-; Nat. Vice-Chair. Labour Party 62-63, Chair 63-64; Sec. of State for the Colonies 64-65; Minister of Overseas Devt. 65-66; Minister of Housing and Local Govt. 66-.
House of Commons, London, S.W.1; Home: 38 Downshire Hill, Hampstead, London, N.W.3, England.

Greenwood, Walter; British writer; b. 17 Dec. 1903; ed. elementary council school, and Labour Coll.
Publs. *Love on the Dole* 33 (play 34, film 41), *His Worship the Mayor* 34, *Standing Room Only* 35, *The Secret Kingdom* 37, *The Cleft Stick* 38, *Only Mugs Work* 38, *How the Other Man Lives* 39, *Give us This Day* (play) 40, *Something in my Heart* (novel) 44, *Six Men of Dorset* (film script) 44, *The Village that Voted the Earth was Flat* (Rudyard Kipling: film script) 45, *Cure for Love* (play) 45, *So Brief the Spring* (play) 45, *Eureka Stockade* (film script) 47, *Lancashire* (County Books) 50, *Cure for Love* (film script) 49, *Chance of a Lifetime* (film script) 49, *So Brief the Spring* (novel) 51, *Too Clever for Love* (play) 51, *Saturday Night at the Crown* (play) 54, *What Everybody Wants* (novel) 54, *Down By The Sea* (novel) 56, *Saturday Night at the Crown* (novel) 58, *Happy Days* (play) 59, *The Secret Kingdom* (T.V. serial) 60, *This is Your Wife* (play) 63, *There Was a Time* (autobiography) 67.
Whitegates, Cannan Avenue, Kirk Michael, Isle of Man.

Greer, Rt. Rev. William Derrick Lindsay, M.A., D.D.; British ecclesiastic; b. 28 Feb. 1902; ed. St. Columba's Coll., and Trinity Coll., Dublin.
Asst. Principal, Min. of Home Affairs, N. Ireland 25-29; Curate 29-32, Vicar 32-35 of St. Luke's Church, Newcastle-on-Tyne; Gen. Sec. Student Christian Movement of Great Britain and N. Ireland 35-44; Principal of

Westcott House, Cambridge 44-47; Bishop of Manchester 47-; took seat in House of Lords 55.
Bishopscourt, Bury New Road, Manchester 7, England.
Telephone: Broughton 2096.

Gregh, François-Didier; French public servant; b. 26 March 1906; ed. Lycée Janson-de-Sailly, Faculty of Law and Letters, Ecole Libre des Sciences Politiques, Paris.
Inspector of Finances 30-35, Financial Controller 35-43; Dir. of the Budget, Ministry of Finance 44-49; Dir. Crédit Lyonnais 49-53; Dir. of Int. Bank for Reconstruction and Development (Asian and Middle East Div.) 53-55; Asst. Sec.-Gen. for Economy and Finance, NATO 55-59, Deputy Sec.-Gen. 59-67; Insp.-Gen. of Finances (French Govt.) 59-; Commdr. Légion d'Honneur, several foreign decorations.
9 rue Michel Ange, Paris 16, France.
Telephone: AUT 79-24.

Grégoire, Henri; Belgian classical and Byzantine scholar.
Prof. of Greek and Byzantine History, Brussels Univ.; Sather Prof. Univ. of Calif. 38; Co-Founder Ecole Libre des Hautes Etudes N.Y.; Vice-Dean Faculty of Letters 41-45, Pres. 44; Asst. Prof. of History, New School for Social Research, N.Y.; Pres. Asscn. Int. des Byzantinistes; Editor *Byzantion, Corpus Bruxellense Historiae Byzantine, La Nouvelle Clio, Ta Kyprin*; Co-Founder and Joint Editor of *Le Flambeau* 18-; *Renaissance* 42-; Pres. Centre Nat. de Recherches byzantines, and Editor of its publs.; assoc. mem. Acad. des Inscriptions et Belles Lettres, Paris, and Accad. Nazionale dei Lincei, Rome; mem. Brussels, Bucharest, Copenhagen, Mainz, Munich and Palermo Acads., Medieval Acad. of America, Slav Insts. of Prague and of Belgrade; Chair. Acad. of Mythological and Religious Research, Bulgarian Historical Society, Byzantine Insts. of Providence, R.I. Paris and Istanbul, etc.; Dr. h.c. (Paris, Athens, Thessalonika, Algiers, Sofia, Cairo).
Publs. *Digenis Akritas, the Byzantine Epic in History and Poetry* (with P. Morphopoulos) 42, *Dans la montagne grecque* 48, *Asklepios, Apollon Smintheus et Rudra* (with R. Goossens and M. Mathieu), *La base historique de l'épopée médiévale* 50, *Les Persécutions dans l'Empire romain* (with P. Orgels, J. Moreau and A. Maricq) 51, *Euripides Tragédies* III-VII, *Les Perles de la Poésie Slave* 60.
45 rue des Bollandistes, Brussels, Belgium.

Grégoire, Pierre; Luxembourg politician; b. 9 Nov. 1907; ed. secondary and higher education, Luxembourg.
Administrative career 29-33; Editorial staff *Luxemburger Wort* 33-59; mem. Govt. 59-, now Minister of Foreign Affairs, Armed Forces and Cultural Affairs; Pres. Asscn. of Catholic Writers; in concentration camp 40-45; numerous Luxembourg and foreign decorations.
Publs. *Drucker, Gazettisten and Zensoren* (4 vols.) 64, *Le Baiser d'Europe* 67, and about thirty other works (literary, poetry, history, criticism, etc.).
Strassen, 177 route d'Arlon, Grand Duchy of Luxembourg.
Telephone: Luxembourg 478-461.

Gregor, Antonín, LL.D.; Czechoslovak diplomatist; b. 9 Sept. 1908; ed. Law Faculty, Charles Univ., Prague.
Minister of Foreign Trade 48-52; Amb. to People's Repub. of China 55-57; First Deputy Minister of Foreign Affairs 57-67; Amb. to Poland 67-; Order of Labour 65.
Embassy of Czechoslovak Socialist Republic, Al Róż 16, Warsaw 10, Poland.

Gregory, Bernard Paul, PH.D.; French physicist; b. 19 Jan. 1919; ed. Ecole Polytechnique, Paris, and Massachusetts Inst. of Technology, U.S.A.
Professor of Physics, Ecole des Mines, Paris 53-58; Prof. of Physics, Ecole Polytechnique, Paris, also Deputy Dir. of Physics Laboratory 59-65; Directorate mem. for Research, European Org. for Nuclear Research (CERN) 64-65; Dir.-Gen. of CERN Jan. 66-; Croix de Guerre 39-45; Chevalier Légion d'Honneur; Officier Ordre Nat. du Mérite.
Publs. articles on high-energy nuclear physics, in particular works on the discovery of new particles by means of cosmic rays and high-energy accelerators.
European Organization for Nuclear Research (CERN), 1211 Geneva 23; Home: 12 Chemin de Velours, 1211 Geneva, Switzerland.
Telephone: 41-98-11.

Gregory, Horace Victor, B.A.; American writer; b. 10 April 1898; ed. Milwaukee and Univ. of Wisconsin.
Freelance in New York 24-; awarded Young Poet's Prize for Poetry (Chicago) 28, Helen Haire Levinson Poetry Award 34, Russell Loines Award (American Inst. Arts and Letters) 42, Guggenheim Fellowship 51, Union League Civic and Arts Foundation Prize for Poetry (Chicago) 51; Acad. of American Poets Award 62, Bollingen Prize Yale 65; elected mem. Inst. of Arts and Letters 64; mem. English Faculty, Sarah Lawrence Coll., Bronxville 34-62; Lecturer New School for Social Research 55-56; contrib. to *New Republic, New Masses, Herald Tribune, Poetry, Saturday Review of Literature, Partisan Review, New York Times, Book Review, The Commonweal,* etc.
Publs. *Rooming House* (poems) 32, *Poems of Catullus* (translation) 33, *D. H. Lawrence: Pilgrim of the Apocalypse* 33, *No Retreat* (poems) 33, *Chorus for Survival* (poems) 35, *Poems 1930-40* 41, *The Shield of Achilles, Essays on Beliefs in Poetry* 44, *A History of American Poetry 1900-1940* (with Marya Zaturenska) 46, *Selected Poems of Horace Gregory* 51; *Ovid's Metamorphoses: an adaptation into modern verse* 58, *Amy Lowell: An Historical Portrait* 58, *The World of James McNeill Whistler* 59, *Medusa in Gramercy Park* (poems) 61, *Collected Poems* 64; Editor: *New Letters in America* 37, *The Triumph of Life* (anthology of devotional and elegaic verse) 43, *The Portable Sherwood Anderson* 49, *The Snake Lady and Other Stories* by Vernon Lee 54, *Robert Browning's Selected Poems* 56, *The Mentor Book of Religious Verse* 56; *The Crystal Cabinet* (with Marya Zaturenska) 62, *Love Poems of Ovid* (new English verse adaptation) 64, *The Silver Swan: An Anthology* (with Marya Zaturenska) 66, *Dorothy Richardson: An Adventure in Self-Discovery* 67.
Palisades, Rockland County, N.Y., U.S.A.
Telephone: 914-EL9-4362.

Greindl, Josef; German singer; b. 23 Dec. 1912.
Studies with Paul Bender 32-36; with Krefeld Stadttheater 36, Städtische Bühnen, Düsseldorf 38, Berlin State Opera 42, Deutsche Oper Berlin 48-, Vienna State Opera 56-59, 65-; sang at Bayreuth Festival 43, 44, 52-68, Salzburg Festival 49-52, Lucerne Festival 51, Zürich Festival 51-54; Dir. Opera and Music School, Saarbrücken 61-; has frequently sung at foreign opera houses, including Metropolitan Opera, New York, La Scala, Milan and in Rome, Naples, Venice, Paris, Lisbon, Amsterdam, Chicago, Tokyo, Buenos Aires, San Francisco and Mexico City, numerous European concert tours and recordings; Berlin Art Prize 55; Bundesverdienstkreuz (1st Class).
Küchelstr. 1a, Munich 55, German Federal Republic.
Telephone: 744506.

Grenfell, Joyce Irene, O.B.E.; British entertainer and writer; b. 10 Feb. 1910.
Radio Critic *Observer* 36-39; first stage appearance in Farjeon's *Little Revue* April 39-April 40; appeared in *Diversion* Wyndham's Theatre Oct. 40-April 41, *Light and Shade* Ambassadors Theatre Sept. 41; Welfare Officer Canadian Red Cross 41-43; entertained troops, and in hospitals in N. Africa, the Middle East, India and Italy 44-45; appeared in Noel Coward's revue *Sigh No More* 45-46, *Tuppence Coloured* 47-48, *Penny*

Plain 49-50, *Joyce Grenfell Requests the Pleasure*, London 54-55, New York 55; Toured U.S. and Canada with solo programme 56, 58, 60, and in Sydney, Australia 59, Switzerland and Canada 63, London 65; mem. Pilkington Cttee. on Radio and TV 60-62; appeared in Australia, New Zealand, Hong Kong and Singapore 63; Pres. Soc. of Women Writers and Journalists; films include: *Poet's Pub, The Happiest Days of Your Life, Stage Fright, Galloping Major, Laughter in Paradise, The Magic Box, The Pickwick Papers, Genevieve, The Million Pound Note, Forbidden Cargo* 53, *Belles of St. Trinians* 54, *The Pure Hell of St. Trinians, The Americanisation of Emily* 63, *The Yellow Rolls-Royce* 64; Radio: own series *A Note With Music, The How Series* in collaboration with Stephen Potter, and T.V. appearances, etc.
c/o Christopher Mann Ltd., 140 Park Lane, London, W.1, England.

Gresford, Guy Barton, B.SC., F.R.A.C.I.; Australian science administrator; b. 7 March 1916; ed. Hobart High School, Royal Melbourne Technical Coll., Trinity Coll., Univ. of Melbourne, and School of Administration, Harvard Univ.
Officer in Charge, Australian Scientific Liaison Office, London 42-46; Asst. Sec. (Australian) Commonwealth Scientific and Industrial Research Org. 47-52, Sec. (Physical Sciences) 52-59, Sec. 59-66; Dir. for Science and Technology, UN 66-; Sec. UN Advisory Cttee. for Application of Science and Technology to Devt. 66-; Harkness Fellow, Commonwealth Fund of New York 57.
United Nations, New York, N.Y., U.S.A.

Gresford Jones, Rt. Rev. Edward Michael, K.C.V.O., M.A., D.D.; British ecclesiastic; b. 21 Oct. 1901; ed. Rugby School, and Trinity Coll., Cambridge.
Curate, St. Chrysostom's, Victoria Park, Manchester 26-28; Chaplain, Trinity Coll., Cambridge 28-33; Vicar of Holy Trinity, South Shore, Blackpool 33-39; Rural Dean of the Fylde 38-39; Vicar of Hunslet, Leeds 39-42; Bishop Suffragan of Willesden 42-50; Lord Bishop of St. Albans 50-; Chair. Church of England Moral Welfare Council 51-61; Lord High Almoner to H.M. Queen Elizabeth II 53.
Abbey Gate House, St. Albans, Herts., England.
Telephone: St. Albans 53305.

Gressitt, J(udson) Linsley, B.S., M.S., PH.D., F.R.E.S.; American entomologist; b. 16 June 1914; ed. Stanford and California Univs.
Asst. in Zoology Cal. Univ.; Instructor Lingnan Univ. (Canton and Hong Kong) 39-41; interned 41-43; Lieut. U.S.N. Medical Research Unit No. 2 45-46; Asst. Prof. Lingnan Univ. 46. Assoc. Prof. 48-51; mem. U.S. Nat. Research Council (Pacific Science Board) 51-52; Entomologist Bishop Museum, Honolulu 53-, Chair. Dept. of Entomology 56-; L. Allen Bishop Distinguished Chair. of Zoology 63-; Chair. Standing Cttee. on Pacific Entomology (Pacific Science Asscn.) 53-57; field work in Far East 29-51, South Pacific 51-, Antarctica 59-66; Guggenheim Fellowship 55-56, Fulbright Fellowship (Australia) 60-61; Polar Research Cttee. Nat. Acad. of Sciences 65-.
Publs. *Longicorn Beetles of Hainan Island* 40, *Longicorn Beetles of China* 51, *Filth-inhabiting Flies of Guam* (with G. Bohart) 51, *Tortoise-beetles of China* 52, *Coconut Rhinoceros Beetle* 53, *Insects of Micronesia—Introduction* 54, *Cerambycidae* 56, *Hispine Beetles from the South Pacific* 57, *Longicorn Beetles from New Guinea* Vol. I 59, *Bibliographic Introduction to Antarctic-Subantarctic Entomology* 60, *Problems in the Zoogeography of Pacific and Antarctic Insects* 61, *Chrysomelidae of China and Korea* (with S. Kimoto) 61, 63, *Insects of Campbell Island* 64, *Land Anthropods of Antarctica* 65, *Bibliography of New Guinea Entomology* (with J. Szent-

Ivany) 68, Editor *Entomology of Antarctica* 67, etc. Bishop Museum, Honolulu, Hawaii 96819, U.S.A.
Telephone: 855951 (Office); 554757 (Home).

Gresson, Sir Kenneth Macfarlane, K.B.E., LL.B., P.C.; New Zealand judge; b. 18 July 1891; ed. Wanganui Collegiate School, and Univ. of New Zealand.
In practice as lawyer, Christchurch 18-47; Dean, Faculty of Law, Canterbury Univ. Coll. 36-47; Judge of the Supreme Court of New Zealand 47-; Pres. New Zealand Court of Appeal 58-63, Judicial Cttee. of Privy Council 63.
54 Aurora Terrace, Wellington, New Zealand.

Grewe, Wilhelm G.; German university professor and diplomatist; b. 16 Oct. 1911; ed. Univs. of Berlin, Freiburg, Frankfurt and Hamburg, and The Acad. of International Law, The Hague.
Taught in Berlin and Göttingen Univs. 41-47; Prof. of Law, Freiburg Univ. 47-55; Chief of Legal Division, Foreign Office 53-54, of the Political Division 55-58; Ambassador to U.S.A. 58-62, Perm. Rep. to North Atlantic Treaty Organisation (NATO) 62-; mem. Perm. Court of Arbitration, The Hague.
Publs. *Gnade und Recht* 36, *Ein Besatzungsstatut für Deutschland* 48, *Deutsche Aussenpolitik der Nachkriegszeit* 60.
North Atlantic Treaty Organisation (NATO), Evère, Brussels, Belgium.
Telephone: Brussels 41-44-80.

Grey, Beryl Elizabeth (Mrs. S. G. Svenson); British prima ballerina; b. 11 June 1927; ed. Dame Alice Owens School, London, Madeline Sharp School, Royal Ballet School, and de Vos School of Dance.
Debut Sadler's Wells Co. 41; Prima Ballerina with Royal Ballet until 57; freelance int. prima ballerina since 57; first full-length ballet *Swan Lake* on 15th birthday; has appeared since in leading roles of classical and numerous modern ballets including *Giselle, Sleeping Beauty, Sylvia, Casse Noisette, Les Sylphides, Checkmate, Donald of the Burthens, Dante Sonata, Three Cornered Hat, Ballet Imperial, Lady and the Fool, Les Rendezvous*; American, Continental, African, Far Eastern tours with Royal Ballet since 45; guest artist European Opera Houses in Norway, Finland, Sweden, Denmark, Belgium, Rumania, Germany, Italy, etc.; guest artist South and Central America, Middle East, Union of South Africa, Rhodesia, Australasia; first foreign guest artist ever to dance with the Bolshoi Ballet in Russia 57-58 (Moscow, Leningrad, Kiev, Tiflis) and first to dance with Peking Ballet and Shanghai Ballet 64; Dir.-Gen. of Arts Educational Trust, London 66-68.
Publs. *Red Curtain Up* 58, *Through the Bamboo Curtain* 65.
78 Park Street, London, W.1, England.
Telephone: 01-629-0477.

Grey, Sir Ralph Francis Alnwick, G.C.M.G., K.C.V.O., O.B.E., LL.B.; British civil servant; b. 15 April 1910; ed. Wellington Coll., Auckland Univ. Coll., Pembroke Coll., Cambridge.
Barrister and Solicitor, Supreme Court of New Zealand 32; Judge's Assoc. N.Z. 32-36; Cadet, Colonial Admin. Service, Nigeria 37, Asst. Financial Sec. 48, Admin. Officer (First Class) 51, Development Sec. 52, Sec. to the Gov.-Gen. and Council of Ministers 54; Chief Sec. Fed. of Nigeria 55-57; Deputy Gov.-Gen. 57-59; mem. Council of Ministers, Fed. of Nigeria 55-57, and mem. Council of Ibadan Univ. Coll.; Gov. and C.-in-C. British Guiana 59-64; Gov. and C.-in-C. Bahamas 64-, also Gov. Turks and Caicos Islands 65-; Knight of St. John.
Government House, Nassau, Bahamas; Overbrook, Naunton, Glos., England.
Telephone: Guiting Power 263.

Gribachov, Nikolai Matveevich; Soviet poet and journalist; b. 1910; ed. Coll. of Land Reclamation.
Land Surveyor in Northern regions; Editor-in-Chief

Soviet Union; mem. C.P.S.U. 43-; candidate mem. Central Cttee. C.P.S.U.; State Prizewinner 48, 49; Lenin Prize 60, Order of Lenin 67.
Publs. *The Bolshevik Collective Farm* 47, *Spring in the Pobeda* 48, *Poems and Verses* 51, *After Thunderstorm* 52, *My Dear Fellow-Countrymen* 54, *Thoughtful Mood* 55, *Face to Face with America* 61, *Orbit of Century* 61, *Selected Works* (3 vols.) 61, *America, America* 61, *I am Going* 62, *Night Thunderstorm* (novel) 64, *White-Black* (poetry) 65, *Love and Anxiety and Battle* (poetry) 67.
Union of Writers of U.S.S.R., 52 Vorovsky Street, Moscow, U.S.S.R.

Gribbin, George H.; American advertising executive; b. 13 Aug. 1907; ed. Bay City Junior Coll. (Mich.), Univ. of Wisconsin and Stanford Univ.
Copywriter, Young and Rubicam 35-42, Copy Supervisor 42, 46-51; U.S. Army 42-46; Vice-Pres. (Radio-TV Commercials), Young and Rubicam 51-54, Vice-Pres. (Print and Radio-TV Copy) 54-56, Senior Vice-Pres. 56-58, Pres. 58-63, Chair. of Board 63-65, Chief Exec. Officer 65-; mem. social and philanthropic orgs.
Young and Rubicam Inc., 285 Madison Avenue, New York City 17, N.Y., U.S.A.

Gridley, John Crandon, C.B.E.; British company director; b. 28 May 1904; ed. Queen's Coll., Taunton.
Chair. Mobil Oil Co. Ltd. 49-; Dir. Powell Duffryn Ltd.; mem. Univ. Grants Cttee. 54-63; Pres. Inst. of Petroleum 62-64; Court of London Univ. 62-.
Mobil Oil Co. Ltd., Caxton House, Tothill Street, London, S.W.1; and 71 Melbury Court, London, W.8; Home: Cwrt-yr-Ala, Dinas Powis, Glamorgan, Wales.

Grieg, Harald, M.A.; Norwegian publisher; b. 3 Aug. 1894; ed. Univ. of Oslo.
Journalist with *Tidens Tegn* 14; war corresp. in Finland 18; Man. Dir. of publishing house Gyldendal Norsk Forlag 21-; arrested by the Nazis and interned in Grini concentration camp 41; resumed business 45; Chair. of Board, Norwegian Publishers' Asscn. 36-62; Foundation mem. Scandinavian Publishers' Council 35-; Chair. Board of Nat. Theatre 39-62; Chair. Swedish-Norwegian Foundation 49-64.
Publs. *Bjørnson and the Book Trade* 32, *Publishing as a Vocation* 45, *The Blessing of Reading* 45, *Kielland and the Wicked Robbers* 49, *Speeches in the Theatre, Back to Norway, Out Fishing with Hemingway* 50, *A Publisher's Reader* 52, *Hamsun* 54, *En Dansk Forlegger og Fire Norske Diktere* 55, *Nordahl my Brother* 56, *A Publisher's Memoirs I-II* 58, *Underveis* 65.
Home: Benneches vei 4b, Bygdöy, Oslo; Office: Gyldendal Norsk Forlag, Universitetsgt. 16, Oslo, Norway.

Griera, Antoni, LITT.D.; Spanish university professor; b. 87; ed. Univs. of Halle, Zürich and Paris.
Prof. of History of Spanish Literature, Gran Seminario de Barcelona; Prof. of Christian Culture, Escuela Superior de Bellas Artes de Barcelona; Prof. of Romance Philology, Univ. of Barcelona; mem. Higher Council of Scientific Research, Madrid; mem. Real Acad. de Buenas Letras, Barcelona, Real Acad. de Bellas Artes de San Jorge, Barcelona; Royal Gustav Adolfus Acad., Uppsala, Royal Literary and Royal Historic and Ancient Literature Acads. Stockholm; Accad. di Scienze, Bologna, Pontificia Accad. Romana di Archeologia; Dr. h.c. (Würzburg and Louvain).
Publs. *Tresor de la Llengua, de les Tradicions et de la Cultura popular de Catalunya,* 14 vols. 35-47, *Atlas lingüístic de la Catalunya,* 8 vols., *Boletín de Dialectologia catalana-española,* 45 vols., 13-66, *Atlas lingüístic d'Andorra* 60, *Vocabulario Vasco* 60, *Memories* 63, *Consueta jueva* 66, *Liturgia Popular* 67, *Homonímies* 67, *Els Ormeigs de pescar dels rius i costes de Catalunya* 68, *Homonímies d'Andorra* 68, *Los Atlas lingüísticos y la*

interpretación de sus mapas 68, *La Casa Catalana* 68, *Trilogia de la Vida* 68.
Instituto Internacional de Cultura Románica, Abadia de San Cugat del Vallés, Barcelona, Spain.
Telephone: S. Cugat del Vallés 44.

Grierson, John, M.A., LL.D.; British film producer; b. 26 April 1898; ed. Glasgow, Durham and Chicago Univs.
Served R.N. 14-18 war; Film Officer, Empire Marketing Board 28-33, G.P.O. 33-37; Film adviser, Canadian Govt., Scotland Film Cttee., Imperial Relations Trust; mem. Cinematograph Films Council 38; Canadian Govt. Film Commr. 39-45; Gen. Man. Canadian Wartime Information Board 43-45; Controller of Film Activities, C.O.I. 48-50; Dir. Mass Communications and Public Information UNESCO 47-48.
Films include *Drifters* 29, *Song of Ceylon* 35, *Night Mail* 36, *The World in Action* Series under the auspices of Nat. Film Board 41-45, *The Brave Don't Cry* 52, *Man of Africa* 53; Television: *This Wonderful World* 61.
Publs. *The Cinema in the Arts Today* 35, *The Course of Realism* 38, *Grierson on Documentary* 46.
Tog Hill, Calstone, Calne, Wiltshire, England.

Griffin, Charles Donald; American naval officer; b. 12 Jan. 1906; ed. U.S. Naval Acad., and Univ. of Michigan.
U.S. Navy 27-, Vice-Admiral 60, Admiral 63; Duty in Battleships and Destroyers 27-30, U.S.S. *Enterprise* 37-40, Flight Test Officer, Naval Air Station, Anacostia 40-42, Commdr. Carrier Air Group 9, U.S.S. *Essex* 42-43; mem. Joint War Plans Cttee., Joint Chiefs of Staff 44, Commanding Officer, U.S.S. *Croatan* 45-46, Plans Officer, U.S. Atlantic Fleet 46-47, Strategic Plans Div., Operations Navy 48-50, Plans Officer, U.S. Pacific Fleet 51-53, Commanding Officer, U.S.S. *Oriskany* 53-54, Special Asst. to Chair., Joint Chiefs of Staff 55-56, Commdr. Carrier Div. 4, 57-58, Dir. Strategic Plans, Navy Dept. 59-60, Commdr. Seventh Fleet 60-Oct. 61, Dep. Chief of Naval Operations for Fleet Operations and Readiness Dec. 61-63, C.-in-C. U.S. Naval Force in Europe 63-65; C.-in-C. Allied Forces, Southern Europe 65-68.
4610 Dexter Street, S.W., Washington, D.C. 20007, U.S.A.

Griffin, Robert P.; American lawyer and politician; b. 6 Nov. 1923; ed. Central Michigan Coll., and Univ. of Michigan.
Admitted to Michigan Bar; mem. law firm Williams, Griffin, Thompson and Coulter, Traverse City 50-56; mem. U.S. Congress 56-66; U.S. Senator from Michigan 66-; Republican.
U.S. Senate, Washington, D.C., U.S.A.

Griffith, Ernest Stacey; American political scientist and research director; b. 28 Nov. 1896; ed. Hamilton Coll., and Univ. of Oxford.
Instructor in Economics, Princeton 20-21; Warden, Univ. Settlement and David Lewis Club, Liverpool 23-28; Lecturer in Social Studies Univ. of Liverpool 26-28; Assoc. Prof. Syracuse Univ. 28-29; Visiting Prof. Harvard 29-30; Dean and Prof. of Political Science, Syracuse 30-35, and American Univ. Washington 35-40; Dir. Legislative Reference Service, Library of Congress 40-58; Fulbright Prof., Oxford 51-52, and Lecturer in Birmingham, Manchester, Swansea and Oslo; Dean, School of Int. Service, American Univ., Wash. 58-65; Consultant Editor Praeger Series U.S. Govt. Depts. and Agencies 66-; Pres. Nat. Acad. of Econs. and Political Science 58-63.
Publs. *The Impasse of Democracy* 39, *The Modern Government in Action* 42, *Research in Political Science* 48, *Congress: Its Contemporary Role* 51, 61, *The American System of Government* 54, 59, 62.
Home: 1941 Parkside Drive N.W., Washington 12, D.C., U.S.A.

Griffith, Harold Melvin; American steel executive; b. 4 July 1904; ed. Chicago Technical Coll. and Harvard Univ.

Steel works metallurgist, Bethlehem Steel Co. 26-30; Jones & Laughlin Steel Co. 30-36; with Steel Co. of Canada Ltd. 36-, Vice-Pres. 53-64, Exec. Vice-Pres. 64-66, Pres. 66-, also Dir.; Dir. Toronto, Hamilton & Buffalo Railway Co., Royal Trust Co.; mem. American Iron & Steel Inst., American Inst. of Mining, Metallurgical and Petroleum Engineers.

Steel Company of Canada Ltd., Wilcox Street, Hamilton, Ontario, Canada.

Griffith, Thomas, A.B.; American editor; b. 30 Dec. 1915; ed. Univ. of Washington.

Reporter, then Asst. Editor *Seattle Times* (Wash.) 36-41; Pacific Northwest Corresp. *Collier's Weekly* 40-41; Nieman Fellow, Harvard 42; Contributing Editor, then Assoc. Editor *Time* magazine 43-46, Senior Editor 46, Nat. Affairs Editor 49-51, Foreign Editor 51-60, Asst. Man. Editor, *Time* 60-63; Senior Staff Editor, all Time Inc. Publs. 63-67; Editor *Life* magazine 68-.

Publ. *The Waist-High Culture* 58.

Time & Life Building, Rockefeller Center, New York City 10020; Home: 25 East End Avenue, New York City 10028, U.S.A.

Telephone: LL6-3871 (Office); RE4-7625 (Home).

Griffith-Jones, Sir Eric (Newton), K.B.E., C.M.G., Q.C.; British company director and former colonial civil servant; b. 1 Nov. 1913; ed. Cheltenham Coll.

Barrister-at-Law 34; Advocate and Solicitor, Straits Settlements and Johore 35, Crown Counsel, Straits Settlements 39, Malayan Union 46; Senior Federal Counsel, Fed. of Malaya 48; Legal Adviser, Selangor 48-49, Perak 49-51; Solicitor-Gen., Kenya 52-55; Dep. Speaker and Chair. of Cttees. Kenya Legislative Council 54-55; Attorney-Gen. and Minister for Legal Affairs, Kenya 55-61 (at times Acting Chief Sec.), Deputy Gov. 61-63 (at times Acting Gov.); Chair. The Guthrie Corpn. Ltd. 65-, Guthrie Estates Ltd. 64-, Landairsy Investments Ltd. 64-, Calderdale Developments Ltd. 65-, Guthrie Industries Ltd. 66-, Lintafoam Industries Ltd. 66-, Lintafoam Ltd. 66-, Wm. Symington & Son Ltd. 66-, Property Holdings (Pennine) Ltd. 66-, Sutcliffe Mitchell (Insurances) Ltd. 66-; Dir. Provident Mutual Life Assurance Asscn. 64-, Provident Clerks' Benevolent Fund 64-; Mil. Service 41-46.

Office: 52-54 Gracechurch Street, London, E.C.3; Home: The Combe, Rogate, Near Petersfield, Hants., England.

Telephone: 01-626-1301 (Office).

Griffiths, Rt. Hon. James, P.C., C.H., J.P., M.P.; British politician; b. Sept. 1890; ed. elementary school, and Labour Coll.

Labour Party Agent 22-25; Miners' Agent 25-36; Pres. South Wales Miners' Fed. 33-36; mem. Nat. Exec. Miners' Fed. of Great Britain 34-36; Labour M.P. for Llanelly Div. of Carmarthen 36-; mem. Nat. Exec. Labour Party 39-59; Minister Nat. Insurance Aug. 45-Feb. 50; Sec. of State for the Colonies 50-51; Chair. of Labour Party 48; mem. B.B.C. Gen. Advisory Council 52; Deputy Leader Parl. Labour Party 56-59; Sec. of State for Wales 64-66; Hon. LL.D., Univ. of Wales.

House of Commons, London, S.W.1, England.

Griffiths, Sir Percival Joseph, Kt., C.I.E., M.A., B.SC.; British civil servant (India) and businessman; b. 15 Jan. 1899; ed. Peterhouse, Cambridge.

Served with Indian Civil Service 22-37; Adviser to the Indian Tea Asscn., Calcutta 37-47; mem. Indian Legislative Assembly 37-47; publicity adviser to Govt. of India during Second World War; adviser to the Indian Tea Asscn. (London) and Pakistan Tea Asscn. (London); Pres. India, Pakistan and Burma Asscn.; company director.

Publs. *The British in India* 46, *The British Impact on India* 52, *Modern India* 57, *The Changing Face of Communism* 61, *The Road to Freedom* 64.

St. Christopher, East Drive, Wentworth, Virginia Water, Surrey, England.

Grigorenko, Alexei Semyonovich; Soviet politician; b. 1915; ed. Kiev Industrial Inst.

Design Engineer, Head of Technological Bureau, Man. of several shops at Konotop Locomotive and Wagon Repair Factory 39-52; First Sec., Konotop Town Cttee. of the C.P.S.U., Sec., Sumy Regional Cttee. of C.P.S.U., Official, Central Cttee. Ukrainian C.P. 52-58; Second Sec., Chernovtsy Regional Cttee., Ukrainian C.P. 58, First Sec. 63-; Exec. mem. Ukrainian C.P.; Deputy to U.S.S.R. Supreme Soviet; mem. C.P.S.U. 45-, Legislative Proposals Cttee. Soviet of Union.

Chernovtsy Regional Committee of the Communist Party of the Ukraine, Chernovtsy, U.S.S.R.

Grigorieff, Serge; British (b. Russian) ballet dancer and régisseur; b. 18 Oct. 1883; ed. Imperial School of Drama and Ballet, St. Petersburg.

Mem. of Mariinsky Theatre ballet company 1900-12; régisseur to Serge de Diaghilev's ballet company 09-29; formed own ballet company to perform at Monte Carlo theatre 29-31; régisseur to de Basil's ballet company 31-52; revived ballets from the Diaghilev repertory for the Royal Ballet, Covent Garden and La Scala, Milan; awarded Les Palmes Académiques in Paris 09, The Queen Elizabeth II Coronation Award 66.

Publ. *The Diaghilev Ballet* 1909-1929.

c/o Royal Opera House, Covent Garden, London, W.C.2; Home: 77 Stafford Court, Kensington High Street, London, W.8, England.

Telephone: 01-937-8887 (Home).

Grigoriev, Andrei Alexandrovich; Soviet geographer; b. 1 Nov. 1883; ed. St. Petersburg, Heidelberg and Berlin Univs.

Lecturer in Geography, High Pedagogical Coll., St. Petersburg 14-19; Prof. Geographical Inst., Leningrad 18-36; Prof. Leningrad Univ. 25-36; Dir. Inst. of Geomorphology, Leningrad 31-34; Dir. Inst. of Geography, Moscow 34-51, Chief of Dept. of History of Geography 51-; mem. C.P.S.U. 46-; mem. U.S.S.R. Acad. of Sciences 39-, Deutsche Akademie der Naturforscher 61-; State Prize, Order of Red Banner of Labour, Order of Lenin, Great Gold Medal of the Geographical Soc. of the U.S.S.R. 65, etc.

Publs. *An Experiment of Analytical Characterization of Composition and Structure of Physical-Geographical Envelope of the Earth* 37, *Subarctic, An Experiment of Characterization of Basic Types of Physical Geographical Environment* 46, *Some Problems of Physical Geography* 51, *Development of Theoretical Problems of Soviet Physical Geography* 1917-37 65, *Regularities of the Structure and Revolution of Natural Environment* 66, etc.

Institute of Geography, Academy of Sciences of the U.S.S.R., Staromonetny pereulok 29, Moscow, U.S.S.R.

Grigorov, Mitko; Bulgarian politician; b. 20; ed. Sofia State Univ.

Member Workers Youth Union 39, Bulgarian Communist Party 40-; political imprisonment 42-44; Head of Dept. and Sec. of Sofia City Cttee. of Communist Party 45-50; Head of Propaganda and Agitation Dept. of Central Cttee. of Bulgarian Communist Party 50-54, 57: First Sec. Varna Regional Cttee. of C.P. 54-57; mem. Central Cttee. of Bulgarian Communist Party 57-, Sec. 58-, mem. Politburo 61-66; Minister, Bulgarian People's Republic 62-.

Central Committee of Bulgarian Communist Party, Sofia, Bulgaria.

Grigorovich, Yuri Nikolaevich; Soviet ballet-master; b. 2 Jan. 1927; ed. Leningrad Choreographic School and Lunarcharski Inst. of Theatrical Art, Moscow.

Troupe of Kirov Theatre 46, Soloist until 62, Ballet-

Master, Kirov Theatre 62-63; Chief Ballet Master, Bolshoi Theatre, Moscow 64-; People's artist of R.S.F.S.R. Ploshchad Sverdlova, Moscow, U.S.S.R.

Grigoryev, Pyotr Mikhailovich; Soviet politician; b. 1921; ed. Omsk Teachers' Training Inst. and Higher Party School of C.P.S.U. Central Cttee.
Teacher 38-39; mil. service 39-43; Party Official 44-62; Chair. Omsk Regional Soviet of Working People's Deputies; Deputy to U.S.S.R. Supreme Soviet; mem. C.P.S.U. 42-, Public Health Cttee. Soviet of Union.
Omsk Regional Soviet of Working People's Deputies, Omsk, U.S.S.R.

Grigoryeva, Nadezhda Nikolayevna; Soviet trade union official; b. 13; ed. Ivanovo Medical Inst.
Pediatrician, later Asst. Head, Ivanovo City Health Dept. 40-43; party work, Ivanovo 44-47; Head, City, later Regional, Health Dept., Ivanovo 47-52; Dep. Minister of Health, R.S.F.S.R. 52-62; Chair. Central Cttee. of Medical Workers' Trade Union 62-; mem. All-Union Council of Trade Unions 62-; mem. C.P.S.U. Order of Lenin, Red Banner of Labour, etc.
Central Committee of the Medical Workers' Trade Union, 42 Leninsky Prospekt, Moscow, U.S.S.R.

Grigson, Geoffrey; English poet; b. 2 March 1905; ed. Univ. of Oxford.
Founder and one-time Editor of the English periodical *New Verse.*
Publs. *Several Observations: Thirty-five Poems* 39, *Under the Cliff and Other Poems* 43, *The Isles of Scilly and other Poems* 46, *Samuel Palmer* (biography) 47, *The Harp of Aeolus* (criticism) 48, *Places of the Mind* 49, *Poems of John Clare's Madness* 49, *The Crest on the Silver* (autobiography) 50, *The Victorians* 50, *Selected Poems of William Barnes* 50, *Selected Poems of John Clare* 50, *Essays from the Air* 51, *Gardenage* 52, *Freedom of the Parish* 54, *The Englishman's Flora* 55, *English Drawings* 55, *Painted Caves* 57, *The Three Kings, Art Treasures of the British Museum* 58, *A Herbal of All Sorts* 59, *The Cherry Tree* 59, *English Excursions* 60, *Samuel Palmer's Valley of Vision* 60, *Christopher Smart* 61, *Collected Poems* 63, *Poems of Walter Savage Landor* 64, *Shapes and Stories* (with Jane Grigson) 64, *The Shell Country Alphabet* 66, *A Skull in Salop and Other Poems* 67, *The English Year* 67, *Poems and Poets* 68.
Broad Town Farm, nr. Swindon, Wiltshire, England.

Grimes, Joseph Rudolph, B.A., LL.B., M.I.A.; Liberian lawyer, diplomatist and politician; b. 31 Oct. 1923; ed. Coll. of West Africa, Liberia Coll., Law School Harvard Univ. and Columbia Univ.
Cadet, Bureau of Public Health and Sanitation 38-42; Clerk, Exec. Mansion 42-47; Counsellor, Dept. of State 51-56; Dir. Louis Grimes School of Law, Liberia Univ. 54-58; Under-Sec. of State 56-60, Sec. of State 60-; mem. Liberian Del. to Asian African Conf., Bandung 55, to Heads of African States Conf. 61, to 16th Session of UN Gen. Assembly; Most Venerable Order of the Pioneers, Knight Great Band, Humane Order of the African Redemption and other honours.
Department of State, Monrovia, Liberia.

Grimes, William Francis, C.B.E., D.LITT., F.S.A., F.M.A.; British archaeologist; b. 31 Oct. 1905; ed. Univ. of Wales.
Asst. Keeper of Archæology, National Museum of Wales 26-38; Asst. Archæology Officer, Ordnance Survey Office 38-45, Acting Archæology Officer 45; seconded to Ministry of Works, Ancient Monuments Dept., for investigation of historic monuments threatened with destruction 39-45; Dir. of London Museum 45-56; Hon. Dir. of Excavations, Roman and Medieval London Excavation Council 47-; Sec. Council for British Archæology 49-54, Pres. 55-59; Pres. London and Middlesex Archæological Society 50-59; Vice-Pres. Society of Antiquaries of London 53-57; Vice-Pres. Prehistoric

Soc. 57-60, Soc. for Medieval Architecture 57-64; Pres. Royal Archaeological Inst. 57-60; Chair., London Topographical Society 61-; Dir. Inst. of Archaeology and Prof. of Archaeology, Univ. of London 56-; Chair. Faculty of Archaeology, History and Letters, British School at Rome 63-66; Pres. Cambrian Archaeological Asscn. 63-64; Chair. Royal Comm. on Ancient Monuments (Wales and Monmouthshire) 67-.
Publs. *Holt, Denbighshire: The Works-Depot of the Twentieth Legion at Castle Lyons* (Y Cymmrodor, Vol. XLI, 1931), *The Prehistory of Wales, Charterhouse* (with Prof. M. D. Knowles), *Excavations in Defence Sites 1939-45, 1 Brooke House, Hackney* (with W. A. Eden, M. Draper, A. Williams), *The Excavation of Roman and Medieval London* 68.
Institute of Archæology, 31-34 Gordon Square, London, W.C.1, England; 1 Elsworthy Court, Elsworthy Road, London, N.W.3, England.

Grimond, Rt. Hon. Joseph, P.C., M.P.; British politician; b. 29 July 1913; ed. Eton and Balliol Coll., Oxford.
Barrister; served Fife and Forfar Yeomanry 39-45; fmr. Dir. of Personnel, European Office of UNRRA; Sec. Nat. Trust for Scotland 47-49; Liberal M.P. for Orkney and Shetland 50-; Liberal Chief Whip 51-57, Leader of Parl. Party 57-67.
Publs. *The Liberal Future* 59, *The Liberal Challenge* 63.
Old Manse of Firth, Kirkwall, Orkney, Scotland; The House of Commons, London, S.W.1, England.

Grin, Edmond, DR.THEOL.; Swiss theologian; b. 11 Sept. 1895; ed. Lausanne, theological faculties Lausanne, Zürich, Strasbourg and Marburg, philosophical faculty, Paris.
Pastor, Chesalles-sur-Moudon 22-26, Echallens 26-32; Extraordinary Prof. of Theology, Lausanne Univ. 32-38, Prof. 38-66, Dean of the Faculty 38-40, 46-50, Rector 56-58, now Hon. Prof.; Pres. Conf. of Swiss Rectors 58, Comm. théologique des Eglises protestantes de la Suisse 63; Dr. h.c. Basle Univ.; Diploma Hautes Etudes de philosophie Univ. de Paris à la Sorbonne.
Publs. *Charles Secrétan et la philosophie de Schelling* 25, *La morale chrétienne sur la base de la foi réformée* 29, *Les origines et l'évolution de la pensée de Charles Secrétan* 30, *Morale de la conscience et morale de la grâce* 33, *La notion protestante des oeuvres* 37, *Le salut par la foi et les oeuvres du chrétien* 38, *Expérience religieuse et témoignage du Saint-Esprit* 47, *Les exigences de l'Evangile et la question sociale* 50, *J. Chr. Blumhardt* 52, *Existentialisme et morale chrétienne* 56, *La pensée théologique de Bonhoeffer* 60, *De Calvin à Ch. Secrétan* 60, *La Christologie de D. Bonhoeffer* 61, *D. Bonhoeffer et l'interprétation "non-religieuse" des notions bibliques* 62, *L'actualisation du message biblique chez D. Bonhoeffer* 63, *Une discipline ecclésiastique aujourd'hui?* 64, *Théologie systématique en Suisse romande, continuité d'une tradition* 66, *Un grand théologien méconnu: Emile Brunner* 67.
2 Chemin de Longeraie, 1006 Lausanne, Switzerland. Telephone: 021-23-92-32.

Griñán Núñez, Alba; Cuban diplomatist; b. 14 June 1926; ed. Univ. de Oriente and Univ. de Paris à la Sorbonne.
Worked in planning and inspection of primary schools, Municipal Dept. of Educ., Havana 60; mem. several Cuban dels. to UN, Del. to Comm. on Status of Women, Geneva 61; Observer at Pan African Women's Conf., Dar-es-Salaam 64; Head, UN Dept., Ministry of Foreign Affairs, Havana 64-65; Ambassador to U.K. 65-.
Embassy of Cuba, 22 Mount Street, London, W.1, England.

Grishin, Ivan Timofeyevich; Soviet foreign trade official; b. 1911; ed. Higher Party School.
Member C.P.S.U. 31-; Party and Komsomol Leader 35-41; Chair. Novosibirsk Regional Cttee. of C.P. 41-45; Second, later First, Sec., Volgograd Regional Cttee. of C.P. 48-55; Amb. to Czechoslovakia 55-59; Deputy

Minister of Foreign Trade 59-; Order of Lenin (three times), Order of Red Banner of Labour (three times).
Ministry of Foreign Trade, 32/34 Smolenskaya-Sennaya Ploshchad, Moscow, U.S.S.R.

Grishin, Konstantin Nicolayevich; Soviet politician; b. 1908; ed. Higher Party School, Moscow.
Member C.P.S.U. 31-; shoemaker and salesman 28-32; teacher 32-33; party work 38-55; First Sec. Vladimir District Cttee. C.P.S.U. 55-60, Ryazan District Cttee. 60-; Cand. mem. Central Cttee. C.P.S.U. 56-61, mem. 61-; Deputy to U.S.S.R. Supreme Soviet; mem. Budget Comm. Soviet of Union.
District Committee C.P.S.U., Ryazan, U.S.S.R.

Grishin, Viktor Vasilievich; Soviet trade union official; b. 14; ed. Moscow Railway Inst.
Fmr. railway engine driver and locomotive depot chief; mem. C.P.S.U. 39-; Sec. Serpukhov City Cttee. C.P.S.U. 42-50; Sec. Moscow Region Cttee. C.P.S.U. 50-56, Cand. mem. Pres. Central Cttee. of C.P.S.U. 61-66, Alt. mem. Politburo 66-; Chair. All-Union Cen. Council of Trade Unions 56-67; First Sec. Moscow City Cttee. of C.P.S.U. 67-; Deputy to Supreme Soviet; mem. Soviet Parl. Del. to U.K. 56; Order of Lenin, Badge of Honour.
Moscow City Committee of C.P.S.U., Moscow, U.S.S.R.

Grishmanov, Ivan Aleksandrovich; Soviet engineer and politician; b. 06; ed. Leningrad Inst. of Civil Engineers.
Member C.P.S.U. 29-; Deputy to Supreme Soviet of R.S.F.S.R. 55; Head Construction Dept., Central Cttee. of Communist Party of U.S.S.R. 56-; Chair. State Cttee. for Construction Materials, Council of Ministers, U.S.S.R. 61-65; Minister of Building Materials Industry 65-; mem. Central Cttee. C.P.S.U.; Deputy, U.S.S.R. Supreme Soviet; Order of Red Banner of Labour.
Ministry of Building Materials Industry, Moscow, U.S.S.R.

Grist, Reri; American coloratura soprano; ed. Music and Art High School, New York City and Queen's Coll.
First major part Consuelo in *West Side Story* 57; with Santa Fe Opera Co. and New York City Opera 59, Washington Opera Soc. 60, 62, Vancouver Opera Asscn. 62, 64, San Francisco Opera 63, 64, 65, 66, Chicago Lyric Opera 64, Montreal debut as Gilda, *Rigoletto* 66, Metropolitan Opera debut as Rosina, *Barber of Seville* 66; has sung in numerous opera houses and festivals in Europe including debut as Queen of the Night, *Magic Flute* in Cologne, Glyndebourne 62 as Despina, *Cosi fan Tutti* and Zerbinetta, *Ariadne*, Naples 63, Holland Festival 63, Piccola Scala, Milan 63, Bordeaux Opera 64, Munich State Opera 65; regular appearances with Zurich Opera 60-, Covent Garden 62, 66, Vienna State Opera 63-, Salzburg Festival 64-.
c/o Metropolitan Opera Association, 147 West 39th Street, New York City, N.Y., U.S.A.

Griswold, Erwin Nathaniel, A.M., LL.D., S.J.D., L.H.D., D.C.L.; American lawyer; b. 14 July 1904; ed. Oberlin Coll., and Harvard Law School.
Worked in the office of the Solicitor Gen. 29-34; Asst. Prof. of Law, Harvard Law School 34-35, Prof. of Law 35-46, Dean and Langdell Prof. of Law 46-67; mem. U.S. Civil Rights Comm. 61-67; Pres. Asscn. American Law Schools 57-58; Dir. American Council of Learned Socs.; Solicitor Gen. of the U.S. 67-; mem. American Philosophical Soc., etc.
Publs. *Spendthrift Trusts* 36, 47, *Cases on Federal Taxation* 40-66, *Cases on Conflict of Laws* (with others) 64 (5th edn.), *The Fifth Amendment Today* 54, *Law and Lawyers in the United States* 64.
Office of the Solicitor General, Washington, D.C. 20530, U.S.A.
Telephone: REpublic 7-8200, Ext. 2201.

Gritschin, Pyotr Alexandrovich; Soviet foreign trade official; b. 1912; ed. Saratov Inst. of Motor Roads and Acad. of Foreign Trade.
Member C.P.S.U. 42-; Deputy Commercial Rep., then Commercial Rep., of U.S.S.R. in Austria 46-51; Deputy Chair. *Raznoimport* 51-52; Official, Ministry of Foreign Trade 52-53; Official, Head Dept., Soviet Property Abroad 53-56; Chair. *Autoexport* 56-60, *Tractoroexport* 66-; U.S.S.R. Commercial Rep. in German Fed. Repub. 60-66; Order of Red Banner of Labour, Badge of Honour.
Tractoroexport, Ministry of Foreign Trade, 32-34 Smolenskaya-Sennaya Ploshchad, Moscow, U.S.S.R.

Grivas, Lieut. Gen. George; Cypriot-born Greek officer; b. 98.
Adopted Greek nationality 19; officer in Infantry Corps, Asia Minor campaign 19-22; infantry school, Versailles and fire-training school, Chalons-sur-Marne; staff officer 28; War Coll., Paris; lecturer in Tactics, Salonika Training School; Chief of Staff, II Division 40; founded and led "X" underground organisation in Athens during German occupation in Second World War; returned to Cyprus 51; organised and led, under the name "Dighenis", EOKA movement 55-58; returned to Greece after Cyprus settlement 59; organized the Cypriot army and C.-in-C. Greek and Cypriot mil. forces June 63-Nov. 67; Freedom and Gold Medal, City of Athens; Gold Medal, Athens Acad.; Grand Cross, Order of George I, Commdr., Order of Military Merit.
Publs. *Memoirs* 64, *Guerilla Warfare* 64.
Aristidou 3, Halandri, Athens, Greece.
Telephone: 683375.

Grobbelaar, James Arthur; South African trade union leader; b. 1925; ed. Pretoria Junior High School and Observatory Boys' High School, Cape.
Boilermaker by trade; Branch Official of S. African Boilermakers' Soc. 49-55, Nat. Organizer 55-59, Area Sec. 59-62, Admin. Sec. 62-64; Gen. Sec. Trade Union Council of S. Africa 64-.
P.O. Box 5592, Johannesburg; and 417 Union Centre, 31 Pritchard Street, Johannesburg, Transvaal, South Africa.

Groeben, Hans von der, DIP.JUR.; German Member Commission European Communities; b. 1907; ed. Charlottenburg Engineering Coll., Berlin, Bonn and Göttingen Univs.
With Dept. of Agriculture, Berlin 33-39; military service 39, 42-45; Lower Saxony Finance Dept. 45-52; Dir. E.C.S.C. Div., Fed. Dept. of Economy 52-58; Co-rapporteur Spaak Report (on setting up of E.E.C.); Chair. working party for drawing up E.E.C. Treaty 56; mem. Comm. of European Econ. Community 58-67; mem. Comm. European Communities 67-; Dr. h.c. rer. pol.
European Communities Commission, 23 Avenue de la Joyeuse Entrée, Brussels, Belgium.
Telephone: 35-00-40.

Groenman, Sjoerd, LITT.D., PHIL.D.; Netherlands sociologist; b. 28 Nov. 1913; ed. Gymnasium Winschoten and Universiteit van Amsterdam.
Sociologist, Community at Emmen 38, Northern Econ. Technological Org. 40, Econ. Technological Inst., Overijssel 41, Board of North-Eastern Polder (Zuiderzeeworks) 43; Prof. of Sociology, Utrecht State Univ., Dean, Faculty of Social Sciences 63-; Prof. of Applied Sociology, Univ. of Leiden 56-60; Chair. Int. Social Science Council 60-; mem. Int. Cttee. on Documentation of Social Sciences 64-; mem. Board of Dirs. European Centre for Coordination and Documentation in Social Sciences, Vienna 63-; Chair. Advisory Cttee. Ministry of Social Work 56-66; Officer, Order of Orange Nassau 63.
Publs. *Methoden der Sociografie* (Methods of Social Research) 50, 66, *Kolonisatie op nieuw land* (Colonisation

on New Land) 53, *Ons deel in de ruimte* (Our Part in Space) 59.
Anna Paulownalaan 188, Zeist near Utrecht, Netherlands.

Groepper, Horst; German diplomatist; b. 17 June 1909.
Entered German Foreign Service 38; served Moscow 39-41; First Counsellor, Moscow 56-60; Deputy Head, Eastern Dept., Ministry of Foreign Affairs, Bonn 60-62; Ambassador to U.S.S.R. 62-66, to Turkey 66-.
Embassy of the German Federal Republic, Atatürk Bulvarı 114, Ankara, Turkey.

Groh-Kummerlöw, Grete; German politician; b. 6 Feb. 1909; elementary education.
Textile worker, domestic service, etc. 24-40; Communist youth movement 27-33; Communist mem. Saxon Parl. 30-33; illegal anti-fascist activity 33-44; mem. of Secretariat and Exec. Cttee. of Free German Trade Unions (F.D.G.B.); mem. Saxon Parl. 46-49, Praesidium 54-; Deputy Pres. of Volkskammer; Clara-Zetkin Medal and other awards.
Volkskammer der D.D.R., Luisenstrasse 58, 104 Berlin, Germany.

Grollet, Louis Jean Alfred, M.D.; French doctor; b. 14 July 1899; ed. Univ. de Paris à la Sorbonne.
Former urologist, Faculty of Medicine, Paris, and Medical Asst., Hopital Broca; Medical Superintendent, Ecole Nationale Vétérinaire d'Alport (Seine); Sec.-Gen. Soc. of Comparative Pathology and Int. Cttee. of Congress of Comparative Pathology; Founder Sec.-Gen. of Asscn. for Clean Air 56; Founder Sec.-Gen. of Medical Centre specialising in biological and electronic research; Editor-in-Chief *Revue de Pathologie Comparée*; mem. New York Acad. of Sciences; Officier Légion d'Honneur and other decorations.
4 rue Théodule-Ribot, Paris 17e, France.

Gromaire, Marcel; French painter; b. 24 July 1892.
Member Salon d'Automne, Soc. of French Painters and Engravers; collaborated in revival of French tapestry 38-42; exhibitions of tapestry in Paris, Brussels, Amsterdam, London, and New York; exhibition of recent paintings in Louis Carré gallery 47; exhibition in L. Carré Gallery N.Y. 49; juryman Carnegie Prize Competition Pittsburgh 50; exhibition *New York vu par Gromaire*, Louis Carré Gallery. Paris 51, exhibition in Maison de la Pensée française, Paris, June-Oct. 57; Commdr. Légion d'Honneur, Commdr. des Arts et des Lettres; 2nd Prize, Carnegie Int. Award 52, Guggenheim Prize for France 56, Grand Prix Nat. des Arts, Paris 59; one-man exhbn. at Musée Nat. d'Art Moderne, Paris 63.
Paintings include *Le repas paysan* 21, *La loterie foraine* 23, *Le faucheur flamand* 24, *Les Travaux de la Terre* (Paris Museum), *Les lignes de la Main*, *La Forêt* (Museum of Modern Art, Paris); Paintings in Oslo, Copenhagen, Gothenburg and Basle Galleries and in Paris Int. Exhbn. 37; Engravings to illustrate *Macbeth* 58.
47 rue Sarrette, Paris 14e, France.
Telephone: GOB 6734.

Gromashevsky, Lev Vasilievich; Soviet microbiologist; b. 1887; ed. Novorossiysk Univ.
Practising epidemiologist 11-14; Army surgeon 14-17; Junior Research Assoc., Head of Chair, Rector Medical Inst., Odessa 20-27; Dir. Sanitary-Bacteriological Inst. 28-31; Prof. Cen. Inst. of Postgraduate Medical Training 31-48; Dir. Cen. Inst. of Epidemiology and Biology 31-33; Head Sanitary-Epidemiological Laboratory 33-38; Soviet Army 41-42; Dir. Inst. of Infectious Diseases 48-51; mem. U.S.S.R. Acad. of Medical Sciences 44-; Head of Chair, Medical Inst., Kiev 48-; Deputy Dir. Inst. of Epidemiology and Parasitology 53-; Badge of Honour (twice).

Publs. Over 200 works on epidemiology of various infectious diseases and rickettsiosis.
Institute of Epidemiology, Microbiology and Parasitology, 4 Spusk Razina, Kiev, U.S.S.R.

Gromyko, Andrei Andreevich; Soviet diplomatist; b. 6 July 1909; ed. Minsk Agricultural Inst. and Moscow Inst. of Economics.
Member C.P. 31-; worked as senior research scientist at Acad. of Sciences; in charge of American Div. of Nat. Council of Foreign Affairs 39; Counsellor at Washington Embassy 39-43; Amb. to U.S.A. and Minister to Cuba 43-46; Soviet Rep. on UN Security Council 46-49; Deputy Foreign Minister 46-49; 1st Deputy Minister of Foreign Affairs 49-52, 53-57, Minister of Foreign Affairs 57-; Ambassador to Great Britain 52-53; Deputy to Supreme Soviet 46-; Cand. mem. Central Cttee. Communist Party 52-56, mem. 56-; took part in Teheran, Yalta and Potsdam Confs., Chair. Del. to Dumbarton Oaks Conf. on Post-War Security 44; Alt. mem. C.P.S.U. Central Cttee. 52-56, mem. 56-; Chair. Comm. for Publ. of Diplomatic Documentation; four Orders of Lenin and other decorations.
Ministry of Foreign Affairs, 32-34 Smolenskaya-Sennaya Ploshchad, Moscow, U.S.S.R.

Gronchi, Giovanni; Italian politician; b. 10 Sept. 1887; ed. Pisa Univ.
Early mem. of Don Sturzo's movement; active in reorganisation of Italian trade unionism; served in army 14-18; a founder of Italian Popular Party; Mem. Parl. 19-; Under-Sec. of State for Industry and Commerce 22-23; retired from public life 23-42; Sec. of State for Commerce, Industry and Labour 44-46; Pres. Christian Democrat Parl. Group 46-48; Speaker, Chamber of Deputies 48-55, President of Italian Republic 55-62.
Publ. *Autobiography* 62.
Senato della Repubblica, Rome; and Via Carlo Fea 7, Rome, Italy.

Groningen, Bernhard A. van, D.LITT., PH.D.; Netherlands university professor; b. 20 May 1894; ed. Athénée Royal and Brussels and Groningen Univs.
Classics Teacher 19-26; Rector, Assen Gymnasium 26-29; Asst. Prof. of Greek Papyrology, Univ. of Groningen 25-29; Prof. of Greek Language, Literature and Greek Antiquities, Univ. of Leiden 29-64; mem. Royal Acad. of Netherlands 35-, Pres. 49-63; Knight Order of the Lion, Commdr. Order Orange-Nassau (Netherlands); Hon. D.Litt. (Belfast) and Ph.D. (Thessaloniki).
Publs. *Le Gymnasiarque des métropoles de l'Egypte romaine* 24, *Aristote, le second livre de l'Economique* 33, *Papyrological Primer* (in collaboration with M. David) 40, 46, 52, 64, *Short Manual of Greek Palaeography* 40, 55, 63, 67, *Basileus* 41, *The Warren Papyri* (in collaboration) 41, *Herodotus, with commentary in Dutch* 45-55, *A Family Archive from Tebtunis* 50, *In the Grip of the Past* 53, *La Poésie verbale grecque* 53, *Homerus* 54, *La composition littéraire archaïque grecque* 58, *Le Dyscolos de Ménandre, Etude critique du texte* 60, *Traité d'Histoire et de Critique des Textes Grecs* 63, *Théognis I, Commentaire* 66, *Aristote, les 3 economiques* 68, *Euphorion* 68.
20 van Beuningenlaan, Leiden, Netherlands.
Telephone: 01710-53501.

Gronouski, John Austin, PH.D.; American economist and government official; b. 26 Oct. 1919; ed. Oshkosh State Teachers Coll., Oshkosh, Wis., and Univ. of Wisconsin.
U.S. Army Air Corps 42-45; Prof. Univ. of Maine 48-50; Research Assoc. Fed. Tax Administrators 52-56; Research Assoc. Univ. of Wisconsin 56-57; Prof. Wayne State Univ. 57-59; Research Dir. Wisconsin Dept. of Taxation and Univ. of Wisconsin Tax Impact Study 59; Exec. Dir. Revenue Survey Comm., Wisconsin 59-60; Commr. of Taxation, Wisconsin; Postmaster-Gen. of the United States 63-65; Ambassador to Poland

65-68; mem. Exec. Board, Nat. Asscn. Tax Administrators, Editorial Advisory Board *Nat. Tax Journal*, etc.; Trustee, John F. Kennedy Library; Democrat.
6133 Thirty-Third Street, N.W., Washington, D.C. 20015, U.S.A.

Groote, Paul De; Belgian engineer and politician; b. 05; ed. Athénée Royal de Bruxelles and Univ. of Brussels.
Gen. Sec. of Permanent Cttee. for Co-ordination of Transport in Congo 27, Chief Engineer for Otraco operation 30; Lecturer Brussels Univ. 34; Prof. 45; Adviser to Min. of Communications 44; Vice-Chair. Nat. Office for Transport Regulation 44; mem. Board of Belgian Railways 44; mem. Exec. Board E.C.I.T.O. 45; Min. of Economic Co-ordination and Nat. Re-equipment Mar. 47-49; mem. Euratom Comm. 58-67; Pres. Brussels Univ. 60-61; Belgian Labour Party.
Publs. *La Co-ordination des Transports en Belgique* 45, *Unité d'exploitation des Transports* 46.
249 Dieweg, Brussels, Belgium.

Grootjans, Frans; Belgian politician; b. 24 Jan. 1922. Started as journalist; mem. Parl. for Antwerp 54-; Minister for Nat. Educ. 66-; Pres. Antwerp branch, Parti de la Liberté et du Progrès (P.L.P.), Partij voor Vrijheid en Vooruitgang (P.V.V.).
Ministry of National Education, Wetstraat 151, Brussels, Belgium.

Gropius, Walter; German architect; b. 18 May 1883; ed. Univs. of Charlottenburg (Berlin) and Munich.
With Peter Behrens, Berlin 07-10, own practice since 10; Dir. Bauhaus Weimar (later Bauhaus Dessau) 18-28; in practice with Maxwell Fry in London 34-37; Prof. of Architecture, Harvard Univ., 37-52; Chair. of Dept. of Architecture 38-52, Emeritus 52-; Chair. Educational Cttee., Int. Congresses of Modern Building 48-53; Visiting Cttee., School of Architecture and Planning, M.I.T. 53-55; Vice-Pres. Int. Congresses of Modern Building, Zürich 29-57; Hon. degrees from Harvard Univ., R.S.A. (London), Western Reserve Univ., Ohio, Sydney Univ., Univ. of Brazil, Rio de Janeiro and N. Carolina State Coll.; Howard Myers Award 51; Int. Architecture Prize of Matarazzo Foundation, Brazil 53; Hanseatic Goethe Prize 56; Royal Gold Medal (R.I.B.A.); Berlin Reuter Medal 56; Grosses Bundesverdienstkreuz mit Stern 58; Fellow American Acad. of Arts and Letters, American Inst. of Architects; Gold Medal American Inst. of Architects 59; Grand State Prize Düsseldorf, Fellow Royal Soc. of Arts 60; D.H.L. (Columbia), Goethe Prize, Frankfurt, Kaufmann Award 61, Hon. Doctor of Fine Arts, Pratt Inst., New York 61; Gold Albert Medal, Royal Soc. of Arts, London; Hon. Senator, Hochschule für Bildende Künste, Berlin 62; Hon. D.H.L. (Williams Coll.), Dr. Phil. h.c. (Freie Univ., Berlin) 63; Assoc. Nat. Acad. of Design, New York; Hon. Academician of Royal Acad. of Arts, London; Hon. Dr. of Arts, Stonehill Coll., Mass. 67; Hon. Dr. of Fine Arts, Univ. of Ill.
Publs. *Staatliches Bauhaus* 23, *Internationale Architektur* 25, *Bauhausbauten in Dessau* 30, *New Architecture and the Bauhaus* 35, *The Bauhaus 1919-1928* 38, *Rebuilding our Communities* 46, *Scope of Total Architecture* 55.
Home: Baker Bridge Road, Lincoln, Mass.; Office: 46 Brattle Street, Cambridge, Mass., U.S.A.
Telephone: Clearwater 9-8098 (Home); UN 8-4200 (Office).

Gropper, William; American artist; b. 3 Dec. 1897; ed. Nat. Acad. of Design and New York School of Fine and Applied Arts.
16 one-man shows New York 36-58; further one-man shows Paris, Detroit, Warsaw, Moscow, Mexico City, etc.; rep. in perm. collections of New York Metropolitan Museum of Art and Museum of Modern Art, Chicago Art Inst., Whitney Museum of American Art, Paul Sachs Collection, Library of Congress, Walker Art Center, Pushkin Museum, Moscow, Nat. Museum, Prague, etc.; awards include Young Israel Prize, John Herron Prize for Lithography, Guggenheim Fellowship, Carnegie Int. Painting Prize, etc.
Publs. *Gropper* (drawings), *The Little Tailor*, *Caprichios*, *Caucasian Studies*, *Lest We Forget*; also much book illustration.
Mt. Airy Road, Croton-on-Hudson, N.Y., U.S.A.

Gros, André; French judge at International Court of Justice; b. 19 May 1908; ed. Univs. of Lyons and Paris. Assistant Law Faculty Paris 31, Asst. Prof. Univ. Nancy 35, Toulouse 37, Univ. Prof. Public Law 38-; seconded to Ministry of Foreign Affairs 39; Prof. Political Science Rio de Janeiro Univ. 39, 41-42; served France 40; legal Counsellor to French Embassy in London; French rep. on War Crimes Comm., London 45; legal adviser to French Del. Council of Foreign Ministers and Peace Conf. Paris 46; Legal Adviser Ministry of Foreign Affairs 47-; Prof. Ecole Nationale d'Administration Paris 47-; mem. Permanent Court of Arbitration, The Hague 50; del. to Comm. for the Rhine 50; Agent to Int. Court of Justice 50-60; Conseiller d'Etat 54-; Judge, Int. Court of Justice 64-; mem. Inst. of Int. Law 65; mem. UN Int. Law Comm. 61-; Commdr. Légion d'Honneur, Croix de Guerre (39-45).
Publs. *Survivance de la Raison d'Etat* 32, *Problèmes Politiques de l'Europe* 42-44 (Spanish transl. 43), *La Convention de Genève sur les pêcheries* 59, *Traités et Documents diplomatiques* (with Paul Reuter) 60, *La protection diplomatique* (in *Encyclopédie française*) 64.
6 Alexanderstraat, The Hague, Netherlands; and 12 rue Beaujon, Paris 8e, France.

Gross, Bernhard, DIPL.ING., DR. RER. NAT.; German-born Brazilian physicist; b. 05; ed. Tech. Univ. Stuttgart, and Univ. of Berlin.
Research asst. Dept. of Physics, Stuttgart 31-33; staff mem. Nat. Inst. of Technology, Rio de Janeiro 34-, Dir. Electricity Div. 46-47; Dir. Physics Div. Brazilian Nat. Research Council 51-54; Prof. of Physics Univ. of Federal District, Brazil 34-37; Prof. of Electrical Measurements Catholic Univ., Rio de Janeiro 55; fmr. mem. Scientific Advisory Cttee. I.A.E.A.; Brazilian rep. to U.N. Scientific Advisory Cttee. 58-60; mem. Brazilian Del. to UN Scientific Cttee. on Effects of Atomic Radiation 57-59; Dir. Div. of Scientific and Technical Information, Int. Atomic Energy Agency, Vienna 61-67; Dir. of Research, Nat. Nuclear Energy Comm. of Brazil 67-.
Publs. *Mathematical Structure of Theories of Viscoelasticity* 53, *Charge Storage Effects in Solid Dielectrics* 64, and over 100 papers.
Commissão Nacional de Energia Nuclear, Rio de Janeiro, Brazil.

Gross, Boone; American business executive; b. 4 March 1905; ed. Milwaukee Acad.
Motor Vehicle Corpn., Lansing 28-34, Hiram Walker Inc. 35-39, Pres. Gooderham and Worts (Hiram Walker) 39-42; Vice-Pres., Gillette Safety Razor Co., Boston 46-52; Pres. Razor Div., Vice-Pres. Gillette Co. 52-58, Pres. Gillette Co. 58-65, Dir. 58-; Dir. American Optical Co., Goodrich Rubber Co., P. R. Mallory Co., American Tobacco Co., Employers' Group of Insurance Cos.
Gillette Park, Boston 6, Mass.; Home: 1 Invergordon Drive, Scottsdale, Arizona, U.S.A.

Gross, Courtlandt S.; American businessman; b. 21 Nov. 1904; ed. Harvard Univ.
Clerk and Salesman, Lee Higginson & Co., Boston 27-29; Buyer, Dir. Viking Flying Boat Co., New Haven 29-32; Eastern Rep., Lockheed Aircraft Corpn., New York City 32-40, Vice-Pres., Gen. Man., Dir., Burbank 43-52, Exec. Vice-Pres. 52-56, Pres. 56-61, Chair. 61-67, Chair. Finance Cttee. 67-; Pres., Dir. Vega Aircraft,

Burbank 40-43; Dir. Lockheed Air Terminal, Burbank, Southern Calif. Gas Co.; Overseer, Harvard Coll.
Home: 3131 Antello Road, Los Angeles 24, Calif.; Office: 2555 Hollwood Way, Burbank, Calif., U.S.A.

Gross, Evgeny Fedorovich; Soviet physicist; b. 1897; ed. Moscow Univ.
Postgraduate, Research Assoc., Asst. Prof. Moscow Univ. 24-; Assoc. Ioffe Physico-Technical Inst., U.S.S.R. Acad. of Sciences 44-; Corresp. mem. U.S.S.R. Acad. of Sciences 46-; State Prize 46.
Publs. Works on spectroscopy of solid bodies.
U.S.S.R. Academy of Sciences, 14 Lenin Prospekt, Moscow, U.S.S.R.

Gross, Gerald Connop, B.S.; American communications engineer; b. 27 Dec. 1903; ed. Haverford Coll., Pennsylvania.
Communications Engineer, U.S. Bureau of Standards 26-28; Asst. Chief Engineer, Fed. Radio Comm. and Fed. Communications Comm. 28-45, Sec. Interdepartmental Radio Cttee. 33-40; joined Int. Telecommunication Union secretariat 45, Acting Sec.-Gen. June 58-Dec. 59, Sec.-Gen. Dec. 59-65; Pres. Telecommunication Consultants Int., Inc. 66-; Fellow Inst. of Radio Engineers, mem. American Inst. of Electrical Engineers, American Rocket Soc.
Publ. Telecommunications (with J. M. Herring) 36.
1028 Connecticut Avenue, N.W., Washington, D.C. 20036; Home: 4100 Cathedral Avenue, N.W., Washington, D.C. 20036, U.S.A.
Telephone: 659-1155 (Office); 362-1955 (Home).

Gross, Ludwik, M.D.; American (b. Polish) cancerologist; b. 11 Sept. 1904; ed. Uniwersytet Jagiellonski, Cracow.
Intern and Resident St. Lazar Hospital, Cracow 29-32; clinical training, Salpêtrière Hospital, Univ. de Paris à la Sorbonne 32-39; cancer research, Pasteur Inst., Paris 32-39, Christ Hospital, Cincinnati, Ohio, U.S. 41-43; Capt. to Major, Medical Corps, U.S. Army 43-46; Chief, Cancer Research Unit, Veterans Admin. Hospital, New York 46-; Consultant, Sloan-Kettering Inst. 53-56, Assoc. Scientist 57-60; mem. American MedicalAsscn., American Soc. of Hematology, American Asscn. of Cancer Research and other socs.; Fellow American Coll. of Physicians, New York Acad. of Sciences, American Asscn. for the Advancement of Science, Int. Soc. of Haematology; Diplomate, American Board of Internal Medicine; awards include Prix Chevillon 37, R. R. de Villiers Int. Award for Leukemia Research 53, Walker Prize, Royal Coll. Surgeons, England 62, Pasteur Silver Medal, Pasteur Inst. Paris 62, L. W. Ewing Award, James Ewing Soc., N.Y. 62, WHO UN Prize 62, Bertner Foundation Award, Univ. Texas 63, Albert Einstein Centennial Medal 65.
Publs. Oncogenic Viruses 61 and over 150 papers on experimental cancer and leukemia.
Veterans Administration Hospital, 130 West Kingsbridge Road, Bronx 68, New York, U.S.A.
Telephone: 212-LU4-9000, Ext. 227.

Grosul, Yakim Sergeyevich; Soviet historian; b. 1912; ed. Tiraspol State Pedagogic Inst.
Member C.P.S.U. 39-; secondary school teacher 41-44; Lecturer, Moldavian Pedagogic Inst. 44-46; Chair. Moldavian base of U.S.S.R. Acad. of Sciences 47-50; Vice-Chair. and later Chair. Presidium of Moldavian Branch of U.S.S.R. Acad. of Sciences 50-61; mem. and Pres. Moldavian Acad. of Sciences 61-; Corresp. mem. U.S.S.R. Acad. of Sciences 66-; Orders and Medals of U.S.S.R.
Presidium of the Moldavian Academy of Sciences, 1 Lenin Prospekt, Kishinev 1, U.S.S.R.

Groszkowski, Janusz, DR.ING., F.I.E.E.E.; Polish university professor; b. 21 March 1898.
Lecturer, Warsaw Technical Univ. 22-29, Prof. 29-;

Dir. Radio Inst. (later State Inst. of Telecommunications), Warsaw 29-50; mem. Polish Acad. of Sciences 52-, Vice-Pres. 57-62, Pres. 63-; Chair. Govt. Council Science and Technology 63-; Chair. Nat. Comm. Int. Scientific Radio Union 59-; Vice-Pres. Int. Scientific Radio Union 66-; mem. Bulgarian, Czechoslovak, Hungarian, Romanian, U.S.S.R. Acads. of Sciences; Dr. h.c. Warsaw and Łódź Technical Univs.; State Prize 1st Class 51, 52.
Publs. The Interdependence of the Frequency Variation and Harmonic Content and Constant Frequency Oscillators 32, On the Temperature Coefficient of Inductance 35, The Fundamentals of Frequency Stabilization 38, Frequency Generation and Stabilization (in Polish, Russian, Rumanian, Chinese) 47, 58, High Vacuum Technology (in Polish, Russian) 48, 57, Frequency of Self-Oscillations (in English) 64.
Palace of Culture and Sciences, Warsaw, Poland.

Grote, Ludwig, DR. PHIL.; German art historian; b. 8 Aug. 1893; studied architecture at Brunswick Tech. Univ. and art history at Halle Univ.
Provincial Curator of Sachsen-Anhalt and Gallery Dir. in Dessau 24-33; self-employed as writer on art 33-51; first Dir. German Nat. Museum, Nuremberg 51-58, Gen. Dir. 58-61; Hon. Prof. Univ. of Erlangen 56-; Grosses Bundesverdienstkreuz.
Publs. Georg Lemberger 33, Deutsche Stilfibel 37, Die Brüder Olivier und die deutsche Romantik 38, C.D. Friedrichs Skizzenbücher aus den Jahren 1806 und 1818 42, Deutsche Kunst im 20. Jahrhundert 53, Hier bin ich ein Herr, Dürer in Venedig 56.
c/o Nationalmuseum, Nuremberg, German Federal Republic.

Groth, Wilhelm E., DR. RER. NAT.; German university professor; b. 9 Jan. 1904; ed. Munich Technical High School, Univs. of Munich and Tübingen.
Asst. Hanover Technical High School 27-32; Asst. Hamburg Univ. 32-39, Lecturer 39-45, Asst. Prof. 45-48, Prof. 48-50; fmr. Deputy Dir. Inst. for Physical Chemistry, Univ. of Hamburg; Prof. Bonn Univ. 50-; Dir. Inst. for Physical Chemistry, Univ. of Bonn; Rector Univ. Bonn 65-66.
Rheinische Friedrich-Wilhelms-Universität, Institut für Physikalische Chemie, 53 Bonn, Wegelerstrasse 12, German Federal Republic.

Grouès, Henri (called **Abbé Pierre**); French ecclesiastic and philanthropist; b. 5 Aug. 1912; ed. Collège des Jésuites and Univ. of Lyons.
Entered Capuchin Order 30; left for health reasons 38; almoner at the hospital of La Mure and in charge of the Groupements de Jeunesse and the Orphanage of the Cote Ste. André 40, vicar of Grenoble 41; founded an escape organisation through the Alps and the Pyrenees, thus saving a great number of people; founded a laboratory for forged identity papers; captured by the Italians and the Germans and escaped both times; carried Jacques de Gaulle (brother of the General), who was paralysed, through the Swiss frontier to escape the Gestapo; created Maquis of Chartreuse and Vercors; published and distributed the clandestine papers L'Union Patriotique Indépendante, Résistance and Cahiers du Témoignage Chrétien; founded the cttee. against forced labour; joined Free French Forces in Algiers as Almoner to the Fleet 44; Dep. for Meurthe-et-Moselle 46-51; organised help for the destitute and the homeless and created the Centre d'Emmaüs through an appeal to public opinion; founded the revue Faim et Soif 54; Chevalier de la Légion d'Honneur, Croix de Guerre (2 citations avec palmes), Médaille de la Résistance, Médaille des Evadés, Médaille des Combattants Volontaires, Médaille des Maquisards Belges.
Publs. 23 mois de vie clandestine, Vers l'Homme,

Feuilles Eparses (poems), *L'Abbé Pierre vous Parle*, *Emmaüs* 59, *Pleine Vie*.
2 avenue de la Liberté, Charenton (Val de Marne 94), France.
Telephone: 368-62-44.

Groussard, Serge, L. ès L.; French writer and journalist; b. 18 Jan. 1921; ed. Lycée La Rochelle and Lycée Gourand, Rabat, Ecole Nat. d'Administration, Ecole Libre des Sciences Politiques, and Univ. de Paris à la Sorbonne.
Chief Reporter *Le Figaro* 54-62, *L'Aurore* 62-; Chevalier Légion d'Honneur, Croix de Guerre, Prix Claude Blanchard 48, Prix du Grand Réportage 48, Prix du Roman populiste 49, Prix Fémina 50, Prix de la Nouvelle 51.
Publs. *Crépuscule des vivants* 46, *Pogrom* 48, *Solitude Espagnole* 48, *Des gens sans importance* 49, *La Femme sans passé* 50, *Talya* 51, *La Ville de joie* 52, *Un officier de tradition* 54, *Demain est là* 55, *Une chic fille* 56, *La Belle Espérance* 58, *Quartier chinois* 58, *La Passion du Maure* 59, *Le Prêtre dans la nuit* 59, *Jeunesse sauvage* 60, *Une espionne doit mourir* 62, *Les Chacals* 64.
5 rue de Koufra, Boulogne-sur-Seine 92, Seine, France.
Telephone: Val d'Or 17-43.

Grover, Anthony Charles; British underwriter; b. 13 Oct. 1907; ed. Westminster School.
Served in Coldstream Guards, rising to rank of Major (mentioned in despatches) 40-45; Chair. Lloyd's Underwriters' Assen. 54-56; Deputy Chair. and Treas. Lloyd's Register of Shipping 56-57, Chair. 63-; Deputy Chair. Lloyd's 58, Chair. 59-60; Chair. Lifeguard Assurance Ltd.; Dir. F. Bolton & Co. (Holdings Ltd.), Bolton Ingham Agency, William France, Fenwick Co. Ltd., Grover-Bolton & Co. Ltd.
Lloyd's Register of Shipping, 71 Fenchurch Street, London, E.C.3
Telephone: 01-709-9166.

Groves, Wallace, M.A., B.SC., LL.B., LL.M.; American financier; b. 20 March 1901; ed. Georgetown Univ., Washington, D.C.
Admitted Maryland Bar 25; private legal practice 25-31; fmr. Pres. and Chair. Phoenix Securities Corpn.; Founder of Freeport, Bahamas; Pres. Grand Bahama Port Authority, Freeport Medical Authority, Freeport Educational Authority, Freeport Trust Company; Founder Wallace Groves Foundation (charitable organisation).
P.O. Box 5, Freeport, Grand Bahama, Bahamas.
Telephone: BIZ 6611.

Grubb, Sir Kenneth George, Kt., C.M.G.; British public servant; b. 9 Sept. 1900; ed. Marlborough Coll.
Missionary S. America 23-28; Editor Survey Application Trust 28-39; Head Latin American Section, Min. of Information 39-41, Controller of Overseas Publicity 41-46; Sec.-Gen. Hispanic Council 46-54; Consultant J. Arthur Rank Organisation 56-59; Pres. Church Missionary Soc. 44-67; Chair. Churches' Comm. on Int. Affairs 46-, House of Laity Church Ass., Burge Memorial Trust, Royal Court of St. Katharine, Asia Christian Colleges Asscn., British Council of Churches Int. Dept. 46-56, etc.; Chair. Inst. for Strategic Studies 58-63, Vice-Pres. 63-; Vice-Chair. Inst. of Race Relations; Dir. C. S. Services (Public Relations firm) 67-; Hon. LL.D. Muhlenberg (Pennsylvania) 51; Hon. Fellow and Trustee St. Peter's Coll., Oxford.
Publs. *Lowland Indians of Amazonia* 28, *Amazon and Andes* 30, *From Pacific to Atlantic* 33, *Religion in the Republic of Spain* 33, *The Republic of Brazil* 32, *World Christian Handbook* 49, 52, 57, 62.
The Moot Farm, Downton, Wiltshire, England.

Grüber, Arthur; German conductor; b. 21 Aug. 1910; ed. Hochschule für Musik, Cologne.
Conductor in Frankfurt-am-Main 32-38; Dir. Opera

Wuppertal 38-39; Conductor, Berlin Opera House, 39-44; Dir. of Music, Halle 44-47; Chief Conductor, Hamburg State Opera 47-51 and Komische Opera, Berlin 47-53; Gen. Music Dir. in Brunswick 55-62; Gen. Music Dir. in Karlsruhe and Dir. of Conductors' Section, Badische Hochschule für Musik 62-.
Compositions: comic opera, *Trotz wider Trotz*, first performed 48, *Hölderlin-Ode* 54.
Badisches Staatstheater, Karlsruhe, German Federal Republic.

Grüber, Heinrich K. E., D.D., PH.D., L.H.D.; German ecclesiastic; b. 24 June 1891; ed. Univs. of Bonn, Berlin and Utrecht.
Clergyman in Dortmund 20, Dir. Inst. for Juvenile Delinquents; Clergyman in Düsseldorf 25, Templin 26; dismissed by Nazis 33; Clergyman in Berlin-Kaulsdorf 34; Founder and Dir. "Buro Grüber" (Relief Cttee. for Victims of Nuremberg Laws) 37; inmate of Sachsenhausen and Dachau Concentration Camps 40-43; Dean of Berlin 45-; mem. Berlin City Council; Rep. Council of Protestant Church of Germany; Pres. Protestant Relief Cttee. for Victims of Nuremberg Laws; Vice-Pres. British-German Fellowship; Rep. Protestant Relief Comm. of Berlin and East Zone of Germany; Rep. Council of Protestant Church to Govt. of German Democratic Republic 48-58; Pres. Deutsch-Israelische Gesellschaft; hon. degrees; Ossietzky Medal 65; Commdr. Orange-Nassau 66; Albert Schweitzer Prize 67.
Publs. *Dona Nobis Pacem* 51, *Leben in Spannungen* 58, *An der Stechbahn* 60, *Durchkreuzter Hass* 61, *Fürchtet euch nicht* 62, *Pro Israel* 63, *Leben an der Todeslinie-Dachauer Predigten*, *Der Gerechte unter den Nationen* 66.
1 Berlin 37, Teltower Damm 124, Germany.
Telephone: 80-24-95 and 84-38-46.

Gruber, Karl J., DR. JUR.; Austrian politician; b. 3 May 1909; ed. Univs. of Innsbruck and Vienna.
Austrian resistance leader 38-45; Gov. of the Tyrol May-Oct. 45; Under-Sec. of Foreign Affairs 45-46; Minister of Foreign Affairs 46-53; Ambassador to U.S.A. 54-57; mem. of Parl. 46; Lecturer in Economics, Vienna Univ. 46-61; fmr. Vice-Pres. O.E.E.C.; Special Adviser to Int. Atomic Energy Agency 58-60; Ambassador to Spain 61-66, to German Fed. Repub. 66; Sec. of State May 66-; Hon. LL.D. (Univ. of S. Calif.) 46; Austrian People's Party.
Publs. *Die Politik der Mitte* 45, *Voraussetzungen der Vollbeschäftigung* 46, *Zusammenhang zwischen Grösse, Kosten und Rentabilität industrieller Betriebe* 48, *Zwischen Befreiung und Freiheit* 53.
1030 Vienna, Rennweg 6A, Austria.

Grubiakov, Vasily Fedorovich; Soviet diplomatist; b. 1911; ed. Saratov Univ., Higher Diplomatic School.
Second, First Sec., Soviet Embassy in Turkey 43-45; Consul-Gen. in Istanbul 45-47; Adviser and Senior Adviser, Soviet Del. at UN 53-57; Chief First European Dept., Foreign Ministry 62-65; Amb. to Belgium 67-.
U.S.S.R. Embassy, 66 Avenue De Fré, Brussels, Belgium.

Gruen, Victor; American (b. Austrian) architect; b. 18 July 1903; ed. Vienna Technological Inst., and Acad. of Fine Arts.
Designer, Supervisor and Co-ordinator with Melcher & Steiner, Vienna 24-33; independent practice in Vienna, executing a large number of residential and commercial projects 33-38; designer in New York and Los Angeles 38-48; in independent practice as Senior Partner, Victor Gruen Associates 48-; has lectured widely at univs., colls., clubs, etc.; Fellow, American Inst. of Architects; mem. American Inst. of Planners, etc.; has exhibited in Washington, Brussels (World Fair), New York, Mexico City, Moscow, Berlin, etc.
Projects include: about 50 regional shopping centres, several near Detroit, Minneapolis, Philadelphia,

Chicago; Wilshire Terrace luxury apartments; various office buildings; Midtown Plaza, Rochester, N.Y.; revitalization plans for Fort Worth, Fresno, Boston and Green Bay (Wis.).

Publs. *How To Live With Your Architect, The Planning of Shopping Centers, Shopping Towns U.S.A.* (with Larry Smith), *The Heart of Our Cities*; numerous articles on design, architecture and planning.

Office: 6330 San Vicente Boulevard, Los Angeles; Home: 315 N. Beverly Glen Boulevard, Los Angeles 24, Calif., U.S.A.

Telephone: 937-4270 (Office).

Gruenberg, Benjamin Charles, B.S., A.M., PH.D.; American biologist and educationist; b. 15 Aug. 1875. Sugar chemist 95-02; Instructor in Biology New York City High Schools 02-22; mem. staff U.S. Public Health Service 20-22 and 38-39; Urban Motion Pictures 22-23; Educational Editor Viking Press 29-32; Lecturer Coll. of City of New York, Brooklyn Coll., Univ. of Colorado, Univ. of Denver, Colorado, Coll. of Education; Research Consultant Nat. Resources Cttee.; Editor various publs. for U.S. Public Health Service, Nat. Health Council, Fed. Child Study (later Child Study Asscn. of America), and American Asscn. for Medical Progress; Associate in Science, American Asscn. for Adult Education; Fellow and hon. life mem. American Asscn. for Advancement of Science; co-founder and hon. life mem. Nat. Asscn. of Biology Teachers; Research Consultant Comm. on Secondary Education and American Public Health Asscn.; Special Consultant U.S. Public Health Service; Consulting Economist Social Security Board, Nat. Resources Comm.; Consulting Editor Nat. Health Council; Consultant in revision of American Oxford Encyclopedia; Outstanding Achievement Award Univ. of Minnesota 57.

Publs. *Elementary Biology* 19, *Manual of Suggestions for Teachers of Elementary Biology* 20, *Parents and Sex Education* 23, 35, *Biology and Human Life* 25, *The Story of Evolution* 29, *Science and the Public Mind* 35; *Science in Our Lives* 38, *Activities in General Science* 39 (both with S. P. Unzicker), *Instructional Tests in Electricity, Instructional Tests in Machinery* 43, *Biology and Man* (with N. E. Bingham) 44, *Workbook for Students of Biology* (with Emily E. Snyder and Jesse V. Miller) 46, *Teachers Manual for Biology and Man* (with N. E. Bingham), *How Can We Teach About Sex?* 46, *Children for the Childless* (co-author) 54, *An Analysis of the Kinsey Report* (co-author) 54, *Your Breakfast and the People Who Made It* (with Leona Adelson) 54, *The Wonderful Story of You* (with S. M. Gruenberg) 60, etc. 100 Central Park South, New York, N.Y. 10019, U.S.A.

Gruening, Ernest, A.B., M.D.; American journalist and politician; b. 6 Feb. 1887; ed. Hotchkiss School (Lakefield, Conn.), and Harvard Univ.

Man. Editor *The Nation* 20-23, Editor 33-34; Founder Editor, *Portland* (Me.) *Evening News* 27-32; Editor *New York Evening Post* 34; Dir. Department of the Interior (U.S. Govt.) Territories and Island Possessions Division 34-39; Admin. Puerto Rico Reconstruction Admin. 35-37; Gov. of Alaska 39-53; Senatorial Rep. from Alaska 56-58; U.S. Senator from Alaska 58-; Hon. LL.D. Alberta, Alaska and Brandeis Univs.; Democrat.

Publs. *Mexico and Its Heritage* 28, *The Public Pays* 31, *The State of Alaska* 54, *An Alaska Reader* 67, *The Battle for Alaska Statehood* 67; Editor *These United States*.

7926 West Beach Drive, Washington, 12, D.C.; P.O. Box 1001, Juneau, Alaska, U.S.A.

Gruenther, General Alfred M.; American army officer (retd.); b. 3 March 1899; ed. U.S. Military Acad.

Routine peacetime assignments 19-41; Chief of Staff, Third Army 41-42; Deputy Chief of Staff, Allied Force H.Q. (London, North African campaign, Algiers) 42-43; Chief of Staff, Fifth Army (Italian campaign) 43-44;

Chief of Staff, 15th Army Group (Italian campaign) 44-45; Deputy Commanding-Gen. U.S. Forces in Austria 45; Deputy Commandant, Nat. War Coll. 45-47; Dir. Joint Staff, Joint Chiefs of Staff 47-49; Deputy Chief of Staff for Plans and Combat Operations, Army Gen. Staff 49-51; Chief of Staff, SHAPE 51-53; Gen. Aug. 51; Supreme Allied Commdr. Europe 53-56; Pres. American Red Cross 57-64; Chair. English-Speaking Union of U.S. 66-; Dir. Pan American World Airways, N.Y. Life Insurance Co., Rexall Drug and Chemical Co., Federated Dept. Stores, Inc.; mem. The Business Council; D.S.M. (with two Oak Leaf Clusters) (U.S.); Hon. C.B. (U.K.); Grand Cross Légion d'Honneur, Médaille Militaire (France); Grand Cordon, Order of Leopold (Belgium), and numerous other international decorations; Hon. Degrees from 37 Univs.

Publs. *The Referee's Analysis of the Decisive Hands of the Lenz-Culbertson Match* 31, *Duplicate Contract Bridge Complete* 33.

Cathedral Apartments, 4101 Cathedral Avenue, N.W., Washington, D.C. 20016, U.S.A.

Telephone: 201-244-7693.

Grumman, Leroy Randle; American aeronautical engineer; b. 4 Jan. 1895; ed. Cornell Univ.

Aeronautical Engineer, Loening Aeronautical Engineering Corpn., N.Y.C. 20-29; Pres. Grumman Aircraft Corpn. 30-46, Chair. Board of Dirs. 46-66, Hon. Chair. 66-; Presidential Medal for Merit 45, Daniel Guggenheim Medal 48, Frank M. Hawks Memorial Award 58; Hon. Eng. D. Brooklyn Polytechnic Inst., Hon. LL.D. Adelphi Coll.

Grumman Aircraft Engineering Corporation, Bethpage, Long Island, New York, U.S.A.

Telephone: 516-LR5-3301.

Grünbaum, Henry; Danish economist and politician; b. 27 July 1911; ed. Københavns Universitet.

Former engraver; Sec. Econ. Council Danish Labour Movement 38-40; Statistician of Trade Unions Congress 40-48; mem. Resistance Movements Liaison Cttee., Stockholm 44-45; Econ. and Political Columnist on *Social-Demokraten* (daily, now *Aktuelt*) 49-56; Econ. Adviser to Danish Gen. Workers Union 56-64, and Editor-in-Chief of Danish Gen. Workers Union biweekly periodical 62-64; Minister of Econ. and Scandinavian Affairs 64-65, Minister of Finance 65-68, mem. of Parl. Nov. 66; mem. Board Econ. Soc. 59-65.

Publs. *Industrial Democracy, Consumers Price-Index and Wages.*

Torvegade 47, 1400 Copenhagen, Denmark.

Grundig, Max; German industrialist; b. 7 May 1908; ed. Friedrich-Alexander-Univ. Erlangen-Nürnberg.

Owner of Grundig Elektro-mechanische Fabrik und Versuchs-anstalt, Fürth, Grundig Werke G.m.b.H., Grundig Verkaufs G.m.b.H., Grundig Bürotechnik G.m.b.H., Grundig Wohnungsbau G.m.b.H.; Chair. Triumph Werke A.G., Adlerwerke A.G., Grundig-Bank G.m.b.H.; mem. Landesbeirat der Bayerischen Hypotheken- und Wechselbank, Dresdner Bank; official of other Grundig firms in Germany and abroad; Dr. rer. pol. h.c.; Grosses Bundesverdienstkreuz, German Fed. Repub.; Bayrischer Verdienstorden.

Grundig Werke G.m.b.H., 8510 Fürth (Bay), Kurgartenstrasse 37; Home: 8510 Fürth-Dambach, Holzackerstrasse 50, German Federal Republic.

Grundy, Gordon Edward; Canadian automobile executive; b. 12; ed. Halifax Acad. and Dalhousie Univ.

Brokenshire, Scarff & Co., Chartered Accountants, Windsor, Ontario 30-32; Clarkson, Gordon & Co., Chartered Accountants, Windsor and Toronto 32-36; Internal Auditor and Chief Cost Accountant, Hiram Walker-Gooderham and Worts Ltd., Walkerville, Ontario 36-41; Dep. Chief, Prices Div., Wartime Prices and Trade Boards 41-46; Comptroller and Asst. Sec., The Studebaker Corpn. of Canada Ltd., Hamilton,

Ontario 46-53; Vice-Pres., Comptroller and Asst. Sec. Studebaker-Packard of Canada Ltd. 53-58, Pres. and Gen. Manager Studebaker of Canada Ltd. 58-.
Studebaker of Canada Ltd., Hamilton, Ontario, Canada.

Grunebaum, Gustave E(dmund) von, DR.PHIL.; American university professor; b. 1 Sept. 1909; ed. Univs. of Vienna and Berlin.
Asst. Prof. Arabic and Islamic Studies, Asia Inst., N.Y. City 38-42, Chair. Dept. of Arabic 42-43; Asst. Prof. of Arabic, Univ. of Chicago 43-46, Associate Prof. 46-49, Prof. 49-57; Prof. of Near Eastern History, and Dir. Near Eastern Center, Univ. of Calif., Los Angeles 57-; mem. Advisory Cttee. 1965 Int. Congress of Int. Asscn. for History of Religions; mem. American Oriental Soc. and Vice-Pres. 54-55; hon. mem. Islamic Research Asscn. Bombay; mem. Accad. del Mediterraneo, Palermo; Fellow Middle East Inst., American Acad. for Arts and Sciences; Foreign Assoc. Accademia Nazionale dei Lincei; Charter mem. American Soc. for Study of Religion; mem. Board of Trustees, Exec. Cttee. American Asscn. for Middle East Studies; Vice-Pres. 63-64, 64-65; Pres. American Research Center in Egypt 66-; Hon. Pres. Middle East Studies Asscn. 67; corresp. mem. Advisory Cttee. Dairatul-Ma'arif-il-Osmania (Hyderabad, India); Editor *Bibliothek des Morgenlandes* (Switzerland); Dr. h.c. Univ. of Frankfurt.
Publs. include: *Die Wirklichkeitweite der früharabischen Dichtung: Eine literaturwissenschaftliche Untersuchung* 37, *Medieval Islam: A Study in Cultural Orientation* 46, *A Tenth-Century Document of Arabic Literary Theory and Criticism: The sections on poetry of al-Bāqillāni's I'jāz al-Qur'ān* (translated and annotated) 51, *Muhammadan Festivals* 51, *Islam—Essays in the Nature and Growth of a Cultural Tradition* 55, *Kritik und Dichtkunst: Studien zur arabischen Literaturgeschichte* 55, *Az-Zarnūji: Instruction of the Student—The Method of Learning* (translated, with an introduction together with T. M. Abel) 47; co-operated on *Palestine: A Study of Jewish, Arab and British Policies* 47; ed. and contrib. *Unity and Variety in Muslim Civilisation* 55, *Classicisme et déclin culturel dans l'histoire de l'Islam* 57, *Dirasat fi'l adab al 'arabi* 59, *Shu Arā' 'Abbāsiyyūn* 59; Ed. and contributor *Universität und moderne Gesellschaft* 59, *Klassizismus und Kulturverfall* 60, *Modern Islam* 62, *Der Islam in Propyläen Weltgeschichte, V* 63, *French African Literature* 64, *Islam: Experience of the Holy and Concept of Man* 65, *Der Islam in seiner klassischen Epoche, 622-1258*, 66, co-Editor and contributor *The Dream and Human Societies* 66.
Near Eastern Center, University of California, Los Angeles 24, Calif., U.S.A.

Grüneberg, Gerhard; German politician; b. 29 Aug· 1921; ed. elementary school and building studies.
Builder 39-41, 45-46; war service and prisoner-of-war 41-45; official in Socialist Unity Party, (S.E.D.) 46-; First Sec. Frankfurt/Oder District Cttee. 52; mem. and Sec. Central Cttee. S.E.D. 58-, Candidate mem. Politburo 63-66, mem. 66-; mem. Agricultural Council of Council of Ministers 63-; mem. Volkskammer 58-, mem. Comm. for Foreign Affairs 58-63; mem. Nat. Council of Nat. Front 58-; Vaterländischer Verdienstorden in Silber 59, in Gold 64.
Sozialistische Einheitspartei Deutschlands, 102 Berlin, 2 Werderscher Markt, Germany.

Grunewald, Admiral Augusto Hamann Rademacker; Brazilian naval officer and politician; b. 11 May 1905; ed. naval school.
Sub-Lieut. 27, rose to Admiral of the Fleet 64; fmr. Asst. Commdr. of N.E. Naval Force; Dir. Centre of Naval Armaments; Deputy Chief of Operations, Naval Gen. Staff; Commdr. Fifth Naval District; Head of Cen. Command of Atlantic Defence Zone; mem. Revolutionary Command 64; Minister for Navy, Trans-

port and Public Works 64; Minister for Navy 67-; numerous decorations.
Ministry for the Navy, Brasilia, Brazil.

Grunitsky, Nicolas; Togolese politician; b. 5 April 1913; ed. Lycée Millet, Aix-en-Provence, and Public Works School, Paris.
Civil Servant, Public Works Dept., Dahomey, later Togo; Head "Combat" Movement 40; founder, later Gen. Sec., Togolese Progress Party; Dep. Togolese Territorial Assembly 51 and 56; mem. French Nat. Assembly 51 and 56; Prime Minister of Togo 58-60; formed Union Démocratique des Populations Togolaises 59; Pres. of Togo 63-67; Minister of Foreign Affairs, Interior, and Nat. Defence 63-65; Head of the Govt. and Minister of Nat. Defence 66-67; Grand Croix de la Légion d'Honneur.
Lomé, Togo, West Africa.

Grushetsky, Ivan Samoilovich; Soviet politician; b. 1904; ed. Higher Party School, Moscow.
Soviet and party work 22-; Soviet Army 41-44; First Sec. Chernovitsy District Cttee. and Town Cttee., Ukrainian C.P. 40-41, Lvov District and Town Cttee. 44-48, Lvov District Cttee. 50-51, Volyn District Cttee. 51-61, Lvov District Cttee. 61-65; Sec. Cen. Cttee. C.P. Ukraine; Deputy Chair. Council of Ministers Ukrainian S.S.R.; Deputy to Supreme Soviet U.S.S.R.; Chair. Cttee. for Party-State Control, Ukrainian S.S.R.; mem. C.P.S.U. 28-; mem. Cen. Cttee. of C.P.S.U. 61-66; Alternate mem. Politburo Cen. Cttee. C.P. Ukraine.
Committee for Party-State Control of Ukrainian S.S.R., Kiev, U.S.S.R.

Grushin, Petr Dmitriyevich; Soviet aviation specialist; b. 1906; ed. Moscow Aviation Inst.
Member C.P.S.U. 31-; leading engineer in aircraft industry 32-; Dean of Dept. Moscow Aviation Inst. 48-51; Dir. Aircraft Plant 53-; mem. Cen. Cttee. C.P.S.U. 66-; corresp. mem. U.S.S.R. Acad. of Sciences 62-66, mem. 66-; Hero of Socialist Labour; Lenin Prize.
Publs. Works on aerodynamics and aircraft construction.
U.S.S.R. Academy of Sciences, 14 Lenin Prospekt, Moscow, U.S.S.R.

Grut, Aage, M.D., D.P.H., D.I.H.; Danish health officer; 23 Dec. 1906; ed. Copenhagen Univ.
Medical Inspector of Factories 40-48; Chief Industrial Hygiene Division and Industrial Hygiene Adviser, I.L.O., Geneva, 48-53; Medical Officer of Health 54; Senior Medical Inspector of Labour 55-; Asst. Sec.-Gen. Int. Conf. of Experts on Pneumoconiosis, Sydney 50; I.L.O. missions to 10 countries 50-53; Univ. Medal 36, Hon. mem. Argentine Soc. of Industrial Medicine 51, Cuban Soc. of Industrial Medicine 53.
Publs. Many papers in medical periodicals.
Hambros allé 20, Hellerup, Denmark.

Grzybowski, Stefan Mieczysław, D.IUR. HABIL.; Polish jurist and university professor; b. 16 Nov. 1902; ed. Jagiellonian Univ., Cracow, School of Politics, Cracow, Berlin and Paris Univs.
Judge 26-37; Asst. Jagiellonian Univ. Cracow 30-36, Docent and Lecturer in Civil Law 37-49, Asst. Prof. 49-57, Prof. 58-; Prof. School of Social Sciences, Cracow 46-49; Prof. School of Econs., Cracow 49-61; Head of Civil Law Dept. Jagiellonian Univ. Cracow 49-, Rector, School of Econs. 49-52, Dean, Faculty of Law 56, Pro-Rector Jagiellonian Univ. 56-58, Rector 58-62; mem. Cttee. for Legal Science of Polish Acad. of Sciences 60-; mem. Sociological Comm. Polish Acad. of Sciences 59-; Editor-in-Chief *Studia;* Prisoner of War 39-45; Commdr. Order of the Southern Cross, Officer, Order of Polonia Restituta.
Publs. (Polish) *The Legal Character of Partnership* 28; *Hay, a study of the peasant soul* 30, *Copyright* 31, *Legal Protection of the Author's Personal Interests after his*

Death 33, *Divisibility of Marriage as a Codification Problem* 35, *Legal Protection of Inventions, Designs, and Trade Marks* 36, *Personal Interests* 36, *Marital Law* 46, *An Introduction to the Study of Labour Law* 48, *The Road to Development of the Trade Unions* 48, *An Introduction to Political Science* 48, *Civil Law* Vols. I, II 52, *Law of Maintenance* 55, 56, 57, *Inventor's Rights* 56, 65, *Basic Problems of Property Relations in the System of Law of Water Supply* 57, *Protection of Personal Interests*, 57, *Normative Utterance and its Formal Structure* 61, *Patent Act—Studies* 63, *Civil Law Principles of Social Coexistence—Studies* 64, *The Administrative Act as the Source of Obligatory Relations* 67, *The Civil Law Relations and the State Property* 66, *Copyright in Moving Picture Films* 66, *Transfer* 67, *The Know-How Contracts* 68.
Michalowskiego 9/6, Cracow, Poland.
Telephone: 38523.

Gschnitzer, Franz, DR. JUR.; Austrian university professor; b. 19 May 1899; ed. Univs. of Innsbruck, Vienna and Tübingen.
Extraordinary Prof. of Roman Law and Austrian Private Law, Univ. of Innsbruck 27; Ordinary Prof. of Austrian Private Law 28; Rector of Univ. of Innsbruck 46-48; mem. Austrian Fed. Council, Austrian People's Party 62-65; Pres. Liechtenstein Supreme Court 45-; Austrian State Sec. for Foreign Affairs 56-61; mem. Austrian Acad. of Science.
Publs. *Der Inn* 47, *Kommentar zum Allgemeinen Bürgerlichen Gesetzbuch* (2nd edn.) 48-, *Tirol, Geschichtliche Einheit* 57, 58, 59, 60, *Lehrbuch des österreichischen bürgerlichen Rechts 1-6*, 63-68.
Weiherburggasse 23, Innsbruck, Austria.
Telephone: 8145.

Guardini, Mgr. Romano, TH.D.; Italian-born German ecclesiastic; b. 17 Feb. 1885; ed. Tübingen, Munich, Berlin and Freiburg Univs.
Ordained priest 10; Prof. of Christian Philosophy, Breslau, Berlin, Tübingen and Munich Univs.; Domestic Prelate 52; German Booksellers' Peace Prize 52, Munich Gold Medal 55; Orden Pour le Mérite 58; Erasmus Prize 61; Grosses Verdienstkreuz mit Stern 65; Hon. Dr. Phil. Freiburg Univ.; promoter German Catholic Youth Movement.
Publs. A large number of religious and philosophical works including *Der Gegensatz, Versuche zu einer Philosophie des Lebendig-Konkreten* and *Der Herr* (life of Christ trans. into English, French, Italian, Spanish, Dutch, Greek and Japanese).
Merzstrasse 2, Munich 27, German Federal Republic.

Guareschi, Giovanni; Italian journalist and novelist; b. 1 May 1908.
Editor *Il Corriere Emiliano* 29; fmr. Chief Editor *Bertoldo*; Dir. *Candido* 45-61.
Publs. *Il Piccolo Mondo di Don Camillo, Don Camillo e la sua Gregge, Diario Clandestino, Lo Zibaldino, Il Compagno Don Camillo*.
Via Righi 6, Milan, Italy.

Guayasamín Calero, Oswaldo; Ecuadorean painter; b. 19; ed. School of Fine Arts, Quito.
First exhibition 40; toured United States 42; visited Russia and China; paints portraits and murals; Bienal de España Prize 55, Mexican prize 60.
c/o School of Fine Arts, Quito, Ecuador.

Guazzugli Marini, Giulio, DR. PH.; Italian atomic energy administrator; b. 14; ed. Rome Univ.
Assistant Professor of Philosophy, Rome Univ. 37-47; Personal Sec. to Signor Carlo Sforza. Minister of Foreign Affairs 49-53; official at Council of Europe, Strasbourg 49-53; Dir., Secretariat, Council of Coal and Steel Community 53-57; Exec. Sec. Euratom Commission 58-67; Dir.-Gen. European Community Joint Research Centre 68-.

European Community, 51-53 rue Belliard, Brussels, Belgium.
Telephone: 13-40-90.

Gubanov, Mikhail Vasilievich; Soviet trade corporation official; b. 19; ed. Kazan Aviation Inst. and Foreign Trade Acad.
Foreman, Shop Supt., Designing Engineer, Scientific Research Inst. 43-46; trade missions, Korean People's Democratic Republic 49-52, Czechoslovakia 54-57; Dep. Chair. *Mashinoimport* 52-54, 57-59; Chair. *Tekhnopromimport* (equipment for power stations and chemical factories) 59-63; trade representative of U.S.S.R. in Japan 63-68; mem. C.P.; numerous decorations.
Trade Representation of U.S.S.R. in Moscow, U.S.S.R.

Guber, Alexander Andreevich; Soviet historian; b. 1902.
Professor, Moscow Univ. 37-; Prof. Acad of Social Sciences of Central Cttee. of C.P.S.U. 46-; Corresp. mem. U.S.S.R. Acad. of Sciences 53-66, mem. 66-; Senior Assoc., Inst. of History, U.S.S.R. Acad. of Sciences 57-; mem. Editorial Board *Novaya i noveshayna istoriya* (Modern and Current History); Chair. Nat. Cttee. of Soviet Historians 57-; Vice-Pres. Int. Cttee. of Historical Sciences 60-; specializes in history of S.E. Asia; Order of Red Banner of Labour (twice).
U.S.S.R. Academy of Sciences, 14 Lenin Prospekt, Moscow, U.S.S.R.

Gudeman, Edward, B.A.; American businessman and government official; b. 9 Oct. 1906; ed. Harvard Univ.
Vice-President (Merchandising) Sears Roebuck & Co. 52-61; Under-Sec., Commerce Dept. 61-63; Partner, Lehman Bros. (investment bankers) 63-; Democrat.
142 East 56th Street, New York, U.S.A.

Güden, Hilde; Austrian opera singer; b. 15 Sept. 1922; ed. High School, and Acad. of Music.
Member, Vienna State Opera, La Scala, Milan 47-, Metropolitan Opera, New York 51-; Festivals Salzburg, Edinburgh, Glyndebourne, etc.; toured Europe, U.S.A., Canada; Grand Cross for Science and Art 59, Cross of Order of Dannebrog 62; awarded Decca Golden Record 58, Vienna Phil. Orch. Silver Rose 59, Golden Oscar of Acad. du Disque Français 61.
Gerlasse 2, Vienna III, Austria.

Gudmundsson, Gudmundur I., CAND. IURIS; Icelandic lawyer and politician; b. 17 July 1909; ed. Reykjavík Coll., and Univ. of Iceland.
Law practice 34-45; Supreme Court Attorney 39-45; District Judge, Hafnarfjoerdur 45-56; mem. Althing 42-65; Minister for Foreign Affairs 56-65; Ambassador to U.K., Netherlands, Spain and Portugal 65-; Commdr. with Star Order of Icelandic Falcon, Grand Cross White Rose (Finland), Grand Cross St. Olav (Norway), Hon. K.B.E., and many other decorations; Labour.
Icelandic Embassy, 1 Eaton Terrace, London, S.W.1, England.
Telephone: 01-730-5131.

Gudmundsson, Kristinn; Icelandic politician; b. 14 Oct. 1897; ed. Reykjavík Grammar School, Univs. of Berlin and Kiel.
Began business career in Hamburg and Reykjavík 26-29; teacher, Akureyri Grammar Coll. 29-44; Tax Dir., Akureyri 44-53; Minister of Foreign Affairs 53-56; Minister in London 56-57, Ambassador 57-61, also accredited as Ambassador to the Netherlands 56-61; Ambassador to the U.S.S.R. 61-, concurrently Minister to Rumania and Hungary, Ambassador to Romania and Bulgaria 65-, and Hungary 66-; Grand Cross of Dannebrog (Danish), Vasa (Swedish), White Rose (Finnish); Commdr. (1st Class) of Icelandic Falcon, and other foreign decorations.
Icelandic Embassy, Moscow, U.S.S.R.

Gudmundsson, Kristmann; Icelandic writer; b. 23 Oct. 1901.

Writes in Icelandic and Norwegian; his novels have been translated into 36 languages; Icelandic Falcon Order.

Publs. *Poems of Twilight* 22, *Icelandic Love* 26, *The Bridal Gown* 27, *Armann and Vildis* 28, *Morning of Life* 29, *Sigmar* 30, *The Blue Coast* 31, *The Sacred Mountain* 32, *Early Spring* 33, *White Nights* 34, *Children of Earth* 35, *The Lamp* 36, *The Goddess and the Bull* 38, *The Sneering Stonemonster* 43, *Comrade Woman* 47, *An Evening in Reykjavík* 48, *Scarlet Mist* (2 vols.) 50-52, *The Tragedy at Osterby* 55, *Poems from Kristmann* 55, *History of World Literature* (2 vols.) 55-56, *The Little Café* 58, *A Voyage to the Stars* 59, *Adventures in Space* 59, *Autobiography* (4 vols.), *The Black Isolde* 59, *Norwegian Idyll* 60, *My Botanical Garden* 61, *The White Flame* 61, *The Golden Isolde* 62, *Playthings* 62, *The Centre* 65, *Winter Days* 66.

P.O.B. 615, Reykjavík, Iceland.

Telephone: 15648.

Guédira, Ahmed Réda; Moroccan politician; b. 22.

Former Cabinet Minister under Mohammed V, Minister of State in charge of Franco-Moroccan negotiations; Dir.-Gen. Ro al Cabinet 61-; Minister of Agriculture 61-Nov. 63, of the Interior 61-June 63; Dep. for Casablanca May 63-; Minister for Foreign Affairs Nov. 63-64; mem. Front for the Defence of Constitutional Institutions.

c/o Ministry for Foreign Affairs, Rabat, Morocco.

Guéhenno, Jean (*pseudonym* of Marcel Guéhenno); French writer and educationist; b. 25 March 1890; ed. Ecole Normale Supérieure.

Served French Army 14-18; teacher, various Paris lycées. Chief Editor of review *L'Europe* until 36; supervised collection *Ecrits* for Librairie Grasset; Dir. of weekly *Vendredi* 36; after Liberation wrote for *Figaro* and *Figaro Littéraire*; Gen. Insp. of Nat. Educ. 45-61, Hon. Insp. 61-; Commdr. de la Légion d'Honneur, Croix de Guerre, Médaille de la Résistance, Prix des Ambassadeurs, Paris Literature Prize, Eve Delacroix Prize; mem. Académie Française 62-.

Publs. *L Evangile Eternel, Caliban Parle, La Conversion à l'Humain, Le Journal d'un Homme de Quarante Ans* 34, *Journal d'une Révolution* 38, *Dans la Prison, La France et le Monde* 46, *Journal des Années Noires* 47, *Jean Jacques, en Marge des Confessions* 48, *La Part de la France* 49, *Jean Jacques: roman et vérité* 50, *Voyages: tournée américaine, tournée africaine* 52, *Jean Jacques; grandeur et misère d'un esprit* 52, *Aventures de l'esprit, La France et les Noirs, La part de la France, La foi difficile, Sur le Chemin des Hommes, Changer La Vie, Ce que je crois* 64.

35 rue Pierre-Nicole, Paris 5e, France.

Guellal, Cherif; Algerian diplomatist; b. 18 Aug. 1932; ed. Univ. de Paris à la Sorbonne, and in Algeria and England.

Propagandist for Nat. Front of Liberation (F.L.N.) at outbreak of Algerian Revolution, F.L.N. rep. in Tunisia, rep. of Gen. Union of Algerian Workers, Tunis 56, Cairo 57; Foreign Affairs Adviser to Pres. Ben Bella 61-63; Amb. to U.S.A. 63-67, accred. also to Canada and Mexico.

c/o Ministry of Foreign Affairs, Algiers, Algeria.

Guéna, Yves; French civil servant; b. 6 July 1922; ed. Ecole Nat. d'Administration.

Official in Morocco 47; Maître des Requêtes, Conseil d'Etat 57; Dir. de Cabinet to M. Debré (Minister of Justice) 58-59, Dep. Dir. de Cabinet to M. Debré (Prime Minister) Jan.-July 59; High Commr. Ivory Coast 59-60, Envoy Extraordinary (Dean of Diplomatic Corps) 60-61; Deputy for Dordogne 62-; Minister of Posts and Telecommunications 67-68, of Information

May 68-; Officier Légion d'Honneur, Croix de Guerre, Médaille de la Résistance.

186 avenue Victor Hugo, Paris 16e, France.

Guérin, André Paul; French journalist; b. 1 Dec. 1899; ed. Collège de Flers, Lycée de Rennes, Caen Univ., and Ecole Normale Supérieure, Univ. of Paris.

On staff of *L'Oeuvre* 22-39; Editor *L'Aurore* 46-; Officier de la Légion d'Honneur, Croix de Guerre.

Publs. *Manuel des Partis Politiques en France* 28, *Normandie Champ de Bataille de la Libération* 54, *Vacances en Normandie* 57, *Opération Bergère* 61, "1871" *La Commune* 66.

171 rue Saint-Honoré, Paris 1er, France.

Guérin, Daniel; French writer; b. 19 May 1904; ed. Lycée Louis-le-Grand.

Journalist, writer, sociologist, historian; Founder, Centre laïque des Auberges de jeunesse; Cultural Adviser, Théâtre des Nations; mem. French Inst. of Sociology, Comité Ben Bella, Comité Ben Barka.

Publs. *Le Livre de la dix-huitième année* 22, *L'enchantement du Vendredi-Saint* 25, *La Vie selon la chair* 28, *La Peste brune a passé là* 33, *Fascisme et grand capital* 36, *La Lutte de classes sous la 1ère République* 46, *Où va le peuple américain?* 51, *Au service des colonisés* 54, *Kinsey et la sexualité* 55, *Les Antilles décolonisées* 56, *Jeunesse du socialisme libertaire* 59, *Shakespeare et Gide en correctionnelle?* 59, *Eux et Lui* 62, *Front Populaire révolution manquée* 63, *Décolonisation du Noir américain* 63, *Sur le fascisme* 65, *Un jeune homme excentrique* 65, *L'Anarchisme* 65, *L'Algérie qui se cherche, L'Algérie caporalisée?* 64, 65, *Ni Dieu ni Maître* 66; Plays: *Le Grain sous la Neige* 61, *Vautrin* 62.

13 rue des Marronniers, Paris 16e, France.

Telephone: 224-67-08.

Guéron, Jules; French atomic scientist; b. 2 June 1907; ed. Lycée Charlemagne, Paris, and Univ. de Paris à la Sorbonne.

Lecturer, Univ. of Strasbourg 38, Asst. Prof. 46- (on leave since 47); with Tube Alloys 41-46; Head of Service Commissariat of Atomic Energy 46-49, Dir. Commissariat of Atomic Energy 49-58, Dir. Centre de Saclay 51-54, Dir. of Gen. Programme 54-58, Head Physical-Chemistry Dept. 49-58; Dir.-Gen. Research EURATOM 58-; Lecturer, Conservatoire Nat. des Arts et Métiers 51-61; mem. and Sec. Comm. on Atomic Weights, Int. Union of Pure and Applied Chemistry 60-; Chevalier Légion d'Honneur; Prix Adrian, Chemical Soc. of France 35.

Publs. About 70 scientific and gen. publications.

15 rue de Siam, Paris 16e, France; and 51 avenue Général de Gaulle, Brussels, Belgium.

Telephone: 870-09-89.

Guerra, Ruy Teixeira; Portuguese lawyer and diplomatist; b. 02; ed. Univ. of Lisbon and School of Public Administration, Harvard Univ.

Practised law, Lisbon 25-32; Portuguese Foreign Service 32-, Canada, Germany, U.S.A., U.K., France; Head Portuguese Del. to OEEC until Jan. 56, Chair. Exec. Cttee. OEEC 55-56; Dir.-Gen. Economic Affairs, Ministry of Foreign Affairs 56-60; Ambassador to Switzerland and Perm. Rep. to EFTA and GATT 60-67; several decorations.

c/o Ministry of Foreign Affairs, Lisbon, Portugal.

Guerrero, León María; Philippine diplomatist; b. 24 March 1915; ed. Ateneo de Manila, Philippine Law School, Manila.

Assoc. Editor, Philippines Free Press 35-40; with Office of Solicitor-Gen. 40; served army 40-45; Chief of Protocol, Dept of Foreign Affairs 46; Legal and Legislative Counsel, Philippines Senate 48; Under-Sec. of Foreign Affairs 54; Ambassador to Great Britain (concurrently Minister to Norway, Sweden, Finland and Denmark) 54-61, to Spain 61-66, to India 66-; Chair.

Philippine Trade Mission to Western Germany 55; Amb. Extraordinary to Independence Celebrations of Ghana 57; Del. UN Gen. Assembly 59; Vice-Chair. Int. Sugar Council 59, Chair. 60.

Publs. *Twilight in Tokyo* 46, *Passion and Death of the USAFFE* 47, *Report from Europe* 50, *The Young Rizal* 52, *Our Foreign Relations* 52, *Alternatives for Asians* 57, *An Asian on Asia* 58, *Noli Me Tangere* (translation) 60, *El Filibusterismo* (translation) 61, *El Si y El No* 63, *The First Filipino* 63.

Philippine Embassy, 3rd Floor, Thapar House, Janpath, New Delhi, India.

Guerrero, Dr. Gustavo A.; Nicaraguan economist and banker; b. 26 Aug. 1923; ed. Univ. of Texas and American Univ., Washington, D.C.

Chief of Econ. Studies, Ministry of Economy, Nicaragua 49-55; training at Int. Monetary Fund 52; Dir. of Budget, Nicaragua 55-57; Dir. of Internal Revenue 57-60; Vice-Minister of Economy 60-63, Minister of Economy 62-63; Vice-Minister of Finance 63-65; Pres. Central American Bank for Econ. Integration 65-68; Pres. and Gen. Man. Inst. de Fomento Nacional 68-; Dir. Nat. Devt. Inst. (Nicaragua) 53-65, Central Bank of Nicaragua 60-65, Corinto Port Authority 63-65, Booth Nicaragua (commercial fishing) 62-65, Hercasa (chemical enterprise) 64-65; mem. Central Customs Cttee. of Nicaragua 56-65; Exec. Sec. Nat. Econ. Council of Nicaragua 60-65; mem. Board of Dirs. Latin American Planning Inst. 65-67, 67-69; Del. to numerous int. confs; Commdr. Order of Quetzal (Guatemala); Grand Cross Nat. Order of José Matías Delgado (El Salvador).

Instituto de Fomento Nacional, Managua, Nicaragua.

Guerrero, Manuel Flores León; American (Guam) politician; b. 25 Oct. 1914; ed. Guam schools.

Guam Government 30-48, 50-; Asst. Sec. Guam 56-60, Sec. 61-63; Gov. of Guam 63-; Vice-Pres. Guam Commercial Corpn. 46-48; Fiscal Adviser, Controller 48-49; Chair. Finance Cttee. and Alt. U.S. Commr. S. Pacific Comm. 62-64, U.S. Commr. 64-.

Governor's Office, Agana, Guam; and P.O. Box 223, Agana, Guam.

Telephone: 7945.

Guerrero Gutiérrez, Lorenzo, M.D.; Nicaraguan doctor and politician; b. 13 Nov. 1900; ed. Instituto Nacional de Oriente and Univ. Nacional de Oriente y Mediodía.

Secretary, School of Medicine, Univ. Nac. Oriente y Mediodía 26; elected Asst. Mayor 30; Local Health Chief 31; Mayor 32; Minister of Public Instruction and Physical Educ. 34-37; Amb. to Mexico 37; mem. Nicaraguan Del. to Instituto Indigenista Interamericano, Mexico 42; Minister to Mexico for Second Interamerican Agriculture Conf. 42; Private Sec. to Presidency 43; Chief, Special Mission to Cuba 44, Costa Rica 44; Amb. to Mexico 45; Minister of Educ. 46; Chief, Special Mission on Transfer of Power, Mexico 52; Amb. to Costa Rica 53; Senator 57-; Del., Cen. American Interparl. Meeting 58; Head Del. First American Interparl. Conf., Peru 59; Vice-Pres. Nicaragua 63-67; Minister of Home Affairs 63; Constitutional Pres. of Nicaragua Aug. 66-May 67; Minister of Foreign Affairs 67-; mem. scientific orgs. in Nicaragua and abroad; Orden Nac. del Aguila Azteca 45; Orden de Rubén Darío 66; orders from El Salvador 66, Peru and Honduras 67.

Publ. *El Yatrén en la Terapéutica de los Estímulos y Cooperación Interamericana.*

Ministerio de Relaciones Exteriores, Managua, Nicaragua.

Guerriero, Augusto; Italian magistrate and journalist; b. 93; ed. Univ. of Naples.

Hon. Pres. Corte di Conti (Italian Exchequer); Foreign Affairs columnist *Corriere Della Sera* and *Epoca*; Cavaliere di Gran Croce; Commandeur de la Légion

d'Honneur; Grosses Verdienstkreuz of German Federal Republic.

Viale XXI Aprile 81, Rome, Italy.

Guerry, Mgr. Emile, DR. en D. (Grenoble), DR. en THÉOLOGIE (Gregorian Univ.); French ecclesiastic; b. 28 Sept. 1891; ed. Lycée de Grenoble, Grenoble Univ., Gregorian Univ., Rome.

Called to Bar Grenoble; entered Grand Séminaire de Saint-Sulpice 12; served French Army 14-19; diocesan seminary Maylan 20-21; ordained Priest 23; Curate Saint-Laurent de Grenoble 25-27; Prof. of Fundamental Theology and later Prof. of Dogma, Grand Séminaire, Grenoble 27-32; Vicar-Gen. in charge of Action Catholique 32-40; Sec. to perm. comm. of Cardinals and Archbishop of France; Archbishop of Cambrai 52-66; Chevalier Légion d'Honneur; Croix de Guerre, Médaille Militaire, Military Medal (G.B.).

Publs. *Les Syndicats Libres Feminins de l'Isère* 21, *Code de l'Action Catholique* 28, *L'Action Catholique* 36; *Vers le Père* 37, *L'Eglise Catholique en France sous l'Occupation* 47, *Dans le Christ Total* 52, *L'Evêque* 54, *La doctrine sociale de l'Eglise* 57, *L'Eglise et la communauté des peuples* 58, *Eglise catholique et communisme athée* 60, *L'Eglise dans la melée des peuples* 61, *Le Laïcat ouvrier* 63.

Nivolas-Vermelle (Isère), France.

Guest, Douglas, M.A., MUS.B., F.R.C.M.; British organist and conductor; b. 9 May 1916; ed. Reading School, Royal Coll. of Music and King's Coll., Cambridge (Organ Scholar).

War Service as Major, Royal Artillery 39-45; Dir. of Music, Uppingham School 45-50; Organist and Master of Choristers, Salisbury Cathedral 50-57, Worcester Cathedral 57-63; Conductor of The Three Choirs Festival; Organist and Master of Choristers Westminster Abbey 63-; Prof. Royal Coll. of Music 63-; Hon. R.A.M., Hon. F.R.C.O.

Composition: *Missa Brevis* 57.

8 The Little Cloister, Westminster Abbey, London, S.W.1, England.

Telephone: 01-222-6222.

Guest, Raymond Richard; American diplomatist; b. 25 Nov. 1907; ed. McGill and Yale Univs.

Horse breeder, cattle farmer, King George, Virginia 31-; U.S. Navy 41-47; Asst. to Sec. of Defense 45-47; mem. Va. Senate 47-53; Dir. Bessemer Securities Inc. 47-65; mem. Virginia State Comm. on Fisheries and Game 59-65; Amb. to Ireland 65-June 68.

Home: Powhatan Plantation, King George, Virginia 22485, U.S.A.

Guevara Arze, Walter, DR.JUR.; Bolivian lawyer and politician; b. 12; ed. Univ. La Paz.

Professor of Economics, Univ. of La Paz; Prof. of International Law, Cochabamba Univ.; former Congressman and National Senator; Sec. of State for Foreign Affairs 52-56, 67-; Minister of Govt. 57-59; Presidential candidate 60; Leader of the Partido Revolucionario Auténtico-PRA 60-.

Partido Revolucionario Auténtico, La Paz, Bolivia.

Gueye, Lamine; Senegalese lawyer and politician; b. 20 Sept. 1891.

Formerly advocate Dakar Court of Appeal and Prof. William Ponty Coll.; Mayor of Dakar 45-; Senegalese Counsellor 47-; Dep. Senegal Constituent Assembly 58-59; Senegalese Rep. in Senate of French Community 59; Pres. Senegal Nat. Assembly 61-; Grand Croix de l'ordre nat. de la république du Sénégal, Grand Officier Légion d'Honneur.

[Died, 10 June 1968.]

Guggenheim, Harry F., B.A., M.A.; American executive; b. 23 Aug. 1890; ed. Yale Univ., Pembroke Coll., Cambridge Univ.

American Smelting & Refining Co., Mexico 07; Guggen-

heim Bros. 16-23; U.S. Del. Int. Conf. Civil Aeronautics, Washington 28; Amb. to Cuba 29-33; served First and Second World Wars; Senior Partner Guggenheim Brothers; Pres. Daniel and Florence Guggenheim Foundation; Chair. Foundation Comm. Daniel and Florence Guggenheim Jet Propulsion Centers, Princeton Univ. and Calif. Inst. of Technology; Chair. Daniel and Florence Guggenheim Aviation Center, Cornell Univ.; Pres. Solomon R. Guggenheim Foundation; Pres. and Editor-in-Chief *Newsday*; Pres. Harry Frank Guggenheim Foundation.
120 Broadway, New York City, N.Y. 10005, U.S.A.

Guggenheim, Paul, LL.D.; Swiss international lawyer; b. 15 Sept. 1899; ed. Coll. for Classical Studies, Zürich, and Univs. of Geneva, Rome and Berlin.
Lecturer Geneva Univ. 28-31; Asst. Prof. 31-40 and full Prof. 40, Graduate Inst. of Int. Studies; Prof. of Int. Public Law Geneva Univ. 55; mem. of the Permanent Court of Arbitration, The Hague 51-; Agent and Counsel for Switzerland and other countries in different cases before the Int. Court of Justice and European Court of Human Rights, mem. and Pres. several Conciliation Comms.; Lecturer at The Hague Acad. of Int. Law 32, 49, 52 and 58; mem. of the UN Cttee. for elaborating the Constitution of Erythrae 51-52; Pres. Swiss Soc. of Int. Law; hon. mem. American Soc. of Int. Law; mem. Inst. of Int. Law, four Int. Conciliation Comms.; Dr. h.c., Univs. of Louvain, Dijon, Kiel, Paris and Rome.
Publs. *Traité de droit international public*, Vol. I 53, Vol. II 54, and many publications on International Law.
1 Route de Bout du Monde, 1206 Geneva, Switzerland. Telephone: 36-56-71.

Guggenheim, Peggy; American art collector; b. 26 Aug. 1898; ed. Jacobi School, New York.
Opened Guggenheim Jeune Art Gallery, London 38-39; Art of this Century Gallery, New York 42-46; Museo Palazzo Venier dei Leoni, Venice 51-; exhibitions of private collection throughout Europe 51-, London 65.
Publs. *Out of this Century* 46, *Una Collezionista Ricorda* 56, *Confessions of an Art Addict* 60.
Palazzo Venier dei Leoni, 701 San Gregorio, Venice, Italy.

Gugina, Yelizaveta Fyodorovna; Soviet trade union official; b. 19; ed. Moscow Inst. of the Food Industry, Univ. of Marxism-Leninism and Ordjonikidze Inst.
Bolshevik biscuit factory 43-59; Sec. Party Cttee. 57-59; Dir. Rot-Front confectionery factory 59-61; Chair. Central Cttee. of Trade Union of Food Industry Workers 62-; mem. C.P.S.U. and All-Union Council of Trade Unions; Red Banner of Labour and other decorations.
Central Committee of the Trade Union of the Food Industry Workers, 42 Leninsky Prospekt, Moscow, U.S.S.R.

Guha, Mrs. Phulrenu, D.LITT.; Indian social worker; b. 13 Aug. 1911; ed. Calcutta Univ. and Univ. de Paris à la Sorbonne.
Participated in Freedom Movement since early days; social worker, West Bengal, for over thirty years, actively assoc. with relief, social and children's welfare, family planning, defence aid, moral and social hygiene; undertook relief work during Bengal famine 43, Noakhali 46, Calcutta 47-; Sec. United Council of Relief and Welfare, West Bengal; now Vice-Chair. All India Women's Conf.; mem. Rajya Sabha 64-; Union Minister of State for Social Welfare March 67-.
Ministry of State for Social Welfare, New Delhi, India.

Gui, Luigi; Italian politician; b. 26 Sept. 1914.
War service, Italy and Russia 41-43; Christian Democrat underground movement 43-45; elected to Constituent Assembly 46, re-elected 48, 53, 58, 63; fmr. Sec. of the Parl. Comm. on Agriculture and Under-Sec.

Ministry of Agriculture and Forestry; Minister of Labour 57-58, of Educ. 62-68, of Defence June 68-.
Ministry of Defence, Rome, Italy.

Gui, Vittorio; Italian conductor and composer; b. 14 Sept. 1885; ed. Conservatorio di Musica, Santa Cecilia, Rome.
Conductor Teatro Adriano 07, Società dei Concerti Sonfonici, Milan 24, Teatro di Torino, Turin 25-27; founded Orchestra Stabile, Florence 28, Conductor 28-43; subsequently conducted in Rome, Naples, Milan, Lisbon, Leningrad, Moscow, London, Edinburgh and Glyndebourne Festivals; Artistic Counsellor and Dir. of Music, Glyndebourne Festival Opera (England) 60-; Gold Medal for Culture (Italy) 57, and many foreign decorations.
Villa S. Maurizio, Fiesole, Italy.

Guichard, Baron Olivier Marie Maurice; French politician; b. 27 July 1920; ed. Univ. de Paris and Ecole libre des sciences politiques.
Member Rassemblement du peuple français, and Principal Sec. Gen. de Gaulle 47-48; Press Officer Atomic Energy Commissariat 55-58; Asst. Dir. Office of Gen. de Gaulle 58, Technical Adviser to the Pres. 59-60; Del. Gen. of Org. des régions sahariennes 60-63; Gen. Asst. Office of the Prime Minister 63-66; Del. for Regional and Territorial Affairs 63-67; mem. Nat. Assembly 67; Minister of Industry 67-May 68, of Econ. Planning May 68-; Dir. Compagnie nationale du Rhône 66-; mem. Council of Admin. Radiodiffusion-Télévision française 64-; Médaille militaire, Chevalier Légion d'Honneur, Croix de Guerre.
Publ. *Aménager la France* 65.
12 avenue Bugeaud, Paris 16e, France.

Guido, Dr. José María; Argentine politician; b. 10; ed. Univ. of La Plata.
Joined Radical Civic Union 36; mem. Constituent Convention, Rio Negro Province 57-58, mem. of Senate 58-; Leader, Radical Civic Union 58; Provisional Pres. of Senate 58-62; Pres. of Argentina 62-63.
Buenos Aires, Argentina.

Guidotti, Gastone, F.R.S.A.; Italian diplomatist; b. 29 Sept. 1901.
Head of Dept. Ministry of Foreign Affairs 35; First Sec., Belgrade 38, Stockholm 42; Italian Rep. to Allied Govts., London 45; in charge Legation, Prague 45, Athens 46; Head of Liaison Office, Ministry of Foreign Affairs with Allied Govt. in Trieste 47; Gen. Dir. Political Affairs, Ministry of Foreign Affairs and mem. various dels. to NATO confs. 48; Head of Italian Del. to UN 51; Ambassador to Yugoslavia 55, to Austria 58, to German Fed. Republic 61, to U.K. Sept. 64-.
Italian Embassy, 4 Grosvenor Square, London, W.1, England.
Telephone: 01-629-8200.

Guild, Walter; American advertising executive; b. 04; ed. High School, Lincoln, Nebraska.
Radio Dir. Sidney Garfield Advertising, San Francisco 38-43; Partner, Gardner and Guild Advertising, San Francisco 43-49; Founder and Pres. Guild, Bascom and Bonfigli Advertising, San Francisco 49-65, Chair. 64-65; Vice-Chair. Advertising Fed. of America 61-62.
Publ. *How to Market Your Product Successfully* 56.
910 Avon Street, Belmont, Calif. 94002, U.S.A.

Guillabert, André; Senegalese lawyer, politician and diplomatist; b. 15 June 1918; ed. Lycée Faidherbe, St. Louis-du-Sénégal, Faculté des Lettres, Bordeaux, and Faculté de Droit, Toulouse.
Lawyer, Dakar Court of Appeal 45-; Vice-Pres., Conseil Général du Sénégal 47-52; First Vice-Pres. Territorial Assembly, Senegal 52; Counsellor, Assembly of French Union 57-58; Senator (France) 58-59, Senator (French Community) 59-61; Vice-Pres. Constituent Assembly, Senegal 58-59, First Vice-Pres. Legislative Assembly 59,

Nat. Assembly 60-62; Amb. to France 60-62, 66-; Minister of Foreign Affairs, Senegal 62; Keeper of the Seals and Minister of Justice 62-63; Deputy and Vice-Pres. Nat. Assembly, Senegal 63-66; Grand Officier Légion d'Honneur and many other decorations.
Ambassade du Sénégal, Square Pétrarque 2, Paris 16e, France; 30 corniche de Faun, Dakar, Senegal.

Guillaumat, Pierre L. J.; French civil servant; b. 5 Aug. 1909; ed. Prytanée Militaire, La Flèche and Ecole Polytechnique.
Chef du Service des Mines, Indochina 34-39, Tunisia 39-43; Dir. of Carburants 44-51; Admin.-Gen. Atomic Energy Comm. 51-58; Pres. Petroleum Research Bureau 45-58; Minister of the Armies, de Gaulle Cabinet, June 58-Jan. 59, Debré Cabinet Jan. 59-Feb. 60; Minister attached to Prime Minister's Office Feb. 60-April 62; Minister of Education (a.i.) Nov. 60-Feb. 61; Pres. Union Générale des Pétroles 62-65, Electricité de France 64-66, Entreprise de Recherches et d'Activités Pétrolières 65-, Soc. Nat. des Pétroles d'Aquitaine 66-; Commdr. de la Légion d'Honneur, Croix de Guerre.
2 rue Louis-Murat, Paris 8e, France.

Guillemin, Henri; French writer and university professor; b. 19 March 1903; ed. Ecole Normale Supérieure, Paris.
Teaching posts, various lycées, France 28-36; Prof. of French Literature, Univ. of Cairo, Egypt 36-38; Prof. of French Language and Literature, Univ. of Bordeaux 38-42; Cultural Counsellor, French Embassy, Berne 45-62; Prof., Univ. of Geneva 63-; Chevalier, Légion d'Honneur; Grand Prix de la Critique, Paris 65.
Publs. Over thirty volumes of literary history and history.
58 faubourg de l'Hôpital, Neuchâtel, Switzerland.

Guillén, Nicolás; Cuban poet; b. 10 July 1902; ed. Camagüey Inst.
Legal studies 21; poet and author 22-; Spanish war correspondent for *Mediodía* magazine 37-38; Mayoral Candidate for Camagüey 40 (Popular Socialist, later Cuban C.P.); Candidate for Senate, La Habana Province 48; Pres. Cuban Union of Writers and Artists (UNEAC); Amb. of Cuba; Lenin Peace Prize 54; Order of Merit of Haiti.
Poetry: *Motivos de son* 30, *Sóngoro cosongo* 31, *West Indies Ltd.* 34, *España* 37, *Cantos para soldados y sonos para turistas* 37, *El son entero* 47, *La paloma de vuelo popular* 58, *Elegías* 58, *Tengo* 64, *Poemas de Amor* 64, *Gran Zoo*; essays on violinist Brindis de Salas 35; chronicles: *Prosa de Prisa* 62.
Unión de Escritores y Artistas de Cuba, Calle 17 No. 351, Vedado, Havana, Cuba.

Guinness, Sir Alec, Kt., c.b.e.; British actor; b. 2 April 1914; ed. Pembroke Lodge, Southbourne and Roborough, Eastbourne.
Entered Advertising Agency as Copywriter 33; Scholarship to Fay Compton Studio of Dramatic Art 34; First Stage appearance April 34; played in seasons for John Gielgud and Old Vic Theatre Co.; *Hamlet* in modern dress 38; served R.N.V.R. 40-44; began film career 45; Hon. Dr. Fine Arts (Boston Coll.); films include: *The Lavender Hill Mob, Kind Hearts and Coronets, Father Brown, The Man in the White Suit, The Bridge on the River Kwai* 57 (Oscar 58), *The Horse's Mouth* 58, *The Scapegoat* 59, *Our Man in Havana* 59, *Tunes of Glory* 60, *Lawrence of Arabia* 62, *The Fall of the Roman Empire* 64, *Hotel Paradiso* 65, *Dr. Zhivago* 66, *The Comedians* 67; plays include: *Hamlet* 51, *The Prisoner* 54, *Hotel Paradiso, Ross, Exit the King, Dylan, Incident at Vichy, Macbeth, Wise Child* 67, *The Cocktail Party* 50, 68.
Kettlebrook Meadows, Steep Marsh, Petersfield, Hants., England.

Guinness, Henry Samuel Howard; British banker; b. 22 June 1888; ed. Winchester and Balliol Coll., Oxford.

Banking educ. in U.S.A. and Germany; Hon. financial adviser at Foreign Office 19-20; Guinness Holdings Ltd. (fmrly. Guinness Mahon & Co.) 23-, Senior partner 37-, now Chair.; Senior Dir. Guinness & Mahon, Dublin, Guinness Mahon Representation Co., New York.
3 Gracechurch Street, London, E.C.3, England.
Telephone: 01-626-6141.

Guiringaud, Louis de; French diplomatist; b. 12 Oct. 1911; ed. Lycée Buffon, Lycée Saint Louis, Univ. de Paris à la Sorbonne, and Ecole des Sciences politiques.
Staff of Minister for Foreign Affairs 36; entered Diplomatic Service 38-; Attaché Ankara 38-39; First Sec., London 46-49; Political Dir. French High Comm. in Germany 49-52; Consul-Gen. San Francisco 52-55; Deputy Rep. to UN Security Council 55-57 Ambassador to Ghana 57; Dir. Dept. of Moroccan and Tunisian Affairs, Ministry for Foreign Affairs 60; Deputy High Commr. in Algeria 62; Gen.-Inspector Diplomatic Posts 63-66; Ambassador to Japan 66-; Commdr. Légion d'Honneur, Croix de Guerre, etc.
Ambassadeur de France au Japon, 44-11-4 Chomé Minami Azabu, Minato-ku, Tokyo, Japan.
Telephone: 473-0171-9.

Guirola, Carlos Alberto; Salvadorean banker; b. 1894; ed. Hitchcock Military Acad., California, Univ. of California, Coll. of Agriculture, Davis, California, and Heald's Business Coll., San Francisco.
President, El Salvador Nat. Legislative Assembly 31; Dir. Banco Salvadoreño 28-35, Pres. 36, 38, 40, 42, 44, 46-.
Banco Salvadoreño, 2A Ave. Norte 129, San Salvador, El Salvador.

Guissou, Henri; Upper Voltan diplomatist; b. 10; ed. Ecole Primaire Supérieure, Ouagadougou, Ecole Normale William-Ponty, Dakar-Gorée.
Accountant, Office of Public Works, Abidjan 35-38; Head of Temporary Financial Office, Bobo-Dioulasso 42-43; Counsellor-Gen. of Upper Volta 48; Senator of Ivory Coast 47-48; Deputy of Upper Volta 48-56; Deputy to Nat. Assembly from Upper Volta 59; Amb. to France 61-63, to German Fed. Repub. 64-66, to France 66-.
Embassy of Upper Volta, rue de Général-Foy 21, Paris 8e, France.

Guitton, Jean Marie Pierre; French university professor; b. 18 Aug. 1901; ed. Ecole Normale Supérieure.
Former teacher in schools at Troyes, Moulins, Lyon, and Univs. of Montpellier and Dijon; Prof. of Philosophy and History of Philosophy, Univ. of Paris 55-; mem. Programmes Cttee. Radiodiffusion et Télévision Française (ORTF) 65-; mem. Académie Française 61-; Observer at 2nd Vatican Council 63.
Publs. *Le temps et l'éternité chez Plotin et Saint Augustin, La philosophie de Newman, L'existence temporelle, Essai sur l'Amour humain, Le Problème de Jésus, Le Nouvel Art de Penser, Le travail intellectuel, Portrait de Monsieur Pouget, Jésus, Apprendre à vivre et à penser, Le Cardinal Saliège, La vocation de Bergson, L'Eglise et l'Evangile, Journal, Problème et Mystère de Jeanne d'Arc, Journal Oecuménique, Le Clair et l'Obscur vers l'Unité, Les Portraits.*
Faculté de Lettres de Paris, 47 rue des Ecoles, Paris 5e, France.

Gulbenkian, Nubar Sarkis, M.A., LL.B., F.R.G.S.; Turkish (formerly Iranian) philanthropist; b. 2 June 1896; ed. Harrow, Bonn Univ., Trinity Coll., Cambridge, and Middle Temple, London.
Attached French Ministry of Supply (Petroleum Section) 17-21; Dir. Iraq Petroleum Co. 17-25, 28-38; with Royal Dutch Shell Group 22-25; engaged in Middle East oil negotiations 26-28 and 48-54; worked with his father in oil and finance 25-55; Iranian Commercial Attaché, London 26-51, 56-65; Hon. Turkish Counsellor,

London 66-; Hon. Pres. Armenian Church Trustees 55-; Hon. Pres. Asscn. of Econ. Reps. 56-; Legion of Honour (Knight 19 and Commdr 28), Order of St. Gregory the Illuminator (with diamonds) 57; Order of Taj 62.
Publ. *Pantaraxia* (Autobiography) 65.
c/o St. James' Club, Piccadilly, London, W.1, England, and Domaine des Colles, o6 Valbonne, France.

Gülek, Kasim, B.SC. (COM.), PH.D.; Turkish politician, economist and farmer; b. 10; ed. Robert Coll., Ecole des Sciences Politiques, Paris, Columbia, Cambridge, London, Berlin and Hamburg Univs.
Member of Parl. 40; Chair. Cttee. on Commerce 43; Minister of Public Works 47; Minister of Communications 48; Minister of State 49; Del. to Council of Europe 49, 50, 51, 58, 60, 61, 62; Chair. UN Comm. on Korea; fmr. Sec.-Gen. People's Republican Party 51-59; mem. Constituent Assembly 60; Vice-Pres. Council of Europe 61-62; expelled from Republican People's Party for one year Dec. 62.
Publs. *Development of Economically Backward Countries* 32, *Development of Banking in Turkey* 33, *Democracy Takes Root in Turkey* 51.
B. Evler, Ankara, Turkey.

Gullion, Edmund Asbury, A.B.; American diplomatist; b. 2 March 1913; ed. Princeton Univ.
Vice-Consul, Marseilles 37; Dept. of State 38; Vice-Consul, Salonika 39; Third Sec. London 42-43; Algiers 42; Chargé d'Affaires, Helsinki 43; Second Sec. Stockholm 44; Dept. of State, Washington 45; Counsellor, Saigon 50; Dept. of State, Washington 52-56; Foreign Service Insp. 57; Dept. of State 60; Acting Dep. Dir. U.S. Disarmament Admin. 60, Dep. Dir. 61; Ambassador to the Congo (Léopoldville) 61-64; Dean Fletcher School of Law and Diplomacy; mem. American Foreign Service Asscn., American Acad. of Arts and Science, Council on Foreign Relations (N.Y.), World Peace Foundation, World Affairs Council (Boston).
Tufts University, Fletcher School of Law and Diplomacy, Medford, Mass., U.S.A.

Gulyam, Gafur, Soviet poet; b. 1903; ed. Tashkent Agricultural Institute.
Member Uzbek Acad. of Sciences 43-; mem. C.P.S.U. 46-; Deputy Uzbek Supreme Soviet; State Prize 46; Orders of Lenin (twice), Red Banner of Labour (twice), and other decorations.
Publs. *Dynamo* (collection) 31, *China pictures* 32, *Yagdar* (novel) 38, 62; collection of verses: *I'm going from the East* 43, *Light of Uzbekistan* 47, *Festival in Yanghi-Ev* 57, *Selected verses* 61, *Lenin and the East* 61, Collections in 5 vols. 65, *Spring of the World* 63, *Meeting the Future* 66, *Selected Lyrics* 66, *The Result* 67; translated into Uzbek verses by A. S. Pushkin, M. Y. Lermontov, V. V. Mayakovsky and other Russian poets, also *Othello* by W. Shakespeare.
Uzbek Writers' Union, Tashkent, U.S.S.R.

Guna-Kasem, Jote, B. COMM.; Thai banker; b. 03; ed. Birmingham Univ., England.
Railway Scholarship for study in England 22; Asst. Accountant, Royal State Railways of Thailand 28, Traffic Inspector 29, Hotels and Catering Man. 32, Dir. Passenger Service 34; joined Siam Commercial Bank 36, Chief Accountant 48; Lecturer in Commerce and Accountancy, Chulalongkorn Univ. 39; with Bangkok Brokerage Co. 50; Man. Dir. Eastern Int. Development Corpn., Superintendent, Govt. Lottery Bureau 51; M.P. for Bangkok 52-56; Man. Thai Military Bank 57-59; Gov. Bank of Thailand 58-59; Minister of Finance 59. Bangkok, Thailand.

Gunawardena, Philip; Ceylonese politician.
Founder mem. Lanka Sama Samaja Party which has formed an alliance with the Sri Lanka Freedom Party

under the name of Mahajana Eksath Peramuna; mem. of Parl. since 36; Leader, Viplavakari Sama Samaja Party; Minister of Agriculture 56-59.
130 Reid Avenue, Colombo 4, Ceylon.

Gundersen, O. C., CAND. JUR.; Norwegian lawyer and politician; b. 17 March 1908; ed. Oslo Univ.
Qualified as solicitor 31, High Court barrister 39; Town Councillor Trondheim 38, dismissed by Nazis 41; escaped to Sweden, attached to Norwegian Legation Stockholm; summoned to London 42 and apptd. Dir. of State Insurance Office and Chair. Insurance Council; Town Councillor and Alderman Trondheim; Minister of Justice Nov. 45-53; Justice of the Supreme Court; Chair. UN Special Advisory Board 57-; Ambassador to U.S.S.R. 58-61; Minister of Commerce and Shipping 62-63, of Justice 63-65; Judge of Supreme Court 67-.
c/o Ministry of Justice, Oslo, Norway.

Gundevia, Yezdezard Dinshaw, B.A.; Indian civil servant and diplomatist; b. 19 June 1908; ed. Wilson Coll., Bombay.
Called to the bar, Middle Temple, London; entered Indian Civil Service 31; held various posts United Provinces 31-45; Sec. to Govt. of India Rep. in Burma 45-47; Counsellor, Indian Embassy, Rangoon 48; Joint Sec. and Controller-Gen. of Emigration, Ministry of External Affairs 48-50; Minister-Counsellor, Moscow 50-53; Ambassador to Switzerland, concurrently Minister to Austria and the Vatican 53-54; Deputy High Commr. to Great Britain 54-57; High Commr. in Ceylon 57-60, 67-; Special Sec. Ministry of External Affairs 60, Commonwealth Sec. 61-64, Foreign Sec. to Minister for External Affairs 64-65; Sec. to Pres. 65-67.
Indian High Commission, 7 Kollupitiya Station Road, P.O.B. 882, Colombo, Ceylon.

Gunewardene, Ratnakirti Senerat Serasinghe; Ceylonese lawyer and diplomatist; b. 99; ed. Ceylon and Univ. of London.
Advocate Supreme Court of Ceylon; mem. Ceylon State Council 36 until its dissolution in 47; sometime Minister of Local Administration; mem. of (first Ceylon) Parl. 47-52, briefly Minister without Portfolio and Chief Govt. Whip; Minister to Italy 52-54; Leader Ceylon Del. to FAO 52-53; Gov. World Bank 54-58; Perm. Rep. to UN 56-58; High Commr. in Canada 57-58; Ambassador to U.S.A. 54-July 61, to France and Switzerland July-Oct. 61; High Commr. in U.K. 61-63; High Commr. to Canada 63-67 and Perm. Rep. to UN 63-65.
7 Vayira Lane, Colombo 5, Ceylon.

Gunn, Sir William Archer, K.B.E., C.M.G.; Australian grazier and company director; b. 1 Feb. 1914; ed. The King's School, Parramatta, New South Wales.
Chairman Australian Wool Board 63-67, Int. Wool Secr. 61-67, The Wool Bureau Inc., New York, Queensland Advisory Board, Devt. Finance Corpn.; Man. Dir. Tipperary Land Corpn., Elsey Pastoral Pty. Ltd., The Elsey Station Ltd., Hodgson Downs Ltd., Gunn Rural Management Pty. Ltd., Gunn Devt. Pty. Ltd., The Douglas Pastoral Co. Pty. Ltd.; Dir. Rothmans of Pall Mall (Australia) Ltd., Amagraze Ltd., Queensland Board of Nat. Mutual Life Asscn. of Australasia Ltd., Grazcos Co-operative Ltd., Queensland Meat Producers Co-operative Asscn. Ltd., Clausen Steamship Co. (Australia) Pty. Ltd., Walter Reid & Co. Ltd.; mem. Commonwealth Bank Board 52-59, Reserve Bank Board 59-67, Australian Meat Board 53-66, Australian Wool Bureau 51-63 (Chair. 58-63), Australian Wool-growers Council 47-60 (Chair. 56-57), Graziers Fed. Council of Australia 51-60 (Pres. 51-54), Australian Woolgrowers and Graziers Council 60-66, Export Devt. Council 62-65, Exec. Council, United Graziers Asscn. of Queensland 44-67 (Pres. 51-59), Australian Wool Testing Authority 58-63, Exec. Int. Wool Secr. 58-63 (Chair.

61-63); Golden Fleece Achievement Award (Nat. Asscn. of Wool Manufacturers of America) 62.
Office: Gunn Rural Management Pty. Ltd., Wool Exchange, 69 Eagle Street, Brisbane; Home: 35 Junction Road, Clayfield, Brisbane, Queensland, Australia. Telephone: Brisbane 2-0472 (Office); Brisbane 6-4146 (Home).

Gunneng, Arne, LL.B.; Norwegian diplomatist; b. 1 Dec. 1914; ed. Oslo Katedralskole, Oslo Univ.
First Sec. Embassy, Washington 45-48; Ministry of Foreign Affairs, Oslo 48-50; Chargé d'Affaires, Warsaw 50-51; Counsellor, Stockholm 51-52; Dep. Perm. Rep. North Atlantic Council, Paris 52-55; Ambassador to Canada 55-59; Dir.-Gen. of Political Affairs, Ministry of Foreign Affairs, Oslo 59-62; Ambassador to Sweden 62-66, to U.S.A. 66-.
Norwegian Embassy, Washington, D.C., U.S.A.

Gunness, Robert Charles, B.S., D.SC.; American oil executive; b. 28 July 1911; ed. Univ. of Massachusetts and Massachusetts Inst. of Technology.
Assistant Dir. of Research, Standard Oil Co. (Indiana) 43-45, Assoc. Dir. 45-47, Man. of Research 47-52, Asst. Gen. Man. of Mfg. 52-54, Dir. 53-, Gen. Man. Supply and Transportation 54-56, Exec. Vice-Pres. 56-65, Pres. 65-; Vice-Chair., Research and Devt. Board, Dept. of Defense, Washington, D.C. 51.
Standard Oil Company (Indiana), 910 South Michigan Avenue, Chicago, Ill. 60680, U.S.A.

Gunter, Rt. Hon. Raymond Jones, P.C., M.P.; British trade unionist and politician; b. 30 Aug. 1909; ed. elementary school.
Member of Parl. 45-51, 59-; Treas. Transport Salaried Staffs Asscn. 53, Pres. 56-64; mem. Nat. Exec. Labour Party 55-; Chair. Labour Party Org. Cttee. 63-; Vice-Chair. Labour Party 63-64, Chair. 64-65; Minister of Labour 64-68; Minister of Power April-June 68-.
House of Commons, London, S.W.1, England.

Gunther, John, PH.B.; American journalist; b. 30 Aug. 1901; ed. Univ. of Chicago.
Foreign corresp. *Chicago Daily News* 24-36, successively at Paris, Rome, Geneva, Berlin, Moscow, Vienna 30-35, London corresp. 35-36; travelled widely India, China, Japan 37-38, Latin America 40-41, London 41, covered Mediterranean War 43; Commentator for Nat. Broadcasting Co., New York 39-42, for Blue Network 42-45.
Publs. *The Red Pavilion* 26, *The Golden Fleece* 29, *The Bright Nemesis* 32 (novels), *Inside Europe* 36, 37, 38, 39, 40, *Inside Asia* 39, 42, *The High Cost of Hitler* 39, *Inside Latin America* 41, *D-Day* 44, *The Troubled Midnight* 45, *Inside U.S.A.* 47, *Death Be Not Proud* 49, *Behind the Curtain* 49, *Roosevelt in Retrospect* 50, *The Riddle of McArthur* 51, *Eisenhower: The Man and the Symbol* 52, *Alexander the Great* 53, *Inside Africa* 55, *Inside Russia Today* 58, *Taken at the Flood* 60, *Inside Europe Today* 61, *The Story of the "Inside" Books* 62, *A Fragment of Autobiography* 62, *Meet Soviet Russia* 64, *The Lost City* 64, *Procession* 65, *Inside South America* 67.
1 East End Avenue, New York N.Y. 10021, U.S.A.

Gupta, Chandra Bhanu, M.A., LL.B.; Indian politician; b. 14 July 1902; ed. Lucknow Univ.
Lawyer 25; mem. A.I.C.C. 26-; Municipal Board, Lucknow 28-31; Pres. Congress Cttee., Lucknow 29-44; mem. U.P.P.C.C. 33-; Legislative Assembly, Uttar Pradesh 37-57, 60-; Parl. Sec. to Chief Minister 46; Minister of Food and Civil Supplies 47-48, of Health 48, of Planning and Industry 54-57; Chief Minister of Uttar Pradesh 60-63, 67, concurrently Minister of Gen. Admin. and Home Affairs 67.
Seva Kutir, Pan Dariba, Lucknow, Uttar Pradesh, India.

Gurmani, Hon. Nawab Mushtaq Ahmad; Pakistani farmer and politician; b. 05; ed. M.A.O. Coll., Aligarh and privately.

Mem. Legislative Council, Punjab 30-36, Punjab Legislative Assembly and Parl. Sec. to Min. for Education and Health, Punjab 37-42; mem. Board of Economic **Inquiry, Punjab, Joint Development Board, Punjab,** N.W. Railway Advisory Cttee., etc.; Dir. of Technical Recruitment and Publicity, Govt. of India 42-45; Dir.-Gen. of Resettlement and Employment and Joint Sec. to Govt. of India 45-47; Del. to Int. Labour Conf., Montreal 46; Prime Minister of Bahawalpur State, Pakistan 47-48; Minister for Kashmir Affairs, Govt. of Pakistan 49-51; Minister for Home Affairs and States and Frontier Regions, Govt. of Pakistan 51-54, Gov. of Punjab 54-55, West Pakistan 55-57, retd. 57; Chair. Board of Dirs. of the Universal Life and Gen. Insurance Co. Ltd.
44 G. Gulberg, Lahore, West Pakistan.

Gurov, Yevgeni Petrovich; Soviet trade corporation official; b. 14; ed. Moscow Mechanical and Machine-Building Inst.
Employee *Stankoimport* (machinery) 37-41, 46-47; trade missions to Sweden 41-42, U.K. 42-45, Canada 45-46, Netherlands 51-56; Ministry of Foreign Trade 47-51; Chair. *Soyuznefteexport* (oil) 56-67; Trade Rep. in Greece 68-; mem. C.P.S.U. 40-; Order of Red Banner of Labour.
U.S.S.R. Trade Representation, Athens, Greece.

Gürsan, İhsan; Turkish politician; b. 1903; ed. Faculty of Political Science, Istanbul Univ.
Former Asst. Dir.-Gen. of Public Revenue, Ministry of Finance, and Dir.-Gen. of Agricultural Tools Enterprise; mem. Nat. Assembly 61-; fmr. Minister of Commerce, and Minister of Finance; Minister of Finance 65-66; Justice Party.
National Assembly, Ankara, Turkey.

Gurupadaswamy, M. S., M.A., LL.B.; Indian journalist and politician; b. 8 Jan. 1923; ed. Univs. of Mysore and Lucknow.
Practising lawyer 46-48; Editor *Prajamatha*, Bangalore 47-52; Pres. Mysore State Journalists Asscn. 50-51; mem. House of People 52-57; mem. Nat. Exec. Praja Socialist Party 57-63; Chair. Mysore State Praja Socialist Party 58-60; Sec. Parl. Group Praja Socialist Party 52-64; mem. Council of Studies 60-; Editor *Parliament Studies* 55-67; Union Minister of State for Atomic Energy 67, now Minister of State for Food and Agriculture.
Publs. *International Studies, Political Pilgrimage, Communalism.*
Ministry of Food and Agriculture, New Delhi, India.

Gusenkov, Pyotr Vasilyevich; Soviet chemist and politician; b. 1905; ed. training as technical chemist.
Deputy Minister of Health of U.S.S.R. (in charge of Medical Industry Enterprises) 53-67; U.S.S.R. Minister of Medical Industry 67-.
Ministry of Medical Industry, Moscow, U.S.S.R.

Gustaf VI Adolf; King of Sweden; b. 11 Nov. 1882.
Married (1) June 15, 1905, Princess Margaret (b. January 15, 1882, died May 1, 1920), daughter of Prince Arthur, Duke of Connaught; (2) November 3, 1923, Lady Louise Mountbatten (b. July 13, 1889, died March 7, 1965); succeeded to throne on death of his father 19 Oct. 50; heir: grandson, Crown Prince Carl Gustaf, b. 30 April 1946.
Royal Palace, Stockholm, Sweden.

Gustafson, Torsten, PH.D.; Swedish physicist; b. 8 May 1904; ed. Lund, Göttingen and Copenhagen Univs.
Professor of Theoretical Physics, Lund Univ. 39-; mem. Swedish Atomic Energy Research Council 45-64, Swedish Atomic Energy Del. 56-; del. European Organization for Nuclear Research 53-64; Dir. Nordic Inst. for Theoretical Atomic Physics 57-58, Chair. 63;

Govt. Advisory Del. on Research 63-; mem. of numerous Scandinavian Acads. of Science.
Publs. Papers on flow round airfoil-like bodies 27-36, on inertia currents in the oceans 36, on divergencies in quantum electrodynamics 37-47, on atomic nuclei 47-.
Gyllenkroks allé 13, Lund, Sweden.

Gustafsson, Carl Åke Torsten, PH.D.; Swedish geneticist; b. 8 April 1908; ed. Lunds Universitet, and in Stockholm and U.S.
Docent, Univ. of Lund 35, Research Assoc. 44; Prof. Univ. of Stockholm 47; Head, Inst. of Forest Genetics, Royal Coll. of Forestry, Stockholm 47, Prefect 67-; Guest Lecturer at various insts. and univs. throughout Europe, and in U.S.A., Thailand, India, Philippines, etc.; mem. Royal Physiographic Soc., Royal Acad. of Forestry and Agriculture, Royal Acad. of Sciences (all in Sweden), and Leopoldina Acad. of Natural Sciences (Germany), Royal Acad. of Sciences (Denmark), Nat. Acad. of Sciences (U.S.), etc.
Publs. 200 scientific articles; books of prose and poetry.
Kungl. Skogshögskolan, Stockholm 50, Sweden.

Gustov, Ivan Stepanovich; Soviet politician; b. 1911; ed. Higher Party School of the C.P.S.U. Central Cttee. and Velikie Luky Inst. of Agriculture.
Chairman Collective Farm and Dir. of a machine and tractor station 30-36; Head of a district Land Dept., Chair. of a district Soviet of Working People's Deputies, First Sec. of a District Cttee. of C.P.S.U. in Novosobirsk Region 36-49; Sec. Velikie Luky Regional Cttee. C.P.S.U. 50-55; First Vice-Chair., then Chair., Velikie Luky Regional Soviet 55-57; Second Sec., Pskov Regional Cttee. of C.P.S.U. 57-61, First Sec. 61-; Alt. mem. of C.P.S.U. Central Cttee. 61-; Deputy to U.S.S.R. Supreme Soviet; mem. C.P.S.U. 32-.
Pskov Regional Committee of C.P.S.U., Pskov, U.S.S.R.

Gut, H.E. Cardinal Benno; Swiss ecclesiastic; b. 1 April 1897; ed. Coll. of St. Anselm, and Bible Inst., Rome.
Ordained Priest 21; Prefect and Prof., Classical School, Einsiedeln; Prof. and Master of Choir of St. Anselm, Rome; Abbot 47; Superior-Gen. Benedictines, Rome 59-; created Cardinal by Pope Paul VI 67.
Collegio S. Anselmo, Rome, Italy.
Telephone: 5740372.

Guthrie, Douglas, M.D., D.LITT., F.R.C.S. (Edin.), F.R.C.P. (Edin.), F.R.S.E.; British surgeon; b. 8 Sept. 1885; ed. Univs. of Edinburgh, Jena and Paris.
Surgeon, Ear, Nose and Throat Dept., Royal Hospital for Sick Children 19-34; Lecturer on Diseases of Ear, Nose and Throat, School of Medicine, Edinburgh 20-45; Lecturer on History of Medicine, Univ. of Edinburgh 45-56; served as Major in R.A.M.C. in First and Second World Wars; Pres. Scottish Otological Society 25, Otology Section, Royal Society of Medicine 36-37; British Medical Asscn. (Edinburgh Branch) 36, Royal Physical Society of Edinburgh 37-46; Pres. and Founder, Scottish Society of the History of Medicine 48; Pres. Section of Medical History of Royal Soc. of Medicine 56; Curator and Librarian, Royal Society of Edinburgh; hon. mem. Otolaryngological Societies of Paris, Poland and Hungary, and of Spanish, American and Peruvian Societies of the History of Medicine; Fellow of Society of Antiquaries of Scotland.
Publs. *A History of Medicine* 45, *Lord Lister, His Life and Doctrine* 49, *From Witchcraft to Antisepsis* 54, *Janus in the Doorway* 63.
21 Clarendon Crescent, Edinburgh, Scotland.
Telephone: Dean 1820.

Guthrie, Sir Giles Connop McEacharn, Bt., O.B.E., D.S.C., J.P.; British airline executive; b. 21 March 1916; ed. Eton and Magdalene Coll., Cambridge.

Winner (with C. W. A. Scott) Portsmouth-Johannesburg Air Race 36; Traffic Officer, British Airways 38-39; Fleet Air Arm, Second World War 39-46; fmr. Managing Dir. Brown Shipley and Co. Ltd.; fmr. Dep. Chair. North Central Finance Ltd.; fmr. Dir. Prudential Assurance Co. Ltd., Radio Rentals Ltd. and other companies; Chair. and Chief Exec. B.O.A.C. 64-Dec. 68; Dir. B.E.A. 59-.
Office: B.O.A.C., London (Heathrow) Airport, Hounslow, Middx., England.

Guthrie, Malcolm, PH.D., B.SC.; British university professor; b. 10 Feb. 1903; ed. Northgate School, Ipswich, and Imperial Coll., London.
Missionary in Africa 32-41; Lecturer in Bantu Languages, School of Oriental and African Studies 42-47; Reader in Bantu Languages, Univ. of London 47-50; now Prof. of Bantu Languages, Univ. of London, and Head of Dept. of the Languages and Cultures of Africa, School of Oriental and African Studies, London.
Publs. *The Classification of the Bantu Languages* 48, *Bantu Word-Division* 48, *The Bantu Languages of Western Equatorial Africa* 53, *Bantu Sentence Structure* 61.
Brambletye, Cowden, nr. Edenbridge, Kent, England.

Guthrie, Randolph Hobson, B.S., LL.B.; American lawyer and business executive; b. 1905; ed. The Citadel, Charleston and Harvard Law School.
Senior Partner of Nixon, Mudge, Rose, Guthrie, Alexander and Mitchell and predecessor firms since 43; Chair. Board of Studebaker-Worthington, Inc. 63-.
Office: 20 Broad Street, New York, N.Y. 10005; Home: 157 Lake Drive, Mountain Lakes, New Jersey, U.S.A.
Telephone: 212-422-6767.

Guthrie, Robin (Robert Craig); British portrait and landscape painter; b. 15 June 1903; ed. Slade School, Univ. of London.
Worked as painter in France, Neths., Italy, U.S.A. and Canada; exhibitor at Goupil, Leicester and other London Galleries, New English Art Club, and with Royal Society of Portrait Painters (mem.) and Royal Acad.; One-Man exhibitions, London 26, 28, 38, 46; took representative exhibition of British Art to Bordeaux for French Ministry of Fine Arts 45; Dir. Museum School of Fine Art, Boston, Mass. 31-33; fmr. Instructor at Royal Coll. of Art; Instructor at the City and Guilds of London Art School, St. Martin's School of Art 36-65; work acquired by Tate Gallery, Nat. Portrait Gallery, British Museum, Manchester Art Gallery, Manchester Whitworth Inst., Bristol Municipal Art Gallery, Nat. Gallery of N.S.W., Nat. Gallery of Canada, Fogg Art Museum, Cambridge, Mass., Stoke-on-Trent Art Gallery, Carlyle Art Gallery, Victoria and Albert Museum, Ashmolean Museum, Worthing Art Gallery, etc.; executed Panel for Roman Catholic Hall, Chiswick; mem. Soc. of Mural Painters, Royal Portrait Soc. 60-.
1 Sydney Close, 76 Fulham Road, London, S.W.3, England.

Guthrie, Sir (William) Tyrone, Kt., M.A.; British theatrical producer; b. 2 July 1900; ed. Wellington Coll., and St. John's Coll., Oxford.
Producer Oxford Repertory Theatre 24, B.B.C. Belfast 25, Scottish Nat. Players 26, Cambridge Repertory Theatre 29; produced *The Anatomist* Westminster Theatre London 31 and thereafter many productions in London, including several seasons of classical plays at the Old Vic.; Dir. Old Vic and Sadler's Wells Theatres London 39-45; Dir. Northern Ireland Festival Co. 51; Dir. Old Vic 51-52; Artistic Dir. Shakespeare Festival, Stratford, Ontario 52-55; Tyrone Guthrie Theatre, Minneapolis; recent productions: *Gideon* (New York), *H.M.S. Pinafore, The Pirates of Penzance* (both in

London), *The Skin of Our Teeth, As You Like It, Dance of Death* (Minnesota), *Tartuffe, Volpone* (London), *The Anatomist* (Glasgow); Chancellor, Queen's Univ., Belfast 63-; Hon. Fellow, St. John's Coll. Oxford, Hon. D.Litt. from univs. and colls. in U.K., U.S. and Ireland.

Publs. *Squirrels' Cage and Other Microphone Plays* 31, *Theatre Prospect* 32, *Top of the Ladder* 50, *A Life in the Theatre* 60, *A New Theatre* 64, *In Various Directions* 66.

Annagh ma Kerrig, Doohat, Newbliss, Co. Monaghan, Ireland.

Gutiérrez, Julio César, DR. ECON.; Paraguayan economist and banker; b. 11 Feb. 1920; ed. Escuela Nacional de Comercio, Asunción, Universidad Nacional, Asunción, and Centro de Estudios Monetarios Latinamericano, Mexico.

Superintendent of Banks, Paraguay 50-56; Financial Adviser to Ministry of Finance 57-58; Nat. Financial Controller, Paraguay 59-62; Dir. of Seminary, Faculty of Econ. Sciences, Asunción 57-60, Univ. Prof. 60-62; Econ. Counsellor, Paraguayan Embassy, Washington 62-; Exec. Dir. Inter-American Devt. Bank (IDB) 64-.

Inter-American Development Bank, 808 17th Street, N.W., Washington, D.C. 20577; Home: 4000 Tunlaw Road, N.W., P.O.B. 326, Washington, D.C. 20007, U.S.A.

Gutiérrez Cano, Joaquín; Spanish international bank official; b. 20; ed. Univ. of Madrid.

Spanish Diplomatic Service 47-57; Pres. Spanish Fruit Producers' and Exporters' Asscn. 58; M.P. 58-; mem. Council of Inst. of Fiscal Studies 60-; Perm. Counsellor, National Economy; mem. Board Bank of Spain 62-, Bank of Industrial Credit 62-; Exec. Dir. for Spain, Italy, Greece and Portugal, International Bank for Reconstruction and Development (World Bank) 63-.

International Bank for Reconstruction and Development, 1818 H Street, N.W., Washington, D.C. 20433, U.S.A.

Gutiérrez Gómez, José, D.IUR., D.RER.POL.; Colombian diplomatist; b. 09; ed. Antioquia Univ.

Man. Cali Agricultural, Industrial and Mining Credit Bank 32-35, Uribe Angel Laboratories, Medellín 35-46; Chair. Nat. Asscn. of Industrialists (ANDI) 46-57; mem. Govt. Economic Cttee. 47-48, Economic Mission to Washington 48; del., with rank of Ambassador, Ninth Gen. Assembly of U.N. 52, Fourth Extraordinary Session, Inter-American Economic and Social Council, Rio de Janeiro 54; Mayor of Medellín 57; Ambassador to U.S. and to Council of the Organization of American States 57-60; Dir. Corporación Financiera Nacional 61-; Hon. D.Econ. (Antioquia Univ.).

Corporación Financiera Nacional, Medellín, Colombia.

Gutiérrez-Olivos, Sergio; Chilean lawyer and diplomatist; b. 26 July 1920; ed. Sacred Heart School, Santiago, Catholic Univ. of Chile and Inter-American Law Inst., New York.

Associate Professor of Civil Law, Catholic Univ. of Chile 45-51, Prof. of International Public Law 51-59, Dir. School of Law 51-54; Chilean Del. to numerous conferences 55-; Pres. Chilean Management Asscn. 58-59; Ambassador to Argentina 59-62, to United States 63-65; assoc. law firm Gutiérrez and Siebel 51-; now counsellor or mem. board several enterprises engaged in int. business including Westinghouse Electric Int. Co., American Screw (Chile) S.A., Williamson, Balfour & Co. S.A., Duncan Fox & Co. Ltd., Pan American Foundation, Gildemeister, S.A.C., Grace & Co. (Chile) S.A., Gibbs & Co. S.A.C., Ford Foundation, Industrias Kaiser (Argentina) S.A., and various domestic corpns.

Publs. *El Contrato de Transacción ante la Doctrina y la Jurisprudencia* 45, *Mar Territorial y Derecho Moderno* 55, *Alberdi* 62, *Subdesarrollo, Integración y Alianza*

63, *El Drenaje de Recursos Humanos: problema nacional e internacional* 65, *The Chilean Development Banks* 65.

Huérfanos 1376, Santiago, Chile.

Gutiérrez Roldán, Pascual; Mexican financier and oil executive; b. 03; ed. Nat. School of Agriculture and School of Economy of Nat. Univ. of Mexico.

Federal Currency Comptroller 33-41; Dir.-Gen. Banco Capitalizador de Ahorros 41-51, Altos Hornos de México 51-58, Petróleos Mexicanos 58-64; Prof. of Credit and Monetary Theory and of Credit Institutions and Operations, Nat. Univ. of Mexico 36-40; French Legion of Honour 60, Venezuelan Order of the Liberator 60; Federal German Order of Merit 61, Chilean Order of Merit 61, Italian Order of Merit 61, Brazilian Nat. Order of the Southern Cross 62.

Monte Olimpo 110, Mexico City, Mexico.

Gutt, Camille, LL.D.; Belgian barrister; b. 14 Nov. 1884; ed. Brussels Univ.

Barrister and journalist 06; volunteer in Belgian Army 14-18; Sec.-Gen. of Belgian War Material Purchasing Comm. London 16; Sec.-Gen. of Belgian Del. to Reparations Comm. 19; Chief Sec. to Minister of Finance 20; Asst. Del. to Reparations Comm. 24; Asst. to M. Francqui, Chancellor of the Exchequer 26; Minister of Finance 34; in Pierlot Cabinet Feb. 39; arrived in London Aug. 40; Min. of Finance 39-45; Nat. Defence and Communications 40-42; Economic Affairs 40-45; Managing Dir. Int. Monetary Fund 46-51; mem. Board Banque Lambert, Brussels; decorations include Grand Cordon of Order of Leopold, of Order of Orange Nassau (Neths.), of Order of Crown of Oak (Luxembourg), Grand Officier de la Légion d'Honneur (France), Ordre pour le Mérite (Austria), etc.

70 Avenue Bel Air, Brussels, Belgium.

Guttenberg, Hermann von, D.PHIL.; German botanist; b. 13 Jan. 1881; ed. Graz, Vienna and Leipzig Univs.

Asst. Botanical Inst. Graz 08, Berlin 10, Prof. Berlin 12; Prof. of Botany, Dir. Botanical Inst. and Garden, Rostock Univ. 23-58, Prof. Emeritus 58-; mem. Leopoldina Acad. of Natural Sciences, New York Acad. of Science; co-editor *Planta, Botanische Studien*; Hon. D.Med., Hon. Senator.

Publs. *Das Bewegungsgewebe* 26, *Der primäre Bau der Angiospermenwurzel* 40, *Der Gymnospermenwurzel* 41, *Die Physiologischen Scheiden* 43, *Lehrbuch der Allgemeinen Botanik* (6th edition) 63, *Die Histogenese höherer Pflanzen I* 60, *II* 61, *III* 65, *Pflanzenanatomie* 66.

Zelckstrasse 2, 25 Rostock, German Democratic Republic.

Telephone: Rostock 23945.

Gutton, André Henry Georges; French architect and town planner; b. 8 Jan. 1904; ed. Ecole nationale supérieure des beaux arts and Inst. d'Urbanisme de l'Univ. de Paris.

Architect for private buildings and nat. palaces 36-; Prof. Inst. of Town Planning, Sorbonne 43-49; Prof. of Theory of Architecture, Nat. School of Fine Arts 49-58, of Town Planning 58-; Technical Counsellor, Govt. of Syria 51; mem. Exec. Cttee. Union internationale des architectes 49-, Pres. Town Planning Comm. 51; Consultant Town-Planner Canton of Geneva 60; Pres. Parisian Order of Architects 61-; Vice-Pres. Congress of Architects 65; mem. Acad. of Architecture, Royal Acad. of Belgium; Hon. Fellow American Inst. of Architects; Int. Prize for plan for Place des Nations, Geneva 58; Officier Légion d'Honneur, Knight, Order of Orange-Nassau, of Dannebrog; Officier des Arts et Lettres.

Major works: Architectural Plans for Institut de France 43, Post Office Buildings, Paris 44, The Opera 50, Post Office Buildings at Versailles, Nancy, Besançon, Chateauroux, Roanne, Neuilly-sur-Seine and schools

and offices in France; Town Planning: Plans for Nancy 38, Dakar (Senegal), Boulogne, Issy 45, Aleppo (Syria) 52, Sihanoukville (Cambodia) 60.
Publs. *Charte de l'Urbanisme* 41, *Conversations sur l'Architecture*: (*L'edifice dans la cité, La maison des hommes, les églises et les temples, les universités, L'urbanisme au service de l'homme*).
Office: Institut de France, 1 rue de Seine, Paris 6e; Home: 23 *bis* quai Conti, Paris 6e, France.
Telephone: Danton 59-56.

Guttuso, Renato; Italian painter; b. 2 Jan. 1912.
Mem. of the "Corrente" group 40-42; one of the founders of the group "Fronte Nuovo delle Arti" 47; rep. at Dunn Int. Exhbn., London 63; Prize for Young Artists 24th Biennale, Venice, one-man show at 26th Biennale, Second Int. Prize for "La Spiaggia" 28th Biennale; Titular Prof. of Design, Liceo Artistico Rome.
Ciancaleoni 1, Rome, Italy.

Guy, William Lewis, B.S., M.S.; American farmer and politician; b. 30 Sept. 1919; ed. North Dakota State Univ., Minnesota Univ.
Lieutenant U.S. Navy 42-46; Asst. County Agent, Cass County 46; Livestock Salesman 47; co-owner Guy-Bean Farm Supply 48; farmer 48-; State Rep. Cass County 59; Gov. North Dakota 61-; Chair. Missouri River States Comm. 61-; Democrat.
1111 4th Street, Bismarck, North Dakota, U.S.A.

Guyon, Edouard Félix, L. en DROIT; French diplomatist; b. 24 Feb. 1902; ed. Ecole des Sciences Politiques, Paris.
Entered diplomatic service 27; Counsellor in Berne 45, Minister 46; Minister in Tel-Aviv 49-52, Ambassador 52; Ambassador to Uruguay 52-57; Ambassador to Luxembourg 57-62; post in Ministry of Foreign Affairs 62-, special leave 65-; Officier de la Légion d'Honneur.
40 boulevard Gouvion-Saint-Cyr, Paris 17e; and 98 boulevard de Cimiez, Nice, France.

Guzenko, Partenty Vasilievich; Soviet politician; b. 1913; ed. Agricultural Inst. in Ordjonikidze.
Agronomist, Krasnodar Territory 33-41; Soviet Army 41-45; mem. C.P.S.U. 41-; work at Krasnodar Territory, C.P.S.U.; First Sec., Arkhangelsk District Cttee., C.P.S.U.; First Sec., Brukhovetsk District Cttee., C.P.S.U. 45-49; work at Cen. Cttee., C.P.S.U. 49-56; Sec. Kemerovo District Cttee., C.P.S.U. 56-62; Chair., Exec. Cttee., Kemerovo Regional Soviet of Workers' Deputies 62-; Deputy, Supreme Soviet of the U.S.S.R.
Kemerovo Regional Soviet of Workers' Deputies, Kemerovo, U.S.S.R.

Guzmán, Martín Luiz; Mexican writer, journalist and politician; b. 6 Oct. 1887; ed. Escuela Nacional Preparatoria and Mexico Univ.
Editorial Staff, *El Imparcial* 08; took part in Mexican Revolution 13; Co-founder *El Honor Nacional* 13; Counsellor to Minister of War 14; exile 14-20; Editor-in-Chief *El Heraldo de México* 20; Founder *El Mundo* 22; mem. Chamber of Deputies 22-24; lived in Spain 24-30; Founder and Man. Dir. *Tiempo* (Mexico) 42-; Pres. Comisión Nacional de los Libros de Texto Gratuitos 59.
Publs. *La querella de México* 15, *A orillas del Hudson* 22, *El águila y la serpeinte* 28, *Aventuras democráticas* 29, *La sombra del caudillo* 29, *Javier Mina* 32, *Filadelfia, paraiso de conspiradores* 33, *El hombre y sus armas* 38, *Campos de batalla* 39, *Panoramas políticos y la causa del pobre* 40, *Memorias de Pancho Villa* 51, *Muertes históricas* 58, *Otras páginas* 59, *Academia e Islas Marías* 59, *Axkaná González en las elecciones* 60, *Maestros rurales y Piratas y Corsarios* 60, *Necesidad de cumplir*

las leyes de Reforma 63, *Febrero de 1913* 63, *Crónicas de mi destierro* 63.
Tiempo, General Prim 38, Apdo. 1122, Mexico, D.F., Mexico.

Guzmán Neyra, Alfonso; Mexican politician and judge; b. 06; ed. National Univ. of Mexico.
President, Supreme Tribunal of Justice, Veracruz; Dep. for First District, Veracruz; Pres. Fed. Cttee. for Conciliation and Arbitration; Dir. Govt. Works in Fed. District; Pres. Regional Cttee. of Partido Revolucionario Institucional (P.R.I.); Pres. Supreme Court of Justice 59-66, Judge Fourth Chamber 66-.
Supreme Court of Justice, Mexico, D.F., Mexico.

Gvati, Chaim; Israeli farmer and politician; b. 29 Jan. 1901; ed. Vilna, Poland, and Russian university.
Emigrated to Israel 24; mem. Kibbutz 24-, mem. Kibbutz Meuchad Central Cttee. 42-45; Chair. Security and Farming Cttees. of The Agricultural Centre 45-49; Dir.-Gen. Ministry of Agriculture 50-57; Sec. Ichud Hakvutzot Veakibbutzim 59-62; Sec. Federation of Kibbutz Movement 63-64; Minister of Agriculture Nov. 64-; Mapai.
Kibbutz Yifat, and Ministry of Agriculture, Jerusalem, Israel.

Gwinn, William Persons; American aircraft executive; b. 22 Sept. 1907; ed. Gunnery Preparatory School, Washington, Conn.
Joined Pratt & Whitney Aircraft Div. of United Aircraft Corpn. 27, Sales Dept. 27-37, W. Coast rep. 37-42, Asst. Gen. Man. 42, Gen. Man. 43, Vice-Pres. 46, Pres. and Chief Admin. Officer 56-, and mem. Exec. Cttee.; Dir. United Aircraft Corpn., United Aircraft of Canada Ltd., United Aircraft Int., Hartford Nat. Bank & Trust Co., Soc. for Savings, Conn. Mutual Life Ins. Co., Phoenix Ins. Co., Transportation Asscn. of America, Hartford Hospital; Trustee, Rensselaer Polytechnic Inst., Trinity Coll. (Life), etc.; Hon. Dr. Eng. (Rensselaer Polytechnic Inst.), D.Sc. (Trinity Coll.) 64.
60 Ledyard Road, West Hartford, Conn., U.S.A.

Gwira, Kobina Daniel; Ghanaian barrister and diplomatist; b. 2 Jan. 1923; ed. St. Peter's School, Sekondi, Adisadel Coll., Cape Coast, Trinity Coll., Dublin, and King's Inn, Dublin.
Ghana Bar 54-61; High Commr. for Ghana in Sierra Leone 61-66; Amb. to Yugoslavia 66-67, to Bulgaria 67-.
Embassy of Ghana, Sofia, Bulgaria; and P.O.B. 104, Sekondi, Ghana.

Gwynn, Denis Rolleston, B.A., D.LITT., F.R.HIST.S.; Irish university professor; b. 6 March 1893; ed. National Univ. of Ireland.
Edited weekly *New Ireland* 15; served in France First World War 17; journalism in France and London 20-26; author, journalist and publisher, Literary Dir., Burns Oates & Washbourne, and editor *Dublin Review* 33-39; Prof. of Modern Irish History, Univ. of Cork 47-63; Ed. Cork Univ. Press 54-63; mem. Royal Irish Acad. and Irish Acad. of Letters.
Publs. *The Struggle for Catholic Emancipation* 29, *The Life of John Redmond* 33, *Life and Death of Roger Casement* 32, *The Second Spring* 42, *Young Ireland and 1848* 48, *Cardinal Wiseman* 50, *The History of Partition* 50, *Father Luigi Gentili* 51, *Thomas Francis Meagher* 62, etc.
Rosenallis, Seamount Road, Malahide, Co. Dublin, Ireland.

Gyani, Lt.-Gen. Prem Singh, O.B.E.; Indian army officer; b. 10; ed. Rashtra Indian Military Coll., Dehra Dun, and R.M.A., Woolwich.
Commissioned and joined Regt. of Artillery 32; passed Staff Coll., Quetta 41; commanded Field Regt. Burma

theatre 44-46; Dir. of Artillery, Army H.Q. 47-50; attended Imperial Defence Coll., London 51; commanded Infantry Brigade 52-54; alternate del. (military), Int. Comm. for Truce Supervision and Control, Laos 54-55; Commdt. Defence Services Staff Coll., Wellington, India 55-59; G.O.C. Infantry Div. 59; Commdr. UN Emergency Force Gaza Dec. 59-64; UN Observer in Cyprus 64; Commdr. UN Cyprus Force March 64-June 64; Pres. Birla Inst. of Technology, Ranchi 65-.
3H Sector 5, Chandigarh, Punjab, India.

György, Paul, M.D.; American physician; b. 7 April 1893; ed. Univ. of Budapest.
Prof. of Pediatrics, Heidelberg Univ. 27-33; Visiting Research worker, Cambridge Univ. 33-35; Visiting Asst. Prof. of Pediatrics, Western Reserve Univ., Cleveland 35-37; Assoc. Pediatrist, Babies' and Children's Hospital, Cleveland 35-44; Assoc. Prof. of Pediatrics, **Univ. of Pa. 44-46, Prof. of Clinical Pediatrics 46-50,** Prof. of Nutrition in Pediatrics 50-54; Prof. of Pediatrics 54; Dir. of Pediatrics, Philadelphia General Hospital 57-63, Prof. Emeritus 58-; Hon. M.D. (Heidelberg); discoverer and co-discoverer of the vitamins Riboflavin, Pyridoxine, Vitamin H (Biotin).
201 Curwen Road, Rosemont, Pa. 19010, U.S.A.

Gyselynck, Léon, D.LL.; Belgian university professor; b. 11 July 1891; ed. Athénée Royal, Antwerp, and Univ. of Brussels.
Member Bar of Antwerp 19-47; Hon. Deputy Judge Court of 1st Instance; Hon. lecturer Inst. Supérieur de Commerce de l'Etat, Antwerp 32; lecturer Int. Law, Brussels Univ. 35, Prof. 44, now Hon. Prof.; founder and mem. Board Inst. Royal des Relations Internationales, Brussels 46; Pres. Asscn. Belge des Banques, Antwerp; Hon. Chair. Board Banque d'Anvers; Pres. Amis de la Maison de Rubens; Pres. Fonds de Dotation Musée Plantin Moretus, etc.; Chevalier Ordre de Léopold; Grand Officer Order of the Belgian Crown; Grand Officer Order of Léopold II, Commdr. Order of Merit, Italy.
Publ. *L'Enseignement des Relations internationales* 52.
37 Berkenlaan, Antwerp, Belgium.

H

Haack, Robert William; American financial executive; b. 15 Feb. 1917; ed. Hope Coll. and Harvard Business School.
Naval service, Second World War; with Robert W. Baird & Co. (Milwaukee securities firm) until 64, Partner 50-64; Pres. Nat. Asscn. of Securities Dealers, Washington 64-67; Pres. New York Stock Exchange 67-.
New York Stock Exchange, 11 Wall Street, New York 5, N.Y., U.S.A.

Haak, Jan Friedrich Wilhelm; South African lawyer and politician; b. 20 April 1917; ed. Prince Albert School and Univ. of Stellenbosch.
Attorney, Bellville, Cape Town 45-48; Advocate, Cape Bar 60; Mayor of Bellville 49-52; M.P. 53-; Deputy Minister of Econ. Affairs 61-64, Deputy Minister of Mines June 62-64, Deputy Minister of Planning Dec. 62-64; Minister of Mines and Planning Aug. 64-67, of Econ. Affairs Jan. 67-; mem. Chief Council of Nationalist Party 51-.
9047, Cape Town, Republic of South Africa.
Telephone: 34156.

Hába, Alois; Czechoslovak composer; b. 21 June 1893; ed. Kromeritz School and Conservatoires of Prague, Vienna and Berlin.
Professor, Acad. of Music and Dramatic Arts, Prague 45-51; mem. Czechoslovak Acad. and Société Internationale pour la Musique Contemporaine; Honoured Artist 63.
Written many works, including *Cesta života, Fantaisie Symphonique*, etc.; and three operas: *Matka, Nová země* and *Přijd Království Tvé*; publ. a number of books on music.
c/o U družstva Práce 59, Prague 4, Podolí, Czechoslovakia.

Habe, Hans; American (b. Austrian) writer; b. 12 Feb. 1911; ed. Franz Joseph Gymnasium, Vienna, and Univs. of Vienna and Heidelberg.
Former newspaperman and reporter, Vienna; fmr. Editor-in-Chief *Der Morgen*, Vienna; fmr. League of Nations Corresp. *Prager Tagblatt*, Geneva; served in French and U.S. Armies, Second World War; Editor-in-Chief *Die Neue Zeitung* after Second World War, later Founder and Editor-in-Chief *Münchner Illustrierte* and *Echo der Woche* (Munich); numerous decorations; Fellow, Boston Univ.
Publs. *Three Over the Frontier* 36, *A Time Collapses* 38, *Sixteen Days* 39, *A Thousand Shall Fall* (film *Cross of Lorraine*) 41, *Kathrine* 43, *Aftermath* 47, *Walk in Darkness* (also play) 48, *Black Earth* 52, *Our Love Affair with Germany* 52, *All My Sins* 55, *Off Limits* 56, *The Devil's Agent* 57, *Ilona* 60, *The Countess* 62, *Anatomy of Hatred* 64, *The Mission* 65, *Im Jahre Null* 66, *Christopher and his Father* 67, *Gentlemen of the Jury* 67.
Casa Acacia, Via Muraccio, Ascona, Ticino, Switzerland.
Telephone: Ascona 22383.

Habeck, Fritz, DR.IUR.; Austrian writer; b. 8 Sept. 1916; ed. Univ. of Vienna.
Served in German Army during Second World War; Asst. Man. Josefstadt Theatre, Vienna 46; radio producer in Vienna 53-; Goethe Award of City of Vienna, City Prize of Vienna, Austrian State Prize, Handel-Mazzetti Prize, Vienna Children's Book Prize 60, 61, 63, 67, State Children's Book Prize 63, 67, Wildgans Prize of Austrian Industry 64.
Publs. Novels: *Der Scholar vom linken Galgen* 41, *Der Tanz der sieben Teufel* 50, *Das Boot kommt nach Mitternacht* 51, *Das zerbrochene Dreieck* 53, *Ronan Gobain* 56,

Der Ritt auf dem Tiger 58, *Der Kampf um die Barbacane* 60, *Die Stadt der grauen Gesichter* 61, *Der verliebte Oesterreicher* 61, *Der einäugige Reiter* 63, *In eigenem Auftrag* (Selections) 63, *Der Piber* 65, *Die Insel über den Wolken* 65, *König Artus* 65, *Aufstand der Salzknechte* 67, *Salzburg-Spiegel* 67, *Marianne und der Wilde Mann* 68; Plays: *Zwei und zwei ist vier* 48, *Baisers mit Schlag* 50, *Marschall Ney* 54.
Armbrustergasse 10, 1190 Vienna, Austria.
Telephone: 0222-36-57-593.

Haberler, Gottfried, DR.RER.POL., D.IUR.; Austrian-born American economist; b. 20 July 1900; ed. Vienna Univ.
Graduate student London, Harvard and other Univs. 27-29; lecturer, later Prof. of Economics and Statistics, Vienna Univ. 28-36; Visiting lecturer, Harvard Univ. 31-32; attached to Financial Section, League of Nations, Geneva 34-36; settled in U.S.A. 36; Prof. of Economics, Harvard Univ. 36-; Assoc. Board of Govs., Fed. Reserve System, Washington 43; Pres. Int. Economic Asscn. 50-51, Hon. Pres. 53-; Pres. Nat. Bureau of Economic Research 55; mem. American Economic Asscn. (Vice-Pres. 48), Royal Economic Soc.; Charter mem. Econometric Soc.; Pres. American Econ. Asscn. 63-.
Office: Littauer Center 326, Harvard University, Cambridge, Mass. 02138; Home: 2 Mercer Circle, Cambridge, Mass. 02138, U.S.A.

Habib-Deloncle, Michel, L. ès L., L. en D.; French lawyer and politician; b. 26 Nov. 1921; ed. Ecole libre des Sciences Politiques, Paris and Faculties of Law and Letters (Sorbonne), Univ. of Paris.
Resistance Movement 41-45; Journalist, *France Catholique* 45-53; Sec.-Gen. Parl. Group Rassemblement du Peuple Français 48-54; mem. Asscn. of the French Union 54-58; Deputy 58-; Sec. of State to the Ministry of Foreign Affairs 62-66, to the Ministry of Educ. 66-67; mem. European Parl. 67-; Int. Relations Del., Exec. Cttee. Union Démocratique pour la Ve République 68-.
17 rue Margueritte, Paris 17e, France.
Telephone: 924-57-65.

Hachette, Jean-Louis, LIC. en DR.; French publisher; b. 30 June 1925; ed. Collège Stanislas, Paris, and Faculté de Droit, Paris.
Joined Librairie Hachette (founded by great-grandfather in 1826) 46; entire career spent with Librairie Hachette.
8 rue de Presbourg, Paris 16e, France.

Hachey, Henry Benedict, M.B.E., E.D., M.SC., LL.D., F.R.S.C.; Canadian oceanographer; b. 7 June 1901; ed. St. Francis Xavier and McGill Univs.
Lecturer, St. Francis Xavier Univ. 22-23; Nat. Research Council Grant, McGill Univ. 23-25; Asst. McGill Univ. 25-26; Prof. of Physics, Univ. of New Brunswick 26-28; Oceanographer, Fisheries Research Board of Canada 28-46, Principal Oceanographer 46-51, Dir. 51-; Officer-in-Charge Hudson Bay Fisheries Expedition 30; Lieut.-Col., army 40-46; Hon. Lecturer, Univ. of New Brunswick 50-59; fmr. Chief Oceanographer, Fisheries Research Board of Canada, Sec. Canadian Cttee. on Oceanography; Consultant Oceanographer 64-; Board of Govs., St. Francis Xavier Univ. 64-; Fellow, Royal Soc. of Canada.
Publs. Scientific papers chiefly on hydrography and hydrodynamics of Canadian waters.
132 Edward Street, St. Andrew's, New Brunswick, Canada.
Telephone: 529-3144.

Hacker, Louis Morton, M.A., LL.D.; American university professor and administrator; b. 17 March 1899; ed. Columbia Univ.

Taught history and econs. at Ohio State, Wis., Hawaii, Pa. State, Cambridge, Yeshiva, Fairleigh Dickinson Univs., Utah State Agricultural, Army War, Nat. War Colls., and New School for Social Research, New York; Lecturer, Columbia Univ. 35-48, Prof. of Econs. 48-; Dean, School of Gen. Studies 49-58; Harmsworth Prof. of American History, Oxford Univ. and Fellow, Queen's Coll. 48-49; Editor and contributor of *New Int. Encyclopaedia, Encyclopaedia of Social Sciences, Columbia Encyclopaedia*; Editor *The American Century* Series; Hon. LL.D. (Hawaii).

Publs. *The United States since 1865* (with B. B. Kendrick) 32, *The Farmer is Doomed* 33, *A Short History of the New Deal* 34, *The United States: A Graphic History* 37, *American Problems of Today* 39, *Triumph of American Capitalism* 40, *The United States and its place in World Affairs* (with others) 43, *Shaping of the American Tradition* 47, *New Industrial Relations* (with others) 49, *The United States in the Twentieth Century* (with H. S. Zahler) 52, *Government Assistance to Universities in Great Britain* (with others) 52, *Capitalism and the Historians* (with others) 53, *Alexander Hamilton in the American Tradition* 57, *American Capitalism* 57, *Larger View of the University* 61, *Documents in American Economic History* (2 vols.) 61, *The World of Andrew Carnegie, 1865-1901* 68.

430 West 116th Street, New York, N.Y. 10027; and Columbia University, New York, N.Y. 10027, U.S.A. Telephone: 212-666-9252.

Hackett, Gen. Sir John Winthrop, G.C.B., C.B.E., D.S.O., M.C., B.LITT., M.A., LL.D.; British army officer; b. 5 Nov. 1910; ed. Geelong Grammar School (Australia) and New Coll., Oxford.

Commissioned 31; Palestine 36; Transjordan Frontier Force 37-39, Syria 41; Sec. Comm. of Control, Syria and Lebanon; G.S.O. 2, 9th Army, Western Desert 42; G.S.O. 1, Raiding Forces, G.H.Q., Middle East Land Forces; Commdr. 4th Parachute Brigade 43; Italy 43; Arnhem 44; Commdr. Transjordan Frontier Force 47; D.Q.M.G., British Army of the Rhine (B.A.O.R.) 52; Commdr. 20th Armoured Brigade 54; G.O.C. 7th Armoured Div. 56-58; Commandant, Royal Mil. Coll. of Science 58-61; G.O.C. in C., Northern Ireland Command 61-63; Deputy Chief of Imperial Gen. Staff 63-64; Deputy Chief of Gen. Staff, Ministry of Defence 64-66; C.-in-C. British Army of the Rhine (B.A.O.R.) 66-68 and Commdr. Northern Army Group 66-68; Principal Designate, King's Coll., London (68-).

Commander-in-Chief's House, H.Q. B.A.O.R., B.F.P.O. 40. Telephone: Rhine Army 2222.

Hackworth, Green H., A.B., LL.B.; American lawyer; b. 23 Jan. 1883; ed. Valparaiso, Georgetown and George Washington Univs.

Barrister 12; Attorney State Dept. 16-25; mem. Advisory Cttee. on Research in Int. Law of Harvard Law School; mem. Permanent Court of Arbitration The Hague 37; mem. U.S. Del. Tripartite Conf. Moscow 43; U.S. Del. Int. Security Conversations Dumbarton Oaks, Washington, D.C. 44; Adviser to Sec. of State Inter-American Conf. on Problems of War and Peace, Mexico City 45; Chair. United Nations Comm. of Jurists, Washington, D.C. 45; Adviser U.N. Conf., San Francisco 45; mem. Int. Court of Justice 46-61, Pres. 55-58; Senior Adviser to first part of first session of Gen. Assembly and meetings of Security Council U.N. held in London 46: mem. Inst. de Droit International; Hon. LL.D. (Univs. of Kentucky, Valparaiso and Calif.). Publ. *Digest of International Law* (8 vols.).

3714 Morrison Street, N.W., Washington, D.C., U.S.A. Telephone: Woodley 6-2487.

Hadari, Dr. Osman El; Sudanese diplomatist; b. 20; ed. Gordon Coll., Khartoum, Khartoum School of Science and Faculty of Medicine, Univ. of Alexandria. Houseman, Alexandria Hospitals 49-50; private medical practice 50-56; Ambassador to Pakistan 56-59, to U.S.A. 59-64, to United Arab Republic 64-.

Embassy of the Sudan, Cairo, United Arab Republic.

Haddow, Sir Alexander, Kt., F.R.S., F.R.S.E., F.R.S.M., M.B., CH.B., PH.D., M.D., D.SC.; British pathologist; b. 18 Jan. 1907; ed. Broxburn High School, and Univ. of Edinburgh.

Carnegie Research Student and House Physician, Royal Infirmary of Edinburgh; later Davidson Research Fellow and Lecturer in Bacteriology, Univ. of Edinburgh; Laura de Saliceto Student Univ. of London; Prof. of Experimental Pathology, Univ. of London 46-; Dir. Chester Beatty Research Inst., Royal Cancer Hospital London; Chair. B.B.C. Science Consultative Group; fmr. lay mem. Press Council; Pres. Medical Asscn. for the Prevention of War; Past Pres. Int. Union against Cancer; mem. Grand Council, Scientific Advisory Cttee., British Empire Cancer Campaign, Soc. for Study of Growth and Devt. (U.S.), Exec. Council Ciba Foundation; life mem. Royal Medical Soc. of Edinburgh; Fellow, N.Y. Acad. of Sciences; mem. Pathological Soc. of G.B. and Ireland, Chemical Soc., Genetical Soc., Acad. royale de médecine de Belgique; Hon. mem. Czechoslovak Medical Soc.; Foreign mem. American Acad. of Arts and Sciences, Acad. of Medical Sciences of U.S.S.R.; Chevalier de la Légion d'Honneur; Officer Order of Don Carlos Finlay (Cuba); Gold Medal, Worshipful Soc. of Apothecaries of London; Hon. M.D. (Perugia Univ.) 57.

Chester Beatty Research Institute, Institute of Cancer Research, Royal Cancer Hospital, Fulham Road, London, S.W.3, England. Telephone: 01-352-8133.

Hadj, Messali Ahmed bin; Algerian politician; b. 98. Service in French Army, First World War; f. independence movement L'Etoile Nord-Africaine 25, banned and imprisoned 29, 34, 35; f. *Al Oumma* (The Nation) 29; f. Algerian People's Party and imprisoned for subsequent disturbances 36, 39-41, sentenced to sixteen years' hard labour 41, pardoned, placed in enforced residence 43-45; restored as nationalist leader but then sent to Brazzaville 45-47; f. Movement for the Triumph of Democratic Liberties (M.T.L.D.) (later split into M.N.A. and F.L.N.) 47; placed in enforced residence, France 52-62; fmr. Pres. M.N.A. Algiers, Algeria.

Hadley, Morris, A.B., LL.B.; American lawyer; b. 21 March 1894; ed. Groton School, Yale Univ., and Harvard Law School.

Army service (Major) in Europe 17-19; legal practice in New York City 21-; Trustee, Carnegie Corpn. 47-67 (Chair. 55-66); Partner, Milbank, Tweed, Hadley & McCloy; Trustee, N.Y. Public Library (Pres. 43-58); Hon. LL.D. (Yale, Univ. of Nevada). Publs. *The Citizen and the Law* 41, *Arthur Twining Hadley* 48.

1 Chase Manhattan Plaza, New York, N.Y., U.S.A. Telephone: 212-422-2660.

Hadow, Reginald Michael, C.M.G.; British diplomatist; b. 17 Aug. 1915; ed. Berkhamsted School and King's Coll., Cambridge.

Indian Civil Service 37-48; Foreign Office 48-52; Private Sec. to Minister of State for Foreign Affairs 49-52; Head of Chancery, Mexico City 52-54; Foreign Office 55, Head of Levant Dept. and Counsellor 58; Counsellor, Paris 59-62; Head of News Dept., Foreign Office 62-65; Ambassador to Israel 65-.

British Embassy, Tel-Aviv, Israel.

Haedens, Kléber Gustave; French writer and critic; b. 11 Dec. 1913; ed. Prytanée Militaire de La Flèche, Inst. Montesquieu de Libourne and Ecole Supérieure de Commerce et d'Industrie de Bordeaux.
Literary and Film Critic *Présent*; Drama Critic *Paris-Soir*; Sport Critic *Action Française* and *Figaro* 37-45; Theatre and Film Critic *L'Epoque*; Literary Editor *Samedi-Soir*; Literary Critic *Paris-Presse* 51-, *Nouveau Candide* 62-, *le Journal du Dimanche* 68-; Prix Interallié 66.
Publs. Essays: *Gérard de Nerval* 39, *Paradoxe sur le roman* 41, *Une histoire de la littérature francaise* 43; Novels: *l'Ecole des parents* 37, *Magnolia Jules* 38, *Une jeune Serpente* 40, *Salut au Kentucky* 47, *Adieu à la rose* 55, *L'été finit sous les tilleuls* 66.
Domaine de la Bourdette, Aureville, 31 Castanet-Tolosan, France.
Telephone: 85-21-61.

Haekkerup, Hans; Danish politician; b. 25 Dec. 1907. Entered Ministry of Finance 34; appointed Chief of Bureau 50; mem. of Parl. (Social Democrat Party) 45-; Minister of Justice 53-64, of Interior 64-67.
C. F. Richs V.58, Copenhagen F, Denmark.

Haekkerup, Per; Danish politician; b. 25 Dec. 1915; ed. Univ. of Copenhagen.
Member, City Council of Copenhagen 46-50; mem. *Folketing* (Parl.) 50-; Pres. Social-Democratic Youth Movement 46-52; Gen. Sec., Int. Union of Socialist Youth 46-54; mem. Consultative Assembly, Council of Europe 53-62; Econ. Editor *Aktuelt* 56-61; Minister of Foreign Affairs 62-66; Parl. Spokesman and Floor Leader of Social Democratic Party Nov. 66-.
Publ. *Danmarks Undenrigs-politik* 65.
Folketinget, Christiansborg, Copenhagen K; Home: Niels Juelsgade 13, Copenhagen K, Denmark.
Telephone: Minerva 301.

Haferkamp, Wilhelm; German Common Market official; b. 1 July 1923; ed. Universität zu Köln.
Head of Social Policy Dept. of Deutscher Gewerkschaftsbund (German Trade Union Fed.) 50, mem. Exec. Cttee. and Head of Econ. Dept. 62-67; Socialist mem. Landtag of North Rhine-Westphalia 58-66, 67; mem. Combined Comm. of European Communities July 67-; mem. Board Volkswagen Foundation; mem. Supervisory Board Hoesch A.G., Thyssen Röhrenwerke A.G.
Commission of the European Communities, 23 Avenue de la Joyeuse Entrée, Brussels, Belgium.

Hafez, Maj.-Gen. Amin El; Syrian army officer and politician; b. 11.
Former Military Attaché in Argentina; took part in the revolution of March 1963; Dep. Prime Minister, Mil. Gov. of Syria and Minister of Interior March-Aug. 63; Minister of Defence and Army Chief of Staff July-Aug. 63; Pres. of Revolutionary Council and C.-in-C. of Armed Forces July 63; Prime Minister Nov. 63-May 64, Oct. 64-Sept. 65; Chair. of Presidency Council 65-66.
Damascus, Syria.

Hafstein, Jóhann; Icelandic politician; b. 19 Sept. 1915; ed. Univ. of Iceland.
Law studies in England 38-39; Man., later Gen. Man., Independence Party 39-52; Gen. Man. Fisheries Bank of Iceland 52-63; Town Councillor, Reykjavík 46-58; mem. Althing 46-; Minister of Justice and Industry 63-.
Ministry of Justice, Reykjavík, Iceland.

Haftmann, Werner, DR. PHIL.; German art historian and writer; b. 28 April 1912; ed. Univs. of Berlin and Göttingen.
First Asst. Inst. of History of Art, Florence 35-40; Dozent in Art History, State High School for Fine Arts, Hamburg 51-55; Freelance writer 56-66; Dir. Nat. Gallery, Berlin 66-; Lessing Prize, City of Hamburg 62; Goethe-Plakette (Hesse) 64.

Publs. *Das italienische Säulenmonument* 39, *Paul Klee Wege bildnerischen Denkens* 50, 61, *Malerei im XX. Jahrhundert* (2 vols.) 54, 56, 62, 65, *Emil Nolde* 58, *E. W. Nay* 60, *Skizzenbuch: Zur Kultur der Gegenwart* 61, *Nolde-Ungemalte Bilder* 63, *Wols-Aufzeichnungen* 63.
Berlin-Charlottenburg, Knesebeckstr. 33, Germany.

Hag-Ali, Nasr El-, B.A.; Sudanese university official; b. 07; ed. Gordon Memorial Coll. and American Univ. of Beirut.
On staff of Gordon Memorial Coll. 35-47; Vice-Principal, Inst. of Education, Ruda 47-51; Asst. Dir. (Personnel), Ministry of Education 51-54, Dep. Dir. 54-56, Dir. 56-58; Vice-Chancellor, Univ. of Khartoum 58-62; mem. Board of Dirs., Barclays Bank, D.C.O., Khartoum 62-; Assoc. Univ. of London Inst. of Educ. 50; Hon. LL.D. Univ. of Khartoum 67.
c/o Barclays Bank, Gamhouria Avenue, Khartoum, Sudan.
Telephone: 80137.

Hagberg, Erik Rudolf; Swedish journalist and politician; b. 17 March 1891.
Man. Dir. and Editor-in-Chief *Skånska Aftonbladet* and *Helsinborgs-Posten* 26-50; M.P. 33-63; Conservative; Dir. Swedish Nat. Debt Office; Del. to UN 52, 53, 55, 62, 63; Chair. Cttee. Swedish Film Industry.
Fridhemstorget 22, Malmö, Sweden.

Hagelstange, Rudolf; German author; b. 14 Jan. 1912; ed. Humanistisches Gymnasium, Nordhausen.
Journalist 35-40; war correspondent 40-45; professional author 45-; Vice-Pres. Darmstadt Acad. of Speech and Poetry; German Critics' Prize 52; German Schiller Stiftung 55; Julius Campe Prize 58; Grosses Verdienstkreuz 59; Olympic Diploma 64.
Publs. *Es spannt sich der Bogen* 43, *Venezianisches Credo* 45, *Strom der Zeit* 48, *Meersburger Elegie* 50, *Ballade vom verschütteten Leben* 51, *Zwischen Stern und Staub* 53, *Tragödie des Orpheus* 55, *Die Nymphe von Fiesole* (poetry) 57, *Die Nacht* 54, *Es steht in unserer Macht* 53, *How do you like America?* 57, *Lied der Muschel* 58, *Spielball der Götter* 59, *Nacht Mariens* 59, *Viel Vergnügen* 60, *Huldigung* 60, *Römisches Olympia* 61, *Lied der Jahre* 61, *Reise nach Katmandu* 62, *Farbiges Deutschland* 62, *Die Puppen der Puppe (Eine Russlandreise)* 63, *Corazón (Gedichte aus Spanien)* 63, *Zeit für ein Lächeln* 65, *Heitere Prosa* 66.
(7777) Unteruhldigen, Bodensee, German Federal Republic.

Hagen, Uta Thyra; American (b. German) actress; b. 12 June 1919; ed. Univ. of Wisconsin High School, Royal Acad. of Dramatic Art, London, and Univ. of Wisconsin.
Debut as Ophelia in *Hamlet*, Dennis, Mass. 37; Teacher (and Co-Founder) Herbert Berghof Studio (School of Acting) 47-.
Plays acted in include: *The Seagull, Arms and the Man, The Latitude of Love, The Happiest Days, Key Largo, Othello, The Master Builder, Angel Street, A Streetcar Named Desire, The Country Girl, Saint Joan, Tovarich, In Any Language, The Lady's not for Burning, The Deep Blue Sea, Cyprienne, A Month in the Country, The Good Woman of Setzuan, The Affairs of Anatol, The Queen and the Rebels, Who's Afraid of Virginia Woolf?, The Cherry Orchard.*
Herbert Berghof Studio, 120 Bank Street, New York City, N.Y., U.S.A.

Hager, Kurt; German politician; b. 10 Aug. 1912; ed. Oberrealschule, Stuttgart.
Membr Kommunistische Partei Deutschlands (K.P.D.) until 45, Sozialistische Einheitspartei Deutschlands (S.E.D.) 45-; fmr. journalist; fought in Spanish Civil War 37-39, Dir. of Radio Madrid; interned in U.K. in Second World War; posts in S.E.D. 45-54; Prof. of Philosophy, Humboldt Universität zu Berlin 49; mem.

Central Cttee. S.E.D. 54-, Sec. for Propaganda of Central Cttee. 55-, mem. Politburo 63-, Sec. and Leader of Ideological Comm., Politburo 63-; mem. Volkskammer 58-; Vaterländischer Verdienstorden in Silber.
Sozialistische Einheitspartei Deutschlands, Am Werderschen Markt, Berlin C.2, Germany.

Hagerty, James C.; American radio and television executive; b. 9 May 1909; ed. Blair Acad., New Jersey, and Columbia Univ.
Became reporter on *New York Times* 34; Legislative Corresp. in Albany 38-43; appointed Press Sec. by Gov. Thomas E. Dewey 43; joined Eisenhower forces 52; appointed Press Sec. to Gen. Eisenhower, after Eisenhower's nomination as Pres. candidate, and served in that capacity during the 52 campaign and until 61; Vice-Pres. for news, American Broadcasting Co. 61-63; Vice-Pres. (Corporate Relations) American Broadcasting Companies Inc. 63-.
Office: American Broadcasting Companies Inc., 1330 Avenue of the Americas, New York, N.Y.; Home: 7 Rittenhouse Road, Bronxville, N.Y. 10708, U.S.A. Telephone: Deerfield 7-5424.

Hägg, Gunnar, DR. PHIL.; Swedish university professor; b. 14 Dec. 1903; ed. Univs. of Stockholm, London, and Jena.
Lecturer, Univ. of Stockholm 29-36; Prof. of Gen. and Inorganic Chemistry, Univ. of Uppsala 36-; mem. Royal Swedish Acad. of Science 42, Royal Society of Science of Uppsala 40, Royal Physiographical Society of Lund 43, Royal Neths. Acad. of Science 50, Royal Danish Society of Science 56, Royal Swedish Acad. of Engineering Sciences 57, Leopoldina German Acad. of Scientists 60, Norweg. Acad. of Science 61; Vice-Pres. Int. Union of Crystallography 60; mem. Nobel Cttee. for Chemistry, Royal Swedish Acad. of Science 65.
Publs. *Kemisk Reaktionslära* 40, *Die Theoretischen Grundlagen der Analytischen Chemie* 50, *Teoría de la Reacción Química* 62, *Allmän och Oorganisk kemi* 63; and numerous works mainly dealing with X-ray crystallography and its applications to inorganic chemistry.
Institute of Chemistry, The University, Uppsala; Home: Thunbergsvägen 24, Uppsala, Sweden.
Telephone: 018-139460 (Office); 018-136989 (Home).

Hägglöf, Gunnar; Swedish diplomatist; b. 15 Dec. 1904; ed. Uppsala Univ.
Entered diplomatic service 26, served Paris, London, Moscow; Sec. Disarmament Conf., Geneva 32-34; Minister without Portfolio 39; led dels. to Berlin and London during 39-45 war; Minister to Belgian and Dutch Govts. 44, to Miscow 46; Perm. Del. to UN 47; Amb. to Great Britain 48-67, to France 67-.
11 avenue d'Iéna, Paris 16e, France.

Hägglöf, Ingemar; Swedish diplomatist; b. 20 April 1912; ed. Uppsala Univ.
Law practice 34; joined Ministry of Foreign Affairs 34; served in London 35, Paris 36, Berlin 38, Stockholm 41, Moscow 43, Stockholm 45-49; Counsellor Embassy, Washington 49-51, Dep. Head, Commercial Dept. 51-53; Del. to O.E.E.C., Paris 53; Council of Europe 53; EFTA, Geneva 60; Perm. Swedish Rep. to O.E.E.C., Paris 53-61; Ambassador 57-61, to O.E.C.D. 61-63; Ambassador to Finland 64-.
Swedish Embassy, Esplanadikatu 7B, Helsinki, Finland.

Hagihara, Yusuke, DR. SC.; Japanese astronomer; b. 28 March 1897; ed. Tokyo, Cambridge and Harvard Univs.
Assistant, Tokyo Univ. 21, Asst. Prof. 23, Prof. of Astronomy 35-57; Rockefeller Fellowship 28-29; Harvard Observatory Research Assoc. 38; Dir. of Tokyo Astronomical Observatory 46-57 (Visiting Prof. Chicago Univ. 52), Emeritus 57; Prof. of Astronomy, Tohoku Univ. 57-60; Consultant Smithsonian Astrophysical

Observatory 61-; Pres. Utsunomiya Univ. 60-64; mem. Science Council of Japan 49-59, Japan Acad. 43-, F.R.A.S. 28-; Pres. Physico-Mathematical Soc. of Japan 42; Pres. Astronomical Soc. of Japan 49-53; mem. Standing Cttee. of Int. Astronomical Union 28-, Vice-Pres. 61-; Chair. of Comm. on Celestial Mechanics 61-; official mem. Int. Scientific Radio Union 50-60; H.I.M. Decoration for Cultural Merit 54, Watson Medal (Nat. Acad. of Sciences of U.S.A.) 60; Lecturer Yale Univ. Summer Inst. on Dynamical Astronomy 60, 61, 62, 64, 65.
Publs. *Foundation of Celestial Mechanics I* 47, *Beyond Nebulae* 49, *General Astronomy* 55, *Astronomy* 56, *Stability in Celestial Mechanics* 57, *The Stability of the Solar System* (in *The Solar System*, vol. 3, ed. Kuiper) 61. Himonya 6-chome, 3-7 Meguro-ku, Tokyo, Japan.
Telephone: 712-7800.

Hagiwara, Kichitaro; Japanese business executive; b. 15 Dec. 1902; ed. Keio Univ., Tokyo.
Mitsui Co. 26-40; Hokkaido Colliery and Steamship Co. 40-, Dept. Chief, Secretarial Dept. 43-47, Dept. Chief, Personnel Dept. 45-47, Man. Dir. 47-55, Pres. 55-; Chair. Japan Coal Asscn. 61-.
No. 36-4, Taira-machi, Meguro-ku, Tokyo, Japan.

Hagman, (Erik Richard) Ragnar, LL.B.; Swedish banker; b. 14 Nov. 1908; ed. Uppsala Univ.
Began his career as a lawyer; Man. Dir. Negotiation Board of Swedish Banks 42-48, Chair. 53-57; Dir. Svenska Handelsbanken 48-57; Man. Dir. and Sec. Swedish Iron and Steel Works' Employers' Asscn. 57-; Chair. AB Järnbruksförnödenheter; mem. Stockholm City Council; Conservative.
Järnbruksförbundet, Hovslagargatan 3, Stockholm C, Sweden.

Hague, Sir (Charles) Kenneth (Felix), Kt., C.ENG., F.I.E.E.; British engineer; b. 17 Sept. 1901; ed. New Coll. School, Oxford, and Leeds Univ.
Joined Babcock & Wilcox Ltd. 24, held various positions on engineering and sales staffs, Dir. 40-42, Deputy Man. Dir. 42-44, Man. Dir. 45-58, Deputy Chair. 50-60, Chair. 60-; mem. Iron and Steel Board 59-64; Deputy Chair. Power Securities Corpn., Tersons 66-; Chair. James Kilpatrick 66-; Dir. other companies; mem. U.K. Management/Labour Del. to U.S.A. 41; British Rep. on Public Utilities Cttee. of Combined Production and Resources Board, Washington 44; mem. Engineering Advisory Council 47-52, Heavy Electrical Plant Consultative Council 44-45; Past Pres. British Engineers' Asscn.; Pres. Inst. Mechanical Engineers 61-62; Pres. Engineering and Allied Employers' Nat. Fed. 58-60; Chair. Engineering Institutions Joint Council 63-64; Hon. LL.D. (Glasgow), Hon. M.I.Mech.E., Hon. M.I.Struct.E.
Home: Poland Mill, Odiham, Hants.; Office: Babcock House, 209 Euston Road, London, N.W.1, England.

Haguiwara, Toru; Japanese diplomatist; b. 25 May 1906; ed. Tokyo Imperial Univ.
Entered diplomatic service 28; Chief of several sections of the Ministry of Foreign Affairs 40-46; Dir. Treaties Bureau, Ministry of Foreign Affairs 46-50; Chief of Japanese Govt. Overseas Agency, Paris 50-52; Minister to France 52; Envoy and Minister to Switzerland 52, Ambassador 55-57; Ambassador to Canada 57-61, to France 61-67.
Publs. include two books on Diplomatic History of World War II 49, and the Peace Treaty 51.
c/o Ministry of Foreign Affairs, Tokyo, Japan.

Hahn, E. Adelaide, A.M., PH.D.; American college professor and classicist; b. 1 April 1893; ed. Hunter Coll., and Columbia Univ.
Hon. Fellow Hunter Coll. 15-16, Instructor 17, Asst. Prof. 25, Associate Prof. 33, Prof. of Latin and Greek

and Chair. Classics Dept. 36-63, Prof. Emer. 63-; Drisler Fellow Columbia Univ. 16-17; Hon. Fellow Yale Univ. 34-35. 36-37; Pres. Linguistic Society of America 46; Prof. Linguistic Inst. Univ. of Michigan 47; Collitz Prof. Linguistic Inst. Univ. of Calif. 51; Vice-Pres. American Oriental Soc. 52-53; Pres. Alumni Asscn. Hunter Coll. 58-62; Vice-Pres. Classical Asscn. of Atlantic States 58-60, Pres. 60-62; Sec. and Treas. New York Classical Club 26-39, Pres. 39-41; Vice-Pres. 9th Int. Congress of Linguists 62.
Publs. *Coordination of Non-Coordinate Elements in Vergil* 30, *Subjunctive and Optative: Their Origin as Futures* 53; and many articles in classical and linguistic journals.
640 Riverside Drive, New York, N.Y. 10031, U.S.A. Telephone: Wadsworth 6-8071.

Hahn, Kurt Matthias, C.B.E.; British (b. German) educationalist; b. 5 June 1886; ed. Univs. Berlin, Freiburg, Göttingen, Christ Church, Oxford.
Lector of English newspapers for German Foreign Office, then Supreme Command 14-18; Private Sec. to Prince Max of Baden (last Imperial Chancellor) 18-19; helped Prince Max found co-ed. school at Salem, Baden 20, Headmaster 20-33; emigrated to Britain (British subject 38) and founded Gordonstoun School in Scotland 33, Headmaster 33-53; Co-founder, Outward Bound 41; Co-founder, Atlantic Coll. 62; Hon. LL.D. (Edinburgh), Hon. Dr. phil. (Göttingen, Tübingen, Berlin); Grosses Bundesverdienstkreuz (German Fed. Repub.).
7777 Salem, Baden, German Federal Republic; and Brown's Hotel, Dover Street, London, W.1, England. Telephone: Pfullendorf 07552-476; 01-493-6020 (London).

Hahn, Otto, PH.D.; German radiologist; b. 8 March 1879; ed. Univs. of Marburg and Munich.
Member Ramsay Laboratory, London 04-05, Rutherford Laboratory Montreal 05-06 and Chemical Institute of Berlin Univ. 06-; Prof. at Kaiser Wilhelm Inst. for Chemistry 12-, Dir. 28-; mem. Prussian Acad. of Science 24-, and other Acads.; research worker in radioactivity and applied radio chemistry; discoverer of radioactive substances, Radiothor, Mesothorium, Protactinium (with Lise Meitner), Uranium and Thorium fission (with F. Strassmann); awarded Nobel Prize for Chemistry 44; Pres. Max Planck Gesellschaft 46-60, Hon. Pres. 60-; Foreign mem. Royal Soc. 57; Orden Pour le Mérite, Enrico Fermi Award 66.
34 Göttingen, Bunsenstrasse 10; Home: 34 Göttingen, Jervinusstrasse 5, German Federal Republic. Telephone: 44051.

Hahnloser, Hans Rob., PH.D.; Swiss art historian; b. 13 Dec. 1899; ed. Winterthur Gymnasium, Basel, Zürich and Vienna Univs.
Asst. to Prof. von Schlosser, Vienna 27; Lecturer, Vienna 34; Prof. Berne 34; Dean Philosophy Faculty, Berne Univ. 38-39, 45-46, Rector 56-57, Pro-Rector 57-58; Hon. mem. Société d'Histoire de l'Art en Suisse; Treas. Int. Council for Philosophy and Humanistic Studies; Treas. Int. Art History Cttee.; Trustee, Kunstmuseum, Berne, Graphische Sammlung, Eidgen. Tech. Hochschule, Swiss Inst., Rome, German Inst. of History of Art, Florence; mem. Swiss Council for Scientific Research, Acad. of Science, Vienna, Pontificia Accademia Romana di Archeologia, Soc. Nat. Antiquaires de France; Officer Arts and Letters.
Publs. *Das Musterbuch von Wolfenbüttel* 29, *Villard de Honnecourt* 34, *Das Kluniazenserpriorat Rüeggisberg* 47, *Chorfenster und Altäre des Berner Münsters* 50, *Scolae et Artes cristellariorum de Veneciis*, *Werke aus der Sammlung Hahnloser* 56, *Urkunden zur Bedeutung des Bronzetürrings* 59, *H. Manguin* 64, *La Pala d'Oro di San Marco*

a Venezia 65, *Vom Impressionismus zu den Nabis und Fauves* 65, *P. Bonnard* 65.
3013 Berne, Sonnenbergrain 8, Switzerland. Telephone: 41-49-40.

Hahr, Henrik A. A., .MA.; Swedish broadcasting official; b. 10 Jan. 1911; ed. Uppsala and Stockholm Univs.
Radio Reporter Swedish Broadcasting Corpn. 34-38; Foreign Corresp. (London, Brussels, Rome) *Svenska Dagbladet* 38-42; Swedish Broadcasting Corpn., Head External Relations 42-47, Programme planning 47-50, Current Affairs 50-55, Programme Dir. Sound Broadcasting 55-56, then Television 56-59, Co-ordinating Dir. Radio-TV, Dir. Int. Dept. and Asst. to Dir.-Gen. 59-64; Dir. Admin. Office and Sec.-Gen. European Broadcasting Union (E.B.U.). Geneva 64-; mem. Swedish UNESCO Cttee. 50-64; mem. Board Swedish Inst. of Journalism 61-64; Pres. Code-of-Practice Cttee. Swedish Broadcasfing Corpn. 60-64, and other Broadcasting Cttees.; Knight Nordstjärnan Order, Légion d'Honneur, Dannebrog Order, Knight Commdr. al Merito della Repubblica Italiana, and other decorations. Publs. *Vår Radio och Andras* 45, *Nordisk Radio and TV* 63.
European Broadcasting Union, 1 rue de Varembé, 1211 Geneva 20, Switzerland. Telephone: 33-24-00.

Haidar, Salim, IUR.D.; Lebanese lawyer and diplomatist; b. 11; ed. Baalbek Elementary School, Nat. Coll., Aley, Lycée Français, Beirut, and Univ. of Paris.
Judge, Mount Lebanon Tribunal 38-43; Pres. Beirut Tribunal 43-45; Counsellor, Court of Appeal 45-46; Minister to Iran 46; Minister of Nat. Education, Public Health, Social Affairs and Posts, Telegraphs, and Telecommunications 52; mem. Lebanese Parl. 53; Minister of Agriculture and Posts, Telegraphs and Telecommunications 54-55; Ambassador to Morocco 58-63, to U.S.S.R. 63-66; Commandeur, Ordre du Cèdre and foreign decorations.
Publs. *La Prostitution et la Traite des Femmes et des Enfants* 37, *Afaak* (Arabic poems), *Alsinat-Al-Zaman* (Arabic verse play), *Hawl-Ashshi'r* (Arabic studies on poetry), *Ashwaak* (Arabic poems).
Corniche El-Mazraa, Imm. Dr. Barbir, Beirut, Lebanon.

Haider, Michael Lawrence, B.S.; American business executive; b. 1 Oct. 1904; ed. Stanford Univ.
Standard Oil Co. (New Jersey) and affiliates 29-; Carter Oil Co., Tulsa 29-38; Manager, Research and Engineering Dept., Standard Oil Development Co., New York City 38-45; Exec., Producing Dept., Standard Oil Co. (N.J.) 45-46; Gen. Manager of Exploration and Production, Vice-Pres. and Dir. Imperial Oil Ltd., Toronto 46-48, Dep. Co-ordinator of Producing Activities, Standard Oil Co. (N.J.) 52-54; Pres. and Dir. International Petroleum Co. Ltd. 54-59; Standard Oil Co. (N.J.), New York City 59-, Vice-Pres. 60-61, Exec. Vice-Pres. 61-63, Pres. 63-65, Chair. and Chief Exec. Officer and Chair. Exec. Cttee. 65-; Past Pres. American Inst. of Mining, Metallurgical and Petroleum Engineers; Hon. LL.D., Univ. of Miami 62, Instituto de Cultura Hispanica 62.
River Road, Essex, Conn., U.S.A.

Haikal, Yusuf, PH.D., D. en DROIT; Jordanian diplomatist; b. 15 Aug. 1912; ed. Arab Coll., Jerusalem and Univs. of London and Paris.
Gen. Inspector of Awqaf (Moslem Public Properties in Palestine); District Judge (Palestine) 43-45; Mayor of Jaffa 45-48; Minister to U.S.A. 49-53; Chief Jordan Del. with Mixed Armistice Comm., Jerusalem 53-54; Ambassador to Great Britain 54-56, to France 56-57, to U.S.A. 57-62, to France 62-64, to Repub. of China 64-65; Istiqlal Medal 1st Class.

Publs. include (in French) *The Prime Minister and the Evolution of the Parliamentary System, The Dissolution of Parliament*; (in Arabic) *The Palestine Problem, Towards Arab Unity*.
c/o Ministry of Foreign Affairs, Amman, Jordan.

Haile Sellassie I, His Imperial Majesty; Emperor of Ethiopia, K.G. (original name Ras Tafari Makonnen); b. 23 July 1892.
Proclaimed Regent and Heir to Imperial Throne 16; invested with Grand Cordon of the Order of Solomon; took Ethiopia to League of Nations 23; proclaimed abolition of slavery 24; proclaimed King 28; proclaimed Emperor after death of Empress Zauditu 30; established Constitution 31; following invasion by Italy 35 forced to quit Addis Ababa 36; appeared personally before League of Nations 36; lived in England till 40; rallied refugee patriots in Kenya and Sudan and crossed the frontier 41; reinstated in capital 41; reorganised Government, reopened Parliament, reinstituted State Bank of Ethiopia 42; proclaimed new currency, established airlines, opened roads, reorganised army, navy and air force, built numerous schools, expanded industry and agriculture, founded the University Coll. of Addis Ababa and other colleges, organised a judiciary system, codified law and revised the Constitution 55, entered into diplomatic relations with most of the important nations of the world; secured reintegration of Eritrea 52; Grand Cross of the Order of the Legion of Honour; of the Annunziata; of Leopold, Belgium; of the Lion d'Or de la Maison de Nassau, Luxembourg; Netherlands Order of Orange-Nassau; Danish Order of the Elephant; Brazilian Order of San Sebastian Guillaume; Mexican Order of the Aztec Eagle, Order of Military Merit of the Federal Republic of Germany; Order of the Star of Yugoslavia; Order of Military Merit of France; Order of Mohammed Ali of Egypt; Swedish Order of the Seraphim; Norwegian Order of St. Olaf; Greek Order of the Saviour; Order of Merit of the Italian Republic; Order of Suvorov U.S.S.R.; 1st Class Military Order of the White Lion Czechoslovakia; Ribbon of the Grand Cross of the Three Orders Portugal; Sudan Order of the Republic 1st Class; K.G., G.C.B. (Hon.); G.C.M.G. (Hon.); G.C.V.O. (Hon.); LL.D. (Hon.) Cantab., Columbia, Howard, McGill, Montreal, Michigan, Athens, Laval, Banaras, Moscow, Charles; D.C.L. (Hon.) Oxford; Hon. LL.D. (Ag.) Bonn.
The Imperial Palace, Addis Ababa, Ethiopia.

Hailes, Baron; **Rt. Hon. Patrick Buchan-Hepburn,** C.H., G.B.E., P.C., M.A.; British politician and administrator; b. 2 April 1901; ed. Harrow and Cambridge Univ.
Attaché British Embassy Constantinople 26-27; Conservative M.P. for East Toxteth Div. of Liverpool 31-50, for Beckenham 50-57; Parl. Private Sec. to the Rt. Hon. Oliver Stanley 31-39; Asst. Govt. Whip 39; Junior Lord of the Treasury 39-40 and 44-45; war service with R.A., and on the Staff 40-43; Dep. Conservative Chief Whip July 45-48, Chief Whip 48-51; Parl. Sec. to the Treasury and Govt. Chief Whip 51-55; Minister of Works 55-57; Gov.-Gen. Fed. of The West Indies 58-62; Chair. Historic Buildings Council for England 63-.
c/o Lloyds Bank Ltd., 16 St. James Street, London, S.W.1, England.

Hailey, 1st Baron, cr. 36, of Shahpur and Newport Pagnell; **William Malcolm Hailey,** P.C., O.M., G.C.S.I., G.C.M.G., G.C.I.E.; b. 15 Feb. 1872; ed. Corpus Christi Coll., Oxford.
Joined Indian Civil Service 95; Colonisation Officer Jhelum Canal Colony 1900; Sec. Punjab Govt. 07; Chief Commr. Delhi 12-18; Finance mem. Council Govt. of India 19-20; Home mem. Council of Govt. of India 22-24; Gov. Punjab 24-28, United Provinces 28-34; Dir. African Research Survey 35-38; mem. LN Perm. Mandates Comm. 36-39; toured West, East and Central

Africa to study native admin. 40, and again in 46, 47 and 50; Chief economic mission Belgian Congo 40; Chair. School of Oriental and African Studies 41-46; Chair. Colonial Research Cttee. 42-47; mem. Rhodes Trust 42-63; Pres. Royal Central Asian Soc. 43-47; Deputy Chair. Royal African Soc. 44-57; Chair. Int. African Inst. 44-47; Pres. Research Defence Soc. 47-53; Pres. East India Asscn. 50-54; Hon. Pres. Indian Civil Service Asscn. (Retd.); Hon. Fellow Corpus Christi Coll., Oxford, and School of Oriental and African Studies, London; hon. degrees (Lahore, Allahabad, Lucknow, Oxford, Cambridge, Bristol, Toronto, Witwatersrand, Leiden, London and Sheffield Univs.).
Publs. *An African Survey* 38, *Britain and Her Dependencies* 43, *The Future of Colonial Peoples* 43, *Native Administration in the British African Territories* (5 vols.) 50-52, *An African Survey* (Revised) 56, *Republic of South Africa and the High Commission Territories* 63.
2 Ross Court, Putney Hill, London, S.W.15, England.

Haissinsky, Moïse; French physico-chemist; b. 4 Nov. 1898; ed. Univ. degli Studi, Rome.
Chemical Industry, Paris 28-30; with Laboratoire Curie 30-, scholar 30-35; Research Asst. Centre national de la Recherche Scientifique (C.N.R.S.) 35-45, Researcher C.N.R.S. 45-55, Research Dir. 55-58, Scientific Dir. 62-; Assoc. Prof. Sorbonne 58-59, Prof. Radio Chemistry 59-62; Hon. mem. Accad. Ligure di Scienze e Lettere, Genoa 61; Prix Hébert, Acad. des Sciences, Paris 38.
Publs. *Atomistique moderne et la chimie* 32, *La Chimie nucléaire et ses applications* 57, *Dictionnaire de radiochimie* 65, and more than 200 papers on Radio Chemistry, Inorganic Chemistry, etc.
Laboratoire Curie, 11 rue Pierre Curie, 75 Paris 5e, France.
Telephone: 633-0871.

Hait, James (Merritt), M.E.; American engineer and business executive; b. 19 April 1906; ed. Rensselaer Polytechnical Inst.
Chief Engineer, Peerless Pump Co., Los Angeles 29-40; Man. and Chief Engineer, Procurement and Engineering Div., Food Machinery Corpn., Los Angeles 40-46; Vice-Pres. and Dir. of Engineering, Food Machinery and Chemical Corpn. 46-60, Head, Ordnance Div. 51, Dir. 52-, Pres. 60-66, Chair. FMC Corpn. (fmrly. Food Machinery and Chemical Corpn.) 66-.
FMC Corporation, 1105 Coleman Avenue, San José, Calif.; Home: 11199 Canon Vista Drive, San José, Calif. 95127, U.S.A.
Telephone: 258-5743.

Hajarnavis, Ramchandra Martand; Indian lawyer and politician; b. 24 Feb. 1908; ed. Patwardhan High School, Nagpur, Morris Coll., Nagpur, and Univ. Coll. of Law, Nagpur.
Advocate, Bombay High Court and Supreme Court, now Senior Advocate, Supreme Court; Lecturer in Constitutional Law and Equity, Univ. Coll. of Law, Nagpur 51-54; Head of Dept. of Studies in Law, Nagpur Univ. 54; Treas. Univ. of Nagpur 56; Chair. Janata Co-operative Housing Soc. 56-; Dep. Minister of Law, India 58-61; Dep. Minister of Mines and Fuel 62-63; Minister of State for Home Affairs 63-64, Minister of State in Ministry of Supply 64; Minister of State for Cultural Affairs 64-65.
Publ. *Law of Agricultural Tenancy and Village Service Lands in the Central Provinces* 48.
89 Shahjahan Road, New Delhi 11, India.
Telephone: 383765.

Hájek, Jiří; Czechoslovak diplomatist and politician; b. 6 June 1913; ed. Charles Univ., Prague.
Imprisoned 39-45; Lecturer, Coll. of Political and Social Sciences, Prague 47-48, Prof. 48-52; Prof. of Int. Relations, Charles Univ. 52-55; Dep. to Nat.

Assembly 45-54, Chair. Foreign Relations Cttee. 52-54; Ambassador to U.K. 55-58; Dep. Minister of Foreign Affairs 58-62; Perm. Rep. to UN 62-65; Minister of Educ. and Culture Nov. 65-67, Minister of Educ. Jan. 67-68, Minisetr of Foreign Affairs 68-; mem. Central Cttee. C.P. of Czechoslovakia 48-, Ideological Comm. Central Cttee. C.P. of Czechoslovakia 66-; Corresp. mem. Czechoslovak Acad. of Sciences 65-; Order of the Repub. 60.
Ministry of Foreign Affairs, Prague, Czechoslovakia.

Hakim, George, M.A., L. en D.; Lebanese diplomatist; b. 13; ed. American Univ., Beirut, and Univ. St. Joseph. Appointed Adjunct Prof. of Economics, American Univ., Beirut 43; mem. of several advisory govt. cttees. on economic and financial questions 42-46; appointed alternate del. of Lebanon to Economic and Social Council of U.N. 46; Chief Del. 49; Counsellor Lebanese Legation, Washington, D.C. 46-52; Chargé d'Affaires 48 and 51; apptd. by Pres. of Republic of Lebanon as Minister of Finance, of Nat. Economy and of Agriculture 52-53; Minister of Foreign Affairs and of Economy 53; Deputy Sec.-Gen. Ministry of Foreign Affairs Mar.-July 55; Minister to German Fed. Republic July 55-58; concurrently Minister of Nat. Economy Mar.-June 56; represented Lebanon at numerous int. confs.; Board of Govs. of the Int. Bank for Reconstruction and Development and the Int. Monetary Fund 47-50; Vice-Chair. Economic and Financial Cttee., U.N. 49; Chair. Group of Experts on economic development of under-developed countries, apptd. by Sec.-Gen. of U.N. Feb.-May 51; Ambassador to German Fed. Republic 58; Perm. Rep. to UN 59-65; Minister of Foreign Affairs July 65-.
Ministry of Foreign Affairs, Beirut, Lebanon.

Haksar, Sundar Narain; Indian diplomatist; b. 4 Dec. 1909; ed. St. Stephen's Coll., Delhi.
Indian Civil Service 33-48; Foreign Service 48-; Counsellor, Cairo 48-49; Joint Sec. Ministry of External Affairs 50-53; Minister, Washington 53-54; Ambassador to Turkey 54-56, to Afghanistan 57-60, to Italy 60-64, to United Arab Repub. 64; Deputy High Commr. in U.K. until 67; Sec. to Prime Minister May 67; Amb. to Netherlands 67-.
Indian Embassy, Buitenrustweg 2, The Hague, Netherlands.

Halaby, Najeeb E., A.B., LL.B.; American lawyer, government official and executive; b. 19 Nov. 1915; ed. Stanford Univ., Michigan Law School, and Yale Univ. Law School.
Served as test pilot, U.S. Navy, Second World War; admitted to California Bar 40, law practice Los Angeles 40-42; Foreign Affairs Adviser to Sec. of Defense 48-53, Dep. Asst. Sec. of Defense 52-54; with L. S. Rockefeller and Bros. 53-56; Vice-Pres. Servomechanisms Inc. 56-58, Exec. Vice-Pres. and Dir. 59-61; Sec.-Treas. The Aerospace Corpn. 59-61; Pres. American Technology Corpn; Administrator, Federal Aviation Agency 61-65; Senior Vice-Pres. and Dir. Pan American World Airways 65-68, Pres. 68-; Trustee Aerospace Corpn. 65-; Democrat.
Office: Pan American World Airways, Pan Am Building, New York, N.Y. 10017; Home: 1120 Fifth Avenue, New York, N.Y. 10028, U.S.A.

Hald, Knut; Norwegian industrialist; b. 10 Jan. 1902. Apprentice, Fed. of Norwegian Industries 21-28, Sec. 28-42, Dir.-Gen. 42-43, resgnd. during Quisling régime. Man. Dir. 45-65; mem. Board Norwegian Industries Fair, Norwegian Chamber of Commerce in Italy.
Pilestredet 94D, Oslo, Norway; and Drammensvn 40, Oslo, Norway.

Halecki, Oskar, PH.D.; Polish historian; b. 26 May 1891; ed. Vienna and Cracow Univ.
Lecturer, Cracow Univ. 16-18; Prof. History, Warsaw Univ. 19-39; Dean Faculty of Arts Warsaw Univ. 20-21 and 30-31; Prof. Int. Relations Warsaw School of Political Sciences 31-39; Expert Polish Del. at Peace Conf. 19; mem. L.N. Secretariat 21-24; Sec. League Cttee. of Intellectual Co-operation 22-24; Inst. of Intellectual Co-operation 25-26; mem. Polish Acad. 29; Vice-Chair. Catholic Union of Int. Studies 30-39; Chair. Union of Catholic Writers and Polish Heraldic Soc. 31-39; Dr. h.c. Univs. Lyons 34, Montreal 43, De Paul Univ. 45, Fordham Univ. 61, St. Peter's Coll. 67; corresp. mem. Royal Historical Soc., London 35, Inst. de France 37; Dir. Polish Inst. Arts and Sciences N.Y. 42-52, Pres. 53-64, Hon. Pres. 64-; Prof. History Fordham Univ. 44-61; Prof. History Montreal Univ. 44-51; Gov. Coll. of Europe, Bruges 50-; Privy Papal Chamberlain 53-; Visiting Prof. History, Columbia Univ. 55-61, Loyola Univ., Rome 62, Fribourg Univ. 63, Univ. of California, Los Angeles 63, Good Counsel Coll., White Plains 64-; mem. Papal Cttee. on Historical Sciences 66; Knight 53, Grand Cross of Grace and Devotion Order of Malta 58, Grand Cross Polonia Restituta 66.
Publs. *Consensus Sendomiriensis* 15, *History of the Polish-Lithuanian Union* (2 vols.) 19-20, *Poland in the Time of the Jagellons* 28, *Un Empereur de Byzance à Rome* 30, *La Pologne de 963 à 1944* 33, *Rome et Byzance au temps du grand schisme d'occident* 37, *The End of the Middle Ages* 38, *History of Poland* 42, *The Crusade of Varna* 43, *The Limits and Divisions of European History* 50, *E. Pacelli, Pope of Peace* 51, *Borderlands of Western Civilisation* 52, *Grenzraum des Abendlandes* 57, *Europa-Grenzen v. Gliederung seiner Geschichte* 57, *From Florence to Brest (1439-1596)* 58, *The Millenium of Europe* 63, *The Millenium of Catholic Poland* 66, *Das Europäische Jahrtausend* 66, *Storia della Polonia* 67.
35 Barker Avenue, White Plains, N.Y. 10601, U.S.A.

Halefoğlu, Vahit M., M.A.; Turkish diplomatist; b. 19 Nov. 1919; ed. Antakya Coll. and Univ. of Ankara. Turkish Foreign Service 43-, served Vienna, Moscow, Ministry of Foreign Affairs, London 46-59; Dir.-Gen., First Political Dept., Ministry of Foreign Affairs 59-62; Ambassador to Lebanon 62-65, concurrently accred. to Kuwait 64-65, Amb. to U.S.S.R. 65-66, to Netherlands 66-; Greek, Italian, German and Spanish decorations.
Turkish Embassy, Prinsessegracht 29, The Hague, The Netherlands.
Telephone: 070-112958.

Haley, Sir William John, K.C.M.G., LL.D.; British journalist and administrator; b. 24 May 1901; ed. Victoria Coll., Jersey.
Joint Man. Dir. *Manchester Guardian* and *Evening News* Ltd. 39-43; Dir. Reuters and Press Asscn. 39-43; Editor-in-Chief B.B.C. 43-44; Dir.-Gen. 44-52; Editor *The Times* 52-66; Chair. Times Newspapers Ltd. 67; Editor-in-Chief *Encyclopaedia Britannica* 68-; Chevalier Légion d'Honneur; Grand Officer, Order of Orange-Nassau.
Encyclopaedia Britannica Inc., 425 North Michigan Avenue, Chicago, Illinois 60611, U.S.A.
Telephone: 312-321-6904.

Halim, Mustapha Ben; Libyan engineer and politician; b. 21; ed. The Egyptian Univ., Alexandria.
Began career with Egyptian engineering firm; Minister of Works and Communications in first Cyrenaican Govt. 50; Minister, Province of Cyrenaica 52-54; Federal Minister of Communications 54; Prime Minister 54-57, simultaneously Minister of Foreign Affairs April 55-Nov. 56; Special Adviser to the King 57-59; Ambassador to France 59; private business 59-.
Tripoli, Libya.

Halkin, Simon, B.A., M.A., D.H.L.; American Hebrew scholar and author; b. 30 Oct. 1899; ed. N.Y. City Coll., Chicago, New York and Columbia Univs.

Instructor in Hebrew, Hebrew Union School for Teachers, New York City 24-32; Lecturer in Bible, Jewish History and Sociology and Modern Jewish History, Chicago Coll. of Jewish Studies 40-43; Prof. of Hebrew and Hebrew Literature, Jewish Inst. of Religion, New York City 43-49; Assoc. Prof. of Hebrew Literature, Hebrew Univ. of Jerusalem 49-56, Prof. and Head of Dept. 56-; Visiting Prof. Univ. of Calif. 54-55, Jewish Theological Seminary, New York; mem. Acad. of Hebrew Language; Pres. Israel PEN Club; Tchernichovsky Prize for translation (of Whitman) 53, Binlik Prize for Poetry 68.
Publs. *Yehiel Hagri* (novel) 28, *Arai va-Keva* (collected essays) 43, *Ad Mashber* 45, *Al Haiy* (collected poems) 46, *Modern Hebrew Literature: Trends and Values* 50, *Maavar Yabok* (collected poems); translations of Shakespeare, Maeterlinck, Whitman, etc.
5 Redak Street, Jerusalem, Israel.
Telephone: Jerusalem 3-3069.

Hall, Sir Arnold Alexander, Kt., M.A., F.R.S., D.ENG., D.SC., C.ENG.; British aviation engineer and administrator; b. 23 April 1915; ed. Alsop High School, Liverpool and Clare Coll., Cambridge.
Research Fellow in Aeronautics of Company of Armourers and Braziers 36-38; Royal Aircraft Establishment, Farnborough 38-45; Zaharoff Prof. of Aviation, Univ. of London 45-51; Dir. Royal Aircraft Establishment, Farnborough 51-55; Dir. Hawker Siddeley Group Ltd. 55-, Lloyds Bank Ltd. 66-; Man. Dir. Bristol Siddeley Engines Ltd. 58-63; Vice-Chair. and Man. Dir. Hawker Siddeley Group Ltd. 63-67, Chair. and Man. Dir. 67-; Pro-Chancellor, Univ. of Warwick 64-; mem. Advisory Council on Technology (Ministry of Technology) 64, Electricity Supply Research Council 64-; Pres. British Electrical and Allied Manufacturers' Asscn. March 67-68; Fellow, Imperial Coll. of Science and Technology; mem. Council, Confederation of British Industry 67-; Hon. F.R.Ae.S., Hon. A.I.A.A., Hon. A.C.G.I., Hon. M.I.Mech.E.
Hawker Siddeley Group Ltd., 18 St. James's Square, London, S.W.1, England.

Hall, Floyd D., B.S.; American airline executive; b. 4 April 1916; ed. Univ. of Colorado and Univs. of Michigan and California (Los Angeles).
General Man. U.S. Operations, Trans-World Airlines Inc. 57-58, Gen. Man. System Flight Operations 58-59, Vice-Pres. Flight Operations 59, Vice-Pres. and Gen. Transportation Man. 59-61, Senior Vice-Pres. and System Gen. Man. 61-63; Pres. and Chief Exec. Officer Eastern Air Lines Inc. Dec. 63-67, Chair. and Chief Exec. Officer 68-.
Eastern Airlines Inc., 10 Rockefeller Plaza, New York, N.Y. 10020; Home: 35 Sutton Place, New York, N.Y. 10022, U.S.A.

Hall, George Edward, A.F.C., E.D., M.S.A., M.D., PH.D., D. ès SC., F.R.S.C.; Canadian educationalist and business executive; b. 10 Oct. 1907; ed. Lindsay Collegiate Inst., Ontario Agricultural Coll., Univs. of Toronto and Ghent.
Research Assoc. Dept. of Medical Research, Banting Inst., Toronto Univ. 35-36, Asst. Prof. 36-37, Assoc. Prof. 37-39, Prof. 39; Service with Royal Canadian Air Force 39-45; Dean, Faculty of Medicine, Univ. of Western Ontario, London 45-47; Pres. and Vice-Chancellor of the Univ. 47-67; Pres. Asscn. of Univs. and Colls. of Canada 56-57; Chair. Asscn. of Commonwealth Univs. 63-65; mem. Ontario Research Council 47-53, Nat. Cancer Inst. 47- (Pres. 50-51), Nat. Research Council 50-56, Canadian Forces Medical Council 51-66 (Chair. 62-66), Canada Council 60-66, Royal Comm. on Fluoridation 60, Nat. Productivity Council 62-64, Ontario Council of Health 66-; Chair. Comm. of Inquiry on Pollution 67-68, Northern Life Assurance

Co.; Dir. Int. Business Machines Co. Ltd., Labatt Industries Ltd.; Life Hon. mem. Canadian Medical Asscn.; American Legion of Merit; Hon. LL.D. (several), Hon. D.Sc.
Northern Life Assurance Co., London, Ontario; Home: 114 Fritton's Road, Orellia, Ont., Canada.
Telephone: 439-0171 (Office); 326-2179 (Home).

Hall, Joseph Bates, PH.B.; American business executive; b. 13 July 1899; ed. Univ. of Chicago.
Bookkeeper, Morris & Co., Chicago 21-23; Gordon Strong & Co., Real Estate, Chicago; Pres. Hamilton Bond & Mortgage Co., Chicago, Exec. Sec. Chicago Mortgage Bankers' Asscn., and Asst. Man. Real Estate Dept., Continental-Ill. Bank & Trust Co., Chicago 23; Gen. Man. Real Estate Dept., The Kroger Co. 31, Man. St. Louis Branch 35, Eastern Div. Man. 37, Vice-Pres. (Manufacturing) 42, Treas. 43, Exec. Vice-Pres. 44, Pres. 46-62, Chair. 62-; Chair. Selective Insurance Co.; Dir. Armco Steel Corpn., Cincinnati & Suburban Bell Telephone Co., Tenneco, Market Research Corpn. of America, Little Miami R.R. Co., Transit Casualty Co., St. Louis, U.S. Plywood-Champion Papers Inc., Goodyear Tire and Rubber Co.; Pres. Cincinnati Redevelopment Corpn.; mem. Business Council; Trustee, Ohio Univ.
Office: 105 West Fourth Street, Cincinnati, Ohio 45202; Home: 3 Grandin Terrace, Cincinnati 8, Ohio, U.S.A.

Hall, Sir Noel, M.A., A.M.; British economist and college principal; b. 23 Dec. 1902; ed. Bromsgrove School, Brasenose Coll., Oxford, Princeton Univ.
Commonwealth Fund Fellow 25-27; Lecturer in Political Economy and Civil Service Tutor, Univ. of London, Univ. Coll. 27-29, Senior Lecturer 29; Prof. of Political Economy 35-38; Sec. Fellowship Advisory Cttee. Rockefeller Foundation for Social Sciences in Great Britain and Ireland 30-36; Dir. Nat. Inst. of Economics and Social Research 38-43; Joint Dir. Ministry of Economic Warfare 40-41; Minister attached to Embassy Washington, D.C. 41-43; West African Development Adviser 43-45; Principal Admin. Staff Coll., Greenlands, Henley-on-Thames 46-61; Principal Brasenose Coll. Oxford 61-; created knight 57; New York Univ. Medal 58; Hon. LL.D. (Lancaster) 64.
Publs. *The Economist in the Witness Box* (with Stephen King-Hall) 33, *The Exchange Equalisation Account* 35, *The Making of Executives, The Modern Challenge* 58.
Homer End, Ipsden, Oxon., England.

Hall, Peter Reginald Frederick, C.B.E., M.A.; British theatre and film director; b. 22 Nov. 1930; ed. Perse School and St. Catharine's Coll., Cambridge.
Produced and acted in over 20 plays at Cambridge; first professional production Windsor 53; produced in repertory at Windsor, Worthing and Oxford Playhouse; two Shakespearean productions for Arts Council; Artistic Dir. Elizabethan Theatre Co. 53; Asst. Dir. London Arts Theatre 54, Dir. 55-56; formed own producing company, Int. Playwright's Theatre 57; Dir. Royal Shakespeare Theatre, Stratford-on-Avon and Aldwych Theatre, London 60-68; Assoc. Prof. of Drama, Warwick Univ. 66-.
Productions: *Blood Wedding, Immoralist, The Lesson, South, Mourning Becomes Electra, Waiting for Godot, The Burnt Flowerbed, Waltz of the Toreadors, Camino Real, Gigi, Wrong Side of the Park, Love's Labours Lost, Cymbeline, Twelfth Night, A Midsummer Night's Dream, Coriolanus, Two Gentlemen of Verona, Troilus and Cressida, Ondine, Romeo and Juliet, Becket, The Collection, Cat on a Hot Tin Roof, The Rope Dancers* (on Broadway), *The Moon and Sixpence* (opera), *Henry VI* (parts 1, 2 and 3), *Richard III, Richard II, Henry IV* (parts 1 and 2), *Henry V, Eh?, The Homecoming, Moses and Aaron* (opera), *Hamlet, The Government*

Inspector, The Magic Flute (opera), *Staircase, Work is a Four Letter Word* (film).
18 Buckingham Street, London, W.C.2; Avoncliffe, Stratford-on-Avon, Warwicks., England.

Hall, Sir Robert Lowe, K.C.M.G., C.B., B.A., B.ENG.; British economist; b. 6 March 1901; ed. Univ. of Queensland and Magdalen Coll., Oxford.
Lecturer in Economics, Trinity Coll., Oxford 26-27; Fellow of Trinity Coll., Oxford 27-49; temporary civil servant 39-45; Dir. Economic Section, Cabinet Office 47-53; Economic Adviser to Her Majesty's Govt. 53-61; mem. of Economic Planning Board 47-61; Vice-Pres. Royal Economic Soc. (Pres. 58-60); Advisory Dir. Unilever Ltd. 61-; Principal, Hertford Coll., Oxford 64-67.
Publs. *Earning and Spending* 34, *The Economic System in a Socialist State* 36, *The Place of the Economist in Government* (Sidney Ball Lecture, Oxford) 56.
34 Maunsel Street, London, S.W.1, England.
Telephone: 01-834-6108.

Hall, Wilfred Newman, B.A.SC.; Canadian chemical engineer and business executive; b. 29 July 1908; ed. Vancouver public and high schools and Univ. of British Columbia.
Canadian Industries Ltd. 29-45; Vice-Pres. (Operations) Standard Chemical Co., Toronto 45-50; Vice-Pres. Dominion Tar and Chemical Co. Ltd. (name changed to Domtar Ltd. 65) 50-55, Exec. Vice-Pres. 55-57, Pres. and Dir. 57-66; Dir. Montreal Trust Co.
2315 Place Ville Marie, Montreal, Quebec; Home: P.O. Box 38, Como, Quebec, Canada.
Telephone: 866-8161 (Office); 453-6404 (Home).

Halleck, Charles Abraham, A.B., LL.B.; American lawyer and politician; b. 22 Aug. 1900; ed. Indiana Univ.
Prosecuting Attorney, Jasper-Newton Circuit, Ind. 24; mem. U.S. House of Reps. from 2nd Ind. District 35; majority leader in House, 80th and 83rd Congresses; minority leader 86th, 87th and 88th Congresses 59-64; Republican.
Rensselaer, Ind., U.S.A.

Hallowes, Odette Marie Céline, G.C., M.B.E.; British (b. French) wartime agent; b. 28 April 1912; ed. Convent of Ste. Thérèse, Amiens, and privately.
Worked as British agent with Special Forces in France 42-43 when captured by the Gestapo; sentenced to death 43; endured imprisonment and torture until 45 when she left Ravensbruck Concentration Camp; Vice-Pres. Mil. Medallists' League; mem. Royal Soc. of St. George; Légion d'Honneur 50; Vice-Pres. Women's Transport Services (F.A.N.Y.).
2 Balfour Mews, London, W.1, England.
Telephone: 01-493-5497.

Hallstein, Walter, DR.IUR.; German international politician; b. 17 Nov. 1901; ed. Univs. of Bonn, Munich and Berlin.
Assistant Faculty of Law, Berlin Univ. 25; with Inst. of Foreign and Private Int. Law, Berlin 27; Asst. Prof. of Law, Berlin Univ. 29; Prof. of Rostock Univ. 30-41; Prof. Univ. of Frankfurt 41-44, Rector 46-48; Visiting Prof. Georgetown Univ., Washington 48-49; Chair. German Comm. UNESCO 49-50; led German Del. to Schuman Plan Conf. 50; Sec. of State, Foreign Office 51-58; Pres. Commission of the European Economic Community (EEC) 58-67; Pres. European Movement 68-; Dr. h.c. Georgetown Univ., Washington; Hon. Doctor of Law (Univ. of Padua, Tufts Univ., Colby Coll. Maine, Adelphi Univ. New York, Harvard Univ., Nebraska Univ., Columbia Univ., Johns Hopkins Univ., and Univs. of Liège, Sussex, Nancy, Louvain, Hamburg and Tübingen; Grand Cross of Merit and Vatican, Italian, Greek, Argentine, Brazilian, Icelandic,

Thai, Iranian, Austrian, Peruvian, Mexican, Swedish, Chilean, Belgian, Liberian, Bolivian, Luxembourg, German, Cuban, Venezuelan, Togolese, Niger and other African decorations; Charlemagne Prize 61.
Publs. *Die Aktienrechte der Gegenwart* 31, *Die Berichtigung des Gesellschaftskapitals* 42, *Wiederherstellung des Privatrechts* 46, *Wissenschaft und Politik* 48, *United Europe: Challenge and Opportunity* 62.
Home: 5439 Rennerod, Oberwesterwaldkreis, German Federal Republic.

Hallström, Björn; Swedish journalist; b. 4 March 1906; ed. Germany, Sweden and Institut Monnier, Switzerland.
Contributor to *Stormlockan* 23-38; Editor of *Norrskensflamman* 30-38; Foreign News Editor of *Eskilstuna-Kuriren* 38-39; London Corresp. of the Christian Press of Norway 39-, *Skånska Dagbladet* 46-.
Publs. *Secret Journey Through Spain* 48, *Glött bak jernteppet* 48, *Jag trodde på Stalin* 52, *I Believed in Moscow* 53, *Formosa i blickpunkten* 55, *William Wilberforce, Slavenes Venn* 55.
37 Dunstan Road, London, N.W.11, England.
Telephone: 01-455-2448.

Halm, William Marmon Quao; Ghanaian diplomatist; b. 02; ed. Wesleyan Boys' High School, Freetown, Sierra Leone, American Univ., Washington.
Former Chair. Ghana Industrial Devt. Corpn.; fmr. Pres. Black Star Shipping Line; fmr. Treasurer United Gold Coast Convention Party, later Treasurer, Convention People's Party; Ambassador to Israel 58-59, to U.S.A. 59-62; Gov. of Bank of Ghana 62-65.
c/o Bank of Ghana, Accra, Ghana.

Halperin, Tulio, D.PHIL.; Argentine historian; b. 27 Oct. 1926; ed. Univ. de Buenos Aires, Ecole pratique des Hautes Etudes, Paris.
Professor, Univ. Nac. del Litoral (Rosario, Argentina) 55-61; Prof. Univ. de Buenos Aires 59-66; Lecturer, History Dept. Harvard Univ. 67-.
Publs. *El Pensamiento de Echeverria* 51, *Un Conflicto Nacional: Moriscos y Cristianos Viejos en Valencia* 55, *El Rio de la Plata al Comenzar el Siglo XIX* 60, *Tradicion Política Española e Ideologia Revolucionaria de Mayo* 61, *Historia de la Universidad de Buenos Aires* 62, *Argentina en el Callejon* 64.
Committee on Latin American Studies, Harvard University, 77 Dunster Street, Cambridge, Mass., U.S.A.

Halstead, Eric Henry, E.D., M.A., B.COM., F.P.A.N.Z., A.C.I.S.; New Zealand politician and company director, chartered accountant; b. 26 May 1912; ed. Auckland Univ. Coll. and Teachers' Training Coll.
Major N.Z. Forces 39-45; head of Commercial and Accountancy Dept., Seddon Memorial Technical Coll. 45-49; Member of Parliament (mem. of National Party) 49-57; Minister of Social Security and Minister-in-Charge of Tourist and Health Resorts 54-56; Minister-Asst. to the Prime Minister 54-57; concurrently Minister of Industries and Commerce and of Customs 56-57; partner Mabee, Halstead and Co.; Pres. Auckland Savings Bank; Dir. Air New Zealand Ltd.; mem. Council Univ. of Auckland.
Publs. *Modern Bookkeeping, Junior Commercial Practice.*
5 Pere Street, Remuera, Auckland 5, New Zealand.
Telephone: 545-083.

Halusa, Arno; Austrian diplomatist; b. 13 Aug. 1911; ed. Ecole Libre des Sciences Politiques, Paris, and Universität Wien.
Foreign Service 33-, served in Europe, North and South America and South East Asia 33-54; Minister to Thailand, Indonesia, Philippines and Cambodia 54-58; Amb. to India and Minister to Ceylon and Nepal

58-62; Dir.-Gen. Foreign Office, Vienna 62-64; Head of Austrian Perm. Del. to Org. for Econ. Co-operation and Devt. (OECD) 64-.
Austrian Delegation to OECD, 3 rue Albéric Magnard, Paris 16e, France.
Telephone: 870-74-45.

Hambro, Edvard; Norwegian lawyer and diplomatist; b. 22 Aug. 1911; ed. Oslo Univ. and in Geneva.
Secretariat, League of Nations before Second World War; Norwegian Ministry of Foreign Affairs, London, during Second World War; Head of Legal Dept., UN Secr. 45-46; Registrar, Int. Court of Justice, The Hague; Prof. at Norwegian School of Econs. and Business Admin. 59-66; mem. Storting 61-66; Perm. Rep. of Norway to UN 66-; mem. Perm. Court of Arbitration, The Hague.
Permanent Mission of Norway to the United Nations, 757 Third Avenue, New York, N.Y. 10017, U.S.A.

Hambro, Jocelyn Olaf, M.C.; British banker; b. 7 March 1919; ed. Eton and Trinity Coll., Cambridge.
In Coldstream Guards 39-45; with Hambros Bank Ltd. 45-, Man. Dir. 47-, Chair. 65-; Deputy Chair. Western American Bank (Europe) 67-; Dir. Phoenix Assurance Co. Ltd., Charter Consolidated Ltd., British Empire Investment Trust Ltd. and Diamond Devt. Co. Ltd.
Coopersale House, Epping, Essex; and 43 Wilton Crescent, London, S.W.1, England.

Hamburger, Christian; Danish doctor; b. 19 Feb. 1904; ed. Københavns Universitet.
Scientific Asst., Inst. for Gen. Pathology, Univ. of Copenhagen 32-35; Head, Hormone Dept. Statens Seruminstitut, Copenhagen 34-; mem. Advisory Panel Ciba Foundation 49-; mem. Advisory Panel on Biological Standardisation, World Health Org. (WHO) 52-; Pres. Danish Soc. for Endocrinology 47-; Chief editor *Acta Endocrinologica* 60-; Alfred Benzon Prize 60, Pfizer Prize 64, Thorvald Madsen Prize 66.
Publs. *Studies on gonadotropic hormones from the hypophysis and chorionic tissue* 33, *Hypophyseal, gonadal and adrenal hormones* 50.
62 Slotsvej, Copenhagen-Charlottenlund, Denmark.
Telephone: OR 3116.

Hameed, Col. Subhi Abdul; Iraqi army officer and politician; b. 31 Jan. 1924; ed. Mil. Coll. and Staff Coll., Baghdad, and Staff Coll., Camberley, England.
Graduated Mil. Coll. of Baghdad 48; Iraqi Army Service 48-63; Instructor, Staff Coll., Baghdad 59-Feb. 63; Dir. of Mil. Operations Feb. 63; Minister of Foreign Affairs Nov. 63, of Interior 64-65; participated in July 58, Feb. 63 and Nov. 63 Revolutions; arrested July 66; Rafidain Order (1st Class) and foreign decorations.
Yarmook 107-29, Baghdad, Iraq.

Hamelin, Jean Achille; French newspaper executive; b. 2 Dec. 1918; ed. Lycées Henri IV and Louis-le-Grand, Univ. de Paris à la Sorbonne, and Univ. de Lyon.
Court of Accounts 46-47; Recorder various Govt. Depts. 47-49; Technical Counsellor, Office of Under-Sec. of State for Finance, Econ. Affairs and Office of Ministry of Merchant Navy 49-50; Referendary Court of Accounts 50-52; Vice-Dir. *Le Progrès de Lyon* 52-59, Deputy Dir. 59-61; Dir. *Paris-Match* and *Marie-Claire* 61-; Dir. Société d'Exploitation Industrielle des Tabacs et Allumettes 61-; Pres.-Dir. Gen. Société *Le Figaro* 65-; Croix de Guerre.
Publ. *Le Contrôle des Finances Publiques* 49.
Figaro, 14 Rond-Point Champs-Elysées, Paris 8e; and 9 *bis* avenue Pierre-Grenier, 92 Boulogne-Billancourt, France.

Hamid, Abdul Rana, B.A., LL.B.; Pakistani lawyer and politician; b. 07; ed. Muslim High School, Lahore, Government Coll., Lahore, Forman Christian Coll., Lahore, Law Coll., Lahore, Muslim Univ., Aligarh, and Punjab Univ., Lahore.

Barrister, Montgomery Dist., W. Pakistan; mem. Montgomery Dist. Board 31; Chair. Debt Conciliation Board, Montgomery 39-45; mem. Punjab Legislative Assembly 46; Minister for Development, Pakistan 54-55; Minister for Food and Agriculture and Rehabilitation and Works 62; Pres. Pakistan Olympic Asscn.
Rana Abdul Hamid Khan, Civil Lines, Montgomery, West Pakistan.

Hamid, Agha Abdul; Pakistani United Nations official; b. 2 Aug. 1912; ed. Govt. Coll., Lahore, and Emmanuel Coll., Cambridge.
Joined Indian Civil Service 35, Asst. Commr. 37; Deputy Dir.-Gen. All-India Radio 42-45; Deputy Registrar, later Registrar of Co-operative Socs. 45-47; Sec. to late Liaquat Ali Khan, Prime Minister of Pakistan 48-51; Prime Minister of Kalat State 51-53, Baluchistan State Union 53-54; Joint Sec. to Central Cabinet 54-55, Joint Sec. in charge of Ministry of Information and Broadcasting 55-56; Joint Sec. Cabinet 56-58, Cabinet Sec. 58, 66-68; Commr. in Peshawar 59-60; Administrator 60-61; Dir. Civil Service Acad. 61-66; Chair. Central Public Service Comm. 66; Asst. Sec.-Gen. for Public Information, UN 68-; Founder, later Sec. and Chair. Karachi Fine Arts Soc.; fmr. Chair. Pakistan Arts Council; Pres. Pakistan Section of Int. Asscn. of Art Critics; Sitara Quaid-i-Azam.
Publs. *Majlis, Scrutiny*.
UN Secretariat, New York City, N.Y., U.S.A.

Hamilton, Duke of; **Douglas Douglas-Hamilton,** K.T., P.C., G.C.V.O., A.F.C., LL.D., F.R.G.S.; British officer; b. 3 Feb. 1903; ed. Eton and Balliol Coll., Oxford.
Cons. M.P. for Eastern Div. of Renfrewshire 30-40; Chief Pilot Houston Mt. Everest Flight Expedition 33; served Royal Air Force 39-45; Gov. British Linen Bank; Dir. Scottish Aviation Ltd., Scottish Union and Norwich Union Life Society; Hereditary Keeper, Palace of Holyrood House; Chancellor, Univ. of St. Andrews 58-; The Queen's Commr. to the Church of Scotland 53-55 and 58; Pres. Air League of the British Empire 59; Pres. Building Societies Asscn.; Chair. Cttee. on Air Pilot Training 62-63.
Publ. *The Pilot's Book of Everest* (with Group Captain McIntyre).
Lennoxlove, Haddington, East Lothian, Scotland.

Hamilton, Charles Denis, D.S.O.; British newspaper director and editor; b. 6 Dec. 1918; ed. Middlesbrough High School.
With *Evening Gazette*, Middlesbrough, and *Evening Chronicle and Journal*, Newcastle 36-39; served Infantry 39-46; Personal and Editorial Asst. to Viscount Kemsley 46-50; Editorial Dir. Thomson (fmrly. Kemsley) Newspapers Ltd. 50-66; Editor *The Sunday Times* 60-67; Editor-in-Chief *The Times* and *Sunday Times*, and Chief Exec. Times Newspapers Ltd. 67-; Dir. Newcastle Chronicle and Journal Ltd., North Eastern Evening Gazette Ltd., Reuters Ltd.; Founder mem. Nat. Council for the Training of Journalists, Chair. 58-59; mem. Council NPA, Press Council, Exec. Int. Press Inst. (Great Britain).
Home: Weston House, Nutbourne, Nr. Chichester, Sussex; and 25 Roebuck House, Palace Street, London, S.W.1; Office: Thomson House, 200 Gray's Inn Road, London, W.C.1, England.
Telephone: 01-828-0410 (Home).

Hamilton, Fowler; American lawyer; b. 7 May 1911; ed. Univ. of Missouri and Oxford Univ.
Private legal practice 35-38; Special Asst. to Attorney-Gen. 38-42; Dept. of Justice 42; Econ. Warfare Div., American Embassy, London 43; Chief Enemy Branch, Foreign Econ. Admin. 42-43; U.S.A.A.F. 43-44; Chief Legal Consultant, U.S. Dept. of Justice 45; Partner, Cleary, Gottlieb, Steen and Hamilton, New York City 46-61 and 63-; Gen. Counsel Sub-Cttee. of Air Force,

Senate Armed Forces Cttee. 56; Dir. N.Y. County Lawyers Asscn.; mem. Council of Foreign Relations, Foreign Policy Asscn., American Coll. of Trial Lawyers; Admin. U.S. Agency for Int. Devt. 61-62; Democrat.
Office: 52 Wall Street, New York, N.Y. 10005; Home: 14 Sutton Place South, New York, N.Y. 10022, U.S.A.

Hamilton, Francis Alvin George, P.C., B.A.; Canadian politician; b. 30 March 1912; ed. Univ. of Saskatchewan. Collegiate Teacher 38-40; R.C.A.F. (Overseas) Flight Lieutenant; Collegiate Teacher 45-48; Provincial Organizer for Progressive Conservative Party in Saskatchewan 48-57; Provincial Leader of P.C. Party 49-57; mem. Federal House of Commons 57-; Minister of Northern Affairs and National Resources 57-60, of Agriculture 60-63.
4, Kitoman Crescent, Manotick, Ontario, Canada.

Hamilton, Hamish, M.A., LL.B.; British publisher; b. 15 Nov. 1900; ed. Rugby and Cambridge.
Called to Bar Inner Temple 26; European Rep. Harper & Bros. New York 26-31; founded Hamish Hamilton Ltd., Publishers 31, Managing Dir. 31-; served Army 39-41; mem. staff American Div.; Ministry of Information 41-45; a Gov. British Inst. Florence; Hon. Sec. Kinsmen Trust 42-56; Chevalier de la Légion d'Honneur.
Publs. *Decade* 41, *Majority* 52.
43 Hamilton Terrace, London, N.W.8, England.

Hamilton, Hon. William McLean, P.C., B.SC.COM.; Canadian executive and politician; b. 23 Feb. 1919; ed. Montreal High School and Sir George Williams Univ. Gen. Man. Advertising and Sales Executives' Club of Montreal 49-57; City Councillor, Montreal 50-57; mem. of Parl. 53-62; Postmaster-Gen. of Canada 57-62; Pres. Canadian Park & Tilford Distilleries Ltd. 63-66, British Columbia Int. Trade Fair 66-67; Dir. Spilsbury & Tindall Ltd., Pacific Controls Ltd. 66-; Vice-Pres. Murzo Holdings Ltd. 67-; Chair. Fidelity Life Assurance Co., Century Insurance Co. of Canada 68-.
1110-1111 West Hastings, Vancouver 1, B.C.; Home: 6212 Wiltshire Street, Vancouver 13, B.C., Canada. Telephone: 684-3268 (Office); 263-4055 (Home).

Hammad, Tewfik Hammad; Sudanese politician; b. 04; ed. Gordon Memorial Coll. Khartoum.
Joined Finance Dept. 24 and became Inspector of Accounts, Dept. of Agriculture 46; left Govt. 47 to manage father's farm in the Gezira; former Man. Watania Cinema Co., Khartoum 50; founder mem. Graduates Congress; Sec. Nat. Front Party until formation of Nat. Unionist Party of which he became exec. mem. 52; mem. House of Reps. for Messelemiya 54-58; Minister of Finance and Economics 54-56, of Communications Feb.-July 56; resigned from Nat. Unionist Party and took part in creation of People's Democratic Party of which he became Supervisor-Gen.; Minister of Commerce, Industry and Supply, July 56-Mar. 58; mem. of Senate Mar.-July 58; Man.-Dir. Agricultural Bank of Sudan Aug 58-.
Agricultural Bank of Sudan, P.O. Box 1363, Khartoum, Sudan.

Hammadi, Sadoon Lawlah, PH.D.; Iraqi politician; b. 30; ed. Karhala High School, American Univ. of Beirut and Univ. of Wisconsin.
High school teacher 53; Univ. of Baghdad 57-58; Chief Editor, *Jumhuria* 58; Minister of Agrarian Reform 63.
Publ. *About the Present Crisis of Communism* 59.
c/o Ministry of Agrarian Reform, Baghdad, Iraq.

Hammarskjöld, Knut Olof Hjalmar Akesson; Swedish diplomatist; b. 16 Jan. 1922; ed. Stockholm Univ.
Entered Foreign Service 46, served Paris, Vienna, Moscow, Bucharest, Kabul, Sofia 47-55; Head of Foreign Relations Dept., Royal Board of Civil Aviation, Stockholm 57-59; Dep. Head, Swedish Del. to O.E.E.C.,

Paris 59-60; Dep. Sec.-Gen., European Free Trade Asscn. (EFTA) 60-66; Dir.-Gen. of Int. Air Transport Asscn. (IATA), Montreal 66-.
IATA, 1155 Mansfield Street, Montreal 3, P.Q., Canada. Telephone: 866-1011.

Hammerich, Louis L., PH.D., LITT.D.; Danish philologist; b. 31 July 1892; ed. Univ. of Copenhagen.
Sec. Danish Red Cross, P.O.W. Dept. 15-17, 18-19; teacher 19-21; Sec. Schleswig Frontier Comm. 20; Prof. of Germanic Philology Univ. of Copenhagen 22-58; editor of publs. of Royal Danish Acad. of Science and Letters; Pres. Int. Asscn. of Germanists 55-60, Int. Fed. for Modern Languages and Literatures 57-60, Int. Academic Union 65; Hon. degrees Utrecht, Nancy, Groningen, Kiel, Ghent; Goethe Medal, Frankfurt 58, Konrad Duden Prize, Mannheim 66, Grimm Brothers Prize, Marburg 59.
Publs. Books on philological and literary subjects.
Solbakkevej 66, Gentofte, Denmark.
Telephone: GE 4616.

Hammett, Louis Plack, A.B., PH.D.; American chemist; b. 7 April 1894; ed. Harvard Coll., Columbia Univ., Technische Hochschule, Zürich.
Civilian chemist, U.S. Army 17-19; with Columbia Univ. as Instructor, Asst. Prof., Assoc. Prof., Prof. since 20; on leave 41-45 for work under direction of Office of Scientific Research and Development, U.S. Govt.; Chair. Div. of Chemistry and Chemical Technology, Nat. Research Council 46-47; Consulting Ed. Int. *Chemical Series* 40-55; Chair. Bd. of Directors, American Chemical Soc. 61; Mitchill Prof. Emer. of Chemistry, Columbia Univ. 61-; Visiting Senior Chemist, Brookhaven Nat. Laboratory 62; Distinguished Visiting Lecturer Univ. of South Carolina 62, Pennsylvania State Univ. 64, Purdue Univ. 64; Hon. Fellow Chemical Soc. (London) 65; awarded William H. Nichols Medal 57, James Flack Norris Award 60, Priestly Medal, Willard Gibbs Medal 61, James Flack Norris Award in Physical Organic Chemistry 66, Gilbert Newton Lewis Medal 67, Nat. Medal of Science, Charles Frederick Chandler Medal 68; D.Sc. (Hon.) Columbia Univ. 62.
Publs. *Solutions of Electrolytes* 29, *Physical Organic Chemistry* 40, *Introduction to the Study of Physical Chemistry* 52.
R.D.4, Box 310, Newton, N.J. 07860, U.S.A.
Telephone: 383-272, Area Code 201.

Hammond Innes (Ralph); British author; b. 15 July 1913.
Financial News 34-40; Royal Artillery 40-46.
Publs. *Wreckers Must Breathe* 40, *The Trojan Horse* 40, *Attack Alarm* 41, *Dead and Alive* 46, *The Lonely Skier* 47, *Killer Mine* 47, *Maddon's Rock* 48, *The Blue Ice* 48, *The White South* 49, *The Angry Mountain* 50, *Air Bridge* 51, *Campbell's Kingdom* 52, *The Strange Land* 54, *The Mary Deare* 56, *The Land God Gave to Cain* 58, *Harvest of Journeys* 60, *The Doomed Oasis* 60, *Atlantic Fury* 62, *The Strode Venturer* 65, *Sea and Islands* 67, *The Conquistadors* 69; Films: *Snowbound, Hell Below Zero, Campbell's Kingdom, The Wreck of the Mary Deare.*
Ayres End, Kersey, Suffolk, England.
Telephone: Hadleigh (Suffolk) 3294.

Hamouz, František; Czechoslovak politician; b. 15 Aug. 1919; ed. Commercial Acad., Teplice.
North Bohemian Oil Works, Ustí n/Labem; Foreign Trade Service 48-, Oleaspol Co., later in Foreign Trade Corpn.; Chief. Man. Foreign Trade Corpn., Motokov 51-53; Dep. Minister for Foreign Trade 53-54; Dep. Sec. Council for Mutual Econ. Assistance, Moscow 54-58; First Dep. Minister for Foreign Trade 59-63, Minister for Foreign Trade 63-68; Deputy Prime Minister 68-; Perm. Rep. of Czechoslovakia to COMECON 68-;

Deputy to Nat. Assembly 64-; mem. State Planning Comm. 65-; Award for Merit in Construction 61.
Office of the Deputy Prime Minister, Prague, Czechoslovakia.

Hamperl, Herwig; Austrian pathologist; b. 12 Sept. 1899; ed. Universität Wien.
Assist. Prof. Vienna Univ. 31-35; Assoc. Prof. Berlin Univ. 35-40; Prof. and Dir. of Inst. Prague 40-45; Dir. Pathological Inst. Salzburg 46-49; Prof. and Dir. of Inst. Marburg Univ. 49-54, Bonn 54-; Hon. mem. Royal Soc. of Medicine, Acad. nacional de Medicina de Mexico, Soc. Española de Anatomia Patologica; mem. Royal Soc. of Sciences (Uppsala); Corresp. mem. German Acad. of Sciences (Berlin), Soc. of Physicians of Vienna, Soc. of Physicians Duodecim (Helsinki), American Asscn. for Cancer Research; Co-editor *Virchow's Archiv, Zeitschrift für Krebsforschung, Berichte der Pathologie.*
Publ. *Lehrbuch der Pathologie.*
53 Bonn, Ahornweg 4, German Federal Republic.
Telephone: 28-19-12.

Han Che-yi; Chinese administrator.
Mem. of North China Administrative Council and Dir. of Finance Dept. 54; Asst. Chair. of Finance and Economic Committee; Vice-Chair. State Budget Committee 54-56; Dir. Administrative Bureau and Vice-Chair. State Economic Commission 56; Alt. Sec. East China Bureau, Chinese Communist Party 62-.
East China Bureau of Chinese Communist Party, Peking, China.

Han Suyin, M.B., B.S., L.R.C.P., M.R.C.S.; British medical practitioner and author; b. 12 Sept. 1917; ed. Yenching Univ., Peking, Univ. of Brussels, Belgium, Royal Free Hospital, London Univ.
Born in China, educated in Peking and Brussels 35-38; in London 42-48; employed Queen Mary Hospital, Hong Kong 48-52, Johore Bahru Hospital, Malaya 52-55; private medical practice 55-63; Lecturer in Contemporary Asian Literature, Nanyang Univ., Singapore 60-63.
Publs. *Destination Chungking* 42, *A Many-Splendoured Thing* 52, . . . *And the Rain My Drink* 56, *The Mountain is Young* 58, *Cast but One Shadow* 62, *Winter Love* 62, *The Four Faces* 63, *The Crippled Tree* (autobiog.) 65, *A Mortal Flower* (autobiog.) 66, *China in the Year 2001* 67.
c/o Jonathan Cape, 30 Bedford Square, London, W.C.1, England.

Hanan, Josiah Ralph; New Zealand lawyer and politician; b. 13 June 1909; ed. Southland and Waitaki Boys High Schools and Otago Univ.
Private Law Practice 35-; Mayor of Invercargill 38-41; mem. of Parl. 46-, Minister of Health 54-57, of Justice, of Maori Affairs, in Charge of the Electoral Office, and Attorney-Gen. 60-, Minister of Island Territories 63-.
260A, Tinakori Road, Wellington, New Zealand.
Telephone: 45-896.

Hanania, Anastas; Jordanian diplomatist; b. 03; ed. American Univ., Beirut.
Lawyer in Jerusalem 26-48; joined Jordan Govt. 50; Minister of Posts and Telegraphs 51; of Development and Reconstruction 52; of Foreign Affairs 52; of Justice 53, 59; of Agriculture 53; Dep. Pres. of Development Board 58-59; Ambassador to U.K. 59-65.
c/o Ministry of Foreign Affairs, Amman, Jordan.

Hancock, John Walker, Jr.; American businessman; b. 11 April 1909; ed. Long Beach City Coll. and Southwestern Univ.
Joined Refining Dept. Hancock Oil Co. 24, Exec. Vice-Pres. 47-53, Pres. 53-58; Pres. and Dir. Belmont Aviation Corpn., Walker Development Co., Newport Development Co.; Vice-Chair. and mem. Advisory

Board, Long Beach State Coll.; Dir. R. M. Pyles Boys Camp, Western Oil and Gas Asscn. (Pres. 56), Independent Petroleum Asscn. of America, Calif. Natural Gasoline Asscn.
Office: 4201 North Long Beach Boulevard, Long Beach 7, Cal.; Home: 258 Roycroft Avenue, Long Beach 3, Cal., U.S.A.

Hancock, Sir (William) Keith, K.B.E., Kt., M.A., LITT.D., F.B.A.; British university professor; b. 26 June 1898; ed. Univ. of Melbourne and Balliol Coll., Oxford.
Fellow of All Souls Coll. Oxford 23; Prof. of Modern History, Univ. of Adelaide, Australia 26-33; Lecturer in Modern History, Balliol Coll., Oxford 30; Prof. of History Univ. of Birmingham 33; Chichele Prof. of Economic History, Univ. of Oxford 44-49; Supervisor of Civil Histories, War Cabinet Office 41-46; Prof. Commonwealth Affairs, Univ. of London, and Dir. Inst. of Commonwealth Studies 49-56; Dir. of Research School of Social Sciences 57-61; Prof. of History, Australian Nat. Univ., Canberra 57-65, Univ. Fellow 66-67, Emeritus Prof. 68-; Govt. expert to examine constitutional questions in Uganda 54; (Civil) Editor of British Official War Histories; Hon. D.Litt. (Rhodes, Oxford, Cape Town, Birmingham); Hon. Litt.D. (Cambridge, Melbourne, A.N.U.); Order of Merit, Italy; Foreign Hon. mem. American Acad. of Arts and Sciences.
Publs. *Ricasoli* 26, *Australia* 30, *Survey of British Commonwealth Affairs* 37-42, *Argument of Empire* 42, *Politics in Pitcairn* 47, *British War Economy* 49, *Wealth of Colonies* 50, *Country and Calling* 54, *War and Peace in This Century* 61, *Smuts: The Sanguine Years 1870-1919* Vol I 62, *Selections from the Smuts Papers* Vols. I-VI (edited with Dr. J. van der Poel), *Smuts: The Fields of Force 1919-50* Vol. II 68.
c/o Australian National University, Canberra; Home: 14 Liversidge Street, Acton, Canberra, A.C.T., Australia.
Telephone: 4-4593.

Hancock, Patrick Francis, C.M.G.; British diplomatist; b. 25 June 1914; ed. Winchester Coll. and Trinity Coll., Cambridge.
Foreign Service 37-, Principal Private Sec. to Foreign Sec. 55; Head of Western Dept., Foreign Office 56-59; Ambassador to Israel 59-62, to Norway 63-65; Asst. Under Sec. Foreign Office 65-.
Foreign Office, London, S.W.1; Home: 7 Paultons Street, London, S.W.3, and The Old Vicarage, Affpuddle, Dorset, England.
Telephone: 01-352-9088 and Puddletown 315.

Hand, Lloyd N., B.A., LL.B.; American lawyer; b. 31 Jan. 1929; ed. Charles M. Hilby High School, Houston and Univ. of Texas.
With U.S. Navy 52-55; Asst. to Senator Lyndon B. Johnson 57-61; Partner Allbritton, McGee and Hand, Houston 61-; Chief of Protocol of the U.S.A. 65-; Dir. several Corpns. in Los Angeles; mem. Board of Dirs. Continental Air Services; Pres. Worldwide Consultants, Inc.; mem. Board of Foreign Scholarships; Dir. Continental Air Lines Inc., MTRW (Mitsubishi Electric Co.—TRW, U.S.).
Office: 9808 Wilshire Boulevard, Calif.; Home: 507 North Sierra Drive, Beverly Hills, Calif., U.S.A.
Telephone: 274-6639 (Office); 273-3653 (Home).

Handfield-Jones, S. J.; Canadian (b. England) economist; b. 26 Dec. 1925; ed. Yale Univ. and New Coll., Oxford.
Economic Research Div., London School of Econs. and Political Science 50; Dept. of Trade and Industry, Nova Scotia, Canada 51-55; in Research Dept., Bank of Canada, Ottawa 55-, rising to Asst. Chief of Dept.; Alt. Exec. Dir. Int. Monetary Fund (IMF) and Int. Bank for Reconstruction and Devt.—World Bank (IBRD) 64-65; Exec. Dir. IMF 65-.
International Monetary Fund, Washington, D.C. 20431, U.S.A.

Handley, William J., B.A.; American diplomatist; b. 17 Dec. 1918; ed. Univs. of London and Maryland, American Univ.
With War Production Board 42-44, Foreign Econ. Admin. 44; joined Foreign Service 44, served on numerous posts in Middle East; Labor Admin., Bureau of Near Eastern, South Asian and African Affairs 49; New Delhi 51-52; transferred to U.S. Information Agency 53; Chief Near Eastern Policy Staff 55; Dep. Asst. Dir. Near East, South Asia and Africa 56, Asst. Dir. 57; Dir. Information Center Service 60; Ambassador to Mali 61-64; Deputy Asst. Sec. of State for Near Eastern and S. Asian Affairs 64-.
3424 North Venice Street, Arlington, Virginia, U.S.A.

Hanemann, Wilhelm; German economist; b. 30 Sept. 1910; ed. Univs. of Frankfurt, Berlin and Heidelberg.
Central Statistical Office, Berlin 34-35; Fed. of Trade, Berlin 35-40; Ministry of Transport, Nordrhein Westfalen 46-49; Fed. Central Statistical Office, Wiesbaden 49-51; Fed. Ministry for Econ. Affairs, Bonn 51-56; Alt. Exec. Dir. Int. Monetary Fund, Washington 56-59; Fed. Ministry for Econ. Affairs, Bonn 59-61; Exec. Dir. for Germany, Int. Monetary Fund, Washington 62-64; Asst. Sec.-Gen., Org. for Econ. Co-operation and Devt. (OECD) 64-66; Deputy Asst. Sec. Fed. Ministry for Econ. Affairs, Bonn 66-.
Bündesministerium für Wirtschaft, 53 Bonn-Duisdorf, German Federal Republic.
Telephone: 306-3734.

Hang Ou-tung; Chinese administrator; b. 07.
Chairman Liaoning Prov. People's Govt. 48; Sec. C.C.P. Mukden Municipal Cttee. and Vice-Mayor, Mukden 49-52; Mayor 52; Sec., First Sec. C.C.P. Liaoning Prov. Cttee. 54-58, Second Sec. 58-; Chair. Liaoning Cttee., People's Political Consultative Conf. 55-58; Gov. Liaoning 58-; Deputy from Mukden, Nat. People's Congress 54-; Alternate Mem. C.C.P. Central Cttee. 56-.
Governor's Residence, Shenyang, Liaoning, People's Republic of China.

Hanga, Sheikh Abdulla Kassim; Tanzanian politician; b. 31; ed. London School of Economics and Patrice Lumumba Univ., Moscow.
Member Afro Shirazi Party; Prime Minister of People's Republic of Zanzibar Jan. 64-April 64; Minister of Industry, Mines and Power, Tanzania 64, Minister of State for Union Affairs 65-.
Ministry of Union Affairs, Dar es Salaam, Tanzania.

Hani, Nasir Al-; Iraqi diplomatist; b. 20 March 1920; ed. Baghdad Univ., Univ. of Cairo and London Univ.
Former Asst. Prof. Baghdad Univ.; Dir. of Educ. Mission, Ministry of Educ.; Cultural Attaché, Washington; Lecturer, School of Oriental and African Studies, Univ. of London; Dir.-Gen. of Public Relations, Ministry of Foreign Affairs; fmr. Ambassador to Lebanon; Ambassador to Syrian Arab Republic 63; Under-Sec. Ministry of Foreign Affairs, Baghdad 63-64; Amb. to U.S.A. 64-67, to Lebanon 67-.
Publs. *Naqd Wa'Dab* 53, *Criticism and its Influence on the Early Abbasid Poets* 54, *Jamil Az-zahawi* 54, *Literary Terms of European Literature* 58, *Diwan Ar-ra'i Al-numairi* 64.
Embassy of Iraq, Ramlat al-Baida, Imm. Ali Arab, Beirut, Lebanon.

Haniel, Klaus; German business executive; b. 14 Jan. 1916; ed. Wilhelm-Gymnasium, Munich, and in Aachen, Berlin and Dortmund.
Chairman of Advisory Board Gutehoffnungshütte Aktienverein, Gutehoffnungshütte Sterkrade A.G.; mem. Advisory and Management Boards of numerous other firms.
Gutehoffnungshütte Aktienverein, 4200 Oberhausen (Rheinl.), German Federal Republic.

Hankey, 2nd Baron, cr. 39, of The Chart; **Robert Maurice Alers Hankey,** K.C.M.G., K.C.V.O., B.A.; British diplomatist; b. 4 July 1905; ed. Rugby and New Coll., Oxford.
Travelling Fellow, Queen's Coll., Oxford 26-27; entered Diplomatic Service 27; served in Berlin 27, Paris 28, Foreign Office, London 30; Private Sec. to Rt. Hon. Anthony Eden 33-36; served Warsaw 36, Bucharest 39, Cairo 41, Teheran 42, Foreign Office 43-45; Counsellor, British Embassy, Warsaw 45-46; Head of Northern Dept., Foreign Office 46-49; British Chargé d'Affaires, Madrid 49-51; Minister to Hungary 51-53; Ambassador to Sweden 54-60; Perm. Rep. to OEEC and Official Chair. 60; Perm. Del. to OECD and Chair. of Econ. Policy Cttee. 61-65; retd. from British Diplomatic Service 65; Vice-Pres. European Inst. of Business Admin. (INSEAD), Fontainebleau 62; mem. Int. Council of the Atlantic Colls., Council of Int. Baccalaureate Org.
Hethe House, Cowden, Kent, England.
Telephone: Cowden 538.

Hanley, Edward James, B.S., M.B.A.; American steel executive; b. 27 Feb. 1903; ed. Phillips Acad., Massachusetts Inst. of Technology and Harvard Business School.
General Electric Co. 27-36; Sec. Allegheny Ludlum Steel Corpn. 36-41, Treas. 41-46, Vice-Pres. (Finance) 46-49, Dir. 47-, Exec. Vice-Pres. 49-51, Pres. 51-67, Chair. and Chief Exec. Officer 67-; Dir. of other companies.
Allegheny Ludlum Steel Corporation, Oliver Building, Pittsburgh, Pa. 15222, U.S.A.

Hanley, James; British novelist; b. 01.
Publs. *Drift* 30, *The German Prisoner* 30, *Boy* 31, *Men in Darkness* 31, *Ebb and Flood* 31, *Aria and Finale*, *Captain Bottell* 33, *The Furys* 34, *The Maelstrom* 35, *Stoker Bush* 35, *The Secret Journey* 36, *Half an Eye* 37, *Grey Children* 37, *Broken Water* (autobiography) 37, *Hollow Sea* (novel) 38, *Soldiers Wind* (essays) 38, *People are Curious* (stories) 38, *Between the Tides* 39, *Our Time is Gone* 39, *The Ocean* 41, *Sailor's Song* 44, *No Directions*, *What Farrar Saw*, *Emily* (novels); *Crilley* (stories); *Collected Stories* 48; *Winter Song* (novel) 50; *A Walk in the Wilderness* (stories) 50; *The Closed Harbour* (novel) 52; *Don Quixote Drowned* (essays) 53; *The Welsh Sonata* (novel) 54, *Levine* (novel) 55, *An End and a Beginning* (novel) 58, *Say Nothing* (play) 62, *Plays One* (containing *The Inner Journey* and *The Stone Flower*) 68.
c/o David Higham Associates Ltd., Dean Street, London, W.1, England.

Hannah, John Alfred, B.S.; American university official; b. 9 Oct. 1902; ed. Grand Rapids Junior Coll., Univ. of Michigan and Michigan State Univ.
Secretary, State Board of Agriculture 35-41; Pres. Michigan State Univ. 41-, Nat. Asscn. of State Univs. and Land-Grant Colls. 48-49, Chair. of its Exec. Cttee. 49-51; Asst. Sec. of Defense 53-54; Chair. U.S. Section, Perm. Joint Board on Defense, Canada-U.S. 54-64, U.S. Comm. on Civil Rights 57-, American Council on Educ. 66-; Dir. Fed. Reserve Bank of Detroit 51-53, 56-60; mem. Int. Devt. Advisory Board 50-52, Rhodes Scholarship Selection Cttee. 61-62; numerous awards and hon. degrees.
Cowles House, West Circle Drive, East Lansing, Michigan 48823, U.S.A.

Hannaberry, Patrick Joseph, O.B.E., B.C.E.; Australian engineer; b. 12 Sept. 1904; ed. Melbourne Univ.
With Victorian Railways 23-34; joined Commonwealth Railways Dept. 34; Engineer of Way and Works 40; Chief Civil Engineer 44; Asst. Commr. 48; Commonwealth Railways Commr. 48-60; Railway Consultant 60-.
623 Collins Street, Melbourne, C.1, Australia.

Hannover, Georg Wilhelm, Prinz von, DR.IUR.; German educationist; b. 25 March 1915; ed. Hameln/ Weser High School, Marlborough Coll., Schule Schloss Salem, Univs. of Vienna and Göttingen.
Head, Salemer Schulen 48-59, now mem. Board of Dirs.; Chair. Outward Bound Mountain School (Austria); King Edward VII Foundation (German side); mem. Inst. for Town Planning; Hon. Pres. European Asscn. of Saving for Building Banks; mem. German Soc. for European Educ.; Pres. Int. Olympic Acad.
8166 Neuhaus bei Schliersee, Georgihaus, Upper Bavaria, German Federal Republic.

Hansen, Alvin Harvey, PH.D., LL.D., M.A.; American economist; b. 23 Aug. 1887.
Prof. Univ. of Minnesota 19-37; Lucius N. Littauer Prof. of Political Economy Harvard Univ. 37-60, Emer. 60-; Economist State Dept., Washington 34-35; Special Economic Adviser, Fed. Reserve System, Washington 40-45.
Publs. *Cycles of Prosperity and Depression* 21, *Business Cycle Theory* 27, *Fiscal Policy and Business Cycles* 41, *America's Role in the World Economy* 45, *Monetary Theory and Fiscal Policy* 49, *Business Cycles and National Income* 51, *A Guide to Keynes* 53, *The American Economy* 57, *Economic Issues of the 1960s*, *The Dollar and the International Monetary System* 65.
56 Juniper Road, Belmont, Mass., U.S.A.
Telephone: 484-4721.

Hansen, Bennet C. K.; Danish shipowner; b. 3 Aug. 1914.
Business experience with shipping firms in Britain and Germany; partner in shipping firm of C. K. Hansen and Copenhagen Stevedoring Co.; Chair. Steamship Co. Dantank Ltd., C. K. Hansen and Dannebrog Pension Scheme, C. K. Hansen Trust; Dir. Copenhagen Bunker Coal Depot Ltd., and Steamship Co. Dannebrog Ltd.
Amaliegade 35, Copenhagen, Denmark.

Hansen, Bent, FIL. DR.; Danish-born Swedish economist; b. 1 Aug. 1920; ed. Univs. of Copenhagen and Uppsala.
Civil servant, State Dept., Copenhagen 46; Lecturer Uppsala Univ. 47-48 and 50-51, Gothenburg 48-50; Reader, Uppsala 51-55; Prof. and Head of Konjunkturinst. (National Inst. of Economic Research), Stockholm 55-64, Consultant, Inst. of Nat. Planning, Cairo 62-65; Special Consultant for OECD, Paris 65-67; Prof. of Political Economy, Stockholm Univ. 67-.
Publs. *A Study in the Theory of Inflation* 51, *The Economic Theory of Fiscal Policy* 58, *Foreign Trade Credits and Exchange Reserves* 61, *Development and Economic Policy in the UAR (Egypt)* 65.
Stockholms Universitet, Drottninggatan 16, Stockholm, Sweden.

Hansen, Charles L.; Danish mechanical engineer and businessman; b. 27 Sept. 1891.
Fmrly. with Elsinore Ship and Engine-building Yard, East Asiatic Co. A/S, Engineer Burmeister and Wain Oil Engine Co. Ltd. Glasgow 13, Vacuum Oil Co. New York 15; Chief Engineer Scandinavian Vacuum Oil Co. 20, European Technical Manager 22; Commercial Dir. Vacuum Oil Co. A/S Copenhagen 26, mem. Board 35; Asst. Manager Socony-Vacuum Oil Co. Inc. New York 37-47; Exec. Man. 47-55; Chair. of Board of Burmeister and Wain American Corpn. 49; Dir. Socony Bunker Oil Co. Ltd. 47-56; mem. New York Acad. of Sciences 61; Pres. Rebild Nat. Park Soc. Inc. 63; Knight Cross 1st Class of the Order of Dannebrog.
Villa San Zeno, Lamone, Ticino, Switzerland (all mail); and 180 Central Park South, New York City 19, N.Y., U.S.A.

Hansen, Clifford Peter, B.S.; American banker, rancher and politician; b. 16 Oct. 1912; ed. Univ. of Wyoming.
Vice-President, Jackson State Bank 53-; Trustee Univ.

of Wyoming 46-, Pres. Board 56-63; fmr. Chair. Advisory Cttee. on Livestock Research and Marketing to Sec. of Agriculture; former Vice-Pres. Northwest Devt. Asscn.; Gov. of Wyoming 63-66; Senator from Wyoming 67-; mem. Wyoming Stock Growers' Asscn., Pres. 53-55; mem. American Nat. Cattlemen's Asscn., Sec. and Vice-Pres. 56-57; mem. Exec. Cttee. Nat. Govs. Conf. and Western Govs. Conf. 65-; Hon. LL.D. (Univ. Wyoming) 65; Republican.
2801 New Mexico Avenue, N.W., Washington, D.C., U.S.A.
Telephone: 202-337-3140; 202-225-3424.

Hansen, Hans Christian Poul; Danish politician; b. 27 Feb. 1913.
Sec. Social Democratic Youth Organisation 33-37, Chair. 37-42; on editorial staff *Fyns Social-Demokrat* 42-45; Sec. Information Centre of the Labour Movement 45-55, Social Democratic Organisation 55-56; Editor *Verdens Gang* 47-52; mem. Folketinget 45-, Sec. Social Democratic Parl. Group 47-50; mem. Parl. Defence Cttees. 46, 55, Chair. 56-58, Scandinavian Defence Cttee., Affairs Cttee. 53-56; Minister of Defence 56-62, Minister of Finance 62-65; mem. Social Democratic Party.
Publs. *Marchen til venstre* 45, *Danish Politicians* 49, *En bygning vi rejser* (co-author) 54-55.
Bredevej 3, Virum, Denmark.

Hansen, Hellmut; German mining industrialist; b. 23 Feb. 1896; ed. Univ. of Göttingen and Mining Coll., Clausthal.
Plant Man. Friedrich-Heinrich AG., Camplintfort 25-35; Dir. and Works Man. Heinitz/Saar Colliery (Saargruben AG) 35-45 (subsidiary of Frankenholz/Saar 42-); Dir. and mem. Management Bd. all Hoesch AG collieries, Essen-Altenessen 46-52; mem. Exec. Bd. Hoesch-Werke AG (Hoesch AG)., Dortmund 52-63; Chair. State Fed. of Ind. Employers Asscns. (North-Rhine Westphalia), Düsseldorf, Lippeverband, Essen; mem. Presidium, German Fed. of Employers, Cologne; Chair. Advisory Bd. Hoesch-AG Bergbau, Essen Altenessen; Fed. Labour Judge, Fed. Labour Court, Kassel 53-63; mem. Social Advisory Board, Fed. Ministry of Labour and Social Order until 63; Chair. German Inst. for Industry, Cologne; mem. Exec. Board, Econ. Asscn. for Mining, Bad Godesberg 63-64.
9 Limbecker Postweg, Dortmund-Hoechsten, German Federal Republic.

Hansen, Irwin Roy; American businessman; b. 16 Aug. 1913; ed. Univ. of Wisconsin.
With Haskins & Sells (C.P.A.'s) 36-44; joined Minn. Mining & Mfg. Co., St. Paul 44, Gen. Auditor 44-50, Asst. Controller 50-54, Asst. Treas. 54-57, Treas. 57-63, Vice-Pres. (Finance) 63-; Dir. and Vice-Pres. Salisbury Cruises Ltd.; Dir. 3M Foundation; Treas. Big Rock Stone and Material Co., Prehler Electric Insulating Co.; Dir. Mutual Broadcasting Co., Business Products Sales Inc., Wonewok Lodge Inc., First Nat. Bank of St. Paul.
2501 Hudson Road, St. Paul 19, Minn., U.S.A.

Hansen, Kurt, DR.ING.; German businessman; b. 11 Jan. 1910; ed. Technische Hochschule, Munich.
With I. G. Farbenindustrie A.G./Farbenfabriken Bayer A.G., Leverkusen 36-; Man. Uerdingen Factory, Farbenfabriken Bayer Jan. 55, Wuppertal-Elberfeld Factory April 56-57; mem. Bd. of Management, Farbenfabriken Bayer 57-61, Chair. 61-; Chair. Supervisory Board Agfa-Gevaert A.G.; mem. Supervisory Board Allianz Versicherungs-Aktiengesellschaft, Erdölchemie G.m.b.H., Hamburg-Amerika Linie, Siemens A.G., Otto Wolff A.G.; Prof.
Farbenfabriken Bayer A.G., 509 Leverkusen-Bayerwerk, German Federal Republic.
Telephone: 30-6530.

18

Hansen, Victor Georg; Danish lawyer; b. 29 Aug. 1889.
Employed in Min. of Justice 17-27; Judge in Court of Copenhagen 27-37; Judge in High Court of Copenhagen 37-41; Judge in Supreme Court 41-59; Legal Adviser to Min. of Health; Pres. Danish Labour Court of Arbitration 53-60; Hon. Ph.D. (Univ. of Copenhagen).
Publs. Twenty-two vols. on Danish beetles in *Danmarks Fauna*; *Retsplejen ved Höjesteret* (Organisation and Procedure of the Danish Supreme Court).
I.E. Ohlsensgade 4, Copenhagen, Denmark.
Telephone: Øbro 6863.

Hanson, Howard; American music teacher, conductor and composer; b. 28 Oct. 1896; ed. Luther Coll. Conservatory, Univ of Nebraska, Inst. of Musical Art of New York and Northwestern Univ., Evanston, Illinois.
Prof. of Music and Dean of Conservatory of Fine Arts, Coll. of the Pacific 19-21; winner of Prix de Rome when Fellow of American Acad. in Rome 21-24; Dir. Eastman School of Music, Rochester, N.Y. 24-64; Dir. Inst. of American Music, Univ. of Rochester 64-; guest conductor of numerous American and foreign symphony orchestras; Fellow Swedish Royal Acad. of Music; mem. Nat. Inst. of Arts and Letters; over thirty Honorary Doctorates; Pulitzer Prize, Peabody Award, Freedom Award, Huntington Hartford Foundation Award, etc.
Works include: (orchestra) six symphonies, *Elegy in Memory of Serge Koussevitzky*, *Mosaics*, *Summer Seascape*, Concerto for Organ, Strings and Harp; (choral) *Songs from "Drum Taps"* (after Walt Whitman), *The Cherubic Hymn*, *Song of Democracy*, *Song of Human Rights*; (opera) *Merry Mount*; (chamber) Quintet for piano and strings, *Concerto da Camera* for piano and strings, String Quartet, *Bold Island Suite*, *Concerto for Piano and Orchestra*, *Four Psalms* for baritone and strings, *Summer Seascapes* Nos. 1 and 2; piano music and songs.
Publ. *Harmonic Materials of Modern Music*.
362 Oakdale Drive, Rochester, N.Y. 14618, U.S.A.
Telephone: BR1-9009.

Hanuszkiewicz, Adam; Polish actor and theatre director; b. 16 June 1924; ed. State High School of Drama, Łódź, and State High School of Drama, Warsaw.
Debut as actor 45, acted in Cracow, Poznań and Warsaw; debut as dir. 53, directed in Poznań and Warsaw; Artistic Dir. Polish Television 56-63; Dir. and Producer, Popular Theatre, Warsaw 63-, visited, with theatre company, Prague 64, 66, Moscow 65, London 66, Paris 66; acted in 50 major roles in theatre; directed 30 plays in theatre, 100 television plays; State Award (First Class) for TV work; City of Warsaw Award for theatre work; Theatre Critics' Prize 64.
Principal roles include: Hamlet (*Hamlet*) 51-59, Tytus (*Berenicia*, Racine) 62, Prospero (*The Tempest*, Shakespeare) 63, Raskolnikov (*Crime and Punishment*, Dostoevsky) 64, Don Juan (*Don Juan*, Molière) 65.
Plays directed include: *The Wedding* (Wyspiański), *Crime and Punishment* (Dostoevsky), *Coriolanus* (Shakespeare), *Don Juan* (Molière), *Platonov* (Chekhov), *The Columbus Boys* (Bratny).
Teatr Powszechny, Warsaw, Zamojskiego 20, Poland.

Harada, Ken; Japanese diplomatist and Grand Master of Ceremonies; b. 6 Dec. 1892; ed. Tokyo Univ.
Ministry of Foreign Affairs 19-56; mem. League of Nations Secretariat 20-38; Counsellor of Embassy, Paris 40, Minister 42; Ambassador to Vatican 42-46; Dir.-Gen. and Vice-Pres. U.N.A. of Japan 47-52; Ambassador to Italy 52-55; Grand Master of Ceremonies to H.M. Emperor of Japan 57-; Grand Cross: Order of Sacred Treasure, Order of Pius X (Holy See), Order of Merit (Italy), Order of Homayoun (Iran), Order of Merit (Peru), Order of Leopold II (Belgium), Order of Crown (Thailand), Hon. K.B.E., and numerous other decorations.
Imperial Palace, Tokyo, Japan.

Harcourt, 2nd Viscount; **William Edward Harcourt,** K.C.M.G., O.B.E., M.A., D.L.; British banker; b. 08; ed. Eton Coll. and Christ Church, Oxford.
Served in Royal Artillery and on the Staff in Middle East and Mediterranean Theatres 39-45; H.M. Minister (Economic) British Embassy and Head of U.K. Treasury Del., Washington 54-57; U.K. Exec. Dir. of Int. Bank for Reconstruction and Development and of Int. Monetary Fund 54-57; Chair. Messrs. Morgan Grenfell & Co. Ltd., Legal and General Assurance Society Ltd., Gresham Life Assurance and Fire Insurance Societies, British Commonwealth Insurance Co. Ltd.; Dir. Plessey Co. Ltd.; mem. Departmental (Radcliffe) Cttee. on Monetary and Credit Policy 57-59; mem. Plowden Cttee. on Representational Services Overseas; Adviser, Int. Finance Corpn. 62-; Rhodes Trustee; Chair. of Trustees London Museum; Chair. Board of Govs. Museum of London.
Stanton Harcourt, Oxford; and 23 Culross Street, London, W.1, England.

Harden, Donald Benjamin, O.B.E., M.A., PH.D., F.S.A., F.M.A.; British museum official; b. 8 July 1901; ed. Westminster School, Trinity Coll., Cambridge, and Univ. of Michigan.
Senior Asst., Dept. of Humanity, Univ. of Aberdeen 24-26; Commonwealth Fund Fellow 26-28; Asst. Keeper, Dept. of Antiquities, Ashmolean Museum, Oxford 29-45, Keeper 45-56; Leverhulme Research Fellowship 53; Vice-Pres. Soc. of Antiquaries, London 49-53, 64-67; Pres. Council for British Archaeology 50-54; Pres. Oxford Architectural and Historical Society 52-54; Pres. Section H, British Asscn. 55; Dir. London Museum 56-; Pres. Museums Asscn. 60-61; Pres. London and Middlesex Archaeological Soc. 59-64, Royal Archaeological Inst. 66-; mem. governing bodies British Schools of Archaeology in Jerusalem and Iraq, London Univ. Inst. of Archaeology, Soc. for Medieval Archaeology, Ancient Monuments Board for England, Royal Comm. on Historical Monuments (England).
Publs. *Roman Glass from Karanis* 36, *The Anglo-Saxon Cemetery at Abingdon, Berks.* (with E. T. Leeds) 36; *The Phoenicians* 62. Editor *Dark-Age Britain* 56, and *Medieval Archaeology* (annually).
12 St. Andrew's Mansions, Dorset Street, London, W.1; and London Museum, Kensington Palace, W.8, England.

Harder, Howard Charles; American food products executive; b. 15 May 1916; ed. Univ. of Texas and Harvard Univ.
With Corn Products Refining Co. (now Corn Products Co.), New York City 37-, successively accountant, Asst. Treas., Asst. Comptroller, Exec. Asst. to Exec. Vice-Pres. 37-57, Treas. 57-58, Comptroller 58-, Vice-Pres. (Finance) 59-61, Senior Vice-Pres. 61-64, Exec. Vice-Pres. (Admin.) 64-65, Pres. 65-, also Dir.; Dir. Otis Elevator Co., People's Trust Co. of Bergen County 67-, Carrier Corpn. 68-; mem. Trust Board, First Nat. City Bank; U.S. Army 42-46.
Corn Products Co., 717 Fifth Avenue, New York, N.Y. 10022; Home: 170 Boulevard, Mountain Lakes, N.J., U.S.A.

Harders, Friedrich Eugen, DR. ING., DR. PHIL., DIPL. CHEM.; German iron and steel executive; b. 09; ed. Gymnasium (Mannheim, Leipzig, Dortmund) and Martin Lüther-Universität, Halle-Wittenberg, Westfälische Wilhelms-Universität, Münster, and Bergakademie Clausthal-Technische Hochschule, Clausthal-Zellerfeld.
Member of Management Board, Dortmund-Hörder Hüttenverein A.G., Dortmund 46; Technical mem.

Management Board, Hüttenwerk Hörde A.G., Dortmund-Hörde 47; Technical mem. Management Board, Dortmund-Hörder Hüttenunion A.G., Dortmund 52-62, Chair. Management Board 62-.
Dortmund-Hörder Hüttenunion A.G., Rheinische Strasse 173, 46-Dortmund, German Federal Republic.

Harding, Lt.-Col. George Richardson, D.S.O., M.B.E.; British industrialist; b. 15 Sept. 1884; ed. Brighton.
Civil engineer, England 01-07, Canada 07-14; served First World War 14-19; Chair. Maconochie Bros. Ltd. 26-42; Dir. Aplin & Barrett 43-60, Chair. 56-; Pres. Food Manufacturers' Federation Inc. 37-43; mem. Consultative Cttee. on A.R.P., Home Office 39-43; mem. Nat. Advisory Council on Fire Prevention 41-43; mem. Council, Hon. Treas. 38, 39, Deputy Chair. 40, Chair. 41-43, Vice-Pres. 43-, London Chamber of Commerce; Chair. Food Manufacturers' Export Group 40; mem. Food Prices Control Cttee. 40-; Chair. British Food Manufacturing Industries Research Asscn. 48-52; mem. Postmaster-General's Advisory Council 46-65; Vice-Pres. Asscn. of British Chambers of Commerce 49-55; mem. Council of Foreign Bondholders 44-56, and Board of Referees 53-65.
Wildwood, Abbots Drive, Virginia Water, Surrey, England.
Telephone: Wentworth 2137.

Harding of Petherton, 1st Baron, cr. 58, of Nether Compton; **Field Marshal John Harding,** G.C.B., C.B.E., D.S.O., M.C.; British army officer; b. 1896; ed. Ilminster Grammar School.
Served with Territorial Army and Machine Gun Corps, First World War 14-19; Lieut. Somerset Light Infantry 20, Capt. 23; Brigade Major, British Force, Saar Plebiscite; p.s.c. 28; Brevet Major 35, Brevet Lieut.-Col. 38, Lieut.-Col. 39, Brigadier 42, Major-Gen. 42, Lieut.-Gen. 43, Gen. 49; served Second World War 39-45; G.O.C. Central Mediterranean Forces 46-47; G.O.C.-in-C. Southern Command 47-49; C.-in-C. Far East Land Forces 49-51; C.-in-C. British Army of the Rhine 51-52; Chief Imperial Gen. Staff 52-55; A.D.C. to late King 50-52, to Queen 52-53; Gov. and C.-in-C. Cyprus 55-57; Dir. Nat. Provincial Bank 57-, Standard Bank 65-, Western Gazette Co. 58-; Gold Stick to H.M. The Queen 57-64; Dir. The Plessey Co. 62-64, Deputy Chair. 64-67, Chair. 67-; Chair. Horserace Betting Levy Board 61-67, Williams (Hounslow) Ltd. 62-, Assoc. Tees-side Stores Ltd. 62-; Hon. D.C.L. (Durham Univ.).
Lower Farm, Nether Compton, Nr. Sherborne, Dorset, England.

Hardy, Sir Alister Clavering, Kt., F.R.S., M.A., D.SC., LL.D.; British zoologist; b. 10 Feb. 1896; ed. Oundle School and Exeter Coll., Oxford.
Lieut. and Capt. First World War 15-19; Royal Engineers Asst. Camouflage Officer 18; Asst. Naturalist, Fisheries Dept., Min. of Agriculture and Fisheries 21-24; Chief Zoologist *Discovery* Expedition 24-28; Prof. Zoology and Oceanography, Univ. Coll. of Hull 28-42; Regius Prof. Natural History, Aberdeen 42-45; Linacre Prof. Zoology and Comparative Anatomy, Oxford 45-61. Publs. *The Open Sea: the World of Plankton* 56, *The Open Sea: Fish and Fisheries* 59, *The Living Stream* 65, *The Divine Flame* 66, *Great Waters* 67.
7 Capel Close, Oxford, England.
Telephone: Oxford 54381.

Hare, Raymond Arthur, A.B.; American diplomatist; b. 3 April 1901; ed. Grinnell Coll.
Instructor, Robert Coll., Constantinople 24-27; Exec. Sec. American Chamber of Commerce for Levant 26-27; Clerk, later Vice-Consul, U.S. Consulate-Gen., Constantinople 27-28; Language Officer, Paris, 29, 31, also Vice-Consul 31; Sec. in Diplomatic Service and Vice-Consul, Cairo 31; Vice-Consul, Beirut 32; Third Sec. and Vice-Consul, Teheran 33; Dept. of State 35; Second Sec., Cairo 39, also at Jeddah 40-44, also Consul, Cairo

40; Second Sec., later First Sec. and Consul, London 44; Dept. of State 46; Nat. War Coll. 46-47; Chief, Div. of Middle East, Indian and South Asian Affairs 47; Deputy Dir. Office of Near East and African Affairs 48; Deputy Asst. Sec. of State for Near East, S. Asian and African Affairs Oct. 49; Ambassador to Saudi Arabia and Minister to Yemen 50-53; Ambassador to the Lebanon 53-54; Dir.-Gen. U.S. Foreign Service 54-56; Ambassador to Egypt 56-58, Ambassador to U.A.R. 58-60, also Minister to Yemen 59; Deputy Under-Sec. of State (Political Affairs) 60-61; Ambassador to Turkey 61-65; Asst. Sec. of State (Near Eastern and S. Asian Affairs) 65-66; Pres. Middle East Inst. 66-.
Middle East Institute, 1761 N. Street, N.W., Washington, D.C. 20016; Home: 3214 39th Street, N.W., Washington, D.C. 20016, U.S.A.
Telephone: 202-244-4877.

Harewood, The Earl of; **George Henry Hubert Lascelles;** British musical administrator; b. 7 Feb. 1923; ed. Eton Coll. and King's Coll., Cambridge.
Captain, Grenadier Guards 42-46; prisoner of war 44-45; A.D.C. to Earl of Athlone, Gov.-Gen. of Canada 45-46; Counsellor of State during absence of the Sovereign 47, 54 and 56; mem. Board of Dirs. Royal Opera House, Covent Garden 51-53, Admin. Exec. 53-60; Dir.-Gen. Leeds Musical Festival 58-; Artistic Dir. Edinburgh Int. Festival 61-65; Chair. British Council Music Advisory Cttee. 56-66, Arts Council Music Panel 66-; Pres. English Opera Group, Royal Manchester Coll. of Music, British Italian Soc. 56-; Pres. English Football Asscn. 64-; Chancellor, York Univ. 66-67; Editor *Opera* 50-53, *Kobbé's Complete Opera Book* 54; Austrian Great Silver Medal of Honour 59.
Harewood House, Leeds, Yorks.; and 121 Hamilton Terrace, London, N.W.8, England.

Harhoff, Preben; Danish shipowner; b. 29 Nov. 1911; ed. Copenhagen Univ. and in Germany, England and France.
Partner C. K. Hansen, Copenhagen 50-, Copenhagen Stevedoring Co. 50-; Dir. The Copenhagen Bunker Coal Depot Ltd. 46, Dannebrog Steamship Co. Ltd. 50, Dantank Steamship Co. Ltd. 52-65; Chair. Dantank 65-; Chair. Vendila Steamship Co. Ltd. 63-; Dir. Dansk Transatlantisk Rederi Ltd. 57-65, Chair. 65-; Dir. Int. Paints Ltd., Copenhagen 46-53, Chair. 53-; Subsidiary Dir. Exec. Cttee. The Baltic and Int. Maritime Conf. 51-63, Dir. 63, Vice-Chair. 65, Subsidiary Dir. of its Board of Dirs. 53; Dir. Copenhagen Marine Insurance Asscn. Ltd. 58, British Import Union, Copenhagen 58, Dansk Radio Aktieselskab 60, Elektromekano Ltd. 60, Selskabet Orlogsmuseets Venner 65, Whitbread & Co. (Scandinavia) Ltd. 65, and numerous other companies; Hon. Consul-Gen. for Tunisia in Copenhagen 62; several decorations.
Office: C. K. Hansen, 35 Amaliegade, 1256 Copenhagen K; Home: Olaf Poulsensvej 12, 2920 Copenhagen-Charlottenlund, Denmark.
Telephone: HE 6262.

Harington, Sir Charles Robert, K.B.E., F.R.S., M.A., PH.D.; British biochemist; b. 1 Aug. 1897; ed. Malvern Coll., Magdalene Coll., Cambridge, and Univ. of Edinburgh.
Research Asst. Dept. of Therapeutics Edinburgh Univ. 20-22; Lecturer in Pathological Chemistry Univ. Coll. Hospital Medical School London 22; Dir. Graham Laboratories, Univ. Coll. Hospital Medical School 37-42; Reader in Pathological Chemistry, London Univ. 28-31; Prof. of Pathological Chemistry 31-42; Editor *Biochemical Journal* 30-42; mem. Medical Research Council 38-42; Dir. Nat. Inst. for Medical Research 42-62; mem. Agricultural Research Council 41-45; Croonian Lecturer and Royal Medal, Royal Soc. 44; Hon. Fellow, Magdalene Coll., Cambridge 44, Royal Soc. of Medicine

59, Royal Coll. of Physicians 63; Hon. Sc.D., Hon. F.R.C.P.

Publ. *The Thyroid Gland: its Chemistry and Physiology* 33.

6 Waverley Court, Beaumont Street, London, W.1, England.

Harkavy, Rabbi Zvi, B.A., M.A., TH.D.; Russian-born Israeli author and librarian; b. 1 Feb. 1908; ed. Inst. of Admin., Bibliography and Booklore in Russia, Jerusalem Teachers' Seminary, Haifa Technion, Hebrew Univ. of Jerusalem, Petach Tivka Yeshiva, C.S.R.A.

Leader in Zionist underground in Russia; emigrated to Palestine 26; schoolmaster and lecturer Jerusalem Teachers' Seminaries 30-; Dir. Eretz Yisrael Publishing House 35-; Chaplain in Israeli Army 48-49; Dir. Dept. of Refugees in Ministry of War Casualties and later Editor of Ministry of Religious Affairs *Monthly* 49-53; Dir. Central Rabbinical Library of Israel 53-68; Editor *Hasefer* 54-; mem. Exec. Union of Israel Librarians 55-; Visiting Prof. Yeshira Univ., N.Y. 59; lectured in U.S.S.R. Acad. of Sciences, Leningrad 62; Editor of *Yad Lakorei*; Founder Religious Writers Org., then Chair.; one of the founders of the Religious Academics Org. and fmr. Chair.; an Editor of the *General Encyclopaedia* and of numerous periodicals and books; Del. to numerous congresses abroad; Komemiyut, Mishmar and Hagana Medals.

Publs. Biographies: *Rambam, Rabbi Shmuel Strashun, Rabbi Mateth Strashun, S. Rosanes, Rabbi I. M. Pines, Professor Simcha Assaf, A. E. Harkavy, Rabbi Reuven Katz (Chief Rabbi of Petach Tikvat); Research into Famous Families; The Family Maskil L'eitan, The Family Harkavy, Jews of Salonica, The Jewish Community of Ekaterinoslav; Scepticism of Pascal; The Man, The Plant, The Animal, Inorganic Nature; The Secret of Happy Marriage, Sexual Hygiene from the Religious and Scientific Viewpoint; Judaicainin Russen*, etc. (62 books); also about a thousand articles and papers on bibliography, Rabbinics, theology, philosophy, philology, history and the Dead Sea Scrolls.

P.O. Box 7031, 7 Haran Street, Jerusalem, Israel. Telephone: 32963.

Harker, David, B.S., PH.D.; American scientist; b. 19 Oct. 1906; ed. Univ. of Calif., Calif. Inst. of Technology.

Research Asst., Atmospheric Nitrogen Corpn., Solvay, N.Y. 30-33; Instructor in Chemistry Johns Hopkins Univ. 36-39, Assoc. in Chemistry 39-41; Assoc., Research Laboratory, Gen. Electric Co., Schenectady, N.Y. 41-49, Head Crystallography Div. 49-50; Dir. The Protein Structure Project, Polytechnic Inst. of Brooklyn 50-59; Adjunct Prof. of Physics 53-56; Prof. of Crystallography, Polytechnic Inst. of Brooklyn 56-59; Head Biophysics Dept. Roswell Park Memorial Inst. 59-; Research Prof. of Biophysics, State Univ. of N.Y., Buffalo 60-, Professorial Lecturer 59-; Visiting Prof. of Biophysics, Univ. of Rochester 65-; Adjunct Prof. of Physics, State Univ. Coll. at Buffalo, N.Y. 66-; mem. U.S. Nat. Comm. on Crystallography, Nat. Research Council 51-56, 58-63, Chair. 54-55; Chief American Del. to Int. Congress on X-ray Crystallography, London 46; Del. to Gen. Assembly, Int. Union of Crystallography, Stockholm 51, Paris 54, Montreal 57 and Cambridge 60; fmr. mem. Electron Microscope Soc. of America (Pres. 46, 47); mem. American Society for X-ray and Electron Diffraction (Pres. 46), Société Française de Minéralogie et de Crystallographie, American Crystallographic Asscn., Biophysical Soc., and A.A.A.S.; Fellow, American Inst. of Mining and Metallurgical Engineers, New York Acad. of Sciences, American Physical Soc.; consultant on X-ray Diffraction to X-ray Dept. of Gen. Electric Co. 53-, to Carborundum Co. 62-; Advisory Editor, Trans. Russian Journal *Crystallography* 58-; Dir. Center for Crystallographic Research, Roswell Park Div. of Health Research, Inc., Buffalo 65-; mem. Advisory Board Russian Trans., American Inst. Physics; Del. VIIth Gen. Assembly, Int. Congress and Symposium, Int. Union Crystallography 66.

Home: 23 High Street, Buffalo, N.Y. 14203; Office: Roswell Park Memorial Institute, Buffalo, N.Y. 14203, U.S.A.

Telephone: 886-2666.

Harkness, Hon. Douglas Scott, P.C., G.M., E.D., B.A.; Canadian farmer and politician; b. 29 March 1903; ed. Central High School, Calgary and Univ. of Alberta.

High School teacher 26-39; active service with Canadian Army in Europe 39-45, Lieut.-Col.; farming and livestock business; mem. House of Commons 45-; Minister of Northern Affairs and Nat. Resources June 57-Aug. 57; Minister of Agriculture Aug. 57-Oct. 60, of Nat. Defence Oct. 60-63; Progressive Conservative.

4232 Elbow Drive, Calgary, Alberta; and House of Commons, Ottawa, Canada.

Harkness, Col. R. Dickson, D.S.O., M.C., K.G.ST.J., B.SC., L.L.D.; Canadian electrical engineer; b. 23 Dec. 1892; ed. Cornwall High School and Queen's Univ., Kingston, Ontario.

Served First World War 14-19; Dir. Northern Electric Co. 38-67, Vice-Pres. and Gen. Man. 38, Pres. 48, Chair. of Board 61-62; Dir. Montreal Trust Co.; Hon. Dir. Dominion Bridge Co.; Dir. Bell Telephone Co. of Canada 51-63, Cominco 53-66, Howard Smith Paper Mills 47-61, Domtar 61-68, Royal Bank of Canada 52-56, Sun Life Assurance Co. of Canada 54-68; mem. Defence Research Board of Canada 47-50, 53-56; Chair. Board of Trustees, Queen's Univ., Kingston, Ont.; mem. Engineering Inst. of Canada, Corps of Engineers, Quebec.

Braeside, R.R.I., Kingston, Ont., Canada. Telephone: 544-1441.

Harkort, Peter Guenther, DR.RER.POL.; German diplomatist; b. 1 Sept. 1905; ed. Städt. Real-Gymnasium Hagen i W., Univs. of Heidelberg, Berlin, Bonn, Kiel.

Reich Statistical Office, Ministry of Nat. Economy; Württemberg-Baden Ministry of Nat. Economy; bizonal Admin. of Nat. Economy; German Bureau for Peace Questions; Rep. to ECA, Washington 49-52; Foreign Service 52-, Ministerial Dir., Head of Commercial Dept., Bonn 58-61; Ambassador and Perm. Rep. to the EEC and EURATOM, Brussels 61-65; Ministerial Dir., Head, Dept. Commerce and Devt., Bonn 65-.

Mecklenburgerstr. 3, 532 Bad Godesberg, German Federal Republic.

Telephone: Bad Godesberg 7-57-33.

Harlan, John Marshall, M.A., LL.B.; American lawyer; b. 20 May 1899; ed. Princeton Univ., Balliol Coll., Oxford (Rhodes Scholar) and New York Law School.

Admitted to New York Bar 25; joined firm of Root, Clark, Buckner & Howland (later Root, Ballantine, Harlan, Bushby & Palmer) as an assoc. 23; mem. of firm 31-54; Judge, U.S. Court of Appeals, Second Circuit 54-55; Justice of Supreme Court of the U.S.A. Mar. 55-; Chief Counsel, N.Y. State Crime Comm. 51; Col. U.S. Army Air Force 43-45; Legion of Merit, Croix de Guerre (France, Belgium); Hon. LL.D. (Brandeis, Evansville, N.Y. Law School, Princeton, Columbia, Oberlin, Michigan, Harvard).

1677 31st Street, N.W., Washington, D.C., U.S.A.

Harland, Sydney Cross, D.SC., F.R.S., F.R.S.E.; British cotton geneticist; b. 19 June 1891; ed. King's Coll., London Univ.

Head Botanical Dept. British Cotton Industry Research Asscn. Manchester 20-23; Prof. of Botany Imperial Coll. of Tropical Agriculture Trinidad 23-26; Chief Geneticist Empire Cotton Growing Corpn. 26-35; gen.

adviser Brazilian State Cotton Industry 35-39; Dir. Institute of Cotton Genetics, Nat. Agricultural Society Peru 39-50; Harrison Prof. of Botany, Univ. of Manchester 50-58, Emeritus 58-; mem. Agric. Research Council 50.
Cliff Grange, Snainton, Scarborough, Yorks., England.

Harlech, 5th Baron (cr. 1876); **William David Ormsby Gore,** P.C., K.C.M.G.; British diplomatist; b. 20 May 1918; ed. Eton and New Coll., Oxford.
War Service 39-45; Conservative M.P. 50-61; Parl. Private Sec. to Minister of State for Foreign Affairs 51-56; Parl. Under-Sec. of State for Foreign Affairs 56-57; Minister of State for Foreign Affairs 57-61; Amb. to U.S.A. Oct. 61-65; Deputy Leader Conservative Party, House of Lords 66-67; Chair. Harlech Television 67-; Pres. British Board of Film Censors 65-; Chair. Kennedy Memorial Trust; Pres. The Pilgrims of Great Britain; Hon. LL.D. (New York, Farleigh Dickinson and Manchester Univ.); Hon. D.C.L. (Pittsburgh Univ.); Hon. D.IUR (Brown Univ., Providence, and Coll. of William and Mary, Williamsburg).
Publ. *Must the West Decline?* 66.
Woodhill, Oswestry, Shropshire, England.
Telephone: Oswestry 3134.

Harlem, Gudmund, M.D.; Norwegian doctor and politician; b. 24 July 1917; ed. Medical School, Oslo Univ.
Assistant Physician Hygiene Inst., Oslo Univ. 46-48; Senior Physician State Rehabilitation Centre, Oslo 53-; studied rehabilitation in Great Britain 47, 48 and 50, in U.S.A. 49-50; as UN Technical Expert on Rehabilitation went on missions to Egypt 54, Greece and Italy 55; Deputy Chair. Oslo Labour Party 52-, mem. Central Cttee. Labour Party 53-57; mem. Norwegian Nat. Research Council 49-57; Chair. Rehabilitation Council 55-57; Minister of Health and Social Affairs 55-61, of Defence 61-65; Resident, Oslo Univ. Hospital 65-66; Pres. Int. Soc. for Rehabilitation of the Disabled 66-; Lasker Award 60; Labour.
State Rehabilitation Institute in Oslo, Sinsenvn. 76, Refstad, Oslo 5, Norway.
Telephone: 02-227760.

Harman, Avraham, B.A.; Israeli diplomatist; b. 14; ed. Oxford Univ.
Emigrated to Israel 38; held posts in Jewish Agency 38-48; Deputy Dir. Govt. Information Bureau 48-49; Consul-Gen. Montreal 49-50, New York, and Counsellor Del. to UN 50-53; Consul-Gen. in New York 53-55; Asst. Dir.-Gen. Ministry of Foreign Affairs 55-56; Dir. Information Dept. Jewish Agency 57-59; Ambassador to the U.S.A. 59-68.
3 Disraeli Street, Talbiah, Jerusalem, Israel.

Harmel, Pierre Charles José Marie, D. EN D.; Belgian university professor and politician; b. 11.
Prof., Faculty of Law, Univ. of Liège 47-; mem. and fmr. Vice-Pres. Chamber of Reps.; Minister of Public Instruction and Fine Arts June 50-54; Minister of Justice 58; Minister of Cultural Affairs 59-60; Minister of Admin. 60-61; Prime Minister July 65-66; Minister of Foreign Affairs 66-; Croix de Guerre with palms 40.
Publs. *Principes non bis in idem et les droits d'enregistrement* 42, *La Famille et l'Impôt en Belgique* 44, *Culture et Profession* 44, *Les Sources et la Nature de la Responsabilité Civile des Notaires, en droit Belge de 1830 à 1962* 64.
Mont St. Martin 54, Liège, Belgium.

Harmer, Frederic Evelyn, C.M.G.; British shipping executive; b. 3 Nov. 1905; ed. Eton and King's Coll., Cambridge.
Treasury 39, Temporary Asst. Sec. 43-45, served Washington 44, 45; Dir. Peninsular and Orient Steam Navigation Co. 55-57, Deputy Chair. 57-; Govt. Dir. British Petroleum Co. Ltd.; Dir. Westminster Bank

Ltd.; Vice-Chair. of Governors, London School of Econs.; Chair. Cttee. of European Shipowners.
Stanny, Aldeburgh, Suffolk, England.

Harms, Hans, DR. ING.; German chemical executive; b. 3 Sept. 1906; ed. Technische Hochschule, Darmstadt, and Universität Freiburg/Breisgau.
Chairman of Management Board, E. Merck A.G.; Vice-Pres. Asscn. of German Chemical Industry; mem. Management Board Fed. Asscn. of Pharmaceutical Industry; mem. Commercial Political Cttee. of Asscn. of Chemical Industry; mem. U.S.S.R. Dept. of Trade Council for Foreign Trade, Chair. China Dept.; Pres. Int. Group of Pharmaceutical Industries of European Common Market Countries, Brussels; mem. Regional Advisory Cttee. for Hesse of Deutsche Bank A.G., Frankfurt; mem. Advisory Council of Frankfurter Versicherungs A.G., Frankfurt; Chair. Board of Dirs. Elektrochemische Werke München A.G.
61 Darmstadt, Dieburger Strasse 209, German Federal Republic.

Harper, Heather, C.B.E. (Mrs. Leonard Buck); British soprano; b. 8 May 1930; ed. Trinity Coll. of Music, London.
Promenade Concert recitalist every season since 57; has sung at music festivals throughout the world, and given concerts in the United States, Middle East and Asia; Soprano role in Britten's *War Requiem* in U.K., Europe and Australia; has sung principal roles at Covent Garden, Glyndebourne, Sadler's Wells and Beyreuth.
15 Lancaster Grove, Hampstead, London, N.W.3, England.

Harper, John D.; American electrical engineer and business executive; b. 6 April 1910; ed. High School and Univ. of Tennessee.
Aluminum Co. of America (ALCOA) 33-, Asst. Dist. Power Man. 43-51, Man. Rockdale Works 51-55, Asst. Gen. Man. Smelting Div., Pittsburgh 55-56, Gen. Man. Smelting Div. 56-60, Vice-Pres. (Smelting and Fabricating) 60-62, Vice-Pres. (Production) 62, Exec. Vice-Pres. 62-63, Dir. 62, Pres. 63-, Chief Exec. Officer 65-, Chair. Exec. Cttee. 66-; Pres. Aluminum Asscn.; Dir. Foreign Policy Asscn., Inc., Metropolitan Life Assurance Co., etc.; Trustee, Cttee. on Econ. Devt., Nat. Industrial Conf. Board, Carnegie Inst. of Technology, Council for Latin America; mem. American Inst. of Electrical Engineers, American Soc. of Mechanical Engineers, Engineers' Soc. of Western Pennsylvania; Hon. Dr. Eng. (Lehigh Univ., Maryville Coll., Tenn. and Rensselaer Polytechnic Inst., N.Y.); Nathan W. Dougherty Award of Univ. of Tenn., Professional Engineers' Distinguished Service Award of Penn. Soc. of Professional Engineers 66.
Aluminum Company of America, 1501 Alcoa Building, Pittsburgh, Penn. 15219; Home: 880 Old Hickory Road, Pittsburgh, Pennsylvania 15216, U.S.A.

Harper, Marion, Jr.; American advertising executive; b. 14 May 1916; ed. Phillips Acad., Yale Univ.
McCann-Erickson, Inc., N.Y.C. 39-, Dir. 46-, Pres. 48-67, Chair. 58-67; Chair. and Pres. The Interpublic Group of Companies Inc., 61-67; Chair. American Asscn. of Advertising Agencies 62-63; Cruzeiro do Sul 55.
Publ. *Getting Results from Advertising* 48.
Home: Ridge Acres, Langdon Avenue, Irvington-on-Hudson, N.Y., U.S.A.

Harper, Roy W.; American judge; b. 26 July 1905; ed. Univ. of Missouri.
Admitted to Bar 29; mem. Tax Insurance Claims Dept., Shell Petroleum Corpn., St. Louis 29-30; private legal practice 31-34; mem. Ward & Reeves, Caruthersville 34-47; U.S. District Judge of Missouri, Eastern and Western Districts 47-, Chief Judge, Missouri, Eastern

District 59-; Chair., Missouri State Democrat Cttee. 46-47.
315 U.S. Court House and Custom House, St. Louis, Missouri 63101, U.S.A.

Harrar, J. George, A.B., M.S., PH.D.; American foundation executive; b. 2 Dec. 1906; ed. Oberlin Coll., Ohio, Iowa State Univ. and Univ. of Minnesota.
Professor of Biology, Univ. of Puerto Rico 29-30, Head of Dept. 30-33; Instructor, Plant Pathology, Univ. of Minn. 34-35; Asst. Prof. of Biology, Virginia Polytechnic Inst. 35-37, Assoc. Prof. 37-41, Prof. 41; Prof. and Head, Dept. of Plant Pathology, Washington State Univ. 41-42; Field Dir. for Agriculture, Rockefeller Foundation (Mexico) 43-52; Deputy Dir. for Agriculture, Rockefeller Foundation (N.Y.) 52-55, Dir. 55-58; Vice-Pres. Rockefeller Foundation 59-61, Trustee and Pres. 61-; mem. Board of Trustees, Oberlin Coll., Ohio 62-, Advisory Board, Inst. of Nutrition Sciences, Columbia Univ. 64-, President's Gen. Advisory Cttee. on Foreign Assistance Programs 65-, Mayor's Science and Technology Advisory Council, New York City 66-, and many other advisory cttees.; Fellow American Phytopathological Soc. and American Asscn. for the Advancement of Science; mem. American Acad. of Arts and Sciences, American Philosophical Soc., Nat. Acad. of Arts and Sciences, Italian Nat. Acad. of Agriculture, Nat. Acad. of Sciences, etc.; Hon. LL.D. (Oberlin Coll. and Univ. of Calif.), Hon. D.Sc. (Univ. of Florida, and West Virginia and Ohio State Univs.), Dr. h.c. (Univs. of the Andes, Bogotá and Colombia and Central Univ., Quito); Hon. Prof. (Univ. of San Carlos, Guatemala and Catholic Univ. of Chile); Hon. D.Sc. Clemson Univ. and Univ. of Illinois; Order of the Golden Heart, Philippines 64; numerous other awards and honours.
Publs. (with E. S. Harrar) *Guide to Southern Trees* 46, (with E. C. Stakman) *Principles of Plant Pathology* 57, *Strategy for the Conquest of Hunger* 63, 67.
The Rockefeller Foundation, 111 West 50th Street, New York City, N.Y. 10020, U.S.A.
Telephone: 212-CO 5-8100.

Harriman, E(dward) Roland; American banker; b. 24 Dec. 1895; ed. Yale Univ.
In banking in New York 20-; Partner Brown Brothers Harriman & Co. 31-; Chair. Board of Dirs. Union Pacific Railroad 46-; Dir. Delaware and Hudson Railroad; mem. Board of Managers, Delaware and Hudson Co.; Dir. American Bank Note Co., Anaconda Co., Centennial Insurance Co.; Trustee Atlantic Mutual Insurance Co., Mutual Life Insurance Co. of N.Y.; Chair. American Nat. Red Cross; mem. Advisory Finance Cttee., Albany Insurance Co., Atlas Assurance Co., Ltd., U.S. Branch, Royal Exchange Assurance of America, Inc.
59 Wall Street, New York City, N.Y. 10005, U.S.A.

Harriman, Sir George, Kt., C.B.E.; British industrialist; b. 3 March 1908.
Joined Austin Motor Co. 40, Works Dir. 45; Deputy Man. Dir. British Motor Corpn. 52-56, Deputy Chair. and Joint Man. Dir. 56-58, Deputy Chair. and Man. Dir. 58-61, Chair. and Man. Dir. 61-66, Chair. 66; Chair. Pressed Steel Co. 65-; Chair. British Motor Holdings Ltd. 66-, British Leyland Motor Corpn. 68-; Chair. Soc. of Motor Manufacturers and Traders 67-.
British Leyland Motor Corpn., Longbridge, Birmingham, England.
Telephone: Birmingham Priory 2101.

Harriman, Lewis G., M.S., LL.D.; American banker; b. 24 March 1889; ed. Trinity Coll.
Trust Officer Guaranty Trust Co. of New York 17; Vice-Pres. Fidelity Trust Co. of Buffalo 19; Pres. 24; Pres. Manufacturers and Traders Trust Co. of Buffalo

25, Chair. 54-65; Pres. Buffalo Chamber of Commerce 27, 28; fmr. Dir. N.Y. Telephone Co., Nat. Gypsum Co., Cornell Aeronautical Laboratory, Chair. Univ. of Buffalo Foundation; Trustee, Buffalo Museum of Science, Millard Fillmore Hospital, Buffalo Historical Society and Buffalo Foundation; Republican.
5400 S.W. 98th Terrace, Miami, Florida 33156, U.S.A. Telephone: 305-665-2616.

Harriman, William Averell, HON. LL.D. (New York); American industrialist, banker, diplomatist, and government official; b. 15 Nov. 1891; ed. Groton School and Yale Univ.
Vice-Pres. in charge of Purchases and Supplies Union Pacific R.R. Co. 15-17; Chair. of Board Merchant Shipbuilding Corpn. 17-25; Chair. of Board W. A. Harriman & Co. Inc. 20-30; partner Brown Brothers, Harriman & Co. (merger) Jan. 31-; Chair. Exec. Cttee. Illinois Central R.R. Co. 31-42, Dir. 15-46; Dir. Union Pacific R.R. Co. 13-46, Chair. of Board 32-46; Dir. Guaranty Trust Co. of New York 15-40; at one time Dir. of Western Union Telegraph Co. and Weekly Publications Inc. (publishers of *Newsweek* Magazine); mem. N.Y. State Fair Comm. 15-17; Admin. Div. II N.R.A. Jan.-Mar. 34; Special Asst. Admin. Mar.-May 34; Admin. Officer 34-35; mem. Business Advisory Council Dept. of Commerce 33-; Chair. 37-40; served with Office of Production Management June 40-Jan. 41; special rep. of Pres. Roosevelt in Great Britain with rank of Minister Mar. 41, U.S.S.R. with rank of Ambassador Aug. 41; rep. in London of Combined Shipping Adjustment Board Feb. 42; mem. London Combined Production and Resources Board July 42; Ambassador to U.S.S.R. Oct. 43-Feb. 46; Ambassador to Great Britain April-Oct. 46; U.S. Sec. of Commerce Oct. 46-April 48; U.S. Special Rep. in Europe for E.C.A. April 48-June 50; Special Asst. to the Pres. July 50-Oct. 51; Dir. for Mutual Security Oct. 51-Jan. 53; Gov. of New York 55-59; Ambassador-at-Large Jan.-Nov. 61, Feb. 65-; Asst. Sec. of State for Far Eastern Affairs Nov. 61-63, Under-Sec. for Political Affairs 63-65; Chief American negotiator Nuclear Test Ban Treaty, Moscow 63; took part in negotiations on war in Viet-Nam, Paris 68; Democrat.
Publ. *Peace with Russia?* 60.
Department of State, Washington 25, D.C., and 16 East 81st Street, New York City 28, N.Y., U.S.A.

Harrington, Fred Harvey, A.B., M.A., PH.D.; American historian and university president; b. 24 June 1912; ed. Cornell and New York Univs.
Instructor in History, Washington Square Coll. of New York Univ. 36-37, Univ. of Wisconsin 39-40, Asst. Prof. 39-40; Prof. and Chair. of History and Political Science, Univ. of Arkansas 40-44; Assoc. Prof. of History, Univ. of Wisconsin 44-47, Prof. 47-, Chair. of Dept. 52-55, Special Asst. to Pres. 56-58, Vice-Pres. of Academic Affairs 58-62, Vice-Pres. 62, Pres. 62-; Visiting Prof. W. Virginia Univ. 42, Cornell Univ. 44, Univ. of Pennsylvania 49, Univ. of Colorado 51, Oxford Univ. 55, Univ. of Kyoto (Japan) 62; Frederic Courtland Penfield Fellow in Diplomacy and Int. Relations, New York Univ. 33-36; Fellow John Simon Guggenheim Memorial Foundation 43-44; Ford Foundation Faculty Fellow 55-56; Hon. LL.D. (New York Univ. and Univ. of Calif.); Hon. L.H.D. (Univ. of Maine, De Paul and Miami Univs.).
Publs. *God Mammon and the Japanese: Dr. Horace N. Allen and Korean-American Relations (1884-1905)* 44, *Fighting Politician: Major-General N. P. Banks* 48, *An American History* (2 vols., with Curti and Shyrock, and Cochran) 50, *Hanging Judge, Isaac C. Parker and the Indian Frontier* 51, *A History of American Civilization* 53.
University of Wisconsin, Madison, Wisconsin; Home: 130 N. Prospect Avenue, Madison, Wisconsin, U.S.A.

Harrington, Milton E.; American tobacco executive; b. 19 Sept. 1908; ed. Duke Univ.
Liggett & Myers Tobacco Co. 34-, successively Factory Man., Leaf Buyer, Leaf Supervisor, Man. of Leaf Dept., Dir. 55-, Vice-Pres. (Leaf) 60-64, Exec. Vice-Pres. 63-64, Pres. April 64-, Chief Exec. Officer July 64-; mem. Exec. Cttee. and Board of Dirs. The Tobacco Inst.; mem. Board of Dirs. Grocery Manufacturers of America; mem. various cttees. of Duke Univ.; U.S. Army, Second World War.
Liggett & Myers Tobacco Company, 630 Fifth Avenue, New York, N.Y. 10020, U.S.A.

Harris, Marshal of the R.A.F. Sir Arthur Travers, Bt., G.C.B., O.B.E., A.F.C.; British officer; b. 13 April 1892.
Joined 1st Rhodesian Regt. 14, served S.W. Africa R.F.C. 15, served First World War and with R.A.F. India, Iraq, and Middle East; Head, R.A.F. mission to U.S. and Canada 38; Air Officer Commanding R.A.F. Palestine and Transjordan 38-39; Air Officer Commanding No. 5 Group 39-40; Deputy Chief of Air Staff 40-41; Head R.A.F. Del. U.S.A. 41, and R.A.F. mem. Joint Chiefs of Staff; Air Officer Commanding-in-Chief Bomber Command 42-45; Man. Dir. South African Marine Corpn. 46-53; awards include Order of Suvorov (U.S.S.R.) 1st Class 44, Grand Cross Polonia Restituta (Poland), Chief Commdr. Legion of Merit (U.S.A.), D.S.M. (U.S.A.), Grand Cross Order of Southern Cross (Brazil), Grand Officier Légion d'Honneur, Croix de Guerre avec Palme, Freeman of Honiton 45, Chipping Wycombe 45; Hon. LL.D. (Liverpool).
Publ. *Bomber Offensive* 46.
The Ferry House, Goring-on-Thames, Oxon., England.

Harris, Fred R., B.A., LL.B.; American lawyer and politician; b. 13 Nov. 1930; ed. Walters High School and Univ. of Oklahoma.
Private legal practice until 64; mem. Oklahoma State Senate 56-64; Senator from Oklahoma 64-; Democrat.
254 Senate Office Building, Washington, D.C.; and 1120 Cherry Street, Lawton, Oklahoma, U.S.A.

Harris, Geoffrey Wingfield, C.B.E., M.A., SC.D., M.D., D.M., F.R.S.; British physiologist and anatomist; b. 4 June 1913; ed. Dulwich Coll., Emmanuel Coll., Cambridge and St. Mary's Hospital Medical School, London.
Demonstrator in Anatomy, Cambridge Univ. 40-47, Lecturer 47-48, Lecturer in Physiology 48-52; Senior Lecturer in Experimental Neuroendocrinology, Univ. of London 52-53; Fitzmary Prof. of Physiology, Univ. of London (Inst. of Psychiatry, Maudsley Hospital, London) 53-62; Dr. Lee's Prof. of Anatomy, Univ. of Oxford 62-; Visiting Prof. of Anatomy, Univ. of Calif., Los Angeles 53, Berkeley 54-55; Visiting Prof. Rockefeller Univ., New York 67; Hon. Dir. Medical Research Council Neuroendocrinology Research Unit 62-; Hon. D.Sc. (Detroit).
Publs. *The innervation and actions of the neurohypophysis; an investigation using the method of remote control stimulation* 47, *Functional grafts of the anterior pituitary gland* 52, *Neural Control of the Pituitary Gland* 55, *Sex Hormones, Brain Development and Brain Function* 64, *Pituitary Gland* (co-editor with B. T. Donovan) 3 vols. 66.
Department of Human Anatomy, South Parks Road, Oxford; Home: Campsfield Wood, Woodstock, Oxford, England.
Telephone: Oxford 58686 (Office); Woodstock 354 (Home).

Harris, George Bernard; American judge; b. 16 Aug. 1901; ed. Univ. of San Francisco.
Admitted to California State Bar 26; Judge, California State Courts 41-, U.S. District Court 46-, now Chief Judge, U.S. District Court, California 94102, Northern District; Knight of Malta and Knight Order of St. Gregory the Great.
Federal Building and U.S. Court House, 450 Golden Gate Avenue, San Francisco, California, U.S.A.
Telephone: 556-3710.

Harris, Michael Saul; American international official; b. 15 July 1916; ed. public schools, Philadelphia.
Steelworkers' Organising Cttee., Congress of Industrial Orgs. (C.I.O.), Berwick, Pa. 37, Sub. Regional Dir. Philadelphia 38-41; District Dir. and mem. Int. Exec. Board United Steelworkers of America, Philadelphia 42-48; Econ. Cooperation Admin. (E.C.A.) Special Mission to France 48, Chief E.C.A. Special Mission to Sweden 49-51, to Germany 51-53; U.S. Minister (Econ. Affairs), Bonn 53-55; with Ford Foundation 55-63; Dep. Sec.-Gen. Organisation for Economic Co-operation and Development (OECD) Sept. 63-67.
25 Patrick Road, Westport, Conn., U.S.A.

Harris, Oren; American lawyer and politician; b. 20 Dec. 1903; ed. Henderson State Coll. and Cumberland Univ.
Admitted to Arkansas Bar 30, U.S. Supreme Court Bar 43; Dep. Prosecuting Attorney, Union County, Arkansas 33-36; Prosecuting Attorney, 13th Judicial Circuit 36-40; mem. U.S. House of Representatives 40-65; Fed. Judge, Arkansas 65-; Chair. Cttee. on Interstate and Foreign Commerce; Democrat.
U.S. Court House, Little Rock, Arkansas, U.S.A.

Harris, Mrs. Patricia Roberts, A.B., IUR.D.; American lawyer and diplomatist; b. 31 May 1924; ed. George Washington Univ. Law School, Howard Univ., Univ. of Chicago and American Univ., Washington, D.C.
Program Dir. Young Women's Christian Asscn. of Chicago 46-49; Asst. Dir. American Council on Human Rights 49-53; Exec. Dir. Delta Sigma Theta 53-59; Trial Attorney, U.S. Dept. of Justice 60-61; Assoc. Dean of Students and Lecturer in Law, Howard Univ. 61-63, Assoc. Prof. of Law 63-67, Prof. 67-; Amb. to Luxembourg 65-67; Alt. U.S. del. to Gen. Assembly of UN 66, 67 and Chair. Plenary Session Econ. Comm. for Europe 67; mem. U.S.-Puerto Rican Comm. on Status of Puerto Rico; mem. Comm. on Revision of Columbia District Criminal Code 68; mem. Nat. Advisory Cttee. on Reform of Fed. Penal Code 68-; Admin. Conf. of the U.S. 68.
Faculty of Law, Howard University, 2400 Sixth Street, N.W., Washington, D.C. 20001, U.S.A.
Telephone: 202-797-1783.

Harris, Poul Joachim; Danish business executive; b. 28 March 1907.
Manager, W. Hellesen and Co.'s Dental Depot 31-47; Gen. Man. Dental A/S of 1934 Aarhus and Copenhagen 48-60, mem. Board 60-62; Joint Partner and Gen. Man. Rahr's Tekniske Forretning A/S, Aarhus 60-; Vice-Pres. Conseil Internationale des Employeurs du Commerce 62, Pres. 63-; Vice-Chair., Asscn. of Dental Depots in Denmark 46-47; Chair. Danish Trade and Office Employers' Asscn. 62; mem. Den Danske Provinsbank A/S 64-66; Hon. Consul for the Netherlands.
Tammerisvej 24, Risskov, Denmark.

Harris, Roy Ellsworth; American composer; b. 12 Feb. 1898; ed. California Univ.
Studied under Arthur Farwell and Nadia Boulanger; Guggenheim Fellow 28-30, Pasadena Music and Art Asscn. Fellow 30-33; Composer in residence, Cornell Univ. 41-42, Colorado Coll. 42-48, Utah State Univ. of Agriculture and Applied Science 48-; Fellow, Nat. Inst. of Arts and Letters; Pres. Fellowship of American Composers 46-50; Coolidge Medal 42; Hon. Mus.D. (Rutgers and Rochester Univs.).
Compositions: six symphonies, three string quartets, string and piano quintets, choral, piano, band and school compositions.
139 East 1st North Street, Logan, Utah, U.S.A.

Harris, Seymour, A.B., PH.D.; American professor and political adviser; b. 9 Aug. 1897; ed. Harvard Univ. Instructor, Lecturer, Littauer Professor of Political Economy, Harvard Univ. 22-64, Emeritus 64-; Adviser, Governor Stevenson 52, 56; Democratic Advisory Council 57-60, Adviser to Senator, later Pres. Kennedy 60-63; Managing Editor, *Review of Economics and Statistics* 43-62, Editor 62-; Advisory Editor *Journal of Sociology of Education* 63-; Chair. Dept. of Econs. and Prof. of Econs., Univ. of Calif. 64-; mem. Board of Trustees, John F. Kennedy Library; Hon. LL.D.; Democrat.
Publs. *The Assignats* 30, *The New Economics* 47, *The Market for College Graduates* 48, *Higher Education in the United States: The Economic Problems* 60, *An Economist on Higher Education* 61, *The Economics of American Medicine* 64, *Economics of the Kennedy Years* 64, and 30 other books.
Department of Economics, Univ. of California (San Diego), P.O. Box 109, La Jolla, Calif. 92037, U.S.A. Telephone: 453-2000.

Harrison, Sir Cyril Ernest, Kt., M.A.; British company director; b. 14 Dec. 1901; ed. Burnley Grammar School. Chairman English Sewing Cotton Co. Ltd.; Chair. North-West Regional Council, F.B.I. 57-59, Christie Hospital and Holt Radium Inst. 59-61; Pres. Manchester Chamber of Commerce 58-60, F.B.I. 61-63; mem. Court of Govs. Manchester Univ. 58-; Pres. The Cotton Silk and Man-Made Fibres Research Asscn.; mem. Nat. Econ. Devt. Council (N.E.D.C.) 62-64, mem. of Council Manchester Business School, mem. British Nat. Export Council 65-67; Joint Deputy Chair. Williams Deacon's Bank Ltd.; Chair. Board of Govs. United Manchester Hospitals 67-; Dir. Royal Bank of Scotland and Cheadle Royal (Industries) Ltd.; part-time mem. North Western Electricity Board; Fellow British Inst. of Management, Chartered Inst. of Secretaries; M.A. h.c. (Univ. of Manchester) 60, Companion Textile Inst. 61.
4 Harefield Drive, Wilmslow, Cheshire, England. Telephone: WIL 22186.

Harrison, Rt. Hon. Sir Eric John, P.C., K.C.M.G., K.C.V.O.; Australian politician; b. 7 Sept. 1892; ed. Crown Street School, Sydney.
Served 14-18 war with A.I.F. and 39-45 war as Liaison Officer to U.S. Forces; Liberal mem. Australian House of Reps. 31-56; Minister for the Interior 34; mem. Joint Cttee. Public Works 37-43; Minister without Portfolio 38-39; Postmaster-Gen. and Minister for Repatriation 39-40; Minister for Trade and Customs 40-41; mem. Economic Cabinet 39-41; Deputy Leader Liberal Party 44; Deputy Leader of the Opposition 44-49; Minister for Defence 49-50; Resident Minister for Australia in London, and Minister for the Interior, Australia 50-51; Vice-Pres. Exec. Council, Leader House of Reps., and Minister for Defence Production 51-56; Minister-in-Charge of the Royal Tour 54; Acting Prime Minister and Acting Treasurer 54; Minister for the Army and for the Navy 55-56; Australian High Commr. in the U.K. 56-64. Stoke Lodge, 95 Neerim Road, Castle Cove, Sydney, New South Wales, Australia.

Harrison, Sir Geoffrey (**Wedgwood**), G.C.M.G., K.C.V.O.; British diplomatist; b. 18 July 1908; ed. Winchester and King's Coll., Cambridge.
Entered Foreign Office 32, served Tokyo 35-37, Berlin 37-39; Private Sec. to Parl. Under-Sec., Foreign Office 39-41; First Sec., Foreign Office 41-45; Counsellor, Brussels 45-47; Minister, Moscow 47-49; Head of Northern Dept., Foreign Office 49-51; Asst. Under-Sec., Foreign Office 51-56; Ambassador to Brazil 56-58, to Iran 58-63; Dep. Under-Sec. of State, Foreign Office 63-65; Ambassador to U.S.S.R. 65-68.
British Embassy, Moscow, U.S.S.R.; Home: 6 Ormonde Gate, London, S.W.3, England.

Harrison, George McGregor; American labour leader; b. 19 July 1895; ed. public schools.
Railway clerk 09-17; Chair. various brs. Brotherhood of Railway Clerks 17-22, Pres. Grand Lodge 28-63, Chief Exec. Officer 63-; Dir. Brotherhood of Railway Clerks Nat. Bank; mem. editorial cttee. *Labor*; Vice-Pres. American Fed. of Labor; mem. U.S. Social Security Act Cttee., Industrial Analysis Cttee.; assisted in forming Railroad Retirement Act 37; Dir. Social Science Research Council, Pres. Workers' Education Bureau, Nat. Cttee. on Economic Recovery, Good Neighbor League; mem. Nat. Youth Admin. Population Redistribution Cttee., etc.; del. 3rd World Power Conf.; U.S. Labour mem. I.L.O. Governing Board 36, U.S. Labour Del. I.L.O. Havana 39; mem. Defense Mediation Board 41; mem. Board of Dirs. Roosevelt Nat. Memorial Foundation; Board of Dirs. American Overseas Aid; Board of Dirs. American Arbitration Asscn.; Citizens' Cttee. for Reciprocal World Trade; mem. Advisory Cttee. to the Council of Econ. Advisers to the Pres. of the U.S.; mem. Pres. Advisory Cttee. on Labor-Management Policy, Advisory Cttee., Agency for Int. Development; special Asst. to Dir. Office of Defense Mobilisation, U.S. Govt.; Dir. American Asscn. for UN 58; mem. U.S. del. to 13th Gen. Assembly of UN 59, Advisory Cttee. of Export-Import Bank 59-61, Advisory Cttee. on Foreign Trade Policy; Trustee Harry S. Truman Library Foundation, John F. Kennedy Library Foundation; Chair. Labor Div., Democratic Nat. Cttee.
6300 Elwyne Drive, Silverton, Ohio; and 1015 Vine Street, Cincinnati 2, Ohio, U.S.A.

Harrison, James Merritt, PH.D.; Canadian geologist; b. 20 Sept. 1915; ed. Univ. of Manitoba and Queen's Univ., Kingston, Ontario.
Geologist, Geological Survey of Canada 43-55; Lecturer Queen's Univ. 49-50; Geological Survey of Canada, Chief Precambrian Div. 55-56, Dir. 56-64; Asst. Deputy Minister (Research), Dept. of Mines and Technical Surveys 64-67; Asst. Deputy Minister (Mines and Geosciences), Dept. of Energy, Mines and Resources 67-; mem. Int. Council of Scientific Unions (ICSU) 62, Exec. and Vice-Pres. ICSU 63-65, Pres. 66-; Pres. Int. Union Geological Sciences 61-64; Vice-Pres. Canadian Inst. of Mining and Metallurgy, Pres. 68; Pres. Royal Soc. of Canada 67-68; Kemp Memorial Medal, Columbia Univ.; Blaylock Medal, Canadian Inst. of Minerals and Metals; several hon. degrees.
Department of Energy, Mines and Resources, Ottawa 4; Home: 588 Booth Street, Ottawa 4, Ontario, Canada. Telephone: 613-994-9335.

Harrison, Jay Smolens; American music critic, musicologist and teacher; b. 25 Jan. 1927; ed. New York Univ.
Instructor of Music, New York Univ. 48-55, Asst. Prof. 55-56; Guest Critic, *New York Herald Tribune* 48-52, Assoc. Critic 52, Music Editor 52-60; Editor *Music Mag* 60-61; Dir. Reader's Digest Music Inc. 61-63; scriptwriter for television and radio 54-; assoc. producer, Metropolitan Opera broadcasts 54-; Editor-in-Chief *Musical America* 63-64; Adviser to N.Y. State Council on the Arts 62-; mem. U.S. Nat. Council on the Arts and Govt. 55-; perm. panelist of Metropolitan Opera Quiz radio broadcasts 58-; Dir. Editorial Services, Columbia Records 64-67.
741 West End Avenue, New York, N.Y. 10025, U.S.A. Telephone: 662-0706.

Harrison, Rex Carey; British actor; b. 5 March 1908; ed. Liverpool Coll.
First professional appearance Liverpool 24; first film performance 29; service in R.A.F. 41-44; plays include *French Without Tears, Design for Living, The Cocktail Party, Bell, Book and Candle, Venus Observed, The Love of Four Colonels, Anne of a Thousand Days, Platonov,*

My Fair Lady; films include *Night Train to Munich, Major Barbara, Blithe Spirit, The Rake's Progress, Anna and the King of Siam, Escape, Unfaithfully Yours, King Richard and the Crusaders, The Constant Husband, The Reluctant Debutante, Midnight Lace, Cleopatra, My Fair Lady, The Yellow Rolls-Royce, The Agony and the Ecstasy, The Honey Pot, Dr. Doolittle.*
c/o London International, Park House, Park Street, London, W.1, England.

Harrison, Wallace Kirkman; American architect; b. 28 Sept. 1895.
Director of Office of Inter-American Affairs, Washington 43-45; fmr. Dir. of Planning, United Nations. Principal works include: Rockefeller Center, New York; the UN Headquarters and Lincoln Center Opera House, N.Y.; Presbyterian Church, Stamford; Theme Center, 1939 World's Fair; New York State Capitol, South Mall. 630 Fifth Avenue, New York City, N.Y., U.S.A.

Harrod, Sir (Henry) Roy Forbes, Kt., F.B.A.; British economist; b. 13 Feb. 1900; ed. Westminster School, and New Coll., Oxford.
Lecturer Christ Church 22-24; Student of Christ Church 24-67, Hon. Student 67-; Junior Censor 27-29; Senior Censor 30-31; mem. Hebdomadal Council Oxford 29-35; Bodleian Library Comm. 30-31; Pres. Section F of British Asscn. 38; Statistical Dept. in Admiralty 40; in Prime Minister's Office 40-42 and subsequently part-time; Statistical Adviser in Admiralty 43-45; Joint Editor of *Economic Journal* 45-61; Liberal candidate for Huddersfield 45; Adviser to the Int. Monetary Fund 52; Pres. Royal Econ. Soc. 62-64; Nuffield Reader in Int. Econs., Oxford Univ. 52-67; Hon. Dr. of Law (Poitiers and Penn. Univs.); Hon. LL.D. (Aberdeen); Bern and Harms Prize, Kiel.
Publs. *International Economics* 33, *The Trade Cycle* 36, *A Page of British Folly* 46, *Are these Hardships Necessary?* 47, *Towards a Dynamic Economy* 48, *Life of Lord Keynes* 51, *And So It Goes On* 51, *Economic Essays* 52, *The Dollar* 53, *The Foundations of Inductive Logic* 56, *Policy Against Inflation* 58, *The Prof. (A Personal Memoir of Lord Cherwell)* 59, *Topical Comment* 61, (with D. C. Hague) *International Trade Theory in a Developing World* 63, *The British Economy* 63, *Reforming the World's Money* 65, *Towards a New Economic Policy* 67.
51 Campden Hill Square, London, W.8, England.
Telephone: 01-727-3435.

Harroy, Jean-Paul; Belgian former colonial administrator and university professor; b. 4 May 1909; ed. Univ. Libre de Bruxelles.
Sec. Gov. Cttee. Belgian Congo Inst. of Nat. Parks, Dir. Foundation for popularising scientific studies of Congo Nat. Parks 35-48; Guardian, Albert Nat. Park, Kivu 37-38, Garamba Nat. Park, Uélé 47-48; Sec.-Gen. Inst. for Scientific Research in Central Africa (IRSAC) 48-55; Sec.-Gen. Int. Union for Protection of Nature; Prof. of Colonial Econs., Brussels Univ. 48-; Resident-Gen. Ruanda-Urundi 55-62; Chair. Cttee. of Experts for the Conservation of Nature and Landscape of the Council of Europe; Vice-Chair. Int. Comm. on Nat. Parks; Médaille d'Or Geoffroy St. Hilaire, etc.; Commander, Ordre du Lion.
Publs. *Afrique, terre qui meurt* 44, *Tropiques* (co-author). 9 avenue des Scarabées, Brussels 5, Belgium.

Harsch, Joseph Close, A.B., M.A.; American journalist; b. 25 May 1905; ed. Williams Coll. Williamstown, Mass., and Cambridge Univ., England.
Correspondent *Christian Science Monitor* 29-; Asst. Dir. Inter-governmental Cttee. on Political Refugees 39, returning to *Monitor* on outbreak of war; *Monitor* corresp. Berlin Oct. 39-Jan. 41; *Monitor* war corresp. Southwest Pacific theatre 42; Radio news analyst for Columbia Broadcasting System 43-49; Commentator for B.B.C. 43; Chief, Washington News Bureau, *Christian Science*

Monitor 49-51; Radio News analyst for Liberty Broadcasting System 51-52; foreign affairs columnist *Christian Science Monitor*; News Commentator, Nat. Broadcasting Co. 53-57; Senior European Corresp. N.B.C. 57-65, Diplomatic Corresp. N.B.C., Washington 65-67; A.B.C. Commentator 67-; Hon. C.B.E.
Publs. *Pattern of Conquest* 43, *The Curtain Isn't Iron* 50. 2806 29th Street, N.W., Washington, D.C. 20008; and Highland Drive, Jamestown, Rhode Island, U.S.A.
Telephone: 202-232-0456.

Hart, Cecil Augustus, C.M.G., T.D., D.SC. (Eng.), PH.D., M.I.C.E., M.I.MECH.E., F.R.I.C.S.; British civil engineer; b. 4 Nov. 1902; ed. University Coll., London.
Dover Engineering Works 19-20; Kitchener Scholar, Univ. Coll., London 20-23; Asst. Engineer on Public Works 23-26; Lecturer, Municipal Engineering, Univ. Coll. 26-36, Senior Lecturer Surveying 36-39; Tutor in Engineering, Coll. of Estate Management, London 39; served in R.E. (Survey) with B.E.F. France, War Office, Air Ministry, Middle East, S.E. Asia, and in charge of Air Survey Research 39-46; Prof. of Civil Engineering (Surveying and Photogrammetry) Univ. Coll. London 46-50; Vice-Chancellor Univ. of Roorkee, India 50-53; Rector and Principal Nigerian Coll. of Technology 53-60; Dir. London Master Builders' Asscn. 60-63; mem. Council Royal Inst. of Chartered Surveyors (mem. and Chair. many Cttees.) 47-50, Council, Inst. of Navigation 48-49; Fellow, Inst. of Navigation, Royal Geographical Soc.; mem various Govt. Cttees. and attended several int. confs. 46-; Reporter-Gen. on Radar applied to Geodesy, Int. Union Geodesy and Geophysics, Oslo 48, Brussels 51, Rome 54, Toronto 57; mem. Planning Comm., U.P., India, All-India Engineering Research Board, All-India Council for Technical Studies, Inter-Univ. Board (India), etc.; Pres. Inst. of Surveyors (India) 52-53; mem. Scientific Council for Africa South of the Sahara 58; Leader, Colombo Plan Team to Singapore 64; Consultant to SEATO 64.
Publs. *Principles of Road Engineering* (with Prof. H .J. Collins) 36, *Air Photography applied to Surveying* 39; also a number of research publs., etc.
The Old Greyhound, Akeley, Buckingham, England.
Telephone: Lillingstone Dayrell 260.

Hart, Rt. Hon. (Constance Mary) Judith, P.C., M.P.; British politician; b. Sept. 1924; ed. London School of Economics.
Labour M.P. for Lanark 59-; Joint Parl. Under-Sec. of State for Scotland 64-66; Minister of State for Commonwealth Affairs 66-July 67; Minister of Social Security July 67-.
House of Commons, London, S.W.1; and Ministry of Social Security, 10 John Adam Street, London, W.C.1, England.
Telephone: 01-930-6240, Ext. 896; 01-236-2090.

Hart, George Arnold Reeve, M.B.E.; Canadian banker; b. 2 April 1913; ed. Public and High Schools, Toronto, Ontario.
Bank of Montreal 31-41; Canadian Army 41-46; Bank of Montreal 46-, Sec. to Pres. 46-48, Asst. Supt. Calgary 48, Manager, Edmonton 49-51, Third Agent, New York 51-53, Supt., Head Office 53-54, Asst. Gen. Manager Head Office 54-56, Deputy Gen. Manager 56-57, Gen. Manager 57-58, Vice-Pres. and Dir. 58-59, Pres. and Chief Exec. Officer 59-64, Chair. of Board 64-, Pres. 64-67, Chief Exec. Officer and Chair. of Exec. Cttee. 64-; Dir. numerous companies and official of several commercial and other orgs.; Hon. LL.D. (Univ. of Saskatchewan, Univ. of Montreal), Hon. D.C.L. (Bishop's Univ.), Hon. D.Sc. (Univ. of Sherbrooke).
Office: Bank of Montreal, 129 St. James Street West, Montreal, Quebec; Home: 1700 McGregor Street, Montreal, Quebec, Canada.

Hart, Parker T.; American diplomatist; b. 28 Sept. 1910; ed. Dartmouth Coll., Harvard Univ., and Institut Universitaire des Hautes Etudes Internationales, Geneva.
Translator, Dept. of State 37-38; Foreign Service Officer 38-, served Vienna, Pará (Brazil), Cairo, Jeddah, Dhahran 38-47; Dept. of State 47-49; Consul-Gen. Dhahran 49-51; Nat. War Coll. 51-52; Dir. Office of Near Eastern Affairs, Dept. of State 52-55; Dep. Chief of Mission and Counsellor, Cairo 55-58; Consul-Gen., Damascus 58; Deputy Asst. Sec. of State, Near Eastern and S. Asian Affairs 58-61; Ambassador to Saudi Arabia 61-65, concurrently Ambassador to Kuwait 62-63, Minister to Yemen 61-62; Ambassador to Turkey 65-; mem. Middle East Inst., Royal Geographical Soc., Royal Central Asian Soc., Council of Harvard Graduate Soc.
American Embassy, Ankara, Turkey; and 830 Lincoln Street, Evanston, Ill., U.S.A.

Hart, Philip A., B.A., J.D.; American lawyer and politician; b. 10 Dec. 1912; ed. Georgetown and Michigan Univs.
Law practice in Detroit; Michigan Corpn. and Securities Commr. 49; Dir. of Price Stabilisation 51; U.S. District Attorney, Eastern Michigan 52; Legal Adviser to Gov. Williams 53; Lieut. Gov. of Michigan, Senator from Michigan 58-; mem. Senate Judiciary Cttee.; service with U.S. Army (Lt.-Col.) 41-46; fmr. Pres. Mich. State Bar Foundation; Croix de Guerre and other military honours; Democrat.
Senate Office Building, Washington 25, D.C., U.S.A.

Hartford, Huntington, B.A.; American financier and art patron; b. 18 April 1911; ed. St. Paul's School, and Harvard Univ.
Chairman Oil Shale Corpn. (N.Y.); Founder Huntington Hartford Foundation, Huntington Hartford Theatre, Hollywood 54 and Handwriting Inst., N.Y. 56; Developer Paradise Island (Nassau, Bahamas) 59; Founder, Gallery of Modern Art (including Huntington Hartford Collection) Columbus Circle, N.Y. City 64; Editor *Show Magazine*; Chair. American Cttee. to preserve Abu Simbel 64; mem. U.S. Nat. Cttee. for UNESCO, U.S. Cttee. for UN; Adviser Cultural Affairs to Pres. of Borough of Manhattan 67; Hon. Fellow Nat. Sculpture Soc.; Broadway Asscn. Man of Year Award; served as Lt. U.S. Coast Guard 42-45.
Publs. *Jane Eyre* (play) 58, *Art or Anarchy* 64.
420 Lexington Avenue, New York, N.Y. 10017, U.S.A.
Telephone: MUrray Hill 3-2367.

Hartke, (Rupert) Vance, A.B., J.D.; American lawyer and politician; b. 31 May 1919; ed. Stendal High School, Evansville Coll., Indiana Univ.
Deputy Prosecutor, Vanderburgh County, Ind. 50-51; Pres. Eighth Congressional District Young Democrats, Chair. Vanderburgh County Democratic Cen. Cttee. 52-58; Democratic Senatorial Campaign Cttee.; Mayor of Evansville, Ind. 56-58; mem. U.S. Senate Cttees. on Finance, Commerce, Post Office and Civil Service; U.S. Senator from Indiana 58-; Democrat.
850 Dexter Avenue, Evansville 15, Ind., U.S.A.

Hartke, Werner, D.PHIL.; German university professor; b. 1 March 1907; ed. Berlin Univ.
Lecturer, Königsberg and Göttingen Univs., Prof. of Classical Philology 48-55; Dean, Faculty of Philosophy, Rostock Univ. 49-51, 53-55, Prof. Latin Language and Literature, Humboldt Univ., Berlin 55-, Rector 57-59; Dir. Berlin Inst. for Antiquity Research; mem. Deutsche Akad. der Wissenschaften, Pres. 58-; mem. U.S.S.R. Acad. of Sciences, Hungarian Acad. of Sciences, Bulgarian Acad. of Sciences, Egyptian Inst.; Nat. Prize 58; D.Phil. h.c.
Publs. *De saeculi IV exeuntis historiarum scriptoribus* 32,

Geschichte und Politik im spätantiken Rom 40, *Römische Kinderkaiser* 51.
Deutsche Akademie der Wissenschaften, Otto-Nuschke-strasse 22, 108 Berlin; Kurt-Fischer-Str. 41, 111 Berlin, Germany.

Hartl, Karl, DR.JUR.; Austrian government official; b. 8 Jan. 1912; ed. Vienna Univ.
Legal practice 38-39; military service Second World War 40-45; Judge, Vienna 45-46; Ministry of Educ. 46-49; Asst. Man. Nat. Theatre 49-57, Man. 57-63; Perm. Sec. Ministry of Educ. 63-65; Dir.-Gen. for Fine Arts 65-; Austrian and foreign awards.
Minoritenplatz 5, Vienna I, Austria.

Hartley, Fred L(loyd), B.SC.; American (b. Canadian) oil exec.; b. 16 Jan. 1917; ed. Univ. of British Columbia.
Went to U.S.A. 39, naturalized 50; Engineering Supervisor, Union Oil Co. of Calif. 39-53, Man. Commercial Devt. 53-55, Gen. Man. Research Dept. 55-56, Vice-Pres. (Research) 56-60, Senior Vice-Pres. 60-63, Dir. 60-, Exec. Vice-Pres. 63-64, Pres. and Chief Exec. Officer 64-; Dir. Southern Calif. Symphony Asscn., Union Bank, N. American Rockwell Corpn.; mem. Calif. Natural Gas Asscn. (Pres. 53-54), American Inst. of Chemical Engineers, Los Angeles Chamber of Commerce, American Chemical Soc., Nat. Petroleum Council, Soc. Automotive Engineers, Nat. Petroleum Refiners Asscn., etc.
Union Oil Co. of California, Box 7600, Los Angeles 90054; Home: Palos Verdes Estates, Calif., U.S.A.

Hartley, Brig.-Gen. Sir Harold, G.C.V.O., C.H., C.B.E., M.C., F.R.S.; British chemist; b. 3 Sept. 1878; ed. Dulwich Coll. and Balliol Coll., Oxford.
Tutorial Fellow and Bedford Lecturer, Balliol Coll., Oxford 01-13, Research Fellow, Balliol 31-41, Hon. Fellow 41; Chemical Adviser to Third Army 15-17; Asst. Dir. of Gas Services in France 17-18 and Controller Chemical Warfare Dept. of Ministry Munitions 18-19; fmr. Vice-Pres. London, Midland and Scottish Railway and Dir. of Scientific Research 30-45; Chair. Fuel Research Board, Dept. of Scientific and Industrial Research 32-47; Chair. Int. Exec. Council and British Nat. Cttee. World Power Conf. 35-50, Pres. World Power Conf. 50-56; Dir. *The Times* Publishing Co. Ltd. 36-60; mem. Advisory Council to Cttee. of Privy Council for Scientific and Industrial Research 39-44; mem. Ministry of Supply Advisory Council 39-41; Hon. Adviser to Minister of Fuel and Power on Development of Home-Produced Fuels 39-47; Gen. Treas. British Asscn. 43-46, Pres. 50; Chair. British European Airways Aug. 46-June 47; Chair. B.O.A.C. April-June 47-June 49; Chair. Electricity Supply Research Council of the British Electricity Authority July 49-52; Pres. Inst. Chemical Engineers 51-52 and 54-55; Chair. O.E.E.C. Comm. for Energy 54-55; Chair. of Council of H.R.H. The Duke of Edinburgh's Study Conf. 54-56; Pres. Soc. of Instrument Technology 57-58; Hon. D.C.L. (Oxford); Hon. LL.D. (Edinburgh); Hon. D.Sc. (Birmingham, Princeton, Sheffield).
Publ. *Humphry Davy* 66.
The Manor House, Middleton-on-Sea, Bognor Regis, Sussex, England.
Telephone: 024369-3153.

Hartley, Leslie Poles, C.B.E.; British author; b. 30 Dec. 1895; ed. Harrow and Balliol Coll., Oxford.
Critic for various reviews 23-; James Tait Black Memorial Prize for *Eustace and Hilda* 47, Heinemann Foundation Award for *The Go-Between* 53.
Publs. Novels: *Simonetta Perkins* 25, *The Shrimp and the Anemone* 44, *The Sixth Heaven* 46, *Eustace and Hilda* 47, *The Boat* 50, *My Fellow Devils* 51, *The Go-Between* 53, *A Perfect Woman* 55, *The Hireling* 57, *Facial Justice* 60, *The Brickfield* 64, *The Imperfect Witness* 64, *The Betrayal* 66, *Poor Clare* 68; Short stories: *Night Fears* 24, *The Killing Bottle* 32, *The*

Travelling Grave and Other Stories 51, *The White Wand, Two for the River* 61; Criticism: *The Novelist's Responsibilities* 68.
Avondale, Bathford, Somerset, England.

Hartline, Haldan Keffer, M.D.; American physiologist; b. 22 Dec. 1903; ed. Lafayette Coll., Easton, Pennsylvania, and Johns Hopkins Univ., Baltimore, Maryland.
National Research Fellow in Medical Sciences, Johns Hopkins Univ. 27-29; Eldridge Johnson Traveling Research Scholar, Univs. of Leipzig and Munich 29-31; Fellow in Medical Physics, Eldridge Johnson Research Foundation, Univ. of Pennsylvania 31-36, Asst. Prof. of Biophysics 36-40, 41-42; Assoc. Prof. of Physiology, Cornell Univ. Medical Coll. 40-41; Assoc. Prof. of Biophysics, Univ. of Pennsylvania 43-48, Prof. 48-49; Prof. of Biophysics and Chair. of Dept., Johns Hopkins Univ. 49-53; mem. and Prof. Rockefeller Univ., New York City 53-; mem. Nat. Acad. of Sciences, American Physiological Soc., American Philosophical Soc., American Acad. of Arts and Sciences; Foreign mem. Royal Soc. (U.K.) 66; Howard Crosby Warren Medal 48, Michelson Award 66; Nobel Prize for Medicine 67.
Rockefeller University, 66th Street and York Avenue, New York City, N.Y. 10021; Home: 447 East 65th Street, New York, N.Y. 10021; and Patterson Road, Hydes, Md., U.S.A.
Telephone: 301-592-4602.

Härtling, Peter; German writer and journalist; b. 13 Nov. 1933; ed. Gymnasium (Nürtingen/Neckar).
Childhood spent in Saxony, Czechoslovakia and Württemberg; journalist 53-; Literary Editor *Deutsche Zeitung und Wirtschaftszeitung*, Stuttgart and Cologne; Editor of magazine *Der Monat* 62-, also Co-publisher; Editor, S. Fischer Verlag, Frankfurt; Literaturpreis des Deutschen Kritikerverbandes 64, Literaturpreis des Kulturkreises der Deutschen Industrie 65, Literarischer Förderungspreis des Landes Niedersachsen 65, Prix du meilleur livre étranger, Paris 66.
Publs. *Yamins Stationen* (poetry) 55, *In Zeilen zuhaus* (essays) 57, *Palmström grüsst Anna Blume* (essays) 61, *Spielgeist-Spiegelgeist* (poetry) 62, *Niembsch oder Der Stillstand* (novel) 64, *Janek* (novel) 66.
Walldorf/Hessen, Finkenweg 1, Germany.
Telephone: 06105-6109.

Hartmann, Rudolf; German opera producer and administrator; b. 11 Oct. 1900.
Producer, Altenburg (Court Theatre) 24-28, Nuremberg 28-34, Zürich and Nuremberg 46-52, Berlin State Opera 34-37; Producer, Bavarian State Opera, Munich 37-44, Admin. and Chief Producer 52-67; staged a great variety of operas and very many by Richard Strauss, including first performances of *Friedenstag, Capriccio* and *Die Liebe der Danae*, also first performances of *Die Harmonie der Welt* (Hindemith), *Der Mond* (Orff) and revised version of *Die Bernauerin* (Orff); productions throughout Germany and in London, Edinburgh, Stockholm, Paris, Milan, Rome, Venice, Zürich, Salzburg, Bayreuth and Vienna; mem. Goethe Institut; Grosses Bundesverdienstkreuz and several other awards.
8 Munich 90, Harthauserstr. 48A, German Federal Republic.
Telephone: 638002.

Hartmann, Wilhelm C. B., DIPL. ING.; German civil engineer; b. 13 April 1908; ed. Belgrano School, Buenos Aires, Argentina, Wöhler-Real-Gymnasium, Frankfurt, and Technical Univs. of Darmstadt and Dresden.
Site Man. Ph. Holzmann A.G., Frankfurt 34-35; Chief Engineer, Cía Gen. de Obras Públicas, S.A., Buenos Aires 36-46; Technical Dir. Corpn. Sudamericana de Construcciones S.A., Buenos Aires 46-55; mem. Board of Dirs. Hochtief A.G., Essen 55-; mem. Foreign Com-

merce Council of Ministry of Econs. of German Fed. Republic 63-.
Publs. articles in technical journals.
(43) Essen-Bredeney, Westerwaldstrasse 13, German Federal Republic.

Hartnell, Norman, M.V.O.; British dress designer; b. 12 June 1901; ed. Mill Hill School and Magdalene Coll., Cambridge.
Began dress designing 23; designed new uniform for W.R.A.C. and for Red Cross Nurses; holds Royal Warrant as Dressmaker to H.M. Queen Elizabeth II and H.M. Queen Elizabeth the Queen Mother; Neiman-Marchs Award (U.S.A.) for world influence on fashion.
Publ. *Silver and Gold* (autobiog.) 55.
26 Bruton Street, London, W.1; Lovel Dene, Windsor Forest, Berks., England.

Hartner, Willy R.; German university professor; b. 22 Jan. 1905; ed. Johann Wolfgang Goethe-Universität, Frankfurt, Universitetet i Oslo, and Univ. de Paris à la Sorbonne.
Assistant, China Inst., Frankfurt 28-31, Acting Dir. 40-41; Asst., Observatory, Frankfurt 31-35; Lecturer in Scandinavian Languages and Literatures, Univ. of Frankfurt 31-; Visiting Prof. of History of Science, Harvard Univ. 35-37; Docent, History of Science, Frankfurt Univ. 40-46, Dir. Inst. for History of Sciences 43-, Prof. of History of Science 46-, Dean of Faculty of Science 46-48, 54-55, Rector 59-60; Visiting Prof. Univ. of Chicago 49, 55, Harvard Univ. 61-62, 62-63, 64-; Vice-Pres. Académie Internationale d'Histoire des Sciences, Paris 65-; Assoc. Royal Astronomical Soc.; mem. several scientific socs.
Publs. articles on history of science in numerous int. journals; *Oriens-Occidens* (selected articles 1934-1967) 67.
(638) Bad Homburg, Schopenhauerstrasse 5, German Federal Republic.
Telephone: 06172-23684.

Hartog, Harold Samuel Arnold; Netherlands business executive; b. 21 Dec. 1910; ed. Wiedemann Coll., Geneva.
Joined Unilever 31; mem. Netherlands forces, Second World War; joined Unilever in France after Second World War, later in charge of Unilever companies in Netherlands; mem. Board Unilever N.V. 48-; mem. Unilever Rotterdam Group Management responsible for Unilever activities in Germany, Austria and Belgium 52-60; mem. Unilever Cttee. for Overseas Interests, London 60-62; one of two World Co-ordinators, Unilever's food interests, London 62-66; Chair. Unilever N.V. 66-.
Office: Unilever House, Blackfriars, London, E.C.4; Home: 21 St. James's Place, London, S.W.1, England.
Telephone 01-493-55-58.

Hartog, Jan de; Netherlands writer; b. 14.
Publs. *Het Huis met de Handen* 34, *Ave Caesar* 36, *Oompje Owadi* 38, *Holland's Glory* 40, *God's Geuzen* Vol. I 47, Vol. II 48, Vol. III 49, *Stella* 50, *Mary* 51, *The Lost Sea* 51, *Thalassa* 52, *Captain Jan* 52, *The Little Ark* 54, *The Inspector* 61, *Waters of the New World* 61 (travel), *The Artist* 63, *The Hospital* 65, *The Captain* 67; plays: *De Ondergang van de Vrijheid* 37 (Great Nat. Drama Prize 39), *Mist* 38, *Skipper Next to God* 46, *Death of a Rat* 46, *The Fourposter* 46; detective stories under pseudonym of F. R. Eckman: *Een Linkerbene gezocht* 35, *Spoken te koop* 36, *Ratten op der trap* 37, *Drie Doode Dwergen* 37, *De Maagd en de Moordenaar* 38.
Ship "Rival", Sixhaven, Amsterdam, Netherlands.

Hartung, Hans; German-born French painter; b. 21 Sept. 1904; ed. Leipzig Univ., Leipzig and Dresden Acads. of Fine Art.
First exhibition 31; Foreign Legion in the Second World War; French nationality 46; rep. at Dunn Int. Exhibi-

tion, London 63, Tate Gallery, London 64; mem. Berlin and Munich Acads. of Fine Art; Guggenheim Prize 56, Rubens Prize 57, Grand Prize, Venice Biennale 60; Prix d'Honneur, Ljubljana Graphic Art Exhbn. 67; works rep. in numerous museums and galleries in Europe, Asia, North and South America; Officier de la Légion d'Honneur, Officier des Arts et Lettres, Médaille Militaire, Croix de Guerre.
c/o Musée National D'Art Moderne, 2 rue de la Manutention, Paris 16e, France.

Hartung, Rear-Admiral Teodoro E.; Argentine naval officer and diplomatist; b. 1900.
Commissioned in Navy 16; Aide to Argentine Pres. 41-43; Naval Attaché in London and head of the Argentine Naval Commission in Europe 45-47; retd. from Navy 51; Minister of Marine 55-58; Ambassador to Great Britain 58-63; led Int. Maritime Conf., Copenhagen 45; Orden al Mérito Militar (Guatemala), Gran Cruz Blanca, Mérito Naval de Perú, Commdr. Légion d'Honneur, Gran Oficial Condor de los Andes (Bolivia).
c/o Ministry of Foreign Affairs, Buenos Aires, Argentina.

Hartwell, Baron (Life Peer), cr. 68, of Peterborough Court in the City of London; (**William**) **Michael Berry,** M.B.E., T.D.; British journalist; b. 18 May 1911; ed. Eton Coll. and Christ Church, Oxford.
Served 39-45 war; fmr. Deputy Editor-in-Chief *The Daily Telegraph*, Editor-in-Chief 54-; Editor-in-Chief *The Sunday Telegraph* 61.
Publ. *Party Choice* 48.
18 Cowley Street, London, S.W.1; and Oving House, Whitchurch, nr. Aylesbury, Bucks., England.

Hartwell, Dulcie Marie; South African trade union leader; b. 15; ed. Public Schools in Transvaal and Dominican Convents at Newcastle, Natal, Pietersburg, and Boksburg.
Dress machinist in clothing factories and Chair. Dressmakers' Branch; Vice-Pres. of Garment Workers' Union of South Africa 33-37; Asst. Gen. Sec. of the Union 37-39; Sec. Unemployment Insurance Fund for the Clothing Industry 39-50; Sec. Medical Aid Soc. for Clothing Industry 41-50; joint Gen. Sec. S.A. Trades and Labour Council 51-53, Gen. Sec. 53-54, when this was dissolved Gen. Sec. of the S.A. Trades Union Council 55-64; hon. mem. S.A. Boilermakers, Iron and Steel Workers and Ship Builders' Society 55-.
P.O. Box 5592, Johannesburg; and 517 Union Centre, 31 Pritchard Street, Johannesburg, Transvaal, South Africa.

Hartz, Gustav Emil; Danish civil engineer; b. 18 June 1888; ed. Royal Danish Technical Coll.
Civil engineer; Man. Industrial Asscn., Copenhagen 18; Man. Dir. Fed. Danish Industries 26-46; Man. Dir. Thomas B. Thrige's Foundation (Vice-Chair. 60-66), and Thomas B. Thrige's Works, Odense 47-60; Hon. Pres. Danish Nat. Cttee. for World Power Conf.; mem. Board of Dirs. Danish War Marine Insurance of Goods 39-67; mem. Danish Nat. Cttee. Int. Chamber of Commerce until 67; mem. Board of the Nat. Bank of Denmark 50-67; mem. Central Council Danish Conservative Party 28-67; Joint Founder and mem. Acad. of Technical Sciences; mem. Board of Fed. of Danish Industries 47-66; Chair. Foundation of Faedrelandets Vel; mem. Danish Atomic Energy Comm. 55-56; mem. Royal Electricity Council 35-67; mem. Board of Scandia Wagon Works Ltd. until 66; mem. Brandts Klaedefabrik Ltd. until 67; mem. Thomas B. Thrige, Copenhagen, Ltd. until 66; Chair. Danish Tourist Office 61-66.
Bredstedgade 25, 5100 Odense, Denmark.

Harun, Datu Mustapha bin Datu, O.B.E.; Sabah (Malaysian) administrator; b. 18.
Member Legislative Council of North Borneo 56-63; Chair. Sabah (North Borneo) Nat. Council; Chair. and Leader United Sabah Nat. Org.; Yang Di-Pertuan Negara (Head of State) of Sabah Sept. 63-.
Office of the Yang Di-Pertuan Negara, Jesselton, Sabah, Malaysia.

Harva, Urpo Hemminki, M.A., PH.D.; Finnish university professor; b. 22 May 1910; ed. Univ. of Turku.
Reader in Adult Education, School of Social Sciences. Tampere (now Univ. of Tampere) 40-46, Prof. 46-, Rector 45-48.
Publs. *Die Philosophie von G.I. Hartman* 35, *Kristinusko ja psykologia* (Christianity and Psychology) 40, *Vapaa kansansivistystyö* (Adult Education) 43, *Kansansivistäjä* (The Adult Educator) 48, *Johdatus filosofiaan* (An Introduction to Philosophy) 53, *Yksilö ja Yhteisö* (The Individual and Society) 54, *Moraali ja yhteiskunta* (Morals and Society) 57, *Ihminen etsii itseään* (Man in Search of Himself) 57, *Etiikka* (Ethics) 58, *Systemaattinen kasvatustiede* (Philosophy of Education) 60, *Ihminen Hyvinvointivaltiossa* (Man in the Welfare State) 64.
Tampereen Yliopisto, Tampere, Finland.
Telephone: Tampere 21040.

Harvey, Laurence; British actor; b. 1 Oct. 1929; ed. Meyerton Coll. and Athlone High School, Johannesburg, S. Africa.
With Johannesburg Repertory Co. 43 and 45-46; S. African Army 43-46; studied at R.A.D.A. 46; Manchester Library Theatre 47, London 51, Shakespeare Memorial Theatre 52, 54, New York 55, London 55-56 and 57, New York 57-58, Old Vic Tour of America 58-59 (title role in *Henry V*); has made several television appearances in plays; has played in over 40 films, including *Romeo and Juliet* (Romeo), *I am A Camera* (Christopher Isherwood), *Room at the Top* (Joe Lampton), *Summer and Smoke, The Alamo, Butterfield 8, The Long and the Short and the Tall, The Wonderful World of Brothers Grimm, Walk on the Wild Side, Manchurian Candidate, The Running Man, Of Human Bondage, Life at The Top, The Outrage, Darling, The Spy with the Cold Nose, A Dandy in Aspic,* and produced and acted in *The Ceremony,* acted in *Camelot;* nominated for British Acad. Awards, for American Acad. Award 60; Western Heritage Award 60.
c/o A. R. Lloyd, Esq., Brook House, Park Lane, London, W.1, England.

Harvie-Watt, Sir George Steven, Bt., Q.C., T.D., British politician; b. 23 Aug. 1903; ed. George Watson's Coll., Glasgow and Edinburgh Univs.
Called to Bar Inner Temple Jan. 30; Brevet Major 35, Lieut.-Col. Commanding 31st Battalion R.E., T.A. 38-41; Conservative M.P. for Keighley Div. of Yorkshire 31-35 and for Richmond, Surrey, Feb. 37-59; Parl. Private Sec. to the late Rt. Hon. Euan Wallace when Parl. Sec. to Board of Trade 37-38, and to Rt. Hon. Winston Churchill 41-45; Asst. Govt. Whip 38-40; D.L. Surrey 42, Greater London Council 66; J.P. County of London 44-56; Chair. Consolidated Goldfields; Dir. Midland Bank Ltd., The Standard Bank Ltd., Eagle Star Insurance Co. Ltd.; Chair. Monotype Corpn. Ltd.; mem. of Queen's Bodyguard for Scotland—The Royal Company of Archers; Commdr. 63rd A.A. Brigade 48-50; A.D.C. to H.M. the King 48-52; A.D.C. to H.M. the Queen 52-59.
Earlsneuk, Elie, Fife, Scotland.
Telephone: Elie 506.

Harwood, Raymond Charles, B.C.S.; American publisher; b. 10 June 1906; ed. New York Univ.
Assistant Treas. Harper and Brothers 30-42, Treas. 42-58, mem. Board of Dirs. 43-, mem. Exec. Cttee. 44-, Gen. Man. 45-50, Exec. Vice-Pres. 50-55, Chair. 67- (now Harper Row, Publishers Inc.); Sec. and Treas. Paul B. Hoeber Inc. 35-61; Chair. of Exec. Cttee., Treas.,

Trustee and Chair. Finance Cttee. Princeton Univ. Press.
49 East 33rd Street, New York, N.Y., 10016; Home: 31 Intervale, Roslyn Estates, Roslyn, Long Island, N.Y., U.S.A.

Hasairi, Ahmed Al; Libyan politician.
Nazir of Education in the Tripoli Provincial Govt.; Fed. Minister of Defence 60-62; Minister of Finance 62; Chair. Board of Dirs. Tripoli International Fair 63-.
Tripoli International Fair, P.O. Box 819, Tripoli, Libya.

Hasan, Said, B.A.; Pakistani diplomatist and public administrator; b. 05; ed. Univ. of the Punjab.
Indian Finance Dept. 27; organised small industries for war production 39-45; in charge of the financial partition of the Provinces of Bengal and Assam; Jt. Sec. and Sec. of the Ministry of Economic Affairs, Pakistan 50-56; mem. Pakistan Nat. Planning Board 53-56, Chair. 57-60; Chair. UN Technical Assistance Cttee. 55; Pres. SEATO Economic Cttee. 55; Vice-Pres. UN ECOSOC 56; Perm. Rep. to UN 60-61; Deputy Chair. Pakistan Planning Comm. 61-; Hilal-i-Pakistan 66.
G-78, Clifton, Karachi 6, Pakistan.

Hasani, Baqir Husain, B.SC., LL.B.; Iraqi diplomatist and public administrator; b. 15; ed. Columbia Univ., New York and Baghdad Univ.
Director of Commerce and Registrar of Companies, Iraq Ministry of Econs. 47-51; Dir.-Gen. of Contracts and Econ. Affairs, Development Board 51-54; Dir.-Gen. of Income Tax, Ministry of Finance 54-55; Dir.-Gen. and Chair. of Bd. of Dirs. Tobacco Monopoly Admin. 56-59; Minister, later Ambassador to Austria 59-63; Chair. Board of Govs. Int. Atomic Energy Agency (IAEA) 61-62, Special Adviser to Dir.-Gen. IAEA 63-.
c/o International Atomic Energy Agency, Vienna 1010, Kaerntnerring 11, Austria.
Telephone: 52-45-11.

Hase, Karl-Günther von; German civil servant; b. 15 Dec. 1917.
Military service; German Foreign Service, Bonn and Ottawa; Deputy Chief, later Head of Press Dept., Foreign Office, Bonn 56-61, Head, Western Dept. 61-62; State Sec., Head, Press and Information Office of the Fed. Govt. 62-68; State Sec. Ministry of Defence 68-.
Ministry of Defence, Bonn, German Federal Republic.
Telephone: 20-161.

Haseeb, Dr. Khair-El-Din; Iraqi economist and statistician.
Director-Gen. Iraqi Fed. of Industries 60-63; mem. Planning Board 60-63; Gov. Central Bank of Iraq 63-65; Chair. Social Security Board 63-65, Econ. Establishment 64-65; Asst. Prof. in Econs., Coll. of Econs. and Political Science 66-; mem. Board of Iraq Nat. Oil Co. 67-.
15/18/4, Al-Mansoor, Baghdad, Iraq.
Telephone: 356266.

Hasegawa, Kazuo; Japanese actor; b. 1908.
First film appearance in *Chigo no Kempo* (The Childish Sword Master) 27; more recent films include *Genji Monogatari* (Tales of Genji) 51, *Jigokumon* (Gate of Hell) 53, *Yoshinaka* 55, *Zangiku Monogatari* (Kabuki Elergy) 56, *Naruto Hicho* 57.
c/o Daiei Motion Picture Co. Ltd., 3-8 Kyobashi, Chuo-ku, Tokyo, Japan.

Hasegawa, Norishige; Japanese chemical executive; b. 07; ed. Tokyo Univ.
Sumitomo Chemical Co. 31-, Dir. 51-, Managing Dir. 56, Vice-Pres. 63-65, Pres. 65-; Dir. Univ. of Sacred Heart, Japan Cttee. for Econ. Development, Kansai Cttee. for Econ. Development; mem. Industrial Structure Council of Ministry of Int. Trade and Industry, Inquiry Comm. for Tax System of Ministry of Finance; Chair. Kansai Symphonic Orchestra Asscn.; Chair. Japan Ammonium Sulphate Industry Asscn.
Sumitomo Chemical Co., 15 5-chome, Kitahama, Higashi-ku, Osaka, Japan.
Telephone: Osaka (203) 1231.

Haskell, Arnold Lionel, C.B.E., M.A.; British ballet school governor, author and lecturer; b. 03; ed. Westminster and Trinity Hall, Cambridge.
Member Editorial Board of William Heinemann 29-34; joint founder Camargo Soc. 30; Ballet critic *Daily Telegraph* 34-47; lectured for Ministry of Information and other bodies on Australia 40-45; Gov. Royal Ballet School; Gov. Royal Ballet; Chair. and Trustee, Ballet Benevolent Fund; Vice-Pres. Varna Ballet Competitions, Royal Acad. of Dancing; Council mem. Royal West of England Acad.; travelled and lectured in U.S.A., Australia, Canada, France, Germany, Italy, Spain, Portugal, U.S.S.R., Cuba, etc.; Chevalier de la Légion d'Honneur.
Publs. *Balletomania* 34, *Diaghileff* 35, *Dancing Round the World* 37, *Ballet Panorama* 38, *Ballet: A Complete Guide to Appreciation* 38, *Balletomane's Album* 39, *Waltzing Matilda* 40, *The Australians* 42, *Australia* 42, *The National Ballet* 45, *In His True Centre* (autobiography) 51, *Saints Alive* 54, *The Russian Genius in Ballet* 63, *Ballet Retrospect* 64, *Heroes and Roses* 66.
Beechwood House, Widcombe Hill, Bath, England.
Telephone: Bath 2472.

Haskell, Broderick, B.S.; American banker and industrialist; b. 22 Aug. 1899; ed. Massachusetts Inst. of Technology.
Director Banco de Reserva del Peru 27-28; Vice-Pres. Guaranty Trust Co. of New York 30-53; Dir. Combustion Engineering Inc. 46-56 (Vice-Chair. 53-56), Lummus Co., New York 52-56, Air Preheater Corpn., New York 54-56; mem. Advisory Board, Chase Manhattan Bank 54-56; Dir. Atomic Industrial Forum 54-57; Dir. of Investments, Int. Finance Corpn. 56-61; Partner, Bache & Co. Inc. 62-65, Vice-Pres. 65-; Dir. Foote Mineral Co.
Publ. (with others) *The American Individual Enterprise System.*
Office: 36 Wall Street, New York 5; Home: 36 East 79th Street, New York 21, N.Y., U.S.A.

Haskins, Caryl Parker, PH.D.; American scientist and educationist; b. 12 Aug. 1908; ed. Yale and Harvard Univs.
Member of research staff Gen. Electric Co., Schenectady 31-35; Research Assoc. Mass. Inst. of Technology 35-44; Pres., Dir. and Research Dir. Haskins Laboratories, Inc. 35-55; Research Prof. in Biophysics, Union Coll., Schenectady 37-55; Liaison Officer 40-43, Exec. Asst. to the Chair. 43-44 and Deputy Exec. Officer 44-45, Nat. Defence Research Cttee.; Scientific Adviser to the Policy Council 47 and to the Research and Devt. Board of the National Military Establishment 48-51; Chair. Advisory Cttee. to the Sec. of Defence on special weapons 48-49; Consultant to the Sec. of Defense 48- and to the Sec. of State 50-; mem. President's Science Advisory Cttee. 55-58, Consultant 59; Pres. Carnegie Inst. of Washington D.C. 56-; Presidential Certificate of Merit and King's Medal for Service in the Cause of Freedom 48.
Publs. *Of Ants and Men* 39, *The Amazon, The Life History of a Mighty River* 43, *Of Societies and Men* 51, *Scientific Revolution and World Politics* 64, *The Search for Understanding.*
Carnegie Institution, 1530 P Street N.W., Washington D.C. 20005, U.S.A.
Telephone: DU 7-6400.

Hasluck, Rt. Hon. Paul Meernaa Caedwalla, P.C., M.A., M.P.; Australian historian, diplomatist and politician; b. 1 April 1905; ed. Western Australia Univ.

Mem. Editorial staff *The West Australian*; Lecturer in History Western Australia Univ.; mem. staff Australian Dept. of External Affairs 41-47; Sec. Canberra Conf. Jan. 44; Adviser on Australian del. to Wellington Conf. Nov. 44; Adviser British Commonwealth meeting London April 45; Adviser San Francisco Conf. April 45; Australian del. Exec. Cttee. of United Nations Preparatory Comm. London Aug. 45; alternate del. Preparatory Comm. Nov. 45; del. General Assembly Jan. and Sept. 46; Dir. post-hostilities Div. Australian Dept. of External Affairs April 45; Counsellor Australian Mission U.N. H.Q. Mar. 46; Acting rep. of Australia on Security Council and Atomic Energy Comm. July 46; Research Reader in History, Univ. of W. Australia 48; elected to Commonwealth Parl. as Liberal M.P. Dec. 49-; Minister for Territories, Fed. Cabinet 51-63; Minister of Defence Dec. 63-April 64, of External Affairs April 64-; engaged on official history of Australia in Second World War during 47, 48, 49.
Publs. *Into the Desert* 39, *Black Australians* 42, *Workshop of Security* 47, *The Government and the People, 1939-1941* (Australian Official War History) 52, *Native Welfare in Australia* 53.
Parliament House, Canberra, A.C.T., Australia.

Hasnie, Shujaat Ali, M.SC.; Pakistani civil servant; b. 05; ed. Govt. Coll., Lahore and Univ. of Punjab. Joined Indian Audit and Accounts Service 30; Under-Sec. Finance Dept., Govt. of India 38, Dep. Sec. 40; Joint Financial Adviser, War and Supply 45, later Joint Sec. of Commerce, and held same post in Govt. of Pakistan after independence; Sec. Ministry of Food and Agriculture 52-56, Ministry of Finance and Economic Affairs 57-60; Gov. State Bank of Pakistan 60-67; Chair. UN Food and Agriculture Org. 55-59.
[*Died, 17 March* 1968.]

Hassan II, King of Morocco; 17th Sovereign of the Alaouite dynasty; b. 1930; ed. Bordeaux Univ.
Son of Mohammed V; invested as Crown Prince Moulay Hassan 57; C.-in-C. and Chief of Staff of Royal Moroccan Army 57; personally directed rescue operations at Agadir earthquake disaster 60; Minister of Defence May 60-June 61; Vice-Premier May 60-Feb. 61; Prime Minister Feb. 61-Nov. 63, June 65-; succeeded to throne on death of his father, Feb. 26th, 1961.
Royal Palace, Rabat, Morocco.

Hassan, Hon. Sir Joshua (Abraham), Kt., C.B.E., M.V.O., Q.C.; Gibraltar lawyer and politician; b. 1915; ed. Line Wall Coll., Gibraltar.
Called to Bar, Middle Temple, London 39; mem. Exec. Council, Chief mem. Legislative Council, Gibraltar 50-64; Chief Minister of Gibraltar 64-; Mayor of Gibraltar 45-50, 53-; Deputy Coroner, Gibraltar 41-64; Chair. Cttee of Management Gibraltar Museum 52-65; Chair. Central Planning Comm. 47-, Gibraltar Lottery Cttee. 55-; Pres. Gibraltar Labour Party and Asscn.; Asscn. for the Advancement of Civil Rights.
11/18 Europa Road, Gibraltar.
Telephone: 2295.

Hassan, Syed Muhammad; Pakistani diplomatist; b. 12; ed. Punjab Univ., Lahore, Aitchison Chief's Coll., Indian Mil. Acad., Dehradun.
Several years service in British Indian Army from 34 onwards; Indian Govt. Trade Commr., Teheran 44-47; served as Counsellor in Pakistani Embassies in Iran 47-49, Turkey May-Oct. 49, U.S.S.R. 49-51; Deputy Sec. Ministry of External Affairs 52; Joint Sec. 52-56; Ambassador to Turkey Jan. 57-61, to Sweden 61-62; Dir.-Gen. Ministry of External Affairs 62-63; High Commr. in Malaysia 63-.
Pakistani High Commission, Kuala Lumpur, Malaysia.

Hassel, Kai-Uwe von; German politician; b. 21 April 1913.
Studied farming and trade in Tanganyika; Plantation

trader, E. Africa 35-40, deported to Germany 40; served in Army 40-45, prisoner 45; Mayor of Glücksburg 47 and mem. of County Council; C.D.U. deputy for Schleswig-Holstein Landtag 50-; also elected to Bundestag, but resigned on appointment as Minister-Pres. of Schleswig-Holstein 54-63; Pres. Bundesrat 55-56; Deputy Chair. C.D.U. 56; Minister of Defence, German Fed. Repub. 63-66, for Refugees and Expellees 66-.
Ministry for Refugees, Bonn-Duisdorf, German Federal Republic.

Hassouna, Mohammed Abdel-Khalek al; United Arab Republic (Egyptian) diplomatist; b. 28 Oct. 1898; ed. Cairo Univ. and Cambridge.
Began as lawyer 21; subsequently joined Egyptian Diplomatic Corps; served Berlin 26, Prague 28, Brussels 28, Rome 30, and at Ministry for Foreign Affairs, Cairo 32-39; Under-Sec. of State, Ministry for Social Affairs 39; Gov. of Alexandria 42; Under-Sec. of State, Ministry for Foreign Affairs 48; Minister of Social Affairs 49; Minister of Education 52; Minister for Foreign Affairs 52; Sec.-Gen. Arab League 52-; Grand Cordon of the Order of the Nile; Légion d'Honneur; decorations conferred by Belgium, China, Ethiopia and Italy.
The Arab League, Midan al Tahrir, Cairo, United Arab Republic.

Hastie, William Henry, A.B., LL.B., S.J.D.; American judge; b. 17 Nov. 1904; ed. Amherst Coll. and Harvard Univ.
Member of Faculty, Howard Univ. School of Law 30-37; Asst. Solicitor, U.S. Dept. of Interior 33-37; Judge of Dist. Court of Virgin Islands 37-39; Dean, Howard Univ. School of Law 39-46; Civilian Aide to Sec. of War 40-42; mem. Caribbean Comm. 47-50; Gov. of Virgin Islands 46-49; U.S. Circuit Judge, U.S. Court of Appeals for Third Circuit 49-; Fellow American Acad. of Arts and Sciences.
United States Courthouse, Philadelphia, Pennsylvania 19017, U.S.A.

Hastings, A(lbert) Baird, B.S., PH.D.; American professor of biological chemistry; b. 20 Nov. 1895; ed. Univ. of Michigan and Columbia Univ.
Chemist U.S. Public Health Services 17-21; Asst. Rockefeller Inst. for Medical Research 21-22; Assoc. 22-26; Prof. Physiological Chemistry Univ. of Chicago 26-28, Prof. of Biochemistry 28-35; Hamilton Kuhn Prof. of Biological Chemistry Harvard Medical School 35-58, Em. 58-; mem. Scripps Clinic and Research Foundation 59-66, mem. Emeritus 66-; Lecturer Univ. of Southern Calif. 24; mem. American Acad. of Arts and Sciences, American Philosophical Soc. Nat. Acad. of Sciences, Royal Danish Acad. of Sciences and Letters, Nat. Research Council (mem. of various cttees.); mem. cttee. on Medical Research, Office of Scientific Research and Devt., Washington 41-47; mem. Board of Review, U.S. Atomic Energy Comm. 47; Pres. Soc. for Experimental Biology and Medicine and American Soc. of Biological Chemists 45-47; Syndic, Harvard Univ. Press; Consultant, Div. of Biology and Medicine, U.S. Atomic Energy Comm. 50-62; U.S. del. Int. Conf. on Peaceful Uses of Atomic Energy, Geneva 54; U.S. Public Health Nat. Advisory Cttees. 43-; Walter Reed Army Inst. of Research 56-62, etc.; Trustee Brookhaven Nat. Laboratory, Associated Univs. Inc. 48-51, mem. Visiting Cttee. 56-; Hon. Sc.D. (Michigan, Harvard, Columbia, Boston, Oxford and St. Louis Univs.); President's Medal for Merit 48, Banting Medal of American Diabetes Asscn. 62, and many other awards.
Department of Neurosciences, University of California, San Diego Campus, La Jolla, Calif.; and 5912 Bellevue Avenue, La Jolla, California 92037, U.S.A.

Hastings, John Simpson, B.S., LL.B., LL.D.; American judge; b. 30 June 1898; ed. U.S. Military Acad., West Piont and Indiana Univ.
Admitted to Indiana Bar 24, mem. Hastings, Allen &

Hastings 24-57; Judge, U.S. Court of Appeals, 7th Circuit, Chicago 57-, Chief Judge 59-; Dir. Indiana Univ. Foundation, Vice-Pres. 51-.
219 South Dearborn Street, Chicago, Illinois 60604, U.S.A.

Hatcher, Harlan Henthorne, M.A., PH.D., LIT.D., LL.D., L.H.D.; American author and university president; b. 9 Sept. 1898; ed. Ohio State Univ. and Univ. of Chicago.
Instructor, Ohio State Univ. 22-28; Asst. Prof. 28-32; Prof. of English 32-51, Dean of Coll. of Arts and Sciences 44-48, Vice-Pres. 48-51; Pres. Univ. of Michigan 51-67; served U.S. Army 18, U.S. Navy 42-44; State Dir. Fed. Writers' Project in Ohio 37-39; Editorial Adviser *College English* 38-48.
Publs. *The Versification of Robert Browning* 28, *Tunnel Hill* 31, *Patterns of Wolfpen* 34, *Creating the Modern American Novel* 35, *The Buckeye Country* 40, *The Great Lakes* 44, *Lake Erie* 45, *The Western Reserve* 49, revised edn. 66, *A Century of Iron and Men* 50, *Persistent Quest for Values* 66; Editor: *The Ohio Guide* 40, *Modern Continental, British and American Dramas, with critical introductions* (3 vols.) 41, *Modern Dramas* (shorter edition) 44, *A Modern Repertory* 53, *A Pictorial History of the Great Lakes* 63.
815 South University Avenue, Ann Arbor, Mich., U.S.A.
Telephone: 313-764-6270.

Hatfield, Mark O.; American politician; b. 12 July 1922; ed. Willamette Univ. and Stanford Univ.
U.S. Navy, Second World War; Instructor, Asst. Prof., Assoc. Prof. in Political Science, Willamette Univ. 49-56, Dean of Students 50-56; State Rep., Marion County 51-55, State Senator, Marion County 55-57; Sec. of State, Oregon 57-59, Gov. of Oregon 59-67; U.S. Senator from Oregon 67-, mem. Senate Cttee. on Agriculture and Forestry, Cttee. on Interior and Insular Affairs, and Select Cttee. on Small Business, numerous awards; Republican.
6327 New Senate Office Building, Washington, D.C. 20510, U.S.A.
Telephone: 225-3753.

Hathaway, Earl B.; American rubber executive; b. 11 Feb. 1903; ed. Northwestern Univ.
Firestone Tire & Rubber Co. 27-; Salesman 30-32; Store Man. Alton, Springfield, St. Louis and Chicago 32-36; Asst. Man. Chicago District 36-38, District Man., Detroit 38-41; Wholesale Sales Man., Akron 41-42; Eastern Div. Man. 42-48; Trade Sales Man. 48-57; Vice-Pres. (Trade Sales) 57-59, Vice-Pres. (Sales) 59-62; Dir. 60-; Exec. Vice-Pres. 62-64, Pres. 64-; Dir. Rubber Manufacturers' Asscn. and Automotive Old Timers, Inc.; Hon. L.L.D. Univ. of Akron 65; Alumni Award Northwestern Univ. 66.
Firestone Tire & Rubber Co., 1200 Firestone Parkway, Akron 17, Ohio, U.S.A.

Hathaway, Gail A., B.S.(C.E.); American civil engineer; b. 11 Oct. 1895; ed. Oregon State Univ.
Assistant to State Engineer of Oregon 24; hydraulic engineer with Corps of Engineers, Dept. of Army 28-38; joined Office of Chief of Engineers, Dept. of Army 38-57; Engineering Consultant to Dept. of Technical Operations of International Bank for Development and Reconstruction 57-63; in private practice 63-; Pres. Int. Commission on Large Dams 52-58; Vice-Chair. Internat. Exec. Council, World Power Conf. 52-58, and other engineering comms.; Fellow American Soc. Civil Engineers (Pres. 51), etc.; Pres. citation and Bronze Star.
4316 Van Buren Street, University Park, Hyattsville, Maryland 20782, U.S.A.
Telephone: 927-7857.

Hathi, Jaisukhlal; Indian politician; b. 19 Jan. 1909.
Advocate, Bombay High Court; mem. Constituent Assembly 46-47; mem. Provisional Parl.; Chief Sec.

Saurashtra 48; mem. Rajya Sabha 52-57, 62-, Lok Sabha 57-62; Deputy Minister of Irrigation and Power 52-62; Minister of State for Labour and Employment April-Nov. 62; Minister of Supply 62-64; Minister of State in Ministry of Home Affairs 64-66, also Minister of Defence Supplies 65-66; Minister of State for Defence Nov. 66-March 67; Minister for Labour and Rehabilitation March 67-.
11 Asoka Road, New Delhi, India.
Telephone: 43380; 32864.

Hatta, Mohammad; Indonesian politician; b. 02; ed. Rotterdam School of Economics, Holland.
Nationalist activity from schooldays; Chair. "Perhimpunan Indonesia" (Univ. Students' Asscn.) Holland 26; arrested by Dutch 27; tried and released 28; returned to Indonesia 32 and founded Pendidikan Nasional Indonesia, mass-education political party 32; arrested 34; exiled to Digul 35, later to the Moluccas; released by Japanese 42; elected Vice-Pres. of Republic of Indonesia 45-49, 50-56; Prime Minister and Minister of Defence 48; Prime Minister and Minister of Foreign Affairs 49-50.
57 Djalan Diponegoro, Djakarta, Republic of Indonesia.

Hattori, Motozo; Japanese shipping executive; b. 1 Jan. 1905; ed. Kyoto Imperial Univ.
Kawasaki Kisen Kaisha Ltd., Kobe 31-, Rep. New York Branch 40-41, Sub-Man., Santiago, Chile 41-42, Man. 42-43, Sub-Man., later Man. Operating Section, Kobe 43-46; Gen. Man. Operating and Chartering Dept. 46, Dir. 47-49, Exec. Dir. 49-50, Pres. 50-; Pres. Kawasaki Steamship Co., New York 55-, Kawasaki (London) Ltd. 56-; Pres. The "K" Line Ltd., Kobe 64-; official of other firms and business orgs.
Kawasaki Kisen Kaisha Ltd., 8 Kaigan Dori, Ikuta-ku, Kobe, Japan.

Hauge, Gabriel; American economist and banker; b. 7 March 1914; ed. Concordia Coll., Moorhead, Minnesota, and Harvard Univ.
Instructor in Econs., Harvard Univ. 38-40; Senior Statistician, Fed. Reserve Bank of New York 39; Instructor in Econs., Princeton Univ. 40-42; U.S. Naval Reserve 42-46; Chief, Div. of Research and Statistics, New York State Banking Dept. 47-50; McGraw-Hill Publishing Co. 50-52; Admin. Asst. to Pres. of U.S. for Econ. Affairs 53-56; Special Asst. to Pres. of U.S. (Econ. Affairs) 56-58; mem. Board of Dirs., Chair. Finance Cttee., Manufacturers Trust Co., New York City 58-61; Vice-Chair. of Board, Manufacturers Hanover Trust Co., N.Y. City 61-, Pres. 63-.
Manufacturers Hanover Trust Co., 350 Park Avenue, New York, N.Y. 10022, U.S.A.

Hauge, Jens Chr.; Norwegian lawyer and politician; b. 15 May 1915; ed. Oslo Univ.
Apptd. Judge 38; Tutor Oslo Univ. 40; Head of Price Police in Oslo 40-Aug. 41, arrested; leading member Military Organisation within Home Front Organisation from 41; became Sec. Prime Minister Gerhardsen 45; Minister of Defence Nov. 45-52; practising lawyer 52-; temporary Sec. Labour Party 52; Minister of Justice 55; Chair. of Royal Theatre Comm. 60; Chair. of Board Royal Norwegian Airlines 62- (concurrently S.A.S. 62).
Youngstorget 2, Oslo, Norway.

Haughey, Charles James; Irish politician; b. 16 Sept. 1925; ed. Univ. Coll. and King's Inns, Dublin.
Member Dublin Corpn. 53-55; M.P. 57-; Parl. Sec. to Minister for Justice 60-61, Minister for Justice 61-64; Minister of Agriculture and Fisheries 64-66, Minister for Finance 66-, Fianna Fail Party.
Grangemore, Raheny, Dublin 5, Ireland.

Haughton, Daniel Jeremiah; American aircraft executive; b. 7 Sept. 1911; ed. Univ. of Alabama.
Cost Accountant, Consolidated Aircraft Corpn. 36-39; Lockheed Aircraft Corpn. 39-, Gen. Man. and Vice-

Pres. 52-56, Exec. Vice-Pres. 56-61, Pres. 61-67, Chair. Board of Dirs. 67-; Dir. subsid. companies.
Lockheed Aircraft Corporation, 2555 Hollywood Way, Burbank, California, U.S.A.
Telephone: 213-847-6696.

Haugland, Jens, LL.M.; Norwegian lawyer and politician; b. 16 April 1910; ed. Oslo Univ.
With firm of barristers, Stavanger 37-38; Legal Adviser City Treas., Stavanger 38-40; Junior Judge, Ryfylke District 41; established own practice Kristiansand 43; fled to Sweden where attached to Norwegian Legation 44; resumed practice Kristiansand 45; mem. Storting 54-; Minister of Justice 55-63; Minister of Municipal Affairs and Labour 63-65, mem. Norwegian Labour Party.
The Storting, Oslo, Norway.

Haupt, Arthur Wing, B.SC., PH.D.; American botanist; b. 9 Aug. 1894; ed. Univ. of Chicago.
With U.S. Dept. of Agriculture 18; Prof. of Biology Carthage (Illinois) Coll. 19-20, St. Lawrence Univ. New York 20-23; with Univ. of California at Los Angeles 24-, Prof. of Botany 46-61, Prof. Emer. 61-; Visiting Prof. Univ. of British Columbia 36; mem. Ed. Board *Madroño* (Journal of Western Botany) 35-40; Pres. Pacific Section Botanical Society of America 37-38; botanical exploration Costa Rica 40; Pres. Haupt Botanical Lab. Inc.
Publs. *An Introduction to Botany, Fundamentals of Biology, Plant Morphology.*
832 Hendersonville Road, Asheville, N.C., U.S.A.

Hausen, Hans Magnus, DR.PHIL.; Finnish geologist; b. 84; ed. Helsinki University.
Emeritus Prof. of Geology and Mineralogy Åbo Acad.; mem. of the Finnish Society of Science, Geological Societies of Helsinki and Bonn, Finnish Geographical Soc., Inst. de Estudios Canarios, Tenerife; corresp. mem. Argentine Society of Geographical Studies, Universidad Nacional de La Plata, Inst. del Museo; journeys to Baltic Russia 10-13, Canada, Alaska 13, Argentina, Chile 14-17, Siberia 17-20, Argentina 22-23, Italy 39, Canary Islands 47, 48-50, 53-54, 57, 63 and 66-67.
Publs. 60 books and papers, including: *Materialien zur Kenntnis der pleistozänen Bildungen in den russischen Ostseeländern* 13, *On the Lithology and Geological Structure of the Sierra de Umango Area, Province of La Rioja, Argentina* 21, *Die Apatite* 29, *Geologische Beobachtungen in den Hochgebirgen der Provinzen Salta und Jujuy, N.W. Argentinien* 30, *Zur Kenntnis der Magmengesteine der chilenischen Atacama-Wüste* 37, *Das Halditjokko-Massiv* 42, *Hidrografía de las Islas Canarias* 54; with geological maps: *Contribution to the Geology of Tenerife (Canary Islands)* 56, *On the Geology of Fuerteventura (Canary Islands)* 58, *On the Geology of Lanzarote and adjacent islands (Canarian Archipelago)* 59, *New Contribution to the Geology of Grand Canary* 62.
Armas Lindgrens väg 5, Brändö, Helsinki, Finland.

Hausmann, Manfred, DR. PHIL.; German writer; b. 10 Sept. 1898; ed. Univs. of Göttingen, Munich and Heidelberg.
Served in Army 16-18; merchant in Bremen 22-24; on editorial staff of *Weser-Zeitung* Bremen 24-27, of *Weser-Kurier* 45-52.
Publs. *Frühlingsfeier* 25, *Marienkind (Legendenspiel)* 27, *Lilofee* (drama) 27, *Lampioon* 28, *Salut gen Himmel* 29, *Kleine Liebe zu Amerika* 30, *Abel mit der Mundharmonika* 32, *Abschied von der Jugend* 38, *Das Worpsweder Hirtenspiel* 42, *Das Erwachen* (translations of Greek poems) 49, *Der dunkle Reigen* (drama) 49, *Gedichte* 49, *Martin* 49, *Einer muss wachen* 50, *Liebe, Tod und Vollmondnächte* (translations of Japanese poems) 51, *Der Ueberfall* 52, *Liebende leben von der Vergebung* 53, *Isabel* 53, *Hafenbar* (drama) 53, *Hinter dem Perlen-*

vorhang (translations of Chinese poems) 54, *Die Entscheidung* 54. *Der Fischbecker Wandteppich* (drama) 55, *Was dir nicht angehört* 56, *Andreas* 57, *Aufruhr in der Marktkirche* (drama) 57, *Das Lied der Lieder* (translations of Hebrew poems) 58, *Die Zauberin von Buxtehude* (drama) 59, *Tröstliche Zeichen* (essays) 59, *Irrsal der Liebe* (poems), 60 *Heute Noch* (short story) 62, *Kleiner Stern im Dunklen Strom* 63, *Gelöstes Haar* (translations of Japanese poems) 64, *Sternsagen* 65, *Und wie Musik in der Nacht* 65, *Kassel (Porträt einer Stadt)* 65, *Und es geschah (Gedanken zür Bibel)* 65, *Brüderliche Welt* 65, *Spiegel des Lebens* 66, *Hinter den Dingen* 67.
Dyllenhoff, 2820 Bremen-Roennebeck, German Federal Republic.
Telephone: 0421-608394.

Hautecoeur, Louis, DR. ès L.; French museum curator; b. 11 June 1884; ed. Ecole Normale Supérieure, Ecole Française de Rome.
Research on N. Africa for Ministry of Education and on Tunisia for Acad. of Inscriptions; Prof. French Inst. St. Petersburg 12-13; Head Diplomatic Information Service Lugano 17-18; mem. Comm. of Information, Peace Conf. 19; del. to League of Nations Comm. for Intellectual Co-operation; Prof. Faculty of Arts Caen 19-22; Museum Curator and Prof. Ecole du Louvre 20-40; Prof. Ecole Nationale Supérieure des Beaux Arts 23-40; Dir.-Gen. of Fine Arts Egypt 27-30; Curator Luxemburg Museum 28-40; Dir. of Works of Art, Paris Exhibition 37; Dir. Biennial Exhibitions Venice 32, 34, 36, 38; Sec.-Gen. des Beaux Arts de la France and Counsellor of State 40; dismissed from Paris post by Germans 44; reinstated and retd. at own request 46; Curator of Fine Arts. Geneva, and Prof. Geneva Univ. 46-49; Perm. Sec. Acad. des Beaux-Arts 55-64; Commandeur de la Légion d'Honneur; mem. Inst. de France, Acad. de Saint Luc, Rome, Acad. Royale de Belgique, Acad. d'Architecture.
Palais de l'Institut, 25 quai de Conti, Paris 6e, France.
Telephone: 326-85-40.

Havel, Vaclav; Czechoslovak playwright; b. 5 Oct. 1936; ed. Faculty of Economics, Technical Coll., Prague.
Dramaturg (literary man.), Theatre on the Balustrade, Prague 60-.
Publs. *Garden Party* 63, *The Memorandum* 65, (plays).
Na zábradlí Theatre, Anenské nám 5, Prague 1, Czechoslovakia.

Havelange, Jean Marie Faustin Godefroid; Brazilian sports administrator and lawyer; b. 16.
Head of Imports and Exports, Companhia Siderúrgica Belgo-Mineira 37-41; Vice-Pres. Associação Desportiva Floresta, São Paulo 43-44; Vice-Pres. Federação Paulista de Natação, São Paulo 45-48, Pres. 49-51; Pres. Federação Metropolitana de Natação, Rio de Janeiro 52-56; mem. Brazilian Olympic Cttee. 56-63; Vice-Pres. Brazilian Sports Confederation 57, Pres. 58-; Dir. Pres. Viação Cometa S.A. 47-; Dir. Atlas Comercial, Equipamentos Materiais S.A. 52-; Dir. Banco Brasileiro S.A. 61-.
Avenida Visconde de Albuquerque 473 apto. 302, Rio de Janeiro, Brazil.

Haveman, Bastiaan Wouter, D.SC., LL.D.; Netherlands civil servant; b. 25 Nov. 1908; ed. Technical Univ., Delft and Leiden Univ.
Secretary, High Council of Labour 35-40; Aide-de-Camp, Commdr. of Police Troops, Netherlands Army H.Q. 39-41; mem. Resistance and Editor *Je Maintiendrai* 41-45, Prisoner 45; Sec.-Gen. Employers' Asscn. 41-45; Sec. to the Prime Minister 45-46; Adviser, Del. to UN 46-47; Econ. Adviser, Ministry of Transport and Works 47-51; Govt. Commr. for Emigration 51-62; Pres. Central Court of Arbitration for Agriculture 49-62; Dir. ICEM (Intergovernmental Cttee. for European

Migration), Geneva 62-; Netherlands and foreign honours.

17 Avenue de Budé, apt. 17-33, Geneva, Switzerland. and 5B Frankenslag, The Hague, Netherlands.

Telephone: 34-97-02 (Geneva); and 55-41-89 (The Hague).

Havers, Hon. Sir Cecil Robert, Kt., Q.C., LL.B., M.A.; British judge; b. 12 Nov. 1889; ed. Norwich Grammar School and Corpus Christi Coll., Cambridge.

Served in First World War 14-18; called to the Bar (Inner Temple) 20; K.C. 39; Recorder of Chichester 39-51; Deputy Chair. Advisory Cttee. on Aliens 40-45; Commr. in Gold Coast 44-45; Bencher, Inner Temple 46; Deputy Chair. West Kent Quarter Sessions 47-51; Commr. of Assize, Oxford and Midland Circuits 49; a Justice of the High Court 51-67.

Publ. *Landlord and Tenant Act* 27.

8 Lichfield Road, Kew Gardens, Surrey, England.

Haviland, Denis William Garstin Latimer, C.B.; British industrialist; b. 15 Aug. 1910; ed. Rugby School and St. John's Coll., Cambridge.

London Midland and Scottish Railway 34-39; Army service 40-46; Principal, Control Office for Germany and Austria 46-47; Asst. Sec. Foreign Office, German Section 47-50; Imperial Defence Coll. 50-51; Ministry of Supply 51-59, Under-Sec. 53-59, Dep. Sec. 59; Dep. Sec. Ministry of Aviation 59-64; Dep. Chair. Staveley Industries 64-65, Chair. and Man. Dir. 65-; Deputy Chair. Short Brothers and Harland 68-; Chair. European Launcher Devt. Org. (ELDO) Preparatory Group 62-64. Home: 113 Hampstead Way, London, N.W.11; Office: Portland House, Stag Place, London, S.W.1, England. Telephone: 01-455-2638 (Home); 828-6311 (Office).

Havrevold, Finn; Norwegian author and critic; b. 11 Aug. 1905; ed. Norges Tekniske Høyskole.

Qualified architect 29; book designer and illustrator; author 39; radio critic *Dagbladet* 51-; dramatic critic *Urd* 56-; Damm Prize 55 and 57, Damm-Allers Prize, Film Prize 60.

Publs. novels: *Til de dristige* 46, *Walter den fredsommelige* 47, *Skredet* 49, *Den Ytterste Dag* 63, *De gjenstridige* 65; short stories: *Det raker ikke Andersen* 39; children's books: *Sommereventyret* 52, *Drommeveggen* 53, *Den ensomme kriger* 55, *Marens lille ugle* 57, *Viggo* 57, *Grunnbrott* 60, *Jeg flykter i natt* 63; plays: *Jubileum* 51, *Uretten* 55, *Sommerhuset* 57, *Tomannsboligen* 59, *Stakkars Anton* 61, *Helens dagbok* 64, *Regissøren* 64, *Gruppen* 64; biography: *Helge Krog* 59; radio plays: *Sensommer, Wilhelm og Alice, Eskapade, Katastrofe* 60, *Arabesk, I Kveldingen, Svalene Flyr Lavt, Hjemturen* 61, *Brev til Tom* 62, *Dikterjubileum* 63, *Duellen* 65; TV play: *En Smule Kjaerlighet* 61; film scenarios: *Drapen* 60, *Farlig Kurs* 64.

Thomas Heftyes Gate 64C, Oslo 2, Norway.

Hawke, Hon. Albert Redvers George, M.L.A.; Australian politician (retired); b. 3 Dec. 1900; ed. Kapunda Model School, South Australia.

Mem. South Australia House of Assembly for Burra Burra 24-27; Political Organiser for Labour Party in Western Australia 28; Labour Mem. for Northam 33-68; Minister for Employment, Western Australia 36-39, for Labour 36-43, for Industrial Development 39-47; Deputy Leader of the Opposition 47-52, Leader 52-53; Premier, Treasurer and Minister for Child Welfare, Western Australia 53-59, Leader of the Opposition 59-66.

Walker Street, West Perth, Western Australia. Telephone: 219770.

Hawker, Sir (Frank) Cyril, Kt.; British business executive; b. 21 July 1900; ed. City of London School. Bank of England 20, Deputy Chief Cashier 44-48, Chief Accountant 48-53, Adviser to Governors 53-54, Exec. Dir. 54-62; Chair. The Standard Bank Ltd. 62-,

Standard Bank of West Africa Ltd.; Dir. Head Wrightson & Co. Ltd. 62-, Agricultural Mortgage Corpn. Ltd. 64-, Midland and Int. Banks Ltd.; Chair. Finance Cttee., Nat. Playing Fields Asscn.; High Sheriff of County of London 63.

Home: Pounsley Lodge, Blackboys, Nr. Uckfield, Sussex; Office: Standard Bank Ltd., 10 Clements Lane, London, E.C.4, England.

Hawkes, Charles Francis Christopher, M.A., F.B.A., F.S.A.; British archaeologist; b. 5 June 1905; ed. Winchester Coll., and New Coll., Oxford.

Assistant Dept. of British and Medieval Antiquities, British Museum 28, Asst. Keeper, promoted to 1st Class 38; Ministry of Aircraft Production 40-45; returned to British Museum 45, in charge of Prehistoric and Romano-British Antiquities 46; Prof. of European Archæology, Oxford Univ. 46-; Fellow Keble Coll.; Prof.-in-charge, Inst. of Archæology 61-; elected Nat. Sec. (U.K.) on Council Int. Congress of Prehistoric and Protohistoric Sciences 31, full mem. 48, mem. Exec. Cttee. 50; excavations on various sites in U.K. 25-; Editor *Archæological Journal* London 44-50; Pres. Prehistoric Society 50-54, Council for British Archæology 61-64; Editor *Inventaria Archæologica* for Great Britain 54-.

Publs. *St Catharine's Hill, Winchester* (with J. N. L. Myres and C. G. Stevens) 31, *Archæology in England and Wales, 1914-31* (with T. D. Kendrick) 32, *Winchester College* 33, *The Prehistoric Foundations of Europe* 40, *Prehistoric Britain* (with Jacquetta Hawkes) 43, *Camulodunum: The Excavations at Colchester, 1930-39* (with M. R. Hull) 47.

Institute of Archæology, 35 Beaumont Street, Oxford, England.

Hawkes, Jacquetta, O.B.E., M.A. (wife of J. B. Priestley, q.v.); British author and archaeologist; b. 1910; ed. Perse School and Newnham Coll., Cambridge.

Archaeological activities in Great Britain, Eire, France and Palestine 31-40; Asst. Principal, Post-War Reconstruction Secretariat 41-43; with Ministry of Education, Sec., U.K. Nat. Comm. for UNESCO 43-49 (retd.); Vice-Pres. Council for British Archaeology 49-52; Archaeological Adviser, Festival of Britain 49-51; Gov. British Film Inst. 50-55; mem. Culture Advisory Cttee., UNESCO 66-; Author Editor (with Frankfort and Woolley) *UNESCO History of Mankind* (Vol. I); Archaeological Corresp. *Sunday Times*; Kemsley Award for *A Land* 51.

Publs. *Archaeology of Jersey* 39, *Prehistoric Britain* (with Christopher Hawkes) 44, *Early Britain* 45, *Symbols and Speculations* (poems) 48, *A Land* 51, *Guide to Prehistoric and Roman Monuments in England and Wales* 51, *Dragon's Mouth* (play), *Fables* 53, *Man on Earth* 54, *Journey Down a Rainbow* (with J. B. Priestley) 55, *Providence Island* 59, *Man and the Sun* 62, *Prehistory and the Beginnings of Civilisation* (with Sir Leonard Woolley) 63, *The World of the Past* 63, *King of the Two Lands* 66, *The Pharoes of Egypt* 67, *Dawn of the Gods* 68.

B 3, Albany, London, W.1, England.

Haworth, Leland John, PH.D.; American nuclear physicist; b. 11 July 1904; ed. Indiana Univ. and Univ. of Wisconsin.

High school teacher, Indianapolis 26-28; Instructor in Physics, Univ. of Wisconsin 30-37; Lalor Fellow in Physical Chemistry, Mass. Inst. of Technology 37-38; Assoc. in Physics, Univ. of Illinois 38-39, Asst. Prof. 39-44, Prof. 44-47; Staff mem. Radiation Laboratory, Mass. Inst. of Technology 41-45; Asst. Dir. Brookhaven Nat. Laboratory 47-48, Dir. 48-61; Vice-Pres., Assoc. Univs. Inc. 51-60, Pres. 60-61; mem. U.S. Atomic Energy Comm. 61-63; Dir. Nat. Science Foundation 63-; Adviser, President's Science Advisory Cttee.; Pres. American Nuclear Soc. 58-59; mem. Federal Council for Science and Technology, Nat. Acad. of

Sciences, American Inst. of Physics, etc.; Fellow, American Acad. of Arts and Sciences, American Nuclear Soc., American Physical Soc., New York Acad. of Sciences; numerous hon. degrees.

Publs. Papers in fields of surface structure of metals, secondary electron emission, low temperature research, nuclear physics, high energy physics, especially very high energy accelerators, electronics.

2000 South Eads Street, Arlington, Va. 22202, U.S.A. Telephone: 521-4684.

Hawthorne, William Rede, C.B.E., M.A., SC.D., F.R.S., M.INST.MECH.E., F.R.Ae.S.; British professor of applied thermodynamics; b. 22 May 1913; ed. Westminster School, London, Trinity Coll., Cambridge, and Mass. Inst. of Technology, U.S.A.

Development Engineer, Babcock & Wilcox Ltd. 37-39; Scientific Officer, Royal Aircraft Establishment 40-44; British Air Comm., Washington, D.C. 44; Deputy Dir. of Engine Research, Ministry of Supply (U.K.) 45; Assoc. Prof. of Mechanical Engineering, Mass. Inst. of Technology (M.I.T.) 46; George Westinghouse Prof. of Mechanical Engineering, M.I.T. 48-51; Prof. of Applied Thermodynamics, Univ. of Cambridge 51-; Master of Churchill Coll., Cambridge 68-; Hunsaker Prof. of Aeronautical Engineering, M.I.T. 55-56; Visiting Inst. Prof., M.I.T. 62-63; Foreign Assoc. U.S. Nat. Acad. of Sciences; Medal of Freedom (U.S.A.) 47.

Middlefield, Huntingdon Road, Cambridge, England; and Tideacres, Cedar Street, Duxbury, Mass., U.S.A. Telephone (England): Cambridge 76234.

Hawtrey, Sir Ralph George, C.B., D.SC., F.B.A.; British economist; b. 1879; ed. Eton and Trinity Coll., Cambridge.

Member Staff Admiralty 03-04, Treasury 04-45; Lecturer Vice-Pres. Royal Statistical Society 29-31 and 35-37; Pres. Royal Economic Society 46-48; Price Prof. of Int. Economics Royal Inst. of Int. Affairs 47-52; Hon. Fellow Trinity Coll. Cambridge 59.

Publs. *Currency and Credit* 19, *The Economic Problem* 26, *The Art of Central Banking* 32, *Capital and Employment* 37, *A Century of Bank Rate* 38, *Economic Destiny* 44, *Economic Rebirth* 46, *Bretton Woods, for Better or Worse* 46, *Western European Union* 49, *The Balance of Payments* 50, *Towards the Rescue of Sterling* 54, *Cross Purposes in Wage Policy* 55, *The Pound at Home and Abroad* 61, *Incomes and Money* 67.

29 Argyll Road, London, W.8, England. Telephone: 01-937-3805.

Haxel, Otto Philipp Leonhard, D.RER.NAT.; German physicist; b. 2 April 1909; ed. Tübingen, Munich and Berlin Univs.

Lecturer, Berlin Technical High School 37-45, Max Planck Physics Inst., Göttingen 45-50; Dir. Second Physical Inst., Heidelberg Univ. 50-; mem. German Atomic Comm., Scientific and Technical Cttee. European Atomic Energy Comm., Heidelberger Akad. der Wissenschaften.

Philosophenweg 12, 69 Heidelberg 1, German Federal Republic.

Telephone: Heidelberg 43787.

Hay, Alexandre, L. en D.; Swiss banker; b. 29 Oct. 1919; ed. Univ. of Geneva.

Federal Political Dept. (Financial Affairs), Berne 45-48; Swiss Legation, Paris 48-53; Head of Div., Swiss Nat. Bank, Zürich 53-55; Dir. and Asst. to Head of Second Dept., Swiss Nat. Bank, Berne 55-66, Head of Second Dept. and Vice-Pres. Gen. Management 66-; mem. Cttee. on European Monetary Agreement 50-62; Pres. 62-67.

Office: Swiss National Bank, Bundesplatz 1, Berne; Home: Mayweg 7, Berne, Switzerland. Telephone: 61-42-45 (Office); 45-72-79 (Home).

Hay, David Osborne, C.B.E., D.S.O., B.A.; Australian diplomatist; b. 16; ed. Geelong Grammar School, Brasenose Coll. Oxford and Melbourne Univ.

Joined Australian Dept. of External Affairs 39 and rejoined 46, after army service 39-45; Del. to UN 49 and 50; served Ottawa 50-52; attended Imperial Defence Coll. London 54 Minister to Thailand 55-56, Ambassador 56-57, concurrently Rep. to SEATO; Asst. Sec. Department of External Affairs 57-61; High Commr. to Canada 61-64; Ambassador and Perm. Rep. of Australia to the UN 63-65; Ministry of External Affairs 65-66; Administrator, Territory of Papua and New Guinea 67-.

Government House, Port Moresby, T.P.N.G. Telephone: Port Moresby 4321.

Haya de la Torre, Victor Raúl; Peruvian politician; b. 95; ed. Univs. of Oxford and San Marcos, Lima. Exiled to Mexico 23-30; Founder and Leader Alianza Popular Revolucionaria Americana (A.P.R.A.) 30-; candidate for President 31; imprisoned 32-33; Political Refugee, Colombian Embassy, Lima 48-53; exile in Panama, Mexico, Belgium 54-56; Candidate for President 62, 63.

c/o Alianza Popular Revolucionaria Americana, Lima, Peru.

Hayakawa, Takashi; Japanese politician; b. 16; ed. Tokyo Univ.

Entered Ministry of Warfare, later moved to Home Ministry; founder and Pres. *Kishu Mimpo* (newspaper), Vice-Pres. *Yukan Miyabo* (newspaper); mem. House of Reps.; Minister of Autonomy and Public Safety July 63-64; Liberal Democratic Party.

c/o Ministry of Autonomy and Public Safety, Tokyo, Japan.

Haycraft, Howard; American publisher and author; b. 24 July 1905; ed. Univ. of Minnesota.

University of Minnesota Press 28; H. W. Wilson Co., New York City 29-, Vice-Pres. 40-52, Pres. 53-67, Chair. Board of Dirs. 67-; mem. Pres. Cttee. Employment of Handicapped 63-; mem. Mystery Writers of America Club, Pres. 63.

Publs. as Author, Editor or Joint Editor: *Authors Today and Yesterday* 33, *Junior Book of Authors* 34, *Boys' Sherlock Holmes* 36, *Boys' Book of Great Detective Stories* 38, *American Authors 1600-1900* 38, *Boys' Second Book of Great Detective Stories* 40, *Murder for Pleasure: The Life and Times of the Detective Story* 41, *Crime Club Encore* 42, *Twentieth Century Authors* 42, *Art of the Mystery Story* 46, *Fourteen Great Detective Stories* 49, *British Authors before 1800* 52, *Treasury of Great Mysteries* 57, *Ten Great Mysteries* 59, *Five Spy Novels* 62, *Books for the Blind: A Postscript and an Appreciation* 65.

950 University Avenue, New York 52, N.Y., U.S.A.

Hayden, Carl; American politician; b. 2 Oct. 1877; ed. Leland Stanford Univ.

Treasurer Maricopa County 05-06 and Sheriff 07-11; mem. U.S. Congress 12-27; U.S. Senator from Arizona 27-; Chair. Rules and Admin. Cttee. 49-53; Chair. Cttee. on Appropriations; Democrat.

49 N. Country Club Drive, Phoenix, Ariz., U.S.A.

Hayek, His Beatitude Denys Antoine; Syrian ecclesiastic; b. 14 Sept. 1910; ed. Séminaire Patriarcal, Charfé, Lebanon, Pontifical Coll., Rome, and Oriental Pontifical Inst., Rome.

Ordained priest 33; successively or concurrently Dir. of School, Curate and Vicar-Gen., Aleppo; Archbishop of Aleppo 59-68; Syrian Patriarch March 68-.

Patriarcat Syrien Catholique d'Antioche, Beirut, Lebanon.

Hayek, Friedrich August von, DR.JUR., DR.RER. POL. (Vienna), D.SC. (Econ.) (London), F.B.A.; British (b. Austrian) economist; b. Vienna 8 May 1899; ed. Vienna Univ.

Austrian Civil Service 21-26; Dir. Austrian Inst. for Economic Research 27-31; Lecturer in Economics

Vienna Univ. 29-31; Prof. of Economic Science and Statistics London Univ. 31-50; Prof. of Social and Moral Science, Univ. of Chicago 50-62; Prof. of Economics, Univ. of Freiburg 62-; naturalised British 38.
Publs. *Prices and Production* 31, *Monetary Theory and the Trade Cycle* 33, *Collectivist Economic Planning* 35, *Monetary Nationalism and International Stability* 37, *Profits, Interest and Investment* 39, *The Pure Theory of Capital* 41, *The Road to Serfdom* 44, *Individualism and Economic Order* 48, *J. S. Mill and Harriet Taylor* 50, *The Counter-Revolution of Science* 52, *The Sensory Order* 52, *Capitalism and the Historians* 54, *The Political Ideal of the Rule of Law* 55, *The Constitution of Liberty* 60, *Studies in Philosophy, Politics and Economics* 67.
Rechts- und Staatswissenschaftliche Fakultät der Universität, Werthmannplatz 1, Freiburg-i-B.; Home: Urachstrasse 27, 78 Freiburg-i-B., German Federal Republic.
Telephone: 23851.

Hayek, Heinrich, DR. MED., DR. PHIL.; Austrian anatomist; b. 1900; ed. Univ. of Vienna.
Asst. in Anatomy, Vienna Univ. 23-29, Rostock Univ. 29; Extra. Prof. Univ. of Rostock 36; Prof. of Anatomy, Tung-Chi Univ., Shanghai 35-38; Extra. Prof. Univ. of Würzburg 38-52; Prof. of Anatomy Univ. of Vienna and Dir. Anatomical Inst. 52-; mem. Acad. of Sciences, Vienna, Acad. Leopoldina, Halle, Int. Institute of Embryology; affiliated mem. Royal Soc. of Medicine; Hon. mem. Austrian Tuberculosis Soc.
Publs. *Die menschliche Lunge* 53 (U.S. trans. 60), *Normale Anatomie der Brustorgane* (in *Handbuch der Thoraxchirurgie*) 57; *Anatomischer Atlas* (Toldt-Hochstetter, revision of vols. I-III) 57-61.
Währingerstrasse 13, Vienna IX, Austria.
Telephone: Vienna 431526.

Hayes, Albert John; American machinist and trade unionist; b. 14 Feb. 1900; ed. elementary and High School, Milwaukee, and Univ. of Milwaukee Extension Dept.
International Asscn. of Machinists 19-, Vice-Pres. 44-49, Int. Pres. 49-; Vice-Pres. American Fed. of Labor 53-55; mem. AFL-CIO 55-; official of numerous labour and civic orgs.
International Association of Machinists, Machinists Building, 1300 Connecticut Avenue, N.W., Washington 6, D.C., U.S.A.

Hayes, Alfred, B.A., B.LITT.; American banker; b. 4 July 1910; ed. Harvard and Yale Univs. and New Coll., Oxford.
Investment Analyst, City Bank Farmers Trust Co., New York 33-40; with Bond Dept. Nat. City Bank of New York 40-42; Asst. Sec. Investment Div., New York Trust Co. 42-47, Asst. Vice-Pres. Foreign Div. 47-49, Vice-Pres. (in charge of the Foreign Div.) 49-56; Pres. Fed. Reserve Bank of New York 56-, Vice-Chair. Fed. Open Market Cttee. 56-; mem. Foreign Exchange Cttee. of N.Y. Money Market 53-56; Dir. Bankers' Asscn. for Foreign Trade 53-56; Dir. Netherlands Chamber of Commerce in the U.S. 54-56; Pres. Trustees of Lingnan Univ., China 47-54; mem. Council on Foreign Relations, N.Y., Yale Univ. Council.
Home: Brushy Ridge Road, New Canaan, Conn.; Office: Federal Reserve Bank of New York, 33 Liberty Street, New York, N.Y., U.S.A.

Hayes, John S., B.A.; American communications exec. and diplomatist; b. 21 Aug. 1910; ed. Univ. of Pennsylvania.
Commanding Officer, American Forces Network, U.S. Army 42-45; Exec. Vice-Pres. The Washington Post Co. 47-66; Amb. to Switzerland 66-; Pres. United Community Funds and Councils of America 62-64; Chair. on Int. Broadcasting, Nat. Asscn. of Broadcasters 64; mem. Carnegie Comm. on Educational Television 66; mem. Board of Trustees Springfield

Coll.; Trustee, Fed. City Council of Washington, D.C.; mem. Board of Dirs. Nat. Symphony Orchestra Asscn.; Hon. O.B.E.; Croix de Guerre, U.S. Bronze Star.
Publ. *Both Sides of the Microphone* 38.
United States Embassy, Berne, Switzerland; Homes: 4625 Garfield Street, N.W., Washington, D.C.; 701 Ponte Vedra Boulevard, Ponte Vedre, Florida, U.S.A.

Hayes, Richard James, B.A., LL.D.; Irish librarian; b. 26 June 1902; ed. Clongowes Wood Coll., Kildare, and Trinity Coll., Dublin.
Asst. Librarian Nat. Library of Ireland 24, Senior Asst. Librarian 29, Dir. 40-; mem. Irish Manuscript Comm., Royal Irish Acad., Arts Council; Hon. Librarian, Chester Beatty Library; Hon. D.Litt., Hon. Litt.D.
Publs. *Comparative Idiom* 27, *Clár Litridheacht na Nua-Ghaedhilge* I-III 38-40, *Foclóir Gaedhilge agus Frainncise* 54, *Manuscript Sources for the History of Irish Civilisation* I-XI 66.
20 Shrewsbury Road, Dublin, Ireland.

Haymerle, Heinrich; Austrian diplomatist; b. 10; ed. Univ. of Vienna.
Diplomatic Service, OEEC, Paris 48-51; Chief of Protocol, Dept. of Foreign Affairs 51-53; Austrian Observer at UN 53-55; Austrian Rep. in Madrid 55-56; Head, Political Div., Dept. of Foreign Affairs 56-60; Ambassador to U.S.S.R. 60-64; Head, Political Div., Ministry for Foreign Affairs 64-, Deputy Sec.-Gen. 67-; Gov. of Austria to the IAEA 65-67; Vice-Chair. Board of Govs. of IAEA 66-67.
Ministry for Foreign Affairs, Ballhausplatz 2, Vienna 1, Austria.

Haynes, Sir George Ernest, Kt., C.B.E., B.SC.; British administrator; b. 24 Jan. 1902; ed. Sandbach School and Liverpool Univ.
Warden. Univ. Settlement, Liverpool 28-33; Chief Advisory Officer Nat. Council of Social Service 33-37, Dir. 40-67; Chair. Temporary Int. Council of Educational Reconstruction of UNESCO 47-50, Social Services Cttee. of National Asscn. for Mental Health 55-58, Standing Conf. on British Orgs. for aid to Refugees 53-60, Rural Industries Loan Fund Ltd., Advisory Council of Rural Industries Bureau; Pres. Int. Conf. of Social Work 48-56, Hon. Pres. 56-; Pres. Nat. Birthday Trust; Chair. Invalid Children's Aid Asscn., Nat. Bureau for Co-operation in Child Care, Exec. Cttee. British Conf. on Social Welfare, British Standing Conf. on Econ. and Social Activities of UN; Exec. Cttee. King George VI Foundation; U.K. Del. to Social Comm. of UN 62-67; Réne Sand Award 58.
12 Celia Court, Holmesdale Road, Kew, Surrey.

Haynie, Roscoe George; American business executive; b. 17 April 1910; ed. Cotner Coll., Lincoln, Creighton Univ.
Labourer, Dold Packing Co., Omaha 32-33, Foreman 33-38; Asst. Manager, Beef Division, Wilson & Co. Inc., Omaha 38-39, Manager, Grading Div., Chicago 39-43, Manager, Beef Div. 43-46, Vice-Pres. in charge of Beef Operations 46-55, Vice-Pres. in charge of Meat Operations 55-60, Pres. 60-67, Chief Exec. Officer 63-, Chair. 67-; Chair. Beef Industry Advisory Cttee., Office of Price Admin. 46-47; Chair. Board of Dirs. Wilson Sporting Goods Co. 63-, American Meat Inst. 64-.
Home: 10416 S. Bell Avenue, Chicago 60643; Office: Prudential Plaza, Chicago, Illinois, U.S.A.
Telephone: 312-BE 8-7045.

Hays, Brooks, A.B., LL.B.; American lawyer and government official; b. 9 Aug. 1898; ed. Univ. of Arkansas and George Washington Univ.
Admitted Arkansas Bar 22; held various admin. posts, Arkansas 25-35; served Farm Security Admin.; mem. 78th-85th Congress; Board of Dirs. Tennessee Valley Authority 59-61; Asst. Sec. for Congressional Relations, Dept. of State 61; Special Assistant to Pres. Kennedy

61-63; Assoc. Dir. Community Relations Service 65;
A. T. Vanderbilt Prof. of Public Affairs, Rutgers Univ.
63-65; Visiting Prof. of Public Affairs, Univ. of Mass.
66-.
Little Rock, Arkansas, U.S.A.

Hays, Harry; Canadian politician; b. 1909.
Former livestock breeder; Mayor of Calgary 59-63;
Mem. of Parl. 63-66, of Senate 66-, Minister of Agri-
culture 63-66; Liberal.
The Senate, Ottawa, Ontario; Home: 8944 Elbow Drive,
Calgary, Alberta, Canada.

Hayter, Stanley William, C.B.E., B.SC.; British
painter, engraver and writer; b. 27 Dec. 1901; ed.
Whitgift Middle School and King's Coll., London.
Chemist, Anglo-Iranian Oil Co., Iran 22-25; founded
Atelier 17, Paris 27; paintings and engravings exhibited
France, England, U.S.A., Belgium, Switzerland, S.
America, Japan; paintings in Tate Gallery, London,
Whitney Gallery, N.Y., Musée d'Art Moderne, Paris,
Nat. Gallery of Canada, Montreal, St. Louis City
Museum, and Museum of Modern Art, Santiago, Chile;
Int. First Prize, Tokyo 60; Légion d'Honneur.
Publs. *New Ways of Gravure* 49, *About Prints* 62,
Nature and Art of Motion 64.
36 rue Boissonade, Paris 14e, France.
Telephone: DAN 26-60.

Hayter, Sir William Goodenough, K.C.M.G.; British
diplomatist and college principal; b. 1 Aug. 1906; ed.
Winchester and New Coll., Oxford.
Entered Diplomatic Service 30; served in Foreign Office
30-31, Vienna 31, Moscow 34, Foreign Office 37, China
38, Washington 41, Foreign Office 44; Asst. Under-Sec.
of State 48; Minister in Paris 49-53; Ambassador to
U.S.S.R. May 53-57; Deputy Under-Sec. of State 57-
58; Warden of New Coll. Oxford 58-; Pres. Anglo-
Austrian Soc.; mem. Council G.B.-U.S.S.R. Asscn.
59-; Trustee British Museum 60; Gold Medal for
Services to Austria 67.
Publs. *The Diplomacy of the Great Powers* 60, *The
Kremlin and the Embassy* 66.
New College, Oxford, England.
Telephone: Oxford 48451.

Hayward, Sir Isaac James, Kt., J.P.; British industrial
negotiator and politician; b. 17 Nov. 1884; ed. elementary school.
Trade Union official 18-46; Gen. Sec. Nat. Union of
Enginemen, Firemen, Mechanics and Electrical Workers 38-46; mem. London & Home Counties Joint Electricity Authority 25-49; Dir. British European Airways 46-49; mem. London Electricity Board and Chair.
London Electricity Consultative Council 48-60; fmr.
mem. Ministry of Supply Machine Tool Advisory
Council; Nat. Advisory Council on Employment of
Disabled; mem. State Management Districts Council;
mem. Court, Univ. of London; mem. London County
Council 28-65, Chief Whip, Chair. of various cttees.
32-47, Leader 47-65; Hon. LL.D. (London Univ.) 52;
mem. South Bank Theatre and Opera House Board
62-; Labour.
140 Chudleigh Road, Brockley, London, S.E.4, England.

Hazard, Ellison L.; American business executive; b.
6 Aug. 1911; ed. Univ. of California and Harvard Univ.
Business School.
Continental Can Co. 34-, in charge of aircraft and bomb
parts production during Second World War, later
Plant Man. and Div. Man. of Manufacturing; Vice-
Pres. Central Metal Div., Continental Can Co. 58-62,
Vice-Pres. (Plastics and Closures Operations Group)
62-63, Dir. 62-, Senior Exec. Vice-Pres. 63, Pres. 63-;
Trustee, Cttee. for Econ. Devt.
Continental Can Co. Inc., 633 Third Avenue, New York,
N.Y. 10017; Home: 31 Old Farm Road, Darien, Conn.,
U.S.A.

Hazlett, James Luke; New Zealand sheep farmer and
diplomatist; b. 12; ed. Waitaki Boys' High School.
Sheep farmer, Southland; New Zealand Army, Second
World War; New Zealand High Commr. in Australia 64-.
New Zealand High Commission, Canberra, A.C.T.,
Australia.

Hazlitt, Henry; American journalist; b. 28 Nov. 1894;
ed. Coll. of City of New York.
Mem. staff *Wall Street Journal* 13-16 and New York
Evening Post 16-18; Financial Editor New York
Evening Mail 21-23; editorial writer New York *Herald*
23-24; Literary Editor *The Sun* 25-29; Literary Editor
The Nation 30-33; Editor *American Mercury* 34;
editorial writer *New York Times* 34-46; business
columnist *Newsweek* 46-66; nationally syndicated
newspaper columnist Oct. 66-; Editor *The Freeman*
50-53; Hon. Litt.D. (Grove City Coll.) 58, Hon. LL.D.
(Bethany Coll.) 61.
Publs. *Thinking as a Science* 16, *The Anatomy of Criti-
cism* 33, *A New Constitution Now* 42, *Economics in One
Lesson* 46, *Will Dollars Save the World?* 47, *The Great
Idea* 51 (British title: *Time Will Run Back* 52), *The
Free Man's Library* 56, *The Failure of the "New Economics": An Analysis of the Keynesian Fallacies* 59,
What You Should Know about Inflation 60, *The Founda-
tions of Morality* 64; ed. *A Practical Program for
America* 32, *The Critics of Keynesian Economics* 60.
65 Drum Hill Road, Wilton, Conn. 06897, U.S.A.

Head, 1st Viscount, cr. 60, of Throope in the County
of Wiltshire; **Antony Henry Head,** P.C., G.C.M.G., C.B.E.,
M.C.; British politician; b. 06; ed. Eton and Royal Mil.
Coll., Sandhurst.
Adjutant, Life Guards 34-37; Staff Coll. 39; Brigade
Major 20th Guards' Brigade 40; Asst.-Sec. Cttee.
Imperial Defence 40-41; Guards Armoured Div. 41-42
(G.S.O.2); Army Rep. with Dir. of Plans for Amphibious
Operations 43-45; Conservative M.P. for Carshalton
Div. Surrey 45-60; Sec. of State for War 51-56; Minister
of Defence 56-57; High Commr. in Fed. of Nigeria
October 60-63; High Commr. in Malaysia 63-66.
Throope Manor, Bishopstone, nr. Salisbury, Wilts.,
England.

Heald, Henry Townley, M.S., D.ENG., LL.D., L.H.D.;
American consultant and civil engineer; b. 8 Nov. 1904;
ed. Washington State Coll. and Univ. of Illinois.
Asst. Engineer U.S. Bureau of Reclamation on
construction of McKay Dam 23-24; Designer Bridge
Dept. Illinois Central Railroad 25-26; Structural
Engineer City of Chicago 26-27; Asst. Prof. of Civil
Engineering, Armour Inst. of Technology 27-31; Assoc.
Prof. of Civil Engineering and Asst. to the Dean 31-33,
Dean of Freshmen 33-34; Prof. of Civil Engineering and
Dean of the Inst. 34-38, Acting Pres. 37-38, Pres. 38-40;
Pres. Illinois Inst. of Technology 40-52; Pres. Inst. of
Gas Technology 41-52, Armour Research Foundation
of Ill. Inst. of Technology 36-52; Chancellor New
York Univ. 52-56; Pres. The Ford Foundation 56-65;
Chair. of Heald, Hobson & Assocs. 66-; Special
Adviser Bureau of Naval Personnel U.S. Navy
42-49; Pres. American Society for Engineering Educa-
tion 42-43; mem. Cttee. on Engineering Schools,
Engineers' Council for Professional Development 44-49,
Chair. 47-49; Special Adviser to U.S. Office of Educa-
tion 42-45; Dir. and Vice-Pres. Nat. Safety Council
43-49; Vice-Pres. and Chair. American Asscn. for the
Advancement of Science, Section on Engineering 46-47;
Deputy Chair. Cttee. on Equipment and Materials
of Research and development Board 49-53; mem.
Building Research and Advisory Board of Nat. Re-
search Council 50-53; Chair. American Council on
Education 53-54; Chair. N.Y.S. Comm. on Educational
Finances 54-55, N.Y.S. Comm. on Higher Education
60; mem. Advisory Cttee. on Private Enterprise in

Foreign Aid, A.I.D. Dept. of State 64-65; mem. Hudson River Valley Comm. 65-66; Chair. Case Western Reserve Study Comm. 66-67; Dir. American Telephone and Telegraph Co. 58-, Equitable Life Assurance Soc. of U.S. 53-, United States Steel Corpn. 61-, Lever Brothers Co. 62-; Consultant Agency for Int. Devt. 66-.
Office: 230 Park Avenue, New York, N.Y. 10017; Home: 1 Mitchell Place, New York, N.Y. 10017; and Tuxedo Park, N.Y. 10987, U.S.A.
Telephone: 212-421-6746.

Healey, Rt. Hon. Denis Winston, P.C., M.B.E., M.P.; British politician; b. 30 Aug. 1917; ed. Bradford Grammar School and Balliol Coll., Oxford.
Major, Royal Engineers 45; Sec. Labour Party Int. Dept. 46-51; M.P. 52-; Sec. for Defence 64-.
Publs. *The Curtain Falls* 51, *New Fabian Essays* 52, *Neutralism* 55, *Fabian International Essays* 56, *A Neutral Belt in Europe* 58, *NATO and American Security* 59, *The Race Against the H Bomb* 60, *A Labour Britain and the World* 63.
House of Commons, London, S.W.1, England.

Healy, Robert Edward, B.S., D.C.S.; American advertising executive; b. 15 Aug. 1904; ed. Dwight Preparatory School and Pace Coll.
Salesman, T. J. Adikes 26, Hoover Co. 27-28; Asst. to Vice-Pres. (Sales Promotion), Johns-Manville Co. 29-33; Man. Production Section of Advertising Dept., Colgate-Palmolive Co. 34-36, Asst. Advertising Man. 36-39, Brand Advertising Man. 39-42, Gen. Advertising Man. 42-46, Vice-Pres. (Advertising) 46-52; Vice-Pres., Treas., Dir. McCann-Erickson Inc. 52-53, Vice-Pres., Gen. Man. 53-54, Gen. Man. New York Office 54, Exec. Vice-Pres. 55-58, Vice-Chair. Board of Dirs. 58-61, Chair. Board 60-62, mem. Finance Cttee. 57-61, Chair. Board McCann-Erickson Corpn. (Int.) 56-58; Pres. Interpublic S.A., Geneva, Switzerland 62-65; Exec. Vice-Pres. Interpublic Group of Companies Inc. 65-67, Pres. and Chief Exec. Officer 67-, Chair. of Board 68-; mem. Board of Dirs. Better Business Bureau, Nat. Outdoor Advertising Bureau; Public Inf. Chair., United Negro Coll. Fund; Advertising Industry Chair., N.Y. States Citizens Comm. for Public Schools.
Interpublic Group of Companies Inc., 1271 Avenue of the Americas, New York, N.Y. 10020, U.S.A.
Telephone: TN7-1122.

Heard, Henry Fitz Gerald; British writer; b. 6 Oct. 1889; ed. Sherborne and Gonville and Caius Coll., Cambridge.
Publs. *Narcissus, The Ascent of Humanity, The Social Substance of Religion, The Emergence of Man, This Surprising World, These Hurrying Years, Science in the Making, The Source of Civilisation, Exploring the Stratosphere, The Third Morality, Pain, Sex and Time, The Creed of Christ, The Code of Christ, Man the Master, Preface to Prayer, Taste for Honey, Reply Paid, Desert Dialogue, Gospel According to Gamaliel, The Great Fog, The Eternal Gospel, Doppelgangers, The Thaw Plan, Is God Evident?, The Great Fog and Other Weird Tales, The Lost Cavern, Morals 1900-1950, Is God in History?, The Black Fox, The Book of Wishes, The Human Venture, The Perennial Praxis, Training for a Life of Growth, The Five Ages of Man.*
322 East Rustic Road, Santa Monica, California 90402, U.S.A.

Heard, H.E. Cardinal William Theodore, B.A., PH.D., D.D., D.C.L.; British ecclesiastic; b. 24 Feb. 1884; ed. Fettes Coll. (Edinburgh), Balliol Coll., Oxford and English Coll., Rome.
Fmr. solicitor; ordained priest 18, service at Dockhead, Bermondsey 21-27; Auditor Sacred Roman Rota 27-58; Dean 58-59; Prelate Sacred Congregation of Rites 44; mem. Pontifical Comm. for Interpretation of the Codex 59; created Cardinal by Pope John XXIII 59.
Via Monserrato 45, Rome, Italy.

Hearnes, Warren Eastman, B.A., A.B., LL.B.; American lawyer and politician; b. 23; ed. U.S. Mil. Acad., West Point, and Univ. of Missouri.
U.S. Army until 49; mem. Missouri House of Representatives 58-61, Majority Floor Leader 57-61; Missouri Sec. of State 61-64; Gov. of Missouri 64-; Democrat.
Office: Executive Office, Capitol Building, Jefferson City, Missouri; Home: Executive Mansion, Jefferson City, Missouri, U.S.A.

Hearst, David Whitmire; American newspaper executive; b. 2 Dec. 1915; ed. Princeton Univ.
Classified and Display Advt. Dept. *Los Angeles Evening Herald-Express* 38-44, Business Manager 44-45, Gen.-Man. 45-47, Exec. Publisher 47-50, Publisher 50-60; Vice-Pres. and Dir. Hearst Corpn. 60-.
Office: Hearst Corporation, 270 N. Canon Drive, Beverly Hills, Calif.; Home: 710 N. Beverly Drive, Beverly Hills, Calif., U.S.A.

Hearst, George, Sr.; American newspaper executive; b. 23 April 1904; ed. Univ. of Calif.
Publisher *San Francisco Examiner* 24-27; Vice-Pres. *Los Angeles Examiner* 29-53, now Publisher; Vice-Pres. Dir. of Trustees Board, Hearst Corpn., San Francisco; Pres. and Dir. The Hearst Foundation Inc.; Vice-Pres. and Trustee William Randolph Hearst Foundation; Dir. Hearst Consolidated Publications, Inc. and Hearst Publishing Co., Inc.
Office: Hearst Building, 3rd and Market Streets, San Francisco, also 270 N. Canon Drive, Beverly Hills, Calif., U.S.A.

Hearst, Randolph (Apperson); American newspaper executive; b. 2 Dec. 1915; ed. Harvard Univ.
Assistant to Editor *Atlanta Georgian* 34-38; Asst. to Publisher, San Francisco *Call-Bulletin* 38-41, Exec. Editor 46-50, Publisher 50-53; Pres. and Dir. Hearst Consolidated Publications Inc., and Hearst Publishing Co. Inc. 53-64; Chair. Exec. Cttee. and Dir. The Hearst Corpn. 65-; Trustee, William Randolph Hearst Foundation and The Hearst Foundation.
1018 Hearst Building, San Francisco, Calif. 94103, U.S.A.

Hearst, William Randolph, Jr.; American newspaper executive; b. 27 Jan. 1908; ed. Univ. of California.
Reporter, New York 28; Publisher, *New York Journal American* 37-56, *American Weekly* 45-56; War Corresp. 43-45; Editor-in-Chief, Hearst Newspapers; Vice-Pres. and Dir. The Hearst Foundation, Inc.; Chair. and Dir. The Hearst Corpn.; Vice-Pres. and Trustee William Randolph Hearst Foundation; Vice-Pres. and Dir. Androscoggin Water Power Co., Halifax Power and Pulp Co. Ltd.; Dir. Twentieth Century-Fox Film Corpn.; Pulitzer Prize 56, Overseas Press Club Award 58.
959 8th Avenue, New York City 19, N.Y., U.S.A.

Heath, Rt. Hon. Edward Richard George, P.C., M.B.E., M.P.; British politician; b. 9 July 1916; ed. Chatham House School, Ramsgate, and Balliol Coll., Oxford.
Served in Royal Artillery in Second World War, rising to rank of Lieut.-Col.; Civil Service 46-47; M.P. for Bexley 50-; Asst. Conservative Whip, Lord Commr. of the Treasury 51, Joint Deputy Govt. Chief Whip 52, Deputy Govt. Chief Whip 53-55, Parl. Sec. to the Treasury and Govt. Chief Whip 55-59; Minister of Labour 59-60; Lord Privy Seal with Foreign Office Responsibilities 60-63; Sec. of State for Industry, Trade and Regional Development, Pres. Board of Trade 63-64; Leader, British delegation, Brussels Conf. for Countries seeking entry to the Common Market Oct. 61-63; elected Leader of Conservative Party and of Her Majesty's Opposition 65; Charlemagne Prize 63; Conservative.
Publ. *One Nation: a Tory approach to social problems* (co-author) 50.
House of Commons, London, S.W.1, England.

Heath, Howard Davis; American insurance executive; b. 29 March 1904; ed. Univ. of Washington.
Northwestern Mutual Insurance Co. 23-, Asst. Sec. 38, Asst. Vice-Pres. 44, Man. Eastern Claim Div. (Chicago) 45, Manager Midwestern Dept. 51, Eastern-Southern Div. 59, Vice-Pres. and Dir. 60, Pres. 61-; Dir. Northwestern Security Insurance Co., Seattle, Washington 60-, Pres. 61-; Cream City Mutual Insurance Co., Milwaukee, Wisconsin 60-65, Pres. 61-65; Dir., mem. of Exec. Cttee., Olympic Nat. Life Insurance Co., Seattle 66; Board of Dirs. American Mutual Insurance Alliance, Chicago; mem. Governing Board Improved Risk Mutuals, New York; Trustee and Past Pres. Industrial Conf. Board (Wash. State); Gov. Board and Vice-Pres. Mutual Loss Research Bureau, Chicago 63-66.
Northwestern Mutual Insurance Co., 217 Pine Street, Seattle, Washington 98101, U.S.A.
Telephone: 206-MU2-7200.

Hebb, Donald Olding, F.R.S., M.A., PH.D., D.SC., D.H.L.; Canadian psychologist; b. 22 July 1904; ed. Dalhousie, McGill and Harvard Univs.
Teacher 25-34; Research, Montreal Neurological Inst. 37-39; Lecturer, Queens Univ. 39-42; Research, Yerkes Laboratories of Primate Psychology 42-47; Prof. Psychology, McGill Univ. 47-, Chair. Dept. 48-58; Hon. LL.D. (Dalhousie Univ.) 65, Hon. LL.D. (Queen's Univ.) 67.
Publs. *Organisation of Behaviour* 49, *Textbook of Psychology* 58, revised edn. 66.
Department of Psychology, McGill University, Montreal 2, Canada.
Telephone: 844-6311-1279.

Heber Usher, Albert; Uruguayan business executive and politician; b. 1918.
President of Governing Council of Uruguay 66-67; mem. Blanco Party.
Governing Council, Montevideo, Uruguay.

Hebert, Paul Macarius, A.B., LL.B., J.S.D.; American university professor and lawyer; b. 1 Nov. 1907; ed. Louisiana State Univ., Yale Univ. School of Law.
Admitted to the Bar Louisiana 29; admitted to the Bar U.S. Supreme Court 42; Sterling Fellow Yale Law School 29-30; Prof. of Law Loyola Univ., New Orleans 30-31; Dean 32-36; Asst. Prof. of Law Louisiana State Univ. 31-32; Prof. and Dean of Admin. 36-37; Dean of Law School 37-39; Acting Pres. 39-41; again Dean Law Branch, Judge Advocate General's Office 43-45; Judge Military Tribunals, War Crimes Trials, Nuremberg, Germany 47-48; Dean of Univ. of Louisiana and Prof. of Law 49-51; mem. law firm of Sachse, Wilson and Hebert, Baton Rouge 51-52; Dean Law School and Prof. of Law, Louisiana State Univ. 52-; Sec. Louisiana State Law Inst.
2331 Kleinert Avenue, Baton Rouge, Louisiana, U.S.A.

Heck, Bruno, DR. PHIL.; German teacher and politician; b. 20 Jan. 1917; ed. Tübingen Univ.
Former teacher; Ministry of Education, Württemberg 50-52; Exec. Sec. Christian Democrat Party (C.D.U.) 52-62; mem. Bundestag 57-; Minister of Family and Youth Affairs 63-, also Sec.-Gen. of C.D.U. 67-.
Ministry of Family and Youth Affairs, 532 Bad Godesberg, Kennedy-allee 105-107, German Federal Republic.
Telephone: Bad Godesberg 7061.

Heckmann, Otto, DR. PHIL.; German astronomer; b. 23 June 1901; ed. Univ. of Bonn.
Asst. Bonn Univ. Observatory 25-27, Göttingen 27-35; Asst. Prof. Göttingen 35-39, Acting Dir. Göttingen Observatory 39-41; Dir. Hamburg Observatory 41-62; Dir. European Southern Observatory 62-; Prof. of Astronomy, Univ. of Hamburg 41-; Pres. German

Astronomical Society 52-57; Vice-Pres. Int. Astronomical Union 55-61.
Publ. *Theorien der Kosmologie* 42.
Von Auckeln-Strasse 12, 205 Hamburg-Bergedorf, German Federal Republic.

Heckscher, August; American journalist and author; b. 16 Sept. 1913; ed. St. Paul's School, Concord, Yale and Harvard Univs.
Instructor in Govt., Yale Univ. 39-41; Army service 41-45; Editor *Auburn* (New York) *Citizen-Adviser* 46-48; Chief Editorial Writer *New York Herald Tribune* 48-56; Spl. Consultant, Pres. of U.S.A. on the Arts 62-63; Parks Commr., New York 67-; Dir. Twentieth Century Fund; Gov. Yale Univ. Press; Fellow American Acad. of Arts and Sciences.
Publs. *These Are The Days* 36, *A Pattern of Politics* 47, *The Politics of Woodrow Wilson* 56, *Diversity of Worlds* (with Raymond Aron) 57, *The Public Happiness* 63.
830 Fifth Avenue, New York, N.Y., U.S.A.

Heckscher, Gunnar Edvard, D.PHIL.; Swedish professor and politician; b. 8 July 1909; ed. Uppsala Univ. and King's Coll., Cambridge.
Lecturer of Political Science, Uppsala Univ. 33-41, Stockholm Univ. 41-48, Prof. 48-; Dir. Stockholm School of Social Work and Local Admin. 41-54; Co-Dir. Inst. of Public Admin., Ankara 52-53; Dir. Swedish Inst. for Cultural Relations 54-57; Chair. Bd. of Psychological Defence 54-59; mem. of Riksdag (Lower House of Parl.) 57-65; Parl. Leader and Chair. Conservative Party 61-65; Ambassador to India 65-; mem. Consultative Assembly, Council of Europe 57-65; Chair. Econ. Cttee. 60-65.
Publs. *Démocratie Efficace* 57, *The Study of Comparative Government* 57, etc.
Swedish Embassy, Naya Marg, Chanakyapuri, New Delhi 21, India.

Heeley, Pierre; French engineer and businessman; b. 2 July 1898; ed. Lycée Janson-de-Sailly, Ecole Navale and Ecole Supérieure d'Electricité.
Joined Compagnie des Compteurs 26, fmr. Gen. Man., now Pres. Dir.-Gen.; Pres. and Gen. Man. Carbonisation, Entreprise et Céramique; Chevalier Légion d'Honneur, Croix de Guerre.
Compagnie des Compteurs, 3 rue Dosne, Paris 16e; and 48 avenue Georges-Mandel, Paris 16e, France.
Telephone: KLE 34-90.

Heenan, H.E. Cardinal John Carmel; British ecclesiastic; b. 26 Jan. 1905; ed. Ushaw and English Coll., Rome.
Ordained 30; parish priest in East London 31-47; Superior, Catholic Mission Society 47-51; Bishop of Leeds 51-57; Archbishop of Liverpool, Metropolitan of Northern Province 57-63; Archbishop of Westminster and Metropolitan of the Westminster Province 63-; created Cardinal 65.
Publs. *Priest and Penitent* 36, *Cardinal Hinsley* 45, *Letters from Rush Green* 48, *The People's Priest* 51, *Our Faith* 57, *My Lord and My God* 58, *Council and Clergy* 66.
Archbishop's House, Westminster, London, S.W.1, England.

Heeney, Arnold Danford Patrick, Q.C., M.A., B.C.L., LL.D., D.C.L.; Canadian public servant; b. 5 April 1902; ed. Univ. of Manitoba, St. John's Coll., Oxford, and McGill Univ.
Practising lawyer, Montreal 29-38; Lecturer, McGill Univ. 34-38; Principal Sec. to Prime Minister 38-40; and Sec. Cabinet War Cttee. 39-45; Clerk of Privy Council and Sec. to Cabinet 40-49; Under-Sec. of State for External Affairs 49-52; Ambassador and Permanent Rep. to N.A.T.O. and Rep. to O.E.E.C., Paris 52-53; Ambassador to U.S.A. 53-57, 59-62; Chair. Civil Service Comm. 57-59; Chair. Canadian Section U.S.–

Canada Int. Joint Comm. 62-, Canadian Section, Perm. Joint Board on Defence 67-; Hon. LL.D. (British Columbia, Manitoba, Franklin and Marshall, Michigan State, Rhode Island, Kenyon, McGill); Hon. D.C.L. St. John's Coll., Winnipeg.
International Joint Commission, Suite 850, 151 Slater Street, Ottawa 4; Home 428 Buena Vista Road, Ottawa 2, Canada.
Telephone: 99-2-2417 (Office); 745-5056 (Home).

Hees, Hon. George H.; Canadian politician; b. 17 June 1910; ed. Trinity Coll. School, Royal Mil. Coll., Univ. of Toronto and Cambridge Univ.
Served overseas as Brigade Major, 5th Infantry Brigade; Dir. Woodgreen Community Centre; mem. House of Commons 50-; Minister of Transport 57-60; Minister of Trade and Commerce 60-63; Pres. Montreal and Canadian Stock Exchanges 64-; Progressive Conservative.
484 Avenue Road, Apt. 604, Toronto, Ont., Canada.

Hegen, Josef; German diplomatist; b. 24 April 1907; elementary education.
Mem. Czechoslovak Communist Party 24; Sec. Czechoslovak Communist Youth League 29; joined resistance movement after invasion and occupation of Czechoslovakia; Mauthausen concentration camp; Head of People's Police, Sachsen-Anhalt 48; Chair. Magdeburg City Council 52; State Sec. Ministry of the Interior 53-57; Ambassador to Poland 57-61; Dep. Minister for Foreign Affairs 61; Ambassador to People's Republic of China 61-64; Deputy Foreign Minister 64-66, State Sec. and First Deputy Foreign Minister 66-.
Ministry of Foreign Affairs, Berlin, Germany.

Héger, Charles Emile Victor, D. en D.; Belgian lawyer and politician; b. 26 May 1902.
Mem. of House of Reps. 46-; Minister of Agriculture Aug. 50-54, 61-; mem. Christian Social Party.
155 rue de la Loi, Brussels; and Vedrin (Province de Namur), Belgium.

Hegland, David LeRoy, B.A.; American motor executive; b. 12 June 1919; ed. Whitman Coll., Walla Walla, Washington, U.S.A.
U.S. Navy (Air) 41-45; Man. Dir. Gen. Motors Int. A/S, Copenhagen, Denmark 56-58; Man. Dir. Gen. Motors South African Ltd., Port Elizabeth, S. Africa 58-61; Man. Dir. Gen. Motors-Holden's Pty. Ltd., Melbourne, Australia; Man. Dir. Vauxhall Motors Ltd., Luton, Beds., England Jan. 66-, also Chair. July 66-; mem. Econ. Devt. Cttee. for Motor Manufacturing Industry, etc.
Vauxhall Motors Ltd., Luton, Beds., England.

Heide-Jørgensen, Erling; Danish jurist; b. 18 Dec. 1910; ed. Københavns Universitet.
Civil Servant, Ministry of Justice 36-52, Chief of Section 50-52; Nat. Commr., Danish Police 52-; Del. Int. Criminal Police Org. 53-; mem. Exec. Cttee. 60-63; Pres. Danish Fire Protection Asscn. 59-.
5 Anker Heegaardsgade, 1588 Copenhagen V, Denmark.
Telephone: 01-141448.

Heidegger, Martin, PH.D.; German philosopher; b. 26 Sept. 1889.
Prof. of Philosophy Marburg Univ. 23-28; Prof. Freiburg i. Br. Univ. 28, Rector 33, Emeritus 51-.
Publs. *Die Kategorienlehre des Duns Scotus* 16, *Sein und Zeit* 27, *Vom Wesen des Grundes* 29, *Was ist Metaphysik?* 29, *Kant und das Problem der Metaphysik* 29, *Die Selbstbehauptung der deutschen Universität* 33, *Hölderlin und das Wesen der Dichtung* 36, 51, *Vom Wesen der Wahrheit* 43, *Brief über den Humanismus* 47, *Existence and Being* 49, *Holzwege* 50, *Einführung in die Metaphysik* 53, *Der Feldweg* 53, *Aus der Erfahrung des Denkens* 54, *Was heisst Denken?* 54, *Vorträge und Aufsätze* 54, *Was ist Philosophie?* 56, *Zur Seinsfrage* 56, *Der Satz vom Grund* 57, *J. P. Hebel* 57, *Identität und Differenz* 57, *Unterwegs zur Sprache* 59, *Nietzsche* 61, *Die Frage nach dem Ding* 62, *Kants These über das Sein* 63, *Die Technik und die Kehre* 63.
Rötebuckweg 47, Freiburg i. Br., German Federal Republic.

Heidelberger, Michael, B.S., A.M., PH.D.; American chemist; b. 29 April 1888; ed. Columbia Univ. and Federal Polytechnic Inst., Zürich.
Asst. in Chemistry Summer Sessions Columbia Univ. 09 and 11; Fellow, Asst., Assoc. and Assoc. Mem. of the Rockefeller Inst. for Medical Research 12-27; Chemist to Mount Sinai Hospital 27-28; and Presbyterian Hospital of N.Y. 28-56; Assoc. Prof. of Biological Chemistry, Columbia Univ. 29-45, Prof. of Biochemistry 45-48, Prof. of Immuno-Chemistry 48-56, Emeritus 56-; Visiting Prof. of Immuno-Chemistry, Rutgers Univ. 55-64; Chair. of the Research Council, Public Health Research Inst. of N.Y. City 51-56; Consultant to Sec. of War 42-46; mem. Nat. Acad. of Sciences; foreign mem. Royal Danish Acad. of Sciences 57-, Accademia Nazionale dei Lincei 63-; Adjunct Prof. of Pathology, N.Y. Univ. School of Medicine 64-; Hon. Dr. Univs. of Bordeaux 47, Paris 49, Uppsala 50, Strasbourg 52, Oslo 56, Marseille 59, Nancy 60, Rutgers 61, Ehrlich Silver Medal 33, Lasker Award 52, von Behring Prize 54, Louis Pasteur Gold Medal (Swedish Med. Soc.) 60, T. Duckett Jones Memorial Award 64; Officier Légion d'Honneur 66, Officier, Ordre de Léopold II 53.
Publs. *Advanced Laboratory Manual of Organic Chemistry* 23, *Lectures in Immuno-Chemistry* 56; numerous papers and reviews.
Home: 333 Central Park West, New York 25, N.Y.; Laboratory: Dept. Pathology, N.Y. University School of Medicine, 550 First Avenue, New York, N.Y. 10016, U.S.A.

Heifetz, Jascha; Russian-born American violinist; b. 2 Feb. 1901; ed. Petrograd Conservatoire of Music.
First appearance at age seven; concerts Russia, Germany, Austro-Hungary, Scandinavia, U.S. 17, later England; toured Australia and New Zealand 21, Far East 23, world tour 25-27; 1st Vice-Pres. American Guild Musical Artists; hon. mem. Soc. of Concerts, Paris, Asscn. des Anciens Elèves du Conservatoire, Cercle Int. de la Jeunesse Artistique; hon. Vice-Pres. Mark Twain Society U.S.; hon. Pres. Musicians' Fund of America, Légion d'Honneur.
1520 Gilcrest Drive, Beverly Hills, Calif., U.S.A.

Heikal, Muhammed Hassanein; United Arab Republic (Egyptian) journalist; b. 1923.
Editor *Akher Saa* magazine 52-, *Al Ahram* daily newspaper 57-; Head of Press Dept., Arab Socialist Union Secr. 65-.
Al Ahram Building, 14 Sharia Mazloum, Cairo, United Arab Republic.
Telephone: Cairo 46464.

Heiliger, Bernhard; German sculptor; b. 11 Nov. 1915; ed. Stettin Art School, Berlin Acad. of Fine Arts and in Paris.
Prof. of Plastic Arts, High School of Applied Arts, Berlin-Weissensee 46-, High School of Pictorial Arts, Berlin-Charlottenburg 49-; numerous exhibitions in Europe and elsewhere; works in German and foreign museums and private collections; mem. Berlin Acad. of Arts; Berlin Art Prize 50, Cologne Art Prize 52, Nat. and Int. Prize, Inst. of Contemporary Arts, London and Great Art Prize, Nordrhein-Westfalen.
Notable works include *Flamme* for Ernest-Reuterplatz, Berlin, *Auftakt* for Berlin Philharmonic Orchestra and 15 reliefs in Market Place, Bremen.
Käuzchensteig 12, Berlin-Dahlem, Germany.
Telephone: 76-01-12.

Heiller, Anton; Austrian composer and organist; b. 23; ed. Akademie für Musik und darstellende Kunst, Vienna.

Professor of Music, Music Acad., Vienna 45-; concerts all over the world as organist, also as harpsichordist and conductor; Josef Marx Prize 42, Improvisation Prize, Haarlem 52, Schott prize 54, Kulturpreis der Stadt, Vienna 63.
Compositions: numerous choir compositions and organ works including a Concerto for Organ and Orchestra.
Heuberggasse 26, Vienna XVII, Austria.

Heilmeyer, Ludwig, M.D.; German professor of medicine; b. 6 March 1899; ed. Maximilian Gymnasium, Munich and Universität München.
Assistant and Assoc. Prof., Jena 26-45; Prof. of Pharmacology and Pathological Physiology, Düsseldorf 45-46; Prof. of Internal Medicine, Chair. of Dept. of Internal Medicine and Dir. of Univ. Hospital, Freiburg/Br. 46-; Dir. Foundation Cttee. for Univ. of Ulm, Rector, Univ. of Ulm; Hon. Prof. Univ. of Freiburg; Hon. mem. Faculty of Medicine, Univ. de Santiago de Chile; Dr. h.c. (Athens, Louvain, Frankfurt/Main, Vienna); mem. Deutsche Akademie der Naturforscher Leopoldina, Heidelberger Akademie der Wissenschaften; several medals.
Sonnhalde 100, Freiburg/Br., German Federal Republic.

Heim, Roger Jean, ING. E.C.P., D. ès sciences naturelles, F.R.S.E., F.L.S.; French scientist; b. 12 Feb. 1900.
Curator, Alpine Garden (Faculty of Sciences, Grenoble) 23-25; Demonstrator, Ecole des Hautes Etudes, Paris 26; Asst. at Nat. Museum of Natural History 27-32, Deputy Dir. Cryptogamic Laboratory 32-45, Dir. Laboratory of Mycology and Phytopathology 40-, **Prof. and Dir. Cryptogamic Laboratory** 45-; Dir. Museum of Natural History 51-65; mem. Acad. d'Agriculture 45, Acad. des Sciences 46, Acad des Sciences d'Outre-Mer 47, Acad. Royale de Belgique 48, Acad. Leopoldina 62-; Pres. Soc. de Pathologie végétale 37, Soc. mycologique 45, Soc. Botanique de France 48, Société française de Microscopie 48, Asscn. française pour l'avancement des Sciences 51; Union Int. pour la Conservation de la Nature 54, Société des Océanistes 54; Pres. Fondation-Singer-Polignac 58-; Pres. Académie des Sciences 63; Dr. h.c. Univ. of Uppsala; Commdr. de la Légion d'Honneur, Médaille de la Résistance, Croix de Guerre, etc.
Publs. *Le Genre Inocybe* 31, *Fungi iberici: Observations sur la flore mycologique catalane* 34, *Les champignons toxiques* 38, *Les Lactario—Russulés de Madagascar* 38, *La reproduction chez les plantes* 38, *Etudes sur les Agarics termitophiles africains* 40-52, *La sombre route* 47, *Les champignons, Tableaux d'un monde étrange* 48, *Destruction et Protection de la Nature* 52, *Les Lactaires d'Afrique Intertropicale* 55, *Un Naturaliste autour du monde* 55, *La Langue Française et la Science* 55, *Manuel des Champignons d'Europe* 57, *Les Champignons hallucinogènes du Mexique* (with R. G. Wasson) 58, *Les Champignons toxiques et hallucinogènes* 63, *Nouvelles investigations sur les Agarics hallucinogènes* 67.
Laboratoire de Cryptogamie, 12 rue de Buffon, Paris 5e, France.
Telephone: 402-35-21.

Heimann, Robert Karl, B.A., M.A., PH.D.; American business executive; b. 22 Sept. 1918; ed. Princeton and New York Univs.
Editor *Nation's Heritage* 48-49; Man. Editor and Exec. Editor *Forbes Magazine of Business and Finance* 49-54; Exec. Asst. The American Tobacco Co. 54-60, Asst. to the Pres. The American Tobacco Co. 61-64, Vice-Pres. for marketing and public relations 64-66, Exec. Vice-Pres. 66-.
Publ. *Tobacco and Americans* 60.
The American Tobacco Co., 150 E. 42nd Street, New York City 17, N.Y., U.S.A.

Heineman, Ben Walter, LL.B., LL.D.; American railroad executive; b. 10 Feb. 1914; ed. Univ. of Michigan and Northwestern Univ.
Practising lawyer 36-56; Chair. Exec. Cttee., and Dir. Minneapolis & St. Louis Railway Co. 54-56; Chair. and Dir., Four Wheel Drive Auto Co. 54-57; Chair. Chicago and North Western Railway Co. and Chicago, St. Paul, Minneapolis & Omaha Railroad 56-, now also Pres.; Dir. Asscn. of American Railroads, Packers Car Line, First Nat. Bank of Chicago; Life Fellow American Bar Foundation; Trustee Univ. of Chicago; Order of Coif; Hon. LL.D. Lawrence Coll.
1126 East 48th Street, Chicago 15, Ill., U.S.A.

Heinemann, Gustav W., DR.RER.POL., DR.IUR.; German lawyer and politician; b. 27 July 1899; ed. Realgymnasium, Essen, and Univs. of Münster, Marburg, Munich, Göttingen and Berlin.
Solicitor, Essen 26-; Legal Counsel, Rheinische Stahlwerke, Essen 28-36, Mining Dir. 36-49; Dozent, Univ. of Cologne 33-39; Lord Mayor of Essen 46-49; Minister of Justice, North Rhine Westphalia 47-48; Fed. Minister of Interior 49-50, of Justice Dec. 66-; mem. Bundestag 57-; mem. Council Protestant Church in Germany 45-67; Christian Democrat -57, Social Democrat 57-.
Bundesjustizministerium, 53 Bonn; Home: 43 Essen, Schinkelstrasse 34, German Federal Republic.

Heinen, Reinhold, DR.RER.POL.; German journalist; b. 7 Jan. 1894; ed. Düren Gymnasium and Univs. of Bonn, Königsberg and Breslau.
Editor-in-Chief *Oberschlesischer Kurier* (Königshütte) 17, *Neue Oberschlesische Volkszeitung* (Ratibor) 18, *Volksfreund* (Aachen) 19; Gen. Sec. Kommunalpolitische Vereinigung, Publisher *Kommunal Politische Blaetter* 21; Lecturer in Civic Affairs, Cologne Univ. 30-37; imprisoned 33 and 41-45 (in Sachsenhausen concentration camp 42-45); Landrat, Monschau 45; Publisher *Kölnische Rundschau* and *Bonner Rundschau* 46-, Editor-in-Chief 46-58; Dir. Wasserverband Schwammenauel (dam) 46-66, Hon Dir. 66-; mem. Aufsichtsrat Deutsche Presseagentur G.m.b.H. (DPA) 50, Pres. Verwaltungsrat Vereinigte Wirtschaftsdienste (VWD) 51-; hon. citizen of Heimbach; Marianer Deutscher Ritterorden, Commdr. Papal Commdr. of Sylvester, Officer Order of Orange-Nassau; mem. Christian Democratic Union.
Publs. *Die Fraktion in Gemeindeparlement* 21, 27, etc.
Stolkgasse 25, Cologne and Heimbach/Eifel, German Federal Republic.
Telephone: 20321 (Cologne); 02446/277 (Eifel).

Heinesen, William; Danish (Faroese) author; b. 15 Jan. 1900; ed. commercial schools, Copenhagen.
Writes generally about Faroese subjects; also draws and paints; mem. Danish Literary Acad.; Scandinavian Literature Prize 65.
Publs. Novels: *Noatun* 38, *The Black Pot* 49, *The Lost Fiddlers* 50, *Mother of the Seven Stars* 52, *Windy Dawn* 61, *The Good Hope* 64; stories: *The Enchanted Light* 57, *The Bewitched Gamaliel* 60.
Vardagöta 33, Thorshaven, Faroe Isles.

Heinz, Henry John, II, B.A.; American industrialist; b. 10 July 1908; ed. Yale Univ. and Trinity Coll., Cambridge.
Salesman H. J. Heinz Co. Ltd. London 32-33, in Sales Dept. 34-37, Asst. to Pres. 37-41, Pres. 41-59, Chair. 59-; Dir. Mellon National Bank & Trust Co. Pittsburgh; Trustee, Carnegie Institute, Carnegie-Mellon Univ.; Pres. Nutrition Foundation 48-60; Trustee U.S. Council of Int. Chamber of Commerce; Trustee of Cttee. for Economic Development; Chevalier, Légion d'Honneur, Commdr., Order of Merit (Italy), Cross of Commdrs. Royal Order of the Phoenix.
Home: Goodwood, Sewickley, Pennsylvania; Office: P.O. Box 57, Pittsburgh 30, Pa., U.S.A.

Heinze, Sir Bernard Thomas, Kt., M.A., F.R.C.M.; Australian university professor and conductor; b. 1 July 1894; ed. Univ. of Melbourne, Royal Coll. of Music, London and Schola Cantorum, Paris.
Apptd. to academic staff, Univ. of Melbourne 24; Ormond Prof. of Music, Univ. of Melbourne 25-; Dir.-Gen. of Music for Australian Broadcasting Co. 29-32; Conductor, Royal Melbourne Philharmonic Society 28-; Melbourne Symphony Orchestra 33-46 and now Victorian Symphony Orchestra; Dir. State Conservatorium of N.S.W. 57-; conductor to Australian Broadcasting Comm.; Officer, Order of the Crown (Belgium); Hon. LL.D. (Univ. of British Columbia), Mus. Doc. (Univ. of W. Australia).
101 Victoria Road, Bellevue Hill, Sydney, N.S.W. Australia.

Heisbourg, Georges; Luxembourg diplomatist; b. 10 April 1918; ed. Luxembourg and Univs. of Grenoble, Innsbruck and Paris.
Chief, Govt. Press and Information Service 44-45; Attaché and Sec. to Legation, London 45-51; Sec., Counsellor, Dir. Political Affairs, Ministry of Foreign Affairs 52-58; Ambassador to U.S.A. 58-64; Perm. Rep. to UN 58-61; Minister to Canada 59-60, Ambassador 60-64; Minister to Mexico 59-60, Ambassador 60-64, to Netherlands 64-67; numerous W. European decorations.
Embassy of Luxembourg, 33 avenue Rapp, Paris 7e, France.
Telephone: 468-0004 and 705-4733.

Heisenberg, Werner; German physicist; b. 5 Dec. 1901; ed. Munich and Göttingen Univs.
Dozent Göttingen Univ. 24; Lecturer Copenhagen Univ. 26; Prof. of Theoretical Physics Leipzig Univ. 27-41; Berlin Univ. 41-45; Göttingen 46-58; Munich 59; Dir. Max Planck Institute for Physics and Astrophysics (Kaiser Wilhelm Inst.) 41-; Gifford Lecturer, St. Andrews Univ. 55-56; Foreign mem. Royal Soc. (U.K.); Nobel Prizeman 32; Orden Pour le Mérite; research worker in atomic physics.
Publs. *The Physical Principles of the Quantum Theory* 30, *Wandlungen in den Grundlagen der Naturwissenschaft* 35, *Die Physik der Atomkerne* 43, *Kosmische Strahlung* 43, *Das Naturbild der heutigen Physik* 55, *Physics and Philosophy* 58, *Introduction to the Unified Field Theory of Elementary Particles* 66, *Einführung in die einheitliche Feldtheorie der Elementarteilchen* 67.
Föhringer Ring 6, 8 Munich 23, German Federal Republic.
Telephone: 327-001.

Heiskanen, Weikko A., PH.D.; Finnish geodesist; b. 27 July 1895; ed. State Univ. of Finland, Helsinki, and Göttingen and Berlin Univs.
State Geodesist of Finland 22-28; Prof. of Geodesy Inst. of Technology 28-49, Chair. Surveying Dept. 35-49; Dir. Finnish Geodetic Inst. 49-61; Dir. Isostatic Inst. of IAG 36-; Prof. of Geodesy, Ohio State Univ., U.S.A. 50-65, Dir. Inst. of Geodesy, Photogrammetry and Cartography, Ohio State Univ. 52-65; Establisher and Supervisor of worldwide gravity project, Ohio State Univ. 52-65; mem. Finnish and six foreign Acads. of Sciences, Finnish Parl. 33-36; Bowie Gold Medal A.G.U.; several hon. degrees.
Publs. *Über den Einfluss der Gezeiten auf die säkuläre Acceleration des Mondes* 21, *Untersuchungen über Schwerkraft und Isostasie* 24, *Beobachtung der Schwerkraft, die Lotabweichungen, und Problem der Isostasie* 36, *New Isostatic Tables for Reduction of the Gravity Values Calculated on Basis of Airy's Hypothesis* 38, *The Universe of Stars I* 48, *II* 50, *On the World Geodetic System* 51, *Columbus Geoid* 57, *The Earth and its Gravity Field* 58, (with Prof. F. A. Vening Meinesz), *Present Problems of Physical Geodesy* 65.
Isostaatinen Laitos, Dosentintie 3 A 2, Helsinki 33, Finland.

Heiskell, Andrew; American press executive; b. 13 Sept. 1915; ed. Germany, Switzerland, Univ. of Paris and Harvard School of Business Administration.
Science teacher, Ecole du Montcel; settled in the U.S.A. 35; Reporter, *New York Herald Tribune* 36-37; Editorial staff *Life* magazine 37-39, Asst. Gen. Man. 39-40, Paris office 40-42, Gen. Man. 42-46, Publisher 46-60; Vice-Pres. Time Inc. 49-50, mem. Board of Dirs. 50-, Chair. 60-; mem. Board of Dirs. Inter-American Press Asscn., American Heritage Foundation, Atlantic Council; mem. Visiting Cttee., Jt. Center for Urban Studies, M.I.T./Harvard Univ.
Time & Life Building, Rockefeller Center, New York, N.Y. 10028, U.S.A.

Heisler, Philip Samuel; American newspaperman; b. 8 Sept. 1915; ed. Penn State Coll.
Reporter McKeesport (Pa.) *Daily News* 37-39; Sun-papers War Corresp. 44-45; Ed. *Sunday Sun Magazine*, Baltimore, 45-46; Film Dir. Television Station WMAR-TV, Baltimore 47-49; Reporter *Evening Sun*, Baltimore 39-44, Man. Editor 49-; Owner Rabar Racing Stable.
Home: 4406 Bedford Place, Baltimore 18; Office: The Sunpapers, Baltimore, Md., U.S.A.

Heissenbüttel, Helmut; German broadcasting official and writer; b. 21 June 1921; ed. Kaiser-Wilhelms-gymnasium, Wilhelmshaven, Realgymnasium, Papenburg, Technische Hochschule, Dresden, and Universitäten Leipzig und Hamburg.
Publishers' Reader, Claassen Verlag, Hamburg 55-57; Editor, Süddeutscher Rundfunk, Stuttgart (Chief Editor *Radio-Essay*) 57-; Hugo-Jacobipreis 60.
Publs. *Kombinationen* 54, *Topographien* 56, *Textbuch 1* 60, *Textbuch 2* 61, *Textbuch 3* 62, *Textbuch 4* 64, *Textbuch 5* 65.
Stuttgart-W, Rotebühlstrasse 179, German Federal Republic.

Heitler, Walter, PH.D., F.R.S.; Irish university professor; b. 2 Jan. 1904; ed. Univs. of Berlin and Munich.
Priv. doz. Univ. of Göttingen 29-33; Research Fellow Univ. of Bristol 33-41; Prof. Dublin Inst. for Advanced Studies 41-49, Dir. 46-49; Prof. of Theoretical Physics Univ. of Zürich 49-; mem. Royal Irish Acad., Royal Soc. of Sciences of Uppsala; Hon. D.Sc.
Publs. *Theory of Chemical Bond* 27, *Quantum Theory of Radiation Elementary Wave Mechanics, Der Mensch und die Naturwissenschaftliche Erkenntnis* 61, 4th edn. 66, *Man and Science* 63, and papers on cosmic rays, the Meson theory and Quantum-electrodynamics.
Am Guggenberg 5, 8053 Zürich, Switzerland.
Telephone: 051-531266.

Hekmat, Ali Asghar; Iranian politician, educationist and writer; b. 93; ed. American High School and Univ. of Paris.
Dir.-Gen. of Education 28-30; Acting Minister of Education, Religious Foundations and Fine Arts 33-34; Minister of Education 34-37; Pres. Teheran Univ. 35-38, Prof. of Literature and History of Religions 40-; Pres. Iranian Acad. 38; Minister of the Interior 39-40, of Public Health 41-43, of Justice 43; head of cultural mission to India 44; Pres. Iranian Nat. Comm. for UNESCO 46-54; Minister without Portfolio June 47; Vice-Pres. Iranian Red Cross 48-51; Minister of Foreign Affairs 48-50, 58-59; Ambassador to India, concurrently Minister to Thailand 54-58; leader of several dels.; numerous Persian and foreign decorations; hon. mem. Arab Acad.; Hon. Ph.D.
Publs. *Sarzarmin-e-Hind, Shakuntala,* translations of Shakespeare, *Djami* 43, *Majaless-ol Nafayess* 45, *From Saadi to Djami* (history of Persian literature) 48, *Parsi-el-Naghze* (anthology) 51, *Kashfol Asrar* 52, *The Proverbs of the Koran* 53, *A Short History of Persian Literature* (in English) 57, *Treatise on Navai* 58, *History of Religions* (2 vols.) 60-61.
Fisherabad, Teheran, Iran.

Helaissi, Sheikh Abdulrahman Al-: Saudi Arabian diplomatist; b. 24 July 1922; ed. Univs. of Cairo and London and in Islamic Religious Law.
Official at Ministry of Foreign Affairs; Secretary to Embassy London 47-54; Under-Sec. Ministry of Agriculture 54-57; Rep. to UN, and at conferences on Health, Agriculture, Wheat, Sugar and Locusts; Head of Del. to FAO 55-61; Amb. to Sudan 57-60; Del. to Conf. of Non-Aligned Nations, Belgrade 61; Amb. to Italy and Austria 61-66, to U.K. and Denmark July 66-.
Publ. *The Rehabilitation of the Bedouins* 59.
Embassy of Saudi Arabia, 27 Eaton Place, London, S.W.1, England.

Helders, Gerardus Philippus, LL.D.; Netherlands civil servant and politician; b. 9 March 1905; ed. Leiden Univ.
Employed in the former Netherlands East Indies, rising to grade of Finance Inspector 30-40; at Ministry of Finance 46-48; Dir. Nationale Trust Maatschappij, Amsterdam 48-57; Minister for Overseas Affairs 57-59; Counsellor of State; Knight Order of the Netherlands Lion, War Cross and other decorations for service in the army (Gen. Staff) and Netherlands East Indies, Grand Cross Order of Homayoun (Iran).
Storm van 's-Gravesandeweg 71, Wassenaar, Netherlands.
Telephone: 01751-5575.

Hélion, Jean; French painter; b. 21 April 1904.
Abstract painter until 39; Prisoner-of-War 40-42 when he escaped; figurative painter 43-; first one-man exhbn. 32, later in America and Europe; designed sets and costumes for *King Lear*, Television Production 65; numerous group exhbns. and works in numerous museums.
Retrospective exhbns.: Abstracts, Galerie Louis Carré, Paris 62, General, Gallery of Modern Art, New York 64, Drawings, Galerie Yvon Lambert, Paris 64, General, Leicester Galleries, London 37-66, Galerie du Dragon, Paris 66, Galleria Il Fante di Spade, Rome, 68.
Publ. *They Shall Not Have Me* 43.
4 rue Michelet, Paris 6e, France.
Telephone: Odéon 49-41.

Heller, John Roderick, B.S., M.D.; American medical research administrator; b. 27 Feb. 1905; ed. Clemson Coll. and Emory Univ.
Public Health Clinician and Admin. Georgia State Dept. of Health 30-31; Venereal Disease Clinician, U.S. Public Health Service, Ark. 31-32; V.D. Control Officer, Tenn. State Dept. of Health 32-34; entered U.S. Public Health Service 34, States Relations Admin. 34-43, Chief Dir. of Venereal Diseases 43-48; Dir. Nat. Cancer Inst. 48-60; Professional Lecturer George Washington Univ. School of Medicine 48-60; Asst. Surgeon Gen. U.S. Public Health Service 57-60 (retd.); Pres. and Chief Exec. Officer Sloan-Kettering Cancer Center 60-64; Clinical Prof. Preventive Medicine, Cornell Medical Coll., New York, N.Y. 62-; Special Consultant on Int. Medical and Scientific Affairs, American Cancer Soc. Inc. 64-; Special Consultant, Nat. Cancer Inst., Bethesda, Md. 65-; Hon. Sc.D. (Clemson Coll.) 58, Hon. LL.D. Hahnemann Medical Coll. 60, M.D. h.c. Perugia Univ. 61.
Publs. *The Control of Venereal Disease* (with Vonderlehr) 46, and many papers.
National Cancer Institute, Bethesda, Maryland 20014; Home: 5604 McLean Drive, Bethesda, Md 20014, U.S.A.

Heller, Walter Wolfgang, A.B., M.A., PH.D.; American economist and government adviser; b. 27 Aug. 1915; ed. Oberlin Coll., Ohio, and Univ. of Wisconsin.
Asst. Dir. of Tax Research, U.S. Treasury 42-46; Assoc. Prof. of Economics, Univ. of Minnesota 46-50, Prof. 50-60, 64-67, Regents' Prof. 67-; Chair. of Econs. Dept. 57-61, Chief Internal Finance, U.S. Mil. Govt., Germany 47-48; mem. E.C.A. Mission on German Fiscal Problems 51; Tax Adviser to Gov. of Minnesota 55-60; Consultant to Cttee. for Econ. Devt. 48-49, 54-57, to U.S. Census Bureau 58-61, to UN (on fiscal problems of newly-developing countries) 52-60, to Royal Comm. on Taxation, Jordan 60; Chair. President's Council of Econ. Advisers 61-64; Dir. Int. Milling Co. 65-, Nat. City Bank of Minneapolis 64-, Nat. Bureau of Econ. Research 65-, Northwestern Nat. Life Insurance Co.; mem. Oberlin Coll. Board of Trustees 66-; mem. Cttee. for Econ. Devt. Research Advisory Board 65-; Consultant to Exec. Office of the Pres. 65-; Chair. OECD Group of Fiscal Experts 67-; several hon. degrees.
Publs. *Taxes and Fiscal Policy in Under-developed Countries* (co-author) 54, *State Income Tax Administration* (co-author) 59, *New Dimensions of Political Economy* 66, *Revenue Sharing and the City* (co-author) 68, *Perspective in Economic Growth* (editor) 68.
University of Minnesota, Minneapolis, Minnesota 55455; Home: 2203 Folwell Street, Saint Paul, Minn. 55108, U.S.A.
Telephone: 612-645-2258.

Hellman, Lillian; American playwright; b. 20 June 1905; ed. New York and Columbia Univs.
With Horace Liveright Inc., publishers 24-25; theatrical play reader 27-30; book reviewer *New York Herald Tribune* 25-28; scenario writer 35-; mem. Screen Writers Guild, Dramatists Guild, American Acad. of Arts and Sciences, American Inst. of Arts and Letters.
Plays: *The Children's Hour* 34, *Days to Come* 36, *The Little Foxes* 39, *Watch on the Rhine* 41, *The Searching Wind* 44, *Another Part of the Forest* 46, adaptation E. Roble's *Montserrat* 49, *The Autumn Garden* 52, adaptation of Anouilh's *The Lark* 55, *Toys in the Attic* 60; *Candide*, an operetta with Leonard Bernstein and Richard Wilbur 56, *My Mother, My Father and Me* 63; film scenarios: *The Dark Angel* 35, *These Three* 35-36, *Dead End* 37, *The Little Foxes* 40, *The North Star* 43, *The Searching Wind* 45.
63 East 82nd Street, New York, N.Y., U.S.A.

Hellwege, Heinrich Peter; German politician; b. 18 Aug. 1908; ed. Athenaeum, Stade.
Served in German Army 39-45; mem. Landtag of Lower Saxony 47; Chair. Deutsche Partei 46-60; mem. Fed. Parl. 49; Minister for Fed. Council Affairs 49-55; Minister Pres. Lower Saxony 55-59.
2152 Neuenkirchen 45, Post Horneburg/Niederelbe, German Federal Republic.

Hellwig, Fritz, DR.PHIL.HABIL.; German economist and European politician; b. 3 Aug. 1912; ed. Marburg, Vienna, Berlin Univs.
Staff mem. of the Saarbrücken Chamber of Industry and Commerce 33-39; Dir. of the Saarwirtschaftsarchiv 33-39; Man. of the District Organisations of the Iron and Steel Industry at Düsseldorf and Saarbrücken, 40-43; war service 43-47; Econ. Adviser and Dir. of Deutsches Industrieinstitut, Cologne 51; Substitute delegate, Consultative Assembly of Council of Europe 53-56; mem. of Bundestag 53-59; Chair. of the Econ. Affairs Cttee. of the Bundestag 56-59; mem. of European Parl. 59; mem. of High Authority of the European Coal and Steel Community, Luxembourg 59-67; Vice-Pres. of the Comm. of the European Communities, Brussels.
Publs. *Westeuropas Montanwirtschaft, Kohle und Stahl beim Start der Montan-Union* 53, *Saar zwischen Ost und West, Die wirtschaftliche Verflechtung* 54, *10 Jahre Schumanplan* 60, *Gemeinsamer Markt und Nationale Wirtschaftspolitik* 61, *Montanunion Zwischen Bewährung und Belastung* 63, *Politische Tragweite der europäischen Wirtschaftsintegration* 66.
Office: Commission of the European Communities,

23-27 avenue de la Joyeuse Entrée, Brussels, Belgium; Home: Klosterbeigstr. 117c, Bad Godesberg, German Federal Republic.

Hellyer, Hon. Paul Theodore; Canadian engineer and politician; b. 6 Aug. 1923; ed. Waterford High School, Curtiss Wright Technical Inst., California, and Univ. of Toronto.
Fleet Aircraft, Fort Erie 42-, Group Leader 43-; Royal Canadian Air Force 44-46; Owner, Mari-Jane Fashions, Toronto 45-56; Treas. Curran Hall Ltd. 50-, Pres. 51-62; Pres. Trepil Realty Ltd. 51-62; Pres. Hendon Estates Ltd. 59-62; mem. House of Commons 49-57, 58-, Parl. Asst. to Minister of Nat. Defence 56-57, Assoc. Minister April-June 57, Minister of Nat. Defence 63-67, of Transport 67-; Liberal.
1982 Rideau River Drive, Ottawa, Ontario, Canada.

Helm, Harold Holmes, B.A., LL.D.; American banker; b. 9 Dec. 1900; ed. Ogden Coll. and Princeton Univ.
Credit Department, Chemical Bank New York Trust Co. (fmrly. Chemical Nat. Bank) 20, Junior Officer 26, Vice-Pres. 29, Dir. 41, First Vice-Pres. 46, Pres. 47-56, Chair. 56-66, now Chair. Exec. Cttee.; Chair. Exec. Cttee. of Fed. Hall Memorial Assocs.; Dir. Associated Dry Goods Corpn., Home Indemnity Co., Equitable Life Assurance Soc. of the U.S.A., Uniroyal, F. W. Woolworth Co., Bethlehem Steel Corpn., Western Electric Co., Cummins Engine Co., Corn Products Corpn., Home Insurance Co., Colgate Palmolive Corpn., McDonnell Douglas Corpn., etc.; Chair. Finance Cttee. Princeton Univ.; Commdr. Order of St. Olav, Hon. D.C.S. (New York Univ.), Hon. LL.D. (Centre Coll.), Hon. D.C.L. (Univ. of the South).
Chemical Bank New York Trust Company, 277 Park Avenue, New York, N.Y., U.S.A.
Telephone: 212-922-6338.

Helmis, Dimitri; Greek politician and banker; b. 94; ed. Univ. of Athens.
Deputy for Athens and Under-Minister of Finance 33-35; Minister of Transport to Hellenic Govt. in exile in Egypt 44-46; Minister of Finance, and Minister of Supply and Nat. Economy 46-50, of Econ. Co-ordination 56-58; Pres. of Nat. Monetary Council 56-58; Gov. of Nat. Bank of Greece 58-64; fmr. Chair. Ethniki Insurance Co.; mem. Board of Industrial Development Organisation; dir. other companies; Grand Commdr. of the Royal Order of George I.
15 Rigilis Street, Athens, Greece.

Helms, Richard M.; American government official; b. 30 March 1913; ed. high schools in France and Germany, and Williams Coll.
Worked for United Press and *The Indianapolis Times* 35-42; joined U.S. Navy 42, in Office of Strategic Studies, Second World War; Central Intelligence Group 47-49, Central Intelligence Agency 49-, Deputy Dir. for Plans Plans 62, Deputy Dir. 65, Dir. June 66-.
Central Intelligence Agency, Washington, D.C., U.S.A.

Helou, Charles; Lebanese lawyer, journalist and politician; b. 11; ed. St. Joseph (Jesuit) Univ. and Ecole Française de Droit, Beirut.
Barrister, Court of Appeal and Cassation, Beirut 36; founded newspaper *L'Eclair du Nord*, Aleppo, Syria 32; founded *Le Jour*, Beirut 34; Political Dir. *Le Jour* until 47; Lebanese Minister to Vatican 47; Minister of Justice and Health, Lebanon 54-55, of Educ. Feb.-Sept. 64; Pres. of Lebanon Sept. 64-; fmr. Sec.-Gen. Catholic Action of Lebanon.
Office of the President, Beirut, Lebanon.

Helpmann, Sir Robert Murray, Kt., C.B.E.; British dancer, actor and choreographer; b. 9 April 1909; ed. Prince Alfred's Coll., Adelaide.
With Sadler's Wells Ballet Company 33-50; danced in *The Sleeping Princess, Les Sylphides, Giselle. Lac des Cygnes, Coppelia, Apparitions, Comus, Hamlet, Check-*mate, *Miracle in the Gorbals, Don Juan, Job, Prospect Before Us, The Rake's Progress, Le Spectre de la Rose, A Wedding Bouquet, Adam Zero, Carnival;* Choreographer for: *Hamlet, Comus, The Birds, Miracle in the Gorbals, Adam Zero, The Red Shoes* (film) *and Electra;* acted in Old Vic and Stratford productions of Shakespeare's plays, and in *The Insect Play, The White Devil, He who Gets Slapped,* and *The Millionairess;* American Tour 54, Australian Tours 55, 58, Australian and South American Tours 61-62; Films: *One of our Aircraft is Missing, Caravan, Henry V, The Red Shoes, Tales of Hoffman, Iron Petticoat, Big Money, 55 Days at Peking,* Directed: *Murder in the Cathedral* (Old Vic) and *Duel of Angels* (U.S.A.); Produced operas: *Butterfly, Coq d'Or* (Covent Garden); plays: *The Tempest, As You Like It, Antony and Cleopatra* (Old Vic), *Nekrassov* (Edinburgh Festival 57 and Royal Court), *Nude with Violin* (Globe) 58, *Marriage Go Round, Aladdin* (London) 59; Co-artistic Dir. Australian Ballet 65-; Guest artist, Royal Ballet 58; Knight, Northern Star (Sweden), Order of the Cedar (Lebanon); Queen Elizabeth II Coronation Award, Royal Acad. of Dancing 60; Australian of the Year 65.
c/o The Royal Ballet, Covent Garden, London, W.C.2; Home: 72 Eaton Square, London, S.W.1, England.
Telephone: 235-2235.

Helsby, Sir Laurence Norman, G.C.B., K.B.E.; British civil servant (retired and cr. Life Peer April 68); b. 27 April 1908; ed. Sedbergh and Keble Coll., Oxford.
Lecturer in Econs., Univ. Coll. of South-West 30-31, Durham Colls. in Univ. of Durham 31-45; Asst. Sec. Treasury 46; Principal Private Sec. to Prime Minister 47-50; Dep. Sec. Ministry of Food 50-54; First Civil Service Commr. 54-59; Perm. Sec. Ministry of Labour 59-62; Jt. Perm. Sec. to Treasury and Head of Home Civil Service 63-68; Dir. Rank Org., Imperial Tobacco Co., Midland Bank 68-.
Logmore Farmhouse, Dorking, Surrey, England.

Heltzer, Harry, MET.ENG.; American business exec.; b. 22 Aug. 1911; ed. Univ. of Minnesota.
Production Man. Chemolite Plant, Minnesota Mining and Manufacturing Co. 48-52, Gen. Man. Reflective Products Div. 52-59, Div. Vice-Pres. 59-61, Corporate Vice-Pres. Reflective Products Div. 61-66, mem. Board of Dirs. 65, Pres. 66-; Corporate Vice-Pres. Nat. Advertising Co. 61-63; Group Vice-Pres. Advertising Services and Protective Products 63-66; Outstanding Achievement Award, Univ. of Minnesota 66.
Minnesota Mining and Manufacturing Company, 2501 Hudson Road, St. Paul, Minn. 55119, U.S.A.

Hencken, Hugh O'Neill, PH.D., D.LITT.; American archaeologist; b. 8 Jan. 1902; ed. Princeton Univ., Cambridge Univ.
Assoc., Peabody Museum, Harvard Univ. 30-31, Asst. Curator European Archæology 31-32, Curator 32-; Asst. Dir. American School of Prehistoric Research 40-45, Dir. 45-, Chair. 60-; Lecturer London and Oxford 47, Edinburgh 59; excavations in England 28, 30, 31; Dir. Harvard excavations in Ireland 32-36; Dir. American School of Prehistoric Research excavations Morocco 47, Algeria 49; mem. Hon. Cttee., Int. Council of Prehistoric and Protohistoric Sciences 48-; Hon. D.Litt. Nat. Univ. of Ireland; Pres. Archæological Inst. of America 49-51.
Publs. *Archæology of Cornwall* 32, *Ballinderry Crannog* (No. 1) 36, *Cahercommaun* 38, *Lagore Crannog* 50, *Indo-European Languages and Archaeology* 55.
American School of Prehistoric Research, Peabody Museum, Harvard University, Cambridge 38, Mass., U.S.A.

Henderson, Douglas; American diplomatist; b. 15 Oct. 1914; ed. Boston Univ. and Fletcher School of Law and Diplomacy.
Instructor, Tufts Coll. 41-42; Diplomatic Service 42-,

Vice-Consul Nogales 42, Arica 43, Cochabamba 43, Foreign Service Officer 46; Dept. of Commerce 47; Consul 50; Second Sec. and Consul, Berne 50, First Sec. and Consul 54; Asst. Chief, Econ. Defense Div. 56; Counsellor, Econ. Affairs, Lima 60, Counsellor, Lima 61; Ambassador to Bolivia 63-.
American Embassy, Calle Colón, Edificio Banco Popular del Perú, La Paz, Bolivia.

Henderson, Rt. Rev. Edward Barry, D.D., D.S.C.; British ecclesiastic; b. 22 March 1910; ed. Radley, and Trinity Coll., Cambridge.
Ordained 34; Curate, St. Gabriel's, Pimlico 34-36; Priest, All Saints, Pimlico 36-39; Rector, Holy Trinity, Ayr 39-47; Chaplain R.N.V.R. 43-44; Vicar, St. Paul's, Knightsbridge 47-55; Rural Dean of Westminster 53-55; Bishop Suffragan of Tewkesbury 55-60; Bishop of Bath and Wells 60-; sub-Prelate of the Order of St. John of Jerusalem 62.
The Palace, Wells, Somerset, England.

Henderson, Horace Edward; American exec.; b. 30 July 1917; ed. Coll. of William and Mary, Williamsburg, Virginia, and Yale Univ.
Army service, Second World War; Owner, Henderson Real Estate, Williamsburg, Virginia 47-52; Vice-Pres. Junior Chamber Int. 51-52; Nat. Pres. U.S. Junior Chamber of Commerce 52-53; Asscns. Co-ordinator, Nat. Auto Dealers Asscn., Washington 54-55; Vice-Chair. Operation Brotherhood 54-56; Dir. Office of Special Liaison and Special Asst., Deputy Under-Sec. of State 58; U.S. Del. to ILO 59-60, WHO 59-60, UNESCO 60, FAO 59, High Comm. for Refugees 59, ECOSOC 59, U.S. Del. to UN 60; Deputy Asst. Soc. of State, Dept. of State, Washington, D.C. 59-60; Chair. Americans for Asian Security and Freedom 61-62, Cttee. Against Recognition of Red Hungary 62-64; Chair. Republican Party of Virginia 62-64; mem. Republican Nat. Cttee. 62-64; Chair. of Board, Henderson Real Estate Agency, McLean, Virginia 65-; Exec. Dir. World Peace Through Law Center, Geneva 64-65, Dir.-Gen. 65-.
Office: World Peace Through Law Center, 75 rue de Lyon, Geneva, Switzerland; Home: 8001 Chanute Place, Falls Church, Va. 22042, U.S.A.

Henderson, Loy Wesley, B.A.; American diplomatist; b. 28 June 1892; ed. Northwestern Univ., and Denver Univ. Law School.
Mem. Inter-Allied Comm. to Germany for repatriation of prisoners of war 19; mem. American Red Cross Comm. to W. Russia and Baltic States 19-20; in charge A.R.C., Germany 20-21; Vice-Consul, Dublin 22, Queenstown 23; Dept. of State 25; Third Sec. Riga, Kovno and Tallin 27; Second Sec. 29; Dept. of State 30; Moscow 34, First Sec. and intermittently Chargé d'Affaires 35-38; Asst. Chief Div. of European Affairs, Dept. of State 38; Inspector of Diplomatic Missions and Consular Offices 42-43; Counsellor and Chargé d'Affaires U.S.S.R. 42; Minister to Iraq 43-45; Dir. Near-Eastern, South Asian and African Affairs, Dept. of State 48-51; Ambassador to India, also Minister to Nepal 48-51; Ambassador to Iran 51-55; Deputy Under-Sec. of State for Admin. 55-61; Career Ambassador 56; U.S. Observer Baghdad Pact Confs. 56, 57, 59; Gov. American Red Cross 59-61; Prof. of Int. Relations and Dir. Center of Diplomacy and Foreign Policy, The American Univ. 61-; Pres. Washington Inst. of Foreign Affairs 61-; Dept. of State Distinguished Service Award 54, Pres. Award for Distinguished Federal Civilian Service 58; Hon. LL.D. (Northwestern Univ., Bates Coll., Univ. of Ark., Wade Univ.).
2727 29th Street, N.W., Washington, D.C. 20008, U.S.A.

Hendrych, Jiří; Czechoslovak politician; b. 28 Dec. 1913.
Communist Party Official 35-; fmr. Editor *Svoboda*;

detained in Mauthausen concentration camp, Second World War; Head, Ideological Work and later Agitation and Propaganda Dept., Central Cttee. of C.P. 45-52; Leading Sec. Regional Cttee. of C.P., České Budějovice 52-54; mem. Central Cttee. C.P. 46-, Sec. 54-68, mem. Presidium 58-68; Chair. Agricultural Comm., Central Cttee. of C.P. 63-65, Ideological Comm., Central Cttee. of C.P. 65-68; Deputy to Nat. Assembly; Klement Gottwald Order 63; Order of Republic 65.
Central Committee of the Communist Party of Czechoslovakia, Prague 1, náb. Kyjevské brigády 12, Czechoslovakia.

Hendy, Sir Philip, M.A.; British art historian; b. 27 Sept. 1900; ed. Westminster School and Christ Church, Oxford.
Asst. to the Keeper and Lecturer, Wallace Collection, London 23-27; studied Italian painting, Italy 27-30; Curator of Paintings Museum of Fine Arts, Boston. Mass., U.S.A. 30-33; Dir. City Art Gallery Leeds and Temple Newsam 34-45; Slade Prof. of Fine Art Oxford Univ. 36-46; Dir. Nat. Gallery 46-67; Artistic Adviser to Israel Museum, Jerusalem 67-68, Dir. 68-; Pres. Int. Council of Museums 59-65; art critic *Daily Herald* 23-26, *New Statesman* 26-27, *London Mercury* 34-36, *Britain To-day* 45-52.
Publs. *Hours in the Wallace Collection* 26, *Wallace Collection: Catalogue of Paintings and Drawings* 28, *Isabella Stewart Gardner Museum* (*Boston*) *Catalogue of Paintings and Drawings* 31, *Matthew Smith* 44, *Giovanni Bellini* 45, *Spanish Painting* 46, *The National Gallery* 55, *Masaccio* 57.
Israel Museum, Jerusalem, Israel.

Henkel, Konrad, DR. ING.; German chemist and business executive; b. 20 Oct. 1915; ed. Technische Hochschule, Munich and Brunswick, and Freiburg Univ.
Assistant to Prof. Dr. Richard Kuhn, Max-Planck Inst. for Medical Research, Heidelberg 40-46; Chemist, Henkel and Cie. G.m.b.H., Man. 56-61; Chair. Board of Dirs. and Advisory Board, Henkel and Cie. G.m.b.H. 61-; Vice-Pres. Exec. Board and Man. Persil G.m.b.H. 61-; mem. Presidential Cttee. of Asscn. of Chemical Industry in Germany, Admin. Council of Cultural Comm. of Fed. Asscn. of German Industry; dir. many other companies.
Chamissostrasse 9, Düsseldorf, German Federal Republic.

Henkle, Herman Henry, A.B., M.A., D.LITT.; American librarian; b. 26 March 1900; ed. Whittier Coll., California and Chicago Univs.
Served in Biology Library, California Univ. 30-35; Assoc. Library School, Illinois Univ. 36-37; Prof. Library Science and Dir. School of Library Science, Simmons Coll., Boston 37-42; Dir. Process Dept. Library of Congress, Washington D.C. 42-47; Librarian John Crerar Library, Chicago 47-, Exec. Dir. 63-; Lecturer, Graduate Library School, Chicago Univ. 50-.
John Crerar Library, 35 West 33rd Street, Chicago, Illinois 60616, U.S.A.

Henle, Günter, D.IUR.; German businessman; b. 3 Feb. 1899; ed. Würzburg and Marburg Univs.
Diplomatic service 21-36; Partner and Gen.-Man. Klöckner & Co., Duisburg 37-; Chair. Klöckner-Werke A.G., Duisburg, Klöckner-Humboldt-Deutz A.G., Köln-Allianz Versicherungs A.G., Munich, SKF Kugellagerfabriken G.m.b.H., Schweinfurt; Vice-Chair. Deutsche Bank A.G.; mem. Board of Dirs. Siemens A.G., Vereinigte Industrie-Unternehmungen A.G.; Glanzstoff A.G., etc.; founder and owner G. Henle Musikverlag, Munich 47; mem. Frankfurt Econ. Council 47-49; mem. Bundestag 49-53; mem. ECSC Common Assembly 52-53; Pres. German Soc. for Foreign Policy 55; Dr. phil. h.c. (Cologne 64).
Klöcknerhaus, 41 Duisburg, German Federal Republic.

Henley, J. Smith; American judge; b. 18 May 1917; ed. Univ. of Arkansas.
Admitted to Arkansas Bar 41; private legal practice 41-54; Assoc. Gen. Counsel, Fed. Communications Comm. 54-56; Dir. Office Admin. Procedure, Dept. of Justice, Washington 56-58; U.S. District Judge, Eastern District, Arkansas 58-, Eastern and Western Districts 59-, Chief Judge, Eastern District 59-.
U.S. Courthouse, Little Rock, Arkansas, U.S.A.
Telephone: Franklin 2-4361, Ext. 5352.

Henley, William Ballentine, A.M., J.D., M.S. (P.A.), LL.D., SC.D., L.H.D.; American lecturer, educationist and lawyer; b. 19 Sept. 1905; ed. Univ. of Southern California and Yale Univ.
Attorney; Asst. to Co-ordination Officer, Univ. of Southern Calif. 28-29 and 30-33; Public Speaking Instructor, American Inst. of Banking 28-29; Dir. of Religious Education, First Methodist Episcopal Church, New Haven, Conn. 29-30; Exec. Sec. Women's Civic Conf.. Univ. of Southern Calif. 30-36; Asst. to Dean, School of Govt., Univ. of Southern Calif. 33-35, Acting Dean and Acting Co-ordinating Officer 35-37, Dir. Inst. of Govt. 35-37, Dir. of Co-ordination and Assoc. Prof. of Public Admin. 37-40; Pres. Calif. Coll. of Medicine 40-65; Provost, Univ. of Calif., Irvine, Calif. Coll. of Medicine 65-; Pres. Rotary Club Los Angeles 55-56; Gov. District 528 Rotary Int. 59-60; Chair. Host Club Exec. Cttee. for Rotary Int. Convention 62; mem. Los Angeles, Calif. and American Bar Asscns., Asscn. of American Medical Schools, Acad. of Political and Social Sciences, Nat. Education Asscn.; Calif. Governor's Medical Advisory Cttee. on Civil Defense 45-48, American Management Asscn., American Asscn. for History of Medicine, Western Interstate Comm. for Higher Education; Past-Pres. American Asscn. Osteopathic Colls.; Educational Consultant 56-; Gen. Motors Exec. Speakers Panel 56-; on Board of Los Angeles Community Health Org. and of several charitable orgs.; mem. Defense Orientation Conf. Asscn. 65-.
Publs. *The History of the University of Southern California* and many magazine articles.
Office: 1721 Griffin Avenue, Los Angeles, California 90031; Home: 1224 Geneva Street, Glendale, Calif. 91207, U.S.A.
Telephone: 213-223-1381 (Office); 213-245-4406 (Home).

Henneberg, Gerd Michael; German theatre director; b. 14 July 1922; ed. Acad. of Dramatic Art, Leipzig.
Actor, Civic Theatre, Aschaffenburg 40-44, Producer 43-44; Artistic Dir. Civic Theatres Ballenstadt/Harz 46; Asst. Deutsche Theater, Berlin 46; Producer and Actor, National Theatre, Weimar 47-50; Actor, Berlin 53-60; Dir. of Friedrich-Wolf Theatre, Neustrelitz; Gen. Dir. Staatstheater Dresden 62-.
Staatstheater Dresden, Julien-Grimau Allee 27, Dresden A. 1, German Democratic Republic.

Hennessy, Sir Patrick, Kt.; British motor executive; b. 18 April 1898.
Royal Inniskilling Fusiliers 14-18; fmr. mem. Advisory Council, Ministry of Aircraft Production; Chair. and fmr. Chief Exec. Ford Motor Co. Ltd. till 68; Chair. Henry Ford and Sons Ltd., Cork, Ireland; Deputy Pres. Soc. of Motor Manufacturers and Traders.
Larkmead, Theydon Bois, Essex, England.

Henniker-Major, Hon. Sir John Patrick Edward Chandos, K.C.M.G., C.V.O., M.C.; British diplomatist; b. 19 Feb. 1916; ed. Stowe and Trinity Coll., Cambridge.
Entered Foreign Service 38; Army Service 40-45; at Embassy, Belgrade 45-46; Asst. Private Sec. to Sec. of State for Foreign Affairs 48-50; Foreign Office 48-50; at Embassy, Buenos Aires 50-52; Counsellor, Foreign Office, Head of Personnel Dept. 52-60; Ambassador to Jordan 60-62, to Denmark 62-66; Civil Service Comm.

66-67; Asst. Under-Sec. for African Affairs at Foreign Office 67-68; Dir.-Gen. of the British Council 68-.
Decoy Farm, Woodbridge, Suffolk, and 30 Evelyn Mansions, Carlisle Place, London, S.W.1, England
Telephone: Eyke (Woodbridge) 212; also 01-828-4122.

Henningsen, Eigil Juel, M.D.; Danish physician; b. 18 July 1906; ed. Københavns Universitet.
State Epidemiologist, State Serum Inst. 35-40; Deputy Dir.-Gen., Nat. Health Service of Denmark 40-; temporary Dir.-Gen. Danish Red Cross 45; Chair. The Mothers Aid Inst. 45-; Chair. WHO Expert Cttee. on Radiation 62; Gen. Chair. Vth Int. Poliomyelitis Conf., Copenhagen 60; Chair. European Nuclear Energy Agency (ENEA) Health and Safety Cttee. 66; mem. other int. medical cttees.
Office: National Health Service, St. Kongensgade 1, Copenhagen; Home: Havgårdsvej 35, Copenhagen-Hellerup, Denmark.

Henningsen, Sven, DR. PHIL.; Danish historian; b. 2 Feb. 1910; ed. Københavns Universitet.
Lecturer in Modern History and Political Science, Univ. of Copenhagen 43; Asst. Prof. Univ. of Gothenburg, Sweden 44-45; Visiting Prof. Univ. of Minnesota, U.S.A. 48-49; Prof. of Contemporary History and Political Science, Univ. of Copenhagen 53-, Vice-Chancellor 67-; Visiting Rockefeller Prof., Univ. of E. Africa 62; Chair. Danish Council for UN 59-65; mem. Council for European Asscn. of American Studies; Chair. Nordic Asscn. for Study of Int. Relations, Council for Danish Nat. UNESCO Cttee.; Chair. Danish Political Science Asscn.
Publs. *The Polish Corridor and Danzig* 36, *The Far East and the Great Powers* 41, *Studies in Economic Liberalism* 44, *The North Atlantic Treaty* 54, *The Foreign Policy of Denmark* 62, *The Twentieth Century* 65.
Dantes Plads 4, Copenhagen V, Denmark.

Henrichs, Helmut; German theatre director; b. 13 April 1907; ed. Humanistisches Gymnasium and university.
Former Production Asst., Schauspielhaus, Düsseldorf; Theatre Critic, Düsseldorf and Berlin; Producer, Deutsches Theater, Berlin, Staatstheater, Stuttgart, Deutsches Theater, Göttingen; Gen. Intendant Wuppertal; Intendant Bayerisches Staatsschauspiel, Munich.
Munich 55, Ossingerstrasse 79, German Federal Republic.
Telephone: 74-55-44.

Henriksen, Peder Kock, M.SC.; Danish chemical engineer and dairy executive; b. 10 July 1904; ed. Danish Technical Univ.
Director, Minsterley Creameries Ltd., Shropshire, U.K. 35-39; Managing Dir. Canned Cream and Milk Ltd., Odense 40-48; Comm., Fed. of Danish Dairy Asscns. 49-55, Deputy Dir. 55-58, Joint Man. Dir. 58-; Sec.-Gen. 16th Int. Dairy Congress, Copenhagen 62; del. to numerous confs.; Knight Order of Dannebrog.
Publs. *Sales Possibilities of Danish Dairy Products* 50, *Denmark's Share and Possibilities in the International Trade in Dairy Products* 54.
Dalgas Avenue 59, 8000 Aarhus C., Denmark.
Telephone: Aarhus 124624.

Henriksen, Rein; Norwegian business exec.; b. 17 Dec. 1915; ed. Universitetet i Oslo.
Barrister of Supreme Court of Norway; Nat. Income Tax Comm. 43-45; Norwegian Shipowners' Asscn. 45-47; Legal Dept., Aktieselskapet Borregaard (pulp for paper, oils, detergents, etc.) 47-60, Gen. Dir. 60-; Knight of St. Olav; Grand Cross (Austria); Order of Homayoun (Iran).
Borregaard Hovedgård, Sarpsborg, Norway.

Henrion, Robert; Belgian banker and university professor; b. 23 July 1915.
Barrister, Brussels 38-46; Prof. of Political Economy and Financial Affairs, Univ. Libre de Bruxelles; Vice-Pres. Inst. for European Studies; Lecturer, Univ. of Louvain; Vice-Chair. Société Générale de Banque; Minister of Finance 66-68; no party political affiliation.
c/o Ministry of Finance, Brussels, Belgium.

Henry, David Dodds, A.M., PH.D.; American educationist; b. 21 Oct. 1905; ed. Pennsylvania State University.
Instructor, Pennsylvania State Univ. 25-29; Prof. of English and Dir. of School of Liberal Arts Battle Creek (Mich. Coll.) 29-33; Asst. State Supt. of Public Instruction Lansing (Mich.) 33-35; Prof. of English 35-52; Asst. to Exec. Vice-Pres. Wayne State Univ. Detroit 36-39; Exec. Vice-Pres. 39-45, Pres. 45-52; Exec. Vice-Chancellor, N.Y. Univ. 52-55; Pres. Univ. of Illinois Sept. 55-; Pres. Assoc. Urban Univs. 45-46, Nat. Comm. on Accrediting 56-58; Chair. Joint Cttee. on Educational T.V. 54-55; Vice-Chair. Cttee. on Education Beyond High School 56-57; Pres. Nat. Asscn. State Univs. and Land-Grant Colls. 64-65; Dir. Council for Financial Aid to Education 58-63; Chair. American Council on Education 60-61; mem. Pres. Cttee. on Employment of Physically Handicapped 56-, Advisory Cttee., Agency for Int. Devt.-Univ. Relations 65-66, 67-69, Advisory Council Nat. Fund for Medical Educ. 59-, Electoral Coll. Hall of Fame for Great Americans; Hon. LL.D. (Toledo, Louisville and Millikin, Miami, Rhode Island Univs., Knox Coll., Roosevelt, Notre Dame, Butler), Hon. HH.D. (Wayne), Hon. Litt.D. (Albion Coll., Eastern Michigan), Hon. L.H.D. (New York Univ., Rockford, Pittsburgh, Monmouth, DePaul, Lincoln), D.Sc.Ed. (Univ. of Akron), Hon. Ped.D. (Bradley Univ.); Trustee Carnegie Foundation for the Advancement of Teaching 60-, Cttee. on Educational Television, Carnegie Corpn. 65-, Inst. Int. Educ. 65-68, Carnegie Comm. on Future Structure and Financing of Higher Educ.
364 Administration Building, Urbana, Ill. 61801, U.S.A.
Telephone: 333-3070.

Hensel, Witold, PH.D., SC.D.; Polish archæologist; b. 17; ed. Poznań Univ.
Lecturer and Adjunct, Poznań Univ. 46-50, Prof. 51-56, Dean History Faculty 51-53; Prof. Warsaw Univ. 54-; Dir. Polish Acad. of Sciences Inst. for History of Material Culture 54-; has led excavations at Gniezno, Klecko, Ostrów Tumski of Poznań and Kruszwica (near Inowroclaw), Stårmen, Bulgaria and in St.-Jean-Le-Froid, Condorcet and Montaigut, France; mem. Council Int. Cong. of Prehistoric Sciences 56 and Istituto Italiano di Preistoria e Protostoria 61; Pres. Int. Cttee of Research for Origin of Towns 62, Int. Congress Slavonic Archaeology 65-67; Corresp. mem. Polish Acad. Sciences 65; State Prize 55, 66.
Publs. *Studia nad osadnictwem Wielkopolski wczesno-historycznej* (Studies of Settlement in Wielkopolska in the Early Historical Period) Vols. I-IV 48-59, *Słowian-szczyzna wczesnośredniowieczna—Zarys kultury material-nej* (Early Medieval Slav Culture—An outline of Material Culture) 52, 56, 65, *Sztuka społeczeństw paleolitycznych* (The Art of Palaeolithic Societies) 57, *Poznań w zaraniu dziejów* (Poznań in Proto-historic Times) 58, *Najdawniejsze stolice Polski* (Poland's Ancient Capitals) 60, *The Beginnings of the Polish State* 60, *Poland a Thousand Years Ago* 60, 64, 67, *Archeologia o początkach miast słowiańskich* (Origins of Slovene Towns in Light of Archaeology) 63; *Méthodes et perspectives de recherches sur les centres ruraux et urbains chez les Slaves* 63, *Die Slawen im Frühen Mittelalter* 65, *Naissance de la Pologne* 66, *Anfänge der Städte bei den Ost-und Westslawen* 67; Editor *Slavia Antiqua, Archaeo-*

logia Polona, Archaeologia urbium, Swiatowit and *Polskie Badania Archeologiczne* (Polish Archaeological Researches).
Marszalkowska 84/92, Warsaw, Poland.

Henshaw, Kenneth Ralph, M.A.; British oil company exec.; b. 1 Nov. 1918; ed. King's School, Canterbury and Trinity Coll., Oxford.
Senior Vice-Pres. Sinclair and BP Explorations Inc. 59-63; Regional Man. Exploration Dept., British Petroleum Co. Ltd. 63-65; Man. Dir. Kuwait Oil Co. Ltd. 66-; Dir. of Middle East Navigational Aids Service.
Burgan House, 105 Wigmore Street, London, W.1, England.

Henty, Hon. Sir Norman Henry Denham, K.B.E.; Australian (British) merchant and politician; b. 13 Oct. 1903; ed. Launceston C. of E. Grammar School.
Mem staff of T. Norman Henty Pty. Ltd. 17, Gen. Man. 37-50, Chair. of Dirs. 51; Mayor of Launceston 48-49; Senator representing Tasmania 49-; mem. Parliamentary Standing Cttee. on Public Works 51-56; Minister of State for Customs and Excise 56-64; Minister for Civil Aviation 64-66, of Supply, and Leader in Senate 66-; J.P. Tasmania; Liberal.
Office: Ministry of Supply, Canberra, A.C.T.; Home: 30 Penquite Road, Launceston, Tasmania, Australia.
Telephone: 23031.

Henze, Hans Werner; German composer and conductor; b. 1 July 1926; ed. Staatsmusikschule, Brunswick, Kirchenmusikalisches Institut, Heidelberg.
Musical Director Heinz Hilpert's Deutsches Theater in Constance 48; Artistic Dir. Ballet of the Hessian State Theatre in Wiesbaden 50; living in Italy as an independent artist since 53; Prof. of Composition, Mozarteum, Salzburg 61-; Robert Schumann Prize 52, North-Rhine-Westphalia Art Prize 56, Prix d'Italia 54, Sibelius Gold Medal, Harriet Cohen Awards, London 56, Music Critics Prize, Buenos Aires 58, Kunstpreis, Berlin, Niedersächsischer Kunstpreis 62.
Composition: Operas: *Das Wundertheater, Boulevard Solitude, König Hirsch, Der Prinz von Homburg, Elegy for Young Lovers* 61, *Der Junge Lord* 64, *Die Bassariden* 65; Radio Operas: *Ein Landarzt, Das Ende einer Welt*; Ballets: *Jack Pudding, Tancred und Cantylene, Variationen, Labyrinth, The Idiot, Apoll und Hyazinth, Ondine*; Oratorio: *Novae de Infinito Laudes* 62; Cantatas: *Being Beauteous* 63, *Ariosi* 63, *Cantata della Fiaba Estrema* 63; Choral works: *Chor-fantasie* 64, *Musen Siziliens* 66; Oratorio: *Medusa* 68; five Symphonies, Violin and Piano and Violoncello Concertos, Double Concerto for Oboe, Harp and Strings, two String Quartets, Wind Quintet, *Kammermusik 1958* (tenor and ensemble); film music for *Muriel*, etc.
La Leprara, Marino, Rome, Italy.

Hepburn, Audrey; American actress; b. 4 May 1929; ed. Arnhem Conservatoire.
Studied dancing in Amsterdam and London; ballet appearances in London; played in the British films *Laughter in Paradise, The Lavender Hill Mob, Young Wives' Tale*, etc., and in American films *Roman Holiday, Sabrina Fair, War and Peace, Funny Face, Love in the Afternoon, The Nun's Story, Green Mansions, Breakfast at Tiffany's, Paris when it Sizzles, The Children's Hour, Charade, My Fair Lady, How to Steal a Million Dollars and Live Happily Ever After, Two for the Road, Wait Until Dark*; stage appearances in *Gigi* and *Ondine*; Acad. award for *Roman Holiday*.
c/o Kurt Frings, 242 North Canon Drive, Beverly Hills, Calif., U.S.A.

Hepburn, Katharine; American actress; b. 9 Nov. 1909.
Plays in which she has appeared include *The Lake, Philadelphia Story, Without Love, As You Like It, The Millionairess, The Rainmaker, Taming of the Shrew, Measure for Measure, Antony and Cleopatra,* etc.;

films include *Morning Glory, Little Women, Quality Street, Dragon Seed, Pat and Mike, Adam's Rib, Philadelphia Story, Summertime, The Rainmaker, Suddenly Last Summer, Long Day's Journey into Night, Woman of the Year, African Queen, Guess Who's Coming to Dinner*; Gold Medal Venice 34, N.Y. Critics' Award 40 and 59; Acad. Awards for *Morning Glory, Guess Who's Coming to Dinner*.
201 Bloomfield Avenue, West Hartford, Conn., U.S.A.

Hepworth, Dame Barbara, D.B.E.; British sculptor; b. 10 Jan. 1903; ed. Leeds School of Art, Royal Coll. of Art, London.
First exhbn. of sculpture 28; exhibited Lefevre Gallery, London 31-54; main retrospective exhbns.: 25th Biennale, Venice 50, Whitechapel Art Gallery, London 54 and 62, Tate Gallery, London 68; touring exhbns. U.S.A. and Canada 55-56, Fifth São Paulo Bienal 59; commissioned by UN to make abstract bronze (21 ft. high) in memory of Dag Hammarskjöld to stand outside UN Secretariat, N.Y. 63; now exhibits at Gimpel Fils, London, Marlborough Fine Art Ltd. London and N.Y. and Gimpel-Hanover Gallery, Zürich; has also exhibited in France, Italy, Finland, Norway, Netherlands, Belgium, Sweden, Denmark, Canada and U.S.A.; sculpture in the Tate Gallery and Victoria and Albert Museum, London, and in many other museums in U.K., Museum of Modern Art, New York, The Walker Art Center, U.S.A., Detroit Museum of Art, U.S.A., Rijksmuseum Kroller-Müller, Netherlands, the Nat. Galleries of Canada and Australia, Nebraska Museum of Art, Museum Boymans-van Beuningen, Rotterdam, Nat. Gallery of New Zealand, Middleheim Park, Antwerp, Museo de Arte Moderna de São Paulo, Brazil, Museum of Fine Art, Valparaiso, Chile, Gemeente-museum den Haag, Netherlands, Albright Art Gallery, Buffalo U.S.A., Smith Coll. Museum, Northampton, Mass. U.S.A., Yale Univ. Museum, Steinberg Hall, Washington Univ., St. Louis, Missouri, U.S.A.; Int. Grand 1st Prize São Paulo Bienial 59; Hon. D.Litt., Birmingham, Leeds, Oxford and Exeter; Foreign Minister's Award, 7th Biennale, Tokyo.
Trewyn Studio, St. Ives, Cornwall, England.
Telephone: St. Ives 6226.

Herbert, Sir Alan Patrick, Kt., M.A.; British author, journalist, barrister-at-law and politician; b. 24 Sept. 1890; ed. Winchester and New Coll., Oxford.
Called to the Bar (Inner Temple) 18; contributor to *Punch* 10- and mem. staff 24-; served with Royal Naval Div. (Hawke Battalion) 14-17, Gallipoli, France; Independent M.P. for Oxford Univ. 35-50; secured passage his Matrimonial Causes Bill 37; Petty Officer, Royal Naval Auxiliary Patrol 39-45; Thames Conservator 40; Trustee, National Maritime Museum 47; Pres. Soc. of Authors 67; Hon. D.C.L. (Oxford Univ.). Publs. *The Secret Battle, Light Articles Only, Tinker, Tailor . . . , The Old Flame, The Water Gipsies, Holy Deadlock* (novels), *La Vie Parisienne, Helen, Tantivy Towers* and *Derby Day* (opera libretti), *Plain Jane* (verse), *Siren Song, The Trials of Topsy, Misleading Cases, Mr. Pewter Sees It Through, Let Us Be Glum, Bring Back the Bells, Well Anyhow* (humorous essays), *Home and Beauty* (musical comedy), *General Cargo, Less Nonsense!, What a Word!, The Point of Parliament, Topsy Turvy, Mr. Gay's London, Big Ben, Bless the Bride* (opera libretto), *Tough at the Top, Why Waterloo?* 52, *Pools Pilot* 53, *The Right to Marry* 54, *No Fine on Fun* 57, *Made for Man* 58 (play: *Better Dead* 62), *Look Back and Laugh* 60, *Silver Stream* 62, *Bardot, M.P.?* 64, *Watch this Space* 64, *Wigs at Work* 66, *The Thames* 66, *Sundials Old and New* 67, *The Singing Swan* 68.
12 Hammersmith Terrace, London, W.6, England.

Herbert, Jean Jules M. E.; French surgeon; b. 16 July 1905; ed. Lycée de Rennes and Univ. de Paris à la Sorbonne.

Head of clinic, Faculty of Medicine, Paris; Surgeon, Hospital Aix-les-Bains 36-; Chief Surgeon of hospitals Aix-les-Bains; founder surgical centre for osteo-articular surgery and rheumatology; Pres. Centre de Recherches du Rhumatisme; founder of the first French bone bank 48; Editor-in-Chief *Rhumatologie*; mem. Acad. of Surgery, and Int. Soc. of Surgery; Pres. French Soc. of Orthopaedic Surgery and Traumatology; mem. numerous foreign socs. including Royal Soc. London; Officier Légion d'Honneur, Croix de Guerre, Officier de la Santé publique.
Publ. *Chirurgie du rhumatisme*.
11 boulevard de la Roche du Roi, 73 Aix-les-Bains, Savoie, France.
Telephone: 35-07-01.

Herbert, Zbigniew; Polish poet, essayist and playwright; b. 19 Oct. 1924; ed. Cracow, Toruń and Warsaw Univs.
Prize from Polish Inst of Sciences and Arts in America; Lenau Int. Prize for European Literature, Vienna 65.
Publs. Poetry includes: *A String of Light* 56, *Hermes, The Dog and the Star* 57, *The Study of an Object* 61; radio plays and drama include: *The Other Room, The Philosophers' Den, Reconstruction of a Poet, Lalek*; essays: *A Barbarian in the Garden* 63.
Świerczewskiego 95/99 m. 108, Warsaw, Poland.

Herbison, Rt. Hon. Margaret, P.C., M.P.; British politician; b. 11 March 1907; ed. Dykehead Public School, Shotts, Bellshill Acad. and Glasgow Univ.
Former schoolteacher, Glasgow; M.P. 45-; Joint Parl. Under-Sec. of State, Scottish Office 50-51; Minister of Social Security 64-67; Chair. Labour Party 57.
House of Commons, London, S.W.1, England; Home: 61 Shottskirk Road, Shotts, Lanarkshire, Scotland.
Telephone: Shotts 2159.

Herbst, Axel, LL.D.; German diplomatist and European Economic Community official; b. 18; ed. Univs. of Berlin, Cologne and Münster, Acad. of Int. Law, The Hague, and Law Society's School of Law, London.
German Foreign Service 51, German Embassy, Washington; Head, North American Desk, Fed. Ministry of Foreign Affairs 57-60; Dep. Exec. Sec. Comm. of the European Economic Community (E.E.C.) 60-63, Dir.-Gen., External Relations 63-.
European Economic Community Commission, 24 avenue de la Joyeuse Entrée, Brussels 4, Belgium.
Telephone: Brussels 35-00-40.

Herdal, Harald; Danish author; b. 1900; ed. primary schools.
Publs. *Nyt Sind* 29, *Eros og Døden* 31, *Tirsdag* 32, *Bisser* 33, *Nøgne Digte* 33, *Man skal jo leve* 34, *En lidt almindelig Historie* 34, *Løg* 35, *Den første Verden* 36, *Der er noget ivejen* 36, *Mennesket* 37, *Mens vi blir voxne* 37, *En Egn af Landet* 39, *Digte gennem ti Aar* 40, *Blomstrende Tjørne* 41, *Tusmørke* 43, *Nye Digte* 44, *Barndom, Erindringer I* 44, *De unge Aar, Erindringer II* 45, *Læreaar, Erindringer III* 46, *Digte i Vinteren* 46, *Digte 1929-1949, Uhuelige Menneske* 49, *I berøring med livet* 50, *Drømmeren* 51, *Skyede Sommerdage* 52, *Guldspurven og Sølvfuglen* 53, *Jammersminde* 53, *Rast undervejs* 54, *Elise* 55, *Dagens går* 55, *Grevinde Danner* 56, *Det største* 57, *The Tin Boxes* 58; biography: *Danish Authors* 52, *Hegnets Nattergal* 60, *Moderne dansk for udlaendige* 63, *Den Danske Sommer* 63, *Traelene i Nordon* 64, *Bisser* 64.
Rungstedvej 9D, Rungsted, Denmark.

Hereil, Georges Jules Bernard Victor, LL.D.; French aviation executive; b. 28 Aug. 1909; ed. Paris Law Faculty.
Honorary Liquidator Seine Commercial Court; Pres. and Dir.-Gen. SNCASE 46-57; following merger of SNCASE and SNCASO Pres. and Dir.-Gen. Sud-Aviation 57-62, Hon. Chair. 62-; Pres. and Dir.-Gen.

Papeteries de la Chapelle, Hon. Chair. 63; Hon. Pres. Union Syndicale des Industries Aéronautiques; Founder-Pres. Asscn. Int. des Constructeurs de Matériel Aéronautiques; Pres. Lehman Bros. Int., Hon. Chair. 63; Chair. Gen. Man. Automobiles SIMCA; Vice-Pres. Chrysler Int. S.A., Vice-Pres. and mem. Board of Dirs., Chrysler Corpn.; Dir. Barreiros Diesel (Madrid); Dir. Rootes, England; Commdr. Légion d'Honneur, Médaille de l'Aéronautique, etc., Italian, Finnish, Swedish, Belgian, Dutch and German orders.
Home: 65 avenue de Ségur, Paris 7e; Office: 136 avenue des Champs-Elysées, Paris 8e, France.

Herfelt, Jens; Danish judge; b. 16 Jan. 1894; ed. Univ. of Copenhagen.
Official in Ministry of Justice 22-45, Chief of Police Section 39-45; Judge of Court of Appeal of Eastern Denmark 45-46; Custodian of Enemy Property 46-48 and 53-60; Commr. of Police in Copenhagen 48-51; Judge of Supreme Court 51-64; Vice-Pres. Labour Court 53, Pres. 61-64; Grand Cross Order of Dannebrog (Denmark); Commdr. 1st Class of Order of Vasa (Sweden), and of Order of St. Olav (Norway).
Trondhjemsgade 6, Copenhagen, Denmark.
Telephone: TRIA 8600.

Hériat, Philippe (*pseudonym* of Raymond-Gérard Payelle); French writer; b. 15 Sept. 1898; ed. Lakanal and Louis-le-Grand Lycées.
Served French Army 16-19, 39-40; began career as film and stage actor; won Prix Théophraste-Renaudot for novel *L'Innocent* 31; French Technical Adviser (film) Hollywood 37; won Prix Goncourt for novel *Les Enfants Gâtés* 39, and Grand Prix du Roman de l'Académie Française for *Famille Boussardel* 46; drama critic for *La Bataille* 45-47; elected mem. Académie Goncourt January 49; Commdr. Légion d'Honneur.
Other publs. *La Main Tendue* 33, *L'Araignée du Matin*, and *Départ du Valdivia* 34, *La Foire aux Garçons* 34, *Miroirs* 36, *La Bruyère du Cap* 43, *Le Secret de Mayerling* 49, *Retour sur mes Pas*, *Les Grilles d'Or* 59 (novels); *L'Immaculée, Les noces de Deuil, Les Joies de la Famille* 60 (plays); *Piège de lumière, Conte Cruel* (ballets); *Les Hauts de Hurlevent* (opera).
87 avenue de Villiers, Paris 17e, France.

Hering, Erich Martin, DR. PHIL.; German entomologist; b. 10 Nov. 1893; ed. Univs. of Königsberg (now Kaliningrad) and Berlin.
Asst. Zoological Museum, Univ. of Berlin 21-26, Curator of Lepidoptera 26-32, Curator and Prof. 32-57, Emeritus 57-; mem. Exec. Cttee. Int. Congress of Entomology 39; mem. Entomology Section, Int. Union of Biological Sciences 50; Fellow World Acad. of Arts and Science; hon. mem. Int. Congress of Entomology 60, and several foreign entomological socs.; several awards.
Publs. *Biologie der Schmetterlinge* 26, *Oekologie der blattminierenden Insektenlarven* 26, *Die Blattminen Mittel-und Nordeuropas* 35-37, *Biology of the Leaf Miners* 51, *Bestimmungstabellen der Blattminen von Europa* (3 vols.) 57, etc.
Reichensteiner Weg 21, Berlin-Dahlem, Germany.

Herlitz, Nils, DR.PHIL., DR.JUR. h.c.; Swedish jurist; b. 7 Aug. 1888; ed. Uppsala Univ.
Prof. of Public Law Stockholm Univ. 27-55; lectured American Univs. 38; Editor *Nordisk Tidskrift* 21-46, *Förvaltningsrättslig Tidskrift* 38-55; Senator 39-55; Pres. Nordic Council 55; Conservative.
Publs. (over 200) include: *Svensk stadsförvaltning på 1830-talet* 24, *Grunddragen av svenska statsskickets historia* 28, *Om lagstiftning* 30, *Svensk självstyrelse* 33, *Riksdagens finansmakt* 34, *Föreläsningar i förvaltningsrätt* 37-49, *Sweden, A Modern Democracy* 39, *Svensk frihet* 43, *Förvaltningsrättsliga grunddrag* 43, *Förvaltningsförfarandet* 46, *Svenskt författningsliv* 47, *Svenska*

statsrättens grunder 48, *Nordisk offentlig rätt* 58-63, *Swedish Administrative Law* 59, *Tidsbilder* 65.
Eskadervägen 16, Näsbypark, Sweden.
Telephone: Stockholm 7563248.

Hermann, Grover Martin; American industrialist; b. 21 July 1890; ed. public schools at Callicoon, N.Y.
Founder, American Asphalt Paint Co., Chicago 13, Pres., Dir. 13-40, name changed to American-Marietta Co. 40, Pres., Dir. 40-50, Chair. Board of Dirs. 50-61, Hon. Chair. of Board and Dir. 61-, now Martin-Marietta Corpn.; Dir. Consolidated Freightways, Inc., Stainless Steel Products, Inc., Pacific Coast Holdings, Inc., American Nat. Bank and Trust Co. of Chicago, 140 East Walton Place, Chicago, Ill., U.S.A.

Hermann, Henri Xavier, Dr. of Medicine; French university professor; b. 19 Dec. 1892; ed. Univ. of Nancy.
Prof. of Physiology, Univ. of Lyon 33-; Dir. of Physiology Laboratory, Ecole pratique des Hautes Etudes Lyon 42-; Dean Faculty of Medicine and Pharmacy, Univ. of Lyon 43-63; Pres. of Administrative Council of Ecole d'Infirmières (Rockefeller Foundation), Lyon 46-63; Pres. Asscn. of French Physiologists 46; correspondant de l'Institut (Académie des Sciences); mem. Académie nationale de médecine; Pres. Acad. of Lyon 61; Pres. Physiological Section 50, and of Biology Group 57, Nat. Centre of Scientific Research; holder of Croix de Guerre; Commdr. de la Légion d'Honneur.
Publs. *La Circulation du Sang* 42, *Les Glandes Endocrines* 43, *Les phéochromocytons* 63, *Précis de Physiologie* 63.
15 avenue Félix Faure, Lyon 7e (69), France.
Telephone: 72-32-97.

Hernández Terán, Ing. José; Mexican engineer; b. 1921; ed. Escuela Nacional de Ingeniería, Univ. Nacional Autónoma de México.
Engineer with Nat. Irrigation Comm. 44; mem. Exec. Cttee. Rio Fuerte Comm. 55-64; Gen. Man. Naucalpan-Zaragoza-Tlanepantla project; later, Technical Adviser to Fed. Electricity Comm. on "27 de Septiembre" hydro-electric plant 58-60, to Secr. of Public Works on Chihuahua-Pacific Railway 60; Arbiter on El Aguila Co. controversy with El Salvador Govt. 61; Founder-mem. Coplan (firm of heavy construction technical advisers) 62; now Sec. for Hydraulic Resources, Fed. Govt.
Secretaría de Recursos Hidraulicos, Mexico City, Mexico.

Hernelius, (John) Allan, LL.B.; Swedish journalist; b. 19 March 1911; ed. Stockholm Univ.
Sec. Swedish Asscn. of Retail Grocers 39, Man. Dir. 41; Vice-Man. Dir. Swedish Retail Fed. 43; Man. Dir. Swedish Newspaper Publishers' Asscn. 45; Asst. Chief Editor *Svenska Dagbladet* 49, Chief Editor 55-; Adviser, U.N. Conf., Geneva 48; mem. Psychological Defence Cttee. 49; Pres. Swedish Cttee., Int. Press Inst. 51-; mem. of Board, Royal Defence Coll. 52-, Swedish Radio and Television 53-, Stockholm Stock Exchange, *Svenska Dagbladet* 56-; Chair. Stockholm Section, Conservative Party 53-55; Chair. Int. Press Inst. Exec. Board 62-64; mem. of Parl. First Chamber 62-.
Home: Styrmansgatan 1, Stockholm Ö; Office: *Svenska Dagbladet*, Rålambsvägen 7, Box 594, Stockholm, Sweden.
Telephone: 62-07-05 (Home), 22-50-00 (Office).

Heron, Patrick; British painter; b. 30 Jan. 1920; ed. Slade School, London.
Art Critic *New English Weekly* 45-47, *New Statesman and Nation* 47-50; London corresp. *Arts* New York 55, resigned and ceased writing 58, teacher of painting Central School of Arts and Crafts, London 53-55; thirty one-man exhbns. in London, New York, Zürich, Edinburgh, Oslo, Rio de Janeiro, Buenos Aires,

Santiago, Lima, Caracas and Dublin, retrospective exhbns. Wakefield City Art Gallery 52, Demarco Gallery Edinburgh 67, Museum of Modern Art, Oxford 68; represented at São Paulo Bienal 54, 65, and numerous group exhbns. in Europe and America, many organized by British Council; paintings in public galleries including Tate Gallery, British Museum, Victoria and Albert Museum, Arts Council, British Council, Nat. Portrait Gallery, London; Nat. Museum of Wales, Cardiff; Montreal Museum of Fine Art, Toronto Art Gallery; Vancouver Art Gallery; Nat. Gallery of W. Australia, Perth; Brooklyn Museum, N.Y.; Boymans Museum, Rotterdam; etc.; Silver Medal São Paulo Bienal 65.

Publ. *The Changing Forms of Art* 55.

Eagle's Nest, Zennor, near St. Ives, Cornwall; and 12A Edith Mansions, Edith Grove, London, S.W.10, England.

Telephone: Zennor 21.

Héron de Villefosse, René; French archivist; b. 17 May 1903; ed. Ecole des Chartes.

On staff of the Petit Palais, Paris 30; Asst. Keeper 36-42; Keeper 42-47; Keeper-in-chief of Musées de la Ville de Paris and of the Musée de l'Ile de France (Château de Sceaux) Oct. 57-; Prof. Ecole du Louvre; Chevalier Légion d'Honneur, Chevalier des Arts et des Lettres and many other decorations.

Publs. *Paris vivant* 32, *Construction de Paris* 38, *Singularités de Paris* 41, *Bourgeois de Paris* 42, *Prés et Bois Parisiens* 43, *Histoire de Paris* 44, *Trésors méconnus de Paris* 46, *Aux Belles de Paris* 47, *Charles le Sage* 47, *Voyage au temps de la douceur de vivre* 47, *La Rivière Enchantée* 50, *Dames de Paris* 51, *Couronnes de Paris* 52, *A travers les Vignes* 53, *Histoire et Géographie gourmandes de Paris* 56, *Histoire et Géographie galantes de Paris* 58, *Portes maritimes de l'Europe* 61, *La Seine*, *L'Ile de France* 65.

20 avenue Georges V, Paris 8e, France.

Herpin, Guy Louis Auguste; French journalist and government administrator; b. 20 April 1899.

Worked on daily newspapers between demobilisation in 21 and mobilisation in 39; joined Free French Forces Mar. 41; carried out several special missions in France; arrested by Gestapo and imprisoned at Buchenwald and Belsen Mar. 44-April 45; joined Gen. de Gaulle's staff as chief of parliamentary services Sept. 45-Jan. 46; Insp.-Gen. of Tourism Feb. 46-; Commandeur Légion d'Honneur, Croix de Guerre, Resistance Medal, etc.

Laversine par Creil, Oise, France.

Herrera Lane, Felipe; Chilean banker; b. 17 June 1922; ed. Colegio Alemán de Santiago, Escuela Militar, Univs. of Chile and London.

Legal Dept., Central Bank of Chile 43-47; Attorney for Central Bank of Chile, and private law practice 47-52; Prof. of Econs., Schools of Law and Sociology, Univ. of Chile 47-58; Under-Sec. for Economy and Commerce 52, Minister of Finance 53; Gen. Man. Central Bank of Chile 53-58; Alt. Gov. Int. Bank for Reconstruction and Development, Int. Monetary Fund 53-58, Exec. Dir. 58-60; Pres. Inter-American Devt. Bank 60-; numerous awards and hon. degrees.

Publs. *El Banco Central de Chile* 45, *Política Económica* 50, *Los Fundamentos de la Política Fiscal* 51, *Manual de Política Económica* 52, *Elementos de Economía Monetaria* 55, *o Desarrollo Económico o Estabilidad Monetaria?* 58, *América Latina Integrada* 64.

Inter-American Development Bank, 808 17th Street, N.W., Washington, D.C. 20577; and 3041 Normanstone Terrace, N.W., Washington, D.C., U.S.A.

Herrera y Oria, H.E. Cardinal Angel; Spanish ecclesiastic; b. 86.

Ordained priest 40; Suffragan Bishop of Malaga 47-66; created Cardinal 65; mem. Comm. de Fidelium Aposto-lorum, de Scriptis Prelo Edendis et de Spectaculis Moderandis, Ecumenical Council.

Calle Limite, 3 Ciudad Universitaria, Madrid, Spain.

Telephone: 253-40-07; also 233-52-00.

Herridge, Geoffrey Howard, C.M.G.; British oil executive; b. 22 Feb. 1904; ed. Crypt School, Gloucester and St. John's Coll., Cambridge.

Joined Turkish Petroleum Co. Ltd. (later Iraq Petroleum Co. Ltd.) Iraq 26; served in Iraq, Jordan, Palestine 26-47; Gen. Man. in Middle East for Iraq Petroleum Co. and Assoc. Cos. 47-51, Exec. Dir. 53-57, Man. Dir. 57-63, Deputy Chair. 63-65, Chair. 65-; mem. London Cttee., Ottoman Bank 64-; Chair. Petroleum Industry Training Board 67-.

Office: Iraq Petroleum Co. Ltd., 33 Cavendish Square, London, W.1; Home: 22 Albert Hall Mansions, Kensington Gore, London, S.W.7, England.

Telephone: 01-589-2830 (Home).

Herring, Lt.-Gen. the Hon. Sir Edmund Francis, K.C.M.G., K.B.E., D.S.O., M.C., E.D., Q.C., M.A.; Australian officer and lawyer; b. 2 Sept. 1892; ed. Melbourne Grammar School, Trinity Coll., Melbourne, and New Coll., Oxford.

Served first World War 14-19, King Edward's Horse and R.F.A.; called to Bar, Inner Temple 20; admitted Barrister and Solicitor, Melbourne 21; practised as Barrister 21-39; K.C. 36; served A.I.F. 39-44; commanded 6th Div. 41-42; Northern Territory Force 42; New Guinea Force 42-43; 1 Australian Corps 42-44; C.B.E. 41; Greek M.C. (Class 'A') 41; D.S.C. (American) 43; K.B.E. 43; Lieut.-Governor of Victoria 45-; Chief Justice Supreme Court of Victoria 44-64; Chancellor, Diocese of Melbourne 41-; Hon. Fellow New Coll. Oxford; Pres. Boy Scout Asscn. of Victoria 45-, Australian Boy Scouts' Asscn. 59-, Toc H. Australia 47-; Dir.-Gen. Recruiting 50-51; Leader Australia Contingent to Coronation 53; Chair. Australian War Memorial, Canberra 59-; Hon. Bencher Inner Temple 63; Hon. D.C.L. (Oxford); Knight of St. John.

226 Walsh St., South Yarra, Victoria 3141, Australia.

Telephone: Melbourne 261000.

Herron, Hon. Sir Leslie James, K.B.E., C.M.G., Q.C., LL.B., K.ST.J.; Australian judge; b. 22 May 1902; ed, Sydney Grammar School and Sydney Univ.

Called to Bar 25; practised in the Common Law Courts; Acting District Court Judge 39; Supreme Court Judge 41; Chief Justice of New South Wales 62-; Chair. State Govt. Cttee. of Law Reform; mem. of Royal Comm. into Housing Comm. Contracts 58; Pres. N.S.W. and Australian Rugby Union 41-53, Australian Golf Club 44-, St. John Ambulance Asscn.; Trustee Australian Museum.

Supreme Court, Sydney; and "Mevagissey", 6 Mannerim Place, Castle Cove, N.S.W., Australia.

Hersey, John Richard, B.A.; American writer; b. 17 June 1914; ed. Yale Univ. and Clare Coll., Cambridge.

Sec. to Sinclair Lewis 37; writer, corresp. and editor *Time* and *Life* 37-45; corresp. *New Yorker* 45-46; editor and Dir. *'47 Magazine* 47; Vice-Pres. Authors' League of America 48-55; Master, Pierson Coll., Yale Univ. 65-; Hon. M.A. (Yale), LL.D. (Washington, Jefferson), D.H.Litt. (Dropsie Coll., New School for Social Research, Wesleyan); Pulitzer Prize for fiction 45; elected to American Acad. of Arts and Letters 53-; Hon. Fellow, Clare Coll., Cambridge.

Publs. *Men on Bataan* 42, *Into the Valley* 43, *A Bell for Adano* 44, *Hiroshima* 46, *The Wall* 50, *The Marmot Drive* 53, *A Single Pebble* 56, *The War Lover* 59, *The Child Buyer* 60, *Here to Stay* 62, *White Lotus* 65, *Too Far to Walk* 66, *Under the Eye of the Storm* 67.

231 Park Street, New Haven, Conn., U.S.A.

Hershey, Lt.-Gen. Lewis Blaine; American army officer and government official; b. 12 Sept. 1893; ed. Univs. of Indiana and Hawaii and Command and General Staff School, Fort Leavenworth, and Army War Coll., Washington, D.C.
Regular Army Service 11-36; Sec. and Exec. Officer, Jt. Army-Navy Selective Service Cttee. 36; Dir. of Selective System 41-; numerous medals.
Selective Service System, 1724 "F" Street, N.W., Washington D.C., U.S.A.

Hertz, Gustav, DR.PHIL.; German physicist; b. 22 July 1887; ed. Univs. Göttingen, Munich and Berlin.
Asst., Philips Laboratory in Eindhoven before 25; **Prof. Experimental Physics, Univ. of Halle 25-27,** Technische Hochschule, Berlin-Charlottenburg 28-35; Dir. Siemens Research Laboratory 35-45; scientific **work in U.S.S.R. 45-54; Prof. of Physics, Univ. of** Leipzig 55-60; mem. German Acad. of Sciences; hon. mem. Hungarian Acad. of Sciences; corresp. mem. Göttingen Acad. of Sciences; foreign mem. U.S.S.R. Acad. of Sciences; mem. Czechoslovak Acad. of Sciences; Nobel Prize for Physics (jointly with J. Franck) 26, Russian State Prize 51, Planck Medal.
Publs. Papers on *Quantative Exchange of Energy between Electrons and Atoms* (with J. Franck) 14, *Isotope Separation* 33.
Lienhardweg 47, 117 Berlin-Köpenick, Germany.

Hertzog, Albert, B.A., B.C.L., LL.D.; South African advocate and politician; b. 14 July 1899; ed. Stellenbosch, Amsterdam, Oxford and Leyden Univs.
Member of the Council of the Univ. of S. Africa 36-39; mem. Pretoria City Council 44-51; elected M.P. for Ermelo 48, 53, 58, 61 and 66; foundation mem. of Afrikaanse Pers Beperk and Volkskas Beperk; Minister of Posts and Telegraphs 58-68, and Minister of Health 58-.
Publ. *Saaklike Reg en Eiendom.*
10 Edward Street, Waterkloof, Pretoria, South Africa.

Hertzsprung, Ejnar; Danish astronomer; b. 8 Oct. 1873; ed. in St. Petersburg and Leipzig.
Lecturer in Astronomy, Univ. of Göttingen 09, later Observer, Astrophysical Observatory, Potsdam; Asst. Dir. Leiden Observatory 19, Dir. 45; Prof. Univ. of Leiden 20-44; mem. Danish Acad. of Sciences, Netherlands Acad. of Sciences, Royal Astronomical Soc. (U.K.); Corresp. mem. Acad. des Sciences, Paris, Belgian Acad.; Dr. h.c. (Utrecht, Copenhagen and Paris).
Villavej 6, Tølløse, Denmark.

Hervé-Bazin, Jean-Pierre Marie, L. ès L. (**Hervé Bazin**)**;** French writer; b. 17 April 1911; ed. Faculté des Lettres de Paris.
Critic for Newspaper *L'Information*; on staff of Editions Grasset; Vice-Pres., Asscn. of Writers; mem. Acad. Goncourt 58-, PEN Club, Soc. des Gens de Lettres; Chevalier des Arts et des Lettres, des Palmes Académiques; numerous prizes.
Publs. Poetry: *Jours* 47, *A la Poursuite d'Iris* 48, *Humeurs* 53; Novels: *Vipère au Poing* 48, *La Tête contre les Murs* 49, *La Mort du Petit Cheval* 50, *Le Bureau des Mariages* 51, *Lève-toi et Marche* 52, *L'Huile sur le Feu* 54, *Qui j'ose aimer* 56, *La Fin des Asiles* 59, *Au Nom du Fils* 60, *Chapeau bas* 63, *Plumons l'oiseau* 66, *Le Matrimoine* 67.
5 rue de la Prévoyance, Villemomble (Seine-Saint-Denis); and Dumaine du Preuil, Bigny Vallenay (Cher), France.

Herwarth von Bittenfeld, Hans; German diplomatist; b. 14 July 1904; ed. Univs. of Berlin, Breslau and Munich.
Entered Foreign Office 27; Attaché, Paris 30; Second Sec. and Personal Sec. to Ambassador, Moscow 31-39; mil. service 39-45; Govt. Counsellor, Dir., Bavarian State Chancellery 45-49; Ministerialdirigent and Chief of Protocol, Fed. German Govt. 50; apptd. Minister 52;

Ambassador to U.K. 55-61; State Sec., Chief of Office of Fed. Pres. 61-65; Ambassador to Italy 65-; Grand Cross 2nd Class, Order of Merit (Fed. Germany), G.C.V.O. (U.K.) and other decorations.
Embassy of the Federal Republic of Germany, Via Po 25c, 00198 Rome, Italy.
Telephone: 860341.

Herzberg, Gerhard, Dr.Ing., LL.D., D.SC.; Canadian physicist; b. 25 Dec. 1904; ed. Darmstadt Inst. of Technology and Univs. of Göttingen and Bristol.
Lecturer, Darmstadt Inst. of Technology 30-35; Research Prof. of Physics, Univ. of Saskatchewan 35-45; Prof. of Spectroscopy, Yerkes Observatory, Univ. of Chicago 45-48; Dir. of the Div. of Pure Physics, Nat. Research Council, Ottawa 49-; mem. Royal Soc. of Canada (Pres. Section III 51-52), Royal Soc. of London; Hon. Fellow Indian Acad. of Sciences; Univ. of Liège Medal 50; Henry Marshall Tory Medal (Canadian Royal Soc.) 53; Joy Kissen Mookerjee Gold Medal (Indian Asscn. for the Cultivation of Science) 57; Bakerian Lecturer, Royal Soc. 60; Hon. mem. Hungarian Acad. of Sciences 64; Frederic Ives Medal, Optical Soc. of America 64; Academician, Pontifical Acad. of Sciences 64; Hon. Foreign mem. American Acad. of Arts and Sciences 65; Pres. Royal Soc. of Canada 66-; Hon. mem. Optical Soc. of America 68; Hon. Fellow, Chemical Soc. of London 68.
Publs. *Atomic Spectra and Atomic Structure* 37, *Molecular Spectra and Molecular Structure: I. Spectra of Diatomic Molecules* 39, *II. Infra-red and Raman Spectra of Polyatomic Molecules* 45, *III. Electronic Spectra Polyatomic Molecules* 66.
Home: 190 Lakeway Drive, Ottawa 7, Ontario; and Office: Division of Pure Physics, National Research Council, Sussex Drive, Ottawa 2, Ontario, Canada.
Telephone: 746-4126 (Home); 992-2350 (Office).

Herzog, Maurice; French politician and former mountaineer; b. 15 Jan. 1919; ed. Collège Chaptal, Paris, Faculty of Science, Lyon and Faculty of Law, Paris.
Leader, French Himalayan Expedition 50; fmr. Dir. Kléber-Colombes Soc.; High Commr. for Youth and Sport 58-63, Sec. of State 63-66; mem. UN Econ. and Social Council 66-; Sec.-Gen. to High Cttee. on Youth 58, to High Cttee. on Sport 61; Officier, Légion d'Honneur.
Publs. *Annapurna premier 8000, Regards sur L'Annapurna, L'Expédition de l'Annapurna, La Montagne.*
4 rue Jean-Richepin, Paris 16e, France.

Herzog, Paul M., S.B., LL.B., M.A.; American lawyer, university professor and government officer; b. 21 Aug. 1906; ed. Harvard Univ., Univ. of Wisconsin, Harvard Law School, Columbia Law School.
Assistant to Sec. Nat. Labor Board 33-35; practised law in New York 36-37; mem. of New York State Labor Relations Board 37; Chair. New York State Labor Relations Board 42; Lieut. U.S.N.R. 44-45; Chair. Nat. Labor Relations Board 45-53, resigned; Assoc. Dean Graduate School of Public Admin., Harvard Univ. 53-57; Exec. Vice-Pres. American Arbitration Asscn. 58-, Pres. 61-63; Pres. Salzburg Seminar in American Studies 65-; mem. Cttee. of Experts on Application of Conventions ILO (Geneva) 56-68; Vice-Pres. American Soc. for Public Admin. 56-57; mem. N.Y. D.C. and U.S. Supreme Court Bars; Hon. LL.D. Hobart Coll. 59.
14 East 75th Street, New York City 21, N.Y., U.S.A.; also Schloss Leopoldskron, Salzburg, Austria.

Herzog, Raymond Harry; American business executive; b. 15 Sept. 1915; ed. Lawrence Univ.
Chemist, West Virginia Coal and Coke Co. 37-38; Science Teacher, St. Croix Falls, Wisconsin 39-41; Minnesota Mining and Manufacturing Co. 41-, Gen.

Man. Duplicating Products Div. 56-59, Divisional Vice-Pres. 59-61, Corpn. Vice-Pres. 61-63, Group Vice-Pres. 63-, mem. Board of Dirs. 65-.
Home: 23 Shady Woods Road, St. Paul, Minn. 55115; Office: 3M Center, St. Paul, Minn. 55101, U.S.A.
Telephone: 733-1240 (Office).

Hesburgh, Rev. Theodore M., S.T.D.; American university president; b. 25 May 1917; ed. Univ. of Notre Dame, Gregorian Univ., Rome, and Catholic Univ. of America.
Ordained priest of Congregation of Holy Cross 43; joined Univ. of Notre Dame 45, Head of Theology Dept. 48-49, Exec. Vice-Pres. of Univ. 49-52, Pres. 52-; mem. U.S. Comm. on Civil Rights, Nat. Comm. on Humanities, State Dept. Policy Planning Council, Carnegie Comm. on the Future Structure and Financing of Higher Educ., Comm. on the Future of Private and Independent Higher Educ. in New York State, Board of Consultants of Nat. War Coll., Adlai E. Stevenson Inst. of Int. Affairs; Perm. Rep. of Holy See to Int. Atomic Energy Agency, Vienna 57-; Pres. Int. Fed. of Catholic Univs.; Pres. Asscn. of American Colls. 61; Trustee, Rockefeller Foundation, Carnegie Foundation for Advancement of Teaching (Pres. 63-64); fmr. Dir. American Council on Educ.; Dir. Woodrow Wilson Nat. Fellowship Corpn., Nutrition Foundation and other orgs.; Fellow American Acad. of Arts and Sciences; Distinguished Service Medal, U.S. Navy; Presidential Medal of Freedom 64; 21 hon. degrees.
Publs. *Patterns for Educational Growth, God and the World of Man.*
University of Notre Dame, Notre Dame, Indiana, U.S.A.
Telephone: 219-284-6383.

Hess, Gerhard, DR. PHIL.; German university professor; b. 13 April 1907; ed. Basle, Heidelberg and Berlin Univs.
Assistant Prof. Heidelberg Univ. 41, Prof. 48, Dean, Philosophical Faculty 48-49, Rector 50-51; Pres. Rectors' Conf. 50-51; Vice-Pres. Asscn. of Univ. Profs. 51-55; Pres. Deutsche Forschungsgemeinschaft 55-64; Vice-Pres. Alexander von Humboldt-Stiftung 59-64; mem. Heidelberg Acad. of Sciences 51-; Chair. Academic Planning Board, Konstanz Univ. 64-66, Rector, Konstanz Univ. 66-.
Publs. *Alain in der Reihe der französischen Moralisten* 32, *Die französische Philosophie der Gegenwart* 33, *Pierre Gassend: der französische Späthumanismus und das Problem von Wissen und Glauben* 39, *Die Landschaft in Baudelaires "Fleurs du Mal"* 53, *Zur Entstehung der "Maximen" La Rochefoucaulds* 57, *Gesammelte Schriften* 1938-1966; trans. of Leibniz, La Bruyère, de la Fayette.
Säntisstrasse 3, Konstanz, German Federal Republic.

Hess, Walter Rudolf, D.MED.; Swiss physiologist; b. 17 March 1881; ed. elementary and grammar schools; studied medicine at various Swiss and German Univs.
Physician in Zürich, Asst. in Surgery and Ophthalmology, studies in Paris and in practice as oculist 05-12; Asst. and Reader in Physiology in Zürich and Bonn 12-17; Prof. of Physiology and Dir. of Physiological Inst., Univ. of Zürich 17-51, Emeritus 51-; awarded Swiss Marcel Benoist Prize 33, Ludwig Medal of Germany for Circulation Research 38, Nobel Prize for Medicine (with Prof. Egas Moniz) 49; Hon. mem. of Swiss Acad. of Medical Sciences 48, and of other Swiss and foreign learned societies; Dr. Phil. h.c. Univ. of Berne, Dr. Med. h.c. Univ. of Geneva, and Dr. h.c. of Science McGill Univ., Dr. Med. h.c. Freiburg i/Br. Univ.
Publs. *Die Regulierung des Blutkreislaufes* 30, *Die Regulierung der Atmung* 31, *Die Methodik der lokalisierten Reizung und Ausschaltung subkortikaler Hirnab-*

schnitte 32, *Atlas der Stammganglien und des Zwischenhirns der Katze* 37, *Das Zwischenhirn und die Regulation von Kreislauf und Atmung* 38, *Die funktionelle Organisation des vegetativen Nervensystemes* 48, *Das Zwischenhirn* 49, *Diencephalon, Autonomic and Extrapyramidal Functions* 54, *Hypothalamus and Thalamus* (Atlas) 56, *The Functional Organisations of the Diencephalon* 57, *Psychophysiology* 62; Translation, *The Biology of the Mind* 64.
Via Gabbio 6, 6612 Ascona, Switzerland.
Telephone: 093-25406.

Hess, Werner; German broadcasting official; b. 13 Oct. 1914; studies in protestant theology and drama, Giessen, Marburg, Jena and Frankfurt/Main.
Film and Television Dir., Protestant Church in Germany 45-60; Television Dir., Hessischer Rundfunk 60-62, Gen. Dir. 62-.
Bertramstrasse 8, Frankfurt am Main, German Federal Republic.

Hess Estrada, Raúl; Costa Rican economist; b. 10 July 1928; ed. Universidad de Costa Rica.
Member ECLA (UN Econ. Comm. for Latin America) Comm. for Study of Problems of Econ. Development, Santiago, Chile 54; Research Lecturer on Costa Rican Econ. Development, Universidad de Costa Rica 55-64, Prof. of Econ. Development and Contemporary Econ. Theory 56-64; Chair. Board of Dirs. Nat. Production Council 56-57; Minister of Econ. and Finance 57-58, 62-63; Exec. Dir. Inter-American Development Bank 63-64; Coordinator of Panel of Nine, Alliance for Progress 65; Gen. Man. Central Bank of Costa Rica 66-.
Banco Central de Costa Rica, Casilla W, San José, Costa Rica.

Hessellund-Jensen, Aage, D.IUR.; Danish diplomatist; b. 22 April 1911; ed. Aarhus Cathedral School and Copenhagen Univ.
Joined Danish Foreign Service 37; Lecturer in Law, Copenhagen Univ. 40-42, 46-48; Sec. Danish Legation, Stockholm 42-46, Sec. Head, Ministry of Foreign Affairs 46-49, Counsellor, Washington 49-54; attached to NATO Defence Coll., Paris 54-55; Dir. Political Dept., Ministry of Foreign Affairs 56-58, Perm. Rep. to U.N. 58-64; Ambassador to Sweden 64-; Commdr. Order of Dannebrog, Finnish Order of the White Star, Kt. Swedish Order of the Polar Star, Danish and Swedish Red Cross Medals.
Danish Embassy, Gustav Adolfs Torg 14, Stockholm C, Sweden.
Telephone: 23-18-60.

Hester, James McNaughton, B.A., M.A., D.PHIL.; American university official; b. 19 April 1924; ed. Princeton and Oxford Univs.
Japanese language officer, U.S. Marine Corps 43-47; Rhodes Scholar, Oxford Univ. 47-50; Asst. to Sec. to Rhodes Trustees, Princeton 50; duty with U.S. Marine Corps, Quantico, Va. 51-52; Graduate research, Washington 52-53; Jr. Assoc. and Asst. to Pres., Handy Associates, Inc. (Management Consultants) N.Y. 53-54; Account Supervisor, Gallup & Robinson, Inc. (Advertising Research) 54-57; Provost, Brooklyn Center, Long Island Univ. 57-60 (Vice-Pres. Long Island Univ. 58-60, mem. Bd. of Trustees 59-60); Exec. Dean of Arts and Science, Dean Graduate School of Arts and Science, Prof. of History, New York Univ. 60-61, Pres. 62-; Vice-Chair. Governing Cttee., Brooklyn Acad. of Music 58-; Dir. New York World's Fair 1964, Int. House, N.Y.C.; Trustee Brooklyn Inst. of Arts and Science; mem. Advisory Board of Coll. Pres. to Nat. Scholarship Service and Fund for Negro Students.
25 Cleveland Lane, Princeton, N.J., U.S.A.

Hetherington, Hector Alastair, M.A.; British journalist; b. 31 Oct. 1919; ed. Gresham's School, Holt, and Corpus Christi Coll., Oxford.
Served in Royal Armoured Corps 40-46; on staff *The*

Glasgow Herald 46-50; joined (*Manchester*) *Guardian* 50, Foreign Editor 53, Editor 56-.
The Guardian, 192 Gray's Inn Road, London, W.C.1, and 3 Cross Street, Manchester, England.

Hettier de Boislambert, Claude; French diplomatist; b. 26 July 1906; ed. Coll. de Normandie and Ecole des Sciences Politiques.
Joint Dir., Gen. de Gaulle's Cabinet 40-44; Chief of French Liaison Missions with Allied Forces 44-45; Gov. of Rhineland 45-47, Gov. Del.-Gen. of French Repub. for Rhineland and the Palatine 47; Deputy for La Manche 51-60; Ambassador to Senegal 60-62; Chancellor of Order of Liberation 62-; Pres. Int. Hunting Council 49-59; Grand Officier, Légion d'Honneur, Croix de Guerre, Compagnon de la Libération, etc.
36 rue Scheffer, Paris 16e, France.

Hettlage, Dr. Karl Maria; German university professor; b. 28 Nov. 1902; ed. Univs. of Cologne and Münster.
Government Official of Prussian Land 25-30; Financial Adviser, Cologne city admin. 30-31; Financial Dept., Berlin city admin. 31-38; senior bank official 38-51; Prof. of Public Law, Univ. of Mainz 51-, Hon. Prof. of Financial Sciences, Univ. of Bonn 49-; State Sec. Finance Ministry, Fed. German Govt. 58-62, 67-; mem. European Coal and Steel Community (ECSC) High Authority 62-67.
Friedrich Ebert-Strasse 83, 532 Bad Godesberg, German Federal Republic.

Hetzenauer, Franz, LL.D.; Austrian lawyer and politician; b. 25 Feb. 1911; ed. Leopold-Franzens Universität Innsbruck.
Mechanic 29-35; Provincial Sec. Tyrol Branch, Union of Christian Workers and Employees 35-38; practised law, Innsbruck 39; served in Second World War; Deputy Chair. Tyrol Branch, Fed. of Austrian Trade Unions and Fed. of Workers and Employees 55-; mem. Nationalrat 56-; State Sec. Ministry of Justice 63-66; Minister of the Interior April 66-67; People's Party.
c/o Ministry of the Interior, Vienna, Austria.

Heurtematte, Roberto Manuel; Panamanian international official; b. 19 May 1908; ed. Yale Univ.
Commercial, financial, industrial and livestock activities in Panama 31-59; alt. Gov. of Panama for Int. Monetary Fund and Int. Bank 47, Gov. for Int. Bank 51-54, for I.M.F. 51-59; Ambassador to U.S.A. and Permanent Rep. of Panama to O.A.S. 51-54; Comptroller-Gen. of Panama 54-58; Under-Sec., UN 59-62; Assoc. Man. Dir. UN Special Fund 62-65; Assoc. Administrator (Under-Sec.) UN Devt. Programme 66-.
United Nations, 1st Avenue, New York, N.Y., U.S.A.; and Box 293, Panama City, Republic of Panama.

Heusinger, Gen. Adolf Ernst; German army officer and public servant; b. 4 Aug. 1897; ed. Gymnasium in Holzminden and Helmstedt.
Commissioned 15; entered *Reichswehr* 20; posted to Gen. Staff 30; Company Commdr. 34-35, Divisional Gen. Staff 35-37; Gen. Staff Officer 37-44; arrested July 20th 44; Military Adviser of German Fed. Govt. 50; Chair. Joint Chiefs of Staff of German Armed Forces Mar. 57-61; Chair. NATO Military Cttee. in Perm. Session 61-64; retd. 64.
Publ. *Befehl im Widerstreit* (*Schicksalstunden der deutschen Armee 1923-45*) 50.
Bayenthalgürtel, Cologne, German Federal Republic.
Telephone: Cologne 38-61-76.

Heusinger, Bruno, DR.PHIL.; German lawyer; b. 2 March 1900; ed. Göttingen, Berlin Univs.
Served in World Wars I and II; articled 24; Assessor 27; County Court Judge 29; Provincial Court of Appeal Judge 30, Pres. 33; Senatspräsident, Provincial Court of Appeal 35; Pres. Provincial Court of Appeal, Bruns-

wick 48, Celle 55; Pres. Federal Supreme Court, Karlsruhe 60-; Dr. Iur. h.c.; Hon. Senator Technischen Hochschule, Karlsruhe.
Kathe Kollwitz Strasse 46, 75 Karlsruhe/Durlach, German Federal Republic.

Hevesi, Gyula; Hungarian chemical engineer; b. 1890. Foundation mem. Hungarian Communist Party; Ed. *International*; industrial man. Soviet Union 21; Head of Hungarian State Patent Office 48-51; Sec., Dept. of Technical Sciences 51-56; Sec. Acad. of Sciences 56-60, Vice-Pres. 60-, Technological Devt. Cttee.; Hon. Pres. Union of Technological and Natural Science Socs.; mem. Central Cttee. Hungarian Socialist Workers' Party; Kossuth Prize 59.
Publs. *Continuous Production in Industry* 31, *Socialist Relationships between Science and Production* 53, *An Engineer Witnessing Revolution* 59, *Socialist Production* 59.
Academy of Sciences, Budapest V., Roosevelt tér 9, Hungary.

Hewedy, Amin; United Arab Republic (Egyptian) diplomatist; b. 21; ed. Military and Staff Colls., United Arab Republic, and General Staff Coll., Fort Leavenworth, U.S.A., and Press Coll., U.A.R.
Former Army Officer; fmr. Amb. of United Arab Republic to Morocco; Amb. to Iraq 63-66, Minister of State 66-.
Publs. *Speeches in Strategy* 55, *Sun-Tso* 57.
Cairo, United Arab Republic.

Hewitt, William Alexander, A.B.; American manufacturing executive; b. 9 Aug. 1914; ed. Univ. of Calif.
With John Deere Plow Co., San Francisco 48-54, Vice-Pres. 50-54; Dir. Deere & Co., Moline, Ill. 51-, Exec. Vice-Pres. 54-55, Pres. 55-64, Chair. and Chief Exec. Officer 64-; Dir. Continental Illinois Nat. Bank & Trust Co. of Chicago; Int. Pakers Ltd. (Chicago), American Telephone & Telegraph Co., Continental Oil Co.; mem. Board of Govs. American Nat. Red Cross; mem. American Soc. of Agric. Engineers; mem. Nat. Industrial Conf. Board, and many other orgs.; Trustee Cttee. for Econ. Devt., and U.S. Council Int. Chamber of Commerce; Lieut.-Commdr. U.S.N.R. 42-46.
Home: 38th Street and Blackhawk Road, Rock Island, Ill.; Office: John Deere Road, Moline, Ill. 61265, U.S.A.

Hey, Donald Holroyde, D.SC., PH.D., M.SC., F.R.I.C., F.R.S.; British chemist; b. 12 Sept. 1904; ed. Magdalen Coll. School, Oxford and Univ. Coll., Swansea.
Lecturer in Chemistry Manchester Univ. 28-38; Lecturer in Organic Chemistry Royal Coll. of Science, London Univ. 39-41; mem. Council Chemical Soc. 40, 45 and 61-66, Hon. Sec. 46-51, Vice-Pres. 51-54; mem. Council Royal Inst. Chemistry 44-46 and 54-57; mem. Chemical Council 48-50; Dir. of Research, British Schering Research Inst. 41-45; Prof. Chemistry, King's Coll., London Univ. 45-50; Daniell Prof. of Chemistry King's Coll. 50-; Asst. Principal King's Coll., London 62-68, Fellow King's Coll., London; Pres. Section B, British Asscn. for Advancement of Science 65; Visiting Prof. Univ. of Florida 68.
King's College, Strand, London, W.C.2, England.
Telephone: 836-5454.

Heydon, Peter Richard, C.B.E., B.A., LL.B.; Australian diplomatist; b. 9 Sept. 1913; ed. Sydney Univ.
Called to the Bar, N.S.W. 36; entered Diplomatic Service 36; Private Sec., Minister for External Affairs 36-37; Second Sec. Washington 40-42, Moscow 43-44; First Sec. and Counsellor, Dept. of External Affairs, Canberra 45-47; Counsellor London 47-50; Chargé d'Affaires The Hague 50; Minister to Brazil 51-53; High Commr. in N.Z. 53-55, in India 55-58; Asst. Sec. Dept. of External Affairs 59-60, First Asst. Sec. 60-61; Sec.

Dept. of Immigration 61-; mem. Australian del., 3rd Gen. Assembly of UN, Paris, New York 48-49, and 11th Gen. Assembly, New York, 57.

Publ. *Quiet Decision* (A Study of G. F. Pearce) 65.

Home: 18 Tennyson Crescent, Forrest, Canberra, A.C.T.; Office: Department of Immigration, Canberra, A.C.T., Australia.

Heyerdahl, Thor; Norwegian anthropologist and explorer; b. 6 Oct. 1914; ed. Univ. of Oslo.

Specialised in zoology and geography at univ. but changed to anthropology during field researches among Polynesians in Marquesas Is. 37-38; research in N.W. Indian territory of Brit. Columbia (ref. theory of two separate American Indian movements into Pacific) 39-40; served free Norwegian Mil. Forces 41-45; research in Europe and U.S.A. 45-47; led Kon-Tiki expedition from Callao, Peru to Raroia, Polynesia (covering 4,300 miles in 101 days and thus proving Peruvian Indians could have settled in Polynesia) 47; founded (with Knut Haugland) Kon-Tiki Museum, Oslo 49; research and lectures in Europe and U.S.A. 48-52; led Norwegian Archæological Expedition to Galápagos (establishing evidence of pre-European visits by South American Indians) Field Research in Bolivia, Peru and Colombia 54; led Norwegian Archæological Expedition to Easter Island and the East Pacific 55-56; Commdr. of the Order of St. Olav, Officer Servicio del Mérito Distinguido of Peru, Grande Ufficiale dell' Ordine al Merito della Repubblica Italiana, and many other awards including Acad. First Award ("Oscar") for Kon-Tiki film 51; mem. Norwegian Acad. of Science 58, Fellow New York Acad. of Sciences 60; Hon. Ph.D. (Oslo Univ.); Vega Medal (Swedish Soc. of Anthropology and Geography) 62; Lomonosov Medal (Moscow Univ.) 62; Patron's Gold Medal (Royal Geographical Soc., London) 64.

Publs. *På Jakt Efter Paradiset* 38, *Kon-Tiki Ekspedisjonen* (trans. 62 languages) 48, *American Indians in the Pacific: the Theory behind the Kon-Tiki Expedition* 52, *Archæological Evidence of Pre-Spanish Visits to the Galápagos Islands* 56, *Aku-Aku: Påskeøyas Hemmelighet* (trans. 32 languages) 57, *Reports of the Norwegian Archaeological Expedition to Easter Island and the East Pacific*, (Vol. I *Archaeology of Easter Island* 61, Vol. II *Miscellaneous Reports* 65) (with E. N. Ferdon), *Indianer und Alt-Asiaten im Pazific* 66, and many articles.

Colla Micheri, Laigueglia, Italy.

Heymans, Corneille Jean François, M.D.; Belgian university professor; b. 28 March 1892; ed. Univ. of Ghent, Coll. de France, Univ. of Vienna, Univ. Coll., London and Western Reserve Univ., U.S.A.

Professor Emer. of Pharmacology, Pharmacodynamics and Toxicology, and Dir. J. F. Heymans Inst. of Pharmacology and Therapeutics, Univ. of Ghent; titular mem. Pontifical Acad. of Sciences, Royal Acad. of Medicine of Belgium, Physiological Soc. (U.K.), American Pharmacological Soc.; mem. Acad. of Sciences (Inst. de France), Accad. Nazionale dei Quaranta, Rome, French Soc. of Cardiology, Neths. Soc. for Physiology and Pharmacology, Belgian Biological Soc., Soc. Experimental Biology and Medicine, N.Y.; hon. mem. Royal Flemish Acad. for Medicine of Belgium, Royal Acad. of Pharmacy, Madrid, Acad. of Medicine, N.Y., German Pharmacological Soc., etc.; corresp. mem. several foreign socs.; awards include: Nobel Prize for Medicine and Physiology, Alvarenga Prize (Royal Acad. of Medicine of Belgium) Gluge Prize (Royal Acad. of Sciences of Belgium), Bourceret Prize (Acad. of Medicine, Paris), Montyon Prize (Acad. of Sciences, Inst. de France), Pius XI Prize (Pontifical Acad. of Sciences); Grand Officer Order of Léopold, Officer Order of the Crown, Croix de Guerre and other decorations; Prof.

h.c. (Univ. of Montevideo); Dr. h.c. fourteen universities.

University of Ghent Medical School, Department of Pharmacology, 3 Alb. Baertsoenkaai, Ghent, Belgium.

Heyne, Hans, DR. ING.; German engineer and business executive; b. 4 Oct. 1900; ed. Dresden Realgymnasium and Technische Hochschule.

Koch & Sterzel A.G. 28-34, later Vice-Pres. Allgemeine Elektricitätsgesellschaft (A.E.G.); Pres. Telefunken A.G. Berlin 50-64; Pres. A.E.G. Berlin 62-64; fmr. Chair. of Board A.E.G.; Chair. of Board, Telefunken A.G. 65; mem. of Board TELDEC Hamburg 50-, Berlin Disconto-Bank 57-, Grosser Beirat Allianz 64-, A.E.G. Telefunken 66-; Dr. Ing. h.c.

Ernst-Reuter-Platz 7, 1000 Berlin 10, Germany.

Telefunken 66-; Dr.-Ing. E.h.

Heyns, Ockert Stephanus, M.A., D.SC., F.R.C.O.G., F.I.C.S.; South African obstetrician and gynaecologist; b. 27 Nov. 1906; ed. Univs. of Cape Town, London and Edinburgh, Queen's Univ. (Belfast), and Univs. of Manchester and Witwatersrand.

Senior Lecturer, Univ. of Witwatersrand 39, Prof. of Obstetrics and Gynaecology 47-67, with accompanying clinical posts such as Chief Obstetrician and Gynaecologist; Prof. Emer. 68-, and Hon. Consultant to Hospital research in three phases: (i) bony pelvis, (ii) uterine action, (iii) abdominal decompression in labour and pregnancy (improving foetal development); Academician, South African Acad.; Corresp. mem. Soc. Royale Belge; Havenga Prize; David Hillman Fellow, Int. Soc. of Reproductive Biology.

Publs. include monograph on abdominal decompression, book on "Decompression Babies".

Whiteleaf, Hermanus, Cape, South Africa.

Telephone: Hermanus 276.

Heyworth, 1st Baron, cr. 55, of Oxton in the County Palatine of Chester; **Geoffrey Heyworth,** Kt.; British industrialist; b. 18 Oct. 1894; ed. Dollar Acad., Scotland.

Joined Lever Bros. Ltd. Liverpool 12; served Canadian Army 15-18; various positions in Canada and England until 31; Dir. parent co. London 31-; Chair. Unilever Ltd. (Lever Brothers and Unilever Ltd.) 42-60; Chair. Council on Prices, Productivity and Incomes 60-62, Cttee. on Social Sciences 63-65; Pres. Nat. Council of Social Service; Court of Govs. of Admin. Staff Coll.; Hon. Fellow, Nuffield Coll.; Grand Officer Order of Orange Nassau 47; Hon. LL.D. (St. Andrews and Manchester 50, London 62, Bristol and Sussex 66), Hon. D.C.L. (Oxford 57), Hon. D.Litt. (Warwick 67).

29 Sussex Square, London, W.2, England.

Telephone: 01-262-6141.

Heywot, Zaude Gabre; Ethiopian diplomatist; b. 12; ed. Menelik II School, Addis Ababa.

Controller of Customs, Addis Ababa 30-31; with Public Works Dept. 31-34; Asst. Head, Jigjigga Ras Makonnen School 34-36, Ethiopian Refugee School, Somaliland 36-40; Liberation campaign 40-41; Sec.-Gen. Addis Ababa Governorate 41-42, Harar Province 44, Dir.-Gen. 44; Sec.-Gen. Prime Minister's Office 44-45; in London Legation 45-46; mem. Del. to U.N. Gen. Assembly 45-47; Chargé d'Affaires, Stockholm 46-47; Dir.-Gen. Ministry for Foreign Affairs 50; Perm. Rep. of Ethiopia to U.N. 52-56; Ambassador to U.S.S.R. 56-58, to U.S.A. 58-60; Mayor of Addis Ababa 60-.

Residence of the Mayor, Addis Ababa, Ethiopia.

Hibbs, Ben, A.B., D.LITT.; American journalist and editor; b. 23 July 1901; ed. Univ. of Kansas.

News Ed. *Fort Morgan* (Colorado) *Times* 23, and *Pratt* (Kansas) *Tribune* 24; Prof. of Journalism Hays (Kansas) State Coll. 24-26; Ed.-Man. *Goodland* (Kansas) *News-Republic* 26-27; Managing Ed. *Arkansas City* (Kansas) *Traveler* 27-29; Associate Ed. *Country Gentleman* (national magazine) 29-40 and Ed. 40-42; Ed. *The*

Saturday Evening Post. 42-62, Senior Editor 62; mem. Exec. Comm. The Curtis Publishing Co. 40-62; Senior Editor, *The Reader's Digest* 63-.
737 Braeburn Lane, Penn Valley, Narberth, Pa., U.S.A. Telephone: MO4-2125.

Hickenlooper, Bourke Blakesmore, B.SC., J.D.; American lawyer and politician; b. 21 July 1896; ed. Iowa State Coll., and Univ. of Iowa.
Admitted to Iowa Bar 22; practised law Cedar Rapids, with Johnson, Donnelly & Lynch 22-25, in private practice 25-33, formed firm Hickenlooper & Mitvalsky 35, practised with it until 42; mem. Iowa House of Reps. 35-39; Lieut.-Gov. 39-43, Gov. 43-44; Senator from Iowa 45-; Republican.
200 First Avenue, N.E., Cedar Rapids, Iowa, U.S.A.

Hickey, John Joseph, LL.B.; American lawyer and politician; b. 22 Aug. 1911; ed. Rawlins (Wyoming) High School and Wyoming Univ.
Law practice in Rawlins 34-; City Treas., Rawlins 35-40; Attorney, Carbon County 38-42, 46-49; army service (Captain) 42-46; U.S. Attorney for Wyoming 49-52; joined firm of Ellery, Gray & Hickey 52; Democratic State Chair. 54; Gov. of Wyoming 59-61; Senator from Wyoming 61-62; Judge, U.S. Court of Appeals, Tenth Circuit; Democrat.
U.S. Post Office and Courthouse Building, Cheyenne, Wyoming 82001; Home: P.O.B. 1288, Cheyenne, Wyoming 82001, U.S.A.
Telephone: 632-1808.

Hicks, Brig. Sir Cedric Stanton, Kt., C.ST.J., M.SC., M.D., PH.D., F.R.I.C., F.R.S.A.; Australian physiologist; b. 2 June 1892; ed. Otago Univ., N.Z., Trinity Coll., Cambridge, Freiburg, Zürich and Vienna.
Fmrly. Lecturer in Chemistry, Otago Univ., Lecturer in Pathology, Otago Medical School, Clinical Pathologist, Dunedin Hospital, and Govt. Analyst for Otago; mem. Cttee. on Endocrine Diseases, Medical Research Council Great Britain; studied Medical Education and Research in U.S. and Europe 24-26, 29-30 and 34-35; Emeritus Prof. Human Physiology and Pharmacology, Sheridan Research Fellow, Adelaide Univ. 26-58; Editor *Australian Journal of Experimental Biology and Medical Science* 26-; Editorial Board *Excerpta Medica*, Amsterdam 47-66; mem. Australian Nat. Research Council; mem. Commonwealth Nutrition Advisory Cttee. 36-39; mem. Nutrition Cttee., Nat. Health and Medical Research Council 36-39; Pres. Tuberculosis Asscn.; Chair. State Nutrition Cttee. 39-64; served First World War; founder Australian Army Catering Corps, enlisted Lieut. A.I.F., Jan. 40; Col. and Dir. Army Catering, Australian Mil. Forces 40-52; Scientific Mission to Washington, D.C. and U.K. 44; Asst. Commr. St. John Ambulance Brigade (Overseas), S. Australia 40-50; mem. Scientific Advisory Cttee. (Foods), Australian Food Council 42-45; mem. Medical Advisory Cttee. Navy, Army and Air Force 40-45; mem. Nat. Red Cross Nutrition Cttee.; Chair. Commonwealth Defence Food Stuffs Research Cttee. 49-59, Scientific Food Consultant, Army, Australia 52-; Vice-Pres. Nat. Old People's Welfare Council 59-; Editorial Board *International Journal for Vitamin Research;* mem. Australian Asscn. for Gerontology.
Publs. *Molecular Structure and Physiological Action, Chemistry and Pharmacology of Native Poisons, Human Ecology and Food Production, Soil Food and Life, Nutrition and Beri Beri in a Japanese P.O.W. Camp* 62, *Terrestrial Animals in the Cold: Primitive Man* 64, *Nutritional Requirements of Living Things* 68.
University of Adelaide; also Woodley, Glen Osmond, South Australia.
Telephone: 79-1308.

Hicks, Granville, A.M.; American writer; b. 9 Sept. 1901; ed. Harvard Univ.
Instr. Smith Coll. 25-28; Asst. Prof. of English, Rensselaer Polytechnic Inst. 29-35; mem. Editorial staff

New Masses 34-39; Counsellor in American Civilization, Harvard Univ. 38-39; staff mem. radio programme "Speaking of Books" 41-43; Lecturer at Pacific Northwest Writers' Conf. 48; Literary Editor *New Leader* 51-58; Instructor, New School for Social Research 55-58; Berg Prof. of American Literature, New York Univ. 59; Contributing Editor *Saturday Review* 58-; Visiting Prof. Syracuse Univ. 60-.
Publs. *The Great Tradition—an Interpretation of American Literature since the Civil War* 33, 35, *One of Us* (with Lynd Ward) 35, *John Reed—the Making of a Revolutionary* 36, *I Like America* 38, *Figures of Transition* 39, co-editor *Proletarian Literature in the United States* 35, *The Letters of Lincoln Steffens* (with Ella Winter) 38, *The First to Awaken* (with Richard M. Bennett) 40, *Only One Storm* 42, *Behold Trouble* 44, *Small Town* 46, *There Was a Man in Our Town* 52, *Where We Came Out* 54, *The Living Novel* (editor) 57, *Part of the Truth: An Autobiography* 65.
Grafton, N.Y., U.S.A.

Hicks, Henry Davies, M.A., B.SC., B.C.L., Q.C.; Canadian barrister, politician and educator; b. 5 March 1915; ed. Mount Allison Univ., Dalhousie, and Exeter Coll., Oxford.
Admitted to Nova Scotia Bar 41; served Royal Canadian Artillery 41-45; practised law, Bridgetown 46-50; mem. Nova Scotia Legislature 45-60; first Minister of Education 49-55, Provincial Sec. 54-56; Premier of Province of Nova Scotia 54-56; Leader of Her Majesty's Loyal Opposition in Nova Scotia Legislature and leader, Nova Scotia Liberal Party 56-60; Pres. Canadian Nat. Comm. for UNESCO 63-67; Dean of Arts and Science, Dalhousie Univ. 60-61, Vice-Pres. 61-63, Pres. and Vice-Chancellor 63-; Hon. D.Ed., Hon. D.C.L., Hon. LL.D.
6446 Coburg Road Halifax, Nova Scotia, Canada.
Telephone: 429-1420 Local 201 (Office); 422-5575 (Home).

Hicks, Sir John Richard, Kt.; British economist; b. 8 April 1904; ed. Clifton Coll. and Balliol Coll., Oxford. Professor of Political Economy, Univ. of Manchester 38-46; Fellow of Nuffield Coll. Oxford 46-52; Prof. of Political Economy, Univ. of Oxford 52-65; Research Fellow, All Souls Coll. Oxford 65-.
Publs. *Theory of Wages* 32, *Value and Capital* 39, *The Social Framework* 42, *Contribution to the Theory of the Trade Cycle* 50, *A Revision of Demand Theory* 56, *Essays in World Economics* 59, *Capital and Growth* 65, *Critical Essays in Monetary Theory* 67.
All Souls College, Oxford, England.
Telephone: Oxford 49641.

Hidalgo, Alberto; Peruvian poet; b. 97; ed. National Univ. of San Marcos, Lima.
Studied medicine, Lima Univ.; abandoned studies for literature.
Publs. Verse: *Actitud de los Años* 33, *Dimensión del Hombre* 38, *Edad del Corazón* 40, *Anivegral* 52, *Carta al Perú* 53, *Espaciotiempo* 59, *Biografía de Yo mismo* 59, *Patria completa* 60, *Poesía Inexpugnable* 62; Prose: *Los Sapos y Otras Personas* 27, *Diario de mi Sentimiento* 37, *Tratado de Poética* 44, *El Universo está cerca* 45, *Aquí está el Anticristo* 57.
Bermúdez 2412, Olivos, Buenos Aires, Argentina.

Hidayatullah, Mohammed, O.B.E., M.A.; Indian judge; b. 17 Dec. 1905; ed. Government High School, Raipur, Morris Coll., Nagpur, Trinity Coll., Cambridge, and Lincoln's Inn, London.
Advocate, Nagpur High Court 30-46; Advocate-Gen. Madhya Pradesh 43-46; Puisne Judge 46-54; Dean of Faculty of Law, Nagpur Univ. 49-53; Chief Justice, Nagpur High Court 54-56; Chief Justice, Madhya Pradesh High Court 56-58; Judge, Supreme Court of India 58-68; Chief Justice of India 68-.
Publs. *Democracy in India and the Judicial Process,*

The South-West Africa Case, Mullars Mahomedan Law
(editor, 16th edn.).
5 Hastings Road, New Delhi, India.
Telephone: 33317.

Hiernaux, Jean-Robert-Laurent, M.D.; Belgian doctor
and professor; b. 9 May 1921; ed. Athénée Royal de
Charleroi and Univ. Libre, Brussels.
Divisionary physician at the Compagnie Minière des
Grands Lacs Africains 46-49; research worker of the
Institut pour la Recherche Scientifique en Afrique
Central 49-56; Prof. at Université Officielle du Congo
Belge et du Ruanda-Urundi 56-60, and Rector 57-61,
Hon. Rector 63-; Maître de recherche, Centre Nat. de
la Recherche Scientifique, Paris 64-.
Publs. *Les caractères physiques des Bashi* 53, *Caractères
physiques des populations du Ruanda et de L'Urundi* 54,
*Analyse de la variation des caractères physiques humains
en une région de l'Afrique Centrale: Ruanda-Urundi et
Kivu* 56, *La Diversité Humaine en Afrique Sub-
saharienne, Recherches Biologiques* 68.
156 avenue Carsoel, Brussels 18, Belgium.
Telephone: 74-07-94.

Hietanen, Lauri Bernhard; Finnish Co-operative
manager; b. 22 Dec. 1902; ed. secondary school and
commercial inst.
Began work in the Finnish neutral co-operative move-
ment 20, and became managing dir. of several co-
operative societies; mem. exec. staff of SOK (Finnish
Co-operative Wholesale Soc.) 47-, its second and com-
mercial Man. 49-65, Gen. Man. 65-; Pres. Central
Union of Commercial Employers of Finland 54-; Pohja
Insurance Co. 58; mem. Central Cttee. of Int. Co-
operative Alliance 48-, Exec. Cttee. of Int. Co-operative
Alliance 66-; Minister of Soc. Affairs 53; Finance
Minister 57-58; Counsellor of Mining.
Riistavuorenkuja 6 D 32, Helsinki 32, Finland.
Telephone: 571-719.

Higgins, Michael Harold, M.A.; British international
administrator; b. 3 Oct. 1908; ed. privately and at
London, Edinburgh and Cambridge Univs.
Asst. Lecturer, Edinburgh and London Univs. 37-45;
attached to Air Ministry 40-45; Deputy Commandant,
Royal Observer Corps 41-42; Private Sec. to Vice-Chief
of Air Staff 42-45; Asst. to Pres. of Council, Int. Civil
Aviation Organisation 45-49; Deputy Dir. U.N. Trans-
port and Communications Division, New York 49;
mem. Mudaliar U.N. Staff Selection Cttee., New York
52, Bangkok 53, U.N. Staff Selection Board, New York
53-57, Geneva 54-55, Bangkok 56, U.N. Joint Pension
Board 56-57, U.N. Appointment Review and Promotion
Board 57-; Sec. Preparatory Cttee., Inter-Govt. Mari-
time Consultative Organisation 58-59, Exec. Sec. 1st
Assembly, London 59, Dir. of Admin. and External
Relations, IMCO 59-63, Admin. and Financial Services,
UN Office, Geneva 63-.
Home: Mill Vale House, Bratton, Nr. Westbury,
Wilts., England; and Villa Marguerite, 39 chemin de la
Fontaine, 1292 Chambésy, Switzerland; Office: Room
243, Palais des Nations, Geneva, Switzerland.
Telephone: 34-60-11 (Office); 58-11-70 (Home).

Higginson, John, M.D., M.R.C.P.; American professor
of pathology; b. 16 Oct. 1922; ed. Royal Belfast
Academical Inst., Belfast, N. Ireland, and Univ. of
Dublin, Ireland.
Pathologist, S. African Inst. for Medical Research,
Baragwanath Hospital, S. Africa 50-58; Head, Cancer
Registry, S. African Inst. for Medical Research 52-58;
American Cancer Soc. Career Professorship, Univ. of
Kansas 61-66; Prof. of Pathology, Univ. of Kansas
Medical Center 62-66; Dir. Int. Agency for Cancer
Research, Lyon, France 66-.

Publs. over 70 scientific papers in field of geographical
pathology and cancer research.
International Agency for Cancer Research, 16 avenue
Maréchal Foch, Lyons 6e, France.
Telephone: 52-33-26.

Highet, Gilbert, D.LITT., F.R.S.L.; Scottish-born
American scholar and critic; b. 22 June 1906; ed. Hill-
head High School (Glasgow), Glasgow Univ. and Balliol
Coll., Oxford.
Fellow St. John's Coll., Oxford 32-38; Prof. of Greek
and Latin Columbia Univ. 38-50, Anthon Prof. of Latin
Language and Literature 50-; mem. Board of Judges
Book-of-the-Month Club 54-; Chair. Advisory Board
Horizon 58-; Guggenheim Fellowship 51.
Publs. *The Classical Tradition* 49, *The Art of Teaching*
50, *People, Places and Books* 53, *Juvenal the Satirist* 54,
A Clerk of Oxenford 54, *Man's Unconquerable Mind* 54,
The Migration of Ideas 54, *Poets in a Landscape* 57,
Talents and Geniuses 57, *The Powers of Poetry* 60, *The
Anatomy of Satire* 62.
706 Philosophy Hall, Columbia University, New York,
N.Y. 10027, U.S.A.
Telephone: 280-3901.

Hilaly, Agha, M.A., S.Pk.; Pakistani diplomatist; b.
20 May 1911; ed. Madras and Cambridge Univs.
Entered Civil Service 36; apptd. Under-Sec. to Finance
Ministry, Govt. of Bengal; transferred to pre-partition
Govt. of India and served as Under-Sec. in Ministries
of Agriculture, Food and Commerce 41-47; Deputy Sec.
Pakistan Foreign Ministry 47-51, Joint Sec. 51-54;
attended several Int. Confs. as Sec.-Gen. of Pakistan
dels.; Ambassador to Sweden, Norway, Denmark and
Finland 56-59, to U.S.S.R. (concurrently Minister to
Czechoslovakia) 59-61; High Commr. in India and
Ambassador to Nepal 61-63; High Commr. in U.K. and
Ambassador to Republic of Ireland 63-66; Ambassador
to U.S.A. 66-.
Pakistan Embassy, 2315 Massachusetts Avenue, N.W.,
Washington, D.C., U.S.A.

Hildebrand, Joel Henry, SC.D., LL.D., PH.D.; American
professor of chemistry Emeritus; b. 16 Nov. 1881; ed.
Univ. of Pennsylvania and Berlin Univ.
Instructor in Chemistry Univ. of Pennsylvania 07-13;
Asst. Prof. of Chemistry Univ. of Calif. 13; Assoc. Prof.
17, Prof. 18-52; Dean of Coll. of Letters and Science
39-43; Dean Coll. of Chemistry 49-51; Faculty Research
Lecturer 36; Commissioned Capt. U.S. Army 17;
Lieut.-Col. Chemical Warfare Service 18; awarded
D.S.M. 18; Liaison Officer for Office of Scientific Re-
search and Development, U.S. Embassy, London 43-44,
King's Medal (Brit.); Pres. American Chemical Soc.
for 55; Westman Lecturer, Chemistry Inst. of Canada
57; Hon. Fellow Royal Society, Edinburgh, National
Acad. Sciences, American Philosophical Society;
hon. mem. American Inst. of Chemists; hon. Life mem.
Faraday Soc.; Nichols Medal 39; American Chemical
Society Award in Chemical Education 52; Gibbs Medal
53, Jas. F. Norris Award in Chemical Educ. 61, Wm.
Proctor Prize, Scientific Research Soc. of America 62,
Priestley Medal 62 (American Chemical Soc.), Joseph
Priestley Award 65, Hildebrand Hall Laboratory,
Univ. of Calif., Berkeley dedicated in honour 66,
Madison Marshall Award 67.
Publs. *Principles of Chemistry* (with R. M. Powell) 52, 64,
Solubility of Non-Electrolytes (with R. L. Scott) 50,
Reference Book of Inorganic Chemistry (with W. M.
Latimer) 51, *Science in the Making* 56, *Regular Solutions*
(with R. L. Scott) 62, *Is Intelligence Important?* 63, *An
Introduction to Molecular Kinetic Theory* 63; 200 papers.
Department of Chemistry, Univ. of California, Berke-
ley, Calif. 94720; Home: 500 Coventry Road, Berkeley,
Calif. 94707, U.S.A.
Telephone: 415-525-2131.

Hildesheimer, Wolfgang; German writer and artist; b. 9 Dec. 1916; ed. Odenwaldschule, Heppenheim, Germany, Frensham Heights School, Surrey, England, and Central School of Arts and Crafts, London.
British Information Officer, Palestine 43-45; Lecturer, British Inst., Tel-Aviv 45-46; interpreter, War Crimes Trials, Nuremberg 47-49; now freelance writer and artist; Prof. of Poetry at Frankfurt Univ. 67; Radio Play Prize in aid of War Blinded 55; Literaturpreis der Freien Hansestadt Bremen 66.
Publs. include: *Lieblose Legenden* (short stories) 52, *Die Verspätung* 62 (play), *Nachtstück* (one-act play) 63, *Tynset* (novel) 65, *Rivalen* (play) 65, Georg Buchner Preis der Deutschen Akad. für Sprache und Dichtung, Darmstadt 66.
7742 Poschiavo (GR), Switzerland.
Telephone: (082) 50467.

Hildred, Sir William Percival, Kt., C.B., O.B.E., M.A.; British international administrator; b. 13 July 1893; ed. Univ. of Sheffield.
Served First World War 14-18; lectured Social History for Workers' Educational Asscn. Univ. of Sheffield 18; entered Treasury 19; Finance Officer Empire Marketing Board 26-34; Head Special Measures Branch Min. of Agriculture and Fisheries 34-36; Deputy Gen. Man. Exports Credit Guarantee Dept. 36-38; Deputy Dir.-Gen. of Civil Aviation March 38-39; Principal Asst. Sec. in Air Ministry 39-40; with Ministry of Aircraft Production 40-41; Dir.-Gen. Min. of Civil Aviation 41-46; Dir.-Gen. Int. Air Transport Asscn. (IATA) 46-66; Grand Officer Order of Orange-Nassau (Neths.) 46, Commdr. Order of the Crown of Belgium 48; Hon. LL.D. (Univ. of Sheffield and McGill Univ.).
Spreakley House, Frensham, Surrey, England.
Telephone: Frensham 2330.

Hill, Archibald Vivian, C.H., O.B.E., SC.D., LL.D., F.R.S.; British physiologist; b. 26 Sept. 1886; ed. Trinity Coll., Cambridge.
Fellow of Trinity Coll. 10-16, Hon. Fellow 41; Fellow King's Coll. 16-22, Hon. Fellow 27; Foreign mem. Nat. Acad. Sciences, Washington and other Acads. and Societies; Prof. of Physiology Manchester Univ. 20-23 and Univ. Coll., London 23-25; Foulerton Research Prof. of Royal Society 26-51; Trustee British Museum 47-63, British Museum (Natural History) 63-65; Sec. Royal Soc. 35-45, Foreign Sec. 45-46; Ind. M.P. for Cambridge Univ. 40-45; Pres. British Asscn. for the Advancement of Science 52; Pres. Marine Biological Asscn. of U.K. 55-60; Sec.-Gen. Int. Council of Scientific Unions 52-56; Pres. Soc. for Visiting Scientists, London 52-66; Hon. Fellow Univ. Coll., London 48; Nobel Prize for Physiology and Medicine 22; Copley Medal, Royal Soc. 48.
Publs. *Living Machinery* 27, *The Ethical Dilemma of Science* 60, *Trails and Trials in Physiology* 65.
11A Chaucer Road, Cambridge, England.
Telephone: Cambridge 54551.

Hill, Sir Austin Bradford, Kt., C.B.E., PH.D., D.SC., F.R.S.; British university professor; b. 8 July 1897; ed. Chigwell School and London Univ.
Research worker for Industrial Health Research Board and Medical Research Council 23-32; London Univ. Reader in Epidemiology and Vital Statistics at the London School of Hygiene and Tropical Medicine 32-45, Prof. of Medical Statistics 45-61; Hon. Dir. Statistical Research Unit of Medical Research Council 45-61; Civil Consultant in Medical Statistics to the R.N. and R.A.F. and mem. Flying Personnel Research Cttee.; Pres. Royal Statistical Soc. 50-52, Gold Medallist, Royal Statistical Soc. 53; Hon. Fellow American Public Health Asscn. 53, Royal Soc. of Medicine 62; Fellow, Univ. Coll. London 55; Hon. Fellow, Soc. of Occupational Medicine 57, Royal Coll. of Physicians 63, Soc. of Medical Officers of Health 63-; Hon. mem. Inst. of Actuaries 56,

Faculty of Medicine, Univ. of Chile 59; Galen Medal, Soc. of Apothecaries 59, Harben Gold Medal, Royal Inst. of Public Health and Hygiene 61, Heberden Medal 65, Jenner Medal of Royal Soc. of Medicine 65; Hon. D.Sc. Oxford 63, Hon. M.D. Edinburgh 68.
Publs. *Principles of Medical Statistics* (8th edition) 66, *Statistical Methods in Clinical and Preventive Medicine* 62.
Green Acres, Little Kingshill, Great Missenden, Bucks., England.
Telephone: Great Missenden 2380.

Hill, Christopher (*see* Hill, (John Edward) C.).

Hill, David Garrett; American businessman; b. 6 June 1902; ed. Cornell Univ.
Industrial Engineer, Pittsburgh Plate Glass Co. 24-29, Asst. to Vice-Pres. 29-40, Gen. Supt. plate glass factories 40-52, Vice-Pres. 52-55, Dir. 54, Pres. 55-66, Chair. of Board 66-67, Chair. Exec. Cttee. 62-67, mem. 67-; Dir. Pittsburgh Corning Corpn.; Dir. and Pres. S.A. des Glaces de Courcelles; Dir. Bell Telephone Co. of Pennsylvania, Duplate Canada Ltd. and several other companies; Dir. Brockway Glass Co., Inc.; Dir.-Consultant, Presbyterian-Univ. Hospital, Univ. of Pittsburgh
Home: 21 Edgewood Road, Pittsburgh, Pa. 15215; Office: One Gateway Center, Pittsburgh, Pa. 15222, U.S.A.

Hill, John A.; American insurance executive; b. 24 Feb. 1907; ed. Univ. of Denver.
Aetna Life Insurance Co. 28-, Denver 28-30, Manager, Group and Pensions Depts., Detroit 30-33, District Supervisor 33-36, Gen. Agent, John A. Hill & Assocs., Toledo 36-58, Senior Vice-Pres. 58-62, Pres. 62-.
151 Farmington Avenue, Hartford, Connecticut 06115, U.S.A.

Hill, John Anthony, B.A., LL.B.; American lawyer and industrialist; b. 6 May 1904; ed. Amherst Coll. and Columbia Law School.
Lawyer with Shearman and Sterling 28-39; with Air Reduction Co., Inc. 39-, Dir. 47-, Pres. and Chief Exec. Officer 64-; Dir. Air Reduction Canada Ltd., Marine Midland Grace Trust Co., Marine Midland Corpn., Nat. Industrial Conf. Board, Amherst Coll., Presbyterian Hospital, New York City.
Office: 150 E. 42nd Street, New York, N.Y. 10017; Home: 10 Banksville Road, Armonk, N.Y. 10504, U.S.A.
Telephone: Armonk 3-3137.

Hill, (John Edward) Christopher, M.A., D.LITT.; British historian; b. 6 Feb. 1912; ed. St. Peter's School, York, and Balliol Coll., Oxford.
Fellow of All Souls Coll., Oxford 34-38; Asst. Lecturer, Univ. Coll., Cardiff 36-38; Fellow and Tutor in Modern History, Balliol Coll., Oxford 38-65, Master of Balliol Coll. 65-; Army and Foreign Office Service 40-45; Univ. Lecturer in 16th and 17th Century History, Oxford 59-65; mem. Editorial Board *Past and Present*, Yale Edition of Milton's *Complete Prose*; Fellow of British Acad. 66; Hon. D.Litt. (Hull and Sheffield).
Publs. *The English Revolution, 1640* 40, *Lenin and the Russian Revolution* 47, *The Good Old Cause* (documents, edited jointly with E. Dell) 49, *Economic Problems of the Church* 56, *Puritanism and Revolution* 58, *The Century of Revolution, 1603–1714* 61, *Society and Puritanism in Pre-Revolutionary England* 64, *Intellectual Origins of The English Revolution* 65, *Reformation to Industrial Revolution* 67.
Balliol College, Oxford, England.

Hill, John McGregor, B.SC., PH.D., F.INST.P.; British atomic energy official; b. 21 Feb. 1921; ed. Richmond County Grammar School, King's Coll., London, and St. John's Coll., Cambridge.
Flight Lieut., R.A.F., Second World War; research at

Cavendish Laboratory, Cambridge 46-48; Lecturer, London Univ. 48-50; U.K. Atomic Energy Authority 50-, mem. for Production 64-68, Chair. 68-.
United Kingdom Atomic Energy Authority, 11 Charles II Street, London, S.W.1, England.

Hill, Lister, A.B., LL.B.; American lawyer and politician; b. 29 Dec. 1894; ed. Alabama and Columbia Univs.
Admitted to Alabama Bar 15; commenced law practice, Montgomery 16; served with 17th and 71st U.S. Infantry Regiments, First World War 17-19; mem. Congress 23-38, resigned; U.S. Senator from Alabama 38-; Democrat.
1618 Gilmer Avenue, Montgomery, Ala., U.S.A.

Hill, Robert Charles; American diplomatist and politician; b. 30 Sept. 1917; ed. Taft School and Dartmouth Coll.
Vice-Consul Foreign Service 43-45; Asst. Vice-Pres. W. R. Grace & Co., N.Y. 49-53; Clerk, Senate Banking and Currency Cttee. 47-48; Ambassador to Costa Rica 53-54, to El Salvador 54-55; Special Asst. to Under-Sec. of State for Mutual Security Affairs 55-56; Asst. Sec. of State for Congressional Relations 56-57; U.S. Ambassador to Mexico 57-61; mem. N.H. State Legislature 61-62; Consultant, Int. Affairs 61-; Pres. People's Nat. Bank, Littleton, N.H. 66-67; Chair Republican Nat. Cttee. Foreign Policy Task Force 65-; Dir. United Fruit Co., Boston, Merck and Co., Rahway, N.J., Int. Power Co. Ltd., Montreal, Monterey Railway Light and Power Co., Montreal, Northeast Airlines, Boston, etc.; Aztec Eagle, First Class (Mexico), Grand Order of Merit (Peru), and other decorations; Hon. LL.D. (New England Coll., Dartmouth Coll., St. Mary's Univ., San Antonio, Univ. of Dallas, Mexican Acad. Int. Law), etc.
P.O. Box 350, Littleton, New Hampshire 03261; also 240 Bal Bay Drive, Bal Harbour, Florida 33154, U.S.A. Telephone: 603-444-3446; also 305-864-7818.

Hill, Walter, B.SC.(ECON.); British economist; b. 04; ed. London School of Economics.
With *The Economist*, London, becoming Asst. Editor 28-46; First Dir. Economist Intelligence Unit; Asst. Dir. Econ. Dept. Int. Bank for Reconstruction and Development 46-47, Asst. Dir. Loans Dept. 47-48, Special Rep. in Europe and Head of Paris Office 48-55; Sec.-Gen. Int. Chamber of Commerce, Paris 57-.
International Chamber of Commerce, 38 cours Albert 1er, Paris 8e, France.

Hill, William Charles Osman, M.D.; British zoologist and anthropologist; b. 13 July 1901; ed. King Edward VI School, Birmingham and Birmingham Univ.
Assistant Lecturer, Zoology, Birmingham Univ. 24-25, Lecturer in Anatomy 25-30; Prof. of Anatomy, Ceylon Medical Coll. (later Univ. of Ceylon) 30-44, Registrar 38-40; Reader in Physical Anthropology, Univ. of Edinburgh 45-50; Prosector to Zoological Soc. of London 50-62; Editor-in-Chief, *Ceylon Journal of Science* 32-44; Gen. Editor, *Zoo Penguins* 57; Visiting Prof. of Anatomy, Emory Univ., Georgia 57-58; Part-time Lecturer in Morphology, Charing Cross Hospital Medical School 54-62; Assoc. Dir. Yerkes Regional Primate Center, Emory Univ., Atlanta, Ga. 62-.
Publs. *Comparative Anatomy and Taxonomy of The Primates* (6 vols.) 53, 55, 57, 60, 62, 66, *Man's Ancestry* 54, *Man as an Animal* 57.
Moonfleet, Frithsden Copse, Berkhampsted, Herts., England; 1061 Oxford Rd., Atlanta, Ga. 30306, U.S.A. Telephone: 378-1690.

Hill, (William) Martin, M.A.; British United Nations official; b. 8 April 1905; ed. Malvern Coll., Oriel Coll., Oxford, London School of Economics, and Univs. of Vienna and Cambridge.
Entered League of Nations Secretariat 27; mem. Econ.

and Financial Section 27-34, Political Section 34-39, Econ., Financial and Transit Dept. 39-45; Sec. to the Bruce Cttee. 39, to the Econ. and Financial Cttees. 42-45; Asst. to the Sec.-Gen. 45-46; Special Adviser to the Exec. Sec. to the San Francisco Conf. 45; Chief of Administrative and Budgetary Section, Preparatory Comm. of the U.N. 45; joined permanent secretariat of the U.N. 46; Special Adviser to the Sec.-Gen. 46-48; Dep. Exec. Asst. to the Sec.-Gen. and Dir. of Co-ordination for the specialised agencies and econ. and social matters 48-55; Dep. Under-Sec. for Econ. and Social Affairs and Personal Rep. of Sec.-Gen. to the Specialized Agencies 55-66; Asst. Sec.-Gen. for Inter-Agency Affairs 67-.
Publs. *The Economic and Financial Organisation of the League of Nations* 45, *Immunities and Privileges of International Officials* 47, *Commercial Policy in the inter-war Period* 42, *Quantitative Trade Controls* 43.
260 Snowden Lane, Princeton, N.J.; and United Nations, New York, N.Y., U.S.A.
Telephone: WA1-7967; also PL4-1234.

Hill of Luton, Baron (Life Peer), cr. 63; **Charles Hill,** P.C., M.A., M.D., D.P.H., LL.D.; British doctor; b. 15 Jan. 1904; ed. St. Olave's Grammar School, Trinity Coll., Cambridge, and the London Hospital.
Univ. Tutorial Lecturer in Biology 26-30; Sec. British Medical Asscn. 44-50; Pres. World Medical Asscn. 49-50; Liberal-Conservative M.P. 50-63; Parl. Sec., Ministry of Food 51-55; Postmaster-Gen. 55-57; Chancellor of the Duchy of Lancaster 57-61; Minister of Housing and Local Govt. and Minister for Welsh Affairs. 61-62; Dir. Laporte Industries 62-65, Chair. 65-; Dir. Abbey National Building Soc. 64-; Chair. Independent Television Authority 63-67; Chair. of Govs. B.B.C. 67-; Chair. Nat. Joint Council for Local Authorities' Administrative, Professional, Technical and Clerical Services; Pres. Central Council for Health Educ.
Publs. *What is Osteopathy?* 37, *Your Health in Wartime* 41, *Wartime Food for Growing Children* 42, *Wise Eating in Wartime* 43, *When Your Baby is Coming* 43, *Wednesday Morning Early—by the Radio Doctor* 44, *Your Body* 44, *Your Aches and Pains* 45, *The Way to Better Health* 46, *Bringing up Your Child* 50, *Dictionary of Health* 51, *Both Sides of the Hill* 64.
Winch Hill House, Wandon End, nr. Luton, England.

Hillary, Sir Edmund Percival, K.B.E.; New Zealand explorer and bee farmer; b. 20 July 1919; ed. Auckland Grammar School and Univ. of Auckland.
Served R.N.Z.A.F. (on Catalinas in the Pacific) 44-45; went to Himalayas on N.Z. Garwhal expedition 51, when he and another were invited to join the British reconnaissance over Everest under Eric Shipton; took part in British expedition to Cho Oyu 52, and in British Mount Everest Expedition under Sir John Hunt, 53, when he and Tenzing reached the summit on May 29th; Leader N.Z. Alpine Club Expedition to Barun Valley 54; N.Z. Antarctic Expedition 56-58, reached South Pole Dec. 57; Leader Himalayan Expeditions 61, 63, 64; Pres. Volunteer Service Abroad in New Zealand 63-64; built a hospital for Sherpa tribesmen, Nepal 66; Leader climbing expedition on Mount Herschel, Antarctica 67; Polar Medal 58; Gurkha Right Hand (1st Class).
Publs. *High Adventure* 55, *The Crossing of Antarctica* (with Sir Vivian Fuchs) 58, *No Latitude for Error* 61, *High in the Thin Cold Air* (with Desmond Doig) 63, *Schoolhouse in the Clouds* 65.
278A Remuera Road, Auckland, New Zealand.

Hilldring, Major-Gen. John Henry, B.S.; American soldier, business executive and public official; b. 27 March 1895; ed. Columbia Univ. and Univ. of Connecticut.
Commissioned Army Infantry 17; with A.E.F. 18-19; advanced through grades to Major-Gen. 42; assigned War Dept., Gen. Staff July 39; Exec. Officer of per-

sonnel (G-I) Div. Feb. 41; Asst. Chief of Staff, G-I Feb. 42; Commd. 84th Infantry Div. July 42; first Dir. of Civil Affairs Div., Office of Chief of Staff 43-46; Asst. Sec. of State responsible for the formulation of policy in occupied areas 46-47; State Dept. mem. and Chair. State-War-Navy Co-ordinating Cttee.; awards include D.S.C., D.S.M. (with Oak-Leaf Cluster), C.B.E., Commdr. Order of Leopold (Belgium); Pres. U.S. Infantry Asscn. 43-46; Pres. Military Govt. Asscn. 47; Alternate U.S. del. General Assembly, U.N. 47; Gen. Man. Foreign Operations, Gen. Aniline & Film Corpn. and Gen. Dye-stuff Corpn. 50-52, Vice-Pres. in charge Foreign Operations, Gen. Aniline & Film Corpn. 52-55, Pres. and Dir. 55, Chair. of Bd. and Dir. 59-61; Dir. U.S. Industries Inc. 48-; Dir. Ansco Ltd. Canada 51-60; Chemical Developments of Canada Ltd. 51-61; Pres. and Dir. Anilitalia, Milan, Italy 58-61; mem. Advisory Cttee. Bankers' Trust Co. N.Y. 56-; Hon. LL.D. (Lincoln Coll.); Alumnus of the Year, Univ. of Conn. 59.
3150 West Manor Drive, Phoenix, Arizona, U.S.A.

Hillebrecht, Rudolf Friedrich Heinrich, DIPL. ING.; German architect and town planner; b. 26 Feb. 1910; ed. Humanistisches Gymnasium, Hanover, and Technische Hochschulen, Hanover and Berlin.
Worked with Walter Gropius, Berlin 33-34; Building Inspector, Travemünde, Hamburg and Hanover 34-37; Office Manager, architectural practice of Konstanty Gutschow, Hamburg 37-45; worked in Dept. for Replanning of Hamburg 37-44; Army Service 44-45; worked with Werner Kallmorgen, Hamburg 45-46; Deputy Chief, Building Div., British Occupied Zone 46; Sec. for Building Affairs, German Advisory Council of British Zone 46-48; Municipal Town Planner and Architect, City of Hanover 48-; mem. German Acad. for Town and Country Planning and other orgs.; Mitglied des Ordens Pour le Mérite für Wissenschaften und Künste 64, and many other decorations.
Office: Friedrichswall 4, 3 Hanover; Home: Gneiststrasse 7, 3 Hanover, German Federal Republic.

Hilleman, Maurice R., PH.D.; American virologist; b. 30 Aug. 1919; ed. Montana State Coll. and Univ. of Chicago.
Assistant Bacteriologist, Univ. of Chicago 42-44; Research Assoc., Virus Laboratories, E. R. Squibb & Sons 44-47, Chief Virus Dept. 47-48; Medical Bacteriologist and Asst. Chief, Virus and Rickettsial Diseases, Army Medical Service Graduate School, Walter Reed Army Medical Center 48-56; Chief, Respiratory Diseases, Walter Reed Army Inst. of Research, Washington 56-58; Dir. Virus and Cell Biology Research, Merck Inst. for Therapeutic Research, Merck & Co. Inc. 58-66, Exec. Dir. 66-; Visiting Lecturer in Bacteriology, Rutgers Univ. 47; Visiting Investigator, Hospital of Rockefeller Inst. for Medical Research 51; Visiting Prof. Dept. of Bacteriology, Univ. of Maryland 53-57; Consultant, Surgeon-Gen. U.S. Army 58-63; Fellow, American Public Health Asscn., American Acad. of Microbiology, American Asscn. for the Advancement of Science; mem. Expert Advisory Panel on Virus Diseases, World Health Org. 52-, Cttee. on Influenza 52, Cttee. on Respiratory Diseases 58, Scientific Group on Measles Vaccine Studies 63, on Viruses and Cancer 64, on Human Viral and Rickettsial Vaccines 65, on Respiratory Diseases 67; mem. Study Section, Microbiology and Immunology Grants-in-Aid Program 53-61; mem. numerous U.S. and Int. Medical Socs., Editorial Board *Int. Journal of Cancer* 64-, Inst. for Scientific Information 68; recent awards include Distinguished Civilian Service Award given by Sec. of Defense 57; Washington Acad. of Sciences Award for Scientific Achievement in the Biological Sciences 58; Walter Reed Army Medical Center Incentive Award 60; Hon. D.Sc. (Montana) 66.

Publs. Over 200 original publications on virology, immunology and public health.
Merck Institute for Therapeutic Research, Merck & Co. Inc., West Point, Pennsylvania 19486, U.S.A.
Telephone: 215-699-5311.

Hillenbrand, Martin Joseph M.A. PH.D.; American diplomatist; b. 1 Aug. 1915; ed. Univs. of Dayton and Columbia.
Foreign Service Officer 39-; Vice-Consul, Zürich 39, Rangoon 40, Calcutta 42, Lourenço Marques 44, Bremen 44; Consul, Bremen 46; Bureau of German Affairs, State Dept. 50-52; First Sec., Paris 52-56; U.S. Political Adviser, Berlin 56-58; Dir. Office of German Affairs, State Dept. 58-62; Head of "Berlin Task Force" 62-63; Deputy Chief of Mission, Bonn 63-; Chair. Fulbright Comm. for Germany 63-67; Amb. to Hungary 67-.
Publ. *Power and Morals* 48.
c/o American Embassy, Budapest, Hungary.

Hillery, Patrick John; Irish politician; b. 2 May 1923; ed. Miltown-Malbay National School, Rockwell Coll., Cashel and Univ. Coll., Dublin.
Member of Health Council 55-57; Medical Officer, Miltown-Malbay 57-59; Coroner for West Clare 58-59; mem. Dáil 51-; Minister for Educ. 59-65; Minister for Industry and Commerce 65-66, for Labour 66-.
Spanish Point, Co. Clare, Ireland.

Hilsman, Roger, Jr., B.S., M.A., PH.D.; American diplomatist and educator; b. 23 Nov. 1919; ed. West Point and Yale Univ.
U.S. Army 43-53; Center for Int. Studies, Princeton Univ. 53-56; Chief Foreign Affairs Div. of Legislative Reference Service, Library of Congress 56-58, Dep. Dir. (for Research) 58-61; Dir. Bureau of Intelligence and Research, Dept. of State 61-63; Asst. Sec. of State for Far Eastern Affairs 63-64; Prof. of Govt., Columbia Univ. 64-.
Publs. *Strategic Intelligence and National Decisions* 56, co-author *Military Policy and National Security* 56, contributor to *Alliance Policy in the Cold War* 59, *NATO and American Security* 59, *The Guerrilla—and How to Fight Him* 62, *Modern Guerrilla Warfare* 42, *Foreign Policy in the 60s* 65, *To Move a Nation* 67.
448 Riverside Avenue, New York, N.Y.; and Hamburg Cove, Lyme, Conn., U.S.A.

Hilton, Conrad Nicholson; American hotel proprietor; b. 25 Dec. 1887; ed. N.M. Military Acad. and N.M. School of Mines.
Member N.M. House of Reps. 12-13; organized N.M. State Bank of San Antonio 13; officer in U.S. Army 17-19; entered hotel business 19; Founder Hilton Hotels Corpn. 46-, Chair. of Board 60-; Pres. Hilton Hotels Int. Hotel Waldorf-Astoria Corpn. Inns Inc.; Chair. Hilton Credit Corpn.
Publs. *Be My Guest* (autobiography) 57, *Inspiration of an Innkeeper* 63.
9990 Santa Monica Boulevard, Beverly Hills, Calif., U.S.A.

Hilton, Hugh Gerald, B.SC., D.ENG.; Canadian businessman; b. 31 March 1889; ed. Case School of Applied Science, Cleveland, Ohio.
Asst. Supt. of blast furnaces, Steel Co. of Canada 21, Asst. Works Man. 27, Works Man. 34, Vice-Pres. 37, Dir. 41, Exec. Vice-Pres. 43, Pres. 45-57, Chair. and Chief Exec. Officer 57-60, Chair. of the Board 60-66, Chair. Exec. Cttee. 66-; Dir. Canadian Gen. Electric Co. Ltd., Toronto, Hamilton and Buffalo Railway Co.; Hon. Vice-Pres. American Iron and Steel Inst.; mem. American Inst. of Mining and Metallurgical Engineers, British Iron and Steel Inst., Canadian Manufacturers' Asscn., American Asscn. for Advancement of Science, Newcomen Soc., Engineering Inst. of Canada.
17 Inglewood Drive, Hamilton, Ont., Canada.

Himle, Erik; Norwegian economist and politician; b. 10 April 1924; ed. Oslo Univ.
Secretary, Ministry of Commerce 48-49; Int. Bank for Reconstruction and Development, Washington 50; Ministry of Commerce 51-52; Chief of Dept., Ministry of Defence 52-55, Dir. 56-58, Under-Sec. of State 58-60, Sec.-Gen. 61; Under-Sec. of State, Ministry of Transport and Communications 62-63; Ministry of Commerce and Shipping 63-64, of Communications 64-65; Labour.
The Storting, Oslo, Norway.

Himsworth, Sir Harold Percival, K.C.B., M.D., F.R.S., F.R.C.P.; British medical research scientist; b. 19 May 1905; ed. Univ. of London.
Formerly Prof. of Medicine Univ. of London and Dir. Medical Unit Univ. Coll. Hospital Medical School, London 39-49; Sec. Medical Research Council 49-68; Fellow Univ. Coll. London; Consulting Physician Univ. Coll. Hospital; Fellow Royal Society; hon. mem. Swedish Medical Society, and Belgian Royal Acad. of Medicine; mem. Norwegian Medical Society; foreign hon. mem. American Acad. of Arts and Sciences; mem. Royal Soc. Arts and Sciences, Gothenburg; hon. Fellow Faculty of Radiologists; hon. mem. Asscn. of American Physicians; Dr. h.c. (Toulouse); Hon. LL.D. (Glasgow, London, Wales); Hon. D.Sc. (Manchester) 56; Hon. Sc.D. (Cambridge) 64; Hon. D.Sc. (Leeds and Univ. of West Indies) 68; Hon. F.R.C.P. (Edin.) 60; Hon. F.R.S.M. 61; Hon. F.R.C.S. 65.
20 Park Crescent, London, W.1, England.

Hinckley, Robert Henry, A.B.; American business exec.; b. 8 June 1891; ed. Brigham Young Univ.
Instructor in Languages, Brigham Young Univ. 14-16; automobile business, Mt. Pleasant, Utah 16-29; real estate, automobile and aviation business, Ogden, Utah 28-38; mem. Utah State House Reps. 18-20; Assistant Administrator Fed. Emergency Relief Admin. 34; Asst. Admin. Works Projects Admin. 35-38; mem. Civil Aeronautics Authority 38-40, Chair. 39-40; Asst. Sec. of Commerce 39-42, Exec. Sperry Corpn., N.Y. 42-44; Dir. Office of Contract Settlement 44-46; Dir. First Security Corpn., Salt Lake City; Vice-Pres. and Dir. American Paper and Supply Co., Salt Lake City; Dir. and mem. Exec. Cttee. American Broadcasting Companies Inc. 53-.
1283E South Temple, Salt Lake City, Utah, U.S.A.
Telephone: 355-3992.

Hindle, Edward, M.A., PH.D., SC.D., F.R.S.; British zoologist; b. 21 March 1886; ed. Magdalene Coll., Cambridge, Royal Coll. of Science and King's Coll., London, Univ. of California, Berkeley, and Pasteur Inst., Paris.
Charles Kingsley Lecturer and Bye Fellow Magdalene Coll. 13; served First World War 14-19 and Second World War 39-43; Prof. of Biology School of Medicine Cairo 19-24; Milner Research Fellow, London School of Hygiene and Tropical Medicine 24-27; mem. Kala Azar Comm. of Royal Soc. to Northern China 25-27; Beit Research Fellow in Tropical Medicine 28-33; Regius Prof. of Zoology Glasgow Univ. 35-43; Scientific Dir. Zoological Soc. of London 44-51; Pres. Univs. Fed. of Animal Welfare; Founder-Dir. Int. Wildfowl Research Bureau; Founder-Pres. Inst. of Biology; Hon. Vice-Pres. Royal Geographical Soc.; Hon. Fellow, Imperial Coll. of Science and Technology; Hon. Fellow Inst. of Biology; Jt. Editor *Parasitology* and Sectional Editor of *Tropical Diseases Bulletin*: Geoffroy St. Hilaire Gold Medal (Société d'Acclimatation de France) 51; Croix Civique (Belgium) First Class; Rhodesian Gold Medallist.
Publs. *Flies and Disease: Blood-sucking Flies*, and many scientific publications dealing particularly with insect-transmitted infections and general biology.
51 Warwick Avenue, London, W.9, England.
Telephone: 01-286-2603.

Hindus, Maurice Gerschon; American writer; b. 27 Feb. 1891 in Russia; ed. Colgate and Harvard Univs. Freelance writer; visited Russia for *Century Magazine* 23 and since for other journals.
Publs. *The Russian Peasant and the Revolution* 20, *Broken Earth* 26, *Humanity Uprooted* 29, *Red Bread* 31, *The Great Offensive* 33, *We Shall Live Again, Green Worlds* 39, *Sons and Fathers* 40, *To Sing with the Angels* 41, *Russia Fights On* 42, *Russia and Japan* 42, *Mother Russia* 43, *The Cossacks* 45, *In Search of a Future* 49, *Magda* 51, *Crisis in the Kremlin* 53, *House without a Roof* 62, *The Kremlin's Human Dilemma* 67.
Columbia University Club, New York City, U.S.A.

Hine, Maynard Kiplinger, D.D.S., M.S.; American dentist; b. 25 Aug. 1907; ed. Univ. of Illinois.
Instructor at Univ. of Illinois Coll. of Dentistry 30-32; Assoc. 36-38; Asst. Prof. 38-43; Assoc. Prof. and Head of the Div. of Oral Pathology at Indiana Univ. School of Dentistry 44-45; Prof. and Head of the Dept. of Periodontia and Histopathology, Indiana Univ. School of Dentistry 45; Dean of Indiana Univ. School of Dentistry 45-; mem. American Asscn. of Dental Editors, Pres. 49-50; mem. Nat. Dental Advisory Cttee. of U.S. Public Health Service 48-50; mem. Int. Asscn. Dental Research, Pres. 52; mem. Advisory Panel on Medical Sciences, Dept. of Defence; mem. Indiana State Dental Asscn., Pres. 57-58; Editor *Journal of Periodontology* 49-; Pres. American Asscn. of Dental Schools 52; Pres. American Dental Asscn. 66; Regent Nat. Library of Medicine 60-63; mem. Advisory Council of Nat. Inst. for Dental Research; Pres. American Acad. of Periodontology 64.
4580 North Meridan Street, Indianapolis, Indiana, U.S.A.

Hines, Rt. Rev. John Elbridge, D.D.; American ecclesiastic; b. 3 Oct. 1910; ed. Univ. of South and Virginia Theological Seminary.
Ordained 33; Curate, St. Louis 33-35; Rector, Hannibal, Missouri 35-37, Augusta, Georgia 37-41, Houston, Texas 41-45; Bishop Coadjutor of Texas 45-55, Bishop of Texas 55-64; Presiding Bishop, Protestant Episcopal Church of U.S.A. 64-.
Episcopal Church Center, 815 Second Avenue, New York 17, N.Y., U.S.A.

Hinman, Edward B., B.A.; Canadian business executive; b. 10 Dec. 1913; ed. Dartmouth Coll., Hanover, N.H. and Harvard School of Business Administration.
In U.S. Army 43-46; Vice-Pres. Canadian Int. Paper Co. 56-59, Vice-Pres. and Gen. Man. 59-61, Pres. 61-65; Dir. Int. Paper Co. 65-, Pres. Feb. 66-, Pres. and Chief Exec. Officer May 66-.
International Paper Co., 220 East 42nd Street, New York, N.Y. 10017, U.S.A.

Hinshaw, Horton Corwin, A.B., M.A., PH.D., M.D.; American physician; b. 02; ed. Coll. of Idaho, Univs. of Calif. and Pennsylvania.
Asst. Prof. of Parasitology Univ. of Calif. 27-28; Adjunct Prof. of Parasitology, School of Medicine American Univ. of Beirut, Lebanon (Chair. Dept of Parasitology and Bacteriology) 28-31; Instructor in Bacteriology, Univ. of Pennsylvania Medical School 31-33; Fellow and First Asst. in Medicine, Mayo Foundation, Rochester 33-35; fmrly. Assoc. Prof. of Medicine, Mayo Foundation, Univ. of Minnesota, and Consultant in Medicine (Head of Section), Mayo Clinic; Clinical Prof. of Medicine and Head of Div. in Diseases of the Chest, Stanford Univ. School of Medicine 49-59; Clinical Prof. of Medicine, Univ. of Calif. Medical Cen. 60-; Area Consultant U.S. Veterans' Administration, Washington, D.C.; Consultant to Letterman Army Hospital, San Francisco, Oak Knoll Naval Hospital, Oakland, Calif., and Coll. of Idaho; Consultant, Weimar Medical Center, Calif.; Hon. D.Sc. (Idaho Coll.).
450 Sutter Street, Suite 1023, San Francisco, Calif. 94108, U.S.A.

Hinton of Bankside, Baron (Life Peer) cr. 65, of Dulwich; **Christopher Hinton,** K.B.E., F.R.S., M.A., M.I.C.E., M.I.MECH.E., M.I.CHEM.E., M.I.E.E., F.R.S.A., F.INST.F., F.B.I.M.; British engineer; b. 12 May 1901; ed. Trinity Coll., Cambridge.
Engineering apprenticeship, Great Western Railway Co., Swindon 17-23; engineer Imperial Chemical Industries (Alkali) 26-40, and Chief Engineer 31-40; on loan from I.C.I. to Ministry of Supply 40-46; Dep. Dir.-Gen. of Filling Factories 42-46; Dep. Controller for Atomic Energy (Production), Ministry of Supply and later Man. Dir. of the Industrial Group of the United Kingdom Atomic Energy Authority 46-57; Chair. Central Electricity Generating Board 57-64, Int. Exec. Cttee. of World Power Conf.; carried out a study of transport co-ordination 65; Special Adviser to the World Bank; Deputy Chair. Electricity Research Advisory Cttee.; Chancellor Bath Univ.; Hon. D.Sc. (Oxford, Southampton, Durham, Bath), Hon. LL.D. (Edinburgh), Hon. D.Sc. (Eng.) (London), Hon. D.Eng. (Liverpool), Hon. Sc.D. (Cambridge); Hon. Assoc. Manchester Inst. of Science and Technology; Hon. mem. Inst. of Metals, Inst. of Gas Engineers, Inst. of Welding; Hon. Fellow Trinity Coll., Cambridge; Imperial Order of the Rising Sun (2nd Class).
Publs. include lectures and papers on engineering and nuclear power development.
Tiverton Lodge, Dulwich Common, London, S.E.21, England.
Telephone: 01-693-6447.

Hiort, Esbjörn; Danish architect; b. 2 April 1912; ed. Det Kongelige Akademi for de Skønne Kunster.
Practised as Architect 37-52; Sec. Asscn. of Academic Architects 45-52; Sec.-Gen. Nat. Fed. of Danish Architects 52-59; Gen. Manager Perm. Sales Exhibition of Danish Arts and Crafts (Den Permanente) 59-67; Knight Order of Dannebrog, Officier d'Académie (France); Officer, Order of Leopold II (Belgium).
Publs. *Contemporary Danish Architecture* 49, *Housing in Denmark* 52, *Modern Danish Silver* 54, *Modern Danish Ceramics* 55, *Modern Danish Furniture* 56, etc.
Strandvejen 645, Klampenborg, Denmark.
Telephone: Bellevue 537.

Hirasawa, Kô, M.D.; Japanese university official; b. 1900; ed. Faculty of Medicine, Kyoto Imperial Univ.
Assistant Prof., Kyoto Imperial Univ. 25-26; Asst. Prof. Niigata Medical Coll. 26-30, Prof. 30-46; Prof. Kyoto Univ. 46-64, Pres. 57-64; Acad. Prize for Medical Science 51, Takeda Prize 56; mem. Japan Soc. of Neurosurgery, Japan Soc. of Neurology and Psychiatry, Japan Soc. of Anatomy.
Publs. *Der Plexus brachialis der Japaner* 32, *The cortical motor system* 51 and many articles.
43 Shinnyo-cho, Jôdoji, Sakyo-ku, Kyoto, Japan.

Hiratsuka, Masunori, M.A., LITT.D.; Japanese educationist; b. 07; ed. Tokyo Imperial Univ.
Lecturer, Aoyama Gakuin Theological School 31-36, Ferris Seminary 32-36, St. Paul Univ. 36-39, Hiroshima Higher Normal School 39-40, Prof. 40-44; Prof. Faculty of Letters, Kyushu Imperial Univ. 44-49, Faculty of Education 49-, leave of absence 60, Dean of Faculty of Education 54-55, Dir. Research Inst. of Education and Culture 56-60; mem. Nat. Inspection of Education 59-; Dir. Dept. of Education, UNESCO, Paris 60-; Dir. Nat. Inst. for Educational Research 63-; mem. Central Council on Education, Nat. Comm. for UNESCO 63-; Commdr. Palmes Académiques (France) 61.
Publs. *The Educational Thought of the Old Testament* 35 and 57, *History of Education in Japan* 38, *History of Modern Education in China* 44, *Future of Japan and Moral Education* 59.
Kokuritsu Kyoiku Keukyusho, 284 Chojamara Kamiosaki, Shinagawa-ku, Tokyo, Japan.

Hirohito, Emperor of Japan; b. 29 April 1901.
Son of Emperor Taishô, married 24 Princess Nagako Kuni; Regent 21-26; succeeded 26; heir H.I.H. Crown Prince Akihito (Tsugunomiya), b. 33, married Michiko Shoda 59.
Publs. Nine books on coral.
The Imperial Palace, Tokyo, Japan.

Hirota, Hisakazu; Japanese steel executive; b. 7 May 1899; ed. Univ. of Kyoto.
Sumitomo Steel Works 23, Dir. Sumitomo Metal Industries Ltd. 46-, Man. Dir. 47, Senior Man. Dir. 47-49, Pres. 49-62, Chair. 62-; Pres. Kansai Productivity Center; "Ranju Hosho" Decoration.
No. 27-5, 1-chome, Tsukaguchi-cho, Amagasaki-city, Hyogo-ken, Japan.

Hirota, Seiichiro; Japanese business executive; b. 25 Jan. 1905; ed. Hiroshima Univ.
Toyo Rayon Co. 27-; Dir. 56-60, Man. Dir. 60-63, Exec. Vice-Pres. 63-66, Pres. 66-.
Toyo Rayon Co. Ltd., Toray Building, 2-2 Nihonbashi-Muromachi, Chuo-ku, Tokyo, Japan.

Hirsch, Etienne; French civil engineer and administrator; b. 24 Jan. 1901; ed. Ecole des Mines, Paris.
Joined Etablissements Kuhlmann 24, attached to research laboratory 24-29, later factory man., Dir. of Research and Development and Dir. Société Marles-Kuhlmann, Société Technique pour l'Amélioration des Carburants and Société des Produits Chimiques Ethyl-Kuhlmann; joined Free French Forces 40; Asst. Dir. of Armaments, Algiers 43; Pres. French Supply Council, London, French rep. temporary Economic Cttee. for Europe 45; Head, Technical Div., Commissariat-Général au Plan 46-49, Deputy Commr. Gen. 49-52, Commr. Gen. 52-59; participated in negotiations setting up European Coal and Steel Community 50-52, NATO Cttee. of Wise Men 51-52; Pres. Euratom Comm. 59-62; Président, Inst. Technique de Prévision Economique et Sociale 62; Prof. Free Univ. of Brussels 63-; Président, Comité Central du Mouvement Fédéraliste Européen 64-; Commdr. Légion d'Honneur.
10 rue de la Justice, Sèvres (S.-et-O.), France.

Hirsch, Helge Verner; Swedish executive; b. 9 May 1888; studied law at Univs. of Uppsala and Stockholm.
Exec. Vice-Pres. AB. Svenska Telegrambyrân 14-22, Pres. 22-57, Chair. of the Board 58-; Knight Royal Order of Northern Star, Commdr. Royal Order of Vasa, Commdr. Order of the Lion of Finland, and many other awards.
c/o AB Svenska Telegrambyrân, Box 45, Stockholm 1; Home: Ulrikagatan 5, Stockholm No, Sweden.
Telephone: 62-04-42.

Hirsch, Robert; French civil servant; b. 20 Nov. 1912; ed. Lycée Janson-de-Sailly, Paris, and Ecole Polytechnique, Paris.
Sub.-Lieut. French Air Force 34, Lieut. 36, Capt. 40, Commandant 44, Dir. Supply, Accommodation and Transport, Sûreté Nationale 44; Prefect, Charente Maritime 47; Dir.-Gen. Sûreté Nationale 51-54; Prefect Seine Maritime 54-59, Nord 59-63; Admin.-Gen. Atomic Energy Comm. 63-; Commdr. Légion d'Honneur, Croix de Guerre, etc.
33 rue de la Fédération, Paris 15e, France.

Hirst, Sir Edmund Langley, Kt., C.B.E., M.A., D.SC., LL.D., SC.D., F.R.I.C., F.R.S.E., F.R.S.; British professor emeritus of chemistry; b. 21 July 1898; ed. Northgate Grammar School, Ipswich, Madras Coll., St. Andrews, and St. Andrews Univ.
Assistant in Chemistry St. Andrews Univ. 20-23; Asst. Lecturer Manchester Univ. 23-24; Lecturer Armstrong Coll., Univ. of Durham 24-26; Lecturer Birmingham Univ. 27-35; Reader 35-36; Prof. of Organic Chemistry Univ. of Bristol 36-44; Sir Samuel Hall Prof. of Chemistry and Dir. of Chemical Laboratories Victoria Univ.

Manchester 44-47; Forbes Prof. of Organic Chemistry, Univ. of Edinburgh 47-68; Chair. Chemistry Research Board, D.S.I.R. 50-55; Pres. Chemical Society 56-58; Pres. Royal Soc. of Edinburgh 59-64; Hon. M.R.I.A.; Davy Medal, Royal Soc. 48; Longstaff Medal Chemical Soc. 57, Bakerian Lecture, Royal Soc. 59, Gunning Victoria Jubilee Prize, Royal Soc. of Edinburgh 65.
Chemistry Department, The University, West Mains Road, Edinburgh 9, Scotland.
Telephone: NEW 1011 (Edinburgh).

Hitchcock, Alfred; American (b. British) film director; b. 13 Aug. 1899; ed. as engineer.
Fmr. mem. staff Lasky Famous Players Corpn.; Senior Dir. British Int. Pictures.
Films produced under his direction include: *Blackmail, Juno and the Paycock, The Farmer's Wife, Hindle Wakes, Thirty-nine Steps, The Man Who Knew Too Much, Secret Agent, Sabotage, Young and Innocent, The Lady Vanishes, Jamaica Inn, Rebecca, Foreign Correspondent, Mr. and Mrs. Smith, Suspicion, Saboteur, Shadow of a Doubt, Lifeboat, Spellbound, Notorious, The Paradise Case, Rope, Under Capricorn, Stage Fright, Strangers on a Train, I Confess, Dial M for Murder, Rear Window, To Catch a Thief, The Trouble with Harry, The Wrong Man, Vertigo, North by Northwest, Psycho, The Birds, Marnie, Torn Curtain;* television series: *Alfred Hitchcock Presents* 55-61, *Alfred Hitchcock Hour* 62-65.
Publ. *Stories Not for the Nervous* 66.
10957 Bellagio Road, Bel Air, Los Angeles, Calif., U.S.A.

Hitchcock, Henry-Russell, M.A.; American architectural historian; b. 3 June 1903; ed. Harvard Coll., Harvard Graduate School of Design.
Assistant Professor of Art, Vassar Coll. 27-28, Wesleyan Univ. 29-41, Assoc. Prof. 41-47, Prof. 47-48; Prof. of Art. Smith Coll. 48-, Sophia Smith Prof. of Art 61-; Dir. Smith Coll. Museum of Art 49-55; American Council Learned Socs. Award 61.
Publs. *Modern Architecture* 29, *The International Style* 32, 66, *Architecture of H. H. Richardson* 36, 61, 66, *In the Nature of Materials, Buildings of Frank Lloyd Wright* 42, *American Architectural Books* 46, 62, *Early Victorian Architecture in Britain* 54, *Architecture, 19th and 20th Centuries* 58, 63, 68, *The Brothers Zimmermann* 68, *Rococo Architecture Studies* 68.
111 South Street, Northampton, Mass. 01060, U.S.A.
Telephone: 584-6161.

Hitchens, (Sydney) Ivon, C.B.E.; British painter; b. 3 March 1893; ed. Bedales, St. John's Wood Art Schools, Royal Acad. Schools.
Foundation mem. of the "Seven and Five" Group 22; first one-man exhbn. Mayor Gallery, London 25; numerous one-man exhbns. Lefevre, Leicester and Waddington Galleries, London and Poindexter Gallery, New York; retrospective shows Leeds, Sheffield, London, Venice Biennale, Vienna, Munich, Musée Nat. d'Art Moderne, Paris, Stedelijk Museum, Amsterdam, Tate Gallery, London 63; rep. in many int. exhbns. including "Masters of British Painting 1800-1950" Museum of Modern Art, New York 56, Exhbn. Universelle et Int., Brussels 58, XI Premio Lissone, Italy 59, Int. Asscn. of Art Critics 12th Exhbn., Vancouver 59, Exhbn. of British Painting 1720-1960, Pushkin Museum Moscow and Hermitage Leningrad 60, Arts Council 3 Masters of Modern British Painting 61; large mural executed for Cecil Sharpe House, London 53-54; Rural Landscape, Nuffield Coll., Oxford 59; Refectory Mural, Univ. of Sussex 62; works purchased by Tate Gallery, Victoria and Albert Museum, Arts Council, British Council and numerous museums and insts. in Great Britain, U.S.A., Canada, New Zealand, Australia, France and Norway.
Greenleaves, Lavington Common, Petworth, Sussex, England.

Hitti, Philip Khuri, PH.D., B.A.; American orientalist; b. 24 June 1886; ed. American Univ. Beirut, Columbia Univ.
Lecturer Oriental Dept. Columbia Univ. 15-19; Prof. American University Beirut 19-26; Asst. Prof. Semitic Literature Princeton 26-29; Assoc. Prof. 29-36; Full Prof. 36-54; Prof. Emer. 54-; Chair. Dept. of Oriental Languages 44; Dir. Programme in Near Eastern Studies 47-54; mem. American Oriental Soc., etc.; Hon. D.Litt.
Publs. *The Origins of the Islamic State* 16, 66, *The Semitic Languages Spoken in Syria and Lebanon* 22, *The Syrians in America* 24, *Characteristics of Moslem Sects* 24, *Syria and the Syrians* 26, *An Arab-Syrian Gentleman and Warrior in the Period of the Crusades* 29, 64, *The Origins of the Druze People and Religion* 29, *Kitab al I'tibar li- Usamah* 30, *History of the Arabs* 37 (revised edn. 61), *The Arabs* 43-44 (revised edn. 68), *History of Syria, including Lebanon and Palestine* 51, 57, *Lebanon in History* 57, 62, *Syria: A Short History* 59, 65, *The Near East in History* 61, *Islam and the West* 62, *A Short History of Lebanon* 65, *A Short History of the Near East* 64, *A Short History of Syria* 67, *Makers of Arab History* 68.
144 Prospect Avenue, Princeton, N.J., U.S.A.

Hitzinger, Walter; German engineer and industrialist; b. 8 April 1908; ed. Technical Coll., Vienna.
Steyr-Daimler-Puch factory 35-44; Gen. Man. "Flugmotorenwerke Ostmark" 43-45; owner factories Linz and Salzburg 46-; Chair. and Gen. Man. A.G. Vöest 52-61; Chair. and Gen. Man. Daimler-Benz A.G. Stuttgart 61-66.
Hitzinger u. Co., Linz, Austria.

Hjalmarson, Harry; Swedish business executive; b. 19 May 1907.
Member Nat. Pension Fund 59-; mem. Board of Dirs. Commercial Banking Co. of Swedish Savings Banks, Celloplast Co., South Sweden Power Co., Swedish Saltpetre Works, Sentab, Swedish Shaleoil Co. 57-; Chair. of Board Kooperativa förbundet (Swedish Co-operative Union and Wholesale Soc.) 66-; Chair. of Board Konsum Stockholm (Stockholm Co-operative Soc.).
Home: Skinnarviksringen 10, Stockholm SV; Office: Kooperativa förbundet, Stockholm 15, Sweden.
Telephone: 69-66-22.

Hjörne, Harry; Swedish political journalist and Editor-in-Chief; b. 26 April 1893.
Editor *Frisinnad Ungdom* (The Liberal Youth) 20-25; mem. staff *Göteborgs-Posten* (The Gothenburg Post) 18, Editor-in-Chief 26-; Chair. Swedish League of Liberal Youth 23-26; Pres. Swedish Liberal Press Union; mem. of the Board of Svenska Tidningsutgivarefoereningen (Swedish Paperowners' Asscn.), Svenska Pressbyrån (Swedish Press Bureau), Tidningarnas Telegrambyrå (Swedish News Agency, owned by the Swedish Press Bureau).
Publ. *Femte Länken* (The Fifth Link) 37, *Bult and Son* (novel) 45.
Polhemsplatsen 5, Gothenburg, Sweden.

Hjorth-Nielsen, Henning; Danish diplomatist; b. 22 July 1913; ed. Københavns Universitet.
Ministry of Justice 38; Asst. to Gov. of Faroe Islands 39; Danish Mil. Mission, London 44; Ministry for Foreign Affairs 46-51; mem. Danish Del. to North Atlantic Treaty Org. (NATO) 51, to OEEC 54; Commercial Minister, London 59-63; Amb. to Netherlands 63-66, to NATO 66-, to Belgium 67-; Danish and foreign awards.
Royal Danish Embassy, 56 rue Belliard, Brussels 4, Belgium.

Hkio, Sao Hkun, K.S.M., M.A.; Burmese politician; b. 12; ed. Govt. English High School, Maymyo, Framlingham Coll. Suffolk, and Magdalene Coll. Cambridge.

Succeeded to Sawbwaship of Monqmit State 37; elected mem. Constituent Assembly 47; Counsellor for Frontier Areas to Gov. of Burma 47-48; Minister for, and Head of Shan State 48; Acting Foreign Minister 48, Foreign Minister 50-58, 60-62; Dep. Prime Minister 56-58; mem. Defence Mission and Financial Mission to U.K. to negotiate Anglo-Burmese Treaty 47.
15 Windermere Park, Rangoon, Burma.

Hla Maung, U Thado Thiri Thudhamma; Burmese diplomatist; b. 20 Sept. 1911; ed. Rangoon Univ.
Deputy-Sec. Ministry of Foreign Affairs 42-45; founder and a leader of the Anti-Fascist People's Freedom League (A.F.P.F.L.); Parl. Sec. to Minister for Forests and Agriculture, later transferred to Minister for Home and Judicial Affairs 47; mem. Constituent Assembly; then Amb. to Thailand 48-51, concurrently to Indonesia 50-51; Amb. to People's Republic of China 51-58, concurrently Minister to Mongolia 57; Amb. to Israel 58-61, to the U.K. 61-68, concurrently to Norway, Sweden and Denmark 63-68; Amb. to U.S.A. 68-.
Embassy of Burma, 2300 S Street, N.W., Washington 8, D.C., U.S.A.
Telephone: DE 2-9044.

Hlína, Jan; Czechoslovak politician; b. 14 May 1910. Former ironworker and chemical laboratory technician; mem. C.P. of Czechoslovakia 45-, fmr. Party and T.U. official, V. I. Lenin Works; Sec. Regional Cttee. of C.P. of Czechoslovakia, Pilsen 52-53, Chief Sec. 53-62; mem. Nat. Assembly, Czechoslovak Socialist Repub. 60-; mem. Central Cttee. C.P. of Czechoslovakia, Candidate mem. Politburo 58-62; Deputy Chair. Central Control and Revision Comm. of Central Cttee. of C.P. of Czechoslovakia 62-.
Central Committee of the Communist Party of Czechoslovakia, Prague, Czechoslovakia.

Ho Chi-Minh; Viet-Namese political leader; b. 90. Lived in France for some years; mem. French Socialist Party; organised Colonial Fed. and publ. *Pariah Weekly*; went to U.S.S.R. 24; took part in Great Chinese Revolution 25-27; went to Siam 27 and imprisoned for political activities in Hong Kong 31; led struggle for independence in Indo-China during Second World War; declared Pres. Democratic Republic of Viet-Nam 45; refused to recognise Bay of Along Treaty with France 48 and continued guerrilla warfare as leader of Vietminh; Hon. Chair. Nat. Cttee. of Lien-Viet Front (merger of Vietminh and Lien-Viet Leagues) and Chair. Laodong (newly formed Revolutionary Workers' Party) Mar. 51; Pres. and Prime Minister of North Viet-Nam following July 54 Armistice Agreement; relinquished Premiership Sept. 55 but remained Pres., re-elected 60; Order of Lenin 67.
Publs. *Prison Diary, Selected Writings 1920-1966* 66.
Hanoi, Democratic Republic of Viet-Nam.

Ho Lung; Marshal of Chinese army and politician; b. 95.
Formerly Commander N.W. Mil. Region of the People's Liberation Army; Vice-Premier; Chairman Physical Culture and Sports Cttee.; Vice-Chair. Council of Nat. Defence 54-; mem. of Political Bureau of Communist Party of China; Vice-Chair. People's Revolutionary Mil. Cttee.; Marshal of Liberation Army 55; Vice-Premier, State Council 59-.
State Council, Peking, China.

Ho Lu-Ting (Rodin Ho); Chinese composer; b. 03.
During Japanese war taught music at Lu Hsun Academy of Fine Arts, Yenan and conducted Central Symphony Orchestra; Vice-Chair. Union of Chinese Musicians; Pres. of Shanghai Conservatoire of Music.
Composed music for films, orchestra, chorus, popular songs.
Conservatoire of Music, Shanghai, China.

Ho Wei; Chinese diplomat and administrator; b. 08; ed. Honan Province Normal Coll., Yenan Central Communist Party Coll.
During the War, Commissar to the New Fourth Army; Mayor of Kweilin 50; Mayor of Canton 52; Asst. to Minister of Foreign Affairs 54-57; mem. Third Council of Chinese People's Institute of Foreign Affairs 55; Ambassador to Democratic Republic of Viet-Nam Jan. 58-63; Second Sec. Honan Cttee., C.C.P. 63-66; now Minister of Educ.
Ministry of Education, Peking, China.

Hoar, Arthur Stanley George, B.SC. (ECON.); British banker; b. 17 July 1903; ed. Owen's School, London, and Univ. of London.
Staff of Bank of England 23-46; Sec. of League Loans Cttee. (London) 35-46; Comptroller-Gen. of Banking Branch in Control Comm. for Germany (British Element) 45-46; Asst. Loan Dir. Int. Bank for Reconstruction and Development 46-51, Loan Dir. 51-52, Dir. of Operations for Europe, Africa and Australasia 52-55; Gen. Man. Commonwealth Development Finance Co. Ltd. 55-56, Man. Dir. 56-; Dir. C.D.F.C. (Holdings) Ltd., Toronto 63-; Dir. C.D.F.C. Australia Ltd. 64-.
Chevy Chase, Stratton Road, Beaconsfield, Bucks., England.

Hoar, William Stewart, B.A., M.A., PH.D., D.SC., F.R.S.C.; Canadian zoologist; b. 1913; ed. Univs. of New Brunswick, Western Ontario and Boston.
Demonstrator in Zoology, Univ. of Western Ontario 34-36; Histology asst., Boston Univ. Medical School 36-39; Asst. Prof. of Biology, Univ. New Brunswick 39-42; Physiology Research Assoc., Univ. of Toronto 42-43; Prof. of Zoology, Univ. of New Brunswick 43-45; Prof. of Zoology and Fisheries, Univ. of British Columbia 45-64, Prof. and Head, Zoology Dept. 64-; John Simon Guggenheim Fellowship Oxford 58-59; Flavelle Medal Award 65; Hon. D.Sc.
Publs. Articles on physiology and behaviour of fish.
Department of Zoology, University of British Columbia, Vancouver 8, Canada.
Telephone: 228-3168.

Hobby, Oveta Culp (Mrs. William P.); American newspaper proprietor; b. 19 Jan. 1905; ed. public schools, private tutors and Mary Hardin Baylor Coll.
Parliamentarian, Texas House of Representatives 26-31 and 39, 41; joined *Houston Post* as Research Editor 31, became successively Literary Editor, Asst. Editor, Vice-Pres., Exec. Vice-Pres. and Editor, Editor and Publisher; resgnd. 53, returned as Pres. and Editor 55-65; Editor and Chair. of Board Houston Post Co. 65-; Dir. Station KPRC-AM-FM-TV 45-53 and 55-65; Chief, Women's Interest Section, War Dept. Bureau of Public Relations 41-42; apptd. Dir. W.A.A.C. 42; Col. U.S. Army and Dir. W.A.C. 43-45; Fed. Security Admin. 53; Sec. Dept. of Health, Educ. and Welfare 53-55; Hon. LL.D. Baylor Univ. 43, Sam Houston State Teachers' Coll. 43, Univ. of Chattanooga 43, Bryant Coll. 53, Ohio Wesleyan Univ. 54, Columbia Univ. 54, Smith Coll. 54, Middlebury Coll. 54, Univ. of Pa. 55, Colby Coll. 55, Fairleigh Dickinson 56, Western Coll. 56; Hon. L.H.D. Bard Coll. 50, La Fayette Coll. 54; Hon. D.B.A. Southwestern Business Univ. 51; Hon. D.Litt. Colorado Women's Coll. 47; Hon. Dr. of Humanities Mary Hardin Baylor Coll 56; D.S.M. 44; Philippine Mil. Merit Medal 47.
Publs. *Mr. Chairman* (parliamentary law textbook) and syndicated column of same title.
Houston Post, Houston, Texas, U.S.A.

Höcherl, Hermann; German politician; b. 31 March 1912; ed. Univs. of Berlin, Aix-en-Provence and Munich. Assistant Judge, Regensburg 38; served Second World War; Public Prosecutor 50, Senior Judge 51, mem. Bundestag 53-; Fed. Minister of Internal Affairs 61-65,

Minister for Food, Agriculture and Forestry 65-; Christian Socialist Union.
Federal Ministry of Food, Agriculture and Forestry, Bonn, German Federal Republic.

Hochhuth, Rolf; Swiss playwright; b. 33.
Former Publisher's Reader; Resident Municipal Playwright, Basle 63-.
Publs. Plays: *The Representative* 62, *The Employer* 65, *The Soldiers* 66.
c/o Stadtstheater, Basle, Switzerland.

Hochoy, Sir Solomon, G.C.M.G., G.C.V.O., O.B.E.; West Indian civil servant and Governor-General; b. Jamaica 20 April 1905; ed. St. Mary's Coll., Trinidad.
Official Trinidad Port and Marine Dept. 31-44, Labour Dept. 44-46; Dep. Industrial Adviser, Labour Dept. 46-49; Commr. of Labour 49-55; Dep. Chief Sec. 55-56, Chief Sec. 56-60; Gov. Trinidad and Tobago 60-62; Gov.-Gen. of Trinidad and Tobago Aug. 62-.
Governor-General's House, Port-of-Spain, Trinidad.

Hochschild, Walter, B.A.; American industrialist; b. 27 Sept. 1900; ed. Phillips Acad., Andover, Mass., Yale Univ.
Began with The American Metal Co. Ltd. 20, Sec. 34-47, Dir. 28-, Vice-Pres. 42-50, Pres. 50-57, Chair. of Bd. 57-; American Metal Co. Ltd. and Climax Molybdenum Co. merged; Chair. American Metal Climax Inc. 60-65, now Hon. Chair. and Chair. Exec. Cttee.; Dir. Mufulira Copper Mines Ltd., Roan Selection Trust Ltd.; U.S. Council of Int. Chamber of Commerce; served with U.S. Army 42-45; discharged with rank of Major, Air Corps.
Home: Blue Mountain Lake, New York, N.Y. 12812; Office: 1270 Avenue of the Americas, New York, N.Y. 10020, U.S.A.

Hochwälder, Fritz; Austrian playwright; b. 28 May 1911; elementary education and apprenticeship as upholsterer; evening classes at Volkshochschule "Volkheim".
First performances in small Viennese theatres 32, 36; emigrated to Switzerland 38; free-lance writer in Zürich 45-; Literary Prize of City of Vienna 55; Grillparzer Prize of Austrian Acad. of Sciences 56; Anton Wildgans Prize of Austrian Industry 63; Austrian State Prize for Literature 66.
Publs. plays: *Das heilige Experiment* 42, *Hôtel du Commerce* (comedy) 45, *Der Flüchtling* 45, *Meier Helmbrecht* 46, *Der öffentliche Ankläger* 48, *Donadieu* 53, *Die Herberge* 56, *Der Unschuldige* 58, *Donnerstag* 59, *1003* 63, *Der Himbeerpflücker* 64, *Der Befehl* 65.
Am Oeschbrig 27, 8053 Zürich, Switzerland.
Telephone: 53-20-73.

Hocke, Gustav René; German writer and journalist; b. 1 May 1908; ed. Univs. of Berlin, Paris, Bonn.
Literary editor, *Kölnische Zeitung* 34-39; Italian corresp. for several German newspapers 40-; mem. Deutsche Akad. für Sprache und Dichtung; Commdr. Italian Republic and other awards.
Publs. *Das geistige Paris* 37, *Das verschwundene Gesicht* 39, 60, *Der tanzende Gott* (novel) 48, *Die Welt als Labyrinth* 57, *Manierismus in der Literatur* 59, *Magna Graecia* 60, *Das Europäische Tagebuch* 63.
Stampa Estera, Via Mercede 54, Rome, Italy.
Telephone: Rome 9396515.

Hodge, Sir William Vallance Douglas, Kt., M.A., SC.D., F.R.S.; British university professor; b. 17 June 1903; ed. George Watson's Coll., the Univ., Edinburgh and St. John's Coll., Cambridge.
Lecturer in Mathematics Univ. of Bristol 26-31; Fellow of St. John's Coll., Cambridge 30-33; Lecturer in Mathematics, Cambridge Univ. 33-36; Lowdean Prof. of Astronomy and Geometry, Cambridge Univ. 36-; Fellow of Pembroke Coll., Cambridge 35-58; Master of Pembroke Coll., Cambridge 58-; mem. Council of Royal Soc. 44-46, Sec. 57-65; Pres. London Math. Soc. 47-49; Cambridge Philosophical Soc. 47-49; mem. Exec. Cttee. Int. Mathe-

matical Union 52-58, Vice-Pres. 54-58; Pres. Int. Congress of Mathematicians 58; De Morgan Medal (London Mathematical Soc.) 59; Royal Medal (Royal Soc.) 57.
Publs. *The Theory and Applications of Harmonic Integrals* 41, *Methods of Algebraic Geometry* (with D. Pedoe), Vol. I 47, Vol. II 52, Vol. III 54.
The Master's Lodge, Pembroke College, Cambridge, England.
Telephone: Cambridge 53032.

Hodges, Luther Hartwell, A.B., LL.D.; American politician and businessman; b. 9 March 1898; ed. Univ. of North Carolina.
Sec. to Gen. Man. of local mills 19; Gen. Man. Marshall Field & Co.'s mills 38; Vice-Pres. Marshall Field and Co. 43; retd. 50; head of Industry Division, Economic Corpn. Admin. W. Germany 50-51; Lieut.-Gov. of North Carolina 52, Gov. 54, 56-61; U.S. Sec. of Commerce 61-64; Chair. South Regional Education Board; Chair. of Board, Research Triangle Foundation of N.C.; Chair. Financial Consultants Int.; Pres. Rotary Int. 67-; Dir. of several corpns.; Lecturer, Univ. of N.C.; Democrat.
Box H, Research Triangle Park, N.C. 27709, U.S.A.

Hodgkin, Alan Lloyd, F.R.S.; British physiologist; b. 5 Feb. 1914; ed. Gresham's School, Holt, and Trinity Coll., Cambridge.
Scientific Officer (radar), Air Ministry and Ministry of Aircraft Production 39-45; Lecturer, later Asst. Dir. of Research, Cambridge 45-52; Foulerton Research Prof., Royal Soc. 52-; Pres. Marine Biological Asscn. 66-; mem. Medical Research Council 59-63, Royal Danish Acad. of Sciences, Leopoldina Acad., German Democratic Republic; Foreign mem. American Acad. of Arts and Sciences; numerous hon. degrees; Royal Medal, Royal Soc. 58; Copley Medal, Royal Soc. 65; Nobel Prize for Medicine 63.
Publs. papers dealing with the nature of nervous conduction; *Conduction of the Nervous Impulse* 63.
25 Newton Road, Cambridge, England.

Hodgkin, Dorothy Crowfoot (wife of Thomas Hodgkin, q.v.), O.M., F.R.S.; British crystallographer; b. 1910; ed. Sir John Leman School (Beccles) and Somerville Coll., Oxford.
Wolfson Research Prof., Royal Soc. 60-; Fellow Somerville Coll., Oxford; foreign mem. Royal Netherlands Acad. of Science and Letters, American Acad. of Arts amd Sciences, Yugoslav Acad. of Sciences, Ghana Acad. of Sciences, Puerto Rico Acad. of Sciences, Australian Acad. of Sciences; Royal Medal of Royal Soc. 57; Nobel Prize for Chemistry 64; Hon. D.Sc. (Leeds, Manchester, Cambridge, Sussex, Ghana, Hull, East Anglia, London, Delhi and Kent).
Somerville College, Oxford; Home: 20c Bradmore Road, Oxford, England.
Telephone: 57125.

Hodgkin, Thomas Lionel (husband of Dorothy Hodgkin, q.v.); British lecturer and writer; b. 3 April 1910; ed. Winchester Coll. and Balliol Coll., Oxford.
Senior Demy, Magdalen Coll. 32-33; Asst. Sec. Palestine Civil Service 34-36; Educ. Officer, Cumberland Friends' Unemployment Cttee. 37-39; Staff Tutor in North Staffordshire, Oxford Univ. Tutorial Classes Cttee. 39-45; Sec. to Oxford Univ. Delegacy for Extra-Mural Studies, Fellow of Balliol Coll. 45-52; Visiting Lecturer, Northwestern Univ., Illinois 57, Univ. Coll. of Ghana 58; Research Assoc., Inst. of Islamic Studies, McGill Univ., Montreal 58-61; Dir. Inst. of African Studies, Univ. of Ghana 62-65; Lecturer, Govt. of New States, Univ. of Oxford, Senior Research Fellow, Balliol Coll. 65-.
Publs. *Nationalism in Colonial Africa* 56, *Nigerian Perspectives* 60, *African Political Parties* 61.
Balliol College, Oxford, England.
Telephone: Oxford 55250.

Hodgson, Rev. Leonard, M.A., S.T.D., D.D.; British ecclesiastic; b. 24 Oct. 1889; ed. St. Paul's School, Hertford Coll., Oxford, and St. Michael's Coll., Llandaff. Curate, St. Mark's Church, Portsmouth 13-14; Vice-Principal, St. Edmund Hall, Oxford 14-19; Official Fellow and Dean Divinity Magdalen Coll. Oxford 19-25; Prof. of Christian Apologetics Gen. Theological Seminary New York 25-31; Residentiary Canon Winchester Cathedral 31-38; Exam. Chaplain to Bishop of Winchester 31-58; Sec. to Continuation Cttee. World Conf. on Faith and Order 33-48; Theological Secretary World Council of Churches Comm. on Faith and Order 48-52; Canon of Christ Church and Regius Prof. of Moral and Pastoral Theology Oxford 38-44, of Divinity 44-58; Warden, William Temple Coll., Rugby 54-66; Hon. Fellow St. Edmund Hall, Oxford 44-, Selwyn Coll. Cambridge 57-; Hon. D.C.L., Hon. D.D.

Publs. *The Place of Reason in Christian Apologetic* 25, *And was made Man* 28, *Eugenics* 33, *The Lord's Prayer* 34, *Democracy and Dictatorship in the Light of Christian Faith* 35, *The Grace of God in Faith and Philosophy* 42, *Towards a Christian Philosophy* 36, *This War and the Christian* 39, *The Christian Idea of Liberty* 41, *The Doctrine of the Trinity* 43, *Theology in an Age of Science* 44, *Biblical Theology and the Sovereignty of God* 46, *Christian Faith and Practice* 50, *The Doctrine of the Atonement* 51, *For Faith and Freedom* 56, 57, *Church and Sacraments in Divided Christendom* 59, *The Bible and the Training of the Clergy* 63, *Sex and Christian Freedom: An Enquiry* 67.

34 Newbold Terrace, Leamington Spa, Warwickshire, England.
Telephone: Leamington Spa 23619.

Hodin, Dr. Josef Paul; British (b. Czechoslovak) author, art historian and critic; b. 17 Aug. 1905; ed. Kleinseitner Realschule, Neustädter Realgymnasium, Prague, Charles Univ., Prague, London Univ., Art Academies, Dresden and Berlin.

Press Attaché, Norwegian Govt. in London 44-45; Dir. of Studies and Librarian, Inst. of Contemporary Arts, London 49-54; Hon. mem. Editorial Council *The Journal of Aesthetics and Art Criticism*, Cleveland 55-; founder mem. British Soc. of Aesthetics; Editor *Prisme des Arts*, Paris 56-59, *Quadrum*, Brussels 59-; several decorations.

Publs. Monographs on *Sven Erixson* 40, *Ernst Josephson* 42, *Edvard Munch* 48, 63, *Isaac Grünewald* 49, *Art and Criticism* 44, *J. A. Comenius and Our Time* 44, *The Dilemma of Being Modern* 56, *Henry Moore* 56, *Ben Nicholson* 57, *Barbara Hepworth* 61, *Lynn Chadwick* 61, *Oskar Kokoschka* 63, 66, 68, *Walter Kern* 66, *Ruszkowski* 67, *Bernard Leach* 67.

12 Eton Avenue, London, N.W.3, England.
Telephone: 01-794-3609.

Hodja, Enver (see Hoxha, E.).

Hodson, Henry Vincent; British administrator and journalist; b. 12 May 1906; ed. Gresham's School and Balliol Coll., Oxford.

Fellow All Souls Coll. Oxford 28-35; mem. Staff Economic Advisory Council 30-31; Asst. Editor *Round Table* 31-34, Editor 34-39; Dir. Empire Div. Min. of Information 39-41; Reforms Commr. India 41-42; Principal Asst. Sec. Min. of Production 42-45; Assistant Editor *Sunday Times* 46-50, Editor 50-61; Provost of Ditchley Foundation 61-.

Publs. *Slump and Recovery 1929-37* 38, *Economics of a Changing World* 33, *The Empire in the World* (part) 37, *The British Commonwealth and the Future* (Editor) 39, *Twentieth Century Empire* 48.

Ditchley Park, Enstone, Oxfordshire, England.
Telephone: Enstone 310.

Höegh, Leif; Norwegian shipowner; b. 21 April 1896; ed. Oslo Univ. (Degree in Political Economy).

Chairman, Norwegian America Line; mem. of Exec. Cttee. of the Norwegian Shipowners' Asscn.; Board of Dirs. Scandinavian Shipowners' Asscn. (Legal Defence); Vice-Chair. The Nat. Theatre; Del. of Norwegian Govt. to United Maritime Authority 45-46; mem. UN Transport Comm. 46; Chair. Sea Transport Comm. of Int. Chamber of Commerce 45-51; mem. Standing Cttee. Int. Chamber of Shipping 45-66; Vice-Pres. Council of Norwegian NATO Cttee. 55-; Hon. C.B.E. (U.K.).

Home: Prinsessealleen 8, Oslo, Norway; Office: Parkveien 55, Oslo, Norway.
Telephone: 56-35-80.

Hofe, Ernst Vom, D.IUR.; German economic official; b. 30 Jan. 1905; ed. Philipps-Universität, Marburg, and Humboldt-Universität zu Berlin.

Judge, District Court, Berlin-Charlottenburg; Dept. of Money and Credit, Ministry of Econs. 35-, Deputy Asst. Sec. 62-; Exec. Dir. for Germany, Int. Monetary Fund 66-; State Commr., Deutsche Industriebank, Berlin; mem. Board Industriekredit Bank A.G., Düsseldorf, Hotelbetriebsgesellschaft (Hilton), Berlin; Deputy mem. Board European Investment Bank, Brussels.

International Monetary Fund, 19th and H Streets, N.W., Washington, D.C. 20431, U.S.A.

Hoff, Hans, M.D.; Austrian psychiatrist and university professor; b. 97; ed. University of Vienna.

Assistant Prof. 32-36; Head, Neurological Dept., Polyclinic, Vienna 36-38; Prof. of Neurology and Psychiatry, Royal Medical School, Baghdad 38-42; Prof. Columbia Univ., New York and Presbyterian Hospital 42-47; Head, Viennese Mental Hospital, Rosenhugel 49; Extraordinary Prof. of Neurology and Psychiatry and Head of Neurological Inst., Vienna 49, Prof. of Neurology and Psychiatry, Head of Neuro-Psychiatric Univ. Hospital, Vienna 50-; Chair. Fxec. Board W.F.M.H. (London) 54, Vice-Pres. 57-58, Pres. 58-59; Officer, Hon. mem. and mem. of scientific asscns. in Austria, Germany, France, Greece, Turkey, U.S.A., South America, Iran; Austrian decorations.

Publs. *Encephalitis Lethargica* 23, *Malaria Treatment in General Paralysis* 25, *Reflexes of Posture and Position* 25, *Metalues* 25, *Koerperschema* 26, *Hormonal Disturbances and Metabolism of Water* 28, *Sleep* 29, *Cerebral Function of Vision* 30, *Frontal Lobe Function* 30, *Intoxication by Metal Ions* 30, *Thalamic Lesions* 31, *Aphasia* 32, *Brain Surgery* 33, *Brain Tumours* 36, *Phenomenon of "Zeitraffer"* 38, *Multiple Sclerosis* 47, *Psychotherapy* 49, *Epilepsy* 50, *Organic Basis of Psychoses* 50, *Thalamatomy* 52, *Tremor* 53, *Alcoholism* 54, *Temporal Lobe Epilepsy* 55, *Neuroses in Childhood* 56, *Neurosis and Our Time* 56, *Mental Hygiene in Neurology and Psychiatry* 57, *Synthesis of Schizophrenia* 58, *Psychosomatics* 59, *Psychopharmacological Action of Drugs* 60, *Delinquency in Childhood* 60, *Rehabilitation in Neurology and Psychiatry* 60, *Manual of Treatment in Neurology and Psychiatry* 60.

Neuro-Psychiatric University Hospital, Lazarettgasse 14, Vienna IX, Austria.

Hoffa, James Riddle; American trade unionist; b. 14 Feb. 1913.

International Brotherhood of Teamsters 32-, leader in major dispute, car hauling industry, Detroit 33-35; Pres. Teamsters Local (299) 37; Chair. Central Conf. of Teamsters Negotiating Cttee. 40; Pres. Michigan Conf. of Teamsters 42; Pres. Joint Council (43) 46; Trustee, Int. Brotherhood of Teamsters, Vice-Pres. 52-57, Gen. Pres. 57-.

International Brotherhood of Teamsters, Chauffeurs, Warehousemen and Helpers of America, 25 Louisiana Avenue, N.W., Washington 1, D.C., U.S.A.

Hoffman, Karel; Czechoslovak politician; b. 15 June 1924; ed. Coll. of Political and Social Science, Prague. Worked on Central Cttee. of C.P. of Czechoslovakia; Gen. Dir. Czechoslovak Radio 59-67; Minister of

Culture and Information 67-68; mem. Ideological Comm. of Central Cttee. of C.P. of Czechoslovakia 63-, mem. Central Cttee. of C.P. 66-; Order of Labour 65.
Central Committee of Communist Party of Czechoslovakia, Prague, Czechoslovakia.

Hoffman, Michael L., PH.D.; American economist and journalist; b. 13 June 1915; ed. Oberlin Coll., Ohio and Chicago Univ.
Lecturer in monetary theory and international trade at Oberlin Coll. and Trinity Coll., Connecticut; Consultant U.S. Treasury 41; Acting Dir. wartime Foreign Funds Control; U.S. Treasury Rep. Allied Force Headquarters Algiers, London and Paris; European economic correspondent *The New York Times* 45-56; Dir. Economic Development Inst. of the International Bank for Reconstruction and Development (IBRD) 56-61; Dir. Development Advisory Service, IBRD 62-63; Exec. Vice-Pres. and Dir. Lambert Int. Corpn. 63-65; Assoc. Dir. Devt. Services Dept., IBRD 65-.
Office: 1818 Street, N.W., Washington, D.C. 20433; Home: RFD, Vineyard Haven, Mass. 02568, U.S.A.
Telephone: 617-693-1013.

Hoffman, Paul Gray; American international aid administrator and business executive; b. 26 April 1891; ed. Univ. of Chicago.
Salesman for Studebaker dealer, Los Angeles 11-15. Sales Man. of Los Angeles retail branch 15-17, Man. 17; served U.S. Army 17-19; purchased Los Angeles Studebaker branch 19; Vice-Pres. Studebaker Corpn. 25-35. **Pres. 35-48, Chair. 53-54; Chair. Studebaker-Packard Corpn. 54-56;** Administrator for Economic Co-operation 48-50; Pres. Ford Foundation 51-53; U.S. Del. to 11th Gen. Assembly of U.N. 56-57; Chair. Hoffman Speciality Manufacturing Corpn.; Dir. *Encyclopædia Britannica,* Encyclopædia Britannica Films Inc., New York Life Insurance Co.; Dir. Emer. United Air Lines Advisory Dir. Time Inc., Chair. of Board of Trustees, Cttee. for Economic Devt. 42-48; mem. Business Advisory Council, Dept. of Commerce; Trustee, Kenyon Coll., Gambier, Ohio U.S. Council, Int. Chamber of commerce; Chair. Public Policy Cttee., the Advertising Council; Man. Dir. UN Special Fund 59-; Administrator UN Devt. Programme 65-; hon. degrees from many univs.; numerous other awards.
Publs. *Seven Roads to Safety* 39, *Peace Can be Won* 51, *One Hundred Countries—One and a Quarter Billion People* 60, *World Without Want* 62.
United Nations, New York City 17, N.Y., and 8 Sutton Square, New York, N.Y. 10022, U.S.A.

Hoffmann, Gen. Karl-Heinz; German politician; b. 28 Nov. 1910; ed. elementary school and Acad. of Frunze, U.S.S.R.
Member Kommunistische Partei Deutschlands until 45, Sozialistische Einheitspartei Deutschlands (S.E.D.) 45-; apprentice fitter 25-28; official in Communist Youth Org. 26-30; emigrated to U.S.S.R. 35; fought in Spanish Civil War; Kominternschule, U.S.S.R. 41-43; in Germany 45-; Govt. posts, Berlin 45-52; mem. Volkskammer 52-56; Lieut-Gen. of People's Police and Deputy Minister of Interior 52-56; mem. Central Cttee. S.E.D. 52-; Lieut.-Gen. Nat. People's Army 56-59, Col.-in-Chief 59-61, Gen. 61-; Deputy Minister of Nat. Defence 56-60, Minister of Nat. Defence 60-; Rep. of D.D.R. in Supreme Command of Warsaw Pact; Vaterländischer Verdienstorden in Gold.
Ministerium für Nationale Verteidigung, Berlin, Germany.

Hoffmeister, Adolf, LL.D.; Czechoslovak painter and writer; b. 15 Aug. 1902; ed. Law Faculty, Charles Univ., Prague.
Attorney, Prague until 39; Founder-mem. Devětsil Art Union 20; emigrated to U.S. 39; on Editorial Staff, Office of War Information, U.S. 42-45; Chief, Dept. for Cultural Relations, Ministry of Information,

Prague 45-48; Amb. to France 48-51; Prof. Coll. of Fine and Applied Arts, Prague 52-; Chair. Czechoslovak PEN Club 58-, Union of Czechoslovak Artists 65-67; Del. to UNESCO; exhbns. of caricatures and illustrations, Paris, Moscow, Venice, Berlin, London, New York and Havana; Order of the Republic 60, Honoured Artist 62, Nat. Artist 67.
Publs. include *Podoby* (Images) 34, 61, *Americké houpačky* (American Swings) 37, *The Animals are in Cages* 41, Czech trans. 46, *Pohlednice z Číny* (Postcard from China) 54, *Vyhlídka s Pyramid* (The View from the Pyramids) 57, *Made in Japan* 58, *Čas se nevrací* (Time Doesn't Return 65.
College of Fine and Applied Arts, nám. Krasnoarmějců 80, Prague 1, Czechoslovakia.

Hoffmeyer, Erik, D.SC.; Danish banker; b. 25 Dec. 1924; ed. Københavns Universitet.
At Danmarks Nationalbank 51-59, Econ. Counsellor 59-62, Chair. of Board of Govs. 65-; Rockefeller Fellow, U.S. 54-55; Lecturer in Econs., Univ. of Copenhagen 56, Prof. 59-64; Gov. Bikuben Savings Bank 62-64, Chair. of Board 64; Gov. for Denmark to Int. Monetary Fund (IMF) 65-; Pres. Asscn. of Political Economy 51-53; mem. Board of Management, Nat. Econ. Soc. 60-66, Presidium of Econ. Council 62-65, Acad. of Technical Sciences 63, Econ. Council 65, Danish Science Advisory Council 65.
Publs. *Stabile priser og fuld beskæftigelse* 60, *Strukturaendringer på penge-og kapitalmarkedet* 60, *Velfaerdsteori og velfærdsstat* (edited) 62, *Industriel vækst* 63.
Danmarks Nationalbank, Holmens Kanal 17, DK-1093 Copenhagen, Denmark.

Hofland, Hendrik Johannes Adrianus; Netherlands journalist and newspaper editor; b. 20 July 1927.
Chief Editor *Algemeen Handelsblad.*
Algemeen Handelsblad, Nieuwe Zyds, Voorburgwal 234-240, Amsterdam, Netherlands.
Telephone: 229811.

Hofstadter, Richard, B.A., M.A., PH.D.; American historian; b. 6 Aug. 1916; ed. Buffalo and Columbia Univs.
Asst. Prof. of History Univ. of Maryland 42-46, Columbia Univ. 46-52; Assoc. Prof. of History Columbia Univ. 52-54, Prof. of History 54-59, De Witt Clinton Prof. of American History 59-; Lecturer Salzburg Seminar in American Studies 50, Charles A. Walgreen Lecturer in American Civilisation, Univ. of Chicago 52, Commonwealth Lecturer in American History, Univ. Coll. London 55, Pitt Prof. of American History and Insts. Cambridge Univ. 58-59; Haynes Foundation Lecturer, Univ. of Southern Calif. 62; Herbert Spencer Lecturer, Univ. of Oxford 63; Jefferson Memorial Lecturer, Univ. of Calif. (Berkeley) 66; Centennial Prof. Univ. of Toronto 67; Pulitzer Prize in history 56, in general non-fiction 64; Hon. M.A. Cambridge Univ.
Publs. *Social Darwinism in American Thought* 44, *The American Political Tradition* 48, *The Development and Scope of Higher Education in the United States* 52, *The Age of Reform* 55, *The Development of Academic Freedom in the United States* 55, *Great Issues in American History* 58, *The American Republic* 59, *American Higher Education* 61, *Anti-intellectualism in American Life* 63, *The Paranoid Style in American Politics* 65, *The Progressive Historians, Turner, Beard and Parrington* 68.
Columbia University, New York City 27, N.Y., U.S.A.

Hofstadter, Robert, B.S., M.A., PH.D.; American university professor; b. 5 Feb. 1915; ed. City Coll. of New York, Princeton Univ.
Instructor, Univ. of Pennsylvania, City Coll., New York 40-42; Physicist, Nat. Bureau of Standards, Washington, D.C. 42-43; Asst. Chief Physicist, Norden Laboratories Corpn., New York 43-46; Asst. Prof. of Physics, Princeton Univ. 46-50, Assoc. Prof. Stanford

Univ. 50-53, Prof. 54-; Dir. High Energy Physics Lab., Stanford Univ. 67-; Assoc. Editor *Physical Review* 51-53, Review of *Scientific Instruments* 54-56, *Reviews of Modern Physics* 58-61; now Editor *Investigations in Physics*, Assoc. Editor *Il Nuovo Cimento*; mem. Nat. Acad. of Sciences 58-; Fellow American Physical Soc., Physical Soc. of London; mem. Italian Physical Soc.; mem. Board of Govs. Weizmann Inst. of Science, Rehovoth, Israel; Calif. Scientist of Year 59; Nobel Prize Winner in Physics 61, other prizes and awards.
Publs. *Nuclear and Nucleon Structure*, Jt. author *High-Energy Electron Scattering Tables*, over 75 scientific papers, Co-Ed. *Investigations in Physics* 51-, Assoc. Ed. *Reviews in Modern Physics*.
Department of Physics, Stanford University, Stanford, Calif. 94305, U.S.A.
Telephone: 415-321-2300.

Hofstra, Hendrik Jan; Netherlands banker; b. 28 Sept. 1904.
Tax inspector prior to 39; tax consultant 39-45; mem. Second Chamber of States Gen. 45-56; Dir. Central Life Insurance Bank, The Hague and Central Gen. Insurance Co., The Hague prior to 56; Minister of Finance 56-58; Gov. European Investment Bank 56-58; Vice-Pres. Verolme United Shipyards, Rotterdam 61-66; Prof. Leiden Univ. 66-; mem. Labour Party; Knight of the Netherlands Lion; Commdr. Order of Orange-Nassau.
Publ. *Socialistische Belastingpolitiek* 46.
A. Noordewierstraat 67, The Hague, Netherlands.
Telephone: 371620.

Hogan, Hon. Sir Michael Joseph, Kt., C.M.G., Q.C., B.A., LL.D.; British lawyer; b. 15 March 1908; ed. Belvedere Coll., Stonyhurst Coll., and Trinity Coll., Dublin.
Admitted solicitor, Ireland 30, Kenya Bar 31, called to Irish Bar 36; Chief Magistrate, Palestine 36; Attorney-Gen., Aden 45; called to Inner Temple 46; Solicitor-Gen., Palestine 47; attached to Foreign Office 49; Solicitor-Gen., Malaya 50, Attorney-Gen. 50-55; Chief Justice, Hong Kong 55-, Chief Justice of Brunei 64-; mem. Anglo-Japanese Property Comm. (Appointed under Peace Treaty).
Chief Justice's House, Gough Hill Road, Hong Kong.
Telephone: H231321.

Hogan, Patrick, T.D.; Irish politician.
Member of Parl. for Clare 23-38, 43-44, 48-; mem. of Senate 38-43; Dep. Speaker Dáil Eireann (House of Reps.) 28, 32-38, 48-51, Speaker 51-; mem. Council of State; Chair. Civil Service Comm. 51-; Chair. Local Appointment Comm. 51-; Pres. Irish Group, Inter-Parl. Union 51-; deported to England 16 and tried by British Mil. Court for "levying war against the King of England".
Publs. *Camps on the Hearthstone, The Unmarried Daughter;* play: *Roisin's Robe;* also written many songs.
7 Ard-na-Gréine, Ennis, County Clare, Ireland.

Hogben, Lancelot, M.A., D.SC., F.R.S.; British physiologist; b. 9 Dec. 1895; ed. Trinity Coll., Cambridge.
Lecturer in Zoology Imperial Coll. of Science 19-22; Lecturer in Experimental Physiology Edinburgh Univ. 23-25; Asst. Prof. Zoology McGill Univ. 25-27; Prof. Univ. of Capetown 27-30; Prof. of Social Biology in London Univ. 30-37; awarded Keith Prize and Gold Medal, Royal Society of Edinburgh 36; Regius Prof. of Natural History Univ. of Aberdeen 37-41; Mason Prof. of Zoology Birmingham Univ. 41-47; Croonian Lecturer Royal Society 42; Deputy-Dir. Medical Statistics War Office 44-47; Prof. Medical Statistics, Birmingham Univ. 47-61; Vice-Chancellor Univ. of Guyana 63-65; Hon. Senior Fellow in Linguistics, Birmingham Univ. 61-63; Hon. LL.D. (Birmingham) 64, Hon. D.Sc. (Wales) 64.
Publs. *The Comparative Physiology of Internal Secre-*

tions, The Nature of Living Matter, Nature and Nurture, Mathematics for the Million 36, *Science for the Citizen* 38, *Dangerous Thoughts* 39, *Interglossa* 43, *Chance and Choice: An Introduction to Probability* 50, *Statistical Theory* 57, *Mathematics in the Making* 60, *Essential World English* 62, *Science in Authority* 63, *The Mother Tongue* 64, etc.
Tregeiriog, Denbighshire, Wales.
Telephone: Glynceiriog 272.

Hogg, Rt. Hon. Quintin McGarel, P.C., Q.C., M.P.; British politician; b. 9 Oct. 1907; ed. Eton and Christ Church, Oxford.
Fellow All Souls Coll., Oxford 31-; Barrister Lincoln's Inn 32; Q.C. 53, Bencher 56; M.P. 38-50, 63-; mem. House of Lords 50-63; served war 39-45; Parl. Under-Sec to Air Ministry 45; First Lord of Admiralty 56-57; Minister of Education 57; Lord Pres. of Council 57-59, 60-64; Chair. Conservative Party 57-59; Lord Privy Seal 59-60; Minister for Science and Technology 59-64; Sec. of State for Education and Science 64; Minister responsible for dealing with unemployment in the North East 63-64; Leader of House of Lords 60-63, disclaimed title of 2nd Viscount Hailsham Nov. 63; Conservative Spokesman on Home Affairs and mem. Shadow Cabinet; Rector Glasgow Univ. 59-62.
Publs. *The Law of Arbitration* 35, *One Year's Work* 44, *The Law and Employer's Liability* 44, *The Times We Live In* 44, *Making Peace* 45, *The Left was Never Right* 45, *The Purpose of Parliament* 46, *The Case for Conservatism* 47, *The Law of Monopolies and Restrictive Practices* 56, *The Conservative Case* 59, *Interdependence* 61, *Science and Politics* 63.
The Corner House, 13 Heathview Gardens, Putney, London, S.W.15, England.
Telephone: 01-788-2256.

Hoggart, (Herbert) Richard; British university professor; b. 24 Sept. 1918; ed. Leeds Univ.
Royal Artillery 40-46; Staff Tutor and Senior Staff Tutor, Univ. of Hull and Univ. Coll. of Hull 46-59; Senior Lecturer in English, Univ. of Leicester 59-62; Visiting Prof. Univ. of Rochester, New York 56-57; Prof. of English, Birmingham Univ. 62-; mem. Albemarle Cttee. on Youth Services 58-60, Youth Service Development Council 60-62, Pilkington Cttee. on Broadcasting 60-62; Gov. Birmingham Repertory Theatre 63-; Dir. Centre for Contemporary Cultural Studies 64-; mem. B.B.C. Gen. Advisory Council 59-60, 64-; mem. Culture Advisory Cttee. of U.K. Nat. Comm. to UNESCO and Del. to UNESCO Biennial Conf. 66-; Gov. Royal Shakespeare Theatre 66-.
Publs. *Auden* 51, *The Uses of Literacy* 57, *W. H. Auden—A Selection* 61, *Teaching Literature* 63.
Department of English, The University, Edgbaston, Birmingham 15; and 40 Richmond Hill Road, Birmingham 15, England.
Telephone: 021-472-1301 (University); 021-454-3798 (Home).

Hohler, Henry Arthur Frederick, C.M.G.; British diplomatist; b. 4 Feb. 1911; ed. Eton Coll. and Royal Military Acad., Sandhurst.
Served in Grenadier Guards 31-32; entered Diplomatic Service 34; Foreign Office, Budapest, Helsinki, Moscow; Head, Northern Dept., Foreign Office 51-56; Minister in Rome 56-60; Amb. to Repub. of Viet-Nam 60-63; Minister in Paris 63-65; Asst. Under-Sec. of State, Foreign Office 65-67; Amb. to Switzerland 68-.
British Embassy, Berne, Switzerland.
Telephone: 031-44-45-46.

Holan, Vladimír; Czechoslovak poet; b. 16 Sept. 1905.
State Prize 48, 65, Sicilian Prize Etna Taormina 67.
Publs. *Blouznivý vějíř, Triumf smrti, Kolury, Vanutí, Torso, Oblouk, Kameni, přicházíš . . ., Září* 1938, *Sen, Záhřmotí, První testament, Lemuria, Chór, Terezka Planetová, Cesta Mraku, Dík Sovětskému svazu, Pany-*

chida, Havraním brkem, Zpěv tříkrálový, Rudoarmějci, Tobě, První básně, Dokument, Prostě, Bajaja, Tři, Z Dokumentu, Mozartiana, Noční hlídka srdce, Příběhy, etc.

Union of Czechoslovak Writers, Národni třída 11, Prague, Czechoslovakia.

Holas, B. (Théophile); French ethnologist; b. 28 Sept. 1909; ed. Univ. de Paris à la Sorbonne.
Director, Centre des Sciences humaines, Abidjan; Curator, Nat. Museum of Ivory Coast; scientific missions in Africa, North and South America, Far East and Oceania; mem. Acad. des sciences d'outre-mer, Int. African Inst., London, Soc. des Gens de Lettres, Paris; Commdr. de l'Ordre national and several other awards.
Publs. *Mission dans l'Est libérien 52, Les masques kono 52, Le Culte de Zié 55, Les Sénoufo 57, Cultures matérielles de la Côte d'Ivoire 60, Changements sociaux 61, Les Tours 62, La Côte d'Ivoire: passé, présent, perspectives 64, La Sculpture Sénoufo 64, Les religions de l'Afrique noire 64, Le Séparatisme religieux en Afrique noire 65, Industries et cultures en Côte d'Ivoire 65, Arts de la Côte d'Ivoire 66, Craft and Culture in the Ivory Coast 68, L'image du monde bété 68, Les dieux d'Afrique noire 68.*
B.P. 1600, Abidjan, Ivory Coast; and 12 rue Vavin, Paris 6e, France.

Holbrook, David Stearns; American steel executive; b. 17 July 1912; ed. Pittsburg Univ.
Steam Engineer, Carnegie Steel Co., Youngstown 33-35; Project Engineer, Carnegie-Illinois Steel Corpn. 35-40; Asst. Chief Engineer, Homestead Works, Carnegie-Illinois Steel Corpn. 40-44; Asst. Gen. Manager, Algoma Steel Corpn. Ltd., Sault Sainte Marie, Ontario, Canada 44-45, Exec. Asst. to Pres. 45-46, Vice-Pres. 46-49, Exec. Vice-Pres. 49-56, Pres. 56-, Chair. and Pres. 62-; Vice-Pres. and Dir. Cannelton Coal Co.; Dir. Canada Steamship Lines Ltd., Dominion Bridge Co. Ltd., The Royal Bank of Canada, American Iron and Steel Inst., Du Pont of Canada Ltd., Int. Iron and Steel Inst.
Algoma Steel Corporation Ltd., Sault Sainte Marie, Ontario, Canada.
Telephone: 256-2261.

Holford, Baron (Life Peer) cr. 65, of Kemp Town; **William Graham Holford,** Kt., M.A., F.R.I.B.A., M.T.P.I.; British architect; b. 22 March 1907; ed. Diocesan Coll., Rondebosch, and Liverpool School of Architecture.
American Scholar 28; Rome Scholar in Architecture 30; in private practice; Lecturer in History of Architecture 34; Prof. of Civic Design Univ. of Liverpool 36-47; Planning Consultant to North Eastern Trading Estates; Chief Architect hostels and wartime buildings 40; Dir. of Research Min. Town and Country Planning 44; Consultant to Corpn. of London 46; Prof. of Town Planning London Univ. Oct. 47-; Consultant to Cambridge County Council and British Electricity Authority 49; part-time mem. Central Electricity Generating Board 58-; Pres. Royal Inst. of British Architects 60-62; Hon. D.Arch. (Natal), Hon. D.C.L. (Durham), Hon. LL.D. (Liverpool), Hon. D.Litt. (Oxon.).
Publs. *The Great Baroque Masquerade 33, Roman Verona 35, The Future of Merseyside 37, Town and City 43, Reconstruction of the City of London 47, Civic Design 48, Cambridge Planning Proposals 50, Corby New Town 52, Design in Town and Village 53, The Precincts of St. Paul's 56, The Future of Canberra 58.*
20 Eccleston Square, London, S.W.1; also 133 Marine Parade, Brighton, Sussex, England.
Telephone: 01-828-8772; and Brighton 64428.

Hollaender, Alexander, A.B., M.A., PH.D.; German-born American radiation biologist; b. 19 Dec. 1898; ed. Wisconsin Univ.
Asst. in Physical Chemistry, Wisconsin Univ. 29-31; Nat. Research Council Fellow in Biological Sciences 31-

33; Investigator, Rockefeller Foundation 34; Investigator in charge of Nat. Research Council Wisconsin Radiation Project 34-37; Washington Biophysics Inst., Assoc. Biophysicist 37-38, Biophysicist 38-41, Senior and Principal Biophysicist 45-46, Head Biophysicist 46-50; attached to Office of Scientific Research and Development, Atomic Energy Comm. 40-45; Dir. Biology Division, Oak Ridge (Tennessee) Nat. Laboratory 46-66, Senior Research Adviser 67-; Pres. Comité Int. de Photobiologie 54-60, Hon. Pres. 64-; Free mem. of the Exec. Cttee. 60-64; Chair. Nat. Research Council Photobiology Cttee. 55-60; mem. Radiobiology Subcttee.: mem. Genetic Effects of Atomic Radiation Panel, Nat. Acad. of Sciences 56-63; Prof. of Radiation Biology, Tennessee Univ. 55-66, Prof. of Biomedical Sciences 67-; mem. Cttee. on Int. Exchange of Persons, Biology Advisory Cttee. Italian Nat. Nuclear Research Cttee. 57-; Pres. Int. Asscn. for Radiation Research 62-66, Hon. Pres. 66-; mem. Nat. Acad. of Sciences; Sc.D. (Hon.) Univ. of Vermont, 59; Hon. D.Sc. (Univ. of Leeds) 62; Hon. D.Sc. (Marquette Univ.) 67.
Publs. A very large number of papers in learned periodicals 29-.
48 Outer Drive, Oak Ridge, Tennessee 37830, U.S.A. Telephone: 615-483-8611, Ext. 37137 (Office); 615-482-2311 (Home).

Holland, Spessard Lindsey, PH.B., LL.B.; American politician; b. 10 July 1892; ed. Emory Coll. and Univ. of Florida.
Taught in public schools, Warrenton, Ga. 12-14; served with Coast Artillery Corps, U.S. Army, and as aerial observer, Army Air Corps, France, First World War; practised law in Bartow, Florida 16-; Prosecuting Attorney, Polk County, Fla. 19-20, County Judge Polk County 21-29; mem. Fla. State Senate 32-40; Governor of Florida 41-45; U.S. Senator from Florida 46-, re-elected 52, 58; mem. Florida State, and American Bar Asscns.; mem. Exec. Council, Univ. of Fla.; Hon. LL.D. (Rollins Coll. 41, Florida Southern Coll. 41, Emory Univ. 43, Florida State Univ. 56); Hon. D.C.L. (Univ. of Florida); Hon. H.H.D. (Univ. of Tampa); D.S.C.; Democrat.
1005 S. Broadway, Bartow, Florida, U.S.A.

Holland-Martin, Edward; British banker; b. 8 March 1900; ed. Eton Coll. and Christ Church, Oxford.
Martin's Bank 23-33; Dir. Bank of England 33-48; Dir. Bank of London and South America 48, Deputy Chair.; Dir. Agricultural Mortgage Corpn., Sun Alliance and London Insurance Ltd., and Monks Investment Trust; Hon. Treas. Nat. Trust, and Council for the Preservation of Rural England.
28 St. James's Place, London, S.W.1, England.

Hollander, Franciscus Querien den; Netherlands mechanical engineer; b. 31 May 1893; ed. Technical Univ. of Delft.
Trained with Holland Railway Co. 16-17; employed by Netherlands Indies State Railways 18-37; Asst. Man. Govt. Artillery Establishments, Hembrug 38-40, Gen. Man. 40; Perm. Under-Sec., Min. of Economic Affairs 45; Man. Dir. of Traffic, Min. of Transport 45-46; Gen. Man. and Acting Pres. of Netherlands Railway 46-47, Pres. 47-59; Hon. Life Fellow Permanent Way Inst.; F.R.S.A.; hon. mem. Inst. of Transport, Inst. of Railway Signal Engineers, Inst. of Mech. Engineers, London, Royal Inst. of Eng., The Hague, etc.; Knight Order of Netherlands Lion; Grand Officer Order of Orange-Nassau; Officier de la Légion d'Honneur; Commdr. Order Dannebrog, Denmark; Commdr. Order of North Star, Sweden, and many other decorations; Hon. Dr. of Technical Sciences (Delft Technological Univ.).
9A Amersfoortseweg, Maarn, The Netherlands. Telephone: 03432-1355.

Hollenden, Baron; **Geoffrey Hope Hope-Morley,** J.P.; British industrialist; b. 28 Jan. 1885; ed. Eton and Trinity Coll., Cambridge.
High Sheriff County of London 17; Chair. I. & R. Morley Ltd. until 65, Pres. 65-.
Hall Place, Leigh, Tonbridge, Kent, England.

Höllerer, Walter Friedrich, DR. PHIL.; German writer and critic; b. 19 Dec. 1922; ed. Univs. of Erlangen, Göttingen and Heidelberg.
Dozent in German Studies, Frankfurt/Main Univ. 58, Münster Univ. 59; Ord. Prof. of Literature, Berlin Technical Univ. 59-, Dir. Inst. für Sprache im technischen Zeitalter 61-; Steuben Visiting Prof. Univ. of Wisconsin 60; Dir. Literarisches Colloquium, Berlin 63-; Editor *Akzente: Zeitschrift für Dichtung* 54 (now co-publisher), *Sprache im technischen Zeitalter* 61 (now publisher); publisher *Literatur als Kunst*; mem. German PEN Club, Akad. für Sprache und Dichtung, Berlin Acad. of Arts, Group 47, Comunità Europea degli Scrittori, Schutzverband der Schriftsteller deutscher Sprache; Literature Prize of Cultural Circle of German Industry; Fontane Prize.
Publs. *Der andere Gast* (poems) 52, 64, *Transit: Lyrikbuch der Jahrhundertmitte* (anthology) 56, *Zwischen Klassik und Moderne: Lachen und Weinen in der Dichtung einer Übergangszeit* (essays) 58, *Junge Amerikanische Lyrik* 61, *Spiele in einem Akt* 62, *Gedichte* 64, *Theorie der Modernen Lyrik* 65, *Modernes Theater auf Kleinen Bühnen* 66, *Ein Gedicht und sein Autor* (poems and essays) 67, *Ausserhalb der Saison* (poems) 67.
Heerstr. 99, 1 Berlin 19; Arndt-Str. 25, Frankfurt/Main, German Federal Republic.
Telephone: 304-58-79.

Holliday, Gilbert Leonard Gibson, C.M.G.; British diplomatist; b. 10 April 1910; ed. Rydal School and The Queen's Coll., Oxford.
Entered Foreign Service 32, has served in Buenos Aires, Valparaiso, Santiago, Katowice, Los Angeles, New York, Warsaw, Paris, Berne and Stockholm; Ambassador to Laos 56-58; Head, European Economic Organisations Dept., Foreign Office 58-60; Ambassador to Bolivia 60-64, to Morocco 65-.
British Embassy, Rabat, Morocco; also c/o Records Section, D.S.A.O., King Charles Street, London, S.W.1, England.
Telephone: 209-05.

Hollings, Ernest F., B.A., LL.B.; American lawyer and politician; b. 1 Jan. 1922; ed. The Citadel and Univ. of S. Carolina.
Admitted to S. Carolina Bar 47; mem. S. Carolina House of Reps. 48-54, Speaker *pro tem.* 50-54; Lieut.-Gov. of S. Carolina 55-59, Gov. of S. Carolina 59-63; law practice, Charleston 63-66; Senator from S. Carolina 67-; mem. Hoover Comm. on Intelligence Activities 54-55, President's Advisory Comm. on Intergovernmental Relations 59-63; Democrat.
U.S. Senate, Washington, D.C.; Home: 120 S. Battery, Charleston, S. Carolina, U.S.A.

Hollis, Rt. Rev. Arthur Michael, M.A., B.D.; British ecclesiastic; b. 23 June 1899; ed. Trinity Coll., Oxford.
Ordained Deacon 23, Priest 24; Curate St. Andrew's Huddersfield 23-24; Chaplain and Lecturer Hertford Coll. Oxford 24-31, Fellow 26-31; Examining Chaplain to Bishop of Ripon 26-31; Lecturer St. Peter's Leeds 31; S.P.G. Missionary, Bishop's Theological Seminary, Nazareth, Tinnevelly 31-37; Bishop of Madras 42, Bishop in Madras, Church of South India 47-54, Moderator 48-54; Prof. United Theological Coll. Bangalore 55-60; Visiting Prof., Vanderbilt Divinity School, Nashville 60; Luce Prof. World Christianity, Union Theological Seminary N.Y. 61; Rector of Todwick 61-64; Asst. Bishop of Sheffield 63-66, of St. Edmondsbury and Ipswich 66-.

Publs. *Paternalism and the Church, The Significance of South India, Mission, Unity and Truth.*
72 Rembrandt Way, Bury St. Edmunds, Suffolk, England.

Hollister, John Baker, A.B., LL.B.; American lawyer and administrator; b. 7 Nov. 1890; ed. Yale, Univ. of Munich and Harvard Law School.
Capt. Artillery, U.S. Army 17-19; served with American Relief Admin. in Poland and Lithuania 19; organised law firm of Taft, Stettinius and Hollister 23, senior partner 41-; Mem. House of Reps. 31-36; Exec. Dir. Hoover Comm. 53-55; Dir. Int. Co-operation Admin. 55-57.
1831 Keys Crescent, Cincinnati, Ohio, U.S.A.; and Taft, Stettinius and Hollister, 603 Dixie Terminal Building, Cincinnati, Ohio 45202, U.S.A.

Holiom, Jasper Quintus; British banker; b. 16 Dec. 1917; ed. King's School, Bruton.
Entered Bank of England 36, Dep. Chief Cashier 56-62, Chief Cashier 62-66, Exec. Dir. 66-.
Tiryns, Forest Road, Wokingham, Berks., England.
Telephone: Wokingham 1527.

Holloway, J. E., B.A., D.SC. (ECON.), LL.D., D.COM.; South African businessman and diplomatist; b. 4 July 1890; ed. Victoria Coll., Ghent Univ. and London School of Economics.
Lecturer Grey Univ. Coll. 19; Lecturer and later Prof. of Economics, Transvaal Univ. Coll.; Dean Commerce Faculty of South African Univ. 21-25; Dir. of Census and Statistics 25-33; Chair. Native Economic Comm. 30-32 and Customs Tariff Comm. 34-35; mem. S.W. Africa Comm. 35-36, Adviser Ottawa Conf. 32, World Econ. Conf. 33, Imperial Conf. 37, Montreal Conf. 58; Economic Adviser to Treasury 34-37; Permanent Head of Treasury 37-50; Del. Monetary Conf. Bretton Woods 44; Chair. Cttee. Gold Mining Taxation 45; Alternate Gov. Int. Monetary Fund 48-52; Leader, South African Del., Int. Conf. on Trade and Employment, Geneva 47, Havana 48; Dir. of Barclays Bank D.C.O. (South African Board), South Africa Mutual Fire and Gen. Insurance Co., Int. Computers and Tabulators S.A. (Pty.) Ltd., African Batignolles Construction (Pty.) Ltd., French Corpn. of S.A. Ltd., Swiss-Union Trust for S.A. (Pty.) Ltd., Anglo-Alpha Cement Ltd., Union Liquid Air Co. Ltd., Delfos and Atlas Copco (Pty.) Ltd.; Chair. S.W. Africa Financial Comm. 51; Univs. Financial Comm. 51-53 and Comm. on univ. facilities for non-Europeans 53-54; mem. Comm. regarding Europeans in Transkei; Council Univ. of Pretoria, S.A. Foundation, Simon van der Stel Foundation; Ambassador to U.S.A. 54-56; High Commr. in United Kingdom 56-58; Leader, South African Trade Mission to Europe 61; Hutchison Research Medallist.
P.O. Box 1156, Johannesburg, South Africa.
Telephone: 838-8281.

Holloway, Admiral James Lemuel, Jr., B.S.; American naval officer; b. 20 June 1898; ed. U.S. Naval Acad. and Naval War Coll.
Commissioned Ensign, U.S.N. 18, and advanced through grades to Rear-Admiral 43; served in various assignments afloat and ashore; during Second World War commanded Destroyer Squadron Ten during first African invasion. Operation "Torch"; Commdr. Destroyer and Destroyer Escort Training Group; Dir. of Training, Bureau of Naval Personnel, Navy Dept.; commanded fast battleship *Iowa* 44-45, during Luzon strikes and bombardment of Japanese homeland; commanded Fleet Training Commd., Pacific Fleet, and Asst. Chief of Naval Personnel until 47; Pres. Board establishing Navy's Holloway Plan (Navy NROTC); Supt. U.S. Naval Acad., Annapolis, Md. 47-50; Commdr. Battleship-Cruiser Force, U.S. Atlantic Fleet 50-53; Vice-Admiral and Chief of Naval Personnel 53-58; Admiral and C.-in-C., U.S. Naval Forces, Eastern Atlantic and

Mediterranean 58-59; Gov. U.S. Naval Home, Philadelphia 62-66; U.S.N. Distinguished Service Award; Legion of Merit with gold star; Grand Officer, Order of Leopold (Belgium); Order of Merit (Cuba); Naval Order of Merit (Brazil), etc.; Hon. LL.D. (Muhlenberg and Notre Dame); Hon. L.H.D. (Villanova).
1517 Duke of Windsor Road, Virginia Beach, Va. 23454, U.S.A.

Holloway, Philip Everett; British steel executive; b. 9 June 1907; ed. Sherborne School, Dorset.
Cargo Fleet Iron Co. 24-32; Assistant Works Man., Lancashire Steel Corpn. Ltd., Irlam Works 32-36, Works Man. 36-45, 45-50; mem., Allied Control Comm., Germany 45-46; Dir. Lancashire Steel Corpn. Ltd. 50-, Man. Dir. Lancashire Steel Mfg. Co. Ltd. 58-61, Chair. and Gen. Man. Dir. Lancashire Steel Corpn.; Dir.-in-Charge, Lancs. Div. Scottish and Northwest Group British Steel Corpn.
Rixton Old Hall, Rixton, Warrington, Lancashire, England.
Telephone: 061-775-2329.

Hollowood, A. Bernard, M.SC.(ECON.), F.R.S.A.; British economist and journalist; b. 3 June 1910; ed. Hanley High School, St. Paul's Coll., Cheltenham, London Univ.
Lecturer in Economics, Stoke and Loughborough Coll. 32-43; on staff of *The Economist* 44-45; Editor *Pottery and Glass* 44-50; Research Officer, Council of Industrial Design 46; Editor *Punch* 57-; broadcaster since 39, and television appearances; Hon. M.A. (Keele).
Publs. *Direct Economics* 43, *Money is No Expense* 46, *An Innocent at Large* 47, *Britain Inside-Out, Scowle and Other Papers, Poor Little Rich World* 48, *Pottery and Glass, The Hawksmoor Scandals* 49, *Cornish Engineers* 51, *The Story of Morro Velho* 54, *Tory Story* 64.
Blackmoor Paddock, Shamley Green, Surrey, England.
Telephone: Bramley 2118.

Holm, Tryggve O. A.; Swedish business executive; b. 5 Feb. 1905; ed. Royal Inst. of Technology, Stockholm, and Carnegie Inst. of Technology, Pittsburgh, U.S.A.
Engineer, AB Bofors, Sweden 29-30, Hess Bright Manufacturing Co., Philadelphia 30-31; Engineer, Steel Works, AB Bofors 32-36, Chief Engineer and Man. 36-39; Pres. AB Svenska Järnvägsverkstäderna, Linköping 40-50, Saab Aktiebolag Linköping 50-67; Chair. Swedish Metal Trades Employers' Asscn. 55-67; Chair. Swedish Employers' Confederation 67-; Chair. of Board Gusums Bruk AB 64-, Hexagon AB 65-; Chair. of Board Skandinaviska Träimport AB 67-; Chair. of Board Vegete Insurance Co. 68-; mem. Board AB Svenska Järnvagsverkstäderna 40-, Saab Aktiebolag 47-, Östergötlands Enskilda Bank 52-, Aeronautical Research Institute of Sweden 54-, Holmens Bruks och Fabriks AB 55-, Nat. Pension Insurance Fund 59-; Danish Consul 49-; several decorations.
Office: Nygatan 54, Linköping; Home: Vasavägen 13, Linköping, Sweden.
Telephone: 013-10-08-20 (Office); 013-12-58-16 (Home).

Holmblad, Niels Erik, D.SC.(ENG.); Danish telecommunications executive; b. 24 July 1905; ed. Danmarks Tekniske Hojskole.
Joined Danish Post and Telegraphs 29, Engineer-in-Chief 37-54; Gen. Man. Great Northern Telegraph Co., Denmark 54-; work on Int. Telecommunications Union (I.T.U.) and Int. Electrotechnical Cttee.G (I.E.C.); mem. Danish Electrotechnical Cttee., Pres. 55-62, and mem. Danish Acad. of Technical Sciences, Pres. 62-; many articles on telecommunications; Commdr. of the Order of Dannebrog, Commdr. Order of St. Olav, and of Swedish Royal Order of Vasa.
Tranevænget 8, 2900 Hellerup, Denmark.
Telephone: 12-00-88 (Office); HE 7088 (Home).

Holmboe, Vagn; Danish composer; b. 20 Dec. 1909; ed. Royal Danish Music Conservatory.
Teacher at Royal Inst. for Blind 40-49; music critic *Politiken* 47-55; Prof. of Composition and Orchestration, Royal Danish Music Conservatory 55-66; mem. Board of Danish Composers' Asscn.; Kt. of Dannebrog; mem. Royal Swedish Acad. of Music; various prizes.
Compositions: 9 symphonies, 14 concertos, 9 quartets, oratorios, chamber and orchestral music, choral works, etc.
Ramlöse, 3200 Helsinge, Denmark.
Telephone: 03299-45.

Holmes, Dyer Brainerd; American engineer; b. 24 May 1921; ed. Newark Acad., Carteret School, Cornell Univ., Bowdoin Coll., and Massachusetts Inst. of Technology.
Service in U.S. Naval Reserve; Bell Telephone Laboratories and Western Electric Co. 45-53; Radio Corpn. of America 53-61, engaged as Project Manager of Talos (ground-to-air-missile) and electronic count-down system for Atlas Intercontinental Ballistic Missile; Program Manager of Ballistic Missile Early Warning System (B.M.E.W.S.), Greenland, Alaska and England, Gen. Manager Defense Systems Div., Moorestown, N.J. 61; Manager Apollo Project (N.A.S.A.) to send astronauts to moon 61-63; Senior Vice-Pres., Dir. Raytheon Co. 63-.
72 White Oak Road, Wellesley, Mass., U.S.A.

Holmes, Admiral Ephraim Paul; American naval officer; b. 14 May 1908; ed. Downsville High School and U.S. Naval Acad., Annapolis.
Commissioned 30, Capt. 48; Commanded destroyer *U.S.S. Stockham* 44; Commanding Officer *U.S.S. Northampton* 55-57; Special Asst. to Deputy Chief of Naval Operations (Plans and Policy), Dept. of Navy 57-58; Commdr. Cruiser Div. Four 58-60; Asst. Chief of Naval Operations (Gen. Planning) and Dir. Gen. Planning Group, Dept. of Navy 60-63; Vice-Admiral, Commdr. Amphibious Force, Pacific 63-64; Commdr. First Fleet 64; Dir. Navy Program Office, Chief of Naval Operations 64-67; Supreme Allied Commdr., Atlantic (NATO) June 67-.
U.S. Naval Base, Norfolk, Virginia 23511, U.S.A.
Telephone: 444-6626 and -6236.

Holmqvist, Eric Bertil; Swedish politician; b. 2 Feb. 1917.
Member of Parl. 48-; Minister of Agriculture 61-.
Kanslihuset, Mynttorget, Stockholm 2, Sweden.

Holroyd, Sir Ronald, Kt., M.SC., PH.D., F.R.S.; British chemist and company director; b. 26 April 1904; ed. Holgate Grammar School, Barnsley, Yorks., and Univ. of Sheffield.
Lindley Research Fellow, Sheffield Univ. 25-26; Scientific Officer, Safety in Mines Research Board 26-28; Research Chemist, Imperial Chemical Industries Ltd. 28-46, Research Dir., I.C.I. Billingham Div. 46-52; Dir., I.C.I., responsible for research 52-57, Deputy Chair. 57-67; Dir. Canadian Industries Ltd. 55-60, African Chemicals and Explosives Ltd. 60-, I.C.I. (Australia and New Zealand) Ltd. 60-67, British Nylon Spinners Ltd. 57-67 (Chair. 64-67); Chair. Home Office Enquiry into U.K. Fire Services 66-; Hon. D.Sc. (Oxford, Sheffield, Dublin and Hull Univs.), Hon. D.Tech. (Bradford) 67.
Old Timbers, 375 Cockfosters Road, Hadley Wood, Nr. Barnet, Herts., England.

Holroyd-Reece, John; British publisher; b. 30 April 1897; ed. Stancliffe Hall, Matlock, Repton and King's Coll., Cambridge (but did not go into residence).
Served with Dorset Yeomanry, 5th Cavalry Brigade and 5th Cavalry Div. Egypt 15-19; Military Gov. of Zahle and Moallaka 18; official expert on Collotype, first Int. Mixed Arbitral Tribunal 20; founded the

Pegasus Press, Man. Dir. 25-; Dir. Pantheon Casa Editrice, Florence 30; founded the Albatross Continental Library 31; Dir. Musée Ethnographique du Trocadéro, Paris; Man. Dir. Editions des Bibliothèques Nationales de France and the Publishing Holding Co., Luxembourg; acquired control Tauchnitz Editions 34; Vice-Chair. and Man. Dir. Edizioni Continentali, Rome; mem. Royal Inst., London; Knight Commdr. Order of the Crown of Italy.
Publs. English trans. of Keyserling, Meier-Graefe, etc. The Keep, Chilham Castle, Chilham, Kent, England.
Telephone: Chilham 363.

Holt, Homer Adams, A.B., LL.B.; American lawyer; b. 1 March 1898; ed. Greenbrier Mil. School and Washington and Lee Univ.
Instructor in Mathematics Washington and Lee Univ. 20-23, Asst. Prof. of Law 23-24, Assoc. Prof. of Law 24-25; practised law, Fayetteville, W. Va. 25-33; Attorney-Gen. of W. Va. 33-37; Gov. of W. Va. 37-41; resumed law practice as mem. of firm of Brown, Jackson & Knight, Charleston 41-46; Gen. Counsel, Union Carbide & Carbon Corpn. (now Union Carbide Corpn.), N.Y. 47-53, Vice-Pres. 49-53, Dir. 44-55, mem. Exec. Cttee. 50-53; Dir. Acacia Mutual Life Insurance Co., Washington, D.C. 41-; mem. American Bar Asscn. 29-, West Virginia Bar Asscn. (Pres. 43-44) 25-, West Virginia State Bar 47-, Fayette County (West Virginia) Bar Asscn. 25-, Charleston Bar Asscn.(now Kanawha County Bar Asscn.) 41-, N.Y. State Bar Asscn. 52-53, Asscn. of the Bar of the City of N.Y. 52-, Bar Asscn. Nassau County, N.Y., Inc. 48-53, etc.; resumed law practice with Jackson, Kelly, Holt & Moxley (now Jackson, Kelly, Holt, and O'Farrell), Charleston, W. Va. 53-; Chair. W. Va. Comm. on Constitutional Revision 57-63; Dir. Kanawha Valley Bank 54-; Trustee and mem. Exec. Cttee. Washington and Lee Univ.; Hon. LL.D. (West Virginia Univ. 37 and Bethany Coll 40).
1521 Bridge Road, Charleston 4, W. Va., U.S.A.
Telephone: 346-1169.

Holt, Victor, Jr.; American business executive; b. 8 May 1908; ed. Oklahoma Univ.
Sales posts, The Goodyear Tire & Rubber Co. 29-36, Manager, Goodyear Service Store, Miami 36-37; Manager Sales Promotion Dept., Akron 37-38; Manager LifeGuard Sales Dept. 38-39; District Manager, Harrisburg 39-41, Philadelphia 41-42; Sales Dept., Akron 42-56; Vice-Pres. (Renewal Tire Sales) 56-58, Vice-Pres. (Sales) 58, Dir. 58-, Exec. Vice-Pres. 58-64, Pres. 64-.
The Goodyear Tire and Rubber Company, 1144 E. Market Street, Akron 16, Ohio, U.S.A.

Holtedahl, Olaf, PH.D.; Norwegian geologist; b. 24 June 1885; ed. Universitetet i Oslo.
Docent Univ. of Oslo 14, Prof. 20-55, Prof. Emeritus 55-; Geological investigations in Norway, Spitsbergen, Bear Island, Novaya Zemlya, W. Antarctic and Sub-Antarctic Islands; Pres. Norsk Geologisk Forening 15, 32, Det Norske Geografiske Selskab 39-45; Pres. and Vice-Pres. Det Norske Videnskaps-Akademie i Oslo 46; Assoc. mem. Acad. Royale de Belgique; Foreign mem. Royal Soc. (U.K.); Foreign or Corresp. mem. numerous geological socs.; numerous medals.
Publs. About two hundred geological papers.
Institutt for Geologi, Blindern, Oslo 3, Norway.

Holten, Cai, M.D.; Danish physician; b. 15 Nov. 1894; ed. Univ. of Copenhagen.
Chief Physician, Aalborg County Hospital 31-38; Chief Physician, Aarhus Municipal Hospital 38-; Prof. of Internal Medicine, Univ. of Aarhus 39-, Vice-Chancellor 47-49, mem. of Senate 58; Head of Dept., Univ. of Aarhus Medical Dept.; mem. Board of Danish Rheumatism Asscn. 43-; Advisory mem. Acad. of Human Rights 52-; hon. mem. American Rheumatism Asscn. 48; mem. N.Y. Acad. of Sciences 60; Pres. Scandinavian Congress

Rheumatology, Copenhagen 62; Chair. Danish Soc. for Research into Rheumatism 62; Hon. mem. Medical Soc. of Jutland 63, Danish Soc. Internal Medicine 66.
Publs. Various medical publications, mainly on metabolism, haematology, anti-coagulant therapy, and renal diseases.
22 Strandparken, Aarhus, Denmark.
Telephone: 121178.

Holten Eggert, Christian D., LL.M.; Danish diplomatist; b. 18 April 1912; ed. Metropolitanskolen and Univ. of Copenhagen.
Danish Foreign Service 37-, Asst. Chief of Section, Foreign Office 46; Dep. Perm. Rep. to UN, New York 49; Chief of Section, Foreign Office 53; Minister to Egypt and Syria 56-58, Ethiopia and Lebanon 56-61, Iraq 56-60, Jordan and Sudan 58-61; Ambassador to U.A.R. 58-61, concurrently to Iraq 60-61; Ambassador to U.S.S.R. 61-66, to Spain 66-; Chair. Danish Govt. dels. for negotiating trade and payment agreements abroad 46-49, 53-56.
Royal Danish Embassy, Serrano 63, Madrid 6, Spain.
Telephone: 226-82-96.

Holter, Heinz, DR. PHIL.; Danish biologist; b. 5 June 1904; ed. Univ. of Vienna.
Asst. Chemical Institute Univ. of Vienna 28-30; Dept. of Chemistry Carlsberg Laboratory, Copenhagen 32-42; Chief of Dept. of Cytochemistry 42-56; Chief of Dept. of Physiology 56-; mem. of Danish Acad. of Sciences 42, Royal Soc. of Sciences, Uppsala 60, Royal Physiographical Soc. of Lund 62.
Publs. Various scientific papers in the fields of organic chemistry, enzyme chemistry, cytochemistry and cell physiology.
10 Gamle Carlsbergvej, 2500 Copenhagen Valby, Denmark.
Telephone: Asta 2220.

Holthusen, Hans Egon, D.PHIL.; German writer; b. 15 April 1913; ed. Tübingen, Berlin and Munich Univs.
Served in the army 39-45; writer 45-; Dir. Goethe House, New York 61-64; Del. Biennale Int. de Poésie, Knokke (Belgium) 51-52; Kiel Kulturpreis 56.
Publs. *Rilkes Sonette an Orpheus—Versuch einer Interpretation* 37, *Hier in der Zeit* (poems), *Der späte Rilke* 49, *Der unbehauste Mensch* (essays) 51 and 55, *Labyrintische Jahre* (poems) 52, *Ja und Nein* (essays) 54, *Das Schiff* (novel) 56, *Das Schöne und das Wahre* (essays) 58, *R. M. Rilke in Selbstzeugnissen und Bilddokumenten* (biography) 58, *Kritisches Verstehen* (essays) 61, *Avantgardismus* (essay) 64, *Plädoyer für den Einzelnen* (essays) 67.
Agnesstr. 48, Munich 13, German Federal Republic.
Telephone: 372161.

Holthusen, Hermann, M.D.; German radiologist; b. 22 Sept. 1886; ed. Hamburg Johanneum, Heidelberg, Munich and Berlin Univs.
Asst., Heidelberg Univ. Medical Clinic 10; Head Physician St. Georg Hospital Radiology Inst., Hamburg 21, Supernumerary Medical Dir. 47; Prof of Radiology, Hamburg Univ. 51, Emer. 54-; Grosses Bundesverdienstkreuz mit Stern 57; Hon. Dr. Rer. nat. (Heidelberg and Hamburg Univs.).
Publs. *Lehrbuch der Dosimetrie* (with Braun) 33, *Einführung in die Röntgenologie* (with Haenisch and Liechti) 5th edition 51.
Badestr. 25, 2 Hamburg 13, German Federal Republic.

Holtrop, Marius Wilhelm, DR.ECON.; Netherlands banker; b. 2 Nov. 1902; ed. Public Commercial Training School, Amsterdam, and Univ. of Amsterdam.
With Royal Dutch Blast Furnaces and Steel Works 29-36, Man. Dir. 39-46; Vice-Pres. Shell Chemical Co. at San Francisco 36-39; Pres. De Nederlandsche Bank, Amsterdam 46-67; Pres. and Chair. of Board Bank for Int. Settlements, Basle until June 67; Gov. Int

Monetary Fund, Washington; Knight Order of the Netherlands Lion, Grand Cross Order of the Crown (Belgium), Grand Cross Order of Orange-Nassau; Dr. h.c. Netherlands School of Econs., Rotterdam, and Univ. of Basle.
Home: Zomerzorgerlaan 2, Bloemendaal, Netherlands.

Holtsmark, Johan Peter, DR.PHIL.; Norwegian physicist; b. 13 Feb. 1894; ed. Oslo, Leipzig, Würzburg and Göttingen Univs., and King's Coll., London.
Lecturer in Oslo Univ. 20; Prof. of Physics Trondheim Technical Univ. 23; Prof. of Physics Univ. of Oslo 42-64; mem. Det Norske Videnskaps Akademi i Oslo and Det Kgl. Norske Videnskabers Selskab, Trondheim; Fellow, Acoustical Soc. of America.
Publs. numerous papers in Norwegian and foreign journals.
P.O.B. 229, Blommenholm, Norway.
Telephone: Oslo 548677.

Holub, Miroslav, M.D., C.SC.; Czechoslovak writer and poet; b. 13 Sept. 1923; ed. Charles Univ., Prague.
Scientific worker, Microbiological Inst., Czechoslovak Acad. of Sciences 53-, Public Health Research Inst. N.Y. 65-67; mem. Central Cttee. Union of Czechoslovak Writers 63-.
Publs. Poetry: *Denní Služba* (Day Shift) 58, *Achiles a želva* (Achilles and the Tortoise) 60, *Slabikář* (The Primer) 61, *Jdi a otevři dveře* (Go and Open the Door) 61, *Zcela nesoustavná zoologie* (Entirely Unsystematic Zoology) 63, *Kam teče krev* (Where Blood Flows) 63, *Tak zvané srdce* (So-called Heart 63, *Anamnesa* (Selected Poems 1958-63) 64, 67; Prose: *Anděl na kolečkách* (Angel on Wheels—report of trip through U.S.A.) 63, *Tři kroky po zemi* (Three Steps on the Ground) 65; Scientific works: *Experimental Morphology of Antibody Formation* 58, *Mechanisms of Antibody Formation* 60 (editor), *The Lymphocyte and The Immune Response* 67.
Microbiological Inst. CSAV, Prague 4 Krc, Czechoslovakia.
Telephone: 438-341-394.

Hołuj, Tadeusz; Polish writer; b. 23 Nov. 1916; ed. Jagiellonian Univ., Cracow.
Studied law and philosophy at Jagiellonian Univ., Cracow; Co-Editor 36-39; soldier 39, underground 39-42; prisoner in Auschwitz, organizer of Int. Resistance Movement 42-45; journalist 46; Pres. and Sec. Int. Auschwitz Cttee. 57-67; mem. Exec. Cttee. Polish Writers Union; City of Cracow Prize 46-58; Ministry of Arts Prize and Editorial Prize 62; State Literary Prize 66.
Publs. *The Test of Fire* 45, *A Kingdom Without a Land* 54-56, *The End of Our World* 58, *A Tree Bears Fruit* 63; *Poems* 45, 60.
Cracow, Ul. Emaus 14/1, Poland.
Telephone: 209-81.

Holyoake, Rt. Hon. Keith Jacka, C.H., P.C., M.P.; New Zealand politician and farmer; b. 11 Feb. 1904; ed. Tauranga, Hastings, Motueka.
Nelson Provincial Pres. Farmers' Union 30-41; Pres. N.Z. Hop Marketing Cttee. 38-41; Dominion Vice-Pres. Farmers' Union 49-50; mem. Dominion Exec. Farmers' Union 40-50; mem. N.Z. Tobacco Growers' Fed. and N.Z. Fruit Exporters' Asscn.; M.P. 32-; Deputy Leader of Opposition 47; Deputy Prime Minister and Minister of Agriculture 49-57; Prime Minister Sept.-Dec. 57; Leader of Opposition 57-60; Prime Minister and Minister of External Affairs 60-; N.Z. Rep. at Farmers' World Conf., London 46; Chair. Gen. Council F.A.O. 55; National Party.
41 Pipitea Street, Wellington N.I., New Zealand.

Holzmeister, Clemens, DR.ENG.; Austrian architect; b. 27 March 1886; ed. Vienna Technical High School.
Prof. Düsseldorf Acad. of Arts 29-33; fmr Prof. and Rector Vienna Acad. of Creative Arts, again Prof. 54-;

mem. Austrian State Council 34-38; Prof. of Architecture at Technical Univ., Istanbul, Turkey, until 50; Pres. Austrian Kunstsenat 54-.
Works include designs for the Vienna Crematorium, Salzburg Festival Theatre and extensions, Govt. buildings Ankara, Dollfuss Memorial Vienna, churches, hotels, schools, etc., in Austria, Germany and Italy; new broadcasting house, Vienna, Parl. Bldg., Ankara, Belo Horizonte Cathedral (Brazil), etc.
Association of Austrian Technical Engineers & Architects, Vienna; Home: 1060 Vienra, Esterhazygasse 11, Austria.
Telephone: 56-12-13 (Vienna).

Homann, Heinrich, DR.PHIL.; German politician; b. 6 March 1911; ed. Gymnasium and law studies.
Military service, Second World War (Prisoner-of-War); Co-Founder, Free Germany 43; mem. Nat. Democratic Party (N.D.P.D.) 48-, Political Man. 49-52, Dep. Chair. 52-; mem. Volkskammer 50-, Vice-Chair. 54-63; Deputy Chair. State Council of German Democratic Republic 60-; mem. Presidium of the Nat. Council of the Nat. Front of Democratic Germany; mem. Presidium of German Peace Council; Order of Merit of the Fatherland in Silver; German Peace Prize; Ernst-Moritz-Arndt Medal.
National-Demokratische Partei Deutschlands, Friedrichstrasse 65, Berlin, W.8, Germany.

Hommel, Nicolas; Luxembourg diplomatist; b. 8 Oct. 1915.
Called to the Bar 39; Foreign Service 46-; mem. Luxembourg Military Mission, Berlin 46-48; Perm. Rep. to Org. for European Econ. Co-operation (OEEC) 49-58, to North Atlantic Treaty Org. (NATO) 53-58; Amb. to Belgium 58-62, to France 62-67; several Luxembourg and foreign decorations.
c/o Ministry of Foreign Affairs, Luxembourg.

Honda, Chikao; Japanese newspaper executive; b. 99; ed. Waseda University.
Joined *Osaka Mainichi* 24, Editor in Chief 45-48, Pres. Mainichi Newspapers 48-; fmr. Pres. Japanese Newspaper Publishers' and Editors' Asscn. (Nihon Shinbun Kyokai).
126 Hara-machi, Bunkyo-ku, Tokyo, Japan.

Honda, Soichiro; Japanese business executive; b. 17 Nov. 1906.
Garage apprentice 23, opened own garage 28; Owner and Head, Piston Ring Production Factory 39; started producing motor cycles 48, now Pres. Honda Motor Co.
Honda Motor Company, 5-5 Yaesu, Chuo-ku, Tokyo, Japan.

Hone, Sir Evelyn Dennison, G.C.M.G., C.V.O., O.B.E., British official; b. 13 Dec. 1911; ed. Wellington Coll.; Rhodes Univ. (S. Africa) and Oxford Univ.
Administrative Officer, Tanganyika 35; Sec. to Govt. of the Seychelles 44; Asst. Sec. Palestine 46; Colonial Sec. British Honduras 48-53; Chief Sec. to the Govt. of Aden 53-57; Chief Sec. Northern Rhodesia 57-59, Gov. 59-64; Adviser, West Africa Cttee. 67.
The Mill House, North Marston, Bucks., England.
Telephone: North Marston 268.

Hone, Major-Gen. Sir Herbert Ralph, K.C.M.G., K.B.E., M.C., T.D., K.ST.J., Q.C., LL.B.; British lawyer and colonial administrator; b. 3 May 1896; ed. Varndean Grammar School, Brighton and London Univ.
Joined London Irish Rifles 15, Lieut. 16, Capt. 18, served with B.E.F. France 16, 17-18; Staff Capt. Ministry of Munitions 18-20; called to Bar, Middle Temple, practised S.E. Circuit 23-24; Registrar Zanzibar High Court 25, Resident Magistrate 28, Crown Counsel Tanganyika 30; Attorney-Gen. Gibraltar 33-36; Attorney-Gen. Uganda 37-40; Commdt. Uganda Defence Force 40; Chief Legal Adviser Political Branch

G.H.Q. Middle East 41, Chief Political Officer 42-43; attached Gen. Staff War Office 43-44; Chief Civil Affairs Officer, SEAC 45-46; Sec.-Gen. to Gov.-Gen. of Malaya 46-48; Deputy Commr.-Gen. S.E. Asia 48-49; Gov. and C.-in-C. North Borneo 49-54; Head Legal Division, Commonwealth Relations Office 54-61; resumed private practice 61-; Draftsman, S. Rhodesia Constitution 61, Bahamas Constitution 63; Constitutional Adviser, Kenya 62, South Arabia 65, Bermuda 66.
Office: 1 Paper Buildings, Temple, London, E.C.4.; Home: 56 Kenilworth Court, London, S.W.15, England.
Telephone: 01-788-3367.

Honecker, Erich; German politician; b. 12.
Member, German Communist Party 29-46; imprisoned for anti-fascist activity 35-45; Youth Sec., Central Cttee of German Communist Party 45; mem. Central Cttee., German Communist Party 46; mem. Man. Cttee., Socialist Unity Party 46-; Chair. Central Cttee., Free German Youth 46-55; mem. Volkskammer 49-; mem. Politburo, Central Cttee. of Socialist Unity Party, Sec. Central Cttee.; Order of Merit of the Fatherland in Gold; Medal for Fascist Resistance 33-45.
Socialist Unity Party, Am Werderschen Markt, Berlin, C.2, Germany.

Honecker, Margot; German politician; b. 17 April 1927.
Co-Founder Anti-Fascist Youth Cttee., Halle 45; Sec. in Freie Deutsche Jugend (F.D.J.) Cttee., Sachsen-Anhalt; Leader, Young Pioneers, later Sec. in Central Council, F.D.J. 49-54; mem. Volkskammer 50-; mem. Central Cttee. Sozialistische Einheitspartei Deutschlands (S.E.D.) 50-; training in U.S.S.R. 53-54; Teacher Training Dept., Ministry of Educ. 55-58, Deputy Minister of Educ. 58-63, Minister of Educ. 63-.
Ministerium für Volksbildung, Berlin, Germany.

Hongladarom, Sunthorn, B.A.; Thai politician and economist; b. 23 Aug. 1912; ed. Thepsirin School, Bangkok, Weymouth Coll., England and Cambridge Univ.
Chief of Foreign Div. Dept. of Information 43-46; Asst. Sec.-Gen. of Council of Ministers 48-50; Sec.-Gen. of Nat. Econ. Council 50-57; Amb. to Fed. of Malaya 57-59; Minister of Econ. Affairs 59; Minister of Finance 59-65; Deputy Minister of Nat. Devt. 63; Minister of Econ. Affairs 65-68; Amb. to the U.K. 68-; Rector of Chiengmai Univ. 66; Fellow of Econ. Devt. Inst., Int. Bank of Reconstruction and Devt.
Royal Embassy of Thailand, Queen's Gate, London, S.W.7, England.

Hönsvald, Nils; Norwegian politician; b. 4 Dec. 1899; ed. Nordic Acad., Geneva.
Became journalist 19; Editor various Labour Party newspapers 22-; mem. Sarpsborg City Council 32-(Exec. mem. 35-47); mem. Storting 45-, Deputy Pres. 58-61; Chair. State Social Insurance Authority 46-; Minister of Supply 48-50; Parl. Leader Labour Party 55-64; Pres. Lagting (Upper Chamber) 61-65, Odelsting (Lower Chamber) 65-.
Odelsting, Oslo, Norway.

Hont, Ferenc, CAND. LITT., D.PHIL.; Hungarian theatrical producer; b. 07; ed. Szeged.
Producer at Odeon Theatre Paris 25-28, at various Hungarian theatres 28-44; edited dramatic papers 34-38; Sec. of Histrionic Soc. 36-; escaped to Russia 44, returned 45; Dir. Acad. of Dramatic Art 45; Dir. Madách Theatre 46; Artistic Dir. of Hungarian Nat. Film Company 48; Dir. Youth Theatre 50, Museum of Theatrical History 52; Pres. Council of Theatrical History of the Hungarian Acad. of Sciences 67; Pres. Inst. of Theatrical and Film Science 57, Hungarian Centre Int. Theatrical Inst. 57; Dir. Inst. for Theatrical Sciences 59-; instigator of open-air Summer Festival Plays of Szeged; Kossuth Prize 49.

Publs. *A Színjáték, Színház és Munkásosztály, A Színészi képzelet fejlesztése, Az eltünt magyar színjáték, Költészet a dobogón, A rendező munkája, A színjátszó munkája, Valóság a színpadon, From a Director's Notebook.*
Institute for Theatrical Sciences, Krisztina körut 57, Budapest I, Hungary.
Telephone: 354-536.

Hoo Chi-Tsai, Victor (Hu-Shih-tse), LL.B., LL.D.; Chinese diplomatist; b. 16 Nov. 1894; ed. Paris.
Asst. Sec. Chinese Del. Peace Conf. 19; Chargé d'Affaires in Berlin 24; Sec. Min. of Foreign Affairs 28; Dir. of Asiatic Affairs in Foreign Office 30-31; Dir. Permanent Office of Chinese Del. to L.N. 31-40 and concurrently Min. to Switzerland 32-42; Vice-Min. Foreign Affairs 42-45; Asst. Sec.-Gen. for Trusteeship, UN 46-54; Under-Sec. for Conference Services, UN 55-61; Commr. for Technical Assistance, UN 62-.
3 Borghild Avenue, Yonkers, N.Y., U.S.A.

Hook, Sidney, PH.D.; American philosopher and author; b. 20 Dec. 1902; ed. Coll. of City of New York and Columbia Univ.
Instructor of Philosophy, New York Univ. 27-32, Asst. Prof. of Philosophy 32-34, Assoc. Prof. and Chair. of Dept. 34-39, Prof. 39-, Head All-Univ. Dept. of Philosophy 50-; Dir. N.Y. Univ. Inst. of Philosophy and Editor of its *Proceedings*; Dr. of Humane Letters, Univ. of Maine 60, LL.D. Univ. of Calif. 66.
Publs. *The Metaphysics of Pragmatism* 27, *Towards the Understanding of Karl Marx* 33, *From Hegel to Marx* 36, *Reason, Social Myth and Democracy* 39, *The Hero in History: A Study in Limitation and Possibility* 45, *Education for Modern Man* 47, *Heresy Yes, Conspiracy No* 53, *Common Sense and the Fifth Amendment* 58, *Political Power and Personal Freedom* 59, *The Ambiguous Legacy: Marx and the Marxists* 60, *The Quest of Being* 61, *The Paradoxes of Freedom* 62, *The Fail-Safe Fallacy* 63, *Religion in a Free Society* 67.
c/o Department of Philosophy, New York University, Washington Square, New York, N.Y. 10003, U.S.A.

Hooper, Frank Arthur; American judge; b. 21 April 1895; ed. Georgia Inst. of Technology and Atlanta Law School.
Admitted to Georgia Bar; Sec. to Judge, Georgia Court of Appeals 17; private legal practice 19-43; Judge, Georgia Court of Appeals 33; Instructor, Atlanta Law School 34-43; Asst. City Attorney, Atlanta 40-43; Judge, Superior Court, Atlanta Judicial Circuit 43-49; Chief Judge, N. District, Georgia 49-.
U.S. Courts, Northern District of Georgia, Atlanta 1, Georgia, U.S.A.

Hooper, Sir Robin William John, K.C.M.G., D.S.O., D.F.C.; British diplomatist; b. 26 July 1914; ed. Charterhouse and The Queen's Coll., Oxford.
Entered Foreign Office 38; served R.A.F. 40-44; Second Sec., Paris 44-47, First Sec., Lisbon 47-49. Head of Personnel Dept., Foreign Office 50-53, Counsellor, Baghdad 53-56, Head of Perm. Under-Sec.'s Dept., Foreign Office 56-60; Asst. Sec.-Gen. (Political Affairs) NATO 60-66; Amb. to Tunisia 66-68, to People's Repub. of S. Yemen 68-.
British Embassy, Aden, People's Repub. of S. Yemen.

Hoover, Calvin Bryce, A.B., PH.D.; American economist; b. 14 April 1897; ed. Monmouth Coll., Univ. of Minnesota, Univ. of Wisconsin.
Served Artillery U.S. Army 17-19; Instructor School of Business Univ. of Minnesota 23-25; Asst. Prof. Duke Univ. 25-27, Prof. 27-; Dean, Graduate School 38-47; Economic Adviser U.S. Dept. of Agriculture 33-34; Consumers Counsel A.A.A. 35; Consultant Nat. Resources Planning Board 37; Consultant, Advisory Cttee. to Council of Nat. Defence 40-41; Economic Adviser O.S.S. 41-44; Economic Adviser U.S. Control Council

for Germany 45; Research staff Cttee. for Economic Development 44-45; mem. President's Cttee. on Foreign Aid 47; Economic Adviser to U.S. Special Rep. in Europe for European Economic Recovery 48; **Pres. Southern Economic Asscn. 37;** Vice-Pres. **American** Economic Asscn. 40, Pres. 53; Pres. Asscn. for Comparative Econs. 64; Distinguished Fellow, American Econ. Asscn. 65; Hon. Litt.D. from Columbia Univ. and Monmouth Coll.; awarded U.S. Medal of Freedom 47. Publs. *The Economic Life of Soviet Russia* 31, *Germany Enters the Third Reich* 33, *Dictators and Democracies* 37, *International Trade and Domestic Employment* 45, *Impact of Federal Policies on the Economy of the South* 49, *Economic Resources and Policies of the South* (jointly) 51, *The Economy, Liberty and The State* 59, *Economic Systems of The Commonwealth* 62, *Memoirs of Capitalism, Communism and Nazism* 65.
Duke University, Durham, North Carolina, U.S.A.

Hoover, Herbert, Jr., B.A., M.B.A.; American engineer and public servant; b. 4 Aug. 1903; ed. Stanford Univ. and Harvard.
Teaching Fellow, California Inst. of Technology 34-35; Pres. United Geophysical Co. 35-53, Chair. 52-53; Pres. Consolidated Engineering Corpn. 36-46; Consultant to Govts. of Venezuela, Iran, Brazil, Peru, etc. 40-53; Special Adviser to Sec. of State 53-54; Under-Sec. of State 54-57; Dir. Southern Cal. Edison Co.; hon. degrees New York Univ., Temple Univ., Rutgers (56), Univ. of Southern California (57); Kemp Medal in Geology, Columbia Univ. 56; Hoover Medal in Engineering 57.
70 Park Drive, Bal Harbour, Florida 33154, U.S.A. Telephone: 864-8865.

Hoover, Herbert William, Jr., A.B.; American executive; b. 23 April 1918; ed. Rollins Coll.
Exec. Sales, The Hoover Co. 41-43; 2nd Lt. U.S. Army 43-45; Dir. of Public Relations, The Hoover Co. 45-48, Dir. 45-, Asst. Vice-Pres. 48-52, Sales Vice-Pres. 52-53; Exec. Vice-Pres. 53-54, Pres. 54-66, Chair. 59-66; Dir. Hoover Co., Canada 52-66, Pres. 54-66; Dir. Hoover (Great Britain) Ltd. 54-66, Pres. 56-66; Dir. and Pres. Hoover (America Latina) S.A., Panama 55-66, Hoover Mexicana, Mexico 55-66; Hoover Inc., Panama, Hoover Industrial y Comercial S.A. Colombia 60-67; Pres. and Chair. Hoover Worldwide Corpn. 60-66; Pres. Dir.-Gen. S.A. Hoover, France 65; fmr. Regional Vice-Chair. U.S. Cttee. for UN; Dir. The Harter Bank and Trust Co. Canton, Ohio; Hon. LL.D. Mount Union Coll.; Chevalier de la Légion d'Honneur.
P.O. Box 2151, North Canton, Ohio 44720, U.S.A.

Hoover, John Edgar, LL.M.; American lawyer and civil servant; b. 1 Jan. 1895; ed. George Washington Univ. Clerk, Library of Congress 13; entered U.S. Dept. of Justice 17, Special Asst. to Attorney-Gen. 19, Asst. Dir. Bureau of Investigation 21, Dir. Fed. Bureau of Investigation 24-; honours include Presidential Medal of Merit from Pres. of Nicaragua 46, Medal of Merit from Pres. of U.S. 46, Hon. K.B.E. (Great Britain) 47; Hon. LL.D. (George Washington Univ., Pa. Mil. Coll., N.Y. Univ., Westminster Coll., Okla. Baptist Univ., Georgetown Univ., Drake Univ., Univ. of Notre Dame, St. John's Univ. Law School, Rutgers Univ., Univ. of Ark., Seton Hall Coll., Holy Cross Coll., Pace Coll., Marquette Univ., Morris Harvey Coll. and the Catholic Univ. of America); Hon. D.Sc. (Kalamazoo Coll.), Hon. D.C.L. (Univ. of the South), Nat. Security Medal 55, Pres. Award for Distinguished Fed. Civilian Service 58, Humanitarian of the Year Award 59, Distinguished Service Citation of Reserve Officers' Asscn. 60, United Service Orgs. Award 61, Mutual of Omaha Criss Award 61, Freedoms Foundation's George Washington Award 62, Distinguished Service Award of Order Knights of Pythias 62, Gold Medal of Merit of the Jewish War Veterans of the U.S.A. 62, Pro Deo et Juventute Award, Nat. Catholic Youth Org. 63; Brotherhood

Award, Brotherhood of Washington Hebrew Congregation 63, Sword of Loyola Award 64, Gold Medal of the Pennsylvania Soc. 64, Grand Cross of Honour Award, Supreme Council 33°, Scottish Rite 65.
Publs. *Persons in Hiding* 38, *Masters of Deceit* 58, *A Study of Communism* 62.
Federal Bureau of Investigation, Ninth Street and Pennsylvania Avenue, Washington D.C. 20535, U.S.A.

Hoover, Paul Edward; American banker; b. 7 June 1898; ed. schools in Kalispell, Mont.
With First and Conrad Nat. Banks, Kalispell 19-21; Nat. Bank Examiner, Office of Comptroller of Currency, Nat. Banking Dept. 7th and 9th Fed. Reserve Dist. 21-25, Commissioned Nat. Bank Examiner, H.Q. Minneapolis 25; Vice-Pres. N.W. Bancorporation, Minneapolis 29-33; Vice-Pres. Anglo-Calif. Nat. Bank, San Francisco (now Crocker-Citizens Nat. Bank) 33-51, Pres. 51-62, Chair. of Board and Principal Officer 62-; Dir. The Greyhound Corpn., American President Lines Ltd., Nat. Industrial Conf. Board Inc., San Francisco Symphony Asscn., San Francisco Stock Exchange Club; Trustee and Treas. San Francisco Bay Area Council Inc.; Consulting Prof. of Banking in Graduate School of Banking, Stanford Univ.
Office: 1 Montgomery Street, San Francisco 20, Calif.; Home: 459 Roblar Avenue, Hillsborough, Calif., U.S.A.

Hooykaas, Reijer, D.SC.; Netherlands university professor; b. 1 Aug. 1906; ed. Utrecht Univ.
Chemistry teacher, Christelijke Hoogere Burgerschool A, Amsterdam 30, Christelijk Lyceum, Zeist 32; Extraordinary Prof. of History of Science, Free Univ. of Amsterdam 45-48, Prof. 48-66, Prof. of History of Science, Univ. of Utrecht 67-; mem. Royal Netherlands Acad. of Sciences and Letters, Int. Acad. of History of Science, Hollandsche Maatschappij der Wetenschappen; assoc. mem. Comité belge d'Histoire des Sciences; foreign mem. Royal Flemish Acad. of Sciences and Acad. da Cultura Portuguesa; Vice-Pres. Int. Comm. History Geological Sciences, Moscow; Knight Order of Nederlandse Leeuw; Commdr. Order of Polonia Restituta.
Publs. *The Concept of Element, its historical-philosophical development* 33, *Robert Boyle: a study in Science and Christianity* 43, *The Chemical Revolution: A. L. Lavoisier* 52, *Humanisme, Science et Réforme, Pierre de la Ramée* 58, *The Principle of Uniformity in Geology, Biology and Theology* 59, 63; *Physik und Mechanik in historischer Hinsicht* 63, *Introdução à Historia das Ciências* 65; numerous articles in international historical and scientific journals.
Krullelaan 35, Zeist, Netherlands. Telephone: 03404-12488.

Hope, Alec Derwent; Australian poet; b. 21 July 1907; ed. Sydney and Oxford Univs.
Former Lecturer Sydney Teachers' Coll. and Senior Lecturer Melbourne Univ.; Prof. of English Canberra Univ. Coll. 50-60, Australian Nat. Univ. 60-; Arts Council Prize 65, Britannica-Australia Award 66.
Publs. *The Wandering Islands* 55, *Poems* 60, *The Cave and the Spring* 65, *Collected Poems* 66; verse and criticism in numerous magazines, including *Meanjin, Southerly, M.U.M., Hermes, Quadrant* and *The Southern Review.*
Australian National University, Canberra, A.C.T.; 66 Arthur Circle, Canberra, A.C.T., Australia. Telephone: Canberra U1342.

Hope, Bob; American (b. British) comedian; b. 1904. First film 38; since then has appeared in numerous films and radio and television productions; American Congressional Medal of Honor 63; films include *College Swing* 38, *Road to Singapore* 40, *Caught in the Draft* 41, *Road to Morocco* 42, *Let's Face It* 43, *Road to Rio* 46, *Paleface* 47, *Fancy Pants* 49, *My Favourite Spy*

51, *Road to Bali* 52, *Casanova* 53, *That Certain Feeling* 56, *Beau James* 57, *Paris Holiday* 58, *Alias Jesse James* 59, *The Facts of Life* 60, *The Road to Hong Kong* 61, *Call Me Bwana* 62, *A Global Affair* 64, *I'll Take Sweden* 65, *Boy, did I get a Wrong Number!* 66.
Publs. *I Never Left Home, They Got Me Covered, So This Is Peace, Have Tux, Will Travel, I Owe Russia $1200* 63, *Five Women I Love* 67.
c/o Paramount Pictures, 5451 Marathon Street, Hollywood, Calif. U.S.A.

Hope, Charles Peter, B.SC. C.M.G. T.D.; British diplomatist; b. 22 May 1912; ed. Oratory School and Imperial Coll. London.
Joined War Office 38; service with Royal Artillery 39-46; entered Foreign Service 46, served Paris 46-50; Asst. Head, U.N. Dept., Foreign Office 50-53; served as Counsellor, High Comm. Germany, later at Embassy, 53-56; Head of News Dept., Foreign Office 56-59; Minister, Madrid 59-62; Consul-Gen. Houston, U.S.A. 63-64; Alternate Rep., UN 64-68; Amb. to Mexico 68-.
British Embassy, Mexico City, Mexico.

Hopf, Heinz, DR. PHIL.; Swiss mathematician; b. 19 Nov. 1894; ed. König-Wilhelms-Gymnasium Breslau and Univs. of Breslau, Heidelberg, Berlin and Göttingen.
Privatdozent Univ. of Berlin 26-31; Rockefeller Fellow, Princeton Univ. 27-28; Prof. Eidgenössische Technische Hochschule (Swiss Fed. Inst. of Technology), Zürich 31-65; Pres. Int. Mathematical Union 55-58; mem. Heidelberg Acad., Nat. Acad. of Sciences (U.S.A.), Leopoldina Acad., Halle, American Acad. of Arts and Sciences, American Philosophical Soc., Accademia Nazionale dei Lincei, Acad. Göttingen; Gauss-Weber Medal, Göttingen; Dr. h.c. (Princeton, Freiburg-im-Breisgau, Manchester, Paris, Brussels and Lausanne).
Publ. (with Paul Alexandroft) *Topologie I* 35.
Alte Landstrasse 37, Zollikon (Zürich), Switzerland.

Hopkinson, (Henry) Thomas, C.B.E., M.A.; British journalist and author; b. 19 April 1905; ed. St. Edward's School and Pembroke Coll., Oxford.
Asst. Editor *Weekly Illustrated* 34-38; Editor *Picture Post* 40-50, *Lilliput* 41-46; Features Editor *News Chronicle* 54-56; Editor *Drum* 58-61; Dir. for Africa, Int. Press Inst. 63-66; Senior Fellow in Press Studies Univ. of Sussex 67-; contributor to *The Observer*, and British and American magazines.
Publs. *A Wise Man Foolish* 30, *A Strong Hand at the Helm* 33, *The Man Below* 39, *Mist in the Tagus* 46, *The Transitory Venus* 48, *Down the Long Slide* 49, *Love's Apprentice, George Orwell* 53, *The Lady and the Cut-Throat* 58, *In the Fiery Continent* 62, *South Africa* 64.
Flat 9, 2 Grand Avenue, Hove, Sussex, England.
Telephone: OBR3-777137.

Hoppé, E. O., F.R.P.S.; British photographer and author; b. in Germany 78; ed. Paris and Vienna.
Travelled extensively in Europe, America, Australia, Africa and the Far East; works in nat. and municipal art galleries and museums; perm. collection in Japan.
Publs. *The Russian Ballet, Picturesque Great Britain, In Gypsy Camp and Royal Palace, Romantic America, Cities Time Has Passed By, Bali, The Fifth Continent, The Book of Fair Women* (with Richard King), *Across the World with a Camera, Unknown London, Hundred Thousand Exposures, Island of Song and Laughter, Rural London, London Tapestry, The Life of Famous Pirates, Legends of the Balkan Gipsies, Jamaica— Island of Many Waters.*
The Savage Club, Carlton House Terrace, London, S.W.1; and Triangle, Wildhern, near Andover, Hampshire, England.
Telephone: Hathenden 228.

Hoppenot, Henri; French diplomatist and writer; b. 25 Oct. 1891; studied Law and Philosophy at Paris and Oxford.
Entered diplomatic service 14; Sec. and Chargé d'Affaires in Switzerland, Brazil, Iran, Chile, Germany, Syria, and China; Dir. of European Affairs at Ministry of Foreign Affairs 38-40; Minister Plenipotentiary in Uruguay until resignation in 42; represented French Cttee. of Nat. Liberation in the Antilles 43; Del. of the French Provisional Govt. in Washington 43-44; Ambassador to Switzerland 45-51; Permanent Del. to Security Council and U.N. 52-55; High Commissioner to Viet-Nam 55-56; Pres. Control Comm. for referendum and general elections in Algeria 58; Grand Officier Légion d'Honneur 55; Conseiller d'Etat 56-; Pres. Cour Arbitrale de la Communauté 59-61; mem. Haut-Tribunal Militaire 61-62; Hon. Conseiller d'Etat 64.
Publs. *Trois Poèmes* 11, *Moharem* 23, *Continent Perdu* 27-47.
42 Quai des Orfèvres, Paris, France.
elephone: 033-36-30.

Hopson, Sir Donald (Charles), K.C.M.G., D.S.O., M.C., T.D.; British diplomatist; b. 31 Aug. 1915; ed. Christ's Hospital and Univ. Coll., Oxford.
Kelsall & Kemp Ltd. (woollen manufacturers), Rochdale 38-39; British Army, France and Belgium 40, Sicily and Italy 43, France, Belgium, Holland and Germany 44-45; Diplomatic Service 45-, served Copenhagen 46-48, Saigon 48-50, Budapest 50-52, Buenos Aires 55-57; Amb. to Laos 62-65; Chargé d'Affaires *en titre*, Peking 65-, concurrently Amb. to Mongolia 65-66.
c/o Diplomatic Service Mail Office, King Charles Street, London, S.W.1; Home: 16 Chelsea Embankment, London, S.W.3, England.
Telephone: 01-352-4262 (Home).

Horák, Jiří; Czechoslovak folklorist and literary historian; b. 4 Dec. 1884; ed. Charles Univ., Prague.
Lecturer Charles Univ. of Prague 19; Prof. of History of Slavonic Literatures and Folklore, Masaryk Univ. Brno 23-26; Prof. Prague Univ. 26-51; Czechoslovak Amb. to U.S.S.R. 45-48; Dir. Inst. of Ethnography, Czechoslovak Acad. of Sciences 57-64, leading mem. 64-; mem. of Czechoslovak Acad.; mem. Serbian Acad. Belgrade and Warsaw Scientific Soc.; Collaborator, Polish Acad. Cracow; Hon. Fellow Royal Anthropological Inst. of G.B. and Ireland, Hungarian Ethnographical Soc.; Légion d'Honneur.
Publs. *Národopis československý, Masaryk a Dosotjevskij, Z dějin literatur slovanských, Naše lidová píseň, Humor, vtip a satira v české lidové písni, České legendy, Český Honza, Běloruské pohádky, České ponádky, Slovenské ľudové balady, Pohádky a písně Lužických Srbů, The Feudal Survivals in Slovak Popular Balladry, Zbojnícke piesne slovenského ludu.*
Na Ořechovce 71, Prague 6, Czechoslovakia.
Telephone: 35-20-34.

Horenstein, Jascha; American (b. Ukraine) conductor; b. 6 May 1899; ed. Universität Wien.
Conductor, Vienna Symphony Orchestra 23-25, Berlin Symphony Orchestra 25-28; Musical Dir. Düsseldorf Opera 29-33; has conducted with principal orchestras throughout the world; Grand Prix du Disque (three times).
12 Chemin du Coteau, Lausanne-Pully, Switzerland.

Horgos, Dr. Gyula; Hungarian mechanical engineer and politician; b. 20; ed. Budapest Technical Univ.
Engineer, Csepel Machine Tool Plant 43-49; postgraduate studies 49-53; Chief Engineer, Csepel Metal Works 54, later Vice-Pres. Nat. Planning Office, later Technical Dir. Csepel Metal Works; Dep. Minister of Foundry and Machine Industry 60-63, Minister 63-; mem. Communist Party 45-.
Minister of Foundry and Machine Industry, Budapest, Hungary.

Horikoshi, Teizo, LL.B.; Japanese business executive; b. 13 Dec. 1898; ed. Tokyo Imperial Univ.
Entered Bank of Japan 24, Dir. 47-; Deputy Dir. Econ. Stabilization Agency 47; Sec.-Gen. Japanese Nat. Cttee. of Int. Chamber of Commerce 50; Exec. Dir. and Sec.-Gen. Fed. of Econ. Orgs. 54-; Auditor, Toho Mutual Life Insurance Co. 59-; Pres. Securities and Exchange Council, Ministry of Finance 61-; Pres. Nippon Usiminas Co. Ltd. 65-; Hon. C.B.E. (U.K.) 66.
270 Kyodo-machi, Setagaya-ku, Tokyo, Japan.

Horn, Maj.-Gen. Carl Von; Swedish officer; b. 15 July 1903; ed. Stockholm.
Aide to Count Bernadotte in repatriation operations 43-45; Mil. Attaché in Oslo 47, in Copenhagen 48; Col.-in-Chief, Kronobergs Reg. 50-57; Commdr. Malmo Defence Area 57-58; Chief of Staff of UN Truce Supervisory Org. (Palestine) 58-60, 61-63; Commdr. UNOC (UN Operations in the Congo) 60-61; Head UN Mission to Yemen June-Aug. 63 (resigned).
Publ. *Soldiering for Peace* 66.
c/o Jordberga, Klagstorp, Sweden.
Telephone: Ohio 26512.

Hornby, Robert A.; American businessman; b. 1900; ed. Univ. of Calif.
President and Director Pacific Lighting Corpn.; Chair. of Bd. and Dir. Pacific Lighting Gas Supply Co.; Dir. United Calif. Bank; Dir. and Treas. Calif. State Chamber of Commerce; Trustee Univ. of S. Calif.; Trustee St. Francis Memorial Hospital (San Francisco); mem. or official of several other social and professional bodies.
Home: 2515 Scott Street, San Francisco 15; Office: 600 California Street, San Francisco 8, Calif., U.S.A.

Horne, Lena; American singer; b. 30 June 1917.
Dancer, Cotton 34; tours and recordings with Noble Sissle Orchestra 35-36, with Charles Barnett's Band 40-41; star of several films, including *Cabin in the Sky*, *Stormy Weather*; numerous television performances.
Publ. *Lena* (autobiog.) 66.
300 West End Avenue, New York City, New York, U.S.A.

Horner, Horace Mansfield, B.S.; American aircraft executive; b. 12 Sept. 1903; ed. Yale Univ.
Joined Prutt & Whitney Aircraft (now a div. of United Aircraft Corpn.) 26; held various positions incl. Asst. Treas., Asst. Sec., Asst. Sales Manager, Asst. Gen. Man., Gen. Man. 40; Vice-Pres. United Aircraft 42, Vice-Pres. in Charge of Manufacturing 43, Pres. 43-56, Chair. and Chief Exec. 56-; Dir. Hartford Nat. Bank & Trust Co., Southern New England Telephone Co., First Nat. City Bank of New York, Travelers Insurance Co., United Aircraft of Canada.
United Aircraft Corpn., 400 Main Street, East Hartford, Conn., U.S.A.

Horner, Richard Elmer, B.S., M.S.E.; American aviation research administrator; b. 24 Oct. 1917; ed. Univ. of Minnesota and Princeton Univ.
U.S. Air Force 40-49; civilian aeronautical development engineer, Air Force Flight Test Centre, Edwards Air Force Base, Calif. 49-53, Technical Dir. 53-55; Deputy for Requirements to Asst. Sec. of Air Force for Research and Development 55-57; Asst. Sec. to A.F. for Research and Development 57-59; Assoc. Administrator, Nat. Aeronautics and Space Admin. 59-60; Senior Vice-Pres. (Technical) Northrop Corpn. 60-; Gen. Man. Norair Div., Northrop Corpn.; Fellow American Inst. of Aeronautics and Astronautics, American Ordnance Asscn., American Astronautical Soc., Soaring Soc. of America; Silver Star, Air Medal with 4 clusters, Presidential Unit Citation.
Northrop Space Laboratories, 3901 West Broadway, Hawthorne, Calif.; Home: 2226 Stradella Road, Los Angeles, Calif. 90024, U.S.A.

Hornig, Donald Frederick; American chemist and government official; b. 17 March 1920; ed. Harvard Univ.
Research Assoc. Woods Hole (Mass.) Oceanographic Inst. 43-44; Scientist, Los Alamos Lab., New Mexico 44-46; Pres. Radiation Instruments Co. 45-47; Asst. Prof. of Chemistry Brown Univ. 46-49, Assoc. Prof. 49-51, Prof. 51-57, Dir. Metcalf Research Lab. 49-57; Assoc. and Acting Dean, Graduate School, Brown Univ. 52-53; Prof. of Chemistry Princeton Univ. 57-63, Chair. Dept. 58-63, Donner Prof. of Science 59-63; Dir. W. A. Benjamin, Inc. 62-64; Dir. Office of Science and Technology, Exec. Office of Pres. 64-; mem. American Chemical Soc., American Physical Soc., etc.; Hon. mem. Nat. Acad. of Sciences U.S.A., American Acad. of Arts and Sciences, etc.; numerous awards and hon. degrees.
Office of Science and Technology, Executive Office of the President, White House, Washington 25, D.C., U.S.A.

Horowitz, David; Israeli economist; b. Feb. 1899; ed. Vienna and Lwów.
Member Exec. Cttee. Gen. Fed. of Jewish Labour 23; journalist and writer; Economic Adviser and Sec., American Economic Cttee. for Palestine 32-35; Dir. Economic Dept. of Jewish Agency for Palestine; mem. various Govt. Cttees. under Mandatory Regime, and dir. various enterprises 35-48; fmr. Dir.-Gen. Ministry of Finance (resgnd. 52), Gov.-Designate Bank of Israel 52-54, Gov. 54-; Lecturer at High School for Law and Economics, Tel-Aviv; Liaison Officer to U.N. Special Cttee. on Palestine 46; mem. Jewish Del. to Lake Success 47; Head of Israel Del. to Econ. Survey Comm. of UN 48; Head of Israel Del. Financial Talks on Sterling Releases between Israel and Great Britain, London 49, and in negotiations between Israel and Great Britain on economic and financial affairs in connection with termination of the Mandate; Gov. (for Israel) Int. Development Asscn., Int. Finance Corpn., and Int. Bank for Reconstruction and Development; Chair. Board of Dirs., The Eliezer Kaplan School of Econ. and Soc. Sciences, Hebrew Univ.; mem. State Council for Higher Education; Head, Israel Del. to UN Conf. on Trade and Development, Geneva 64.
Publs. *Aspects of Economic Policy in Palestine* 36, *Jewish Colonisation in Palestine* 37, *Economic Survey of Palestine* (with Rita Hinden) 38, *Palestine Jewry's Economic War Effort* 42, *Postwar Reconstruction* 42, *Palestine and the Middle East, An Essay in Regional Economy* 43, *Prediction and Reality in Palestine* 45, *State in the Making* 53, *Anatomie unserer Zeit* 64, *Hemispheres North and South* 66, *The Economics of Israel* 67; and several publs. in Hebrew.
Home: 4 Halamed Hé Street, Jerusalem; Office: Bank of Israel, Mizpah Building, Jerusalem, Israel.

Horowitz, Vladimir; American pianist; b. Russia 1 Oct. 1904.
Studied under Felix Blumenfeld and Sergei Tarnowsky; first appearance 17; début U.S. with N.Y. Philharmonic Orchestra 28; soloist N.Y. Symphony Orchestra, Philadelphia Orchestra, N.B.C. Symphony Orchestra, Cleveland, Boston, Chicago, Detroit and St. Louis and other orchestras.
c/o Columbia Records, 51 West 52nd Street, New York, N.Y. 10019, U.S.A.

Horrocks, Lt.-Gen. Sir Brian Gwynne, K.C.B., K.B.E., D.S.O., M.C.; British army officer; b. 7 Sept. 1895.
Served First World War 14-18; Commd. 44th (H.C. Div.), 9th Armoured Div., 13 Corps, 10 Corps in Egypt and Africa, 9 Corps in Tunis, 30 Corps in B.L.A. 39-45; G.O.C.-in-C. Western Command 46-48; G.O.C.-in-C. British Army of the Rhine 48-49; Gentleman Usher of The Black Rod, House of Lords 49-63;

Dir. Bovis Holdings 63-; Pres. Electronic Rentals Asscn. 63-; Hon. LL.D.
Publ. *A Full Life* 60.
Manor Farm, East Compton, Shepton Mallet, Somerset, England.

Horsey, Outerbridge, B.A.; American diplomatist; b. 1 Oct. 1910; ed. Downside School and Trinity Coll., Cambridge.
U.S. Nat. Emergency Council 34-36; joined Dept. of State 38, served Naples, Budapest, Belgrade, Madrid and Lisbon; Asst. Chief, Div. of West European Affairs 47; First Sec., Rome 47, and Counsellor 50; Dep. Dir. Office of British Commonwealth and North European Affairs 54, Dir. 55; Minister Tokyo 56, Minister Rome 59; Amb. to Czechoslovakia 63-67.
c/o Department of State, Washington, D.C., U.S.A.

Horsfall, Frank Lappin, Jr., B.A., M.D., C.M.; American scientist; b. 14 Dec. 1906; ed. Univ. of Washington and McGill Univ.
Assistant Rockefeller Inst. 34-37, mem. and Prof. 41-60, Vice-Pres. Clinical Studies 55-60; Asst. Resident Physician, Hospital of the Rockefeller Inst. 34-37, Physician 41-55, Physician-in-Chief 55-60; Medical Corps. U.S. Naval Reserve 42-46; Pres. and Dir. Sloan-Kettering Inst. for Cancer Research 60-; Prof. of Medicine, Cornell Univ. Medical Coll. 60-; Dir. and Prof. of Microbiology, Sloan-Kettering Div., Graduate School of Medical Sciences, Cornell Univ. Medical Coll. 60-; Trustee, Memorial Sloan-Kettering Cancer Center 60-, Dir. of Research 65-; Dir. of Research, Memorial Hospital for Cancer and Allied Diseases 65-; mem. Nat. Research Council Cttee. Advisory to U.S. Army Chemical Corps 57-59; mem.-at-Large, Defense Science Board 57-62, mem. Cttee. on Science and Public Policy, Nat. Acad. of Sciences 63-66; mem. numerous nat. medical councils and cttees.; Hon. Ph.D. (Uppsala), Hon. LL.D. (Univ. of Alberta), Hon. D.Sc. (McGill).
Sloan-Kettering Institute for Cancer Research, New York, N.Y. 10021, U.S.A.

Horst, Karl August, DR.PHIL.; German writer; b. 10 Aug. 1913; ed. Univs. of Munich, Berlin, Göttingen, Bonn.
Interpreter and wireless operator in Second World War 40-45; asst. under E. R. Curtius, Univ. of Bonn 45-48; self-employed as writer 48-; literary critic *Merkur.*
Publs. *Ich und Gnade, eine Studie über Friedrich Schlegels Bekehrung* 51, *Zero* (novel) 51, *Ina Seidel, Wesen und Werk* 56, *Die deutsche Literatur der Gegenwart* 57, *Das Spektrum des modernen Romans* 59, *Kritischer Führer durch die Deutsche Literatur der Gegenwart* 62, *Der Skorpion, Erzählungen* 63, *Das Abenteuer der Deutschen Literatur im Zwanzigsten Jahrhundert* 64.
Ried/Benediktbeuern 51, German Federal Republic.

Hörstadius, Sven (Otto); Swedish zoologist; b. 18 Feb. 1898; ed. Univ. of Stockholm.
Reader in Zoology, Univ. of Stockholm 28-32; Assoc. Prof. 32-42; Head of Dept. of Developmental Physiology and Genetics, Wennergren Inst. of Experimental Biology 38-42; Prof. of Zoology, Uppsala Univ. 42-64; research work at several marine biological stations all over the world; received Prix Albert Brachet of Belgian Royal Acad. of Science 38; Pres. Int. Union of Biological Sciences 53-58; Pres. Sveriges Ornitologiska Forening 47-68; Pres. Int. Council Scientific Unions 62-63; Chair. European Section of Int. Council for Bird Preservation; Fellow Royal Swedish Acad. of Science, Royal Soc. of Science, Uppsala, Royal Danish Acad. of Science, Acad. Pontificio, Rome; foreign mem. Royal Soc., London, Finnish Soc. of Science, Zoological Soc., London; hon. mem. Belgian Royal Zoological Soc., British Ornithologists' Union, Société Philomatique

Paris, Royal Inst. of Gt. Britain, etc.; Gen. Sec., Congress of Ornithology, Uppsala 50; Dr. h.c. Univs. of Paris and Cambridge.
Zoologiska Institutionen, Uppsala, Sweden.
Telephone: 018-111818 (Inst.); 018-22202 (Home).

Horton, Alexander Romeo; Liberian banker; b. 20 Aug. 1923; ed. B.W.I. Inst. Coll. of West Africa, Morehouse Coll., Atlanta, U.S.A. and Wharton School of Finance and Commerce, Pennsylvania Univ.
Founder and President, Bank of Liberia 54-; Asst. Econ. Adviser to Liberian Govt. 54-63; Chair. Steering Cttee. of Conf. of African Businessman 60; Chair. ECA Cttee. of Nine African Countries on Development Bank for Africa 62; Sec. of Commerce and Industry, Liberia 64-; has attended numerous int. confs.; decorations include Knight Commdr. Order of African Redemption, Officier Nat. Order of Ivory Coast, Grand Commdr. Order of Star of Africa, Grand Band Order of Star of Africa, Grand Cross Order of Orange Nassau.
The Bank of Liberia, P.O.B. 131, Monrovia, Liberia.

Horton, Jack King; American businessman; b. 27 June 1916; ed. Stanford Univ. and Oakland Coll. Law School.
Admitted to Calif. Bar 41; Treasury Dept. Shell Oil Co. 37-42; private law practice 42-43; Attorney, Standard Oil Co. 43-44; Sec., Legal Counsel, Coast Counties Gas & Electric Co. 44-57, Pres. 51-54; Vice-Pres. Pacific Gas & Electric Co., San Francisco 54-; Pres. S. Calif. Edison Co. 59-, Chief Exec. Officer 65-.
Home: 315 South Windsor Boulevard, Los Angeles, Calif. 90005; Office: P.O. Box 351, Los Angeles, Calif. 90053, U.S.A.
Telephone: 213-624-7111 (Office).

Horwitz, Abraham, M.D., M.P.H.; Chilean physician; b. 10; ed. Univ. of Chile and Johns Hopkins Univ., U.S.A.
Professor of Epidemiology and Infectious Diseases, School of Nursing of Chilean Ministry of Welfare and Social Assistance, Prof. of Social Medicine, Univ. of Chile, and Prof. of Infectious Diseases at School of Medicine of Catholic Univ. of Chile 45-50; with Pan American Sanitary Bureau 50-53; Dir., School of Public Health, Univ. of Chile 53-54; Asst. Dir., Nat. Health Service, Santiago, Chile 54-59; Prof. of Preventive Medicine, Univ. of Chile 57-59; Dir. Pan American Health Org., Regional Office of World Health Org. 59-; mem. and fmr. Pres. Chilean Soc. of Public Health; Vice-Pres., American Public Health Asscn. 58-59.
Pan American Health Organization, 1501 New Hampshire Avenue, N.W., Washington, D.C. 20036, U.S.A.

Hoskins, Halford Lancaster, A.B., A.M., PH.D.; American historian and administrator; b. 25 March 1891; ed. Univs. of Chicago, Pennsylvania and Harvard.
Instructor in History Friends Univ. Wichita, Kan. 15-17; Asst. Prof. European History Trinity Coll. (now Duke Univ.) 18-19; Asst. Prof. History Tufts Coll. 20-24, Dickson Prof. of History 24-49, Head of Dept. 25-34; Organiser, Dean and Prof. of Diplomatic History, Fletcher School of Law and Diplomacy 33-44; mem. American Co-ordinating Comm. of Int. Studies Conf. 36-39, etc.; Consultant, Dept. of State 42-44; co-organiser and Dir. School of Advanced Int. Studies, Johns Hopkins Univ. 44-49; Organiser and Dir. The Middle East Institute 46-50; Senior Specialist in Int. Relations, Legislative Reference Service, Library of Congress 49-64; mem. Planning Board and Prof. of Middle Eastern Studies, School of Int. Service, American Univ. 64-; mem. American Historical Asscn., American Political Science Asscn., American Acad. of Arts and Sciences, Council on Foreign Relations, Washington Inst. of Foreign Affairs; Hon. LL.D.
Publs. *Preliminaries of the World War* 18, *Guide to Latin-American History* 22, *An Outline of Modern European History* 25, *British Routes to India* 28, *Euro-*

pean Imperialism in Africa 30, *The New Orient* 32, *The Atlantic Pact* 49, *Middle East Oil in United States Foreign Policy* 50, *The Middle East: Problem Area in World Politics* 54; Editor *Aiding Underdeveloped Areas Abroad* 50.
(*Deceased*).

Hotelling, Harold, A.B., M.SC., PH.D., LL.D., SC.D.; American university professor; b. 29 Sept. 1895; ed. Princeton, Chicago, Univ. of Washington, and Rothamsted Experimental Station, England.
Instructor in Mathematics Princeton 22-24; Junior Research Associate and Research Associate, Food Research Inst., Stanford Univ. 24-27; Associate Prof. of Mathematics, Stanford 27-31; Professor of Economics, Columbia Univ. 31-46; Prof. of Mathematical Statistics Univ. of North Carolina 46-66; organiser and head of Statistical Research Group at Columbia Univ. doing war research 42-45; Consultant to Nat. Recovery Admin. 33; Treasury Div. of Tax Research 43, Bureau of the Budget 44-49; N.Y. State Public Service Comm. 49-50; Nat. Science Foundation 52-54; Pres. Econometric Soc. 36 and 37, Inst. of Mathematical Statistics 41, Elisha Mitchell Scientific Society 49-50; Assoc. Editor *American Journal of Economics and Sociology*; Hon. LL.D. (Univ. of Chicago 55), Hon. Sc.D. (Univ. of Rochester 63); awarded medal by Université Libre de Bruxelles 51; Hon. Fellow, Royal Statistical Soc. (London); mem. Int. Statistical Inst.
Department of Statistics, University of North Carolina, Chapel Hill, North Carolina, U.S.A.
Telephone: Chapel Hill 942-2167.

Hotson, Leslie, A.B., A.M., PH.D., M.A., LITT.D. (Cantab.), F.R.S.L.; American literary scholar; b. 16 Aug. 1897; ed. Harvard Univ.
Travelling Scholar and Fellow 22-25 and Instructor Harvard Univ. 24-25; Senior Research Fellow Yale Univ. 26-27; Assoc. Prof. of English New York Univ. 27-31; Prof. of English Haverford Coll. 31-42; Capt. U.S. Army Signal Corps 43-46; Fulbright Senior Research Fellow, England 49-50; Research Assoc., Yale Univ. 53; Fellow, King's Coll., Cambridge 54-60.
Publs. *The Death of Christopher Marlowe* 25, *The Commonwealth and Restoration Stage* 28, *Shelley's Lost Letters to Harriet* 30, *Shakespeare versus Shallow* 31, *I, William Shakespeare* 37, *Shakespeare's Sonnets Dated* 49, *Shakespeare's Motley* 52, *Queen Elizabeth's Entertainment at Mitcham* 53, *The First Night of Twelfth Night* 54, *Shakespeare's Wooden O* 59, *Mr. W. H.* 64.
White Hollow Road, Northford, Conn., U.S.A.

Hotter, Hans; German singer; b. 19 Jan. 1909; ed. Munich.
Concert début 29, opera début 30; mem. Vienna, Hamburg and Munich Opera companies; has appeared at concerts and in operas in major cities in Europe, Australia and the U.S., and at Festivals at Salzburg, Bayreuth and Edinburgh; renowned for Wagnerian roles.
München-Solln, Dittlerstrasse 26, German Federal Republic.

Hottinguer, Baron Rudolphe; French banker; b. 16 Oct. 1902; ed. Ecole des Hautes Etudes Commerciales.
Associate Hottinguer & Cie., Bankers; Pres. Asscn. Professionnelle des Banques; Vice-Pres. Paris Cttee. of Ottoman Bank; Pres. French Nat. Cttee. of Int. Chamber of Commerce; Censeur, Crédit Foncier de France; Dir. Schneider S.A., Kléber Colombes, Chatillon Commentry, Tréfimétaux, Union Européenne Industrielle et Financière Mines et Fonderies de la Vieille Montagne; Commdr. Légion d'Honneur; Officier de l'Ordre Nat. du Mérite; Chevalier des Palmes Acadé-

miques; Croix de Guerre (39-45); Commdr. du Mérite Commercial et de l'Economie Nationale.
Office: 38 rue de Provence, Paris 9e; Home: 4 rue de la Baume, Paris 8e, France.

Hou Teh-pang, PH.D., D.SC.; Chinese industrial chemist; b. 90; ed. Massachusetts Institute of Technology and Columbia Univ., U.S.A.
Vice-Chair. All-China Fed. of Scientific Societies 50-; Vice-Minister of Chemical Industry 57-; Pres. China Chemistry and Chemical Engineering Soc. 59-.
Publs. *Manufacture of Soda*, etc.
17 Wai Chiao Pu Street, East City, Peking, China.

Houdet, Roger; French politician; b. 14 June 1899; ed. Inst. Nat. Agronomique, Ecole Nat. du Génie Rural, Ecole Supérieure d'Electricité, Paris.
Inspector Gen., Génie Rural; Technical Counsellor and Sec. to various former Ministers of Agriculture; Sec. of State, Ministry of Agriculture 52; Senator 52-; Minister of Agriculture, Laniel Cabinet 53-54, Mendès-France Cabinet 54-55, de Gaulle Cabinet June 58-Jan. 59, Debré Cabinet 59-60; Mayor of Luneray (Seine Maritime); mem. Consultative Assembly of Council of Europe; Officier, Légion d'Honneur, Médaille de la Résistance, Commdr. Mérite Agricole.
Palais du Luxembourg, Paris; Villa Santa Lucia, Luneray (Seine-Maritime), France.
Telephone: ODEon 9500; Luneray 85-31-69.

Houghton, Amory, A.B.; American industrialist; b. 27 July 1899; ed. Harvard Univ.
With Corning Glass Works 21-, Exec. Vice-Pres. 28-30, Pres. 30-41, Chair Board 41-61, Chair. Exec. Cttee. 61-64, Hon. Chair. of Board 64-; Dir. Pittsburgh-Corning Corpn., First Nat. City Bank 37-68, Dow Corning Corpn., Metropolitan Life Insurance Co. 38-; Dir.-Gen. of Operations, War Production Board 42; Deputy Chief Economic Affairs Mission, London 44; Ambassador to France 57-61; mem. Business Advisory Council Dept. of Commerce 43-; U.S. Council, Int. Chamber of Commerce 45-, Chair. 62-64, Vice-Chair. U.S. Council 62-64; mem. of Exec. Comm. U.S. Council 64; Pres. Boy Scouts of America 46-51, Hon. Vice-Pres. 51-; Dir. Nat. Educ. Television & Radio Center 61-67, Atlantic Council of the U.S. France America Soc., Fédération des Alliances Françaises aux Etats-Unis, American Soc. of the French Legion of Honour; Dir. Int. Exec. Service Corpn. 64-; mem. Advisory Trust Board, First Nat. City Bank 68-, Advisory Council, State Univ. of N.Y.; Trustee, Inst. for Advanced Study, Princeton, N.J.; Hon. LL.D. (Hobart and William Smith Colls., Geneva (N.Y.), Colgate and Alfred Univs., New York and N.Y. Univ.); Hon. D.Eng. (Rensselaer Polytechnic Inst.); Order of Merit Bernardo O'Higgins (Chile); Grand Cross of the Legion of Honour (France).
The Knoll, Corning, N.Y.; Corning Glass Works, Corning, N.Y. 14830, U.S.A.
Telephone: 607-936-3111.

Houghton, Amory, Jr., M.B.A.; American executive; b. 7 Aug. 1926; ed. Harvard Univ., Business School.
Served in U.S. Marine Corps 45-46; joined Corning Glass Works 51, Dir. 55, Staff Vice-Pres. 57, Pres. 61-64, Chair. and Chief Exec. Officer 64-; Chair. of Board and Dir. Corning Glass Works of Canada Ltd.; Dir., Dow Corning Corpn., Pittsburgh Corning Corpn., B.F. Goodrich Co., Corhart Refractories Co., New York Telephone Co., Corning Fibre Box Corpn.; Trustee Corning Glass Works Foundation, The Corning Museum of Glass, Episcopal Theological School (Cambridge, Mass.), Nat. Security Industrial Asscn.; mem. Board Nat. Industrial Conf.
33 East 3rd Street, Corning, New York, U.S.A.

Houghton, Arthur Amory, Jr.; American executive; b. 12 Dec. 1906; ed. St. Paul's School, Concord (N.H.) and Harvard Univ.

Corning Glass Works, Manufacturing Dept., 29, Treas. Dept. 29-30, Asst. to Pres. 30-32, Vice-Pres. 35-42; Pres. Steuben Glass; Dir. U.S. Steel Corpn., Past Dir. Nat. Book Cttee. Inc.; Vice-Pres. Corning Museum of Glass; Curator of Rare Books, Library of Congress 40-42; Hon. Consultant in English Bibliography; Chair. Copper Union N.Y., Wye Inst. Inc.; Past Chair. Parsons School of Design, N.Y., Philharmonic Symphony Soc. of N.Y., Inst of Int. Educ.; Past Vice-Chair. Lincoln Center for the Performing Arts, N.Y.; Vice-Pres. Pierpont Morgan Library, Vice-Chair. Fund for the Advancement of Educ.; Dir.-at-large Empire State Foundation; Pres. Metropolitan Museum of Art; Trustee N.Y. Public Library, Modern Language Asscn., Rockefeller Foundation, U.S. Trust Co.; Dir. N.Y. Life Insurance Co., U.S. English-Speaking Union; mem. American Revolution Bicentennial Comm.; service in U.S. Air Force (Lieut.-Col.) 42-45; Friedsam Industrial Art Medal 53; Officier, Légion d'Honneur; Senior Fellow Royal Coll. of Art; Fellow Royal Soc. of Arts, Assoc. Commdr. (Brother) Most Venerable Order of the hospital of St. John of Jerusalem.
Office: 715 Fifth Avenue, New York, N.Y. 10022; Home: 3 Sutton Place, New York City; Wye Plantation, Queenstown, Md., U.S.A.
Telephone: 212-PL2-1441 (Office).

Houghton, Rt. Hon. Arthur (Leslie Noel) Douglas, C.H., P.C., M.P.; British trade unionist and politician; b. 11 Aug. 1898; ed. Derbyshire County Secondary School.
General Sec. Inland Revenue Staff Fed. 22-60; mem. Gen. Council, Trades Union Congress 52-60; mem. Civil Service Staff Whitley Council 23-58, Chair. 54-56; Alderman, London County Council 47-49; M.P. 49-, Chair. Public Accounts Cttee., House of Commons 63-64; Chancellor, Duchy of Lancaster 64-66; Minister without Portfolio 66-67; Chair. Parl. Labour Party Liaison Cttee. April 67-; Labour.
House of Commons, London, S.W.1; Home: 110 Marsham Court, London, S.W.1, England.
Telephone: 01-834-8181.

Houghton, Mrs. Hiram Cole, B.A.; American public servant; b. 90; ed. Wellesley Coll.
President Iowa Federation of Women's Clubs; Pres. Gen. Fed. of Women's Clubs 50-52; Dep. Dir. Int. Co-op. Admin. 53-56; mem. Nat. Cttee. UNESCO and 18 other cttees.; Pres. Electoral Coll. 56, Hon. Life-Pres.; Italian, Greek, German and Netherlands honours; Nansen Refugee Award; four hon. degrees.
Hotel Johnson, Red Oak, Iowa, U.S.A.

Hougron, Jean (Marcel); French writer; b. 1 July 1923; ed. Faculty of Law, Univ. of Paris.
Schoolmaster 43-46; commercial employment in export-import firm, Saigon 46-47, lorry driver 47-49, translator in American Consulate 50, news editor Radio France Asie 51; returned to France to write 52; bookseller in Nice 53-54; lived in Spain 58-60; Grand Prix du Roman, Acad. Française 53; Prix Populiste 65.
Publs. *Tu récolteras la Tempête* 50, *Rage Blanche* 51, *Soleil au ventre* 52, *Mort en Fraude* (film) 53, *Les Portes de l'Aventure* 54, *Les Asiates* 54, *Je reviendrai à Kandara* (film) 55, *La Terre du Barbare* 58, *Par qui le scandale* 60, *Le Signe du Chien* 61, *Histoire de Georges Guersant* 64, *Les Humiliés* 65.
34 rue Greneta, Paris 2e, France.

Houin, Roger; French professor of law; b. 17 Aug. 1912; ed. Univ. de Paris à la Sorbonne and Ecole des Sciences politiques.
Lecturer, Univ. of Lille 39; Prof. Univ. of Rennes 41-57, Dean of Faculty 55-57; Sec.-Gen. Comm. for Reform of Civil Law 45-65; Prof. Faculty of Law, Univ.

of Paris 57-, Inst. of Political Studies 58-; Councillor of State; mem. of numerous legal orgs. and legal expert on Cttees. of European Econ. Community; Founder-Dir. quarterly *Revue de droit commercial* 48; Co-Dir.-Founder quarterly *Revue de droit européen* 65; Dir. *Bibliothèque de droit commercial* (13 vols.); Chevalier, Légion d'Honneur and other decorations; Dr. h.c. Univs. of Ghent and Brussels.
Publs. *Précis de droit commercial* (2 vols.) 4th edn. 64, *Cours de droit commercial* 65, *Jurisclasseur de la responsabilité civile et des assurances* (3 vols.) 41, *Les grands arrêts et la jurisprudence commerciale* 63.
6 rue Coëtlogon, Paris 6e, France.
Telephone: 222-49-61.

Houle, Cyril O., PH.D.; American educationist; b. 26 March 1913; ed. Univ. of Florida and Univ. of Chicago.
Department of Education, Univ. of Chicago 39-, Dean of Univ. Coll. 44-52, Prof. of Education 52-; mem. U.S. Nat. Comm. for UNESCO 59-64, mem. Int. Cttee. for Advancement of Adult Education (UNESCO) 61-63; Hon. LL.D. (Syracuse) and (Florida), D.H.L. (Rutgers).
Publs. *Adult Education* (with F. W. Reeves and T. Fansler), *The Armed Services and Adult Education* (with others), *Libraries in Adult and Fundamental Education*, *The University*, *The Citizen and World Affairs* (with C. A. Nelson), *The Effective Board*, *The Inquiring Mind*, *Continuing Your Education*.
Department of Education, University of Chicago, Chicago 37, Illinois, U.S.A.

Houmann, Borge Kruuse; Danish journalist; b. 26 March 1902; ed. Denmark and Derby Grammar School, England.
Sailor 20; started writing poems and short stories 23; economic dir. of Riddersalen Theatre 33; Man. Dir. of publishing firm Arbejderforlaget 35; mem. of Danish Freedom Council (underground) 43-45; mem. Danish Parliament 45-46; mem. Danish Radioraadet (Danish Broadcasting Council) 46-50; Chief Editor of Communist daily *Land og Folk*; Communist 45-54; Dir. publishing firm of Sirius 57.
Publs. *Huset ved Havet* 23, translation of Whitman's *Leaves of Grass* 27, *Lystgas* (a novel) 32, *Forlis* (poems) 34, *Martin Andersen Nexø, Selected Speeches and Articles*, Vols. 1-3 (Editor) 54, *Drømmen om en ny verden*, *Martin Andersen Nexø og hans forhold til Sovjetunion* 57, *Martin Andersen Nexø Bibliography* (with notes) Vol. I-II, 61, 67, and many translations from English and German.
Aage Bergsvej 19, Risskov, Denmark.
Telephone: (06) 179549.

Houphouet-Boigny, Félix; Ivory Coast politician; b. 18 Oct. 1905; ed. School of Medicine, Dakar.
President Syndicat Agricole Africain 44; mem. Constituent Assembly 45-46; mem. Nat. Assembly Nov. 46-, re-elected 51 and 56; successively Territorial Councillor for Korhogo, Pres. Territorial Assembly, Ivory Coast, *Grand Conseiller* for French West Africa; Minister attached to the Prime Minister's Office 56-57; Minister of Health 57-58; Minister of State (Pflimlin Cabinet) May 58, (de Gaulle Cabinet) June 58-Jan. 59, (Debré Cabinet) Jan.-May 59; Pres. Assembly, Ivory Coast Republic 58-59, Pres. Council May 59-Nov. 60; Pres. of the Republic Nov. 60-, concurrently Minister of Foreign Affairs 61, of Interior, Defence, Education and Agriculture 63-; now Pres. of Council of Ministers and in Charge of Economy and Finance and Nat. Defence; Minister-Counsellor to French Govt. 59-60; Pres. Parti Démocratique de la Côte d'Ivoire.
Présidence de la République, Abidjan, Ivory Coast, West Africa.

Housiaux, Albert, D.RER.POL.; Belgian journalist; b. 14; ed. Athénée Royal, Ixelles, Brussels Free Univ.
Joined staff of *Le Peuple* 37; news bulletin editor I.N.R.;

Editorial Sec. *Socialisme*; served in the army and captured during the Second World War; Inspector-Gen. Ministry of Imports 45; Dir.-Gen. *Le Peuple* 48-54, Political Dir. (later Ed.) 54-; mem. Bureau Belgian Socialist Party (with vote); Chevalier Ordre de Léopold, Ordre de la Couronne, Officer of the Order of Merit (Italy).
Office: *Le Peuple*, 29 rue des Sables, Brussels 1; Home: 201 Avenue Rommelaere, Jette-St.-Pierre, Brussels 9, Belgium.

Houssay, Bernardo Alberto, M.D.; Argentine physiologist; b. 10 April 1887; ed. Buenos Aires.
Prof. Physiology, Veterinary School, Buenos Aires 10-19, Medical School, Buenos Aires 19-43, 45-46, 55-57; Prof. Univ. of Calif. 48; Dir. Inst. de Biología y Medicina Experimental; Research Prof. Univ. of Buenos Aires 57-68; Hon. Prof. 15 Univs. in S. America; Pres. Nat. Council for Scientific and Technical Investigation, Argentine Biological Soc.; Past Pres. Council Int. Union of Physiological Sciences; mem. Argentine Acads. of Medicine, Letters, Science (Buenos Aires and Córdoba), Political and Moral Sciences, Pontifical Acad. of Science, Accad. Naz. dei XL Rome, Cttee. Balzan Foundation Prizes; foreign mem. Acads. of Science U.S.A., Germany, Sweden, Paris, Lima, Royal Soc. (London), American Philosophical Soc., Medical Acads. of Paris and Belgium, Accad. Naz. dei Lincei, Biological Soc. of Paris; Hon. mem. Medical Acads. of Madrid, Rio de Janeiro, Mexico, New York, Lombardy, Bogotá, Washington; Physiological Soc., American Physiological Soc., American Acad. of Arts and Sciences, Royal Soc. Edinburgh, Harvey Soc., Museo de La Plata, N.Y. Acad. of Sciences, Indian Academy of Science and Socs. of Medicine, Biology, Cardiology, Physiology, Endocrinology, etc., in America and Europe; corresp. mem. Acads. of Medicine Rome, Romania, Valladolid, Havana; Acads. of Science Turin, Brazil, Bolivia, Acad. of Pharmacy Paris, Acad. of Letters Uruguay, and numerous socs.; Nat. Prize for Sciences 23, Charles Mickle Fellowship, Toronto 45, Banting Medal, American Diabetes Asscn. 46, Research Award, American Pharmaceutical Manufacturers Asscn. 47, Baly Medal, Royal Coll. of Physicians, London 47, James Cook Medal, Australia 48, Nobel Prize for Physiology and Medicine 47; Dale Medal (London) 60; Weizmann Prize in Science and Humanities 67; Hon. M.D. 16 Univs., Hon. D.Sc. 11 Univs., Hon. LL.D.; numerous decorations.
Publs. *Fisiologia Humana*, papers on internal secretions, hypophysis, adrenal, thyroid, diabetes, snake and spider venoms, hypertension, etc.
Viamonte 2790, Buenos Aires; and Instituto de Biología y Medicina Experimental, Obligado 2490, Buenos Aires, Argentina.

Houston, Clifford Granville, A.M., PH.D.; American educational psychologist; b. 5 March 1903; ed. Univ. of Colorado and Univs. of Columbia and Chicago.
Professor of Education and Psychology, State Junior Coll., Grand Junction 29-31, Pres. 31-37; Dir. Extension Div. and Dean of Summer School Univ. of Colorado 37-42; Dean Extramural Activities, Univ. of Colorado, Boulder 46-47; Dean of Students and Dir. of Student Personnel and Prof. of Education, Univ. of Colorado, Boulder 47-57, Prof. of Education 57-; Pres. Board of Reps. 51-52; Chair. Academic Council Western Personnel Inst. 51-53; mem. Governor's Human Relations Comm. and Chair. of its Research Cttee. 51-53; Ford Fund for the Advancement of Education 51-53; mem. Nat. Advisory Council, Nat. Students' Asscn. 53-58; mem. Nat. Educational Advisory Council, Nat. Asscn. of Manufacturers 54-57; mem. Consulting Cttee. in Management Training, U.S. Veterans Admin., Washington, D.C. 57-60.
3840 Armer Drive, Boulder, Colo., U.S.A.

Houston, William Vermillion, B.A., B.S. in ED., S.M., PH.D.; American physicist; b. 19 Jan. 1900; ed. Ohio State Univ. and Univ. of Chicago.
Nat. Research Fellow, Calif. Inst. of Technology 25-27; Guggenheim Fellow 27-28; mem. of Faculty, Calif. Inst. of Technology 27-31; Prof. of Physics 31-46; on leave of absence to Columbia Univ., Div. of War Research 41-45; Prof. of Physics and Pres. of Rice Inst. 46-61; Visiting Prof. Rockefeller Inst. 63-; Hon. Chancellor Rice Univ. 61-; mem. Nat. Science Board 57-66, Nat. Acad. of Sciences; Hon. D.Sc. (Ohio State Univ.) 50, Hon. LL.D. (Univ. of Calif.).
Publs. *Principles of Mathematical Physics* 34, *Principles of Quantum Mechanics* 51.
Rice University, Houston 1, Texas, U.S.A.
Telephone: JA8-4141.

Houten, Hans Rudolf van, DR. JUR.; Netherlands diplomatist; b. 13 Aug. 1907; ed. Univ. of Leyden.
Attaché, Neths. Legation, Copenhagen 32-33, Stockholm 33-34, Copenhagen 34-35; Sec. Berlin 35-40; Counsellor Washington 40-45, Brussels 45-48; Head of Foreign Service Dept., Ministry of Foreign Affairs (rank of Minister) 48-51; Minister to Mexico 51-54, Ambassador 54-58; Dir. Gen. for Political Affairs, Ministry of Foreign Affairs 58-59; Under-Sec. of State for Foreign Affairs 59-63; Ambassador to Austria 64-; Commdr. Order of Orange-Nassau; Knight Order of the Netherlands Lion; Grand Cross Leopold II of Belgium; Grand Officer of the Belgian Crown; Grand Cross Order of Merit, Austria; and numerous other decorations.
Publ. *International Status of Egypt* 30.
Royal Netherlands Embassy, Jacquingasse 10, A-1030 Vienna, Austria.
Telephone: 73-35-01; also 73-24-77.

Houtte, Jean van, D. en D.; Belgian university professor and politician; b. 17 March 1907; ed. Univ. of Ghent.
Prof. Univ. of Liège 31, and Univ. of Ghent 37; Head of Secretariat, Ministry of the Interior 44-45; co-opted Senator 49-; Minister of Finance 50-52; Prime Minister Jan. 52-54; Minister of Finance 58-61; Minister of State 66-; mem. Christian Social Party; various Belgian and foreign decorations.
Publs. *Traité des sociétés de personnes à responsabilité limitée* 35, 50, 62, *La responsabilité civile dans les transports aériens* 40, *La réparation des dommages de guerre aux biens privés* 48, *Formulierboek voor notarissen* 47, *Principes de droit fiscal belge* 58, 66.
54 Boulevard St. Michel, Brussels, Belgium.
Telephone: 33-62-94.

Hovde, Frederick Lawson, B.CH.E., B.A., M.A.; American educational administrator; b. 7 Feb. 1908; ed. Minnesota and Oxford Univs.
Assistant Director, General Coll., Univ. of Minnesota 32-36; Asst. to Pres., Univ. of Rochester, New York 36-41; Head, London Mission, Office of Scientific Research and Development 41-42; Exec. Asst. to Chair. Nat. Defense Research Cttee., OSRD 42-43; Chief of Rocket Ordnance Research Div., NDRC, OSRD 43-46; Pres. Purdue Univ. 46-; Chair. Cttee. on Guided Missiles, Research and Development Board 47-49; Hon. D.Sc., Hon. D.Eng., Hon. D.H.L., Hon. D.C.L. (Oxon.), Hon. LL.D.; Rhodes Scholarship 29-32; King's Medal for Service in the Cause of Freedom (Gt. Britain) 48; President's Medal for Merit (U.S.A.) 48; Brazilian Order of Southern Cross 68.
Purdue University, Lafayette, Indiana; Home: 515 South Seventh Street, Lafayette, Indiana 47901, U.S.A.

Hoveyda, Amir Abbas, E.M.A., PH.D.; Iranian diplomatist, business executive and politician; b. Feb. 1919; ed. Univs. of Paris and Brussels.
Ministry of Foreign Affairs 42-58, served Paris, Fed. Germany, Teheran, UN, Geneva, Ankara; mem. Board

of Dirs. and Head of Admin., Nat. Iranian Oil Co. 58-64; Minister of Finance 64-65; Prime Minister 65-. Office of the Prime Minister, Teheran; Home: No. 5 Kh. Cyrus Ehteshamieh, Darrous, Teheran, Iran. Telephone: 68-801.

Hoving, Thomas Pearsall Field, PH.D., M.F.A.; American art gallery director; b. 15 Jan. 1931; ed. The Buckley School, New York, Eaglebrook School, Deerfield, Mass., Exeter Acad., Exeter, N.H., The Hotchkiss School, Lakeville, Conn., and Princeton Univ.
Curatorial Asst., Medieval Art and The Cloisters, Metropolitan Museum of Art 59-60, Asst. Curator 60-63, Assoc. Curator 63-65, Curator of Medieval Art and The Cloisters 65; Commr. of Parks, New York City 66; Admin. of Recreation and Cultural Affairs, New York City 67; Dir., The Metropolitan Museum of Art April 67-; Fellowship, Nat. Council of Humanities 55, Kienbusch and Haring Fellowship 57; Distinguished Citizen's Award, Citizen's Budget Cttee. 67; Hon. LL.D. (Pratt Inst.) 67.
Publs. *Guide to the Cloisters* 62, *Metropolitan Museum of Art Calendar* 66.
150 East 73rd Street, New York City, N.Y. 10021, U.S.A.

Howald, Prof. Oskar, DR. SC. TECH., DIPL. ING. AGR.; Swiss agricultural economist and professor; b. 2 March 1897; ed. Fed. Technical High School, Zürich.
Deputy Dir. Swiss Farmers' Union 29-39; Dir. 39-49, scientific consultant, Tutor in Agricultural Economics, Fed. Technical High School 28-35; Prof. of Farm Management, Farm Accountancy and Agrarian Policy 36-67; Vice-Pres. European Confederation of Agriculture (CEA) 49-59; Pres. Swiss Home Works Corpn., Agricultural Information Services Asscn., Dr. h.c. Hochschulen Vienna 57, Stuttgart 62; Editor *Agrarpolitische Revue*, *Wirz's Landwirtschaftlicher Taschenkalender* 46-, etc.
Publs. include: *Die Dreifelderwirtschaft im Kanton Aargau* 26, *Besteuerung des ldw. Besitzes u. Einkommens u. der ldw. Organisationen* 27, *Die Organisation der Schlachtviehverwertung im Ausland und in der Schweiz* 29, *Überschuldung und Entschuldung der Schweiz. Landswirtschaft* 34, *Einführung in die Agrarpolitik* 46, *Fünfzig Jahre Schweizerischer Bauernverband* 47, *ABC für Agrarpolitik und Agrarwirtschaft* 51, 65, *Schriftenfolge über Landarbeitstechnik in der Schweiz* (11 vols.) 47-66, *Entwicklung und Stand der Forschung aus dem Gebiete der Wirtschaftslehre des Landbaus* 51, *Zukunftsaussichten des bäuerlichen Familienbetriebes* 55, *Die Kleinbauernfrage in Europa* 55, *Bewertung, Buchhaltung und Kalkulation in der Landwirtschaft* 57, *Strukturwandel in der Landwirtschaft* 62, *Bauer und Landwirt in der Heutigen Volkswirtschaft* 62, *Landwirtschaftliche Betriebslehre für bäuerliche Verhältnisse* 17e. 67, *Schweizerische Landwirtschaft und Schweizer Bauerntum* (Monograph) 63, *Betrachtungen zur Lehre vom bäuerlichen Familienbetrieb* 67, etc.
Stäblistrasse 19, 5200 Brugg, Switzerland.

Howard, George Wren, M.A., M.C.; British publisher; b. 24 March 1893; ed. Marlborough Coll. and Trinity Coll., Cambridge.
British Army 14-19, serving France, Belgium, Italy; Medici Society Ltd., London 19-20; joint founder firm of Jonathan Cape (Publishers) 21; Treasurer Publishers' Asscn. 35-37; Treas. Int. Publishers' Congress, London 36 Pres. Publishers' Asscn. 37-39; Chair. Jonathan Cape Ltd.; Dir. Book Centre Ltd., Duralin Book-Binding Products Ltd., Australasian Publishing Co. Ltd.
3 Hampstead Way, London, N.W.11, England.

Howard, Harry Nicholas, A.B., M.A., PH.D.; American historian; b. 19 Feb. 1902; ed. Univs. of Missouri and California.

Gregory Fellow in History Univ. of Missouri 26-27; Research Asst. in Modern European History Univ. of California 28-29; Asst. Prof. History Univ. of Oklahoma 29-30; Associate Prof. History, Miami Univ. 30-37, Prof. 40-42; Lecturer Contemporary Problems, Univ. of Cincinnati 37-42; Head, East. European Unit Div. of Ter. Studies, Dept. of State 42-44; mem. Div. Int. Org. Aff. 44-46; Tech. Expert, U.S. Del., UNCIO 45; Adviser, Special Interrogation Comm., Germany 45; Chief N.E. Branch, Div. of Research for N.E. and Africa 46-47; Adviser, Div. of Greek, Turkish, and Iranian Affairs 47-49; Adviser U.S. Del., UNGA 47-50; UN Adviser, Dept. of State, Bureau of Near East, S. Asian and African Affairs 49-56; Acting U.S. Rep. Advisory Comm. UNRWA, Beirut 56-61; Special Asst. to Dir. of UNRWA 62-63; Adviser U.S. Del. UN Balkan Comm. 47-50; Prof. of Middle East Studies, School of Int. Service, American Univ., Washington, D.C. 63-; Chair. Middle East Program, Foreign Service Inst., Dept. of State 67; Reserve Consultant, Dept. of State 67-; Assoc. Editor *Middle East Journal* 63-; Chief Consultant, Middle East, Cincinnati World Affairs Council 68-69.
Publs. *The Partition of Turkey, A Diplomatic History 1913-1923*, 31, *Military Government in the Panama Canal Zone* 31 (with Prof. R. J. Kerner), *The Balkan Conferences and the Balkan Entente* 30-35, *A Study in the Recent History of the Balkan and Near Eastern People* 36, *The Problem of the Turkish Straits* 47, *The United Nations and the Problem of Greece* 47, *The General Assembly and the Problem of Greece* 48, *Yugoslavia* (co-author) 49, *Soviet Power and Policy* (co-author) 55, *The King-Crane Commission* 63.
Home: 6508 Greentree Road, Bradley Hills Grove, Bethesda, Md. 20034; Office: American University, Washington, D.C., U.S.A.
Telephone: 365-3693 (Home).

Howard, Jack Rohe; American newspaper and broadcasting executive; b. 31 Aug. 1910; ed. Yale Univ.
Journalist, Tokyo, Shanghai, Indianapolis, Washington 32-35; with radio companies, Knoxville, Washington and New York (now Scripps-Howard Broadcasting Co.) 36-39; Asst. Exec. Ed. Scripps-Howard Newspapers 39-42, 45-48, Gen. Ed. Man. 48-; U.S. Navy 42-45; Pres. E. W. Scripps Co. 53-; Pres., Dir. and mem. Exec. Cttee. Scripps-Howard Broadcasting Co.
200 Park Avenue, New York, N.Y. 10017, U.S.A.

Howard, Hon. Mabel Bowden, J.P.; New Zealand politician; b. 1894.
Started as stenographer in father's office (he was Sec. of Gen. Labourers' Union); apptd. Sec. of the Union 19 (first woman in N.Z. to hold such a position); made frequent appearances as Advocate before the Arbitration Court and Conciliation Council; was for twelve years mem. of Christchurch City Council; mem. of N.Z. Parl. 43-; apptd. to Cabinet as Minister of Health May 47-49 (first woman Cabinet Minister in N.Z.); Minister of Social Security and Minister of Child Welfare 57-60; during Second World War organised Women's War Service Auxiliary; mem. N.Z. Labour Party.
147 Pages Road, Christchurch, New Zealand.

Howard, Trevor Wallace; British actor; b. 29 Sept. 1916; ed. Clifton Coll., Bristol.
Service in 1st Airborne Division 40-43; plays include various Shakespeare plays at Stratford-upon-Avon and The Old Vic, London, *The Devil's General, The Cherry Orchard, Two Stars for Comfort, The Father*; films include *Brief Encounter, The Third Man, An Outcast of the Islands, The Heart of the Matter, Les Amants du Tage, Cockleshell Heroes, The Key, Roots of Heaven, Sons and Lovers, Mutiny on the Bounty, Von Ryan's Express, The Liquidator, Danger Grows Wild* 66, *Triple Cross* 67, *The Long Duel* 67.
Rowley Green, Arkley, Herts., England.

Howe, Harold II; American educator; b. 1918; ed. Yale and Columbia Univs., Univ. of Cincinnati, and Harvard Univ.

History teacher, Darrow School, New Lebanon, New York 40-42; Lt. U.S. Naval Reserve 42-45; History teacher, Phillips Acad., Andover, Mass. 47-50; Principal, Andover High School and Junior High School 50-53; Principal, Walnut Hills High School, Cincinnati, Ohio 53-57; Principal, Newton High School, Newton, Mass. 57-60; Supt. of Schools, Scarsdale, N.Y. 60-64; Exec. Dir. Learning Inst. of N. Carolina, Chapel Hill, N. Carolina 64-65; U.S. Commr. of Educ. Dec. 65-.

U.S. Office of Education, 400 Maryland Avenue, S.W., Washington, D.C. 20202, U.S.A.

Howe, Quincy, A.B.; American editor; b. 17 Aug. 1900; ed. Harvard Univ. and Christ's Coll., Cambridge.

Mem. staff Atlantic Monthly Co. 22-28; Editor *Living Age* 29-35, Contributing Editor 35-36; Editor Simon and Schuster Inc., publishers; News commentator Station WQXR New York 39-41, Columbia Broadcasting System 41-49; with C.B.S. Television 49-50; Assoc. Prof. School of Journalism, Univ. of Ill. 50-54; News Analyst American Broadcasting Co. 54-63; Radio New York World Wide 66-; Editor of *Atlas: The Magazine of the World Press* 61-65; Pres. Nat. Board of Review of Motion Pictures.

Publs. *World Diary* 29-34, *England Expects Every American To Do His Duty* 37, *Blood is Cheaper than Water* 39, *The News and How to Understand it* 40, *A World History of Our Own Times*, Vol. I 49, Vol. II 53.

108 East 82nd Street, New York, 28, N.Y., U.S.A.

Howells, Herbert Norman, C.B.E., D.MUS. (Oxon.), F.R.C.O., F.R.C.M., HON. R.A.M., HON. F.T.C.L.; British composer; b. 17 Oct. 1892; ed. Royal Coll. of Music.

Prof. Royal Coll. of Music; Dir. of Music St. Paul's Girls' School 36-62; first John Collard Fellow 31; King Edward Prof. of Music, Univ. of London 54-64; Pres. Royal Coll. of Organists 59; Fellow Royal Coll. of Music; Pres. Incorporated Soc. of Musicians 52; Pres. of Mediaeval and Plainsong Soc. 58; Master of Worshipful Company of Musicians 59; Fellow Royal School of Church Music 63; Hon. D.Mus. Cambridge 61.

Works include *Sir Patrick Spens* (for chorus and orchestra), *Requiem* (for unaccompanied choir and soloists), *Sine Nomine, Procession, Puck's Minuet* (all for orchestra), *Pageantry* (suite for brass band), *Hymnus Paradisi* (for soprano and tenor solo, chorus and orchestra), *Missa Sabrinensis* (for four soloists, chorus and orchestra) 54, piano concerto, 'cello concerto, clarinet quintet, and many other chamber music works, songs, organ works; recent works include concerto for strings, *Howell's Clavichord,* and a new series of church works; *Music for a Prince* (for orchestra); *A Kent Yeoman's Wooing Song* (chorus and orchestra), *An English Mass, Missa "Collegium Regale"* 56, *Missa Aedes Christi* 57, *Three Figures* (brass band) 60, *A Sequence for St. Michael* (chorus, strings and organ) 61, *Stabat Mater* (tenor solo, chorus and orchestra) 63.

3 Beverley Close, Barnes, London S.W.13; and Royal College of Music, London, S.W.7, England.

Telephone: 01-876-5119.

Howes, Frank Stewart, C.B.E., F.R.C.M.; British journalist and music critic; b. 2 April 1891; ed. St. John's Coll., Oxford, and Royal Coll. of Music.

On staff *The Times* 25-60; Music Critic 43-60; Lecturer, Royal Coll. of Music 38-; Editor *Journal of English Folk Dance and Song Society* 27-46; Chair. Musicians' Benevolent Fund 38-56; Pres. Royal Musical Asscn. 48-59; Hon. R.A.M.

Publs. *The Borderland of Music and Psychology* 26, *Byrd* (in Masters of Music series) 28, *Key to the Art of Music* 35, *Key to Opera* (with Philip Hope-Wallace) 39, *Full Orchestra* 42, *Man, Mind and Music* 48, *The Music of R. Vaughan Williams* 54, *Music and its Meanings* 58,

The Fontana Guide to Orchestral Music (revised version of *Full Orchestra*) 58, *The Music of William Walton* 65, *The English Musical Renaissance* 66.

Newbridge Mill, Standlake, nr. Witney, Oxon., England.

Howick of Glendale, 1st Baron (cr. 60); **Evelyn Baring,** G.C.M.G., K.C.V.O.; British administrator; b. 29 Sept. 1903; ed. Winchester and New Coll., Oxford.

Entered Indian Civil Service 26, Sec. to Agent of Govt. of India in S. Africa 29, retd. 34; Gov. of Southern Rhodesia 42-44; High Commr. in the Union of South Africa, and High Commr. for Basutoland, the Bechuanaland Protectorate, and Swaziland 44-51; Gov. and C.-in-C. Kenya 52-59; Chair. East Africa High Comm. 52-59; Chair. Colonial Development Corpn. 61-62, Commonwealth Devt. Corpn. 62-; mem. Natural Environment Research Council 65-; Dir. Swan, Hunter and Wigham Richardson, Baring Brothers & Co. Ltd.; Queen's Commendation for Brave Conduct 59.

Howick, Alnwick, Northumberland, England.

Howitt, Sir Harold Gibson, G.B.E., D.S.O., M.C., D.C.L., LL.D., F.C.A., J.P., D.L.; British chartered accountant; b. 5 Oct. 1886; ed. Uppingham.

Served First World War 14-18; partner Peat, Marwick, Mitchell & Co. 11-61; mem. Council Inst. of Chartered Accountants 32-61 (Pres. 45), Council Toynbee Hall 22-51, Boys' Hostels Asscn. 26-51, Benevolent Cttee. of British Legion 32-49; Chair. British North Borneo Comm. 26, London Civil Airports Comm. 39, Wool Marketing Comm. 44-45; Chair. Board of Finance, Air Training Corps 40-46; Dir. United Services Trust 44-66, Chair. 52; Chair. and Deputy British Overseas Airways Corpn. 43-48; Chair. Building Materials Board 42-43; Financial Adviser Ministry of Works 43-44; Pres. 6th Int. Congress on Accounting, London 52; Chair. Hampstead Bench 50-58; Comm. of Enquiry on the Powers of the Crown over unpatented inventions 55; hon. mem. Soc. of Incorporated Accountants and Auditors 53; Hon. D.C.L. (Oxford), Hon. LL.D. (Nottingham), mem. Council on Productivity, Prices and Incomes 57-59.

1 Cressy House, Queen's Ride, Barnes, London, S.W.13, England.

Telephone: 01-789-3715.

Howson, Hon. Peter; Australian politician; b. 22 May 1919; ed. Stowe School and Trinity Coll., Cambridge.

Fleet Air Arm and R.N.V.R. 40-46; Staff Man. Foy and Gibson Stores Ltd. 50, Dir. 51-55; Dir. Eagley Mills Ltd. 55, Cleckheaton (Yorkshire) Ltd. 61-64; mem. House of Reps. 55-; Minister for Air 64-68; Minister assisting the Treas. 66-68; Liberal.

Parliament House, Canberra, A.C.T.; Home: 40 Kensington Road, South Yarra, Melbourne, Victoria, Australia.

Hoxha, Enver; Albanian politician; b. 16 Oct. 1908; ed. Gjirokastra and Korça (Albania) and Faculty of Natural Sciences, Montpellier, France.

Teacher, Tirana and Korça 36-39; founder and leader, Communist Party of Albania Nov. 41, Sec.-Gen. 43-48; led national liberation struggle 39-44, achieved national independence 44; Prime Minister and Supreme Commdr. of Albanian Armed Forces 44-54; Minister of Foreign Affairs 46-53; Sec.-Gen. Party of Labour of Albania 48-54, First Sec. Central Cttee. 54-; Chair. Gen. Council of Democratic Front; mem. Presidium People's Assembly of Albania; Hero of the People (twice); Hero of Socialist Labour; Order of Suvorov (First Class) and other decorations.

Party of Labour of Albania, Tirana, Albania.

Hoyle, Fred, F.R.S., M.A.; British astronomer and mathematician; b. 24 June 1915; ed. Bingley Grammar School and Emmanuel Coll. and St. John's Coll., Cambridge Univ.

Fellow of St. John's Coll. 39; Univ. Lecturer in Mathematics, Cambridge 45-58; Staff mem. of Mount Wilson and Palomar Observatories, California, U.S.A. 56-; Plumian Prof. Astronomy and Experimental Philosophy, Cambridge Univ. 58-, Dir. Inst. of Theoretical Astronomy 67; Visiting Prof. of Astrophysics at Calif. Inst. of Technology, Pasadena 58; Hon. mem. American Acad. of Arts and Sciences 64.

Publs. *Recent Research in Solar Physics* 49, *Nature of the Universe* 50, *Decade of Decision* 53, *Frontiers of Astronomy* 55, *The Black Cloud* 57, *Ossian's Ride* 58, *A for Andromeda* (radio play with John Elliot) 62, *Rockets in Ursa Major* (play) 62, *Astronomy* 62, *Fifth Planet* (with Geoffrey Hoyle) 63, *Of Men and Galaxies* 64, *Galaxies, Nuclei and Quasars* 65, *October First is too late* 66, *Man in the Universe* 66.

Institute of Theoretical Astronomy, Madingley Rise, Madingley Road, Cambridge, England.

Hrabal, Bohumil, LL.D.; Czechoslovak writer; b. 28 March 1914; ed. Universita Karlova, Prague.
Lawyer's clerk, railway worker, insurance agent, travelling salesman, foundry worker, paper salvage worker, stage hand and stage extra 39-62; professional writer 62-.

Publs. short stories: *Perlička na dně* (Pearl at the Bottom, some stories filmed) 63, *Pábitelé* 64, *Inzerát na dům, ve kterém už nechi bydlet* (An Ad. for a House in Which I Don't Want to Live Any More) 65, *Automat svět* (selected stories, some filmed) 66; short novels: *Tanečni hodiny pro starší a pokročilé* (Dancing Lessons for Adults and Advanced) 64, *Ostře sledované vlaky* (Closely Watched Trains, film 66) 65.

Union of Czechoslovak Writers, Národní třída 11, Prague 1, Czechoslovakia.

Hromádka, Josef L., PH.D., D.D., DR.HIST.; Czechoslovak theologian; b. 8 June 1889; ed. Vienna, Basle, Heidelberg, Aberdeen, Prague Univs.
Pastor, Evangelical Church of Czech Brethren 12-20; Chaplain, Austro-Hungarian Army 18; Prof. of Systematic Theology, John Hus Theological Faculty 20-39; Guest Prof. of Apologetics and Christian Ethics, Princeton Theological Seminary 39-47; returned to Prague 47; Vice-Chair. Czechoslovak Peace Cttee. 49; Dean Comenius Faculty 50-66; mem. Exec. Cttee. World Council of Churches 54; Pres. Christian Peace Conf. 61; mem. World Peace Council; Czechoslovak Peace Prize 53; Order of the Repub. 54, 59; Lenin Peace Prize 58; Dr. h.c. (Humboldt Univ., Berlin).

Publs. *Catholicism and the Struggle for Christianity* 25, *Masaryk* 30, *Dostoevski and Masaryk* 31, *Christianity in Thought and Life* 31, *Calvin* 36, *Don Quixote of Czech Philosophy* 43, *Doom and Resurrection* 45, *From the Other Shore* 46, *Masaryk between Yesterday and To-morrow* 46, *Between the East and the West* 46, *Unity of the People in Truth* 49, *Theology and the Church* 49, *From the Reformation to Tomorrow* 56, *The Church and Theology in Today's Troubled Times* 56, *Theology between Yesterday and Tomorrow* 57, *Evangelium für Atheisten* 58, *The Gospel on the Way to Man* 58, *Sprung über die Mauer* 61, *An der Schwelle des Dialogs* (in Czech) 64, (in German) 65.

45 Moravská, Prague 2 Vinohrady, Czechoslovakia.
Telephone: 25-33-87.

Hrubín, František; Czechoslovak poet and writer; b. 17 Sept. 1910; ed. Universita Karlova, Prague.
Worked at Prague Municipal Library 35-45; professional writer 46-; State Prizes 54, 58; Honoured Artist 60; Order of Labour 65, Nat. Artist 66.

Publs. *Hrajte si s námi* (Play with Us, poems for children, State Prize) 53, *Mánesův orloj* 53, *Kuřátko a obilí* (The Chick and the Grain) 53, *Můj zpěv* (My Song, poems, State Prize) 56, *Proměna* (Metamorphosis) 57, *Srpnová neděle* (A Sunday in August, play and film) 58, *Zlatá reneta* (The Golden Rennet Apple) 63 (film 65).

Union of Czechoslovak Writers, Národní třída 11, Prague 1, Czechoslovakia.

Hruska, Roman Lee, LL.B.; American politician; b. 16 Aug. 1904; ed. Univ. of Omaha, Univ. of Chicago, and Creighton Univ.
Admitted to Nebraska Bar 29; practised law, Omaha; County Commr. Douglas County, Nebraska 44-52; mem. House of Reps. 53-54; U.S. Senator from Nebraska 54-; Hon. LL.D.; Republican.
2139 South 38th Street, Omaha, Nebraska, U.S.A.

Hryniewiecki, Jerzy; Polish architect; b. 08; ed. Warsaw Polytechnic.
Senior Asst. Warsaw Polytechnic 38-39; prisoner of war 39-45; Deputy Prof., Warsaw Polytechnic 45, Prof. 59; Head of Section, Warsaw Reconstruction Bureau 45; Prof. Szczecin Higher School of Engineering 48; Pres. Polish Asscn. of Architects 58-; State Prize, 1st Class.
Works include many industrial, sports and exhibition buildings such as Polish Printing Centre, Tenth Year Stadium (both in Warsaw) and pavilions, etc., Exhibition of Regained Territories (Wrocław).
Skolimowska 6, Warsaw, Poland.

Hsi Chung-hsun; Chinese administrator; b. 12.
Joined Chinese Communist Youth League 26; imprisoned 27; took part in guerilla warfare in Shensi; undertook defence of Shensi-Kansu-Ninghsia Border Region during Japanese War; Vice-Chair. N.W. Mil. and Administrative Council 49; Vice-Chair. Educational Council 52; mem. State Planning Commission 52; Vice-Chair. N.W. Administrative Council 53; Dir. Propaganda Board of Central Cttee. of C.P.C. 53; Sec.-Gen. of State Council 54-59, Vice-Premier, State Council 59-65.
c/o State Council, Peking, China.

Hsi-jao-chia-ts'o; Chinese politician and administrator.
Chairman, Chinese Buddhist Association, Peking 55-; Vice-Gov., Chinghai Province 49-.
Office of the Vice-Governor, Sining, Chinghai (N.W. China), People's Republic of China.

Hsia Kang-nung; Chinese novelist.
Founded Chun Chao Press with Chang Yu-sung and edited *Chun Chao Monthly*; Vice-Chair. Nationalities Cttee., Southwest Military and Administrative Council; Vice-Principal Southwest Nationalities Academy; Dir. preparatory cttee. of Szechwan Province Working Cttee. of Chinese Peasants and Workers Democratic Party 53; Szechwan del. to N.P.C. 54; mem. Secr. China Scientific and Technical Asscn. 58-.
China Scientific and Technical Association, Peking, China.

Hsia Nai (Shiah Nae), PH.D.; Chinese archaeologist; b. 1910; ed. Tsinghua and London Univs.
Director, Institute of Archaeology, Academia Sinica; fmr. Prof. of Archaeology, National Peking Univ.; excavated at Anyang 35, Tunhuang, Hueihsien, Changsha and abroad, etc.; excavated a Ming Royal tomb near Peking 58; mem. Cttee. Dept. Philosophy and Social Sciences, Standing Cttee. Acad. Sinica 55; Del. from Shantung to Second Nat. People's Congress 59.
Publs. Many articles on archæology.
Institute of Archæology, Academia Sinica, Peking, China.

Hsia Yen; Chinese playwright; b. 1900; ed. School of Industry and in Japan.
Active in Northern Expedition, in May 4th movement 19; began writing 27; among original organisers League of Left Writers and Left Dramatists; Assoc. Ed. of newspaper in Shanghai, etc.; Vice-Minister of Culture 54-.
Publs. *Under the Eaves of Shanghai*, *The Germs of Fascism*, etc.
Union of Chinese Writers, Peking, China

Hsiang Shu-hsiang; Chinese industrialist and politician; ed. Tsinghua Univ., Britain and U.S.A.
Formerly Asst. Man. Tientsin-Chekiang Industrial Bank, Prof. in Nankai Univ. and later Gen. Man. Chekiang Industrial Bank; mem. Standing Cttee. All-China Fed. of Industry and Commerce 53; mem. Standing Cttee. of Central Cttee. of China Democratic National Construction Assoc. 55; Sec.-Gen. All-China Fed. of Industry and Commerce 56-.
All-China Federation of Industry and Commerce, Peking, China.

Hsiao Chien; Chinese journalist and man of letters; b. 11.
In second World War journalist in Europe covering Western Front; now associate ed. *Literary Gazette* and head of foreign literature section.
Publs. Translations of Fielding, Lamb, Hasek, *Etching of a Tormented Age, Spinners of Silk,* etc.
Wen Yi Pao, Peking, China.

Hsiao Hua; Chinese army officer and politician; b. 1915.
Director Org. Section, 115th Div. Political Dept.; later Political Dir. Hopei-Shantung Region; Command posts in Shantung-Hopei-Honan Mil. Region, S. Manchuria and Liaotung 40-49; Deputy Dir. of Cadres Dept., Headquarters of People's Liberation Army 49-54, Dir. 54; later Deputy Dir. Gen. Political Work Dept., People's Liberation Army, Dir. 63-; Chair. Political Work Conf. 66; mem. Central Cttee. Chinese C.P. 54-.
Army Headquarters, Peking, People's Republic of China.

Hsieh Chueh-tsai; Chinese politician; b. 81.
Joined Kuomintang 24; Editor Hunan *Min Pao* (People's Newspaper) 26; joined Communist Party, worked in Party School and edited peasant newspaper 31-32; Sec. Central Govt. 33; Chief Judicial Dept., North China Govt. 48; Minister of the Interior 49-59; Pres. Supreme People's Court 59-65; Vice-Chair. Chinese People's Political Consultative Conf. (C.P.P.C.C.) 65-; Vice-Premier 65-.
Chinese People's Political Consultative Conference, Peking, China.

Hsieh Fu-chih, Gen.; Chinese officer; b. 1908; ed. Red Army College.
Former mil. commdr. in Yunnan and head of Yunnan C.P. 54-58; mem. Central Cttee. Chinese C.P. 56-; mem. Nat. Defence Council; Minister of Public Security 59-, also Dir., Gen. Office for Internal Affairs; Vice-Premier of China 65-; fmr. Dir., Gen. Office for Political and Legal Affairs.
General Office for Internal Affairs, Peking, People's Republic of China.

Hsieh Fu-min; Chinese (Chuang) politician; b. 09; ed. Kwangsi Provincial Normal Coll.
Joined C.C.P. at college; in Yu-chiang revolution 29; with Red Army on Long March 34; Vice-Chair. Nationalities Cttee. of N.P.C. 55-65, Chair. 65-; mem. standing cttee. of N.P.C.
c/o National People's Congress, Peking, China.

Hsing Hsi-ping; Chinese Marxist theoretician and politician; b. 02; ed. Berlin Univ. and Moscow.
Joined European branch of C.C.P.; during the war assisted Chou En-lai as liaison officer between Kuomintang and Communist Army; Mayor of Tsinan 48; Deputy-Dir., United Front Work Dept., Central Cttee. of Chinese Communist Party 49-65, Dir. 65-; Exec. Vice-Chair. C.P.P.C.C. Nat. Cttee.
United Front Work Department, Central Committee of Chinese Communist Party, Peking, China.

Hsiung Fo-hsi; Chinese playwright; b. 1900; ed. Yenching Univ., Columbia Univ. Theatrical Dept.
Lectured on literature at Yenching Univ.; Dir. Thea-

trical Section, People's Educn. Movement, Ting-hsien; mem. All-China Fed. of Literary and Art Circles 49; head of Theatrical School, Shanghai, 49; Principal, East China branch of Central Academy of Dramatic Art 55.
Publs. Numerous plays dealing mostly with rural life.
East China Academy of Dramatic Art, Shanghai, China.

Hsiung Shih-I; Chinese author; b. 14 Oct. 1902; ed. Teachers Coll., Nat. Univ. Peking.
Assoc.-Man. Chen Kwang Theatre, Peking 22; Prof. Agricultural Coll., Nanchang 23; Editor, Commercial Press, Shanghai 26, Special Editor 28; Prof. Chung Shan Univ., Nanchang 27; Man.-Dir. Pantheon Theatres Ltd., Shanghai 29; Prof. Min Kuo Univ., Peiping 30; Sec. China Society, London 33, Hon. Sec. 35; Chinese Del. to Int. P.E.N. Congress 34, 35, 38, 39, 40, 47; to Int. Theatre Inst. Congress 48; Lecturer, Cambridge Univ. 50-53; Dean, Coll. of Arts, Nanyang Univ. 54-55; Managing Dir. Pacific Films Co. Ltd., Hong Kong 55-; Hon. Ph.D.
Publs. in English: *Lady Precious Stream* 34, *The Romance of Western Chamber* 35, *The Professor from Peking* 39, *The Bridge of Heaven* 43, *The Life of Chiang Kai-Shek* 48, *The Gate of Peace* 49, *The Story of Lady Precious Stream* 50, *Book of Chinese Proverbs* 53; translations into Chinese of B. Franklin's *Autobiography* 23, of Barrie's and Shaw's plays, and Hardy's novels 26-33.
Staverton House, Oxford, England; and Pacific Films Co. Ltd., Hong Kong.

Hsü Hsiang-chien, Marshal; Chinese soldier; b. 02; ed. Taiyüan Normal School and Whampoa Mil. Acad.
Joined Communist Party of China in 26; commanded the Fourth Division of the Red Army; C.-in-C. Fourth District of the Red Army 31; led Red Army to establish a new Soviet Area in Szechuan 32; Second-in-C. 129th Division of Eighth Route Army 37; Second-in-C. North-West Area of People's Liberation Army 46; mem. North China People's Govt. 48; Chief of Staff and Second-in-C. North China Mil. Area 49; Vice-Chair. People's Revolutionary Mil. Cttee. 54; Vice-Chair. Council of Nat. Defence 54-; Vice-Chair. Standing Cttee. of Nat. People's Congress.
National People's Congress, Peking, China.

Hsu Peh-Yuan; Chinese banker and economist; b. 02; ed. National Southeastern Univ. and Univs. of Chicago, Illinois and California.
Assistant Gen. Manager China Electric Corpn. 33; Dep. Dir.-Gen. Postal Remittances and Savings Bank 34-35; Manager, Bank of Communications, Peking, Tientsin, Kunming 35-39; Dep. Sec.-Gen., Sec.-Gen. Joint Board Four Govt. Banks 39-48; Chair. Board of Dirs. Bank of Taiwan 51-52; Commissioner of Finance, Taiwan Provincial Govt. 53-54; Minister of Finance 54-58; Chair. Foreign Exchange and Trade Control Comm., Exec. Yuan 55-58, 63-; Chair. Finance Cttee., China Kuomintang Party 54-; Chair. Bank of China 49-61; Governor Central Bank of China 60-; Gov. for China (Taiwan) Int. Monetary Fund 64-; Order of Brilliant Star, First Class.
Central Bank of China, 21 Paoching Road, Taipei, Republic of China (Taiwan).

Hsü Teh-heng; Chinese scholar and politician; b. 94; ed. Peking Univ. and Univ. of Paris.
Has been Head of Depts. of History and Sociology at Peking Univ., Univ. of China, Sun Yat-sen Univ. and Tsinan Univ.; mem. Standing Cttee. of Univ. Affairs Cttee. of Peking Univ. 49; Minister of Marine Products 56-; Chair. Chiu San Society; mem. Asian Solidarity Cttee. of China.
Publs. Works, some translated, on sociology.
Ministry of Marine Products, Peking, China.

Hsü Ti-hsin; Chinese economist; b. 07; ed. Inst. of Commerce of the Central Univ.
Joined Communist Youth League in 25; Vice-Chair. Financial and Economic Cttee. of East China Military and Admin. Council 50; mem. China Cttee. for the Promotion of Internat. Trade 52; Vice-Chair. All-China Fed. of Industry and Commerce 53-; Dir. Central Bureau for Admin. and Supervision of Industry and Commerce 54-.
All-China Federation of Industry and Commerce, Peking, China.

Hsueh Mu-chiao; Chinese economist.
During war at Hua-chung Kang-Jih Univ.; Prof. at Shantung Univ. 43; Cttee. mem. and Sec. Financial and Economic Commission and Dir. of Bureau of Private Industry 49; on Cttee. for Advancement of Foreign Trade and Dir., State Statistical Bureau 52-; Kiangsu del. to N.P.C. 54; Vice-Chair. State Planning Commission 54-; on Cttee. Dept. of Philosophy and Social Sciences Academia Sinica 55; Sec. Scientific Planning Commission 56.
Publs. *Introduction to Chinese Village Economy*, etc.
State Statistical Bureau, Peking, China.

Hu Chiao-mu; Chinese journalist and historian; b. 05; ed. Tsinghua Univ.
Succeeded Chen Po-ta as Political Secretary of Mao Tse-tung; Head of General Press Office 49; Sec.-Gen. of Cultural and Educational Cttee. 49; Dir. Hsinhua News Agency 52-54; Alt. mem. Secr., Central Cttee. of Chinese Communist Party 56-; Chair. Cttee. for the Reform of the Written Language 55.
Publs. *Thirty Years of the Communist Party of China*, etc.
Secretariat of Central Committee of Chinese Communist Party, Peking, China.

Hu Yü-chih; Chinese politician; b. 95; ed. Hangchow English Language Institute and Univ. of Paris.
Student of international politics and an Esperantist; Head of General Office of Publications 49; Vice-Pres. Chinese People's Institute of Foreign Affairs 49; Sec.-Gen. China Democratic League 63; Vice-Chair. Cttee. for the Reform of the Written Language 54; Vice-Pres. Sino-Indonesian Friendship Asscn.
Publ. *Impressions of Moscow*.
China Democratic League, Peking, China.

Huan Hsiang; Chinese politician and diplomatist; b. 10; ed. Chiao Tung Univ.
Journalist and editor since 36; Deputy Sec.-Gen. Chinese People's Political Consultative Conf. 49, mem. Nat. Cttee. 49-54; Head of Dept. of Western and African Affairs, Ministry of Foreign Affairs 50-54; Chargé d'Affaires of People's Republic of China to Great Britain 54-62; Asst. to Minister of Foreign Affairs 64-.
c/o Ministry of Foreign Affairs, Peking, People's Republic of China.

Huang Chen; Chinese diplomatist.
Deputy Dir. 18th Div., Shansi-Hopei-Shantung Border Region Army 44; after war Deputy Political Dir. in mil. admin. areas; Ambassador to People's Republic of Hungary 50-54; Ambassador to Republic of Indonesia 54-61; Dep. Foreign Minister 61-64; Ambassador to France 64-; rep. at the Afro-Asian Conference 55.
Embassy of the People's Republic of China, 104 boulevard Bineau, Neuilly-sur-Seine, France.

Huang Shao-ku; Chinese politician; b. *c.* 1900; ed. National Peking Normal Univ.
Secretary-Gen. of Exec. Yuan 49-54; Vice-Premier, Repub. of China 54-58, 66-; Minister of Foreign Affairs, later Amb. to Spain 58-62.
Office of the Vice-Premier, Taipei, Republic of China.

Huang Yen; Chinese administrator.
Man. Dir. of Tientsin-Pukow Railway 41; Asst. Sec. of N. Anhwei Regional Cttee. of the Communist Party of China 49; Vice-Chair. Anhwei Provincial People's Govt. and Second-in-C. Anhwei Mil. Region 52; Gov. of Anhwei Province 55-.
The Anhwei Provincial Government, Hofei, Anhwei, China.

Huant, Ernest Albin Camille; French doctor, philosopher and sociologist; b. 29 Oct. 1909; ed. Lycée de Charleville and Univ. de Paris à la Sorbonne.
Medical radiologist, Paris hospitals 43; Pres. Centre d'Etudes des Problèmes de l'Homme 60; mem. Soc. d'Economie Politique, Paris 58-; Scientific Adviser to Laboratories 57-; mem. Int. Cttee. and French Del. to Int. Soc. for Cybernetic Medicine 65; Lauréat de l'Institut de France 64-65; Chevalier Légion d'Honneur; Carnegie Foundation Medal (U.S.A.); Prix de l'Acad. de Médecine for *Les Traitements Milotiques du Cancer* 58, *Les Maladies de Société* 61; Prix de l'Acad. des Sciences Morales et Politiques for *Florence et Rome* 65; Pres. de la Société d'études philosophiques des Sciences de la nature 67; Pres. du Centre Internationale de Cyto-Cybernétique 67.
Publs. *Les Radiations et la Vie* 42, *Déterminisme et Finalités* 46, *Connaissance du Temps* 51, *Biologie et Cybernétiques* 54, *Credo de Jean Rostand* 57, *L'Anti-Masse* 57, *Du Biologique au Social* 57, *Milieu et Adaptation* 59, *Les Maladies de Société* 61, *Le Péché contre la Chair* 61, *Naître ou ne pas Naître* 63, *A.D.N. Recherches expérimentales et Cliniques* 64, *Florence et Rome* 64, *Economie et Cybernétique* 65, *Voyage en Assuro-Socyalie* 65, *Masses-Morale-Machines* 67, *Le Troisième Triumvirat* 67.
9 avenue Niel, Paris 17e, France.
Telephone: 380-28-72.

Huber, Paul; Swiss physicist; b. 1 Oct. 1910; ed. Seminar Wettingen, Swiss Inst. of Technology, Zürich.
Lecturer Eidgenössische Technische Hochschule, Zürich 41; Prof. of Physics and Dir. Physical Inst. of Univ. of Basle 42-; Rector Univ. of Basle 58; mem. Swiss Atomic Energy Comm.; Vice-Pres. Swiss Council of Science; Pres. Federal Comm. for control of radioactive fall-out, Swiss Acad. of Sciences; Pres. IUPAP Comm. Low Energy Nuclear Physics.
Publs. *Introduction to Physics* Vol. 1 51, Vol. 2 58; also various publications on nuclear physics and general science.
Office: Klingelbergstr. 82, 4000 Basle; Home: Hungerbachweg 13, Riehen, Basle, Switzerland.

Huberman, Leo, B.S., M.A.; American economic historian; b. 17 Oct. 1903; ed. Newark State Normal School, New York Univ. and London School of Economics.
Teacher public and private schools 22-33; Teacher Bryn Mawr Summer School 34, New York Univ. Teachers' Training Summer School 35; Assoc. Editor *Scholastic* magazine 34-35; mem. Comm. on Human Relations 35-37; Assoc. and Chair. Social Science Dept. New Coll. Columbia Univ. 38-39; Labor Editor *P.M.* 40; Columnist *U.S. Week* 41; Dir. Public Relations and Education, Nat. Maritime Union 42; Assoc. Editor Reynal & Hitchcock, publishers 45-; Co-Editor *Monthly Review* 49-.
Publs. *We the People* 32, *Man's Worldly Goods* 36, *The Labour Spy Racket* 38, *America Incorporated* 40, *The Great Bus Strike* 41, *Storm Over Bridges* 41, *The Truth About Unions* 46, *The Truth About Socialism* 50, *Cuba: Anatomy of a Revolution* (with Paul M. Sweezy) 60, *P. A. Buran: A Collective Portrait* (with Paul M. Sweezy) 65, *Fifty Years of Soviet Power* 68.
66 Barrow Street, New York 14, N.Y., U.S.A.

Huchel, Peter; German writer; b. 3 April 1903; ed. Humboldt-Universität zu Berlin, Albert-Ludwigs-Universität, Freiburg-im-Breisgau and Universität Wien.

Freelance writer 25-45, 62-; lived in France 26-28; travelled in Balkans and Turkey 30-32, U.S.S.R., England, Netherlands, Belgium, Italy, Bulgaria, Czechoslovakia and Poland 52-60; Dir. and Arts Dir. Berliner Rundfunk 45-48; Chief Editor *Sinn und Form* (literary magazine) 49-62; mem. Group 47; mem. German Acad. of Arts, Berlin; Ehrenmitglied der Freien Akademie der Künste, Hamburg; Mitglied der Akademie der künste, West Berlin; Lyrikpreis der Zeitschrift *Kolonne* 32, Nationalpreis 51, Theodor-Fontane-Preis der Mark Brandenburg 55, Plakette der Freien Akademie der Künste, Hamburg 59, Berliner Kunstpreis für Literatur (Fontane-Preis) 63, Preis der jungen Generation, Hamburg 65.
Publs. include: *Poems* 48, *Poems* 49, *Dvanact Noci* 58, *Poems* 59, *Chausseen, Chausseen* 63, *Silnice, Silnice* 64, *Die Sterneureuse* 67, *Wiersze* 67.
Potsdam/Wilhelmshorst, Hubertusweg 43/45, Germany.
Telephone: Michendorf 394.

Huddleston, Rt. Rev. Trevor, M.A.; British ecclesiastic; b. 15 June 1913; ed. Christ Church, Oxford.
Ordained Deacon 36, Priest 37; Curate, St. Mark's, Swindon 36-39; professed Community of the Resurrection, Mirfield 41; Prior and Priest-in-Charge, Sophiatown, Orlando, and Pimville, Johannesburg 43, Provincial of the Community of the Resurrection, South Africa 49-56; Novice-Master, Community of the Resurrection, England 56-58; Prior, London Community of the Resurrection 58-60; Bishop of Masasi 60-68; Suffragen Bishop of Stepney 68-; Hon. D.D. (Aberdeen Univ.).
Publs. *Naught for Your Comfort* 56, *The True and Living God* 64, *God's World* 66.
c/o Fulham Palace, London, S.W.6, England.

Hudon, L. Denis, M.A.; Canadian financial executive; b. 21 Dec. 1924; ed. Laval Univ., Quebec City, and Toronto Univ.
Economic Policy Div., Dept. of Finance, Ottawa 48-51; Sec. (Financial), Perm. Canadian Mission to North Atlantic Treaty Org. (NATO) 52-54; Int. and Econ. Div. (Int. Programmes and Contributions), Dept. of Finance, Ottawa 54-60; Dir. Policy and Planning Coordination, External Aid Office 60-61; Alt. Dir. Int. Monetary Fund, Int. Bank for Reconstruction and Devt., Int. Devt. Asscn. 61-64, Exec. Dir. for Canada, Ireland and Jamaica 65-; Financial Counsellor, Canadian Embassy, Washington 61-64; Dir. Int. Programmes Div., Dept. of Finance, Ottawa 64-66.
Assistant Director General, External Aid Office, Ottawa, Canada.
Telephone: 996-2033.

Hudson, Sir William, K.B.E., F.R.S., B.SC.(Eng).; British engineer; b. 27 April 1896; ed. Nelson Coll., New Zealand, Univs. of London and Grenoble.
Former Engineer, Sir W. G. Armstrong-Whitworth & Co. Ltd., Public Works Dept., New Zealand, Sir Alexander Gibb & Partners, Metropolitan Water, Sewerage and Drainage Bd., Sydney; Commr. Snowy Mountains Hydro-Electric Authority, Cooma, New South Wales 49-; Australasian Engineer Award 57, Kernot Memorial Medal 59; Fellow, Univ. Coll. London 61-; Hon. mem. Australasian Inst. of Mining and Metallurgy 61-; Hon. mem. of the Institution of Engineers, Australia; LL.D. h.c (Australian Nat. Univ.) 62; Hon. Fellow the Royal Australian Inst. of Architects 68.
39 Flanagan Street, Garran, A.C.T., Australia.
Telephone: 815137.

Huerta, Commodore Roberto; Argentine air force officer; b. 7 April 1917; ed. Military Coll., Buenos Aires.
Sub-Lieut. (Army) 37; served in 1st and 2nd Infantry Regiments; 1st-Lieut. Military Air Force 45; held numerous important posts, retd. 51; returned to active service 55; Minister for Air 57-58, Sec. of State for Air 58; Pres. and Gen. Dir. Industria Automotriz Santa Fe S.A., Auto-Union DKW 59-63; Pres. Banco de la Provincia de Rio Negro; Dir. numerous companies; Minister for Economy, Rio Negro Province.
Vedia 1671 Buenos Aires; and Ministerio de Economía, Viedma (Prov. de Rio Negro), Argentina.
Telephone: Buenos Aires 70-4890; Viedma 201.

Huet, Pierre, D. en D.; French civil servant; b. 12 Nov. 1920; ed. Paris Law Faculty and Ecole des Sciences Politiques.
Special Asst., French Govt. Refugee Del. 40, Asst. to Sec. of State, Ministry of Food 44; Junior mem. Conseil d'Etat, mem. Legal Cttee. of French Union 46; Asst. to Sec. Gen., Cttee. for European Economic Co-operation 47; Legal Adviser, OEEC 48; Senior mem. Conseil d'Etat 54; Gen. Counsel, OEEC 56; Dir. European Nuclear Energy Agency 58-62, Dir.-Gen. 62-64; Council of State 64-; Chair. Board, Asscn. Technique pour l'Energie Nucléaire 65; Commdr. Ordre de Léopold (Belgium); Grosses Goldene Ehrenzeichen für Verdienste (Austria), Chevalier, Légion d'Honneur.
162 boulevard Haussmann, Paris 8e, France.

Huggins, Charles B., B.A., M.D.; American (b. Canadian) professor of surgery and cancerologist; b. 22 Sept. 1901; ed. Acadia and Harvard Univs.
Houseman in surgery, Univ. of Michigan 24-26, Instructor 26-27; Instructor in Surgery, Univ. of Chicago 27-29, Asst. Prof. 29-33, Assoc. Prof. 33-36, Prof. 36-; Dir. Ben May Laboratory for Cancer Research 51-; William B. Ogden Distinguished Service Prof. 26-; mem. Nat. Acad. of Sciences 49, American Philosophical Soc. 62; Hon. mem. Royal Soc. of Medicine 56; Hon. Fellow, Royal Coll. of Surgeons, Edinburgh 58, England 59; Hon. Fellow American Coll. of Surgeons 63; Orden Pour le Mérite (German Federal Republic), Orden El Sol del Perú; numerous gold medals and prizes from American Scientific and Cancer Socs., and British Hospitals; Charles L. Mayer Award, Nat. Acad. of Sciences 44, Francis Amory Prize 48, Ferdinand Valentine Award 62; Gold Medal Soc. Int. d'Urologie 47, Walker Prize, Royal Coll. of Surgeons, England 61, Albert Lasker Award for Clinical Research 63, Gold Medal in Therapeutics, Worshipful Soc. of Apothecaries of London 66, Gairdner Award, Toronto 66, Nobel Prize for Medicine 66.
Ben May Laboratory for Cancer Research, University of Chicago, 950 East 59th Street, Chicago, Illinois 60637, U.S.A.

Huggins, Edwin Virgil, PH.B., LL.B.; American business executive; b. 28 Sept. 1907; ed. Yale Coll., Yale Law School.
Admitted to Bar, N.Y. State 34; Assoc. Attorney, N.Y. 32-40, Attorney, Philadelphia 40-43; Joined Westinghouse Electric Corpn. as Attorney 43, Head N.Y. Office Law Dept. 45-51, Corporate Sec. 48-51, 54-57, Vice-Pres. 53-61, Chair. Exec. Cttee. 58-61, Exec. Vice-Pres. Associated Activities 61-63, Dir. 51-; Chair. and Dir. Westinghouse Broadcasting Co. Inc. and subsidiaries; Dir. and mem. Exec. Cttee. Canadian Westinghouse Co. Ltd.; Dir. Canadian Westinghouse Int. Co. Ltd.; Dir. and Vice-Chair. Industria Eléctrica de México, S.A.; Pres., Trustee and mem. Exec. Cttee., Nat. Security Industrial Asscn.
Office: 120 Broadway, New York, U.S.A.

Hughes, Rt. Hon. Cledwyn, P.C., M.P., LL.B.; British politician; b. 14 Sept. 1916; ed. Holyhead Grammar School and Univ. Coll. of Wales, Aberystwyth.
Solicitor 40; R.A.F.V.R. 40-45; mem. Anglesey County Council 46-52; M.P. Anglesey 51-, Chair. Welsh Parl.

Party 53-54, Welsh Labour Group 55-56, mem. Cttee. of Public Accounts 57-64; Minister of State for Commonwealth Relations 64-66; Sec. of State for Wales 66-68; Minister of Agriculture, Fisheries and Food April 68-; Labour.
House of Commons, London, S.W.1, England; and Ty Gwyn, Holyhead, Anglesey, Wales.

Hughes, Howard Robard; American executive, aviator and film producer; b. 24 Dec. 1905; ed. Rice Inst., Houston and California Inst. of Technology.
Established in plane of his own design land-plane speed record 35, U.S. transcontinental record 37, world flight record 38; world's largest plane 47; Pres. Hughes Tool Co., Hughes Aircraft Co.; owns extensive property in Nevada; films produced include *Scarface, Hell's Angels, The Outlaw*; Harmon Trophy 38, Collier Trophy 39, Octave Chanute Award 40, Congressional Medal 41.
Humble Building, Houston 2, Texas, U.S.A.

Hughes, Richard, O.B.E.; British writer; b. 19 April 1900; ed. Charterhouse and Oriel Coll., Oxford.
Poet, playwright, novelist and literary critic; co-founder Portmadoc Players; sometime Vice-Chair. Welsh Nat. Theatre Ltd.; sometime Gresham Prof. in Rhetoric; author world's first radio play; mem. American Acad. and Inst. 63; Hon. D.Litt. (Univ. of Wales). Publs. *The Sisters' Tragedy* 22, *The Man Born to be Hanged* 23, *A Comedy of Good and Evil* 23, *Danger* 24, *Gipsy-Night and Other Poems* 22, *Confessio Juvenis* (collected poems) 26, *Plays* 24, *A Moment of Time* (collected stories) 26, *A High Wind in Jamaica or The Innocent Voyage* (novel) 29, *The Spider's Palace* (children's stories) 31, *In Hazard* (novel) 38, *Don't Blame Me!* (children's stories) 41, *The Administration of War Production* (in *Official History of the War*) (with J. D. Scott) 56, *The Human Predicament* (Vol. I, *The Fox in the Attic*) (novel) 61, *Gertrude's Child* (children's story) 66, *Hong Kong* 67.
c/o Chatto and Windus, 40-42 William IV Street, London, W.C.2, England.

Hughes, Richard, LL.B.; American lawyer and politician; b. 9 Aug. 1909; ed. St. Charles Coll., St. Joseph's Coll. and New Jersey law school.
Private law practice, Trenton 32-39; Asst. U.S. Attorney for New Jersey 39-45; Mercer County Judge 48-53, Superior Court of N.J. 53-57, Judge, Appellate Div., New Jersey 57; private law practice 57; Gov. of New Jersey 62-; LL.D. h.c. (St. Joseph's Coll., Rutgers Univ., Seton Hall Univ., St. Peter's Coll., Jersey City); Democrat.
State Capitol, Trenton, New Jersey, U.S.A.

Huh Chung; Korean politician; b. 96; ed. Korean Univ.
Took part in Korean revolution 19; in exile 19-45; Sec.-Gen. Democratic Party 45; Minister of Transport 45-47; Dir.-Gen. Korean Coal and Shipping Corpns. 47-50; Minister of Social Affairs 50-51, Acting Prime Minister 51 (resigned); Mayor of Seoul, Head Korean Del. Japanese Negotiations 59; Acting President, Republic of Korea 60-61; Minister of Foreign Affairs 60-61.
Seoul, Republic of Korea.

Hui Yu-yu; Chinese administrator; b. 06.
Political Commissar, People's Liberation Army; Chair. N. Kiangsu People's Administrative Council 49; Sec., C.C.P., Nanking Municipal Cttee. 53; mem. Kiangsu Prov. People's Govt. 53-; Mayor of Nanking 54; Dep. Sec. C.C.P. Kiangsu Prov. Cttee.; Gov. Kiangsu 55-67; Deputy from Kiangsu, Nat. People's Congress 54-.
Nanking, Kiangsu, People's Republic of China.

Hull, Gen. John Edwin; American army officer; b. 24 May 1895; ed. Miami Univ. (Ohio), Graduate Infantry School, Command & Staff School, War Coll.
Commissioned U.S. Infantry 17, served through all

grades to General 51, Brigadier Gen. 45, Major Gen. 48; War Dept. Gen. Staff 42-44, Asst. Chief of Staff 44-46; Commanding Gen., Army Forces Pacific and Hawaiian Dept. 46-48 (also C.O. Task Force 7 responsible for Atomic Tests at Eniwetok 47-48); Commanding Gen. U.S. Army Pacific 48-49; Dir. Weapons System Evaluation, Defense Dept., Washington 49-51; Vice-Chief of Staff 51-53; C.-in-C. Far East Command, C.-in-C. U.N. Forces in the Far East and Gov. Ryukyu Islands 53-55; Pres. Manufacturing Chemists' Asscn. 55-63; decorations include D.S.M., Silver Star, Legion of Merit, Hon. C.B.E., Hon. D.Mil.Sc. (Pennsylvania), Hon. LL.D. (Miami Univ., Ohio).
3133 Connecticut Avenue, Washington, D.C., U.S.A. Telephone: NOrth 7-5325.

Hull, Field-Marshal Sir Richard Amyatt, G.C.B., D.S.O., M.A., D.L.; British army officer; b. 7 May 1907; ed. Charterhouse and Trinity Coll., Cambridge.
Joined 17th/21st Lancers 28; Commanded 17th/21st Lancers 41, 12th Infantry Brigade 43, 26th Armoured Brigade 43, 1st Armoured Div. 44, 5th Infantry Div. 45; Commdt. Staff Coll., Camberley 46-48; Dir. of Staff Duties, War Office 48-50; Chief Army Instructor, Imperial Defence Coll. 50-52; Chief of Staff, G.H.Q., Middle East Land Forces 52-54; G.O.C. British Troops in Egypt 54-56; Deputy C.I.G.S. 56-58; C.-in-C. Far East Land Forces 58-61; Chief, Imperial Gen. Staff 61-65; A.D.C. (Gen.) to the Queen, Dec. 61-64; Chief of Defence Staff 65-67; Col. Commdt. R.A.C. 68; Pres. Army Benevolent Fund 68; Dir. Whitbread and Co. Ltd.
Beacon Downe, Pinhoe, Nr. Exeter, Devon, England.

Hull, Roger; American insurance executive; b. 07; ed. Mississippi State Coll. and Kentucky Wesleyan Coll.
Mutual Life Insurance Co. of New York 28-; Agent Meridian, Mississippi 28-32, District Manager 32-35; Manager Nashville, Tennessee 35-38; Asst. Supt. of Agencies 38-41, Vice-Pres. and Man. of Agencies 41-50; Exec. Vice-Pres. 50-59, Pres. 59-67, mem. Board of Trustees 50-, Chair. 67-; Dir. Life Insurance Asscn. of America; Vice-Chair. and Life Trustee American Coll. of Life Underwriters; Dir. Health Insurance Inst., Dun & Bradstreet, Inc., Hart Schaffner and Marx; Dr. h.c. Kentucky Wesleyan Coll., Wheaton Coll., Illinois and Houghton Coll., New York; John Newton Russell Memorial Award.
1740 Broadway, New York 10019, U.S.A.

Hulme, Hon. Alan Shallcross, F.C.A.; Australian politician; b. 14 Feb. 1907; ed. North Sydney Boys' High School.
Honorary Treas. King's Univ. Coll. 44-49; Pres. Queensland Div. Liberal Party of Australia 46-49, 62-63; mem. House of Reps. 49-61, 63-; mem. Commonwealth Parl. Public Accounts Cttee. 53-58; Chair. Special Commonwealth Cttee. investigating Depreciation under Income Tax Acts 55, Commonwealth Immigration Planning Council 55-58; Dir. Chandlers (Aust.) Ltd., J. B. Chandler Investment Co. Ltd. 52-58, 62-63; Postmaster-Gen. 63-; Vice-Pres. of Exec. Council 66-.
Ridley Road, Aspley, Queensland, Australia.

Hulst, Hendrik Christoffel van de, PH.D.; Netherlands astronomer; b. 19 Nov. 1918; ed. Utrecht Univ.
Post-Doctoral Fellow Chicago Univ. 46-48; Lecturer in Astronomy Leiden Univ. 48-52, Prof. of Astronomy 52-; Pres. Comm. 34 (Interstellar Matter) Int. Astronomical Union 52-58, Nederland Astronomen Club 53-56, Cttee. on Space Research (COSPAR) 58-62; Chair. Netherlands Comm. for Geophysical and Space Research; Vice-Chair. European Space Research Org. (ESRO) 60-65, Chair. 68-; mem. Royal Neths. Acad. of Sciences; Eddington Medal Royal Astronomical Soc.

(U.K.) 55, Draper Medal Nat. Acad. of Sciences (U.S.A.) 56, Rumford Medal Royal Soc. (U.K.) 64.
Publs. *A Course of Radio Astronomy* 51, *Phaenomenologie en Natuurwetenschap* (with C. A. van Peursen) 53, *Light Scattering by Small Particles* 57; numerous articles and papers, particularly on interstellar matter. The Observatory, Sterrewacht 8, Leiden, Netherlands.

Hultgren, Most Rev. Gunnar, D.D.; Swedish ecclesiastic; b. 19 Feb. 1902; ed. Uppsala.
Curate in Charge, Husby-Oppunda 26; Rector, Björklinge 34; Lecturer in Systematic Theology, Uppsala Univ. 40; Rector and Dean, Härnösand 40; Bishop of Visby 47, of Härnösand 50; Archbishop of Uppsala 58-67.
Skuttunge prästgärd, Björklirge, Sweden.
Telephone: 018-741-60.

Hulton, Sir Edward George Warris, Kt.; British periodical publisher and writer; b. 29 Nov. 1906; ed. Harrow, Brasenose Coll., Oxford.
Conservative candidate 29, 31; called to Bar Inner Temple; created Knight 57; Freeman of the City of London; Chair. and Man. Dir. Hulton Publications Ltd.; Editor-in-Chief *European Review, Conflicts* 66.
Publs. *The New Age* 43, *When I Was a Child* 52.
22 Edwardes Square, London, W.8, England.

Hulubei, Horia; Romanian scientist; b. 1896; ed. Univs. of Jassy and Paris.
Director research, Centre Nat. Recherches Scientifiques, Paris 33-40; Prof. of the Structure of Matter, Jassy Univ. 38; Prof. of Atomic Physics, Bucharest Univ. 39; Rector of Bucharest Univ. 39-44; Dir. Nuclear Physics Inst. of R.S.R. Acad. 49-; full mem. R.S.R. Acad. 55-; Pres. and Chair. R.S.R. Nuclear Energy Cttee.; mem. Scientific Council, Joint Nuclear Research Inst., Dubna, U.S.S.R.; corresp. mem. and laureate, Acad. of Sciences, Paris, corresp. mem. Acad. of Sciences Lisbon, Acad. of Sciences of New York.
Institute of Atomic Physics, Magurele, Bucharest, Romania.
Telephone: 146332.

Hulugalle, Herbert, M.V.O.; Ceylonese company director and journalist; b. 10 March 1899; ed. St. Thomas' Coll., Colombo, and Ceylon Law Coll.
Editor, Ceylon Daily News 31-48; Dir. of Information, Ceylon Govt. 48-54; Amb. to Italy 54-59; Chair. of Comm. on Information and Broadcasting 66; Grand Officer Italian Order of Merit; Knight Grand Cross of St. Silvester (Vatican).
Publs. *British Governors of Ceylon, Ceylon of the Early Travellers, Introducing Ceylon, Life and Times of D. R. Wijewardene, History of Colombo.*
4 Greenlands Lane, Colombo 5, Ceylon.

Humason, M. L.; American astronomer; b. 19 Aug. 1891.
Asst. Astronomer, Mount Wilson Observatory 19-48; Asst. Astronomer and Sec. Mount Wilson and Palomar Observatories 48-54, Astronomer and Sec. 54-57; mem. American Astronomical Society, and Astronomical Society of Pacific; Foreign Assoc. mem. Royal Astronomical Society; Hon. Ph.D. (Lund Univ. Sweden) 50.
Box 165, Mendocino, California 95460, U.S.A.

Hume-Rothery, William, O.B.E., PH.D., D.SC., M.A., F.R.S.; British scientist; b. 15 May 1899; ed. Cheltenham Coll., Royal Military Acad., Woolwich, Magdalen Coll., Oxford, and London Univ.
Royal Society Armourers and Brasiers Research Fellowship 29-32; Royal Soc. Warren Research Fellow 32-42, 43-55; Lecturer in Metallurgical Chemistry, Oxford Univ. 38-55; George Kelley Reader in Metallurgy, Oxford Univ. 55-57; Isaac Wolfson Prof. of Metallurgy 58-66; Professorial Fellow, St. Edmund Hall 58-66; Fellow, Magdalen Coll. 38-43; Hon. Fellow of St.

Edmund Hall; many British and foriegn medals and awards.
Publs. *The Metallic State* 31, *Structure of Metals and Alloys* 36 (and with G. V. Raynor 44, 54, 62,), *Atomic Theory for Students of Metallurgy* 46, 52, 60, *Electrons, Atoms, Metals and Alloys* 48, 63, *Metallurgical Equilibrium Diagrams and Experimental Methods for their Determination* (with J. W. Christian and W. B. Pearson) 52, *Elements of Structural Metallurgy* 61, 66, *The Structures of Alloys of Iron: An Elementary Introduction* 66, and numerous scientific papers.
Cherry Orchard, Abberbury Road, Iffley, Oxford, England.
Telephone: Oxford 79259.

Humo, Avdo; Yugoslav politician; b. 14; ed. Mostar and Belgrade Univ.
Mem. Fed. Exec. Council and fmr. Chair. Cttee. Nat. Development Plan of Fed. Exec. Council; Chair. Cttee. for Econ. Relations with Foreign Countries of Fed. Exec. Council 62-; mem. Parl., Central Cttee. Yugoslav League of Communists, Fed. Cttee. for Nuclear Energy 60-; Maj.-Gen of Reserve; 1941 Partisan Commemoration Medal, Orders of Nat. Hero, Nat. Liberation, Meritorious Service to the People, 1st Class, Bravery.
Committee for Economic Relations with Foreign Countries, Belgrade, Yugoslavia.

Humphrey, George Duke, M.A., PH.D., LL.D., D.LITT.; American university president; b. 30 Aug. 1897; ed. Blue Mountain Coll. (Miss.), Univ. of Chicago, Ohio State Univ.
Teacher, Supt. and Principal in Public and High Schools 15-24; County Supt. of Education, Tippah Co. (Miss.) 24-30; Supt. Kosciusko City Schools 31-32; State High School Supervisor (Miss.) 32-33; Pres. Mississippi State Coll. 34-45; Pres. Univ. of Wyoming 45-64; Pres. Southern Asscn. of Colls. and Secondary Schools 42-45; part-time public mem. Fourth Regional War Labour Board 43-45; mem. Exec. Cttee. Asscn. Land Grant Colls. and Univs. 44-46, Chair. of its Cttee. on Irrigated Agriculture and Water Resources 48-55, Sec. of its Council of Presidents 55-56 and Chair. 56-57; mem. Nat. Science Foundation Board 50-62; Vice-Pres. Asscn. of American Colls. 58, Pres. 59; Vice-Pres. Nat. Asscn. of State Univs. 59-60, Pres. 60-61; mem. Nat. Comm. on Accrediting 61-64; Pres. Emer. and Administrator, School of American Studies, Univ. of Wyoming 64-.
Home: 1410 Bridger, Laramie, Wyoming 82070; Office: Box 3067, University Station, Laramie, Wyoming 82070, U.S.A.
Telephone: 742-2972.

Humphrey, George Magoffin; American executive; b. 8 March 1890; ed. Univ. of Michigan.
Admitted to Mich. Bar 12; practised law at Saginaw, Mich. 12-17; joined M. A. Hanna & Co., Cleveland, as Gen. Counsel 17, Partner 20-22, Vice-Pres. The M. A. Hanna Co. 22-24, Exec. Vice-Pres. 24-29, Pres. 29-52, Chair. Board 52-53; resigned all corporate offices to become Sec. of Treasury 53-57; Hon. Chair. Board, Dir. M. A. Hanna Co. 57-65; Dir. Nat. Steel Corpn.; Hon. mem. American Inst. of Mining, Metallurgical and Petroleum Engineers, American Ordnance Asscn.; mem. American Iron and Steel Inst., Business Council; Hon. Trustee Cttee. for Econ. Devt.; mem. Advisory Council of Effective Citizens Org.; official of numerous other business and civic orgs.; Hon. LL.D. (Western Reserve, Rochester, Wesleyan, Michigan, John Carroll, Brown, Pittsburgh, West Virginia, Williams, Yale, Harvard, Notre Dame and Lehigh Univs.); Hon. D.Eng. (Case Inst. of Technology); Republican.
100 Erieview Plaza, Cleveland 14, Ohio, U.S.A.
Telephone: 523-3232.

Humphrey, Hubert Horatio, Jr., A.M.; American politician; b. 27 May 1911; ed. Denver Coll. of Pharmacy, Univ. of Minnesota and Louisiana State Univ.
State Dir. War Production Training and Re-employment 41; State Chief of Minnesota War Service Programme 42; Asst. Dir. War Manpower Comm. 43; Prof. Political Science, Macalester Coll. 43-44; former Vice-Pres. American Political Science Asscn.; radio news commentator 44-45; Mayor, City of Minneapolis 45-49; U.S. Senator from Minnesota 49-64; American del. to UN 56; Chair. Senate Sub-Cttee. on Disarmament 55-64; Vice-Pres. of the United States 65-; Chair. Nat. Aeronautics and Space Council; Chair. Peace Corps Advisory Council; mem. Nat. Security Council; mem. Board of Regents, Smithsonian Inst., etc.; Democratic-Farmer-Labor Party.
Publs. *The Cause is Mankind* 64, *School Desegregation: Documents and Commentaries* 64, *War on Poverty* 65.
Home: 3216 Coquelin Terrace, Chevy Chase, Md.; Office: Senate Office Building, Washington, D.C., U.S.A.

Humphrey, John Peters, B.COM., B.A., B.C.L., PH.D;. Canadian lawyer and university professor; b. 30 April 1905; ed. Rothesay Coll., Mount Allison Univ., McGill Univ. and Univ. de Paris.
Called to Montreal Bar 29, practised law with Wainwright, Elder & McDougall 30-36; Lecturer in Roman Law, McGill Univ. 36, Sec. of Law Faculty 37-46, Gale Prof. of Roman Law and Dean of Law Faculty 46, Prof. of Law and Political Science 66-; Carnegie Fellow in Int. Law, Paris 36-37; Dir. Div. of Human Rights, UN Secr. 46-66; Exec. Sec. UN Conf. on Freedom of Information 48, Refugees 51, Status of Stateless Persons 54, Slavery Conf. 56; Principal Sec. UN Fact-Finding Mission to S. Viet-Nam 63; Hon. Chair. Montreal Branch, UN Asscn. in Canada 66-; mem. UN Sub-Comm. on Prevention of Discrimination and Protection of Minorities 66; mem. Board of Dirs. Int. League for the Rights of Man 66-; Rapporteur, Cttee. on Human Rights, Int. Law Asscn. 66-; Pres. Canadian Comm., Int. Year for Human Rights 68; Hon. Dr. Soc. Sciences (Ottawa); Int. Co-operation Year Citation (Canada) 65, World Jewish Congress Citation 66.
Publ. *The Inter-American System: A Canadian View* 42.
1455 Sherbrook Street West, Montreal, P.Q., Canada.

Humphreys, Christmas (*see* Humphreys, (Travers) C.).

Humphreys, Sir Olliver William, Kt., C.B.E., B.SC., F.INST.P., M.I.E.E., F.R.Ae.S.; British physicist; b. 4 Sept. 1902; ed. Univ. Coll., London Univ.
Joined scientific staff of the G.E.C. Research Laboratories 25; Dir. G.E.C. Research Laboratories 49-61; Dir. G.E.C. 53-; Vice-Chair. 62-68; Chair. G.E.C. (Research) Ltd. 62-68; mem. Board Assoc. Semiconductor Mfrs. Ltd. 62-; mem. Board of Trade Cttee. on the Org. and Constitution of the British Standards Inst. 49-50; mem. Board of Inst. of Physics 51-59 and Pres. 56-58; mem. British Standards Inst. Gen. Council 53-56, and mem. of Exec. Cttee. 53-60; mem. Council Inst. Electrical Engineers 52-55, Vice-Pres. 59-64, Pres. 64-65; Chair. D.S.I.R. Radio Research Board 57-62; Chair. Int. Special Cttee. on Radio Interference 53-61; mem. British Nat. Cttee. of the Int. Electrotechnical Comm.; mem. of Board of British Nuclear Energy Conf. 55-58; Chair. Council of British Electrical and Allied Industries Research Asscn. 58-61; Pres. Electrical Engineering Asscn. 62-64; Chair. Conf. of Electronics Industry 63-68, mem. Nat. Electronics Research Council 63-68; Fellow of Univ. Coll., London 63.
Publ.: Include lectures and papers on scientific and engineering subjects.
5 Branksome Cliff, Branksome Park, Poole, Dorset, England.
Telephone: Westbourne 66195.

Humphreys, (Travers) Christmas, Q.C.; British lawyer; b. 15 Feb. 1901; ed. Malvern Coll., Trinity Hall Cambridge.
Junior Counsel to Treasury 32; Junior Counsel to Treasury at Central Criminal Court 34; Recorder of Deal 42-56; Senior Prosecuting Counsel to the Crown at Central Criminal Court 50-59; Recorder of Guildford 56-; Judge, Central Criminal Court 68-; Founder, Pres. Buddhist Lodge, London (now Buddhist Soc.) 24; Pres. The Shakespearean Authorship Soc. 55.
Publs. *The Great Pearl Robbery of 1913* 28, *What is Buddhism?* 28, *Concentration and Meditation* 35, *The Development of Buddhism in England* 37, *Studies in The Middle Way* 40, *Poems of Peace and War* 41, *Seagulls, and other Poems* 42, *Karma and Rebirth* 43, *Shadows and other Poems* 45, *Walk On* 47, *Via Tokyo* 48, *Zen Buddhism* 49, *The Way of Action* 60, *Zen Comes West* 60, *The Wisdom of Buddhism* 60, *Poems I Remember* 60, *A Popular Dictionary of Buddhism* 62, *Zen, A Way of Life* 62.
3 Temple Gardens, Temple, London, E.C.4, England.

Hund, Friedrich, DR. PHIL; German physicist; b. 4 Feb. 1896.
Asst. Göttingen Univ. 25; Extra. Prof. Rostock Univ. 27 and Prof. 28; Prof. of Mathematical Physics Leipzig Univ. 29-46; Prof. of Theoretical Physics Jena Univ. 46-51; Prof. of Theoretical Physics, Frankfurt (Main) Univ. 51-56; Prof. of Theoretical Physics Göttingen Univ. 56-64, Emeritus 64-; mem. German Acad. of Sciences, Acad. of Sciences Göttingen; Dr. phil. nat. h.c.
Publs. on Quantum Theory of atoms, molecules and solids: *Linienspektren* 27, *Einführung in die theoretische Physik* (5 vols.) 45-50, *Materie als Feld* 54, *Theoretische Physik* (3 vols.) 56-57 and additional editions, *Theorie des Aufbaues der Materie* 61, *Geschichte der Quanten Theorie* 67.
Merkelstrasse 55, 34 Göttingen, German Federal Republic.
Telephone: (0551) 58589.

Hunold, Albert Conrad; Swiss business and public executive; b. 4 July 1899; ed. Univs. of Zürich, Geneva and London.
Secretary, Zürich Stock Exchange Asscn. 30-45; Sec. Asscn. of Zürich Insts. of Credit 39-45; Joint Dir. Crédit Suisse 45-46; Marketing Dir. Swiss Fed. of Watch Manufacturers 47-49; Founder and mem. Board Econ. Section, Swiss Inst. of Int. Studies, Zürich 50-58, Exec. mem. of Board 58-.
Publs. include *The Swiss Stock Exchanges* (in German) 49, *The Industrial Development of Switzerland* (in English) 54, *Social Peace in Switzerland* 64; edited *Full Employment, Inflation and Planning* 51, *Economy without Miracles* 53, *Convertibility of European Currencies* 54, *The Free World in the Cold War* 55, *The Problem of the Masses in Democracy* 56, *Education for Freedom* 58, *Underdeveloped Countries* 61, *Latin America—Land of Trouble and of Future* 62, *Inflation and International Monetary Order* 63, *Africa and its Problems* (all in German).
CH-7064, Tschiertschen GR, Switzerland.

Hunsaker, Jerome C., D.SC.; American aeronautical engineer; b. 26 Aug. 1886; ed. U.S. Naval Acad. and Massachusetts Inst. of Technology.
Officer in Navy 08-26; Asst. Vice-Pres. Bell Telephone Laboratories, New York 26-28; Vice-Pres. Goodyear Zeppelin Corpn., Akron 28-33; Head Dept. of Mechanical Engineering of Massachusetts Inst. of Technology 33-47, Head Dept. of Aeronautical Engineering 33-51; Hon. Fellow Royal Aeronautical Society of Great Britain, Inst. of the Aeronautical Sciences, and Imperial Coll. of Science and Technology, London; hon. mem. Inst. of Mechanical Engineers and American Society of Mechanical Engineers; Regent, Smithsonian Inst.; Guggenheim Medal, Franklin Medal, Navy Cross,

Medal for Merit, Legion of Honour, Wright Trophy, Langley Medal, Gold Medal (Royal Aeronautical Soc. of Gt. Britain); Prof. Emer. Mass. Inst. of Technology. 10 Louisburg Square, Boston, Mass. 02108, U.S.A.
Telephone: Boston, LA3-1094.

Hunt, Baron (Life Peer, cr. 66), of Llanvair Waterdine; **John Hunt** (brother of Hugh Hunt, *q.v.*), Kt., C.B.E., D.S.O.; British mountaineer; b. 22 June 1910; ed. Marlborough Coll. and Royal Mil. Coll., Sandhurst.
Took part in expeditions to Karakoram 35 and to S.E. Himalayas 37 and 40; led Brit. Expedition to Mount Everest, when Hillary and Tenzing reached the summit on May 29th 53; Brit. expedition to Caucasus 58, to N.E. Greenland 60; British-Soviet Expedition to the Pamirs 62; Asst. Commandant Staff College, Camberley 53-55; Pres. The Alpine Club 56-58; Chair. Mount Everest Foundation 56-57; Dir. The Duke of Edinburgh's Award Scheme 56-66; Rector, Aberdeen Univ. 63-66; Chair. Parole Board 68-; Indian Police Medal, Indian Everest Medal; Founder's Medal of Royal Geographical Soc.; Order (1st Class) of Gurkha Right Hand of Nepal; Hon. D.C.L. (Durham Univ.), Hon. LL.D. (Aberdeen and London Univs.).
Publs. *The Ascent of Everest* 53, *Our Everest Adventure* 54, *The Red Snows* (with Christopher Brasher) 60.
Highway Cottage, Aston, Henley-on-Thames, England.

Hunt, Sir David W. S., K.C.M.G., O.B.E.; British diplomatist; b. 25 Sept. 1913; ed. St. Lawrence Coll., Ramsgate and Wadham Coll., Oxford.
Served in the Middle East, Greece, N. Africa and Italy during the Second World War; Commonwealth Relations Office 47-, service in S. Africa, Pakistan, Nigeria 47-50, 52-62; Dep. High Commr., Lagos, Nigeria 60-62; Private Sec., Office of the British Prime Minister 50-52, 60; British High Commr. in Kampala, Uganda Oct. 62-65, in Nicosia, Cyprus April 65-66, in Lagos, Nigeria 67-.
British High Commission, Lagos, Nigeria; and c/o D.S.A.O., King Charles Street, London, S.W.1, England.

Hunt, Herold Christian, A.B., M.A., ED.D.; American professor and politician; b. 9 Feb. 1902; ed. Univs. of Michigan and Chicago and Teachers' Coll., Columbia Univ.
Teacher, Hastings High School, Michigan 23-27; Principal, St. Johns High School 27-28 and 29-31; Asst. Cashier, St. Johns Nat. Bank 28-29; Superintendent, St. Johns Public Schools 31-33, Kalamazoo Schools, Michigan 34-37, New Rochelle, N.Y. 37-40, Kansas City, Missouri 40-47, Chicago 47-53; Charles William Eliot Prof. of Education, Harvard Univ. 53-; Under-Sec. U.S. Dept. of Health, Education and Welfare 55-57; Pres. American Assen. of School Administrators 47-48; Chair. American Council of Education 48-49, Educational Testing Service 49-50; Hon. M.A. (Harvard Univ.), LL.D. (Park Coll., Western Michigan Coll., Univ. of Wisconsin, and St. Louis Univ.); American Education Award 58.
Publ. *The Practice of School Administration* (co-author), *The School Personnel Administrator* (co-author).
5 Lantern Lane, Lexington 73, Mass., U.S.A.

Hunt, Hugh Sydney (brother of Lord Hunt, *q.v.*), M.A.; British theatrical director; b. 25 Sept. 1911; ed. Marlborough Coll., Sorbonne, Heidelberg Univ. and Magdalen Coll., Oxford.
Producer, Maddermarket Theatre, Norwich 34, Croydon Repertory Theatre 34, Abbey Theatre Dublin 35-38; served Second World War 39-45; directed Bristol Old Vic Company 45-49; Dir. Old Vic Company 49-53; Dir. Elizabethan Theatre Trust, Sydney, Australia 55-60; Dir. Sadler's Wells Opera Trust; Prof. of Drama, Univ. of Manchester 61-; mem. Independent Television Authority; Dir. Sadler's Wells Trust and Liverpool Playhouse.

Publs. *Old Vic Prefaces, The Director in the Theatre* 34, *The Living Theatre* 61.
Brant Wood, Red Lane, Disley, Cheshire, England.
Telephone: Disley 2127.

Hunt, John Joseph Benedict; British civil servant; b. 23 Oct. 1919; ed. Downside School and Magadalene Coll., Cambridge.
Served in R.N.V.R. 40-46; joined Home Civil Service (Dominions Office) 46; Private Sec. to Parl. Under-Sec. 47; Second Sec., Colombo 48; Directing Staff, Imperial Defence Coll. 51-52; First Sec., Ottawa 53-56; Private Sec. to Sec. of Cabinet and Head of Civil Service 56-58; Asst. Sec. Commonwealth Relations Office 58-60; Cabinet Office 60-62; H.M. Treasury 62-67, Under-Sec. 65, Deputy Sec. 68-; First Civil Service Commr. Jan. 68-.
Hale House, Churt, Surrey, England.
Telephone: Headley Down 2238.

Hunt, Col. John Philip, T.D.; British company director; b. 27 April 1907; ed. Malvern Coll.
Director, Philblack Ltd., Hallamshire Steel Co. Ltd., Wellington Tube Holdings Ltd., Midland Bank Ltd., Newton Chambers and Co. Ltd., Cooper and Turner Ltd., and several other companies.
Holme Hall, Bakewell, Derbyshire, England.

Hunt, Reed Oliver; American business executive; b. 12 Oct. 1904.
Joined Crown Zellerbach Corpn. at Port Angeles as clerk 27, Asst. Office Man. 30, Office Man., West Linn. and Camas, Asst. to Corpn. Vice-Pres. for Manufacturing 43-47, Asst. Gen. Man. for Manufacturing 47-50, Gen. Man. 50-52, Vice-Pres. in charge of manufacturing 52-54, Vice-Pres. for operations 54-56, Exec. Vice-Pres 56-59, Pres. and Chief Exec. Officer 59-63, Chair. of Board and Chief Exec. Officer 63-; mem. Board of Dirs., Zellerbach Paper Co.; Pres. St. Francisville Paper Co.; Pres. and Dir. Crown Simpson Pulp Co., San Francisco; Dir. Canadian Imperial Bank of Commerce, Toronto, Gen. Reinsurance Co., N.Y., Pacific Gas & Electric Co., San Francisco, Crocker Citizens Nat. Bank, Pacific Nat. Bank, Union Oil Co., and many firms and civic cttees.; Hon. LL.D. (Pacific Univ.).
2518 Pacific Avenue, San Francisco, Calif. 94115, U.S.A.

Hunter, Croil; American airline executive; b. 18 Feb. 1893; ed. Yale Univ. and Sheffield Scientific School.
Treasurer, Fargo Mercantile Co. 15-28; served in U.S. Army 17-19; N.Y. Man. First Bancredit Corpn. 28-32; Traffic Man. Northwest Airlines 32, Vice-Pres. and Gen. Man. 33-37, Pres. and Gen. Man. 37-53, Chair. of Board 53-.
Office: Northwest Airlines Inc., St. Paul 11, Minnesota; Home: 427 Portland Avenue, St. Paul 2, Minn., U.S.A.

Hunter, Sir Ernest John, Kt., C.B.E., D.SC., D.L.; British shipbuilder; b. 3 Nov. 1912; ed. Oundle School and Cambridge and Durham Univs.
Apprentice, Swan, Hunter & Wigham Richardson, 30-35, Drawing and Design Offices, Wallsend 35-37; Barclay, Curle & Co. Ltd. 37-39; Asst. Man., Dry Docks Dept. Swan, Hunter & Wigham Richardson, Ltd. 39-41, Asst. Gen. Man. 41-43, Gen. Man. 43-57, Dir. 45-, Chair. 57-66; Chair. and Man. Dir. Swan Hunter Group Ltd. 66-; Chair. Swan Hunter (Dry Docks) Ltd., Swan Hunter and Tyne Shipbuilders Ltd., M. W. Swinburne & Sons Ltd., Brims & Co. Ltd., Barclay Curle & Co. Ltd., Wallsend Slipway & Eng. Co. Ltd., Merchandise Presentations Ltd.; Dir. many other companies; Pres. Shipbuilding Employers' Fed. 56-57; Pres. British Employers' Confederation 62-64; Chair. Central Training Council 64-.
Swan Hunter Group Ltd., P.O. Box 1, Wallsend,

Northumberland; Home: "The Dene", Stocksfield, Northumberland, England.
Telephone: Wallsend 623121 (Office); Stocksfield 3124.

Hunter, Evan, B.A.; American author; b. 15 Oct. 1926; ed. Cooper Union and Hunter Coll.
Publs. *The Blackboard Jungle* 54, *Second Evening* 56, *Strangers When We Meet* 58 (screenplay 59), *A Matter of Conviction* 59, *Mothers and Daughters* 61, *The Birds* (screenplay) 62, *Happy New Year, Herbie* 63, *Buddwing* 64, *The Easter Man* (play) 64, *The Sentries* (as Ed. McBain) 65, *The Paper Dragon* 66, *A Horse's Head* 67, *Last Summer* 68; 87th Precinct Mysteries under *pseudonym* Ed McBain: *Cop Hater* 56, *The Mugger* 56, *The Pusher* 56, *The Con Man* 57, *Killer's Choice* 57, *Killer's Payoff* 58, *Lady Killer* 58, *Killer's Wedge* 59, *'Til Death* 59, *King's Ransom* 59, *Give the Boys a Great Big Hand* 60, *The Heckler* 60, *See Them Die* 60, *Lady, Lady, I Did It* 61, *Like Love* 62, *The Empty Hours* (three novelettes) 62, *Ten plus One* 63, *Ax* 64, *He Who Hesitates* 65, *Doll* 65, *Eighty Million Eyes* 66, *Fuzz* 68.
c/o Scott Meredith Literary Agency Inc., 580 Fifth Avenue, New York City 36, N.Y., U.S.A.

Huong, Tran Van; Viet-Namese politician; b. 1904. Former schoolteacher; participated in Viet-Minh resistance against French; Mayor of Saigon on two occasions; Prime Minister 64-65, May 68-.
Office of the Prime Minister, Saigon, Republic of Viet-Nam.

Hurcomb, 1st Baron; **Cyril William Hurcomb,** G.C.B., K.B.E., M.A.; British civil servant; b. 18 Feb. 1883; ed. St. John's Coll., Oxford.
Entered Sec.'s Office in Post Office 06, Private Sec. to Permanent Sec. 10 and to Postmaster-Gen. 11; Deputy Dir. and later Dir. Commercial Services of Min. of Shipping during First World War 15-18; Perm. Sec. to Min. of Transport 27-37; Chair. Electricity Comm. 38-47; Pres. Inst. of Transport 35-36; Dir.-Gen. Ministry of Shipping 39-41, Ministry of War Transport 41-45; Chair. Main Cttee. of Confs. for European Inland Transport 44-45; Senior British Del. to United Maritime Exec. Board; Chair. British Transport Comm. 47-53; mem. of the Nature Conservancy 53-62, Chair. 61-; Trustee British Museum 60-63; Vice-Pres. Union Int. pour la Conservation de la Nature; Pres. Royal Soc. for Protection of Birds 61-66; Chair. Int. Trust for Zoological Nomenclature; Hon. Fellow, St. John's Coll., Oxford; Silver Medal, Zoological Soc., London 65.
47 Campden Hill Court, London, W.8, England.
Telephone: 01-937-6902.

Huré, Francis, L. ès L.; French diplomatist; b. 5 Oct. 1916; ed. Faculté des lettres de Paris and Ecole libre des sciences politiques.
In Algiers 43; Attaché, French Embassy in Moscow 44-45; Foreign Office, Paris 45-46, 50; First Sec., Tokyo 47-49; Adviser French Del. to UN 53; Counsellor, London 54-58; Chargé d'Affaires, Guinea 59; Amb. to Cameroon 65-; Officier Légion d'Honneur; Prix Cazes 63.
Publ. *Le Consulat du Pacifique.*
5 boulevard Jean-Mermoz, Neuilly-sur-Seine, France; and Marine de Pino, Corsica.

Huré, Joseph Marie Paul Eugène; French industrialist; b. 21 Jan. 1899; ed. Abbeville Coll., Ecole Bossuet, Ecole Polytechnique and Ecole des Mines de Paris.
Army service 17-20; Engineer Corps des Mines 22-25; joined Société Française des Pétroles B.P. (then Société Générale des Huiles de Pétrole) 25, Man. 31, Dir. 36, Dir. and Asst. Gen. Manager 43-46, Vice-Pres., Gen. Man. 46-54, Pres., Gen. Man. 54-64, Chair. of the Board 64-; Dir. several other companies; Hon. C.B.E.; Commandeur de la Légion d'Honneur; Croix de Guerre.
Office: Société Française des Pétroles B.P., 10 quai

Paul Doumer, 92-à Courbevoie (Hauts-de-Seine); Home: 11 rue Porto Riche, 92-Meudon (Hauts-de-Seine), France.
Telephone: ALMa 48-00 (Office); OBServatoire 12-42 (Home).

Hürlimann, Martin, D.PHIL.; Swiss publisher and writer; b. 1897; ed. Univs. of Zürich, Leipzig and Berlin.
Founded the Atlantis Verlag 30; Dir. of Atlantis Verlag. Publs. consist of a series *Orbis Terrarum, France* 27, *India* 28, *Indochina* 28, *Germany* 31, *Switzerland* 31, *France* 37, *Paris* 51, *Spain* 51, *Italy* 51, *Athens* 56, *London* 56, *Istanbul* 57, *Europe* 57, *Moscow and Leningrad* 58, *Traveller in the Orient* 60, *Kyoto* 61, *Hongkong* 62, *Bangkok* 63, *Delhi* 64, *The World* 65.
Witellikerstrasse 9, 8702 Zollikon, Zürich, Switzerland.

Hurok, Sol; Russian-born American impresario; b. 9 April 1888.
Went to U.S. 06, naturalised 14; has contracted numerous famous artistes and companies for American engagements, including Pavlova, Chaliapin, Russian Ballet, Rubinstein, Piatigorsky, Stern, The Old Vic, Markova, Segovia, Victoria de los Angeles, Sadler's Wells, Barrault, Comédie Française, Bolshoi Ballet, Marian Anderson, Nathan Milstein, Richter, Gilels, Callas; Dr. h.c. Boston and Wayne Univs.; Hon. C.B.E., Officer of the Legion of Honour.
Publs. *Impresario* (autobiography), *S. Hurok Presents.*
730 Fifth Avenue, New York City, N.Y., U.S.A.

Hurwitz, Jerard, PH.D.; American research scientist; b. 20 Nov. 1928; ed. Coll. of City of New York, Indiana Univ. and Western Reserve Univ., Cleveland, Ohio.
Research Asst., Dept. of Biochemistry, Western Reserve Univ. 49-50; Instructor in Microbiology, Washington Univ., St. Louis 56-58; Asst. Prof. in Microbiology, New York Univ. School of Medicine 58-60, Assoc. Prof. of Microbiology 60-63; Prof. of Molecular Biology, Albert Einstein Coll. of Medicine, New York 63-65, Prof. Developmental Biology and Cancer 65-; mem. Biochemical Soc. of England, American Soc. of Biological Chemists; American Cancer Soc. Research Prof.; Eli Lilly Award in Biochemistry 62.
Department of Developmental Biology and Cancer, Albert Einstein College of Medicine, Yeshiva University, 1300 Morris Park Avenue, Bronx, New York, N.Y. 10461, U.S.A.

Hurwitz, Stephan; Danish academic lawyer; b. 20 June 1901; ed. Univ. of Copenhagen.
Prof. of Law, Univ. of Copenhagen 35, Vice-Chancellor 53; Parl. Commr. (State controller, Ombudsman) 55-; Chief Danish Refugee Admin. in Sweden 43; mem. Danish Mil. Comm., London 44-45; Danish rep. on UN War Crimes Comm. 45; Pres. Danish Asscn. of Criminologists 43; Pres. Int. Cttee. of Nordic Asscns. of Criminologists 52; Pres. Royal Permanent Penal Cttee. of Denmark 60; Chief Editor *Scandinavian Journal of Criminal Science* 49; Gold Medal of Univ. of Copenhagen; D.Jur. 33; D.Jur. h.c. Stockholm 60, Oslo 61, Helsinki 63.
Publs. *The Press Treatment of Court Proceedings* 37, various works on law of procedure in Criminal and Civil Cases, *Criminology* 48 (English, Italian and Spanish editions), *Danish Criminal Law* 50-55.
Dalsvinget 7, Hellerup, Denmark.

Husain, Akhtar, M.A., LL.B.; Pakistani civil servant and diplomatist; b. 10 Jan. 1907; ed. Univs. of Allahabad and Agra.
Administrative posts in U.P. (India) and Ajmer Marwara 33-41; served Govt. of India Dept. of Supply 41-45; Sec. Devt. Board, Cawnpore, U.P. 45-47; served Govt. of India Dept. of Supply and later Dept. of External Affairs 47-48; Deputy Sec. Govt. of Pakistan

Ministry of Foreign Affairs and Commonwealth Relations 48; Adviser and Sec.-Gen., Del. to UN Gen. Ass. 48; Amb. to Italy 53-56, to U.S.S.R. 56-59, to Iran 60-63, to Algeria 64-65, to Austria 65-67 (retired).
162/F, Block III, P.E.C.H.S., Karachi-29, Pakistan.

Husain, Akhter, H.PK.; Pakistani administrator; b. 02; ed. Hakimia High School, Burhanpur, M.A.O. Coll., Aligarh, and St. John's Coll., Cambridge.
Apptd. to Indian civil service in Punjab 26; various admin. posts 30-43; Sec. Post-War Reconstruction Dept. 44; Chief Sec. Govt. Punjab 46-47; Financial Commr. and Sec. to Govt., West Punjab 47-53; mem. Tenancy Inquiry Cttee. 51, Liaquat Ali Assassination Inquiry Cttee. 51; special duty at Karachi for re-organisation of Karachi Admin. 51; Chair. Lord Boyd Orr's Expert Cttee. 53; Sec. Ministry of Defence, Govt. Pakistan 53-57; Chair. Karachi Admin. Cttee. 55; Gov. West Pakistan 57-60; Minister of Information, Nat. Reconstruction and Kashmir Affairs 60, of Kashmir Affairs 60-61, of Education and Scientific Research, Minority Affairs 61-62; Chair. Land Reforms Comm. 58, Land Comm. and Provincial Admin. Comm. 59; Chief Election Commr. (Pakistan) 62-64; Chair. Nat. Press Trust 65, Investment Corpn. of Pakistan 66; mem. Advisory Council of Islamic Ideology; Dir. Agric. Devt. Bank of Pakistan 67; Chair. Water Allocation and Rate Cttee. of W. Pakistan 68.
29a Sunset Boulevard, Defence Housing Society, Karachi, Pakistan.

Husain, Altaf, M.A.; Pakistani journalist; b. 1900; ed. Cotton Coll. Gauhati and Univ. of Dacca.
Lecturer in English, Univ. of Dacca 23, Islamia Coll. Calcutta 26; Prof. of English, Intermediate Coll. Chittagong 27; Prof. and Head of English Dept., Islamia Coll. Calcutta 34; Principal, Intermediate Coll. Dacca 37; Dir. of Public Information, Bengal Govt. 38; Press Censor, Indian Govt. 42; Dir. of Public Information, Bengal Govt. 43; resigned from Govt. Service 45; Editor *Dawn*, Delhi 45-47, Karachi 47-65; Minister for Industries and Natural Resources 65-.
Publs. *Complaint and Answer* (translation) 42, *India: The Last Ten Years* 47, *A Fortnight in Moscow* 52.
(*Died 25 May* 1968)

Husain, Mahmud, PH.D., D.LITT.; Pakistani historian; b. 1907; ed. Islamia High School, Etawah, India, Jamia Millia Islamia, Delhi, India and Heidelberg Univ., Germany.
Reader in Modern History, Univ. of Dacca 33, Prof. of Int. Relations 48; mem. Constituent Assembly 46-49; Deputy Minister, Ministry of Defence States and Frontier Regions and Deputy Minister of Foreign Affairs and Commonwealth Relations 49; Cabinet Minister for Kashmir Affairs 51; Minister of Educ. 52-53; Prof. of History, Karachi Univ. 53-, Dean of Faculty of Arts 66-; Vice-Chancellor Dacca Univ. 60-63; Chair. Board of Editors *History of Freedom Movement of Muslims in Indo-Pakistan Sub-Continent* 52; Editor *Jamia Educational Quarterly* 60-; Founder-Pres. Council of Nat. Educ. 52-; Pres. Pakistan Museum Asscn. 55-58, Pakistan Library Asscn. 56-64; Chair. Improved Syllabus Cttee. for Darul Ulum and Arabic Madarsas 60; Visiting Prof. of South-Asian History, Univ. of Heidelberg 64, Columbia Univ. 64-65, of Political Science, Pennsylvania Univ. 64-65; mem. Pakistan Sterling Balance Del. to London 48, Grosses Verdienstkreuz; Hon. D.Litt.
Publs. *Quest for Empire* 37; Urdu trans. of Rousseau's *The Social Contract* and Izzddin's *Arab Dunia*; English trans. of *Dreams of Tipu Sultan;* Edited *Fath-ul-Mujahedeen* by Tipu Sultan and *Treatise on Causes of Mutiny* by Sir Syed Ahmad Khan.
41/N. 6, P.E.C.H.S., Karachi, Pakistan.

Husain, Maqbool Fida; Indian painter; b. 17 Sept. 1915.
Joined Progressive Artists Group, Bombay 48; first one-man exhbn., Bombay 50, later at Rome, Frankfurt, London, Zürich, Prague, Tokyo, New York, New Delhi, Calcutta, Kabul and Baghdad; mem. Lalit Kala Akademi, New Delhi 54; mem. Gen. Council Nat. Akademi of Art, New Delhi 55; First Nat. Award for Painting 55; Int. Award, Biennale Tokyo 59.
Major works: Murals for Air India Int. at Hong Kong, Bangkok, Zürich and Prague 57, and WHO Building, New Delhi 63; Mural in Mosaic for Lever Bros. and Aligarh Univ. 64; working on High Ceramic Mural for Indian Govt. Building, New Delhi; Exhibitor "Art now in India" exhbn., London 67.
Film: *Through the Eyes of the Painter* 67 (Golden Bear Award, Berlin 67).
6 Zeenat Manzil L. Jamshedji Road, Mahim, Bombay 16, India.

Husain, Mohamed Arshad, B.A.; Pakistani diplomatist; b. 9 Jan. 1910; ed. St. Catharine's Coll., Cambridge, and Middle Temple, London.
Dep. Sec. Ministry of Foreign Affairs 50-54; Counsellor and Chargé d'Affaires, Embassy of Pakistan, Brussels 54-56; Dep. High Commr. India 56; Jt. Sec. Ministry of Foreign Affairs 57-59; Ambassador to Sweden, Norway, Denmark and Finland 59-61, to U.S.S.R. and Czechoslovakia 61-63, to Nepal 63-65; High Commr. to India Oct. 63-68; Minister of Home Affairs 68-.
Home: 51/3 Lawrence Road, Lahore, Pakistan.

Husain, Muhammad Afzal, M.A., M.SC.; Pakistani professor; b. 89; ed. Govt. Coll. Lahore and Christ's Coll. Cambridge.
Prof. of Zoology and Entomology, Punjab Agricultural Coll. 19-38, Principal 33-38; on staff Research Inst. Lyallpur and Entomologist to Govt. of Punjab 19-38; Officiating Imperial Entomologist, Agricultural Research Inst., Pusa, Bihar 25-27; Locust Research Entomologist to Imperial Council of Agricultural Research, India 30-33; Vice-Chancellor Univ. of the Punjab 38-44; Agricultural Adviser to Govt. of Bengal 44; mem. Bengal Famine Comm. 44-45; mem. Punjab and N.W.F.P. Joint Public Service Comm. 45-47, Chair. 47-48; Chair. Pakistan Public Service Comm. 48-52; Vice-Chancellor Univ. of the Punjab 54-58; Chair. Pakistan Sugar Comm. 57-59; Chair Agricultural Research Council of Pakistan Nov. 65-; Gen. Pres. Indian Science Congress 46, Pakistan Asscn. for the Advancement of Science 48-; Fellow Nat. Inst. of the Sciences of India, Pakistan Acad. of Sciences (and its first Pres.); Fellow, Entomological Soc. of India; awarded Hilal-i-Quaid-i-Azam 58; Hon. D.Sc.; Hon. LL.D.
Publs. numerous papers on entomology, desert locusts and cotton, fruit, vegetable pests and agricultural and educational problems.
51/3 Lawrence Road, Lahore, Pakistan.

Husain, Syed Munir, M.A.; Pakistani civil servant and radio executive; ed. Government Coll., Lahore.
Formerly Lecturer in Econs., Punjab Univ.; joined Civil Service of Pakistan 52; Asst. Commr. of Abbottabad, of Peshawar, then of Nowshera 54-57; Deputy Sec., Devt. and Irrigation Dept. of W. Pakistan 57-58; Deputy Commr. of Abbottabad 59-61, of Karachi 61-64; Information Sec., Govt. of W. Pakistan 64-66; Dir.-Gen. of Radio Pakistan Jan. 66-.
Radio Pakistan, 71 Garden Road, Karachi, Pakistan.

Husain, Zakir, M.A., PH.D.; Indian educator and administrator; b. 8 Feb. 1897; ed. Islamia High School, Etawah, M.A.O. Coll., Aligarh and Berlin Univ.
Vice-Chancellor, Jamia Millia Islamia, Delhi 26-48; Pres. Hindustani Talimi Sangh, Sevagram 38-50; Vice-Chancellor, Aligarh Muslim Univ. 48-56; mem. Univ.

Educ. Comm. 48-49, Indian Press Comm. 52-54; Chair. World Univ. Service, Geneva 55-57; mem. UNESCO Exec. Board, Paris 56-58; Gov. of Bihar 57-62; Vice-Pres. of India 62-67, Pres. of India 67-; Chair. Rajya Sabha 62-67; Padma Vibhushan 54; Bharat Ratna 63; Hon. D.Litt. Delhi, Calcutta, Aligarh, Allahabad and Cairo Univs.
Publs. *Capitalism: An Essay in Understanding, Educational Discourses* (in Urdu), *Shiksha* (in Hindi), *Principles of Educational Reconstruction* (Patel Memorial Lectures), *Scope and Method of Economics* (Hindustani Acad. Lectures), *Ethics and the State* (Mavalankar Memorial Lecture); translations into Urdu of Plato's *Republic*, List's *National System of Economics* and Cannan's *Elements of Economics*; *The Dynamic University, Abbo Khan ki Bakri and other Stories* (Urdu).
Rashtrapati Bhavan, New Delhi, India.

Husák, Gustav, LL.D., C.SC.; Czechoslovak politician; b. 10 Jan. 1913; ed. Law Faculty, Comenius Univ., Bratislava.
Junior lawyer, Bratislava 38-42; office worker 43-44; took part in Slovak Nat. Rising; Commr. of Interior 44-45; Commr. for Transport and Technology 45-46; Chair. of Board of Commrs. 46-50, concurrently Commr. for Agriculture 48; Dept. Head at Central Cttee. of C.P. of Slovakia 50-51; political imprisonment 51-60; Building Works, Bratislava 60-63; Scientific Worker, Inst. of Law, Slovak Acad. of Sciences 63-68; Deputy Premier 68-; mem. 5th illegal Central Cttee. of C.P. of Slovakia, mem. of Central Cttee. and Presidium, Deputy Chair. of C.P. of Slovakia 43-44; mem. Central Cttee. and Presidium of Central Cttee. of C.P. of Slovakia 45-50; mem. Central Cttee. of C.P. of Czechoslovakia 45, 49-51; mem. Presidium of Slovak Nat. Council 43-45; mem. Slovak Nat. Council 45-50; mem. Nat. Assembly 45-51; numerous Czechoslovak and foreign decorations, including Klement Gottwald Order (Czechoslovakia) 68.
Publs. *On the Agricultural Problem in Slovakia* 48, *The Struggle for Tomorrow* 48, *Evidence on Slovak National Rising* 64.
Presidium of the Government, Prague 1, nábř, kpt. Jaroše 4, Czechoslovakia.

Husein, Abdul-Aziz; Kuwaiti diplomatist; b. 21; ed. Teachers Higher Institute, Cairo and University of London.
Former Dir. "House of Kuwait", Cairo, Dir-Gen. Dept. of Educ., Kuwait; Ambassador to the U.A.R. 61-62; Perm. Rep. to Arab League Council; appointed State Minister in Charge of Cabinet Affairs 63-64.
Publ. *Lectures on Arab Society in Kuwait* 60.
c/o Ministry of Cabinet Affairs, Kuwait, Persian Gulf.

Hussein, Abdirizak Haji; Somali politician; b. 20. Joined Somali Youth League 44, Pres. 55-56; Minister of Interior, later of Works and Communications 60-64; Prime Minister 64-67; Pres. Univ. Inst.
Somali Youth League, Mogadishu, Somalia.

Hussein, Amin Ahmed, G.C.V.O., O.B.E.; Sudanese diplomatist; b. 13; ed. Gordon Memorial Coll., Khartoum. Joined Ministry of Interior (Police), rose to Commr. of Police 54; Dep. Under-Sec. for Security, Ministry of Interior 57; Dep. Perm. Under-Sec., Ministry of Foreign Affairs Sept. 57-61; Ambassador to U.K. 61-65, to U.S.A. 65-67; Grand Officer of the Star of Ethiopia; Long Distinguished Service Decoration.
Ministry of Foreign Affairs, Khartoum, Sudan.

Hussein ibn Talal, King of Jordan; b. 14 Nov. 1935; ed. Victoria Coll., Alexandria, Harrow School, and Royal Military Academy, Sandhurst, England.
Succeeded his father August 11th, 1952; came to power May 2nd, 1953; married 55, Princess Dina, d. of Abd-el-Hamid Aoun of Saudi Arabia (marriage dissolved); married 61, Antoinette Gardiner (assumed name of

Muna el Hussein), sons, Prince Abdullah b. 62, Prince Feisal b. 63, twin daughters, Princess Zein and Princess Ayeshia, b. April 68.,
Publ. *Uneasy Lies the Head* 62.
Royal Palace, Amman, Jordan.

Hussein, Major Kamal El-Din; United Arab Republic (Egyptian) soldier and politician; b. 21; ed. Cairo Univ. and Mil. Coll.
Army service 39-52; mem. Revolutionary Council 53; Minister of Social Affairs 54, of Educ. 54-58; Minister of Educ. in U.A.R. 58-61; Pres. Exec. Council of Egyptian Region 60-61; Vice-Pres. of U.A.R. in charge of Public Services, concurrently Minister of Local Administration and Housing 61-62, member Presidency Council 62-64.
c/o Council of Ministers, Cairo, United Arab Republic.

Hussein, Taha, DR. LITT.; United Arab Republic (Egyptian) writer; b. 89; ed. University of Cairo and University of Paris.
Professor of Arabic Literature, Fouad I Univ. Cairo 20-32; fmr. Dean of the Faculty of Arts, Fouad I Univ., Under-Sec. of State at Ministry of Educ., Rector Farouk I Univ. Alexandria; Minister of Educ. 50-52; fmr. Senator; now Vice-Pres. Acad. of Arabic Language; corresp. mem. Acad. des Inscriptions et Belles Lettres Paris, Accad. dei Lincei Rome, Acads. of Mainz, Teheran, Damascus, Baghdad, and Royal Acad. of History, Madrid; many awards and decorations, including Grande Médaille de l'Univ. de Paris, Grand Officier de la Légion d'Honneur (France), Commdr. Order of the Nile (Egypt), Grand Cross Order of the Phoenix (Greece); Dr. h.c. (Univs. of Lyon, Montpellier, Rome, Oxford, Athens, Madrid).
Publs. Over 40 works, translations from French and Ancient Greek into Arabic, studies on Arabic literature, on educational problems of modern Egypt, etc., and including *The Stream of Days* (2 vols.).
Academy of the Arabic Language, 26 Sharia Mourad, Giza, U.A.R.

Husseini, H.E. Haj Amin; Grand Mufti of Palestine; ed. Jerusalem and Al-Azhar Univ. Cairo.
Officer in Ottoman Army during First World War 14-18; became Mufti 21; elected Pres. of Supreme Muslim Council for life 22; elected Pres. World Moslem Conf. Jerusalem 31 and Pres. Arab Higher Cttee. for Palestine 36; left Palestine after disagreement with Mandate Govt. over policy of establishing Jewish Nat. Home in Palestine 37; in Lebanon 37-39, Iraq 39-41, in Persia and Europe 41-45, France 45-46; on return from Europe 46, re-elected Pres. Arab Higher Cttee. for Palestine; in Egypt as guest of King Farouk 46; elected Pres. Assembly and Supreme Council All-Palestine Govt. 48; Pres. World Moslem Conf., Karachi 51, Baghdad 62, Moslem Ulama Conf., Karachi 52, Exec. Cttee. World Moslem Conf.. Karachi 52; Chair. Palestine Arab Del. to Asiatic-African Conf. Bandung 55.
Beirut, Lebanon.

Husson, Jean Henri; French writer; b. 26 Feb. 1923. Fire technician, Régiment de Sapeurs Pompiers de Paris; Palmes académiques; Grand Prix du Roman, Académie Française 65.
Publs. *La Brouillerie* 57, *Les Malles* 59, *La Bête noire* 63, *Le Cheval d'Herbeleau* 65.
1 place Jules Renard, Paris 17e, France.
Telephone: GAL 90-76.

Hustich, Väinö Ilmari, PH.D.; Finnish professor; b. 11 Aug. 1911; ed. Helsinki Univ.
Professor of Econ. Geography 50-, Rector of Swedish School of Econs., Helsinki 66-; mem. State Scientific Board 60-65; Chair. Comm. Archipelago Devt. 61-66; Minister of Trade and Industry 61-62; mem. State Foreign Trade Board 62-, State Comm. for Devt. Areas 63-; Corresp. mem. Arctic Inst. of N. America 67-.

Publs. on economics, political geography, Canadian and Finnish forests, etc.
Hollandarvagen 1, Munksnas, Helsinki 33, Finland.

Huston, John; Irish (b. American) film writer and director; b. 5 Aug. 1906.
Joined Warner Bros. Studio as writer 38; directed *The Maltese Falcon* 41, *In This Our Life* 42, *Key Largo* 48; writer and director Metro-Goldwyn-Mayer 49-; other films include *The Red Badge of Courage, Beat the Devil, Treasure of Sierra Madre* 48, *The Asphalt Jungle* 50, *Moby Dick* 56, *The Roots of Heaven* 58, *The Unforgiven, The Misfits* 60, *The Bible* 66, *Casino Royale* 67, *Reflections in a Golden Eye* 68; has also directed stage productions of *A Passage to Bali* 39, *No Exit* 45, *The Mines of Sulphur* 67; Screen Writers' Laurel Award 63; numerous awards for films and plays directed.
St. Clerans, Craughwell, Co. Galway, Ireland.

Hutcheson, Joseph C., Jr., LL.B.; American lawyer; b. 19 Oct. 1879; ed. Virginia and Texas Univs.
Barrister 1900-18; Chief Legal Adviser City of Houston 13-17 and Mayor 17-18; Judge, U.S. District Court, Southern District of Texas 18-31; Judge, U.S. Court of Appeals 31-; Chief Judge Fifth Circuit 48-58; American Chair. Anglo-American Cttee. Enquiry on Palestine 45-46.
Publs. *Law as Liberator, Judgement Intuitive.*
Post Office Building, Houston, Texas, U.S.A.

Hutchins, Robert Maynard, A.B., A.M., LL.B., LL.D.; American lawyer and former university official; b. 17 Jan. 1899; ed. Oberlin Coll. and Yale Univ.
Sec. Yale Univ. 23-27, Acting Dean Yale Law School 27-28, Dean 28-29 and Prof. of Law 27-29; Pres. Univ. of Chicago 29-45, Chancellor 45-51; Dir. Encyclopædia Britannica Inc., Encyclopædia Britannica Ltd., and Encyclopædia Britannica Films 43-. and Chair. Board of Editors *Encyclopædia Britannica* 46-; Chair. The Great Books Foundation 47-50; Chair. Board of Editors *Measure* 49-51; Assoc. Dir. Ford Foundation 51-54; Pres. Fund for the Republic 54-; mem. American and Connecticut Bar Asscns.; hon. mem. Chicago Bar Asscn.
Publs. *No Friendly Voice* 36, *The Higher Learning in America* 36, *Education for Freedom* 43, *St. Thomas and the World State* 49, *Morals, Religion and Higher Education* 50, *The Great Conversation* 52, *The Conflict in Education* 53, *The University of Utopia* 53, *Freedom, Education and the Fund* 56, *Some Observations on American Education* 56.
Fund for the Republic Inc., Santa Barbara, California, U.S.A.

Hutchinson, Edmond C., M.A., PH.D.; American government official; b. 23 Nov. 1913; ed. Southwestern Univ. and Univ. of Virginia.
Economist, Analyst, Railroad Retirement Board 38-42; Management Analyst, War Production Board 42-44; Provisional Dir.-Gen. of Finances, Iranian Govt. 44-46; Management Analyst, Civil Production Admin. 46, Dept. of Commerce 46-47; Budget Analyst, Dept. of Army, Japan 47-52; Budget Examiner, Dep. Divisional Chief, Bureau of Budget 53-58; Chief, Loan Operations 58-60; Asst. Dep. Man. Dir. for Operations, Development Loan Fund 60-61; Asst. Administrator for Africa, Agency for Int. Devt. Dept. of State 61-66; Chair. Exploration Devt. Group, Research Analysis Corpn. 67-.
9619 Hillridge Drive, Kensington, Maryland, U.S.A.

Hutchinson, Sir Joseph Burtt, Kt., C.M.G., F.R.S., SC.D.; British professor of agriculture; b. 21 March 1902; ed. Ackworth and Bootham Schools, and St. John's Coll., Cambridge.
Formerly worked at Cotton Research Station, Trinidad, later at Inst. of Plant Industry, Indore, India; Dir. of Cotton Research Station, Namulonge, Uganda 49-57;

Drapers Prof. of Agriculture, Cambridge Univ. 57-; Chair. Council of Makerere Coll., Uganda 53-57; Fellow St. John's Coll., Cambridge, Linnean Soc.; Pres. British Asscn. for Advancement of Science 65-66; mem. Nature Conservancy 62-; Hon. Fellow Makerere Coll.; Royal Medal of the Royal Soc. 67; Hon. D.Sc., Nottingham.
Publs. *The Genetics of Gossypium* 58, *Genetics and the Improvement of Tropical Crops* 58, *Application of Genetics to Cotton Improvement* 59; Editor *Essays on Crop Plant Evolution* 65.
School of Agriculture, Downing Street, Cambridge, England.
Telephone: Cambridge 58381.

Hutchinson, Ray Coryton, M.A., F.R.S.L.; British author; b. 23 Jan. 1907; ed. Monkton Combe and Oriel Coll., Oxford.
Publs. *Thou Hast a Devil* 30, *The Answering Glory* 32, *The Unforgotten Prisoner* 33, *One Light Burning* 35, *Shining Scabbard* 36, *Testament* 38, *Last Train South* (play) 38, *The Fire and the Wood* 40, *Interim* 44, *Elephant and Castle* 49, *Recollection of a Journey* (U.S. title *Journey with Strangers*) 52, *The Stepmother* 55, *March the Ninth* 57, *Image of My Father* 61 (U.S. title *The Inheritor*), *A Child Possessed* 64.
Dysart, Bletchingley, Redhill, Surrey, England.
Telephone: Caterham 45041.

Hutchison, James Seller; British business executive; b. 15 Oct. 1904; ed. Greenock Acad. and Glasgow Univ.
Chartered Accountant 28; Chair. The British Oxygen Co. Ltd. 50-.
The British Oxygen Co. Ltd., Hammersmith House, Hammersmith, London W.6, England.

Hutton, Edward; British writer; b. 12 April 1875; ed. Blundell's School, Tiverton.
Mem. Council of British Inst. of Florence 17-54; Editor *Anglo-Italian Review*; British Acad. Gold Medallist in Italian Studies; mem. Cardinal Hinsley's Cttee. for Decoration of Westminster Cathedral; Cavalier of the Crown of Italy; Commdr. Italian Order of Merit 58; Italian Medaglia Culturale d'oro 65; designed and built Cosmati pavements in Westminster Cathedral and Buckfast Abbey.
Publs. *Rome, Florence, Venice and Venetia, Assisi and Umbria, Cities of Spain, Highways and By-Ways in Somerset, A Glimpse of Greece, Giovanni Boccaccio: a Biography, A History of Ravenna, Catholicism and English Literature, The Cosmati*; and many volumes of Italian travel, history and criticism; Editor Dennistoun's *Dukes of Urbino* and Crowe and Cavalcaselle's *History of Painting in Italy*.
114 Clifton Hill, London, N.W.8, England.
Telephone: 01-624-1747.

Hutton, John Henry, C.I.E., M.A., D.SC.; British anthropologist; b. 27 June 1885; ed. Chigwell School and Worcester Coll., Oxford.
Asst. Magistrate, Eastern Bengal 09; Asst. Commr., Naga Hills, Assam 12; Political Officer, Kuki operations 17; Census Commr., Govt. of India 29; Deputy Commr., Naga Hills, Assam 34; retd. 36; Lecturer in Social Anthropology, Cambridge 36; William Wyse Prof. of Social Anthropology, Cambridge 37-50; Frazer Lecturer at Oxford 38; Rivers Memorial Medal 29; Royal Society of Arts Silver Medal 31-32; Annandale Gold Medal of Royal Asiatic Society of Bengal 37; High Sheriff of Radnorshire 43; Hon. Fellow St. Cath. Coll. Cambridge 51.
Publs. *The Angami Nagas* 22, *The Sema Nagas* 22, *Report on the Census of India 1931* 33, *A Primitive Philosophy of Life* (Frazer Lecture) 38, *Caste in India* 46, 63.
[*Died May* 1968]

Hutton, Sir Maurice Inglis, Kt., C.M.G., M.A.; British company director; b. 3 Aug. 1904; ed. Kelvinside Acad., Glasgow Univ., Balliol Coll., Oxford, and Yale Univ. With Buckmaster & Moore, Stockbrokers, and O. T. Falk & Co., Investment Bankers, London 29-39; Ministry of Food 39-41; mem. British Food Mission to N. America 41-44, Head of Mission, U.K. Rep. Int. Wheat Council, U.K. mem. Combined Food Board (subsequently Int. Emergency Food Council) 44-48; U.K. Alternate Dir., Int. Bank for Reconstruction and Development 46-47; Head of British Supply Mission in U.S.A. 47-48; Head of Int. Bank/F.A.O. Mission to Uruguay 50-51; Chair. Chancellor's Cttee. on Purchase Tax 52-53; Managing Dir. Anglo-Australian Corpn. (Pty.) Ltd. 55-; Chair. London Australia Investment Co. Ltd., Power Cables of Australia Pty. Ltd., Food Machinery (Australia) Ltd.; Dir. numerous other companies; Order of Leopold (Belgium) 48.
Greenways, Terrara Road, Vermont, Victoria, Australia.

Huvelin, Paul; French engineer; b. 22 July 1902.
Engineer in charge of production, Société Métallurgique de Normandie 24-27; Chief Engineer, Sec. and Man. l'Electrique Lille-Roubaix-Tourcoing and Chemin de fer de l'Est de Lyon 28-36; Man. Soc. Industrielle de Gérance et d'Exploitation, later Manager Soc. Gén. d'Exploitations Industrielles (SOGEI) 36-47, Chair. of Board and Pres. 47-; Chair. and Pres. Energie Electrique du Nord de la France 40-46, Cie. Electrique de la Loire et du Centre 45-46; Vice-Chair. Soc. Gén. d'Entreprises; Chair. and Pres. Soc. de Pneumatiques et Caoutchouc Manufacturé Kléber-Colombes; Dir. Cie. Financière de Suez et de l'Union Parisienne, Cie. Pechiney, Cie. Thomson-Brandt.
56 rue du St. Honoré, 75-Paris 8e, France.
Telephone: ANJ 12-40.

Hüvös, Sándor; Hungarian aviation administrator; b. 11; ed. Budapest Univ.
Study tours in Austria, Germany, France; mem. Hungarian Meteorological Soc., Hungarian Automobile Club, Exec. Cttee. British Section of Hungarian Chamber of Commerce, Board of Dirs. Ibusz Ltd.; Dir.-Gen. Board of Civil Aviation, Ministry of Communications and Posts.
Dob u. 75-81, Budapest VII, Hungary.

Huxley, Andrew Fielding, F.R.S.; British physiologist; b. 22 Nov. 1917; ed. Univ. Coll. School, Westminster School and Trinity Coll., Cambridge.
Operational Research, Anti-Aircraft Command 40-42, Admiralty 42-45; Fellow of Trinity Coll., Cambridge 41-60, Dir. of Studies 52-60; Demonstrator, Dept. of Physiology, Cambridge Univ. 46-50, Asst. Dir. of Research 51-59, Reader in Experimental Biophysics 59-60; Jodrell Prof. of Physiology, Univ. Coll. London 60-; Foreign Hon. mem. American Acad. of Arts and Sciences 61; Nobel Prize for Medicine 63; Hon. D.Sc. (Sheffield); Hon. M.D. (Saar); Hon. D.Sc. (Leicester) 67.
Manor Field, Grantchester, Cambridge, England.
Telephone: Trumpington 2207.

Huxley, Elspeth Josceline, C.B.E., J.P.; British author; b. 23 July 1907; ed. Reading and Cornell Univs.
Assistant Press Officer, Empire Marketing Board 29-32; extensive travels in America, Africa and elsewhere with her husband Gervas Huxley; farms in Wiltshire but visits Africa every year; mem. B.B.C. Advisory Council 52-59; Justice of the Peace for Wiltshire; mem. Monckton Commission on Central Africa 60.
Publs. *White Man's Country, Lord Delamere and the Making of Kenya* (2 vols.) 33, *Red Strangers* (novel) 39, *The Walled City* (novel), *The Sorcerer's Apprentice* (travel) 48, *Four Guineas* (travel) 52, *A Thing to Love* (novel) 54, *The Red Rock Wilderness* (novel) 57, *The Flame Trees of Thika* (autobiography) 59, *A New Earth* 60, *The Mottled Lizard* 62 *The Merry Hippo* 63, *A Man*

from Nowhere 63, *Forks and Hope* 64, *Back Street New Worlds* 64, *Brave New Victuals* 65, *Their Shining Eldorado* (travel) 67; also three detective novels 34-38.
Woodfolds, Oaksey, nr. Malmesbury, Wilts., England.

Huxley, Sir Julian Sorell, Kt., M.A., D.SC., F.R.S.; British biologist and writer; b. 22 June 1887; ed. Eton and Balliol Coll., Oxford.
Lecturer in Zoology Balliol Coll. 09-11; Asst. Prof. at the Rice Inst., Houston, Texas, U.S.A. 12-16; Fellow New Coll. and Senior Demonstrator in Zoology at Oxford Univ. 19-25; Prof. and Hon. Lecturer in Zoology at King's Coll. London 23-35; Fullerian Prof. of Physiology at Royal Inst. 26-29; Sec. Zoological Society London 35-42; on B.B.C. Brains Trust from its inception; Comm. on Higher Education in W. Africa 44-45, Nat. Parks Cttee. 45; Exec. Sec. UNESCO (Prep. Comm.) 46, Dir.-General 46-48; mem. of Editorial Board *New Naturalist, The African Naturalist,* Aldus Books; Darwin Medallist, Royal Soc. 57; Lasker Award, N.Y. 59; hon. mem. Acad. des Sciences, Paris, New York Acad. of Arts and Sciences; recipient of several hon. degrees and other awards.
Publs. include *Essays of a Biologist, Religion Without Revelation, Problems of Relative Growth, Africa View, The Captive Shrew* (poems), *Animal Biology* (with J. B. S. Haldane), *The Science of Life* (with H. G. and G. P. Wells), *Elements of Experimental Embryology* (with G. R. de Beer), *Simple Science* (with E. N. da C. Andrade), *We Europeans* (with A. C. Haddon), *Scientific Research and Social Needs, Ants, Bird Watching and Bird Behaviour, The Uniqueness of Man, The Private Life of the Gannets* (film with R. M. Lockley; Hollywood award 36), *Democracy Marches, Evolution: the Modern Synthesis* (2nd edn.) 63, *T.V.A.: Adventure in Planning, On Living in a Revolution, Ethics and Evolution, Man in the Modern World* (Essays) 47, *Soviet Genetics and World Science* 49, *Evolution in Action* 52, *From An Antique Land* 54, 66, *New Bottles for New Wine* 57, *Biological Aspects of Cancer* 57, *The Story of Evolution* 58, *The Humanist Frame* (Editor) 61, *The Conservation of Wild Life in Central and East Africa* 61, *Essays of a Humanist* 64; (with H. B. D. Kettlewell) *Charles Darwin and His World* 64; supervised numerous biological and educational films; edited *The New Systematics* and *Evolution as a Process.*
31 Pond Street, London, N.W.3, England.

Huxley, Sir Leonard George Holden, K.B.E., M.A., D.PHIL., PH.D., F.A.A.; Australian public official; b. 29 May 1902; ed. The Hutchins School, Hobart, Tasmania Univ. and New Coll., Oxford.
On scientific staff, C.S.I.R., Sydney 29-30; Lecturer, Univ. Coll., Nottingham, England 30-32; Head, Physics Dept., Univ. Coll., Leicester, England 32-40; Principal Scientific Officer, Telecommunications Research Establishment M.A.P. 40-46; Reader in Electromagnetism, Birmingham Univ., England 46-49; Elder Prof. of Physics, Adelaide Univ. 49-60; Vice-Chancellor, Australian Nat. Univ. 60-67; Pres. Australian Inst. of Physics 62-65; Fellow, Australian Acad. of Science 54-; Chair. Radio Research Board of Australia 58-63, Radio Frequency Allocation Cttee. 60-64, Australian Nat. Standards Comm. 53-65, Gen. Council Encyclopaedia Britannica Australia 64-; mem. U.S. Education Foundation in Australia 60-64; mem. Nat. Library Council 60-, Exec. Commonwealth Scientific and Industrial Research Org. (C.S.I.R.O.) 60; mem. Australian-American Educ. Foundation 65-; Chair. Gen. Council Australia-Britannica Awards Scheme 64-.
Publs. *Wave Guides* 47, numerous papers on gaseous electronics, electromagnetism, ionosphere and upper atmosphere.
19 Glasgow Place, Hughes, Canberra, A.C.T. 2605, Australia.
Telephone: Canberra 815560.

Huyghe, René; French art critic and historian; b. 3 May 1906; ed. Ecole du Louvre and Faculty of Letters, Paris.

On staff of Musée du Louvre 27; Asst. Keeper 30; Keeper of Paintings 37; Head Keeper of Paintings and Drawings 45; Prof. Ecole du Louvre; Prof. of Psychology of Plastic Arts, Coll. de France 50-; mem. French Museum Council 52, Vice-Pres. 64; Dir. of art review *L'Amour de l'Art* 30-; founder and dir. of review *Quadrige* 45-; has collaborated or organised numerous exhibitions, including French Art, London 31, Van Gogh and Masterpieces of French Art, Paris 37, Modern Painting, Rio de Janeiro 45, etc.; has made three art films, including *Rubens and His Age* (Venice Festival Prize); mem. and fmr. Pres. Académie Septentrionale; Commdr. Légion d'Honneur, Commdr. Ordre de Léopold; mem. Acad. Française 60-; Erasmus Prize 66. Publs. *Histoire de l'Art Contemporain* 34, *Cézanne* 36, *La Peinture française: le portrait* (2 vols.) 37, *Les Dessins de Van Gogh* 37, *Les Contemporains* 39, *La Peinture actuelle* 45, *La Poétique de Vermeer* 48, *Le Dessin français au XIXe siècle* 49, *Univers de Watteau* 50, *Gauguin et Noa-Noa* 51, *Le Carnet de Gauguin* 52, *La Peinture d'Occident* 52, *Dialogue avec le Visible* 55, *L'Art et l'Homme*, Vol. I 57, Vol. II 58, Vol. III 61, *Van Gogh* 58, *Gauguin* 59, *L'Art et l'Ame* 60, *Peinture française aux XVIIe et XVIIIe Siècles*, 62, *Delacroix ou le Combat Solitaire* 63, *Les Puissances de L'Image* 65, *Sens et Destin de l'Art* 67.

3 rue Corneille, Paris 6e, France.

Hvass, Frants, B.L.; Danish diplomatist; b. 29 Aug. 1896; ed. Univ. of Copenhagen.

Entered foreign service 22; served Hamburg 27, Ministry of Foreign Affairs 30, London 33; Min. Foreign Affairs 36, Vice-Head of Section, Economic Div. 39, Head, Chief Admin. Div. 40, Chief Political and Judicial Div. 41; Permanent Under-Sec. of State for Foreign Affairs 45-49; Head of Military Mission, Berlin, and Head of Mission to Allied High Comm. Bonn 49; Amb. to Germany 51-66; Sec. Danish Del. to Disarmament Conf. Geneva 32, Danish Cttee. for Scandinavian Econ. Collaboration 37-39; mem. Del. to UN Paris 48, New York 49; mem. Scandinavian Defence Cttee. 48-49; Vice-Pres. Int. Inst. of Admin. Sciences 47, Pres. 56, Hon. Pres. 62; Grand Cross and Cross of Honour, Order of Dannebrog, Grand Cross Order of Nordstjaernan (Sweden), St. Olav (Norway), of Léopold II (Belgium); Grand Officier Légion d'Honneur. c/o Ministry of Foreign Affairs, Copenhagen, Denmark.

Hyde, Rosel Herschel; American government official; b. 12 April 1900; ed. Utah Agricultural Coll. and George Washington Univ.

Assistant Gen. Counsel, Broadcast Bureau 42-45, Gen. Counsel 45-46, Commr. Fed. Communications Comm. 46-, Vice-Chair. 52-53, Chair. 53-54, 66-; mem. President's Task Force on Communications Policy 67-; mem. Council for Admin. Conf. of U.S. 68-; official at numerous int. confs.; Gold Medal of Int. Radio and Television Soc. 65; Ballington and Maud Booth Award by Volunteers of America 67.

Federal Communications Commission, Washington, D.C. 20554, U.S.A.

Telephone: 632-6336 (Office).

Hyder, Sajjad, B.A.; Pakistani diplomatist; b. 20; ed. Govt. High School, Jullundur, D.A.V. Coll., Jullundur, and Indian Mil. Acad., Dehradun.

Served Burma, Siam and Malaya, Second World War; joined Indian Foreign Service 47, opted for Pakistan, served New Delhi, Washington, Karachi, London, Karachi 47-57; Dep. High Commr., New Delhi 57-59, London 59-61; Ambassador to Iraq 61-65, to United Arab Republic 65-.

Embassy of Pakistan, Cairo, United Arab Republic.

Hyman, Joe; British textile executive; b. 14 Oct. 1921; ed. North Manchester Grammar School.

Entered father's General Textile Merchanting Co. 37; founder Portland Woollen Co. 46; owner Melso Fabrics Ltd., now Gainsborough Cornard Ltd. (Cornard Knitting Mills Ltd., Fine Jersey Ltd., and Cooper Bros.) 57; Gainsborough Cornard and William Hollins Ltd. merged to form Viyella Int. Ltd. 61, Chair. 62-.

Stone Court, Kingston Gorse, East Preston, Sussex, England.

Hytten, Torleiv, C.M.G., M.A.; Australian economist of Norwegian origin; b. 17 Feb. 1890; ed. Tasmania Univ.

Came to Australia 10; journalist 19-26; Lecturer in Economics Tasmania Univ. 26, Prof. 29-35; Dir. Tutorial Classes 28-32; Economic Adviser to Tasmanian Govt. 29-35; Chair. Tasmanian State Employment Council 32; Economic Adviser to Bank of New South Wales 35; Australian Del. L.N. Assembly 35, Int. Chamber of Commerce Congresses 35, 37 and 53; Int. Management Congress, Stockholm 43, and Congress of British Universities, Cambridge 53; Chair. Australian Nat. Cttee. Int. Chamber of Commerce 49; Vice-Chancellor Univ. of Tasmania 49-57; Chair. Cttee. of Inquiry into Parl. Salaries (Adjustment Bill) Tasmanian Govt. 51; Chair. Commonwealth-State Consultative Cttee. on Railways 51; mem. Commonwealth Bank Board 54-59; Vice-Chair. Cttee. on Commonwealth Public Service Recruitment 57-58, Enquiry into Transport Problems in Queensland 58; Knight, 1st Class, Order of St. Olav (Norway); Chevalier, Order of the Crown (Belgium).

Balvenie, Cults, Aberdeen AB1 9SS, Scotland.

Telephone: Aberdeen 47276.

Hyuga, Hosai; Japanese metals executive; b. 06; ed. Univ. of Tokyo.

Head Office, Sumitomo Group 31-41; Govt. Service 41; Sumitomo Group 41-, Dir. Sumitomo Metal Industries Ltd. 49-, Man. Dir. 52-58, Senior Man. Dir. 58-60, Exec. Vice-Pres. 60-62, Pres. 62-.

No. 51-2, Matsuhama-cho, Ashiya-city, Hyogo-ken, Japan.

I

Iakovos (*see* James).

Ibáñez-Martín, José, L. en D., PH.D., D.LITT.; Spanish diplomatist; b. 96.
Prov. Deputy for Murcia, later Vice-Pres. and Pres. of Deputation 23-30; mem. Gen. Assembly 27-30; Prof. History and Geography, San Isidro Inst., Madrid 28; Deputy to Cortes 33-36; Pres. Higher Council of Scientific Research 39-; Minister of Education 39-51; Pres. Council of State 51-56; Ambassador to Portugal 58-; Grand Cross Carlos III, Order of Isabel the Catholic, Grand Cross Alfonso X and numerous foreign orders.
Publs. *A History of Spain, A History of the World, Geography, Economics and Politics.*
Consejo Superior de Investigaciones Científicas, Serrano 117, Spain; Estrada de Benfica 39, Lisbon, Portugal.

Ibiam, Francis Akanu; Nigerian medical missionary and politician; b. 29 Nov. 1906; ed. Hope Waddell Training Inst., Calabar, King's Coll., Lagos and Univ. of St. Andrews (Scotland).
Medical Missionary, Church of Scotland Mission, Calabar, Nigeria 36-, built Abiriba Hospital 36-45, Medical Supt. C.S.M. Hospital, Itu 45-48, Uburu 52-57; mem. Board of Govs. Hope Waddell Training Inst. 45-57, Principal 57-60; mem. Legislative Council, Nigeria 47-52, Exec. Council 49-52, Privy Council, E. Region of Nigeria 54-59, Gov. E. Nigeria 60-66; Adviser to Mil. Gov. of E. Nigeria 66, now Adviser to Head of State of Biafra; Pres. Christian Council of Nigeria 55-58; Chair. Provisional Cttee. of All-Africa Church Council 58-62, Council of Univ. Coll., Ibadan 58-61; one of six Pres. World Council of Churches 61-; official of many other religious and medical bodies.
1 Mount Street, Enugu, Eastern Nigeria, Nigeria.

Ibrahim, Wing Commdr. Hassan; United Arab Republic (Egyptian) air force officer and politician; b. 17; ed. Egyptian Mil. Coll. and Egyptian Air Force Coll.
Served Egyptian Air Force 39-52; mem. Revolutionary Council 52; Minister for Presidency and for Production 54-56; Pres. Economic Development Organisation Mar. 57- Oct. 59; Chair. El Nasr Co. for Pencil and Graphite Production 57-61; Pres. and Man. Dir. Paints and Chemical Industries S.A.E. 57-61; mem. Presidential Council 62-64; Vice-Pres. U.A.R. 64-66; holder of the Collar of the Nile.
6 Khartoum Street, Heliopolis, Cairo, U.A.R.

Ibrahim, Sir Kashim, K.C.M.G., C.B.E.; Nigerian politician; b. 10 June 1910; ed. Bornu Provincial School, Katsina Teachers' Training Coll.
Teacher 29-32; Visiting Teacher 33-49; Education Officer 49-52; Central Minister of Social Service 52-55; Northern Regional Minister of Social Development and Surveys 55-56; Waziri of Bornu 56-62; Gov. of Northern Nigeria 62-66; Chair. Nigerian Coll. of Arts, Science and Technology 58-62, Provincial Council of Ahmadu Bello Univ. 61-62; Adviser to Mil. Gov. of Northern Nigeria 66-; Chancellor, Ibadan Univ. 67-; Grand Cross Order of the Niger.
Publs. *Kanuri Reader Elementary I-IV, Kanuri Arithmetic Books I-IV for Elementary Schools.*
State House, Kaduna, Northern Nigeria, Nigeria.

Ibrahim, Sid Moulay Abdullah; Moroccan politician; b. 18; ed. Ben Youssef Univ., Marrakesh and the Sorbonne, Paris.
Mem. Istiqlal (Independence) Party 44-59; mem. Editorial Cttee. *Al Alam* (Istiqlal organ) 50-52; imprisoned for political reasons 52-54; Sec. of State for Information and Tourism, First Moroccan Nat. Govt. 55-56; Minister of Labour and Social Affairs 56-57; Prime Minister and Minister of Foreign Affairs Dec. 58-May 60; leader Union National des Forces Populaires 59-.
Union National des Forces Populaires, B.P. 747, Casablanca, Morocco.

Ibrahim, Waziri; Nigerian politician; b. 26; ed. Elementary School, Damaturu, Middle School, Bornu and Kaduna Coll.
United Africa Co. Ltd. 48-52, Labour and Staff Man. 53-55, Haberdashery Sales and Area Man. 56-57, Branch Man. Mallam Maduri 57, District Man. Kaduna 59; Fed. Minister of Health 59-61, of Econ. Devt. 62-66.
Lagos, Nigeria.

Ibrahimov, Gadji Aga Halil ogly; Soviet party politician; b. 1923; ed. Azerbaijan State Univ. and Higher Party School of Central Committee C.P.S.U.
Soviet Army 41-46; in Young Communist League and Party Official, Azerbaijan 46-61; First Sec. Nakhichevan Regional Cttee. of C.P. of Azerbaijan 61-; mem. Central Cttee. of C.P. of Azerbaijan; Deputy to U.S.S.R. Supreme Soviet; mem. Budget Cttee. Soviet of Union; mem. C.P.S.U. 48-.
Nakhichevan Regional Committee, Communist Party of Azerbaijan, Nakhichevan, U.S.S.R.

Ibrahimov, Mirza Aidjarogly; Soviet politician and writer; b. 1911.
Mem. Acad. of Sciences of Azerbaijan; Minister of Educ., Azerbaijan 42-47; Vice-Chair. Azerbaijan S.S.R. Council of Ministers 47-52; Chair. Azerbaijan S.S.R. Union of Writers 48-54, First Sec. 65-; Chair. of the Supreme Soviet of the Azerbaijan S.S.R. 54-58; Deputy of the Supreme Soviet of the U.S.S.R. 58; State prizewinner 51; awarded Order of Lenin 67.
Publs. plays: *Hayat* 37, *Madrid* 38, *Mahabbeth* 42, *The Country Girl* 62, *A Good Man* 65; novels: *The Day Will Come* 51, *Beyuk Dayag* 57; scientific works: *Beyuk democrat* 39, *Hayat ve edebijyath* 47, *Halgilik ve realizm jabhesinden* 62, *According to Laws of Beauty* 64, *Collected Works* (10 vols.) 64.
Academy of Sciences, Baku, Azerbaijan, U.S.S.R.

Ibuka, Masaru; Japanese industrialist; b. 11 April 1908; ed. Waseda Senior High School and Waseda Univ.
Research Engineer, Photo-Chemical Laboratory 33-37; Man. Radio Telegraphy Dept., Japan Audio Optical Industrial Corpn. 37-40; Man. Dir. Japan Measuring Apparatus Co. Ltd. 40-45; Organiser, Tokyo Telecommunications Engineering Corpn. 45- (Sony Corpn. since 58), Pres., Man. Dir. 50-; Chair. Japan Cttee. for Econ. Development; mem. Econ. Council; dir. several industrial asscns.; Blue Ribbon Medal 60.
5, I-chome Shimomeguro, Megoru-ku, Tokyo, Japan.

Icaza, Jorge; Ecuadorean writer; b. 10 July 1906; ed. Colegio San Gabriel, Colegio Nacional Mejia, and Universidad Nacional, Quito.
Actor and Theatre Dir. 29-32; playwright, civil servant and businessman 33-44; Founder and Titular mem. Cultural Council, Organiser and first Sec.-Gen. Union of Writers and Artists 44-60; Dir. Nat. Library 60-; del. to various Latin American Cultural Congresses; mem. numerous foreign literary socs.; awards include First Prize for Latin American Novel of *La Revista Americana de Buenos Aires* 36, and First Prize for Ecuadorean Novel.
Publs. Plays: *El Intruso* 29, *La Comedia sin Nombre* 30, *Por el Viejo* 31, *Cual Es?* 31, *Como Ellos Quieren* 32, *Sin Sentido* 32, *Flagelo* 36; short stories: *Barro de la Sierra* 33, *Seis Relatos* 52, *Viejos Cuentos* 60; novels: *Huasipungo* 34, *En las Calles* 35, *Cholos* 37, *Media vida*

Deslumbrados 42, *Huairapamushcas* 48, *El Chulla Romero y Flores* 58.
Biblioteca Nacional, Plaza España 233, Quito, Ecuador.

Ichikawa, Kon; Japanese film director.
Films include: *Poo-San* 53, *A Billionaire* 54, *The Heart* 54, *Punishment Room* 55, *The Burmese Harp* 56, *The Men of Tohoku* 56, *Conflagration* 58, *Fires on the Plain* 59, *The Key* 59, *Bonchi* 60, *Her Brother* 60, *The Sin* 61, *Being Two Isn't Easy* 62, *The Revenge of Yuki-No-Jo* 63, *Alone on the Pacific* 63, *Tokyo Olympiad* 64.
271 Seijo, Setagaya-ku, Tokyo, Japan.

Ichimada, Hisato; Japanese financier and politician; b. 12 Aug. 1893; ed. Tokyo Univ.
Served with Bank of Japan 18-54, Pres. 46-54; mem. of Japanese Del. to San Francisco Peace Conf. 51; Minister of Finance 54-56, 57-58; mem. House of Reps. 55-; Chair. Overseas Economic Co-operation Special Cttee. of Liberal Democratic Party 59-; Hon. Ph.D. (Syracuse Univ.), Hon. Ph.D. (International Christian Univ.).
5-30, 3-chome, Nishi-Azabon, Minato-ku, Tokyo, Japan.
Telephone: (401) 1628, 0082.

Idemitsu, Sazo; Japanese business executive; b. 85; ed. Kobe Coll. of Commerce.
Founded Idemitsu Firm 11; Pres. Idemitsu Kosan Co. Ltd. 40-; Adviser, Kyushu Asahi Broadcasting Co. 60-; Blue Ribbon Medal 59.
502 8-chome, Kamimeguro, Meguro-ku, Tokyo, Japan.

Idenburg, Philippus Jacobus, DR. JUR.; Netherlands statistician and educationist; b. 01; ed. Univs. of Amsterdam and Leiden.
Secretary of a Govt. Efficiency Cttee. 27-28; Chief of a Div. of Netherlands Central Bureau of Statistics 29-38; Dir. of Bureau of Statistics 39-45; Dir.-Gen. of Educ. 46; Dir.-Gen. of Statistics 47-66; Prof. of Educ., Univ. of Amsterdam; Pres. Comparative Educ. Soc. in Europe, Netherlands Arts Council, Netherlands Foundation for Research in Educ., Netherlands Foundation for Statistics; Hon. D.Litt. (Durban).
Publs. Books and articles on statistics and education.
18 Mesdagstraat, The Hague, Netherlands.

Idham Chalid, Dr. Kjai Hadji; Indonesian politician; b. 5 Jan. 1921; ed. Islamic Teachers Coll., Ponorogo, East Java.
Teacher at Islamic schools 43-47; Indonesian Navy 47; local politics 48-50; mem. Indonesian Parl. 50, mem. Constituent Assembly 56; Second Deputy Prime Minister 57-59; mem. Supreme Advisory Council 59; mem. Provisional People's Consultative Assembly 60-, Deputy Chair. 60, Minister and Deputy Chair. 60, 62, 64-; First Minister of People's Welfare 67-; Leader Religious Teachers Party.
Ministry of People's Welfare, Djakarta, Indonesia.

Idris I (Sayyid Muhammad Idris as-Sanusi); King of Libya; b. 90.
Son of Sayyid Muhammad al-Mahdi; succeeded his uncle, Sayyid Ahmad Asharif Idris as-Sanusi, in charge of affairs of the Senusiya Order 16; became Amir of Cyrenaica; proclaimed King of Libya Dec. 2nd, 50.
Royal Diwan, Benghazi, Libya.

Iduarte Foucher, Andrés, LL.D., D.PHIL.; Mexican writer; b. 1 May 1907; ed. Nat. Univ. of Mexico, Univ. of Paris, Central Univ. of Madrid and Columbia Univ., N.Y.
Asst. Prof. of History, Nat. Univ. of Mexico 30-32; First Sec., Ibero-American Section, Ateneo, Madrid 35; Instructor in Spanish, Columbia Univ., N.Y. 39-45; Asst. Prof. of Spanish American Literature 45-50, Acting Dir. Univ. Hispanic Inst. 49, Assoc. Prof. 50-60, Full Prof. 60-, Asst. Dir. 55-67; mem. Cttee. for Rómulo Gallegos Int. Novel Contest 67; Dir.-Gen. Nat. Inst. of Fine Arts, Mexico 52-54; mem. Cuban Acad. of History 46; several literary prizes; Orders of Céspedes (Cuba) 46;

Dr. h.c. (Univ. de San Nicolás de Hidalgo Mexico); C.B.E. 53; Pres. Int. Inst. of Ibero-American Literature 57-59.
Publs. *Himno a la Sangre* 28, *El Caballero Matón* 32, *Martí Escritor* 45, *Sarmiento a través de sus mejores páginas* 49, *Prosas de Martí* 50, *Pláticas Hispano-americanas* 51, *Un Niño en la Revolución Mexicana* 51, *Veinte Años con Rómulo Gallegos* 54, *La Isla sin Veneno* 54, *Sarmiento, Martí y Rodó* 55, *Alfonso Reyes, el Hombre y su Mundo* 56, *Gabriela Mistral, santa a la jineta* 58, *Martín Luis Guzmán en sus libros* 60, *Don Pedro de Alba y su Tiempo* 62, *México en la nostalgia* 65, *Tres escritores mexicanos* 67.
521 Philosophy Hall, Columbia University, New York 27, N.Y., U.S.A.

Idzumbuir, Théodore; Congolese diplomatist; b. 9 Nov. 1930; ed. Lovanium-Kisantu Inst., Mayidi Seminary and Inst of International Studies, Geneva.
Minister Plenipotentiary, Perm. Rep. of the Dem. Repub. of Congo to the UN 63-; Vice-Pres. UN Gen. Assembly 67; Nat. Order of Leopard 66.
Permanent Mission of the Democratic Republic of Congo (Kinshasa) to the United Nations, 757 Third Avenue, New York City 17, N.Y., U.S.A.

Iengar, H. V. R.; Indian banker and industrialist; b. 23 Aug. 1902.
Held several posts in the Indian Civil Service including Sec. Ministry of Commerce and Industry; Chair. State Bank of India 55-57; Gov. Reserve Bank of India 57-62; Chair. and Managing Dir. E.I.D.-Parry Ltd.; Chair. Indian Aluminium Co. Ltd. 67, Herdillia Chemicals Ltd.
c/o Parry and Co. Ltd., P.O.B. 12, Madras 1; Home: "Bens Garden", Chamiers Road, Madras 28, India.
Telephone: Madras 71418.

Ifeagwu, Chukuemeka Okeke, B.A., PH.D.; Nigerian diplomatist; b. 21; ed. Dennis Memorial Grammar School, Onitsha, Pepperdine Coll., Los Angeles, and Univ. of Southern California.
District Officer, Aba, E. Nigeria 57; Nigerian Diplomatic Service 57-; First Sec. Perm. Mission of Nigeria to UN 60-61, Counsellor 61-62; Head Africa, Asia and Euro-Western Div., Ministry of External Affairs, Lagos 62-63; Ambassador to U.S.S.R. 63-.
Nigerian Embassy, Ul Kachalova 13, Moscow, U.S.S.R.

Ignacio-Pinto, Louis, D. ès D., D. ès L.; Dahomeyan diplomatist; b. 03; ed. Ecole St. Gènes, Bordeaux and Univs. of Bordeaux and Paris.
Office-Cadet 31-32; engaged in starch manufacture 33-36; junior counsel, Paris Court of Appeal 37-39; war service in Lorraine 39-40; Counsel, Conakry 40-46; resistance worker; Rep. of Dahomey to French Senate 46-56; Vice-Pres. Comm., France d'Outre Mer 46-56; Minister of Econs. Commerce and Industry, Dahomey 57-58, Minister of Justice 58-59; returned to legal profession 59; Counsellor, French Embassy, Vatican City 60; Ambassador of Dahomey to UN, New York 60-67, Amb. of Dahomey to U.S.A. 60-67; Pres. of Supreme Court of Dahomey 67-; Judge, Admin. Tribunal of UN.
Supreme Court of Justice, Cotonou, Dahomey.

Ignar, Stefan; Polish politician and economist; b. 08; ed. Poznań and Łódź Univs.
Ed. *Chłopskie Życie Gospodarcze* ("Peasant Economic Life"); during the war, a Lieut.-Col. of the Peasants Battalions in the resistance; mem. of the Seym (Parliament); Deputy Chair. State Council 52-56, Council of Ministers 56-; Chair. United Peasant Party 56-62, Polish Acad. of Sciences Cttee. for Research on Regions being industrialized 61-; mem. Presidium 62-; Prof. of Agricultural Econs. Warsaw Central School of Agriculture.
Urząd Rady Ministrów, Al. Ujazdowskie 1-3, Warsaw, Poland.

Ignatieff, George, B.A.; Canadian diplomatist; b. 16 Dec. 1913; ed. Jarvis Coll. Inst., Toronto, Univs. of Toronto and Oxford.

Department of External Affairs, Ottawa 40-; Third Sec., London 40-44; Dept. of External Affairs, Ottawa 44-45; Adviser, Canadian Del., UN Atomic Energy Comm. 46, UN Assembly 46-47; Alt. Rep. UN Security Council 45-49; Chair. Admin. and Budgetary Cttee., UN Gen. Assembly 49; Counsellor, Washington 49-53; attended Imperial Defence Coll., London 53-54; Head of Defence Liaison (First Div.) Dept. of External Affairs, Ottawa 55; Ambassador to Yugoslavia 56-58; Dep. High Commr., London 59-60; Asst. Under-Sec., Dept. of External Affairs, Ottawa 60-62; Perm. Rep. and Ambassador to NATO 62-66; Perm. Rep. to UN 66-. Permanent Mission of Canada to UN, 866 United Nations Plaza, New York 17, N.Y., U.S.A. Telephone: 751-5600.

Ignatius, Paul Robert; American government official; b. 11 Nov. 1920; ed. Univ. of Southern California and Harvard Business School.

Instructor in Business Admin., Harvard Business School 47-50; Vice-Pres., Dir. Harbridge House Inc. (management consultants), Boston 50-61; Asst. Sec. of Army for Installations and Logistics 61-63; Under-Sec. of Army 64; Asst. Sec. of Defence 64-67; Sec. of Navy 67-; U.S. Naval Reserve 43-46.

Department of the Navy, The Pentagon, Washington 25, D.C.; Home: 3650 Fordham Road, Washington 16, D.C., U.S.A.

Iida, Keizo; Japanese retail executive; b. 13 April 1900; ed. Keio Univ.

Osaka Branch, Takashimaya Dept. Store 26, Man. 41, Dir. Takashimaya 42-, Managing Dir. 43-52, Pres. 52-60, now Chair.

Takashimaya Co. Ltd., Namba, Minami-ku, Osaka, Japan.

Ikebe, Ryo; Japanese actor; b. 18.

First film appearance in *Togyo* (Fighting Fish) 41; other films include *Aoi Sanmyaku* (Blue Mountains) 49, *Akatsuki no Dasso* (Escape at Dawn) 50, *Geisha Konatsu* 54, *Byaku-fujin no Yoren* (The Legend of the White Serpent) 56, *Yukiguni* (Snow Country) 57.

c/o Toho Film Co. Ltd., 1-6 Yuraku-cho, Chiyoda-ku, Tokyo, Japan.

Ikeda, Daisaku; Japanese religious leader; b. 2 Jan. 1928; ed. Toyo Commercial High School and Taisei Gakuin Coll.

Chief of Staff, Youth Division, Soka Gakkai 54-58, Gen. Exec. 58-60, Pres. of Soka Gakkai 60-; Owner Seikyo Press; Pres. Minon Concert Asscn.; Hon. Dir. Oriental Inst. of Academic Research.

Publs. *Lectures on Buddhism,* Vols. 1-13 61-65, *Essays on Buddhism,* Vol. 1 62, Vol. 2 64, *Lecture on Piety in Buddhism* 64, *Lectures on the Opening of the Eyes* Vols. 1-2, 64-65, *Science and Religion* 65, *Politics and Religion* 65, *The Human Revolution* (novel) Vols. 1-2 65-66; other writings on Buddhism.

c/o The Soka Gakkai, 32 Shinamo-machi, Shinjuku-ku, Tokyo, Japan.

Ilangaratne, Tikiri Bandara; Ceylonese politician, writer, playwright, novelist; b. 27 Feb. 1913; ed. St. Anthony's Coll., Kandy.

Clerical Servant until 47; mem. of Parl. for Kandy 48, for Galaha 52; Gen. Sec. Sri Lanka Freedom Party 54-; mem. of Parl. for Hewaheta 56; Minister for Social Services and Housing 56-59, of Home Affairs 59, of Trade, Commerce, Food and Shipping 61-63, of Finance 63-64, of Trade and Supplies 64-65.; Vice-Pres Sri Lanka Freedom Party 66, mem. of Parl. for Kdonnawa 67, responsible for nationalizing foreign oil companies in Ceylon.

Publs. (in Sinhalese). Novels: *Wilambeeta, Denuwara,*

Kathava, Thilaka, La Sanda, Thilaka and Thilaka, Nedeyo; Plays: *Häramitiya, Manthri Hamuduruwo, Jataka Natyaya, Rangamandala, Handahana, Ambaryaluwo;* Short stories: *Onchillawa.*

37 Abdul Caffoov Mawatha, Colombo 3, Ceylon. Telephone: 79499.

Ileo, Joseph; Congolese politician; b. 22; ed. philosophy and sociology in Europe.

Held post in African Territories Division of Belgian Gov.-General's Office; active in movement for independence, signatory of the "Memorandum of the Sixteen" 58; passed periods in jail and exile; formed Congolese National Movement Party with Patrice Lumumba; joined Abako Party 59; former Editor *The African Conscience;* Head of Congolese Senate July 60- Sept. 60; Premier Sept. 60-Aug. 61; Minister of Information and Cultural Affairs Aug. 61-62; Minister without Portfolio in charge Katangese Affairs 63-64.

Lubumbashi, South Katanga, Congo Democratic Republic.

Iliff, Sir William (A.B.), Kt.; British international banker; b. 2 Oct. 1898.

Financial Counsellor at British Embassy in Teheran; Financial Adviser to Gov. of Burma; U.K. Treasury Rep. in Middle East 44-48; Dir. Loan Dept. of International Bank 48-51, Asst. to Pres. of Bank 51-56, Vice-Pres. of Bank 56-62; Dir. De La Rue Co. Ltd., Power Securities Corpn. Ltd.; served in 14-18 and 39-45 wars.

c/o Travellers' Club, London, S.W.1, England.

Ilku, Pál; Hungarian politician; b. 12; ed. Beregszász State Grammar School and Bratislava Teachers' Training Coll.

Former village teacher; fmr. Ed. *New Epoch* (educ. journal); fmr. First Sec. Pécs Urban Party Cttee.; Dep. Minister of Culture 58, Minister of Culture and Education 61-; mem. Central Cttee. of Hungarian Socialist Workers Party; Alt. mem. Political Cttee. Hungarian Socialist Workers Party 62-.

Ministry of Culture, Budapest, Hungary.

Illés, Béla; Hungarian author and political writer; b. 22 March 1895; ed. Budapest Univ.

Member Revolutionary Army Council 18; illegal political and Party activity Western Ukraine 20-21; Sec. Soviet Writers' Union; later, Gen. Sec. World Org. of Proletarian Writers in Moscow; in Second World War served in the Red Army; after the war, settled again in Hungary; edited *Uj Szo,* later *Irodalmi Ujság* (literary weekly); fmr. Board mem. Nat. Union of Hungarian Writers; Vice-Pres. Hungarian PEN; Kossuth Prize 50, 55.

Publs. *Nikolaj Suhaj, Generalprobe, Minden ut Moszkvaba vezet (Alle Wege führen nach Moskau), Kárpáti Rapszodia, Heuriger Wien, Hirtenfeuer auf dem Verhovina, Szkipetarok, Kézfogások, A zene szava, Poèmes choisis* (Poems, in French), *Malom a Seden.*

Association of Hungarian Writers, Bajza-u. 18, Budapest VI; Home: Virányos ut 15/b, Budapest XII, Hungary.

Illia, Arturo Umberto; Argentine physician and politician; b. 01.

Former Provincial Senator; fmr. Vice-Gov. Córdoba Province; Pres. of Argentina Oct. 63-June 66; mem. People's Radical Civic Union.

Cruz del Eje, Córdoba, Argentina.

Illyés, Gyula; Hungarian author; b. 2 Nov. 1902; ed. Budapest, Prague, Milan, Paris, Brussels, Berlin, Warsaw, London, etc.

Former editor of *Nyugat, Magyar Csillag* and *Válasz;* Vice-Pres. Union of Hungarian Writers; awarded Kossuth Prize 48 and 53, Grand Prix de Poésie, Knokke (Belgium).

Publs. *Puszták Népe, Petöfi, Magyarok, Lélek és Kenyér,*

Kora tavasz, A tü foka, Hunok Párizsban, Lélekbúvár, Osszes Versei, Az Ozorai Példa, Fáklyaláng, Dózsa, Kézfogások, Uj Versek, Ebéd a kastélyban, Nem volt elég, Másokért egyedül, Nyitott kapu, Szives kalauz, Poèmes Choisis, Hommage a G.I., Ingyen Lakoma, Dölt Vitorla, Poètes d'aujourd'hui, Poharaim.
Józsefhegyi u. 9, Budapest II, Hungary.

Ilnitsky, Yuri Vasilyevich; Soviet politician; b. 1924; ed. Higher Party School of the C.P. of the Ukraine.
Agricultural official 39-45; Party Official in the Ukraine 45-59; Second Sec. Transcarpathian Regional Cttee. of the Ukranian C.P. 59-62, First Sec. 62-; mem. Central Cttee. C.P. of the Ukraine; Deputy to U.S.S.R. Supreme Soviet; mem. C.P.S.U. 45-.
Transcarpathian Regional Committee, Communist Party of the Ukraine, Uzkgorod, U.S.S.R.

Ilsley, Rt. Hon. James Lorimer, P.C., D.C.L., LL.D.; Canadian judge; b. 3 Jan. 1894; ed. Acadia and Dalhousie Univs.
Called to Bar Nova Scotia 16, K.C. 28; in practice Kentville and Halifax 16-35; mem. House of Commons for Hants-Kings 26-35, for Digby-Annapolis-Kings 35-48; Min. of Nat. Revenue Mackenzie King Cabinet Oct. 35-July 40; Min. of Finance July 40-Dec. 46; Min. of Justice Dec. 46-June 48; mem. Imperial Privy Council Jan. 46; resgnd. from Govt. June 48 and resumed law practice as partner in law firm of Ilsley, Duquet & MacKay, Montreal; Dir. Royal Bank of Canada and Toronto Gen. Trusts Corpn. 48-49; Puisne Judge of Supreme Court of Nova Scotia May 49, Chief Justice of Nova Scotia Jan. 50-.
5889 Inglis Street, Halifax, Nova Scotia, Canada.

Ilvessalo, Yrjö, DR.PHIL.; Finnish forester; b. 1 Dec. 1892; ed. State Academy for Science and Arts.
Asst. Forester 14-18; Lecturer, Univ. of Helsinki 18-22; Prof. of Forest Management, Finnish Forest Research Inst. 22-48; Lecturer, Technical High School 22-48; Prof. State Acad. of Finland 48-62; mem. Acad. of Science 26-, Chair. 48-49; Hon. Chair. Soc. of Forestry in Finland; mem. Trustees and Hon. mem. Geographical Soc. of Finland (Chair. 39-41); Hon. mem. Swedish Forestry Asscn., Finnish Union of Foresters; foreign mem. Swedish Royal Acad. of Agriculture, Norwegian Acad. of Science; mem. Perm. Comm. of Int. Union of Forest Research Orgs. 33-36, Section Leader 48-56; Chair. State Board for agriculture-forestry Research; Hon. degrees from Univs. of Zürich, Fribourg and Aas; Prizes for scientific work.
Publs. *Concerning Methods of Forest Mensuration, Forest Surveys and Forest Management, Growth and Yield of Forests, Forest Site Types and Forest Resources* 16-68.
Runeberg St. 26, Helsinki 10, Finland.

Ilyashenko, Kirill Fedorovich; Soviet politician; b. 15; ed. Tiraspol Pedagogical Inst.
Soviet Army 40-45; mem. Communist Party of Soviet Union 45-; Chair. State Cttee. for Co-ordination of Scientific and Research Work, Council of Ministers of Moldavian S.S.R. and Deputy Chair. of Council of Ministers of Moldavian S.S.R. 62-63; Chair. of Presidium of Supreme Soviet of Moldavian S.S.R. 63-; mem. Buro of Central Cttee. of C.P. of Moldavian S.S.R. 63-; mem. Central Auditing Comm. C.P.S.U.; Deputy Chair. Presidium of Supreme Soviet of U.S.S.R.
Presidium of Supreme Soviet of Moldavian S.S.R., Kishinev, Moldavian S.S.R., U.S.S.R.

Ilyichev, Ivan Ivanovich; Soviet diplomatist; b. 1905; ed. higher historical school.
Diplomatic Service 48-; Deputy Head, Third European Dept., U.S.S.R. Ministry of Foreign Affairs 48-49; Deputy Political Counsellor to Soviet Control Comm. in Germany 49-52; Head of U.S.S.R. Diplomatic Mission to German Democratic Republic 52-53; High Commr.

and Ambassador to Austria 53-55, Ambassador to Austria 55-56; Head of Scandinavian Countries Dept., U.S.S.R. Ministry of Foreign Affairs 56-, Head of Third European Dept. 56-66; Amb. to Denmark 66-.
U.S.S.R. Embassy, Kristianiagade 5, Copenhagen, Denmark.
Telephone: Tria 5585.

Ilyichev, Leonid Fyodorovich; Soviet journalist and politician; b. 15 March 1906; ed. North Caucasian Communist Univ. and Inst. of Red Profs., Moscow.
Worker at a factory, Krasnodar 18-24; Young Communist League work 24-27; student and assistant teacher, North Caucasian Communist Univ. 30-31; party work 31-34; Sec. *Bolshevik Journal* 38-40; mem. staff *Pravda* 40-44; Editor-in-Chief *Izvestia* 44-48; on staff C.P.S.U. Central Cttee. 48-49; Deputy Editor-in-Chief, later Editor-in-Chief *Pravda* 49-52; Dir. Press Dept., Ministry of Foreign Affairs 53-58; Dir. C.P. Agitation and Propaganda Service 58-61; Sec. Central Cttee. of C.P.S.U. 61-65, mem. Central Cttee. 61-66; Deputy Foreign Minister of U.S.S.R. 65-; mem. U.S.S.R. Acad. of Sciences 62-; Lenin Prize 60.
Ministry of Foreign Affairs, 32-34 Smolenskaya-Sennaya ploshchad, Moscow, U.S.S.R.

Ilyin, Vitaly Sergeyevich; Soviet biochemist; b. 1904; ed. First Leningrad Medical Inst.
Research worker, Inst. of Natural Sciences 27-40; Senior Research Worker, Leningrad Inst. of Blood Transfusion 33-39; Head of Dept., Deputy Dir. Tajik Medical Inst. 40-45; Senior Research Worker, Pavlov Inst. of Physiology 45-50; Head, Dept. of Biochemistry, Leningrad Inst. of Stomatology 45-51; Head of Dept., Inst of Experimental Medicine, U.S.S.R. Acad. of Medical Sciences, and Head of Dept., Leningrad Inst. for Postgraduate Medical Training 51-; Editor of Chemistry Dept. of *Great Medical Encyclopaedia* and mem. Editorial Boards of *Evolutional Biochemistry and Physiology*, *Biochemistry* and *Aspects of Medical Chemistry;* Order of Red Banner of Labour 51.
Publs. Over 100 works on cellular and molecular mechanisms of hormonal and nervous regulation of metabolism.
Institute of Experimental Medicine, Kirovsky Prospekt 69/71, Leningrad, U.S.S.R.

Ilyushin, Sergei Vladimirovich; Soviet aircraft designer; b. 94; ed. Air Force Engineering Acad.
Lt.-Gen. in the engineering-technical service; Prof. at the N.E. Zhukovsky Air Force Engineering Acad.; Deputy to U.S.S.R. Supreme Soviet; Designer-Gen. of U.S.S.R. Ministry of Aircraft Industry; Corresp. mem. U.S.S.R. Acad. of Sciences; State prize winner (seven times); Hero of Socialist Labour (twice); Lenin Prize 60. Principal designs: the TsKB-30 twin-engine plane 36, the IL-2 armoured attacker 39, the IL-12 twin-engine passenger plane 46, the IL-18 (*Moscow*) turbo-prop passenger plane 57, the IL-62 turbo-jet passenger plane 62.
Ministry of Aircraft Industry, Moscow, U.S.S.R.

Imai, Kenji; Japanese architect; b. 11 Jan. 1895; ed. Architectural Dept., Waseda Univ., Tokyo.
Assistant Prof. Waseda Univ. 20-37, Prof. 37-65, Hon. Prof. 65-; Prof. Kantö Gakuin Univ., Yokohama 66-; Hon. Counsellor Tama Fine Arts Univ., Tokyo 65-; studied in Europe and America 26-27; mem. Catholic Art Soc. 49-; Rep. of Japan Branch of Gaudi Friend Circle 56, participated in 10th Anniversary of Antonio Gaudi Friend Circle, Barcelona 63; Hon. mem. Rudolf Steiner Goetheanum 63; one-man exhbn. of European sketches 64; Prize of Architectural Inst. of Japan 59, 62; Marquis Ohkuma Academic Prize, Waseda Univ. 62; Japan Art Acad. Prize 66.
Major works include: Waseda Univ. Library 25, Waseda Univ. Museum of Drama 28, Aeroplane

Monument, Tokyo 41, Ohtakimachi Town Office, Chiba Prefecture 59, Memorial Centre for Japanese 26 Martyrs 62, Chapel for Sisters of the Visitation Convent (Kamakura) 65, *Toka Gakudo*—The Empress' Memorial Music Hall, Imperial Palace 66, Marquis Ohkuma Memorial Hall, Saga Prefecture 66.
Publs. *Gunnar Asplund* 30, *Das Vorbild der Katholischen Gattin—Architecture and Humanity* 54, *Öryo Sobyö* (Sketch of Travel through Europe) 63, *Tabiji* (Voyage) 67; collection of artistic works in commemoration of 70th birthday 68.
4-12-28, Kitazawa, Setagaya-ku, Tokyo, Japan.
Telephone: 468-2708 (Tokyo).

Imbert, Bertrand Sainclair Marie; French hydrographic engineer and naval officer; b. 23 Oct. 1924; ed. Collège Saint-Martin de France and Collège Sainte Geneviève.
Entered Free French Navy, Ecole Navale 43; served in Indo-China Campaign 45-47; Antarctic expeditions 51, 56 and 57; Principal Marine Nationale; Chief of French Antarctic Expeditions of the Int. Geophysical Year 56-59; mem. Atomic Energy Comm. 59-; Croix de Guerre, Chevalier, Légion d'Honneur.
8 rue de l'Odéon, Paris 6e, France.

Imoudu, Michael Atokhamen Ominius; Nigerian trade unionist; b. 04; self-educated.
Nigerian Railways 28-, Chargeman 45; organised Railway Workers Organisation 31, Railway Workers Union 40; imprisoned, later detained 42-45; Life-Pres. Railway and Ports Workers' Union 47-, Pres. All-Nigerian Trade Union Fed. 47-58, Nigerian Trade Union Congress 59-61; Leader Marxist-Leninist Party of All Nigerian Toilers.
65 Simpson Street, Ebute-metta, Lagos, Nigeria.

Imru, Ras Haile Selassie; Ethiopian diplomatist; b. 92; ed. Menelik II School, Addis Ababa.
Deputy Gov. Harar Province 18-29, Wollow Province 29-32, Gojjam Province 32-35; C.-in-C. Ethiopian Army 35-36; later C.-in-C. of all Ethiopian Forces; subsequently captured by Italians, freed 43; Gov.-Gen. Begemdir and Simen 44; Minister to Washington 46-49, Ambassador 49-53; Ambassador to India 54-60.
P.O.B. 1170, Addis Ababa, Ethiopia.

Imshenetsky, Alexander Alexandrovitch; Soviet microbiologist; b. 8 Jan. 1905; ed. Voronezh State Univ.
Teacher of Microbiology, Leningrad Chemico-Technological Inst. 32-34; Senior Scientific Worker, Inst. of Microbiology, U.S.S.R. Acad. of Sciences 32-41, Head of Dept. 41-, Dep. Dir. 45-49, Dir. 49-; Prof. of Microbiology, Piscicultural Faculty, Timiryazevsky Agricultural Acad. 35-37; mem. U.S.S.R. Acad. of Sciences 62-; First Pres. (and Founder) U.S.S.R. Microbiological Soc. 60; Editor *Microbiology*; Order of Lenin, Order of Red Banner of Labour (twice).
Publs. *The Structure of Bacteria* 40, *Microbiological Processes at High Temperatures* 44, *Microbiology of Celluloses* 53, *Morphology of Bacteria* 62, *Perspectives for the Development of Exobiology* 63.
Institute of Microbiology of the U.S.S.R. Academy of Sciences, Profsoyuznaya ul. d. 7, Moscow; Leninsky Prospekt 13 app. 107, Moscow, U.S.S.R.
Telephone: 13-2-51-56.

Inagaki, Hiroshi; Japanese film director; b. 05.
Began career in films as actor, script-writer, etc. 14; Asst. to Teinosuke Kinugasa 27; Director 28-; at present under contract to Toho Film Co.; mem. Board Motion Picture Directors' Asscn. of Japan; Ministry of Education Awards for *Edo Saigo No Hi* 42 and *Te O Tsunagu Kora* 48; Ministry of Welfare Award for *Wasurevareta Kora* 50; American Motion Picture Acad. Award for *Samurai* (a different film from *The Seven Samurai*) 56; Venice Film Festival Grand Prix, Tokyo

Gold Prize and Sankei Silver Star Prize for *Muhomatsu No Issho* 57.
Films include *Tenka Taiheiki*, *Edo Saigo No Hi* (The Last Days of Edo), *Te O Tsunagu Kora* (Children Holding Hands Together), *Wasurevareta Kora* (Neglected Children), *Samurai*, *Muhomatsu No Issho* (The Rickshaw Man).
861 Seijomachi, Setagaya-ku, Tokyo, Japan.

Inayama, Yoshihiro; Japanese steel executive; b. 2 Jan. 1904; ed. Tokyo Univ.
Yawata Iron and Steel Works 27-, Man. Dir. 50-60, Vice-Pres. 60-61, Pres. 61-; also Chair. Japan Iron and Steel Federation.
Yawata Iron and Steel Co. Ltd., 1-1 Marunouchi, Chiyoda-ku, Tokyo, Japan.

Inchyra, 1st Baron (cr. 62), of St. Madoes in the County of Perth; **Frederick Robert Hoyer Millar,** G.C.M.G., C.V.O.; British diplomatist; b. 6 June 1900; ed. Wellington Coll. and New Coll., Oxford.
Honorary Attaché Brussels 22; entered Diplomatic Service 23; served as Third Sec. Berlin and Paris, Second Sec. Cairo; Asst. Private Sec. to Sec. of State for Foreign Affairs 34-38; First Sec. Washington 39, Counsellor 41-42; Sec. British Civil Secr., Washington 43; Counsellor, Foreign Office 44, Asst. Under-Sec. 47; Minister, British Embassy, Washington 48; U.K. Dep. NATO 50-52; U.K. Perm. Rep. North Atlantic Council 52-53, U.K. High Commr. in Germany 53-55, Ambassador to German Fed. Repub. 55-57; Perm. Under-Sec. of State 57-61; retired 62; Dir. Shell Transport and Trading Co. Ltd., Gen. Accident, Fire and Life Assurance Corpn., Stockholders Investment Trust, Rootes Motors, British Linen Bank; Chair. Exec. Cttee. British Red Cross Soc.
57 Eaton Place, London, S.W.1, England.

Incze, Jenő; Hungarian engineer, politician and diplomatist; b. 01; ed. Budapest Technical Univ.
Former Asst. Lecturer Budapest Technical Univ.; Engineer, Ganz Works 26-45, later Chief Engineer, Dep. Dir. 45-48; Deputy Dir. *Nikex* (heavy machinery, shipbuilding and diesel engines trading corporation) 49-53; Dept. Head, Ministry of Foreign Trade 54-55, Dep. Minister of Foreign Trade 55-57, Minister of Foreign Trade 57-63; Ambassador to U.K. 63-.
Hungarian Embassy, 35 Eaton Place, London S.W.1, England.
Telephone: 01-235-4048.

Indra, Alois; Czechoslovak politician; b. 17 March 1921.
Former Head of Planning, Finance and Foreign Trade Dept., Central Cttee. of Czechoslovak C.P.; Minister-Chair. State Planning Comm. 62-63; Minister of Transport 63-68; mem. Secr. of Central Cttee. and Sec. of Central Cttee. of C.P. of Czechoslovakia 68-; mem. State Planning Comm. 65-; mem. Central Cttee. of C.P. of Czechoslovakia 62- (Econ. Comm. 63-66); Deputy to Nat. Assembly.
Prague, Czechoslovakia.

Ingalls, Daniel Henry Holmes, A.B., M.A.; American orientalist; b. 4 May 1916; ed. Harvard Univ.
Junior Fellow, Harvard Univ. 39-42 and 46-49; Office of Strategic Services 42-44, U.S. Army 44-46; Asst. Prof. Harvard Univ. 49-54, Assoc. Prof. 54-58, Wales Prof. of Sanskrit 58-; Editor *Harvard Oriental Series*; Pres. American Oriental Soc. 59-60; Dir. Virginia Hot Springs, Inc. 46-57, Pres. 57-63, Chair. of Board 63-.
Publs. *Materials for the Study of Navya-nyaya Logic* 50, *An Anthology of Sanskrit Court Poetry* 64.
Widener Library 273, Harvard University, Cambridge, Mass. 02138, U.S.A.

Ingarden, Roman, PH.D.; Polish philosopher; b. 94; ed. Lwów Univ., Göttingen Univ. and Freiburg-im-Breisgau Univ.
Fmr. Prof. John Casimir Univ., Lwów 33; Prof.

Jagiellonian Univ., Cracow 45; mem. Polish Acad. of Sciences and Letters; mem. Polish Acad. of Sciences, Institut Int. de Philosophie, Paris, Wrocław Scientific Soc., American Soc. for Aesthetics, Soc. Française d'Esthétique.

Publs. *Die Intuition und Intellekt bei Heinrich Bergson, Essentiale Fragen, Spór o istnienie świata* (The Controversy over the Existence of the World), *Das Literarische Kunstwerk, O poznawaniu dziela literackiego* (Cognition of Works of Literature), *Studia z estetyki* (Studies in Aesthetics), *Untersuchungen zur Ontologie der Kunst, Z badán nad filozofia współczesna* (Studies in Contemporary Philosophy), *Time and Modes of Being, Der Streit um die Existenz der Welt* (Vols. I, II), *Przeżycie-Dzieło-Wartość Experience* (Work of Art Value), numerous papers and articles.
Biskupia 14, Cracow, Poland.

Inge, William, A.B., A.M.; American playwright; b. 3 May 1913; ed. Univ. of Kansas and Peabody Teachers' Coll.
Taught at Stephens Coll. for Women 38-43; critic on *St. Louis Star-Times* 43-46; Lecturer Washington Univ. 46-49; Pulitzer Prize, Critics' Prize and Donaldson Award for *Picnic* 53.
Plays. *Farther Off From Heaven* 47, *Come Back Little Sheba* 50, *Picnic* 53, *Bus Stop* 55, *The Dark at the Top of the Stairs* 57, *A Loss of Roses* 59, *Natural Affection* 63, *Where's Daddy* 66; Film: *Splendour In the Grass.*
c/o Random House Inc., 457 Madison Avenue, New York City 22, N.Y., U.S.A.

Ingersoll, Ralph McAllister, B.S.; American journalist and newspaper publisher; b. 8 Dec. 1900; ed. Hotchkiss School, Lakeville, Conn., Yale and Columbia Univs.
Fmr. mining engineer; reporter *New York American* 23-24; freelance journalist 24-25; reporter *New Yorker* 25, Man. Editor 25-30; Associate Editor *Fortune* 30, Man. Editor 30-35; Vice-Pres. and Gen. Man. Time, Inc., publishing *Time, Life, Fortune* and *Architectural Forum* 35-40, publisher *Time* 37-40; Founder and Editor N.Y. daily newspaper *P.M.* 40-46; joined U.S. Army as private 42, rose to Col. Gen. Staff Corps; served in Africa, England, France, Italy, Belgium and Germany on staff of Gen. Devers, Field-Marshal Montgomery and Gen. Bradley 43-45; Pres. The R.J. Co. Inc. (newspaper investments) 49-58, Capitol City Publishing Co., Inc.; owner *Middletown* (N.Y.) *Times Herald* and *Port Jervis* (N.Y.) *Union Gazette*; Vice-Pres. and Dir. of New England Newspapers Inc. 49-58; awarded Legion of Merit, Assault Landing Arrowhead, Belgian Order of the Crown (Officer).
Publs. *In and Under Mexico* 23, *Report on England* 40, *America's Worth Fighting For* 41, *Covering all Fronts* 42, *The Battle is the Pay Off* 43, *Top Secret* 46, *The Great Ones* 48, *Wine of Violence* 51, *Point of Departure* 61.
Cornwall Bridge, Connecticut, U.S.A.

Ingersoll, Robert Stephen; American businessman; b. 28 Jan. 1914; ed. Phillips Acad. and Sheffield Scientific School, Yale Univ.
With Armco Steel Corpn. 37-39; with Ingersoll Steel & Disc Div. (later Ingersoll Products Div.), Borg-Warner Corpn., Chicago 39-41, 42-54, Pres. Ingersoll Products Div. 50-54, Admin. Vice-Pres. Borg-Warner Corpn. 53-56, Pres. 56-61, Pres. and Chief Exec. Officer 58-61, Chair. and Chief Exec. Officer 61-; Dir. Borg-Warner Ltd., Letchworth, Eng.; Dir. 1st Nat. Bank of Chicago, Container Corpn. of America, Kelsey-Hayes Co.
200 S. Michigan Avenue, Chicago, Ill. 60604, U.S.A.

Inglés, José D.; Philippine lawyer and diplomatist; b. 24 Aug. 1910; ed. Univ. of the Philippines, Santo Tomás Univ., Manila, and Columbia Univ., New York. Attorney 32-36; Legal Asst., Pres. of the Philippines 36-39; Asst. Solicitor-Gen. 40; Judge First Instance 41-43; Prof. Philippine Law School 45-46; mem.

Philippine Del. to UN 46-56, 62-65, mem. numerous UN Cttees.; Minister to German Fed. Rep. 56-58, Amb. 58-62; Amb. to Thailand 62-66; Rep. South East Asia Treaty Org. (SEATO) 62-66; mem. Standing Cttee. Asscn. of South East Asia (ASA) 63-66; Under-Sec. of Foreign Affairs 66-; Grosskreuz des Verdienstordens der Bundesrepublik Deutschland, Order of the Crown of Thailand, Most Exalted Order of the White Elephant, Gran Cruz del Order de Mayo, Grand-Croix de l'Ordre de Leopold II.
Publs. numerous papers on economics and int. affairs.
21 Vinzons Street, Heroes' Hill, Quezon City, Philippines. Telephone: 93808.

Inglin, Meinrad; Swiss writer; b. 28 July 1893; ed. Univs. of Neuchâtel, Geneva and Berne.
Awarded Schiller Prize of Swiss Schiller Foundation 48; Hon. Dr. Phil. (Zürich), Grosser Literaturpreis der Innerschweiz 53, Gottfried Keller Preis 65.
Publs. *Die Welt in Ingoldau* 22, *Jugend eines Volkes* 33, *Die graue March* 35, *Schweizerspiegel* 38, *Güldramont* 43, *Die Lawine* 47, *Werner Amberg* 49, *Ehrenhafter Untergang* 52, *Urwang* 54, *Verhexte Welt* 58, *Besuch aus dem Jenseits* 61, *Erlenbuel* 65.
6430 Schwyz, Switzerland.

Ingold, Sir Christopher Kelk, Kt., D.S.C., A.R.C.S., F.R.I.C., F.R.S.; British chemist; b. 28 Oct. 1893; ed. Univ. Coll. Southampton, and Imperial Coll. of Science and Technology, London.
Research Chemist Cassel Cyanide Co. 18-20; Lecturer in Chemistry Imperial Coll. of Science and Technology 20-24; Prof. of Organic Chemistry Univ. of Leeds 24-30; Prof. of Chemistry Univ. Coll. London Univ. 30-37; Dir. Chemical Laboratories 37-61; Baker Lecturer Cornell Univ. 50; Davy Medal of Royal Soc. 46; Longstaff Medal of Chemical Soc. 48; Royal Medal, Royal Soc. 52; Pres. Chemical Soc. 52-54; Paracelsus Medal of Swiss Chemical Soc.; Hon. Fellow Univ. Coll., London 63; Faraday Medal of Chemical Soc. 62; James Flack Norris Award of American Chemical Soc. 64; Hon. mem. New York and Corresp. mem. Spanish Royal Acad. of Sciences, Foreign Hon. mem. American Acad. of Arts and Sciences; mem. Royal Irish Acad., Acad. of Bologna, Hon. Fellow Weizmann Inst., Israel; Fellow Imperial Coll.; Hon. Ph.D. (Oslo Univ.); Hon. D.Sc. (Bologna, Paris, Montpellier, McMaster, Southampton, Leeds, Sheffield Univs. and Nat. Univ. of Ireland); Hon. Sc.D. (Oxford and Dublin).
University College, Gower Street, London, W.C.1; and 12 Handel Close, Edgware, Middlesex, England. Telephone: 01-952-3837.

Ingrand, Henry, M.D.; French doctor, civil servant and diplomatist; b. 18 Aug. 1908; ed. Univ. of Paris. Head of a Surgical Clinic, Paris until 39; active in French Resistance Movement during 39-45 war; Commr. for Auvergne Region 44; High Commr. for Tourism 46; Chair. Tourism Cttee. O.E.E.C. 49-52; Pres. Union Internationale des Organismes officiels de Tourisme 51-52; entered Ministry of Foreign Affairs 52; Del. to UNRWA Beirut 52-55; Ambassador to Colombia 55-59; Sec.-Gen. for Algerian Affairs Jan.-Dec. 59; Ambassador to Venezuela 61-63; Ministry of Foreign Affairs 63; Pres. Admin. Council of Houillères, Provence 64-; Commdr. Légion d'Honneur, Compagnon de la Libération, Croix de Guerre, Hon. C.B.E. (U.K.).
34 avenue de la Motte Picquet, Paris 7e, France.

Ingstad, Helge Marcus; Norwegian author and explorer; b. 30 Dec. 1899; ed. Universitetet i Oslo.
Practised law as barrister, Levanger, Norway 22-25; lived as trapper N.E. of Great Slave Lake, Arctic Canada 26-30; Norwegian Gov., N.E. Greenland 32-33; Norwegian Gov. of Svalbard (Spitsbergen) 33-55; studied Apache Indians, Arizona, and made expedition to Sierra Madre Mountains, Mexico, in search of some

primitive Apache Indians 36-38; studied eskimo group *Nunamiut*, Brooks Range, N. Alaska 49-50; made expedition with wife to W. Greenland to study old Norse settlements 53; made six expeditions to N. America, where at N. tip of Newfoundland (L'Anse aux Meadows) a Norse pre-Columbian site was discovered and excavated 60-66; numerous awards including Franklin L. Burr Award (Nat. Geographic Soc., Washington) 64, Fridtjof Nansen Award, Univ. of Oslo 65; Hon. D.Sc. (Saint Olaf Coll., Minnesota) 65.
Publs. *Pelsjegerliv blant Nord-Kanadas Indianere* (Land of Feast and Famine) 31, *Øst for Den Store Bre* (East of the Great Glacier) 35, *Apache—Indianerne. Jakten pa den tapte stamme* 39, *Klondyke Bill* (Klondyke Bill) 45, *Siste Båt* (play) 46, *Landet med De Kalde Kyster* 48, *Nunamiut. Blant Alaskas Innlands-eskimoer* (Nunamiut—Among Alaska's Inland Eskimoes) 51, *Landet under Leidarstjernen* (Land under the Pole Star) 59, *Vesterveg til Vinland* (Westwards to Vinland) 65 (deals with discovery and excavation of a pre-Columbian settlement in N. Newfoundland).
Vettalivei 24, Vettakollen, Oslo, Norway.

Ingvaldsen, Bernt; Norwegian electrical engineer and politician; b. 12 Oct. 1902; ed. Norges Tekniske Høgskole, Trondheim.
Manager, factories of Nat. Industry Ltd., Drammen 32-49, Man. Dir. of Nat. Industry Ltd. 49-; Vice-Chair. Conservative Party 54-62; Del. to UN Gen. Assembly 59; mem. Storting 45-, Chair. Mil. Cttee. 61-65, Pres. of Storting Oct. 65-.
Stortinget, Oslo, Norway.
Telephone: 41-38-10.

Inman, 1st Baron, cr. 46, of Knaresborough; **Philip Inman,** P.C., J.P.; British administrator; b. 12 June 1892; ed. Harrogate and Headingley Coll. and Leeds Univ.
President Charing Cross Hospital; Chair. Hotels Exec. of British Transport 48-51; Chair. of Publishing, Hotel and Commercial companies; Lord Privy Seal with seat in Cabinet April-Oct. 47; Chair. Board of Govs. of B.B.C. Dec. 46-April 47; underwriting mem. of Lloyds; Pres. St. Mary's School, Gerrard's Cross; mem. Council King Edward's Hospital Fund, and of Royal Albert Hall.
Publs. *The Human Touch, The Silent Loom, The Golden Cup, Oil and Wine, Straight Runs Harley Street, No Going Back* (autobiography).
Knaresborough House, Warninglid, Haywards Heath, Sussex, England.

Innocenti, Luigi; Italian industrialist; b. 19 Dec. 1923; ed. Massimo Coll., Rome and School of Engineering, Rome.
Manager, Innocenti 48-51, Gen. Vice-Dir. 51-58, Vice-Chair. 58-66, Chair. 66-.
Via Senato 19, Milan, Italy.

Inönü, Gen. Ismet; Turkish politician; b. 24 Sept. 1884; ed. Military and Staff Colls.
Attached 2nd Army Edirne 06; organised local patriotic society Party of Union and Progress; Gen. Staff 4th Army Edirne 08; mem. expeditionary force against insurgents, Arabia 10; Major, Chief of Gen. Staff Yemen Army 12; Dir. 1st section Gen. Staff Istanbul April 13; military adviser Turkish Del. Turko-Bulgarian peace negotiations Aug. 13; Lieut.-Col. 14; Col., Chief of Gen. Staff 2nd Army Eastern Thrace 15; Comm. 4th Army Corps, Russian front 16, 20th Army Corps 17, 3rd Army Corps Syria 17; Under-Sec. for War 18; joined Mustafa Kemal 20; Deputy for Edirne Nat. Assembly, Min. and Chief of Gen. Staff 20; comm. Western Front and victor Battles of Inönü 21; promoted Brig.-Gen. 21, Lieut.-Gen. 22, Gen. 26-27, retd.; Min. of Foreign Affairs 22; signed Treaty of Lausanne 23; fmr. Vice-Pres. Republican People's Party, Leader 38-; Prime Min. 23-24 and 25-37; Pres. of Turkish Republic 38-50; Dep. for Malatya 50-60, 61-, and Leader of the Opposition 50-60, 65-; Prime Minister 61-65.
Office of the Republican People's Party, Ankara, Turkey.

Inoue, Toshio; Japanese banker and business executive; b. 10 Jan. 1902; ed. Univ. of Tokyo.
Bank of Japan 24-59, Vice-Gov. 54-59; Chair. Council of Securities Transactions, Ministry of Finance 59-61; Pres. Tokyo Stock Exchange 61-67; Adviser, Japan Securities Finance Co. Ltd. 61-, Tokyo Securities Dealers' Asscn. 62-; Dir. Shinetsu Chemical Industry Co. Ltd. 60.
5-25-7, Koengi-minami, Suginami-ku, Tokyo, Japan, Telephone: (Tokyo) 312-3458.

Inoue, Yuichi; Japanese artist; b. 16.
Co-founder "Bokujin-kai" group of calligraphers 52-; rep. travelling exhibition of Japanese Calligraphy, Europe 55, São Paulo Bienal 57, Brussels Int. Exhibition 58, Kassel Int. Exhibition 59, Pittsburgh Int. Exhibition 61, São Paulo Bienal 61.
3003 Hishinuma, Chigasaki, Kanagawa-ken, Japan.

Inouye, Daniel Ken; American lawyer and politician; b. 7 Sept. 1924; ed. Univ. of Hawaii and George Washington Univ. Law School.
U.S. Army 43-47; Majority Leader, Territorial House of Reps. 54-58, mem. Territorial Senate 58-59; mem. U.S. Congress 59-62; U.S. Senator from Hawaii 63-; Democrat.
U.S. Senate, Washington, D.C.; and The Ilikai, 1777 Ala Moana Boulevard, Honolulu, Hawaii, U.S.A.

Inozemtsev, Anatoly Fyodorovich; Soviet foreign trade official; b. 1912; ed. Inst. of Foreign Trade.
Member C.P.S.U. 31-; Official, Ministry of Foreign Trade 37-42, Deputy Chief of Section 44-46; Soviet Army 42-44; Deputy U.S.S.R. Commercial Rep., Hungary 46-47; Deputy Chair. *Raznoexport* Trust 47-51; U.S.S.R. Commercial Rep., Romania 51-55; Deputy Chief of Dept., Ministry of Foreign Trade 55-63; U.S.S.R. Commercial Rep., Bulgaria 66-; Order of Red Banner of Labour, Order of Red Star, Honour Badge.
U.S.S.R. Trade Representation, Sofia, Bulgaria.

Insiseinmay, Thao Leuam; Laotian politician; b. 17. War Service in Indochina; mem. Govt. 48-; Deputy of Nat. Ass. 50-; Minister of Nat. Educ., Fine Arts, Sport and Youth 62-; Vice-Pres. of the Council 65-; Officier Légion d'Honneur, and Grand Croix, Million d'Eléphants et du Parasol Blanc.
Ministry of National Education, Vientiane, Laos.

Ioana; Rumanian painter; b. 29; ed. School of Fine Arts, Bucharest, and Paris.
Travelled in France, Latin America and Far East 48-52; exhibited: Rome, Venice, Florence, Caracas, Paris, Munich, Luxembourg, Duisburg 59; Florence, Paris, Liège, Brussels, Milan and Florence 60; Brasilia Bienal, Copenhagen 61; Morbihan, Biarritz, Palette du Nord de la France, Arras, Paris 62, Madrid, London, Paris 64.
Via della Croce 67, Rome, Italy.

Ioannisiani, Bagrat Konstantinovich; Soviet designer; b. 21.
Chief designer of the Vavilov State Inst. of Optics; awarded Lenin Prize for designing new astronomical instruments 57.
Principal works: ASI-4 astro-photo-camera, meniscus telescope with 70 cm. aperture and 98 cm. mirror (Abastumani Observatory, Georgia), 50-metre nebular spectrograph (Crimean Observatory).
State Institute of Optics, Leningrad, U.S.S.R.

Iofan, Boris Mikhailovich; Soviet architect; b. 91; ed. Odessa School of Art, Architectural Dept. of the Rome Higher Inst. of Fine Arts.

State prize winner 39, 41; awarded Order of Red Star, Order of the Red Banner of Labour (twice); mem. C.P.S.U. 26-.
Designs include: first draft of the Palace of Soviets in Moscow; the U.S.S.R. Pavilions at the World Fairs in Paris 37, New York 39, the Baumann underground station in Moscow, design of reconstruction of city of Novorossiysk; regional plan and supervision of re-development of Pervomaysky Borough, Moscow, also Sverdlovsky Borough, Moscow; design and construction of Inst. of Physical Culture, Moscow; Oil Scientific Research Inst., Lenin Ave., Moscow; sixteen-storey blocks of flats, Moscow; experimental block of flats with extensive use of plastics.
U.S.S.R. Academy of Building and Architecture, 24 Pushkinskaya Street, Moscow, U.S.S.R.

Ioganson, Boris Vladimirovich; Soviet artist; b. 13 July 1893; ed. Moscow School of Art and Architecture. President U.S.S.R. Acad. of Arts 58-62; Dir. Tretyakovskaya Gallery 51-54; First Sec. of Board, Union of Soviet Artists 65-; Deputy of Supreme Soviet of the U.S.S.R.; Hon. mem. German Acad. of Arts; People's Artist of U.S.S.R.; Gold Medal, Brussels World Fair 58; State Prize winner; two orders of Lenin.
Principal works: *Studens* 28, *Interrogation of Communists* 33, a diorama *The Canal* 35-37, *At an Old Urals Factory* 37, *Lenin Speaking at the Komsomol Third Congress* 50.
Union of Soviet Artists, 25/9 Gorky Street, Moscow, U.S.S.R.

Ionesco, Eugène; Romanian-born French playwright; b. 13 Nov. 1912; ed. Bucharest and Paris.
Lecturer and critic in Bucharest before finally settling in Paris 38; Chevalier Légion d'Honneur.
Publs. Plays: *The Bald Prima Donna* (first produced Paris 50, London 57), *Jacques, The Lesson* (Paris 51, London 55, New York 58), *The Chairs* (Paris 52, London 57, New York 58), *Amedée* (Paris 54, London 57), *Victims of Duty* (Cambridge 57), *The New Tenant* (London 56, Paris 57), *Le Rhinocéros* (Düsseldorf 59, Paris 60, London 60), *The Killer, L'Impromptu de l'Alimat, The Picture, Le Piéton de l'air* (Paris 62), *Chemises de Nuit* 62, *Le roi se meurt* 63, *La Soif et la Faim* 64, *Peste* 67; radio play: *Le Salon de l'Automobile;* short stories: *Oriflamme* (adapted as the play *Amedée*), *La Photo du Colonel* 62 (adapted as the play *The Killer*); ballet: *Jeune Homme à Marier* (with Flemming Flindt) 65; Essays: *Notes et contre notes, Entretiens avec Claude Bonnefoy; Journal en miettes* (autobiog. journal) 67.
c/o Editions Gallimard, 5 rue Sebastien-Bottin, Paris 7e, France.

Iordan, Iorgu, D. ès L.; Romanian romance philologist; b. 29 Sept. 1888; ed. Liceul Internat, Jassy, and Jassy, Bonn, Berlin and Paris Univs.
Secondary school teacher 11; Prof. Jassy Univ. 26-46, Dean, Faculty of Literature 38-39; Prof. Bucharest Univ. 46-, Dean, Faculty of Philology 47-50, 56-57, Rector 57-58; Dir. Jassy Nat. Theatre 28-30; Pres. Rumanian Antifascist Asscn. 34; Ambassador to U.S.S.R. 45-47; Pres. UNESCO Nat. Comm. 56-57, Vice-Pres. 58-66; Titular mem., Vice-Pres., Pres. Philological Sciences Section, Dir. Linguistic Inst., Acad. of Romanian Socialist Repub.; Corresp. mem. Saxon Acad. of Sciences, Leipzig, German Acad. of Sciences, Berlin, Austrian Acad. of Sciences, Vienna, Bavarian Acad. of Sciences, Munich; founding mem. Soc. de Linguistique Romane, Paris; mem. Soc. de Linguistique, Paris, Int. Cttee. for Onomastic Sciences (CISO), Junta Directiva Asoc. Int. de Hispanistas, Counsellor Board Soc. Linguistic Romane, Comité Int. des Linguistes (CIPL); European Cultural Soc., Venice; State Prize, First and Second Class; Order of Labour, First Class; Star of the Romanian People's Repub., First Class; Romanian Order 23 August; Dr. h.c. Humboldt Univ., Berlin,

Univs. Montpellier, Jassy, Ghent (Belgium); mem. Romanian Workers' Party 44-.
Publs. *Diftongarea lui "e" si "o" accentuaţi în poziţiile "ă", "e"* 21, *Rumänische Toponomastik* 24-26, *Introducere în studiul limbilor romanice* 32 (English trans. 37), *Gramatica limbii române* 37 (2nd ed. 46, Russian trans. 50), *Limba română actuală. O gramatică a "greşelilor"* 43 (2nd ed. 48), *Stilistica limbii române* 44, *Nume de locuri romanesti în Republica Populară Romănă* (Vol. I) 52, *Limba română contemporană* 54 (2nd ed. 56), *Cronica lui Neculce* (edition of an XVIII-century chronicle, with introductory study and glossary) 55 (2nd edn. 59), *Lingvistica romănică, Evoluţie. Curente. Metode* 62, *Toponimia romănească* 63, *Istoria limbii spaniole* 63.
Str. Sofia 21, Bucharest, Romania.
Telephone: 33-18-86.

Iordanoglou, Hippocrates; Greek politician; ed. Univ. of Athens.
Practised law 32-67; Sec.-Gen. Union of Salonica lawyers 52-55; Deputy 61, and in Salonica for Nat. Radical Union 63, 64-; Minister for Commerce 67.
c/o Ministry of Commerce, Athens, Greece.

Iran, Shah of (*see* Pahlavi, Mohammad Reza).

Ireland, Charles T., Jr.; American lawyer and business executive; b. 14 April 1921; ed. Bowdoin Coll. and Yale Law School.
Associate White and Case 48-51; Sec. and Counsel Alleghany Corpn. 51-54; Sec. New York Central Rail Road Co. 54-59; Exec. Vice-Pres. Alleghany Corpn. 59-61, Pres. 61, 63-68; Vice-Pres., Exec. Asst. to Chair. and Pres. Int. Telephone & Telegraph Corpn. 68-; Consultant to Allan P. Kirby 61-63; Chair. Exec. Cttee. Investors Diversified Services Inc. 65-; Dir. Int. Telephone & Telegraph Co. (ITT), Calif. Western States Life Insurance Co.; Overseer, Bowdoin Coll.
55 Deepwood Drive, Chappagua, New York, N.Y., U.S.A.

Iribarrén Borges, Ignacio; Venezuelan lawyer and diplomatist; b. 12; ed. Don Bosco Coll., Valencia and Central Univ., Caracas.
District Attorney, Valencia 36; Judge, Primary Court of Claims, Valencia 36-39; Prof. of Roman Law, Miguel José Sanz School of Law, Valencia 38-39; Asst. Prof. of Civil Law, Cen. Univ., Caracas 40-44; Counsellor Cen. Univ. City Inst. 45-47; mem. Univ. Council 46-47; later Pres. Nat. Hotel Corpn. (Compañía Conahotu Ltda.); Sec. Governing Junta (under Presidency of Dr. Edgard Sanabria) 58-59; Ambassador to Great Britain 59-64; Minister of Foreign Affairs 64-67; Grand Cordon, Order of the Liberator.
Cerro Quintero, Urbanización Las Mercedes, Caracas, Venezuela.

Irmler, Heinrich, D.IUR; German banker; b. 27 Aug. 1911; ed. Realgymnasium, Leipzig, Allgemeine Deutsche Creditanstalt, Leipzig, and Univ. of Leipzig.
Deutsche Reichsbank 37-48; Army Service 39-45; Bank Deutscher Länder, Frankfurt 48-53; mem. Board of Managers and Vice-Pres. Landeszentralbank von Niedersachsen (Lower Saxony), Hanover 53-57; Vice-Pres. Landeszentralbank in Nordrhein-Westfalen (North Rhine-Westphalia), Düsseldorf 58-62; Pres. Landeszentralbank in Niedersachsen, Hanover 62-64; mem. Board of Dirs. Deutsche Bundesbank, Frankfurt 64-.
Frankfurt am Main, Taunusanlage 4-6, German Federal Republic.
Telephone: 268360.

Irvine, Sir Arthur James, Kt., Q.C., M.P.; British Solicitor-General; b. 14 July 1909; ed. Edinburgh Acad., Edinburgh Univ. and Oriel Coll., Oxford.
President Oxford Union 32; called to Bar 35; Sec. to Lord Chief Justice of England 35-40; Army Service

40-45; M.P. for Edgehill (Liverpool) 47-; Recorder of Colchester 65-67; Solicitor-Gen. 67-; Labour.
4 Paper Buildings, Temple, London, E.C.4; 20 Wellington Square, Chelsea, London, S.W.3, England.
Telephone: 01-236-8408; 01-730-3117.

Irving, K. C.; Canadian oil executive; b. 14 March 1899; ed. Dalhousie Univ. and Acadia Univ.
President Irving Oil Co. Ltd. 29-; Pres. Irving Pulp & Paper Ltd., K. C. Irving Ltd., Chair. Irving Refining Ltd.
Irving Oil Co., Golden Bell Building, St. John, New Brunswick, Canada.

Irwin, Raymond, M.A., F.L.A.; British librarian and professor; b. 14 March 1902; ed. King's Coll., Taunton and Oxford Univ.
County Librarian, Northants. 24-34; County Librarian, Lancashire 34-44; Hon. Treas., Library Asscn. 47-54, Vice-Pres. 54-58, Pres. 58-, Hon. Fellow 63; Prof. Library Studies London Univ. 57-; Dir. School of Librarianship and Archives, Univ. Coll., London 44-.
Publs. *The National Library Service* 47, *Librarianship: Essays on Applied Bibliography* 49, *British Bird Books: An Index to British Ornithology* 51, *British Birds and their Books: Catalogue of the Exhibition for the National Book League* 52, *The Origins of the English Library* 58, *The Heritage of the English Library* 64, *The English Library: Sources and History* 66.
University College London, Gower Street, London, W.C.1; Home: 13 Furzefield Crescent, Reigate, Surrey, England.
Telephone: Reigate 42508.

Irwin, William Arthur, B.A.; Canadian journalist and diplomatist; b. 98; ed. Univs. of Manitoba and Toronto.
Sometime Rodman Canadian Northern Railway Construction; later Reporter, *Toronto Mail and Empire*, and subsequently Reporter, Corresp. (Parl. Press Gallery, Ottawa) and Editorial Writer *Toronto Globe*; Assoc. Editor *Maclean's Magazine* 25-42, Man. Editor 43-45, Editor 45-50; served in France during First World War; Chair. Nat. Film Board 50-53; High Commr. in Australia 53-56; Ambassador to Brazil 57-59, to Mexico 60-64; Publisher *Victoria Daily Times*; Vice-Pres. Victoria Press Ltd. 64-.
Publs. *The Wheat Pool* 29, *Motor Vehicle Transportation Briefs* (Royal Comm. on Railways and Transportation 32, Royal Comm. on Transportation in Ontario 37), *The Machine* 38.
3260 Exeter Road, Victoria, British Columbia, Canada.

Iryani, Sheikh Qadi Abdul Rahman; Yemeni religious and political leader.
Took part in abortive revolution 48; imprisoned 48-54; took part in uprising 55; mem. Revolutionary Council 62-; Minister of Justice 62-63; Vice-Pres. Exec. Council 63-64; mem. Political Bureau Jan. 64-; Chair. Peace Cttee. set up after Khamer Peace Talks May 65; Head of State of Yemen Nov. 67-; leader of Zaidi (Shia) sect.
Office of Chief of State, Sana'a, Yemen.

Isaacs, Jacob, M.A.; British literary historian; b. 96; ed. Exeter Coll. Oxford.
Asst. Lecturer Univ. Coll. of N. Wales 21-24 and King's Coll. London 24-28; Lecturer Sorbonne, British Inst. Paris, Workers' Education Asscn. and Univ. Extension; Lecturer in English Language and Literature, King's Coll. London 28-42; Prof. of English Language and Literature, Univ. of Jerusalem 42-45; Prof. of English Language and Literature, Queen Mary Coll. London 52-; Gen. Ed. English Library Reprints; Joint-Editor *Contemporary Movements in European Literature*.
Publs. *Shakespeare as Man of the Theatre* 27, *Production and Stage Management at the Blackfriars Theatre* 33, *Shakespeare Scholarship* and *Later Shakespeare Criticism* (in *Companion to Shakespeare Studies*) 33, *Dramatic Criticism* (in *Encyclopædia Britannica*); edited *Chester*

Play of the Deluge 24, Milton's *Paradise Lost* 37, *An Assessment of Twentieth Century Literature* 51, *The Background of Modern Poetry* 51, *Shakespeare's Earliest Years in the Theatre* 53, *William Poel's Prompt Book of "Fratricide Punished"* 56.
Little Court, Court Yard, Eltham, London, S.E.9, England.

Isaacson, Sir Robert Spencer, K.B.E., C.M.G.; British diplomatist; b. 11 Nov. 1907; ed. Radley Coll.
Kuala Muda Rubber Estates, Malaya 26-32; Welbecson Press, London 32-39; British Embassy, Rio de Janeiro 40-47, British Legation, Bucharest 48, British Embassy, Athens 48-52, Washington 52-55, Paris 55-59, Rio de Janeiro 59-63; Ambassador to Guatemala 63-64, to Switzerland 64-67.
c/o Foreign Office, London, S.W.1, England.

Isaev, Vasily Yakovlevich; Soviet engineer and politician; b. 17; ed. Leningrad Engineering-Construction Inst.
Administrative work in construction orgs. 37-55; mem. C.P.S.U. 39-; Chief Board of Housing, Civil and Industrial Construction in Leningrad 55-61; Deputy Chair., then Chair. Exec. Cttee. Leningrad City Council of Working People's Deputies (Mayor of Leningrad) 62-64; Deputy of Supreme Soviet U.S.S.R.; Deputy Chair. of Gosplan U.S.S.R. 65-; Alt. mem. Central Cttee. C.P.S.U.
U.S.S.R. Gosplan, Moscow, U.S.S.R.

Isakovsky, Mikhail Vasilyevich; Soviet poet; b. 1900; ed. high school.
Editor of a provincial newspaper 21-31; then worked on other papers -66; has written words for popular songs: including *Katyusha* (Soviet army marching song in Second World War); mem. Supreme Soviet, R.S.F.S.R.; mem. C.P.S.U. 18-; State Prizes 43, 49; Order of Lenin (twice); Order of Red Banner of Labour (twice).
Publs. *Wires in Straw* 27, *The Province* 30, *Four Wishes* 36, Book of songs and poems 49, *The Lay of Russia* (verse) 58, *The Poet's Skill* (criticism) 60, *Collections* (2 vols.) 62, *You Are Walking Along the Country* 64.
Writers' Union, 52 Vozovsky Street, Moscow, U.S.S.R.

Isano, Masashi; Japanese business executive; b. 15 Sept. 1899; ed. Kyoto Univ.
President Kawasaki Dockyard 64-; Dir. Kawasaki Aircraft Ltd.; Governing Dir. Japan Fed. of Employers' Asscns.
2-14 Higashikawasaki-cho, Ikuta-ku, Kobe, Japan.

Isard, Walter, A.B., M.A., PH.D.; American regional scientist; b. 19 April 1919; ed. Temple, Harvard and Chicago Univs.
Instructor Wesleyan Univ. 45, Mass. Inst. of Technology 47; Visiting Lecturer Tufts Coll. 47; Assoc. Prof. of Economics, Assoc. Dir. of Teaching, Inst. of Econs., American Univ. 48-49; Research Fellow and Lecturer, Harvard Univ. 49-53; Assoc. Prof. of Regional Economics, Dir. Urban and Regional Studies, Mass. Inst. of Technology 53-56; Prof. of Economics, Chair. Dept. of Regional Science, Univ. of Pa. 56-; Visiting Prof. of Regional Science, Yale Univ. 60-61; Consultant, Tenn. Valley Authority 51-52, Resources for the Future Inc. 54-58, Ford Foundation 55-56, O.E.E.C. Economic Productivity Agency (and Chair. Conf. on Regional Economics and Planning, Bellagio, Italy) 60; Pres. Regional Science Asscn. 59, Hon. Chair. 60-; Exec. Sec. Peace Research Soc. (Int.) 65-; Ford Foundation Fellow (Econs. and Business Admin.) 59-60; Consultant, Nat. Science Foundation 60-61.
Publs. *Atomic Power: An Economic and Social Analysis* 52 (Japanese edn. 54), *Location Factors in the Petrochemical Industry* 55, *Location and Space Economy* 56, *Municipal Costs and Revenues resulting from Community Growth* 57, *Industrial Complex Analysis and Regional Development* 59, *Methods of Regional Analysis* 60, *Regional Economic Development* 61.
3218 Garrett Road, Drexel Hill, Pa., U.S.A.

Isaza Calderón, Baltasar, D.PHIL., D.LITT.; Panamanian professor; b. 04; ed. National Inst., Panama, Pedagogical Inst., Santiago de Chile, Central Univ. of Madrid.
Secretary, Gen. Inspectorate of Primary Educ. 26-27; Prof., Nat. Inst. of Panama 34-39, Univ. of Panama 37-62; Dean, Faculty of Philosophy, Letters and Educ. Univ. of Panama 43-48; Dir. Panamanian Acad. 60-.
Publs. *El Retorno a la Naturaleza* 34, *Estudios Literarios* 57, *Estampas de Viaje* 59, *La Doctrina Gramatical de Bello* 60.
Apartado Postal 7286, Panama City, Panama.

Isenov, Mukhambet Aituyevich; Soviet politician; b. 1909; ed. Moscow Gubkin Oil Inst.
Member C.P.S.U. 37-; employed in the oil industry of Kazakhstan 37-41; Soviet Army 41-43; at U.S.S.R. Ministry of Oil Industry 44-47; Party and trade union official, Kazakhstan 47-64; First Sec. Guryev Regional Cttee., C.P. of Kazkhstan 64-; mem. Central Cttee., C.P. of Kazakhstan; Deputy to U.S.S.R. Supreme Soviet.
Guryev Regional Committee, Communist Party of Kazakhstan, Guryev, U.S.S.R.

Isherwood, Christopher; American (b. British) writer; b. 26 Aug. 1904; ed. Repton School, Corpus Christi Coll., Cambridge and King's Coll., London (Medical School).
Publs. Novels: *All the Conspirators* 28, *The Memorial* 32, *Mr. Norris Changes Trains* 35, *Good-bye to Berlin* 39, *Prater Violet* 45, *The World in the Evening* 54, *Down There on a Visit* 62, *A Single Man* 64, *Lions and Shadows* autobiography 38; plays (with W. H. Auden): *The Dog Beneath the Skin* 35, *Ascent of F.6* 36, *On the Frontier* 38; travel: *Journey to a War* (with W. H. Auden) 39, *The Condor and the Cows* 49; translations: *The Bhagavad-Gita* (with Swami Prabhavananda) 45, Shankara's *Crest-Jewel of Discrimination* (with Swami Prabhavananda) 47, Baudelaire's *Intimate Journals* 47, *The Yoga Aphorisms of Patanjali* (with Swami Prabhavanada) 53, *Ramakrishna and His Disciples* (biography) 65, *Ex-humations* (stories, articles, verses) 66, *A meeting by the river* (novel) 67.
145 Adelaide Drive, Santa Monica, California, U.S.A.

Ishibashi, Shojiro; Japanese company director; b. 25 Feb. 1889; ed. Kurume Commercial School.
Pres. Bridgestone Tyre Co. Ltd. 31, Chair. 63; Chair. Prince Motors Ltd. 51; Pres. Japan Synthetic Rubber Co. Ltd 57, Chair 65; Exec. Dir. Nat. Fed. of Econ. Orgs. 49, Japan Fed. of Employers' Associations 52; Dir. Kurume Univ. 51; Pres. Bridgestone Gallery 52; Councillor, Nat. Museum of Modern Art 52, Society for International Cultural Relations 57, Nat. Museum of Occidental Art 59, Nat. Museum of Tokyo 59; Chair. Ishibashi Foundation 56; Dark Blue Ribbon Medal 37, 39, 57, 59, Green Ribbon Medal 40, Blue Ribbon Medal 58; Hon. Citizen Kurume City 56; Légion d'Honneur 60; Grand Officer of Order of Merit of the Italian Republic 61; Second Order of Sacred Treasure 64; and other honours.
No. 1 Azabu-Nagasaka-cho, Minato-ku, Tokyo, Japan.

Ishibashi, Tanzan; Japanese editor and politician; b. 84; ed. Waseda Univ.
Joined *Tokyo Mainichi Shimbun* newspaper 08; joined *Oriental Economist* 11, Pres. 39; Adviser, Japan Liberal Party 45; Minister of Finance in first Yoshida Cabinet 46; concurrently Dir.-Gen. Economic Stabilisation Board and Dir.-Gen. of Price Board 47; elected to House of Reps. 47; removed from public office May 47 until June 51; elected to House of Reps. 52; Rector Rissho Univ. 52-; Chair. Party Policy Council, Liberal Party 53-; Minister for Int. Trade and Industry 54-56; Prime Minister 56-57; Pres. Liberal-Democratic Party 56-57.
Publs. *Advocating a New Agricultural Policy* 27, *Effects of Lifting of Gold Embargo and Counter Measures* 29, *Theory and Practice of Inflation* 32, *Japan's Recent Economy and Finances* 34, *Japan's Monetary History* 36, *Japanese Economy in Drastic Transition* 37, *Impressions of Manchurian Life and Korean Industries* 41, *Life and Economy* 42, *My Recollections* 51, *Ishibashi Finances* 52, *Directing the Course of Japanese Economy* 59.
1712 Yonchome, Shimo-Ochiai, Shinjuku-ku, Tokyo, Japan.

Ishida, Hirohide; Japanese politician; b. 14; ed. Waseda Univ.
Chugai Shogga Shimpo; Kitashika Civil Engineering Asscn.; House of Reps. 38-; Dir. of Cabinet Secretariat 56-57; Minister of Labour 57-58, 60-61, 64-65; Liberal Democrat.
Publs. *Wasurerareta Kodomotachi* (Forgotten Children), *Ijoji-To Sono Sakuhin* (Abnormal Children and Their Works).
c/o Ministry of Labour, Tokyo, Japan.

Ishida, Kazuto, LL.B.; Japanese judge; b. 03; ed. Tokyo Imperial Univ.
Judge, Tokyo District Court 28-41, Presiding Judge 41-47, Chief Judge 56; Dir., Personnel Affairs Bureau, Gen. Sec. Supreme Court 47-50; Dep. Sec.-Gen., Supreme Court 50-56, Sec.-Gen. 60; Pres. Tokyo High Court 62; Assoc. Justice, Supreme Court 63; Vice-Pres. Int. Legal Soc. in Japan 60-62; Dir. Japan Bar Asscn. 59-.
1644 2-chome, Oohara-Machi, Meguro-ku, Tokyo, Japan.

Ishida, Reisuke; Japanese businessman and state transport official; b. 20 Feb. 1886; ed. Tokyo Coll. of Commerce.
Representative, Seattle Branch, Mitsui & Co. Ltd. 16-21, Manager Bombay, Calcutta, Dairen and New York Branches 21-33, Dir. 33-36, Exec. Manager Dir. 36-39, Rep. Exec. Dir. 39-41; Pres. Trade Corpn. 43-46; Chair. and mem. Inquiry and Audit Cttee., Japanese Nat. Railways 56-62; Pres. Japanese Nat. Railways 63-; mem. Metropolitan Transport Council, Japan Electric Power Survey Cttee., Railway Construction Council and Civil Aeronautics Council; Counsellor, Japan Productivity Centre and Japan Atomic Industrial Forum.
2064 Kozu, Odawara City, Kanagawa Prefecture, Japan.

Ishida, Taizo; Japanese automobile executive; b. 16 Nov. 1888; ed. Shiga Prefectural Daiichi Junior High School.
President, Toyoda Automatic Loom Works Ltd. 48-; Pres. Toyota Motor Co. Ltd. 50-61; Dir. Toyota Motor Sales U.S.A., Inc. 57-61; Chair. Board Toyota Motor Co. Ltd. 61-; Pres. Textile Machinery Manufacturers Asscn.; Blue Ribbon Medal 57, 58.
6-78 Hachiman-cho, Kariya-shi, Aichi, Japan.

Ishii, Mitsujiro, B.A.; Japanese politician; b. 89; ed. Kobe Higher Commercial School and Tokyo Higher Commercial School.
Entered Higher Civil Service 13; Sec. to Gov.-Gen. of Formosa, concurrently Councillor of Govt.-Gen. of Formosa 15; Dir. *Asahi* (Newspaper Publishing Co.) 25, Man. Dir. 40-45; Pres. Asahi Movie Manufacturing Co. 37-41; joined Japan Liberal Party 46; elected to House of Reps. 46; Minister of Commerce and Industry, Yoshida Cabinet 47; Pres. Asahi Broadcasting Co. 51-52; Dir. Nishi Nippon Railroad Co. Ltd. 51-; Minister of Transportation Nov. 52-54; Chief Sec. of Liberal Party 54-55, Chair. Exec. Board of Liberal Democratic Party 55-56, 60-; Dep. Prime Minister 57-58; Minister of Trade and Industry 60, of Justice 65-66.
c/o Ministry of Justice, Tokyo, Japan.

Ishikawa, Shigeru, D.ECON.; Japanese economist; b. 7 April 1918; ed. Tokyo Univ. of Commerce (now Hitotsubashi Univ.).
Attached to Jiji News Agency 45-56, Hong Kong

Corresp. 51-53; Asst. Prof., Inst. of Econ. Research, Hitotsubashi Univ. 56-63, Prof. 63-.
Publs. *National Income and Capital Formation in Mainland China* 65, *Economic Development in Asian Perspective* 67.
149, 3 chome Kugayama, Suginami-ku, Tokyo, Japan. Telephone: 391-8376.

Ishizaka, Taizo, LL.B.; Japanese businessman; b. 3 June 1886; ed. Tokyo Imperial Univ.
Director and Man. Daiichi Life Insurance Co. 21-34, Man. Dir. 34-38, Pres. 38-46, Counsellor 52-; Dir. Tokyo Shibaura Electric Co., Ltd. 40-49, Pres. 49-57, Chair. 57-65, Counsellor 65-; Counsellor, Japan Devt. Bank 51-, Japan Airlines 53-, Bank of Japan 56-, Mitsui Bank 59-, Tokyo Express Railway Co. 59-, Chamber of Commerce and Industry of Japan 56-; Pres. Fed. of Econ. Orgs. 56-; Chair. Arabian Oil Co. Ltd. (Japan) 58-, Nippon Atomic Industry Group Co. Ltd. 58-, Japanese Business and Industry Advisory Cttee. to OECD, Ministry of Finance, Insurance and Nat. Property, Central Councils; Dir. Tokyo Electric Power Co. Ltd. 56-, Japan Atomic Power Generation Co. Ltd. 57-; Chair. Int. Asscn. for Protection of Industrial Property; Pres. Japan Asscn. for 1970 World Exposition 65-; mem. Int. Advisory Cttee., Chase Manhattan Bank 67-; Hon. LL.D. (Loyola Univ. and Univ. of Hawaii); many national and foreign decorations, including Hon. K.B.E. (U.K.).
Tokyo Shibaura Electric Company Limited, 1, 1-chome, Uchisaiwaicho, Chiyoda-ku, Tokyo, Japan.

Ishkov, Alexander Akimovich; Soviet government official; b. 29 Aug. 1905; ed. State Pedagogical Inst., Rostov-on-Don.
Fish industry 30-; People's Commissar for fishing industry 40-46; U.S.S.R. Minister of Fish Industry 48-50, 54-57; Head, Fish Industry Dept., U.S.S.R. State Planning Cttee. (Gosplan) 57-60, Chief, Main Admin. of Fishing Economy (Gosplan) 60-62; Chair. State Cttee. on the Fishing Econ. 62-65; Minister of Fisheries 65-; Alt. mem. Central Cttee. of C.P.S.U., mem. C.P.S.U. 27-; Deputy to U.S.S.R. Soviet; Order of Lenin (thrice), Order of Red Banner, Order of Red Banner of Labour.
U.S.S.R. Ministry of Fisheries, 12 Rozhdestvensky Boulevard, Moscow K-45, U.S.S.R.

Ishlinsky, Aleksandr Yulevich; Soviet applied mathematician; b. 6 Aug. 1913; ed. Moscow Univ.
Professor, Moscow Univ. 35-48; mem. Ukrainian Acad. of Sciences 48-; Dir. Inst. of Mathematics, Ukrainian Acad. of Sciences 48-55; Prof. Kiev Univ. 49-55; Prof. and Head of Dept., Moscow Univ. 55-66; Dir. Inst. of Problems of Mechanics U.S.S.R. Acad. of Sciences 64-; mem. U.S.S.R. Acad. of Sciences 60-; Deputy Chair. U.S.S.R. Nat. Comm. of Mechanics, Regional mem. Int. Fed. Scientific Workers. Hero of Socialist Labour, Order of Lenin (twice), Order of the Red Banner of Labour, Order of Honor, Lenin Prize.
Publs. *The Dynamics of Ground Masses* 54, *The Theory of the Horizon Compass* 56, *On the Equation Problems determining the Position of Moving Objects by using a Gyroscope and measuring Acceleration* 57, *The Mechanics of Gyroscopic Systems* 63.
Institute of Problems of Mechanics, U.S.S.R. Academy of Sciences, Leningrad Prospekt 7, Moscow A-40, U.S.S.R.

Işik, Hasan Esat; Turkish diplomatist and politician; b. 21 Oct. 1916; ed. Ankara Univ.
Ministry of Foreign Affairs 40-; Consulate-Gen., Paris 45-49; Head of Section, Dept. of Commerce and Econ. Affairs, and Dept. of Int. Econ. Relations 49-52; staff of Perm. Turkish Del. to European Office of UN, Geneva 52-54; Dir.-Gen. of Dept. of Commerce and

Commercial Agreements, Ministry of Foreign Affairs 54-57; Asst. of Econ. Affairs to Sec.-Gen. of Ministry of Foreign Affairs 57-62; Ambassador to Belgium 62-64, to U.S.S.R. 64-65, 66-; Minister of Foreign Affairs 65.
Embassy of Turkey, Moscow, U.S.S.R.

Iskenderov, Mamed Abdul ogly; Soviet engineer and politician; b. 1915; ed. Azerbaijan Industrial Inst.
Secondary school teacher at Khanlyg; served with Red Army Engineering Corps during Second World War; worked in oil industry after the war; Sec. Cen. Cttee. Communist Party of Azerbaijan 53-59; Chair. Council of Ministers Azerbaijan S.S.R. 59-62; Chair. of Presidium of Supreme Soviet of Azerbaijan S.S.R. 62-; Dep. Chair. Presidium of Supreme Soviet of U.S.S.R. 62-; mem. Central Auditing Comm. C.P.S.U. 66-.
Presidium of Supreme Soviet of Azerbaijan S.S.R., Baku, Azerbaijan S.S.R., U.S.S.R.

Iskhakov, Bakhtzhan Iskhakovich; Soviet politician; b. 1918; ed. Moscow Inst. of Municipal Construction Engineers.
Engineer, Alma Ata City Soviet 41-42; with Council of People's Commissars of Kazakh S.S.R. 42-44; mem. C.P.S.U. 43-; Consultant at U.S.S.R. Council of Ministers 44-45; Senior Consultant for Perm. Representation of Kazakh S.S.R. to U.S.S.R. Council of Ministers 45-49, 51-53, 56-61; Deputy Dir. of Kazakhstan Pavilion at Exhbn. of Nat. Econ. Achievements 49-51; with Moscow Metro contruction org. 53-56; Deputy Perm. Rep. of Kazakh S.S.R. Council of Ministers to U.S.S.R. Council of Ministers 61-63, Perm. Rep. 63-.
Permanent Representation of Kazakh S.S.R. Council of Ministers to U.S.S.R. Council of Ministers, Chistoprudny Boulevard 3A, Moscow, U.S.S.R.

Isles, Keith Sydney, C.M.G., B.COM., M.A., M.SC.; Australian economist; b. 4 Aug. 1902; ed. Univs. of Tasmania and Cambridge.
Lecturer in Political Economy, Univ. of Edinburgh 31-37; Prof. of Economics, Univ. Coll., Swansea 37-39; Prof. of Economics, Univ. of Adelaide 39-45; Prof. of Economics, Queen's Univ., Belfast 45-57, and Dean Faculty of Economics 45-53; Vice-Chancellor, Univ. of Tasmania 57-67; Economic Adviser to Rationing Comm. 42; Army service 44-45; Joint Local Sec. of British Asscn. for the Advancement of Science 52; Hon. LL.D. (St. Andrews), Hon. D.Litt. (Tasmania).
Publs. *Wages Policy and the Price Level* 34, *Money and Trade* 35, *Compulsory Saving* (with B. R. Williams) 42, chapters in *Ulster under Home Rule* (ed. Wilson) 55, *An Economic Survey of Northern Ireland* (with Norman Cuthbert) 57.
91 Esplanade, Lindisfarne, Hobart, Tasmania 7015. Telephone: 438580.

Isliukov, Semyon Matveyevich; Soviet politician; b. 1915; ed. Kazan Juridical Inst., Higher Party School.
Member C.P.S.U. 39-; party work 41-47; Sec. Chuvask Regional Cttee. C.P.S.U. 47, 50-55; Chair. Council of Ministers, Chuvash Autonomous Republic 55; First Sec. Chuvash Regional Cttee. C.P.S.U. 55-; Candidate mem. Central Cttee. C.P.S.U. 56-; Deputy to U.S.S.R. Supreme Soviet.
Chuvash Regional Committee of C.P.S.U., Cheboksary, U.S.S.R.

Ismagilov, Zagir Garipovich; Soviet composer; b. 1917; ed. Moscow Conservatoire.
Executive mem., U.S.S.R. Composers' Union, Chair. Bashkir Branch; Honoured Worker of Arts of R.S.F.S.R. 55, People's Artist of Bashkir Autonomous S.S.R. 63, Red Banner of Labour, People's Artist of R.S.F.S.R. 68, other decorations.
Principal compositions: Lenin Cantata 50, Symphonic Overture 51, Vocal-Choreographic Suite 53, *Salavat*

Yulayev (opera) 54, *Kodasa* 59; vocal and instrumental works.
Bashkir Section, R.S.F.S.R. Composers' Union, Ufa, U.S.S.R.

Ismailov, Ramazan Akper ogly; Soviet politician; b. 1928; ed. Erevan Veterinary Inst. and Higher Party School C.P.S.U.
Member C.P.S.U. 52-; Veterinary, then Chief Veterinary Surgeon to Ministry of Agriculture, Nakhichevan Autonomous S.S.R. 61-62; Chair. Nakhichevan Area Soviet of Working People's Deputies 62-64; Chair. Council of Ministers, Nakhichevan Autonomous S.S.R. 64-; mem. Central Cttee. C.P. of Azerbaijan; Deputy to U.S.S.R. Supreme Soviet.
Council of Ministers, Nakhichevan Autonomous S.S.R., Nakhichevan, U.S.S.R.

Ismailov, Rustum Gadjievich; Soviet chemist; b. 1909; ed. Azerbaijan Oil Inst.
Member C.P.S.U. 41-; in Azerbaijan oil industry 46-; Minister of Oil Refining and Petro Chemical Industry of Azerbaijan; mem. Azerbaijan Acad. of Sciences 62-, Pres. 67-; State Prize, Hero of Socialist Labour, Orders of Lenin (3), other decorations.
Presidium of Azerbaijan Academy of Sciences, 10 Kommunisticheskaya ulitsa, Baku, U.S.S.R.

Ispahani, Mirza Abol Hassan, LL.B., M.A.; Pakistani diplomatist; b. 23 Jan. 1902; ed. Cambridge.
Called to Bar (Inner Temple) 24; joined family business in India 25; mem. Calcutta City Corpn. 33-36 and 40-47; mem. Bengal Legislative Assembly 37-47; Joint Sec. Bengal Provincial Muslim League 36-37; Treas. 36-47; Pres. Muslim Chamber of Commerce. Calcutta 45-47; mem. Indian Constituent Assembly 46; Pakistan Constituent Assembly 47; Vice-Chair. Pakistan Del. to UN Gen. Assembly 47; Chair. Pakistan Del. to UN Conf. on Trade and Employment, Havana 47; Vice-Chair. Pakistan Del. to UN Security Council in connection with Kashmir question 48; has led other dels. to int. confs.; Ambassador to U.S.A. 47-52; High Commr. for Pakistan in Great Britain 52-54; Minister of Commerce and Industries 54-55 (resigned), reverted to business.
Publs. *27 Days in China, Leningrad to Samarkand, Qaid-é-Azam Jinnah As I knew him.*
2 Reay Road, Karachi, Pakistan.
Telephone: 50665.

Issa, Abdullahi; Somali politician; b. 22; ed. Koran School and an Italian Government School.
Italian Govt. service 37-42; in business, Belet Uen 42; joined Somali Youth League 44, Sec.-Gen. 47; Prime Minister and Minister of Justice, Somalia 56-59; Prime Minister and Minister of Interior 59-60; Minister of Foreign Affairs, Repub. of Somalia 60-64; Minister of Health, Veterinary Affairs and Labour 64-66; Minister of Industry and Commerce 66-67.
Republic of Somalia, East Africa.

Issigonis, Alec Arnold Constantine, C.B.E., F.R.S.; British engineer and designer; b. 1905; ed. Battersea Polytechnic, London.
Draughtsman, Rootes Motors Ltd. 33-36; Suspension Engineer, British Motor Corpn. 56, Chief Engineer 57-61, Technical Dir. 61-; designed the Morris Minor 48, the Mini Minor and Austin Seven 59, Morris 1100 62; Leverhulme Medal, Royal Society 66.
British Motor Corporation, Longbridge, Birmingham, England.

Istomin, Eugène George; American pianist; b. 26 Nov. 1925; ed. under Kyriena Silote, Rudolf Serkin and at Curtis Inst., Philadelphia.
Concert pianist 43-; toured with Adolf Busch Chamber Players 44-45; first European appearance 50; charter mem. Casals Prades and Puerto Rico festivals 50-; several world tours; founded Trio with Isaac Stern and

Leonard Rose 61; numerous recordings of solo, orchestral and chamber works.
c/o Sol Hurok Attractions, 730 5th Avenue, New York, N.Y., U.S.A.

Italiaander, Rolf Bruno Maximilian; German (b. Netherlands) writer and explorer; b. 20 Feb. 1913.
Explorer in Africa for over thirty years; Visiting Prof. Inst. for European Studies, Univ. of Vienna 59, Univ. of Michigan 61, Hope Coll., Michigan 61, Kalamazoo Coll. Michigan 61, American Negro Univs. 62, Universidade de Bahia and Instituto Joaquim Nabuco, Recife, Brazil 67; Co-Founder and Hon. Sec. Free Acad. of Art, Hamburg 48-; Founder German Translators Union 54, Hon. Pres. 60-; Co-founder Fed. Int de Traducteurs, Paris; Hon. Consul of Senegal 64; Pres. Int. Translators Congress, Hamburg 65; mem. American Acads.; Hans Henny Jahn Award; several decorations.
Publs. *Der ruhelose Kontinent* 58, *The New Leaders of Africa* 60, *Schwarze Haut im roten Griff* 62, *Die neuen Männer Asiens* 64, *Immer wenn ich unterwegs bin* 63, *König Leopolds Kongo* 64, *Dappers Afrika 1668* 64, *The Challenge of Islam* 64, *In Namen des Herrn im Kongo* 65, *Die Friedensmacher* 65, *In der Palmweinschenke* 66, *Rassenkonflikte in der Welt* 66, *Frieden in der Welt* 57, *Lebensentscheidung für Israel* 67, *Heinrich Bath* 67, *Aufstieg und Sturz des Oscar Wilde* 67, *Terra Dolorosa (Indoamerica)* 68; Biography and Bibliography: *Unterwegs mit Rolf Italiaander* 63.
Heilwigstrasse 39, 2 Hamburg 20, German Federal Republic.

Ito, Jirozaemon; Japanese business executive; b. 5 July 1902; ed. Keio Univ.
Former Pres. ceramics companies; Pres. Matsuzakaya Dept. Store Chain 47-; fmr. Pres. Nagoya Chamber of Commerce; mem. Standing Cttee. Japan Fed. of Employers' Asscn.
Matsuzakaya Department Stores, No. 16-1, Sakae-3-chome, Naka-ku, Nagoya, Japan.

Ito, Shinsui; Japanese painter; b. 98; ed. Kiyokata Art School, Tokyo.
Has exhibited many pictures of women incl. *A Mirror* (Nat. Acad. of Art Prize 46); organiser of Jitsugetsu Sha, and art league of young painters of promise; has about 100 disciples; mem. Council of the Nat. Art Exhibition; Sec. Japan Fed. of Art Societies.
Kita-Kamakura, Kanagawa Prefecture, Japan.

Itoh, Kyoichi; Japanese textile exec.; b. 27 May 1914; ed. Kobe Univ.
Director Kureha Spinning Co. Ltd. 56, Man. Dir. 56-63, Exec. Dir. 63-64, Pres. 64-66; Pres. Kureha Ansonia Co. Ltd. 63-; Chair. Ritto Textile Mfg. Co. Ltd. 60-; Dir. Ishikawa Machine Works 60-, Japan Lactam Co. Ltd. 63-, Japanese Fed. of Econ. Orgs. and Fed. of Man. Asscns. 64-; Exec. Vice-Pres. Toyobo Co. Ltd. 66-; Dir. Kureha Chemical Industries Ltd., Toyo Pulp Co. Ltd., Nippei Sangyo Ltd.; Hon. Consul of El Salvador, Osaka 58-.
Kureha Spinning Co. Ltd., 2 Chome, Homma-chi, Higashi-ku, Osaka; and 1845 Kuegazaka, Sumiyoshi-cho, Higashinada-ku, Kobe, Japan.

Itokawa, Hideo; Japanese aeronautic engineer; b. 12; ed. Tokyo Univ.
Engineer, Nakajima Aircraft Co. 39-41; Asst. Prof. of Engineering at Tokyo Univ. 41-48, Prof. 48-67; Exec.-Dir. Space Engineering Dept., Inst. of Industrial Science 55-; Pres. Japanese Rocket Soc. 56-58; Convener Nat. Cttee. on Space Research, Japan Science Council 56-; mem. Nat. Space Council 60-.
1077, 3-chome, Matsubara, Setagaya-ku, Tokyo, Japan.

Iturmendi Bañales, Antonio; Spanish lawyer and politician; b. 07; ed. Univ. of Deusto (Bilbao).
Successively Clerk of the Court in Logroño and Bilbao,

Legal Adviser to the Local Govt. of Vizcaya, Deputy Mayor of Bilbao, Gov. of Tarragona and Zaragoza; Dir.-Gen. of Local Administration and mem. Nat. Council 39-41; Under Sec. for Home Affairs 41; Minister of Justice 51-64; Pres. of Cortes (Parliament) 65-; numerous decorations.

Serrano 40, Madrid, Spain.

Iue, Toshio; Japanese business executive; b. 28 Dec. 1902; ed. senior elementary school.

Matsushita Co. 18-47; founded Sanyo Electric Machinery Co. 47, later Sanyo Electric Co. 50, Pres. 50-.

Sanyo Electric Co., 2-18 Keihan Hondori, Moriguchi City, Osaka Prefecture, Japan.

Ivanov, Semyon Pavlovich; Soviet stereocinematographer; b. 06.

Works in field of stereoscopic cinema; invented and developed perspective grating light-absorbing screen without glasses 35; the high-speed lens grating screen 42; basis of equipment for integral stereoscopic picture 60; State Prize winner 41; Order of Red Banner of Labour.

Publs. include *On Stereoscopic Cinematography* 48, *On Colour Stereoscopic Photography* 51, *Second Journey into the Micro-World* 59, *Features of Integral Stereosurvey and Projection* 63.

Film and Photo Research Institute, 47 Leningradsky Prospekt, Moscow, U.S.S.R.

Ivanov, General Vladimir Dimitrievich; Soviet army officer; b. 1900; ed. Frunze Military Acad.

Soviet army service 18-; mem. C.P.S.U. 19-; Military Acad. of Gen. Staff 30-35; Central Apparatus, U.S.S.R. Ministry of Defence 35-; Dep. Chief of Gen. Staff, U.S.S.R. Forces 60-65; Chief Military Acad. of Gen. Staff 65-; Orders of Lenin (thrice), Kutuzov, Suvorov (thrice), Red Banner (thrice), Red Star, etc.

Ministry of Defence, 34 Maurice Thorez Embankment, Moscow, U.S.S.R.

Ivanov-Smolensky, Anatoly Grigorievich; Soviet pathophysiologist; b. 95; ed. Mil. Medical Acad.

Assistant in Inst. of Psychiatry and Psychiatric Clinic of Military Medical Acad. 18-21; worked in field of pathophysiology and psychiatry in laboratory of I. P. Pavlov 21-45; Head of Moscow Dept. of I. P. Pavlov Inst. of Physiology 45-50; Dir. Inst. of Higher Nervous Activity of Acad. of Sciences of U.S.S.R. 52-57; mem. Acad. of Medical Sciences; Pavlov and State prizewinner.

Publs. *Methods of investigation of Conditional Reflexes in Man* 28, 33, *Fundamental Problems in Pathological Physiology of the Higher Nervous Activity of Man* 33, *Essays on the Patho-physiology of Higher Nervous Activity* 49, 52, *I. P. Pavlov's Teaching and Pathological Physiology* 52, *Experience of the Objective Study of the Work and Interaction of the First and Second Signal Systems of the Brain* 61, etc.

U.S.S.R. Academy of Medical Sciences, 14 Solyanka Street, Moscow, U.S.S.R.

Ivchenko, Alexandr Georgievich; Soviet aircraft engine designer; b. 1903; ed. Kharkov Machine-Building Inst.

Worked in heavy industry 20-24; mem. C.P.S.U. 24-, party work 24-30; with aircraft industry 35-, engineer, engine designer and constructor, Chief of Designing Office, Chief Designer of the Works 45-; designed and constructed many original aircraft engines, including IL-18 Ilyushin passenger plane (Lenin Prize 60).

Ministry of Aircraft Industry, Moscow, U.S.S.R.

Iveroth, C. Axel; Swedish business executive; b. 4 Aug. 1914; ed. Stockholm School of Economics.

Producer, Swedish Broadcasting Corpn. 37-41; Sec. Industrial Inst. for Econ. and Social Research 39-44; Industrial Counsellor, Swedish Embassy, Washington 44-45; Ed.-in-Chief *Industria* 46; Chair. and Founder, Industrial Council for Social and Econ. Studies 48-60;

Man. Cementa 47-52; Chair. and Man. Dir. Cembureau (Cement Statistical and Technical Asscn.) 52-57; Chair. Advisory Board European Productivity Agency, Paris 54-56; Dir.-Gen. Fed. of Swedish Industries 57-; Sec.-Gen. Business and Industry Advisory Cttee., OECD 62-63; Chair. Swedish Productivity Council, Swedish-American New Exchange; Chair. Integration Cttee. of European Ind. Feds. 58-; Knight of the Vasa Order (Sweden), C.B.E., Officier de l'Ordre de la Couronne (Belgium), Commendatore dell'Ordine "Al Merito della Repubblica Italiana".

Federation of Swedish Industries, Artillerigatan 34, Stockholm O, Sweden.

Iversen, Dr. Carl; Danish economist; b. 5 March 1899; ed. Copenhagen and Harvard Univs.

Journalist, *Börsen* (The Exchange) 20-30; joined Staff of Copenhagen Univ. 27; Prof., Economics 39-67; Vice-Chair., Danish Nat. Bank 51; econ. adviser to Chile 50, Iraq 53, Ceylon 56, Visiting Prof., Univ. of Washington, Seattle 52, Johns Hopkins Univ., Baltimore 54; Rector of Copenhagen Univ. 58-66; Chair. Danish Council of Econ. Advisers 62-.

Publs. *Aspects of the Theory of International Capital Movements* 35, *Monetary Problems of Iraq* 54.

Amaliegade 40A, Copenhagen K, Denmark.

Telephone: BYEN 2470.

Ives, Burl Icle Ivanhoe; American actor and singer; b. 14 June 1909.

Began stage career 38; has appeared in the musicals *The Boys from Syracuse, I Married An Angel, Heavenly Express, This is the Army, Sing Out Sweet Land, Knickerbocker Holiday, Paint Your Wagon, Show Boat;* the stage plays *The Man Who Came to Dinner, She Stoops to Conquer, Cat on a Hot Tin Roof, Joshua Beene and God;* the films *Smokey, Green Grass of Wyoming, Station West, So Dear to my Heart, Sierra, East of Eden, The Power and the Prize, Desire Under the Elms, The Big Country, The Everglades, Cat on a Hot Tin Roof, The Day of Outlaw, Our Man in Havana, The Spiral Road, Summer Magic, The Brass Bottle, Mediterranean Holiday, Ensign Pulver, Pt. Barnum's Rocket to the Moon;* American Motion Picture Award for best supporting actor (*The Big Country*) 59; Hon. LL.D. (Fairleigh Dickinson Coll., Rutherford, N.J.).

Publs. *The Wayfaring Stranger, The Wayfaring Stranger's Notebook, Sailing on a Very Fine Day, Burl Ives' Tales of America;* ed. *The Burl Ives Song Book, The Burl Ives Book of Sea Songs, The Burl Ives Book of Irish Songs, America's Musical Heritage* (six records with sing-along book), *Song in America—A New Song Book, Albad the Oaf.*

c/o William Morris Agency, 1350 Avenue of the Americas, New York City, N.Y., U.S.A.

Ivy, Andrew Conway, PH.D.; M.D.; American physiologist; b. 25 Feb. 1893; ed. Univ. of Chicago.

Instructor in Physiology Univ. of Chicago 17-19; Associate Prof. of Physiology Loyola Univ. 19-23; Associate Prof. of Physiology Univ. of Chicago 23-25; Chair. Dept. of Physiology and Pharmacology Northwestern Univ. Medical School 25-46; Vice-Pres. Univ. Illinois in charge of Chicago Professional Schools of Clinical Science 46-53, Distinguished Prof. of Physiology, Head of Dept. of Clinical Science 46-61, Distinguished Prof. Emer. 61-; Director U.S. Naval Medical Research Institute 42-43; Consultant Nuremburg trials of war criminals; Exec. Dir. Nat. Advisory Cancer Council 47-51; Prof. Emer. Biochemistry and Dir. Medical Research Laboratory, Roosevelt Univ., Chicago 63-; Fellow American Coll. of Physicians; mem. American Medical Asscn. (Chair. Physiology and Pathology Section 32-33); Pres. Society of Internal Medicine, Inst. of Medicine of Chicago; mem. American Asscn. of Univ. Profs., American Gastro-Enterology Asscn. (Pres.), American Physiology Society (Pres.),

Society for Experimental Biology, American Inst. of Nutrition, Asscn. for Study of Internal Secretions; Hon. D.Sc. (Univ. of Nebraska, Grinnell Coll. Iowa 47, Boston Univ. 48, Hastings Coll. 51, Coe Coll. 57), LL.D. (Loyola Univ.) 50.
Publ. *Peptic Ulcer.*
178 W. Randolf, Chicago, Ill., 60601, U.S.A.
Telephone: 372-6005.

Iwai, Akira; Japanese railwayman and trade unionist; b. 22; ed. Matsumoto High Elementary School, Nagano Prefecture.
Kamisuwa Engine Section, Nat. Railway 37-42; Military Service 42-46; Engine Driver, Kamisuwa Engine Section, Nat. Railway 46; Chief Joint Struggle Dept., Nat. Railway Workers' Union 50-51, Chief of Planning Dept. 51-55; Gen. Sec. Gen. Council of Trade Unions of Japan (SŌHYO) 55-.
Publs. *We, born in Taisho Era, The Workers.*
Sohyo Kaikan, Shiba Park, Minato-ku, Tokyo, Japan.

Iwasa, Yoshizane; Japanese banker; b. 6 Feb. 1906; ed. Tokyo Univ.
Manager, Kanagawa Branch, Yasudu Bank 44-45, Man. Loan Dept. (Head Office) 45-46, Personnel Dept. 46-47, Chief Man. Personnel Dept. 47-48; Dir. Yasuda Bank 48; Vice-Chair. Fuji Bank 48-57, Deputy Chair. 57-63, Chair. and Pres. 63-.
Fuji Bank Ltd., 1-chome, Otemachi, Chiyoda-ku, Tokyo, Japan.

Iwashita, Fumio, LL.B.; Japanese businessman; b. 30 Dec. 1891; ed. Tokyo Imperial Univ.
Director, Tokyo Shibaura Electric Co. Ltd. 45-47, Man. Dir. 47-50, Senior Man. Dir. 50-53, Vice-Pres. 53-57, Pres. 57-65, Chair. 65-; Chair. Tokyo Denki Co. Ltd. 57-, Shibaura United Engineering Co. Ltd. 59-, Toshiba Steel Tube Co. Ltd. 60-; Gov. Dir. Japan Fed. of Employers' Asscns. 57-, Fed. of Econ. Orgs. 58-; Pres. Electronics Industries Asscn. of Japan 58, Japan Electric Industry Devt. Asscn. 65-, Japan Electric Machine Industry Asscn.; Blue Ribbon Medal (Japan); Order of Sacred Treasure (Second Class).

Tokyo Shibaura Electric Company Limited, 1, 1-chome, Uchisaiwaicho, Chiyoda-ku, Tokyo; 2407 Nirazoki-cho, Nirazaki-shi, Yamanashi-ken, Japan.

Iwaszkiewicz, Jarosław; Polish writer; b. 94; ed. Kijow Univ.
Sec. Polish Embassies, Copenhagen and Brussels 32-35; Editor *Zycie Literackie* 45-46, *Nowiny Literackie* 47-48, *Twórczość* 55-; Pres. Union of Polish Writers 45-50, 59; Chair. Defenders of Peace Polish Cttee. 52-58; two First Class State Prizes, L. Reynal Prize 37.
Publs. Verse: *Oktostychy* 19, *Dionizje* 22, *Powrót do Europy* (Return to Europe) 31, *Lato 1932* (Summer 1932) 33, *Ody olimpijskie* (Olympic Odes) 48, *Ciemne ścieżki* (Dark Paths) 57; Short Stories: *Panny z Wilka* (The Girls from Wilko) 33, *Mlyn nad Utrata* (Mill on the Utrata) 36, *Nowa miłość* (New Love) 46, *Nowele włoskie* (Italian Stories) 47, *Tatarak* 60; Novels: *Zmowa mezczyzn* (Conspiracy of Men) 30, *Czerwone tarcze* (Red Shields) 34, *Pasje Bledomierski* (Bledomierski Passions) 38, *Slawa i chwala* (Fame and Glory) Vol. I 56, Vol. II 58, Vol. III 62; Plays: *Lato w Nohant* (Summer in Nohant) 37, *Maskarada* (Masquerade) 39, *Wesele pana Balzaka* (M. Balzac's Wedding) 59; Biographies: *Fryderyk Chopin* 38, 53, 66, *Jan Sebastian Bach* 51.
Twórczość, ul. Wiejska 16, Warsaw, Poland.

Izmerov, Nikolai F., M.D.; Soviet doctor; b. 19 Dec. 1927; ed. Tashkent Medical School and Moscow Central Inst. for Advanced Medical Training.
Worked as doctor in Khavast rural areas, Tashkent District; Postgraduate training, Moscow 52-53; Senior Insp. U.S.S.R. Ministry of Health 53-55; Postgraduate training (Municipal Hygiene) 55-58; doctor in Moscow City Sanitary Epidemiological Station 56-59; Deputy Dir. (Int. Health), Dept. of External Relations, U.S.S.R. Ministry of Health 60-62; Vice-Minister of Health of R.S.F.S.R., Moscow, and Chief Sanitary Insp. 62-64; Asst. Dir.-Gen. World Health Org. 64-.
World Health Organization, Avenue Appia, 1211 Geneva, Switzerland.

J

Jablonski, Henryk, PH.D.; Polish historian and politician; b. 09; ed. Univ. of Warsaw.
Professor Warsaw School of Political Sciences 46-50, Warsaw Univ. 50-; mem. Seym (Parliament) 47-, Nat. Council 45-47; Dep. Minister of Educ. 47-53; Sec. Polish Socialist Party 46-48; mem. Cen. Cttee. Polish United Workers' Party 48-; Minister of Higher Educ. 65-66; Minister of Educ. and Higher Educ. 66-; corresp. mem. Polish Acad. of Sciences 52-56, mem. 56-, Gen. Sec. 55-65, Vice-Pres. 66-; corresp. mem. Acad. of Romanian Socialist Repub. 65-; mem. Czechoslovakian Acad. of Sciences 65-; foreign mem. U.S.S.R. Acad. of Sciences 66-; State Prize 55, 64; Hon. L.H.D. (Moscow).
Publs. *The Military Criminal Court in 1794* 35, *Aleksander Waszkowski—Warsaw's Last Military Chief in the Insurrection of 1863-64* 37, *Public Opinion, Parliament, and the Press, At the Origins of the Present Day* 47, *Polish National Autonomy in the Ukraine in 1917-18* 48, *The Policy of the Polish Socialist Party during the First World War* 53, and numerous articles on history and current affairs.
Ministry of Education, Warsaw, Poland.

Jaccard, Pierre, TH.D., D.ès.L.; Swiss university professor; b. 14 Sept. 1901; ed. Univs. of Lausanne, Strasbourg, Paris, and Union Theological Seminary, New York.
Prof. of French, Wooster Coll., Ohio 29-34; Prof. of Systematic Theology at Neuchâtel Univ. 34-40; Prof. of Psychology, Sociology and Social Ethics, Lausanne Univ. 40-; Pres. Lausanne Univ. Graduate School of Social and Political Sciences 54-60.
Publs. *Le Sens de la Direction et l'Orientation lointaine chez l'Homme* 32, *Trois Contemporains: Mauriac, Chardonne, Montherlant* 45, *Essais sur la Peinture: Breughel, Le Nain, Vermeer* 48, *La Dignité du Travail* 51, *Travail et Salaire* 51, *Politique de l'emploi et de l'éducation* 57, *Histoire sociale du travail* 60, *La Formation des Elites* 61, *Sociologie de l'Education* 62, *Investir en Hommes* 64, *Psycho-sociologie du travail* 66.
Avenue de Chailly 31, Lausanne, Switzerland.

Jackling, Sir Roger William, K.C.M.G.; British diplomatist; b. 10 May 1913; ed. Felsted School and Law Soc.
Admitted as Solicitor, Supreme Court 35; Acting Vice-Consul, New York 40-42; Commercial Sec., Quito 42-43; Second, then First Sec., Washington 43-47; Foreign Office 47; Asst. Sec. Cabinet Office 50-51; Commercial Counsellor, British Legation, The Hague 51-53; Econ. Adviser, British High Comm., West Germany 53-55; Minister (Econ.), Bonn Embassy 55-57; Counsellor, Washington 57-59; Asst. Under-Sec. of State 59-63; Deputy Perm. Rep. to UN 63-67; Deputy Under-Sec. of State 67-68; Amb. to German Fed. Repub. 68-.
Publ. *Federal Republic of Germany: Economic Survey* 55.
37 Boundary Road, St. John's Wood, London, N.W.8, England.

Jackson, Eric Stead, C.B., M.A.; British civil servant; b. 27 Aug. 1909; ed. Corpus Christi Coll. Oxford.
On Air Ministry Staff 32-40; Private Sec. to Minister of Aircraft Production 42, to Minister Resident in Washington 43; Dir.-Gen. Aircraft Branch, Control Comm., Germany 45; Deputy Pres. Economic Sub-Comm., Berlin 47; British Head of Delegation from Western Zone of Germany to O.E.E.C., Paris 48; Under-Sec. Ministry of Supply 50; Dir.-Gen. Atomic Weapons,

Ministry of Supply 56-59; Under-Sec. Ministry of Aviation 59-67, Ministry of Technology 67-.
48 Canonbury Park North, London, N.1, England.

Jackson, Gordon Noel, C.M.G., M.B.E.; British diplomatist; b. 25 Dec. 1913.
Political Officer, Sharjah 47, Kuwait 49-50; Consular Service, St. Louis, Basra, Lourenço Marques 53-60; Consul-Gen. Benghazi 60-63; Ambassador to Kuwait 63-67; Amb. to Ecuador 67-.
c/o Lloyds Bank, G2 Section, 6 Pall Mall, London, S.W.1, England.

Jackson, Henry M.; American lawyer and politician, b. 31 May 1912; ed. Univ. of Washington.
Practising lawyer 35-; mem. House of Reps. for Washington 41-52; Senator (Democrat, Washington) 53-; Chair. Democratic Nat. Cttee. July 60-Jan. 61; Hon. LL.D. (Alaska).
3602 Oakes Avenue, Everett, Washington, U.S.A.

Jackson, Sir Richard Leofric, Kt., C.B.E., B.A.; British police official; b. 12 July 1902; ed. Cheam School, Eton, Trinity Coll., Cambridge.
Called to Bar, Middle Temple 27; on staff of Director of Public Prosecutions 33-46; Sec. of Metropolitan Police office 46-53; Asst. Commissioner, Criminal Investigation Dept. 53-63; Pres. International Criminal Police Org. (INTERPOL) 60-Sept. 63; Dir. and Joint Vice-Chair. Securicor Ltd. 63-.
Publ. *Occupied with Crime* (memoirs) 67.
10 Persfield Mews, Ewell, Surrey, England.

Jackson, Commdr. Sir Robert Gillman Allen, Kt., K.C.V.O., C.M.G., O.B.E.; British planning consultant; b. 8 Nov. 1911.
Royal Australian Navy 29-37; Royal Navy 37-45; H.M. Treasury 45-; Senior Dep. Dir. UNRRA 45-47; Asst. Sec.-Gen. for Co-ordination in UN 48; Perm. Sec. Ministry of Nat. Devt., Australia 50-52; Adviser to Govts. of India and Pakistan on Devt. Plans 52; Chair. Preparatory Comm. for Volta River Project, Gold Coast 53-56; Chair. Devt. Comm., Ghana 57-63; Adviser to Pres. of Liberia 61-; Senior Consultant UN Special Fund 62-65, UN Devt. Programme 66-; mem. of and Consultant to Volta River Authority, Ghana 62-; mem. Comm. on Mekong Project 61-; Adviser to Planning Comm., Govt. of India 63; Hon. LL.D. (Syracuse).
Barclays Bank D.C.O., Oceanic House, Cockspur Street, London, S.W.1, England.

Jackson of Burnley, Baron (Life Peer), cr. 67, of Burnley; **Willis Jackson,** Kt., D.SC., D.PHIL., M.I.E.E., M.I.MECH.E., F.INST.P., F.R.S.; British electrical engineer; b. 29 Oct. 1904; ed. Manchester and Oxford Univs.
Lecturer in Electrical Engineering, Bradford Technical Coll. 26-29, Manchester Coll. of Technology 30-33, Oxford Univ. 33-36; with Metropolitan Vickers Electrical Co. Ltd., Manchester 29-30, 36-38; Prof. of Electrotechnics, Manchester Univ. 38-46; Prof. of Electrical Engineering, Imperial Coll., Univ. of London 46-53, 61-; Dir. of Research and Education, Metropolitan Vickers Electrical Co. Ltd. July 53-61; Pres. Inst. of Electrical Engineers 59-60; mem. Radio Research Board 44-48, 50-54, Scientific Advisory Council, B.B.C. 48-53, 61-, Central Advisory Council for Educ. (England) 44-48; mem. Council British Asscn. 53-57, 64-; mem. Royal Comm. on the Civil Service 53-55, Univ. Grants Cttee. 54-64, Inter-Univ. Council for Higher Educ. Overseas 56-58 and 62-, Research Council Dept. of Scientific and Industrial Research 56-61; Advisory Council on Scienti-

fic Policy 61-, Scientific Manpower Cttee. 62-64; Chair. Cttee. on Manpower Resources for Science and Technology 64-; mem. Council for Scientific Policy 64-; Chair. Ministry of Educ. Cttee. on Technical Teachers 56-57, Governing body Royal Coll. of Advanced Technology, Salford 57-62; Chair. Television Advisory Cttee. 63-, Gov. Body Mil. Coll. of Science 64-; Pres. British Asscn. Commercial and Industrial Educ. 62-; Vice-Pres. Manchester Coll. of Science and Technology 62-; Pres. British Asscn. Advancement of Science 66-67; Pro-Rector Imperial Coll. 67-; Hon. D.Sc. Tech. (Zürich), D.Sc.Eng. (Bristol), Hon. D.Sc. (City Univ. London), D.Eng. (Sheffield), LL.D. (Aberdeen), Hon. D.T. (Bradford), Hon. D.Sc. (Dublin).
Publs. *High Frequency Transmission Lines* 46,*Applications of Communications Theory* 53, *Insulation of Electrical Equipment* 54.
Electrical Engineering Dept., Imperial College, South Kensington, London, S.W.7; Home: 25 Manor Road, Cheam, Surrey, England.
Telephone: 01-642-1611.

Jacob, Lieut.-Gen. Sir Edward Ian Claud, G.B.E., C.B., B.A.; British soldier and broadcasting administrator; b. 27 Sept. 1899; ed. Wellington Coll., Royal Mil. Acad. Woolwich, and King's Coll., Cambridge.
2nd Lieut. Royal Engineers 18; Capt. 29; Maj. 38; Col. 43; T/Maj.-Gen. 44; Mil. Asst. Sec. to Cttee. of Imperial Defence 38 and to War Cabinet 39-46; attended Confs. at Atlantic Meeting, Washington, Casablanca, Quebec, Moscow, Yalta, Potsdam,; retd. July 46; Controller European Services of B.B.C. 46-47; Dir. Overseas Services B.B.C. 47-52, Dir.-Gen. B.B.C. 52-59; Pres. European Broadcasting Union 50-52 and 54-60; Chair. Covent Garden Market Authority 60-66; Dir. Fisons and E.M.I.; Trustee Imperial War Museum 66-.
The Red House, Woodbridge, Suffolk, England.

Jacob, Ernest Fraser, M.A., D.PHIL., F.B.A., F.S.A., F.R.HIST.S.; British historian; b. 12 Sept. 1894; ed. Winchester and New Coll., Oxford, Paris, Heidelberg. Fmr. Prof. Medieval History, Manchester Univ., and Pro-Vice-Chancellor; Chichele Prof. Modern History, Univ. of Oxford 50-61, Prof. Emeritus 61, and Fellow All Souls Coll.; mem. Royal Comm. on Historical MSS.; Lecturer in Medieval History, King's Coll., London 22-24; Student and Tutor, Christ Church, Oxford 24-29; elected to Bureau of Int. Historical Congress 60; Church Commr. 48-; Librarian of All Souls Coll. 60-; Hon. Vice-Pres. Royal Historical Soc., Historical Asscn.; Hon. Litt.D.
Publs. *Illustrations to the Life of St. Alban* 24, *Studies in the Period of Baronial Reform and Rebellion* 25, *The Legacy of the Middle Ages* 26, *Innocent III and Henry III of England* (*Cambridge Medieval History*), *The Register of Archbishop Chichele* (4 vols.) 38-47, *Essays in the Conciliar Epoch* 53, *Henry V and the Invasion of France* 47, *Italian Renaissance Studies* 60, *England: The Fifteenth Century* 61, *Archbishop Henry Chichele* 67, *Studies in Later Mediaeval History* 68.
205 Woodstock Road, Oxford, England.
Telephone: 55386.

Jacob, François, M.D., D.SC.; French professor of genetics; b. 17 June 1920; ed. Lycée Carnot and Univ. de Paris à la Sorbonne.
Officer Free French Forces 40-45; with Institut Pasteur 50-, Asst. 50-56, Head of Laboratory 56-60, Head of Microgenetic Service 60-; Prof. of Cellular Genetics Coll. de France 64-; Foreign mem. Acad. Royale des Lettres et Sciences du Danemark 62, American Acad. of Arts and Sciences 64; Prix Charles Léopold Mayer, Acad. des Sciences 62; Nobel Prize for Medicine (jointly with A. Lwoff and J. Monod) 65; Dr. h.c. Univ. of Chicago; Croix de la Libération, Commdr. Légion d'Honneur.
Institut Pasteur, 28 rue du Dr. Roux, Paris 15e, France.

Jacobs, Robert Allan, A.B.; American architect; b. 16 Sept. 1905; ed. Amherst, Columbia Architectural School.
Worked with Le Corbusier 34-35, with Harrison and Fouilhoux 35-38; in partnership with E. J. Kahn under the name of Kahn and Jacobs 40-; designed buildings for World's Fair, N.Y. 64; Fellow, American Inst. of Architects, Associated Architects on U.S. Mission to the UN; mem. Beaux Arts Inst. Architectural League of New York and New York Building Congress; Hon. Master of Fine Arts, Amherst Coll. 57.
Home: 1065 Lexington Avenue, New York, N.Y. 10021; Office: 2 Park Avenue, New York 16, N.Y., U.S.A.

Jacobsen, Arne; Danish architect; b. 11 Feb. 1902; ed. Royal Danish Acad.
Fellow of American Inst. of Architects; Hon. corresp. mem. Royal Inst. of British Architects (R.I.B.A.); Extraordinary mem. Akademie der Künste, Berlin; mem. Accademia Nazionale di San Luca, Rome, Académie Serbe des Sciences et des Arts, Belgrade; Hon. D.Litt., (Oxford); exhbns. in London 59, Stedelijk Museum, Amsterdam 59, Paris 61, Zürich 62, Hanover 62, Vienna 63, Dortmund 63; Gold medal Royal Danish Acad. 28, Eckersberg Medal 36, Prize of Honour São Paulo, Brazil 54, C. F. Hansen Medal 56, Grand Prix, Architecture d'aujourd'hui 60, Akademisk Arkitektforening's Medal of Honour 62, Prince Eugen Medal, Sweden 62, R.I.B.A. Bronze Medal 65.
Major works include: villas, town halls, banks, commercial structures, Royal Hotel, Copenhagen, St. Catherine's College, Oxford, Nat. Bank of Denmark, project of Parliament Building, Islamabad, Pakistan. Strandvej 413, Klampenborg, Denmark.
Telephone: Ordrup 7010.

Jacobsen, Frithjof Halfdan, B.LL.; Norwegian diplomatist; b. 14 Jan. 1914; ed. Oslo Univ., London School of Economics and Political Science.
Entered Norwegian Foreign Service 38, served Paris, Moscow and London; Dir.-Gen. Political Affairs Dept. of the Norwegian Foreign Ministry 55-59; Ambassador to Canada 59-61, to Soviet Union 61-66; Under-Sec. of State for Foreign Affairs 66-.
Ministry of Foreign Affairs, Oslo, Norway.

Jacobson, Herbert Laurence, B.A.; American United Nations official; b. 7 April 1915; ed. Erasmus Hall and Columbia Coll.
Editor-in-Chief *World News*, N.Y. (magazine) 37-40; Head, Radio Dept., MCA, Chicago 40-41; U.S. Army Officer, Mediterranean 41-46; Dir.-Gen. Radio Network, Free Territory, Trieste 46-52; U.S. High Comm., Germany 53-55; U.S. Embassy, Rome 55-57; Foreign Business Man., Mondadori Publs., Milan 57-58; Export Man., Squibb of Italy, Rome 59-60; Dir., S. Europe, Cotton Council Int., Rome, Barcelona, St. Gall 60-64; Dir., Int. Trade Centre, UNCTAD/GATT 64-; Editor-in-Chief *International Trade* (UNCTAD/GATT) 64-; mem. Advisory Board Waterloo Lutheran Univ., Ontario 67-.
International Trade Centre, UNCTAD/GATT, Palais des Nations, Geneva; Home: 10 Chemin de Tavernay, Geneva, Switzerland.
Telephone: 34-60-11 (Office); 33-97-83 (Home).

Jacobson, Sydney, M.C.; British journalist; b. 26 Oct. 1908; ed. Strand School, London, and King's Coll., Univ. of London.
Editor *The Leader* Magazine 48-49; Political Editor *Daily Mirror* 54-64; Editor *Daily Herald* 62-64, *The Sun* 64-65; Editor Dir. *The Sun* 65-; Chair. Odhams Newspapers 68-.
c/o International Publishing Corporation Ltd., New Fetter Lane, London, E.C.4, England.

Jacottet, Carl Maurice; Swiss industrialist; b. 7 Feb. 1904; ed. Gymnasium, Hildesheim, and Philipps Univ., Marburg.

Behring-Werke, Marburg 22-29; Sandoz Ltd., Basle, Switzerland 29-, Sub-Man. 39-44, Deputy Man. 44-49, Man. 49-, mem. Exec. Cttee. 56-, Man. Dir. 60-, Vice-Chair. 63-67, Chair. 68-, Pres. Exec. Cttee. 68-; Dir. Dr. A. Wander A.G., Berne, Glaro S.A., Fribourg, Union Bank of Switzerland; mem. Board of Trustees Foundation for the Advancement of Teaching and Research, Basle Univ., Art Comm. Basle, Soc. for Research in Nat. Economy of St. Gall Graduate School of Econs., Business and Public Admin.; Vice-Pres. Swiss American Soc. Basle; Treas. Inst. Henry Dunant, Geneva; Hon. Dr. Rer. Pol. Basle Univ. 62.
Sandoz Limited CH-4002 Basle; Home: 34 Therwiler-strasse, CH-4153 Reinach BL, Switzerland.
Telephone: (Basle) 44-00-11 (Office); 46-55-20 (Home).

Jacquemard, Simonne; French novelist, journalist and traveller; b. 6 May 1924; ed. "Les Oiseaux" and Univ. of Paris.
Teacher of Music, Latin and French; collaborator, Laffont-Bompiani Dictionaries; contributor to *Figaro Littéraire, La Table Ronde*; travelled in U.S.S.R.; Egypt, Greece, Italy, N. Africa and Spain; Prix Renaudot 62.
Publs. *Les Fascines* 51, *Sable* 52, *La Leçon des Ténèbres* 54, *Judith Albarès* 58, *Planant sur les Airs* 60, *Compagnons Insolites* 61, *Le Veilleur de Nuit* 62, *L'Oiseau* 63, *L'Orangerie* 63, *Les Derniers Rapaces* 65, *Dérive au Zénith* 65, *Exploration d'un corps* 65, *Navigation vers les îles* 67; studies on music (with Lucette Descave), and on bird life and observation of wild animals.
35 rue de la Harpe, Paris 5e, France.

Jacques, Thomas Reginald, C.B.E., M.A., D.MUS., F.R.C.M.; British conductor; b. 13 Jan. 1894; ed. Grammar School, Ashby-de-la-Zouche, and Queen's Coll., Oxford.
Served in First World War; Organist, SS. Philip and James Church, Oxford 18-22; Dir. of Music and Conductor, Eglesfield Musical Society Concerts, Queen's Coll., Oxford 26-36; Conductor Oxford Harmonic Soc. 23-30, Oxford Orchestral Soc. 30-36; Music Adviser to the L.C.C. 36-42; Dir. of Music, C.E.M.A. (now Arts Council of Great Britain) 40-45; Silver Medal R.S.A. 45, elected Fellow 46; Founder Conductor Jacques Orchestra 38-60; Dir. of Music to Bach Choir 32-60; Founder and Conductor The Cantata Singers; guest conductor, choral and orchestral concerts; has conducted B.B.C. and all established symphony orchestras in Great Britain.
Publs. *Voice Training and Conducting in Schools, The Thirty Song Book, The Forty Song Book, The Oxford S.A.B. Song Book, The Oxford S.A.B. Carol Book, Carols for Choirs* (with David Willcocks); songs, choral and orchestral arrangements.
c/o Barclays Bank Ltd., Melbury Court, Kensington High Street, London W.8., England.

Jacquet, Marc; French politician and industrialist; b. 17 Feb. 1913.
Deputy to Nat. Assembly 51-55, 58-; mem. Gen. Council of Melun-Sud 51-58; Sec. of State to the Presidency of the Council in Charge of the Associated States 53; Vice-Pres. Finance Comm., Nat. Assembly Jan.-Oct. 59, *Rapporteur général* 59-62; Minister of Public Works and Transportation 62-66; Mayor of Barbizon; Pres. New Soc. for Building Industry.
26 boulevard Raspail, Paris 7e, France.

Jacquinot, Louis, D.IUR.; French lawyer and politician; b. 16 Sept. 1898; ed. Coll. de Bar-le-Duc.
Served French Army 14-19; called to Paris Bar; Dep. 32-40, 45-; Under-Sec. for Interior 39-40; served French Army 40; escaped and joined Gen. de Gaulle; Commr. for Navy 43; Minister of War 44-45; Pres. Gen. Council of the Meuse 45-; Minister of State 45, for Navy 45-47, for Overseas Territories 51-53; Presidential candidate 54; Minister of State 58-61; Minister for Overseas

Territories 61-66; Commdr. de la Légion d'Honneur, Croix de Guerre (14-18, 39-45), Rosette de la Résistance, and other medals.
31 avenue Charles Floquet, Paris 7e, France.

Jacquinot, Pierre, D.SC.; French physicist; b. 18 Jan. 1910; ed. Université de Nancy.
Research Scientist, Centre Nat. de la Recherche Scientifique 33-42; Faculty of Science, Université de Clermont-Ferrand 42-46; Pres. French Physical Soc. 58-59; Prof. Univ. de Paris à la Sorbonne 46-; Dir.-Gen. Centre Nat. de la Recherche Scientifique 62-; mem. Académie des Sciences 66; Holweck Prize (Physical Soc. of London and French Physical Soc.) 50; Jaffé Prize (Institut de France) 62.
16 rue Pierre Curie, Paris 5e, France.

Jacquot, Pierre Elie; French army officer; b. 16 June 1902; ed. Ecole Speciale Militaire de St.-Cyr, Ecole Supérieure de Guerre.
Rose from Capt. to Lt.-Gen. 39-54; G.O.C.-in-C. Indo-China 55-56; G.O.C.-in-C. French forces in Germany 56-59; General 57; Insp.-General French Land Forces 59-61; C.-in-C. Allied Forces Central Europe 61-63; Grand-Croix, Légion d'Honneur 61.
Publs. *Essai de Stratégie Occidentale* 53, *La Stratégie Périphérique devant la Bombe Atomique* 53.
15 avenue de Villars, Paris 7e, France.
Telephone: 468-70-45.

Jaeger, H.E. Cardinal Lorenz; German ecclesiastic; b. 23 Sept. 1892; ed. Wipperfurth Gymnasium, Philosophisch-Theologische Akademie, Paderborn and Univs. of Munich and Münster.
Ordained Priest 22; Curate in Oebisfelde 22-26, teacher, Herne Oberrealschule 26-33, Hindenburg-Realgymnasium 33-41; Army Chaplain 39-41, Archbishop of Paderborn 41-; created Cardinal 65; Editor *Zeitschrift für den Religionsunterricht an höheren Schulen*; decorations include Iron Cross (1st Class), Grand Cross Knights of Malta, Knights of the Holy Sepulchre; Asst. at the Papal Throne; Dr. theol. h.c.
Publs. *The Ecumenical Council, the Church and Christendom* 60, *A Stand on Ecumenism, the Council's Decree* 65.
479 Paderborn, Kamp 38, German Federal Republic.
Telephone: 22310 (Paderborn).

Jaeger, Richard, DR.IUR.; German politician; b. 16 Feb. 1913; ed. Maximilian Gymnasium, Munich, Ludwig-Maximilians Universität, Munich, Humboldt-Universität zu Berlin and Rheinische Friedrich-Wilhelms-Universität, Bonn.
Military Service, Second World War 39-45; Govt. Counsel, Bavarian Ministry of Educ., Munich 47-48; Lord Mayor, Eichstätt, Bavaria 49; mem. Bundestag 49-, Vice-Pres. Bundestag and Chair. Defence Cttee. 53-65; Fed. Minister of Justice 65-66; Vice-Pres. Bundestag 67-; Pres. German Atlantic Asscn. 57-; Vice-Pres. Atlantic Treaty Asscn. 58-66; Grosses Bundesverdienstkreuz and other decorations.
Publs. *Soldat und Bürger—Armee und Staat* 56, 63, *Sicherheit und Rüstung* 62.
Bundeshaus, 53 Bonn, German Federal Republic.
Telephone: Bonn 16-29-12.

Jaenicke, Joachim; German diplomatist; b. 2 Aug. 1915; ed. Univ. of Geneva, Graduate Inst. of Int. Studies, Geneva, Haverford Coll., Haverford, U.S.A., and Fletcher School of Law and Diplomacy, U.S.A.
Teacher of Modern Languages and History, Westtown School, Pennsylvania 41-46; Asst. Prof. of History and German, Earlham Coll., Richmond, Indiana 46-48; returned to Germany 48; German Foreign Service 50-; Vice-Consul, New York 51; Second Sec., Washington 51-55; Chief, American Section, Fed. Press Office, Bonn 55-56; Chief of Press Section and Spokesman of German Foreign Office, Bonn 56-58; Counsellor, Ottawa 59-62; Far East Desk, Foreign Office 62-63; Dir. in

Div. of Political Affairs, North Atlantic Treaty Organization (NATO), Paris 63-65, now Asst. Sec.-Gen for Political Affairs, NATO.
North Atlantic Treaty Organization, Brussels 39, Belgium.

Jaffar, Khalid Mohammad; Kuwaiti diplomatist; b. 12 June 1922; ed. Mubarakia School, Kuwait.
Schoolteacher 40-43; Chief Cashier, Kuwait Municipality 43-45; Kuwait Oil Co. 45-61; mem. of Goodwill Mission to Latin American Countries 61; Lord Chamberlain to Amir of Kuwait 61-62; Head of Cultural and Press Dept., Foreign Office, Kuwait 62; mem. del. to U.N.; deputised for Under-Sec. of State, Ministry of Foreign Affairs 62-63; Amb. to U.K. 63-65, to Lebanon 65-68, to Turkey 68-; Chair. Kuwait Investment Board in London 64-65.
Embassy of the State of Kuwait, Ankara, Turkey.

Jagan, Cheddi (husband of Mrs. Janet Jagan, *q.v.*), B.SC., D.D.S.; Guyanese politician; b. 22 March 1918; ed. Queen's Coll., British Guiana, Howard Univ., Washington, Y.M.C.A. (now Roosevelt) Coll., Chicago and Northwestern Univ. Dental School, Chicago.
Mem. Legislative Council 47-53; Leader of People's Progressive Party, formed 50; Minister of Agriculture, Lands and Mines and Leader of House of Assembly April-Oct. 53; six months' political imprisonment 54; Minister of Trade and Industry 57-61; Leader of the P.P.P. Majority Party 57-61; First Premier of British Guiana and Minister of Development and Planning 61-64; Leader of the Opposition 64-.
Publs. *Forbidden Freedom* 54, *Anatomy of Poverty in British Guiana* 64, *The West on Trial* (autobiog.) 66.
65 pln, Bel Air, E.C.D., Guyana.

Jagan, Mrs. Janet (wife of Cheddi Jagan, *q.v.*); Guyanese (b. American) politician; b. 20 Oct. 1920.
General Sec. People's Progressive Party 50-68; Editor *Thunder* 50-55; Deputy Speaker House of Assembly 53; six months' political imprisonment 54; Minister of Labour, Health and Housing 57-61; Minister of Home Affairs 63-64.
65 Pln. Bel Air, E.C.D., Guyana.

Jagielski, Mieczysław, DR. ECON.; Polish economist and politician; b. 12 Jan. 1924; ed. Social Sciences Inst., Central Cttee. of Polish United Workers' Party.
Member Youth Fighting Union 45-; mem. Polish Workers' Party 47-48, Polish United Workers' Party 48-, mem. Central Cttee. 59-, Deputy mem. Political Office of Central Cttee. 64-; Vice Minister of Agriculture 57-59, Minister of Agriculture 59-.
30 Wspólna Street, Warsaw, Poland.

Jahn, Gunnar; Norwegian economist and statistician; b. 10 Jan. 1883; ed. Oslo Univ.; graduate in Law and Economics.
Lecturer Oslo Univ. 13-20; Dir. Cen. Rationing Board 18-20; Dir. Cen. Statistical Bureau 20-45; Chair. Exchange Comm. 25 and Financial Cttee. 32; Chair. Clearing Cttee. 34-40; Chair. Nobel Peace Prize Cttee. 42-; mem. L.N. Economic Cttee. 28-30; Minister of Finance 34-35; mem. L.N. Cttee. of Statistical Experts 34 and I.L.O. Cttee. of Statistical Experts 35; mem. Norwegian Acad. of Science; hon. mem. and Vice-Pres. Int. Inst. of Statistics 47-51; mem. Admin. Council 40; Minister of Finance in Gerhardsen Govt. June-Oct. 45; Gov. Bank of Norway 46-54; Gov. of Int. Bank for Reconstruction and Development and of Int. Monetary Fund 46-54; Chair. Norwegian Joint Cttee. of Research Councils 54-60, Norwegian Whaling Council 54-60; Chair. Econ. Asscn. of Norway 34-37 and 54-60; mem. of Statistical Comm. U.N. Economic and Social Council 46-54; Hon. Fellow Royal Statistical Society, London 55.
Publs. *Houses and Types in the Rural Districts of Norway* 20, *Statistical Methods* 37, *How to Make Trout Flies* 38, *The Longbow* 38, *Miscellany* 49.
Husebyvegen 12, Smestad, pr. Oslo, Norway.

Jain, Shanti Prasad, B.SC.; Indian industrialist; b. 12; ed. Banaras Hindu Univ. and Agra Univ.
Controls a chain of industries in Bihar, U.P., Rajasthan, West Bengal and Kashmir; Chair. and Dir. Sahu Jain Ltd.; Chair. Rohtas Industries Ltd., The Jaipur Udyog Ltd., Pres. Shri Ahimsa Prachar Samity, Calcutta, Bihar Industries Asscn., Patna; formerly President Federation of Indian Chamber of Commerce and Industry, New Delhi, All-India Org. of Industrial Employers, New Delhi, Indian Chamber of Commerce, Calcutta, Indian Paper Mills, Asscn., Calcutta, Indian Sugar Mills Asscn., Calcutta, Bihar Chamber of Commerce, Patna, Employers' Asscn., Calcutta, Rajasthan Chamber of Commerce and Industry, Jaipur, Eastern U.P. Chamber of Commerce, Allahabad, Marwari Relief Soc., Calcutta; Founder, Baharatiya Jnanpith (Acad.), Benares.
11 Clive Row, Calcutta, India.

Jaipur, Maharani of (Gayatri Devi); Indian politician and social worker.
Wife of His Highness the Maharajah of Jaipur, G.C.S.I., G.C.I.E. (ruler of the former State of Jaipur, Rajpramukh of Rajasthan 49-56); a leader of the Swatantra Party 59-; mem. of the Lok Sabha 62-.
The Palace, Jaipur, Rajasthan; Lok Sabha, New Delhi, India.

Jakobovits, Rabbi Immanuel, B.A., PH.D.; British (b. Germany) Rabbi; b. 8 Feb. 1921; ed. Jews' Coll. London and Yeshivah Etz Chaim, London.
Minister of Brondesbury Synagogue, London 41-44, of South East London Synagogue 44-47, of Great Synagogue, London 47-49; Chief Rabbi of Ireland 49-58; Rabbi of Fifth Avenue Synagogue, New York 58-67; Chief Rabbi of the United Hebrew Congregations of the British Commonwealth of Nations, London 66-.
Publs. *Jewish Medical Ethics* 59, rev. edn. 67, *Journal of a Rabbi* 66, *Jewish Law Faces Modern Problems* 66.
Office of the Chief Rabbi, Adler House, Tavistock Square, London, W.C.1, England.

Jakobsen, Frode, M.A.; Danish politician; b. 21 Dec. 1906; ed. Univ. of Copenhagen.
Agricultural worker until 25; Lecturer in Philosophy and Literature until 40; Leader, Resistance Movement 41-45; founder-mem. Danish Freedom Council (illegal govt. during occupation) 43-45; Chief of all armed underground forces 43-45; mem. Cabinet May-Nov. 45; mem. Parl. 45-; Civil Chief of Home Guard 48-; mem. Consultative Assembly, Council of Europe 49-64, Vice-Pres. 53-54; mem. Govt. Cttee. for Foreign Affairs; Pres. European Movement in Denmark; Social Democratic Party; mem. Danish Defence Cttee., Govt. Cttee. on Disarmament Questions 66-; Danish Del. to UN 56-57, 61, Head of Del. 62-65; Int. Council, Congress for Cultural Freedom 60-66.
Publs. *Nietzsches Kamp med den kristelige Moral* 40, *The European Movement and the Council of Europe* 50, *Europe—and Denmark* 53, *Standpunktev* 66.
107 Ravnsnaesvej, Birkerød, Denmark.
Telephone: 810743.

Jakobson, Max; Finnish journalist and diplomatist; b. 1923.
Journalist until 53; Press Attaché, Finnish Embassy, Washington 53-59; Chief of Press Dept., Ministry of Foreign Affairs 59-62; Asst. Dir. for Political Affairs, Ministry of Foreign Affairs 59-62, Dir. 62-65; Perm. Rep. of Finland to UN 65-.
Publs. include *The Diplomacy of the Winter War*.
Permanent Mission of Finland to the United Nations, 866 United Nations Plaza, New York, N.Y. 10017, U.S.A.

Jakobson, Roman, PH.D.; American philologist; b. 11 Oct. 1896; ed. Lazarev Inst. of Oriental Languages, Moscow Univ. and Prague Univ.
Prof. of Russian Philology, Masaryk Univ. Brno 33-

39; Visiting Lecturer, Univs. of Copenhagen, Oslo, Uppsala 39-41; Prof. Ecole Libre des Hautes Etudes, New York 41-46; Prof. Columbia Univ. 43-49; Samuel Hazzard Cross Prof. of Slavonic Languages, Literatures and Gen. Linguistics, Harvard Univ. 49-; Inst. Prof. at the Mass. Inst. of Technology 57-; mem. Polish Acad. Sciences, Norwegian Acad. of Sciences, Danish Royal Acad. of Sciences, American Acad. of Arts and Sciences, Serbian Acad. of Sciences, Netherlands Acad. of Sciences, Irish Acad. of Sciences; Pres. Linguistic Soc. of America 56; Vice-Pres. of the Int. Cttee. of Slavicists; Fellow Center for Advanced Study in the Behavioral Sciences 58-59, 60-61; hon. mem. Int. Phonetic Asscn. and Finno-Ugric Soc., Helsinki; American Council of Learned Socs. Award 60; Dr. h.c. Cambridge, Oslo, Uppsala, Michigan, New Mexico, Grenoble, Nice, Rome, Yale and Chicago Univs.
Publs. *Novejshaja russkaja poezija, O ceshskom stikhe: Nejstarsi ceske pisne duchovni, Remarques sur l'évolution phonologique du russe, K kharakteristike evrazijskogo jazykovogo sojuza, Beitrag zur allgemeinen Kasuslehre, Kindersprache, Aphasie und allgem. Lautgesetze, La Geste d'Igor, Preliminaries to Speech Analysis* (with G. Fant and M. Halle), *Ivan Fedorov's Primer, Fundamentals of Language* (with M. Halle), *Selected Writings I* 62, *II* 68, *IV* 66, *Essais de Linguistique générale* 63, *Sofonija's Tale of the Russian-Tatar Battle* (with D. S. Worth) 63.
Harvard University, Boylston Hall 301, Cambridge, Mass. 02138, U.S.A.
Telephone: 617-868-7600, Ext. 665.

Jakopp, Heinrich, DIPL. ING.; German (b. Austrian) business exec.; b. 4 July 1901; ed. Technical Univ., Graz and Graz Univ.
Former Chair. Management Board Klöckner Humboldt-Deutz AG, Cologne; Chair. Supervisory Board Veith Pirelli, Höchst-Odenwald, Deutsch-Atlantische Telegraphengesellschaft (DAT), Cologne; mem. Supervisory Board Preussisch-Rheinische Dampfschiffahrts- Gesellschaft, Cologne, L. Schuler, Goeppingen, Central Krankenversicherung AG, Cologne, European Enterprises Devt., Paris, J.M. Voith AG, St. Pölten, Vienna, Brevillier & Co. and A. Urban & Söhne, Vienna; Pres. Gov. Council Deutsches Krankenhaus-institut E.V., Düsseldorf; mem. Presidium Ibero-Amerika Verein e.V., Hamburg, Deutscher Handelskammer, Vienna.
Leyboldstrasse 56, Cologne-Marienburg, German Federal Republic.

Jakovos (*see* James).

Jakubowski, Janusz Lech; Polish scientist; b. 9 Dec. 1905.
Professor of High Voltage Technology, Warsaw Polytechnic; mem. Presidium, Polish Acad. of Sciences 52-; Dir. Center Pol. Acad. Sciences in Paris 59-61; corresp. mem. Acad. des Sciences, Inscriptions et Belles Lettres de Toulouse 62; UNESCO Project Man. Ecole Nat. Poly., Alger 67; State Prize 50.
Iganska 9, Warsaw, Poland.

Jalan, Nand Kishore; Indian industrialist; b. 8 March 1921; ed. privately.
Entered business 39; Man. Moon Mills, Ltd. (Cotton Mill), Bombay 44, Oriental Gas Co., Ltd., Calcutta and Bombay Gas Co., Ltd., Bombay 46; Partner-Man. and Dir. of Soorajmull Nagarmull, Bengal Jute Mill Co. Ltd., The Elphinstone Spinning and Weaving Mills Co. Ltd.; Chair. Calcutta Jute Fabrics Shippers' Asscn.; Dir. Bombay Gas Co. Ltd., Asiatic Textiles Co. Ltd., Moon Mills Ltd., W. H. Harton & Co., Ltd., The Ganges Manufacturing Co. Ltd., East India Jute and Hessian Exchange Ltd., Madaripur Trading Co., Ltd., Shahjahanpur Electric Supply Co., Ltd., Bombay Gas Co. (Prop.), Ltd., Jute Baling and Trading Co., Ltd., Eastern Bengal Jute Trading Co., Ltd., Western Bengal Co., Ltd., J. K. Chemicals Ltd., etc.; Pres.

Indian Soc. for Quality Control 61-65; mem. Indian Jute development council.
Soorajmuli Nagarmull, 8 Dalhousie Square (East), Calcutta, India.
Telephone: 22-6851.

Jallow, Momadou Ebrima; Gambian trade unionist; b. 28; ed. St. Augustine School and Co-operative Coll., Ibadan.
Clerk, Civil Service, later Secretariat, Income Tax Div.; founder-mem. Gambia Workers Union 57-; Sec.-Gen. AFRO, African Regional Organisation of International Confederation of Free Trade Unions (ICFTU) 64-.
African Regional Organisation, AFRO, Day Spring House. P.O. Box 1038, 85 Simpson Street, Ebute-Metta, Nigeria.

James (Jakovos), Archbishop; American ecclesiastic; b. 29 July 1911; ed. Theological School of Halki, Istanbul.
Deacon 34; ordained priest in U.S.A. 40; Dean Cathedral of the Annunciation, Boston 42-54; Bishop of Malta 54; Rep. of Patriarch of Constantinople to World Council of Churches, Geneva 55; Orthodox Archbishop of North and South America 59-; Pres. World Council of Churches 59-.
Orthodox Cathedral of the Holy Trinity, New York, N.Y., U.S.A.

James, Edwin Oliver, D.LITT., PH.D., D.D., F.S.A.; British university professor; b. 30 March 1888; ed. Univ. Coll. School, London, Exeter Coll. Oxford, and Univ. Coll. London.
Prof. of the History and Philosophy of Religion, Univ. of Leeds 33-45; Wilde Lecturer in Comparative Religion. Univ. of Oxford 39-42; University Prof. of the History and Philosophy of Religion, Univ. of London, and Fellow of Univ. Coll. and King's Coll., London 45-55, Emeritus Prof. 55-; Forwood Lecturer Univ. of Liverpool 49-50; Editor of *Folk-Lore* 32-58; Pres. Folk-Lore Soc. 30-32; Vice-Pres. of VIIth Int. Congress for the History of Religion, Amsterdam 50; Pres. Anthropological Section, British Asscn. for Advancement of Science 52; Chaplain All Souls Coll., Oxford 60-; Hon. D.D. (St. Andrews).
Publs. *Primitive Ritual and Belief* 17, *Introduction to Anthropology* 19, *Origins of Sacrifice* 33, *Christian Myth and Ritual* 33, *Old Testament in the light of Anthropology* 35, *Social Function of Religion* 40 (French trans. 50), *Comparative Religion* 38, *The Beginnings of Religion* 48 (Spanish trans. 56), *The Concept of Deity* 50, *Marriage and Society* 52, *The Nature and Function of Priesthood* 55 (German trans.), *The History of Religions* 56, *Prehistoric Religion* 57 (French, German, Italian editions), *Myth and Ritual in the Ancient Near East* 58, *The Cult of the Mother Goddess* 59, *The Ancient Gods* 60, *Seasonal Feasts and Festivals* 61, *Sacrifice and Sacrament* 62, *The Worship of the Sky-God* 63, *From Caves to Cathedrals* 64, *The Tree of Life* 66, *Christianity and other Religions* 67.
Hidsfield House, Cumnor Hill; and All Souls College, Oxford, England.
Telephone: Cumnor 2040.

James, F(rank) Cyril, PH.D., D.SC., (Econ.), F.R.S.C.; Canadian economist; b. 8 Oct. 1903; ed. Hackney Downs School, London School of Economics, Univ. of Pennsylvania.
Clerk, Barclays Bank, London 21-23; Instructor in Finance and Transportation, Univ. of Pennsylvania 24-27, Asst. Prof. of Finance 27-33, Associate Prof. 33-35, Prof. 35-38, Chair. Graduate Faculty in Social Science 36-37, Prof. of Finance and Economic History 38-39; Prof. of Political Economy, McGill Univ. 39-62; Dir. School of Commerce, McGill Univ. 39-40, Principal and Vice-Chancellor 39-62, Principal Emer. 62-; Gov. of Birkbeck Coll., London 66-; mem. Nat. Bureau of Economic Research (N.Y.) Conf. on Financial Research;

Chair. Canadian Govt. Advisory Cttee. on Reconstruction 41-44; Vice-Pres. Nat. Conf. of Canadian Univs. 46-48, Pres. 48-50; mem. Exec. Council Asscn. of Univs. of British Commonwealth 46-53 (Chair. 49); mem. Exec. Board, Int. Asscn. of Univs. 55-, Pres. 60-65; Hon. Sec. Oxfam 66-; mem. Univ. Advisory Cttee. Training of Veterans, Ottawa; Hon. LL.D. (Queen's, Ursinus, Syracuse, New York, Saskatchewan, Toronto, London, Manitoba, McMaster, New Brunswick, Punjab, Birmingham, Cambridge, Glasgow, Rochester, British Columbia, Princeton, Northwestern, Alberta, Ottawa), D.Sc. (Clarkson), D.C.L. (Bishop's and Kansas), D.Sc. (Econ.) (Laval, Pennsylvania), Hon. D.Litt. (Punjab, McGill), Docteur de l'Université de Montréal; Chevalier de la Légion d'Honneur; Fellow, Royal Soc. of Canada.
Publs. *Cyclical Fluctuations in the Shipping and Shipbuilding Industries* 27 *The Economics of Money, Credit and Banking* 30, 35, 40, *England Today: A Survey of her Economic Situation* 31. *The Road to Revival* 32, *The Meaning of Money* (with others) 35, *The Economic Doctrines of J. M. Keynes* (with others) 38, *The Growth of Chicago Banks* (2 vols.) 38, *Economic Problems in a Changing World* (with others) 39, *Report of the Advisory Committee on Reconstruction, Canada* (joint author) 44, *On Understanding Russia* 59.
Pipers Croft, Devonshire Avenue, Amersham, Bucks., England.
Telephone: Amersham 2936.

James, Sir John Morrice Cairns, K.C.M.G., C.V.O., M.B.E.; British diplomatist; b. 30 April 1916; ed. Bradfield, Oxford Univ.
Joined Dominions Office 39; Royal Navy, Royal Marines Second World War; staff of United Kingdom High Commission in South Africa 46-47; Commonwealth Relations Office, London 47-52; Dep. U.K. High Commr., Lahore 52-53, Karachi 55-56; Dep. U.K. High Commissioner, India 58-61, U.K. High Commissioner, Pakistan 61-65; Deputy Under-Sec. of State, Commonwealth Office, London 66-68, Perm. Under Sec. of State 68-.
34 Hans Place, London, S.W.1, England.
Telephone: 01-584-2621.

James, Philip, C.B.E.; British arts administrator; b. 31 Oct. 1901; ed. Sherborne School and University Coll., London Univ.
Sub-Librarian Middle Temple, London 23-25; Asst. Keeper, Victoria and Albert Museum 25-35; Keeper of the Library, Victoria and Albert Museum 35-39; Ministry of Home Security 39-41; with Council for the Encouragement of Music and the Arts (CEMA) 41; Art Dir. CEMA 42; Art Dir. Arts Council of Great Britain 46-58; Dir. Waddesdon Manor (Nat. Trust) 58-60; Sec. and Editor Museums Asscn. 60-64; Commdr. of the Order of the Aztec Eagle (Mexico); Chevalier de l'Ordre de la Couronne (Belgium); Commdr. of the Order of the Lion (Finland); Commdr. Order of Merit (Fed. Republic of Germany); Fellow of University Coll., London 61; Hon. F.M.A.
Starveacre, Seer Green, Bucks., England.
Telephone: Jordans 2265.

James of Rusholme, Baron (Life Peer); cr. 59; Kt. (cr. 56); **Eric John Francis James,** M.A., B.SC., D.PHIL. (Oxon.), LL.D. (McGill); British educationist; b. 09; ed. Taunton's School, Southampton and Queen's Coll., Oxford.
Assistant Master Winchester Coll. 35-45; High Master The Manchester Grammar School 45-62; Vice-Chancellor, Univ. of York 62-; mem. Univ. Grants Cttee. 48-58; Chair. Headmasters' Conf. 53 and 54; mem. Central Advisory Council for Educ. 57; Fellow Winchester Coll. 63; mem. Press Council 64-, Social Science Research Council 65-; Hon. Fellow Queen's Coll., Oxford 60.

Publs. *Elements of Physical Chemistry* (in part) 38, *Science and Education* (in part) 42, *An Essay on the content of Education* 49, *Education and Leadership* 51.
The University of York, Heslington, York, England.

Jameson, (Margaret) Storm, M.A.; British novelist; b. 94; ed. Leeds Univ. and King's Coll., London.
Pres. English P.E.N. Club 38-45; Hon. D. Litt.
Publs. *The Lovely Ship* 27, *Farewell to Youth* 28, *The Voyage Home* 29, *A Richer Dust* 31, *That Was Yesterday* 32, *A Day Off* 33, *No Time Like the Present* 33, *Company Parade* 34, *Love in Winter* 35, *In the Second Year* 36, *None Turn Back* 36, *Delicate Monster* 37, *Civil Journey* 39, *Farewell Night, Welcome Day* 39, *Europe to Let* 40, *Cousin Honoré* 40, *The Fort* 42, *Then We Shall Hear Singing* 42, *Cloudless May* 43, *The Journal of Mary Hervey Russell* 45, *The Other Side* 45, *Before the Crossing* 47, *The Black Laurel* 48, *The Moment of Truth* 49, *The Writer's Situation and Other Essays* 50, *The Green Man* 52, *The Hidden River* 55, *The Intruder* 56, *A Cup of Tea for Mr. Thorgill* 57, *A Ulysses Too Many* 58, *Last Score* 61, *Road from the Monument* 62, *A Month Soon Goes* 63, *The Aristide Case* 64, *The Early Life of Stephen Hind* 66.
c/o Macmillan & Co., Little Essex Street, London, W.C.2, England.

Jamieson, John Kenneth, B.S.; American (b. Canadian) oil executive; b. 28 Aug. 1910; ed. Univ. of Alberta and Massachusetts Inst. of Technology.
Plant Engineer, later Foreman, Northwest Stellarene, Canada; Foreman, Engineer, Manager of Refineries, British American Oil Co., Canada 34-48; Assoc. Manager (Coordination and Econs.), Imperial Oil Co. Ltd., Toronto 48-49, Manager, Engineering and Development, Sarnia 49-50, Dir. 50-53, Vice-Pres. 53-58; Pres. Int. Petroleum Co. Ltd., Florida 59-61; Vice-Pres. and Dir. Humble Oil and Refining Co., Houston, Texas 61-62, Exec. Vice-Pres. and Dir. 62-63, Pres. and Dir. 63-64; Exec. Vice-Pres. and Dir. Standard Oil Co. (N.J.), New York 64-65, Pres. and Dir. 65-; Dir. Chase Manhattan Bank 65-.
Office: Standard Oil Co. (N.J.), 30 Rockefeller Plaza, New York, N.Y. 10020; Home: 1310 Flagler Drive, Mamaroneck, N.Y. 10543, U.S.A.

Janberg, Hans, D.IUR.; German business executive; b. 17 April 1909.
Member of Management Board, Deutsche Bank A.G.; Chair. and mem of Advisory Board of several undertakings; Chair. of Management Board, Asscn. of Banks and Bankers in Rhineland and Westphalia.
Königsallee 45/47, Düsseldorf, German Federal Republic.

Jankovcová, Mrs. Ludmila, Ing.; Czechoslovak politician; b. 8 Aug. 1897.
Member of Exec. Cttee. Social Dem. Party, active in resistance movement during the war; Deputy to Nat. Assembly 46-63; Minister of Industry 47-48; Minister of Food 48-54; Co-Deputy Premier 54-63; mem. State Comm. for Finance, Prices and Wages 65-; mem. Central Cttee. C.P. of Czechoslovakia; Order of the Repub. 57.
Obrángů míru 90, Prague 7, Czechoslovakia.

Janne, Henri, D.PHIL. ET LETTRES; Belgian university professor and sociologist; b. 20 Feb. 1908; ed. Athénée Royal d'Ixelles, Univ. of Brussels.
Directed a number of govt. economic and social services, including Dir. Office National des Vacances Ouvrières 36, Dir.-Gen. Rééquipement National 47, Dir.-Gen. Coordination Economique (Prime Minister's Office) 49; *Chef du Cabinet*, Ministries of Economic Affairs, Supplies, and Economic Co-ordination 45-49; Pres. Defence Production Board, NATO 49-51; Pres. Belgian del. to UN Economic and Social Council 54 session; Prof. of Sociology, Univ. of Brussels 51-; Dir. Institut de Sociologie Solvay 53-56; Pres. Conseil Nat. du Travail,

Prof. Coll. of Europe, Bruges 52-; mem. Senate; Minister of Nat. Educ. and Culture 63-65; Vice-Pres. Nat. Council for Scientific Policy; mem. Int. Cttee. for Social Sciences Documentation, Int. Cttee. of UNESCO for Social Science Terminology 54, Libre Académie de Belgique, Inst. de Sociologie de France; mem. Acad. Royale de Belgique des Sciences et des Lettres; Rector Brussels Univ. 56-59; Pres. d'honneur de l'Association Int. des Sociologiques de langue français, Croix de Guerre Française avec palme, Officier Ordre de Léopold, Officier Légion d'Honneur, Commandeur de l'Ordre de Léopold II.

Publs. *L'Antialcibiade* 46, *Sociologie et Politique Sociale dans les pays occidentaux* 62, *Technique, Développement économique et Technocratie* 63, *Le Système; Social Essai de Thèorie Générale* 68.

244 avenue Louise, Brussels, Belgium.
Telephone: 47-13-12.

Janne d'Othée, Xavier, PH.D., LL.D.; Belgian jurist; b. 83; ed. Liège Univ.
Lecturer, Liège Univ. 20, Prof. of Law 30-53 (Dean 30-31), Prof. Emeritus 53-; Prof. Acad. of Int. Law, The Hague; Bâtonnier Ordre des Avocats Verviers 36; fmr. Vice-Pres. Féd. des Avocats Belges; mem. Int. Law Asscn. London, American Law Asscn., Société de Législation Comparée Paris; Vice-Pres. Henri Capitant Asscn. for Juridical Science Paris; mem. Int. Diplomatic Acad.; corresp. mem. Inst. of Comparative Law and Legislative Studies, Rio de Janeiro; mem. Acad. of Jurisprudence, Madrid; founder Janne-Zurstrassen Prize, Liège Univ.; mem. d'Honneur Asscn. Amitiés Belgo-Canadiennes; Dr. h.c. (Montpellier, Montreal, Laval); Created Chevalier Dec. 66.
10 rue de la Banque, Verviers, Belgium.

Jánossy, Lajos, DR. PHIL.; Hungarian physicist; b. 2 March 1912; ed. Vienna and Berlin Univs.
On staff of Manchester Univ. 39-47; Senior Prof. and Dept. Head, School of Cosmic Rays, Dublin 47-50; Prof. L. Eötvös Univ., Budapest 50-57, Head, Dept. of Atomic Physics 57-; Dir. Central Research Inst. for Physics, Budapest; Vice-Chair. Hungarian Nat. Atomic Energy Comm.; Vice-Pres. Hungarian Acad. of Sciences; mem. Central Cttee. Hungarian Socialist Workers' Party; Vice-Chair. IAEA Board of Govs. 61-63; mem. Scientific Council, Joint Inst. of Nuclear Research, Dubna; mem. numerous foreign acads. of science; Kossuth Award 51.
Publs.: *Cosmic Rays* 48 (Russian 49), *Cosmic Rays and Nuclear Physics* 48 (Italian 54), *Introduction to Cosmic Ray Research* 54 (German 55, Polish 56), *Philosophical Problems of the Theory of Relativity* (Hungarian) 63, *Theory and Practice of the Evaluation of Measurements* 65 (Russian 65, English 65), *Theory of Relativity and Physical Reality* 68 (German 69).
Central Research Institute for Physics, P.O.B. 49, Budapest 114, Hungary.
Telephone: 166-255.

Janot, Raymond Marcel Louis, L. en D., L. ès L.; French civil servant; b. 9 March 1917; ed. Coll. Stanislas, Lycée Henry-IV, Paris Univ. and Ecole Libre des Sciences Politiques.
Auditeur, Conseil d'Etat 46, Maître des Requêtes 48-; Legal Counsellor, Présidence de la République 47-51; Economic Counsellor French High Comm. in Indo-China 51-52; Dir. du Cabinet, Minister for Relations with Associated States 52-53; Sec.-Gen. Conseil d'Etat 56-59; Technical Counsellor, Gen. de Gaulle June 58-Jan. 59; Sec.-Gen. French Community Feb. 59-60; Dir.-Gen. Radiodiffusion-Télévision Française 60-62; Conseil d'Etat 62-; Officier Légion d'Honneur, Croix de Guerre, Médaille des Evadés.
Conseil d'Etat, place du Palais-Royal, Paris 1er, France.

Janow, Seymour J.; American government official; b. 22 Jan. 1913; ed. Univ. of California (Berkeley).

Statistician, Economist, Business Exec., Social Worker California State Relief Admin. 36-38; Economist, Dept. of Agriculture 39-41; mem. Intelligence Analysis Board of Econ. Warfare 42; Principal Econ. Analyst, Import-Export Bank, Washington; War Dept. foreign trade Economist in Japan 47-48; Vice. Pres. U.S. Consultants Inc., U.S. Consultants Overseas Inc. 49-61; Admin. for Far East Region, Agency for Int. Devt. 62-63; U.S. Consultants, Inc. since 64, Pres. of U.S. Consultants, Inc., Tokyo, Japan.
1327 33rd Street N.W., Washington, D.C., U.S.A.
Telephone: 337-1220.

Japan, Emperor of (*see* Hirohito).

Jargalsaikhan, Bayaryn; Mongolian diplomatist; b. 15.
Diplomatic service 41-, First Sec., Moscow, Dir. to Dept., Ministry of Foreign Affairs, Ambassador to People's Republic of China; Dep. to Grand People's Hural 51-; Perm. Rep. of Mongolian People's Republic to the UN 61-64; Amb. to Czechoslovakia, U.A.R. and France.
Embassy of the Mongolian People's Republic, Paris, France.

Jarman, Walton Maxey; American business executive; b. 10 May 1904; ed. Massachusetts Inst. of Technology.
Secretary-Treasurer, Jarman Shoe Co. 25-32; Pres. Gen. Shoe Corpn. 32-49, Chair. 49- (name changed to Genesco Inc.); Dir. Freedoms Foundation, H. & M. Rayne Ltd., S. H. Kress & Co., Nat. Shoe Manufacturers Asscn., Fed. Reserve Bank of Atlanta 60-66; Trustee Mutual Life Insurance Co. of New York, Moody Bible Inst., Greenfield Real Estate Investment Inst.; Vice-Pres. American Bible Soc.; Hon. Dr. Laws (Stetson Univ., Florida).
Publ. *A Businessman Looks at the Bible* 64.
111 Seventh Avenue North, Nashville, Tenn., U.S.A.

Jarnik, Vojtěch, DR. RER. NAT., D.SC.; Czechoslovak mathematician; b. 22 Dec. 1897.
Professor of Physical and Mathematical Sciences, Charles Univ., Prague; mem. Czechoslovak Acad. of Sciences 52-; has worked mainly in field of analytical theory of numbers; State Prize 52; Order of Labour, Silver Plaque of Czechoslovak Acad. of Sciences, Order of the Republic 67.
Publ. *Introduction to Integral and Introduction to Differential Mathematics.*
Charles University, Prague, Czechoslovakia.

Jarosinski, Witold; Polish politician; b. 18 Sept. 1909; ed. Uniwersytet Warszawski.
Member Communist Union of Polish Youth 29; fought and wounded Sept. 39; worked in Warsaw refrigerating plant 42-44; mem. Polish Workers' Party Voivodship Cttee., Katowice 45-47; Sec. Voivodship Cttee., Wrocław 47-48; Sec. Polish United Workers Party (P.Z.P.R.) Voivodship Cttee., Cracow 49; First Sec. Voivodship Cttee., Warsaw 50-51, Deputy Head of Organizational Dept. of P.Z.P.R. Central Cttee 51; Minister of Educ. 51-56; Sec. of P.Z.P.R. Central Cttee. 56-; First Sec. Warsaw Cttee. of P.Z.P.R. 57-60; Alt. mem. P.Z.P.R. Central Cttee. 49-54, mem. 54-; mem. Seym 52-; decorations include Order of Banner of Labour, First Class 54, 64.
Polska Zjednoczona Partia Robotnicza, Nowy Świat 6, Warsaw, Poland.

Jaroszewicz, Piotr; Polish politician; b. 09.
Schoolmaster before, and in U.S.S.R. during Second World War; joined Polish army in U.S.S.R. 43; Deputy Commdr. in charge of political affairs, First Polish Army 45; Vice-Minister of Defence 45-50; Deputy Chair. State Comm. for Economic Planning 50-52; Vice-Premier 52-; Perm. Rep. to Council for Mutual Econ. Aid (COMECON) 57-; Chair. Cttee. for Econ. Co-operation with Foreign Countries 58-; mem. Central

Cttee. and Deputy mem. of Political Bureau of Polish United Workers' Party; mem. Polish Diet.
1/3 Aleje Ujazdowskie, Warsaw, Poland.
Telephone: 28-90-01.

Jarring, Gunnar, PH.D.; Swedish diplomatist; b. 12 Oct. 1907; ed. Lund Univ.
Assoc. Prof. Turkic Languages Lund Univ. 33-40; Attaché Ankara 40-41; Chief Section B Teheran 41; Chargé d'Affaires a.i. Teheran and Baghdad 45, Addis Ababa 46-48; Minister to India 48-51, concurrently to Ceylon 50-51, to Persia, Iraq and Pakistan 51-52; Dir. Political Div. Ministry of Foreign Affairs 53-56; Perm. Rep. to U.N. 56-58; rep. on Security Council 57-58; Ambassador to U.S.A. 58-64, to U.S.S.R. 64-, and to Mongolia 65-; Special Envoy of UN Security Council on Middle East situation Nov. 67-; Knight Commdr. Order of the North Star.
Publs. *Studien zu einer osttürkischen Lautlehre* 33, *The Contest of the Fruits—An Eastern Turki Allegory* 36, *The Uzbek Dialect of Qilich*, *Russian Turkestan* 37, *Uzbek Texts from Afghan Turkestan* 38, *The Distribution of Turki Tribes in Afghanistan* 39, *Materials for the Knowledge of Eastern Turkestan* (Vols. I-IV) 47-51, *An Eastern Turki-English Dialect Dictionary* 64.
Swedish Embassy, Ul. Vorovskovo 44, Moscow, U.S.S.R.

Järvi, Osmo Henrik, M.D.; Finnish pathologist; b. 1 Jan. 1911; ed. Helsinki and Utrecht Univs. and Karolinska Inst., Stockholm.
Assistant, Anatomy Dept., Helsinki Univ. 32-38; Asst., Dept. of Pathological Anatomy 38-44; Lecturer, Microscopical Anatomy, 40-44, Prof. of Pathological Anatomy, Turku Univ. 44-; Dean, Faculty of Medicine 45-54, Rector 54-60; Chair. Finnish Medical Research Council 61-67; mem. Finnish Acad. of Science and Letters 60, Finnish Medical Soc. "Duodecim", Finnish Medical Asscn.; Hon. mem. Swedish Medical Soc., Finnish Asscn. of Pathologists (Chair. 56-62), Scandinavian Asscn. of Pathologists, Pathological Soc. of Great Britain and Ireland, American Soc. of Clinical Pathologists, Int. Acad. of Pathology, N.Y. Acad. of Sciences, Cancer Asscn. of Finland, Cancer Foundation of Finland (Chair. 60-), etc.
Publs. Works on secretion process and Golgi apparatus, morbid pathology of respiratory and intestinal tract, exfoliated cytology; *Pohdintaa* (Meditations) 67.
Yliopistonkatu 2K, Turku, Finland.

Jarvis, Alan Hepburn, B.A.; Canadian art gallery director and sculptor; b. 26 July 1915; ed. Univs. of Toronto and Oxford, and New York Univ.
With Ministry of Aircraft Production 41-45; Sec. to Sir Stafford Cripps 45; Dir. of Public Relations, Council of Industrial Design 45-47; Dir., Pilgrim Pictures Ltd. 47-50; Head, Oxford House, Bethnal Green, and Chair. of Governors, Group Theatre 50-55; Dir., Nat. Gallery of Canada 55-59; Chair. Soc. of Art Publications 59-; Dir. Canadian Conf. on the Arts, Toronto 60-.
Publs. *Democracy Alive* (edited collected speeches of Sir Stafford Cripps) 46, *The Things We See* series (Editor), *Indoors and Out*, *How to Buy Furniture* (with Sir Gordon Russell) 53.
541 Manor Road, Rockcliffe Park, Ottawa, Ont., Canada.

Jarvis, Porter Maxwell, B.S.; American business executive; b. 6 Nov. 1902; ed. Iowa State Univ.
Provision Dept., Swift & Co., South St. Joseph, Mo. 26-28, Chicago office 28-33, Asst. to Vice-Pres. in Charge Pork Div. 33-38, Asst. to Pres. 38-41, Vice-Pres. 41-49, Dir. 49-, Exec. Vice-Pres. 49-55, Pres. 55-64, Chair. 64-68; Dir. American Meat Inst., Int. Harvester, Int. Livestock Exhbn., Chicago Asscn. of Commerce and Industry, Ill. Central Railroad, Continental Ill. Nat. Bank; Trustee Univ. of Chicago Cttee. for Econ.

Devt. and Nutrition Foundation Inc., Museum of Science and Industry.
Home: 400 E. Randolph, Chicago, Ill. 60643; Office: 115 West Jackson Blvd., Chicago, Ill. 60604, U.S.A.

Jaspers, Karl, M.D.; German professor of philosophy; b. 23 Feb. 1883; studied medicine.
Extraordinary Prof. of Philosophy, Heidelberg 20; Ordinary Prof. of Philosophy 21; declined appointments in Greifswald, Kiel and Bonn; Ordinary Prof. of Philosophy, Basle 48-; Dr. ès Lettres h.c. (Lausanne, Geneva); Dr. Phil. h.c. (Heidelberg); Dr. h.c. (Paris); Dr. Med. h.c. (Basle); hon. mem. Netherlands Soc. for Psychiatry and Neurology; mem. Heidelberg Acad. of Sciences; Peace Prize, German Booksellers Asscn. 58, Erasmus Prize 59.
Publs. *Allgemeine Psychopathologie* (6th edition) 53, *Psychologie der Weltanschauungen* 19, *Die geistige Situation der Zeit* 31, *Philosophie* (3 vols.) 32, *Vernunft und Existenz* 35, *Nietzsche* 36, *Descartes* 37, *Die Schuldfrage* 46, *Nietzsche und das Christentum* 46, *Von der Wahrheit* 47, *Der philosophische Glaube* 47, *Vom Ursprung und Ziel der Geschichte* 49, *Einführung in die Philosophie* 50, *Vernunft und Widervernunft in unserer Zeit* 50, *Rechenschaft und Ausblick* (speeches and essays) 51, *Zur Frage der Entmythologisierung* 54, *Schelling* 55, *Die grossen Philosophen* 57, *Philosophie und Welt* 58, *Die Atombombe und die Zukunft des Menschen* 58, *Freiheit und Wiedervereinigung* 60, *Die Idee der Universität* 61, *Der philosophische Glaube angesichts der Offenbarung* 62, *Kleine Schule des philosophischen Denkens* 64, *Hoffnung und Sorge* 65, *Aus dem Ursprung denkende Metaphysiker* 66, *Wohin treibt Die Bundesrepublik?* 66, *Antwort* 67, *Schicksal und Wille* 67, *Aneignung und Polemik* 68.
Austrasse 126, 4000 Basle, Switzerland.

Jastrun, Mieczysław, PH.D.; Polish writer; b. 03; ed. Cracow Univ.
State Prize, First Class for *Mickiewicz*.
Publs. *Spotkanie w Czasie* (Meeting in Time), *Dzieje nieostygłe* (History Still Fresh), *Strumień i milczenie* (The Stream and Silence), *Godzina strzeżona* (The Guarded Hour), *Rzecz ludzka* (Human Affairs), *Genezy* (Genesis); biographical novel *Mickiewicz*, *Spotkanie z Salomeą* (Meeting with Salomea) (on J. Słowacki), *Poeta i dworzanin* (Poet and Courtier) (on J. Kochanowski), *Między słowem a milczeniem* (Between Word and Silence; Essays) 60, *Większe od życie* (Larger than Life; Poems) 60; *Piękna Choroba* 61, *Schöne Krankheit* 61, essays and translations from French, Russian and German poetry; *Mit śródziemnomorski* (Mediterranean Myth; Essays) 62, *Intonationen* 62, *Strefa owoców* (Zone of Fruits) 64, *Poezja i rzeczywistość* (Poetry and Truth; Essays) 66, *Poezje* (a selection of poems) 66.
ul. Iwicka 8a m.9, Warsaw 36, Poland.

Jaszczuk, Bolesław; Polish diplomatist and politician; b. 13; ed. Warsaw Polytechnic.
Active mem. Union of Polish Youth before Second World War; mem. resistance movement Bialystok and Warsaw 39-42; arrested and imprisoned in Oswiecim and Mauthausen concentration camps; Economic Sec. Warsaw Cttee. Polish Workers' Party 45; later Vice-Pres. Warsaw City Council, Chair. Katowice People's Council; Minister of Power 51-59; Vice-Chair. Planning Comm., Council of Ministers 57-59; Ambassador to U.S.S.R. 59-63; Sec. Cen. Cttee. Polish United Workers' Party 63-, also Deputy mem. Political Bureau.
Central Committee of the Polish United Workers' Party, Warsaw, Poland.

Jatti, Shri Basappa Danappa, B.A., LL.B.; Indian politician; b. 10 Sept. 1912; ed. Bijapur Govt. High School, Rajaram Coll. and Sykes Law Coll., Kolhapur.
Bar practice at Jamkhandi 40-45; mem. Jamkhandi State Legislature; Minister and subsequently Chief Minister Jamkhandi State until its merger with Bombay State 48; mem. Bombay State Legislative Assem-

bly, Parl. Sec. to Chief Minister 50-52; Deputy Minister for Health and Labour, Bombay State 52; Chief Minister of Mysore 58-62, Minister of Finance 62-65, Minister for Food, Mysore 65-.
Vidhana Soudha, Bangalore 1, Mysore, India.

Javits, Jacob Koppel, LL.B.; American lawyer and politician; b. 18 May 1904; ed. New York Univ. Law School.
Admitted to the American bar 27; Asst. to the Chief of Chemical Warfare Service 39-42; Asst. to the Chief of Operations, Chemical Warfare Service, Europe 43, Pacific 44; resumed law practice 45; elected to 80th Congress from N.Y. 46; re-elected 48, 50, 52; mem. of Cttee. on Foreign Affairs and Chair. Sub-Cttee. on Foreign Economic Policy; Attorney-Gen. of N.Y. 54-56; Senator from N.Y. 57-; partner in Javits, Trubin, Sillocks, Edelman and Purcell 58-; Legion of Merit and Army Commendation Ribbon; Republican.
Publs. *A Proposal to Amend the Anti-Trust Laws* 39, *A Liberal Political Philosophy for the Republican Party* 46, *Discrimination, U.S.A.* 60, *Order of Battle, A Republican's Call to Reason* 64.
911 Park Avenue, New York 21, N.Y., U.S.A.

Jawara, Hon. Sir Dauda (Kairaba), M.P., Kt., M.R.C.V.S., D.T.V.M.; Gambian politician; b. 11 May 1924.
Former Principal Veterinary Officer, Gambian Civil Service; entered politics 60; Minister of Educ. 60-61; Premier 62-63; Prime Minister 63-.
Office of the Prime Minister, Bathurst, Gambia.

Jay, Rt. Hon. Douglas Patrick Thomas, P.C., M.P.; British journalist and politician; b. 23 March 1907; ed. Winchester Coll. and New Coll. Oxford.
Mem. staff *The Times* 29-33, *Economist* 33-37; City Editor *Daily Herald* 37-41; Fellow All Souls Coll. Oxford 30-37; Ministry of Supply 41-43; Principal Asst. Sec. Board of Trade 43; Personal Asst. to Prime Minister 45-46; M.P. 46-; Economic Sec. to Treasury 47-50; Financial Sec. to the Treasury 50-51; President of Board of Trade 64-67; Dir. Courtaulds 67-; Labour.
Publs. *The Socialist Case* 37, *Who is to Pay for the War and the Peace?* 41, *Socialism in the New Society* 62, *After the Common Market* 68.
12 Well Road, London, N.W.3, England.

Jayaratne, Merenna Francis de S.; Ceylonese diplomatist; b. 04; ed. Univ. of Ceylon and Univ. of London.
Ceylon Civil Service 27-; Dir. of Commerce and Dir. Tourist Bureau, Ceylon 48-49; Acting Dir. of Education 49-51; Perm. Sec. Ministry of Commerce and Trade 53-57, of Transport and Power 53-57, 59-60; Perm. Sec. Ministry of Defence 60, later Adviser to Prime Minister; Ambassador to United States 63-65; Perm. Rep. to UN, New York 65-67.
c/o Ministry of Foreign Affairs, Colombo, Ceylon.

Jayewardene, Junius Richard; Ceylonese lawyer and politician; b. 17 Sept. 1906; ed. Royal Coll., Univ. Coll., and Law Coll., Colombo.
Mem. Colombo Municipal Council 41; mem. State Council 43; mem. House of Representatives 47-; Minister of Finance 47-53; Hon. Sec. Ceylon Nat. Congress 40-47; Hon. Treasurer United Nat. Party 47-48 and Vice-Pres. 53; Leader of the House of Representatives and Minister of Agriculture and Food 53-56; Minister of Finance, Information, Broadcasting, Local Govt. and Housing Mar. 60-July 60; Deputy Leader of Opposition July 60-65; Minister of State, and Parl. Sec. to Minister of Defence, External Affairs and Planning 65-.
Publs. *Buddhist Essays, In Council* (speeches), *Buddhism and Marxism.*
66 Ward Place, Colombo, Ceylon.
Telephone: Colombo 95028.

Jean, H.R.H. Grand-Duke of Luxembourg, Prince of Nassau, Prince of Bourbon-Parma; b. 5 Jan. 1921.
Married Princess Josephine-Charlotte of Belgium

April 53; Lieut.-Rep. of Grand Duchess 61-64; became Grand-Duke of Luxembourg on abdication of Grand Duchess Charlotte Nov. 64.
Grand-Ducal Palace, Luxembourg.

Jeanmaire, Renée Marcelle (Zizi), (wife of Roland Petit, *q.v.*,); French actress, dancer and singer; b. 29 April 1924.
Student, Paris Opera Ballet 33-40, Dancer 40-44; with Ballets de Monte-Carlo, Ballets Colonel de Basil, Ballets Roland Petit; leading roles in *Aubade, Piccoli, Carmen, La Croqueuse de Diamants, Rose des Vents, Cyrano de Bergerac, La Dame dans la Lune*; films: *Hans Christian Andersen, Anything Goes, Folies Bergères, Charmants Garçons, Black Tights*; musical: *The Girl in Pink Tights* (Broadway); music hall appearances.
12 rue de la Paix, Paris 2e, France.

Jeanneney, Jean-Marcel, L. ès L., D. en D.; French economist and politician; b. 13 Nov. 1910; ed. Ecole Libre des Sciences Politiques, Paris.
Prof. of Political Economy, Grenoble Univ. 37-51, Dean of Law Faculty 47-51; Prof. of Social Economics, Paris Univ. 51-56, of Financial Economics 57-59; Dir. du Cabinet of his father, Jules Jeanneney, Minister of State, de Gaulle Provisional Govt. 44-45; mem. Admin. Council, Ecole Nat. d'Admin. 45-58; Dir. Economic Activity Study Service, Fondation Nat. des Sciences Politiques 52-58; Consultant to OEEC 53; mem. Rueff Cttee. 58; Rapporteur and del. to numerous Confs.; Minister of Industry, Debré Cabinet Jan. 59-62; Ambassador to Republic of Algeria 62-63; Chair. French Cttee. on Co-operation with Developing Countries 63; mem. and French Rep. to UN Econ. and Social Council 64-66; Prof. Political Econ., Paris Univ. 63; Minister of Social Affairs 66-May 68.
Publs. *Essai sur les mouvements des prix en France depuis la stabilisation monétaire (1927-1935)* 36, *Economie et Droit de l'Electricité* (with C. A. Colliard) 50, *Les Commerces de détail en Europe occidentale* 54, *Forces et Faiblesses de l'Economie française 1955-1956* 56, *Textes de droit économique et social français 1789-1957* (with Perrot), *Tableaux statistiques relatifs à l'économie française et l'économie mondiale* 57, *Documents économiques* (2 Vols.) 58, *Economie Politique* 59; seven published courses of lectures on political, social and financial economy 52-58.
102 rue d'Assas, Paris 6e, France.

Jedrychowski, Stefan, D.IUR.; Polish politician and economist; b. 19 May 1910; ed. Wilna Univ.
Active in progressive youth movement; imprisoned for political reasons 37; one of the organisers of the Polish "Kosciuszko" Division in the U.S.S.R. during the Second World War; Dir. Dept. of Information and Propaganda, Nat. Liberation Cttee. 44; later successively Ambassador to U.S.S.R. and to France, Minister of Marine and Foreign Trade, Deputy Chair. State Economic Planning Cttee., Deputy Chair. Council of Ministers; Chair. Planning Comm. at the Council of Ministers; mem. Seym (Parliament) and Political Bureau, Polish United Workers Party 56-.
Planning Commission of the Council of Ministers, Warsaw, Poland.
Telephone: 28-73-27.

Jeejeebhoy, Sir Jamsetjee, Bt., J.P., B.A.; Indian industrialist; b. 10 May 1909; ed. Cathedral and John Cannon High School, Bombay and Gonville and Caius Coll. Cambridge.
Mem. Bombay Municipal Corpn. 34-39; J.P. 34; Hon. Presidency Magistrate Dec. 35; active in Boy Scout Movement, later resigned as a sequel to the Baden-Powell dispute; Commdr. Bombay Civic Guards, Northern Div. 40; Chair. Board of Trustees Sir J. J. Charity Funds, Sir J. J. Parsee Benevolent Inst., N. M. Wadia

Charities, The Bombay Pinjrapole, the District Benevolent Soc., etc.; Trustee Sir J. J. School of Art, Deccan Coll., Nowrosjee Wadia and Motlibai Wadia Hospital, etc.; Dir. of a number of Joint Stock Companies; Chair. Royal Western India Turf Club 48-52.
Sett Minar, Pedder Road, Bombay 26, India.
Telephone: 364421.

Jeffreys, Sir Harold, Kt., M.A., D.SC., F.R.S.; British astronomer; b. 22 April 1891; ed. Rutherford Coll., Newcastle, Armstrong Coll., Newcastle and St. John's Coll., Cambridge.
Lecturer in Mathematics, Cambridge Univ. 23-31, Reader in Geophysics 31-46, Prof. of Astronomy 46-58; Pres. Royal Astronomical Society 55-57, Pres. Int. Seismological Asscn. 57-60; Fellow St. John's Coll. Cambridge 14-; Copley and Royal Medals of the Royal Soc., Gold Medal, Royal Astronomical Soc., Vetlesen Prize 62, Guy Medal, Royal Statistical Soc., Wollaston and Murchison Medals, Geological Soc.
Publs. *The Earth, Methods of Mathematical Physics, Scientific Inference, Theory of Probability, Asymptotic Approximations.*
160 Huntingdon Road, Cambridge, England.

Jeleň, Lieutenant-Gen. Oskár; Czechoslovak diplomatist; b. 4 Sept. 1904; ed. State Teachers' Coll., Bratislava.
Deputy to Nat. Assembly and Slovak Nat. Council; mem. Central Cttee. of C.P. of Czechoslovakia; mem. Central Cttee. C.P. of Slovakia; mem. Bureau of Central Cttee. of C.P. of Slovakia; Chief of Main Political Admin. of Ministry of Nat. Defence 51; Deputy Minister of Interior 52-54; Deputy Chair. Slovak Board of Commrs., and Commr. of Interior 54-60; Amb. to Polish People's Repub. 60-67 (retd.); Order of 25th Feb. 1948, First Class; Order of Labour 64; resistance decorations.
c/o Ministry of Foreign Affairs, Prague, Czechoslovakia.

Jellicoe, 2nd Earl, (cr. 25); George Patrick John Rushworth Jellicoe, P.C., D.S.O., M.C.; British diplomatist and politician; b. 4 April 1918; ed. Winchester and Trinity Coll., Cambridge.
Military Service 39-45; joined Foreign Office 47; First Sec. Washington, Brussels, Baghdad; Dep. Sec.-Gen. Baghdad Pact; Jt. Parl. Sec., Ministry of Housing and Local Govt. 61-62; Minister of State, Home Office 62-Oct. 63; First Lord of Admiralty Oct. 63-April 64; Minister of Defence for the Royal Navy 64; Deputy Leader of the Opposition, House of Lords 67-; Croix de Guerre; Légion d'Honneur; Greek Mil. Cross.
Tidcombe Manor, Tidcombe, Nr. Marlborough, Wilts., England.

Jenkins, Baron (Life Peer) cr. 59; David Llewelyn Jenkins, P.C., M.A. British judge; b. 8 April 1899; ed. Charterhouse and Balliol Coll.
Called to Bar by Lincoln's Inn 23; K.C. 38; Bencher of Lincoln's Inn 45; Attorney-Gen. Duchy of Lancaster 46-47; a Justice of the High Court of Justice April 47-49; a Lord Justice of Appeal 49-59; Lord of Appeal in Ordinary 59-63; Privy Councillor 49-; Chair. Company Law Cttee. 59; Hon. Fellow Balliol Coll. Oxford 50.
24 Ashley Gardens, London, S.W.1, England.

Jenkins, Elizabeth; British writer; ed. Newnham Coll. Cambridge.
Publs. *Lady Caroline Lamb: a Biography* 32, *Portrait of an Actor* 33, *Harriet* (Femina Vie Heureuse Prize) 34, *The Phoenix Nest* 36, *Jane Austen—a Biography* 38, *Robert and Helen* 44, *Young Enthusiasts* 46, *Henry Fielding,* English Novelists Series 47, *Six Criminal Women* 49, *The Tortoise and the Hare* 54, *Ten Fascinating Women* 55, *Elizabeth the Great* 58, *Elizabeth and Leicester* 61, *Brightness* 63.
8 Downshire Hill, London, N.W.3, England.

Jenkins, Rt. Hon. Roy Harris, P.C., M.P.; British politician and writer; b. 11 Nov. 1920; ed. Abersychan Grammar School and Balliol Coll., Oxford.
Royal Artillery 39-46; mem. Staff of Industrial and Commercial Finance Corpn. 46-48; Labour M.P. 48-; Parliamentary Private Sec. to Sec. of State for Commonwealth Relations 49-50; Gov. British Film Inst. 55-58; mem. Cttee. of Management, Soc. of Authors 56-60; Chair. Fabian Soc. 57-58; mem. Council, Britain in Europe; Dep. Chair. Common Market Campaign; Dir. of Financial Operations, John Lewis Partnership Ltd. 63-64; Minister of Aviation 64-65; Sec. of State for Home Dept. 65-Nov. 67; Chancellor of the Exchequer Nov. 67-.
Publs. *Purpose and Policy* (Editor) 47, *Mr. Attlee: An Interim Biography* 48, *New Fabian Essays* (contributor) 52, *Pursuit of Progress* 53, *Mr. Balfour's Poodle* 54, *Sir Charles Dilke: A Victorian Tragedy* 58, *The Labour Case* 59, *Asquith* 64, *Essays and Speeches* 67.
11 Downing Street, London, S.W.1, England.

Jenkins, William Maxwell, A.B., M.B.A.; American banker; b. 19 April 1919; ed. Everett High School, Univ. of Washington and Harvard Graduate School of Business Admin.
Assistant cashier, Asst. Vice-Pres., Asst. Manager of Metropolitan Branch (Seattle), Seattle-First Nat. Bank 45-53; First Nat. Bank of Everett 53-61, Pres. 57-61; Chair. Everett Trust and Savings Bank 56-61; Exec. Vice-Pres. and Man., Everett Div., Seattle-First Nat. Bank 61-62; Chair. of Board and Chief Exec. Officer Seattle-First Nat. Bank 62-; Dir. other companies.
Seattle-First National Bank, Box 3586, Seattle, Washington 98124; and Home: 3008 Webster Point Road N.E., Seattle, Washington 98105, U.S.A.

Jenks, Clarence Wilfred, M.A., LL.D.; British lawyer; b. 7 March 1909; ed. Gonville and Caius Coll. Cambridge and Geneva School of International Studies.
Member Legal Section ILO 31, Legal Adviser 40, Asst. Dir.-Gen. 48-64, Deputy Dir.-Gen. 64-67, Principal Deputy Dir.-Gen. 67-; Adviser to Venezuelan Govt. on labour legislation 38; mem. ILO dels. to UN Conf. on Int. Org., San Francisco 45, Gen. Assembly and Econ. and Social Council of the UN and other int. confs. and cttees.; mem. Inst. of Int. Law, Int. Acad. of Comparative Law; Corresp. mem. Int. Acad. of Astronautics.
Publs. *The Headquarters of International Institutions* 45; *The International Protection of Trade Union Freedom* 57, *The Common Law of Mankind* 58, *Human Rights and International Labour Standards* 60, *International Immunities* 61, *The Proper Law of International Organisations* 62, *Law, Freedom and Welfare* 63, *The Prospects of International Adjudication* 64, *Space Law* 65, *Law in the World Community* 67, *The World beyond the Charter* 68; Editor of *The International Labour Code* 39 and 51, *Constitutional Provisions Concerning Social and Economic Policy* 44.
Office: International Labour Office, Geneva, Switzerland; Home: 3 rue de Contamines, Geneva, Switzerland.
Telephone: 32-62-00 (Office); 35-42-35 (Home).

Jenks, Downing Bland, B.S. in Industrial Engineering; American railroad executive; b. 16 Aug. 1915; ed. St. Paul Acad. and Yale Univ.
Asst. on Engineer Corps., Pennsylvania Railroad 37-38; Trainmaster, Div. Engineer, Roadmaster, Great Northern Railway 38-47, Div. Supt. 47; Vice-Pres. and Gen. Man., Chicago & Eastern Illinois Railroad 48; Asst. Vice-Pres. Rock Island Lines 50, Vice-Pres. operation 51, Exec. Vice-Pres. 53, Pres. 56-60; Pres. Missouri Pacific Railroad Co., Texas and Pacific Railroad and subsidiaries 61-; Dir. Asscn. of American Railroads, First Nat. Bank in St. Louis, Bankers Life Co., Transportation Asscn. of America; U.S. Army service,

North Africa, Italy, France, Germany, Lieut.-Col. Military Railway Service 42-45; Bronze Star Medal.
8 Greenbriar, St. Louis, Missouri 63124, U.S.A.

Jenny, Mgr. Henri Martin; French ecclesiastic; b. 11 July 1904; ed. Grand séminaire de Cambrai and Pontificia Universitas Gregoriana, Rome.
Professor of Holy Scripture, Grand Séminaire, Cambrai 29-49; Leading Curate, Saint-Géry Cambrai 50-53; Arch-Priest Douai 53-59; Auxiliary Bishop of Cambrai 59-65, Co-adjutor Bishop 65-66, Archbishop of Cambrai 66-; mem. Preparatory Comm. and mem. Comm. on Liturgy, Ecumenical Council.
Publs. *Les dimanches de l'année chrétienne, Le Mystère pascal dans l'année liturgique, La Messe, Les Actes des apôtres.*
Office of the Archbishop, B.P. 134, Cambrai 59; and Rue de Noyon, Cambrai 59, France.
Telephone: 81-34-96.

Jens, Walter, D.PHIL.; German philologist and novelist; b. 8 March 1923; ed. Hamburg and Freiburg im Breisgau Univs.
Assistant, Hamburg and Tübingen Univs. 46-50; Docent, Tübingen Univ. 50-56, Prof. of Classical Philology and Rhetoric 56-67, Dir. of Inst. für Allgemeine Rhetorik, Tübingen Univ. 67-; mem. German PEN, Berliner Akademie der Künste, Deutsche Akademie für Sprache und Dichtung; Lessingpreis der Hansestadt Hamburg 68.
Publs. *Nein—Die Welt der Angeklagten* (novel) 50, *Der Blinde* (novel) 51, *Vergessene Gesichter* (novel) 52, *Der Mann, der nicht alt werden wollte* (novel) 55, *Das Testament des Odysseus* (novel) 57, *Die Götter sind sterblich* (Diary of a Journey to Greece) 59, *Statt einer Literaturgeschichte* (Essays on Modern Literature) 57, *Moderne Literatur—moderne Wirklichkeit* (essay) 58, *Die Stichomythie in der frühen griechischen Tragödie* 55, *Hofmannsthal und die Griechen* 55, *Deutsche Literatur der Gegenwart* 61, *Zueignungen* 62, *Herr Meister* (Dialogue on a Novel) 63.
Sonnenstrasse 5, 74 Tübingen, German Federal Republic.

Jensen, Carl P.; Danish trade unionist and politician; b. 3 Jan. 1906; ed. as plumber and gas fitter.
Secretary to Plumbers' Asscn. 36-43; Sec. to Fed. of Danish Trade Unions 43-60; Minister of Housing 60-64, Minister for Greenland 64-67; mem. Folketing 53-; Social Democrat.
Ejderstedgade 14, Copenhagen V, Denmark.

Jensen, Eiler; Danish trade unionist; b. 14 April 1894.
Worked as sailor, messenger and warehouseman; Chair. Copenhagen Warehouse Workers' Union 25-36; mem. Exec. Bd. Nat. Union of Gen. and Special Workers 35-36; Sec. Danish Fed. of Trade Unions 36-39, Vice-Pres. 39-42, Acting Pres. 42-43, Pres. 43-; mem. Danish Parl. 45-52; Vice-Pres. ICFTU 49.
Danish Federation of Trade Unions, Rosenørns Alle 14, Copenhagen V, Denmark.

Jensen, Hans Daniel; German physicist; b. 25 June 1907.
Dozent Univ. of Hamburg 37-41; Prof. Inst. of Technology, Hanover 41-49; Prof. of Theoretical Physics, Heidelberg Univ. 49-, Dir. Inst. for Theoretical Physics, Heidelberg Univ. 49-; Nobel Prize for Physics 63.
Institute for Theoretical Physics, Heidelberg University, Heidelberg, German Federal Republic.
Telephone: Heidelberg 43645.

Jensen, Kai Adolf, M.D.; Danish doctor; b. 16 July 1894; ed. Københavns Universitet.
Assistant, State Serum Inst. 24, Head of Tuberculosis Dept. 31; Prof. of General Pathology, Univ. of Copenhagen 40-65, Emeritus 65-; mem. Acad. of Technical Sciences 43, Royal Danish Soc. of Sciences 46; Pres. Conf. of Int. Union against Tuberculosis 50-52, Chair.

Sub-Cttee. of Laboratory Methods 53-57; Editor *Acta Pathologica et Microbiologica Scandinavica* 62-65.
Malmögade 2, Copenhagen Ö, Denmark.
Telephone: Tr. 287.

Jensen, Kai Arne, DR. PHIL.; Danish chemist; b. 27 March 1908; ed. Københavns Universitet.
Chemical Laboratory, Univ. of Copenhagen 33-, Assoc. Prof. of Chemistry 43-50, Prof. 50-, Head of Chemical Laboratory II; Chair. Comm. on Nomenclature of Inorganic Chemistry of Int. Union of Pure and Applied Chemistry (IUPAC); mem. Royal Danish Acad. of Sciences and Letters, Danish Acad. of Technical Sciences; Knight Order of Dannebrog; Julius Thomsen Gold Medal.
Chemical Laboratory II of the University of Copenhagen, The H. C. Örsted Institute, Universitetsparken 5, 2100 Copenhagen Ø; Home: Bøgehøj 64, Copenhagen-Hellerup, Denmark.
Telephone: (01-) 35-31-33 (Office); Søborg 9375 (Home).

Jensen, Lars P.; Danish politician; b. 23 April 1909. Business manager, Co-operative Soc. 36; mem. Folketing 45-; Minister of Commerce 60, 64-66, of Interior 61; Social Democrat.
Serridslevvej 8, Copenhagen, Denmark.

Jephcott, Sir Harry, Bt., M.SC., F.R.I.C., F.P.S.; British company director; b. 15 Jan. 1891; ed. King Edward's Grammar School, Birmingham, and West Ham Technical Coll., London.
Called to Bar (Middle Temple) 25; Chair. Glaxo Laboratories Ltd. 45-63; Chair. Council of D.S.I.R. 56-61; Pres. Royal Inst. of Chemistry 53-55; Chair. Asscn. of British Chemical Manufacturers 47-52, President 52-55; mem. Advisory Council Scientific Policy 53-56; Chairman Committee on Detergents 53-55; Chairman School of Pharmacy, Univ. of London 48-; Gov. London School of Economics 52-; Gov. N. London Collegiate School 57; Hon. D.Sc. (Birmingham); Hon. Fellow Royal Soc. Medicine 61.
Weetwood, 1 Cheney Street, Pinner, Middlesex, England.
Telephone: 01-866-0305.

Jeppesen, Knud; Danish musician and composer; b. 15 Aug. 1892; ed. Univs. of Copenhagen and Vienna (PH.D. in Music).
Organist at St. Stefans Church, Copenhagen 17-32; at Holmens Church, Copenhagen 32-47; Prof. of Theory of Music in the Royal Conservatory, Copenhagen 20-47; Prof. of Musicology, Univ. of Aarhus 46-57; Dir. Royal Conservatory of Music, Copenhagen 32-47; mem. Royal Danish Acad. of Sciences; Pres. of the Int. Society for Musical Research 49-52; Hon. R.A.M. (London); mem. Royal Swedish Acad. of Music; Hon. mem. Accademia Nazionale di S. Cecilia, Accademia Nazionale dei Lincei (Rome); Premio Internazionale Forte dei Marmi 67; Editor *Acta Musicologica* 31-54.
Publs. *The Style of Palestrina and the Dissonance* 25, *Der Kopenhagener Chansonnier* 27, *Counterpoint* 30, *Dania sonans I* 33, *Die mehrstimmige italienische Laude um 1500* 35, *Die italienische Orgelmusik am Anfang des Cinquecento* 43, 60, *La Flora*, Vols. I-III 49, *Le Messe mantovane di Palestrina*, Vols. I-II 54, *Italia Sacra Musica*, Vols. I-III 62, *Balli Antichi Veneziani* 62; (compositions) *Reformationskantate* 36, *Lave og Ion* 37, *Te Deum Danicum* 45, motets and other works (mainly choral), *Rosaura*, opera in 3 Acts (Royal Opera, Copenhagen 50).
Lyngvej, Risskov pr. Aarhus, Denmark.
Telephone: Aarhus 179770.

Jepson, Selwyn; British novelist and screen writer; b. 99; ed. St. Paul's School.
Served First and Second World Wars (Mil. Intelligence and S.O.E.).
Publs. Novels: *The Qualified Adventurer* 21, *The King's*

Red-Haired Girl 23, *Rogues and Diamonds* 25, *The Death Gong* 28, *I Met Murder* 30, *Rabbit's Paw* 32, *Heads or Tails* (with Michael Joseph) 33, *Keep Murder Quiet* 40, *Man Running* 48, *The Golden Dart* 49, *The Hungry Spider* 50, *Man Dead* 51, *The Black Italian* 54; *The Assassin* 56, *Noise in the Night* 57, *The Laughing Fish* 60, *Fear in the Wind* 63, *The Third Possibility* 65, *The Angry Millionaire* 67.
Play: *Dark Horizon* (with Lesley Storm); screen plays: *Going Gay, For the Love of You* 32, *Irresistible Marmaduke, Monday at Ten* 33, *The Love Nest, The Riverside Murders* 34, *White Lilac, Hyde Park Corner* 35, *The Scarab Murder, Toilers of the Sea* (adapted and directed) 36, *Sailing Along* 37, *Carnet de Bal, Double Crime on the Maginot Line* 38, *Stage Fright* (*Man Running*) 50; television plays: *Thought to Kill, Dialogue for Two Faces* 53, *Face of the Law, The Last Moment* 54, *The Interloper* 55; radio plays: *The Hungry Spider, The Bath that Sang* 58, *Noise in the Night* 59, *Small Brother, Uncle Murderer, Art for Art's Sake, Death of a Guardian* 60, *Greymail* 62, *Dark Corners* 63; numerous television plays.
The Far House, Liss, Hants., England.

Jerome, Frank Edward; American banker; b. 22 Jan. 1905; ed. Seattle parochial and public schools and Pacific Coast Banking School.
Joined Seattle First Nat. Bank 19, Asst. Cashier 38-40, Asst. Vice-Pres. and Man. Credit Dept. 40-44, Vice-Pres. 44-53, Pres. 54-60, Vice-Chair. Board 60-; official of financial, commercial and philanthropic orgs.
1665 Broadmoor Drive, Seattle 2, Washington, U.S.A.

Jerusalem, Patriarch of (*see* Benedictos).

Jespersen, Iver, CAND. PHIL.; Danish publisher; b. 21 Oct. 1904.
Trained as bookseller and publisher in Boghallen Alfr. G. Hassing, Copenhagen; Naville et Cie., Geneva; Houghton Mifflin Co., Boston, Mass.; Doubleday's Book Shop at Lord & Taylor's, New York; Lars Hökerbergs Bokförlag, Stockholm; with Jespersen and Pio 27-, owner 52; Vice-Pres. Danish Publishers' Asscn. 47-52; Pres. 53-59; Pres. Booksellers' School 61; mem. Scandinavian Publishers' Council 53-; mem. Cttee. of Int. Publishers' Asscn. 53-.
Publs. *Goethe og haus Forläggere* (*Goethe and his Publishers*) 65, *Weimar 1806* 68.
Valkendorfsgade 22, 1151 Copenhagen K, Denmark.
Telephone: 01-129642.

Jespersen, Kaj Thomas, M.D.; Danish physician; b. 6 April 1898; ed. Københavns Universitet.
Assistant Supt., Mil. Hospital, Copenhagen 31; Chief Physician, Rigshospitalet, Copenhagen 39-65; Vice-Chair. Soc. of Danish Physicians 38-43; mem. Central Cttee. Danish Medical Asscn. 50-54, Vice-Chair. 52-54; Danish Del. European League against Rheumatism 47-57; Chair. Danish Org. of Physicians of Physical Medicine 38-48, Danish Soc. for Investigation of Rheumatic Diseases 51-53; Hon. mem. Danish Org. of Physicians of Physical Medicine 63; Knight Order of Dannebrog.
Publ. *Forholdet mellem Febris rheumatica og rheumatoid artritis* 40.
Skovdvaget 9, Bagsvaerd, Denmark.

Jessen, Borge, DR. PHIL.; Danish mathematician; b. 19 June 1907; ed. Univ. of Copenhagen.
Docent, Royal Veterinary and Agricultural Coll., Copenhagen 30-35; Prof. Technical Univ. of Denmark, Copenhagen 35-42; Prof. Univ. of Copenhagen 42-; mem. of the Royal Danish Acad. of Sciences and of Acad. of Technical Sciences; Dir. Carlsberg Foundation 50-63, Pres. 55-63.
Dantes Plads 3, Copenhagen V, Denmark.

Jessen, Knud, DR. PHIL.; Danish botanist; b. 29 Nov. 1884; ed. Univ. of Copenhagen.
Botanist with Geological Survey of Denmark 14; Prof. of Botany Univ. of Copenhagen, and Dir. Univ. Botanical Gardens 31-55; Pro-Rector of Univ. 40-41; mem. Board of Carlsberg Foundation 37-59 of Rask-Ørsted Foundation 39-55; Chair. Scientific Cttee. of Danish Soc. for the Protection of Nature 31-; Dr. h.c. (Trinity Coll., Dublin) 47, (Univ. of Cambridge) 56; Albrecht Penk Medal 62.
Publs. *Moseundersøgelser i det nordøstlige Sjælland* 20; *Planterester fra den ældre Jernalder i Thy* 33; *Archæological Dating in the History of North Jutland's Vegetation* 35, *The Composition of the Forests in Northern Europe in Epipalaeolithic Time* 35; (with V. Milthers) *Stratigraphical and Palæontological Studies of Inter-glacial Fresh-water Deposits in Jutland and North-west Germany* 28; (with A. Farrington) *The Bogs at Ballybetagh near Dublin, with remarks on late glacial conditions in Ireland* 38; (with H. Helbæk) *Cereals in Great Britain and Ireland in Prehistoric and Early Historic Times* 44; *Studies in Late Quaternary Deposits and Flora History of Ireland* 49; (with S. Th. Andersen and A. Farrington) *The Interglacial Deposits near Gort, Co. Galway, Ireland* 59.
The University Botanical Museum, Gothersgade 130, Copenhagen, Denmark; and Aabrinken 56, Virum, Denmark.
Telephone: 01-85-17-20.

Jessup, Philip C., B.A., L.C.D., LITT.D., J.D., LL.D., PH.D.; American international lawyer and professor; b. 5 Jan. 1897; ed. Hamilton Coll. and Columbia and Yale Univs.
Lecturer, Asst. Assoc. Prof. Int. Law, Columbia Univ. 25-35, Prof. 35-46, H. Fish Prof. of Int. Law and Diplomacy 46-61; mem. Staff Office of Foreign Relief and Rehabilitation Operations, Dept. of State 43; Asst. Sec.-Gen. UNRRA 43; Asst. Tech. Sec.-Gen. UNO Bretton Woods Conf. 44; Asst. U.S. Delegation San Francisco Conf. 45; Assoc. Dir. Naval School of Military Govt. and Admin. 42-44; Dep. U.S. rep. to UN Security Council 48-49; apptd. Ambassador-at-Large Mar. 49, resgnd. Jan. 53; Judge, Int. Court of Justice 61-; mem. Curatorium Hague Acad. of Int. Law, American Acad. Arts and Sciences, American Philosophical Soc., Inst. de Droit Int., Governing Council Int. Inst. for Unification of Private Law 64-67; several hon. degrees.
Publs. *The Law of Territorial Waters and Maritime Jurisdiction* 27, *American Neutrality and International Police* 28, *The U.S. and the World Court* 29, *International Security* 35, *Neutrality, Its History, Economics and Law:* Vol. I *The Origins* (with Francis Deák) 35, Vol. IV *To-day and To-morrow* 36, *Elihu Root* (2 vols.) 38, *International Problem of Governing Mankind* 47, *A Modern Law of Nations* 48, *Transnational Law* 56, *Parliamentary Diplomacy* 56, *The Use of International Law* 59, *Controls for Outer Space and the Antarctic Analogy* (with Howard J. Taubenfeld) 59.
International Court of Justice, Peace Palace, The Hague, Netherlands; Home: Norfolk, Connecticut 06058, U.S.A.

Jewkes, John, C.B.E., M.COM., M.A.; British economist; b. 29 June 1902; ed. Barrow Grammar School and Manchester Univ.
Asst. Sec. Manchester Chamber of Commerce 25-26; Lecturer in Economics, Manchester Univ. 26-29; Rockefeller Foundation Fellow 29-30; Prof. of Social Economics and Dir. of Economics Research Section 36-48; Prof. of Economic Organisation, Univ. of Oxford 48-; Dir. Economic Section, War Cabinet Secretariat 41; Dir.-Gen. of Statistics and Programmes, Ministry of Aircraft Production 43; Principal Asst. Sec., Office of Ministry of Reconstruction 44; Hon. Prof. Johns Hopkins Univ. 58-.
Publs. (With A. Winterbottom) *An Industrial Survey of Cumberland and Furness, Juvenile Unemployment;* (with E. M. Gray) *Wages and Labour in the Cotton*

Spinning Industry; (with Sylvia Jewkes) *The Juvenile Labour Market; The Genesis of the British National Health Service; Value for Money in Medicine;* (with Sawers and Stillerman) *The Sources of Invention; Ordeal by Planning, Public and Private Enterprise, The New Ordeal by Planning.*
Entwood, Boars Hill, Oxford, England.
Telephone: Oxford 35104.

Jha, Chandra Shekhar, O.B.E., M.SC., LL.B., I.C.S.; Indian diplomatist; b. 09; ed. Patna Univ. and London School of Oriental Studies.
Joined Indian Civil Service 33; Asst. Magistrate and Collector, Bihar and Orissa 33-36; Under-Sec. Finance Department, Bihar 36-39, Deputy Commr. 39; later Controller and Sec. Supply and Transport Dept., Orissa; Deputy Sec. Commonwealth Relations Dept., Govt. of India 46-47; Joint Sec. Ministry of External Affairs 47-50; Chargé d'Affaires, Ankara 50-51; Ambassador to Turkey 51-54; Joint Sec. Ministry of External Affairs 54-57; Ambassador to Japan 57-59; Perm. Rep. to UN 59-62, Chair. Human Rights Comm. 61-62; High Commr. in Canada 62-64; Commonwealth Sec., Ministry of External Affairs 64-65, Foreign Sec. Feb. 65-67; Amb. to France 67-.
Embassy of India, 15 rue Alfred Dehodencq, Paris-16, France.
Telephone: TRO-39-30.

Jha, Lakshmi Kant, M.B.E.; Indian civil servant; b. 22 Nov. 1913; ed. Hindu Univ., Banaras and Trinity Coll., Cambridge.
Under-Secretary, Govt. of Bihar, Local Self Govt. Dept. 41-42; Dep. Sec. Supply Dept., Govt. of India 42-46; Del. to UN Maritime Conf.; Chief Controller of Imports and Exports 47-50; former Special Sec. Ministry of Commerce and Industry: Chair. G.A.T.T. (General Agreement on Tariffs and Trade) 59-60, UN Cttee. on Int. Commodity Arrangements 61-62; Sec. Ministry of Finance, Dept. of Econ. Affairs 60-64; Dir. Reserve Bank of India and State Bank of India; Alt. Gov. Int. Bank for Reconstruction and Devt. 60-64; Sec. to Prime Minister 64-67; Gov. Reserve Bank of India 67-.
Publ. *India's Foreign Trade,* Parts I and II.
Reserve Bank of India, Mint Road, Bombay 1; Home: 9 Race Course Road, New Delhi 11, India.

Jha, Veni Shanker, PH.D.; Indian educationist; b. 99; ed. Model High School and Robertson Coll., Jabalpore, India, and Univ. Coll., London.
Assistant Prof. Philosophy, Maroris Coll., Nagpur 20-31; Inspector of Schools, Dep. Dir. of Public Instruction, Central Provinces 31-46, Dir. 46-48; Sec. to Govt. of Madhya Pradesh 48-53; Chair., Public Service Comm., Madhya Pradesh 53-56; Vice-Chancellor, Banaras Hindu Univ. 56-60; Dir. Commonwealth Education Liaison Unit, London 60-63.
Wright Town, Jabalpore, Madhya Pradesh, India.

Jisr, Hussein El; Lebanese lawyer and diplomatist.
Administrator, Mont-Liban District 43-47; mem. Higher Council for Common Interests of Lebanon and Syria 47-50; Plenipotentiary Minister 50; Ambassador to Saudi Arabia 55-59, to Belgium 59-60, to U.K. 60-62, to Morocco 62-65.
rue Sursock, Beirut, Lebanon.

Job, Jakob, D.PHIL.; Swiss radio director and writer; b. 14 Dec. 1891; ed. Zürich Univ.
Dir. Swiss School, Naples 23-28: Dir. Swiss Foreign Secretariat, Berne 30-31; Dir. Radiogenossenschaft, Zürich 32-57.
Publs. *Jakob Bosshart als Erzähler* 23, *Vom Gestern zum Heute Gedichte* 26, *Neapel, Reisebilder und Skizzen* 28, *Gedichte aus Italien* 30, *Die Schweizerschulen im Ausland* 30, *Die Jugend in der neueren deutschen Dichtung* 32, *Scusate Signor . . . 32, Im Dienst der Heimat* 35,

Möglichkeiten und Grenzen der Erziehung durch Radio 38, *Briefe von Jakob Bosshart* 38, *Weg des Herzens* 39, *Italienische Städte* 41, *Heimat in der Fremde* 42, *Sardinienfahrt* 44, *Herbst in Paris* 45, *Röntgen und die Schweiz* 48, *Unter südlichem Himmel, Geschichten und Anekdoten aus Italien* 48, *25 Jahre Radio Zürich* 49, *Portugal, Land der Christusritter* 51, *Wanderrast: Gedichte, Reise und Städtebilder* 51, *Dome, Türme und Paläste, Ein Italienbuch* 54, *Sardinien: Ein Reisebuch* 56, *Neapel* 59, *Sizilien* 61, *Burg Weissenstein, Ferientage im Bayrischen Wald* 61, *Tenuta di Ricavo, Im Hügelland des Chianti* 63, *Die rosenrote Stadt der Wüste* 64, *Umbrien und Toskana* 65, *Bei Simeon dem Säulenheiligen* 65, *Autostrada del Sole* 65, *Am Mittelmeer* 66.
Zollikerstrasse 23, 8008 Zürich, Switzerland.
Telephone: 051-345194.

Joboru, Magda, Dr.; Hungarian politician and educationist; b. 18; ed. High School, Budapest Univ.
Teacher, Mezotur 41-46; Dir. Ilona Zrinyi People's Coll. 46-48; Gen. Sec. Hungarian Democratic Women's Union 48-50; Dep. Minister of Education 50-58, M.P. 47-51; Dir.-Gen., Nat. Library 58; Chair. Hungarian Nat. Cttee. on UNESCO and mem Exec. Board; Vice-Pres. Exec. Board UNESCO 66-; Amb. and Head of Perm. Delegation of Hungary at UNESCO 66-; Kossuth Medal, Order of Labour.
Publs. *Life and School, The Grammar School in the Horthy Period, Education in the Capitalist Countries from 1918 until Now.*
Országos Széchenyi Könyvtár, Muzeum krt. 14/16, Budapest VIII, Hungary.

Jochum, Eugen; German conductor; b. 1 Nov. 1902; ed. Gymnasium St. Stephan, Augsburg, and Akad. der Tonkunst, Munich.
First Conductor, Kiel Opera House 26-29, Mannheim Nat. Theatre 29-30; Gen. Musical Dir. Duisburg 30-32, Radio Berlin 32-34, Staatsoper and Philharmonic Orchestra, Hamburg 34-49, Bayerischer Rundfunk 49-61; Chief Conductor Concertgebouw Amsterdam 61-63; Guest Conductor all over Europe 26-, U.S.A., Canada and Japan 58-; Regular Conductor Berlin Philharmonic Orchestra; tours with Berlin Philharmonic Orchestra, Concertgebouw, Bayerischer Rundfunk, Detroit Symphony Orchestra, Los Angeles Symphony Orchestra; now Perm. Guest Conductor with Concertgebouw, Amsterdam, West Berlin State Opera and Philharmonic Orchestra, Chicago Opera; Brahms and Bruckner Medals; Record Prizes, Bayerischer Verdienstorden, etc.
Records (Deutsche Grammophon and Philips): include all Beethoven, Brahms, all Bruckner symphonies.
Munich 19, Brunhildenstrasse 2, German Federal Republic.

Jodłowski, Jerzy, D.IUR.; Polish politician and lawyer; b. 09; ed. Warsaw Univ.
Active in socialist youth movement before Second World War; during German occupation lectured in law in "underground" univ. courses; imprisoned in Gross-Rosen and Mauthausen concentration camps 44-45; mem. Exec. Cttee. Democratic Party 45-; Deputy to Nat. Council and later to Seym 46-; Vice-Marshal of the Seym 57-61; Pres. Comm. of Justice of Seym 57-65; Prof. Warsaw Univ., Dean Faculty of Law 61-65; Prof. Int. Faculty of Comparative Law, Strasbourg 62-; Dr. h.c. (Univ. of Dijon) 65.
16, al. I Armii, Warsaw, Poland.
Telephone: 28-15-76.

Jodoin, Marie Joseph Paul Claude; Canadian trade unionist; b. 25 May 1913; ed. Ste. Marie Coll. and Jean de Brebeuf Coll. Montreal.
Joined Int. Ladies' Garment Workers Union staff 37; Asst. Man. Dressmakers' Union, Montreal 40, Man. 47; Vice-Pres. Quebec Fed. of Labor 41; Vice-Pres. Montreal Trades and Labor Council 40-42, Pres. 47; Vice-

Pres.; Trades and Labor Congress of Canada 49-54, Pres. 54-56; Pres. Canadian Labor Congress 56-; mem. Exec. Board Int. Confederation of Free Trade Unions 49-; City Councillor in Montreal 40-42 and 47-54; mem. Quebec Legislature for Montreal-St. James 42-44; Dir. Canadian Centenary Council, Religion-Labour Council of Canada; mem. Nat. Research Council, Central Council of Canadian Red Cross, Canadian Trade Cttee., Economic Council of Canada, Vice-Chair. Canadian Highway Safety Council.
Home: 40 Riverside Drive, P.O. 281, Manotick, Ont.; Office: 100 Argyle Avenue, Ottawa, Ont., Canada.

Jogjakarta, Sultan of; Hamengku Buwono IX; Indonesian ruler; b. 22 April 1912; ed. Univ. of Indology, Leiden.
Inaugurated Sultan of Jogjakarta 40; Mil. Gov. of Special Territory (with rank of Maj.-Gen. of the Army) 45-49; Head of Special Territory 46; Gov., Head of Special Territory 59; mem. Provisional People's Consultative Assembly Aug. 59, Titular Gen. of the Army 60; Minister of State Oct. 46-49; Minister of Defence and Co-ordinator of Domestic Security Aug.-Dec. 59; Defence Minister, Cabinet of the Repub. of the United States of Indonesia Dec. 49, 53; Deputy Prime Minister 50-April 51; Curator Univ. of Gadja Mada Dec. 51; Chair. Supervisory Comm. for the Apparatus of the State Aug. 59; Minister and Head, Body for Controlling State Finance 64; First Minister for Econ. and Financial Affairs in the Presidium and Deputy Prime Minister 66-; Chair. Indonesian Olympic Cttee. 51, Tourist Inst. 56, Asian Games Fed. 58, Indonesian Tourist Council 62-; Chair. Session, Econ. Comm. for Asia and the Far East (ECAFE) 57, Nat. Preparatory Cttee. for New York World Fair 63; Chief Del. of Indonesia, Pacific Area Travel Asscn. (PATA), U.S. 58, UN First World Conf. of Int. Travel and Tourism, Rome 63; Medal of the Guerilla, Medal of Loyalty to the Independence and the Order of the White Elephant (Thailand); Hon. titles of Maha Purta (Spes Patria) and Pramuka Agung (Supreme Boy Scout).
The Presidium, Jogjakarta, Indonesia.

Johannes, Herman; Indonesian engineer, professor and politician; b. 13.
High School teacher 40; Lecturer, Medical Faculty, Djakarta Univ. 43; Lecturer, Technical Faculty, Gadjah Mada Univ., Jogjakarta 46, Prof. of Physics 48-, Dean Physics and Mathematics Faculty 49-, Rector 61-; Minister of Public Works and Power, Republic of Indonesia Sept. 50-April 51; mem. Exec. Board UNESCO 54-56; mem. Council for Sciences of Indonesia 56-63; mem. Planning Council 58-63.
Publs. *Analysis of the Critical Depth* 39, *Flexure Factors Method* 53.
Gadjah Mada University, Bulaksumur, Jogjakarta, Indonesia.

Johansson, Albin; Swedish business executive; b. 11 Feb. 1886.
Mem. Board of Swedish Co-operative Wholesale Society 17-57, Man. Dir. 20-57; mem. Board of Internat. Co-operative Alliance 19-64; Pres. Board for Royal Theatres 33-40, mem. of Board 45-57; Vice-Pres. Nordisk Andelsforbund 20-32, Pres. 32-58; Trustee, Swedish State Railways 26-58; Pres. Swedish Inventors' Asscn. 40-59; Pres. Int. Co-operative Petroleum Asscn. 46-59; Hon. Dr. Econ. in Stockholm 56.
Fiskargatan 9, Stockholm, Sweden.

Johansson, Rune; Swedish politician; b. 12 Feb. 1915; ed. Ljungby.
Worked as a baker; held positions in Ljungby Town Council; M.P. 51; mem. of Cttee. on Death Duties; Minister of the Interior 57-; Social Democratic Labour.
Kungl, Inrikesdepartementet, Stockholm 2, Sweden.

John, Admiral of the Fleet Sir Caspar, G.C.B.; British naval officer; b. 22 March 1903; ed. Royal Naval Coll., Dartmouth.
Joined R.N. 16, Captain Home and Mediterranean Fleets 41, Rear-Admiral 51, Flag Officer Commanding Third Aircraft Carrier Squadron and Heavy Squadron 51-52, Dep. Controller Aircraft 53-54, Vice-Admiral 54, Flag Officer Air 55-57, Vice-Chief of Naval Staff 57-60, First Sea Lord and Chief of Naval Staff 60-63; Chair. Housing Corpn. 64-.
13 Woodlands Road, London, S.W.13, England.
Telephone: 01-876-5596.

John, David Dilwyn, C.B.E., T.D., D.SC.; British museum director; b. 20 Nov. 1901; ed. Univ. Coll. of Wales.
Zoologist, engaged in oceanographical research in Antarctic seas 25; Asst. Keeper, Natural History, British Museum 35, Deputy Keeper 48; Dir. Nat. Museum of Wales, Cardiff 48-; Polar Medal.
7 Cyncoed Avenue, Cardiff, Wales.

John, DeWitt, B.A., M.A., M.S.; American newspaper editor; b. 1 Aug. 1915; ed. Principia Coll., Elsah, Ill., Univ. of Chicago, and Columbia Univ.
Editorial page writer, *St. Petersburg Times* (Florida) 38-39; mem. staff *Christian Science Monitor* 39-, Editor 64-; Man. Christian Science Cttees. on Publs. 62-64; U.S. Naval Reserve 42-45.
Publ. *The Christian Science Way of Life* 62.
The Christian Science Monitor, 1 Norway Street, Boston, Mass. 02115; Home: Old Concord Road, Lincoln, Mass. 01773, U.S.A.

John, Michael; Indian politician, industrialist and trade unionist; b. 03; ed. Dufton Coll., Madras.
Member Bihar Legislative Assembly 46-52; mem. Rajya Sabha, Nat. Productivity Council, Central Advisory Council of Industries; Dir. Hindustan Steel Co. Ltd., Hindustan Shipyard Ltd.; Pres. Indian Nat. Trade Union Congress 52, 60, 61, 63, 64; now Pres. Indian Nat. Iron and Steel Workers' Fed.
27 K Road, Jamshedpur, Bihar, India.

Johns, Jasper; American painter; b. 15 May 1930; ed. Univ. of South Carolina.
Works in following collections: Tate Gallery, London Museum of Modern Art, New York City, Albright-Knox Art Gallery, Buffalo, N.Y.; one-man exhibitions: Leo Castelli, N.Y. 58, 60, 61, 63, Galerie Rive Droite, Paris 59, 61, Galleria d'Arte del Naviglio, Milan 59, Columbia Museum of Art, Columbia, South Carolina 60, Ileana Sonnabend, Paris 62, Jewish Museum, New York City 64, Whitechapel Gallery, London 64, Pasadena Museum, Calif. 65; Prize, Pittsburgh Int. 58.
Edisto Beach, South Carolina, U.S.A.

Johnson, Axel Ax:son; Swedish industrialist and shipowner; b. 4 Oct. 1910; ed. Royal Inst. of Technology, Stockholm.
Man. Dir. Rederi AB Nordstjernan (Johnson Line); Chair. Avesta Jernverks AB, AB Karlstads Mekaniska Werkstad, AB Motala Verkstad, A. Johnson & Co. Inc., New York, AB Nynäs Petroleum, Axel Johnson Inst. for Industrial Research, Norbergs Grufförvaltning, Norbergs Gruf AB, A. Johnson and Co. (Canada) Ltd. and other companies; Board mem. Stockholm's Enskilda Bank AB, Swedish Shipowners' Asscn., Shipowners' Asscn. of Stockholm, Fed. of Swedish Industries, Swedish Ironmasters' Asscn., Swedish Export Asscn., Swedish Chamber of Commerce of the U.S.A.; Thule Group of Insurance Companies.
Stureplan 3, Stockholm, Sweden; and Karlavägen 85, Stockholm Ø, Sweden.

Johnson, Celia (Mrs. Peter Fleming), C.B.E.; British actress; b. 18 Dec. 1908; ed. St. Paul's Girls' School, Royal Acad. of Dramatic Art.
First stage appearance, Huddersfield 28; first London

appearance as Currita (*A Hundred Years Old*) 29; subsequent roles include Loveday Trevelyan (*Debonair*) 30, Phyl (*After All*) 31, Ophelia (*Hamlet*) (New York) 31, Anne Hargraves (*The Wind and the Rain*) 33, Elizabeth Bennet (*Pride and Prejudice*) 36, Mrs. de Winter (*Rebecca*) 40, Jennifer (*The Doctor's Dilemma*) 42, Joan (*St. Joan*) 48-49, Viola (*Twelfth Night*) 50, Olga (*The Three Sisters*) 51, Sheila Broadbent (*The Reluctant Debutante*) 55, Isobel Cherry (*Flowering Cherry*) 57-58, Aline (*The Master Builder*) 64, Mme Ranyevskaya (*The Cherry Orchard*), Chichester 66, *Relatively Speaking* London 67, *Hay Fever* 68; films include *In which We Serve, Dear Octopus, Brief Encounter, This Happy Breed, The Holly and the Ivy, The Captain's Paradise, A Kid for Two Farthings, The Good Companions*.
Merrimoles House, Nettlebed, Oxfordshire, England.

Johnson, Hon. Daniel, B.A., LL.L.; Canadian lawyer and politician; b. 9 April 1915; ed. Sacred Heart Elementary School, Seminary of St. Hyacinthe and Univ. of Montreal.
Called to Bar 40; fmr. Pres. Univ. of Montreal Students' Asscn., Canadian Fed. of Catholic Students, and French Section of Young Catholic Union of Canada; Vice-Pres. Pax Romana (Asscn. of Catholic Students from 39 countries) 38; fmr. Legal Adviser to Central Council of Nat. Trade Unions of Montreal and French Language Weekly Newspapers Asscn.; mem. Quebec Legis. Assembly 46-; Parl. Asst. to Prime Minister of Quebec (Maurice Duplessis) 54; Chair. of Cttees. and Deputy Speaker of Legis. Assembly (Quebec) 56; Minister of Hydraulic Resources, Quebec 58; Leader, Nat. Union Party 61-; Prime Minister of Quebec June 66-, also Minister of Federal-Provincial Affairs and Minister of Natural Resources; mem. Queen's Privy Council for Canada 67-.
Publ. *Egalité ou Indépendance* 65.
Parliament Buildings, Quebec City, Quebec, Canada.

Johnson, David Gale; American economist; b. 10 July 1916; ed. Iowa State Coll., Univs. of Wisconsin and Chicago.
Research Assoc. Iowa State Coll. 41-42, Asst. Prof. of Econs. 42-44; Dept. of Econs., Univ. of Chicago 44-, Asst. Prof. 44-54, Prof. 54-, Assoc. Dean Div. of Social Studies 57-60, Dean 60-; Economist, Office of Price Admin. 42, Dept. of State 46, Dept. of Army 48; Office of the President's Special Rep. for Trade Negotiations 63-; Agency for Int. Development 61-62; RAND Corpn. 54-; Dir. Social Science Research Council 54-57; Pres. American Farm Econ. Asscn. 64-65, Nat. Opinion Research Center 62-; mem. President's Nat. Advisory Comm. on Food and Fibre 65-.
Publs. *Forward Prices for Agriculture* 47, *Trade and Agriculture* 50, *Grain Yields and the American Food Supply* 63.
5617 S. Kenwood Avenue, Chicago, Illinois 60637, U.S.A.

Johnson, David Moffat, B.C.L.; Canadian diplomatist and lawyer; b. 02; ed. McGill and Oxford Univs.
Called to Inner Temple 26, to Bar of Province of Quebec 27; practised law with Stairs, Dixon & Claxton, Montreal 26-36; Solicitor to Dept. of Finance, Ottawa 36-46, on loan to Dept. of External Affairs (in London) 41; served Canadian Army 43-45; joined Dept. of External Affairs 47; Sec. Canadian Section, Permanent Board on Defence 47-48; Acting High Commr., Dublin 49; High Commr. to Pakistan 50-51; Permanent Rep. to UN, New York 51-55; Canadian Commr. Int. Supervisory Comm. for Viet-Nam 55-56; Ambassador to the U.S.S.R. 56-60; Rep. in Nigeria of UN Technical Assistance Board 61-.
Technical Assistance Board, United Nations, New York City, N.Y., U.S.A.

Johnson, Earl Dallam, A.B.; American aviation executive; b. 14 Dec. 1905; ed. Univ. of Wisconsin.
Instructor, Graduate Course in X-Ray Analysis, Univ. of Wisconsin 28-29; Investment Financial Consultant, Waller, Carson and Co., Milwaukee 30-31; Investment Consultant, Loomis, Sayles and Co. (Boston), Chicago 33, Milwaukee 33, Dir. 38, Vice-Pres. in charge New York Office 41, Vice-Pres. and Dir. 46-50; U.S. Air Transport Command 42-46; Asst. Sec. Army Manpower and Reserve Forces 50-52, Under-Sec. of Army 52-54; Chair. of Board Panama Canal Co. 53-54; Pres. Air Transport Asscn. 54-55, Air Cargo Inc. 54-55; Senior Vice-Pres. (Fiscal Affairs and Operations) Gen. Dynamics Corpn. 55-57, Dir. 55-63, Exec. Vice-Pres. 55-57, Pres. 59-62, Vice-Chair. of Board 62-63; Exec. Vice-Pres. and Dir. Delta Air Lines Inc. 63-.
Delta Air Lines Inc., Atlanta Airport, Atlanta, Georgia, U.S.A.

Johnson, Earl Jaquins; American editor; b. 13 April 1900; ed. South-Western Coll., Winfield, Kansas, and Univ. of Kansas.
Reporter *Winfield Daily Courier* 16-17; City Editor Winfield Free Press 17-18; Reporter United Press, Chicago 21; United Press Bureau Manager in Cleveland, Columbus, Chicago, New York and London 23-35; Vice-Pres. and Gen. News Man. of United Press Asscn. (later United Press Int.) 35-; Achievement Award, Univ. of Kansas 51; Trustee, William Allen White (Journalism) Foundation.
Publ. *Readability in News Writing* 45.
Home: 455 East 57th Street; Office: 220 East 42nd Street, New York City, N.Y., U.S.A.

Johnson Ernest R., B.S., M.S.; American steel executive; b. 25 Dec. 1899; ed. Univ. of Michigan.
Central Steel Co. (later Republic Steel Corpn.) 22-29; Asst. Chief Metallurgist, Republic Steel Corpn., Massillon, Ohio 29-44, Chief Metallurgist 44-46, Asst. Dist. Manager 46-52, Dist. Manager 52-53, Asst. Vice-Pres (Operations), Cleveland, Ohio 53-54, Vice-Pres. (Operations) 54-60, Asst. Pres. and First Vice-Pres. 60-.
Republic Steel Corporation, 1706 Republic Building, Cleveland, Ohio 44101, U.S.A.

Johnson, Eyvind; Swedish novelist; b. 29 July 1900; ed. primary school.
Worked in a quarry, lumber trade, brickyard 14-19; in Stockholm 19-21; began writing in Stockholm; went to Germany 21, later to France for six years; lived in Switzerland and England 47-50; mem. Swedish Acad. 57-; Nordic Council Prize for Literature, Helsinki 62; Ph.D. h.c. (Gothenburg) 53.
Publs. About 30 vols. of novels and stories including: *Romanen om Olof* (autobiographical) 34-37, *Grupp Krilon* 41, *Krilons resa* 42, *Krilon sjalv* 43, *Strändernas svall* 46, *Drömmar om Rosor och eld* 49, *Molnen över Metapontion* 57, *Hans nades tid* 61, *Livsdagen lang* 64; *Sju liv* (short stories in one volume) 44.
Vitsippsvägen 8, Saltsjöbaden 2, Sweden.

Johnson, Frank Minis, Jr.; American judge; b. 30 Oct. 1918; ed. Gulf Coast Military Acad., Massey Business Coll. and Univ. of Alabama.
Admitted to Alabama Bar 43; U.S. Army service 43-46; private legal practice 46-, mem. Curtis, Maddox and Johnson 46-53; U.S. District Attorney, Northern District, Alabama 53-55, U.S. District Judge, Middle District, Alabama 55-.
Federal Building, Montgomery 1, Alabama, U.S.A.

Johnson, G. Griffith; American government official; b. 15 Aug. 1912; ed. Harvard Univ.
Treasury Dept. 36-37, 38-39; National Defense Admin. Comm. 40-41; Office of Price Admin. 41-46; Dir. Economic Stabilisation Div., Nat. Security Resources Board 48-49; Asst. Chief, Fiscal Div., Chief Economist, Bureau of Budget 49-50; Asst. Admin. Economic Policy,

Economic Stabilisation Agency 50; Economist, Motion Picture Asscn. of America 52, Vice-Pres. 52-62; Consultant, Int. Economics, Dept. of State 62, Asst. Sec. of State for Econ. Affairs 62-65; Exec. Vice-Pres. Motion Picture Asscn. of America 65-.

Publs. *The Treasury and Monetary Policy* 39, *Economic Effects of Federal Public Works Expenditures* (with J. K. Galbraith) 40.

6412 Garnett Place, Chevy Chase, Maryland, U.S.A.

Johnson, Gerald W., A.B.; American journalist; b. 6 Aug. 1890; ed.Wake Forest Coll. and Toulous Univ.

Newspaper work in North Carolina 11-24; Prof. of Journalism, North Carolina Univ. 24-26; mem. staff Baltimore *Evening Sun* 26-43; American Correspondent London *Sunday Express* 46-47; Hon. LL.D., Litt.D., and D.C.L.

Publs. *Andrew Jackson* 27, *Randolph of Roanake* 29, *By Reason of Strength* 31, *Secession of the Southern States* 33, *Number Thirty-Six* (novel) 33, *An Honourable Titan* 36, *The Sunpapers of Baltimore* (with H. L. Mencken, Frank R. Kent and Hamilton Owens) 37, *A Little Night-Music* 37, *The Wasted Land* 37, *America's Silver Age* 39, *Roosevelt: Dictator or Democrat?* 41, *American Heroes and Hero-Worship* 43, *Woodrow Wilson* 44, *The First Captain* 47, *Liberal's Progress* 48, *Our English Heritage* 49, *Incredible Tale* 50, *This American People* 51, *Pattern for Liberty* 52, *Lunatic Fringe* 57, *Peril and Promise* 58, *The Lines are Drawn* 58, *America: A History for Peter* (3 vols.) 59-60, *The Man Who Feels Left Behind* 61, *Hod-Carrier* 64, *Communism: An American's View.*

1310 Bolton Street, Baltimore, Md. 21217, U.S.A.

Johnson, Gen. Harold K.; American army officer; b. 22 Feb. 1912; ed. U.S. Mil. Acad., West Point.

Second Lieut. 33; Prisoner of War 42-45; served Korea 50-51; Nat. War Coll. 53; Dept. of Army, Washington 53-56; Asst. Div. Commdr., 8th Div. 56-58; Chief of Staff, Seventh Army, Stuttgart 59; Chief of Staff, Central Army 59-60; Commdt., U.S. Army Command and Gen. Staff Coll., Fort Leavenworth, Kansas 60-63; Army Gen. Staff, Washington 63-, Deputy Chief of Staff (Mil. Operations) 63-64, Chief of Staff 64-68; several awards.

Department of the Army, Washington 25, D.C., U.S.A.

Johnson, Harry Gordon, M.A., PH.D., LL.D.; Canadian economist; b. 26 May 1923; ed. Toronto, Cambridge and Harvard Univs.

Instructor, Toronto Univ. 46-47; Asst. Lecturer, Cambridge Univ. 49, Lecturer and Fellow of King's Coll. 50-56; Prof. of Economic Theory, Manchester Univ. 56-59; Prof. of Econs., Chicago Univ. Oct. 59-, London School of Econs. and Political Science 66-; Visiting Prof. Toronto Univ. 52, Northwestern Univ. 55, 66, Stanford Univ. 55, Indiana Univ. 63, Centennial Prof., Toronto Univ. 67, Wicksell Lecturer 68; Asst. Editor *Review of Economic Studies* 51-59; Editor *The Manchester School* 56-59, *Review of Economic Studies* 59-61, *Journal of Political Economy* 60-66; Fellow American Acad. of Arts and Sciences 64-.

Publs. *International Trade and Economic Growth* 58 (Japanese edn. 59), *Money, Trade and Economic Growth* 62, *Canada in a Changing World Economy* 62, *The Canadian Quandary* 63, *The World Economy at the Crossroads* 65, *Economic Policies Towards the Less Developed Countries* 67, *Essays in Monetary Economics* 67.

London School of Economics, Houghton Street, London, W.C.2; also 91 Bedford Court Mansions, Bedford Avenue, London, W.C.1, England; University of Chicago, 1126 East 59th Street, Chicago 60637; and 5825 South Dorchester Avenue, Chicago 60637, U.S.A. Telephone: 01-580-7491.

Johnson, Sir Henry Cecil, Kt., C.B.E.; British railwayman; b. 11 Sept. 1906; ed. Bedford Modern School, Bedford.

General Man., Eastern Region of British Railways 58-62, Chair. and Gen. Man., London Midland Region 62-June 67; Vice-Chair. British Railways Board June 67-Jan. 68; Chair. British Railways Board Jan. 68-.

"Rowans", Harewood Road, Chalfont St. Giles, Bucks.; 7 Chalfont Court, Baker St., London, N.W.1, England. Telephone: OCH-04-2409; 01-486-4268 (London).

Johnson, Howard Albert, B.A., B.D., S.T.M.; American ecclesiastic; b. 8 Oct. 1915; ed. Univ. of California, Protestant Episcopal Theological Seminary, Virginia, Princeton Univ. and Union Theological Seminary, New York City,

Ordained priest, Protestant Episcopal Church 40; served in parishes in Calif. and Washington 40-45; Fellow American-Scandinavian Foundation, Univ. of Copenhagen 46-48; Assoc. Prof. Systematic Theology, Univ. of the South, Sewanee 49-53; Fellow, St. Augustine's Central Coll. of Anglican Communion, Canterbury 53-54; Canon Theologian Cathedral of St. John the Divine 54-64; Asst. Prof. Religion, Columbia 54-58; Editor: *Preaching the Christian Year, This Church of Ours*; Co-Editor: *A Kierkegaard Critique* 62.

Publs. *Kierkegaard no Rikaino Kagi* 53, *Man in the Middle* (with James A. Pike) 56, *Global Odyssey* 63. Cathedral Heights, New York, N.Y. 10025, U.S.A.

Johnson, Howard C.; American financial official; b. 7 Feb. 1909; ed. Swarthmore Coll. and Harvard Business School.

Investment Banking with Lazard Frères & Co., subsequently with Morgan Stanley & Co. 33-41; U.S. Navy in Second World War, Asst. to Sec. of Joint Chiefs of Staff 43-45; Chief of Div. of Int. Security Affairs, later Advisor on Planning, Bureau of UN Affairs, State Dept. 45-52; with Ford Foundation 52-55; Asst. to Chair. of Board, U.S. Steel Corpn. 55-60, Dir. Stockholder Relations Dept. 60-63; Man. of Portfolio Sales and Participations, Marketing Dept., Int. Bank for Reconstruction and Development and Int. Finance Corpn. (IFC) 63, Dir. of New York Office, Int. Bank and IFC Nov. 63-68; Pres. and Chief Exec. World Banking Corpn., Nassau, Bahamas 68-.

World Banking Corporation Ltd., P.O.B. 100, Nassau, Bahamas.

Johnson, Howard Wesley, M.A.; American educator; b. 2 July 1922; ed. Central Coll., Univ. of Chicago and Glasgow Univ.

U.S. Army 43-46; Assoc. Prof. and Dir. of Management Research, Univ. of Chicago 48-55; Assoc. Prof., Assoc. Dean, Alfred P. Sloan School of Management, Mass. Inst. of Technology, 55-59, Prof., Dean 59-66; Exec. Vice-Pres., Federated Dept. Stores 66, mem. Board of Dirs. 65-; Dir. Hitchiner Mfg. Co. 61-, Putnam Funds 62-; mem. Council on Foreign Relations, President's Advisory Cttee. on Labor-Management Policy 66-; Pres. Mass. Inst. of Technology 66-; Dir. Fed. Reserve Bank of Boston 67-68, Chair. 68-; Dir. John Hancock Mutual Life Insurance Co. 68-; Fellow American Acad. of Arts and Sciences, Fellow American Asscn. for Advancement of Science.

Massachusetts Institute of Technology, Cambridge, Massachusetts 02139, U.S.A. Telephone: 617-864-6900.

Johnson, John H.; American publisher; b. 19 Jan. 1918; ed. DuSable High School and Chicago and Northwestern Univs.

Asst. Editor (36), later Man. Editor of employees' publication, Supreme Liberty Life Insurance Co.; founded *Negro Digest* 42, *Ebony* 45, *Tan* 50, *Jet* 51, *Hue* 53; first Negro businessman to be selected as one of the "ten outstanding young men of the year" by U.S. Junior Chamber of Commerce 51; accompanied Vice-Pres.

Nixon at Ghana Independence celebrations 57, Appointed Special Amb. representing the U.S. at Ivory Coast Independence celebrations 61; Dir. Supreme Liberty Life Insurance Co., Nat. Soc. for Crippled Children and Adults Inc., Nat. Conf. of Christians and Jews, United Negro Coll. Fund, etc.; Trustee, Tuskegee Inst., Howard and Fisk Univs.; Dir. Chicago Asscn. of Commerce; Hon. LL.D. (Central State Coll., Shaw Univ. and North Carolina Coll.).
Johnson Publishing Co. Inc., 1820 South Michigan Avenue, Chicago, Ill., U.S.A.

Johnson, Keith; Jamaican civil servant and diplomatist; b. 29 July 1921; ed. Columbia Univ., N.Y., and Univ. of London.
Jamaican Civil Service 40-48; Research Asst., Bureau of Applied Social Research, Columbia Univ. 48; Population Div., Dept. of Econ. and Social Affairs, UN Secr. 49-62; Consul-Gen. of Jamaica in New York 62-67; Perm. Rep. of Jamaica to UN 67-.
Permanent Mission of Jamaica to the United Nations, 235 East 42nd Street, New York, N.Y. 10017, U.S.A.

Johnson, General Leon William, M.S.; American air force officer; b. 13 Sept. 1904; ed. U.S. Mil. Acad., U.S. Army Advanced Flying School, Calif. Inst. of Technology.
Army 26; Air Force 29; commdr. Heavy Bombardment Group and Wing in Europe 42; Deputy Chief of Staff for personnel services, H.Q., A.A.F. 45-46; Deputy Asst. Chief of Staff for personnel H.Q., U.S.A.F. 46-47; Commanding Gen. 15th Air Force 47-48, 3rd Air Division and 3rd Air Force (England) 48-52, and Continental Air Command 52-56; U.S.A.F. Rep. Mil. Staff Cttee. U.N. 52-56; U.S. Rep. Mil. Cttee and Standing Group NATO 56-58; Air Deputy SHAPE 58-61; Dir. Net Evaluation Subcommittee, Security Council 61-65; awarded Congressional Medal of Honor, D.S.M., Silver Star, Distinguished Flying Cross (with oak leaf cluster), Air Medal (with 3 oak leaf clusters), Legion of Merit, D.F.C. (British), Légion d'Honneur, Croix de Guerre.
1129 Litton Lane, McLean, Va., U.S.A.

Johnson, Lyndon Baines; American politician; b. 27 Aug. 1908; ed. public school, Johnson City, Texas, South-West State Teachers Coll., San Marcos, Texas, and Georgetown Univ.
Teacher, public schools in Texas 30-31; Sec. to U.S. Congressman Richard Kleburg 31-35; Texas Dir., Nat. Youth Admin. 35-37; mem. U.S. House of Reps. 37-49; U.S. Navy 41-42; U.S. Senator from Texas 49-61, Senate Majority Whip 51-53, Senate Minority Leader 53-55, Senate Majority Leader 55-61; Vice-Pres. of the United States 61-Nov. 22nd, 63; Pres. of the United States Nov. 22, 63-; numerous hon. degrees; Democrat.
Publs. *My Hope for America* 64, *A Time of Action* 64.
The White House, Washington, D.C., U.S.A.

Johnson, Pamela Hansford (Lady (C. P.) Snow), F.R.S.L.; British novelist and critic; b. 29 May 1912; ed. Clapham County Secondary School.
Arts and Letters Fellow, Timothy Dwight Coll., Yale 61; Fellow, Center for Advanced Studies, Wesleyan Univ. 61; Hon. D.Litt. (Temple Univ., Philadelphia and York Univ., Toronto).
Publs. Novels include: *This Bed Thy Centre* 35, *World's End* 37, *Winter Quarters* 44, *The Trojan Brothers* 45; the trilogy: *Too Dear for My Possessing* 40, *An Avenue of Stone* 47, *A Summer to Decide* 48, *The Philistines* 49, *Catherine Carter* 52, *An Impossible Marriage* 54, *The Last Resort* 56, *The Unspeakable Skipton, The Humbler Creation* 59, *An Error of Judgement* 62, *Night and Silence Who is Here?* 63, *Cork Street, Next to the Hatter's* 65, *The Survival of the Fittest* 68; *Thomas Wolfe, a Critical Study* 47; *I. Compton-Burnett, a Critical Essay* 51; *Six Proust Reconstructions* 58; *On Iniquity* (Social Criticism) 67; play: *Corinth House* 48; and Proustian Reconstructions broadcast 49-55.
199 Cromwell Road, London, S.W.5, England.
Telephone: 01-373-5235.

Johnson, Paul Burney, LL.B.; American lawyer and politician; b. 23 Jan. 16; ed. Columbia Military Acad. and Univ. of Mississippi School of Law.
Law Practice 40-48; Asst. U.S. Attorney, S. District, Mississippi 48-51; Lt.-Gov. of Mississippi 60-64, Gov. 64-68; Democrat.
Jackson, Mississippi, U.S.A.

Johnson, Philip Cortelyou, A.B.; American architect; b. 8 July 1906; ed. Harvard Univ.
Dir. Dept. of Architecture and Design, Museum of Modern Art 32-54; works include the Annexe and Sculpture Court, Museum of Modern Art, and the Glass House, New Canaan, Connecticut, Lincoln Center Theater; assoc. with Mies van der Rohe in design of Seagram Building, New York City.
Publs. *The International Style, Architecture since 1922* (with H. R. Hitchcock, Jr.) 32, *Machine Art* 34, *Mies van der Rohe* 47, *Architecture 1949-1965* 66.
Home: Ponus Street, New Canaan, Conn.; Office: 375 Park Avenue, New York, N.Y., U.S.A.

Johnson, Robert Wood, Jr.; American business executive; b. 9 Sept. 1920; ed. Milbrook School and Hamilton Coll.
Johnson and Johnson 41-42, 46-, Vice-Pres. (Merchandising, Advertising, Personal Products Corpn.) 53-54, mem. Exec. Cttee. 54-, Exec. Vice-Pres. (Marketing) 55-59, Exec. Vice-Pres. and Gen. Man. 59-60, Pres. 61, Chair. 63; U.S. Army 42-46.
Johnson and Johnson, New Brunswick, New Jersey, U.S.A.

Johnson, Thor, A.B., D.MUS., LL.D., LITT.D.; American musician; b. 10 June 1913; ed. Univs. of North Carolina, Michigan, Mozarteum Acad., Salzburg, Conservatoire of Music, Leipzig, and Berkshire (U.S.A.) Music Center.
Assistant Prof. Univ. of Michigan 37-42; conductor Grand Rapids Symphony 39-42; conductor Univ. of Michigan Little Symphony, Univ. Symphony and Choral Union 37-42; Army Soldier Symphony 42-44; Prof. of Conducting and conductor of orchestra Juilliard School of Music, N.Y.C. 46-47; Music Dir. Cincinnati Symphony Orchestra 46-58; Co-conductor N.B.C. Symphony on tour in Orient 55; prof. and head of orchestral activities, Northwestern Univ., Ill. 58-64; Dir. Interlochen Arts Acad. 64-67; Music Dir., Nashville Symphony Orchestra 67-; mem. Advisory Cttee. on the Arts to U.S. Govt. 60-; Conductor, Chicago's Little Symphony 60-; Guest Conductor Europe, Asia 55-; numerous awards.
823 Cammack Court, Nashville, Tennessee, U.S.A.

Johnson, U. Alexis; American diplomatist; b. 17 Oct. 1908; ed. Occidental Coll., Los Angeles, and Georgetown Univ., Washington, D.C.
Entered foreign service 35; served Tokyo 35, Seoul 37, Tientsin, China 39, Seoul 39, Manchuria 40, Rio de Janeiro 42, U.S. Army Civil Affairs Training Schools 44, Manila 45; Staff Political Adviser to S.C.A.P., Japan 46; Consul, Yokohama 46; Deputy Dir. Office North-East Asian Affairs, Dept. of State 49-51, Dir. 51; Deputy Asst Sec. of State for Far-Eastern Affairs 51-53; Ambassador to Czechoslovakia 53-58; U.S. Rep. Geneva Conf. June-July 54, and in subsequent talks with People's Republic of China 55-57; Ambassador to Thailand 58-61; Dep. Under Sec. of State for Political Affairs 61-64; Deputy Ambassador to Republic of Viet-Nam 64-65; Under-Sec. of State for Political Affairs 65-66; Amb. to Japan 66-; Medal of Freedom, Career Service Award of Nat. Civil Service League, Rockefeller Public Service Award.
American Embassy, Tokyo, Japan.

Johnson, Uwe; German writer; b. 20 July 1934. Resident in German Democratic Republic 49-59, in West Berlin 59-; Fontane Prize 60; Int. Publishers' Asscn. Prize 62.

Publs. *Mutmassungen über Jakob* 59, *Das dritte Buch über Achim* 61, *Karsch, und andere Prosa* 64, *Zwei Ansichten* 65.

c/o Suhrkamp Verlag, Postfach 2446, Frankfurt/Main; Postfach 11, Berlin, German Federal Republic.

Johnson, Walter, M.A., PH.D.; American university professor; b. 27 June 1915; ed. Dartmouth Coll. and Univ. of Chicago.

Instructor Univ. of Chicago 40-43, Asst. Prof. 43-49, Assoc. Prof. 49-50, Prof. and Chair. Dept. of History 50-66, Preston and Sterling Morton Prof. of History 63-66; Writing Fellow Newberry Library of Chicago 45; Dir. of Edward R. Stettinius Manuscripts 48-49; Chair. Fulbright Board of Foreign Scholarship 50-53; accompanied Gov. Adlai Stevenson on world tour 53; Harmsworth Prof. of American History, Oxford Univ. 58-59; Prof. of History, Univ. of Hawaii 66-.

Publs. *Battle against Isolation* 44, *William Allen White's America* 47, *Selected Letters of William Allen White* (Editor) 47, *United States' Experiment in Democracy* (co-author) 47, *How We Drafted Adlai Stevenson* 55; Editor: *Roosevelt and the Russians: The Yalta Conference*, by Edward R. Stettinius 49; *Turbulent Era*, by Joseph C. Grew, *1600 Pennsylvania Avenue* 60.

University of Hawaii, Honolulu, Hawaii, U.S.A.

Johnson, Warren C., B.S., M.S., PH.D.; American chemist; b. 22 Sept. 1901; ed. Kalamazoo Coll., Clark and Brown Univs.

Research Instructor in Chemistry, Brown Univ. 25-27; Instructor in Chemistry, Univ. of Chicago 27-28; Asst. Prof. 28-32, Associate Prof. 32-43, Prof. 43-, Chair. of Dept. of Chemistry 45-55; Assoc. Dean, Physical Sciences Div. 46-55, Dean 55-59, Vice-Pres. 58-; Dir. Chemistry Div., Clinton Laboratories, Oak Ridge, Tenn. 43-45; Dir. Oak Ridge Inst., Nuclear Studies 53-; Chair. Section 9-3 of Nat. Defense Research Cttee. 40-43; Consultant U.S. Atomic Energy Comm.; mem. Gen. Advisory Cttee., Atomic Energy Comm.; Fellow, American Asscn. for the Advancement of Science; Hon. D.Sc. (Kalamazoo Coll. and Brown Univ.); U.S. Atomic Energy Comm. Citation 61.

Publs. *Qualitative Analysis and Chemical Equilibrium* 37, *Chemical Equilibrium as Applied to Qualitative Analysis* 41.

University of Chicago, Chicago 37, Ill., U.S.A.

Johnson, William Summer; American chemist; b. 24 Feb. 1913; ed. Amherst Coll. and Harvard Univ. Instructor, Amherst Coll. 36-37; Research Chemist, Eastman Kodak Co., summers 36-39; Instructor, Univ. of Wisconsin 40-42, Asst. Prof. 42-44, Assoc. Prof. 44-46, Prof. 46-60; Prof., Exec. Head Dept. of Chemistry Stanford Univ. 60-; mem. Board of Editors, *Journal of American Chemical Soc.* 56-; Sec. Int. Congress of Pure and Applied Chemistry 51; Fellow, London Chemical Soc.; mem. Swiss Chemical Soc., American Chemical Soc., Nat. Acad. of Sciences, American Acad. of Arts and Sciences.

Department of Chemistry, Stanford University, Stanford; 191 Meadowood Drive, Portola Valley, California, U.S.A.

Johnston, Sir Charles Hepburn, K.C.M.G.; British diplomatist; b. 11 March 1912; ed. Winchester and Balliol Coll., Oxford.

Entered Diplomatic Service 36; Third Sec., Tokyo 39; First Sec., Cairo 45, Madrid 48; Counsellor, Foreign Office 51, Bonn 55; Ambassador to Jordan 56-60; Gov. and C.-in-C. Aden 60-63; High Commr. in Aden and Fed. of South Arabia 63; Deputy Under-Sec. in charge of Econ. Affairs, Foreign Office 63-65; High Commr. in Australia 65-.

Publ. *The View from Steamer Point* 64.

British High Commission, Canberra, A.C.T., Australia.

Johnston, Denis (*see* Johnston, William Denis).

Johnston, Sir John (Baines), K.C.M.G.; British diplomatist; b. 13 May 1918; ed. Banbury Grammar School and Queen's Coll., Oxford.

Army service 40-46; Asst. Principal, Colonial Office 47, Principal 48; Asst. Sec. West African Council, Accra 50-51; U.K. Liaison Officer, Comm. for Technical Co-operation in Africa South of the Sahara 52; Principal Private Sec. to Sec. of State for Colonies 53, Asst. Sec. 56, Head of Far Eastern Dept., Colonial Office 56; transferred to Commonwealth Relations Office 57, Dep. High Commr. in S. Africa 59-61; High Commr. in Sierra Leone 61-63, in Fed. of Rhodesia and Nyasaland 63, in Rhodesia 64-65; Asst. Under-Sec. of State, Commonwealth Office 66-68, Deputy Under-Sec. of State 68-.

Commonwealth Office, Downing Street, London, S.W.1; and 16 Kennington Palace Court, London S.E.11, England.

Telephone: 01-735-7300.

Johnston, Logan T., B.S.; American steel executive; b. 1 Sept. 1900; ed. Carnegie Inst. of Technology.

Salesman, Columbia Steel Co., Butler, Pennsylvania (acquired by Armco Steel Corpn. 27) 25-47, Gen. Man. of Sales, Armco Steel Corpn. 47-52, Vice-Pres. of Sales 52-56, Vice-Pres. of Distribution 56-58, Exec. Vice-Pres. and Dir. 58-60, Pres. 60-65, Chair. 65-; Trustee Carnegie Mellon Univ., Miami Univ.

Armco Steel Corporation, Middletown, Ohio 45042, U.S.A.

Telephone: 513-425-2981.

Johnston, (William) Denis, O.B.E., M.A., LL.M.; Irish-born barrister-at-law, broadcaster and dramatist; b. 18 June 1901; ed. St. Andrew's Coll., Dublin, Merchiston Castle School, Edinburgh, Christ's Coll., Cambridge, and Harvard Law School, U.S.A.

Barrister-at-Law, Inner Temple and King's Inns; Dir. Dublin Gate Theatre 31-35; B.B.C. Feature Programme writer and producer 36; B.B.C. War Corresp. Middle East, Italy, France and Germany 42-45; Television Programme Dir. 46-47; Prof. of English, Mount Holyoke Coll., U.S.A. 50-61; Chair., Theatre Dept., Smith Coll., U.S.A. 61-66; Visiting Prof. Amhurst Coll. 66-67, Univ. of Mass. 67-68; Guggenheim Fellow 55.

Plays (with dates of production): *The Old Lady Says "No"* 29, *The Moon in the Yellow River* 31, *A Bride for the Unicorn* 33, *Storm Song* 34, *The Golden Cuckoo* 39, *The Dreaming Dust* 46, *A Fourth for Bridge* 49, *Strange Occurrence on Ireland's Eye* 56, *The Scythe and the Sunset* 58, *Nine Rivers from Jordan* (autobiography) 53, *In Search of Swift* 59 (biography), *John Millington Synge* 65.

Dept. of English, Univ. of Mass., Amhurst, Mass., U.S.A.

Johore, H.H. The Sultan of; Tunku Ismail, C.M.G.; Malayan ruler; b. 94.

Colonel Commandant, Johore Military and Volunteer Services; succeeded his father, Sultan Ibrahim, May 59; Hon. K.B.E. (U.K.), Darjah Karabat, Order of the Crown of Johore, Order Sri Manjku Negara, Order of Crown of Kelantan and foreign decorations.

Istana Bukit Serene, Johore Bahru, Malaya, Malaysia.

Jolinon, Joseph, LL.D., POL. SC.D.; French novelist; b. 9 Dec. 1885; ed. Lille, Paris and Dijon Univs.

Former advocate at Court of Appeal, Lyon; Laureate of Renaissance Prize 29, Prix de Littérature régionaliste 38; Grand Prix du roman, Acad. française 50, Grand Prix de la Société des Gens de Lettres.

Publs. *Le Joueur de Balle* 22, *Le valet de gloire* 23, *La*

tête brûlée 24, *Le Meunier* 25, *La paroissienne* 26, *La Foire* 28, *Les Revenants dans la Boutique* 30, *Képi Pompon* 31, *Marie Bourgogne* 31, *Dame de Lyon* 32, *L'Arbre Sec* 33, *Imagerie du Curé d'Ars* 34, *Le Bât d'Argent* 35, *Imagerie du Bandit Mandrin* 35, *Fesse-Mathieu le soldat inconnu* 36, *Les Coquines* 37, *Guerillas 1808* 41, *Le chat du second* 42, *Charme de Lyon* 42, *Les malandries du beaujolais* 43, *Le pacifiste sanguinaire* 45, *La belle auberge* 47, began publ. of series of 12 novels under general title *Les Provinciaux* 48, *I Quatre gibus, II Le Jubilé, III Ecus d'or, IV Dernières ombrelles, V Pantalons rouges, VI Robes de flamme* 55, *Pauline Jaricot* 57, *Garibaldi* 60, *Encyclopédie du Football par l'image* 61.
28 Montée des Carmélites, Lyon (Rhône); Frontigny, Briant (Saône-et-Loire), France.

Jolivet, André; French composer; b. 8 Aug. 1905; ed. Lycée Colbert, Ecole Normale supérieure.
Orchestral leader; Prof. Conservatoire Nat. de Paris; Dir. of Music, Comédie-Française and Prof. of Composition 45-; Vice-Pres. Nat. Cttee. for Music; Tech. Adviser to Direction Générale des Arts et des Lettres 60-62; Hon. Pres. Syndicat Nat. des artistes, musiciens de France et d'outre-mer; Prés. des Concerts Lamoureux 63; Croix de Guerre, Grand Prix Musical de la ville de Paris, Grand Prix du Disque, Officier Légion d'Honneur, Officier de l'Ordre des Arts et Lettres.
Principal works 34-66: 50 chamber music compositions, 11 vocal works, 26 symphonies, 3 ballets, 1 opera-ballet, 1 opera-buffa, music for 16 plays and 19 films, 2 oratorios.
Publ. *Ludwig van Beethoven.*
6 rue Meissonier, Paris 17e, France.
Telephone: CArnot 62-64.

Jolivet, Henri; French engineer and business executive; b. 8 June 1904; ed. Ecole Nationale Supérieure des Mines de Saint-Etienne.
Président Directeur Général, Ugine Kuhlmenn; Président, Soc. des Tôles Spéciales & Inoxydables Ugine-Gueugnon; Vice-Pres. Chambre Syndicale des Aciers Fins & Spéciaux; Admin. Irsid, Ugine-Carbone, Plastugil, Carbone-Lorraine, Hauts Fourneaux & Forges d'Allevard, Savoie-Acheson; Officier de la Légion d'Honneur.
10 rue du Général Foy, Paris 8e, France.

Jonas, Franz; Austrian politician; b. 4 Oct. 1899; ed. evening classes.
Former compositor; served on Russian and Italian fronts in Austrian Army, First World War; Sec. Florisdorf Section, Austrian Socialist Party 32-34; arrested 35; worker in locomotive works, Second World War; Mayor of Floridsdorf (District of Vienna) 46-48; Dep. Leader Vienna Branch Socialist Party 45-49, Leader 49-65; Deputy Chair. party inner council 49-65; Head of Food Supply Dept., City of Vienna 48-49, of Housing Dept. 49-51; Mayor and Gov. of Vienna 51-65; Federal Pres. of Austria 65-.
Hofburg, Vienna I, Austria.

Jonathan, Chief Joseph Leabua; Basuto politician; b. 30 Oct. 1914; ed. Mission School, Leribe.
Worked in mines in South Africa 34-37; returned to Basutoland 37; Court Pres. 38; entered politics 52; mem. District Council 54; mem. Nat. Council 54, mem. Panel of 18 56-59; founded Basutoland Nat. Party 59, leader 59-; mem. Legislative Council 60-64; Del. at Constitutional Conf. 64; Prime Minister of Basutoland (now Lesotho) and Minister of External Affairs 65-.
Prime Minister's Office, P.O. Box 527, Maseru, Lesotho.

Jonckheer, Efrain; Netherlands (Antilles) politician; b. 17; ed. in Netherlands Antilles.
Dir. of several companies in Curaçao; first Pres. Democratic Party 44-; mem. of all Round Table Confs. leading to full autonomous status of Netherlands

Antilles 47-54; mem. Staten (legislative assembly) 45-; Leader Democratic Party Group in Staten 45-54; mem. Island Council of Curaçao 51-53; Prime Minister of Netherlands Antilles and Minister of General Affairs 54-; Min. of Transport and Communications 54-56; Min. of Social Affairs 56-57; Commdr. Order Orange-Nassau.
Asteroidenweg 11, Willemstad, Curaçao, Netherlands Antilles, West Indies.

Jones, Rt. Hon. Aubrey, B.SC.; British politician and industrialist; b. 20 Nov. 1911; ed. London School of Econs.
On foreign and editorial staff *The Times* 37-39 and 47-48; served with Army Intelligence Staff, War Office and Mediterranean 40-46; joined British Iron and Steel Fed. as Special Asst. to Chair. 49, Economic Dir. 54 and Gen. Dir. 55; M.P. for Birmingham (Hall Green) 50-65; Minister of Fuel and Power 55-57; Minister of Supply 57-59; fmr. Dir. Guest, Keen & Nettlefolds Steel Co. Ltd., fmr. Chair. Staveley Industries Ltd., fmr. Dir. Courtaulds Ltd.; Chair. Nat. Board for Prices and Incomes 65-; mem. Nat. Econ. Devt. Council 65-; Hon. Fellow London School of Econs. 59, mem. Court of Govs. 64; Gov. Nat. Inst. Econ. and Social Research 67; Hon. Vice-Pres. Consumers' Asscn. 67; Conservative.
Publs. *The Pendulum of Politics* 46, *Right and Left* 44, *Industrial Order* 50.
116 Oakwood Court, London, W.14, England.

Jones, Charles S.; American oil executive.
Chairman and Dir. Richfield Oil Corpn.; Dir. Douglas Aircraft Co., Inc., Pacific Mutual Life Insurance Co.
555 S. Flower Street, Los Angeles 17, Calif., U.S.A.

Jones, Rt. Hon. Sir (Frederick) Elwyn, Kt., P.C., Q.C., M.P.; British lawyer and politician; b. 24 Oct. 1909; ed. Llanelly Grammar School, Univ. Coll. of Wales, Aberystwyth, and Gonville and Caius Coll., Cambridge.
Called to Bar, Gray's Inn 35; Deputy Judge Advocate 43-45; M.P. 45-; Recorder of Merthyr Tydfil 49-53, of Swansea 53-60, of Cardiff 60-64; Parl. Private Sec. to Attorney-Gen. 46-51; Attorney-Gen. 64-; mem. Bar Council 56-59; Chair. Soc. of Labour Lawyers 57-60; Treas. of Justice, British Section, Int. Comm. of Jurists 59-64; Labour.
Publs. *Hitler's Drive to the East* 37, *The Battle for Peace* 38, *The Attack from Within* 39.
House of Commons, London, S.W.1; 5 Gray's Inn Square, London, W.C.1, England.

Jones, Ernest Cyril Brieley; Liberian administrator and politician; b. 96; ed. Tuskegee Institute, Tuskegee, Alabama, U.S.A.
Vocational Arts Instructor, Prairie View State Coll., Texas, U.S.A. 21-22; Dir. of Trades School, St. John A & I School, Robertsport, Liberia 22-25; Asst. Plantations Man., Firestone Plantations Co., Liberia 26-28; engaged in private enterprise 28-31; entered politics and apptd. a County District Commr. 32, First Class District Commr. 37, Provincial Commr. 44; Chief of the Bureau of Tribal Affairs 46; Asst. Sec. of Interior 48; Cabinet Minister, Sec. of Defence 49-60; Ambassador to Ivory Coast Republic 60-; Chair. Exec. Immigration Comm., Monrovia; Knight Commdr. Star of Africa (Liberia); Commdr. Star of Benin (France); mem. National True Whigs Party.
Liberian Embassy, 17 ave. Chardy, Abidjan, Ivory Coast Republic.

Jones, George Lewis; American diplomatist; b. 18 Jan. 1907; ed. Boys' Latin School, Baltimore, Harvard Univ., Christ's Coll., Cambridge, and London School of Econs.
Clerk to U.S. Commercial Attachés 30-32; at Cairo 32-34; Asst. Trade Commr., Athens 35-41; Acting Commercial Attache Cairo 41-42; Near Eastern Div., Dept. of State 42-45; Asst. Chief, Div. of Near Eastern Affairs 45-46; Second Sec. London 46-47, First Sec.

47-49; Nat. War Coll. 49-50; mem. Policy Planning Staff, Dept. of State 50; Dir. Office of Near Eastern Affairs 50-52; Consul-Gen., Tunis 52-53; Counsellor, Cairo 53-55, Teheran, with personal rank of Minister 55-56; Amb. to Tunisia 56-59; Asst. Sec. of State for Near Eastern and S. Asian Affairs 59-61; Minister, London 61-64; Co-ordinator, Senior Seminar in Foreign Policy, Dept. of State 64-.
1644 Avon Place, Washington 7, D.C., U.S.A.

Jones, Geraint Iwan; British organist; b. 16 May 1917; ed. Caterham School and Royal Acad. of Music. Concert organist, Nat. Gallery Concerts 40-44; Conductor, Purcell's *Dido and Aeneas*, Mermaid Theatre 50-53; Founder, Geraint Jones Singers and Orchestra 51; Musical Dir. Lake District Festival 60-, Kirckman Concert Soc. 63-; Prof., Royal Acad. of Music; Grand Prix du Disque 59.
Frequent harpsichord recitals with violinist wife Winifred Roberts; frequent tours of Europe and America 48-; complete organ works of Bach in London 45-46 and 55; has recorded on most historic organs in Europe.
Missenden House, Little Missenden, Amersham, Bucks., England.

Jones, Sir Glyn Smallwood, G.C.M.G., M.B.E., B.A.; British colonial civil servant; b. 9 Jan. 1908; ed. King's School, Chester, and St. Catherine's Soc., Oxford Univ.
Colonial Service, N. Rhodesia 31, District Commr. 39; Commr. for Native Development 50; Provincial Commr. 56; Minister for Native Affairs 58; Chief Sec., Nyasaland 60; Gov. of Nyasaland 61-64; Governor-Gen. of Malawi 64-66.
17 Iverna Gardens, London, W.8, England.
Telephone: 01-937-1349.

Jones, Gwyneth, A.R.C.M.; British soprano; b. 7 Nov. 1936; ed. Twmpath School, Pontypool, Royal Coll. of Music, London, Accad. Chigiana, Siena, Zürich Int. Opera Centre and under Maria Carpi, Geneva.
With Zürich Opera House 62-63; with Royal Opera House, Covent Garden 63-; guest performances in numerous opera houses throughout the world including La Scala, Milan, Rome Opera, Vienna State Opera, Berlin State Opera, Munich State Opera, Paris, Marseilles and Dallas Opera, Teatro Colon, Buenos Aires, Tokyo, Bayreuth Festival, Edinburgh Festival and Welsh Nat. Opera; known for many opera roles including Leonora, *Il Trovatore*, Desdemona, *Otello*, Aida, *Aida* (Verdi), Leonora, *Fidelio* (Beethoven), Octavian, *Der Rosenkavalier* (Strauss), Senta, *Fliegender Holländer* (Wagner), Medea, *Medea* (Cherubini), Sieglinde, *Walküre* (Wagner), Lady Macbeth, *Macbeth* (Verdi), Elizabeth, *Don Carlos* (Verdi); recordings for Decca.
Pen-y-Lan, 127 Brunswick Road, Ealing, London, W.5, England.

Jones, Sir Henry Frank Harding, K.B.E., M.A., M.I.C.E., M.I.CHEM.E.; British engineer; b. 13 July 1906; ed. Harrow School and Pembroke Coll., Cambridge.
Army Service 39-45; fmr. Deputy Chair. Watford and St. Albans Gas Co., Wandsworth and District Gas Co.; fmr. Dir. South Metropolitan, South Suburban and other gas companies; Chair. East Midlands Gas Board 49-52; Dep. Chair. Gas Council 52-60, Chair. 60-; Hon. mem. Inst. of Gas Engineers, Pres. 56-57; Birmingham Medal, Inst. of Gas Engineers 64.
Pathacres, Weston Turville, Aylesbury, Buckinghamshire, England.

Jones, Howard Mumford, M.A.; American university professor; b. 16 April 1892; ed. Univs. of Wisconsin and Chicago.
Adjunct Prof. of General Literature and English, Univ. of Texas 16-17; Asst. Prof. of English, State Univ. of Montana 17-19; Assoc. Prof. of Comparative Literature, Univ. of Texas 19-25; Assoc. Prof. of English, Univ. of North Carolina 25-30; Prof. of English, Univ. of Michigan 30-36; Prof. of English, Harvard Univ. 36-62, Emer. 62-; Dean Graduate School of Arts and Sciences 43-44; Abbot Lawrence Lowell Prof. of the Humanities 60; Chair. American Council of Learned Socs. 55-59; Editor-in-Chief John Harvard Library 59-; Jusserand Medal; Guggenheim Fellow; Research Assoc. Henry E. Huntington Library; American Acad. of Arts and Sciences (Pres. 44-51); Fellow Center for Advanced Studies in Behavioral Sciences 57-58; Weil Lecturer 67; numerous hon. degrees; Pulitzer Prize 64.
Publs. *A Little Book of Local Verse* 15, *Gargoyles* (poems) 18, *The Shadow* (play) 17, *A Bibliography of Works and MSS. of Byron* (with R. H. Griffith) 24, *America and French Culture (1750-1848)* 27, *The Romanesque Lyric* (with P. S. Allen) 28, *The Life of Moses Coit Tyler* 33, *They Say the Forties* 37, *The Harp That Once* 37, *Ideas in America* 44, *Education and World Tragedy* 46, *The Theory of American Literature* 48, *The Bright Medusa* 52, *The Pursuit of Happiness* 53, *The Frontier in American Fiction, American Humanism* 57, *Reflections on Learning* 58, *One Great Society* 59, *Guide to American Literature Since 1890* 59, *History and The Contemporary* 64, *O Strange New World* 64, *Jeffersonionism and the American Novel* 66, *Belief and Disbelief in American Literature* 67.
14 Francis Avenue, Cambridge, Mass. 02138, U.S.A.
Telephone: TR-6-1656.

Jones, Howard Palfrey, LITT.B.; American diplomatist and educator; b. 2 Jan. 1899; ed. Univ. of Wisconsin, Columbia Univ. and Univ. of Michigan.
Newspaper work 21-29; with Nat. Municipal League 29-39; Lect. Prof. Graduate School of Journalism, Columbia Univ. 33-39; Civil Service Commr., N.Y. State 39-43; Deputy Comptroller 43; Dept. of State 47, served Germany, China 47-54; Chief of Mission, U.S. Foreign Operations Mission to Indonesia 54-55; Deputy Asst. Sec. of State for Far Eastern Econ. Affairs 55-58; Ambassador to Indonesia 58-65; Chancellor East-West Center, Honolulu 65-; Hon. LL.D. Farleigh Dickinson Univ.
East-West Center, Honolulu, Hawaii, 96822, U.S.A.
Telephone: 944-8955.

Jones, J. Wesley, A.B.; American diplomatist; b. 4 June 1907; ed. George Washington Univ.
Vice-Consul, Mexico 30-32; Calcutta 32-35; Consul, Rome 35-41; Asst. Chief, Div. S. European Affairs, State Dept. 41-45; First Sec., Embassy, Rome 45-48; Counsellor, Embassy Nanking 48-49; Madrid 49-53; Dir. W. European Office, State Dept. 53-57; Dep. Asst. Sec. of State 57-58; Amb. to Libya 52-63, to Peru 63-.
American Embassy, Lima, Peru.

Jones, James; American writer; b. 6 Nov. 1921; ed. High School, Robinson, Illinois, Hawaii and New York Univs.
Purple Heart Medal, Bronze Star Medal, National Book Award.
Publs. *From Here to Eternity* 51, *Some Came Running* 58, *The Pistol* 59, *The Thin Red Line* 62, *Go to the Widow-maker* 67.
Home: 10 Quai d'Orléans, Ile Saint Louis, Paris 4e, France; Office: c/o Dell Publishing Co. Inc., 750 Third Avenue, New York City, N.Y. 10017, U.S.A.

Jones, Marvin, A.B., LL.B.; American lawyer and politician; ed. Southwestern and Texas Univs.
Admitted to Texas Bar 07, practised Amarillo; Chair. Board Legal Examiners, 7th Supreme Judicial District Texas 13; mem. Congress from Texas 17-41, Chair. House Cttee. on Agriculture 31-40; Judge U.S. Court of Claims 40-43; Agricultural Adviser to Dir. Economic Stabilisation Office 43; Pres. First Int. Conf. on Food

and Agriculture, Hot Sprngs, Va., May 43; War Food Admin. June 43-July 45; Chief Justice, U.S. Court of Claims 47-64, Active Senior Judge 64-; Democrat.
2807 Hughes Street, Amarillo, Texas, U.S.A.

Jones, Norman Edward; Australian metals executive; b. 2 Aug. 1904; ed. Hamilton and Cooks Hill High Schools, and Newcastle Technical Coll.
The Broken Hill Proprietary Co. Ltd. 21-, Chemist and Metallurgist 21-34, Asst. and Acting Open Hearth Supt. 34-37, Technical Asst. to Gen. Man., Melbourne 38, Asst. Gen. Man. 43-50, Chief Gen. Man. 50-52, Man. Dir. 52-67, now Dir.; Dir. The Nat. Bank of Australasia Ltd., Australia Paper Manufacturers Ltd., The Colonial Mutual Life Assurance Soc. Ltd.
136 Kooyong Road, Toorak 3142, Victoria, Australia. Telephone: 20-3365.

Jones, Roger Warren, A.B., M.A., LL.D.; American government official; b. 3 Feb. 1908; ed. Cornell and Columbia Univs.
Instructor, Coral Gables, Mil. Acad. 28-29; in commerce 29-31; Asst. Exec. Officer, Central Statistical Bd., Washington 33-39; Admin. Officer, Budget Bureau, 39-42; Col. in U.S. armed forces 42-45; Budget Examiner, and subsequently Asst. Dir. for Legislative Reference and Dep. Dir. Bureau of the Budget 45-59; Chair., Civil Service Comm. 59-61; Dep. Under-Sec. of State for Admin. 61-62; Senior Consultant, Budget Bureau 62-; mem. Comm. on Political Activity of Govt. Personnel 67-.
Bureau of the Budget, Washington 25, D.C.; Home: 3912 Leland Street, Chevy Chase, Md. 20015, U.S.A.

Jones, Thomas Victor; American aircraft executive; b. 22 July 1920; ed. Pomona Junior Coll. and Stanford Univ.
Engineer, El Segundo Div., Douglas Aircraft Co. 41-47; Tech. Adviser, Brazilian Air Ministry 47-51; Prof., Head of Dept., Brazilian Inst. of Technology 47-51; Rand Corpn. 51-53; Asst. to Chief Engineer, Northrop Aircraft Inc. 53, Dep. Chief Engineer 54-56, Dir. Development Planning 56-57, Corporate Vice-Pres. 57, Senior Vice-Pres. 58-59, Pres. 59-, Chief Exec. Officer 60-, Chair. of Board 63-.
Publ. *Capabilities and Operating Costs of Possible Future Transport Airplanes* 53.
Northrop Corporation, 9744 Wilshire Boulevard, Beverly Hills, Calif.; Home: 1050 Moraga Drive, Los Angeles, Calif. 90049, U.S.A.

Jong, Petrus J. S. de, D.S.C.; Netherlands naval officer and politician; b. 3 April 1915; ed. Royal Naval Coll.
Entered Netherlands Royal Navy 31, commissioned 34; submarine commander during Second World War; Adjutant to Minister for Navy 48; Staff Officer on staff Allied Commander-in-Chief, Channel, Portsmouth 53; Adjutant to Queen of Netherlands 55; Commander of destroyer *Gelderland* 58; State Sec. for Defence 59-63; Minister of Defence 63-67; Prime Minister and Minister of Gen. Affairs 67-; Catholic Party.
Office of the Prime Minister, The Hague, Netherlands.

Jongh, Samuel Elzevier de, DR. MED.; Netherlands pharmacologist; b. 98; ed. Univs. of Utrecht and Amsterdam.
Professor of Pharmacology Univ. of Leiden 35-37 (dismissed by the Germans during war), Emeritus 63; adviser to pharmaceutical firm of Organon Ltd.; and to medical section of Nat. Defence Org.; mem. Royal Acad. of Sciences 50-, Royal Flemish Acad. of Medicine 62-; hon. mem. Flemish Soc. for Advancement of Medicine, Netherlands Soc. of Endocrinology; Dr. h.c. (Ghent) 53.
Publs. with several others: *Het autonome zenuwstelsel* 34, *Aanwinsten op diagn. en therap. gebied* 35, *Contribution to the knowledge of the influences of gonadotropic*

and sex hormones on the gonads of rats (with J. H. Gaarenstroom) 46, *Hormonologie* (with E. Laqueur and M. Tausk) 48, *Inleiding tot de Algemene Farmacologie* 59 (2nd edn. 64).
Boerhaavelaan 33, Leiden, Netherlands.

Jonker, Willem, D.IUR.; Netherlands business executive; b. 2 July 1907; ed. Gymnasium, The Hague, and Univ. of Leiden.
Lawyer 31; City Councillor, The Hague 39; Managing Dir. Centraal Bureau voor de Rijn—en Binnenvaart 39-45, Pres. 45; mem. Economic and Social Cttee., European Economic Community (E.E.C.) and Euratom 58-, Vice-Chair. 62-64; mem. Comm. on Int. Affairs, Netherlands Social and Econ. Council 60-; Transport Cttee. Int. Chamber of Commerce; Managing Dir. N.V. Nederlandsche Rijnvaartvereeniging, Rotterdam; Officer, Order of Orange-Nassau 63.
12 Zuidwerflaan, The Hague, Netherlands.

Jonkman, Jan Anne, LL.D.; Netherlands politician; b. 13 Sept. 1891; ed. Utrecht, Toulouse and Leiden.
Joined Netherland-Indies Civil Service (Judicature) 19; mem. of Legislative Assembly Batavia 27-31; Public Prosecutor, High Court of Justice at Macassar (Celebes) 31, at Semarang (Java) 38; Speaker of Legislative Assembly 39-42; imprisoned by Japanese army of occupation in Java 42-45; Min. for the Overseas Territories of the Kingdom of the Netherlands July 46-Aug. 48; mem. Parl. 48-66; Pres. Senate 51-66; Labour. Publ. *The National-Indonesian foundations of education for the Indonesian population* 18.
61 Schoutenstraat, The Hague, Netherlands. Telephone: 070-245223.

Jónsson, Emil; Icelandic engineer and politician; b. 27 Oct. 1902; ed. Reykjavík Grammar School and Technical Univ. of Copenhagen.
Municipal Engineer, Hafnarfjördur 26-37; Mayor of Hafnarfjördur 30-37; mem. Parl. 34-; State Dir. of Lighthouses and Harbours 37-44, 49-57; Man. Dir. Nat. Bank of Iceland 57-58; Minister of Communications 44-47, of Commerce and Communications 47-49; Minister of Foreign Affairs, a.i. 56; Speaker of the Althing 56-58; Prime Minister 58-59; Minister of Social Affairs and Fisheries 59-65; Minister of Foreign Affairs 65-; Chair. Labour (Social Democratic) Party 57-.
Ministry of Foreign Affairs, Reykjavík, Iceland.

Jonsson, John Erik; American industrialist; b. 6 Sept 1901; ed. Rensselaer Polytechnic Inst., Troy, N.Y.
Aluminum Co. of America 22-27; Dumont Motor Car Co. 27-29; Aluminum Co. of America 29-30; Texas Instruments Inc. 30-, Hon. Chair. 67-; Chair. Board of Govs. Southwest Centre of Advanced Studies; Dir. Educational Facilities Laboratories, Equitable Life Assurance Soc. (U.S.) 58-, Republic Nat. Bank of Dallas, Texas 58-, American Man. Asscn. 56-, Neiman Marcus Co.; mem. Board of Trustees Rensselaer Polytechnic Inst., Skidmore Coll., Saratoga Springs, N.Y., American Assembly N.Y.C. 67; Nat. Industrial Conf. Board, New York City 59-; Mayor of Dallas 4-; mem. Nat. Planning Council and Asscn. 58-, Soc. of Exploration Geophysicists. 30-; Chair Board of Visitors, Tulane Univ. 68-; Hon. D.Eng. (Rensselaer Polytechnic Inst., N.Y.), Hon. D.Sc. (Hobart, William Smith and Austin Colls.), LL.D. (Southern Methodist Univ.).
3300 Republic Bank Tower, Dallas, Texas 75201, U.S.A

Jónsson, Magnus; Icelandic politician; b. 7 Sept. 1919; ed. Univ. of Iceland.
Former attorney; Officer in Ministry of Finance 47-53; mem. Althing 51-; Gen. Sec. Independence Party 53-60; Gen. Man. Agricultural Bank of Iceland 61-65; Minister of Finance 65-.
Ministry of Finance, Reykjavík, Iceland.

Jooss, Kurt; balletmaster and choreographer of German origin; b. 12 Jan. 1901; ed. Württemberg Music Acad., Stuttgart and Laban School of Dance, Hamburg.
Producer Münster Municipal Theatre 24; Dir. Dance Dept. Folkwang Municipal School Essen 27, 49, 56-; founded Folkwang Studio (Ballets Jooss) 32; Ballet Dir. Essen Opera House 30; Ballet School Dartington Hall, Devon 34-40; Maître de Ballet and chief choreographer Düsseldorf Opera 54-56; Dir. Ballets Jooss and Prof. of Choreography and Dir. Inst. Tanz, Folkwang Hochschule, Essen 63-.
Works include libretti and choreography for ballets: *Die Brautfahrt* 25, *Tragödie* 26, *Drosselbart* 29, *Pavane for a Dead Infanta* 29, *The Green Table* 32, *Big City* 32, *The Prodigal Son* 33, *Chronica* 39, *Company at the Manor* 43, *Pandora* 44, *Juventud* 48, *Journey in the Fog* 52, *Night Train* 52, Purcell's *Faërie Queene* 59.
Bredeneyerstr. 141, 43 Essen-Bredeney, Germany.
Telephone: Essen 42127.

Jooste, Gerhardus Petrus, M.A.; South African diplomatist; b. 5 May 1904; ed. Univ. of Pretoria.
Entered Union Public Service 24; apptd. Private Sec. to Hon. N. C. Havenga, Minister of Finance 29; joined Dept. of External Affairs 34; Sec. of Legation and Chargé d'Affaires a.i., Brussels 37, Chargé d'Affaires to Belgian Govt.-in-Exile, London 40-41; Head of Economic Div., Dept. of External Affairs, Pretoria 41, Head of Political and Diplomatic Div. 46; Ambassador to U.S.A. and Permanent Del. to U.N. 49-54; Alternate Del. U.N. Gen. Assembly, Paris 48, Leader S. African Del., N.Y. 49, Leader and Deputy Leader, N.Y. 50, Dep. Leader, Paris 51-52, 58, Leader, N.Y. 52, 53, 54 and 63; High Commr. in Great Britain 54-56; Sec. for External Affairs, Pretoria 56-, Ex-officio mem. of Atomic Energy Board 56-66; Sec. for Foreign Affairs 61-66; Special Adv. on Foreign Affairs to the Prime Minister and Minister of Foreign Affairs July 66; mem. Comm. Water Matters 66-; Leader UN Gen. Assembly, N.Y. 66.
Private Bag 343, Pretoria, Republic of South Africa.
Telephone: 22167.

Jorda, Enrique; Spanish conductor; b. 24 March 1911; ed. under Paul Le Flem (harmony and composition) and Marcel Dupré (organ).
Debut as conductor with Paris Symphony Orch. 38; permanent conductor Madrid Symphony Orch. 40-45; guest conductor leading European orchestras 45-47; conductor Cape Town Orch. 47-52; permanent conductor San Francisco Orch. 54-64; numerous tours in many parts of the world; Conde de Cartagena Prize 41, Order of Alfonso X El Sabio 56.
1140 Filbert Street, San Francisco, California, U.S.A.

Jordan, B. Everett; American textile manufacturer and politician; b. 8 Sept. 1896; ed. Trinity Coll., North Carolina.
Served with U.S. Tank Corps 18-19; organised Sellers Manufacturing Co. 27; later Sec.-Treas., Gen. Man. and official of numerous other textile firms; Chair. North Carolina Democratic Exec. Cttee. 49-54; N.C. Democratic Nat. Committeeman 54-58; Senator from North Carolina 58-; Vice-Pres. Board of Methodist Colls. 52-56; Chair. Board of Trustees, Alamance County Gen. Hospital; Trustee Duke Univ., Elon Coll.; Democrat.
Senate Office Building, Washington 25, D.C., U.S.A.

Jordan, Len B.; American politician; b. 15 May 1899; ed. Univ. of Oregon.
U.S. Army, First World War; Dir. Circle C Ranch and Jordan Motor Co.; mem. Idaho Legislature 47; Gov. of Idaho 51-55; mem. Int. Joint Comm. 55-57; Int. Advisory Board 58-59; U.S. Senator from Idaho Aug. 62-; U.S. Adviser to UN Comm. on the Peaceful Uses of Outer Space; Republican.
U.S. Senate, Washington, D.C., U.S.A.

Jordan, Maurice; French engineer and business executive; b. 24 Aug. 1899; ed. Ecole des Roches, Verneuil-sur-Avre.
Vice-President, Dir.-Gen. Peugeot Motors, Pres. and Gen. Manager Oct. 64-; Dir. Peugeot Land and Finance Soc., of Gen. Motors Co. (France), and of Soc. of Alimentary and Dietetic Products.
Peugeot S.A., 75 avenue de la Grande-Armée, Paris 16e, France.

Jordan, Pascual, DR. PHIL.; German physicist; b. 18 Oct. 1902; ed. Univ. of Göttingen.
Extraordinary Prof., Univ. of Rostock 29-35, Ordinary Prof. 35-44; awarded Planck Medal of German Physical Society 42; Ordinary Prof. of Theoretical Physics and Dir. of Inst. of Theoretical Physics Berlin 44; Visiting Prof. Univ. of Hamburg 47-53, Ordinary Prof. 53-; Gauss Medal 55; mem. of Bundestag 57-61.
Publs. incl. *Anregung von Quantensprüngen* (with J. Franck) 28, *Elementare Quantenmechanik* (with M. Born) 30, *Statistische Mechanik auf quantentheoretischer Grundlage* 30, *Anschauliche Quantentheorie* 36, *Die Physik des 20. Jahrhunderts* 36, *Das Bild der modernen Physik* 47, *Schwerkraft und Weltall* 52, (2nd edition 55), *Der Naturwissenschaftler vor der religiösen Frage* 63, *Die Expansion der Erde* 66.
Isestrasse 123, 2 Hamburg 13, German Federal Republic.
Telephone: Hamburg 473226.

Jorge Zubiri, Horacio; Argentine politician; b. 27; Minister of Public Works, Provincial Govt. of Buenos Aires 58-61; Unión Cívica Radical Intransigente (UCRI), Minister of Public Works 62-63; Chair. Dirección Nacional de Vialidad.
Avenida 9 de Julio 1925, Buenos Aires, Argentina.

Jorgensen, Albert N., LL.D., LITT.D., PH.D., SC.D.; American university president; b. 20 March 1899; ed. Coe Coll., Iowa, State Univ. of Iowa.
Assoc. Dir. Bureau of Research, State Univ. of Iowa 25-27; Prof. and Dir. Educational Admin. and Research, Eastern Michigan Coll. 27-31; Prof. Educational Admin., Univ. of Buffalo 31-35; Pres. Univ. of Connecticut 35-63; Dir. Washington Office, Inst. of Int. Education 63-.
Publs. *Use and Interpretation of Educational Tests* 29, *Use and Interpretation of Elementary School Tests* 35, *Use and Interpretation of High School Tests* (all with H. A. Greene) 36, *Measurement and Evaluation in the Elementary School* (with Greene and Gerberich) 42, 53, *Measurement and Evaluation in the Secondary School* 43, 54, *Evaluation in Education* 62.
Office: 2601 Woodley Place, N.W., Washington D.C.; Home: Springhill, Storrs, Connecticut 06268, U.S.A.

Jorio, H.E. Cardinal Alberto di; Italian ecclesiastic; b. 18 July 1884.
Ordained priest 08; Sec. of the Conclave of Oct. 58 which elected Pope John XXIII; created Cardinal by Pope John XXIII Oct. 58; Pro-Pres. Pontifical Commission Vatican State Aug. 61-; mem. Sacred Congregations of Sacraments, of the Council, De Propaganda Fide, of the Fabric of St. Peter's and of Seminaries and Universities; mem. Cardinal Comms. Amministrazione Speciale della Santa Sede, Amministrazione dei Beni della Santa Sede, Vigilanza dell'Istituto per le Opere di Religione, etc.
Vatican City, Italy.
Telephone: 6982-SCV.

Jorn, Asger; Danish artist; b. 3 March 1914.
Studied with Léger and collaborated with Le Corbusier on the "Temps Nouveaux" pavilion, Paris Universal Exhibition 37; co-founder of the "Cobra" international group; rep. at first Exhibition of Experimental Art, Amsterdam 49, at Brussels Int. Exhibition 58, at Dunn Int. Exhibition, London 63 and at numerous other exhbns. (Cologne 67); executes paintings, engravings, sculpture and ceramics.
28 rue du Tage, Paris 13e, France.

Joseph, Dov, B.A., B.C.L., PH.D.; Israeli politician; b. 99; ed. McGill and London Univs.
Legal Adviser, Jewish Agency for Palestine 36-45, mem., Exec. 45-47, Treas. 57-61; mem. (for Mapai) of Knesset 49-; Minister of Supply and Rationing 49-50, Agriculture 49-50, Transport and Communications 50-51, Trade and Industry 51-52, Justice 51-52, Development 53-55, Health 55, Justice 61-66.
Publs. *Nationality—its Nature and Problems, British Rule in Palestine, The Faithful City (The Siege of Jerusalem)* 48.
22 Alharizi Road, Jerusalem, Israel.
Telephone: 39032.

Joseph, Rt. Hon. Sir Keith Sinjohn, Bt., M.P.; British politician; b. 17 Jan. 1918; ed. Harrow School and Magdalen Coll., Oxford.
Military service 39-46; Barrister, Middle Temple 46; Councilman, City of London 46, Alderman 46-49; fmr. Underwriter, Lloyd's; Dir. Bovis Holdings Ltd. 51-59, Chair. Bovis Ltd. 58-59, Deputy Chair. 64-; Conservative M.P. 56-; Parl. Private Sec. to Parl. Under-Sec. of State, Commonwealth Relations Office 57-59; Parl. Sec. Ministry of Housing and Local Govt. 59-61; Minister of State, Board of Trade 61-62; Minister of Housing and Local Govt. and Minister for Welsh Affairs 62-64; Fellow, All Souls Coll., Oxford 46-60.
23 Mulberry Walk, London, S.W.3, England.

Josephson, Erland; Swedish actor and theatre director; b. 15 June 1923.
At Municipal Theatre, Helsingborg 45-49, Gothenburg 49-56, Royal Dramatic Theatre, Stockholm 56-; Dir. of Royal Dramatic Theatre, Stockholm June 66-.
Publs. include: *Cirkel* 46, *Spegeln och en portvakt* 46, *Spel med bedrövade artister* 47, *Ensam och fri* 48, *Lyssnarpost* 49, *De vuxna barnen* 52, *Utflykt* 54, *Sällskapslek* 55, *En berättelse om herr Silberstein* 57, *Kungen ur leken* 59, *Doktor Meyers sista dagar* 64, *Kandidat Nilssons första natt* 64.
Royal Dramatic Theatre, Stockholm, Sweden.

Jost, Nestor; Brazilian politician and bank official; b. 10 Jan. 1917; ed. Anchieta High School, Pôrto Alegre.
Local govt. work 39-45; fmr. Mayor of São Laurenco do Sul; State Deputy 47; mem. Legis. Assembly of Rio Grande do Sul 47-50; Fed. Deputy, Partido Demo-crático (P.S.D.) 51; Sec.-Gen. P.S.D., Rio Grande do Sul Div. 48-49; later Dir. Industrial Credit Section and Agricultural Credit Section, Bank of Brazil; Pres. Bank of Brazil 67-.
Banco do Brazil S.A., Brasília, Brazil.

Jouhandeau, Marcel; French novelist; b. 26 July 1888.
Publs. include *La Jeunesse de Théophile* 20, *Les Pincen-grain* 24, *M. Godeau intime* 25, *Les Terébinthe* 26, *Ximinès Malinjoude* 27, *Opales* 28, *Brigitte ou la Belle au bois dormant, Le parricide imaginaire* 29, *Le journal du coiffeur* 30, *Eloge de l'imprudence* 32, *Elise Véroni-cœana* 33, *M. Godeau marié* 33, *Chaminadour* (2 vols.) 34, *Images de Paris* 34, *Algèbre des valeurs morales* 35, *Le Saladier* 36, *Chroniques maritales* 38, *Le Jardin de Cordoue* 38, *De l'Abjection* 39, *L'Arbre de visages Trip-tyque, Requiem, Et lux* 40, *Les miens, Minos et moi, Nouvelles chroniques maritales* 42, *L'oncle Henri* 43, *Chronique d'une passion* 44, *Petit bestiaire* 44, *Essai sur moi-même* 46, *Animaux familiers, Annotations en marge de la Genèse, Carnets de Don Juan* 47, *Don Juan, récit* 48, *Mémorial I: Le livre de mon père* 48, *II Ménagerie domestique* 48, *La Faute plutôt que le scandale* 49, *L'Imposteur* 50, *Un Monde* 50, *Mémorial III: Le Fils du Boucher* 51, *Ces Messieurs* 51, *Contes Rustiques* 51, *Elise architecte* 51, *La Paroisse du Temps Jadis* 52, *Eloge de la Volupté* 52, *De la Grandeur* 52, *Galande ou Convalescence au Village* 53, *Derniers Jours et Mort de Véronique* 53, *Endymion illustré par P. Y. Trémois* 53, *Mémorial IV: Apprentis et Garçons* 53, *Anna de Mme*

Apremont, Eléments pour une Ethique, Mémorial V: Le langage de la tribu 54, *Contes de l'Enfer* 55, *Nouvelles Images de Paris* 56, *Jeunesse* 56, *Réflexions sur la Vieillesse et la Mort* 56, *Théâtre sans spectacle, Carnets de l'écrivain, St. Philippe Néri, Correspondance avec André Gide* 57, *Mémorial VI: les Chemins de l'Adolescence, Réflexions sur la Vie et le Bonheur* 58, *Les Argonautes* 59, *L'Eternel Procès* 60, *L'Ecole des Filles* 61, *Ani-maleries* 61, *Descente aux Enfers* (illustrated by Georges Braque); *Journaliers I-VII, Divertissements, Journaliers VIII* 66, *Journaliers IX* 67, *Journaliers X, Le gourdin d'Elise* 67.
8 Av. Ducis, Parc de la Malmaison, Rueil, S.-et-O., France.

Joukhdar, Mohammed Saleh, B.A., M.A.; Saudi Arabian economist; b. 1932; ed. Univs. of California and Southern California.
Economic Consultant to Directorate-Gen. of Petroleum and Minerals, Saudi Arabia 58; Govt. Rep., Supervisory Cttee. for Expenditure and Purchasing, Arabian Oil Co. 61, Dir. 61-66; Sec.-Gen. Org. of the Petroleum Exporting Countries (OPEC) 67-; mem. American Soc. of Economists.
Organization of the Petroleum Exporting Countries, Dr. Karl Lueger Ring 10, Vienna 1010, Austria.

Journet, H.E. Cardinal Charles; Swiss ecclesiastic; b. 26 Jan. 1891.
Professor of Divinity, Grand Séminaire, Fribourg; Dir. of review *Nova et Vetera*; consecrated Archbishop 65; created Cardinal 65.
Publs. *Exigences chrétiennes en politique, Destinées d'Israël, Connaissance et Inconnaissance de Dieu, l'Eglise du verbe incarné, La Messe, Présence du Sacrifice de la Croix, Théologie de l'Eglise,* and many other theological publications.
Grand Séminaire, Fribourg, Switzerland.

Jousset, Bernard; French business executive; b. 27 May 1899; ed. Lycées Janson-de-Sailly and Condor-cet, Coll. Stanislas and Ecole Supérieure de la Metallur-gie et des Mines, Nancy.
Served French Army 18-19; founded and became Pres., Dir.-Gen. of Société Parisienne de Cémentation; Hon. Pres. Groupement Inter-Professionnel Patronal Courbe-voie Colombes; Pres. Comm. du Régime Légal des Entreprises, Conseil National du Patronat Français; Hon. Pres. French Catholic Employers; Chevalier, Légion d'Honneur, Commandeur de St.-Sylvestre.
Publs. *L'Accession des Travailleurs au Capital, Vers un salaire humain* (with Hyacynthe Dubreuil).
26 Avenue du grand Veneur, 78 Le Vesinet, France.

Jouve, Géraud Henri; French journalist and diplo-matist; b. 5 July 1901; ed. Univs. of Strasbourg and Paris.
Attached Lycée de Cahors 29, Institut Français, Berlin 30; corresp. for Havas Agency in Budapest, Warsaw, Berlin, Amsterdam, Bucharest 31-40; Free French Del. to Turkey and the Balkans 40-42; Dir. Radio-Brazza-ville 43-44, and of Agence France-Presse (Algeria-Paris) 44-45; Consul-Gen. Ministry of Foreign Affairs 46; mem. Nat. Assembly 46-51; Permanent French Del. to Council of Europe 51-55; Ambassador to Finland 55-60; French del., U.N. High Comm. for Refugees 60-66; Pres. Asscn. syndicale des Rédacteurs en chef; Officier Légion d'Honneur, Médaille de la Résistance 46.
Publs. *La Remontée de Munich à Brazzaville* 45, *Voici l'âge atomique* 46.
104, Boulevard Arago, Paris 14e, France.

Jouve, Pierre Jean; French writer and poet; b. 11 Oct. 1887; ed. Collège d'Arras, Lycée de Lille, and Lille, Paris and Poitiers Univs.
Poetic writing began 25 with *Les Mystérieuses Noces*; essays on music, painting and poetry; Mil. Hospital service 14-18; voluntary exile in Switzerland working

for Resistance and Allies 39-45; Commandeur de la Légion d'Honneur; Premio Poesia "citta di Firenze", Florence 60; Grand Prix National des Lettres, Paris 62; Grand Prix de Poésie, Acad. Française 66, Dr. h.c. Univ. Basel 66.

Publs. Poetry: *Le Paradis Perdu* 29, *Les Noces* 31, *Sueur de Sang* 35, *Matière Céleste* 37, *Kyrie* 38, *La Vierge de Paris* 40-44, *Hymne* 47, *Diadème* 49, *Ode* 50, *Langue* 54, *Lyrique* 56, *Mélodrame* 57, *Inventions* 58, *Moires* 62, *Ténèbre* 65 (collected edn. of poetical works, vols. I, II, III, IV) 64-67; novels: *Paulina 1880* 25, *Le Monde Désert* 27, *Hécate* 28, *Vagadu* 31, *Histoires Sanglantes* 32, *La Scène Capital* 35; collected edn. of novels 59-63; *Proses* 60; essays: *Le Don Juan de Mozart* 44, *Wozzeck* 53, *En Miroir* 54, *Tombeau de Baudelaire* 58; translations of Shakespeare: *Roméo et Juliette* 37, *Les Sonnets* 56, *Macbeth* 59, *Othello* 61.
7 rue Antoine-Chantin, Paris 14e, France.
Telephone: 532-97-32.

Jouven, Pierre; French industrialist; b. 29 March 1908; ed. Ecole Polytechnique, Paris, and Ecole Nationale Supérieure des Mines de Paris.
State Civil Mining Service 31-42; Péchiney 43-, Man. of Plants 45-58, Man. 48-60, Gen. Man. 60-, Chair. of Board 68-, Dir. other companies; Officier, Légion d'Honneur.
Péchiney, 23 rue Balzac, Paris 6e, France.

Jovanovich, William Iliya; American publisher; b. 6 Feb. 1920; ed. Univ. of Colorado and Harvard and Columbia Univs.
Harcourt, Brace & World Inc., New York City 47-, Assoc. Editor Coll. and High School Textbooks 47-53, Vice-Pres., Dir. 53-54, Pres. and Dir. 55-; Pres. Longmans Canada Ltd. 61-63, Chair. 63-.
Publ. *Now, Barabbas* 64.
757 Third Avenue, New York City 17, N.Y., U.S.A.

Joxe, Louis, L. ès L.; French diplomatist and politician; b. 16 Sept. 1901; ed. Lycée Lakanal and Faculty of Arts, Paris.
Mem. French del. League of Nations 32, 33, 39; Deputy Chief of Secretariat to Minister for Air and mem. French del. to Conf. for Reduction of Armaments 33-34; attached to Information Service, League of Nations 33-39; Sec.-Gen. Centre d'Etudes de Politique Etrangère, Paris Univ.; Inspector of Foreign Services, Agence d'Information 35-39; Sec.-Gen. of Cttee. for Nat. Liberation 43-44; Sec.-Gen. of Govt. 44-46, Councillor of State 44; in charge of cultural relations Ministry of Foreign Affairs, Paris 46-52; Ambassador to U.S.S.R. 52-56, to Germany 56; Sec.-Gen. Ministry of Foreign Affairs 56-59; Sec. of State, Prime Minister's Office 59-60; Minister of Nat. Education July-Nov. 60; Minister of State in charge of Algerian Affairs Nov. 60-Dec. 62, for French Admin. Reform 62-67; Minister of Justice 67-May 68; mem. French del. to UNESCO Conf. 46, 47, 49, 50, 51; Commdr. Légion d'Honneur, Médaille de la Résistance.
39, quai de l'Horloge, Paris 1er, France.

Joyce, Eileen; Australian concert pianist; ed. Loreto Convent, Perth, Leipzig Conservatoire, studied in Germany under Teichmuller and Schnabel.
Concert debut, London, at Promenade Concerts under Sir Henry Wood; numerous concert tours, radio performances and gramophone recordings; during Second World War played in asscn. with London Philharmonic Orchestra; concerts with all principal orchestras in U.K., Berlin Philharmonic Orchestra, Conservatoire and Nat. Orchestras, France, Concertgebouw Orchestra, Netherlands, La Scala Orchestra, Italy, Philadelphia Orchestra, Carnegie Hall, New York and Royal Philharmonic Society; concert tours, Australia 48, South Africa 50, Scandinavia and Netherlands 51, South America, Scandinavia and Finland 52, Yugoslavia 53, New Zealand 58, U.S.S.R. 61, India 62; contributed to sound tracks of films, including *The*

Seventh Veil and *Brief Encounter*; appeared in films, including *Wherever She Goes* (autobiographical); gramophone recordings include first recording of John Ireland's Pianoforte Concerto.
Chartwell Farm, Westerham, Kent, England.

Juan, Prince, Count of Barcelona; Pretender to the Spanish throne; b. 20 June 1913.
Went into exile with his father King Alfonso April 31; recognised as King of Spain by his father 41; married Princess Maria Mercedes of Bourbon-Sicily 35.
Villa "Giralda," Estoril, Portugal.
Telephone: Lisbon 261091.

Jube, Albert Riordan, B.S., LL.B.; American industrialist and lawyer; b. 26 July 1888; ed. Amherst Coll., Columbia Univ. Law School, and N.Y. Law School.
Began law practice N.Y. City 13; served in U.S. Navy, First World War; resumed law practice N.Y. City 18; also practice in Newark, N.J. 17; now Vice-Chair. Board of Dirs. and Dir. Collins & Aikman Corpn.; Dir. Firemen's Insurance Company, Newark, N.J., and Chair. of its Finance and Exec. Cttee., also Dir. of its subsidiary companies; Dir. First Nat. State Bank, Newark, N.J., McGraw-Edison, Elgin, Ill., Bush Terminal Buildings Co. N.Y.; Pres. and Commr. Palisades Interstate Park Comm.; mem. American Bar Asscn., N.Y. State Bar Asscn., N.Y. County Lawyers' Asscn., etc.
Home: 226 Elmwynd Drive, Orange, New Jersey; Office: 210 Madison Avenue, New York 16, and 120 Broadway, New York 5, N.Y., U.S.A.

Judge, Edward Thomas, M.A.; British steel executive; b. 20 Nov. 1908; ed. Worcester Royal Grammar School and St. John's Coll., Cambridge.
Dorman, Long & Co. Ltd. 30-, Chief Technical Engineer 37-44, Special Dir. and Chief Engineer 44, Dir. 47; Asst. Managing Dir. Dorman, Long (Steel) Ltd. 59-60, Jt. Managing Dir. 60-61; Chair. and Gen. Manager Dorman, Long & Co. Ltd. 61-67; Chair. Redpath, Brown & Co. Ltd. 61-; Chair. Teesside Bridge & Engineering Works Ltd. 61-; Pres. British Iron and Steel Fed. 65-66; Chair. Darlington & Simpson Rolling Mills Ltd., and part-time Chair. of several companies; Dir. Pilkington Bros. Ltd., North Sea Marine Engineering Construction Co. Ltd., etc.; Vice-Pres. Iron and Steel Inst.
The Red House, Nunthorpe, Middlesbrough, Yorks., England.
Telephone: Middlesbrough 36283.

Juglas, Jean-Jacques, L. ès L.; French professor and politician; b. 10 June 1904; ed. Collège de Bergerac and Univ. of Bordeaux.
Taught at various lycées; Prof. of Geography at Ecole Normale Supérieure de l'Enseignement Technique and Ecole Nationale des Arts et Métiers Paris; Sec.-Gen. for Information at Ministry of French Overseas Territories; served French Army 39-40; worked with Resistance during Occupation; one of founders of M.R.P. (Catholic Party) in west of Paris; mem. of both Constituent Assemblies; Deputy for Paris 46-51, Lot et Garonne 51-56; del to Franco-Vietnamese Conf. Fontainebleau 46, and to U.N. 50, 51 and 54; Pres. Comm. for Overseas Territories in the Nat. Assembly 46-55; Minister for Overseas Territories Jan.-Feb. 55; Dir. 56-60, Pres. Council of Admin. Office of Scientific and Technical Research Overseas 60-63; Prof. Econ. Geography, Conservatoire Nationale des Arts et Métiers; Pres. Cttee. for Scientific Research and Tropical Techniques; mem. Académie des Sciences d'Outre-Mer.
Publ. *Traité de Géographie Economique.*
137 rue de la Tour, Paris 16e, France.
Telephone: 870-25-40 (Paris).

Julia, Gaston Maurice, D. ès s.; French university professor; b. 3 Dec. 1893; ed. Ecole Normale Supérieure.
Lecturer, Ecole Normale Supérieure 19-28; Lecturer

at the Sorbonne 20-25; Titular Prof. of Higher Analysis at the Sorbonne 25-64; Tutor at the Ecole Polytechnique 20-36; Prof. of Geometry, Ecole Polytechnique 36-64; mem. Acad. des Sciences (fmr. Pres.), Pontifical Acad. of Sciences; Grand Officier Légion d'Honneur (mil.); Croix de Guerre (14-18).
Publs. Sixteen volumes and 200 monographs on analysis, geometry, and mechanics 24-47.
4 *bis* rue Traversière, Versailles, France.

Julia, Roger Antoine; French engineer and business executive; b. 29 May 1898; ed. Ecole Polytechnique.
War service 14-18; entered Société Alsacienne de Constructions Mécaniques (SACM) 34; Pres. Dir. Gen. Groupement Atomique Alsacienne Atlantique (G.A.A.A.) and Vice-Pres. Dir. Gen. Société Industrielle de Combustible Nucléaire (S.I.C.N.) (branches of SACM); Pres. Dir. Gen. ALCATEL 63-; Vice-Pres. Société Hispano-Alsacienne (formerly SACM); Dir. Société Lille-Bonnières and Colombes and Société ALSTHOM; mem. EURATOM Scientific and Technical Cttee.; Officier Légion d'Honneur; Croix de Guerre 1914-18.
Société ALCATEL, 32 rue de Lisbonne, 75 Paris VIII, France.
Telephone: 522-17-09.

Juliana, Queen of the Netherlands, Princess of Orange Nassau, Duchess of Mecklenburgh, Princess of Lippe-Biesterfeld; b. 30 April 1909.
Daughter of Queen Wilhelmina and Prince Henry of Mecklenburg-Schwerin; married Prince Bernhard of Lippe-Biesterfeld Jan., 37; daughters Princess Beatrix Wilhelmina Armgard, b. Jan. 38, Princess Irene Emma Elisabeth, b. Aug. 39, Princess Margriet Francisca, b. Jan. 43, Princess Maria Christina, b. Feb. 47; went to Canada after German occupation 40; in England 44; returned to Netherlands 45; Princess Regent 48; Queen of Netherlands Sept. 48-.
Palace of Soestdijk, Baarn, Netherlands.

Julien, A. M. (pseudonym of Aman Maistre); French theatrical director and administrator; b. 24 July 1903; ed. Inst. St. Joseph, Toulon.
Founder, Compagnie des Quinze; Asst. to Cavalcanti; Artistic Dir., Radio-Cité, Editor *Vedettes* 42-44; Producer, Théâtre Sarah-Bernhardt 44, Dir. 47-59, 62-; Dir.-Gen. Paris Drama Festival 54-; Dir.-Gen. Théâtre des Nations 58-65; Admin. Paris Opéra and Opéra Comique 59-62; Vice-Pres. Syndicat des Dirs. de Théâtre; Officier Légion d'Honneur.
Théâtre Sarah-Bernhardt, 15 avenue Victoria, Paris 1er, France.

Juma, Midhet; Jordanian diplomatist; b. 19 Aug. 1920; ed. Cairo Univ.
Attaché to Arab League, Cairo 45-47; First Sec. and Counsellor, Cairo 47-52; Counsellor and Chargé d'Affaires, London 52-53; Minister to Pakistan 53-55; Chief of Protocol, Royal Palace Amman 56; Under-Sec. for Press and Broadcasting 56-58; Amb. to the U.S.A. 58-59, to Morocco 59-62, to Federal German Republic 62-65, to Lebanon 65-67, to U.K. 67-; numerous decorations.
Embassy of Jordan, 6 Upper Phillimore Gardens, London, W.8, England.
Telephone: 01-937-3685.

Juma, Saad; Jordanian diplomatist; b. 16; ed. Syrian Univ., Damascus.
Civil Service for 29 years; Dir. Press and Publicity; Chief Censor; Sec. to Prime Minister; Perm. Under-Sec., Govt. of Amman; Under-Sec. for Foreign Affairs; Ambassador to Syrian Arab Republic 62, to U.S.A. 62-65; Prime Minister April 67-Oct. 67; honours from Jordan, Iran, Syria, Italy and China.
Amman, Jordan.

Jumblatt, Kamal; Lebanese politician and hereditary Druse chieftain; b. 19.
Former Minister of National Economy; Pres. Socialist Progressive Party of Lebanon; Minister of Education and Fine Arts 60-61; Minister of State for the Interior and Planning Services 61-64; Minister of Public Works and Transport 66-67.
Beirut, Lebanon.

Jundi, Sami; Syrian dentist, politician and diplomatist; b. 24.
Dir.-Gen. of Information, United Arab Repub. 58-61; imprisoned 61-62; Minister of Culture and Nat. Guidance, Syrian Arab Repub. March-May 63; Minister of Information 63-64; Ambassador to France 64-66, to Spain 66-67; fmr. mem. Baath Party; founded Socialist Unity Party March 63.
c/o Ministry of Foreign Affairs, Damascus, Syrian Arab Republic.

Jung, Nawab Mir Nawaz (M. Mir Khan), B.A., LL.B., M.SC.; Pakistani financier and diplomatist; b. 1914; ed. Nizam's Coll., Hyderabad and Univs. of London, Paris and Geneva.
In service of Hyderabad State, holding posts of Cabinet Sec., Sec. Railways and Civil Aviation, Sec. Finance, Official Dir. State Bank, Deccan Airways, Coal Mines Co., etc.; prior to partition was Hyderabad's Envoy in London; Minister of Pakistan to Sweden, Norway, Denmark and Finland 51-53; Amb. to the UN 54-57, Pres. Econ. and Social Council of the UN 57-58; Amb. to France and to the Vatican 57-59; Amb.-at-Large to African States 60; Regional Rep. of UN to N.W. Africa, Dakar 61-65; UN Rep., Tunis 65-.
Publs. *Federal Finance* 36, *Central Banking* 45, *Five Year Appraisals* (1960-64) *of UN and Agencies* (co-author).
United Nations, 61 Boulevard Farchat Hached, Tunis, Tunisia.

Jung, Richard, DR.MED.; German neurologist; b. 27 June 1911; ed. Vienna, Freiburg, Paris, Berlin and Munich Univs.
Assistant, Neuro-psychiatric Clinic, Freiburg i. Br. Univ. 35-36, 38-48; Rockefeller Fellow, London and Zürich 36-37; at Hirnforschungsinst., Berlin-Buch 37-38; Dozent, Freiburg i. Br. Univ. 41, Extraordinary Prof. 47, Dir. Dept. of Clinical Neurophysiology 48, Ordinary Prof. of Neurology and Clinical Neurophysiology 51-, Dean Medical Faculty 54-55; hon. mem., Soc. de Neurologie (Paris), Soc. Italiana d'Elettroencefalografia; corresp. mem., American Neurological Asscn.; mem. Akademie der Wissenschaften, Mainz 60.
Publs. *Eine Methodik der Ableitung lokalisierter Potentialschwankungen aus subcorticalen Hirngebieten* (with A. E. Kornmüller) 38, *Physiologische Untersuchungen über den Parkinsontremor und andere Zitterformen beim Menschen* 41, *Über rasch wiederholte Entladungen der Motoneurone und die Hemmungsphase des Beugereflexes* (with J. F. Tönnies) 48, *Mikroableitungen von einzelnen Neuronen im optischen Cortex der Katze: Die lichtaktivierten B-Neurone* (with R. von Baumgarten and G. Baumgartner) 52, *Neuronal Discharge* 53, *Allgemeine Neurophysiologie* 53, *Korrelationen von Neuronentätigkeit und Sehen* 61.
Hansastrasse 9, Freiburg i. Breisgau, German Federal Republic.
Telephone: 32211.

Jung Bahadur, Nawab Ali Yavar, B.A.; Indian diplomatist; b. 05; ed. Nizam Coll., Hyderabad, Queen's Coll., Oxford.
Professor of History, Osmania Univ. 27-34; Dir. of Information, Hyderabad Govt. 34-36; Sec. for Constitutional Affairs, Information and Broadcasting 36-42, for Constitutional Affairs, Police, Education, Religious Affairs and Justice 42-45; Vice-Chancellor, Osmania

Univ. 45-46 and 48-52; Minister for Constitutional Affairs, Local Govt., Police, Public Health and Education 46-47; resigned from Hyderabad Govt. 47; Del. and Deputy Chair. to many UN sessions; Amb. to Egypt, Minister to Lebanon and Libya 54-58; Chair. UN Cttee. SUNFED 56-57; Amb. to Yugoslavia and Greece and Minister to Bulgaria 58-61, Amb. to France 61-65; Vice-Chancellor Muslim Univ. Aligarh 65-68; Amb. to U.S.A. 68-; Hon. LL.D. Osmania Univ. 56; awarded Padma Bhushan 59.
Publs. *Hyderabad in Retrospect, External Relations of Hyderabad.*
Embassy of India, 2700 Macomb Street, N.W., Washington D.C., U.S.A.
Telephone: 265-1471; 265-5050.

Jungalwalla, Nowshir K., O.B.E., M.B.B.S., M.R.C.S., M.R.C.P.; Indian (b. Burma) public health official; b. 1 Dec. 1912; ed. Univ. of Rangoon and Johns Hopkins Univ., U.S.A.
Indian Army Medical Services 39-46; Deputy Public Health Commr., Minister of Health 46-50; Regional Adviser, Regional Office for S.E. Asia, World Health Org. (WHO) 50-52, Rep. in Indonesia 52-55, Dir. Public Health Services, Geneva April 67-; Deputy Dir.-Gen. of Health Services, India 55-57, 60-65, Additional Dir.-Gen. 65-67; Dir. All-India Inst. of Hygiene and Public Health 57-60; Hon. Fellow American Public Health Asscn.; Fellow Acad of Medical Sciences (India); Deputy Dir.-Gen. of Health Services 63-65.
Division of Public Health Services, World Health Organization, Avenue Appia, 1211 Geneva 27, Switzerland.

Jünger, Ernst; German writer; b. 29 March 1895; ed. Hanover; studied zoology and philosophy in Leipzig and Naples.
Served in German Army in both World Wars; awarded Pour le Mérite in First War; involved in July 20th 1944 plot while on Staff of Gen. Stülpnagel in Paris; Literary Award of City of Bremen 56, Goslar 56, Grand Cross of Merit 59, Culture Award, Fed. of German Industries 60, Immermann Award of Düsseldorf 65.
Publs. *In Stahlgewittern* 20, *Das Abenteuerliche Herz* 29, *Der Arbeiter* 32, *Auf den Marmorklippen* 39, *Gärten und Strassen* 42, *Der Friede* 45, *Sprache und Körperbau* 48 *Atlantische Fahrt* 48, *Heliopolis* 49, *Strahlungen* 49, *Über die Linie* 50, *Der Waldgang* 51, *Besuch auf Godenholm* 52, *Der Gordische Knoten* 53, *Das Sanduhrbuch* 54, *Am Sarazenenturm* 55, *Rivarol* 56, *Gläserne Bienen* 57, *Jahre der Okkupation, An der Zeitmauer* 59, *Der Weltstaat* 60, *Ein Vormittag in Antibes* 60, *Sgraffiti* 60, *Werke* (collected works, 10 vols.) 60-65, *Das spanische Mondhorn* 62, *Typus, Name, Gestalt* 63, *Sturm* 63, *Grenzgänge* 65, *Im Granit* 67, *Subtile Jagden* 67.
7941 Wilflingen über Riedlingen, Württ., German Federal Republic.

Junker, Werner E., DR.JUR.; German diplomatist; b. 5 Nov. 1902; ed. Univs. of Freiburg, Königsberg and Kiel.

Joined Foreign Service 27; Attaché in Vienna 31-33; Sec., later Counsellor, Peking and Nanking 33-37; Counsellor in Belgrade 43-45; Ambassador to Argentina 56-63; Ambassador to Republic of South Africa 63-; Kt. Commdr. Order of Merit (German Fed. Rep.); Crown of Thailand; Commdr. Corona d'Italia, Coroana României, Grand Cross May-Order of Merit, Grand Cross Order of San Martin (Argentina).
Embassy of the German Federal Republic, (P.O.B. 2023), Pretoria, Republic of South Africa.
Telephone: Pretoria 74-5931.

Junor, John Donald Brown, M.A.; British journalist; b. 15 Jan. 1919; ed. Glasgow Univ.
Served Fleet Air Arm 40-45; political columnist *Sunday Express* 48-50; Asst. Editor *Daily Express* 51-53; Deputy Editor *Evening Standard* 53-54; Editor *Sunday Express* 54-, Dir. 56-; Dir. Beaverbrook Newspapers 60-.
Publs. *Proletariat of Westminster* 49, *Equal Shares* 50.
Wellpools Farm, Charlwood, Surrey, England.
Telephone: Norwood Hill 370.

Juráček, Pavel; Czechoslovak film director and scriptwriter; b. 2 Aug. 1935; ed. Acad. of Music and Dramatic Arts, Prague.
With Film Studio, Barrandov 62-; awards at Oberhausen and Mannheim Festivals 64, Fipresci Award at Karlovy Vary Festival 66, Special Jury Prize at Youth Film Festival, Cannes.
Directed films: *Joseph Kilian* 63, *Every Young Man* 65.
Krakovská 5, Prague 1, Czechoslovakia.
Telephone: 225725.

Jurgens, R. G.; Netherlands business executive; b. 1904; ed. Universiteit van Amsterdam.
Joined Anton Jurgens' Vereenigde Fabrieken N.V. 27, later merged with Unilever; with Unilever in Germany until 36, in U.K. 36-46, mem. Board Unilever Ltd. 41-, Unilever N.V., Rotterdam 45-; Vice-Chair. Unilever N.V., Rotterdam 63-; Knight Order of Netherlands Lion; Gran Cruz del Merito Civil (Spain).
Unilever N.V., Burg. S'Jacobplein 1, Rotterdam, Netherlands.

Jurinac, Sena; Yugoslav-born Austrian singer; b. 24 Oct. 1921; studied under Maria Kostrencíc.
First appearance as Mimi, Zagreb 42; mem. Vienna State Opera Co. 44-; has sung at Salzburg, Glyndebourne, etc., Festivals; sang in *Der Rosenkavalier,* Covent Garden 66; appointed Austrian State Kammersängerin 51; numerous tours and recordings; Ehrenkreuz für Wissenschaft und Kunst 61; Grosses Ehrenzeichen für Verdienste um die Republik Österreich 67.
State Opera House, Vienna I, Austria.

Juxon-Smith, Colonel Andrew; Sierra Leone army officer; b. 1933; ed. Royal Mil. Acad., Sandhurst, U.K., and Joint Services Staff Coll., U.K.
Creole from Freetown; has served with a British Regiment; Chair. Nat. Reformation Council, Sierra Leone March 67-April 68.
Freetown, Sierra Leone.

K

Kabachnik, Martin Izrailevich; Soviet organic chemist; b. 9 Sept. 1908; ed. Moscow Higher Chemicotechnical School.
Associate of Inst. of Organic Chemistry 39-54; Assoc. of Inst. of Elemental-Organic Compounds, U.S.S.R. Acad. of Sciences 54-; Corresp. mem. U.S.S.R. Acad. of Sciences 53-58, mem. 58-; State Prize 46.
Publs. *Investigation in the Field of Organo-Phosphorus Compounds* 46-, *Some Problems of Tautomerism* 56, *Dual Reaction Capacity and Tautomerism* 60, *Conjugation in Non-Coplanar Systems* 62.
Institute of Elemental-Organic Compounds, U.S.S.R. Academy of Sciences, 14 Ul. Yavilowa, Moscow; Ul. Gubkina 4, kv. 11, B-333, Moscow, U.S.S.R.

Kabalevsky, Dmitri Borisovich; Soviet composer; b. 30 Dec. 1904; Moscow Conservatoire.
Studied under N. Y. Myaskovsky and A. B. Goldenweiser; Prof. Moscow Conservatoire 39-; Sec. Union of Soviet Composers 51-; mem. Communist Party 40-; mem. World Peace Council 55-; Deputy to U.S.S.R. Supreme Soviet; People's Artist of the U.S.S.R.; State Prize 46, 49 and 51; R.S.F.S.R. State Prize 66; Badge of Honour 40; Order of Lenin 64, of Red Banner of Labour 66.
Works include four symphonies, two string quartets, three piano concertos 29, 35, 52; violin and 'cello concertos 48, 49, 64; cantata: *Great Motherland* 42; operas: *Colas Brugnon* 37, *Under Fire* 43, *Tara's Family* 50, *Nikita Vershinin* 54; music for films: *Petersburg Nights* 33, *Shchors* 39, *Marusya's First Year at School* 48, *Mussorgsky* 50, *Volnitsa* 56, *Sisters* 57, *18th Year* 58, *Gloomy Morning* 59; 10 Shakespeare sonnets for bass with pianoforte accompaniment 53-55; *Romeo and Juliet* (symphonic suite) 56, *Song of Morning, Spring and Peace* (children's cantata), *Spring Sings* (operetta) 57, *Lenintsy* (cantata) 59, *Sonata for 'Cello and Piano* 62, *Requiem* (oratorio) 64.
c/o Union of Soviet Composers, 8/10 Nezhdanova Street, Moscow, U.S.S.R.

Kabaloyev, Bilar Emazayevich; Soviet politician; b. 1917; ed. Moscow V. I. Lenin State Pedagogical Inst. and the Higher Party School of the Central Cttee. of C.P.S.U.
Teacher 39-42; Party and Young Communist League Official, North Osetia 42-52; Sec. North Osetian Regional Cttee., C.P.S.U. 52-61, First Sec. 61-; Alt. mem. C.P.S.U. Central Cttee.; Deputy to U.S.S.R. Supreme Soviet; mem. C.P.S.U. 40-.
North Osetian Regional Committee, C.P.S.U., Ordjonikidze, U.S.S.R.

Kabanda, Pierre Célestin; Rwandese diplomatist; b. 1936; ed. Petit Séminaire de Kabgayi, Grand Séminaire de Nyakibanda, and Univ. of Lovanium, Kinshasa.
Formerly in charge of Legislative Bureau of Office of Pres. of Rwanda; Sec.-Rapporteur of Cabinet; Amb. to U.S.A. and Canada 64-; Perm. Rep. of Rwanda to UN 66-.
Permanent Mission of the Rwandese Republic to the United Nations, 120 East 56th Street, New York, N.Y. 10022, U.S.A.

Kabir, Humayun, M.A., M.P.; Indian politician and writer; b. 22 Feb. 1906; ed. Calcutta and Oxford.
Taught at Univs. of Calcutta and Andhra; Leader Peasants' Party Bengal Legislative Council; Secretary and Librarian, Union Society, Oxford; mem. Indian Railway Enquiry Cttee. 47; Pres. Indian Philosophical Congress, All-India Writers Convention, first Asian Writers Conf. 56, Indian Council for Cultural Relations 58-64, All-India Educ. Conf. 55; Indian Science Congress 63-64; Consultant Fund for the Advancement of Educ., N.Y.; Editor *Chaturanga* 39-; Minister of Civil Aviation 57-58; Minister for Scientific Research and Cultural Affairs 58-63; Minister of Petroleum and Chemicals 63-65; Pres. Int. Congress of Orientalists 64; Herbert Spencer Lecturer, Oxford 67; Tagore Memorial Lectures, Univ. of Wis. 67.
Publs. *Swapna Sadh, Poems, Kant on Philosophy in General, Immanuel Kant, Dharabahik, Poetry, Monads and Society, Sarat Chandra Chatterjee, Muslim Politics 1906-42, Mahatma and other Poems, Banglar Kavya, Men and Rivers, The Indian Heritage, Three Stories, Of Cabbages and Kings, Marx Vad, Nadi-O-Naree, Science, Democracy and Islam, Education in New India, Indian Philosophy of Education,* etc.
54 Ganeshchandra Avenue, Calcutta; 8 Ashoka Road, New Delhi, India.
Telephone: Calcutta 24-5713 and New Delhi 47650.

Kabkov, Yakov Ivanovich; Soviet politician; b. 1908; ed. Odessa Mechanical and Technical Inst.
Member C.P.S.U. 30-; food exec. 37-40; Apparatus, Central Cttee. C.P., Ukraine 40-41, 43-50, 57-58; Soviet army service 41-43; First Dep. Minister of Trade, Ukraine 50-55, Minister of Fishing Industry 55-57; Dept. Head Central Cttee. C.P.S.U. 58-62, 65-; Head of Dept., Cttee. for Party-State Control 62-65, mem. Cttee. 63-; mem. Central Auditing Comm. C.P.S.U. 61-.
C.P.S.U. Central Committee, 4 Staraya ploshchad, Moscow, U.S.S.R.

Kachkeyev, Kadyrkul; Soviet politician; b. 1905; ed. Central Asia Communist Univ. and Higher Party School.
Member C.P.S.U. 29; with office of the Public Prosecutor 34-41; Sec. Issyk Kul Regional Cttee. C.P.S.U. 41-43; Chair. Osh Regional Soviet 45-50; Minister for Cotton Growing of the Kirghiz S.S.R. 50-53; Perm. Rep. Kirghiz S.S.R. Council of Ministers to the U.S.S.R. Council of Ministers 53-; mem. Central Cttee. Kirghiz C.P. 48-; Deputy to Supreme Soviet of Kirghizia; Order of the Red Banner of Labour (four times), Badge of Honour and other honours.
Office of the Permanent Representative of the Kirghiz S.S.R. Council of Ministers to the U.S.S.R. Council of Ministers, Ploshchad Revolutsii 1-3, Moscow, U.S.S.R.

Kadár, Ján; Czechoslovak film director; b. 1 April 1918; ed. Faculty of Law, Charles Univ. of Prague, and Photography and Film School under Prof. Karel Plicka, Bratislava.
Imprisoned during Second World War; Scriptwriter and Asst. Dir. at Barrandov Feature Film Studio 47-; Awards include State Prize 2nd Class 60, Gold Prize, Moscow Int. Film Festival 63, State Prize 64, Grand Prix, Karlovy Vary Int. Film Festival 64, U.S. Acad. Award Oscar 65, New York Film Critics Award 66, Selznik Prize, U.S. 66; David Di Donatello Prize 67; Honoured Artist 65; Co-Dir. with Elmar Klos (*q.v.*): *Únos* (Kidnapped) 52, *Smrt si říká Engelchen* (Death is Called Engelchen) 63, *Obžalovany* (The Accused) 64, *Obchod na korze* (The Shop on Main Street) 65 (all award-winning films).
Pařížská 5, Prague 1, Czechoslovakia.
Telephone: 272022.

Kádár, János; Hungarian politician; b. 22 May; 1912 ed. secondary school.
Mem. Young Communist Workers Fed. 31, illegal

Communist Party 32; helped to organise resistance movement Second World War; Deputy Police Chief 45; Sec. Greater Budapest Party Cttee. 45-46; Asst. Gen. Sec. Communist Party 47, reappointed on merger of Communist and Social Democratic Parties to become Hungarian Working People's Party 48; Mem. Parl. 45-; Minister of Internal Affairs 48; Hon. Sec. 47-50; First Sec. Socialist Workers' Party 56-; Prime Minister 56-58, 61-65; mem. Presidential Council 65-; Minister of State 58-61.
Publ. *Firm People's Power—Independent Hungary* 58.
Socialist Workers' Party, Budapest, Hungary.

Kadlec, Vladimír, LL.D., D.SC.; Czechoslovak economist and politician; b. 4 Oct. 1912; ed. Law Faculty, Charles Univ., Prague.
Ministry of Finance 38-42; Nat. Bank 45-46; Cen. Admin. of Banks 46-48; Office of Pres. of Repub. 48-52; Asst. Prof., Czech Technical Univ., Prague 52-62; Prof. at School of Econs., Rector 62-; Minister of Educ. 68-; mem. Econ. Comm. of Cen. Cttee. of C.P. of Czechoslovakia 63-; mem. Cen. Cttee. of C.P. of Czechoslovakia 66-; mem. Inst. of Management Sciences, Inst. Int. des Finances Publiques.
Publs. *Surplus of Purchasing Power* 46, *Currency Stability* 48, *Mathematical Methods in Economic Planning* (trans. into German) 59, *Practical Application of Linear Planning Methods* 62, *Application of Computers iu Socialist Agriculture* 62, *Linear Programming in Transport* 63, *Optimalization of Production Plans in Agricultural Enterprises* 67, *Economic Calculations on Computers in Industrial Practice* 67, etc.
Ministry of Education, Prague; Home: Prague 3-Vinohrady, Čapajevovo nám 18, Czechoslovakia.

Kadomtsev, Boris Borisovich; Soviet physicist; b. 26; ed. Moscow State Univ.
Senior Research Scientist Kurchatov Inst. of Atomic Energy, U.S.S.R. Academy of Sciences 56-; Corresp. mem. U.S.S.R. Acad. of Sciences 62-.
U.S.S.R. Academy of Sciences, 14 Lenin Prospekt, Moscow, U.S.S.R.

Kadoorie, Horace, O.B.E., J.P.; Hong Kong business executive; b. 02; ed. Cathedral School, Shanghai, Ascham St. Vincents, Eastbourne, and Clifton Coll., Bristol.
Partner, Sir Elly Kadoorie and Sons, Hong Kong; Chair. and Dir. numerous public companies incl. Hong Kong & Shanghai Hotels Ltd., China Light and Power Co. Ltd., Amalgamated Rubber Estates, Java Consolidated Estates Ltd., Hong Kong and Kowloon Wharf and Godown Co. Ltd., Hong Kong and Whampoa Dock Co. Ltd., Peak Tramways Co. Ltd., "Star" Ferry Co. Ltd.; Dir. Rubber Trust Ltd., Green Island Cement Co. Ltd., Hong Kong Carpet Manufacturers Ltd., Humphreys Estate & Finance Ltd.; mem. and official numerous Hong Kong civic orgs.; Chevalier de la Légion d'Honneur; Ramon Magsaysay Award 62, Order of Leopold 66, Solomon Schechter Award 59.
Publ. *The Art of Ivory Sculpture in Cathay* (7 vols.).
Sir Elly Kadoorie and Sons, Lane Crawford House, 5th Floor, Des Voeux Road, Central, Hong Kong.
Telephone: 220337.

Kadoorie, Lawrence; Hong Kong business executive; b. 2 June 1899; ed. Cathedral School, Shanghai, Ascham St. Vincents, Eastbourne, Clifton Coll., Bristol and Lincoln's Inn, London.
Partner, Sir Elly Kadoorie and Sons, Hong Kong; Chair. China Light and Power Co. Ltd., Hong Kong Engineering and Construction Co. Ltd., Franki Piling and Engineering Co. Ltd., Hong Kong Carpet Manufacturers Ltd., Island Dyeing and Printing Co. Ltd., Int. Dress Corpn., Major Contractors Ltd., Nanyang Cotton Mill Ltd.; Dir. numerous other public companies; mem. and official numerous Hong Kong civic orgs.; Solomon Schechter Award 59; Chevalier de la

Légion d'Honneur; Officier de l'Ordre de Leopold 66; Ramon Magsaysay Award 62.
Sir Elly Kadoorie and Sons, Lane Crawford House, 5th Floor, Des Voeux Road, Central, Hong Kong.
Telephone: 229517.

Kadosa, Pál; Hungarian composer and pianist; b. 1903; ed. Budapest Acad. of Music, under Zoltán Kodály and Arnold Székely.
Teacher, Fodor Music School 27-43, Goldmark Music School 44; Prof. 45-, then mem. of Directors' Council, Budapest Acad. of Music; mem. Board, later, Acting Chair. Fed. of Hungarian Musicians; Pres. Nat. Copyright Office; Kossuth Prize 50, Erkel Prize 55, 62, Eminent Artist of the Hungarian People's Repub. 63; Hon. mem. Royal Acad. of Music (London) 67.
Compositions: for orchestra, symphonies, string quartets, violin and piano concertos, cantatas, choruses, songs; opera, *Huszti Kaland*.
Hungarian Academy of Music, Liszt Ferenc Place 8, Budapest VI; and Budapest V, Marcius 15 ter. 8, Hungary.
Telephone: 181398.

Kaeckenbeeck, Georges Silvain François Charles, D.C.L. (Oxon.); Belgian jurist; b. 30 May 1892; ed. Univ. of Brussels and Oxford.
Asst. Legal Adviser to Belgian Foreign Office 18-20; mem. Legal Section of Gen. Secretariat of L.N. 20-22; Pres. Upper Silesian Arbitral Tribunal 22-37; Prof. at Hague Acad. of Int. Law and at the Graduate Inst. of Int. Studies, Geneva 37-39; jurisconsult of Belgian Ministry for Foreign Affairs in London during Second World War; Minister Plenipotentiary represented Belgium at the Peace Conf., at Sessions of UN Gen. Assembly and before the Court of Int. Justice; mem. of the Permanent Court of Arbitration 46-65; mem. of the Institut de Droit International; Sec.-Gen. of the Int. Authority for the Ruhr 49-53; Chair. UN Special Advisory Board 53-57; Chair. Conf. on the status of forces in Germany 55-59; mem. Franco-German Arbitration Court for the Saar 57-63.
Publs. *International Rivers* 18, *La Protection internationale des droits acquis* 37, *De la guerre à la paix* 40, *Le Règlement conventionnel des conséquences de remaniements territoriaux* 40, *The International Experiment in Upper Silesia* 42, *La Charte de San Francisco dans ses rapports avec le droit international* 47.
Les Oiselets, 8 chemin de Cotterd, avenue de Naye, 1842 Territet, Switzerland.
Telephone: (021)613994.

Kafai, Djafar: Iranian diplomatist; b. 09; ed. Univ. of Paris.
Former Secretary, Supreme Court; Ministry of Foreign Affairs; Attaché, Iranian Embassy, France; Second Sec. Cairo; mem. Constituent Assembly; Consul-Gen., Geneva; Dir. of Information and Publication, Ministry of Foreign Affairs; Perm. Rep. to European Office of UN; Under-Sec., Ministry of Foreign Affairs; Ambassador to Greece; Ambassador to Pakistan and Ceylon 63-65, to Turkey 65-; Homayoun Award Class II, Grand Award of St. George (Greece).
Imperial Iranian Embassy, Tahran Cad. 10, Ankara, Turkey.

Kafarov, Victor Viacheslavovich; Soviet chemist; b. 1914 ed. Kirov Chemical Technology Inst., Kazan.
Engineer at designing org. in aniline industry 38-40; Postgraduate, Research Assoc. Colloid-Electrochemical Inst. U.S.S.R. Acad. of Sciences 40-44; Asst. Prof., Prof., Head of Chair, Mendeleyev Inst. of Chemical Technology; mem. C.P.S.U. 52-; Corresp. mem. U.S.S.R. Acad. of Sciences 66-.
Publs. Works on chemical technology, mathematical modelling of chemical technology processes.
U.S.S.R. Academy of Sciences, 14 Lenin Prospekt, Moscow, U.S.S.R.

Kafka, Alexandre; Brazilian professor of economics; b. 25 Jan. 1917.
Prof. of Econs., Univ. of São Paulo 41-46; Adviser to Brazilian Del. to Preparatory Cttee. and Conf. of Int. Trade Org. 46-48; Asst. Div. Chief, Int. Monetary Fund (IMF) 49-51, Temp. Alt. Gov. 54-55, Exec. Dir. 66-; Adviser, Superintendency of Money and Credit (now Central Bank of Brazil); Dir. of Research, Brazilian Inst. of Econs. 51-54, Dir. 61-63; Chief Financial Inst. and Policies Section, UN 56-61; Prof. of Econs., Univ. of Virginia, U.S. 63-64; Adviser to Brazilian Minister of Finance 64.
International Monetary Fund, 19th and H Streets, Washington, D.C. 20431, U.S.A.
Telephone: DUI-3048 (Office).

Kaganovich, Lazar Moiseyevich; Soviet politician; b. 93.
Member Communist Party 11-62; worked in the Ukraine; Pres. District Council in Gomel, Oct. 17; afterwards mem. Cttee. on Red Army Organisation; Sec. Central Cttee. of the Communist Party of the Ukraine 25-28; fmr. Sec. and Second Sec. Central Cttee. of the All-Union Communist Party; Sec. All-Union Council of Trades Unions 28; mem. Union Central Exec. Cttee.; Chief of Comm. of Party Control in Communist Party; Commissar of Railways 35 and 43-44; Commissar for Oil 35-41; mem. Presidium of Supreme Council, Deputy Commr. for Heavy Industries Jan. 38-July 40; became mem. Politburo 38, State Defence Cttee. 42-43; Deputy Chair. Council of Ministers 45-53; First Deputy Chair. Council of Ministers and mem. Presidium of Central Cttee. of Communist Party 53-57; Exec. for Building Materials and Industry in the Urals; Chair. Advisory Cttee. to Council of Ministers on Labour Problems 55-56; retired 63; awarded title Hero of Soviet Labour and Order of Lenin Nov. 43.
R.S.F.S.R. Ministry of Social Security, 14 Shabolovka, Moscow, U.S.S.R.

Kahaneman, Rabbi Joseph; Lithuanian-born Israeli religious leader; b. 88.
Formerly Jewish Min. of Ponevez (Lithuania) and Dean of the Ponevez Yeshiva; Dep. to Lithuanian Parliament before Second World War; Founding Pres. and Dean Ponevez Yeshiva at Bnei-Brak, Israel 44- (numerous affiliated foundations including the Batei-Avot Refugee Children's Settlement, Satinsky Talmudic Library, Archives of Lithuanian Jewry, etc.), Founder Kiryat Hayeshiva Ashdod 64; mem. High Council, Israeli Religious Leaders.
Ponevez Yeshiva, P.O. Box 26, Bnei-Brak, Israel.

Kaharov, Abdulakhad; Soviet politician; b. 13; ed. Leninabad Pedagogical Inst.
Trade Union, Komsomol, Soviet and party work, Tajikistan 33-47; mem. C.P.S.U. 39-; Second Sec. Leninabad Regional Cttee., C.P. of Tajikstan 47-54; Chair. Exec. Cttee. Leninabad Regional Soviet of Workers' Deputies 54-55; Dep. Chair. Council of Ministers, Tajikstan 56-58; Chair. *Gosplan*, Tajikstan 57-61; Chair. Council of Ministers, Tajikstan 61-; Cand. mem. Central Cttee. of C.P.S.U. 61-; mem. Presidium of Central Cttee. of C.P. of Tajikistan.
Council of Ministers of Tajikstan, Dushanbe, Tajik S.S.R., U.S.S.R.

Kahhar, Abdullah; Soviet writer; b. 1907; ed. Central Asian State Univ.
Lived in orphanage 19-25, worked in Young Communist League Organisations, Kokand City, 25-26; Univ. Preparation Course, Tashkent Univ. 26-35; Sec. *Soviet Literature* magazine, Tashkent 35-38; Literary Translator and Editor, various publishing houses, Tashkent 38-54; Chair., Uzbek Writers Union 54-56; mem. Writers' Union of U.S.S.R., full-time writer 56-; Badge of Honour, Two Orders of Labour (Red Banner), State Prize; mem. Communist Party of Soviet Union.

Publs. *Collected Short Stories, Mirage* 37, 59, *Koschinar's Lights* 48, *On the New Land* 51, *The Aching Teeth* 54, *Selected Works in Three Volumes* 57, *The Tiny Bird* 59, *Voice from the Tomb* 61, *Stories and Novels* 65.
Union of Writers of the Uzbek S.S.R., Tashkent, Uzbek S.S.R., U.S.S.R.

Kähler, Erich Ernst, DR.PHIL.; German mathematician; b. 16 Jan. 1906; ed. school in Leipzig and Universität Leipzig.
Lecturer Hamburg 30; Prof. Univ. Königsberg 36; Prof. (with Chair) Univ. Leipzig 48; Prof. Technische Univ. Berlin 58; Prof. Univ. Hamburg and Hon. Prof. Technische Univ. Berlin 64-; mem. Sächsische Akad. der Wissenschaften and Deutsche Akad. der Naturforschen Leopoldina; Foreign mem. Accad. Nazionale dei Lincei 61-.
Publs. *Einführung in die Theorie der Systeme von Differentialgleichungen* 34, *Geometria Aritmetica* 58, *Der innere Differentialkalkul* 63, *Wesen und Erscheinung als Mathematische Prinzipen der Philosophie* 65.
1 Berlin 46, Waldmannstrasse 23; 2 Hamburg 13, Rothenbaumchaussée 67, German Federal Republic.
Telephone: Berlin 73-75-78.

Kähler, Otto: German bank official; b. 17 April 1905; ed. Classical High School.
Junior Bank Officer, Deutsche Reichsbank 31-38; Reichsbank, Berlin 41; mem. Berlin Stock Exchange; Dir. Deutsche Reichsbank 48-; Dir., mem. Management Board, Landeszentralbank, Kiel 51-58; Vice-Pres. Landeszentralbank Hessen, Frankfurt 58-59; Pres. Landeszentralbank, Schleswig-Holstein 60-; mem. Federal Bank Council.
10 Luisenweg, 23 Kiel 1, German Federal Republic.
Telephone: Kiel 51391.

Kahn, Baron (Life-Peer), cr. 65, of Hampstead; **Richard Ferdinand Kahn,** C.B.E., M.A.; British economist; b. 10 Aug. 1905; ed. St. Paul's School and King's Coll., Cambridge.
Employed in various government depts. 39-46; Prof. of Economics, Cambridge Univ. 51-; on leave of absence to work in U.N. Economic Comm. for Europe 55; Fellow of King's Coll., Cambridge, British Acad.
King's College, Cambridge, England.

Kahn, Ely Jacques, A.B.; American architect; b. 1 June 1884; ed. Columbia Univ. and Ecole des Beaux Arts, Paris.
Prof. of Architecture, Cornell Univ. 15; in partnership with R. A. Jacobs 40-, with whom he designed the U.N. Secretariat Building, New York; responsible for numerous govt. projects and New York skyscrapers; Fellow, American Inst of Architects; Benjamin Franklin Fellow, Royal Soc. of Arts.
Publs. *Design and Art in Industry* 37, articles in *Encyclopædia Britannica*, etc.
1185 Park Avenue, New York, N.Y. 10028, U.S.A.

Kahn, Herman, B.A., M.S.; American mathematician; b. 15 Feb. 1922; ed. Univ. of California (Los Angeles) and California Inst. of Technology.
Mathematician, Douglas Aircraft 45-46, Northrup Aviation 47; Research Analyst, RAND Corpn. 47-59; Lecturer, Center for Int. Studies, Princeton 59; Dir., Hudson Inst. 61-; Consultant to Boeing Aircraft, Office of Defense Mobilisation, System Development Corpn., Planning Research Cttee., Stanford Research Inst., Scientific Advisory Board to U.S. Air Force etc.
Publs. *On Thermonuclear War* 60, *Thinking about the Unthinkable* 62, *On Escalation* 65 (with Anthony Wiener), *The Year 2000* 67.
19 Birch Lane, Chappaqua, New York, U.S.A.

Kahn, Louis I.; American (b. Estonia) architect; b. 20 Feb. 1901; ed. Central High School and Univ. of Pennsylvania.
Came to U.S. 05; designer in various firms 24-31;

Organizer and Dir. Architectural Research Group 32-33; ind. practice 35-; Exhbn. of Architecture in Govt. Housing, Museum of Modern Art, New York 36; Consultant Architect for Philadelphia Housing Authority 37, for U.S. Housing Authority 39, for Philadelphia City Planning Comm. 46-52; Chief Critic of Architectural Design, Yale Univ. 47; Prof. of Architecture, Yale Univ. 48-57; Resident Architect, American Acad. in Rome 50-51; Albert Farwell Bemis Prof. at School of Architecture and Planning, Mass. Inst. of Technology 56; Consultant Architect, Philadelphia City Planning Comm. 61; Prof. of Architecture, Univ. of Pa. 57-; one-man Retrospective Exhbn., Museum of Modern Art, N.Y. 66; Fellow American Inst. of Architects; mem. Nat. Inst. of Arts and Letters, N.Y.; mem. Royal Swedish Acad. of Fine Arts; Arnold Brunner Prize, Nat. Inst. of Arts and Letters, New York 60, Medal of Honour of Danish Architectural Asscn. 65, and other medals; Hon. Dr. Arch. (Polytechnic Inst. of Milan) 64, Hon. Dr. Hum. (Univ. of N. Carolina) 64; Dr. Fine Arts (Yale) 65, Hon. LL.D. (La Salle Coll.) 67. Publs. *Why City Planning is Your Responsibility* 43, *You and Your Neighbours* 44 (both with Oscar Stonorov); and numerous articles.
Office: 1501 Walnut Street, Philadelphia 2; Home: 921 Clinton Street, Philadelphia, Pa., U.S.A.
Telephone: LOcust 3-9844 (Office).

Kahnweiler, Daniel-Henry; French (born German) art historian and art dealer; b. 25 June 1884.
Opened gallery in Paris, helping Derain, Vlaminck, Picasso, Braque, Gris, and Léger 07; gallery seized by French authorities 14 and all pictures sold; with André Simon founded Gallery Simon 20; Gallery Simon, which was Jewish property was bought by sister-in-law (Louise Leiris) to save it from Germans in 39-45 war; Co-Dir. Louise Leiris Gallery 45.
Publs. *Der Weg zum Kubismus* 20 (English translation 49), *Juan Gris, sa vie, son oeuvre, ses écrits* 46 (English translation 47, German translation 65), *Les Sculptures de Picasso* 49 (English translation 49), *La Céramique de Picasso* 57 (English, French and German), *Mes Galeries et mes Peintres, Entretiens avec Francis Crémieux* 61 (German translation 61, Czech translation 64, Polish translation 67, Swedish and Finnish translations 68), *Confessions Esthétiques* 63 (French) (German edn. 67), *Entretiens avec Picasso* (Italian translation 64), *Asthetisches Bekenntnis* 68 (German).
53 bis Quai des Grands Augustins, Paris 6e, France.
Telephone: ODE-1861.

Kahuda, František; Czechoslovak politician and scientist; b. 3 Jan. 1911; ed. Faculty of Sciences, Charles Univ., Prague.
Former Prof. of Science, Charles Univ., Prague; worked for Comenius Pedagogical Research Inst., Prague; Minister of Education 54-56, of Education and Culture 56-63, First Deputy Minister of Educ. and Culture 63-66, First Deputy Minister of Educ. 67; Prof. of Sociology, Charles Univ., Prague 68-.
Prague 5, K Mechurce 4, Czechoslovakia.
Telephone: 52-36-71.

Kai, Fumihiko; Japanese diplomatist; b. 17 May 1912; ed. Tokyo Univ.
Consul-Gen., Djakarta 52-55; Deputy Rep. of Japan to 9th Session of ECAFE Conf., Bandung 53; Counsellor, The Hague 53-55; Consul-Gen., Berlin 55-57, Hamburg 57-58; Dir. Japan External Trade Org. 58-61; Counsellor, Ministry of Foreign Affairs 61, Dir. Econ. Co-operation Bureau, Ministry of Foreign Affairs 61; now Ambassador to Malaysia; Panglima Mangku Negara (Malaysia); Gran Oficial Al Merito (Argentina).
174 Jalan Ampang, Kuala Lumpur, Malaya, Malaysia.

Kairov, Ivan Andreevich; Soviet educationist; b. 1893; ed. Moscow Univ.
Immediately after the Revolution of 17 he dealt with

the question of agricultural education in Moscow and the Moscow region, later at the Ministry of Education, R.S.F.S.R.; was Prof. of Higher Pedagogical Courses at the Timiriazev Agricultural Acad. and Dir. of the Agro-Pedagogical Inst. of the Acad.; Head, Dept. of Education at Moscow Univ. 37-49; Minister of Education R.S.F.S.R. 49-56; Pres. of the R.S.F.S.R. Acad. of Pedagogical Sciences 56-66; Pres. of the U.S.S.R. Acad. of Pedagogical Sciences 66; awarded Orders of Lenin and Orders of the Red Banner of Labour; Hero of Socialist Labour.
Academy of Pedagogical Sciences, 58, B. Poljanka, Moscow, U.S.S.R.

Kaiser, Edgar F.; American industrialist; b. 29 July 1908; ed. Univ. of Calif.
With affiliated Kaiser companies 30-; Gen. Man., Pacific Northwest yards in Portland area 42-45; Gen. Man. automotive plant, Willow Run, Mich. 45; now Pres. and Chief Exec. Officer Kaiser Industries Corpn—the parent firm of more than sixty companies; Chair and Pres. Nat. Steel and Shipbuilding Co.; Chair. Henry J. Kaiser Co. (Canada) Ltd., Willys-Overland Export Corpn., Kaiser Center, Inc., Kaiser Aluminium & Chemical Corpn., Kaiser Steel Corpn.; mem. President's Missile Sites Labor Comm.; Hon. Dr. of Laws (Univ. of Portland and Pepperdine Coll.); Commdr. Nat. order Southern Cross, Brazil 65; Industrialist of the Year Award 66; Family of Man Award 66.
Kaiser Industries Corporation, 300 Lakeside Drive, Oakland, Calif. 94604, U.S.A.
Telephone: 415-271-2211.

Kaiser, Khwaja Muhammad; Pakistani diplomatist; b. 13 Sept. 1918; ed. Dacca Univ.
Indian Police Service 41-50; Second Sec. Dep. High Comm. for Pakistan, Calcutta 50; Dep. Sec. Ministry of External Affairs, Dacca 50-51; Dep. Sec. Ministry of External Affairs, Karachi 51-55; Counsellor, Peking 55-57; Consul-Gen., New York 57-60; Minister, Washington 60-62; High Commr. in Australia and New Zealand 62-65; Dir.-Gen. Ministry of Foreign Affairs, Pakistan 65-66; Amb. to Sweden, Norway, Denmark, Finland 66-; awarded Sitara-e-Quaid-e Azam 62.
c/o Ministry of Foreign Affairs, Islamabad, Pakistan.

Kaiser, Philip M., A.B., M.A.; American diplomatist; b. 12 July 1913; ed. Univ. of Wisconsin and Balliol Coll., Oxford.
Federal Reserve System 39-42, Board of Econ. Warfare 42-46; joined Research Planning Div. Dept. of State 46; Exec. Asst. to Asst. Sec. of Labor (Int. Labor Affairs) 46-47; Dir. Office of Int. Labor Affairs, Dept. of Labor 47-49; Asst. Sec. of Labor 49-53; Labor Adviser, Comm. for Free Europe 53-54; Special Asst. to Gov. of New York 55-58; Prof. of Int. Labor Relations, American Univ. 58-61; Ambassador to Senegal and Mauritania 61-64; Minister American Embassy in London 64-.
Office: American Embassy, London, England; Home: 9133 McDonald Drive, Bethesda, Md. 20015, U.S.A.

Kaissouni, Abdel Moneim, B.COM., B.SC., PH.D.; United Arab Republic (Egyptian) financial administrator and politician; b. 16; ed. Univ. of Cairo and London School of Economics.
With Barclays Bank, England 42-43; Lecturer and Asst. Prof. of Economics, Univ. of Cairo 44-50; Adviser to Council of Ministers for Post-War Affairs 44-45; Deputy Dir.-Gen. of Foreign Affairs in Ministry of Nat. Economy 49-50; Dir. Middle East Dept. Int. Monetary Fund, Washington, and later Chief Technical Rep. in Middle East 46-50; with Nat. Bank of Egypt 50-54; Dep. Min. Finance and Economy 54, Min. Sept. 54-58; mem. Nat. Assembly 57; Minister of Economy and Commerce for Egypt in U.A.R. 58; Minister of Economy, U.A.R. Central Govt. 58-62, Minister of Treasury and Planning 62-64; Chair. Board of Econ. Org. 59-; Dep. Prime Minister for Econ. Affairs and Finance and

Minister of Econ. and Foreign Trade 64-65; Deputy Prime Minister for Financial and Econ. Affairs 65-66; Minister of Planning 67-68; Orders of the Nile (Repub. of Egypt), Merit (Syria), St. Mark 2nd Grade (Greece) El Kawkab 1st Grade (Jordan), Nat. Cedar (Lebanon); 10 Tolumbat Street, Garden City, Cairo, U.A.R.

Kaitila, Esa Heikki; Finnish economist and politician; b. 22 April 1909.
Professor of Economics, Helsinki Univ.; Cabinet Minister 53-54, 57; Minister of Finance 64-66; Gen. Man. State Treasury Office 62-; Vice-Chair. Liberal People's Party.
Vanamotie 8, Helsinki 93, Finland.
Telephone: 334240.

Kalamkarov, Vartan Aleksandrovich; Soviet engineer; b. 06; ed. Azerbaijan Polytechnical Inst.
Engineer, Oil Industry 41-45; Dep. U.S.S.R. Commissar, Oil Industry 45-46, Dep. Minister U.S.S.R. Oil Industry 46-55; State Planning Comm. (Gosplan) 55, Head of Dept. (Gosplan) 57-63; Deputy Chair. U.S.S.R. Council of Nat. Econ., Minister of U.S.S.R. 63-65; Deputy Chair. State Cttee. for Material and Equipment Supply, U.S.S.R. Council of Ministers 65-; mem. C.P.S.U. 39-; State Prize, Lenin Prize.
State Committee for Material and Equipment Supply, Moscow, U.S.S.R.

Kalanda, Auguste Mabika; Congolese politician; b. 26 Nov. 1932.
Administrator in Colonial Civil Admin.; fmr. mem. Coll. of Commrs.; fmr. Lecturer, Nat. School of Law and Admin.; Minister of Foreign Affairs, Congo (Léopoldville) April-Dec. 63; Dir.-Gen. Nat. School of Law and Admin.
Publs. *Baluba et Lulua* 60, *Tabalayi* 63, *La Remise en Question*.
B.P. 3357, Kinshasa-Kalina, Republic of the Congo.

Kalatozov, Mikhail Konstantinovich; Soviet film director; b. 03.
Began his career in Georgian State Cinema Industry 23, cameraman 26-29, Dir. 29; worked at Leningrad film studios 39-41; worked at Moscow film studios 42-48, at Mosfilm 49-; mem. C.P.S.U. 39-; important films include *Courage* 39, *Valery Chkalov* 41, *Conspiracy of the Doomed* 50, *True Friends* 54, *First Wave* 55, *The Cranes are Flying* 57, *The Letter That Has Never Been Sent* 60, *I'm—Cuba*; State Prize for *Conspiracy of the Doomed* 51 and for *True Friends* 54; First Prize, Cannes Int. Film Festival for *The Cranes are Flying* 58; Order of the Red Star, People's Artist of R.S.F.S.R.
Mosfilm Studio, 1 Mosfilmovskaya ul., Moscow, U.S.S.R.

Kalbitzer, Hellmut; German merchant and politician; b. 17 Nov. 1913; ed. Hamburg-Lichtwerkschule.
Imprisoned for anti-Nazi activity 36-38; active in re-establishment of Trade Unions and Social Democratic Party, Hamburg 45; mem. Bundestag 49-65; mem. and Vice-Pres. European Parl. 57-61.
Publ. *Entwicklungshilfe und Weltmächte* 61.
Rheingoldweg 46, 2 Hamburg 56, German Federal Republic.

Kalchenko, Nikifor Timofeevich; Soviet (Ukrainian) politician; b. 06; ed. Poltava Inst. of Agronomy.
Agronomist and Dir. of a machine and tractor station; elected to Odessa Regional Soviet 38; Minister for Industrial Crops, Minister of State Farms and Minister of Agriculture of the Ukraine 45-52; First Deputy Prime Minister of the Ukraine 52-54, 61-; Prime Minister of the Ukraine 54-61; Minister for State Purchases, Ukraine 61-; mem. Politburo of Cen. Cttee. of Ukraine C.P.; Cand. mem. C.P.S.U. Cen. Cttee. 61-; Deputy to U.S.S.R. Supreme Soviet; mem. C.P.S.U. 32-; awarded

Order of Lenin (three times), two Czechoslovak honours, four Polish Orders.
Council of Ministers of the Ukraine S.S.R., Kiev, Ukraine, U.S.S.R.

Kalchenko, Stepan Vlasovich; Soviet politician; b. 08; ed. Timiryazev Agricultural Inst.
Member C.P.S.U. 31-; agronomist, and successively Dir. State Grain Farm, Chief, Agricultural Admin. Board 28-48; First Dep. Chair. Exec. Cttee. Kurgun Regional Council of Workers' Deputies 48-54; Dep. Minister of State Farms, Dep. Minister of Agriculture U.S.S.R. 54-58; Chair. Exec. Cttee. Kirov Regional Council of Workers' Deputies 58-59; Minister of Agriculture R.S.F.S.R. 59-60; Chair. Exec. Cttee. Altai Rural Council of Workers' Deputies 60-64; Chair. Exec. Cttee. Altai Regional Council of Workers' Deputies 64-66; First Deputy Dir. Exhbn. of Soviet Economy Achievements 66; Cand. mem. Cen. Cttee. C.P.S.U. 61-66.
Moscow, U.S.S.R.

Kaldor, Nicholas, M.A., F.B.A., B.SC(ECON.); British economist; b. 12 May 1908; ed. Model Gymnasium, Budapest and London School of Economics.
Asst. Lecturer, Lecturer and Tutor, and Reader, London School of Economics 32-47; war service U.S. Strategic Bombing Survey, British Bombing Survey Unit; Dir. Research and Planning Division U.N. Econ. Comm. for Europe 47-49; Lecturer, later Reader and now Prof. of Econs. Cambridge Univ. 49-; Fellow of King's Coll., Cambridge 49-; mem. Royal Comm. in the Taxation of Profits and Income 50-55; Survey on Indian Tax Reform, Govt. of India 56; Taxation Adviser, Govt. of Ceylon 58; Fiscal Adviser, Govt. of Mexico 60; Econ. Adviser Govt. of Ghana 61; Fiscal Adviser Govt. of British Guiana 61, Govt. of Turkey 62, Reserve Bank of Australia 63; Special Adviser to Chancellor of Exchequer 64-; Dr. h.c. (Dijon).
Publs. *An Expenditure Tax* 55, and with S. Silverman *A Statistical Analysis of Advertising Expenditure* 46, *Essays in Value and Distribution* 60, *Essays in Economic Stability and Growth* 60, *Ensayos sobre Desarollo Economico* (Mexico) 61, *Essays on Economic Policy* (2 Vols.) 64.
King's College, Cambridge, England.

Kalecki, Michal; Polish economist; b. 22 June 1899.
With Department of Economics, Cambridge (England) Univ. 37, Oxford Univ. Inst. of Statistics 39-45, U.N. Econ. Dept. 47-54; Adviser to Chair. of Planning Cttee., Warsaw 57-64; now Prof. Main School of Planning and Statistics; mem. Polish Acad. of Sciences.
Publs. About 200 items (some in English), including *Essays in the Theory of Economic Fluctuations, Studies in Economic Dynamics, Theory of Economic Dynamics, Essay on the Theory of Growth of a Socialist Economy*.
Aleja I Armii Wojska Polskiego 11, Warsaw, Poland.
Telephone: 21-15-34.

Kalinnikov, Trofim Georgiyevich; Soviet trade union official; b. 07; ed. All-Union Inst. of Journalism and Higher Party School.
State Farm worker, Voronezh Region 22-27; Editor, Soviet Press 29-42; Sec. Khabarovsk Territorial Cttee. of C.P.S.U. 43-52; Kamchatka Regional Cttee. 52-55; Instructor, Central Cttee. of C.P.S.U. 55-60; Chair. Central Cttee. of Cultural Workers' Trade Union 60-66; on Staff Central Cttee. of C.P.S.U. 66-; mem. C.P.S.U.; four medals.
Central Committee of C.P.S.U., Moscow, U.S.S.R.

Kalinowsky, Lothar Bruno, M.D.; German-born American neuropsychiatrist; b. 28 Dec. 1899; ed. Berlin, Heidelberg and Munich Univs.
Asst. in Neuropsychiatry at hospitals in Berlin, Hamburg, Breslau, Vienna 22-32, Rome 33-39; Clinical

Prof. of Psychiatry, N.Y. Medical Coll.; Assoc. Prof. of Neuropsychiatry, N.Y. School of Psychiatry; Consultant Psychiatrist, St. Vincent's Hospital, N.Y. 57-.
Publ. *Somatic Treatments in Psychiatry* (with Paul H. Hoch and Brenda Grant) 61.
115 East 82nd Street, New York 28, N.Y., U.S.A.

Kalita, Fyodor Illarionovich; Soviet politician; b. 1917; ed. Higher Party School of the C.P.S.U.
Teacher 37-38; Soviet Army service 38-46; Party Official, Ukraine 46-61; First Sec. Volyn Regional Cttee., C.P. of Ukraine 61-; mem. Central Cttee., C.P. of Ukraine; Deputy to U.S.S.R. Supreme Soviet; mem. C.P.S.U. 39-.
Volyn Regional Committee, Communist Party of the Ukraine, Lutsk, U.S.S.R.

Kállai, Gyula; Hungarian journalist and politician; b. 10 June 1910; ed. Budapest Univ.
As a student, joined illegal Communist Party 31; helped to initiate pre-war March Front Movement; mem. Editorial Board of *Nepszava*, organ of Social Democratic Party, in Second World War; continued work in resistance movement; mem. Central Leadership of Communist Party 45, 56; Pres. of the Nat. Council of the Hungarian People's Patriotic Front 58-; mem. Central Cttee. and Political Cttee. Hungarian Socialist Workers Party 56-; Sec. of State 45; Foreign Minister 49-51; Dep. Minister of Culture 55-56; Minister of Culture 56-58; Minister of State 58-60; First Dep. Prime Minister 60-65; Prime Minister June 65-67; Speaker of Parl. 67-.
Publs. *The Hungarian Movement for Independence 39-45*, *For Socialist Culture* 58, *Socialism and Culture* 62.
The National Assembly, Budapest, Hungary.

Kallen, Horace Meyer, PH.D., L.H.D., LITT.D.; American philosopher; b. 11 Aug. 1882; ed. Harvard, Princeton, Oxford and Paris Univs.
Asst. and Lecturer in Philosophy Harvard Univ. 06-10; Lecturer in Logic Clark Univ. 10; Instructor in Philosophy and Psychology Univ. of Wisconsin 10-18; Prof. New School for Social Research 19-52, Emeritus 52-, Research Prof. in Social Philosophy 53-; Dean Graduate Faculty of Political and Social Science 44-46: mem. President's Nat. Comm. on Higher Education 46-; mem. Board of Trustees, Inst. of Church and State 48-; Fellow Jewish Acad. of Arts and Sciences 57-; Pres. Soc. for Scientific Study of Religion 60-.
Publs. *William James and Henri Bergson, Creative Intelligence* (with John Dewey and others), *The Book of Job as a Greek Tragedy, The Structure of Lasting Peace, The League of Nations Today and Tomorrow, The International Mind—its Nature and Conditions, Culture and Democracy in the United States, Education, the Machine and the Worker, The Philosophy of William James, Why Religion, Frontiers of Hope, The Warfare of Religion Against Science, Judaism at Bay, Indecency and the Seven Arts, Individualism—An American Way of Life, A Free Society, American Philosophy Today and Tomorrow* (jointly), *Freedom in the Modern World, The Decline and Rise of the Consumer, Of War and Peace, Art and Freedom* (2 vols.), *The Liberal Spirit, Ideals and Experience, The Education of Free Men, Patterns of Progress, Democracy's True Religion, Human Beings and Psychological Systems, "Of Them Which Say They are Jews", Secularism is the Will of God, Cultural Pluralism and the American Idea, Utopians at Bay, A Study of Liberty, Philosophical Issues in Adult Education, Freedom, Tragedy and Comedy.*
66 West 12th Street, New York, N.Y., U.S.A.

Kallós, Ödön; Hungarian commercial official; b. 17.
Commercial Attaché, Egypt 48, later Trade Counsellor until 55; Deputy Dir. MOGURT Hungarian Trading Co. for Motor Vehicles 55-56; Commercial Counsellor and Head of Hungarian Trade Comm. to India 56-59; Pres. Hungarian Chamber of Commerce 59-.
Hungarian Chamber of Commerce, Rosenberg hp.-u. 17, Budapest V, Hungary.

Kalmbach, Leland J.; American insurance executive; b. 30 April 1901; ed. Univ. of Michigan.
Joined Cleveland Life Ins. Co. 23; with Lincoln Nat. Life Insurance Co., Fort Wayne, Ind. 24-47; Vice-Pres. 39-47, 1st Vice-Pres. 47, Dir. 37-47; Vice-Pres. Mass. Mutual Life Insurance Co., Springfield, Mass. 48-50, Pres. 50-62, Chair. 62-; Dir. Sheraton Corpn. of America; Dir. N.E. Telephone and Telegraph Co.; official of several professional and civic orgs.
1295 State Street, Springfield 9, Mass., U.S.A.

Kalmyk, Nikolai Iosifovich; Soviet politician; b. 1913; ed. Bogodukhov Agricultural Coll. and Higher Party School of the C.P.S.U.
Agronomist 31-36, 38-39; Soviet Army 36-38; Agronomist and Dir. of a machine and tractor station, Tula Region 39-43; Party Official, Tula Region 43-51; at Head Offices, C.P.S.U. Central Cttee. 51-55; Sec. Smolensk Regional Cttee. C.P.S.U. 55-62, Second Sec. 62-63, First Sec. Jan. 63-.
Smolensk Regional Committee C.P.S.U., Smolensk, U.S.S.R.

Kalmykov, Valeri Dmitrievich; Soviet politician; b. 08; ed. Moscow Inst. of Energetics.
Minister of Radio Technical Industry U.S.S.R. 54, Chair. State Cttee. for Radioelectronics 57-65; U.S.S.R. Minister of Radio Industry 65-; Cand. mem. Central Cttee. of C.P.S.U. 56-61, mem. 61-.
U.S.S.R. Ministry of Radio Industry, Kitaiskii proezd 7, Moscow K-74, U.S.S.R.

Kalnberzin, Janis Eduardovich; Soviet politician; b. 93; ed. Communist Univ. of Moscow, Inst. of Red Professors.
Joined Communist Party 17; took active part in establishment of Soviet power in Latvia 19; went to Soviet Russia after fall from power of Soviet in Latvia; fought in the Civil War; returned to Latvia 36, conducted underground activities; arrested and sent to prison 39; after establishment of Soviet power in Latvia, became First Sec., Central Cttee. of Latvian Communist Party 40-59; alt. mem. Central Cttee. of C.P.S.U. 41-52, mem. 52-; Vice-Chair. Presidium of Supreme Soviet of U.S.S.R. 60-; Chair. Presidium of Supreme Soviet of Latvian S.S.R. 59-; mem. Presidium Latvian C.P.; Deputy to U.S.S.R. and Latvian S.S.R. Supreme Soviets; Hero of Socialist Labour, Order of Lenin (three times), Order of the Patriotic War (First Class), and other decorations.
Supreme Soviet of Latvian S.S.R., Riga, Latvia, U.S.S.R.

Kalonji-Ditunga, Albert; Congolese politician; b. 1929; ed. secondary and technical schools.
Mulopwe of the Baluba tribe in Kasai Province; teacher of agronomy; insurance broker; mem. Legislative Council, Brussels 59-60; nat. legislator 60-; supported Congolese Nationalist Movement 58; Pres. M.N.C.-Kalonji 59-; ruler of S. Kasai 60-62; detained by Central Govt. 62, released and reached S. Kasai Sept. 62, in exile 62-64; Minister of Agriculture (Congo) 64-65; now maker of industrial ice and exporter of coffee.
M.N.C.-Kalonji Party, P.O. Box 1736, Kinshasa, Democratic Republic of the Congo.
Telephone: 5725 (Kinshasa).

Kalra, Hari Chand; Indian civil engineer; b. 06; ed. Government Coll., Lahore, and Roorkee Univ.
Punjab Public Works Dept. (Irrigation Branch) 29-54; Ministry of Irrigation and Power 54-, Superintending Engineer, Dep. Sec., Chief Engineer and Consultant 59-60, Commr. for Indus Waters and Joint Sec. to

Govt. of India; Rep. of India on Perm. Indus Comm. 61-; Vice-Pres. Central Board of Irrigation and Power 63-.
Commissioner for Indus Waters, Ministry of Irrigation and Power, Central Secretariat, New Delhi 1, India; c/o Mr. M. R. Chhabra, 15 Mandeville Gardens, Flat No. 1, Calcutta 19, India.

Kamaladevi; Indian political and social worker; b. 3 April 1903; ed. Mangalore, Bedford Coll. and London School of Economics, London Univ.
Joined Congress; elected to A.I.C.C. 27; Organizing Sec. and Pres. All-India Women's Conf.; imprisoned 30, 32, 34 and 42; founded Indian Co-operative Union to re-habilitate refugees on a co-operative basis 48; Chair. All-India Handicrafts Board 52-; Vice-Chair. Sangeat Natak Akad.; Pres. Theatre Centre of India; helped to found World Crafts Council and is its Senior Vice-Pres.; Indian and Foreign awards.
Publs. *In War-torn China, Japan: Its Weakness and Strength, Socialism and Society, America, the Land of Superlatives, Uncle Sam's Empire, Indian Handicrafts, Carpets and Floor Coverings of India.*
2 Canning Place, New Delhi; and Flat No. 6, Chateau Marine, Marine Drive, Bombay, India.
Telephone: New Delhi 48908; Bombay 241189.

Kamalov, Kallibek; Soviet politician; b. 1926; ed. Teacher-Training Inst.
Teacher and Young Communist League Official 42-51; Local Govt. and Party Official 51-53; Minister of Municipal Econ., then Minister for Road Transport and Highways, Karakalpak Autonomous S.S.R. 53-59; Chair. Council of Ministers, Karakalpak Autonomous S.S.R. 59-63; First Sec. Karakalpak Regional Cttee. of C.P. of Uzbekistan 63-; mem. Central Cttee. C.P. Uzbek-istan; Deputy to U.S.S.R. Supreme Soviet; mem. C.P.S.U. 46-.
Karakalpak Regional Committee, Communist Party of Uzbekistan, Nukus, U.S.S.R.

Kamanga, Reuben Chitandika; Zambian politician; b. 26 Aug. 1929; ed. Munali.
Imprisoned several times for political reasons 52-60; lived in Cairo 60-62; Deputy Pres. United Nat. Ind. Party; fmr. Minister of Labour and Mines; Minister of Transport and Communications 64; Vice-Pres. 64-67; Leader of House, Legislative Assembly 64-; Minister Foreign Affairs 67-.
Ministry of Foreign Affairs, Lusaka, Zambia.

Kamanin, Col.-Gen. Nikolai Petrovich; Soviet air force officer; b. 1908; ed. Zhukovsky Air Force Acad. and Acad. of the Armed Forces General Staff.
Entered Soviet Army 27; commanded a detachment for *S.S. Chelyuskin* crew rescue 34; commanded forma-tions of aviation attack 47-54; Deputy Chief of Air Force H.Q. and Head of Soviet Cosmonaut Training Programme 58-; Hero of the Soviet Union 34, awarded 23 Soviet and foreign medals and orders.
Ministry of Defence, 34 Maurice Thorez Embankment, Moscow, U.S.S.R.

Kamaraj, K.; Indian politician; b. 03; ed. Virud-hunagar, Madras.
Entered public life during Salt Satyagraha 21, sentenced to two years; mem. Working Cttee., Tamil Nad Con-gress 31, Sec. 35, Pres. 39-54; sentenced to one year 32; mem. Madras Legislative Assembly 37-; detained, Satyagraha Movement 41, 42-45; mem. Constituent Assembly of India 47, All-India Congress Working Cttee., 49; Leader, Madras Legislature Congress Party 54-; Chief Minister, Madras 54-August 63; Pres. Indian Nat. Congress 63-68.
Indian National Congress, 7 Jantar Mantar Road, New Delhi, India.

Kamarck, Andrew Martin, B.S., M.A., PH.D.; American international bank official; b. 10 Nov. 1914; ed. Harvard Univ.
International Section, Fed. Reserve Board 39-40; Con-fidential Asst. to Sec. of U.S. Treasury 40-42; U.S. Army 42-44; Cen. Banking Advisor, Allied Control Comm., Italy 43-44; Chief, Financial Intelligence, Deputy Dir. Finance Div., and American Deputy on Allied Finance Directorate, Allied Control Council, Germany 45; Office of Int. Finance, U.S. Treasury, Chief of Nat. Advisory Council on Int. Monetary and Financial Problems (N.A.C.) Div., Financial Policy Cttee. preparing Marshall Plan 45-46; U.S. Treasury Rep., Chief of Finance Div. of Econ. Co-operative Admin. Mission, Financial Attaché U.S. Embassy, Rome 48-50; Chief of Africa Section, Econ. Dept., World Bank 50-52; Econ. Adviser, Dept. of Operations, Europe, Africa and Australasia, World Bank, Chief of Econ. Missions to 14 countries, Chief Economist, Uganda Survey Mission 52-64; Dir. Econ. Dept., World Bank and Int. Devt. Asscn. 65-; mem. American Econ. Asscn., Council on Foreign Relations, Policy Board, Econ. Inst. of American Econ. Asscn. 62-65; Fellow, 58, and Dir. African Studies Asscn. 61-64; Regents Prof., Univ. of Calif. 64-65; Council, Soc. for Int. Devt. 67-.
Publs. *The Economic Development of Uganda* (co-author) 61, *The Economics of African Development* 67.
International Bank for Reconstruction and Develop-ment, Washington, D.C. 20433, U.S.A.

Kamath, Hari Vishnu, B.SC.; Indian politician; b. 13 July 1907; ed. Mangalore and Presidency Coll., Madras.
Joined Indian civil service in London 29; served I.C.S. 30-38; resigned for political reasons; joined Congress and then the Forward Bloc as Sec.-Gen.; in prison 40-41, 42-45; mem. Constituent Assembly 46-49, and mem. Nagpur Provincial Congress Cttee.; mem. Provisional Parl. 50-52; Praja Socialist Member of Lok Sabha 55-57, 62-; Chair. Praja Socialist Party, Madhya Pradesh 58-60; mem. Nat. Exec. Praja Socialist Party 53-; Chair. Central Parl. Board, Praja Socialist Party 65-; mem. Admin. Reforms Comm., Govt. of India 66-.
Publ. *Communist China colonises Tibet, invades India* 59.
Dhantoli, Nagpur, Maharashtra; and Western Court, New Delhi, India.
Telephone: 22359 (Nagpur); 40989 (New Delhi).

Kambona, Oscar; Tanzanian politician; b. 1928; ed Middle Temple, London.
Former schoolmaster; Org. Sec. Tanganyika African Nat. Union (T.A.N.U.) 54-56; studied law, Middle Temple, London 56-60; Sec.-Gen. T.A.N.U. 60-67; Minister of Educ., Tanganyika 61-62, of Home Affairs 62-63, of Foreign Affairs and Defence 63-64, of External Affairs, Tanzania 64-65, of Regional Admin. 65-67, of Local Govt. and Rural Devt. 67; resigned June 67, left Tanzania Aug. 67.
c/o Ministry of Local Government, Dar es Salaam, Tanzania.

Kamel, Hassan; United Arab Republic (Egyptian) diplomatist and administrator; b. 6 Sept. 1907; ed. Univs. of Montpellier, Cairo and Paris à la Sorbonne.
Member Mixed Bar 30-36; Lecturer, Admin. Law, High Coll. of Police and Admin. 36-37; joined Ministry of Foreign Affairs 37, served in several countries in-cluding Italy, Iran, France, Syria, Portugal, Switzer-land, Libya, Argentina, Turkey and Hungary until 59; Legal Adviser, Govt. of Qatar 60; Dir.-Gen. Govt. of Qatar 61-; Adviser of several dels. to UN and rep. on numerous int. confs.; numerous legal articles.
Office of the Director-General of the Government, Doha, Qatar.

Kamel, Mostafa, LL.B.; United Arab Republic (Egyptian) diplomatist; b. 27 Oct. 1908; ed. Univ. of Cairo and the Sorbonne.

Govt. Observer, Summit Conf., Geneva 55; Ambassador of Egypt to India 55-58; Ambassador of U.A.R. to U.S.A. 58-67, to Belgium and Luxembourg 67-.
Embassy of the United Arab Republic, 2 Avenue Victoria, Brussels, Belgium.

Kamimura, Eisuke, B.A.; Japanese petroleum executive; b. 11 March 1900; ed. Tokyo Imperial Univ.
Joined Nippon Oil Co. 25; with Japan Oil Transportation Co. 46-49; Dir. Nippon Oil Co. 49-50, Man. Dir. 50-58, Vice-Pres. 58-61, Pres. 61-; Dir. Nippon Petroleum Refining Co. 51-61, Pres. 61-; Chair. Japan Oil Transportation Co. 58-; Dir. Nippon Petrochemicals Co. 61-, Nisseki Real Estate Co. 59-, Nippon Petroleum Gas Co. 61-, Nippon Hodo Co. 60-, Nippon Speciality Lubricants Co. 60-; Chair. and Pres. Nippon Oil (Delaware) Ltd. 61-; Exec. Dir. Fed. of Econ. Orgs. 61-, Japan Fed. of Employers' Asscns. 61-.
2, 5-chome, Den-enchofu, Ohta-ku, Tokyo, Japan.

Kaminska, Ida; Polish actress and theatrical producer and manager; b. 99.
First stage appearance 09; organiser and dir. of Jewish theatre companies Warsaw 18, Wilno, Lwów 33-41; since the Second World War in Łódź and Wrocław; now Dir. State Jewish Theatre, Warsaw; roles include Nora (Ibsen's *The Doll's House*), Glikl Hameln, Mother (Gergely's *The Case of Pawel Eszterag*), Ethel (Kruczkowski's *Julius and Ethel*), *Mother Courage* (Brecht), Madame Frank (Dürenmatt's *Frank V.*); appeared in Czechoslovak film *The Shop in the High Street*.
Panstwowy Teatr Zydowski, Warsaw; Al. Jerozolimskie 101.m. 11, Warsaw, Poland.

Kamitatu, Cleophas; Congolese politician; b. 31; ed. Jesuit Seminary.
Worked for nationalist movement in Kwilu Region; member of Constitutional Round Table Conference, Brussels 58; founded (with Gizenga) Parti Solidaire Africain (P.S.A.) 59; delegate Conference of Congolese leaders Madagascar 61; Pres. Léopoldville Province 61-62; Minister of the Interior 62-63, of Planning and Industrial Development 63-64, of Foreign Affairs and External Commerce 65, of Middle Classes 65; sentenced to five years imprisonment July 66.
Kinshasa, Congo Republic.

Kamitz, Reinhard, DR. RER. MERC.; Austrian economist; b. 18 June 1907; ed. Hochschule für Welthandel, Vienna.
Worked in paper industry and later in iron industry; on staff Austrian Inst. for Econ. Research 34-38; leading positions Austrian Chamber of Commerce 39-52; Minister of Finance 52-60; Pres. Austrian Nat. Bank 60-68; Hon. Prof. Vienna Univ.
Austrian Company for Industrial Credit Ltd., Postfach 83, 1096 Vienna, Austria.
Telephone: 0222-4282-12-13.

Kammhuber, General Josef; German air force officer; b. 19 Aug. 1896; ed. Ludwigsgymnasium, Munich.
Volunteer 14, transferred to regular army and served through all ranks to Major-Gen. 40, Lieut.-Gen. 41 and Gen. of the *Luftwaffe* 43; Chief of the German Air Force 56-62; Lieut.-Gen. 56-61; Gen. 61-, Iron Cross, I and II Class, Ritterkreuz and Grosses Bundesverdienstkreuz mit Stern und Schulterband.
Schwindstrasse 24, 8000 Munich 13, German Federal Republic.
Telephone: 55-46-59.

Kamov, Nikolai Ilyich, D.SC.; Soviet aircraft designer; ed. Tomsk Inst. of Technology.
Chief Designer, U.S.S.R. Ministry of Aircraft Engineering; Co-Designer KASKR-1 Autogyro 29; Designer of helicopters: KA-8 in 45, KA-15 in 52, KA-18 in 56,

KA-20, KA-22 and KA-26 in 65; Orders of Lenin, Red Banner of Labour and other decorations.
U.S.S.R. Ministry of Aircraft Industry, Moscow, U.S.S.R.

Kampmann, Viggo; Danish economist and politician; b. 21 July 1910; ed. Univ. of Copenhagen.
Economist, Statistical Dept. 34-44; Deputy Chief, Secretariat-General, Government's Employment Office. 44-46; Adviser, Dept. of Taxes 46-47; Head, Government's Economic Secretariat 47-50; Pres. and Chair. Royal Mortgage Bank of Denmark 50-53; Minister of Finance 50, 53-60, Prime Minister 60-Aug. 62; Pres. State Life Insurance Co. 62-.
Luganovej 12, Copenhagen S, Denmark.
Telephone: Su. 156.

Kanamaru, Tomio; Japanese business executive; b. 24 Feb 1896; ed. Kyoto Univ.
Railway Ministry 24-43, Chief of Second Section, Railway Research Dept., Railway Board 37-43; Nippon Express Co. 43-, Pres. 55-61, Chair. 61-; dir. of other companies and econ. orgs.
Nippon Express Co., 1-chome, Kanda-Hatagocho, Chiyodaku, Tokyo, Japan.

Kanari, Masuhiko; Japanese business executive; b. 4 May 1904; ed. Tokyo Univ.
Chairman, Tokyo Hatsudoki; Pres. Fuji Electric Manufacturing Co.; Vice-Chair. The Japan Electric Asscn.
28 Komagome-Akebono-cho, Bunkyo-ku, Tokyo, Japan.

Kandahl, Torolv; Norwegian journalist; b. 17 Aug. 1899; ed. Oslo Univ.
Began journalistic career 28; Chief Editor *Drammens Tidende*, Drammen 45-61, *Aftenposten*, Oslo 61-; mem. Norwegian Parl. 50-54; Chair. Norwegian Press Asscn. 38-41; Norwegian Editors' Asscn. 50-56; mem. Board, Int. Press Inst. 60-62; Pres. World League of Norsemen 63-; Knight, Order of St. Olav; Conservative.
Rosenborggaten 5, Oslo 3, Norway.
Telephone: Oslo 69-37-83.

Kandrenkov, Andrei Andreyevich; Soviet politician; b. 15; ed. Moscow Veterinary Acad.
Agronomist 37-38; Soviet army service 38-39, 43-45; mem. C.P.S.U. 39-; party work 45-56; Perm. Staff Central Cttee. C.P.S.U. 56; Second Sec. Kaluga Regional Cttee. C.P.S.U. 57-61; Chair. Exec. Cttee. Kaluga Regional Soviet of Workers' Deputies 61; First Sec. Kaluga Rural Cttee. C.P.S.U. 61-65, Kaluga Regional Cttee. C.P.S.U. 65-; Cand. mem. Central Cttee. C.P.S.U. 61-; Deputy to U.S.S.R. Supreme Soviet; mem. Mandate Cttee. Soviet of Union.
Kaluga Regional Committee of C.P.S.U., Kaluga, U.S.S.R.

Kanellopoulos, Panayotis; Greek politician; b. 02.
Fmr. Prof. of Sociology Athens Univ.; served Albanian front 41; Deputy Prime Minister and Min. of Defence 42-43; Min. Finance and Reconstruction 44; Prime Minister Nov. 45; M.P. March 46-; Min. Without Portfolio April 46; Min. of Air 47; Minister of War 49-50; Mem. Parl. 50; Deputy Prime Minister and Minister of Defence in Venizelos Govt. March-April 50; in Jan. 51 formed with S. Stephanopoulos the Populist Unionist Party (LEK); at Gen. Election Sept. 51 joined forces with Marshal Papagos; Minister of Nat. Defence 52-55; Dep. Prime Minister 54-55, 59-63; Prime Minister and Minister of Foreign Affairs 67; co-leader of Populist Party 58, Leader Nat. Radical Union Dec. 63-; Prof. of Social Sciences, Athens Acad. 59-.
Publs. *League of Nations* 26, *Social Progress and Social Policy* 27, *Sociology of the Imperialist Phenomena* 27, *Karl Marx* 31, *Society in our Days* 32, *Progress of Technique and Economy* 33, *Man and the Social Conflicts* 34, *Philosophical and Sociological Problems of History* 36, *Simple Sounds* (Verse) 39, *History of the European*

Spirit (two vols.) 41-47, *I Shall Tell You the Truth* 45, *The Cycle of Sonnets* (Verse) 46, *The 20th Century* 50, *Christianity and Our Era* 52, *Prolegomena to Metaphysics* 55, *Athenian Dialogues* 56, *The End of Zarathustra* 56, *I Was Born in 1402* 57.
Xenokratous 15, Athens, Greece.

Kaneshige, Kankuro; Japanese engineer; b. 5 April 1899; ed. Tokyo Imperial Univ.
Technician, Kanegafuchi Spinning Co. 23-25; Asst. Prof. of Mechanical Engineering, Tokyo Imperial Univ. 25-42; Prof. of Mechanical Engineering, Univ. of Tokyo 42-60; Dir. Inst. of Industrial Science, Univ. of Tokyo 51-54; Dir., Nat. Aeronautical Laboratory 55-57; Pres. Science Council of Japan 58-60; Full-time Commr. of Atomic Energy Comm. of Japan 60-65; Chair. Nat. Space Activities Council 60-67; mem. UN Advisory Cttee. on the Application of Science and Technology to Development 64-; Full-time mem. Council for Science and Technology 65-.
5-46-25 Asagayakita, Suginami-ku, Tokyo, Japan.
Telephone: 03-337-4991.

Kang Ke-ching; Chinese woman political leader; b. 13. Joined army of Arn Teh, duties in southern front line 28; married Chu Teh 29; joined C.C.P. 31; Dir. of Youth Education; Commander of Guard of General Staff; Commander of Women's Voluntary Corps 32; studied in Red Army Mil. Acad. 32; in Long March in Chu Teh's forces 34; in Shensi entered Red Army Acad. and studied politics and military science; finished education in Yenan Anti-Japanese Univ.; on Standing Cttee. of All-China Democratic Women's Fed. 49; Sec.-Gen. Chinese People's National Cttee in Defence of Children; Honan del. to N.P.C. 54; Vice-Chair. All-China Democratic Women's Fed. 57-.
All-China Democratic Women's Federation, Peking, China.

Kang Sheng; Chinese politician; b. c. 1904.
Member Central Cttee. of Chinese Communist Party, mem. Secr. 62-; mem. Standing Cttee. of Politburo 66-; Alt. mem. Political Bureau; Vice-Chair. N.P.C. Standing Cttee. 65-.
Politburo of the Central Committee of the Chinese Communist Party, Peking, People's Republic of China.

K'ang Yung-ho; Chinese trade union leader; b. 15. On executive cttee. Chinese Fed. of Trade Unions 48; Chair. Working Cttee. North China branch of the Fed. 53; mem. Presidium of the Congress of the Fed. 53-; Shansi del. to N.P.C. 54; mem. Secr. All-China Fed. of Trade Unions 57-.
All-China Federation of Trade Unions, 1 Fu Chien Street, Peking, China.

Kano, Hyakuri; Japanese banker; b. 8 March 1898; ed. Tokyo Imperial Univ.
Director Bank of Japan 46-54; Vice-Gov. Export and Import Bank of Japan 54-58; Pres. Tokyo Int. Trade Centre Corpn. 58-64; Pres. Maruzen Petrochemical Co. Ltd. 64-.
No. 13, Azabu Roppongi-cho, Minato-ku, Tokyo, Japan.

Kantol Norodom, H.H. Prince; Cambodian diplomatist and politician; b. 15 Sept. 1920; ed. Saigon, Phnom-Penh and Univ. of Nancy, France.
Successively Chief Gov. Municipality of Phnom-Penh; Chef du Cabinet at Ministry of Finance; First Sec. Cambodian Embassy, Wash.; Minister Plenipotentiary, Tokyo; Pres. of the Council of Ministers and Foreign Minister; now Vice-Pres. of Throne High Council, Dir.-Gen. for Royal Palace Officers, Pres. of High Board of Justice and mem. Council for Royal Family.
Royal Palace, Phnom-Penh, Cambodia.
Telephone: 2-3861.

Kantorovich, Leonid Vitalovich; Soviet mathematician; b. 1912; ed. Leningrad Univ.
Instructor, Leningrad Inst. of Industrial Construction Engineering 30-39; Instructor, Leningrad Univ. 32-34, Prof. 34-; Deputy Dir. Laboratory for Use of Statistical and Mathematical Methods in Econs., Siberian Dept., U.S.S.R. Acad. of Sciences; Corresp. mem. U.S.S.R. Acad. of Sciences 58-64, mem. 64-; State Prize 49.
Laboratory for Use of Statistical and Mathematical Methods in Economics, Siberian Department, U.S.S.R. Academy of Sciences, Novosibirsk, U.S.S.R.

Kantorowicz, Alfred, DR.JUR.UTR.; German university professor and writer; b. 12 Aug. 1899; ed. Univs. of Berlin, Freiburg, Munich, Erlangen.
Army service 17-18; literary critic and foreign corresp. *Vossische Zeitung* 25-32; exile in Paris; escaped to U.S.A. 41; Dir. CBS listening station, New York; returned to Germany 46; publisher of monthly magazine *Ost und West*, Berlin 47-49; Prof. of History of German Literature, and Dir. Germanistisches Inst., Humboldt Univ. 50-57; went to Federal Republic 57; mem. German Communist Party 31-57.
Publs. *In unserem Lager ist Deutschland* (essays) 36, *Portraits* 47, *Deutsche Schicksale* 49, *Spanisches Tagebuch* 49, *Suchende Jugend* 49, *Vom Moralischen Gewinn der Niederlage* 49, *Die Verbündeten* (play) 51, *Heinrich und Thomas Mann* 56, *Meine Kleider* (stories) 57, *Deutsches Tagebuch, Vol. I* 59, *Vol. II* 61, *Spanisches Kriegstagebuch* 66, *Im 2. Drittel unseres Jahrhunderts* 67; edited critical edn. of works of H. Mann 51-57.
Sierichstr. 148, 2 Hamburg 39, German Federal Republic.

Kantrowitz, Adrian, M.D.; American heart surgeon; b. 4 Oct. 1918; ed. New York Univ. and Long Island Coll. of Medicine.
Cleveland Teaching Fellow in Physiology, Western Reserve Univ. School of Medicine 51-52; Instructor in Surgery, New York Medical Coll. 52-55; Asst. Prof. of Surgery, New York Downstate Medical Center 55-57; Assoc. Prof. of Surgery 57-64, Prof. of Surgery 64-; Adjunct Surgeon, Montefiore Hospital, Bronx, N.Y. 51-55; Dir. (full-time) Cardiovascular Surgery, Maimonides Hospital 55-64; Attending Surgeon, Maimonides Medical Center 55-; Dir. Surgical Services (full-time), Maimonides Medical Center and Coney Island Hospital, Brooklyn 64-; Pres. Brooklyn Thoracic Soc. 67-68; Pres.-elect, American Soc. of Artificial Internal Organs 67-68; mem. Editorial Board *Journal of Biomedical Materials Research* 66-, mem. Scientific Review Board *Medical Research Engineering* 66-; Henry L. Moses Research Prize 49; N.Y. State Medical Soc., First Prize, Scientific Exhibit 52, First Prize Maimonides Hospital Research Soc. for work in Bladder Stimulation 63, Gold Plate Award, American Acad. of Achievement 66, Max Berg Award for Outstanding Achievement in Prolonging Human Life 66, Brooklyn Hall of Fame Man of Year Award for Science 66, Theodor and Susan B. Cummings Humanitarian Award, American Coll. of Cardiology 67.
Publs. Numerous articles and films on heart surgery.
Maimonides Medical Center, 4802 Tenth Avenue, Brooklyn, N.Y. 11219, U.S.A.
Telephone: 212-UL6-2426, Ext. 251.

Kanungo, Nityanand, B.A., B.L.; Indian politician; b. 1900; ed. Ravenshaw Coll., Cuttack and Univ. Coll., Calcutta.
Minister for Housing, Law, Industries and Agriculture, Govt. of Orissa 37-52; Dep. Minister of Commerce and Industries, Central Govt. 54-55; Minister of State for Industries 55-56, for Consumer Industries 56-57, for Commerce 57-62, for Industries 62-64, for Civil Aviation 64-65; Gov. of Gujerat 65; Dir. State Co-operative Bank, Orissa; Gov. of Bihar.
Patna, Bihar, India.

Kanza, Thomas; Congolese diplomatist; b. 34; ed. Catholic Univ., Louvain, Coll. of Europe, Bruges and Harvard Univ., U.S.A.

Official, European Econ. Community, Brussels; returned to Léopoldville 60, Rep. to UN 60-62; Chargé d'Affaires in United Kingdom 62-64; a leader of M.N.C. Lumumba.

Publs. *Congo 1961* 62, *Without Rancour* (novel).

c/o M.N.C. Lumumba, Juba, S. Sudan.

Kao Chung-min; Chinese administrator and jurist; b. 92.

On exec. cttee. Northeast Administrative Council 46; Vice-Chair. Governing Council of the Joint Exec. Office of Northeast Provincial Cities 46; on general section Northeast branch Democratic League 46; Vice-Chair. Northeast People's Government, Dir. of Northeast People's Law Courts; del. for Northeast Liberated Areas to C.P.P.C.C.; on State Council 49; Vice-Chair. Northeast People's Government 52; Vice-Chair. Northeast Administrative Council 53; on direction of Chinese Politics and Law Society; Vice-Chair. China Democratic League 53; del. for Heilungkiang to N.P.C., Vice-Chair. and on standing cttee. 54; released from legal posts in Northeast 54; represented Democratic League on 2nd C.P.P.C.C. 54; 2nd term as member and Vice-Chair. of Democratic League 56-.

Chinese Democratic League, Peking, China.

Kao Teng-pang; Chinese administrator.

Exec. Chief Ministry of Railways 54; Dir. General Planning Office Ministry of Railways 55; Dir. Bureau of Government Offices Administration 56-.

Bureau of Government Offices Administration, Peking, China.

Kapfer, Hans, D.JUR.; Austrian lawyer; b. 5 Sept. 1903; ed. Vienna Univ.

Served in Law Courts 26-46, Judge 30; entered Ministry of Justice 46, Sektionsrat 46, Ministerialrat 48, Sektionschef 53; Minister of Justice 55-56; Pres. Oberlandesgericht Vienna 58; Vice-Pres. Supreme Court 63-65, Pres. Supreme Court 66-.

Publs. (Editor) *Allgemeines bürgerliches Gesetzbuch* 48, 51, 55, 60, 61, 63, 64, *Angestelltengesetz, Arbeitsgerichtsgesetz, Wechsel-und Scheckgesetz* 47, 48, 53, 57, 61.

Schmerlingplatz 11, Vienna I, Austria.

Kapitonov, Ivan Vasilyevich; Soviet politician; b. 15; ed. Moscow Municipal Engineering Inst.

Managerial, Party and Govt. work 38-54; First Sec. Moscow Regional Party Cttee. 54-59, Ivanovo Regional Party Cttee. 59-64; Head of Dept. of Party Agencies, Central Cttee. of C.P.S.U. for R.S.F.S.R. 65; mem. Central Cttee., C.P.S.U. 52-, Sec. 65-; mem. Presidium of U.S.S.R. Supreme Soviet 54-62; Deputy to U.S.S.R. Supreme Soviet; mem. C.P.S.U. 39-.

Central Committee of C.P.S.U., Staraya ploshchad 4, Moscow, U.S.S.R.

Kapitza, Peter Leonidovich, PH.D., F.R.S.; Soviet physicist; b. 9 July 1894; ed. Petrograd Polytechnic.

Lecturer Leningrad Polytechnic 19-21; Asst. Dir. of Research in Magnetism, Cavendish Laboratory, Cambridge 24-32; Fellow of Trinity Coll. Cambridge 25-36; Messel Research Prof. of Royal Society and Dir. of Royal Society Mond Laboratory 30-35; Dir. Inst. for Physical Problems, Acad. of Sciences of U.S.S.R. 35-46; Editor Journal of Experimental and Theoretical Physics, U.S.S.R.; mem. Acad. of Sciences of the U.S.S.R.; Dir. Inst. for Physical Problems 55-; hon. mem. Inst. of Metals 43, Franklin Inst. 44, Danish Royal Acad., N.Y. Acad. of Science 46, Royal Irish Acad. 48; Foreign Assoc. American Nat. Acad. of Sciences 46; hon. Fellow Indian Acad. of Science 48, Indian Nat. Inst. of Sciences 57, Trinity Coll., Cambridge, England 66-; Foreign mem. Polish Acad. of Sciences 62-, Royal Acad. of Science, Sweden 66-;

State Prize 41, 43, Faraday Medal of Inst. Electrical Engineers 42, Order of Lenin 43, 44, 45, 64, Medal of Franklin Inst. 44, Hero of Socialist Labour 45, Order of the Red Banner of Labour 54, Sir Devaprasad Sarbadhikari Gold Medal (Univ. of Calcutta) 55; mem. German Acad. of Naturalists "Leopoldina" 58, Kothenius Gold Medal 59; Lomonosov Gold Medal of U.S.S.R. Acad. of Sciences 59, Great Gold Medal, Exhibition of Econ. Achievements, U.S.S.R. 62, Int. Niels Bohr Gold Medal of Dansk Ingeniørvorening 64, Rutherford Medal of Inst. of Physics and Physical Soc. of England 66.

Vorobyevskoe Chaussée 2, Moscow, U.S.S.R.

Kaplan, Rabbi Jacob, L. EN PHIL.; French Rabbi; b. 7 Nov. 1895; ed. Séminaire Israélite de France.

Rabbi of Mulhouse 22; Rabbi in Paris 29; Auxiliary Rabbi to Chief Rabbi of France 39; Chief Rabbi of Paris 50; Chief Rabbi of France 55-; lecturer at l'Inst. d'Etudes Politiques de Paris; mem. Acad. des Sciences Morales et Politiques, Paris 67-; Commandeur de la Légion d'Honneur, Croix de Guerre (twice); Doctor h.c. Theological Seminary of New York; citation by Mayor of New York for distinguished service.

Publs. *Le Judaïsme et la Justice Sociale* 37, *Racisme et Judaïsme* 40, *French Jewry under the Occupation* (American Jewish Year Book) 45-46, *Le Judaïsme dans la Société Française Contemporaine* 48, *Témoignages sur Israël* 49, *Les Temps d'Epreuve* 52.

1 rue Andrieux, Paris 8e, France.

Telephone: 522-33-97.

Kaplan, Joseph, B.S., A.M., PH.D.; American physicist; b. 8 Sept. 1902 in Hungary; ed. Johns Hopkins Univ.

Instructor in Physics Johns Hopkins Univ. 26; Nat. Research Fellow in Physics Princeton Univ. 27-28; Asst. Prof. Univ. of California 28-35, Assoc. Prof. 35, Prof. 40-, and Chair. Dept. of Physics 38-44, Dept. of Meteorology 40-44; Acting Dir., Inst. of Geophysics, Univ. of California, Dir. 46-47; mem. Comm. Int. Astronomical Union 22; Chief Operations Analysis Section 2nd Air Force 43-45, Air Forces Weather Service, Jan.-Sept. 45; mem. Board of Dirs. Microdot, Inc., New World Fund, Inc.; Adviser, Axe Science and Electronics Corpn.; Fellow Physical Soc. and Local Sec. for Pacific Coast; mem. Exec. Cttee. Int. Asscn. of Terrestrial Magnetism and Electricity; Chair. Mixed Cttee. on Upper Atmosphere TMS and (IAIAM) and U.S. Cttee. for the Int. Geophysical year; Fellow, The Meteoritical Soc. (Councillor 46-50); Pres. Int. Asscn. of Geomagnetism and Aeronomy, Int. Union of Geodesy and Geophysics; Chair. U.S. Nat. Cttee for the Int. Geophysical Year; mem. Nat. Acad. of Sciences; Fellow, Inst. of the Aeronautical Sciences; mem. Astronomical Society, Astronomical Society of the Pacific, Int. Geophysical Union, Inst. Aeronautical Sciences, Optical Society of America, American Geophysical Union, Board of Govs. Hebrew Univ. of Jerusalem, Weizmann Inst. of Science at Rehovoth; Hon. D.Sc. (Univ. of Notre Dame, Carleton Coll.); Hon. L.H.D. (Yeshiva Univ., Jewish Theological Seminary and Hebrew Union Coll.).

1565 Kelton Avenue, Los Angeles, Calif. 90024, U.S.A. Telephone: 213-4738839.

Kapp, Edmond X., B.A.; British artist; b. 5 Nov. 1890; ed. Christ's Coll., Cambridge, London, Paris, Berlin and Rome.

First exhibition of drawings London 19, 10th retrospective and first of oil paintings, Wildenstein, London 39, 29th, Milan 54; 30th, Leicester Galleries, London 56; retrospective exhibition, Whitechapel Art Gallery, London 61; contributed drawings to *Observer, Sunday Times, Manchester Guardian, Studio, Time and Tide, New Statesman, Querschnitt*, and other publications; commissioned by British Museum and National Portrait Gallery to make 27 lithographs at L. of N.,

Geneva 33-35; official war artist 40-45; invited as Official Artist to UNESCO, Paris 46-47; Exhibition at UNESCO, Paris 46; represented in "British Art since Whistler", Nat. Gallery, London 45; Works acquired by many galleries and private collectors; six portraits reproduced as stained glass windows in Yale Univ. Law School; Commissioned to make seven portraits for Gonville and Caius Coll., Christ's Coll., Cambridge and Merton Coll., Oxford 65-66; retrospective exhbn. Royal Festival Hall, London 68.
Publs. Collections of drawings, *Ten Great Lawyers*, *Minims*, *Personalities*, *Reflections*, *Pastiche*, *The Nations at Geneva*, etc.
2 Steele's Studios, Haverstock Hill, London, N.W.3, England.
Telephone: 01-722-3174.

Kapp, Eugen Arturovich; Soviet composer; b. 1908; ed. Leningrad Conservatoire.
Professor, Tallin Conservatoire; Chair. Estonian Composers' Union, People's Artist of Estonia, People's Artist of the U.S.S.R., State Prize 46, 49, 52; Order of Lenin 50; Order of Red Banner of Labour (twice).
Principal compositions: Trio for Piano 30, *The Avenger* (Symphonic poem) 31, Concerto for Strings 35, Sonata No. 1 for Violin and Piano 36, *Kalevipoeg* (The Son of Kalev) (Overture) 38, Symphony No. 1 39, Sonata No. 2 for Violin and Piano 43, *Fires of Vengeance* (Opera) 44, *Kalevipoeg* (Ballet) 47, Sonata for 'Cello and Piano 48, *Tallin Scenes* 49, *Bard of Freedom* 50, Symphony No. 2 54, Overture on Finnish Themes 57, *Leningrad Suite* 57, *Winter's Tale* (Opera) 58, *Children's Day* (Cycle of children's songs) 58.
Estonian Composers' Union, Boulevard Estonia 4, Tallin, U.S.S.R.

Kappel, Frederick R., B.S.E.; American businessman; b. 14 Jan. 1902; ed. Univ. of Minnesota.
Joined Bell System as groundman Northwestern Bell Telephone Co. 24, Asst. Vice-Pres. (Operations) 39, Vice-Pres. (Operations) and Dir. 42; Asst. Vice-Pres. (Operation and Engineering) American Telephone and Telegraph Co. 49, Vice-Pres. (Long Lines) 49, (Operation and Engineering) 49, Pres. Western Electric Co. 54, Pres. American Telephone and Telegraph Co. 56-67, Chair. 61-67, Chair. Exec. Cttee. 67-; responsible for *Telstar* communications satellite July 62; Dir. American Telephone and Telegraph Co., Chase Manhattan Bank, Metropolitan Life Insurance Co., Gen. Foods Corpn., Acad. of Political Sciences; Trustee N.Y. Presbyterian Hospital, Grand Central Art Galleries, Cttee. for Econ. Devt., Boys' Clubs of America; mem. of Advisory Board Salvation Army; mem. The Business Council, Smith. 63-64; Trustee Columbia Univ., Minn. Univ., Inst. of Electrical and Electronics Engineers 23-; Outstanding Achievement Award (Minn. Univ.) 54; Dir. Standard Oil Co. (N.J.), Int. Paper Co., etc.; Chair. President's Comm. on Postal Org. 67-68; numerous hon. degrees and awards.
195 Broadway, New York City 7, N.Y., U.S.A.

Käppeli, Robert, DR. RER. POL.; Swiss industrialist; b. 21 July 1900; ed. Kantonsschule, Lucerne, and Universität Basel.
Institut für Weltwirtschaft und Seeverkehr, Univ. of Kiel 29-30; M. M. Warburg & Co., Hamburg 30-34; CIBA Ltd., Basle 34-; Chair. of Board of Dirs. 56-; Dr. h.c. tech. sci. Swiss Fed. Inst. of Technology; Dr. h.c. polit. econ. Univ. of Fribourg.
CIBA Ltd., Basle, Switzerland.

Kaprio, Leo, M.D., M.P.H., D.P.H.; Finnish public health officer; b. 28 June 1918; ed. Helsingen Yliopisto-Helsingfors Universitet and Harvard Univ.
Finnish Army Medical Corps during Second World War; with Public Health Service 45-56, Chief, Div. of Public Health, Nat. Health Service 52-56; Regional

Officer, Eastern Mediterranean and Europe, World Health Org. (WHO) 56-63, Dir. Div. of Public Health Services 63-67, Regional Dir. for Europe Feb. 67-.
European Regional Office, World Health Organization, 8 Scherfigsvej, Copenhagen, Denmark.

Kapur, Balraj Krishna; Indian diplomatist; b. 1910. Joined Indian Political Service and served in North West Frontier Province 36-45; dep. Sec. Min. of External Affairs 46-50, Jt. Sec. 50-51; Sec. Indian Del. to U.N. 46; Chargé d'Affaires, Iran 51-52; Political Officer, Sikkim 52-55; Chargé d'Affaires, Netherlands 55-56, Ambassador 56-57; High Commr., Ghana 57-60, Nigeria 57-60, Ceylon 60-65; Special Sec. Ministry of External Affairs 65-66; Ambassador to Sweden 66-.
Indian Embassy, Stockholm, Sweden.

Kapwepwe, Simon; Zambian politician; b. 12 April 1922; ed. Lubwa Mission.
Former teacher; studied in India and United States; Nat. Treas., United Nat. Independence Party; mem. Parl. 62-; fmr. Minister of Agriculture; Minister of Home Affairs Jan.-Oct. 64; Minister of Foreign Affairs Oct. 64-Sept. 67; Vice-Pres. of Zambia Sept. 67-.
Office of the Vice-President, Lusaka, Zambia.

Karageorghis, Vassos, PH.D., F.S.A.; Cypriot archaeologist; b. 29; ed. Pancyprian Gymnasium, Nicosia, Univ. Coll., and Inst. of Archæology, London Univ.
Assistant Curator, Cyprus Museum 52-60, Curator 60-63, Acting Dir., Dept. of Antiquities, Cyprus 63-64, Dir. 64-; Vice-Pres. Council of Soc. for Cypriot Studies, mem. Governing Body, Cyprus Research Centre; Fellow, Soc. of Antiquaries, London, Corresp. mem. Archaeological Soc., Athens, German Archaeological Inst., Berlin.
Publs. *Treasures in the Cyprus Museum* 62, *Nouveaux Documents pour l'Etude du Bronze Récent à Chypre* 64, *Corpus Vasorum Antiquorum* 64, 65, *Sculptures from Salamis*, vol. I 64, vol. II 66, *Excavations in the Necropolis of Salamis*, vol. I 67, and articles in German, American, English and French journals.
c/o Cyprus Museum, Nicosia, Cyprus.

Karajan, Herbert von; Austrian conductor; b. 5 April 1908; ed. Salzburg Gymnasium and Mozarteum, Vienna Univ. and Conservatoire.
Successively Musical Dir. Ulm, Opera and Gen. Musical Dir. Aachen, Kapellmeister, Berlin State Opera, Conductor, Berlin Philharmonic Orch.; Dir. Berlin Staatskapelle 41-45; concert tours in Europe, U.S.A. and Far East 45-; Artistic Dir. Berlin Philharmonic Orchestra 55-56, Vienna State Opera 56-64; mem. Board of Dirs., Salzburg Festival 65-; Dir. Gesellschaft der Musikfreunde, Vienna; conducted at Salzburg and Lucerne Festivals; Mozart Ring 57; Commdr. First Class, Order of White Rose (Finland).
c/o Vienna State Opera, Vienna, Austria.

Karakeyev, Kurman Karakeyevich; Soviet historian; b. 1913; ed. Higher Party School.
Mem. C.P.S.U. 38-; C.P. work 49-60; mem. and Pres. Kirghiz Acad. of Sciences 60-; Deputy to U.S.S.R. Supreme Soviet; Orders and medals of U.S.S.R.
Presidium of Kirghiz Academy of Sciences, 78 Pushkin Street, Frunze, U.S.S.R.

Karamanlis, Constantinos G.; Greek lawyer and politician; b. 07; ed. Univ. of Athens.
Practising lawyer since 32; Deputy since 35; Minister of Labour 46, of Transport 47, of Social Welfare 48-50, of Nat. Defence 50-52; re-elected Deputy for Serrai 51 and 52; Minister of Public Works 52-54, of Communications and Public Works 54-55, Prime Minister Oct. 55-Mar. 58 and May 58-Sept. 61 and Nov. 61-June 63; National Radical Union.
24 Karneadou Street, Athens, Greece.

Karami, Rashid; Lebanese politician; b. 21; ed. Fuad al-Awal Univ., Cairo.
Minister of Nat. Economy and Social Affairs 54-55;

Prime Minister and Minister of the Interior Sept. 55-Mar. 56; Prime Minister Sept. 58-May 60, 65-66, Dec. 66-68; Minister of Finance, Economy, Defence and Information Oct. 58-Oct. 59, of Finance and Defence Oct. 59-May 60; Prime Minister and Minister of Finance Oct. 61-April 64.
Beirut, Lebanon.

Karan Singh, Maharaja, M.A., PH.D.; Indian politician; b. 9 March 1931; ed. Doon School, Univ. of Jammu and Kashmir, and Delhi Univ.
Son of Lieut.-Gen. H.H. Maharaja Sir Hari Singhji, G.C.S.I., G.C.I.E., G.C.V.O., and Maharani Tara Deviji, C.I.; married, 5 March 1950, Princess Yasho Rajya Lakshmi of Nepal; appointed Regent of Jammu and Kashmir 49; elected Sadar-i-Riyasat (Head of State) by Jammu and Kashmir Legislative Assembly Nov. 52; recognised by Pres. of India and assumed office 17 November 1952, re-elected 57 and 62, Gov. 65-67; Union Minister for Tourism and Civil Aviation 67-; Chancellor, Univ. Jammu and Kashmir State; Chancellor, Banaras Hindu Univ.; Chair. Central Sanskrit Board.
Ministry for Tourism, New Delhi, India.

Karandash, pseudonym of **Rumyantsev, Mikhail Nikolaevich**; Soviet circus actor; b. 06.
People's artist of the R.S.F.S.R.; awarded the Order of the Red Banner of Labour.
Films include *Karandash on Ice, Self-Confident Karandash, The Girl with Temper, Old Courtyard, High Reward, Ivan Nikulin.*
All Union Association of State Circuses, 4 Pushechnaya Street, Moscow, U.S.S.R.

Karanja, Dr. J. N., PH.D.; Kenyan diplomatist; b. 5 Feb. 1931; ed. Alliance High School, Kikuyu, Makerere Coll., Univ. of Delhi and Princeton Univ.
Lecturer in African Studies, Fairleigh Dickinson Univ., New Jersey, U.S.A. 61-62; Lecturer in African and Modern European History, Univ. of East Africa 62-63; High Commr. for Kenya in U.K. 63-, also accred. to Holy See 66-.
Kenya High Commission, 45 Portland Place, London, W.1; Home: Harambee House, Winnington Road, Hampstead, London, N.2, England.
Telephone: 01-636-2371.

Karaosmanoğlu, Yakup Kadri; Turkish writer and diplomatist; b. 89; ed. Univ. of Istanbul.
University Prof. 15-18; active in War of Independence; early collaborator of Kemal Ataturk; Chief Editor *Ikdam* 23-33; People's Party Dep. from Manisa 23-34; Diplomatic Service 34-56, Minister to Switzerland 42-49, 51-53, Ambassador to Iran 49-51, to Switzerland 53-56; Chief Leader Writer *Ulus* until 62; resigned from Republican People's Party 62.
c/o Ministry of Foreign Affairs, Ankara, Turkey.

Karavaeva, Anna Alexandrovna; Soviet writer; b. 93.
Member C.P.S.U.; State Prizewinner 50, two orders of Red Banner of Labour.
Publs. stories: *The Household* 26; *The Sawmill* 28, triology of novels: *Fires* 43, *On the Run* 46-48, *Native Hearth* 50, *Collected Works* in 5 vols. 57-58, *Facts of Life* 63; *World of Yesterday* (reminiscences) 64.
U.S.S.R. Union of Writers, Ul. Vorovskogo 52, Moscow, U.S.S.R.

Karavayev, Georgi Arkadievich; Soviet banker; b. 13; ed. Leningrad Water Transport Engineering Inst.
Member C.P.S.U. 40-; worker in building enterprises and ministries 35-57; Dep. Chair. Sverdlovsk Nat. Econ. Council for Construction 57-59; First Dep. Chair. State Cttee. for Construction 59-61; Chair. Stroibank (All-Union Capital Investment Bank) 61-63; First Dep. Chair. U.S.S.R. State Cttee. for Construction 63-67; Minister for Construction 67-; State Prize 50.
Ministry for Construction, Moscow, U.S.S.R.

Karayev, Kara Abulfas ogly; Soviet composer; b. 1918; ed. Moscow Conservatoire.
Member C.P.S.U. 49-; Chair. Azerbaijan Composers' Union; Sec. Soviet Composers' Union; mem. Azerbaijan Acad. of Sciences; State Prize 46, 48; People's Artist of the U.S.S.R. 59; Lenin Prize 67; Order of Red Banner of Labour (twice).
Principal compositions: *Song of the Heart* (Cantata for choir, symphony orch. and dance group) 37, Azerbaijan Suite for Symphony Orch. 39, First Symphony 44, *Veten* (Opera) 45, Second Symphony 46, *Leili and Medjun* (Symphonic poem) 47, *Seven Beauties* (Ballet) 52, *Albanian Rhapsody* 52, Choreographic Sketches for Symphony Orch. 53, *Viet-Nam* (Symphonic suite) 55, Prelude for Piano 57, *Thunder Path* (Ballet) 57, Three Nocturnes for Jazz Band 58, Sonata for Violin and Piano 60; incidental music for plays: *Masquerade, The Dancing Teacher, Othello, A Winter's Tale, The Crank, An Optimistic Tragedy;* incidental music for film, *Story of Caspian Oil Workers*, and others.
Azerbaijan Composers' Union, 58 Nizami Street, Baku, U.S.S.R.

Karch, George Frederick; American banker; b. 1 May 1907; ed. St. Lawrence Univ., Cleveland Law School and Rutgers Univ. Graduate School of Banking.
Cleveland Trust Co. 26-, mem. Exec. Cttee. 54-, Exec. Vice-Pres. 60-62, Pres. 62-66, Chair. and Pres. 66-; official of many other companies.
916 Euclid Avenue, Cleveland 1, Ohio, U.S.A.

Kardelj, Edward; Yugoslav politician; b. 27 Jan. 1910.
Qualified as teacher; later studied economics and political science; hon. mem. Slovene Acad. of Sciences and Art 49-; active mem. of Workers' Movement and of illegal Communist Party; imprisoned 30-32; lived abroad 34-37; helped organise Liberation Front of Slovenia and Yugoslavia 41; mem. G.H.Q. Nat. Army of Liberation 41; elected first Vice-Pres. of Nat. Cttee. of Liberation 43; entered Tito Govt. as Vice-Pres. and Min. for Constituent Assembly; Vice-Premier and Pres. Control Comm. 45-48; Vice-Premier 48; Chair. Foreign Affairs Cttee. 48-54, Co-ordination Cttee. 54-63; Vice-Pres. Fed. Exec. Council 53-63; Pres. Fed. Assembly 63-67; Sec. Cen. Cttee. of League of Communists of Yugoslavia 48-66; mem. of the Presidency of Cen. Cttee. of League of Communists 66-; mem. Council of Fed. 67-; Del. to Peace Conf. Paris 46; Head of Yugoslav Del. to UN Gen. Assembly 46, 48, 49, 50, 51; mem. Serbian Acad. of Science and Art 60.
Publs. *Development of the Slovene National Problem* 39 (revised and enlarged edn. 57), *The Paris Conference, The Road of New Yugoslavia, The Problems of Socialistic Development* (6 vols.), *Problems of Socialist Policy in the Countryside* 59, *Socialism and War* 60, *The New Constitution of Socialist Yugoslavia* 62, *Notes on Social Criticism in Yugoslavia.*
Council of the Federation, Belgrade, Yugoslavia.

Kardos, Tibor, PH.D.; Hungarian historian and philologist; b. 2 Aug. 1908; ed. Univs. of Pécs and Rome.
Pécs Teachers' Training Inst. 45; Dir. Hungarian Inst. in Rome 46; Prof. Italian Language and Literature, Lóránd Eötvös Univ. Budapest 59; mem. Hungarian Acad. of Sciences 53; mem. Exec. Council European Soc. for Culture; Kossuth Prize 56; Vice-Pres. Assoc. Int. Studi Lingua e Letteratura Italiana 65; Gold Medal 600th Anniversary of Dante.
Publs. *A laikus mozgalom magyar bibliája, Magyar Renaissance Irók, A magyar humanizmus kezdetei, Deákmüveltség és magyar renaissance, Az Albertiek Édenkertje, Per la filologia umanistica, Mattia Corvino re umanista, Középkori kultura, középkori költészet, A magyarság antik hagyományai, A trufa, A huszita biblia keletkezése, A magyarországi humanizmus kora, Dante alkotó képzelete, On the Historical Origins of "In Praise*

of Folly", Régi Magyar Drámai Emlékek I-II, Francis Bacon between two worlds, A Renaissance Magyarordgon, The Tragic Dilemma of Sir Thomas More, Dante összes müvei, L'umanesimo di Dante tra Medioevo e Rinascimento, Petrarca e la formazione dell'umanesimo ungherese, Az Argirus-széphistórica, Studi e ricerche umanistiche italo-ungheresi I.
Lóránd Eötvös University, Pesti Barnabás u. 1, Budapest, and Budapest V, Stollár B-u. 3/a, Hungary.
Telephone: 115-119.

Karefa-Smart, John Musselman, B.A., B.SC., M.D., C.M., D.T.M., M.P.H., M.R.S.H.; Sierra Leonean politician and physician; b. 17 June 1915; ed. Fourah Bay and Otterbein Colls., McGill and Harvard Univs.
Lecturer, Union Coll., Bunumbu 36-38; ordained Elder of Evangelical United Brethren Church 38; Medical Officer, R.C.A.M.C. 43-45; Sierra Leone Missions Hospitals 46-48; Lecturer, Ibadan Univ. Coll. (Nigeria) 49-52; Health Officer, W.H.O. 52-55, Leader Del. to W.H.O. 56 and 59; mem. House of Reps. 57-64; Minister of Lands and Survey 57-59; Africa Consultant, World Council of Churches 55-56; Minister for External Affairs 60-64; Asst. Prof. Columbia Univ. 64-65; Asst. Dir.-Gen. World Health Org., Geneva 65-; Commdr. Order of Star of Africa (Liberia); Knight Grand Band, Order of African Redemption (Liberia); Grand Cordon, Order of the Cedar (Lebanon); Hon. LL.D. (Otterbein); Hon. LL.D. (McGill); Hon. LL.D. (Boston); Sierra Leone All People's Congress.
Publ. *The Halting Kingdom* 59.
World Health Organisation, Geneva, Switzerland.
Telephone: 34-60-61(022).

Karelskaya, Rimma Klavdievna; Soviet ballet dancer; b. 1927; ed. Moscow Ballet School of Bolshoi Theatre.
Joined Bolshoi Ballet 46; has toured with Bolshoi Ballet in Britain, Australia, Belgium, China, Netherlands, New Zealand, United Arab Republic, Poland, German Federal Republic, France, Czechoslovakia and Japan; Honoured Artist of R.S.F.S.R. 62.
Main roles include: Raymonda (*Raymonda* by Glazunov), Laurencia (*Laurencia* by Krein), Lilac Fairy (*Sleeping Beauty* by Tchaikovsky), Sovereign of the Dryads and Street Dancer (*Don Quixote* by Minkus), Mirta (*Giselle* by Adan), Odette-Odille (*Swan Lake* by Tchaikovsky), Zaremba (*Fountains of Bakhchisarai* by Asafyev), Firebird (*Firebird* by Stravinsky), the Servant Girl (*Thunder Road* by Kara Karayev), Tsar Devitsa (*Humpbacked Horse* by Pugni), the Swan (*Dying Swan* by Saint-Saëns).
State Academic Bolshoi Theatre of U.S.S.R., Ploshchad Sverdlova 1, Moscow, U.S.S.R.

Kargin, Valentin Alekseevich; Soviet chemist; b. 23 Jan. 1907; ed. Moscow State Lomonosov Univ.
Research staff, Karpov Physico-Chemical Inst. 27-36; Chief of Laboratory of Colloid Chemistry 37-55; Corresp. mem. U.S.S.R. Acad. of Sciences 46-53, mem. 53-; Prof. Moscow State Univ. 54-; Chief of Chair. of Macromolecular Compounds 55-; Ed. in Chief Soviet Journal of Polymer Chemistry and Physics 59-; mem. Macromolecular Comm., Int. Union of Pure and Applied Chemistry (IUPAC) 57-; Chair. Scientific Council on Macromolecular Compounds, U.S.S.R. Acad. of Sciences 63-; Order of Lenin (twice), Order of Red Banner of Labour (twice), State Prize Laureate (three times), Lenin Prize, Hero of Socialist Labour 66-.
Publs. *Brief Essays on the Physical Chemistry of Polymers* 60, over 400 papers.
Karpov Institute for Physical Chemistry, Ulitsa Obukha 10, Moscow, U.S.S.R.

Kargopolov, Mikhail Ivanovich; Soviet mathematician; b. 1928; ed. Urals Univ.
Postgraduate, Lecturer Perm Univ. 53-60; Senior Research Assoc. Inst. of Mathematics, Siberian branch U.S.S.R. Acad. of Sciences 60-; Prof. 64; mem. C.P.S.U. 65-; Corresp. mem. U.S.S.R. Acad. of Sciences 66-.
U.S.S.R. Academy of Sciences, 14 Lenin Prospekt, Moscow, U.S.S.R.

Karjalainen, Ahti, PH.D.; Finnish economist and politician; b. 10 Feb. 1923; ed. Helsinki Univ.
Prime Minister's Sec. 50-56; Minister of Finance 57-58, of Trade and Industry 59-61, of Foreign Affairs 61-62, Prime Minister 62-63; mem. Board of Govs., Bank of Finland 58-; Minister of Foreign Affairs 64-; mem. Parl. 66-.
Ministry of Foreign Affairs, Helsinki 17, Finland; Home: Perustie 13, Helsinki 33, Finland.
Telephone: 48-45-48.

Karlgren, Klas Bernhard Johannes, DR.PHIL.; Swedish orientalist; b. 5 Oct. 1889; ed. Uppsala and Paris.
Prof. of Far Eastern Languages Göteborg Univ. until 39; Prof. and Dir. Museum of Far Eastern Antiquities Stockholm 39-59; mem. Acad. of Sciences Stockholm, Acad. of History and Belles-Lettres Stockholm, Acad. of Sciences Copenhagen, Oslo; hon. mem. Royal Asiatic Society of Great Britain and Ireland, Société Asiatique Paris; corresp. mem. Acad. des Inscriptions Paris.
Publs. *Etudes sur la Phonologie Chinoise* 15-26, *Analytic Dictionary of Chinese, Sound and Symbol in Chinese* 23, *Philology and Ancient China* 26, *Yin and Chou in Chinese Bronzes* 36, *New Studies on Chinese Bronzes* 37, *Grammata Serica* 40, *Huai and Han* 41, *Glosses on the Odes* (1-3) 42, 44, 46, *The Book of Odes* 44, 45, *Some Weapons and Tools of the Yin Dynasty* 45, *Legends and Cults in Ancient China* 46, *Glosses on the Book of Documents I* 48, *II* 49, *The Book of Documents* 50, *Notes on the Grammar of Early Bronze Décor* 51, *Excursions in Chinese Grammar* 51, *A Catalogue of the Chinese Bronzes in the Alfred F. Pillsbury Collection* 52, *Compendium of Phonetics in Ancient and Archaic Chinese* 54, *Grammata Serica Recensa* 57, *Marginalia on some Bronze Albums* I, II, 59, 60, *Some Characteristics of the Yin Art* 62, *Loan Characters in pre-Han Texts* I-III, 63-65.
c/o Museum of Far Eastern Antiquities, Stockholm 100, Sweden.

Karling, John S., M.A., PH.D., F.R.S.A.; American mycologist; b. 2 Aug. 1899; ed. Univ. of Texas and Columbia Univ.
Dean, Texas Wesleyan Coll. 20; Instructor, Univ. of Texas 21; Columbia Univ. Fellow in Botany; Asst. Prof. 26-35; Assoc. Prof. 35-48; Prof. of Botany and Chair. Dept. of Biological Sciences, Purdue Univ. 48-59, John Wright Distinguished Prof. of Biological Sciences 59-65, Emeritus Prof. 65-; Physiologist, Tropical Research Foundation 25-27; Dir. Chicle Research Experimental Station, British Honduras 27-32; Field Dir. Exploration Dept. U.S. Govt. Rubber Development Corpn., Brazil 42-43; Bermuda Biological Research Fellow 42; Prof. of Botany, Columbia Univ.; Consulting Botanist, American Chicle Co.; Sec. Botanical Soc. of America 45-50; Vice-Pres. 50-51; Sec. Union of American Biological Socs. 46-48; Vice-Pres. American Asscn. for Advancement of Science 50; Chair. Section G, A.A.A.S. 50; Research Fellow Int. Indian Ocean Expedition 63; Visiting Sir C. V. Raman Lecturer, Univ. of Madras 65; Fulbright Research Fellow, New Zealand 65-66; Dir. Ross Biological Reserve, Purdue Univ.
Publs. *The Plasmodiophorales* 42, *The Simple Biflagellate Halocarpic Phycomycetes* 42, *Synchytrium* 63.
Home: 1219 Tuckahoe Lane, West Lafayette, Ind., U.S.A.

Karmen, Roman Lazarevich; Soviet film director and cameraman; b. 06; ed. Moscow Cinematographic Inst.
State prize winner, Lenin prize winner 60, Order of Lenin, People's Artist of R.S.F.S.R. 65, People's Artist of U.S.S.R. 66.

Principal films: *Spanish Events* 36-37, *Spain* 39, *China Struggles* 39, *Day of the New World* 40, *War-time Leningrad* 42, *Judgment of the Nations* 46, *People's Court* 46, *Soviet Turkmenistan* 51, *Viet-Nam* 55, *India's Morning* 56, *Vast is my Land* 58, *Subjugators of the Sea* 59, *Guest from Island of Freedom* 63, *Great Patriotic War* 65.
Studio of Documentary Films, 6 Likhov Street, Moscow, U.S.S.R.

Karnes, William George; American businessman; b. 24 March 1911; ed. Univ. of Ill. and Northwestern Univ.
Admitted to Ill. bar 36; Attorney, Law Dept., Beatrice Foods Co. 36-39, Head, Employee Relations Dept. 39-43, Asst. to Pres. 43-47, Dir. 47-, Exec. Vice-Pres. 48-52, Pres. 52-; Dir. Borg-Warner Corpn., Vaughan Seed Co., Inland Life Insurance Co., La Salle National Bank Motta S.p.A.
120 S. La Salle Street, Chicago 3, Ill. (Office); Butterfield Lane, Flossmoor, Ill., U.S.A.

Karp, David, B.S.S.; American writer; b. 5 May 1922; ed. City Coll. of the City of New York.
Continuity Dir. Station W.N.Y.C., New York 48-49; free-lance writer 49-; Guggenheim Fellowship for creative writing 56-57; mem. editorial board *Television Quarterly* 65-; mem. Council, Writers' Guild of America, West, Inc. 67-; Pres. Leda Productions, Inc. 68-; Emmy Award by Acad. of Television Arts and Sciences 64-65.
Publs. *One* 53, *The Day of the Monkey* 55, *All Honorable Men* 56, *Leave me Alone* 57, *The Sleepwalkers* 60, *Vice-President in Charge of Revolution* (with M. D. Lincoln) 60, *The Last Believers* 64, *Café Univers* (play) 67; also contributed many articles and reviews to magazines and has written for radio, cinema and television.
1116 Corsica Drive, Pacific Palisades, Calif. 90272, U.S.A.

Karpenko, Mikhail Panteleyevich; Soviet politician; b. 1908; ed. Omsk Inst. of Agriculture.
Member C.P.S.U. 38-; Agronomist 28-40; Party Official, Kazakhstan 40-61; First Sec. Semipalatinsk Regional Cttee., C.P. of Kazakhstan 61-; mem. Central Cttee., C.P. of Kazakhstan; Deputy to U.S.S.R. Supreme Soviet.
Semipalatinsk Regional Committee, Communist Party of Kazakhstan, Semipalatinsk, U.S.S.R.

Karpinski, Zygmunt, LL.D.; Polish economist; b. 92.
Former Man. Dir. Bank of Poland, Chief of Foreign Dept.; Chair. Foreign Exchange Control Cttee. 36-39; Man. Nat Bank of Poland 46-50; mem. Polish Del. to Int. Conf., Bretton Woods 44, Savannah (Ga.) 46; Adviser to Pres. of Nat. Bank of Poland 50-.
Narodowy Bank Polski, Warsaw, Poland.

Karpova, Yevdokia Fyodorovna; Soviet politician; b. 1923; ed. Moscow Textile Inst.
Member C.P.S.U. 52-; Chief, textile laboratory 49-54; trade-union worker 54-56; Second, then First Sec. Yegoryevsk City Cttee. of C.P., Moscow Region 56-61; in Moscow Regional Cttee. of C.P. 61-63; in Central Cttee. C.P.S.U. 63-65; Deputy Minister of Light Industry 65-66; Vice-Chair. Council of Ministers of R.S.F.S.R. 66-; Candidate mem. Central Cttee. C.P.S.U. 66-; Deputy to R.S.F.S.R. Supreme Soviet.
Council of Ministers of R.S.F.S.R., 3 Delegatskaya Street, Moscow, U.S.S.R.

Karrer, Paul, PH.D.; Swiss chemist; b. 21 April 1889; Univ. of Zürich.
Professor of Chemistry, Zürich Univ. 18-; Prof. Emer., Univ. of Zürich 59-; Foreign mem. Royal Soc. (U.K.); awarded Nobel Chemistry Prize for Research on Carotinoides and Flavins and Vitamins A and B2 37.
Publs. *Einführung in die Chemie der polymeren Kohlenhydrate* 25, *Lehrbuch der organischen Chemie* 30, 54,

59, *Carotinoide* 48, and numerous publs. on vitamins, plant dyes, alkaloids and other natural products.
Spyristeig 30, Zürich, Switzerland.

Karsh, Yousuf; Canadian (b. Armenian) photographer; b. 23 Dec. 1908; ed. Sherbrooke, Quebec and School of Art and Design, Boston, Mass.
Photo apprenticeship to John Garo of Boston; arrived in Canada from Armenia-in-Turkey 23; specialised in portrait photography; Citizen 46; LL.D. (Queen's Univ., Kingston, Ont., and Carleton Univ.), Hon. D.H.L. (Hanover and Ohio); Canada Council Medal 65.
Publs. *Faces of Destiny* 46, *This is the Mass* (English and French editions), *This is Rome* 59, *Portraits of Greatness* 59, *This is the Holy Land* 61, *In Search of Greatness* (autobiog.) 62, *These are the Sacraments* (co-author) 63, *The Warren Court* 64 (co-author), *Karsh Portfolio* 67.
130 Sparks St., Ottawa, Ont., Canada.

Karsten, Christian Friedrich, DR. ECON.; Netherlands banker; b. 17; ed. Netherlands Economic Univ.
Posts in insurance and industry 40-45; Economist, Rotterdamsche Bank N.V. 45-48, Sec. to Managing Dirs. 48-52, Asst. Managing Dir. 52-55, Managing Dir. 55-65, Amsterdam-Rotterdam Bank 65-; Dir. other companies; Knight, Order of Netherlands Lion.
Publs. *Het Amerikaanse Bankwezen* 52, *Banking without Cheques* 58, *Competition between Commercial Banks and Other Financial Institutions* 60, *De rol van de banken bij de industriefinanciering* 62, *EWG-Perspektiven des Bankwesens* 63, *Transfer Systems* 64, *Should Europe Restrict U.S. Investments?* 65.
Amsterdam-Rotterdam Bank N.V., Coolsingel 119, Rotterdam, Netherlands.

Kartavykh, Alexander Grigorovich; Soviet politician; b. 24.
Worked in Kuznetsk Metallurgical Combine 40-; mem. Communist Party of Soviet Union 53-; mem. Presidium of Supreme Soviet of U.S.S.R. 58-66; Hero of Socialist Labour.
Novokuznetzk Iron and Steel Works, U.S.S.R.

Karttunen, Osmo P., LL.LIC.; Finnish businessman and politician; b. 8 Nov. 1922; ed. Lyceum of Kuopio and Univ. of Helsinki.
Assistant Dir. H. Saastamoinen & Pojat Oy 46-51, Man. Dir. 52-; Man. Dir. H. Saastamoinen Oy 61-, Chair. 66-; Chair. Finnish Wholesalers' Asscn. 60-, Admin. Board, Tukkukauppojen Oy 62-, Admin. Board Eläkevakuutus Oy Ilmarinen 63-, Oy Uusi Suomi 63-; Minister of Finance 62-63; Pres. Finnish Football Asscn.; Finnish Liberty Cross, Commdr. of the Order of the White Rose of Finland, German Eagle Order, Stella Della Solidarietä, Gran Croce dell' Ordine Al Merito (Italy).
Kumpusaair, Kuopio, Finland.
Telephone: 14780 and 81555.

Karume, Sheikh Abeid Amani; Tanzanian politician; b. 06.
Former boatboy, Zanzibar waterfront; joined British Seamen's Union; Pres. Afro-Shirazi Party; Pres. of People's Republic of Zanzibar Jan-April 64; First Vice-Pres. of United Republic of Tanzania April 64-.
Office of the First Vice-President, United Republic of Tanzania, Dar es Salaam, Tanzania.

Kasatkina, Natalia Dmitrievna; Soviet ballet dancer; b. 1934; ed. Bolshoi Theatre Ballet School.
Joined Bolshoi Theatre Ballet Company 54.
Main roles include: Etruscan Dance (*Spartacus*), Gypsy Girl (*Don Quixote*), and in *Legend of Love*, *Nutcracker Suite*.
Author (with V. Vasilyov) of Bolshoi Ballets: *Vanina Vanini* 62, *Heroic Poem* 64, *Rites of Sacred Spring* 65.
State Academic Bolshoi Theatre of U.S.S.R., 1 Ploshchad Sverdlova, Moscow, U.S.S.R.

Kasatonov, Admiral Vladimir Afanasievich; Soviet naval officer; b. 1910; ed. Naval Acad.
Naval service 27; Commanding and Staff posts 31-; with Gen. Staff 45-55; Commdr. Black Sea and N. Fleets 55-56; First Deputy C.-in-C. Soviet Navy 64-; Deputy to U.S.S.R. Supreme Soviet.
Ministry of Defence, 34 Maurice Thorez Embankment, Moscow, U.S.S.R.

Kasavubu, Joseph; Congolese politician; b. 1913; ed. Roman Catholic mission schools, Belgian Congo.
Studied for the priesthood at Mbata-Keila and Kabwe Seminaries, but later abandoned his studies and subsequently worked as a teacher 41-59, an agronomist and a civil servant; Editor *Le Droit du premier occupant*; Pres. Abako (Asscn. of the Lower Congo) 55-; Mayor of Dendale (Léopoldville) 58-59; arrested following Jan. 59 riots and imprisoned for two months; Pres. Congo (Léopoldville) June 60-65; Senator for Life 66-; C.-in-C. Congolese Nat. Army 60-65.
Publ. *Manifesto Abako* 56.
Boma, Congo (Kinshasa).

Kaschnitz, Marie Luise von; German poet and writer; b. 31 Jan. 1901; ed. girls' colls. Potsdam and Berlin.
Member P.E.N., Deutsche Akademie für Sprache und Dichtung, Akademie der Wissenschaften und der Literatur, Mainz; Büchnerpreis 55, Immermannpreis 57, Preis des Kulturkreises der deutschen Industrie.
Publs. *Liebe beginnt* (novel) 33, *Elissa* (novel) 36, *Griechische Mythen* (essays) 42, *Von Menschen und Dingen* (essays) 46, *Totentanz und Gedichte* 48, *Courbet* (biography) 49, *Zukunftsmusik* (poems) 52, *Ewige Stadt* (poems) 52, *Engelsbrücke: Römische Betrachtungen* 55, *Haus der Kindheit* 56, *Neue Gedichte* 57, *Lange Schatten* (short stories) 60, *Dein Schweigen, Meine Stimme* (poems) 62, *Uberallnie* 66; Radio plays 62, *Wohin denn ich* 63, *Ein Wort weiter* (poems) 65, *Ferngespräche* (short stories) 66, *Beschreibung eines Dorfes* 66.
Wiesenau 8, Frankfurt/Main, German Federal Republic.

Käser, Helmut Alfred; Swiss lawyer and sports administrator; b. 12; ed. Commercial High School, Neuchâtel, and Univs. of Berne and Zürich.
Lawyer, Zürich court; fmr. lawyer, Ministry of Economics; Gen. Sec., Swiss Football Asscn. 42-60; Gen. Sec. Fédération Internationale de Football Association (FIFA) 61-.
Publ. *Untersuchungen über den Begriff des Ersatzwertes in der Versicherung* 37.
Hitzigweg 11, 8032 Zürich, Switzerland.

Kašlik, Václav; Czechoslovak composer and conductor; b. 28 Sept. 1917; ed. Faculty of Philosophy, Charles Univ., Prague, Prague Conservatoire and Conductors' Master School, Prague.
Conductor, E. F. Burian Theatre, Prague 40-41; Asst. Dir. Nat. Theatre, Prague 41-43; Chief of Opera Ensemble, Opera of May 5th 45-48; Conductor, Smetana Theatre, Prague 52-62; tours include New York, Leningrad, Moscow, Vienna, Munich; Klement Gottwald State Prize 56; Honoured Artist 58.
Works: Operas: *Robbers' Ballad* 44, *Calvary* 50, *Krakatit* 60; ballets: *Don Juan* 39, *Janošík* 51, *Prague Carnival* 52; Dir. of operas: *The Water Nymph* (Dvořák), Vienna 65, *Julietta* (Martinu), Hanover 66, *Albergo dei Poveri* (Testi), Milan 66; work for TV, Magic Lantern Theatre: *Hoffman's Tales* 62.
National Theatre, Prague, Czechoslovakia.

Kasman, Leon; Polish journalist and politician; b. 05.
Member Central Cttee. Polish United Workers' Party; Editor *Trybuna Wolności* (Liberty Tribune), later Manager publishing co-operative 45-48; Deputy Chair. Central Office of Planning 48-54; Deputy Minister of Light Industry 54; First Deputy Manager, State Cttee.

of Econ. Planning 55-56; Chief Editor *Trybuna Ludu* (People's Tribune) 57-Dec. 67; mem. Seym 61.
Trybuna Ludu, 7/9 Starynkiewicz Square, Warsaw, Poland.

Kassák, Lajos; Hungarian writer and painter; b. 1887.
Founded cultural magazines *Tett* and *Ma*; emigrated to Vienna, returned to Hungary 27; Kossuth Prize.
Publs. *The Life of Man* (Autobiographical novel in 8 vols.); *Angyalföld, Menekülök, Egy Kosár gyümölcs, Emberek, Sorsok* (novels); *Boldogtalan testvérek* (Unhappy Brothers).
c/o Association of Hungarian Writers, Bajza u. 18, Budapest VI, Hungary.

Kassimatis, Grigorios, D. EN D., DR.RER.POL.; Greek professor and politician; b. 16 March 1906; ed. Univ. of Athens and Univ. de Paris à la Sorbonne.
Practised law 27-37; Under-Sec. for Finance (resigned) 36; in concentration camp during Second World War; Assoc. Prof. Salonica Law School, then Prof. Panteios School 37-46; Assoc. Prof. of Civil Law, Law School of Univ. of Athens 39, Prof. of Civil and Labour Law and Social Politics 41; Prof. of Social Studies and Labour Law, Higher Industrial School, Athens 59; Assoc. Prof. Univ. of Paris; Minister of Finance and Public Welfare and Acting Minister for Labour and Justice in Govts. of P. Voularis and Archbishop Damaskinos, then Minister of Finance and Acting Minister of Agriculture in P. Kanellopoulos Govt. 45; Minister without Portfolio as Under-Sec. of Press and Information and Acting Minister of Justice and Finance, then Minister of Labour and Acting Minister for Public Works 50, Minister of Industry 51, of Labour 51-52; Minister without Portfolio and Acting Minister for Co-ordination 56-58; Minister of Educ. and Religion 61-63, of Educ. 67; Deputy of Athens 46, and as an Independent 50, for Liberal Party 51; for Nat. Radical Union 56, 58, 61, 63, 64-; Head of Greek Cttee. to UN 56-57; Rep. of Greece to Int. Bank of Reconstruction and Devt.—World Bank (IBRD) 57, 58; Dr. h.c. Univs. of Aix and Bari.
Publs. Several books and articles.
c/o Ministry of Education, Athens, Greece.

Kassirsky, Iosif Abramovich; Soviet internist and hematologist; b. 1898; ed. Saratov Univ.
Service in Red Army 19-20; Intern, Asst., Prof. Medical Faculty, Cen. Asia Univ. 21-34; Head of Dept., Consulting Prof., Cen. Inst. for Postgraduate Medical Training 34-; Corresp. mem. U.S.S.R. Acad. of Medical Sciences 57-63, mem. 63-; mem. of Boards of All-Union and Moscow Socs. of Internists; Chair. Hematological Section of Moscow Soc. of Internists; mem. Exec. Cttee. of Int. Soc. for Hematology; Order of Lenin 51, 61; Badge of Honour 45; Honoured Scientist of Uzbek S.S.R.
Publs. Over 210 works on hematology, rheumatology and cardiology.
Central Institute for Postgraduate Medical Training, Vosstaniya Square 1/2, Moscow, U.S.S.R.

Kastler, Alfred; French physicist; b. 3 May 1902; ed. Ecole Normale Supérieure.
Taught in lycées at Mulhouse, Colmar, Bordeaux 26-31; Asst. at the Faculty of Sciences, Univ. of Bordeaux 31-36, Prof. 38-41; Lecturer Faculty of Science, Univ. of Clermont-Ferrand 36-38; Prof. of Physics, Ecole Normale Supérieure, Paris 41-; at Univ. of Louvain, Belgium 53-54; mem. Management Board, Centre Nat. de la Recherche Scientifique (CNRS), Dir. of its atomic clock laboratory; mem. Inst. de France; Officier Légion d'Honneur; Holweck Medal and Prize, Physical Soc., U.K. 54, Nobel Prize for Physics 66; Dr. h.c. Univs. of Louvain, Pisa, Oxford and Edinburgh.
1 Rue du Val-de-Grâce, Paris 5e, France.
Telephone: 326-17-88.

Kästner, Erhart, DR. PHIL.; German librarian and author; b. 13 March 1904; ed. Humanistisches Gymnasium St.-Anna, Augsburg, Albert-Ludwigs-Universität, Freiburg im Breisgau, and Universität Leipzig.
Staatsbibliothek, Dresden 28-45; Sec. to Gerhart Hauptmann 36-38; War Service and Prisoner-of-War 40-47; Dir. Herzog August Bibliothek, Wolfenbüttel 50-; Immermann Preis 55; Literaturpreis der Stadt Köln 57.
Publs. *Zeltbuch von Tumilad* 49, *Studentrommel vom heiligen Berg Athos* 53, *Ölberge, Weinberge* 56, *Die Lerchenschule* 64.
Herzog August Bibliothek, 334 Wolfenbüttel, Postfach 227, German Federal Republic.
Telephone: 05331-22561 and 05331-26652.

Kästner, Erich, DR. PHIL.; German author; b. 23 Feb. 1899; ed. Univs. of Berlin, Leipzig and Rostock.
Publs. Poems: *Herz auf Taille* 28, *Lärm im Spiegel* 29, *Ein Mann gibt Auskunft* 30, *Gesang zwischen den Stühlen* 32, *Dr. Erich Kästners Lyrische Hausapotheke* 36, *Bei Durchsicht meiner Bücher* 46, *Die 13 Monate* 55, *Eine Auswahl* 56, *Let's Face It* 63; children's books (stories and verse): *Emil und die Detektive* 28, *Pünktchen und Anton* 31, *Der 35 Mai* 31, *Arthur mit dem langen Arm* 32, *Das verhexte Telefon* 32, *Das fliegende Klassenzimmer* 33, *Emil und die drei Zwillinge* 34, *Till Eulenspiegel* 38, *Das doppelte Lottchen* 49, *Der gestiefelte Kater* 50, *Münchhausen* 51, *Die Schildbürger* 54, *Don Quichotte* 56, *Gullivers Reisen* 61, *Das Schreien beim Friseur* 62, *Der Klein Mann* 63, *Gullivers Reisen* 64, *Der Kleine Mann und die Kleine Miss* 67; novels: *Fabian* 31, *Drei Männer im Schnee* 34, *Die verschwundene Miniatur* 35, *Georg und die Zwischenfälle* 38; other works: *Leben in dieser Zeit* (radio and stage play) 30, *Kurz und Bündig* (epigrams) 48, *Der tägliche Kram* (songs and prose) 48, *Die Konferenz der Tiere* (picture-book) 49, *Die Kleine Freiheit* (songs and prose) 52, *Die Schule der Diktatoren* (play) 56, *Als ich ein kleiner Junge war* (autobiography) 57, *Gesammelte Schriften* 59, *Notabene* 45, 61, *Kästner für Erwachsene* 66.
Flemingstrasse 52, Munich 81, German Federal Republic.

Kasum-Zade, Mamed Dzhavad Sulaiman Ogly, M.ENG.; Soviet engineer; b. 1911; ed. Azerbaijan Industrial Inst. and Moscow Oil Academy.
Soviet army service 36-38; with Azneft (Azerbaijan Oil Corpn.) 38-54; mem. C.P.S.U. 41-; Dep. Minister Oil Industry, Azerbaijan 56-58, First Dep. Minister 58-59; Dep. Dir. of Research, Azerbaijan Research Inst. of Oil Extraction 59-; Lenin Prize 61.
Azerbaijan Research Institute of Oil Extraction, Baku, Azerbaijan S.S.R., U.S.S.R.

Kataev, Valentin Petrovich; Soviet novelist; b. 1897; ed. Odessa.
Served army 15-17, Red Army 18-20; began full-time literary work in Moscow 22; mem. Praesidium, Union of Soviet Writers 53-; State prize 46; Order of Lenin, Order of Red Banner of Labour 57.
Publs. *Otets* (Father) 25, *Rastratchiki* (The Embezzlers) 26, *Vremya vperyod!* (Forward, O Time!) 32, *Beleet parus odinokii* (Lone White Sail) 36, *Ya syn trudovogo naroda* (I, Son of the Working People) 37, *Syn Polka* (Son of the Regiment) 45, *Za vlast Sovetov* (For Soviet Power) 49, 51, *The Hamlet in the Steppe* 56, *Winter Wind* 60; plays: *Kvadratura Kruga* (Squaring the Circle) 28, *Avangard* (The Vanguard) 29, *Peace to Huts, War to Palaces* 60, *Waves of the Black Sea* 61, *Time of Love* 62, *Hearths of the People* 62, *Werewolf* 63, *Small Iron Door in a Wall* 64.
Union of Soviet Writers, Ul. Vorovskogo 52, Moscow, U.S.S.R.

Kataoka, Takenobu; Japanese business executive; b. 16 March 1902; ed. Keio Univ.
Asahi Silk Weaving Co. 30, later Japan Nitrogen Chemical Co.; Dir. Asahi Chemical Industry Co. 47-, then Manager Dir., Pres. 49-62, Chair. 62-.
Asahi Chemical Industry Co., Shin Osaka Building, 25-1 Dojimahamadori 1-chome, Kita-ku, Osaka, Japan.

Katari, Vice-Admiral Ram Dass; Indian naval officer; b. 8 Oct. 1911; ed. Mahboob Coll., Secunderabad, Niazm Coll., Hyderabad and Training Ship *Dufferin*, Bombay.
Served with Hooghly River Survey; joined Indian navy; war service in Atlantic and Indian Ocean; Chief of Personnel Naval H.Q. 49-51; Imperial Defence Coll., London 53; Deputy Chief of Naval Staff, Indian Navy 54-55; Flag Officer (Flotilla), Indian Fleet 56-58; Chief of Naval Staff 58-62; Chair. Andhra Pradesh State Road Transport Corpn. 62-64; Ambassador to Burma 64-.
Indian Embassy, Rangoon, Burma.

Katayama, Tetsu; Japanese lawyer and politician; b. 87; ed. Law Coll. of Imperial Univ.
Lecturer at Tokyo Women's Coll.; helped to organise Social Democratic Party 26, and its successor, the Social Mass Party 31; elected eight times to House of Representatives before 56; protested against invasion of Manchuria and continuation of war in China; was compelled by the Govt. to retire from politics until defeat of Japan; Sec.-Gen. of Nippon Shakai To (Social Democratic Party) Nov. 45; Chair. of same Feb. 47; elected to the Diet 46; re-elected April 47; Prime Minister of Japan May 47-March 48; Chair. Nat. League for Safeguarding New Constitution 47-.
Publs. *The Development of the Socialist Movement in Japan,* and *The Legal Status of Women,* etc.
2-48 Todoroki-cho, Tamagawa, Setagaya-ku, Tokyo, Japan.

Katchalsky, Aharon; Polish-born Israeli chemist; b. Sept. 1914; ed. Hebrew Univ. of Jerusalem.
Asst. Hebrew Univ. of Jerusalem 40-46; research in Switzerland with Prof. Werner Kuhn 46-47; on staff of Weizmann Inst. of Science 48-, now Head Polymer Dept.; Prof. of Physical Chemistry Hebrew Univ. of Jerusalem 52; Pres. Israeli Acad. of Science 62-; Vice-Pres. Int. Union for Pure and Applied Biophysics, Pres. 64; Fellow New York Acad. of Science; foreign mem. American Acad. of Arts and Sciences; mem. Int. Council for Macromolecular Research, Editorial Board *Journal of Polymer Science* and *Biochim. Biophys. Acta*; Hon. D.S. (Clarkson Coll); Weizmann Prize 54; Israel Prize 62.
Publs. numerous papers.
Weizmann Institute of Science, Rehovoth, Israel.
Telephone: 952721.

Katchen, Julius, B.A.; American concert pianist; b. 15 Aug. 1926; ed. Haverford Coll., Penn.
First concert (with Eugene Ormandy and Philadelphia Orch.) 37; European debut at UNESCO Festival, Paris 46; toured throughout the world; first pianist to play complete works of Brahms in four recitals.
3 bis avenue Franco-Russe, Paris 7e, France.

Katenga, Bridger Winston; Malawi (b. Zambia) social worker and diplomatist; b. 1926; ed. Ndola Govt. School, and Jan Hofmeyr School of Social Science, Johannesburg.
Social Welfare Officer, Ndola Municipality, N. Rhodesia 51; Vice-Pres. Municipal Workers' Trade Union of N. Rhodesia 51; later Probation Officer, Kitwe, N. Rhodesia; studied social services in U.K. 58-59; Social Welfare Officer, Ministry of Social Devt., Zomba 59, later Sec. for Community and Social Devt.; Amb. of Malawi to Ethiopia 64-66; Perm. Rep. of Malawi to UN 66-.
Permanent Mission of Malawi to the United Nations, 777 Third Avenue, New York, N.Y. 10017, U.S.A.

Katilungu, Simon; Zambian diplomatist; b. 1 Nov. 1924; ed. Kasama, Munali Secondary School, Lusaka. Formerly with Rhokana Corpn. Ltd.; fmr. Senior Research Asst., Rhodes-Livingstone Inst., N. Rhodesia; staff of U.S. Information Service, N. Rhodesia; posts in United Nat. Ind. Party (U.N.I.P.) 61-64; High Commr. of Zambia in U.K. 64-67, also accred. to Holy See 65-67.
c/o Department of Foreign Affairs, Lusaka, Zambia.

Kato, Goichi; Japanese shipbuilding executive; b. 26 Aug. 1891; ed. Tokyo Univ.
Chief, Chinan Branch, Mitsui Products Co. 18, later transferred to Mitsui Shipbuilding Co., Chief, Shanghai Yard, Pres. 47-60, Chair. 60-; Financial Dir. Japan Employers' Asscn.
Mitsui Shipbuilding and Engineering Co., 2-1-1 Muro-machi, Nihonbashi, Chou-ku, Tokyo, Japan.

Kato, Tadao; Japanese diplomatist; b. 13 May 1916; ed. Tokyo Univ. and Cambridge Univ.
Consul, Singapore 52; First Sec., London 53; Counsellor, Econ. Affairs Bureau, Foreign Office 56-59; Counsellor, Wash. 60-63; Deputy Dir. Econ. Affairs Bureau, Foreign Office 63-66, Dir. 66-67; Amb. to Org. for European Co-operation and Devt. (OECD) 67-.
54 avenue Sainte-Foy, Neuilly (Hauts-de-Seine), France.
Telephone: 722-28-06.

Katona, János; Hungarian diplomatist; b. 11.
Leather worker and Chair. Leather Workers Union before 39; active in resistance during 39-45 war; apptd. Lord Lieut. of Györ-Moson County 45, later Deputy Mayor of Budapest; has worked for Ministry of Foreign Affairs since 49; Counsellor in Washington 49-50; Chargé d'Affaires to Sweden, Norway and Denmark 50-52, Minister 52-53; Minister to Great Britain 53-57; Ambassador to Poland 57-60, to Kenya, Tanzania and Uganda 65-; Order of Labour and Order of Liberty; Order of the Red Banner.
Hungarian Embassy, Nairobi, Kenya.

Katushev, Konstantin Fyodorovich; Soviet politician; b. 1927; ed. Gorky Zhdanov Polytechnic Inst.
Member C.P.S.U. 52-; at Gorky Motor Works 51-57; Party Official 57-63; First Sec. Gorky City Cttee., C.P.S.U. 63-65, Gorky Regional Cttee., C.P.S.U. 65-68; Sec. for Cen. Cttee. of C.P. responsible for relations with other Communist countries 68-; mem. Cen. Cttee. C.P.S.U.; Deputy to U.S.S.R. Supreme Soviet.
Central Committee of C.P.S.U., Moscow, U.S.S.R.

Katz, Benzion, PH.D. (*pseudonym* Benshalom); Israeli university professor; b. 1 Feb. 1907; ed. Univ. of Cracow, Poland.
Lecturer Univ. of Cracow 29-39, Inst. of Judaica, Warsaw 37-39; Dir. Youth Dept. Jewish Agency, Jerusalem 40-63; Lecturer, Univ. of Tel Aviv 56-61, Assoc. Prof. 61-63, Prof. 63-, Dean, Faculty of Humanities 59-64, Vice-Rector 60-64, Rector 64-; Pres. P.E.N. Centre in Israel; mem. Council of Higher Educ., Israel 60-; Chernichovsky Prize for translation of Aeschylus.
Publs. in Hebrew, *In the Storm on a Tempestuous Day* 44, *The Prosody of Bialik* 45, *The Spondee in the Hebrew Hexameter* 59, *Greek Epigram* 60, *Hebrew Literature between the Two World Wars* 53, *Sunsets over Jerusalem* (poetry) 65, *The Ways of Literary Creation* 66; numerous translations into Hebrew from Greek, Latin and Persian including *Prometheus Bound* and *Persians*, Aeschylus, Poems from the Greek Anthology and *Rubáiyát of Omar Khayyám*.
42 Be'eri Street, Tel-Aviv, Israel.
Telephone: 254924.

Katz, Katriel; Israeli diplomatist; b. Poland 16 Oct. 1908; ed. Herzliya Gymnasium and Warsaw Univ.
Came to Palestine 24; Head, Dept. of Propaganda and Education, Haganah 42-43; spokesman of the Haganah 48; spokesman, Public Relations Office, Israel Defence Army 49; on staff of Ministry of Foreign Affairs 49-; former Head, Div. of Political Research; Chargé d'Affaires, Budapest 53-56; Minister to Poland 56-58; Sec. to the Govt. 58-62; Consul-Gen., New York 62-65; Amb. to U.S.S.R. 65-67.
Ministry of Foreign Relations, Jerusalem, Israel.

Katz, Milton, A.B., LL.B.; American professor of law; b. 29 Nov. 1907; ed. Harvard Univ.
Member anthropological expedition to Central Africa 27-28; various official posts U.S. Govt. 32-39; Lecturer on Law Harvard Univ. 39-40, Prof. of Law 40-50; Solicitor War Production Board 41-43; U.S. Exec. Officer, Combined Production and Resources Board 42-43; Office of Strategic Services 43-44; Lieut.-Commdr. U.S.N.R. on active duty 44-46; Ambassador of the U.S. and U.S. Special Rep. in Europe 50-51; U.S. mem. Defence Financial and Economic Cttee. under North Atlantic Treaty 50-51; U.S. Rep. Economic Comm. for Europe (UN) 50-51; Assoc. Dir. Ford Foundation 51-54; Dir. Int. Legal Studies and Henry L. Stimson Prof. of Law, Harvard Univ. 54-; Fellow and Councillor American Acad. of Arts and Sciences; Legion of Merit; Trustee Carnegie Endowment for Int. Peace (Exec. Cttee.), World Peace Foundation (Exec. Cttee.), Inter-American Univ. Foundation, Citizens Research Foundation; Dir. Int. Friendship League; Trustee Brandeis Univ.; Chair. Cttee. on Manpower, White House Conf. on Int. Co-operation 65; Trustee Int. Legal Center; mem. Corpn. Boston Museum of Science; Trustee, Case Western Reserve Univ.
Publs. *Cases and Materials on Administrative Law* 47 *Government under Law and the Individual* (with others) 56, *The Law of International Transactions and Relations: Cases and Materials* (with Kingman Brewster, Jr.) 60, *The Things that are Caesar's* 66, *The Relevance of International Adjudication* 68.
Home: 6 Berkeley Street, Cambridge, Mass.; Office: Harvard Law School, Cambridge, Mass., U.S.A.
Telephone: KIrkland 7-0057 (Home); 868-7600 (Office).

Katz, Mindru; Israeli (b. Rumanian) pianist; b. 3 June 1925; ed. Bucharest Acad. of Music.
First public recital 31; first public concert with Bucharest Philharmonic Orchestra 47; tours of E. Europe 47-, U.K. 58-, South and East Africa 60, 62, Far East, Australia, New Zealand and S. America 61; has played in France, Germany, Portugal, Denmark, Sweden and Turkey; settled in Israel 59-; Prizewinner, Berlin, Prague, Bucharest Int. Piano Competitions 51, 53.
45 Hanassi Street, Herzliya, Nof-Yam, Israel.

Katzenbach, Nicholas deBelleville; American lawyer and government official; b. 17 Jan. 1922; Philips Exeter Acad., Princeton and Yale Univs. and Balliol Coll., Oxford.
U.S. Army Air Force 41-45; admitted to N.J. Bar 50, Conn. Bar 55; with firm Katzenbach, Gildea and Rudner, Trenton, N.J. 50; Attorney-Adviser, Office of Gen. Counsel, Air Force 50-52, part-time Consultant 52-56; Assoc. Prof. of Law, Yale Univ. 52-56; Prof. of Law, Univ. of Chicago 56-60; Asst. Attorney-Gen., U.S. Dept. of Justice 61-62, Deputy Attorney-Gen. 62-64, Attorney-Gen. 65-66; Under-Sec. of State 66-; mem. American Bar Asscn., American Judicature Soc., American Law Inst.; hon. degrees from Rutgers Univ., Univ. of Bridgeport (Conn.), Tufts Univ., Georgetown Univ.; Democrat.
Publs. *The Political Foundations of International Law* (with Morton A. Kaplan) 61, *Legal Literature of Space* (with Prof. Leon Lipson) 61.
Home: 3141 Highland Place, N.W., Washington, D.C.; Office: Department of State, Washington, D.C. 20008, U.S.A.

Katzer, Hans; German politician; b. 31 Jan. 1919; ed. Volksschule, Realgymnasium and Höhere Fachschule für Textil.

National and Mil. Service 39-45; employed in Labour Office, Cologne 45-49; Man. Dir. Social Cttee. of Christian Democratic Employees Asscn. of Germany 50-63, Chair. 63-, publisher of political monthly *Soziale Ordnung*; Man. Chair. of Jakob Kaiser Foundation 63-65; mem. Union of Transport Workers; mem. Christian Democratic Union (C.D.U.) 45-; mem. Cologne City Council 50-57; mem. Bundestag 57-; Chair. Parl. Cttee. for Fed. Econ. Assets 61-65; mem. Fed. Exec. Cttee. of C.D.U. 60-; Fed. Minister of Labour and Social Welfare 65-.

Office: Bundesministerium für Arbeit und Sozialordnung, 5300 Bonn; Home: 5000 Köln-Marienburg, Kastanienallee 7, German Federal Republic.

Katzin, Colonel Alfred G.; South African army officer and United Nations official (retd.); b. o6.

Before the Second World War engaged in South African industrial enterprises; mem. Exec. Board, South African Fed. Chamber of Industries, Vice-Pres. Cape Chamber of Industries; served with South African Army 40-43, with British Army 43-45; Deputy Dir.-Gen. for Finance and Admin. UNRRA European Regional Office 45, Deputy Dir.-Gen. and Chief Exec. Officer UNRRA Headquarters, Washington 46-47; Special Consultant to Sec.-Gen. UN 48; Fund-Raising Co-ordinator UNICEF 49; Special Rep. of UN Sec.-Gen. in Korea 50, UN Collective Measures Cttee. 51 and 52; Dir. of Personnel, UN 54; Deputy Under-Sec. UN Dept. of Public Information 56; Special Asst. to Sec.-Gen. for clearance of Suez Canal Oct. 56; Acting Head of Office of Public Information 58-60; Exec. Sec. UN Conf. on New Sources of Energy 61; Exec. Sec. UN Conf. on Science and Technology 62-63.

12 Chemin des Eglantiers, Grange Canal, Geneva, Switzerland.

Katz-Suchy, Juliusz, DR. JUR.; Polish journalist and diplomatist; b. 12; ed. Cracow, Prague and Warsaw Univs.

Editor and editorial writer of several socialist publications in Poland 34-38; in exile as political refugee in Czechoslovakia 38-39; during Second World War exile in England and employed as factory war worker 40-44; Deputy Dir. Polish Press Agency London 44-45; Press Attaché, Polish Embassy, London 45; Deputy Chief of Section Ministry of Foreign Affairs 45-46; Acting Rep. of Poland to Security Council U.N. 47; Permanent Rep. of Poland to the U.N. with rank of Minister, and Poland's Rep. on Economic and Social Council until 51; Del. to 2nd-6th and 8th-11th sessions U.N. Gen. Assembly (Vice-Pres. 2nd part, 3rd session 49); Del. to 9th-13th sessions Economic and Social Council (Chair. Del. to 13th session); apptd. Dir. Polish Inst. of Int. Affairs, Special Adviser on int. confs. to Minister of Foreign Affairs (rank of Minister) and Prof. of Int. Law, Warsaw Univ.; Head of Chair of Int. Relations and Diplomatic History 64-; Acad. of Diplomatic Service, Warsaw, 51; Alternate Del. to UN 53-54; Vice-Chair. Econ. Comm. for Europe (ECE) 55, 56; Chair. Polish Del. to foundation conf. of Int. Atomic Energy Agency 56; Ambassador to India 57-62 (accredited concurrently to Ceylon and Nepal).

Faculty of Law, University, Warsaw, Poland.

Kauffmann, Johannes, D.PHIL.; German professor; b. 30 March 1896; ed. Berlin, Munich and Kiel Univs.

Assistant, Staatliche Museen zu Berlin 19-20; Asst. to Dr. C. Hofstede de Groot, The Hague 20-22; Lecturer in the History of Art, Berlin Univ. 22-29, Prof. 29-36; Sen. Prof. and Dir. Inst. of History of Art, Cologne Univ. 36-57, Rector 55-56; Sen. Prof. and Dir. Inst. of History of Art, Freie Univ., Berlin 57-; mem. Research Asscn., Düsseldorf.

Publs. *Rembrandts Bildgestaltung* 22, *Albrecht Dürers Rhythmische Kunst* 24, *Donatello* 35, *Über "Rinascere", "Rinascità" und einige Stilmerkmale der Quattrocento Baukunst* 41, *Die fünf Sinne in der Niederländ. Malerei des 17 Jahrhunderts, Die Kölner Domfassade* 48, *Romgedanken in der Kunst Berninis* 54, *Jacob Burckhardts "Cicerone"* 61, *Bildgedanke und Künstlerische Form* 62, *Berliner Baukunst von Schlüter bis Schinkel* 63, *Zweckbau und Monument: zu Fr. Schinkels Museum am Lustgarten* 63, *Adolph Goldschmidt* 64, *Firenze nell' Interpretazione Tedesca* 65, *Die Schützenbilder des Frans Hals* 65, *Fr. Schinkel und seine Stellung in der Architekturgeschichte* 65, *Der Werdegang den Theresagruppe von G. L. Bernini* 67.

Spanische Alle 19, 1 Berlin 38, Germany.
Telephone: 84-48-52.

Kaul, Prince Mohan, M.B., B.S., D.P.H., F.R.C.P., F.I.A.M.S.; Indian physician and health official; b. 1 March 1906; ed. Punjab Univ. and Guy's Hospital, London.

Teacher, Infectious Diseases, and Medical Officer, Campbell Medical School, Calcutta 33-34; commissioned Indian Medical Service 34; army service, rose to Acting Col. 34-45; Dep. Public Comm. Govt. of India 46; Dep. Dir.-Gen. Health Services, Ministry of Health; Dir. WHO Epidemiological Intelligence Station, Singapore 47-49; Dir. WHO Liaison Office to UN, New York 50-52; Dir. Div. External Relations and Technical Assistance 53-56; Asst. Dir.-Gen. UN World Health Org. (WHO) 56-.

WHO, Avenue Appia, Geneva, Switzerland.
Telephone: 34-60-61.

Kaul, Triloki Nath; Indian diplomatist; b. 8 Feb. 1913; ed. Univs. of Punjab, Allahabad, London.

Joined Indian Civil Service 37; served in United Provinces as Joint Magistrate and Collector 37-47; Sec., Indian Council of Agricultural Research, New Delhi 47; First Sec. Indian Embassy, Moscow 47-49, Washington 49-50, Counsellor 50-52, and Minister 52-53, Peking; Joint Sec., Ministry of External Affairs, New Delhi 53-57; Chair., International Commission for Supervision and Control, Viet-Nam 57-58; Ambassador to Iran 58-60; Deputy High Commissioner, United Kingdom 60-61, Acting High Commr. 61-62; Ambassador to U.S.S.R. and Mongolia 62-66; Sec. to Govt. of India, Ministry of External Affairs, New Delhi, June 66-.

Ministry of External Affairs, New Delhi, India.
Telephone: 32014 (Office), 618066 (Home).

Kaunda, Kenneth David; Zambian politician; b. 28 April 1924; ed. Lubwa Training School and Munali Secondary School.

Schoolteacher at Lubwa Training School 43, Headmaster 44-47; Sec. Chinsali Young Men's Farming Asscn. 47; welfare officer, Chingola Copper Mine 48; school teaching 48-49; Founder-Sec. Lubwa branch, African Nat. Congress 50, district organiser 51, provincial organiser 52, Sec.-Gen. for N. Rhodesia 53; broke away to form Zambia African Nat. Congress 58; Pres. United Nat. Independence Party 60-; Minister of Local Govt. and Social Welfare, N. Rhodesia 62-64; Prime Minister of N. Rhodesia Jan.-Oct. 64; Pres. Pan-African Freedom Movement for East, Central and South Africa (PAFMECSA) 63; First Pres. of Zambia Oct. 64-; Order of the Collar of the Nile; Knight of the Collar of the Order of Pius XII, Order of the Queen of Sheba; Hon. Dr. of Laws (Fordham Univ., Dublin, Windsor (Canada) and Sussex Univs. and Univs. of York and Chile).

Publs. *Black Government* 61, *Zambia Shall be Free* 62, *A Humanist in Africa* (with Colin Morris) 66.

State House, P.O. Box 135, Lusaka, Zambia.
Telephone: 72365 (Lusaka).

Kaup, Karl; German mining engineer and executive; b. 13 May 1906; ed. Humanistisches Gymnasium, Wattenscheid, Munich Technical High School and Clausthal Mining Acad.

Man. Dir. Fortuna Mines, Salzgitter 35-39; Dir. of Mines for Cen. Germany, Raw Materials Section, Vereinigte Stahlwerke G.m.b.H. 39-44, Man. at Siegen 44-53; mem. Board, Barbara Erzbergbau G.m.b.H. 53-54, Pres. 54-; Pres. Rohstoffhandel G.m.b.H., Düsseldorf 59;- Chair. Unternehmensverband Eisenerzbergbau e.V., Düsseldorf; Pres. Gewerkschaft Exploration, Düsseldorf; mem. Board Wirtschaftsvereinigung Bergbau e.V., Bad Godesberg, and of numerous other mining and engineering companies; Hon. Dr.rer.nat.

c/o Barbara Erzbergbau G.m.b.H., 4 Düsseldorf, Steinstrasse 20, German Federal Republic.
Telephone: Düsseldorf 84-971.

Kaur, Prabhjot; see Prabhjot Kaur.

Käutner, Helmut; German film director, theatre director and playwright; b. 25 Aug. 1908; ed. Univ. of Munich and Acad. of Arts, Cologne.

Film director 39-; films incl. *Romanze in Moll* 43, *Unter den Brücken* 44, *Nachts auf den Strassen* 52, *Die letzte Brücke* 54, *Der Hauptmann von Köpenick* 56; theatre director of plays by Anouilh, Wilder, Arthur Miller, Ustinov in Hamburg, Bochum, Berlin; opera director: *König Pausole*, *Der Prinz von Homburg*, Hamburg State Opera.

18c Königsallee, Berlin 33, Germany.

Kavun, Vasili Mikhailovich; Soviet politician; b. 28; ed. Agricultural Inst., Uman.

Member C.P.S.U. 54-; Collective Farms, Ukraine 53-; Chair. Collective Farm of 22nd Congress of C.P.S.U., Vinnitsa District, Ukraine 58-; mem. Central Cttee. of C.P.S.U. 61-; mem. Presidium of Supreme Soviet 62-; Hero of Socialist Labour 62, and other decorations.
Presidium of Supreme Soviet, Moscow, U.S.S.R.

Kavur, Kemal Najat; Turkish diplomatist; b. 02. Served Diplomatic Service, Athens, Sofia, Berlin, Helsinki; fmr. Ambassador to U.S.S.R.; Ambassador to Japan 60-62, to U.K. 62-63, to Switzerland 63-67.
c/o Ministry of Foreign Affairs, Ankara, Turkey.

Kawabata, Yasunari, B.A.; Japanese writer; b. 1899; ed. Tokyo Univ.

On Editorial Staff of journal *Bungei Shunjü* 25; Dir. PEN Club; Bungei Konwa Kai Prize 37, Goethe Medal 59.

Publs. include *Izu-no-Odoriko* (Dancers of Izu Province) 25, *Asakusa Kurenai-dan* (Red Group of Asakusa), *Yuki Guni* (Snow Country).

264 Hase, Kamakura-shi, Kanagawa Prefecture, Japan.

Kawamata, Katsuji; Japanese business executive; b. 1 March 1905; ed. Tokyo Univ. of Commerce.

Japan Industrial Bank 29-47, Branch Man. Hiroshima 46-47; Managing Dir. Nissan Motor Co. 47-57, Pres. 57-; Chair. Nissan Diesel, Nissan Shakai Koki.
Nissan Motor Co., 2 Takaracho, Kanagawa-ku, Yokohama, Japan.

Kawamura, Otojiro; Japanese business executive; b. 1890; ed. Hitotsubashi Univ.

Entered Mitsubishi Goshi Kaisha 15; transferred to Mitsubishi Shoji Kaisha 15, Man. Sydney Branch Office 31-35, London Branch Office 35-42, Chief of Industrial Div. 42-43; Exec. Man. Dir. Kirin Brewery Co. 43-51, Pres. 51-56, Chair. of Board of Dirs. 66-; Rep. Dir. Japanese Brewers' Asscns. 54; Dir. Fed. of Econ. Orgs., Japan Fed. of Employers Asscns.; Blue Ribbon Medal 57; Third Class Order, Order of Sacred Treasure 64.
Kirin Brewery Company Ltd., Kashiwabara Building, Kyobashi, Tokyo, Japan.

Kawasaki, Kunio; Japanese business executive; b. 23 Sept. 1907; ed. Tokyo Univ.

Japan Woollen Spinning Co. Ltd. 32-34, Toyobo Co. Ltd. (after merger) 42-, Dir. 56-, Man. Dir. 57-61, Senior Man. Dir. 61-63, Vice-Pres. 63-66, Pres. 66-; Dir. Japan Exlan Co. Ltd. (acrylic fibres) 59-, Pres. 63-; Dir. Great Eastern Textiles Ltd. (Hong Kong) 64-, Kansai Cttee. for Economic Devt. 66-.

Toyobo Co. Ltd., 8 Dajima Hamadori 2-chome, Kitaku, Osaka; Home: 2-115 Nagaoyama, Kirihata, Takarazuka City, Hyugo Prefecture, Japan.

Kawata, Shige; Japanese business executive; b. 25 July 1887; ed. Tokyo Univ.

Nippon Kokan Kabushiki Kaisha (Japan Steel and Tube Corpn.) 18-, Auditor 42-, Dir. 42-, Man. Dir. 45-47, Pres. 47-63, Chair. 63-; Pres. Kokan Mining Industry Co., Nippon Kokan Light Steel Co.; Dir. Japan Usiminas Co., Arabian Oil Co.; Managing Dir. Japan Iron and Steel Fed.; Blue Ribbon Medal 58.
Nippon Kokan Kabushiki Kaisha, Otemachi, Chiyodaku, Tokyo, Japan.

Kawawa, Rashidi Mfaume; Tanzanian politician; b. 29; ed. Tabora Secondary School.

Former Pres. of the Tanganyikan Fed. of Labour; Minister of Local Government and Housing 60-61; Minister without Portfolio 61-62; Prime Minister Jan.-Dec. 62, Vice-Pres. Dec. 62-64; Second Vice-Pres., United Republic of Tanzania 64-; Vice-Pres. of T.A.N.U. (Tanganyika African Nat. Union) mem. T.A.N.U. Central Cttee. and T.A.N.U. Nat. Exec. Cttee.
Office of the Second Vice-President, Dar es Salaam, Tanzania.

Kaya, Seiji, D.SC.; Japanese scientist; b. 98; ed. Tohoku Imperial Univ.

Lecturer Tohoku Imperial Univ. 24, Asst. Prof. and mem. Research Inst. for Iron, Steel and Other Metals 26-28, Prof. of Physics 30-31; studied physics in Germany, Italy and U.S.A. 28-30; Prof. Hokkaido Imperial Univ. 31-43; mem. Nat. Research Council 39; Prof. Tokyo Inst. of Technology 41-48; Prof. of Physics, Tokyo Imperial Univ. 43-58, Dean of Science Faculty 49-51; Dir. Science Education, Ministry of Education 48-49; mem. Science Council of Japan 49-, Vice-Pres. 51-54, Pres. 54; mem. Japan Acad.; mem. Japanese Del. to Gen. Conf. UNESCO 54, mem. Japanese Comm. for UNESCO 56; Pres. Tokyo Univ. 58; Imperial Acad. Prize; Japanese Cultural Medal 64.

Publs. *Kyojisei-Kesshotai* (Ferro-magnetic Crystals) 35, *Kyojiseitai-ron* (Theory of Ferro-magnetism) 40, *Kyojisei* (Ferro-magnetism) 51.
20 Aoba-cho, Shibuya-ku, Tokyo, Japan.

Kayanda, David Mathew; Kenyan diplomatist; b. 1930; ed. Alliance High School (Kikuyu).

Government employee, Kitale 51; East African Branch, Royal Dutch Shell Co. 52-56; mem. African Advisory Council, Mombasa 57, Councillor 58; mem. Mombasa Municipal Council 58-63; Deputy Mayor of Mombasa 61-62, Mayor and Chair. Mombasa Cttee. of Social Services and Welfare 62-63; Amb. to U.S.S.R. 66-.
Embassy of Kenya, Bolshaya Ordinka, Dom 70, Moscow, U.S.S.R.
Telephone: 33-86-65.

Kayani, Malikur Rehman; Pakistani politician and judge; b. 1900; ed. Aligarh Univ.

Active in political life of North-West Frontier; mem. N.W.F.P. Legislative Council 32; elected to first Provincial Assembly 37, and again 49; joined Muslim League Assembly Party 38, becoming mem. of Provincial and later of All-India Muslim League Councils; Parl. Sec. to Minister for Information 43-45; renounced title of Khan Sahib in 46, becoming leader of Muslim League Civil Disobedience Movement in southern districts N.W.F.P. 47; Parl. Sec. to Chief Minister N.W.F.P. 49-51; Gen. Sec. Provincial Muslim League 51; served as Minister for Health and Information, and as Minister for Works in N.W.F.P. Cabinets; Minister for Com-

munications, Pakistan Central Govt. 55-56; Chief Justice, West Pakistan, 58-63.
c/o The Supreme Court, Lahore, Pakistan.

Kaye, Danny; American actor; b. 18 Jan. 1913. Stage appearances include *Straw Hat Revue* 39, *Lady in the Dark* 40, *Let's Face It* 41; films include *Up in Arms* 43, *Secret Life of Walter Mitty* 46, *A Song is Born* 47, *The Inspector General* 48, *Hans Christian Andersen* 52, *Knock on Wood, White Christmas* 54, *Court Jester* 55, *On the Double* 61, *The Man from the Diner's Club* 63; Amb.-at-Large for UN Children's Fund; Pres. Lear Jet Corpn. 66-.
Box 750, c/o J. Lefkowitz & Co., 9171 Wilshire Blvd., Beverly Hills, California, U.S.A.

Kayibanda, Gregoire; Rwandan journalist and politician; b. 1 May 1924; ed. Kabgayi and Nyakibanda, Ruanda (Rwanda since 1962).
Teacher Kigali 49-53; Information Officer Kabgayi 53-55; Editor *L'Ami* 53-55, *Kinyamateka* 55-58; Founder Ruanda Co-operative Movement 52, Hutu Social Movement 57, Democratic Republican Movement 59; Pres. TRAFIPRO Co-operative, Kabgayi; Pres. Democratic Republican Movement; President of Ruanda Oct. 60-June 62, Rwanda July 62-.
Kavumsburg/Gitarama B.P. 54, Rwanda, Central Africa.

Kayla, Ziya; Turkish banker; b. 12; ed. School of Political Sciences, Istanbul.
Ministry of Finance 34-63, Asst. Inspector, Inspector and Chief Inspector of Finance 34-60; Deputy Minister of Finance 60-63; Chair. Board of Dirs. and Dir.-Gen. Central Bank of Turkey 63-66; Alternate Gov. for Turkey, of Int. Bank for Reconstruction and Development 61-65; Pres. Banks' Asscn. of Turkey 63-66; Sec.-Gen. Comm. of Regulation of Bank Credits 63-66; Head of Foreign Investment Encouragement Cttee. 63-66; mem. Board of Controllers of the Prime Ministry 66-.
Publ. *Emission's movements in Turkey* 67.
T.C. Yüksek Denetleme Kurulu Bakanliklar, Ankara; and Kavaklidere Caddesi 21/5, Ankara, Turkey.
Telephone: 123010.

Kayra, Cahit; Turkish civil servant and diplomatist; b. 17; ed. Univ. of Istanbul.
Inspector of Finance 42-50; Counsellor, Gen. Directorate of Finance 50-55; private financial adviser 55-59; Head of Foreign Trade Dept., Ministry of Trade 59-60; Head of Turkish Perm. Del. to Gen. Agreement on Tariffs and Trade (G.A.T.T.) 60-63; Deputy Under-Sec. of State to Minister of Finance 63-64; Head of Turkish Del. to Org. for Econ. Co-operation and Development (O.E.C.D.) 64-.
Publs. *Middle Eastern Oil* 53, *A Guide to the Turkish System of Taxation* 57, *Import Policy in Turkey* 63.
Organisation for Economic Co-operation and Development, Château de la Muette, 2 rue André-Pascal, Paris 16e, France.

Kaysen, Carl, A.B., M.A., PH.D.; American economist; b. 5 March 1920; ed. Overbrook High School, Philadelphia, Univ. of Pennsylvania and Harvard Univ.
National Bureau of Econ. Research 40-42; Office of Strategic Services, Washington, D.C. 42-43; U.S. Army (Intelligence) 43-45; Consultant, Rand Corpn., Calif. 47-; Teaching Fellow in Econs. Harvard Univ. 47, Asst. Prof. in Econs. 50-55, Assoc. Prof. 55-57, Prof. 57-66, Assoc. Dean, Graduate School of Public Admin. 60-66, Lucius N. Littauer Prof. of Political Economy 64-66; Dir. Inst. of Advanced Study, Princeton July 66-; Senior Fulbright Research Scholar, London School of Econs. 55-56; Econ. Consultant to Judge Wyzanski, Fed. District Court of Mass. 50-52; Deputy Special Asst. to Pres. for Nat. Security Affairs 61-63.
Publs. *United States v. United Shoe Machinery Corporation, an Economic Analysis of an Anti-Trust Case* 56, *The American Business Creed* (with others) 56, *Anti-Trust Policy* (with D. F. Turner) 59, *The Demand for Electricity in the United States* (with Franklin M. Fisher) 62.
97 Olden Lane, Princeton, N.J. 08540, U.S.A.
Telephone: 921-7154.

Kayser, Elmer Louis, B.ED., M.A., LLD., PH.D.; American historian; b. 27 Aug. 1896; ed. George Washington Univ., Johns Hopkins Univ., and Columbia Univ.
Assistant in History, George Washington Univ. 14-17, Instructor 17-20, Asst. Prof. 20-24, Assoc. Prof. 24-32, Prof. of European History 32-67, Prof. Emeritus 67-; Asst. Librarian 14-18, Recorder 18, Sec. 18-29, Dir. of Univ. students 30-34, Dean 34-62, Dean Emeritus 67-; Univ. Marshal 32-53, Univ. Historian 62-; Sec.-Treas. 18-24, Vice-Pres. 47-50, Pres. 50-53, Gen. Alumni Asscn.; Historian Nat. Capital Sesquicentennial Comm.; Lay Chair. Cttee. for Improvement of Admin. of Justice in D.C.; Vice-Chair. Board of Trustees, Mount Vernon Seminary; Dir. American Peace Soc.; Assoc. Chair. School of Govt., George Washington Univ. 57-58; mem. Bd. of Govs. Nat. Cathedral School; Assoc. Editor *World Affairs*; Candidate Officer, Field Artillery, U.S. Army 18; Radio Commentator on foreign affairs 39-45; Sec. Navy's Advisory Cttee. on Naval History; Treas. American Historical Asscn.; Alumni Achievement Award, George Washington Univ. 41; Commdr. Nat. Order of Merit, Ecuador.
Publs. *The Grand Social Enterprise* 32, *A Manual of Ancient History* 37, *Contemporary Europe* 41 (co-author), *Washington's Bequest to a National University* 65, *The George Washington University 1821-1966* 66, *Luther Rice, Founder of Columbian College* 66.
Office: The George Washington University, Washington D.C. 20006, Home: 2921 34th Street, Northwest, Washington, D.C. 20008, U.S.A.
Telephone: 202-676-6535.

Kayser, Paul; American fuel executive; b. 10 Feb. 1887; ed. Baylor Univ. and Univ. of Texas (correspondence).
Principal, High School, Gatesville, Texas 09-11; admitted to Texas Bar 13, legal practice 13-29; Pres. El Paso Natural Gas Co., Houston 29-60, Chair. and Chief Exec. Officer 60-65, Hon. Chair. of the Board 65-; Pres. Western Natural Gas Co. 35-63.
1006 Main Street, Houston, Texas, 77002, U.S.A.
Telephone: CA-3-4491.

Kazakov, Marshal Konstantin Petrovich; Soviet army officer; b. 02; ed. Frunze Military Acad.
Soviet Army 21-, Artillery posts, Second World War; Senior mem. Ministry of Defence 58-63; Marshal of Artillery 62-; Commdr. of Rocket and Artillery Ground Forces Nov. 63-; mem. C.P.S.U. 20; Order of Lenin (thrice), Order of Suvorov (twice), Order of Kutuzov (twice), Order of Red Banner (thrice).
Ministry of Defence, 34 Maurice Thorez Embankment, Moscow, U.S.S.R.

Kazakov, Gen. Mikhail Ilich; Soviet army officer; ed. Frunze Military Acad. and General Staff Acad.
Joined Soviet army 20; Chief of Staff Mil. District 37-41; Chief of Staff, Army 44-45; Chief of Staff, Deputy Commdr.-in-Chief and Commdr.-in-Chief several Mil. Districts 45-56; Deputy Commdr.-in-Chief Ground Forces 56; Commdr. Southern Group 56-60; Commdr. Leningrad Mil. District 60-65; Chief of Staff Warsaw Pact Countries 65-; First Deputy Chief of Gen. Staff; cand. mem. Cen. Cttee. of C.P.S.U.; Deputy to U.S.S.R. Supreme Soviet; Order of Lenin (twice), Suvorov (twice), Kutuzov; Order of Red Banner (thrice), Red Star (twice).
c/o Ministry of Defence, 34 Maurice Thorez Embankment, Moscow, U.S.S.R.

Kazan, Elia; American (of Greek extraction) stage and film director; b. 7 Sept. 1909; ed. Williams Coll. and Yale Dramatic School.
Apprentice and Stage Man. with Group Theatre; acted on stage 35-41 in *Waiting for Lefty, Golden Boy, Gentle People, Fire-Alarm Waltz, Liliom* and in two films *City for Conquest* and *Blues in the Night* 41; Stage Dir. *Skin of our Teeth* (Drama Critics Award), *One Touch of Venus, Harriet, Jacobowsky and the Colonel* (Drama Critics Award), *Streetcar Named Desire, Death of a Salesman* (Drama Critics Award), *Tea and Sympathy, Cat on a Hot Tin Roof* (Drama Critics Award), *The Dark at the Top of the Stairs, J.B., Sweet Bird of Youth,* for Lincoln Center Repertory Theater *After the Fall, But for Whom Charlie, The Changeling;* film dir. *Tree Grows in Brooklyn, Gentlemen's Agreement* (Academy Award), *Boomerang, Panic in the Streets, Pinky, Streetcar Named Desire, Viva Zapata, Man on a Tightrope, On the Waterfront* (Acad. Award), *East of Eden, Baby Doll, A Face in the Crowd, Wild River, Splendor in the Grass,* Novels: *America, America, The Arrangement,* fmr. Dir. of Actors Studio.
1545 Broadway, New York City, N.Y., U.S.A.

Kazanets, Ivan Pavlovich; Soviet politician; b. 1918; ed. Siberian Metallurgical Inst.
Electrician, Head of Workshop, Kuznetsk Metallurgical Factory 37-44; mem. C.P.S.U. 44-; Shift Foreman, Trainee Electricians Factory, Yenakievo, Rep. Sec. Factory Cttee. 44-52; First Sec. Yenakievo City Cttee. C.P. Ukraine, later First Sec. Makeyev City Cttee. C.P. Ukraine 52-53; First Sec. District Cttee., Donetsk 53-60; Sec. and mem. Central Cttee., C.P. of Ukraine 60-62, Chair. Council of Ministers of Ukraine 63-65; Minister of Ferrous Metallurgy, U.S.S.R. 65-; Candidate mem. Central Cttee. C.P.S.U. 56-61, mem. 61-; Deputy to U.S.S.R. Supreme Soviet.
Ministry of Ferrous Metallurgy, 2/5 Ploshchad Nogina, Moscow, U.S.S.R.

Kazansky, Boris Alexandrovich; Soviet chemist; b. 1891; ed. Moscow Univ.
Post-Graduate student, Moscow Univ. 18-21, Lecturer in Chemistry 21-35, Prof. 35-; Senior Research Worker, Inst. of Organic Chemistry, Acad. of Sciences of U.S.S.R. 35-37, Dir. of Laboratory 37-54, Dir. of Inst. 54-66; Corresp. mem. U.S.S.R. Acad. of Sciences 43-46, mem. 46-; mem. Bureau of Int. Union of Pure and Applied Chemistry (IUPAC) 55-57, Exec. Cttee. 57-61; U.S.S.R. State Prize 49, Order of Lenin, Order of Red Banner of Labour.
Publs. 310 scientific papers and 2 monographs in the field of chemistry of hydrocarbons and their catalytic transformations.
Institute of Organic Chemistry of Academy of Sciences of U.S.S.R., Lenin Prospekt 47, Moscow, U.S.S.R.

Kazansky, Igor Alexandrovich; Soviet sports administrator; b. 1924; ed. Central School of Central Cttee. of Young Communist League and Novozybkovskiy Pedagogical Inst.
Worker, then technician in Mednogorsk 41-44; mem. C.P.S.U. 44-; Sec. Brijansk All-Union Young Communist League 46-50; Deputy Dir. then Sec. Party Cttee., Cen. School of Young Communist League Youth Dept.; Deputy Chief Editor *Molodoy Communist* (magazine) 53-61; mem. staff Cen. Cttee. of C.P.S.U. 61-64; Deputy Chair. Cen. U.S.S.R. Union of Sporting Socs. and Orgs. 64-.
Central Cttee. of U.S.S.R. Union of Sporting Societies and Organizations, 4 Skatertniy pereulok, Moscow, U.S.S.R.

Kazin, Alfred, M.A.; American writer; b. 5 June 1915; ed. New York City Coll. and Columbia Univ.
Began his career as free-lance literary reviewer 34; Instructor in English Literature successively at New York City Coll., Queen's Coll., New School 37-41;

Literary Ed. *New Republic* 42, Assoc. Ed. *Fortune;* War Corresp. in Great Britain 45; Prof. of American Studies, Amherst Coll. 55-58; Berg Prof. of Literature, New York Univ. 57; Distinguished Prof. of English, State Univ. of New York 63-; mem. Nat. Inst. of Arts and Letters.
Publs. *On Native Grounds: An Interpretation of Modern American Literature* 42, *A Walker in the City* 51, *The Inmost Leaf* 55, *Contemporaries* 62, *Starting Out In The Thirties* 65; edited: *The Portable Blake* 46, *F. Scott Fitzgerald: The Man and His Work* 51, *The Stature of Theodore Dreiser* 55, *Melville's Moby Dick* 56, *Ralph Waldo Emerson: A Modern Anthology* 58, *The Open Form: Essays for our Times* 61; Editor *The Short Stories of Nathaniel Hawthorne* 66.
c/o Atlantic Monthly Press, 8 Arlington Street, Boston, Mass.; and 440 West End Avenue, New York 24, N.Y., U.S.A.

Kaznin, Georgi Vladimirovich; Soviet lawyer; b. 1922; ed. U.S.S.R. Correspondence Inst. of Law.
Chairman of Regional Court, Pskov, N.W. Russia until 61; mem. Collegium of Ministry of Justice of R.S.F.S.R. 61-63; on staff of Central Cttee. of C.P.S.U. 62-63; mem. U.S.S.R. Supreme Court 65-.
U.S.S.R. Supreme Court, Moscow, U.S.S.R.

Kearney, Hon. Mr. Justice John D., M.C., Q.C., B.A., B.C.L.; Canadian judge; b. 93; ed. Loyola Coll. and McGill Univ.
Served Field Artillery 16-18; assoc. for many years with legal firm of Ralston, Kearney, Duquet & Mackay, now Duquet & Mackay, Montreal; created a King's Counsel 31; joined diplomatic service 41; High Commr. to Republic of Ireland 41-45; Minister to Norway 45-46 and to Denmark 46; High Commr. to India 46-49; Ambassador to Argentina 49-51; Judge of the Exchequer Court of Canada 51-; Chair. of Board of Transport Commrs. for Canada 51-57.
Supreme and Exchequer Courts Building, Ottawa, Ont., Canada.

Kearton, Sir Christopher Frank, Kt., O.B.E., F.R.S.; British scientist and textiles executive; b. 17 Feb. 1911; ed. Hanley High School and St. John's Coll., Oxford.
Imperial Chemical Industries, Billingham Div. 33-40; Atomic Energy Project, U.K. and U.S.A. 40-45; Courtaulds Ltd. 46-, in charge Chemical Engineering 46, Dir. 52-, Deputy Chair. 61, Chair. 64-; part-time mem. U.K. Atomic Energy Comm. 55-; mem. Electricity Supply Research Council 54-, Chair. 60-; mem. Govt. Advisory Council on Technology 64-, Nat. Econ. Development Council 65-; Chair. Industrial Reorganisation Corpn. 66-; Hon. LL.D. (Leeds).
The Old House, Whitchurch, nr. Aylesbury, Bucks., England.

Keating, Kenneth B., A.B., LL.B.; American lawyer and politician; b. 18 May 1900; ed. Rochester and Harvard Univs.
Law practice in Rochester, N.Y. 23-; mem. law firm of Harris, Beach, Keating, Wilcox, Dale and Linowitz; mem. U.S. House of Reps., New York 38th District 46-58; mem. U.S. del. to Consultative Assembly of Council of Europe 51; mem. U.S. del. Interparliamentary Union Confs., Washington 53, Vienna 54, Helsinki 55, Bangkok 56, London 57, Rio de Janeiro 58, Senate Observer at Commonwealth Parliamentary Association Conf., Canberra 59; mem. U.S. del. ICEM Confs. 56, 57 and 59; Senator from New York 58-64; service with U.S. Army (Sergeant) in First World War; Col. and Exec. Asst. to Deputy Supreme Commdr., Southeast Asia Command in Second World War; mem. Rochester, New York State and American Bar Asscns.; Hon. LL.D. Rochester Univ. 54, Le Moyne and Hobart Colleges 59; Legion of Merit with Oak Leaf Cluster, Hon. O.B.E.; Republican.
3500 Elmwood Avenue, Rochester 10, N.Y., U.S.A.

Keating, Stephen Flaherty, B.S., J.D.; American business executive; b. 6 May 1918; ed. Univ. of Minnesota.
Admitted to Minn. Bar 42; Special Agent, F.B.I., Norfolk, Va., Detroit 42-43; U.S. Naval Reserve 43-46; Assoc. Otis, Faricy & Burger, St. Paul 46-48; Man. Mil. Contracts, Aero Div., Honeywell Inc. 48-54, Div. Vice-Pres. 54-56, Vice-Pres. 56-62, Exec. Vice-Pres. 61-65, Pres. 65-; Dir. First Bank Stock Corpn., Gen. Mills Inc., Toro Manufacturing Corpn., Dayton Corpn.
2701 Fourth Avenue South, Minneapolis, Minnesota 55408, U.S.A.

Kebin, Iohannes Gustavovich; Soviet politician; b. 1905; ed. Inst. of Red Professors.
Member C.P.S.U. 24-; Chair. of a village soviet 27-31; party functionary 31-36; student, later Instructor, Inst. of Red Profs. 36-41; party work in Estonia 41-48; Sec. of the Cen. Cttee. of the Estonian C.P. 48; First Sec. of the Cen. Cttee. of the Estonian C.P. 50-; mem. C.P.S.U. Cen. Cttee. 52-; Deputy to U.S.S.R. and Estonian S.S.R. Supreme Soviets; mem. Budget Cttee. Soviet of Union; awarded Order of Lenin, Order of the Red Banner of Labour, and other awards.
Central Committee of the Communist Party of Estonia, Tallinn, Estonia, U.S.S.R.

Keck, George Edwin; American airline executive; b. 26 Feb. 1912; ed. Univ. of Illinois.
Industrial Engineer, Swift & Co. 33-37; successively Industrial Engineer, Plant Control Supervisor, Acting Plant Manager Owens-Illinois Can Co. 37-42; Army service 42-46; Dir. of Industrial Engineering, United Air Lines 46-53; Consulting Engineer, A. T. Kearney Co. 53-54; Asst. to Senior Vice-Pres., Engineering and Maintenance, United Air Lines 54-59, Vice-Pres., Base Maintenance 59-61, Exec. Vice-Pres. for Operations and Dir. 61-62, Exec. Vice-Pres., Gen. Manager 62-63, Pres. 63-.
Home: 117 N. Dewey Road, Palatine; Office: P.O. Box 8800, Chicago, Illinois 60666, U.S.A.

Kedah, H.R.H. The Sultan of; Tunku **Abdul Halim Mu'azzam Shah ibni Almarham Sultan Badlishah,** D.U.K., D.K., S.P.M.K., D.M.N.; Kedah Ruler, Malaysia; b. 28 Nov. 1927.
Succeeded his father July 58.
Alor Star, Kedah, Malaysia.

Kedrov, Bonifatiy Mikhailovich; Soviet philosopher; b. 1903; ed. Kharkov Univ. and Inst. of Red Professors.
Member staff Central Cttee. of C.P.S.U. 35-37; scientific posts 38-41; Soviet Army 41-45; Prof. of Dialectical and Historical Materialism, R.S.F.S.R. Acad. of Social Sciences 46-55; at Inst. of History of Natural Sciences, U.S.S.R. Acad. of Sciences 55-, Dir. 63-; Corresp. mem. U.S.S.R. Acad. of Sciences 60-66, mem. 66-.
U.S.S.R. Academy of Sciences, 14 Lenin Prospekt, Moscow, U.S.S.R.

Kedrov, Mikhail Nikolaevich; Soviet actor and producer; b. 1893; ed. Moscow Art Theatre Studio School.
Has played at the Moscow Art Theatre 24-; Editor, Writings of Stanislavsky; People's Artist of the U.S.S.R.; State Prize (four times), Order of Red Banner of Labour, Order of Lenin, Badge of Honour.
Principal roles: Manilov (*Dead Souls* by Gogol), Zakhar Bardin (*Enemies* by Gorky), Karenin (*Anna Karenina* by Tolstoy), Miron Gorlov (*Front* by Korneichuk); plays staged include: *Deep Reconnaissance* (Kron), *Uncle Vanya* (Chekhov), *Wood* (Ostrovsky), *Strange Shadow* (Simonov), *Fruits of Education* (Tolstoy), *The Third Pathetic* (Pogodin).
Moscow Art Theatre, 3 Proyezd Khudozhestvennovo Teatra, Moscow, U.S.S.R.

Keefler, Ralph Holley, C.B.E., D.S.O., E.D., B.A.SC., LL.D.; Canadian business executive; b. 12 Sept. 1902; ed. Univ. of Toronto.

Bell Telephone Co., Montreal 24, District Man., Kingston 29-30, Gen. Commercial Engineer 30-40; Army Service, rising to Maj.-Gen. 40-46; Eastern Div. Man. Bell Telephone Co. 46-49, Asst. to Pres., Ottawa 49-53, Gen. Man., Eastern Area, Montreal 53-54, Vice-Pres. (Public Relations) 54-56, Vice-Pres. (Operations) 56-58, Vice-Pres. (Finance) 58-61; Pres. Northern Electric Co. Ltd. 61-67, Chair. of Board 63-; Pres. Canadian Chamber of Commerce 65-66; Dir. Bell Telephone Co. of Canada, Canadian Int. Paper Co., Guardian-Union of Canada Insurance Group; Dir. Royal Bank of Canada; Légion d'Honneur, Croix de Guerre.
Office: 1600 Dorchester Boulevard West, Montreal 25, Quebec; Home: 21 Barat Road, Westmount, Quebec, Canada.

Keeler, William Wayne; American petroleum executive; b. 5 April 1908; ed. Bartlesville High School and Univ. of Kansas.
Joined Phillips Petroleum Co. while at Univ. 28, employed at refineries at Kansas City, Odessa and Borger as chemist, process engineer, night supt., and Chief Process Engineer 28-41; Technical Asst. to Vice-Pres. of Refining Dept. 41-45; Man. of Refining Dept. 45-47, Vice-Pres. of Refining Dept. 47-51; Vice-Pres., Exec. Dept. 51-54, Dir. 51-; mem. Exec. Cttee. 54-56; Exec. Vice-Pres. 56-62, Chair. Exec. Cttee. 62-67; Pres. and Chief Exec. Officer, Phillips Petroleum Co. 67-; Dir. of Refining, Petroleum Admin. for Defense, Wash. D.C. 52-53; Chair. Mil. Petroleum Advisory Board 54-62; Chair. U.S. Del. to Inter-American Indian Conf., Quito, Ecuador 64; mem. Nat. Advisory Cttee. on War on Poverty Program 65, President's Cttee. on Econ. Opportunity 67-; official of numerous business and civic orgs.
Phillips Petroleum Company, Phillips Building, Bartlesville, Okla. 74003, U.S.A.

Keen, Sir Bernard A., Kt., F.R.S., D.SC.; British physicist and agriculturalist; b. 5 Sept. 1890; ed. Univ. Coll., London.
Andrews Scholar 08; Trouton Research Scholar 11; Carey Foster Research Prizeman 12; Soil Physicist, Rothamsted Experimental Station 13; served (Gallipoli and Palestine) First World War 14-17; Research Dept. Woolwich Arsenal 18; Soil Physicist, Rothamsted 19; Dir. Imperial Inst. of Agricultural Research, India 30-31; Asst. Dir. and Head Soil Physics Dept., Rothamsted Experimental Station 23-47; Scientific Adviser Middle East Supply Centre, Cairo 43-45; Adviser on rural development, Palestine 46; Chair. U.K. Govt. Mission to W. Africa 46; Adviser on agricultural policy in E. Africa 47; Dir. East African Agriculture and Forestry Research Organisation 47-55; Dir. of Research, Baird and Tatlock (London) Ltd. 56-63; Pres. Royal Meteorological Society 38, 39; Cantor Lecturer, Royal Society of Arts 42; Fellow, Univ. Coll., London 24.
Publs. *The Physical Properties of the Soil* 31, *The Agricultural Development of the Middle East* 46.
72 Eaton Square, London, S.W.1, England.

Keenan, Joseph D.; American trade unionist; b. 96.
Representative of American Federation of Labor on Nat. Defense Council 40; Assoc. Dir. War Production Board; Labor Adviser to Gen. Lucius D. Clay 45; Labor Adviser, Nat. Production Administration and Defense Production Authority 50-53, Office of Defense Mobilisation 53-58; Int. Sec., Int. Brotherhood of Electrical Workers 54-; Special Asst. to Dir. for Labor, Consultant to Office of Emergency Planning; Vice-Pres. and mem. Exec. Council A.F.L.-C.I.O.; mem. Pres. Advisory Council on Labor Management Policy; Medal of Freedom, Award of Merit.
International Brotherhood of Electrical Workers, 1200 15th Street, N.W., Washington 5, D.C., U.S.A.

Keener, Jefferson Ward, A.B., M.A.; American business executive; b. 6 Aug. 1908; ed. Birmingham Southern Coll., Ohio State Univ. and Univ. of Chicago.
Instructor, later Asst. Prof. of Economics, Ohio Wesleyan Univ. 29-37, 38-39; Dir. of business research, B. F. Goodrich Co. 39-44, asst. to financial Vice-Pres., asst. to Pres. 44-46, Vice-Pres. 46-56, Exec. Vice-Pres. 56, Pres. and Dir. 57, Pres., Chief Exec. Officer and Dir. 58-; Dir. other Goodrich cos., British Geon Ltd.; Dir. Goodrich-Gulf Chemicals Inc.; mem. Nat. Industrial Conf. Board; Dir. Rubber Manufacturers' Asscn.; served Office of Price Administration and War Production Board in Second World War; also other public service posts; mem. advisory cttee. on civilian personnel, U.S. Army 54-56; U.S. Army Medal for Exceptional Civilian Achievement 56; Hon. LL.D. Birmingham Southern Coll., Ohio Wesleyan Univ.; Hon. D.C.S. Millikin Univ.
Publ. *Cutting the Cost of Bank Loans* 30.
Office: B. F. Goodrich Co., 500 Main Street, Akron 11; Home: 265 Hampshire Road, Akron, Ohio 44313, U.S.A.

Keenleyside, Hugh Llewellyn, PH.D., LL.D., D.SC.; Canadian diplomatist and administrator; b. 7 July 1898; ed. Univ. of British Columbia, Vancouver and Clark Univ., Worcester, Mass., U.S.A.
Served with C.F.A. First World War; Lecturer in History, Univ. of B.C. 25-27; entered Dept. of External Affairs Ottawa 28; went to Tokyo as First Sec. and opened First Canadian Mission in Japan 29, promoted to Counsellor 40; Asst. Under-Sec. of State for External Affairs 41; Canadian Ambassador to Mexico 44-47; Deputy Minister of Mines and Resources 47-50; Dir.-Gen. U.N. Technical Assistance Admin. 50-59; U.N. Under-Sec. for Public Administration 59; Chair. British Columbia Power Comm. and Adviser to Govt. of British Columbia on Resource Devt. Policies 59-62; Chair. British Columbia Hydro and Power Authority 62-; Pres. Columbia Power Co. Ltd.; mem. numerous wartime cttees., including Canada-U.S. Joint Board on Defence 40-45 and War Technical and Scientific Development Cttee. 41-45; Dir. and one of founders of Arctic Inst. of N. America; Dir. Toronto-Dominion Bank; mem. Vancouver Advisory Board, Canada Permanent Companies; hon. degrees from numerous Canadian and U.S.A. Univs.; Haldane Medal of Royal Inst. of Public Admin. 54, Vanier Medal 62.
Publs. *Canada and the United States, International Aid History of Japanese Education* (with A. F. Thomas).
Office: British Columbia Hydro and Power Authority, 970 Burrard Street, Vancouver, B.C.; Home: 3470 Mayfair Drive, Victoria, B.C., Canada.
Telephone: 382-9394.

Keeton, George Williams, M.A., LL.D., F.B.A.; British lawyer and educationist; b. 22 May 1902; ed. Gonville and Caius Coll. Cambridge and Gray's Inn, London.
Reader in Law and Politics Hong Kong Univ. 24-27; Senior Law Lecturer Manchester Univ. 28-31; Reader in Law 31-37, Prof. English Law 37-, Dean Law Faculty 39-54, Univ. Coll. London; Pres. and Treasurer London Inst. of World Affairs 38-; Dean of Faculty of Laws, London Univ. 42-46; Vice-Provost, Univ. Coll., London 66-.
Publs. *The Development of Extra-territoriality in China* 28, *The Law of Trusts* 34, *National Sovereignty and International Order* 39, *Russia and Her Western Neighbours* 42, *China, the Far East and the Future* 43, *Making International Law Work* (with Dr. Schwarzenberger) 46, *Extra-territoriality in International and Comparative Law* 49, *The Passing of Parliament* 52, *Social Change in the Law of Trusts* 58, *Trial for Treason* 59, *Trial by Tribunal* 60, *Guilty but Insane* 61, *The Modern Law of Charities* 62, *Lord Chancellor Jeffreys and the Stuart Cause* 65, *The Norman Conquest and the Common Law* 66, *Shakespeare's Legal and Political Background* 67.

Picts Close, Picts Lane, Princes Risborough, Bucks., England.
Telephone: Princes Risborough 94.

Kefaloyannis, Emmanuel; Greek politician; b. 23 April 1916; ed. Univ. of Athens and Higher School of Economics and Commercial Studies.
Deputy for Popular Party 50, for Nat. Radical Union 56, 58, 61, 63, 64-; Sec.-Gen. Greek Parl. 53-56; Under-Sec. for Housing 58-61; Minister for Merchant Marine 67.
Athens, Greece.

Keilberth, Joseph; German conductor and musical administrator; b. 19 April 1908; ed. Karlsruhe Conservatoire.
Répétiteur, Karlsruhe State Theatre 25, Gen. Musical Dir. 29; Dir. German Philharmonic Orchestra, Prague 40; Dir. Dresden State Opera 45-50; principal conductor, Berlin State Opera 48-50; Gen. Musical Dir., City of Hamburg, and Artistic Dir., Hamburg Philharmonic State Orchestra 50-59; Conductor-in-Chief, Bamberg Symphony Orchestra (successor to German Philharmonic Orchestra of Prague) 50-59; extended concert tours with Bamberg Symphony Orchestra, concert and operatic engagements in numerous European cities; conducted at Bayreuth Festivals 52-56; Resident Conductor Bavarian State Opera Aug. 59-; permanent guest conductor, Hamburg State Opera.
Bayerische Staatsoper, Munich, German Federal Republic.

Keir, Sir David Lindsay, Kt., M.A.; British historian. b. 22 May 1895; ed. Glasgow Univ. and New Coll; Oxford.
Fellow Univ. Coll. Oxford 21-39, Dean 25-33, Estates Bursar 35-39, Univ. Lecturer in English Constitutional History 31-39, Chair. Examiners Hons. School of Modern History Oxford 32, Chair. Board Faculty 38-39; Exchange Tutor Harvard Univ. 23-24; Donnellan Lecturer, Trinity Coll., Dublin 42; Pres. and Vice-Chancellor Queen's Univ., Belfast 39-49; Master Balliol Coll. Oxford 49-65; Chair. Medical Education Enquiry Cttee., Univ. of Malaya 53; Chair. Council for Overseas (former Colonial) Coll. of Arts, Science and Technology 53-62; Pres. Asscn. of Technical Institutions 56-58, Scottish History Soc. 57-61; Chair. Cttee. on Technical Education, Northern Rhodesia 60; Vice-Pres. Ulster Soc. for Irish Historical Studies; Hon. Fellow, Univ. Coll. and New Coll., Oxford; Hon. A.R.I.B.A.; Hon. LL.D. Glasgow, Dublin, Queen's (Ont.), New Brunswick and Queen's (Belfast); Hon. D.C.L. (Oxford), Hon. D.Litt. (Sussex).
Publs. *Cases in Constitutional Law* (with F. H. Lawson) 28 (5th edn. 67), *Constitutional History of Modern Britain* 38 (8th edn. 66).
Hillsborough, Boars Hill, Oxford, England.

Keita, Fadiala; Guinean jurist and diplomatist; b. 1927.
Lawyer, Paris Court of Appeal 51-55; law practice at Kankan, Guinea 55-58; Adviser to Court of Appeal, Conakry 58-61; Pres. Court of Appeal, Conakry, and Supreme Court of Cassation, Guinea 61-62; Attorney-Gen., Court of Appeal and Supreme Court of Cassation 62-67; Amb. to U.S.S.R. 67-; mem. Perm. Sec. Asian-African Legal Consultative Cttee.; mem. Exec. Cttee. Guinea Nat. Confederation of Labour.
Embassy of Guinea, Ul. A. Tolstovo 13, Moscow, U.S.S.R.

Keita, Madeira; Mali politician; b. 17; ed. William Ponty School, Senegal.
Served in French Army; archivist Dakar, Senegal and Conakry, Guinea; Gen. Sec., Democratic Party of Guinea 47-52; Minister of Home Affairs, Sudan Territorial Govt. 59-60, Minister of Home Affairs, National Defence and Security, Republic of Mali 60-61, of Home

Affairs and Information 61-62; Minister of State for Justice 62-68; Minister for Justice and Labour 68-; mem. Comité Nat. de Défense de la Revolution.
Ministry of Justice, B.P. 97 Bamako, Mali, West Africa.
Telephone: 26-51 and 24-36.

Keita, Modibo; Mali politician; b. 4 June 1915; ed. William Ponty Lycée, Dakar.
Conseiller Général, French Sudan; Sec.-Gen. Union Soudanaise; Councillor, Union Française 53-56; Deputy to French Nat. Assembly from Sudan 56-58, Vice-Pres. 56; Pres. Constituent Assembly, Dakar 58-60; Président du Conseil, Sudanese Republic, Mali Fed. 59-60, Mali 60-; President of Mali 60-; Minister of Nat. Defence 61-; Lenin Prize Peace 62.
President's Office, Bamako, Mali, West Africa.

Keita, Moussa Léo; Mali diplomatist; b. 1 July 1927; ed. Ecole Normale de Katibougou, and foreign service training courses in Paris, Geneva and New York.
Assistant Sec.-Gen., Ministry of Foreign Affairs 61, Head of Office 61-62, Sec.-Gen. 62-64; Ambassador of Mali to the U.S.A. 64-, and Perm. Rep. to UN 66-.
Embassy of Mali, 2130 R Street, Washington, 20008 D.C., U.S.A.

Keith, Kenneth Alexander; British banker; b. 30 Aug. 1916; ed. Rugby and Dresden.
Trained as Chartered Accountant, London 34-39; Army Service 39-45; Asst. to Dir.-Gen. Political Intelligence Dept., Foreign Office 45-46; Asst. to Managing Dir. Philip Hill & Partners, London 46-48, Dir 47; Dir. Philip Hill Investment Trust 49, Managing Dir. 51; Managing Dir. Philip Hill, Higginson & Co. Ltd. 51-59, Philip Hill, Higginson, Erlangers Ltd. 59-62, Chair. 62-65; Deputy Chair. and Chief Exec. Hill Samuel & Co. 65-; Deputy Chair. British European Airways; Dir. Beecham Group Ltd., Nat. Provincial Bank Ltd., Times Newspapers Ltd., and other companies; mem. Nat. Econ. Devt. Council.
80 Eaton Square, London, S.W.1, England.

Kekkonen, Urho Kaleva; Pres. of Republic of Finland; b. 3 Sept. 1900; ed. Univ. of Helsinki.
Jurist, Fed. of Rural Communities 27-31; Admin. Sec. Ministry of Agriculture 33-36; M.P. (Agrarian) 36-56; Minister of Justice 36-37, 44-46; Minister of the Interior 37-39; Director, Central Bureau of Evacuees 40-43, Office of Rationalisation 43-46; Speaker of the Diet 48-50; mem. Board of Managers Bank of Finland 46-56; Prime Minister and Minister of the Interior 50-51; Prime Minister 51-52, 53, 54-56; Minister of Foreign Affairs 52-53, 54; Pres. of Finland 56-; LL.D. (Helsinki); Finnish decorations: Grand Cross with Chain, Order of the White Rose, Grand Cross of the Cross of Liberty, Grand Cross Order of the Lion, Grand Cross of the Holy Lamb, Olympic Cross (First Class) of Merit, Gold Cross (First Class) Merit of Finnish Sports; numerous foreign decorations; Dr. h.c. Univs. of Moscow, Aix-en-Provence, Waterloo (Ontario), Warsaw and Delhi.
Presidential Palace, Helsinki, Finland.

Keldysh, Mstislav Vsevolodovich; Soviet mathematician; b. 10 Feb. 1911; ed. Moscow Univ.
Specialist in aerodynamics and the theory of functions of complex variables; corresp. mem. U.S.S.R. Acad. of Sciences 43; mem. U.S.S.R. Acad. of Sciences 46-, Pres. 61-; Prof. Moscow Univ.; Sec. Physics and Mathematics Section, U.S.S.R. Acad. of Sciences 53-; mem. Communist Party 48-, mem. Central Cttee. of C.P.S.U., Deputy to the Supreme Soviet; Hon. mem. American Acad. of Arts and Sciences; two State Prizes; Lenin Prize; Order of Lenin, Hero of Socialist Labour (twice).
Publs. *O razreshimosti i ustoichivosti zadachi Dirikhle* 40, *O predstavlenii funktsii komplexnogo peremennogo ryadami polinomov v zamknutykh oblastyakh* 45, *O sobstvennykh znacheniyakh i sobstvennykh funktsiyakh nekotorykh klassov nesamosopryazhennykh upravlenii* 51, *Vibratsii v vozdushnom potoke kryla s podkosami* 38,

Prilozhenic Teorii funktsii komplexnogo peremennogo k gidrodinamike i aerodinamike (with L. I. Sedov) 64.
U.S.S.R. Academy of Sciences, Lenin Prospekt 14, Moscow, U.S.S.R.

Keleti, Márton; Hungarian film director; b. 26 April 1905.
Outstanding and Merited Artist of the Republic.
Films: *Erkel, A Strange Marriage, Mickey Magnate, Two Confessions, Penny, A New Steps from the Border, Yesterday, Daybreak, The Story of my Folly, A Study on Women;* Kossuth Prize (three times).
Hunnia Film Studio, Gyarmat u. 39, Budapest XIV, Hungary.
Telephone: 297-250.

Kelfa-Caulker, Richard Edmund, B.A., M.A.; Sierra Leonean diplomatist; b. 14 March 1909; ed. Sierra Leone, Otterbein Coll., Ohio, Oberlin Graduate School and Teachers Coll., Columbia Univ.
Headmaster, Albert Academy, Sierra Leone to 59; Commissioner to the United Kingdom 59, Acting High Commissioner 61; Ambassador to U.S.A. 61-63; Ambassador and Permanent Delegate UN 63-64; High Commr. in U.K. 64-66.
1 New Motor Road, Freetown, Sierra Leone.

Keller, Hans Gustav, PH.D., LL.D.; Swiss librarian and historian; b. 12 Nov. 1902; ed. Berne, Vienna, Clermont-Ferrand, Heidelberg, Berlin and Basle Univs.
Librarian Zürich Municipal Museum of Applied Art 34-37, Swiss Nat. Library, Berne 37-44; Dir. Cen. Fed. Library, Berne 44-67; Lecturer in Modern History, Univ. of Berne 48-63, Prof. 63-.
Publs. *Die politischen Verlagsanstalten und Druckereien in der Schweiz 1840-1848* 35, *Das "Junge Europa" 1834-1836* 38, *Das Historische Museum im Schloss Thun 1887-1937* 38, *Der Brudermord im Hause Kiburg* 39, *Das Leben und Leiden Jesu Christi* 40, *"La Chartreuse"* 41, *Minister Stapfer und die Künstlergesellschaft in Bern* 45, *Einigen* 46, *Vom Staatsgedanken und von der Sendung der Schweiz* 47, *Thun* 49, *Legislative und Exekutive in den Vereinigten Staaten von Amerika* 51, *Hutten und Zwingli* 52, *Chr. von Graffenried und die Gründung von Neu-Bern in Nord-Carolina* 53, *Die Wurzeln der amerikanischen Demokratie* 58, *Die Quellen der amerikanischen Verfassung* 58, *Unitarismus und Föderalismus im Werk der amerikanischen Verfassunggebenden Versammlung* 58, *Der "Virginia-Plan"* 60, *Die Idee der Unabhängigkeit* 62, *Pitt's "Provisional Act"* 62, *Die Metaphysik Montesquieus* 65, *Montesquieu's "Esprit des Lois"* 68.
Zumbachstr. 30, 3028 Spiegel b. Bern, Switzerland.

Keller, Hans K. E. L., DR. IUR., DR. OEC. PUBL., DR. EN DROIT; German international lawyer; b. 2 Jan. 1908; ed. Munich, Bordeaux and Kiel Univs.
Int. law research in France, Germany, U.S.A., Italy and England 30-35; founder European Union 31, renamed Nationalist Int. 34; Chair. Int. Congress of Nationalists Berlin 34, London 35, Oslo 36; Pres. Acad. for the Rights of Nations 36; advocated representation of nationalities in L.N. 35, in UN 47; Editor *Corpus Iuris Gentium;* Fellow, Maximilianeum; Fellow, Rockefeller Foundation; founder and Hon. Sec.-Gen. Int. Grotius Foundation for the Propagation of the Law of Nations; Alderman of the City of Munich; Knight Commdr. Sovereign Order of St. John and St. Thomas.
Publs. *Droit Naturel et Droit Positif en Droit International Public* 31, *Das dritte Europa* 34, *Das Rechtliche Weltbild* 35, *Why "The Nationalist International"?* 36, *Das Recht der Völker* 38-41, *Der Kampf um die Völkerordnung* 39, *Völkerrecht beginnt bei Dir!* 52, *Völkerrecht und Völkerpflicht* 54, *Völkerrecht und Weltwirtschaft* 57, *Ein Passionsspiel* 59, *Jumelages* 62.
c/o Grotius Foundation, Munich 27; and Grotianum, Erding via Munich, German Federal Republic.
Telephone: Munich 484084.

Keller, Helen Adams, A.B.; American author and welfare worker; b. 27 June 1880; ed. Radcliffe Coll.
Deaf and blind 81-; Counsellor on nat. and int. relations to American Foundation for the Blind and to American Foundation for Overseas Blind; Org. of Helen Keller World Crusade for the Blind; has undertaken a very large number of lecture tours in U.S.A., Europe, Asia, Africa and Australasia; Trustee American Hall of Fame, Nat. Inst. of Arts and Letters; recipient of numerous awards including Roosevelt Medal 36, Gold Key Nat. Education Assen. 38, Scroll of Honour Fed. of Women's Clubs 41, Distinguished Service Medal American Assen. of Workers for the Blind 51, Gold Medal Nat. Inst. of Social Sciences 52; Nat. Motion Picture Acad. Award for documentary film 55; Chevalier Légion d'Honneur and other foreign decorations; hon. degrees from Temple, Glasgow, Witwatersrand, Delhi, Berlin Free and Harvard Univs.
Publs. *Story of My Life* 02, *Optimism* 03, *The World I Live In* 08, *The Song of the Stone Wall* 10, *Out of the Dark* 13, *My Religion* 27, *Midstream: My Later Life* 30, *Peace at Eventide* 32, *Helen Keller's Journal* 38, *Let us Have Faith* 41, *Teacher* 55, *The Open Door* 57.
[*Died* 1 *June* 1968]

Keller, Paul Victor, DR. JUR.; Swiss banker; b. 1 June 1898; ed. Univs. of Zürich, Geneva, Berlin, Paris.
Asst. Prof. Univ. of Zürich 26-30; Prof. of Economics, St. Gall Business School 30-37; Swiss Civil Service as Del. for Int. Commercial Arrangements 37-46; Pres. Swiss Nat. Bank 47-56; Deputy Chair. Swiss Reinsurance Co., Zürich 57, Chair. 58-64, Vice-Chair. 64-; Liberal.
Winkelwiese 6, Zürich 1, Switzerland.

Kellner, Béla, M.D.; Hungarian oncopathologist; b. 20 March 1904; ed. Univ. of Pécs, Hungary.
Privat Docent, Tumour Pathology, Pécs 36; Chief of Pathological Dept., Jewish Hospital, Budapest 41; Prof. of Pathological Anatomy and Dir. of Inst. of Pathological Anatomy, Univ. of Debrecen 47-54; Prof. and Dir. of Oncopathological Research Inst., Budapest 54-; Corresp. mem. Hungarian Acad. of Sciences 49-; Pres. Hungarian Cancer Soc. 64; mem. Scientific Council of Int. Agency for Cancer Research 65-; State Prize.
Publs. *Lymphkontengeschwülste* 65, and numerous articles on cancer and related subjects.
Office: Research Institute of Oncopathology, Budapest XII, Ráth Gy u. 5; Home: Budapest II, Eszter u. 21, Hungary.
Telephone: 157-190.

Kellock, Roy Lindsay, B.A., LL.D., D.C.L.; Canadian barrister; b. 12 Nov. 1893; ed. McMaster Univ., Osgoode Hall, Toronto.
Practised in Toronto 20-42; Judge Court of Appeal, Ontario 42; Judge Supreme Court of Canada 44-58; resumed practice in Toronto (Blake, Cassels & Graydon) 58-; Chancellor McMaster Univ., Ontario 56-60; Dir. North American Life Assurance Co., Canada Permanent Trust Co.
25 King Street West, Toronto, Canada.

Kellogg, Arthur Remington, M.A., PH.D.; American biologist; b. 5 Oct. 1892; ed. Univs. of Kansas and California.
Assistant Biologist 20-24 and Assoc. Biologist 24-28 Bureau Biological Survey, U.S. Dept. Agriculture; Asst. Curator 28-40 and Curator 41-48; Dir. U.S. Nat. Museum 48-62; Asst. Sec. Smithsonian Inst. 58-62; Research Assoc. 62-; Research Assoc., Carnegie Inst., Wash. 21-43; Chair. Int. Conf. for Regulation of Whaling, Washington 46; Vice-Chair. Int. Whaling Comm. 49-51, and Chair. 52-54; U.S. Commr. Int. Whaling Comm. 55-; U.S. del. to establish Int. Hylean Amazon Inst., Belém-do-Para, Brazil 47; mem. Nat.

Acad. of Sciences; American Philosophical Soc.; Fellow Zoological Society of London; mem. American Soc. of Naturalists; American Assen. of Anatomists, Geological Soc. of America, Paleontological Soc. of America, American Soc. of Mammalogists, American Acad. of Arts and Sciences.
5305 28th Street, N.W., Washington 15, D.C., U.S.A.

Kellou, Mohamed; Algerian lawyer and diplomatist; b. 27 March 1931; ed. Univs. of Algiers and Montpellier.
Lawyer, Algiers; fmr. Vice-Pres. Union Générale des Etudiants Musulmans Algériens (U.G.E.M.A.) (in charge of Foreign Affairs); Front de Libération Nationale (F.L.N.) Rep. in U.K. 57-61; Chief of Provisional Govt. of Algeria Diplomatic Mission to Pakistan 61-62; Chief of Africa-Asia-America Div., Ministry of Foreign Affairs, Republic of Algeria 62-63; Ambassador to U.K. 63-64, to Czechoslovakia 64-.
Algerian Embassy, Prague, Czechoslovakia; 40 blvd. des Martyrs, Algiers, Algeria.
Telephone: 60-00-55.

Kelly, Edna Flannery, B.A.; American politician; b. 20 Aug. 1906; ed. Hunter Coll., New York.
Associate Dir. of Research, Democratic Del. in New York State Legislature 42-44, Dir. 44; mem. Democratic Exec. Cttee. King's County, Brooklyn, N.Y.; mem. U.S. House of Reps. 49-; mem. House Cttee. on Foreign Affairs, Chair. Sub-cttee. on Europe; del. to 18th Gen. Assembly of UN; Chair. Canada-United States Inter-parliamentary Group; hon. D.Hum. Litt. Russell Sage Coll., Troy, N.Y.
1247 Carroll Street, Brooklyn, New York 11213, U.S.A.

Kelly, Gene Curran; American dancer and actor; b. 23 Aug. 1912; ed. Univ. of Pittsburgh.
Has appeared in *Leave it to Me* 38, *Time of Your Life* 40, *One for the Money* 39, *Pal Joey* 41; staged: *Billy Rose's Diamond Horseshoe* 40, *Best Foot Forward* 41; Dir. of dances for films: *Anchors Aweigh* 44, *The Pirate* 48, *Living in a Big Way* 47; appeared in films: *Me and My Girl* 42, *The Pirate* 48, *The Three Musketeers* 50, *An American in Paris* 50, *The Devil Makes Three* 52, *Brigadoon* 54, *Inherit the Wind* 60, *Gigo* 61, *The Young Girls of Rochefort* 67; Co-Dir. *On the Town* 49, *Singin' in the Rain* 51, *It's Always Fair Weather* 55; Dir. *Invitation to the Dance* 53, *What a Way to Go* 64; Producer and Dir. *The Happy Road* (France) 56, *Flower Drum Song* 58, etc.
Publ. *Take Me Out to the Ball Game* 48.
725 N. Rodeo Drive, Beverly Hills, Calif., U.S.A.

Kelly, Sir Gerald Festus, K.C.V.O., P.P.R.A., R.H.A., B.A.; British painter; b. 9 April 1879; ed. Eton and Trinity Hall, Cambridge.
Pictures at Marseilles, Brussels, Dublin, Cork, Johannesburg, Pietermaritzburg, Ottawa, Toronto, Sydney, Bradford, Hull, Manchester, Oldham, Paisley, Wolverhampton, Rochdale, Melbourne, Newport and the Tate Gallery; painted State portraits of King George VI and Queen Elizabeth; mem. Royal Fine Art Comm. 38-43; Keeper of Royal Acad. 43-45; Hon. Surveyor Dulwich Gallery 45-; Pres. Royal Acad. 49-54; Commdr. Légion d'Honneur (France); Commdr. Order of Orange Nassau (Neths.); Dr. h.c. (Cambridge and Trinity Coll., Dublin); corresp. mem. Real Academia San Fernando, Madrid; corresp. mem., Section de Peinture, Acad. des Beaux-Arts de l'Institut de France.
117 Gloucester Place, London, W.1, England.
Telephone: 01-935-0148.

Kelly, Rev. John Norman Davidson, M.A., D.D.; British ecclesiastic, scholar and university official; b. 13 April 1909; ed. Univs. of Glasgow and Oxford.
Ordained Deacon 34 and Priest 35; Curate, St. Lawrence's, Northampton 34-35; Chaplain and Tutor, St. Edmund Hall, Oxford 35-37, Vice-Principal, Fellow and Trustee 37-51, Principal 51-; Oxford Univ. Lecturer in

Patristic Studies 48-; Pro-Vice-Chancellor 64-66; during World War II did part-time work for Chatham House; Canon at Chichester Cathedral 48-; Hon. D.D. (Glasgow) 58; F.B.A. 65.
Publs. *Early Christian Creeds* 50, *Rufinus: A Commentary on the Apostles' Creed* 55, *Early Christian Doctrines* 58, *The Pastoral Epistles* 63, *The Athanasian Creed* 64.
Principal's Lodgings, St. Edmund Hall, Oxford, England.
Telephone: Oxford 41039.

Kemal, Yashar; Turkish writer and journalist; b. 22; ed. self-educated.
Publs. *Memed, My Hawk* 61, *The Wind from the Plain* 63; novels, short stories, plays, and essays in Turkish.
Basınköy, Küçükçekmece, Istanbul, Turkey.

Kemball-Cook, Denis Basil; American oil executive; b. 10; ed. Shrewsbury School and Balliol Coll., Oxford.
Director, Compañía Shell de Venezuela, Caracas 51-57; Dir. and Vice-Pres. Shell Caribbean Petroleum and Asiatic Petroleum Corpn., New York 57-58; Exec. Vice-Pres. and Dir. Shell Oil Co., New York 58-, mem. Exec. Cttee. 62-; Dir. American Petroleum Inst.
Shell Oil Co., 50 West 50th Street, New York City, N.Y., U.S.A.

Kemoularia, Claude de; French international administrator; b. 30 March 1922; ed. Coll. Carnot, Fontainebleau, Univ. de Paris Faculty of Law and Ecole Libre des Sciences Politiques.
Early career with Ministry of Interior 45, Office of Gov.-Gen. French Zone of Occupied Germany 46-47, Ministry of Finance 48; Parl. Sec. to Paul Reynaud 48-56; Personal Asst. to Sec.-Gen. of UN, Dag Hammarskjöld 57-61, in charge of World Refugee Year 59-60; Dir. European Inf. Services of UN 61; entered private business 62; Exec. Dir. Forges de Chatillon-Commentry 62-; Special Adviser to Administrator, UN Devt. Programme 64-; Private Adviser to Prince Rainier of Monaco 65-67; Chair. Soc. Panafricaine d'Etudes et de Réalisations 65-; financial adviser for int. operations (Banque de Paris et des Pays-Bas).
41 boulevard du Commandant Charcot, Neuilly-sur-Seine, Seine, France; 7 rue de l'Athénée, Geneva, Switzerland.
Telephone: TRI 0082.

Kempe, Rudolf; German conductor; b. 14 June 1910; ed. Dresden Staatskapelle.
Member Leipzig Gewandhaus Orchestra 29, Conductor 36; First Conductor, Chemnitz State Theatre 42, Gen. Musical Dir. 46; Gen. Musical Dir. Nat. Theatre, Weimar 48, Sächsisches Staatstheater, Dresden 49, Bavarian State Opera, Munich 52-54; guest conductor New York, London, Vienna Operas, etc., 54-; Chief Conductor, Royal Philharmonic Orchestra London 61-, Artistic Dir. 64-; Chief Conductor Tonhalle Orchestra, Zürich 65-, Artistic Dir. 65-; Gen. Music Dir. Munich Philharmonic Orchestra 67-.
8184 Duernbach/Tegernsee, Bavaria, German Federal Republic.

Kempff, Wilhelm Walter Friedrich; German pianist and composer; b. 25 Nov. 1895; ed. Viktoria Gymnasium, Potsdam, Berlin Univ. and Conservatoire.
Professor and Dir. Stuttgart Staatliche Hochschule für Musik 24-29; since then concert tours as pianist throughout the world; mem. Prussian Acad. of Arts; Mendelssohn Prize, Artibus et Litteris Medal (Sweden), etc.
Compositions include two symphonies, four operas, piano concertos and chamber, vocal and choral music.
Publs. *Unter dem Zimbelstern, Das Werden eines Musikers* (autobiography).
8193 Ammerland, Oberbayern, German Federal Republic.

Kemula, Wiktor, DR. PHIL., DR. CHEM.; Polish university professor; b. 6 March 1902.
Asst. Univ. of Lwów 23-32, Lecturer 32-36, Extra. Prof. 36-39, Prof. 39-45; Prof. of Inorganic Chemistry Univ. of Warsaw 45-, Dean of Faculty of Science 47-50; Dir. Chemical Inst. of Faculty of Mathematics, Physics and Chemistry 52-; mem. Societas Scientiarum Leopoldiensis 36-, Societas Scientiarum Varsoviensis 47- (Sec. of Section III 48-51); Chief Editor *Roczniki Chemii* 50-, *Chemia Analityczna* 56-; Pres. Polish Chemical Soc. 55-60; mem. Polish Acad. of Sciences 56-; mem. New York Acad. of Sciences 60-; Vice-Rector, Univ. of Warsaw 56-59; Hon. mem. Soc. de Chimie Industrielle, Paris 59; mem. Deutsche Akademie der Naturforscher Leopoldina 60; J. Sniadecki Medal of the Polish Chemical Soc. for Scientific Achievements 65; Hon. mem. Czechoslovak Chemical Soc. 66-; J. Hanuš Medal of Czechoslovak Chem. Soc. 66-.
Publs. Numerous scientific works in photochemistry, chromato-polarography, polarography, and analytical chemistry.
Ul. Pasteura 1, Warsaw 22, Poland.
Telephone: 22-23-75.

Kendall, Donald; American business executive; b. 16 March 1921; ed. Western Kentucky State Coll.
Air Corps, U.S. Naval Reserve 42-47; Vice-Pres. Pepsi-Cola Co. 52-57; Pres. Pepsi-Cola Int. 57-63, Pepsi-Cola Co. 63-65; Pres. and Chief Exec. Officer, PepsiCo Inc. 65-; Dir. of: Alaska Airlines, Daytona Int. Speedway Corpn., Sinclair Oil Corpn., Prudential Lines Inc., etc.; Pres. ACCION Int.; Trustee Council for Latin America.
Office: PepsiCo Inc., 500 Park Ave., New York, N.Y. 10022; Home: Porchuck Road, Greenwich, Connecticut, U.S.A.
Telephone: 212-MU8-4500 (Office); 203-661-7040 (Home).

Kendall, Edward C., C.M.S., PH.D.; American research chemist; b. 8 March 1886; ed. Columbia Univ., New York City.
Research chemist for Parke-Davis & Co. 10, where he began thyroid research, continued at St. Luke's Hospital New York 11-14; Head of Biochemistry Section, Mayo Clinic 14-46, Prof. of Physio-Chemistry 21-51, Emeritus; engaged on work on hormones of the adrenal cortex 20 years; associated with experiments leading to commercial cortisone and its early use; awards include: Lasker Award (American Public Health Asscn.) 49, Cameron Award (Univ. of Edinburgh) 51, Kober Medal (Asscn. of American Physicians) 52 and Nobel Prize for Physiology and Medicine (with Dr. Hench and Prof. Reichstein) 50; Visiting Prof. in Chemistry, James Forrestal Research Center, Princeton Univ.
3 Queenston Place, Princeton, New Jersey 08540, U.S.A.

Kendall, James, M.A., D.SC., F.R.S.; British chemist; b. 30 July 1889; ed. Edinburgh Univ. and Stockholm Nobel Inst.
Prof. of Chemistry, Columbia Univ., New York 13-26, N.Y. Univ. 26-28, Edinburgh Univ. 28-59, Dean of Science Faculty 53-54 and 57-59; Pres. Royal Society of Edinburgh 49-54; Vice-Pres. British Asscn. for Advancement of Science 51; fmr. Chair. New York Section, American Chemical Society, and Dean of Graduate School, New York Univ.; Hon. LL.D.
Publs. *At Home Among the Atoms, Breathe Freely, The Truth About Poison Gas, Great Discoveries by Young Chemists, Humphry Davy: Pilot of Penzance, Michael Faraday: Man of Simplicity.*
200 Colinton Road, Edinburgh, Scotland.

Kendall, Maurice George, M.A., SC.D.; British statistician; b. 6 Sept. 1907; ed. Central School Derby, and St. John's Coll. Cambridge.
Permanent Civil Servant with Min. of Agriculture and Fisheries 30-40; Statistician to the Chamber of Shipping of the U.K. 40-49, Joint Asst. Gen. Man. 47-49; Prof. of Statistics Univ. of London 49-61; Dir. of Scientific

Services, Corpn. for Econ. and Industrial Research 61-, Man. Dir. 62-, Chair. 67-; Fellow American Statistical Asscn., Inst. of Mathematical Statistics; mem. Int. Statistical Inst.; Silver and Gold Medallist of the Royal Statistical Soc.; Vice-Pres. Market Research Soc.; fmr. Pres. Operational Research Soc., Royal Statistical Soc. Publs. *An Introduction to the Theory of Statistics* (with G. Udny Yule), 15th edn. 55, *The Advanced Theory of Statistics* (with A. Stuart), Vol. I, 2nd edn. 63, Vol. II, 2nd edn. 67, Vol. III, 1st edn. 66, *Contributions to the Study of Oscillatory Time-Series* 46, *Rank Correlation Methods*, 3rd edn. 62, *A Dictionary of Statistical Terms* (with W. R. Buckland), *A Course in Multivariate Analysis* 57, *The Geometry of n dimensions* 61, *Geometrical Probability* 63 (co-author), *Bibliography of Statistical Literature* Vols. 1-3 63-66 (co-author).
1 Frank Dixon Close, London, S.E.21, England.
Telephone: 01-693-6076.

Kendall, William Hersey; American railway executive; b. 24 March 1910; ed. Dartmouth Coll., and Thayer School of Civil Engineering.
Maintenance Engineer, Pennsylvania Railroad 33-48; Exec. Officer, Atlantic Coast Line Railroad 48-50, Clinchfield Railroad 50-54, now Dir. and mem. Exec. Cttee.; Exec. Officer, Louisville and Nashville Railroad 54-, Vice-Pres., Gen. Manager 57-59, Pres. 59-; official of other railroads.
Louisville and Nashville Railroad, 908 W. Broadway, Louisville 1, Kentucky, U.S.A.

Kendrew, Maj.-Gen. Sir Douglas Anthony, K.C.M.G., C.B., C.B.E., D.S.O., K.ST.J.; British army officer and administrator; b. 22 July 1910; ed. Uppingham School.
Second Lieutenant, Royal Leicestershire Regt. 31, Major 41; Brigade Major, N. Africa 42, Cmmdr., 6th Batt., York and Lancaster Regt., North Africa and Italy 43, Brigade Cmmdr., Italy, Middle East, and Greece 43-46; Commdt. School of Infantry, Rhine Army 46-48; Commdt. Army Apprentice School, Harrogate 48-50; Chief of Staff, Northern Ireland Dist. 50-52; Commdr., 29th Infantry Brigade, Korea 52-53; Imperial Defence Coll. 54; Brigadier Admin., H.Q. Northern Command 55; Gen. Officer Commanding, Cyprus District, and Dir. of Operations 56-58; Dir. of Infantry, War Office 58-60; Head of British Defence Liaison Staff, Australia 60-63; Gov. of W. Australia 63-.
Government House, Perth, Western Australia.

Kendrew, John Cowdery, C.B.E., SC.D., F.R.S.; British molecular biophysicist; b. 24 March 1917; ed. Dragon School, Oxford, Clifton Coll. and Trinity Coll. Cambridge.
Ministry of Aircraft Production 40-45; Fellow of Peterhouse, Cambridge 47-; Medical Research Council 47-, Dep. Chair. Medical Research Council Laboratory of Molecular Biology, Cambridge 53-; Reader, Davy-Faraday Lab., Royal Inst. 54-; Scientific Adviser (part-time), Ministry of Defence 60-63; mem. Council for Scientific Policy 65-; Editor-in-Chief *Journal of Molecular Biology*; Nobel Prize for Chemistry 62; Royal Medal, Royal Soc. 65.
Publ. *The Thread of Life* 66.
Guildhall, Church Lane, Linton, Cambridgeshire, England.
Telephone: Linton 545.

Kendrick, Sir Thomas Downing, K.C.B., D.LITT., LITT.D., F.B.A., F.S.A.; British antiquarian; b. 95.
Fmr. Keeper of British Antiquities in the British Museum; Dir. and Principal Librarian May 50-59.
Publs. *The Lisbon Earthquake* 56, *Saint James in Spain* 60, *Great Love for Icarus* 62, *Mary of A'greda* 67.
Organford Farm House, nr. Poole, Dorset, England.

Keng Piao; Chinese soldier, diplomatist and politician; ed. Chinese Officers' Acad.
Ambassador to Sweden 50-56, to Pakistan 56-59; Dep.

Minister of Foreign Affairs 60-63; Ambassador to Burma 63-.
Embassy of the Chinese People's Republic, Rangoon, Burma.

Kennan, George Frost, A.B.; American diplomatist and scholar; b. 16 Feb. 1904; ed. Princeton Univ.
Vice-Consul Hamburg 27, Tallin 28; Third Sec. Riga, Kovno and Tallin 29; Language Officer Berlin 29; Third Sec. Riga 31; Moscow 34; Consul Vienna 35; Second Sec.35; Second Sec. Moscow 35; Dept. of State 37; Second Sec. Prague 38; Consul 39; Second Sec. Berlin 39, First Sec. 40; Counsellor Lisbon 42; Counsellor to U.S. Del. European Advisory Comm. London 44; Minister-Counsellor Moscow 45; Deputy for Foreign Affairs, Nat. War Coll., Washington 46; Policy Planning Staff, Dept. of State 47; Chief, Policy Planning Staff, Dept. of State 49-50; on leave, at Inst. for Advanced Study, Princeton, N.J. 50-51, Prof. 56; Ambassador to U.S.S.R. 52-53; retd. from Foreign Service 53; Charles R. Walgreen Foundation Lecturer, Univ. of Chicago 51; Stafford Little Lecturer, Princeton 54; George Eastman Visiting Prof. Oxford Univ. 57-58; Reith Lecturer on *Russia, The Atom and the West* 57; Visiting Lecturer, History, Harvard Univ. 60, Yale Univ. 60; Ambassador to Yugoslavia 61-63; Prof. Inst. for Advanced Study, Princeton 63-, Princeton Univ. 64-; Pres. Nat. Inst. of Arts and Letters 65-; Univ. Fellow in History and Slavic Civilizations, Harvard Univ. 66-; Nat. Book Award, Bancroft Prize, Pulitzer Prize history 56, biography 68, Francis Parkman Prize; LL.D. h.c. (Yale, Dartmouth, Colgate, Notre Dame, Kenyon, New School for Social Research, Princeton, Michigan, Northwestern, Brandeis, Denison, Harvard, Rutgers, Wisconsin Univs.).
Publs. *American Diplomacy 1900-1950* 52, *Das Amerikanisch-Russische Verhältnis* 54, *Realities of American Foreign Policy* 54, *Soviet-American Relations 1917-1920*, Vol. I, *Russia Leaves the War* 56, Vol. II, *The Decision to Intervene* 58, *Russia, The Atom and the West* (Reith Lectures) 58, *Soviet Foreign Policy 1917-45* 60, *Russia and the West under Lenin and Stalin* 61, *On Dealing with the Communist World* 63, *Memoirs 1925-1950* 67, *Democracy and the Student Left* 68.
Office: Institute for Advanced Study, Princeton, N.J.; Home: 146 Hodge Road, Princeton, N.J., U.S.A.

Kennedy, David Matthew, A.B., M.A., LL.B.; American banker; b. 21 July 1905; ed. Weber Coll., George Washington Univ., and Stonier Graduate School of Banking, Rutgers Univ.
Special Asst. to Chair. Board, Fed. Reserve System 30-46; Vice-Pres. in charge Bond Dept. Continental Ill. Nat. Bank and Trust Co. of Chicago 46-53, Pres. 56-59, Chair. of Board and Chief Exec. Officer 59-; asst. to Sec. of Treasury, Washington 53-55; Chair. Exec. Board Comm. for Econ. and Cultural Development of Chicago, Chicago Clearing House Assocn.; Dir. Abbott Laboratories, Int. Harvester Co., Commonwealth Edison Co., Pullman Co., Swift and Co., Radio New York Worldwide Communications Satellite Corpn., United States Gypsum Co.; Trustee, Univ. of Chicago, Presbyterian-St. Luke's Hospital, Equitable of Iowa, Brookings Inst., George Washington Univ.; Republican.
231 South La Salle Street, Chicago 90, Illinois, U.S.A.

Kennedy, Donald D., B.S., M.A., PH.D.; American economist; b. 9 June 1900; ed. Pittsburgh, Pennsylvania Univs.
Professor, Newark Univ. 37-42; Office of Price Administration 42-44; Foreign Relations Officer, Dept. of State 46-60; Foreign Service Officer 55-60; Head, U.S. Dels. to numerous int. confs.; Dep. Chief of Mission, New Delhi 54-55; American Consul-Gen., Sydney 55-57; Dep. Asst. Sec. of State, Bureau of Near Eastern and South Asian Affairs 57-60; Special Asst. for Indus

Basin Affairs, Int. Bank for Reconstruction and Development 60-63, Econ. Consultant 63-.
4301 Massachusetts Avenue, N.W., Washington 16, D.C., U.S.A.

Kennedy, Edward Moore, A.B., LL.B., (brother of late Pres. John F. Kennedy); American lawyer and politician; b. 22 Feb. 1932; ed. Milton Acad., Harvard Coll. and Univ. of Virginia Law School.
Reporter, Int. News Service, N. Africa 56; Manager Western States, John F. Kennedy Presidential Campaign 60; fmr. Asst. District Attorney, Mass.; U.S. Senator from Mass. 63-; Pres. Joseph P. Kennedy Jr. Foundation; Trustee, Boston Univ.; Board mem. Fletcher School of Law and Diplomacy; Hon. L.H.D. (Emmanuel Coll.) and many other hon. degrees; Democrat.
U.S. Senate, Washington, D.C., U.S.A.

Kennedy, Jacqueline Lee Bouvier (Mrs. John F. Kennedy); b. 28 July 1929; ed. Vassar Coll., George Washington Univ., U.S.A. and the Univ. of Paris.
Photographer *Washington Times-Herald* 52; initiated and supervised historical reconstruction of décor of the White House 61-63; Rep. of the late Pres. Kennedy on tour of India 62.
1040 Fifth Avenue, at 85th Street, New York City, U.S.A.

Kennedy, Joseph Patrick, A.B., (father of late Pres. John F. Kennedy); American businessman and diplomatist; b. 6 Sept. 1888; ed. Boston Latin School and Harvard Univ.
Bank Examiner for Massachusetts 12-14; Pres. Columbia Trust Co. Boston 14-17; Asst. Gen. Man. Fore River (Massachusetts) plant, Bethlehem Shipbuilding Corpn. 17-19; Man. Hayden-Stone Co. (investment bankers) Boston branch 19-24; Pres. and Chair. Board of Dirs. Keith-Albee-Orpheum Theatres Corpn. 28-29; Pres. and Chair. Board Film Booking Offices of America 26-29; Chair. Board Dirs. Pathé Exchange Inc. 29-30; Corpn. Finance 30-34; mem. Securities Exchange Comm. July 34, Chair. 34-35; resigned; Chair. U.S. Maritime Comm. 37; Ambassador to Great Britain 37-40, resgnd.; Chair. Special Comm. to establish Dept. of Commerce in Mass. 45; Trustee Notre Dame Univ.; mem. Comm. on Organisation of Exec. Branch Federal Government 47, 53; founder, Joseph P. Kennedy Jr. Foundation; Knight of Malta, Grand Knight of Pius X, Knight of Equestrian Order of Holy Sepulchre; Hon. LL.D. (Manchester, Dublin, Edinburgh, Liverpool, Bristol, Cambridge, Catholic Univ. Washington, D.C., Oglethorpe, Notre Dame, Colby Coll.); Democrat.
North Ocean Boulevard, Palm Beach, Fla., U.S.A.

Kennedy, Robert Francis (brother of late Pres. John F. Kennedy); American lawyer and politician; b. 20 Nov. 1925; ed. Harvard, Univ. of Virginia Law School.
War correspondent in Palestine for the *Boston Post*; Attorney, Criminal Division, U.S. Department of Justice 51; Asst. Counsel Hoover Commission on Organization of the Exec. Branch of Federal Govt. 53-54; Chief Counsel U.S. Senate Permanent Sub-Cttee. on Investigations 54-61; Chief Counsel to the U.S. Senate Select Cttee. on Improper Activities in the Labor or Management Field 57-61; Attorney-Gen. 61-64; Senator from New York 65-; Democrat.
Publs. *The Enemy Within* 60, *Just Friends and Brave Enemies* 62, *Pursuit of Justice* 64, *To Seek a Newer World* 67.
[*Assassinated; Died 6 June* 1968]

Kennedy, Sylvester Michael; American businessman; b. 21 Nov. 1894; ed. Pace Inst., New York City, Walton School of Commerce, Chicago and DePaul Univ.
Accountant, William W. Thompson & Co. (C.P.A.'s),

Chicago 19-26, 37-39; Vice-Pres., Sec.-Treas. Nat. Grocers Co. Ltd., Toronto, Ontario 26-31; Gen. Man. Almar Stores Corpn., Philadelphia 31-34; Pres. The Fargason Co., Memphis 34-37; Vice-Pres. and Dir. Consolidated Foods Corpn., Chicago 39-47, Pres. 47-62, Vice-Chair. of Board, Chair. Finance Cttee. 62-67, Chair. of Board, mem. Board of Dirs. 67-; Dir. Nat. Boulevard Bank of Chicago 61-62, Vice-Chair. 62-.
135 S. La Salle Street, Chicago 3, Ill., U.S.A.

Kennet, (2nd Baron) cr. 35, of the Dene; **Wayland Young;** British writer and politician; b. 2 Aug. 1923; ed. Stowe School, Trinity Coll., Cambridge, Perugia and Harvard Univs.
Royal Navy 42-45; Foreign Office 46-47, 49-51; mem. Parl. Assembly Council of Europe and Western European Union 62-65; Chair. British Cttee. for International Co-operation 65; Parl. Sec., Ministry of Housing and Local Govt. 66-.
Publs. *The Italian Left* 49, *The Deadweight* 52, *Now or Never* 53, *Old London Churches* (with Elizabeth Young) 56, *The Montesi Scandal* 57, *Still Alive Tomorrow* 58, *Strategy for Survival* 59, *The Socialist Imagination* (with Elizabeth Young) 60, *Disarmament: Finnegan's Choice* (with Elizabeth Young) 61, *The Profumo Affair* 63, *Eros Denied* 65; Editor *Disarmament and Arms Control* 63-65.
100 Bayswater Road, London, W.2, England.
Telephone: 01-723-2020.

Kenny, Sean; Irish designer; b. 23 Dec. 1929; ed. St. Flannan's Coll., Co. Clare, School of Architecture, Dublin, Frank Lloyd Wright Fellowship U.S.A.
Designer of sets for stage productions: *Shadow of a Gunman* 57, *Bloomsday* 58, *Hamlet* 58, *Coriolanus* 59, *Lock up your Daughters* 59, *The Hostage* 59, *Cock-a-Doodle-Dandy* 59, *Glimpse of the Sea* 59, *Julius Caesar* 60, *Treasure Island* 60, *The Lily White Boys* 60, *Henry V* 60, *Great Expectations* 60, *Here is the News* 60, *Tchin-Tchin* 60, *Oliver* 60, *Laughing Academy* 60, *Why the Chicken* 61, *The Devils* 61, *Altona* 61, *The Miracle Worker* 61, *Stop the World, I want to get off* 61, *Arms and the Man* 61, *Romeo and Juliet* 61, *Blitz* 62, *King Priam* (opera) 62, *Uncle Vanya* 62, *Pickwick* 63, *The Beggar's Opera* 63, *Hamlet* 63, *Maggie May* 64, *The Flying Dutchman* 65, *Roar of the Greasepaint . . .* 65; sets for television and films: *Windmill near a Frontier* 60, *I Thank a Fool* 62; architecture and interior design: Quinn House, Londonderry 53, Theatre for the Casino de Liban 65 and Casino de Paris, Las Vegas 63, 67, Univ. of Sussex Fine Arts Centre Theatre 66, Gyrotron Spectacular Ride and Section One of the British Pavilion, Expo 67, Montreal 67, Welsh Mobile Theatre 68, Winter Garden Theatre 68; Antoinette Perry (Tony) Award for set for *Oliver* 63.
13 Manette Street, London, W.1, England.
Telephone: 01-437-4286.

Kent-Hughes, Col. The Hon. Sir Wilfrid Selwyn, K.B.E., M.V.O., M.C., E.D., M.A.; Australian politician; b. 12 June 1895; ed. Christ Church, Oxford.
Member Victoria Parl. 27-49; M.H.R. for Chisholm, Victoria 49-; Hon. Minister 32, Minister of Transport and Labour 34-35; Deputy Leader Opposition (United Australia Party) 35-39; Minister of Transport and Education 47-48; Deputy Leader Liberal Party 48; Minister of Transport and Electricity, and Deputy Premier 48-49; mem. Federal Parl. 49; Minister for Interior and Works 51-56; Chair. Foreign Affairs Cttee. 56-61; Dir. Ramsay Ware Publishing Proprietary Ltd.; Chair. 1956 Olympic Games Melbourne; Pres. Victorian Olympic Council and Victorian A.A.A.; war service 14-19, 39-46; Hon. LL.D. (China) 66.
Publs. *Modern Crusaders* 18, *Slaves of the Samurai* 46.
4 Selborne Road, Kew, Melbourne, Australia.
Telephone: 81-5646.

Kenter, Ayşe Yildiz; Turkish actress and producer; b. 28; ed. State Conservatoire.

Worked in State Theatre for eleven years, playing almost forty parts; Rockefeller Fellowship in Dramatic Art; teacher of Dramatic Art, State Conservatoire; now acting and producing independently; twice awarded Iskender Prize for best performance of the year. Ihlamur Cad. Kuyulu bostan Sokak No. 31/5 Nişantaş, Istanbul, Turkey.

Kentner, Louis Philip; British (born Hungarian) pianist; b. 19 July 1905; ed. Royal Acad. of Music, Budapest.

Studied with Arnold Székely, Leo Weiner and Zoltan Kodály; concert pianist at age of 14, and has since performed in many parts of the world; took up residence in England 35; gave first performance of Bartók's Second Concerto under Otto Klemperer's direction; world tour 53; gave several complete performances of Beethoven's Piano Sonatas and Violin and Piano Sonatas with Yehudi Menuhin 54-55; gave first performance of Michael Tippett's Piano Concerto in Birmingham Oct. 56; toured South America 56; five tours of U.S.A. and Canada 56-; tours of U.S.S.R. 63, 64, 67; Pres. Liszt Soc. 65-.

Compositions: *3 Sonatinas for Piano.*
1 Mallord Street, London, S.W.3, England.

Kenyatta, Jomo (Johnstone); Kenyan politician; b. 20 Oct. 1891; ed. Dagoretti Scottish Mission and London School of Economics.

Worked for Nairobi Municipality; returned to Kenya from studies in London 46; Pres. Kenya African Union 47; convicted of managing Mau Mau movement and sentenced to imprisonment 53, released April 59, restricted to Lodwar April 59-April 61; restricted to Maralal April-Aug. 61; Pres. Kenya African Nat. Union (KANU) Aug. 61-, Leader KANU Del. to London Constitutional Conf. Feb.-March 62; mem. Legislative Council 62-; Minister of State for Constitutional Affairs and for Econ. Planning April 62-63; Prime Minister also Minister for Internal Security and Defence and Foreign Affairs 63-64, Pres. 64-; Hon. Fellow London School of Econs.; Hon. LL.D. (East Africa).

Publs. *Facing Mount Kenya, Kenya, the Land of Conflict, My People of Kikuyu, Harambee!*
Office of the President, P.O.B. 30510, Nairobi; State House, P.O.B. 530, Nairobi, Kenya; Home: Gatundu, Kenya.

Kenyon, Kathleen Mary, C.B.E., D.LITT., D.LIT., L.H.D., F.B.A., F.S.A.; British archaeologist; b. 5 Jan. 1906; ed. St. Paul's Girls' School and Somerville Coll., Oxford.

Sec. Inst. of Archæology 35-48, Council for British Archæology 44-49; Lecturer Univ. of London Inst. of Archaeology 48-62; Dir. British School of Archaeology in Jerusalem; Principal, St. Hugh's Coll., Oxford Aug. 62-; has participated in and directed numerous excavations in U.K. and Middle East.

Publs. *Excavations at the Jewry Wall, Leicester* 48, *Samaria-Sebaste I* 42, *III* 57 (joint author), *Beginning in Archaeology* 54, *Digging up Jericho* 57, *Excavations at Jericho I* 60, *II* 65, *Archaeology in the Holy Land* 60, *Amorites and Canaanites* 66, *Jerusalem* 67.
St. Hugh's College, Oxford, England.

Keogh, Eugene J.; American politician; b. 30 Aug. 1907; ed. School of Commerce, New York Univ. and School of Law, Fordham Univ.

Member, N.Y. State Assembly 36; mem. U.S. House of Reps. 37-67, fmr. mem. Cttee. on Ways and Means, Adv. Comm. on Inter-governmental Relations; Chair. Franklin D. Roosevelt Memorial Comm.; partner, Halpin, Keogh and St. John, New York City; Trustee and Counsel, The East New York Savings Bank; Dir. Bank of North America, City Title Insurance Co.; New York World's Fair Corpn. 64-65; Athlone Industries Inc.; Democrat.
Office: 30 Rockefeller Plaza, N.Y.C. 20; Home: 1247 Hancock Street, Brooklyn 21, U.S.A.

Keppel, Francis, A.B.; American educational administrator; b. 10 Dec. 1916; ed. Harvard Coll., American Acad. Rome.

Secretary, Joint Army and Navy Cttee. on Welfare and Recreation, Washington 41-44; U.S. Army 44-46; Asst. to Provost, Harvard 46-48, Dean, Harvard Graduate School of Education 48-62; U.S. Commr. of Education, U.S. Dept. of Health, Education and Welfare Dec. 62-Oct. 65, Asst. Sec. (for Educ.) Oct. 65-; mem. Board of Foreign Scholarships, U.S. Nat. Comm. for UNESCO 63-; Fellow American Acad. of Arts and Sciences.
Publ. *The Necessary Revolution in American Education* 66.
Office: 3 East 54th Street, N.Y.C. 10022; Home: 1100 Park Avenue, N.Y.C. 10028, U.S.A.

Kerby, William Frederick; American editor and business executive; b. 28 July 1908; ed. Univ. of Michigan.

Staff Corresp., United Press Asscn., Washington, D.C. 30-32; *Wall Street Journal*, Washington 33-35, New York 37-42, Managing Editor 43-44; Exec. Editor Dow Jones publications 45-51, Vice-Pres. Dow Jones and Co. Inc. 51-60; Exec. Vice-Pres. Dow Jones and Co. Inc. and Editorial Dir. Dow Jones publications 61-66, Pres. Dow Jones and Co. Inc. 66-.
253 Hicks Street, Brooklyn 1, N.Y., U.S.A.

Kerensky, Alexander Fedorovitch; Russian-born politician and writer, now living in U.S.A.; b. 4 May 1881; ed. Tashkent and St. Petersburg Univ.

Called to St. Petersburg Bar 04; mem. of Fourth State Duma (Parliament) 12-17; Minister of Justice in Provisional Govt. Mar.-April 17, Minister of War and Navy May-Sept. 17, Minister-Pres. July-Nov. 17, Commdr.-in-Chief Sept.-Nov. 17; thereafter lived in France and England until 1940 and since then in U.S.A., as writer, editor of newspapers and magazines, lecturer and visiting professor.

Publs. include *The Prelude to Bolshevism, Soviet Russia in the Autumn of 1919* 19, *Allied Policy Towards Russia* 20, *The Catastrophe* 29, *The Crucifixion of Liberty* 34, *Provisional Government of 1917 in Documents* (three vols.) 61, *Russia and History's Turning Point* 65.
109 East 91st Street, New York 28, N.Y., U.S.A.

Keresztury, Dezsö, PH.D.; Hungarian literary historian and writer; b. 6 Sept. 1904; ed. Budapest, Vienna and Berlin.

Lecturer and librarian in Hungarian Inst. of Berlin Univ. 28-36; lecturer in Hungarian Literature, Eötvös Coll. Budapest 35-45, Dir. of Coll. 45-48; Minister of Education 45-47; Chief Librarian of Hungarian Acad. 48-51; Head of Historical Collections in Nat. Széchényi Library; Vice-Pres. Soc. of Hungarian Literary History; edited selected speeches of Mihály Babits, Géza Laczkó, Károly Pap, the complete works of János Batsányi and János Arany.

Publs. *Arany János, Ungarn, A német irodalom kincsesháza, Balaton, Helyünk a világban, A magyar irodalom képeskönyve, A magyar zenetörténet képeskönyve, A német elbeszélés mesterei, A német lira kincsesháza, Dunántuli hexameterek, Lassul a szél, Emberi Nyelven.*
c/o National Széchenyi Library, Muzeum-krt. 14/16, Budapest VIII, Hungary.
Telephone: 134-400.

Kerimov, Jangir Ali Abasovich; Soviet lawyer; b. 1923; ed. U.S.S.R. Corresp. Law Inst.

Service in the Army 41-46; mem. C.P.S.U. 44-; Postgraduate, Lecturer, Head of Chair Kalinin Law Inst., Leningrad 47-54; Postgraduate Inst. of Law U.S.S.R. Acad. of Sciences 54-56; Head of Chair Leningrad Univ·

56-57; Prof. Ulbricht Acad. of State and Legal Sciences at Berlin Univ., D.D.R. 57-59; Head of Chair, Prorector Leningrad Univ. 65-; Corresp. mem. U.S.S.R. Acad. of Sciences 66-.
Publs. Works on theory of socialist state, etc.
U.S.S.R. Academy of Sciences, 14 Lenin Prospekt, Moscow, U.S.S.R.

Kerner, Otto, B.A., J.D.; American lawyer and politician; b. 15 Aug. 1908; ed. Trinity Coll., Cambridge, Northwestern Univ. School of Law and Brown Univ.
Called to Bar 34; Law practice 34-47; Armed Forces (Maj.-Gen.) 34-54; Attorney North Dist. Illinois 47-54; County Judge 54-60; Gov. of Illinois 60-; Democrat.
State Capitol, Springfield, Illinois 62706, U.S.A.

Kerouac, Jack (Jean-Louis); American author; b. 12 March 1922; ed. Horace Mann School, New York and Columbia Univ.
Service in U.S. Navy and Merchant Marine; has travelled widely in N. and Central America, N. Africa and Europe.
Publs. *The Town and the City* 50, *On the Road* 57, *The Dharma Bums* 58, *The Subterraneans* 58, *Doctor Sax* 59, *Maggie Cassidy* 59, *Mexico City Blues* (poems) 59, *Tristessa* 60, *Lonesome Traveler* 60, *Vision of Cody* 60, *Book of Dreams* 61, *Scripture of the Golden Eternity* 61, *Big Sur* 62, *Visions of Gerard* 63, *Desolation Angels* 65, *Satori in Paris* 66, *Vanity of Duluoz* 68.
The Sterling Lord Agency, 75 East 55th Street, New York City, N.Y. 10022, U.S.A.

Kerr, Alexander Enoch, B.A., B.D.; Canadian university president (retired); b. 24 Feb. 1898; ed. Dalhousie Univ., Pine Hill Divinity Hall, Halifax, N.S., Union Theological Seminary, New York.
Served with R.A.F. 18; Asst. Minister St. Andrew's Church, Sydney, N.S. 21; Asst. Minister Park Avenue Presbyterian Church, New York 22; Assoc. Minister American Presbyterian Church, Montreal 23-24; Minister St. Andrew's Presbyterian (later United) Church, Vancouver 24-29; Minister Augustine United Church, Winnipeg 29-39; Principal Pine Hill Divinity Hall, Halifax, N.S. 39-45; Pres. Dalhousie Univ. Halifax 45-63; Pres. Maritime Conf., United Church 65-66; Hon. D.D. (United Coll., Winnipeg) 39, (Acadia Univ.) 48, (Glasgow Univ.) 51, (Pine Hill, Halifax) 60; Hon. LL.D. (Mount Allison Univ.) 46, (Univ. of New Brunswick) 50, (Dalhousie) 64.
Publs. *A Preface to Christmas* 51, *In the Last Analysis* 58, *The Ten Words* 60.
c/o Dalhousie University, Halifax, N.S., Canada.

Kerr, Chester Brooks, B.A.; American publisher; b. 5 Aug. 1913; ed. La Villa, Lausanne (Switzerland), Univ. School, Cleveland (Ohio) and Yale Univ.
Editor Harcourt, Brace & Co. 36-40; Dir. Atlantic Monthly Press 40-42; Chief Book Div., Office of War Information and Dept. of State 42-46; Vice-Pres. Reynal & Hitchcock 46-47; Sec. Yale Univ. Press 49-59; Dir. 59-; Sec.-Treas. Asscn. of American Univ. Presses 57-59, Pres. 65-67; Consultant to Dept. of State 51, to Ford Foundation 57-65; Dir. New Haven Public Library 54-67; Democrat.
Publs. *A Report on American University Presses* 49, *American University Publishing* 55.
421 Humphrey Street, New Haven, Conn., U.S.A.
Telephone: 865-1820.

Kerr, Clark, A.B., M.A., PH.D.; American university president; b. 17 May 1911; ed. Swarthmore Coll., Stanford Univ., and Univ. of Calif. (Berkeley).
Asst., later Assoc. Prof. of Industrial Relations, Univ. of Wash. 40; Assoc. Prof., later Prof. of Industrial Relations, Univ. of Calif. (Berkeley) 45, Chancellor 52; Pres. Univ. of Calif. 58-67; head of major study of future structure and financing of American higher educ., Carnegie Foundation 67-; Marshall Lecturer,

Cambridge 67-68; has held various public service posts, mainly in field of labour relations; Hon. LL.D.
Publs. *Unions, Management, and the Public* (with E. W. Bakke) 48, *Causes of Industrial Peace under Collective Bargaining* (with G. Halverson) 49, *The Uses of the University* 64, *Labor and Management in Industrial Society* 64.
6300 Buckingham Drive, El Cerrito, California 94530, U.S.A.

Kerr, James R.; American business executive; b. 23 Sept. 1917; ed. Pasadena City Coll.
U.S. Air Force 42-54; Dir. West Coast Office, Avco Corpn. 54-56, Vice-Pres. (Defense Planning), New York Office 56-57, Pres. Lycoming Div. 57-, Research and Advanced Development Div. 58-60, Dir. 59-, Exec. Vice-Pres. 60-61, Pres. and Chief Operating Officer 61-; Chair. Arco Broadcasting Corpn. 64; Dir. Arco Delta, Lehman Corpn., etc.; Trustee, Nat. Safety Council; mem. Defense Advisory Council 61, Advisory Cttee. on Finances, Nat. Capital Transportation Agency.
Office: Avco Corporation, 750 Third Avenue, New York, N.Y. 10017, Home: 5941 La Jolla Messa Drive, La Jolla, Calif. 92037, U.S.A.
Telephone: YU 6-5600.

Kerr, Jean (wife of Walter Kerr, q.v.); American writer; b. 1923; ed. Catholic Univ. of America.
Publs. *Jenny Kissed Me* (play) 49, *Touch and Go* (play) 50, *King of Hearts* (with Eleanor Brooke) 54, *Please Don't Eat the Daisies* 57, *The Snake has all the Lines* 60, *Mary, Mary* (play) 62, *Poor Richard* (play) 63.
1 Beach Avenue, Larchmont, N.Y., U.S.A.

Kerr, Walter (husband of Jean Kerr, q.v.), M.A., B.S.; American dramatic critic; b. 8 July 1913; ed. Northwestern Univ.
Assoc. Prof. Catholic Univ. of America 39-49; Drama Critic *The Commonweal* 49-51, *New York Herald Tribune* 51-66, *New York Times* 66-; Pres. New York Critics Circle 55-56; Hon. LL.D. (St. Mary's, Notre Dame), Hon. D.Litt. (La Salle Univ.).
Publs. Plays: *Sing Out Sweet Land* 45, *Touch and Go* (with Jean Kerr) 50, *Goldilocks* (with Jean Kerr) 58; also *How Not To Write A Play* 55, *Criticism and Censorship, Pieces at Eight* (essays) 57, *The Decline of Pleasure* 62, *The Theatre in Spite of Itself* 63, *Tragedy and Comedy* 67.
Office: 230 West 41st Street, New York 10018, U.S.A.

Kerschbaum, Hans, DR.PHIL.; German physicist and businessman; b. 19 Nov. 1902; ed. Stuttgart Inst. of Technology and Munich Univ.
Assistant Munich Univ.; physicist and engineer with Siemens & Halske A.G. 29-, mem. Board of Management 42-, Chair. 56-67; Deputy Chair. Metallgesellschaft A.G., Vice-Pres. Albiswerke Zürich A.G.; mem. Senate Max Planck Soc.
Almeidaweg 23, 813 Starnberg am See, German Federal Republic.
Telephone: 08151-2833.

Kertész, Istvan; German (b. Hungarian) conductor; b. 28 Aug. 1929; ed. Franz Liszt Acad. of Music, Budapest, and Accademia di Santa Cecilia, Rome.
Began conducting at Budapest State Opera; went to Germany 57, later Musical Dir. Augsburg Opera; Gen. Musical Dir. Cologne Opera 64-; Principal Conductor London Symphony Orchestra 65-; has conducted numerous orchestras throughout the world; appeared at Salzburg, Vienna, Lucerne and Edinburgh Festivals.
Hoffman-v.-Fallerslebenstrasse 4, Cologne-Marienburg, German Federal Republic.

Kessel, Joseph; French writer; b. 10 Feb. 1898; ed. Sorbonne, Paris.
Served French army 14-18 war; wrote for *Le Matin, Figaro* and *Paris Soir*; joined Free French 40; Commandeur de la Légion d'Honneur; Lauréat de l'Aca-

démie Française 27, mem. Académie Française 62-; Prix des Ambassadeurs 58.
Publs. *La Steppe Rouge, Les Captifs, Belle de Jour, L'Equipage, Vent de Sable, Les Rois Aveugles, Fortune Carrée, Les Enfants de la Chance, Le Bataillon du Ciel, Le Tour du Malheur, L'Armée des Ombres, Les Coeurs Purs, Mermoz, La Piste Fauve, La Vallée du Rubis, Témoin parmi les Hommes, Le Lion, Les Mains du Miracle* 60, *Les alcooliques anonymes* 60, *Tous n'étaient pas des Anges* 63, *Pour l'honneur* 64, *Le Coup de grâce* 65, *Terre d'amour et de feu* 65, *Les Cavaliers* (novel) 67.
15 boulevard Lannes, Paris 16e, France.

Kessler, Jean Baptiste August; Netherlands company director; b. 16 June 1888; ed. Technical Univ. of Delft.
Director Anglo-Saxon Petroleum Co. 22-61; Dir. Royal Dutch Petroleum Co. 24-61, Dir.-Gen. 47-49, Chair. 49-61; Dir. Shell Transport & Trading Co. 29-61; also Chair. Bataafsche Petroleum Maatschappij 49-61; fmr. Dir. Shell Petroleum Co.; C.B.E., Knight of Order of Neths. Lion; Commdr. of Crown of Belgium; Commdr. of Crown of Italy; Officier de la Légion d'Honneur; Grand Officer Order of Orange-Nassau.
c/o Shell Centre, South Bank, London S.E.1, England.

Kesten, Hermann; American (b. German) writer; b. 28 Jan. 1900; ed. Erlangen, Frankfurt and Rome Univs.
Chief Editor Gustav Kiepenheuer Verlag, Berlin 27-33, Allert de Lange Verlag, Amsterdam 33-40; Kleist Prize 28, Nuremberg Prize 55.
Publs. *Josef Breaks Free* 27, *Happy Man* 31, *Ferdinand and Isabella* 36, *I The King, Philip II* 38, *The Children of Guernica* 39, *The Twins of Nuremberg* 46 (novels), *Copernicus and His World* 45, *Casanova* 52 (biography), *Die fremden Götter* 49, *Ein, Sohn des Glücks* 56, *Abenteuer eines Moralisten* 61, *Die Zeit der Narren* 66 (novels), *Dichter im Café* 59, *Meine Freunde di Poeten* 60, *Filialen des Parnass* 61 (essays), *Die 30 Erzählungen* 62, *Deutsche Literatur im Exil* 64; plays and poetry; edited many anthologies and works of Lessing, Heine, Joseph Roth, Rene Schickele and others.
c/o Gina Strauss, 3g 499 Fort Washington Avenue, New York City 33, N.Y., U.S.A.

Ketelaar, Jan Arnold Albert, PH.D.; Netherlands university professor; b. 21 April 1908; ed. Univ. of Amsterdam, and California Inst. of Technology, Pasadena.
Priv. doz. Chemical Crystallography, Univ. of Leiden 36-40, Lecturer in Physical Chemistry 40-41; Prof. of Physical Chemistry and Chemical Thermodynamics, Univ. of Amsterdam 41-60; Visiting Prof. of Chemistry, Brown Univ., Providence, R.I. 58-59; Prof. of Electrochemistry, Univ. of Amsterdam 60-; Co-ordinator Research K. N. Zoutindustrie-Ketjen, Hengelo.
Publs. *Monomorphe overgangen in de kristalstructuren van zilverkwikjodide, natriumnitraat en aluminium fluoride* 33, *De Chemische Binding* 47, 52 and 66, *Physische Scheikunde* 50, *Chemical Constitution* 53, 58, *Liaisons et propriétés chimiques* 60, *Chemische Konstitution* 64.
Markeloseweg 91, Ryssen, Netherlands.
Telephone: 05400-53241 (Office); 05480-2841 (Home).

Keynes, Sir Geoffrey Langdon (father of Richard Keynes, *q.v.*), M.A., LL.D., D.LITT., M.D., F.R.C.P., F.R.C.S., F.R.C.O.G.; British surgeon and bibliographer; b. 25 March 1887; ed. Rugby and Pembroke Coll., Cambridge.
Served in R.A.M.C. 14-18; Chief Asst. St. Bartholomew's Hospital 20; Hunterian Prof. Royal Coll. Surgeons 23, 29 and 45; mem. Council R.C.S. 44-52; Hon. Librarian, R.C.S.; Consulting Surgeon St. Bartholomew's Hospital, New End Thyroid Clinic and City of London Truss Society; Sir Arthur Sims Travelling Commonwealth Prof. 56; Acting Air Vice-Marshal and Consultant in Surgery, R.A.F. 39; Trustee Nat. Portrait Gallery 42-66,

Chair. 58; Pres. Bibliographical Soc. of London 53-54; Harveian Orator, Royal Coll. of Physicians 58-67; Wilkins Lecturer, Royal Soc. 67; James Tait Black Memorial Prize 66, Osler Orator Royal Coll. of Physicians 68.
Publs. *Blood Transfusion* 22 and 49, *Bibliography of John Donne* 14, 32 and 58, *Bibliography of William Blake* 21, *Bibliography of Sir Thomas Browne* 24 and 68, *Bibliography of William Harvey* 28 and 53, *Bibliography of Jane Austen* 29, *Bibliography of William Hazlitt* 31, *Bibliography of John Evelyn* 37 and 68, *Bibliography of John Ray* 50; Editor of writings of William Blake 25, 27, 57 and 66, Sir Thomas Browne 28 and 64 and Izaak Walton 29, *Bibliography of Rupert Brooke* 54, 59, *Bibliography of Robert Hooke* 60, *Bibliography of Siegfried Sassoon* 62, *Dr. Timothie Bright* 62, *Life of William Harvey* 66, *Letters of Rupert Brooke* (editor) 68.
Lammas House, Brinkley, Newmarket, Suffolk, England.
Telephone: Stechworth 268.

Keynes, Richard Darwin (son of Sir Geoffrey Keynes, *q.v.*), M.A., PH.D., SC.D., F.R.S.; British scientist; b. 14 Aug. 1919; ed. Oundle School and Trinity Coll., Cambridge.
Temporary Experimental Officer, Anti-Submarine Establishment and Admiralty Signals Establishment 40-45; Demonstrator, later Lecturer in Physiology, Univ. of Cambridge 49-60; Research Fellow, Trinity Coll., Cambridge 48-52; Fellow of Peterhouse, Cambridge, and Dir. of Studies in Medicine 52-60; Head of Physiology Dept., Agricultural Research Council Inst. of Animal Physiology, Babraham 60-65, Dir. of Inst. 65-; Extraordinary Fellow of Churchill Coll., Cambridge 61-, Fellow of Eton 63-.
3 Herschel Road, Cambridge, England.

Keys, Ancel, M.A., PH.D.; American university professor; b. 26 Jan. 1904; ed. California and Cambridge Univs.
Research Fellow, Copenhagen 30-31; Cambridge Univ. 31-33; Instructor Biochemical Sciences, Harvard Univ. 33-36; Asst. Prof. Biochemistry, Mayo Foundation 36-37; Assoc. Prof. of Physiology, Univ. of Minnesota 37-39, Prof. and Dir. Physiological Hygiene 39-46; Prof. School of Public Health 46-; Consultant to WHO, UNESCO, FAO.
Publs. *Biology of Human Starvation* (2 vols.) 50, *Eat Well and Stay Well* (with M. H. Keys) 59.
3270 Lake Owasso Heights, St. Paul 55112, Minn., U.S.A.

Keys, David Arnold, PH.D., D.SC., LL.D., F.R.S.C.; Canadian physicist; b. 4 Nov. 1890; ed. Upper Canada Coll., Univs. of Munich and Toronto (Trinity Coll.), Harvard Univ. and Corpus Christi Coll. Cambridge.
Fellow in Physics Univ. of Toronto 15-16; Physicist, British Admiralty 18-19; Austin Teaching Fellow, Harvard Univ. 19-20; Sheldon Travelling Fellow (to Cambridge) 20-21; Asst. Cavendish Laboratory 21-22; Asst. Prof. McGill Univ. 22-26, Associate Prof. 26-29, Prof. 29-41, Macdonald Prof. of Physics 41-47; Dir. of R.C.A.F. Radio Course at McGill Univ. 41-43, ditto Army Course 43-44; mem. of Council, Nat. Research Council, Ottawa 45-55; Vice-Pres. Scientific Nat. Research Council of Canada in charge of Atomic Energy Project, Chalk River 47-55; Scientific Adviser to the Pres., Atomic Energy of Canada Ltd. 53-65; Hon. D.Sc. (McMaster, McGill, Toronto and Ottawa Univs.); LL.D. (Mount Allison Univ.); Hon. Fellow Trinity Coll. Toronto; Doctor of Humanities, Lawrence Inst. of Technology 59; Hon. mem. Engineering Inst. of Canada 59; Hon. Fellow Chemical Inst. of Canada 60; Canadian Assen. of Physicists 1964 Gold Medal; Hon. mem. Royal Canadian Inst. 67; Canadian Service Medal 68.
Publs. *Applsed Geophysics* (with A. S. Eve) 29 (revised

edn. 54), *College Physics* (with others) 35 (revised edn., with Sutton 55).
P.O.B. 452, Deep River, Ont., Canada.

Khachaturov, Tigran Sergeevich; Soviet economist; b. 1906; ed. Moscow Univ.
Department of Transport, U.S.S.R. Central Statistical Office 26-29; at Research Inst. of Rail Transport Econs. 29-33; at All-Union Research Inst. of Rail Transport 42-49; Dir. Inst. of Complex Transport Problems, U.S.S.R. Acad. of Sciences 54-60; Senior Assoc., Inst. of Econs., U.S.S.R. Acad. of Sciences 60-; Corresp. mem. U.S.S.R. Acad. of Sciences 43-66, mem. 66-.
U.S.S.R. Academy of Sciences, 14 Lenin Prospekt, Moscow, U.S.S.R.

Khachaturyan, Aram Ilych; Soviet composer; b. 6 June 1903; ed. Gnesin Music School (Moscow) and Moscow Conservatoire.
Studied cello and composition under M. F. Gnesin and N. Y. Myaskovsky; Sec. Union of Soviet Composers; Hon. Academician of Acad. St. Cecilia (Rome) 60; Hon. Prof. of Conservatoire in Mexico; mem. of the Acad. of Sciences of the Armenian S.S.R.; Corresp. mem. of the Acad. of Arts of the German Democratic Repub.; mem. Presidium Union of Soviet Socs. of Friendship and Cultural Relations with Foreign Countries; Pres. Soviet Asscn. of Friendship and Cultural Relations with Latin America; Deputy to U.S.S.R. Supreme Soviet until 66; State Prizes 41, 43, 46, 50, 65; People's Artist of the U.S.S.R. 54; Lenin Prize 59; Order of Lenin (twice), Order of Red Banner of Labour (twice).
Works include: *Poem for Piano* 27, *Trio for Piano, Violin and Clarinet* 32, *Toccata* 32, *Violin and Piano Sonata* 32, *Dance Suite* 33, *Piano Concerto* 36, *Poem to Stalin* 38, *Violin Concerto* 40, *First Symphony* 34, *Second Symphony* 43, *Gayane* 43, *Masquerade Suite* 44, *Cello Concerto, Three Concert Arias for Soprano and Orchestra* 46, *Symphony Poem* 47, composed music for film *Battle of Stalingrad* 49, *Suite from the music to "Valencian Widow"* 49, *Solemn Poem* 50, *Spartacus* (ballet) 54, *Ode of Joy* (soloist, chorus and orchestra) 56, *Suite from the music to the play "Lermontov"* 57, *Sonatina for Piano* 58, *Rhapsody for Violin and Orchestra* 60, *Ballade for Bass with Orchestra* 60 *Ballad about the Homeland* 61, *Piano Sonata* 61, *Concerto and Rhapsody for Cello and Orchestra* 65.
Union of Soviet Composers, 8-10 Nezhdanova Street, Moscow, U.S.S.R.

Khachaturyan, Karen Surenovich; Soviet composer; b. 1920; ed. Moscow Conservatoire.
Member Exec. Cttee., Soviet Composers' Union; participated in int. festivals.
Principal compositions: Sonata for Violin and Piano 47, Sinfonietta 49, *By the Lonely Willow* (Cantata) 50, Youth Overture 51, Symphony No. 1 54, *A Simple Girl* (Operetta) 59, *Friendship* (Overture for symphony orchestra) 61, Sonata for 'Cello and Piano 62; incidental music for cartoon films.
R.S.F.S.R. Composers' Union, 8-10 Nezhdanova Street, Moscow, U.S.S.R.

Khadduri, Majid, B.A., PH.D.; Iraqi educationist and writer; b. 27 Sept. 1909; ed. American Univ. of Beirut and Univ. of Chicago.
Sec.-Treas. Baghdad P.E.N. Club; mem. American Society of Int. Law; Iraqi Del. to the 14th Conf. of the P.E.N. Clubs in Buenos Aires 36; Adviser to the Iraq Del. at the San Francisco Conf. 45; Visiting Lecturer in Near Eastern History at Indiana Univ. 47-48; former Prof. Modern Middle-Eastern History at the Higher Teachers' Coll., Baghdad, Iraq 48-49; taught Middle East politics at Chicago and Harvard Univs. 49-50; Prof. Middle East Studies, Johns Hopkins Univ. 50-; Dir. of Research and Education, Middle East Inst. 50-; Visiting

Middle East Prof., Columbia Univ.; mem. American Pol. Science Asscn. and Shaybani Society of Int. Law (Göttingen); Order of Rafidain (Iraq).
Publs. *The Liberation of Iraq from the Mandate* (in Arabic) 35, *The Law of War and Peace in Islam* 41, *The Government of Iraq* 44, *The System of Government in Iraq* (in Arabic) 46, *Independent Iraq* 51, *War and Peace in the Law of Islam* 55, *Islamic Jurisprudence* 61, *Modern Libya* 63, *The Islamic Law of Nations* 66.
4454 Tindall Street, N.W., Washington 16, D.C., U.S.A.
Telephone: 244-4454.

Khaidarov, Ashur; Soviet politician; b. 1917; ed. Samarkand Agricultural Inst. and Republican Party School.
Agricultural Technician 29-41; Komsomol Leader 41-46; Sec. of District Cttee., C.P. Uzbekistan, then of Regional Cttee. C.P. Uzbekistan; Chief, Regional Agricultural Dept., Andizhan Regional Soviet Working People's Deputies, then Chair. of Exec. Cttee.; later, Sec. Central Cttee. C.P. Uzbekistan 47-63; First Sec. Andizhan Regional Cttee. C.P. Uzbekistan 63-; mem. Central Cttee. C.P. Uzbekistan; Deputy to U.S.S.R. Supreme Soviet; mem. Mandate Cttee. Soviet of Nationalities; mem. C.P.S.U. 42-.
Andizhan Regional Committee of Communist Party of Uzbekistan, Andizhan, U.S.S.R.

Khain, Victor Yefimovich; Soviet geologist; b. 1914; ed. Azerbaijan Industrial Inst.
Geologist at oil fields, Azerbaijan, 35-39; Assoc., Azerbaijan Oil Research Inst. 39-41; Service in the Army 41-45; mem. C.P.S.U. 43-; Assoc., Inst. of Geology, Acad. of Sciences, Azerbaijan S.S.R. 45-54; Head of Dept. Museum of Agriculture, Moscow Univ. 52-; Senior Assoc., Vernadsky Inst. of Geochemistry and Analytical Chemistry, U.S.S.R. Acad. of Sciences 57-; Prof. Geology Dept., Moscow Univ. 60-; Corresp. mem. U.S.S.R. Acad. of Sciences 66-.
U.S.S.R. Academy of Sciences, 14 Lenin Prospekt, Moscow, U.S.S.R.

Khalaf, Kadhim M.; Iraqi diplomatist; b. 1922; ed. American Univ. of Beirut and Inst. des Hautes Etudes Internationales, Paris.
Member staff Perm. Mission of Iraq to UN 48; Del. to numerous confs.; Dir.-Gen. UN Dept., Ministry of Foreign Affairs, Iraq 62-64; Under-Sec. of Ministry of Foreign Affairs 64-66, 67-68; Perm. Rep. of Iraq to UN 66-67; Amb. to U.K. 68-.
Embassy of Iraq, 21 Queen's Gate, London, S.W.7, England.

Khalatbary, Abbas Ali, PH.D.; Iranian diplomatist and administrator; b. 12; ed. Univ. of Paris.
Ministry of Finance 40-42; Ministry of Foreign Affairs 42-, served Teheran, Berne, Warsaw, Paris; Ambassador to Poland and Rumania 59-; Sec.-Gen. Central Treaty Organization (CENTO) 62-67.
c/o Ministry of Foreign Affairs, Teheran, Iran.

Khalidi, Ismail Raghib, B.A., M.A., PH.D.; Saudi Arabian United Nations official; b. 13 Nov. 1916; ed. St. George's School and Govt. Arab Coll., Jerusalem, American Univ. of Beirut, Michigan Univ. and Columbia Univ., U.S.A.
Assistant Script Editor, Radio Arabic Desk, U.S. Office of War Information, New York 42-44; Sec.-Gen., Inst. of Arab-American Affairs, New York 44-47; New York Corresp. for *Al Misri* (Cairo daily) 46-47; Assoc. Dir. Asia Inst. for Arabic Studies, New York 47-48; Adviser to Saudi Arabian Del., UN 49; mem. UN Secretariat 49-, UN Mission to Libya 50-52, UN Observer, British N. Cameroons 60-61; Senior Political Affairs Officer, UN Security Council Affairs Div. 55-; Principal Sec. UN Comm. for Unification and Rehabilitation of Korea (UNCURK) 62-65.
Publ. *Constitutional Development in Libya* 56.
121 Lorraine Ave., Mount Vernon, N.Y. 10553, U.S.A.

Khalifa, Ser el Khatim; Sudanese educationalist and politician; b. 17; ed. Gordon Coll., Khartoum.
Former teacher, Gordon Coll., Khartoum and Bakhter-Ruda Inst.; Head Khartoum Technical Inst. 60-64, 65-66; Deputy Under-Sec. Ministry of Educ. 64; Prime Minister 64-65; Amb. to Italy 66-68, to U.K. 68-.
Embassy of Sudan, Cleveland Row, London, S.W.1, England.

Khalil, Mohamed Kamal El-Din; United Arab Republic (Egyptian) diplomatist.
Formerly Dir. of Research Dept., U.A.R. Ministry of Foreign Affairs; Chargé d'Affaires, London 60-61; Dir. North American Dept., U.A.R., Ministry of Foreign Affairs 61-64; Ambassador to Jordan 64-66, to Sudan 66-.
Publ. *The Arab States and the Arab League* (2 vols.) 62.
Embassy of the United Arab Republic, Khartoum, Sudan.

Khalil, Mostafa, M.SC., PH.D.; United Arab Republic (Egyptian) civil engineer and politician; b. 20; ed. Faculty of Engineering, Cairo Univ., and Illinois Univ., U.S.A.
Entered service of Egyptian State Railroads 41; sent by Govt. to U.S.A. 47; training with Chicago-Milwaukee Railroad 47; studied for M.Sc. and Ph.D., Univ. of Illinois 47-51; resumed service with Egyptian State Railroads 51-52; lecturer in Railroad and Highway Engineering, Ein Shams Univ. 52-; Technical Consultant to Transport Cttee., Permanent Council for Nat. Production 55-; U.A.R. Minister of Communications 56-64; Dep. Prime Minister for Communications and Transport 64-65, for Industry, Mineral Wealth and Electricity 65-66; mem. American Soc. of Civil Engineers, American Railway Engineering Asscn., etc.
c/o Ministry of Industry, Cairo, United Arab Republic.

Khama, Sir Seretse, K.B.E., B.A., M.P.; Botswana politician and farmer; b. 1 July 1921; ed. Fort Hare Univ., Witwatersrand Univ., South Africa, Balliol Coll., Oxford.
Legal studies, London; son of Sekgoma II (d. 25), Chief of Bamangwato Tribe, Bechuanaland Protectorate; his uncle, Tshekedi Khama, Regent of Bamangwato Tribe in Seretse Khama's minority 26-50; dispute over Chieftancy of Bamangwato Tribe resulted in Seretse Khama's banishment 50; returned to Bechuanaland and renounced all claim to Chieftancy 56; Pres. Bechuanaland Democratic Party; mem. Legislative Council and Executive Council 61-65; mem. Legislative Assembly and Prime Minister of Bechuanaland 65-66; mem. of Parl. and Pres. of the Republic of Botswana 66-; Hon. LL.D., Hon. LL.B.
Private Bag 1, Gaberones, Botswana.

Khamal, Yadunath; Nepalese diplomatist; b. 14; ed. Trichandra Coll., Katmandu and Calcutta Univ.
Professor Trichandra Coll. 43-56; Home Sec. 56; mem. Nepalese del. United Nations 59-60; mem. Tribhuvan Univ. Senate and Syndicate 60-62; Foreign Sec. 61-62; Ambassador to India 63-; Gorkha Dakshina Bahu (First Class), Hon. K.C.V.O.
Publs. *Principles of Criticism* (Nepalese), *Reflections on Nepal-India Relations* (English).
Royal Nepalese Embassy, Barakhamba Road, New Delhi 1, India.

Khampan, H.R.H. Tiao; Laotian administrator and diplomatist; b. 08; ed. Lycée Albert Sarraut, Hanoi, Lycée de Montpellier, Inst. Agricole Maison Carrée, Algeria.
Gov. Sayaboury Province 46-50, Luang-Prabang Province 50-52; Minister to Thailand 52-55; Ambassador to the United Kingdom 55-58; Ambassador to Thailand 58-61, to United States 61-, Perm. Rep. of Laos to UN 63-; Grand Officier Ordre du Million d'Eléphants, Légion d'Honneur, and other decorations.
Permanent Mission of Laos to the United Nations, 321 East 45th Street, New York 17, N.Y., U.S.A.

Khan, Vice-Admiral A. R.; Pakistani naval officer; b. 1921; ed. Command and Staff Coll., Quetta, and Joint Services Staff Coll., U.K.
Joined Royal Navy 38, commissioned 40; active service in Royal Navy, Second World War; later in Indian Navy, transferring to Pakistan Navy 47; C.-in-C. Pakistan Navy 59-66; Minister of Defence, Pakistan 66-.
Ministry of Defence, Rawalpindi, Pakistan.

Khan, Abdul Monem, LL.B.; Pakistani lawyer and politician; b. 02; ed. Dacca Coll. and Calcutta Univ.
Called to the Bar 27; Asst. Sec. Mymensingh District Anjuman-e-Islamia 28-32, Sec. 32-33; founded Mymensingh District Muslim League, Sec. 33-36, 47-55; Pres. District School Board, Mymensingh 46-54; mem. Constituent Assembly, Pakistan 50-54; mem. Nat. Assembly 63-; Minister of Health, Labour and Social Welfare June-Oct. 62; Gov. of East Pakistan Oct. 62-.
Government House, Dacca, Pakistan.

Khan, Abdul Sabur; Pakistani politician; b. 11; ed. Univ. of Calcutta.
Joint Sec. Bengal Provincial Moslem League 40-47; Moslem League mem. Pre-Independence Bengal Provincial Legislature; Pres. Khulna District Branch Moslem League 45-58; Minister of Communications, Pakistan 63-; leader Moslem League Parl. party.
Ministry of Communications, Rawalpindi, Pakistan.

Khan, Alauddin, D.MUS.; Indian musician; b. 7 Oct. 1862.
Former Principal, Govt. Music Coll., Maihar, now Hon. Principal; Dir. Maihar Orchestra; exponent on many Indian musical instruments; invented Indian musical instruments Chadra Sarang, Sur Setar and Brihit Sarang; performances in India and Europe, Dir. of Music Uday Shankar Ballet while in Paris; awarded Brarat Gourav, Sitare Hind, Sangit Nayak, Padma Bhushan and Deshikottam; Govt. of India centenary celebration 62.
Compositions: *Raga Hemant*, *Madan Manjri* and *Prabha Kali*.
Shanti Kutir, Maihar, Madhya Pradesh, India.

Khan, Ali Akbar; Indian musician; b. 1922.
Concert Recitals on Sarode, in India since 36, and all over the world since 55; Founder Ali Akbar Coll. of Music, Calcutta 56; Musical Dir. of many films and numerous contributions on All India Radio; Lecture Recitals at Montreal and McGill Univs., Canada; first long-playing gramophone record introduced by Yehudi Menuhin; Pres. of India Award 63.
c/o Basil Douglas Ltd., 8 St. George's Terrace, Regent's Park Road, London, N.W.1, England.

Khan, Ghulam Ishaq; Pakistani civil servant; b. 1915; ed. Islamia Coll., Peshawar, and Punjab Univ.
North-West Frontier Province (N.W.F.P.) Civil Service (India) 40-47, Sub-Divisional Officer, Treasury Officer and Magistrate First Class 40-44, Bursar and Sec. to Council of Management of Islamia Coll., Peshawar; Sec. to Chief Minister, N.W.P.F. 47; Home Sec. Food and Dir. Civil Supplies to Govt. N.W.F.P. 48; Devt. and Admin. Sec. for Agriculture, Animal Husbandry, Forests, Industries, Co-operatives and Village Aid 49-52; Devt. Commr. and Sec. to Devt. Dept., N.W.F.P. 53-56; Sec. for Devt. and Irrigation, Govt. of W. Pakistan 56-58; mem. W. Pakistan Water and Power Devt. Authority 58-61, Chair. 61-66; mem. Land Reforms Comm. 58-59; Sec. Finance, Govt. of Pakistan 66-; Tamgha-i-Pakistan 59; Sitara-i-Pakistan 62; Hilal-i-Quaid-i-Azam 68.
Secretary, Ministry of Finance, Government of Pakistan, Islamabad; Home: 161 F. 6/3, Islamabad, Pakistan. Telephone: 20515 (Office); 20824 (Home).

Khan, Lieut.-Gen. Mohammad Azam; Pakistani soldier and politician; b. 08; ed. Royal Indian Mil. Coll., Dehra Dun, and Sandhurst, England.
Brigade Commdr., Kashmir 48-49; Admin. in Lahore 52; Refugee Minister 58; Gov. of East Pakistan 60-62.
c/o Ministry of Defence, Rawalpindi, Pakistan.

Khan, Field Marshal Mohammed Ayub; Pakistani soldier and politician; b. 14 May 1907; ed. Muslim Univ. Aligarh, India and Sandhurst, England.
Commissioned 28; served in 14th Punjab Regiment; Brigadier 47; Major-Gen. and Commdr. in East Pakistan 48; Adjutant-Gen. 50; C.-in-C. Pakistan Army 51-; Minister of Defence 54-56; Chief Martial Law Administrator 58; President of Pakistan and Minister of Defence 58-.
Publ. *Friends not Masters* (autobiography) 67.
President's House, Rawalpindi, Pakistan.

Khan, Sultan Mohammad, B.A.; Pakistani diplomatist; b. 19; ed. Ewing Christian Coll. and Allahabad Univ.
Commissioned Indian Army 42; Indian Political Service 46; Pakistan Diplomatic Service 47-; Pakistan High Comm., New Delhi 47, Cairo and Rome 48-50; Ministry of External Affairs, Karachi 50-53; Embassy, Peking and Ankara 53-57; Dep. High Commr. London 57-59; Ministry of External Affairs, Karachi 59-61; High Commr. in Canada 61-, concurrently accredited as High Commr. in Jamaica 63-, Trinidad and Tobago 63-, Ambassador to Cuba 64-.
Office of the High Commissioner for Pakistan, Ottawa, Ont., Canada.

Khan, Gen. Yahya; Pakistani army officer; b. 1917; ed. Punjab Univ. and Indian Military Acad.
Service on N.W. Frontier before Second World War; service in Middle East and Italy, Second World War; set up Pakistan Staff Coll. 47, later Chief of Staff, Pakistan Army; Chair. Capital Comm. 59; G.O.C. East Pakistan 62; Commdr. Infantry Div. 65; C.-in-C. Pakistan Army Sept. 66-.
c/o Ministry of Defence, Rawalpindi, Pakistan.

Khanlari, Parviz N., PH.D.; Iranian writer and politician; b. 14; ed. Teheran Univ. and Univ. of Paris.
Professor of Iranian Linguistics, Teheran Univ. 48; Editor *Sokhan* (literary monthly) 43- and *Sokhan* (scientific monthly) 62-; Deputy Minister of Interior 55; Minister of Educ. 62-64; Co-founder Mardom Party 47; Gen. Sec. Imperial Foundation for Iranian Cultural Studies.
Hafez Avenue, Zomorrod Passage, P.O. Box 984, Teheran, Iran.

Khanna, Mehr Chand; Indian politician; b. 1 June 1897.
Finance Minister North-West Frontier Province 46-47; Adviser to Minister of Rehabilitation, Central Govt. 48-54; Minister of Rehabilitation 54-62; Minister of State for Works, Housing and Supply 62-64, for Works and Housing 64-66; Minister for Works, Housing and Urban Devt. 66-67.
7 Race Course Road, New Delhi 11, India.

Khanolkar, Vasant Ramji, B.SC., M.D.; Indian physician; b. 13 April 1895; ed. Bombay and London Univs.
University Coll. Medical School, London 20-23; Prof. of Pathology, Grant Medical Coll., Bombay 24-25, Seth G.S. Medical Coll., Bombay 25-41; Dir. of Laboratories and Research, Tata Memorial Hospital, Bombay 41-51, of Indian Cancer Research Centre, Bombay 52-63; Vice-Chancellor, Univ. of Bombay 60-63; Nat. Research Prof. in Medicine 63-; Chair. Int. Cancer Research Comm. 50; mem. UN Scientific Cttee. on the Effects of Atomic Radiation 56-, Vice-Chair. 58-; Pres. Int. Union against Cancer 58-62; Hon. LL.D. (Melbourne); Hon.

F.R.C.P. (Edin.), F.A.Sc., F.N.I., Hon. LL.D. (Bombay), Hon. M.D. (Perugia); Fellow and Pres. Indian Acad. of Medical Sciences, Pres. Nat. Inst. of Sciences 65-, mem. Acad. of Medical Sciences, U.S.S.R., Hon. Fellow Royal Soc. of Medicine, London; Padma Bhushan.
Publs. include *Cancer in India in Relation to Habits and Customs, Pathology of Leprosy, A Look at Cancer.*
66 Padmalaya, Sion East, Bombay 22, India.

Kharas, Jamshed Gustadji, B.SC.; Pakistani diplomatist; b. 19.
Joined Indian civil service 42; Dep. Sec. to Govt. of Pakistan 51; Jt. Sec. 55; attended Imperial Defence Coll., London 58; High Commr. for Pakistan in Australia and New Zealand 60-62; Dir.-Gen. Ministry of External Affairs, Karachi 62-63; Amb. to Spain 63-67 and to Holy See 66-67; Amb. to Yugoslavia and Greece 67-.
Embassy of Pakistan, Belgrade, Yugoslavia.
Telephone: 51-377 (Residence); 50-208 (Chancery).

Kharchenko, Boris Ivanovich; Soviet foreign trade official; b. 1914; ed. Kharkov Aviation Inst.
Member C.P.S.U. 39-; Engineer 41-44; Official, Ministry of Foreign Trade 47-52, 57-59; Vice-Chair. *Intourist* Joint Stock Soc. 54-57; U.S.S.R. Commercial Rep. in Sweden 59-63; Chair. *Aviaexport* Trust 64-; Order of Red Banner of Labour, Honour Badge.
Aviaexport Trust, 32/34 Smolenskaya-Sennaya Square, Moscow, U.S.S.R.

Khariton, Yuliy Borisovich; Soviet physicist and physical chemist; b. 04; ed. Leningrad Polytechnical Inst.
Research worker, Leningrad Polytechnical Inst. 21-27; worked in England with Lord Rutherford 27-28; Assoc. of Inst. of Chemical Physics, U.S.S.R. Acad. of Sciences 31-; Corresp. mem U.S.S.R. Acad. of Sciences 43-53, mem. 53-; Dep. to U.S.S.R. Supreme Soviet 54, 58, 62, 66.
Publs. *The Problem of Chain Decay of the Basic Uranium Isotope* 39, *On the Chain Decay of Uranium under the Action of Slow Neutrons* 40, *The Problem of Impact Detonation* 40.
Institute of Chemical Physics, U.S.S.R. Academy of Sciences, 26 Vorobyevskoe Shosse, Moscow, U.S.S.R.

Kharlamov, Mikhail Averkievich; Soviet politician; b. 13; ed. Moscow Inst. of History, Philosophy and Literature and Higher Party School of Central Cttee. of C.P.S.U.
Former teacher; mem. Communist Party of Soviet Union 40-; Staff, Central Cttee. of C.P.S.U. 42-48; journalistic work and with Ministry of Foreign Affairs 48-62; Chair. State Cttee. for Radio and Television under U.S.S.R. Council of Ministers 62-64; Deputy Editor-in-Chief Politizdat (main political publishing house) 64-.
Politizdat, 7 Miusskaya ploshchad, Moscow, U.S.S.R.

Kheir, Ahmed Mohamed; Sudanese politician; ed. Gordon Memorial Coll., and Khartoum School of Law.
Advocate 44; mem. Sudan del. which negotiated Sudan's future 46; fmr. Vice-Pres. and Pres. of Nat. Cttee. for the Constitution; Minister of Foreign Affairs 58-64, and Mineral Resources 62-64.
Publs. (Arabic) *The Struggle of a Generation, Calamities of the British in the Sudan* (English), *Sudan Appeals to U.N.O.*
c/o Ministry of Foreign Affairs, Khartoum, Sudan.

Khene, Abderrahman, M.D.; Algerian doctor, politician and administrator; b. 6 March 1931; ed. Univ. of Algiers.
Secretary of State, Provisional Govt. of Algeria (G.P.R.A.) 58-60; Dir. of Political Affairs, Ministry of Interior, G.P.R.A. 60-61; Dir. of Cabinet, Ministry of Finances, G.P.R.A. 61-62; Pres. of Technical Org. for

Exploiting Wealth of Saharan Sub-Soil (l'Organisme Saharien) Sept. 62-Dec. 65, Pres. Electricité et Gaz d'Algérie (E.G.A.) July-Oct. 64, Organisme Coopération Industrielle (O.C.I.) Jan. 66-; Minister of Public Works and Construction Sept. 66-.

Immeuble "Le Colisée", rue Zéphirin Rocas, Algiers, Algeria.

Khiary, Mahmoud; Tunisian politician and United Nations official; b. 11; ed. Ecole Normale, Tunis.
Teacher 31-55; Sec.-Gen. Tunisian Union of Teachers 41-52; Pres. Gen. Fed. of Tunisian Officials 47-58; fmr. Sec.-Gen., Gen. Union of Tunisian Workers; fmr. Minister of Posts and Telegraphs; fmr. Minister of Agriculture; mem. Nat. Constituent Assembly; Chief, UN Civil Operations in the Congo 61-62.
Gammarth, La Marsa, Tunisia.

Khilnani, Khemchand Rewachand Fatehchand, M.M., F.R.E.S.; Indian diplomatist; b. 6 Feb. 1913; ed. Bombay and Cambridge Univs., Lincoln's Inn, London.
Senior Counsel, Chief Court of Sind 37-48; Under-Sec. Ministry of External Affairs 48-49; Asst. Commr.-Gen. for Europe, Paris 49; First Sec., Prague; Under-Sec. Ministry of External Affairs 51-53; First Sec. Colombo 53-55, Rome 55-57; Counsellor, Cairo 57-59; Jt. Sec. to Govt. in charge of Foreign Trade 59-61; Consul-Gen. to Ruanda-Urundi 61; Commr. in East and Central Africa 61-63; Ambassador to Romania and Bulgaria 63-67; Chair. ECAFE Cttee. on Trade 61; Leader India's Trade dels. to Western Asian and Eastern European countries 59-61, High Commissioner of India to Gambia and Amb. to Senegal, Ivory Coast, Upper Volta and Mauritania June 67-.
Indian Embassy, Dakar, Senegal.

Khim Tit; Cambodian politician; b. 96; ed. Ecole d'Administration Cambodgienne, Phnom-Penh.
Entered Govt. service 25; provincial Gov. in Kratie 35, Kg-Speu 39, Siem-Reap 40-42, Kampot 42-45; Minister of Defence, of Public Works and of Public Health in Son Ngoc Thanh Cabinet 45; Minister of Public Works and Health in Monireth Cabinet 45-46; mem. Council of the Kingdom 48; Minister of Works and Telecommunications, Oum Chneangsun Cabinet 51; Gov. of Kandal 51-52; Under-Sec. Ministry of Interior, in charge ground defences 52-53; Royal Del. to Kg-Cham 53; Minister of Defence, Chan Nak Cabinet, till Apr. 54; Minister of the Interior in two of the Penn-Nouth Cabinets; life mem. Royal High Council; Chief of Staff for operations against subversive activities in Kg-Speu and Kg-Chhang provinces 55; Vice-Pres. in 3rd Sangkum Govt.; Prime Minister, Pres. of the Council and Minister of Planning and Rehabilitation in the 4th Sangkum Govt. 56; Ambassador to U.S.S.R. 60-61, to Czechoslovakia 61-65; Grand Cross, Royal Order of Cambodia; Inter-Allied Medal 1914-18, etc.
c/o Ministry of Foreign Affairs, Phnom Penh, Cambodia.

Khitrov, Stepan Dmitriyevich; Soviet politician; b. 1910; ed. All-Union Polytechnic Inst.
Member C.P.S.U. 32-; Soviet Army service 33-35; Deputy Chief Engineer of state farm, later construction technician, then Editor of newspaper on construction, Voronezh 35-38; Party work 38-47; Sec., then Second Sec. Voronezh Regional Cttee. of C.P., then Chair. Exec. Cttee. of Voronezh Regional Soviet of Working People's Deputies 47-59; Official, Central Cttee. C.P.S.U. 59-60; First Sec. Voronezh Regional Cttee. of C.P. 60-67; Minister of Agricultural Construction of U.S.S.R. 67-; Alt. mem. Central Cttee. C.P.S.U. 61-66, mem. 66-; Deputy to U.S.S.R. Supreme Soviet.
U.S.S.R. Ministry of Agricultural Construction, Moscow, U.S.S.R.

Khlamov, Grigory Sergeevich; Soviet government official; b. 03; ed. Moscow Motor and Tractor Inst.
Former Director Gorky Automobile Works, developed

Pobeda car (State Prize 50); Minister of Automobile and Tractor Industry 50-53; Dep. Minister of Medium Machine Building 53-55; Minister of Tractor and Agricultural Machine Building 55-57; Dept. Head, State Planning Comm. 57-60; Dir. Central Dept. of State Material Reserves, U.S.S.R. Council of Ministers 60-; mem. C.P.S.U. 26-; Order of Lenin 53.
Central Dept. of State Material Reserves, Council of Ministers, 12 Prospekt Marxa, Moscow, U.S.S.R.

Khokhlov, Boris Ivanovich; Soviet ballet dancer; b. 22 Feb. 1932; ed. Bolshoi Theatre Ballet School.
Joined Bolshoi Theatre Ballet Company 51; Honoured Artist of R.S.F.S.R.
Chief roles include: Prince Desire (*Sleeping Beauty*), Siegfried (*Swan Lake*), the Prince (*Cinderella*), the Poet (*Chopiniana*), Basil (*Don Quixote*), Albert (*Giselle*), Vatshar (*Bakhchisavai Fountain*).
State Academic Bolshoi Theatre of U.S.S.R., 1 Ploshchad Sverdlova, Moscow, U.S.S.R.

Khokhlov, Rem Victorovich; Soviet physicist; b. 1926; ed. Moscow Univ.
Postgraduate, Assoc., Asst. Prof., Prof. Moscow Univ. 49-; mem. C.P.S.U. 51-; Corresp. mem. U.S.S.R. Acad. of Sciences 66-.
Publs. Works on radiophysics and radio engineering.
U.S.S.R. Academy of Sciences, 14 Lenin Prospekt, Moscow, U.S.S.R.

Kholov, Maxmadulla; Soviet politician; b. 1920.
Soviet Army 40-47; mem. Communist Party of Soviet Union 47-; party and political work in Tadzhik S.S.R. 54-63; Chair. of Presidium of Supreme Soviet of Tadzhik S.S.R. 63-; mem. Presidium of Central Cttee. of C.P. of Tadzhik S.S.R.; Deputy Chair. Presidium of Supreme Soviet of U.S.S.R.; mem. Central Auditing Comm., C.P.S.U.; Deputy to Supreme Soviet of Tadzhik S.S.R.
Presidium of Supreme Soviet of Tadzhik S.S.R., Dushanbe, Tadzhik S.S.R., U.S.S.R.

Khoman, Thanat; Thai diplomatist and politician; b. 9 May 1914; ed. Assumption Coll., Thailand and Univs. of Bordeaux and Paris.
Thai Foreign Office 41-, Second Sec. Thai Embassy, Tokyo, Japan 42-43; Chargé d'Affaires, Washington 46-47, Ambassador 57-59; Chargé d'Affaires, Thai Legation, New Delhi 47-49; Dir.-Gen. Dept. of Econ. Affairs, UN 50-52, Dir.-Gen. Dept. of UN Affairs 50-51; Dep. Acting Perm. Rep. of Thailand to UN 52-57; Chair. UN Int. Law Comm. 57, UN Cttee. on S.W. Africa 57, UN Gen. Assembly Trusteeship Cttee. 57; Minister of Foreign Affairs, Thailand 59-; Knight Grand Cordon Order of Crown, Thailand; Knight Grand Cordon, Order of White Elephant.
Ministry of Foreign Affairs, Bangkok, Thailand.

Khomenkov, Leonid Sergeevich; Soviet sports administrator; b. 1913; ed. Kaluzhsky School of Mechanics and State Central Inst. for Physical Culture.
Instructor in Physical Culture, Central Section, Track and Field Athletics, Voluntary Sporting Soc. *Sovetov* 34-42; Pres. Cen. Voluntary Sporting Soc. *Krybia Sovetov* 42-46; State Cen. Inst. for Physical Culture 46-47; Asst. Chair. Cttee. for Physical Culture and Sports to Moscow Soviet Exec. Cttee. 47-49; State trainer, Dept. Chief of Track and Field Athletics; Chief Editor *Legkaya Athletida*; Asst. Dir. then Dir. Dept. of Mass Sports of Cttee. for Physical Culture and Sports to U.S.S.R. Council of Ministers 49-59; mem. Presidium and Pres. Bureau of Mass Sports, U.S.S.R. Cen. Council of Sporting Soviets and Orgs.; mem. C.P.S.U. 43-; Orders of Red Banner of Labour, Red Star, Badge of Honour, and medals.
Central Council of U.S.S.R. Union of Sporting Societies and Organisations, 4 Skatertniy pereulok, Moscow, U.S.S.R.

Khorava, Akaki Alexeyevich; Soviet actor; b. 95; ed. Theatre Studio of the Rustavelli Theatre in Tbilisi 21-22.
Acted with the Rustavelli Theatre Co. 22; Dir. of the theatre's studio 35-39; Dir. of the Rustavelli State Theatrical Inst. 39-49; mem. Soviet Peace Cttee. 47; teacher at the Rustavelli State Theatrical Inst. 49; People's Actor of U.S.S.R.; State prize winner 41, 43, 46, 51 (twice); awarded Order of Lenin (twice).
Principal stage roles: Bersenev (*Breaking Point* by Lavrenev), Karl Moor (*The Robbers* by Schiller), Ivan the Terrible (*The Mighty Sovereign* by Sovolyov), Othello (*Othello* by Shakespeare), Oedipus (*Oedipus Rex* by Sophocles); has also acted in films.
Rustavelli Theatre, Tbilisi, Georgian S.S.R., U.S.S.R.

Khoshkish, Youssof; Iranian banker; b. 06; ed. Univs. of Teheran and Paris.
Bank Melli Iran 34-39, 61-; Insp. Ministry of Finance, Europe 39-40; Govt. Rep. (Financial Affairs) India 40-44; Vice-Pres. Bank Sepah 45-61; Pres. Bank Melli Iran 61-.
Bank Melli Iran, Khiaban Ferdowsi, Teheran, Iran.

Khosla, Dr. Ajudhia Nath; Indian public servant, engineer, educationist and administrator; b. 11 Dec. 1892; ed. D.A.V. Coll., Lahore and Thomason Coll. of Engineering, Roorkee.
Chairman Cen. Water and Power Comm.45-53; Founder Pres. Int. Comm. on Drainage and Irrigation 50, Hon. Pres. 54-; Vice-Pres. World Power Conf., Int. Comm. on Dams, Int. Asscn. for Hydraulic Research; Vice-Chancellor Roorkee Univ. 54-59; mem. Rajya Sabha (Parl.) 58-59, Planning Comm. 59-62; Gov. of Orissa 62-68; Pres. Inst. of Engineers 49-50, Cen. Board of Irrigation and Power 46-48, 51-, of Geophysics (India) 50-53, Nat. Inst. of Science 61-62; Chair. Boards of Consultants for Bhakra, Beas, Sabarigiri, Ramganga, Yamuna, and Balimela projects; Hon. Life mem. Inst. of Engineers (India); Hon. degrees from various Univs.
Publs. *Design of Weirs on Permeable Foundations, Silting of Reservoirs, Rainfall and Runoff, Pressure Observations under Dams.*
15 Jangpura-B, Mathura Road, New Delhi, India.

Khosla, Jagan Nath, B.A., B.SC., PH.D.; Indian diplomatist; b. 28 Jan. 1906; ed. Srinagar, Lahore, London and Paris.
Called to Middle Temple Bar 31; practised Lahore and Srinagar High Courts 32-34; lecturer in Law and Political Science, Punjab Univ. 32-48, Principal 47-48; Head of Consular Department, Indian High Commission, London 48-51; Chargé d'Affaires, Rome and (concurrently) Prague 51-52; Dir. Historical Div., Ministry of External Affairs 53-54, Indian Inst. of Public Admin. 64-; Pres. Viet-Nam Int. Comm., Laos Int. Control and Supervision Comm. 54-55; Minister and subsequently Ambassador to Czechoslovakia 55-58, concurrently Ambassador to Rumania 58; Personal Rep. of Prime Minister in Hungary 56; Ambassador to Indonesia 58-61, to Yugoslavia, Bulgaria and Greece 61-64; Alt. Del. to UN Gen. Assembly 61 and 62; Pres. Indian Political Science Asscn. 47; mem. Exec. Cttee. Int. Sociological Asscn. 49-51, Int. Political Asscn. 49-52; has represented India at several int. confs.; mem. Punjab Admin. Reforms Comm. 64-66; mem. Exec. Cttee. of Int. Union of Local Authorities 66-.
Indian Institute of Public Administration, Indraprastha Estate, New Delhi 1; c/o Bank of India Ltd., Jan Path, New Delhi 1, India.
Telephone: 272581 (Office); 274103 (Home).

Khosravani, Attaollah; Iranian politician; b. 19; ed. Univ. of Teheran and Univ. of Paris.
Former Labour Attaché, France; fmr. Govt. Supervisor to Workers Social Insurance Org., later Head; Founder and Dir. newspaper *Afkare Iran*; fmr. Under-Sec. (Admin.), Ministry of Labour and Under-Sec. (Parl.),

Ministry of Labour; Sec.-Gen. Iran Novin party 65-; Minister of Labour and Social Affairs 61-; Order of Homayoun (twice).
Ministry of Labour, Teheran, Iran.

Khosravani, Khosrow; Iranian diplomatist; b. 16 June 1914; ed. Iran and England.
Former Geologist, Dept. of Mines; Foreign Service, served Ministry of Foreign Affairs, UN, Washington; later Sec., Ministry of Nat. Economy; Ambassador to Turkey 63-65, to U.S.A. 65-, Delegate to Gen. Assembly UN; Managing Dir. Foreign Transaction Co., Chair. Board of Inspectorate, National Iranian Oil Co.
c/o Ministry of Foreign Affairs, Teheran, Iran.

Khotsialov, Evgeny Sergeyevich; Soviet foreign trade official; b. 1908; ed. Nizhegorodsk Technical School of Water Transport.
Official, Soviet Purchasing Comm., U.S. 42-47; Deputy Chief, then Chief of Section, Main Dept. of Soviet Property Abroad 47-49; Dir. of Office, then Deputy Chair. *Mashinoexport* Trust 49-51; Vice-Chair. *Transmashimport* Trust 51-53; Chair. *Sudoimport* Trust 54-60; U.S.S.R. Commercial Rep. in Finland 60-; mem. C.P.S.U. 48-; Order of Lenin, Order of Red Banner of Labour, Order of Red Star, Honour Badge.
U.S.S.R. Trade Representation, Helsinki, Finland.

Khotsianov, Lev Kupriyanovich; Soviet hygiene specialist; b. 1889; ed. Military Medical Acad.
Army Surgeon 12-18; hygiene specialist 20-31; Research Assoc., Asst. Prof., Prof. Head of Chair, Cen. Inst. of Postgraduate Medical Training 31-56; Head of Dept. Inst. of Labour Hygiene and Occupational Diseases 51-56; Corresp. mem. U.S.S.R. Acad. of Medical Sciences 46-60, mem. 60-; Consultant 66-; Order of Red Banner (twice).
Publs. Over 120 works; monographs: *Labour Hygiene and Industrial Sanitation, Labour Hygiene in Machine-building Industry.*
Institute of Labour Hygiene and Occupational Diseases, 31 Meyerovsky Proyezd, Moscow, U.S.S.R.

Khrapchenko, Mikhail Borisovich; Soviet literary critic; b. 1904.
Bureau mem. and Deputy Acad. Sec., Dept. of Literature and Language, U.S.S.R. Acad. of Sciences 60-63, Sec. 63-; Corresp. mem U.S.S.R. Acad. of Sciences 58-66, mem. 66-; Order of Red Banner of Labour 64.
Publs. *Works of Gogol* 54, *Dead Souls by N. V. Gogol* 61, *Leo Tolstoi as Artist* 63.
U.S.S.R. Academy of Sciences, 14 Lenin Prospekt, Moscow, U.S.S.R.

Khrennikov, Tikhon Nikolayevich; Soviet composer; b. 1913; ed. Moscow Conservatoire.
General Sec. Soviet Composers' Union 48-57, First Sec. 57-; Deputy to U.S.S.R. Supreme Soviet; mem. C.P.S.U. 47-; State Prize 42, 46, 51, 67, People's Artist of the R.S.F.S.R. 55, of the U.S.S.R. 63; Order of Lenin 63, Red Banner of Labour 67.
Principal compositions: Five Pieces for Piano 33, Three Pieces for Piano 35, Suite for Orchestra from Music for *Much Ado About Nothing, In the Storm* (Opera) 39, Second Symphony 41, incidental music for play *Long Ago* 42, *Frol Skobeyev* (Opera) 50, *Mother* (Opera) 56, Concerto for Violin and Orchestra 59, *A Hundred Devils and One Girl* (Operetta) 61, *White Nights* (Operetta) 67.
Composers' Union of the U.S.S.R., Nezhdanova Street 8/10, Moscow, U.S.S.R.

Khristianovich, Sergei Alexeevich; Soviet mechanical engineer; b. 1908; ed. Leningrad Univ.
Specialist in field of hydrodynamics and gas dynamics; corresp. mem. U.S.S.R. Acad. of Sciences 39, mem. 43-; Sec. Technical Sciences Section, U.S.S.R. Acad. of Sciences 53-56; thrice State prize laureate; Zhukovsky prize of U.S.S.R. Acad. of Sciences 42; Dir. Inst. of

Theoretical and Applied Mechanics, Siberian Div. 57-65.
U.S.S.R. Academy of Sciences, Department of Physical and Engineering Problems of Energetics, 14 Lenin Prospekt, Moscow, U.S.S.R.

Khrushchev, Nikita Sergeyevich; Soviet politician; b. 17 April 1894; ed. Moscow Industrial Acad.
Joined Communist Party 18; active in Party affairs in Moscow and the Ukraine; Sec. Moscow City Cttee. of Communist Party 32-34; First Sec. Moscow Regional and City Party Cttees. 35-38; mem. Cen. Cttee. Communist Party of the Soviet Union 34; First Sec. Cen. Cttee. Ukrainian C.P. 38-49; mem. Political Bureau, Cen. Cttee. C.P.S.U. 39-52; during the Second World War a mem. of Military Councils of the Kiev Special Military District, South-Western direction, Stalingrad, Southern and First Ukrainian fronts; Chair. Ukrainian Council of Ministers 47; Sec. Cen. Cttee. C.P.S.U. and First Sec. Moscow Regional Cttee. 49-53, mem. Presidium 52-64, First Sec. 53-64; Chair. Council of Ministers of the U.S.S.R. (Prime Minister) 58-64, retired 64; Hero of Socialist Labour (thrice), Order of Lenin (five times), Order of Suvorov, 1st and 2nd Class, Order of Kutuzov, 1st Class, Order of Red Banner of Labour, Hammer and Sickle Gold Medal (thrice), Order of the Patriotic War, 1st Class, International Lenin Peace Prize laureate, Hero of the Soviet Union, etc.
Publs. *For a Lasting Peace and Peaceful Coexistence* 58, *To Victory in Peaceful Competition with Capitalism* 59, *A World Without Arms—A World Without War, Let Us Live in Peace and Friendship* 59, *Peace and Happiness to the Peoples, For Peace, Disarmament and Freedom of the Peoples* 60, *Foreign Policy of the Soviet Union* 61, *Communism is Peace and Happiness of the Peoples* 62, *The Building of Communism in the U.S.S.R. and Development of Agriculture* 62-63 (8 vols.), *Lofty Mission of Soviet Literature and Art* 63, *To Prevent War, to Safeguard Peace* 63.
Ministry of Social Security, 14 Shabolovka, Moscow, U.S.S.R.

Khvostov, Vladimir Mikhailovich; Soviet historian; b. 1905.
Member C.P.S.U. 43-; Collegium mem. and Board Head, U.S.S.R. Ministry of Foreign Affairs 45-57; Head, Chair. of Int. Relations, Acad. of Social Sciences of Central Cttee of C.P.S.U. 46-54; Dir. Inst. of History and Deputy Acad. Sec., Dept. of History, U.S.S.R. Acad. of Sciences 59-67; Corresp. mem. U.S.S.R. Acad. of Sciences 53-64, mem. 64-; Pres. Acad. of Pedagogical Sciences of U.S.S.R. 67-; State Prize (twice).
U.S.S.R. Academy of Sciences 14, Lenin Prospekt, Moscow, U.S.S.R.

Kibalnikov, Aleksandr Pavlovich; Soviet sculptor; b. 1912; ed. Saratov Art School.
Exhibition of first works 39; designed monuments to Mayakovsky in Moscow; works in the Tretyakov Gallery, Moscow; mem. Soviet Acad. of Arts; State Prize for statue of Chernyshevsky 49, 51, Lenin Prize 59, People's Artist of U.S.S.R. 63.
Academy of Artists, 21 Kropotkin Street, Moscow, U.S.S.R.

Kielmansegg, General Johann Adolf, Graf von; German army officer; b. 30 Dec. 1906; ed. Monastic School, Rossleben.
Army Service 26-, Officer 30; War Acad., Berlin 37-39; Gen. Staff, 1st and 6th Panzer Div. 39-42; OKH (High Command of the Army) 42-44, C.O. Infantry Regiment III 44-45; journalistic activities 45-50; Defence Ministry 50-55; Mil. Rep. of German Fed. Republic to SHAPE, Paris 55-58; Second-in-Command, 5th Panzer Div. 59-60, later C.O. 10th Panzer Div.; Defence Ministry, Bonn until 63; C.-in-C. Allied Land Forces, Central

Europe 63-66; C.-in-C. Allied Forces, Cen. Europe 66-68.
H.Q. Allied Forces Central Europe, Brunssum, The Netherlands.

Kienle, Johann (Hans) Georg, DR.PHIL.; German astronomer; b. 22 Oct. 1895; ed. Ludwig-Maximilians-Universität, Munich.
Assistant and later Observer, Munich Observatory 18-24; Prof. and Deputy Dir. Univ. Observatory, Göttingen 24-27, Prof. and Dir. 27-39; Dir. Astrophysical Observatory, Potsdam 39-50; Prof., Univ. of Heidelberg, and Dir. Heidelberg Observatory 50-, now Prof. Emer.; mem. Acad. of Sciences, Göttingen, Berlin and Heidelberg; Orden Pour le Mérite für Wiss. und Künste.
Heidelberg, Ziegelhäuser Landstrasse 31, German Federal Republic.
Telephone: 23889.

Kiesinger, Kurt Georg; German lawyer and politician; b. 6 April 1904; ed. Tübingen and Berlin Univs.
Lawyer, Berlin 35-45, Tübingen 48; mem. Bundestag 49-58, Chair. Cttee. for Foreign Affairs 54-58; mem. Consultative Assembly, Council of Europe 50-58, Vice-Pres. 55-58, Chair. Christian Democratic Group 56-58; mem. WEU Assembly 56-58; Minister-Pres., Baden-Württemberg 58-66; Pres. Bundesrat 62-63; Fed. Chancellor 66-; Chair. Christian Democratic Union 67-; Dr. Iur. h.c. (Cologne and New Delhi); Grand Cross Order of Merit of German Fed. Repub., Grand Cross Order of Merit of Italian Repub., Grand Officier de la Légion d'Honneur, Palmes Académiques, Bavarian Order of Merit and several other foreign decorations; Christian Democratic Union.
Bundeskanzleramt, Adenauerallee 141, Bonn, German Federal Republic.

Kihara, Hitoshi; Japanese scientist; b. 93; ed. Hokkaido Univ.
Former Prof., Kyoto Univ.; has specialised in genetics and applied botany; studied cellular heredity of wheat, Germany 29; Del. Int. Congress of Genetics, Stockholm 48; Dir. Kihara Inst. for Biological Research 42; Dir. Nat. Inst. of Genetics 55; mem. Japanese Acad; Foreign Assoc. American Acad. of Arts and Sciences.
41 Otsuka-Naka Machi, Bunkyo-ku, Tokyo, Japan.

Kikawada, Kazutaka; Japanese business executive; b. 23 Aug. 1899; ed. Tokyo Univ.
With Tokyo Electric Light Co. (now Tokyo Electric Power Co.) Vice-Pres. 54-62, Pres. 62-.
2-9 Uchisaiwaicho, Chiyodaku, Tokyo, Japan.

Kikoin, Isaak Konstantinovich; Soviet physicist; b. 08; ed. Kalinin Polytechnical Inst. Leningrad.
Instructor, Higher Technical Education establishments Leningrad, Sverdlovsk 31-44; Prof. of Physics, Engineering Inst. U.S.S.R. Acad. of Sciences 44-; Corresp. mem. U.S.S.R. Acad. of Sciences 43-53, mem. 53-; State Prize 42.
Publs. co-author *The Physics of Metals* 34, *Holl's Coefficient and Electrical Resistance of Ferrous Magnetics* 64, *Magnetic Influence on Resistance of Ferrous Magnetics* 64.
Physical and Engineering Institute, ulitsa Kirova 21, Moscow, U.S.S.R.

Killian, James Rhyne, Jr., B.S.; American technologist, government official and college administrator; b. 24 July 1904; ed. Duke Univ. and Massachusetts Inst. of Technology.
Assistant Managing Ed. *The Technology Review*, M.I.T. 26-27, Managing Ed. 27-30 and Ed. 30-39; Exec. Asst. to Pres. M.I.T. 39-43, Exec. Vice-Pres. 43-45, Vice-Pres. 45-48, Pres. 48-59, Chair. of Corpn. M.I.T. 59-; Special Asst. to President Eisenhower for Science and Technology 57-59; Chair. President's Foreign Intelligence Advisory Board 61-63; Dir. General Motors Corpn. 59-,

Polaroid Corpn. 59-, Cabot Corpn. 63-, American Telephone and Telegraph Co. 63-; Officer of the French Legion of Honour 57; Hoover Medal 63; numerous hon. degrees.
77 Massachusetts Avenue, Cambridge, Mass. 02139, U.S.A.
Telephone: 864-6060.

Killion, George Leonard; American shipping executive; b. 15 April 1901; ed. Univ. of Southern California and Univ. of California.
Editorial Staff, West Coast Newspapers 25-30; Public Relations, Financial Consultant, Safeway Stores, Oakland, Calif. 30-35, Public Relations and Legislative Consultant 35-39; Dir. of Finance, State of California 40-43; Asst. to Petroleum Admin. for War, Washington 43; Asst. to Treasurer, Democratic Nat. Cttee. 44, Treas. 45-47; Pres. and Dir. American President Lines 47-; Chair. Board, Metro-Goldwyn-Mayer 57-63, 63-; Dir. Pacific Nat. Bank 60-, Communications Satellite Corpn. 62-, Dir., mem. Exec. Cttee. 63-; Dir. various other companies.
Office: 333 Montgomery Street; Home: 1090 Chestnut Street, San Francisco, U.S.A.

Kim Il; Korean politician.
Member, Presidium of Central Committee of Workers' Party of Korea; Vice-Premier, Democratic People's Republic of Korea 56-57, First Vice-Premier 57-.
Office of First Vice-Premier, Pyongyang, Democratic People's Republic of Korea.

Kim Il Sung; Korean politician; b. 12.
Joined Communist Youth League 27, Sec. East Manchurian Special Area 29; joined Communist Party 31; organised and led Korean People's Revolutionary Army in struggle against the Japanese 31-45; founded Fatherland Restoration Asscn. 35; Sec.-Gen. Organising Cttee. Korean Communist Party 45; Chair. North Korean People's Cttee. 47, Cen. Cttee. Workers' Party 48-; Premier of the Democratic People's Republic of Korea 48-; Commdr.-in-Chief 50; Marshal and Hero of the Democratic People's Republic of Korea, Order of Nat. Flag (1st Class) (three times), Order of Freedom and Independence (1st Class), Hero of Labour.
Publs. *Selected Works* (4 vols.), etc.
Pyongyang, Democratic People's Republic of Korea.

Kimball, Dan A.; American industrialist; b. 1 March 1896; ed. Soldan High School, St. Louis.
Los Angeles Man., Tire and Rubber Co. of Akron, Ohio 20-, Vice-Pres. 42-; Exec. Vice-Pres. Aerojet Engineering Corpn. of Azusa, Calif. 44-, Pres. 53, now Chair. of Board; Asst. Sec. of the Navy Mar. 49, Under-Sec. 49-51; Sec. of Navy 51-53; Democrat.
2120 S. Street N.W., Washington 20008, U.S.A.

Kimberly, John Robbins; American businessman; b. 13 April 1903; ed. Phillips Andover Acad. and Mass. Inst. Technology.
Joined Kimberly-Clark Corpn., Neenah Wis. 24, Vice-Pres. (Sales) 43-53 Pres. 53-55, Chair. 55-; Chair. Spruce Falls Power & Paper Co. Ltd.; Dir. and Trustee of various orgs.
Office: Kimberly-Clark Corpn., N. Lake Street, Neenah, Wis.; Home: Box 512, Neenah, Wis., U.S.A.

Kimny, Nong; Cambodian diplomatist; b. Jan. 1912; ed. Sisowath Coll., Phnom-Penh and Lycée Chasseloup-Laubat, Saigon.
Entered Cambodian Admin. 32, Gov. of Kompong-Speu Province 40; Chief of King's Cabinet and Sec.-Gen. of Govt. 41-45; studied in France 46-50; Minister to United States 51-52, Ambassador 52-54, 56-64; mem. Cambodian Del. to Geneva Conf. on Indo-China 54; Vice-Pres. Council of Ministers and Minister of Foreign Affairs March-Aug. 56; Perm. Rep. to UN 56-64; Ambassador to India 64-.
Embassy of Cambodia, New Delhi, India.

Kimura, Otokichi; Japanese machinery executive; b. 2 July 1897; ed. Osaka Univ.
Director, Sumitomo Metal Industries Ltd. 49, Man. Dir. 51-54, Chief Man. Dir. 54-55; Chair. of Board, Sumitomo Machinery Co. Ltd. 55-56, Pres. 56-.
Sumitomo Machinery Co., Sumitomo Building, 5-15 Kitahama, Higashiku, Osaka, Japan.

Kindersley, 2nd Baron, cr. 41, of West Hoathly; **Hugh Kenyon Molesworth Kindersley,** C.B.E., M.C.; British company director; b. 7 May 1899; ed. Eton.
Served Scots Guards 17-19; Dir. Lazard Bros. and Co. Ltd.; Gov. Royal Exchange Assurance; Chair. Rolls-Royce Ltd.; Dir. Bank of England, British Match Corpn., Atlas Assurance Co. Ltd., Cierva Autogiro Co. Ltd.; served in Scots Guards (Temp. Brig.) in Second World War; Vice-Pres. Officers' Asscn., Chair. Govt. Review Body for Doctors' and Dentists' Pay.
Ramhurst Manor, nr. Tonbridge, Kent, England.

King, Cecil Harmsworth, M.A.; British company director; b. 20 Feb. 1901; ed. Winchester Coll. and Christ Church, Oxford.
Director *Daily Mirror* 29; Deputy Chair. *Sunday Pictorial* 42; Dir. Anglo-Canadian Pulp and Paper Mills 44-61; Chair. Overseas Newspapers Ltd. 48-64; Chair. Daily Mirror Newspapers Ltd. and Sunday Pictorial Newspapers Ltd. 51-63; Dir. Reuters Ltd. 53-59; Chair. Scottish Daily Record and Sunday Mail Ltd. 56-58; Chair. Fleetway Publications Ltd. 59-61; Chair Newspaper Proprietors Asscn. 62-68, Int. Publishing Corpn. 63-68, Reed Paper Group 63-Dec. 68, Wall Paper Manufacturers Ltd. 65-67; Dir. Bank of England 65-68; Part-time mem. Nat. Coal Board 66; Chair. Iliffe-N.T.P. Inc. 66-68; mem. Nat. Parks Comm. 66-; Chair. Butterworth & Co. Ltd. until June 68.
Home: "The Pavilion", Hampton Court, East Molesey, Surrey, England.

King, Charles Tyrell O'Connor, B.A.; Liberian lawyer and civil servant; b. 06; ed. Coll. of West Africa and Liberia Coll. (now Univ. of Liberia).
County Attorney, Montserrado County 42-44; Asst. Sec. of State 44-48; Judge 6th Judicial Circuit Court, Montserrado County 48-50; Admin. Asst. to Pres. of Liberia 50-55; Perm. Rep. to U.N. 55-59; Ambassador to Nigeria 61-; Chair U.N. Comm. on Togoland under French Admin.; Commdr. Légion d'Honneur, Knight Crown of Italy, Order of Orange Nassau, and Liberian decorations.
Liberian Embassy, Lagos, Nigeria.

King, Frank Lester; American banker; b. 5 Aug. 1897; ed. Sparta (Ill.) High School and Northwestern Univ.
Asst. Cashier First Nat. Bank Sparta, Ill. 16-18; service in U.S. Army 19; Nat. Bank Examiner 20-25; Asst. Cashier Chicago Mutual Nat. Bank 26-27; Comptroller Continental Illinois Nat. Bank and Trust Co. 28-42; Exec. Vice-Pres. United Calif. Bank 43-44, Pres. 45-48, Chair. 59-; Chair. Western Bancorporation, Los Angeles 59-; Pres. and Dir. United Calif. Bank Int., N.Y.; Dir. Cyprus Mines Corpn. U.S. Borax and Chemical Corpn., Pacific Indemnity Co., Pacific Mutual Life Insurance Co., Times-Mirror Co., El Paso Natural Gas Co.; Trustee, Univ. of Southern Calif.; mem. Asscn. of Reserve City Bankers, Asscn. Registered Bank Holding companies; mem. American Bankers Asscn.
10375 Wilshire Boulevard, Los Angeles, Calif. 90024, U.S.A.

King, Rt. Hon. Horace Maybray, P.C., B.A., PH.D., LL.D., D.C.L., F.K.C., M.P.; British politician; b. 25 May 1901; ed. Stockton Secondary School and King's Coll., Univ. of London.
Head of English Dept., Taunton's School, Southampton

25-46; Headmaster Regents Park School, Southampton 47-50; M.P. 50-; Speaker's Panel, Chair. 53-64; Chair. of Ways and Means 64-65; Speaker of House of Commons 65-; Vice-Chair. Cultural Cttee., Council of Europe 60.

Publs. *Selections from Macaulay* 33, *Selections from Homer* 40, *Selections from Sherlock Holmes* 48, *Parliament and Freedom* 51, *State Crimes* 67.

37 Manor Farm Road, Southampton, Hants. and Speaker's House, Palace of Westminster, London, S.W.1, England.

Telephone: Southampton 55884.

Kings Norton, Baron (Life Peer), cr. 65, of Wotton Underwood; **Harold Roxbee Cox,** Kt., PH.D., D.I.C., B.SC.(ENG.), M.I.MECH.E., F.INST.F., F.R.AE.S., F.I.AE.S. (U.S.A.); British engineer and scientist; b. 1902; ed. Kings Norton School, Imperial Coll. of Science and Technology.

Engineer on construction of airship R.101 24-29; Chief Technical Officer, Royal Airship Works 31; investigations in wing-flutter and stability of structures 31-35; Principal Scientific Officer, Aerodynamics Dept., R.A.E. 35-36; Head of Air Defence Dept. R.A.E. 36-38; Chief Technical Officer, Air Registration Board 38-39; Supt. of Scientific Research, R.A.E. 39-40; Deputy Dir. Scientific Research, Ministry of Aircraft Production 40-43; Dir. of Special Projects, M.A.P. 43-44; Chair. and Man. Dir. of Power Jets (Research and Devt.) Ltd. 44-46; Dir. Nat. Gas Turbine Establishment 46-48; Chair. Gas Turbine Collaboration Cttee. 41-44, 46-48; Chief Scientist, Ministry of Fuel and Power 48-54; Chair. Civil Aircraft Research Cttee. 53-58; Dir. Wilmot Breeden Ltd. 54-60; Chair. Coll. of Aeronautics; Vice-Chair. Air Registration Board 59-66, Chair. 66-; Deputy Chair. The Metal Box Co. 59-61, Chair. 61-67; Dir. Boulton Paul Aircraft Co. Ltd. 58-; Ricardo and Co. Engineers (1927) Ltd. 65-; Steel Company of Wales Ltd. 65-; Chair. Nat. Council for Technological Awards 60-64; Chair. of Council for Scientific and Industrial Research 61-65; Chair. Council for Nat. Academic Awards 64-; Pres. Royal Aeronautical Soc. 47-49; Chair. Naval Education Advisory Cttee. 56-60; Medal of Freedom (U.S.A.) with Silver Palm; Hon. D.Sc. (Birmingham Univ.).

3 Upper Harley Street, London, N.W.1; and Idle House, Wotton Underwood, Aylesbury, Bucks., England.

Kingsbury-Smith, Joseph; American journalist; b. 20 Feb. 1908; ed. Friends' School Poughkeepsie and London Univ.

Int. News Service 24-26; United Press 26-27; I.N.S. London 27-31; Washington 31-36; Man. London Bureau 36-38; Washington 40-44; European Gen.-Dir. 44-55; Pres. and Gen. Man. I.N.S. 55-57; Vice-Pres., Assoc. Gen. Manager, United Press Int. 58-59; Trustee Hearst Estate and Fordham Univ.; Publisher *N.Y. Journal-American* 59-; Vice-Pres. and Dir. Hearst Corpn. 65-; various journalistic awards, and Chevalier de la Légion d'Honneur, mostly in recognition of an exchange of correspondence with Stalin (1949) during the blockade of Berlin; Pulitzer Prize 56 for Int. Reporting.

100 avenue Raymond Poincaré, Paris 16, France.

Kinoshita, James Otoichi; Japanese author; b. 3 June 1889; ed. Univs. of California and Southern California. Fmr. Correspondent Washington Disarmament Conf.; Editor *Tsingtao Leader* (English daily), Sec.-Gen. Tokyo Press Asscn. and Dir. Liberal News Agency; Exec. Dir. Japan Trade Promotion Asscn. 30, Pres. 48; Founder The Friends of the U.N. 48 (now The Friends of the World), Managing Dir. 52-, Vice-Pres. 62-; Pres. Nippon Mutual Development Co. Ltd. 63.

Publs. *Is the World Growing Better?, World: A Spiritual System, Religion of Love* (trans.), *The Child Welfare*

Movement, Thrice Around the World, Rationalisation of American Industry.

2056 Izumi, Komae-machi, Kita-tamagun, Tokyo, Japan.

Telephone: 489-1300.

Kinoshita, Keisuke; Japanese film director; b. 12; ed. Hamamatsu Industrial Coll.

Began his career in Shochiku Studio, Kamata; directed first film *Hanasaku Minato* 43; Henrietta Award for *Nijushi no Hitomi* 55, Golden Globe Award of Hollywood Foreign Press for *Taiyo to Bara* 57.

Films include *Hanasaku Minato* (Port of Flowers) 43, *Yabure Daiko* (Torn Drum), *Carmen kokyo ni Kaeru* (Carmen Comes Home) 49, *Nippon no Higeki* (The Tragedy of Japan) 53, *Nijushi no Hitomi* (Twenty-Four Eyes) 54, *Nogiku no Gotoki Kimi Nariki* (My First Love Affair) 55, *Yuyakegumo* (Farewell to Dreams), *Taiyo to Bara* (The Rose of his Arm) 56, *Yorokobi-mo Kanashimi-mo Ikutoshitsuki* (The Lighthouse), *Fuzen no Tomoshibi* (Danger Stalks Near) 57, *Narayama-bushi Ko* (Ballad of the Narayama), *Kono ten no Niji* (The Eternal Rainbow) 58, *Kazahana* 59, *Sekishuncho, The River Fuefuki* 61, *Eien no Hito* (Bitter Spirit) 62.

1366 Tsujido, Fujisawa, Kanagawa Prefecture, Japan.

Kintner, Robert Edmonds, B.A.; American radio administrator; b. 12 Sept. 1909; ed. Swarthmore Coll. Reporter and later Washington corresp. *New York Herald Tribune,* Columnist (with Joseph Alsop) for North American Newspaper Alliance and later for *New York Herald Tribune* 31-41; with U.S. Army Bureau of Public Relations (Lieut. Col.) 41-44; joined American Broadcasting Co. 44, Exec. Vice-Pres. 46-49, Pres. 49-57; Exec. Vice-Pres. National Broadcasting Co. 57, Pres. 58-66, also Chair. 65-66; Special Asst. on White House Staff 66-67.

Publs. (with Joseph Alsop) *Men Around the President, American White Paper.*

817 Fifth Avenue, New York City, N.Y., 10022, U.S.A.

Kipphardt, Heinar, DR.MED.; German writer; b. 8 March 1922; ed. medical studies, Düsseldorf.

Former Asst. doctor, Universitäts-Nerven-Klinik der Charité, Berlin; Chief Dramatist and Dir., Deutsches Theater, Berlin 50-59; freelance writer 59-; Deutscher Nationalpreis 53; Schiller Gedächtnispreis 62; Gerhard Hauptmann Preis 64; Adolf Grimme Preis 64; Fernsehpreis (TV. Prize) der Deutschen Akad. der darstellenden Künste 64.

Publs. *Shakespeare dringend gesucht* (satire) 53, *Der Aufstieg des Alois Piontek* (farce) 56, *Die Stühle des Herrn Szmil* (satire) 60, *Der Hund des Generals* (play) 62, *In der Sache J. Robert Oppenheimer* (play) 64, *Joel Brand, Die Geschichte eines Geschäfts* (play) 65, *Die Nacht in der der Chef geschlachtet wurde* (comedy) 67, *Die Soldaten* (edited) 68, *Die Ganovenfresse* (short stories) 68.

München-Untermenzing, Gotboldstrasse 54, German Federal Republic.

Telephone: 832600.

Kipping, Sir Norman Victor, G.C.M.G., K.B.E., J.P.; British industrial administrator; b. 11 May 1901; ed. Univ. of London.

Transmission engineer, Int. Western Electric Co. 21-26; Standard Telephones & Cables Ltd. 27-42; Ministry of Production 42-45; Hon. D.Sc. (Loughborough); Dir.-Gen. Fed. of British Industries 46-65; mem. Inst. Electrical Engineers, Inst. Production Engineers; Hon. Fellow British Inst. Management; Dir. Joseph Lucas (Industries) Ltd., Pilkington Brothers Ltd.; Chair. of Govs. Univ. Coll. School; foreign orders.

Fosters, Wykeham Rise, Totteridge, London, N.20, England.

Kirby, Allan Price; American businessman; b. 31 July 1892; ed. Wyoming Seminary (Kingston, Pa.), Lawrenceville School (N.J.), Lafayette Coll., Easton, Pa.

Man. Bathurst (New Brunswick, Canada) Lumber Co. 14-15; Pres. Jenkins-Kirby Packing Co. 15-22, Kirby-Davis Co. 22-34; Vice-Pres. Second Nat. Bank of Wilkes-Barre, Pa. 24-34; Pres. Imperial Motor Corporation 34-40, Alleghany Corporation 39-61; Dir. F. W. Woolworth & Co., Int. Telephone and Telegraph Corpn., Hotel Waldorf-Astoria Corpn., New York Cen. Railroad (Chair. Exec. Cttee.); Dir. and Chair. of Board Alleghany Corpn. 63-67; Trustee, Lafayette Coll., Wyoming Seminary, Lawrenceville School, Angeline E. Kirby Memorial Health Center, Wilkes-Barre, Pa., Wyoming Valley (Pa.) Historical and Geological Soc.; Hon. D.H.L. (Lafayette Coll.), Hon. LL.D. (St. Joseph's Coll.).
17 DeHart Street, Morristown, N.J., U.S.A.

Kirby, Sir Arthur Frank, K.B.E., C.M.G., M.INST.T.; British transport administrator; b. 13 July 1899; ed. Sir William Borlase's School, Marlow and London Univ. Served in France and Belgium in First World War 17-18; with Great Western Railway 18-28; Asst. Sec. Takoradi Harbour, Gold Coast 28-35; Traffic Manager Gold Coast Railways 35-38; Asst. Supt. of the Line, Kenya and Uganda Railways 38-42; Gen. Manager Palestine Railways 42-48; Supt. of the Line, E. African Railways and Harbours 48-51; Asst. Commr. for Transport, E. Africa High Comm. Jan. 51, Acting Commr. 52; Gen. Manager E. African Railways and Harbours 52-57; Commr. E. African Common Services Org., London 58-62; Chair. British Transport Docks Board 63-; Chair. Nat. Ports Council 67-.
6 Baltimore Court, The Drive, Hove. Sussex, England.

Kircher, Donald Peter; American businessman; b. 28 April 1915; ed. Univ. of Minn. and Columbia Univ. Admitted to New York State Bar 39, private law practice 39-48, with Winthrop, Stimson, Putnam and Roberts 39-41, 46-48; Asst. to Pres. Singer Co. 48-49, Asst. Vice-Pres. 49-52, Vice-Pres. 52-58, Pres. 58-; Pres. Singer Sewing Machine Co.; Dir.-Gen. Cable Corpn., Bristol-Myers Co., Lehman Corpn., Morgan Guaranty Trust Co., N.Y., Metropolitan Life Insurance Co.; Silver Star with Oak Leaf Clusters, Bronze Star, Purple Heart with Oak Leaf Cluster, Presidential Unit Citation, Chevalier, Order of Léopold, and Croix de Guerre (Belgium).
Office: 30 Rockefeller Plaza, New York City, N.Y. 10020, U.S.A.

Kirchwey, Freda, A.B., LITT.D.; American journalist; b. 26 Sept. 1893; ed. Barnhard Coll., Columbia Univ. Reporter New York *Morning Telegraph* 15-16; mem. Editorial Staff *Every Week* N.Y. 17-18, *Sunday Tribune* 18; with *The Nation* 18-, Managing Editor 22-28, Literary Editor 28-29, Editor 32-55, Publisher 37-55, Contrib. 55-; mem. UN Corresps. Asscn.; Dr. Humane Letters, Rollins Coll. 44; mem. Women's Int. League for Peace and Freedom, Int. League for Rights of Man; Chevalier, Légion d'Honneur 46.
390 First Avenue, New York City, N.Y. 10010, U.S.A. Telephone: SP7-4171.

Kirichenko, Alexei Illarionovich; Soviet politician; b. 08; ed. Azov-Black Sea Inst. of Socialist Agricultural Engineers.
Joined Communist Party 30; held various posts under Central Cttee. of Ukrainian Communist Party 38-41; Sec. of Central Cttee., Ukrainian Communist Party 41; during Second World War, mem. Mil. Councils for the South-Western front and for the Stalingrad, Don, Southern, and Fourth Ukrainian fronts; returned as Sec. of Central Cttee., Ukrainian Communist Party 44; Second Sec. 49-53, First Sec. 53-57; mem. Presidium, Central Cttee. of C.P.S.U. 56-60; Sec. Central Cttee. of C.P.S.U. 57-60; 1st Sec. Rostov Region Communist Party May-June 60; Dir. Penza Motor Cycle Plant 60-63; retired 63; awarded Order of Lenin (three times),

Order of the Red Banner (twice), Order of Kutuzov (Second Class), and other decorations.
c/o Ministry of Social Security of R.S.F.S.R., 14 Shabolovka, Moscow, U.S.S.R.

Kirichenko, Nikolai Karpovich; Soviet politician; b. 1923; ed. Kharkov Pedagogical Inst.
Member C.P.S.U. 44-; Soviet Army service 41-45; Young Communist League Official, Ukraine 45-55; Second Sec. Central Cttee. Young Communist League, Ukraine 55-60; Sec. Poltava Regional Cttee. of C.P., then Chair. Poltava Regional Soviet of Working People's Deputies 60-63; First Sec. Kirovograd Rural Regional Cttee. of C.P. and Chair. Kirovograd Regional Soviet of Working People's Deputies 63-65; First Sec. Kirovograd Regional Cttee. C.P. of the Ukraine 65-; mem. Central Cttee. C.P. of the Ukraine; Deputy to U.S.S.R. Supreme Soviet; mem. Budget Cttee., Soviet of Union. Kirovograd Regional Committee, Communist Party of the Ukraine, Kirovograd, U.S.S.R.

Kirilenko, Andrei Pavolich; Soviet politician; b. 1906; ed. Higher Technical School.
Fitter 25-29; Young Communist League 29-30; mem. C.P.S.U. 31-; Engineer 36-38; Sec. District, later Regional Cttee.; Zaporozhe Regional Cttee., C.T.S.U. 38-41, 43-47; Soviet Army 41-43; First Sec. Nicolaev City and Regional Cttee., C.P.S.U. 47-50, Dnepropetrovsk Regional Cttee. 50-51, Sverdlovsk Regional Cttee. 55-62; Cand. mem. Presidium of Cen. Cttee. of the C.P. of the U.S.S.R. 57-61, mem. 62-66, Sec. 66-; mem. Politburo 66-; First Vice-Chair. Bureau for the R.S.F.S.R. 62-.
Politburo of Central Committee of the Communist Party of the U.S.S.R., Moscow, U.S.S.R.

Kirillin, Vladimir Alekseevich; Soviet thermophysicist; b. 1913; ed. Power Engineering Inst. Moscow.
Lecturer 38-41, 43-52; Prof. Moscow Power Engineering Inst. 52-53; Corresp. mem. U.S.S.R. Acad. of Sciences 53-62, mem. 62-, Vice-Pres. 63-; U.S.S.R. Dep. Minister of Higher Education 54-55; Head, Dept. of Science, Higher Education Inst. and School, Central Cttee. of C.P.S.U. 55-63; mem. Central Auditing Comm. C.P.S.U. 56-61; Cand. mem. C.P.S.U. Central Cttee. until 66, mem. 66-; Deputy to U.S.S.R. Supreme Soviet; Chair. State Cttee. for Science and Engineering 65-; Vice-Chair. U.S.S.R. Council of Ministers 65-; State Prize 51, Lenin Prize 59.
Publs. *Cycles of Turbines of Internal Combustion* 49, *Fundamentals of Experimental Thermodynamics* 50, *Steam in Power* 53, *Thermodynamics of Solutions* 56, *Thermodynamic Properties of Gases* 53, *Investigation of Thermodynamic Properties of Substances* 63.
State Committee for Science and Engineering, 11 Gorky Street, Moscow, U.S.S.R.

Kirk, Grayson, PH.D.; American university president; b. 12 Oct. 1903; ed. Miami Univ., Clark Univ., Ecole Libre des Sciences Politiques, Paris, Univ. of Wisconsin, London School of Economics.
Instructor in Political Science, Univ. of Wisconsin 29-30, Asst. Prof. 30-36, Assoc. Prof. 36-38, Prof. of Political Science 38-40; Assoc. Prof. of Govt., Columbia Univ. 40-43; Research Assoc., Yale Inst. of Int. Studies 43-44; Prof. of Govt., Columbia Univ. 43-47, Prof. of Int. Relations 47-49, Provost 49-50, Vice-Pres. and Provost 50-53, Acting Pres. 51, Pres. and Trustee 53-; Bryce Prof. of the History of Int. Relations, Columbia Univ. 59-; Head of Security Section, Div. of Political Studies, State Dept. 42-43; mem. U.S. Del. Dumbarton Oaks 44; Exec. Officer, Third Comm. (Security Council), San Francisco Conf. 45; mem. Board of Dirs. Acad. of Political Science, Council on Foreign Relations (Pres.), Mobil Oil Co., Int. Business Machines Corpn. Inc., Nation-Wide Securities Co., Dividend Shares Inc., Japan Society, Belgian American Educational Foundation Inc., France-America Society; mem. of Board of

Dirs. Morningside Heights Inc. Chair., Consolidated Edison Co. of N.Y.; Trustee Asia Foundation, Carnegie Foundation for the Advancement of Teaching, Greenwich Savings Bank, Inst. of Int. Educ., Lycée Français of N.Y. (Chair.), Asia Soc.; Commdr. Order of Orange Nassau (Netherlands), Hon. K.B.E., Commdr. Légion d'Honneur, Knight St. John, Officer, Order of Grand Cross of George I (Greece), Order of the Sacred Treasure, 1st Class (Japan), and Italian and Iranian decorations, Commdr. de l'Ordre des palmes académiques (France); Hon. LL.D. (Miami, Waynesburg, Brown, Union, Princeton, Wisconsin, Syracuse, Williams, Pennsylvania, Harvard, Tennessee, Washington, New York, Clark, Puerto Rico, Johns Hopkins, Columbia, Amherst, Dartmouth Coll., Northwestern Univ., Jewish Theol. Seminary, St. Lawrence Univ., Denver, Notre Dame, Bates Coll., Univ. of Michigan, Waseda (Japan), Sussex, Venezuelan Univs. and Univs. in India and Thailand), Hon. Ph.D. (Bologna); D.C.L. (Univ. of King's Coll., Halifax, Nova Scotia); Hon. L.H.D. (Univ. of N. Dakota).

Publs. *Philippine Independence* 36, *Contemporary International Politics* (with W. R. Sharp) 40, *War and National Policy, Syllabus* (with R. P. Stebbins) 41, *The Study of International Relations in American Colleges and Universities* 47.

Home: 60 Morningside Drive, New York, 10027; Office: Columbia University, New York 10027, N.Y., U.S.A. Telephone: 280-2825.

Kirk, Norman E.; New Zealand politician; b. 6 Jan. 1923; ed. Linwood Avenue School.

Formerly engine driver; Mayor of Kaiapoi 53-57; M.P. for Lyttleton 57-; Vice-Pres. N.Z. Labour Party 63-64, Pres. 64-66, Leader Parl. Labour Party Dec. 65-.

19 Hillsborough Terrace, Christchurch, New Zealand.

Kirkaldy, Harold Stewart, C.B.E., M.A., LL.B.; British university professor (retd.); b. 27 Dec. 1902; ed. Grove Acad., Broughty Ferry, and Univ. of Edinburgh.

Asst. Sec. British Employers' Confederation 29-39; Gen. Sec. Iron and Steel Trades Employers' Asscn. 39-45; mem. British Del. Int. Lab. Conf. 29-44; Prof. of Industrial Relations, Cambridge Univ. 44-63, Fellow of Queens' Coll. 44-, Vice-Pres. 65-; mem. of Cttee. of Experts on the Application of Int. Lab. Conventions 46-; Chair. of various Wages Councils under Wages Councils Acts 46-62; Deputy Chair. Royal Comm. on Nat. Incomes 62-65; Chair. of various Comms. of Inquiry, etc.; Perin Memorial Lecturer, Jamshedpur, India 46; mem. Admin. Board Staff Pensions Fund of ILO 46-, Chair. 60-; Chair. UN Joint Staff Pensions Board 60-62; mem. Industrial Disputes Tribunal 52-59; Pres. Mauritius Trade Disputes Arbitration Tribunal 59; mem. Cttee. on Remuneration of Ministers and M.P.s 63-64; Barrister-at-Law.

Queens' College, Cambridge, England.

Kirkconnell, Watson, M.A., PH.D., LL.D., D.LITT., D. ès L., L.H.D., D.P.EC., D.C.L.; Canadian classical scholar; b. 16 May 1895; ed. Queen's Univ. (Kingston, Ontario), and Lincoln Coll., Oxford.

Lecturer in English Wesley Coll. 22, Asst. Prof. 23, Associate Prof. 24, Prof. 31; Prof. of Classics United Coll. 34-40; Prof. of English, McMaster Univ., Hamilton Ont. 40-48; Pres. Acadia Univ. 48-64, Prof. of English 64-; Knight Commdr. Order of the Falcon (Iceland), Knight Polonia Restituta, Fellow, Royal Soc., Canada, hon. mem. Petöfi Soc., Hungary; Hon. Fellow, Icelandic Soc. of Letters; Silver Laurel, Polish Acad. of Literature; foreign mem. Kisfaludy Soc., Hungary; Medal of Honour, P.E.N. Club of Hungary; mem. London School of Slavonic Studies; mem. Shevchenko Soc. of Sciences; Pres. Canadian Authors' Asscn. 42-44, 56-58; Chair. Writers' War Cttee. for Canada 42-44; Humanities Research Council of Canada 43-46; Lorne Pierce Gold Medal, Royal Society of Canada; Nova

Scotia Drama League Trophy 56, Shevchenko Medal and Plaque, Gold Medal of Freedom (Magyars in Exile) 64, George Washington Medal, American Hungarian Studies Foundation 67.

Publs. *International Aspects of Unemployment* 23, *European Elegies* 28, *Icelandic Verse* 30, *The European Heritage* 30, *The Magyar Muse* 33, *The Eternal Quest* 34, *Canadian Overtones* 35, *Polish Lyrics* 36, *Death of Buda* (from Magyar) 37, *Canada, Europe and Hitler* 39, *Titus the Toad* 39, *Ukrainian Canadians and the War* 40, *The Flying Bull and Other Tales* 40, *Canadians All* 41, *Twilight of Liberty* 41, *Seven Pillars of Freedom* 44, *The Quebec Tradition* (with Séraphin Marion) 46, *The Humanities in Canada* (with A. S. P. Woodhouse) 47, *Little Treasury of Hungarian Verse* 47, *Liberal Education in the Canadian Democracy* 48, *The Crisis in Education* 48, *The Celestial Cycle* 52, *Cultural Stratification in Canadian Place-Names* 54, *The Mod at Grand Pré* 55, *The Place of Slavic Studies in Canada* 58; verse translation of the Polish epic *Pan Tadeusz* 32, *The Ukrainian Poets* (with C. H. Andrusyshen) 63, *Complete Poetical Works of Taras Sherchenko* (with C. H. Andrusyshen) 64, *The Invincible Samson* 64, *Centennial Tales and Other Poems* 65, *A Slice of Canada: Memoirs* 66. Box 460, Wolfville, Nova Scotia, Canada.

Kirkpatrick, Ralph, D.MUS.; American harpsichordist; b. 10 June 1911; ed. Harvard Coll.

Harpsichord, clavichord and early piano exponent, tours throughout America and Europe 33-; Prof. of Music, Yale Univ. 40-; recordings of much classical music including Bach's harpsichord concertos 58-60 and complete clavier works 56-67; Editor of J. S. Bach's *Goldberg Variations* 38, and Domenico Scarlatti's *Sixty Sonatas* 53; Fellow American Acad. of Arts and Sciences, mem. American Philosophical Soc., Order of Merit Italian Republic.

Publ. *Domenico Scarlatti* 53.

Old Quarry, Guilford, Connecticut, U.S.A.

Kirkpatrick, Williams Stafford, B.A.SC., F.C.I.C.; Canadian engineering executive; b. 28 Oct. 1903; ed. Kingston Collegiate Inst., Upper Canada Coll., Toronto Royal Mil. Coll., Kingston, Ont., Toronto Univ.

Consolidated Mining and Smelting Co. (now Cominco Ltd.) 26-40, Asst. to Gen Man. 43-45, Asst. Gen. Man. 45-51 (all at Trail, B.C.), Vice-Pres. Montreal 51, Dir. 53-, Exec. Vice-Pres. 56-59, Pres. 59, Chair. 64-, Chief Exec. Officer 66-; fmr. Pres. Canadian Chamber of Commerce; Chair. West Kootenay Power and Light Co. Ltd.; Dir. Consolidated Paper Corpn., Deloro Smelting and Refining Co. Ltd., Henry Gardner and Co. Ltd. (England), Amalgamated Metal Corpn. Ltd. (England), Royal Trust Co., Bank of Montreal, Hawaiian Western Steel Co., Canadian Investment Fund Ltd., Canadian Fund Ltd.; Pres. The Mining Asscn. of Canada (fmrly. Canadian Metal and Mining Asscn.) 65-; Freeman City of Trail, B.C. 60.

Office: Room 3100, 630 Dorchester Boulevard, Montreal 2, P.Q.; 2820 Hill Park Road, Montreal 25, Canada.

Kirkup, James, B.A.; British writer; b. 23 April 1918; ed. Durham Univ.

Gregory Fellow in Poetry, Leeds Univ. 50-52; Visiting Poet, Bath Acad. of Art 53-56; travelling lectureship from Swedish Ministry of Education 56-57; Prof. of English Language and Literature, Salamanca (Spain) 57-58; Prof. of Eng. Lit., Tohoku Univ. 59-61; Visiting Prof. of Eng. Lit., Japan Women's Univ., Tokyo 64-; Visiting Prof. and Poet in Residence, Amherst Coll. Mass. 68-; Literary Editor *Orient-West Magazine*, Tokyo 63-65; Atlantic Award in Literature (Rockefeller Foundation) 59, F.R.S.L. 62, First Prize, Japan P.E.N. literary contest 65, Mildred Batchelder Award, A.L.A., 68.

Publs. *The Cosmic Shape* 47, *The Drowned Sailor* 48, *The Creation* 50, *The Submerged Village* 51, *A Correct*

Compassion 52, *A Spring Journey* 54, *Upon This Rock, The Dark Child, The Triumph of Harmony* 55, *The True Mystery of the Nativity, Ancestral Voices, The Radiance of the King* 56, *The Descent into the Cave, The Only Child* (autobiography) 57; TV plays: *The Peach Garden, Two Pigeons Flying High, Sorrows, Passions and Alarms* (autobiography) 60, *The True Mystery of the Passion, The Prodigal Son* (poems) 56-60, *These Horned Islands* (travel) 62, *The Love of Others* (novel) 62, *Tropic Temper* (travel) 63, *Refusal to Conform, Last and First Poems* 63, *The Heavenly Mandate* 64, *Japan Industrial*, Vols. I and II 64-65, *Tokyo* (travel) 66, *Bangkok* (travel) 67, *Paper Windows: Poems from Japan* 67, *Michael Kohlhaas* 67, *Filipinescas* (travel) 68, *Russia Inside Out* (travel) 68, and numerous trans. from French and German.
2-8-1 Mejiro-dai, Bunkyo-ku, Tokyo, Japan, and Dept. of English, Amherst College, Amherst, Mass., U.S.A.

Kirkwood, Robert Campbell; American retail executive; b. 19 Nov. 1904; ed. schools in Provo, Utah.
Joined F. W. Woolworth Co. 23, rose to Exec. Officer in charge development self-service stores, Vice-Pres. and Dir., Exec. Vice-Pres 55-58, Chief Exec. Officer 58-, Pres. 58-65, Chair. 65-; Pres. F. W. Woolworth & Co. Ltd., Canada, F. W. Woolworth & Co., Mexico; Chair. Woolworth Española, S.A.; Dir. F. W. Woolworth & Co. England, F. W. Woolworth (Japan) Ltd., Irving Trust Co., New York City.
Office: 233 Broadway, New York City, N.Y., U.S.A.

Kirloskar, Shantanu L., B.SC.; Indian industrialist; b. 28 May 1903; ed. Massachusetts Inst. of Technology, U.S.A.
Kirloskar Brothers 26-; Chair. Kirloskar Oil Engines Ltd., Poona, Kirloskar Pneumatic Co. Ltd., Poona, Kirloskar Consultants Ltd., Poona, Kirloskar Cummins Ltd., Poona, Swastik Rubber Products Ltd., Poona, Padamjee Pulp and Paper Mills Ltd., Poona, Kirloskar Bearings Ltd., Kirloskar Brothers Ltd., The Central Pulp Mills Ltd.; Dir. numerous other companies; Pres. Mahratta Chamber of Commerce and Industries, Poona, Fed. of Indian Chambers of Commerce and Industry, New Delhi 65-66; Padma Bhushan 65, Chair. Cttee. for Econ. Devt. in India.
Office: Kirloskar Oil Engines Ltd., Elphinstone Road, Kirkee, Poona 3; Home: "Lakaki", Poona 16, India.

Kirnasovsky, Boris Efremivich; Soviet diplomatist; b. 1918; ed. Moscow Inst. of Railway Engineering.
Diplomatic posts 50-; Second Sec. New Delhi 53-55, First Sec. 55-; Asst. Head Dept. for South Eastern Countries, Ministry of Foreign Affairs 55-58; Counsellor, Indonesia 58-62; Ambassador to Laos 64-.
U.S.S.R. Embassy, Vientiane, Laos.

Kironde, Apollo K.; Ugandan diplomatist; b. 15; ed. King's Coll., Budo, Makerere Coll., Kampala and Adams Coll., Natal, and Univ. of S. Africa (Fort Hare).
Teacher, King's Coll., Budo 43-50; Middle Temple, London 50-52; legal practice, Uganda 52-55; Asst. Minister of Social Services 55-58; Minister of Works and Transport 58-60; Founder, United Nat. Party 60, merged with Uganda Nat. Congress (U.N.C.) 61, Leader U.N.C. 61-; fmr. Ambassador to U.S.; Perm. Rep. to UN 62-67; Special Asst. in African Problems, Dept. of Political and Security Council Affairs, UN 67-; High Commr. in Canada 64-67.
UN Secretariat, New York City, N.Y., U.S.A.

Kirschbaum, Emil, DR. ING.; German engineer; b. 25 July 1900; ed. Technical Colls., Vienna and Brunswick.
Employed by M.A.N. at Nuremberg and Krupp-Grusonwerk at Magdeburg-Buckau as engineer 23-28; Prof. and Dir. of Inst. of Apparatus Construction and Chemical Engineering, Technische Hochschule (now Universität), Karlsruhe 28-, now Emeritus; mem. N.Y. Acad. of Science.
Publs. *Die Wärmeaustauschapparate* 33, *Destillier- und*

Rektifiziertechnik 40, 49, 60, *Trockentechnik*; and approx. 180 other publs.
Badenwerkstrasse 7, 75 Karlsruhe, German Federal Republic.
Telephone: Karlsruhe 21429.

Kirst, Hans Hellmut; German writer; b. 5 Dec. 1914; ed. Volksschule and Gymnasium, Osterode.
Began his career as a farmer; has been a free-lance writer since 47, mem. PEN Club, Author's Guild U.S.A.; Edgar Allan Poe Special Award, U.S.A. 65.
Publs. include *Galgenstrick* 51, *08/15* (trilogy) 54, *Keiner kommt davon* 57, *Fabrik für Offiziere* 60, *Nacht der Generale* 62, *Aüfstand der Soldaten* 65, *Die Wölfe* 67; books translated into 28 languages.
Feldafing am Starnberger See, Bavaria, German Federal Republic.
Telephone: Feldafing 319.

Kirstein, Lincoln; American ballet promoter; b. 4 May 1907; ed. Harvard Univ.
Editor *Hound and Horn* (literary periodical) 27-34; Editor *The Dance Index* 41-47; established School of American Ballet, New York City, and Dir.; Dir. New York City Ballet Co.; Dir.-Gen. American Ballet.
Publs. *A Short History of Theatrical Dancing* 35, *Blast at Ballet* 38, *Low Ceiling* (poems) 35, *Ballet Alphabet* 39, *Rhymes of a P.F.C. (Private First Class)* (poems) 64, *Rhymes and more Rhymes of a P.F.C.* 66, *The Hampton Album* 66, *Three pamphlets collected* 67.
130 West 56th Street, New York City, N.Y., U.S.A.
Telephone: 799-2256.

Kirsten, Robert, B.A., LL.B.; South African diplomatist; b. 06; ed. Transvaal Univ. Coll., Pretoria Univ.
Joined Dept. of Justice 27, Dept. of External Affairs 29; served Lourenço Marques 34, Stockholm 36, Rome 38, Dept. of External Affairs, Pretoria 40, Lisbon 44, Rome 47; Head of Economic, Trade and General Division, Dept. of External Affairs, Pretoria 54; High Commr. in the Federation of Rhodesia and Nyasaland 56-59, in Canada 59-60; Under Sec., Dept. of Foreign Affairs 61-.
Department of Foreign Affairs, 793 Government Avenue, Arcadia, Pretoria, South Africa.
Telephone: 744465.

Kisch, Isaak, D.IUR.; Netherlands professor; b. 05; ed. Amsterdam and Paris Law Faculties, London School of Economics.
Called to Amsterdam Bar 32; Hon. Judge, Amsterdam Court 35; Asst. Lecturer, Law Faculty, Amsterdam Univ. 30, Lecturer 35, Asst. Prof. 38, Prof. of Comparative Law and Philosophy of Law 45-; Dir. Int. Law Inst., The Hague 49-60, Centre for Foreign Law, Amsterdam; fmr. Judge, Supreme Court of the Netherlands; mem. State Cttee. on Conflict of Law; Assoc. mem. Inst. of Int. Law; Order of the Coif, Louisiana, U.S.A.
Publs. *Rights in rem and in personam* 32, *Foreign Marriages* 35; various publications on civil law, comparative law, conflict of law, philosophy of law, legal history, etc.
Schubertstraat-10, Amsterdam Z., Netherlands.

Kiselev, Ivan Ivanovich; Soviet engineer and politician; b. 17; ed. Gorky Technical Inst.
Technician, Head of Bureau, Insp., Workshop Foreman, Gorky Automobile Factory 37-57, Chief Engineer 54-58, Dir. 58-; mem. C.P.S.U. 44-, mem. Central Cttee. of C.P.S.U. 61-.
Gorky Automobile Factory, Gorky, R.S.F.S.R., U.S.S.R.

Kiselev, Tikhon Yakovlevich; Soviet politician; b. 1917; ed. Gomel Pedagogic Inst. and Higher Party School, Moscow.
Member C.P.S.U. 40-; engaged in full-time work for the Byelorussian C.P. 44-45, Sec. Cen. Cttee. C.P. of Byelorussia 55-59; Deputy Chair. U.S.S.R. Supreme

Soviet Council of Nationalities 58-62; Chair. Byelorussian Council of Ministers 59-; mem. Cen. Cttee. of C.P.S.U. 61-; Deputy Supreme Soviet of the U.S.S.R. Council of Ministers of Byelorussian S.S.R., Minsk, Byelorussian S.S.R., U.S.S.R.

Kisfaludi-Strobl, Zsigmond; Hungarian sculptor; b. 1884; ed. Coll. of Applied Arts, under Lajos Mátrai and Antal Loránfi and in Vienna and Paris.
Former Prof. High School of Fine Arts 61; Kossuth Prize, Eminent Artist of the Hungarian People's Repub.; Hon. mem. Soviet Acad. of Arts.
Works: Hussar Monument in Sopron, Heroes Monument in Kecskemét, Freedom Statue and central figure of Kossuth Monument in Budapest; *The Lizzard* (nude figure); and sculptures of G. B. Shaw, Iványi Grünwald, E. Petrovics, Marshal Voroshilov, Maria Gyurkovics.
Népstadion ut 20, Budapest XIV, Hungary.

Kishan, Ram; Indian politician; b. 1913.
Detained during Quit India Movement; Commr., Lahore Municipal Corpn. 46; Municipal Commr., Jullundur City 48-51; mem. Punjab Legislative Assembly 52-57, 62; Gen. Sec. Pradesh Congress; Deputy Minister Punjab 56-57; Minister of State, Punjab 62-63; mem. All-India Congress Cttee., Nat. Devt. Council 64-; Chief Minister, Punjab 64-67.
Chandigarh, Punjab, India.

Kisházi, Ödön; Hungarian politician; b. 1900.
Toolmaker; mem. Communist Party 22-; posts in Iron and Steel Workers Trade Union 20-45; Pres. Central Council of Trade Unions, Asst. Gen. Sec. Iron and Steel Workers Trade Union 45-48; econ. work 48-52; imprisoned 52-55; Asst. Gen. Sec. Central Council of Trade Unions 56-57; Minister of Labour 57-63; Deputy Pres. Presidential Council 63-; mem. Central Cttee. Hungarian Socialist Workers' Party 62-; mem. Presidium Central Council of Trade Unions, Presidium Patriotic People's Front.
Office of the Deputy President, Presidential Council, Budapest, Hungary.

Kishi, Nobusuke; Japanese politician; b. 96; ed. Tokyo Imperial Univ.
Clerk of Ministry of Agriculture and Commerce 20; Chief of Industrial Administration Section, Industrial Affairs Bureau 32; concurrently Sec. to Ministry of Foreign Affairs 33; Chief of Archives Section, Ministry of Commerce and Industry 33; Sec. of Temporary Industrial Rationalization Bureau and Dir. of Industrial Affairs Bureau 35-36; served in various administrative capacities in Govt. of Manchoukuo 36-39; Vice-Minister of Commerce and Industry 39-41 and Oct.-Nov. 43; Minister of Commerce and Industry Oct. 41-April 42; elected mem. of House of Representatives 42; Minister of State without Portfolio Oct. 43-July 44; purged from public service Dec. 47; apptd. Chair. Board of Dirs. of Toyo Pulp Mfg. Co. Ltd. 49; re-elected mem. of House of Representatives 53 and 55; Chair. of Railway Construction Council 55; Minister of Foreign Affairs Dec. 56; Prime Minister 57-60; Pres. Liberal Democratic Party 57-60 (re-elected 59).
45 Nampeidai, Shibuya-ku, Tokyo, Japan.

Kishkin, Sergei Timofeevich; Soviet metallurgist; b. 1906; ed. Moscow Higher Technical School.
Member C.P.S.U. 39-; Prof. Moscow Inst. of Aviation Technology; Corresp. mem. U.S.S.R. Acad. of Sciences 60-66, mem. 66-.
U.S.S.R. Academy of Sciences, 14 Lenin Prospekt, Moscow, U.S.S.R.

Kisielewski, Stefan; Polish writer, composer and musicologist; b. 7 Mar. 1911.
Journalist on *Tygodnik Powszechny;* mem. Seym 57-61, 61-65.
Publs. *Sprzysiezenie* (Conspiracy) 45, *Zbrodnia w dzielnicy północnej* (Crime in the Northern Quarter) 47;

criticism: *Polityka i sztuka* (Politics and Art) 48; essays: *Rzeczy male* (Small Things) 56, *Opowiadania i Podroze* (Travel and Short Stories) 60; several books on music and politics.
Al. I Armii W.P. 16m 11., Warsaw, Poland.
Telephone: 28-96-53.

Kiss, Árpád; Hungarian politician; b. 28 Aug. 1918.
Engineer, Ganz Electrical Appliances Factory; Minister of Light Industry 50-54; Minister of Chemical Industry and Power Supply 54-56; Chair., Nat. Planning Office 56-61; Pres. State Office of Technical Devt. 61-; mem. Central Cttee., Hungarian Socialist Workers' Party.
State Office of Technical Development, V. Akadémia u. 17, Budapest, Hungary.
Telephone: 316-560.

Kiss, Károly; Hungarian politician; b. 03.
Leather worker; mem. Political Cttee., Hungarian Communist Party 45-53; Chair. Cen. Control Comm. 46-56; fmr. Minister for Foreign Affairs; Vice-Pres., Presidential Council 49-51, 58-61, Sec. of Presidential Council 61-67; Vice-Pres. Cabinet Council 52-53; Cen. Council of Trade Unions 67-; mem. Cen. Cttee. Hungarian Socialist Workers' Party.
Central Council of Trade Unions, Dozsa György u. 84/b, Budapest VI, Hungary.

Kissinger, Henry, M.A., PH.D.; American (German-born) professor; b. 27 May 1923; ed. George Washington High School and Harvard Univ.
Went to U.S.A. 38; Army service 43-46; Consultant Operations Research Office 50, Psychological Strategic Board 52-53; Dir. Study Group on Nuclear Weapons and Foreign Relations 50-; Special Studies Project, Rockefeller Foundation 56-58; Consultant, Weapons System Evaluation Group, Joint Chiefs of Staff 56-60; Consultant, Nat. Security Council 61-63; Assoc. Dir. Harvard Univ. Center for Int. Affairs 57-60; Exec. Dir. Harvard Int. Seminar 51-; Faculty mem., Harvard Center for Int. Affairs 60-; Dir. Harvard Defense Studies Program 58-, Assoc. Prof. Dept. of Govt. 59-62, Prof. of Govt. 62-.
Publs. *Nuclear Weapons and Foreign Policy* 56, *A World Restored: Castlereagh, Metternich and the Restoration of Peace 1812-22* 57, *The Necessity for Choice: Prospects of American Foreign Policy* 61, *The Troubled Partnership: A Reappraisal of the Atlantic Alliance* 65.
Center for International Affairs, 6 Divinity Avenue, Cambridge, Mass. 02138; 419 Beacon Street, Boston, Mass., U.S.A.
Telephone: 617-868-7600, Extn. 2125.

Kistiakowsky, George B(ogdan), DR. PHIL.; American chemist; b. Kiev 18 Nov. 1900; ed. Univ. of Berlin.
Int. Research Fellow, Princeton 26-28; Asst. Prof. 28-30; Asst. Prof. Harvard Univ. 30-33, Assoc. Prof. 33-37 Abbott and James Lawrence Prof. of Chemistry 37-; on leave 41-45; Chief, Explosives Div., Nat. Defence Research Cttee. 41-43; Leader, Explosives Div., Los Alamos Project of the Manhattan District, U.S.A. 44-45; Special Asst. to Pres. Eisenhower for Science and Technology 59-61; Vice. Pres. Nat. Acad. of Sciences; American Philosophical Society, American Acad. of Sciences; Foreign mem. Royal Society 60; Medal for Merit 46; Nichols Medal of American Chemical Society 47; King's Medal for Service in the Cause of Freedom 47; Willard Gibbs Medal 60; Medal of Freedom 61; C. L. Parsons Award of American Chemical Soc. 61; Hon. D.Sc. Harvard, Pennsylvania, Rochester, Oxford and Williams Univs., Carnegie Inst. of Technology, Princeton Univ. and Case Inst. of Technology; Hon. Fellow, The Chemical Soc (London).
Publ. *Photochemical Processes* 29.
Gibbs Memorial Laboratory, Harvard University, 12 Oxford Street, Cambridge 02138, Massachusetts, U.S.A.

Kitagawa, Kazue, DR. ENG.; Japanese business executive; b. 26 July 1904; ed. Tokyo Univ.
Director of Sumitomo Electric Industries Ltd. 46-, Managing Dir. 47, Senior Managing Dir. 47-56, Pres. 56-66, Chair. 66-; Orders of Blue Ribbon and Purple Ribbon.
Publs. *Condenser for Electric Power* 42, *Agohige no Oshie* 58, *Sohzoteki Hakai no Seishin* (Creative thinking).
46-35 Aza-Masuzuka Kashio, Takarazuka City, Hyogo, Japan.

Kittel, Wolfgang A.; German travel executive; b. 11 Nov. 1899; ed. Technische Hochschulen, Munich and Berlin.
Army Service, First World War; with Lohman Syndicat 24-28, Colombian Airline SCADTA 28-38; Lufthansa 38-43, 55-64, Far East and Africa 38-43, interned Sierra Leone 43; industrial posts 45-55; General Manager for N. and Central America, Lufthansa, New York 55-59; mem. Exec. Board of Lufthansa 59-64; Exec. Dir. Deutsche Zentrale für Fremdenverkehr (German Nat. Tourist Asscn.) 64-; Dwight Eisenhower Peace Medal 59, Prof. of Communications, Tech. Faculty of Univ. of Bogotá 64; Bundesverdienstkreuz mit Stern 65.
Office: Deutsche Zentrale für Fremdenverkehr, Beethovenstrasse 69, Frankfurt/Main; Home: Tannenwaldallee 27, 638 Bad Homburg v.d.H., German Federal Republic.

Kittikachorn, Gen. Thanom; Thai officer and politician; b. 11; ed. Wat Kokplu School (Tak) and Military Acad. Bangkok.
Entered Military Survey Dept. as student officer 31, assigned to Planning Section 34; Lieut. in Mil. Education Dept. 35, Instructor 36-38, 39-41, 44-46; Capt. 38, student officer in Infantry School, active service in Shan State 41; Major 43, Lieut.-Col. 44; Instructor Mil. Acad. technical branch 46-47; Commdr. 21st Infantry Regt. 47; Colonel, Commdr. 11th Infantry Regt. 48; Deputy Commdr. 1st Infantry Division 49, Commdr. 50; Major-Gen., Dep. Commdr. 1st Army 51; Commdr. 1st Army 54; Lieut.-Gen., mem. Defence Coll. 55; Dep. Minister of Co-operatives 55; Asst. C.-in-C. of Army 57; Dep. Minister of Defence April 57, Minister Sept. 57; Prime Minister, Minister of Defence, General 58; Dep. Prime Minister and Minister of Defence 59-63, Prime Minister 63-; Special A.D.C. to King.
Government House, Bangkok; 808 Keskomol Bridge, 35 Ranong Soi 2, Rama V Road, Bangkok, Thailand.

Kivimaa, Arvi; Finnish writer; b. 6 Sept. 1904; ed. Univs. of Helsinki and Greifswald.
Journalist and literary critic 22-32 and 34-37; Lecturer in Finnish, Univ. of Greifswald 32-34; Dir. Tampere Theatre 37-40; Dir. People's Theatre 40-49, and Finnish Nat. Theatre 49-50; Gen. Dir. Nat. Theatre 50-; Chair. Finnish P.E.N. 36 and 54-57; Vice-Chair. Asscn. Finnish Writers 41-45; Pres. Scandinavian Theatre Council; mem. Exec. Cttee. of Int. Theatre Inst. 55-65, Vice-Pres. 57-65; mem. Finnish Cttee. of UNESCO 57-, Prof. h.c. 58; Commdr. Order of the Lion of Finland, Commdr. Order of the Arts and Letters (France), Officier Légion d'Honneur, Commdr. Order of Nordstjärnan (Sweden), etc.
Publs. Selected Poems: *Airut* (Herald) 47, *Passacaglia* 50, *Sydämen levottomuus* (Restless Heart) 54; Plays: *Paula Seijes* 45, *Syntymäpäivä* (Birthday) 55; Other works: *Lähto ja kotiinpaluu* (Farewell and Return) 38-39, *Katu nousee taivaaseen* (The Street to Heaven) 28, *Teatterivaeltaja* (Pilgrim of the Theatre) 37, *Näyttämön lumous* (Magic of the Stage) 52, *To Greece* 56, 57, *The Most Beautiful Poems* (selection) 58, *Manhattan* 59, *Joenrannan Puu* 61, *Nike of Samothrake* (poems) 64; and contributions to many foreign publs.
Suomen Kansallisteatteri, Helsinki, Finland.

Kiwanuka, Kabimu Mugumba Benedicto, LL.B.; Ugandan barrister-at-law and politician; b. 22; ed. Pius XII Univ. Coll., Basutoland, London Univ., Gray's Inn, London.
Called to the Bar 56, Pres.-Gen., Uganda Democratic Party; Minister without portfolio and Leader of the House April-July 61; Chief Minister of Uganda July 61-March 62; Prime Minister of Uganda March-May 62; arrested Dec. 63, charges subsequently withdrawn.
Kampala, P.O. Box 2962, Uganda, East Africa.

Kjartansson, Hannes; Icelandic diplomatist; b. 1917; ed. Menntaskolinn, Reykjavík, and Univ. of Iceland.
Member Icelandic Del. to UN Gen. Assembly 60-65; Consul-Gen. of Iceland in New York 60-; Perm. Rep. of Iceland to UN 65-.
Permanent Mission of Iceland to the United Nations, c/o Consulate-General of Iceland, 551 Fifth Avenue, New York, N.Y. 10017, U.S.A.

Kjellin, Tor Helge, PH.D.; Swedish professor of art; b. 24 April 1885; ed. Uppsala and Lund Univs.
Dozent of Art History, Lund Univ. 17-29; Prof. of Art History, Dorpat Univ. 21-24; Riga Univ. 29-31; Inspector Karlstad Art and Ethnographic Museum 28-50; expert on Church restoration, Swedish art, and Russian icons; mem. Swedish and foreign scientific societies.
Publs. *Uno Troili 1815-1875* 17, *Medeltida gravvårdsformer i Norden* 18, *Två Pietro Longhi-målningar i Sverige* 23, *Gust. Rydberg, Skånes målare* 25, *En gotl. fabeldjursfunt på Ösel* 26, *Marie gloria, en kretensisk ikon* 26, *Några romanska gravmonum, i Skåne* 27, *Ernst Norlinds konst* 27, *Die Kirche zu Karris auf Ösel und ihre Beziehungen zu Gotland* 28, *Die Hallenkirchen Estlands und Gotlands* 28, *Stilriktn. o. skolor inom det ryska ikonmåleriet* 28, *Aristoteles o. Phyllis* 28, *Vergilius i korgen o. som trollkarl* 29, *Om symboler o. emblem å gamla gravvårdar* 30, *Lettlands moderna måleri* 30, *Latviešu maksla* 32, *Icones russes* 33, *Chr. Erikssons liv och bildkonst* 34, *Två grek-byz. ikoner från Paleologtiden* 34, *Karlstads Stads 350-årsjubileum, en Minneskrönika* 34, *Lettiska bildhuggare* 35, *Glava Kyrkas Historia och Gamla Minnen* 36, *Gamla Värmländska Allmogehem och deras Möblering* 36, *Thor Fagerkvist, mästaren i Persberg* 39, *Värmlands odlingshistoria under 6,000 år* 39-41, *Wermlands Brandstods Bolag 1843-1943* 43, *Från Vänern till Västerhavet* 47, *Värmländsk konst och värmländska konstnärer* 47, *Prolog vid Hammarö köpings tillblivelse Nyårsnatten 1949* 49, *Värmlands och Dalslands kyrkor och kyrkliga konst* 52, *Christian Eriksson* 53, *Ryska ikoner i svensk och norsk ägo* 56, *Nya bidrag till Hammarö kyrkors historia (stavkyrka och blockhuskyrka)* 57, *Gravfynden i Köla kyrka* 58, *Isac Schiulström, en värmländsk bildsnidare* 58, *Nedre Ulleruds Kyrkor* 59, *Erik Jonaeus, den värmländske kyrko-målaren* 59.
Engelbrektsgatan 6, Gåvle, Sweden.

Klaasesz, Jan, K.C.V.O.; Netherlands politician; b. 07; ed. Univs. of Groningen and Paris.
Admin. Officer UNESCO in London and Paris 46-47; Burgomaster of Wageningen 47-49; Gov. of Surinam (Dutch Guiana) 49-56; Queen's Commr. of the Province of South Holland, The Hague 56-.
3 Groen Van Prinstererlaan, Wassenaar, Netherlands.

Klaiber, Manfred, DR. JUR.; German diplomatist; b. 8 June 1903; ed. Univs. of Tübingen and Berlin.
Legation Sec. German Embassy, Paris 29; Legation Sec. and Counsellor in German diplomatic missions to South Africa, Netherlands East India and Turkey; Govt. Dir. and Ministerial Councillor in Württemberg State Ministry 47; Rep. Württemberg-Baden in Admin. Council of United Economic Area; Ministerial Dir. and Chief of German Fed. Presidential Office; State Sec. 53-

57; Ambassador to Italy 57-63; Ambassador to France 63-.
Embassy of the German Federal Republic, 13-15 avenue Franklin D. Roosevelt, Paris 8e, France.

Klaus, Josef, LL.D.; Austrian lawyer and politician; b. 15 Aug. 1910; ed. Univs. of Vienna, Marburg/Lahn. Secretary Vienna Chamber of Labour 34-38 (Deputy-Chair. of Political Economy Dept.); with timber trade firm, Vienna 38-39; war service 39-45 (prisoner of war); lawyer, Hallein, Salzburg 45-49; Governor of Salzburg 49-61; Federal Minister of Finance 61-63; Federal Chancellor Feb. 64-; Austrian People's Party.
Office of the Federal Chancellor, Vienna. Austria.

Klauser, Theodor, DR.THEOL.; German university professor and priest; b. 25 Feb. 1894; ed. Freiburg Univ., Münster Univ., Pontificio Istituto di Archeologia Cristiana.
Vicar at Detmold 20; Rector at Brakel 27; Dozent, Bonn Univ., Catholic Theological Faculty 31; Asst. German Archæological Inst., Rome 31; Extraordinary Prof. of Ecclesiastical History, Bonn 37; Prof., Bonn 45-; Rector Bonn Univ. 48-50; Chair. Deutscher Akademischer Austauschdienst 51-54; mem. Deutsches Archaeologisches Inst. and Arbeitsgemeinschaft für Forschung, Düsseldorf; Corresp. mem. Göttingen Akad. der Wissenschaften; Dir. F. J. Dölger Inst., Bonn Univ.
Publs. *Die Kathedra im Totenkult der heidnischen und christlichen Antike* 27, *Das römische Capitulare evangeliorum* 35, *Doctrina duodecim apostolorum, Barnabae epistula, Recensuit vertit adnotavit* 40, *Kleine abendlandische Liturgiegeschichte* 47 (5th edn. 65), *Der Ursprung der bischöflichen Insignien und Ehrenrechte* 49, *Die römische Petrustradition im Lichte der neueren Ausgrabungen unter der Peterskirche* 56, *Frühchristliche Sarkophage in Bild und Wort* 66; Co-editor of the *Reallexikon für Antike und Christentum* 41-, *Jahrbuch für Antike und Christentum* 58-, *Theophaneia* 40-, and *Florilegium Patristicum* (with B. Geyer) 40-.
Kurfürstenstrasse 15, Ippendorf bei Bonn, German Federal Republic.
Telephone: Bonn 28-34-13.

Klauson, Valther Ivanovich; Soviet politician; b. 1914; ed. Road Engineering Inst. and Higher Party School.
Economic work 33-41; Soviet Army 41-44; mem. C.P.S.U. 43-; Chief Mechanic, later Head of Highways Dept. 44-53; Minister of Roads and Transport Economy, Estonia 53-54; Dep. Chair. Council of Ministers, Estonia 54-61, Chair. 61-; mem. Presidium Central Cttee. of C.P. of Estonia; Cand. mem. Central Cttee. of C.P.S.U. 61-; Deputy to U.S.S.R. and Estonian S.S.R. Supreme Soviets.
Council of Ministers of Estonia, Tallinn, Estonian S.S.R., U.S.S.R.

Klaveness, A. Fredrik (Anton Fredrik); Norwegian shipowner; b. 8 Nov. 1903.
With A. F. Klaveness and Co. A/S 23-, Chair. 47-; Chair. Overseas Shipping Co., San Francisco, A. F. Klaveness & Co. Inc., San Francisco, Forsikringsaktieselskapet Vega 58-, Framnaes Mek, Vaerksted; Board of Reps A/S Sydvaranger, Andresens Bank; Chair. Board of Dirs. A/S Norske Shell; Chair. Board of Reps. Otto Thoresen Shipping Co. A/S; Knight, First Class, Order of St. Olav, Knight, Order of Vasa (Sweden), Officer, Order of Orange Nassau (Neths.).
Lagaasen, Lysaker, Norway.

Klebe, Giselher; German composer; b. 28 June 1925; ed. Berlin Conservatoire and with Boris Blacher.
Composer in Berlin until 57; Prof. of Composition and Theory of Music, Nordwestdeutsche Musik-Akademie, Detmold 57-; mem. Acad. of Arts, Berlin and Hamburg; several prizes for composition.
Principal works: Operas: *Die Räuber* (Schiller 57), *Die*

tödlichen Wünsche (Baizac) 59, *Die Ermordung Cäsars* (Shakespeare) 59, *Alkmene* (Kleist) 61, *Figaro lässt sich scheiden* (Ödön von Horvath) 63, *Jakobowsky und der Oberst* (Werfel) 65.
Ballets: *Signale* 55, *Menagerie* 58.
Orchestral Works: *Zwitschermaschine* 50, *Deux Nocturnes* 52, *Adagio und Fuge* (with theme from Wagner's *Walküre*) 62, *Dritte Sinfonie* 67; Songs: *Fünf Lieder* 62, *Vier Vocalisen für Frauenchor* 63; Masses: *Miserere Nobis* 64, *Stabat Mater* 64, *Gebet einer armen Seele* 66; Chamber Music: 2 String Quartets 49, 63, Piano Trio *Elegia Appassionata* 55, *Introitus, Aria et Alleluja* for Organ 64, Quintet for Piano and Strings *quasi una fantasia* 67.
Quellenstrasse 618, 4931 Pivitsheide V.L., German Federal Republic.

Kleberg, Robert Justus, Jr.; American cattle farmer and breeder; b. 29 March 1896; ed. Wisconsin Univ.
President King Ranch Inc., John B. Ragland Mercantile Co., Buck and Doe Run Valley Farms Co., Coatesville, Pennsylvania; Dir. Kleberg First Nat. Bank, Kingsville, Texas, Missouri Pacific Railroad, Corpus Christi State Nat. Bank, King Ranch (Australia) Pty. Ltd., King Ranch Pastoral Co. Pty. Ltd. (Australia), King Ranch Argentina, S.A., King Ranch do Brazil, etc.; mem. Exec. Cttee. Texas and Southwestern Cattle Raisers' Asscn.; Santa Gertrudis Breeders Int.; Pres. King Ranch Farm, Lexington, Kentucky; mem. and Dir. the Jockey Club, N.Y.; Trustee, New York Racing Asscn.; Hon. Dr. of Agricultural Science (Texas A & M Univ. and Wisconsin Univ.).
King Ranch, Kingsville, Texas, U.S.A.

Klecatsky, Dr. Hans, D.IUR.; Austrian lawyer and politician; b. 6 Nov. 1920.
In Air Force, Second World War; Clerk in Admin. Courts 48; Constitutional Dept. of Chancellery 51; rose to rank of Hofrat in Admin. Courts 59; Lecturer in Constitutional Law and Politics, Innsbruck Univ. 64, Prof. of Public Law, Faculty of Jurisprudence and Political Science 65; Deputy mem. Court of Constitutional Law 65; Minister of Justice 66-.
Publs. *Österreichisches Staatskirchenrecht* (with H. Weiler) 58, *Das österreichische Bundesverfassungsrecht* (with L. Werner) 61-62, *Das österr. Zollrecht* (with A. Kobzina) 66, and other publs.
Innsbruck, Reithmannstrasse 20, Austria.

Klecki, Paul; Polish-born Swiss conductor; b. 21 March 1900; ed. Warsaw Conservatoire and Berlin Acad. of Music.
Teacher of Composition Scuola Superiora di Musica, Milan 35; Principal Conductor Kharkov Philharmonic Orch. 37; worked for Red Cross in Geneva during Second World War; Dir. Lucerne Festival, Lausanne Composition Master Classes 44-45; Guest Conductor Vienna and Salzburg Festivals, numerous European countries, U.S.A., Israel, Australia and South America 45-, La Scala Inaugural concerts 46; Musical Dir. Dallas (Tex.) Symphony Orchestra 58-67; Musical Dir. Suisse Romande Orchestra 67-; Hon. Prof. Lausanne Conservatoire.
Compositions: 3 symphonies, Sinfonietta for Strings, Violin Concerto, Piano Concerto, miscellaneous orchestral works, 3 string quartets, piano works and songs.
Montreux-Territet, Switzerland.

Kleffens, Eelco Nicolaas van, LL.D.; Netherlands diplomatist; b. 17 Nov. 1894; ed. Leyden Univ.
Post-war work on shipping questions 19; mem. L.N. Secretariat 19-21; Sec. Board of Dirs. Royal Dutch Petroleum Co. 21-22; Deputy-Chief Legal Section Ministry of Foreign Affairs 22-27, Diplomatic Section 27-29; Chief of Section 29-39; Minister to Switzerland 39; Minister of Foreign Affairs 39-46; leader del. to San Francisco Conf. 45; Minister without Portfolio and Netherlands Rep. UN Security Council and Econ.

and Social Council 46-47; Ambassador to U.S.A. 47-50; Minister of State 50; Minister to Portugal 50-56; Pres. Arbitration Tribunal between France, Germany, U.K. and U.S.A. (Bonn-Paris Agreements) 52-54; Perm. Rep. on NATO Council 56-58; Pres. 9th Session UN Gen. Assembly 54; Chief Rep. in the United Kingdom of the European Coal and Steel Community 58-67.
Publs. *The Relations between the Netherlands and Japan from 1605* 19, *The Rape of the Netherlands* (also in Spanish, Dutch and German) 40, *Sovereignty in International Law* 53.
Casal de Sta. Filomena, Almocagême, Colares, Portugal.

Klein, George, M.D.; Swedish (b. Hungarian) tumour biologist; b. 28 July 1925; ed. medical schools at Pécs, Szeged and Budapest, Hungary, and Stockholm, Sweden.
Instructor Histology, Budapest Univ. 45, Pathology 46; Research Fellow, Karolinska Inst. 47-49, Research Assoc. Cell Research 51-57, Prof. of Tumour Biology and Head Inst. for Tumour Biology 57-; Guest Investigator Inst. for Cancer Research, Philadelphia, Pa. 50; mem. Research Council Swedish Cancer Soc. 56, mem. Board of Trustees 61-, Vice-Chair. 63-; mem. WHO Expert Advisory Council on Cancer 65-; mem. American Asscn. of Cancer Research; Fellow New York Acad. of Science, mem. Int. Cttee. Int. Soc. for Cell Biology, and various other scientific asscns. in Sweden and abroad.
Publs. 100 papers in field of experimental cell research.
Kottlavägen 10, Lidingö, Sweden.

Kleiner, Sighardus, DR. THEOL.; Austrian-born ecclesiastic; b. 7 Oct. 1904.
Priest 28; Cistercian Monk in Abbey of Mehrerau, Austria 28; Prior of Hauterive, Switzerland 39; Gen. Procurator of Cistercian Order 50, Abbot Gen. 53-.
Piazza Tempio di Diana 14, Rome, Italy.
Telephone: 573-694.

Klemensiewicz, Zenon, D.PHIL.; Polish philologist; b. Sept. 1891; ed. Uniwersytet Jagielloński, Cracow.
Military service 14-19; Teacher in high school, coll., then univ., Cracow 19-39; Prof. of Polish Language, Jagiellonian Univ. 45-61, Prof. Emeritus 61-; mem. Polish Acad. of Sciences 61-, also Vice-Pres. of its Linguistic Cttee. and Head of Cracow Section; Pres. of Board, Polish Asscn. of Teachers, and Head of Scholarship Section; Founder-Adviser, Workshop of Polish Syntax, Cracow; Editor *Język Polski* (The Polish Language); Honours and decorations include Golden Cross of Merit, Banner of Labour, 2nd Class, Distinguished Teacher of the Polish Republic, Golden Badge of the City of Cracow and Ministry of Higher Educ. Prize.
Publs. *Składnia opisowa współczesnej polszczyzny kulturalnej* (Descriptive Syntax of Contemporary Standard Polish) 37, *Gramatyka współczesnej polszczyzny kulturalnej* (Grammar of Contemporary Standard Polish) 38, *Zarys składni polskiej* (Outline of Polish Syntax) 53, *Gramatyka historyczna języka polskiego* (Historical Grammar of the Polish Language) (with T. Lehr-Spławinski and S. Urbańczyk) 55, *Wybrane zagadnienia z zakresu nauczania gramatyki* (Selected Problems in the Teaching of Grammar) 55, 59, *Podstawowe wiadomości z gramatyki języka polskiego* (Fundamentals of Polish Grammar) 61, *Historia języka polskiego* (History of the Polish Language) vol. I 61, vol. II 65, *On the Literary and Artistic Language-Selected Writings* (W kręgu języka literackiego i artystycznego) 61.
Al. Słowackiego 15/V, m 11, Cracow, Poland.

Klemm, Wilhelm Karl, DR. PHIL.; German chemist; b. 5 Jan. 1896; ed. Real Gymnasium, Grünberg, and Univ. of Breslau.
Assistant, Wilhelm Biltz Technische Hochschule, Hanover 23; Privat Docent 27, Titular Prof. 29; Full Prof. and Dir. Inst. of Inorganic Chemistry, Danzig 33, Univ. of Kiel 47, Univ. of Münster 51, Prof. Emeritus

65-; Rector, Univ. of Münster 57-58; Pres. Int. Union of Pure and Applied Chemistry 65; Vice-Pres. Int. Council of Scientific Unions 66; mem. Acads. of Halle, Munich, Göttingen, Vienna and Düsseldorf; Hon. mem. Gesellschaft Deutscher Chemiker (Pres. 52-54), Soc. Chimique de France, Verein Österreichischer Chemiker, Indian Nat. Acad. of Sciences (Allahabad); Liebig-Denkmünze 51, Moissan-Médaille 53, Carl-Duisberg-Plakette 63, Lavoisier Médaille 65; Dr. h.c. (Technische Hochschule, Darmstadt, Univs. of Bordeaux and Dijon); Fed. German Order of Merit 66.
Publs. *Magnetochemie* 36, *Inorganic Chemistry* (13th edition) 64, *Experimentelle Einführung in die Anorganische Chemie* (with H. Blitz and W. Fischer) 66; Editor *Chemisches Zentralblatt*; also 200 published papers concerning many fields of inorganic chemistry: investigations of fused salts; chemistry of so-called rare elements (especially rare earths); application of magnetic properties on chemical problems; compounds of alkaline metals with non-metals, semi-metals and metals, chemistry of the transition metals; substances with anomalous valency (especially fluorine and oxygen compounds with high valency); transition of metals to semi-metals; preparation of compounds of alkaline metals with noble metals.
44 Münster/Westf., Theresiengrund 22, German Federal Republic.

Klemperer, Otto; German conductor; b. 15 May 1885; ed. in Frankfurt and Berlin.
Conductor at German Nat. Theatre, Prague 07-10, Hamburg Opera House 10-13, Barmen Opera 13-15, Strasbourg Opera 15-17; Conductor in Cologne 17-24, Gen. Music Dir. 23-24; in Wiesbaden 24-27; First Conductor Berlin State Opera, and Conductor of Philharmonic Choir 27-32; Dir. Los Angeles Symphony Orchestra 33-46; guest conductor in Europe, Canada, Australia and North and South America since 46; principal conductor Philharmonia Orchestra (England) 59; Hon. Pres. New Philharmonia Orchestra (England); frequent tours of Europe and the Americas.
Publ. *Minor Recollections* 64; Compositions: *Missa Sacra, Lieder, Symphony in Two Movements.*
Dufourstrasse 104, Zürich, Switzerland.

Klenk, Ernst, D.SC.; German physiological chemist; b. 14 Oct. 1896; ed. Öberrealschule, Tübingen, and Eberhard-Karls-Universität, Tübingen.
Began work in physiological chemistry, Tübingen 23, Asst. Prof. Tübingen 31-36; Full Prof. Univ. of Cologne, and Dir. of Physiological Chemistry Inst., Univ. of Cologne 36-; mem. Leopoldina German Acad. of Science; Norman Medal 53, Heinrich-Wieland Prize 64, AOCS Award 65, Stouffer Prize 66; Dr. h.c. (Univ. of Cologne).
Köln-Lindenthal, Kermeterstrasse 18, German Federal Republic.

Kliks, Rudolf Rigoldovich; Soviet architect; b. 25 June 1910; ed. Kharkov Inst. of Constructional Engineers.
Assistant Chief Architect for U.S.S.R. Agricultural Exhbn. 45-56; Chief Architect and Chief Artist U.S.S.R. Econ. Achievements Exhbn. 56-60; Chief Architect for U.S.S.R. Chamber of Commerce 60-.
Principal works include: stadium to seat 10,000 in Orjonikidze 37; general plan for the reconstruction of the U.S.S.R. Agricultural Exhbn. 50-54; designs, displays and interiors of pavilions for about 40 exhbns. in the U.S.S.R. and other countries including: Czechoslovakia 48, Yugoslavia 55, Leipzig, German Democratic Republic 56, Science section of the Soviet Pavilion, Brussels World Exhbn. 58, Helsinki, Finland 59, New Delhi Int. Agricultural Exhbn. 60, Damascus Int. Fair 61, Pavilion at Trade and Industry Exhbn. in London 61, Rio de Janeiro 63, Nehru Commemorative

Exhbn., Moscow 63, Izmir Int. Fair 64, Pavilion at Montreal Expo 67.
Publ. *Architecture of the U.S.S.R. Agricultural Exhibition 54.*
U.S.S.R. Chamber of Commerce, Kuibyshev Street 6, Moscow, U.S.S.R.

Klimaszewski, Mieczyslaw, PH.D.; Polish scientist and politician; b. 08; ed. Uniwersytet Jagiellónski, Cracow. Scientific Research Work 31-; Population and Social Welfare Office, Cracow 39-45; Prof. Extraordinary, Wroclaw Univ. 46-49; Prof. Jagiellonian Univ., Cracow 49-, Rector of Jagiellonian Univ., Cracow 64-; mem. Seym 65-; mem. Council of State 65, Vice-Pres. 65-; Corresp. mem. Polish Acad. of Sciences, Leopoldina Acad. (German Democratic Republic), Netherlands Geographical Soc., Soviet Geographical Soc.; Dr. h.c. (Univ. of Jena).
Publs. *Geomorphological Development of W. Carpathians* 34, 48, 65, 66, *Problems of Geomorphological Mapping* 56, 60, 63, *Geomorphological Studies of Spitsbergen* 60, *Geomorfologia Ogólna* 61.
Council of State, Warsaw, Poland.

Klimenko, Vasili Konstantinovich; Soviet politician; b. 06; ed. Kiev Polytechnical Inst.
Member Communist Party of Soviet Union 29-; Engineer, Workshop Foreman, Dir. Slavinsk Insulator Factory 35-41; party work, Ukraine and Bashkiria 41-51; First Sec. Lugansk Regional Cttee. Communist Party of Ukraine 51-61; Chair. Ukrainian Republican Council of Trade Unions 61-; mem. All-Union Council of Trade Unions and its Praesidium 62-; mem. Cen. Cttee. of C.P.S.U. 56-; mem. Cen. Cttee. Ukraine C.P. (and Political Bureau); Deputy to U.S.S.R. Supreme Soviet; Orders of Lenin (twice), Red Banner of Labour, Badge of Honour and other decorations.
Ukraine S.S.R. Council of Trade Unions, Kiev, Ukraine S.S.R., U.S.S.R.

Klimov, Alexander Petrovich; Soviet retailing official; b. 25 Aug. 1914; ed. Higher Pedagogical Inst. of Applied Econ. and Trade.
Teacher 32-38; Chief of the Education Service of Consumers' Co-operatives 38-48; Dep. Chair. Man. Board *Centrosoyuz* of U.S.S.R. (Central Union of Consumers' Socs.) 48-53; Dep. Minister U.S.S.R. Trade Ministry 53-54; Chair. Management Board *Centrosoyuz* 54-; alt. mem. Central Cttee. C.P.S.U.; mem. of Board U.S.S.R. Ministry of Trade; Vice-Pres. Int. Co-operative Alliance 54-; Deputy of the Supreme Soviet 66-; Vice-Pres. U.S.S.R.-Great Britain Soc.; mem. Soviet Peace Cttee.
Centrosoyuz of the U.S.S.R., 15/17 Bolshoi Cherkassky Pereulok, Moscow, U.S.S.R.

Kline, Alian B., B.S.; American agriculturist; b. 10 Oct. 1895; ed. Morningside Coll. and Iowa State Coll.
Consultant, U.N. Conf., San Francisco 45; del. to Conf. for establishment of Int. Fed. of Agricultural Producers, London 46, to first meeting of this Fed., the Netherlands 47; Pres. American Farm Bureau Fed. 47-55; Dir. Fed. Reserve Bank of Chicago 47-53; mem. Advisory Board of Export-Import Bank and of U.S. Trade Negotiating Team at Geneva 55; Pres. Int. Fed. of Agricultural Producers 54-55; Chair. Farm Foundation; mem. Board of Dirs. J. I. Case Co. 54-, Inst. for American Strategy; Trustee Eisenhower Exchange Fellowship Inc.; mem. Board of Trustees American Assembly 52-; mem. U.S.-Mexican Joint Chamber of Commerce Cttee.; LL.D. Morningside Coll., Sc.D. Iowa State Univ., Litt.D. Parsons Coll.; Great Living American Award 58.
4209 Grove Avenue, Western Springs, Ill., U.S.A.

Kline, Nathan Schellenberg, B.A., M.A., M.D.; American psychiatrist; b. 22 March 1916; ed. Swarthmore Coll., Harvard Univ., New York Univ. Coll. of Medicine,

New School of Soc. Research, Princeton Univ., Rutgers Univ. and Clark Univ.
Intern and Resident St. Elizabeth's Hospital, Washington, D.C. 43-44; U.S. Public Health Service 44-46; Child Psychiatrist, Union County Mental Hygiene Soc. Clinic 46-47; Veterans Admin. Hospital, Lyons, N.J. 46-50; Assoc., Columbia Greystone 47-50; Dir. of Research, Worcester State Hospital, Worcester, Mass. 50-52; private psychiatric practice, New York 52-; Dir. of Research, Rockland State Hospital, Orangeburg, New York 52-; Dir. of Div. of Psychiatry, Bergen Pines County Hospital, Paramus, N.J. 63-; Asst. Prof. of Clinical Psychiatry, Coll. of Physicians and Surgeons, Columbia Univ. 57-; Pres. Int. Cttee. against Mental Illness 61-; Chair. Board Psychiatric Research Foundation 62-; Contributing Editor *Excerpta Medica* 55-; numerous awards, including Albert Lasker Clinical Research Award 57, 64.
Rockland State Hospital, Orangeburg, N.Y., U.S.A.

Kliszko, Zenon; Polish politician; b. 08; ed. Warsaw Univ.
Active before the war in trade union and workers' movement; mem. Polish Communist Party; one of the founders of the resistance movement and Nat. People's Council and P.W.P. 40-45; mem. Cen. Cttee. Polish Workers' Party and United Workers' Party 45-49; removed from office; returned to active political life 56, and again mem. Central Cttee. Polish United Workers' Party; Vice-Marshal of the Seym (Parliament) and Sec. Cen. Cttee. Polish United Workers' Party 57-.
4/6 Wiejska, Warsaw, Poland.

Klochek, Vassily Ivanovich; Soviet foreign trade official; b. 1912; ed. Moscow Economic Inst. and Acad. of Foreign Trade.
Member C.P.S.U. 40-; Chief of Section Ministry of Foreign Trade 46-47; Deputy Commercial Rep. in Hungary 47-50; Deputy Chief of Dept., Ministry of Foreign Trade 50-53; Commerical Rep. in Austria 53-58; Chief of Dept., Ministry of Foreign Trade 58-63; Commercial Rep. in German Democratic Republic 63-; Order of Lenin, Badge of Honour, etc.
U.S.S.R. Trade Representation, Berlin, Germany.

Klompé, Margaretha Albertina Maria, CH.D.; Netherlands politician; b. 16 Aug. 1912; ed. Univ. of Utrecht. Teacher at Nijmegen 32-49; mem. of Netherlands Del. to U.N. Gen. Assembly 47, 48, 49, 50, 52; mem. of Second Chamber 48-56, of Consultative Assembly of Council of Europe 49-56, of Coal and Steel Assembly 52-56; Minister of Social Welfare 56-63; mem. Second Chamber States Gen. 63-66; Minister of Culture, Recreation and Social Welfare 66-; Hon. LL.D. 64; Roman Catholic People's Party.
5 Smidswater, The Hague, Netherlands.
Telephone: 070-606080.

Kloos, Andries Hein; Netherlands trade unionist; b. 12 Aug. 1922; ed. secondary school.
In accountant's office 39-42; Netherlands Fed. of Trade Unions 46-, in admin. depts. 46-51, Econ. Adviser 51-54, Deputy Dir. of Scientific Research Bureau 54-56, Sec. Editor of Netherlands Fed. of Trade Unions, also in charge of social-econ. activities 56-62, Vice-Pres. 62-65, Pres. 65-.
Nederlands Verbond van Vakverenigingen, Postbus 8110, Amsterdam, Netherlands.

Klos, Elmar; Czechoslovak film director; b. 26 Jan. 1910; ed. Faculty of Law, Charles Univ., Prague.
Director, Short Film Studios 46-47; Head of Creative Art Staff, and Scriptwriter, Barrandov Feature Film Studio 48-; Prof. of Film and TV. Acad. of Prague 56-; Awards include State Prize 2nd Class 60, Gold Prize, Moscow Int. Film Festival 63, State Prize 64, Grand Prix, Karlovy Vary Int. Film Festival 64, U.S. Acad.

Award Oscar 65, New York Film Critics Award 67, Selznik Prize, U.S. 66; Honoured Artist 65.
Co-Dir. with Ján Kadár (*q.v.*): *Únos* (Kidnapped) 52, *Smrt si říká Engelchen* (Death is Called Engelchen) 63, *Obžalovaný* (The Accused) 64, *Obchod na korze* (The Shop on Main Street) 65 (all award-winning films).
Barrandov 346, Prague 5, Czechoslovakia.

Klosovsky, Boris Nikodimovich; Soviet physiologist and neurosurgeon; b. 1898; ed. Azerbaijan Univ.
Postgraduate, Leningrad Brain Research Inst. 25-30; Asst. Head of Laboratory and Clinic, Inst. of Pediatrics 27-; Head of Dept., Inst. of Neurosurgery 33-48; Corresp. mem., U.S.S.R. Acad. of Medical Sciences 52-62, mem. 62-; mem. Int. Soc. for Parkinsonism Study, Int. Brain Research Org.; mem. of Board U.S.S.R.-Austria Friendship Soc.; Order of Red Banner of Labour 52; State Prize 52.
Publs.: Over 210 works on structure and function of brain, anatomy of nerves, and physiology of vestibular apparatus; Klosovsky was first to perform *bulbotomy*.
Institute of Pediatrics, Lomonosovsky Prospekt 2/40, Moscow, U.S.S.R.

Klotzbach, Günter, DR.ING.; German engineer and metals executive; b. 16 Feb. 1912; ed. Goethe Gymnasium, Essen, Univ. de Lausanne and Technische Hochschule, Aachen.
With Fried. Krupp Gussstahlfabrik, Essen 37-46; Asst. to Tech. Direction Friedrich-Alfred-Hütte, then Hüttenwerk Rheinhausen AG, Rheinhausen 46-59, Technical Man. Nov. 59-63; mem. Directorate, Fried. Krupp, Essen 63-65; Chair. Management Board Fried. Krupp Hüttenwerke AG 66-.
Office: Fried. Krupp Hüttenwerke AG, 463 Bochum, Alleestrasse 165; Home: 433 Mülheim-Speldorf, Tannenstrasse 27, German Federal Republic.
Telephone: Bochum 502700 (Office); Mülheim 50813 (Home).

Klusák, Milan, LL.D.; Czech diplomatist; b. 8 June 1923; ed. Univ. of Brno.
Diplomatic Service 48-; Czechoslovak Embassy, Moscow 50-53; Ministry of Foreign Affairs, Prague 54-60; Perm. Rep. of Czechoslovakia to European Office of UN, Geneva 60-63; Head of Dept. of Int. Orgs., Ministry of Foreign Affairs, Prague 63-65; Perm. Rep. to UN, N.Y. 65-, Pres. UN Econ. and Social Council 67; Vice-Chair. UN Special Cttee. on Peacekeeping Questions; External Lecturer in Int. Relations, School of Econs., Univ. of Prague 64-65.
Permanent Mission of Czechoslovak Socialist Republic to the United Nations, 1109-1111 Madison Avenue, New York 28, N.Y., U.S.A.
Telephone: LE5-8814.

Kluthe, Hans Albert; German publisher and editor; b. 15 July 1904; ed. Univs. of Munich, Berlin and Cologne.
Official, German Works Management Asscn. 28-34; District Man. Insurance Co. 34-36; political refugee in England working as lecturer, free-lance journalist, Editor *Das wahre Deutschland* (German Freedom Party monthly), Asst. Editor *Neue Auslese* 36-47; returned to Germany 47; publisher *Werra-Rundschau* (daily newspaper) 48-, *Frankfurter Illustrierte* 48-, co-owner and man. of Frankfurter Societäts-Druckerei; Vice-Pres. Liberal Int.; Pres. German Magazine Publishers' Asscn.; Hon. Pres. Féd. Int. de la Presse Périodique; Pres. German Group, Liberal Int.; Pres. German Cttee., Int. Press Inst.; Vice-Pres. Europa-Union; mem. German Council European Movement, German Cttee. UNESCO, German Press Council; awarded Grand Cross German Order of Merit; Chevalier, Légion d'Honneur.
Obere Friedenstrasse 19, Eschwege (Werra); and Frankenallee 71-81, Frankfurt a.M., German Federal Republic.
Telephone: (05651) 3792 and (0611) 230501.

Klychev, Annamuchamed; Soviet politician; b. 1912; ed. Higher Party School.
Soviet Army 41-45; mem. Communist Party of Soviet Union 47-; managerial work 47-51; party and political work 53-63; Chair. Presidium of Supreme Soviet of Turkmenian S.S.R. 63-; mem. Presidium of Central Cttee. of C.P. of Turkmenian S.S.R.; Deputy Chair. Presidium of Supreme Soviet of U.S.S.R.; mem. Central Auditing Comm., C.P.S.U.; Deputy to Supreme Soviet of Turkmenian S.S.R.
Presidium of Supreme Soviet of Turkmenian S.S.R., Ashkhabad, Turkmenian S.S.R., U.S.S.R.

Knapp, J. Burke; American banker; b. 25 Jan. 1913; ed. Stanford Univ. and Oxford Univ.
Joined Brown Harriman and Co., Ltd. (an int. investment firm) 36-40; economist of the Federal Reserve Board, Washington 40-44; economic adviser to the American Mil. Govt. in Germany 44-45; Special Asst. on Int. matters to the Chair. of the Board 45-48; Dir. of Office of Financial and Development Policy, Dept. of State 48-49; Asst. Economic Dir. of the World Bank 49-50; economic adviser to the U.S. NATO del. in London 50-51; U.S. Chair. of the Joint Brazil-U.S. Economic Development Comm., Rio de Janeiro 51-52; Dir. of the World Bank's operations in Latin America 52-56; Vice-Pres. of the Int. Bank for Reconstruction and Development 56-.
Office: International Bank for Reconstruction and Development, 1818 H Street, N.W., Washington D.C.; Home: 3701 Curtis Court, Chevy Chase, Maryland, U.S.A.
Telephone: OLiver 2-3488.

Knapp, Stefan; British (born Polish) artist; b. 21; ed. Lwów High School, Cen. School of Art, London, Slade School of Art, London Univ.
Imprisoned in Siberia 39-42; fighter pilot in R.A.F. 42-45; student 45-50; Exhibitions: One-Man Shows London 47, 54, 55, Paris (paintings) 56, Milan 57, Pierre Matisse Gallery, New York and Caracas (painting and sculpture) 58, Middelheim (Belgium) Biennale 59, Museo de Bellas Artes, Caracas 60; Lissone Prize, Milan 57; inventor of technique of large-scale painting on copper and steel for architectural use; murals include those at Hallfield School, Paddington (London) 55, Seagram Building, New York, St. Anne's Coll., Oxford 59, Univs. of Brunswick and Freiburg 64, New York 66, Queens Coll., New York 66, Columbia Univ., New York 66, Rowney Office Bldg., Berks, 67, Detroit Art Inst. 67.
Publ. *The Square Sun* (autobiography) 56.
Studio 4, 396 King's Road, London, S.W.10, England.
Telephone: 01-352-6173.

Knappstein, K. Heinrich; German diplomatist; b. 15 April 1906; ed. Univs. of Cologne, Berlin, Bonn, Cincinnati.
Editorial Staff *Frankfurter Zeitung* 36-43; Dep. State Minister for Reconstruction and Liberation, Govt. of Hesse 45-49; Consul-Gen. Chicago 51-56; Ambassador to Spain 56-58; Dep. State Sec., Foreign Ministry, Bonn 58-60; German Observer to the United Nations 60-62; Ambassador to the United States 62-; numerous decorations.
Embassy of the German Federal Republic, 4645 Reservoir Road, N.W., Washington, D.C. 20007, U.S.A.

Knight, Douglas Maitland, PH.D.; American university president; b. 8 June 1921; ed. Yale Univ.
Instructor of English, Yale 46-47; Asst. Prof. of English Literature, Yale 47-53; Morse Research Fellow 51-52; Pres., Lawrence Coll., Appleton, Wisconsin 54-63; Pres. Duke Univ., Durham, N. Carolina 63-; mem. Board of Dirs. Soc. for Religion in Higher Educ., Rockefeller Brothers Theological Fellowship Program, Nat. Merit Scholarship Corpn., American Council on Educ.; mem. Int. Asscn. of Univ. Presidents, and other orgs.; Chair.

Nat. Library Comm. Sept. 66-Sept. 67; numerous hon. degrees.
Publs. *Alexander Pope and the Heroic Tradition* 51; Editor and contrib.: *Medical Ventures and the University* 67; Editor: *The Federal Government and Higher Education* 60; Joint Editor Twickenham edn. of *Iliad* and *Odyssey* (trans. by Alexander Pope) 65.
Duke University, Durham, North Carolina 27706, 1508 Pinecrest, Durham, North Carolina, U.S.A.
Telephone: 684-2424 (Office).

Knight, John Shively; American newspaper publisher; b. 26 Oct. 1894; ed. Cornell Univ.
Served in Motor Transport Corps, 113th Inf., and in Army Air Corps, A.E.F. 17-19; newspaper reporter and exec. 20-25; Man. Editor *Akron Beacon Journal* 25-33, Editor 33-; Editorial Dir. *Springfield Sun* 25-27, *Massillon Independent* 27-33, Pres. 33-37; Chair. of Board and Publisher, *Miami Herald* 37-; Pres. Beacon Journal Publishing Co., Knight Newspapers, Inc.; purchased and discontinued *Miami Tribune* 37; owner, publisher, editor *Detroit Free Press* 40; fmr. owner, editor, publisher *Chicago Daily News* 44-59; Chief Liaison Officer U.S.-Brit. censorships, London 43-44; mem. and Past Pres. American Soc. of Newspaper Editors, and Inter-American Press Asscn.; fmr. Dir. and Officer of Assoc. Press; Hon. LL.D. (Akron, Northwestern, Ohio State and Kent State Univs.).
Office: Miami Herald Publishing Co., Herald Plaza, Miami 36, Fla.; Home: 80 N. Portage Path, Akron, Ohio 44309, U.S.A.

Knight, Dame Laura, D.B.E., R.A., R.W.S., R.E.; British artist; b. 1877; ed. Brincliffe, Nottingham and St. Quentin, France; studied Nottingham School of Art.
Subjects vary from backstage, circus and theatre to portraits and landscape; hon. mem. Royal Portrait Soc.; Hon. LL.D. (St. Andrews), Hon. D.Litt. (Nottingham). Works in Tate Gallery, British Museum, Victoria and Albert Museum, Imperial War Museum, National Portrait Gallery and other public galleries in England, S. Africa, New Zealand, Australia, U.S.A., Canada, etc.; one-man exhbn. Royal Academy, London 65.
Publs. *Oil Paint and Grease Paint* 36, *A Proper Circus Omie* 62, *The Magic of a Line* 65.
16 Langford Place, London, N.W.8, England.
Telephone: 01-624-4098.

Knight, Ridgway Brewster, B.S., PH.B., M.B.A.; American diplomatist; b. 12 June 1911; ed. Univ. of Paris and Harvard Univ.
Assistant to Pres. Cartier Inc. 31-35; Vice-Pres. and Treas. Bellows Co. Inc. 36-41; U.S. Army 43-45; Second Sec., Paris 45-50; Dept. of State 50-53; Dep. Asst. High Commr. for Germany 54-55; Political Adviser, Supreme Allied Commdr., Europe 55-57, Minister, Karachi 57-59; Minister, Consul-Gen., Damascus 60-61; Ambassador to Syrian Arab Republic 61-65, to Belgium 65-; numerous decorations.
American Embassy, Brussels, Belgium.

Knipper, Lev Konstantinovich; Soviet composer; b. 1898; ed. Gnesin School of Music, Moscow.
Honoured Worker of Art of Buryat Autonomous S.S.R. 58, State Prizes of the U.S.S.R. 46, 49, Order Badge of Honour and other decorations.
Principal Compositions: *Tales of Budda* (Symphony) 25, *Candide* (Opera-Ballet) 27, *North Wind* (Opera) 29, *Mountain Serenade* (Songs) 45, *Soldiers' Songs* 48; about ten symphonies and a large number of lyric songs.
Moscow Branch, Composers' Union of the U.S.S.R., 4/6 Third Miusskaya Street, Moscow, U.S.S.R.

Knoke, Karl Hermann; German diplomatist; b. 9 Aug. 1909; ed. Ludwig-Maximilians-Universität, Munich, Sorbonne, Paris, Friedrich-Wilhelms-Universität, Berlin, and Georg-August-Universität zu Göttingen.
Reichs Kreditgesellschaft A.G., Berlin; War Service 39-45; Land Govt., Hanover 45-47; Local Govt. Fallingbostel 47-50; Consul, First-Sec., Counsellor Athens 50-54, Chargé d'Affaires a.i., Athens 52-53; South Eastern European Desk, German Foreign Office 54-56, Head of Eastern Dept. German Foreign Office 56-58; Minister, Moscow 58-60, Paris 60-65; Amb. to Netherlands 65-68, to Israel 68-; Commandeur Légion d'Honneur; Grand Officier Ordre du Mérite; Grand Officer Order of Phoenix (Greece); Knight Commander Order of Merit (Fed. Rep. of Germany).
Embassy of the German Federal Republic, 16 Sutin Street, Tel Aviv, Israel.

Knoll, Florence Schust; American architect; b. 24 May 1917; ed. Cranbrook Acad., Architectural Asscn., London, and Illinois Inst. of Technology, Chicago.
Design Dir. Knoll Associates Inc., Knoll International Ltd.; architect, interior and furniture designer 43-65.
Home: 1801 West 27th Street, Sunset Island 2, Miami Beach, Florida, U.S.A.

Knopf, Alfred A., B.A.; American publisher; b. 12 Sept. 1892; ed. Columbia Coll.
President, Alfred A. Knopf Inc. 18-57, Chair. 57-; publisher of Borzoi books; Hon. D.Hum.Litt., Yale Univ. 58, Columbia Univ. 59, Bucknell Univ. 59, Coll. of William and Mary 60, Lehigh 60; Hon. LL.D., Brandeis Univ. 63, Adelphi Univ. 66, Univ. of Chatanooga 66.
501 Madison Avenue, New York 22, N.Y, U.S.A.

Knowland, William Fife, A.B.; American publisher and politician; b. 26 June 1908; ed. public schools of Alameda and Univ. of Calif.
Mem. Calif. State Assembly 33-35, Senate 35-39; mem. Republican National Cttee. 38; Chair. Republican Exec. Cttee. 41-42; served in U.S. Army as enlisted man and officer (in U.K., France, Belgium and Germany); still overseas when appointed U.S. Senator (Republican, California) 45; elected Senator from California 46-58; Majority Floor Leader 53-55, Minority Floor Leader 55-58; Pres., Publisher, Editor and Gen. Man. *Oakland Tribune.*
Oakland Tribune, 401 13th Street, Oakland, Calif., U.S.A.
Telephone: 415-273-2200.

Knowles, Rev. David (name in religion of **Michael Clive**), O.S.B., LITT.D., F.S.A., F.B.A.; British priest and historian; b. 29 Sept. 1896; ed. Downside, Christ's Coll., Cambridge and Collegio Sant' Anselmo, Rome.
Entered novitiate, Downside 14, Priest 22; Editor *Downside Review* 30-34; Univ. Lecturer in History, Cambridge 46; Fellow of Peterhouse, Cambridge 44-63; Prof. of Medieval History, Univ. of Cambridge 47-54, Regius Prof. of Modern History 54-63; Pres. Royal Historical Soc. 56-60; Hon. D.Litt. (Oxford and London Univs.), Hon. Fellow, Christ's Coll. and Peterhouse, Cambridge.
Publs. *The Monastic Order in England* 40, *The Religious Houses of Mediaeval England* 40 (enlarged edition with N. Hadcock 53), *The Religious Orders in England,* 3 vols. 48, 55, 59, *The Monastic Constitutions of Lanfranc* 51, *The Episcopal Colleagues of Archbishop Thomas Becket* 51, *Monastic Sites* 52, *Charterhouse* (with F. W. Grimes) 54, *The English Mystical Tradition* 61, *Saints and Scholars* 62, *The Evolution of Mediæval Thought* 62, *The Historian and Character* 63, *Great Historical Enterprises* 64, *From Pachomius to Ignatius* 66, *What is Mysticism?* 67, *The Christian Centuries 600-1500* 68.
9 Old House Close, Wimbledon, London, S.W.19, England.
Telephone: 01-946-0010.

Knowles, William Charles Goddard, C.B.E.; British businessman; b. 12 Jan. 1908; ed. Christ's Hospital, Trinity Coll., Cambridge.
Butterfield and Swire 29-, London, Hankow, Tientsin,

Shanghai, Hong Kong 47-, Man. 57-64; Chair. Hong Kong and Shanghai Bank 63-64; Exec. Dir. *Lloyd's Register of Shipping* 65-; served in Indian Army during Second World War; mem. Hong Kong Legislative Council; 60-65, Exec. Council 63-65; Chair. Hong Kong Chamber of Commerce 61-63; Vice-Chancellor Hong Kong Univ. 64-65; mem. Governing Body, School of Oriental and African Studies, London Univ. 65-; Hon. LL.D.
Lloyd's Register of Shipping, Lloyd's House, London, E.C.3, England.

Knox, Edmund George Valpy (*nom-de-plume* Evoe); British journalist and essayist; b. 81; ed. Oxford Univ. Humorist in verse and prose; mem. the *Punch* table since 20 and Editor 32-49; contrib. to *Observer, New Statesman, Morning Post, Spectator* and *London Mercury*; Hon. M.A. (Oxon.) 43.
Publs. *The Brazen Lyre, A Little Loot, Parodies Regained, These Liberties, Fiction as She is Wrote, An Hour from Victoria, Fancy Now, It Occurs to Me, Gorgeous Times, Quaint Specimens, Awful Occasions, Poems of Impudence, I'll Tell the World, Wonderful Outings, Here's Misery, Blue Feathers, This Other Eden, Slight Irritations, Folly Calling;* Editor *Anthology of Humorous Verse;* articles on Horace and Parody in the *Encyclopaedia Britannica.*
110 Frognal, London, N.W.3, England.

Knox, Sir Thomas Malcolm, Kt., M.A., LL.D., D.LITT.; British university principal (retired); b. 1900; ed. Liverpool Inst. and Pembroke Coll., Oxford.
In business 23-31; Fellow and Tutor, Jesus Coll., Oxford 33-36; Prof. of Moral Philosophy, St. Andrews Univ. 36-53, Principal 53-66; Hon. Fellow, Pembroke Coll., Oxford; Gifford Lecturer, Aberdeen 65-66, 67-68.
19 Victoria Terrace, Crieff, Perthshire, Scotland.
Telephone: Crieff 2808.

Knudsen, Semon Emil; American automobile executive; b. 2 Oct. 1912; ed. Dartmouth Coll. and Mass. Inst. of Technology.
With Gen. Motors Corpn. 39-68, Vice-Pres. and Gen. Man. Pontiac Motor Div. 56-61, Chevrolet Div. 61-65, Group Vice-Pres. in charge of Overseas and Canadian Group 65-68, also responsible for domestic non-automotive divs. 66-68, Exec. Vice-Pres. (Int. Operations) 67-68; Pres. Ford Motor Co. 68-.
Ford Motor Co., Dearborn, Michigan, U.S.A.

Knuth, Count Eggert Adam; Danish diplomatist; b. 19 April 1901.
Vice-Consul Sydney 29-32; Sec. Legation Reykjavík 35-36; Sec. Legation London 36-43, First Sec. 43-45; Head Div. Min. for Foreign Affairs 45-51; Counsellor, Embassy, London 51, Minister 52-56; Ambassador to Iceland 56-59, to Belgium and Luxembourg 61-67, to Italy 67-.
Via Adolfo Cancani 6, Rome, Italy; Home: Krengerup, Glamsbjerg, Denmark.

Knuth-Winterfeldt, Count Kield Gustav, LL.D.; Danish diplomatist; b. 17 Feb. 1908; ed. Univ. of Copenhagen.
Danish Foreign Service 31-, Hamburg, Tokyo; Sec. Ministry for Foreign Affairs 39-45, Dep. Chief of Section 45, Chief 50; Minister, Argentina 50; Chief, Commercial Information Dept., Ministry of Foreign Affairs, Dep. Dir. Economic Division 56; Ambassador to U.S.A. 58-65, to France 65-66, to German Federal Republic 66-; Grand Officer, Order of Dannebrog, Officer, Order of George I (Greece), Knight, Order of North Star (Sweden), Grand Officer, Order of Merit (Argentina), Grand Officer, Order of Merit (Chile).
Danish Embassy, Bonn, Pfälzer Strasse 14, German Federal Republic.

Knuynants, Ivan Lyudvigovich; Soviet organic chemist; b. 06; ed. Moscow Higher Technical School.
Research worker, Moscow Higher Technical School 28-31; Assoc. Inst. of Organic Chemistry, U.S.S.R. Acad. of Sciences 31-54, mem. C.P.S.U. 41-; Chief of Laboratory, Inst. of Elementary Organic Compounds, Acad. of Sciences 54-; Corresp. mem. U.S.S.R. Acad. of Sciences 46-53, mem. 53-; State Prizes 43, 48, 50; Hero of Socialist Labour.
Publs. *Methods of Introducing Fluorine into Organic Compounds* 47, *The Interaction of Aliphatic Oxides with Hydrogen Fluoride* 47, *Modern Experimental Methods in Organic Chemistry* 60, and other works.
Institute of Elementary Organic Compounds, U.S.S.R. Academy of Sciences, 14 ul. Vavilova, Moscow, U.S.S.R.

Knyazev, Filipp Kirillovich; Soviet politician; b. 1916; ed. Voronezh Pedagogical Inst. and Kuibyshev Regional Party School.
Teacher and Young Communist League (Y.C.L.) officer 34-41; with the Soviet Army 41-42; mem. C.P.S.U. 40-; Officer Y.C.L. then Party Official in Kurgan region 42-59; Chair. Kurgan Regional Soviet of Working People's Deputies 59-66; First Sec. Kurgan Regional Cttee. C.P.S.U. 66-; Alt. mem. Central Cttee. C.P.S.U.; Deputy to Supreme Soviet of the U.S.S.R.; mem. Budget Cttee. Soviet of Union.
Kurgan Regional Committee of the C.P.S.U., Kurgan, U.S.S.R.

Kobayashi, Koji, D.ENG.; Japanese business executive; b. 1907; ed. Tokyo Imperial Univ.
Managing Dir. Nippon Electric Co. Ltd. 56-61, Senior Man. Dir. 61-62, Exec. Vice-Pres. 62-63, Pres. 64-; Pres. Nippon Aviotronics Co. Ltd. 63-; Vice-Pres. Japan Electronics Industry Devt. Asscn. 65-; Dir. Japan Management Asscn. 48; Prime Minister's Prize for Export Promotion 64; Blue Ribbon Medal 64.
Publ. *Carrier Transmission Telephone Equipment* 37.
15-5 Denenchofu 7-chome, Ohta-ku, Tokyo, Japan.

Kobayashi, Takeji; Japanese politician; b. 99; ed. Tokyo Univ.
Ministry of Communications 24, Chief of Secretarial Section 37; later, Dir. General Affairs Bureau, Dir. Kumamoto Communications Bureau, Vice-Dir. Communications Board; Gov., Shizuoka Prefecture 46; mem. House of Councillors 53-; Minister of Welfare July 63-64, of Posts and Telecommunications 66-; Pres. Postal Workers' Relief Org.
House of Councillors, Tokyo, Japan.

Koch, Mrs. Bodil Thastum; Danish politician; b. 25 Oct. 1903; ed. Copenhagen Univ.
Pres. Folkevirke 44-; Editor *Folkevirke* (formerly *Idag*) 46-54; mem. Copenhagen Educational Cttee. 46-53; Member of Folketing 47-; Minister for Ecclesiastical Affairs 50 and 53-66; Ingrid Jesperson Scholarship 52; Minister for Cultural Affairs 66-68; Social-Democrat.
8 Vodroffsvej, Copenhagen V, Denmark.

Kochemasov, Vyacheslav Ivanovich; Soviet politician; b. 1918; ed. Gorki Inst. of Water Transport Engineers.
Member C.P.S.U. 42-; Komsomol worker 42-48; Second Sec. then First Sec. Gorki Regional Cttee. of Young Communist League (Y.C.L.) 43-48; Vice-Chair. then Chair. Antifascist Cttee. of Soviet Youth 48-54; Sec. Central Cttee. Y.C.L. 54-55; Counsellor Berlin 55-60; Deputy Chief of Section Ministry of Foreign Affairs 60-61; Vice-Chair. then First Vice-Chair. State Cttee. on Cultural Ties with Foreign Countries 62-63; Vice-Chair. R.S.F.S.R. Council of Ministers 63-; Alt. mem. Central Cttee. C.P.S.U. 66-; Deputy to Supreme Soviet of the U.S.S.R.
R.S.F.S.R. Council of Ministers, 3 Delegatskaya St., Moscow, U.S.S.R.

Kochetov, Vsevolod Anisimovich; Soviet writer; b. 7 Feb. 1912; ed. Agricultural Coll.
Agronomist 31-38; Journalist 38-48; Chief Editor *Literaturnaya Gazeta* 55-59; Chief Editor *Oktyabr* 61-;

mem. C.P.S.U. 44-; mem. Central Auditing Comm. C.P.S.U. 56-66; Order of Lenin 67.

Publs. *The Brothers Yershov, Beneath the Motherland's Sky, Lake Nero, Family of Zhurbins, Youth is With Us, Secretary of Regional Committee of Communist Party, Streets and Trenches.*

Union of Soviet Writers, 52 Vorovskovo ulitsa, Moscow, U.S.S.R.

Kochina, Pelageya Yakovlevna; Soviet mechanical engineer; b. 13 May 1899; ed. Petrograd Univ.

In Central Geophysical Observatory 19-24, Inst. of Railway Engineers 24-30, Civil Aviation Engineers 30-35; worked in Mathematics Inst. then Inst. of Mechanics, Acad. of Sciences of the U.S.S.R. 35-59; Inst. of Hydrodynamics 59-; Corresp. mem Acad. of Sciences of the U.S.S.R. 46-56, mem. 56-; main works dedicated to theory of filtration, of dynamic meteorology, of the steadiness of plates, of floods in basins; Chair. Comm. Acad. of Sciences for Utilization and Protection of Water Resources in Siberia; State Prize U.S.S.R. 46.

Institute of Hydrodynamics, 90 Akademgorodok, Novosibirsk, U.S.S.R.

Kochinyan, Anton Yezvandovich; Soviet (Armenian) politician; b. 25 Oct. 1913; ed. Erevan C.P. School, Higher Party School.

Held leading posts in the Young Communist League of Armenia 37; mem. C.P.S.U. 38-; Sec. of the Cen. Cttee. of the C.P. of Armenia 46, First Sec. 66-; Chair. of the Council of Ministers of the Armenian S.S.R. 52-66; Cand. mem. Cen. Cttee. of C.P.S.U. 61-66, mem. 66-.

Central Committee of Communist Party of the Armenian S.S.R., Erevan, Armenia, U.S.S.R.

Kochman, Mohamed Nassim; Mauritanian lawyer, diplomatist and international banker; b. 25 Oct. 1932; ed. Van Vollenhoven Lycée, Dakar, Senegal, Marcel Gambier Coll., Lisieux, France, Caen Univ. and Inst. of Political Studies, and Faculty of Law and Economic Sciences, Grenoble, France.

Lawyer, Court of Appeal, Dakar 58-61; First Sec., Embassy of Mauritania, Washington, and Mauritanian Perm. Mission to UN 61; First Counsellor, later Chargé d'Affaires, Washington 62-64; Chargé d'Affaires a.i. Perm. Mission of Mauritania to UN 64; Alt. Dir. Int. Bank for Reconstruction and Devt. (IBRD), Int. Finance Corpn. (IFC), and Int. Devt. Asscn. (IDA) 62-64; Exec. Dir. for Cameroon, Central African Republic, Chad, Congo (Brazzaville), Dahomey, Gabon, Ivory Coast, Malagasy Republic, Mauritania, Niger, Rwanda, Senegal, Somalia, Togo and Upper Volta, IBRD, IFC and IDA 64-.

International Bank for Reconstruction and Development, 1818 H. Street, N.W., Washington, D.C., U.S.A. Telephone: DU1-3662.

Kock, Karin, D.SC. (ECON.); Swedish economist; b. 2 July 1891; ed. Stockholm Univ.

Statistician and economist, Skandinaviska Banken, Stockholm 18-32; Reader (Docent) in Economics, Stockholm Univ. 33; Acting Prof. of Economics, Stockholm Univ. 38-46, now Prof. h.c.; Chief of Section, Ministry of Commerce 47; Minister without Portfolio 47-48; Minister of Supply 48-49; Dir.-in-Chief Central Bureau of Statistics 50-57; Chair. Economic Comm. for Europe 50-53, Swedish Statistical Asscn. 53-54; Research Prof. Inst. for Int. Economic Studies, Stockholm Univ. 63-; mem. Gov. Board UNESCO Inst. for Social Sciences 51-60; Fellow, American Statistical Asscn. 56; mem. Int. Statistical Inst.; Hon. mem. Statistical Asscns. of Sweden and Finland; mem. Soc. Democratic Party.

Publs. *A Study of Interest Rates* 92, *Svenskt bankväsen i våra dagar* 30, *Skånska Privatbanken* 31, *Skånska Cement A.B.* 32, *Sveriges handelsekonomiska läge* 34, *Konjunkturuppsvingets förlopp och orsaker* 35, *Smålands Bank* 37, *National Income of Sweden 1861-1930* (together

with Erik Lindahl and Einar Dahlgren) 37, *Kvinnoarbetet i Sverige* 38, *Statistiska Centralbyrån 100 år* 58, *Kreditmarknad och Räntepolitik I* 61, *II* 62.

Jakob Westinsg. 1A, Stockholm K, Sweden. Telephone: 53-08-68.

Kodaira, Hisao; Japanese business executive and politician; b. 1910; ed. Tokyo Univ. of Commerce.

Formerly with Mitsui Mine Co.; fmr. Pres. Kodaira Heavy Industries Co.; fmr. Pres. Kodaira Industrial Co., Tochigi Isuzu Motorcar Co.; mem. House of Reps. 47-; Minister of Labour June 65-66; Liberal Democrat.

c/o Ministry of Labour, 1-7 Otemachi, Chiyoda-ku, Tokyo, Japan.

Kodama, Tadayasu; Japanese shipping executive; b. 29 July 1898; ed. Kyoto Imperial Univ.

Nippon Yusen Kabushiki Kaisha (Japan Mail Steamship Co.) 22-, Dir. 47-, Man. Dir. 51-58, Vice-Pres. 58-61, Pres. 61-, now Chair.

Nippon Yusen Kaisha, 20-1, 2-chome, Marunouchi, Chiyoda-ku, Tokyo, Japan.

Koditsa, Ivan Sergeyevich; Soviet politician; b. 99; ed. Communist Univ. for Western Nat. Minorities.

On the staff of the Central Cttee. of the Agricultural Workers' Union 30-34; Exec. Sec. of the Central Cttee. of the Union of Workers on Fur-Breeding and State Farms 34-37; Head of a Dept. in the Russian Central Confectionery Administration 38-41; at the Head Office of the Central Cttee. of the Moldavian C.P. 41-50; Minister for Local Industries of Moldavia 51-63; Chair. of the Presidium of the Supreme Soviet of Moldavia 51-63, mem. 63-; Vice-Chair. Presidium of Supreme Soviet of U.S.S.R. 54-66; mem. Central Revisionary Comm. of C.P.S.U. 61-66.

Presidium of Supreme Soviet of Moldavian S.S.R., Kishinev, U.S.S.R.

Kodolányi, János; Hungarian writer; b. 1899.

Suffered privation in 1920s in devoting himself to writing; travelled to Finland 36, 38; many of his works are trans. into English, French, German, Italian and Serbo-Croat.

Publs. include: Historical novels: *Julianus barát* (Friar Julianus), *Boldog Margit* (Blessed Margaret), *Vas fiai* (Iron Sons); Biblical novel: *Az égő csipkebokor* (Burning Bush); Tragedy: *Pogány tüz* (Pagan Fire).

Balatonakarattya, Hungary.

Koenig, Gén. Marie-Pierre; French officer; b. 10 Oct. 1898; ed. Ste. Marie de Caen, Caen.

Lieut. 18, Capt. 32, Maj. 40, Lieut.-Col. 40, Col. 41, Gén. de Brigade 41, de Division 43, de Corps d'armée 44, d'armée 46; joined Gen. de Gaulle after escaping from France 40; served Western Desert (Bir-Hacheim) and Tunisia 42-43; Commdt. Supérieur, French Forces in Great Britain and Mil. Del. French Cttee. of Nat. Liberation 44; Mil. Gov., Paris 44-45; French C.-in-C. in Germany 45- 49; Inspector Land, Sea and Air Forces in N. Africa 49-51; Vice-Pres. Conseil Supérieur de la Guerre 50-51; mem. Inst. de France; Dep. for Bas-Rhin 51-58; Minister of Nat. Defence June-Aug. 54 and Feb.-Oct. 55; official of several companies; Grand Croix de la Légion d'Honneur, Compagnon de la Libération, Médaille Militaire, Croix de Guerre and many other awards.

3 rue Ernest-Hébert, Paris 16e, France.

Koestler, Arthur, F.R.S.L., M.INST.P.I.; British (naturalised) author; b. 5 Sept. 1905; ed. Vienna Univ.

Foreign corresp. in Middle East, later Paris, of *Vossische Zeitung* 26-30; mem. editorial staff Ullstein's, Berlin 30-32; corresp. U.S.S.R., travelled Soviet Central Asia 32-33; free lance, Paris, London, Zürich 33-36; *News Chronicle* Special Corresp. Spanish Civil War, Egypt, Palestine, etc. 36-38; served as Private in French and British Armies; Sonning Prize, Univ. of Copenhagen 68.

Publs. *Spanish Testament* 38, *The Gladiators* 40,

Darkness at Noon 41, *Scum of the Earth* 41, *Arrival and Departure* 43, *The Yogi and the Commissar* 45, *Twilight Bar* (play) 45, *Thieves in the Night* 46, *Insight and Outlook* 48, *Promise and Fulfilment* 49, *The God that Failed* (jointly) 50, *The Age of Longing* 50, *Arrow in the Blue* 52, *The Invisible Writing* 54, *The Trail of the Dinosaur* 55, *Reflections on Hanging* 56, *The Sleepwalkers* 59, *The Lotus and the Robot* 60, *Suicide of a Nation?* (editor) 63, *The Act of Creation* 64, *The Ghost in the Machine* 67, *Drinkers of Infinity* 68.

c/o A. D. Peters, 10 Buckingham Street, London, W.C.2, England.

Koga, Issac, PH.D.; Japanese radio engineer; b. 5 Dec. 1899; ed. Univ. of Tokyo.

Assistant Prof. Tokyo Inst. of Technology 29-39, Prof. 39-58; Prof. Univ. of Tokyo 44-60, Dean of Engineering 58-60; Vice-Pres. Int. Scientific Radio Union, Brussels 57-63, Pres. 63-66; Pres. Inst. of Elect. Communication Engineers of Japan 47-48; Pres. Inst. of Electrical Engineers of Japan 57-58; mem. Technical Advisory Cttee. Nat. Broadcasting Corpn. 51-; mem. Advisory Cttee. for Radio and Tele-Communications, Ministry of Posts and Tele-Communications 63-; Fellow Inst. of Electrical and Electronics Engineers, New York 57; Hon. mem. Inst. of Electrical Communication Engineers of Japan 64, Inst. of Electrical Engineers of Japan 65; Order of Cultural Merit 63.

Major works include: invention of crystal plates of zero frequency-temperature coefficient, investigation on piezoelectric oscillating crystal and quartz crystal circuit (Japan Acad. of Sciences Prize) 48, frequency demultiplier by means of a vacuum tube circuit.

254 8-chome, Kami-Meguro, Tokyo, Japan.
Telephone: (Tokyo) 461-3395.

Kogan, Leonid Borisovich; Soviet violinist; b. 1925; ed. Moscow Conservatoire under Abram Yampolsky.

Professor Moscow Conservatoire; plays music of Bach, Mozart, Vivaldi, Brahms, Tchaikovsky, Prokofiev, Shostakovich; numerous world tours; Honoured Artist of the R.S.F.S.R. 55; People's Artist of the U.S.S.R.; Lenin Prize 65.

State Concert Association of the U.S.S.R., 15 Neglinnaya, Moscow, U.S.S.R.

Kohler, Foy D., B.S.; American diplomatist; b. 15 Feb. 1908; ed. Toledo and Ohio State Univs.

Joined Foreign Service 31; Vice-Consul Windsor (Canada) 32, Bucharest 33-35, Belgrade 35; Legation Sec. and Vice-Consul Bucharest 35-36, Athens 36-41, Cairo 41; Specialist Dept. of State 41-44, Asst. Chief Div. of Near Eastern Affairs 44-45; London Embassy and Adviser to U.S. Del. UNRRA Council 44; Political and Liaison Officer to U.S. Del. San Francisco Conf. 45; Sec.-Gen. U.S. Greek Elections Mission 45-46; studies at Cornell Univ. and Nat. War Coll. 46; 1st Sec. Moscow 47, Counsellor 48, Minister '48; Chief Int. Broadcasting Div. Dept. of State 49; Dir. Voice of America 49-52; Counsellor Ankara 53-56; seconded to Int. Co-operation Admin. (ICA) 56-58; Dep. Asst. Sec. of State 58-59, Asst. Sec. of State (European Affairs) 59-62; Ambassador to U.S.S.R. 62-66; Deputy Under-Sec. of State 66-68; Prof., Univ. of Miami 68-; D. Hum. (Ohio State Univ.), LL.D. (Univ. of Toledo, Ohio).

University of Miami, Coral Gables, Fla., U.S.A.

Kohn, Hans, DR. JURIS.; American historian and political scientist; b. 15 Sept. 1891; ed. Prague German Univ.

Prisoner in Asiatic Russia during First World War; Lecturer New School for Social Research New York 33-; Prof. Modern History Smith Coll., Northampton, Mass. 34-41; Sydenham Clark Parsons Prof. of History Smith Coll. 41-49; Prof. of History City Coll. of N.Y. 49-62, Prof. Emer. 62-; John Simon Guggenheim Fellow 40-41; mem. Inst. for Advanced Study, Princeton 48 and 55; mem. Center for Advanced Studies, Wesleyan Univ.

63-64; Editor-Adviser *Encyclopædia Britannica*, Editor *Smith Coll. Studies in History* 45-50; Editorial Board *Journal of History of Ideas*, and *Orbis;* D.H.L., h.c., LL.D. h.c.

Publs. *Nationalismus* 22, *Sinn und Schicksal der Revolution* 23, *Martin Buber, sein Werk und seine Zeit* 29, *A History of Nationalism in the East* 29, *Nationalism and Imperialism in the Hither East* 32, *Nationalism in the Soviet Union* 33, *Orient and Occident* 34, *Western Civilization in the Near East* 36, *Force or Reason* 37, *Revolutions and Dictatorships* 39, *Not by Arms Alone* 40, *World Order in Historical Perspective* 42, *The Idea of Nationalism* 44, *Prophets and Peoples* 46, *The Twentieth Century* 49, *Pan-Slavism, its History and Ideology* 53, *German History: Some New German Views* 54, *Making of the Modern French Mind* 55, *The Mind of Modern Russia* 55, *Nationalism, its Meaning and History* 55, *Nationalism and Liberty, The Swiss Example* 56, *American Nationalism* 57, *A Basic History of Modern Russia* 57, *Is the Free West in Decline?* 57, *The Mind of Germany* 60, *The Age of Nationalism, The First Era of Global History* 62, *Reflections on Modern History* 63, *Living in a World Revolution* 64, *Prelude to Nation-States: The French and German Experiences 1789-1815* 67.

2100 Walnut Street, Philadelphia, Pa. 19103.
Telephone: LO3-3624.

Kohnstamm, Max: Netherlands international civil servant; b. 14; ed. Univ. of Amsterdam and American Univ. of Washington, D.C.

Private Sec. to Queen Wilhelmina 45-48; Netherlands Foreign Office 48-52; Sec. to High Authority of European Coal and Steel Community (ECSC) 52-56; Vice-Pres. Action Cttee. for United States of Europe 56-; Pres. European Community Inst. for Univ. Studies 59-; Commdr. Order of House of Orange.

12 avenue Casalta, Brussels 18, Belgium.

Kohrt, Günter; German diplomatist and politician; b. 11 March 1912.

Posts concerned with public educ., City Council of Greater Berlin 45-49; Ministry of Foreign Affairs, German Democratic Republic 49-; Ambassador to People's Republic of China 64-66; Sec. of State and First Deputy Foreign Minister 66-.

Ministry of Foreign Affairs, Berlin, Germany.

Koht, Paul; Norwegian diplomatist; b. 7 Dec. 1913; ed. Oslo Univ.

Entered foreign service 38; served Bucharest 38-39, Ministry of Foreign Affairs 39-40, London 40, Tokyo 41-42, New York 43-46, Ministry of Foreign Affairs 46-50, 53-56, Lisbon 50-51, Paris 51-53, Denmark 56-58; Ambassador to U.S.A. 58-63, to German Fed. Republic 63-68, to U.K. 68-.

Norwegian Embassy, 25 Belgrave Square, London, S.W.1, England.

Koike, Konosuke; Japanese investment executive; b. 99; ed. Tokyo and Oxford Univs.

President, The Koike Bank 25-34; Auditor, Oji Paper Co. Ltd. 25-46; Pres. Koike Shokan K.K. 34-43; Chair. Maruko Securities Co. Ltd. 45-47; Pres. Yamaichi Securities Co. Ltd. 43-54, Chair. 54-; Chair. Japan Fed. of Securities Dealers' Asscns. 53-, Tokyo Securities Dealers' Asscn. 53-; official of numerous business and financial orgs.; Medal of Honour with Blue Ribbon.

154 2-chome, Kitazawa-cho, Setagaya-ku, Tokyo, Japan.

Koike, Shinzo; Japanese politician; b. 03; ed. Tokyo Univ.

Ministry of Communications 28, later Chief, Accounting Section, Ministry of Transportation Secr., Dir. Sapporo Communications Bureau, Electric Power Bureau, Ministry of Commerce and Industry; Chief Dir. Central Japan Industrial League 50-63; mem. House of

Councillors 50-; Parl. Vice-Minister of Int. Trade and Industry 50-54; Minister of Postal Services July 63-64; Liberal-Democratic Party.
Publ. *An Outline of the Electric Power Control Decree.*
House of Councillors, Tokyo, Japan.

Koinange, Mbiyu; Kenyan politician; b. 07; ed. Buxton School, Mombasa, Alliance High School, Kikuyu, Ohio Wesleyan Univ., Columbia Univ. New York and postgraduate work.
Founder Kenya Teachers Coll., Githunguri 39, Principal 48; Co-founder Kenya African Union 46, Rep. in Europe 51-59; Dir. for Eastern, Central and South Africa, Bureau of African Affairs, Ghana 59-60; fmr. Sec.-Gen. Pan African Freedom Movement for East, Central and South Africa (PAFMECSA); Minister of State for Pan-African Affairs, Kenya 63-65; Minister for Educ. 65-66, Minister of State, Office of the Pres. 66-.
Ehothla Farm, P.O. Box 9799, Nairobi, Kenya.
Telephone: Riara Ridge 208.

Koirala, Bisweswar Prasad; Nepalese politician; b. 15; ed. Benares and Calcutta Univs.
President Nepali Congress Party; Minister for Home Affairs 51; Prime Minister May 59-61.
Katmandu, Nepal.

Koirala, Matrika Prasad; Nepalese politician and diplomatist; b. 1 Jan. 1912; ed. Benares and Patna, India.
Former President, Nepalese Congress Party; Prime Minister and Minister of Gen. Admin. and Foreign Affairs 51-52, 53-55; nominated to Upper House of Parl.; Ambassador to U.S. 62-64; Perm. Rep to UN 62-64.
c/o Ministry of Foreign Affairs, Katmandu, Nepal.

Koivisto, Mauno Henrik, PH.D.; Finnish banker and politician; b. 25 Nov. 1923; ed. Turku Universitet.
Office keeper 48-51; temp. school teacher 51-53; Vocational Guide City of Turku 54-57; Man. Dir. Savings Bank, Helsinki 59-67; Minister of Finance 66-67; Gov. Bank of Finland Jan.-Mar. 68; Prime Minister 68-; Gov. for Finland, Int. Bank for Reconstruction and Devt. 68.
Office of the Prime Minister, Helsinki, Finland.

Koizumi, Junta; Japanese politician; b. 04; ed. Nihon Univ.
Private Sec. to Minister of Finance 41; Dir. Toho Seikei Tsushin (Eastern Political and Econ.) News Company; Parl. Counsellor of Home Affairs 45; business appointments 50; mem. House of Reps.; Head, Defence Agency 64-65; Liberal-Democrat.
c/o Defence Agency, Tokyo, Japan.

Kojima, Kiyoshi, PH.D.; Japanese economist; b. 22 May 1920; ed. Tokyo Univ. of Commerce and Economics, Leeds Univ. (U.K.) and Princeton Univ. (U.S.A.).
Assistant Prof. of Int. Economics, Hitotsubashi Univ. 43-45, Prof. 53-; Secretariat (Dir.) for UN Conf. on Trade and Development 63; British Council Scholarship 52-53, Rockefeller Foundation Fellowship 53-55.
Publs. (in Japanese): *Theory of Foreign Trade* 50, *Japan's Economic Development and Trade* 58, *Japan in the World Economy* 62, *The Economics of EEC* 62, *Trade Expansion for Developing Countries* 64; Editor *Papers and Proceedings of a Conference on Pacific Trade and Development* 68; also articles in English on int. trade.
3-24-10 Maehara-cho, Koganei-shi, Tokyo, Japan.

Kok, Dr. Jan; Netherlands biochemist; b. 13 June 1899; ed. Amsterdam Univ.
Pharmacist, Amsterdam 25-27; Dir. Pharmaceutical firm, Amsterdam 27-45; Extra Prof. Univ. of Amsterdam 45-49, Full Prof. 49-, Rector 60-65; Managing Dir. Laboratory of Biochemistry, Toxicology and Galenics, Univ. of Amsterdam; Knight of the Netherlands Lion, Hon. Officer of Orange Nassau.

Publs. *Pharmacotherapeutical Vademecum, Handbook of the Science of Prescriptions.*
Gerrit van der Veenstraat 115, Amsterdam Z, Netherlands.
Telephone: 020-723866.

Kokarev, Alexandr Akimovich; Soviet politician; b. 09; ed. Industrial Inst., Zoporozhe.
Member C.P.S.U. 38-; Dept. Head, Workshop Foreman, Dep. Dir. factories in Zoporozhe, Krasnoyarsk 33-45; Dep. Sec. Krasnoyarsk Town Cttee. C.P.S.U. 45-46; Dir. Agricultural Machinery, Krasnoyarsk 46-50; First Sec. Krasnoyarsk Town Cttee. C.P.S.U. 50-54, Second Sec. 54-58; First Sec. Krasnoyarsk Area Cttee. C.P.S.U. 58-; mem. Central Cttee. of C.P.S.U. 61-; Deputy to U.S.S.R. Supreme Soviet; mem. Comm. for Legislative Proposals, Union Soviet of U.S.S.R. Supreme Soviet.
Krasnoyarsk Area Committee of C.P.S.U., Krasnoyarsk, U.S.S.R.

Kokoschka, Oskar, C.B.E.; British artist and writer; b. 1 March 1886 in Austria; ed. Vienna School of Industrial Art.
Worked in Vienna from 06, where he taught at an Industrial school, then in various towns of Switzerland and in Berlin; joined the "Sturm" group in Berlin; cavalry officer on Russian and Italian fronts 15-17; Prof. Dresden Art Acad. 18-24; has travelled in Europe, Asia Minor and Northern Africa; emigré; paintings include landscapes, portraits and compositions; represented in principal European art galleries until 39, when works, as "degenerate," were sold by Nazis; paintings in U.S.A.: *Polperro, Cornwall*, presented to Tate Gallery, London, by Pres. Beneš 41, *A Woman Bathing*, presented to Nat. Gallery Edinburgh 42; Retrospective Exhbn., Tate Gallery, London 62; rep. at Dunn Int. Exhibition, London 63; Exhbn. of portraits, Badischer Kunstverein, Karlsruhe 66; Erasmus Prize 60; Hon. D.Litt. Oxford.
Publs. Plays: *Mörder, Hoffnung der Frauen* 07, *Der brennende Dornbusch* 11, *Hiob* (music by Hindemith 21) 11, *Orpheus und Eurydice* (music by Křenek 26) 16; short stories: *A Sea Ringed with Visions* 62.
Villeneuve, Vaud, Switzerland.

Kolář, Václav; Czechoslovak diplomatist; b. 19 March 1908.
Ministry of Foreign Affairs 59-; Head, Admin. Dept., Ministry of Foreign Affairs 59-64; Amb. to German Democratic Republic 64-.
Botschaft der Tschechoslowakischen Sozialistischen Republik, 1054 Berlin, Schönhauser Allee 103, Germany.

Kolbetskaya, Maria Andreyevna; Soviet trade union official; b. 12; ed. Moscow Textile Inst.
Weaver, later Chief Engineer, Textile Mill 28-43; Party work, Moscow 43-61; Head, Wool and Silk Industries Dept., Moscow Regional Econ. Council 61-62; Chair. Central Cttee. of Trade Union of Workers of Textile and Light Industries 62-; mem. C.P.S.U. 37-; mem. Praesidium All-Union Council of Trade Unions 68-; mem. Cen. Auditing Comm. of C.P.S.U.; Order of Red Banner of Labour.
Central Committee of the Trade Union of the Workers of the Textile and Light Industries, 42 Leninsky Prospekt, Moscow, U.S.S.R.

Kolder, Drahomír; Czechoslovak politician; b. 29 Dec. 1925.
Miner, Ostrava 40-45; various posts in Czechoslovak Youth Union and C.P. in Northern Moravian Region, Chief Sec. Karviná District Cttee., C.P. of Czechoslovakia; Chief Sec. Ostrava City Cttee. of Czechoslovakia 51-52; worked for Central Cttee., C.P. of Czechoslovakia 52-58; Chief Sec. Ostrava Regional Cttee., C.P. of Czechoslovakia 58-62; Cand., Cen. Cttee. C.P. of Czechoslovakia 58-61; mem. Cen. Cttee. C.P. of

Czechoslovakia and cand. of Cen. Cttee. Presidium 61-62; mem. Cen. Cttee. C.P. of Czechoslovakia and mem. of Cen. Cttee. Presidium 62-; Sec. Cen. Cttee. 62-; mem. Secr., Cen. Cttee. 62-; Chair. Econ. Comm., C.P. of Czechoslovakia 63-; Deputy, Nat. Assembly 60-; Order of 25th February 1948 49, Order for Merits in Construction 58.
Central Committee, Communist Party of Czechoslovakia, nábr. Kyjevské brigády 12, Prague 1, Czechoslovakia.

Kolfschoten, Henri Anthony Melchior Tieleman; Netherlands politician; b. 17 Aug. 1903; ed. St. Willibrordus Coll., Katwijk, and Amsterdam Univ. (Law).
Deputy Sec., Roman Catholic State Party 27-38, Dir. 38-41; Private Sec. to Jonkheer Ruys de Beerenbrouck 28-33; representative of State Party in Politiek Convent and Vaderlandsche Comité; Min. of Justice in Schermerhorn-Drees Govt. 45-46; mem. of Eerste Kamer (First Chamber) 46-48, 49-52; Burgomaster of Eindhoven Sept. 46-Feb. 57; Burgomaster of The Hague 57-68 (retd.); Knight Order of the Dutch Lion, Commdr. Order of Orange-Nassau, Officier Légion d'Honneur; Hon. Knight Commdr. R.V.O.; Knight Commdr. Léopold II of Belgium and other foreign decorations.
7 Nieuwe Duinweg, The Hague, Netherlands.

Koliševski, Lazar; Yugoslav politician; b. 12 Feb. 1914.
Former metal worker; mem. Yugoslav Communist Party 35-; partisan, Sec. Provincial Cttee. of C.P. of Macedonia, and leader of Provincial Mil. Staff 41; imprisoned 41-44; Pres. Govt. of Macedonia 45; Sec. Central Cttee. of League of Communists of Macedonia until 63; mem. Exec. Cttee. Central Cttee. of League of Communists of Yugoslavia 52-; fmr. Pres. Macedonian Assembly and Chair. Socialist Alliance of Working People of Macedonia; Chair. Central Board of Socialist Alliance of Working People of Yugoslavia 63-67; mem. Council of Federation 67-.
Sobranie na SRM 320 no. 1, Skopje, Yugoslavia.

Kollek, Theodore; Israeli (b. Austrian) public administrator; b. 27 May 1911; ed. secondary school.
Founder mem. Kibbutz Ein Gev 37; Political Dept. Jewish Agency for Palestine 40; established Jewish Agency office, Istanbul, for contact with Jewish underground in Europe 42; Mission to U.S.A. for Haganah 47-48; Head of U.S. Div., Israel Foreign Ministry 50; Minister, Washington 51-52; Dir.-Gen. of Prime Minister's Office, Jerusalem 52-65; Chair. Israel Govt. Tourist Corpn. 55-65; Chair. Israel Govt. Water Desalination Joint Project with U.S. Govt. 64-; Chair. of Board Israel Museum, Jerusalem 64-, Africa-Israel Investment Co. Ltd. 64-65, Mayor of Jerusalem 65-.
City Hall, Jerusalem; Home: 6 Rashba Street, Rechavia, Jerusalem, Israel.
Telephone: 24651 (Office); 33147 (Home).

Koller, Herbert Josef, IUR.D.; Austrian business executive; b. 11; ed. elementary and secondary schools, Melk, and Univ. of Vienna.
Law practice and business appointments 35-44; Military Service and Prisoner-of-War 44-47; Vereinigte Österreichische Eisen und Stahlwerke (Vöest) 47-; Works Man., Hütte Krems 55-61; Gen. Man. and Chair. of Board of Dirs., Vöest 61-; Chair. Wiener Brückenbau- and Eisen-Konstruktions A.G., Vienna, Hütte Krems G.m.b.H.; Pres. of Board of Management Vöest Italiana, Milan, Vöest Zürich, BOT Zürich; Chair. Board of Management Importkohle Vienna, Ister Reederei, Bremen, Vöest Frankfurt, Ferrum Montage Oslo; Chair. Board of Dirs. Ferrum Copenhagen, Ferrum London; Austrian and German decorations.
Vereinigte Österreichische Eisen-und Stahlwerke A.G., Muldenstrasse 5, Linz/Donau, Austria.

Koller, Simon, LL.D.; Austrian diplomatist; b. 12; ed. Classical High School and Univ. of Graz.
Central Agencies of Economy, County Admin. of Carinthia; Austrian Foreign Service 47-, Germany, UN, Council of Europe; Dep. Dir. of Political Dept. Foreign Office 57-61; Dir. for South Tyrolian Affairs, Foreign Office 60-61; Minister to Hungary 62-, now Ambassador; Vice-Pres. Danube Comm. 63-; Grand Cross, Fed. German Order of Merit.
Austrian Embassy, Bençzur utca 16, Budapest VI, Hungary.

Kollias, Constantine; Greek politician; b.1901; ed. Athens Univ.
Prosecutor, Court of Appeal 45-46; Vice-Prosecutor, Supreme Court 46-62; Prosecutor, Supreme Court, Athens 62-67; Prime Minister 67-Nov. 67; Attorney-Gen. of Greece Jan. 68-.
124 Vassil. Sophias Street, Ampelokipi, Athens, Greece.

Kolman, Arnošt (Ernest), PH.D., D.SC.; Czechoslovak mathematician and philosopher; b. 6 Dec. 1892; ed. Prague Univ.
Chief, Science Dept. of Moscow Cttee. of Communist Party; Prof. of Mathematics Moscow until 45; Prof. of Philosophy, Charles Univ., Prague 45-48; mem. Inst. for History of Sciences and Technology and Cybernetic Scientific Council, Acad. of Sciences, U.S.S.R.; Dir. Inst. of Philosophy, Czech. Acad. of Sciences 59-62; mem. Czech. Acad. of Sciences 60-; Order of Labour 62, Order of Red Banner of Labour 67.
Publs. *The Present Crisis in the Mathematical Sciences* (in *Science at the Cross-roads*) 31, *Eine neue Grundlegung der Differentialrechnung durch Karl Marx* (in *Verhandlungen des internationalen Mathematiker-Kongresses* 32, *On the Problem of a Unified Physical Theory of Matter* (in *Phil. of Science*) 35, *Subject and Method of Modern Mathematics* 36, *Critical Account of the Symbolic Method of Modern Logic* 48, *Bernard Bolzano* 55, *The Great Russian Thinker N.I. Lobachevski* 55, *Cybernetics* 56, *Infinity in Greek Mathematics* 56, *Life and Scientific work of Rudger Boshkovich* 56, *Philosophical Problems of Modern Physics* 57, *On the Categories of Materialistic Dialectics* 57, *Critique of the Contemporary "Mathematical" Idealism* 57, *Gnosiology of Bertrand Russell* 57, *Logic* 58, *Is there a God?* 58, *Some Unsolved Problems of the History of Ancient Mathematics* 58, *Marx and the Natural Sciences* 58, *Lenin and Modern Physics* 59, *The Man of the Cosmic Age* 60, *Cybernetics Paradox and Self-Knowledge of the Brain* 61, *Space, Time, Matter and Motion in Cosmology* 61, *Overcoming of Infinity* 62, *An Outlook in the Future* 62, *Philosophy and Cybernetics* 62, *Expanding Mathematical Methods in New Spheres of Knowledge* 64, *Finite and Infinite in the Universe* 64, *Considerations about the Certainty of Knowledge* 65, *Philosophical and Social Problems of Cybernetics* 66, *Dialectical Development of Contemporary Physics* 67, *Recent Discovery of Plurality of Mathematics and its Philosophical Significance* 67.
Alabyana 40/1 bl. 6, fl. 151, Moscow, A80, U.S.S.R.

Kolmogorov, Andrei Nikolaevich; Soviet mathematician; b. 1903; ed. Moscow Univ.
Instructor, Moscow Univ. 25-31, Prof. 31-, Head, Chair. of Theory of Probability 37-, Dean of Faculty of Mechanics and Mathematics, Moscow Univ. 54-57; mem. U.S.S.R. Acad. of Sciences 39-, Head of Dept. of Theory of Probability and Mathematical Statistics, Inst. of Mathematics of U.S.S.R. Acad. of Sciences 39-59; Editor-in-Chief *Theory of Probability and its Application*; Hon. mem. Polish Acad. of Sciences; mem. Rumanian Acad. of Sciences, German Leopoldina Acad., American Acad. of Sciences and Arts, Nat. Acad. of Sciences (U.S.A.), Royal Statistical Soc. (U.K.); mem. Presidential Board, U.S.S.R.-France Friendship Soc.; Hero of Socialist Labour; State Prize 41; Lenin Prize; Order of Lenin (thrice) etc.

Publs. include *Basic Concepts of the Theory of Probability* 36; co-author *Algebra* 39.
Institute of Mathematics, U.S.S.R. Academy of Sciences, 19 Lenin Prospekt, Moscow, U.S.S.R.

Kolomiets, Fyodor Stepanovich; Soviet politician; b. 1910; ed. All-Union Correspondence Inst. for Food Industry.
Soviet Army 30-37; mem. C.P.S.U. 39-; Food industry 37-55; Deputy Minister of Food Industry, R.S.F.S.R. 56-57; Sec. Krasnodar Territorial Cttee. of C.P.S.U. 57-60; Chair. Krasnodar Territorial Exec. Cttee. of Workers' Deputies 60-63; First Sec. Tselinny Territorial later Regional Cttee. of C.P.S.U. 63-65; First Deputy Minister of Food Industry of U.S.S.R. 65-; Cand. mem. C.P.S.U. Central Cttee. 61-66; Deputy to U.S.S.R. Supreme Soviet until 66; Hero of Socialist Labour.
U.S.S.R. Ministry of Food, Moscow, U.S.S.R.

Kolosov, Mikhail Nikolayevich; Soviet chemist; b. 1927; ed. Lomonosov Inst. of Fine Chemical Technology.
Postgraduate Lomonosov Inst. of Fine Chemical Technology 48-51; Research Assoc. Inst. of Biological and Medical Chemistry, U.S.S.R. Acad. of Medical Sciences 51-59; Inst. of Chemistry of Natural Compounds, U.S.S.R. Acad. of Sciences 59-; Corresp. mem. U.S.S.R. Acad. of Sciences 66-; mem. C.P.S.U. 63-.
Publs. Works on chemistry of biopolymers and other natural compounds.
U.S.S.R. Academy of Sciences, 14 Lenin Prospekt, Moscow, U.S.S.R.

Kolosovsky, Igor Konstantinovich; Soviet diplomatist; b. 1920; ed. Moscow Aviation Inst.
Mem. C.P. of Soviet Union 46-; at Ministry of Foreign Affairs 46-50; First Sec., Asst. Head of Dept. of Latin American Countries at Ministry 50-54; Asst. to Deputy Foreign Minister of U.S.S.R. 54; Counsellor at Soviet Embassy, Buenos Aires 54-58; Consultant-Expert to Editorial Staff of Comm. for Publication of Diplomatic Documents, Ministry of Foreign Affairs 58-59, Deputy Head, First African Dept. 59-62; Counsellor, Washington 62-65; Amb. to Uruguay 65-; Badge of Honour, other decorations.
U.S.S.R. Embassy, Montevideo, Uruguay.

Kolotyrkin, Yakov Mikhailovich; Soviet physico-chemist; b. 1910; ed. Moscow Univ.
Research Assoc., Dir. Karpov Physico-Chemical Inst. 38-; mem. C.P.S.U. 40-; Corresp. mem. U.S.S.R. Acad. of Sciences 66-.
U.S.S.R. Academy of Sciences, 14 Lenin Prospekt, Moscow, U.S.S.R.

Kolozsvári-Grandpierre, Emil; Hungarian novelist; b. 15 Jan. 1907; ed. Secondary School in France, Pécs Univ.
Publisher's reader 41-44; Dir. of literature dept. of the Hungarian Radio 46-49; József Attile Literary Prize 64.
Publs. *A Rosta, Dr. Csibráky szerelmei, A Nagy Ember, Alvajárók, A sárgavirágos leány, Tegnap, Szabadság, Lófő és kora, Az értelem dicsérete, Lelkifinomságok, Mérlegen, A Csodafurulya, A Csillagszemü, A Törökfejes kopja, Elmés mulatságok, A büvös kaptafa, A tisztesség keresztje, Foltonfolt Királyfi, A boldogtalanság miüvészete, Legendák nyomában, Csinnadári, Gyalogtündér, Egy szereplö visszatér, Párbeszéd a Sorssal, A lóvátett sárkány, Csendes rév a háztetön, A Burok, Aquincumi Vénusz, Változatok hegedüre.*
Palánta-u 20/a, Budapest II, Hungary.
Telephone: 350-049.

Kolpakova, Irena Alexandrovna; Soviet ballerina; b. 22 May 1933; ed. Leningrad Choreographic School.
Prima Ballerina, Kirov Theatre of Opera and Ballet, Leningrad; People's Artist of the R.S.F.S.R.; Grand Prix de Ballet, Paris 66.
Principal Roles; Aurora (*Sleeping Beauty*), Juliet (*Romeo and Juliet*), Desdemona (*Othello*), Tao Khao

(*The Red Poppy*), Maria (*Fountain of Bakhchisarai*), Giselle, Zolushka, Raymonda; first performer of part of Katerina (*The Stone Flower*) and Shirin (*Legends of Love*).
Kirov Theatre of Opera and Ballet, 1 ploshchad Iskusstv, Leningrad, U.S.S.R.

Komai, Kenichiro; Japanese business executive; b. 17 Dec. 1900; ed. Coll. of Technology, Tokyo Imperial Univ.
Hitachi Ltd. 25-, Man. of Hitachi Works 46-50, Dir. 46-55, Man. Dir. 55-57, Senior Man. Dir. 57-61, Pres. 61-; Exec. Dir. Japan Fed. of Econ. Organisations 62-; Gov. Dir. Japan Fed. of Employers' Asscns. 62-; Pres. Electronic Machinery Industry Associations 65-; Chair. Japan Consulting Inst. 65-.
20-8, 3-chome, Tamagawa Todoroki-cho, Setagaya-ku, Tokyo, Japan.

Komarov, Nikolai Dmitrievich; Soviet foreign trade official; b. 1918; ed. Moscow Aviation Inst. and Acad. of Foreign Trade.
Member C.P.S.U. 45-; engineer 37-46; Official, Main Dept. for Soviet Property Abroad 51-55; Chief of Section, Deputy Chief of Dept., Chief of Dept., Ministry of Foreign Trade 55-65; Deputy Minister of Foreign Trade 65-; Order of Red Banner of Labour, Badge of Honour.
U.S.S.R. Ministry of Foreign Trade, 32/34 Smolenskaya-Sennaya Square, Moscow, U.S.S.R.

Komiakhov, Vasili Grigorievich; Soviet politician; b. 11; ed. Agricultural Inst., Odessa.
Member Communist Party of Soviet Union 41-; army service 41-45; econ. work 45-49; Chair. Exec. Cttee., Kirovgrad District Council of Workers Deputies 49-53; First Sec. Sumy District Cttee., Ukraine Communist Party 53-55, Crimea 55-61, Poltava 61-62; mem. Politburo of Central Cttee. and Sec. Central Cttee., C.P. of Ukraine, Chair. Bureau of Central Cttee. of C.P. of Ukraine for Agricultural Management 62-; Cand. mem. Central Cttee., C.P.S.U. 56-61, mem. 61-.
Central Committee of the Communist Party of the Ukraine, Kiev, Ukrainian S.S.R., U.S.S.R.

Komócsin, Zoltán; Hungarian politician; b. 23.
Former clerk; fmr. Asst. Sec. Szeged Party Cttee.; fmr. Head, Propaganda Dept., Central Cttee. Hungarian Socialist Workers Party, later First Sec. Party Cttee., Hajdu County; mem. Central Cttee. Hungarian Socialist Workers Party 57-; First Sec. Hungarian Young Communist League 57-61; Head, Editorial Board *Népszabadság* (Hungarian Socialist Workers Party daily) 61-65; mem. Political Cttee. Hungarian Socialist Workers Party Nov. 62-, Sec. Central Cttee 65-.
Central Committee of Hungarian Socialist Workers Party, Széchenyi rakpart 19, Budapest, V., Hungary.

Kondakov, Ivan Petrovich; Soviet educator and librarian; b. 1905; ed. Gorky State Univ. and C.P.S.U. Higher Party School.
Director of a secondary school, Gorky Region 27-32; mem. C.P.S.U. 30-; Deputy Dir. Gorky Political Educ. Inst. and Regional Advanced Teachers' Training Inst. 32-41; Head, Gorky Region Dept. of Educ. 41-42; Deputy Head, later Head of Dept., Gorky Regional Cttee. of C.P.S.U. 42-43; Deputy Head of Dept., Central Cttee of C.P.S.U. 43-46; First Deputy Minister of Educ. of R.S.F.S.R. 46-53; First Deputy Minister of Culture of R.S.F.S.R. 53-59; Dir. State Lenin Library of U.S.S.R. 59-; Vice-Chair. Council for Library Work of U.S.S.R. Ministry of Culture; Honoured Worker of Culture; Order of Red Banner of Labour (twice).
State Lenin Library of U.S.S.R., 3 Kalinin Prospekt, Moscow, U.S.S.R.

Kondrashin, Kirill Petrovich; Soviet musician; b. 14; ed. Moscow Conservatoire.
Assistant Conductor, Nemirovich-Danchenko Musical

Theatre, Moscow 34-37; Conductor, Maly Opera Theatre, Leningrad 38-42; Bolshoi Theatre, Moscow 43-56; Conductor, All-Russia Symphony Orchestra Touring Concert Company 56-60; Chief Conductor, Moscow Philharmonic Orchestra 60-; State Prize 48, 49; Honoured Artist of R.S.F.S.R.
Moscow State Philharmonia, Ulitsa Gorkogo 31, Moscow, U.S.S.R.

Kondratiev, Victor Nikolaevich; Soviet scientist; b. 1 Feb. 1902; ed. Polytechnic Inst., Leningrad.
Chief, Laboratory of Elementary Processes, Inst. of Chemical Physics, Moscow 31-, Vice-Dir., Inst. of Chemical Physics 48-, Chief, Dept. of Kinetics and Combustion 56-; Prof. Polytechnic Inst. Leningrad 34-41, Moscow State Univ. 49-51, Moscow Engineering Physical Inst. 51-57; mem. C.P.S.U. 53-; Corresp. mem. U.S.S.R. Acad. of Sciences 43-53, mem. 53-, mem. Chemical Dept. Bureau, U.S.S.R. Acad. of Sciences 57-; mem. IUPAC Bureau and Exec. Cttee. 61-, Vice-Pres. 65-; State Prize.
Publs. *Spectroscopic Studies of Chemical Gas Reactions* 44, *Structure of Atoms and Molecules* (3rd edn.) 60, *Kinetics of Chemical Gas Reactions* 58.
Institute of Chemical Physics, Moscow V-334, U.S.S.R.

Kondratieva, Maria Victorovna; Soviet ballet dancer; b. 1934; ed. Bolshoi Theatre Ballet School.
Joined Bolshoi Ballet Co. 53; People's Artist of R.S.F.S.R.
Main roles include: Cinderella (*Cinderella*), Maria (*Fountain of Bakhchisarai*), Aurora (*Sleeping Beauty*), Juliet (*Romeo and Juliet*), Katerina (*Stone Flower*), Giselle (*Giselle*), Gayane (*Gayane*), Odette-Odile (*Swan Lake*), Shirin (*Legend of Love*).
State Academic Bolshoi Theatre of U.S.S.R., 1 Ploshchad Sverdlova, Moscow, U.S.S.R.

Koné, Jean-Marie; Mali politician; b. 1913; ed. William Ponty School.
Teacher, Coll. de Jeunes Filles, Sikasso, French Sudan; Territorial Councillor from Sikasso 46-; Sec. Gen. Council, French Sudan 52; Prime Minister, Sudanese Republic (French West Africa) 57-60; Vice-Pres., Minister of Justice and the Civil Service, Sudan, Mali Fed. 60; Minister of State for Justice, Mali 60-62, Minister for Planning and Rural Economy 62-; Pres. Rassemblement Démocratique Africain (R.D.A.) group in Sudan Gen. Council; Chevalier de l'Etoile Noire du Bénin, Paris Silver Medal; mem. Union Soudanaise (R.D.A.).
Ministry for Planning, Bamako, Mali, West Africa.

Koné, Lompolo; Upper Voltan politician; ed. William Ponty School.
Has worked at a home for Creoles, Bingerville, and at William Ponty School; fmr. organiser of Cultural Centres, High Commission, Dakar; fmr. Dir. School of Administration, Republic of Upper Volta; fmr. Sec. for Foreign Affairs; Minister of Foreign Affairs 61-66.
c/o Ministry of Foreign Affairs, Ouagadougou, Upper Volta, West Africa.

Könecke, Fritz, D.RER.POL.; German businessman; b. 16 Jan. 1899; ed. Göttingen, Hamburg and Hanover Univs.
Joined Continental-Gummiwerke A.G., Hanover 20, Sales Man. 28, Dir. 34, Chair. and Gen. Man. 38; Dir. Hamburger Gummiwarenfabrik Phoenix A.G. 49; Asst. Chair. Daimler-Benz A.G., Stuttgart-Untertürkheim 52, Chair. 53, Gen. Man. 54-61; Grand Cross of the Fed. Republic of Germany; Hon. D.Eng.
Am Bismarckturm 54, Stuttgart-N, German Federal Republic.

Koniev, Ivan Stapanovich, Marshal of Soviet Union; Soviet officer; b. 97; ed. Frunze Military Acad.
Joined Communist Party 18, Red Army 18; fought in Civil War; fmr. Commdr. 2nd Far Eastern Front;

military leader in the war against Germany 41-45; served on the Smolensk sector Aug. 41; Col.-Gen. Sept. 41; recaptured Kalinin Dec. 41; C.-in-C. Kalinin front 42; Army-Gen. Aug. 43; C.-in-C. Steppe Front Troops 43; liberated Orel and Byelgorod Aug. 43, Poltava Sept. 43; C.-in-C. 2nd Ukrainian Front Troops winter Campaign 43-44; liberated Kirovograd Jan. 44; apptd. C.-in-C. First Ukrainian Front Troops (July 44) which invaded Silesia, Saxony and Czechoslovakia; Soviet Rep. Allied Control Council for Austria 45; C.-in-C. Soviet Army 46-60; deputy to Supreme Soviet 46-; candidate-mem. Central Communist Party Cttee. 39-52, mem. 52-; candidate-mem. Bureau Communist Party of Ukraine 53-; C.-in-C. Joint Armed Forces set up under Eight Nation Treaty, June 55-60; C.-in-C. Soviet Forces in E. Germany Aug. 61-April 62; Gen. Inspector Ministry of Defence 62-; awarded title Marshal of Soviet Union Feb. 44, Orders of Suvorov (twice), Kutuzov (twice), Red Star, Red Banner (thrice), Weapon of Honour with a Coat-of-Arms in gold and other awards.
Ministry of Defence, 34 Maurice Thorez Embankment, Moscow, U.S.S.R.

König, H.E. Cardinal Franz; Austrian ecclesiastic; b. 3 Aug. 1905; ed. Univs. of Rome, Vienna and Lille.
Dozent, Vienna Univ. 46; Prof. of Moral Theology, Salzburg 48; Titular Bishop of Livias 52; Archbishop of Vienna 56-; created Cardinal by Pope John XXIII 58; Chaplain for Austria 59-; mem. Sacred Congregations of the Consistory, of Seminaries and Univs. of Study and of the Fabric of St. Peter's; Pres. Secretariat for Non-Believers.
Publs. include *Christus und die Religionen der Erde, Religionswissenschaftliches Wörterbuch, Zarathustras Jenseitsvorstellungen und das Alte Testament* 64.
Rotenturmstrasse 2, Vienna I, Austria.

König, René, PH.D.; German sociologist; b. 5 July 1906; ed. Univs. of Vienna, Berlin and Paris.
Member Faculty Zurich Univ. 38; apptd. to Chair of Sociology Cologne Univ. 49-; Sec. First World Congress of Sociology, Zurich 50; Dir. Sociological Research Inst. Cologne 53; Editor *Kölner Zeitschrift für Soziologie und Sozialpsychologie* 55; Pres. Int. Sociological Asscn. 62-66; Guest Prof. Univs. of Mich. 57, Calif. 57, 59, 60, 64, 65, Columbia Univ. 59, Colo. 62; Rockefeller Fellow 52, Commendatore del Ordine di Merito della Repubblica Italiana.
Publs. *Naturalistische Ästhetik in Frankreich* 31, *Niccolo Macchiavelli* 41, *Materialien zur Soziologie der Familie* 46, *Soziologie heute* 49, *Soziologie* 57, 67, *Grundformen der Gesellschaft: Soziologie der Gemeinde* 58 (English trans. *The Community* 67), *Das Buch der Mode* 58, 67, *Handbuch der empirischen Sozialforschung* (2 vols.) 62, 68.
Forschungsinstitut für Soziologie der Universität zu Köln, 5 Köln-Sülz, Zülpicher Strasse 182; 5021 Widdersdorf, Marienstrasse 9, German Federal Republic.
Telephone: Cologne 2024, 2409 (Office); Cologne 50-86-13 (Home).

Konjovic, Petar; Yugoslav composer and conductor; b. 5 May 1883; ed. Prague Conservatoire.
Former Director National Theatre, Novi Sad and Osijek; fmr. Dir. Min. of Public Instruction and Zagreb Opera; fmr. Pres. Yugoslav Section Int. Society for Contemporary Music, Zagreb, and Society of Friends of Slavic Music, Belgrade; fmr. Dir. Inst. of Musicology and Sec. to Dept. for Arts and Music in Serbian Acad. of Sciences; fmr. Rector and Prof. Acad. of Music, Belgrade; Fellow of Serbian Acad. of Sciences and Arts.
Works include *Vilin Veo-Ženidba Miloševa, Knez od Zete, Koštana, Majka Jugovića—La Patrie* (operas), *Seljaci* (folk opera), *Moja Zemlja,* 100 Yugoslav folk songs arranged for voice and piano; *Lyric,* 24 songs, *Makar Chudra,* symphonic poem for complete orchestra;

Koštana, symphonic tryptichon, *Sonata* for violin and piano; *Na Selu* (In the Country) symphonic variations; *Capriccio adriatico* concerto for violin and orchestra; songs and folk songs; symphony orchestra and chamber music works (two string quartets); *Musica Divina, Liturgies, Psalms, Hymns* and 20 other works for choirs.
Publs. *Personalities in Theatre and Music, Serbian and Slav Music, Miloje Milojević, Stevan Mokranjac—a musical portrait* 56.
Prvog maja 32/III, Belgrade, Yugoslavia.

Konnov, Vladimir Kuzmich; Soviet trade union official; b. 14.
Worker in Moscow automobile factory 31-44, rose to Chief of Dept.; mem. Communist Party of Soviet Union 39-; Inspector, Moscow Transport Organisation 55-63; Chair. Communication, Automobile Transport and Highway Workers' Union 63-; mem. Central Revision Comm. 63-68, All-Union Cen. Council of Trade Unions 68-; Order of Red Banner of Labour etc.
Central Committee, Communication, Automobile Transport and Highway Workers' Union, 42 Leninsky Prospekt, Moscow, U.S.S.R.

Kono, Fumihiko, B.ENG.; Japanese business executive; b. 22 Nov. 1896; ed. Tokyo Univ.
Aircraft Designer, Mitsubishi Internal Combustion Engine Mfg. Co. Ltd. 21-45; Gen. Man. First Engineering Works, Mitsubishi Heavy-Industries Ltd. 45, Kawasaki Engineering Works 45-50; Dir. and Gen. Man. Kawasaki Engineering Works, Mitsubishi Nippon Heavy-Industries Ltd. 50-52, Man. Dir. 52-56, Vice-Pres. 56-61, Pres. 61-64; Exec. Vice-Pres. Mitsubishi Heavy Industries Ltd. 64-65, Pres. 65-; Dir. Mitsubishi Shoji Kaisha Ltd., Mitsubishi Steel Co. Ltd., Mitsubishi Atomic Power Industries Inc.; Vice-Pres. Fed. of Econ. Orgs.; Governing Dir. Japan Fed. of Employers' Asscns., The Shipbuilders' Asscn. of Japan; Vice-Pres. The Machinery Fed.; Blue Ribbon Medal.
Mitsubishi Heavy Industries Ltd., 10, 2-chome, Marunouchi, Chiyoda-ku, Tokyo, Japan.

Konoe, Hidemaro; Japanese musician; b. 98; ed. Peers' School, Univ. of Tokyo and in Germany.
Founder and conductor Japanese New Symphony Orchestra (now Japanese Broadcasting Co. Orchestra); Dir. Japanese Philharmonic Society; sometime guest conductor Philadelphia Orchestra, N.B.C. (New York), B.B.C. (London), Berlin Philharmonic, and in Rome, Brussels, Vienna, Prague, Helsinki, Sofia; founded Joho Symphonic Orchestra 45, Konoe Music Research Inst. 45; mem. Japan Acad.
Compositions include symphonies, concert-overtures, *Coronation Cantata*; orchestral transcriptions of old Japanese Court Music, Schubert Quintet, Chopin Concertos.
26 Dai-machi, Akasaka, Minato-ku, Tokyo, Japan.

Konorski, Jerzy, M.D.; Polish neurophysiologist; b. 1 Dec. 1903; ed. Univ. of Warsaw.
Physician in Psychiatric Hospital 29-31; Visiting Scientist in Pavlov's Laboratory, Leningrad 31-33; Scientific Worker, Nencki Inst. of Experimental Biology, Warsaw 34-39; Head, Physiological Dept., Biological Station, Soukchoumi, Caucasus 41-44; Prof. of Physiology, Łódź Univ. 45-55; Dep. Dir. and Head of Dept. of Neurophysiology, Nencki Inst. 46-68, Dir. 68-; corresp. mem. Polish Acad. of Sciences 56, full mem. 66; foreign assoc. Nat. Acad. of Sciences of U.S.A.; Hon. mem. Romanian Acad. of Sciences 65; State Prize 49, 64.
Publs. *Les Principes fondamentaux de la théorie physiologique des mouvements acquis* (with S. Miller) 33, *Conditioned Reflexes and Neuron Organisation* 48, *Integrative Activity of the Brain.*

3 Pasteur Street, Warsaw 22, and 8 Kubanska Street, Warsaw 33, Poland.
Telephone: 222250; 178178.

Konotop, Vassily Ivanovich; Soviet politician; b. 16; ed. Kharkov Machine-Building Inst.
Member Communist Party of Soviet Union 44-; worked Kolomna Engineering Works 42-52; party work, Moscow District 52-59; Chair. Exec. Cttee. Moscow District Council for Deputies of Labour 59-; Cand. mem. Central Cttee. of C.P.S.U. 61-64, mem. 64-; mem. Presidium of Supreme Soviet 66-; Deputy to U.S.S.R. Supreme Soviet.
Moscow Regional Executive Committee of Workers' Deputies, ul. Gorky, 13, Moscow, U.S.S.R.

Konovalov, Nikolai Leontyevich; Soviet politician; b. 1914; ed. Mogilyov Road-Building Technical School and All-Union Forestry Inst. in Leningrad.
Employee of Umsk forestry combine 35-45; mem. C.P.S.U. 40-; consecutively Deputy Sec., Sec., Second Sec., First Sec. Kandalakski City Cttee. of the C.P. 45-51; Sec. Murmansk Regional Cttee. of the C.P. 51-59; Chair. Exec. Cttee. Murmansk Regional Soviet of Workers' Deputies 59-66; First Sec. Murmansk Regional Cttee. of C.P. 66-; Dep. to R.S.F.S.R. Supreme Soviet.
Murmansk Regional Committee of the C.P.S.U., Murmansk, U.S.S.R.

Konovalov, Nikolai Semyonovich; Soviet politician; b. 1907; ed. Higher Party School of the Central Committee of C.P.S.U.
Member Communist Party of Soviet Union 29-; party work, Udmurtsk Autonomous Republic 30-42; Perm. Staff of Central Cttee., C.P.S.U. 43-46, 48-49, 51-55; First Sec. Kalinin Regional and City Cttees. 49-51; Second Sec. Kaliningrad District Cttee. C.P.S.U. 55-61, First Sec. 61-; mem. Central Cttee. C.P.S.U. 61-; Deputy to U.S.S.R. Supreme Soviet.
Kaliningrad District Committee of C.P.S.U., Kaliningrad, U.S.S.R.

Konovalov, Nikolai Vasilyevich; Soviet neuropathologist; b. 1900; ed. Moscow State Univ.
Teacher, Moscow Nervous Diseases Clinic 24-34; Prof. Nervous Diseases, Moscow Medical Inst. 34-36; Dir. Neurological Dept. of Central Clinic 36-47; mem. U.S.S.R. Acad. of Medical Sciences 50-, Vice-Pres. Acad. of Medical Sciences 50-53; Dir. Inst. of Neurology of U.S.S.R. Acad. of Medical Sciences 48-; Lenin Prize 61.
Publs. *Clinical Disseminated Sclerosis* 30, *The Patho-Physiology and Pathology of the Cerebellum* 39, *The Nosological Relationship Between Pseudo-Sclerosis and Wilson's Disease* 27, *Hepatolenticular Degeneration* 37, 38, 40, 48, *Hepatocerebral Dystrophy* 60, *Poliomyelitis Anterior subacuta* 64.
Academy of Medical Sciences, U.S.S.R., 14 Ulitsa Solyanka, Moscow, U.S.S.R.

Konovalov, Sergey, M.A., B.LITT.; British (Russian-born) Slavonic scholar; b. 31 Oct. 1899; ed. Classical Lycée in Moscow and Exeter Coll., Oxford.
Prof. Russian Language and Literature Birmingham Univ. 29-45; Lecturer Slavonic Studies Oxford Univ. 30-45; Hon. Lecturer London Univ. (School of Slavonic Studies) 31-32, 40-41; Prof. Russian Oxford Univ. 45-67, Emeritus 67-; Emeritus Fellow New Coll., Oxford 45.
Publs. *Anthology of Contemporary Russian Literature* 32; editor and contrib. *Birmingham Russian Memoranda* 31-40, co-editor *Birmingham Polish Monographs* 36-39; article on *Soviet Union, Encyclopædia Britannica Year Book* 41; *Russo-Polish Relations—an Historical Survey* (in collaboration) 45; *Oxford and Russia* (Inaugural Lecture) 47; Editor and contributor *Blackwell's Russian Texts* 45-, *Oxford Slavonic Papers* 50-, and *Oxford Russian Readers* 51-.
175 Divinity Road, Oxford, England.

Konrad, Nikolai Josifovich; Soviet philologist; b. 91; ed. Univ. of St. Petersburg.

Lecturer, Kiev Commercial Inst. 13-14; graduate work in Japan and Korea 14-17; Lecturer and then Rector, Orel Univ. 18-21; Prof. Japanese Philology, Univ. of Leningrad and Inst. of Oriental Languages 22-38; mem. Inst. of Oriental Studies, U.S.S.R. Acad. of Sciences 31-; corresp. mem. Acad. of Sciences 34-57, mem. 58-; Prof. Moscow Inst. of Oriental Studies 41-49; two Orders of the Red Banner, two Orders of Lenin.

Numerous publs. on Japanese and Chinese language, literature and history 13-64.

U.S.S.R. Academy of Sciences, Leninski Prospekt 14, Moscow, U.S.S.R.

Konstantinov, Boris Pavlovich; Soviet physicist; b. 10; ed. Leningrad Polytechnical Inst.

Research worker, Leningrad Electrophysical Inst. and elsewhere 30-40; Physicotechnical Inst. U.S.S.R. Acad. of Sciences 40-; Prof. Leningrad Polytechnical Inst. 47-; Corres. mem. U.S.S.R. Acad. of Sciences 53-60, mem. 60-, Vice-Pres. 66-; Dir. Physicotechnical Inst. U.S.S.R. Acad. of Sciences 58-; Vice-Pres. Acad. of Sciences U.S.S.R. 66-; Chief Editor *Technical Physics* 58-; Lenin Prize 59; Hero of Socialist Labour.

Publs. *Some Applications of the Power Continuity Equation in Acoustics, Autovibrations and Sound Formation of Tongue of Harmony, Absorption Sound Waves in Reverberation by Solid Border,* etc.

Physicotechnical Institute, U.S.S.R. Academy of Sciences, Polytechnicheskaya ulitsa 28, Leningrad, U.S.S.R.

Konstantinov, Fedor Vasilevich; Soviet philosopher; b. 1901; ed. Inst. of Red Professors.

Teacher and party worker 32-41; Soviet Army 42-45; Assoc. Inst. of Philosophy, U.S.S.R. Acad. of Sciences 45-62, Dir. 62-; Rector, Acad. of Social Sciences of Central Cttee. of C.P.S.U. 54-55; Head, Dept. of Propaganda and Agitation, Central Cttee. of C.P.S.U. 55-58; Cand. mem. Central Cttee. of C.P.S.U. 56-61; Corresp. mem. U.S.S.R. Acad. of Sciences 53-66, mem. 66-; Academic Sec. Philosophy and Law Branch, Acad. of Sciences U.S.S.R.; Chief Editor *Encyclopaedia of Philosophy*; Order of Lenin.

Institute of Philosophy of U.S.S.R. Academy of Sciences, Volkhonka 14, Moscow, U.S.S.R.

Kony, Mohammed Awad El; United Arab Republic (Egyptian) diplomatist; b. 06.

Consulate, Rome 29-32; Attaché, Washington 37-39; Ministry of Foreign Affairs 39-41; Consul, Bombay 41-43; Second Sec. Moscow 44-46; Ministry of Foreign Affairs 46-49; Counsellor, Washington 49-52; Dir. Political Dept. Ministry of Foreign Affairs 52-55; Ambassador to U.S.S.R. 55-61; Ambassador to U.K. 61-64; Perm. Rep. of U.A.R. to United Nations 64-.

Permanent Mission of the United Arab Republic to the United Nations, 900 Park Avenue, New York 21, N.Y., U.S.A.

Koo, Vi Kyuin Wellington, B.A., M.A., PH.D.; Chinese diplomatist and judge; b. 29 Jan. 1888; ed. Columbia Univ.

Secretary to Pres. of China; Councillor in Foreign Office; Minister to U.S.A. 15; attended Versailles Peace Conf. as China's Plenipotentiary, and later as Head of Chinese Del. 19; Del. to the Assembly and China's Rep. on Council of the L.N. 20-22; Min. to Great Britain 21; Plenipotentiary to Washington Conf. 21-22; Min. of Foreign Affairs, Peking 22-24; Finance Min. 26; Prime Min. and Min. of Foreign Affairs 26-27; mem. of the Int. Court of Arbitration at The Hague 27 and 33; Min. of Foreign Affairs 31; Chinese Assessor to the Comm. of Inquiry of the L.N. 32; Min. to France 32-35; Ambassador to France 36-41; Chinese Rep. on the Council of the L.N. 32-34; Chief Del. to the 13th and 14th Assemblies of the L.N. and to the Special Assem-bly of the L.N. 32-33; Del. to the World Monetary and Economic Conf., London 33; Chief Del. to Assem-blies of the L.N. 35-36 and 38; Del. to Conf. for Reduc-tion and Limitation of Armaments at Geneva 33; Pres. of the 96th Session of League Council 37; Del. to Sessions of League Council 37-39; Chief Del. to Brussels Conf. Nov. 37; Special Ambassador to Belgium 38, the Vatican 39, Portugal 40; Ambassador to Great Britain 41-46; Chinese Ambassador to U.S.A. 46-49, Chinese (Taiwan) Ambassador to U.S.A. 49-56; Del. to the Dumbarton Oaks Conf. 44; Acting Chair. of the Chinese Del. to the San Francisco Conf.; Chair. Chinese Del. to the Preparatory Comm., and the First Session of the UN Gen. Assembly 45-46; Acting Chair. Chinese Del. to UN Assembly 47; Judge, Int. Court of Justice 57-66, Vice-Pres. 64-66; decorations from China, Belgium, Brazil, Chile, France, Greece, Mexico, Portugal, Vatican; Hon. LL.D. from Columbia and Yale Univs., and Univs. of St. John's, Aberdeen, Birmingham, Manchester; L.H.D. (Rollins).

1050 Park Avenue, Apartment 9D, New York, N.Y. 10028, U.S.A.

Köpeczi, Bela; Hungarian publisher and historian of literature; b. 1921; ed. Budapest and Paris Univs.

Publisher 49-53; Vice-Pres., Hungarian Council of Publishing 53-55, Pres. 55-61; Chair., Hungarian Board of Publishing 55; Head, Cultural Dept., Hungarian Socialist Workers' Party 64-66; Prof. Univ. of Budapest; mem. Hungarian Acad. of Sciences.

II Tulipán-u. 5, Budapest, Hungary.

Koper, Daniş; Turkish politician; b. 19 Dec. 1908; ed. Ankara Lycée and Munich Coll. of Technology.

With Water Works Dept. until 48; Technical Dir. Garanti Construction Co. 48-51; Dir. Provincial Bank 50-51; Dir.-Gen. Highways Admin. 51-56; Under-Sec. Ministry of Public Works 56-57; Technical Dir. Verdi Ltd. 57-59; Chair. Asscn. of Chambers of Engineering and Architecture 58-59, Chair. Turkish Airlines 59-60; Minister of Public Works 60; mem. Constitutional Assembly 61; Pres. Kuyas Construction Co. and Bormak Ltd. 60-; Chair. of Ereğli Steel and Iron Factories Co. 61-; Chair. Trustee Middle East Technical Univ., Ankara 59-60, 62-66; Chair. Trustee Ankara Koleji 62-; Chevalier Légion d'Honneur 59.

6 Sokak Nr. 37, Bahçelievler, Ankara, Turkey.
Telephone: 131646 (Ankara).

Kopylov, Alexander Alexandrovich; Soviet conductor; b. 1926; ed. Erevan Conservatoire.

Toured Japan, China, Egypt, America, Canada and Europe with company of Moscow ballet dancers; Conductor, Novosibirsk Theatre of Opera and Ballet 53-63; a conductor of Bolshoi Theatre 63-; Merited Actor of R.S.F.S.R.

State Academic Bolshoi Theatre of the U.S.S.R., 1 Ploshchad Sverdlova, Moscow, U.S.S.R.

Kørbing, Johannes Alfred; Danish company director; b. 16 Nov. 1885; ed. Royal Naval Coll. in Copenhagen, and Technical High School, Charlottenburg.

Lieutenant Engineer 07; Commanding Engineer 12; Sub-Dir. Naval Dockyard 19-21; Technical Dir. The United Steamship Co. 21, Managing Dir. 34-55, Chair. 55-64; Chair. Nat. Bank of Denmark 46-67, The United Breweries Ltd., Tuborg Foundation; Vice-Chair. The Harbour Board of Copenhagen 46-67; mem. Ice Breaking Council 37-55, Danish Acad. Technical Sciences; Chair. and Dir. various other companies and insts.; Chair. Danish Shipping Board 39-49, Danish Shipowners' Asscn. 39-46, Maritime Council 39-46; Knight Commdr. 1st Class Order of Dannebrog, Silver Cross of Order of Dannebrog, Knight Commdr. of Belgian Order of Leopold, of Norwegian Order of St. Olav and of Swedish Nordstjerne Order.

Vestagervej 17, Copenhagen Hellerup, Denmark.
Telephone: Rsyvang 383.

Kordlewski, Kazimierz, D.PHIL.; Polish astronomer; b. 11 Oct. 1903; ed. Univ. of Poznań and Jagellonian Univ. Cracow.
Assistant at Cracow Observatory 24-34, Adjunct 34-39, 45-55, Docent 55-; mem. Int. Astronomical Union 28-; Dir. of Scientific Instruments Section (ZAN) and of Nat. Astronomical Copernicus Inst. (NIA) 39-51; mem. Polish Astronomical Soc. 48-; Pres. Cracow Branch Polish Astronautical Soc. 56-; Chief of Cracow Observation Station for Artificial Satellites 58-; Editor *Eclipsing Binaries Circulars* 60-; discovered new star in 1926 in Corvus constellation, designated today as T-Corvi; discovered two cloud satellites of the Earth 56; discovered dust ring around the Earth 66.
Publs. Approximately 120 papers on astronomy.
Ul. Kopernika 27, Cracow, Poland.
Telephone: Cracow 259-19 and 274-19.

Koren, Stephan, D.ECON.; Austrian university professor and politician; ed. High School and Univ. of Vienna.
Member Austrian Inst. of Econ. Research 45-65; Prof. of Econs. Univ. of Innsbruck 65-; Under-Sec. of State for Econ. Questions, Fed. Chancellery 67-68; Minister of Finance 68-.
Artariastrasse 6, 1170 Vienna, Austria.
Telephone: 463697.

Koretsky, Vladimir Mikhailovich, DR., JUR.; Soviet international lawyer; b. 90; ed. Moscow and Kharkhov Univs.
Scientific research worker and lecturer, Kharkov Univ. 16-20, Prof. of Int. Law and Legal History, Kharkov Law Inst. 20-48; legal adviser of U.S.S.R. dels. to General Assembly of U.N., Council of Foreign Ministers, Paris Peace Conf. 46, and to Security Council; U.S.S.R. rep. on Cttee. on the Progressive Development of Int. Law and its Codification; mem. of Acad. of Sciences Ukrainian S.S.R. 48-, Int. Law Comm. 49-50 (Vice-Chair. 49), Ukrainian S.S.R. del. U.N. Conf. on Law of the Sea 58, 60; Judge, Int. Court of Justice 61-, Vice-Pres. Int. Court of Justice 67-; Vice-Pres. Soviet Asscn. for Int. Law; Order of Lenin.
Publs. Over fifty works on int. law and legal history.
International Court of Justice, The Hague, Netherlands.

Kôri, Yuichi, LL.B.; Japanese politician; b. 16 March 1902; ed. Tokyo Univ.
Governor, Ishikawa Prefecture 47; Deputy Chief Sec. of Cabinet 48-50; mem. House of Councillors 50-; Minister of Home Affairs 57-58; Chair. Discipline Cttee., Liberal Democratic Party 60-62; Minister of Posts and Telecommunications June 65-66.
Publs. *Lectures on New Election System* 48, *Lectures on Secret Protection Law* 54.
19-5, Otsuka 4-chome, Bunkyo-ku, Tokyo, Japan.
Telephone: Tokyo 946-3000.

Korinek, Franz, D.IUR.; Austrian lawyer; b. 20 May 1907; ed. Vienna Univ.
Practised law in Vienna 31-34, 38-47; Leading Sec. Provincial Union of Trades and Commerce of Carinthia 34-38; Rep. Sec.-Gen. Fed. Chamber of Commerce 47-48, Sec.-Gen. 50-66; Minister of Finance 63-64; Dir. Vienna Chamber of Commerce 48-50; Vice-Chair. Pensionsversicherungs-anstalt der Angestellten 48-63; Vice-Pres. Hauptverband der Österreichischen Sozialversicherungsträger 49-63, Chair. Board of Examiners of 2nd and 3rd State Examination, Hochschule für Welthandel, Vienna; Grand Golden Order of Merit of the Austrian Republic; Grand Cross Order of St. Silvester; Commdr. Order of Merit of the Italian Republic, Commdr. Order of the Lion (Finland), Commdr. Order of Orange-Nassau, Grand Cross, 2nd Class, Order of Merit of German Fed. Repub., Grand Officer's Cross Order of Merit of Italian Repub., etc.; People's Party.
A-1060 Vienna, Esterhazygasse 32, Austria.
Telephone: 57-40-105.

Kornberg, Arthur, M.D., D.SC., LL.D., L.H.D.; American biochemist; b. 3 March 1918; ed. City Coll. of New York and Univ. of Rochester.
Commissioned Officer, U.S. Public Health Service 41-42; Nat. Insts. of Health, Bethesda, Md. 42-52; Prof. and Chair. Dept. of Microbiology, Washington Univ. School of Medicine 53-59; Prof. and Head, Dept. of Biochemistry, Stanford Univ. School of Medicine 59-; mem. Nat. Acad. of Sciences, American Philosophical Soc., American Acad. of Arts and Sciences; Nobel Prize in Medicine and Physiology (with Prof. Ochoa) 59; Hon. LL.D., City Coll. of New York 60; D.Sc. (Univs. of Rochester and Pennsylvania), L.H.D. (Yeshiva Univ.) 62.
Publs. Numerous original research papers and reviews on subjects in biochemistry, particularly enzymatic mechanisms of biosynthetic reactions.
Office: Department of Biochemistry, Stanford University School of Medicine, Palo Alto, Calif.; Home: 365 Golden Oak Drive, Portola Valley, Calif., U.S.A.

Korneichuk, Alexander Evdokimovich; Soviet writer and politician; b. 05; ed. Kiev Inst. of Education.
Deputy to Supreme Soviet 37-; Chair. Union of Soviet Writers of Ukraine 38-41, 46-53; Deputy People's Commissar of Foreign Affairs 43-44; People's Commissar of Foreign Affairs, Ukrainian S.S.R. 44; Chair. Cttee. of Cultural Affairs, S.S.R. 44-45; mem. Foreign Affairs Comm., Council of Union 54-; joined Communist Party 40, mem. Central Cttee. 52-; mem. Bureau of Central Cttee. Communist Party of the Ukraine 53-; Chair. Supreme Soviet Ukrainian S.S.R.; mem. Ukrainian Acad. of Sciences 39-; mem. U.S.S.R. Acad. of Sciences 66-; Deputy to U.S.S.R. and Ukrainian S.S.R. Supreme Soviets; Vice-Chair. Union of Nationalities, U.S.S.R. Supreme Soviet; mem. Presidium World Peace Council; mem. Presidential Council U.S.S.R.-France Friendship Soc.; Int. Lenin Prize 60; five State prizes, two Orders of Lenin; Hero of Socialist Labour 67.
Plays: *Stone Island* 29, *Storm* 31, *Death of the Squadron* 33, *Platon Krechet* 34, *Truth* 37, *Bogdan Khmelnitsky* 39, *In the Steppes of the Ukraine* 41, *Front* 42, *Makar Dubrava* 48, *The Hawthorn Grove* 50, *Wings* 54, *Why the Stars Smiled* 57, *Above the Dnieper* 60, *Old Diaries* 64.
Supreme Soviet of Ukrainian S.S.R., Kiev, Ukraine, U.S.S.R.

Kornev, Pyotr Georgievich; Soviet surgeon and tuberculosis specialist; b. 1883; ed. Kiev and Moscow Univ.
Physician, Asst., Prof. 09-35; mem. U.S.S.R. Acad. of Medical Sciences 44-; Head of Dept., Consulting Prof., Leningrad Inst. for Postgraduate Medical Training 32-; Dir. Scientific Dir., Leningrad Inst. of Surgery for Tuberculosis 30-; mem. Editorial Boards *Problems of Tuberculosis, Surgical Review, Orthopedics, Traumatology and Prosthetics*; Hon. mem. Boards of All-Union and All-Russia Scientific Socs. of Phthisiologists; mem. of Board of All-Union Soc. of Surgeons; Hon. mem. of Presidium of Pirogov Surgical Soc.; Hon. Chair. of Leningrad Scientific Soc. of Traumatologists and Orthopedists; mem. Int. Union Against Tuberculosis and Int. Coll. of Surgeons; Order of Lenin 60; Red Banner of Labour 57, 64; Patriotic War, First Class, 45; Honoured Scientist of R.S.F.S.R. 40.
Publ. Over 200 works on complex treatment of bone-and-joint tuberculosis with application of surgery methods; monographs: *Bone-and-Joint Tuberculosis* 51, *Surgery for Bone-and-Joint Tuberculosis* 64.
Institute of Surgery for Tuberculosis, Institutskaya 5, Leningrad, U.S.S.R.

Korniyets, Leonid Romanovich; Soviet politician; b. 1901.
Soviet Army 22-25; mem. Communist Party 26-; Party activity 25-33; Second Sec. Dnepropetrovsk Regional Cttee. C.P. of Ukraine; Chair. Presidium of Ukrainian

S.S.R. Supreme Soviet 38-39; Chair. Ukrainian S.S.R. Council of People's Commissars 39-44, First Deputy 44-50; Cand. mem. Central Cttee. of C.P.S.U. 52-; U.S.S.R. Minister of Procurement 53-56; Deputy Supreme Soviet 54-; Minister of Grain Products 56-61; First Deputy Chair. State Cttee. for Agricultural Supplies 61-63, Chair. 63-; Order of Lenin, Order of Red Banner, Order of Red Banner of Labour, etc.
State Committee for Supplies, 12a Chistoprudny Boulevard, Moscow, U.S.S.R.

Korobin, Leonid Arkadyevich; Soviet diplomatist; b. 1916; ed. Moscow State Librarians' Inst.
Member C.P. Soviet Union 39-; Counsellor, Counsellor-Minister, Soviet Embassy, New Delhi 61-64; Consultant-Expert, Ministry of Foreign Affairs, Moscow 64-65; Amb. to Ceylon 65-.
U.S.S.R. Embassy, Colombo, Ceylon.

Korom, Mihály, LL.D.; Hungarian lawyer and politician; b.1927; ed. Hungarian Socialist Workers' Party Univ.
Farmhand until 45; various police posts 45; mem. Hungarian Socialist Workers' Party 46-; later Dept. Head, Ministry of Interior; Maj.-Gen. and Nat. Commdr. Frontier Guard Force 60-63; Admin. Sec. Central Cttee. Hungarian Socialist Workers' Party 63-66, mem. 63-; Minister of Justice 66-.
Ministry of Justice, Budapest, Hungary.

Korotchenko, Demyan Sergeyevich; Soviet politician; b. 1894; ed. party schools.
Party work 36-38; Chair. Council of People's Commissars, Ukraine 38-39; Sec. Central Cttee. of Ukraine Communist Party 39-47; Chair. Council of Ministers, Ukraine 47-53; Chair. Presidium of Supreme Soviet of Ukraine 54-; mem. C.P.S.U. 18-, mem. Cen. Cttee. of C.P.S.U. 39-; mem. Politburo of Ukraine C.P. 40-, Deputy Chair. Presidium of Supreme Soviet of U.S.S.R.; Hero of Socialist Labour.
Presidium of Ukrainian S.S.R. Supreme Soviet, Kiev, U.S.S.R.

Korry, Edward M.; American journalist and diplomatist; b. 7 Jan. 1922; ed. Washington and Lee Univ. and Harvard Graduate School of Business Management.
National Broadcasting Company 42; United Press, New York 43-47, London 47, Chief Corresp. for U.N. 48, for Eastern Europe (Belgrade) 48-50, Man. for Germany 51, for France 52, Chief European Corresp. 54; European Editor, *Look* magazine 55-60; Asst. to Gardner Cowles and Pres. Cowles Magazine and Broadcasting Inc. 60-63; Amb. to Ethiopia 63-67, to Chile 67-; apptd. by Pres. Johnson to review U.S. policies in Africa 66.
American Embassy, Santiago, Chile.

Korth, Fred, A.B., LL.B.; American banker, lawyer and government official; b. 9 Sept. 1909; ed. Texas and George Washington Univs.
Admitted to Bar 35; law practice Fort Worth 35-62; Dep. Counsellor, Dept. of the Army 51-52, Asst. Sec. of Army 52-53; Consultant to Sec. of Army 53-60; Exec. Vice-Pres. Continental Nat. Bank, Fort Worth 53-59, Pres. 59-62; Sec. of the Navy 62-64; fmr. Dir. All States Life Insurance Co., Bell Aerospace Corpn., T. & P. Railway; mem. American Bar Asscn., American Law Inst., American Bankers' Asscn., Nat. Council Nat. Planning Asscn; recipient of Exceptional Civilian Service Award, Army Dept. 53; Dir. Fischbach and Moore, Southwest Nat. Bank of El Paso, American Air Filter Co.
407 Barr Building, Farragut Square, Washington, D.C. 20006, U.S.A.
Telephone: 202-223-3630.

Korthals, Hendrik Albertus; Netherlands politician; b. 3 July 1911; ed. Rotterdam Economic High School.
Editor *Nieuwe Rotterdamse Courant* 36-40; official,

Ministry for Trade, Shipping and Industry 40-45; mem. of Parl. 45-59; mem. Cons. Assembly of Council of Europe 49-59; Parl. Coal and Steel Community and European Parl. 49-59; Deputy Premier and Minister of Transport and Waterways 59-63; mem. Council of State; Chair. of Board Netherlands Org. for Int. Assistance; Liberal.
63 Witte Singel, Leiden, Netherlands.

Kortner, Fritz; Austrian actor and theatrical director; b. 12 May 1892; ed. Akad. f. Musik u. darstellende Kunst, Vienna.
Former mem. Berlin Schauspielhaus Company; European tours 33-38; in U.S.A. 38-48; returned to Germany 47; roles include Shylock, Hamlet, Othello, Macbeth, Richard III; has directed productions of *Don Carlos, The Rose Tattoo, Minna von Barnhelm, Tod des Handelsreisenden, Waiting for Godot, Das Dunkel ist licht genug, Julius Caesar, Hamlet, Faust, Twelfth Night,* etc.; has appeared in the German films *Die Brüder Karamasoff, Atlantik, Die Affaire Dreyfus, Der Ruf,* and also in American films; dir. the films *Der brave Sünder, So ein Mädel vergisst man nicht, Die Stadt ist voller Geheimnisse, Um Thron und Liebe;* has acted and produced in Munich and Berlin since return to Germany; Grosses Bundesverdienstkreuz mit Stern 57.
Publs. Play: *Waves of the Danube, Autobiography.*
St.-Anna-Platz 2, Munich, German Federal Republic.

Kortunov, Alexei Kirillovich; Soviet politician; b. 07; ed. Novocherkass Engineering Inst.
Member C.P.S.U. 39-; econ. work 36-41; Soviet army service 41-48; with Ministry of Oil Industry 48-50, 53-55; Dep. Minister of Oil Industry 50-53; Dep. Minister, Oil Industry Building Enterprises 55, Minister 55-57; Chief, Gas Industry Board, U.S.S.R. 57-65; Minister of Gas Industry 65-; Cand. mem. Central Cttee. C.P.S.U. 61-; Deputy to U.S.S.R. Supreme Soviet; Hero of the Soviet Union 45.
U.S.S.R. Ministry of Gas Industry, 13 Kirova ulitsa, Moscow, U.S.S.R.

Korytkov, Nikolai Gavrilovich; Soviet politician; b. 10; ed. Agricultural Inst., Leningrad.
Agronomist 31-37; econ. work 37-41, 45-56; Soviet Army 41-45; Sec., Second Sec. Leningrad District Cttee., C.P.S.U. 56-60; First Sec. Kalinin District Cttee., C.P.S.U. 60-; mem. C.P.S.U. 39-. mem. Central Cttee. of C.P.S.U. 61-; Deputy to U.S.S.R. Supreme Soviet; mem. Mandate Cttee., Soviet of Union.
Kalinin Regional Committee of the Communist Party of the Soviet Union, Kalinin, U.S.S.R.

Koryukin, Nikolay Ivanovich; Soviet diplomatist; b. 1915; ed. Gorky Pedagogic Inst.
Diplomatic Service 44-; Deputy Head First European Dept. 48-49, 60-62; Counsellor, Switzerland 49-52, France 52-53; Deputy Head Dept., Ministry of Foreign Affairs 53-57; Counsellor-Minister, France 57-59; Ambassador to Switzerland 59-60, to Greece 62-.
U.S.S.R. Embassy, Irodu Attiku 7, Athens, Greece.

Korzhinskii, Dmitrii Sergeevich; Soviet geologist; b. 13 Sept. 1899; ed. Leningrad Mining Inst.
Geologist, All-Union Geological Inst., Leningrad 25-37; Asst. Prof., Prof. Leningrad Mining Inst. 29-40; Senior Scientific Collaborator, Inst. of the Geology of Ore Deposits, Petrography, Mineralogy and Geochemistry (I.G.E.M.), Acad. of Sciences of U.S.S.R. 37-, Head of Section of Matasomatism and Metamorphism, I.G.E.M. 56-; Corresp. mem. U.S.S.R. Acad. of Sciences 43-53, mem. 53-; Hon. Fellow Geological Soc. of America 59; mem. Geological Soc. of London 62; Vice-Pres. Int. Mineralogical Asscn. 65; Vice-Pres. U.S.S.R. Mineralogical Soc. 64-; U.S.S.R. State Prize for Science 46, Lenin Prize 58.
Publs. *Factors of Mineral Equilibria and Mineralogical Facies of Depth* 40, *Regularities of Mineral Associations*

in Archean Rocks of E. Siberia 45, *Formation of Skarn Deposits* 45, *Bimetasomatic Phlogopite and Lazurite Deposits of the Archean of Baikal Region* 47, *Petrology of Turja Skarn Deposits of Copper* 48, *Outline of Metasomatic Processes* 53, 55, *Physicochemical Basis of the Analysis of the Parageneses of Minerals* 57, 59.
Institute of the Geology of Ore Deposits, Petrography, Mineralogy and Geochemistry (I.G.E.M.) of U.S.S.R. Academy of Sciences, Staromonetny per. 35, Moscow, Zh-17 U.S.S.R.

Kos-Anatolsky, Anatoli Iosifovich; Soviet composer; b. 1909; ed. Lvov Conservatoire.
Chairman Lvov Branch Ukrainian Composers' Union; mem. Board Ukrainian Composers' Union; Merited Worker Arts Ukraina, Orders of Red Banner of Labour 51, of Lenin 60, State Prize 51.
Principal compositions: Opera: *Dawn* 57; Ballets: *Dovbush's Shawl* 51, *The Jay's Wing* 57; Choral Works include: *New Verkhovina, From Moscow to the Carpathians, In the Carpathian Mountains, Encounter in the Field, Gutsuli Waltz;* Other works include: Concerto for harp and orchestra, *Transcarpathian Rhapsody for Violin and Piano, Cheerful Daydreams* (Operetta).
Lvov Branch, Ukrainian Composers' Union, 7 Tchaikovsky Street, Lvov, U.S.S.R.

Kosaka, Zentaro; Japanese politician; b. 23 Jan. 1913; ed. Tokyo Univ. of Commerce.
Mitsubishi Bank 35-39; Dir. Shinetsu Chemical Industry Co. 40-45; elected to House of Reps. 46; Parl. Vice-Minister of Finance 47; Chair. Budget Cttee. 50; Adviser, Policy Research Council, Liberal Party 51, Dep. Chair. Liberal Party Diet Members' Council 51; Minister of Labour 53; Minister of Foreign Affairs July 60-July 62; Liberal-Democrat.
No. 26, 2-Chome, Denenchofu, Oja-Ku, Tokyoto, Japan.

Koschnick, Hans Karl-Heinrich; German politician; b. 2 April 1929; ed. Mittelschule.
Worked in Ministry of Labour concerning prisoners of war 45; local Govt. official, Bremen 45-51 and 54-63; Trade Union Sec. of the Union of Public Employees, Transport and Communications 51-54; mem. Social-Democratic Party 50-; mem. Provincial Diet (Landtag) and City Admin. 55-63; Senator for the Interior 63-67; Deputy of the Fed. Council (Bundesrat) 63-65; Mayor of Bremen 65-; Pres. of the Senate, Bremen 67-.
28 Bremen, Meinkenstrasse 1, German Federal Republic.
Telephone: 320011.

Koshevoi, General Pyotr Kirillovich; Soviet army officer; b. 04; ed. Frunze Military Acad.
Soviet army 20-; mem. C.P.S.U. 25-; Div. and Corps Commdr. 41-45; First Dep. C.-in-C. Soviet Forces, German Democratic Republic 55-57, C.-in-C. 65-; Area Military Commdr. 57-65; Cand. mem. Central Cttee. C.P.S.U. 61-66, mem. 66-; Deputy to U.S.S.R. Supreme Soviet; Hero of Soviet Union (twice); Order of Lenin (five times), Suvorov, Kutuzov (twice), Bogdan Khmelnitsky, Red Banner (twice).
Ministry of Defence, 34 Maurice Thorez Embankment, Moscow, U.S.S.R.

Koske, Theophilus; Kenyan teacher and diplomatist; b. 28; ed. Alliance High School and Makerere Coll.
Science teacher 57-61; commenced political work 60; Clerk County Council 62-63, Ambassador to the U.A.R. Dec. 63-.
Embassy of Kenya, 7 Ahmed El-Melehy Street, Dokki, Cairo, United Arab Republic.

Koskimies, (Kaarlo) Rafael; Finnish literary critic; b. 9 Feb. 1898; ed. Helsinki State Univ.
Lecturer in Finnish Literature, Helsinki Univ. 26-38, Prof. of Aesthetics and Modern Literature 39-61, Prof. Emeritus 61-; mem. Board Otava Publishing Co. 43-, of Finnish Nat. Theatre, Chair. 48-60, of Society of Finnish Literature 46-; mem. Finnish Acad. of Science and Letters, Pres. 63-64; Emil Aaltonen Foundation Prize 50.
Publs. *Fredrik Cygnaeus* 23, 25, *Raunioiden romantiikka* (The Romantic Ruins) 30, *Walter Scott* 31, *Theorie des Romans* 35, *Saksalaisen kirjallisuuden historia* (A History of German Literature) 36, *Yleinen runousoppi* (General Poetics) 37, *Elävä kansalliskirjallisuus* (Living National Literature) 44, 46, 49, *Suomen Kansallisteatteri* (Finnish National Theatre) 53, *Helsinki ja Härjänvatsa* 53, *Porthanin aika* (The Times of Porthan) 56, *Maailman kirjallisuus* (World Literature) 63-65, *Der nordische Faust* 65, *Yrjö Koskinen* 68, *Der nordische Dekadent* 68.
12 Luther Str., Helsinki 10, Finland.

Košler, Zdeněk; Czechoslovak conductor; b. 25 March 1928; ed. Acad. of Music and Dramatic Arts, Prague.
In concentration camp during Second World War; Guest Conductor, Prague Nat. Theatre 51-; Artistic Dir. Olomouc Opera 58-60; Chief, Ostrava Opera 61-; Asst. Conductor, New York Philharmonic Orchestra 63-64; F.O.K. Orchestra, Prague 66-67; Chief Conductor Berlin Comic Opera 67-; Award for Outstanding Work 58; First Prize in young conductors' competition, Besançon 56, First Prize and Gold Medal, D. Mitropoulos Int. Competition, New York 63.
c/o Komische Oper, Berlin, Germany; Prague 4, M. Pujmanove 882, Czechoslovakia.
Telephone: Berlin 22-23-80 and 22-57-61; Prague 435-80-32.

Kospanov, Shapet Kospanovich; Soviet politician; b. 1914; ed. Alma Ata Veterinary Inst.
Member C.P.S.U. 44-; Veterinary Surgeon 36-57; at Kazakhstan Ministry of Agriculture 57-59; Sec., then Second Sec. Kustanai Regional Cttee. 59-61; First Sec. Urals Regional Cttee. Kazakhstan C.P. 61-; mem. Central Cttee. Kazakhstan C.P.; mem. C.P.S.U. Central Cttee. 66-; Deputy to U.S.S.R. Supreme Soviet; mem. Cttee. of U.S.S.R. Parl. Group.
Urals Regional Committee, Communist Party of Kazakhstan, Uralsk, U.S.S.R.

Kostandov, Leonid Arkadyevich; Soviet chemical engineer and politician; b. 1915; ed. Moscow Inst. of Chemical Engineering.
Formerly worked at large chemical combines, Central Asia; Chair. State Cttee. for Chemical Industry until 65; Minister of Chemical Industry 65-; Deputy to U.S.S.R. Supreme Soviet; Alternating mem. C.P.S.U. Cen. Cttee.; State and Lenin prizes and other decorations.
Ministry of Chemical Industry, Moscow, U.S.S.R.

Kostelanetz, André; American (Russian-born) conductor; ed. St. Peter's School, and Conservatoire, St. Petersburg.
Conductor of his own orchestra for the Columbia Broadcasting System; organised and conducted tours of army orchestras in North Africa, Persian Gulf area and Italy 44, China, Burma and India 44-45; Guest Conductor with New York Philharmonic, Boston Symphony, Philadelphia, San Francisco Symphony and numerous other leading orchestras in the U.S.A., Canada, Europe, Israel and South America; Hon. Mus.D. (Albion Coll., Michigan, Cincinnati Conservatory of Music).
c/o Columbia Broadcasting System, 485 Madison Avenue, New York 22, N.Y., U.S.A.

Kostenko, Mikhail Polievktovich; Soviet electrical engineer; b. 1899; ed. Petrograd Polytechnical Inst.
Petrograd Polytechnical Inst. 18-30; Prof. at Central Asian Industrial Inst. 41-44; Corresp. mem. U.S.S.R. Acad. of Sciences 39-53, mem. 53-; Dir. Leningrad Branch, U.S.S.R. Acad of Sciences Inst. of Automation and Telemechanics 50-55; Hon. Scientific and Technical Worker of Uzbek S.S.R. 44-; Deputy to U.S.S.R. Supreme Soviet 58; Dir. Inst. of Electromechanics,

U.S.S.R. Acad. of Sciences 56-; State Prize 49, 51, Lenin Prize 58; Order of Lenin (twice), Red Banner of Labour (twice).
Publs. *Alternating Current Commutator Machines* 33, *Electrical Machines* 44-49, *Electrical Machine Building* 53 and numerous other publications.
Institute of Electromechanics, 18 Dvorzovaya Embankment, Leningrad, U.S.S.R.

Koster, Henri Johan de, M.P.; Netherlands industrialist; b. 5 Nov. 1914; ed. Amsterdam Univ. and in London, Dublin and New York.
With Meelfabriek De Sleutels 37-, Managing Dir. 39-; Netherlands Commr. in New York, Food Purchasing Bureau 45; Pres. Federation of Netherlands' Employers, Union des Industries de la Communauté Européenne (UNICE); Bronzen Leeuw, Officer Order of Orange-Nassau.
Office: Lange Voorhout 35, The Hague; Home: Deroemer, Wassenaar, Netherlands.
Telephone: The Hague 184085 (Office); Wassenaar 9898 (Home).

Koster, Willem, DR. ECON.; Netherlands economist; and banker; b. 24 Sept. 1911; ed. Neths. School of Economics, Rotterdam.
Civil servant Neths. and Neths. East Indies Govts., The Hague and Batavia 36-46; Alternate Exec. Dir., Int. Bank for Reconstruction and Development and of Int. Monetary Fund for the Netherlands, Norway and the Union of South Africa 46-49; Treasurer-Gen. of the Neths., The Hague 49-51; Int. Bank for Reconstruction and Development 51-53; Gen. Man. Netherlands Bank of South Africa Ltd. 53-65; Lecturer Econs., Univ. of Natal, Durban 66-67; Econ. Adviser The Hague; Knight Order of Netherlands Lion.
7 Sÿzenlaan, The Hague, Netherlands.
Telephone: 070-394189.

Kostiuk, Platon Grigorievich; Soviet physiologist; b. 1924; ed. Kiev Univ., Kiev Medical Inst.
Research Assoc. Head of Dept. Inst. of Physiology at Kiev Univ. 46-58; Head of Dept. Bogomolets Inst. of Physiology, Acad. of Sciences, Ukrainian S.S.R. 58-; mem. C.P.S.U. 47-; Corresp. mem. U.S.S.R. Acad. of Sciences 66-.
U.S.S.R. Academy of Sciences, 14 Lenin Prospekt, Moscow, U.S.S.R.

Kostousov, Anatoly Ivanovich; Soviet politician; b. 1906; ed. Moscow Machine Tool and Instrument Building Inst.
Member C.P.S.U. 25-; with machine toolbuilding enterprises 33-46; Deputy Minister Machine Tool Bldg. 46-49; Minister 49-53; Deputy Minister Machine Bldg. 53-54; Minister Machine Toolbuilding and Instruments Industries 54-57; Chair. Moscow Econ. Council 57-59; Chair. State Cttee. for Automation and Machinebuilding 59-65; Minister of Machine Tool Bldg. and Tool-Making Industry 65-; mem. Cen. Cttee. of C.P.S.U.; Deputy to U.S.S.R. Supreme Soviet.
Ministry of Machine Tool Building, 20 Gorki Street, Moscow, U.S.S.R.

Kostrzewski, Józef, PH.D.; Polish archæologist; b. 25 Feb. 1885; ed. Wrocław, Cracow and Berlin Univs.
Prof. Lwów Univ. 18, Poznań Univ. 19; organised Inst. of Prehistory, Poznań Univ.; in hiding during German occupation; Prof. Poznań Univ. 45-50, 56-60; mem. fmr. Polish Acad. of Learning; mem. Polish Acad. of Sciences, Warsaw and Poznań Scientific Socs.; Founder Pres. Polish Archaeological Soc.; Dr. h.c. Jagiellonian Univ., Cracow, Mickiewicz Univ., Poznań.
Publs. *Wielkopolska w Pradziejach* (Wielkopolska in Prehistory) 14, *Od mezolitu do wędrówek ludów* (From the Mesolithic Age to the Migrations of Peoples) 39-48, *Les Origines de la Civilisation polonaise* 47, *Pradzieje Polski* (Prehistory of Poland) 49, *Kultura Łużycka*

na Pomorzu (Lusatian Culture in Pomerania) 58, *Zur Frage der Siedlungsstetigkeit in der Vorgeschichte Polens* 64.
Poznań 15, Biskupinska 1, Poland.

Kosygin, Alexei Nikolaevich; Soviet politician; b. 20 Feb. 1904; ed. Leningrad Textile Inst. and Leningrad Co-operative Technical School.
Worked in Irkutsk Regional Co-operative Union and other co-operative organisations 24-29; Shop Superintendent Zhelyabov Factory, Leningrad 35-37; Dir. October Textile Mills, Leningrad 37-38; Man. Industrial and Transport Dept., C.P.S.U. Leningrad Regional Cttee. 38; Chair. Leningrad City Soviet of Workers' Deputies 38-39; People's Commissar of Textile Industry 39-40; Vice-Chair. Council of People's Commissars 40-46; Chair. Council People's Commissars R.S.F.S.R. 43-46; Minister of Finance 48; Minister of Light Industry 48-53; Minister of Consumer Goods Production 53-54; mem. Communist Party 27-; candidate-mem. Politburo 46-48 mem. Politburo 48-52, mem. Central Cttee. 39-; Deputy Supreme Soviet 38-; mem. of Presidium of Central Cttee. Communist Party until 66, Politburo 66-; Vice-Chair. U.S.S.R. Council of Ministers 57-60, 1st Vice-Chair. 60-64, Chair. 64-; Chair. State Planning Comm. 59-60; Order of Lenin (thrice), Order of Red Banner, Hero of Socialist Labour.
Council of Ministers, The Kremlin, Moscow, U.S.S.R.

Kotarbinski, Tadeusz, DR. PHIL.; Polish university professor; b. 31 March 1886; ed. Univ. of Lwów.
Lecturer in Philosophy, Univ. of Warsaw 18, Extraordinary Prof. 19-29, Ordinary Prof. 29-, Dean of Faculty of Letters 29; Rector Univ. of Łódź 45-49; Pres. Polish Acad. of Sciences 57-62; Pres. Polish Philosophical Soc.; Dr. Phil. h.c., Univs. of Brussels, Łódź, Cracow and Florence; mem. of Moscow, Sofia and Ulan Bator Acads. of Science, British Acad., Acad. Serbe; Commdr. Légion d'Honneur.
Publs. *Szkice praktyczne* (Practical Sketches) 13, *Elementy teorii poznania, logiki formalnej i metodologii nauk* (Elements of the Theory of Cognition, Formal Logic and Methodology of Science) 29, 61, *Traktat o dobrej robocie* (Tractate on Efficiency) 55, 58, 65; *Wykłady z dziejów logiki* (Lectures on the History of Logic) 57, *Wybór pism* (Selected Works) Vol. I 57, Vol. II 58, *Kurs logiki* (Manual of Logic) 51, 53, 55, 60, 61, 63, *Sprawność i Błąd* (Efficiency and Error) 56, 57, 60, 66, *Leçons sur l'histoire de la logique* 64, *Praxiology* 65, *Gnosiology* 66, *Medytacjl o zycin godziwym* (On the Right Way of Living) 67.
Ul. Karowa 14/16 m. 18, Warsaw 1, Poland.
Telephone: 26-57-33.

Kotchian, A. Carl, B.S., M.B.A.; American aircraft executive; b. 17 July 1914; ed. Stanford Univ.
Accountant, Price, Waterhouse & Co., Los Angeles 36-40; Budget Man., Vega Airplane Co., Burbank, Calif., 41-43; Budget Man., Chief Cost Accountant, Lockheed Aircraft Corpn. 43-51, successively Dir. Financial Operations, Dir. Admin., Asst. Mfg. Man., Asst. Gen. Man. Georgia Div. 51-56, Vice-Pres. and Gen. Man. Georgia Div. 56-59; Group Vice-Pres., Lockheed Aircraft Corpn. 59-65, Exec. Vice-Pres. 65-67, Pres. 67-.
Lockheed Aircraft Corporation, 2555 N. Hollywood Way, Burbank, Calif. 91503; Home: 283 Bel Air Road, Los Angeles, Calif. 90024, U.S.A.
Telephone: 213-847-6591 (Office).

Kotelawela, Col. the Rt. Hon. Sir John Lionel, K.B.E., C.H., P.C., J.P.; Ceylonese politician; b. 4 April 1897; ed. Christ's Coll., Cambridge, and Royal Coll., Colombo.
Mem. State Council 31; helped in foundation of United National Party, Pres. until 58; Minister for Agriculture and Lands 33; Minister for Communications and Works 35; Minister for Transport and Works 47-53; Leader of the House, Parl. of Ceylon 50-56; Prime Minister and

Minister of Defence 53-56; Privy Councillor 54; Grand Cross Legion of Honour and numerous other decorations; Hon. LL.D. (Univ. of Ceylon).
Publ. *An Asian Prime Minister's Story* 56.
Kandawala, Kotelawalapura, Ratmalana, Ceylon; Brogues Wood, Biddenden, Kent, England.

Kotelnikov, Vladimir Aleksandrovich; Soviet radio and electronics engineer; b. 08; ed. Power Engineering Inst., Moscow.
Instructor and Dean, Radio Engineering Faculty, Moscow Power Engineering Inst. 31-47, Head, Chair. of Radio Engineering Principles, Moscow Power Engineering Inst. 47-; Deputy Dir. Inst. of Radio Engineering and Electronics, U.S.S.R. Acad. of Sciences 53-54, Dir. 54-; mem. U.S.S.R. Acad. of Sciences 53-; Foreign mem. Czechoslovak Acad. of Sciences; Editor-in-Chief *Radio-engineering and Electronics*; State Prize 43, 46; Lenin Prize 64.
Institute of Radio Engineering and Electronics, U.S.S.R. Academy of Sciences, 18 Prospekt Marxa, Moscow, U.S.S.R.

Kothris, Emmanuel; Greek politician; b. 26 Nov. 1904; ed. Athens Univ. Law School.
Ministry of Justice 25; lawyer, Athens 26-; Pres. Panhellenic Liberal Youth Org. 28-35; political imprisonment 35; mem. Resistance 40-44; escaped to Cairo 44; Head of Political Bureau of Prime Minister 44; Deputy for Liberal Party 46-61, Centre Union 61-; Under-Sec. to Prime Minister's Office and for Press 51; Minister of Transport 51; Minister to Prime Minister and Minister of Social Welfare 65; Minister of Commerce 65-66; Pres. Greek-Czechoslovak League; Vice-Pres. Greek-American Cultural Inst.
c/o Ministry of Commerce, Athens, Greece.

Kotsonis, Archbishop Ieronymos; Greek ecclesiastic.
Former Prof. of Canon Law, Univ. of Salonica; Chaplain to Greek Royal Family 49-; Archbishop of Athens and Primate of Greece, May 67-.
Archiepiscopal Palace, Philotheis 21, Athens, Greece.

Kott, Jan., PH.D.; Polish literary critic; b. 27 Oct. 1914.
Professor of History of Polish Literature, Univ of Warsaw; Visiting Prof. at Yale; Visiting Prof. at Univ. of Calif. 67-68; Herder Award, Vienna 64, Hon. mem. Modern Language Asscn.
Publs. *Mitologia i realizm* (Mythology and Realism) 46, *Szkoła klasyków* (The School of the Classics) 49, *Jak wam się podoba* (As You Like It) 55, *Postęp i głupstwo* (Progress and Folly) 56, *Szkice o Szekspirze* (Essays on Shakespeare) 61, *Shakespeare, notre contemporain* (French trans.) 62, *Miarka za miarkę* (Measure for Measure) 62, *Shakespeare, Our Contemporary* (English trans.) 64, *Szekspir Wspołczesny* 65, *Aloes* 66.
Aleja Róz 6, Warsaw, Poland.

Kotzina, Vinzenz, LL.D.; Austrian lawyer and politician; b. 30 March 1908; ed. Universität Wien and Université de Fribourg, Switzerland.
Lawyer's assistant 33-35; Secr. of Lower Austrian Branch, Fed. of Austrian Trade Unions 35; Leader of Upper Austrian Branch, Traders' Fed. 35; Mil. service 41-45; Man. Dir. Upper Austrian Chamber of Commerce 46-62; mem. Nationalrat 62-; State Sec., Ministry of Trade and Reconstruction 63-66; Minister without Portfolio 66, Minister of Works and Technology 66-; People's Party.
Ministry of Works and Technology, Stubenring 1, A-1010 Vienna, Austria.
Telephone: 57-56-55.

Koucky, Vladimir; Czechoslovak politician; b. 13 Dec. 1920; ed. Secondary School, Jaroměř.
Member C.P. of Czechoslovakia 38-; with underground Party orgs. 39-45; mem. illegal Central Cttee., C.P. of Czechoslovakia 44; mem. Central Cttee., C.P. of Czechoslovakia 45-48, 53-; Deputy Editor-in-Chief *Rudé právo* 45-53, Editor-in-Chief 55-58; Sec. Central Cttee., C.P. of Czechoslovakia 58-68; Chair. Ideological Comm. of Central Cttee. 63-65, Legal Comm. of Central Cttee. 64-68; mem. Ideological Comm. of Central Cttee. 63-68; Amb. to U.S.S.R. 68-; Deputy, Nat. Assembly 45-; mem. Presidium, Nat. Assembly 60-68; Order of Labour 57, and other decorations.
Embassy of Czechoslovakia, Ul. Iuliusa Fuchika 12/14, Moscow, U.S.S.R.

Koun, Karolos; Greek theatre producer, director and actor; b. 13 Sept. 1908; ed. Robert Coll., Constantinople, and Univ. of Paris.
Professor of English Literature, Athens Coll. 29; Founder *Laiki Skini* (popular stage) 34-36; Theatre Dir. Athens 39-41, Greek Nat. Theatre 50-53; Founder *Theatron Technis* (Art Theatre) 42, Dir. and Producer 42-; World Theatre Season, London; Produced Aristophanes' *Birds* 64-65, Aeschylus' *Persae* 65 and Aristophanes' *Frogs* 67; Dir. *Romeo and Juliet*, Stratford-upon-Avon 67; Royal Order of Golden Phoenix.
Art Theatre, Stadium Street, Athens, Greece.

Kounzika, Emmanuel; Angolan politician; b. 25; ed. Salvation Army School, Athénée Royal, Léopoldville, Collège Albert I and Institut National d'Etudes Politiques (both Léopoldville).
Commercial Sec. 48-63, Gen. Sec. Etablissements Madail 57-63; Vice-Pres. Democratic Party of Angola (P.D.A.), Vice-Pres. Revolutionary Gov. of Angola in Exile (GRAE) 63-; Publisher *Mondo*.
P.O. Box 1541, Kinshasa, Congo Republic.

Kourganoff, Vladimir, D.SC.; Russian-born French astronomer; b. 12; ed. Lycée Saint-Louis, Sorbonne, Astrophysical Insts. of Paris and Oslo.
Scholar, Centre Nat. de la Recherche Scientifique 38-42, Research Fellow 42-52; Exchange Prof. Oslo Univ. 46-48; Dir. Astronomical Laboratory, Science Faculty, Lille Univ. 52-61, Prof. Univ. of Paris (Orsay) 61-.
Publs. *La part de la mécanique céleste dans la découverte de Pluton, L'ion H– dans le Soleil, Basic methods in transfer problems, La Recherche Scientifique, Astronomie Fondementale Elémentaire, Initiation à la Théorie de la Relativité, Introduction à la Théorie générale du Transfert des Particules.*
20 Avenue Paul Appell, Paris 14e, France.
Telephone: 402-5366 (Paris).

Kouyoumzelis, Theodore; Greek physicist; b. 1 Dec. 1906; ed. Univs. of Athens, Munich, Manchester and Heidelberg.
Assistant Prof. Physics, Athens Univ. 37-49, Prof. Extraordinary 49-58; Prof. Royal Naval Acad. 47-; Prof. Physics, Athens Nat. Tech. Univ. 58-, Dean 61-; Sec.-Gen. Greek Atomic Energy Comm. 53-60; Perm. Rep. of Greece to CERN; Commdr. Orders of Phoenix and of George I.
Publs. *Alternating Currents* 45, 58, *Nuclear Physics* 47, *Theoretical Electricity* 48, 57, *Wave Theory* 48, *Elements of Nuclear Physics* 60, *Elements of Physics* (3 vols. with S. Peristerakis) 60-62; articles in learned journals.
Office: National Tech. University, Athens 147; Home: Pindou 23, Philothei, Athens, Greece.
Telephone: 61-92-379 (Office); 684-993 (Home).

Kovács, Dénes; Hungarian violinist; b. 1930; ed. Budapest Acad. of Music under Ede Zathureczky.
First Violinist, Budapest State Opera 51-60; leading Violin Prof. at Budapest Music Acad. 57-, Dir. of Budapest Music Acad. 67-; concert tours all over Europe, in China and Japan; Kossuth Prize 63.
Music Academy, Budapest VI, Liszt Ferenc tér 2; Home: Budapest IX, Tolbuhin Körut 5, Hungary.
Telephone: 224-446 (Office); 183-822 (Home).

Kovács, Imre; Hungarian politician; b. 1914; ed. secondary school.
Started work as baker; entered Trade Union and Working-Class Movements 37; imprisoned for participation in independence movement 42; joined armed resistance 44; mem. Hungarian C.P. 45-; Gen.-Sec. Food Industry Workers' Union 45-49; Deputy Minister of Food 50, then of Supply; Minister of Food 57-67; Order of Labour 64.
c/o Ministry of Food, Budapest, Hungary.

Koval, Ivan Grigorievich; Soviet politician; b. 13; ed. Communist Agricultural Inst.
Member C.P.S.U. 38-; party and econ. work 37-41; Soviet army service 41-46; party work 46-; Apparatus, Central Cttee. C.P.S.U. 54-61; Second Sec. Central Cttee. C.P. Tadjikstan 61-; Cand. mem. Central Cttee. C.P.S.U. 61-; Deputy to U.S.S.R. Supreme Soviet.
Central Committee of the Communist Party of Tadjikstan, Dushanbe, U.S.S.R.

Kovalenko, Aleksandr Vlasovich; Soviet politician; b. 1909; ed. Agricultural Communist Univ. Kharkov.
Member C.P.S.U. 31-; Dep. Dir., Dir. Motor Traction Station, Kharkov District 37-39; Parl. work 39-41; Partisan Sec. Underground Regional Cttee. C.P. Ukraine, Kharkov 41-43; party work 44-55; Parl. work 55-60; First Sec. Belgorod District Cttee. C.P.S.U. 60-62, Orenburg Agricultural Cttee., C.P.S.U. 62-64, Orenburg District Cttee. C.P.S.U. 64-; mem. Central Cttee. of C.P.S.U. 61-; Hero of Socialist Labour.
Orenburg District Committee of C.P.S.U., Orenburg, U.S.S.R.

Kovalev, Andrei Efimovich; Soviet diplomatist; b. 23 Feb. 1915; ed. Moscow State Univ.
Diplomatic Service 46-; Head of Dept. for Scandinavian Countries, U.S.S.R. Ministry of Foreign Affairs 62-65; Ambassador to Finland 65-.
U.S.S.R. Embassy, Tehtaenkatu 1B, Helsinki, Finland. Telephone: 61866.

Kovanov, Pavel Vasilievich; Soviet politician; b. 1907; ed. Lenin State Pedagogical Inst. and Higher Party School.
Chairman, Collective Farm, Moscow Region 30-31; with Commissariat of Educ. 31-42; mem. C.P.S.U. 40-; Soviet army service 42-44; Perm. Staff Cen. Cttee. C.P.S.U. 44-56; Second Sec. Cen. Cttee. C.P. Georgia 56-63; Deputy Chair. Cttee. for Party-State Control, Cen. Cttee. of C.P.S.U. and Council of Ministers of U.S.S.R. 63-65, Chair. U.S.S.R. Cttee. of People's Control 65-; Cand. mem. Cen. Cttee. C.P.S.U. 61-66, mem. 66-; Deputy to U.S.S.R. Supreme Soviet; mem. Cttee. of U.S.S.R. Parl. Group.
U.S.S.R. Committee of People's Control, Ulitsa Kuibistseva 21, Moscow, U.S.S.R.

Kovanov, Vladimir Vasilyevich; Soviet surgeon; b. 1909; ed. Moscow Univ.
Postgraduate, Asst., First Moscow Medical Inst. 31-41; Soviet Army Medical Officer 41-45; Instructor, Head of Section, Deputy Head of Dept., C.P.S.U. Cen. Cttee. 45-50; Head of Dept., First Moscow Medical Inst. 46-; Pro-rector, First Moscow Medical Inst. 50-56, Rector 56-66; Corresp. mem. U.S.S.R. Acad. of Medical Sciences 60-63, mem. 63-; Vice-Pres., U.S.S.R. Acad. of Medical Sciences 66-; mem. Presidium Soviet Peace Cttee.; Order of Lenin 61, 65, Red Banner 43, Red Star 42, Patriotic War, First Class 44, Patriotic War, Second Class 44, Honoured Scientist of R.S.F.S.R. 65, Spasokukotsky Prize.
Publ. Over 90 works on treatment of thoracic cage wounds, traumatic shock, surgical anatomy of extremities, cardiac surgery, and transplantation of organs.
U.S.S.R. Academy of Medical Sciences, Solyanka 14, Moscow, U.S.S.R.

Kowarski, Lew, D. ès sc.; French atomic scientist; b. 10 Feb. 1907; ed. Ecole de Chimie Industrielle de Lyon and Univ. of Paris.
Came from Russia to Belgium and then to France; technical sec. (part-time) at Aciéries et Usines à Tubes de la Sarre 29-37; did biochemical research in hospital laboratory; personal sec. to Joliot-Curie 36; worked on neutron emission in uranium fission with Joliot-Curie and Halban; with Halban brought French stocks of heavy water experimental records to England 40; in charge of construction of first Canadian atomic pile 44; returned to France after Liberation and worked for Commissariat for Atomic Energy, of which he became Scientific Dir.; adviser to French del. to UN Atomic Energy Comm. 46-48; in charge of construction of first (47-48) and second (49-52) French atomic piles; Lecturer on Nuclear Physics, Conservatoire des Arts et Métiers 51-53; Dir. Laboratory Group 52-54, Scientific and Technical Services Div. 54-60, Data Handling Div. 61-64, Senior Physicist 65-, European Org. for Nuclear Research (CERN); Scientific adviser to European Nuclear Energy Agency, OEEC 56-61, OECD 61-; Visiting Prof. in Nuclear Engineering, Purdue Univ. Lafayette, Indiana 63-65; Prof. Inst. Nat. des Sciences et Tech. Nucléaires 66-; Prof. Univ. of Texas 68-; Officier de la Légion d'Honneur; Hon. Fellow American Nuclear Soc.
Office: European Organisation for Nuclear Research, Geneva 23, Switzerland; Home: 40 avenue William Favre, Geneva, Switzerland.
Telephone: Geneva (022) 36-59-73.

Kožešník, Jaroslav, DR.ING.; Czechoslovak scientist; b. 8 June 1907.
Former Dir. Combined Research Inst. of the Škoda Works; head of research and development work in heavy engineering industry; Prof. of Czech Technical Univ., Prague; Corresp. mem. Czechoslovak Acad. of Science 53, Academician 60, and First Vice-Pres. 62; Polish Acad. of Sciences 66-; Dir. Inst. of the Theory of Information and Automation; State Prize 59, 67; mem. State Planning Comm. 65-; Order of Labour.
Publs. *Physical Similarity, Mechanics of Models, Dynamics of Machines, Mechanics of Electrical Rotating Machines, Theory of Configurations.*
Náměsti Jos. Machka 6, Prague 5, Czechoslovakia. Telephone: 523-213.

Kozhevnikov, Fedor Ivanovich; Soviet jurist; b. 03; ed. Moscow Univ.
Fmr. Prof. of Int. Law and Dean of the Law Faculty, Moscow Univ.; fmr. Pres. Legal Section U.S.S.R. Soc. for Cultural Relations and mem. Legal Science Experts Cttee., Ministry of Culture; mem. Int. Law Comm. of U.N. 52-53; Judge, Int. Court of Justice 53-61; mem. Editorial Board *The Soviet State and the Law* (Soviet Acad. of Sciences Inst. of Law).
Publs. *Russian State and International Law* 47, *Soviet State and International Law* 48, *Great Patriotic War of the Soviet Union and Some Problems of International Law* 57.
Institute of Law, U.S.S.R. Academy of Sciences, 10 Ulitsa Frunze, Moscow, U.S.S.R.

Kozhevnikov, Yevgeny Fyodorovich; Soviet politician; b. 05; ed. Leningrad Inst. of Railway Engineers.
Various exec. posts on a number of construction projects 28-43; exec. work with State Planning Commr. and later for U.S.S.R. Council of Ministers 45-54; Minister of Transport Construction 54-; mem. Central Cttee. of C.P.S.U. 61-; Deputy to Supreme Soviet of the U.S.S.R.; Order of Lenin (thrice), Order of Red Banner of Labour (twice), Order of Red Star.
Ministry of Transport Construction, 21 Sadovaya Spasskaya ulitsa, Moscow, U.S.S.R.

Kozintsev, Grigori Mikhailovich; Soviet film director; b. 1905; ed. High Art School.
Director of Lenfilm studios in Leningrad 24-; People's

Artist of the U.S.S.R.; State Prize winner 41, 48; awarded Order of Lenin, Order of the Red Banner of Labour, Lenin Prize 65.
Principal films (co-dir. S. L. Trauberg): *The Greatcoat* 26, *The New Babylon* 29, *Maxim's Youth* 35, *Vyborg Side* 38, *Pirogov* 47, *Don Quixote* 57, *Hamlet* 64; productions for stage: *King Lear, Othello, Hamlet* (in Leningrad theatres).
Lenfilm Studio, Leningrad, U.S.S.R.

Kozirev, Semen Pavlovich; Soviet diplomatist; b. 1907; ed. Moscow Legal Inst.
Diplomatic Service 39-; Asst. Gen. Sec. State Cttee. for Foreign Affairs 39-43, Gen. Sec. 43; Counsellor London 43; Counsellor, France 43-45; Head of First European Dept., Ministry of Foreign Affairs 45-49; Envoy to Egypt 50-53; Chief, Division of Personnel, Ministry of Foreign Affairs 53-57; Ambassador to Italy 57-66; Deputy Minister of Foreign Affairs 66-.
Ministry of Foreign Affairs, 32-34 Smolenskaya-Sennaya ploshchad, Moscow, U.S.S.R.

Kozlov, Grigori Ivanovich; Soviet politician; b. 1912; ed. Veterinary Coll., Leningrad Region and Leningrad Higher Veterinary Training Courses.
Member C.P.S.U. 43-; Veterinary 32-34; at Leningrad Regional Cttee. C.P.S.U. 44-46; Head, Regional Dept. of Agriculture 46-61; Chair. Leningrad Regional Soviet of Working People's Deputies 61-63, Dec. 64-; First Sec. Leningrad Regional Cttee. C.P.S.U. 63-64; Alt. mem. C.P.S.U. Central Cttee.; Deputy to U.S.S.R. Supreme Soviet; mem. Legislative Proposals Cttee., Soviet of Union.
Leningrad Regional Soviet of Working People's Deputies, Leningrad, U.S.S.R.

Kozlov, Nikolai Timofeyevich; Soviet politician; b. 1925; ed. Moscow Timiryazev Acad. of Agriculture.
Mem. C.P.S.U. 46; Soviet Army service 43-47; Official, Moscow Regional Cttee. of C.P.S.U. 52-58, 59-60; Head of Statistics Dept., Moscow Region 58-59; First Vice-Chair. Moscow Regional Soviet of Working People's Deputies 60; Sec. Moscow Regional Cttee., C.P.S.U. 60-63; Chair. Moscow Regional Soviet of Working People's Deputies 63-; Alt. mem. C.P.S.U. Central Cttee.; Deputy to U.S.S.R. Supreme Soviet.
Moscow Regional Soviet of Working People's Deputies, Moscow, U.S.S.R.

Kozlov, Vladimir Yakovlevich; Soviet mathematician; b. 1914; ed. Moscow Univ.
Postgraduate Moscow Univ. 37-40; Army Service 40-46; mem. C.P.S.U. 41-; Research Assoc., Asst. Prof., Prof. Inst. of Mathematics, Moscow Univ. 46-; Corresp. mem. U.S.S.R. Acad. of Sciences 66-.
U.S.S.R. Academy of Sciences, 14 Lenin Prospekt, Moscow, U.S.S.R.

Kozlowski, Roman; Polish palaeontologist; b. 1 Feb. 1889; ed. Fribourg (Switzerland) and Paris Univs.
Prof. and Dir. Oruro State (Bolivia) Mining Engineering School 13-21; Dr. Sorbonne, Paris 21-23; Warsaw Free Univ. 23-27, Warsaw Univ. 27-; Founder and Editor *Palaeontologia Polonica* 29-, *Acta Palaeontologica Polonica* 55-; mem. Polish Acad. of Sciences and Corresp. mem. Acad. des Sciences and many foreign scientific socs.; State Prize, First Class 49; Mary Clark Thompson Medal, Nat. Acad. of Sciences, Washington 59, Wollaston Medal, Geological Soc. London 61.
Publs. *Fossiles dévoniens de Parana* 13, *Les Brachiopodes du Carbonifère supérieur de Bolivie* 14, *Faune devonienne de Bolivie* 23, *Les Brachiopodes gothlandiens de la Podolie polonaise* 29, *Les Graptolites et quelques nouveaux groupes d'animaux du Tremadoc de la Pologne* 48-49, *Les Hydroides ordoviciens à squelette chitineux* 59, *Crustoidea—nouveau groupe de Graptolites* 62, *On the Structure and relationships of Graptolites* 66.
Wilcza 22, Warsaw, Poland.

Krag, Jens Otto; Danish politician; b. 15 Sept. 1914. With Directorate of Supply 40-45; Chair. of economic council of labour movement 45-47; mem. of Parl. 47-; Minister of Commerce, Industry, and Shipping 47-50; Economic Counsellor, Danish Embassy, Washington, D.C. 50-52; Minister of Economy and Labour 53-57; Minister of External Economic Affairs 57-58; Minister of Foreign Affairs 58-62; Prime Minister 62-68, also Minister of Foreign Affairs 66-67; Pres. North Atlantic Council 66-67; Charlemagne Prize 66; Chair. of Social Democratic Party.
Publs. *Kooperationen, Fremtiden og Planökonomien* 45; joint author of: *Krigsökonomi og Efterkrigsproblemer* 44, *England bygger op* 47, *Danmark besat og befriet* 47, *Tidehverv og Samfundorden* 54, *Hans Hedtoft: Mandomsgerning* 55, *Wirtschaftspolitik und Socialdemokratie der skandinavischen Länder* 58.
Egernvej 61, Copenhagen F., Denmark.

Krajčír, František; Czechoslovak politician; b. 12 June 1913.
Former Minister of Domestic Trade; Minister of Foreign Trade 59-63; Deputy Prime Minister 63-68; mem. Comm. of Cen. Cttee. of C.P. of Czechoslovakia for Questions of Standard of Living 63-66; mem. Cen. Cttee. of C.P. of Czechoslovakia 46-; Deputy to Nat. Assembly 46-; Order of Feb. 25, 1948 49, Order of Labour 63; several decorations for Resistance heroism in Second World War; Bulgarian, Cambodian and Ethiopian decorations.
Prague, Czechoslovakia.

Krakhmaliev, Mikhail Konstantinovich; Soviet politician; b. 14; ed. Saratov Motor Roads Coll. and All-Union Party School.
Member C.P.S.U. 39; party work 42-; Perm. Staff, Central Cttee. of C.P.S.U. 53-54; Cand. mem. Central Cttee. of C.P.S.U. 56-61, mem. 61-; First Sec. Bryansk Rural District Cttee. C.P.S.U. 60-64, Bryansk District Cttee. C.P.S.U. 64-; Deputy to U.S.S.R. Supreme Soviet.
Bryansk District Committee of C.P.S.U., Bryansk, U.S.S.R.

Kralj, Tone; Yugoslav painter and sculptor; b. 1900; ed. Prague.
Rep. thirty exhibitions Yugoslavia, Venice Biennial Exhibitions 26, 28, 30, 54, six exhibitions Paris, one London, two Amsterdam, two Antwerp, one Strasburg (1st Prize), one Saarbrücken, one Leipzig, three Vienna, three Prague, one Berlin, one Barcelona, four U.S.A., one Copenhagen, three Italy, etc.; works in Yugoslav galleries, Vienna, Prague; private collections U.S.A.
Works include frescoes in thirty churches in Yugoslavia and Italy.
Gerbičeva 11, Ljubljana, Yugoslavia.

Kramer, Erwin, DIPL.ING.; German engineer and politician; b. 22 Aug. 1902; ed. Technical Univ., Berlin. Communist Party 29-; emigrated to U.S.S.R. 32; International Brigade, Spain 37-39; interned, France 39; Socialist Unity Party (SED) 46-; Dir.-Gen. German State Railways 49; Minister of Transport 54-; mem. Central Cttee. SED 54-; National Prize for Science and Technology II Class 58.
Ministry of Transport, 108 Berlin, Voss-strasse 33, Germany.

Kramer, Stanley, B.SC.; American film producer-director; b. 29 Sept. 1913; ed. New York Univ.
M.G.M. Research Dept.; film cutter for three years and film editor; film and radio writer; served U.S. Signal Corps; formed own film production co. to produce *This Side of Innocence*; formed and is Pres. Kramer Pictures. Films incl. (assoc. producer) *So Ends Our Night, Moon and Sixpence*; (producer) *So This is New York, Home of the Brave, Cyrano de Bergerac, Death of a Salesman, High Noon, The Happy Time, Eight Iron Men, Caine Mutiny*; (producer-dir.) *Not As a Stranger, Pride and*

the Passion, The Defiant Ones, On The Beach, Inherit the Wind, Judgment at Nuremberg, It's a Mad, Mad, Mad, Mad World, Ship of Fools, Guess Who's Coming to Dinner.
1438 N. Gower, Hollywood 28, Calif., U.S.A.

Krämer, Werner, DR. PHIL.; German archaeologist; b. 8 March 1917; ed. Univs. of Munich, Frankfurt, Kiel, Marburg.
Curator and Departmental Dir. Bavarian State Office for Preservation of Monuments 47-56; First Dir. and Prof. Roman-German Comm. of German Archæological Inst. Frankfurt 56-.
Palmengartenstrasse 10-12, Frankfurt am Main, German Federal Republic.
Telephone: Frankfurt 776039.

Kranidiotis, Nicos; Cypriot scholar, journalist and diplomatist; b. 25 Nov. 1911; ed. Pan Cyprian Gymnasium, Cyprus, Athens Univ. and Harvard Univ. Center for Int. Affairs.
Worked as schoolmaster in Cyprus; Dir. of *Hellenic Cyprus* (official political organ of Cyprus Ethnarchy) 49; Gen. Sec. Cyprus Ethnarchy 53-57, Councillor 57-60; Amb. to Greece 60-67, to Italy 67-; Sec. of 2nd and 3rd Cyprus Nat. Assemblies 54, 55; Founder, Dir. (with others) of *Kypriaka Grammata* (Cyprus Literature), a literary magazine 34-, Editor 46-56.
Publs. *Chronicles* (short stories) 45, *The Neohellenic Theatre* (essay) 50, *Studies* (poems) 51, *Forms of Myth* (short stories) 54, *The Poet G. Seferis* (essay) 55, *The National Character of Cyprus Literature* 58, *Cyprus in her Struggle for Freedom* (history) 58, *Introduction to the Poetry of G. Seferis* (essay) 65, *Cyprus-Greece* (essay) 66.
16 Promitheus Street, Nicosia, Cyprus.
Telephone: 2907 (Nicosia).

Krapf, Franz; German diplomatist; b. 1911.
Diplomatic Service 38-; formerly Legation Cairo, Embassy Moscow and Paris; later Minister German Del. to NATO, Paris; Head, Eastern Dept., Ministry of Foreign Affairs 61-63; Ministerial Dir. and Head of Political Dept. for East-West Affairs 63-66; Amb. to Japan 66-.
Embassy of German Federal Republic, 5-10, 4-chome, Minanis-Azatu, Minato-ku, Tokyo, Japan.
Telephone: 473-0151-0157.

Krapiva, pseudonym of **Aprakhovich, Kondrat Kondratyevich;** Soviet writer; b. 1906; ed. Byelorussian Univ.
People's Writer of Byelorussia; mem. Byelorussian S.S.R. Acad. of Sciences; State prizewinner 41, 50; awarded Order of Lenin (twice), Order of the Red Banner of Labour.
Publs. fables and sketches: *Nettles* 25, *Fables* 27; plays: *Who Laughs Last* 39, *The Larks Sing* 51, *Men and Devils* 58; satirical poem *The Bible* 26; *Collected Works* (4 vols.) 63, etc.
Writers' Union of Byelorussia, Minsk, Byelorussia, U.S.S.R.

Kraske, Konrad, DR. PHIL.; German politician; b. 5 June 1926; ed. Berlin, Göttingen and Freiburg Univs.
Member of the Nat. Office of the Christian Democratic Union 53-, Gen. Sec. 58-; Mem. of the Bundestag (Parl.).
Nassestrasse 2, Bonn, German Federal Republic.

Krasovskaya, Vera Mihailovna; Soviet (Russian) historian and ballet critic; b. 1915; ed. Choreographical School, Leningrad and Inst. of Theatre, Music and Cinematography, Leningrad.
Ballet Dancer, Kirov Ballet 33-41; Senior Scientific Worker Inst. of Theatre, Music and Cinematography 53-; mem. Union of Soviet Writers 66.
Publs. *Vachtang Chabukiani* 56, 60, *Russian Ballet Theatre from the Beginning to the Middle of the XIX*

Century 58, *Leningrad's Ballet* 61, *Russian Ballet Theatre of the Second Half of the XIX Century* 63, *Anna Pavlova* 64, 65.
12 Povarshoy, appt. 12, Leningrad D-25, U.S.S.R.

Krayevsky, Nikolai Alexandrovich; Soviet pathologist; b. 1905; ed. Moscow Univ.
Assistant, Moscow Univ. 28-30; Asst., Inst. of Occupational Diseases 30-32; Asst., Lecturer, Prof., Second Moscow Medical Inst. 31-54; Head of Laboratory, Cen. Inst. of Hematology and Blood Transfusion 39-51; Head of Dept., Cen. Inst. for Postgraduate Medical Training 54-60; Corresp. mem. U.S.S.R. Acad. of Medical Sciences 53-60, mem. 60-; Academician-Sec. U.S.S.R. Acad. of Medical Sciences 60-62; Head of Dept., Inst. of Experimental and Clinical Oncology, U.S.S.R. Acad. of Medical Sciences 62-; Chair. of Board of All-Union Scientific Soc. of Pathologists; mem. WHO Expert Advisory Panel; mem. Editorial Board of *Archives of Pathology*; Order of Red Star 44, Patriotic War, First Class 45, Badge of Honour, Lenin Prize 63.
Publs. Over 110 works on gastric pathology, morbid anatomy of hemotransfusional complications, and radiation complications in oncology.
Institute of Experimental and Clinical Oncology, Kashirskoye Shosse 6, Moscow, U.S.S.R.

Krebs, Sir Hans (Adolf), M.D., M.A., F.R.S.; British biochemist; b. 25 Aug. 1900; ed. Univs. of Göttingen, Freiburg, Munich, Berlin, Hamburg and Cambridge.
Priv. doz., Univ. of Freiburg 32-33; Demonstrator in Biochemistry, Cambridge Univ. 34; Lecturer in Pharmacology, Sheffield Univ. 35-45, in charge of Dept. of Biochemistry 38-45, Prof. of Biochemistry 45-54; Whitley Prof. Oxford Univ. 54-67; foreign mem. Accad. Nazionale dei Lincei, Academie de Médecine and Société de Biologie; Foreign Assoc. U.S. Nat. Acad. of Sciences; hon. degrees from Paris, Chicago, Freiburg-im-Breisgau, Glasgow, Sheffield, London, Leicester, Jerusalem, Berlin (Humboldt), Granada, Leeds, Wales, Bordeaux and Pennsylvania Univs.; Lasker Award 53 and Nobel Prize (jointly) for Physiology 53; Copley Medal, Royal Soc. 61, Gold Medal, Royal Soc. of Medicine 65.
27 Abberbury Road, Iffley, Oxford, England.

Kreisky, Bruno, LL.D.; Austrian diplomatist and politician; b. 22 Jan. 1911; ed. Univ. of Vienna.
Active mem. Austrian Social Democratic Party to 34; arrested and imprisoned 35 and again 38, when escaped to Sweden; mem. scientific staff Stockholm Co-operative Society 39-46; joined Austrian Foreign Service 46; Austrian Legation, Stockholm 46-51; Austrian Fed. President's Office 51-53; State Sec. for Foreign Affairs in Fed. Chancellery 53; elected to Parl. 56; Minister of Foreign Affairs 59-66; Chair. Socialist Party of Austria 67-; initiator and Vice-Pres. Theodor Körner Fund for Promotion of Arts and Sciences; Vice-Chair. of Board, Inst. for Advanced Studies and Scientific Research, Vienna; Pres. Vienna Inst. for Devt.; Gold Grand Cross of Honour and twenty-three foreign awards.
Publ. *The Challenge*.
Löwelstrasse 18, 1014 Vienna; also Armbrustergasse 15, 1190 Vienna, Austria.
Telephone: 63-27-31 and 26-14-36.

Krejča, Otomar; Czechoslovak actor and director; b. 23 Nov. 1921; ed. Charles Univ., Prague.
Member Prague Nat. Theatre 51-, Art Chief, Nat. Theatre Drama Section 56-61; Head of *Divadlo za branou* (Theatre Beyond the Gate) 65-; Honoured Artist 58, State Prize 51.
Plays directed include: *The Seagull* (Chekhov), *Romeo and Juliet* (Shakespeare), *Hamlet* (Shakespeare); Guest Dir. *Hamlet* and *The Seagull*, Nat. Theatre, Brussels 65, 66.
Prague 8, Kubišova 26, Czechoslovakia.

Krejčí, Josef; Czechoslovak engineer and politician; b. 29 Jan. 1912; ed. secondary school, Rakovník, and Prague Coll. of Machine and Electrical Engineering. Formerly in machine tool design dept., Skoda Works, Prague; later Lecturer, Czech Technical Univ., Prague; also worked in State Inst. for Testing Engines and Motors; Skoda Works, Plzeň 37-45, Pipe-Rolling Plant, Chomutov 45-49, Dir. of Production 49-52, Chief Engineer 54-56, Dir. 56-61, also Dir. of Steel Works, Most; First Deputy Minister of Metallurgy and Ore Mines 61-62, Minister 62-65; Deputy Premier and Minister of Heavy Industry 65-68, Minister of Heavy Industry 68-; Cand. mem. Central Cttee. of C.P. of Czechoslovakia 62-64, mem. 64-, mem. Econ. Comm. 63-66; Deputy to Nat. Assembly 64-; Order of Labour 52, 59.
Ministry of Heavy Industry, Prague 1, Na Františku 32, Czechoslovakia.
Telephone: 217.

Krekeler, Heinz L., DR. PHIL.; German diplomatist; b. 20 July 1906; ed. Univs. of Freiburg, Munich, Göttingen and Berlin.
Chemical engineer with different firms 30-46; mem. Lippe Diet 46, Diet of North Rhine-Westphalia 47-50, Fed. Assembly 49; partner and fmr. Dir. F. Eilers-Schünemann Verlag (Publishers), Bremen 48-; Consul-Gen. in N.Y. 50-51; Chargé d'Affaires, Fed. Republic of Germany, Washington, D.C. 51-53, Ambassador 53-58; mem. Euratom Comm. 58-64; Kt. Commdr.'s Cross of Order of Merit (Germany); Grande Ufficiale dell'Ordine al Merito 59; Commendatore con Placca dell'Ordine S. Gregorio il Grande; Grand Officier de l'ordre de Léopold; Hon. LL.D. Xavier and Univ. of South Carolina.
Publs. *Die Diplomatie* 65, *Die Aussenpolitik* 67.
Gut Lindemannshof, 4912 Post Sylbach in Lippe, German Federal Republic.
Telephone: Bad Salzuflen 8-17-57.

Kremer, Jean Pierre; Luxembourg diplomatist; b. 8 March 1903.
Secretariat-General, League of Nations 31; Sec. of Legation 44; Ministry of Foreign Affairs, Luxembourg, and Perm. Del. to Econ. Comm. for Europe 46; Counsellor of Legation, Brussels 48; Ministry of Foreign Affairs and Perm. Del. to Council of Europe 53; Ambassador to Netherlands 55-61, German Fed. Republic 61-.
Martinstrasse 20, Cologne, German Federal Republic.

Krenek, Ernst; American composer; b. 23 Aug. 1900 in Austria; ed. Univ. of Vienna and Acads. of Music in Vienna and Berlin.
Lived in Switzerland 23-25; Asst. to Dir. of Staatstheater, Kassel 25-27; lived in Vienna 27-37; emigrated to U.S.A. 37; Prof. of Music, Vassar Coll. 39-42; Prof. of Music and Dean of Fine Arts, Hamline Univ., St. Paul, Minn. 42-47; Grosses Bundesverdienstkreuz 65; Hamburg Bach Prize 66.
Compositions include operas: *Der Sprung über den Schatten* 23, *Orpheus und Eurydike* 23, *Jonny Spielt Auf* 25-26, *Dark Waters* 50; *Karl V* 30-33, *Symphonies No. 1* 21, *No. 2* 22, *No. 3* 22, *No. 4* 47, *No. 5* 49, *Piano Concertos No. 3* and *No. 4* 46 and 56, *Pallas Athene* 52-55, *Golden Ram* 62, *Sestina* 57, *Quaestio Temporis* 59.
Publs. *Music Here and Now* 39, *Studies in Counterpoint* 40, *Musik im goldenen Westen* 49, *Zur Sprache gebracht* 58, *Gedanken unterwegs* 59, *Glauben und Wissen* 67.
10424 Pinyon Avenue, Tujunga, Calif. 91042, U.S.A.

Krenz, Jan; Polish conductor and composer; b. 26. ed. Warsaw and Łódź.
Conductor Łódź Philharmonic Orch. 45; Dir. Poznań Philharmonic Orch. 48-49; Dir. and First Conductor Polish Radio Symphony Orch., Katowice 50-; tours in Hungary, Rumania, Czechoslovakia, France, U.S.S.R., Germany, Italy, U.K., etc.; State Prize 55.
Compositions include Symphony, two String Quartets,

Nocturnes for Orchestra, *Rozmowa dwóch miast* (Conversation of Two Towns) (cantata), Rhapsody for Strings, xylophone, harmonium and percussion, Concertino for Piano and Small Symphony Orchestra; orchestral transcriptions of three fugues from *The Art of Fugue* (J. S. Bach).
27 Rynek Starego Miasta, Warsaw, Poland.

Kreps, Evgeny Mikhailovich; Soviet physiologist; b. 1899; ed. Military Medical Acad.
Post graduate student and Junior Instructor, Mil. Med. Acad. 25-31; Head, Physiological Lab. Murmansk Biological Station 23-33; worked in England 30-31; mem. Emergency Rescue Cttee., U.S.S.R. Navy 31-51; Prof. Leningrad Univ. 34-37; Head, Lab. of Comparative Physiology and Biochemistry, Pavlov Inst. of Physiology, U.S.S.R. Acad. of Sciences 36-60; Dir. Inst. of Evolutionary Physiology, U.S.S.R. Acad. of Sciences 60-; Corresp. mem. U.S.S.R. Acad. of Sciences 46-66, mem. 66-; Academic Sec. Physiology Branch, U.S.S.R. Acad. of Sciences 66-.
Institute of Evolutionary Physiology, U.S.S.R. Academy of Sciences, Leningrad, U.S.S.R.

Kresge, Stanley Sebastian; American business executive; b. 11 June 1900; ed. Univ. of Michigan and Albion Coll., Michigan.
Trainee, S. S. Kresge Co. 23-27, Store Manager 27-28, mem. Gen. Office Staff, Detroit 30-50, Dir. 50-, Vice-Pres., Admin. Asst. to Pres. 51-52, Vice-Chair. of Board 53-66, Chair. 66-; Vice-Pres. Kresge Foundation 31-52, Pres. 52-66, Chair. of Board 66-.
The Kresge Foundation, 211 Fort Street West, Detroit, Michigan 48226, U.S.A.

Kreuder, Ernst; German writer; b. 29 Aug. 1903; ed; Frankfurt Univ.
Mem. Akad. der Wissenschaften und der Literatur, Mainz, and Deutsche Akad. für Sprache und Dichtung, Darmstadt; mem. P.E.N.; Georg Büchner Prize 53.
Publs. Novels: *Die Gesellschaft vom Dachboden* 46, *Schwebender Weg* 47, *Die Unauffindbaren* 48, *Herein ohne anzuklopfen* 54, *Agimos oder die Weltgehilfen* 59, *Spur unterm Wasser* 63, *Tunnel zu Vermieten* 66; poems: *Sommers Einsiedelei* 56.
Mühltalstrasse 135, 61 Darmstadt-Mühltal, German Federal Republic.
Telephone: 79535.

Kreyberg, Leiv, M.D.; Norwegian pathologist; b. 22 May 1896.
Professor of Pathology, Oslo Univ. 38-64, Emeritus Prof. 64-; mem. Acad. Science and Letters, Oslo; cancer research and experimental pathology; Chair. Biological Soc. Oslo 28-30, Union of Pathologists 46-47; Vice-Pres. (Europe) Int. Union against Cancer 54-58; hon. mem. Indian Asscn. Pathologists; Soc. Française d'Angiologie and Swedish Medical Asscn., Austrian Cancer Soc., Belgian Pathological Soc., Pathological Soc. of Great Britain and Ireland; Consultant in Cancer, WHO; Dr. h.c. (Perugia) 65; Commdr. of Royal Order of St. Olav.
Munkedams vei 79, Oslo, Norway.

Krieger Vasena, Adalbert, DR. ECON.; Argentine economist and politician; b. 11 Feb. 1920; ed. Univ. de Buenos Aires.
Dir. Banco Central 56-57; Minister of Finance 57-58; negotiated Argentina's membership of Int. Monetary Fund 56; former Head of Argentine Rep. at Gen. Agreement of Tariffs and Trade; Minister of Economy 67-, also Minister of Labour.
Ministry of Economy, Buenos Aires, Argentina.

Krim, Belkacem; Algerian soldier and politician; b. 21. Former Corporal, French Army; outlaw, Algeria 47-57; Founder-mem. National Liberation Front (F.L.N.) 54-; Commander Kabylia Region 54-57; Dep. Prime Minister in general charge of Military Operations 58-62; Minister

of Foreign Affairs 60-61; Minister of Interior 61-62; Leader of Algerian Provisional Govt. Del. to talks at Evian, May 61; Vice-Premier, Algerian Provisional Govt. 62; now living in Italy.
Rome, Italy.

Kripalani, Acharaya Jiwatram Bhagwandas, M.A.; Indian politician; b. 1888.
Professor in Bihar under Calcutta Univ. 12-17; worked with Gandhi 17-18, with Pandit Madan Mohan Malaviya 18; Prof. of Politics, Benares Hindu Univ. 19-20; active in Khadi and village work and Dir. Gandhi Ashram, U.P. 20-; Principal of Gujarat Vidyapith 22-27; imprisoned 42-45; Pres. Indian Nat. Congress 46-47; mem. Constituent Assembly 46-51; formed Congress Democratic Front 51; founded *Vigil*, political weekly 50; formed Kisan Mazdoor Praja Party 51; mem. Lok Sabha (Parl.) 52-62, 63-.
Publs. *The Gandhian Way, The Non-Violent Revolution, The Indian National Congress, The Politics of Charkha, The Future of the Congress, The Fateful Year, Gandhi the Statesman, Basic Education.*
Shri Gandhi Ashram, Meerut, Uttar Pradesh, India.

Kripalani, Mrs. Sucheta, M.A.; Indian politician; b. 1908; ed. Lahore and Delhi.
Lecturer Hindu Univ. Benares 31-39; Sec. Foreign Affairs Dept. A.I.C.C. 39-40; Sec. Women's Dept. A.I.C.C. 41-42; imprisoned 40-41 and 43-45; Org. Sec. Kasturba Memorial Trust 45; mem. Constituent Assembly 46 and M.P.; del. Gen. Assembly U.N.O. 49; resigned from Congress 50 and joined Kisan Mazdoor Praja Party and became mem. Nat. Exec.; mem. Nat. Exec. Praja Socialist Party after merger of K.M.P.P. and the Socialist Party; mem. Lok Sabha 52-57, 57-63; rejoined Congress 57, Gen. Sec. Nat. Exec. 59-60; Minister for Labour Development and Small Industries, Uttar Pradesh 60-63, Chief Minister of Uttar Pradesh 63-67.
11 Gautam Palli, Lucknow, Uttar Pradesh, India.

Krips, Joseph; Austrian conductor; b. 8 April 1902; ed. Vienna Conservatoire.
Assistant Conductor, Vienna Volksoper 21-24; Conductor, Aussig/Elbe 24-25, Dortmund 25-26; Gen. Musical Dir. Karlsruhe State Theatre 26-33; Prof. Vienna Conservatoire 33-38; Conductor, Vienna State Opera 45-50, Belgrade Opera 38-39; Dir. Vienna Hofkapelle 45-; Conductor, London Symphony Orchestra 50-54; Perm. Conductor Buffalo Philharmonic Orchestra 54-63; Conductor, San Francisco Symphony Orchestra 62-; frequent appearances as guest conductor at concerts and in opera houses; Mozart Ring 65 and several other awards.
c/o Harold Holt Ltd., 122 Wigmore Street, London, W.1, England; Montreux, Vaux, 6 Riant Château, Switzerland; Vienna 2, Karmeliberg. 7, Austria.

Krishna Menon, Vengalil Krishnan; Indian barrister and diplomatist; b. 3 May 1897; ed. Presidency Coll. and Law Coll., Madras, London School of Economics and Univ. Coll., London.
Called to Bar (Middle Temple); practised as barrister; has also been teacher, journalist and publicist; Sec. India League 29-47; Borough Councillor, St. Pancras 34-47; Chair. Arts Council St. Pancras; Labour Party candidate for Dundee 39-42; represented Indian Nat. Congress on international congresses and missions from 38; First Editor *Pelican Books*; Editor *20th Century Library* (Bodley Head); High Commissioner of India in U.K. 47-52, concurrently Ambassador to Irish Republic; Mem. Indian Del. to U.N. 46, Deputy Chair. 52, Chair. 53-62; mem. Lok Sabha (Parl.) 52-; Minister without Portfolio 56; Minister of Defence 57-62, of Defence Production 62; LL.D. h.c. (Glasgow, Saugor); Congress Party.
Publ. *Condition of India* (with Ellen Wilkinson).
Lok Sabha, New Delhi, India.

Krishna Moorthi, C. S.; Indian civil servant; b. 21; ed. Madras Univ.
Ordnance Officer, Indian Army 43-46; Asst. Commr. Refugees, Punjab 47-48; Sub-Collector and Joint Magistrate, Madras State 48-52; Board of Revenue, Madras 52-53; Ministry of Finance 54-58; Counsellor, Indian Comm.-Gen. for Econ. Affairs, Washington 58; Alt. Exec. Dir. Int. Bank for Reconstruction and Devt. and Int. Finance Corpn. 58; Minister (Econ.) Indian Embassy, Washington 61-63, Exec. Dir. for India, Int. Bank for Reconstruction and Development, Int. Finance Corpn. and Int. Development Asscn. 62-63; Joint Sec. Dept. of Econ. Affairs, Ministry of Finance, New Delhi 63-.
Ministry of Finance, New Delhi, India.

Krishnamachari, Tiruvallur Thattai; Indian politician; b. 26 Nov. 1899; ed. Madras Christian Coll.
Entered business 21; mem. Madras Legislative Assembly 37-42; mem. Central Assembly 42-46, Constituent Assembly 46-48, Lok Sabha 48-; Minister of Commerce and Industry Central Govt. 52-56, of Iron and Steel 55-57, of Finance 56-58; Minister without Portfolio (for Econ. and Defence Co-ordination) 62-63, of Finance 63-65; represented India at the Commonwealth Prime Ministers' Conference in London, July 64; mem. Drafting Cttee. for Indian Constitution.
Staff Colony, Agaran Road, Tambaram, Madras, India.
Telephone: 89488.

Krishnan, Rappal Sangameswara, D.SC., PH.D.; Indian physicist; b. 1911; ed. Univ. of Madras, St. Joseph's Coll., Trichy, Indian Inst. of Science, and Trinity Coll., Cambridge.
Research Asst. Indian Inst. of Science 35-38; 1851 Exhibition Overseas Scholar, Univ. of Cambridge 38-41; Lecturer in Physics, Inst. of Science 42-45, Asst. Prof. 45-48, Prof. and Head of Dept. of Physics 48-; Fellow of Inst. of Physics, London, of American Physical Society, of Indian Academy of Sciences, and of Nat. Inst. of Sciences; Pres. Physics Section, Indian Science Congress 49; specialist in colloid optics, Raman effect in crystals, crystal physics and nuclear physics.
Publ. *Progress in Crystal Physics*, Vol. I 58.
Physics Department, Indian Institute of Science, Bangalore 12, South India.
Telephone: Bangalore 26901.

Krishnaswamy, K. S., PH.D.; Indian international bank official; b. 1920; ed. Univ. of Mysore and London School of Economics.
Lecturer in Econs., Univ. of Bombay 46-47; Research Officer, Planning Comm., New Delhi; Research Officer, Research Dept., Reserve Bank of India, Bombay 52-54, Deputy Dir. of Research, Research Dept. 54-56; Staff mem. Econ. Devt. Inst. (World Bank), Wash., D.C. 56-59; Deputy Chief, Industrial Finance Dept., Reserve Bank of India 59-61; Chief, Econ. Policy Section, Planning Comm. 64-67; Dir. Econ. Devt. Inst., Int. Bank for Reconstruction and Devt. 67-.
Economic Development Institute, International Bank for Reconstruction and Development (World Bank), Washington, D.C. 20433, U.S.A.

Kriss, Anatoli Evseevich; Soviet microbiologist; b. 16 Sept. 1908; ed. Leningrad Medical Inst.
Scientific worker, Inst. of Microbiology, U.S.S.R. Acad. of Sciences 35-; Dr. of Biological Sciences 47; Head of Marine Microbiology Dept., Inst. of Microbiology 48-; Head of Electron Microscopy Laboratory, U.S.S.R. Acad. of Sciences 46-; microbiological research, Antarctic 67-; awarded title of Prof. of Microbiology 50; Lenin Prize 60.
Publs. *The Variability of Actinomycetes* 37, *Deep-Sea Microbiology* 59 (German edn. 61, English edn. 63, Japanese edn. 63), *Microbial Population of the World Ocean* 64, and over 150 scientific papers.
U.S.S.R. Academy of Sciences, Moscow, U.S.S.R.

Kristensen, Sven Möller, DR. PHIL.; Danish writer; literary critic and editor; b. 12 Nov. 1909; ed. Copenhagen Univ.

Literary and Theatre Critic, *Land og Folk* 45-53; Editor *Athenæum* (literary magazine) 45-49, *Dialog* 50-53, Prof. of Scandinavian Literature Aarhus Univ. 53-64, Copenhagen Univ. 64-; mem. Danish Acad. 60.

Publs. *Æstetiske studier i dansk fiktionsprosa 1870-1900* 38, *Digteren og samfundet I-II* 42, 45; *Amerikansk litteratur 1920-1940* 42, *Dansk Litteratur 1918-1950* 50, *En musaik af moderne dansk litteratur* 54, *Digtningens Teori* 58, *Digtning og Livssyn* 59, *Vurderinger* 61, *Den dobbelte Eros* 66.

Copenhagen University; Vingaards alle 53, Hellerup, Denmark.

Telephone: Hellerup 1521.

Kristensen, Thorkil; Danish business economist; b. 9 Oct. 1899; ed. High School, Askov and Univ. of Copenhagen.

Teacher at Commercial Acad., Aarhus 27; Inspector of Savings-Banks 28-35; Asst. Lecturer Univ. of Copenhagen 36-38; Prof. of Business Economics, Univ. of Aarhus 38; Copenhagen School of Economics 48; Minister of Finance 45-47, 50-53; mem. of Board of Court of Conciliation in Labour questions 40-45; mem. of Folketing 45-60; mem. Acad. of Technical Sciences 46-; Sec.-Gen. OEEC 60-61; Chair. Preparatory Cttee. Organisation for Economic Co-operation and Development (OECD) 60-61, Sec.-Gen. 61-.

Publs. *Danmarks Driftsregnskab* 30, *Undersøgelser af det kommunale Skattespørgsmaal* 35, *Faste og variable Omkostninger* 39, *Haandbog i Kredit og Hypotek foreningsforhold* 44, *The Economic World Balance* 60.

OECD, 2 rue André Pascal, Paris 16e, France.

Kristensen, Tom; Danish writer; b. 4 Aug. 1893 in London; ed. Henrik Madsens School, Copenhagen Univ.

Literary critic of *Politiken* 24-27 and 31-63; mem. Exec. Cttee. Danish Society of Authors 41-44, The Danish Acad. 60; Knight of Dannebrog 59; awarded Holberg Medal 45, Aarestrup Medal 54.

Publs. *Fribytterdrømme* (poems) 20, *Livets Arabesk* (novel) 21, *Mirakler* (poems) 22, *Paafuglefjeren* (poems) 22, *En Anden* (novel) 23, *En Kavaler i Spanien* (prose and poems) 26, *Verdslige Sange* (poems) 27, *Sophus Claussen* 29, *Haervaerk* (novel) 30, *En Fribytters Ord* (poems) 33, *Vindrosen* (short stories) 34, *Mod den yderste Rand* (poems) 36, *Digte i Døgnet* (poems) 40, *Harry Martinson* 41, *Mellem Scylla og Charybdis,* (collected poems from the twenties) 43, *Mellem Krigene* (essays) 46, *Hvad er Heta?* (short stories) 46, *En Omvej til Andorra* (prose) 47, *Den syngende busk* (poems) 49, *Rejse i Italien* (prose) 50, *De forsvundne Ansigter* (poems) 53, *Til Dags Dato* (essays) 53, *En Bogorms Barndom* (autobiography) 53, *Den sidste Lygte* (poems) 54, *Det skabende Øje* (essays) 56, *Oplevelser med Lyrik* (essays) 57, *Den evige Uro* (essays) 58, *Hvad er Heta og andre fortaellinger* (short stories from Copenhagen) 59, *Harlekin Skelet* (detective story) 62, *I min Tid* (essays), *Udvalgte digte* (selected poems) 63, *Kriliher eller anmelder* (essays) 66, *Abenhyerlige Forliesen* (autobiog.) 66, *Bøger, bøger, bøger* (essays) 67.

Torelore, Thurø, Denmark.

Telephone 205059.

Kristiansen, Erling (Engelbrecht); Danish diplomatist and government official; b. 31 Dec. 1912; ed. Herning Gymnasium, Univs. of Copenhagen and Geneva, Paris and London.

Danish Civil Service, Ministry of Labour 41, with Free Danish Legations Stockholm 43, Washington 44, London 45; Commercial Sec. Danish Legation, London 45-47; Head, Del. to Org. for European Economic Co-operation (OEEC) 48-50; Sec., Economic Cttee. of Cabinet 50-51; Asst. Under-Sec. of State, Ministry of Foreign Affairs 51-53, Dep. Under-Sec. 54-64; Ambassador to Great Britain, concurrently to Ireland 64-; Chair. Danish Dels. to major econ. confs. 54-63; Knight Commdr. Order of Dannebrog, Grand Officier Légion d'Honneur, Knight Grand Cross, Order of Falcon of Iceland and other decorations.

Publ. *Folkeforbundet* (The League of Nations) 38.

Royal Danish Embassy, 29 Pont Street, London, S.W.1; 1 Cadogan Square, London, S.W.1, England.

Telephone: 01-235-4696.

Kristiansen, Georg; Norwegian diplomatist; b. 4 March 1917; ed. Univ. of Oslo.

Army Service 40-45; Sec., Ministry of Foreign Affairs 46-47; Attaché Paris 47-52; Sec. later Counsellor, Ministry of Foreign Affairs 52-57; Instructor Nat. Defence Coll., Oslo 57-59; Dir. later Dir.-Gen. Political Affairs, Ministry of Foreign Affairs 59-64; Perm. Rep. to NATO 64-67, and OECD 64-.

92 avenue Henri-Martin, Paris 16e, France.

Krleža, Miroslav; Yugoslav writer; b. 7 July 1893. Director, Yugoslav Lexicographical Inst.

Publs. include *The Return of Phillip Latinovicz, On the Verge of Reason, A Banquet in Blithonamia, Flags* (novels); *God Mars of Croatia, 1001 Deaths* (short stories); *In Agony, Golgotha, The Glembaj Cycle, Aretaeus* (plays); *The Ballads of Petrica Kerempuh, Beisetzung in Theresienburg* 64, *Europäisches Alphabet* 64, *Essays* (6 vols.), *Collected Poems* (7 vols.), *Legends* (7 plays: *Michelangelo, Christopher Columbus,* etc.).

c/o Yugoslav Lexicographical Institute, Zagreb; Strossmayer trg. 4, Zagreb, Yugoslavia.

Krock, Arthur, A.M.; American newspaperman; b. 16 Nov. 1887; ed. Lewis Inst., Chicago, Princeton Univ.

Reporter, Louisville 07; Washington Corresp, *Louisville Times* and *Courier-Journal* 10-15; Editorial Man. *Louisville Times* and *Louisville Courier-Journal* 15-19, Editor *Louisville Times* 19-23; Asst. to Pres. *New York World* 23-27; joined *New York Times* 27, Washington Corresp. 32-53, Washington commentator 53-; Pulitzer Prize 35, 38, 50; Commandant Légion d'Honneur and other foreign awards.

Publ. *The Editorials of Henry Watterson* 23, *In the Nation* 66.

1701 K Street, Washington, D.C. 20006, U.S.A.

Telephone: NA8-3016.

Krohn-Hansen, Rt. Rev. Wollert; Norwegian bishop; b. 28 Dec. 1889.

Chaplain, Tromsø diocese 15; parish priest in Værøy (Lofoten) 15; in Ofoten 22; in Narvik 29; in Tromsø 36; Bishop of Hålogaland 40-; during German occupation of Norway resigned Bishopric; arrested 42; sent to South Norway 43; worked secretly with the Church during the occupation; resumed duties as Bishop of Hålogaland 45-52, of South Hålogaland 52-60; Commdr. Order of St. Olav (Norway); Commdr. 1st Class Order of White Rose (Finland).

Publ. *Den brente jord—dagboksopptegnelser fra krigen og kirkekampen i Nord-Norge* 45.

Fosswinckelsgaten 32A, Bergen, Norway.

Krol, H.E. Cardinal John Joseph; American ecclesiastic; b. 26 Oct. 1910; ed. St. Mary's Seminary, Cleveland, and Pontificia Univ. Gregoriana.

Ordained Priest 37; Private Chamberlain 45; Domestic Prelate 51; Parish Asst. 37-38; Prof. Diocesan Seminary, also Chaplain, Jennings Home for the Aged 42-43; Vice-Chancellor, Cleveland Diocese 43-51, Chancellor 51-53; Auxiliary Bishop to Bishop of Cleveland, also Vicar-Gen., Diocese of Cleveland 53-61; Archbishop of Philadelphia 61-; created Cardinal by Pope Paul VI 67.

Office: 225 North 18th Street, Philadelphia 3; Home: 5700 City Avenue, Philadelphia 31, Pa., U.S.A.

Kroll, Leon; American artist; b. 6 Dec. 1884; ed. Nat. Acad. of Design, and in Paris under Jean Paul Laurens. President American Soc. of Painters, Sculptors and Gravers 31-35; elected mem. American Acad. of Arts and Letters 48, Dir. 59-; Works purchased by various museums; two murals in new Justice Building, Washington. D.C., war memorial murals Worcester, Mass.; mural paintings in the Senate Chamber, Indiana 52-53; memorial domed ceiling in mosaic; *Normandy Beachhead*; mural paintings in Johns Hopkins Univ.; Légion d'Honneur; Pres. U.S.A. Cttee. Int. Asscn. of Plastic Arts 54-; National Academician; various prizes and medals.
15 W. 67th Street, New York, N.Y. 10023, U.S.A.
Telephone: Trafalgar 7-4964 and Susquehanna 7-0100.

Krolow, Karl; German poet and essayist; b. 11 May 1915; ed. Univs. of Göttingen and Breslau.
Writer 42-; mem. Deutsche Akad. für Sprache und Dichtung, Mainzer Akad. der Wissenschaften und der Literatur; Acad. of Fine Arts of Bavaria, PEN Club; Georg Buchner Prize 56, Grosser Niedersächsischer Kunstpreis 65.
Publs. Poetry: *The Signs of the World* 52, *Wind and Time* 54, *Days and Nights* 56, *Foreign Bodies* 59, *Selected Poems* 62, *Invisible Hands* 62, *Collected Poems* 65, *Landscapes for Me* 65; Essays: *Aspects of Contemporary German Lyric Poetry* 61, *Schattengefecht* 64; Trans.: *Contemporary French Lyric Poetry* 57, *Spanish Poems of the 20th Century* 62; Essays: *Poetisches Tagebuch* 66.
61 Darmstadt, Alexandraweg 5, German Federal Republic.

Krombholc, Jaroslav; Czech conductor; b. 30 Jan. 1918; ed. Conservatoire and Charles Univ., Prague. Guest Conductor, Prague National Theatre and Czech Philharmonic Orchestra 40; mem. Board of Trustees, Prague Nat. Theatre Opera House 45-49; Conductor, Prague Nat. Theatre 49-62, First Conductor 63-; toured U.S.S.R. with Nat. Theatre 55, visited Berlin 56, Brussels 58, staged *Jejî pastorkyna* (*Jenufa*, Janáček), Vienna Opera 47, *Bartered Bride* (Smetana), Budapest 49, *Catherine Ismailovna* (Shostakovich) 65; guest conductor in Romania, Bulgaria, Rio de Janeiro, Copenhagen, Vienna, Warsaw, Poznań, France, London; State Prize 49, 55; Honoured Artist 58; Nat. Artist 66.
National Theatre, Divadelní 6, Prague, Czechoslovakia.

Kronacker, Baron Paul Georges, O.B.E., DR.SC.; Belgian Minister of State and industrialist; b. 97; ed. Univ. of Brussels.
Lieut.-Col Reserve; served army 15-19; Chair. and Dir. various industrial concerns, particularly in sugar industry; led Belgian Economic Mission in Netherlands 39; enlisted again 39; escaped to England 40; for Belgian Govt. (London) missions abroad 40-43; Mil. Attaché in London 43-44; Senator for Louvain 39-46, mem. House of Reps. 46-; successively Minister of Imports, Minister for Supplies 44-47; mem. House of Reps. 46-68, Speaker 58-61; mem. Govt. Comm. for Peaceful Atomic Energy Devt.; late Chair. Int. Sugar Council; Pres. of Belgian Del. at Int. Sugar Council; Chair. Nat. Permanent Comm. for Agricultural Industries (Brussels); Honorary Chair. International Commission for Agricultural Industries (Paris); mem. Control Comm. of Ecole Nationale Supérieure d'architecture et des arts Visuels; mem. Board Les Amis des Musées Royaux des Beaux Arts de Belgique; awards include Grand Croix de l'Ordre de la Couronne, Grand Officier de l'Ordre de Léopold, Croix de Guerre (Belgium) 14-18 and 40-45, Officer of the Legion of Merit (Mil.) (U.S.A.), Commdr. de la Légion d'Honneur (France), Officier Order of Orange Nassau (Holland), Officier de l'Ordre du Mérite Hongrois (Hungary), Commdr. Orden Nacional de Mérito Carlos Manuel de Céspedes (Cuba), Gran Cruz, Placa de Plata Orden del Mérito Juan Pablo Duarte (Dominican Republic), Grand Croix de l'Ordre du Tadj (Iran), Gran Cruz Orden de San Martin (Argentina), Grand Cordon de l'Ordre de la Trinité (Ethiopia), Grand Croix Ordre Eléphant Blanc (Thailand).
Home: 101 avenue Franklin Roosevelt, Brussels 5; Country: Wolvenbosch, Kapellen, Antwerp, Belgium.
Telephone: 72-78-10 and 72-58-99.

Kronberger, Hans, C.B.E., F.R.S., B.SC., PH.D., F.INST.P.; British physicist; b. 28 July 1920; ed. Univs. of Durham and Birmingham.
Dept. of Scientific and Industrial Research working on tube alloys, wartime atomic energy project 44-46; Atomic Energy Research Establishment, Harwell 46-51; working on development of Diffusion Plant Research and Development Laboratories, Capenhurst 51 and later Head of Laboratories; Chief Physicist U.K. Atomic Energy Authority (Industrial Group) Risley 55-58 and Dir. of Research and Development (Development and Engineering Group) 58-60, Dep. Man. Dir. Reactor Group 60-64, Scientist-in-Chief 64-.
Smith's Lawn, Holly Road South, Wilmslow, Cheshire, England.
Telephone: Wilmslow 27897.

Krone, Heinrich; German politician; b. 1 Dec. 1895. Former Deputy Sec.-Gen. Catholic Centre Party; mem. Reichstag 25-33; Editor *Zeit im Querschnitt*, until its suppression by Nazis; travelling salesman 33-45; co-founder Caritas Notwerk (relief organisation for victims of Nazism); under arrest 44; helped found Christian Democratic Union in Berlin; mem. Bundestag 49-; Chair. Bundestag C.D.U. 55-; Minister for Special Tasks Nov. 61-64, Chancellor's Deputy in Defence Council of German Federal Republic 63-64, Chair. Federal Defence Council 64-66; Minister for Special Affairs at the Chancellor's Office 66-Dec. 66.
Kaiser-Friedrich-Str. 6, Bonn, German Federal Republic.

Kroner, Richard, PH.D.; German philosopher; b. 8 March 1884; ed. Breslau, Berlin, Heidelberg and Freiburg i. Br. Univs.
Lecturer in Philosophy Freiburg i. Br. Univ. 12; Prof. Freiburg Univ. 19, Dresden Technical Inst. 24 and Kiel Univ. 29; Research Prof. Berlin 34; Editor *Logos* 10-34; Pres. Int. Hegel League 30-35; refugee Oxford 38; Gifford Lecturer, St. Andrews 39-40; Prof. in Philosophy of Religion, Union Theological Seminary, New York 41-52, Emeritus 52-; Temple Univ., Philadelphia 44-64; Hon. Pres. Int. Asscn. for the Study of Hegel 62-.
Publs. *Von Kant bis Hegel* 21-24, *Die Selbstverwirklichung des Geistes* 28, *Kulturphilosophische Grundlegung der Politik* 31, *The Religious Function of Imagination* 41, *The Primacy of Faith* 43, *How Do We Know God?* 43, *Hegel's Early Theological Writings* 48, *Culture and Faith* 51, *Speculation in Pre-christian Philosophy* 56, *Kant's Weltanschaung* 56, *Selbstbesinnung* 58, *Speculation and Revelation in the Age of Christian Philosophy* 59, *Speculation and Revelation in Modern Philosophy* 61, *Between Faith and Thought* 66.
Institut Oecuménique, Chateau de Bossey, 1298 Céligny, Switzerland.
Telephone: 022-762531.

Kropotkin, Petr Nikolayevich; Soviet geologist; b. 1910; ed. Moscow Geology Prospecting Inst.
Geology Engineer, East Siberia 32-36; Research Assoc. Inst. of Geology U.S.S.R. Acad. of Sciences 36-; Corresp. mem. U.S.S.R. Acad. of Sciences 66-.
U.S.S.R. Academy of Sciences, 14 Lenin Prospekt, Moscow, U.S.S.R.

Krotkov, Fyodor Grigorievich; Soviet hygiene specialist, b. 1896; ed. Military Medical Acad.
Member C.P.S.U. 19-; Army Service 26-46; mem. U.S.S.R. Acad. of Medical Sciences 44-; U.S.S.R.

Deputy Minister of Health 46-47; Academician-Sec. U.S.S.R. Acad. of Medical Sciences 47-50; Head, Dept. of Hygiene, Cen. Inst. for Postgraduate Medical Training 37-57; Vice-Pres. U.S.S.R. Acad. of Medical Sciences 53-57; Head, Dept. of Radiation Hygiene, Cen. Inst. for Postgraduate Medical Training 51-; Chair. of Board of All-Union Scientific Soc. of Hygienists; Editor of *Hygiene* and *Sanitation*; mem. WHO Expert Cttee. on Radiation Hygiene; Order of Lenin 43, 45, 66; Red Star 35; Red Banner 45, 50; Badge of Honour 39; Patriotic War, First Class 45; Hero of Socialist Labour 66.
Publs. Over 110 works on mil. and gen. hygiene, nutritional hygiene and epidemiology.
Central Institute for Postgraduate Medical Training, Vasstaniya 1/2, Moscow, U.S.S.R.

Krüger, Christian Martin, D.SC.ENG. (Rand), DR.ING. E.H. (Aachen)., D.ENG.H.C. (Rand); South African engineer and business executive; b. 1 May 1905; ed. Ermolo and Middelburg High Schools, Transvaal and Univ. of the Witwatersrand, Johannesburg.
With South African Iron and Steel Industrial Corpn., Ltd. (I.S.C.O.R.) 31-, Technical Asst., Roll Designing Section 33-34, Roll Designer 34-38, Manager, Rolling Mills Div. 38-48, Mills Consultant, I.S.C.O.R. 48-52, Technical Manager 52-53, Gen. Works Manager 53-55, Gen. Manager 55-, Dir. 59-, Managing Dir. 64-; Chair. several I.S.C.O.R. subsidiaries; Hon. Prof. of Metallurgy and Metallurgical Engineering, Univ. of Pretoria 64-; Gold Medal of Honour for Scientific Achievement in the Field of Engineering, Akademie vir Wetenskap en Kuns 59; Hon. Vice-Pres. Iron and Steel Inst. (England) 65-.
210 Anderson Street, Brooklyn, Pretoria, South Africa.
Telephone: 74-2086.

Krüger, Hans; German lawyer and politician; b. 6 July 1902; ed. legal studies at Jena, Greifswald and Bonn.
Judge, Stargard 38-40, Konitz 40-43; Coastal Artillery 43-45; came as refugee to Westphalia 45; lawyer, Olpe Westphalia 52-; Pres. of Asscn. of Refugees 58-63; mem. Bundestag 57-; Federal Minister for Refugees Oct. 63-Jan. 64; Christian Democratic Union (C.D.U.).
Am Alten Forsthaus 26, 5301 Röttgen bei Bonn, German Federal Republic.

Krul, Wilhelmus Franciscus Johannes Maria; Netherlands engineer; b. 4 Dec. 1893; ed. Royal Military Academy.
Lieut. on Military Engineering Staff 14; Engineer of State Institute for Water Supply 21 and Dir. 22-58; Prof. in Sanitary Engineering, Technological University Delft 58-64; mem. Royal Inst. of Engineers (Holland), Bataafsch Genootschap Proefondervindelijke Wijsbegeerte; panel of experts of World Health Organisation; Maatschappij der Nederlandsche Letterkunde; Fellow American Asscn. for the Advancement of Science; Hon. mem. New England Waterworks Asscn, British Waterworks Asscn., Int. Water Supply Asscn., Water Pollution Control Fed., etc.; Commdr. Order of Orange-Nassau; Knight, Order of Dutch Lion.
Frankenslag 345, The Hague, Netherlands.
Telephone: 070-552470.

Krupkowski, Aleksander, ENG.D.; Polish metallurgist; b. 1894; ed. Petersburg Polytechnic School.
Professor Acad. of Mining and Metallurgy, Cracow 30-; Vice-Pres. Polish Acad. of Sciences 62-; author of theory of distillation and rectification of metals; research on plastic deformation of metals.
Publs. include *Badania nad Stopami niklu z miedzią* (Investigations into nickel and copper alloys) 30, *Zasady nowoczesnej metalurgii w zarysie* (Basis of Modern Metallurgy in Outline) 51, *Zasady termodynamiki i ich Zastosowanie w metalurgii i metaloznastwie*

(Principles of thermodynamics and their application in metallurgy) 58.
12b Smolki-str., Cracow, Poland.
Telephone: 623-77.

Kruppa, Erwin; Austrian mathematician; b. 85; ed. Graz and Vienna Technical Universities, Vienna Univ.
Lecturer, Czernowitz Univ. 11, Graz Technical Univ. 18, Prof. of Mathematics, Vienna Technical University 22, Prof. of Geometry 29; now Prof. Emeritus; Dr.Rer. Nat. h.c. (Karlsruhe Technical Univ.).
Publs. *Lehrbuch der darstellenden Geometrie* (with E. Müller) 36, *Analytische und konstruktive Differentialgeometrie* 57.
Schweizertalstrasse 21a, Vienna XIII, Austria.

Kruschev, Nikita S. (*see* Khrushchev, Nikita S.).

Krutch, Joseph Wood, PH.D.; American essayist; b. 25 Nov. 1893; ed. Tennessee and Columbia Univ.
Instructor, Columbia Univ. 17-18; Asst. Prof. Brooklyn Polytechnic Inst. 21-24; Associate Editor *The Nation* 25-33 and mem. Board 33-37; Drama Critic 37-; Lecturer, Columbia School of Journalism 26-32; Prof. English, Columbia Univ. 37-43, Brander Mathews Prof. of Dramatic Literature 43-52; Hon. Sec. Arizona-Sonora Desert Museum (Tucson) 54-; mem. American Acad. Arts and Letters; Fellow American Acad. Arts and Sciences; Fellow California Acad. of Sciences; Litt.D. (Columbia) 54, D.H.L. (Northwestern Univ.) 57, (Arizona Univ.) 60; Ettinger Medal of Rockefeller Inst. 66; Thorean-Emerson Medal, American Acad. of Arts and Sciences 67.
Publs. *Edgar Allan Poe: A Study in Genius* 26, *The Modern Temper* 29, *Five Masters* 30, *Experience and Art* 32, *Was Europe a Success?* 35, *The American Drama since 1918* 39, *Samuel Johnson* 44, *Henry David Thoreau* 48, *The Twelve Seasons* 49, *Great American Nature Writing* 51, *The Desert Year* 52, *Modernism in Modern Drama* 53, *The Best of Two Worlds* 53, *The Measure of Man* 54, *The Voice of the Desert* 55, *The Great Chain of Life* 57, *Grand Canyon: Today and All its Yesterdays* 58, *Human Nature and the Human Condition* 59, *The Gardener's World* (anthology) 59, *The Forgotten Peninsula* 61, *The World of Animals* (anthology) 61, *More Lives than One* (autobiography) 62, *If You Don't Mind My Saying So* 64, *Herbal* 66, *And Even If You Do* (essays) 66.
5041 East Grant Road, Tucson, Arizona, U.S.A.

Krutikov, Konstantin Alexandrovich; Soviet diplomatist; b. 1920; ed. Moscow Foreign Languages Teachers' Training Inst.
Diplomatic Service 43-; Asst. to Head of Far Eastern Dept., U.S.S.R. Ministry of Foreign Affairs 53-54; Consul-Gen. in Shanghai 54-55; Counsellor, Peking 55-58; Consultant, Deputy Head of Far Eastern Dept., U.S.S.R. Ministry of Foreign Affairs 58-61; Ambassador to Cambodia 61-65; on staff of Ministry of Foreign Affairs 65-.
Ministry of Foreign Affairs, 32-34 Smolenskaya-Sennaya ploshchad, Moscow, U.S.S.R.

Krutina, Vratislav; Czechoslovak politician; b. 29 June 1913.
Minister of Agriculture 55, later Deputy Minister; Minister of Agriculture, Forestry and Waterways 61-63, of Food Industry Sept. 63-67; Chair. Central Co-operative Council 67-; Deputy to Nat. Assembly 54; mem. Central Cttee. C.P. Czechoslovakia 62-; mem. Agricultural Comm., Central Cttee. C.P. of Czechoslovakia 63-66, Central Cttee. of Int. Co-operative Alliance, Exec. of I.C.A. Agricultural Cttee. 67-; Order of the Republic 63, Order of Feb. 25, 1948, 1st Class.
Central Co-operative Council, Těšnov 5, Prague 1, Czechoslovakia.
Telephone: 621-51.

Krylov, Alexei Georgievich; Soviet engineer and politician; b. 08; ed. Mechanical Engineering Inst., Moscow.
Technical, later Chief Technician and Dep. Chief Engineer, ZIL (formerly ZIS) Motor Works 32-42; machine building industry 42-44; Rep. of Ministry of Motor and Tractor Industry, U.S.S.R., Dep. Head *Stankoimport*, U.S.A. 44-48; Chief Engineer, later Dep. Dir. ZIL Motor Works 49-52; Dep. Minister of Motor and Tractor Industry 52-53; Dir. ZIL Motor Works, Moscow 54-63; in Council for Mutual Econ. Aid 63-; mem. Central Cttee. of C.P.S.U. 61-; State Prize 51.
Council of Mutual Economic Aid, 10 Petrovka, Moscow, U.S.S.R.

Krylov, Marshal Nikolai Ivanovich; Soviet army officer and politician; b. 03.
Joined Soviet Army 19; mem. C.P.S.U. 27-; Head of Staff of Army, later Commdr. of Army Second World War; Deputy Commdr. various military areas 45-60; Commdr. Moscow Military Area 60-63; Deputy Minister of Defence and C.-in-C. Military Strategic Rocket Forces 63-; mem. Central Cttee. of C.P.S.U. 61-; Deputy to U.S.S.R. Supreme Soviet; Marshal of the Soviet Union 62; Hero of the Soviet Union (twice); Order of Lenin (four times), October Revolution, Red Banner (four), Suvorov, and Kutuzov, Badge of Honour with a Coat-of-Arms in gold and other decorations.
Ministry of Defence, 34 Maurice Thorez Embankment, Moscow, U.S.S.R.

Krzyzanowski, Julian, PH.D.; Polish literary historian; b. 92; ed. Cracow Univ.
Prof. Univ. of London 26-30, Riga 31-33, Warsaw 34-; Visiting Lecturer, Columbia Univ. 58; mem. Polish Acad. of Sciences.
Publs. *Polish Romantic Literature* (in English), *Historia literatury polskiej* (History of Polish Literature), *Od Sredniowiecza do Baroku* (From the Middle Ages to the Baroque), *Polska bajka ludowa w ukladzie systematycznym* (Polish Folk-tales in a Systematic Arrangement), *Kalendarz zycia i twórczości H. Sienkiewicza* (Journal of the Life and Works of H. Sienkiewicz), *Madrej glowie dość dwie słowie* (A Word to the Wise), *W wieku Reja i Stanczyka* (In the Age of Rej and Stanczyk); Editor of complete editions of Słowacki, Mickiewicz and Sienkiewicz.
c/o Polish Academy of Sciences, Palace of Culture and Sciences, Warsaw, Poland.

Ku Chieh-kang; Chinese historian; b. 93; ed. Peking Univ.
Prof. of History at Peking, Amoy, Chung Shan and Yenching Univs.; on editorial staff Commercial Press; Fellow of Institute of History and Linguistics, Academia Sinica, etc.; pioneer in modern critical handling of early historical texts; specially invited to Chinese People's Political Consultative Conf. 54; central cttee. of Assoc. for Promotion of Democracy.
Publs. *Ku-shih pien* (discussions on early texts) 7 vols.; edited *Yü-kung* (journal of historical geography), etc.
Academia Sinica, Peking, China.

Ku Mu; Chinese politician.
Senior Vice-Minister, State Econ. Comm. until 65; Chair. State Capital Construction Comm. 65-.
State Capital Construction Commission, Peking, People's Republic of China.

Kuang Jen-nung; Chinese administrator.
Director, China Civil Aviation Administration 55-; awarded Liberation Medal, First Class 55.
China Civil Aviation Administration, Peking, China.

Kubadinski, Pencho; Bulgarian politician; b. 18; ed. High School and Higher Party School.
Young Communist League 34-40, Communist Party 40-; Local leader, later Central Cttee., Young Communist League 45-51; First Sec. Rousse District Party Cttee.

52-58; Sec. Central Cttee. of Communist Party 58, Cand. mem. Political Bureau 62-, now mem.; Deputy Prime Minister 62-; mem. Nat. Assembly.
Council of Ministers, Sofia, Bulgaria.

Kubar (*see* Coobar).

Kubelik, Rafael; Czechoslovak musician; b. 29 June 1914; ed. Prague Conservatorium.
Conductor, Czech Philharmonic Society, Prague 36-39; Head of Opera, Brno 39-41; Chief Conductor, Czech Philharmonic, Prague 41-48; Musical Dir. Chicago Symphony Orchestra 50-53; Musical Dir. Royal Opera House, Covent Garden 55-58; Chief Conductor Bayerischer Rundfunk, Munich 61-; Guest Conductor, North and South America, Europe and Australia; tours and concerts with Vienna Philharmonic, Concertgebouw Orchestra, Amsterdam and Bavarian Radio Symphony Orchestra; Festivals at Edinburgh, Salzburg, Lucerne, Venice, Besançon, Montreux, Festival of Holland, etc. 48-.
Compositions include: 4 operas, 2 symphonies with chorus, 4 string quartets, 2 violin concertos, concerto for piano, concerto for violoncello, songs, piano, violin music, requiem *Pro Memoria Uxoris* and cantatas *Pro Memoria Patris, Libera Nos*.
Kastanienbaum, Haus im Sand, Switzerland.

Kubitschek de Oliveira, Juscelino; Brazilian politician; b. 02; ed. Minas Gerais, Paris, Vienna and Berlin.
Qualified as doctor 27, travelled in Europe and Middle East studying surgery; on return to Minas Gerais appointed Medical Officer to various govt. services; Sec. to Gov. 33; Fed. Deputy for Minas Gerais 34-37; later Mayor of Belo Horizonte (and in charge of urban development programme) 34; Rep. for Minas Gerais to Nat. Assembly 46, Gov. 50-54; President of Brazil 56-60; established new capital of Brasilia; produced study of Alliance for Progress 63; voluntary exile 64-65.
Rio de Janeiro, Brazil.

Kubota, Tozo; Japanese business executive; b. 3 Nov. 1897; ed. Waseda Univ.
Kubota Iron and Machinery Works 21-, Chair. 55-.
Kubota Iron and Machinery Works Ltd., Funadecho, Naniwaku, Osaka, Japan.
Telephone: 06-631-1121.

Kubota, Yutaka, DR. ENG.; Japanese engineer and company director; b. 90; ed. Tokyo Univ.
President and Dir. Nippon Koei Co., Ltd.; Chair. Engineering Consulting Firms Asscn. of Japan, Inc.; Chair. Japan Industrial Rehabilitation Engineering Asscn.; Chair. Yaku Island Electric Industrial Co. Ltd.; Adviser to Board of Science and Technology Agency, Japanese Govt.; fmr. Chief Engineer, Dir. and Pres. Korea Power Co. Ltd. and Yalu River Power Development Co.; Managing Dir. Japan Nitrogenous Fertilizer Co., Ltd.; planned, designed and supervised Balu Chaung Hydro-Electric Project for Burmese Govt. 54-, Da Nhim Hydro-electric Project for Vietnamese Govt. 56-, Kali Brantas Multipurpose Project for Indonesian Govt. 61-, Nam Ngum Multipurpose Project for UN 61-, Upper Se San Multipurpose Project in Viet-Nam for UN 62-, Karnali Hydro-electric Project in Nepal for UN 58-; consultant to E.C.A.F.E. (Econ. Comm. for Asia and the Far East) for development of Mekong River 51.
Publs. *The Fusenko Hydroelectric Power Plant* (Tokyo World Power Conf.) 29, *Water Power Generation and Dam Building* (in *An Outline of Civil Engineering*) 40-45.
1459 Yoyogi-Tomigaya, Shibuya-ku, Tokyo, Japan.

Kubrick, Stanley; American film writer and director; b. 26 July 1928; ed. City Coll. of New York.
Staff photographer *Look* 46-50; produced, directed and photographed documentaries for RKO (*Day of the Fight, Flying Padre*) 51, feature films *Fear and Desire* and *Killer's Kiss* for United Artists 52, 54; wrote and directed *The Killing* (U.A.) 56, wrote (with Calder

Willingham) and directed *Paths of Glory* (U.A.); directed *Spartacus* (Universal Int.), *Lolita* (M.G.M.) 62, *Dr. Strangelove* (also wrote and produced) 64, *2001: A Space Odyssey* 66; various film awards for *Paths of Glory*.
c/o Louis C. Blau, 9777 Wilshire Boulevard, Beverly Hills, Calif., U.S.A.

Kučera, Bohuslav, LL.D.; Czechoslovak politician; b. 26 March 1923; ed. Law Faculty, Charles Univ., Prague.
Clerk, Velveta Nat. Enterprise, Varnsdorf 48-49; Chief of Dept., Nopako Nat. Enterprise, Nová Paka 49-50; Sec. of Club of Deputies of Czechoslovak Socialist Party 50-54; Sec. of Presidium of Czechoslovak Socialist Party 54-60, Gen. Sec. 60-68; Chair. Socialist Party 68-, Minister of Justice 68-; mem. Cen. Cttee. of Nat. Front; Deputy to Nat. Assembly; Deputy Chair. Constitutional and Legal Cttee. of Nat. Assembly; several decorations.
Ministry of Justice, Prague; Home: Prague 10- Vršovice, Jerevanská 7, Czechoslovakia.

Kuchel, Thomas; American lawyer and politician; b. 15 Aug. 1910; ed. Univ. of Southern California.
Practising lawyer 35-46; State Legislator, California 37-46; served U.S. Navy 42-45; State Controller 46-53; Republican Senator from California 53-, Asst. Republican leader, U.S. Senate.
315 S. Claudina, St. Anaheim, California, U.S.A.

Kuchmin, Maksim Fedorovich; Soviet diplomatist; b. 1915; ed. Saratov State Univ.
Ministry of Foreign Affairs 46-; Counsellor, Brussels 53-59; Ministry of Foreign Affairs, Moscow 59-64; Counsellor, Berne 64-64; Ambassador to Central African Republic 64-.
U.S.S.R. Embassy, Bangui, Central African Republic.

Küchük, Fazil, M.D.; Turkish Cypriot politician; b. 06; ed. Istanbul and Lausanne Univs.
Owner and Editor *Halkin Sesi* (daily) 41-60; Leader, Cyprus Turkish National Union Party 43-; Chair. Evcaf High Council 56-60; Vice-Pres. Cyprus Aug. 60-.
P.O. Box 339, Nicosia, Cyprus.

Kuczynski, Jürgen, DR.PHIL.; German economist; b. 17 Sept. 1904; ed. Berlin and Heidelberg Univs., and in U.S.A.
Refugee during the Nazi régime; Prof. of Econ. History, Humboldt Univ., Berlin; mem. D.D.R. Statistical Del. to COMECON; mem. Deutsche Akad. der Wissenschaften; Fellow Royal Statistical Soc.; Nat. Prize; Dr. h.c. rer. oec.
Parkstrasse 94, 112 Berlin, Germany.

Kudriatsev, Sergei Mikhailovich; Soviet diplomatist; b. 1915; ed. Moscow Foreign Languages Inst.
Journalist; Tass Corresp. in Berlin 40-41; Diplomatic Service, mem. Staff Soviet Diplomatic Representations in Canada, U.K., Austria, German Federal Repub., France; Amb. to Cuba 60-62; participated in numerous int. confs. and meetings; Amb. to Cambodia 68-.
U.S.S.R. Embassy, Pnom Penh, Cambodia.

Kudrna, Josef; Czechoslovak politician; b. 1 Sept. 1920; ed. Party Coll., Moscow.
First Deputy Minister of Interior 56-65; Minister of Interior 65-March 68; Cand. mem. Central Cttee. C.P. of Czechoslovakia 62-66, mem. 66-, mem. Legal Comm. 66-.
c/o Ministry of Interior, Obráncu míru 85, Prague 7-Holesovice, Czechoslovakia.

Kudsi, Nazem El, PH.D.; Syrian politician; ed. American Coll., Beirut.
Leader, Populist Party; held no political office during U.A.R. régime 58-61; President of the Syrian Arab Republic 61-63.
Damascus, Syrian Arab Republic.

Kuei Pi; Chinese political leader of Mongolian descent.
On Council of People's Government of Inner Mongolian Autonomous Area and Minister; on Mil. Council of Suiynan and Vice-Chair. Suiynan People's Government; on Central Cttee., C.C.P. branch in Inner Mongolia; on C.P.P.C.C. 49; on Standing Cttee. Nationalities State Council 49; reappointed Vice-Chair. Suiynan Gov. 53; Vice-Chair. Inner Mongolian Autonomous Area Govt. and on Standing Cttee and Organisation Chief of Inner Mongolian Branch C.C.P.; Inner Mongolian del. to N.P.C., and on Nationalities Cttee. 54; Vice-Chair. 2nd C.P.P.C.C.; Vice-Chair. Nationalities Cttee. 56-; Vice-Chair. 3rd N.P.C. 56.
Nationalities Affairs Commission, N.P.C., Peking, China.

Kugelberg, Bertil, B.A., LL.B.; Swedish business official; b. 31 June 1900; ed. Kungliga Universitetet i Uppsala.
Assistant Judge of Assize 23-27; in Superior Court and Ministry of Educ. and Ecclesiastical Affairs 27-28; Man. Dir. Swedish Private Banks Asscn. for Collective Negotiations 37-42; Man. Dir. Swedish Insurance Companies Asscn. for Collective Negotiations 42; Vice-Man. Dir. Swedish Employers' Confederation 42-47, Man. Dir. and mem. Board 47-; Judge of Labour Court 49-; official of numerous other business orgs., retired 66.
Leksandsvägen 25, Bromma, Sweden.

Kühn, Alfred, PH.D., DR. h.c. (Oslo), DR.MED. h.c. (Göttingen), Dr. Rer. Nat. h.c. (Freiburg); German biologist; b. 22 April 1885.
Extra. Prof. of Zoology and Comparative Physiology Freiburg i. Br. Univ. 14; Lecturer Berlin Univ. 18; Prof. Göttingen Univ. and Dir. Zoological Inst. 20-37; Dir. Max-Planck Biological Inst. Tübingen 37-58; Prof. Tübingen Univ. 45-67.
Publs. *Anleitungen zu tierphysiologischen Grundversuchen* 17, *Die Orientierung der Tiere im Raum* 19, *Morphologie der Tiere in Bildern* I 21, II 26, *Grundriss der allgemeinen Zoologie* 16th edn. 67, *Grundriss der Vererbungslehre*, 4th edn. 65, *Genetische und entwicklungsphysiologische Untersuchungen* (with K. Henke) I-VII 29, VIII-XII 32, XIII-XIV 36, *Lehrbuch der Zoologie* (with K. Grobben) 32, *Goethe und die Naturforschung* 33, *Über hormonale Genwirkungen* (with E. Caspari and E. Plagge) 35, *Vorlesungen über Entwicklungsphysiologie* 2nd edn. 65, *Versuche zur Entwicklung eines Modells der Genwirkungen* 56, *Über die Wirkungsweise von Erbfaktoren* 58, *Genetisch bedingte Mosaikbildungen* 59, *Parabiosen als Mittel aur Aufklärung von Genwirkungen* (with B. Berg) 62, etc.
Spemannstr. 34, 34 Tübingen, German Federal Republic.
Telephone: 323247.

Kuhn, Ferdinand, A.B.; American journalist; b. 10 April 1905; ed. Columbia Univ.
Reporter *New York Times* 25-28, London staff 28-36, chief London correspondent 37-39, Editorial writer 39-40; Asst. to U.S. Sec. of Treasury 40; Head British Div. Office of War Information 42; Dir. Interim Int. Information Service (U.S. State Dept.) 45; Staff writer *Washington Post* 46-53; at present magazine writer and lecturer on international affairs.
Publs. *Commodore Perry and the Opening of Japan* 55, *The Story of the Secret Service* 57, *Borderlands* 62, *The Philippines: Yesterday and Today* 65.
2915 Audubon Terrace, Washington, D.C., U.S.A.

Kühn, Heinz; German politician; b. 18 Feb. 1912; ed. Univs. of Cologne, Prague and Ghent.
Member Catholic Youth Movement "Neudeutschland", Socialist Youth Movement of Germany 28; mem. Socialist Party (S.P.D.) 30; Chair. of Socialist Student Group, Cologne; political emigration and studies at Univs. of Prague and Ghent 33; Area Chair. Mittelrhein Area, S.P.D. 45; mem. Party Management

Cttee., S.P.D. 45; mem. Landtag, North Rhine-Westphalia 48-54, 62-, Chair. S.P.D. Parl. Party 62-67; mem. Bundestag, mem. S.P.D. Parl. Management Cttee., Bundestag Foreign Affairs Comm. and Chair. Bundestag Comm. on German Schools and Insts. Abroad 53-62; mem. Assembly, Western European Union; Deputy Chair. Council of Admin. Westdeutscher Rundfunk, Cologne 54-; Chair. S.P.D. North Rhine-Westphalia 62-; mem. Presidium S.P.D. 66-; Minister-Pres. of North Rhine-Westphalia, Düsseldorf Dec. 66-.
Der Ministerpräsident des Landes Nordrhein-Westfalen, Düsseldorf, Haroldstrasse 2; Home: 5 Köln-Dellbrück, Roteichenweg 5, German Federal Republic.

Kuhn de Chizelle, Bernard; French engineer; b. 11 Aug. 1897; ed. Lycée d'Amiens and Ecole nationale supérieure d'electro-technique et d'hydraulique, Grenoble.
Engineer, Thomson-Houston Co. 21-25; Dir. of Var and Alpes-Maritime Industrial Energy System 26-35; Dir. Heat and Light Soc., Grenoble 35-44; Dir.-Gen. *Gaz du Lyon* 44, Dir. of Mixed Distribution, *Electricité de France, Gaz de France* 54, Dir.-Gen. *Gaz de France* 59-64, Hon. Dir.-Gen. 64-; Pres., Dir.-Gen. Cie. d'Etudes et de Réalisations de Cybernétique Industrielle (CERCI); Officier, Légion d'Honneur.
8 Avenue de New York, Paris 16e, France.

Kuhns, William Rodney, LITT.B.; American economist; b. 21 Jan. 1897; ed. Denison and Columbia Univs.
Reporter Paris *Herald* 21; United Press corresp. New York, London, Paris 21-24, Far East 24-28; Financial Feature Editor Associated Press, N.Y. 28-30; Associate Editor American Bankers' Asscn. Journal 30-33; Man. Editor *Banking* 32-37, Editor 37-62, Editorial Consultant 62-; Editor Year Book *Present-day Banking* 47-48, 49-50, 50-51; Editor *The Return of Opportunity* 44; Editor *Banking's Newsletter* 42-; mem. American Economic Asscn., American Statistical Asscn., Dir. Public Relations Council, American Bankers' Asscn. 53-57, Senior Deputy Manager 57-62.
Klinesville Road, Flemington, N.J., U.S.A.

Kuiper, Gerard Peter, BSC., PH.D.; American astronomer; b. Netherlands 7 Dec. 1905; ed. Univ. of Leiden.
Research Asst. in Astronomy, Univ. of Leiden 28-33; mem. Neths. Eclipse Expedition to Sumatra 29; Research Fellow, Lick Observatory, Univ. of Calif. 33-35; Lecturer, Harvard Univ. 35-36; Asst. Prof. of Astronomy, Univ. of Chicago 36-37, Assoc. Prof. 37-43, Prof. 43-60; Research Prof. Univ. of Arizona 60-; Dir. Yerkes and McDonald Observatories 47-49 and 57-60; Dir. Lunar and Planetary Lab., Univ. of Arizona 61-; naturalised U.S. citizen 37; Commdr. Order of Orange Nassau (Neths.); mem. of Nat. Acad. of Science; Amer. Acad. of Arts and Sciences; Int. Astronomical Union; Amer. Astr. Soc.; Astr. Soc. of Pacific; Royal Astr. Soc. of London (Assoc.); Neths. Soc. of Science (foreign mem.); Royal Neths. Acad. of Science (foreign mem.).
Publs. Editor and co-author *The Atmospheres of the Earth and Planets* 49, 52, *Photographic Lunar Atlas* 60, *Orthographic Lunar Atlas* 61, *Rectified Lunar Atlas* 63; editor *The Solar System*, 4 vols. 53-61, *Stars and Stellar Systems*, 7 vols. 60-.
721 N. Sawtelle Ave., Tucson, Arizona, U.S.A.
Telephone: 602-326-6998.

Kukarkin, Boris Vasilievich, D.SC.; Soviet astronomer; b. 30 Oct. 1909.
Professor, Moscow Univ. 51-, Head of Dept. of Stellar Astronomy, Moscow Univ. 60-; Dir. Shternberg State Astronomical Inst. 52-56; Vice-Pres. Int. Astronomical Union 55-66.
Publs. *Preliminary Catalogue of Mean Colour Equivalents of 1207 Stars* 37, *Physical Variable Stars* 39, *Visual Observations of 55 Cepheides with Long Periods* 40,

Variable Stars and Methods of their Observation 47, *Investigation of the Structure and Development of Stellar Systems on the Basis of the Study of Variable Stars* 49, *General Catalogue of Variable Stars* (jointly) 58.
Moscow State University, Moscow B-234, U.S.S.R.
Telephone: AV-9-33-18.

Kukiel, Lieut.-Gen. Marian, K.C.B., PH.D.; Polish officer and historian; b. 15 May 1885; ed. Lwów Univ.
Mem. Secret Military Organisation 08; Officer in Polish Legions 14, Commdg. Officer Infantry Brigade 20; Brig.-Gen. Commdg. Infantry Div. 23; Dir. historical section of Gen. Staff 25-26; Lecturer in Modern and Military History Cracow Univ. 27-39; Dir. Czartoryski Museum and Library 30-39; mem. Polish Acad. 37; Deputy Min. of War 39, G.O.C. 1st Polish Corps Scotland 40-42; Min. of Nat. Defence 42-49; Chair. Polish Historical Society in Great Britain.
Publs. *Dzieje wojska polskiego w dobie napoleonskiej* 12, *Próby powstańcze po trzecim rozbiorze* 12, *Zarys historji wojskowości w Polsce* 22, *Maciejowice* 29, *Wojna 1812 roku* 37, Chapters in *Cambridge History of Poland* 41, *Six Years of War for Independence* 47, *Czartoryski and European Unity* 55, *Dzieje Polski Porozbiorowe (1795-1921)* 61.
c/o Polish Institute and Sikorski Museum, 20 Princes Gate, London, S.W.7., England.
Telephone: 01-589-9249.

Kulakov, Fyodor Davydovich; Soviet politician; b. 18; ed. All-Union Agricultural Inst.
Member C.P.S.U. 40-; section leader, sugar beet industry, agronomist 38-43; party, econ. and Soviet work 43-55; Deputy Minister of Agriculture, R.S.F.S.R. 55-59, Minister of Grain Products, R.S.F.S.R. 59-60; First Sec. Stavropol Area Cttee., C.P.S.U. 60-64; Head of Agricultural Dept., Central Cttee. of C.P.S.U. 64-65; mem. Central Cttee. of C.P.S.U. 61-, Sec. 65-; Deputy Supreme Soviet.
Central Committee of the Communist Party of the Soviet Union, 4 Staraya ploshchad, Moscow, U.S.S.R.

Kulatov, Turabay; Soviet politician; b. 1908; ed. Kzyl-Kiysk Soviet-Party School and Higher Party School.
Trade union official 34; mem. Bureau of the Central Cttee. of the C.P. of Kirghizia 38; Chair. of the Council of People's Commissars of Kirghizia 38-45; Chair. of the Presidium of the Supreme Soviet of Kirghizia 45-; Vice-Chair. of the Presidium of the Supreme Soviet of the U.S.S.R. 46-; mem. Central Auditing Comm., C.P.S.U.; Deputy to U.S.S.R. and Kirghizian S.S.R. Supreme Soviets; mem. Central Cttee. C.P. Kirghizian S.S.R., and mem. Politburo; awarded Order of Lenin (four times).
Supreme Soviet of Kirghizia, Frunze, Kirghizia, U.S.S.R.

Kulazhenkov, Anatoly Georgievich; Soviet diplomatist; b. 1911; ed. Moscow Teachers' Training Inst.
Diplomatic Service 37-; U.S.S.R. Minister in Switzerland 46-50; Head of Protocol Dept., U.S.S.R. Ministry of Foreign Affairs 50-53; Amb. to Mexico 53-57; Perm. Rep. to UNESCO 59-61; Amb. to Tunisia 62-64; Export Consultant, Dept. of Int. Orgs., U.S.S.R. Ministry of Foreign Affairs 64-66; Amb. to Senegal 66-68; on staff of Ministry of Foreign Affairs 68-.
U.S.S.R. Ministry of Foreign Affairs, 32-34 Smolenskaya-Sennaya ploshchad, Moscow, U.S.S.R.

Kulczyński, Stanislaw; Polish scientist and politician; b. 95; ed. Jagiellonian Univ., Cracow.
Prof. of Systematics and Morphology, Lwów Univ. 24, Dean of Mathematical and Nat. Sciences Faculty 36, Rector 36; resigned for political reasons; Rector, Wroclaw Univ. and Polytechnic 45-52; now Prof. of Biology, Wroclaw Univ.; mem. of the Seym (Parliament); Chair. Seym Foreign Affairs Cttee. 52-56; Deputy

Chair. Council of State 57-; Chair. Polish Democratic Party; Pres. Polish Peace Cttee. 58-; mem. Polish Acad. of Sciences.
Stronnictwo Demokratyczne, Warsaw, Poland.

Kulichenko, Leonid Sergeyevich; Soviet politician; b. 1913; ed. Volgograd Inst. of Mechanics and C.P.S.U. Higher Party School.
Teacher 36-42; mem. C.P.S.U. 40-; party and local govt. official, Volgograd Region 42-61; Chair. Volgograd Soviet of Working People's Deputies 62-65; First Sec. Volgograd Regional Cttee. of C.P.S.U. 65-; mem. Central Cttee. of C.P.S.U. 66-; Deputy to U.S.S.R. Supreme Soviet.
Volgograd Regional Committee of C.P.S.U., Volgograd, U.S.S.R.

Kulikov, Vasily Vasilievich; Soviet lawyer; b. 12; ed. Kazan Inst. of Soviet Law.
Member Communist Party of Soviet Union 39- successively Investigator, Asst. to Procurator, Dept. Procurator, Dept. Head, Deputy Chief Procurator 32-50; on staff of Central Cttee. C.P.S.U. 50-58; Deputy Gen. Procurator of U.S.S.R. 58-62; First Deputy Chair. Supreme Court of U.S.S.R. 62-; Order of Red Star.
Supreme Court of U.S.S.R., 13 Ulitsa Voroskogo, Moscow, U.S.S.R.

Kulisiewicz, Tadeusz; Polish artist; b. 99; ed. Warsaw Acad. of Fine Arts.
Prof. Warsaw Acad. of Fine Arts 46-; First Prize, Int. Wood Engraving Exhibition, Warsaw 33, State Prizes, First Class 52 and 56, UNESCO Award 54; rep. at exhbns. Prague, Rome, Milan, Vienna, Paris, Brussels, The Hague 53, Germany 55 and 56, Mexico 57, and at XXXVII Venice Biennale 54.
Works include the Sziembark drawings, the China, India and Mexico drawings, the *Caucasian Chalk Circle* (Brecht) drawings.
7 Mazowiecka, Warsaw, Poland.

Kulyebakin, Victor Sergeyevich; Soviet electronic scientist; b. 91; ed. Moscow Higher Tech. Inst.
Teacher, Moscow Energetics Inst. 16-30, Prof. 32-52, Vice-Dir. 32-34; Vice-Dir. State Experimental Electro-Technical Inst., Moscow 21-30; Prof. Zhukovsky Air Academy 23-60; Dir. Inst. of Automation and Tele-mechanics, Soviet Acad. of Sciences 39-41; mem. U.S.S.R. Acad. of Sciences; Head of the Laboratory of Inst. of Automation and Tele-mechanics 60-; Chair. Cttee. of Scientific and Engineering Terminology U.S.S.R. Acad. of Sciences; Order of Lenin (twice), Yablochkov Prize (Soviet Acad. of Sciences) 61, State Prize.
Publs. include: *Start and Control Rheostats* 29, *Testing of Electric Machines and Transformers* 35, *Electrical Equipment* 32, *Cinetics of Excitation of Syncro Motors* 34, *Electrical Equipment of Aeroplanes* 45, *Electrification of Aeroplanes* 52, *Semiconductors in Automation* 63.
U.S.S.R. Academy of Sciences Committee of Scientific and Engineering Technology, 4 ulitsa Griboedov, Moscow, U.S.S.R.

Kumaramangalam, Gen. Paramasiva Prabhaker; Indian army officer; b. 1913; ed. Eton Coll. and Royal Mil. Acad., Woolwich, U.K.
Artillery officer; fought with Indian Forces in Middle East, Second World War; Commandant, Defence Services Staff Coll., Wellington (India) 59-63; Deputy Chief of Army Staff 64-65, Vice-Chief 65-66, Chief of Staff June 66-.
Army Headquarters, New Delhi 11, India.

Kumykin, Pavel Nikolayevich; Soviet politician; b. 01; ed. Moscow State Univ.
Soviet army 20-23; mem. C.P.S.U. 27-; with Ministry of Foreign Trade 24-; Deputy Minister, later First Deputy Minister of Foreign Trade U.S.S.R. 49-51, Minister

51-53; Dep. Minister of Foreign Trade U.S.S.R. 53-; Cand. mem. Central Cttee. C.P.S.U. 52-65; Orders of Lenin (twice), Red Banner of Labour (four times), etc.
Ministry of Foreign Trade, 32-34 Smolenskaya-Sennaya ploshchad, Moscow, U.S.S.R.

Kunayev, Dinmohammed Akhmedovich; Soviet (Kazakh) politician and mining engineer; b. 1912; ed. Moscow Inst. of Non-Ferrous Metals.
Former Dir. Kounrad Mine, Kazakh S.S.R.; Vice-Chair. Council of Ministers Kazakh S.S.R. 45-52, Chair. 52-60, 62-; First Sec. Kazakh Communist Party 60-62, 64-; Alt. mem. Politburo Central Cttee. of C.P.S.U. April 66-; Deputy to Supreme Soviet of the U.S.S.R. and Supreme Soviet of the Kazakh S.S.R.; mem. Presidium of Supreme Soviet of U.S.S.R.; mem. C.P.S.U. Central Cttee. 56-; mem. and fmr. Pres. Acad. of Sciences of the Kazakh S.S.R.
Central Committee of Communist Party of the Kazakh S.S.R., Alma-Ata, Kazakh S.S.R., U.S.S.R.

Kuncewiczowa, Maria; Polish writer; b. 1899; ed. Warsaw.
Member Int. P.E.N. Club; Founder, Centre Writers in Exile; Prof. of Polish Literature, Univ. of Chicago 62-65.
Publs. *Przymierze z dzieckiem*, *Twarz mezczyzny* (trans. into French and Italian), *Miłość Panienska*, *Dwa Ksiezyce*, *Dylizans Warszawski*, *Cudzoziemka* (The Stranger) (trans. into Czech, French, Italian, Dutch, Estonian, English, Spanish, Finnish), *Dni Powszednie Panstwa Kowalskich*, *Miasto Heroda*, *Klucze* (The Keys) (trans. into English, French, Czech), *Zmowa Nie-obecnych* (The Conspiracy of the Absent) (trans. into English) 50, *Lesnik* (The Forester) (trans. into English, Italian) 54; *Thank You for the Rose* (play) 55, *W Domn i w Polsce* (At Home and in Poland) 58, *Odkrycie Patusanu* 59, *Gaj Oliwny* (The Olive Grove) 61, *The Modern Polish Mind* (anthology) 62.
7 Park Avenue, Apt. 18B, New York City 16, U.S.A.

Kundera, Milan; Czechoslovak writer; b. 1 April 1929; ed. Film Faculty, Acad. of Music and Dramatic Arts, Prague.
Assistant, later Asst. Prof., Film Faculty, Acad. of Music and Dramatic Arts, Prague 52-; mem. Cen. Cttee. Union of Czechoslovak Writers 56-, mem. Presidium of Cen. Cttee. 63-67; mem. Editorial Board *Literární noviny* 56-59, 63-67, 68-; Czechoslovak Writers' Publishing House Prize 61; Klement Gottwald State Prize 63; Union of Czechoslovak Writers' Prize 67.
Publs. Poetry: *Man a Broad Garden* 53, *The Last May* 55, *Monologues* 57; Drama: *The Owners of the Keys* 62 (produced in German Fed. Repub., U.S.S.R., Hungary, Bulgaria, Uruguay, U.K. and Switzerland); Short stories: *Ridiculous Loves* 63, *The Second Book of Ridiculous Loves* 65; Novel: *The Joke* 67.
Film Faculty, Academy of Music and Dramatic Arts, Prague 1, Smetanovo nábř. 2, Czechoslovakia.

Kuneralp, Zeki; Turkish diplomatist; b. 5 Oct. 1914; ed. Univ. of Berne.
In Switzerland 23-38; Ministry of Foreign Affairs, Turkey 41-, served Bucharest 43-47, Ankara 47-49, Prague 49-52, NATO (Paris) 52-57; Ambassador to Switzerland 62-64, to U.K. 64-66; Sec.-Gen. Ministry of Foreign Affairs 66-.
Ministry of Foreign Affairs, Ankara, Turkey.

Kunitz, Stanley J., M.A.; American writer and educator; b. 29 July 1905; ed. Harvard Univ.
Editor *Wilson Library Bulletin* 28-42; service with U.S. Army, rising to rank of Staff Sergeant 43-45; Prof. of Literature, Bennington Coll. (Vt.) 46-49; Dir. of Seminar, Potsdam Summer Workshop in Creative Arts 49-53; Lecturer and Dir. of Poetry Workshop, New School for Social Research, New York 50-58; Dir. Poetry Workshop, The Poetry Center, New York,

58-62; Lecturer, Columbia Univ. 63-66; Adjunct. Prof. Graduate School of Writing (Columbia) 67-; mem. Nat. Inst. of Arts and Letters; awards include Garrison Medal for Poetry 26, Blumenthal Prize 41, Levinson Prize 56, Harriet Monroe Award 58, Pulitzer Prize for Poetry 59; Brandeis Creative Arts Poetry Medal 65; Hon. Litt. D. (Clark Univ.) 61.

Publs. Verse: *Intellectual Things* 30, *Passport to the War* 44, *Selected Poems* 58; Editions: *Living Authors* 31, *Authors Today and Yesterday* 33, *Junior Book of Authors* 34, *British Authors of the XIX Century* 36, *American Authors 1600-1900* 38, *XX Century Authors* 42, *British Authors Before 1800* 52, *XX Century Authors* (First Supplement) 55, *Poems of John Keats* 64, *European Authors 1000-1900.* 67.

157 West 12th Street, New York 11, N.Y., U.S.A.

Kuno, Hisashi, DR.SC.; Japanese university professor; b. 7 Jan. 1910; ed. Univ. of Tokyo.

Associate Prof. Univ. of Tokyo 39-55; Prof. of Petrology 55-; Temp. Visiting Prof. Univ. of Minnesota 64; Pres. Int. Asscn. of Volcanology 63-67; Foreign Assoc. U.S. Acad. of Sciences; studies in geology and petrology of Hakone volcano and adjacent regions in Japan, origin of magmas and their differentiation process in Circum-Pacific region and Hawaii and in crystallization of pyroxenes from magmas; Japan Acad. prize for study of pyroxenes in rocks 54.

Publs. Scientific articles: *Volcanoes and Volcanic Rocks* 53.

129 1-chome, Seki-Machi, Nerima-ku, Tokyo, Japan.

Kunstler, Charles; French historian, poet, essayist and art critic; b. 22 Sept. 1887.

Vice-President of the Société des Gens de Lettres; Pres. Syndicat de la Presse Artistique, Assoc. des Ecrivains de Champagne, Dir. des Journalistes et des Nouvellistes Parisiens; Hon. Pres. Maison des Journalistes; mem. de l'Institut (Acad. des Beaux-Arts), P.E.N. Club, Conseil Supérieur des Beaux-Arts, Conseiller de la Caisse Nationale des Lettres, Asscn. des Ecrivains (anciens) Combattants.

Publs. *Paul-Emile Pissarro* 28, *Coubine* 29, *Lucien Mainssieux* 29, *La Peinture Indépendante en France* 29, *La Gravure Originale en France* 30, *Jane Poupelet* 29, *Camille Pissarro* 30, *Forain* 31, *Gauguin* 34, *Les Amours de François Villon* 34, *La Fontaine aux Trois Miracles* 35, *Watteau* 36, *Les Arts de l'Amérique Précolombienne* 38, *La Vie Privée de Marie-Antoinette* 38, *La Vie Privée de l'Impératrice Joséphine* 39, *Renoir* 41, *Gauguin* 42, *Marie-Antoinette* 43, *L'Enseigne de Gersaint* 43, *La Politique des Rois, par eux-mêmes* 43, *Le Testament de François Villon et Maurice L'Hoir* 45, *Pierre Prins* 45, *Fersen et son Secret* 47, *Fersen et les Femmes* 47, *Gauguin* 47, *Mondzain* 48, *La Vie Quotidienne sous Louis XVI* 50, *La Douceur d'Aimer* 51, *Précis d'Histoire Générale de l'Art* 52, *La Vie Quotidienne sous Louis XV* 53, *Paris souterrain* 53, *Solitudes* 54, *L'Art au XIXe siècle* 55, *A mes Amis* 56, *Trois Peintres* 56, *Louis et le Grand-Théâtre de Bordeaux* 56, *Sur les Mémoires de Mme. de Remusat* 57, *Hommage à Georges Duhamel* 57, *Mme. de Pompadour* 60, *Fersen et Marie-Antoinette* 61, *La Vie Quotidienne sous la Régence* 61, *Rois, Empereurs et Présidents de la France* 61, *La Sculpture en France de Rodin à nos Jours* 61, *La Verte Vieillesse de M. de Voltaire* 63, *Eugène Delacroix et la Critique* 63, *Hommage à René Maran* 65, *Elvire ou Le Songe de Don Juan* 66, *Pissarro, Villes et Campagnes* 67, *Rencontre d'un artiste parisien avec les abeilles* 68.

29 rue Hippolyte-Maindron, Paris 14e, France.

Kunz, Erich; Austrian opera singer; b. 20 May 1909; ed. High School for Music, Vienna

With Staatsoper, Vienna 41-; Mozart Medal, Verdienstkreuz, 1st Class, for Arts and Sciences.

Grinzingerstrasse 35, 1190 Vienna, Austria.

Telephone: 32-22-01.

Kunze, Emil, DR.PHIL.; German archaeologist; b. 18 Dec. 1901; ed. Universität Wien and Universität Leipzig.

Studentship, German Archaeological Inst. 26-29; Asst., German Archaeological Inst., Athens 29-33; Studentship, Prussian Acad., Berlin 33-35; Asst., Museum of Casts of Classical Sculpture, Munich 35-37; Lecturer, Univ. of Marburg 36-37; Munich 37-42; Field Dir. Olympia Excavation 37-42, 52-; Prof. of Classical Archaeology, Univ. of Strasbourg 42-45; Univ. of Munich 46-51; Dir. German Archaeological Inst., Athens 51-67; mem. German and Austrian Archaeological Insts.; mem. Bavarian Acad.; Corresp. mem. Acad. of Göttingen and Royal Acad. of Sciences, Copenhagen; Hon. mem. Soc. of Hellenic Studies, London, Hellenic Archaeological Soc., Athens; Federal German Order of Merit.

Publs. *Kretische Bronzereliefs* 31, *Orchomenos II and III* 31, 34, *Zeus und Ganymedes* 40, *Archaische Schildbänder* 51, *Berichte über die Ausgrabungen in Olympia* (Vol. II seq.) 38-, *Drei Bronzen der Slg. H. Stathatos* 53.

Athens, Palaeon Phaleion, Dimitros 5, Greece; Home: 8021 Grosshesselohe bei München, Immergrünstrasse 1, German Federal Republic.

Telephone: Munich 796244; Athens 982346.

Kunze, Horst, DR. PHIL.; German librarian; b. 22 Sept. 1909; ed. Sächsische Landesbibliothek, Dresden and Deutsche Bücherei, Leipzig.

Research Librarian, Landesbibliothek, Darmstadt 39-47; Dir. Universitäts-und Landesbibliothek Sachsen-Anhalt, Halle 47-50; Provisional Gen. Dir. Öffentliche Wissenschaftliche Bibliothek (now Deutsche Staatsbibliothek) 50-51, Gen. Dir. Deutsche Staatsbibliothek 51-; Dir. Inst. of Library Science and Scientific Information, Humboldt-Univ. Berlin 55-; Full Prof. of Library Science, Univ. of Berlin 54-; Chair. Arbeitsgemeinschaft für das Kinder- und Jugendbuch 59-; Pres. Deutscher Bibliotheksverband 64; Prof. in ord. 66.

Publs. *Lieblingsbücher von dazumal* 38 (reprint 65), *Wege zum wissenschaftlichen Buch* (2nd edn.) 55, *Wissenschaftliches Arbeiten* (2nd edn.) 59, *Gelesen und geliebt* (2nd edn.) 63, *Über das Registermachen* 64 (3rd edn. 68), *Willst Du Bibliothekar werden?* (2nd edn.) 65, *Dunkel war's, der Mond schien helle* (7th edn.) 65, *Schatzbehalter vom Besten aus der älteren deutschen Kinderliteratur* (3rd edn.) 68, *Grundzüge der Bibliothekslehre* (3rd edn.) 66.

Regatta-Strasse 246, 118 Berlin-Grünau, Germany.

Telephone: 67-48-09.

Kunzru, Pandit Hriday Nath, B.A., B.SC., D.LITT.; Indian politician; b. 87; ed. Allahabad Univ. and London School of Economics and Political Science.

Joined Servants of India Society (national missionaries pledged to devote their lives to the service of India) 09, Pres. 36-; mem. Indian Legislative Assembly 27-30, Council of State 37-47, Constituent Assembly 46-50, Provisional Parl. 50-52, Upper House, Indian Parl. 52-62; Leader Indian Del. Inter-Parliamentary Union 56-61; Pres. East African Nat. Congress 29; Pres. Nat. Liberal Fed. 34; mem. Defence Consultative Cttee. 42-46; Leader, Govt. of India's del. to South Africa 50; visited numerous countries to study condition of Indians settled in these places; mem. of Govt. of India's Del. to Malaya 46; Gen. Sec. All India Seva Samiti, Allahabad; Chair. Nat. Cadet Corps Cttee. 46-47; mem. Armed Forces Re-organisation Cttee. 46-47; of State Re-organisation Comm 53-55; Univ. Grants Comm. 53-66; Pres. Indian Council of World Affairs 49-; Chair. Indian School of Int. Studies 55-, of Railway Accidents Inquiry Cttee. 61-63; Pres. Indian Asscn. for Advancement of Urdu 62-; Chair. Railways Study Team of Admin. Reform Comm. 67-.

Indian Council of World Affairs, Sapru House, Barakhamba Road, New Delhi 1, India.

Telephone: 40243.

Kuo Mo-jo; Chinese poet, historian and politician; b. 92; ed. Kyushu Imperial Univ. Japan.

Deputy Head Gen. Political Dept., Nat. Revolutionary Army 26-27; took part in Nanchang Revolution, after defeat in exile in Japan 27-37; Dir. 3rd Dept., Political Training Board, Nat. Military Council 38-40; Chair. of its Cultural Work Cttee. 40-45; mem. Nat. Cttee. of Chinese People's Political Consultative Conf. 49-; Vice-Chair. of its Standing Cttee.; mem. Central People's Govt. Council 49-54; Vice-Premier of Govt. Admin. Council 49-54; Vice-Chair. Standing Cttee. Nat. People's Congress 54-; State Peace Prize 52; Vice-Chair. Lenin Int. Peace Prize Cttee.; Pres. Academia Sinica 49-; Foreign mem. Czechoslovak Acad. of Sciences; Chair. China Peace Cttee., All-China Fed. of Literary and Art Circles.

Publs. *The Goddess, Starry Canopy* (poems), *Three Women Rebels* (play), *On the Study of Ancient Society in China, Chu Yuan* (play) 41, *Ten Critical Essays, The Age of Bronze* (essays).

Chinese Academy of Sciences, Peking, China.

Kuprevich, Vasili Feofilovich; Soviet botanist; b. 1897; ed. Inst. of Advanced Pedagogical Qualifications.

At Inst. of Botany of U.S.S.R. Acad. of Sciences 31-52, Dir. 49-52; Pres. Byelorussian Acad. of Sciences 52-; Editor-in-Chief *Botanical Journal* 58-64, *Transactions of the Byelorussian Academy of Sciences* 58-, *Limnology and Phytopathology* 61-; Corresp. mem. U.S.S.R. Acad. of Sciences 53-; mem. C.P.S.U. 45-; awards, orders and medals of U.S.S.R.

Presidium of Byelorussian Academy of Sciences, 66 Lenin Prospekt, Minsk, U.S.S.R.

Kuprianov, Alexei Andreevich; Soviet sports administrator; b. 1908; ed. Trainers' School at State Central Inst. of Physical Culture.

Textile worker and civil aviation worker 25-34; Exec. Sec. Presidium of Cen. Board of Sporting Soc. *Dynamo* 25-52, Deputy Pres. 52-; mem. Man. Cttee. Int. Union of Cyclists; Vice-Pres. Int. Amateurs' Fed. of Cyclists; Pres. U.S.S.R. Fed. of Cycling Sport; U.S.S.R. Merited Master of Cycling Sport; mem. C.P.S.U. 39-.

U.S.S.R. Union of Sporting Societies and Organizations, 4 Skatertny pereulok, Moscow, U.S.S.R.

Kuraishi, Tadao; Japanese industrialist and politician; b. 1900; ed. Hosei Univ. and Univ. of London.

Entered Fujokai Co. Ltd. as Dir. 34-37; Managing Dir. Southern Japan Chemical Industry Co. Ltd. 37; mem. House of Reps. 47-; Minister of Labour 55-56, 58-59, of Agriculture and Forestry 66-Feb. 68; Chair. Diet Policy Cttee., Liberal Party 52, House of Reps. Budget Cttee. 53.

17 Nijukki-cho, Shinjuku-ku, Tokyo, Japan.

Kural, Adnan; Turkish diplomatist; b. 9 April 1910; ed. Ankara Univ.

Entered Foreign Service 35; served Rome, Moscow, Ministry of Foreign Affairs, Rome 38-45; del. to U.N. 45-51; Ministry of Foreign Affairs 51-55; Ambassador to Syria 55-58, to Greece 60; Perm. Rep. to UN 62-64; Amb. to Switzerland 64-65, to Italy 65-66, to Spain 67-. Turkish Embassy, Madrid; Residence: Monte Esquinza 48, Madrid 4, Spain.

Telephone: Madrid 2-24-87-96; also 2-57-02-35.

Kurata, Chikara; Japanese business executive; b. 1 March 1889; ed. Sendai Higher Technical School.

Hitachi Ltd. (then Kuhara Mining Co.) 12-, Dir. 41-47, Man. Dir. 47, Pres. 47, Chair. of Board and Pres. 47-61, Chair. of Board 61-67, Counsellor 67-; Chair. Japan Science Foundation 60-, Japan Machinery Industry Fed. 54-; Man. Dir. Japan Fed. of Econ. Org. 50; Adviser, Ministry of Int. Trade and Industry 60-, Science and Technology Agency 56-.

22, 1-chome, Higashida-cho, Suginamiku, Tokyo, Japan.

Telephone: 311-0635.

Kurath, Hans, A.B., PH.D., L.H.D.; American linguist; b. 13 Dec. 1891; ed. Univs. of Wisconsin, Texas and Chicago.

Instructor in German Univ. of Texas 14-16 and 17-19; Fellow Univ. of Chicago 16-17 and 19-20; Instructor in German Northwestern Univ. 20-22, Asst. Prof. 22-27; Prof. of German and Linguistics Ohio State Univ. 27-31; Prof. of Germanic Languages and General Linguistics and Chair. Dept. of Germanic Languages Brown Univ. 31-46; Prof. of English, Univ. of Michigan 46-62, Emeritus 62-; Editor and Dir. *Linguistic Atlas of the United States and Canada* 31; Editor *Middle English Dictionary* 46; Dir. Linguistic Inst. 47-50.

Publs. *American Pronunciation* 28, *Handbook of the Linguistic Geography of New England* 39, *Linguistic Atlas of New England* (3 vols.) 39-43, *A Word Geography of the Eastern U.S.* 49, *Middle English Dictionary* 52-61, *The Pronunciation of English in the Atlantic States* 59-61, *A Phonology and Prosody of Modern English* 64, *Lautgestalt einer Kartner Mundart* 65.

1125 Spring Street, Ann Arbor, Michigan, U.S.A.

Kuratowski, Kazimierz, PHIL. D.; Polish mathematician; b. 96; ed. Glasgow and Warsaw Univs.

Docent Warsaw Univ. 21; Prof. Lwów Polytechnic 27, Dean 29-30; Prof. of Mathematics Warsaw Univ. 34; Editor *Fundamenta Mathematicae* and *Monografie Matematyczne* and *Bulletin* (Polish Acad. of Sciences); Vice-Pres. Polish Acad. of Sciences; Vice-Pres. Comm. of Prizes Balzan Int. Foundation; fmr. Pres. and Hon. mem. Polish Mathematical Soc.; fmr. Dir. Mathematical Inst. of Polish Acad. of Science; Polish Nat. Prize 49 and 51; foreign Hon. mem. Soviet Acad. of Sciences, Hungarian Acad. of Sciences, Austrian Acad. of Sciences; Hon. F.R.S. (Edinburgh), Hon. Dr. (Prague), Hon LL.D. (Glasgow), Hon. Dr. Maths. (Wrocław), Hon. Dr. (Austrian Acad. of Sciences); Balzan Golden Medal (Czechoslovak Acad. of Sciences).

Publs. *Topologie I* 33, *II* 50, *Calculus* 48, *Set Theory* (with Mostowski) 52, *Introduction to Set Theory and Topology* 55, and about 150 short publications.

Kielecka 42, m. 3, Warsaw 12, Poland.

Telephone: 44-25-30.

Kurbanov, Rakhmankul; Soviet teacher and politician; b. 1912; ed. Bukhara Pedagogical Inst. and Higher Party School, Moscow.

Member C.P.S.U. 40-; teacher 37-42; Party Worker 43-61; Chair. Council of Ministers Uzbek S.S.R. 61-; mem. Central Cttee. of C.P.S.U. 61-; Deputy to U.S.S.R. Supreme Soviet; Order of Lenin (twice), Order of Red Banner of Labour, two Badges of Honour, etc.

26 Uezdnaya ulitsa, Tashkent, Uzbek S.S.R., U.S.S.R.

Kurdgeldiyev, Mahmed Geldiyevich; Soviet politician; b. 1912; ed. Planning and Economic Inst.

Instructor, Ashkhabad Trade and Co-operative Coll. 29-37, Dir. 38-41; mem. C.P.S.U. 41-; Vice-Chair. Peoples' Commissars of Turkmenian S.S.R. 41-42; Business Man. Presidium of Supreme Soviet of Turkmenian S.S.R. 42-43; Attaché, New Delhi 47-50; Dir. Turkmenistan Pavilion, Exhbn. of Nat. Econ. Achievements 50-52; mem. staff Central Cttee. of C.P. of Turkmenistan 52-57; Perm. Rep. of Turkmenian S.S.R. Council of Ministers to U.S.S.R. Council of Ministers 57-; Deputy to Supreme Soviet of Turkmenistan; Badge of Honour.

Permanent Representation of Turkmenian S.S.R. Council of Ministers to U.S.S.R. Council of Ministers, Aksakov pereulok 22, Moscow, U.S.S.R.

Kurdiani, Archil Grigorevich; Soviet (Georgian) architect; b. 03; ed. Georgian Polytechnic Inst.

Chief Architect, Tbilisi 36-44; Chief Admin. on Architecture, Georgian Council of Ministers 44-53; Chair. Union of Architects of Georgian S.S.R.; Merited Worker of Arts, Georgian S.S.R.; State Prize 41; Order of Lenin and Red Banner of Labour.

Main works: Dynamo stadium, Tbilisi 37, Pavilion of Georgian S.S.R., U.S.S.R. Econ. Achievement Exhibition 39, Didybinsky Bridge 54, Television station, Tbilisi 54, Hotels, etc.
Union of Architects, Tbilisi, Georgian S.S.R., U.S.S.R.

Kurdjumov, Georgy Vecheslavovich; Soviet (Russian) metallurgist; b. 02; ed. Leningrad Polytechnical Inst. Research with X-rays on quenched and tempered steel 24-32; Head, Phase Transformation Lab., Physical Tech. Inst., Dniepropetrovsk 32-44; Prof. Metal Physics, Dniepropetrovsk Univ. 33-41; Dir. Inst. of Metallography and Metal Physics, Central Research Inst. of Ferrous Metallurgy, Moscow 44-; Dir. Lab. of Metal Physics, Ukraine Acad. of Sciences, Kiev 46-51; mem. Ukraine Acad. of Sciences 39-, Soviet Acad. of Sciences 53-; mem. American Acad. of Mining, Metallurgical and Oil Engineers; State Prize 49, Orders of the Red Banner 45, 58, Orders of Lenin 54-62.
Publs. *Crystal Structure of Martensite* 27, *Theory of the Hardening and Tempering of Steel* 40, *Martemsitic Transformations* 48, *Nature of the Hardness of Quenched Steel* 54, *Phenomena of Quenching and Tempering of Steels* 60, *Strengthening of Metal Alloys* 61.
Institute of Metallography and Metal Physics, Central Research Institute of Ferrous Metallurgy, 2-Baumanskaya ulitsa 9/23, Moscow, U.S.S.R.

Kurita, Jun-ichi, B.A.; Japanese petroleum executive; b. 88; ed. Tokyo Imperial Univ.
With Lactose Co. 18-19, Hoden Oil Co. 19-21; Joined Nippon Oil Co. 21, Dir. 42-46; Man. Dir. 46-47, Senior Man. Dir. 47-51, Vice-Pres. 51-58, Pres. 58-61, Chair. 61-; Pres. Nisseki Real Estate Co. 59-, Nippon Petroleum Gas Co. 58-; Dir. Nippon Petrochemicals Co. 55-, Calpis Food Industrial Co. 57-, Nippon Specialty Lubricants Co. 60-; Consultant, Productivity Center 58-, Mitsui Bank Ltd. 59-; fmr. Exec. Dir. Japan Fed. of Econ. Orgs., Fed. of Employers Asscns.; fmr. Pres. Japanese Nat. Cttee., World Petroleum Congress, Nippon Oil (Delaware) Ltd., Petroleum Asscn. of Japan, Nippon Petroleum Refining Co.
Publs. *Outline of Oriental History* 13, *Forty Days Travelling America and Europe* 55, *Not Becoming a Priest* 58, *My Personal History* 59 (all in Japanese).
300, 3-chome, Kami Osaki Shinagawa-ku, Tokyo, Japan.

Kurmazenko, Alexander Kirillovich; Soviet foreign trade official; b. 1917; ed. Dnepropetrovsk Metallurgical Inst. and Acad. of Foreign Trade.
Member C.P.S.U. 45-; Official, Main Dept. of Soviet Property Abroad 48-56; Official, Ministry of Foreign Trade 56-58; Deputy U.S.S.R. Commercial Rep. in Italy 58-61; U.S.S.R. Commercial Rep. in Turkey 61-65; Chair. *Tekhmashexport* Trust 66-; Badge of Honour (twice).
Tekhmashexport Trust, 35 Mosfilmovskaya Street, Moscow, U.S.S.R.

Kurnakowicz, Jan; Polish actor; b. 01.
First stage appearance, Vilno 21; since then at Letni, Boguslawski, Polski Theatres, Warsaw; now at Teatr Narodowy (People's Theatre), Warsaw; guest appearances Paris and Moscow; roles include Bottom (Shakespeare's *Midsummer Night's Dream*), Doolittle (Shaw's *Pygmalion*), The Grand Prince (Slowacki's *Kordian*), Horodniczy (Gogol's *The Government Inspector*), etc.
Teatr Narodowy, Warsaw, Poland.

Kurokawa, Noriaki, B.TECH., M.TECH.; Japanese architect; b. 8 April 1934; ed. Kyoto and Tokyo Univs.
Member Kenzo Tange's Team 57-62; own atelier for architecture and urban design 62-; Prof. Tokai Women's Coll. 65-; Contributing Editor annual, *World Architecture* 63-; works include Project for Helix City 61, Sagae City Hall 67; Hishino New Town 67, Aichi-ken Handicapped People's Town 67; award for design 58 and 64.

Publs. *Prefabrication of Houses* 60, *Metabolism (Proposition for Future Environment)* 60, *Prefabrication in Future* 63, *Urban Design* 64, *Action Architecture* 67, *Metabolism in Architecture and City Planning* 67.
Park Avenue Building, 1-20, Sendagaya, Shibuya, Tokyo, Japan.

Kurosawa, Akira; Japanese film director; b. 10; ed. Keika Middle School.
Joined Toho Film Co. as asst. dir. 36; dir. his first film *Sugata Sanshiro* 43; First Prize, Venice Film Festival for *Rashomon*, Silver Lion for *The Seven Samurai*, American Motion Picture Acad. Award for *Rashomon*.
Films: *Sugata Sanshiro, Ichiban Utsukushiku, Torano Owofumu Otokotachi, Waga Seishun ni Kuinashi, Subarashiki Nichiyobi, Yoidore Tenshi, Shizukanaru Ketto, Norainu, Rashomon, Hakuchi, Ikiru, The Seven Samurai, Ikimono no Kiroku, Kumonosu Jio, Donzoko, Kakushi Toride no San Akunin, The Hidden Fortress, Throne of Blood, Yojimbo, The Bad Sleep Well, Sanjuro, High and Low, Akahige.*
1755 Nichome Matsubara-machi, Setagaya-ku, Tokyo, Japan.

Kuroyedov, Vladimir Alexeyevich; Soviet politician; b. 1906; ed. Gorky Teachers' Training Inst.
Teacher, Secondary School Dir., Deputy Head of Dept. of Educ., Gorky 28-34; Dir. Gorky Automechanical Technical Coll. 34-39; mem. C.P.S.U. 36-; Instructor, Gorky Regional Cttee. of C.P.S.U. 39-40; Dept. Head, Central Cttee. of C.P. of Lithuania 40-41; Sec. Gorky City Cttee. C.P.S.U. and Editor *Gorkovskaya Kommuna* (regional newspaper) 41-46; Dept. Head, Central Cttee. of C.P.S.U. 46-49; Sec. Sverdlovsk Regional Cttee., C.P.S.U. 49-59; Chair. of Council for Russian Orthodox Church of U.S.S.R. Council of Ministers 60-66; Chair. of U.S.S.R. Council of Ministers' Council for Matters of Religion 66-; Order of Red Banner of Labour.
Council for Matters of Religion, U.S.S.R. Council of Ministers, 11/2 Smolensky Boulevard, Moscow, U.S.S.R.

Kursanov, Andrei Lwovich, SC.D.; Soviet plant physiologist; b. 8 Nov. 1902; ed. Moscow Univ.
Central Inst. of Sugar Industry 29-34; A. N. Bakh Inst. of Biochemistry 34-54; Dir. K. A. Timiriazev Inst. of Plant Physiology and Head of Lab. of Translocation of Substances 52-; mem. U.S.S.R. Acad. of Sciences 53-, Leopoldin.-Carolin German Acad. of Natural Science 58-, Acad. of Agriculture of France 64-, Polish Acad. of Science; Hon. mem. German Botanical Soc. 61-, American Acad. of Arts and Sciences 62-; Order of Lenin, Commdr. Ordre de Léopold II (Belgium).
Publs. *The Reversible Action of Enzymes in Living Grown Cells* 40, *Synthesis and Transformation of the Tannins in Tea Leaves* 53, *The Root System as an Organ of Metabolism* 57, *The Interaction of Physiological Processes in Plants* 60, *Metabolism and the Transport of Organic Substances in the Phloem* 63, *Competition of Sugars for Penetrations into Cells* 64, *Biochemical basis of transport and accumulation of Sucrose in the Sugarbeet plant.*
K. A. Timiryasev Plant Physiology Institute, Academy of Sciences, 33 Leninsky Prospekt, Moscow; and Fl. 5, M. Yakimanka Str. 3, Moscow, U.S.S.R.

Kurtág, György; Hungarian composer; b. 1926; ed. Budapest Music Acad. and in Paris.
Erkel Prize (twice).
Compositions: Concerto for Viola 54, String Quartet 59, Quintet for Wind Instruments 59, *Signs* (for solo viola) 61.
Budapest VI, Rózsa Ferenc utca 46, Hungary.
Telephone: 420-819.

Kurti, Nicholas, M.A., DR.PHIL., F.R.S.; British (Hungarian born) physicist; b. 14 May 1908; ed. Minta Gymnasium, Budapest, Paris and Berlin Univs.
Asst. Breslau Technical University 31-33; attached to

Clarendon Laboratory, Oxford 33-40, U.K. Atomic Energy Project 40-45; Demonstrator in Physics, Oxford Univ. 45-60, Reader 60-67, Prof. 67-; Senior Research Fellow, Brasenose Coll. 47-67, Professorial Fellow 67-. Publs. Papers on Low Temperature Physics and Magnetism.
Office: Clarendon Laboratory, Parks Road, Oxford; Home: 38 Blandford Avenue, Oxford, England.
Telephone: 59291 (Office); 56176 (Home).

Kurylowicz, Jerzy, PH.D.; Polish philologist; b. 26 Aug. 1895; ed. Lwów and French Univs.
Lecturer, Lwów Univ. 26-28, Extraordinary Prof. 28-34, Prof. 34-; mem. Polish Acad. of Sciences, Danish Acad., Irish Acad., Norwegian Acad., Serbian Acad., Institut de France, American Acad. of Arts and Sciences; Polish rep. Comité Int. Permanent des Linguistes; State Prize, First Class 55, 64; Prix Volney; Hon. Dr. Celtic Philology (Nat. Univ. of Ireland); Hon. Dr. (Sorbonne, Austrian Acad., Dublin, Vienna, Chicago, Ann Arbor). Publs. *Etudes indo-européennes* 35, *L'accentuation des langues indo-européennes* 52, *L'apophonie en indo-européen* 56, *Esquisses linguistiques* 60, *L'apophonie en sémitique* 61, *Inflectional Categories of Indo-European* 64. Podwale 1, Cracow, Poland.
Telephone: 228-20.

Kusch, Polykarp, M.S., PH.D.; American physicist; b. 26 Jan. 1911; ed. Case Inst. of Technology and Univ. of Illinois.
Asst. in Physics, Univ. of Illinois 31-36; Research Asst. Univ. of Minnesota 36-37; Instructor in Physics, Columbia Univ. 37-41; Vacuum Tube Engineer, Westinghouse Electric Corpn. 41-42; staff mem. Division of War Research, Columbia Univ. 42-44; mem. Technical staff, Bell Telephone Laboratories 44-46; Assoc. Prof. of Physics, Columbia Univ. 46-49, Prof. 49-; research in atomic, molecular and nuclear physics; awarded Nobel Prize in Physics (jointly with Prof. W. E. Lamb) 55; mem. Nat. Acad. of Sciences; Hon. D.Sc. (Case, Ohio, Ill., Colby).
450 Riverside Drive, New York, N.Y. 10027, U.S.A.

Kusunoki, Naomichi, B.ENG.; Japanese business executive; b. 11 May 1900; ed. Tokyo Imperial Univ.
Automobile Dept., Tokyo Ishikawajima Shipbuilding and Engineering Co. Ltd. 24-29, Dept. separated, firm finally became Isuzu Motors Ltd., Exec. Dir. Isuzu Motors Ltd. 43-46, Managing Dir. 46-62, Pres. 62-; Pres. Yamato Motor Co. Ltd. 62-; Dir. Diesel Kiki Co. Ltd. 51-, Jidosha Kiki Co. Ltd. 55-, Steel Press Works Corpn. 62-, Japan Motor Industrial Fed. 49-; Pres. Soc. of Automotive Engineers of Japan Inc. 53-56; Blue Ribbon Medal 62.
23 Nakane-cho, Meguro-ku, Tokyo, Japan.

Kutyrev, Boris Mikhailovich; Soviet trade corporation official; b. 15; ed. Bauman Mechanical Engineering Inst. and Acad. of Foreign Trade, Moscow.
Engineer 38-46; Derunaft Stock Co., German Dem. Repub., Asst. Soviet Trade Rep., German Dem. Repub. 49-56; Vice-Chair. *Auto-export* (motor vehicles) 56-61; Chair. *Traktoroexport* (tractors, etc.) 61-65; Soviet Trade Rep. in People's Republic of China 65-; mem. Communist Party; numerous decorations.
U.S.S.R. Trade Representation, Peking, People's Republic of China.

Kuwabara, Takeo, B.A.; Japanese writer; b. 10 May 1904; ed. Kyoto Univ.
Lecturer, Kyoto Univ. 31-42; Asst. Prof., Tohoku Univ. 43-48; Prof. Kyoto Univ. 48-68; Dir. Univ. Inst. of Humanistic Studies 59-63; mem. Science Council of Japan 50-, Vice-Pres. 60-.
Publs. *Fiction and Reality* 43, *Reflections on Contemporary Japanese Culture* 47, *Some Aspects of Contemporary French Literature* 49, *Introduction to Literature* 50, *Conquest of Mount Chogolisa* 59, *Studies on J.-J.*

Rousseau 51, *Studies on the Encyclopédie* 54, *Studies on the French Revolution* 59, *Studies on Chomin Nakae* 66, *Selected Works in 7 vols.* 68-69.
421, Tonodan-Yabunosita, Kyoto, Japan.
Telephone: 231-0261.

Kuwait, H.H. The Ruler of (*see* Sabah, Emir Sabah Al Salem Al).

Kuzmich, Anton Savvich; Soviet politician; b. 20 Dec. 1908; ed. Moscow Mining Inst.
Coal industry 31-45; Mine section superintendent, Trust manager, Chief engineer and Dir. of group of mines; Deputy Minister of Coal Industry of E. Areas of U.S.S.R., Deputy Minister of Coal Industry of U.S.S.R., Minister and Deputy Minister of Coal Industry of Ukraine 46-57; Chair. Lugansk Econ. Council 57-60; Chair. Ukrainian Econ. Council 60-63; Deputy Chair. State Cttee. of Fuel Industry attached to U.S.S.R. Gosplan 63-65; Deputy Dir. A. A. Skochinsky Mining Inst. of U.S.S.R. Acad. of Sciences 65-; Alt. mem. Central Cttee. of C.P.S.U. 62-66; Deputy to U.S.S.R. Supreme Soviet 59-66; several decorations.
A.A. Skochinsky Mining Institute, Lyubertsy 4, Moscow Region; Gorky Street 8, app. 147, Moscow, U.S.S.R.
Telephone 29-82-95.

Kuzmin, Iosif Iosifovich; Soviet engineer, politician and diplomatist; b. 19 May 1910; ed. Leningrad Electrical Engineering Inst.
Engineer, later Chief Engineer, Moscow projector factory; mem. Party Control Comm., Cen. Cttee. Communist Party of the Soviet Union (Kuibyshev Region) 40; Deputy Chair. Party Control Comm., C.P.S.U. 40-46; mem. Bureau of Agriculture and Storage 47-50, Deputy Chair. 50-52; mem. Council of Ministers of U.S.S.R. 47-57, Deputy Chair. 57-59; on staff of Cen. Cttee., C.P.S.U. 52-57; Chair. State Planning Cttee. of U.S.S.R. 57-59; Chair. Scientific Economic Council with rank of Minister 59-60; Ambassador to Switzerland 60-63; Expert Consultant in Dept. of Int. Econ. Orgs., Ministry of Foreign Affairs 63-.
Ministry of Foreign Affairs, 32-34 Smolenskaya-Sennaya ploshchad, Moscow, U.S.S.R.

Kuzmin, Mikhail Romanovich; Soviet foreign trade official; b. 1907; ed. Inst. of Foreign Trade.
Member C.P.S.U. 31-; in People's Commissariat for Heavy Industry 30-42; mem. Collegium, Chief of Export Dept. People's Commissariat for Foreign Trade 42-43; Deputy People's Commissar for Foreign Trade 43-46; Deputy Minister of Foreign Trade 46-65; First Deputy Minister of Foreign Trade 65-; Order of Lenin (thrice), Order of Red Banner of Labour.
U.S.S.R. Ministry of Foreign Trade, 32-34 Smolenskaya-Sennaya, Moscow, U.S.S.R.

Kuznets, Simon, M.A., PH.D.; American economist and statistician; b. 30 April 1901; ed. Columbia Univ.
Mem. staff, Nat. Bureau of Economic Research, N.Y. City 27-; Prof. of Economics and Statistics, Univ. of Pa. 36-54; Assoc. Dir. Bureau of Planning and Statistics, W.P.B., Washington, D.C. 42-44; Economic Adviser, Nat. Resources Comm. of China 46; Adviser, Nat. Income Cttee. of India 50-51; Prof. of Political Economy, Johns Hopkins Univ. 54-60, Prof. of Economics, Harvard Univ. 60-; Fellow, American Asscn. for the Advancement of Science, American Statistical Asscn.; mem. Int. Statistical Inst., American Philosophical Soc., Econometric Soc., Royal Acad. of Sciences, Sweden; Hon. Ph.D., Hebrew University of Jerusalem; Hon. Fellow, Royal Statistical Soc. (England); Hon. Sc.D. (Princeton, Pennsylvania, Harvard), D.H.L. (Columbia).
Publs. *Cyclical Fluctuations in Retail and Wholesale Trade* 26, *Secular Movements in Production and Prices* 30, *Seasonal Variations in Industry and Trade* 34,

Commodity Flow and Capital Formation 38, *National Income and its Composition* 41, *National Product Since 1869* 46, *Upper Income Shares* 53, *Economic Change* 54, *Six Lectures on Economic Growth* 59, *Capital in the American Economy* 61, *Modern Economic Growth* 66.
Department of Economics, Harvard University, Cambridge; 67 Francis Avenue, Cambridge 38, Mass., U.S.A.

Kuznetsov, Vasili Vasilievich; Soviet politician and diplomatist; b. 01; ed. Leningrad Polytechnical Inst. and in U.S.A.
Worked as Engineer, Makayevka Steel Works 27-31; Engineer, Elektrostal Works, Moscow 34-37; Engineer and later Chief Engineer of Glavspetstal 37-40; Vice-Chair. State Planning Cttee. (Gosplan) 40-43; mem. State Defence Cttee. 41-45; Chair. Central Cttee. Steel-workers' Union 44; Chair. All-Union Central Council of Trade Unions 44-54; Vice-Pres. World Federation of Trade Unions 45-53; Deputy Minister of Foreign Affairs and Ambassador to China 53-55; 1st Deputy Foreign Minister 55-; Head Soviet Del. to UN 55; joined Communist Party 27, mem. of Central Cttee. 52, mem. Praesidium 52-53; Deputy to Supreme Soviet 46-; State Prize 41; four Orders of Lenin, Red Banner of Labour.
Ministry of Foreign Affairs, 32-34 Smolenskaya-Sennaya ploshchad, Moscow, U.S.S.R.

Kuznetsov, Yuri Alexeyevich; Soviet geologist; b. 1903; ed. Tomsk Univ.
Postgraduate, Research Assoc. Tomsk Univ. 25-27; Research Assoc., Siberian Geology Prospecting Inst. 30-33; Asst. Prof. Tomsk Industrial Inst. 33-38; Prof. Head of Chair Tomsk Polytechnical Inst. 38-58; Head of Lab., Inst. of Geology and Geophysics, Siberian Branch U.S.S.R. Acad. of Sciences 58-; Corresp. mem. U.S.S.R. Acad. of Sciences 58-66, mem. 66-.
Publs. Works on stratigraphy, tectonics, petrology and metalogeny of Altai, Kusnetski Ala-Tau, Eastern Sayans and Yenisei Ridge.
U.S.S.R. Academy of Sciences, 14 Lenin Prospekt, Moscow, U.S.S.R.

Ky, Gen. Nguyen Cao; Viet-Namese air force officer and politician; b. 1930; ed. High School, Hanoi, and Officers Training School, Hanoi.
Flight Training, Marrakech until 54; commanded Transport Squadron 54, later commander Tan Son Nimt Air Force Base, Republic of Viet-Nam; spent six months at U.S. Air Command and Staff Coll., Maxwell Field, Alabama, U.S.A.; later, Commdr. Air Force, Republic of Viet-Nam; Prime Minister 65-67; Vice-Pres. of Viet-Nam Sept. 67-.
Office of the Vice-President, Saigon, Republic of Viet-Nam.

Kyaruzi, Vedast Kyalakishaija, M.B., Ch.B., D.P.H.; Tanzanian civil servant; b. 21 Feb. 1921; ed. Primary School and Secondary School, Tanganyika; Makerere Coll., Uganda and Edinburgh Univ.
Medical Officer, Tanganyikan Govt. Medical Service 49-61; Perm. Rep. to UN 61-62; Perm. Sec. External Affairs and Defence 62-63; UNICEF Dir. for Africa South of the Sahara 63-.
UNICEF, P.O.B. 1282, 26-28 Marina, Lagos, Nigeria.

Kyes, Roger Martin; American executive; b. 6 March 1906; ed. Culver Mil. Acad., Culver, Ind., Rayen School, Youngstown, O., and Harvard Univ.
Asst. to Pres. of Glenn L. Martin Co. 28-30; Asst. to Vice-Pres. of Black & Decker Mfg. Co. 30-32; Vice-Pres. Empire Plow Co., Cleveland, O. 32-41; Exec-Vice-Pres. and Gen. Man. Ferguson-Sherman Mfg. Corpn. 41-43; Pres. Harry Ferguson Inc. 43-47; Exec. in charge of Procurement and Schedules Staff, Gen. Motors Corpn. 48-49; Asst. Gen. Man. Truck and Coach

Div. 49-50, Gen. Man. and Vice-Pres. Gen. Motors Corpn. 50-53; Deputy Sec. of Defense Feb. 53-54; rejoined Gen. Motors Corpn. 54, Vice-President, Dir. and Exec.-in-Charge of Dayton, Household Appliance and G.M.C. Truck and Coach Divisions, General Motors Corpn. 54-59, Group Exec. in charge of Accessory Group 59-65, Group Exec. in charge of Automotive Components and Defense Group 65-66, Exec. Vice-Pres. in charge of Car and Truck, Body and Assembly and Automotive Components Group 67-; numerous honours include Medal of Freedom; Republican.
"Bellwood", 945 Cranbrook Road, Bloomfield Hills. Mich., U.S.A.

Kyllingmark, Håkon Olai; Norwegian politician; b. 19 Jan. 1915.
Army Service 34-45; Commanding Officer, Home Guard, District of Nord Hålogaland 45-53; has operated own business, Svolvaer 46-; mem. Svolvaer City Council 45-47, 51-63; mem. Storting 54-; Second Deputy Chair. Nat. Cttee. of Conservative Party 58; Minister of Defence 63; Minister of Transport and Communications 65-.
Ministry of Transport and Communications, Oslo, Norway.

Kyo, Machiko; Japanese actress; b. 24.
Began her career as a dancer with the Shochiku Girls' Opera Co., Osaka; film début in *Saigo ni Warau Otoko* (Last Laughter) 49; later films: *Rashomon* 50, *Ugetsu Monogatari* 53, *Gate of Hell* 54, *Story of Shunkin* 55, *Akasen Chitai* (Street of Shame), *Teahouse of the August Moon* 56, *Yoru no Cho* (Night Butterflies) 57, *Odd Obsession* 59, *Floating Weeds* 59, *A Woman's Testament* 60; Best Actress Award for *Rashomon* 50; Jussie (Finland) Award 57.
Seijo-machi, Setagaya-ku, Tokyo, Japan.

Kyprianou, Spyros; Cypriot lawyer and politician; b. 32; ed. City of London Coll. and Gray's Inn, London.
Barrister; mem. Cyprus Ethnarchy Secr. London 54-59; Minister of Justice 60; Minister of Foreign Affairs 60-.
Ministry of Foreign Affairs, Nicosia, Cyprus.

Kyril, Patriarch of Bulgaria, D.D. (Constantine Marcov); Bulgarian ecclesiastic; b. 01; ed. Czernovits, Vienna, Berlin and Belgrade.
Sec. Ryla Monastery 26; teacher, Training Coll. for Priests 26-31; ordained Friar 31; Archimandrite and Chief of Cultural-Educational Dept. with Holy Synod 32; Gen. Sec. of Holy Synod 35-; ordained Bishop 36; Archbishop of Plovdiv 38-53; Patriarch of Bulgaria and Archbishop of Sofia 53-; Pres. Holy Synod Bulgarian Orthodox Church; Vice-Pres. Nat. Council for Protection of Peace in Bulgaria; mem. Council for World Peace; Hon. D.D. (Theol. Acads., Sofia, Moscow and Czernovits).
Publs. Many sermons and works on ecclesiastical, cultural and historical subjects, including *Panaret of Plovdiv* 50, *Nathaniel of Plovdiv* 52, *The Word of Life* 53, *The Resistance against the Treaty of Berlin: The Rising of Kresna* 55, *Exarch Anthimos I (1816-88)* 56, *The Way of God* Vol. I 57, Vol. 59, Vol. III 61, Vol. IV 63, Vol. V 65, *Earl Ignatiew and the Bulgarian Church Question* 58, *Bulgarian-Moslem Settlements in the Southern Rhodope Mountains* 60, *Contribution to the Bulgarian Ecclesiastical Problems* 61, *Catholic Church Propaganda Amongst the Bulgarians in the Middle 19th Century* 63.
Sofia Holy Synod, Sofia, Bulgaria.

Kyrollos VI, Mena el-Matwahhed; United Arab Republic (Egyptian) ecclesiastic; b. 02.
Pope of Alexandria and Patriarch of the See of St. Mark in all Africa and the Near East (116th in line of succession).
St. Mark's Patriarchate Cathedral, Azbakiya, Cairo, United Arab Republic.

L

Labarca Hubertson, Amanda Pinto de, PH.D.; Chilean educationalist; b. 86; ed. Univ. of Chile, Columbia Univ. and Sorbonne, Paris.
Assistant School Dir. 06-09, Dir. 16-28; Extra. Prof. of Psychology in Pedagogical Inst. of Univ. of Chile 22-23, Prof. of Philosophy 23-28; Dir.-Gen. of Secondary Education in Chile 31-32; Govt. rep. on Council of Univ. of Chile 34-52; Pres. Nat. Council of Women; Pres. Exec. Cttee. Chilean Comm. on Intellectual Co-operation 36; Pres. Asscn. Univ. Women 44-46; Pres. Nat. Fed. Women's Institutions 44-; Del. to Gen. Assembly of U.N. Sept.-Dec. 46; Chief of Section on Status of Women U.N. Feb. 48-June 49; Head, Dept of Extension Courses, Univ. of Chile 49-56; Pres. Asscn. for Cultural Freedom 59-; Pres. P.E.N. Club, Chile 61-62.
Publs. *Impresiones de juventud* 09, *Actividades femeninas en los Estados Unidos* 14, *En tierras extrañas* 16, *La escuela secundaria en los Estados Unidos* 19, *La lámpara maravillosa* 21, *Lecciones de filosofía* 26, *A dónde va la mujer?* 34, *Historia de la Enseñanza en Chile* 39, *Bases para una política educacional* 43, *Desvelos en el Alba* 45, *Realidades y problemas de nuestra enseñanza* 53, *Women and Education in Chile* 53.
Casilla 9, Santiago, Chile.

Labbé, Roland Georges Joseph Marie, L. ès D.; French industrialist; b. 17 Sept. 1899.
Président, Société Lorraine-Escaut, Société des hauts-fourneaux et forges, de Saulnes et Gorcy, Chambre Syndicale de la Sidérurgie de l'Est de la France, Union des Industries Métallurgiques et Minières; Vice-Pres. Chambre Syndicale de la Sidérurgie Française, Société Aciéries de Longwy; Hon. Pres., Société Métallurgique de Gorcy, Société Longométal; Commdr., Légion d'Honneur; Officier, Ordre de Léopold (Belgium).
198 avenue Victor Hugo, Paris 16e, France.

Labis, Attilio; French ballet dancer and choreographer; b. 5 Sept. 1936; ed. Ecole de Danse académique de l'Opéra, Paris.
Member Corps de Ballet at the Paris Opera 52, Premier Danseur 59, Principal Premier Danseur 60-; Guest Dancer in London, Paris, Washington, Tokyo, Moscow, Kiev, Leningrad, Rome, Berlin, Munich, Stuttgart, and Sydney; Chief Choreographer at the Paris Opera.
105 rue de la Convention, Paris 15e, France.

Labisse, Félix Louis Victor Léon; French painter and theatrical designer; b. 9 March 1905; ed. Coll. St. Jean, Douai and Lycée Michelet, Paris.
Lived in Ostend 27-32, in Paris area since 32; mem. Cttee. Salon de Mai, in charge of Surrealist and Fantastic Art Rooms; one-man exhbns. in Paris, Brussels, Liège, Antwerp, Rio de Janeiro, São Paulo, Buenos Aires, Milan, Cologne, London, New York, etc., Retrospective Exhbn. Knokke-Le-Zoute 60; mem. Institut de France, Acad. des Beaux-Arts; mem. Higher Council for Teaching of Fine Arts; mem. Comm. for Artistic Creation, Ministry of Arts and Letters; Chevalier Légion d'Honneur, Officier Ordre des Arts et Lettres, Officier Ordre de la Couronne de Belgique, Cruzeiro do Sul do Brasil, Commandeur de l'Ordre Nationale de la Côte d'Ivoire; Grand Prix Bienal of São Paulo for theatre decors 57.
Works in: Musée d'Art Moderne, Paris, Musée d'Art Moderne, Ville de Paris, Musée de Lille, and museums in Douai, Liège, Tel-Aviv, Rio de Janeiro, Ostend, and Museum of Modern Art, New York.
Major theatre decors and costumes for: *Hamlet, Les Nuits de la Colère, Le Procès* (Kafka), *Zadig, Noë, Elisabeth la Femme sans homme, L'Orestie, Le Séducteur, Fabien, Le Martyre de Saint Sebastien, Le Château*

(Kafka), *Le Médium, Le Château de Barbe-Bleue, Le Mariage de Monsieur Mississippi, Partage de Midi, Le Diable et le bon Dieu, Faust, Piège de lumière, The Prisoner, Liliom, L'Amérique* (Kafka), *Padmovati, Le Roi d'Ys, Le Révélation, Lazare, Irène Innocente, Le Sabre de mon père,* etc.
21 rue Saint James, Neuilly-sur-Seine 92, France.

Labouchere, Sir George Peter, G.B.E., K.C.M.G.; British diplomatist; b. 2 Dec. 1905; ed. Charterhouse and Univ. of Paris.
Entered diplomatic service 29; served Madrid, Cairo, Rio de Janeiro, Rome, Stockholm, Nanking, Buenos Aires and Vienna; Counsellor 46; Minister to Hungary 53-55; Ambassador to Belgium 55-60, to Spain 60-66.
c/o Foreign Office, London, S.W.1, England.

Labouisse, Eve Denise (Mrs. Henry R. Labouisse, née Curie); American writer, journalist and lecturer; b. 6 Dec. 1904; ed. Coll. Sévigné, Paris.
Went to London from France 40; war corresp. Libya, Russia, Burma, China 42; Lieut. Women's Aux. Forces, Free French Army 43-44; returned to Paris 44; co-publisher *Paris-Presse* 45-49; special adviser to Sec.-Gen. NATO, Paris 52-54; American citizen since 56.
Publs. *Madame Curie* 37 (trans. into 35 languages), *Journey among Warriors* 43.
1 Sutton Place South, New York, N.Y. 10022, U.S.A.

Labouisse, Henry R., B.A., LL.B.; American United Nations official; b. 11 Feb. 1904; ed. Princeton and Harvard Univs.
Attorney-at-law N.Y.C. 29-41; Asst. Chief Division of Defence Materials, Dept. of State 41-43 and Chief of Division 43; Deputy Dir. Office of Foreign Economic Co-ordination 43; Chief Eastern Hemisphere Division 44; Minister, Economic Affairs, U.S. Embassy, Paris 45; Special Asst. to Asst. Sec. of State for Economic Affairs 46; Special Asst. to Dir., Office of European Affairs 46; Head U.S. del. E.E.C. 48; Co-ordinator for Foreign Aid and Assistance 48; Dir. Office of British Commonwealth and Northern European Affairs 49; Chief Special Mission to France of Economic Co-operation Admin. 51-54; Chief Mutual Security Agency Special Mission to France 52; Dir. U.N. Relief and Works Agency for Palestine Refugees 54-58; Consultant, Int. Bank for Reconstruction and Development 59-61; Head of IBRD Mission to Venezuela 59; Dir. Int. Co-operation Admin. 61-62; U.S. Ambassador to Greece 62-65; Exec. Dir. United Nations Children's Fund (UNICEF) 65-; Hon. LL.D. (Univ. of Bridgeport) 61, (Princeton Univ.) 65, (Lafayette Coll.) 66, (Tulane Univ.) 67.
Office: UNICEF, New York City; Home: 1 Sutton Place South, New York, N.Y. 10022, U.S.A.
Telephone: PL4-1234 (Office); 751-4156 (Home).

Lacalle Larraga, Lt.-Gen. José; Spanish air force officer and politician; b. 97.
Former Commdr., Spanish Air Force, Pyrenees Region; Minister of Aviation.
Ministry of Aviation, Madrid, Spain.

Lacarte, Julio Antonio; Uruguayan diplomatist; b. 1918; ed. Inst. de Bordeaux.
Attaché and later Sec. Uruguayan Embassy London 40-46; Deputy Dir. Div. of Int. Trade and Balance of Payments, UN and Deputy Exec. Sec. GATT 46-48; Minister Counsellor Washington 49-51; Minister to Ecuador 51-54; Amb. to Bolivia 54-56, to U.S.A. and Rep. to Org. of American States 56-60; Amb. to German Fed. Repub. 60-67; Rep. to European Econ. Communities 63-; First Vice-Pres. GATT 64-; Ecuadorean

and Bolivian decorations; corresp. mem. Uruguayan Acad. of Economics.

Publs. *New Principles in World Trade* 49, *Uruguay and the General Agreement on Tariffs and Trade* 51, *Foreign Economic Policy of Uruguay* 55, Ministry of Foreign Affairs, Montevideo, Uruguay.

Lacassagne, Antoine Marcellin Bernard; French scientist; b. 19 Aug. 1884; ed. Lycée Ampère de Lyon, Univ. of Lyon and Institut Pasteur, Paris.

Resident doctor in hospitals in Lyon 08-12; Faculty of Medicine, Lyon 13-19; Laboratory Chief, Institut Pasteur 19-; Dir. Inst. du Radium (Institut Pasteur) 37; Hon. Chef de Service, Institut Pasteur; Prof. Coll. de France 41-55; Hon. Prof. 55.

Institut du Radium, 26 rue d'Ulm, Paris 5e, France.

Lacerda, Carlos; Brazilian politician, writer and publisher; b. 30 April 1914.

Writer, Students Column *Diário de Noticias* 29; journalist on *Diário Carioca, O Jornal, Agência Meridional, Observador Econômico e Financeiro* and *Correio de Manhã;* founder *Tribuna da Imprensa;* fmr. Federal Dep., Leader of the Opposition; Gov. of Guanabara State 61-65; Leader, Nat. Democratic Union; Nat. Democratic Union Candidate for Pres. of Brazil; Maria Moors Cabot Prize, Columbia Univ., Mergenthaler Award, Interamerican Press Soc.

R. Carmo 27-4°, Rio de Janeiro, Guanabara, Brazil.
Telephone: 31-5830.

Lacerda, Flávio Suplicy de; Brazilian civil engineer and politician; b. 03.

Rector of Univ. of Paraná 50-64; Fed. Minister of Education and Culture 64-66.

c/o Ministry of Education and Culture, Brasilia, Brazil.

Lachs, Manfred, LL.M., LL.D., D.SC., D. de L'UNIV.; Polish international lawyer; b. 21 April 1914; ed. Uniwersytet Jagielloński, Cracow, Univ. de Nancy and London School of Economics.

Director, Legal and Treaties Dept., Ministry for Foreign Affairs 47-60; Prof. Acad. of Political Sciences, Warsaw 49-50; Prof. of Int. Law, Univ. of Warsaw 52-66; Minister 56-60, Amb. 60-66; Judge, Int. Court of Justice, The Hague 67-; Polish Del. Paris Peace Conf. 46; mem. Polish Del. to UN Gen. Assembly 46-52, 55-60, 62-64; Rep. of Poland to UN Disarmament Cttee. 62-64; Chair. Legal Cttee., UN Gen. Assembly 49, 51, 55, Vice-Chair. 52; mem. UN Int. Law Comm. 62-, Rapporteur 62, Chair. of its sub-cttee. on Succession of States and Govts., Special Rapporteur on sub-cttee.; Coresp. mem. Polish Acad. of Sciences, Acad. of Moral Sciences Bologna; involved with various other UN orgs. and cttees.; Lecturer various acads., univs. and insts. in Europe and North and South America; Hon. mem. Int Acad. of Astronautics; Hon. Dr. jur. et pol. sc. (Univ. of Budapest).

Publs. Numerous essays and articles and *War Crimes, An Attempt to Define the Issues* 45, *The Geneva Agreements on Indochina* (in Polish) 55 (Russian trans. 56), *Les développements et Fonctions des Traités Multilatéraux: Recueil des Cours* 57, *The Multilateral Treaties* (in Polish) 58 (Russian, Hungarian and Spanish trans.), *The Polish-German Frontier* (in English and French), *The Law of Outer Space, A Law in-the-making: Recueil des Cours* 64.

The International Court of Justice, The Hague, Netherlands.
Telephone: The Hague 392344.

Laclavère, Georges; French geophysicist; b. 28 June 1906; ed. Ecole Polytechnique, Paris.

Service Géographique Paris 34; geodetic and astronomical operations in France and in Overseas Territories 36-40; Inst. Géographique National 40-; Sec. Gen. Int. Union of Geodesy and Geophysics 51-63; mem. Int. Cttee. for the Int. Geophysical Year 53-59; Chief Dept. of Cartography, Inst. Géographique National, Paris 57-

63, Dir. 63-; mem. Bureau des Longitudes 57; Pres. Scientific Cttee. for Antarctic Research 58-63, French Nat. Cttee. for Antarctic Research; Treas. Int. Council of Scientific Unions 61-; Sec.-Gen. Comité Int. de Géophysique 59-65; mem. Centre Nat. de la Recherche Scientifique 60; Dir. of Programme UN Conf. on Science and Technology 61-63; Officier Légion d'Honneur, Croix de Guerre, Legion of Merit.

Publs. *Traité de Géodésie* (with P. Tardi) 54, and numerous articles in scientific journals.

53 ave. de Breteuil, Paris 7e, France.
Telephone: 734-94-26.

Lacombe, Américo Jacobina; Brazilian teacher; b. 7 July 1909; ed. Colégio Jacobina, Rio de Janeiro, Colégio Arnaldo (Belo Horizonte), and Univ. of Rio de Janeiro.

Secretary, Nat. Council of Educ. 31-39; Dir. Casa de Rui Barbosa 39-61; Prof. at Pontifical Univ. of Rio de Janeiro; mem. Comm. on Historical Texts, Board of Sociedade Brasileira de Cultura Inglesa; mem. numerous Historical Insts.

Publs. *Mocidade e Exilio de Rui Barbosa* 34, *Paulo Barbosa e a Fundação de Petrópolis* 40, *Um Passeio Pela História do Brasil* 42 (trans. *Brazil: A Brief History* 54), *O Pensamento Vivo de Rui Barbosa* 44, *Brasil—Período Colonial* 56.

Rua Dezenove de Fevreiro 105, Rio de Janeiro, GB; Pontifícia Universidade Católica do Rio de Janeiro, rua Marquês de São Vicente 263, Rio de Janeiro, Brazil.

Lacombe, Henri; French oceanographer; b. 24 Dec. 1913; ed. Lycée de Nice, Lycée Saint-Louis, Paris, and Ecole Polytechnique, Paris.

Marine hydrographical engineer 35-55; Prof. of Physical Oceanography, Museum de Paris 55-, Dir. of scientific expeditions in the sea—in the Mediterranean and Strait of Gibraltar; Officier Légion d'Honneur, Croix de Guerre, Commdr. Etoile d'Anjouan, etc.

Publs. *Etudes Acoustique sous-Marine* 46, *Ouvrage sur courants de Marée* 53, *Mission Hydrographique Maroc* 59; various studies on the movement of the sea 61-68: *Cours d'Océanographie Physique* 65, *Les Energies de la Mer* 68.

Laboratoire d'Océanographie Physique du Museum, 57 rue Cuvier, Paris 5e; Home: 20 bis avenue De Lattre de Tassigny, 92 Bourg-La-Reine, France.
Telephone: 707-85-44, Ext. 19-00 (Office); 702-23-22 (Home).

Lacoste, Robert; French politician; b. 5 July 1898.

Began career in Ministry of Finance; Sec.-Gen. Féd. générale des Fonctionnaires and Editor *Tribune des Fonctionnaires* before 39; during occupation founder mem. Libération-Nord, mem. Executive Libération-Sud, co-founder Mouvements Unifiés de la Résistance; with Provisional Govt. 44; mem. both Constituent Assemblies 45-46; Socialist Deputy for the Dordogne 46-58, 62-; Minister for Industrial Production 44-47, for Industry Oct.-Nov. 47, for Industry and Commerce 47-50; Resident Minister Algeria Feb. 56-May 58; Pres. Conseil Supérieur de l'Electricité, Gaz de France 50-66; Officier Légion d'Honneur, Croix de Guerre, Rosette de la Résistance.

4 rue Casimir-Périer, Paris 7e, France.

La Coste-Messelière, Pierre Frotier, Marquis de, D. ès L.; French archaeologist; b. 3 March 1894.

Member of French School at Athens 21; Lecturer, Ecole des Hautes Etudes 27, Dir. 32; scientific missions in Greece 26-61; mem. Acad. des Inscriptions et Belles Lettres (Inst. de France) 44-.

Publs. *Sculptures grecques de Delphes* 27, 29, *Fouilles de Delphes: Trésors ioniques* 28, *Fouilles de Delphes: Sculpture des Temples* 31, *Au Musée de Delphes* 36, *Delphes* 43, *Sculptures du Trésor des Athéniens* 57.

Château des Ousches, par Melle (Deux-Sèvres); and 1 rue de la Planche, Paris 7e, France.

Lacretelle, Jacques de; French writer; b. 14 July 1888. Winner Grand Prix (Novel) of Acad. Française 30, mem. Acad. Française 36-; Président-Directeur Général, Soc. fermière du Figaro; Commdr. de la Légion d'Honneur.

Publs. Novels: *Silbermann* (Fémina Prize) 22, *La Bonifas* 25, *Lettres Espagnoles* 29, *Amour nuptial* 30, *Les Hauts Ponts*, 4 vols.: *Sabine, Les Fiançailles, Années d'Espérance, La Monnaie de Plomb* 32-35, *L'Ecrivain public* 36, *Croisés en eaux troublées* 39, *Le Demi-dieu ou le Voyage de Grèce, Libérations* 45, *Le pour et le contre* 46, *Idées dans un chapeau* 46, *Deux Coeurs Simples* 53, *Tiroir Secret, les Maîtres et les Amis, la Galerie des Amants, Talleyrand* 64; trans. into French: *Precious Bane* (Mary Webb), *Wuthering Heights* (Emily Brontë).
49 rue Vineuse, Paris 16e, France.

Lafaurie, Jean; French numismatist; b. 31 Nov. 1914. Prof. Ecole pratique des Hautes Etudes de la Sorbonne; Keeper, Cabinet des médailles, Nat. Library, Paris 46-; hon. mem. Int. Numismatic Comm.; Dir. *Revue Numismatique* 58-, Past Pres. French Numismatic Soc.; Dir. Soc. for the Study of the History of Paper Money; Hon. mem. Swiss, Belgian and Netherlands Numismatic Socs.; Royal Numismatic Soc. Medal.
3 rue de l'Abbé Guilleminault, Nogent-sur-Marne 94, France.
Telephone: TRE 15-72.

Lafay, Bernard, D. ès sc., Docteur en Médecine; French physician and politician; b. 05; ed. Lycée Buffon and Paris Univ.
Practised as a doctor 31-45; Sec.-Gen. of Radical party 46-48; Vice-Pres. of Paris Municipal Council 48-49; Deputy 51-58; Sec. of State 52; Sec. of State for Economic Affairs 53-54; Pres. Paris Municipal Council 54-55; Minister of Public Health 54-56; Senator 59-; Commdr. Légion d'Honneur; Croix de Guerre.
123 rue de Longchamp, Paris 16e, France.

Lafer, Horacio; Brazilian industrialist and politician; b. 1900; ed. Univ. of São Paulo.
Pres. São Paulo Industry Centre; founded several industrial concerns; Brazilian del. to L. of N. before 30; mem. Federal Constituent Assembly 34, 45; Federal Rep. 34-55, 58; Minister of Finance 51-53; Chair. Joint Brazil-U.S.A. Comm. for Economic Development; Chair. Conf. of I.M.F. and I.B.R.D. 52; Chair. Int. Conf. of Economic Comm. for Latin America 53; mem. Board of Govs. I.B.R.D. 51-53; Minister of Foreign Affairs 59-61; Chair. Museum of Modern Art of São Paulo.
Avenida Atlántica 910, Rio de Janeiro, Brazil.

Lagasse, Raphael; Belgian international official; b. 1927; ed. Catholic Univ. of Louvain.
Secretary-General, Int. Org. of Employers 60-; Belgian Civic and Military Orders.
98 rue de St. Jean, 1201 Geneva, Switzerland.
Telephone: 022-31-73-50.

Lagerfelt, Baron Karl-Gustav; Swedish diplomatist; b. 21 Nov. 1909.
Foreign Service 35-, Helsinki, London, Foreign Office, London, Paris, Tokyo 35-56; Amb. to European Coal and Steel Community 57-63, to Euratom and European Econ. Community 59-63; Amb. to Austria 64-.
Swedish Embassy, Vienna, Austria.

Lagerkvist, Pär; Swedish writer; b. 23 May 1891.
Member Swedish Acad. 40; awarded Hon. Ph.D. 41; Nobel Prize for Literature 51.
Publs. Poems, novels, plays: *The Eternal Smile, The Hangman, The Man who lived his Life Again, Let Man Live, The Man without a Soul, The Marriage Feast, Guest of Reality, The Dwarf, The Philosopher's Stone, Midsummer Dream in the Workhouse, Barabbas, The Sibyl, The Death of Ahasuerus, Pilgrim at Sea, The Holy Land, Mariamne,* etc.
Lidingö, Sweden.

Lagos, Lt.-Gen. Julio Alberto; Argentine army officer and diplomatist; b. 01; ed. Argentine Military Coll.
Second-Lieutenant, Engineer Corps 20; Prof. Argentine Military Coll. 25-30; Gen. Staff 35; Prof. Higher Military Coll. 35-40; Dir.-Gen. of Posts and Telecommunications 44-45; Military Attaché, Argentine Embassy, Chile 46-47; Brig-Gen. and Mil. Gov. of Comodoro Rivadavia 49; Gen. Commdr. of Army of Andes 51-55; C.-in-C. Argentine Army 55; Pres. Argentine Del. to Inter-American Defense Council, Washington 56-58; Co-ordinator, Argentine National Oilfields (YPF) 60-62; Ambassador to Spain 62-64; decorations from Brazil, Chile, Peru, Mexico and Paraguay.
c/o Ministry of Foreign Affairs, Buenos Aires, Argentina.

Lagrange, Maurice, L. en D.; French lawyer; b. 14 May 1900; ed. Lycée Charlemagne, Paris, Paris Univ., and Ecole Libre des Sciences Politiques.
Auditeur, Conseil d'Etat 24, Maître des Requêtes 34; Conseiller d'Etat 45-, Section des Travaux Publics 64-; Legal Expert, French Del. during negotiations setting up ECSC 50; Advocate-Gen., ECSC Court 52-58, 58-64; Court of the European Communities 58-64; Commdr. de la Légion d'Honneur.
Publs. *La Cour de Justice de la Communauté Européenne du Charbon et de l'Acier* 54, *L'Ordre Juridique de la CECA vu à travers la Jurisprudence de sa Cour de Justice* 58, *Les Pouvoirs de la Haute Autorité* 61 (all in *Revue du Droit Public et de la Science Politique*), *The Role of the Court of Justice as seen through its Case Law* 61.
18 avenue de la Bourdonnais, Paris 7e, France.
Telephone: 468-59-42.

Lahr, Rolf; German diplomatist; b. 6 Nov. 1908; ed. Univs. of Berlin, Giessen, and Freiburg/Br.
Foreign Trade Div., Ministry of Econs. 34-42; mil. service 42-45; Man. Fruit and Vegetable Processing Industry Asscn. for Schleswig-Holstein 45-49; Foreign Trade Div., Ministry of Econs. 49-51, Counsellor 51-53; Foreign Office 53-61; Ambassador and Del. in German-French negotiations 56, German-Soviet negotiations 57-58, German-Netherlands negotiations 58-60, German-Scandinavian air traffic 59-60; Perm. Rep. to European Econ. Community, Brussels 61; State Sec. for Foreign Affairs 61-; Iron Cross (1st Class) 43; Officer, Grand Cross (2nd Class) of the Order of Merit 63, and other foreign orders.
Foreign Office, 5 Wörthstrasse, Bonn, German Federal Republic.

Lai Chi-fa; Chinese politician.
Former Vice-Minister of Building Construction; Minister of Building Materials 65-.
Ministry of Building Materials, Peking, People's Republic of China.

Laín Entralgo, Pedro; Spanish physician; b. 08; ed. Univs. of Zaragoza, Valencia, Madrid and Vienna.
Prof. of History of Medicine, Madrid Univ. 42-, Rector of Univ. 51; mem. of Real Acad. de Medicina 46, Real Acad. Española 54, Real Acad. de la Historia 62; Dr. h.c. Univ. San Marcos, Lima, Toulouse Univ.; Hon. Prof. Univ. of Santiago, Chile, and mem. of Akademie der Wissenschaften, Heidelberg.
Publs. *Menéndez Pelayo* 44, *La Generación del Noventa y Ocho* 45, *La Historia Clínica* 50, *Historia de la Medicina* 54, *Mind and Body* (London 55), *España como Problema* 56, *La espera de la esperanza* 56, *La curación por el palatre en la Antigüedad clásica* 58, *Teoría y Realidad del otro* 61.
José Ortega y Gasset, 11, Madrid, Spain.

Laing, Hon. Arthur, M.P.; Canadian business executive and politician; b. 04; ed. Richmond High School and Univ. of British Columbia.
Manager, Fertilizers Dept., Vancouver Milling and Grain Co. Ltd. 26-33; Man. Agricultural Chemicals Div., Buckerfields Ltd. 33-51; M.P. 49-53, 63-; Leader British Columbia Liberal Party 53-62; Minister for

Northern Development and Nat. Resources 63-65, of Indian Affairs and Northern Affairs 65-; Liberal.

Department of Indian Affairs and Northern Development, Ottawa; Home: 5937 Angus Drive, Vancouver 13, Canada.

Laing, Sir (John) Maurice, Kt.; British building and civil engineering contractor; b. 1 Feb. 1918; ed. St. Lawrence Coll., Ramsgate.

Laing Group of Companies 35, Man. Dir. 57-, Deputy Chair. 58-, Dir. John Laing & Son (Canada) Ltd., and Grosvenor-Laing Holdings Ltd., Bank of England 63-; Chair. Export Group for Constructional Industries 57-59, Fed. of Civil Engineering Contractors 59-60, Vice-Pres. 60-; Vice-Pres. British Employers' Confederation 60-64, Pres. 64-65; First Pres. Confederation of British Industry 65-66; mem. Grand Council, Fed. of British Industries 56-65, Export Guarantees Advisory Council 59-63, Ministry of Labour Nat. Joint Advisory Council 60, Nat. Econ. Devt. Council (N.E.D.C.) 62-.

"Reculver", Totteridge, London, N.20, England.

Laing, R(obert) Stanley, B.S.MECH.ENG., M.B.A.; American business executive; b. 1 Nov. 1918; ed. Univ. of Washington and Harvard Business School.

National Cash Register Co., Dayton, Ohio 47-; Special Asst. in Exec. Office 47-49; Asst. to Comptroller 49; Gen. Auditor 50-53; Asst. Comptroller 53-54; Comptroller 54-60; Vice-Pres. (Finance) 60-62, Exec. Vice-Pres. 62-64, Pres. 64-; Dir. N.C.R., Fed. Reserve Bank of Cleveland, etc.; Trustee, Financial Exec. Research Foundation; mem. Harvard Univ. Advisory Cttee., Council on Foreign Relations.

The National Cash Register Company, Main and K Streets, Dayton, Ohio 45409; Home: 245 W. Thruston Boulevard, Dayton, Ohio 45419, U.S.A.

Telephone: 513-449-2250 (Office).

Laithwaite, Sir John Gilbert, G.C.M.G., K.C.B., K.C.I.E., C.S.I., M.A.; British civil servant; b. 5 July 1894; ed. Clongowes and Trinity Coll., Oxford.

Served in France 17-18 (wounded); India Office 19; Private Sec. to Parl. Under-Sec. 22-24; Asst. Private Sec. to Secs. of State 24, Principal 24; attached to Prime Minister for Second Indian Round Table Conf. 31; Sec. Indian Franchise Cttee. 32, Indian Delimitation Cttee. 35-36; Private Sec. to Viceroy of India 36-43; Sec. to Gov.-Gen. of India 37-43; Asst. Under-Sec. of State for India 43; an Under-Sec. (Civil) of the War Cabinet 44-45; Deputy Under-Sec. of State for Burma 45-47, for India 47; Deputy Under-Sec. of State for Commonwealth Relations 48-49; U.K. Rep. to Republic of Ireland 49-50, Ambassador 50-51; High Commr. for the U.K. in Pakistan Sept. 51-54; Permanent Under-Sec. of State for Commonwealth Relations 55-59 (retd.); Chair. Council of Royal Central Asian Soc. 64-66, Vice-Pres. 67-; Pres. Hakluyt Soc. 64-, Royal Geographical Soc. 66-; Dir. and Deputy Chair. Inchcape and Co. Ltd. 60-64, Dir. 64-; Hon. Fellow, Trinity Coll., Oxford 55; Hon. LL.D. (Dublin) 57; Freeman, City of London 60; Knight of Malta 60.

Publs. *The Laithwaites, Some Records of a Lancashire Family* 41, *Miscellaneous Genealogical Notes* 43.

c/o National and Grindlays Bank Ltd., 13 St. James's Square, London, S.W.1, England.

Laking, George Robert, LL.B.; New Zealand diplomatist; b. 15 Oct. 1912; ed. Auckland Grammar School, and Auckland and Victoria Univs.

Prime Minister's and External Affairs Depts. 40-49; Counsellor, New Zealand Embassy, Washington 49-54, Minister 54-56; Dep. Sec. of External Affairs, Wellington 56-58; Acting High Commr. for New Zealand in London 58-61; Ambassador to European Economic Community (E.E.C.) 60-61, to U.S.A. 61-67; Sec. of External Affairs 67-.

Department of External Affairs, Parliament Building, Wellington, New Zealand.

Lalbhai, Kasturbhai; Indian industrialist; b. 19 Dec. 1894; ed. Gujerat Coll., Ahmedabad.

Vice-Pres. Ahmedabad Millowners' Asscn. 23-26; Pres. 33-36; mem. Central Legislative Assembly 23-26; Del. Int. Labour Conf. Geneva 29 and 34; Pres. Fed. of Indian Chambers of Commerce 34-35; Consultative mem. British Indian Trade Del. to U.K. 37; Dir. Reserve Bank of India; Adviser to Govt. of India in Indo-Burman Trade Negotiations 40; mem. Scientific and Industrial Research Board 40; mem. Textile Control Board 43; mem. Indian Del. to Cairo Cotton Conf. 43; Rep. of Govt. of India on Textile Cttee. of Combined Production and Resources Board, Washington 46; Head Indian Del. to Int. Cotton Textile Industry Conf. Manchester 52; Head Indian Del. to Russia 54; one of the leaders and Pres. of Jain Community in India; now Dir. in twenty concerns: textiles, insurance, electricity, steamship and motor companies, etc., mem. Central Advisory Council, Govt. of India 53-; Chair. Nat. Research and Development Corpn. 54-; Chair. Western Regional Cttee., All India Council for Technical Educ. 55-; Chair. Inst. of Technology, Bombay; mem. Senate Gujarat Univ.; Chair. Indian Cotton Mills Fed. 56.

Pankore's Naka, Ahmedabad, India.

Lall, Arthur; Indian diplomatist; b. 14 July 1911; ed. Punjab and Oxford Univs.

Appointed to Indian Civil Service and served in the Punjab and with central Govt.; Commercial Counsellor, High Comm., London 47-51; Consul-Gen., with rank of Minister, New York 51-54; Permanent Rep. to U.N. 54-59; Chair. U.N. Mission to Samoa 59; Ambassador to Austria 59-63; Lecturer, Cornell Univ. 63-; Prof. of International Relations, Columbia Univ., New York 65-; Consultant, UN Inst. for Training and Research, New York; Del. to UN Econ. and Social Council and Trusteeship Council; Del. to numerous econ. confs.

Publ. *How Communist China Negotiates* 68.

c/o Center for International Studies, Cornell University, Ithaca, N.Y., U.S.A.

Lalla Aicha, H.R.H. Princess; Moroccan diplomatist. Eldest daughter of late King Mohammed V; Ambassador to U.K. 65-; Pres. Moroccan Red Crescent; Grand Cordon of Order of the Throne.

Royal Moroccan Embassy, 49 Queen's Gate Gardens, London, S.W.7, England.

Lalouette, Roger, L. ès L., L. ès D.; French diplomatist; b. 8 Sept. 1904; ed. Ecole des Sciences Politiques.

Attaché, Berne 30; Sec. Vienna 31, Prague 35, Berlin 36; Head, Cabinet of Ministry of Foreign Affairs 39-42, at French Residence, Morocco 42-44, at Dublin (French Cttee. of Nat. Liberation) 44; Rep. to Nuremberg Trials 46; Dep. Dir. of Personnel and Accountancy 48-50; Dep. High Commr. to Austria 50, Minister 51-55; Minister, Rabat 55-56; Ambassador to the Republic of Viet-Nam 58-64, to Czechoslovakia 64-; Commdr. Légion d'Honneur; Croix de Guerre.

French Embassy, Prague, Czechoslovakia; Home: 67 rue du Maréchal Foch, Versailles, France.

La Malfa, Ugo, B.D.S.; Italian economist and politician; b. 16 May 1903; ed. Univ. of Venice.

Member Consultative Assembly 45-46, Constituent Assembly 46-48, Chamber of Deputies 48-; Pres. Parl. Finance Board 48-50; Minister of Transport 45, of Reconstruction 46, of Foreign Trade 46; Minister without Portfolio in charge Public Corporations 50-51; Minister of Foreign Trade 51-53; Minister of the Budget 62-63; Pres. Parliamentary Budget Commission 64-66; Sec. Italian Republican Party 65-; mem. Assembly European Coal and Steel Community, Pres. Treaties Comm.; Vice-Gov. Int. Monetary Fund.

Viale Cristoforo Colombo 179, Rome, Italy.

Telephone: 512-73086.

LaMarsh, Julia Verlyn, P.C., Q.C., LL.D.; Canadian politician; b. 24; ed. Stamford, Hamilton Normal School, Univ. of Toronto and Osgoode Hall.

Canadian Women's Army Corps 43-45; Member of Parliament 60; Minister of Nat. Health and Welfare 63-65; Sec. of State 65-; fmr. Vice-Pres. Ontario Asscn. of Rural-Urban Municipalities; mem. Planning Asscn. of Canada, Int. Parliamentary Union, Commonwealth Parliamentary Asscn.; Liberal.
Home: 1992 Corwin Avenue, Niagara Falls; Office: House of Commons, Ottawa, Ontario, Canada.

Lamb, William Kaye, B.A., M.A., PH.D.; Canadian librarian and archivist; b. 11 May 1904; ed. Univs. of British Columbia, Paris and London.
Librarian and Archivist, Provincial Library and Archives of British Columbia, Victoria 34-40; Superintendent, Public Library Comm., British Columbia 36-40; Librarian, Univ. of British Columbia 40-48; Dominion Archivist, Public Archives of Canada, Ottawa 48-, and also Nat. Librarian, Nat. Library of Canada, Ottawa 53-; Fellow and Past Pres. Royal Soc. of Canada; Past Pres. Canadian Library Asscn., Canadian History Asscn., etc.; several hon. degrees; Tyrrell Medal.
Office: Public Archives of Canada, 395 Wellington Street, Ottawa 4, Ont.; Home: 7 Crescent Heights Ottawa 1, Ont., Canada.
Telephone: 992-2473 (Office); 235-6298 (Home).

Lamb, Willis Eugene, Jr., PH.D., SC.D.; American physicist; b. 12 July 1913; ed. Univ. of Calif.
Instructor, Columbia Univ. 38, Prof. of Physics 48-52; Prof. of Physics, Stanford Univ. 51-56; Wykeham Prof. of Physics and Fellow, New Coll., Univ. of Oxford 56-62; Henry Ford II Prof. of Physics, Yale Univ. 62-; Loeb Lecturer, Harvard 53-54; mem. Nat. Acad. of Sciences; awarded Rumford Premium (American Acad. of Arts and Sciences) 53; Nobel Prize in Physics (shared with Prof. P. Kusch) 55; Research Corpn. Award 55.
Department of Physics, Yale University, New Haven, Conn., U.S.A.

Lambert, Sir Anthony Edward, K.C.M.G.; British diplomatist; b. 7 March 1911; ed. Harrow School and Balliol Coll., Oxford.
Foreign Service 34-, Brussels 37, Ankara 40, Beirut and Damascus 42, Brussels, 44, Stockholm 49, Athens 52, Minister to Bulgaria 58-60, Ambassador to Tunisia 60-63, to Finland 63-66, to Portugal 66-.
British Embassy, Lisbon, Portugal; and c/o DSAO, King Charles Street, London, S.W.1, England.

Lambert, Baron Léon Jean Gustave; Belgian banker; b. 2 July 1928; ed. Canterbury School, Yale Coll., Oxford Univ., Univ. of Geneva and Inst. of International Studies, Geneva.
Président du Conseil de gérance de la Banque Lambert, Brussels 50-; Prés. Compagnie Lambert pour l'Industrie et la Finance, Brussels 66-; Dir. various companies in Europe, U.S.A. and Canada; Chevalier de l'Ordre de Léopold (Belgium); Commdr. de l'Ordre à la Valeur (Cameroon).
Banque Lambert, 24 avenue Marnix, Brussels, Belgium.
Telephone: 13-81-81.

Lambert, Hon. Marcel Joseph Aimé, P.C., M.P.; Canadian lawyer and politician; b. 19; ed. St. Joseph's High School, Edmonton, Alberta, Univ. of Alberta, and Hertford Coll., Oxford.
Royal Canadian Army Corps. 41-45; legal practice 51-; M.P. 57-; Parl. Asst. Minister of Nat. Defence 57-58; Parl. Sec. Ministry of Nat. Revenue 59-62; Speaker, House of Commons 62-63; Minister of Veterans' Affairs 63; Progressive Conservative.
85 Range Road, Ottawa, Ontario, Canada.

Lambert-Ribot, Alfred, LL.D.; French industrialist; b. 1 Dec. 1886.
Chief of Cabinet to Ministry of Labour 13, to Ministry of Public Works 17; Prés. d'Honneur du Centre National pour l'Amélioration de l'Habitation; Pres. de la Société

Immobilière Thionvilloise; Prés. Caisse industrielle d'assurance mutuelle, Hon. Pres.; Pres. Caisse de Prévoyance des Industries métallurgiques, Caisse Foncière de Crédit pour l'amélioration du logement dans l'Industrie; Vice-Pres. Cie. d'Assurances La Union et le Phénix Espagnol, Cie. Financière et Immobilière d'Investissement, Cie. du Chemin de Fer de Paris à Orléans; Admin. Société de Wendel; Dir. Compagnie d'Assurances La Préservatrice.
49 rue de Monceau, Paris 8e, France.

Lambetti, Ellie; Greek actress; b. 30; ed. Athens Gymnasium.
First appeared in Marika Kotopouli's company in *Hannele* (Hauptmann) 45; subsequently played leading roles in *Blood Wedding* (Lorca) 47, *The Glass Menagerie* (Tennessee Williams), *Antigone* (Anouilh) 48, *The Heiress* 49, *Shadow and Substance* (P. V. Carroll) 50, *Peg o' My Heart* 51; formed own company with Dimitri Horn 53 and has appeared in *The Deep Blue Sea* (Rattigan) 53, *The Moon is Blue* (Herbert) 54, *Hamlet* 55, *The Rainmaker* (R. Nash), *Gigi* 57, *The Fourposter* (J. de Hartog) 58, *Two for the Seesaw*, *La Dame aux Camélias* 59; headed own Theatre Group 60-; has appeared in a number of films including *Windfall in Athens* 54, *A Girl in Black* 56, *A Matter of Dignity* 58 (all directed by Michael Cacoyannis).
Sina 56, Athens, Greece.

Lambo, (Thomas) Adeoye, O.B.E., M.D., F.R.C.P., D.P.M.; Nigerian neuro-psychiatrist; b. 29 March 1923; ed. Baptist High School, Akeokuta, and Birmingham Univ.
Medical Officer Nigerian Medical Services 50-; Govt. Specialist-in-charge, Aro Hospital for Nervous Diseases; Consultant Physician, Univ. Coll., Ibadan; Prof. and Head of Dept. of Psychiatry and Neurology, Univ. of Ibadan 63, Dean of Medical Faculty 66; convened first Pan-African Conf. of Psychiatrists 61; founded Asscn. of Psychiatrists in Africa 61; Vice-Chancellor Univ. of Ibadan 68-; Chair. Scientific Council for Africa, UN Advisory Cttee. for Prevention of Crime and Treatment of Offenders; mem. Advisory Cttee. for Mental Health, WHO, Exec. Cttee. Council for International Org. for Medical Sciences, UNESCO; mem. Royal Medico-Psychological Asscn. Great Britain.
Publs. Numerous articles in various medical journals.
Vice-Chancellor's Lodge, University of Ibadan, Nigeria.
Telephone: 23248 (Office); 21165 (Residence).

Lambrakis, Chrestos; Greek journalist and newspaper proprietor; b. 24 Feb. 1934; ed. London School of Economics.
Publisher and Editor weekly *Tachydromos* (Courier) 55-; succeeded father as proprietor of dailies *To Vima* (Tribune), *Ta Nea* (News) and the weeklies *Economicos Tachydromos* (Economic Courier) 57, *Omada* (The Team) 58; Publisher monthly *Epoches* 63-; Pres. Greek Section, Int. Press Inst.; in prison (Folgentros Prison Island) Nov. 67.
Lambrakis Press, Christou Lada 3, Athens, Greece.
Telephone: 230-221; 237-283.

Lambrechts, Peter, PH.D., LL.D.; Belgian university professor and administrator; b. 28 June 1910; ed. Athénée Royal, Ostend, and Ghent Univ.
Asst. Univ. of Ghent 37; Prof. Liège Univ. 44; Dir. of Higher Education Ministry of Education 45-48; Prof. of Brussels Univ. 45; Prof. Ghent Univ. 48- and Rector 57-61, and Pres. of Board of Admin.; mem. of Belgian Senate 65; Commdr. de l'Ordre de Léopold; Commdr. Order of Orange Nassau.
Publs. *La composition du Sénat romain au deuxième siècle de notre ère* 36, *La composition du Sénat romain au troisième siècle de notre ère* 37, *Contributions à l'étude des divinités celtiques* 42, *Wat Hellas en Rome ons gaven* 50,

L'exaltation de la tête dans la pensée et dans l'art des Celtes 54.
19 Gaverland, Baarle-Drongen, Belgium.
Telephone: 09-523659.

Lamizana, General Sangoule; Upper Volta army officer and politician; b. *c.* 1916.
Served in French Army in Second World War, and later in Indo-China; Chief of Staff, Army of Upper Volta 61, Lt.-Col. 64; Pres., Prime Minister, Minister of Defence, War Veterans, Foreign Affairs, Information, Youth and Sports, Upper Volta Jan. 66-.
Office of the President, Ouagadougou, Upper Volta.

Lamming, George William; West Indian novelist and poet; b. 27; ed. Combermere School, Barbados.
Schoolmaster in Trinidad 46-50; came to England and worked in London factories 50; Broadcaster B.B.C. Colonial Service 51; Guggenheim Fellowship tour of America 54; Somerset Maugham Award 57.
Publs. *In the Castle of My Skin* 53, *The Emigrants* 54, *Of Age and Innocence* 58, *The Pleasures of Exile, Season of Adventure* 60, poems in periodicals and broadcasts.
115 Mansfield Road, London, N.W.3, England.

Lamonica, Roberto de; Brazilian artist; b. 27 Oct. 1933; ed. Escola de Belas Artes de São Paulo and Museu de Arte Moderna, Rio de Janeiro.
Professor School of Fine Arts, Lima 61-62, Univ. of Chile and Catholic Univ. of Chile 62-63, School of Fine Arts, Viña del Mar 63-64; Prof. of Printmaking, Museum of Modern Art, Rio de Janeiro 64-; has exhibited in Graphic Art Exhbns. all over the world; illustrations and covers for several books; numerous prizes.
Rua Anibal de Mendança 180, A.P. 202, Rio de Janeiro ZC-37, Brazil.

Lamontagne, Hon. Maurice, P.C., M.P., M.SC., F.R.S.C., F.R.S.A.; Canadian politician; b. 1917; ed. Rimouski Seminary, Quebec, Laval and Harvard Univs.
Professor of Econs., Dir. Dept. of Econs., Laval Univ. 49; Asst. Deputy Minister, Dept. of Northern Affairs and Nat. Resources, Ottawa 54; Econ. Adviser to Privy Council 55-57, Pres. 63-; Prof. of Econs., Ottawa Univ. 57, Dean of Faculty of Social Sciences 58; Leader of the Opposition 58; Sec. of State and Registrar-Gen. 64-65; Liberal.
Parliament Buildings, Ottawa; 18 Lakeview Terrace, Ottawa 1, Ontario, Canada.

LaMotte, Louis Howell; American corporation executive; b. 29 March 1896; ed. Harvard Univ.
Joined Int. Business Machines Corpn. (I.B.M.) 22, Vice-Pres. 53-54, Dir. 52-, Exec. Vice-Pres. 54-59, Chair. Exec. and Finance Cttee. 59-65.
Casey Key, Route 1, Box 448, Nokomis, Florida, U.S.A.

Lamour, Philippe, L. en DR.; French businessman; b. 12 Feb. 1903.
President and Gen. Man. Compagnie Nat. d'Aménagement de la Région du Bas-Rhône-Languedoc 55-; Pres. Conseil Nat. de L'Aménagement du Territoire, Conseil Supérieur du Plan, Féd. Nat. des Vins de Qualité Supérieure; Vice-Pres. Féd. des Asscns. Viticoles de France; mem. Conseil Nat. du Crédit, Conseil Nat. de la Productivité, Centre national du commerce extérieur; Mayor of Ceillac.
Publ. *60 Millions de Français.*
Mas Saint Louis, la Perdrix, Bellegarde du Gard (Gard), France.

Lampe, William Frederick Meinhardt; Netherlands lawyer and politician; b. 96; ed. High School, Netherlands Antilles.
Registrar, Court of Justice, St. Eustatius 17; Postmaster, St. Martin (Netherlands Antillian Part) 19; Acting Lieut.-Gov. Saba 22; Gov. Netherlands Windward Islands 27-30; held various posts, including Attorney for the Netherlands Antilles 30-45; Public Notary, Aruba 46; Minister of Justice and Vice-Premier, Netherlands Antilles 51-55; Minister for the Netherlands Antilles to the Netherlands 55-62; Acting Gov. of the Netherlands Antilles 67-; mem. Windward Islands Progressive Party; Commdr. Order of Orange Nassau 66; Bearer Grand Cross (Peru and Argentina).
Mozart Straat 7, Oranjestad, Aruba.

Lampert, Maj.-Gen. James Benjamin; American army officer and military engineer; b. 14; ed. U.S. Military Acad., Massachusetts Inst. of Technology, Army Engineers' School and National War Coll.
Military Service, South and South-West Pacific 42-45, Exec. Officer, Manhattan Project 46-47, Armed Forces Special Weapon Project 47-49, Army District Engineer, South Carolina and Oklahoma 49-52, Officer-in-Charge Army Atomic Energy Comm. Nuclear Power Program 52-57, Military Asst. Advisory Group, Saigon, Viet-Nam 58-60, Dir. Military Construction, Office of Chief Engineers, U.S. Army 61-63, Supt., U.S. Mil. Acad., West Point, New York 63-66; Deputy Asst. Sec. of Defence (Manpower) 66-; mem. Soc. American Military Engineers, American Soc. of Civil Engineers; D.S.M., Silver Star, Legion of Merit, Bronze Star Medal, Army Commendation Medal.
The Pentagon, Washington, D.C. 20301, U.S.A.

Lamping, Arnold T.; Netherlands diplomatist; b. 17 June 1893.
Military service 14-18; Ministry for Foreign Affairs 19; Consulate, Kleef, Germany 20; Consulate Gen., Antwerp 20-22; Acting Consul-Gen., Smyrna 22-24; Ministry for Foreign Affairs 24-27; mem. Netherlands Del. to Econ. World Conf., Geneva 27; Chargé d'Affaires, Santiago de Chile 27-32; Dir. Trade Agreements 32-44; Sec.-Gen. various Ministries of the Netherlands Govt. in London 40-45; Minister Plenipotentiary, Head of the Econ. Section of the Netherlands Embassy in London, Netherlands rep. UNRRA; Conseil Tripartite Netherlands, France, Belgium and Luxembourg, and in charge first negotiations Benelux 44; Ambassador Extraordinary and Plenipotentiary, India 47-50; Special Mission to Nepal 50; Netherlands High Commissioner, Indonesia 50-52; Ambassador Extraordinary and Plenipotentiary to the German Federal Republic 53-60; left Diplomatic Service Jan. 60; Netherlands Lion (Knight), Orange Nassau (Commander), Léopold, Belgium (Grand Cross), Order of Merit, Germany (Grand Cross), Order Left Hand Nepal (Grand Cross), and many other honours.
Jozef Israelsplein 13, The Hague, Netherlands.

Lancaster, Burt(on) Stephen; American actor; b. 2 Nov. 1913; ed. New York Univ.
Acrobat 32-39; shop asst. and salesman 39-42; army service 42-45; appeared in the play *A Sound of Hunting* (New York) 45; films include *The Killers* 46, *Desert Fury* 47, *All My Sons* 48, *The Flame and the Arrow* 50, *Ten Tall Men* 51, *The Crimson Pirate* 52, *His Majesty O'Keefe, From Here to Eternity, The Rose Tattoo* 55, *Trapeze, The Rainmaker* 56, *Gunfight at O.K. Corral, Sweet Smell of Success* 57, *Separate Tables* 58, *The Devil's Disciple* 59, *The Unforgiven, Elmer Gantry* 60 (Acad. Award for Best Actor 1960), *Judgement at Nuremberg* 61, *Birdman of Alcatraz* 62, *The Leopard* 62, *A Child is Waiting* 62, *Seven Days in May* 64, *The Train* 64, *The Professionals* 66, *The Scalphunters* 68, *The Swimmer* 68; Dir. Hecht-Hill-Lancaster Productions Inc.
830 Linda Flora, Beverly Hills, Calif., U.S.A.

Lancaster, Osbert, C.B.E.; British artist and writer; b. 4 Aug. 1908; ed. Charterhouse, Lincoln Coll., and Slade School, London.
Cartoonist, *Daily Express* 39-; News Dept., Foreign Office 40; British Embassy, Athens 44-46; Sydney Jones Lecturer in Art, Liverpool Univ. 47, Hon. Litt.D. (Birmingham).
Designed sets for *Pineapple Poll*, Sadler's Wells 51,

Bonne Bouche, Covent Garden 52, *Love in a Village*, English Opera Group 52, *High Spirits*, Hippodrome 53, *Rake's Progress*, Edinburgh (for Glyndebourne) 53, *All's Well That Ends Well*, Old Vic 53, *Don Pasquale*, Sadler's Wells 54, *Coppelia*, Covent Garden 54, Napoli Festival Ballet 54, *Falstaff*, Edinburgh (for Glyndebourne) 55, *Zuleika*, Saville 57, *L'Italiana in Algeri*, Glyndebourne 57, *Tiresias*, English Opera Group 58, *Candide*, Saville 59, *La Fille mal gardée* Covent Garden 60, *She Stoops to Conquer*, Old Vic 60, *La Pietra del Paragone*, Glyndebourne 64, *L'Heure Espagnole*, Glyndebourne 66.
Publs. *Progress at Pelvis Bay* 36, *Our Sovereigns* 36, *Pillar to Post* 38, *Homes, Sweet Homes* 39, *Classical Landscape with Figures* 47, *The Saracen's Head* 48, *Drayneflete Revealed* 49, *Façades and Faces* 50, *Private Views* 56, *The Year of the Comet* 57, *Études* 58, *Here, of All Places* 59, *Signs of the Times* 61, *All Done from Memory* (autobiography) 64, *Graffiti* 64, *A Few Quick Tricks* 65, *With an Eye to the Future* 67.
12 Eaton Square, London, S.W.1, England.

Lanctot, Gustave, B.LITT., LL.M., D.LITT., Q.C.; Canadian archivist and writer; b. 83; ed. Montreal Coll. and Univ. and Oxford and Paris Univs.
Called to Bar 07; entered Dominion Archives 12; special work U.S.A. 13; served First World War, mem. Canadian Special Mission to France; Asst. Dir. War Trophies 18; Chief French Archivist, Canada 23; K.C. 25; Joint Sec. to Dominion Provincial Conf., Ottawa 27; del. Colonial Historical Exhibition, Paris 29; Canadian rep. Int. Cttee. of Historical Sciences; fmr. Deputy Minister and Dominion Archivist 37-48; formerly Pres. Canadian Writers' Foundation, Chair. Military Museum Board; Pres. Canadian Folk-Lore Society; Past-Pres. Canadian Catholic Historical Asscn.; Pres. Alliance Française; Pres. Ottawa Historical Society; Pres. Union des Alliances françaises du Canada; Pres. Royal Soc. of Canada, Canadian Historical Soc.; Hon. LL.D.
Publs. *Contes populaires canadiens* 23, *Français Xavier Garneau* 24, *Les Archives du Canada* 26, *L'Administration de la Nouvelle-France* 29, *Le Canada d'hier et d'aujourd'hui* 34, *Les Canadiens Français et leurs voisins du Sud* 41, *Situation politique de l'Eglise canadienne* 42, *Montréal au temps de la Nouvelle France* 42, *Trois ans de guerre* 43, *Cartier's First Voyage to Canada in 1524* 44, *Une Accusation contre Mgr. de Laval* 45, *Jacques Cartier devant l'histoire* 47, *Faussaires et faussetés en histoire canadienne* 48, *L'Œuvre de la France en Amérique du Nord* 51, *Réalisations françaises de Cartier à Montcalm* 51, *Filles de joie ou Filles du Roi* 52, *Une Nouvelle-France inconnue* 54, *Histoire du Canada des Origines au Régime Royal* (Vol. I 59, II 63, III 64), *Le Canada et la Révolution américaine* 65, *Montréal sous Maisonneuve* 66.
5642 Woodbury Avenue, Montreal, Canada.

Land, Edwin Herbert; American scientist; b. 7 May 1909; ed. Norwich Acad., and Harvard Univ.
Founder Polaroid Corpn., Cambridge, Mass. 37, later Pres., Chair., and Dir. of Research; invented camera which delivers finished photograph immediately after exposure 47; Consultant on missiles to U.S. Navy 41-45; research on polarisation of light; mem. President's Science Advisory Cttee.; numerous medals; Fellow, Photographic Soc. of America; mem. American Acad. of Arts and Sciences (past-Pres.), etc.
730 Main Street, Cambridge, Massachuse s, U.S.A.

Landau, Moshe, LL.B.; Israeli judge; b. Danzig 12; ed. London Univ.
Went to Israel 33; called to Palestine Bar 37, Magistrate of Haifa 40, District Court Judge, Haifa 48, Justice, Supreme Court, Jerusalem 53-.
The Supreme Court, Jerusalem, Israel.

Landau, Rom; British writer and Islamicist.
Sculptor and art critic; R.A.F. Liaison Officer 39, later Air Gunner and Flight-Lieut.; mem. Arab Cttee. Political Intelligence Dept., Foreign Office 41-44; Prof. Islamic and North African Studies, American Acad. of Asian Studies, San Francisco 52-58, and Univ. of the Pacific 55-; mem. Board of Dirs. Islamic Center, San Francisco 55-58; Dir. of Area Studies, Peace Corps Morocco Project 62-63; Commdr. of the Ouissam Alaouite Order of Morocco 56.
Publs. *Minos the Incorruptible* 25, *Pilsudski: Hero of Poland* 29, *Paderewski* 34, *God is my Adventure* (1st edn.) 35, *Seven* 36, *Thy Kingdom Come* 37, *Search for Tomorrow* 38, *Arm the Apostles* 39, *Love for a Country* 39, *Of No Importance* 40, *We Have Seen Evil* 41, *Hitler's Paradise* 41, *The Fool's Progress* 42, *Letter to Andrew* 43, *Islam To-day* (with Prof. A. J. Arberry) 43, *The Brother Vane* 44, *The Wing* 45, *Sex, Life and Faith* 46, *The Merry Oasis* 47, *Odysseus* 48, *Human Relations* 49, *Personalia* 49, *Invitation to Morocco* 50, *The Sultan of Morocco* 51, *The Beauty of Morocco* 51, *Moroccan Journal* 52, *Morocco* (survey for Carnegie Endowment for Int. Peace) 52, *Portrait of Tangier* 52, *France and the Arabs* 53, *Among the Americans* 54, *The Arabesque* 55, *Moroccan Drama, 1900-55* 56, *Outline of Moroccan Culture* 57, *Mohammed V, King of Morocco* 57, *Arab Contribution to Civilisation* 58, *Islam and the Arabs* 58, *The Philosophy of Ibn Arabi* 59, *Morocco Independent* (English and Arabic) 61, *The Arab Heritage of Western Civilization* 62, *Hassan II, King of Morocco* 62, *The Moroccans—Yesterday and Today* 63, *The History of Morocco in the 20th Century* 63, *God is My Adventure* (14th edn.) 64, *Morocco: Fez, Rabat and Marrakesh* 67.
2001 Pierce Street, San Francisco; and University of the Pacific, Stockton 4, Calif., U.S.A.

Landázuri Ricketts, H.E. Cardinal Juan, D.C.L.; Peruvian ecclesiastic; b. 13; ed. Univs. of Arequipa and Antonianum, Rome.
Franciscan Friar; Teacher of Canon Law; Archbishop Coadjutor to Cardinal Guevara, Archbishop of Lima; Primate of Peru; Kt. Commdr. of Order of Malta and many honours.
Palacio Arzobispal, Plaza de Armas, Lima, Peru.

Landowski, Marcel François Paul; French composer; b. 18 Feb. 1915; ed. Lycée Janson-de-Sailly and Conservatoire nationale de musique de Paris.
Director Conservatoire, Boulogne-sur-Seine 60-65; Dir. of Music, Comédie Française, Paris 62-; Insp.-Gen. of Musical Studies 64; Dir. of Music, Ministry of Cultural Affairs 66-; Chevalier Légion d'Honneur, Croix de guerre.
Compositions include: *Rhythmes du monde* (Oratorio), *Jean de la peur* (Symphony), *Le Rire de Nils Halérius*, *Le Fou*, *Le Ventriloque*, *Les Adieux* (Operas); two cantatas, chamber music, film music, music for *Cyrano de Bergerac* at Comédie Française.
10 rue Max-Blondat, Boulogne-sur-Seine, Seine, France.

Landquist, John, PH.D.; Swedish writer; b. 3 Dec. 1881; ed. Uppsala Univ.
Literary Critic *Dagens Nyheter* 11-18, and *Afonbladet* 24-; Editor *Aftonbladet* 32-35; Prof. of Phychology Lund Univ. 35-46, Emeritus 47-.
Publs. *The Will* 08, *Essays* 13, *Gustav Froding* 16, *Knut Hamsun* 17, *The Living Past* 19, *Knowledge of Man* 20, *Erik Gustav Geijer* 24, *Henri Bergson* 28, *Modern Swedish Literature in Finland* 29, *Humanism* 31, *The Unity of the Soul* 35, *Psychology* 40, *History of Pedagogy* 41, *As I remember them* 49, *In Youth* 57, *Charles Darwin, Life and Work* 59.
Villavägen 19, Stocksund, Sweden.

Landré, Guillaume (Louis Frédéric); Netherlands composer; b. 24 Feb. 1905; ed. Univ. of Utrecht (Doctor in Law), composition under Willem Pijper.
Teacher, Amsterdam 30-47; Gen.-Sec. Arts Council

47-57, Pres. Music Dept. 57-; Hon. Life Pres. Netherlands Composers' Guild 61; Hon. Life Pres. 2nd Fed. of Conf. Int. des Socs. d'Auteurs et Compositeurs (Cisac) 64; mem. Artistic Board Concertgebouw Orchestra; Vice-Pres. Netherlands Opera Foundation; Officer Orange-Nassau; Officer Polar Star (Sweden); Sweelinck Prize (Music Prize of the Netherlands).
Compositions: 4 Symphonies 33, 41, 51, 54, Concerto for Clarinet and Orchestra 57, *Permutazioni sinfoniche* 57, *Anagrams for Orchestra* 60, *Variazioni senza Tema per orchestra* 67-68, 4 String Quartets 29, 42, 51, 65, 2 Wind Quartets 30, 60, *Jean Lévecq* (one-act Opera) 64, *La Symphonie pastorale* (Opera) 66.
Molenweg 34, Amstelveen, Netherlands.
Telephone: 13284.

Lane, Sir Allen; British publisher; b. 21 Sept. 1902; ed. Bristol Grammar School.
Apprenticed to John Lane at The Bodley Head 19, later becoming Man. Dir.; resgnd. and founded Penguin Books Ltd. 36; began publication of Pelican Books 37; Chair. and Man. Dir. Penguin Books Ltd.; Dir. Royal Insurance Group (London), Penguin Books Australia Ltd., Penguin Books Inc.; Hon. Fellow, Royal Coll. of Art; Hon. M.A. (Bristol); Hon. LL.D. (Manchester and Birmingham); Hon. D.Litt. (Oxford and Reading).
Penguin Books, Harmondsworth, Middlesex; Home: The Old Mill House, Mill Road, West Drayton, Middlesex, England.
Telephone: West Drayton 2997 (Home).

Lang, André; French dramatist and journalist; b. 12 Jan. 1893.
Publs. include Plays: *Fantaisie Amoureuse* 25, *Les trois Henry* 30 (produced at Comédie Française), *La Paix est pour demain* 37, *L'Impure* 48; novels: *Le Responsable* 21, *Fausta* 22, *Mes deux Femmes* 31; essays: *Voyage en zigzags dans la République des Lettres* 22, *Déplacements et Villégiatures Littéraires* 23, *Tiers de Siècle* 35, *L'Homme libre, ce prisonnier* (crowned by French Acad.) 46, *Le tableau blanc* (cinema) 48, *Le Crime du Roi* (radio play, with Pierre Lafue) 52, *Fernand Ledoux* 54, *Le Voyage à Turin* (play) 56, *Le Septième Ciel* (novel) 58, *Une Vie d'orages: Germaine de Staël* (biography) 58, *Bagage à la Consigne* (autobiography) 60, *Le Sac* (play) 62, *La Dame de Coppet* (play) 64, *Pierre Brisson* (biography) 67.
15 rue La Kanal, Paris 15e, France.
Telephone: 828-45-46.

Lang, Fritz; American film producer, director and writer; b. Austria 5 Dec. 1890.
Fmrly. artist selling picture postcards in Brussels café; fmr. fashion designer Paris; joined Decla Film Co. after First World War, then UFA Berlin, Fritz Lang Film Co., later Nero Film Co.; collaborated in scenario writing with his fmr. wife, Thea von Harbou; freelance producer and director; Commdr. Cross Order of Merit (Fed. Republic of Germany) 66; Officier des Arts et des Lettres (France) 66.
Produced and directed *Dr. Mabuse, Destiny, Niebelling Saga, The Girl in the Moon, The Spy, Metropolis, "M", The Testament of Dr. Mabuse, Lilion, Fury, You Only Live Once, You and Me, The Return of Frank James, Western Union, Manhunt, Hangmen Also Die, Ministry of Fear, The Woman in the Window, Scarlet Street, Cloak and Dagger, Secret Beyond the River, House by the River, An American Guerilla in the Philippines, Chuck-a-Luck, Clash by Night, Blue Gardenia, The Big Heat, Human Desire, Moonfleet, While the City Sleeps, Beyond a Reasonable Doubt, Das indische Grabmal, Der Tiger von Eschnapur, Die 1000 Augen des Dr. Mabuse;* starred as himself in *Le Mépris* by Jean-Luc Godard.
1501 Summitridge Drive, Beverly Hills, Calif., U.S.A.

Lang, Paul Henry, PH.D.; American (Hungarian-born) musicologist; b. 28 Aug. 1901; ed. Budapest Royal Acad. of Music, Heidelberg, Paris and Cornell Univs.
Settled in U.S.A. 28, naturalised citizen 34; Asst.

Prof. of Music Vassar Coll. 30-31; Assoc. Prof. of Music Wells Coll. 31-33; Prof. of Musicology Columbia Univ. 33-; music critic for *New York Herald Tribune* 54-66; Fellow American Acad. of Arts and Sciences; Pres. Int. Musicological Soc.; mem. French, Netherlands and Belgian Musicological Socs.; Editor *The Musical Quarterly.*
Publ. *Music in Western Civilisation* 41.
33 Aldridge Road, Chappaqua, N.Y., U.S.A.

Långbacka, Ralf Runar, M.A.; Finnish theatre director; b. 20 Nov. 1932; ed. Åbo Akademi, Universität München, and Freie Univ., Berlin.
Editor of Finnish Radio literary programmes 55-56; Asst. and Dir. Lilla Teatern, Helsinki 58-60; Manager and Artistic Dir. Swedish Theatre, Turku 60-63; Dir. Finnish Nat. Theatre 63-65; Artistic Dir. Swedish Theatre, Helsinki 65-67; The Critics Spurs 63.
Koivikkotie 20 O 15, Helsinki, Finland.
Telephone: 740848.

Langdon, Jervis, Jr.; American railroad executive; b. 28 Jan. 1905; ed. Cornell Univ., and Univ. of Dijon.
Assistant Gen. Attorney, Chesapeake and Ohio Railway 36-38, Gen. Attorney 38-41, Asst. Vice-Pres. (Traffic) 41-42; U.S. Army Air Force 42-45; Special Counsel, Asscn. of Southeastern Railroads 47-53, Chair. 53-56; Gen. Counsel, Baltimore and Ohio Railroad 56-61, Pres. 61-64; Chair. Chicago, Rock Island and Pacific Railroad 64-65, Chair. and Pres. May 65-; Legion of Merit.
Chicago, Rock Island and Pacific Railroad Co., La Salle Street Station, Chicago 5, Illinois, U.S.A.

Langdon, Michael; British bass singer; b. 12 Nov. 1921; ed. Bushbury Hill School, Wolverhampton.
Principal bass, Royal Opera House, Covent Garden 51-; sang in *Gloriana* (Britten) at Royal Command Performance 53; Promenade Concerts, Royal Albert Hall 53-; int. engagements since 61; engaged to sing at Teatro Colón, Buenos Aires Sept. to Nov. 67; known for leading bass roles in *Fidelio, Der Rosenkavalier, Il Seraglio, Don Carlos, Wozzeck, Don Giovanni, Faust, Das Rheingold, Die Walküre, Götterdämmerung, Magic Flute* and *Falstaff;* particularly well known as Baron Ochs in *Der Rosenkavalier.*
49 Banstead Road South, Sutton, Surrey, England.

Lange, Gunnar, PH.D.; Swedish government official and politician; b. 9 March 1909; ed. Stockholm Univ.
Served in Board of Agriculture 35-38; Asst. Prof. Agriculture and Economics, Univ. of North Carolina, U.S.A. 41-43; Chief of Bureau, Swedish Food Comm. 43-46; Sec. of State Ministry of Agriculture 47-50, Ministry of Finance 50-54; Minister of Civil Service 54-55; Minister of Commerce and Industry 55-; mem. of First Chamber of Parliament 53-; Chair. Ministerial Council of European Free Trade Asscn. 59-60, 63, 67; Pres. of Swedish Football Asscn. 53-; Social Democratic Labour.
Office: K. Handelsdepartement, Rosenbach, Stockholm 1; Home: Stopvägen 84, Bromma, Stockholm, Sweden.
Telephone: 224500 (Office); 08-259980 (Home).

Lange, Halvard Manthey, M.A.; Norwegian lecturer, historian and politician; b. 16 Sept. 1902; ed. Univs. of Oslo and Geneva, London School of Economics.
Asst. Sec. Int. Fellowship of Reconciliation London 23-25; Univ. studies 25-29; teacher of Economic History, Oslo High School of Commerce 30-35; Sec. Norwegian Workers' Educational Asscn. and Lecturer Modern History, Univ. of Oslo 35-36; Warden Norwegian Central T.U. Coll. and Soermarka Workers' High School 38-40; mem. Exec. Norwegian Labour Party 33-39 and 45-; imprisoned by Gestapo Aug. 40-June 41 and Aug. 42–May 45; Minister of Foreign Affairs 46-Aug. 63 and Sept. 63-65; Chair. NATO Council 60; Hon. LL.D. (Birmingham); Labour.
Publs. (All in Norwegian): *History of Norwegian Trade*

Unions 33; *Nazis and Norway* 34, *Political Labour Internationals 1914-1934* 35, *History of World Political Labour Movement 1914-1936* (2 Vols.) 36 and 37, *History of Norwegian Labour Party 1887-1914* (2 Vols.) 37 and 39, *Norwegian Foreign Policy since 1945* 52, *From Sect to Party* 62, *Norway's Road to NATO* 66. Drammensveien 102*i*, Oslo 2, Norway.

Lange, Horst; German writer; b. 6 Oct. 1904; ed. Univs. of Berlin and Breslau.

Freelance writer, Berlin 31-40; Army service 40, wounded with loss of left eye 41; freelance writer 41-; Poetry Prize of *Die Kolonne* (periodical) 32, Fed. of German Industries Culture Prize 56, Bavarian Acad. Award 58, Esslingen Literature Prize 60, Bavarian Acad. Literature Prize 63.

Publs. *Schwarze Weide* (novel) 37, *Ulanen Patroville* (novel) 40, *Das Irrlicht* (short stories) 43, *Die Leucht Kugeln* (short stories) 44, *Der Traum von Wassilkowa* (play) 46, *Die Frau, die sich Helena wähnte* (monologue) 46, *Gedichte aus zwanzig Jahren* (poetry) 48, *Ein Schwert zwischen uns* (novel) 52, *Verlöschende Feuer* (novel) 56, *Aus dumpfen Fluten kam Gesang* (poetry) 58. 8 Munich 49, Züricherstrasse 104, German Federal Republic.

Lange, Per; Danish writer; b. 30 Aug. 1901.

Free-lance translator and literary critic; former book critic of *Berlingske Tidende*; on staff of *Sind og Samfund* 32-37; Literary adviser *Gyldendals Forlag*, Copenhagen 46-.

Publs. Poems: *Kaos og Stjaernen* 26, *Forvandlinger* 29, *Orfeus* 32, *Relieffer* 43; *Spejlinger* (essays) 53, *Ved Musikkens Tærskel* (essays) 57, *Samtale med et Aesel* (essays) 61, *Om Krig og Krigsmoend* (essays) 66; also numerous translations of English, French and American authors.

Maria Kirkeplads 6 ,IV, 1707 Copenhagen 5, Denmark. Telephone: (01) Ve 10056.

Langemeijer, Gerard Eduard, DR. JUR.; Netherlands lawyer; b. 03; ed. Leiden Univ.

Called to the Bar 28; District Attorney, Rotterdam 29-34; The Hague 34-39; Judge, Amsterdam 39-46; Prof. of Law, Leiden Univ. 46-58; Asst. Attorney-Gen. 47-57, Attorney-Gen. 57-; Pres. Royal Netherlands Acad. of Sciences and Letters 63; Co-editor of *Nederlands Juristenblad* (Law Review).

Cornelis Jolstraat 70, The Hague, Netherlands.

Langenhove, Fernand Van; Belgian diplomatist; b. 30 June 1889; ed. Univ. of Brussels.

Sec. Inst. of Sociology, Brussels 10; Dir. Min. of Econ. Affairs, Belgium 17; Prof. Univ. of Brussels 20; Dir. Min. of Foreign Affairs 22; Chief of Cabinet of the Min. of Foreign Affairs 27; Sec.-Gen. of the Min. of Foreign Affairs 29; Ambassador 36; Perm. Belgian Rep. to UN 46-57; Pres. Inst. Royal des Relations Int. 58; mem. Acad. Royale de Belgique 61, Acad. Royale des Sciences d'Outremer; Grand Cross of Order of Crown (Belgium), of Order of Netherlands Lion, of Order of Southern Cross (Brazil), of Order of Merit (Portugal), of Order of Crown (Italy); Grand Officier de la Légion d'Honneur (France), etc.

Publs. *La Nationalité Albanaise* 13, *Comment naît un cycle de légendes* 16, *Le dossier diplomatique de la question belge* 17, *L'action du Gouvernement belge en matière économique pendant la guerre* 21, *Le problème de la protection des populations aborigènes aux Nations Unies* 56, *La crise du système de sécurité collective des Nations Unies* 58, *Consciences Tribales et Nationales en Afrique Noire* 60, *Le rôle proéminent du Secrétaire Général dans l'opération des Nations Unies au Congo* 64.

67 Avenue de la Floride, Brussels 18, Belgium. Telephone: 74-12-87.

Langer, William Leonard, A.M., PH.D., LL.D., DR.PHIL., L.H.D., LITT.D.; American historian; b. 16 March 1896; ed. Harvard and Vienna Univs.

Instructor in Modern Languages, Worcester Acad. 15-17; Asst. Prof. of History, Clark Univ. 23-25; Associate Prof. 25-27; Asst. Prof. of History, Harvard Univ. 27-31; Associate Prof. 31-36, Coolidge Prof. 36-64, Prof. Emeritus 64-; Prof. Fletcher School of Diplomacy, Medford, Mass. 33-34, 36-41; mem. American Historical Asscn., Mass. Historical Society, Council on Foreign Relations, American Acad. of Arts and Sciences, American Philosophical Society, etc.; mem. editorial board *Journal of Modern History* 29-33, *American Historical Review* 36-39, *Foreign Affairs* 55-; mem. Advisory Board *Historical Abstracts* 55-; editorial adviser to Houghton, Mifflin Co.; Chief Research and Analysis Branch, Office Strategic Services 41-45; Dir. Office of Intelligence Research and Liaison, Dept. of State 45-46; Special Asst. to Sec. of State for Research and Intelligence 46; Dir. for Nat. Estimates, Central Intelligence Agency 50-51; mem. President's Foreign Intelligence Advisory Board 61-; mem. American Historical Asscn. (Pres. 57); Fellow, Center for Advanced Study in the Behavioral Sciences 59-60; Medal for Merit.

Publs. *The Franco-Russian Alliance of 1890-94* 29, *European Alliances and Alignments* 31, *The Diplomacy of Imperialism* 35, *Foreign Affairs Bibliography* 33, *Our Vichy Gamble* 47, *The Challenge to Isolation* (with S. E. Gleason) 52, *The Undeclared War* (with S. E. Gleason) 53, *Gas and Flame in World War I* 65.

1 Berkeley Street, Cambridge 38, Mass., U.S.A.

Langsam, Walter Consuelo, B.S., M.A., PH.D., LITT.D., SC.D. in ED., L.H.D., SC.D., LL.D.; American historian and university administrator; b. 2 Jan. 1906; ed. City Coll. of New York and Columbia Univ.

Tutor in History, Coll. City of N.Y. 26; Instructor in History Columbia Univ. 27; Asst. Prof. Columbia Univ. 35; Prof. of History Union Coll. 38; Visiting Prof. British Columbia, Duke, Ohio State, Columbia, N.Y. and Colorado Univs.; radio news commentator Station WGY Schenectady 41-43; Office of Strategic Services 44-45; Pres. Wagner Coll., N.Y. 45-52; Pres. of Gettysburg Coll., Pa. 52-55, of Univ. of Cincinnati 55-; mem. Council on Foreign Relations, American Historical Asscn.; Trustee, Hamma School of Theology, Endicott Junior Coll.; Chair. Comm. on Colls., North Central Asscn.; Dir. Cincinnati Chamber of Commerce; Vice-Pres. Board of Theological Education, Lutheran Church in America; mem. Exec. Cttee., Region Four, Boy Scouts of America; mem. Board of Dirs. Spindletop Research Center, North Central Asscn. of Colls. and Secondary Schools and U.S. Playing Card Co.; mem. Education Cttee., Robert A. Taft Inst. of Government; Townsend Harris Medallist (City Coll. of New York) Bronze Medal, Freedoms Foundation at Valley Forge.

Publs. *The Napoleonic Wars and German Nationalism in Austria* 30, *The World since 1914* 33 (6th edn. 48), *Major European and Asiatic Developments since 1935* 39, *In Quest of Empire, the Problem of Colonies* 39, *Documents and Readings in the History of Europe since 1918* 39 (rev. edn. 51), *Since 1939—A Narrative of War* 41, *Francis the Good, the Education of an Emperor (1768-1792)* 49, *The World since 1919* 54, *Franz der Gute: Die Jugend eines Kaisers* 54, *Historic Documents of World War II* 58, *World History since 1870* 63; contr. *The American Historical Association's Guide to Historical Literature* 61; contributor to *Virtute Fideque: Festschrift für Otto von Habsburg zum fünfzigsten Geburtstag* (ed. Emil Franzel) 65; *While Freedom Exists* 67.

University of Cincinnati, Cincinnati, Ohio 45221, U.S.A. Telephone: 475-2201.

Laniel, Joseph; French manufacturer and politician; b. 12 Oct. 1889; ed. Ecole Gerson, Lycée Janson de Sailly, and Univ. of Paris.

Deputy, Nat. Assembly 32-58; mem. Comité Nat. de la Résistance; founded Parti Républicain de la Liberté

(P.R.L.) 46; Sec. of State for Finance Mar. 40, July 48; Minister for Posts, Telegraph and Telephones Aug. 51; Minister of State Oct. 52-Jan. 53, Prime Minister June 53-54; Officier de la Légion d'Honneur; Croix de Guerre (14-18, 39-45); Médaille de la Résistance avec Rosette.
15 rue Leroux, Paris 16e, France.

Lanier, Edmond Raoul Henri; French shipping executive; b. 1 March 1906; ed. Univ. de Paris à la Sorbonne, and Ecole Libre des Sciences Politiques.
Compagnie Générale Transatlantique 32-, Gen. Sec. 45-58, Gen. Manager 58-64, Pres. and Chair. 64-; Officier Légion d'Honneur, Médaille Militaire, Croix de Guerre, and several foreign awards.
Publs. *De la pêche à la morue au paquebot "France"* 63, *Un décret parmi tant d'autres.*
Compagnie Générale Transatlantique, 6 rue Auber, Paris 9e; 33 avenue Georges Mandel, Paris 16e, France.

Lanocita, Arturo; Italian journalist; b. 4 June 1904; ed. Univ. degli Studi, Pavia.
Editor newspaper *L'Ambrosiano* 23-30, *La Stampa* 30; Editor *Corriere della Sera* 30-45, Vice-Editor-in-Chief 45-62, Cinema Critic 46, Editor-in-Chief 62-68; mem. Int. Jury Venice Cinema Festival 48, 50, 52, 62, Pres. 63; mem. Int. Jury San Sebastian Cinema Festival 59; Commendatore della Repubblica Italiana; Golden Pen of Cinema Critics 51, Borselli Prize 66.
Publs. *Attrici e attori in pigiama* 26, *Scrittori del tempo nostro* 28, *Quaranta milioni* 32, *Quella maledettissima sera* 39, *Salvateli dalla ghigliottina* 43, *Il Croce a sinistra* 45, *Il ragazzo che doveva mentire* 46, *Cinema, fabbrica di sogni* 50, *Gratis* 59, *Sofia Loren* 66.
Via Alessandro Volta 7, Milan, Italy.

Lanoux, Armand; French writer; b. 24 Oct. 1913.
Former teacher, painter; infantry officer 39-40; professional writer 46-; Sec.-Gen., Université Radiophonique et Télévisuelle Internationale; Vice-Pres. Société des Auteurs Dramatiques; Chevalier de la Légion d'Honneur, Croix de Guerre 39-40, Officier des Arts et Lettres; Prix Interallié 56, Prix Goncourt 63.
Publs. biographies: *Bonjour, Monsieur Zola* 54, *Maupassant, le Bel Ami* 67; novels: *Le Commandant Watrin* 56, *Le Rendez-Vous de Bruges* 58, *Quand la Mer se Retire* 63, *Margot, l'enragée* 64.
7 route de Malnoue, Champs-sur-Marne, Seine et Marne, France.
Telephone: 957-21-89.

Lansdowne, 8th Marquess of; George John Charles Mercer Nairne Petty-Fitzmaurice, P.C.; British politician; b. 27 Nov. 1912; ed. Eton Coll., and Christ Church, Oxford.
Army service 39-45, Major 44, served with Free French Forces; Private Sec. to Rt. Hon. A. Duff Cooper, Ambassador to France 44-45; Lord-in-Waiting to H.M. The Queen 57-58; Joint Parl. Under-Sec. of State, Foreign Office 58-62; Chair. Intergovernmental Cttee. Malaysia Aug.-Dec. 62; Minister of State for Colonial Affairs 62-64; Conservative.
Bowood, Calne, Wiltshire, England.

Lantier, Raymond François; French archaeologist; b. 11 July 1886; ed. Ecole pratique des Hautes Etudes, Ecole du Louvre, and Ecole des Hautes Etudes Hispaniques, Madrid, Univ. of Caen.
With Musées Nationaux 11-14; military service 14-18; Inspector of Antiquities and Arts Tunisia 21-26; Asst. Keeper Musée des Antiquités Nationales 26-32, Keeper 33-56, Hon. Keeper 56-; Prof. of Nat. and Prehistoric Antiquities, Ecole du Louvre 27-51; mem. Acad. de la Historia, Madrid 33, Acad. des Inscriptions et Belles-Lettres, Inst. de France 46, Akad. der Wissenschaften und Litteratur, Mainz 47, New York Acad. of Sciences 58; Co-Dir. *Revue archéologique* 33-65; Chief Editor *Préhistoire* 32-67.
Publs. *El santuario ibérico de Castellar de Santisteban*

(Jaen) 17, *Inventaire des monuments sculptés préchrétiens de la Péninsule ibérique, 1ère partie: Lusitanie* 18, *Bronzes votifs ibériques* 35, *Recueil des bas-reliefs, sculptures et bustes de la Gaule romaine* (Vols. XII, XIII, XIV, XV, 47, 49, 54, 65), *Les origines de l'art français, Des temps préhistoriques à l'époque carolingienne* 47, *Guide illustré du Musée des Antiquités Nationales au château de Saint-Germain-en-Laye* 48, *Les Hommes de la Pierre Ancienne* (with H. Breuil) 51, 59, *La vie préhistorique* 52, 57, 65, *L'Art Préhistorique* 61, *L'Art Celtique* 65.
8 rue Armagis, Saint-Germain-en-Laye, 78 Yvelines, France.

Lanusse, Ing. Antonio R.; Argentine politician.
Minister of Transport Nov. 66; Minister of Defence 67-March 68.
c/o Ministry of Defence, Buenos Aires, Argentina.

La Paz, Lincoln, A.B., A.M., PH.D.; American mathematician; b. 12 Feb. 1897; ed. Harvard and Chicago Universities.
Instructor in Mathematics, Harvard Univ. 21-22, Dartmouth Coll. 22-25; Nat. Research Fellow 28-29; Instructor, Chicago Univ. 29-30; Asst. Prof. 30-35, Assoc. Prof. 35-42, Prof. of Mathematics, Ohio State Univ. 42-45; Research Mathematician, Office of Scientific Research and Development 42-44; Technical Dir. Operations Analysis Section, H.Q. 2nd Air Force 44-45; Head, Dept. of Mathematics, and Dir. Inst. of Meteoritics, Univ. of New Mexico 45-53; Dir. Div. of Astronomy 53-62, Inst. of Meteoritics 53-66; Vice-Pres. and Fellow Meteoritical Society; Fellow American Asscn. for the Advancement of Science; mem. New York Acad. of Sciences, Int. Astronomical Union, British and Canadian Astronomical Societies, Mathematical Asscn., etc.
Publs. *Advances in Geophysics, Vol. IV* (co-author) 58, *Space Nomads* (co-author) 61.
3400 Wilway Drive, Albuquerque, New Mexico, U.S.A.

Lapesa, Rafael; Spanish author and university professor; b. 08; ed. Instituto Cardenal Cisneros and Madrid Univ.
Engaged in research work at Centro de Estudios Históricos, Madrid, under guidance of Ramón Menéndez Pidal 27-39; Prof. at Madrid Univ. 47-; has lectured as guest Prof. in Univs. of Princeton, Yale, Harvard, California, Pennsylvania, Wisconsin, La Plata and Buenos Aires; mem. of Real Academia Española; mem. of Hispanic Society of America; corr. mem. Acad. Argentina de Letras; hon. mem. Modern Language Asscn. of America and American Asscn. of Teachers of Spanish and Portuguese; Dr. h.c. Toulouse Univ.
Publs. *Historia de la Lengua Española* 42, 51, 55, 59, *Asturiano y Provenzal en el Fuero de Avilés* 48, *La trayectoria poética de Garcilaso* 48, *La obra literaria del Marqués de Santillana* 57.
Residencia de Profesores 3, Calle de Isaac Peral, Madrid 15, Spain.

Lapie, Major Pierre Olivier, K.B.E., M.C.; French lawyer and administrator; b. 2 April 1901.
Barrister-at-Law; Deputy for Meurthe-and-Moselle 36, 58; Liaison Officer with B.E.F. 39; volunteer, Norwegian Expedition; as Capt. in Foreign Legion participated in capture of Narvik; joined Gen. de Gaulle's Free French Forces June 40; Gov. of Chad Territory Nov. 40; served Libyan and Tunisian campaigns; Sec. of State for Foreign Affairs 46; Del. UN Gen. Assemblies 47, 48, 49, 51 and 54; Del. to Council of Europe since 49; Minister of Education 50-51; Del. UNESCO Conf. 56; Vice-Pres. Nat. Assembly and mem. Foreign Affairs Cttee. 57; Chair. Franco-British Parl. Cttee.; mem. High Authority of European Coal and Steel Community 59-67; Chair. Franco-German Co-operative Cttee. Croix de Guerre 40, and Légion d'Honneur 54; Hon. K.B.E., M.C. (both U.K.); Dr. h.c. Edinburgh Univ.
Publs. *Certitudes Anglaises* 36, *The Foreign Legion in*

Narvik 1940, *Chad* 42, *Cromwell* 48, *Lisos ou de l'action* 56, *Les Trois Communautés* 60, *Heniot*, etc.
11 rue de Bellechasse, Paris 7e, France.
Telephone: INV-19-23.

Lapin, Sergei Georgievich; Soviet diplomatist and journalist; b. 1912; ed. Univ. of Leningrad.
Journalist, editor, Vice-Chair. Radio Cttee. 45-55; Diplomatic Service 55-; Head, Third European Dept., Ministry of Foreign Affairs 55-56; Ambassador to Austria 56-60; Vice-Chair. State Comm. for Cultural Relations with Foreign Countries 60; Minister of Foreign Affairs of R.S.F.S.R. 60-62; Deputy Minister of Foreign Affairs 62-65; mem. C.P.S.U. Central Cttee. 66-; Amb. to People's Republic of China 65-67; Dir. of Tass 67-.
Tass, Moscow, U.S.S.R.

La Pira, Giorgio; Italian lawyer, politician and philanthropist; b. 9 Jan. 1904; ed. Florence Univ.
University prof., theological lecturer and social organizer; mem. of the Constituent Assembly; mem. East-West Round Table Conf.; fmr. mem. of Parl.; fmr. Under-Sec. of State to the Minister of Labour and Social Welfare; Pres. of the Tuscan Council, San Vicenzo de'Paoli Organization; Pres. Int. Congress for Peace and Christian Civilization 52-, Mediterranean Congress of Florence 58-; Mayor of Florence 51-64.
Via Lamarmora 5, Florence, Italy.

Lapointe, Hon. Hugues, P.C., Q.C., B.A., LL.D.; Canadian politician; b. 3 March 1911; ed. Univ. of Ottawa, and Laval Univ., Quebec.
Member of Parl. for Lotbinière 40-57; apptd. Parl. Asst. to Minister of Nat. Defence 45; Parl. Asst. to Sec. of State for External Affairs 49; Privy Councillor and Solicitor-Gen. of Canada 49; del., Gen. Assembly, UN, Paris 48, Lake Success 49, 50 (Vice-Chair. Canadian del. 50); Minister of Veterans' Affairs 50-57; concurrently Postmaster-Gen. 55-57; private legal practice 57-62; Agent Gen. for Quebec in London 61-66; Lt.-Gov. of Quebec 66-; Liberal.
Office of the Lieutenant-Governor, Montreal, Quebec, Canada.

Laporte, William F., A.B., M.B.A.; American business executive; b. 3 Sept. 1913; ed. Princeton Univ., and Harvard Coll. of Business Administration.
President, Whitehall Pharmacal Co. 50-57; Vice-Pres. American Home Products Corpn. 57-60, Dir. 57-, Pres. 60-, Chair. of Board and Pres. 65-; Dir. Manufacturers Hanover Trust Co. 65-; Dir. Nat. Starch and Chemical Corpn. 66-; Trustee, Dime Savings Bank of Brooklyn 66-.
American Home Products Corporation, 685 Third Avenue, New York, N.Y. 10017; Home: 941 Park Avenue, New York, N.Y. 10028, U.S.A.
Telephone: RE 4-1919.

Lappas, Vice-Admiral Pirros; Greek naval officer; b. 11 Jan. 1900; ed. Naval Cadet Coll.
Commissioned in Royal Greek Navy 20; held various appointments both at sea and on shore; C.O. *King George I* 41, and later (after joining Free Greek Forces) *Samos*; participated in landing operations of Italy and Southern France; Commdr. 12th Destroyer Flotilla 44; Chief of Personnel, Admiralty 46, and later Chief of Technical Services; Commodore in charge of Light Vessels and Submarines 47; Deputy Chief of Naval Gen. Staff 49; Rear-Admiral 49; Chief of Naval Commands and Gen. Inspector of the Royal Hellenic Navy 49; C.-in-C. Royal Hellenic Fleet 50, Vice-Admiral 52; Chief of Naval Gen. Staff 52-58; Chief of military household to H.M. the King 58-60, Hon. General A.D.C. to H.M. the King 60-; Hon. C.B.E.; Grand Commdr. Royal Order of George I and Grand Cross of Order of Phoenix, War Cross, D.S.M. and bars; Hon. Sec.

Hellenic Olympic Cttee.; mem. Int. Olympic Cttee.
26 Tsakaloff Street, Athens, Greece.
Telephone: Athens 613-221.

Laprade, Albert; French architect; b. 29 Nov. 1883; ed. Lycée de Châteauroux and Ecole nationale supérieure des beaux-arts.
French consular architect, Morocco 15-19; Hon. Insp.-Gen. of Fine Arts, mem. Académie des Beaux-Arts (Vice-Pres. 64, Pres. 65); mem. Inst. de France (Pres. 65); mem. Académie d'Architecture and des Sciences d'Outre-mer.
Major works: The French Residency, Rabat; Musée de la France d'outre-mer, Paris; French Embassy, Ankara.
Publs. include *Carnets de Croquis, Lyautey urbaniste, François d'Orbay, Architecte de Louis XIV, Vies des Architectes.*
27 rue Lhomond, Paris 5e, France.

Lara Bustamante, Fernando; Costa Rican lawyer and politician; b. 12 Jan. 1911; ed. Liceo de Costa Rica and Escuela de Derecho.
Graduated in law 34; Police Official, San José 32-37; Official in Ministry of Educ. 37-40; Dir. *Jurisprudencia* (law magazine) 33-36; Deputy to Nat. Assembly 42, re-elected 46; mem. Editorial Comm. for Political Constitution 48; Prof. Faculty of Law 40-52; Deputy, First Sec., Legislative Assembly 49; Minister of Foreign Affairs 49-52, 66-; Pres. Coll. of Lawyers of Costa Rica 54-55; Deputy to Legislative Assembly 58-62, 66-, Pres. 60-61; Sec. Gen. Unión Nacional Party 58-66; decorations from Mexico, El Salvador, Panama, France, Italy, Vatican, Ecuador, Republic of China and Cuba.
Ministerio de Asuntos Exteriores, San José, Costa Rica.

Laraki, Moulay Ahmed; Moroccan diplomatist and politician; b. 1930; ed. Univ. de Paris.
With Ministry of Foreign Affairs 56-57; Perm. Rep. to UN 57-59; medical affairs 59-62; Amb. to Spain 62-65, to Switzerland 65-66, to U.S.A. and concurrently accred. to Mexico, Canada and Venezuela 66-67; Minister of Foreign Affairs 67-.
Ministry of Foreign Affairs, Rabat, Morocco.

Lardinois, P. J.; Netherlands politician; b. 13 Aug. 1926; ed. Wageningen Agricultural Coll.
Various agricultural posts until 60; entered Ministry of Agriculture and Fisheries Feb. 60; Agricultural Attaché, London Embassy May 60-Sept. 63; mem. Second Chamber 63-; mem. European Parl. Oct. 63-; Minister of Agriculture 67-.
Ministry of Agriculture, The Hague, Netherlands.

Larkin, Arthur E., Jr., B.A.; American food executive; b. 7 March 1917; ed. Blake School and Dartmouth Coll.
Served U.S. Navy 40-45; with Geo. A. Hormel & Co. 46-58, Vice-Pres. and Dir. 53-58; joined Gen. Foods Corpn. 58, Maxwell House Marketing Man. 58-59, Maxwell House Gen. Man. 59-62, Vice-Pres. Gen. Foods Corpn. 60, Exec. Vice-Pres. Operations 62-65, Dir. Gen. Foods Corpn. 63-, Exec. Vice-Pres. 65-66, Pres. and Chief Operating Officer Oct. 66-; Dir. Gillette Co.
General Foods Corporation, 250 North Street, White Plains, N.Y. 10602, U.S.A.

Larkin, Frederick George, Jr.; American banker; b. 28 Dec. 1913; ed. Univ. of Washington, Stanford Univ., and Graduate School of Banking.
President and Dir., Security First Nat. Bank 61-; Dir. of Tidewater Oil Co. 62-; official of civic, religious and philanthropic orgs.
526 South Arden Boulevard, Los Angeles 5, California, U.S.A.

Larock, Victor J. L.; Belgian sociologist and politician; b. 04.
Prof. Inst. des Hautes Etudes, Ghent 36-40; Editor of *Le Peuple* 44-54; Mem. of Parl. 49-; Minister of Foreign Trade 54-57; Minister of Foreign Affairs 57-58; Minister

of Nat. Educ. and Culture 61-63; Chair. of Bureau (Exec. Cttee.) of Socialist Int. 64-.

Publs. *Essai sur la Valeur Sociale des Personnes dans les Sociétés Inférieures* 32, *La Pensée Mythique* 45, *La Grande Cause* 53.

18c rue des Champs-Elysées, Brussels, Belgium.

Larraona, Cardinal Arcadio; Vatican ecclesiastic; b. 87; ed. Pontifical Lateran and Gregorian Univs.

Entered Congregation of Claretian Missionaries 03; normal theological studies 03-11; studied law in Rome 11-18; Prof. of Roman Law, Lateran Univ. 18-59; Sub-Sec. Sacred Congregation of Religious 43-50, Sec. 50; Consultor for the Oriental Church; mem. Comm. for Codification of Oriental Canon Law and Comm. for Interpretation of Canon Law; named Cardinal Deacon Nov. 59; founded review *Commentarium pro Religiosis et Missionariis* 20; Prefect Sacred Congr. of Rites 62-68.

Via Serristori 10, Rome, Italy.

Larraz López, José, LL.D.; Spanish economist and politician; b. 04; ed. Madrid Univ.

Advocate 24; Advocate of State 26; Chief Counsellor Bank of Spain 30; Vice-Pres. Nat. Economic Council and Gen. Commissar for Wheat 35; Chief Nat. Banking, Monetary and Exchange Service 38; Min. of Finance Aug. 39-May 41; Academician, Real Academia de Ciencias Morales y Políticas 43-.

Publs. *La evolución económica de Bélgica* 30, *La Hacienda Pública y el Estatuto Catalán* 32, *El ordenamiento del mercado triguero en España* 35, *La época del Mercantilismo en Castilla (1500-1700)* 43, *La Meta de dos Revoluciones* 46.

Espalter 3, Madrid, Spain.

Larrazábal, Rear Adm. Wolfgang; Venezuelan naval officer and politician; b. 11.

Commissioned 32; Dir. Naval Acad. 45-47; Naval C.-in-C. 47-49; Naval Attaché Washington 49-51; del. Inter-American Defense Board 51; Pres. Governing Junta after overthrow of Pérez Jiménez régime Jan.-Nov. 58; resigned to stand as Presidential candidate in elections of Dec. 58; Ambassador to Chile 59-66.

c/o Foreign Office, Caracas, Venezuela.

Larre, René J.; French civil servant; b. 21 Feb. 1915; ed. Faculté de Droit and Ecole des Sciences Politiques, Paris.

Inspector of Finance 42-45; External Relations Dept., Ministry of Economic Affairs 46-50; Asst. Exec. Sec. Int. Materials Conf. 51; Technical Counsellor, French Embassy, Washington 52-54; Technical Adviser, Office of Minister of Finance 55; Dir. Office of Sec. of State for the Budget 56; Exec. Dir. Int. Bank for Reconstruction and Development 57, 58; Dir. of Int. Monetary Fund 64-67; Dir. of Finance, France 67-; Dir. Office of Minister of Finance 57; fmr. Dir. European Investment Bank.

31 boulevard du Commandant Charcot, Neuilly-sur-Seine, France.

Larsen, Peter; Danish farmer and politician; b. 29 June 1924.

Member Folketing 53-; mem. Agricultural Comm. of 1960 60-68, Govt. Comm. on Land Settlement 64-68; Minister of Agriculture 68-; Liberal Party (Venstre).

Ministry of Agriculture, 10 Slotsholmsgade, 1216 Copenhagen K; Home: Østrup pr. 5450 Otterup, Fyn, Denmark.

Larsen, Roy Edward, A.B.; American publisher; b. 20 April 1889; ed. Boston Latin School, and Harvard Univ.

With N.Y. Trust Co. 21-22; Time Inc. 22-, Circulation Man. *Time* 22, Vice-Pres. Time Inc. 27-39, *March of Time* radio 31, *March of Time* cinema 34, Dir. Time Inc. 33, Publisher *Life* 36-46, Pres. Time Inc. Sept. 39-60, Chair. Exec. Cttee. 60-; Chair. U.S. Advisory Cttee. on the Arts; Vice-Chair. U.S. Advisory Cttee. for Int. Cultural and Educational Affairs; Trustee, Ford Foundation; Trustee and Vice-Pres. N.Y. Public Library; Trustee Cttee. for Economic Development, etc.; Chevalier de la Légion d'Honneur (France); Hon. LL.D. (Marietta Coll., Dartmouth, Bucknell, New York, Harvard, Tufts Univs.); Hon. L.H.D. (Bard Coll., Kalamazoo Coll., Temple Univ.).

Home: 4900 Congress Street, Fairfield, Conn.; Office: Time and Life Building, Rockefeller Center, New York, N.Y. 10020, U.S.A.

Telephone: 556-4192.

Larson, Arthur, M.A., D.C.L., LL.D.; American lawyer, university professor and politician; b. 4 July 1910; ed. Augustana Coll., Univ. of South Dakota and Pembroke Coll., Oxford.

Practised law Milwaukee, Wisconsin 35-39; Asst. Prof. of Law, Univ. of Tennessee 39-41; Division Counsel, Office of Price Administration, Washington 41-44; Head Scandinavian Branch, Foreign Economic Administration, Washington 44-45; Prof. of Law, Cornell Law School 45-53; Dean Univ. of Pittsburgh Law School 53-54; Under Sec. of Labour, Washington 54-56; Dir. U.S. Information Agency 56-57; Special Asst. to the Pres. 57-58, Special Consultant 58-61; Dir. Rule of Law Research Centre; Prof. of Law, Duke Univ., Durham N.C. 59-; Consultant, U.S. Dept. of State; Consultant to Pres. on Foreign Affairs; Hon. Fellow Pembroke Coll., Oxford.

Publs. *Towards World Prosperity* (joint author) 47, *Cases on Corporations* (with R. S. Stevens) 47, *The Law of Workmen's Compensation*, 2 vols. 52, *Know Your Social Security* 55, 59, *A Republican Looks at His Party* 56, *What We Are For* 59, *The International Rule of Law* 61, *When Nations Disagree* 61, *A Warless World* 63, *Propaganda: Towards Disarmament in the War of Words* (with J. B. Whitton) 64, *Sovereignty Within the Law* (ed. and contrib.) 65, *Vietnam and Beyond* (with D. R. Larson) 65, *Eisenhower: The President Nobody Knew* 68.

The Law School, Duke University, Durham, N.C., U.S.A.; Home: 3408 Dover Road, Durham, N.C., U.S.A. Telephone: 919-684-3518 (Office); 919-489-9002 (Home).

Larsson, Joel; Swedish industrialist; b. 10 Dec. 1895; ed. Royal Inst. of Technology, Stockholm, Sheffield Univ., and Carnegie Inst. of Technology.

Entered AB Svenska Kullagerfabriken (SKF), Gothenburg 23, Asst. Gen. Man. 41-53, Gen. Man. 53-61; Dir. SKF affiliates in England, France, Germany, Netherlands, Canada; Dir. SKF, AB Bofors, Bolidens Gruv AB, Elektriska Svetsnings AB, Stora Kopparbergs Bergslags AB, Eriksberg Mek. Verkstad, Rederi AB Svenska Lloyd, Kohlswa Jernverks AB; K.V.O. 1st Class.

Nya Allén 6B, Gothenburg, Sweden.

Larsson, Lars-Erik; Swedish musician; b. 15 March 1908; ed. Stockholm, Vienna and Leipzig.

At Royal Swedish Opera 30-31; music critic 33-37; conductor Swedish Broadcasting Co. 37-54; Prof. Kungl. Musikhögskolan 47-59; Dir. of Music, Uppsala 61-; mem. Council Swedish Asscn. of Composers.

Compositions include two symphonies, two concert overtures, sinfonietta for string orchestra; serenade for strings, saxophone concerto, music to Shakespeare's *The Winter's Tale*; the opera *The Princess of Cyprus*; chamber music and songs.

Jaktstigen 4, Lidingö, Sweden.

Lascelles, Rt. Hon. Sir Alan Frederick, P.C., G.C.B.; G.C.V.O., C.M.G., M.C., M.A.; British palace official; b. 11 April 1887; ed. Marlborough Coll., and Trinity Coll., Oxford.

Served with Bedfordshire Yeomanry 14-18, Capt. 16; A.D.C. to Lord Lloyd when Gov. of Bombay 19-20; Asst. Private Sec. to Prince of Wales 20-29; Sec. to Gov.-Gen. of Canada 31-35; Asst. Private Sec. to the King 35-43, Private Sec. 43-52, to the Queen 52-53, Keeper of the King's Archives 45-52, Queen's Archives 52-53; Chair. Pilgrim Trust 54-60; Chair. Historic

Buildings Council for England 58-63; Dir. Midland Bank, Royal Acad. of Music; LL.D. (Hon.) Bristol and Durham; Hon. D.C.L. (Oxford) 63.
Kensington Palace, London, W.8, England.

Lasdun, Denys Louis, C.B.E., F.R.I.B.A.; British architect; b. 8 Sept. 1914; ed. Rugby School, and Architectural Association, London.
Architectural practice in assoc. with Wells Coates until 39; Royal Engineers 39-45; practised with Tecton & Fry, Drew 45-59; own architectural practice 60-; Hoffman Wood Prof. of Architecture, Univ. of Leeds 62-63.
Principal works: housing schemes and schools for Bethnal Green and Paddington, London; new store for Peter Robinson, London; luxury flats, St. James's Place, London; Ghana Nat. Museum, Accra; Royal Coll. of Physicians, London; new coll. for Fitzwilliam, Cambridge; Devt. Plan for Univ. of East Anglia; extensions to Christ's Coll., Cambridge and Royal Inst. of Chartered Surveyors, London; architect to South Bank Board for Nat. Theatre London; Hon. A.I.A.
25 Dawson Place, London W.2, England.
Telephone: 01-486-4761.

Laskorin, Boris Nikolayevich; Soviet chemist; b. 1915; ed. Kiev Univ.
Research Assoc. Inst. of Chemical Industry 38-52; mem. C.P.S.U. 45-; U.S.S.R. Inst. of Chemical Technology 52-; Corresp. mem. U.S.S.R. Acad. of Sciences 66-.
Publs. Works on chemistry and production technology of non-organic materials.
U.S.S.R. Academy of Sciences, 14 Lenin Prospekt, Moscow, U.S.S.R.

Laskov, Haim; Israeli army officer and administrator; b. April 1919; ed. Reali School, Haifa, and St. Antony's Coll., Oxford.
Guide to British Army units in Palestine 38-39; served with British Army (major) 41-46; Commdr. of Israeli forces in capture of Nazareth and Upper Galilee 48; G.O.C. Training Command and Dir. Mil. Training 48-51; Air Officer Commanding, Israel Air Force 51-53; Dep. Chief of Staff and Dir. of Operations 55; Commdr. Armoured Forces, Sinai Campaign 56; G.O.C. Southern Command 57-58; Vice-Chief of Staff, Israel Defence Force 55-56, Chief of Staff 58-60; Gen. Dir. of Port Authorities 61-.
Israel Port Authorities, P.O.B. 20121, Tel-Aviv, Israel.
Telephone: 38911.

Lassen, Bengt; Swedish judge and publisher; b. 22 Sept. 1908; ed. Lund University.
Assistant Judge 33-36; Asst. to Mil. Ombudsman 36-43; Asst. Judge Court of Appeal Malmö 43-45; Head Law Office, Ministry of Justice 45-48; Judge, Court of Appeal Gothenburg 48-53; Managing-Dir. P. A. Norstedt and Sons 53-; Pres. Swedish Publishers Asscn.; mem. Board Swedish Book Printers; Asst. Editor and Editor Swedish Law Journal *Svensk Juristtidning* 46-61; mem. Exec. Cttee. and Int. Comm. Int. Publishers Asscn.; Commdr. Order of Vasa and Order of North Star.
14 Moravägen, Bromma, Stockholm, Sweden.
Telephone: 228040 (office); 258525 (home).

Lassus Saint-Geniès, Anne Henri Jacques de; French engineer; b. 24 March 1889; ed. Lycée Carnot, Ecole Centrale.
Engineer with Société Générale 19, Soc. Financière pour l'Industrie 22; Sec. of various enterprises, incl. Compagnie de l'Electricité Industrielle, Soc. des Usines Gallus, Soc. d'Aérotopographie 24-33; Consultant to Compagnie Française Thomson-Houston 33-54; Chevalier Légion d'Honneur, Croix de Guerre (1914-18); Silver Medal (Office Nat. des Recherches Scientifiques et Industrielles) 24, Prix Jean Barrès 27, Gold Medal of Schroeder Foundation.
Publs. Large number of works on Mechanics, Thermo-

dynamics, Optics and Photography, incl. *L'Optique du Film Gauffré.*
14 rue Saint-Guillaume, Paris 7e; Azas (Haute-Garonne), France.

Lassus Saint-Geniès, Baron Etienne de; French industrialist; b. 7 June 1887.
Director and Hon. Pres. Compagnie Française Thomson-Houston; Pres. Compagnie des Lampes; Vice-Pres. Soc. Générale des Constructions Electriques et Méchaniques, Usines du Pied-Selle; Dir. Soc. Centrale de Dynamite, Compagnie Universelle d'Acétylène et Electro-métallurgie, Soc. des Grands Travaux de Marseille, Soc. Centrale pour l'Industrie; Grand Officier Légion d'Honneur, Croix de Guerre (1914-18).
63 avenue Kléber, Paris 16e, France.

Lasswell, Harold Dwight, PH.D.; American political scientist; b. 13 Feb. 1902; ed. Chicago, Geneva, Paris, London, Berlin Univs.
Political Science Asst. Chicago Univ. 22-24, Instructor 24-27, Asst. Prof. 27-32, Associate Prof. 32-38; Visiting Prof. Syracuse Univ. 26, Western Reserve Univ. 29, Univ. of California 35, Yenching (Peking) Univ., Yale Univ. 38-46; Political Scientist, Washington School of Psychiatry 38-39; Dir. War Communications Research, Library of Congress 39-45; Prof. of Law, Yale School of Law, Yale Univ. 46-, and of Political Science 52-; Visiting Prof. Univ. of Tokyo 55; Fellow, Center for Advanced Study in the Behavioral Sciences, Stanford 54-; Visiting Prof. Mass. Inst. of Technology 60-61.
Publs. *Propaganda Technique in the World War* 27, *Psychopathology and Politics* 30, *World Politics and Personal Insecurity* 35, *Politics: Who Gets What, When, How* 36, *World Revolutionary Propaganda: A Chicago Study* (with D. Blumenstock) 39, *World Politics Faces Economics* 46, *Analysis of Political Behaviour* 48, *Power and Personality* 48, *Language of Politics* (with N. Leites) 49, *National Security and Individual Freedom* 50, *Power and Society: A Framework for Inquiry* (with A. Kaplan) 50, *World Revolution of our Time* 51, *Comparative Study of Symbols* (with others) 51, *Comparative Study of Elites* (with others) 51, *The Policy Sciences* (with D. Lerner), *In Defense of Public Order* (with R. Arens) 61, *The Future of Political Science* 63, *Power, Corruption and Rectitude* (with A. Rogow) 63, *The Public Order of Space* (with others) 63, *World Handbook of Social and Economic Indicators* (with others) 64, *World Revolutionary Elites* (with others) 65, *The Sharing of Power in a Psychiatric Hospital* (with R. Rubenstein) 66.
Yale Law School, 127 Wall Street, New Haven 11, Conn., U.S.A.
Telephone: State 73131.

Laštovička, Bohuslav; Czechoslovak politician and journalist; b. 29 April 1905; ed. Military Acad.
Editor *Rudé právo* 34-35; Commdr., Czechoslovak Volunteer Anti-aircraft Battery, Spain (civil war); in U.K. 39-45; Dir. of Czechoslovak Radio 45-48; Czechoslovak Ambassador to U.S.S.R. 48-50; Deputy Minister of Nat. Defence 50-52; Editor-in-Chief *Nová mysl* 57-61; Head of Int. Dept. of Central Cttee. of C.P. of Czechoslovakia 61-64; Deputy to Nat. Assembly 64-, Chair. 64-68; mem. Central Cttee of C.P. of Czechoslovakia 45-52, 57-, mem. Presidium 64-68; mem. Ideological Comm. Central Cttee., Czechoslovak Communist Party 63-65; Order of White Lion 1st Class 48, Order of the Repub. 60, Klement Gottwald Order 65, Order of the Red Star 66.
Prague, Czechoslovakia.

László, Andor; Hungarian banker and economist; b. 24 Dec. 1914; ed. Budapest and Vienna Univs.
Hungarian Gen. Credit Bank, Budapest 36; Office of State Banks until 48; directed establishment of Hungarian Savings Bank System 48; Deputy Chief,

Credit Dept. Nat. Bank of Hungary 48-49; Chief Banking and Credit Dept., Ministry of Finance 49-54; Prof. Károly Marx Univ., Budapest 50-; Gen. Man. Nat. Savings Bank 54-61; Pres. Nat. Bank of Hungary 61-; Sec. of State 68-; various Hungarian honours.
8-9 Szabadság-tér, Budapest V, Hungary.
Telephone: 112-600.

Latham, Sir Joseph, Kt., C.B.E., F.C.A., COMP.I.E.E.; British business executive; b. 1 July 1905; ed. Stand Grammar School.
Dir. and Sec. Manchester Collieries Ltd. 41-46; Dir.-Gen. Finance, Nat. Coal Board 46-55, mem. Finance Cttee. 55-56, Dep. Chair. 56-60; Dir. Assoc. Electrical Industries Ltd. 60, Finance Dir. 61, Vice-Chair. 64, Deputy Chair. 65, Deputy Chair. and Man. Dir. 67-68; Chair. Metal Industries Ltd. 68-; other directorships include George Wimpey & Co. Ltd., Thorn Electrical Industries Ltd., Black and Decker Ltd., Black and Decker Manufacturing Ltd., U.S.A.; mem. Export Credit Guarantees Advisory Council.
Brook House, Park Lane, London, S.W.1; Home: Ovington, The Mount, Leatherhead, Surrey, England.
Telephone: 01-493-6770 (Office); Leatherhead 2433 (Home).

Lathbury, General Sir Gerald, G.C.B., D.S.O., M.B.E.; British army officer; b. 14 July 1906; ed. Wellington and Royal Military Acad., Sandhurst.
Commissioned into Oxfordshire and Buckinghamshire Light Infantry; fmr. Commdt., Staff Coll.; fmr. C.-in-C. East Africa; fmr. G.O.C.-in-C. Eastern Command; Quarter-Master Gen., War Office 61-65; A.D.C. Gen. to the Queen 62-65; Gov. of Gibraltar Aug. 65-; awarded D.S.C. by U.S.A.
The Convent, Gibraltar; Home: Lock's House, Wokingham, Berks., England.

Latourette, Kenneth Scott, B.S., M.A., PH.D.; American ecclesiastic; b. 9 Aug. 1884; ed. Linfield Coll., McMinnville, Ore., Yale Univ.
Member of the Faculty Coll. of Yale in China 10-12; Lecturer in History, Reed Coll. 14-15, Asst. Prof. 15-16, Assoc. Prof. of History, Denison Univ. 16-17, Prof. 17-21, Chaplain 18-21; Prof. of Missions, Yale Univ. 21-27, of Missions and Oriental History 27-53, Emeritus 53-; Visiting Prof. and Lecturer, Union Theological Seminary, N.Y. 55-64; Curator, Day Missions Library 32-35; mem. Board of Mans. American Baptist Foreign Mission Society 21-25, 35-44, and 47-55; Pres. 46-47; Pres. American Baptist Convention 51-52; Pres. Japan Int. Christian Univ. Foundation 51-; Pres. American Historical Asscn. 48; Pres. Far Eastern Asscn. 55; Hon. LL.D. (Denison), Hon. D.D. (McMaster, Univ. of Wales, Colgate, Oxford, Yale, Linfield), Hon. Litt.D. (Baylor, Princeton, Wm. Jewell, Boston, Shurtleff), Hon. S.T.D. (Glasgow), Hon. L.H.D. (Kalamazoo and Int. Christian Univ. Tokyo), Hon. D.Sc.Rel. (Marburg).
Publs. *Development of China* 17, *Early Relations Between the United States and China (1787-1844)* 17, *Development of Japan* 18, *The Christian Basis of World Democracy* 19, *A History of Christian Missions in China* 29, *The Chinese: Their History and Culture* 34 (Spanish translation 50, Japanese 43, 4th ed. 64), *Missions To-morrow* 36 (Chinese translation 37), *A History of the Expansion of Christianity*, 7 vols. 37-45, *Toward a World Christian Fellowship* 38, *Anno Domini* 40, *The Unquenchable Light* 41, *A Short History of the Far East* 46 (4th ed. 64), *The United States Moves Across the Pacific* 46, *Tomorrow is Here* (with W. R. Hogg) 47, *The Christian Outlook* 48, *The Emergence of a World Christian Community* 49, *These Sought a Country* 50, *The American Record in the Far East 1947-1952* 52, *A History of Christianity* 53, *The Christian World Mission in Our Day* 54, *A History of Modern China* 54, *Challenge and Conformity* 55, *Introducing Buddhism*

55, *World Service* 57, *Desafío a los Protestantes* 57, *Christianity in a Revolutionary Age*, vols. I, 58, II 58, III 60, IV 61, V 62, *China* 64, *A Short History of Christianity* 65, *Christianity Through the Ages* 65, *Beyond the Ranges* 67.
409 Prospect Street, New Haven, Conn., U.S.A.
Telephone: State 73131-667.

La Tramerye, Raymond de, L. ès L., L. ès D.; French industry executive; b. 6 May 1901; ed. Univ. of Paris. Founder and Président-Directeur Général, Société Tubest and Assoc. Companies 28-; Chevalier de la Légion d'Honneur; Croix de Guerre (39-45); French and Polish Resistance Medals; American Silver Star, etc.
6 rue Quentin-Bauchart, Paris 8e, France.

Latreille, André; French historian and university professor; b. 29 April 1901; ed. Lycée Ampère de Lyon, and Univ. de Lyon.
Prof. Lycées de Clermont Ferrand, Marseille and Lyon 24-37; Prof. Univ. of Poitiers 37-44; with Ministry of the Interior 44-45; Prof. of Modern History, Univ. of Lyon 45-; Prof. Institut d'Etudes Politiques (Paris, Lyon, Grenoble); mem. Comité Consultatif des Universités; historical editor *Le Monde*; corresp. L'Institut de France; hon. Dr. Laval Univ.
Publs. *Napoléon et le Saint-Siège* 35, *Le Catéchisme Impérial de 1806* 35, *L'Eglise Catholique et la Révolution Française* (2 vols. 46 and 50), *Les Forces Religieuses et la Vie Politique* 51 (with A. Siegfried), *Histoire de Lyon*, Kleinclausz (Vol. III), *Cahiers d'Histoire des Universités de Lyon, Grenoble, Clermont* 56; *Histoire du Catholicisme en France* (with J. R. Palanque, E. Delaruelle and R. Rémond) (3 vols.) 57-62, *La Seconde Guerre Mondiale* 66.
18 rue Pierre Dupont, 69 Lyon, France.
Telephone: 28-35-53.

Lattimore, Owen; American educator and writer; b. 29 July 1900; ed. St. Bees School, Cumberland, and Harvard Univ.
Business and journalism China 19-25; research work for Social Science Research Council in Manchuria 29-30, for Harvard-Yenching Inst. Peiping 30-31, for Guggenheim Foundation 31-33; research, China and Mongolia to 37; awarded Cuthbert Peek Grant, Royal Geographical Society 30, gold medal Geographical Society of Philadelphia 33, Patron's Medal Royal Geographical Soc. 42; Fellow Royal Geographical Soc.; Hon. mem. American Geographical Soc., mem. American Philosophical Soc., Royal Central Asian Soc.; Editor of *Pacific Affairs* 34-41; special political adviser to Generalissimo Chiang Kai-shek 41-42; Dir. Pacific Operations, Office of War Information 43-44; mem. Vice-Pres. Wallace's mission in Siberia and China 44; Economic Adviser Amer. Reparations Mission in Japan 45-46; Chief UN Technical Aid Exploratory Mission to Afghanistan 50; travelled in Mongolia 61, 64, 66; Prof. of Chinese Studies, Leeds Univ. 63-.
Publs. *The Desert Road to Turkestan* 28, *High Tartary* 30, *Manchuria: Cradle of Conflict* 32, *The Mongols of Manchuria* 34, *Inner Asian Frontiers of China* 40, *Mongol Journeys* 41, *America and China* 43, *The Making of Modern China* (with Eleanor Lattimore) 44, *Solution in Asia* 45, *China, A Short History* (with Eleanor Lattimore) 47, *The Situation in Asia* 49, *Pivot of Asia* 50, *Ordeal by Slander* 50, *Nationalism and Revolution in Mongolia* 55, *Nomads and Commissars* 62, *Studies in Asian Frontier History* 62.
The University, Leeds 2, England.

Lattre, André Marie Joseph de; French financial administrator; b. 26 April 1923; ed. Univs. de Paris à la Sorbonne and Grenoble, and Ecole libre des sciences politiques.
Inspector of Finance 46; with Ministry of Finance 48-; Dept. of External Finance 49-54, Sub-Dir. 55-58. Financial Adviser to Pres. of the Republic 58-60; Perm;

Sec. Ministry of Finance 60-61; Dir. of External Finance 61; Censor, Bank of France 62, Vice-Gov. 66-; Prof. Inst. d'études politiques, Paris 58-; Alt. Extraordinary Dir. Int. Monetary Fund 54; Mission to India for Pres. of World Bank 65; Vice-Gov. Bank of France; Chevalier Légion d'Honneur and foreign awards.
3 rue de La Vrillière, Paris 1er, France.

Latymer, Baron; **Thomas Burdett Money-Coutts,** M.A.; British banker; b. 6 Aug. 1901; ed. Radley Coll., and Trinity Coll., Oxford.
Entered Banking House of Messrs. Coutts & Co., London 24; Chair. London Cttee. of Ottoman Bank; Chair. Investment Trust Corpn., Metropolitan Trust Co. Ltd., London Maritime Investment Trust, North Atlantic Securities Corpn., Anglo-American Securities Corpn. Ltd., London and Thames Haven Oil Wharves Ltd.; mem. of Board of Mercantile Investment Trust Ltd., U.K. Provident Instn., Messrs. Coutts & Co., Claverhouse Investment Trust Ltd., and Nat. Provincial Bank; mem. Council of Foreign Bondholders; Vice-Chair. Middlesex Hospital.
Cinderhill Farm, Mayfield, Sussex, England.

Laufberger, Vilém, M.D., D.SC.; Czechoslovak doctor and physiologist; b. 29 Aug. 1890.
Former Prof. of Physiology Charles Univ., Prague; Academician 52-; Vice-Pres. Czechoslovak Acad. of Sciences 52-61; Dir. Laboratory of Graphical Diagnostics 52-; experiments transforming the larva of axolotl into an adult animal 13, explanation of the mechanism of insulin effects 24, discovering ferritine and preparing it in crystalline form 37; Laureate of the State Prize 54; Order of the Repub. 55; Medal of J. E. Purkyně 56; Polonia Restituta Order 57.
Publs. *Hidden Facets of Life* 62, *Spatiocardiography* 64. Vostrovská 12, Prague 6, Czechoslovakia.

Laugier, Henri, M.D., D.SC.; French physiologist; b. 5 Aug. 1888; ed. French univs.
Prof. of Industrial Physiology, Conservatoire des Arts et Métiers 28-37; Prof. of Gen. Physiology, Sorbonne 37, and Dir. Nat. Centre of Scientific Research until 40, dismissed; fmr. Chef de Cabinet to Min. of Education; fmr. Prof. of Physiology, Montreal Univ.; Asst. Sec.-Gen. in charge of Social Affairs, UN 46-51; mem. High Cttee. for Protection and Development of the French Language 66; Commdr. de la Légion d'Honneur; Croix de Guerre.
55 rue de Babylone, Paris, France.

Laun, Rudolf von, LL.D.; German jurist and philosopher; b. 1 Jan. 1882; ed. Vienna and Paris Univs.
Lecturer in Public Law, Vienna Univ. 08; Ministry of Commerce, Vienna 08; Extra. Prof. Vienna Univ. 11; attached to Austro-Hungarian Ministry of War 16, to Austrian Prime Minister's Office 17, to Ministry of Foreign Affairs, Vienna 18; mem. Del. to St. Germainen-Laye 19; Prof. of Public Law Hamburg Univ. 19, Rector 24-26; Judge Hamburg Supreme Court of Administration 22-33; Dean of Hamburg Law School 45, Pro-Rector of Univ. 45-47, 49-51, Rector 47-49; Pres. Constitutional Court of Bremen 49-56.
Publs. *Das freie Ermessen und seine Grenzen* 10, *Das Recht der Meerengen und Kanäle* 18, *Recht und Sittlichkeit* 24, *Les Actes de Gouvernement* 31, *Der Wandel der Ideen, Staat und Volk als Aeusserung des Weltgewissens* 33, 65, *La Démocratie* 33, *Le Pouvoir discrétionnaire* 34, *Stare Decisis* 38, *Der Satz vom Grunde* 42, 56, *Studienbehelf Allgemeine Staatslehre* 45, 50, 64, *Grundlagen der Erkenntnis* 46, *Die Haager Landkriegsordnung* 46, 50, *Der dauernde Friede* 47, *Die Menschenrechte* 48, *Allgemeine Rechtsgrundsätze* 48, *Die Lehren des Westfälischen Friedens* 49, *Zweierlei Völkerrecht* 49, *Das Recht auf die Heimat* 51, *Das Völkerrecht und die Verteidigung Deutschlands* 51, *Voraussetzungen für demokratische Wahlrechtssysteme* 53, *Freies Ermessen und Détourne-*

ment de Pouvoir 54, *Naturrecht und Völkerrecht* 54, *Nationalgefühl und Nationalismus* 54, *Mehrheitsprinzip Fraktionszwang und Zweiparteiensystem* 54, *Altösterreich als Vorbild* 55, *Zum Problem der Behandlung der nationalen Frage durch internationale Organisation* 55, *L'Autonomie du droit et le droit international* 56, *Le droit des peuples de disposer d'eux-mêmes* 58, *Das Recht der Völker auf die Heimat der Vorfahren* 58, *Grenzen von 1959 oder Demokratie?* 59, *Wozu ein Friedensvertrag?* 59, *Rechtsfragen einer Integration Europas* 60, *Freiheit und Selbstbestimmung* 61, *Allgemeine Staatslehre im Grundriss* 61, 65.
Vossberg 2, 207 Ahrensburg-Holstein, German Federal Republic.

Launoit, Comte Paul de; Belgian industrialist; b. 15 Nov. 1891; ed. Ecole des Hautes Etudes Commerciales et Consulaires, Liège.
Pres. BRUFINA (Société de Bruxelles pour la Finance et l'Industrie); Vice-Pres. Société Cockerill-Ougrée; Pres. Société Minière et Métallurgique de Rodange; Pres. Société Belge de l'Azote et des Produits Chimiques du Marly; Commr.-Gen. Liège Water Exhbn. 39; Pres. Chapelle Musicale de la Reine Elisabeth; Concours Musical Int. Reine Elisabeth de Belgique; honours from Belgium, France, the Netherlands, Luxembourg, Sweden, Italy, Austria and Greece.
19 Avenue Franklin Roosevelt, Brussels 5, Belgium.

Laurent, Jacques Charles Henri; French industrialist; b. 11 March 1896; ed. Ecole des Sciences Politiques, Paris.
Pres. Council Cultures Company of the Ivory Coast 27; Dir. Cie. Delmas-Vieljeux 35; mem. Gen. Council Bank of France 39; Dir. Union Maritime et Financière, Société de Combustibles Delmas-Vieljeux; Légion d'Honneur; Croix de Guerre 14-18 and 39-40; Polish Croix de Guerre.
7 rue de Talleyrand, Paris 7e, France.

Laurila, Erkki Aukusti, M.SC., PH.D.; Finnish physicist; b. 20 Aug. 1913; ed. Helsinki Univ.
Assistant, Institute of Physics, Univ. of Helsinki 36-40; Head, Valmet instruments factory, Tampere 42-46; Military Service 39-40, 41-42 (Capt.); Prof. of Technical Physics, Finnish Inst. of Technology 45-63; mem. Finnish Acad. 63-; Chair. Finnish Atomic Energy Comm. 58-; Wihuri Foundation Prize 52, Kordelin Foundation Prize 60.
Publs. Two textbooks, scientific papers.
Mantytie 17 b 20, Helsinki, Finland.

Lauritzen, Ivar; Danish shipowner; b. 25 March 1900; ed. Coll. of Commerce and training with various firms in England, France, Spain and Germany.
Joint proprietor with Knud Lauritzen of J. Lauritzen Steamship Co. 32; Chair. Esbjerg Ropeworks Ltd., Esbjerg; Dir. Rederiet "Ocean" A/S, A/S D/S "Vesterhavet", Copenhagen, Aalborg Shipyard, Aalborg, Scandinavian Canning Co., Esbjerg, Atlas Engineering Works, Baltica Insurance Co., Baltica Life Co.; Dir. Baltic and Int. Maritime Conf.; Chair. Fanø Nautical School Jubilee Fund, Esbjerg Old Seamen's Fund; Dir. J.-L. Fund, Copenhagen.
Home: Øster Allé 27, Copenhagen; Office: Hammerensgade 1, Copenhagen, Denmark.

Lauritzen, Knud; Danish shipowner; b. 12 April 1904; ed. Coll. of Commerce, and training with various firms in England, France, Spain and Germany.
Became joint proprietor with Ivar Lauritzen of J. Lauritzen Steamship Co. 32; Consul for Chile 37-50; Chair. Rederiet "Ocean" A/S, Copenhagen, Scandinavian Canning Co., Esbjerg, Aalborg Shipyard, Aalborg, Atlas Engineering Works, Copenhagen; Dir. A/S D/S "Vesterhavet", Copenhagen, and Esbjerg Ropeworks Ltd., Esbjerg; Chair. J.-L. Fund, Atlas Bonus-Arrangement (profit-sharing) 50-56, and Hygiene

Cttee. of the Danish Merchant Navy, all in Copenhagen.

Hammerensgade 1, Copenhagen, Denmark.

Telephone: 11-12-22.

Lauritzen, Lauritz, D.IUR.; German lawyer and politician; b. 20 Jan. 1910; ed. Albert-Ludwigs-Univ. Freiburg and Christian-Albrechts-Univ. Kiel.

Lawyer and later Head of Dept. of Commercial Org., Berlin 37; Magistrate in Berlin after Second World War; Head of Presidential Office to Pres. of Schleswig-Holstein; Provincial Dir., Ministry of Interior, Schleswig-Holstein 46-50, in partial retirement 50-51; Head of Dept., Lower Saxony Ministry of Interior 51-54; Mayor of Cassel 54-63; Minister of Justice and Fed. Affairs, Hesse 63-66; Fed. Minister of Housing and Reconstruction 66-; Social Democrat.

Bundesministerium für Wohnungswesen und Städtebau, 532 Bad Godesberg, German Federal Republic.

Lauro, Achille; Italian shipowner and politician; b. 19 June 1887.

Pres. Asscn. of Shipowners, Naples; Vice-Pres. Confed. of Italian Shipowners; Mayor of Naples; Senator for Campania 54; Dep. 58-; founded Partito Monarchico Popolare 54 and leader 54-59; Joint leader Partito Democratico Italiano (merger of two former Monarchist parties) 59-, fmr. Pres.

Palazzo Lauro, Via Nuova Marittima, Naples, Italy.

Lausche, Frank John; American politician; b. 14 Nov. 1895; ed. John Marshall School of Law.

Practised law, Cleveland 20-32; Judge Municipal Court, Cleveland 32-35, Common Pleas Court 35-41; Mayor of Cleveland 41-44; Gov. of Ohio 45-46 and 49-56; elected U.S. Senator from Ohio 56-; mem. Cleveland Bar Asscn.; Democrat.

New Senate Office Building, Washington, D.C., U.S.A.

Lautner, Julius Georg, LL.D.; Swiss jurist; b. 30 Dec. 1896.

Lecturer, Graz Univ. 21 and Extra. Prof. 26; Prof. Mannheim Commercial High School 29; Prof. Zürich Univ. since 30.

Publs. *Die richterliche Entscheidung und die Streitbeendigung im altbabylonischen Prozessrecht* 22, *Die Interrogatio in iure im klassisch-römischen Recht* 25, *Geltendes und künftiges Angestelltenvertragsrecht* 27, *Probleme der Tarifrechtsreform* 29, *Altbabylonische Personenmiete und Erntearbeiterverträge* 36, *Grundsätze des Gewährleistungsrechtes* 37, *Studien zum Miteigentum im altbabylonischen Recht: Rechtsverhältnisse an Grenzmauern, Gesellschaftsverhältnisse* 39, *System des schweizerischen Kriegswirtschaftsrechts*, vols. I-II 42-45, *Straftatbestand und Geltung des Verbotes "übersetzter Gewinne" im Preiskontrollrecht der Kriegswirtschaft* 46, *Die kriegswirtschaftliche Preiskontrolle in der Schweiz (Kriegs-u. Ubergangszeit)=System* vol. III 50, *Preisüberwachung und Reaktivierung der Preisreglementierung* 51, *Die Instandstellungsvereinbarung und die Rechtsnatur der Instandstellungsentschädigung des Mieters* 53.

Hadlaubstr. 96, Zürich 6, Switzerland.

Laver, James, C.B.E., B.A., B.LITT., HON. R.E., F.R.S.A., F.R.S.L.; British art historian and administrator; b. 14 March 1899; ed. Liverpool Inst., and New Coll., Oxford.

Joined staff Victoria and Albert Museum 22, Keeper of Prints, Drawings and Paintings 36-59.

Publs. *A Stitch in Time* 27, *History of British and American Etching, French Painting and the Nineteenth Century* 37, *Whistler* 30, *Ladies' Mistakes* 33, *Nymph Errant* 32, *Background for Venus* 34, *Winter Wedding* 34, *Laburnum Tree* 35, *Tommy Apple* 35, *Panic Among Puritans* 36, *James Tissot* 36, *Taste and Fashion* 37, *Poems of Baudelaire* 39, *Nostradamus* 42, *Fashions and Fashion-plates* 43, *Letter to a Girl on the Future of Clothes* 46, *British Military Uniforms* 47, *Homage to Venus* 48, *Titian* 49, *The Shape of Things: Dress* 50,

Style in Costume 50, *Tudor Costume* 51, *Holkham Hall* 51, *Children's Fashions of the XIXth Century* 51, *Drama: Its Costume and Decor* 51, *Pleasures of Life: Dress* 52, *The First Decadent* 54, *Victorian Vista* 54, *Fragonard* 56, *Edwardian Promenade* 58, *Between the Wars* 61, *Museum Piece* 63, *Costume in the Theatre* 64, *Women's Clothes in the Age of Jazz* 64, *The Age of Optimism* 66, *Victoriana* 66, *Dandies* 68, *Modesty in Dress* 68.

4/10 The Glebe, London, S.E.3, England.

Telephone: 01-852-3905.

Lavergne, Bernard, LL.D.; French economist; b. 15 Dec. 1884.

Prof. of Political Economy Paris Univ.; Dir. *L'Année Politique et Economique* and *Revue des Etudes Coopératives*.

Publs. *Le principe des nationalités et les guerres* 21, *Les Coopératives de consommation en France* 23, *L'Ordre Coopératif* 26, *Le gouvernement des Démocraties modernes* 33, *Essor et décadence du Capitalisme* 38, *La crise et ses remèdes* 38, *Munich défaite des démocraties* 39, *Le problème des Nationalisations* 45, *Une révolution dans la politique coloniale de la France* 48, *Suffrage universel et autorité de l'Etat* 49, *La Révolution Coopérative ou le socialisme de l'Occident* 49, *Le Plan Schuman* 51, *La chimère de "l'Europe Unie"* 52, *L'Armée dite Européenne* 52, *Les accords de Londres et de Paris* 55, *Afrique du Nord et Afrique Noire* 56, *Problèmes africains* 56, *La France trahie (Euratom et Marché Commun)* 57, *L'Hégémonie du Consommateur: Vers la rénovation de la science économique* 58, *Individualisme contre Autoritarisme* 59, *Pourquoi le Conflit Occident—Union Soviétique?* 62, *Les idées politiques en France de 1900 à nos jours—souvenirs personnels* 66, *Le problème religieux à l'heure actuelle* 67.

19 quai Bourbon, Paris 4e, France.

Lavon, Pinhas; Israeli politician; b. 04 in Poland; ed. Lwów Univ.

Settled in Israel 29; Sec. Mapai Party 35-37; mem. Exec. Cttee. Mapai and Histadrut (Gen. Fed. of Labour) 42-; Chair. Board of Dirs. Solel Boneh Contracting Corpn. 47-49; mem. Knesset 49-; Sec. Gen. Histadrut 49-50, 56-61; Minister of Agriculture 50-51; Minister of Defence 51-54; Minister without Portfolio 54-55; mem. Zionist Actions Cttee.

Publ. *Yesodot* (Foundation).

85 Gordon Street, Tel-Aviv, Israel.

Lavrentiev, Mikhail Alexeyevich; Soviet mathematician; b. 1900; ed. Moscow Univ.

Professor of Mathematics, Moscow Univ. 31-41; Dir. Inst. of Mathematics, Acad. of Sciences of the Ukraine 39-48; Vice-Pres. Acad. of Sciences of the Ukraine 45-48; Dir. Inst. of Precise Mechanisms and Computing Technique, Acad. of Sciences of the U.S.S.R. 50-53; Sec.-Academician Dept. of Physico-Mathematical Sciences, Acad. of Sciences of the U.S.S.R. 51-53, 55-57; Vice-Pres. and Chair. of Council of Siberian Dept. U.S.S.R. Acad. of Sciences; mem. U.S.S.R. Acad. of Sciences 46-; Chair. Siberian Dept. of the U.S.S.R. Acad. of Sciences 57; Vice-Pres. Int. Mathematical Union 67-; Deputy to U.S.S.R. Supreme Soviet; mem. C.P.S.U. Central Cttee.; Foreign mem. Czechoslovak Acad. of Sciences; Lenin and State prize winner 46-49; Hero of Socialist Labour 67; Order of Lenin (twice), Order of Red Banner of Labour (thrice).

Publs. include: *Fundamental Theorem of the Theory of Quasi-Conformal Depictions of Plane Areas* 48, *On Theory of Conformal Depictions* 37, *On Some Properties of Single Leaf Functions Applied to Theory of Jets* 48, *Course of Variational Calculations* 38, *Problems of Mechanics of Continuous Media* 61, *Methods of Calculations of Rail Chains by Electronic Computers* 63.

Siberian Dept., U.S.S.R. Academy of Sciences, 20 Sovietskaya Street, Novosibirsk, U.S.S.R.

Telephone: E5-40-50.

Lavrov, Boris Alexandrovich; Soviet biologist; b. 1884; ed. Moscow Univ.

School teacher 09-19; Lecturer, Moscow Univ. 19-32; Prof. and Head of Dept., Moscow Polytechnical Inst. 19-29; Head of Dept., All-Union Research Inst. of Vitaminology; Head, State Vitamin Control Station; Dir., Head of Dept., Consultant, All-Union Research Inst. of Vitaminology 30-; mem. U.S.S.R. Acad. of Medical Sciences 45-; Deputy Chair. Problem Comm. on Vitaminology U.S.S.R. Acad. of Medical Sciences; Order of Lenin 53, Red Banner of Labour 44, Badge of Honour 61.

Publs. Over 110 works on physiology and role of vitamins in metabolism.

All-Union Institute of Vitaminology, Kvartal 35, Novye Cheremushki, Moscow, U.S.S.R.

Lavrov, Ivan Mikhailovich; Soviet diplomatist; b. 1912; ed. Leningrad Inst. of Journalism.

Member C.P. of Soviet Union 37-; at Ministry of Foreign Affairs 41-44; Asst. to Head, Third European Dept., Ministry of Foreign Affairs 44-46; Asst. to Minister for Foreign Affairs 46-49; Asst. to Vice-Chair., U.S.S.R. Council of Ministers 49-55; Senior Asst. to Minister of Foreign Affairs 55-56; Senior Asst. to First Vice-Chair. of U.S.S.R. Council of Ministers 56-57; Counsellor, Embassy, Vienna 57-60; Deputy Head, Third European Dept., Min. of Foreign Affairs 60-62; Counsellor-Minister, Embassy, Bonn 62-65; Amb. to Mauritania 65-; Red Banner of Labour (twice) and other awards of U.S.S.R.

U.S.S.R. Embassy, Nouakchott, Mauritania.

Lavrov, Vladimir Sergeyevich; Soviet diplomatist; b. 1919; ed. Moscow energet Inst.

Diplomatic Service 47-; First Sec., London 52-53; Asst. to Deputy Minister of Foreign Affairs of U.S.S.R. 53-56; Counsellor, Washington 56-59; Chargé d'Affaires *ad interim* in Yemen 59-60; Deputy Head Second European Dept. of U.S.S.R. Ministry of Foreign Affairs 60-62, Head 62-64; Amb. to Kenya 64-67, to Netherlands 67-.

U.S.S.R. Embassy, The Hague, Netherlands.

Lavrushin, Vladimir, D.SC.; Soviet chemist; b. 15 May 1912; ed. Kharkov State Univ.

Worked in shoe factory 27-30; Kharkov State Univ. 30-35; postgraduate course 35; Army Service 41-45; research and educ. work, Kharkov 45-48; Prof. of Chemical Technology, later Organic Chemistry, Kharkov State Univ. 48-, Asst. Rector 56-61, Rector 61-66, Dir. Inst. of Chemistry 67-; Order of Lenin, Order of Red. Star; Hon. D.Sc. (Manchester).

Publs. contributions to the study of the halocromism of organic compounds.

Kharkov A.M. Gorky State University, Ploshchad Dzerzhinskogo 4, Kharkov, Ukrainian S.S.R., U.S.S.R.

Law, Phillip Garth, C.B.E., M.SC., D.APP.SC., F.A.I.P.; Australian scientist, antarctic explorer and educationist; b. 21 April 1912; ed. Ballarat Teachers' Coll., and Univ. of Melbourne.

Science master in secondary schools 33-38; Tutor in Physics Newman Coll., Melbourne Univ. 40-47 and Lecturer in Physics 43-47; Research Physicist and Asst. Sec. Scientific Instrument and Optical Panel, Ministry of Munitions 40-45; Scientific Mission to New Guinea battle areas for the Australian Army 44; Senior Scientific Officer Australian Nat. Antarctic Research Expeditions 47-49, Leader 49-66; Dir. Antarctic Div., Dept. of External Affairs 49-66; Australian Observer Norwegian-British-Swedish Antarctic Expedition 50; led expeditions to estab. first permanent Australian research station at Mawson, MacRobertson Land 54 and at Davis, Princess Elizabeth Land 57; exploration of coast of Australian Antarctica 54-66; mem. gov. councils Melbourne and La Trobe Univs.; Vice-Pres. Victoria Inst. of Colleges 66-; Chair. Australian Nat. Cttee. on

Antarctic Research 66-; Pres. Royal Soc. of Victoria 67, 68; Founder's Medal Royal Geographical Society 60.

Publs. *ANARE* (with Bechervaise) 57, also numerous articles on antarctic exploration and research and papers on cosmic rays, thermal conductivity, optics and education.

16 Stanley Grove, Canterbury, Victoria, Australia. Telephone: 82-5630.

Lawrence, Arnold Walter, M.A., F.S.A.; British archaeologist; b. 2 May 1900; ed. City of Oxford School, and New Coll., Oxford.

Ur excavations 23; Craven Fellow Oxford 24; Student of British Schools of Rome and Athens; Reader in Classical Archæology Cambridge 30; Literary executor of T. E. Lawrence 35; Mil. Intelligence Middle East 40; Scientific Officer R.A.F. 42; with Min. of Economic Warfare 43; Prof. of Classical Archæology Cambridge Univ. 44-51; Fellow of Jesus Coll. Cambridge 44-51; Prof. of Archæology, Univ. Coll. of Gold Coast and Dir. Nat. Museum of the Gold Coast 51-57; Hon. Sec. and Conservator, Monuments and Relics Comm., Gold Coast 52-57.

Publs. *Later Greek Sculpture and its Influence* 27, *Classical Sculpture* 29, *Herodotus annotated* 35, *T. E. Lawrence by his Friends* 37, *Greek Architecture* 57, 67, *Letters to T. E. Lawrence* 62, *Trade Castles and Forts of West Africa* 63, etc.

c/o Martins Bank, 68 Lombard Street, London, E.C.3, England.

Lawrence, David; American journalist; b. 25 Dec. 1888; ed. Princeton Univ.

Mem. staff Associated Press 10-16; Washington correspondent New York *Evening Post* 16-19; Pres. Consolidated Press Association, Washington D.C. 19-33; Founder-Pres. *United States Daily* 26-33; Pres. and Editor *United States News* 33-48, and *World Report* 46-48, *U.S. News and World Report* 48-59, Chair. of Board and Editor 59-; writer of a despatch on nat. and world affairs syndicated to daily newspapers 16-.

Publs. *True Story of Woodrow Wilson* 24, *The Other Side of Government* 29, *Stumbling into Socialism* 35, *Nine Honest Men* 36, *Supreme Court or Political Puppets?* 37.

1241 24th Street, N.W., Washington, D.C. 20037, U.S.A.

Lawrence, Hon. Harry Gordon, Q.C., B.A., LL.B.; South African lawyer and politician; b. 17 Oct. 1901; ed. Rondebosch and Univs. of Capetown and South Africa.

Called to Bar Cape Town 26; M.P. for Salt River 29-38, for Woodstock 38-43, Salt River 43-61; joined United Party 33; Minister of Labour Union Govt. 38-39, of Interior and Public Health 39-43; Minister of Welfare and Demobilisation 43-45; Minister of Justice, and of Social Welfare and Demobilization Nov. 45-47, Minister of Justice, of Interior and Demobilization 48 until defeat of Govt. May 48; resigned from United Party Sept. 59; elected Nat. Chair. and Parl. Leader, Progressive Party Nov. 59; defeated as Progressive Candidate Oct. 61; Dir. Consolidated Diamond Mines of South West Africa, Western Holdings, Springbok Colliery.

The Cotswolds, Kenilworth, Cape Province; and Temple Chambers, Wale Street, Cape Town, S. Africa. Telephone: 77-3278 and 41-0019.

Lawrence, J. Dudley; Liberian lawyer and diplomatist; b. 19 April 1909.

Ministry of Foreign Affairs 28-; Clerk to Supreme Court, Administrative Officer, Elections Comm. 41-49; Chief of Protocol, Dir. Int. Confs. 49-52; Minister to Spain 52-54, Ambassador 54-56, Ambassador to France 54-64, concurrently Minister to Holy See 56-, Ambassador to Switzerland 61-; Ambassador to Great Britain 64-; mem. Liberian Del. to UN 51-58, Chair. 55; Great Band of the Order of African Redemption, Knight Grand Commander of the Order of Pioneers, Grand

Cross of Civil Merit (Spain), Grand Cross of St. Gregorius Magnus (Vatican), Grand Officer, Legion of Honour, Grand Golden Cross of Honour (Austria), Grand Cross National Order of Merit (France), Commdr. National Order (Madagascar).
Liberian Embassy, 21 Princes Gate, London, S.W.7, England.
Telephone: 01-589-9405.

Lawrence, William Howard; American journalist; b. 12 Jan. 1916; ed. Univ. of Nebraska.
Reporter, Lincoln, Neb. *Star* 33-35; Corresp. Assoc. Press, Neb. 35-36, United Press, Chicago, Detroit and Washington 36-41; Corresp. in Washington, *New York Times* 41-43; Chief Corresp. *New York Times*, Moscow 43-45; War Corresp. Pacific 45, Korea 50, Nat. Corresp. 47-61; Political Ed. American Broadcasting Co. 61-; Pres. Nat. Press Club, Washington 59-60; Peabody Award for T.V. Reporting 64; Hon. Dr. Litt. (Grinnell Coll., Iowa) 67.
3001 Veazey Terrace, N.W., Washington, D.C. 20008, U.S.A.
Telephone: 202-362-4343.

Lawson, Frederick Henry, D.C.L., F.B.A.; British university professor; b. 14 July 1897; ed. Queen's Coll., Oxford, and Göttingen Univ.
Served in Royal Artillery 16-19; called to the Bar Gray's Inn 23; Lecturer in Law, Univ. Coll., Oxford 24-25; Junior Research Fellow, Merton Coll., Oxford 25-30; Official Fellow and Tutor in Law, Merton Coll. Oxford 30-48; All Souls Reader in Roman Law 31-48; Temporary Principal Ministry of Supply 43-45; Prof. of Comparative Law Univ. of Oxford and Fellow of Brasenose 48-64; Sec.-Gen. Int. Asscn. of Legal Science 64-; Part-time Lecturer in Law, Univ. of Lancaster 64-; Maurice Frankel Prof. of Law, Univ. of Houston 67-68; Jt. Editor *Journal of Comparative Legislation* 48-52; *Int. and Comparative Law Quarterly* 52-55; Editor *Journal of the Society of Public Teachers of Law* 55-62; Dr. h.c. (Louvain, Paris and Ghent Univs.), Dr. jur. h.c. (Frankfurt-am-Main Univ.), Hon. LL.D. (Glasgow Univ.).
Publs. *Cases in Constitutional Law* (with Sir D. L. Keir) 28, *Negligence in the Civil Law* 50, *The Rational Strength of English Law* (Hamlyn Lectures) 51; revisions of various works on Constitutional and Roman Law; contributions to *Law and Government in Principle and Practice* (Ed. J. L. Brierly), and latest edn. of *Chambers's Encyclopaedia; A Common Lawyer Looks at the Civil Law* 55, *Introduction to the Law of Property* 58, *The Oxford Law School 1850-1965* 68.
High Cliff, Eden Park, Lancaster, England.
Telephone: Lancaster 66598.

Lawther, Sir William, Kt., J.P.; British trade union official and politician; b. 20 May 1889; ed. Colliery School, Central Labour Coll., London.
Fmr. Pres. Nat. Union Mineworkers; Vice-Chair. Gen. Council T.U.C. 48-49, 49-50; mem. Coal Production Council 40-; contested South Shields 22, 23, 24; Labour M.P. for Barnard Castle 29-31; mem. Nat. Labour Party Exec. Cttee. 23-26; mem. Industrial Mission to U.S.A. 41; mem. Trade Union Mission to Italy 44, Anglo-French Trade Union Council 45; mem. Anglo-American Council of Productivity; Pres. T.U.C. 49-50; Sec. Miners Int. Fed. 47-57; Pres. All-American Miners Conf., Peru 57; Chevalier de la Légion d'Honneur.
6 Grange Close, Marden Cullercoats, North Shields, Northumberland, England.
Telephone: North Shields 72589.

Laxness, Halldor; Icelandic writer; b. 23 April 1902. Many of his novels have been translated into English; Nobel Prize for Literature 55.
Publs. include *The Great Weaver of Cashmere* 27, *Salka Valka* 34, *Independent People* 39, *The Atom Station,*

Paradise Reclaimed, The Fish Can Sing, etc.; translated into Icelandic Hemingway's *Farewell to Arms*, Voltaire's *Candide*, Gunna Gunnarsson's works, etc.
P.O.B. 664, Reykjavík, Iceland.

Layton, Robert Geoffrey, B.COM.; American business executive; b. 16 May 1923; ed. public school and Inst. of Chartered Accountants of England and Wales, Univ. of London.
Chartered Accountant, London and Birmingham 39-48; Chief Accountant, Caracas Petroleum S.A., Caracas, Venezuela 48; Controller, Van Reekum Paper Inc., New York 48-50; Financial Analyst, Ford Motor Co., Detroit 50-54; Dir. of Finance, Ford Mexico 54-57; Dir. of Finance Ford-Werke AG, Cologne 57-63, Deputy Gen. Man. 63-65, Gen. Man. and Chair. Man. Cttee. 65-67; mem. Supervisory Board Friedrich Krupp Hüttenwerke AG, Rheinhausen, Friedrich Simon Bank KG, Düsseldorf, Gerling Konzern, Cologne; Vice-Pres. Sales, Ford of Europe Inc. 67.
Ford of Europe Inc., Warley, Brentwood, Essex, England.
Telephone: 01-592-7300.

Lazareanu, Alexandru; Romanian diplomatist; b. 13; ed. Bucharest Faculty of Letters and Philology.
Journalist 31-46; Cultural and Press Counsellor, Washington 46-48; Dir. Ministry of Foreign Affairs 49-51; First Counsellor, Chargé d'Affaires a.i., Paris 51-53; Dir., mem. Collegium, Ministry of Foreign Affairs 53-56; Deputy Minister, Ministry of Foreign Affairs 56-61; Minister to Great Britain 61-64, Ambassador 64-66; Dir. Ministry of Foreign Affairs 66-; Order of Star of Republic, Order of Labour.
Ministry of Foreign Affairs, Bucharest, Romania.

Lazareff, Hélène (see Gordon-Lazareff).

Lazareff, Pierre; French journalist; b. 16 April 1907.
Editor *Paris-Soir* until 40; Head of French Section Office of War Information, New York and London 41-44; Gen. Manager *France-Soir, France Dimanche, Elle, Journal du Dimanche, Nouveau Candide, Scoop Agency*; mem. Exec. Bd. *Paris-Presse-l'Intransigeant, Jardin des Modes, Réalités, Femmes d'Aujourd'hui, Lectures d'Aujourd'hui, Télé 7 Jours, Régie Presse;* Publisher *Air du Temps* (books); Producer *5 Colonnes à la Une* (French T.V.); Commdr. Légion d'Honneur.
Publs. *Dernière Edition, De Munich à Vichy,* (with Hélène Lazareff) *L'U.R.S.S. à l'heure Malenkov.*
100 rue Réaumur, Paris 2e, France.

Lazarev, Viktor Nikitich; Soviet art scholar; b. 97; ed. Moscow Univ.
Pushkin State Museum of Fine Arts 24-36; Prof. Moscow Univ. 35-; Scientific Worker, Inst. of History of the Arts 45-61; Corresp. mem. U.S.S.R. Acad. of Sciences 43; Hon. mem. Florence Acad. of Drawing; Corresp. mem. British Acad., Serbian Acad. of Sciences and Arts, Venice Inst. of Sciences, Literature and Arts; Order of Red Banner of Labour (three times); etc.
Publs. inc. *Johannes Vermeer of Delft* 33, *The Le Nain Brothers* 36, *The Portrait in 18th-Century European Art* 37, *Chardin* 47, *The Art of Novgorod* 47, *History of Byzantine Painting* in 2 vols. 47-48, *Leonardo da Vinci* 52, *Origins of the Italian Renaissance* (3 vols.) 56-59, *Andrei Rublev,* 60, *Frescoes of the Old Ladoga* 60, *Mosaics of Sophia of Kiev* 60, *Feofan Grek and His School* 61, *Old Russian Art in 15th and Early 16th Centuries* 63.
Moscow University, 18 Marx Prospekt, Moscow, U.S.S.R.

Lazarsfeld, Paul Felix; American (b. Austrian) sociologist; b. 13 Feb. 1901; ed. Universität Wien.
Director Radio Research, Princeton Univ. 37-40; Prof. Sociology, Columbia Univ. 40-62; fmr. Pres. American Asscn. for Public Opinion Research; Quetelet Prof. of Social Science, Columbia Univ. 63-; fmr. Pres. American

Sociological Asscn.; Hon. L.H.D. (Yeshiva Univ.); Hon. LL.D. (Univ. Chicago).
Publs. include: *The Unemployed of Marienthal* 32, *Radio and the Printed Page* 40, *The People's Choice* 48, *Organizing Educational Research* (with Sam D. Sieber) 64, *Latent Structure Analysis* (with Neil Henry) 67.
610 W. 110th Street, New York, N.Y. 10025, U.S.A.
Telephone: 212-RI9-0044.

Lazarus, Fred, Jr.; American corporation executive; b. 29 Oct. 1884; ed. Ohio State Univ.
F. & R. Lazarus & Co., Columbus, Ohio (later merged into Federated Dept. Stores, Inc.) 03-28, Pres. Shillito's 28-47; Pres. Federated Dept. Stores, Inc. 45-57, Chair. of Board 57-67, of Exec. Cttee. 67-.
Federated Department Stores, Inc., 222 West Seventh Street, Cincinnati, Ohio 45202, U.S.A.
Telephone: 513-721-7600.

Lazarus, Ralph; American businessman; b. 30 Jan. 1914; ed. Dartmouth Coll.
Vice-Pres. F. & R. Lazarus & Co. 47-51; Exec. Vice-Pres. Federated Department Stores, Cincinnati 51-57, Pres. 57-67, Chair. of Board 67-.
Home: 3849 Washington Avenue; Office: 222 West 7th Street, Cincinnati, Ohio, U.S.A.

Lazebny, Nikolai Semyonovich; Soviet politician; b. 1909; ed. Siberian Inst. of Metallurgy 47 and C.P.S.U. Higher Party School.
Member C.P.S.U. 42-; Soviet Army service 41-43; geological expeditions in Altai area 47-51; Party Official 51-64; First Sec., Gorno-Altai Regional Cttee. C.P.S.U. 64-; Deputy to U.S.S.R. Supreme Soviet.
Gorno-Altai Regional Committee, Communist Party of the Soviet Union, Gorno-Altaisk, U.S.S.R.

Lazell, Henry George Leslie; British business executive; b. 23 May 1903; ed. L.C.C. Elementary School.
Clerk until 30; Accountant, Macleans Ltd. 30, Sec. 30, Dir. and Sec. 36; Sec. Beecham Group Ltd. 39; Man. Dir. Macleans Ltd., and Dir. Beecham Group Ltd. 40; Man. Dir. Beecham Group Ltd. 51-58, Chair. 58-68; Dir. Imperial Chemical Industries Ltd. 66-68; Chair. Govs. Ashridge Management Coll. 63-; Chair. Appeal Cttee. British Heart Foundation.
Home: Clyde Cottage, Dawes Green, Leigh, nr. Reigate, Surrey, England.
Telephone: Dawes Green 225 (Home).

Lazurenko, Mikhail Konstantinovich; Soviet politician; b. 1908; ed. Higher Party School of the Communist Part of the Ukraine.
Member C.P.S.U. 31-; railway worker 27-31; Party Official 31-41; Soviet Army service (mem. of partisan detachment in Ukraine) 41-44; Party Official, Ukraine 44-61; First Sec. Zhitomir Regional Cttee. Communist Party of the Ukraine 61-; mem. Central Cttee. C.P. of the Ukraine; Deputy to U.S.S.R. Supreme Soviet, Budget Cttee. Soviet of Union.
Zhitomir Regional Committee, Communist Party of the Ukraine, Zhitomir, U.S.S.R.

Leach, Bernard Howell, C.B.E.; British (b. in Hong Kong) potter, author and artist; b. 5 Jan. 1887; ed. Beaumont Coll., Slade School of Art, and London School of Art.
Studied pottery in Japan and visited Korea and China 09-20; started (with Shoji Hamada) Leach Pottery at St. Ives, Cornwall 20; exhibited widely, taught, wrote and lectured 20-68; started small pottery at Dartington Hall, Devon; initiated first Int. Craft Conference of Potters and Weavers, Dartington Hall 52; exhibited, travelled and lectured, Japan 52-54, 61; U.S. lecture tours 50, 52, 60; Retrospective Exhibitions, Arts Council, London, Tokyo and Osaka 61; Exhbns.: Japan 66-67, Hamburg 67; Binns Medal, American Ceramic Soc.; Hon. Assoc., Manchester Coll. of Art 60, Hon.

D.Litt., Exeter Univ. 61; Second Order of the Sacred Treasure (Japan) 66.
Publs. *A Potter's Book* 40, *A Potter's Portfolio* 50, *A Potter in Japan* 60, *Kenzan and his Tradition* 67.
The Leach Pottery, St. Ives, Cornwall, England.
Telephone: 6398.

Leach, Edmund Ronald, M.A., PH.D.; British social anthropologist; b. 11 Nov. 1910; ed. Marlborough Coll., Clare Coll., Cambridge, and London School of Economics.
Commercial Asst., Butterfield and Swire, Shanghai 32-37; Graduate Student, London School of Econs. 38-39, 46-47; Military Service, Burma Army 39-45; Lecturer (later Reader) in Social Anthropology, London School of Econs. 47-53; Lecturer, Cambridge Univ. 53-57, Univ. Reader in Social Anthropology 57-; Fellow of King's Coll., Cambridge 60-66, Provost 66-; Fellow of Center for Advanced Study in Behavioral Sciences, Stanford 61; Senior Fellow, Eton Coll. 66-; Malinowski Lecturer 59, Henry Myers Lecturer 66; B.B.C. Reith Lecturer 67; Field Research Formosa 37, Kurdistan 38, Burma 39-45, Borneo 47, Ceylon 54-56; Vice-Pres. Royal Anthropological Inst. 64-66; Chair. Asscn. of Social Anthropologists 66-; Curl Essay Prize 51, 57; Rivers Medal 58.
Publs. *Social and Economic Organization of the Rowanduz Kurds* 40, *Social Science Research in Sarawak* 50, *Political Systems of Highland Burma* 54, *Pul Eliya: A Village in Ceylon* 61, *Rethinking Anthropology* 61.
Provost's Lodge, King's College, Cambridge, England.
Telephone: Cambridge 50411.

Leader, George Michael, B.S.; American politician and business executive; b. 17 Jan. 1918; ed. Univ. of Pennsylvania.
Dem. Committee-man, York Co. 40-42; Sec. York Co. Dem. Cttee. 42-46; served with U.S. Navy 42-46; Chair. York Co. Dem. Cttee. 46-50; mem. Pa. State Senate 50-54; Gov. of Pa. 55-59; Vice-Pres. W. A. Clarke Mortgage Co., Philadelphia 59-61; Exec. Vice-Pres. Bankers Bond and Mortgage Co., Philadelphia 61-64; Exec. Vice-Pres. Capitol Products Corpn., Harrisburg 64-; Chair. of Board and Chief Exec. Officer, Citation Life Insurance Co. 65-; LL.D. h.c. from Temple Univ., Lincoln Univ., La Salle Coll., etc.
Office: 7 Penn Center Plaza, Philadelphia, Pennsylvania; Home: 1010 Black Rock Road, Gladwyne, Pennsylvania, U.S.A.

Leakey, Louis Seymour Bazett, M.A., PH.D., F.B.A.; British archaeologist; b. 7 Aug. 1903; ed. Weymouth Coll., St. John's Coll., Cambridge.
Fellow, St. John's Coll., Cambridge 30-35; Leader of East African Archæological Expeditions 26-27, 28-29, 31-32, 34-35; Munroe Lecturer, Edinburgh Univ. 36; C.I.D., Nairobi during Second World War; Curator of Coryndon Memorial Museum 45-61, Hon. Keeper of Palaeontology and Prehistory 61, 62; Hon. Dir. of Law Univ. of California 63; Hon. Dir. of Nat. Museum Centre for Prehistory and Palaeontology, Nairobi; Hon. D.Sc. (Oxford), LL.D. (Calif.); Royal Medal, Royal Geographical Soc. London.
Publs. include *Stone Age Culture of Kenya*, *Stone Age Races of Kenya*, *Stone Age Africa*, *Adam's Ancestors*, *Olduvai Gorge*, *White African*, *Kenya Contrasts and Problems*, *Mau Mau and the Kikuyu*, *Defeating Mau Mau*, *Animals in Africa* (with Ylla), *Some East African Pleistocene Fossil Suidae*, *First Lessons in Kikuyu Language*, *Olduvai 1951-1961*, *The Progress and Evolution of Man in Africa*, etc.
P.O.B. 15028, Langata, Nairobi, Kenya.

Lean, David, C.B.E.; British film director; b. 25 March 1908; ed. Leighton Park School, Reading.
Entered industry with Gaumont-British as number-board boy 28; editor for Gaumont Sound News and British Movietone News; edited *Escape Me Never,*

Pygmalion, 49th Parallel: co-directed with Noel Coward *In Which We Serve*; directed *This Happy Breed, Blithe Spirit, Brief Encounter, Great Expectations, Oliver Twist, The Passionate Friends, Madeleine, The Sound Barrier, Hobson's Choice, Summer Madness* (American title *Summertime*), *The Bridge on the River Kwai, Lawrence of Arabia* 62, *Dr. Zhivago* 65.
146 Piccadilly, London, W.1, England.

Learned, Stanley; American business executive; b. 5 Nov. 1902; ed. Univ. of Kansas.
Joined Phillips 24, Vice-Chair. Phillips Operating Cttee. 44, Chair. Cttee. 44-49, Vice-Pres., Dir. and mem. Exec. Cttee. 49-51, Exec. Vice-Pres. and Asst. to Pres. 51-62, Pres. Phillips Petroleum Co. 62-64, Pres. and Chief Exec. Officer 64-67, Vice-Chair. 67-; mem. of numerous petroleum asscns.; Distinguished Service Award, Univ. of Kansas.
18-C1 Phillips Building, Bartlesville, Oklahoma; 821 Johnstone Avenue, Apt. 123, Bartlesville, Oklahoma, U.S.A.

Learson, T. Vincent; American business executive; b. 26 Sept. 1912; ed. Harvard Univ.
Joined IBM, Boston 35, Vice-Pres. 54, Dir. 61-, Pres. April 66-; Dir. Carborundum Co., Niagara Falls, N.Y., Chemical Bank New York Trust Co., American Arbitration Asscn.; mem. Exec. Board American Red Cross in Greater New York; mem. Harvard Business School Visiting Cttee.; Trustee, Nat. Industrial Conf. Board.
IBM Corporation, Old Orchard Road, Armonk, N.Y.; Home: North Manursing Island, Rye, N.Y., U.S.A.

Leathers, 2nd Viscount, cr. 54; **Frederick Alan Leathers,** M.A.; British company director; b. 4 April 1908; ed. Brighton Coll., and Emmanuel Coll., Cambridge.
Mem. Baltic Exchange; underwriting mem. of Lloyd's; mem. Court Worshipful Co. of Shipwrights, Court Watermen's and Lightermen's Co.; Fellow Inst. of Chartered Shipbrokers; mem. Inst. Petroleum; Chair. Wm. Cory & Son, Ltd., Cory Mann George Ltd., R. & J. H. Rea Ltd., Hull Blyth and Co. Ltd., St. Denis Shipping Co. Ltd.; Dir. Afsa Ltd., Cory and Strick Ltd., General Cttee. of Lloyds Registrar of Shipping, New Zealand Cement Holdings Ltd., Laporte Industries Ltd., Tunnel Portland Cement Co. Ltd., Westminster Bank Ltd.; Fellow Royal Philatelic Soc.
Hills Green, Kirdford, Sussex, England.
Telephone: Kirdford 202.

Leavis, Frank Raymond, PH.D.; British university lecturer and writer; b. 14 July 1895; ed. Perse School, Cambridge, Emmanuel Coll., Cambridge.
University teacher 24-; editor *Scrutiny* 32-53; Univ. Lecturer in English, Cambridge 37-60, Reader 60-62; Visiting Prof. Univ. of York 65-67; Hon. Visiting Prof. Univ. of York 67-68; fmr. Fellow and Dir. of English Studies, Downing Coll., Cambridge.
Publs. *For Continuity* 33, *New Bearings in English Poetry* 32, *Revaluation: Tradition and Development in English Poetry* 36, *Education and the University* 43, *The Great Tradition* 48, *The Common Pursuit* 52, *D. H. Lawrence, Novelist* 55, (with Denys Thompson) *Culture and Environment* 33, *Mill on Bentham and Coleridge* 50 (editor), *Two Cultures? The Significance of C. P. Snow* 62, *Scrutiny: A Retrospect* 63, *"Anna Karenina" and Other Essays* 67, *A Selection from Scrutiny* 68 (editor).
12 Bulstrode Gardens, Cambridge, England.
Telephone: Cambridge 52530.

Lebedev, Aleksandr Alekseyevich; Soviet physicist; b. 2 Nov. 1893; ed. St. Petersburg Univ.
Research in optical glass, developed theoretical basis for establishing temperature controls in tempering optical glass 19-31; designed polarisation interferometer based on light waves passing through double refraction lenses, also electronograph using focusing properties of magnetic lenses 31; Prof. Electrophysics Leningrad State Univ.; State Prize for first Soviet-designed electron microscope 47, for designing camera to investigate types of electrical phenomena 49; mem. U.S.S.R. Acad. of Sciences 43-; Chief Editor, *Izvestiya Akademii Nauk S.S.S.R.*; Hero of Socialist Labour, Order of Lenin.
Publs. *On Polymorphism and Glass Tempering* 21, *The Polarisation Interferometer and its Application* 31, *On Structure Transformation in Glass* 53.
Leningrad State University, 33 Tenth Line, Leningrad U.S.S.R.

Lebedev, Evgeny Alexeevich; Soviet actor; b. 1917; ed. Moscow Theatre School.
Tbilisi Russian Theatre for Youth 40-49; Leningrad Theatre of Lenin Young Communist League 49-56; Leningrad Bolshoi Drama Theatre 56-; People's Artist of R.S.F.S.R. 62; People's Artist of U.S.S.R. 68.
Main roles: Mitya (*Poverty is No Vice*), Tikhon (*Thunderstorm* by A. N. Ostrovsky), Paval Korchagin (*How the Steel Hardened* by N. Ostrovsky), Monakhov (*Barbarians* by M. Gorky), *Arturo Ui* (Brecht), etc.
Leningrad Bolshoi Drama Theatre, 1 Ploshchad Iskusstv, Leningrad, U.S.S.R.

Lebedev, Polikarp Ivanovich; Soviet art gallery director; b. 1904; ed. Moscow Univ.
Member C.P.S.U. 24-; Head of Literature Dept., *Izogiz* (Fine Arts Publishing House) 34-38; Deputy Dir. State Tretyakov Art Gallery, Moscow 38-39, 53-54, Dir. 49-51, 54-; Deputy Head of Dept., Central Cttee. of C.P.S.U. 41-45, Head of Dept. 45-48; Chair. Cttee. for Arts of U.S.S.R. 48-51; Senior Scientific Editor *Great Soviet Encyclopaedia* 51-53; Corresp. mem. U.S.S.R. Acad. of Arts; Honoured Art Worker of U.S.S.R.; Order of Red Banner of Labour.
State Tretyakov Art Gallery, Lavrushensky pereulok 9, Moscow, U.S.S.R.

Lebedev, Sergei Alekseyevich; Soviet electronic engineer; b. 02; ed. Bauman Higher Technical Coll., Moscow.
Expounded theory of artificial stability in synchronised machines, specialist in electro-automation and electronic digital computers, designed and built high-speed computers BESM I and II and M-20; Dir. Inst. of Precision Mechanics and Computing Equipment of the U.S.S.R. Acad. of Sciences 53-; mem. Ukrainian S.S.R. Acad. of Sciences 45-; mem. U.S.S.R. Acad. of Sciences; State Prize, Hero of Socialist Labour.
Publs. works on automation and computer technique.
Leninski Prospekt 51, Moscow, U.S.S.R.

Lebègue, Raymond; French university professor and writer; b. 16 Sept. 1895; ed. Lycée Louis-le-Grand and Univ. de Paris à la Sorbonne.
Teacher, Brest 19, Clermont-Ferrand 20-23; Prof. Univ. of Rennes 23-42, Univ. of Paris 42-65; mem. Institut de France 55; Pres. Association Internationale des Etudes Françaises and Soc. des Textes Français Modernes; Officier Légion d'Honneur.
Publs. *Le Mystère des Actes des Apôtres* 29, *La Tragédie religieuse en France* 29, *Les Correspondants de Peiresc dans les anciens Pays-Bas* 43, *La Tragédie française de la Renaissance* 44, *Ronsard* 50, *La Poésie française de 1560 à 1630* 51, Editor of Collections by Ronsard, Malherbe, R. Garnier, and Stendhal.
13 rue Bobierre de Vallière, 92 Bourg-la-Reine, France.
Telephone: ROB 20-97.

Leber, Georg; German bricklayer and politician; b. 7 Oct. 1920; ed. primary and commercial schools in Limburg (Lahn).
Soldier 39-45; joined trade union and Social Democrat Party (SPD) 47; trade union leader, Limburg 49; Chair. of local branch of SPD 51; Editor *Der Grundstein* (trade union paper) 52; mem. Management Cttee. Bau-

Steine-Erden Trade Union 53-57, Chair. 57; mem. Management Cttee. Fed. of German Trade Unions 57; mem. Management Cttee. of Int. Federation of Building and Timber Workers and Pres. Joint Cttee. of Trade Unions of Building and Timber Trade in European Common Market 57; mem. Bundestag 57-; mem. European Parl. 58-59; mem. Management Cttee. SPD Faction in Bundestag 61-, mem. Party Management 61-; Federal Minister of Transport Dec. 66-.
Der Bundesminister für Verkehr, 53 Bonn, Sternstrasse 100, German Federal Republic.
Telephone: 302-2100.

Leber, Maj.-Gen. Walter Philip; American army officer and govt. official; b. 12 Sept. 1918; ed. Missouri School of Mines and George Washington Univ.
Served in Second World War, Regular Army Comm. 42; Chief, X-10 Project, Manhattan District, Oak Ridge 46, Technical Branch, Mil. Liaison Cttee. to Atomic Energy Comm., Washington 47-49; Asst. to District Engineer, Seattle District, then District Exec. Officer, Walla Walla District, North Pacific Div., Corps of Engineers 49-50; Engineer Bn. Commdr., and later, Group Commdr. Fort Sill 51; Dept. of Army Gen. Staff, Washington 52-55; Commanding Officer, 2nd Engineer Group (Construction) Eighth Army, Korea 56-57; Exec. Officer to Chief of Engineers, Washington 58-61; Lt.-Gov. Canal Zone and Vice-Pres. Panama Canal Co. 61-63; Ohio River Div. Engineer, Cincinnati 63-66; Dir. of Civil Works, Office Chief of Engineers, Washington 66; Gov. Canal Zone and Pres. Panama Canal Co. 67-; Legion of Merit and other awards.
Balboa Heights, Panama Canal Zone, Central America.

Le Bigot, Guillaume Charles René; French shipping executive; b. 24 Feb. 1909; ed. Ecole des Hautes Etudes Commerciales.
Chief of Budgetary and Financial Section, Ministry of Armed Forces 47-50; Chief of Liaison Mission with Allied Forces 50-51; Chief of Div. of Budget and Finance, Quartermaster Dept., Allied Forces in Europe 51-58; attached to Ministry of Armed Forces for Admin. of Navy 58; Ministerial Sec. for the Navy 59-61; Chair. Compagnie des Messageries Maritimes 61-66; Dir. Union des Transports Aériens (U.T.A.); Commdr. Légion d'Honneur; Commdr. Palmes Académiques; Commdr. Legion of Merit.
Union des Transports Aériens, 3 boulevard Malesherbes, Paris 8e; Home: 9 boulevard Suchet, Paris 16e, France.

Leblanc, Félix A. E. J. G.; Belgian economist and university official; b. 26 May 1892; ed. Université Libre de Bruxelles.
Served in First World War 14-18; Asst. Man. Ministry of Econ. Affairs 19, Man. 20; official of numerous industrial and financial firms 20-27; joined staff, Université Libre de Bruxelles 27, Ordinary Prof., Admin. 47-52, Vice-Pres. 52-58, Pres. 58-65, now Prof. Emer.; Hon. Pres. Fed. des Entreprises des Fabrications métalliques (Fabrimetal) 65; Admin. Fed. of Belgian Industries; Pres. European Cttee. of Co-operation of Machine-Tool Industries; Croix de l'Yser (14), Grand Officier de l'Ordre de Léopold and other Belgian and foreign awards.
84 avenue Franklin Roosevelt, Brussels 5, Belgium.

Leburton, Edmond-Jules-Isidore; Belgian politician; b. 18 April 1915; ed. Liège Univ.
Principal Controller of Labour 36-46; Chef de Cabinet, Ministry of Labour and Social Welfare 45-46; Commandant of Secret Army and mem. various resistance groups 39-45; mem. Chamber of Representatives 46-; mem. Socialist Party Council 47-; Burgomaster of Waremme 46-; Prof. Ecole Provinciale de Service Social, Liège, and Ecole Provinciale d'Infirmières, Herstal; Dir. of Studies at Institut d'Etudes Sociales de l'Etat, Brussels; Minister of Public Health and Family Welfare 54-58, Minister of Social Security 61-65; Minister-Vice-Pres., Co-ordinator of Infrastructure Policy 65-March 66; Socialist Party; awards include: Commdr. de l'Ordre de Léopold, Grand Cross Order of Orange-Nassau, Croix de Guerre avec palmes, Commdr. l'Ordre de la Santé Publique (France).
Publs. *Précis de Sécurité Sociale, Traité d'Economie Politique.*
c/o Parti Socialiste Belge, 17 place E. Vandervelde, Brussels; Home: Clos de Hesbaye, Waremme, Belgium.

Lecache, Bernard; French journalist; b. 16 Aug. 1895; ed. Univ. of Paris.
Journalist 16-; regular contributor to leading newspapers and magazines in France and other countries; Founder and Dir. *Droit de Vivre* (anti-racial newspaper) 30-; Dir. *Journal du Dimanche* 50-; Founder and Pres. Int. League Against Racialism and Anti-Semitism 27-; deported for acts of resistance 40-42, joined Free French Army; Reuter's Correspondent, Paris 44-46; Légion d'Honneur (Military), Croix de Guerre, Médaille de la Résistance.
Publs. *Jacob* 25, *Quand Israel Meurt* 27, *Les Porteurs de Croix* 30, *Séverine* 31, *Les Ressuscités* 33.
Office: 100 rue Réaumur, Paris 2e; Home: 6 rue Ballu, Paris 9e, France.
Telephone: 236-92-01 (Office).

Lecanuet, Jean Adrien François; French politician; b. 4 March 1920; ed. Lycée Corneille, Rouen, Lycée Henri IV, Paris, and Univ. of Paris.
Master of Requests, Council of State; Inspector Gen., Ministry of Information 44; Dir. of the Cabinets of Ministry of Information, Merchant Marine, Nat. Econ., Interior 46-51; Dep. to Nat. Assembly 51-55; Sec. of State, Presidency Council 55-58; First Asst. to Mayor of Rouen 58; Senator 59-, mem. Senate Cttee. on Foreign Affairs; Nat. Pres., Centre Démocrate; Chevalier, Légion d'Honneur, Commdr. Ordre St. Grégoire le Grand.
Le Sénat, Palais du Luxembourg, 15 rue de Vaugirard, Paris 6e, France.

Le Carré, John (*see* Cornwell, David John Moore).

Lechi, Hadji (Haxhi Lleshi): Albanian politician; b. 13. Fought with resistance against Italian and German occupations 39-45; mem. provisional Govt. 44; Minister of the Interior 44-46; Major-Gen. Albanian Army; Pres. Presidium of the People's Assembly (Head of State) 53-; mem. Cen. Cttee. Albanian Workers' Party 53-.
The People's Assembly, Tirana, Albania.

Lechín Oquendo, Juan; Bolivian politician and diplomatist; b. 15.
Former professional footballer; fmr. Minister of Mines; President Bolivian Mine Workers' Confed.; fmr. Pres. of Senate; Vice-Pres. of Repub. 60-64; Ambassador to Italy 62-63; exiled May 65; Leader, Left Sector of Movimiento Nacionalista Revolucionario (MNR); sought asylum in Chile June 67.

Leckwijck, William Peter Edward Joseph van; Belgian geologist; b. 16 Nov. 1902; ed. Clifton Coll. Bristol and Univ. de Liège.
Geological investigations and mapping in Morocco, Greece, Bulgaria, Finland, Italy, France, Luxembourg, Belgium 30-38; work on brown coalfields for the Tunisian Govt. 39-40; investigations on mineral deposits in Belgium 41-46; geological, palaeontological and sedimentological work in coalfields 47-; fmr. Pres. three Geological Socs. of Belgium; fmr. Officer Int. Asscn. of Sedimentology; fmr. Officer Perm. Cttee. Carboniferous Congresses; fmr. Pres. Int. Subcommission on Carboniferous Stratigraphy; fmr. Vice-Pres. Int. Comm. on Stratigraphy; Officer Geological Council of Belgium; Dir. Belgian Nat. Research Station for Geology of Coalbearing Strata 50-; Sec.-Gen. Int. Union of Geological Sciences (IUGS) 64-; Prof. Geology

and Stratigraphical Palaeontology, Univ. of Louvain 64-; Wetrems Prize and van Ertborn Prize, Royal Acad. Belguim; van Waterschoot van der Gracht Medal of Royal Dutch Geological and Mining Soc.; Officier Ouissan Alouite for Geological work in Morocco.

Publs. 110 papers on geological sciences in many foreign publs.

Koninklijk Instituut voor Natuurwetenschappen, Vautierstraat 31, Brussels 4 (Office); Geologisch Instituut, St. Michielsstraat 6, Louvain; Mechelse Steenweg 206, Antwerp, Belgium (Home).

Telephone: Antwerp 03-382766; Brussels 02-480475; Louvain 016-31253.

Le Clézio, Jean Marie Gustave; French-British writer; b. 13 April 1940; ed. Lycée and Univ. de Nice.

Travelled in Nigeria 48, England (studied at Bristol and London Univs.), U.S.A. 65; Prix Renaudot 63.

Publs. *Le Procès-Verbal* (The Interrogation) 63, *La Fièvre* (Fever) (short stories) 65, *Le Déluge* 66, *L'Extase Matérielle* 67, *Terra amata* (novel) 67.

c/o Editions Gallimard, 5 rue Sébastien-Bottin, Paris 7e, France.

Lecompte-Boinet, Jacques Henri Marie; French diplomatist; b. 26 April 1905; ed. Ecole Libre des Sciences Politiques.

Mem. Nat. Council of the Resistance 43-45; mem. Provisional Consultative Assembly 43-45; Provisional Sec.-Gen., Ministry of Public Works 44; Vice-Pres. Comm. for Nat. Re-equipment of the Consultative Assembly 44-45; Minister, later Ambassador, to Colombia 46-50; Minister to Finland 50, Ambassador 54-55; permanent French Del. Council of Europe 55-61; French Ambassador to Norway 61-65; Croix de la Libération, Officier de la Légion d'Honneur, etc.

6 rue Fréville-le-Vingt, Sèvres (Seine et Oise), France.

Lecourt, Robert, D. en D.; French lawyer and politician; b. 19 Sept. 1908; ed. Caen Univ.

Resistance leader during Second World War; Deputy to Constituent Assemblies 45, 46; Deputy to Nat. Assembly from Paris 46-58, from Hautes Alpes 58-; Minister of Justice 48-49, 57; Minister of State, with special responsibility for relations between the Republic and the French Community (Debré Cabinet) Jan. 59-Feb. 60, for Overseas Territories, Overseas Departments and Sahara Feb. 60-61; mem. for France, European Community Court of Justice 62-, Pres. 67; Pres. M.R.P. group in Nat. Assembly 49-58; Chevalier, Légion d'Honneur, Croix de Guerre, Officier de la Résistance.

29 rue Marie-Adélaïde, Luxembourg; and 17 avenue de Tourville, Paris, France.

Leddy, John M.; American government official; b. 29 June 1914.

Former Special Asst. to Under-Sec. of State, Douglas Dillon; Asst. Sec. U.S. Treasury 61-62; U.S. Rep. to Organisation for Economic Co-operation and Development (OECD) 62-65; Asst. Sec. for European Affairs 65-; Democrat.

State Department, Washington, D.C. 25, U.S.A.

Lederberg, Joshua, B.A., PH.D.; American geneticist; b. 23 May 1925; ed. Columbia and Yale Univs.

Professor of Genetics and Biology, Stanford Univ. 59-; Dir. Kennedy Laboratory for Molecular Medicine, Stanford Univ.; Nobel Prize in Medicine (with Beadle and Tatum) 58.

Publs. Numerous papers and articles in various scientific and lay publications.

School of Medicine, Stanford University, Palo Alto, Calif., U.S.A.

Ledesma, Oscar, A.B., LL.B.; Philippine politician and diplomatist; b. 3 April 1902; ed. Ateneo, Manila and Univ. of the Philippines.

Mayor, Iloīlo City 40-41; Congressman 41-49; Sec. for Commerce and Industry 54-57; mem. Senate 57-63;

Amb. to the U.S.A. 64-67; Knight of St. Sylvester. 8th Street, Quezon City, Philippines.

Telephone: 7-26-68.

Ledingham, George Aleck, M.B.E., M.SC., PH.D., F.R.S.C., F.C.I.C.; Canadian microbiologist; b. 03; ed. Univs. of Saskatchewan and Toronto.

Research Asst. in Pathology, Univ. of Saskatchewan 27; Asst. in Botany, Univ. of Toronto 32; Research Asst. Laboratories of Cryptogamic Botany, Harvard Univ. 32; Mycologist, Nat. Research Council, Ottawa 33-47; Dir. Prairie Regional Laboratory, Nat. Research Council, Saskatoon 47-.

Publs. include papers on soil fungi 29-36, on the Trail Smelter Question 34-39, on Production and Properties of **2, 3**-Butanediol 44-49, studies on plant rusts 50-61.

936 University Drive, Saskatoon, Sask., Canada.

Ledoux, Albert Frédéric Edmond; French diplomatist; b. 5 June 1901; ed. Bowdoin Coll., Brighton Coll., Lycée Janson de Sailly, and Ecole des Hautes Etudes Commerciales.

Attaché Constantinople 27-28; Sec., Rio de Janeiro, Madrid, Brussels, Montevideo 28-40; Gen. de Gaulle's Personal Rep. in S. America 40-41; Del. of French Nat. Cttee. for Argentina, Brazil, Chile, Paraguay and Uruguay 42-43; Dir. of Staff Accounts, Foreign Ministry 44-45; Ambassador to Peru 45-49, to Uruguay 49-52, to Norway 55-57; Diplomatic Adviser to Govt. 59-62; Amb. to Denmark 62-66; Commdr., Légion d'Honneur, Médaille de la Résistance, Grand Cross of St. Olav (Norway), El Sol (Peru).

41 boulevard Commandant Charcot, Neuilly-sur-Seine, France.

Ledoux, Jean-Paul; French engineer; b. 23 Oct. 1904; ed. Ecole Centrale des Arts et Manufactures, Paris.

President, Dir.-Gen., Antar (Pétroles de l'Atlantique) and of Antargaz; Pres., Socal S.A., Lausanne; Administrator, Société Française commerciale et maritime; Pres. Centre Professionnel des Lubrifiants Pechelbronn S.A.E.M., Societé des Transports Maritimes Pétroliers; Chevalier, Légion d'Honneur; Commdr. de l'Economie nationale du Mérite commercial.

98 rue de Courcelles, Paris 17e, France.

Ledovskiy, Andrei Mefodyevich; Soviet diplomatist; b. 1914; ed. Astrakhan Teachers' Training Inst.

Diplomatic Service 42-; Consul, Lanchow, China 43-44; Consul-Gen., Peking 46-47; Deputy Head of Far Eastern Dept., U.S.S.R. Ministry of Foreign Affairs 52-55; Counsellor, Washington 55-59; Amb. to Burma 59-66; mem. staff, Ministry of Foreign Affairs 66-.

U.S.S.R. Ministry of Foreign Affairs, Smolenskaya-Sennaya ploshchad 32/34, Moscow, U.S.S.R.

Leduc, François Jacques; French diplomatist; b. 10 Nov. 1912; ed. Lycée Louis-le-Grand, Univ. de Paris à la Sorbonne, and King's Coll., Cambridge.

Economic Section, Ministry of Foreign Affairs 45-47; Resident, Tunis 47-50; Ministry of Nat. Defence 51-54; Minister-Councillor, Bonn 55-57, 58-60, Brussels 57-58; Dir. Admin. and Consular Affairs. Ministry of Foreign Affairs 60-65; Pres. Supervisory Council of Compagnie européenne de radiodiffusion et de télévision (CERT) 63-65; Ambassador to Canada 65-; Officier Légion d'Honneur, Medal of Freedom.

Embassy of France, 42 Sussex Drive, Ottawa, Canada; 2 rue Huysmans, Paris 6e, France.

Lee, Rt. Hon. Sir Frank Godbould, P.C., G.C.M.G., K.C.B.; British civil servant and college principal; b. 26 Aug. 1903; ed. Brentwood School and Downing Coll. Cambridge.

Joined Civil Service 26; mem. Treasury Del. Washington 44-46; Dep. Sec. Ministry of Supply 47; Minister, Washington 48; Perm. Sec. Ministry of Food 49-51, Board of Trade 51-59; Jt. Perm. Sec. Treas. 59-62; Master of Corpus Christi Coll., Cambridge 62-; mem.

Econ. Planning Board 51-61, Chair. 60-61; mem. London Advisory Cttee., Union Corporation; Dir. Bowater Paper Corpn. 63-; Trustee, *The Economist* 63-; Gov. London School of Econs.; Hon. Fellow Downing Coll. Cambridge; Fellow, London Graduate School of Business Studies.
The Master's Lodge, Corpus Christi College, Cambridge, England.

Lee, Rt. Hon. Frederick, P.C., M.P.; British politician; b. 3 Aug. 1906; ed. Langworthy Road School.
Former Engineer, Chair. Works Cttee. Metro-Vickers Ltd., Trafford Park, Manchester; mem. Nat. Cttee. Amalgamated Engineering Union 44-45; M.P. 45-; fmr. Parl. Private Sec. to Chancellor of Exchequer; Parl. Sec., Ministry of Labour 50-51; Minister of Power 64-66; Sec. of State for Colonies 66-67; Chancellor of Duchy of Lancaster 67-, taking special responsiblity for the North Oct. 67-; Labour.
House of Commons, London, S.W.1, England.

Lee, Sir Henry Desmond Pritchard, Kt., M.A., D.LITT.; British schoolmaster; b. 30 Aug. 1908; ed. Arden House, Repton School, Cambridge Univ.
Tutor, Cambridge Univ. 35-48; Lecturer, Faculty of Classics 37-48; Regional Commrs. Office (Civil Defence) 40-44; mem. Council of Senate, Cambridge Univ. 44-48; Headmaster, Clifton Coll. 48-54, Winchester Coll. 54-68; Chair. Headmasters' Conf. 59-60, 67; Research Fellow Univ. Coll. Cambridge 68-; Hon. D.Litt. (Nottingham).
Publs. *Zeno of Elea* (text and trans.) 35, Aristotle's *Meteorologica* 52, Plato's *Republic* 55, Plato's *Timæus* 65.
University College, Cambridge, England.

Lee, General Honkon; Korean army officer and diplomatist; b. 20; ed. Japanese Imperial Mil. Acad.
Superintendent, Korean Mil. Acad. 46-48; Mil. Attaché, Washington 49; Commdg. Gen., Eighth Republic of Korea Army Division 49-50, Third Army Corps 50-51, First Army Corps 52-54; UN Command Del. to Korean Armistice 51-52; Chair. Jt. Chiefs of Staff 54-56, Chief of Staff 56-58; Nat. Pres. Korean Veterans Asscn. 58-61; Amb. to Philippines 61-62, to U.K. 62-67; numerous decorations.
c/o Ministry of Foreign Affairs, Seoul, Republic of Korea.

Lee, Rt. Hon. Jennie, P.C., M.A., LL.B., M.P. (widow of late Rt. Hon. Aneurin Bevan); British politician; b. 3 Nov. 1904; ed. Edinburgh Univ.
M.P. for North Lanark 29-31, Cannock 45-; Parl. Sec. Ministry of Public Building and Works 64-65; Minister for the Arts and Under-Sec. of State, Dept. of Educ. and Science 65-67, Minister for the Arts and Minister of State, Dept. of Educ. and Science 67-; Dir. *Tribune*; mem. Central Advisory Cttee. on Housing; mem. Nat. Exec. Cttee., Labour Party 58-, Chair. 67-.
Publs. *Tomorrow is a New Day* 39, *Our Ally, Russia* 41, *This Great Journey* 63.
Asheridge Farm, Chesham, Bucks., England.

Lee Kuan Yew, M.A.; Singapore politician; b. 16 Sept. 1923; ed. Raffles Coll. Singapore and Cambridge Univ.
One of the founders of the Socialist Peoples' Action Party 54, Sec.-Gen. 54-; mem. Legislative Assembly 55-; (first) Prime Minister 59-; mem. Singapore Internal Security Council 59-; (first) Prime Minister Republic of Singapore 65-; mem. Bureau of the Socialist Int. 66.
Prime Minister's Office, St. Andrew's Road, Singapore 6.

Lee, Laurie, M.B.E.; British author and poet; b. 26 June 1914; ed. Slad Village School, and Stroud Central School.
Script-writer with Crown Film Unit 40-43; editor, Ministry of Information publications 44-46; film-making in India 46-47; caption-writer-in-chief, Festival of Britain 50-51; travelling and writing 51-; Atlantic Award 47, William Foyle Poetry Prize 56, W. H. Smith and Son Award 60.
Publs. *The Sun My Monument* (poems) 44, *The Bloom of Candles* (poems) 47, *The Voyage of Magellan* (radio play) 48, *A Rose for Winter* (travel) 55, *My Many-Coated Man* (poems) 55, *Cider with Rosie* (autobiography) 59, *The Firstborn* (essay) 64.
49 Elm Park Gardens, London, S.W.10, England.

Lee, Manfred B. (co-writer with Frederic Dannay, *q.v.*, under pseudonym **Ellery Queen**); American writer; b. 11 Jan. 1905.
Co-Editor Ellery Queen's Mystery Magazine; Co-Founder Mystery Writers of America; fmr. Co-Pres. Crime Writers Asscn.
Publs. Crime and mystery novels and short stories.
Roxbury, Connecticut 06783, U.S.A.
Telephone: 203-354-4700.

Lee, Rensselaer Wright, A.B., PH.D.; American art historian; b. 15 June 1898; ed. Princeton Univ.
Instructor of English, Princeton Univ. 22-23, 25-28, Chair. Dept. of Art and Archaeology 55-64, Marquand Prof. 61-66; Assoc. Prof. History of Art and Chair. of Dept., Northwestern Univ. 31-34, Prof. 34-40; Prof. Smith Coll. 41-48, Columbia Univ. 48-54, New York Univ. 54-55; Editor-in-Chief *Art Bulletin* 42-44; mem. Inst. for Advanced Study 39, 42-44, 46-47; Chair. Cttee. on Research and Publication in the Fine Arts 42-44, Protection of Cultural Treasures in War Areas 44-46; Pres. Coll. Art Asscn. of America 44-46; mem. Board of Dirs. American Council of Learned Socs. 53-61; mem. Board of Dirs. and Trustee, Renaissance Soc. of America 60-; Harris Lecturer, Northwestern Univ. 66; Trustee, American Acad. in Rome 58-; Vice-Pres., Int. Fed. of Renaissance Socs. and Insts. 61-; Pres. Union Académique Internationale 62-65; Vice-Pres. Int. Council for Philosophy and Humanistic Studies 65-; Fellow American Acad. of Arts and Sciences.
Publs. *Ut pictura poesis: The Humanistic Theory of Painting* 40, new edition 67.
120 Mercer Street, Princeton, New Jersey, U.S.A.
Telephone: 924-2401.

Lee, General Robert Merrill; American air force officer; b. 09; ed. U.S. Military Acad., West Point, Air Corps Primary Flying School, Air Corps Tactical School and Nat. War Coll.
35th Pursuit Squadron 32-37, First Cavalry(Mechanized) 37-38, 12th Observation Squadron 38-40, Commdr. 40-41, Chief of Corps Aviation 41-42, Commdr. 73rd Observation Group 42-43, Chief of Staff, 1st Air Support Command 43-44, Dep. Commd. Gen. for Operations and Chief of Staff, Ninth Air Force, Western Europe 44-45, Air Section, Theater Gen. Board, Europe 45, Chief of Staff, Tactical Air Commd. Virginia 46; Nat. War Coll. 46-47; Dep. Commd. Gen., Tactical Air Comnd., Langley Field, Virginia 47-48, Commd. Gen. 48-50, Commdr. Air Task Group 3.4 for Atomic Bomb Tests *Greenhouse* 50-51, Dep. Dir. of Plans, Dep. Chief of Staff for Operations, Headquarters USAF 51-53, Commdr. Fourth Allied Tactical Air Force 53-57, of Twelfth United States Air Force in Europe 53-56, Commdr. Ninth Air Force Tactical Air Command 57-58, Chief of Staff, United Nations Command, United States Forces, Korea 58-59, Vice-Commdr. Air Defense Command 59-61, Commdr., Air Defense Command 61-63, Air Deputy to Supreme Allied Commdr. Europe, NATO 63-66; Distinguished Service Medal, Legion of Merit, Commdr. Legion of Honour (France), Hon. C.B.E. and other decorations.
318 Pine Avenue, Colorado Springs, Colo. 80906, U.S.A.

Lee Soo Young; Korean diplomatist; b. 28 Dec. 1921; ed. Waseda Univ., Japan, and Military Acad. of Korea.
Teacher of English and English Literature, Ewha High

School 46-48; Lecturer, Seoul Nat. Univ. 47-48; Army Service 48-53; Dir. Information Bureau, Ministry of Foreign Affairs 53-54, Int. Relations Bureau 55-56; Chargé d'Affaires *a.i.*, Paris 56-57; Counsellor, London 57-59, Korean Mission to UN 59-60; Vice-Minister of Foreign Affairs 60; Amb., Korean Mission to UN 61; Special Envoy of Pres. of Korea to African Countries 62-65; Chief of Econ. Mission to Canada 62; Minister of Information 64; Amb. to France, concurrently to Spain, Luxembourg, Netherlands, Portugal, Cameroon, Congo (Kinshasa), Madagascar, Niger, Togo, Dahomey, Gabon, Upper Volta, Senegal and Chad 65-; numerous decorations.
Publ. *With Hope and Confidence* (speeches) 65.
Embassy of Republic of Korea, avenue Mozart 33, Paris 17e, France; Home: 340-15 Shindang Dong, Seoul, Korea.
Telephone: 52-6701 (Home).

Lee Tong-Won; Korean diplomatist and politician; b. 2 Aug. 1925; ed. Rio Grande Coll., Kent State Univ., Columbia Univ. and Oxford Univ.
President Int. Research Center, Seoul 58; Publisher-Editor *Koreana Quarterly* 58; Prof. Seoul Nat. Univ., Nat. Defence Coll. 58-62; Sec.-Gen. to the Pres. of Repub. of Korea 62; Ambassador to Thailand 63-64; Minister of Foreign Affairs 64-66; Most Noble Order of White Elephant, and of the Crown (Thailand), Order of the Crown of Malaysia.
c/o Ministry of Foreign Affairs, Seoul, Republic of Korea.

Lee Tsung-Dao, PH.D.; Chinese physicist; b. 26; ed. National Chekiang Univ., National Southwest Univ. (China) and Univ. of Chicago.
Research Assoc. in Astronomy, Univ. of Chicago 50; Research Assoc. and Lecturer in Physics, Univ. of California 50-51; mem. Inst. for Advanced Study, Princeton, N.J. 51-53; Asst. Prof. of Physics Columbia Univ. 53-55; Assoc. Prof. 55-56 and Prof. 56-60, 63-; Prof. Princeton Inst. for Advanced Study 60-63; mem. Nat. Acad. of Sciences; Nobel Prize in Physics 57; Albert Einstein Award in Science 57.
Publs. consist of articles in physical journals.
25 Claremont Avenue, New York, N.Y. 10027, U.S.A.

Leemans, Victor; Belgian writer and politician; b. 1901.
Member Belgian Senate 49-, European Parl. 49-58; Pres. European Parl. 65-66; Christian Democrat.
Prins Albertlei 8, Antwerp, Belgium.

Leer-Andersen, Rt. Rev. Jens Bagh; Danish ecclesiastic; b. 25 Nov. 1910; ed. Stenhus Coll., Holboek, and Univ. of Copenhagen.
Minister Groendals Church, Copenhagen 36-40, Blistrup 40-47; Sec. Church Fund of Copenhagen 47-50, Exec. Sec. 50-56; Minister of St. Olaf's Church, Elsinore 56-61; Bishop of Elsinore 61-.
Heslehøj Alle 4, Copenhagen Hellerup, Denmark.
Telephone: HE-9312.

Le Fanu, Admiral Sir Michael, G.C.B., D.S.C.; British naval officer; b. 2 Aug. 1913; ed. Bedford School.
Served in H.M. Ships *Aurora, Howe* and U.S. 3rd and 5th Fleets 39-45; Commander H.M.S. *Eagle* 57-58; Third Sea Lord and Controller of the Navy 61-65; Commander-in-in-Chief, Middle East 65-68; First Sea Lord and Chief of Naval Staff Aug. 68-; U.S. Bronze Star 45.
17 Stonehill Road, London S.W. 14, England.
Telephone: 01-876-1477.

Lefèbvre, H.E. Cardinal Joseph, TH.D.; French ecclesiastic; b. 15 April 1892; ed. Fribourg Univ., and Gregorian Univ., Rome.
Successively parish priest, Diocesan Dir. and Vicar-Gen. Diocese of Poitiers; Bishop of Troyes 38-43; Archbishop of Bourges 43-; created Cardinal by Pope John XXIII 60; Officier Légion d'Honneur.
Archevêché de Bourges, 4 rue du 95e-de-Ligne, Bourges (Cher), France.

Lefèbvre, René, M.A., DIP. AGR.; Belgian agricultural engineer and farmer; b. 93; ed. Athénée Royal, Tournai, Univ. of Brussels and Institut agronomique de l'Etat, Gembloux.
Burgomaster of Lamain (Hainault) 21-; Deputy for the County of Tournai 19-35; Counsellor for Hainault province 29-35; mem. of Belgian Parl. for county of Tournai 36-; detained as political hostage by German occupation forces June 44; Minister of Agriculture 45-47 and 54-58, of Interior 58-61; mem. of State Economic Council for Agriculture 25-; Vice-Pres. Liberal Party 61; Pres. Belgian Nat. League of Agricultural Professional Unions for districts of Hainault and Tournai.
131 Ferme de la "Grande Barre", Near Lamain, Province of Hainault, Belgium.

Lefèvre, Théo; Belgian lawyer and politician, b. 14; ed. St. Joseph and St. Liévin Colls., Ghent, and Univ. of Ghent.
Member of the Resistance 40-45; Editor, Flemish newspaper *Vrij*; mem. of Chamber of Reps. 46-; Pres. Christian Social Party 50-61; mem. Parl. Assembly, ECSC 50-59, European Parl. 59-61; Minister of State 58; Pres. Int. Union of Christian Democrats 59; Prmie Minister, in charge of Econ. Co-ordination and Scientific Policy 61-65; Minister without Portfolio in Charge of Politics and Scientific Programme June 68-.
43 rue Savaen, Ghent, Belgium.

Le Fèvre de Montigny, Gillis Johannis; Netherlands army officer; b. 01; ed. Breda Royal Mil. Acad., General Staff Coll.
2nd Lieut. Artillery 22; until 32 with Garrison Artillery Regiment, and 1st and 2nd Field-Artillery Regiments; Staff Coll. 32-35; A.D.C. to Chief of Gen. Staff 37-38; Chief of Staff 4th Div. 39-40; prisoner of war in Germany 42-45; attached to Mil. Cabinet of Ministry of War 45-47; Asst. Chief of Staff, G.5 (Training) 47-50; Chief of Staff 1 (NL) Corps. 50-53; Deputy Chief of Staff, Allied Forces in Central Europe (N.A.T.O. H.Q.) 53; Deputy Chief of Staff (Operations and Intelligence), Royal Netherlands Army 55; Vice-Chief of Gen. Staff Apr. 57, Chief of Gen. Staff, C.-in-C., Netherlands Land Forces 57- 62; Chair. Joint Chiefs of Staff 62-65; A.D.C. Extraordinary of H.M. Queen Juliana 62-.
Hasseltse Straat 19, The Hague, Netherlands.
Telephone: 553328.

Lefol, Lucien, D. en D.; French industrialist; b. 21 April 1891; ed. Ecole Polytechnique, Ecole du Génie Maritime.
Naval engineer 13; joined Société des Ateliers & Chantiers de France as engineer 21, Chief Engineer 23, Dir. 25, Dir.-Gen. 29, Pres. 43, now Prés. d'Honneur; Administrateur Prés. d'Honneur Cie. des Forges et Aciéries de la Marine et de Saint-Etienne; Vice-Pres. Admin. Council Sidelor, and Chamber of Shipbuilders and Marine Engineers; mem. Admin. Council Cie. Auxiliaire de Navigation, Cie. de Construction Mécanique Sulzer, Technical Maritime and Aeronautical Asscn., Ateliers & Forges de la Loire, Soc. des Mines et Usines de Redange-Dilling, Charbonnages de Beeringen, Aciéries et Forges de Firminy, Forges & Chantiers de la Gironde; mem. Inst. of Naval Architects, Soc. of Naval Architects, Soc. of Naval Architects and Marine Engineers; corresp. mem. Acad. de la Marine; Commdr. de la Légion d'Honneur; Croix de Guerre 14-18; Commdr. du Mérite Maritime.
4 rue Mignard, Paris 16e, France.

le Fort, Gertrud Petrea Elsbeth Mathilde Augusta von; German-Swiss authoress; b. 11 Oct. 1876; ed. Univs. of Heidelberg, Marburg and Humboldt Univ., Berlin.

Member Bavarian Acad. of Fine Arts; mem. Acad. of Arts, Berlin; extraordinary mem. German Acad. for Language and Literature, Darmstadt; Hon. Pres. Droste Soc.; Grosses Verdienstkreuz 53, Münchner Dichterpreis 47, Badischer Staatspreis 48, Gottfried Kellerpreis, Genf 52, and Grosser Kunstpreis des Landes Nordrhein-Westfalen 55, Bayrischer Verdienstorden 59, Dr. h.c. (Munich); Stein Zum Grossen Verdienstkreuz 66.

Publs. include *Hymnen an die Kirche* 24, *Das Schweisstuch der Veronika*, Vol. I: *Der römische Brunnen* 28, *Der Papst aus dem Ghetto* 30, *Die Letzte am Schafott* 31, *Das Reich des Kindes* 33, *Die ewige Frau* 34, *Die Opferflamme* 38, *Die Abberufung der Jungfrau von Barby* 40, *Das Schweisstuch der Veronika*, Vol. II: *Der Kranz der Engel* 46, *Gedichte* 49, *Die Vöglein von Theres* 50, *Die Tochter Farinatas* 50, *Aufzeichnungen und Erinnerungen* 51, *Gelöschte Kerzen (Die Verfemte, Die Unschuldigen)* 53, *Am Tor des Himmels* 54, *Die Frau des Pilatus* 55, *Gesamtausgabe des Erzählenden Werkes* (three vols.) 56, *Der Turm der Beständigkeit* 57, *Die letzte Begegnung* 59, *Die Frau und die Technik* 59, *Das fremde Kind* 61, *Aphorismen* 63, *Die Tochter Jephtas* 64, *Hälfte des Lebens* 65, *Erzählungen* 66, *Das Schweigen* 67. Im Haslach, 9 Oberstdorf, Allgäu, Bavaria, German Federal Republic.
Telephone: 970.

Lefschetz, Solomon, M.E., PH.D.; American mathematician; b. 3 Sept. 1884; ed. Ecole Centrale, Paris, and Clark Univ.
Teacher Univ. of Nebraska 11-13; Univ. of Kansas 13-25; Assoc. Prof. Princeton Univ. 25-28, Prof. 28-32, H.B. Fine Research Prof. 33-53, Emeritus 53-, Chair. Dept. of Mathematics 45-; Prof. Mexico Univ. 45; mem. Nat. Acad. of Sciences, American Philosophical Soc., Bohemian Soc. of Science; Corresp. mem. Acad. des Sciences, Paris; former Pres. American Mathematical Soc.; foreign mem. Royal Soc., London; Editor *Annals of Mathematics*; Dr. h.c. (Prague, Mexico, Clark); Feltrinelli Int. Prize 56.
Publs. *L'Analyse Situs et la Géométrie Algébrique* 24, *Surfaces et variétés algébriques* 27, *Topology* 30, *Algebraic Topology* 42, *Topics in Topology* 42, *Introduction to Topology* 49, *Algebraic Geometry* 53, *Differential Equations: geometric theory* 58.
11 Lake Lane, Princeton, N.J., U.S.A.

Le Gallienne, Eva; American actress, director and author; b. in London 11 Jan. 1899; ed. Coll. Sévigné, Paris.
Debut in London in *The Laughter of Fools* 15; in N.Y. starred in *Liliom* 22, *The Swan* 23; founded Civic Repertory Theatre in N.Y. City 26; played and produced there some 40 plays, including Ibsen's *Master Builder*, *Hedda Gabler*, *John Gabriel Borkman*, Chekhov's *The Cherry Orchard*, *The Seagull*, Sierra's *The Cradle Song*, Giraudoux' *Siegfried*, Dumas' *Camille*, Shakespeare's *Romeo and Juliet* and *Twelfth Night*, Barrie's *Peter Pan*, Molière's *Would-be Gentleman*, Carroll's *Alice in Wonderland*, etc.; subsequently appeared on Broadway in Rostand's *L'Aiglon*, Job's *Uncle Harry*, Shakespeare's *Henry VIII*, Ibsen's *Rosmersholm* and *Ghosts*, Williams' *The Corn is Green*; Elizabeth I in Schiller's *Mary Stuart* in New York and on tour 58-60, and in Maxwell Anderson's *Elizabeth The Queen* on tour 61-62; on tour in Chekhov's *The Seagull* and Anouilh's *Ring Round the Moon* 62-63 and in *The Trojan Women* and *The Mad Woman of Chaillot* 65-66; Man. Dir. of American Rep. Theatre 46-47; Hon. M.A. (Tufts Univ.), Litt.D. (Russell Sage and Mt. Holyoke Colls.), D.H.L. (Smith Coll. and Univ. of N. Carolina), Litt.D. (Brown Univ. and Univ. of Fairfield), Gold Medal Society of Arts and Sciences, Medal of Honour Town Hall Club of N.Y., Gold Medal American Acad. of Arts and Letters, Cross of St. Olav (Norway).

Publs. *At 33* (autobiography) 34, *Alice in Wonderland* (stage version, French edn.), *Flossie and Bossie* 49, *With a Quiet Heart* 53, *Six Plays by Henrik Ibsen* (translation) 58, *Seven Plays by H. C. Andersen* (trans.) 59, *The Wild Duck and other Plays by Ibsen* (trans.) 61, H. C. Andersen's *The Nightingale* (trans.) 65, *The Mystic in the Theatre: Eleonora Duse* 66.
Hillside Road, Weston, Conn., U.S.A.

Legaz Lacambra, Luis; Spanish university professor; b. 06; ed. Colegio de Escolapios, Saragossa, Univs. of Saragossa, Madrid, Grenoble, Munich, Vienna, and Acad. de Droit Internat., The Hague.
Doctor of Law 32; Asst. Prof. Univ. Saragossa 32; Prof. Univ. La Laguna 35, Univ. Santiago de Compostela 35, Rector, Univ. Santiago de Compostela 42-60; Univ. of Madrid 60; Under-Sec. Ministry of Nat. Education; award from Coimbra Univ.; mem. Inst. Int. de Sociologie, Inst. de Estudios Políticos, Madrid, Real Acad. de Ciencias Morales y Políticas, Madrid, Fac. Int. pour l'Enseignement du Droit Comparé, Strasbourg, Int. Acad. for Comparative Law.
Publs. *Kelsen: Estudio Crítico* 33, *El Estado de Derecho* 35, *Introducción a la Ciencia del Derecho* 43, *Horizontes del Pensamiento Jurídico* 47, *Derecho y Libertad* 52, *Filosofía del Derecho* 53, *Justicia, Derecho y seguridad* 54, *La Obligación Política* 56, *La Función del Derecho en la Sociedad Contemporánea* 56, *Political Obligation and Natural Law* 57, *Lógica y pensamiento jurídico* 57, *Humanismo, Estado y Derecho* 59, *La Realidad del Derecho* 63, *Rechtsphilosophie* 65.
Ministro Ibáñez Martín 4, Madrid 15, Spain.
Telephone: 2432571.

Le Genissel, Charles Edouard; French diplomatist; b. 23 Dec. 1905; ed. Univs. of Algiers and Paris, and Ecole Libre des Sciences Politiques.
Ministry of Foreign Affairs 30-, New York, Rio de Janeiro, Algiers, Mexico, Tokyo, Rio de Janeiro 30-58; French Consul-Gen. in Monaco 58-60; Ambassador to Haiti 60-; Officier, Légion d'Honneur.
French Embassy, 51 place des Héros-de-l'Indépendance, Port-au-Prince, Haiti.

Legentilhomme, Gen. Paul Louis, K.C.B. (HON.) 46; French officer; b. 26 March 1884; ed. St. Cyr, Ecole Supérieure de Guerre.
Attached to 23rd Colonial Infantry Regt., took part in operations against last pirate chief Indo-China 09; École Supérieure de Guerre 12-14; served First World War, prisoner of war, promoted Capt. 15, attached H.Q. French Forces in Levant, part of Allenby's Egyptian Expeditionary Force 18; École Supérieure de Guerre 19-20; attached to Staff Indo-China 20-22; Company Commdr. 23rd Colonial Infantry Regt. 22; direction Colonial Troops Min. of War 23; Major, Head of Gen. Staff, Madagascar 26; in command battalion 23rd Colonial Infantry Regt. 28, promoted Lieut.-Col.; suppressed Communist riots Annam 31; Col. of Senegalese Regt. Toulon 32; 2nd-in-Command Special Military School St. Cyr 37; Gen. 38; Centre de Hautes Études Militaires 38; organised defences French Somaliland 39; joined Gen. de Gaulle's Free French Forces; Officer Commanding Free French Forces Eritrea Feb. 41; formed 1st Free French Div. Palestine; Officer Commanding Allied Forces which took Damascus 41; C.-in-C. Africa 41; Nat. Commr. for War 41; sentenced to death by Vichy authorities 41; Nat. Commr. for Madagascar 42; Commr. for Nat. Defence Sept.-Nov. 43; G.O.C. 3rd Military Region 44-45; Military Gov. of Paris 45-47; Councillor of French Union; Médaille Militaire, Grande Croix de la Légion d'Honneur, Croix de la Libération, Croix de Guerre, etc.; American Commdr. Legion of Merit; Belgian Grand Officier de la Couronne et Croix de Guerre; Czech Grand Officer Order

of White Lion; Polish Virtuti Militari (3rd Class); Brazilian Grand Officer Order of Southern Cross.
27 avenue Chanzy, La Varenne, St. Hilaire, Val de Marne, France.
Telephone: GRA 11-78.

Leger, Alexis, L. en D. (*pseudonym* Saint-John Perse); French writer and diplomatist; b. 31 May 1887; ed. Bordeaux and Paris Univs.
Joined Foreign Service 14; Sec. Peking 16-21; Chef de Cabinet, Ministry of Foreign Affairs 25-32, Asst. Dir. Asiatic and Pacific Section 25-27, Dep. Dir. Political and Commercial Section 27-29, Dir. 29-33, Ambassador and Sec.-Gen. to the Ministry 33-40; Grand Officer Légion d'Honneur 39, Commdr. Order of the Bath 40; mem. American Acad. and Bavarian Acad. 50, American Acad. of Arts and Sciences 63; Dr. h.c. Yale Univ. 59; Grand Prix National des Lettres 59, Nobel Prize for Literature 60.
Publs. *Eloges, La Gloire des Rois, Anabase, Exil, Vents, Amers, Chronique, Oiseaux* (poetry), *Pour Dante.*
1621 34th Street, N.W., Washington, D.C., U.S.A.; and "Les Vigneaux", Giens (var), France.

Léger, Jules; Canadian civil servant; b. 4 April 1913; ed. Univs. of Montreal and Paris.
Served on editorial staff *Le Droit*, Ottawa 38-40; Asst. Press Censor 40; joined Dept. of External Affairs 40; served Santiago 43, London 47; seconded to Prime Minister's Office, Ottawa 49-50; Head European Div., Dept. of External Affairs 50-51, Asst. Under-Sec. of State for External Affairs 51-53; Ambassador to Mexico 53-54; Under-Sec. of State for External Affairs 54-58; Perm. Rep. for Canada to NATO 58-62; Ambassador to Italy 62-64, to France 64-.
Canadian Embassy, 35 avenue Montaigne, Paris 8e, France.

Leger, H.E. Cardinal Paul Emile, L.TH., J.C.L.; Canadian ecclesiastic; b. 26 April 1904; ed. Grand Séminaire of Montreal and Paris.
Ordained at Montreal May 29; Prof. Issy Séminaire (near Paris) 31-32; Asst. Master of Novices, Saint-Sulpice, Paris 32-33; Founder-Superior at Fukuoka Seminary, Japan 33-39; Prof. Montreal Seminary of Philosophy 39-40; Vicar-Gen. and Cathedral Pastor Valleyfield 40-47; Rector of Canadian Coll., Rome 47-50; elected to Episcopal See 50 and enthroned as Archbishop of Montreal May 50, resigned as Archbishop of Montreal Nov. 67 to become missionary among lepers; elevated to Cardinal, with title of St. Mary of the Angels 53; D. Th. (Univ. of Laval) 51, D. ès. L. (Collège de l'Assomption, Mass.) 54; D.Iur. (McGill Univ.) 60, (Ottawa Univ. and St. Francis Xavier Univ.) 61; D.D. (Ottawa Univ.) and other Hon. degrees; papal legate to the closing of the Marian Year at Lourdes 54, crowning of statue of St. Joseph 55, St. Anne de Beaupré Tercentenary 58; Knight Grand Cross Legion of Honour and other decorations.
Dakar, Senegal.

Legorreta, Agustín; Mexican banker; b. 13; ed. Newman High School, Lakewood, New Jersey, U.S.A., and Ecole des Hautes Etudes Commerciales, France.
J. P. Morgan and Co., New York 30-32; Banco Nacional de Mexico 32-, now Pres.
Banco Nacional de Mexico S.A., Isabel la Católica 44, Apdo. 14 *bis*, Mexico D.F., Mexico.

Lehel, György; Hungarian conductor; b. 10 Feb. 1926; studied composition with Pál Kadosa and conducting with Laszló Somogyi.
Conductor Symphonic Orchestra of Hungarian Radio 47-62, Chief Conductor 62-; propagates contemporary Hungarian music; has conducted in Czechoslovakia, Poland, Switzerland, Austria, Soviet Union, Italy, Romania, France, Belgium, German Democratic

Republic, German Fed. Republic., Yugoslavia, Great Britain and Japan; Liszt Prize 55, 62.
Symphonic Orchestra of Hungarian Radio, Bródy Sándor u 5-7, Budapest VIII; Home: 7 Rumbach S.U. 20/22, Budapest, Hungary.
Telephone: 427-484.

Lehman, Robert; American banker; b. 29 Sept. 1892.
Partner, Lehman Bros., investment bankers, New York; Chair. of Board Lehman Corpn.; Dir. Gimbel Bros., 20th Century Fox Film Corpn., Pan American Airways, Associated Dry Goods Corpn., Metropolitan Opera Asscn., United Fruit Co.; mem. New York Stock Exchange; Trustee, New York Univ., Metropolitan Museum, Yale Univ. Art Gallery.
1 William Street, New York, N.Y., U.S.A.

Lehmann, John Frederick (brother of Rosamond Lehmann, q.v.), C.B.E., F.R.S.L.; British author and editor; b. 2 June 1907; ed. Eton and Trinity Coll., Cambridge.
Founder and Ed. of *New Writing* (including *The Penguin New Writing* and *New Writing and Daylight*) and of *Orpheus*; Partner and Gen. Man. The Hogarth Press 38-46; Man. Dir. John Lehmann Ltd. 46-53; Advisory Ed. *The Geographical Magazine* 40-45; Ed. *New Soundings* (B.B.C.) 52-53; Ed. *The London Magazine* 54-61; Pres. Alliance Française in Great Britain 54-63; Vice-Pres. European Community of Writers 62-; Pres. Royal Literary Fund 66-; Grand Officier Etoile Noire, Officier Légion d'Honneur, Officier Ordre des Arts et des Lettres, Commdr. Order of George I (Greece); William Foyle Poetry Prize 64.
Publs. *A Garden Revisited* 31, *Evil was Abroad* 38, *Down River* 39, *New Writing in Europe* 40, *The Age of the Dragon* 51, *The Open Night* 52, *The Whispering Gallery* (autobiography) 55, *I Am My Brother* (autobiography 2) 60, *Ancestors and Friends* 62, *Collected Poems* 63, *Christ the Hunter* 65, *The Ample Proposition* (autobiography) 66, *A Nest of Tigers* 68, and editor of many anthologies and symposia.
85 Cornwall Gardens, London, S.W.7. England.

Lehmann, Lotte; American singer; b. 27 Feb. 1888.
Sang at Vienna State Opera, Metropolitan Opera, New York, Covent Garden, London and in most countries of Europe, and throughout the U.S.A. and South America and Australia; Hon. Pres. Music Acad. of the West, Santa Barbara and Dir. of the Vocal Dept.; Golden Palm of France, Officer of the Legion of Honour, Golden Medal of Sweden, Golden Medal of Austria, Cross of Honour First Class (Austria), Great Cross of Germany; four honorary degrees.
Publs. *Midway in my song, More than singing, My many lives, Eternal Flight, Five operas and Richard Strauss.*
4565 via Huerto, Hope Ranch, Santa Barbara, Calif., U.S.A.

Lehmann, Maurice; French theatrical director; b. 19 Jan. 1895; ed. Paris Conservatoire.
Former Pensionnaire Comédie Française; Dir. at several Paris theatres, and of numerous films; Gen. Admin. Réunion des Théâtres Lyriques (Opéra and Opéra Comique) 51-55, Hon. Dir. 55-; mem. Council, Ordre des Arts et des Lettres: Commdr. Légion d'Honneur, Croix de Guerre (1914-18), Grand Croix du Nicham-Iftikhar, etc.
15 rue d'Andigné, Paris 16e, France.
Telephone: TRO-88-42.

Lehmann, Rosamond Nina (sister of John Lehmann, q.v.); British novelist; ed. Girton Coll., Cambridge.
Publs. *Dusty Answer* 27, *A Note in Music* 30, *Invitation to the Waltz* 32, *The Weather in the Streets* 36, *No More Music* (play) 39, *The Ballad and the Source* 44, *The Gypsy's Baby* 46, *The Echoing Grove* 53, *The Swan in the Evening* 67.
70 Eaton Square, London, S.W.1, England.

25

Lehmann, Wilhelm, D.PHIL.; German writer; b. 4 May 1882; ed. Univs. of Tübingen, Strasbourg, Berlin and Kiel.
Soldier 17-19; teacher in various schools; Kleistpreis 23; Kunstpreis Schleswig-Holstein 52; Lessingpreis Hamburg 53; Grosses Verdienstkreuz; Schiller Gedächtnispreis 59, Kulturpreis der Stadt Kiel 63.
Publs. novels and stories: *Der Bilderstürmer* 17, *Die Schmetterlingspuppe* 18, *Weingott* 21, *Vogelfreier Josef* 22, *Der Sturz auf die Erde* 23, *Der bedrängte Seraph* 24, *Verführerin Trösterin* 47, *Ruhm des Daseins* 53, *Der stumme Laufjunge* 56, *Der Überläufer* 64; poetry: *Antwort des Schweigens* 35, *Der grüne Gott* 42, *Entzücker Staub* 46, *Noch nicht genug* 50, *Überlebender Tag* 54, *Meine Gedichtbücher* 57, *Abschiedslust* 62, *Reclamauswahl* 63; autobiography: *Mühe des Anfangs* 52; critical: *Dichtung als Dasein* 56, *Kunst des Gedichts* 61; essays: *Bukolisches Tagebuch* 48, *Bewegliche Ordnung* 56, *The Complete Works* (3 vols.) 62, *Dauer des Staunens* 63, *Sichtbare Zeit* 67.
Lützowweg 5, 233 Eckernförde, Schleswig-Holstein, German Federal Republic.

Lehnartz, Emil Friedrich Robert, C.B.E., M.D.; German university professor; b. 29 June 1898; ed. Cologne, Frankfurt a.M., and Freiburg i.Br.
Asst. Physiological-Chemical Inst., Frankfurt a.M. 26; Reader of Physiology 29, Extra. Prof. 35; Chief Asst. Physiological Inst., Göttingen 35; Dir. of Physiological-Chemical Inst., Münster i.W. 39-66, Prof. 46; Rector, Münster Univ. 46-49; Chair. Deutsche-Englische Gesellschaft; Dr. Phil. h.c. and Dr. h.c.
Publs. *Die chemischen Vorgänge bei der Muskelkontraktion* 33, *Lehrbuch der Physiologie für Studierende der Zahnheilkunde* (with E. Fischer) 34, *Einführung in die Chemische Physiologie* (11th edition) 59; collaborated in *Ernährungslehre* (Editor W. Stepp) 39, *Handbuch der Biologie* (Editor L. v. Bertalanffy) and *Die Ernährung* (Editors K. Lang and R. Schön); Joint Editor: *Physiologische Chemie* (with B. Flaschenträger), Hoppe-Seyler/Thierfelder *Handbuch der Physiologisch- und Pathologisch-Chemischen Analyse* (10th edn., with K. Lang and G. Siebert), *Klinische Wochenschrift* (co-editor), *Medizinische Klinik* (co-editor), *Deutsches Medizinisches Journal* (co-editor).
Maldmedyweg 11, 44 Münster i.W., German Federal Republic.
Telephone: 45415.

Lehto, Reino Ragnar; Finnish civil servant and politician; b. 2 May 1898; ed. Helsinki Univ.
Solicitor, Turku 22-32; Sec. to Chancellor of Justice 33-34; Solicitor to Landed Property Bank 34-36; Cabinet Counsellor and Sec.-Gen. Ministry of Commerce and Industry 36- (leave of absence 63-64); Chief Sec. Delegation for War Reparation Industries 44-48; Dir. Outokumpu Oy, Valmet Oy, Neste Oy, Oy Rego AB, Merikiito Oy, Orijärvi Oy; Prime Minister 63-64; Gov. of Uusimaa 64-; several decorations.
Nuorimichenkatu 11A, Helsinki, Finland.

Lei Jen-min; Chinese administrator; b. 10; ed. Tanyuan People's Normal School and France.
Joined Chinese Communist Party 28; post in North China People's Govt. 48; Head, Exec. Dept., Internal Affairs, Central Govt. 49, Vice-Dir. Trade Dept.; on China Cttee. for the Promotion of International Trade; Vice-Minister of Foreign Trade 52-; All-China Fed. of Industry and Commerce 53; Vice-Chair. China Cttee. for the Promotion of International Trade 55-.
China Committee for the Promotion of International Trade, Peking, China.

Leibholz, Gerhard, DR. JURIS., DR. PHIL.; German scholar; b. 15 Nov. 1901; ed. Berlin and Heidelberg.
Asst. Judge 26; Referent Inst. for Public Law, Berlin 26; Lecturer in Constitutional and Int. Law, Berlin 28; Judge 28; Prof. of Public Law and Political Science,

Greifswald 29-31, Göttingen 31-35, Prof. Emeritus Jan. 36-58; Fellowship World Council of Churches, and Magdalen Coll., Oxford 39-48; Prof. Göttingen 58-, Coll. of Europe, Bruges 54-; Assoc. Justice Fed. Constitutional Court (Germany) 51-; Editor *Jahrbuch des öffentlichen Rechts* 51-.
Publs. *Fichte und der demokratische Gedanke* 21, *Zu den Problemen des faschistischen Verfassungsrechts* 28, *Die Auflösung der liberalen Demokratie und das autoritäre Staatsbild* 33, *Il Secolo XIX e lo Stato totalitario* 38, *Syndicalisme, Corporatisme et Etat Corporatif* 39 (2nd ed. 58), *Christianity, Politics and Power* 42, *Macht und Ideologie im 20 Jahrhundert* 49, *Staat und Gesellschaft in England* 50, *Der Strukturwandel der Demokratie* 52, *Demokratie und Rechtsstaat* 57 (3rd edn. 67), *Volk, Nation, Staat im 20 Jahrhundert* 58 (3rd edn. 67), *Strukturprobleme der modernen Demokratie* 58 (3rd edn. 67; Korean trans. 62), *Die Gleichheit vor dem Gesetz* (2nd edn. 59), *Das Wesen der Repräsentation* (3rd edn.) 66, *Verfassungsrecht und Arbeitsrecht* 60, *Verbot des Ermessensmissbrauches im Völkerrecht* (2nd edn.) 64, *Conceptos fundamentales de la Politica* 64, *Politics and Law* 65, *Kommentar zum Bonner Grundgesetz* 66 (3rd edn. 68) (with Dr. Rinck), *Stellung der Industrie-und Handels kammern* 66, *Demokratie und Erziehung* 67.
Federal Constitutional Court, Rheingoldstrasse 19, 75 Karlsruhe; Dahlmannstrasse 6, Göttingen, German Federal Republic.
Telephone: Karlsruhe 26888; also Göttingen 57040.

Leimena, Johannes; Indonesian physician and politician; b. 05; ed. Medical School, Djakarta.
Asst. in Govt. and private hospitals 30-42; Doctor-in-charge Govt. Hospitals, Purwakarta and Tanggerang 42-45; Minister of Health 46-53 and 55-56; Minister of Social Affairs 57; Third Deputy Prime Minister 57; Senior Adviser, Ministry of Health 53-55 and 56-59; Third Vice-Premier 59; Dep. Chief Minister and Minister of Distribution 59-64; Second Vice-Premier and Minister of Distribution 64; mem. Christian Political Party.
Djakarta, Indonesia.

Leimgruber, Oscar, DR. JUR.; Swiss public servant; b. 5 July 1886; ed. Fribourg, Berne and Vienna Univs.
Co-Dir. Cantonal Office of Arts and Crafts (Industrial Museum, Fribourg) 08-12; founder and Ed. *L'artisan et commerçant romands* 09-25; Ed. *Liberté* and *Freiburger Zeitung* 07-09; Cantonal advocate Uri; entered Federal State Service 12, first as mem. then Deputy Chief, Legal Dept. 12-19; Gen. Sec. Federal Post and Railways Dept. 19-25; founder and mem. Board Int. Middle Class Union 23; founder int. review *La Classe Moyenne*; organiser and Sec. first Int. Middle-Class Congress Berne and Interlaken 24; Gen. Commissar Congress, World Union of mems. of Parliaments 24; Founder and Deputy Pres. Int. Middle-Class Inst. 03; Founder-Pres. Int. Inst. of Admin. Sciences 30; Pres. a.i. World Union of Int. Orgs.; Deputy Chancellor of Swiss Confederation 25-43, Chancellor 44-52; mem. Int. Acad. of Political Sciences, Swiss Section UNESCO, Central Cttee. Swiss Conservative People's Party and of Swiss Roman Catholic People's Union; Founder and Hon. Pres. Swiss Soc. for Nat. Admin.
Publs. *Le problème social et la classe moyenne, Les buts et les tâches de l'Union Internationale des Classes moyennes, Bericht über den ersten Internationalen Mittelstandskongress* 24, *Rationalisierung und Mittelstand, Gott und der Staat, Volk und Staat, Die Rationalisierung in Staat und Gemeinde, Christliche Wirtschaftsordnung und Mittelstand, Der Dienstvertrag nach schweizerischem Recht, Was Gläubiger und Schuldner von der Schuldbetreibung wissen müssen, Der Nachlassvertrag nach schweiz. Recht, Die Rationalisierung in den öffentlichen Verwaltungen, Dictionnaire populaire du droit usuel suisse, Manuel de droit civil à l'usage de l'hôtelier suisse, etc.*
Südbahnhofstrasse 17, Berne, Switzerland.

Leinsdorf, Erich; American (b. Austrian) musician; b. 4 Feb. 1912; ed. Univ. of Vienna and State Acad. of Music, Vienna.

Assistant Conductor, Salzburg Festival 34-38; U.S.A. 37-; Conductor, Metropolitan Opera 37-43; Music Dir. and Conductor Cleveland Orchestra 43; Music Dir. Philharmonic Orchestra, Rochester 47-56; Dir. New York City Center Opera 56, Metropolitan Opera 57-62; Music Consultant, Metropolitan Opera Management 58-62; Music Dir. Boston Symphony Orchestra 62-; Dir. Berkshire Music Center, Festival 63-; mem. Exec. Cttee. John F. Kennedy Center for the Performing Arts; Guest Conductor, Philadelphia Orchestra, New Orleans, Concertgebouw Amsterdam, San Francisco Orchestra, Vienna Opera, London Symphony and Israel Philharmonic Orchestras, etc.; Bayreuth, Holland and Prague Festivals; Fellow American Acad. of Arts and Sciences; Hon. music degrees (Rutgers Univ. and Baldwin-Wallace and Williams Colls.).
Symphony Hall, Boston, Mass. 02115, U.S.A.
Telephone: 617-266-1492.

Leiper, Henry Smith, B.A., D.D., M.A.; American ecclesiastic; b. 17 Sept. 1891; ed. Blair Acad., Amherst Coll., Columbia Univ., and Union Theological Seminary. Travelling Sec. Student Volunteer Movement 13-14; ordained Presbyterian Church 15; transferred to Congregational Church 20; acting Pastor Rutgers Presbyterian Church New York City 14-16; served with Army Y.M.C.A. Siberia 18; missionary American Board of Commrs. for Foreign Missions Tientsin 18-22, Asst. Sec. of the Board N.Y. 22-23; mem. Gov. Board China Int. Famine Comm. 19-20; mem. Chinese Int. Friendship Del. to Japan 21; Editor Congregational Nat. Council's Comm. on Missions 23-29; Assoc. Corresp. Sec. American Missionary Asscn. 24-27; Acting Pastor American Church, Paris 32; special preacher St. Paul's Cathedral, London 43; co-founder World Communion Sunday Observance; mem. American Famine Comm. to India 46, Official Church Visitor Australian Jubilee 51; World Council Faith and Order Conf. Lund, Sweden 52; Chair. Vellore Medical Coll. Board, N.Y. 53-59; Gen. Sec. American Conf. of World Council of Churches in America 48-52; Assoc. Gen. Sec. World Council of Churches 48-52; Consultant, World Council of Churches Assembly 54; Minister and Exec. Sec., Missions Council of Congregational Christian Churches 52-59; Sec. American and Foreign Christian Union 35-, Friends of the World Council of Churches 48-; Dir. Dept. of Religion, Chautauqua 59-; Special Sec. American Bible Soc. 59-; mem. Council on Foreign Relations; Editor *Ecumenical Courier* 48-52; contrib. *Encyclopaedia Britannica*.
Publs. *Blind Spots—Experiments in Cure of Race-Prejudice* 29, *The Ghost of Caesar Walks: The Conflict of Nationalism and World Christianity* 35, *Christ's Way and the World's: in Church, State, and Society* 36, *World Chaos or World Christianity* 38; jointly: *Younger Churchmen Look at the Church, The Church Through Half a Century, Protestantism, U-Boat to Pulpit, Pilgrimage to Amsterdam, Protestant Thought in the 20th Century* (co-author) 51, *We Believe in Prayer* (co-author) 59, *In Memoriam Dietrich Bonhoeffer* 63, *The World in Miniature* 63; Edited world symposium *Christianity Today* 47, *Herald of the Evangel—60 Years of American Christianity* (co-author) 65, *S. Parkes Cadman—Ecumenical Prophet and Advocate* 67.
1 Paulin Boulevard, Leonia, N.J., U.S.A.
Telephone: 944-8136.

Leiper, Robert Thomson, C.M.G., D.SC., M.D., LL.D., F.R.S., F.R.C.P., J.P.; British helminthologist; b. 17 April 1881; ed. Birmingham and Glasgow Univs.
Mem. Egyptian Govt. Survey, Uganda 07; Helminthologist, Grouse Diseases Inquiry Cttee. 09; Dir. Prosectorium, Zoological Gardens London 19-21; Consultant

Parasitologist Royal Army Medical Corps; Bilharzia Missions, Egypt 15-16 and 28; awarded West London Triennial Gold Medal, Straits Settlement Gold Medal, Mary Kingsley Medal; mem. Colonial Office Advisory Medical Cttee. 40-45; mem. Council of Royal Society, London 39-41; former Pres. Tropical Diseases and Comparative Medicine Sections, Royal Society Medicine; corresp. mem. Helminthological Society, Washington, Belgian Society Tropical Medicine, etc.; Prof. Emeritus of Helminthology Univ. of London; Dir. Dept. Parasitology London School of Hygiene and Tropical Medicine 17-46; mem. Council Royal Society of Tropical Medicine and Hygiene 16-22; Dir. Inst. of Agricultural Parasitology, St. Albans 23-46; Dir. Commonwealth Bureau of Helminthology 46-58; Founder *Journal of Helminthology*; Hon. mem. American Soc. of Parasitologists, Nat. Inst. of Sciences of India, British Veterinary Asscn., British Soc. for Parasitologists; corresp. mem Soc. Pathologie Exotique, Paris; Order of Ismail (2nd Class) Egypt, Bernhard Nocht Medal, Hamburg 61.
Normansland Farm, Wheathampstead, Herts., England.

Leitão da Cunha, Vasco; Brazilian diplomatist and politician; b. 2 Sept. 1903; ed. Univ. do Brasil.
Diplomatic Service 29-, Minister 43; Consul-Gen., then Chargé d'Affaires in Rome 45-46; Ambassador to Belgium, Cuba, U.S.S.R., and Portugal 54-64; Minister of Foreign Affairs 64-65; Ambassador to U.S.A. 65-; numerous Brazilian and foreign decorations.
Brazilian Embassy, 3007 Whitehaven Street, N.W., Washington, D.C., U.S.A.

Leith-Ross, Sir Frederick William, G.C.M.G., K.C.B.; British financial administrator; b. 4 Feb. 1887; ed. Merchant Taylors' School, and Balliol Coll., Oxford.
Appointed to Treasury 09; Private Sec. to Prime Minister 11-13; Asst. Sec. to Treasury 19 and to Cabinet 20; British mem. of Finance Board of Reparations Comm. 20-25; Deputy Controller of Finance in Treasury 25-32; Chief British Expert at Hague Conf. 30 and Lausanne Conf. 32; Chief Econ. Adviser to the Govt. 32-46; Del. World Econ. Conf. 33; mem. War Debts Mission to U.S. 33; Chair. Industrial Property Conf. 34; negotiated financial agreements with Germany 34, Italy 35; financial mission to China 35; Del. Int. Sugar Conf. London 37; Dir.-Gen. Min. of Economic Warfare Sept. 39-Mar. 42; British rep. and Chair. Inter-allied Cttee. on Post-War Requirements 41; Deputy Dir. European Regional Office U.N.R.R.A. 44-45; Chair. European Cttee. U.N.R.R.A. 45-46; Gov. Nat. Bank of Egypt May 46-51; Deputy Chair. Nat. Provincial Bank Ltd.; Dir. Standard Bank Ltd. and Nat. Discount Co. 51-66.
Publ. *Money Talks* 68.
St. Olaves, Bowring Road, Ramsey, Isle of Man.
Telephone: Ramsey 2451.

Leitz, Guenther; German businessman; b. 14 Oct. 1914.
Managing Dir. Ernst Leitz G.m.b.H., Wetzlar, Ernst Leitz (Canada) Ltd., Midland, Ontario.
Burweg 8, Wetzlar, German Federal Republic; and Ruby Street, Midland, Ont., Canada.

Leivo-Larsson, Tyyne; Finnish politician; b. 3 March 1902.
Member Child Welfare Board 34-49; Chair. 45-59; Chair. Social Democratic Women's League 47-59, 65-; mem. and Deputy Chair. Helsinki City Council 47-56; mem. of several State cttees.; Minister of Social Affairs 48-50 and 54-57, 58; Dep. Prime Minister 58; Dir. Social Museum, Helsinki 40-58; Vice-Pres. Finnish Red Cross Org. 50-54; mem. Del. to UN 56-57, 66; Head Del. to Econ. and Soc. Council, UN 57-58; Amb. to Norway 58-65, and to Iceland 59-65; re-elected mem. of Parl

66-; mem. of Parl. Del. to the Congress of I.P.U. 66-67; mem. Nordic Councils Finnish Groups 66-67, 68.
Temppelikatu 15, Helsinki, Finland.
Telephone: Helsinki 499353.

Lejeune, Jules Nicolas Gaston Jean-Marie, D. ès SC., D. ès SC. COM.; Belgian university professor; b. 10; ed. Univs. of Paris and Liège and London School of Economics.
Deputy Prof. of Statistics, Univ. of Liège 36, Prof. 42-; Pres. and Prof. of Statistics, Ecole Supérieure des sciences commerciales; Pres. Admin. Council of *Review of Economic Sciences*, Liège; mem. Int. Inst. of Statistics; Vice-Pres. Belgian Statistical Soc., Nat. Bookkeeping Soc.; mem. Belgian Higher Cttee. for Statistics, Comm. on Price Indices and Nat. Revenue Comm. Scientific Council of Inst. for Economic and Social Study of the Middle Class, New York Acad. of Sciences, American Statistical Asscn. (Washington), Paris Statistical Soc.; Pres. Belgian UNA; Chevalier Légion d'Honneur, Civic Medal 1st Class, Officier Ordre de Léopold, Commdr. de l'Ordre de la Couronne.
Publs. *Les Méthodes de Construction des Index Numbers* 35, *Cours de Statistique professé à l'Université de Liège* 47, 61.
Université de Liège, Place du XX-Août 7, Liège, Belgium.

Lejeune, Michael L.; American (b. British) banking official; b. 22 March 1918; ed. Cate School, Carpinteria, Calif., Yale Univ., and Yale Univ. Graduate School.
Teacher St. Paul's School, Concord, New Hampshire 41; Volunteer in King's Royal Rifle Corps in British Army 42-46; Int. Bank for Reconstruction and Devt. 46-, Personnel Officer 48-50, Asst. to Loan Dir. and Sec. Staff Loan Cttee., Loan Dept. 50-52, Chief of Div., Europe, Africa and Australasia Dept. 52-57, Asst. Dir. of Operations, Europe, Africa and Australasia 57-63, Asst. Dir. of Operations, Far East 63-64; Dir. of Admin., Int. Bank for Reconstruction and Devt., Int. Devt. Asscn. and Int. Finance Corpn. 64-67, Dir. Middle East and North Africa Dept. 67-.
International Bank for Reconstruction and Development, Washington, D.C. 20433, Home: 626 Chain Bridge Road, McLean, Virginia 22101, U.S.A.
Telephone: EX3-6360 (Office); JA 8-0292 (Home).

Lekic, Danilo; Yugoslav diplomatist; b. 13; ed. Univ. of Belgrade.
Fought in Spanish Civil War 37-39; Army Service 41-56, Military Attaché, Washington 52-54; fmr. Army Commdr. and Insp.-Gen. of Armed Forces; Secretariat of State for Foreign Affairs 56; Yugoslav Ambassador to Brazil 57-61; Asst. Sec. of State for Foreign Affairs 61-63; Perm. Rep. of Yugoslavia to UN 63-67; Amb. to U.A.R. 67-; People's Hero Order and other Decorations.
Yugoslav Embassy, 33 Rue El Mansur Mohamed, Cairo, U.A.R.

Leloir, Luis Federico; Argentine biochemical researcher; b. 6 Sept. 1906; ed. Univ. of Buenos Aires.
Early career as research worker in U.K., Argentina, and U.S.A., Research at Inst. of Biology and Experimental Medicine, Buenos Aires 46; Dir. Inst. of Biochemical Research, Campomar 47-; Head, Dept. of Biochemistry, Univ. of Buenos Aires 62-; Chair. Argentine Asscn. for Advancement of Science 58-59; mem. Directory, Nat. Research Council 58-64; mem. Nat. Acad. of Medicine 61; Foreign mem. Nat. Acad. of Sciences, U.S.A., American Acad. of Arts and Sciences, and American Philosophical Soc.; several prizes and Dr. h.c. Univ. of Paris.
Major research includes: isolation of glucose diphosphate 48, of uridine diphosphate glucose 50, of uridine diphosphate acetylglucosamine 53, mechanism of glycogen 59, of starch biosynthesis 60, isolation of adenosine nucleotides from corn grains 64.

Instituto de Investigaciones Bioquímicas, "Fundación Campomar", Obligado 2490, Buenos Aires 28, Argentina.
Telephone: 76-2871.

Lemaignen, Robert; French businessman; b. 15 March 1893; ed. Ecole Militaire de Saint-Cyr.
War service 14-18; entered Société Commerciale d'Affrètements et de Commission 18, Pres. 42-; fmr. Man. Compagnie de Mokta el Hadid, Tharsis Sulphur Co., Cie. Salins du Midi et de Djibouti and of other commercial and industrial enterprises in North and Central Africa; Pres. Cie. Optorg, Union Financière Internationale pour le Développement de l'Afrique, Société Marocaine Métallurgique; fmr. rep. overseas territories on the council of Air France; fmr. Pres. Cttee. of French Africa, Int. Chamber of Commerce and Hon. Pres. 58, Exec. Cttee. as Pres. of the Budget; fmr. Pres. Comm. of Economic Co-operation, fmr. Vice-Pres. of the Patronat Français; fmr. Pres. Cttee. France Actuelle; mem. EEC Comm. 58-61; Pres. Groupe d'Outre-mer; mem. Acad. of Colonial Sciences; Commdr. of the Légion d'Honneur; Croix de Guerre; Médaille de la Résistance, and many foreign decorations.
Publ. *L'Europe au berceau* 64.
22 avenue Friedland, Paris 8e, France.

Lemaire, Maurice; French politician; b. 25 March 1895; ed. Ecole Polytechnique.
District Head, Northern Railways 21-37, Chief of Railway Systems, Alsace-Lorraine 37-38, Head, Fixed Installations Service 38, Dep. Dir. Eastern Railway Network 39-44, Dir. Northern Network 44; Dir.-Gen. Société Nationale des Chemins de Fer 46-49; Exec. Pres. Union Internationale des Chemins de Fer 46-51; Dep. to Nat. Assembly 51-, Minister of Construction and Building 53, 53-54, Nov. 54-Feb. 55, Sec. of State for Industry and Commerce 56-57, Pres. of Nat. Assembly Cttee. on Production and Trade 59-; Commandeur, Légion d'Honneur, Officier de l'Ordre de Léopold de Belgique.
National Assembly, Paris 7e, France; and 15 avenue de La Bourdonnais, Paris 7e, France.

Lemass, Sean F.; Irish politician; b. 15 July 1899; ed. Christian Brothers' Schools.
Fought with I.R.A. 16-22 several times imprisoned; mem. of Dáil Éireann 24-; Minister for Industry and Commerce in De Valera Govt. 32-39, Minister of Supplies 39-45, for Industry and Commerce 41-48; Tanaiste (Deputy Prime Minister) 45-48; Tanaiste and Minister for Industry and Commerce June 51-54 and 57-59; Taoiseach (Prime Minister) 59-66; Chair. Ronald Lyon Estates Dec. 66-; Managing Dir. Irish Press Ltd. 48-51; Grand Cross Order of St. Gregory the Great 48; LL.D. h.c. (Iona Coll., New Rochelle, New York) 53; D. Econ.Sc. h.c. (Nat. Univ., Ireland); LL.D. (Dublin Univ., Villa Nova Univ., Pa.).
Hillside Drive, Rathfarnham, Dublin, Ireland.

LeMay, General Curtis; American air-force officer (retd.); b. 15 Nov. 1906; ed. Ohio State Univ.
Held various mil. posts until outbreak of Second World War; in command of 305th Bombardment Group in England 42; Commanding Gen. Third Bombardment Div. 43-44; transferred to Pacific theatre of war in command 20th Bomber Command 44-45; Commdr. of the Mariana-based 21st Bomber Command 45; Deputy Chief of Air Staff Research and Development 45-47; Commdr. U.S. Air Forces in Europe 47-48; C.-in-C. Strategic Air Command 48-57; Vice-Chief of Staff U.S. Air Force 57-61, Chief of Staff 61-64, now Chair. Networks Electronic Corpn.; Distinguished Service Cross, Distinguished Service Medal with two Oak Leaf Clusters, Silver Star, Distinguished Flying Cross with two Oak Leaf Clusters, Air Medal with three Oak Leaf Clusters, Medal for Humane Action and the Mackay Trophy, etc.; foreign decorations: British D.F.C.,

Commdr. Legion of Honour and Croix de Guerre with Palm Leaf (France), Belgian Croix de Guerre with Palm Leaf, Brazilian Order of the Southern Cross, Commdr. Moroccan Order of the Ouissam Alaouite Chérifien, Russian Order of Patriotic War, Argentine Order of Aeronautical Merit; several honorary degrees.
Networks Electronic Corpn., 9750 De Soto Ave., Chatsworth, Calif., U.S.A.

Lemberger, Dr. Ernst; Austrian diplomatist; b. o6; ed. Univ. of Vienna.
Served Paris 46, Foreign Office, Vienna 48-50, Washington 48-55, Foreign Office 55-58, Ambassador to Belgium 58-63, to European Economic Community (EEC) 60-65, to U.S.A. 65-.
Austrian Embassy, 2343 Massachusetts Avenue, N.W., Washington, D.C., U.S.A.

Leme, Hugo de Almeida; Brazilian agricultural specialist; b. 17; ed. Escola Superior de Agricultura Luiz de Queiroz.
Associate Prof., Escola Superior de Agricultura Luiz de Querioz, Piracicaba, (Univ. of São Paulo) 39-40, Prof. 40, Full Prof. 44, 46-, Vice-Dir. 58-60, Dir. 60-64; Minister of Agriculture 64-66; mem. Council for Agricultural Reform, State of São Paulo; has attended and organised numerous confs.; Ford Motor Company Prize for work on the mechanization of agriculture 61.
c/o Ministerio da Agricultura, Rio de Janeiro, Brazil.

Lemieux, Raymond Urgel, B.SC., PH.D., F.R.S.; Canadian chemist; b. 16 June 1920; ed. Univ. of Alberta, Edmonton, and McGill Univ., Montreal.
Research Fellow, Ohio State Univ. 47; Asst. Prof., Univ. of Saskatchewan 48-49; Senior Research Officer, Nat. Research Council 49-54; Prof., Univ. of Ottawa 54-61; Fellow, Chemical Inst. of Canada 53, Royal Society of Canada 55, Royal Society (London) 67; Chemical Inst. of Canada Medal 64; C. S. Hudson Award, American Chemical Soc. 66; Hon. D.SC. (Univ. of New Brunswick).
Publs. over 100 research papers mostly appearing in *Canadian Journal of Chemistry*.
7602 119th Street, Edmonton, Alberta, Canada.

Lemke (von Soltenitz), Helmut, DR. IUR.; German lawyer and politician; b. 29 Sept. 1907; ed. Univs. of Kiel, Tübingen and Heidelberg.
Naval officer in Second World War; Public Prosecutor; Mayor of Eckernförde, Schleswig, Lübeck; Barrister at Law; Minister of Educ., Schleswig-Holstein 54-56, Minister of Interior 55-63; Pres. German Fed. Council 66-67 (as such for a time Acting Pres. German Federal Republic); mem. State Diet 55-, mem. Bundesrat 55-; Minister-Pres. of Schleswig-Holstein 63-; Grand Cross of Fed. German Order of Merit and other decorations; Chair. Christian Democratic Union (C.D.U.) in Schleswig-Holstein.
Landeshaus, Kiel, Schleswig-Holstein, German Federal Republic.
Telephone: 5961.

Lemmer, Ernst; German journalist and politician; b. 28 April 1898; ed. Marburg Univ.
Secretary-General of the German Democratic Trade Union (Gewerkschaftsring) 22; member of the Reichstag (Democratic Party) for province of Pomerania 24-33; Berlin corresp. of Swiss *Thurgauer Zeitung* and *Neue Zuercher Zeitung* 33; Joint Chair. Christian Dem. Union, Berlin, Dec. 45; elected Soviet Zone Free German Trade Union Feb. 46 (resgnd.); Second Chair. Christian Dem. Union June 46 (temporarily not in action by order of the SMA); Chief Editor of the Berlin evening paper *Der Kurier* May 49; mem. West Berlin House of Reps. and Leader of C.D.U. Party in Berlin; mem. German Fed. Parl., Bonn, Council of Europe, Strasbourg; Postmaster-Gen. 56-57; Fed. Minister for All-German Affairs 57-62, for Refugee Affairs 64-65;

Deputy Chair. of C.D.U. Party in Bundestag 62-65; Special Rep. of Fed. Chancellor in Berlin.
1 Berlin 30, Schaffenbergstr. 14, Germany.
Telephone: 132112; also 2126360.

Lemnitzer, Gen. Lyman L.; American army officer; b. 29 Aug. 1899; ed. U.S. Military Acad.
Commissioned 20; pupil Coast Artillery School 20-21; served Fort Adams, R.I. 21-23; served Philippines 24-26; Instructor, U.S. Mil. Acad. 26-30; pupil, Coast Artillery School 30-31; served in Philippines 31-34; Instructor, U.S. Mil. Acad. 34-35; pupil, Commd. and Gen. Staff School 35-36; Instructor, Coast Artillery School 36-39; pupil, Army War Coll. 39-40; Bn. Commdr. 70th Coast Artillery 40; served with War Dept. Gen. Staff 41; Commdr. 34th A.A. Brigade 42; served in Europe and North Africa 42-45; with Joint Chiefs of Staff 45-47; Deputy Commdt. Nat. War Coll. 47-49; Asst. to Sec. of Defence 48 (part-time) 49-50 (full-time); pupil, Airborne Course Ft. Benning 50; Commdr. 11th Airborne Div. 51; 7th Infantry Div. (in Korea) 51-52; Deputy Chief of Staff (Plans and Research) 52-55; Commdr. U.S. Army Forces, Far East and Eighth U.S. Army April 55; C.-in-C. Far East and U.N. Commands and Gov. of the Ryukyu Islands June 55-July 57; Vice-Chief of Staff, U.S. Army 57-59, Chief of Staff 59-60; Chair. Joint Chiefs of Staff 60-62; C.-in-C. U.S. Forces in Europe 62-; Supreme Allied Commdr. in Europe (NATO) 63-; D.S.M., Silver Star, Legion of Merit, Legion of Merit (Officer's Degree), C.B. (Great Britain), C.B.E., Grand Croix Légion d'Honneur, Croix de Guerre (with Palm), and Brazilian, Polish, Italian, Czechoslovak, Yugoslav, Ethiopian, Korean, Colombian, Thai, Chilean, Chinese, Philippine and Japanese decorations.
SHAPE, B. 7010, Belgium.

Le Moal, Henri Jean Alain; French university rector; b. 21 Dec. 1912; ed. Lycée La Tour d'Auvergne, Quimper and Univ. of Rennes.
Military service 38-44; Asst., Faculty of Science, Univ. of Rennes 45-47, Chef de Travaux 47-53, Asst. Prof. 53-57, Prof. of Gen. Chemistry 57, Dean 58-60, Rector, Acad. of Rennes 60-; Chevalier, Légion d'Honneur, Commdr. des Palmes Académiques, Commdr. de l'Ordre National de la République de la Côte d'Ivoire, Commdr. de l'Ordre du Mérite Sportif; Hon. DD.L. Univ. of Exeter.
Home: 19 Boulevard de Sévigné, Rennes, France.

Lemus, Lieut.-Col. José Maria; Salvadorean army officer and politician; b. 11; ed. School and Acad. of Military Staff, San Salvador, and Military Staff School, Camp Lee, U.S.A.
Under-Sec. of Defence 48-49; Minister of the Interior 49-55; Pres. of the Republic of El Salvador 56-60, deposed Oct. 60; Gran Cordon Orden del Libertador (Venezuela), Gran Cruz Orden del Mérito Civil (Spain).
Publs. many military and political works, including *Pensamiento Social de Don Bosco, Simón Bolívar, Símbolos Patrios*, etc.
Guatemala City, Guatemala.

Lenárt, Jozef; Czechoslovak politician; b. 3 April 1923; ed. Party Coll. Moscow.
Member Czech underground movement, Second World War; took part in Slovak rising 44; mem. C.P. of Czechoslovakia 43-; mem. Central Cttee. C.P. of Slovakia 51-; Leading Sec. Bratislava Regional Cttee. C.P. of Slovakia 56-58; Central Cttee. C.P. of Czechoslovakia 58-; Sec. Central Cttee. Slovak C.P. 58-62; Chair. Slovak Nat. Council 62-63; Prime Minister of Czechoslovakia 63-68; Alt. mem. Presidium of Central Cttee. of Czechoslovak C.P. 68-; Decoration for Merit in Construction 58; Order of the Nile 65.
Prague, Czechoslovakia.

Leness, George John; American investment banker; b. 17 May 1903; ed. Mass. Inst. of Technology and Harvard Univ.

Member Buying Dept., Harris Forbes & Co., N.Y.C. 27-31, later Chase Harris Forbes Corpn. 31-34; with First Boston Corpn. 34-43, Vice-Pres. 39-43; Pres. Merrill Lynch, Pierce, Fenner & Smith Inc. 61-65, Chair. & Chief Exec. 65-; Dir. Sinclair Oil Corpn.

Merrill Lynch, Pierce, Fenner & Smith Inc., 70 Pine Street, New York City 5, U.S.A.

Le Ngoc Chan; Vietnamese barrister and diplomatist; b. 1 July 1915; ed. Faculty of Law, Hanoi.

Member Leadership Cttee. of Viet-Nam Quoc-Dan-Dang (Viet-Nam Nationalist Party), arrested several times 47-49; Barrister, Saigon Court of Appeal 52-; Founder-mem. Leadership Cttee. Nat. Solidarity Peace Movement 53; Sec. of State for Nat. Defence 54; Counsellor to French Union Assembly 55; then mem. Tu-Do Tien-Bo (Democracy and Progress) Bloc; detained Nov. 60-Aug. 63; Amb. to Tunisia 65-67, to U.K. 67-.

Office: Embassy of Republic of Viet-Nam, 12 Victoria Road, London, W.8; Home: Clock House, 4 Windmill Road, London S.W.19, England.

Lengyel, Menyhért Melchior; Hungarian writer and dramatist; b. 12 Jan. 1880.

First success with play *The Great Prince* 07; lived in Switzerland 14-18; theatre dir., Budapest 29; moved to London 31, to U.S.A. 37; now lives in Italy; Grand Prix, Rome 63.

Works include: libretto for Bartók's pantomime *The Miraculous Mandarin; Typhoon* (play) 07; film scripts for Hollywood: *To Be or Not to Be, Angel, Cat, Ninochka* (with Greta Garbo).

Via Porta Pinciana 16a, Rome, Italy.

Lennep, Jonkheer Emile van, DR.JUR; Netherlands lawyer and economist; b. 20 Jan. 1915; ed. Amsterdam Univ.

Foreign Exchange Inst. 41-45; Netherlands Bank 45-48; Financial Counsellor to High Commr., Indonesia 48-49; Head of Financial Dept. of Netherlands High Commr. in Indonesia 49-50; Netherlands Bank 50-51; Treasurer-Gen. in Netherlands Ministry of Finance 51-; mem. Board of Dirs. of K.L.M., and of Nat. Investment Bank of the Netherlands (Herstelbank); Chair. Monetary Cttee. E.E.C.; Knight, Order of Netherlands Lion, Officer, Order of Orange Nassau; Grand Officier Ordre de la Couronne du Chêne (Luxembourg); Knight Commdr's. Cross (Star) of the Order of Merit of the Federal Republic of Germany.

34 Van der Burchlaan, The Hague, Netherlands.

Lenz, Hans; German politician; b. 12 July 1907; ed. Univs. of Tübingen, Paris, London, Berlin and Reykjavík.

Director, Publishing Houses for Scientific Literature, Breslau, Brno and Vienna 36-43; served Second World War, severely wounded 43-45; Acting Dir. Acad. of Music, Trossingen 47-51; Admin. Dir. Hohner Foundation 51-53; mem. Free Democratic Party (F.D.P.) 48-; mem. Bundestag 53-, mem. Budget Cttee., Vice-Chair. F.D.P. Parl. Group 57-; Vice-Chair. F.D.P. Fed. Exec. Board 60-; Fed. Minister of Fed. Property 61-62, for Atomic Energy and Power 62-65.

Trossingen/Württ., Karpfenstrasse 10, German Federal Republic.

Lenz, Siegfried; German writer; b. 17 March 1926; ed. High School, Samter, and Univ. of Hamburg.

Cultural Editor *Die Welt* 49-51; freelance writer 52-; Gerhart Hauptmann Prize 61, Bremer Literaturpreis 62. Publs. novels: *Es waren Habichte in der Luft* 51, *Duell mit dem Schatten* 53, *So Zärtlich War Suleyken* 55, 62, *Der Mann im Strom* 57, 58, *Brot und Spiele* 59, *Stadtgespräch* 63; stories: *Jäger des Spotts* 58, *Das Feuer-*

schiff 60; plays: *Zeit der Schuldlosen* 61, *Das Gesicht* 63, *Haussuchung* (radio plays) 67.

Oberstrasse 72, Hamburg 13, German Federal Republic.

León-Portilla, Miguel, M.A., PH.D.; Mexican anthropologist and historian; b. 26; ed. Loyola Univ. of Los Angeles and Nat. Univ. of Mexico.

Secretary-General, Inter-American Indian Inst. 55-59, Asst. Dir. 59-60, Dir. 60-66; Asst. Dir. Seminar for Náhuatl Culture, Nat. Univ. of Mexico 56-; Dir. *América Indígena* 60-; Dir. Inst. of History, Nat. Univ. of Mexico 63-; Adviser, Int. Inst. of Different Civilisations 60-; mem. American Anthropological Asscn. 60-, Mexican Acad. of the Language 62-, Corresp. to Royal Spanish Acad. 62-.

Publs. *La Filosofía Náhuatl* 56, *Visión de los Vencidos* 59, *Los Antiguos Mexicanos* 61, *The Broken Spears, Aztec Account of the Conquest of México* 62, *Rückkehr der Götter* 62, *Aztec Thought and Culture* 63, *Literaturas Precolombinas de México* 64, *Imagen del México Antiguo* 64, *Le Crépuscule des Aztèques* 65, *Trece Poetas del Mundo Azteca* 67, *Pre-Columbian Literatures of Mexico* 68.

Alberto Zamora 103, Coyoacán, Mexico 21, D.F., Mexico.

Leone, Giovanni; Italian professor and politician; b. 3 Nov. 1908.

Professor of Law, Univ. of Naples; elected to Constituent Assembly 46, to Chamber of Deputies 48 and 53; Vice-Pres., Chamber of Deputies 48-49, Pres. 55-63; Prime Minister 63-Nov. 63, June 68-; Christian Democrat.

Chamber of Deputies, Rome, Italy.

Leonhardt, Rudolf Walter, DR. PHIL.; German journalist; b. 9 Feb. 1921; ed. Berlin, Leipzig, Bonn, Cambridge and London.

Lecturer in German, Cambridge Univ. 48-50; Foreign Corresp. *Die Zeit*, London 53-55, Cultural Editor *Die Zeit*, Hamburg 57-.

Publs. *The Structure of a Novel* 50, *Notes on German Literature* 55, *77 x England* 57 (trans. into Spanish 64), *Der Sündenfall der deutschen Germanistik* 59, *Leben ohne Literatur?* 61, *x-mal Deutschland* 61 (trans. into English, Italian, Spanish 64), *Zeitnotizen* 63, *Junge Deutsche Dichter für Anfänger* 64, *Reise in ein Fernes Land* (with Marion Gräfin Dönhoff and Theo Sommer) 64 (trans. into Japanese 65); *Kästner für Erwachsene* 66.

Elbchaussee 81, Hamburg, German Federal Republic. Telephone: 388157.

Leoni, Raúl, DR. RER. POL.; Venezuelan lawyer and politician; b. 05; ed. Bogotá, Colombia.

Founder mem. ORVE political movement 35; Founder mem. Nat. Democratic Party 37, now Acción Democrática; Minister of Labour 45-48; in exile 49-58; Pres. Acción Democrática 58-; Pres. of Venezuela 64-.

Office of the President, Caracas, Venezuela.

Leonov, Col. Alexei Arkhipovich; Soviet cosmonaut; b. 34; ed. Chuguevsky Air Force School for Pilots and Zhukovsky Air Force Engineering Academy.

Pilot 56-59; cosmonaut training 60; took part in flight of space-ship *Voskhod 2*, and moved 5 metres into space outside space-ship; mem. C.P.S.U. 57-; Pilot-Cosmonaut of U.S.S.R.; Hero of the Soviet Union.

Zvezdny Gorodok, Moscow, U.S.S.R.

Leonov, Arseni Alexandrovich; Soviet politician; b. 1901; ed. Timiryazev Agricultural Acad.

Member C.P.S.U. 21-; Head of an agricultural school, Moscow Region 25-30; mem. staff Moscow Regional Planning Cttee. 30-40; Vice-Chair. State Planning Cttee. of Estonian S.S.R. 40-41, 43-59, Chair. 48-51; Perm. Rep. of Estonian S.S.R. Council of Ministers to U.S.S.R. Council of Ministers 51-; Deputy to Estonian Supreme Soviet; Red Banner of Labour (twice), Badge of Honour and other awards.

Permanent Representation of Estonian S.S.R. Council of Ministers to U.S.S.R. Council of Ministers, Sobinovsky pereulok 5, Moscow, U.S.S.R.

Leonov, Leonid Maximovich; Soviet writer; b. 1899; ed. Moscow Univ.
Deputy to Supreme Soviet; State Prize 42, Lenin Prize 57, Order of Lenin 46, 59, Hero of Socialist Labour 67. Publs. *Bazsuky* 24, *The Thief* 27, *Sotj* 30, *Skutazevsky* 32, *Road to the Ocean* 36, *The Ordinary Man* 41, *Lenushka* 43, *The Fall of Velikoshumsk* 44, *The Golden Car* 46, *Sazancha* 59, *Mr. McKinley's Flight* 61, *Evgenia Ivanovna* 63, *Plays* 64.
Union of Soviet Writers, 52 Vorovsky Street, Moscow, U.S.S.R.

Leonov, Pavel Artyomovich; Soviet politician; b. 1918; ed. Moscow Bauman Higher Technical School.
Member C.P.S.U. 44-; technologist 42-45; party official 45-61; First Sec. Sakhalin Regional Cttee. C.P.S.U. 60-; Alt. mem. Central Cttee. of C.P.S.U. 61-; Deputy to U.S.S.R. Supreme Soviet.
Sakhalin Regional Committee, Communist Party of the Soviet Union, Yuzhno-Sakhalinsk, U.S.S.R.

Leontovich, Mikhail Alexandrovich; Soviet theoretical physicist; b. 03; ed. Moscow Univ.
Works in field of electro-dynamics, optics, statistical physics and radio-physics; worked at the Inst. of Physics of Moscow Univ. 29; mem. U.S.S.R. Acad. of Sciences; the Lebedev Inst. of Physics 34-52; Inst. of Atomic Energy; awarded Popov Gold Medal 52, Lenin prizewinner 58.
Publs. *Statistical Physics* 44, *Introduction to Thermodynamics* 52.
Atomic Energy Institute, U.S.S.R. Academy of Sciences, Ul. Kurchatova 46, Moscow, D-182, U.S.S.R.

Léopold III; fmr. King of the Belgians; b. 3 Nov. 1901. Son of King Albert; married Princess Astrid (died 35), niece of King Gustav V of Sweden 26; succeeded 34; Commander-in-Chief Armed Forces May 40; married Mlle. Mary Lilian Baels Sept. 41; abdicated July 16, 1951, in favour of his son, King Baudouin, b. 30.
Domaine Royal d'Argenteuil, Poste Waterloo, Belgium.

Lepeshinskaya, Olga Vasilievna; Soviet ballerina; b. 16; ed. Moscow School of Choreography.
Danced with the Bolshoi Theatre Ballet Company 33-62; ballet teacher 62-; People's Artist of U.S.S.R. 54; State prize-winner 41, 46, 47, 50.
Principal rôles: Cinderella (*Cinderella* by Prokofiev), Jeanne (*Flames of Paris* by Asafiev), Swanhilda (*Coppelia* by Delibes), Tao Tkhoa (*Red Poppy* by Glière).
State Academic Bolshoi Theatre of the U.S.S.R., Ploshchad Sverdlova, Moscow, U.S.S.R.

Lépine, Pierre Raphaël, M.D., L.SC.; French scientist; b. 15 Aug. 1901; ed. Univ. of Lyons.
Instructor of Parasitology 24; Doctor of Medicine 25; Prof. of Pathology, American Univ., Beirut 25-26; Asst. Coll. de France 27; Chief of Lab., Institut Pasteur 28; Dir. Institut Pasteur Hellénique, Athens 30-35; Chief, Rabies Div., Institut Pasteur 36, Chief of Virus Research 40-; Visiting Prof. Institut de Microbiologie et d'Hygiène, Univ. of Montreal 47-53; Pres. European Asscn. against Poliomyelitis 52; mem. WHO Experts Panel on Rabies, Influenza and Polio; Fellow N.Y. Acad. of Sciences; mem. Nat. Acad. of Medicine, Paris; mem. Acad. of Sciences, Paris, Pontifical Acad. of Sciences; Hon. foreign mem. Acad. Royale de Médecine de Belgique; Commdr. de la Légion d'Honneur.
Institut Pasteur, 25 rue du Dr. Roux, Paris 15e, France.

Le Portz, Yves; French financial executive; b. 30 Aug. 1920; ed. Univ. de Paris à la Sorbonne, Ecole des Hautes Etudes Commerciales, and Ecole Libre des Sciences Politiques.
Attached to Gen. Inspectorate of Finances 43, Ministry of Finance and Econ. Affairs 51; French Del. to Econ. and Social Council of UN 57-58; Dir.-Gen. of Finance for Algeria 58-62; Dir.-Gen. Bank for Devt. of Algeria 59-62; Vice-Chair. European Investment Bank 62-.
European Investment Bank 2 place de Metz, Luxembourg; Home: 127 avenue Wagram, Paris 17e, France.

Leprette, Jacques; French diplomatist; b. 22 Jan. 1920; ed. Univ. of Paris and Ecole Nationale d'Administration.
Ministry of Foreign Affairs (European Div.) 47-49, Counsellor, Council of Europe 49-52; Head, Political Div., French Military Govt.; Counsellor, French Embassy, U.S.A. 55-59; Ministry of Foreign Affairs (African Div.) 59-61; Ambassador to Mauritania 61-64; Dir. Int. Liaison Service for Information 64-65; Minister-Counsellor, Washington 66-; Chevalier de la Légion d'Honneur, Croix de Guerre, Bronze Star Medal.
8 Allée du Grand Tulipier, Ville d'Avray, S.-et-O., France; French Embassy, 2535 Belmont Road, N.W., Washington D.C., U.S.A.

Leprince-Ringuet, Louis; French scientist; b. 27 March 1901; ed. Lycée Louis-le-Grand, Ecole Polytechnique and Ecole Supérieure d'Electricité et des P.T.T.
Worked as engineer and did research on cosmic rays and fundamental particles physics; Prof. at Ecole Polytechnique 36-; Pres., Société française de physique 56; mem. Académie des Sciences (Physics) 49-; mem. Académie Française 66-; Dir. of Laboratory at Ecole des Hautes Etudes Pratiques; mem. Atomic Energy Comm.; Prof. of Nuclear Physics at Collège de France 59-; Vice-Pres. CERN Scientific Council, Pres. 64-.
Publs. *Rayons Cosmiques, Les Inventeurs Célèbres, Les Grandes Découvertes du XXe siècle, Des Atomes et des Hommes, La Science Contemporaine.*
Ecole Polytechnique, 17 rue Descartes, Paris 5e, France.

Leray, Jean, D. ès sc.; French mathematician; b. 7 Nov. 1906; ed. Ecole Normale Supérieure.
Professor Faculty of Sciences, Nancy 36-41, Paris 41-47; Prof. of Differential and Functional Equations, Collège de France 47-; mem. Inst. de France; Foreign Assoc. Nat. Acad. of Sciences (U.S.A.); Foreign mem. U.S.S.R. Acad. of Sciences, and Acad. of Sciences of Boston, Brussels, Göttingen, Palermo and Turin; Officier Légion d'Honneur.
Publs. papers on mathematics and mechanics.
12 rue Pierre Curie, 92-Sceaux, France.

Lercaro, H.E. Cardinal Giacomo; Italian ecclesiastic; b. 20 Oct. 1891.
Ordained priest 14; Archbishop of Ravenna and Cervia 47-52, of Bologna 52-68; created Cardinal by Pope Pius XII 53; mem. Sacred Congregations of the Council, of Religious and of Seminaries and Univs. of Study; mem. Pontifical Comm. for Biblical Studies; Moderator Ecumenical Council 63-65; Pres. Consilium ad Exsequendam de Sacra Liturgia until Jan. 68.
Vatican City, Rome, Italy.

Lerner, Alan Jay; American theatrical writer and producer; b. 31 Aug. 1918; ed. Bedales, England, Choate, U.S.A., Harvard Univ.
Free-lance radio script-writer 41-.
Productions: Stage: *The Patsy* 42, *What's Up?* 43, *The Day Before Spring* 45, *Brigadoon* 47, *Love Life* 48, *Paint Your Wagon* 61, *My Fair Lady* 56, *Camelot* 60, *On a Clear Day You Can See Forever* 64; Films: *A Royal Wedding* 51, *An American in Paris* 51, *Brigadoon* 54, *Gigi* 58.
4 West 58th Street, New York City, N.Y., U.S.A.

Lerner, Max, A.B., A.M., PH.D.; American writer; b. 20 Dec. 1902; ed. Yale and Washington (St. Louis) Univs., Robert Brookings Graduate School of Economics and Govt.

Asst. Editor *Encyclopædia of the Social Sciences* 27, later Managing Editor; mem. Social Science Faculty Sarah Lawrence Coll. Bronxville (N.Y.) 32-36; Chair. Faculty Wellesley Summer Inst. 33-35; Dir. Consumers' Div. Nat. Emergency Council 34; Lecturer Dept. of Govt. Harvard Univ. 35-36; Editor *The Nation* 36-38; Prof. of Political Science Williams Coll. 38-43; Contrib. Editor *New Republic* 40-45; Editorial Dir. *PM* New York 43-48; Columnist *N.Y. Star* 48-49; radio commentator *WOR* 44-47; Columnist *New York Post* 49-; Prof. of American Civilisation, Brandeis Univ. 49-; Ford Foundation Prof. American Civilisation, School of Int. Studies, New Delhi, India 59-60; Internationally-syndicated newspaper columnist 59-; Ford Foundation Research and Study Grant, Paris 63-64.
Publs. *It is Later Than You Think* 38, *Ideas Are Weapons* 39, *Ideas for the Ice Age* 41, *The Mind and Faith of Justice Holmes* 43, *Public Journal* 45, *The World of the Great Powers* 47, *Actions and Passions* 48, *America as a Civilisation* 57, *The Unfinished Country* 59, *Essential Works of John Stuart Mill* 61, *Education and a Radical Humanism* 62, *The Age of Overkill* 62, *Tocqueville's Democracy in America* 66, *The Life and Thought of Thomas Jefferson* 67.
445 East 84th Street, New York City, N.Y., U.S.A.
Telephone: Regent 7-3416.

Lernet-Holenia, Alexander; Austrian novelist and playwright; b. 21 Oct. 1897.
Publs. *Ollapotrida* 26, *Das Geheimnis Sankt Michaels* 27, *Die Abenteuer eines jungen Herrn in Polen* 31, *Jo und der Herr zu Pferde* 33, *Die Standarte* 34, *Die Neue Atlantis* 35, *Die Goldene Horde* 35, *Die Auferstehung des Maltravers* 36, *Der Baron Bagge* 36, *Der Mann im Hut* 37, *Strahlenheim* 38, *Ein Traum in Rot* 39, *Beide Sizilien* 41, *Die Trophae* 46, *Mars in Widder* 47, *Germanien* 47, *Der 20 Juli* 47, *Spanische Komödie* 48, *Der Graf von Saint-Germain* 48, *Das Feuer* 49, *Die Wege der Welt* 52, *Die Inseln unter dem Winde* 52, *Die drei Federn* 53, *Der junge Moncada* 54, *Der Graf Luna* 55, *Das Finanzamt* 55, *Das Goldkabinett* 57, *Die vertauschten Briefe* 58, *Die Schwäger des Königs* 58, *Die wahre Manon*, *Der wahre Werther* 59, *Prinz Eugen* 60, *Mayerling* 60, *Naundorff* 61, *Das Halsband der Königin* 62, *Das Bad an der belgischen Küste* 63, *Götter und Menschen* 64, *Drei Gesellschaftsstücke* 65, *Die Weisse Dame* 65, *Pilatus* 67.
Hofburg, Vienna I, Austria.
Telephone: 52-40-333.

Le Roux, Pieter Mattheus Kruger; South African politician; b. 11 Nov. 1904; ed. Outeniqua High School, Univ. of Stellenbosch.
Farmer; Chair. Klein Karoo Agricultural Co-operative Soc.; Dir. Kango Tobacco Co-operative Soc.; M.P. 42 and 48-; Chief Whip 55; Minister of Agriculture, Technical Services and Water Affairs 58-66, of Interior 66-.
17 Bryntirion, Pretoria, South Africa.

Lesage, Jean, P.C., M.P.P., Q.C., LL.D., B.A.; Canadian lawyer and politician; b. 10 June 1912; ed. Laval Univ.
Practised law, Quebec Bar; Crown Attorney 39-44; mem. Parl. for Montmagny-l'Islet 45-58; Parl. Asst. to Sec. of State for External Affairs 51, to Minister of Finance 53; Minister of Resources and Development Sept.-Dec. 53, of Northern Affairs and National Resources Dec. 53-57; Canadian Rep. to U.N. Gen. Assembly 50 and 52; led Canadian Del. to ECOSOC, Geneva 51, New York 52; Pres. U.N. Technical Asst. Conf. Paris 52; Leader Liberal Party in Quebec 58; Premier of Quebec 60-66, concurrently Minister of Finance and Minister of Federal-Provincial Affairs 61-66; D.Iur. h.c. 61.
Quebec Liberal Party, Montreal, Quebec, Canada.

Lesch, George H., B.S.; American business executive; b. 10 Oct. 1909; ed. Monmouth Coll., Illinois, and Univ. of Illinois.

Accountant, Arthur Andersen and Co. (Chicago) 31-32, Colgate-Palmolive Co. 32-39; Office Man. Colgate-Palmolive S.A. (Mexico) 39-48, Exec. Vice-Pres. and Gen. Man. 48-55; Vice-Pres. Colgate-Palmolive Int. 55-57, Pres. 57-60; Pres. Colgate-Palmolive Co. 60-61, Chair. Board and Pres. 61-.
Colgate-Palmolive Co., 300 Park Avenue, New York 22, N.Y., U.S.A.

Lesechko, Mikhail Avksentyevich; Soviet engineer and government official; b. 1909; ed. Moscow Aviation Inst.
Former turner, technologist and factory man. 36-45; with Council of Ministers State Cttee. for Introduction of New Equipment 46-48; Dir. Moscow Counting-Analytical Equipment 48-54; First Deputy Minister of Machine Instrument Making 54-56; Minister of Instrument Making and Automation 56-57; First Vice-Chair. Ukrainian S.S.R. State Planning Cttee. 57-58; First Vice-Chair. State Planning Cttee. 58-60; Chair. of Comm. for Foreign Econ. Affairs, attached to Presidium of Council of Ministers 60-62, Deputy Chair. U.S.S.R. Council of Ministers 62-; mem. C.P.S.U. 40-, Central Cttee. C.P.S.U. 61-; Deputy to U.S.S.R. Supreme Soviet; mem. Cttee. of Parliament Group, Inter-parliamentary Union; State prizewinner 57.
U.S.S.R. Council of Ministers, The Kremlin, Moscow, U.S.S.R.

Lesieux, Louis; French airline official; b. 16 May 1907; ed. Ecole Polytechnique and Ecole Nationale des Ponts et Chaussées.
Engineer and Chief Engineer of Roads and Bridges, Niort, Lille and Nice; Dir.-Gen. of Paris Airport 48-55, Dir. 55-; Dir.-Gen. of Air France 55-67, Hon. Dir.-Gen. 67-; Commdr. Légion d'Honneur; several foreign decorations.
Office: Compagnie Générale d'Electricité, 54 rue Laboétie, Paris 8e; Home: 61 avenue Kléber, Paris 16e, France.
Telephone: KLE 06-59.

Lesky, Albin, D.PHIL.; Austrian university professor; b. 7 July 1896; ed. Akademisches Gymnasium, Graz and Univs. of Graz and Marburg.
Privatdozent, Univ. of Graz 24-31; Prof., Vienna Univ. 32-35; Prof. Innsbruck Univ. 36-49; Prof. of Classics, Vienna Univ. 49-67, Prof. Emeritus 67-; Sec. Austrian Acad. of Sciences 59-63, Vice-Pres. 63-; Vice-Pres., Int. Thesaurus Cttee. 67-; Hon. mem. Dublin Acad., Corresp. Fellow British Acad., Corresp. mem. Bavarian Acad., Acad. des Sciences morales et politiques, Heidelberg Acad., Acad. of Athens and Acad. of Stockholm; Wilhelm Hartel Prize, Austrian Acad. of Sciences 59, Österreichisches Ehrenzeichen Pro Litteris et Artibus, Purkyně Medal, Univ. of Brno, Dr. h.c. (Innsbruck, Athens, Ghent, Glasgow), Hon. Senator (Vienna).
Publs. *Alkestis, der Mythos und das Drama* 25, *Die griechische Tragödie* 38 (4th edn. 68, English trans. 65, Spanish trans. 66), *Der Kommos der Choephoren* 43, *Thalatta: Der Weg der Griechen zum Meer* 47, *Aristainetos* 50, *Die Tragische Dichtung der Hellenen* 56 (2nd edn. 64), *Geschichte der griechischen Literatur* 57-58 (Italian, Greek and English trans., 2nd edn. 63), *Göttliche und menschliche Motivation im homerischen Epos* 61, *Homeros* 66.
Alserstrasse 69/17, A-1080 Vienna VIII, Austria.
Telephone: 42-30-115.

Leslie, John Charles, B.S., M.S.; American airline executive; b. 21 July 1905; ed. Phillips Exeter Acad., Princeton Univ., and Mass. Inst. of Technology.
Fokker Aircraft Co. of U.S. 28; Asst. to Chief Engineer, Pan American World Airways 29, Asst. Div. Engineer, Miami 29-35, Div. Engineer, Pacific Div., San Francisco 35-38, Div. Operations Man. 38-41, Man. Atlantic Div., New York 41-45, Vice-Pres. System Office 46, Vice-

Pres. Admin. and Dir. 50, Vice-Pres. and Asst. to Pres 59-64, Vice-Pres. and Asst. to Chair. 64-.
Home: 8 Murray Hill Road, Scarsdale, N.Y.; Office: Pan American World Airways, Pan Am Building, New York, N.Y. 10017, U.S.A.

Leslie, Sir John Randolph (Shane Leslie), Bt., LL.D.; British author; b. 85; ed. Eton and Cambridge Univ. Publs. incl. *The Isle of Columcille, The End of a Chapter, Doomsland, The Greek Anthology, The Anglo-Catholic, The Cantab, The Epic of Jutland, The Oxford Movement, The Passing Chapter, The Script of Jonathan Swift, The Skull of Swift, Mrs. Fitzherbert* (play), *Men Were Different: Studies in Late Victorian Biography* 37, *Sir Evelyn Ruggles-Brise* 38, *Sublime Failures, The Life and Letters of Mrs. Fitzherbert* (2 vols.) 49, *Salutation to Five* 51, *Lives of Cardinal Manning and Cardinal Gasquet* 54, *Shane Leslie's Ghost Book* 55, *Long Shadows* 65.
Castle Lesley, Glaslough, Ireland; 5 Morpeth Mansions, London, S.W.1, England.

Lesser, Most Rev. Norman Alfred, M.A., TH.D., D.D.; British ecclesiastic; b. 16 March 1902; ed. Liverpool Collegiate School, Fitzwilliam House and Ridley Hall, Cambridge.
Curate, Anfield 25-26, Formby 26-29; Curate-in-Charge Norris Green 29-30; Chaplain of Cathedral, Liverpool 30-31; Vicar, Barrow-in-Furness 31-39; Hon. Canon, Rector and Sub-Dean, All Saints Cathedral, Nairobi 39-47; Provost of Nairobi 42-47; Bishop of Waiapu 47-; Primate and Archbishop of New Zealand 61-.
Bishop's Court, Napier, New Zealand.

Lessing, Doris May; British writer; b. 22 Oct. 1919; ed. Roman Catholic Convent, and Girls' High School, Salisbury, Southern Rhodesia.
Somerset Maugham Award 54.
Publs. include: *The Grass is Singing* 50, *This was the Old Chief's Country* 51, *Martha Quest* 52, *Five* 53, *A Proper Marriage* 54, *Retreat to Innocence* 56, *Going Home* 57, *The Habit of Loving* 58, *Each His own Wilderness* (play) 58, *A Ripple from the Storm* 58, *In Pursuit of the English* (reportage) 60, *The Golden Notebook* 62, *Play With a Tiger* (play) 62, *A Man and Two Women* 63, *African Stories* 64, *Landlocked* 65, *Winter in July* 66, *Particularly Cats* 67, *The Four Gated City* 68.
60 Charrington Street, London, N.W.1, England.

Lesz, Mieczysław, DR. ING.; Polish politician; b. 20 May 1911; ed. Polytechnic School, Lwów.
Member Resistance Movement, Second World War; Econ. Admin. 45-53; Deputy Chair. Planning Comm., Council of Ministers 54-57; Minister of Home Trade 57-; mem. Polish Workers' Party 45-48, Polish United Workers' Party 48-, Deputy mem. Central Cttee. 59-65; First Deputy Chair. Cttee. of Science and Technology 66-.
1 Plac Powstańców Warszawy, Warsaw; Krakowskie-Przedmiescie 1, Warsaw, Poland.

Leszczycki, Stanisław Marian, PH.D.; Polish geographer; b. 07; ed. Jagiellonian Univ., Cracow.
Assistant, Jagiellonian Univ., Cracow 28-39; imprisoned in Dachau and Sachsenhausen concentration camps during Second World War; Deputy to Seym Parliament) 45-49; Extraordinary Prof. of Anthropogeography, Jagiellonian Univ., Cracow 45-47; Prof. of Economic Geography, Warsaw Univ. 48-; Vice-Minister of Foreign Affairs 46-50; Pres. Polish Geographical Soc. 50-53; Pres. Nat. Geographical Cttee.; Pres. Cttee. of Space Econ. and Regional Planning Polish Acad. of Sciences 58-; Dir. Geographical Inst., Polish Acad. of Sciences 53-; mem. Council of Polish Acad. of Sciences 52-; Vice-Pres. Int. Geographical Union 64-; Hon. mem. many European Geographical Societies; fourteen foreign and Polish decorations.
30 Krakowskie Przedmieście, Warsaw, Poland.
Telephone: 260328.

Letavet, Avgust Andreyevich; Soviet hygienist; b. 1893; ed. Moscow Univ.
Army Physician 17-18; physician in Kursk Region 18-19; Head of Sanitary Inspectorate, Senior Asst., Head of Section, Head of Lab., Dir., Inst. of Occupational Hygiene and Occupational Diseases 19-; Corresp. mem., U.S.S.R. Acad. of Medical Sciences 45-50, mem. 50-; Head of Dept., Central Inst. for Postgraduate Medical Training 31-55; Academician-Sec., Dept. of Hygiene and Microbiology, U.S.S.R. Acad. of Medical Sciences 57-66; Chair. All-Union Soc. of Hygienists; Deputy Chair., Comm. for Prevention of Silicosis; Vice-Pres. Int. Fed. for Hygiene and Preventive Medicine; Hon. mem. Purkyně Medical Soc. (Czechoslovakia); Order of Lenin 51, 63, Red Banner of Labour 45, 49, 54, Badge of Honour 61, State Prize 49.
Publs. Over 100 works on Hygiene of Labour, particularly on microclimate at industrial enterprises, physiology of labour and radiation hygiene.
Institute of Occupational Hygiene and Occupational Diseases, Meyerovsky proyezd 31, Moscow, U.S.S.R.

Leünberger, Hermann; Swiss trade union official; b. 15 July 1901; ed. secondary school.
Union of Commercial, Transport and Food Workers 28, Gen. Sec. 33; Pres. Int. Union of Food and Drink Workers 39-49; mem. Swiss Parliament 39-; Pres. Union of Commercial, Transport and Food Workers 42; Pres. Swiss Fed. of Trade Unions 58-; Vice-Pres. European Regional Org. of ICFTU 61-.
Schweizerischer Gewerkschaftsbund, Monbijoustrasse 61, Berne, Switzerland.

Leusse, Comte Pierre de; French diplomatist; b. 24 Dec. 1905.
Attaché, French Embassy, Berne 31, Washington 33; Sec. in Vienna 35, Prague 38; Chief Sec. High Commission, Beirut 38; Aide-de-Camp to Gen. Weygand 39; Consul, Lugano 41; office revoked by Vichy Govt. 42; rep. of French Cttee. of National Liberation in Switzerland 42; Counsellor, London 44; Dir. Dept. for German and Austrian Affairs, Paris 45; Dir. Central Europe Dept. 46; Dir. Press and Information Services 50; Ambassador to Poland 54-56; Perm. Rep. to NATO 59-62; Ambassador to Morocco 62-65; Perm. Rep. to NATO 65-67; Amb. to Algeria 67-; Mayor of Reichshoffen; Commdr. de la Légion d'Honneur.
Home: 4 rue de Talleyrand, Paris 7e; Office: Embassy of France, 8 rue Sahara, Hydra, Algiers, Algeria.

Leussink, Hans, DR.ING., DIPL.ING.; German university professor; b. 2 Feb. 1912; ed. Technische Hochschule, Dresden, and Technische Hochschule, Munich.
Manager, Soil Mechanics Inst., Technische Hochschule, Munich 39-46; Construction eng. office 46-54; Prof. and Dir. of Inst. for Soil Mechanics and Rock Mechanics, Univ. of Karlsruhe 54-, Rector Technische Hochschule, Karlsruhe 58-61; Pres. West German Conf. of Univ. Rectors, Bad Godesberg 60-62; at Council of Europe, Strasbourg 62-; mem. German Scientific Council 64-, Chair. 65-; mem. Advisory Council for Science Policy of Fed. Govt. 67-, Board of Dirs. Krupp Foundation 67-.
75 Karlsruhe-Durlach, Strählerweg 45, German Federal Republic.
Telephone: Karlsruhe 42668.

Levard, Georges; French trade union official; b. 24 March 1912; ed. Conservatoire National des Arts et Métiers.
Member of Nat. Cttee. for Productivity; mem. Econ. Council 47-59, Vice-Pres. 59-; mem. Higher Council of the Plan; mem. several other councils; mem. Federal Bureau and Vice-Pres. of French and Democratic Confederation of Labour (C.F.T.C.) 46-48, Asst. Sec.-Gen. 48-53, Sec.-Gen. 53-61, Pres. 61-67; Dir. Banque Nationale de Paris; Conseiller d'Etat 66-.

Publs. *L'âme du syndicalisme chrétien, Eléments d'action syndicale, Rapport sur la Réforme de l'entreprise.*
c/o French and Democratic Confederation of Labour, 26 rue de Montholon, Paris 9e, France.

Lévárdi, Dr. Ferenc; Hungarian mining engineer and politician; b. 19; ed. Grammar School, Esztergom, and Sopron Technical Univ., Candidate in Technical Science. Assistant Lecturer in Geophysics and Mine Metrology, Sopron Technical Univ. 44-47; Mining Engineer, later Chief Engineer, Production Man., and Dir. Dorog Coal Mining Trust 47-58; First Dep. Minister of Heavy Industry 58-63, Minister 63-; mem. Communist Party 47-; Pres. Hungarian Mining and Metallurgical Soc. 60-66; Pres. Mining Cttee., Hungarian Acad. of Sciences.
Ministry of Heavy Industry, Markó-U. 16, Budapest V, Hungary.
Telephone: 115-400.

Levasseur, Francis; French diplomatist; b. 29 Aug. 1914; ed. Inst. Saint-Aspais, Melun, Lycée de Nice, Law Faculty, Univ. of Paris, and Ecole Libre des Sciences Politiques.
Chef de Cabinet to French Resident-Gen., Rabat 45-48; Sub-Dir., Personnel Dept. Ministry of Foreign Affairs 49-53; Counsellor, Rio de Janeiro 53; Dir. du Cabinet, French Resident-Gen., Rabat 54-55; Counsellor, Ottawa 56-61; Sub-Dir. for African and Madagascan Affairs, Ministry of Foreign Affairs 62-63, Asst. Dir. 63; Ambassador to Upper Volta 63-; Officier, Légion d'Honneur, Croix de Guerre.
French Embassy, B.P. 504, Ouagadougou, Upper Volta.

Lever, Sir Ernest (Harry), LL.D., F.I.A.; British industrialist; b. 22 Nov. 1890.
Former Chair. Richard Thomas & Baldwin's Ltd., Steel Co. of Wales Ltd.; Dir. Lloyds Bank Ltd.; Chair. Monks Hall & Co. Ltd., Tinplate Conf. (1925) Ltd., The Whitehead Thomas Bar & Strip Co., Welsh Plate and Sheet Manufacturers' Asscn.; fmr. Dir. British Sheet Trading Co. Ltd., African Metals Ltd.; fmr. Joint Sec. Prudential Assurance Co. Ltd.
Blackbrook Farm, Dorking, Surrey, England.
Telephone: Dorking 6422.

Levesque, Very Rev. Father Georges Henri; French-Canadian ecclesiastic; b. 03; ed. Ecole des Frères Maristes (Roberval), Séminaire de Chicoutimi, Couvent d'Etudes des Dominicains (Ottawa) and Catholic Univ. of Lille.
Dominican Novitiate 23-24, ordained Priest 28; in Europe 30-33; Lecturer, Coll. des Dominicains d'Ottawa 33-38, Univ. of Montreal 35-38, Laval Univ. 36-; first Dir. Faculté des Sciences Sociales, Laval Univ., and Prof. 38; Founder-Pres. Quebec Co-operative Council 39; exec. on Advisory Council to Minister of Labour 41-51; Prédicateur Général of his Order 43; mem. Royal Comm. on the development of art, sciences and letters in Canada 49; Pres. Canadian Political Science Asscn. 51; Co-Dir. in India of the Int. Seminar of the World Univ. Service; Rector of La Maison Montmorency 55-; Vice-Chair. Canada Council 57; mem. Canadian Royal Soc.; hon. degrees from Univs. of British Columbia, Manitoba, Antigonish, Toronto, Saskatchewan, Ottawa, St. Joseph and Western Univ.; Légion d'Honneur.
Publs. include: *Capitalisme et Catholicisme* 36, *Le pluralisme démocratique, condition de l'unité canadienne* 48, *Culture et Civilisation* 50, *Humanisme et Sciences Sociales* 52, *Le Chevauchement des Cultures* 55, *Service Social, Industrialisation et Famille* 56, *Youth and Culture To-day* 61, *Les Universités* 61.
La Maison Montmorency, 2490 avenue Royale, Courville, Quebec 5, Canada.

Levey, Michael Vincent, M.V.O., M.A. (husband of Bridgid Brophy, *q.v.*); British art historian; b. 8 June 1927; ed. Oratory School and Exeter Coll., Oxford.
Officer, British Army 45-48; Asst. Keeper Nat. Gallery 51-66, Deputy Keeper 66-68, Keeper 68-; Slade Prof. of Art Cambridge Univ. and Fellow of King's Coll. Cambridge 63-64.
Publs. Edited Nat. Gallery Catalogues: *18th Cent. Italian Schools* 56, *The German School* 59, *Painting in XVIIIth c. Venice* 59, *From Giotto to Cézanne* 62, *Later Italian Pictures in the Royal Collection* 64, *Dürer* 64, *Rococo to Revolution* 66, *Fifty Works of English and American Literature We Could do Without* (with Brigid Brophy and Charles Osborne) 67, *Brozino* 67, *Early Renaissance* 67.
185 Old Brompton Road, London, S.W.5, England.

Levi, Carlo; Italian writer and artist; b. 29 Nov. 1902. Left medical profession for painting; banished to Southern Italy during Fascist régime; Dir. *L'Italia Libera* (daily), Rome 45-46; contrib. articles and drawings to *L'Italia Socialista* 47-48 and *La Stampa* 49-.
Publs. *Cristo si è fermato a Eboli* (Christ Stopped at Eboli) 45, *Paura della libertà* 46, *L'Orologio* 50, *Le Parole sono Pietre* 55, *Il Futuro Ha Un Cuore Antico* 56, *La Doppia Notte Dei Tigli* 59, *Tutto il Mièle e Finito* 64, etc.
Via Di Villa Ruffo 31, Rome, Italy.
Telephone: Rome 359988.

Levi, Doro, PH.D.; Italian archæologist; b. 98; ed. Florence and Rome Univs.
Member Italian Archæological School, Athens 21-23; conducted excavations in Crete 24 and in Chiusi, Vetulonia, Volterra, Massa Marittima 26-31; Insp. of Antiquities in Florence 26, later Dir.; Organiser Italian Mission in Mesopotamia 30, first expedition to Kakzu (Assyria) 33; Lecturer Florence Univ. 31; Prof. of Archæology and History of Classical Art in Univ. of Cagliari 35; Dir. of Art and Antiquities in Sardinia; Dir. Museums of Cagliari and Sassari 35-38; mem. Inst. for Advanced Study, Princeton, N.J.; lectureships at Princeton and Harvard Univs. 39-45; Guggenheim Fellow 41-43; Dir. Italian Archæological School at Athens and Dir. Italian Archæological Expeditions in the Levant 47-; conducted excavations at Phaistos, Gortyna, Crete, Anatolia, Cyrene, etc.; mem. Accad. dei Lincei, Rome, The N.Y. Acad. of Sciences, etc.
Publs. *Arkades, Una Città Cretese all'alba della civiltà ellenica* (Annuario Scuola It. di Atene X-XII), *La necropoli etrusca del Lago dell' Accesa* (in *Monumenti Antichi Lincei XXXV*) 33, *Corpus Vasorum Antiquorum: Florence, I-II, Il Museo Civico di Chiusi* 35, *Early Hellenic Pottery of Crete* 45, *Antioch Mosaic Pavements* 47, *L'ipogeo di S. Salvatore di Cabras in Sardegna* 49, *L'arte romana* 50, *L'archivio di cretule a Festos,* etc. (*Annuario Scuola Atene XXXV-XXXVI,* 57-58) and other papers in *Annuario, Bollettino d'Arte, La Parola del Passato, The Recent Excavations at Phaistos* 64.
56 Amalias Avenue, Athens, Greece.

Levi, Edward Hirsch; American lawyer and university professor; b. 26 June 1911; ed. Univ. of Chicago and Yale.
Assistant Prof. Univ. of Chicago Law School 36-40, Prof. of Law 45-, Dean of Law Faculty 50-65, Provost 62-, Pres. of Univ. of Chicago 68-; Special Asst. to Attorney-Gen. U.S. Washington 40-45; mem. Research Advisory Board, Cttee. for Econ. Devt. 51-54, Citizens' Comm. on Graduate Medical Educ. 64-66; Chair. Council on Educ. in Professional Responsibility 66-; Fellow American Acad. of Arts and Sciences; Fellow American Bar Foundation; mem. Council of American Law Inst. 65-; Board of Dirs. Int. Legal Center.
Publs. *Introduction to Legal Reasoning* 49, *Four Talks on Legal Education* 52, Editor *Gilbert's Collier on Bankruptcy* (with J. W. Moore) 36, *Elements of the Law* (with R. S. Steffen) 50.
The University of Chicago, 5801 S. Ellis Avenue, Chicago, Illinois, U.S.A.

Levi Sandri, Lionello, LL.D.; Italian politician and government official; b. 5 Oct. 1910.
Former Prof. of Labour Law, Univ. of Rome; fmr. official in Ministry of Labour and Transport; del. to numerous int. labour confs.; Pres. of Section, State Council; mem. Comm. of the European Econ. Community Brussels 61-64, Vice-Pres. 64-67, Vice-Pres. Combined Comm. of EEC, ECSC and Euratom 67-.
Publs. *I controlli dello Stato sulla produzione industriale* 38, *Gli infortuni sul lavoro* 52, *Linee di una teoria giuridica della previdenza sociale* 53, *La tutela dell'igiene e della sicurezza del lavoro* 54, *Lezioni di diritto del lavoro* 62, *Istituzioni di legislazione sociale* 66.
Commission of the European Economic Community, 23-27 Avenue de la Joyeuse Entrée, Brussels 4, Belgium.

Lévi-Strauss, Claude; French university professor and writer; b. 28 Nov. 1908; ed. Lycée Janson de Sailly, Paris, and Univ. de Paris à la Sorbonne.
Professor Univ. of São Paulo Brazil 35-39; Visiting Prof. New School for Social Research, New York 42-45; Cultural Counseller, French Embassy to U.S.A. 46-47; Assoc. Dir. Musée de l'Homme, Paris 49-50; Dir. of Studies, Ecole Pratique des Hautes Etudes, Paris 50-; Prof. Collège de France 59-; Prix Paul Pelliot 49, Huxley Memorial Medal 65, Officier Légion d'Honneur; Foreign mem. Royal Acad. of the Netherlands, Norwegian Acad. of Sciences and Letters, American Acad. of Arts and Sciences, British Acad.; Foreign Assoc. U.S. Nat. Acad. of Sciences; Hon. mem. Royal Anthropolical Inst. and American Philosophical Soc.
Publs. *La Vie familiale et sociale des Indiens Nambikwara* 48, *Les Structures élémentaires de la parenté* 49, *Tristes Tropiques* 55, *Anthropologie Structurale* 58, *le Totémisme aujourd'hui* 62, *La Pensée Sauvage* 62, *Le Cru et le Cuit* 64, *Du miel aux cendres* 67, *L'Origine des Manières de Table* 68.
Laboratoire d'Anthropologie Sociale, 11 place Marcelin-Berthelot, 75 Paris 5e; Home: 2 rue des Marronniers, Paris 16e, France.
Telephone: 633-78-10 (Office); 288-34-71 (Home).

Levichkin, Klement Danilovich; Soviet diplomatist; b. 07; ed. Leningrad Technological Inst.
Diplomatic Service 36-; Union Control Comm., Bulgaria 45-47; Counsellor, Sofia 47-49; Deputy Head of Dept. for Balkan Affairs, Ministry of Foreign Affairs 49-52; Envoy and later Ambassador to Bulgaria 52-55; Deputy Head of Fifth European Dept., Ministry of Foreign Affairs 55-57; Deputy Perm. Rep. to UN 57-59; Head of Fifth European Dept., Ministry of Foreign Affairs 55-57; Deputy Perm. Rep. to UN 57-59; Amb. to Denmark 59-66; Deputy Minister of Foreign Affairs of R.S.F.S.R. 66-.
Ministry of Foreign Affairs of R.S.F.S.R., Prospekt Mira 79, Moscow, U.S.S.R.

Levin, Harry (Tuchman), A.B.; American teacher and writer; b. 18 July 1912; ed. Univs. of Harvard and Paris.
Instructor in English at Harvard Univ. 39-44; Associate Prof. 44-48, Prof. 48-55; Prof. of English and Comparative Literature 55-60; Chair. Dept. of Comparative Literature 46-51, 53-54, 63-; Chair. Div. of Modern Languages 51-52, 55-61; Irving Babbitt Prof. Comparative Literature 60-; Visiting Prof. Univ. of Paris 53, Salzburg Seminar in American Studies 53, Univ. of Tokyo 55, Univ. of Calif. (Berkeley) 57, Princeton Univ. 61, Indiana Univ. 67, Cambridge Univ. 67; Vice-Pres. Int. Comparative Literature Asscn. 64-67; Pres. American Comparative Literature Asscn. 65-68; mem. American Inst. Arts and Letters 60, American Acad. of Arts and Sciences 50-, American Philosophical Soc. 61-; Award of the American Inst. of Arts and Letters 47; Chevalier of the Legion of Honour 53; Award of American Council of Learned Socs. 62; Hon. Litt.D., LL.D., L.H.D.

Publs. *The Broken Column: A Study in Romantic Hellenism* 31, *James Joyce: A Critical Introduction* 41, *The Overreacher: A Study of Christopher Marlowe* 52, *Symbolism and Fiction* 56, *Contexts of Criticism* 57, *The Power of Blackness: Hawthorne, Poe, Melville* 58, *The Question of Hamlet* 59, *The Gates of Horn: A Study of Five French Realists* 63, *Refractions: Essays in Comparative Literature* 66.
400 Boylston Hall, Harvard University, Cambridge, Mass. 02138, U.S.A.

Levin, Theodore; American judge; b. 18 Feb. 1897; ed. Univ. of Detroit.
Admitted to Michigan State Bar 20; private legal practice, Detroit 20-46; U.S. District Judge, Eastern District, Michigan 46-59, Chief Judge 59-.
Federal Building, Detroit 26, Michigan, U.S.A.

Levina, Zara Alexandrovna; Soviet composer; b. 1906; ed. Odessa Conservatoire and Moscow Conservatoire.
Member Board Moscow branch, U.S.S.R. Composers' Union; mem. editorial councils of State Music Publishing House and U.S.S.R. Radio and TV Cttees; Merited Worker of Arts 67.
Compositions include: lyrical and vocal music settings for the verse of Russian, Soviet and Oriental poets, over 200 songs for children and 23 romances.
Moscow Branch, Composers' Union of the U.S.S.R., 4/6 Third Miusskaya Street, Moscow, U.S.S.R.

Levine, Jack; American artist; b. 3 Jan. 1915; studied with Dr. Denman W. Ross, and H. K. Zimmerman.
One Man exhibition Downtown Gallery, New York City 38; Artists 1942 Exhibition, Museum of Modern Art, New York City 43; exhibited at Jeu de Paume, Paris 38; Carnegie Int. Exhibitions 38, 39, 40; Retrospective Exhibitions Inst. of Contemporary Art, Boston 53, Whitney Museum of American Art N.Y. 55, Palacio de Bellas Artes, Mexico 60; Dunn Int. Exhibition, Tate Gallery London 63; pictures in Museum of Modern Art, William Hayes Fogg Museum (Harvard), Addison Gallery, Andover, Mass., etc.; mem. Nat. Inst. of Arts and Letters, American Acad. of Arts and Sciences; D.F.A. Colby Coll., Maine.
231 West 11th Street, New York City, N.Y., U.S.A.
Telephone: Yukon 9-5990.

Levis, John Preston; American businessman; b. 30 July 1901; ed. Cornell Univ.
Joined Ill. Glass Co. 24, company acquired by Owens-Ill. Glass Co. 29, Pres. 41-50, Chair. 50-; Dir. Toledo Trust Co.; mem. Board of Trustees, American Red Cross; Trustee, Nutrition Foundation.
Home: 3773 Hillandale Road East, Toledo 43606; Office: Owens-Illinois Building, Toledo, Ohio, U.S.A.

Lévis Mirepoix, Antoine Pierre Marie François Joseph, Duc de Lévis Mirepoix et de San Fernando Luis; French writer; b. 1 Aug. 1884; ed. Univ. de Paris.
Elected mem. Acad. Française 53; Président du Cincinnati de France; Gobert History Prize; Commdr. de la Légion d'Honneur; Croix de Guerre.
Publs. Novels: *Le papillon noir, Le nouvel apôtre, Le baiser de l'Antéchrist, Le seigneur inconnu, Le voyage de Satan, La vie des poupées*; historical novel: *Montségur*; memoirs: *La Touche Tréville à Naples, La Politesse*; historical works: *François Ier, Philippe le Bel, Les Trois femmes de Philippe Auguste, Sainte Jeanne de France, La France de la Renaissance, Les guerres de Religion, Le coeur secret de Saint-Simon, Vieilles races et temps nouveaux, Aventures d'une famille française, Grandeur et Misère de l'Individualisme Français, Le Roi n'est mort qu'une fois.*
30 rue de Berri, Paris 8e; and Léran, Ariège, France.

Levitin, Yury Abramovich; Soviet composer; b. 1912; ed. Leningrad Conservatoire.
Member Board Moscow Branch R.S.F.S.R. Composers' Union; State Prize 52; Merited Worker of Arts 65.

Compositions include: Suite *My Ukraine* 43, eight Quartets 40, 42, 43, 46, 48, 51, 52, 58, Sonata for violin and piano 58, Sonata for 'cello and piano 59, Sonata for flute and piano 58; Concertos: for piano and string orchestra 44, for clarinet and bassoon 49, for oboe and orchestra 60, for French horn and orchestra 61; Concertino for 'cello and orchestra without strings 62, Sinfonietta 51, three ballet suites 46, two dance suites 49, Cantatas: *Lenin Lives* 60, *Happy Beggars* 63, Oratorios: *The Sacred War* 42, *Fatherland* 47, *Requiem for Fallen Heroes* 46, *Lights Over the Volga* 47, Operas: *Monna-Marianne* 39, *Moidodyr* 55, *Memorial* 63.
Moscow Branch, R.S.F.S.R. Composers' Union, 4/6 Third Miusskaya Street, Moscow, U.S.S.R.

Levy, Hyman, M.A., D.SC., F.R.S.E.; British mathematician; b. 7 March 1889; ed. Edinburgh, Göttingen and Oxford Univs.
Mem. Aerodynamics Research Staff of the Nat. Physical Laboratory 16-20; Asst. Prof. Royal Coll. of Science 20-23; Prof. of Mathematics Imperial Coll. of Science and Technology 23-54, Emeritus 54-; Dean Royal Coll. of Science 46-52; mem. Council London Mathematical Society 29-33, Vice-Pres. 31-32; Chair. Science Advisory Cttee. of Labour Party 24-30; Editor *Proceedings of the 7th Int. Congress for Applied Mechanics* 48; Hon. A.R.C.Sc.; Hon. Fellow, Imperial Coll.; Chas. Beard Lecturer, Ruskin Coll., Oxford 62.
Publs. *Aeronautics in Theory and Experiment, Science in Perspective, Science in the Changing World, The Universe of Science, Science in Edwardian England, Makers of the Modern Spirit—Newton, Science in an Irrational Society, The Web of Thought and Action, Numerical Studies in Differential Equations* 34, *Thinking* 35, *Elements of the Theory of Probability* 36, *A Modern Philosophy* 38, *Modern Science* 39, *Elementary Mathematics* 42, *Science: Curse or Blessing?* 40, *Elements of Statistics* 44, *Social Thinking* 45, *Literature for an Age of Science* 52, *Jews and the National Question* 58, *Finite Difference Equations* 59, *Changed Lives* 67.
25 Home Park Road, London, S.W.19, England.

Levy, Walter James, LL.D.; American oil consultant; b. 21 March 1911; ed. Univs. of Berlin, Freiburg, Munich, Hamburg, Heidelberg and Kiel.
Assistant to Editor, Petroleum Press Bureau, London 37-41; Special Asst. and Chief, Petroleum Section, Office of Strategic Services; mem. of Enemy Oil Cttee. under Joint Chiefs of Staff 42-44; Special Asst. Office of Intelligence Research, Dept. of State 45-48; Consultant, Office of Dep. Admin., Chief of Oil Branch, Economic Co-operation Admin. 48-49; Economic Consultant N.Y. Sept. 49-; Consultant E.C.A. 49-50; Consultant, President's Materials Policy Comm. 51-; U.S. Oil Adviser, missions to Iran, July-Sept. 51; Consultant, Nat. Security Resources Board 52; and Policy Planning Staff 52-53; Consultant to Int. Co-operation Admin. 56-57, to Dept. of State and Office of Civil and Defense Mobilization 60, to Dept. of State, Office of Under-Sec. and Asst. Secs. 60-; Oil Adviser to the Special Emissary of Pres. Kennedy to the Pres. of Indonesia 63; Adviser to the European Econ. Community 65.
30 Rockefeller Plaza, New York, N.Y. 10020, U.S.A.
Telephone: 212-JU6-5263.

Lewandowski, Bohdan; Polish diplomatist; b. 29 June 1926; ed. Acad. of Political Sciences, Warsaw.
Polish Foreign Service in United States 46-48; Head, N. America Section, Ministry of Foreign Affairs 51-56; Dep. Dir. Dept. for U.K. and America 56-60; Polish Rep. UN Security Council 60; Perm. Rep. of Poland to UN 60-66.
c/o Ministry of Foreign Affairs, Warsaw, Poland.

Lewanika, Sir Mwanawina, III, K.B.E.; Barotseland Paramount Chief; b. c. 96; ed. Lovedale Coll. S. Africa.
Paramount Chief of Barotseland (Litunga of Barotseland Protectorate) 45-; K.B.E. (U.K.) 59.

Lealui, Barotseland Protectorate, Zambia, Central Africa.

Lewis, Anthony Carey, C.B.E., M.A., MUS.B.; British professor of music; b. 2 March 1915; ed. Wellington Coll. and Peterhouse, Cambridge.
On music staff, B.B.C. 35-46 (Music Supervisor, Third Programme 46); Peyton and Barber Prof. of Music, Univ. of Birmingham 47-68, Dean Faculty of Arts 61-64; Principal, Royal Academy of Music 68-; Chair. Music Panel, Arts Council 54-65; Pres. Royal Musical Asscn. 64-; Chair. Advisory Music Panel, British Council 66-; Founder and Gen. Editor *Musica Britannica;* Gov. Wellington Coll.; Hon. Sec. Purcell Soc.; Hon. R.A.M.
Works: Compositions: *A Tribute of Praise* (for Unaccompanied Chorus), Concerto for Trumpet and Orchestra, Concerto for Horn and Strings; Editor: *Venus and Adonis* (Blow), *The Fairy Queen* (Purcell), *Apollo and Daphne* and *Athaliah* (Handel).
Royal Academy of Music, Marylebone Road, London N.W.1, England.
Telephone: 01-935-5461.

Lewis, Bernard, B.A., PH.D., F.B.A., F.R.HIST.S.; British university professor; b. 31 May 1916; ed. Univs. of London and Paris.
Lecturer in Islamic History, School of Oriental Studies, Univ. of London 38; served R.A.C. and Intelligence Corps 40-41; attached to Foreign Office 41-45; Prof. of History of the Near and Middle East, Univ. of London 49-; Visiting Prof. of History, Univ. of California at Los Angeles 55-56, Columbia Univ. 60, Indiana Univ. 63, Princeton Univ. 64, Univ. of Calif. at Berkeley 65.
Publs. *The Origins of Ismā'ilism* 40, *Turkey Today* 40, *British Contributions to Arabic Studies* 41, *Handbook of Diplomatic and Political Arabic* 47, 56, *Land of Enchanters* (Editor) 48, *The Arabs in History* 50, 54, 56, 58, 60, 64, 66, *Notes and Documents from the Turkish Archives* 52, *The Emergence of Modern Turkey* 61, 62, 65, 68, *The Kingly Crown* 61, *Historians of the Middle East* (co-editor with P.M. Holt) 62, *Istanbul and the Civilization of the Ottoman Empire* 63, *The Middle East and the West* 64, *The Assassins* 67.
School of Oriental and African Studies, University of London, London, W.C.1, England.
Telephone: 01-580-9021.

Lewis, D. B. Wyndham, F.R.S.L.; British writer; b. 91.
Publs. *A London Farrago* 22, *At the Green Goose* 23, *At the Sign of the Blue Moon* 24, *At the Blue Moon Again* 25, *On Straw and other Conceits* 27, *François Villon* 28, *The Anatomy of Dandyism* (trans. from Barbey D'Aurevilly) 28, *A Christmas Book* (with G. C. Heseltine) 28, *King Spider: Louis XI of France* 30, *The Stuffed Owl —an Anthology of Bad Verse* (with Charles Lee) 30, *Emperor of the West* (Charles V) 32, *Take it to Bed* 44, *Ronsard* 44, *The Hooded Hawk* 47, *Four Favourites* 48, *The Soul of Marshal Gilles de Raiz* 52, *The Terror of St. Trinian's* 54, *Doctor Rabelais* 57, *A Florentine Portrait* 59, *Molière: The Comic Mask* 59, *The Shadow of Cervantes* 62.
c/o A. D. Peters, 10 Buckingham Street, Adelphi, London, W.C.2, England.

Lewis, David, B.A.; Canadian barrister and politician; b. 23 June 1909; ed. McGill Univ., Canada, and Oxford Univ.
Admitted to Bar in Canada 36; Nat. Sec. Co-operative Commonwealth Fed. of Canada 37-50, Vice-Chair. 50-54, Chair. 54-58, Pres. 58-61; mem. law firm of Jolliffe, Lewis & Osler, Toronto; helped found New Democratic Party, elected Nat. Vice-Pres. 61; M.P. 62-63, 65-.
Publ. *Make This Your Canada* (co-author).
Home: 138 Rodney Crescent, Ottawa 5; Office: Jolliffe, Lewis and Osler, Suite 1105, 85 Richmond Street W., Toronto 1, Ont., Canada.

Lewis, David Sloan, Jr., B.S.; American business executive; b. 6 July 1917; ed. Univ. of S. Carolina and Georgia Inst. of Technology.
Aerodynamicist, Glenn L. Martin Co., Baltimore 39-46; McDonnell Aircraft Corpn., St. Louis 46-, Chief Preliminary Design 52-55, Sales Man. 55-57, Vice-Pres. and Project Man. 57-60, Senior Vice-Pres. Operations 60-61, Exec. Vice-Pres. 61, Vice-Pres. and Gen. Man. 61-62, Pres. 62-67; Pres. McDonnell Douglas Co. and Chair. Douglas Aircraft Co. Div. 67-.
1451 North Amalfi Drive, Los Angeles, California, U.S.A.

Lewis, Sir Edward Roberts, Kt.; British stockbroker and businessman; b. 19 April 1900; ed. Rugby School, and Trinity Coll., Cambridge.
Member of the London Stock Exchange 25-; Chair. Decca Ltd.; Chair. The Decca Record Co. Ltd. 57-; The Decca Navigator Co. Ltd. 45-; Chair. Decca Radar Co. Ltd. 50-.
23 Rutland Gate, London, S.W.7, England.

Lewis, Hobart Durbin; American magazine executive; b. 19 Dec. 1909; ed. Princeton Univ.
Instructor Mercer Junior Coll., Princeton 34-38; Advertising Copy Writer N. W. Ayer and Son, Philadelphia 38-42; joined *Reader's Digest* 42, Exec. Editor, Vice-Pres. 61-64, Exec. Editor, Pres. 64-.
Reader's Digest, Pleasantville, New York, U.S.A.

Lewis, J. O'Neil, B.COM.; Trinidad civil servant and diplomatist; b. 4 Aug. 1919; ed. Queen's Royal Coll., Port of Spain, London School of Economics, and St. Catherine's Coll., Oxford.
Former journalist; Asst. to Economic Adviser, Govt. of Trinidad 50-53; studies in England 53-56; Asst. Economic Adviser, Planning Div., Prime Minister's Office, Trinidad 56-60, Dep. Sec. 60-61, Perm. Sec. 61-62; Head of Civil Service and Perm. Sec. Ministry of Finance 62-64; Rep. to E.E.C. 63; High Commr. of Trinidad in U.K. 64; mem. Industrial Court 65-.
5-7 Grenada Avenue, Federation Park, Port of Spain, Trinidad.

Lewis, John Llewellyn; American labour executive; b. 12 Feb. 1880; ed. public schools.
Legislative agent United Mine Workers of America 09-11; Rep. of American Fed. of Labor 11-17; Vice-Pres. United Mine Workers of America 17-18, Acting Pres. 19, Pres. 20-60, Pres. Emeritus 60-; Chair. Nat. Coal Policy Conf. 62-63; mem. Labor Advisory Board and Nat. Labor Board of Nat. Recovery Admin.; fmr. Pres. Congress of Industrial Organisations; Hon. LL.D., West Virginia Univ.; Hon. D.H.L., Georgetown Univ.
United Mine Workers' Building, Washington D.C., U.S.A.

Lewis, Neville, R.P.; South African painter; b. 8 Oct. 1895; ed. S. African Coll. School, Slade School, London.
Served First World War France, Belgium, Italy; painted native life S. Africa, portraits Spain, U.S.A. and England; works acquired by Tate Gallery, Nat. Gallery of Modern Art Madrid, Imperial War Museum, and Oldham, Manchester, Liverpool, Sheffield, Belfast, Leeds, Bradford, Birmingham and other Municipal Galleries, S.A. National Gallery, Johannesburg Art Gallery, Durban Art Gallery; mem. Royal Society Portrait Painters, New English Art Club; official artist to S. African Defence Force 40-43.
Works include portraits of Gen. Smuts, Solly Joel, Sir Winston Churchill, the King of Spain, the King of Greece, F.M. Viscount Alexander, F.M. Viscount Montgomery and Lord Tedder.
42 Rowan Street, Stellenbosch, South Africa.

Lewis, Richard, C.B.E., F.R.A.M., F.R.M.C.M., L.R.A.M.; British opera singer; ed. Royal Manchester Coll. of Music, Royal Acad. of Music.
English debut in *Rape of Lucretia*, Glyndebourne; created Troilus (*Troilus and Cressida* by Walton); sang in première of Stravinsky's *Canticum Sacrum*; guest appearances at Covent Garden, Edinburgh Festival, San Francisco Opera, Glyndebourne, Vienna State Opera and Teatro Colón, Buenos Aires; appearances in oratorio and recitals in Europe, America, Australia and New Zealand; numerous broadcasts and recordings.
Casuarina, Harrington Sound, Bermuda.

Lewis, Roger; American business executive; b. 11 Jan. 1912; ed. Stanford Univ.
Lockheed Aircraft Corpn. 34-47; Vice-Pres. (Sales) Canadair Ltd., Montreal 47-50; Vice-Pres. Curtiss-Wright Corpn. 50-53; Asst. Sec. of Air Force 53-55; Exec. Vice-Pres., Dir. and mem. Exec. Cttee. Pan American World Airways 55-62; Chair. of Board, Pres. and Dir. Gen. Dynamics Corpn. 62-, Dir. Canadair Ltd. (subsid.); mem. Council on Foreign Relations; Medal of Freedom.
General Dynamics Corporation, 1 Rockefeller Plaza, New York City 20, N.Y., U.S.A.

Lewis, Wilfrid Bennett, C.B.E., M.A., PH.D., F.R.S., F.R.S.C.; British physicist; b. 24 June 1908; ed. Haileybury Coll., and Gonville and Caius Coll., Cambridge Univ.
Research Fellow Gonville and Caius Coll. 34-40; Univ. Demonstrator Cambridge 35-37, University Lecturer 37-39; Senior Scientific Officer, Bawdsey Research Station, Air Ministry (later became Telecommunications Research Establishment, Malvern) 39, Chief Supt., T.R.E., Malvern 45-46; Dir. Atomic Energy Research Div. of Nat. Research Council of Canada 46-52; Vice-Pres. Research and Development, Atomic Energy of Canada Ltd. 52-63, Senior Vice-Pres. Science 63-; research in Nuclear Physics at Cavendish Laboratory, Cambridge 30-39; research and development of radar for air operations 39-46; Canadian Rep. UN Scientific Advisory Cttee.; mem. Scientific Advisory Cttee. IAEA 58-, UN Sec.-Gen.'s Cttee. of Experts on Implications of Atomic Weapons 67; Fellow and Pres. American Nuclear Soc. 61-62; Govt. of Canada Outstanding Achievement in Public Service Award 66, Atom for Peace Award 67, U.S. Medal of Freedom (Silver Palms); C.C. (Companion of the Order of Canada) 67; hon. D.Sc. Queen's Univ., Kingston 60, Saskatchewan Univ. 64, McMaster Univ., Hamilton, Ont. 65, Dartmouth Coll., New Hampshire 67, Hon. LL.D. Dalhousie Univ., Halifax 60, Carleton Univ., Ottawa 62.
Publ. *Electrical Counting* 42.
13 Beach Avenue, Deep River, Ontario, Canada.
Telephone: 613-584-3561.

Lewis, Sir William Arthur, Kt., PH.D., B.COM., M.A., L.H.D., LL.D.; West Indian economist; b. 23 July 1915; ed. St. Mary's Coll., St. Lucia, and London School of Economics.
Lecturer at the London School of Economics 38-47; Stanley Jevons Prof. of Political Economy in the Univ. of Manchester 48-58; Dep. Man. Dir U.N. Special Fund 59-60; Principal Univ. Coll. of the West Indies 59-62; Vice-Chancellor, Univ. of W. Indies 62; Prof. of Public and Int. Affairs, Princeton Univ. 62-; mem. Colonial Development Corpn. 51-53; Econ. Adviser to Govt. of Ghana 57-58; Hon. L.H.D. Columbia; Hon. LL.D. Toronto, Wales, Williams, Bristol, Dakar, Leicester; Hon. Fellow London School of Econs.; Foreign Fellow American Acad. of Arts and Sciences; Hon. Fellow Weizmann Inst., Israel.
Publs. *Overhead Costs* 49, *Economic Survey, 1919-1939*, 49, *The Principles of Economic Planning* 49, *Industrial Development in the Caribbean* 50, *Theory of Economic Growth* 55, *Politics in West Africa* 65, *Development Planning* 66; co-author of UN Report *Measures for the Economic Development of Under-Developed Countries* 51.
Woodrow Wilson School, Princeton University, Princeton, New Jersey, U.S.A.

Ley, Hellmut, DR.-ING.; German business executive; b. 23 Dec. 1909; ed. Innsbruck Univ. and Technische Hochschule, Darmstadt.
Chairman of the Board Metallgesellschaft A.G., Frankfurt/Main; Chair., Advisory Board Lurgi Ges. für Wärme- und Chemotechnik, Frankfurt/Main, Norddeutsche Affinerie, Hamburg, "SACHTLEBEN" A.G., Cologne, Karl Schmidt G.m.b.H., Neckarsulm, Vereinigte Deutsche Metallwerke A.G., Frankfurt/Main; mem. Advisory Board, Bergmann Elektrizitätswerke A.G., Berlin, "Berzelius" Metallhütten-Ges. m.b.H., Duisburg, Degussa Deutsche Gold- und Silber-Scheide-Anstalt, Frankfurt/Main, Dresdner Bank A.G., Frankfurt/Main, Kernreaktor-Finanzierungs-Ges., Frankfurt/Main, Lurgi Apparatebau G.m.b.H., Frankfurt/Main, Lurgi Ges. für Chemie und Hüttenwesen m.b.H., Frankfurt/Main, Lurgi Ges. für Mineraloeltechnik m.b.H., Frankfurt/Main, Lurgi Verwaltung G.m.b.H., Frankfurt/Main, Pigment-Chemie G.m.b.H., Cologne, VDO-Tachometer-Werke Adolf Schindling G.m.b.H., Frankfurt/Main; mem. Board Stifterverband für die deutsche Wissenschaft, Essen, and DECHEMA Deutsche Ges. für Chemisches Apparatewesen e. V., Frankfurt/Main; Past Pres., Soc. of German Chemists.
Reuterweg 14, Frankfurt/Main, German Federal Republic.
Telephone: 5-90-91.

Ley, Hermann Hubert, DR.HABIL.; German philosopher and politician; b. 11; ed. Helmholtz School and Leipzig Univ.
Professor of Theoretical Pedagogics, Leipzig Univ. 47-48, of Dialectics and Historical Materialism, Dresden Tech. High School 48-56; Dir.-Gen. State Cttee. for Broadcasting and Television 56-62; Prof. of Relations of Nat. Science and Philosophy, Humboldt Univ. Berlin; Silver Patriotic Order of Merit 59, National Prize 60.
Publs. *Avicenna* 52, *Mittasch* 53, *Zur Entwicklungsgeschichte der europäischen Aufklärung* 55, *Bemerkungen über Kant* 54, *Bemerkungen zum Wesen echter Menschlichkeit (Auseinandersetzung mit Jakob Hommes)* 56, *Vorreformatorische Bewegung in Deutschland* 56, *Studie zur Geschichte des Materialismus im Mittelalter* 58, *Dialektischer Widerspruch zu Lakebrink* 58, *Dämon Technik* 60, *Einige erkenntnistheoretische Probleme in Naturwissenschaft und Technik* 63, *Geschichte der Aufklärung und des Atheismus I* 67.
Ernst-Grube-Strasse 41c, Berlin-Köpenick, Germany.

Leydon, John; Irish business executive; b. 17 Jan. 1895; ed. St. Mel's Coll., Longford, and St. Patrick's Coll., Maynooth.
Entered British Civil Service, War Office 15; transferred to Irish Civil Service 23; mem. staff Dept. of Finance 23-32; Sec. Dept. of Industry and Commerce 32-55, Dept. Supplies 39-45; Sec. Economic Cttee. 28; mem. Electricity Supply Board 29; mem. Comm. of Inquiry on Derating 30; corresp. mem. L.N. Economic Cttee.; Chair. Aer Rianta Tta. 37-49, Aer Lingus Tta. 37-49; and Irish Shipping Ltd. 41-49; Chair. Insurance Corpn. of Ireland Ltd., Asbestos Cement Ltd., Wm. & P. Thompson Ltd., Dollar Exports Advisory Cttee. 50, Capital Investment Advisory Cttee. 56, Nat. Bank of Ireland Ltd., Aerlinte Eireann (Irish Airlines) 58-60; Pres. Inst. of Public Admin. 57-60; Dir. Cement Ltd., Asbestos Pipes Ltd., Central Bank of Ireland, Bank of Ireland; mem. Council and of Exec. Cttee. of Irish Management Inst. 57; mem. Board of Govs. Nat. Gallery of Ireland 61; Kt. Commdr. Order of St. Gregory the Great; LL.D. h.c. Dublin Univ. 60.
58 Ailesbury Road, Dublin, Ireland.
Telephone: 693535.

Li Ching-chuan; Chinese politician; b. 08.
Vice-Political Commissar, Southwest China Mil. Dist., People's Liberation Army 49; Chair. West Szechwan Admin. Area 50-52; Chair. Szechwan Prov. People's Govt. 53-54; mem. Southwest China Admin. Cttee. 50-54; Sec. Szechwan Prov. Cttee. C.C.P. 53-; Chair. Szechwan Prov. Cttee., People's Consultative Conf. 55-; mem. C.C.P. Central Cttee. 56-, Politburo 58-; Vice-Chair. Standing Cttee. of Nat. People's Congress 65-; First Sec. C.C.P. South West Bureau 65-.
The Politburo of the Central Committee of the Chinese Communist Party, Peking, People's Republic of China.

Li Choh-Ming, C.B.E., M.A., PH.D.; American (b. Chinese) educator and university professor; b. 17 Feb. 1912; ed. Univ. of Nanking, China, and Univ. of California (Berkeley).
Professor of Economics, Nankai, Southwest Associated and Nat. Central Univs., China 37-43; Dep. Dir. Gen. Chinese Nat. Relief and Rehabilitation Admin. (CNRRA) 45-47; Chief Del. of Republic of China to UN Economic Comm. for Asia and the Far East 47-49; Chair. Board of Trustees for Rehabilitation Affairs, Nat. Govt. of China 49-50; Expert on the UN Population Comm. and Statistical Comm. 52-57; Lecturer, Assoc. Prof. and Prof. of Business Admin. and Dir. of Centre for Chinese Studies, Univ. of Calif. (Berkeley) 51-63; Vice-Chancellor Chinese Univ. of Hong Kong 63-; Vice-Pres. Assen. of Southeast Asian Insts. of Higher Learning; mem. Editorial Boards *Asian Economic Review, Asian Survey, Modern Asian Studies, China Quarterly;* Life Fellow, Royal Econ. Soc., London; mem. American Econ. Asscn., Asscn. for Asian Studies (U.S.A.) and other socs.; Dr. of Laws h.c. Univs. of Hong Kong and Michigan.
Publs. *Economic Development of Communist China* 59, *Statistical System of Communist China* 62; Editor: *Industrial Development in Communist China* 64.
Office of the Vice-Chancellor, Chinese University of Hong Kong, 677 Nathan Road, Kowloon, Hong Kong.
Telephone: 814455.

Li Fan-wu; Chinese politician and administrator.
Member, Chinese Communist Party; Gov., Heilungkiang Province 58-67.
Harbin, Heilungkiang Province (Manchuria), China.

Li Fu-chun; Chinese administrator and politician; b. 01; ed. in France.
Joined French branch of Communist Party of China in 22; Vice-Chair. N.E. People's Govt. 49; Vice-Premier State Council 55-; Chair. State Planning Comm. 54-; mem. Standing Cttee. Political Bureau of C.P. of China.
State Planning Commission, Peking, China.

Li Hsien-nien; Chinese soldier and politician; b. 08.
Commanded 5th Division New Fourth Army 41; Vice-Premier; Minister of Finance 54-; mem. Political Bureau of Communist Party of China; Vice-Chair. South Central Mil. and Admin. Cttee. 49; Sec. Hupeh Provincial Cttee. of Communist Party 49; Chair. Hupeh Provincial People's Govt. 49-54; Mayor of Wuhan 52; mem. National Defence Cttee. 54.
Ministry of Finance, Peking, China.

Li Hsueh-feng; Chinese politician.
Vice-Chair. Nat. People's Congress Standing Cttee. 65-; First Sec. Chinese C.P. North China Bureau.
Office of the Standing Committee of National People's Congress, Peking, People's Republic of China.

Li Kwoh Ting, B.S.; Chinese government official; b. 28 Jan. 1910; ed. Nat. Central Univ., China, and Cambridge Univ., England.
Superintendent of Tze Yu Iron Works, Chungking 42-45; Pres. Taiwan Shipbuilding Corpn. 51-53; mem. Industrial Development Comm., Econ. Stabilisation Board 53-58; Sec.-Gen. Council for U.S. Aid, Convener of Industrial Planning and Co-ordination Group of Ministry of Econ. Affairs, Head of Industrial Development and Investment Center 58-63; Vice-Chair. Council for Int. Econ. Cooperation and Development 63-,

Minister of Econ. Affairs 65-; mem. Nat. Security Council 67-; Vice-Chair. Nat. Reconstruction Planning Cttee. 67-.
Publs. *Symposium on Nuclear Physics, British Industries, Japanese Shipbuilding Industry, The Growth of Private Industry in Free China, Economic Policy and Economic Development.*
3 Lane 44, Linyi Street, Taipei, Taiwan, Republic of China.
Telephone: 28525.

Li Li; Chinese politician.
Former mem. Standing Cttee. Chinese C.P. Central-South Bureau; fmr. Sec. Honan Province Cttee.; Sec. Kweichow Province Cttee. 65-; Gov. of Kweichow 65-67.
Kweichow Province, People's Republic of China.

Li Szu-kuang; Chinese palaeontologist and geologist; b. 89; ed. Birmingham Univ., England (doctorate).
Dir. Geological Research Inst., Acad. Sinica 30-33; Prof. and Dir. Geology Dept., Peking Nat. Univ. 33; lectured in England 35; Vice-President, Academia Sinica 51-; Vice-Chair. Second Nat. Cttee. Political Consultative Conf.; All-China Fed. of Scientific Societies; Vice-Chair World Asscn. of Scientific Workers; Vice-Chair. Chinese People's Nat. Cttee. in Defence of Children; Minister of Geology 52-.
Publs. *Geology of the Yangtze Gorge, Structural Types of Eastern Asia, The Fundamental Causes of the Evolution of the Surface Features of the Earth, Geology of China.*
Ministry of Geology, Peking, China.

Li Ta-chang; Chinese administrator; b. 10.
Director of Propaganda Taihang Sub-Cttee., C.C.P., Sino-Japanese War; Dep. Dir. Propaganda, C.C.P., Northeast China Bureau 45-49; Chair. South Szechwan People's Administrative Council 49-52; Vice-Chair. Szechwan Prov. People's Govt. 52-54; Dep. Sec. C.C.P., Szechwan Prov. Cttee. 53; mem. South West China Admin. Cttee. 53-54, later Sec. C.C.P. South West Bureau; First Sec. Kweichow C.C.P. Province Cttee. 65; Gov. Szechwan Province 55-; Deputy from Szechwan, N.P.C. 54-; Alt. mem. C.C.P. Central Cttee. 56-.
Governor's Residence, Chengtu, Szechwan, China.

Li Teh-chuan (Li te-ch'üan); Chinese welfare worker.
Widow of Marshal Feng Yü-hsiang; in war directed Women's Welfare Society; on Sino-Soviet Cultural Cttee.; after war, chaired Women's Fed. and worked with children; worked in the China Welfare Fund, Chinese Red Cross, on int. welfare and educational activities; Vice-Pres. All-China Democratic Women's Fed. 49; Pres. Chinese Red Cross Society 52; del. for Hupeh in the 1st N.P.C. 54; Vice-Chair. Chinese People's Nat. Cttee. in Defence of Children 55; Minister of Public Health 49-65; Vice-Chair. Chinese People's Political Consultative Conf. (C.P.P.C.C.) 65-.
Chinese People's Political Consultative Conference, Peking, China.

Li Ti-Tsun, B.A., M.A., PH.D.; Chinese diplomatist; b. 01; ed. Tsing Hua Coll. of Peiping, Univs. of Wisconsin, Harvard and Chicago.
Prof. of Political Science, Central Political Inst. 29-30; Nat. Central Univ. 30-31; Co-founder and Editor *Current Events Monthly* 29-39; Section Chief and Asst. Dir., Ministry of Foreign Affairs 29-33; Dir. Dept. of Information, Ministry of Foreign Affairs 33-39; Minister to Cuba 39-47; concurrently Minister to Venezuela, Colombia and Dominican Repub. 42-47; Expert on Nat. Resources Comm., Nanking 35-37; Foreign Relations Cttee. of Supreme Nat. Defence Council of Chungking 38-39; Ambassador on special mission to Indonesia 46-47; Ambassador to Turkey 47-57; Ambassador to Brazil May 57-63; Del. UNESCO Conf., New Delhi 56; Rep. 16th Session UN Gen. Assembly N.Y. 61; Adviser Ministry of Foreign Affairs 63-66; Chair. Dept. of English, Coll. of Chinese Culture 63-66; Prof. of

Latin American History, Nat. War Coll. 63-66; Ambassador to Chile 66-; numerous decorations.
Publ. *Political and Economic Theories of Dr. Sun Yat-sen 29.*
Embassy of the Republic of China, Avenida Pedro Valdivia 522, Santiago, Chile.

Li Yu-wen; Chinese administrator; b. 08; ed. Moscow Univ.
Former Deputy Sec. C.C.P., Northeast China Bureau; Sec. Gen. Northeast China People's Govt. 49-53; Chair. Kirin Prov. People's Govt. 53-55; Gov. Kirin 52-67; Deputy from Kirin, Nat. People's Congress 54-.
Changchun, Kirin, China.

Lian, Camille Constant; French heart specialist; b. 4 Jan. 1882; ed. Lycée Jacques-Amyot, Auxerre, and Univ. de Paris à la Sorbonne.
Hospital Doctor in Paris 19-23; Prof. Agrégé Faculty of Medicine, Paris 22-42, Prof. 42, now Hon. Prof.; mem. Acad. Nationale de Médecine 49; medical military service two World Wars; founder and fmr. Pres. Soc. française de Cardiologie; Doctor mem. Hôpitaux de Paris; Commdr. Légion d'Honneur.
Publs. many treatises on heart diseases including *L'Angine de poitrine, Phonocardiographie, Guide d'électrocardiographie.*
19 rue de Bourgogne, Paris 7e, France.

Liang Szu-cheng; Chinese architect; b. 01; ed. Tsinghua Univ., Pennsylvania Univ., M.A. (Architecture), Princeton Univ.
Son of Liang Chi-chao; Head Architectural Dept., Northeast Univ.; Dir. of Research, Society of Chinese Architects; Vice-Chair. City Planning Board, Peking 52; Deputy Dir. Society of Chinese Architects 53; Peking del. to 1st N.P.C. 54; mem. of advisory Committee on Wuhan bridge over Yangtze 55; mem. Central Cttee. Democratic League; on Commission for Conservation of Historical Monuments; mem. Standing Cttee. N.P.C. 65-; Hon. Dr. Princeton Univ.
Publs. on architecture and history of architecture.
Architectural Society of China, Peking, China.

Liang Yuen-Li (Liang Yun-li), LL.B., DR.JUR.; Chinese lawyer; b. 04; ed. Nanyang Univ. Comparative Law School, Harvard and Geneva Univs.
Editor *China Law Review* 24-26; Lecturer Comparative Law School and Legal Editor *Commercial Press* 26-27; Sec. to Minister of Foreign Affairs 27 and Minister of Justice 28; Judge Shanghai Provisional Court 28; Prof. of Law Comparative Law School 28-29; Sec. Washington Legation 29-33; Carnegie Teachers Fellow in Int. Law Harvard 30-31; Counsellor of Exec. *Yuan* 33; Senior Sec. of Ministry of Foreign Affairs 34; senior mem. Treaty Comm. of Ministry of Foreign Affairs and Prof. Central Univ. 36-37; contrib. Editor *China Critic*; First Sec. Embassy London 39-42; Counsellor 43-46; mem. Chinese del. to Dumbarton Oaks and San Francisco Conf. 44-45; Chair. Cttee. of Experts, Security Council 46; Visiting Prof., Univ. of Michigan, Summer Session 47; Prof. Hague Acad. of Int. Law 48; Lecturer, New York Univ. Law School 47-48 and 49-50, Adjunct Assoc. Prof. 51-60, Adjunct Prof. 60-; Dir. Legal Dept. United Nations 46-; elected Assoc. Inst. of Int. Law 50.
Publs. *The First Year of the Far Eastern Crisis, International Government, Sociology of Law, China 46, Le Développement et la Codification du Droit international 48.*
United Nations, 1st Avenue, New York, N.Y., U.S.A.

Liao Cheng-chih; Chinese politician; b. 08; ed. Japan, Lingnan Univ.
Took part in the Shameen demonstration 25; Dir. of Communist Publishing Press at Yenan 35; Vice-Chair. and Sec.-Gen. Chinese People's Cttee. for World Peace 53; on standing cttee. C.P.P.C.C.; Pres. Hsin Hwa News Agency; Vice-Chair. Asian Solidarity Cttee. 56, Chair.;

Chair. Overseas Chinese Affairs Comm. 59-; Chair. of Chinese Cttee. for Afro-Asian Solidarity.
Overseas Chinese Affairs Commission, Peking, China.

Liao Lu-yen; Chinese administrator; b. *c.* 97.
Asst. dir. Counsellors' Office, Central People's Government 49; gen. sec. Policy Research Office 49; asst. sec. State Council and dir. Counsellor's Office 52; Vice-Minister, Dept. of Agricultural Work 53-56; Kiangsu del. to N.P.C. 54; Minister of Agriculture 54-.
Ministry of Agriculture, Peking, China.

Liatis, Alexis S., LL.M.; Greek diplomatist; b. 18 March 1908; ed. Univ. of Lyons.
Diplomatic Service 29-; Netherlands 34-36, U.S. and Canada 38-48, Cyprus 49-50, Egypt 50-53, Turkey 53-54; Foreign Office 54-58 (Head, Econ. Dept. 54-55, Adviser to Foreign Sec. 55-56, Head, Div. of African, Middle East, S. and S.E. Asian Affairs 54-58); Ambassador to U.S. 58-62, to Japan 62-65; Perm. Rep. to UN 65-67; decorations from many countries.
c/o Ministry of Foreign Affairs, Athens, Greece.

Libby, Willard Frank, B.S., PH.D.; American scientist; b. 17 Dec. 1908; ed. Univ. of California.
Instructor of Chemistry, Univ. of Calif. 33, Asst. Prof. 38, Assoc. Prof. 45, Prof. 59-; mem. Columbia Univ., War Research Div. 41-45; Prof. Dept. of Chemistry, Inst. for Nuclear Studies, Univ. of Chicago 45-54; mem. U.S. Atomic Energy Comm. 54-59; Prof. of Chemistry Univ. of Calif. at Los Angeles 59-; Dir. Inst. of Geophysics and Planetary Physics, Univ. of Calif. 62-; Univ. of Calif., Boulder-Distinguished Visiting Prof. of Chemistry, Physics and Astrophysics 67-; Guggenheim Fellowship 41-42 and 60-63; Research Corpn. Award (for radiocarbon dating technique) 51; mem. Plowshare Advisory Cttee. of A.E.C. 59, Cttee. of Selection of Guggenheim Memorial Foundation 59, Air Resources Board, State of California 67; mem. American Chemical Soc., Nat. Acad. of Sciences, American Acad. of Arts and Sciences, American Nuclear Soc., American Physical Soc., Mich. and Heidelberg Acads. of Sciences; American Asscn. for the Advancement of Science, American Philosophical Society, Bolivian Soc. of Anthropology, Royal Swedish Acad. of Science, Washington Acad. of Science, American Geophysical Union; Pres. Isotope Foundation; Chandler Medal (Columbia Univ.) 54; American Chemical Soc. Award for nuclear applications in chemistry 56; Elliot Cresson Medal, Franklin Inst. 57, Willard Gibbs Medal 58, Day Medal, Geological Soc. of America 61; Calif. Alumnus of the Year Award 63; Fellow American Nuclear Soc. 67; Hon. Sc.D. (Wesleyan Univ. 55, Syracuse Univ. 57, Trinity Coll. Dublin 57, Georgetown Univ. 62, Manhattan Coll. 63, Newcastle upon Tyne 65; Dr. h.c. (Carnegie Inst. Technology) 59; Albert Einstein Medal 59; Nobel Prize for Chemistry 60.
Publs. *Radiocarbon Dating* 52 (2nd edn. 55) and articles.
Chemistry Department, UCLA, 405 Hilgard, Los Angeles, Calif. 90024, U.S.A.
Telephone: 272-8911, extension 2866 or 3169.

Liberman, Yevsei Grigorievich; Soviet economist; b. 7 Oct. 1897; ed. Univ. of Kiev.
Lecturer, Kharkov Engineering and Econs. Inst., later Kharkov Univ., Prof. 57-.
Publs. include: *Structure of the Balance of an Industrial Undertaking* 48, *Economic Accounting in a Factory* 50, *Ways of Raising the Profitability of Socialist Enterprises* 56, *Main Problems of Composite Mechanization and Automation of Production* 61, *Plan, Profit, Bonuses* 62, *The Economic Methods to Raise the Efficiency of Socialistic Enterprises* 67.
Kharkov State University, 4 Ploshchad Dzerzhinskogo, Kharkov, U.S.S.R.

Libya, King of (*see* Idris I, Sayyid Muhammad Idris as-Sunasi).

Lichtenberger, Rt. Rev. Arthur Carl, B.PHIL., B.D.; American ecclesiastic; b. 8 Jan. 1900; ed. Kenyon Coll., Ohio, and Episcopal Theological School, Cambridge, Massachusetts.
Professor of New Testament, St. Paul's Divinity School, Wuchang, China 25-27; Rector, Grace Church, Cincinnati 28-33; Rector, St. Paul's Church, Brookline, Mass. 33-41; Lecturer on Pastoral Care, Episcopal Theological School 38-41; Dean, Trinity Cathedral, Newark, N.J. 41-48; Prof. of Pastoral Theology, Gen. Theological Seminary, New York 48-51; Bishop Coadjutor of Missouri 51-52, Bishop 52-59; Presiding Bishop of Protestant Episcopal Church 58-64; Prof. Pastoral Theology, Episcopal Theological School, Cambridge, Mass. 65-; several hon. degrees.
Publ. *The Day is at Hand.*
13 St. John's Road, Cambridge, Mass. 02138, U.S.A.

Lichtenstein, Roy; American painter and sculptor; b. 1923; ed. Ohio State Univ.
Served in Second World War; taught painting at Ohio State Coll. and Rutgers Coll., N.J. until 62; has since concentrated on pop painting based on comic strips and advertising illustrations; one-man exhbn. Tate Gallery, London 68.
New Jersey, U.S.A.

Liddell Hart, Sir Basil Henry, Kt.; British military historian; b. 31 Oct. 1895; ed. Cambridge Univ.
Served First World War 14-18; retired 27; military corresp. *Daily Telegraph* 25-35; military corresp. and adviser on defence to *The Times* 35-39; Military Editor *Encyclopædia Britannica*; Lees-Knowles Lecturer, Cambridge Univ. 32-33, Leverhulme Fellow 34; personal adviser to War Minister Hore-Belisha in reorganisation of Army 37-38; Distinguished Visiting Prof. Univ. of Calif., Davis 65-66; Hon. D.Litt., Oxford, Hon. Fellow, Corpus Christi Coll., Cambridge.
Publs. Over 30 books, including *New Methods of Infantry Training, Paris or the Future of War, Scipio Africanus, The Remaking of Modern Armies, Sherman, Foch, The British Way in Warfare, A History of the World War, The Future of Infantry, The Ghost of Napoleon, T. E. Lawrence—In Arabia and After, The War in Outline, Europe in Arms, The Defence of Britain, Dynamic Defence, The Current of War, The Strategy of Indirect Approach, Thoughts on War, Why Don't We Learn from History? The Revolution in Warfare, The Other Side of the Hill, Defence of the West, The Tanks* 59, *Deterrent or Defence* 60, *Memoirs,* Vols. I and II 65.
States House, Medmenham, Buckinghamshire, England.

Lidin, Vladimir Germanovich; Soviet writer; b. 1894; ed. Moscow Univ.
Member Union of Soviet Writers; Order of Red Banner of Labour 67.
Publs. *Nord, Idut Korabli* (The Ships Are Sailing), *Otstupnik* (The Apostate), *Iskateli* (The Seekers), *Mogila niezvestnogo soldata* (The Tomb of the Unknown Soldier) *Velikiy ili Tichiy* (The Pacific Ocean), *Syn* (The Son), *Bolshaya reka* (Great River), *More* (The Sea), *Road to the West* 40, *Winter 1941* 42, *Prostaya Zhizn* 43, *Izgnanie* 47, *Izbrannoe* (Selected Works) 48, *Dve Zhizni* (Two Lives) 50, *Svezhiy veter* (A Fresh Wind) 52, *Rasskazi, povesti, vospominania* (Stories, Recollections) 54, *Dalnyevostochnie povesty* (Far East Stories) 54, *Dalyekiy drug* (A Far-Away Friend) 56, *People I Have Met* 57, 61, *Povesti i rasskazi* (stories) 58, *Notchnie poezda* (Night Trains) 59, *Slovo o Tchechove* (A Word about Chekhov) 59, *Doroga Zhuravley* (Way of Cranes) 61, *Books, My Friends* 62, *Shum Dozhdya* (The Rustle of the Rain) 63, *Povesti i rasskazi* (Stories) 63, *Serdza Svoego Tyen* (The Shade of One's Own Heart) 65, *A Cloudy Day Over the Sea* 67.
Union of Soviet Writers, 52 Vozovsky Street, Moscow, U.S.S.R.

Lidman, Sara; Swedish writer; b. 30 Dec. 1923; ed. Uppsala Universitet.
First four books deal with life in sparsely populated N. Sweden; in S. Africa and wrote *Jag o min son* 60; in Kenya 62-64, in N. Viet-Nam 65.
Publs. include: *Tjärdalen* 53, *Hjortronlandet* 55, *Aina* 56, *Regnspiran* 58, *Bära mistel* 60, *Jag o min son* 61, *Med fem diamanter* 64.
Jungmansgrand 2, Stockholm SV, Sweden.

Lidorenko, Nikolai Stepanovich; Soviet electrochemist; b. 1916; ed. Novocherkassk Polytechnical Inst.
Engineer 40-50; Dir. U.S.S.R. Inst. of Sources of Electric Current; Corresp. mem. U.S.S.R. Acad. of Sciences 66-; Merited Scientist of R.S.F.S.R. 66.
Publs. Works on transformation of energy.
U.S.S.R. Academy of Sciences, 14 Lenin Prospekt, Moscow, U.S.S.R.

Lie, Trygve Halvdan; Norwegian lawyer and diplomatist; b. 16 July 1896; ed. Oslo Univ.
Asst. to Sec. of Norwegian Labour Party 19-22; legal adviser, Trade Union Fed. 22-35; Exec. mem. Labour Party 26; Minister of Justice in Govt. of John Nygaardsvold 35-39; mem. Norwegian Parl. 35; re-elected 45; Minister of Trade, Industry, Shipping, and Fishing 39, of Supply 39-40; escaped to England with Govt. June 40; Acting Foreign Minister 40; Foreign Minister 41; evolved provisional measures that saved Norwegian Fleet for Allies; Chair. Norwegian del. to U.N. Conf., San Francisco, April 45 (Chair. Comm. III for drafting Charter of Security Council); resgnd. as Foreign Minister June 45, re-appointed Oct. 45; Chair. Norwegian del. UN Gen. Assembly, London 46; Sec.-Gen. of the United Nations 46-53; Gov. Oslo and Akershus 55-63; Chair. Foreign Industry Cttee. 59-63; Minister of Industries 63-64, of Commerce 64-65; Hon. LL.D. (Yale, Princeton, Santo Domingo, Manitoba, Harvard, Maine, Chattanooga, Wisconsin, Columbia, Quito Central, Syracuse, Nebraska Univs., Uppsala, Lafayette, Swarthmore Coll., New School for Social Research, N.Y.), Hon. D.C.L. (Boston Univ.), Hon. L.H.D. (Wagner Coll., Univ. of Vermont), Dr. h.c. (Brussels, Louvain, Manchester Univs.).
Publs. *In the Cause of Peace* 54, *Live or Die, Norway at War* 55, *With England in the Front Line* 56, *Homeward Bound* 58.
Hoffsveien 30, Sköyen, Oslo 2, Norway.
Telephone: 558850.

Liebaert, Henri Marcel; Belgian industrialist and politician; b. 95; ed. Koninklijk Athenaeum, Ghent and Höhere Technische Schule, Krefeld, Germany.
Member of Parl. (Liberal) 39; Minister of Econ. Affairs 46-47 and of Finance 49-50; Pres. Belgian Liberal Party 53-62; Minister of Finance 54-58; Grand Officier Ordre de Léopold, Grand Croix Ordre de la Couronne, Croix de Guerre, etc.
453 Avenue Louise, Brussels, Belgium; and La Hêtraie, Renipont par Genval, Belgium.

Lieberich, Heinz, D.IUR.; German archivist and legal historian; b. 29 Jan. 1905; ed. Humanistisches Gymnasium, Munich, Univ. of Munich, and School of Archives, Munich.
Bavarian State Archive Service 31-, Speyer 34-38, Central Archives, Munich 38-, Gen. Dir. Bavarian State Archives 59; Hon. Prof. of Legal History, Univ. of Munich 55-; Chair. of Comm. for Bavarian History, Bavarian Acad. of Sciences 60-; mem. Exec. Cttee. Int. Council of Archives 61-.
Publs. *Rechtsgeschichte Bayerns u. der bayerischen Schwaben* 52, *Zur Feudalisierung der Gerichtsbarkeit in Bayern* 54, *Kaiser Ludwig der Bayer als Gesetzgeber* 59, *Landherren und Landleute* 64; (with Mitteis) *Deutsche Rechtsgeschichte* (10th edn.) 66, *Deutsches Privatrecht* (5th edn.) 68.
8 Munich 13, Adalbertstr. 44/IV, German Federal Republic.

Liebermann, Rolf; Swiss composer; b. 14 Sept. 1910; ed. Zürich Conservatoire, and Univ. of Zürich.
Mem. Musical Dept. Swiss Radio Corpn. 45-50; Head of Orchestra Dept. Swiss Radio Station Beromünster 50-57; Musical Dir. N. German Broadcasting System, Hamburg 57-59; General Man. State Opera, Hamburg 59-.
Works, operatic: *Leonore* 52, *Penelope* 54, *School for Wives* 55; orchestral: *Furioso* 47, *The Song of Life and Death* 50, *Concerto for Jazzband and Symphony orchestra* 54.
Staatsoper, Hamburg, German Federal Republic.

Lieftinck, Pieter, DR. JUR.; Netherlands economist and politician; b. 30 Sept. 1902; ed. Utrecht Univ.
Fellow Rockefeller Foundation; economist Dept. of Economic Affairs and Gen. Sec. Economic Council 32-34; Lecturer Neths. School of Economics at Rotterdam 34; mem. Supreme Council for Labour matters; Minister of Finance in Schermerhorn Govt. June 45-July 46; same in Beel Govt. July 46-Aug. 48, and in Drees Govt. Aug. 48-51, 51-52; Special Rep. and Chief of Missions, I.B.R.D. 52-56; Exec. Dir. I.B.R.D., and Int. Monetary Fund 56-.
3229 Idaho Av. N.W., Washington 16, D.C., U.S.A.

Liénart, H.E. Cardinal Achille, DR. en THEOLOGIE, L. en PHILOSOPHIE; French ecclesiastic; b. 7 Feb. 1884; ed. Coll. Saint-Josef, Lille and Grand Séminaire de Saint Sulpice.
Ordained Priest 07; Prof. of Holy Scripture Grand Séminaire de Cambrai; Prof. of Holy Scripture Grand Séminaire de Lille; served as Chaplain to French Army in First World War; Vicar-Dean of Saint-Christophe de Tourcoing 26-28; Bishop of Lille 28-; created Cardinal by Pope Pius XI 30; mem. Sacred Congregations of the Council, of Seminaries and Univs. of Study and of the Fabric of St. Peter's; mem. of Pontifical Comm. for Biblical Studies; Chancellor Catholic Faculties of Lille; Pres. Assemblée de Cardinaux et Archevêques de France; Grand Officier de la Légion d'Honneur, Croix de Guerre.
68 rue Royale, Lille, France.

Liepa, Maris-Rudolf Eduardovich; Soviet ballet dancer; b. 1936; ed. Moscow Ballet School.
Soloist with Latvian Theatre of Opera and Ballet, Riga 55-56; soloist with Moscow Stanislavsky and Nemirovich-Danchenko Theatre Ballet Co. 56-59; soloist with Bolshoi Theatre Ballet; Honoured Artist of R.S.F.S.R.
Main roles include: Jean de Brien (*Raimonde*), Konrad (*Corsair*), Siegfried (*Swan Lake*), Vatslev (*Fountain of Bakhchiserai*), Feb (*Esmeralda*), the Poet (*Straussiana*), Basil (*Don Quixote*), Albert (*Giselle*), Armen (*Gayane*), Spartacus (*Spartacus*), Prince Desire (*Sleeping Beauty*), Romeo (*Romeo and Juliet*), Farkhad (*Legend of Love*).
State Academic Bolshoi Theatre of the U.S.S.R., 1 Ploshchad Sverdlova, Moscow, U.S.S.R.

Lifar, Serge; Russian ballet dancer, choreographer and writer; b. 2 April 1905.
Left Russia as refugee and joined Diaghilev company, Paris 23; studied under Cecchetti; created *Apollon* (Stravinsky), *Fils Prodigue* (Prokofiev), etc.; debut as choreographer Stravinsky's *Renard* 29; produced *Prométhée*, Opera House, Paris 29; first London appearance in *Cimarosiana* and *Les Fâcheux*, Coliseum 24; Cochran's *1930 Revue*, London Pavilion 30; returned to Paris and produced and danced in *Bacchus and Ariadne*, *Le Spectre de la Rose*, and *Giselle* 31, *Icare* 35, *David Triomphant* 36, *Le Chevalier et la Demoiselle* 41, *Jean de Zarissa* 42, *Suite en Blanc* 43, *Chota Roustaveli*,

Dramma per Musica 46, *Lucifer* 48, *Septuor, Le Cheva-lier Errant, Phèdre* 50, *Blanche Neige* 51, *Fourberies de Scapin* 52, *Noces Fantastiques* 55, *Roméo et Juliette* (Prokofiev) 55, appeared in film *Le Testament d'Orphée* (Cocteau) 60; founder-Dir. Inst. choréographique at Opera House, Paris 47-; premier maître de ballet and premier danseur of Théâtre Nat. de l'Opéra, Paris 47-58, 62-63.
Publs. *Traditional to Modern* 38, *Diaghilev, a Biography* 40, *Traité de la Danse académique* 50, *Histoire du Ballet Russe* 51, *Vestris* 51, *Réflexions sur la Danse* 52, *Traité de Choréographie* 52, *The Three Graces* 59.
6 place de Mexico, Paris 16e, France.

Lifshitz, Evgeny Mikhailovich (brother of Ilya Lifshitz, *q.v.*); Soviet physicist; b. 1915; ed. Kharkov Inst. of Mechanics and Machine-building.
Ukraine Physical Inst., Kharkov 34-38; Senior Research Scientist, Inst. of Physical Problems, U.S.S.R. Acad. of Sciences 39-; Corresp. mem. U.S.S.R. Acad. of Sciences; State Prize 54, Lenin Prize 62.
Publs. *Mechanics, Theory of Fields, Quantitive Mecha-nics, Statistical Physics, Solid State Mechanics, Solid State Electrodynamics,* etc.
Institute of Physical Problems, U.S.S.R. Academy of Sciences, Vorobyevskoye Chaussée 2, Moscow, U.S.S.R.

Lifshitz, Ilya Mikhailovich (brother of Evgeny Lifshitz, *q.v.*); Soviet physicist; b. 1917; ed. Kharkov State Univ.
Ukraine Physical Inst., Kharkov 39-; Corresp. mem. U.S.S.R. Academy of Sciences.
Publs. works on solid state theory and electronic theory of metals.
Physical and Technical Institute, Tchaikovskaya str., Kharkov, U.S.S.R.

Ligachov, Igor Kuzmich; Soviet party official and politician; b. 1920; ed. Moscow Inst. of Aviation and C.P.S.U. Higher Party School.
Engineer 43-49; joined C.P.S.U. 44; Party and Local Govt. Official Novosibirsk 49-55; Vice-Chair. Novo-sibirsk Regional Soviet of Working People's Deputies 55-58; Sec. Novosibirsk Regional Cttee. C.P.S.U. 59-61; with Central Cttee. C.P.S.U. 61-65; First Sec. Tomsk Regional Cttee. C.P.S.U. 65-; Candidate mem. Central Cttee. C.P.S.U. 66-; Deputy to Supreme Soviet.
Tomsk Regional Committee, Communist Party of the Soviet Union, Tomsk, U.S.S.R.

Ligeti, Louis, D.PHIL., D.LIT.; Hungarian orientalist; b. 28 Oct. 1902; ed. Budapest Univ. and Coll. Eötvös, Budapest.
Lecturer, Budapest Univ. 31, Prof. 38; Lecturer, Ecole des Langues Orientales, Paris 34-35; visits to Mongolia 28-31, Afghanistan 36-37, Japan 40; Prof., Chair. of Central Asia; Eötvös Lóránd Univ. Budapest; mem. Hungarian Acad. 36-, Vice-Pres. 49-; mem. Mongolian Acad. of Sciences; hon. mem. Turkish Soc. of Language, Société Asiatique, Royal Asiatic Soc.; corresp. mem. Finno-Ugrian Soc. Sächsische Akad. d. Wissenschaft; Acad. des Inscriptions et Belles Lettres; Kossuth Prize 49.
Publs. *Rapport préliminaire d'un voyage d'exploration fait en Mongolie Chinoise* 33, *Les voyelles longues en turc* 38, *Catalogue du Kanjur mongol imprimé* 42-44, *Le Subhasitaratnanidhi mongol* 48, *L'Histoire Secrète des Mongoles* 62.
Belgrád-rkp. 26, Budapest, Hungary.
Telephone: 187-529.

Lightfoot-Boston, Sir Henry Josiah, K.ST.J., G.C.M.G., M.A., LL.B., B.C.L.; Sierra Leone fmr. Governor-General; b. 19 Aug. 1898; ed. Sierra Leone Grammar School, Fourah Bay Coll., Durham and London Univs., Lincoln's Inn, London.
Civil Service, Sierra Leone 20-23; founded Boston and Boston (solicitors) 26; Police Magistrate 46-54, Registrar Gen. 54-55, Senior Police Magistrate 55; Acting Judge, Supreme Court of Sierra Leone 45-57, Judge 57; Speaker, House of Reps. 57-62; Gov.-Gen. and C.-in-C. 62-67.
Freetown, Sierra Leone.

Lightner, Edwin Allen, Jr.; American diplomatist; b. 8 Dec. 1907; ed. Taft School, and Princeton Univ.
Joined Foreign Service 30, served Venezuela, Chile, Brazil, Argentina 30-38; Sec. Legations Riga, Oslo, Moscow, Stockholm 38-43; Asst. Political Adviser to European Advisory Comm. 44-45; Asst. Chief, Div. of Central European Affairs, State Dept. 45-47, Assoc. Chief 47-48; Deputy Dir. Office of Political Affairs, U.S. High Comm., Frankfurt 49-51; Counsellor, Korea 51-53; Consul-Gen., Munich 53-56; Deputy Asst. Sec. of State for Public Affairs 56-59; Minister, Berlin 59-63; Amb. to Libya 63-65; State Dept. Rep., Water Resources Task Force 65-66; Deputy Commdt. Foreign Affairs, Nat. War Coll. 66-.
Quarters 15a, Fort Lesley J. McNair, Washington, D.C. 20315, U.S.A.

Lilar, Albert J., LL.D.; Belgian lawyer and professor; b. 21 Dec. 1900; ed. Athénée Royal Antwerp, and Univ. of Brussels.
Admitted to Antwerp Bar 22; Pres. of Young Lawyers' Congress Antwerp 38; Asst. at Univ. of Brussels 36; Prof. of Comparative Commercial, Private Int. Law and Maritime Law, Univ. of Brussels 44; Senator; Min-ister of Justice 46-47, 49-50, 54-58, 60-61; Deputy Prime Minister 58-60; Head of the Antwerp Bar 64-66; Pres. Asscn. Belge de Droit Maritime 47-; Fed. of Belgian Lawyers 47-, Int. Maritime Cttee. 47-; Liberal.
Publs. *Communications d'ordre juridique, Eloge de l'Humanisme* 36.
33 rue Jordaens, Antwerp, Belgium.
Telephone: 394262; 394617.

Lilienfeld, Abraham M., A.B., M.D., M.P.H.; American epidemiologist; b. 13 Nov. 1920; ed. Johns Hopkins Univ., and Univ. of Maryland.
Associate Public Health Physician, N.Y. State Dept. of Health 49-50; Dir. Southern Health District, Baltimore 50-52; Asst. Prof. of Epidemiology, Johns Hopkins Univ. 52-54; Prof. and Chair. Dept. of Chronic Diseases 58-; Chief Dept. of Statistics and Epidemiological Research, Roswell Park Memorial Inst., Buffalo 54-58, Assoc. Prof. Medical Statistics Univ. of Buffalo 54-58; mem. Nat. Advisory Heart Council 62-66; mem. Research Advisory Council, American Cancer Soc. 65-; mem. Scientific Council, Int. Agency for Cancer Research 65-.
Publs. *Prenatal Factors in Cerebral Palsy* 51, *Prenatal Factors in Childhood Neuropsychiatric Disorders* 51-56, *Tobacco Use and Bladder Cancer* 56, *Epidemiological Methods* 57, *Epidemiology of Cancer* 54-65, *Chronic Diseases and Public Health* 66, *Cancer Epidemiology: Methods of Study* 67.
6200 Gist Avenue, Baltimore, Md. 21215, U.S.A.
Telephone: 301-FL8-1464.

Lilienthal, David Eli, A.B., LL.B.; American public servant, business executive and writer; b. 8 July 1899; ed. De Pauw Univ., and Harvard.
Admitted to Ill. Bar 23, Tenn. Bar 24; law practice in Chicago 23-31; mem. Wis. Public Service Comm. 31-33; Dir. Tennessee Valley Authority 33, Chair. 41-46; Chair. U.S. Atomic Energy Comm. Oct. 46-Feb. 50; Chair. U.S. State Dept. Board of Consultants on Int. Control of Atomic Energy 46; Consultant to Pres. of Colombia; Chair. Development and Resources Corpn. 55-; mem. American Acad. of Arts and Sciences; Pro-gressive Farmer Award for services to agriculture 45; Catholic Cttee. of the South Award 46: Public Welfare Award, Nat. Acad. of Sciences 51; Freedom House Award 49, Comendador de la Orden El Sol del Perú 64.

Publs. *TVA: Democracy on the March* 44, *This I Do Believe* 49, *Big Business: A New Era* 53, *Change, Hope and the Bomb* 63, *The Journals of David E. Lilienthal* (Vols. I and II) 64, (Vol. III) 66, *Management: A Humanist Art* 67.
1 Whitehall Street, New York, N.Y., U.S.A.; and 88 Battle Road, Princeton, N.J., U.S.A.

Lilje, Johannes Ernst Richard, DR.THEOL.; German ecclesiastic; b. 20 Aug. 1899; ed. Göttingen, Leipzig and Zürich Univs.
Students' Chaplain, Technical Acad., Hanover 24-26; Gen. Sec. of German Christian Student Movement, and Vice-Pres. World Student Christian Movement 27-34; Gen. Sec. Lutheran World Convention 35-44; Pres. Central Cttee. for Inner Mission in Germany 45-57; Bishop of Evangelical Lutheran Church of Hanover 47-; mem. Central Cttee. World Council of Churches 48; Member Evangelical Church Council, Germany; Pres. Lutheran World Fed. 52-57; Presiding Bishop of the United Evangelical Lutheran Church Germany; Hon. D.Theol. (Göttingen and Helsinki Univs.), Hon. D.D. (Edinburgh Univ., Augusta and Oberlin Colls.), Hon. L.H.D. (Muhlenberg and Concordia Colls.), Hon. LL.D. (Wittenberg Coll.).
Publs. *The Technical Era* 28, *Luther's Conception of History* 32, *The Last Book of the Bible* 40, *Luther Now* 46, *The Valley of Shadow* 47, *Martin Luther* 64.
Calenberger Strasse 34, Hanover 3, German Federal Republic.
Telephone: (0511) 15312.

Lilley, Tom; American industrialist; b. 13 Aug. 1912; ed. Harvard Univ.
Associate Professor and Assistant Dir. of Research, Harvard Business School 42-48; entered Ford Motor Co. 48, Asst. Divisional Controller 51, Asst. Gen. Man., Ford International Division 54, Vice-Pres. and Gen. Man., Int. Div. 57-59, Vice-Pres. Ford Int. Staff 60-65; Dir. Export-Import Bank of Washington 65-.
Office: Export-Import Bank, 811 Vermont Avenue, N.W., Washington, D.C. 20571, U.S.A.

Lillie, Beatrice (Lady Peel); British actress; b. 29 May 1898; ed. St. Agnes' Coll., Belleville, Ont., Canada.
Numerous appearances in revues and cabarets, London and New York 14-; first One-Woman Show, Summer Theater, New York 52, second (*Beasop's Fables*) U.S.A. 56; *An Evening with Beatrice Lillie*, London and Florida 56; appeared at Ziegfeld Follies, New York 57; played leading role in *Auntie Mame*, London 58; appeared in the films *Exit Smiling* 27, *Doctor Rhythm* 38, *On Approval* 44, *Around the World in Eighty Days* 56, *Thoroughly Modern Millie* 67; Donaldson Award 45, Antoinette Perry Award 53, etc.
55 Park Lane, London, W.1, England.

Lim, Manuel, A.B., LL.B., LL.M., D.C.L.; Philippine lawyer and politician; b. 6 Aug. 1899; ed. Univ. of Philippines and Univ. of Santo Tomás.
Lawyer 21-41, 45-47, 48-57, 59-60, 62-; Dean and Prof. Coll. of Law, Ateneo de Manila 36-41, 47-59; Prof. of Law, Univ. of Santo Tomas 38-41; judicial posts 41-48; Pres. Realty Investments Inc. 50-; Chair. Mindanao Mother Lode Mines Inc. 49-60; Pres. Tax Service of Philippines Inc. 57-59; Acting Sec. of Educ., Govt. of Philippines 57-59; Sec. of Commerce and Industry 60-62; Vice-Pres. and Gen. Counsel Philippine American Life Insurance Co. 62-; Chair. Comm. on Asian and Far Eastern Affairs—Int. Chamber of Commerce 67-; mem. Labour-Management Advisory Council 63-; mem. numerous legal and other associations and official of numerous industrial companies.
Philippine American Life Insurance Company, Manila, Philippines.

Lim, Robert Kho-Seng, M.B., CH.B., PH.D., D.SC.; American (b. Chinese) physiologist; b. 15 Oct. 1897; ed. Univ. of Edinburgh.

Lecturer Physiology, Univ. of Edinburgh 19-23; Prof. Peking Union Medical Coll., Peking 24-37; Man. Editor, *Chinese Journal of Physiology* 27-41; mem. Comm. for Biological Standardization, League of Nations 35-39; Dir. Chinese Red Cross Relief Corps 37-42; Insp.-Gen. Medical Service, Chinese Army 42-44, Deputy Surgeon-Gen. 44-45, Surgeon-Gen. 45-49; Organizing Dir. Inst. of Medicine, Academia Sinica 45, Nat. Defence Medical Centre 46; mem. Cttee. Int. Congress of Physiology 47-53; Prof. and Head Dept. of Physiology and Pharmacology, Creighton Univ., Nebraska 50-51; Dir. Medical Sciences Research Laboratory, Miles Laboratories Inc., Elkhart, Indiana 52-, now Emer.; Hon. mem. Deutsche Akad. der Naturforscher, Halle; Corresp. mem. Royal Acad. of Sciences Bologna, Fellow Academia Sinica; Yun Hui Order 1st Class, Legion of Merit, Medal of Freedom.
Publs. numerous scientific papers in the field of gastric secretion, central control of automatic function, and neuropharmacology.
738 Marine Avenue, Elkhart, Indiana 46514, U.S.A.
Telephone: JA2-3327.

Lim Yew Hock, Tun; Singapore politician and diplomatist; b. 14; ed. Raffles Institution.
Junior clerk; Sec. Singapore Clerical and Administrative Workers' Union; British Council scholarship to England 47, studied trade union and co-operative movements; nominated mem. Singapore Legislative Council 48-51, elected mem. 51-63; visited U.S.A. with U.S. Information Services grant 51; Minister of Labour and Welfare 55-59; Chief Minister 56-59; founder and Chair. Singapore People's Alliance 58; High Commr. in Australia 63-; led Constitutional Del. to London Mar.-April 57; Hon. Dr. Jur. (Univ. Malaya); awarded title Seri Maharaja Mangku Negara 58.
High Commission of Singapore, Canberra, A.C.T., Australia.

Lima, Francisco Negrão de; Brazilian politician.
Ambassador to Belgium, Paraguay, Venezuela and Portugal; Minister of Justice 51-52; Minister of Foreign Affairs 58-59; later Mayor of Rio de Janeiro; Gov. of Guanabara Oct. 65-; Partido Social Democrata.
Palacio Guanabara, Rio de Janeiro, E. Guanabara, Brasil.

Lima, Francisco R., LL.D.; Salvadorean lawyer and diplomatist; b. 13 Feb. 1917; ed. Saint Michel School, Brussels, Lycée Lakanal, Paris, Quernmore School, London, and Univ. of El Salvador.
Rockefeller Foundation Fellowship, Inst. of Anthropology and Social Sciences, Univ. of Mexico 41-45; practicing lawyer 45-56; Chief of Dept. of Statistics, Dept. of Labour 46; Chief of Social Security Comm., El Salvador 47-49; Alt. Rep. to UN 56-59; Rep. on Exec. Board UNICEF 57-59; Ambassador of El Salvador to United States and Rep. to Organization of American States (OAS) 62-64; Vice-Pres. Council of American States 61-62; Pres. OAS Cttee. on Econ. and Social Affairs 64-65.
c/o Ministry of Foreign Affairs, San Salvador, El Salvador.

Lima, Hermes; Brazilian lawyer, historian and politician; b. 02; ed. Univ. of Bahia.
Former Lecturer, Law Faculty, Univ. of Bahia, Univ. of São Paulo; fmr. Prof., Nat. Faculty of Law, Univ. of Brazil; fmr. Dir. School of Econs. and Law, Univ. of the Fed. Dist.; fmr. Legal Dir. Soc. for Agricultural and Industrial Research; Rep. UN Gen. Assembly 51, 52; Rep. to Pan-American Conf., Caracas 54; Head of the Civilian Cabinet of Presidential Affairs 61-62; Minister of Labour 62; Prime Minister Sept. 62-Jan. 63; Minister of Foreign Affairs Jan. 63-June 63.
Publs. *Introdução a Ciência do Direito, Tobias Barreto—a época e o homen, Notas á vida brasileira, Lições da Crise.*
c/o Ministry of Foreign Affairs, Rio de Janeiro, Brazil.

Lin Feng; Chinese politician; b. o6; ed. U.S.S.R. Joined C.C.P. 27; Political Commissar, Sino-Japanese War; mem. C.C.P. Central Cttee. 45-; Chair. Northeast China People's Govt. 49; mem. Nat. Cttee., People's Political Consultative Conf. 49-54, and Central People's Govt. Council 49-54; Dir. Second Office, State Council 54-59; Dep. from Mukden and mem. Standing Cttee., Nat. People's Congress 54-, Vice-Chair., Standing Cttee. 59-; Vice-Chair. Asscn. to Eliminate Illiteracy 56-; Head Spare Time Educ. Cttee., State Council 60-; Head of Higher Party School 63-.
Standing Committee, National People's Congress, Peking, China.

Lin Piao, Marshal; Chinese soldier and politician; b. o8; ed. Whampoa Military Acad.
In Northern Expedition in 4th Army; joined Communist Youth 25; Mem. Chinese C.P. 26-; at Chin-kang-shan and a founder of the Red Army 28; Commdr. First Red Army 32-36; Pres. of Red Army Acad. 36-37, Dir. 37; Dir. of Political Training; various mil. commands during campaigns; Commdr. Northeast People's Liberation Army 45, later Commdr. 4th Field Army; Mem. C.C.P. 45-; Commdr. Communist Forces in N.E. China 45-50; Vice-Chair. Council of Nat. Defence 54; del. to the N.P.C.; decorated for war services 55; mem. Political Bureau C.C.P. 56, Vice-Chair. Central Cttee., mem. Standing Cttee. of Politburo; Vice-Premier 59-; Minister of Nat. Defence Sept. 59-; Vice-Chair. Politburo 58-; named as heir to Mao Tse-tung.
Ministry of National Defence, Peking, China.

Lin Yutang, M.A., PH.D., HON. D.LITT.; Chinese author and philologist; b. 10 Oct. 1895; ed. St. John's, Harvard and Leipzig Univs.
Professor of English Philology Peiping Nat. Univ. 23-26; fmr. Dean of Arts Amoy Univ.; Research Fellow in Philology and English Editor Acad. Sinica 30-35; Sec. Ministry of Foreign Affairs 27; Chancellor Nanyang Univ., Singapore 54-55; contrib. Editor *China Critic*, Shanghai 30; inventor Chinese index system and collaborator in official romanization plan; founder and Editor *Lun Yu*, Shanghai 32, *This Human World* 34, *Yuchoufeng* 36; Del. Cttee. on Intellectual Co-operation; Head, Arts and Letters Dept., UNESCO 48.
Publs. *My Country and My People* 36, *The Importance of Living* 37, *Movement in Peking* 40, *With Love and Irony* 41, *A Leaf in the Storm* 42, *Wisdom of China and India* 42, *Between Tears and Laughter* 43, *The Vigil of a Nation* 45, *The Gay Genius* 47, *Chinatown Family* 48, *On the Wisdom of America* 50, *Peace is in the Heart* 50, *Widow, Nun and Courtesan* 51, *Famous Chinese Short Stories* 52, *Vermilion Gate* 53, *The Unexpected Island* 54, *Lady Wu* 57, *Secret Name* 59, *From Pagan to Christian* 60, *Importance of Understanding* 61, *Red Peony* 62, *The Pleasures of a Non-conformist* 63, *Juniper Loa* 64, *Flight of the Innocents* 65, *The Chinese Theory of Art* 67.
315 East 65th Street, New York 21, N.Y., U.S.A.

Linares Aranda, Francisco, M.S., PH.D.; Guatemalan diplomatist; b. 21; ed. Univ. of San Carlos, Guatemala City, and School of Foreign Service, Georgetown Univ., U.S.A.
Second Sec. Washington 43-45, First Sec. 45-47, Counsellor 47-50, Chargé d'Affaires a.i. 47-48, 49; Del. to Int. Civil Aviation Conf. Chicago 44, World Fund and Bank, Savannah, Ga. 46, F.A.O. Fifth Int. Conf. Washington 49 and other Int. Confs. in U.S.A. 44-49, 57, Vienna 61, Mexico 65; Alternate Rep. on Board of Dirs. Pan American Union 47-48, on Council Organisation of American States 48-50; Minister to Great Britain 50-53; Minister to France 53-54; Chief of Protocol, Ministry of Foreign Affairs, Guatemala 54-58; Under-Sec. of State Foreign Affairs Sept. 58-59, Acting Sec. Sept.-Oct. 58; Ambassadorial rank 57; Ambassador to German Federal Republic Dec. 59-62,

to Chile 62-63, to Mexico Sept. 63-Aug. 66, to U.S.A. Canada and O.A.S. 66-.
Embassy of Guatemala, 2220 R. St., N.W., Washington, D.C., U.S.A.
Telephone: DE 2-2865.

Linares Cerda, Julio; Nicaraguan judge, writer and poet; b. 26 May 1902; ed. Instituto de Rivas, Nicaragua, Instituto Ramírez Goyena, Managua, School of Law, Managua.
Secretary of Exec. Cttee., Managua Nat. District 30-33; Head of Legal Dept., Ministry of Labour 45-48; Prof. of Law, Managua Nat. Univ. 52; Pres. Higher Tribunal of Labour 50-56; Magistrate, Supreme Court of Justice 57-61; Pres. Supreme Court of Justice 62-63, Judge Supreme Electoral Tribunal 63-; mem. Acad. Nicaragüense; several awards for poetry.
Publs., mainly poetry, include *Poemas Cortos, Primavera y Otoño, Modesto Barrios* (biography), *El Mundo Fantasma, Caña de Azúcar, Antología Poética, Paisajes de Tierra y Alma, Letras nicaragüenses.*
3a-Avenida S.O. No. 1002, Managua, Nicaragua.
Telephone: 4044.

Linari Sespón, Jorge Oscar; Argentine journalist; b. o6; ed. Colegio Nacional Bartolomé Mitre.
Secretary *Revista América* 23; Managing Dir. *Suplemento Semanal* S.A. 24-46; Co.-Dir. *La República* 36-38; Managing Dir. *El Diario* 38-43; Dir.-Gen. Empresa Periodística Jorge Oscar Linari y Cia. S.R.L. (newspaper publishers) 43-62; mem. Consejo Directivo del Hogar Policial de la Seccional 19 de Buenos Aires 44-; Pres. and Dir.-Gen. Empresa Periodística Linari S.A.C. 62-; Founder-Pres. C.I.P. (Centro de Informaciones de Publicidad) 65-68; founder and Pres. Asociación Representantes Prensa Interior; founder and Pres. Asociación Promotores Publicitarios de la Argentina; Vice-Pres. Asociación Diarios y Periódicos del Interior; Dir. de Junta y Pres. Comisión de Promoción de A.D.E.P.A. (Asociación de Entidades Periodísticas Argentinas).
Mansilla 2450 (1° P.B.); and Esmeralda 358 (5° Piso), Buenos Aires, Argentina.
Telephone: 40-6920, 40-7293 and 46-6227.

Lindberg, Kai; Danish trade union leader and politician; b. 10 Dec. 1899.
Formerly skilled craftsman in shipbuilding and leader of the Engineering Workers' Trade Union; Sec. of Danish Fed. of Labour 41; mem. of upper house for short period 47; mem. of *Folketing* (lower house) 47-; Minister for Greenland 55-60, for Public Works 55-66.
Lundeborgv. 16, Hellerup, Denmark.

Lindberg, Stig; Swedish designer and ceramic artist; b. 17 Aug. 1916; ed. Stockholm State School of Arts and Crafts.
Began work at Gustavsberg potteries 37; founded with Prof. Kage Gustavsberg Studio 43, Art Dir. 49-58; textile designer for Nordiska Kompaniet, Stockholm 47-; Chief Instructor, Stockholm State School of Arts and Crafts 57; now working in pottery, porcelain and textile design, posters, drawings and sculpture; invented and introduced enamel painting for murals on steel sheet 49; many exhibitions, including Stockholm 41, Zürich 47, Copenhagen 49, Berlin 52, New York 51 and 57, Tokyo 59, London 61, 66, Cologne 65, Amsterdam 68; rep. at Victoria and Albert Museum (London), Museum of Modern Art (N.Y.), Museum für angewandte Kunst (Vienna), Stockholm Nat. Museum, Kunstindustrimuseum (Copenhagen) etc.; Grand Prix Milan Triennali 51 and 54; Swedish State Art Award 67, 68; Gold Medals: Cannes 55, Prague 62, Ljubljana 65, Munich 66.
Principal Works: Terma flameware 55, ceramic wall decoration at Saltsjöbaden 49, playing-card design 48, service in bone china for Stockholm town hall 59, stoneware fountain for Stockholm Folksam Building 60;

big murals: Alfa Laval Tumba 65, Nacka Hospital 66,
Kabi Imt 67.
Gustavsberg, Sweden.
Telephone: 0766-30297.

Lindbergh, Charles Augustus, A.F.C., D.S.C.; American
aviator; b. 4 Feb. 1902; ed. Univ. of Wisconsin and
Lincoln Flying School.
First flight 22; first flight as Air Mail pilot, Chicago to
St. Louis, April, 26; record coast to coast flight of 21
hours 20 minutes in 27; first non-stop solo transatlantic
flight from New York to Paris 27; Chair. Technical
Cttee. of Trans-Continental and Western Air Transport
31-35; Technical Adviser to Pan-American Airways;
left United States to avert possibility of second son
being kidnapped Dec. 35; on active service U.S. Air
Corps 39; Col. U.S. Army Corps Reserve to 41, resigned;
mem. Nat. Advisory Cttee. for Aeronautics until 39,
resigned; civilian expert doing research work for War
Dept. 42-45.
Publs. *Of Flight and Life* 48, *The Spirit of St. Louis*
(Pulitzer Prize) 53.
Scott's Cove, Darien, Conn., U.S.A.

Lindebraekke, Sjur, LL.D.; Norwegian banker and
politician; b. 6 April 1909; ed. Univ. of Oslo.
Assistant Manager Bergens Privatbank, Bergen 40-45,
Jt. Managing Dir. 45-59, Gen. Managing Dir. 59-; Pres.
Governmental Reparations Directorate 45-46; Pres.
Norwegian Bankers Asscn. 54-60; mem. Parliament
45-53; Vice-Chair. Conservative Party 50-54, Chair. 62-;
Cttee. mem. The Christian Michelsen Inst. for Science
and Intellectual Freedom; Knight First Class St. Olav
Order 60.
Publs. *Transfer of Ownership by Voluntary Transfer of
Personal Property* 40, *Negotiable Documents, Norwegian
Indemnification Law, Documentary Credit Law, Owner-
ship and Seizure in Bankruptcy Proceedings* 46,
Confidence and Political Confidence 53, *At a New Era* 65.
Bergens Privatbank, Torvalmenning 2, Bergen, Norway.

Lindemann, Erich, PH.D., M.D.; American (b. German)
psychiatrist; b. 1 May 1900; ed. Univs. of Marburg and
Giessen, Univ. Hospital of Cologne Medical Coll., and
Univ. of Heidelberg, Germany.
University of Iowa 29-53; Rockefeller Research Fellow
in Physiology and Psychiatry, Harvard Univ. 35-36;
Assoc. in Psychiatry, Harvard Medical School 41-48;
Lecturer, Dept. of Social Relations, Harvard Univ.
47-53; Lecturer in Psychoanalysis, Boston Psycho-
analytic Inst. 44-50; Assoc. Prof. of Mental Health,
Harvard Univ. School of Public Health 51-54; Prof. of
Psychiatry, Harvard Univ. Medical School 54-65; in
charge Psychiatric Out Patient Dept., Mass. Gen.
Hospital 38-46, Psychiatrist-in-Chief 54-65; Founder
and Dir. Wellesley Project 49-65; Visiting Prof. of
Psychiatry, Stanford Univ., Calif.
Publs. recent works: *The Biological and Social Sciences
in an Epidemiology of Mental Disorder* 42, *Modifications
in ego Structure and Personality Reactions under Drugs*
52, *Use of Psychoanalytic Constructs in Preventive
Psychiatry* 52, *The Wellesley Project for the Study of
Community Mental Health* 53, *The Nature of Mental
Health Work as a Professional Pursuit* 57, *Psycho-social
Factors as Stressor Agents* 60, *Preventive Intervention in
Situational Crisis* 62, *Mental Health and the Urban
Environment* 63.
Stanford Univ. Medical Center, Stanford, Calif. 94305;
Home: 2808 Greer Road, Palo Alto, Calif., U.S.A.

Linder, Harold Francis; American banker and govern-
ment official; b. 13 Sept. 1900; ed. Columbia Univ.
President, Cornell, Linder and Co. 25-33; Partner, Carl
M. Loeb, Rhoades and Co. 33-38; philanthropic work
and corporate directorships 38-61; U.S. Navy 41-45;
Pres. Gen. American Investors Co. Inc. 48-51; Deputy

Asst. Sec. of State for Econ. Affairs 51, Asst. Sec. 52-53;
Pres. and Chair. Export-Import Bank 61-; Democrat.
Export-Import Bank, Washington, D.C. 20571, U.S.A.
Telephone: Republic 7-7890.

Lindh, Sten, LL.B., B.A.; Swedish diplomatist and
industrialist; b. 24 Oct. 1922; ed. Kalmar Grammar
School, Stockholm Univ., and Stockholm Business
School.
Entered Swedish Foreign Service 45, served Washington,
Paris, London, Geneva and Brussels; Ministry of Finance
50-51; Head of Dept., Ministry of Foreign Affairs 59,
61-63; Head of EFTA Secr., Geneva 60; Ambassador
to the European Econ. Communities and Perm. Rep.
to Council of Europe 64-67; Amb. en disponibilité 68;
Pres. Skånska Cement A.B. and A.B. Iföverken 68-.
Fridhemsvägen 4, S-217 74 Malmö, Sweden.

Lindhardt, Poul Georg, D.TH.; Danish university professor; b. 12 Dec. 1910; ed. Univ. of Copenhagen.
Ordained 34, Minister in various parishes 34-42; Asst.
Lecturer Univ. of Copenhagen 39-41, Aarhus Univ.
41-42; Prof. of Church History, Aarhus Univ. 42-,
Dean of Faculty of Divinity 44, 48, 53, 57, 62; Minister
of Our Lady's Church, Aarhus 45.
Publs. *Konfirmationens Historie i Danmark* 36, *Dan-
mark og Reformkoncilierne* 42, *Bibelen og det danske
Folk* 42, *Den nordiske Kirkes Historie* 45, *Dines Pon-
toppidan* 48, *Morten Pontoppidan I* 50, *II* 53, *Grundtvig,
An Introduction* 51, *Vækkelser og kirkelige retninger* 51,
Det evige Liv 53, *En dansk Sognepræst* 54, *Fem Aalborg-
Bisper* 54, *Religion og Evangelium* 54, *Kirken igaar og
idag* 55, *15 Prædikener* 56, *Danmarks kirkehistorie 1849-
1901, To Højkirkemænd, Repliker, Helvedsstrategi* 58,
Vækkelse og kirkelige retninger (2nd ed.), *F. C. Krarups
Breve til Lyder Brun* 59, *Stat og kirke* 60, *Biskop Chr.
Ludwigs visitatsdagbog* 60, *Paaskud og Prædikener* 63,
Grundtvig 64, *Det religiøse liv i senmiddelalderen* 66, *Den
danske reformations historie* 66, *Den danske kirches
historie 1901-65* 66, *Stat og kirke* (2nd edn.) 67, *Den
nordiske kirkes historie* (2nd edn.) 67.
The University, Aarhus, Denmark.

Lindley, Sir Arnold Lewis George, Kt., C.G.I.A.,
M.I.MECH.E., M.I.E.E.; British electrical manufacturing
executive; b. 13 Nov. 1902; ed. Woolwich Polytechnic.
Chief Engineer, British Gen. Electric Co. (B.G.E.C.),
South Africa 33-45, Dir. and Man. 45-49; Dir. East
Rand Eng. Co. 43-49; Gen. Man. Erith Works, Gen.
Electric Co. (G.E.C.), England 49-58, Dir. G.E.C. 53-64,
Asst. Man. Dir. 58-59, Vice-Chair. 59-61, Chair. and
Managing Dir. 61-63, Chair. 63-64; Chair. Engineering
Industry Training Board 64; Deputy Chair. Motherwell
Bridge (Holdings) Ltd. 65-.
The Crest, Raggleswood, Chislehurst, Kent, England.
Telephone: 01-467-2159.

Lindo, Sir Henry Laurence, Kt., C.M.G.; Jamaican
diplomatist; b. 13 Aug. 1911; ed. Jamaica Coll.,
Jamaica, and Keble Coll., Oxford.
Inspector of Schools Jamaica 35; Asst. Information
Officer 39-43; Asst. Sec. Colonial Secretariat 45-50,
Principal Asst. Sec. 50-52; Administrator, Dominica,
Windward Islands 52-59; Acting Gov. Windward Is-
lands 57, 59; Governor's Sec., Jamaica 60-62; High
Commr. for Jamaica in U.K. 62-; Amb. to France 66-.
6-10 Bruton Street, London, W.1, England.

Lindon, Jérôme; French publisher; b. 9 June 1925.
Président-Directeur Général, Editions de Minuit 48-,
has published novels of the "nouveau roman" (Beckett,
Robbe-Grillet, Butor, Nathalie Sarraute, Simon, Pinget,
etc.); had nine books seized in his opposition to the
Algerian war.
Publ. *Jonas* 55.
Editions de Minuit, 7 rue Bernard Palissy, Paris 6e,
France.

Lindsay, Jack (son of Norman Lindsay, *q.v.*), B.A., F.R.S.L.; British author; b. 20 Oct. 1900; ed. Queensland Univ.

Earlier work mainly verse; began series of translations of Greek and Latin poets; came to England 26; Man. and Editor Fanfrolico Press until 30; began novel-writing and direct historical work in 30's; first historical novel 34; served in Signals and in War Office 41-45; Fellow, Royal Soc. of Literature.

Publs. Historical novels: *Rome for Sale, Caesar is Dead, Last Days with Cleopatra, The Barriers are Down, Thunder Underground,* and others on the ancient world; *1649, Lost Birthright, Men of Forty-eight, Fires in Smithfield,* and others on English history; biographies of Mark Antony, John Bunyan, George Meredith, Charles Dickens and J. M. W. Turner; various critical works and trans., including *I am a Roman, Medieval Latin Poets,* and *Song of a Falling World* (Latin poets A.D. 350-650); *Byzantium into Europe, Betrayed Spring, Rising Tide, Moment of Choice, Arthur and his Times, Life Rarely Tells, The Roaring Twenties* and *Fanfrolico and After* (autobiography), *Meeting with Poets;* works on Roman Britain and Roman Egypt; art-criticism, *The Death of the Hero, A Short History of Culture, The Clashing Rocks.*
Castle Hedingham, Halstead, Essex, England.
Telephone: Hedingham 259.

Lindsay, John Vliet; American politician; b. 24 Nov. 1921; ed. The Buckley School, St. Paul's School, Concord, Yale Univ., and Yale Law School.

Admitted to New York Bar 49; mem. Webster, Sheffield, Fleischmann, Hitchcock and Chrystie, New York 53-; Exec. Attorney to U.S. Attorney-Gen. 55-57; mem. U.S. House of Reps. 59-65; Mayor of New York 66-; Republican.
Publ. *Journey Into Politics* 67.
Gracie Mansion, New York City, N.Y., U.S.A.

Lindsay, Norman (father of Jack Lindsay, *q.v.*); Australian artist and writer; b. 23 Feb. 1879; ed. Creswick Grammar School.

Chief Cartoonist Sydney *Bulletin;* represented at Exhibition of Australian Art London; illustrated works of Theocritus, Boccaccio, Casanova, Petronius, Hugh McCrae's *Satyrs and Sunlight, Columbine,* Banjo Paterson's *The Animals that Noah Forgot,* etc.; joint founder the Endeavour Press.

Publs. include *The Pen Drawings of Norman Lindsay, A Curate in Bohemia* 13, *The Magic Pudding* 19, *Creative Effort* 20, *Redheap* 31, *Saturdee* 33, *Pan in the Parlour* 34, *Age of Consent* 38, *The Cousin from Fiji* 45, etc.
Bangslappers, Castle Hedingham, Halstead, Essex, England.

Lindsay, Lieut.-Gen. Richard Clark, (retd.); American air force officer; b. 31 Oct. 1905; ed. Univ. of Minn.

Commissioned Second Lieut. Air Corps, U.S. Army 29, advancing through grades to Major-Gen. 48; various peacetime assignments 29-41; Asst. Chief and Chief European-African Section, Air Plans, War Dept., Washington, D.C. 41-42; Staff Asst. and Chief of Combined Subjects Section, Operations Div., War Dept. Gen. Staff 42-43; Army Air Force Mem. Joint War Plans Cttee. of Joint Chiefs of Staff 43-44; Army Air Force mem. Joint Staff Planners of Joint Chiefs of Staff Organisation 44-45; Asst. Chief of Staff, Plas. (A-5), H.Q. U.S. Army Strategic Air Forces 45, at Guam and Pacific Air Commd., Manila 45; commd. 316th Bombardment Wing (VH), 8th Air Force, Okinawa 46; Asst. Chief of Staff, A-2, H.Q. F.E.A.F. 47; Chief, Policy Div., Directorate of Plans and Operations and Air Planner, H.Q. U.S.A.F., Washington, D.C. 47-48; Deputy Dir. Plans and Operations, Office of DCS/O 48-49; Deputy Dir. for Strategic Plans, The Joint Staff, Joint Chiefs of Staff 49-51; Standing Group

Liaison Officer to NATO 51-52; Commdg. Gen. 3650th Air Force Indoctrination Wing, Sampson Air Force Base, N.Y. 53-54; Dir. Plans, DCS/O 54-57; Asst. Deputy Chief of Staff, Operations Feb.-Aug. 57; Commdr. Allied Air Forces, Southern Europe 57-60; retd. from active service April 60; Res. Consultant The Rand Corpn. 61-63, Consultant 64-; Asst. to Pres. Electronic Communications Inc. 63-64; Asst. to Pres. and Dir. European Staff, Litton Systems European Div. 64-, Exec. Asst. to Pres. Econ. Dev. Div. 65; Gen. Man. Central Econ. Dev. Org., Washington 66-; decorations include D.S.M. (U.S.), Hon. C.B.E.
Fort Ward Towers, 2500 North Van Dorn, Alexandria, Va. 22302, U.S.A.
Telephone: 202-931-5564.

Lindskog, (Claes) Folke; Swedish business executive; b. 18 Jan. 1910; ed. Royal Inst. of Technology, Stockholm.

Managing Dir. The SKF Ball Bearing Co. (Pty.) Ltd., Johannesburg, S. Africa 57-60, The Skefko Ball Bearing Co. Ltd., Luton, England 60-64; Man. Dir. and mem Board Aktiebolaget Svenska Kullagerfabriken, Gothenburg, Sweden 64-.
Office: Aktiebolaget Svenska Kullagerfabriken, Hornsgaten 1, Gothenburg N.; Home: Lyckans väg 2, Gothenburg S., Sweden.

Lindström, Mrs. Ulla; Swedish politician; b. 15 Sept. 1909; ed. Univ. of Stockholm.

Teacher 33; Editor teachers' weekly publ. 34-46; Editor weekly publ. on housing 34-44; elected Stockholm Municipal Council 42; elected Senate 46-; Chair. Govt. Cttees. on the Furniture Industry, the Shoe Industry, and on the Distribution of Consumer Goods 46, 48, 55; Expert, Trade Dept. 46-54; Minister without Portfolio 54-66; mem. Swedish Del. to UN 47-66; Labour Party.
Fleminggatan 56, Stockholm, Sweden.

Lindt, Auguste Rudolph, LL.D.; Swiss diplomatist; b. 5 Aug. 1905; ed. Univs. of Geneva and Berne.

Special news corresp. in Manchuria, Liberia, Palestine, Jordan, the Persian Gulf, Tunisia, Rumania and Finland 27-40; served in Swiss Army 40-45; special del. of the Int. Red Cross, Berlin 45; Press Attaché and Counsellor Swiss Legation, London; Permanent Observer from Switzerland to the U.N. 53-56; fmr. Chair. U.N.I.C.E.F.; Pres. U.N. Opium Conf. 53; U.N. High Commissioner for Refugees 56-60; Swiss Ambassador to U.S.A. 60-63; Del. Swiss Federal Council for Technical Co-operation 63-66; Swiss Amb. to U.S.S.R. 66-; Hon. Dr. Univ. of Geneva.
Embassy of Switzerland, Moscow, U.S.S.R.

Lindtberg, Leopold; Swiss theatre producer and film director; b. 1 June 1902; ed. Realgymnasium Wien, and Universität Wien.

Actor, Berlin, Vienna, Düsseldorf 24-, later producer Berliner Staatstheater, Piscator-Buehne; Artistic Dir. Zürich Schauspielhaus 33-, Dir. 65-; Prof. at Univ. of Zürich; more than 150 theatrical productions; stage producer Habimah Theatre, Tel Aviv 34, 35; also film director 38-; theatrical productions at Vienna Burgtheater, Hamburg Schauspielhaus, Munich Kammerspiele, Israel theatres, Salzburg Festival; opera productions Staatsoper, Vienna and Hamburg, Municipal Opera, Frankfurt and Zürich; numerous awards.
Principal productions: *Faust,* Salzburg Festival 60-65; first performances at Zürich of Faulkner, Wilder, Sartre, Brecht, Zuckmayer, Frisch, Dürrenmatt; films: *Marie Louise* 43, *The Last Chance* 46, *Four in a Jeep* 50, *The Village* 53, *Profile of a Miracle* 58.
Publ. *Shakespeare's History Plays* 62.
Schuerbungert 36, Zürich, Switzerland.

Linen, James Alexander, III; American magazine executive; b. 20 June 1912; ed. The Hotchkiss School and Williams Coll.

Joined *Time* magazine 34, worked New York and Detroit 34-38; on *Life* magazine, New York 38-40, Advertising Man. *Life* 40-42; Office of War Information 42-45; Publisher *Time* 45-60, Pres. Time Inc. 60-; official of numerous civic, welfare and educational orgs.; Hon. L.H.D. (Long Island and Coll. of New Rochelle); Hon. LL.D. (Adelphi Univ.) 66.
Time and Life Building, Rockefeller Center, New York, N.Y. 10020; Home: John Street Greenwich, Conn., U.S.A.

Ling, James J.; American business executive; b. 22; ed. St. John's Collegiate Prep. School, Shreveport.
President Ling Electrics 46-58; Chair. Ling Electronics 58-60; Pres., Chair. Exec. Cttee. Ling Temco Electronics 60-61; Chair. Exec. Cttee. Ling-Temco-Vought Inc. 61-63, Chair. of Board and Chief Exec. Officer 63-; Dir. Graduate Research Center of Southwest, Nat. Bank of Commerce; Horatio Alger Award 62.
Ling-Temco-Vought Inc., P.O. Box 5003, Dallas, Texas 75222, U.S.A.

Linklater, Eric, C.B.E., T.D., LL.D.; British novelist; b. 8 March 1899; ed. Aberdeen Grammar School and Univ.
Private, The Black Watch 17-19; Asst. Editor *Times of India* 25-27; Asst. to Prof. of English Literature Aberdeen Univ. 27-28; Commonwealth Fellow in U.S.A. 28-30; Major Royal Engineers 39, Gen. Staff (Public Relations) War Office 41-45; Rector Aberdeen Univ. 45-48; Temporary Lieut.-Col., Korea 51.
Publs. *Whitemaa's Saga* 29, *Poet's Pub* 29, *A Dragon Laughed* (verse) 30, *Juan in America* 31, *Ben Jonson and King James* 31, *The Men of Ness* 32, *Mary Queen of Scots* 33, *The Crusader's Key* 33, *Magnus Merriman* 34, *The Revolution* 34, *Robert the Bruce* 34, *The Devil's in the News* (play) 34, *Ripeness is All* 35, *The Lion and the Unicorn* 35, *God Likes them Plain* 35, *Juan in China* 37, *The Sailor's Holiday* 37, *The Impregnable Women* 38, *Judas* 39, *The Man on My Back* (autobiography) 41, *The Cornerstones* 42, *Socrates Asks Why* 42, *The Great Ship* 43, *Crisis in Heaven* (play) 44, *The Wind on the Moon* (for children) 44, *Private Angelo* 46, *The Art of Adventure* 47, *Sealskin Trousers* 47, *The Pirates in the Deep Green Sea* (for children) 49, *Love in Albania* (play) 49, *A Spell for Old Bones* 49, *Two Comedies* 50, *Mr. Byculla* 50, *The Atom Doctor* (play) 50, *Laxdale Hall* 51, *The Italian Campaign* (Official History) 51, *A Year of Space* 53, *The House of Gair* 53, *The Faithful Ally* 54, *The Ultimate Viking* 55, *The Dark of Summer* 56, *A Sociable Plover* 57, *Position at Noon* 58, *Breakspear in Gascony* (play) 58, *The Merry Muse* 59, *Edinburgh* 60, *Roll of Honour* 61, *Husband of Delilah* 62, *A Man over Forty* 63, *Orkney and Shetland* 65, *The Prince in the Heather* 65, *The Conquest of England* 66, *A Terrible Freedom* 66, *The Survival of Scotland* 68, *The Stories of E. L.* (collected stories) 68.
Pitcalzean House, Easter Ross, Scotland.

Linner, Carl Sture, M.A.; Swedish international civil servant; b. 15 June 1917; ed. Stockholm and Uppsala Univs.
Associate Prof. of Greek, Uppsala Univ. 43; Del. to Int. Red Cross, Greece 43-45; Dir. A.B. Electrolux, Stockholm 45-50; Dir. Swedish Employers' Confederation 50-51; Exec. Vice-Pres. A.B. Bahco, Stockholm 51-57; Pres. Swedish Lamco Syndicate 57; Exec. Vice-Pres. and Gen. Man. Liberian-American-Swedish Minerals Co., Monrovia 58-60; Chief UN Civilian Operations, later UN Mission, in the Congo 60-61; Special Rep. of UN Sec.-Gen. in Brussels and London 62; UN Rep. in Greece, Turkey, Israel and Cyprus 62-65, in London 65-; mem. Royal Acad. of Arts and Sciences, Uppsala; Star of Africa, Order of Phoenix, Prince Carl Medal.
Publs. *Syntaktische und Lexikalische Studien zur Historia Lausiaca des Palladios* 43, *Giorgos Seferis* 63, *Roms*

Konungahävder 65, *Fredrika Bremer i Grekland* 65, *W. H. Humphreys' First Journal of the Greek War of Independence* 66.
c/o United Nations Office, 14-15 Stratford Place, London, W.1, England.
Telephone: 01-629-3816.

Linnik, Vladimir Pavlovich; Soviet physicist; b. 89; ed. Kiev Univ.
Professor, Leningrad Univ. 26-41, Prof. State Optical Inst. 26-; mem. U.S.S.R. Acad. of Sciences 39-; State Prizes 46, 50; two Orders of Lenin.
Publs. *Instrument for Interferential Investigation of Reflecting Objects under the Microscope, Instrument for Interferential Investigation of Surface Microprofile*, papers on constructing optical instruments.
U.S.S.R. Academy of Sciences, 14 Lenin Prospekt, Moscow, U.S.S.R.

Linnik, Yuri Vladimirovich; Soviet mathematician; b. 1915; ed. Leningrad State Univ.
Postgraduate, Moscow State Univ. 38-40; Soviet Army 41-42; Research Work, Leningrad Section, U.S.S.R. Acad. of Sciences, Steklov Mathematical Inst. 42-(now Chief of Laboratory); Prof. Leningrad State Univ. 44-; Corresp. mem. U.S.S.R. Acad. of Sciences 53-64, mem. 64-; State Prize.
Publs. Works on theory of figures, theory of probabilities, and mathematical statistics.
U.S.S.R. Academy of Sciences, 14 Lenin Prospekt, Moscow, U.S.S.R.

Linowitz, Sol Myron, LL.B.; American lawyer and business executive; b. 7 Dec. 1913; ed. Hamilton Coll., and Cornell Univ. Law School.
Assistant Gen. Counsel, Office of Price Admin., Washington 42-44; Officer, Office of Gen. Counsel, Navy Dept. 44-46; Fmr. Partner, Harris, Beach, Wilcox, Dale & Linowitz, Gen. Counsel, Chair. of Board and Chair. of Exec. Cttee., Xerox Corpn.; Trustee, John F. Kennedy Center for Performing Arts, American Assembly, Cornell Univ., Univ. of Rochester, Hamilton Coll.; Mem. Freedom House, American Jewish Cttee.; mem. Regent's Advisory Cttee. on Educational Leadership, American Bar Asscn. Cttee. on Int. Law; U.S.A. Amb. to the Org. of American States 66-; U.S.A. Rep. on the Inter-American Cttee. of the Alliance for Progress.
2204 Wyoming Avenue, Washington, D.C., U.S.A.
Telephone: 483-9086.

Linsenmeyer, John Cyril, B.S.; American manufacturing executive; b. 5 Feb. 1904; ed. Univ. of Detroit.
Engineer, McColl, Snyder and McLean, Detroit 25-31; American Radiator and Standard Sanitary Corpn. 31-, Plant Man. 39-46, Works Man. 46-53, Pres. Subsidiary Co. 53-57, Exec. Vice-Pres. and Dir. (Corporative Development) 57-.
American Radiator and Standard Sanitary Corporation, 40, West 40th Street, New York 18, N.Y.; Home: 15 East 91st., New York 28, N.Y., U.S.A.

Linthorst Homan, Johannes, LL.D.; Netherlands official; b. 28 Aug. 1903; ed. Leiden Univ.
Mayor of Vledder 32; Queen's Commissioner, Province of Groningen 37-41; Pres. Nat. Office for Town and Country Planning 47; Dir. European Integration, Ministry of Economic Affairs 52; Head Netherlands del. Brussels Conf. 55-57; Pres. Netherlands Olympic Cttee. 51-59; Ambassador, Head Netherlands Mission to the European Economic Community and European Community for Atomic Energy 58; mem. High Authority, ECSC 62-67; Nederlandse Leeuw, Grande Croix de l'Ordre de Léopold II (Belgium), Grande Croix de l'Ordre Grand-Ducal de la Couronne de Chêne (Luxembourg), Grand Croix de l'Ordre Royal du Phénix (Greece) and other orders.
Publs. *The Birth of Local Community in the Province of*

Drenthe 34, *History of Drenthe* 46, *European Agricultural Policy* 50, *European Integration* 55.
2 Place de Metz, Luxembourg.

Linton, Sir Andrew, K.B.E.; New Zealand farmer; b. 93; ed. schools in Otago and Southland, New Zealand. New Zealand Dairy Board 35-, Chair. 56-; fmr. Chair. New Zealand Dairy Research Inst.; Chair. New Zealand Veterinary Council 47-57; Chair. Superannuation Board 52; mem. New Zealand Meat Board 58; Dir. Freezing Co. 41.
Glenavon, Greytown, Wairarapa, New Zealand.

Lintott, Sir Henry (John Bevis), K.C.M.G.; British diplomatist; b. 23 Sept. 1908; ed. Edinburgh Acad., Edinburgh Univ., and King's Coll., Cambridge.
Customs and Excise Dept. 32-35; Board of Trade 35-48; Ministry of Econ. Warfare 39-40; Office of Minister of State, Cairo 41; Dep. Sec.-Gen. OEEC 48-56; Dep. Under-Sec. of State, Commonwealth Relations Office 56-63; High Commr. in Canada 63-.
British High Commission, Ottawa, Ontario, Canada.

Lipchitz, Jacques; American (Lithuanian-born) sculptor; b. 22 Aug. 1891.
Worked in Paris 09-40, in U.S.A. 40-; works include *Prometheus Strangling the Vulture* (for Paris Int. Exhibition 37) *Mother and Child* and *Virgin* commissioned for Dominican church at Assy (France), casts of which are also in Iona Abbey (Scotland) and shrine at New Harmony (Ind.).
c/o Fine Arts Associates, 44 Walker Street, New York City, N.Y., U.S.A.

Lipiński, Edward; Polish economist; b. 88; ed. Leipzig and Zürich Univs.
Lecturer, Cen. School of Econ. Warsaw 23, Prof. 29; Founder Dir. Inst. for Study of Markets and Prices, Warsaw 27-39; Prof. Łódź Univ. 45; Chair. Warsaw Inst. of Economics 45-48; Prof. Warsaw Univ. 50; Pres. Bank Gospodarstwa Krajowego (Bank of Nat. Economy) 47-50; Deputy Chair. Economic Council 57-; mem. Polish Acad. of Sciences and several foreign scientific Socs.; State Prize, First Class 53.
Publs. *Ruch robotniczy w Polsce* (The Workers' Movement in Poland), *Inspekcja Pracy* (Work Inspection) 16, *Statystyka dotyczaca robotników miejskich* (Statistics Relating to Urban Workers) 18, *Historią myśli ekonomicznej* (History of Economic Thought) 56, *Rewizje* (Reassessments) 57, *Studia nad historią polskiej myślć ekonomicznej* (Studies on the History of Polish Economic Thought) 55, *Teoria ekonomii a rzeczywistoći* (Economics and Economic Reality) 61, *Histoire de la pensée économique en Pologne* 61.
Rakowiecka 6, Warsaw, Poland.

Lipmann, Fritz (Albert), M.D., PH.D., SC.D.; American biochemist; b. 12 June 1899; ed. Univs. of Koenigsberg and Berlin.
Research Asst. Kaiser Wilhelm Inst., Berlin and Heidelberg 27-31; research Fellow Rockefeller Inst. for Medical Research, N.Y.C. 31-32; research Assoc. Biological Inst. of Carlsberg Foundation, Copenhagen 32-39; research Assoc. Dept. of Biological Chemistry, Cornell Univ. Medical School, N.Y.C. 39-41 ; research Fellow in Surgery, Harvard Medical School, Boston 41-43 and Assoc. in Biochemistry 43-49; Prof. of Biological Chemistry Harvard Medical School, Massachusetts Gen. Hospital, Boston 49-57; Prof. of Rockefeller Univ., New York City 57-; has done outstanding work on energy metabolism, the metabolic function of B vitamins, and has discovered coenzyme A; Foreign mem. Royal Soc. (U.K.); Nobel Prize in Medicine and Physiology 53; Nat. Medal of Science 66; Hon. Sc.D.
The Rockefeller University, New York, N.Y. 10021; and 150 East 18th Street, New York, N.Y. 10003, U.S.A.

Lippmann, Walter; American journalist; b. 23 Sept. 1889; ed. Harvard Univ.
Former Assoc. Editor *New Republic*; Asst. to Sec. of War 17; Sec. of org. to prepare data for Peace Conf.; Editor *New York World* until 31; special writer for *New York Herald-Tribune* 31-67; Overseer Harvard 33-39; mem. Inst. of Arts and Letters, Acad. of Arts and Letters; Gold Medal, American Inst. of Arts and Letters 65; Commdr. Légion d'Honneur, Order of Orange Nassau; Officer, Order of Leopold; Kt. Cross Order of St. Olav; Hon. LL.D., Hon. Litt.D.
Publs. *A Preface to Politics* 13, *Drift and Mastery* 14, *The Stakes of Diplomacy* 15, *The Political Scene* 19, *Liberty and the News* 20, *Public Opinion* 22, *The Phantom Public* 25, *Men of Destiny* 27, *American Inquisitors* 28, *A Preface to Morals* 29, *The United States in World Affairs* (with William O. Scroggs), 2 vols., 32, 33, *The Method of Freedom* 34, *The New Imperative* 35, *Interpretations* (2 vols.) 32, 35, *The Good Society* 37, *Some Notes on War and Peace* 40, *U.S. Foreign Policy: Shield of the Republic* 43, *U.S. War Aims* 44, *Cold War* 47, *Isolation and Alliances* 52, *The Public Philosophy* 55, *The Communist World and Ours* 59, *The Coming Tests with Russia* 61, *Western Unity and the Common Market* 62, *The Essential Lippmann* 63, *Poems by Paul Mariett* (Editor).
1021 Park Avenue, New York, N.Y. 10028, U.S.A.

Lipton, Seymour; American sculptor; b. 6 Nov. 1903; ed. Columbia Univ.
Teacher, New School for Social Research, New York City 39-58, Cooper Union Art School, N.Y.C. 43-45, New Jersey State Teachers' Coll., Newark 44-45; One-Man shows New York City 38-58, Washington 51; Visiting critic, Yale Art School 57-59; rep. Venice Biennale 58; Guggenheim Award 60, Ford Foundation Award 61 and others; represented in over 160 museums throughout the world.
302 West 98th Street, New York City, N.Y., U.S.A.

Lisette, Gabriel; Chad politician; b. 2 April 1919; ed. Lycée Carnot (Point-à-Pitre, Guadeloupe), Lycée Henri IV (Paris) and Ecole Nat. de la France d'Outremer.
Admin. France d'Outre-mer 44-46; Dep. from Chad to Nat. Assembly, Paris 46-51, 56-59; Territorial Counsellor, Chad 52-59; Pres. Chad Govt. Council 57-58; Deputy Chad Legislative Assembly 59-60; Pres. Council of Ministers, Repub. of Chad 58-59, Vice-Pres. 59-60; Minister-Counsellor to French Govt. 59-60; Admin.-in-Chief of Overseas Affairs (France); Mayor of Fort-Lamy 56-60; French Govt. Perm. Rep. Econ. Comm. for Latin America (ECLA); Pres. Mutualité d'Outre-mer et de l'Extérieur 63; fmr. Vice-Pres. Rassemblement Démocratique Africain (R.D.A.); fmr. Joint leader Parti Progressiste Tchadien; First Citizen of Honour of Chad; Chevalier Légion d'Honneur; Commdr. de l'Ordre Nat. de la République de Côte d'Ivoire.
French Delegation to ECLA, Sainte-Rose, Guadeloupe, Antilles; 3 boulevard des Courcelles, Paris 8e, France.

Lissák, Kálmán; Hungarian university professor; b. 13 Jan. 1908; ed. Univ. of Budapest.
Assistant, Physiological Inst., Debrecen Univ. 33-37, Reader 37-41, Prof. 41-43; Prof. of Physiology, Medical Univ. of Pécs; Dean of Medical Faculty, Univ. of Pécs 46-47, 50-51, 56-57, Rector 47-48, 48-49; mem. Hungarian Acad. of Sciences; Kossuth Prize 54; mem. Deutsche Akad. der Naturforscher Leopoldina 67; Hon. mem. Purkinje Medical Soc. of Czechoslovakia.
Publs. *Neurophysiology and Neuro-Endocrine Regulation of Behaviour;* numerous articles in Hungarian, English, American, German and Russian medical journals.
Physiological Institute, Rákoczi ut. 80, Pécs, Hungary. Telephone: 12-63.

Lissouba, Pascal; Congolese politician; b. 10 Nov.
1931; ed. secondary education in Nice, France, and
Ecole Supérieure d'Agriculture, Tunis.
Former agricultural specialist; Prime Minister of Congo
(Brazzaville) Dec. 63-66, concurrently Minister of Trade
and Industry and Agriculture.
Brazzaville, Republic of the Congo.

Lister, Sir (Charles) Percy, Kt., D.L.; British company
director; b. 15 July 1897; ed. Mill Hill School, and
Royal Military Coll., Sandhurst.
Chair. and Man. Dir. R. A. Lister Co. Ltd. until Sept. 67;
Chair. Blackstone & Co. Ltd.; Dir. Broom & Wade Ltd.,
Armstrong Whitworth (Engineers) Ltd., Harrison
Lister Engineering, Hawker Siddeley Group Ltd.; Pres.
R. A. Lister & Cie. Brussels; mem. Capital Issues Cttee.,
Western Hemisphere Exports Council; mem. Iron and
Steel Board 53-57.
Stinchcombe Hill House, Dursley, Gloucestershire,
England.
Telephone: Dursley 2030.

Listov, Konstantin Yakovlevich; Soviet composer;
b. 1900; ed. Tsaritzin Musical School.
Order of Red Star 43, Honoured Worker of the Arts of
R.S.F.S.R. 50.
Principal compositions: Operettas: *Coralina* 48, *Dream-
ers* 50, *Ira* 51, *Song of the Volgograders* 55, *Rustle of Our
Forests* 57, *Sebastopol Waltz* 61; Operas: *Olesya* 57,
Daughter of Cuba 61; Romances and songs, settings
of verse by Russian and Soviet poets, many musical
pieces for radio and theatre productions.
Moscow Branch, Composers' Union of the R.S.F.S.R.,
4/6 3rd Miusskaya Street, Moscow, U.S.S.R.

Listowel, Earl of; **William Francis Hare,** P.C., G.C.M.G.,
PH.D.; British philosopher and politician; b. 28 Sept.
1906; ed. Eton and Balliol Coll., Oxford, and London
Univ.
Labour mem. London County Council for East Lewis-
ham; Chief Whip Labour Party and Deputy Leader
House of Lords, Parl. Under-Sec. of State India Office
44-45; Postmaster-Gen. Aug. 45-April 47; Sec. of State
for India and Burma April-Aug. 47; Sec. of State for
Burma, Aug. 47-Dec. 48; Minister of State for the
Colonies Jan. 48-50; Joint Parl. Sec., Ministry of Agri-
culture and Fisheries 50-51; Gov.-Gen. of Ghana 57-60.
Publs. *The Values of Life* 31, *A Critical History of
Modern Esthetics* 33.
31 Old Church Street, London, S.W.3, England.

Little, Clarence C., B.A., M.S., D.SC., LL.D., LITT.D.,
L.H.D., ED.D.; American geneticist and pathologist; b.
6 Oct. 1888; ed. Harvard Univ.
Research Asst. in Genetics, Harvard Univ. 10-13, Asst.
Dean 15-18 and Associate in Comparative Pathology
16-19; Pres. Univ. of Maine 22-25; Pres. Univ. of
Michigan 25-29; Dir. R. B. Jackson Memorial Labora-
tory 29-56, Emer. 56-; Man. Dir. American Soc. for
Control of Cancer 29-45; Pres. American Eugenics
Society 30; Pres. American Cancer Research 31-40;
Scientific Director Tobacco Industrial Research Cttee.
54-; Fellow Nat. Acad. of Sciences, American Asscn. for
the Advancement of Science and American Acad. of
Arts and Sciences; Pres. American Birth Control
League, American Euthanasia Society 39-43.
Publs. *The Awakening College* 30, *Civilization Against
Cancer* 40, *Genetics, Biological Individuality and Cancer*
54, *The Inheritance of Coat Color in Dogs* 56.
R.F.D. 1, Ellsworth, Maine, U.S.A.

Little, Henry G.; American advertising executive; b.
01; ed. Hollywood High School, Hollywood, California.
Vice-Pres. Lord and Thomas, Chicago 36-40; Vice-Pres.
and Man. Roy S. Durstine, Cincinnati 40-41; Advertising
Man., Nash-Kelvinator Corpn. 41-44; Gen. Man.

Campbell-Ewald Co. 44-45, Exec. Vice-Pres. 45-52,
Pres. 52-58, Chair. of Board 53-.
Campbell-Ewald Company, General Motors Building,
Detroit, Michigan 48202, U.S.A.

Littler, Emile; British theatrical impresario, producer,
author and company director; b. 9 Sept. 1903; ed.
Stratford-on-Avon.
Served apprenticeship working on theatre stages;
Asst. Man. Theatre in Southend 22; subsequently
worked as Asst. Stage Man., Birmingham Repertory
Theatre; in U.S.A. 27-31; became Man. and Licensee
Birmingham Repertory Theatre for Sir Barry Jack-
son 31; began personally in management 33; theatrical
productions include *Victoria Regina, 1066 and All That,
The Maid of the Mountains, The Night and the Music,
Claudia, The Quaker Girl, Lilac Time, The Barretts of
Wimpole Street, Song of Norway, Annie Get Your Gun,
Blue for a Boy, Zip Goes a Million, Love from Judy, Book
of the Month, The Lovebirds, The Happiest Millionaire,
Signpost to Murder, The Right Hon. Gentleman*; Chair.
and Man. Dir. Palace Theatre, London, Cambridge
Theatre, London, London Entertainments Ltd., Emile
Littler Ltd., Keith Prowse Ltd., Theatres Mutual
Insurance Co. Ltd.; a Gov. of Royal Shakespeare
Theatre, Stratford-on-Avon; Dir. Westward Television,
Eagle Star Insurance.
Publs. (joint author) *Cabbages and Kings, Too Young
to Marry, Love Isn't Everything*; and ten Christmas
pantomines.
31 St. Martin's Lane, London, W.C.2, England.

Littlewood, Joan; British theatrical director; ed.
Royal Acad. of Dramatic Art, London.
Began career with Manchester Repertory Theatre;
founded Theatre Union 37; free-lance work for B.B.C.
39-45; founded Theatre Workshop 45, tours in Great
Britain and Europe 45-53, established in Theatre
Royal, Stratford (London) 53-61, 63-64, 67-; at work at
Cultural Centre, Hammamet, Tunisia 66-67; productions
include *Uranium 235, The Good Soldier Schweik,
Lysistrata, Richard II, Volpone, The Quare Fellow, The
Hostage, A Taste of Honey, Fings ain't Wot They Used
T'be, Make Me an Offer, Sparrers Can't Sing* (film 63),
Oh What a Lovely War 63, *A Kayf Up West* 64, *Macbird*
67, *Intrigues and Amours* 67, *Mrs. Wilson's Diary* 67,
The Marie Lloyd Story 67; East Berlin Gold Medal
(for *Lysistrata*) 58, Best Production Award, Théâtre
des Nations (Paris) 59, Olympic Award Taormina 59,
Challenge Trophy, Grand Prix Théâtre des Nations
(Paris) 63.
c/o Theatre Royal, Stratford, London, E.15, England.

Littlewood, John Edensor, M.A., LL.D., D.SC., SC.D.,
F.R.S., F.R.A.S.; British mathematician; b. 9 June 1885;
ed. St. Paul's School, and Trinity Coll., Cambridge.
Senior Wrangler 05; Richardson Lecturer Manchester
Univ. 07-10; Lecturer Trinity Coll. 10-28 and Rouse
Ball Prof. of Mathematics Cambridge Univ. 28-50;
Fellow Trinity Coll. 08-; Fellow Cambridge Philoso-
phical Society; Foreign mem. Royal Danish Acad.,
Royal Neths. Acad. and Royal Swedish Acad.; corresp.
mem. Paris Acad., Gesellschaft der Wissenschaften zu
Göttingen; Royal Medal Royal Society 29, De Morgan
Medal, London Mathematical Society 39, Sylvester
Medal Royal Society 43, Copley Medal, Royal Society 58.
Publs. *The Elements of the Theory of Real Functions,
Lectures on the Theory of Functions, A Mathematician's
Miscellany*.
Trinity College, Cambridge, England.

Liu Chang-sheng; Chinese trade union leader.
Joined Communist Youth in Vladivostok 24; went to
Yenan 36; on Northern Exec. Bureau of All-China Fed-
erated Trade Unions; in Japanese War underground work
in Shanghai; additional member of Central Cttee. 7th
Congress C.C.P. 45; on exec. of All-China Federated

Trade Unions and dir. East China Office; Chair. Shanghai Federated Trade Unions; on C.P.P.C.C. 49; on East China Mil. and Administrative Council, on Financial and Economic Cttee. and head Labour Dept. 50; on standing cttee. C.P.P.C.C. 53; Vice-Chair. All-China Fed. of Trade Unions 53-; Shantung del. to N.P.C. 54; on Central Cttee. 8th Congress C.C.P. 56; Chair. China-Africa Friendship Asscn.
All-China Federation of Trade Unions, 1 Fu Chien Street, Peking, China.

Liu Chieh; Chinese diplomatist; b. 16 April 1906; ed. Oxford and Columbia Univs.
Foreign Service 31-; Chinese Del. to League of Nations 32-39; Counsellor, Chinese Embassy, London 33-40, Minister, Washington 40-45; Vice-Minister for Foreign Affairs 45-47; Ambassador to Canada 47-63; mem. Chinese Del. to UN 46-; Pres. UN Trusteeship Council 48; mem. Int. Law Comm. 61-66; Perm. Rep. of China to UN 62-.
Permanent Mission of Republic of China (Taiwan) to the United Nations, 201 East 42nd Street, 15th Floor, New York City, N.Y. 10017, U.S.A.
Telephone: MU7-2022.

Liu Chieh; Chinese politician.
Honan Prov. People's Govt. 49-54; Dir. Dept. of Industry, Chinese Mil. and Admin. Cttee. 51-52, Vice-Chair. Cttee. of Finance and Economic Affairs 51-54; Vice- Minister of Geology, Central People's Govt. 52-58; Deputy Dir., 3rd Office, State Council 55-58; Vice-Minister, First Ministry of Machine Building 58-60, Minister, Second Ministry of Machine Building 60-.
Second Ministry of Machine Building, Peking, China.

Liu Hsiao; Chinese diplomatist.
On executive cttee. of 2nd All-China Congress of Soviets at Juichin 34; sec. of Kiangon Provincial Cttee. 42; additional mem. Central Cttee. at 7th Congress C.C.P. 45; 2nd sec. Shanghai City Council 49; cttee. mem. and dir. of supervisory cttee. of East China Mil. and Admin. Council 49-53; on East China Area Council 53; del. to and on standing cttee. of C.P.P.C.C. 2nd session 54; mem. Central Cttee. Chinese Communist Party; Ambassador to U.S.S.R. 55-62; Vice-Foreign Minister 63-.
Central Committee of the Chinese Communist Party, Peking, China.

Liu Hsiu-feng; Chinese Communist official and administrator; b. 11.
Joined Chinese Communist Youth 24; leader of student movement; arrested and imprisoned at Paoting 26; on release Sec. of Wan District Party; later worked in Tientsin area, arrested and imprisoned, released 35, became Dir. Organisation Dept., Hopei Cttee.; in Japanese War organised a Volunteer Force and in guerilla activity; in Yenan 32; Sec. Chang-thia-kon City C.C.P. Cttee; Vice-Mayor Tientsin City government 49; Vice-Chair. North China Administrative Council 53-54; positions on North China Bureau of C.C.P. 53-54; Vice-Minister of Building 54, Minister 58-65; on 2nd C.P.P.C.C. 54.
c/o Ministry of Building, Peking, China.

Liu Ke-ping; Chinese political official of Hui nationality.
On State Council and Vice-Dir. Nationalities Cttee. 49; on Electoral Law Drafting Cttee. 53; Vice-Dir. Central Institute of Nationalities 54; Tientsin del. to 1st. N.P.C.; on standing cttee. and dir. Nationalities Cttee. 54; Asst. Dir. Central United Battle Front work 54-56; mem. Central Cttee. C.C.P. 56- and mem. Central Control Cttee.; fmr. Chair. Cttee. of Nationalities, Nat. People's Congress.
Central Committee of Chinese Communist Party, Peking, China.

Liu Lan-Tao; Chinese government official and administrator.
Additional mem. Central Cttee. 7th Congress C.C.P. 45; Dir. Bureau for Northern Affairs Central People's Government 50; exec. mem. Cttee. for Administration for North, State Council 52, Chair. 53; on Cttee. for Draft Electoral Law 53; 3rd Sec. Northern Office, Central People's Government 53-54; Hopeh del. to N.P.C. 54; released for duty with Northern Office; on Standing Cttee. N.P.C. 54; Asst. Sec.-Gen. C.C.P. 55-65; Deputy Chair. Chinese People's Political Consultative Conf. 65-; posts in secr. and Cen. Control Cttee., C.C.P.
Chinese People's Political Consultative Conference, Peking, China.

Liu Ning-Yi; Chinese trade union organiser; b. 05.
Led labour movements in Peking, Tientsin, etc.; imprisoned 32-37; organised labour in Shensi-Kansu-Ningsia border areas 43; active in Nanking and Shanghai 46; standing cttee. of C.P.P.C.C. 49; Electoral Law Drafting Cttee. 53; Chair. Congress of Chinese T.U.s; del. for Shantung at 1st N.P.C., and elected to standing cttee. 54; Sec.-Gen. and Vice-Chair. of Asian Solidarity Cttee. of China 56; Chair. All-China Fed. of Trade Unions 58-; Vice-Chair. and Sec.-Gen. N.P.C. Standing Cttee. 65-; mem. Secr. of Central Cttee. of C.C.P. 66-.
All-China Federation of Trade Unions, 1 Fu Chien Street, Peking, China.

Liu Pai-yu; Chinese short story writer; b. 15.
In Yenan during war; reporter for Hsin Hwa Agency; President, Yenan branch, National Writers' Anti-Aggression Association; edited *Ta-chung wen-i*; on Cttee. of Chinese Writers' Association 53; del. for Honan in 1st N.P.C. 54; on editorial board *Wen-i pao* 55; Sec. of Union of Chinese Writers 56.
Union of Chinese Writers, Peking, China.

Liu Po-cheng; Marshal of the Chinese Army and politician; b. 92; ed. Red Army Mil. Acad., Soviet Mil. Acad.
Revolutionary activity in Szechwan in 11; joined C.C.P. 26; took part in Nanchang rising 27; studied in U.S.S.R. 28-30; on Gen. Staff, Red Army; active in Border Areas 32; Cttee. of 7th Congress C.C.P. 45; Commander Central Forces, P.L.A. 46; first to cross Yellow River 47; took Nanking 49; Chair. Southwest Mil. Government Council; Dir. People's Liberation Army Mil. Acad. 51; del. for People's Liberation Army to 1st N.P.C. and on standing cttee. 54; Vice-Chair. Council of Nat. Defence 54-; decorated for war services 55; mem. Political Bureau 56-; Vice-Chair. Standing Cttee. Nat. People's Congress 61-.
Council of National Defence, Peking, China.

Liu Shao-chi; Chinese Marxist scholar, trade unionist and politician; b. 98; ed. Far Eastern Univ., Moscow.
Joined Communist Party 21; with Secretariat, China Labour Union 22; Vice-Chair. All-China Fed. of Trade Unions 25, Sec.-Gen. 26; mem. Central Cttee. Communist Party 27, Central Control Cttee. 28; mem. Exec. Bureau Int. Congress of Trade Unions in Moscow 30-31; mem. Political Bureau of Central Cttee. C.P. 31-, mem. Standing Cttee.; returned to China to serve in Trade Unions Dept. of Central Cttee.; in Long March to Northwest 34 and apptd. Head Political Dept. 3rd Army Corps.; Sec. North China Bureau of Central Cttee. C.P. 36, Central Plain Bureau 38; Political Commissar New 4th Army 41; Vice-Chair. Chinese People's Revolutionary Mil. Council 43; Pres. Nat. Conf. on Agrarian Work 47; Vice-Chair. Central People's Govt. 49-; Vice-Chair. People's Revolutionary Mil. Council 49; Hon. Pres. All-China Fed. of Trade Unions 49-; Vice-Pres. World Fed. of Trade Unions 49; Chair. Standing Cttee. 1st Nat. People's Congress 54; Chair. Chinese People's Republic 59-.

Publs. *How to be a Good Communist* and other theoretical works.
Office of the Chairman of the Chinese People's Republic, Peking, China.

Liu Tzu-hou; Chinese administrator.
Director of Finance, Honan-Hupeh Border Admin. Sino-Japanese War; mem. Cttee. of People's Control, Central-South China Mil. and Admin. Cttee. 49, Hupeh Prov. People's Govt. 49-51, Vice-Chair. 51, Gov. Hupeh 54-56, Gov. Hopei 58-; Second Sec. C.C.P. Hupeh Prov. Cttee. 53; mem. Secretariat C.C.P. Hopei Prov. Cttee.; Dep. from Hopei Nat. People's Congress 58-; Alternate mem. C.C.P. Central Cttee. 58-.
Governor's Residence, Tientsin, Hopei, China.

Liu Wen-hui; Chinese politician; b. 95; ed. Paoting Military Academy.
Commdr. Nationalist 24th Army 27-46; Gov. Szechwan 29-35; Gov. Sikang 39-49; Vice-Chair. Southwest China Mil. and Admin. Cttee. 50-54; mem. Nat. Cttee. People's Political Consultative Conf. 51-, Standing Cttee., Nat. Cttee. of People's Political Consultative Conf. 54-; Vice-Chair. Szechwan Prov. Cttee., Political Consultative Conf. 55-; Minister of Forestry 59-; Dep. from Szechwan, Nat. People's Congress 54-; mem. Nat. Defence Council 54-; mem. Central Standing Cttee., Revolutionary Cttee. of Kuomintang 56-.
Ministry of Forestry, Peking, China.

Liuzzi, Giorgio; Italian army officer; b. 30 Aug. 1895; ed. Turin Military Acad.
Entered army 13; Brigadier-General 43; in command of a brigade 48; Major-General 50; in command of a division 51; Lieut.-Gen. in command of army corps 53; Chief of Staff of Italian Army 54-59; columnist and and military critic, *Corriere della Sera;* two Bronze and one Silver military medals; Commdr. Order of the Italian Crown, Officer Order of Saints Maurice and Lazarus, Great Cross Italian Order of Merit, Grand Officier Legion of Merit, Commdr. Légion d'Honneur, Great Cross of the Order of Mil. Merit (Argentina and Spain), Gran Oficial do Ordem de Merito Militar do Brasil, Great Cross for Merit with Star and Sash of the German Fed. Repub. Order of Merit, Order of Homa-youn (1st Class) of Iran, Ulehi Distinguished Service Medal of South Korea.
Publs. include: *L'Artiglieria Italiana* 23-24, *Compendio di Arte Militare* 32, *Il servizio Aereo di Artiglieria* 32, *L'osservazione aerostatica* 34, *Contributo dell'osservazione e della fotografia aerea alla preparazione topografica del tiro* 34, *Individuazione degli obiettivi e tiro con osserva-zione aerea* 35, *Esplorazione con truppe celeri* 32, *L'aviazione da osservazione terrestre* 33, *Questioni d'impiego dell'Aviazione per l'Esercito* 34, *La brevità degli ordini d'operazioni* 35, *L'Esplorazione aerea stra-tegica per l'Esercito* 35, *L'aviazione ed i servizi* 36, *La divisione celere nell'esplorazione in rapporto all'esplora-zione aerea* 37, *Carri armati e unità corazzate* 50, *Il volo verticale, necessità dell'Esercito* 51, *L'Esercito di Vittorio Veneto e l'Esercito di oggi* 58, *Italia difesa?* 63.
via Dell 'Arcadia 43, Rome, Italy.

Livanov, Boris Nikolaevich; Soviet actor; b. 04; ed. Moscow Art Theatre 4th Studio.
With the Art Theatre Co. 24-; State Prize 41, 42, 47, 49, 50; 3 Orders of Red Banner of Labour; People's Actor of the U.S.S.R.
Principal roles: Solyony, Astrov (*Three Sisters, Uncle Vanya* by Chekhov), Nozdrev (*Dead Souls* by Gogol), the sailor Shvandya (*Lyubov Yarovaya* by Trenev), King Lear (*King Lear* by Shakespeare), Mitya Kara-mazov (*Brothers Karamazov* by Dostoievsky), Egor Bulychov (*Egor Bulychov* by Gorky), Zabelin (*The Chimes of the Kremlin* by Pogodin).
Moscow Art Theatre, 3 Proyezd Khudozhestvennovo Teatra, Moscow, U.S.S.R.

Livi, Livio, LL.D.; Italian statistician and sociologist; b. 2 Jan. 1891.
Prof. of Statistics, Univ. of Modena 15-20, Univ. of Trieste 21-25; Prof. of Demography, Rome Univ. 26-28; Prof. of Statistics, Florence Univ. 29-48; Rome Univ. 48-, Dean Faculty of Econs. and Commerce 61-66; mem. Int. Statistical Inst.; Pres. Italian Statistical and Demo-graphic Soc. 38-42; Pres. Inst. of Social Sciences 28-35, Vice-Pres. Int. Union for the Scientific Study of Popu-lation 49-54; mem. Higher Council of Statistics 26-56; nat. mem. Accad. Nazionale dei Lincei 50; Pres. Istituto Italiano di Antropologia 53-56; mem. Nat. Council of Economy and Labour; Dir. Centro per la Statistica Aziendale.
Publs. *Gli Ebrei alla luce della statistica,* 2 vols. 18, 20, *Principi di Statistica* 26, *Il Darwinismo sociale e la Critica dei fatti* 30, *Lezioni di Statistica degli Affari* 33, *La Previsione delle Crisi e la Disciplina dell'Attività Produttiva* 34, *Lezioni di Demografia* 35, *I Fattori bio-demografici dell'ordinamento sociale* 40, *Le Leggi naturali della Popolazione* 41, *Storia Demografica di Rodi* 44, *La Rilevazione della Ricchezza e del Reddito Nazionale* 52, *Elementi di Statistica* (15th edn.) 68, *La vecchia e la nuova sociologia generale positiva* 57, *Previsioni economiche* 59, *Corso di Statistica Economica* 59, *Il Consumo del pesce nell'economia alimentare del 1 sec. d.C.,* 65, *La durata normale della vita degli italiani* 66, *Sulla distribuzione della proprietà fondiaria sotto Traiano* 68.
Via A. Baldesi 18, Florence, Italy.
Telephone: 51866.

Livingston, Homer John, LL.B.; American banker; b. 30 Aug. 1903; ed. Grant Grammar School, Crane High School, and John Marshall Law School, Chicago.
With First National Bank of Chicago 22-, Law Clerk 22, Asst. Attorney 30, Attorney 34, Counsel 44, Vice-Pres. 45, Dir. 48-, Pres. 50-60, Chief Exec. Officer 55-, Chair. 60-; Pres. Nat. Safe Deposit Co.; Vice-Pres. First Chicago Corpn.; Dir. Continental Casualty Co., Continental Assurance Co., Sears Roebuck and Co., Armour and Co., Standard Oil Co. (Ind.), Inland Steel Co.; mem. American Bankers Asscn. (Pres. 54-55); Pres. Fed. Advisory Council of Fed. Reserve System 59-61; Trustee Univ. of Chicago (Chair. Investment Cttee.); Hon. LL.D. Washington and Jefferson Coll. 52.
38 South Dearborn Street, Chicago 60603, Ill.; Home: 1425 Ashland Avenue, River Forest, Ill., U.S.A.
Telephone: Fr. 2-6800.

Lleras Camargo, Alberto; Colombian journalist, politician and writer; b. 3 July 1906.
Editorial staff of *El Espectador* and *El Tiempo,* Bogotá 25-30; Sec.-Gen. of Liberal Party and Editor of *La Tarde* 30; Chair. of House of Reps. 32; Sec. of Colom-bian Del. to Pan-American Conf. Montevideo 34; Sec.-Gen. of exec. branch of Colombian Govt. 34-35; Minister of Govt. 35; Del. to Inter-American Conf. for Main-tenance of Peace Buenos Aires 36; Minister of Educa-tion 36; Minister of Govt. 36-38; Editor of *El Liberal* 38-43; elected Senator 43; Ambassador to U.S.A. and Minister of Govt. 43; Minister of Foreign Affairs 45; head of Colombian Del. to Conf. of Chapultepec Mexico and U.N. Conf., San Francisco 45; Pres. of Colombia Aug. 45-Aug. 46; Editor of *Semana* 46-47; Sec.-Gen. of Organisation of American States June 47-54; Pres. Univ. of the Andes 54-55; Pres. of Colombia 58-62; produced study of Alliance for Progress 63; Hon. Ph.D. Universidad de los Andes 57, Hon. Degree Johns Hopkins Univ. 60; Hon. LL.D. (Harvard).
Bogotá, Colombia.

Lleras Restrepo, Carlos; Colombian lawyer and politician b. 12 April 1908.
Lawyer 30-; Deputy 31; Minister of Treasury 38-43; Prof. of Public Finance, Law Faculty, Univ. Nacional 39; Pres. of Nat. Liberal Party 41, 48-50; mem.

Triumvirate 50, Leader 61-; Senator 42-52, 58-59, 62-; Pres. Colombian Del. to Bretton Woods Conf. 44; mem. various Colombian Dels. to UN Comms.; Vice-Pres. Econ. and Social Council, UN 46; in Europe 59-60; Pres. Colombian Del. to Geneva Conf. 64; Pres. of Colombia 66-.
Office of the President, Bogotá, Colombia.

Llewellyn, Frederick John, PH.D., D.SC., LL.D., F.R.I.C., F.N.Z.I.C., F.R.S.A., F.R.S.N.Z.; British administrator; b. 29 April 1915; ed. Dursley Grammar School, Univ. of Birmingham.
Scientific Officer, Fuel Research Station, Greenwich 38-39; Lecturer in Chemistry, Birkbeck Coll. 39-45; Dir. Ministry of Supply Research Team 41-46; I.C.I. Research Fellow, Birmingham Univ. 46-47; Prof. of Chemistry, Auckland Univ. Coll. (N.Z.) 47-55; Vice-Chancellor and Rector, Univ. of Canterbury (N.Z.) 56-61; Chair. Univ. Grants Cttee. (N.Z.) 61-66; Chair. New Zealand Broadcasting Corpn. 62-65; Chair., Nat. Council of Adult Educ. 61-66, N.Z. Commonwealth Scholarships and Fellowships Cttee. 61-66; mem. N.Z. Council for Technical Educ. 61-66, Council of Scientific and Industrial Research, N.Z. 58-62, Council of Asscn. of Commonwealth Univs. 66-; Vice-Chancellor, Exeter Univ. 66-.
The University, Exeter, Devon, England.
Telephone: Exeter 77911.

Llewelyn-Davies, Baron (Life Peer), cr. 63, of Hastoe in the County of Hertford; **Richard Llewelyn-Davies,** M.A., F.R.I.B.A., M.T.P.I.; British architect; b. 24 Dec. 1912; ed. Trinity Coll., Cambridge, and Ecole des Beaux Arts, Paris.
Director of Div. for Architectural Studies, Nuffield Foundation 53-60; Prof. of Architecture, Univ. of London, and Head of Bartlett School of Architecture, Univ. Coll. 60-; also senior partner Llewelyn-Davies Weeks Forestier-Walker and Bor; R.I.B.A. Bronze Medal.
Principal architectural works include: new buildings for *The Times,* London, The Stock Exchange, London, new village at Rushbrooke, Suffolk, new hospitals in U.K. and overseas; Planning work includes studies and master plans for new cities in England, at Swindon, Milton Keynes and Washington, and urban renewal redevelopment projects in U.S.A.
Publs. *Design of Research Laboratories* 57, *Children in Hospital* 58, *Psychiatric Services and Architecture, Hospital Planning and Administration* (with H. M. C. Macaulay) 66.
36 Parkhill Road, London, N.W.3, England.
Telephone: 01-485-6576.

Lloyd, Harold (Clayton); American film actor; b. 20 April 1894; ed. High Schools, Denver and San Diego. Began film career with Edison Co. 19; acted in and produced 300 films, the last being *Professor Beware* 39. 1225 Benedict Canyon, Beverly Hills, California, U.S.A.

Lloyd, Rt. Hon. (John) Selwyn Brooke, P.C., C.H., C.B.E., T.D., Q.C., M.P.; British politician; b. 28 July 1904; ed. Fettes and Magdalene Coll., Cambridge.
Barrister 30-, Master of the Bench, Gray's Inn 51; served army 39-45; elected as Conservative M.P. for Wirral Div. of Cheshire 45, re-elected 50, 51, 55, 59, 64 and 66; Recorder of Wigan 48-51; Minister of State Foreign Office 51-54; Minister of Supply 54-55, of Defence 55; Sec. of State for Foreign Affairs 55-60; Chancellor of the Exchequer 60-62; Chair. Nat. Econ. Devt. Council 62; Lord Privy Seal and Leader of the House of Commons Oct. 63-Oct. 64; Dir. Alliance Assurance, Sun Alliance Insurance 62-63, 65-, Rank Org. 63, 65-, English and Caledonian Investment Co. Ltd. 65-; Legion of Merit, Hon. D.C.L. (Oxford).
House of Commons, London, S.W.1, England.

Lloyd, Seton, C.B.E., M.A., F.B.A., F.S.A., A.R.I.B.A.; British archaeologist; b. 30 May 1902; ed. Uppingham and Architectural Asscn.
Assistant to Sir Edwin Lutyens, P.R.A. 27-28; excavated for Egypt Exploration Soc., Egypt 29-30, for Oriental Inst., Univ. of Chicago in Iraq 30-37, for Univ. of Liverpool in Turkey 37-39; Technical Adviser, Govt. of Iraq, Directorate-Gen. of Antiquities 39-49; Dir. British Inst. Archæology in Ankara 49-61; Prof. of Western Asiatic Archæology, London Univ. 62-.
Publs. *Mesopotamia* 34, *Sennacherib's Aqueduct at Jerwan* 35, *The Gimilsin Temple* 40, *Presargonid Temples* 42, *Ruined Cities of Iraq* 42, *Twin Rivers* 43, *Foundations in the Dust* 48, *Early Anatolia* 56, *Art of the Ancient Near East* 61, *Beycesultan* 62, *Mounds of the Near East* 63.
Woolstone Lodge, Faringdon, Berkshire, England.
Telephone: Uffington 248.

Lloyd, Woodrow Stanley, B.A.; Canadian politician; b. 13; ed. Univ. of Saskatchewan.
Principal of Biggar Schools, Biggar, Saskatchewan; Minister of Educ. 44-60; Provincial Treas. 60-62; Premier of Saskatchewan 62-May 64; Leader of Official Opposition and Provincial Leader Co-operative Commonwealth Federal Party.
Publ. *The Role of Government in Canadian Education* 59.
Legislative Building, Regina, Saskatchewan, Canada.

Lloyd-Jones, Peter Hugh Jefferd, M.A., F.B.A.; British classical scholar; b. 21 Sept. 1922; ed. Lycée Français du Royaume-Uni (London), Westminster School, and Christ Church, Oxford.
Fellow Jesus Coll. Cambridge 48-54; Fellow and E.P. Warren Prælector in Classics Corpus Christi Coll. Oxford 54-60; Regius Prof. of Greek and Student of Christ Church 60-; Chancellor's Prize for Latin Prose, Ireland and Craven Scholarships 47; J. H. Gray Lecturer, Cambridge 61; Visiting Prof. Yale Univ. 64-65, 67-68; Fellow Samuel F. B. Morse Coll., Yale Univ.
Publs. Appendix to *Aeschylus* (Loeb Classical Library) 57, *Menandri Dyscolus* (Oxford Classical Texts) 60; *Greek Studies in Modern Oxford* 61; translated *Greek Metre* 62; edited *The Greeks* 62, *Tacitus* 64; articles and reviews in classical periodicals.
Christ Church, Oxford; Gateways, Harterton Mead, Oxford, England.
Telephone: Oxford 62393 and 48737.

Lo Jui-ching; Chinese army officer; b. 07; ed. Officers' Acad., Whampoa.
In Northern Expedition; after split of Kuomintang and Communists active on Hupeh in 1st Army (under Hsu Chi-sheu); on exec. cttee. 2nd Sino-Soviet Conf. 34; Commissar at Yenan Anti-Japanese Univ. 37; Commissar in Shantung Mil. Area; on Central Cttee. C.C.P. and Dir. Propaganda Dept. 18th Army Group; Vice-Dir. Anti-Japanese Univ. 44; additional mem. Central Cttee. 7th Congress C.C.P. 45; held post in Taiynan area and in Peking City government, etc. 49; on cttee. Central School for Political Leaders 54; Hopeh del. to N.P.C. 54; on Council of Nat. Defence 54; decorated; appointed General in Liberation Army 55; Central Cttee. 8th Congress C.C.P.; Minister of Public Security Sept. 59; Vice-Premier 59-66; Chief of Staff of Armed Forces 59-66; mem. Secr. Central Cttee. of Chinese C.P. 62-66; Vice-Chair. Nat. Defence Council 65-66.
Peking, China.

Lo Su Yin, (Peter Lo), LL.B.; Malaysian politician; b. 19 May 1923; ed. St. Mary's School, Sandakan, St. Anthony's Boys School, Singapore and Victoria Univ., Wellington.
Called to New Zealand Bar 56, law practice 57-64; mem. Town Board 58-64; mem. Legislative Council 62, mem. Parl. 63-67; Fed. Minister without Portfolio 64; Chief Minister Sabah 65-67; Chair. Sabah Chinese Asscn. 65-.
Kota Kinabalu, Sabah, Malaysia.

Loane, Most Rev. Marcus Lawrence, M.A., TH.D., D.D.; Australian ecclesiastic; b. 14 Oct. 1911; ed. The King's School, Parramatta, Univ. of Sydney, and Moore Theological Coll., Sydney.

Resident Tutor and Chaplain, Moore Theological Coll., Sydney 35-38, Vice-Principal 39-53, Principal 54-58; Canon, St. Andrew's Cathedral 49-58; Bishop Coadjutor, Diocese of Sydney 58-66; Archbishop of Sydney and Metropolitan of New South Wales 66-.

Publs. *Oxford and the Evangelical Succession* 51, *Cambridge and the Evangelical Succession* 52, *Masters of the English Reformation* 55, *History of Moore Theological College* 55, *Life of Archbishop Mowl* 59, *Pioeers of the Reformation in England* 63, *Sons of the Covenant* 63, *The History of the China Inland Mission in Australia and New Zealand* 65, *Makers of Our Heritage* 67, *Do You Now Believe* 67.

Diocesan Church House, George Street, Sydney, New South Wales, Australia.

Lobanok, Vladimir Eliseevich; Soviet politician; b. 1907; ed. Byelorussian Agricultural Inst., and Higher Party School, Moscow.

Member C.P.S.U. 30-; Agronomist 32-41; Soviet army service 41-44; Chair. Exec. Cttee., Polotsk Regional Council of Workers' Deputies 44-46; Second Sec. Polessye Regional Cttee. C.P. Byelorussia 46-48, First Sec. 48-53; Chair. Gomel Regional Council of Workers' Deputies 54-56; First Sec. Vitebsk Regional Cttee. C.P. Byelorussia 56-62; First Deputy Chair. Council of Ministers of Byelorussian S.S.R. 62-; mem. C.P.S.U. Central Auditing Comm. 61-; mem. Central Cttee. of C.P. Byelorussia; Deputy to U.S.S.R. and Byelorussian S.S.R. Supreme Soviets; Hero of the Soviet Union 43.

Council of Ministers, Minsk, Byelorussian S.S.R., U.S.S.R.

Lobanov, Paval Pavlovich; Soviet agriculturalist and politician; b. 1902; ed. Timiryazev Agricultural Acad., Moscow.

Director Voronezh Agricultural Inst.; R.S.F.S.R. People's Commissar of Agriculture; U.S.S.R. People's Commissar of State Farms; First Deputy U.S.S.R. People's Commissar of Agriculture 25-53; Deputy Chair. U.S.S.R. Council of Ministers 55-56; Deputy Chair. State Planning Comm. 61; mem. Central Cttee. of Communist Party of Soviet Union 61-66; Pres. All Union Acad. of Agricultural Sciences 65-; Deputy to U.S.S.R. Supreme Soviet; mem. U.S.S.R. Parliamentary Group and Cttee. for Agriculture, Soviet of Union. All Union Academy of Agricultural Sciences, Bolshoi Kharitonevsky per. 21, Moscow, U.S.S.R.

Lobe, Dr. Fernando; Brazilian diplomatist and politician; b. 96.

Entered Brazilian Ministry of Foreign Affairs and served in many posts at home and abroad 18-35; First Sec. 35-38 and Minister Counsellor, Washington 42-46; Sec. Brazilian del. League of Nations, Geneva 22; mem. Efficiency Comm. of Ministry of Foreign Affairs 38; Dir. of Secretariat of Third Consultation Meeting of Foreign Ministers of the American Republics, Rio de Janeiro 42; Consultant and Alt. Brazilian del. U.N.R.R.A., Atlantic City 46; Chief Dept. of Admin, Ministry of Foreign Affairs 46-50; Dep. Sec.-Gen. Conf. of Rio de Janeiro 47; Sec.-Gen. Brazilian del. Gen. Assembly of U.N., Paris 48 and Alt. del. New York 50; Ambassador to Venezuela 50-53; Chair. Brazilian del. Third Extraordinary Meeting of the Inter-American Economic and Social Council, Caracas 53; Brazilian Rep. Council of the Organization of American States 53; del. Tenth Inter-American Conf., Caracas 54; Chair. Brazilian del. Special Inter-American Conf. on Preservation of Natural Resources, Ciudad Trujillo 56; Chair. Council Organization of American States 56-57; Brazilian Ambassador to the Organization of American States 58-61; Minister of Foreign Affairs 61-62; Great Cross of

the Order of Boyacá 57; Great Cross of the Order of D. Vasco Nuñez de Balbôa 57.

c/o Ministry of Foreign Affairs, Rio de Janeiro, Brazil.

Lobov, Admiral Semen Mikhailovich; Soviet naval officer; b. 1913; ed. Frunze Higher Naval School in Leningrad.

Railway and factory worker 29-33; Naval Service 33-; Captain of various ships 37-; Chief of of Staff, Cmmdr. Naval Foundation, First Deputy Cmmdr. Northern Fleet 55-65; Cmmdr. Northern Fleet 64-; mem. C.P.S.U. 40-; Alt. mem. Central Cttee. of C.P.S.U.; Dep. to U.S.S.R. Supreme Soviet.

Ministry of Defence, 34 Maurice Thorez Embankment, Moscow, U.S.S.R.

Loc, Nguyen van, LL.M.; Viet-Namese lawyer, writer and politician; b. 24 Feb. 1922; ed. Univ. de Montpellier.

Lawyer, Saigon Court of Appeal 55; Teacher, Nat. Inst. of Admin. 65; Chair. People and Armed Forces Council 66, People and Armed Forces Council Political Cttee. 66; Vice-Chair. Constituent Assembly Electoral Law Preparation Cttee.; mem. Barristers Fraternity 61-67; Del. in charge of campaigning, Cttee. for Aid to War Victims (Viet-Nam Red Cross); Counsellor, Viet-Nam Asscn. for Protection of Human and People's Rights; Sec.-Gen., Inter-Schools Asscn. 65-67; Prime Minister of Repub. of Viet-Nam Nov. 67-May 68.

Publs. *Rank* 48, *New Recruits* (novel) 48, *Uprising* (novel) 46,, *Poems on Liberation* (collection) 49, *Recollections of the Green Years* 60, *Free Tribune* (collection) 66.

7 Thong-Nhat-Saigon, Republic of Viet-Nam.

Lochen, Einar; Norwegian lawyer and diplomatist; b. 18; ed. Oslo Univ., London School of Economics, Chicago Univ., Calif. Univ.

Assistant judge 45-46; Lawyer 46-49; Asst. Adviser to Norwegian Ministry of Foreign Affairs 49-51; Fellow of Chr. Michelsens Institutt, Bergen 51-55; Counsellor to Norwegian Ministry of Foreign Affairs 55-58; Perm. Rep. to Council of Europe 58-63; Sec. Norwegian Del. to Nordic Council.

Publs. *Norway's Views on Sovereignty* 55, *A Comparative Study of Certain European Parliamentary Assemblies* 58, *Det Europeiske Økonomiske Fellesskap* 61.

Otto Ruges vei 1, Oslo, Norway.

Lochner, Louis P., B.A., LI:T.D.; American journalist; b. 22 Feb. 1887; ed. Wisconsin Univ.

Member Berlin staff Associated Press of America 24-42; Chief of Bureau 28-42; U.S. War Corresp. in Europe 44-46; Pres. Foreign Press Asscn. of Berlin 28-31 and 34-37; Pres. American Chamber of Commerce in Germany 35-42; mem. Hoover Comm. to Germany and Austria 47; Pres. Overseas Press Club of America 50 and 55; Chair. Overseas Rotary Fellowship 56-; mem. P.E.N. Club; winner Pulitzer Prize (foreign corresp.) 39; American mem. U.N. Expert Cttee. on Public Information 58; Dir. American Council on Germany 59-; Commentator, Broadcast Editorial Reports 60-63; mem. Editorial Board, *The Lutheran Witness* 51-; Chair. Eyes Right, Inc. (Eye Restoration Service) 50-67; Trustee Corresps' Fund Inc. 64-; Trustee, Overseas Press Clubs Foundation 66-; Commdr's Cross of the German Order of Merit 67.

Publs. *America's Don Quixote* 23, *Das amerikanische Nachrichtenwesen* 31, *What About Germany?* 42, *The Goebbels Diaries* 48, *Fritz Kreisler* 50, *Tycoons and Tyrant* 54, *Always the Unexpected* 56, *Herbert Hoover and Germany* 60, *New York* 60 and contributions to many American magazines.

32 Buena Vista Avenue, Fair Haven, N.J. 07701, U.S.A. Telephone: 201-741-9013.

Locke, Edwin Allen, Jr., A.B.; American industrialist, banker and diplomatist; b. 8 June 1910; ed. Harvard Univ.

With Paris Branch, Chase Nat. Bank, N.Y. 33-35, London Branch 35-36, New York 36-40; served in Office of Co-ordinator of Purchases, Advisory Comm. to Council of Nat. Defense 40-41; Asst. Deputy Dir. Priorities Div., Office of Production Management 41; Deputy Chief Staff Officer Supply Priorities and Allocation Board 41-42; Asst. to Chair. War Production Board 42-44; Exec. Asst. to Personal Rep. of the Pres. 44-45; Personal Rep. of the Pres., Washington and China 45-46, Special Asst. to the Pres. March-Dec. 46; Vice-Pres. of the Chase Nat. Bank, New York 47-51; apptd. Special Rep. of Sec. of State, with personal rank of Ambassador to co-ordinate economic and technical assistance programmes in the Near East Nov. 51-53; Pres. and Dir. Union Tank Car Co. 53-63; mem. special mission to Liberia and Tunisia; Pres. and Dir. Modern Homes Construction Co. 63-, Coastal Products Corpn. 63-.
404 Terrace Boulevard, Valdosta, Georgia, U.S.A.

Locke, Eugene Murphy, B.A., LL.B.; American lawyer and diplomatist; b. 6 Jan. 1918; ed. North Dallas High School, Univ. of Texas and Yale Law School.
Admitted to Texas Bar 40, practised various Fed. Courts, Fifth Circuit Court of Appeals, U.S. Supreme Court; U.S. Navy Second World War; a Senior Partner, Locke, Purnell, Boren, Laney & Neely, Attorneys, Dallas, Texas 46-66; Amb. to Pakistan 66-67; Deputy Amb. to Repub. of Viet-Nam 67-68; official of numerous business, civic and educational orgs. 58-67.
Locke, Purnell, Boren, Laney & Neely, 3600 Republic National Bank Tower, Dallas, Texas 75201, U.S.A.

Lockhart, Sir Robert Bruce, K.C.M.G.; British author; b. 3 Sept. 1887; ed. Fettes Coll., Edinburgh.
Member Consular and Commercial Diplomatic Services 11-23; acting Consul-Gen. Moscow 14-17; Head of Special British Mission to Bolshevik Govt. 18; arrested and imprisoned 18 but later exchanged for Litvinov, who was arrested by British Govt. as hostage; banking in Central Europe 22-28; mem. editorial staff *Evening Standard* 28-37; mem. Political Intelligence Dept., Foreign Office 39-40; British Rep. Provisional Czechoslovak Govt. 40-41; Deputy Under-Sec. of State, Foreign Office, and Dir.-Gen. of Political Warfare Exec. 41-45.
Publs. *Memoirs of a British Agent* 32, *Retreat from Glory* 34, *Return to Malaya* 36, *My Scottish Youth* 37, *Guns or Butter* 38, *Comes the Reckoning* 47, *My Rod My Comfort* 49, *The Marines Were There* 50, *Jan Masaryk: A Personal Memoir* 51, *Scotch* 51, *My Europe* 52, *Your England* 55, *Friends, Foes and Foreigners* 57, *The Two Revolutions* 57, *Giants Cast Long Shadows* 60.
St. James' Club, Piccadilly, London, W.1, England.

Lockspeiser, Sir Ben, K.C.B., M.A., D.SC., M.I.MECH.E., F.R.S.A., F.R.Ae.S., F.R.S.; British scientist; b. 9 March 1891; ed. Sidney Sussex Coll., Cambridge.
Asst. Dir. Scientific Research, Min. of Aircraft Production 39, Deputy Dir. 41, Dir. 43-; Dir.-Gen. Scientific Research (Air) Min. of Supply 46; chief scientist to Min. of Supply Dec. 46-49; Sec. Dept. of Scientific and Industrial Research 49-56; Dir. Staveley Industries Ltd., Ricardo and Co. Ltd.; Pres. European Org. for Nuclear Research 55-57.
Birchway, Waverley Road, Farnborough, Hants., England.

Lockwood, Sir Joseph Flawith, Kt.; British businessman; b. 14 Nov. 1904.
Man. of flour mills in Chile 24-28; Techn. Man. Henry Simon Ltd. in Paris and Brussels 28-33; Dir. Henry Simon Ltd., Manchester 33; Dir. Henry Simon, Buenos Aires and Chair. Henry Simon (Australia) Ltd., etc. 45; Chair. Electric and Musical Industries Ltd. 55-; Dir. Smiths Industries Ltd., Beecham Group Ltd., The Hawker-Siddeley Group Ltd.; Chair. Board of Govs., Royal Ballet School; Chair. of Govs. Central School of Speech and Drama; Dir. South Bank Theatre Board 68-;

mem. Arts Council Industrial Reorganization Corpn.
Publs. *Provender Milling: the Manufacture of Feeding Stuffs for Livestock* 39, *Flour Milling* (in English, French, Spanish, German and Serbo-Croat) 45.
Flat 18, 33 Grosvenor Square, London, W.1, England.

Lodge, George Cabot (son of Henry Cabot Lodge, Jr., *q.v.*); American politician; b. 7 July 1927; ed. Harvard Coll.
United States Naval Reserve, Second World War; on staff of *Boston Herald* 50-54; Dir. of Information, U.S. Dept. of Labor 54-58; Asst. Sec. of Labor for Int. Affairs 58-61; Pres. Governing Body, Int. Labour Org. (ILO) 60-61; Lecturer, Harvard Business School 63-; cand. for U.S. Senate 62; Republican.
Publ. *Spearheads of Democracy* 62.
275 Hale Street, Beverly, Mass., U.S.A.

Lodge, Henry Cabot, Jr., A.B. (brother of John Davis Lodge, *q.v.*); American politician; b. 5 June 1902; ed. Harvard Coll.
With *Boston Evening Transcript* 24-25; mem. editorial staff *New York Herald Tribune* 25-31; mem. House and Senate Press Galleries; mem. Nat. Press Club; elected Representative to Gen. Court of Mass. 32, 34; U.S. Senator from Massachusetts 36; Major U.S. Army, served with 1st American tank detachment, Libya 42; re-elected to Senate Nov. 42, resigned from Senate in order to go on active service with Army Feb. 44; served Mediterranean and Europe until 45; Senator from Mass. 46-53; Chair Resolutions Cttee. Republican Nat. Convention 48; U.S. Rep. to U.N.; Rep. on Security Council 53-60; Republican candidate for Vice-Pres. 60; Trustee, Int. Inst. of Educ. 61; Dir.-Gen. Atlantic Inst., Paris 61-63; Amb. to Repub. of Viet-Nam 63-64, 65-67; Amb. to German Fed. Repub. 68-; Special Consultant to Pres. of U.S. on Viet-Nam Crisis 65; Hon. LL.D., D.C.L., D. ès L.; Legion of Merit Medal, Légion d'Honneur and Croix de Guerre avec palme.
American Embassy, Bonn, German Federal Republic.

Lodge, John Davis, LL.B. (brother of Henry Cabot Lodge, Jr., *q.v.*); American lawyer and diplomatist; b. 03; ed. Middlesex School, Concord, Harvard Coll., Harvard Law School and Ecole de Droit, Paris.
Naval Officer U.S. Navy, Mediterranean Theatre 42-46; Congressman from 4th District of Connecticut 46-50; mem. Cttee. on Foreign Affairs; Gov. of Connecticut 50-55; Ambassador to Spain 55-61; Chair. Cttee. Foreign Policy Research Inst., Univ. of Pennsylvania; Pres. Junior Achievement Inc. 63-64; Chevalier de la Légion d'Honneur, Croix de Guerre avec palme; Grand Cross of Noble Order of Charles III (Spain); Grand Officer, Order of Merit of the Repub. of Italy; Order Polonia Restituta (Poland); numerous other foreign decorations; hon. degrees many U.S. colls. and univs.; Republican.
129 Easton Road, Westport, Conn., U.S.A.

Lods, Marcel; French architect; b. 16 Aug. 1891.
With Eugène Beaudoin pioneered use of industrialized building at Champ-des-Oiseaux, Bagneux; designed Cité de la Muette, Drancy 32-35, open-air school, Suresnes 35, Maison du peuple, Clichy 37-39; recent work includes residential area, Marly-les-Grandes-Terres (Paris Region); founded, with Soc. Saint-Gobain, Groupement pour l'étude d'une architecture industrialisée (G.E.A.T.); Grand Prix du Cercle d'Etudes Architecturales 67.
90 avenue Niel, Paris 17e, France.

Loeb, James Isaac; American diplomatist; b. 18 Aug. 1908; ed. Dartmouth Coll., and Northwestern Univ.
Teacher, Romance Languages, Northwestern Univ. 30-36, Townsend Harris High School, New York City 37-41; Nat. Dir. Union for Democratic Action 45-47, Americans for Democratic Action 47-51; Consultant to Pres. Truman's Special Council 51-52; Exec. Asst. New York Gov. W. Averell Harriman 52; Co-Publisher,

Editor *Adirondack Daily Enterprise*, Saranac Lake, New York 53-; Co-Publisher *Lake Placid News* 60-; Ambassador to Peru 61-Nov. 62; Consultant to State Dept. Nov. 62-June 63; Ambassador to Guinea 63-65. c/o Department of State, Washington, D.C. 25, U.S.A.

Loeb, Robert Frederick, M.D., F.R.A.C.P., F.R.C.P., M.A.C.P.; American professor of medicine; b. 14 March 1895; ed. Harvard Univ.
Instructor, later Prof., in Medicine, Coll. of Physicians and Surgeons, Columbia Univ. 21-47; Internship Massachusetts General Hospital 19-20; Asst. Residency, Johns Hopkins Hospital, Baltimore, Md. 20-21; Bard Prof. of Medicine, Columbia Univ. 47-60; Dir. Dept. of Medicine, Presbyterian Hospital, New York City 47-60, Consultant 60-; fmr. Chair. Medical Fellowship Board, Nat. Research Council 47; fmr. Chair. Board of Review, U.S. Atomic Energy Comm; mem. Nat. Acad. of Sciences, American Acad. Arts and Sciences, American Philosophical Soc., Nat. Science Foundation Board 50-64; Pres. American Soc. for Clinical Investigation 36, Harvey Soc. 50-51, Asscn. of American Physicians 55; mem. Presidential Science Advisory Cttee. 59-63; Hon. Sc.D. (Chicago 51, New York 55, Kenyon Coll. 57, Columbia 61, Dartmouth 62, Trinity Coll., Dublin 62), LL.D. (Univ. of Wales 53, Amherst 61), D.Sc. (Oxford 61), Dr. h.c. (Strasbourg 51, Paris 52); Trustee, Rockefeller Univ., Vice-Pres. Board of Trustees 61-; Trustee, Rockefeller Foundation 47-60; F.R.C.P. (London) 57; Hon. F.R.A.C.P. 53; Hon. Fellow, Royal Soc. of Medicine 60; Foreign corresp. mem. British Medical Asscn. 57, Asscn. of Physicians of Great Britain and Ireland, Belgian Royal Acad. of Medicine, etc.; Overseer Harvard Univ. 61-67.
Publs. on adrenal glands, nephritis, diabetes, and Addison's Disease; fmr. co-editor *Cecil—Loeb Textbook of Medicine*; Co-editor *Martini's Principles and Practice of Physical Diagnosis*.
950 Park Avenue, New York City, N.Y. 10028, U.S.A.
Telephone: RE4-8362.

Loesser, Frank; American composer; b. 29 June 1910; ed. Manhattan Public School, Townsend-Harris High School, Student Coll., New York City.
Newspaper reporter, New York, then City Editor of small publ. 29; Exploitation Rep., Tiffany Pictures Inc. 30; Co-writer original screenplay *Priorities on Parade;* Composer of scores for films *The Rents of Pauline, Variety Girl, Hans Christian Andersen;* wrote music and lyrics for shows *Guys and Dolls, The Most Happy Fella;* composer of many songs for films; Academy Award for Best Film Song 48; Co-recipient Pulitzer Prize for Drama 62.
119 West 57th Street, New York, N.Y. 10019, U.S.A.

Loewe, Frederick; American (Austrian-born) composer; b. 10 June 1901.
Studied piano with Ferruccio Busoni and Eugène d'Albert, composition and orchestration with Nicholas Reznicek; went to U.S.A. 24; composer musical comedies: *Salute to Spring, Great Lady, Life of the Party, Day before Spring, Brigadoon, Paint your Wagon, Camelot;* collaborator (with Alan Jay Lerner) music for *My Fair Lady;* composer score for film *Gigi* 59.
Palm Springs, Calif., U.S.A.

Loewy, Raymond Fernand; American (French-born) industrial designer; b. 5 Nov. 1893; ed. Chaptal Coll., Ecole de Lanneau and Univ. de Paris à la Sorbonne.
Captain, Corps of Engineers 5th Army, France 14-18; Art Dir., Westinghouse Electric 29; started private org. of industrial design 29; liaison officer A.E.F., Second World War; Head, Raymond Loewy Assocs. 45-61; Founder, Compagnie de l'Esthetique Industrielle, Paris 52; Chair. Raymond Loewy/William Snaith Inc. 61-; mem. President's Cttee. on Employment of the Handicapped 65-; Hon. Designer to Industry, Fellow

British Royal Soc. of Arts; Commdr., Légion d'Honneur and many honours and awards.
Publs. *The Locomotive, Its Aesthetics* 37, *Never Leave Well Enough Alone* 51.
900 Fifth Avenue, New York; Tierra Caliente, Palm Springs, Calif., U.S.A.; Manoir de la Cense, Rochefort-en Yvelines, France.
Telephone: Murray Hill (N.Y.) 8-2-500; Paris POI-2660.

Loga-Sowinski, Ignacy; Polish politician and trade union official; b. 20 Jan. 1914.
Active in revolutionary work from early age; imprisoned several times for his work in Lodz branch of Communist Youth Union; released from prison 39; took part in defence of Warsaw; helped organise underground group during the occupation; joined Polish Workers' Party 42; became mem. of its Central Cttee., working in Supreme Command of People's Guard and later in P.W.P. Secretariat; dismissed from party's Central Cttee. on charge of right wing nationalist deviation 48; worked for several years as Chair. of Area Council of Trade Unions in Wrocław, and later in Central Council of Trade Unions; mem. Central Cttee. 43-54 and Political Bureau of Polish United Workers' party 56-; Chair. Central Council of Polish Trade Unions 56-; Vice-Chair. World Fed. of Trade Unions 57-; Deputy Pres. Council of State 65-.
Ul. Kopernika 36/40, Warsaw, Poland.

Logan, Sir Douglas (William), Kt., M.A., D.PHIL., D.C.L., LL.D.; British barrister-at-law and university administrator; b. 27 March 1910; ed. Liverpool Collegiate School, Univ. Coll., Oxford, and Harvard Law School.
Asst. Lecturer, London School of Economics 36-37; called to the Bar 37; Fellow of Trinity Coll., Cambridge 37-43; served Ministry of Supply 40-44; Clerk of Court, Univ. of London 44-47; Principal of Univ. of London 48-; Pres. British Univs. Sports Fed. 62-; Trustee of City Parochial Foundation 53-67; Vice-Chair. Athlone Fellowship Cttee. 59-; mem. Commonwealth Scholarships Comm. 60-; mem. Marshall Scholarship Comm. 61-; Vice-Chair. Asscn. of Univs. of the British Commonwealth 61-63, Chair. 62; Gov. Old Vic theatre; mem. Nat. Theatre Board; Gov. Bristol Old Vic; Rede Lecturer 63; Hon. Bencher, Middle Temple; Hon. A.R.I.B.A.; Hon. Fellow, London School of Econs.; Hon. F.D.S., R.C.S. Eng.; Chevalier, Légion d'Honneur 57.
University of London, The Senate House, London, W.C.1, England.
Telephone: 01-386-1911.

Loganathan, Chelliah, B.COM.; Ceylonese banker; b. 19 Sept. 1913; ed. Hartley Coll. and Jaffna Coll., Jaffna, and Univ. Coll., Colombo.
Former mem. Nat. Planning Council; fmr. mem. Comm. of Inquiry into Employee Participation in Profits; fmr. Chair. Cttee. of Tourism; Gen. Manager and Chief Exec., Bank of Ceylon; Dir. Devt. Finance Corpn. of Ceylon; Chair. Ceylonese Nat. Chamber of Int. Chamber of Commerce; Vice-Chair. Comm. on Asian and Far Eastern Affairs of Int. Chamber of Commerce; mem. Ceylon Devt. Advisory Council.
Publs. *Development Savings Bank, Asia's Dilemma—Private Sector in Economic Development*.
75 Green Path, Colombo 3, Ceylon.

Loginov, Vitali Abramovich; Soviet diplomatist; b. 1910; ed. Moscow Literary Inst.
Diplomatic Service 44-; Sec. Asst. Deputy Head 2nd European Dept., Ministry of Foreign Affairs 44-54, 56-59; Counsellor, Ottawa 54-56; Chargé d'Affaires, London 59-63; Amb. to Australia 63-66; Ministry of Foreign Affairs 66-.
Ministry of Foreign Affairs, 32-34, Smolenskaya-Sennaya ploshchad, Moscow, U.S.S.R.

Loginov, Marshall Yevgeny Fedorovich; Soviet air force officer and politician; b. 1907; ed. Acad. of the General Staff.
Joined Armed Forces 26; Commdr. Air Div., Air Corps 41-45; Head of Command Faculty, Acad. of Air Forces 50-54; Commdr. Air Force 54-56; Deputy C.-in-C. Soviet Air Force 57-59; Head, Main Board, Civil Air Fleet, U.S.S.R. Council of Ministers 59-64; Minister of Civil Aviation 64-; Candidate mem. Central Cttee. C.P.S.U.; Deputy to U.S.S.R. Supreme Soviet; Order of Lenin (thrice), Red Banner of Labour (thrice) and other decorations.
Ministry of Civil Aviation (Aeroflot.), Leningradsky Prospekt 39, Moscow, U.S.S.R.

Lohmann, Johannes; Netherlands civil engineer; b. 5 Oct. 1908; ed. Delft Technical Univ.
Civil Engineer, Netherlands Railways 30-52, Chief Civil Engineer 52-54, Chief Operating Officer 54-58, Gen. Man. 58-59, Pres. 59-.
N.V. Nederlandse Spoorwegen, Utrecht, Netherlands.

Lohmann, Karl, DR.MED., DR.PHIL.; German university professor; b. 10 April 1898; ed. Univs. of Münster and Göttingen (chemistry), Univ. of Heidelberg (medicine).
Rockefeller scholarship 23-24; asst. at Kaiser-Wilhelm-Institut für Biologie 24-29, later senior asst. for medical research; studied medicine at Heidelberg 31-35; Prof. Berlin Univ. and Dir. Physiological-Chemical Inst. of Berlin Univ. 37-51; mem. Deutsche Akad. der Wissenschaften 49-; Emer. Pres. of its Inst. of Nutrition and Dir. of its Inst. for Biochemistry; mem. Deutsche Akad. der Naturforscher Leopoldina, Halle; Nat. Prize 51; Vaterländischer Verdienstorden 58; Dr. Agr. h.c. Humboldt Univ. Berlin 61; Hervorragender Wissenschaftler des Volkes 63; Dr. Med. h.c. Humboldt Univ. Berlin 66.
Lindenberger Weg 78, 1115 Berlin-Buch, Germany. Telephone: 56-98-51.

Lohr, Lenox Riley; American engineer; b. 15 Aug. 1891; ed. Cornell Univ., and Clare Coll., Cambridge.
Dir. Montgomery Ward & Co.; Dir. and Exec. Sec. Society of American Military Engineers and Editor of its journal, *The Military Engineer* 22-29; Gen. Man. Century of Progress Exposition, Chicago 1933 29-35; Pres. Nat. Broadcasting Co. Inc. 35-40; Dir. R.C.A. Manufacturing Co. Inc. 37-40; Trustee, Museum of Science and Industry, Chicago. Ill. 35-, Pres. 40-; Pres. Chicago Railroad Fair 48-49; Pres. Centennial of Engineering, 1952, Inc.; Chair. Illinois Comm. on Higher Education 54-59; Dir. Cook County Metropol. Fair and Exposition Authority; Hon. D.Eng. (Ill. Inst. Technology), Hon. LL.D. (Knox Coll., Bradley Univ., Loyola Univ.), Hon. C.E. (Rensselaer Polytechnic Inst.), Hon. D.Sc. (Shurtleff Coll.); Fellow, Inst. of Medicine of Chicago; Hon. LL.D. (De Paul Univ. Chicago) 58.
Publs. *Magazine Publishing* 32, *Television Broadcasting* 40, *Fair Management* 52, *A History of the Centennial of Engineering* 53.
[*Died June* 1968.]

Loiseau, Louis Marie Jean; French museum curator (hon.); b. 9 July 1890; ed. Ecole polytechnique, Paris.
Artillery officer 13-18; naval artillery engineer 18-23; engaged as engineer in manufacture of telegraphic material 23-32; curator of the Museum of the Nat. Conservatory of Arts and Crafts, Paris 35-58, hon. curator 58-; Officer Legion of Honour; Inter-Allied Medal and Croix de Guerre 14-18.
29 rue Madame, Paris 6e, France. Telephone: 222-49-37.

Lokanathan, Palamadai Samu, M.A., D.SC.; Indian economist; b. 10 Oct. 1894; ed. Univ. of Madras and London School of Economics and Political Science.

Professor of Econs., Univ. of Madras 41-42; Editor *Eastern Economist*, New Delhi 43-47; Exec. Sec. UN Econ. Comm. for Asia and the Far East (ECAFE), Bangkok 47-56; Dir.-Gen. Nat. Council of Applied Econ. Research, New Delhi 56-; Chair. Nat. Productivity Council 58-63, 64-66, Asian Productivity Org., Tokyo 63 (Dir. for India 62-66), Mettur Chemical and Industrial Corpn. Ltd., Mettur Dam, S. India and Int. Perspective Planning Team (for devt. of small industries) 63; Vice-Chair. Exec. Council of Central Inst. of Research and Training in Public Co-operation; Vice-Pres. Indian Council on World Affairs; Consultant to Inst. of Nat. Planning, Cairo 60; mem. Governing Council of Asian Inst. of Econ. Devt. and Planning, Bangkok, Nat. Savings Central Advisory Board at Ministry of Finance, Board of Trade, Export-Import Advisory Council of Industries, Panel of Economists on Planning Comm.; Visiting Prof., Dept. of Business Management and Industrial Admin., Univ. of Delhi; Hon. Fellow London School of Econs. and Political Science; Most Noble Order of the Crown of Thailand First Class.
Publs. *Industrial Welfare in India, Industrial Organization in India, Indian Industry, Indian Economic System*, and many other economic and industrial surveys and reports.
5B Pusa Road, New Delhi 5, India.

Lollobrigida, Gina; Italian actress; b. 4 July 1932; ed. Liceo Artistico, Rome.
First leading screen role in *Campane a Martello* 48; has since appeared in numerous films including *Cuori senza Frontiere* 49, *La Città si difende, Achtung, banditi! Enrico Caruso* 51, *Altri Tempi, Moglie per una Notte, Fanfan la Tulipe, La Provinciale, Les Belles de la Nuit* 52, *Pane, amore e fantasia* 53, *Pane, amore e gelosia, La Romana, Il Grande Gioco* 54, *Trapeze, La Donna più Bella del Mondo* 55, *Notre Dame de Paris* 56, *Solomon and Sheba* 59, *Never So Few* 60, *Go Naked in the World* 61, *She Got What She Asked For* 63, *Woman of Straw* 64, *Le Bambole* 65.
120 Inglewood Drive, Toronto, Ontario, Canada.

Lomako, Pyotr Fadeevich; Soviet metallurgist and government official; b. 1904; ed. Moscow Inst. of Non-Ferrous Metals and Gold.
Member C.P.S.U. 25-; Engineer, Dir. of Plant, Man. of Trust in Non-Ferrous Metallurgy 32-39; Deputy Minister of Non-Ferrous Metallurgy 39-40, Minister 40-48, 50-53, 57; Deputy Minister of Metallurgical Industry 48-50, 53-57; Chair. Krasnoyarsk Nat. Econ. Council 57-61; Deputy Chair. C.P.S.U. Central Cttee. Bureau for R.S.F.S.R. 61-62; Deputy Chair. U.S.S.R. Council of Ministers and Chair. State Planning Cttee. (Gosplan) 62-65; Minister of Non-Ferrous Metal Industry 65-; mem. C.P.S.U. Central Cttee. 61-; Deputy to U.S.S.R. Supreme Soviet.
U.S.S.R. Ministry of Non-Ferrous Metal Industry, 5-7 Nogin Square, Moscow, U.S.S.R.

Lomax, Alan; American collector of folk songs; b. 31 Jan. 1915; ed. Univ. of Texas, Harvard and Columbia Univs.
American Folk Music Library of Congress 37-42; C.B.S. 39-44; Decca 47-49; Research at Univ. of W. Indies 62, Columbia 63-; Dir. Cantometrics Project, Dept. of Anthropology, Columbia Univ. 63-; many lectures and radio programmes.
Publs. *Harriett and her Harmonium, Mister Jelly Roll, The Rainbow Sign, Folk Songs of North America, Penguin Book of American Folk Songs, Folk Song Style, Song Structure and Social Structure;* (with J. A. Lomax): *Cowboy Songs and other Frontier Ballads, Negro Folk Songs as Sung by Lead Belly, American Ballads and Folk Songs, Folk Songs U.S.A., Our Singing Country, Phonotactique Du Chant Populaire l'Homme* 64, *Special*

Features of the Sung Communication, Essays on the Verbal and Visual Arts 67.
215 West 98th Street, 12-E, New York 25, N.Y., U.S.A.

Lombardo, Ivan Matteo; Italian politician; b. 22 May 1902.
Editor, Labour Section, *Avanti!* 20-22; in business 25-45; Industrial Commr. Lombardy Liberation Cttee. 45; mem. Consulta Nazionale, Under-Sec. of State for Industry and Commerce 45-46; elected to Constituent Nat. Ass. 46; Chief Italian Del. for negotiations with France 46; Sec.-Gen. Partito Socialista Italiano di Unità Proletaria (P.S.I.U.P.) 46; Chief Italian del. U.S.A. Treaty negotiations 47; mem. Nat. Ass. 48-53; Minister of Industry and Commerce 48-49, of Foreign Trade 50-51; Chief Italian del. E.D.C. Conf.,Paris 51-54; Co-Pres. Italian American Council for Marketing 51-52; Pres' Nat. Productivity Council (C.N.P.) 55-67; Pres. Nat. Handicrafts Devt. Co. (C.N.A.), Florence 48-61, Milan Triennial Exhbn. 49-61, Italian Chamber of Commerce for the Americas 51-, Italian Atlantic Cttee. 55-, Atlantic Treaty Asscn. (London) 59-61; mem. Council of Govs., Institut Atlantique; Chair. Squibb S.p.A.; Knight Grand Cross, Italian Order of Merit, Officier Légion d'Honneur, Knight of Orden de Mayo (Argentina), Milan Gold Medal, Grand Cross, Portuguese Order of Infante Henrique.
Piazza Stefano Jacini 5, Rome, Italy.
Telephone: 320-326.

Lombardo Toledano, Vicente, PH.D., LL.D.; Mexican labour leader; b. 94; ed. Nat. Univ.
For many years Prof. of Philosophy, Labour Laws and Economics, Nat. Univ. of Mexico; twice Dir. of Nat. Preparatory School and Central School of Plastic Arts; Founder and Dir. of Workers' Univ. (Universidad Obrera de México) 36-; fmr. Gov. of State of Puebla and of Congress of the Union; organiser and Sec.-Gen. of Confederation of Mexican Workers (CTM) 36-41; Pres. of Confederation of Latin-American Workers (CTAL) 38-63; Vice-Pres. W.F.T.U. 45-62; Founder and Pres. Partido Popular Socialista June 48; Rep. to Congress of Union 64-67.
Publs. *Public Law and the New Philosophical Currents, Syndical Liberty in Mexico, Bibliography of Labour and Social Foresight in Mexico, The Monroe Doctrine and the Labour Movement, Journey to the World of the Future* (with V. M. Villaseñor); over 100 studies on politics, economics, history, philosophy, etc.
Flores 506, Villa Obregón, D.F., Mexico.

Lomonosov, Vladimir Grigorevich; Soviet politician; b. 28; ed. Moscow Steel Inst.
Foreman, Moscow Hammer and Sickle Iron Works 53-57, Party Work 57-58; Head, Central Asian Bureau, C.P.S.U. Dec. 62-64; Second Sec. Central Cttee. of C.P. of Uzbekistan 65-; mem. C.P.S.U. Central Cttee. 66-; Deputy to U.S.S.R. Supreme Soviet.
Central Committee of Communist Party of Uzbekistan, Tashkent, Uzbek S.S.R., U.S.S.R.

Lomský, General Bohumír; Czechoslovak army officer and politician; b. 22 April 1914; ed. Military Acads., Hranice and Moscow.
Organized Czechoslovak troops in U.S.S.R. during Second World War, Chief-of-Staff, First Czechoslovak Brigade and of Czechoslovak Corps in U.S.S.R. 43-44; various posts in Army in Czechoslovakia 45-53; First Deputy Minister of Nat. Defence 53-56, Minister 56-68; mem. Central Cttee., C.P. of Czechoslovakia 58-68; Deputy, Nat. Assembly 60-; Order of White Lion for Victory 48, Order of Labour 55, 64, and other Czechoslovak and foreign decorations.
c/o Ministry of National Defence, nám. Svobody 471, Prague 6, Dejvice, Czechoslovakia.

Long, Cyril Norman Hugh, D.SC., M.D.; American professor of physiology; b. 19 June 1901; ed. Manchester and McGill Univs.

Demonstrator in Physiology, Univ. Coll., London 23-25; Lecturer, Dept. of Medicine, McGill Univ. 25-29, Asst. Prof. 29-32; Dir. Geo. S. Cox Medical Research Inst. and Asst. Prof. of Medicine, Univ. of Pennsylvania 32-36; Prof. of Physiological Chemistry, School of Medicine, Yale Univ. 36-38, Sterling Prof. of Physiological Chemistry 38-52, Chair. Dept. of Physiological Chemistry 36-52; Sterling Prof. of Physiology 52-, Chair. Dept. of Physiology 52-64; Dean School of Medicine 47-52; mem. Nat. Acad. of Sciences, American Philosophical Soc., Asscn. of American Physicians, American Acad. of Arts and Sciences, Endocrine Soc.; Hon. D.Sc. (Princeton, McGill Univs.), Hon. M.A. (Yale Univ.), Hon. M.D. (Univ. of Venezuela).
Department of Physiology, 333 Cedar Street, New Haven, Conn. 06510, U.S.A.

Long, Edward V.; American politician, lawyer and banker; b. 18 July 1908; ed. Missouri Univ.
Attorney Pike County Missouri 37-41; City Attorney Bowling Green 41-45; elected to Missouri State Senate 45; Lieut. Gov. Missouri 56-60; Senator from Missouri 60-; U.S. Senate Del. to NATO Parliamentarian Conference, Paris 61, to Interparliamentary Union, Canberra 66; mem. Senate Judiciary Comm., Senate Banking and Currency Comm.; Dir. Rotary International; Democrat.
3107 New Senate Office Building, Washington, D.C. 20510, U.S.A.
Telephone: 202-225-5721.

Long, Franklin Asbury; American chemist and government official; b. 27 July 1910; ed. Montana State Univ., and Univ. of California (Berkeley).
Fellow in Chemistry, Univ. of California (Berkeley) 33-34; Instructor in Chemistry, Univ. of Chicago 36-37; Faculty mem. Chemistry Dept., Cornell Univ. 37-43, 45-62; Research, Carnegie Inst. of Technology 43-45; Consultant, Nat. Defense Research Cttee. 41-45; Consultant, Nat. Bureau of Standards 57, Dept. of Army 53-62, Dept. of Air Force 57-62, of Defense 59-62; Asst. Dir. U.S. Arms Control and Disarmament Agency 62-63, Consultant 63-; Visiting Chemical Consultant, Brookhaven Nat. Laboratory 46-62; mem. President's Science Advisory Cttee. 61-66; Vice-Pres. Research and Advanced Studies, Cornell Univ. 63-; Trustee, Assoc. Univs. Inc. 46-.
303 Day Hall, Cornell University, Ithaca, N.Y.; Home: 429 Warren Road, Ithaca, N.Y., U.S.A.
Telephone: 607-272-6383.

Long, Gerald; British journalist; b. 22 Aug. 1923; ed. St. Peter's School, York, and Emmanuel Coll., Cambridge.
Reuters 48-, Corresp. in Turkey 53-54, News Editor, Paris 55-56, Chief Rep. in Germany 56-60, Asst. Gen. Man. (with special responsibility for Europe) 60-63, Gen. Man. 63-.
17 Southwood Avenue, Highgate, London, N.6, England.
Telephone: 01-340-4543.

Long, Olivier, D.EN D., D.ES SC.POL.; Swiss diplomatist; b. 1915; ed. Univ. de Paris à la Sorbonne and Univ. de Genève.
With Int. Red Cross 41-46; Foreign Affairs Dept., Berne 46-49; Washington Embassy 49-53; Div. of Commerce, Berne 53-55; Govt. Del. for Commercial Agreements 55-66; Head of Swiss Del. to European Free Trade Asscn. (EFTA) 60-66; Prof. Graduate Inst. of Int. Studies Geneva 62-; Amb. to United Kingdom and Malta 67-68; Dir. Gen. GATT 68-.
Villa le Bocage, Palais des Nations, Geneva, Switzerland

Long, Russell B.; American lawyer and politician; b. 3 Nov. 1918; ed. Fortier High School and Louisiana State Univ.
Served U.S. Navy 42-45; in private legal practice 45-48,

Exec. Counsel to Gov. of Louisiana 48-; U.S. Senator from Louisiana 48-, Senate Majority Whip 65-; Chair. Finance Cttee. 66; Democrat.
Senate Office Building, Washington, D.C., U.S.A.; and 1112 Steele Boulevard, Baton Rouge, La., U.S.A.

Longchambon, Henri F. M., D. ès SC.; French university professor and politician; b. 27 July 1896; ed. Ecole Normale Supérieure.
Professor of Mineralogy, Univ. of Lyon, Dean of the Science Faculty; fmr. Minister (Scientific Research); Hon. Commr. of the Republic; Senator representing French people resident overseas; mem. Rassemblement Gauche Démocratique; Officier de la Légion d'Honneur; Croix de Guerre.
Palais du Luxembourg, Paris 6e, France.

Longford, 7th Earl of (cr. 1785); **Francis Aungier Pakenham** (cr. Baron 45), P.C., M.A.; British politician; b. 5 Dec. 1905; ed. Eton and New Coll., Oxford.
Tutor, Univ. Tutorial Courses, Stoke-on-Trent 29-31; with Conservative Party Economic Research Dept. 30-32; Lecturer in Politics, Christ Church, Oxford 32; Student in Politics, Christ Church 34-46 and 52-; Prospective Parl. Labour Candidate for Oxford City 38; served Bucks. Light Infantry 39-40; personal asst. to Sir William Beveridge 41-44; Lord-in-Waiting 45-46; Parl. Under-Sec. to War Office 46-47; Chancellor of the Duchy of Lancaster 47-48; Minister of Civil Aviation 48-51; First Lord of the Admiralty May-Oct. 51; Lord Privy Seal and Leader of House of Lords 64-65, 66-68; Sec. of State for Colonies 65-66; Chair. Nat. Bank Ltd. 55-62.
Publs. *Peace by Ordeal* (*The Anglo-Irish Treaty of 1921*), *Born to Believe* 53, *The Causes of Crime* 58, *Five Lives* 63.
Bernhurst, Hurst Green, Sussex, England.

Longo, Luigi; Italian politician; b. 15 March 1900.
Univ. student 20; Sec. of Piedmontese Communist Group which founded the Italian Communist Party 21; mem. Central Cttee. Young Communist Federation 21; del. to Fourth Congress of the Comintern 22; Editor of *L'Avanguardia* (organ of Young Communist Federation) 23; arrested and imprisoned for political activities 23-24; del. of Young Communists at Third Congress of Italian Communist Party 26; mem. Young Communists' International 26-27; responsible for youth work at Foreign Centre of Communist Party in Paris 27; del. to Sixth Congress of Comintern 28; illegal political activity in Italy; two years in Moscow 32-34; Inspector-Gen. of Int. Brigades in Spain 36-39; after end of Spanish war returned to France; imprisoned in France 39-41; in Italy 42-43; organised popular resistance to the Germans in Rome Sept. 43; Vice-Commdr of Volunteer Liberation Corps, Commdt.-Gen. "Garibaldi" Brigades; Deputy Constituent Assembly 46, Nat. Assembly 48, 53, 58, 63, 68; Deputy Sec.-Gen. of Italian Communist Party 45-64, Sec.-Gen. 64; U.S. Bronze Star; Stella d'oro Garibaldina.
Publs. *Un popolo alla macchia* 47, *Sulla via dell'insurrezione nazionale* 54, *Le Brigate Internazionali in Spagna* 56, *Revisionismo nuovo e antico* 57, *Il miracolo economico italiano e la critica marxista* 62.
Via Botteghe Oscure 4, Rome, Italy.
Telephone: 684101.

Longuet-Higgins, Hugh Christopher, F.R.S., F.R.I.C., M.A., D.PHIL.; British university professor; b. 11 April 1923; ed. Winchester Coll., and Balliol Coll., Oxford.
Research Fellow Balliol Coll. 47-48; Research Assoc. Univ. of Chicago 48-49; Lecturer and Reader in theoretical chemistry, Victoria Univ. of Manchester 49-52; Prof. of Theoretical Physics King's Coll., London Univ. 52-54; Fellow, Corpus Christi Coll. and Prof. of Theoretical Chemistry, Univ. of Cambridge 54-67; Editor *Molecular Physics* 58-61; Harrison Memorial

Prize 50; F.R.S. 58; Foreign mem. American Acad. of Arts and Sciences 61.
Publs. include about 120 papers on theoretical physics and chemistry in scientific journals.
26 Dundas Street, Edinburgh 3, Scotland.
Telephone: 031-556-4146.

Longwell, Chester Ray, M.A., PH.D.; American geologist; b. 15 Oct. 1887; ed. Univ. of Missouri and Yale Univ.
Assistant Geologist, Okla. Geological Survey 16; Capt., Field Artillery, U.S. Army 17-19; Asst. Prof. of Geology; Yale Univ. 20, Assoc. Prof. 26, Prof. 29-56, Emer. 56; Chair. Div. of Geology and Geography, Nat. Research Council 37-40; Chair. Dept. of Geology, Yale Univ. 38-46; U.S. Geological Survey 20-; Pres. Geological Soc. of America 49, American Geological Inst.; mem. Nat. Acad. of Sciences 35-; American Philosophical Society, American Acad. of Arts and Sciences; Chair. Cttee. on Tectonic Map of U.S. 34-44.
Publs. *Geology of the Muddy Mountains, Nevada* 28, *Geology from Original Sources* (with W. M. Agar and R. F. Flint) 29, *Textbook of Geology* (with A. Knopf and R. F. Flint) 32, 3rd edn. 48, title changed to *Physical Geology, Introduction to Physical Geology* (with R. F. Flint) 55 (revised 62, rewritten with R. F. Flint and J. E. Sanders 68); and many articles and monographs.
Office: Dept. of Geology, Stanford University, Stanford, Calif.; Home: 1820 Mark Twain, Palo Alto, Calif., U.S.A.
Telephone: Palo Alto 321-8141 (Home).

Löns, Josef, D.IUR.; German diplomatist and lawyer; b. 14 Nov. 1910; ed. law studies.
Head of Legal Dept., Insurance Co.; served in Second World War; Attorney 45; Gen. Sec. C.D.U., British Zone 45-48; Dep. Mayor, Cologne 48-52; Ministerial Dir. of Foreign Office 53; Head of Personnel and Administration, Foreign Office 53-58; Ambassador to the Netherlands 59-63, to Austria 63-.
Embassy of the German Federal Republic, Vienna, Metternichgasse 3, Austria; 4 Krautwig Strasse, Cologne/Lindenthal, German Federal Republic.

Lonsdale, Dame Kathleen, D.B.E., F.R.S., D.SC., LL.D.; British crystallographer; b. 28 Jan. 1903; ed. Bedford Coll., and Univ. Coll., Univ. of London.
Research Asst., Royal Institution, London 23 and 32; Leverhulme Research Fellow 35; elected F.R.S. 45; Dewar Research Fellow 45; Special Research Fellow U.S.A. Fed. Health Service 47; Reader in Crystallography, Univ. of London 46-49, Prof. of Chemistry, Univ. Coll., London 49-68; Gov. and Fellow of Bedford Coll., London; Fellow of Univ. Coll., London; Gen. Sec. British Asscn. for the Advancement of Science 60-64, Pres. Section A 66-67, Pres. 67-68; Vice-Pres. Royal Soc. 61; Pres. Int. Union Crystallography 66; Hon. D.Sc. (Wales, Manchester, Leicester, Lancaster), Hon. LL.D. (Leeds).
Publs. *Structure Factor Tables* 36, *Crystals and X-Rays* 49, *Quakers visit Russia* 52, *International Tables for X-Ray Crystallography*, Vol. I 52, Vol. II 59, Vol. III 62, *Removing the Causes of War* 53, *Is Peace Possible?* 57.
125A Dorset Road, Bexhill, Sussex, England.
Telephone: Bexhill 3405.

Loomis, Alfred Lee, A.B., LL.B., M.SC.; American physicist; b. 4 Nov. 1887; ed. Phillips Acad., Andover, Mass., Yale and Harvard.
Admitted to New York Bar, and began practice New York City; mem. law firm of Winthrop and Stimson 16-20; Vice-Pres. Bonbright and Co. 19-33; Dir. (physicist) Loomis Laboratories 28-41; Pres. Loomis Inst. of Scientific Research 30-65; Chief of Div. 14 Nat. Defence Research Cttee. 40-47; served as Major in U.S. Army in charge experimental work 17-19; Trustee Carnegie Inst. of Washington, Mass. Inst. of Technology; mem. American Physical Society, American

Chemical Society, Nat. Acad. of Sciences, Royal Astronomical Society, etc.
610 Park Avenue, New York, N.Y. 10021, U.S.A.

Loomis, Cecil Edward; American businessman; b. 12 May 1906; ed. Ohio State Univ.
Clerk, Ohio Fuel Gas Co. 28-35; engineer, Columbia Gas System Service Corpn. 35-50, Asst. Vice-Pres. 50, Vice-Pres., Dir. 51-56, Senior Vice-Pres. 56-60, Pres. 60-61, Vice-Chair. 61-64, Chair. 64-; Asst. Vice-Pres. Columbia Gas System Inc., New York City 50-51, Vice-Pres. 51-56, Senior Vice-Pres. 56-60, Dir. 56-, Pres. 60, Vice-Chair. 61-64, Chair. 64-; Dir. Columbia Hydrocarbon Corpn., Columbia Gas of New York Inc., United Fuel Gas Co., and numerous other companies.
Home: Braxmar Drive South, Harrison, N.Y. 10524; Office: 120 East 41st Street, New York City 17, N.Y., U.S.A.

Loos, Anita; American writer; b. 26 April 1893; ed. High School, San Diego, Calif.
Scenario writer with D. W. Griffith (five years), Douglas Fairbanks (three years), Constance Talmadge (two years).
Publs. (novels) *Gentlemen Prefer Blondes* 25, *But Gentlemen Marry Brunettes* 28, (with John Emerson) *The Whole Town's Talking, The Fall of Eve, Cherries are Ripe, The Social Register, A Mouse is Born* 50, *This Brunette Prefers Work* 56, *Gentlemen Still Prefer Blondes, No Mother to Guide Her* 61, *A Girl Like I* (autobiog.) 66; (films) *Red Headed Women, Blossoms in the Dust, I Married an Angel, The Pirate*; (plays) *Happy Birthday* 46, *Gentlemen Prefer Blondes* 49.
c/o Avon Books, 959 Eighth Avenue, New York 19, N.Y., U.S.A.

Lopes-Graça, Fernando; Portuguese composer and writer; b. 17 Dec. 1906; ed. Lisbon Conservatoire, Univs. of Lisbon, Coimbra and Paris.
Prof. Instituto de Música (Coimbra) 32-36, Acad. de Amadores de Música (Lisbon) 40-54.
Compositions include: two piano concertos 40, 53, four piano sonatas 34, 39, 52, 61, *Glosas* (piano) 49-50, four *Canciones de Federico García Lorca* (for baritone and chamber instrumental ensemble) 54, *Trois Danses Portugaises pour Orchestre* 41, *Sinfonia per Orchestra* 44, *Estelas Funerárias* 48, *Suite Rústica No. 1* (for Orchestra) 50, *24 Preludes* (piano) 52-58, *Trovas* 55, *Canções Populares Portuguesas* (for voice and piano, and for voices "a cappella") 55, *Concertino* (for piano, brass, strings and percussion) 56, *Divertimento for Wind Instruments, Percussion, Cellos and Double-basses* 57, *Melodias Rústicas Portuguesas* (piano) 57, *5 Nocturnes* (piano) 59, *História Trágico-Marítima*, for baritone, fem. chorus and orch. 43-60, Cycles for tenor and piano 59, 60, *Pequeno Cancioneiro do Menino Jesus* for fem. voices and instr. chamber ensemble 59, *Petit Triptyche* for violin and piano 60, *Gabriela, Cravo e Canela* (overture) 60, *Prelude and Fugue* (violin solo) 61, *Canto de Amor e de Morte* (orch.) 61, *Poema de Dezembro* (orch.) 61, *Para uma Criança que vai Nascer* (for strings) 61, *Mar de Setembro* (cycle for voice and piano) 62, *Concertino for Viola and Orchestra* 62, *Cosmorama* (piano) 63, *In Memoriam Bela Bartok* (7 suites for piano) 59-64, *String Quartet* 64, *9 Cantigas de Amigo* (for voice and chamber instrumental ensemble) 64, *Four Sketches* (for strings) 65, *Suite Rústica No. 2* (for string quartet) 65, *Concerto da camera col violoncello obligato* 65, *Quatorze Anotações* (for string quartet) 66, *Sete Lembranças para Vieira da Silva* (for wind quintet) 66.
Publs. include *Reflexões sobre a Música* 41, *Introdução à Música Moderna* 42, *Música e Músicos Modernos* 43, *A Música Portuguesa e os Problemas* (vol I) 44, *Tali Euterpe e Terpsicore* 45, *Visita aos Músicos Franceses* 48, *Viana de Mota* 49, *Bela Bartok* 53, *A Canção Popular Portuguesa* 54, *Em Louvor de Mozart* 56, *Dicionário de Música* (Vol I) 56, (Vol. II) 58, *Igor Stravinsky and Bela Bartok* 59, *A Música Portuguesa e os seus Problemas* 2nd vol. 59, *Musicalia* 60, *Nossa Companheira Música* 64, *Paginas Escolhidas de Crítica e Estética Musical* 67 and translations of Rousseau, Mann, Keller, Mörike, Percy Buck, Alan Bush, Haskell, Romain Rolland.
El Mio Paraiso, 2° Ave. da Republica, Parede, Portugal. Telephone: 2472824.

López, Salvador P.; Philippine journalist, diplomatist and politician; b. 11; ed. Univ. of the Philippines.
Columnist, Magazine Editor and Assoc. Editor *Philippines Herald* 33-41; Radio News Commentator 40-41; Philippine Army Service 42-46; Diplomatic Service 46-; Adviser on Political Affairs, Philippine Mission to UN 46-48, Senior Adviser 48-49, Chargé d'Affaires a.i. 50-52, Acting Perm. Rep. to UN 53-54; Minister to France 55-56 concurrently Minister to Belgium and Netherlands 55-56, to Switzerland 57-58, Ambassador to France 56-62, concurrently Perm. Rep. to UNESCO 58-62, Minister to Portugal 59-62; Under-Sec. of Foreign Affairs, Philippines 62-63; Sec. of Foreign Affairs 63-64; Perm. Rep. to UN 64-, concurrently Amb. to U.S.A. 68-; numerous decorations.
Publs. *Literature and Society* 51, *Freedom of Information* 53, *English for World Use* 54, *The United States—Philippines Colonial Relationship* 66.
Philippine Mission to the United Nations, 13 East 66th Street, New York 21, N.Y., U.S.A.

López Arellano, Gen. Oswaldo; Honduran air force officer and politician; b. 21; ed. School of Mil. Aviation and Flight Training, U.S.A.
Joined armed forces 39, Lieut. 47, Col. 58; mem. Mil. Junta, Chief of Mil. Govt. of Honduras, Minister of Nat. Defence, Minister of Public Security, and Chief of Armed Forces Oct. 63-66; Pres. of Honduras 66-; several decorations.
Office of the President, Tegucigalpa, Honduras.

López Bravo, Gregorio; Spanish politician; b. 23.
Former Dir. Constructora Naval Co.; fmr. Head, Foreign Exchange Inst.; Minister of Industry 62-.
Ministry of Industry, Madrid, Spain.

López Mateos, Adolfo; Mexican politician; b. 26 May 1910; ed. Col. Francés, Mexico City, Toluca Scientific and Literary Inst. and Mexican Nat. Univ.
Successively Librarian, Professor and Dir. Toluca Scientific and Literary Inst.; Official in Inst. of Fine Arts; Senator; Leader Del. to U.N. Economic and Social Council, Geneva; Sec. Gen. Partido Revolucionario Institucional, Pres. Programme Comm.; fmr. Minister of Labour; Pres. of Mexico Dec. 58-64.
c/o Palacio Presidencial, Mexico City, D.F., Mexico.

López Otero, Modesto; Spanish architect; b. 85.
Medallist of Fine Arts Exhibition, Madrid 12; First Prize winner in competition for monument of "Las Cortes de Cadiz"; Hon. Dir. Spanish School of Architecture and of Acad. of Fine Arts; Architect in charge of Madrid new Univ. City; mem. Acad. of History, Nat. Council of Architecture, Nat. Council of Education, International Cttee. of Architects.
Publs. *Influence of Spanish Architecture in the Spanish Mission in California, Conservation of Monuments.*
Paseo de la Castellana 102, Madrid, Spain.

López Rodó, Laureano; Spanish lawyer and government official; b. 20; ed. Univ. de Madrid.
Professor of Admin. Law, Univ. de Santiago de Compostella 45-53, Univ. de Madrid 53-; Technical Sec.-Gen. Office of the Pres. 56-62; Pres. and founder Centro de Formacion y Perfeccionamiento de Funcionarios; Commr. for the Development Plan 62-, also Minister without Portfolio July 65-; mem. Exec. Cttee. Int. Inst. of Admin. Sciences; del. to numerous int. congresses; mem. Real Academia de Ciencias Morales y Políticas;

Councillor Consejo Superior de Investigaciones Cientí-ficas; mem. Opus Dei; several decorations.
Presidencia del Gobierno, El Ministro y Comisario del Plan de Desarrollo Económica y Social, Castellana 3, Madrid, Spain.
Telephone: 2-19-03-00.

López Villamil, Humberto; Honduran lawyer and diplomatist; b. 20 March 1917; ed. Academy for Inter-national Law, The Hague.
Alternate Rep. of Honduras to UN 55-56; Ambassador to Netherlands 57-59; fmr. Prof., Honduras Nat. Univ.; Perm. Rep. to UN 65-.
Publs. include: *Statement of the Law of Honduras, The Central American Court of Justice and International Politics.*
Permanent Mission of Honduras to the United Nations, 290 Madison Avenue, Room 603, New York, N.Y. 10017, U.S.A.

Lora Tamayo, Manuel; Spanish chemist and politi-cian; b. 04.
Professor of Organic Chemistry, Seville 33-43, Madrid 43; Minister of Educ. 62-; Chair. Nat. Comm., UNESCO 67-68; mem. Supreme Council for Scientific Research, Royal Acad. of Science, hon. mem. Lisbon Acad. of Science; Dr. h.c. Paris.
c/o Ministry of Education, Madrid, Spain.

Lorain, Maurice; French banker; b. 16 Oct. 1897; ed. Lycée Lacanal à Sceaux, Faculté de Droit de Paris.
At Société Générale since 26, Dir.-Gen. 43-58, Pres. 58-67, Hon. Pres. 67-; mem. Cttee. for Econ. and Financial Reform 58; Pres. Cttee. for studying Finance-ment of Investments 62-63; Vice-Pres. Professional Bankers' Asscn. 63-; mem. Econ. and Social Council 65-; Grand Officier Légion d'Honneur; Croix de Guerre.
17 rue de Valois, Paris 1er, France.

Lorant, Stefan; American (born Hungarian) author and editor; b. 22 Feb. 1901.
Started career as film cameraman in Vienna; mem. Editorial Staff *Das Magazin* Berlin 25; Editor *Bilder Courier* Berlin 25, *Ufa Magazin* Berlin 25-26, *Münchner Illustrierte Presse* 26-33; placed in "protective custody" following Hitler's accession to "power; upon release came to England where he founded *Weekly Illustrated*, *Lilliput* (Editor 37-40), *Picture Post* (Editor 38-40); now in U.S.A.; LL.D. (Knox Coll.), M.A. (Harvard).
Publs. *I Was Hitler's Prisoner* 35, *Chamberlain and the Beautiful Llama* 40, *The United States* (ed.) 40, *Lincoln: His Life in Photographs* 41, *The New World* 46, *F.D.R.: a pictorial biography* 50, *The Presidency* 51, *Lincoln, a Picture Story of Life* 52, *The Life of Abraham Lincoln* 54, *The Life and Times of Theodore Roosevelt* 59, *Pittsburgh: The Story of an American City* 64, *The Glorious Burden: The American Presidency* 68.
"Farview", Lenox, Mass., U.S.A.
Telephone: 413-637-0666.

Lord, Cyril, LL.D.; British businessman and textile technologist; b. 12 July 1911; ed. Manchester Univ., and Coll. of Technology.
Laboratory controller Scott Son and Co. Ltd., London 33-36; laboratory controller H. Ledgard Ltd., London 36-39; Dir. Hodkin and Lord Ltd., London 40; tech-nical adviser Cotton Board of England, Manchester 40-43; worked in Northern Ireland on the development of long staple fibres for flax machinery 43-45; Chair. Cyril Lord Ltd. and of fifteen subsidiary companies 45-68.
1 Harley Street, London, W.1, England; and Wayside, Donaghadee, Co. Down, Northern Ireland.
Telephone: 01-580-7755 (Office).

Loren, Sophia (wife of Carlo Ponti, *q.v.*); Italian actress; b. 20 Sept. 1934.
First screen appearance as an extra in *Quo Vadis*; has appeared in many Italian and other films including *E Arrivato l'Accordatore* 51, *Africa sotto i Mari* (first leading role), *La Tratta delle Bianche, La Favorita* 52, *Aida, Il Paese dei Campanelli, Miseria e Nobiltà, Tempi Nostri* 53, *Carosello Napoletano, L'Oro di Napoli* 54, *Attila, Peccato che sia una canaglia, Il Segno di Venere, La Bella Mugnaia, La Donna del Fiume* 55, *Boccacio' 70, Matrimonio All'Italiana*; and in the following American films: *The Pride and the Passion* 55, *Boy on a Dolphin, Legend of the Lost* 56, *The Key, Desire Under the Elms* 57, *Houseboat, The Black Orchid, That Kind of Woman* 58; Venice Festival Award for *The Black Orchid* 58, *It Started in Naples, Heller in Pink Tights* 60, *The Millionairess, Two Women, El Cid, Madame Sans Gêne, Yesterday, Today and Tomorrow* 63, *The Fall of the Roman Empire* 64, *Lady L* 65, *Opera-tion Crossbow* 65, *Judith* 65, *A Countess from Hong Kong* 65, *Arabesque* 66, *More than a Miracle* 67; Cannes Film Festival Award for best Actress (*Two Women*) 61.
Palazzo Colonna, Piazza d'Aracoeli 1, Rome, Italy.

Lorentz, Stanisław, PH.D.; Polish art historian and museum administrator; b. 28 April 1899; ed. Warsaw Univ.
Lecturer, Vilno Univ. 30-35, Warsaw Univ. 37-39; Dir. Nat. Museum, Warsaw 35-39, 45-; Dir.-in-Chief, Museums and Conservation of Monuments Department, Ministry of Culture and Art 45-52; Prof. of Art History, Warsaw Univ. 47-; del. UNESCO Congress, Paris 49; Montevideo 54, New Delhi 56, Paris 58, 60, 62, 64; del. Int. Congress of History of Art, New York 61, 64; Int. Council of Monuments and Sites 65; mem. Presidium Int. Union of Art Historians, Int. Comm. of Museums (ICOM); Pres. Polish Nat. ICOMOS Cttee.; mem. Polish Acad. of Sciences; mem. of Parl. 65-.
Publs. *Victor Louis à Varsovie* 58, *Musées et Collections en Pologne* in French, German, English and Russian, *Natolin* 48, *Relazioni artistiche fra l'Italia e la Polonia* 61, and numerous other works in Polish, French and English.
3 Aleje Jerozolimskie, Warsaw, Poland.
Telephone: 218195.

Lorenz, Konrad, D.MED., ET. PHIL.; Austrian etholo-gist; b. 7 Nov. 1903; ed. Univ. of Vienna.
Assistant Inst. of Anatomy, Vienna 28-35; Lecturer in Comparative Anatomy and Animal Psychology, Vienna 37-40; Head, Dept. of Psychology, Königsberg 40-45; Physician in the German Army 42-44; Dir. Max Planck Inst. for Physiology of Behavior; Foreign mem. Royal Soc. (U.K.).
Publs. *King Solomon's Ring* 52, *Man Meets Dog* 54, *Das Sogenannte Böse* 63, *Über tierisches und men-schliches Verhalten* 65, *Evolution and Modification of Behavior* 65.
8131 Seewiesen, German Federal Republic.
Telephone: 08157-8121.

Loridan, Walter, DR. POL. SC.; Belgian diplomatist; b. 22 Feb. 1909; ed. Brussels Univ.
Sec. Belgian Legation, Warsaw 36; Chargé d'Affaires, Spain 37-39, Mexico 40-43; Personal Asst. to the Minister of Foreign Affairs 44-47; Prof. Brussels Univ. 45; Dir.-Gen. Political Dept., Ministry of Foreign Affairs 48-51; Minister to Mexico 51-54; Ambassador to Mexico 54-55; Ambassador to U.S.S.R. 55-59; Perm. Rep. to UN 59-65; Ambassador to German Fed. Repub. 65-.
Embassy of Belgium, Bonn, Kaiser-Friedrich Str. 22, German Federal Republic.

Losey, Joseph, B.A., M.A.; American film and theatre director; b. 09; ed. Dartmouth Coll., New Hampshire, and Harvard Graduate School of Arts and Science.
Freelance journalist 31; stage manager, later theatre producer, Broadway 32-40; writer, producer and editor of radio documentaries 38-; film director 38-; settled in U.K. 55; numerous film awards.
Films include: *A Child went Forth* 41, *A Gun in His Hand* 45, *The Boy with Green Hair* 48, *The Lawless* 49, *The Prowler* 50, *M* 50, *The Big Night* 51, *Stranger on*

the Prowl 51, *The Sleeping Tiger* 54, *A Man on the Beach* 55, *The Intimate Stranger* 55, *Time Without Pity* 56, *The Gypsy and the Gentleman* 57, *Blind Date* 59, *The Criminal* 60, *The Damned* 61, *The Servant* 63, *King and Country* 64, *Modesty Blaise* 65, *Accident* 66, *Boom* 67. c/o London International, Park House, Park Street, London, W.1, England.
Telephone: 01-629-8080.

Loshakov, Alexandr Ivanovich; Soviet diplomatist; b. 1910.
Diplomatic Service 42; Asst. Deputy Minister of Foreign Affairs 47-48; Counsellor, Budapest 54-56; U.S.S.R. Ministry of Foreign Affairs 56-60; Ambassador to Mali 60-62, to Switzerland 63-66; U.S.S.R. Ministry of Foreign Affairs 66-.
U.S.S.R. Ministry of Foreign Affairs, Moscow, U.S.S.R.

Loshchenkov, Fyodor Ivanovich; Soviet politician; ed. Moscow Inst. of Aviation and C.P.S.U. Cttee. Higher Party School.
Industrial worker 32-36; Soviet Army service 36-38; Student 38-43; Engineer 43-46; Party Official 46-61; First Sec. Yaroslavl Regional Cttee. C.P.S.U. and Alt. mem. C.P.S.U. Central Cttee. 61-; mem. C.P.S.U. 43-; Deputy to U.S.S.R. Supreme Soviet.
Yaroslavl Regional Committee, Communist Party of the Soviet Union, Yaroslavl, U.S.S.R.

Losonczi, Pál; Hungarian politician; b. 19.
Agricultural labourer; set up Red Star Co-operative Farm, Barcs 48; mem. Communist Party 45-; mem. of Parliament 53-; Minister of Agriculture 60-67; Chair. Nat. Council of Co-operative Farms 65-67; Pres. of Presidential Council 67-; mem. Central Cttee. Hungarian Socialist Workers' Party; Kossuth Prize 56; Hero of Socialist Labour and Order of Hungarian People's Republic 54.
The Presidential Council, Budapest, Hungary.

Lotz, Kurt; German business executive; b. 18 Sept. 1912; ed. August-Vilmar-Schule, Homberg.
Joined Brown Boveri and Cie. 46, Chair. of Management Board 58; mem. Board of Dirs. A. G. Brown Boveri & Cie., Baden, Switzerland (parent company) 61, Del. mem. Board of Dirs. 63; Deputy Chair. Management Board Volkswagenwerk A.G. June 67-April 68, Chair. April 68-; mem. Fed. of German Industries, Central Fed. of Electronics Industry, Asscn. of German Machine Tool Manufacturers; Hon. Senator Heidelberg Univ.; Dr. rer. pol. h.c. (Wirtschaftshochschule, Mannheim) 62.
Volkswagenwerk A.G., 3180 Wolfsburg, German Federal Republic.

Loubatières, Auguste Louis; French professor of pharmacology and pharmacodynamics; b. 28 Dec. 1912; ed. Coll. d'Agde, Univs. of Montpellier and Marseilles.
Assistant Lecturer in Physiology, Univ. of Montpellier 41-44, Lecturer 44-46, Prof. 46-52, Prof. of Applied Physiology and Pharmocodynamics 52-66, Pharmacology and Pharmacodynamics 66-; mem. Institut de France, Académie des Sciences, Acad. of Sciences of New York, Nat. Acaf. of Medicine of Buenos Aires, Royal Soc. of Medicine of London, Acad. Nat. de Médecine de Paris, Soc. of Biology, Soc. of Biological Chemistry, and Soc. of Therapeutics and Pharmacodynamics; Corresp. mem. Acad. Royale de Médecine de Belgique; Hon. mem. British Diabetic Asscn., Purkinje Medical Soc., Prague, European Soc. for Study of Diabetics; Vice-Pres. Foundation for French Medical Research; French rep. at Advisory Panel on the CIBA Foundation (London); numerous scientific and cultural missions overseas; Chevalier Légion d'Honneur, Officier Ordre du Mérite, Officier d'Académie, Officier des Palmes Académiques.
Major research: Discovery of the Cardiotonic Action

and Cardiatic Analeptics of Heptaminol 38, Discovery of the action and mechanism of action of Hyperglycaemic and antidiabetic Sulphonamides 46-67.
Publs. about 350 publications on physiology, pharmacology and fundamentals of applied pharmacodynamics.
Institut de Biologie, boulevard Henri IV, 34 Montpellier; and Allée des Sophoras, Résidence des Sophoras, 34 Montpellier, France.
Telephone: Montpellier 92-41-74.

Louchheim, Mrs. Katie S.; American government official; b. 28 Dec. 1903; ed. Rosemary Hall, and Columbia Univ.
Assistant to Dir. of Public Information, UNRRA 42-46; Democratic Nat. Committeewoman D.C. 56-61; Dir. Women's Activities, Democratic Nat. Cttee. 53-60; Vice-Chair. Democratic Nat. Cttee. 56-60; Special Consultant to Promote the Role of Women in Int. Cultural Exchange Matters, State Dept. 61-62; Dep. Asst. Sec. of State for Public Affairs 62-63; mem. Defense Advisory Cttee. on Women in the Armed Services 55-62; Deputy Asst. Sec. of State for Community Advisory Services 64-66, for Educational and Cultural Affairs 66-; American Nat. Red Cross 66-; mem. Arthur and Elizabeth Schlesinger Library on History of Women in America, Radcliff Coll. 64-; mem. First Lady's Cttee. on Beautification 65-; Chair. Fed. Woman's Award 62-68.
Publ. *With or Without Roses* 66.
Department of State, Washington 25, D.C.; and 2824 "O" Street, N.W., Washington, D.C. 20007, U.S.A.
Telephone: 212-337-1096.

Loudon, Jonkheer John Hugo; Netherlands oil executive; b. 27 June 1905; ed. Univ. of Utrecht.
Joined N.V. De Bataafsche Petroleum Mij., The Hague 30, served Venezuela, The Hague, U.S.A. 30-44; Gen. Man. Royal Dutch/Shell interests, Venezuela 44-47; Man.-Dir. Royal Dutch Petroleum Co., N.V. De Bataafsche Petroleum Mij., Shell Petroleum Co. Ltd. 47; Pres. Royal Dutch Petroleum Co. 52-65, Dir. 65-; Chair. Board Shell Oil Co. U.S.A. 57-65; Chair. Shell Caribbean Petroleum Co.; Dir. other companies; Hon. K.B.E. (U.K.), Knight, Order of Netherlands Lion; Order of Liberator (Venezuela).
35 Grosvenor Square, London, W.1, England; Koekoeksduin, Aerdenhout, Netherlands.

Louis, Pierre, D. ès L.; French professor and university official; b. 1 Aug. 1913; ed. Lycée Henri IV, Univ. of Paris and Fondation Thiers.
Former Dir. of Studies, Faculty of Letters, Rennes, Faculty of Letters, Lyon; fmr. Prof., Faculty of Letters, Lyon; fmr. Rector, Académie de Clermont-Ferrand; Rector, Univ. of Lyon 60-; Officier de la Légion d'Honneur, Commandeur Ordre des Palmes Académiques.
Université de Lyon, 30 rue Cavenne, Lyon 7, France.

Loum, Seymi Amadou; Senegalese diplomatist; b. 4 April 1924; ed. Faculté de Droit and Institut d'études politiques, Paris.
Lawyer, Court of Appeal, Paris 50-53, Abidjan (Ivory Coast) 54-60; Dir. of Studies in Constitutional Law and Political Institutions, Institut de Droit, Abidjan 58-60; Amb. to Ghana 61-63, to U.S.S.R. 63-67.
Ministry of Foreign Affairs, Dakar, Senegal.

Lourie, Arthur, M.A., LL.B.; Israeli diplomatist; b. 19 March 1903; ed. Cambridge and Harvard Univs.
Lecturer in Roman-Dutch Law, Witwatersrand Univ. 27-32; Political Sec. Jewish Agency for Palestine, London 33; Director UN Office, Jewish Agency 47; Consul-Gen. of Israel, New York and Dep. Head, Perm. Del. to U.N. 48-53; Asst. Dir.-Gen. Ministry for Foreign Affairs 53-57, 65-; Ambassador on Special Mission to Emperor of Ethiopia 56; Ambassador to

Canada 57-59; Chair. Del. U.N. Gen. Assembly 59; Amb. to U.K. 60-65; Deputy Dir.-Gen. Ministry of Foreign Affairs 66-.
Ministry of Foreign Affairs, Jerusalem, Israel.

Lourie, Donold Bradford; American food manufacturing executive; b. 99; ed. Princeton Univ.
Executive Vice-Pres. 45-47, mem. Exec. Cttee., Dir. Quaker Oats Co. 47-53, 54-; Pres. 47-53, 54-62, Chair. 62-; Chief Exec. Officer 56-66; Under-Sec. of State for Admin. 53-54; dir. other companies.
Quaker Oats Co., Merchandise Mart Plaza, Chicago 54, Ill. 60654, U.S.A.

Louvel, Jean-Marie-Edmond; French engineer and politician; b. 1 July 1900; ed. Lycée Malherbe, Caen, Ecole Polytechnique and Ecole Supérieure d'Electricité. Did engineering work before war; served French Army 39-40; Deputy for Calvados (M.R.P.) 46-58; Pres. French Higher Council for Electricity and Gas; Minister of Industry and Commerce, Bidault, Queuille, Pléven Cabinets 50, Queuille Cabinet 51; Minister of Industry and Power, Pléven Cabinet 51; Minister of Industry and Commerce, Faure and Pinay Cabinets 52; Minister of Industry, Mayer Cabinet 53; Minister of Commerce, Laniel Cabinet 53-54; Municipal Councillor, Caen 53-; Mayor 59; Senator for Calvados 59-; Dir., Compagnie générale d'électricité 63-65, Pres. 65-.
1 place Maréchal-Foch, Caen (Calvados), France.

Louw, The Hon. Eric Hendrik, B.A., LL.B., D.COMM.; South African politician; b. 21 Nov. 1890; ed. Victoria Coll., Stellenbosch, Rhodes Univ. Coll., Grahamstown.
Admitted as Barrister 17; M.P. 24, 38-63; Trade Commr., U.S.A. and Canada 25-28; High Commr., London 29; Minister, U.S.A. 29-33, Italy 33, France and Portugal 34-37; Minister of Econ. Affairs 48-54, of Finance 55-56, of Foreign Affairs 56-Dec. 63; Rep. to UN Assembly 48, 49, 56, 58, 59, 60, 61, 62; Prime Minister's Rep. to Commonwealth Prime Minister's Meetings, London 48,57, 60; South African Rep. to Commonwealth Econ. Conf. 52; Rep. to many int. conferences.
[Died 24 June 1968].

Love, George Hutchinson; American business executive.
Chairman of Board, Consolidation Coal Co., M.A. Hanna Co.; Chair. Exec. Cttee. Chrysler Corpn. until 66; dir. other companies; Hon. LL.D. (Washington and Jefferson Coll.).
5920 Braeburn Place, Pittsburgh, Pa., U.S.A.

Love, John A., LL.B.; American lawyer and politician; b. 29 Nov. 1916; ed. Cheyenne Mountain School and Denver Univ.
U.S. Naval Air Force 42-45; legal practice, Love, Cole and Mullett, Colorado Springs 45-63; Gov. of Colorado 63-; mem. Colorado State Republican Central Cttee., American Bar Asscn.
The Governor's Mansion, Denver, Colorado, U.S.A.

Loveless, Herschel Cellel; American politician; b. 5 May 1911; ed. high school.
Worked with Chicago, Milwaukee, St. Paul and Pacific Railway 27-39 and 44-47 and with John Morrell and Co., Ottumwa, Ia. 39-44; Supt. of Streets City of Ottumwa 47-49 and Mayor 49-53; Owner-Man. Municipal Equipment Co., Ottumwa 53-56; Gov. of Iowa 57-61; with Renegotiation Board 61-; mem.-at-large Iowa Exec. Council; mem. Exec. Council of Governors' Conf. San Juan, Puerto Rico 59; Chair. Advisory Cttee. on Agriculture, Dem. Nat. Advisory Council 59.
1910 K Street, Washington, D.C., U.S.A.

Lovell, Sir (Alfred Charles) Bernard, Kt., F.R.S., O.B.E., PH.D., M.SC.; British radio astronomer; b. 31 Aug. 1913; ed. Bristol Univ.
Assistant Lecturer in Physics, Univ. of Manchester 36-39; with Telecommunications Research Est. 39-45; Lecturer in Physics, Univ. of Manchester 45-47, Senior

Lecturer 47-49, Reader 49-51, Prof. of Radio Astronomy 51-; Dir. Nuffield Radio Astronomy Laboratories, Jodrell Bank 51-; Fellow, Royal Soc. 55; Hon. Foreign mem. American Acad. of Arts and Sciences 55, Hon. mem. N.Y. Acad. of Sciences 60; Royal Medal of Royal Soc. 60; Hon. Fellow Royal Swedish Acad. 62, Inst. of Electrical Engineers 67; Daniel and Florence Guggenheim Int. Astronautics Award 61; Ordre du Mérite pour la Recherche et l'Invention 62; Maitland Silver Medal, Inst. of Structural Engineers 64; Churchill Gold Medal, Soc. of Engineers 64; LL.D. (Edinburgh), D.Sc. (Leicester), LL.D. (Calgary) 66, D.Sc. (Leeds) 66.
Publs. *Science and Civilisation* 39, *World Power Resources and Social Development* 45, *Radio Astronomy* 52, *Meteor Astronomy* 54, *The Exploration of Space by Radio* 57, *The Individual and the Universe* (The Reith Lectures 58), *The Exploration of Outer Space* 62, *Discovering the Universe* 63; Editor (with Tom Margerison) *The Explosion of Science: The Physical Universe* 67, *The Story of Jodrell Bank* 68.
Nuffield Radio Astronomy Laboratories, Jodrell Bank, Macclesfield, Cheshire; Home: The Quinta, Swettenham, Nr. Congleton, Cheshire, England.
Telephone: Lower Withington 321.

Lovett, Robert Abercrombie; American banker and railroad executive; b. 14 Sept. 1895; ed. Yale and Harvard Univs.
Clerk, Nat. Bank of Commerce, New York City 21; partner, Brown Brothers, Harriman and Co. 26-40, 46-47, 49-50; Special Asst. to Sec. of War Dec. 40-April 41; Asst. Sec. of War for Air 41-45; Under-Sec. of State 47-49; Deputy Sec. of Defense 50-51, Sec. of Defense 51-53; Gen. Partner, Brown Brothers, Harriman and Co. 53-; Special Adviser to Pres. Kennedy 61-63; dir. several financial orgs.; U.S. Presidential Medal of Freedom 63.
Locust Valley, Long Island, New York; and 49 Wall Street, New York, N.Y. 10005, U.S.A.

Lovinescu, Horia, D.ES.L.; Romanian theatre director and playwright; b. 7 Aug. 1917; ed. Universitatea București.
First Press Attaché for Cultural Relations 48-63; Dir. Nottara Theatre, Bucharest 64-; Vice-Pres. Romanian P.E.N. Club 63-, Theatre Council 63-; mem. Leading Board of Writers' Union 65-; State Prize and other Romanian awards.
Publs. *Jean Arthur Rimbaud* (critical study); Plays: *Citadela Sfărîmată* (Destroyed Citadel) 54, *Hanul Dela Rascruce* (Inn at the Crossroad) 55, *Surorile Boga* (Boga Sisters) 57, *Mai Presus de Toate* (Above All) 59, *Febre* (Feber) 60, *Iomul care și-A Pierdut Omenia* (The Man Who Lost his Humanity) 61, *Paradisul* (The Paradise) 62, *Moartea Unui Artist* (The Death of an Artist) 64, *Locțiitorul* (The Man Instead) 66.
Bulevardul Bălcescu 16, Bucharest, Romania.

Lovink, Antonius Hermanus Johannes, B.COMM.; Netherlands diplomatist; b. 02; ed. Rotterdam Commercial Univ., Heidelberg and Mukden Univs.
Fmrly. worked banks and shipping offices London, Hamburg and Paris; attached Consulates Berlin, Frankfurt, Trade Dept. Embassy Paris; attached Chinese Maritime Customs 24-28; Dir. Chinese-Japanese Affairs Bureau for Netherlands East Indies Govt. 28-34; Chief of Bureau for East Asiatic Affairs 35-42; Sec.-Gen. Min. for Co-ordination of Warfare, Netherlands Govt. in London 42-43; Ambassador to China 43-46; Ambassador to U.S.S.R. 46-47; Ambassador Extraordinary and Plenipotentiary Sec.-Gen. of Min. of Foreign Affairs 48-49; Governor-General Indonesia 49, Ambassador to Canada 50-57, 60-68, to Australia 57-60; Grand Officer, Order of Orange-Nassau, Knight Order of Netherlands Lion, Grand Cross, Order of the Brilliant Star (China), Cross of

Merit, Netherlands Grand Cross, Dr. jur. h.c. (Queen's Univ. Kingston, Ontario 56, Univ. of Western Ontario, London, Ontario 64).
2194 Elder Road, Ottawa, Canada.

Løvlein, Emil; Norwegian farmer and politician; b. 22 Sept. 1899.
Secretary of Communist Party 33-46, Chair. 46-65; mem. Parl. 45-49 and 53-.
Grönlandsleret 39, Oslo, Norway.

Low, Alan Roberts, M.A.; New Zealand banker; b. 11 Jan. 1916; ed. Canterbury Univ. Coll.
Joined Reserve Bank of New Zealand 38; Mil. Service 42-44; Econ. Adviser, Reserve Bank of New Zealand 51, Asst. Gov. 60-62, Deputy Gov. 62-67, Gov. 67-.
Reserve Bank of New Zealand, P.O. Box 2498, Feathers-ton Street, Wellington, New Zealand.

Low, Sir Francis, Kt.; British journalist; b. 19 Nov. 1893; ed. Robert Gordon's Coll., Aberdeen.
Member staff *Aberdeen Free Press* 10-22; Editor *Evening News of India* 24, *Times of India* 32-48; Hon. Sec. East India Asscn. 54-66.
High Gardens, Hook Heath, Woking, Surrey, England.
Telephone: Woking 63211.

Low, George Michael; American space scientist; b. 10 June 1926; ed. Rensselaer Polytechnic Inst., Troy, New York.
National Advisory Cttee. for Aeronautics 49-58, research on Aerodynamic Heating, Boundary Layer Theory, Internal Aerodynamics, Space Technology, Chief of Special Projects Branch 56-58; Nat. Aeronautics and Space Admin. (N.A.S.A.) 58-63, assisted with Mercury, Gemini and Apollo manned space flight programmes as Deputy Assoc. Administrator for Manned Space Flight; Deputy Dir. N.A.S.A. Manned Spacecraft Center 64-67; Man. Apollo Spacecraft Programme, N.A.S.A. 67-; Fellow, American Astronautical Soc.; Assoc. Fellow, American Inst. of Aeronautics and Astronautics; Nat. Aeronautics and Space Agency's Outstanding Leadership Medal 62, Arthur S. Flemming Award 63.
504 Clearview Avenue, Friendswood, Texas 77546; and N.A.S.A. Manned Spacecraft Center, Houston, Texas 77058, U.S.A.
Telephone: 713-HU3-4858.

Lowdermilk, Walter Clay, M.A., PH.D.; American soil conservation specialist; b. 1 July 1888; ed. Univs. of Arizona, Oxford and California.
Assistant Forest Ranger 15; Timber Acquisition Officer, American Peace and Liquidation Comms. 17-19; Re-search Officer, Region 1, U.S. Forest Service 19-22; Research Prof. of Forestry, Univ. of Nanking, China 22-27; Project Leader, Erosion Stream Flow Research, Calif. Forest Experimental Station 27-33; Assoc. Chief Soil Conservation Service, U.S. Dept. of Agriculture, Washington, D.C. 33-39, Asst. Chief 39-47, Chief of Research 37-47 retd.; Pres. American Geophysical Union 41-44; survey of land use in soil and water conservation and flood control, Europe and Near East 38-39; Consultant on erosion and flood control Japan 51, to UN Secretariat on water matters 54, to F.A.O. in Israel and Yugoslavia; Visiting Prof. Haifa Inst. of Technology 55-57; consultant and adviser on soil con-servation problems to various foreign govts.; Counsellor Near East Foundation; Chair. Cttee. on Land Erosion, Int. Union Geodesy and Geophysics; mem. Int. Soc. of Soil Science; Fellow, American Geographical Soc., Geological Soc. of America, etc.; Hon. D. Tech. Sc. (Israel Inst. of Technology) 53.
Publs. *Tracing Land Use Across Ancient Boundaries, Palestine—Land of Promise, Eleventh Commandment, Technical Assistance to Less Developed Countries, Re-clamation of a Man-Made Desert* 60.
1620 Le Roy Avenue, Berkeley 4, Calif., U.S.A.
Telephone: 415-845-5253.

Lowe, David Nicoll, O.B.E., M.A., B.SC., F.R.S.E.; British public servant; b. 9 Sept. 1909; ed. High School, Arbroath, and Univ. of St. Andrews, Scotland.
Asst. Sec. of British Asscn. for the Advancement of Science 35-39; seconded for wartime service to the British Civil Service (Cabinet Office) 39-46; Sec. British Asscn. 46-54; Sec. Carnegie U.K. Trust 54-.
Comely Bank, 2 Park Avenue, Dunfermline, Scotland.

Lowell, Ralph, A.B.; American banker; b. 23 July 1890; ed. Harvard Univ.
Joined firm of Curtis and Sanger 13; with First Nat. Bank of Boston 16-17; served in U.S. Army (Lieut. Col.) 17-19; with Lee, Higginson and Co. 19-32; joined Clark, Dodge and Co. 32, Partner 37-43; Chair. Boston Safe Deposit and Trust Co. 43-46, Pres. 46-59, Bd. Chair. 59-66; trustee numerous organizations; Dir. Nat. Fund for Medical Education; Pres. Museum of Fine Arts; Fellow Amer. Acad. Arts and Sciences; Hon. LL.D. (Harvard Univ., Northeastern Univ. and Bates Coll.), Hon. D.Sc. (Lowell Technological Inst.), Hon. L.H.D. (Tufts Univ.).
Home: 228 Fox Hill Street, Westwood, Mass.; Office: 100 Franklin Street, Boston, Mass., U.S.A.

Lowell, Robert (Traill Spence), Jr., A.B.; American poet; b. 1 March 1917; ed. Kenyon Coll., Ohio, and Harvard Univ.
Guggenheim Fellow and Consultant in Poetry, Library of Congress 47-48; Pulitzer Prize and American Acad. of Arts and Letters Prize 47; Winner Nat. Book Award 59.
Publs. *Land of Unlikeness* 44, *Lord Weary's Castle* 46, *The Mills of the Kavanaughs* 51, *Life Studies: New Poems and an Autobiographical Fragment* 59, *Imitations* 61, *The Old Glory* (play) 64, *For the Union Dead* 64, *Benito Cereno* (play) 67, *Near the Ocean* 67.
15 West 67th Street, New York City, N.Y., U.S.A.

Lowenstein, Leon; American business executive; b. 14 June 1883; ed. Coll. of City of New York.
With M. Lowenstein & Sons Inc., New York City 99-, Treas. 18-36, Pres. 36-47, Chair. of Board 47-59, Exec. Chair. 59-; Chair. subsidiary companies.
M. Lowenstein & Sons Inc., 1430 Broadway, New York, City, N.Y., U.S.A.

Löwenthal-Chlumecky, Max, LL.D.; Austrian diplo-matist; b. 08; ed. Vienna Univ.
Entered foreign service, served Prague 32-34, Paris 35, Federal Chancellery, Ministry of Foreign Affairs 35-38; with Continentale Motorschiffahrts A.G. 41-45; re-entered Federal Chancellery, Ministry of Foreign Affairs 45-52, Head Dept. of Political Economy 47; Ambassador to U.S.A. 52-54, to Argentina 54-55, to Italy 55-, concurrently Minister to Tunisia 59-67, and Libya 61-.
Austrian Embassy, Via Pergolesi 3, Rome, Italy.
Telephone: 86-82-41.

Lower, Arthur R. M., M.A., PH.D., LL.D., D.LITT., F.R.S.C.; Canadian university professor; b. 89; ed. Barrie Collegiate Inst., Barrie, Ontario, Toronto and Harvard Univs.
Head, Dept. of History, United Coll., Univ. of Manitoba 29; Douglas Prof. of Canadian History, Queen's Univ. 47-59, Prof. Emer. 59-; Visiting Prof. Univ. of Wisconsin 55-56, Univ. of Glasgow 67; Tyrrell Medal of the Royal Soc. of Canada, two Gov.-Gen.'s Medals; Senior Fellowship Canada Council 59-60; Pres. Royal Soc. of Canada 61-62; Hon. LL.D., Hon. D.Litt., Hon. D.C.L.
Publs. *Documents in Canadian Economic History* (with others) 33, *Settlement and the Forest Frontier in Eastern Canada* 36, *The North American Assault on the Canadian Forest* 38, *Canada and the Far East* 40, *Colony to Nation: a History of Canada* 46, *Canada, Nation and Neighbour* 52, *Unconventional Voyages* 53, *This Most*

Famous Stream: Anglo-Saxon Liberty 54, *Canadians in the Making* 58, *My First Seventy Five Years* 67.
Horizon House, Collins Bay, Ontario, Canada.
Telephone: 389-2546.

Lowry, Bates, PH.B., M.A., PH.D.; American art gallery director; b. 21 June 1923; ed. Univ. of Chicago. Assistant Prof. Univ. of Calif. 54-57; Asst. Prof. New York Univ., Inst. of Fine Arts 57-59; Chair. Art Dept. Pomona Coll. 59-63, Prof. Brown Univ. 63-68, Chair. Dept. of Art 63-68; Dir. Museum of Modern Art, New York, 68-; mem. Board of Dirs. Soc. of Architecural Historians 60-63, 64-67, College Art Asscn. 63-66; Editor-in-Chief, *Art Bulletin* 65-68; Editor College Art Asscn. Monographs Series 59-62, 65-68; Chair. Nat. Exec. Cttee., Cttee. to Rescue Italian Art (CRIA).; Governors award for Fine Arts, Rhode Island 67.
Publs. *The Visual Experience* 61, *Renaissance Architecture* 62.
The Museum of Modern Art, 11 West 53rd Street, New York, N.Y., U.S.A.

Lowry, H(omer) H(iram), M.A., PH.D.; American physical chemist; b. 6 Oct. 1898; ed. Ohio Wesleyan Univ., and Princeton Univ.
With Western Electric Co. 20-25, Bell Telephone Laboratories Inc. 25-30; Dir. of Coal Research Laboratory, Carnegie Inst. of Technology 30-53; Consultant 53-60; Asst. Research Dir. Pittsburgh Coal Research Center, U.S. Bureau of Mines 60-64; Staff Research Co-ordinator, Coal Research, U.S. Bureau of Mines 64-67; mem. American Chemical Soc. (Pittsburgh Award 52), American Gas Asscn., American Inst. of Mining and Metallurgical Engineers, Eastern States Blast Furnace and Coke Oven Asscn., Engineers' Society of Western Pa.; Fellow, American Asscn. for Advancement of Science, Inst. of Fuel (London); hon. mem. American Coke and Coal Chemicals Inst.; Hon. Pres. Fuel, Power and Transport, XIth Int. Congress Pure and Applied Chemistry, London 47; Fellow, Royal Society of Arts; mem. Geochemical Soc., New York Acad. of Sciences; Percy Nicholls Award (A.I.M.M.E.) 59.
321 Marguerite Ave., Wilmerding, Pa. 15148, U.S.A.
Telephone: 412-824-1530.

Lowry, Laurence Stephen, M.A., LL.D., R.A.; British painter; b. 1 Nov. 1887; ed. Manchester School of Art. Early paintings are portrait and landscape, later (after 18) are of industrial scenes; showed at the Lefevre Gallery, London 39, 42, 45, 48, 51, 53, 56, 58, 61 and 64; Retrospective Exhbn., Manchester City Art Gallery 59, rep. at Dunn Int. Exhbn., London 63, Retrospective Exhbn. Tate Gallery 66; B.B.C. Television Film 57.
Works consist of many paintings, including *The Pond* (Tate Gallery) 51, *The Cripples* (Lefevre Gallery) 51, *Industrial Street Scene* (in Canada) 57.
The Elms, Stalybridge Road, Mottram-in-Longdendale, Cheshire, England.

Lowson, Sir Denys Colquhoun Flowerdew, Bart., M.A.; British executive; b. 22 Jan. 1906; ed. Winchester and Christ Church, Oxford.
Called to the Bar (Inner Temple): Hon. Treas. Princess Louise Hospital 38-48; Alderman, City of London 42, Sheriff 39-40; one of H.M. Lieutenants 42; L.C.C. mem. for Cities of London and Westminster 49-52; Lord Mayor of London 50-51; Chair. and Man. Dir. Australian Estates Co. Ltd., British Isles & Gen. Investment Trust, New South Wales Pastoral Co., New Zealand & River Plate Land Mortgage Co., Pacific Atlantic Canadian Investment Co. Ltd., Algoma Central Railway; Dir. Bank of Nova Scotia, British American Insurance Co. Ltd., Canada Perm. Trust Co., Crown Life Insurance Co., Costa Rica Railway Co. Ltd., Gen. Accident Fire & Life Assurance Corpn. Ltd. (London Board), Trust & Agency Co. of Australasia Ltd., etc.; Gov. Univ. Coll. Dundee, Shakespeare Theatre, St. Bartholomew's Hospital; Church Commr. for England 48-62;

High Steward of Stratford-on-Avon 52; Gov. The Hon. The Irish Soc. 58-61; Pres. British Philatelic Asscn. 58-61; Pres. Chartered Inst. of Secretaries 62-63; original mem. Victoria (Australia) Promotion Cttee. 56; Vice-Pres. Royal Overseas League 60; Hon. Freeman of London (Ontario), Nanaimo (Vancouver Island), Granby (Quebec), Halifax (Nova Scotia) and Lewes (Sussex); decorations include Orders of Dannebrog (Denmark), St. Olav (Norway), Orange Nassau (Netherlands) and Finnish Lion, Order of Mercy, Knight of Justice St. John of Jerusalem.
Home: Brantridge Park, Balcombe, Sussex, England; Office: 56 Gresham Street, London, E.C.2, England.

Loyd, Sir Francis Alfred, K.C.M.G., O.B.E.; British overseas civil servant; b. 5 Sept. 1916; ed. Eton Coll., and Trinity Coll., Oxford.
Cadet, Provincial Admin., Kenya 39; Military Service 40-42; Private Sec. to Gov. of Kenya 42-45; Consul, Mega, Ethiopia 45; Dist. Commr., Kenya 47-55; Commonwealth Fund Fellowship to U.S.A. 53-54; Provincial Commr., Kenya 56-62, Perm. Sec., Governor's Office and Sec. to Cabinet 62-63; Commr. for Swaziland 64-.
Government House, Mbabane, Swaziland.

Loyen, André, D. ès L.; French university professor; b. 21 Nov. 1901; ed. Univ. of Rennes, and Ecole des Hautes Etudes, Paris.
Prof. Orléans Lycée 25-37, Sceaux Lycée 37-38, Lecturer Faculty of Letters, Rennes 38-43, Prof. 43-47, Dean 45-47; Rector, Univ. of Poitiers 47-61; Dir. Centre Nat. des Oeuvres Univ. Paris 61-63; Rector Univ. of Toulouse 63-67; Prof. Univ. of Paris 67; Officier Légion d'Honneur; Docteur (h.c.) Univ. Laval, Quebec; Prix Bordin 44; Commdr. de l'Ordre des Palmes Académiques 56, etc.
Publs. *Les Débuts du Royaume Wisigoth de Toulouse* 34, *La Bataille d'Orléans de 463* 35, *Recherches Historiques sur les Panégyriques de Sidoine Apollinaire* 42, *Sidoine Apollinaire et l'esprit précieux en Gaule aux derniers jours de l'Empire* 43 (Prix Bordin), *A la Recherche du Vicus Helena* 44, *Equilibre à établir entre la spécialisation et la culture générale* 55, *Sidoine Apollinaire et les derniers éclats de la culture antique dans les territoires occupés par les Goths* 56, *Sidoine Apollinaire Poêmes* (editor and transl.) 60, *Bourg-Gironde et les Villas d'Ausone* 60, *Résistants et collaborateurs en Gaule à l'époque des Grandes Invasions* 63.
19 Place St. Georges, 31 Toulouse, France.

Loyo, Gilberto; Mexican economist and politician; b. 01; ed. Nat. Univ. of Mexico and Univ. of Rome.
Has held various teaching posts since 23, including Prof. of Mexican and Gen. History, Political Economy, Rural Sociology and Gen. Economic History, Nat. School of Agriculture and Prof. of Demography, Nat. Polytechnic Inst.; founded Chair of Political Demography in Nat. School of Economics; Chief of Central Office of Census 40; organised and directed Nat. Censuses 50; fmr. statistical adviser to Mexican state govts. and to various foreign govts.; fmr. Dir. of Social Welfare, Fed. Labour Dept., Chief of Research, Secretariats of Economy and Finance and Dir.-Gen. of Credit and Statistics in these Secretariats; Minister of Economy 53-58; Dir. Consejo Técnico de los Censos Nacionales; mem. Mexican dels. to Inter-American and int. confs., including UN Gen. Assembly, Paris 48, Int. Statistical Congress, Berne 49, Int. Congress of Sociology, Rome 50, etc.; fmr. Vice-Pres. and Pres. Mexican Society of Geography and Statistics; founder Mexican Cttee. for Study of Population Problems; mem. Statistical Comm. of UN.
Publs. *La Concentración Agraria en el Mundo* 33, *La Política Demográfica de México* 35, *La Concentración Agraria en 28 países* 41, *La Presión Demográfica* 49, *Sobre Enseñanza de la Historia* 50, *La Población de*

México, Estado Actual y Tendencias 1960-1980 60, *Población y Desarrollo Económico* 63, etc.
Gen. León 80, Tacubaya, Mexico D.F. 18, Mexico.
Telephone: 15-31-61.

Lu Cheng-Tsao; Chinese politician.
Former Vice-Minister of Railways; Minister of Railways 65-; mem. Delegation to 10th Ministerial Conf. of Railway Co-operation Org. of Socialist Countries 66.
Ministry of Railways, Peking, People's Republic of China.

Lu Ting-yi; Chinese politician.
Member Central Cttee. of Chinese Communist Party, mem. Secretariat of Politburo 62-, Head, Propaganda Dept., Chinese Communist Party until 66; Vice-Pres. State Council 59-66; Minister of Culture 65-66.
Peking, People's Republic of China.

Lubennikov, Leonid Ignatievich; Soviet politician; b. 10; ed. All-Union Agricultural and Pedagogical Inst. Moscow.
Member C.P.S.U. 39-; Political Officer, Soviet Army 39-46; First Sec. Bobruisk District Cttee., Communist Party of Byelorussia 52-53, Minsk District Cttee. 53-55; Apparatus of Central Cttee. of C.P.S.U. 55, 58-60; First Sec. Central Cttee. of Communist Party of Karelo-Finnish Republic 55-56; First Sec. Karelia District Cttee., C.P.S.U. 56-58; First Sec. Kemerovo District Cttee. of C.P.S.U. 60-64; Deputy Chair. R.S.F.S.R. People's Control Cttee. 65-; mem. Central Cttee. of C.P.S.U. 56-66.
R.S.F.S.R. People's Control Committee, 8 Sadovaya-Chermo-Gryazeskaya ulitsa, Moscow, U.S.S.R.

Lubin, Isador, A.B., PH.D., LL.D.; American economist; b. 9 June 1896; ed. Clark Coll., Univs. of Michigan and Missouri, and Brookings Institution.
Statistician U.S. Food Admin. 18; Expert U.S. War Industries Board 18-19; Asst. Prof. of Economics, Univ. of Michigan 20-22; mem. staff Brookings Inst. 22-33; mem. teaching staff Brookings Graduate School 24-30; Adviser to Education and Labour Cttee., U.S. Senate 28-29; Chair. Labour Advisory Board, Public Works Admin. 33-36; mem. U.S. Central Statistical Board 33-37; Commr. U.S. Bureau of Labour Statistics 33-45; Statistical Asst. to Pres. Roosevelt 41-45; U.S. Assoc. rep. Allied Comm. on Reparations, Moscow 45; U.S. Rep. UN Econ. and Employment Comm. 46-50; U.S. Rep. U.N. Comm. on Reconstruction of Devastated Areas 46; U.S. Rep. U.N. Economic and Social Council 50-53; U.S. Rep. Advisory Cttee. to the U.N. Korean Reconstruction Agency 51-53; Industrial Commr. N.Y. State Dept. of Labor 55-59; Nat. Comm. on Money and Credit 58-61; Pres. American Statistical Asscn. 46; Fellow, Int. Statistical Inst. 48-; mem. Boards of Trustees Brandeis Univ., Weizmann Inst. of Science (Israel), New School for Social Research; Chair. Exec. Cttee. Franklin D. Roosevelt Foundation, Amalgamated Shirt Industry Pension Fund; Prof. Public Affairs. Rutgers Univ. 59-61; Chair. President's Comm. on Railroad Labor Conditions 62; Consultant Jewish Agency Inc. (New York) 60-; Econ. Consultant to Twentieth Century Fund 62-; Consultant, Office of Statistical Standards, U.S. Bureau of the Budget; del. UN Conf. on Application of Science and Technology for the Benefit of the Less Developed Areas 63; mem. Board of Dirs. Eastern Life Insurance Co. (New York).
Publs. *Government Control of Prices during the War* (in collaboration) 19, *Miners' Wages and the Cost of Coal* 24, *The British Coal Dilemma* (with Helen Everett) 27, *The British Attack on Unemployment* 34, *Our Stake in World Trade* 54, *U.S. Stake in the U.N.* 54.
1095 Park Avenue, New York 28, N.Y., U.S.A.
Telephone: LE5-4441.

Lubis, Mochtar; Indonesian journalist; b. 22.
Joined Indonesian Antara News Agency 45; Co-publisher daily *Indonesian Raya* 49-61, Editor 56-61,

66-; published and edited *The Times of Indonesia* 52; Nat. Literary Award 53; Pres. Magsaysay Award for the Press 58, Golden Pen of Freedom, Int. Fed. of Publishers 67.
Publs. *Pers and Wartawan, Tak Ada Esok, Si Djamal* (short stories), *Djalan Ada Udjung, Korean Notebook, Perkenalan Di Asia Tenggara, Melawat Ke Amerika, Stories from Europe, Indonesia Dimata Dunia, Stories from China.*
17 Djalan Bonang, Djakarta III/20, Indonesia.

Lübke, Heinrich; German politician; b. 14 Oct. 1894; ed. Univs. of Bonn, Berlin and Münster.
Director, Agricultural group, Deutsche Bauernschaft 26-33; mem. Prussian Landtag 31-33; deprived of all offices and imprisoned 33-35; housing estate planning 36-45; C.D.U. Mem. of North Rhine Westphalia Landtag 46-53, of Federal Parl., 53-59; Minister of Agriculture, Fisheries and Forestry, North Rhine Westphalia 47-52; Gen. Sec. Deutscher Raiffeisenverband 53; Minister of Food, Agriculture and Forestry, Fed. Govt. 53-59; Pres. German Federal Republic Sept. 59-; Dr. h.c. (Bonn 53, Munich 60).
Haager Weg 69, Bonn-Venusberg, German Federal Republic.

Lucas, Jim Griffing; American journalist; b. 22 June 1914; ed. Univ. of Missouri.
Began career with *Daily Phoenix*, Muskogee, Okla.; reporter *Tribune*, Tulsa, Okla.; Marine Corps combat corresp. 42-45; corresp. Scripps-Howard Newspaper Alliance 45-; Bronze Star Medal 45, Nat. Headliner's Award 45, George Polk Memorial Award, Ernie Pyle Award 53, U.S. 7th Division (Korea) Citation 53, Pulitzer Prize 53, Ernie Pyle Memorial Award 64.
Publs. *Battle for Tarawa* 46, *Dateline: Viet-Nam* 66.
Scripps-Howard Newspaper Alliance, 1013 13th Street, N.W., Washington 5, D.C., U.S.A.

Luce, Mrs. Clare (Clare Boothe); American writer and diplomatist.
Republican mem. 78th and 79th Congress from Fairfield County, Conn. 43-47; fmr. Man. Editor *Vanity Fair*; Ambassador to Italy 53-57; appointed Ambassador to Brazil 59; appointment approved by Senate; resigned before taking up post; Hammarskjöld Prize 66.
Publs. include: plays: *Abide with Me* 35, *The Women* 36, *Kiss the Boys Good-bye* 38, *Margin for Error* 39, *Child of the Morning* 52; and *Stuffed Shirts* 33, *Europe in the Spring* 40.
Sugar Hill, Limestone Road, Ridgefield, Conn., U.S.A.

Luce, Admiral Sir (John) David, G.C.B., D.S.O., O.B.E.; British naval officer; b. 23 Jan. 1906; ed. Royal Naval Coll., Osborne and Dartmouth.
Joined Submarines 27, commd. H.M. Submarine *H.44* 36, *Rainbow* 39-40, *Cachalot* 40-41; R.N. Air Station, Ford 46-48; Dep. Dir., Plans Div., Admiralty 48-51; commd. H.M.S. *Liverpool* 51-52, H.M.S. *Birmingham* 52-53; Dir. R.N. Staff Coll. 53-54; Naval Sec. to First Lord of Admiralty 55-56; Flag Officer (Flotillas), Home Fleet 56-58; Flag Officer, Scotland 58-59; C.-in-C. Far East Station 60-62; First C.-in-C. British Forces in Far East 62-63; U.K. Military Adviser to SEATO (South East Asia Treaty Org.) 61-63; First Sea Lord and Chief of Naval Staff Aug. 63-Feb. 66.
Monastery Garden, Edington, Westbury, Wiltshire, England.
Telephone: Bratton 273.

Luce, Henry III; American journalist; b. 28 April 1925; ed. Brooks School and Yale Univ.
Commissioner's Asst., Hoover Comm. on Org. Exec. Branch of Govt. 48-49; Reporter, Cleveland Press 49-51; Washington Corresp. Time Inc. 51-53, *Time* writer 53-55, Head New Building Dept. 56-60, Asst. to Publisher 60-61, Circulation Dir. *Fortune* and *Archi-*

tectural Forum 61-64, *House and Home* 62-64, Vice-Pres. 64, Chief London Bureau 66-68, Publisher *Fortune* 68-. *Fortune*, Time & Life Building, New York City, N.Y. 10020, U.S.A.

Luce, Sir William Henry Tucker, G.B.E., K.C.M.G.; British diplomatist; b. 25 Aug. 1907; ed. Clifton Coll., and Christ's Coll., Cambridge.
Joined Sudan Political Service 30; Private Sec. to Gov.-Gen. 41-47, Deputy Gov. Equatoria Province 50-51, Gov. of Blue Nile Province and Dir. Sudan Gezira Board 51-53, Adviser to Gov.-Gen. on Constitutional and External Affairs 53-56; Gov. and C.-in-C. Aden 56-Aug. 60; Political Resident Persian Gulf 61-66; Dir. Eastern Bank 66-, Tilbury Overseas Contractors and Gray Mackenzie 67-.
Brook House, Fovant, Near Salisbury, Wiltshire, England.

Lucebert; Netherlands painter and poet; b. 15 Sept. 1924; ed. School of Applied Arts, Amsterdam.
Member of Experimental COBRA group; has lived and worked in Berlin (with Bertolt Brecht) 54, Bulgaria 55, France 64 and Spain 65; First one-man exhbn., Galerie Espace, Haarlem 58, also Stedelÿk Museum, Amsterdam 59, and Marlborough New London Gallery 63; Amsterdam Poetry Prize 54, Premio Marzotto 62, Graphic Art Prize, Biennale Carrara 62, Del Naviglio Prize, Venice Biennale 64.
Publs. Seven books of poetry in Dutch including: *Triangel in de Jungle* 52, *Collected Poems* 65, Editor of own Poems in English trans.
Boendermakerhuis, Bergen/North, Holland, Netherlands.

Lucet, Charles Ernest; French diplomatist; b. 16 April 1910; ed. Ecole libre des sciences politiques.
Attaché, French Embassy, Washington 35, First Sec. 42; Commisariat for Foreign Affairs, Algeria 43; Sec. to Embassy, Ankara 43; Dep. Dir. at Ministry of Foreign Affairs; First Counsellor, Beirut 46; Counsellor, Cairo 47; Head of Cultural Relations, Ministry of Foreign Affairs 50; Minister-Counsellor, Security Council, UN 53; Minister-Counsellor, French Embassy, Washington 55; Dir. of Political Affairs, Ministry of Foreign Affairs 59-65; Ambassador to U.S.A. 65-; Officier, Légion d'Honneur.
French Embassy, 2221 Kalorama Road, Washington, D.C., U.S.A.; Home: 9 rue de Thann, Paris 17, France.

Lucey, Most Rev. Robert Emmet, S.T.D.; American ecclesiastic; b. 16 March 1891; ed. St. Patrick's Seminary, Menlo Park, Calif., and North American Coll., Rome.
Ordained to the priesthood 16; consecrated Bishop of Amarillo, Texas 34; Archbishop of San Antonio, Texas 41-; Papal Asst. to the Pontifical Throne 59-; Exec. Chair. Bishop's Cttee. for the Spanish Speaking.
9123 Lorene Lane, P.O. Box 13190, San Antonio, Texas 78213, U.S.A.

Luciolli, Mario, LL.D.; Italian diplomatist; b. 17 Oct. 1910; ed. Univ. degli Studi, Rome.
Entered Foreign Service 33; Vice-Consul Zurich 34-36, Paris 36-38; Foreign Ministry Rome 38-40; Consul, Melbourne 40; Sec. Berlin 40-42; Consul, San Sebastian 42-44; Foreign Ministry Rome 44-48; Counsellor, then Minister Counsellor, Washington 48-55; Dip. Adviser to Pres. of the Repub., Rome 55-56; Amb. to Chile 56-61, to Turkey 61-64, to German Fed. Repub. 64-.
Italian Embassy, Rolandstrasse 43, Bad Godesberg, German Federal Republic.
Telephone: 65815.

Lücke, Paul; German politician; b. 13 Nov. 1914; ed. Higher Technical School, Berlin.
Local govt. officer (head of Gummersbach Commercial Office) 45; Head of Engelskirchen local government 47-49; mem. of German Federal Parl., Chair. Fed. Parl.

Reconstruction and Housing Cttee. 49-57; Pres. German Local Council 54-; Minister of Housing, Town Planning and Regional Devt. 57-65, of Interior 65-March 68.
Odinweg 36, Bensberg, Cologne, German Federal Republic.

Luckhardt, Wassili; German architect; b. 22 July 1889; ed. Berlin, Munich and Dresden Technical High Schools.
Buildings designed 45-: Hochhaus am Kottbuser Tor (Berlin), Constructa Exhibition Pavilion (Hanover), Mehrfamilienhaus (Hansa quarter of Berlin), Bavarian Social Security Office (Munich), Bremen Parl. Building, Plant Physiology and Veterinary Medicine Insts., Berlin Free Univ., and private houses; mem. Berlin (West) Acad. of Arts; Dr. Ing. h.c. Berlin Technical Univ.; Berlin Culture Prize.
Publs. *Zur neuen Wohnform* 30, *Bauten und Entwürfen Wassili und Hans Luckhardt* 58, *Lichtarchitektur Wassili Luckhardt* 56.
Fabeck Strasse 48, 1 Berlin-33 Dahlem, Germany.

Ludin, Mohammed Kabir; Afghan diplomatist; b. 11; ed. Habibia Coll., Kabul, and Cornell Univ., New York.
Director of Irrigation, Ministry of Public Works 39-44; Under-Sec. of Public Works, Acting Minister of Public Works 44-46, Minister of Public Works 46-49; Chair. Econ. Development Comm. 49-50; Perm. Rep. to UN 52-53; Ambassador to U.S.A. 53-57; Leader of Afghan Del. to Gen. Assembly of UN 52-56; Ambassador to United Kingdom 57-64, to India 64.
c/o Ministry of Foreign Affairs, Kabul, Afghanistan.

Ludwig, Christa (wife of Walter Berry, *q.v.*); Austrian mezzo-soprano opera singer; b. 16 March 1935.
Former cabaret singer; debut as opera singer as Orlowsky at Städtische Bühnen, Frankfurt; joined Vienna State Opera 55; appearances at Festivals in Salzburg, Bayreuth, Lucerne, Holland, Prague, Saratoga, Stockholm; guest appearances in season in Vienna, New York, Chicago, Buenos Aires, Scala Milano, Berlin, Munich; numerous recitals and soloists in concerts often appearing with husband Walter Berry; recordings of Lieder and complete operas including *Norma* (with Maria Callas), *Lohengrin, Così fan tutte, Der Rosenkavalier, Carmen, Götterdämemrung, Die Walküre, Herzog Blaubarts Burg, Don Giovanni, Zauberflöte, Figaros Hochzeit, Capriccio, Fidelio;* winner of Bach-Concours, record award for Fricka in *Walküre;* awarded title of Kammersängerin by Austrian Govt.
Office: Gschwendt 21, Klosterneuburg, Niderösterreich, Austria; Home: Seefeldstrasse 11, Lucerne, Switzerland.

Luft, Friedrich; German journalist; b. 24 Aug. 1911; ed. Univs. of Berlin and Königsberg (Kaliningrad).
Drama and film critic *Die Neue Zeitung* 45-55, *Süddeutsche Zeitung* 55-62, *Die Welt* 55-; weekly commentator on theatre and film for Radio RIAS, Berlin 46-.
Publs. *Luftballons* 39, *Tagesblätter von Urbanus* 47, *Puella auf der Insel* 47, *Köpfe* (with Fritz Eschen) 57, *Altes-Neues Berlin* 59, *Kritische Jahre, Berliner Theater 1945-61* 61, *Luftsprünge* (essays) 61, *Stimme der Kritik* 65, *Fille, Mein Photo—Milien* (editor) 67.
Maienstrasse 4, Berlin 30, Germany.
Telephone: 0311-245873.

Lugeon, Jean, D.SC.; Swiss meteorologist; b. 4 Aug. 1898; ed. Lausanne Univ., and Zürich Fed. Polytechnic.
Engineer Paris 23-24; Meteorologist Nat. Meteorological Inst. Zürich 24-29; Vice-Dir. Polish Nat. Meteorological Inst. 29, Dir. 30-36; Lecturer Zürich Polytechnic 37, Prof. 48; Zürich University 40; fmr. Visiting Prof. Madrid, Warsaw, Chicago, Buenos Aires and Oporto Univs., and Lecturer Paris, Stockholm, London, Washington, Rio de Janeiro, Mexico City, Poona and Switzerland; leader expeditions to the Sahara, Bear Island (N. Spitzbergen) I.G.Y. and Mont Blanc;

Pres. scientific comms. and mem. Int. Meteorological Organisation, Int. Comm. of Aerial Navigation; Vice-Pres. Radio-Scientific Union and other int. scientific asscns.; Pres. Int. Radio-Atmospheric Comm.; Pres. European Asscn. of World Meteorological Organisation 51; hon. mem. Royal Hungarian Meteorological Society 36, Warsaw Geophysical Society 38; Deputy Dir. Swiss Meteorological Office 41-45, Dir. 45-63; Medal of Astronomical Society of Belgium; Dr. h.c. Polytechnic High School, Warsaw 57; Hon. mem. Arctik Klub Tromsoe 58. Publs. More than 180 works, including *Précipitations Atmosphériques, Écoulement et Hydroélectricité* 28, *La nouvelle méthode de sondage* 28-31, *L'Institut National Météorologique de Pologne* 32, *Tables Crépusculaires* 34, 57, *Expédition Année Polaire à l'Ile des Ours* 36, *Poste Aérologique Payerne, nouvelles méthodes de radiosondage* 42, *Echosondage* 53.
avenue Secrétan 35, Lausanne, Switzerland.

Lugli, Giuseppe; Italian archaeologist; b. 18 July 1890; ed. Univ. degli Studi, Rome.
Lecturer, Univ. of Rome 14-23, Prof. of Roman Topography 33-60, Prof. Emeritus 60-; Inspector then Dir. Antichità del Lazio 23-33; Dir. Scuola Nazionale di Archeologia 60-; Foreign Assoc. Inst. of France 51; Corresp. mem. Accad. Nazionale dei Lincei 38, Full mem. and Sec. 46-, and mem. numerous other academies in Europe; numerous awards and prizes including Rome Prize of Accad. d'Italia 41.
Publs. *Le antidie ville-del Suburbis di Roma* 23-29, *Il porto di Roma Imperiale* (with G. Filibeck) 35, *Saggi di esplorazione archaeologica per mezzo della fotografia aerea* 40, *Forma Italiae: Torracine, Circei, Antium* 26-40, *Roma Antica Il Centro Monumentale* 46, *Album di Arte Classica* 56, *La tecnica edilizia Romana* 57, *Mons Palatinus, Fonti e Documenti* 60, and numerous monographs.
Via Ferdinando di Savoia 3, Rome, Italy.
Telephone: Rome 350973.

Luisi, Héctor, LL.D.; Uruguayan lawyer and politician; b. 19 Sept. 1919; ed. Navy School, Univ. of Uruguay and Cambridge Univ.
Corporation lawyer; Asst. Sec.-Gen. and Counsellor to Interamerican Bar Asscn.; Uruguayan Rep. at Int. Convention on Civil Aviation, Montreal 54; mem. Cttee. which drafted Uruguayan Constitution 66; Senator 67-; Minister of Foreign Affairs 67-; Pres. Conf. of Foreign Ministers of Org. of American States (OAS) 67; Hon. Legal Adviser, British Embassy 48-66; Hon. O.B.E. (U.K.) 65; Grand Cross Order of Merit (Chile) 67, Order of Sun (Peru) 67, Order of Isabel la Católica (Spain) 67; Grand Cordon of Order of Brilliant Star (China) 68.
Br. España 2614, Montevideo, Uruguay.
Telephone: 71258.

Lukács, György, PH.D.; Hungarian philosopher and critic; b. 13 April 1885; ed. Univs. of Budapest and Berlin.
Freelance writer until 19; Commissioner for Education, Hungarian Soviet Republic 19; emigrated to Vienna 19-29; worked in Marx-Engels Inst. Moscow 30-31, Berlin 31-33; worked in Inst. of Philosophy of Soviet Acad. Moscow 33-45; returned Hungary 45; Prof. of Philosophy Budapest Univ. 45-; mem. World Peace Council 48-57; mem. of Hungarian Acad.; Corresp. mem. of German Acad. of Sciences, of German Acad. of Arts; hon. mem. Polish Acad. of Science.
Publs. *Esztétikai kultura, Die Seele und die Formen, Zur Soziologie des modernen Dramas, Die Theorie des Romans, Geschichte und Klassenbewusstsein, Lenin, Moses Hess und die Probleme der idealistischen Dialektik, Gottfried Keller, Goethe und seine Zeit, Der junge Hegel, Der russische Realismus in der Weltliteratur, Deutsche Realisten des 19-ten Jahrhunderts, Thomas Mann, Balzac und der französische Realismus, Skizze*

einer Geschichte der neuen deutschen Literatur, Beiträge zur Geschichte der Aesthetik, Wider den missverstandenen Realismus, Irástudók felelőssége, Nagy Orosz Realisták, Nietzsche és a fasimus, A történelmi regény Irodalom és Demokracia, A polgari filozofia valsaga, Uj magyar kulturaért, Existentialisme ou marxisme; in Russian: *Literary Theories of the XIXth Century and Marxism, On the History of Realism; The Meaning of Contemporary Realism* (in English, German, French, Italian, Spanish and Portuguese), *Prolegomena a un' Estetica Marxista, Contributi alla storia dell' estetica, The Destruction of Reason* (in German, Hungarian, Spanish, Japanese, Slovenian, French and Italian), *Die Eigenart des Aesthetischen, Schriften zur Literatursoziologie, Historical Novel* (in seven languages), *Schriften zur Ideologie und Politik, Gespräche mit Georg Lukács.*
Belgrád rakpart 2, Budapest V, Hungary.
Telephone: 185-366.

Lukács, Pál; Hungarian viola player; b. 1919; ed. Acad. of Music, Budapest.
Soloist, Nat. Opera House 47-; Prof. of Singing, Acad. of Music, Budapest 46-47, Prof. of Viola 47-; numerous concerts abroad; mem. jury Int. Geneva Competition 63; Geneva Prize 48; Kossuth Prize 65.
Academy of Music, Budapest; and Budapest VI, Jókai-u. 1, Hungary.
Telephone: 118-776.

Luke, 2nd Baron, of Pavenham; **Ian St. John Lawson Johnston;** British business executive; b. 7 June 1905; ed. Eton Coll., and Trinity Coll., Cambridge.
President, Incorporated Sales Managers Asscn. 53-56, Advertising Asscn. 55-58, London Chamber of Commerce 52-55; Chair. Bovril Ltd., Argentine Estates of Bovril Ltd., Electrolux Ltd., Virol Ltd.; Dir. Ashanti Goldfields Corpn. Ltd., Aktiebolaget Electrolux, Lloyds Bank Ltd., Nat. Provident Inst., Australian Mercantile, Financial, Land and Finance Co. Ltd., I.B.M. United Kingdom Ltd., etc.
Odell Castle, Bedfordshire, England.
Telephone: 02-308-240.

Luke, Sir Harry, K.C.M.G., D.LITT., HON. LL.D.; British colonial servant, traveller and author; b. Dec. 1884; ed. Eton and Trinity Coll., Oxford.
Private Sec. and Aide-de-Camp to Gov. of Sierra Leone 08-11 and to Gov. of Barbados 11; attached to Colonial Office 11; Private Sec. to High Commr. of Cyprus 11-12; Asst. Sec. to Govt. of Cyprus 12; served First World War 14-18; Commr. of Famagusta, Cyprus 18; Political Officer to Admiral of the Fleet, Sir J. de Robeck 19-20; British Chief Commr. Georgia, Armenia and Azerbaijan 20; Asst. Gov. Jerusalem 20-24; Colonial Sec. Sierra Leone 24-28; Chief Sec. Palestine 28-30; Lieut.-Gov. of Malta 30-38; Gov. and Commander-in-Chief Fiji and High Commr. Western Pacific 38-42; British Council Chief Rep. West Indies 43-46; Bailiff Grand Cross, Bailiff of Egle and Registrar, Order of St. John of Jerusalem; Grand Officer of Merit, Sovereign Order of Malta; Hon. Fellow, Trinity Coll. Oxford.
Publs. *The Fringe of the East* 13, *The City of Dancing Dervishes* 14, *Cyprus under the Turks* 21, *Anatolica* 24, *Mosul and its Minorities* 25, *Prophets, Priests and Patriarchs* 27, *In the Margin of History* 33, *An Eastern Chequerboard* 34, *More Moves on an Eastern Chequerboard* 35, *The Making of Modern Turkey* 36, *Britain and the South Seas* 45, *From a South Seas Diary* 46, *Caribbean Circuit* 50, *Cities and Men* (autobiography) Vols. I and II 53, *Queen Salote and her Kingdom* 54, *The Tenth Muse* (cookery) 54 (enlarged 2nd edn. 62), *The Old Turkey and The New* 55, *Cities and Men* Vol. III 56, *Cyprus* 57 (rev. 2nd edn. 65), *Malta* 49 (enlarged 2nd edn. 60), *The Islands of the South Pacific* 62.
8 Bedford Gardens House, Bedford Gardens, London, W.8, England.
Telephone: 01-727-7409.

Luke, Sir Stephen Elliot Vyvyan, K.C.M.G.; British civil servant; b. 26 Sept. 1905; ed. Wadham Coll., Oxford. Asst. Clerk, House of Commons 30; Colonial Office 30; Under-Sec., Cabinet Office 47-50; Asst. Under-Sec. of State, Colonial Office 50-53; Comptroller for Development and Welfare for the West Indies and British Co-Chair. Caribbean Comm. 53-58; Senior Crown Agent, Overseas Govts. and Admins. 59-.
Lyewood House, Ropley, Hants., England.

Lukic, Vojin; Yugoslav politician; b. 19; ed. Faculty of Law, Univ. of Belgrade.
Former State Sec. for Internal Affairs, Republic of Serbia; fmr. mem. Exec. Council, Serbia and Pres. Cttee. for Internal Affairs, Serbia; now Fed. Sec. for Internal Affairs; arrested Dec. 66; mem. Central Cttee. League of Communists for Serbia, Main Board, Socialist Alliance of Working People of Serbia.
Federal Secretariat for Internal Affairs, Belgrade, Yugoslavia.

Lukomsky, Pavel Evgenievich; Soviet internist and cardiologist; b. 1899; ed. Moscow Univ.
Intern, Asst., Lecturer, Prof. and Head of Dept., First Moscow Medical Inst. 23-44; Head of Dept., Chelyabinsk Medical Inst. 44-49; Head of Dept., Chief Internist of U.S.S.R. Ministry of Health 56-64; mem. C.P.S.U. 57-; Corresp. mem. U.S.S.R. Acad. of Medical Sciences 61-63, mem. 63-; Presidium mem. 66-; Chair. of Board of All-Union Soc. of Cardiologists; mem. of Board of All-Union Soc. of Internists; mem. Editorial Board *Soviet Medicine;* Order of Lenin 53, Red Banner of Labour 59.
Publ. Over 100 works on cardiovascular pathology, rheumatism, atherosclerosis, coronary insufficiency, and nonspecific lung diseases.
U.S.S.R. Academy of Medical Sciences, Solyanka 14, Moscow, U.S.S.R.

Lukyanenko, Pavel Panteleymonovich; Soviet agronomist; b. 1901; ed. Kuban Agricultural Inst.
At Kuban-Black Sea Agricultural Research Inst. 26-28; Head, Strain Testing Plot, All-Union Inst. of Applied Botany and New Crops, Leningrad 29-30; Assoc., Krasodar Agric. Research Inst. 30-56; Dir. Dept. of Selection and Seed Growing, Krasnodar Agricultural Inst. 56-; mem. All-Union Lenin Acad. of Agricultural Sciences 49-; mem. U.S.S.R. Acad. of Sciences 66-; Hero of Socialist Labour; Order of Lenin; State Prize; Order of Red Banner of Labour; Lenin Prize.
U.S.S.R. Academy of Sciences, 14 Lenin Prospekt, Moscow, U.S.S.R.

Lulka, Arkhip Mikhailovich; Soviet aircraft jet engine designer; b. 1908; ed. Kiev Polytechnical Inst.
Engineer researching into vapour turbines, Kharkov Turbo-Generator Works 31-33; at Kharkov Aviation Inst. 33-39, created first experimental turbo-compressor air-jet engine 37-39; worked at Leningrad Central Boiler-Turbine Inst. 39-41, other Insts. 41-45; Principal designs 45-: AL-3, AL-5 turbo-jet engines; Prof. Moscow Aviation Inst. 54-; Corresp. mem. U.S.S.R. Acad. of Sciences 60-; mem. C.P.S.U. 47-; State Prizes 48-51; Hero of Socialist Labour 57; Orders of Red Banner of Labour, etc.
U.S.S.R. Academy of Sciences, 14 Lenin Prospekt, Moscow, U.S.S.R.

Lumbard, Joseph Edward, Jr.; American judge; b. 18 Aug. 1901; ed. Harvard Univ., and Harvard Law School.
Assistant U.S. Attorney, Southern District, New York 25-27; Special Asst. Attorney-Gen. New York State 28-29; mem. Fogarty, Lumbard and Quel 29-31; Asst. U.S. Attorney, Criminal Div., Southern District, New York 31-33; mem. Donovan, Leisure, Newton, Lumbard and Irvine 34-53; U.S. Attorney, Southern District, New

York 53-55; U.S. Circuit Judge for Second Circuit 55-59, Chief Judge, U.S. Court of Appeals, Second Circuit 59-; mem. Board of Overseers, Harvard 59-65; Trustee William Nelson Cromwell Foundation; Chair. American Bar Asscn.'s Special Cttee. for the Formulation of Minimum Standards for the Administration of Criminal Justice 64-.
U.S. Court House, Foley Square, New York City, N.Y.; and 417 Park Avenue, New York, New York, U.S.A.

Lund, Svend Aage; Danish editor; b. 18 April 1900; ed. Copenhagen Polytechnic.
Secretary Asscn. of Danish Employers 27, Fed. of Danish Industries 28; Sub-Editor *Berlingske Tidende* 29, Editor-in-Chief *Berlingske Tidende* and *Berlingske Aftenavis* 34-; Chair. Fed. Danish newspapers 58.
Berlingske Tidende, 34 Pilestraede, Copenhagen K; Home: Carl Baggers alle 8, Charlottenlund, Denmark.

Lundberg, Arne S.; Swedish business executive; b. 14 May 1911.
Journalist 29-44; specialist in Ministry of Communications 44-47, Perm. Sec., Ministry of Communications 47-51; Sec.-Gen., Ministry for Foreign Affairs 51-56; with Luossavaara-Kiirunavaara Aktiebolag 56-, Man. Dir. 57-.
Luossavaara-Kiirunavaara Aktiebolag, Regeringsgatan 107, Pa Box 40144, Stockholm 40, Sweden.

Lundberg, Bo Klas Oskar, M.S.; Swedish aeronautical engineer; b. 1 Dec. 1907; ed. Hudiksvalls Läroverk and Royal Inst. of Technology, Stockholm.
Designer, Test Pilot, AB Svenska Järnvägsverkstäderna, Aeroplanavdelningen, Linköping 31-35, Sparmanns flygplanverkstad, Stockholm 35-37; Asst. Inspector of Civil Aviation, Luftfartsmyndigheten, Stockholm 37-38; Chief, Aeronautical Dept., Götaverken, Gothenburg 39; Chief Designer, J-22 Fighter, Royal Air Board 40-44; Chief, Structures Dept., Aeronautical Research Inst. of Sweden 44-47, Dir.-Gen. 47-; Fellow Royal Aeronautical Soc., Hon. Fellow American Inst. of Aeronautics and Astronautics; Thulin Medal, Silver 48, Gold 55, Flight Safety Foundation Air Safety Award 60, Sherman Fairchild Certificate of Merit 63, Monsanto Aviation Safety Award 63.
Publs. include *Aeronautical Research in Sweden* 55, *Notes on the Level of Safety and the Repair Rate with regard to Fatigue in Civil Aircraft Structures* 58, *A Statistical Method for Fail-Safe Design with Respect to Aircraft Fatigue* 60, *Should Supersonic Airliners be Permitted?* 61, *Gedanken zur Einführung des Ueberschallluftverkehrs* 63, *The Supersonic Threat* 63, *Gedanken zum Sicherheitsproblem und über die Dringlichkeit des Ueberschallfluges* 64, *Aviation Safety, Supersonic Transports, and their Effects on Society* 64, *Aviation Safety and the SST* 65, *Supersonic Aviation—a Testcase for Democracy* 65, *The Allotment of Probability Shares— APS—Method, a Guidance for Flight Safety Measures* 66, *The Menace of the Sonic Boom to Society and Civil Aviation* 66.
Baveragen 16, Bromma, Sweden.
Telephone: 08-26-18-47.

Lunde, Ivar, LL.B.; Norwegian politician and diplomatist; b. 18 June 1908; ed. Oslo Univ.
Secretary Norwegian Consulate, Gdynia, Poland 33-35; Attaché, France 35-36; with Legation in U.S.S.R. and concurrently Chargé d'Affaires in Iran 38, transferred to Iran 43; diplomatic posts Turkey, then Portugal 43-45; Chief, Foreign Ministry's First Political Dept. 46-47; Adviser, Perm. Mission of Norway to UN 47-50; Chargé d'Affaires, Greece and Israel 50-52; Minister to Thailand and Indonesia 52-56; Amb. to Turkey (concurrently to Iraq, Pakistan and Iran) 56-61, to Finland 61-65, to U.S.S.R. 66-.
Norwegian Embassy, Moscow, U.S.S.R.

Lundegårdh, Henrik Gunnar, PH.D.; Swedish plant physiologist; b. 23 Oct. 1888; ed. Stockholms Universitet.

Reader in Botany Stockholm Univ. 12-15, Lund 15-26; Prof. and Head of Botany Dept., Experimentalfältet, Stockholm 26-37; Prof. of Plant Physiology, Royal Agricultural Coll. of Sweden, Uppsala 37-55; Dir., Research Laboratory for Plant Physiology, Penningby 47-; Foreign Assoc. U.S. Acad. of Sciences; Linné Gold Medal, Royal Physiographic Soc., Lund 45, Reid Barnes Award, American Soc. of Plant Physiologists 53, Wahlberg Gold Medal, Royal Swedish Acad. of Science 64.

Publs. *Zelle und Zytoplasma* 20, *Der Krieslauf der Kohlensäure in der Natur* 24, *Klima und Boden* 25 (5th edn. 57), *Die Nährstoffaufnahme der Pflanze* 32, *Die quantitative Spektralanalyse der Elemente* 29-34, *Leaf Analysis* 51, *Plant Physiology* 66.

Västerliden 6820, Norrtälje, Sweden.

Telephone: 0176-66036.

Lunding, Franklin Jerome, LL.B.; American businessman; b. 26 Feb. 1906; ed. North Dakota and George Washington Univs.

With Research Dept. U.S. Chamber of Commerce 27-28; Attorney Fed. Trade Comm. 29-31; Gen. Counsel Jewel Tea Co. Inc. (Jewel Companies, Inc. since 66) 31, later Asst. to Pres. and Exec. Vice-Pres., Pres. 42-51, Chair. Exec. Cttee. 51-61, Chair of Board 54-65, Chair. Finance Cttee. 65-; Chair. Exec. Cttee. Lever Bros. Co. 50-57; Chair. Fed. Reserve Bank of Chicago 49-53, 65-; Dir. Thomas Industries Inc., Ill. Bell Telephone Co., United States Steel Corpn., S.A. Supermarches G.B. (Antwerp), S. A. Super Bazars (Belgium), Avimmo (Belgium), Pennsylvania Railroad Co., Pennsylvania Co.; Hon. LL.D. Univ. of North Dakota 49, Marquette Univ. 56.

Publ. *Sharing a Business* 51.

Office: 135 South La Salle Street, Chicago, Ill. 60603; Home: 1630 Sheridan Road, Apt. 9M, Wilmette, Ill. 60091, U.S.A.

Telephone: 312-726-5442.

Lundquist, Evert; Swedish artist; b. 17 July 1904; ed. Royal Acad. of Fine Arts, Stockholm.

Professor, Royal Swedish Acad. of Fine Arts 60-; Exhibitions in London, Paris, New York, Chicago, Pittsburgh, San Francisco, Milan, Venice, Brussels, São Paulo; paintings in Tate Gallery, London, Musée d'Art Moderne, Paris, Museum of Modern Art, New York, Nat. Gallery, Melbourne, Museo de l'Arte Moderna, São Paulo, Moderna Museet, Stockholm; mem. Swedish Royal Acad.; Prince Eugene Medal.

Kanton, Drottningholm, Sweden.

Lundsgaard, Einar, M.D., SC.D.; Danish physiologist; b. 12 Feb. 1899.

Asst. Copenhagen Univ. Inst. of Medical Physiology 28-34, Prof. 34-; foreign mem. Royal Physiographical Society, Lund (Sweden) and Harvey Society New York; Dr. h.c. (McGill and Paris).

Østerled 4, Copenhagen Ø, Denmark.

Lundvall, (Dan) Bjorn (Hjalmar); Swedish electrical engineer and business executive; b. 12 Aug. 1920; ed. Royal Inst. of Technology, Stockholm, and Management Development Inst., Lausanne, Switzerland.

Telefonaktiebolaget L. M. Ericsson 43-, Head of Dept. of Research and Devt. of Carrier Telephone Systems 54-57, Head of Marketing Activities of Long Distance Div. 57-60, Man. of Long Distance Div. 60-63, Deputy Man. Dir. 63-64, Man. Dir. 64-; Knight Order of Vasa; Knight Commdr. of Ordem de Rio Branco.

Office: Telefonaktiebolaget L. M. Ericsson, Stockholm 32; Home: Oskar Baeckströms väg 11, Hägersten, Sweden.

Telephone: Stockholm 19-00-00 (Office); 46-55-30 (Home).

Luneburg, William V., B.SC., M.B.A.; American automobile executive; b. 22 May 1912; ed. New York Univ. and Harvard Business School.

Director of Textile Econs., Bureau of New York 37; Financial Analyst, Ford Motor Co. 49, later Man., Cost Control and Budget Dept., then Man., Rouge Assembly Plant 56-59; Exec. Vice-Pres. Mather Spring Co., Toledo, Ohio 59-63; Vice-Pres. (Finance), American Motors Corpn. 63-65, Vice-Pres. (Automotive Manufacturing) 65-66, Group Vice-Pres. of Automotive Operations 66-67, Pres. and Chief Operating Officer, American Motors Corpn. Jan. 67-.

American Motors Corporation, 14250 Plymouth Road, Detroit, Michigan 48232, U.S.A.

Telephone: 493-2531.

Lunkov, Nikolay Mitrofanovich; Soviet diplomatist; b. 7 Jan. 1919; ed. Lomonosov Technical Inst., Moscow.

Diplomatic Service 43-; Asst. Minister of Foreign Affairs 51-52; Deputy Political Counsellor, Soviet Control Comm. in Germany 52-54; Counsellor, Stockholm 54-57; Deputy Head, Dept. of Int. Orgs., Ministry of Foreign Affairs 57, 3rd European Dept. 57-59; Head of Scandinavian Div., Ministry of Foreign Affairs 59-62; Amb. to Norway 62-68; Head of Dept. of Cultural Relations with Foreign Countries 68-.

U.S.S.R. Ministry of Foreign Affairs, 32-34 Smolenskaya-Sennaya ploshchad, Moscow, U.S.S.R.

Lunn, Sir Arnold, Kt.; British writer; b. 18 April 1888; ed. Harrow and Balliol Coll., Oxford.

Former Sec. Oxford Union and Editor *Isis*; fmr. Pres. Ski Club of Great Britain, Alpine Ski Club, Kandahar Ski Club, Oxford Univ. Mountaineering Club; mem. Cttee. Int. Ski Fed. 34-49; Chair. Int. Cttee. for Downhill Ski Racing 46-49; Invented modern Slalom race; Press Correspondent in Balkans, Chile, Peru 39-45; Lecturer abroad for British Council; Editor *British Ski Year Book* 20-; Dr. Phil h.c. (Zürich) 54; Hon. Citizen of Chamonix 52; Grand Cross of Isabel la Católica (Spain) 59.

Publs. *Guide to Montana* 07, *The Englishman in the Alps* 12, *The Harrovians* 13, *Ski-ing* 13, *The Alps* 14, *Was Switzerland Pro-German?* (*nom de plume* Sutton Croft) 18, *Loose Ends* 19, *Auction Piquet* (*nom de plume* Rubicon) 20, *Cross Country Ski-ing* 20, *The Alpine Ski Guides* (Bernese Oberland) 20, *Alpine Ski-ing* 21, *Roman Converts* 24, *Ski-ing for Beginners* 24, *The Mountains of Youth* 25, *A History of Ski-ing* 27, *Things that have Puzzled Me* 27, *Switzerland* 27, *John Wesley* 28, *The Flight from Reason* 30, *The Complete Ski-Runner* 30, *Family Name* 31, *Venice* 32, (with Rev. R. A. Knox) *Difficulties* 32, *The Italian Lakes and Lakeland Cities* 32, *Within the Precincts of the Prison* 32, (with C. E. M. Joad) *Is Christianity True?* 33, *Public School Religion* 33, *Now I See* 33, *A Saint in the Slave Trade* 34, (with Prof. J. B. S. Haldane, F.R.S.) *Science and the Supernatural* 35, *Within that City* 36, *Spanish Rehearsal* 37, *Communism and Socialism* 38, *Whither Europe?* 40, *Come What May: An Autobiography* 40, *And the Floods Came* 42, *Mountain Jubilee* 43, *The Good Gorilla* 43, *Switzerland and the English* 44, *The Third Day* 45, *Is the Catholic Church Anti-Social* (with C. G. Coulton) 46, *Switzerland in English Prose and Poetry* 47, *Mountains of Memory* 48, *The Revolt against Reason* 50, *The Cradle of Switzerland* 52, *The Story of Ski-ing* 52, *Zermatt and the Valais* 55, *Memory to Memory* 56, *Enigma* 57, *A Century of Mountaineering* 57, *The Bernese Oberland* 58, *And Ever New* 58, *The Swiss and their Mountains* 63, *The Englishman on Ski* 63, *The New Morality* (with Garth Lean) 64, *The Cult of Softness* (with Garth Lean) 65, *Matterhorn Centenary* 65, *Unkilled for So Long* (autobiog.) 68.

c/o The Ski Club of Great Britain, 118 Eaton Square, London, S.W.1, England.

Luns, Joseph Marie Antoine Hubert, G.C.M.G., LL.D.; Netherlands politician; b. 28 Aug. 1911; ed. Amsterdam and Brussels, Univs. of Leiden, Amsterdam, London and Berlin.

Ministry of Foreign Affairs 38-40; Attaché Dutch Legation Berne 40-41, Lisbon 41-42, Second Sec. 42-43; Second Sec. Netherlands Ministry for Foreign Affairs, London 43-44; Second, then First Sec. Dutch Embassy, London 44-49; Perm. Del. to UN 49-52; Co-Minister for Foreign Affairs 52-56; Minister of Foreign Affairs 56-; Pres. NATO Council 58-59; Hon. Fellow, London School of Economics; Officer of the Order of Orange Nassau, Charlemagne Prize 67, and forty-two foreign awards.

Publs. Several studies on Netherlands Navy in British and Portuguese magazines and articles about current political problems in various magazines, e.g., *International Affairs* and *Atlantic Review*.

Ministry for Foreign Affairs, Plein 23, The Hague, Netherlands.

Lunt, Alfred (husband of Lynn Fontanne, *q.v.*); American actor; b. 1893; ed. Carroll Coll., Waukesha, Wisconsin.

First appearance Castle Square Theater, Boston, Mass. 13; plays include *Romance and Arabella* 17, *Sweet Nell of Old Drury* 23, *The Guardsman* 25-29, *Caprice* 29, *Design for Living* 33, *The Taming of the Shrew* 35, *Idiot's Delight* 36, *Amphitryon 38* 37, *The Seagull* 38, *There Shall Be No Night* 39, *O Mistress Mine* 45, *I Know My Love* 50, *Quadrille* 52-55, *The Great Sebastians* 56, *The Visit* 58; Dir. Theatre Guild 35-; American Acad. of Arts and Letters Award 47; Hon. D.Litt. (Milwaukee Univ.), Hon. LL.D. (Dartmouth Univ. and Carroll Coll.).

Genesee Depot, Wis., U.S.A.

Luqman, Muhammad Ali Ibrahim; Arab (Southern Yemen) lawyer and journalist; b. 1898; ed. Aden and India.

Manager, Clayton Ghaleb and Co. Ltd. 18-19, English Pharmacy 21-22; Headmaster Govt. School Aden 24-28; A. Besse (British Somaliland Branches) 32-34; Pleader of the Supreme Court Aden Colony; Ed. *Fatat-ul-Jezirah Newspaper* 40-, and *The Aden Chronicle*.

Publs. *Springs of European Progress* 33, *The British Nation* 40, *Saeed* 40, *Ardh Adhhaher* 45, *Kamla Devi* 47, *The French Revolution* 48, *Lahej Constitution* 52, *Aden Needs Self-Government* 53, *The Story of the Yemen Revolution* (joint editor) 62.

Esplanade Road, Aden Camp, Aden, South Yemen.

Luraghi, Giuseppe; Italian business executive; b. 12 June 1905; ed. Univ. Commerciale Luigi Bocconi, Milan.

Started career in textile industry; with Pirelli Group 30-50, consecutively Central Dir., mem. Board of Dirs. and Chair. of various companies in the group; Asst. Gen. Man. I.R.I. (Istituto per la Ricostruzione Industriale) and mem. Board of S.I.P. (Hydro-electric), then Gen. Man. Finmeccanica 50-56; Chair. and Man. Dir. Lanerossi S.p.A. 56-60; Chair. Alfa Romeo S.p.A. 60-, Compagnia Generale Interscambi Cogis Milan; Vice-Chair. Ente Fiera Campionaria Milan; mem. Board of Dirs. S.I.P. (Telephones) Turin, Siemens Milan, Unione Italiana Constructori Autoveicoli UICA Turin, Società Nuova S. Giorgio Genova—*Il Fabbricone* Prato.

Alfa Romeo, Via Gattamelata 45, Milan; and Via Revere 2, Milan, Italy.

Lusk, Robert Emmett; American advertising executive; b. 25 Feb. 1902; ed. Yale Univ.

Advertising Man. R. H. Macy 28-33; Advertising Exec., Benton & Bowles 33, Dir. 46-, Exec. Vice-Pres., later Pres. 50-56, Chief Exec. Officer 56-65, Chair. of Board 61-.

Benton & Bowles, 666 Fifth Avenue, New York City, N.Y., U.S.A.

Telephone: Judson 2-6200.

Lussier, Rt. Rev. Irénée, B.A., L.TH., L.PH.; Canadian ecclesiastic; b. 18 April 1905; ed. Univ. of Montreal, Grand Seminary of Montreal, Institut Catholique de Paris, and Sorbonne.

Ordained 30; mem. Catholic School Board of Montreal 35; Principal, Pedagogical Inst. Emmélie Tavernier 38; Assoc. Prof., Univ. of Montreal 46, Rector 55-65; Domestic Prelate (H.H. Pope Pius XII) 53; Fellow of the Royal Soc. of Arts, Hon. Prof., Univ. of San Carlos, Guatemala; Hon. D.C.L. (Bishop 56), Hon. LL.D. (Alberta 57, McGill 58, Univ. of British Columbia 58, Toronto 58); Hon. Dr. in Pedagogical Sciences, Univ. of Ottawa 62.

c/o University of Montreal, Montreal 1, P.Q., Canada.

Lustenberger, Louis C.; American business executive; b. 9 Dec. 1904; ed. Carnegie-Mellon Univ.

Trainee and Salesman, White Motor Co., Cleveland 26-27, American Rolling Mill Co. 27-29; Asst. Standards Dept., W. T. Grant Co., New York City 29-32; Asst. Operating Dept., Montgomery Ward and Co., Chicago 32-35, Gen. Personnel Man. 38-39, Vice-Pres. and Personnel Dir. 39-40, Vice-Pres. and Dir. 40; Vice-Pres. and Asst. to Pres. W. T. Grant Co. 40-48, Dir. of Personnel 41-48, Exec. Vice-Pres. 48-59, Gen. Man. 57-59, Pres. 59-68, Chair. Exec. Cttee. 68-; official of other companies and business and educational orgs.

W. T. Grant Co., 1441 Broadway, New York, N.Y. 10018; Home: 103 Fox Meadow Road, Scarsdale, N.Y. 10583, U.S.A.

Telephone: 212-564-1000 (Office); 914-SC3-2863 (Home).

Lustig, Arnošt; Czechoslovak writer; b. 21 Dec. 1926; ed. Coll. of Political and Social Science, Prague.

In concentration camps at Terezín, Auschwitz and Buchenwald, Second World War; Editor *Mladý svět* (weekly) 58-59; screenplay writer 60-; mem. Central Cttee. Union of Czechoslovak Writers 63-, mem. Presidium 63-; Klement Gottwald State Prize 67.

Publs. *Démanty noci* (Diamonds of the Night—short stories, one of which was filmed 64) 58, *Modlitba za Kateřinu Horowitzovou* (A Prayer for Kateřina Horowitz—story, filmed for TV) 65, film script for *Transport z ráje* (Transport from Paradise) 65.

Czechoslovak Film, Jindřišská 34, Prague 1, Czechoslovakia.

Lutak, Ivan Kondratyevich; Soviet politician; b. 19; ed. Kazakh Agricultural Inst.

Member Communist Party of Soviet Union 40-; Soviet Army 42-45; party and political work in Ukraine 45-54; Chair. Exec. Cttee. Cherkassy District Council of Working People's Deputies 54-61; First Sec. Crimea District Cttee. of Ukraine C.P. 61-; mem. Central Cttee. of C.P.S.U. 61-; Deputy to Supreme Soviet of Ukrainian S.S.R. and U.S.S.R.

Crimea District Committee of Communist Party of Ukraine, Simferopol, Ukrainian S.S.R., U.S.S.R.

Lutfi, Ashraf Taufiq, B.A.; Kuwaiti civil servant; b. 1 Jan. 1919; ed. Scots Coll., Safad, Palestine.

Teacher in elementary and secondary schools 38-46, Welfare Officer 46-48; Sec. to State Sec. in Govt. Secr. 48-55, Asst. Sec. of State 55-61; Dir. of Office of Emir of Kuwait 61-64; Adviser on Oil Affairs, Ministry of Finance and Industry 64-65; Sec.-Gen. Org. of Petroleum Exporting Countries (OPEC) 65-Jan. 67; mem. Board Kuwait Nat. Petroleum Co. 61-; Chair. Board Kuwait Aviation Fuelling Co.

Publ. *Arab Oil—A Plan for the Future* 60.

National Petroleum Company, Kuwait.

Lutoslawski, Witold; Polish composer; b. 25 Jan. 1913; studied in Warsaw.
City of Warsaw Music Prize 48, Polish Music Festival Prize 51, State Prizes 52, 55, 64, Prime Minister's Prize for Children's Music 54, Polish Composer's Union's Prize 59, Ministry of Culture's Prize 60, Koussevitzky Int. Recording Award 64; Plaque of the Freie Akad. der Künste, Hamburg 66; Gottfried-von-Herder Prize, Vienna 67; Sonning Music Prize, Copenhagen 67; mem. Swedish Royal Acad. of Music 62-.
Works include *Symphonic Variations* 38, *Variations on a Theme of Paganini* (two pianos) 41, *Folk Melodies* (piano) 45, Symphony 47, Overture (string orch.) 49, *Little Suite* 51, *Silesian Triptych* (voice and orch.) 51, *Bucoliques* 52, *Dance Preludes* (clarinet) 53, *Concerto for Orchestra* 54, *Musique Funèbre* (string orch.) 58, Five Songs (female voice and instruments) 58; *Jeux Vénitiens* 61, *Trois Poèmes d'Henri Michaux* (choir and orch.) 63, *String Quartet* 64, *Paroles Tissées* (tenor and chamber orchestra) 65; *Second Symphony* 67; chamber, piano, vocal and children's music; compositions for theatre, films and radio.
Zwyciezcow 39, Warsaw 33, Poland.
Telephone: 17-79-88.

Luttig, Hendrik Gerhardus, M.A., D.LITT. ET PHIL.; South African diplomatist; b. 26 Oct. 1907; ed. Wepener High School, Grey Univ. Coll., Bloemfontein (now Univ. of Orange Free State) and Univ. of Leiden, Netherlands.
Member staff Africana Museum, Johannesburg 33-34; Principal of a Correspondence Coll. 34-49; mem. Parl. for Mayfair 49-65; Amb. to Austria 65-67, to U.K. 67-.
South African Embassy, Trafalgar Square, London, W.C.2, England.
Telephone: 01-930-4488.

Lutyens, Elisabeth (daughter of architect, late Sir Edwin Lutyens); British composer; b. 9 July 1906; ed. Ecole normale de musique, Paris, and Royal Coll. of Music, London.
First film score 44, radio score 47; exclusive contract with Mills Music Ltd., publishers 59-63.
Major works: *O Saisons, O Châteaux* (cantata for soprano and strings) 46, *The Pit* (dramatic scene) 47, *String Quartet No. 6* 52, *Motet* (Wittgenstein) 53, *Music for Orchestra I* 54, *Valediction* (for clarinet and piano) 56, *Infidelio* (for soprano and tenor soli and seven instruments) 56, *De Amore* (cantata) 57, *Wind Quintet* 60, *Symphonies* (for piano solo, harp and percussion) 61, *Quincunx* (for large orchestra) 60, *Catena* (for soprano and tenor soli and 22 instruments) 62, *Music for Orchestra II* 62, *String Quartet* 63, *Music for Orchestra III* 64, *String Trio No. 2* 64, *Scena* (for violin, viola and percussion) 64, *Hymn of Man* (for men's chorus) 65, *The Valley of Hatsu-se* (for soprano and four instruments) 65, *In the Temple of a Bird's Wing* (song cycle) 65, *Akahotik Rose* (for soprano and instrumental ensemble) 66, *And Suddenly it's Evening* (for Tenor and instrumental ensemble) 66; about 60 film scores and 50 radio scores.
76A Belsize Park Gardens, London, N.W.3, England.
Telephone: 01-722-8505.

Luukka, Eemil Vihtori; Finnish farmer and politician; b. 1 Dec. 1892.
Member of Parl. 36-; Minister of Agriculture and Dep. Minister of Interior 44-46; Minister of Agriculture 50-51, 51-53; Minister of Interior 60-62; Acting Prime Minister July 61; Agrarian Party.
Lapinlahdenkatu 23 B 23, Helsinki, Finland.

Luvsanchultem, Nyamin; Mongolian diplomatist.
Former Sec. of Presidium of Great People's Hural; Ambassador to U.S.S.R. 64-.
Embassy of the Mongolian People's Republic, Ul. Pisemskogo 11, Moscow, U.S.S.R.

Luxembourg, Grand Duke of (*see* Jean).

Luyt, Sir Richard Edmonds, G.C.M.G., K.C.V.O., D.C.M.; b. 8 Nov. 1915; ed. Diocesan Coll., Rondebosch, Univ. of Capetown, and Trinity Coll., Oxford.
Colonial Service, N. Rhodesia 40; War Service 40-45; Colonial Service, N. Rhodesia 46-54; Labour Commr., Kenya 54-57; Perm. Sec. Kenya Govt. 57-61, Sec. to Cabinet 61-62; Chief Sec. Govt. of N. Rhodesia 62-64; Gov. and Commdr.-in-Chief, British Guiana 64-66; Gov.-Gen. of Guyana May-Oct. 66; Principal and Vice-Chancellor Univ. of Capetown 68-.
University of Capetown, Rondebosch, Cape, South Africa.

Luyten, Norbert Alfons, PH.D.; Belgian university professor; b. 8 Aug. 1909; ed. Catholic Univ., Louvain.
Professor of Philosophy, Ghent 39-45; Prof. of Philosophical Psychology, Univ. of Fribourg 45-, Dean of Philosophical Faculty 48-49, 61-63; Rector 56-58; Pres. Philosophical Soc., Fribourg; Pres. Swiss Philosophical Soc.; Assoc. mem. Société Philosophique de Louvain and other learned bodies; Chief editor Naturwissenschaft und Theologie.
Publs. *La condition corporelle de l'homme* 57, *Unsterblichkeit* 57, *Universität und Weltanschauung* 58, *Teilhard de Chardin* 64, *Recherche et culture* 65, *Wetenschap en Geloof* 65.
Albertinum, CH-1700 Fribourg, Switzerland.
Telephone: 037-2-65-10.

Luz, Kadish; Israeli politician; b. 10 Jan. 1895; ed. in Russia.
Mem. Central Supervising Cttee., Gen. Fed. of Jewish Labour in Palestine 35-40, Labour Council, Tel-Aviv 41-42, Secretariat, Hever Haqvoutzot (Union of Agricultural Co-operative Settlements) 49-51; mem. Knesset 51-; Minister of Agriculture 55-59; mem. Central Cttee. Labour Party, Gen. Council Fed. of Jewish Labour 56; Speaker of Knesset 59-.
Publs. *Haqvoutza Ve Hanoar* (The Co-operative Settlement and Social Changes), *Gormei Mesheq Baqvutza Vehatmurot* (The Growth of the Co-operative Settlement and Social Changes), *Gormei Mesheq Haqvoutza* (Household Factors in the Co-operative Settlement), *Darko shel Hever Haqvoutzot, Avnei Derech.*
Deganie B, Jordan Valley, Israel.

Lwoff, André Michel; French scientist; b. 8 May 1902; ed. Lycée Voltaire, Univ. de Paris à la Sorbonne.
Joined Institut Pasteur 25, Asst. 25-29, Head of Laboratory 29-38, Head Dept. of Microbial Physiology 38-; mem. Board of Dirs. 66-; Prof. Microbiology, Univ. de Paris 59-; mem. numerous French and foreign scientific societies including Assoc. mem. New York Acad. of Science and Foreign mem. U.S.S.R. Acad. of Medicine; Nobel Prize for Medicine (jointly with F. Jacob and J. Monod) 65, Einstein Award 67; Médaille de la Résistance, Commdr. Légion d'Honneur.
Publs. include: *Biological Order* 62.
Service de Physiologie Microbienne, Institut Pasteur, 28 rue du Dr. Roux, Paris 15e, France.

Lyashko, Alexandr Pavlovich; Soviet politician; b. 1915; ed. Industrial Inst., Donetsk.
Soviet Army 41-45; mem. C.P.S.U. 42-; engineer and party worker, Donetsk Region 45-60; First Sec. Donetsk District Cttee., C.P. of Ukraine 60-63; Sec. Central Cttee. of C.P. of Ukraine 63-; mem. Politburo Central Cttee., C.P. of Ukraine; Chair. Bureau of Central Cttee. of Ukraine C.P. for Management, Industry and Construction 63-; mem. C.P.S.U. Central Cttee. 61-; Deputy to U.S.S.R. and Ukrainian S.S.R. Supreme Soviets.
Central Committee of the Communist Party of the Ukraine, Kiev, Ukraine S.S.R., U.S.S.R.

Lykova, Lidia Pavlovna; Soviet politician; b. 23 March 1913; ed. C.P.S.U. Acad. of Social Science and Pedagogical Inst.

Member C.P.S.U. 38-; party work 39-47; Perm. staff Central Cttee. C.P.S.U. 47-49; Sec., the Second Sec. Ivanov Regional Cttee. C.P.S.U. 49-55; Second Sec. Smolensk Regional Cttee. C.P.S.U. 58-61; Minister of Social Security, R.S.F.S.R. 61-67; Deputy Chair. Council of Ministers of R.S.F.S.R. 67-; candidate mem. Central Cttee., C.P.S.U. 52-.
Council of Ministers of R.S.F.S.R., 3, Delegatskaya ulitsa, Moscow, U.S.S.R.

Lyle, Sir Ian D., Kt., D.S.C.; British businessman; b. 07; ed. Shrewsbury School and St. John's Coll. Oxford.
Chairman Tate and Lyle Ltd. 54-64, Pres. 64-; Dir. Canada and Dominion Sugar Co. Ltd.; Pres. Aims of Industry.
Home: Barrington Court, Ilminster, Somerset; Office: Tate and Lyle Ltd., 21 Mincing Lane, London, E.C.3, England.
Telephone: 01-626-6525.

Lyle, John; British business executive; b. 26 April 1918; ed. Uppingham School, Clare Coll., Cambridge.
Tate and Lyle Ltd. 45-, Dir. 51-, Vice-Chair 62-64, Chair. 64-.
Tate and Lyle Ltd., 21 Mincing Lane, London, E.C.3, England.

Lymberaki, Margarita; Greek novelist, dramatist and painter; b. 19; ed. Athens Univ.
Publs. novels: *The Trees* 47, *The Straw Hats* 50, *Trois Etés* 50, *The Other Alexander* 52; plays: *Kandaules' Wife* 55, *The Danaids* 56, *L'Autre Alexandre* 57, *Le Saint Prince* 59, *La Lune a Faim* 61, *Sparagamos* 65, *Le Bain de Mer* 67; film scripts: *Magic City* 53, *Phaedra* 61.
2, Strat. Sindesmon, Athens, Greece; and 7 rue de L'Eperon, Paris, France.

Lympany, Moura, F.R.A.M.; British concert pianist; b. 18 Aug. 1916; ed. Belgium, Austria.
First performance, Harrogate 29; has played in U.S.A., Canada, South America, Australia, New Zealand, India and most European countries.
9 East 62nd Street, New York City 21, N.Y., U.S.A.

Lynch, John, B.L.; Irish lawyer and politician; b. 15 Aug. 1917; ed. North Monastery, Cork, Univ. Coll., Cork and Kings Inns, Dublin.
Member of Dáil Éireann (Parl.) 48-; Alderman, Cork Corpn. 50-57; Parl. Sec. to Govt. 51-54; Minister for Educ. 57-59; Minister for Industry and Commerce 59-65, for Finance 65-66; Vice-Pres. Council of Europe 58; Pres. Int. Labour Conf. 62; Taoiseach (Prime Minister) 66-.
21 Garville Avenue, Rathgar, Dublin 6, Ireland.

Lynch, Patrick, M.A.; Irish university professor and public administrator; b. 18; ed. Univ. Coll. Dublin.
Joined Irish Civil Service 41; served Finance Dept. 41-48; Asst. Sec. Dept. of Prime Minister 50-52; Chair. Foreign Trade Cttee. 49-52; retired 52; Lecturer, Nat. Univ. of Ireland 52-66; Chair. Aer Lingus 54-; Capital Investment Advisory Cttee.; mem. of Council Irish Asscn. of Civil Liberty; Vice-Pres. Inst. of Public Admin.; Dir. Provincial Bank of Ireland; Dir. OECD Govt. Surveys on Investment in Educ. and Research and Development 62-; mem. Governing Body, Univ. Coll. Dublin 64-; Fellow Commoner, Peterhouse, Cambridge; Assoc. Prof. of Political Econ. 66-; Chair. Medics Social Research Board 66; mem. Nat. Science Council 67.
Publs. *The Economics of Independence* 59, *Planning for Economic Development* (with C. F. Carter) 59, *Guinness's Brewery in the Irish Economy* (with J. Vaizey) 60, *The Role of Public Enterprises in Ireland* 61.
50 Leeson Park, Dublin, Ireland.

Lynden, Baron Carel Diederic Aernout van, LL.D.; Netherlands economist and politician; b. 23 Aug. 1915; ed. Law Faculty, Univ. of Leiden.
Head of Dept. in Monetary Agreements of Nederlandsche Bank, Amsterdam 45-53; mem. Managing Board of European Payments Union, Paris 50-51; Alternative Head of Dutch del. at Conf. on German External Debts in London 51-52; Asst. Manager Finance Dept. of High Authority of European Community for Coal and Steel, Luxembourg 53-56; Sec.-Gen. Benelux Econ. Union, Brussels 56-; Officer, Order of Orange Nassau (Netherlands); Commdr., Order of the Crown (Belgium), Grand Officer, Order of Merit (Luxembourg), Ufficiale Ordine al Merito della Repubblica Italiana.
39 rue de la Régence, Brussels, Belgium.

Lynen, Feodor, DR. PHIL.; German biochemist; b. 6 April 1911; ed. Luitpold Oberrealschule and Ludwig-Maximilians-Universität, Munich.
Dozent, Univ. of Munich 42-46, Extraordinary Prof. 47-53, Prof. of Biochemistry 53-; Dir. Max-Planck Inst. for Cell Chemistry, Munich 54-; Neuberg Medal, American Soc. of European Chemists and Pharmacists 54; Liebig Award, German Chemical Soc. 55; Carus Medal, Leopoldina Acad. 61; Otto Warburg Medal, Soc. for Physiological Chemistry 63; Nobel Prize for Medicine 64; Dr. med. h.c. (Univ. of Freiburg).
Publ. *Der Weg von der "Aktivierten Essigsäure" zu den Terpenen und den Fettsäuren.*
Office: Max-Planck-Institut für Zellchemie, Munich 2, Karlstrasse 23; Home: 813 Starberg, Schiesstättstrasse 10, German Federal Republic.

Lyng, John Daniel; Norwegian lawyer and politician; b. 22 Aug. 1905; ed. Oslo Univ. and legal studies in Germany and Denmark.
Legal practice 32-42; Judge 45-64; during Second World War, in the Norwegian Govt. service in Stockholm and London; mem. Trondheim Local Council 35-45, Skien Local Council 55-59; mem. Storting (Parl.) 45-53, 58-65; Leader Parl. Conservative Party 58-65; Prime Minister Aug. 63-Sept. 63; Gov. of Oslo and Akershus 64; Minister of Foreign Affairs 65-.
Publs. *The Norwegian Athletic Sports* 37, *The Epoch of Treason* 48, *The Growth of State Power* 58.
Markalleen 41b, Stabekk, Oslo, Norway.

Lyngstad, Bjarne; Norwegian politician; b. 9 Jan. 1901; ed. Norges Landbrukshøgskole, Ås and Friedrich-Schiller-Universität, Jena.
Teacher, Sund Senior Primary School 26-40; mem. Inderöy Municipal Council 30-33, 36-51 (Chair. 45, 46, 48-52), 56-; Chair. Liberal Party, Nord-Tröndelag 53-58, mem. Nat. Cttee. 58-, Deputy Chair. 60-; mem. Storting 61-; Minister of Municipal and Labour Affairs Aug.-Sept. 63, of Agriculture 65-.
Ministry of Agriculture, Oslo, Norway.

Lynne, Seybourn Harris; American judge; b. 25 July 1907; ed. Alabama Polytechnic Inst., and Univ. of Alabama.
Admitted to Alabama Bar 30; private legal practice, Decatur, Alabama 30-34; Judge, Morgan (Alabama) County Court 34-41; Judge, Eighth Judicial Circuit of Alabama 41-42; Staff, Judge Advocate, Central Pacific Base Command 42-46; Judge, U.S. District Court, Northern District, Alabama 46-, Chief Judge 53-.
Federal Building, Birmingham 1, Alabama, U.S.A.

Lyon, Cecil Burton; American diplomatist; b. 8 Nov. 1903; ed. St. Bernard's School, New York, St. George's School, Newport, Rhode Island, and Harvard Univ.
Investment Banker 27-30; Foreign Service Officer 30-; Havana, Hong Kong, Tokyo, Peking, Santiago (Chile), State Dept. 31-43; Second Sec. Cairo 44-46; Chief of Div., River Plate Affairs, State Dept. 46-48; First Sec. Warsaw 48-50; Nat. War Coll. 50; Dir. Berlin Element, Office of U.S. High Commr. for Germany 51-54; Dir.

Office of German Affairs, State Dept. 54; Deputy Asst.
Sec. of State for Inter-American Affairs 55; Ambassador
to Chile 56-58; Deputy Chief of Mission, Paris 58-64;
Ambassador to Ceylon 64-.
American Embassy, Colombo, Ceylon; Home: Hancock,
New Hampshire, U.S.A.
Telephone: 603-525-3375.

Lyons, Dame Enid Muriel, G.B.E., M.P.; Australian
politician; b. 9 July 1897; ed. State School, and Hobart
Teachers' Training Coll.
M.P. (first woman mem. of House of Reps.) for Darwin
43-51; International Vice-Pres. St. Joan's International,
Social and Political Alliance 47-; Vice-Pres. of Exec.
Council Dec. 49-51; newspaper columnist 51-54; mem.
Australian Broadcasting Comm. 51-62; mem. Liberal
Party; Hon. Fellow Australian Coll. of Nursing.
Publ. *So We Take Comfort* 67 (autobiog.).
Home Hill, Middle Road, Devonport, Tasmania,
Australia.
Telephone: Devonport 2-2250.

Lyons, Sir William, Kt.; British businessman; b. 01;
ed. Arnold School, Blackpool.
Founded, in partnership, Swallow Sidecar Co. 22, now
Jaguar Cars Ltd.; Pres. Soc. of Motor Manufacturers
and Traders Ltd. 50-51; Pres. Motor Industry Research
Asscn. 54; Pres. Motor Trades Benevolent Fund 54;
appointed Royal Designer for Industry by the Royal
Soc. of Arts 54; Pres. Fellowship of the Motor Industry
57-58; Chair. and Chief Exec. Jaguar Cars Ltd.,
Coventry, Daimler Co. Ltd.; Chair. Guy Motors
(Europe) Ltd.; Chair. Coventry Climax Engines Ltd.;
Dir. British Motor Holdings Ltd.
Jaguar Cars Ltd., Browns Lane, Coventry, Warwick-
shire; Wappenbury Hall, Wappenbury, nr. Leamington
Spa, Warwickshire, England.

Lysenko, Trofim Denisovich; Soviet scientist; b.
29 Sept. 1898; ed. Uman Agricultural School, and Kiev
Agricultural Inst.
Worked at Gandze Selection Station and later at All-
Union Selection and Genetics Inst., Odessa; Dir. Inst.
of Genetics, U.S.S.R. Acad. of Sciences 40-65; Head of
Laboratory, Inst. of Genetics, U.S.S.R. Acad. of Sciences
65-; Head of Laboratory, Experimental Research
Station "Gorki Leninskyi", U.S.S.R. Acad. of Sciences
66-; mem. Ukrainian Acad. of Sciences 34-; mem. Lenin
All-Union Acad. of Agricultural Sciences 35-, Pres.
38-56, 61; mem. U.S.S.R. Acad. of Sciences 39;
Metchnikov Gold Medal, Acad. of Sciences 50; State
Prizes, 41, 43, 49; seven Orders of Lenin; Red Banner

of Labour Order; Hero of Socialist Labour 45; Silver
Medal, World Peace Council 59.
Publs. *Agrobiology* 48, *Stage Development of Plants* 52,
Selected Works 58.
U.S.S.R. Academy of Sciences, Leninsky Prospekt 33,
Moscow, U.S.S.R.

Lysholm, Alf James; Swedish professor; b. 14 Dec.
1893; ed. Royal Inst. of Technology, Stockholm.
Member of staff of A.B. Ljungstöms Angturbin, Stockholm 17-44, Calculating engineer 17-19, Head of
turbine and calculating depts. 19-28, Chief Engineer
28-44; Consultant Engineer 44; Prof. Royal Inst. of
Technology 50-60, Emer. 60-; mem. Royal Inst.
Technical Research, Sweden, Inst. of Mechanical
Engineers, London, American Soc. of Mechanical
Engineers, and Soc. of Automobile Engineers, U.S.A.;
recipient of several prizes; over a hundred patented
inventions of steam turbines, compressors, etc.
Karlaplan 11, Stockholm, Sweden.

Lysö, Nils; Norwegian politician; b. 3 Sept. 1905.
Served in local government 34-40, 45-54; Sec.-Gen. of
Norwegian Fishermen's Organization 54-55; Minister
of Fisheries 55-Aug. 63; Gov. of Sor Tröndelag Dec.
63-; mem. Norwegian Labour party.
Elvegaten 17, Trondheim, Norway.

Lyttelton, Humphrey Richard Adeane; British bandleader and journalist; b. 23 May 1921; ed. Eton Coll.
Grenadier Guards 41-46; Camberwell Art School 47-48;
formed own band 48; cartoonist for London *Daily Mail*
49-53; freelance journalist and leader of Humphrey
Lytteltons' Band 53-; recorded Parlophone 50-60,
Columbia 60-; contributor *Melody Maker* 54-, *Reynolds
News* 55-62, *Sunday Citizen* 62-67; Compère B.B.C. jazz
programmes: *Jazz Scene, Jazz Club, Jazz 625* (T.V.);
frequent television appearances.
Publs. *I Play as I Please, Second Chorus.*
8 Great Chapel Street, London, W.1; and 235 Regent
Street, London, W.1, England.

Lyzhin, Nikolai Mikhailovich; Soviet politician; b.
1914; ed. Higher Party School.
Consumers' co-operatives 29-36; Soviet Army 36-37;
Young Communist League Official 39-41; mem. Partisan
Movement in Byelorussia 41-45; Student 46-50; Party
Official 51-61; First Sec. Karachayevo-Cherkessy
Regional Cttee., C.P.S.U. 61-; mem. C.P.S.U. 41-;
Deputy to U.S.S.R. Supreme Soviet.
Karachayevo-Cherkessy Regional Committee, Com-
munist Party of the Soviet Union, Cherkessk, U.S.S.R.

M

NOTE: All names beginning Mc and Mac are treated as if they began Mac.

Ma Ssu-tsung (Sitson Ma); Chinese composer; b. 10; ed. Conservatoire de Paris.
Founded Private Canton Conservatoire of Music 28; lectured at Academy of Fine Arts, Central Univ., Nanking; with Ma Kuo-lin founded South China Conservatoire of Music at Kowloon 38; Dir. Central Conservatoire of Music, Peking 49-67; granted political asylum in U.S.A. 67-; Vice-Chair. Union of Chinese musicians.
Publs. Instrumental and vocal music; arrangements of folk music.

Ma Wen-jui; Chinese administrator.
Formerly mem. North-West Bureau of Central Cttee. of C.C.P. and head of Organisation Dept.; mem. North-West Military and Admin. Council 50; Chair. Cttee. of People's Control 50; mem. North-West Admin. Council 53; Asst. Sec. North-West Bureau of Central Cttee. of C.C.P. 53; Minister of Labour 54-.
Ministry of Labour, Peking, China.

Maazel, Lorin; American conductor and musician; b. 6 March 1930; ed. under Vladimir Bakalienikoff and at Univ. of Pittsburgh.
Debut as conductor 38; Conductor, American Symphony Orchestras 39-64; violin recitalist; Asst. Conductor Pittsburgh Symphony Orchestra; European debut 53; festivals include Bayreuth, Salzburg, Edinburgh; tours include South America, Australia, U.S.S.R. and Japan; General-musikdirektor, Deutsche Oper Berlin, and Musical Dir. Radio Symphony Orchestra, Berlin 64-; Hon. D.Mus. (Pittsburgh Univ.) 65.
c/o Deutsche Oper Berlin, Berlin, Germany; and 730 Fifth Avenue, New York 19, N.Y.

Mabe, Manabu; Brazilian (b. Japanese) painter; b. 24.
Abstract painter; exhibitions in countries all over the world; Leiner Prize for Contemporary Arts 57, Braun Prize 59, Best Nat. Painter, São Paulo Bienal 59, Fiat Prize Venice Biennale 60, First Prize American Biennale, Cordoba 62.
Rua das Canjeranas 321, Jabaquara, São Paulo; and c/o Yutaka Sanematsu, Rua Quintino Bocaiuva 291 2°, São Paulo, Brazil.

McAdams, Edward Joseph, PH.B., LL.B., C.P.A.; American chemical, food and industrial products executive; b. 8 Aug. 1902; ed. Univ. of Chicago and Chicago Kent Coll. of Law.
Armour and Co. 23-, Asst. to Pres. 57, Treas. 58, Financial Vice-Pres. and Treas. 59-65, Sec. 59-62, Dir. 62-, Pres. 65-67; Dir. Fed. Sign and Signal Corpn., Blue Island, Illinois; Trustee, Saint Xavier Coll., Chicago.
Armour and Company, 401 N. Wabash Avenue, Chicago, Illinois 60611, U.S.A.

Macapagal, Diosdado; Philippine politician; b. 28 Sept. 1910; ed. Santo Tomás Univ.
Diplomatic Service 46-48, Second Sec., Washington 48; mem. House of Reps. 49-56; Vice-Pres. of the Philippines 57-61, Pres. 62-65; Chair. Liberal Party 57-61.
Malacañang, Manila, Republic of the Philippines.

Macarrón Jaime, Ricardo; Spanish painter; b. 9 April 1926; ed. Escuela Superior de Bellas Artes de San Fernando, Madrid and scholarship in Paris.
Professor of Drawing and Painting, Escuela Superior de Bellas Artes, Madrid; mem. Royal Soc. of Portrait Painters 62; numerous one-man exhbns. in Spain and abroad including two in London and one in New York; represented at Museo de Arte Contemporáneo, Madrid, Univ. of Oslo and Fundación Guell, Barcelona, portraits at the Royal Soc. of Portrait Painters; numerous awards.
Ambros 29, Colonia Iturbe, Madrid 2, Spain.

MacArthur II, Douglas; American foreign service officer; b. 5 July 1909; ed. Milton Acad. and Yale Univ.
United States Army 33-35; Foreign Service 35-; Vancouver 35-36; Foreign Service School 36; Naples 37, Paris 37-40, Lisbon 40, Vichy 40-42; interned by Nazis 42-44; Asst. Political Adviser SHAEF 44; Paris 44-48, Brussels 48-49; Dept. of State 49-51; Counsellor in Paris and Adviser on Int. Affairs to SHAPE 51-52; Counsellor of the Dept. of State 53-56; Ambassador to Japan 57-61, to Belgium 61-65; Asst. Sec. of State for Congressional Relations 65-67; Amb. to Austria 67-.
American Embassy, Boltzmanngasse 16, Vienna, Austria.

McAshan, S. M. Jr.; American advertising executive.
Vice-Pres., Anderson, Clayton and Co. until 59, Pres. 59-, Chair. 66-; Dir. Shell Oil Co.
Cotton Exchange Building, Houston, Texas, U.S.A.

McBride, Katharine Elizabeth, M.A., PH.D.; American college president and educator; b. 04; ed. Bryn Mawr Coll. and Columbia Univ.
Research in Psychology, Philadelphia 29-35 (with Dr. T. Weisenburg 29-34); Lecturer in Educ. Bryn Mawr Coll. 35-36; Asst. Prof. of Educ. and Psychology 36-38, Assoc. Prof. 38-40; Dean Radcliffe Coll. 40-42; Pres. Bryn Mawr Coll. 42-; mem. American Psychological Asscn., American Asscn. of Univ. Women, Cttee. on Relationships of Federal Govt. to Higher Education of American Council on Education, mem. Nat. Advisory Arthritic and Metabolic Diseases Council of the Nat. Insts. of Health, mem. Board Nat. Science Foundation, Educ. Board Pa. State; Dir. of the New York Life Insurance Company; mem.-at-large American Council of Learned Socs.; Trustee Carnegie Foundation for the Advancement of Teaching; Hon. L.H.D., L.L.D., Ed.D.
Publs. *Aphasia* (with Theodore Weisenburg) 35; *Adult Intelligence* (with T. Weisenburg and A. Roe) 36.
907 Wyndon Avenue, Bryn Mawr, Pa., U.S.A.

McBride, Sir Philip Albert Martin, K.C.M.G., P.C., M.P.; Australian politician; b. 18 June 1892; ed. Burra Public School and Prince Alfred Coll.
President Stockowners' Asscn. of S. Australia 30-31; mem. Federal House of Representatives 31-37, 46-; Senator 37-44; mem. War Cabinet 39-40; Asst. Minister for Commerce 39-40; Minister for Army 40, for Supply and Development and Munitions 40-41; Deputy Leader of Opposition 41-43; Minister of the Interior 49-51; Acting Minister for Defence March-Oct. 50; Minister for the Navy and for Air May-July 51; Minister for Defence Oct. 50-58; Liberal.
4 View Street, Burnside, South Australia.

MacBride, Séan, S.C.; Irish barrister and politician; b. 26 Jan. 1904; ed. St. Louis de Gonzague, Paris, Mount St. Benedict, and Nat. Univ. Dublin.
Imprisoned many times for Irish nationalistic activities; Journalist for many years before being called to Bar 37; called to Inner Bar 43; founded Republican Party (Clann na Poblachta) 46; elected to Irish Parl. (Dáil Éireann) 47, re-elected 48, 51, 54 and 57; Minister for External Affairs 48-51; Pres. Council of Ministers, Council of Europe 50; Vice-Pres. Council of O.E.E.C. 48-51; Exec. mem. Pan European Union 50; Chair.

Amnesty International; Irish Rep. to Council of Europe
Assembly, and Rapporteur of Econ. Comm. 54-57;
mem. Ghana Bar; Sec.-Gen. Int. Comm. of Jurists 63-;
Hon. mem. Institut des Sciences Administratives
(Brussels).
Publs. *Civil Liberty* 48, *Our People—Our Money* 51.
International Commission of Jurists, 2 Quai du Cheval-
Blanc, Geneva, Switzerland; Roebuck House, Clonskea,
Dublin, S.4, Ireland.

McCabe, Thomas Bayard, A.B., HON. LL.D.; American
industrialist and banker; b. 11 July 1893; ed. Swarth-
more Coll.
Scott Paper Co., Pennsylvania, Salesman 16-17, Asst.
Sales Man. 19-20, Sales Man. 20-22, Dir. 21-, Sec. and
Sales Man. 22-27, Vice-Pres. 27, Pres. 27-62, Chair. and
Chief Exec. 62-66, Chair. 66-; Dir. Fed. Reserve Bank of
Philadelphia 38-48, Chair. 39-48; mem. Business Ad-
visory Council, Dept. of Commerce 40-, Chair. 44-45;
Exec. Asst. to Commr., Advisory Comm. to Council of
Nat. Defense 40; Deputy Dir., Div. of Priorities, Office
of Production Management 41; Deputy Lend-Lease
Administrator 41-42; Army-Navy Liquidation Commr.
45; Special Asst. to Sec. of State and Foreign Liquida-
tion Commr. 45-46; Chair., Board of Governors of
Federal Reserve System, Washington, D.C. 48-51;
Chair. Board of Trustees Eisenhower Exchange Fellow-
ships; Chair. Board of Trustees of the Marketing
Science Inst.; Trustee Cttee. for Economic Development;
mem. U.S. Associates of the Int. Chamber of Commerce;
American Del. to Congress of Int. Chamber of Com-
merce, Montreux 47; awarded Medal of Merit 46.
Scott Paper Company, Philadelphia 13, Pa., U.S.A.
Telephone: 215-SA 4-2000.

McCain, James Allen, A.B., M.A., ED.D., D.SC.;
American university official; b. 8 Dec. 1907; ed.
Wofford Coll., Duke Univ. and Stanford Univ., Calif.
Asst. Prof. of English and Journalism Colorado State
Univ. 29-34; Asst. to Pres. Colo. State Univ. 34-39, Dean
of Student Personnel 39-41, Dean of Vocational Educa-
tion and Guidance, and Dir. of Summer Session 41-42;
on active duty as officer-in-charge of Enlisted Classifi-
cation Program, U.S. Navy, with rank of Lieut.-
Commdr. 42-45; Pres. Montana State Univ. 45-50;
Dir. Helena Branch Federal Reserve Bank of Minnea-
polis 48-50; Pres. Kansas State Univ. 50-; Dir. Kansas
State Chamber of Commerce 54-57; mem. U.S. Nat.
Comm. for UNESCO 56-58; Eisenhower Internat.
Exchange Fellow 57; Trustee Eisenhower Exchange
Fellowships 60; mem. Advisory Council to Peace Corps
61-, Advisory Cttee. to Export-Import Bank 61-,
Advisory Board to Office of Econ. Analysis; Mid-
America Governors' Transportation Cttee.; Dir. Acad.
for Educational Devt. Inc., Eisenhower Library Comm.,
Kansas Research Foundation, Manhattan Mutual Life
Insurance Co., Security Benefit Life Insurance Co.,
Dunlap and Assocs., Inc.; Hon. LL.D. (Wofford Coll.,
Colorado State Univ., Univ. of Montana); Hon. D.Sc.
Publs. *Vocational Guidance for Vocational Teachers* 42,
Vocational Education (with others) 42, *Education in
the Armed Services* (with others) 42, *Universities . . .
and Development Assistance Abroad* (with others) 67.
Kansas State University Campus, Manhattan, Kansas
66502, U.S.A.
Telephone: 913-532-6222.

McCall, Howard Weaver, Jr., B.A.; American banker;
b. 11 Aug. 1907; ed. the McCallie School, Chattanooga,
Tenn., Univ. of Virginia, and Graduate School of
Banking, Rutgers Univ.
Chemical Bank New York Trust Co. 28-, Asst. Sec.
37-41, Asst. Vice-Pres. 41-45, Vice-Pres. 45-55, Exec.
Vice-Pres. 55-60, First Vice-Pres. 60-61, Vice-Chair.
61-65, Pres. 65-, also Dir.; Dir. Chemical Int. Banking
Corpn., Chemical Int. Finance Ltd., Interchemical
Corpn., Liggett & Myers Tobacco Co. Inc., Lykes Bros.

Steamship Co. Inc.; mem. Boards of Trutees Mutual
Life Insurance Co. of New York.
Chemical Bank New York Trust Co., 20 Pine Street,
New York, N.Y. 10015; Home: 68 Dorchester Road,
Darien, Conn. 06820, U.S.A.

McCance, Sir Andrew, Kt., D.SC., LL.D., F.R.S., D.L.;
British industrialist; b. 30 March 1889; ed. Morrison's
Acad., Crieff, Allan Glen's School and Royal School of
Mines, London.
Asst. Armour Man. W. Beardmore and Co. 10-19;
Founder and Man. Dir. Clyde Alloy Steel Co. Ltd. 19-30;
mem. Scientific Advisory Council Dept. Scientific and
Industrial Research 41-47; fmr. Pres. Inst. Engineering
and Shipbuilders, Scotland, Iron and Steel Inst.
and Glasgow and West Scotland Iron and Steel Inst.,
Glasgow; fmr. Pres. British Iron and Steel Federation;
fmr. Chair. and Man. Dir. Colvilles Ltd., now Hon.
Pres.; Pres. Clyde Alloy Steel Co. Ltd.; Dir. Nat.
Commercial Bank of Scotland Ltd.
The Craigs, Carmunnock, Lanarkshire, Scotland.
Telephone: Glasgow Busby 1757.

McCance, Robert Alexander, C.B.E., M.A., M.D., PH.D.,
F.R.C.P., F.R.S.; British physician; b. 9 Dec. 1898; ed.
Mourne Grange, Co. Down, St. Bees School, Cumberland,
and Sidney Sussex Coll., Cambridge.
Royal Naval Air Service, including service with Grand
Fleet 17-19; undergraduate studies 19-22; Biochemical
research 22-25; qualified in medicine 27; Asst. Physician
in charge of Biochemical Dept., King's Coll. Hospital
34; Reader in Medicine, Cambridge Univ. 38; Prof. of
Experimental Medicine, Cambridge Univ. 45-; Fellow of
Sidney Sussex Coll. Cambridge; Dir. Dept. of Experi-
mental Medicine, Medical Research Council; Triennial
Gold Medal, West London Medico-Chirurgical Society
49; hon. mem. American Pediatric Soc., Asscn. of
American Physicians, Swiss Soc. for Research in
Nutrition; Conway Evans Prize 60, James Spence
Medal, British Paediatric Asscn. 61.
Sidney Sussex College, Cambridge, England.

McCann, Hugh James, B.SC.(ECON.); Irish diplomatist;
b. 8 Feb. 1916; ed. London School of Economics, Univ.
of London, Belvedere Coll., Dublin.
Admin. Officer, Dept. of Industry and Commerce,
Dublin 40-41; Private Sec. to Minister for Industry
and Commerce 41-43; Superintending Officer, Dept. of
Supplies 43-44; Commercial Sec. Office of the High
Commr. for Ireland, London 44-46; First Sec. Dept. of
External Affairs 46-48; Counsellor, Irish Embassy,
Washington, D.C. 48-54; Minister to Switzerland and
Austria 54-56; Asst. Sec. to the Dept. of External
Affairs 56-58; Ambassador to the United Kingdom 58-
63; Sec. Dept. of External Affairs, Dublin 63-.
Department of External Affairs, Iveagh House, 80 St.
Stephen's Green, Dublin; Frankfield, Mart Lane,
Foxrock, Co. Dublin, Ireland.
Telephone: 893682 (home); 52971 (office).

McCann, Most Rev. James, M.A., PH.D., D.D.; British
Protestant ecclesiastic; b. 31 Oct. 1897; ed. Royal
Belfast Academical Inst., Queen's Univ., Belfast and
Trinity Coll., Dublin.
Curate, Ballymena 20-22, Ballyclare 22-24, Cavan 24-
28, Oldcastle 28-30; Rector, Donaghpatrick 30-36, St.
Mary's, Drogheda 36-45; Canon, St. Patrick's Cathedral,
Dublin 44-45; Bishop of Meath 45-59; Archbishop of
Armagh and Primate of All Ireland 59-; Ecclesiastical
History Prize 17, Elrington Theological Prize 30; Hon.
LL.D. (Queen's Univ. Belfast) 66.
Publ. *Asceticism: an historical study* 44.
The Palace, Armagh, Northern Ireland.
Telephone: Armagh 2851.

McCann, Joseph Henry, B.S., M.S.; American business
executive and government official; b. 30 June 1915;
ed. Univ. of Michigan, Wayne State Univ. and Univ.
of Detroit.

Executive Staff, Ford Motor Co. 39-53; Asst. to Pres., Hall Lamp Co. 54, Exec. Vice-Pres. and mem. Board of Dirs. 55-61; Dep. Administrator, St. Lawrence Seaway Devt. Corpn. 61-62, Administrator Jan. 62-; U.S. mem. Nat. Comm. Perm. Int. Asscn. Navigation Congresses; mem. Great Lakes Basin Comm.
31 Windsor Road, Massena, New York, U.S.A.

McCann, H.E. Cardinal Owen, D.D., PH.D.; South African ecclesiastic; b. 26 June 1907; ed. St. Joseph's Coll., Rondebosch and Pontificium Collegium Urbanianum de Propaganda Fide.
Ordained priest 35; Titular Bishop of Stettorio 50; Archbishop of Cape Town 51-; named Asst. at the Papal Throne 60; mem. Comm. De Episcopis et Dioecesium Regimine and Comm. on the Press at the Ecumenical Council; mem. Post Conciliar Comm. De Episcopis et Dioecesium Regimine; created cardinal 65. Archdiocesan Chancery, Cathedral Place, 12 Bouquet Street, Capetown, South Africa.

McCarthy, Sir Edwin, Kt., C.B.E., B.COM.; Australian diplomatist; b. 30 March 1896; ed. Christian Brothers Coll., Melbourne and Melbourne Univ.
Australian Shipping Rep. in U.S.A. 41-44; Sec. Commonwealth Dept. of Commerce 45-50; Controller-Gen. of Food 45-48; Dep. High Commr. in London 50-58; Ambassador to Netherlands 58-62, to Belgium 59-62; Ambassador to European Economic Community 60-64; Chair. Commonwealth Economic Cttee. 64-67.
Commonwealth Secretariat, 10 Carlton House Terrace, London, S.W.1, England.
Telephone: 01-930-7651.

McCarthy, Eugene Joseph, B.A., M.S.; American politician; b. 29 March 1916; ed. St. John's Univ., Collegeville, Minn. and Minnesota Univ.
Successively Prof. of Economics and Education, St. John's Univ., Collegeville, Minn.; Civilian Technical Asst., War Dept. Military Intelligence Division; Acting Chair., Sociology Dept., St. Thomas Coll., St. Paul, Minn.; mem. U.S. House of Reps. (Fourth Minn. district) 48-58; Senator from Minnesota 58-; Cardinal Newman Award 55; Hon. LL.D. St. Louis Univ. 55; Democrat.
Publs. *Frontiers in American Democracy*, *The Limits of Power: America's Role in the World* 67.
2103 Iglehart Avenue, St. Paul, Minn.; Senate Office Building, Washington 25, D.C., U.S.A.

McCarthy, Mary (Mrs. James West); American writer; b. 21 June 1912; ed. Vassar Coll.
Theatre critic *Partisan Review* 37-57; Instructor Bard Coll. 45-46, Sarah Lawrence Coll. 48; *Horizon* award (for *The Oasis*) 48, Guggenheim Fellowships 49 and 59, Nat. Acad. of Arts and Letters award 57.
Publs. *The Company She Keeps* (novel) 42, *The Oasis* (re-issued as *A Source of Embarrassment*) (novel) 49, *Cast a Cold Eye* (short stories) 50, *The Groves of Academe* (novel) 52, *A Charmed Life* (novel) 55, *Venice Observed* 56, *Sights and Spectacles* (theatre criticism) 56, *Memories of a Catholic Girlhood* (memoirs) 57, *The Stones of Florence* 59, *On the Contrary* 62, *The Group* 63 (film 66), *Vietnam* 67; numerous essays, short stories, reviews, etc. in *The New Yorker*, *Harper's*, *Encounter* and other magazines.
141 Rue de Rennes, Paris 6e, France.

McCarthy, Michael W.; American financier; b. 24 May 1903.
Office Man., Mutual Stores, Oakland, Calif.; organised Hagstrom Food Stores, Calif. 32; Merrill Lynch, Pierce, Fenner and Beane, investment brokerage, New York City 40-, Gen. Partner 44-48, Asst. Man. Partner 48-57, Man. Partner, Merrill Lynch, Pierce, Fenner and Smith 57-59, Pres., Merrill Lynch, Pierce, Fenner and Smith Inc. 59-61, Chair., Chief Exec. Officer 61-, Chair. Exec. Cttee. 66-; Dir. Safeways Stores, Calif. 56-; fmr.

Governor, New York Stock Exchange, American Stock Exchange, Asscn. Stock Exchange Firms.
70 Pine Street, New York City 5, N.Y., U.S.A.

Maccas, Leon, LL.D.; Greek journalist, politician and diplomatist; b. 1892; ed. Univ. of Athens.
Journalist 11-22; Chief of Press Bureau, Paris 22-28; M.P. for Athens 28-55; Min. Asst. to Prime Minister; Minister and Gov. of Ionian Islands 44-45; Adviser, Greek Del. to Paris Peace Conf. 46; Pres. European Parliamentary Union 47; Minister of Greek Royal Navy 50-51, of Industry 51, of Commerce 54-55; Perm. Representative to Council of Europe 64-66; Chief Del. Economic Confs. of the European Movement, Brussels 52 and London 53; Commdr. Légion d'Honneur (France), Order of Cedar of Lebanon; Liberal.
Publs. *The Financial Policy of Capodistria* 10, *Greeks and Israelites* 13, *France and Germany before Hellenism* 15, *German Atrocities* 15, *The Venizelos Policy* 16, *Constantine, King of Greece* 17, *The Great War, Nations and Men* 18, *The Hellenism of Asia Minor* 19, *Hellenism and Socialism* 20, *The Greco-Albanian Question* 21, *Democracy in Greece* 24, *French Philhellenism* 26, *The Balkan Federation* 31, *The Labour Question in Greece* 31, *The Greek Problem* 33, *The National Policy of Eleutherios Venizelos* 36, *Roman Violence and Hellenic Spirit* 42, *National Fears and Hopes* 46, *Peaceful Coexistence* 57.
c/o Ministry of Foreign Affairs, Athens, Greece.

McClellan, John Little; American politician; b. 25 Feb. 1896.
Admitted to Arkansas Bar 17; practised law, Sheridan; Prosecuting Attorney 7th Judicial District of Arkansas 27-30; mem. House of Reps. 35-39; Senator from Arkansas 43-; Chair. Govt. Operations Cttee. 55-; George Washington Award (Freedom Foundation) 60; Democrat.
Union Life Building, Little Rock, Arkansas, U.S.A.

McClintock, Robert; American diplomatist; b. 30 Aug. 1909; ed. Stanford Univ.
Entered Foreign Service 31; served Panama City 32, Kobe, Japan 33, Santiago 34-37, Ciudad Trujillo 37-39, Helsinki 39-42, Stockholm 44, Dept. of State 45; Sec. First Cttee. UN Conf. San Francisco 45; Adviser U.S. Del., Preparatory Comm., UN, London 45, with U.S. Dels. to UN Gen. Assembly 46 and 47-48; served Brussels 49; on staff Nat. War Coll. 51-52; Deputy Chief of Mission and Counsellor, Cairo Embassy 52; Chargé d'Affaires, Saigon 53; Ambassador to Cambodia 54-57; mem. Policy Planning Staff, Dept. of State, Jan. 57-Dec. 57; Ambassador to the Lebanon Dec. 57-61; mem. Policy Planning Council 61; Ambassador to Argentina 62-64; State Dept. Adviser, U.S. Naval War Coll. 64-.
c/o State Department, Washington, D.C., U.S.A.

McCloskey, Matthew H.; American newspaper executive, politician and diplomatist; b. 93.
Chairman of Board and Publisher Philadelphia *Daily News*; Treas. Democratic Nat. Cttee. 55-62; Ambassador to Ireland 62-64.
c/o State Department, Washington, D.C., U.S.A.

McCloy, John J., B.A., LL.B.; American lawyer, banker and administrator; b. 31 March 1895; ed. Amherst Coll. and Harvard Law School.
Served Field Artillery, First World War; admitted to N.Y. Bar 21; mem. law firm Cravath, de Gersdorff, Swaine and Wood 35-40; Asst. Sec. of War 41-45; Chair. Civil Affairs Cttee. Combined Chiefs of Staff 43-45; mem. law firm Milbank, Tweed, Hope, Hadley and McCloy 45-47, partner 62-; Pres. Int. Bank for Reconstruction and Devt. 47-49; U.S. Mil. Gov. and High Commr. for Germany 49-52; Chair. Chase Manhattan Bank, N.Y. 53-60; Adviser to Pres. Kennedy on Disarmament Matters 61; Chair. Board Ford Foundation 53-65; Chair. Atlantic Inst. (Paris) 66-; Chair. Council

on Foreign Relations (U.S.); Chair. Int. House, N.Y.; Chair. Board of Trustees, Amherst Coll.; Chair. Exec. Cttee. Squibb Beech-Nut, Inc.; Chair. President's Gen. Advisory Cttee. on Disarmament 62-; mem. Co-ordinating Cttee. on Cuban Crisis 62-63, President's Cttee. to Investigate Assassination of Pres. Kennedy 63-64; Dir. Allied Chemical Corpn.; D.S.M. (U.S.); Presidential Medal of Freedom; Grand Cross of Order of Merit of German Fed. Repub.; Grand Officer of Legion of Honour (France); Grand Officer of Order of Merit of Italy; numerous hon. degrees.
Publ. *The Challenge to American Foreign Policy* 53.
Milbank, Tweed, Hadley and McCloy, 1 Chase Manhattan Plaza, New York City, N.Y. 10005, U.S.A.
Telephone: 212-422-2660.

McCollum, Leonard Franklin, B.A.; American executive; b. 20 March 1902; ed. Univ. of Texas.
Div. Geologist Humble Oil & Refining Co. 27-34; Exploration Manager, Carter Oil Co., Tulsa, Okla. 34-36, Dir. 36-38, Vice-Pres. and Dir. 38-41, Pres. 41-43; Asst. Co-ordinator of Production, Standard Oil Co. (N.J.) and Exec. Vice-Pres., Creole Petroleum Corpn., N.Y. 43-44; Co-ordinator, Producing Activities, Standard Oil Co. (N.J.) 44-47; Pres. and Dir. Continental Oil Co. of Houston, Texas, Dec. 47-64, Chair. and Chief Exec. Officer 64-67, Chair. 67-; Dir. Hudson's Bay Oil and Gas Co. Ltd., Morgan Guaranty Trust Co. of N.Y., mem. Board of Dirs. of Chrysler Motors Corpn. 58; mem. American Petroleum Inst., American Asscn. of Petroleum Geologists, Inst. of Int. Education, American Inst. of Mining and Metallurgical Engineers; Trustee, California Inst. of Technology.
3620 Inverness Drive, Houston 19, Texas, U.S.A.

McConaughy, Walter Patrick, A.B.; American diplomatist and government official; b. 11 Sept. 1908; ed. Birmingham Southern Coll. and Duke Univ.
Teacher 28-30; Dept. of State 31-, Mexico, Japan, Bolivia, Brazil; Consul-Gen. Hong Kong 50-52; Dir. Office Chinese Affairs, Dept. of State 52-57; Ambassador to Burma 57-60, to Republic of Korea 60-61; Asst. Sec. for Far Eastern Affairs, Dept. of State Jan.-Nov. 61; Ambassador to Pakistan 62-66, to Repb. of China 66-.
American Embassy, Taipei, Taiwan, Republic of China.
Telephone: 33551.

McCone, John A.; American business executive; b. 4 Jan. 1902; ed. Univ. of California.
Began as construction engineer, Llewellyn Iron Works; Supt. Consolidated Steel Corpn. 29, Exec. Vice-Pres., Dir. 33-37; Pres. Bechtel-McCone Corpn. (engineers), Los Angeles 37-45; Pres. Dir. Calif. Shipbuilding Corpn. 41-46; Pres., Dir. Joshua Hendy Corpn. 45-58, Chair. 58-; Dir. United Calif. Bank, Los Angeles, Standard Oil Co. of Calif., San Francisco, Int. Telephone and Telegraph Corpn., New York; mem. President's Air Policy Comm. 47-48; Deputy to Sec. of Defence 48; Under-Sec. U.S. Air Force 50-51; Chair U.S. Atomic Energy Comm. 58-60; Dir. Central Intelligence Agency (C.I.A.) 61-65.
Office: 612 South Flower Street, Los Angeles, California 90017; Homes: 1100 Oak Grove Avenue, San Marino, Calif.; and Norcliffe, The Highlands, Seattle, Wash., U.S.A.

McConnell, Albert Joseph, M.A., SC.D.; Irish university official; b. 19 Nov. 1903; ed. Ballymena Acad., Trinity Coll., Dublin, and Univ. of Rome.
Lecturer in Mathematics, Trinity Coll., Dublin 27-30; Prof. of Natural Philosophy, Univ. of Dublin 30-57; Visiting Prof. Univ. of Alexandria 46-47; Provost of Trinity Coll., Dublin 52-; Hon. D.Sc. (Belfast), Hon. Sc.D. (Columbia).
Publ. *Applications of the Absolute Differential Calculus* 31.
Provost's House, Trinity College, Dublin, Ireland.

McConnell, John; Canadian newspaper publisher; b. 11; ed. Lower Canada Coll., Montreal, McGill Univ. and Cambridge Univ.
Chairman, The Montreal Star Co. Ltd., Montreal Standard Publishing Co. Ltd.; Pres. Canada Wide Feature Service, Star Building Ltd., Commercial Trust Co.; Dir. St. Lawrence Sugar Refineries Ltd.
1328 Redpath Crescent, Montreal 25, Quebec, Canada.

McConnell, Gen. John Paul; American air force officer; b. 7 Feb. 1908; ed. Henderson-Brown Coll., Arkansas, and U.S. Military Acad.
Field Artillery 32; flight training 32-33; Air Force Service U.S.A., Hawaii, India, Ceylon, Chungking, Nanking, Washington, England 33-53; Deputy Dir. and Dir. of Plans, Strategic Air Command (SAC) H.Q., Offutt, Nebraska 53-57; Commdr., Second Air Force, Barksdale, Louisiana 57-61; Vice-Commdr.-in-Chief, SAC, Offutt, Nebraska 61-62; Deputy C.-in-C. U.S. European Command 62-64; Vice-Chief of Staff, U.S. Air Force 64-65, Chief of Staff 65-; numerous decorations.
Department of the Air Force, Washington 25, D.C., and Booneville, Arkansas, U.S.A.

McConnell, Joseph Howard, B.A., LL.B.; American executive; b. 13 May 1906; ed. Davidson Coll. and Univ. of Virginia.
Practised law in W. Palm Beach, Fla. 31-32, in Charlotte, N.C. 32-33; NRA, Washington, D.C. 33-35; Assoc. in law firm of Cotton, Franklin, Wright and Gordon (now Cahill, Gordon, Sonnet, Reindel and Ohl), New York City 35-41; various exec. posts with Radio Corpn. of America, including Financial Vice-Pres. and Exec. Vice-Pres. 41-49; Pres., Nat. Broadcasting Co. 49-52; Pres. Colgate-Palmolive Co. 53-55; Exec. Vice-Pres. and Gen. Counsel, Reynolds Metals Co. 55-63, Pres. 63-.
Bellona, Old Gun Road, R.F.D. 1, Midlothian, Virginia, U.S.A.
Telephone: 272-5065.

McConnell, Thomas Raymond, A.M., PH.D.; American college president, dean and professor; b. 25 May 1901; ed. Cornell Coll., Mount Vernon, and Univ. of Iowa.
Instructor in English and Journalism Cornell Coll. 25-26, Instructor, Asst. Prof., and Prof. of Educ. and Psychology 29-36, Dean of Coll. 32-36; Prof. Educ. Psychology Univ. of Minnesota 36-50; Chair. Comm. on Educ. Research 37-47; Assoc. Dean Coll. of Science, Literature and the Arts 40-44, Act. Dean 42-44, Dean 44-50; Chancellor Univ. of Buffalo 50-54; Prof. of Higher Educ. Univ. of California 54-; Chair. Center for the Study of Higher Educ. (Univ. of Calif.) 57-; fmr. mem. Pres. Truman's Comm. on Higher Educ., and Problems and Policies, and Instruction and Evaluation, Comms. of American Council on Educ., Cttee. on Devt. of Youth of the Social Science Research Council; mem. Comm. on Plans and Objectives for Higher Educ., American Council on Educ.; mem. Board of Editors of *Encyclopaedia of Educational Research* 57-59, Chair. 63-; Research Cttee. of Educational Testing Service 56-; mem. Board of Dirs. Inst. for Coll. and Univ. Administrators, Board of Trustees, Cornell Coll.; Founding mem. Nat. Acad. of Educ.
Publs. *Psychology in Everyday Living* (with others) 38, *Educational Psychology* (with others) 48, *A Restudy of the Needs of California in Higher Education* (with H. H. Semans and T. C. Holy), *A General Pattern for American Public Higher Education* 62.
Center for the Study of Higher Education, 4606 Tolman Hall, University of California, Berkeley, California; 775 Creston Road, Berkeley 8, California, U.S.A.

McCormack, John W.; American politician; b. 21 Dec. 1891.
Admitted to Massachusetts Bar 13; practised law, Boston; mem. firm McCormack & Hardy; mem. Mass.

House of Reps. 20-22, State Senate 23-26; mem. House of Reps. 27-, House Majority Leader 55-62, Speaker 62-; Hon. LL.B. (Boston Univ.); Knight of Malta; Democrat.
726 Columbia Road, Boston, Mass., U.S.A.

McCorquodale, 1st Baron, cr. 55; **Malcolm Stewart McCorquodale,** P.C., K.C.V.O., M.A.; British politician; b. 29 March 1901; ed. Harrow and Christ Church, Oxford.
Member of Parliament 31-45, 47-55; Parl. Sec. to Minister of Labour and Nat. Service 42-45; Chair. Industrial Training Council 58-60; Dir. Bank of Scotland; Chair. Nat. Discount Co. Ltd.; fmr. Pres. British Employers' Confederation; Conservative.
Cotswold Park, Cirencester, Glos., England.

McCulloch, Frank Waugh, LL.B.; American lawyer and government official; b. 05; ed. Williams Coll. and Harvard Law School.
Legal Practice 30-35; Industrial Relations Sec., Council for Social Action, Congregational-Christian Churches, Chicago 35-46; Dir. Labor Educ. Div., Roosevelt Univ., Chicago 46-49; Admin. Asst. to U.S. Senator Paul H. Douglas 49-61; Chair. Nat. Labor Relations Board 61-; Hon. LL.D. (Olivet Coll., Chicago Theological Seminary).
National Labor Relations Board, 1717 Pennsylvania Avenue, N.W., Washington, D.C., U.S.A.

McCulloch, Robert; American (b. Scottish) aircraft executive; b. 27 Oct. 1903; ed. Dumbarton Academy. Marine Engineering Apprenticeship, Mathew Paul Co., Dumbarton, Scotland 19-24; Foreman, Beardmore Naval Construction Works, Dalmuir 24-27; arrived in U.S.A. 27, naturalised 34; Production Foreman, Atlantic Aircraft, Teterboro, N.J. 27-32; Factory Manager, North American Aviation Inc. 32-41; Gen. Manager Consolidated Vultee Aircraft 41-43; Gen. Manufacturing Manager, North American Aviation Inc. 43-45; Pres. and Gen. Manager, Temco Aircraft Corpn. 45-60; Chair. of Board and Chief Exec. Officer, Ling-Temco Electronics 60-61, Ling-Temco-Vought Inc. 61-63; Chair. Exec. Cttee. and Dir. Ling-Temco-Vought Inc. 64-; Chair. Board of Govs. Aircraft Industries Manufacturing Council.
Ling-Temco-Vought Inc., P.O. Box 5003, Dallas 22, Texas, U.S.A.

McCune, Francis Kimber; American business executive; b. 10 April 1906; ed. California Univ.
With Gen. Electric Co. 28-67, Asst. Gen. Man., Nucleonics Dept. 49, Gen. Man. Atomic Products Div. 54, Vice-Pres. 54-67, Vice-Pres. Engineering 60, Vice-Pres. Business Studies 65-67; Vice-Pres. and Dir. American Standards Asscn. 65; Hon. Dir. and Past Pres. Atomic Industrial Forum Inc.; Chair. New York State Gen. Advisory Cttee. on Atomic Energy 59-62; Pres. United States of America Standards Inst. 67-; mem. Nat. Acad. Eng.; mem. Woods Hole Oceanographic Inst.
1564 Danny Drive, Sarasota, Florida 33580, U.S.A.
Telephone: 813-755-7177.

McCurdy, Richard Clark; American oil executive; b. 2 Jan. 1909; ed. Stanford Univ.
With Shell Oil Co., Ventura, Calif. 33, Junior Engineer, later Engineer, Los Angeles, Bakersfield, Coalinga, Long Beach 35-42, Washington Office 42-43, Chief Exploitation Engineer, Pacific Coast Production Area 43-45, Acting Div. Man. San Joaquin Production Div. Bakersfield 45-47; Asst. Man., later Man., Western Div. Royal Dutch/Shell Group companies in Venezuela 47-50, Gen. Man. 50-53; Pres. Shell Chemical Co. (div. of Shell Oil Co.) 53-65, Pres. and Chief Exec. Officer Shell Oil Co. 65-; fmr. Chair. Board of Dirs. Manufacturing Chemists' Asscn.; Trustee Stanford Univ., Hood Coll., etc.; mem. Soc. of Chemical Industry, American

Physical Soc., and American Inst. of Mining and Metallurgical Engineers.
Shell Oil Co., 50 West 50th Street, New York 20, N.Y., U.S.A.

McCutcheon, Hon. M(alcolm) Wallace, P.C., C.B.E., Q.C., LL.D.; Canadian lawyer, industrialist and politician; b. 18 May 1906; ed. Univ. of Toronto, Osgoode Hall.
Called to the Bar, Ontario 30; with Wartime Prices and Trade Board 41-46, Dep. Chair. 45-46; Vice-Pres. and Managing Dir. Argus Corpn. Ltd. 45-62; mem. of Senate 62-; Minister without Portfolio 62-63; Minister of Trade and Commerce 63; Chair. Ontario Cancer Inst., Princess Margaret Hosp.; mem. of Board of Govs. Univ. of Toronto, St. Francis Xavier Univ., St. Michael's Hosp.; Past Pres. Canadian Welfare Council; Chair. Nat. Life Assurance Co. of Canada; Dir. Montreal Trust Co., Glens Falls Insurance Co.; Counsel, Shibley, Righton & McCutcheon; Conservative.
The Senate, Ottawa; 522 University Avenue, Toronto 2, Canada.
Telephone: 366-2211.

McDaniel, Boyce Dawkins, PH.D.; American physicist; b. 6 Nov. 1917; ed. Ohio Wesleyan Univ., Case Inst. of Technology and Cornell Univ.
Staff mem. Radiation Laboratory, Mass. Inst. of Technology 43; Los Alamos Scientific Laboratory 43-46; Asst. Prof. of Physics, Cornell Univ. 46-48, Assoc. Prof. 48-56, Prof. 56-; on sabbatic leave at Australian Nat. Univ., Canberra 53-54, Laboratorio Nazionale di Frascati, Italy 59-60; Assoc. Dir. Laboratory of Nuclear Studies 60-67, Dir. 67-; Fulbright Research Award 53, 59; Guggenheim Award 59.
Laboratory of Nuclear Studies, Cornell University, Ithaca, N.Y., U.S.A.
Telephone: 607-275-2301.

MacDermott, Baron (Life Peer), cr. 47, of Belmont; **John Clarke MacDermott,** P.C., LL.D., M.C.; British lawyer; b. 12 April 1896; ed. Queen's Univ., Belfast.
Served with Machine Gun Corps First World War; called to Irish Bar 21; Lecturer in Jurisprudence Queen's Univ. Belfast 31-35; M.P. for Queen's Univ., Northern Ireland Parl. 38-44; Major Royal Artillery 39-40; Min. of Public Security Northern Ireland 40-41, Attorney-Gen. 41-44; Judge Supreme Court Northern Ireland 44-47; Lord of Appeal in Ordinary April 47-51; Lord Chief Justice, Northern Ireland 51-, LL.D. (h.c.) Queen's Univ., Belfast 51, Edinburgh 58.
House of Lords, London, S.W.1; and Glenburn, Cairnburn Road, Strandtown, Belfast, Northern Ireland.

McDermott, Edward Aloysious, B.A., IUR.D.; American lawyer, educator and government official; b. 28 June 1920; ed. Loras Coll. and State Univ. of Iowa.
Professor of Business Law, Loras Coll., Dubuque, Iowa 46-48; Prof. of Economics, Clarke Coll., Dubuque 48-50; Partner law firm O'Connor, Thomas, McDermott and Wright, Dubuque 51-61; Chief Counsel U.S. Senate Subcttee. on Privileges and Elections 50-51; Dep. Dir. Office of Civil and Defense Mobilisation, The White House 60-61; Dir. Office of Emergency Planning, Exec. Office of the Pres. 62-65; mem. Nat. Security Council; Chair. Emergency Planning Cttee.; U.S. Rep. Senior Civil Emergency Planning Cttee., NATO 62-65; mem. President's Cttee. on Economic Impact on Defense and Disarmament; Chair. President's Petroleum Policy Cttee. 63; Partner Law Firm Hogan and Hartson, Washington D.C.; mem. Board of Advisers, Industrial Coll. of Armed Forces, Washington 65-; mem. Board of Regents, Univ. Santa Clara (California); Lynchburg Coll. (Virginia); mem. Board of Dirs. American Irish Foundation; mem. American Bar Asscn. etc.; official of legal, civic and charitable orgs.
5400 Albemarle, N.W., Westmorland Hills, Washington D.C., U.S.A.
Telephone: 301-654-8755.

MacDiarmid, Hugh (pseudonym of Christopher Murray Grieve); British writer; b. 11 Aug. 1892; ed. Langholm Acad., Edinburgh Univ.

One of founders Scottish Nationalist Party; founder Scottish Centre P E N Club; Editor *The Voice of Scotland*; J.P. for County of Angus; Hon. LL.D. (Edin.). Publs. *Annals of the Five Senses, Contemporary Scottish Studies, Albyn, or the Future of Scotland, The Present Condition of Scottish Arts and Affairs, Scottish Scene, At the Sign of the Thistle, Scottish Eccentrics, Robert Burns: Today and Tomorrow, The Handmaid of the Lord* (translated from Spanish of Ramón Maria de Tenreiro), *The Scottish Islands*, etc.; Poetry: *Sangschaw, Penny Wheep, A Drunk Man Looks at the Thistle, To Circumjack Cencrastus, Stony Limits, and other poems, First Hymn to Lenin and other poems, Second Hymn to Lenin and other poems, Cornish Heroic Song for Valda Trevlyn, The Birlinn of Clanranald* (from Gaelic of Alexander MacDonald), *Direadh, Golden Treasury of Scottish Poetry, Lucky Poet* (autobiography), *Speaking for Scotland* (publ. U.S.A. only), *A Kist of Whistles, R. B. Cunninghame Graham, In memoriam James Joyce, Stony Limits and Scots Unbound, The Battle Continues, Aniara* (translated from Swedish of Harry Martinsen, with Elspeth Harley Schubert), *John Davidson: A Selection of His Poems* (with Maurice Lindsay and T. S. Eliot), *The Kind of Poetry I Want, Collected Poems, David Hume, The Company I've Kept* (autobiography), *A Lap of Honour* (poems).

The Cottage, Brownsbank, by Biggar, Lanarkshire, Scotland.

Telephone: Skirling-Biggar 55.

McDiarmid, John, A.M., PH.D.; American UN official; b. 12 Aug. 1911; ed. Texas Christian Univ. and Univ. of Chicago.

Instructor in Government, Texas Christian Univ. 32-33; Research Asst. Nat. Resources Board, U.S. Govt. Washington 35; Instructor in Politics, Princeton Univ. 36-38; Asst. Prof. of Public Admin., Univ. of Southern California 38-42; various positions with U.S. Civil Service Comm. Washington 42-45; Assoc. Prof. of Political Science, Northwestern Univ., Evanston, Ill. 45-46; Official of UN Secretariat, New York, and Deputy Dir. of Personnel, UN 54-57, Act. Dir. of Personnel 57-59, Senior Dir. Technical Assistance Board 59-64, Resident Rep. UN Devt. Programme in India 64-.

Publs. *Government Corporations and Federal Funds* 38, *The Administration of the American Public Library* (with E. W. McDiarmid) 43.

21 Curzon Road, New Delhi, India; and 22 Thayer Pond Road, New Canaan, Conn., U.S.A.

Macdiarmid, Niall Campbell; British steel executive; b. 7 June 1919; ed. Uppingham and Magdalen Coll., Oxford.

Army Service, Second World War; Stewarts and Lloyds Ltd. 46-; Man. Dir. Stanton Ironworks Co. Ltd. (later Stanton and Stavely Ltd.) 57-62, Chair. 62-64; Dir. Stewarts and Lloyds 59-, Chair. Iron and Steel Div. 63-64, Chair. and Gen. Man. Dir. Stewarts and Lloyds Ltd. 64-; Man. Dir. Northern and Tubes Group, British Steel Corpn. 67-; mem. Iron and Steel Board, East Midlands Gas Board; Vice-Pres. Council of Iron and Steel Inst. 66; Dir. The United Steel Cos. Ltd.

Stewarts and Lloyds Ltd., Park House, Park Street, London, W.1; Home: Stibbington Hall, Wansford, Peterborough, Northants., England.

Telephone: Wansford 322 (Home).

McDivitt, James Alton; American astronaut; b. 10 June 1929; ed. Jackson Junior Coll. and Univ. of Michigan.

U.S. Air Force 51-, flew combat missions in Korean War; at U.S. Air Force Experimental Test Pilot School, Edwards Air Force Base 59-60; Experimental Test Pilot 60-62; U.S. Air Force Aerospace Research Pilot Course 61; astronaut 62-; Command Pilot of *Gemini 4* Spacecraft, making 62 orbits of the earth June 3rd-7th 65.

NASA Manned Spacecraft Center, Houston 1, Texas, U.S.A.

McDonald, Alexander Forbes, B.L., D.L.; British business executive; b. 14 Aug. 1911; ed. Hillhead School and Glasgow Univ.

Chartered Accountant 34; Deputy Chair. the Distillers Co. Ltd. 64-67, Chair. 67-; Chair. the Scotch Whisky Asscn. 67-; Dir. Royal Bank of Scotland.

6 Oswald Road, Edinburgh, Scotland.

Telephone: Newington 4246.

MacDonald, Maj.-Gen. Bruce F.; Canadian army officer; b. July 1917; ed. Edmonton and Univ. of Alberta.

Canadian Army 40-, served Normandy; Commdr. Royal Canadian Armoured Corps School, Camp Borden, Ont. 46-49; Directing Staff, Canadian Army Staff Coll., Kingston, Ont. 49-52; H.Q. Central Command, Oakville, Ont. 52-55; Dir. of Armour, Army H.Q. 55-57; Staff Planner, NATO Standing Group, Washington 58-59; Sec. to Chair. of Canadian Joint Staff, Washington 59-62; Commdr. First Canadian Infantry Brigade Group 62-65; Commdr. Nicosia Zone, UN Peace-Keeping Force in Cyprus April-Sept. 65; Chief Officer of UN India-Pakistan Observation Mission (UNIPOM) Sept. 65-66.

c/o United Nations, New York City, N.Y., U.S.A.

McDonald, Admiral David Lamar; American naval officer; b. 20 Sept. 1906; ed. Riverside Military Acad. and U.S. Naval Acad.

Entered U.S. Navy 24, Naval Aviator 31-, Rear Admiral 55; Dir. Air Warfare Div., The Pentagon, Washington 55-57; Deputy Asst. Chief of Staff, Plans and Policy, SHAPE 57-60; Commdr., Carrier Div. 60-61, Commdr. 6th Fleet, Mediterranean 61-63, Commdr., U.S. Naval Forces in Europe April-Aug. 63; U.S. Chief of Naval Operations Aug. 63-67.

Navy Department, Washington D.C. 20350, U.S.A.

McDonald, Denis Ronald, B.A.; Irish diplomatist; b. 22 Feb. 1910; ed. Univ. Coll., Cork.

Minister, later Amb., to Belgium 54-60; Irish Rep. to EEC 59-60; Amb. to France 60-66, to Italy and to Turkey 66-; Head of Irish Del. to OEEC (now OECD) 60-66; Perm. Del to UNESCO 61-66; Kt. Commdr. Order of St. Gregory the Great.

Embassy of Ireland, 9 Via del Circo Massimo, Italy.

MacDonald, Rt. Hon. Malcolm John, P.C., M.A. (son of late J. Ramsay MacDonald); British diplomatist; b. 17 Aug. 1901; ed. Bedales and Oxford Univ.

Labour M.P. for Bassetlaw Div. of Notts. 29-31, and National Labour 31-35 and for Ross and Cromarty 36-45; Parl. Under-Sec. of State for Dominion Affairs in First and Second Nat. Govts. Aug. and Nov. 31-June 35; Sec. of State for the Colonies in reconstructed Cabinet June-Nov. 35; Sec. of State for Dominion Affairs Nov. 35-May 38; Sec. of State for the Colonies May-Oct. 38; Sec. of State for Dominion Affairs and Colonies Oct. 38-Jan. 39, for Colonies Jan. 39-May 40; Min. of Health May 40- Feb. 41; High Commr. in Canada 41-46; Gov.-Gen. of the Malayan Union and Singapore May-July 46; Gov.-Gen. of Malaya and British Borneo 46-48; Commr.-Gen. for U.K. in South-East Asia 48-55; High Commr. in India 55-60; Chancellor Univ. of Malaya 49-61; Co-Chair. Int. Conf. on Laos 61-62; Governor of Kenya Jan.-Dec. 63, Gov.-Gen. Dec. 63-Dec. 64; Visitor, Univ. Coll., Nairobi 63-64; High Commr. in Kenya 64-65; Special Rep. of British Govt. in a number of Commonwealth countries in East and Central Africa 65-, in Africa 66-.

Publs. *Down North* 45, *The Birds of Brewery Creek* 47,

Borneo People 56, *Angkor* 58, *Birds in my Indian Garden* 61, *Birds in the Sun* 62, *Treasure of Kenya* 65.
Box 30283, Nairobi, Kenya and Mbagathi Ridge, Karen, Nairobi, Kenya.
Telephone: Karen 584.

Macdonald, Ray Woodward; American business executive; b. 20 Dec. 1912; ed. Univ. of Chicago School of Business Admin.
Junior Salesman, Burroughs Corpn., Detroit 35, successively Manager Travelling Exhibit Sales Div., in Export Dept., Asst. Export Man., Export Man., Gen. Man. (Int. Activity), Vice-Pres. (Int.) 35-57, Vice-Pres. in charge Int. Div. 57-64, Exec. Vice-Pres. 64-66, Pres. 66-, Chief Exec. Officer 67-; Dir. 59- and Dir. of subsidiaries: Compañía Burroughs de Máquinas, Ltd. (Argentina), Burroughs, Ltd. (Australia), Companhia Burroughs de Brasil, Inc. (Brazil), Burroughs de Colombia, S.A. (Colombia), Burroughs de Centro América S.A. (Costa Rica), Compañía Burroughs Mexicana, S.A. (Mexico), Burroughs de Perú, S.A. (Peru), Burroughs Inc. (Puerto Rico), Burroughs Machines Ltd. (South Africa), Compañía Burroughs de Venezuela, Inc. (Venezuela), Burroughs Adding Machines Ltd. (Great Britain); mem. American Management Asscn., Int. Foreign Trade Council, etc.
Office: 6071 Second Avenue, Detroit, Mich. 48232; Home: 41 Lochmoor Boulevard, Grosse Pointe Shores, Mich. 48236, U.S.A.

Macdonald, Sir Thomas Lachlan, K.C.M.G.; New Zealand politician and diplomatist; b. 14 Dec. 1898; ed. Southland Boys High School, Invercargill, New Zealand.
Union Steamship Co. of New Zealand 15-18; N.Z. Army, Palestine and Egypt 18-19; farming 19-37; M.P. for Mataura 38-40, 43-46, for Wallace 46-57; N.Z. Army, N. Africa 40-43; Minister of Defence 50-57, of Civil Aviation 50-54, of External Affairs 54-57, of Island Territories 54-57; High Commissioner for New Zealand in U.K. 61-68; Amb. to European Econ. Community 61-67; concurrently Amb. to Ireland 66-68; New Zealand National Party.
c/o New Zealand House, Haymarket, London, S.W.1, England.

Macdonald, Hon. William Ross, P.C., Q.C.; Canadian barrister and politician; b. 25 Dec. 1891; ed. Univ. of Toronto and Osgoode Hall.
Served Canadian Expeditionary Force 14-18; mem. firm Macdonald, Brown, Binkley & Leslie; mem. House of Commons for Brantford City 35-53; Deputy Speaker of House of Commons 45-49, Speaker 49-53; Leader of the Govt. in the Senate 53; Solicitor-Gen. 54-57; leader of the Opposition in Senate 57-63; Leader of Senate 63-Jan. 64; mem. Privy Council for Canada 53; Hon. Col. 56th Field Regiment R.C.A.; Liberal.
40 Market Street, Brantford, Ont., Canada.

McDonnell, James Smith, Jr., B.S., M.S. in Aeronautical Engineering; American executive; b. 9 April 1899; ed. Princeton Univ. and Mass. Inst. of Technology.
Aeronautical Engineer and Pilot, Huff Daland Airplane Co., Ogdensburg, N.Y. 24; Stress analyst and draughtsman Consolidated Aircraft Co., Buffalo, N.Y. 25; Asst. Chief Engineer, Stout Metal Airplane Co., Dearborn, Mich. 25, Hamilton Aero Manufacturing Co., Milwaukee 27; Engineering Consultants, McDonnell and Associates, Milwaukee 28; Vice-Pres. Airtransport Engineering Co, Chicago 30-31; Engineer, Test Pilot, Great Lakes Aircraft Corpn., Cleveland 32; Chief Project Engineer for Landplanes, Glenn L. Martin Co., Baltimore 33-38; Founder, Dir. and Chair. McDonnell Aircraft Corpn., St. Louis, Mo. 39-; Chair. and Chief Exec. Officer McDonnell Douglas 62-; Fellow Inst. Aeronautical Sciences; mem. Board of Dirs. Atlantic Council of the U.S.A., UN Asscn. of the U.S.A., Pres. Johnson's Citizens Cttee., Int. Co-operation Year; now Chair. Board of Dirs., Washington Univ. (St. Louis), also

Chair, Washington Univ. Medical School and Assoc. Hospitals; Hon. Dr. of Engineering, Missouri School of Mines and Metallurgy 57, Washington Univ. (St. Louis, Mo.) 58, Hon. LL.D. (Princeton) 60, (Univ. of Arkansas) 65; St. Louis Award 59, Daniel Guggenheim Medal Award 63.
Home: 1 Glenview Road, St. Louis 24, Mo.; Office: Post Box 516, St. Louis 66, Mo., U.S.A.

Macdonnell, Ronald Macalister, B.A.; Canadian diplomatist and international civil servant; b. 11 May 1909; ed. Univ. of Manitoba and Oxford Univ.
Third Sec., Dept. of External Affairs 34; served in Ottawa, Washington and Moscow; Chargé d'Affaires in Czechoslovakia 47; Minister, Canadian Embassy, Paris 50; Asst. Under-Sec. of State for External Affairs 52; Canadian Commr., Int. Supervisory Comm. for Cambodia Aug. 54; returned to post as Asst. Under-Sec. in Ottawa Nov. 54; Deputy Under-Sec. of State for External Affairs 55-57, 58-59; Ambassador to Egypt (subsequently to United Arab Republic) and Minister to Lebanon 57-58; Sec.-Gen. Int. Civil Aviation Organization (I.C.A.O.) 59-64; Ambassador to Indonesia 64-66; High Commissioner to New Zealand 67-.
Canadian High Commission, Wellington, New Zealand.

MacDougall, Sir George Donald Alastair, C.B.E., F.B.A., M.A.; British economist; b. 26 Oct. 1912; ed. Balliol Coll., Oxford.
Assistant Lecturer, Leeds Univ. 36-39; mem. Sir Winston Churchill's Statistical Branch 39-45 and 51-53; Fellow Wadham Coll., Oxford 45-50, Nuffield Coll. 47-64, Hon. Fellow, Wadham Coll. 64-, Nuffield Coll. 67-; Reader in Int. Econs., Oxford 51-52; Econs. Dir. OEEC Paris 48-49; Econ. Dir. Nat. Econ. Devt. Council (N.E.D.C.) 62-64; Dir.-Gen. Dept. of Econ. Affairs Oct. 64-.
Publ. *The World Dollar Problem* 57.
19 Park Town, Oxford, England.
Telephone: Oxford 55794.

McDougall, Sir Malcolm, Kt.; British thread manufacturer; b. 22 Nov. 1899; ed. Camphill School, Paisley.
J. & P. Coats Ltd. (now J. & P. Coats, Patons & Baldwins Ltd.) 14-, Chair. J. & P. Coats Ltd. 60-, Chair. J. & P. Coats, Patons & Baldwins Ltd. 61-, Thomas White & Sons Ltd.; Dir. Westminster Bank Ltd., Scottish Mutual Assurance Soc. Ltd., Bruce Peebles & Co. Ltd.; mem. Board of Trade Advisory Cttee. 53-60.
Moorburn, Auchengreoch Road, Milliken Park, Renfrewshire, Scotland.

McDowall, Robert John Stewart, D.SC. M.D. F.R.C.P. (Edin.); British physiologist; b. 92; ed. Edinburgh Univ.
Asst. and Lecturer in Physiology, Edinburgh Univ. 19-21; Lecturer in Experimental Physiology and Pharmacology, Leeds Univ. 21-23; Lecturer in Applied Physiology, London School of Hygiene 27-29; served in Royal Army Medical Corps 14-18, also 40-41; Prof. of Physiology 23-59, Emeritus 59-; Dean Faculty of Medicine, King's Coll., London Univ.; Deputy Asst. Dir. of Medical Services, Egyptian Exp. Force; Examiner for London, Edinburgh, Bristol, Manchester, Durham, Sheffield, Aberdeen, and Leeds Univs., Royal Coll. of Physicians and Royal Coll. of Surgeons (England, Ireland and Scotland); Pres. Physiology section of British Asscn. 36; Chair. Medical Advisory Cttee. Asthma Research Council; Pres. European Congress of Allergy 59; Parkin Prize 35, Cullen Prize 38; Arris and Gale Lecturer, Royal Coll. of Surgeons 33; Oliver Sharpey Lecturer, Royal Coll. of Physicians 41; Gold Medal, Univ. of Edinburgh 36; Medal of Honour, Univ. of Ghent 51; Hon. Fellow several Allergy Socs.
Publs. *The Science of Signs and Symptoms in relation to Modern Diagnosis and Treatment* (4 edns.), *Handbook of Physiology* (9 edns.), *The Control of the Circulation of*

the Blood 38, *A Biological Introduction to Psychology* 41, *Sane Psychology* 43, *The Whiskies of Scotland* 67.
34 Park Drive, London, N.W.11, England.
Telephone: 01-455-2858.

McDowell, Robert Wright; American oil company executive; b. 9 Aug. 1895; ed. Blackwell High School, Okla., and Spalding's Business School, Kansas City, Mo.
Sales Man. Producers & Refiners Corpn. 22-24; Vice-Pres. and Gen. Man. Hawkeye Oil Co., Waterloo, Iowa 25-27; Asst. to Vice-Pres. in Charge of Marketing, Mid-Continent Petroleum Corpn., Tulsa, Okla. 27-29, Vice-Pres. in Charge of Marketing 30, Dir. 44-, Exec. Vice-Pres. 47, Pres. 49-55; Dir. Western Petroleum Refiners Asscn. Tulsa, American Petroleum Inst.; on merger of Mid-Continent Petroleum Corpn. with Sunray Oil Corpn. became Vice-Chair. of joint Board and Pres. of D-X Sunray Oil Co. 55-60, Chair. of Board 60-62, now Dir.; Chair. Sunray Mid-Continent Oil Co. 60-62.
Home: 2431 East 34th Street, Tulsa 5; Office: Sunray Building, P.O. Box 2039, Tulsa 2, Okla., U.S.A.

MacEachen, Allan J., P.C., M.P., M.A.; Canadian politician; b. 6 July 1921; ed. St. Francis Xavier Univ., Univs. of Toronto and Chicago, and Massachusetts Inst. of Technology.
Professor of Economics, St. Francis Xavier Univ. 46-48, later Head, Dept. of Economics and Social Sciences; mem. House of Commons 53-58, 62-; Special Asst. and Consultant on Economic Affairs to Lester Pearson 58; Minister of Labour 63-65; Minister of Nat. Health and Welfare 65-; Hon. D.Iur., St. Francis Xavier Univ. 64; Liberal.
Ministry of National Health and Welfare, Ottawa; Home: 258 Daly Avenue, Ottawa, Canada.

Mac Eachen, Dr. Roberto Eduardo; Uruguayan diplomatist; b. 15 Oct. 1899; ed. British School of Montevideo, Colegio Uruguayo, Montevideo, and Universidad de Montevideo.
Secretary and Counsellor of Legation, U.S.A. and London 26-40; Minister to Cuba 40; Ambassador to U.K. 44, 61-65; Ambassador to Argentina 48, to Mexico 50; Del. of Uruguay to numerous int. confs.; Gran Cruz y Banda de Primera Clase de la Orden Mexicana del Aguila Azteca, etc.
c/o Ministry of Foreign Affairs, Montevideo, Uruguay.

Macek, Josef, PH.D., D.SC.; Czechoslovak historian; b. 8 April 1922; ed. Charles Univ., Prague, and State Archive School, Prague.
Professor, Coll. of Political and Econ. Sciences 49; Dir. Historical Inst., Czechoslovak Acad. of Sciences 52-; Corresponding mem. Czechoslovak Acad. of Sciences 52-60, mem. 60; Chair. Czechoslovak Soc. for Dissemination of Political and Scientific Knowledge 57-65; mem. Ideological Comm., Central Cttee. C.P. of Czechoslovakia 63-; Deputy to Nat. Assembly 64-; mem. Presidium World Peace Council 62-; Chair. Czechoslovak Peace Cttee. 66-; Cand. mem. Central Cttee. C.P. of Czechoslovakia 62-66, mem. 66-; State Prize 52.
Publs. mainly on history of Hussite Movement in Bohemia, including *Husitské revoluční hnutí* (Hussite Revolutionary Movement) 52 (State Prize), *Renaissance and Reformation*.
Historical Institute, Czechoslovak Academy of Sciences, Jiřská 3, Prague 1—Hrad, Czechoslovakia.

McElroy, Neil H., A.B.; American executive; b. 30 Oct. 1904; ed. Harvard Univ.
Joined Procter & Gamble Co. 25, Man. Promotion Dept. 29, Man. Advertising and Promotion 40, Vice-Pres. and Dir. in charge of Advertising and Promotion 43, Vice-Pres. and Gen. Man. 46, Pres. 48-57, Chair. 59-; Dir. Gen. Electric Co. and Chrysler Corpn.; Dir. Equitable Life Assurance Society of the United States;

Pres. The Soap and Detergent Association 50; Chair. White House Conference on Education 54-55; Trustee Nat. Industrial Conf. Board Inc. 53-57, 60-64; Chair. Council for Financial Aid to Educ. 63-66; Dir. The Atlantic Council of the U.S. Inc.; mem. Exec. Cttee. Business Council; Trustee Nat. Safety Council; Sec. of Defense 57-59; Chair. Cttee. on Univ. Resources, Harvard Univ.; mem. of numerous cttees.
3478 Vista Terrace, Cincinnati, Ohio 45208, U.S.A.

McElvenny, Ralph Talbot; American lawyer and businessman; b. 20 June 1906; ed. Stanford Univ.
Attorney, Guaranty Trust Co., New York 31-33; Nat. Bank Conservator U.S. Treasury Dept., Washington, D.C. 33-34; Asst. Dir. U.S. Securities and Exchange Comm. 34-45; Vice-Pres. and Asst. to Chair. American Natural Gas Co. 45, later Pres. and Dir.; Pres. Mich. Consolidated Gas Co.; Dir. of numerous other companies.
Home: 63 Cloverly Road, Grosse Pointe Farms, Mich. 48236; Office: 1 Woodward Avenue, Detroit, Mich. 48226, U.S.A.
Telephone: WO5-8300.

MacEntee, Sean; Irish politician; b. 22 Aug. 1889; ed. St. Malachy's Coll., Belfast and Belfast Coll. of Technology.
Consulting Elec. Engineer, Co.-Dir. and Registered Patent Agent; sentenced to death by British Court Martial June 16 for participation in Irish Insurrection in that year; sentence commuted to penal servitude for life; released under amnesty June 17; mem. Exec. Cttee. Irish Republican Army 17-21; Republican Deputy and mem. Dáil Éireann 18-22; Fianna Fáil Deputy Co. Dublin 27-; Minister of Finance in First De Valera Govt. 32, and subsequent Govts. 33 and 37 and in first and second Govts. of Eire 37 and 38-39; Min. of Industry and Commerce Sept. 39-Aug. 41, of Local Govt. and Public Health 41-46, of Local Govt. 46-48; Min. of Finance 51-54; Min. of Health 57-65, and Social Welfare 58-61; Tanaiste (Deputy Prime Minister) 59-65; Signatory to London Agreement 38; Nat. Treas. Sinn Fein Organisation 24-26, and Fianna Fáil 26-32; mem. Nat. Exec. Fianna Fáil 26-, Nat. Vice-Pres. 55-; mem. President's Council of State 48-; mem. Consultative Assembly, Council of Europe, Strasbourg 49-51, 67.
Publs. *Poems* 18, *Episode at Easter* 66.
9 Leeson Park, Dublin, and Tignacille, Dunquin, Co. Kerry, Ireland.

Macerata, Dr. Giorgio; Italian lawyer and business executive; b. 13; ed. Univ. of Padua.
Legal-commercial posts, Venice 35-39; Gen. Sec. Serbatoi Montani per Irrigazione ed Elettricità, SAVA Group 39-48; Sec. at President's Office, Montecatini 49-51, Vice-Central Manager 51-53, Managing Dir. Compagnie Néerlandaise de l'Azote et Ammoniaque Synthétique et dérivés, Brussels 54-59, Head, Admin. Services Dept., Montecatini 59-62; Managing Dir. and Gen. Manager Montecatini Group (now Montecatini-Edison) 63-.
Montecatini-Edison, Largo Guido Donegani 1-2, Milan, Italy.
Telephone: 6333 or 6334.

McEwen, Rt. Hon. John, P.C., M.P.; Australian politician; b. 29 March 1900.
Enlisted Australian Imperial Force 18; farmer Stanhope, Victoria 19-; mem. House of Reps. for Echuca Div. 34-37, for Indi Div. 37-49, for Murray 49-; Min. of the Interior 37-39, of External Affairs 40, and of Air and Civil Aviation Oct. 40-41; mem. War Council 41-45; Deputy Leader Country Party 43-58, Leader 58-; Minister of Commerce and Agriculture 49-56, of Trade 56-, and Industry 64-; Deputy Prime Minister 58-.
Office: Parliament House, Canberra, A.C.T.; Home: Chilgala, Stanhope, Victoria, Australia.

McFadzean, Baron (Life Peer), cr. 66, of Woldingham; **William (Hunter) McFadzean,** Kt., F.R.S.A., C.I.E.E.; British chartered accountant; b. 17 Dec. 1903; ed. Stranraer Acad. and High School, and Glasgow Univ. Served articles with McLay, McAllister & McGibbon, Chartered Accountants, Glasgow 22-27; on staff of Chalmers Wade & Co., Chartered Accountants, Liverpool 27-32; joined British Insulated Cables Ltd. as Accountant 32, apptd. Financial Sec. 37, Exec. Manager 42; on amalgamation of British Insulated Cables Ltd. and Callender's Cable & Construction Co. Ltd. in 45 apptd. to the Board of British Insulated Callender's Cables Ltd., and also Exec. Dir.; Deputy Chair. 47, Chief Exec. March 50, Man. Dir. 54-61, Exec. Chair. 54-; Chair. British Insulated Callender's Construction Co. Ltd. 52-64, and British Insulated Callender's (Submarine Cables) Ltd.; Dir. Midland Bank Ltd. 59-68, Chair. 68-; Dir. Midland Bank Exec. & Trustee Co. Ltd. 59-67, English Electric Co. Ltd., Steel Co. of Wales Ltd. 66-67, etc.; mem. Council of Inst. of Dirs., Ministry of Labour Advisory Board on Resettlement of Ex-Regulars 57-60, Board of Trade Advisory Council on Middle East Trade 58-60; Pres. Fed. British Industries 59-61; Chair. Council of Industrial Fed. of European Free Trade Asscns. 60-63, Export Council for Europe 60-64, Hon. Pres. 64-; Pres. British Electrical Power Convention 61-62, British Nuclear Forum 64-66; mem. Minister of Transport's Shipping Advisory Panel 62-64, Advisory Cttee. for Queen's Award to Industry 65, Council Confederation of British Industry 65; Vice-Pres. British/Swedish Chamber of Commerce 63, Middle East Asscn. 65; Chair. British Nat. Export Council 64-66, Pres. 66-68; Chair. Commonwealth Export Council 64-66; mem. Court of British Shippers' Council 64; Vice-Pres. City of London Soc. 65-; mem. Council Anglo-Danish Soc. 65-; Pres. The Coal Trade Benevolent Asscn. 67-; Commdr. Order of the Dannebrog (Denmark) 64.
"Garthland", Woldingham, Surrey; Office: 130 Whitehall Court, London, S.W.1, England.
Telephone: Woldingham 3222 (Home); 01-930-3160.

McFarlane, Alexander N., B.S.; American business executive; b. 12 Nov. 1909; ed. Tufts Univ.
Technical Service Dept., Corn Products Co. 34-36, Technical Sales Dept. 36-39, Asst. Dir. of Research 39-44, Man. of Chemical Sales 44-47, Exec. Asst. to Gen. Sales Man. 47-56, Vice-Pres. (Sales) 56-57, Pres. Corn Products Sales Co. 57-59, Corporate Senior Vice-Pres. (Sales) 59-61, Dir. Corn Products Co. 61-, Exec. Vice-Pres. (Domestic Operations) 62-64, Pres. 64-65, Chair. and Chief Exec. Officer 65-; Dir. Marine Midland Grace Trust Co. of New York, Lehmann Corpn., Chesebrough-Ponds Inc.; mem. Int. Business Advisory Board of Chemical Bank New York Trust Co.; Trustee Tufts Univ.; Chair. Business Council for Int. Understanding, Food and Drug Law Inst. Inc., Nutrition Foundation, and official of other commercial orgs.
Corn Products Company, International Plaza, Englewood Cliffs, N.J. 07632, U.S.A.

MacFarquhar, Sir Alexander, K.B.E.; British United Nations official; b. 6 Nov. 1903; ed. Aberdeen Univ. and Emmanuel Coll., Cambridge.
Indian Civil Service 26-47, Dep. Commr. Ferozepore 30-33, Amritsar 33-36, Settlement Officer Amritsar 36-41, Dep.-Sec. Govt. of India 41, Dep. Dir.-Gen., Directorate-Gen. of Supply 43-46, Dir.-Gen. Disposals 46-47; Commerce and Educ. Sec. Govt. of Pakistan 47-51; Resident Rep. to Pakistan of UN Technical Assistance Bd. (TAB) 52-55, Regional Rep. to Far East, Bangkok 55-60, Special Adviser of UN Sec.-Gen. for Civilian Affairs in the Congo 60-62; Dir. of Personnel, UN 62-Dec. 67.
c/o Lloyds Bank, 6 Pall Mall, London, S.W.1, England.

McGannon, Donald H.; American broadcasting official; b. 9 Sept. 1920; ed. Fordham Coll. and Fordham Law School.
Network Exec. and Gen. Man., Owned and Operated Stations, DuMont Television Network 52-55; Pres. and Chair. Westinghouse Broadcasting Co. Inc. (Ind.), (Md.), (Del.) 55-, Television Advertising Representatives, Inc.; Chair. of Board AM Radio Sales Co.; WBC Productions, Inc.; WBC Program Sales, Inc.; officer of many broadcasting Asscns.; Trustee, Sacred Heart Univ. and others; mem. Conn. Transportation Authority; mem. Advisory Council, Notre Dame Univ., Georgetown Univ.; mem. Pontifical Comm. on Communications Media; Distinguished Service Award, Nat. Asscn. of Broadcasters 64; Hon. Degrees Fordham, Scranton, Creighton and St. Bonaventure Univs.
Westinghouse Broadcasting Co. Inc., 90 Park Avenue, New York, N.Y. 10016, U.S.A.

McGee, Gale, A.B., M.A., PH.D.; American professor and politician; b. 17 March 1915; ed. Nebraska State Teachers' Coll., Univs. of Colorado and Chicago.
Teacher 36-40; History Instructor, Nebraska Wesleyan Univ., Iowa State Coll., Univ. of Notre Dame, Univ. of Chicago 40-46; Prof. (History), Dir. Inst. of Int. Affairs, Univ. of Wyoming 46-58; Senator from Wyoming 58-; Democrat.
Senate Office Building, Washington, D.C.; and 7205 Marbury Road, Washington, D.C. 20034, U.S.A.

McGhee, George C., B.SC., D.PHIL.; American government official; b. 10 March 1912; ed. Southern Methodist Univ. Dallas, Univ. of Oklahoma, Oxford Univ. and Univ. of London.
Subsurface Geologist, The Atlantic Refining Co. 30-31; Geophysicist, Continental Oil Co. 33-34; Vice-Pres. Nat. Geophysical Co., Dallas 37-39; Partner DeGolyer, Mac-Naughton and McGhee 39-41; independent explorer for and producer of oil 40-; Senior Liaison Officer OPM and WPB 41-43; U.S. Deputy Exec. Sec. Combined Raw Materials Board 42-43; Special Asst. to the Under-Sec. of State for Econ. Affairs 46-47; Co-ordinator for Aid to Greece and Turkey; Special Asst. to Sec. of State March-June 49; Asst. Sec. Near East, South Asian and African Affairs 49-51; Ambassador to Turkey 51-53; Adviser N.A.T.O. Council, Ottawa 51; Dir. Inst. of Inter-American Affairs, Inter-American Education Foundation 46-51; Director U.S. Commercial Co. 46; Dir. Foreign Service Educ. Foundation 47; Consultant, Nat. Security Council 58-; Counsellor, Dept. of State and Chair. Policy Planning Council Jan.-Nov. 61; Under- Sec. of State for Political Affairs Nov. 61-63; Ambassador to German Federal Republic 63-68; Owner McGhee Production Co.; Dir. or Trustee, Robert Coll. Istanbul 53-61, Brockings Inst. 54-61, Cttee. for Econ. Development 57-61, Aspen Inst. Humanistic Studies 58-, Vassar Coll. 59-63, Duke Univ. 62-; served in U.S.N.R. in Second World War 43-46; Lieut.-Col. U.S.A.F. Reserve 49-; Hon. LL.D. (Tulane Univ. 57), (Maryland Univ. 65); Hon. D.C.L. (Southern Methodist Univ. 53); awarded Legion of Merit.
Home: Farmer's Delight, Middleburg, Va., U.S.A.
Telephone: 703-687-3451.

MacGillavry, Carolina Henriette, D.SC.; Netherlands crystallographer; b. 22 Jan. 1904; ed. Univ. of Amsterdam.
Asst. Univs. of Leiden and Amsterdam 29-41; Conservatrix, Univ. of Amsterdam 41-47; Lecturer in Crystallography, Univ. of Amsterdam 47-50, Prof. of Chemical Crystallography 50-; mem. Royal Acad. of Sciences Amsterdam 50, Gen. Sec. 61; mem. Bd. of Editors of *Nederlands Tijdschrift voor Natuurkunde* 39-56; mem. Board of Editors of Int. Tables for Crystal Structure Determination 48-66; mem. Exec. Cttee. of Int. Union of Crystallography 54-60; mem. Cttee. for

the Award of Fellowships, Int. Fed. of Univ. Women 52-60, Chair. 55-60; Pres. Board of Child Guidance Clinic, Amsterdam; Knight of Dutch Lion.
Nieuwe Prinsengracht 126, Amsterdam C, Netherlands.
Telephone: 020-224933.

McGinley, Phyllis; American poetess and essayist; b. 21 March 1905; ed. Public Schools, Univ. of Calif. and Univ. of Utah.
Member Inst. of Arts and Letters; Pulitzer Prize for Poetry 61.
Publs. *On the Contrary, One More Manhattan, Pocketful of Wry, Stones from a Glasshouse, A Short Walk from the Station, The Love Letters of Phyllis McGinley, The Province of the Heart, Times Three, Sixpence in Her Shoe, Wonderful Time, A Wreath of Christmas Legends.*
Ladder Hill Road, Weston, Connecticut, U.S.A.

McGovern, George Stanley; American politician; b. 19 July 1922; ed. Dakota Wesleyan Univ. and Northwestern Univ.
Served U.S. Air Force, Second World War; Teacher, Northwestern Univ. 48-50; Prof. of History and Government, Dakota Wesleyan Univ. 50-53; Exec. Sec. South Dakota Democratic Party 53-56; mem. U.S. House of Reps. 56-61, served Agricultural Cttee.; Dir. "Food for Peace" Programme 61-62; Senator from South Dakota 63-.
United States Senate, Washington D.C.; and Mitchell, South Dakota, U.S.A.

McGrath, Raymond, B.ARCH., R.H.A., F.R.I.B.A., F.R.I.A.I., F.S.I.A.; Australian architect; b. 7 March 1903; ed. Univs. of Sydney and Cambridge.
In private practice as architect and industrial designer, London 31-39; Official War Artist 40; Principal Architect, Office of Public Works, Dublin 48-; Appointed architect for Kennedy Memorial Concert and Congress Hall, Dublin 64; architectural work for private housing, exhibitions, restaurants, office and industrial building; industrial design for furniture, glassware and carpets; drawings and paintings; mem. Royal Hibernian Acad.; Fellow Soc. of Industrial Artists; Medallion of the Board of Architects of New South Wales 28.
Publs. *Twentieth Century Houses* (in Basic English) 34, *Glass in Architecture and Decoration* 61.
Somerton Lodge, Rochestown Avenue, Co. Dublin, Ireland.

MacGregor, George Lescher, B.S.; American utilities executive; b. 29 Oct. 1901; ed. Univ. of Texas.
Joined Dallas Power & Light Co. 29, Man., Pres. 40-53, Chair. of Board 44-53, Dir. 53-; Vice-Pres. and Dir. Texas Utilities Co. 45-53, Pres. and Dir. 53-67, Chair. 67-; Dir. Texas Electric Service and Texas Power & Light Co.; Dir. State Fair of Texas; Trustee Texas Research Foundation; Pres. and Trustee Southwestern Medical Foundation; Chair. Board Technical Services Inc.; mem. Advisory Cttee. Edison Electric Inst.; Distinguished Engineering Graduate Award, Univ. of Texas.
Home: 6322 Westchester Drive, Dallas 75205; Office: 1506 Commerce Street, Dallas, Texas, U.S.A.

McGregor, Gordon Roy, O.B.E., D.F.C., F.R.AE.S., Hon. F.C.A.S.I.; Canadian businessman; b. 26 Sept. 1901; ed. St. Andrew's and McGill Univ.
With Bell Telephone Co. of Canada 23-39; served in Royal Canadian Air Force 39-45; Gen. Traffic Manager, Trans-Canada Air Lines (name changed to Air Canada 64) 45-48, Pres. 48-; Board of Man. Montreal Gen. Hospital; Exec. Cttee. Int. Air Transport Asscn.; Order of Orange Nassau (Netherlands), Croix de Guerre (France), Czechoslovak War Cross.
Air Canada, Place Ville Marie, Montreal 2, Canada.
Telephone: 481-8660 (Home); 874-4830 (Office).

McGuigan, His Eminence Cardinal James Charles, D.D., PH.D., LL.D.; Canadian ecclesiastic; b. 26 Nov. 1894; ed. Prince of Wales Coll. and St. Dunstan's Univ., P.E.I., Laval Univ., Quebec, and Catholic Univ. of America.
Ordained 18; Prof. St. Dunstan's Univ. 19; Sec. to Bishop of Charlottetown, P.E.I. 19; to Archbishop of Edmonton 20; Chancellor, Vicar-Gen. and Dean of Edmonton Diocese 22-28; Rector, St. Joseph's Seminary, Edmonton 28; Protonotary Apostolic with title of Monsignor 29; Archbishop of Regina 30; Archbishop of Toronto 34-; Asst. at Pontifical Throne and Roman Count 42-; Cardinal with title of Santa Maria del Popolo Feb. 46; Papal Legate to Marian Congress of Ottawa 47; Gov. St. Augustine's Seminary, Toronto; Dir. St. Francis Xavier Seminary, Toronto; Chancellor Pontifical Inst. of Medieval Studies, Toronto; Chancellor Catholic Church Extension Society of Canada; mem. Sacred Congregations of the Consistory, De Propaganda Fide and of Fabric of St. Peter's.
Archbishop's House, 55 Gould Street, Toronto, Ontario, Canada.

McGuire, Dominic Paul, C.B.E.; Australian diplomatist and writer; b. 3 April 1903; ed. Christian Brothers' Coll., Adelaide, and Univ. of Adelaide.
Former Lecturer in History, Univ. of Adelaide, served Royal Australian Navy 39-45; Adviser, Commonwealth Prime Ministers' Conf., London 51; Del. to UN 53; Minister to Italy 53-58, Ambassador 58-59; Knight Grand Cross of St. Sylvester 59.
Publs. *The Two Men* 32, *The Poetry of Gerald Manley Hopkins* 35, *7.30 Victoria* 35, *Prologue to the Gallows* 35, *Cry Aloud for Murder* 36, *Born to be Hanged* 36, *Burial Service* 37, *W.1* 37, *Restoring All Things* (with J. Fitzsimmons) 38, *Australian Journey* 39, *Spanish Steps* 40, *Westward the Course* 42, *Price of Admiralty* (with F. M. McGuire) 45, *The Three Corners of the World* 48, *Experiment in World Order* 48, *The Australian Theatre* (with B. P. Arnott and F. M. McGuire) 48, *Freedom for the Brave* 49.
136 Mills Terrace, North Adelaide, South Australia.

McGuire, Matthew F.; American judge; ed. Holy Cross Coll., Worcester, Mass., and Boston Univ.
Admitted to Massachusetts Bar 26, private legal practice, Boston; Special Asst. to U.S. Attorney-Gen. 34, 39, Asst. to Attorney-Gen. U.S. 40-41; Chief Judge, U.S. District Court, District of Columbia 62-66; now Senior United States District Judge, etc.
U.S. Court House, Washington, D.C. 2000, U.S.A.
Home: 2701 Connecticut Avenue, N.W., Washington, D.C. 20008, U.S.A.

Machado, Francisco José Vieira, O.B.E.; Portuguese bank official; b. 98; ed. Univ. of Lisbon Faculty of Law.
Member, then Vice-Pres., Admin. Council Banco Nacional Ultramarino 26-34; Under-Sec. of State 34; Minister for Overseas Territories 36-44; Dir. and Pres. Banco Ultramarino Brasileiro 54-61; mem. of Parl. 35-46; Procurator of the Corporative Chamber; Gov. of Banco Nacional Ultramarino; Portuguese, Brazilian, Spanish, British, Belgian and Papal decorations.
Publs. *Grandes Empréstimos de Guerra, Degredo para Africa, Projectos de Decretos, Alguns Discursos proferidos em Africa, Cultura do Arroz em Portugal, Elogio Histórico do Dr. Manual Rodrigues, Os Cem Anos do Banco Nacional Ultramarino, Discursos em Moçambique.*
c/o Banco Nacional Ultramarino, 94 Rua do Comércio, Lisbon, Portugal.

Machado, Luis; Cuban financial officer; b. 25 Sept. 1899; ed. Candler Coll. and Havana Inst.
Delegate to numerous Int. Confs. 19-46, High Commr. of Cuba to New York World's Fair 39; Pres. Nat. Manufacturers Asscn. of Cuba, Dir. of Nat. Safety Council 41; Dir., Inter-American Arbitration Cttee., Inter-

American Intellectual Co-operation Council 42; Exec. Dir., Int. Bank for Reconstruction and Development 46-48, 52-, Gov. for Cuba 49-54, Dir. Int. Finance Corpn. 56-, Dir., Int. Development Asscn. 60-; Pres. Economic Comm. for Latin America 49; Cuban Ambassador to U.S.A. 50-52.

Publs. *La Enmienda Platt-Estudio de su Alcance e Interpretación y Doctrina sobre su Aplicación, Legislación Internacional del Aire, Necesidad de Adoptar Una Política de Comercio Exterior, Ensayo de Economía Cubana, Indice Fiscal Cubano.*

International Bank for Reconstruction and Development, 1818 H Street, N.W., Washington, D.C., U.S.A.

Machavariani, Alexei Davidovich; Soviet composer; b. 1913; ed. Tbilisi Conservatoire.
Chair. Composers' Union of Georgia; Exec. mem. U.S.S.R. Composers' Union; Deputy to Supreme Soviet of U.S.S.R.; Honoured Worker of the Arts of Georgian S.S.R. 50, State Prize 51, People's Artist of the U.S.S.R. 58; Badge of Honour 63, of Lenin 66.
Principal compositions: *Khorumi* (poem for piano) 39, *Mumli Mukhasa* (symphonic suite) 39, *Elegy* (symphonic sketch) 39, *Mother and Son* (opera) 41, *The Bridge* (symphonic suite) 42, Concerto for Piano and Orchestra 44, *Secret of Two Oceans* (symphonic suite) 44, First Symphony 47, *Death of a Hero* (symphonic poem) 49, Concerto for Violin and Orchestra 50, Ten Unaccompanied Choral Pieces 52, *Doluri* (for symphony orchestra) 52, *Doluri* (for unaccompanied violin) 52, *My Country's Day* (oratorio) 53, *Othello* (ballet) 57; incidental music for: *King Lear, Richard III, The Legend of Love*, and for films: *Cradle of the Poet, Mayakovsky*, and others.
Composers' Union of Georgian S.S.R., Rustaveli Prospekt, Tbilisi, U.S.S.R.

McIlraith, Hon. George James, P.C., Q.C., M.P.; Canadian lawyer and politician; b. 08; ed. Osgoode Hall, Toronto.
Member of Parl. 40-; Parl. Asst. to Minister of Reconstruction 45, to Minister of Trade and Commerce 48, to Minister of Defence Production 51; Canadian rep. to UN 46; Minister of Transport 63-64; Pres. of Privy Council and Pres. of Treasury Board 64; Government House Leader 64-, Min. of Public Works 65-; Liberal.
Ministry of Public Works, Ottawa, Canada.

McIlvaine, Robinson, A.B.; American diplomatist; b. 17 July 1913; ed. Harvard Univ.
Commander, U.S. Navy 40-46; Editor-Publisher 46-53; Dep. Asst. Sec. of State and Chair. Caribbean Comm. 53-56; Consul-Gen. Lisbon 56-60, Léopoldville 60-61; Amb. to Dahomey 61-64; Dir. Interdept. Seminar, Washington 64-66; Amb. to Rep. of Guinea 66-.
Department of State, Washington 25, D.C., U.S.A.

McIlwain, Henry, D.SC., PH.D.; British university professor; b. 20 Dec. 1912; ed. King's Coll., Durham Univ. and Queen's Coll., Oxford.
With British Medical Research Council 37-47; Senior Lecturer and Reader in Biochemistry, London Univ. 48-55; Prof. of Biochemistry, Inst. of Psychiatry, London Univ. 55-.
Publs. *Biochemistry and the Central Nervous System* 55, *Chemotherapy and the Central Nervous System* 57, *Practical Neurochemistry* (with R. Rodnight) 62, *Chemical Exploration of the Brain* 63.
73 Court Lane, London, S.E.21, England.
Telephone: 01-693-5334.

MacInnes, Most Rev. Angus Campbell, C.M.G., M.A., D.D.; British ecclesiastic; b. 18 April 1901; ed. Harrow School and Trinity Coll., Cambridge.
Deacon 26; Priest 27; Curate of Peckham 26-28; C.M.S. Missionary, Jerusalem 28-51; Principal, Bishop Gobat School, Jerusalem 30-44; Archdeacon in Palestine and

Transjordan 43-50; Archdeacon in Jerusalem 50-51; Examining Chaplain to Bishop in Jerusalem 43-51; Vicar of St. Michael's, St. Albans 51-54; Rural Dean of St. Albans 53-57; Residential Canon, St. Albans 53-57; Lord Bishop Suffragan of Bedford 53-57; Anglican Archbishop in Jerusalem 57-.
St. George's Close, P.O.B. 18, Jerusalem, Jordan.
Telephone: 2253.

Macintosh, Sir Robert Reynolds, M.A., M.D., F.R.C.S., F.F.A.R.C.S., D.A.; British anaesthetist; b. 17 Oct. 1897; ed. New Zealand and Guy's Hospital.
Professor of Anaesthetics Oxford Univ. 37-65; hon. consultant in Anaesthetics, R.A.F.; Hon. Fellow Pembroke Coll., Oxford, Royal Soc. of Medicine; Hon. D.Sc. (Univ. of Wales), Hon. M.D. (Buenos Aires and Aix-Marseilles); Order of Military Merit (Spain), Order of Liberty (Norway).
Publs. *Essentials of General Anæsthesia, Physics for the Anæsthetist, Local Anæsthesia, Brachial Plexus, Lumbar Puncture and Spinal Analgesia* 50.
Pembroke College, Oxford; Home: 326 Woodstock Road, Oxford, England.
Telephone: Oxford 55471.

McIntyre, H.E. Cardinal James Francis A.; American ecclesiastic; b. 25 June 1886.
Ordained priest 21; Titular Bishop of Cyrene 40; Titular Archbishop of Palto 46; Archbishop of Los Angeles 48-; created Cardinal by Pope Pius XII 53; mem. Sacred Congregations of the Consistory, De Propaganda Fide and of Ceremonies.
Archbishop's Office, 1531 West 9th Street, Los Angeles, Calif., U.S.A.

McIntyre, Sir Laurence Rupert, Kt., C.B.E., M.A.; Australian diplomatist; b. 22 June 1912; ed. Tasmania Univ. and Exeter Coll., Oxford.
Served in London 36, Canberra 40, Washington 42, Canberra (Head of Pacific Division) 47, Singapore 50, Canberra (Asst. Sec.) 51, Singapore (Commr.) 52, London (Minister) 54; Ambassador to Indonesia 57-60, to Japan 60-65; Deputy Sec. Dept. of External Affairs 65-.
Department of External Affairs, Canberra, A.C.T., Australia.

MacIntyre, Malcolm Ames; American executive; b. 28 Jan. 1908; ed. Yale Univ. and Oxford Univ.
Admitted U.S. Bar 34; with Debevoise, Plimpton, Lyons and Gates 48-57; Pres. Chemical Div. Martin Marietta Corpn. 64-; U.S. Air Force 42-46; Under-Sec., U.S.A.F. 57-59; Pres. Eastern Airlines Inc. 59-63; Dir. Schröder Banking Corpn.; Trustee Carnegie Corpn.; Chair. Isochem Inc.; mem. Airways Modernization Board 57-; Mayor, Village of Scarsdale, N.Y. 67-.
60 Mamaroneck Road, Scarsdale, N.Y., U.S.A.

Macintyre, Tan Sri S. Chelvasingam; Malayan lawyer and diplomatist; b. 03; ed. Methodist Boys School, Kuala Lumpur and Trinity Coll., Kandy, Ceylon.
Called to the Bar 27, Advocate and Solicitor, Johore 28-, Personal Legal Adviser to H.H. Sultan of Johore 56-; mem. Batu Pahat Town Council 53-56, Batu Pahat Central Constituency 54-57, Federal Legislative Council 55-57; High Commr. for Fed. of Malaya in India 57-63, for Malaysia 63-64; concurrently in Ceylon 59-64; Ambassador to Nepal 60-64; High Court Judge Sept. 64-; Judge of Fed. Court, Malaysia 68-; Panglima Mangku Negara.
Home: No. 734 Lapangan Terbang, Kuala Lumpur; Office: Federal Court, Kuala Lumpur, Malaysia.
Telephone: 84414 (Office); 21010 (Home).

McIntyre, Thomas James, B.A., LL.B.; American lawyer and politician; b. 20 Feb. 1915; ed. Dartmouth Coll. and Boston Univ. Law School.
Army Service, Second World War; Mayor of Laconia, New Hampshire 49-51; cand. for Congress 54; New

Hampshire State Chair., Sen. Kefauver's campaign for Democratic Pres. nomination 56; Senator from New Hampshire 63-; Democrat.

4917 Rodman Street, N.W., Washington, D.C., U.S.A.

MacIver, Loren; American artist; b. 2 Feb. 1909; ed. Art Students League.

One Man exhibitions, East River Gallery, New York City 38, Pierre Matisse Gallery, New York City 40-44, 49, 56, 61, 66, Museum of Modern Art Travelling Exhbn. 41, Vassar Art Gallery 50, Wellesley Coll. 51, Whitney Museum 53, Dallas Museum of Fine Arts 53 etc.; represented in numerous exhibitions including Fantastic Art, Dada, Surrealism 38, Art in Our Time 39, State Dept. Exhibition in Europe 46, Dunn Int. Exhibition, Tate Gallery, London 63, Venice Biennale 61; First Prize, Corcoran Art Gallery 57; Chicago Art Inst. 61, Univ. of Illinois 62; Ford Foundation Grant 60; mem. Nat. Inst. of Arts and Letters; Purchase Prize, Krannert Art Museum, Univ. of Illinois 63.

61 Perry Street, New York City 14, N.Y., U.S.A.

MacIver, Robert Morrison, M.A., D. PHIL.; American university professor; b. 17 April 1882; ed. Edinburgh and Oxford Univs.

Lecturer in Political Science Aberdeen Univ. 07-15; Prof. Univ. of Toronto 15-27; Prof. Barnard Coll. and Columbia Univ. 27-29; Lieber Prof. of Political Philosophy and Sociology Columbia Univ. 29-50, Emeritus 50-; Special Lecturer in Govt. 50; Dir. City of New York investigation of juvenile delinquency 56-62; Pres. New School for Soc. Research 63-64, Chancellor 65-66; Hon. Litt.D. (Columbia, Harvard, Princeton), Hon. D.Sc. (New School for Soc. Research), Hon. L.H.D. (Yale), Hon. LL.D. (Edinburgh, Toronto).

Publs. *Community* 17, *Elements of Social Science* 21, *The Modern State* 26, *Society, its Structure and Changes* 31, *Social Causation* 42, *The Web of Government* 47, *The Ramparts We Guard* 50, *Democracy and the Economic Challenge* 52, *Academic Freedom in Our Times* 55, *The Pursuit of Happiness* 55, *Life: Its Dimensions and its Bounds* 60, *The Challenge of the Passing Years* 62, *Power Transformed* 64.

Heyhoe Woods, Palisades, New York, U.S.A.

Mack, James S(teven); American retail executive; b. 9 Feb. 1914; ed. William and Mary Coll., Williamsburg, Va., and Harvard Univ.

Joined G. C. Murphy Co. 36, Construction Supervisor 36-38, Real Estate Dept. 38-39, Asst. Store Man. 39-40, Store Man. 40-42, Dist. Store Man. 42-45, Dir. 40, Vice-Pres. (Real Estate and Construction Div.) 45, Vice-Pres. (Finance, Real Estate and Office Management) and Treas. 46-53, Pres. 53-, Chair. of Board, 62-; Dir., Vice-Pres., Treas. Mack Realty Co. (a subsidiary) 46-53, Pres. 53-; official of numerous trade and educational organisations.

Home: 1137 Summitt Street, McKeesport, Pa.; Office: 531 Fifth Avenue, McKeesport, Pa., U.S.A.

McKay, David Oman; American religious leader; b. 8 Sept. 1873; ed. Weber Acad., Utah, Univ. of Utah.

First Assistant General Superintendent, Church-wide Sunday Schools 09-18, Gen. Superintendent 18-34; Pres. European Missions, Church of Jesus Christ of Latter-day Saints, Liverpool 22-24; mem. Council of the Twelve Apostles 06-34, Pres. 50-51; Pres. Church of Jesus Christ of Latter-day Saints 51-, Board of Education 51-, Board of Trustees, Brigham Young Univ. 51-; mem. Council of Twelve Apostles 06-; Director of five corporations; Hon. M.A. (Brigham Young Univ.), Hon. LL.D. (Utah State Agricultural Coll.), Hon. Dr. Hum. (Brigham Young Univ., Weber State Coll.), Hon. D.Lit. (Utah, Temple Univs.); many awards.

Publs. *Ancient Apostles* 18, *Gospel Ideals* 53, *Cherished*

Experiences 55, *Home Memories* 56, *Pathways to Happiness* 57, *Secrets of a Happy Life* 60, *Treasures of Life* 62, *Man May Know For Himself* 67; numerous lesson manuals for the Church of Jesus Christ of Latter-day Saints.

47 East South Temple, Salt Lake City, Utah, U.S.A.

Mackay, Ian Keith, C.M.G.; New Zealand broadcasting executive; b. 19 Oct. 1909; ed. Nelson Coll., New Zealand.

Broadcasting Station Manager, New Zealand 39-43; Senior Exec., Commercial Div., New Zealand Broadcasting Commission 44-50; Production Man., Macquarie Network, Australia 50-61; Dir.-Gen. Nigerian Broadcasting Corpn. 61-64, Adviser, Board of Govs. 63-65; Public Relations Officer, Dept. of Information, Papua, New Guinea 66-; mem. Royal Soc. of Literature, Soc. of Authors.

Publs. *Broadcasting in New Zealand* 53, *Broadcasting in Australia* 57, *Macquarie—the Story of a Network* 60, *Broadcasting in Nigeria* 64, and other articles on broadcasting.

32 Norfolk Street, Killara, Sydney, N.S.W., Australia; and Dept. Information and Extension Services, Konedobu, Papua, New Guinea.

Telephone: 4681 (Office).

Mackay, John Alexander, B.D., M.A., LITT.D.; American clergyman and educationist; b. 17 May 1889; ed. Aberdeen Univ., Princeton Theological Seminary, Univs. of Lima, Madrid and Bonn.

Principal, Anglo-Peruvian Coll., Lima 16-25; Prof. of Philosophy, Nat. Univ. of Peru 25; writer and lecturer, South American Fed. of Y.M.C.A.s 26-32; Sec. Board of Foreign Missions of the Presbyterian Church in the U.S.A. 32-36; Pres. Princeton Theological Seminary 36-59; Pres. Board of Foreign Missions, Presbyterian Church, U.S.A. 45-51; mem. Provisional Cttee. World Council of Churches 46-48, Central Cttee. 48-54; Chair. Int. Missionary Council 47-58, Hon. Chair. 59-61; Pres. World Presbyterian Alliance 54-59; f. theological quarterly *Theology Today*, Editor 44-51, Chair. Editorial Council 51-59; mem. Advisory Council, Dept. of Philosophy, Princeton Univ. 41-59; mem. American Asscn. of Theological Schools, Pres. 48-50; Pres. Emer. Princeton Theological Seminary; Adjunct Prof. American Univ. of Washington 61-64; Hon. D.D. (Princeton, Aberdeen, Debrecen, Presbyterian Coll. Montreal, Serampore Coll.), Hon. LL.D. (Ohio Wesleyan Univ., Albright Coll., Coll. of Wooster, Lincoln Univ.), Hon. L.H.D. (Boston Univ., Lafayette Coll.); Hon. Fellow Stanford Univ.).

Publs. *Mas yo os Digo* 27, *El Sentido de la Vida* 31, *The Other Spanish Christ* 32, *That Other America* 35, *A Preface to Christian Theology* 41, *Heritage and Destiny* 43, *Christianity on the Frontier* 50, *God's Order* 53, *The Presbyterian Way of Life* 60, *His Life and Our Life* 64, *Ecumenics* 64.

3709 Chevy Chase Lake Drive, Chevy Chase 15, Maryland, U.S.A.

Telephone: OL6-6263.

MacKay, Robert Alexander, PH.D.; Canadian university professor and diplomatist; b. 2 Jan. 1894; ed. Univ. of Toronto and Princeton Univ.

Served army 16-19; Lecturer in Politics, Princeton Univ. 24-25; Asst. Prof. of Govt., Cornell Univ. 25-27; Prof. of Govt. and Political Science, Dalhousie Univ. 27-47; mem. Royal Comm. on Dominion-Provincial Relations 37-40; Special Asst. to Under-Sec. of State for External Affairs 43-46, Asst. Under-Sec. 52-54, Deputy Under-Sec. 54; Permanent Rep. to U.N. 55-58; Ambassador to Norway, and to Iceland 58-61; Visiting Prof. Carleton Univ. Ottawa 61-; Pres. Canadian Political Science Asscn. 43-44; Fellow Royal Society of Canada; mem. Canada-U.S. Permanent

Joint Board of Defence 50-55; Hon. LL.D. (Dalhousie Univ.).
Publs. *The Unreformed Senate of Canada* 26 (2nd edn. 63), *Canada Looks Abroad* 38, *Newfoundland Studies* 48.
c/o Ministry for External Affairs, Ottawa, Ont., Canada.

Mackehenie y de la Fuente, Carlos Antonio Ramón; Peruvian diplomatist; b. 1904; ed. in England.
Served Monaco, London, Washington, Paris 31-53; Peruvian Minister to Sweden 53-57; Perm. Rep. to UN 57-; many foreign decorations.
Permanent Mission of Peru to the United Nations, 301 East 47th Street, New York 17, N.Y., U.S.A.

McKeithen, John Julian, B.S., LL.B.; American politician; b. 18; ed. High Point (N. Carolina) Coll., and Louisiana State Univ.
State Rep. 48-52; Public Service Commr. 54-64; Gov. of Louisiana 64-; mem. Louisiana and American Bar Asscn.; mem. Board of Dirs. Caldwell Bank and Trust Co., and Corey Gin Co. Inc.; Democrat.
Governor's Mansion, Baton Rouge, Louisiana 70802; and Governor's Office, State Capitol, Baton Rouge, La. 70804, U.S.A.
Telephone: 389-5281 (Office); 342-5252 (Mansion).

McKell, Rt. Hon. Sir William John, P.C., G.C.M.G., Q.C.; Australian politician; b. 26 Sept. 1891; ed. Public School, Surry Hills, Sydney.
Apprenticed as boilermaker, Morts' Dock and Engineering Co.; Financial Sec. Boilermakers' Union; mem. Legislative Assembly N.S.W. 17, Minister of Justice 20-22, 25-27; Asst. Treas. 25-27; Barrister Supreme Court N.S.W. 25; Financial Mission London, New York 27; Minister of Justice 31-32; Leader of the Opposition N.S.W. 39-41, Premier and Treas. 41-47; Gov.-Gen. and C.-in-C. Australia 47-53; mem. Malayan Constitutional Comm. 56-57; Hon. LL.D. (Sydney).
Goulburn, N.S.W., Australia.

McKelway, Benjamin Mosby; American newspaperman; b. 2 Oct. 1895; ed. Va. Polytechnic Inst. and George Washington Univ.
Reporter, *Washington Times* 16; Editorial Writer and News Editor, *New Britain* (Conn.) *Herald* 19-20; successively reporter, City Editor, News Editor, Man. Editor, Assoc. Editor, *Washington Star* 21-46, Editor 46-63, Editorial Chair. 63; Dir. Evening Star Newspaper Co.; fmr. Pres. Assoc. Press; fmr. Pres. American Soc. of Newspaper Editors; Dir. Evening Star Broadcasting Co.; Trustee, George Washington Univ. (D.C.) Public Library, Nat. Geographic Society, Library of Congress Trust Fund Board.
4920 Palisade Lane, N.W., Washington 16, D.C., U.S.A.

McKenna, Hon. Nicholas, LL.B., F.A.S.A.; Australian barrister and accountant; b. 9 Sept. 1895; ed. Univ. of Melbourne.
On staff of Commonwealth Audit Office 12-24; Accountant, Townsville, Queensland 24-25, Melbourne, Victoria 26-27; Barrister and Solicitor, Melbourne 28-29, Hobart, Tasmania 29-47; Senator Rep. Tasmania in Federal Parl. 44-; Minister for Health and Social Services in Chifley Labour Commonwealth Govt. 46-49; Leader of Labour Party in the Senate 51-66.
18 Elizabeth Street, Hobart, Tasmania; and Parliament House, Canberra, A.C.T., Australia.

McKenna, Siobhán; Irish actress; b. 24 May 1923; ed. St. Louis Convent, Monaghan and Galway Univ.
Semi-professional appearances at An Taibhdearc Theatre, Galway 40-43; Abbey Theatre, Dublin 44-47; first London appearance in *The White Steed*, Embassy 47.
Plays include *Fading Mansions*, Duchess 49, *Ghosts*, Embassy, *Héloïse*, Duke of York's; Stratford-on-Avon 52; *Playboy of the Western World*, Edinburgh and Paris Festivals, *Saint Joan*, Arts 54, St. Martin's 55, *The Chalk Garden*, New York 55, *Saint Joan*, New York

56, *The Rope Dancers*, New York 57; Shakespearean seasons at Stratford, Ontario, and Cambridge Drama Festival; *Captain Brassbound's Conversion*, Philadelphia 61, *St. Joan of the Stockyards*, Dublin Festival 61, London 64, *Play with a Tiger* 62, *Laurette* 64, *The Cavern* (Anouilh) 65, *Juno and the Paycock* 66; films include *Hungry Hill*, *Daughter of Darkness*, *The Lost People*, *The Adventurers*, *King of Kings*, *Playboy of the Western World*, *Dr. Zhivago*.
c/o M.C.A., 598 Madison Avenue, New York, U.S.A.

McKenzie, Sir Alexander, K.B.E.; New Zealand businessman and politician; b. 26 Oct. 1896; ed. Southland Boys' High School.
Began career as farmer; served army 14-18 war; with The Govt. Life Insurance, Invercargill; joined N.Z. Forest Products Ltd. 22, which he helped establish in N.Z., Australia and Great Britain, Business Man. for N.Z. 29; founded own business 32-; a Dir. of 15 companies; mem. N.Z. Nat. Party, fmr. Chair. Auckland Div. of Party; Pres. N.Z. National Party 51-62.
54 Wallace Street, Herne Bay, Auckland, New Zealand.

Mackenzie, Bruce Roy; D.S.O., D.F.C.; Kenyan politician and farmer; b. 20; ed. Hilton Coll., Natal, and Agricultural Coll.
Settled in Kenya 46; fmr. mem. New Kenya Party; Minister of Agriculture 59-61; mem. Kenya African National Union (KANU) 61-; Minister of Agriculture and Animal Husbandry 62-.
P.O. Box 30028, Nairobi, Kenya.

Mackenzie, Chalmers Jack, C.M.G., M.C., B.E., M.C.E., D.ENG., D.SC., LL.D., D.C.L., F.R.S.C., F.R.S.; Canadian engineer; b. 10 July 1888; ed. Dalhousie and Harvard Univs.
Member engineering firm Maxwell & Mackenzie 12-16; served with Canadian Expeditionary Force 16-18; Prof. of Civil Engineering Saskatchewan Univ. 18-39, Dean of Engineering 21-39; Acting Pres. Nat. Research Council of Canada 39-44, Pres. 44-52; Pres. Atomic Energy of Canada Ltd. 52-53, Pres. Atomic Energy Control Board 48-61; Chancellor Carleton Univ., Ottawa 54-; consultant numerous engineering and scientific projects; many hon. degrees; U.S. Medal of Merit, Chevalier Légion d'Honneur, Kelvin Medal 53, R. B. Bennett Empire Prize 54.
210 Buena Vista Road, Rockliffe Park, Ottawa, Ont., Canada.

Mackenzie, Sir Compton, Kt., O.B.E., LL.D., F.R.S.L.; British novelist; b. 17 Jan. 1883; ed. St. Paul's School and Magdalen Coll. Oxford.
Lord Rector, Glasgow Univ. 31-34; Literary Critic to *Daily Mail* 31-35; Founded *The Gramophone;* served with Royal Naval Div. at Gallipoli; Capt. Royal Marines 15; Military Control Officer, Athens 16; Dir. Aegean Intelligence Service 17; Pres. Wexford Festival; Gov.-Gen. Royal Stuart Soc.; Patron, Poetry Soc.; Scottish Nationalist; Hon. R.S.A.; Chevalier Legion of Honour and of Redeemer; Officer White Eagle.
Publs. include: Plays: *The Gentleman in Grey* 07, *Carnival* 12, *Columbine* 20; other works: *Sinister Street* 13-14, *Guy and Pauline* 15, *Sylvia Scarlett* 15 (filmed), *Poor Relations* 19, *Rich Relatives* 21, *The Seven Ages of Woman* 22, *The Parson's Progress* 23, *Vestal Fire* 27, *Extraordinary Women* 29, *Gallipoli* 29, *Athenian Memories* 31, *Water on the Brain* 33, *The Darkening Green*, *Marathon and Salamis* 34, *The Four Winds of Love: The East Wind*, *The South Wind* 37, *The West Wind* 40, *The North Wind* 44-45, *The Red Tapeworm* 41, *Mr. Roosevelt* 44, *Dr. Benes* 46, *Whisky Galore* 47 (filmed), *Hunting the Fairies* 49, *Eastern Epic* (Vol. I) 51, *Echoes* 53, *Thin Ice* 56, *Sublime Tobacco*, *Rockets Galore* 57 (filmed), *The Lunatic Republic* 58, *Greece in my life*, *Cat's Company*, *Mezzotint* 61, *On Moral Courage* 62, *My Life and Times*, *First*

Octave (1883-1891), Second Octave (1892-1900) 63, Paradise for Sale 63, Third Octave (1900-1907) 64, Fourth Octave (1907-1915) 65, Fifth Octave (1915-1923) 66, Sixth Octave 66, Paper Lives 67, Seventh Octave 68.
31 Drummond Place, Edinburgh 3, Scotland, and Pradelles, Les Arques, par Cazals, Lot, France.

Mackenzie, Maxwell Weir, C.M.G., B.COM.; Canadian business executive; b. 30 June 1907; ed. Trinity Coll. School, McGill Univ.
Joined McDonald, Currie & Co., Chartered Accountants, Montreal, and admitted to Society of Chartered Accountants of Prov. of Quebec 29; became partner in firm 35; called to Foreign Exchange Control Board and transferred to Wartime Prices and Trade Board 42, apptd. Deputy Chair. of Board 43; returned to McDonald, Currie & Co. 44; apptd. mem. of Royal Comm. on Taxation of Annuities and Family Corpns. 44; Deputy Minister of Trade and Commerce 45-51; Deputy Minister of Defence Production 51-52; Exec. Vice-Pres. Canadian Chemical & Cellulose Co. Ltd. 52-54; Pres. Canadian Chemical & Cellulose Co. Ltd. 54-59, Chemcell Ltd. 59-63; Chair. Finance Cttee., Chemcell Ltd. and Columbia Cellulose Co. Ltd. 67-; Chair. Royal Comm. on Security 66-; Dir. The Canadian Imperial Bank of Commerce 55-, Celanese Corpn. of America 59-67, The Royal Trust Co. 60-67, Canron Ltd. 61-, Imperial Life Assurance Co. of Canada 62-, RCA Victor Co. Ltd. 63-, Int. Milling Co. Inc. 64-; mem. Econ. Council of Canada 63-.
P.O. Box 128, Como, P.Q., Canada.

MacKenzie, Norman Archibald MacRae, C.M.G., M.M. and Bar, Q.C., B.A., LL.B., LL.M., LL.D., D.C.L., D.SC.SOC., D.LITT., F.R.S.C.; Canadian lawyer and public servant; b. 5 Jan. 1894; ed. Pictou Academy, Dalhousie University, Harvard, St. John's College, Cambridge and Gray's Inn.
Served with Canadian Infantry 14-19; called to Bar N.S. 26; Legal Adviser I.L.O. Geneva 25-27; Assoc. Prof. of Law Univ. of Toronto 27-33, Prof. of Int. and Canadian Const. Law 33-40; Pres. Univ. of New Brunswick 40-44; Pres. Univ. of British Columbia 44-62, Pres. Emer. 62-; Chair. War-time Information Board Canada 43-45, N.B. Reconstruction Comm. 41-44, Conciliatory Boards in Labour Disputes 37-42; Trustee Carnegie Foundation for Advancement of Teaching 51-, Chair. Board of Trustees 58-59; Chair. Doukhobor Consultative Cttee. 50-; mem. Canada Council 57-, Canadian Inst. Int. Affairs, American Soc. Int. Law, etc.; Pres. Canadian Nat. Comm. for UNESCO 57-60; Dir. Bank of Nova Scotia 60-; Pres. Canadian Centenary Council 62-; Hon. LL.D. (Mt. Allison, N.B., Toronto, Ottawa, Bristol, Alberta, Glasgow, Dalhousie and St. Francis Xavier, McGill, Sydney, Rochester, California, Alaska, British Columbia, Royal Mil. Coll. of Canada); Hon. D.C.L. (Whitman Coll., Saskatchewan Univ.); Hon. D.Sc.Soc. (Laval); Hon. D.Litt. (Memorial Univ. of Newfoundland); Hon. LL.D. (Cambridge); Hon. Fellow St. John's Coll. (Cambridge); mem. Senate of Canada 66.
Publs. Legal Status of Aliens in Pacific Countries 37, Canada and the Law of Nations (with L. H. Laing) 38, Canada in World Affairs (with others) 41, Challenge to Education 53, First Principles 54, A Canadian View of Territorial Seas and Fisheries (with Jacob Austin), The Work of the Universities (in Canadian Education—Today) 56.
The Senate, Ottawa; also 4509 West 4th Avenue, Vancouver 8, B.C., Canada.
Telephone: 224-7800 (Home); 992-9966 (Office).

McKeown, Lieut.-Gen. Sean; Irish army officer; b. 3 June 1910; ed. Cadet School, Irish Military Coll.
Commissioned 31; Infantry, and Instructor, Irish Mil. Coll. 31-39; Commdr. Infantry Battalion 39-45; Commandant Cadet School, Irish Mil. Coll. 45-53; Western Command Headquarters 53-57; Commandant, Irish Mil. Coll. 57-60; Army Chief of Staff, Dublin 60-; Commdr. U.N. Forces in the Congo 61-62.
Army H.Q., Parkgate, Dublin 7, Ireland.
Telephone: Dublin 771881.

Mackerras, Charles; British conductor; b. 17 Nov. 1925; ed. Sydney Grammar School, N.S.W. Conservatoire, and Prague Acad. of Music.
Principal Oboist Sydney Symphony Orchestra 45-47; Conductor Sadler's Wells 48-54, B.B.C. Concert Orchestra 54-56; guest conductor in Europe, Canada, Australia, S. Africa 56-66, guest opera conductor at Covent Garden, Sadler's Wells, Berlin State Opera, Hamburg State Opera, etc. 56-66; First Conductor, Hamburg State Opera 66-; musical articles in various magazines. Arrangements: Ballets: Pineapple Poll 51, Lady and the Fool 54, Melbourne Cup 65.
Essex House, 4 The Green, Southgate, London, N.14, England.
Telephone: 01-886-2823.

McKie, Sir William Neil, Kt., M.V.O., M.A., D.MUS.; British musician; b. 22 May 1901; ed. Melbourne Grammar School, Royal Coll. of Music, London and Worcester Coll., Oxford.
Director of Music Clifton Coll., Bristol 26-30; City Organist Melbourne 31-38; Organist, Magdalen Coll., Oxford 38-41; Organist and Master of Choristers Westminster Abbey 41-63; war service R.A.F. 41-45; Dir. of Music, Coronation of Queen Elizabeth II 53; Hon. Sec. Royal Coll. of Organists 63-67; Hon. Fellow Worcester Coll., Oxford 54-; Hon. D.Mus. Univ. of Melbourne; Commdr. with Star Order of St. Olav.
Sugar Hill, Groombridge, Sussex, England.

McKim, Robert James; American businessman; b. 21 Aug. 1895; ed. Tulane Univ.
President, Steward Dry Goods Co., Louisville 30-43; Pres. and Dir. Associated Dry Goods Corpn., New York City 43-59, Chair. 59-67, Chair. Exec. Cttee. and Finance Cttee. 67-; Dir. U.S. Rubber Co., Chemical Bank of N.Y.
417 Fifth Avenue, New York City 16, N.Y., U.S.A.

McKinney, Robert Moody, B.A.; American newspaper publisher and diplomatist; b. 28 Aug. 1910; ed. Univ. of Oklahoma.
Editor and Publisher, The New Mexican; Pres. The New Mexican, Inc.; Chair. New Mexico Development Comm. 49-51; Asst. Sec. U.S. Dept. of Interior 51-52; Chair. Panel to report to Congress on impact of peaceful uses of atomic energy 55-56; Permanent U.S. Rep. to Int. Atomic Energy Agency, Vienna 57-58; U.S. Rep. to 2nd Int. Conf. on Peaceful Uses of Atomic Energy 58; rapporteur, Cttee. on Scientific and Technical Cooperation, Atlantic Congress, London 59; apptd. by Joint Cttee. of U.S. Congress to review int. atomic policies and programmes of U.S.A. 59-60; Ambassador to Switzerland 61-63; Exec. Officer, Presidential Task Force on Int. Investments 63-64; Vice-Chair. Advisory Cttee. on Financial Investments 66; war service U.S. Navy 42-45; Pres. Robert Moody Foundation; Board of Govs. and Vice-Chair. St. John's Coll., New Mexico, Annapolis, Santa Fé; Dir. Martin Marietta Corpn., Copper Range Co., General Public Service Corpn., Trans World Airlines Inc.; Univ. of Okla. Research Inst.; Democrat.
Publs. Hymn to Wreckage: A Picaresque Interpretation of History 47, The Scientific Foundation for European Integration, Reappraising the European Energy Problem, On Increasing the Effectiveness of Western Science and Technology, all 59, The Red Challenge to Technological Renewal 60.
202 East Mercy Street, Santa Fé, New Mexico 87501, U.S.A.
Telephone: 983-3303.

Mackintosh, William Archibald, c.c., c.m.g., ph.d., LL.D., D.C.L., F.R.S.C.; Canadian university professor; b. 21 May 1895; ed. St. Andrew's Coll., Toronto and Queen's and Harvard Univs.
Lecturer in Economics, Brandon Coll. 17-19; Asst. Prof. of Economics, Queen's Univ. 20-23, Assoc. Prof. 23-25, Prof. 25-27, Sir John A. Macdonald Prof. and Head of Dept. 27-51, Vice-Chancellor and Principal 51-61, Vice-Chancellor 61-65; Dir. School of Commerce and Administration 23-51, Dean Faculty of Arts 47-51; Asst. Advisory Board of Tariff and Taxation 26-29; Dir. of Research, Canadian Pioneer Problems Cttee. 29-34; mem. Nat. Employment Comm. 36; Research Asst. Royal Comm. on Dominion-Provincial Relations 38-39; on leave from Queen's Univ. to hold advisory posts in Depts. of Finance and Reconstruction 39-46; Acting Deputy Minister of Finance 45; Pres. Royal Society of Canada 56-57; mem. Comm. on Organisation of Govt. in Ontario 58-59, Royal Comm. on Banking and Finance 61-64; Dir. Bank of Canada 64-; Canada Council Medal 66, Innis-Gerin Medal, Royal Society of Canada 67.
Publs. *Agricultural Co-operation in Western Canada* 24, *Statistical Contributions to Canadian Economic History* (2 vols.) 29, *Economic Background of Dominion-Provincial Relations* 39; Joint Editor *Canadian Frontiers of Settlement* (9 vols.) 34-36 (Author of 2 vols. *Prairie Settlement* and *Economic Problems of Prairie Provinces*).
Alwington Place, Kingston, Ontario, Canada.

McKissick, Floyd Bixler, A.B., LL.B.; American lawyer; b. 9 March 1922; ed. North Carolina Coll.
Lawyer, Durham, North Carolina; Nat. Chair. Congress of Racial Equality (CORE) 63-66, Nat. Dir. 66-.
Congress of Racial Equality, Dayton, Ohio, U.S.A.
Telephone: 212-281-9650.

McKnight, Allan Douglas, c.b.e., LL.B.; Australian administrator; b. 14 Jan. 1918; ed. Fort Street High School and Univ. of Sydney.
Assistant Sec. to Cabinet 51-55; Sec. Dept. of Army 55-58; Exec. Comm. Australian Atomic Energy Comm. 58-64; Gov. for Australia, Board of Govs., Int. Atomic Energy Agency (I.A.E.A.) 59-64, Chair. I.A.E.A. Board of Govs. 61; European Rep. of Australian Atomic Energy Comm. 62-64; Inspector Gen., Int. Atomic Energy Agency, Vienna 64-.
International Atomic Energy Agency, Kaerntnerring, Vienna 1, Austria.
Telephone: 52-45-25, extension 133/134.

McLachlan, Donald Harvey, o.b.e., m.a.; British journalist and newspaper editor; b. 25 Sept. 1908; ed. City of London School, Magdalen Coll., Oxford.
Laming Fellow Queen's Coll., Oxford 32-33; editorial staff of *The Times* 33-36; Asst. Master, Winchester Coll. 36-38; Ed. *The Times Educational Supplement* 38-40; Naval Intelligence 40-45; returned to *The Times* 48-49; Asst. Ed. (Foreign) *The Economist* 47-54; Deputy Ed. *Daily Telegraph* 54-60; Editor *Sunday Telegraph* 61-66.
Publ. *Room 39: Naval Intelligence in Action 1939-45* 68.
65 Roebuck House, London, S.W.1; and Coneycroft, Selbourne, Hants., England.
Telephone: Selbourne 224.

McLain, Marvin Leland, B.S.; American government official; b. 1 Oct. 1906; ed. Iowa State Coll.
Engaged in hardware and farm equipment business 28-30; farmer and landowner 30-52; Chair. Agricultural Adjustment Admin., Poweshiek County 34-44; Pres. and Dir. Malcolm Co-operative Elevator 45-52; Dir. Iowa Farm Bureau Fed. 46-52; Dir. and Vice-Chair. Iowa Dairy Ind. Comm. 44-50; Chair. Iowa ASC State Cttee. 53; Dir. Grain Division U.S. Dept. of Agriculture 53-56, Asst. Sec. of Agriculture 56-60; Asst. Legislature Dir. American Farm Bureau 60-.
4433 31st Street South, Apt. 103, Arlington 6, Va., U.S.A.

McLaren, Norman; Canadian (b. Scotland) film director; b. 11 April 1914; ed. Glasgow School of Art.
With G.P.O. Film Unit 37-39; moved to New York City 39, later produced independently, and for Guggenheim Museum of Non-Objective Art, several abstract colour films; Dir. of Experimental Films, Nat. Film Board of Canada 41-; assignment in China for UNESCO 49-50, in India for UNESCO 52-53; numerous awards including Canada Council Medal 66.
Films include: *Around is Around, Begone Dull Care, Blinkity-Blank, Canon, A Chairy Tale, Christmas Cracker, Dots, Fiddle-De-Dee, Hen Hop, A Little Phantasy on a 19th Century Painting, Loops, Neighbours, New York Lightboard Record, Now is the Time, Opening Speech, Pen Point Percussion, A Phantasy, Rythmetic, Le Merle, Lines-Horizontal, Lines-Vertical Horizontal, Serenal, Short and Suite.*
Publ. *Six Musical Forms* (illustrated).
National Film Board, Box 6100, Montreal 3; Home: Apt. 305, 3590 Ridgewood Avenue, Montreal 26, Canada.
Telephone: 747-5511, Ext. 338 (Office); 731-6210 (Home).

McLaughlin, Donald Hamilton, B.S., A.M., PH.D.; American mining geologist and engineer; b. 15 Dec. 1891; ed. Calif. and Harvard Univs.
Chief Geologist, Cerro de Pasco Copper Corpn. 19-25; Prof. of Mining Geology, Harvard Univ. 25-41; Dean, Coll. of Engineering, Univ. of Calif. 41-43; Vice-Pres. and Gen. Man. Cerro de Pasco Corpn. 43-45; Pres. Homestake Mining Co. 45-61, Chair. 61-; Dir. Homestake Mining Co., San Luis Mining Co., Int. Nickel Co. of Canada; Advisory Dir. Wells Fargo Bank (of San Francisco), Western Air Lines Inc.; Past Pres. American Inst. of Mining and Metallurgical Engineers 50, Soc. of Econ. Geologists, and Mining and Metallurgical Soc. of America 53; mem. Nat. Science Board 50-60; Regent, Univ. of Calif. 51-66; Fellow American Acad. of Arts and Sciences, Geographical Soc. of America; mem. Nat. Science Foundation 50-60; Monell Medal and Prize, Columbia Univ.; Hon. Dr. Eng. (Mich. Inst. of Mining and Technology, S. Dakota Inst. of Mining and Technology, Montana School of Mines, and Colorado School of Mines); LL.D. Univ. of California (Berkeley).
Office: Homestake Mining Co., 650 California Street, San Francisco, Calif., Home: 1450 Hawthorne Terrace, Berkeley, Calif., U.S.A.
Telephone: 981-8150 (Office); 415-848-0699 (Home).

MacLean, Commdr. Andrew Dyas; Canadian journalist; b. 96; ed. Royal Naval Coll.
Member staff *Toronto Daily News* 19; Chair. Hugh C. MacLean Publications Ltd.
Publs. *British Flags on Land and Sea, R. B. Bennett: Prime Minister of Canada.*
81 Dunvegan Road, Toronto, Canada.

Maclean, Major Sir Charles Hector Fitzroy, Bt., K.B.E.; Scottish army officer and scout; b. 5 May 1916.
Served Scots Guards; Boy Scouts Asscn., Chief Commr. for Scotland 54-59, Chief Scout, British Commonwealth and Empire 59-; Lord Lieutenant for Argyllshire 54-; Chief of Clan Maclean.
Duart Castle, Isle of Mull, Scotland.

Maclean, Sir Fitzroy, Bart., C.B.E., M.P.; British politician; b. 11 March 1911; ed. Eton and Cambridge Univ.
Entered Diplomatic Service 33; served Paris 34-37, Moscow 37-39; enlisted in Cameron Highlanders 41; joined 1st Special Air Service Regiment 42; Captain 42, Lt.-Col. 43, Brigadier 43; Commdr. British Military Mission to Yugoslav Partisans 43-45; Conservative M.P. for Lancaster Div. 41-59, for Bute and N. Ayr 59-; Parl. Under-Sec. of State and Financial Sec. War Office 54-57; Chair. Great Britain-U.S.S.R. Asscn. 59-; Croix

de Guerre, Order of Kutuzov (U.S.S.R.), Partisan Star 1st Class.

Publs. *Eastern Approaches* 49, *Disputed Barricade* 57, *A Person from England* 58, *Back to Bokhara* 59.

Strachur House, Argyll, Scotland.

MacLean, Wing Commdr. J. Angus, D.F.C., B.SC., C.D., LL.D., M.P., P.C.; Canadian farmer and politician; b. 15 May 1914; ed. local schools in P.E.I., Mount Allison Acad., Summerside High School, Univ. of British Columbia and Mount Allison Univ.

Served with R.C.A.F. 39-47; candidate Fed. Elections 45 and 49; elected to House of Commons at by-election June 51, re-elected 53, 57, 58, 62, 63 and 65; Minister of Fisheries June 57-63; Pres. Royal Air Forces Escaping Soc. (Canadian Branch); Progressive Conservative.

287 Clemow Avenue, Ottawa 1; Home: Belle Creek R.R.3, Prince Edward Island, Canada.

Telephone: 992-4935 (Business); Murray River 107-3 (Home).

McLean, Robert, LITT.B.; American newspaper proprietor; b. 1 Oct. 1891; ed. Princeton Univ.

Publisher and Chair. Philadelphia *Bulletin* Co.; Dir. Associated Press 24-, First Vice-Pres. 36-37, Pres. 38-57, Chair. 59-; Chair. Santa Barbara News Press 64-; Hon. Litt.D.; Hon. LL.D.; Hon. L.H.D.

Bulletin Building, Philadelphia, Pa., U.S.A.

McLean, William Flavelle; Canadian business executive; b. 16; ed. Univ. of Toronto.

Royal Canadian Air Force 42-46; Canada Packers 46-, Dir. 50-, Vice-Pres. and mem. Executive Cttee. 52-54, Pres. 54-; Dir. Canadian Imperial Bank of Commerce, Canadian Gen. Electric Co. Ltd.

Canada Packers Ltd., 95 St. Clair Avenue West, Toronto 7, Canada.

McLeay, The Hon. Sir John, K.C.M.G., M.M., M.P.; Australian politician; b. 19 Nov. 1893.

Fmr. Mem. House of Assembly, South Australia; Lord Mayor of City of Adelaide and Mayor of City of Unley; Fed. Mem. for Boothby, S. Australia 49-66; Speaker, House of Representatives Aug. 56-67; mem. Liberal Party; former mem. Council of Govs., Adelaide Univ. and Scotch Coll., Adelaide.

188 Cross Road, Malvern, South Australia.

MacLeish, Archibald, B.A., LL.B., M.A., LITT.D., D.C.L., LL.D., L.H.D.; American poet; b. 7 May 1892; ed. Yale and Harvard Univs.

Pulitzer Poetry Prize 32 and 53; Librarian of Congress 39-44; Dir. Office of Facts and Figures 41-42; Asst. Dir. Office of War Information 42; Asst. Sec. of State 44-45, resgnd.; Chair. U.S. Del. UNESCO 45; Dep. Chair. U.S. Del. UNESCO 46; U.S. mem. Exec. Board UNESCO 46-47; Boylston Prof. Harvard Univ. 49-62; Simpson Lecturer, Amherst Coll. 64-67; Pres. American Acad. of Arts and Letters 53-56; Pulitzer Drama Prize for *J.B.* 58; Commdr. Legion of Honour (France); Commdr. Order of The Sun of Peru.

Publs. *The Happy Marriage* 24, *The Pot of Earth* 25, *Nobodaddy* 25, *Streets in the Moon* 26, *The Hamlet of A. MacLeish* 28, *New Found Land* 30, *Conquistador* 32, *Union Pacific* (a Ballet) 34, *Panic* (a play) 35, *Public Speech* 36, *The Fall of the City* (radio verse play) 37, *The Land of the Free* 38, *Air Raid* (radio verse play) 38, *America Was Promises* (verse) 39, *The Irresponsibles* 40, *The American Cause* 40, *A Time to Speak* 41, *A Time to Act* 43, *The American Story* (broadcasts) 44, *Act Five and other Poems* 48, *Freedom is the Right to Choose* 51, *Collected Poems* 52, *This Music Crept By Me Upon the Waters* (verse play) 53, *Songs for Eve* 54, *J.B.* (play) 58, *Poetry and Experience* (prose) 61, *The Eleanor Roosevelt Story* 65 (film 66), *Herakles* (verse play) 67, *A Continuing Journey* 67.

Conway, Mass., U.S.A.

Telephone: 413-369-4338.

Maclennan, Sir Ian Morrison Ross, K.C.M.G.; British diplomatist; b. 30 Oct. 1909; ed. Hymers Coll. Hull and Worcester Coll., Oxford.

Colonial Office 33-37, Dominions Office 37; U.K. High Comm. in Ottawa 38, Pretoria 45; U.K. High Commr. S. Rhodesia 51-53, Fed. of Rhodesia and Nyasaland 53-55, Ghana 57-59; Ambassador to Republic of Ireland 60-64; High Commr. in New Zealand 64-.

British High Commission, P.O. Box 1812, Wellington, New Zealand.

McLennan, Sir Ian Munro, K.B.E., B.E.E.; Australian engineer; b. 30 Nov. 1909; ed. Scotch Coll., Melbourne and Melbourne Univ.

Assistant Gen. Man. Broken Hill Pty. Co. Ltd. 47-50, Gen. Man. 50-56, Dir. 53-, Senior Gen. Man. 56-59, Chief Gen. Man. 59-67, Man. Dir. 67-; Chair. Joint War Production Cttee.; Councillor, Australian Mineral Devt. Laboratories (Chair. 59-67), Australasian Inst. of Mining and Metallurgy (Pres. 51, 57); mem. and Dep. Chair. Immigration Planning Council 49-67; Australasian Inst. of Mining and Metallurgy Medal 59, Inst. of Production Engineers' James N. Kirby Award 64.

Office: 500 Bourke Street, Melbourne; Home: 160 Whitehorse Road, Balwyn, Vic., Australia.

Telephone: 60-0701 (Office); 80-4398 (Home).

MacLeod, Rt. Hon. Iain Norman, P.C., M.P.; British politician; b. 11 Nov. 1913; ed. Gonville and Caius Coll. Cambridge.

Served 39-45 war; joined Conservative Parl. Secretariat 46, Head Home Affairs Research Dept. of Conservative Party 48-50; M.P. for Enfield West 50-; Minister of Health 52-55, of Labour and Nat. Service 55-59; Sec. of State for the Colonies 59-61; Chancellor of the Duchy of Lancaster, Leader of the House of Commons, Chair. of Conservative Party 61-Oct. 63; Editor *The Spectator* Nov. 63-65; Dir. Lombard Banking Nov. 63-.

Publ. *Neville Chamberlain* 61.

The White Cottage, Potters Bar, Middlesex, England.

Mac Liammóir, Micheál; Irish actor, designer and playwright; b. 25 Oct. 1899; ed. privately.

First stage appearance as King Goldfish in *The Goldfish* 11; studied at Slade School 15-16; painter and designer for Irish Theatre and Dublin Drama League 17-21; studied painting abroad 21-27; joined Anew McMaster's Shakespearean Company 27; opened Galway Gaelic Theatre (with Hilton Edwards) with own play *Diarmuid agus Gráinne* 28; founder (with Hilton Edwards) Dublin Gate Theatre 28; has played Hamlet, Robert Emmett in *The Old Lady Says No* 35, Romeo, Othello, Mark Antony, Faust, Raskolnikoff in *Crime and Punishment*, Orin in *Mourning Becomes Electra*, Henry in *Henry IV* (Pirandello), Brack in *Hedda Gabler*, Don Pedro in *Much Ado About Nothing*, Hitler in *The Roses are Real*; compiled one-man entertainment *The Importance of Being Oscar*, Dublin and London 60, *I Must be Talking To My Friends* 63, *Talking about Yeats* 65; plays include *The Ford of The Hurdles* 29, *Dancing Shadow* 41, *Where Stars Walk* 40, *Portrait of Miriam* 47, *The Mountains Look Different* 48, *Home for Christmas* 50, *A Slipper for the Moon* 54; other publs. include, *All for Hecuba* (autobiography) 46, *Put Money in Thy Purse* (diaries) 54, *Each Actor on His Ass* (memoirs) 62, *Blath Agus Taibhse* (poems in Irish) 64, *Ireland* (travel) 66, *The Importance of Not Being Oscar* (autobiography and study of Wilde).

4 Harcourt Terrace, Dublin, Ireland.

Telephone: Dublin 67609.

McLoughlin, Brig. Eduardo F.; Argentine Air Force officer, politician and diplomatist; b. 13 May 1918; ed. Salesians Primary and High School and Military Coll. Air Force Cadet 37-40, promoted through ranks to Brig. (Air Vice-Marshal) 59, Aide-de-Camp to the Pres. of the Republic 55, retired from active service 61; in offices of Dir.-Gen., Air Ministry 53, mem. of Staff 55,

Dir.-Gen. 56; 2nd Dir. *a.i.* Air Force Military Acad. 55; Minister Sec. of State for Air 57, 62; War Minister *a.i.* 57; Air Attaché Washington Embassy 58-61; Amb. to U.K. 66-; mem. Aeronautical Mission to Europe 64, Argentine Del. to Interamerican Defense Board 58-61; Pres. of the Honour Tribunal for Armed Forces 65; U.S. and Peruvian decorations.
Argentine Embassy, 49 Belgrave Square, London, S.W.1, England.

McLucas, John Luther, B.S., M.S., PH.D.; American scientist; b. 22 Aug. 1920; ed. Davidson Coll., Tulane Univ. and Pennsylvania State Univ.
U.S. Navy 43-46; Physicist, U.S. Air Force, Cambridge Research Center 46-47; Physics Dept., Pennsylvania State Univ. 47-49; Electronics Engineer Haller, Raymond and Brown Inc. 49-50, Vice-Pres. and Technical Dir. 50-57; Pres. HRB-Singer Inc. 57-62; Chair. Pennsylvania State Univ. Industrial and Professional Advisory Council 57-62; Deputy Dir. of Research and Engineering (Tactical Warfare Programs) U.S. Dept. of Defense 62-64; Asst. Sec.-Gen. for Scientific Affairs, North Atlantic Treaty Org. (NATO) 64-66; Pres. The Mitre Corpn. 66-; Fellow Inst. Radio Engineers 62; Dept. of Defense Distinguished Civilian Service Award 64; mem. Defense Intelligence Agency Scientific Advisory Cttee. 66, New York Acad. Sciences 67, Air Force Scientific Advisory Board 67, Defense Science Board 68.
Office: P.O. Box 208, Bedford, Mass.; Home: College Road, Concord, Mass. 01742, U.S.A.
Telephone: 271-2575 (Office); 369-2699 (Home).

McLuhan, Herbert Marshall, B.A., M.A., PH.D., LL.D., D.LITT.; Canadian university professor and author; b. 21 July 1911; ed. Univ. of Manitoba and Cambridge Univ.
Teacher, Univ. of Wisconsin 36-37, Univ. of St. Louis 37-44, Assumption Univ. 44-46, St. Michael's Coll., Univ. of Toronto 46-; Dir. Centre for Culture and Technology, Univ. of Toronto 63-; Schweitzer Prof. in Humanities, Fordham Univ., New York 67-68; Gov.-Gen's. Award for Critical Prose (Canada) 63; Fellow Royal Soc. of Canada 64; Carl Einstein Prize, Young German Art Critics of W. Germany 67; Molson Award, Canada Council 67.
Publs. *The Mechanical Bride* 51, *Explorations in Communications* 60, *The Gutenberg Galaxy* 62, *Understanding Media* 64, *Voices of Literature* (2 vols.) 66, *The Medium is The Message* 67, *Counterblast* 68, *Through The Vanishing Point: Space in Poetry and Painting* 68, *War and Peace in the Global Village* 68.
Centre for Culture and Technology, University of Toronto, Toronto 5, Ontario, Canada.
Telephone: 416-928-3328.

McMahon, Rt. Hon. William, P.C., LL.B., B.EC.; Australian lawyer and politician; b. 23 Feb. 1908; ed. Sydney Univ.
Practised as solicitor until 39; served 39-45 war; mem. House of Reps. 49-; Minister for Navy and Air 51-54, for Social Services 54-56, for Primary Industry 56-58, for Labour and Nat. Service 58-66, Treas. 66-; Acting Minister for Trade 56 (in charge C.S.I.R.O. 56), for Labour and Nat. Service 57, Nat. Devt. 59; Acting Attorney-Gen. 60, 61; Acting Minister for Territories 62; Vice-Pres. Executive Council 64-66; Deputy Leader Liberal Party 66-; Leader Australian Del. Commonwealth Parl. Conf. New Delhi 57; Pres. ILO Regional Conf., Melbourne 62; Visiting Minister ILO Conf. Geneva 60, 64; Leader Australian Del. to IMF and World Bank Confs. Washington 66, Rio de Janeiro 67, to Commonwealth Finance Ministers Confs. Montreal 66, Trinidad 67; Gov. Asian Devt. Bank 68-, Chair. 68.
Commonwealth Parliament Offices, Sydney, N.S.W., and Department of the Treasury, Canberra, A.C.T., Australia.

MacMillan, Donald Baxter, B.A., M.A., D.SC.; American explorer; b. 10 Nov. 1874; ed. Bowdoin Coll. and Harvard Univ.
Principal Levi Hall High School, North Gorham 98-00; Head of Classical Dept. Swarthmore Preparatory School 00-03; Instructor Worcester Acad. 03-08; mem. expeditions to Labrador and North Pole and Commdr. 29 expedns. into Arctic Regions 08-55; Tallman Foundation Prof. in Anthropology Bowdoin Coll. 32-33; Dir. Bowdoin Kent's Island Scientific Station; Technical Adviser, Engineering Branch, U.S. Army 41-42; U.S. Navy 41, Commdr. U.S. *Bowdoin,* Greenland Patrol May-Dec. 41; attached to Hydrographic Office, Bureau of Navigation 42-45; mem. Board Research and Development Branch, Office of Quartermaster-Gen. 43-54; Elisha Kent Kane gold medal 27, Congressional Medal for work on Polar Sea 44; Special Gold Medal Chicago Geographic Society 49; Gold Medal Nat. Geographic Society 53; Gold Medal Explorers' Club 53.
Publs. *Four Years in the White North* 18, *Etah and Beyond* 27, *Kah-da* 29, *How Peary Reached the Pole* 34, *The Value of the Arctic Record, Thanksgiving at the Top of the World, Eskimo place names and aid to conversation* 43, *Bibliography of the Arctic* 45.
Provincetown, Mass., U.S.A.

McMillan, Edwin M(attison), M.S., PH.D.; American physicist; b. 18 Sept. 1907; ed. Calif. Inst. of Technology and Princeton Univ.
Nat. Research Fellow Univ. of Calif. 33-34, Research Assoc. 35, Asst. Prof. 36-41, Assoc. Prof. 42-46, Prof. of Physics at Univ. of Calif., Berkeley 46-; mem. Gen. Advisory Cttee. U.S. Atomic Energy Comm. 54-58; Dir. E. O. Lawrence Radiation Laboratory, Univ. of Calif. 58-; mem. High Energy Physics Comm., Int. Union for Pure and Applied Physics 60-66; Research Corpn. Scientific Award 51, Nobel Prize in Chemistry (with G. T. Seaborg) 51; Atoms for Peace Prize (with V. Veksler) 63; D.Sc. (h.c.), Rensselaer Polytechnic Inst. 61, Gustavus Adolphus Coll. 63; Alumni Distinguished Service Award, Calif. Inst. of Technology 66.
University of California, Berkeley, California, U.S.A.

MacMillan, Sir Ernest Campbell, Kt., MUS.D., LL.D., LITT.D., HON. R.A.M., F.R.C.M., F.R.C.O.; Canadian musician; b. 18 Aug. 1893; ed. Toronto and Edinburgh.
Principal Toronto Conservatory of Music 26-42; Dean Faculty of Music, Toronto Univ. 27-52; Conductor Toronto Symphony Orchestra 31-56, Toronto Mendelssohn Choir 42-57; Pres. Composers, Authors and Publishers Asscn. of Canada, Canadian Music Council 47-66; Hon. Pres. Les Jeunesses Musicales du Canada; mem. Canada Council 57-63.
Publs. *England* (ode for chorus and orchestra), *Sketches for String Quartet, Songs, Canadian Song Book, Six Bergerettes du Bas Canada,* etc.
Office: 1263 Bay Street, Toronto 5; Home: 115 Park Road, Toronto, Ont., Canada.
Telephone: 921-4574 (Office); 921-9787 (Home).

MacMillan, Rt. Hon. (Maurice) Harold, P.C., F.R.S.; British politician and publisher; b. 10 Feb. 1894; ed. Eton Coll. and Balliol Coll., Oxford.
Captain in Grenadier Guards 14-18; A.D.C. to Gov.-Gen. of Canada 19-20; Conservative M.P. for Stockton-on-Tees 24-29 and 31-July 45, Bromley Div. of Kent Nov. 45-64; Parl. Sec. Ministry of Supply May 40-Feb. 42; Parl. Under-Sec. of State for Colonies 42; Minister-Resident in N.W. Africa and Central Mediterranean 42-45; Diplomatic Rep. with French Nat. Cttee. 43-44; British mem. Advisory Council for Italy, Chair. 44-45; Sec. of State for Air May-July 45; Minister of Housing and Local Govt. 51-54, of Defence 54-55; Sec. of State for Foreign Affairs 55; Chancellor of the Exchequer 55-57; Prime Minister and First Lord of the Treasury Jan. 57-Oct. 63; Chair. Macmillan (Holdings) 63-; Dir. Pan Books Ltd.; Chancellor Oxford Univ. 60-; Hon.

D.C.L. (Durham and Oxford Univs.); Hon. LL.D. (Cambridge, Sussex).
Publs. *Industry and the State* (with others) 27, *Reconstruction: a plea for a National Policy* 33, *The Next Five Years* 35, *The Middle Way* 38, *Planning for Employment* 38, *Economic Aspects of Defence* 39, *Winds of Change* (autobiography vol. I) 66, *The Blast of War* (autobiography vol. II) 67.
Birch Grove House, Chelwood Gate, Hayward's Heath, Sussex, England.

McMillan, John Lanneau; American politician; ed. Mullins High School and Law School, Univ. of North Carolina.
Member U.S. House of Reps. 39-; Chair., Cttee. on District of Columbia 63-; Democrat.
House of Representatives, Washington, D.C. U.S.A.

MacMillan, Kenneth; British ballet director; b. 11 Dec. 1929; ed. Great Yarmouth Grammar School.
Resident Choreographer, Royal Ballet until 66; Dir. of Ballet, Deutsche Oper, Berlin 66-.
Major Choreography: *Romeo and Juliet, Song of the Earth, Rite of Spring, Las Hermanas, The Invitation, Diversions, Baiser de la Fée, Danses concertantes, Agon, Solitaire, Noctambules, House of Birds, Images of Love, The Seven Deadly Sins, Anastasia.*
Deutsche Oper, Berlin, Germany.

Macmillan, Norman John, Q.C., B.A., LL.B.; Canadian railway executive; b. 8 April 1909; ed. Univ. of Manitoba and Manitoba Law School.
Law Practice, Winnipeg; with Canadian Nat. Railways 37-, instrumental in modernization programme, Exec. Vice-Pres. 57-67, Chair. and Pres. Jan. 67-; assisted Govt. with Commonwealth Air Training Plan during Second World War.
Canadian National Railways, P.O.B. 8100, Montreal 1, Canada.

Macmillan, William M., M.A.; Historian and publicist; b. Scotland 1 Oct. 1885; ed. Stellenbosch, South Africa, Oxford, Aberdeen and Germany.
Lecturer, Rhodes Univ. Coll. 11; Prof. of History, Univ. of Witwatersrand 17-33. Research Fellow in African History and Administration; associate mem. All Souls' Coll. Oxford 26-27, 33; travel in Africa 30-33, 38, U.S.A. and W. Indies 34-35; mem. de l'Institut Colonial Int. (INCIDI) 31; Acting Dir. Empire Intelligence B.B.C. 41-42; British Council Senior Rep. in West Africa 43-46; Dir. Colonial Studies, St. Andrews Univ. 47-54; Advisory Cttee. on Education in Colonies 38-42; Colonial Labour Advisory Cttee. 46-53; South African Lecture Tour 49; Mission for Tanganyika Govt. 50; Observer Mission to Bechuanaland Protectorate 51, African tours 52, 58-59, 62, 64, 67-68; Acting Prof. of History, Univ. Coll. of the West Indies 54-55; Chevalier Order of the Lion (Belgium); Hon. D.Litt. (Oxford) 57, (Univ. of Natal) 62.
Publs. *Economic Conditions in a Non-Industrial South African Town* 15, *The South African Agrarian Problem* 19, *The Cape Colour Question* 27, *Bantu, Boer and Briton* 29 (new edn. 63), *Complex South Africa* 30, *Warning From the West Indies* 36 and 38, *Africa Emergent* 39 and 48, *Europe and West Africa* (jointly) 40, *Democratise the Empire* 41, *The Road to Self-Rule: a Study in Colonial Evolution* 59 (Italian edn. 63).
Long Wittenham, Abingdon, Berks., England.
Telephone: Clifton Hampden 358.

McMillen, Dale Wilmore, Jr., B.A.; American business executive; b. 6 Jan. 1914; ed. Northwestern Univ.
Production Dept., Central Soya Co. Inc., Decatur, Ind. 36-39, Vice-Pres., later Exec. Vice-Pres. 39-46, Vice-Chair. Bd. 46-50, Pres. 54-, Dir. 38-; Dir. Fort Wayne Nat. Bank 47-, Pres. Bd. of Aviation Commrs., Fort

Wayne 59-; Dir. Central Soya-Seriom S.p.A.; official of educational and church orgs.
3415 South Washington Road, Fort Wayne, Indiana, U.S.A.

McMillen, Harold Wilmore; American business executive; b. 29 Sept. 1906; ed. Oberlin Coll. and Purdue Univ.
Vice-President and Dir. of Sales, Central Soya 45-50, Exec. Vice-Pres. 50-53, Chair. of Bd. 53-; Pres. Central Sugar Co. Inc. 39-45; official of several welfare and business orgs.
300 Fort Wayne Bank Building, Fort Wayne, Indiana, U.S.A.

McMullin, Sir Alister Maxwell, K.C.M.G.; Australian politician; b. 14 July 1900.
Mem. the Senate since 51, Pres. 53-; Chair. Gen. Council of Commonwealth Parl. Asscn. 59-60; Dep. Chair. Nat. Library of Australia; Chair. Parl. Library Cttee.; Chancellor Univ. of Newcastle, N.S.W.; mem. Liberal Party.
Home: St. Aubin's, Scone, N.S.W.; Office: Parliament House, Canberra, A.C.T., Australia.
Telephone: Scone 153 (Home).

Macmurray, John, M.C., M.A., LL.D.; British philosopher; b. 16 Feb. 1891; ed. Glasgow and Oxford Univs.
Lecturer in Philosophy Manchester Univ. 19; Prof. Witwatersrand Univ. 21; Classical Tutor, Jowett Lecturer, and Fellow Balliol Coll. Oxford 22; Grote Prof. Philosophy of Mind and Logic, London Univ. 28-44; Prof. of Moral Philosophy, Edinburgh Univ. 44-58; Gifford Lecturer, Univ. of Glasgow 52-54; retired 58.
Publs. *Freedom in the Modern World* 32, *Interpreting the Universe* 33, *Philosophy of Communism* 33, *Some Makers of the Modern Spirit* 33, *Marxism* 34, *Aspects of Dialectical Materialism* 34, *Creative Society* 35, *Reason and Emotion* 35, *The Structure of Religious Experience* 36, *The Clue to History* 38, *The Boundaries of Science* 40, *Challenge to the Churches* 42, *Constructive Democracy* 43, *The Conditions of Freedom* 49, *The Self as Agent* 57, *Persons in Relation* 60, *Religion, Art and Science* 61, *Search for Reality in Religion* 65.
"Hatherly Brake", Jordans, Beaconsfield, Bucks., England.
Telephone: Chalfont St. Giles 4547.

McMurray, Joseph Patrick Brendan; American economist; b. 4 March 1912; ed. Jamaica High School, Queens, N.Y., Brooklyn Coll., and New York School for Social Research.
Economist, Gov. Agencies 40-44; Econ. Consultant, U.S. Senate Labor and Educ. Comm. 45-47; Admin. Asst. to U.S. Senator Wagner 47-48; Consultant and Staff Dir. U.S. Senate Banking and Currency Comm. 48-54; Exec. Dir. N.Y. City Housing Authority 54-55; Commr. of Housing, State of New York 55-59; Pres. Queensborough Community Coll. 59-61; Chair. Fed. Home Loan Bank Board 61-65; Pres. of Queens Coll., Flushing, N.Y. 65-.
Queens Coll., Flushing, N.Y., U.S.A.
Telephone: 516 MA7-1514.

MacNabb, Byron Gordon; American research and development engineer; b. 14 Aug. 1910; ed. Rose Polytechnic Inst., Terre Haute, and Ill. Inst. of Technology.
Worked for Carnegie Steel Corpn., South Chicago 30-43; U.S. Navy officer 43-48; Asst. to Dir. of Research for Sandia Corpn., Albuquerque, working on A-bomb 48-50; Asst. to Dir. of Research, Pullman Standard Car Co. 50-53; Operations Man. for Cambridge Corpn. 53-55; joined Convair-Astronautics (now Gen. Dynamics/Convair) 55, Operations Man. at Air Force Missile Test Center, Cape Canaveral 55-62, Dir. of Operations 62-63; Dir. of Test Engineering, General Dynamics/Astronautics, San Diego 63-65; Operations

Man. Gen. Dynamics/Convair, Cape Kennedy 65-66; responsible for Launch Operations, Atlas/Mercury Manned Orbital Project Mercury, Cape Canaveral (now Cape Kennedy); Man. Tests and Operations, Advanced Interplanetary Programs, Gen. Electric, Missile & Space Div. 66-; Presidential Citation for devt. of first anti-kamakazi anti-aircraft weapon, and other awards. Office: General Electric Co., P.O. Box 8661, Philadelphia, Pa.; Home: P.O. Box 272, Valley Forge, Pa., U.S.A.
Telephone: 215-962-3536 (Office); 215-666-5964 (Home).

McNair, 1st Baron, cr. 55; **Arnold Duncan McNair,** Kt., C.B.E., LL.D., F.B.A., Q.C.; British lawyer; b. 4 March 1885; ed. Aldenham School and Gonville and Caius Coll. Cambridge.
Fellow and Law Lecturer, Gonville and Caius Coll. 12; Sec. Coal Controller's Advisory Board 17-19; Sec. Coal Industry (Sankey) Comm. 19; Tagore Prof. Univ. of Calcutta 31; mem. Inst. of Int. Law, Pres. 48-50; Pres. Society of Public Teachers of Law 33; Whewell Prof. of Int. Law, Cambridge 35-37; Vice-Chancellor Liverpool Univ. 37-45; Prof. Comparative Law, Cambridge 45-46; Bencher Gray's Inn; Treas. Gray's Inn 47; Judge Int. Court of Justice 46-55, Pres. 52-55; Pres. European Court of Human Rights 59-65; Assoc. Belgian Acad.; Hon. LL.D. (Glasgow, Salonika, Birmingham, Liverpool and Brussels), Hon. D.C.L. (Oxon.), Hon. D.Litt. (Reading).
Publs. *Legal Effects of War* 20, 44, 48 and 66, *Law of the Air* 32, 53 and 64, *Roman Law and Common Law* (with Prof. Buckland) 36, *Law of Treaties* 38, 61, *International Law Opinions* (3 vols.) 56, *Expansion of International Law* 62.
25 Storey's Way, Cambridge, England.
Telephone: Cambridge 53595.

McNamara, Robert Strange, A.B., LL.D.; American businessman and government official; b. 9 June 1916; ed. Univ. of Calif. and Harvard Univ.
Asst. Prof. in Business Admin., Harvard Univ. 40-43; served Army Air Force 43-46; Exec. Ford Motor Co. 46-61, Vice-Pres. 55-60, Pres. 60-61; U.S. Sec. of Defense 61-68; Pres. of Int. Bank for Reconstruction and Devt. (World Bank) April 68-; Legion of Merit; U.S. Medal of Freedom 68.
2412 Tracy Place, Washington, D.C., U.S.A.

MacNaught, Hon. J. Watson, P.C., Q.C., M.P.; Canadian lawyer and politician; b. 19 June 1904; ed. Prince of Wales Coll., Charlottetown, Prince Edward Island, and Dalhousie Univ.
Called to Nova Scotia Bar 32, Prince Edward Island Bar 32; King's Counsel 42; Law Clerk to Legis. Assembly of Prince Edward Island 35-42, Clerk 42-45; Crown Prosecutor, Prince County, Prince Edward Island 43-45; mem. House of Commons 45-; Parl. Asst. to Minister of Fisheries 48; Solicitor-Gen. of Canada April 63-65, Minister of Mines and Technical Surveys 65-68; Liberal.
Parliament Buildings, Ottawa, Canada.

Macnaughton, Alan Aylesworth, B.A., B.C.L.; Canadian lawyer and politician; b. 1904; ed. McGill Univ. and London School of Economics.
Lawyer, Montreal; M.P. 49-, Chair. House of Commons Public Accounts Cttee. 58-63, Speaker, House of Commons 63-66; mem. Senate of Canada 66-; Chair. Roosevelt Campobello Int. Park Comm. 66-; Hon. P.C., Hon. Q.C.; Liberal.
635 Dorchester Boulevard, Montreal, Quebec, Canada.
Telephone: 866-9575.

McNee, Sir John (William), Kt., D.S.O., M.D., D.SC., F.R.C.P., F.R.S.E.; British physician; b. 17 Dec. 1887; ed. Glasgow, Freiburg and Johns Hopkins Univs.
Formerly Asst. Prof. of Medicine and Lecturer in Pathology Glasgow Univ., Associate Prof. of Medicine and Associate Physician Johns Hopkins Univ.; Lettsom Lecturer Medical Society of London 31; Croonian Lecturer Royal Coll. of Physicians 32; Vicary Lecturer, Royal Coll. of Surgeons 58, Examiner in Medicine Cambridge, Sheffield, St. Andrews, Edinburgh, Leeds Universities and National University of Ireland; Physician Univ. Coll. Hospital London and Holme Lecturer in Clinical Medicine Univ. Coll. Hospital Medical School; Regius Prof. of Medicine, Glasgow Univ. Sept. 36-53, Emeritus 53-; Physician to H.M. King George VI and later to H.M. Queen Elizabeth II in Scotland 37-54; Consulting Physician to R.N. 35-55; Physician to Western Infirmary, Glasgow; Consulting Physician, Univ. Coll. Hospital, London; Pres. Asscn. of Physicians of Great Britain and Ireland 51-52; Pres. Gastro-Enterological Soc. of Great Britian 50-51; Pres. British Medical Asscn. 54-55; served with Royal Army Medical Corps 14-18, with Royal Navy 39-46; Surgeon-Rear-Admiral and Consulting Physician; Hon. M.D. (Dublin), Hon. LL.D. (Glasgow and Toronto Univs.
Publs. *Diseases of the Liver, Gall-Bladder and Bile Ducts* (with late Sir Humphry Rolleston) 3rd edn. 29, *Textbook of Medical Treatment* (with Dunlop and Davidson) 6th edn. 52.
Barton Edge, Worthy Road, Winchester, Hampshire, England.
Telephone: Winchester 5444.

McNeely, Eugene Johnson, B.S. in E.E.; American engineer and executive; b. 11 Jan. 1900; ed. Missouri Univ.
With Southwestern Bell Telephone Co. 22-48; Engineer, Kansas City, St. Louis, 26-35; Plant Supt., Little Rock, Kansas City, St. Louis 35-47; Gen. Plant Man., St. Louis 47-48; Joined American Telephone and Telegraph Co. as Asst. Vice-Pres. (Personnel) 48; Vice-Pres. (Operations), Northwestern Bell Telephone Co. 49, Pres. 49-52; Vice-Pres. (Personnel) American Telephone and Telegraph Co. 52-54, Vice-Pres. (Operations and Engineering) 54-55, Exec. Vice-Pres. 55-61, Dir. 55-67, Pres. 61-64; Dir. Continental Oil Co. 59-, Manufacturers Hanover Trust Co. 59-66, Travelers Insurance Co. 63, Consolidated Electronics Industries 66-, Honeywell Inc. 66-; Chair. N.Y. State Science and Technology Foundation 65; Trustee E. River Savings Bank 55-; Teachers Coll. Columbia Univ. 56-66; Distinguished Service in Engineering Award (Missouri Univ.) 57; Hon. LL.D. (Missouri 62, and Grinnell Coll., Iowa 64), Hon. L.H.D. (Indiana Cent. Coll.) 63.
Stone Ridge, New York; and 195 Broadway, New York 7, N.Y., U.S.A.

McNeil, Hector, C.B.E., B.E., M.I.E.E., M.I.MECH.E.; British engineering executive; b. 20 July 1904; ed. Univ. of New Zealand.
In Public Works Dept., New Zealand 27-29; State Electricity Comm. of Victoria 29-31; with Babcock and Wilcox Ltd. 31-, Gen. Man. 47, Dir. 50, Man.-Dir. 53; Chair. Babcock and Wilcox (Operations) Ltd., Babcock U.K. Investments Ltd. and Babcock Int. Investments Ltd. 65-, Nuclear Design & Construction Ltd.; Dir. of German, French, Spanish, Australian, Canadian and New Zealand Associated Babcock and Wilcox Cos. and of English Electric, Babcock and Wilcox and Taylor Woodrow Atomic Power Construction Co. Ltd., Babcock and Wilcox Technische Maatschappij, Netherlands, Diamond Power Speciality Ltd., Nat. Bank of New Zealand, Ltd.; Pres. Inst. of Fuel 57-58; mem. Export Council for Europe 60, Chair. 65-.
Bramber, St. George's Hill, Weybridge, Surrey, England.

McNeill, Robert E., Jr.; American banker; b. 20 Jan. 1906; ed. public schools.
Formerly Pres. Atlantic Nat. Bank; Vice-Pres. the Hanover Bank (now Manufacturers' Hanover Trust Co.) 40-50, Pres. and Trustee 50-, Chair. and Chief Exec. 63-; Dir., Trustee and mem. of cttees. American

Smelting and Refining Co., American Title Insurance Co., Chrysler Corpn., Continental Insurance Co. and its N.Y. subsidiaries, Fed. Reserve Bank of N.Y., Florida Power and Light Co., Union Corpn., New York Univ., Univ. of Florida Foundation Inc., etc.
52 Wayside Place, Montclair, N.J.; Office: 350 Park Avenue, New York, N.Y. 10022, U.S.A.

MacNichol, George Pope, Jr.; American glass manufacturer; b. 8 May 1899; ed. Scott High School, Toledo, Univ. of Michigan and Yale Univ.
Assistant Treas. Edward Ford Plate Glass Co. 20-23, Treas. 23-26, Treas. and Sales Man. 26-30; Vice-Pres. (Sales), Libbey-Owens-Ford Glass Co. 30-53, Exec. Vice-Pres. 53, Pres. 53-, later Chair.; Dir. ten other companies; official of civic and business orgs.; retired April 65.
Room 201, Libbey-Owens-Ford Bldg., 811 Madison Ave., Toledo, Ohio 43624; Home: 30217 E. River Road, Perrysburg, Ohio, U.S.A.
Telephone: 382-2518.

McNicol, David Williamson, C.B.E.; Australian diplomatist; b. 20 May 1913; ed. Carey Grammar School, Melbourne, Kings Coll. Adelaide and Adelaide Univ.
Minister to Cambodia, Laos and Vietnam 55-56, Commr. to Singapore 58-60, High Commr. in Pakistan 62-65, in New Zealand 65-68; Amb. to Thailand and Rep. to SEATO 68-.
Australian Embassy, Bangkok, Thailand.

Macomber, William Butts, Jr., M.A., LL.B.; American government official and diplomatist; b. 28 March 1921; ed. Phillips Andover Acad., Yale, Harvard and Chicago Univs.
Lecturer in Govt., Boston Univ. 47-49; with C.I.A., Washington 51-53; Asst. to Special Asst. to Sec. of State 53-54; Special Asst. to Under-Sec. of State 55-57; Asst. Sec. of State for Congressional Relations 57-61; Ambassador to Jordan 61-63; Asst. Admin. Agency for International Development (AID), Washington 64-67; Asst. Sec. of State for Congressional Relations 67-.
4200 Cathedral Avenue, N.W., Washington 16, D.C., U.S.A.
Telephone: 244-6637.

McPherson, Harry Cummings, Jr., B.A., LL.B.; American lawyer and government official; b. 22 Aug. 1929; ed. Tyler High School, Texas, Southern Methodist Univ., Dallas, Univ. of the South, Tennessee, Columbia Univ. and Univ. of Texas Law School.
U.S. Air Force 50-53; admitted to Texas Bar 55; Asst. Gen. Counsel, Democratic Policy Cttee., U.S. Senate 56-59, Assoc. Counsel 59-61, Gen. Counsel 61-63; Deputy Under Sec. for Int. Affairs, Dept. of Army 63-64; Asst. Sec. of State for Educational and Cultural Affairs 64-65; Special Asst. and Counsel to Pres. Johnson 65-; Special Counsel to the President 66-.
Office: The White House, Washington, D.C. 20500; Home: 30 W. Irving Street, Chevy Chase, Maryland, U.S.A.
Telephone: 656-2469.

Macpherson, Sir John Stuart, G.C.M.G., M.A.; retired British colonial servant and businessman; b. 25 Aug. 1898; ed. Watson's Coll., Edinburgh and Edinburgh Univ.
Served with Argyll and Sutherland Highlanders First World War; Malayan Civil Service 21; attached to Colonial Office 33-35; Principal Asst. Sec. Nigeria 37; Chief Sec. Palestine 39-43; Head British Colonies Supply Mission in Washington and mem. Anglo-American Caribbean Comm. 43; British Co-Chair. Caribbean Comm. and Comptroller Devt. and Welfare West Indies 45-48; Gov. and C.-in-C. of Nigeria 48-54; Gov.-Gen. and C.-in-C. Fed. of Nigeria 54-55; Chair. UN Mission

to the Pacific 56; Perm. Under-Sec. for the Colonies 56-59; mem. Court of Univ. of Essex 65-; Chair. Cable and Wireless Ltd. until July 67; Chair. Basildon Devt. Corpn. until Dec. 67; Vice-Pres. Royal Commonwealth Soc.; mem. of Council, Royal African Soc., Voluntary Service Overseas; Hon. Vice-Chair. London Conf. on Overseas Students; Hon. LL.D. (Edinburgh Univ.) 57.
141 Marsham Court, London, S.W.1, England.
Telephone: 01-834-8807.

McQuaid, Most Rev. John Charles, D.D., M.A., D.LITT.; Irish ecclesiastic; b. 28 July 1895; ed. St. Patrick's Diocesan Coll., Cavan, Blackrock Coll., Clongowes Wood Coll., Nat. Univ. of Ireland, and Rome.
Entered Novitiate of Holy Ghost Fathers at Kimmage Manor 13; professed 14; ordained priest 24; Pres. Blackrock Coll., Dublin 31-39; R.C. Archbishop of Dublin and Primate of Ireland 40-; fmr. Chair. Catholic Headmasters' Asscn., mem. Royal Irish Acad.; Fellow Royal Soc. of Antiquaries of Ireland.
Archbishop's House, Dublin 9, Ireland.

McRuer, Hon. James Chalmers; Canadian lawyer; b. Aug. 23 1890; ed. Lycée in Paris, Osgoode Law School.
Called to Bar of Ontario 14, British Columbia 26, Alberta 40; served overseas in R.C.A. 16-19; apptd. K.C. 29; Lectured in the Law School 30-35 (Criminal Procedure); elected a Bencher of the Law Society of Upper Canada 36; mem. Royal Comm. on the Penal System of Canada 37; apptd. to the Court of Appeal of Ontario 44, Chief Justice of High Court of Justice for Ontario 45-64; Chair. Royal Comms. on insanity in criminal cases and on sexual psychopathic offenders; Chair. Ont. Law Reform Comm. 64-; Royal Commr., Enquiry into Civil Rights (Ont.) 64-; Pres. of the Canadian Bar Asscn. 46-47; Hon. LL.D. (Laval and Toronto Univs., Osgoode Hall Law School).
Publs. *The Evolution of the Judicial Process, Trial of Jesus* 64.
9 Deer Park Crescent, Apt. 1005, Toronto 7, Ont., Canada.

McTiernan, Rt. Hon. Sir Edward A., P.C., K.B.E., B.A., LL.B.; Australian lawyer; b. 16 Feb. 1892; ed. Sydney Univ.
Barrister 16; mem. New South Wales Legislature 20-27; Attorney-Gen. 20-22 and 25-27; mem. Federal Parliament 29-30; Justice of High Court of Australia 30-; Privy Chamberlain of Sword and Cape 28.
"Breffni", Chilton Parade, Warrawee, N.S.W., Australia.

Macy, John Williams, Jr.; American public administrator; b. 6 April 1917; ed. Wesleyan Univ., Connecticut and Nat. Inst. of Public Affairs, Washington, D.C.
Admin. Aide Social Security Board Washington 39-40; Personal Asst. Civilian Personnel Div. War Dept. 40-42; Asst. Dir. Civilian Personnel War Dept. 42-43, 46-47; Dir., Personnel and Org. Atomic Energy Comm. Los Alamos 47-51; Asst. to Under-Sec. of Army 51-53; Exec. Dir., U.S. Civil Service Comm. 53-58; Exec. Vice-Pres., Wesleyan Univ., Middletown, Conn. 58-61; Chair. U.S. Civil Service Comm. 61-.
201 North Langley Lane, McLean, Va., U.S.A.

Madan, Bal Krishna, PH.D.; Indian banker and economist; b. 13 July 1911; ed. Univ. of Punjab, Lahore.
Lecturer in Economics, Univ. of Punjab 36-37; Officer for Enquiry into Resources, Punjab Govt. 37-38; mem. Punjab Board for Economic Enquiry 38-40, Sec. 38; Economic Adviser to Punjab Govt. 40-41; Dir. of Research, Reserve Bank of India, Bombay 41-45; Sec. of Indian del. to Bretton Woods 44; Deputy Sec. Indian Tariff Board 45; mem. Indian Legislative Assembly and Assembly Cttee. on Bretton Woods Agreement 46; Alternate Exec. Dir., Int. Monetary Fund 46-48; Int. Bank for Reconstruction and Development 47-48; Exec. Dir. Int. Monetary Fund 48-50, 67-; mem. Indian Del. to

First Commonwealth Finance Ministers' Conf. London 49; Adviser Indian Del. to UN Economic and Social Council 49; mem. UN Cttee. on Domestic Financing of Economic Development 49; Economic Adviser to Reserve Bank of India 50; mem. Finance Comm., Indian Govt. 52; mem. Taxation Enquiry Comm. 53-54; mem. Experts Group on UN Special Fund for Economic Development 55; mem. Foodgrains Policy Cttee., Indian Govt. 57-58; Principal Adviser to Reserve Bank of India 57, Exec. Dir. 59, Deputy Gov. 64-67; mem. Governing Body Indian Investment Centre 60-67; Pres. Indian Econ. Asscn. 61; Vice-Chair. Industrial Development Bank of India 64-67.

Publ. *India and Imperial Preference—A Study in Commercial Policy* 39, *Aspects of Economic Development and Policy* 64.

International Monetary Fund, 19th and H Streets, N.W., Washington, D.C. 20431; Home: 4460 Sedgwick Street, N.W., Washington, D.C. 20016, U.S.A.

Telephone: DUI-3231 (Offce); 362-0130 (Home).

Madariaga, Salvador de; Spanish diplomatist and writer; b. 23 July 1886; ed. Madrid Inst. Cardenal Cisneros, Paris Ecole Polytechnique and Ecole des Mines.

Engineer Northern Spanish Railway Co. 11; Dir. Disarmament Section, L.N. 22-28; Prof. Spanish Studies, Oxford Univ. 28; Prof. Mexico Univ. 31; Deputy Cortes Constituyentes 31; Ambassador, Washington 31; mem. L.N. Council 31-36; Del. L.N. Disarmament Conf. 32; Ambassador to France 32-34; Minister of Education and of Justice in Lerroux Cabinet Mar.-April 34; Chief Spanish Del. to L.N. 31-36; Pres. Cttee. of Five 35; Pres. Cultural Section, European Movement; Hon. Pres. Liberal Int.; Hon. Fellow Exeter Coll., Oxford; D.Litt. h.c. (Arequipa, Lima, Poitiers, Princeton, Liège, Lille); Grand Cross Légion d'Honneur; Hanseatic Goethe Prize 67.

Publs. *Shelley and Calderón, The Genius of Spain, The Sacred Giraffe, Englishmen, Frenchmen, Spaniards* (Ere Nouvelle Prize), *Sir Bob, Disarmament, Americans, The Price of Peace, Anarchy or Hierarchy* 37, *Theory and Practice in International Relations* 38, *The World's Design* 38, *Christopher Columbus* 39, *Hernán Cortés* 42, *Spain* 43, *The Heart of Jade* 44, *The Rise of the Spanish American Empire* 46, *Victors Beware* 46, *The Fall of the Spanish-American Empire* 47, *Bolívar* 52, *Portrait of Europe* 52, *Essays with a Purpose* 54, *A Bunch of Errors* 54, *War in the Blood* 57, *Democracy versus Liberty?* 58, *The Blowing up of the Parthenon* 60, *Latin America Between the Eagle and the Bear* 61, *On Hamlet* 64, *Portrait of a Man Standing* 68.

3 St. Andrews Road, Oxford, England.

Maddox, Lester Garfield; American state governor; b. 30 Sept. 1915.

Industrial supervisor 34; restaurant, then grocery shop, proprietor; Gov. of Georgia 67-; Hon. mem. various Georgian asscns.; Democrat.

State Capitol, Atlanta, Georgia, U.S.A.

Maderna, Bruno; Italian musician; b. 20; studied with Bustini, Malipiero and Scherchen and at Conservatorio di Musica 'Santa Cecilia'.

Conductor and composer; specialises in electronic music 55-.

Compositions: *Studi per il Processo di Kafka* (Orchestra) 49, *Composizione in tre tempi* (Orchestra) 54, *Dark Rapture Crawl* (Orchestra) 57, *Syntaxis* 57, *Continuum* 58.

c/o Conservatorio di Musica "Santa Cecilia", Via dei Greci 18, Rome, Italy.

Madia, Chunilal Kalidas; Indian writer; b. 12 Aug. 1922; ed. Bhagwatsinhji High School, Dhoraji, Gujerat, and H.L. Coll. of Commerce, Ahmedabad.

Writes mainly in Gujerati; Editorial Staff *Prabhat* and *Navsaurashtra* 42-44; Editor *Varta* (short story monthly)

43; Editorial Staff, Janmabhoomi Group of Newspapers, Bombay 45-50; Language Editor, U.S. Information Service, Bombay 50-62; now Editor *Ruchi* (literary and cultural magazine); Literary Editor *Sandesh* (Gujerati daily); Narmad Gold Medal for Best Play Writing 51; Ranajitram Gold Medal for Outstanding Creative Writing 57; numerous other prizes.

Publs. (in Gujerati): novels: *Vyajano Varas, Velavelani Chhanyadi, Liludi Dharati, Kumkum Ane Ashaka;* short stories: *Ghooghavatan Pur, Padmaja, Champo Ane Kel, Tej Ane Timir, Roop-Aroop, Antasrota;* plays: *Rangada, Vishavimochan, Raktatilak, Shoonyashesh;* poems: *Sonnet* (collected sonnets); criticism: *Granthagarima, Shahamrig, Suvarnamrig;* in Malayalam: *Gujarati Kathakal.*

B-213, Chandralok, Manav Mandir Road, Malabar Hill, Bombay 6, India.

Telephone: 36-8245.

Madsen, Rt. Rev. Willy Westergaard; Danish ecclesiastic; b. 16 Jan. 1907; ed. Univ. of Copenhagen.

General Sec. Social Works of the Parishes in Copenhagen 42; Bishop of Copenhagen, Primate of the Lutheran Church of Denmark 61-; editor *Fra Menighedsplejen* 42-60.

Publ. *Din Naeste* 45.

Nørregade 11, Copenhagen K, Denmark.

Telephone: PA-3508.

Maegraith, Brian Gilmore, M.B., B.S., F.R.C.P. (L. & E.), B.SC., M.A., D.PHIL.; Australian university professor; b. 26 Aug. 1907; ed. St. Peter's and St. Mark's Colls., Univ. of Adelaide, Magdalen and Exeter Colls., Univ. of Oxford.

Medical Fellow and Tutor in Physiology, Exeter Coll., Oxford 34-40; Univ. Lecturer and Demonstrator in Pathology, Oxford 37-44, Dean of Medical School 38-44; Lieut.-Col. R.A.M.C., O.C. Malaria Research Unit, War Office 39-45; mem. Medical Research Council Malaria Cttee. 43-46; Tropical Medicine Research Board (Medical Research Council) 59-, Council Royal Society of Tropical Medicine 47-51 (Vice-Pres. 49-51, 57-); Prof. Tropical Medicine, Dean of School, Liverpool School of Tropical Medicine 44-; Physician in Tropical Medicine, Royal Infirmary and Selton General Hospital, Liverpool; Nuffield Consultant in Tropical Medicine, West Africa 49-; mem. Medical Research Council Chemotherapy Cttee. 53-; hon. mem. Belgian Society of Tropical Medicine; Chalmers Gold Medal, Royal Society of Tropical Medicine 51, Le Prince Medal, American Society of Tropical Medicine 55, Bernhard Nocht Medal (Hamburg) 57; Hon. D.Sc. (Bangkok).

Publs. *Pathological Processes in Malaria* 48, *Clinical Tropical Diseases* 53, *Tropical Medicine for Nurses* 54, *Clinical Methods in Tropical Medicine* 62, *Exotic Diseases: Practice* 65.

School of Tropical Medicine, Pembroke Place, Liverpool 3, and 23 Eaton Road, Cressington Park, Liverpool 19, England.

Telephone: 01-709-7611.

Maekawa, Kunio, B.ENG.; Japanese architect; b. 14 May 1905; ed. Tokyo Imperial Univ.

Worked in Le Corbusier's office, Paris 28-30, Antonin Raymond's office, Tokyo 30-35; Pres., Kunio Maekawa Architect's Office 35-; Prof., Nihon Univ., Tokyo; Pres. Japan Architects Asscn. 59-62; mem. Japanese Del., Exec. Cttee. of Int. Union of Architects 59-; numerous prizes.

Buildings include: Yokohama Cultural Centre 52, Kanagawa Prefectural Library 54, Japanese Pavilion, Brussels World Fair 58, Kyoto Cultural Centre 59, Gakushin Univ. 60, Tokyo Metropolitan Festival Hall 61.

Office: 8 Honshio-cho, Shinjuku-ku, Tokyo; Home: Kami-Osaki 3-10-59, Shinagawa-ku, Tokyo, Japan.

Telephone: Tokyo 351-7101 (Office).

Maeo, Shigesaburo; Japanese politician; b. 05; ed. Faculty of Law, Tokyo Imperial Univ.
Former Chief of Taxation Bureau, Pres. Mint Agency of Finance Ministry, Minister of Int. Trade and Industry, Vice-Chair. Policy and other boards of Liberal Party, Chair. Local Admin. Cttee., Chair. Foreign Affairs Cttee., House of Reps.; mem. House of Reps.; fmr. Sec.-Gen. Liberal Democratic Party.
Publs. *Zei no zuihitsu shū* (Essays on Taxation), *Seijika no saijiki* (Memoirs of a Statesman).
Liberal Democratic Party Headquarters, 7 2-chome, Hirakawa-cho, Chiyoda-ku, Tokyo, Japan.

Maevsky, Viktor Vasilevich; Soviet journalist; b. 1921; ed. Moscow Pedagogical Inst.
Headmaster of a Middle School 42-44; mem. *Pravda* staff 47-, mem. C.P.S.U. 47-, Correspondent in London 50-53, Editor Asia and Africa Dept. 55-61, Observer of Int. Affairs 61-; Order of Red Banner of Labour; V. Vorzovsky Prizewinner for Journalism 60.
Publs. *On the British Isles* 55, *On the Japanese Islands* 58, *Malayan Morning* 59, *First or Fifth* 60, *Skyscrapers are not Steady* 62.
Pravda, Ulitsa Pravdi 24, Moscow, U.S.S.R.

Maga, Hubert; Dahomeyan politician; b. 16; ed. Ecole Normale de Gorée.
Headmaster of school at Nabitingou until 51; Gen. Counsellor of Dahomey 47; Grand Counsellor of Art 48-57; Deputy for Dahomey to French Nat. Assembly 51-58; Under-Sec. for Labour, Gaillard Cabinet; Minister of Labour in Dahomey 58-59, Premier 59-63, Pres. 60-63; under restriction Dec. 63-Nov. 65; mem. Dahomeyan Democrat Group; awards incl. Mérite Social and Etoile Noire de Bénin.
20 Avenue Mac-Mahon (XVIIe), Paris, France.

Magalhães, Maj.-Gen. Juracy Montenegro; Brazilian diplomatist; b. 05; ed. Lyceu, State of Ceará, Realengo Military Acad., Gen. Staff School and Superior War Coll.
Former Army Officer; Military Attaché, Washington 53-54; Fed. Interventor, State of Bahia 31-34; Gov. of Bahia 35-37, 59-63; mem. for Bahia, Fed. Chamber of Deputies 46-50, Fed. Senator for Bahia 54, 58-; Pres. Cia. Vale do Rio Doce (iron ore exports) 51-52; Pres. Petrobrás 54; Chair. Nat. Democratic Union (UDN) 57-58; Ambassador to United States 64-65; Minister of Justice and Interior 65-66, of Foreign Affairs 66-67; numerous decorations.
Publs. *Defendendo o meu Govêrno* (In Defence of my Government), *Petróleo, Fonte de Libertação ou de Escravidão* (Petroleum, Source of Liberation or of Enslavement).
c/o Ministry of Foreign Affairs, Brasilia, Brazil.

Magalhães Pinto, José de; Brazilian banker, business executive and politician; b. 28 June 1909; ed. Free School of Law, Belo Horizonte.
Director, Banco da Lavoura, Minas Gerais 29-35; Pres. Assoc. Comercial, Minas Gerais 35-37; Pres. Fed. Comércio, Minas Gerais 37; Founder and Chair. of Board Banco Nacional de Minas Gerais 44; Fed. Deputy 40-60; Gov. of Minas Gerais 60-65; mem. Chamber of Deputies 45-60, Nov. 66-; Minister of Foreign Affairs March 67-; Pres. União Democrática Nacional (U.D.N.); Prof. at Econ. Univ. of Minas Gerais; Dr. h.c. Univ. Rural de Viçosa.
Avenida Atlântica 2016, Apt. 401 Copacabana ZC-07, Rio de Janeiro, GB, Brazil.

Magaloff, Nikita; Swiss (b. Russian) pianist; b. 8 Feb. 1912; ed. Conservatoire national de musique, Paris and with Joseph Szigeti.
Professor of Virtuosity, Geneva Conservatoire 49-; numerous concerts all over the world since 39, including two tours of South America and tour round the world 60; particularly well known as Chopin interpreter;

numerous invitations to play in the major European int. music festivals; frequent mem. of jury in European Int. Piano Competitions.
Compositions include: *Sonatina* for Violin and Piano, *Toccata* for Piano, and Songs.
Vieux Convent, Coppet (Vaud), Switzerland.
Telephone: (022)- 762882.

Magariños, Gustavo; Uruguayan international civil servant; b. 22; ed. Univ. of Montevideo.
Economic Counsellor, Uruguayan Embassy, London, and Economic Adviser, Ministry of Foreign Affairs 54-59; Dir. of Commercial and Economic Dept., Uruguayan Embassy, Buenos Aires 59-62; Dir. of Dept. of Negotiation, Latin American Free Trade Asscn. (LAFTA) 62, Asst. Exec. Sec. LAFTA Dec. 62-67, Perm. Exec. Sec. 67-.
Latin American Free Trade Association, Cebollati 1461, Casilla de Correo 577, Montevideo, Uruguay.

Magariños D., Victor; Argentine painter; b. 10 Sept. 1924; ed. Escuela nacional de artes visuales.
Founded *Grupo Joven* 46; First one-man exhbn. Galería Juan Cristóbal 50, also at Inst. de Arte Moderno 50-51, Pres. Argentine Cttee. of Int. Asscn. for Plastic Arts, UNESCO 58; Scholarship to France 51, to U.S.A. 65; represented at Biennali: São Paulo 51-55, Venice 56; also at Concrete Art Exhbn. Museum of Modern Art 63, El Nuevo Arte Argentino, Walker Art Center, Minneapolis, A Decade of Latin-American Art, Guggenheim Museum 65-66.
Martin Capello 225, Banfield, Argentina.

Magee, Frank Lynn; American businessman; b. 13 April 1896; ed. Bethlehem Preparatory School and Lehigh Univ.
Sergeant in Army Signal Corps in France during First World War; service with Aluminum Co. of America (Alcoa) 17-, Salesman in New Haven, New York and other offices 20-25, Man. Albany office 25, Plant Sales Rep. and Asst. Product Man. Massena works 26-29, District Sales Man. Atlanta 29-37, Gen. Production Man. and Asst. to Vice-Pres. (Operations) 37-46, Vice-Pres. and Gen. Production Man. 46-55, Dir. 52-, Exec. Vice-Pres. 55-57, mem. Exec. Cttee. 56-, Chief Exec. Officer 59-62, Chair. of Board 60-63, Chair. Exec. Cttee. 63-; Dir. Mellon Nat. Bank and Trust Co., Pittsburgh, Westinghouse Air Brake Co., Mohawk Airline; mem. American Inst. of Electrical Engineers, etc.; Trustee Lehigh Univ., Univ. of Pittsburgh, and Cttee. for Econ. Devt.; President's Certificate of Merit 48; Hon. D.Eng. (Lehigh Univ.) 56, Hon. LL.D. (Maryville Coll.) 58, Hon. D.Comm. (Univ. of Pittsburgh) 66.
Home: 128 N. Craig St., Pittsburgh 15213; Office: 1501 Alcoa Building, Pittsburgh 15219, Pa., U.S.A.

Magistrati, Count Massimo, DR. IUR.; Italian diplomatist; b. 5 July 1899; ed. Collegio Nazareno, Rome, and Università degli Studi, Rome.
Minister in Bulgaria 40-43, Switzerland 43-45; Vice-Del. for Marshall Plan in Italy 49-52; Dir.-Gen. for Political Affairs, Foreign Office, Rome 54-58; Ambassador to Turkey 58-61, to United Arab Republic 61-65; numerous decorations.
Publ. *Italia a Berlino* 56.
Via San Nicola dei Cesarini 3, Rome, Italy.
Telephone: 650295.

Magloire, Paul; Haitian officer and politician; b. 07; ed. Cap Haiti High School.
Taught at Lycée National Philippe Guerrier, Cap Haiti 29-30; entered army as cadet 31; Lieut. 31; Head of Military School 34; Asst. District Commdr., Cap Haiti 35-37; Major 38; District Commdr. 38-41; Chief of Police, Port-au-Prince, and Commdr. of Palace Guard 44; mem. provisional Military Govt. and Minister of Interior 46 and 50; Pres. of Haiti 50-56; Orders of "Honneur et Mérite", "Brevet de Mérite", etc.
Port-au-Prince, Haiti.

Magnani, Anna; Italian film actress; b. 7 March 1918; ed. Acad. of Dramatic Art, Rome.
Worked in night clubs and repertory companies; began film career 34 with role in *Blind Woman of Sorrento*; acted in following films: Rossellini's *Open City* 46, *Before Him All Rome Trembled* 47, *Angelini* 47, *Love* 47, *Volcano* 53, *Bellissima* 53, Renoir's *The Gold Coach* 54, *Rose Tattoo* 55, *Suor Letizia* 58, *Awakening* 58, *Nella Città l'Inferno* 59, *The Fugitive Kind* 60, *And the Wild, Wild Women* 61, *Mamma Roma* 63; awards include Venice Film Festival Award, Italian Ribbon of Silver, American Oscar Award 56.
c/o Ercole Graziadei, Via Veneto 96, Rome, Italy.

Magne, Augusto; Brazilian university professor; b. 87; ed. Rome, Innsbruck and Vienna.
Professor of Romance Philology, Univ. of Brazil, and Greek Language and Literature, Catholic Univ. of Rio de Janeiro.
Publs. *The Legend of the Holy Grail, Dictionary of Mediaeval and Classical Portuguese, Etymological Dictionary of the Latin Language and Portuguese Derivations,* etc.
Rua S. Clemente 226, Botafogo, Rio de Janeiro, Brazil.

Magnet, Alejandro; Chilean writer, journalist and diplomatist; b. 28 Oct. 1919; ed. Universidad Católica de Chile.
Founded magazine *Política y Espíritu* 45, Literary Critic 45-52, Commentator on Int. Political Affairs 52-60; Asst. Editor *La Voz* 60-62; Commentator on Int. Affairs, Radio Chilena 54-62, TV Channel 13 62-64; Int. Political Affairs Editor *El Sur* (newspaper), Concepción 58-62, *Mensaje* (magazine) 59-64; Ambassador Rep. of Chile to Org. of American States 64-.
Publs. *Nuestros Vecinos Justicialistas* 53, *El Padre Hurtado* 54, *Nuestros Vecinos Argentinos* 56; children's books: *El Secreto Maravilloso* 44, *La Espada y el Canelo* 58.
Representation of Chile to Organization of American States, 1255 New Hampshire Avenue, N.W., Washington, D.C. 20036, U.S.A.

Magnuson, Warren Grant; American lawyer and politician; b. 12 April 1905; ed. Public School, Minnesota, and Univ. of Washington.
Special Prosecuting Attorney 31; elected to Washington State Legislature 33; Asst. U.S. Dist. Attorney 34; Prosecuting Attorney, King County, Washington 34; elected to 75th, 76th, 77th, and 78th Congresses; served in House of Reps.; Senator from Washington 44-; served as Lieut.-Commdr. in U.S.N.R. during Second World War; Democrat.
Home: Olympic Hotel, Seattle, Washington; Office: 127 Senate Office Bldg., Washington, D.C., U.S.A.

Magnússon, Magnús Vignir; Icelandic diplomatist; b. 10 Oct. 1910; ed. Reykjavík Grammar School and Univ. of Iceland.
Secretary, Ministry of Foreign Affairs 37-41; First Sec., London 41-44, Washington 44-47; Counsellor, Washington 47-51; Sec.-Gen., Ministry of Foreign Affairs 51-56; Ambassador to Sweden and Minister to Finland 56-62, concurrently Minister to Israel 57-62, to Iran 57, to Japan 60; Ambassador to Fed. Rep. of Germany 62-, concurrently to Greece 62-, to Switzerland 62-.
Kronprinzenstrasse 4, Bad Godesberg, German Federal Republic.

Magomayev, Djamal Muslimovich; Soviet politician; b. 1910; ed. Azerbaijan Petroleum Inst.
Mechanic-engineer at oil undertakings in Azerbaijan 32-48; mem. C.P.S.U. 40-; Vice-Chair. Azerbaijan S.S.R. Council of Ministers 48-52, 54-57; Second Sec. Baku Regional Cttee. of C.P. of Azerbaijan 52-53; Minister of Local Industry of Azerbaijan S.S.R. 53-54; First Vice-Chair. State Planning Cttee. of Azerbaijan S.S.R. Council of Ministers 57-62; Perm. Rep. of Azerbaijan

S.S.R. Council of Ministers to U.S.S.R. Council of Ministers 62-; Deputy to Supreme Soviets of Azerbaijan S.S.R. and U.S.S.R.
Permanent Representation of Azerbaijan S.S.R. Council of Ministers to U.S.S.R. Council of Ministers, Gogolevsky boulevard 31A, Moscow, U.S.S.R.

Magowan, Robert Anderson; American businessman; b. 19 Sept. 1903; ed. Kent School and Harvard Univ.
Merchandise Man. R. H. Macy & Co. 27-34; Vice-Pres. N. W. Ayer & Son 34-35; Vice-Pres. Safeway Stores Inc., San Francisco 35-38, Chair. 55-; Chair. Canada Safeway Ltd.; Vice-Pres. Merrill Lynch & Co. Inc. 38-40, Partner Merrill Lynch, Pierce, Fenner and Beane 40-55, Limited Partner 55-; official of several civic orgs.
Home: 2100 Washington Street, San Francisco 9; Office: 4th and Jackson Streets, Oakland 4, Calif., U.S.A.

Magrí, Salvatore; Italian accountant and business executive; b. 97.
Qualified accountant 14; Credito Italiano 14-52; Chair. and Managing Dir. Dalmine Co. 52-60; Chair. and Managing Dir. Finanziaria Meccanica (Finmeccanica) 60-; "Honoris Causa" Degree of Economy and Commerce 54.
Finanziaria Meccanica, Via Torino 48, Rome, Italy.
Telephone: 478-041.

Maguire, Conor A., S.C.; Irish jurist; b. 16 Dec. 1889; ed. Univ. Coll. Dublin.
Solicitor 14; Judge of Republican Courts and Dail Land Settlement Comm. 20-22; Called to Bar 22; Fianna Fáil Deputy for Nat. Univ. and Attorney-Gen. in De Valéra Govt. 32-36; Pres. Irish High Court 36-46; Chair. Irish Red Cross Soc. 40-46; Chief Justice 46-61; mem. European Comm. of Human Rights 62-65, European Int. Court of Human Rights 65-; Hon. LL.D. (Nat. Univ. of Ireland and Univ. of Dublin); Commdr. Légion d'Honneur, Cross St. Raimon de Penafort, Grosses Verdienstkreuz.
St. Alban's, Albany Avenue, Monkstown, Co. Dublin, Ireland.

Mahalanobis, Prasanta Chandra, B.SC., M.A., F.R.S.; Indian scientist; b. 29 June 1893; ed. Calcutta and Cambridge Univs.
Indian Educational Service 15-48; Head Dept. of Physics, Presidency Coll. 22-42, Principal 45-48, Prof. Emeritus 48-; Meteorologist, Calcutta 22-26; Head, Postgraduate Dept. of Statistics, Calcutta Univ. 41-45; Statistical Adviser to Govt. of Bengal 45-48, to the Cabinet, Govt. of India 49-; mem. Planning Comm., Govt. of India 55-; Sec. and Dir. Indian Statistical Inst., Calcutta, since foundation in 31; Founder-Editor *Sankhya* (The Indian Journal of Statistics) 33-; Karmasachiva (Gen. Sec.) Rabindranath Tagore's Visvabharati 21-31; Fellow, Indian Acad. of Sciences, Nat. Acad. of Sciences, India, Royal Statistical Soc., London, American Statistical Asscn., etc.; mem. Int. Statistical Inst. 37, hon. mem. 52-, hon. Pres. 57-; Vice-Pres. Int. Biometric Soc. 47; hon. mem. Pakistan Statistical Asscn. 52; Fellow Econometric Soc.; Pres. Indian Science Congress 50; mem. UN Statistical Comm., ECOSOC 46-, Chair. 48; Chair. UN Sub-Comm. on Statistical Sampling 47-51; Leader Indian Del. World Statistical Congress, Washington 47; Del. UN Scientific Conf. on Conservation and Utilisation of Resources, N.Y. 49; del., rep. or observer several other int. confs.; foreign mem. U.S.S.R. Acad. of Sciences; Hon. Fellow King's Coll., Cambridge 58; Fellow World Acad. of Art and Science 63; Hon. D.Sc.; lecturer, U.S., Canada and many European and Asian countries; awarded Weldon Medal and Prize, Oxford Univ. 44, Sarvadhikary Medal, Calcutta Univ. 57.
204 Barrackpore Trunk Road, Calcutta 35, India; and 8 King George Avenue, New Dehli, India.

Mahdi, Ahmed Abdel Rahman El; Sudanese politician; b. 1933; ed. Victoria Coll., Alexandria and New Coll., Oxford.
Private Sec. to late Imam Abdel Rahman El Mahdi; Leader of *Ansar* movement; Man. Dir. Dairat El Mahdi, comprising Aba Island and White Nile Agricultural Schemes, Estate Co. Khartoum, Agricultural and Commercial Groups of Companies Khartoum; various political and social appointments; Minister of the Interior 65-67; later Minister of Information and Social Affairs; Minister of Defence.
c/o Ministry of the Interior, P.O. Box 282, Khartoum, Sudan.

Mahdi, El Haj Abdul Rahman El; Sudanese religious leader; b. 15; ed. religious schools.
Succeeded his brother, Siddik El Mahdi, as leader of the Ansari sect and spiritual head of the Mahdi movement 61.
Khartoum, Sudan.

Mahdi, Saadik El (Great grandson of Imam Abdul-Rahman El-Mahdi); Sudanese politician; b. 1936; ed. Comboni Coll., Khartoum and St. John's Coll., Oxford.
Son of the late Siddik El Mahdi; Leader, Umma Mahdist Party 61-; Prime Minister 66-67.
Publ. *Problems of the South Sudan.*
c/o Office of the Prime Minister, Khartoum, Sudan.

Maheu, René; French administrator; b. 28 March 1905; ed. Lycée de Toulouse, Lycée Louis-le-Grand, Paris, Sorbonne and Ecole Normale Supérieure, Paris.
Lecturer, Cologne Univ. 31-33; Lecturer in Philosophy, French Inst., London 33-39; Teacher of Philosophy at Coll. Franco-Musulman Moulay-Idriss, Fez, Morocco 40-42; Dir. Features Service France-Afrique, Algiers 43; mem. Civilian Cabinet, French Residency-Gen. in Morocco, Rabat and Paris 44-46; joined UNESCO Sept. 46, Head, Div. Free Flow of Information 46-48, Dir. Office of Dir.-Gen. 49-54, Asst. Dir.-Gen. in Paris 54-55, in New York (at U.N.) 56-58, in Paris 59, Deputy Dir. Gen. 59-61, Acting Dir.-Gen. 61-62, Dir.-Gen. of UNESCO 62-.
Publ. *La civilisation de l'universal* 67.
2 place de Fontenoy, Paris 7e, France.

Mahgoub, Mohammed Ahmed; Sudanese lawyer and politician; b. 08; ed. Gordon Coll. and Khartoum School of Law.
Practising lawyer; fmr. mem. Legislative Assembly; accompanied Umma Party Del. to United Nations 47; mem. Constitution Amendment Comm.; non-party candidate in Gen. Election 54; Leader of the Opposition 54-56; Minister of Foreign Affairs 56-58, 64-65, Prime Minister 65-66, May 67-; practising solicitor 58-64.
Office of the Prime Minister, Khartoum, Sudan.

Mahoney, David Joseph, Jr.; American advertising and business executive; b. 17 May 1923; ed. LaSalle Military Acad., Cathedral High School, New York, and Wharton School of Business, Univ. of Pennsylvania.
Ruthrauff and Ryan 46-51; David J. Mahoney Inc. (advertising agency) 51-56; Pres. Good Humor Corpn. 56-61; Exec. Vice-Pres. Colgate-Palmolive Co. 61-66; Pres. and Chief Exec. Officer Canada Dry Corpn. 66-.
Office: 100 Park Avenue, New York, N.Y. 10017, U.S.A.

Mahtab, Harekrushna, D.LITT., LL.D.; Indian politician and journalist; b. Nov. 1899; ed. Ravenshaw Coll., Cuttack.
Joined non-co-operation movement 21; worker for Indian Nat. Congress 21-; mem. Bihar & Orissa Legislative Council 24; Editor, *Prajatantra* and *Jhankar*; civil disobedience movements 30, 32; Pres. Utkal Provincial Congress Cttee. 30, 37; organised Inchudi Salt Satyagraha, imprisoned 30-31, 32, 42; mem. Congress Working Cttee. 38-46; Leader, Congress Assembly Party, Orissa; Chief Minister, Orissa State

46-50, 56-61; Minister for Commerce and Industry, Govt. of India 50-52; Sec.-Gen. Congress Parl. Party 52-55, Deputy Leader 62-63; Gov. of Bombay 55-56.
Publs. *History of Orissa;* three novels, one play.
Bhuvaneshwar, Orissa, India.

Mai-Bornu, Aliyu; Nigerian banker and administrator; b. 19; ed. Yola Middle School, Kaduna Coll., and Univ. of Bristol, England.
Schoolmaster 42-54; Univ. of Bristol 54-57; Admin. Officer, Northern Nigeria Govt. 57-59; Sec. Central Bank of Nigeria 61-62, Deputy Gov. 62-63, Gov. 63-67; Alt. Gov. of Int. Monetary Fund for Nigeria 63-67.
2 Glover Road, Ikoyi, Lagos, Nigeria.

Maiboroda, Georgi Illarionovich; Soviet composer; b. 1913; ed. Kiev Conservatoire.
Chairman, Ukrainian Composers' Union; Honoured Worker of Arts of the Ukrainian S.S.R. 57; People's Artist of the U.S.S.R. 60; Order of Red Banner of Labour 63.
Principal compositions include: symphonies 40, 52, *Gutsuli Rhapsody* 51, *Friendship of the Peoples* (cantata), *Zaporozhtsy* 54, *Milana* (opera) 56, *The Arsenal* (opera) 60, *King Lear* (suite for symphonic orchestra) 59, *Taras Shevchenko* (opera) 67, also many romances and songs.
Composers' Union of the Ukrainian S.S.R., Shevchenko Prospekt, Kiev, U.S.S.R.

Mailer, Norman Kingsley, B.S.; American writer; b. 31 Jan. 1923; ed. Harvard Univ.
Mem. Editorial Board *Dissent* magazine; co-founder New York weekly *The Village Voice.*
Publs. *The Naked and The Dead* 48, *Barbary Shore* 51, *The Deer Park* 55, *The White Negro* 58, *Advertisements for Myself* 59, *Deaths for the Ladies* (poems) 62, *The Presidential Papers* 63, *An American Dream* 64, *Cannibals and Christians* 66, *The Deer Park* (play script) 67, *Why Are We in Vietnam?* 67, *The Armies of the Night* 68.
128 Willow Street, Brooklyn, N.Y., U.S.A.

Maillart, Ella; Swiss traveller and writer; b. 20 Feb. 1903; ed. Geneva.
Travelled Russia, Turkestan, Manchuria, Tibet, Iran, Afghanistan; in S. India 40; Nepal 51; Fellow Royal Geographical Society London; Hon. mem. Ski Club G.B.
Publs. *Parmi la Jeunesse Russe* 32, *Des Monts Célestes aux Sables Rouges* (Turkestan Solo) 34, *Oases Interdites* (Forbidden Journey) 37, *Gypsy Afloat* 42, *Cruises and Caravans* 42 (pub. in French, German), *The Cruel Way* 47 (pub. in Dutch, Swedish, French, Spanish and German), *Ti-Puss* (in English and German), *The Land of the Sherpas.*
c/o David Higham Associates, 76 Dean Street, London, W.1, England; and 10 ave. Vallette, Geneva, Switzerland.
Telephone: 46-46-57 (Geneva).

Maingot, Rodney, F.R.C.S. ENG.; British surgeon; ed. Ushaw Coll. and St. Bartholomew's Hospital, London.
Served R.A.M.C. 16-19; fmr. House Surgeon, Casualty Officer, Chief Asst. to a Surgical Unit, St. Bartholomew's Hospital, London; Consulting Surgeon to Royal Free Hospital, London, and Southend Gen. Hospital; Fellow, Asscn. of Surgeons of Great Britain; former Pres. Section of Surgery, Royal Society of Medicine; Chair. Editorial Board *London Clinic Medical Journal*; Editor-in-Chief *British Journal of Clinical Practice.*
Publs. *Post-Graduate Surgery* 38, *Technique of Gastric Operations* 41, *War Wounds and Injuries* (part editor) 43, *The Surgical Treatment of Gastric and Duodenal Ulcer* 45, *Techniques of British Surgery* 50, *The Management of Abdominal Operations* (2nd edn.) 57, *Abdominal Operations* (5th edn.) 68, contributor to *Surgery of the Gallbladder and Bile Ducts* 64.
149 Harley Street, London, W.1, England.
Telephone: 01-935-4444.

Maisel, Karl; Austrian politician; b. 90; ed. elementary school and Workers' High School, Vienna.
Engineer in Vienna 04-14; served as Sergeant in Austro-Hungarian Army 14-19; engineer at Siemens Works, Vienna 19-26; Sec. of Metalworkers T.U. 27-34; interned by Austrian Govt. 34; employed as foreman 38-39; in Buchenwald concentration camp 39-40; employed Siemens factory 40-44; in concentration camp 44-45; Chair. Austrian Metalworkers' Union 45-62, Hon. Chair. 62-; Min. of Social Welfare 45-56; Pres. Fed. Austrian Chambers of Labour; Socialist.
Vordere Zollamtsstrasse 11, Vienna III, Austria.

Maisky, Ivan Mikhailovich; Soviet diplomatist, historian and writer; b. 19 Jan. 1884; ed. St. Petersburg and Munich Univs.
Chief of Press Dept. Foreign Office, Moscow 22; Counsellor, Soviet Embassy, London 25-27, Tokyo 27-29; Ambassador to Finland 29-32; Ambassador to Great Britain 32-43; Asst. People's Commissar for Foreign Affairs U.S.S.R. 43-46, mem. U.S.S.R. Acad. of Sciences 46-; Order of Lenin 42, Order of Red Banner of Labour 44, 45, 64.
Publs. *Germany and the War* 16, *Political Germany* 17, *Contemporary Mongolia* 21, *Before the Storm* (reminiscences) 44, *Spain, 1808–1917* 57, *So Near and Yet So Far* (novel) 58, *Mongolia on the Eve of the Revolution* 59, *Reminiscences of a Soviet Ambassador to Britain* 60, *Journey into the Past* (reminiscences) 60, *Who Helped Hitler?* 62, *Spanish Notebooks* 62, *Reminiscences of a Soviet Ambassador* 64-65.
Academy of Sciences of the U.S.S.R., Lenin Prospekt 14, Moscow, U.S.S.R.

Maiti, Abha, B.A., LL.B.; Indian social worker and politician; b. 23 May 1925; ed. Univ. Law Coll., Calcutta.
Joined Quit India Movement 42; Sec. Women's sub-cttee. of West Bengal Pradesh Congress 48-54; mem. West Bengal Pradesh Congress Cttee. 54-59; Pres. Midnapore Congress Cttee. 59; mem. West Bengal Legislative Ass. 52-57; mem. All India Congress Cttee. 52-, Congress Working Cttee. 60-, Gen. Sec. Indian Nat. Congress 60-64; mem. Rajya Sabha 60-; Joint Sec. Paschim Banga Khadi Kendra 57-; Minister of Refugee Relief and Rehabilitation, Relief and Social Welfare and Home (Constitution and Elections) for West Bengal 62-.
P-14 Durga Charran Mitra Street, Calcutta 6, West Bengal; and 97 South Avenue, New Delhi, India.

Maiwandwal, Mohamed Hashim; Afghan diplomatist; b. 23 March 1921; ed. privately in Habibia, Kabul.
Editor of *Ittifâq-i Islam* 42; Dir. Afghan Encyclopaedia 44; Editor of *Anis* 45; Acting Pres. of Press Dept. of the Royal Afghan Govt. 49; Press Adviser of His Afghan Majesty 50; Pres. Press Dept. of Afghan Govt. 51; Counsellor Afghan Embassy in Washington 53; Pres. Press Dept. Afghan Govt. 54; Deputy Foreign Minister 55; Ambassador to United Kingdom 57, to Pakistan 57-58, 63-65, to the U.S.A. 58-63; First Class Star 58; Minister of Press and Information 64; Prime Minister Nov. 65-Oct. 67.
Kabul, Afghanistan.

Majekodunmi, Chief The Hon. Moses Adekoyejo, C.M.G., LL.D., M.A., M.D., F.R.C.P., M.A.O., D.C.H., L.M.; Nigerian doctor and politician; b. 17 Aug. 1916; ed. Abeokuta Grammar School, St. Gregory's Coll., Lagos, Trinity Coll., Dublin.
House Physician, Nat. Children's Hospital, Dublin 41-43; Medical Officer, Nigeria 43-49; Consulting Obstetrician, Massey Street Maternity Hospital and General Hospital and Creek Hospital, Lagos 49-60; Senior Specialist Obstetrician, Nigerian Federal Gov. Medical Services 49-60; Senator and Leader of Senate 60; Minister of State for the Army 60; Fed. Minister of Health 61-65; Fed. Minister of Health and Informa-

tion 65; Admin. for W. Nigeria 62; Pres. 16th World Health Assembly 63; Internat. Vice-Pres., 3rd World Conf. on Medical Education, New Delhi 66.
Publs. *Premature Infants: Management and Prognosis* 43, *Partial Apresia of the Cervix Complicating Pregnancy* 46, *Sub-Acute Insususeption in Adolescents* 48, *Thiopentone Sodium in Operational Obstetrics* 54, *Rupture of the Uterus Involving the Bladder* 55, *Effects of Malnutrition in Pregnancy and Lactation* 57; *Behold the Key* (play) 44; *Medical Education and the Health Services: A Critical Review of Priorities in a Developing Country* 66.
3 Kingsway, Ikoyi, Lagos, Nigeria.

Majerus, Pierre, DR. IUR.; Luxembourg diplomatist; b. 29 Sept. 1909; ed. Athénée and C.S. Luxembourg, and Univ. of Paris.
Barrister, Luxembourg 33; Attaché, Ministry of Foreign Affairs 36, Sec. 44, Counsellor 45; Chamberlain to Grand Duchess of Luxembourg 46, to Grand Duke 64; Chargé d'Affaires, Brussels 44-47; Chief of Political Section, Ministry of Foreign Affairs 48-51; Del. to UN Gen. Assembly 49, 50; Minister to Germany and Chief of Luxembourg Mil. Mission to Berlin 51-56; Ambassador to Fed. Germany 55-61, to Italy 61-, concurrently to Switzerland 63-; several decorations.
Publs. *Le Luxembourg Indépendant* 45, *L'Etat Luxembourgeois* 48 (second edn. 59), *Principes élémentaires de Droit Public Luxembourgeois* 53.
Villa Ardeatina, Via Ardeatina 134-138, Rome, Italy.

Majewski, Stanislaw; Polish government official; b. 15; ed. Uniwersytet Jagielloński, Cracow.
Bank of Commerce, Cracow 37, later at Bank of Co-operative Econ., Bank of Union of Econ. Co-operatives, and Vice-Dir. Bank of Handicraft and Commerce; Dir. of Dept. of Financial Co-ordination and State Budget 60-65; Pres. of Nat. Bank of Poland and Under-Sec. of State to Finance Ministry 65-.
Narodowy Bank Polski, 11/21 Swietokrzyska Street, Warsaw, Poland.

Majid, Abdul, PH.D.; Afghan diplomatist; b. 14 July 1914; ed. Cornell Univ. and Univ. of California (Berkeley).
Member Afghan Inst. of Bacteriology 41, Dir. 41-42; Prof. of Biology and Physiology, Kabul Univ. 40-46, Pres. of Univ 46-48; Minister of Public Health 48-50; Minister of Education 50-56; Ambassador to Japan 56-63, to U.S.A. 63-67, to U.K. 67-; Leader of Afghan del. to UN 66; Order of Educ. First Class 56, Sardar-i Ali 59, A. Haas Award (Univ. of Calif.) 66.
Royal Afghan Embassy, 31 Princes Gate, London, S.W.7, England.
Telephone: 01-589-8891.

Majluta Azar, Jacobo; Dominican accountant and politician; b. 34; ed. Univ. of Santo Domingo.
Assistant, Accounts Dept., R. Esteva and Co. 48; Monte de Piedad (State Credit Bank) 49-55; Insp. of Banks, Ministry of Finance 55-58; Auditor, later Admin. Gen. Chocolatera Industrial 58-62; Minister of Finance 62-63; Partido Revolucionario Dominicano (P.R.D.); Org. Sec. of the Nat. Exec. Cttee. of P.R.D. 62-64; in exile 63-65.
Pina Street 34, Santo Domingo, Dominican Republic.

Major, Louis Charles; Belgian trade union leader; b. 02; ed. Labour Univ. of Brussels.
Secretary of the Dock Workers Trade Union in Ostend 25, and in Antwerp 36; Nat. Sec. of Gen. Fed. of Belgian Trade Unions 40-44, Asst. Gen. Sec. 44-52, Gen. Sec. 52-68; Minister of Labour June 68-; Deputy in the House of Representatives; mem. Exec. Cttee. of the International Confederation of Free Trade Unions, and of the Exec. Cttee. of the Belgian Socialist Party; Pres. Econ. and Social Cttee., European Communities; King's Medal.
42 rue Haute, Brussels, Belgium.

Major, Máté, D.TECH.SC.; Hungarian architect; b. 3 Aug. 1903; ed. Budapest Technical Univ.
Private practice 31-36; employed by state 36-48; Prof. 49-; mem. and Sec. Group of Socialist Painters and Sculptors 33-37; mem. Presidium of Union of Hungarian Architects and Artists 51-, Pres. 55-64; Corresp. mem. Hungarian Acad. of Sciences 49-60, mem. 60-; has edited several periodicals since 46; Hon. Corresp. mem. Royal Inst. of British Architects 63-; Hon. mem. Instituto de Arquitectos do Brasil and Sociedad de Arquitectos Mexicanos 64-; Foreign mem. Serbian Acad. of Arts and Sciences 65-; Kossuth Prize 49; Order of the People's Repub. 50; Golden Order of Labour 64; Order for Socialist Country 67.
Publs. *History of Architecture*, Vols. I-III 54-60, *P.L. Nervi* 66, *Peculiarity of Architecture* 67; *Essays 51-68*, 68.
Vecsey u. 4, Budapest V; Budapest Technical University, Müegyetem rakpart 3, Budapest XI, Hungary.
Telephone: 113-399.

Major, Tamás; Hungarian actor and director; b. 10; ed. Academy of Dramatic Art.
Budapest National Theatre Dir. 45-62, leading Stage Man. 62-; played Tartuffe, Richard III, Iago (*Othello*), etc.; mem. Central Cttee., Hungarian Socialist Workers' Party 57-66; Kossuth Prize (twice), decorated Outstanding Artist of the Hungarian People's Republic.
c/o National Theatre, Budapest VII, Hevesi Sándor tér 2, Hungary.
Telephone: 413-849.

Makarios III, Archbishop; Cypriot ecclesiastic and politician; b. 13 Aug. 1913; ed. Theological Coll. of Athens Univ. and School of Theology, Boston Univ.
Ordained Deacon Greek Orthodox Church 38; studied in Greece 38-43; mem. teaching staff Kykkos Abbey 43-46; ordained Priest 46; studied in U.S.A. supported by World Council of Churches Fellowship 46-48; Bishop of Kition 48-50; Archbishop of Cyprus 50-; Cypriot national leader identified with *Enosis* (Union with Greece) movement; has travelled abroad to promote interest and support for *Enosis*; led negotiations with Sir John Harding, Gov. of Cyprus 55-56; deported to the Seychelles 56; released Mar. 57; in Athens until return to Cyprus March 59; Cyprus Transitional Cttee., March 59, President-Elect 59-60; President of Cyprus 60-; Hon. Dr. of Divinity (Boston Univ.), Hon. LL.D. (Kerala Univ.), and other decorations.
Presidential Palace, Nicosia, Cyprus.

Makarova, Tamara Fyodorovna; Soviet film actress; b. 13 Aug. 1907; ed. Leningrad Inst. of Scenic Arts.
Dozent at the Institute of Cinematography 44-; People's Artist of the U.S.S.R.; State prizewinner 41, 47; awarded Sign of Merit; Rector People's Univ. of Arts 64-.
Principal roles: Dr. Okhrimenko (*Seven Brave People* 35), Natasha Solovyova (*Komsomolsk* 37), collective farmer Shumilina (*The Teacher* 39), Koshevaya (*The Young Guard* 48), Dr. Kazakova (*The Country Doctor* 52), *Memory of the Heart* 58, *Men and Beasts* 62, *The Journalist* 67.
All-Union State Institute of Cinematography, Moscow, U.S.S.R.

Makhmudov, Nasyr; Soviet politician; b. 1913; ed. C.P.S.U. Higher Party School.
Teacher and journalist 31-38; Soviet Army service 36-38; Party Official 38-48; Party and Local Govt. Official, Uzbekistan 50-56; First Sec. Kara-Kalpak Regional Cttee., Communist Party, Uzbekistan 56-63; First Sec. Syr-Darya Regional Cttee. C.P. Uzbekistan 63-; mem. C.P.S.U. 40-; mem. Central Cttee. Communist Party of Uzbekistan; Deputy to U.S.S.R. Supreme Soviet.
Syr-Darya Regional Committee, Communist Party of Uzbekistan, Gulistan, U.S.S.R.

Makhous, Dr. Ibrahim; Syrian politician.
Member of Baath Party's Supreme Command 65; Deputy Prime Minister and Minister of Foreign Affairs Sept. 65-Dec. 65, March 66-.
Ministry of Foreign Affairs, Damascus, Syrian Arab Republic.

Maki, Fumihiko, B.ARCH., M.ARCH.; Japanese architect; b. 6 Sept. 1928; ed. Univ. of Tokyo, Cranbrook School of Art, Mich. and Harvard Univ.
Associate Prof. Washington Univ. 56-62, Harvard Univ. 62-66; Lecturer, Dept. of Urban Engineering, Univ. of Tokyo 64-; Principal Partner, Maki and Associates (architectural firm) 64-; Visiting Lecturer and Critic to various univs. and insts. in Canada and U.S. 60-; awards include Gold Medal of Japan Inst. of Architects 64; major works include Steinberg Hall, Washington Univ. 60, Toyoda Memorial Hall, Nagoya Univ. 60, Lecture Hall, Chiba Univ. 64, and Rissho Univ. Campus 66-.
Publs. *Investigations in Collective Form* 64, *Movement Systems in the City* 65, *Metabolism* 60, *Structure in Art and Science* (contrib.) 65.
16-22, 5-chome Higashi-Gotanda, Shinagawa-ku, Tokyo, Japan.

Makkawi, Abdul Qawi Hassan; Aden politician; b. 18.
Joined A. Besse and Co., successively Manager in Eritrea, Divisional Manager Aden, now Dir. of Company; elected mem. Legislative Council 46; nominated mem. Legislative Council 59; Vice-Chair. Chamber of Commerce 64; Chief Minister of Aden 65-Sept. 65; Sec.-Gen. Revolutionary Council of Front for Liberation of Occupied S. Yemen, Taiz 66-.
Revolutionary Council of Front for Liberation of Occupied S. Yemen, Taiz, Yemen.

Makonnen, Endalkachew, M.A.; Ethiopian politician; b. 27; ed. Haile Selassie I Secondary School, Addis Ababa and Oriel Coll., Oxford.
Ministry of Foreign Affairs 51-58, Acting Head Dept. of Protocol 52-53, Chief of Protocol 53-56, Asst. Minister 56-57, Vice-Minister 57-58; Vice-Minister of Social Affairs 58-59; Ambassador to the U.K. 59-61; Minister of Commerce and Industry 61-66; Chair. Board of Govts. Univ. Coll. Addis Ababa 59, Nat. Coffee Board 62; Perm. Rep. to UN 66-; numerous decorations.
Permanent Mission of Ethiopia to the United Nations, 575 Lexington Avenue, New York, N.Y., U.S.A.

Maksaryov, Yury Yevgenyevich; Soviet politician; b. 10 Aug. 1903; ed. Leningrad Inst. of Technology.
Alternative mem. Cen. Cttee. C.P.S.U. 52-61; Chair. State Cttee. for Science and Technology, Council of Ministers 57-60; Chair. State Cttee. for Inventions and Discoveries 61-; State Prize; Hero of Socialist Labour 43.
State Committee for Inventions and Discoveries, 2 Maly Cherkassky Pereulok, Moscow, U.S.S.R.

Maksymowicz, Stanislaw; Polish diplomatist and politician; b. 13; ed. Jan Kazimierz Univ., Lwów, Handelshochschule, St. Gallen and Freiburg Univ.
Ministry of Navigation and Foreign Trade 45-46; Attaché, later Commercial Counsellor, Polish Embassy, Paris 46-50; Chief Dir. Varimex (Foreign Trade Enterprise) 50-57; Head of a Dept., Ministry of Foreign Trade 57-61; Commercial Counsellor, Polish Embassy, Vienna 61-62; Gen. Sec., Polish Chamber of Foreign Trade 62-.
Polska Izba Zagraniczna, Trebacka 4, Warsaw, Poland.

Malabu, Alhaji Bello; Nigerian politician and diplomatist; b. 12 May 1913; ed. Yola Middle School and Katsina Coll.
Teacher Yola Middle School 33-48, Headmaster 48-49; Asst. Lecturer, School of Oriental and African Studies, London 49-51; Native Schools Man. 51-56; mem.

Nigerian House of Reps. 51-54; mem. Nigerian Ports Authority 54-57, N. Nigerian Regional Legislature 51-60, Nigerian Senate, April-Sept. 60; Ambassador to Cameroon Republic 60-.
Embassy of Nigeria, B.P. 448, Yaoundé, Cameroon.
Telephone: 41-37.

Malaccorto, Dr. Ernesto; Argentine economist and politician; b. 02; ed. Univ. of Buenos Aires.
Under-Secretary of Finance, Argentina 42-43; Organiser and Dir. Income Tax Bureau, Argentina; UN Adviser on Fiscal Matters 52-55; fmr. Minister of Agriculture; Dir. Banco Central de la República Argentina; mem. Cttee. of Nine, Alliance for Progress.
Alliance for Progress, Washington 25, D.C., U.S.A.

Malagodi, Giovanni Francesco, DR.IUR.; Italian banker and politician; b. 12 Oct. 1904; ed. Rome Univ.
Joint Gen. Manager Banca Commerciale Italiana 33, Gen. Manager 47; Gen. Manager Banque Française et Italienne pour l'Amérique du Sud 37; Econ. and Financial Adviser, Ministry of Foreign Affairs 47; Chair. O.E.E.C. Man-power Cttee. 50; Deputy for Milan 53- (re-elected 58 and 63); Sec.-Gen. Partito Liberale Italiano 54-; Vice-Chair. Liberal Int. 56-58, Chair. 58-; Commdr. Ordine al Merito della Repubblica Italiana; Liberal.
Publs. *Le Ideologie Politiche* 27, *Rapporto sull'Emigrazione* 52, *Massa non Mass* 63, *Liberalismo in Commino* 65.
Corso Venezia 40, Milan; Via Frattina 89, Rome, Italy.

Malakul, Mom Luang Peekdhip; Thai diplomatist; b. 06; ed. Debsirindr School and Assumption Coll., Bangkok, the Inner Temple, London.
Attached to Office of Royal Households 32, to Protocol Division, Ministry of Foreign Affairs 35, Chief of Section 39, Chief of Division 42; Sec., Rangoon 49, Chargé d'Affaires 50; Dir. Gen. Dept. of Economic Affairs, Ministry of Foreign Affairs 53, Dir. Gen. Protocol Dept. 54; Deputy Under-Sec. of State for Foreign Affairs 57, Under-Sec. 57; Ambassador to Great Britain 58-62, to Pakistan 64-; rep. of Ministry of Foreign Affairs, Thai Special Goodwill Mission to British Commonwealth in Far East 40; del. Franco-Thai Peace Convention, Tokyo 41, Official Mission to Tokyo 43; Deputy Chief Del. Burma Independence Celebrations 47; Knight Grand Cross of the Orders of the Crown of Thailand and White Elephant; Knight Grand Cross of Royal Victorian Order, Grand Officer Orders of Million Elephants and White Parasol, Hon. C.B.E. (U.K.), Spanish, Netherlands, Danish, Italian, Federal German, French, Belgian and Greek decorations.
Royal Thai Embassy, 36-P Block 6, P.E.C.H.S., Karachi, Pakistan.

Malalasekera, Gunapala Piyasena, O.B.E., D.LITT., PH.D., M.A.; Ceylonese scholar and diplomatist; b. 9 Nov. 1899; ed. St. John's Coll., Ceylon and Univ. of London.
College Vice-Principal and Principal 21-27; Head of Dept. of Oriental Languages, Univ. Coll., Colombo 27-42; Prof. and Head of Dept. of Pali and Buddhist Civilisation, Univ. of Ceylon 42-58; Editor-in-Chief, *Encyclopaedia of Buddhism*; Ambassador of Ceylon to U.S.S.R. 57-61; High Commr. to Canada 61-63, to U.K. 63-66, concurrently Perm. Rep. of Ceylon to UN 61-63; Pres. World Fellowship of Buddhists 50-58, All-Ceylon Buddhist Congress, Ceylon Society of Arts; Chair. Nat. Council of Higher Educ., Ceylon 67-; Gen. Pres. Indian Philosophical Congress 57.
Publs. *Dictionary of Pali Proper Names* (2 vols.) 38, *The Pali Literature of Ceylon, The Buddha and His Teaching* 57, etc.
202 Bullers Road, Colombo, Ceylon and 12 Longden Terrace, Colombo 7, Ceylon.
Telephone: 85808.

Malamud, Bernard, B.A., M.A.; American author; b. April 1914; ed. New York City Coll. and Columbia Univ.
Evening High School teacher, Brooklyn and Harlem 40-49; English Dept., Oregon State Coll. 49-61, Assoc. Prof. 59-; mem. Literature Div. Bennington Coll. 61-; mem. Nat. Inst. of Arts and Letters 64; *Partisan Review* Fiction Fellowship 56, Rosenthal Award (Nat. Inst. of Arts and Letters) and Daroff Memorial Award for *The Assistant* 58, Ford Foundation Grant in Humanities and Letters, Nat. Book Award for *The Magic Barrel* 59, Pulitzer Prize for Fiction for *The Fixer* 67.
Publs. *The Natural* 52, *The Assistant* 57, *A New Life* 61, *The Fixer* 66 (novels); *The Magic Barrel* (short stories) 57, *Idiots First* (short stories) 63; numerous short stories have appeared in *Commentary, Esquire, Partisan Review, The New Yorker,* etc.
Bennington College, Bennington, Vermont, U.S.A.

Malaviya, Keshava Deva, M.P., M.SC.; Indian politician; b. 11 June 1903; ed. Allahabad Univ. and Harcourt Butler Technological Inst., Kanpur.
Joined Congress Movement 21; served various sentences as political prisoner; former Gen. Sec. Uttar Pradesh Provincial Congress Cttee.; actively participated in "Quit India" Movement; Parl. Sec. to Minister for Industries and Development, U.P. Govt. 46; Minister for Industries and Development ,U.P. 47-51; Parl. Sec. to Fed. Minister of Education 52; Deputy Fed. Minister of Natural Resources and Education 52-56; Fed. Minister of Natural Resources 56-57; Minister of State for Mines and Oil 57-62.
7 Raisina Road, New Delhi, India.

Malavolta, Euripedes, D.SC.; Brazilian agricultural biochemist; b. 13 Aug. 1926; ed. E.S.A. Luiz de Queiroz (Universidade do São Paulo) and Univ. of California (Berkeley), U.S.A.
Instructor in Agricultural Chemistry, Univ. of São Paulo 49, Private Docent 51, Prof. of Agricultural Biochemistry 58-; Research Assoc. Univ. of Calif. 52-53, Visiting Prof. 59-60; Vice-Dean, E.S.A. Luiz de Queiroz, Univ. of São Paulo 66-; mem. Brazilian Acad. of Sciences.
Publs. *Elements of Agricultural Chemistry* 54, *Manual of Agricultural Chemistry* 59, 67, *On the Mineral Nutrition of Some Tropical Crops* 62, 64, 67.
Travessa Portugal 146, Piracicaba, São Paulo, Brazil.
Telephone: 3948.

Malayeri, Mahmood; Iranian diplomatist; b. 05; ed. Univ. de Paris à la Sorbonne.
Former Dir.-Gen. Ministry of Interior; fmr. Technical Dir. Library of Ministry of Foreign Affairs until 50, Head of Translating Dept. 50-51; First Sec., London 51-53; Consul-Gen. Baghdad 53-55; Consul-Gen. Basra 55-57; Head of Information and Publs. Dept. 57-59; Head of First Political Dept. 59; Minister Chargé d'Affaires a.i. Baghdad 59-60; mem. High Political Council 60-; Minister Consul-Gen. Hamburg 60-61; Ambassador to Syria 62-64; Admin. Dir.-Gen. Ministry of Foreign Affairs 64-65.
c/o Ministry of Foreign Affairs, Teheran, Iran.

Malbakhov, Timbora Kubatiyevich; Soviet politician; b. 17; ed. State Agricultural Coll., Orjonikidze and C.P.S.U. Higher Party School.
Soviet Army 40-46; First Sec. Kubin District Cttee. of C.P.S.U. 47-49; Sec., later Second Sec. Kabardinian Regional Cttee. of C.P.S.U. 49-52; Chair. Presidium of Supreme Soviet of Kabardinian-Balkar Autonomous Repub. 52-56; First Sec. Kabardinian-Balkar Regional Cttee. of C.P.S.U. 56-; Alt. mem. Cen. Cttee. of C.P.S.U.; Dep. to U.S.S.R. Supreme Soviet; several decorations.
Kabardinian-Balkar Regional Committee of C.P.S.U., Nalchik, Kabardinian-Balkar Autonomous Republic, U.S.S.R.

Malcolm, Dugald, C.M.G., C.V.O., T.D.; British diplomatist; b. 22 Dec. 1917; ed. Eton and New Coll., Oxford.
Armed Forces 39-45; Foreign Service 45-; served Lima, Bonn, Seoul and London; Vice-Marshal of Diplomatic Corps 57-65; Ambassador to Luxembourg 66-; mem. Queen's Bodyguard for Scotland (Royal Company of Archers).
British Embassy, Luxembourg.

Malcolm, George (John), C.B.E., M.A., B.MUS.; British harpsichordist and conductor; b. 28 Feb. 1917; ed. Wimbledon Coll., Balliol Coll., Oxford, and Royal Coll. of Music.
Originally trained as concert pianist; Master of Music, Westminster Cathedral 47-59, trained Boys' Choir for which Benjamin Britten wrote *Missa Brevis* Op. 63; harpsichordist and conductor making frequent tours especially in Europe; Artistic Dir., Philomusica of London 62-66; Cobbett Gold Medal, Worshipful Company of Musicians 60, Hon. mem. Royal Acad. of Music, Hon. Fellow Balliol Coll., Oxford.
38 Cheyne Walk, London, S.W.3, England.

Malcolm, Wilbur George; American business executive; b. 22 June 1902; ed. Univ. of Maryland.
Instructor Univ. of Maryland 22-24; Senior Bacteriologist, Anti-Toxin and Vaccine Labs., Forest Hill, Mass. 30-34; Vice-Pres. and Gen. Man. Lederle Labs. 46-55; Chair. and Chief Exec. Officer American Cyanamid Co. until 66; mem. Int. Coll. of Surgeons, Soc. American Bacteriologists, New York Acad. of Science; Dir. Manufacturing Chemists' Asscn.
125 River Road, Grand View-on-Hudson, N.Y., U.S.A.

Malcuzynski, Witold; Polish pianist; b. 10 Aug. 1914; ed. Warsaw Conservatoire, Warsaw Univ.
International debut, Paris 40, American debut Carnegie Hall 42, London 45; tours throughout world.
Chernex sur Montreaux, Switzerland.

Maldybayev, Abdylas; Soviet composer; b. 1906; ed. Frunze Teachers' Training Inst. and Moscow Conservatoire.
People's Artist of the U.S.S.R.; awarded Order of Lenin, three Orders of Red Banner of Labour, Badge of Honour, medal for work in Second World War, Medal for Distinguished Labour.
Works include the first Kirghiz operas: *Aichurek* 39, *On the Banks of the Issyk Kul* 50; with Vlasov and Fere he composed the music for the anthem of the Kirghiz S.S.R.; *Manas* (opera) 44; choral symphonies: *The Party—Our Happiness* 54, *Glory to the Party, Toktogul* (Opera); over 300 songs, romances and choral pieces.
Office: Union of Composers, Frunze, Kirghizia 1, U.S.S.R.

Malecela, John William Samuel; Tanzanian diplomatist and politician; b. 34; ed. Bombay Univ. and Cambridge Univ.
Administrative Officer, Civil Service 60-61; Consul in U.S.A. and Third Sec. to the UN 62; Regional Commr., Mwanza Region 63; Perm. Rep. to the UN 64-; Order of Merit of First Degree, (United Arab Republic).
Tanzanian Mission to UN, 205 East 42nd Street, New York, N.Y. 10017, U.S.A.

Malecki, Ignacy; Polish scientist; b. 18 Nov. 1912.
Professor of Acoustics, Warsaw Technical Univ; Inst. Dir. for Fundamental Technical Problems, Polish Acad. of Sciences; Pres. and mem. Presidium Polish Acad. of Sciences; mem. Int. Comm. on Acoustics; Dr. R.C. Univ. Budapest; State Prize 66; Mem. Exec. Cttee. Int. Confederation of Scientific Unions, now Vice-Pres.
Nowowiejska 22, Warsaw, Poland.
Telephone: 21-18-66 (home); 26-89-51 (office).

Málek, Ivan, M.D., DR.SC.; Czechoslovak microbiologist; b. 28 Sept. 1909.
Professor of Medical Microbiology, Charles Univ.,
Academician 52, and mem. of Presidium, Czechoslovak Acad. of Sciences 65-; Vice-Pres. 60-65; Dir. Inst. of Microbiology, Czechoslovak Acad. of Sciences; Corresp. mem. German Acad. of Sciences, mem. Perm. Cttee. of Pugwash 64-, mem. of Bureau and Hon. Sec. World Fed. of Scientific Workers 52-, Chief Editor 64, mem. Swedish Royal Technical Acad. 65-; mem. Leopoldina-Halle/Salle German Acad. of Research in Natural Sciences; Vice-Pres. World Acad. of Art and Sciences; Chair. Socialist Acad. Czechoslovakia 65-; mem. Central Cttee. Communist Party of Czechoslovakia 62-; mem. Agricultural Comm. 63-66; mem. Bulgarian Acad. of Sciences 66, Science Advisory Cttee. 67; Laureate of the State Prize 51, 59, winner of the Medal of J. E. Purkyně 56; awarded the Order of Labour 58, Lenin Peace Prize 67; played an important role in the reform of medical studies as well as research, studies in the organisation of the nationalised pharmaceutical industry, and established a number of biological insts.
Publs. *Biology in the Future* 61 (German and Russian edns. 63), *Opened Problems of Science in Czechoslovakia* 67, *Theoretical and Methodological Basis of Continual Culture of Micro-organisms* (editor and co-author) 64 (English edn. 66).
Institute of Microbiology of the Czechoslovak Academy of Sciences, Budějovická 1083, Prague 4, and Na Dolinách 18, Prague 4, Czechoslovakia.
Telephone: Prague 439032 (Institute); Prague 437092 (Home).

Malenkov, Georgi Maximilianovich; Soviet politician; b. 8 Jan. 1903; ed. Moscow Higher Technical Coll.
Political Commissar Eastern and Turkestan Districts during Revolution; fmr. mem. Communist Party; fmr. Sec. Bolshevik Students' Organisation; worked Central Cttee. Communist Party 25-30, Organising Sec. Moscow Section of Party 30, later Head Personnel Dept. of Central Cttee., and mem. of Secretariat; dep. of the Supreme Soviet 37-57; mem. Cttee. for State Defence 41; mem. Cttee. for Economic Rehabilitation of Liberated Districts; Deputy Chair. Council of Ministers 46-53, Chair. 53-55; Deputy Chair. Council of Ministers and Minister of Power Stations 55-57; mem. former Politburo of Communist Party 46-53; mem. Presidium of Central Cttee. 53-57; Manager of Ust-Kamenogorsk Power Station 57-63; awarded title Hero of Socialist Labour 43, Hammer and Sickle Gold Medal, Order of Lenin (twice).
c/o Ministry of Social Security of R.S.F.S.R., 14 Shabolovka, Moscow; Home: Ust-Kamenogorsk, Kazakh S.S.R., U.S.S.R.

Malherbe, Ernst G., M.A., PH.D.; South African educationist; b. 8 Nov. 1895; ed. Stellenbosch and Columbia Univs.
Studied Oxford, The Hague, Amsterdam, Germany; Fellow, Teachers' Coll., Columbia Univ. 23-24; South African rep. British Asscn. Centenary Meeting, London 31; fmrly. teacher Cape Town Training Coll.; Lecturer in Educational Psychology, Stellenbosch Univ.; Senior Lecturer in Education, Cape Town Univ.; Chief Investigator, Education Section, Carnegie Poor White Research Comm. 28-32; mem. Govt. Comm. to Investigate Native Education in South Africa 35; Dir. Nat. Bureau of Educational and Social Research for South Africa 29-39; Dir. of Census and Statistics for Union 39-45; Lt.-Col. Dir. Army Educ. Services 40-45; Dir. Military Intelligence Union Defence Forces 42-45; Principal and Vice-Chancellor Univ. of Natal 45-65; Pres. S. African Asscn. for the Advancement of Science 50-51; Pres. South African Inst. of Race Relations 66-68; Hon. M.A. (Sydney); Hon. LL.D. (Cambridge, Queens, Melbourne, McGill, Cape Town, Natal, Rhodes, Witwatersrand).
Publs. *Education in South Africa 1652 to 1922* 25,

Education and the Poor White 31, *Education in a Changing Empire* 32, *Educational Adaptations in a Changing Society* (Editor) 37, *Entrance Age of University Students in Relation to Success* 38, *Educational and Social Research in South Africa* 39, *The Bilingual School* 43, *Race Attitudes and Education* 46, *Our Universities and the Advancement of Science* 51, *Die Outonomie van ons Universiteite en Apartheid* 57, *Education for Leadership in Africa* 60, *Problems of School Medium in a Bilingual Country* 62, *The Need for Dialogue* 67, *Education and the Development of South Africa's Human Resources* 67, *The Nemesis of Docility* 68.

By-die-See, Salt Rock, Umhlali, Natal, S. Africa.
Telephone: Umhlali 103.

Malietoa, Tanumafili II, H.H., C.B.E.; Samoan politician; b. 13; ed. Wesley Coll., Auckland, New Zealand.
Adviser, Samoan Govt. 40; mem. New Zealand del. to UN 58; fmr. mem. Council of State; Joint Head of State of Western Samoa 61-63, Sole Head 63-.
Government House, Vailima, Apia, Western Samoa, South Pacific.

Malik, Adam; Indonesian diplomatist; b. 17.
Ambassador to U.S.S.R. 59-63; Minister of Trade 63-66; Minister of Foreign Affairs 66-.
Ministry of Foreign Affairs, Djakarta; Djl. Diponegoro 17, Djakarta, Indonesia.

Malik, A. M., M.D.; Pakistani doctor and politician; b. 05; ed. Calcutta Univ., Santiniketan, Bengal and Vienna Univ.
Practised medicine in Calcutta; joined All-India Muslim League 36; former mem. Executive of All-India Trades Union Congress, Secretary of All-India Seafarer's Federation, Pres. Indian Quartermasters' Union and Indian Sailors' Union Calcutta; Pres. of All-Pakistan Trades Union Federation 47; former Minister of Agriculture, Co-operation, Forests, Fisheries and Labour, East Bengal; Minister in charge of Minorities Affairs 50-51; Minister of Labour and Works and Health 49-55; Chair. of Governing Body of I.L.O. 53-54; Amb. to Switzerland 55-58, Chinese People's Republic 58-61, Philippines 61-65, High Commr. in Australia 65-67.
c/o Ministry of External Affairs, Karachi, Pakistan.

Malik, Bidhubhusan, M.A., LL.D., Barrister-at-Law; Indian lawyer; b. 11 Jan. 1895.
Advocate, Allahabad High Court 19; called to Bar, Lincoln's Inn 23; mem. Judicial Cttee. Benares State 41-44; Special Counsel, Income Tax Dept. 43-44; Puisne Judge, High Court, Allahabad 44-47, Chief Justice High Court of Uttar Pradesh, Allahabad Dec. 47-Jan. 55 (acting Gov. U.P. Mar.-April 49); Indian Rep. to Federation of Malaya Constitutional Comm. 56-57; Commr. for Linguistic Minorities 57-62; Senior Advocate, Supreme Court of India; UN Constitutional Adviser for Congo 62; Constitutional Adviser, Kenya Conference, London 62; Adviser to Mauritius Govt. at Mauritius Conf. 65; Vice-Chancellor, Calcutta Univ. 62-.
18A Broad Street, Calcutta 19; 23 Muir Road, Allahabad, U.P., India.
Telephone: 2589.

Malik, Charles Habib, M.A., PH.D.; Lebanese philosopher, educationist and diplomatist; b. 06; ed. American Tripoli Boys' High School, American Univ. of Beirut and Harvard and Freiburg Univs.
Instructor Maths. and Physics, American Univ., Beirut 27-29, Instructor in Philosophy 37-39, Adjunct Prof. 39-43, Assoc. Prof. 43-45, Head of Dept. 39-45, Dean of Graduate Studies and Prof. of Philosophy 55-56; Min. of Lebanon to U.S.A. 45-53, Ambassador 53-55; Minister to Cuba 46-55; mem. and Chair. Del. of Lebanon to UN, N.Y. 45-54, Chair. 56-58; Pres. 13th Session, UN Gen. Assembly 58-59; Chair. of various UN Cttees. and Sub-Cttees.; rep. of Lebanon on Economic and Social

Council, Second-Eighth sessions, and Pres. of Council 48; rep. of Lebanon on Human Rights Comm. and Rapporteur of Comm. 47-54, Chair. of Comm. 51-52;. mem. UN Security Council 53-54, sometime Pres.; Gov. for Lebanon, Int. Bank and Monetary Fund 47-52, Chair. Del. of Lebanon Conf. for Conclusion and Signing Peace Treaty with Japan, San Francisco 51; Minister of Foreign Affairs 56-58, of Nat. Education and Fine Arts Nov. 56-57; M.P. for Al-Koura 57-60; Fellow American Asscn. for Advancement of Science, American Geog. Soc.; mem. American Philos. Asscn., American Philos. Soc., American Acad. of Arts and Sciences, Acad. of Human Rights, etc.; Hon. Litt.D. (Princeton, James Millikin Univs.), Hon. LL.D. (Notre Dame, Brown, Denison, Fairfield, Syracuse, Harvard, Boston, Lehigh, Yale, Georgetown, Washington, Columbia, Ohio, California, Columbia, Dartmouth, St. Mary's Halifax, Wesleyan Univs., Colby, Williams Albright Colls.); Hon. Rector, Univ. Dubuque 51.
Publs. *War and Peace* 50, *Problem of Asia* 51, *Problem of Coexistence* 55, *Christ and Crisis* 62, *Man in the Struggle for Peace* 63.
Ras-Beirut, Beirut, Lebanon.

Malik, Gunwantsingh Jaswantsingh, B.SC., M.A.; Indian diplomatist; b. 29 May 1921.
Royal Air Force 43; Indian Foreign Service 47-, served Brussels, Addis Ababa 48-50; Under-Sec. Ministry of External Affairs 50-52; served Buenos Aires, Tokyo, Singapore 52-59; Special Officer, Frontier Areas, Ministry of External Affairs 59; Ministry of Commerce 60; Counsellor (Commercial) and Asst. Commr. Singapore 60-63; Dir. Ministry of Commerce 63-64; Joint-Sec. Ministry of External Affairs 64-65; Ambassador to Philippines 65-.
Embassy of India, 1856 Nebraska, Malate, Manila, Philippines and 21A Nizamuddin West, New Delhi.
Telephone: 619785 (India).

Malik, Sardar Hardit Singh, C.I.E., O.B.E., B.A.; Indian diplomatist; b. 23 Nov. 1894; ed. Eastbourne Coll., and Balliol Coll., Oxford.
Served in French Army 16, in R.F.C., later R.A.F. 17-18; Asst. Commr. Punjab 22-23, Deputy Commr. 24-30; Deputy Trade Commr. London and Hamburg 31-34; Deputy Sec., Commerce Dept., Govt. of India 34-36, Joint Sec. 37; Indian Govt. Trade Commr., N.Y. and Canada 38; del. to Int. Cotton Conf. Washington 39, I.L.O. Conf. N.Y. 40, U.N. Food Conf. Hot Springs 43, U.N. Relief Conf. Atlantic City 43; Prime Min. Patiala 44-47; leader and mem. of many Indian dels. to int. confs.; High Commr. for India in Canada 47-49; Ambassador to France 48-57, concurrently Indian Minister to Norway 50-57; now dir. of several companies.
28 Golf Links, New Delhi, India.

Malik, Omar Hayat, LL.B., M.A., M.SC., PH.D.; Pakistani diplomatist; b. 94; ed. Univs. of Aligarh, Cambridge and Göttingen.
Fmr. Senior Prof. of Mathematics, Islamia Coll., Peshawar, later Principal; Principal, Islamia Coll., Lahore 43-48; Chief Statistical Officer, Dept. of Supply, Govt. of India, during Second World War; mem. Indian Constituent Assembly 46, Pakistan Constituent Assembly 47; Vice-Chancellor and Dean of Univ. Instruction, Univ. of the Punjab 47; Ambassador to Indonesia 50; Ambassador to German Federal Republic 52-54, to Japan 55-58; High Commr. in India 59-60; Hon. LL.D. (Glasgow Univ.).
c/o Ministry for Foreign Affairs, Karachi, Pakistan.

Malik, Yakov Alexandrovich; Soviet diplomatist; b. 06; ed. Kharkov Inst. of Economics.
Graduated from Inst. for Diplomatic and Consular Officials 37; Asst. Chief, Press Dept., Ministry of Foreign Affairs 37-39; Counsellor, Tokyo 39-42; Ambassador to Japan 42-45; Political Adviser, Allied Council for Japan

46; Deputy Minister of Foreign Affairs 46-53; Permanent Rep. of U.S.S.R. to UN, concurrently U.S.S.R. Rep. on UN Security Council 49-52; Ambassador to Great Britain 53-60; Deputy Minister of Foreign Affairs 60-67; Perm. Rep. to UN, New York 67-; two Orders of Lenin, two Orders of Red Banner of Labour and Medals.

U.S.S.R. Permanent Representation to United Nations, New York, U.S.A.

Malikyar, Abdullah; Afghan diplomatist; b. 09; ed. Isteklal Coll., Kabul, and Franco-Persian Coll., Teheran.

Secretary and Gen. Dir., Prime Minister's Office 31-35; Head, Govt. Purchasing Office, Europe 36-40; Vice-Pres. Central Bank and Deputy Minister of Commerce 41-42; Gov. of Herat 42-47, 51-52; Minister of Communications 48-50; Pres. Hillmand Valley Authority Projects 53-62; Minister of Commerce 55-57, of Finance 57-June 64, Deputy Prime Minister 63-Feb. 64; Acting Prime Minister Feb.-June 64; Ambassador to U.K. 64-67, to U.S.A. 67-; Sardar Ali Reshteen Decoration.

Royal Afghan Embassy, 2001 24th Street, N.W. Washington, D.C., U.S.A.

Malinschi, Vasile; Romanian economist; b. 1 May 1912; ed. Commercial and Industrial Acad., Bucharest and Bucharest Univ.

Official Nat. Bank 38; Prof. of the Econ. Inst. 49-, Chancellor 49-52; Minister for Home Trade 49-54; Vice-Pres. State Planning Cttee. 54-56; mem. Presidium of the Romanian Acad. 55-; Gov. Nat. Bank of the Socialist Repub. of Romania 63-; Vice-Pres. Econs. Soc.; mem. Nat. Comms. for UNESCO and FAO; mem. Int. Law Asscn., Int. Asscn. of Sociology and Int. Asscn. of Agricultural Econ.; mem. Econ. Council, Int. Asscn. of Economists; Vice-Pres. Nat. Cttee. of Sociology.

Publs. *Socialist Economy* 39, *The Land Reform* 47, *The Agrarian Problem* 58, *Agrarian Economy and Rural Sociology* 60, *Studies of Economy* 67, *Agrarian Essays* 68.

Academy of the Socialist Republic of Romania, Calea Victoriei 125, Bucharest; and Strada Pictor Iscovescu 32, Bucharest, Romania.

Malipiero, G. Francesco; Italian composer; b. 18 March 1882; ed. Venice, Vienna.

Member Académie Flamande, Brussels, Institut de France, Royal Acad. of Music, London; composer: 11 symphonies, 7 quartets, sonatas for 3, 4, 5 instruments, 10 works for orchestra, 4 oratorios, 14 operas; Ed. and publisher complete works of Monteverdi and Vivaldi.

696 Forestovecchio, Asolo, Treviso, Italy.

Mallaby, Sir (Howard) George, K.C.M.G., O.B.E.; British civil servant; b. 17 Feb. 1902; ed. Radley Coll. and Merton Coll., Oxford.

Asst. master at various schools 23-35; Headmaster, St. Bees School, Cumberland 35-38; District Commr. Special Area of W. Cumberland 38-39; Deputy N.W. Regional Transport Commr. 39-40; war service in army 40-45; served in mil. secretariat of War Cabinet 42-45, Col. 45; Sec. Nat. Trust 45; Asst. Sec. Ministry of Defence 46; Sec.-Gen. Brussels Treaty Defence Organisation 48-50; Under-Sec. Cabinet Office 50-54; Sec. War Council and Council of Ministers, Kenya 54; Deputy-Sec. Univ. Grants Cttee. 55-57; High Commr. for the U.K. in New Zealand 57-59; First Commissioner U.K. Civil Service 59-64; Legion of Merit.

Publs. *Wordsworth* 32, *Wordsworth: A Tribute* 50, *From My Level* 65.

Down the Lane, Chevington, W. Suffolk, England.

Mallakh, Kamal El, M.A.; United Arab Republic (Egyptian) archaeologist; b. 18; ed. Cairo Univ. and Military Engineering Coll.

Entered Govt. Antiquaries Dept. 44, Dir. of Giza Area and Lower Egypt 45-; worked as illustrator and art critic; art critic, *Al Ahram* 45, *Akhbar el Yom* 50-; art and archaeology commentator, Egyptian (later U.A.R.) Broadcasting Service 50-; Gold Cedar Decoration (Lebanon); held one-man exhibitions 39 and 49; two paintings in Cairo Museum of Modern Art.

Publs. Five books on art, archæology and the discovery of solar boats.

173 Twenty-Sixth of July Street, Zamalek, Cairo, U.A.R.

Mallart, José; Spanish educationist and sociologist; b. 10 June 1897.

Prof. Nat. Psychotechnic Inst. Madrid 27-; founder Spanish Cttee. for scientific organisation of labour 28; Insp.-Gen. of Workers' Education 33; mem. Cttee. for Agricultural Education 34; Prof. Social School Madrid 48, Nat. Inst. for Rationalisation 49; UNESCO expert in Ecuador 57-; mem. Exec. Cttee., International Asscn. of Applied Psychology 64.

Publs. *La educación activa* 24, *Colonias de educación* 30, *La elevación moral y material del Campesino* 33, *Organización científica del trabajo agrícola* 34, *La Organización económica internacional y el problema de la paz* 41, *Organización científica Trabajo* 42, *Orientación Funcional y Formación Profesional* 46, *El Mundo Económicosocial que nace* 47, *Obras de dignificación humana* 48, *Cuadernos de Organización Científica del Trabajo* 54-60.

San Julio 11, Madrid 2, Spain.
Telephone: 2617850.

Malle, Louis; French film director; b. 30 Oct. 1932. Assistant to Commander Cousteau on *La Calypso* 53-55, co-producer *Le Monde du Silence* 55; technical collaborator with Robert Bresson for *Un condamné à mort s'est échappé.*

Films: *Ascenseur pour l'échafaud* 57 (Prix Louis-Delluc 58), *Les Amants* 58 (Special Jury Prize, Venice Film Festival 58), *Zazie dans le métro* 60, *Vie privée* 62, *Le Feu Follet* (special Jury Prize, Venice Film Festival 63), *Viva Maria* 65, *Le Voleur* 66, *William Wilson* 67.

c/o Nouvelles éditions de films, 92 Champs-Elysées, Paris 8e, France.

Mallea, Eduardo; Argentine writer and journalist; b. 14 Aug. 1903; ed. Colegio Nacional and Faculty of Law, Buenos Aires.

Member Board of Dirs. of *Sur* and of *Realidad*; fmr. Pres. Argentine Soc. of Writers; literary editor on staff of *La Nación*; winner of First Nat. Prize for Literature 46.

Publs. *Cuentos para una Inglesa Desesperada* 26, *Nocturno Europeo, Conocimiento y Expresión de la Argentina* 35, *La Ciudad junto al Río Inmóvil* 36, *Historia de una Pasión Argentina* 37, *Fiesta en Noviembre* 38, *Meditación en la Costa* 40, *El Sayal y la Púrpura* 41, *Todo Verdor Perecerá* 41, *La Bahía de Silencio* 40, *Las Aguilas* 41, *Rodeada está de sueño* 44, *El retorno* 46, *El Vínculo* 46, *Los Enemigos del Alma* 50, *La Torre Chaves* 53, *La sala de espera* 53, *Notas de un novelista* 54, *Simbad* 57, *El gajo de enebro* 57, *Posesión* 59, *La razón humana* 60, *La vida blanca* 60, *Las travesías* 62, *La barca de hieto* 67.

Santa Fé 1845, Buenos Aires, Argentina.

Malleson, (William) Miles, B.A.; British playwright and actor; b. 25 May 1888; ed. Brighton Coll. and Emmanuel Coll. Cambridge.

Publs. *Youth, Paddly Pools, The Little White Thoughts, Maurice's Own Idea, D. Co. and Black 'Ell, Young Heaven, Conflict, Merrileon Wise, The Fanatics, Four People, Yours Unfaithfully, Six Men of Dorset, Michael, Last Appearance;* new adaptations of *Tartuffe, The Miser, Le Bourgeois Gentilhomme, The Provincial Lady The Bachelor, The School for Wives, The Misanthrope, Sganarelle, The Bet, Le Malade Imaginaire.*

14 Rugby Street, London, W.C.1, England.

Mallon, Henry Neil, B.A.; American executive; b. 11 Jan. 1895; ed. Yale Univ.
Served in Army First World War; joined U.S. Can Co. as factory worker 20, successively Factory Man., Vice-Pres. and Gen. Man., and Dir.; Pres., later Chair. S.R. Dresser Manufacturing Co. predecessor co. of Dresser Industries Inc.; Chair. Exec. Cttee. and Dir. Dresser Industries Inc.
Home: 2710 Farmers Branch Lane, Farmers Branch, Texas; Office: Republic National Bank Building, Dallas, Texas, U.S.A.

Mallory, Lester D., B.S.A., M.S.A., PH.D.; American diplomatist and bank administrator; b. 21 April 1904; ed. Univ. of British Columbia, Univ. of California.
Appt. to Foreign Agricultural Service 31; served in Marseille and Paris; Dept. of State 39; subsequently Agricultural Attaché Mexico City and Paris, Counsellor Havana and Buenos Aires; Ambassador to Jordan 53-58, to Guatemala 58-59; Dep. Asst. Sec. for Inter-American Affairs, Dept. of State 60; with Inter-American Development Bank 61-63, Regional Rep., Panama and Costa Rica 64-.
Apartado 7297, Panama.

Mallowan, Sir Max Edgar Lucien, Kt., C.B.E., M.A., D.LIT., F.S.A., F.B.A. (husband of Agatha Christie, q.v.); British archaeologist; b. 6 May 1904; ed. Lancing and New Coll., Oxford.
Assistant on staff of British Museum and Museum of Univ. of Pennsylvania Expedition to Ur of the Chaldees 25-30, to Nineveh 31-32; directed excavations on behalf of British Museum and British School of Archaeology in Iraq, at Arpachiyah 33, at Chagar Bazar (Syria) 34-36, Brak (Syria) and in Balikh Valley (Syria) 37-38, at Nimrud on behalf of British School of Archaeology in Iraq 49-58; R.A.F. and seconded to British Mil. Admin., Tripolitania 39-44; Dir. British School of Archaeology in Iraq 47-61, Vice-Chair. 61-65, Chair. 65; Editor *Iraq* 48-; Prof. of W. Asiatic Archaeology, Univ. of London 47-62, Emeritus 62-; Fellow of All Souls Coll., Oxford 62-; Pres. British Inst. of Persian Studies 61; corresp. mem. Arab Acad. Baghdad, German Archaeological Inst.; Foreign mem. Académie des Inscriptions et Belles Lettres (France); Hon. Fellow Metropolitan Museum of Art, New York; Lucy Wharton Drexel Gold Medal, Museum of Univ. of Pennsylvania.
Publs. *Prehistoric Assyria, The Excavations at Arpachiyah* 33, *Excavations at Chagar Bazar* 36-37, *Excavations in the Balikh Valley* 38, *Excavations at Brak and Chagar Bazar* 47, *Early Mesopotamia and Iran* 65, *Nimrud and its Remains* (2 vols.) 66; *Ur Excavations,* vol. IX (with Sir Leonard Woolley) *The Neo Babylonian and Persian Periods* 62.
Winterbrook House, Wallingford, Berks., England.
Telephone: Wallingford 2248.

Malmström, Johan Henning, F.R.S.A.; Swedish painter; b. 12 Aug. 1890; ed. Sweden and Denmark.
Worked in oils until 24, pastels 24-, also sculpture 54-; exhibited Scandinavia, New York, Chicago; rep. in Nat. Museum, Stockholm, Malmö, Lund, Helsingborg, Museum of Art, Cranbrook, U.S.A., and in private collections, etc.
Publs. *Ara Pacis and Virgil's Æneid* 63.
Östergarden, Kvarnby, Sweden.

Malone, Dumas, M.A., PH.D., LL.D., LITT.D., L.H.D.; American historian; b. 10 Jan. 1892; ed. Emory Coll., Yale Univ.
Assoc. Prof. and Prof. of History Univ. of Virginia 23-29; Ed. *Dictionary of American Biography* 29-31 and Ed.-in-Chief 31-36; Dir. Harvard Univ. Press 36-43; Prof. of History, Columbia Univ. 45-59; Man. Editor *Political Science Quarterly* 53-58; Thomas Jefferson Prof. of History, Univ. of Virginia 59-62, Biographer in Residence 62-.

Publs. *Public Life of Thomas Cooper* 25, *Correspondence between Thomas Jefferson and P. S. du Pont de Nemours* 30, *Edwin A. Alderman* (biography) 40; Joint-Editor Vols. IV-VII, Editor Vols. VIII-XX, *Dictionary of American Biography* 29-36, *Jefferson the Virginian* 48, *Jefferson and the Rights of Man* 51, *Story of the Declaration of Independence* 55, *Jefferson and the Ordeal of Liberty* 62, *Thomas Jefferson as Political Leader* 63; Editor *The Jeffersonian Heritage* 53 (with Basil Rauch); *Empire for Liberty* (2 vols.) 60 (6 vol. edn. with individual titles 65).
Alderman Library, University of Virginia, Charlottesville, Va.; Home: 2000 Lewis Mt. Road, Charlottesville, Va. 22903, U.S.A.
Telephone: 703-295-9735.

Malott, Deane Waldo, A.B., M.B.A., LL.D., D.C.S.; American university president; b. 10 July 1898; ed. Kansas and Harvard Univ.
Assistant Dean, Harvard Business School 23-29, Assoc. Prof. of Business 33-39; Vice-Pres. Hawaiian Pineapple Co., Honolulu 29-33; Chancellor, Univ. of Kansas 33-51; Pres. Cornell Univ. 51-63, Pres. Emeritus 63-; Consultant, U.S. Army Air Corps 43-45; mem. Business Council, 44-; Consultant to Asscn. of American Colls. 63-; Dir. General Mills Inc., Citizens Bank, Abilene, The B.F. Goodrich Co., Pitney-Bowes Inc., First Nat. Bank, Ithaca, Owens-Corning Fiberglas Corpn., Lane Bryant, Servomation Corpn., Trustee Teagle Foundation, Corning Museum of Glass, William Allen White Foundation, Univ. of Kansas Endowment Asscn., Pacific Tropical Botanical Garden; Hon. LL.D. (Washburn Univ., Bryant Coll., Hamilton Coll., Univ. of Calif., Juniata Coll., Univ. of N.H., Emory Univ., Univ. of Liberia); D.C.S. (Univ. of Pittsburgh); D.H.L. (Long Island Univ.).
Publs. (with Philip Cabot) *Problems in Public Utility Management* 27, (with J. C. Baker) *Introduction to Corporate Finance* 36, (with J. C. Baker and W. D. Kennedy) *On Going into Business* 36, *Problems in Agricultural Marketing* 38, (with B. F. Martin) *The Agricultural Industries* 39.
322 Wait Avenue, Cornell University, Ithaca, N.Y., U.S.A.
Telephone: 607-275-4010.

Malraux, André; French novelist and politician; b. 3 Nov. 1901.
Served with Republicans, Spanish Civil War; with Tank Div. 39-40; prisoner of war 40, but escaped to unoccupied France; active in resistance movement; Minister of Information 45-46; Minister of State for Information June-July 58, Minister responsible for youth, research and culture July 58-Jan. 59 (De Gaulle cabinet); Minister of State, responsible for Culture (Debré and Pompidou cabinets) Jan. 59-; Pres. Asscn. for the Fifth Republic; Officier Légion d'Honneur, Croix de Guerre (4 palmes), Médaille de la Résistance, D.S.O. (U.K.), and other foreign decorations.
Publs. *Lunes en papier* 21, *La Tentation de l'Occident* 26, *Royaume farfelu* 28, *Les Conquérants* 28, *La Voix royale* 30, *La Condition humaine* 33, *Le Temps du mépris* 35, *L'Espoir* (filmed) 37, *Les Noyers de l'Altenburg* 43, *Esquisse d'une psychologie du cinéma* 46, *Psychologie de l'art* (3 vols.) 47-49, *La Monnaie de l'Absolu* 49, *Les Voix du silence* 51, *Le Musée imaginaire de la sculpture mondiale* 52-55, *La Métamorphose des dieux* 57, *Antimémoires* 67.
19 bis avenue Victor Hugo, Boulogne (Seine), France.

Malraux-Goldschmidt, Clara; French writer.
Fought in Spanish Civil War and with French Resistance in Second World War.
Publs. *Le livre de Comptes* 30, *Portrait de Griselidis* 45, *La maison ne fait pas Crédit, Par de plus longs chemins,*

La Lutte inégale, Le bruit de nos pas 63, *Nos Vingt ans* (2nd vol. of memoirs) 66.
12 square Albin Cachot, Paris, France.

Malta, Eduardo; Portuguese painter and writer; b. 1900; ed. Fine Arts School, Oporto.
Mem. Nat. Acad. of Fine Arts, Lisbon; corresp. mem. Royal Acad. of Arts of San Fernando (Spain); two Prize Medals and two First Medals (Nat. Soc. of Fine Arts, Lisbon); Columbano Prize (Portuguese Govt.); Luciano Freire Prize (Nat. Acad. of Fine Arts, Lisbon); Gold Medal (Int. Exhibition, Paris 37); Dir. Museum of Contemporary Art, Lisbon.
Works include portraits of: *King Alfonso XIII, Primo de Rivera, Getulio Vargas, King Umberto of Italy, Marshal Craveiro Lopes, Oliveira Salazar, Mrs. Winston, Mrs. Guggenheim, Ricardo Espirito Santo, Barão de Saavedra.*
Publs. include: *O papagaio Azul* 25, *Montanhas Russas* 28, *Do meu oficio de pintar* 35, *No Mundo dos Homens* 36, *Retratos e Retratados* 38, *Vários Motivos de Arte.*
30 Rua Victor Cordon, Lisbon, Portugal.

Maltsev, Victor Fyodorovich; Soviet engineer and diplomatist; b. 1917.
With Ministry of Railways 41-61; Chair. Soviet of Irkutsk Region, E. Siberia 61-67; Amb. to Sweden 67-.
U.S.S.R. Embassy, Stockholm, Sweden.

Malvern, 1st Viscount, cr. 55, of Rhodesia and of Bexley in the County of Kent; **Godfrey Martin Huggins,** P.C., C.H., K.C.M.G., F.R.C.S., K.G.ST.J.; Rhodesian surgeon and politician; b. 6 July 1883 (in Great Britain).
In medical practice Salisbury 10-; Army Surgeon in France and Malta First World War; Rhodesia Party mem. of Legislative Assembly 23-53; Prime Minister 33-53; Minister of Native Affairs 33-49 and of Defence 48-53; Prime Minister of the Federation of Rhodesia and Nyasaland 53-56; Fed. M.P. 53-58; Chair. Council, Univ. Coll. of Rhodesia; Dir. of several companies; Hon. D.C.L. (Oxon.), Hon. LL.D. (Witwatersrand, London), Hon. D.L. (Rhodes).
Publ. *Amputation Stumps, their Care and After-Treatment,* and technical papers.
The Craig, P.O. Highlands, Salisbury, Rhodesia.

Malyshev, Aleksandr Evegenievich; Soviet diplomatist; b. 1919; ed. Ivanovo Pedagogical Inst.
U.S.S.R. Foreign Ministry 46-; Counsellor, Soviet Embassy, Belgrade 57-58; Deputy Head Second African Dept., U.S.S.R. Ministry of Foreign Affairs 60-63; Counsellor, Prague 63-64; Ambassador to Tunisia 64-.
U.S.S.R. Embassy, Tunis, Tunisia.

Malyshko, Andrei Samoilovich; Soviet poet; b. 12; ed. Kiev. Inst. of Education.
State prizewinner 47, 50, Order of Lenin.
Principal publs. Poems: *Sons* 45, *Prometheus* 46, *It Happened at Dawn* 48, *Korean poem* 51, *Arsenal, Noon of Age* 60, *Letters at Dawn* 61, *Collected Works* (5 vols.) 62, *Distant Orbits* 62, *Taras Shevchenko* 64.
Union of Soviet Ukrainian Writers, Kiev, Ukraine, U.S.S.R.

Mamadou, Joseph Gilbert; Central African Republic politician and diplomatist; b. 32.
Health Official 46-48; Local Govt. Official 50-54; Asst. Sub Prefect and Postmaster, Paoua 54-57; Minister of Social Affairs, Public Instruction and Health 57-58; Sub-Prefect, Bocaranga 59-60; Head of Mission of Central African Republic to French Community, Paris 60; Asst. to Pres. of Central African Republic 60; Ambassador to France 61-63; Sec.-Gen. Ministry of Foreign Affairs 63-64; Ambassador to China 64-66; Commandeur, Ordre du Mérite Centrafricain, Légion d'Honneur.
Ministry of Foreign Affairs, Bangui, Central African Republic.

Mambetov, Bolot; Soviet politician; b. 1907; ed. Inst. of Water Economy Engineers, Moscow.
Member C.P.S.U. 29-; Engineer, later Head of Irrigation Board, Kirghizia 35-40; Secretary, Central Committee of C.P., Kirghizia 40-45; First Secretary Frunze Regional Cttee., C.P. of Kirghizia 45-51; Dir. Inst. of Water Economy and Power, Kirghizia 53-54; Minister of Water Economy 54-61; Chair. Council of Ministers of Kirghiz S.S.R. 61-; mem. Presidium of Central Cttee. of Kirghiz S.S.R.; Candidate mem. Central Cttee. of C.P.S.U. 61-; Deputy to U.S.S.R. and Kirghiz S.S.R. Supreme Soviets.
Council of Ministers of Kirghizstan, Frunze, Kirghiz S.S.R., U.S.S.R.

Mamedov, Bakhtiyar Mamed Rza ogly, D.SC.; Soviet politician; b. 1925; ed. Azerbaijan Industrial Inst.
Member C.P.S.U. 50-; in oil-industry 48-51, Chief of Oil-Extracting Dept.; Chief, Main Dept., *Glavmorneft* 51-63; Minister of Oil-Extracting Industry, Azerbaijan S.S.R. 65-; Hero of Socialist Labour; mem. Central Cttee. of C.P. of Azerbaijan; Deputy to U.S.S.R. Supreme Soviet.
Council of Ministers of Azerbaijan S.S.R., Baku, U.S.S.R.

Mamert, Jean Albert; French public servant; b. 26 March 1928; ed. Lycée et Faculté de Droit, Montpellier, Institut d'études politiques, Paris, Ecole Nationale d'Administration, Paris.
Auditor 55-, later Master of Requests, Council of State; Technical Counsellor for Constitutional Problems, 58-59; Sec.-Gen. Constitutional Consultative Cttee. 58; Chief of Prime Minister's Office Jan-July 59; Sec.Gen. Econ. and Social Council 59-.
Office: Palais d'Iéna, Paris 16e; Home: 21 avenue de Versailles, Paris 16e, France.
Telephone: 225-35-85 (Office).

Mamoulian, Rouben; American stage and film producer, director, and author; b. in Russia 8 Oct. 1897; ed. Paris Lycée Montaigne, Tiflis Gymnasium, and Moscow Univ.
Produced *Beating on the Door* in London 22; was taken to New York by George Eastman to direct American Opera Co.; Stage Dir. New York 27; Dir. in Hollywood 31-; Film festival *Tribute to Rouben Mamoulian,* New York 67; Festival of films at Nat. Film Theatre, London 68.
Stage Productions include: *Porgy* 27, *Marco Millions* 28, *Wings Over Europe* 28, *R.U.R.* 29, *Month in the Country* 30, *Hand of Fate, Farewell to Arms* 30, *Porgy and Bess* 35, *Oklahoma!* 43, *Sadie Thompson* 44, *Carousel* 45, *St. Louis Woman* 46, *Lost in the Stars* (musical tragedy) 49, *Arms and the Girl* (musical play) 50, *Oklahoma!* for the Berlin Art Festival 51, Hollywood 53, in Paris and in various Italian cities 55; Motion Pictures include: *Applause* 29, *City Streets* 31, *Dr. Jekyll and Mr. Hyde* 31, *Love Me Tonight* 32, *Song of Songs* 32, *Queen Christina* 33, *We Live Again* 34, *Becky Sharp* 35, *The Gay Desperado* 36, *High, Wide and Handsome* 37, *Golden Boy* 39, *Mark of Zorro* 40, *Blood and Sand* 41, *Rings on her Fingers* 42, *Summer Holiday* (based on Eugene O'Neill's *Ah! Wilderness*) 47, *Carousel* 53, *Oklahoma* 55, *Silk Stockings* 57, co-author (with Maxwell Anderson) *The Devil's Hornpipe* (musical, filmed as *Never Steal Anything Small*) 59.
Publs. *Abigayil* 64, *Shakespeare's Hamlet, A New Version* 66 (World Première Performance 66).
1112 Schuyler Road, Beverly Hills, Calif., U.S.A.

Mamoun, Sheikh Hassan; United Arab Republic lawyer and religious and university official; b. 13 June 1894.
Former Judge; fmr. Supreme Judge of the Sudan; Pres. of Supreme Court of Shari'a, Grand Mufti of Egypt 55-61; mem. fmr. Nat. Assembly; mem. Arab Socialist

Union; Grand Imam and Sheikh of Al-Azhar July 64-.
Office of the Grand Sheikh, Administration of Al-Ashar,
Al-Azhar, Cairo, United Arab Republic.

Man, Ivan Alexandrovich; Soviet sailor and polar
explorer; b. 03; ed. Leningrad Naval Polytechnic.
Nat. navigation safety inspector; Commdr. of cargo
steamers *Pravda, Transbalt* in the Arctic Ocean, and of
the liners *Ukraina, Rossia* in the Black Sea; Capt. of
diesel-electric ship *Ob*, flagship of the Soviet Antarctic
Expedition 55; sailed to Mirny in the Antarctic 55, 56,
57; Capt. of liner *Gruzia* 61-62, *Peter Veliki* 62-64;
Chief Specialist in Navigation, Ministry of Merchant
Marine 64-.
Ministry of Merchant Marine, Moscow, U.S.S.R.

Man, Morgan Charles Garnet, C.M.G.; British diploma-
tist; b. 6 Aug. 1915; ed. Cheltenham Coll., and The
Queen's Coll., Oxford.
Joined Consular service 37; Deputy Political Resident,
Bahrain 59-62; Minister, Ankara 62-64; Ambassador to
Saudi Arabia 64-68.
c/o Diplomatic Service Administration Office, King
Charles Street, London, S.W.1.
Telephone: 01-930-8440.

Manandhar, Rama Prasad, M.A.; Nepalese government
official; b. 8 Jan. 1914; ed. Patna Univ., India.
Prof. of English Literature, Tri-Chandra Coll., Kath-
mandu 36-49; Counsellor in London 49-53; rept. Govt.
of Nepal at Council of UNESCO 49, 50, 51; at Int.
Conference on Education at Geneva, 51; at World Power
Conf. in London 50; at F.A.O. Conf. in Rome 51; Foreign
Sec. 53-54; Sec. for Education, Health and Local Self-
Government 55-56; Ambassador to U.K. 56-61, and
concurrently to France, Netherlands, U.S.S.R., Fed.
Germany, and Minister to Switzerland; G.D.B. (Nepal),
Hon. G.C.V.O., C.B.E. (Hon.), Officier de la Légion
d'Honneur, Commdr. of the Order of Orange Nassau.
Peace Grotto, Pyaphal Tole, Katmandu, Nepal.

Manchot, Willy, DR. ING.; German chemist and busi-
ness executive; b. 10 July 1907; ed. Technische
Hochschulen, Munich and Darmstadt.
Chemist and Plant Man., Dr. Alexander Wacker
G.m.b.H., Mückenberg 34-39; Exec. Dir. and Produc-
tion Man. Deutsche Hydrierwerke Rodleben 39; Exec.
Dir. (Chemical and Technical Management) Henkel &
Cie. G.m.b.H. 39-60, Chair. Board and Exec. Dir. Persil
G.m.b.H., Dep. Chair. Board of Dirs. Henkel & Cie.
G.m.b.H. 60-; official numerous other companies.
Postfach 1100, 4 Düsseldorf 1, German Federal Re-
public.

Mancini, Giacomo; Italian politician; b. 21 April
1916; ed. Univ. of Turin.
Member Partito Socialista Italiano (P.S.I.) 43-; Dir.
Socialist Federation of Cosenza 46-48; mem. Chamber of
Deputies 48-; mem. Directorate P.S.I. 53-, Dir. of Party
Organisation 59-; Minister of Public Health 63-64, of
Public Works 64-.
Ministero dei Lavori Pubblici, Rome, Italy.

**Mancroft, 2nd Baron, of Mancroft, Norwich; Stormont
Mancroft Samuel Mancroft,** K.B.E., T.D.; British business
executive; b. 27 July 1914; ed. Winchester and Christ
Church, Oxford.
Called to Bar, Inner Temple 38; Royal Artillery 39-46;
mem. Bar Council 47-51; mem. St. Marylebone Borough
Council 47-53; Chancellor Primrose League 52-54; a
Lord-in-Waiting to the Queen 52-54; Parl. Under Sec;
Home Office 54-57; Parl. Sec. Ministry of Defence 57.
Minister without Portfolio 57-58; Dir. Great Universal
Stores and subsidiaries 58-66; Deputy Chair. Cunard
Line Ltd. 66-, also Dir. Cunard Steamship Co.; Pres.
Inst. of Marketing and Sales Management 59-63, St.
Marylebone Conservative Asscn. 61-66, St. Marylebone

Soc., London Tourist Board; Chair. Cttee. for Exports
to U.S.A.
80 Eaton Square, London, S.W.1, England.
Telephone: 01-235-4684.

Mandela, Nelson Rolihlahla; South African lawyer
and politician; b. 18; ed. Fort Hare, Univ. of the
Witwatersrand.
Son of Chief of Tembu tribe; legal practice, Johannesburg 52; Nat. organiser African Nat. Congress (A.N.C.);
on trial for treason 56-61 (acquitted 61); arrested 62,
sentenced to five years imprisonment Nov. 62; on trial
for further charges Nov. 63-June 64, sentenced to life
imprisonment June 64.
Publ. *No Easy Walk to Freedom* 65.
Robben Island, nr. Cape Town, South Africa.

Mandele, Karel E. van der, DR. ECON.; Netherlands
diplomatist; b. 13 Sept. 1907; ed. Nederlandsche
Economische Hoogeschool, Rotterdam, Université de
Lausanne, Harvard Univ., and Rijksuniversiteit te
Leiden.
Banking 31-38; Vice-Consul, Sydney, New South
Wales 38-43; Sec. Pretoria 43-44, Washington 44-46;
First Sec. Copenhagen 46; UN Division, Ministry of
Foreign Affairs 47-50; Consul-Gen., Hong Kong
50-55; Minister to Ceylon 55-58; Inspector of Foreign
Service 58-63; Ambassador to Denmark 63-; Knight
Order of Netherlands Lion, Officer Order of Orange
Nassau, Commdr. Military Order of Christ, mem.
Order of Dannebrog.
Royal Netherlands Embassy, Amaliegade 42, Copen-
hagen K, Denmark.
Telephone: 15-62-93 (Office); 15-62-62 (Home).

Mandele, Karel Paul van der, LL.D.; Netherlands
banker; b. 1 Nov. 1880; ed. Gynmasium, Delft, and
Univs. of Lausanne and Leiden.
Began career as lawyer 02; Sec. Rotterdamsche Bank
06-10, Gen. Man. 10-40, Pres. 40-55, Vice-Pres. 55-;
Pres. of Rotterdam Chamber of Commerce 38-60, Hon.
Pres. 60-; Hon. Dr.Econ. (Netherlands School of Econo-
mics, Rotterdam).
's-Gravenweg 69, Rotterdam, Netherlands.
Telephone: 123969.

Mandloi, Bhagwantrao Annabhau, B.A., LL.B.; Indian
politician; b. 15 Dec. 1892; ed. Govt. Coll., Jabalpur,
and Univ. School of Allahabad.
Lawyer, Khandwa; Pres. Municipal Cttee., Khandwa
(15 years); mem. Legislative Assembly of Cen. Provinces
and Berar 35-37, of Madhya Pradesh 37-; imprisoned
for political activities 40, 42; mem. Constituent
Assembly and Parl.; Chief Whip, Madhya Pradesh
Assembly Party; mem. Congress Parl. Board 51-52;
Minister for Revenue, Survey and Settlement, Land
Records, Land Reforms and Local Self Govt., Madhya
Pradesh, later for Revenue and Educ. 52-56; Minister
for Revenue and Loval Govt. 56-61, for Revenue and
Industries 61-62; Chief Minister, Madhya Pradesh 62-
August 63; Pres. Madhya Pradesh Congress Cttee.
Nov. 63-.
Bhopal, Madhya Pradesh, India.

Manescu, Corneliu; Romanian politician and diploma-
tist; b. 8 Feb. 1916; ed. Law Coll., Bucharest.
Member Democratic Students' Front; mem. Romanian
Workers' Party (now C.P.) 36-; Ministry of Armed
Forces 48-55; Deputy Chair. State Planning Cttee. 55-
60; Chief of Political Dept. Ministry of Foreign Affairs
60; Ambassador to Hungary 60-61; Minister of Foreign
Affairs March 61-; mem. Central Cttee. of the Romanian
C.P. 65-; Chair. 22nd Session of UN Gen. Assembly
67-68; several orders and medals.
Ministry of Foreign Affairs, Bucharest, Romania.

Manessier, Alfred; French artist; b. 5 Dec. 1911; ed.
Lycée d'Amiens and Paris Schools of Fine Art.
Has designed and executed stained glass for churches

at Bresseux (Jura), Arles, Basle, etc.; rep. at numerous exhibitions, including the Brussels Int. Exhibition 58, Dunn Int. Exhbn., London 63; Caracas Int. Painting Prize, Carnegie Prize 55, Venice Biennale prize 62; Chevalier Légion d'Honneur, Officier des Arts et des Lettres.
203 rue de Vaugirard, Paris 15e, France.

Mange, Michel; French international civil servant; b. 30 May 1898; ed. Stella Matutina, Feldkirch, Austria, Lycée Louis-le-Grand, Paris, Ecole Centrale des Ingénieurs, Paris, and Faculté de Droit, Paris.
Paris-Lyons-Mediterranean Railway Co. 22; Int. Union of Railways 22-24; mem. Int. Railway Comm., Comm. for Reparations Payments, Berlin Office 24-30; Adviser to Romanian State Railways, Bucharest 30-35; Head, Commercial Dept., Société Nationale des Chemins de fer Français (S.N.C.F.) 35-39; Econ. Adviser to French Embassy, Rome 39-40; French Rep. Railway Cttee., Allied Control Authority, Berlin 45-48; Counsellor, Transport and Tourism Division, Org. for European Econ. Co-operation 48-53; Sec.-Gen. European Conf. of Ministers of Transport 53-; Adviser to Portuguese Ministry of Transport, Lisbon 66; Officier Légion d'Honneur, Commdr. Ordre Nat. du Mérite, Grosses Verdienstkreuz der Bundesrepublik Deutschland, Commdr. Star of Romania, Commdr. Crown of Romania.
European Conference of Ministers of Transport, Château de la Muette, 3 rue André Pascal, Paris 16e; Home: 5 rue Philibert-Delorme, Paris 17e, France. Telephone: 622-0383.

Mang'enya, Chief Erasto; Tanzanian diplomatist; b. 15 April 1915; ed. Makerere Coll., Kampala, Uganda.
Ministry of Educ., Tanganyika 38-59; Chief Exec. Officer, District Local Council 59-60; M.P. 60-63, Deputy Speaker Tanganyika Nat. Assembly 61; Parl. Sec. Ministry of Communications, Power and Works 62-63, Ministry of External Affairs and Defence 63; Perm. Rep. of Tanganyika to UN 63-64, of United Republic of Tanganyika and Zanzibar June-Oct. 64, of Tanzania Oct. 64; Minister for Community Devt. and Nat. Culture 64-65; Chair. Perm. Comm. of Enquiry 65.
c/o Permanent Commission of Enquiry, P.O.B. 2643, Dar-es-Salaam, Tanzania.

Mangoldt-Reiboldt, Hans Karl von, DR.JUR.; German banker; b. 2 Aug. 1896; ed. Univs. of Leipzig and Berlin.
Partner of Bank Hardy and Co., Munich 26-34; Dir. Bank Hardy and Co. G.m.b.H., Berlin 35-45; Chief Custodian Bayerische Motoren Werke A.G. (BMW), Munich 46-50; Chief German Permanent Mission O.E.E.C., Paris 48-51; Pres. Man. Board European Payments Union, Paris 50-58; Pres., Man. Bd. European Monetary Agreement, Paris 58-62; Alt. Gov. Int. Monetary Fund, Washington 52-62; Vice-Pres. European Investment Bank, Brussels 58-65; Pres. O.E.C.D. Consortium for the Devt. of Turkey 63-67; Hon. Vice-Pres. European Investment Bank, Brussels 64-; Grosses Bundesverdienstkreuz mit Stern; Commdr. Légion d'Honneur; Grand Cross of the Civil O.M. of Spain; Grand Officer of the Order of the Crown, Belgium.
8120 Weilheim/Obb., Schilcherhof, German Federal Republic.

Mangwazu, Timon Sam; Malawi diplomatist; b. 12 Oct. 1935; ed. Inyati Boys' Inst. (London Missionary Society) Bulawayo, Tegwani Methodist Secondary School, Plumtree, and Ruskin Coll., Oxford.
Nyasaland Civil Service 56; Sec.-Gen. Nyasaland African Civil Servants 61; Asst. Registrar of Trade Unions 63; First Sec. British Embassy in Vienna 64; Amb. of Malawi to German Fed. Repub., later accred.

to Norway, Sweden, Denmark, Netherlands, Belgium, Switzerland, Austria 64-67; Malawi High Commr. in U.K. 67-; Malawi Independence Medal; Malawi Repub. Medal.
Malawi High Commission, 47 Great Cumberland Place, London, W.1, England.
Telephone: 01-723-6021.

Mani, Chandra, M.B., CH.B., M.R.C.S., L.R.C.P., D.P.H., F.A.M.S.; Indian physician and surgeon; b. 03; ed. Birmingham and London Univs.
Joined Indian Medical Service 27; Dep. Dir. Gen. Health Services, Govt. of India; Indian Del. Technical Prep. Cttee. of Economic and Social Council (Paris) 46, Int. Health Conf. (New York) 46, WHO Interim Comm. (Geneva) 46 and 47; WHO Regional Dir. for South-East Asia 49-.
World Health Organisation, Regional Office for South-East Asia, World Health House, Indraprastha Estate, New Delhi, India.

Maniakin, Sergei Iosifovich; Soviet politician; b. 23; ed. Agricultural Inst., Stavropol.
Member C.P.S.U. 45-; Dir. motor tractor station, then Chair. collective farm, Stavropol Territory 48-57; Head, Agricultural Dept., Stavropol Territory Cttee., C.P.S.U. 57-60; Chair. Stavropol Territory Exec. Cttee., Soviet of Workers' Deputies 60-61; Instructor, Central Cttee. of C.P.S.U. 61, mem. 61-; First Sec. Omsk Rural Regional Cttee., C.P.S.U. 61-64; First Sec. Omsk District Cttee. of C.P.S.U. 64-; Deputy to U.S.S.R. Supreme Soviet; mem. Agricultural Comm. Soviet of Union.
Omsk District Committee of the Communist Party of the Soviet Union, Omsk, U.S.S.R.

Manirakiza, Marc; Burundi politician; b. 22 Dec. 1935; ed. Institut Universitaire de Bruxelles, Inst. of Languages, Washington, and Univ. of Michigan, U.S.A.
Founder, Union of Burundi students in Belgium 59; Dir.-Gen. of Planning and Technical Assistance, Burundi 63; Founder, Civil Servants Asscn., Burundi 64, Pres. 64; Minister of Foreign Affairs and Foreign Trade, Burundi 65-66.
B.P. 1041, Bujumbura, Burundi.

Maniusis, Juizas Antonovich, D.SC.; Soviet constructional engineer and politician; b. 1910
Former constructional engineer; Sec. Central Cttee. of C.P. of Lithuanian S.S.R. until 67; Chair. of Council of Ministers of Lithuanian S.S.R. 67-; Deputy to U.S.S.R. Supreme Soviet.
Council of Ministers of Lithuanian S.S.R., Vilnius, U.S.S.R.

Mankiewicz, Joseph Leo, B.A.; American film writer, director and producer; b. 11 Feb. 1909; ed. Columbia Univ.
Asst. Corresp. in Berlin for *Chicago Tribune*; writer, Paramount Pictures 29-33; writer and producer, M.G.M. 33-43; writer, director and producer, Twentieth Century-Fox 43-51; Pres. Screen Director's Guild 50; Acad. of Motion Picture Arts and Sciences Award (Oscar) best screen-play and director 49 and 50; British Film Acad. Award and New York Film Critics' Award (for *All About Eve*) 51.
Works include: Script: *Skippy, Million Dollar Legs, If I Had a Million, Manhattan Melodrama, Forsaking All Others*; Produced: *Fury, Philadelphia Story, Woman of the Year, Keys of the Kingdom*; Script and Dir.: *Dragonwyck, Letter to Three Wives, All About Eve, People Will Talk, The Barefoot Contessa, Guys and Dolls, The Quiet American, The Honey Pot, No Way Out*; Dir.: *Late George Apley, The Ghost and Mrs. Muir, House of Strangers, Five Fingers, Suddenly Last Summer, La Bohème* (at Metropolitan Opera House) 53.
527 Madison Avenue, New York City, N.Y. 10022, U.S.A.

Mankowitz, Wolf, M.A.; British writer and theatrical producer; b. 7 Nov. 1924; ed. East Ham Grammar School, and Downing Coll., Cambridge.

Extensive work in journalism, radio, television and films, and as a theatrical producer; is also an expert in English Ceramics.

Films: *Make me an Offer, A Kid for Two Farthings* 54, *The Bespoke Overcoat* 55 (Venice Film Festival Award, British Film Acad. Award, Hollywood Oscar), *Expresso Bongo, The Long and the Short and the Tall* 59, *The Millionairess, The Day the Earth Caught Fire* 60 (British Film Acad. Award), *Waltz of the Toreadors* 61, *Where the Spies are* 65, *Casino Royale* 66, *The 25th Hour* 67.

Plays: *The Bespoke Overcoat* 53, *The Boychik* 54, *The Mighty Hunter, Expresso Bongo* (musical) 58, *Make Me an Offer* (musical) 59, *Belle* (musical) 61, *Pickwick* (musical) 63, *Passion Flower Hotel* (musical) 65.

Television includes *Conflict* series, *East End West End* series, *The Killing Stones* play-cycle 58, *A Cure for Tin Ear* 65, *The Battersea Miracle* 66.

Publs. (Fiction) *Make Me an Offer* 52, *A Kid for Two Farthings* 53, *Laugh till you Cry, Majollika and Company* 55, *My Old Man's a Dustman* 56, *The Mendelman Fire and Other Stories* 57, *Expresso Bongo* 60, *Cockatrice* 63, *The Biggest Pig in Barbados* 65; (Plays) *The Bespoke Overcoat, Five One-Act Plays* 55, *Expresso Bongo* 61; (Ceramics) *The Portland Vase* 52, *Wedgwood* 53, *A Concise Encyclopedia of English Pottery and Porcelain* 57.

4/10 Piccadilly Arcade, London, S.W.1, England.

Manley, Hon. Norman Washington, M.M., Q.C., B.A., B.C.L.; Jamaican lawyer and politician; b. 4 July 1893; ed. Jesus Coll., Oxford.

Called to the Jamaican Bar 22; practised as advocate since 23; founded People's Nat. Party 38; mem. House of Reps. 49-; Chief Minister of Jamaica 55-59, Premier 59-62; Leader of the Opposition 62-; Founder-Pres. West Indies Fed. Labour Party 56-62.

Mavis Bank, Jamaica.

Mann, Fritz Karl, DR. JURIS., PH.D.; German-American economist; b. 10 Dec. 1883; ed. Freiburg, Munich, Berlin, Paris and London Univs.

Economic Expert to Military Administration of Romania 17; mem. German Supreme Command; Chair. Inter-Allied Danube Comm. 17-18; Lecturer of Political Economy Kiel Univ. 14, Breslau Univ. 19; Prof. Kiel Univ. 20; Prof. Königsberg Univ. and Dir. Inst. for East German Economics 22; Prof. Cologne Univ. 26; Dir. Inst. for Int. Finance 27, Inst. for Fiscal Research 33; Prof. American Univ. Graduate School, Washington, D.C. 36, Brookings Instn. 40-41; Expert of War Dept.; Asst. Dir. and Acting Dir. of Research, Army Indus. Coll. 43-44; Fellow of Library of Congress 43-44; Dir. Institute on Federal Taxes 45-55; Chair. Dept. of Economics, American Univ. 48-54; Prof. Emeritus 56, Dr. rer. pol. h.c.

Publs. *Marschall Vauban und die Volkswirtschaftslehre des Absolutismus* 14, *Überwälzung der Steuer* 28, *Deutsche Finanzwirtschaft* 29, *Die Staatswirtschaft unserer Zeit* 30, *Gründer der Soziologie* 32, *Steuerpolitische Ideale* 37, *The Sociology of Taxation* 43, *The Government Corporation as a Tool of Foreign Policy* 43, *The Socialization of Risks* 45, *The Dual Debt System as a Method of Financing Government Corporations* 47, *The Threefold Economic Functions of Taxation* 47, *The Fiscal Component of Revolution* 47, *Re-orientation Through Fiscal Theory* 49, *Geschichte der angelsächsischen Finanzwissenschaft* 55, *Wirtschaftsgleichgewicht und Wirtschaftswachstum in den Vereinigten Staaten von Amerika* 57, *Die Bekämpfung der Inflationen: Amerikanische Methoden und Erfahrungen* 57, *Bemerkungen über Schumpeters Einfluss auf die amerikanische Wirtschafts-*

theorie 58, *The Romantic Reaction* 58, *Die Finanzwirtschaft als Modell und als System* 58, *Finanztheorie und Finanzsoziologie* 59, *Institutionalism and American Economic Theory: A Case of Interpenetration* 60, *Ideologie und Theorie des Haushaltsgleichgewichts* 61, *Von den Wandlungen und Widersprüchen der Steuerideologie* 61, *Finanzsoziologie* 61, *Vecchie e Nuove Teorie Del Pareggio Del Bilancio* 62, *Physiokratie* 62, *Die konjunktur- und finanzpolitische Lage der Vereinigten Staaten von Amerika; I Problemi dell'Economia Americana* 63, *Economics of Fiscal Decisions in a Pluralistic Society* 64, *Festgabe für F. K. Mann* 63, *Finanzwissenschaftliche Forschung und Lehre an der Universität zu Köln 1927-1935* 67.

3713 Williams Lane, Washington 15, D.C., U.S.A. Telephone: 652-3593.

Mann, Golo, DR.PHIL. (son of Thomas Mann); American (b. German) historian; b. 27 March 1909; ed. Schloss Salem, Univs. of Munich, Berlin and Heidelberg.

Reader in German Literature and History, Ecole Normale Supérieure, St. Cloud 33-35, Rennes Univ. 35-36; Editor *Mass und Wert,* Zurich 37-40; Prof. of Modern History Olivet Coll. (Mich.) 42-43; U.S. Army 43-46; Prof. of History Claremont Men's Coll. (Calif.) 47-57; Visiting Prof. Münster Univ. 58 and 59; Prof. of History, Stuttgart Technische Hochschule 60-64; Mannheim Schillerpreis 64, Berlin Fontane Prize 62.

Publs. *Friedrich von Gentz: Geschichte eines europäischen Staatsmannes* 47, *Vom Geist Amerikas* 54, *Aussenpolitik* (with H. Pross, vol. in *Fischer-Lexikon*) 58, *Deutsche Geschichte des 19. und 20. Jahrhunderts* 58, *Politische Entwicklung Europas und der Vereinigten Staaten 1815-1871* (in *Propyläen Weltgeschichte*) 60, *Geschichte und Geschichten* 61; publisher of *Propyläen Weltgeschichte* 60-64.

Alte Landstrasse 39, Kilchberg am Zürichsee, Switzerland.

Telephone: Zürich 91-46-66.

Mann, Thomas Clifton, B.A., LL.B.; American lawyer and diplomatist; b. 11 Nov. 1912; ed. Baylor Univ.

Member, law firm Mann and Mann, Texas 34-42; Foreign Service, Uruguay, Washington, Athens, Guatemala 42-55; Ambassador to El Salvador 55-57; Asst. Sec. of State for Econ. Affairs 57-60, for Inter-American Affairs 61; Amb. to Mexico 61-63; Asst. Sec. of State for Latin American Affairs 64-65; Under Sec. of State for Econ. Affairs 65-66; Pres. Automobile Manufacturers' Asscn. 67-; Hon. LL.D. (Notre-Dame).

4355 Lowell Street, N.W., Washington, D.C., U.S.A.

Mannheim, Hermann, O.B.E., DR. JURIS.; British criminologist of German origin; b. 26 Oct. 1889; ed. Munich, Freiburg, Strasbourg and Königsberg Univs.

German Civil Service 19-23; Judge Berlin District Court, later Court of Appeal 23-33; Lecturer Berlin Univ., later Prof. Extraordinary of Criminal Law 24-33, retd. 33; emigrated to England, naturalised 40; Lecturer (Criminology) London School of Economics and Political Science 35-46; Leon Fellow London Univ. 36; Reader in Criminology, London Univ. 46-55; Vice-Pres. and fmr. mem. Council and Co-Dir. Inst. for Study and Treatment of Delinquency; fmr. Pres. Scientific Cttee. Int. Soc. of Criminology; Vice-Pres. British Soc. of Criminology; Joint Editor *British Journal of Criminology* and *International Library of Criminology* (till 66); Joint Dir. Int. Course in Criminology, London 54; Chair. Programme Cttee. Int. Congress of Criminology, London 55; Hon. Dir. Criminal Research Unit, London School of Econs. and Political Science 56-62; Hon. Dr. juris. (Utrecht) 57; Hon. Fellow, London School of Econs. 67; Grosses Bundesverdienstkreuz, German Fed. Repub. 65; Golden Medal German Soc. of Criminology 65.

Publs. *Massstab der Fahrlässigkeit* 12, *Lehre von der Revision im Strafverfahren* 25, *Presserecht* 27, *Straf-*

prozessordnung (joint author) 30 and 33, *The Dilemma of Penal Reform* 39, *Social Aspects of Crime in England between the Wars* 40, *War and Crime* 41, *Young Offenders* (joint author) 42, *Criminal Justice and Social Reconstruction* 46, *Juvenile Delinquency in an English Middletown* 48, *Prediction Methods in relation to Borstal Training* (co-author) 55, *Group Problems in Crime and Punishment* 55; chapter on Great Britain in *The University Teaching of Criminology* (UNESCO) 57, *Courts for Adolescents* 58, ed. *Pioneers in Criminology* 60, *Deutsche Strafrechtsreform in englischer Sicht* 60, *Comparative Criminology* (2 vols.) 65; many essays and reviews.
London School of Economics, Houghton Street, W.C.2, England.

Mannin, Ethel (Mrs. R. A. Reynolds); British writer and journalist; b. 11 Oct. 1900.
Associate Editor *The Pelican* 18-20.
Publs. include (Novels) *Sounding Brass, Ragged Banners, Linda Shawn, Venetian Blinds, Men are Unwise, Cactus, The Pure Flame* (sequel to *Cactus*), *Women also Dream, Rose and Sylvie, Darkness my Bride, Julie, Rolling in the Dew, Red Rose, Captain Moonlight, The Blossoming Bough, Proud Heaven, Lucifer and the Child, The Dark Forest, Comrade O Comrade, Late Have I Loved Thee, Every Man a Stranger, Bavarian Story, At Sundown the Tiger, The Fields at Evening, Lover Under Another Name, The Living Lotus, Pity the Innocent, Fragrance of Hyacinths, The Blue-Eyed Boy, Sabishisa, Curfew at Dawn, The Road to Beersheba, The Burning Bush, The Night and its Homing, The Lady and the Mystic;* (Travel and Memoirs) *Confessions and Impressions, South to Samarkand, Privileged Spectator* (sequel to *Confessions*), *Moroccan Mosaic, Land of the Crested Lion, Connemara Journal, German Journey, Jungle Journey, This was a Man* (memories of Robert Mannin), *The Country of the Sea* (Brittany), *Brief Voices* (autobiography), *The Flowery Sword* (Japan), *A Lance for the Arabs, Aspects of Egypt, The Lovely Land* (Jordan), *An American Journey;* (Essays and Miscellaneous) *Common Sense and the Child, Common Sense and the Adolescent, Common Sense and Morality, Women and the Revolution, Christianity—or Chaos, Bread and Roses* (A Survey of Utopias), *Two Studies in Integrity: Francis Mahony* ('Father Prout') *and Gerald Griffin, Rebels' Ride (The Revolt of the Individual), Loneliness: a Study of the Human Condition;* (Short Stories) *No More Mimosa, Green Figs, The Wild Swans* (tales based on the ancient Irish), *So Tiberias* (a novella) *England for a Change* 68.
Oak Cottage, 27 Burghley Road, London, S.W.19, England.

Manning, Hon. Ernest Charles; Canadian politician; b. 20 Sept. 1908; ed. Rosetown, Saskatchewan.
Member Alberta Legislature 35-, Provincial Sec. 35, Minister of Trade and Industry 35, Premier 43-, Provincial Treasurer 44, Minister of Mines and Minerals 52-62, concurrently Attorney-Gen. 56-; mem. Social Credit Party; Hon. LL.D. (Univ. of Alberta).
Legislative Building, Edmonton, Alberta, Canada.

Manning, Robert Joseph; American journalist and government official; b. 25 Dec. 1919; ed. Harvard Univ.
U.S. Army service 42-43; Editor, Press Service 41, Newspaper 61-62; State Dept. and White House Corresp. 44-46, Chief UN Corresp. 46-49; Writer, *Time* magazine 49-55, Senior Editor 55-58, Chief, London Bureau, *Time, Life, Fortune, Sports Illustrated* magazines 58-61; Sunday Editor, *New York Herald Tribune* 61-62; Consultant, Public-Information Office, Dept. of State Feb.-April 62, Asst. Sec. of State for Public Affairs, Dept. of State 62-64; Exec. Editor *Atlantic Monthly* 64-65, Editor 66-.
Office: 8 Arlington Street, Boston, Mass., U.S.A.
Telephone: 159-568.

Manninger, Rezsó Rudolphe; Hungarian veterinary surgeon; b. 7 July 1890; ed. Veterinary Coll., Budapest.
Professor of Infectious Diseases, Veterinary Univ. of Budapest 27-63, Emer. 63-; mem. Hungarian Acad. of Sciences 27-, Vice-Pres. 60-67; Corresp. mem. German Acad. of Agronomic Sciences, G.D.R., Acad. of Agronomic Sciences, U.S.S.R., etc.; mem. Acad. of Sciences, Czechoslovakia, Poland and Bulgaria; Hon. mem. Acad. of Agronomic Sciences, Czechoslovakia, Royal Coll. of Veterinary Surgeons, London, World Veterinary Asscn., etc.; Vice-Pres. Hungarian Microbiologic Soc.; Kossuth Prize (twice); Hon. Dr. med. vet., Leipzig, Budapest, Thessalonika.
Szilágyi Erzsébet fasor 61, Budapest II, Hungary.

Manojlović, Kosta P., B.A.; Yugoslav musician; b. 90; ed. Belgrade Theological Seminary, Munich Conservatoire and Oxford Univ.
Compositions include: *Olče naš, Nalne Zesme, Mnjoga ljeta, Litwegija Opelo, By the Waters of Babylon* (for two choirs, baritone solo and orchestra), *Pesme Zemlje, Tužbalica, Pesme Zemlje Raške, Jugoslovenske narodne pesme;* various songs, etc.
Publs. *Zivot i rad St. Mokranjca, Istorijski pogled na postanak, rad, i ideje Muzičke Skole u Beogradu, Muzičke karakteristike našeg Juga, Debru i Zupi Muzičko delo našega sela, Istoriski pogledu na muz uki Engleskoj, Stevan St. Mokranjac i njegove muzičke studije u Münchena.*
Kralja Milana 84, Belgrade, Yugoslavia.

Mansager, Felix; American business executive; b. 30 Jan. 1911; ed. Colton High School.
General Sales Manager, The Hoover Company 59, Vice-Pres. (Sales) 59-61, Exec. Vice-Pres. and Dir. The Hoover Company 61-63, Hoover Group 63-66, Pres. and Chair. 66-; Hon. LL.D. (Capital Univ., Columbus, Ohio).
The Hoover Company, North Canton, Ohio, U.S.A.

Mansergh, General Sir Robert, G.C.B., K.B.E., M.C.; British army officer; b. 12 May 1900; ed. Rondebosch, S.A., and Royal Military Acad., Woolwich.
Commissioned 20, served U.K. and abroad; mem. Mil. Mission to Iraq 31-35; fmr. Adjutant, Royal Mil. Acad., Woolwich; served Second World War in Middle and Far East; Major-Gen. 46, Lt.-Gen. 48, Gen. 53; C.-in-C. Allied Forces, Netherlands East Indies 46; Dir. Territorial Army and Cadets 47; Military Sec. to Sec. of State for War 48-49; C.-in-C. British Forces Hong Kong 49-51; Col. Commdt. Royal Artillery 50; Deputy C.-in-C. Allied Forces Northern Europe 51-53, C.-in-C. 53-56; C.-in-C. U.K. Land Forces 56-59; retd. 59; Col. Commdt. Royal Horse Artillery 57; A.D.C. to H.M. The Queen 56-59; Master Gunner, St. James's Park 60-; Pres. Westminster Chamber of Commerce 62-63.
66 Abbotsbury Close, London, W.14, England.

Mansfield, Hon. Sir Alan James, K.C.M.G., LL.B.; Australian judge; b. 30 Sept. 1902; ed. Univ. of Sydney.
Admitted to Bar of N.S.W. 24, Queensland 24; Lecturer in Bankruptcy and Company Laws Univ. of Queensland 39; practised as barrister-at-law Queensland 25-40; Judge of Supreme Court of Queensland 40-; mem. Australian War Crimes Board of Enquiry 45; Australian rep. U.N. War Crimes Comm. London 45; Chief Australian Prosecutor Int. Mil. Tribunal for the Far East Jan. 46-Jan. 47; Chair. of Land Appeal Court Queensland 42-45; Chair. Aliens Tribunal 42-45; Chair. Royal Comms. on Queensland Sugar Industry 42, 50; Senior Puisne Judge of Queensland 47-55; Acting Chief Justice of Queensland 50, Chief Justice 56-66; Administrator of Govt. of Queensland 57-58; Chair. Central Sugar Cane Prices Board 55; Warden, Queensland Univ. 56-66, Chancellor, Queensland Univ. 66-; Gov. of Queensland 66-.
Government House, Brisbane, Queensland, Australia.

Mansfield, J(ohn) Kenneth; American government official; b. 1921; ed. Northwestern Univ. and Yale Univ. Instructor in Int. Relations, Yale Univ. 49-50; Chief of Staff, Mil. Applications Sub. Cttee., Joint Congressional Cttee. on Atomic Energy 50-56; combustion engine firm 56-59; Staff. Dir., U.S. Senate Sub. Cttee. on Nat. Policy Machinery 59-62; Insp. Gen. Foreign Assistance, Dept. of State 62-.
Department of State, Washington, D.C. 20520, U.S.A.

Mansfield, Michael Joseph, A.B., A.M.; American politician; b. 16 March 1903; ed. Montana State Univ. Former mining engineer; Prof. of History and Political Science Montana State Univ. 33-42; mem. House of Reps. 43-52, Senator (Democrat, Montana) 52-; Majority Whip 57-61; Leader of Senate 61-.
Missoula, Montana, U.S.A.

Mansholt, Sicco Leendert; Netherlands politician; b. 13 Sept. 1908; ed. School for Tropical Agriculture, Deventer.
Studied agriculture; worked on Dutch farms 24-34, tea plantations in Indonesia 34-36; returned to Netherlands and worked on Wieringermeer Polder from 37; during the German occupation organized important illegal work, particularly for the food supply of western provinces and worked on behalf of concentration camp victims; commanded a section of the forces of the Interior after the capitulation; became Burgomaster of Wieringermeer; Minister of Agriculture, Fisheries and Food in Schermerhorn Cabinet June 45-46; in Beel Cabinet 46-48, in Drees Cabinet 48, 51, 52 and 56-58; Head of the Netherlands Del. to UN for agriculture, and took part in negotiations for creation of Benelux Union 46; prepared *Mansholt Plan* for Agricultural Section of European Econ. Community 53; Vice-Pres. European Econ. Community Comm. 58-67; Vice-Pres. Combined Exec. of EEC, ECSC and Euratom 67-; Dr. h.c. in Agriculture (Inst. of Agriculture, Wageningen, Gembloux); Grand Croix de l'Ordre de la Couronne de Belgique, Commdr. of the Order of the Netherlands Lion and numerous other foreign awards, including Robert Schuman Prize 68.
Home: 95B Avenue Albert Lancaster, Brussels, Belgium; and Communauté Economique Européenne, Avenue de la Joyeuse Entrée, Brussels, Belgium.

Mantilla-Ortega, Jorge, B.S.; Ecuadorean journalist and diplomatist; b. 31 May 1907; ed. Colegio San Gabriel, Quito, The Manlius School, Manlius, N.Y., and Univ. of Maryland.
Editor and Publisher *El Comercio* and *Ultimas Noticias*, Quito; mem. Congress, Ecuador 48-50, Senator 56-60; Counsellor, Perm. Del. of Ecuador to UN 49-52; Dir.-Gen. Inter-American Commercial Arbitration Comm. 58-62; Amb. to Italy 62-64, to U.K. 64-67; Grand Cross of Merit (Ecuador), Grand Cross St. Sylvester (Vatican), Grand Cross of Merit (Italy), Southern Cross (Brazil).
El Comercio, Apdo. Postal 57, Quito, Ecuador.

Manuel, Robert; French actor and producer; b. 7 Sept. 1916; ed. Lycée Carnot and National Conservatoire of Dramatic Art, Paris.
Sociétaire, Comédie-Française; Prof., Nat. Conservatoire of Dramatic Art and Conservatoire de la rue Blanche, Lecturer and Dir. Théâtre Marigny; film actor; Chevalier de la Légion d'Honneur.
Plays produced include: *Les Trois valses, Les Cloches de Corneville, Mamzelle Nitouche, Les Précieuses Ridicules, On ne saurait penser à tout, Mariage forcé, Bidule, Les Croulants se portent bien, La Grève des amoureux, Gigi.*
98 avenue de Villiers, Paris 17e, France.

Manuel Castillo, Carlos, PH.D., M.SC., D.ECON.; Costa Rican economist; b. 19 Dec. 1928; ed. Univ. de Costa Rica, and Univs. of Wisconsin and Tennessee.
Secretary-General Nat. Production Council, Costa Rica 48-49; Chief of Economy and Agricultural Statistics Service, San José 50-51; Economist, Project 39, OAS Technical Co-operation Programme, Havana, Cuba 53-55; Head of Agricultural Section, UN Econ. Comm. for Latin America (ECLA) 56-59, in Mexican Office of ECLA as Sec. of Central American Isthmus Econ. Co-operation Cttee. 59-61, Asst. later Dir. of Office 61-63, 63-66; Secretary-General Perm. Secretariat of General Treaty for Central American Econ. Integration Oct. 66-.
Publs. *Análisis Exploratorio del Sistema de Tenencia de la Tierra en Costa Rica* 53, *La Reforma Agraria y sus Efectos sobre la Tasa de Acumulación de Capital en la Economía* 53, *Problemas Agrícolas e Industriales de México* 54, *El Régimen Agrario y el Funcionamiento de Mercado de los Factores* 55, *La Economía Agrícola en la Región del Bajío* 56, *Growth and Integration in South America Región del Bajío* 56, *Growth and Integration in Central America* 56, *Aspectos Políticos y Administrativos del Desarrollo Económico* 59.
Secretaría Permanente del Tratado General de Integración Económica Centroamericana, Guatemala City, Guatemala.

Manuelli, Ernesto, M.C.S.; Italian financial executive; b. 22 Feb. 1906; ed. Rome Univ.
Banker 23-32; Gen. Sec. Sofindit (Industrial Financial Co.) 32-35; Gen. Inspector, Office of Foreign Trade and Currencies, Rome 35-40; Central Dir., Vice-Pres., Commr., Pres. Bd. of Dirs. Ansaldo S.p.A. Genoa 40-45; Gen. Man., Dir., mem. Exec. Cttee., Finsider S.p.A. Rome 45-58, Chair. Board of Dirs., Man. Dir., mem. Exec. Cttee. 58-; Vice-Pres. Société Financière Italo-Suisse; Dir. Alfa Romeo and other companies; Cavaliere del Lavoro.
Publs. Economic research papers.
495 Via Della Camilluccia, Rome; 122 Viale Castro Pretorio, Rome, Italy.

Manuwa, Chief the Hon. Sir Samuel Layinka Ayodeji, Kt.; The Iyasere (Chief) of Itebu-Manuwa, The Obadugba of Ondo, The Olowa Luwagboye of Ijebu Ode, C.M.G., O.B.E., LL.D., D.SC., D.LITT., M.D., CH.B., F.R.C.S., F.R.C.P., F.A.C.P., F.R.S.(Edin.); Nigerian surgeon and medical administrator; b. 4 March 1903; ed. King's Coll., Lagos, Edinburgh and Liverpool Univs.
Medical Officer and Surgical Specialist British Colonial Medical Service 27-48; Deputy Dir. Medical Services 48-51, Dir. 51, Insp.-Gen. 51-54; Chief Medical Adviser to Fed. Govt. of Nigeria 54-59; mem. Western Nigeria House of Assembly 48-51; mem. Legislative and Exec. Councils 51-52; mem. Governor's Privy Council 52-54; mem. Fed. Privy Council and Public Service Comm. 54-; Pro-Chancellor and Chair. of Council, Univ. of Ibadan 67-; Fellow, Royal Soc. of Arts, London, American Public Health Asscn.; mem. New York Acad. of Sciences; mem. World Health Organisation Expert Panel on Public Health Admin. and Advisory Cttee. on Medical Research; Pres. World Fed. for Mental Health 65-66; Pres. Asscn. of Physicians of W. Africa; Past Pres. Asscn. of Surgeons of W. Africa; Commdr. Order of St. John; John Holt Medal of Liverpool Univ. for Services to Tropical Medicine.
Publs. *History of the Development of our Knowledge of the Endocrine Organs* 24, *Hernia in the West African Negro* 29, *Chronic Splenomegaly in West Africa, Spinal Anaesthesia* 34, *Lymphostatic Verrucosis* 35, *Porocephalosis* 47, *The Estimation of Age in Nigerian Children* 57, *Principles of Planning National Health Programmes in Under-Developed Countries* 61, *Mental Health Programmes in Public Health Planning* 63, *Mental Health is Common Wealth* 67, *The Training of Senior Administrators for Higher Responsibilities in the National Health Services of Developing Countries* 67.
Federal Public Service Commission, Lagos; Pro-Chancellor's Lodge, The University of Ibadan, Ibadan; 2 Alexander Avenue, Lagos, Nigeria.
Telephone: 22014 (Lagos); 21051 (Ibadan).

Manzhulo, Alexei Nikolayevich; Soviet foreign trade official; b. 1913; ed. Inst. of Motor Roads, Acad. of Foreign Trade.
Member C.P.S.U. 40-; Chief of Section, later Deputy Trade Rep. of U.S.S.R. in England 46-51; Official, Ministry of Foreign Trade 51-52; Counsellor, COMECON 52-53; U.S.S.R. Commercial Rep. in Argentina 53-57; Deputy Chief of Dept., Ministry of Foreign Trade, Cuba 60-62; Chief of Dept., Ministry of Foreign Trade 62-; Order of Lenin and Order of Red Banner of Labour.
U.S.S.R. Ministry of Foreign Trade 32-34 Smolenskaya-Sennaya Square, Moscow, U.S.S.R.

Manzini, Raimondo; Italian diplomatist; b. 1913; ed. Univ. degli Studi, Bologna.
Diplomatic Service 40-, served San Francisco, Lisbon, Foreign Ministry, Rome, and London 40-50; Consul-Gen., Leopoldville 50-51, Stuttgart 51-58; Head of Private Office of Foreign Minister 58-65; Italian Rep. to Org. for Econ. Co-operation and Devt. (OECD) 65-.
Organization for Economic Co-operation and Development, Château de la Muette, 2 rue André-Pascal, Paris 16e, France.

Manzù, Giacomo; Italian sculptor; b. 24 Dec. 1908.
Began his career working in a decoration and design studio; Prof. of Sculpture Accad. Brera, Milan 41-54, Salzburg Int. Sommerakademie 54-60; Exhibition of Paintings and Drawings, Hanover Gallery, London 65; Sculpture Prize, Venice Biennale 48; major works include main door of Salzburg Cathedral, *Porta delle Morte*, San Pietro in Vaticano, Rome; Lenin Peace Prize 65.
Publs. *La Porta di San Pietro* 65, *An Artist and the Pope* 67.
Campo del Fico, Ardea, Rome, Italy.

Mao Tse tung (married to Chiang Ching, *q.v.*); Chinese politician; b. 26 Dec. 1893; ed. Hsiang-hsiang Middle School, Ch'angsha, Hunan First Middle School and First Teachers' Training School.
Worked on father's farm 06; in Revolutionary Army 11-12; Library Asst., Peking Univ., Co-Founder of New Citizen's Soc. and teacher at evening school 18; Teacher, Hsiu-yeh Primary School, Ch'angsha, also Organizer, Problem Discussion Group 19; Dir. Primary School Section, First Teachers' Training School 21-22; Founder of Self-Education Coll. (later Hsian Chiang Middle School) and of Hunan branch of Socialist Youth Corps 21; Chair. Asscn. of Trade Unions of Hunan 22, All-China Peasants' Union 27, Special Cttee. Chingkangshan base area 28, Nat. Soviet Govt. 30; Sec. Propaganda Dept., Kuomintang 25; Chief of Peasant Dept., Chinese C.P. 26, Sec. of Front Cttee. 27-28; created Kiangsi Provincial Soviet Govt. 30; war against Japan 37-45; Chair. of Central Cttee. and Politbureau 43-; defeat of Kuomintang 45-49; Chair. Central People's Govt. of Republic of China 49-54, of People's Repub. of China 54-58; Hon. Chair. People's Political Consultative Conf.; fmr. Editor: *Hsiang River Review* and *Hsin Hunan* 19, *Political Weekly* 25.
Publs. *The Great Union of the People* 19, *An Analysis of the Classes in Chinese Society* 26, *Strategic Problems of China's Revolutionary War* 36, *Selected Works of Mao Tse-tung* (4 vols.) 37, *On the Protracted War* 38, *Problems of War and Strategy* 38, *37 Poems of President Mao*, *President Mao's Poetry*, and numerous essays.
Peking, China.

Mao Tun (Shen Yen-ping); Chinese novelist, playwright and critic; b. 96; ed. Hangchow Normal School, National Peking University.
A founder of Society for Literary Research 21; edited *Short Story Magazine* 21-24, when he engaged in revolutionary work; a founder of China League of Left Writers 30; went to Hongkong, editorial work; then Chungking and Sinkiang Univ. 37; Shantung del. to First N.P.C. 54; mem. Dept. of Philosophy, and Social

Sciences, Academia Sinica; Vice-Chair. Asian Solidarity Cttee. of China 56; fmr. Minister of Culture; Editor *Chinese Literature* until March 67; Vice-Chair. All-China Fed. of Literary and Artistic Circles, Chinese People's Political Consultative Conf.
Publs. Many novels and short stories, works on western literature, translations; edited many literary journals.
c/o Ministry of Culture, Peking, China.

Mao Yi-sheng; Chinese engineer; b. 96; ed. Tangshan Engineering Coll., Cornell Univ., Carnegie Inst. of Technology.
Professor Tangshan Engineering Coll. 20; Dean of Coll. of Engineering, Nat. Southeast Univ., Nanking 23; Pres. Peiyang Univ., Tientsin 28; Engineering Dir. Chien Tang River Bridge, Hangchow 33; Pres. China Bridge Co., Chungking 43; Pres. Chiao Tung Univ., Peking 49; Dir. Railways Research Inst., Peking 50; Chair. Board Consulting Engineers, Yangtze river bridge at Hankow 54; Deputy Dir. and Mem. Division of Technical Sciences, Chinese Acad. of Sciences, Peking 54-; mem. Standing Cttee., 1st, 2nd and 3rd Nat. People's Congress 56, 59, 65; Pres. Chinese Civil Eng. Soc. 53-; Vice-Pres. All-China Scientific and Technical Asscn. 58.
Publs. Many articles and books on bridge engineering.
c/o Railways Research Institute, Peking, China.

Marai, Sándor; Hungarian-born American poet and novelist; b. 11 April 1900.
Publs. *Emlékkönyv, Versek, Panaszkönyv, A mészáros, Zendülök, Idegen emberek, Csutora, Egy Polgár vallomásai, Bébi, vagy az elsö szerelem, A szegények iskolája, Bolhapiac, Istenek nyomdában, A féltékenyek, Válás Budán, Kabala, Napnyugati örjárat A négy évszak, A sziget, Müsoron kivül, Sèrbödöttek;* also many novels, plays, etc., published in Czech, German, Finnish, Danish, French, Italian, Dutch, Spanish and Swedish.
100 Park Terrace West, New York 34, N.Y., U.S.A.

Maraini, Dacia (daughter of Fosco Maraini, *q.v.*); Italian authoress; b. 13 Nov. 1936; ed. Collegio S.S. Annunziata, Florence and Rome.
Prix Formentor for *L'Età del Malessere (The Age of Discontent)* 62.
Publs. *La Vacanza* 62, *L'Età del Malessere* 62, *Crudeltá All' Aria Aperta* (poems) 66, *A Memoria* (novel) 67, *La famiglia normale* (one-act play) 67, *Il ricatto a teatro* (play) 68.
Lungotevere Della Vittoria 1, Rome, Italy.
Telephone: 378936.

Maraini, Fosco, D.S.C (father of Dacia Maraini, *q.v.*); Italian writer; b. 15 Nov. 1912; ed. Univ. of Florence.
Asst. Prof., Univ. of Hokkaido, Japan 38-41; Reader in Italian, Univ. of Kyoto 41-43; civil internee (as anti-Fascist) in Japan 43-45; returned to Italy 46; Fellow, St. Antony's Coll., Oxford; writing and research on anthropology and ethnology of Asia.
Publs. *Secret Tibet* 53, *Meeting with Japan* 59, *Karakoram* 61, *Hekura* 62, *Where Four Worlds Meet* 64.
Viale Magalotti 6, Florence, Italy.

Marais, Jean; French actor; b. 11 Dec. 1913; ed. Lycées Condorcet and Janson-de-Sailly, and Conservatoire Maubel.
Appeared in *L'Epervier, Le Scandale, L'Aventurier, Le Bonheur, Dans les Rues, Les Hommes Nouveaux;* also appeared in plays, including *Oedipe Roi, Les Chevaliers de la Table Ronde, Les Parents Terribles, Britannicus, La Machine à Ecrire, L'Avare, Andromaque, Pygmalion, Two For the Seesaw*, etc.; served French Army 39-40 and 44-45; later made more films, including *L'Eternal Retour, Aux Yeux du Souvenir, Le Secret de Mayerling, Orphée, Le Château de Verre, Julietta, Elena et les Hommes, Typhon sur Nagazaky, La Vie à Deux, Amour de Poche, Les Nuits Blanches, Chaque Jour a son Secret, Versailles, Le Bossu, Austerlitz, Le Testament d'Orphée,*

Le Capitan, La Princesse de Clèves, Les Mystères de Paris, Patate, Fantomas, Le Saint Prend l'Affut, etc.
Marnes-la-Coquette (Seine-et-Oise), France.

Maramis, Max; Indonesian diplomatist; b. 5 March 1917; ed. General Bank of People's Credit, Higher Medical School and Land Forces Command and Staff Coll.
Joined Diplomatic Service 50; Indonesian Embassy in U.S., then Chargé d'Affaires in Canada, Austria, Netherlands; Head Press Section, Afro-Asian Conf. Secr. in Bandung; Chief U.S. Section, Foreign Ministry 60-62; Deputy Chief Indonesian Mission at UN Provisional Admin. in West Irian 62-63; Amb. to Tunisia 65-67; Amb. to U.S.S.R. June 67-.
Indonesian Embassy, Novokuznetskaya ul. 12, Moscow, U.S.S.R.

Marañón, Gregorio; Spanish lawyer and administrator; b. 15; ed. England and France.
Legal practice; mem. of the Spanish Cortes; Dir. Inst. of Hispanic Culture 62-; Spanish Delegate to UN; Gran Cruz de Isabel la Católica, Cruz de Honor de San Raimundo de Peñafort y del Mérito Militar, Oficial de la Legión de Honor, etc.
Institute of Hispanic Culture, Avenida Reyes Católicos, Ciudad Universitaria, Madrid, Spain.

Marbo, Camille (*pseudonym* of Mme. Marguerite Borel); French writer; b. 11 April 1883; ed. Sorbonne.
Pres. Société des Gens de lettres de France 37 and 46; Pres. Fémina Jury 51, 60-61; Prix Fémina 13, Grand Prix Barthou 53, Commdr. de la Légion d'Honneur.
Publs. *Hélène Barraux* 11, *La Statue voilée* (Fémina Prize) 13, *Le Survivant* 16, *Cahiers de Francine, Le Perroquet Bleu* 25, *A l'enseigne du Griffon* 28, *A bord de la Croix-du-Sud* 31, *Flammes Juives* 36, *Le buisson de Lilas* 46, *La Maison Bartholène* 46, *Tante Estelle* 47, *L'Idole Offensée* 48, *Le Château condamné* 49, *Sous les Eucalyptus* 50, *La reine de Jolconde* 51, *Monsieur Charles* 52, *Jeux de la Science et de l'Amour* 53, *Le Bel Héritage* 58, *Les Lettres* 60, *La Dernière Nuit* 62, *La Protectrice* 63, *Clara Fontaine* 67, *A Travers Deux Siecles, Souvenirs et Rencontres* 68.
4 rue Froidevaux, Paris 14e, France.
Telephone: 326-5285.

Marca-Relli, Corrado; American artist; b. 5 June 1913.
One man exhibition Niveau Gallery 47, 49, Rome 48, New Gallery 50, Stable Gallery 52, Kootz Gallery (all in New York City) 59; in exhibitions Whitney Museum 53, 55, Yale Univ. Gallery 54, Tate Gallery, London 63; Ford Foundation Award 59.
25 E. 67th Street, New York City, N.Y., U.S.A.

Marceau, Marcel; French mime; b. 22 March 1923; ed. Strasbourg Lycée, and Ecole des Beaux-Arts, Paris.
Dir. Compagnie de Mime Marcel Marceau; creator of the character "Bip"; mimes include *Le Manteau, Exercices de Style* (both filmed), *Mort avant l'Aube, Le Joueur de Flûte, Moriana et Galvau, Pierrot de Montmartre, Les Trois Perruques, Exercices de Style,* etc.; other films: *Pantomime, Un Jardin Public, Le Fabricant de masques, Paris qui rit, Paris qui pleure, Barbarella.*
15 avenue Montaigne, Paris 8e, France.

Marcel, Gabriel Honoré; French philosopher and writer; b. 7 Dec. 1889; ed. Paris Univ.
Held a number of teaching posts 12-41; awarded Grand Prix de Littérature of French Academy 48; mem. Acad. Moral and Political Sciences 52; Goethe Prize, Hamburg Univ. 56, Grand Prix Nat. des Lettres 58, German Booksellers 1964 Peace Prize 64; Grand Prix Littéraire de la Ville de Paris 68; contributed to *Nouvelles Littéraires;* Officier, Légion d'Honneur, Commdr. des Arts et des Lettres, Commdr. des Palmes Académiques.
Publs. Plays: *Le Seuil Invisible* 14, *L'Iconoclaste* 23, *Un Homme de Dieu* 25, *Le Chemin de Crète* 36, *Le Fanal*

36, *La Soif* 38, *L'Horizon* 45, *Vers un autre Royaume* 49, *Rome n'est plus dans Rome* 51; Philosophy: *Journal Métaphysique* 28, *Etre et Avoir* 35, *Du Refus à l'Invocation* 40, *Homo Viator* 45, *Le Mystère de l'être* 51-52, *Théâtre de Religion* 59, *L'Heure Théâtrale: de Giraudoux à Sartre* 59, *Fragments philosophiques, 1909-1914* 63, *Regards sur le Théâtre de Claudel* 64.
21 rue de Tournon, Paris 6e, France.

Marcellin, Raymond, D. en D.; French politician and lawyer; b. 19 Aug. 1914; ed. Meaux Coll., Paris and Strasbourg Univs.
Under-Secretary of State of the Interior 48-49; Sec. of State of Industry 49-52, of the Pres. of the Council 52, of Information 52-57, of Public Functions 57-62; Minister of Public Health and of the Population 62-66, of Industry 66-67; Minister under Prime Minister, Responsible for Plan 67-68; Minister of Interior May 68-; Deputy 46-; Mayor of Vannes 65-; Croix de Guerre, Médaille des Evadés, and many foreign decorations.
71 avenue de Breteuil, Paris 15e, France.

March, Fredric (Frederick McIntyre Bickel), A.B.; American actor; b. 31 Aug. 1897; ed. Univ. of Wisconsin.
Films he has appeared in include *Les Misérables, Anna Karenina, The Barretts of Wimpole Street, A Star is Born, Death Takes a Holiday, Nothing Sacred, The Best Years of Our Lives* (Acad. Award 32), *Dr. Jekyll and Mr. Hyde* (Acad. Award 37), *Inherit the Wind, The Young Doctors, Executive Suite, The Bridges at Toko-Ri, The Desperate Hours, The Man in the Grey Flannel Suit, Alexander the Great, The Middle of the Night, Death of a Salesman, Hombre;* plays: *The Skin of our Teeth, The Autumn Garden, Years Ago, The American Way, An Enemy of the People, Hope for a Harvest, Gideon.*
c/o Roland Mader Inc., 1434 Westwood Blvd., Los Angeles 24, Calif., U.S.A.

Marchal, André; French professor; b. 11 Oct. 1907; ed. Lycée Henri Poincaré, Nancy and Paris Univs.
Lawyer, Nancy Court of Appeal, then at Public Prosecutor's Office 29-35; Asst. Paris Faculty of Law 33-35; Prof. Dijon Faculty of Law 35-39; served French Army 39-40; in charge of course Paris Faculty of Law 42-44; Asst. Prof. 44-45; Prof. 45-; Dir. of Studies, Ecole Pratique des Hautes Etudes 54-.
Publs. *La Conception de l'Economie Nationale et des Rapports Internationaux chez les Mercantilistes Français et chez leurs Contemporains* 31, *L'Action Ouvrière et la Transformation du Régime Capitaliste* 43, *Economie Politique et Technique Statistique* 43, *Le Mouvement Syndical en France* 45, *La pensée économique en France depuis 1945* 53, *Méthode scientifique et Science économique* (2 vols.); *Systèmes et Structures économiques* 59, *L'Europe Solidaire* 64, *L'Intégration Territoriale* 65.
180 rue de Grenelle, Paris 7e, France.

Marchand, André Marius; French painter; b. 10 Feb. 1907; ed. Colls. of Aix-en-Provence, Bouches du Rhône; and studied in Paris.
Has exhibited in Paris since 34; in Holland 36, Cambridge 39, Washington, Boston and Chicago 39, Rio de Janeiro 45, Brussels 45, Canada 46, New York 46, Berne 48, Geneva 48, Stuttgart 48, London, Stockholm, Avignon 49, Innsbruck 50; Bienal in São Paulo 51; exhibition in museums in Holland and Belgium 51, in London (Wildenstein Galleries) 52, in Switzerland and Germany 53; in New York (Wildenstein Gallery) 54, Venice Biennale 54; work on permanent exhibition in Musée d'Art Moderne (Paris), in Grenoble, Arles, Algiers, Toulouse, The Hague, Liège, Eindhoven, Turin, Tokyo; a founder mem. and exhibitor in Salon de Mai (since 45); illustrated (lithographs) *Les Nourritures Terrestres* (André Gide), *Le Visionnaire* (Julien Green), etc. and designed for the works of Darius Milhaud and Jacques Audiberti; Paul Guillaume Prize 37, Arche

Prize for design 52; lithographs for *Petite Cosmogonie Portative* (Raymond Queneau) 55.

31 *bis* rue Campagne Première, Paris 14e, France.

Marchenko, Ivan Tikhonovich; Soviet politician; b. 08; ed. Leningrad Railway Engineering Inst.

Member C.P.S.U. 29-; party and economic work 38-; Chief, Moscow Dept., Western Region Railway 46-51; Second Sec., Moscow City Cttee. C.P.S.U. 54-59; First Sec. Tomsk Regional Cttee. C.P.S.U. 59-65; mem. Central Cttee. of C.P.S.U. 56-61, Cand. mem. 61-66; Minister of Local Industry R.S.F.S.R. 65-; Deputy to U.S.S.R. Supreme Soviet 61-66.

R.S.F.S.R. Ministry of Local Industry, 2 Bolshoy Cherkassky pereulok, Moscow, U.S.S.R.

Marchuk, Ivan Ivanovich; Soviet diplomatist; b. 1922; ed. Univ. of Kiev.

Diplomatic Service 47-; Counsellor, Conakry 59-62; Deputy Head of Press Dept., U.S.S.R. Ministry of Foreign Affairs 62-64; Amb. to Burundi 64-67; on staff of Ministry of Foreign Affairs 67-.

U.S.S.R. Ministry of Foreign Affairs, 32-37 Smolen-skaya-Sennaya Ploshchad, Moscow, U.S.S.R.

Marcks, Gerhard Wilhelm Albert; German sculptor; b. 18 Feb. 1889; ed. Gymnasium in Berlin.

Teacher of sculpture Berlin 18; master at Weimar Bauhaus 19-25; teacher, then head, of studies at Halle Giebichenstein 25-33; private work 33-45; teacher at Hamburg Art School 46-50; Orden Pour le Mérite (German Federal Republic); works include memorials in Hamburg, Cologne, Mannheim, Bochum, Hanover and Lübeck; works on view in New York Museum of Modern Art and other American museums.

Belvedere 149A, Köln-Müngersdorf, German Federal Republic.

Telephone: Cologne 491488.

Marconi, Mario, DR. ECON. AND COMM. SC.; Italian industrialist; b. 14 Feb. 1896; ed. Univ. of Genoa.

Gen. Manager of Vickers Terni Genoa 22-29, of Ansaldo, S. p. A., Genoa 29-35, of "Aquila", Trieste 35-45; **Man. Dir.** Silurificio Whitehead of Fiume 35-45; Vice-Pres. Whitehead-Moto Fides, Leghorn 45-58; Man. Dir. Franco Tosi S. p. a., Milan 46-56; mem. Board of Confederazione Generale Industria Italiana; Chair. Compagnia Italiana Westinghouse, Freni e Segnali, Turin (1951); Chair. Nebiolo S.p.A., Turin; Chair. Rexim-Bugnone, Turin; Vice-Pres. Oerlikon Italiana S.p.A., Milan; mem. Board Ercole Marelli S.p.A., Reinach Oleoblitz S.p.A., Fratelli Borletti S.p.A., etc.; Italian del. to Int. Materials Conf., Washington, D.C. 51-53; Chair. Associazione Nazionale Industria Meccanica Varia ed Affine, ANIMA, Milan 51-54, Hon. Chair. 54-; Chair. Magrini S.p.A. (Bergamo); mem. Comité Européen pour le Progrés Economique et Social; mem. Asscn. pour l'Etude des Problèmes de l'Europe; Cavaliere del Lavoro.

Office: Via dei Cignoli 3, Milan; Home: Via Annunciata 23/1, Milan, Italy.

Telephone: 651-678 (Home); 30-40-65 (Office).

Marcos, Ferdinand E.; Philippines lawyer and politician; b. 1917; ed. Univ. of Philippines.

Lieutenant, later Capt., in Philippines Army; took part in anti-Japanese resistance; Special Asst. to Pres. Manuel Roxas after Second World War; mem. House of Reps. 49-59, Senate 59-66; Pres. of Philippines 66-; mem. Liberal Party until 64, Nationalist Party 64-; Dag Hammarskjöld Award 68; numerous war decorations.

Office of the President, Manila, Philippines.

Marcus, Aage; Danish writer; b. 31 Dec. 1888.

Librarian, Royal Acad. of Fine Arts, Copenhagen 28-58; editor series of works on popular science 25-34 and of several other series e.g. *Danish Classics* 48 and a series of Sacred Books of the East.

Publs. *Mester Eckehart* 17, *Bibliography of Johannes V. Jensen* 33, *Bibliography of the History of Danish Art* 35, *Leonardo da Vinci* 40, *Den blaa Drage* (Chinese Art and Philosophy) 41, *Billedkunsten* (Art History of the World) 42, *Danish Portrait Drawings* 50, *Christian Mysticism* 53, *Rejse i Sverige* 56, *Hellas* 58, *Höduft og Havluft* (essays) 58, *Det hellige Land* (The Holy Land) 59, *Danske Levnedsböger* (Danish Memoirs) 65, *Religionernes Digtning* 67.

Hørsholm, Denmark.

Marcus, Stanley; American business executive; b. 20 April 1905; ed. Amherst Coll., Harvard Univ., and Harvard Business School.

Neiman-Marcus Affiliation 26-, Sec., Treas. and Dir. 28-, Merchandising Manager of all Apparel Divisions 29, Exec. Vice-Pres. 35-50, Pres. 50-; Dir. Republic National Bank, Dallas, New York Life Insurance Co.; Dir. Dallas Symphony Soc., Dallas Council on World Affairs, Dallas Theater Center, Foreign Policy Asscn.; Advisory Dir. Fort Worth Art Asscn.; Trustee Graduate Research Center, Inc., Southern Methodist Univ.; Trustee Cttee. for Economic Development; Board of Trustees, Eisenhower Exchange Fellowships; mem., Advisory Cttee. Dallas Asscn. for the UN, Texas Fine Arts Comm., Cttee. for the Acquisition of American Art for the White House, National Cttee. for Art in the Embassies Program, Advisory Cttee. for Graduate Education, Board for the Center of the Study of Democratic Insts.; mem. Board of Dirs. and Chair. of Resources Cttee., Southwest Center for Advanced Studies; mem. Board of Dirs. Brandeis Univ., Fine Arts Coll.; Chair. Texas Cttee. of Selection for Rhodes Scholarships; Dallas Chair., American Cttee. for Italian Food Relief; Fellow Pierpont-Morgan Library; Orders include Chevalier French Legion of Honour 49; "Star of Italian Solidarity" (Italy) 56; Commdr. of Economic Merit (France) 57; Officer of French Legion of Honour 58; Hon. Order of the British Empire 59; Chevalier of the Order of Leopold II (Belgium) 59; Gold Medal National Retail Merchants Asscn. 61; Commendatore al Merito della Repubblica Italiana 61; Royal Order of Dannebrog (Denmark) 65; The Great Cross of Austria 65; Hon. Dr. of Humanities (Southern Methodist Univ.) 65.

1 Nonsudi Road, Dallas 1, Texas, U.S.A.

Marczewski, Jan; French (b. Polish) university professor; b. 27 May 1908; ed. Lycée Henri Poincaré, Nancy, Univs. of Nancy, Strasbourg and Paris à la Sorbonne.

Early career in Polish Consular Service 26-40; War Service with Polish Army in France; Scientific Dir. Institut de Science Economique Appliquée, Paris, and mem. Higher Council for Nat. Revenue 46-50; Prof. Inst. Political Studies, Paris, Scientific Dir. East European Section of Nat. Foundation of Political Sciences, and Founder and Dir. Preparation Centre, Univ. of Caen 52-59, Hon. Prof. 59-; Prof. Faculty of Law, Univ. of Paris 59-; Vice-Pres. Nat. Council of Accountancy; Scientific Dir. *Europe de l'Est et Union Soviétique* 52-59; Chevalier Légion d'Honneur, Croix de Guerre, Krzyż Walecznych (Poland).

Publs. *Politique monétaire et financière de IIIe Reich* 41, *Planification et croissance économique des démocraties populaires* 56, *La conjoncture économique des Etats-Unis 1850-1960* 61, *L'Europe dans la conjoncture mondiale* 63, *Comptibilité Nationale* 65, *Introduction à l'Histoire Quantitative* 66.

44 *bis*, boulevard Suchet, Paris 16e, France.

Telephone: BAG 49-88.

Marden, George Ernest, M.C.; British business executive; b. 92; ed. Loughton School.

Army Service, First World War; Chairman Wheelock Marden and Co. Ltd. 31-59, Founder Pres. 59-; Chair. Landel Trust Ltd.; Dir. British Merchants Insurance

Co. Ltd., Dominion Insurance Co. Ltd., E. D. Cooke and Partners Ltd., Amore Holdings Ltd., John D. Hutchison (U.K.) Ltd., and other companies.
Fowlers Park, Hawkhurst, Kent, England.

Maree, Willem Adriaan, B.A.; South African politician; b. 7 Aug. 1920; ed. High School Brandfort (Orange Free State), and Univ. of Pretoria.
Nat. Party Organiser 43-45; farmer 45-48; M.P. Newcastle 48-; mem. Native Affairs Comm. 54; Minister of Bantu Educ. 58-66, of Indian Affairs Aug. 61-66, and of Forestry 64-66; Minister of Community Devt., Public Works, Social Welfare and Pensions 66-; Chair. Drakensberg Press, Durban.
P.O.B. 410, Pretoria, Republic of South Africa.

Marei, Sayed; United Arab Republic (Egyptian) politician; b. 26 Aug. 1913; ed. Faculty of Agriculture, Cairo Univ.
Worked on his father's farm after graduation; subsequently with import-export, pharmaceutical, seed, and fertilizer companies; mem. Egyptian House of Commons 45-49; Del. mem. Higher Cttee. for Agrarian Reform 52-; Chair. of Board, Agricultural Co-operative Credit Bank 55-56; initiated "Supervised Credit System"; Minister of State for Agrarian Reform 56-57; Minister of Agriculture and Agrarian Reform 57-58; Central Minister for Agriculture and Agrarian Reform in the U.A.R. 58-61; later Deputy Speaker U.A.R. Nat. Assembly; Man. Dir. Bank Misr, Cairo; Minister of Agriculture June 67-, and of Agrarian Reform 68-.
9 Sh. Shagaret El Dorr, Zamalek, Cairo, U.A.R.
Telephone: 800166.

Marek, Bruno; Austrian politician; b. 23 Jan. 1900.
Director of Vienna Int. Trade Fair 45-65; mem. Vienna District Council and Chair. of Finance Cttee. 45-; First Pres. Vienna Provincial Parl. 49-65; mem. Exec. Cttee. Austrian Socialist Party 65-; Provincial Head and Mayor of City of Vienna June 65-; mem. Bundesrat June 65-; Chair. Fed. of Austrian Cities; Austrian, German, Greek and French decorations.
Vienna VI, Capistrangasse 5/1, Austria.

Marella, H.E. Cardinal Paulo, S.T.D., J.C.D.; Italian ecclesiastic; b. 25 Jan. 1895; ed. Roman Seminary, Apollinaris, and Royal Univ., Rome.
Ordained 18; official in Sacred Congregation of Propaganda Fide 21; Counsellor, Apostolic Del. Washington 23; Titular Archbishop of Doclea 33-66, Hon. Bishop of Doclea 66-; Apostolic Del. to Japan 33, to Australia, New Zealand and Oceania 48-53, to France 53-59; Archpriest of St. Peter's Basilica, Prefect of Sacred Congregation 60-; cr. Cardinal 59.
The Vatican, Vatican City, Italy.

Maremont, Arnold Harold; American industrialist; b. 24 Aug. 1904; ed. Chicago Univ.
President, Maremont Corpn. 52-; Chair., Allied Paper Corpn., Phillips-Eckhardt Electronic Corpn.; Chair., Exec. Cttee., M. and B. American Machine Co. Inc.; Dir. Daco Lowell Shops, Gabriel Co.; Chair., Illinois Public Aid Comm.; Trustee, American Fed. of Arts, Lyric Opera of Chicago; mem. Advisory Council of Dem. Nat. Cttee.
168 North Michigan Avenue, Chicago 1, Illinois, U.S.A.

Maretskaya, Vera Petrovna; Soviet actress; b. 31 July 1906; ed. Vakhtangor Studio and Zavadsky Studio.
At the Rostov Drama Theatre 36-40, Mossoviet Theatre, Moscow 40-; People's Artist of U.S.S.R.; State Prizewinner 42, 46, 48, 51.
Principal roles: Yarovaya, Marina (*Lyubov Yarovaya, On the Banks of the Neva* by K. A. Trenev), Mashenka (*Mashenka* by A. N. Afinogenov), Mirandolina (*The Innkeeper's Wife* by Goldoni), Masha (*The Seagull* by Chekhov), Mukelene (*The Revolt of Women* by Sanderbu), Lady (*Orpheus Descending* by Tennessee Williams), Moskalyova (*The Uncle's Dream* by

Dostoevsky); Films: Sokolova (*The Member of the Government*), Varvara (*The Village Teacher*).
Office: Mossoviet Drama Theatre, 16 Bolshaya Sadovaya ulitsa, Moscow, U.S.S.R.

Marette, Jacques, L. ès D., DR. SC. ECON.; French politician; b. 21 Sept. 1922; ed. Ecole Libre des Sciences Politiques.
Journalist, *France-soir* and *Combat*; Technical Adviser to Ministry of Industry and Commerce 58-59; Dep. Sec.-Gen., Union pour la Nouvelle République 59; Municipal Councillor, Paris 59; Gen. Councillor, Seine 59; Senator 59-; Political Dir. *Courrier de la Nouvelle République*; fmr. mem. of Supreme Council of Electricity and Gas Authority; Minister of Posts and Telecommunications 62-67; Croix de Guerre (39-45); Médaille de la Résistance.
2 avenue du Colonel-Bonnet, Paris 16e, France.

Margai, Sir Albert Michael, Kt.; Sierra Leone lawyer and politician; b. 10 Oct. 1910; ed. Catholic Schools, Bonthe and Freetown, and Middle Temple, London.
Nurse and Druggist 32-44; called to the Bar 47; mem. Sierra Leone Protectorate Assembly 49, Sierra Leone Legislative Council 51; Minister of Education and Welfare, and Local Government 51-57, of Finance 62-64; Prime Minister of Sierra Leone 64-March 67; mem. Sierra Leone People's Party 51-58; founder-mem. People's Nat. Party 58-; Knight of the Grand Cross of St. Gregory the Great.
Freetown, Sierra Leone.

Margain, Hugo B.; Mexican lawyer and diplomatist; b. 13 Feb. 1913; ed. Univ. Nacional Autónoma de México.
Professor Nat. Univ. of Mexico 47-51; Dir.-Gen. Sales Tax Bureau 51, Income Tax Bureau 52-59; Asst. Sec. for Admin. Ministry of Industry and Commerce 59-61; Under-Sec. for Industry and Commerce 61-64; Pres. Nat. Comm. for Distribution of Profits 63-64; Chair. Nat. Comm. on Profit Sharing 63; Ambassador to the U.S.A. 64-.
Publs. *Importance of Fiscal Law in the Economic Development* 60, *An Adequate Public Administration* 61, World Tax Series *Taxation in Mexico* 57, and numerous financial and taxation articles.
Embassy of Mexico, 2829 16th Street, N.W., Washington, D.C. 20009, U.S.A.

Margaret, H.R.H. The Princess, Countess of Snowdon, C.I., G.C.V.O., G.C.ST.J.; b. 21 Aug. 1930.
Sister of H.M. Queen Elizabeth II; married Antony Armstrong-Jones (now 1st Earl of Snowdon) 60; son, Viscount Linley, b. 61; daughter, Lady Sarah Frances Elizabeth, b. 64.
Chancellor, Univ. of Keele; Pres. Royal Ballet; Grand Cross Order Crown of Belgium; Hon. D.Mus. (London), Hon. LL.D. (Keele).
10 Kensington Palace, London, England.

Margaritis, Lieut.-Gen. Constantine; Greek air force officer; b. 1914; ed. Royal Hellenic Air Force Acad.
Commissioned Second Lieut. 36 and rose through ranks to Lieut.-Gen. 57; Commanding Officer, 336 R.H.A.F. Fighter Squadron, Middle East 43-44, First R.H.A.F. Wing 46-49; Deputy Asst. Chief of Staff, Plans and Operations, Gen. Air Staff, R.H.A.F. 49-53; Air Attaché, Washington 53-55; Chief of Air Staff 55-; awards include Commdr. Royal Order of George 1st (Greece), Flying Cross, Air Force Cross, and various war medals; D.F.C. (U.K.); Legion of Merit (U.S.A.).
Platonos Street 6, New Psichico, Athens, Greece.

Margerie, Christian Jacquin de; French diplomatist; b. 14 May 1911; ed. Collège Stanislas, Univ. de Paris à la Sorbonne, and Ecole libre des sciences politiques.
Attaché Rome 37-39; Sec. San Franciso Conf. 45; First Sec. Madrid 46-48; Counsellor, Washington 48-51, Vatican 51-53; mem. French Govt. Del., Berlin 53-55; Minister, Bonn 55-57; Dir. Econ. Affairs Cen.

Admin., Paris 58-63; Ambassador to Argentina 63-; Officier Légion d'Honneur, Croix de Guerre, Commdr. Ordre du Mérite.
French Embassy, Cerrito 1373 Buenos Aires, Argentina; and 37 rue de Babylone, Paris 7e, France.

Margerie, Roland Jacquin de; French diplomatist; b. 6 May 1899; ed. Ecole libre des sciences politiques, and Sorbonne.
Sous-Lieut., Chasseurs Alpins 19; Sec. French Embassy Brussels 21, Berlin 23-33; Counsellor London 33-39; Capt. 152nd Infantry Regt. 39-40; Dir. of Secretariat of Minister of Foreign Affairs April-June 40; Consul-Gen. Shanghai 40-44; Chargé d'Affaires Peking 44-46; Dir. Africa and Near East Office, Ministry of Foreign Affairs 49-50; Deputy Dir. of Political Affairs (with rank of Minister) 50-55; Dir.-Gen. 55-56; Ambassador to the Holy See 56-59, to Spain 59-62, to German Federal Republic 62-65; Counsellor of State 65-; Commdr. de la Légion d'Honneur; C.V.O. (U.K.), etc.
14 rue Saint Guillaume, Paris 7e, France.

Margerit, Robert; French author; b. 25 Jan. 1910; ed. Collège de Brive, and Lycée de Limoges.
Prix Théophraste Renaudot 51, Grand Prix du Roman 63; Chevalier, Légion d'Honneur, Chevalier des Arts et des Lettres.
Publs. *L'Ile des perroquets, Mont-Dragon, Le Vin des vendangeurs, Par un été torride, Le Dieu nu, La Femme forte, Le Château des bois noirs, La Malaquaise, Les Amants, La Terre aux loups, L'Amour et le temps, Les Autels de la peur, Un Vent d'acier, Waterloo.*
46 rue Spontini, Paris 16e, and Thias, par Isle, Hte.-Vienne, France.

Margue, Nicolas Albert; Luxembourg politician; b. 2 Jan. 1888; ed. Munich, Paris, Strasbourg and Fribourg.
Prof. of History Luxembourg Athenæum 10, Diekirch 12-17, Luxembourg Athenæum 17-37; Municipal Councillor for City of Luxembourg 24-37; Min. of Public Instruction, Agriculture, Industry and Commerce 37-40; mem. Catholic Party; interned after German occupation 40; Minister of Nat. Educ., Agriculture, Arts and Science 45-48; mem. of Parl. 48-59; mem. Consultative Assembly of Council of Europe and Assembly of Western European Union 49-59; mem. Assembly European Coal and Steel Community 52-59; mem. Council of State 59-.
Publs. *Biographie de J. B. Nothomb, Gegenwartsgeschichte aus der römischen Kaiserzeit, Manuel d'histoire nationale du Luxembourg, Entwicklung des Luxemburger Nationalgefühls, Mouvements contrerévolutionnaires dans le Luxembourg 1831-32, Jean Beck 48, Die Warte 54, Histoire Sommaire de la Ville de Luxembourg 63.*
Rue Goethe 24, Luxembourg.
Telephone: Luxembourg 23227.

Margulies, Robert; German politician and administrator; b. 29 Sept. 1908; ed. High School.
Business Manager 33-36, Agent 37-39, Manager 45-52; mem. State Constitutional Assembly, Württemberg-Baden 46; mem. Württemberg-Baden Landtag 47; mem. Bundestag 49-, European Parl. 58-; Pres. Mannheimer Produktenbörse; mem. Presidium Gen. Asscn. of German and Wholesale Foreign Trade, Bonn; mem. Comm. of European Atomic Energy Community (EURATOM) 64-67; Bundesverdienstkreuz, First Class.
c/o European Atomic Energy Community, 51-53 rue Belliard, Brussels 4, Belgium.

Mariam, Tashoma Haile, B.C.L.; Ethiopian diplomatist; b. Dec. 1927; ed. Univ. Coll. of Addis Ababa and McGill Univ., Canada.
Codification Dept., Ministry of Justice, Addis Ababa 59-60; Dir.-Gen. of Legal Div., Private Cabinet of Emperor Haile Sellassie 60-64; Attorney-Gen. 64-65; Ambassador to U.S.A. 65-67; mem. UN Comm. of Enquiry into Congo 61.
c/o Ministry of Foreign Affairs, Addis Ababa, Ethiopia.

Maridakis, Georges; Greek lawyer; b. 1890; ed. Univ. of Athens.
Professor of Int. Private Law, Univ. of Athens; fmr. Minister of Justice; mem. Comm. for the drawing up of the Greek Civil Code; Counsel, Court of Cassation; mem. Permanent Court of Arbitration, The Hague; Greek Del. to 8th Private Int. Law Conf., The Hague 56; Judge European Court for Human Rights, Council of Europe; Assoc. of Inst. of Int. Law; Rector, Univ. of Athens 57-59; mem. Acad. of Athens; Dr. h.c. (Paris).
Publs. *Le droit civil dans les Novelles des Empéreurs Byzantins* 22, *Les tendances modernes de droit international privé* 27, *Le divorce selon le droit grec* 38, *Traité de droit international privé* (Vol. I 50, Vol. II 56), *Les principaux traits de la récente codification Hellénique touchant le droit international privé* 54, *Introduction au droit international privé* 62.
Thiras Street 60, Athens, Greece.

Mariere, Samuel Jereton; Nigerian Chief and politician; b. 1907; ed. Church Missionary Society School, Warri.
Olorogun of Evwreni and Onisogene of Aboh; Schoolmaster, Okpari 27-28; clerk, later Business Man. Mukoro Mowoe and Co. 29-38; Clerk-in-Charge, John Holt Station, Agbor 39-61; Foundation mem. Urhobo Progress Union 31, Sec.-Gen. 35-38; mem. Asaba Div. Council 53-55; mem. House of Reps. 54-64; mem. Nat. Exec. Cttee. Nat. Convention of Nigerian Citizens (N.C.N.C.) 54-60, Treas. N.C.N.C. Fed. Parl. Party 60-63; Deputy Administrator and Commr. for Chieftaincy Affairs, Midwest Interim Admin. 63-64; Gov. Midwestern Nigeria 64-66; Adviser to Mil. Gov. of Midwestern Region 66-.
Military Governor's Office, Benin City, Midwestern Nigeria, Nigeria.

Marijnen, V. G. M.; Netherlands politician; b. 21 Feb. 1917; ed. Nijmegen Univ.
Formerly in Ministry of Economic Affairs; mem. of Council for Rehabilitation 45-49; Sec. Horticulture Section, Foundation for Agriculture 49; Dep. Head of Foreign Trade Relations 51; Head of Dept. for Export Promotion of Ministry of Agriculture, Fisheries and Food 53; Minister of Agriculture and Fisheries 59-63; Prime Minister 63-65.
14 A. Prinsenlaan 14, Schiedam, Netherlands.

Marin, Gheorghe Gaston; Romanian politician; b. 18; ed. Institut Polytechnique, Grenoble, France.
Assistant, Institut Polytechnique, Grenoble, 40-44; French resistance 40-44; mem. Communist Party of Romania 45-48, Central Cttee. of Romanian Workers' Party 60-; Sec.-Gen. later Dep. Minister of Industry 47-49; Minister of Electric Power 47-49; First Vice-Pres., later Pres., State Planning Cttee. 54-65; Deputy Chair. Council of Ministers 62.
Council of Ministers, Bucharest, Romania.

Marin, Jean (*pseudonym* of Morvan, Yves); French journalist; b. 24 Feb. 1909; ed. Britanny and Paris.
Director Gen. Agence France Presse 54, elected Pres. Dir.-Gen. 57, re-elected 60; Pres. European Alliance of Information Agencies 61-; Chevalier Légion d'Honneur, Croix de Guerre, and other honours.
Agence France Presse, 13 Place de la Bourse, Paris 2e, France.

Marinatos, Spyridon, DR. PHIL.; Greek university professor; b. 01; ed. Univs. of Athens, Berlin and Halle.
Asst. to Antiquities Dept. Heracleion Museum, Crete 19, Conservator 25, Dir. of Museum and Antiquities 29; Dir. Antiquities Service, Ministry of Education 37; Prof. of Archæology, Univ. of Athens 39-, Head of Antiquities Dept. 54, Rector 58-59, Pro-Rector 60-62; Dir. of Antiquities and Historic Monuments of Greece 56, 67-; mem. Acad. of Athens, Austrian and German Archæological Insts.; foreign mem. Archæological

Inst. of America; corresp. mem. Society for Promotion of Hellenic Studies and Royal Anthropological Society, Acad. of Brussels; Hon. mem. Acad. of Vienna; Dr. h.c. Univ. of Palermo; Order of King George, Légion d'Honneur and other foreign awards.
Publs. include *Cretan Civilisation* 27, *Greece and Greek Civilisation as the Results of Economic Expansion* 46, *Thermopylae: a Guide* 51, *Kreta und das Mykenische Hellas* 59, (English edn. *Crete and Mycenae* 60).
47 Polyla Street, Athens 9, Greece.

Marinello, Juan; Cuban professor and politician; b. 2 Nov. 1898; ed. Havana and Madrid Univs.
Professor, Inst. of Modern Languages, Univ. of Havana; edited *Revista de Avance* 27-30; imprisoned for political activity; Del. to Constituent Ass. 40; Rep. to Nat. Chamber 42; mem. Nat. Council of Culture and Minister without Portfolio 43; Pres. Socialist Popular Party; Vice-Pres. Senate 44; mem. World Peace Council 49; mem. Bd. for the Lenin Peace Prize 62; Rector, Univ. of Havana 62-Nov. 63; Cuban Del. to UNESCO 63-; mem. Presidency World Peace Council 66.
Publs. *Poética, Ensayos* 37, *Literatura Hispanoamericana* 37, *Momento Español* 39, *Martí, Escritor Americano, Ocho Notas sobre Aníbal Ponce* 59, *Meditación Americana* 59, *Conversación con nuestros pintores abstractos* 60, *Guatemala Nuestra* 61, *Once Ensayos Martianos* 65, *Contemporáneos* 65, *Imagen de Silvestre Resultas* 66.
Loma, Flat 684 entre Lombillo y Avenida de Colón, Nuevo Vedado, Havana, Cuba.

Marinescu, Teodor; Romanian journalist and diplomatist; b. 22 Sept. 1922; ed. Ştefan Gheorghiu Higher Party School of Romanian Communist Party.
General Dir. of Agerpres (Romanian news agency) 58-60; Editor-in-Chief *Scînteia* (C.P. organ) 60-65; Chair. State Radio and Television Cttee. 65-66; Ambassador to U.S.S.R. 66-; Deputy to Grand Nat. Assembly, fmr. Head Foreign Policy Cttee.; mem. Central Cttee. Romanian C.P.
Romanian Embassy, Mosfilmovskaya ul. 40, Moscow, U.S.S.R.

Marinho, Ilmar Penna, D.IUR; Brazilian diplomatist; b. 13.
Diplomatic Service 34-; Sec., Rome, Quito, Brussels; Counsellor, Warsaw, Paris; Chargé d'Affaires, Greece 40-45; Rep. to Peace Conf. 46; Rep. to UN Gen. Ass. 48; Rep. to Inter-Governmental Cttee. for European Migration (ICEM), Geneva 58; Ministry of External Affairs, Rio de Janeiro (Head of Consular Dept., Admin. Dept., later Under-Sec. of Ministry); Perm. Rep. to the Org. of American States (OAS) 61.
Permanent Mission of Brazil to the OAS, Pan American Union, Washington 6, D.C., U.S.A.

Marini, Marino; Italian sculptor; b. 27 Feb. 1901; ed. Acad. of Fine Arts of Florence.
Prof. Scuola d'Arte de Villa Reale, Monza 29-40; Titular Prof. of Sculpture, Acad. of Fine Arts of Brera, Milan 40-; has exhibited works in many cities of Europe, America and Canada; Grand Prix Quadriennale Romana 35-; Prix de Sculpture, Paris 37; Grand Prix de Sculpture, Venice Biennale 52; Int. Grand Prix Accademia dei Lincei, Rome 54; mem. Accademia Fiorentina delle Arti, Accademia Albertina di Bologna, Académie Royale Flamingue of Brussels, Akademisches Kollegium of Munich, Royal Acad. of Fine Arts of Stockholm, Accad. Nazionale di San Luca, etc.
Accademia di Belle Arti, Palazzo di Brera, Via Brera 28, Milan, Italy.

Mariolopoulos, Elias, M.A., D.U.P., D. ès SC.; Greek meteorologist; b. 1900; ed. Univs. of Athens, Cambridge, London and Paris.
Chief, Meteorological Dept. Nat. Observatory, Athens 25-28; Prof. of Meteorology, Univ. of Thessaloniki 28-39; Prof. of Meteorology, Univ. of Athens 39-, Rector,

Univ. of Athens 59-61; mem. of the Academy of Athens; Dir. Nat. Observatory, Athens 42-; Pres. Nat. Cttee. of Geophysics and Geodesy; mem. Int. Climatological Comm.; several Greek and foreign decorations.
Publs. *Climate of Greece* (Greek), *Atlas Climatique de la Grèce* (French), *Distribution des Eléments météorologiques en Grèce, Climate of Athens, Dodecanese, Climate of Different Regions of Greece.*
National Observatory, Athens; 9 Viziinou Street, Athens 902, Greece.
Telephone: 880024.

Mariotti, Luigi; Italian politician; b. 12.
Secretary Florentine Socialist Provincial Fed., mem. Cen. Cttee. Italian Socialist Party 48-52; mem. Senate 53-, Sec. Socialist Parl. Group 58, mem. Standing Cttee. for Finance and the Treasury 63, Chair. Socialist Group in Senate 63; Minister of Health 64-.
Ministero della Salute, Rome, Italy.

Maritain, Jacques, PH.D., S.T.D.; French philosopher; b. 18 Nov. 1882; ed. Sorbonne.
Prof. of Philosophy, Inst. Catholique, Paris 16-39; Prof. Inst. of Mediæval Studies, Toronto; Visiting Prof. of Philosophy Columbia Univ. and Princeton Univ. 4c-44; Ambassador to Holy See 45-48; Prof. of Philosophy, Princeton Univ. 48-52; Emeritus 52-; Grand Prix National des Lettres 63.
Publs. include *Art and Scholasticism* 30, *An Introduction to Philosophy* 30, *Religion and Culture* 31, *The Angelic Doctor* 31, *The Degrees of Knowledge* 37, *True Humanism* 38, *France My Country* 41, *Redeeming The Time* 43, *Education at the Crossroads* 43, *Christianity and Democracy* 44, *Anti-Semitism* 44, *The Rights of Man and Natural Law* 44, *Existence and the Existent* 49, *Man and the State* 51, *The Range of Reason* 52, *Creative Intuition in Art and Poetry* 53, *Approaches to God* 54, *On the Philosophy of History* 57, *Reflections on America* 58, *The Sin of the Angel* 60, *The Responsibility of the Artist* 60, *On the Use of Philosophy* 61, *Moral Philosophy* 64, *The Mystery of Israel, The Peasant of the Garonne.*
c/o Brothers of Charles de Foucauld, Toulouse, France.

Marjolin, Robert Ernest; French economist; b. 27 July 1911; ed. Univ. of Paris and Yale Univ.
Asst. to Prof. Charles Rist, Scientific Inst. of Economic and Social Research 34-37; Chief Asst. 38-39; joined Gen. de Gaulle London 41; head of French Supply Mission to U.S.A. 44; Dir. of External Economic Relations, Min. of Nat. Economy 45; Deputy High Commr. of Modernisation and Equipment Plan 46; Sec.-Gen. O.E.E.C. 48-55; Prof. of Economics, Nancy 55-58; Vice-Pres. Comm., European Econ. Community 58-67; Prof. Faculty of Law and Econ. Sciences, Univ. of Paris 67-; Foreign Hon. mem., American Acad. of Arts and Sciences; Dr. h.c., Yale Univ., Harvard Univ. and Univ. of East Anglia; Officier de la Légion d'Honneur; American Medal of Freedom; King's Medal, etc.; Hon. C.B.E. (U.K.).
Publs. *L'Evolution du Syndicalisme aux Etats-Unis de Washington à Roosevelt* 36, *Prix, Monnaie, Production: Essai sur les Mouvements Economiques de Longue Durée* 45, *Europe and the United States in the World Economy* 53.
64 avenue de la Motte-Picquet, Paris 15e, France.
Telephone: Ségur 95-74.

Marjoribanks, Sir James Alexander Milne, K.C.M.G., M.A.; British diplomatist; b. 29 May 1911; ed. Edinburgh Acad., Edinburgh Univ., Strasbourg Univ., and Univ. degli Studi, Florence.
Foreign Office 34-; Early service in Peking, Hankow, Marseille, Jacksonville, Florida, New York, Bucharest, Canberra 34-52; Deputy Head Del. to High Authority of European Coal and Steel Community 52-55; Cabinet Office, London 55-57; Econ. Minister, Bonn 57-62;

Asst. Under-Sec., Foreign Office 62-65; Ambassador to the European Econ. Communities and Head of Del. 65-.
21 avenue Henri Pirenne, Brussels, Belgium; and 13 Regent Terrace, Edinburgh 7, Scotland.

Markel, Lester, LITT.D., L.H.D.; American journalist and newspaper editor; b. 9 Jan. 1894; ed. Columbia School of Journalism.
Reporter 14-15, Night City Ed. and Night Ed. 15-19, Asst. Man. Ed. 19-23 *New York Tribune*; Sunday Ed. *New York Times* 23-64, Assoc. Ed. 64-; Assoc. in journalism, Columbia Univ.; Ed. and contributor Public Opinion and Foreign Policy; mem. American Society of Newspaper Editors, Council on Foreign Relations; founder Int. Press Inst.; Hon. Litt.D., Hon. L.H.D.
Publ. *Background and Foreground.*
135 Central Park; and 229 W. 43rd Street, New York City, N.Y., U.S.A.
Telephone: 556-1741.

Markelius, Sven Gottfrid, Swedish architect; b. 25 Oct. 1889; ed. Stockholm, Germany, France, Italy and U.S.A.
Hon. corresp. mem. Royal Inst. of British Architects, American Inst. Architects, Town Planning Inst., London, Int. Inst. of Arts and Letters, World Acad. of Art and Science, Akad. Arkitektforening, Copenhagen, etc.; mem. Swedish Royal Acad. of Fine Arts 42; fmr. Town Planning Dir., Stockholm; mem. Advisory Cttee. for UN H.Q., Manhattan 47, UNESCO H.Q., Paris 52-58; Visiting Prof. Yale Univ. School of Architecture 49, Massachusetts Inst. of Technology 62, Univ. of California, Berkeley 62; mem. UNESCO H.Q. Art Cttee. 54-; Pres. Fed. of Swedish Architects Soc. 53-56; Howland Memorial Prize, Yale Univ. 49; Gold Medal, R.I.B.A. 62; Dr. Ing. h.c. 66.
Works include: Halsingborg Concert Hall, Stockholm, Univ. of Technology Student Corps Building, Collective House, Stockholm 35, Structure for Stockholm Building Asscn. 36, Swedish Pavilion, World's Fair, New York 39; interior of ECOSOC chamber of UN H.Q., N.Y. 52; Trade Union Centre, Linköping 52; Trade Union Centre, Stockholm 60; Bürgerhaus, Giessen, G.F.R. 66; Park Hotel and Swedish House, Stockholm 68; Housing and Town Planning work.
Home: Kevinge Strand 5, Danderyd 1, Sweden; Office: Floragatan 11, Stockholm, Sweden.
Telephone: 755-63-85; and 755-44-66.

Markevitch, Igor; Italian violinist and conductor; b. 27 July 1912; ed. Coll. de Vevey, Switzerland and Conservatoire de Paris.
Leader of Orchestra of Florence and Maggio Musicale 44-46; International Conductor since 46; Permanent Conductor, Stockholm Philharmonic Orchestra 52-55, Havana Philharmonic Orchestra 57-58, Montreal Symphony Orchestra 56-60, Lamoureux Orchestra, Paris 57-61; Perm. Conductor Spanish Radio-Television Orchestra 65-; Head of Orchestral Conducting Classes at Salzburg 47-54, Mexico Panamerican Courses 57-58, Moscow 63, Santiago de Compostela 66; mem. Royal Swedish Acad.; Chevalier Légion d'Honneur; Commdr. des Arts et Lettres.
Compositions: *Piano Concerto* 29, *Cantata on words by Cocteau* 29, *Rebus* 31, *Icare* 32, *Psalm* 33, *Paradise Lost* 35, also chamber music.
Publs. *Made in Italy* 46, *Point d'Orgue* 61.
L'Aiglerie, 1884 Villars-sur-Ollon, Switzerland.

Markezinis, Spyros, LL.D.; Greek lawyer and politician; b. 1909; ed. Univ. of Athens.
Legal Adviser to late King George II of the Hellenes 36; served in Greek Nat. Resistance 41-44; mem. Parl. for the Cyclades 46, for Athens 51-; founded New Party 47 (dissolved 51); Minister without Portfolio 49; Minister for Co-ordination and Economic Planning till

54; formed Progressive Party Feb. 55; Knight, Gold Cross George I, D.S.M., Knight Commdr. St. Saba; Grand Cross of following: Order of Phoenix (Greece), Légion d'Honneur, Al Merito della Repubblica Italiana, Merit (Germany).
Publs. *From War to Peace* 49, *The Supreme Ruler in Contemporary Democracies, The King, the Royal Family and their Private Lives, The King as International Representative.*
5 Mackenzie King Street, Athens, Greece.

Marklund, Bror Hjalmar; Swedish sculptor; b. 3 Dec. 1907; ed. Royal Acad. of Art, Stockholm, and in France and Italy.
Professor of Drawing, Royal Acad. of Art, Stockholm; exhibitions in Norway, Denmark, Yugoslavia, Italy and U.S.A.; A. Norrland Culture Prize 60, Eugen Prize 62, Sergel Sculpture Prize 65.
Major works: bronze doors of Museum of Nat. Antiquities, Stockholm 39-50; The Sibbarp Stone 47; *Figure in a Storm* (bronze for Trelleborg town) 64; main entrance to police headquarters, Stockholm.
Royal Academy of Art, Fredsgatan 12, Stockholm, Sweden.

Marko, Miloš, LL.D., C.SC.; Czechoslovak journalist and broadcasting official; b. 4 March 1922; ed. Comenius Univ., Bratislava.
Journalist on various Slovak dailies; Asst. Editor-in-Chief *Pravda* 48-52, Editor-in-Chief 53-58; Editor-in-Chief *Predvoj* 58-60; Correspondent of Czechoslovak News Agency in Moscow 60-64; Asst. Prof. of Journalism, Comenius Univ., Bratislava 62-; Regional Dir. Czechoslovak Radio, Bratislava 64-67; Gen. Dir. Czechoslovak Radio, Prague Feb. 67-; mem. Ideological Comm., Central Cttee. of C.P. of Slovakia 66-.
Czechoslovak Radio, Vinohradská 12, Prague 2, Czechoslovakia.

Markov, Dmitry Fedorovich; Soviet philologist; b. 1913; ed. Kharkov Univ.
School Teacher 36-38; Postgraduate 38-41; Army Service 41-44; Head of Chair, Pedagogical Inst. Sumy 44-56; mem. C.P.S.U. 48-; Senior Research Assoc. Head of Sector Inst. of Slav Studies, U.S.S.R. Acad. of Sciences 56-63; Corresp. mem. U.S.S.R. Acad. of Sciences 66-.
U.S.S.R. Academy of Sciences, 14 Lenin Prospekt, Moscow, U.S.S.R.

Markov, Moisey Alexandrovich; Soviet theoretical physicist; b. 1908; ed. Moscow, Univ.
Assoc., Physics Inst., U.S.S.R. Acad. of Sciences 34-; Dir. Inst. of Semi-Conductors, U.S.S.R. Acad. of Sciences until 62; Corresp. mem. U.S.S.R. Acad. of Sciences 53-66, mem. 66-.
U.S.S.R. Academy of Sciences, 14 Lenin Prospekt, Moscow, U.S.S.R.

Markova, Dame Alicia, D.B.E. (Lilian Alicia Marks); British prima ballerina; b. 1 Dec. 1910; ed. privately.
First appeared in *Dick Whittington* at the Kennington Theatre 20; studied under Astafieva and appeared with Legat Ballet Group 23; taken into Russian Ballet by Serge Diaghilev 24, studied under Enrico Cecchetti and toured with the company till Diaghilev's death in 29 (*Song of a Nightingale* created for her); first Prima Ballerina of Vic-Wells (now the Royal Ballet) 33-35; formed Markova-Dolin Ballet Company 35 and toured U.K. till 38; with Ballet Russe de Monte Carlo 38-41; and Ballet Theatre 41-44; toured North and Central America with Markova-Dolin group 44-45; many guest appearances 46-47; concerts with Dolin in United States, Far East and South Africa 47-49; formed Festival Ballet company with Dolin 50-52; guest artist with Teatro Colón in Buenos Aires 52, Sadler's Wells, Ballet Theatre, Marquis de Cuevas Ballet and Metropolitan Opera 53; with de Cuevas

Ballet in London 54; with Royal Danish Ballet 55; Scala Milan; Municipal Theatre Rio de Janeiro 56; Royal Ballet Covent Garden 57; Italian Opera Season, Drury Lane; Festival Ballet Tour 58, and Season 59; appearances with Royal Ballet and Festival Ballet 60; with the Metropolitan Opera Company 54-58; Dir. Metropolitan Opera Ballet of New York 63-; Vice-Pres. Royal Acad. of Dancing 58-; Hon. Dr. Music (Leicester Univ.) 66.
Publ. *Giselle and I* 60.
Metropolitan Opera, New York, U.S.A.; c/o Barclay's Bank, 451 Oxford Street, London, W.1, England.

Marks, Derek John; British journalist; b. 15 Jan. 1921; ed. Seaford Coll.
Royal Air Force 40-46; *Huddersfield Examiner* 46-48; *East African Standard* (Nairobi) 48-49; *Yorkshire Post* (London) 50-52; *Daily Express* 52, later Deputy Editor *Evening Standard*, Editor *Daily Express*, London, and Dir. Beaverbrook Newspapers July 65-.
Daily Express, 121-128 Fleet Street, London, E.C.4, England.
Telephone: 01-353-8000.

Marks, Leonard Harold, B.A., LL.B.; American lawyer and government official; b. 5 March 1916; ed. Univ. of Pittsburgh, and Univ. of Pittsburgh Law School.
Faculty Fellow, Univ. of Pittsburgh Law School 38-39, Asst. Prof. 39-42; Asst. Prof. Nat. Univ. Law School, Washington, D.C. 43-50; Asst. to Gen. Counsel, Fed. Communications Comm., Washington, D.C. 43-46; Partner, Cohn and Marks (law firm), Washington, D.C. 46-65; Dir. Communications Satellite Corpn. 63-65; Dir. U.S. Information Agency 65-; Pres. Broadcasters' Club of Washington, Nat. Home Library Foundation.
2833 McGill Terrace, N.W., Washington, D.C. 20008, U.S.A.
Telephone: 232-7214.

Marlin, Ervin R.; American government official; b. 09; ed. Trinity Coll., Dublin.
Personnel Officer, Farm Credit Admin., Washington, D.C. 35-36, Social Security Board 36-39; Asst. Dir. of Personnel, Federal Security Agency 39-42; Special Asst. to U.S. Minister, Dublin, to U.S. Ambassador, London 42-44; Administrative Analyst, Bureau of the Budget, Washington, D.C. 44-45; External Relations Officer and Director, Technical Assistance Bureau, Int. Civil Aviation Org., Montreal 45-62; Senior Dir., UN High Commissioner for Refugees, Geneva 62-65; Special Asst. to Asst. Sec. of State, Washington D.C. 65-.
3702 Leland Street, Chevy Chase, Md., U.S.A.

Maron, Karl; German politician and civil servant; b. 27 April 1903.
Worked for *Berliner Morgenpost*; emigrated to Soviet Union 34; Chief Editor *Freies Deutschland* 43-45; mem. Berlin City Assembly (Socialist Unity Party) 46; Chief Editor *Neues Deutschland* 49-50; fmr. Head of People's Police, D.D.R.; fmr. Minister of the Interior.
c/o Innenministerium, Berlin, Germany.

Marotta, Domenico; Italian chemist; b. 28 July 1886; ed. Univ. degli Studi, Palermo.
President Accad. Nazionale dei XL 62-; mem. Accad. Nazionale dei Lincei; Pres. Italian Chemical Soc.; Admin. *Gazzetta Chimica Italiana, Annali di Chimica, Rendiconti Accademia Nazionale dei XL*; Cavaliere Gran Croce Ordine al Merito della Repubblica, Commedatore Ordine Equestre de S. Agata, Officier Légion d'Honneur, Hon. C.B.E.
Publs. Numerous scientific works and translations of German scientific works into Italian; Editor of the works of *Stanislao Cannizzaro* 26, *Raffaele Piria, lavori scientifici e scritti vari* 32, *Emanuele Paterno—scritti e ricordi editi e inediti* 65; translation of Bacon's *La Nuova Atlantide* 37.
Via Giusue Borsi 3, Rome, Italy.

Marples, Rt. Hon. Ernest, P.C., M.P.; British politician; b. 9 Dec. 1907; ed. Stretford Grammar School.
London Scottish 39; 2nd-Lt. Royal Artillery 41, Capt. 41; M.P. 45-; Parl. Sec. Ministry of Housing and Local Govt. 51-54; Joint Parl. Sec. Ministry of Pensions and Nat. Insurance 54-55; Postmaster-Gen. 57-59; Minister of Transport 59-64; Conservative.
Publ. *The Road to Prosperity* 47.
House of Commons, Westminster, London, S.W.1, England.

Marquand, Rt. Hon. Hilary Adair, P.C., M.A., D.SC.; British economist; b. 24 Dec. 1901; ed. Cardiff High School, Univ. Coll., Cardiff, and Wisconsin and Chicago Univs., Brookings Graduate School.
Rockefeller Foundation Fellow in U.S.A. 25-26; Lecturer in Economics, Birmingham Univ. 26-30; Prof. of Industrial Relations, Univ. Coll., Cardiff 30-45; Dir. First and Second Industrial Surveys of South Wales 31 and 36; an Acting Principal, Board of Trade, London 40-41; Deputy Controller, Wales Region, Ministry of Labour 41-42; Labour Adviser, Ministry of Production 42-44; Labour M.P. 45-61; Sec. for Overseas Trade 45-47; Paymaster-Gen. 47-48; Minister of Pensions 48-51; Minister of Health Jan.-Oct. 51; mem. Consultative Assembly, Council of Europe and W.E.U. Assembly 57-59; Cttee. Man. Inter-Parl. Union 57, Commonwealth Parl. Asscn. 52-61; Deputy Chair. Nat. Board for Prices and Incomes 65; Dir. Int. Inst. for Labour Studies, Geneva 61-65; Deputy Chair. Nat. Board for Prices and Incomes 65-68.
Publs. *The Dynamics of Industrial Combination* 31, *An Industrial Survey of South Wales* (joint author) 32, *Industrial Relations in the U.S.A.* 34, *South Wales Needs a Plan* 35, *Second Industrial Survey of South Wales* (joint author) 37, *Organized Labour in Four Continents* (joint author) 39.
9 Grove Court, Drayton Gardens, London, S.W.10, England.

Marquez, Vernon O.; Canadian business executive; b. 15 Sept. 1908; ed. St. Mary's Coll., Trinidad.
Joined Northern Electric Co. Ltd. 29, Public Relations Man. 46-56, Marketing Man. 56-57, Gen. Man. Sales Div. 57-60, Vice-Pres. 60-63, Exec. Vice-Pres. 63-67, Dir. 63-, Pres. March 67-; mem. Canadian Export Advisory Council.
Northern Electric Co. Ltd., 1600 Dorchester Boulevard West, Montreal, Quebec; Home: 5 Lancaster Drive, Pointe Claire, Quebec, Canada.
Telephone: 931-5711 (Office); 695-3689 (Home).

Marquina Barredo, Ignacio; Mexican architect and archæologist; b. 13; ed. Colegio Soriano, National Preparatory School, and National Acad. of Fine Arts, National Univ. of Mexico.
Professor of Composition, Nat. Acad. of Fine Arts, Nat. Univ. of Mexico; Prof. of Prehispanic Architecture, Nat. School of Anthropology and History; Dir. of Prehistoric Monuments; Adviser to Nat. Indian Inst.; Dir. numerous explorations; Dir. Nat. Inst. of Anthropology and History 47-56; Sec.-Gen. Pan-American Inst. of Geography and History 56-65; Chair. Exec. Council for building of Nat. Museum of Anthropology 63-.
Publs. *Estudio Arquitectónico de los Monumentos de Teotihuacán* 22, *Arquitectura Cristiana en el Valle de Teotihuacán* 22, *Estudio Arquitectónico Comparativo de los Monumentos Arqueológicos de México* 28, *Tenayuca, La Orientación de las Pirámides de México* 31, *Tenayuca, Estudio Arqueológico de la Pirámide* 32, *Arquitectura Prehispánica* 51.
Cádiz Sur 24, Mixcoac-Insurgentes, Mexico 20, D.F., Mexico.

Marrian, Guy Frederic, D.SC., F.R.I.C., F.R.S., F.I.BIOL.; British biochemist; b. 3 March 1904; ed. Tollington School, and Univ. Coll., London.
Lecturer Univ. Coll. London 30-33; Associate Prof.

Univ. of Toronto 33-35; Prof. Univ. of Toronto 35-38; Prof. of Chemistry in Relation to Medicine, Univ. of Edinburgh 39-59; Dir. of Research, Imperial Cancer Research Fund 59-68.
Home: 43 Oakleigh Avenue, Whetstone, N.20, England.
Telephone: 01-445-4120 (Home).

Marrou, Henri Irénée, D. ès L.; French historian; b. 12 Nov. 1904; ed. Lycée de Marseille, Ecole Normale Supérieure, Paris, Ecole Française de Rome.
Prof. Inst. Français de Naples 32; Prof. Cairo Univ. 37; Univ. de Nancy 38; Univ. de Montpellier 40; Univ. de Lyon 41; Univ. de Paris 45-; mem. Exec. Cttee. and critic *Esprit* 34; mem. Acad. Charles Cros 47; Pres. Institut Scientifique Franco-Canadien 50; mem. Cttee. International Balzan Foundation 62; Corresp. Fellow British Acad. 65; mem. Acad. Inscriptions 67; Chevalier Légion d'Honneur.
Publs. (under pseudonym Henri Davenson) *Fondements d'une Culture Chrétienne* 34, *Traité de la Musique selon l'esprit de Saint Augustin* 42, *Le Livre des Chansons* 44, *Les Troubadours* 61; under own name *Saint Augustin et la fin de la Culture Antique* 38 (4th ed. 58), *Histoire de l'Education dans l'Antiquité* 48 (6th ed. 65), *A Diognète* 52 (2nd edn. 65), *De la Connaissance Historique* 54 (5th edn. 66), *Saint Augustin et l'Augustinisme* 56 (3rd edn. 60), *Clément d'Alexandrie, Le Pédagogue* 60-65, *Nouvelle Histoire de l'Eglise,* vol I. 63.
19 rue d'Antony, Chatenay-Malabry 92, France.

Marschak, Jacob; American economist; b. 23 July 1898; ed. Kiev Technological Inst. and Heidelberg Univ. Lecturer Heidelberg Univ. 30; Dir. Statistical Inst. and Reader in Statistics, Oxford Univ. 35; mem. All Souls Coll., Oxford; fmr. Prof. New School for Social Research N.Y.; Prof. Univ. of Chicago 43-55, Yale Univ. 55-60, Univ. of Calif. (Los Angeles) 60-; Pres. Econometric Soc. 46-47; Dir. American Statistical Asscn. 45-46; Fellow Inst. of Mathematical Statistics; Joint Editor *Behavioral Science* and *Management Science*; Fellow, Center for Advanced Behavioral Studies 55-56; Ford Research Prof. Carnegie Inst. of Technology, Pittsburgh 58-59; Hon. Fellow Royal Statistical Soc.; mem. American Acad. of Arts and Sciences, Int. Statistical Inst.; Distinguished Fellow, American Econs. Asscn.; Dr. h.c. rer. pol. (Univ. of Bonn).
968 Stonehill Lane, Los Angeles, Calif. 90049, U.S.A.
Telephone: 213-472-5394.

Marsh, Daniel L., B.A., M.A., S.T.B., PH.D., D.D., LITT.D., SC.D., L.H.D., LL.D., J.U.D., D.C.L.; American educationist; b. 12 April 1880; ed. Northwestern, Chicago, Boston, Pittsburgh, Geneva and Oxford Univs.
Methodist Pastor 08-13; Gen. Superintendent Methodist Church Union of Pittsburgh 13-26; Pres. Boston Univ. 26-51, Chancellor 51-, also Trustee; Fellow, American Acad. Arts and Sciences; Chair. American Council on Educ., Cttee. on Academic Costumes and Ceremonies; Trustee of American Automobile Asscn. Foundation for Traffic Safety; mem. and Pres. Trustees of Massachusetts State Library 40-62; Trustee, Massachusetts Bible Society, etc.; Republican Presidential Elector 52.
Publs. *The Challenge of Pittsburgh* 17, *The Faith of the People's Poet* 20, *The Youth of America* 23, *Higher Education Plus the Highest Education* 27, *The Art of Fine Living* 29, *The Patriotism of a Mature Mind* 35, *The Indispensible Element in Genuine Education* 36, *Co-ordination in Education* 37, *The Essence of Education* 38, *The American Canon* 39, *Invisible Weapons in the Minds and Hearts of Fighting Men* 43, *Men to Match the New Era* 46, *Can Education's Virtue Counteract War's Vice?* 47, *Proper Bostonian Self-Expression* 48, *The Charm of the Chapel* 50, *The True Church* 58, *The Function of Religion in Higher Education* 62, *A Life-Lesson* 65.
[*Died 20 May 1968*].

Marsh, Ernest Sterling; American railroad executive; b. 10 Jan. 1903; ed. High School, Clovis, N.M., and Harvard Business School.
Clerk Atchison, Topeka & Santa Fé Railways Co. 18, various positions 18-40, Chief Clerk to Pres., Chicago 42, Asst. to Pres. 44, Exec. Asst. to Pres. 45, Vice-Pres Finance 48, Dir. 56, Pres. 57, Pres. and Chief Exec. Officer 58, Pres., Chief Exec. Officer and Chair. Exec. Cttee. 59-; Pres. Santa Fe System 57-66, Chair. 66-; Dir. Harris Trust & Savings Bank, Montgomery Ward & Co., Asscn. of American Railroads; mem. various cttees.
Home: 233 East Walton Place, Chicago 11; Office: 80 East Jackson Boulevard, Chicago 4, Ill., U.S.A.

Marsh, Dame Ngaio, D.B.E.; New Zealand novelist and theatrical producer; b. 23 April 1899; ed. St. Margaret's Coll., New Zealand, and Canterbury Univ. Coll. School of Art, Christchurch, New Zealand.
Joined English theatrical company touring New Zealand; on stage for two years; Red Cross Transport Unit, Second World War; Producer, D. D. O'Connor Theatre Management, N.Z. 44; Hon. D.Litt. (Canterbury, N.Z.).
Publs. *A Man Lay Dead* 34, *Enter a Murderer* 35, *Nursing Home Murder* (with H. Jellett) 36, *Death in Ecstasy* 37, *Vintage Murder* 37, *Artists in Crime* 38, *Death in a White Tie* 38, *Overture to Death* 39, *Death at the Bar* 40, *Surfeit of Lampreys* 41, *Death and the Dancing Footman* 42, *Colour Scheme* 43, *Died in the Wool* 45, *Final Curtain* 47, *Swing Brother Swing* 48, *Opening Night* 51, *Spinsters in Jeopardy* 53, *Scales of Justice* 55, *Off With His Head* 57, *Singing in the Shrouds* 59, *False Scent* 60, *Hand in Glove* 62, *Dead Water* 64, *Black Beech and Honey Dew* (autobiography) 66, *Death at the Dolphin* 67.
c/o Hughes Massie Ltd., 18 Southampton Place, London, W.C.1, England.

Marsh, Rt. Hon. Richard William, P.C., M.P.; British politician; b. 14 March 1928; ed. Jennings School, Swindon, Woolwich Polytechnic and Ruskin Coll., Oxford.
Health Services Officer, Nat. Union of Public Employees 51-59; mem. Clerical and Admin. Whitley Council for Health Service 53-59; M.P. for Greenwich 59-; Parl. Sec. Ministry of Labour 64-65; Joint Parl. Sec. Ministry of Technology 65-66; Minister of Power 66-68, of Transport 68-; Labour.
House of Commons, London, S.W.1; and 17 Glenshiel Road, Eltham, London, S.E.9, England.

Marshall, David Saul, LL.B.; Singapore politician; b. 08; ed. Raffles Institution, Middle Temple and Univ. of London.
Worked in Singapore as sharebroker, salesman and sec. to a shipping co. 24-32; then studied law in England and began legal career in Singapore 37-; joined Singapore Volunteer Corps 38; imprisoned by Japanese 42-45; founder Sec. War Prisoners Asscn.; Pres. Jewish Welfare Board; fmr. mem. Labour Front; Chief Minister of Singapore 55-56; mem. Singapore Legislative Assembly 61-.
8/10 Bank of China Chambers, Singapore 1.

Marshall, Herbert, O.B.E.; Canadian statistician; b. 87; ed. Univ. of Toronto.
Served in First World War; Lecturer in Economics, Univ. of Toronto 20-22; Prices Statistician, Dominion Bureau of Statistics 22-26, Chief of Internal Trade Branch 26-42, Asst. Dominion Statistician 42-45, Dominion Statistician 45-56; Statistical Adviser, West Indies Fed. 58-59; Canadian rep. International Inst. of Statistics meeting New Delhi 51; Sec. British Commonwealth Statisticians' Conf. 35; Canadian rep. (and Chair. 47) of U.N. Statistical Comm.; Pres. American Statis-

tical Asscn. 54; Pres. Inter-American Statistical Inst. 55-62; Vice-Pres. Int. Statistical Inst. 60; Pres. Canadian Political Science Asscn. 52.
Box 506 R.R.I., Rothwell Heights, Ottawa, Canada.
Telephone: 749-2752.

Marshall, J. Howard, II, A.B., LL.B.; American business executive; b. 24 Jan. 1905; ed. George School, Haverford Coll., and Yale School of Law.
Instructor and Asst. Cruise Dir. Floating Univ. Inc. 26-27, Cruise Dir. 28-29; Asst. Dean and Asst. Prof. of Law, Yale School of Law 31-33; Special Asst. to Attorney-Gen. and Asst. Solicitor, U.S. Dept. of Interior, and mem. Petroleum Admin. Board 33-35; Counsel, Standard Oil Co. of Calif. 35-37; Assoc., Pillsbury, Madison and Sutro (Corporate Attorneys) 37-38, Partner 38-44; Dir., Pacific City Lines, Inc. 38-41; Vice-Pres. and Dir. Long Beach Oil Development Corpn. 39-42, 59-; Chief Counsel and Asst. Deputy Administrator, Petroleum Administration for War 41-44; mem. Military Petroleum Advisory Board 44-50, 54-59; Pres. Ashland Oil and Refining Co., Allied Ashland Tankers Inc.; Pres. and Dir. Union Texas Natural Gas Corpn. 61-62; Pres. Union Texas Petroleum Division of Allied Chemical Corpn. 62-, Dir. Allied Chemical Corpn. 62-, Exec. Vice-Pres. 65-; Dir. and Chair. Minnesota Pipe Line Co., Great Northern Oil Co.; Vice-Pres. and Dir. Wyoming Nebraska Pipe Line Co., Signal Oil and Gas Co. 52-59, Exec. Vice-Pres. 59-61; Pres. and Dir. Union Texas Natural Gas Corpn. 61-62; Consultant to Sec. of the Interior on Petroleum Defense Program 50-52; Sec. Treas. and Dir. Great Northern Oil Purchasing Co.; Dir. The Fund for the Repub., Frontier Refining Co., Long Beach Oil Devt. Ltd., Nat. Industries Inc., M.K.T. Railroad, Nat. Bank of Commerce (Houston); mem. American Petroleum Inst., Nat. Petroleum Council, Independent Petroleum Asscn., fmr. Consultant.
Union Texas Petroleum, 3000 Richmond Avenue, Houston 5, Texas, U.S.A.
Telephone: 713-529-3271.

Marshall, Rt. Hon. John Ross, P.C., B.A., LL.M.; New Zealand lawyer and politician; b. 5 March 1912; ed. Victoria Univ. Coll., Univ. of N.Z.
Admitted barrister and solicitor of Supreme Court of N.Z. 36; served with N.Z. Expeditionary Force in Pacific and Italy (Major, Infantry), Second World War 41-46; elected M.P. 46-; Lecturer in Law, Victoria Univ. Coll. 48-51; Minister Assisting the Prime Minister and Minister for State Advances Corpn., Public Trust Office and Census and Statistics 49-54; also Minister of Health 51-54, of Information and Publicity 51-57; Minister of Justice and Attorney-Gen. 54-57; New Zealand Rep. Colombo Plan Conf., New Delhi 53, Commonwealth Prime Ministers Conf. 62, GATT Conf., Geneva 61, 63, 67; Econ. Comm. for Asia and the Far East (ECAFE) Conf., Tokyo 62, Teheran 64, Chair. ECAFE Wellington 65, New Delhi 66, Canberra 68; Deputy Prime Minister 57; Deputy Leader of Opposition 58-60; Deputy Prime Minister and Minister of Industries and Commerce and Overseas Trade 60-; Minister of Customs 60-62; National Party.
Publ. *Law Relating to Watercourses*.
Parliament Buildings, Wellington, C.1, New Zealand.

Marshall, Thurgood; American lawyer and government official; b. 2 July 1908; ed. Lincoln Univ., Pennsylvania, and Howard Univ. Law School, Washington, D.C.
Director-Gen. Nat. Asscn. for Advancement of Colored People Legal Defense and Educ. Fund 40-62; Judge, Second Circuit Court of Appeals 62-65; Solicitor-Gen. of U.S.A. 65-67; Assoc. Justice, U.S. Supreme Court 67-; Springarn Medal 46; Living History Award.
U.S. Supreme Court, Washington, D.C., U.S.A.

Marterer, Emile; French industrialist; b. 12 March 1883.
Former Pres. Compagnie Générale de l'Electricité, now Prés. d'Honneur; Dir. (fmr. Vice-Pres. and Gen. Man.) Mines de Blanzy; Grand Croix Légion d'Honneur.
Le Bourget du Lac (Savoie), France.

Martin, Archer John Porter, C.B.E., M.A., PH.D., F.R.S.; British chemist; b. 1 March 1910; ed. Bedford School, and Peterhouse, Cambridge.
Research, Cambridge, Physical Chemical Lab., Nutritional Lab. 32-38; Wool Industries Research Asscn., Leeds 38-46; Boots' Pure Drug Co. Research Dept., Nottingham 46-48; mem. staff Medical Research Council 48-52; Head of Physical Chemistry Div., Nat. Inst. for Medical Research, Mill Hill, London, 48-56; Chemical Consultant 56-59; Dir. Abbotsbury Laboratories Ltd. 59-; Extraordinary Prof. Eindhoven Technological Univ., Holland 64; Berzelius Gold Medal of Swedish Medical Society 51; shared Nobel Prize in Chemistry 52; John Scott Award 58, John Price Wetherill Medal 59, Franklin Inst. Medal 59, Leverhulme Medal 63.
Abbotsbury, Barnet Lane, Elstree, Herts., England.

Martin, David Christie, C.B.E., B.SC., PH.D., F.R.I.C., F.R.S.E.; British administrator; b. 7 Oct. 1914; ed. Univ. of Edinburgh.
Asst. Sec. Royal Society of Arts 39-45, seconded to Ministry of Supply for wartime duties; Gen. Sec. The Chemical Society; Exec. Secretary The Royal Society 47-; Recorder Chemistry Section British Asscn. for the Advancement of Science 53-58; mem. Council of British Asscn. for the Advancement of Science 59-.
The Royal Society, 6 Carlton House Terrace, London, S.W.1., England.

Martin, Edmund Fible, B.S.; American steel executive; b. 1 Nov. 1902; ed. Stevens Inst. of Technology.
With Bethlehem Steel Corpn. mills, Bethlehem 22-, Supt. 28-39, Asst. Supt. Saucon Div. Bethlehem plant 39-46, Asst. Gen. Manager Lackawanna, N.Y., plant of Bethlehem Steel 46-50, Gen. Manager 50-58; Vice-Pres. Steel Div., Bethlehem Steel Corpn. 58-60; Dir. Bethlehem Steel Corpn. 58-, Pres. 60-63, Vice-Chair. 63-64, Chair. and Chief Exec. 64-; Trustee Nat. Industrial Conf. Board 66-, Stevens Inst. of Technology, Lehigh Univ., Automotive Safety Foundation, National Safety Council, St. Luke's Hospital Bethlehem, United States Council, Int. Chamber of Commerce Council for Latin America; Dir. American Iron and Steel Inst. (Chair. and Chief Exec. Officer 67-), Morgan Guaranty Trust Co. of New York, Bituminous Coal Operators' Asscn.; Dir. Int. Iron and Steel Inst., Brussels 67-; Hon. Dr. Eng. (Univ. of Buffalo) 61, Hon. LL.D. (Moravian Coll.) 64, Hon. LL.D. (Lehigh Univ.) 66; Knight Commdr., Royal Order of the North Star, Sweden; Grand Band of the Order of the Star of America.
c/o Bethlehem Steel Corporation, Bethlehem, Pa. 18016, U.S.A.

Martin, Edwin McCammon; American government official; b. 21 May 1908; ed. Northwestern Univ.
Economist, Central Statistical Board 35-38, Bureau of Labor Statistics 38-40; Exec., War Production Board 40-44; Asst. Chief, and Dep. Chief of Div., Office of Strategic Services 44-45; Chief, Japanese and Korean Economic Affairs, Dept. of State 45-47, Chief of Div. for Occupied Area Economic Affairs 47-48, Dep. Dir., Office of Int. Trade Policy 48-49, Dir., Office for European Regional Affairs 49-52; Special Asst. to Sec. of State for Mutual Security Affairs 52-53; Alternate Perm. Rep. to NATO 53-57; Minister for Economic Affairs, American Embassy, London 57-59; Asst. Sec. of State for Economic Affairs 60-62, Asst. Sec. of State for Inter-American Affairs, Dept. of State 62-63; Asst. Sec. of State for

Interamerican Affairs 62-64; Amb. to Argentina 64-68; Chair. Devt. Assistance Cttee. OECD, Paris 68-.
16 Villa Saïd, Paris 16e, France.
Telephone: KLE 3633.

Martin, Frank; Swiss composer; b. 15 Sept. 1890; studied music in Geneva.
Mozart Medal 65.
Works include: *4 Ballades* (for saxophone, flute, trombone, piano and orchestra), *Le Vin Herbe* (for 12 voices and 8 instruments, text of Joseph Bedier) 41, *In Terra Pax* 44, *Golgotha* 48 (oratorios), *Der Cornet* (for contralto and orchestra, text of R. M. Rilke) 43, *6 Monologe aus Jedermann* (for baritone and orchestra, text of Hugo v. Hofmannsthal) 43, *Petite symphonie concertante* 45, *Musique et choeurs pour Athalie* 46, *8 Preludes* for piano 48, *Concerto* for seven wind instruments 49, *Ballade* for violoncello and piano (or orchestra) 49, *Concerto* for violin and orchestra 51, *Concerto* for harpsichord and orchestra 52, *Der Sturm* (opera from Shakespeare's *The Tempest*) 55, *Etudes* (for string orchestra) 56, *Ouverture en hommage à Mozart* (for small orchestra) 56, *Ouverture en Rondeau* (full orchestra) 58, *Psaumes* (for mixed choir, children's choir, orchestra and organ) 58, *Mystère de la Nativité* (9 soloists, 2 mixed choirs and orchestra, text of Arnoul Gréban (1450) 59, *Drei Minnelieder* (for soprano and piano) 60, *Monsieur de Pourceaugnac* (comic opera, text of Molière) 62, *Passacaille* (for full orchestra) 63, *Les 4 Eléments* (symphonic studies for full orchestra) 63, *Le Cornette* 64.
Bollelaan 11, Naarden (N.H.), Netherlands.

Martin, Graham (Anderson), A.B.; American government official and diplomatist; b. 22 Sept. 1912; ed. Wake Forest Coll.
Washington newspaper corresp. 32-33; Aide to Dep. Admin. Nat. Recovery Admin. 33-36; Asst. to Chair., Social Security Board 36-37, Dist. Man. 37-41; U.S. Army service 42-46; Chief of Bureau, War Assets Admin. 46-47; U.S. Foreign Service 47-, Attaché, France 47-50, Counsellor 51-55, Asst. Chief of Mission 53-55; Dept. of State Adviser, Air War Coll. 55-57; Special Asst. to Under Sec. of State for Econ. Affairs 57-59; Special Asst., Under Sec. of State 59-60; Consul Gen. Geneva and Ambassador to UN Geneva 60-62; Dep. Asst. Admin. Agency for Int. Development 62-63; Amb. to Thailand 63-67; Rep. to U.S. Council to SEATO 63-; U.S. Perm. Rep. to ECAFE 63-.
c/o Department of State, Washington, D.C., U.S.A.

Martin, John Bartlow; American writer and diplomatist; b. 4 Aug. 1915; ed. DePauw Univ.
Reporter, *Indianapolis Times* 37-38; freelance writer, Chicago 38-62; U.S. Army 44-46; contributor to *Saturday Evening Post, Harper's Bazaar, Reader's Digest* and others; mem. election campaign staff of Adlai Stevenson 52, 56, John F. Kennedy 60, Lyndon B. Johnson 64; Amb. to Dominican Repub. March 62-65.
Publs. *Call it North Country: The Story of Upper Michigan* 44, *Indiana: An Interpretation* 47, *Butcher's Dozen* 51, *My Life in Crime* 52, *Adlai Stevenson* 52, *Why Did They Kill* 53, *Break Down the Walls* 54, *The Deep South Says Never* 57, *The Pane of Glass* 59, *Jimmy Hoffa's Hot* 59, *Overtaken by Events* 66.
185 Maple Avenue, Highland Park, Illinois, U.S.A.

Martin, John Edward; American business executive; b. 11 Dec. 1904; ed. Bryson Coll.
Sales Engineer, Link Belt Co., Chicago 27-33, Manager, Stoker Div. 33-41; U.S. Army Ordnance Dept. 42-43; Gen. Manager Link Belt Ordnance Co. Chicago 44-45; Vice-Pres. (Operations), Dir. American Type Founders Inc. 45-47; Pres. and Dir. Firestone Steel Products Co. 48-52; Exec. Vice-Pres. Dana Corpn., Toledo 52-53, Pres., Dir. 54-; Chair. of Board Hayes-Dana Ltd., Canada 62-64, Dir. 64-; Chair. Board Dana Corpn. 66-.
Dana Corporation, 4100 Bennett Road, Toledo, Ohio, U.S.A.

Martin, Sir John Miller, K.C.M.G., C.B., C.V.O.; British civil servant and diplomatist; b. 15 Oct. 1904; ed. The Edinburgh Acad., and Corpus Christi Coll., Oxford.
Assistant Principal, Dominions Office 27; seconded to Malayan Civil Service 31-34; Principal, Colonial Office 35; Sec., Palestine Royal Comm. 36-37; Private Sec. to Prime Minister, Rt. Hon. Winston Churchill 40-41, Principal Private Sec. 41-45; Asst. Under Sec. of State, Colonial Office 45-56, Deputy Under Sec. of State 56-65; High Commr. in Malta 65-67.
Diplomatic Service Administration Office, Great George Street, London, S.W.1, England.

Martin, H.E. Cardinal Joseph Marie Eugène; French ecclesiastic; b. 9 Aug. 1891; ed. Pontificia Univ. Gregoriana.
War Service 14-18; Ordained Priest 20; Chaplain to Catholic Students of Univ. de Bordeaux 24-38; Vicar-Gen. Bordeaux 38; Mil. Chaplain 39-40; Consecrated Bishop of Puy-en-Velay 40-48; Archbishop of Rouen 48-; Primate of Normandy; mem. Roman Secr. for Christian Unity 60, and Pres. French Secr. for Christian Unity 60-; created Cardinal 65; Croix de Guerre, Officier Légion d'Honneur.
Bishop's House, 2 rue des Bonnetiers, Rouen, Seine Maritime, France.

Martin, (Basil) Kingsley, M.A.; British journalist; b. 28 July 1897; ed. Mill Hill School, Magdalene Coll., Cambridge, and Princeton Univ.
Asst. Lecturer, London School of Economics 23-27; mem. editorial staff *Manchester Guardian* 27-30; Editor *New Statesman and Nation* 31-60, Dir. *New Statesman* 61-62, Editorial Consultant 62-.
Publs. *The Triumph of Lord Palmerston, A Study of Public Opinion before the Crimean War* 24, *The British Public and the General Strike* 27, *French Liberal Thought in the Eighteenth Century* 29 (revised edn. 55), *Low's Russian Sketch Book* (with David Low) 32, *The Magic of Monarchy* 37, *Propaganda's Harvest* 41, *Truth and the Public* 45, *The Press the Public Wants* 47, *Harold Laski: A Memoir* 53, *Critic's London Diary* 60, *The Crown and the Establishment* 62, *Father Figures* (autobiog.) 66, *Editor* (autobiog.) 68.
Hilltop, Rodmell, Lewes, Sussex, England.

Martin, Sir (John) Leslie, Kt., M.A., PH.D., F.R.I.B.A.; British architect; b. 17 Aug. 1908; ed. Manchester Univ. School of Architecture.
Asst. Lecturer, Manchester Univ. 30-34; Dir. Hull School of Architecture 34-39; Principal Asst. Architect, L.M.S. Railway 39-48; Deputy Architect, London County Council 48-53, Architect 53-56; Prof. of Architecture, Cambridge Univ. 56-; Fellow, Jesus Coll., Cambridge; Fellow, Royal Inst. of British Architects, Council mem. 52-58, Vice-Pres. 55-57; mem. Royal Fine Art Comm.; awards include Soane Medal 30 and London Bronze Architectural Medal 54; R.I.B.A. Distinction in Town Planning.
The King's Mill, Great Shelford, Cambridge, England.
Telephone: Shelford 2399.

Martin, Ludwig; German lawyer; b. 25 April 1909; ed. Munich.
Assessor, Munich High Court 37-39; Scientific Assistant, Reich Court, Leipzig 39; Military Service 39-45; Chair. Sonthofen Court 46-50; Civil Rights Dept., Fed. Ministry of Justice 50-; Fed. Attorney 52-53; Fed. Judge, Fed. High Court 53-63; Fed. Solicitor-Gen. 63.
Herrenstrasse 45A, Karlsruhe, German Federal Republic.

Martin, The Hon. Paul, P.C., Q.C., M.P., B.A., M.A., LL.M.; Canadian lawyer; b. 1903; ed. St. Alexandre Coll., St. Michael's Coll., Osgoode Hall Law School, Toronto, Univ. of Toronto, Harvard Law School, Trinity Coll., Cambridge, and Geneva School of International Studies.

Lecturer in Political Science, Univ. of Western Ontario 31-34; senior partner firm of Martin, Laird, Easton & Cowan 34-63; mem. of Parl. for Windsor-Walkerville (Windsor, Ont.) 35-; K.C. 37; Del. to L.N. Assembly 38; Parl. Asst. to Min. of Labour 43; Chair. Canadian Govt. Del. and Chair. Employment Comm. I.L.O. Conf. Philadelphia 44; Sec. of State of Canada 45-46; Minister of Nat. Health and Welfare 46-57, of External Affairs 63-68; Senior Minister without Portfolio April 68-; Del. to 1st, 4th, 7th, 10th, 18th, 19th and 20th Gen. Assemblies of the UN, to 1st Session of Econ. and Social Council (London) 46 and to 3rd and 5th Sessions (New York 46 and 47); Pres. North Atlantic Council 65-66; Del. Consultative Cttee., Colombo Plan, Wellington, N.Z. 56; Hon. LL.D. (Michigan, Dalhousie, Toronto, Ottawa, Laval, Assumption, Queen's, Montreal, Dartmouth, John Carroll, St. Thomas, Loyola, British Columbia, Waterloo); Hon. D.C.L. (Western Ontario, Bishop's); Hon. Dr. of Humanities (Wayne State); Christian Culture Award 56; Liberal.
2021 Ontario Avenue, Windsor, Ontario; and Parliament Buildings, Ottawa, Ontario, Canada.

Martin, Pierre, French agriculturalist; b. 19 May 1903; ed. Ecole and Lycée, Bordeaux.
President, Cave Coopérative (Wine-Cellars Organisation), Rauzon, Confédération Nat. de Caves Coopératives, Nat. Fed. of Agricultural Cooperatives, Gironde Chamber of Agriculture; mem. Gen. Council of Bank of France, representing Agriculture 59-; Vice-Pres., Wine-Growers of France; Econ. Councillor 47-59; Vice-Pres. Econ. Council 50-59; Vice-Pres. Econ. and Social Council, representing Agricultural Co-operation 59-.
1 avenue d'Iéna, Paris 16e, France.

Martin, Roger Léon René; French businessman; b. 8 April 1915; ed. Ecole Polytechnique and Ecole Nat. Supérieure des Mines.
Ingénieur des Mines, Nancy 41-42; Asst. to Steel Industry Dir., Dept. of Industry (French Govt.) 42-46; Lecturer Ecole Nat. des Mines 42-53; joined Compagnie de Pont-à-Mousson 48, Asst. Gen. Man. 53, Gen. Man. 59-64, Pres. and Gen. Manager 64-; Chair. Union Sidérurgique Lorraine (SIDELOR); Deputy Chair. De Wendel-Sidelor-Mosellane Jan. 68-; Dir. Soc. des Fonderies de Pont-à-Mousson, Soc. des Mines de Saizerais, Soc. Commerciale d'Affrètements et de Combustibles (SCAC), Soc. Nancéienne de Crédit, Charbonnages de Beeringen (Belgium), HADIR (Luxembourg), A.G. der Dillinger Hütten-Werke (German Fed. Republic); Chevalier Légion d'Honneur.
Office: Compagnie de Pont-à-Mousson, Place Camille Cavallier, Nancy; Home: 38 sur la Carrière, Nancy, and 86 rue d'Assas, Paris 6e, France.

Martin, Thomas, M.SC., F.INST.P.; British scientist; b. 26 July 1893; ed. Alleyn's School, and Univ. Coll., London.
War Service 14-19 and 39; engaged in metallurgical research 20-23; Sec. British Empire Exhibition Cttee. of Royal Society 23-25; Organising Sec. Optical Convention 26; Sec. Inst. of Physics 27-29 and Editor *Journal of Scientific Instruments* 28-29; Gen. Sec. Royal Inst. of Great Britain 29-50; Asst. and Deputy Dir. of Instrument Production, Min. of Supply 39-46; Principal Scientific Officer Home Office 51-64, Chair. Cinematograph Equipment Allocation Cttee. 41-46; mem. Anglo-American Mission to European Countries on Instrument Requirements 46; Chair. Film Sub-Comm. UNESCO Comm. on Technical Needs, Paris 47; Vice-Pres. British Society for the History of Science 54-57, 58-60, Pres. 62-64; Consultant, Navy Dept., Ministry of Defence 64-65.
Publs. *Faraday*; edited *Faraday's Diary*; *Faraday's Discovery of Electro-Magnetic Induction.*
8 Bramerton Street, London, S.W.3, England.
Telephone: 01-352-1116.

Martin, William McChesney, Jr., B.A.; American financier; b. 17 Dec. 1906; ed. Yale and Columbia Univs., Benton College of Law, St. Louis.
Fed. Reserve Bank of St. Louis 28-29; head statistical dept. A. G. Edwards and Sons, St. Louis 29-31, partner 31-38; mem. N.Y. Stock Exchange 31-38, Gov. 35-38, Chair. Comm. on Constitution 37-38, Sec. Conway Comm. to reorganise the Exchange 37-38; Chair. of Board and Pres. *pro tem.* May-June 38, Pres. 38-41; published and edited *Economic Forum* 32-34; drafted as private, U.S. Army 41; attained rank of Col. 45; Asst. to Exec., President's Soviet Protocol Cttee. and Munitions Assignments Board 42; Dir. Export-Import Bank of Washington 45, Chair. and Pres. 46; Asst. Sec. of the Treasury 49-51; Chair. Federal Reserve Board 51-; U.S. Exec. Dir. Int. Bank 49-52; Trustee Foreign Service Educational Foundation, Washington, Berry Schools, Rome, Georgia and The Johns Hopkins Univ.; Alumni Fellow, Yale Corpn., Nat. Geographic Soc.; LL.D. (Temple, Tulane, Washington, Trinity, Pennsylvania, Yale, Tufts, Columbia, Washington and Lee, Hamilton and Rutgers Univs., Amherst, Bowdoin and Marietta Colls.); Legion of Merit.
2861 Woodland Drive, N.W., Washington 8, D.C., U.S.A.

Martin-Artajo, Alberto; Spanish politician; b. 05; ed. Univs. of Madrid, Nijmegen, Louvain, Fribourg and Milan.
Pres. Catholic student del. to Paris 32, to Washington 39; chief editorial writer of *El Debate* and *Ya*; Foreign Minister 45-57; Gen. Sec. Council of State 57-; mem. Cortes, Royal Acad. of Politics; Pres. Board of Dirs. Editorial Católica.
Publs. *Doctrina Social-Católica, Como organizar el régimen corporativo en España, La misión social de la familia, según la doctrina pontificia, Hacia una Comunidad Hispánica de Naciones, Doctrina Política de los Papas, La Conciencia Social de los Españoles.*
Calle Mayor 79, Madrid, Spain.

Martin du Gard, Maurice; French writer; b. 7 Dec. 1896.
Essayist and critic; founder *Les Nouvelles Littéraires* 22; Municipal Councillor, Versailles; Officier, Légion d'Honneur, Chevalier Ordre de Léopold, Officier du Christ du Portugal.
Publs. *Impertinences* 24, *Feux tournants* 25, *H. Bremond* 27, *Vérités du Moment* 28, *Carte rouge* 30, *Courrier d'Afrique* 31, *Moralités libérales* 32, *Soirées de Paris* 32, *Terres Divines* 33, *Le Voyage de Madagascar* 34, *Un Français en Europe* 35, *Caractères et Confidences* 36, *Harmonies critiques* 36, *Pour l'Empire* 37, *La fenêtre ouverte* (play) 38, *Suite de Maximes et Caractères* 44, *La Chronique de Vichy* 47, *La carte impériale* 49, *Les Mémorables* (I) 57, (II) 60, *Climat Tempéré* 64, *Les Libéraux* 67.
34 rue des Missionnaires, 78 Versailles, France.
Telephone: 950-53-71.

Martineau, Hon. Paul, P.C., Q.C.; Canadian lawyer and politician; b. 10 April 1921.
Former Crown Attorney for District of Pontiac, Quebec; M.P. 58-65; Parl. Asst. to Prime Minister 59-61; Deputy Speaker of House of Commons 62-63; Minister of Mines and Technical Surveys 62-63; mem. Royal Comm. on Admin. of Justice 67; Progressive Conservative.
Office: 102 Main Street, Hull, Quebec; Home: Mountain Road, Lucerne, Quebec, Canada.
Telephone: 827-2065 (Home).

Martinelli, Mario; Italian politician; b. 12 May 1906; ed. commercial coll.
Commercial adviser; sometime Pres. Youth Fed., Diocese of Como; mem. P.P.I. (People's Party) 22-26; active resistance movement 43-45; Sec. Como Christian

Democrat Party 45-46; Deputy (for Como-Sondrio-Varese) to Constituent Assembly, later Chamber of Deputies 46-62; Senator 63-; mem. Nat. Council of the Christian Democratic Party 49-51, 58-60, 62-, of Cen. Cttee. 50-51, 65-; Under-Sec., Treasury 51, Ministry of Foreign Trade 53; Minister of Foreign Trade (Scelba Govt.) 54-55; Pres. Transport Section of European Assembly 58-, Finance and Treasury Cttee., Chamber of Deputies 58-60; Minister of Foreign Trade 60-62, Minister of Finance 63; Vice-Pres., Finance and Treasury Cttee., Senate 64-.
Via Dante 60, Como, Italy.

Martínez Durán, Carlos; Guatemalan university professor and pathologist; b. 96; ed. Univ. of San Carlos, Guatemala and Berlin Univ.
Professor, Univ. of San Carlos, Guatemala 32-64, Prof. Emer. 64-, Rector 45-50, 58-62; formerly Pres. Union of Latin American Univs.; Order of Merit, Italy.
Publs. *Synthesis of Colonial Medicine in Guatemala* 36, *Typhoid Epidemics in Guatemala* 40, *Spain in Central America* 41, *Medical Science in Guatemala*, etc.
Apartado 422, Guatemala City, Guatemala.

Martínez Manaotou, Dr. Emilio; Mexican medical officer and politician; b. 30 July 1919; ed. Faculty of Medicine, Nat. Autonomous Univ. of Mexico.
Postgraduate studies in New York and Massachusetts; Professional career in Matamoros, Dir. of Civil Hospital and Pres. of Medical Asscn.; Federal Deputy to 43rd Legislature; Party Del. to various orgs.; Senator 58-64, attended Inter-Parliamentary Assemblies in Guadalajara and Washington; now Sec. to the Presidency.
Secretaría de la Presidencia, Mexico City, Mexico.

Martínez Sotomayor, Carlos; Chilean lawyer, politician and diplomatist; b. 29; ed. Universidad de Chile, Santiago.
Member, Chilean Del. to UN Gen. Assembly 60; Minister for Foreign Affairs, Chile 61-63; Perm. Rep. of Chile to UN Nov. 63-65.
c/o Ministry of Foreign Affairs, Santiago, Chile.

Martini, Fritz, DR. PHIL. HABIL; German university professor; b. 5 Sept. 1909; ed. Univs. of Zürich, Graz, Heidelberg, Grenoble, Berlin.
Extraordinary Prof. of Literary Science and Aesthetics, Technical Univ., Stuttgart 43-49, Ordinary Prof. 49-; mem. Presidium Deutsche Akad. für Sprache und Dichtung, Darmstadt.
Publs. incl. *Heinrich von Kleist und die geschichtliche Welt* 39, *Deutsche Literaturgeschichte*, *Das Wagnis der Sprache, Das Zeitalter des Realismus* 60.
Grüneisenstrasse, 5 Stuttgart, German Federal Republic.

Martini, Herbert, D.IUR.; German banker; b. 4 July 1903.
Managing Dir. Kreditanstalt für Wiederaufbau, Frankfurt-am-Main; Dir. European Investment Bank, Brussels, Deutsche Lufthansa AG, Cologne, Hoesch AG, Dortmund, and many other companies; Grosses Bundesverdienstkreuz.
Kreditanstalt für Wiederaufbau, Lindenstr. 27, Frankfurt-am-Main, German Federal Republic.
Telephone: 720681.

Martino, Edouardo; Italian European Common Market official; b. 20 April 1910; ed. Università di Pisa.
Chairman Higher Inst. of Science of Public Opinion, Int. Univ. of Social Studies 52-56; mem. Chamber of Deputies 48-67; mem. European Parl. Assembly 57-59, Pres. Political Comm. 64-67; Under-Sec. of State in Prime Minister's Office 47-53; Under-Sec. of State for Defence 53-54, 58-60; Under-Sec. of State for Foreign Affairs 62-63; mem. Comm. of European Communities 67-.
Commission of European Communities, 23 avenue de la Joyeuse Entrée, Brussels 4, Belgium.

Martino, Enrico; Italian diplomatist; b. 29 Jan. 1907; ed. Univ. of Genoa.
Prefect of Genoa 45; Deputy to Constituent Assembly 46; Under-Sec. of State for War 46-47; Minister in Belgrade 47-53; Admin. of Somalia 53-55; Amb. to Montevideo 55-58, to Irish Republic 59-61, to Austria 61-67; Perm. Rep. to the Int. Atomic Energy Agency 61-67.
Publ. *Two Years in Somaliland.*
Italian Ministry of Foreign Affairs, Rome, Italy.

Martino, Joseph A.; American business executive; b. 1900; ed. Columbia Univ.
Started with Nat. Lead Co. 16, Dir. 44, Comptroller 45, Exec. Vice-Pres. 46, 47-64, Pres., Dir., and Chair. of Exec. Cttee. 64-65, Chair. Board of Dirs. 65-; Dir. Baker Castor Oil Co., Allegheny Ludlum Steel Corpn., Chase Manhattan Bank, American Broadcasting-Paramount Theatres, Inc., Chemetron Corpn., etc.; Commr., The Port of New York Authority.
111 Broadway, New York, N.Y. 10006, U.S.A.

Martinon, Jean; French conductor and composer; b. 10 Jan. 1910; ed. Conservatoires at Lyons and Paris.
Associate Conductor London Philharmonic Orchestra 49; Chief Conductor Lamoureux Orchestra 51-57; Artistic Dir. Philharmonic Orchestra of Israel 58-59; guest conductor in many countries; Dir.-Gen. of Music Düsseldorf 60-65; Artistic Dir. Chicago Symphony Orchestra 63-68; Artistic Dir. Orchestre Nat. de France (O.R.T.F.) 68-; Grand Prix de la Ville de Paris 43; Prix Béla Bartók 48; Officier Légion d'Honneur, Chevalier des Arts et des Lettres.
Works include *Hécube* (opera), 4 Symphonies and choral, orchestral and chamber music.
52 avenue de Breteuil, Paris 7e, France.
Telephone: BRE-0600.

Martins, Rudolf, LL.D.; Austrian diplomatist; b. 9 Feb. 1915; ed. Humanistisches Gymnasium (Vienna XIII), and Universität Wien.
With Federal Chamber of Commerce, Vienna 46-47; Austrian Trade Commr. for Switzerland and Liechtenstein and Sec. of Austrian Chamber of Commerce for Switzerland, Zürich 47-49; with Fed. Chamber of Commerce, Vienna 49-59; Counsellor, Adviser on Multilateral Trade and Commerce, Minister of Foreign Affairs 59-63; Counsellor, Head of Dept. for Multilateral Trade and Commerce Questions, Minister of Trade and Reconstruction 63-65; Amb. and Perm. Austrian Rep. to Office of UN and UN Specialized Agencies, Geneva, and Leader of Austrian Del. to European Free Trade Asscn. (EFTA) 65-; Goldenes Ehrenzeichen für Verdienste um Republik Österreich.
2 Avenue Calas, CH—1206 Geneva, Switzerland.

Martinson, Harry Edmund; Swedish writer; b. 6 May 1904; ed. Jamshog.
Went to sea for six years; books translated into English, French and German; awarded Froding Prize for Writers 47; mem. Swedish Acad. 49.
Gustavsberg, Gnesta, Sweden.

Martinuzzi, Napoleone; Italian sculptor; b. 31 May 1892.
Works include *War Memorial* (exhibited Venice Biennial Exhibition), *Vittoria*, in honour of D'Annunzio, *Vittoria* (Vidor War Memorial Church), *Grande lampadario a fontana* (Venice Biennial Exhibition), Design for the tomb of D'Annunzio's mother, Equestrian statue in Gov.'s Palace, Grosseto, Decorations for Post and Telegraph Buildings in Ferrara and Palermo; sculptures in Rome and Venice galleries; a group of Mermaids in bronze for the town of Ostia, a bust of Tintoretto for the church of the Madonna dell' Orto, Venice, a Monumental Gate for the Palace of the I.N.A., Rome; War Memorial 1940-45, Univ. of Ca' Foscari, Venice; marble statue *L'Eroismo* (Palazzo della Civiltà Italiana, Rome); bronze statue of Pope

Pius X, St. Mark's, Venice; bronze statue *Il Vetraio*, Murano, marble *Ospitalità*, Hotel Danieli, Venice, bronze bust of Count Volpi di Misurata, Palazzo Gambara, Venice; bronze bust of Claudio Monteverdi, Basilica dei Frari, Venice; architecture and sculpture of the Lepanto Chapel in the Basilica di S. Antonio, Padua, etc.; mem. Insigne Accademia di S. Luca, Rome, Coll. Accademico artistico di Venezia, Accademico Tiberino, Rome; Commissione Edilizia di Venezia; Prize for sculpture in glass, Venice Biennale 52.
Campo S. Ternita Castello 3059, Venice, Italy.

Martola, Lieut.-Gen. Armas Eino Iimari; Finnish army officer and United Nations official; b. 12 May 1896.
Attended Nat. War Coll., Paris 19-21; Officer in Finnish Army; mem. Defence Revision Cttee. 23-24; mem. Disarmament Comm., Geneva 26-34; Finnish Military Attaché, Paris 28-31; Div. Commdr., Karelian Isthmus 39-40; Army Commdr. 41-44; Deputy Min. for Foreign Affairs 44; later Gov. of Uusimaa Province until 46; later Man.-Dir. Paper Office, Finnish Paper Mills Asscn.; Personal Adviser to UN Sec.-Gen. on Military Matters Relating to UN Emergency Force 56-57; Commdr. UN Forces in Cyprus (UNFICYP) 66-; Pres. Finnish Red Cross.
Headquarters, UN Forces in Cyprus, Nicosia, Cyprus; Home: Marikatu 5, Helsinki 14, Finland.
Telephone: 639921 (Home).

Marty, Archbishop François, D.THEOL.; French ecclesiastic; b. 17 May 1904; ed. Petit Séminaire de Graves (Aveyron), Grand Séminaire de Rodez (Aveyron) and Inst. Catholique de Toulouse.
Ordained 30; Priest, Villefranche and Rodez 32-40, Curé, Boumazel, Rieupeyroux and Millau 40-51; Vicar-Gen., Rodez 51-52; Bishop of Saint-Flour 52; Titular Archbishop of Emese and Coadjutor of Mgr. Marmottin, Archbishop of Rheims 59-60; Archbishop of Rheims 60-68; Archbishop of Paris 68-; Chevalier Légion d'Honneur.
Archevêché, 26 rue Barbet de Jouy, 75-Paris 7e, France.
Telephone: 705-90-70.

Martyn, David Forbes, D.SC., F.R.S.; British physicist; b. 27 June 1906; ed. Royal Coll. of Science, Univ. of London.
Houldsworth Fellow, Univ. of Glasgow 27-29; Radio Research Board, Australia 30-; mission on behalf of Commonwealth Govt. to U.K. initiating radar development in Australia 39; Chief Radiophysics Laboratory, Sydney 39-41; Dir. Operational Research, Australian Fighting Services 42-44; Chief Scientific Officer, Radio Research Laboratories, Commonwealth Scientific and Industrial Research Organisation 47-58, Chief Officer-in-Charge Upper Atmosphere Section 58-; Lyle Medal, Australian Nat. Research Council 46; Sidey Medal, Royal Society, N.Z. 47; Walter Burfitt Medal, Royal Society, N.S.W. 51; Charles Chree Medal, Physical Society of London 55; Assoc. Ed. *Planetary and Space Science*; Chair. Australian Nat. Cttee. Space Research, Australian Acad. of Science; Chair. UN Scientific and Technical Cttee. on the Peaceful Uses of Outer Space; mem. Exec. Cttee. Int. Council Scientific Unions.
Coresearch, Camden, N.S.W., Australia.
Telephone: Camden 68-183.

Martynov, Boris Petrovich; Soviet trade corporation official; b. 04; ed. Bauman Higher Technical School.
Draughtsman, later Dir., Krasnaya Roza Plant 30-39; trade missions to Germany 39-40, Yugoslavia 40-41, German Dem. Repub. 49-55, Ministry of Foreign Trade 41-49; Chair. *Mashinoimport* (mining, electrical and industrial machinery, railway rolling-stock) 56-; mem. Communist Party 31-; Order of Lenin (twice), Order of Red Banner of Labour (twice), etc.
V/O Mashinoimport, Ministry of Foreign Trade, 32-34 Smolenskaya-Sennaya Square, Moscow, U.S.S.R.

Martynov, Nikolai Vasilievich; Soviet politician; b. 1910; ed. Moscow Energy Inst.
Member C.P.S.U. 32-; Engineer 34-41; Deputy Commissar for Munitions U.S.S.R. 41-46; Deputy Minister then First Deputy Minister of Agricultural Machine Building, U.S.S.R. 46-53; Dept. Head, Ministry of Automobile, Tractors, and Agricultural Machine Building 54-55, Deputy Minister 55-57; First Deputy Chair. Tashkent Nat. Econ. Council 57-59, Chair. 59-60; Chair. Uzbekistan Nat. Econ. Council 60-63; Sec. Central Cttee. of C.P. of Uzbekistan 63-65; First Deputy Chair. U.S.S.R. Council of Ministers State Cttee. for Material and Equipment Supplies 65-; Deputy to Supreme Soviet.
U.S.S.R. Council of Ministers State Committee for Material and Equipment Supplies, 4 Djakovsky Pereulok, Moscow, U.S.S.R.

Marusi, Augustine Raymond; American food processing executive; b. 30 Nov. 1913; ed. Rensselaer Polytechnic Inst.
Sales Engineer, Chemical Div. of Borden Co., N.Y.C. 39-42, S. Regional Man. 45-47, Dir., Gen. Man. Alba S.A., São Paulo, Brazil 47-52, Vice-Pres. (Chem. Div.) 52-54, Pres. Chem. Div. 54-64, Vice-Pres. Borden Co. 55-64, Exec. Vice-Pres. 64-67, Pres. and Chief Exec. 67- (name changed from The Borden Co. to Borden Inc. April 68); official of other orgs.
Borden Inc., 350 Madison Avenue, New York, N.Y. 10017, U.S.A.

Marvel, Carl Shipp, M.S., M.A., D.SC., PH.D.; American professor of organic chemistry; b. 11 Sept. 1894; ed. Illinois Wesleyan Univ., and Univ. of Illinois.
Instructor Univ. of Illinois 20, Assoc. 21-23, Asst. Prof. 23-27, Assoc. Prof. 27-30, Prof. of Organic Chemistry 30-53, Research Prof. 53-61, Emeritus 61-; Prof. of Chemistry, Arizona Univ. 61-; Pres. American Chemical Society 45; mem. of Board for the Co-ordination of Malarial Studies 44-46, Nat. Advisory Health Council U.S. Public Health Service 45-57, Nat. Acad. of Sciences 38-; American Philosophical Society 45-; American Academy of Arts and Sciences; mem. Materials Advisory Cttee. Nat. Research Council 54-64, Chair. 62-64; Chair. of the Comm. of Int. Union in dealing with *Encyclopaedia Compendia* 47-50; Assoc. Editor *Journal of the American Chemical Society* 43-52; mem. of Editorial Board *Journal of Organic Chemistry* 36-56; Editor Vols. V and XI *Organic Syntheses* 25 and 31; Advisory Board *Journal of Polymer Science*; awarded Nichols Medal N.Y. Section American Chemical Society 44; Willard Gibbs Medal, Chicago Section, American Chemical Society 50; Gold Medal American Inst. of Chemists 55; Priestley Medal, American Chemical Soc. 56, Int. Award, Soc. of Plastic Engineers 64 and numerous other awards.
Department of Chemistry, University of Arizona, Tucson, Arizona 85721; 2332 East 9th Street, Tucson, Arizona 85719, U.S.A.
Telephone: 884-1915.

Marvin, Cloyd Heck, M.A., PH.D., LL.D.; American university president; b. 22 Aug. 1889; ed. Stanford, Southern Calif., and Harvard Univs.
Instructor in Economics, Univ. of Southern Calif. 14-15; Asst. Prof., Summer 16; Thayer Fellow, Harvard Univ. 16-17; Asst. Prof. Commerce, Univ. of Calif. at Los Angeles 19-20, Assoc. Prof., Asst. Dir., and Dean 20-22; Prof. Business Admin., Columbia Univ., Summers 20-21; Prof. of Economics, also Pres., Univ. of Arizona 22-27; Pres. George Washington Univ. 27-59; Lecturer Int. Inst., Geneva 30; Pres. National Parks Asscn. 33-35; Chair. of U.S. del. to 7th Pan-American Scientific Congress 35; Chair. Advisory Cttee. to the Comm. on Educ. of the House of Reps. 44-45; Capt. Aviation Service U.S. Army 17-19; Lt.-Col., Specialist, Reserve

Corps 21-42; Asst. to Secretary of War 47-48; in charge of Research 47-48; Sec. Nat. Comm. on Accrediting 49-56; Civilian Aide to Sec. of the Army for the D.C. 56; Pres. Emer. George Washington Univ. 58-.
2540 Massachusetts Avenue, N.W., Washington, D.C. 20008, U.S.A.
Telephone: 202-NO-6248.

Marx, Groucho (Julius); American actor; b. 2 Oct. 1895.
Appeared with his brothers in music hall shows, musical plays and the films *Animal Crackers, Monkey Business, Horsefeathers, Duck Soup, A Night at the Opera, A Day at the Races, A Day at the Circus, The Marx Brothers Go West, The Big Store, A Night at Casablanca, The Story of Mankind,* etc.; appearances in his own T.V. programme *You Bet Your Life*; Nat. Acad. Television Arts and Sciences Award.
Publs. *Many Happy Returns* 42, *Groucho and Me* 59, *Groucho's Letters* 67, *Tune for Elizabeth* (play with Norman Krasna).
c/o United Artists, Hollywood, Calif., U.S.A.

Marx, William Thomas; American communications executive; b. 15 March 1915; ed. Coll. of City of New York, Pace Coll., and Columbia Univ.
Accountant, Celanese Corpn. of America 37-42, Personnel Manager 45-52, Asst. in Org. and Exec. Development to Vice-Pres. of Org. and Planning 52-55, Corporate Personnel Dir. 55-57; Dir. Personnel Relations, Raytheon Manufacturing Co. 57-59, Dir. Employee Relations and Organisation and Planning 59; Senior Vice-Pres. Int. Telephone and Telegraph Co. 59-63; First Vice-Pres. Great Lakes Carbon Corpn. 63-; Senior Vice-Pres., Dir. Int. Standard Electric Corpn.
Office: 18 East 48th Street, New York 17, N.Y., U.S.A.

Marzotto di Valdagno Castelvecchio, (Count) Gaetano; Italian business executive; b. 11 Oct. 1894; ed. Univ. of Pisa.
President Manifattura Lane Gaetano Marzotto e Figli, Compagnia Italiana Alberghi Turistichi S.A., Società Fondiaria Agricola Industriale, Industria dei Marmi Vicentini; Finances Marzotto Prize; Cavaliere del Lavoro, Cavaliere Gran Croce of the Italian Republic.
Publs. *Bolshevism or Freedom, The Agrarian Reform.*
Via Gaetano Marzotto, Valdagno, Vicenza, Italy.

Masani, Minoo, M.P.; Indian politician and business consultant; b. 20 Nov. 1905; ed. Elphinstone Coll., Bombay, and London School of Economics.
Barrister of Lincoln's Inn; one of the founders of Congress Socialist Party and Sec. till 39; Mayor of Bombay 43-44; mem. Constituent Assembly and Provisional Parl. of India 47-52; Ambassador of India in Brazil 48-49; mem. UN Sub-Comm. on Discrimination and Minorities 47-52; mem. Lok Sabha (Parl.) 63-; mem. Exec. Cttee., Int. Assn. for Cultural Freedom; Pres. Management Consultants Asscn. of India; Chair. Public Accounts Cttee.; Dep. Leader Swatantra Group in Lok Sabha.
Publs. *Our India, Socialism Reconsidered, Your Food, Picture of a Plan, Plea for the Mixed Economy, Our Growing Human Family, Communist Party of India—a Short History.*
Personnel and Productivity Services, 148 Mahatma Gandhi Road, Bombay 1, India.

Mascherini, Marcello; Italian artist; b. 06; ed. Trieste Industrial Inst.
Sculptor in stone, wood and bronze; designer of theatrical décors and costumes; has also executed lithographs and decorative works for the Milan Triennale and Italian liners, decorations of Padua and Trieste Univs.; first exhibited 25, since exhibited in Italy and abroad; Prize for Sculpture Venice Biennale 60.
Trieste, Italy.

Maschwitz, Eric, O.B.E.; British writer and producer; b. 10 June 1901; ed. Repton School and Gonville and Caius Coll., Cambridge.
Editor group Hutchinson's magazines 22-23; joined B.B.C. 26, Editor *Radio Times* 27-33; Variety Dir. 33-36; with Metro-Goldwyn-Mayer, Hollywood 37-38; War Service 39-45; Intelligence Corps Lieut.-Col. 45; Head of Light Entertainment, B.B.C. Television 58-61; Asst. and Adviser to Controller of TV Programmes, B.B.C. 61-63; Producer, Associated Rediffusion 63-.
Plays include *Gay Hussar, Good Night, Vienna, Balalaika, Magyar Melody, New Faces, Starlight Roof, Carissima, Belinda Fair, Zip Goes a Million, Love from Judy, Summer Song, Passion Flower*; screen plays include *Invitation to the Waltz, Good-bye, Mr. Chips*; songs include *These Foolish Things, A Nightingale Sang in Berkeley Square, A Pair of Silver Wings, Room 504, The World is Mine*; autobiog. *No Chip on my Shoulder* 57.
8 Queen Anne Street, London, W.1, England.

Masefield, Peter Gordon, M.A. (Eng.), C.ENG., F.R.Ae.S., M.INST.T.; British aeronautical administrator; b. 19 March 1914; ed. Westminster School, Chillon Coll., Switzerland, and Jesus Coll., Cambridge.
On Design Staff, Fairey Aviation Co. Ltd. 35-37; Asst. Technical Editor *The Aeroplane* 37-39, Technical Editor 39-43; war corresp. and air corresp. *The Sunday Times* 40-43; Personal Adviser on Civil Air Transport to Lord Privy Seal and Sec. of Civil Aviation Cttee. of War Cabinet 43-45; British Civil Air Attaché, British Embassy, Washington, D.C. 45-46; Dir.-Gen. of Long-Term Planning and Projects, Ministry of Civil Aviation 47-48; Chief Exec. and mem. of Board British European Airways 49-56; Man. Dir. Bristol Aircraft Ltd. 56-60, British Executive and General Aviation Ltd., Beagle Aircraft Ltd. 60-67 (Chair. 68-); Dir. Pressed Steel Fisher Ltd. 60-67; Pres. Inst. of Transport 55-56; mem. Aeronautical Research Council 56-60, Pres. Royal Aeronautical Soc. 59-60; Chair. Air Transport Section, London Chamber of Commerce 62-65; Chair. British Airports Authority 65-; Hon. Fellow Inst. Aeronautics and Astronautics (U.S.A.).
Rosehill, Doods Way, Reigate, Surrey, England.
Telephone: Reigate 42396.

'Maseribane, Chief Sekhonyana Nehemia; Basuto Chief; b. 4 May 1918; ed. Eagles Park Coll., Basutoland.
Prominent Trader in Quthing District; descendant of First Paramount Chief of Basutoland, Chief Moshoeshoe I, Chief of Mount Moorosi; mem. Econ. Planning Council of Basutoland; Pres. Basuto Courts 47, and Assessor to Basutoland High Court; mem. Econ. Mission to U.S.A. 62; Prime Minister of Basutoland May-July 65, Deputy Prime Minister and Minister of Internal and External Affairs, and Leader of the House July 65-Jan. 66; Deputy Prime Minister and Minister of Internal Security and Home Affairs Jan. 66-; Vice-Pres. Nat. Party.
Ministry of Internal Security, Maseru, Lesotho.

Mashayekh Faridani, Mohammed Hossein, M.A., P.H.D.; Iranian diplomatist and educationist; b. 14; ed. Pahlavi Coll., Darolfonoon Coll. and Teheran Univ.
Lecturer in Literature and Philosophy, Teheran 40-44; Technical Inspector, Teheran Secondary Schools 44-46; Dir. of Cultural Dept., Ministry of Education 46; Editor, Education and Instruction Magazine 46; Cultural Counsellor, Karachi 48-52, New Delhi 52-55; Cultural Adviser, Ministry of Foreign Affairs 55-56; Dir. of Cultural Relations, Ministry of Foreign Affairs 57, Dir. of Public Relations and Editor of Magazine 57, Dir. Asian Countries Dept. 58; Min. Counsellor, Baghdad 59-63, Amb. to Iraq 63-64, to Saudi Arabia 64-.
Imperial Iranian Embassy, Jeddah, Saudi Arabia.

Masherov, Pyotr Mironovich; Soviet politician; b. 13 Feb. 1918; ed. Vityebsk Pedagogical Institute.
Member C.P.S.U. 43-; Partisan Movement, Byelorussia,

Second World War; Komsomol work 44-54; Second Sec., Minsk Regional Cttee., C.P. Byelorussia 54-55; First Sec., Brest Regional Cttee., C.P. Byelorussia 55-59; Sec., Second Sec., Central Cttee. C.P. Byelorussia 59-65; First Sec., Central Cttee. C.P. Byelorussia 65-; mem. Central Cttee. C.P.S.U. 64-, mem. Presidium of Supreme Soviet 66-; Alt. mem. Politburo 66-; Deputy to the Supreme Soviet of the U.S.S.R.; Hero of the Soviet Union; Order of Lenin 68.
Central Committee of the Communist Party of Byelorussia, Minsk, Byelorussian S.S.R., U.S.S.R.

Mashin, Yury Dimitrievich; Soviet sports officer and social leader; b. 1932; ed. S. Ordjonikidze Aviation Inst., Moscow.
Engineer, Central Aircraft Motors Inst. 56-57; Sec. Young Communist League of Inst. 57-59; mem. C.P.S.U. 59-; Leading Communist Youth Work 59-62; Sec. Kalininsky District Cttee., Moscow 59-60; Sec. City Cttee. 60-62; Chair. Central Council, U.S.S.R. Union of Sports Socs. and Orgs. 62-; mem. Moscow City Cttee. of C.P.S.U. 61-63; mem. Central Cttee. Young Communist League 62-.
Central Council U.S.S.R. Union of Sports Societies and Organizations, 4 Skatertny pereulok, Moscow, U.S.S.R.

Mashour, Ahmed Mashour; United Arab Republic (Egyptian) engineer; b. April 1918; ed. Cairo Univ., Staff Officers' Coll., U.K., and Fort Belvoir, U.S.A.
With Min. of Transport 41; Army Engineer 42; Lecturer, Egyptian Acad. of War 48-52; Staff Officer, Egyptian Corps of Engineers; Dir. of Transit, Suez Canal Authority 56; mem. Board of Dirs. Timsah Shipbuilding Co., Ismailia; Chair. and Man. Dir. Suez Canal Authority 65-; various decorations.
Suez Canal Authority, Ismailia, United Arab Republic.

Masina, Giulietta; Italian actress; b. 22 Feb. 1921; ed. Univ. of Rome.
Began acting career in radio plays.
Films: *Senza Pietà, Luci del Varietà, Persiane Chiuse, Cameriera Bella Presenza Offresi . . ., Europa 51, Wanda la Peccatrice, Lo Sceicco Bianco, Sette Ore di Guai, Il Romanzo della mia Vita, Ai Margini della Metropoli, Donne Proibite, Via Padova 46, Cento Anni d'Amore, La Strada, Il Bidone, Buonanotte Avvocato!, Le Notti di Cabiria, Fortunella, Nella Città l'Inferno 59, Juliet of the Spirits 65.*
Via Archimede 141a, Rome, Italy.

Masiq, Hussain; Libyan politician.
Minister of Foreign Affairs Jan. 64-March 65; Prime Minister March 65-July 67.
Tripoli, Libya.

Masmoudi, Mohamed; Tunisian politician; b. 21; ed. Tunis and Univ. of Paris.
Member of Tunisian Nationalist Movement 30-; Minister of State in Govt. negotiating Tunisian independence 53-55; Ambassador to France 56-58, 65-; Minister of Information 58-61; assoc. with *Action*, later re-named *Afrique Action.*
Ambassade de Tunisie, 25-27 rue Barbet-de-Jouy, Paris 7e, France.

Mason, Basil John, D.SC., F.R.S.; British meteorologist; b. 18 Aug. 1923; ed. Fakenham Grammar School and Univ. Coll., Nottingham.
Commissioned, Radar Branch, R.A.F. 44-46; Shirley Research Fellow, Univ. of Nottingham 47; Asst. Lecturer in Meteorology, Imperial Coll., London 48-49, Lecturer 49; Warren Research Fellow, Royal Soc. 57; Visiting Prof. of Meteorology, Univ. of Calif. 59-60; Prof. of Cloud Physics, Imperial Coll. of Science and Technology, Univ. of London 61-65; Dir.-Gen. Meteorological Office 65-; Hugh Robert Mill Medal, Royal Meteorological Soc. 59; Charles Chree Medal and Prize, Physical Soc. 65.

Publs. *The Physics of Clouds* 57, *Clouds, Rain and Rainmaking* 62.
The Meteorological Office, London Road, Bracknell, Berks.; and 64 Christchurch Road, East Sheen, London, S.W.14, England.
Telephone: 876-2557 (Home); Bracknell 20243 (Office).

Mason, Birny, Jr., B.CHEM.; American chemical engineer and executive; b. 27 Feb. 1909; ed. Cornell Univ.
Joined Union Carbide Corpn. 32, Man. Industrial Relations staff 52-55, Sec. 55, Pres. Union Carbide Development Co. 56; Vice-Pres. Union Carbide Corpn. and mem. Appropriations Cttee. 57-58, Exec. Vice-Pres. 58-60, Dir. 58-, Pres. 60-, now Chair.; Dir. Metropolitan Life Insurance Co., New York, Manufacturers Hanover Trust Co., New York; Public Gov. New York Stock Exchange.
Union Carbide Corporation, 270 Park Avenue, New York, N.Y. 10017, U.S.A.

Mason, James Neville, M.A.; British actor; b. 15 May 1909; ed. Marlborough Coll., and Peterhouse, Cambridge.
Acted in plays and films in England 31-46; principally engaged as actor and film producer in U.S.A. 46-; notable films include *I Met a Murderer, The Man in Grey, The Seventh Veil, Odd Man Out, Rommel—Desert Fox, Five Fingers, Julius Caesar, A Star is Born, Bigger than Life, Journey to the Centre of the Earth, A Touch of Larceny, Lolita, Tiara Tahiti, The Fall of the Roman Empire, The Pumpkin Eater, Lord Jim, Les Pianos Mécaniques, Georgy Girl, The Deadly Affair, Duffy.*
Publ. (with Pamela Kellino) *The Cats in Our Lives* 49.
c/o Al Parker, 50 Mount Street, London, W.1, England.

Mason, Philip, C.I.E., O.B.E.; British writer and administrator; b. 19 March 1906; ed. Sedbergh, Oxford Univ.
Member Indian Civil Service 28-47; Under-Sec., War Dept. 33-36; Dep. Commr., Garhwal 36-39; Dep. Sec., Defence Co-ordination and War Depts. 39-42; Sec., Chiefs of Staff Cttee., India, and Head of Conf. Secretariat, S.E. Asia Command 42-44; represented War Dept., Central Assembly 46; Jt. Sec., War Dept. 44-47; Dir. of Studies in Race Relations, Chatham House, London 52-58, Dir. Inst. of Race Relations, London 58-; Chair. Nat. Cttee. for Commonwealth Immigrants 64-65, B.B.C. Advisory Council for Immigrants 65.
Publs. (as Philip Woodruff): *Call the Next Witness* 45, *The Wild Sweet Witch* 47, *Whatever Dies* 48, *The Sword of Northumbria* 48, *The Island of Chamba* 50, *Hernshaw Castle* 50, *Colonel of Dragoons* 51, *The Men Who Ruled India: Vol. I The Founders* 53, *Vol. II The Guardians* 54; (as Philip Mason): *An Essay on Racial Tension* 54, *Christianity and Race* 56, *The Birth of a Dilemma* 58, *Year of Decision* 60, *Common Sense about Race* 61, *Prospero's Magic* 63.
The Lyon House, Sherfield English, Romsey, Hants., England.
Telephone: West Wellow 273.

Mason, Roy, M.P.; British politician; b. 18 April 1924; ed. Carlton Junior School, Royston Senior School, and London School of Economics (T.U.C. Course).
Branch official, Nat. Union of Mineworkers 47-53; mem. Yorkshire Miners' Council 49-53; M.P. for Barnsley 53-; Minister of State (Shipping), Board of Trade 64-67; Minister of Defence (Equipment) 67-68; Postmaster-Gen. April-June 68; Minister of Power June 68-; Labour.
House of Commons, London, S.W.1, England.

Massamba-Debat, Alphonse; Congolese (Brazzaville) politician; b. 21; ed. Teacher Training Coll., Brazzaville.
Teacher, primary school, Fort Lamy, Chad 40; Sec.-Gen. Asscn. des Evolués du Tchad 45-47; Headmaster, primary schools, Mossendjo and Brazzaville; fmr. mem.

Congo Progressive Party; mem. Democratic Union for Defence of Interests of Africa (U.D.I.A.) 56-; Asst. to Minister of Educ.; mem. Legislative Assembly 59-61, Pres. 59-61; fmr. Minister of Planning and Equipment; Head of Provisional Govt. and Minister of Defence Aug.-Dec. 63; Pres. Dec. 63-.
Office of the President, Brazzaville, Republic of Congo.

Massand, Bhagwan Khemchand, B.SC., LL.B.; Indian diplomatist; b. 10 Sept. 1913; ed. D. J. Sind Coll. and S.C.S. Law Coll., Karachi, and Univ. of Bombay.
Legal Practice, later in business; High Comm. of India, Karachi 47-49, Colombo 50-53, Indian Embassy, Ankara 53-55, Washington 56-57, Cairo 57-59; Counsellor and Chargé d'Affaires, Budapest 59-62; High Commr. in Australia and New Zealand 62-65; Ambassador to Chile, concurrently to Peru and Colombia 65-.
Embassy of India, Santiago, Chile.

Massart, Edward Marie Lucien; Belgian biochemist and university professor; b. 08; ed. Royal Atheneum, Antwerp, and Univ. of Brussels.
Asst. and first Asst. Prof. of Biochemistry, State Univ. of Ghent, and Prof. 34-; Vice-Pres. Ghent Univ. 61-62; Dir. Biochemical Laboratory of the Faculty of Sciences and of the Veterinary Coll., Ghent Univ. 58; Pres. Nat. Council on Scientific Politics 59; mem. Royal Flemish Acad. of Medicine of Belgium; Francqui Award in Natural Sciences 57, etc.
Rysschenbergstraat 46B, Ghent, Belgium.

Massé, Pierre, DR. ès SC.; French engineer; b. 13 Jan. 1898; ed. Ecole Polytechnique.
Began career as electrical engineer 28; Dir. (Electrical Equipment) Electricité de France 46, Dep. Dir. Gen. 48; Commr. Gen. du Plan d'Equipement et de la Productivité 59-65; Pres. Electricité de France 65-; Assoc. Prof., Univ. of Paris; Grand Officier Légion d'Honneur; Commdr. Croix de Guerre (1914-18).
Publs. *Les Réserves et la Régulation de l'Avenir* 46, *Le Choix des Investissements* 59 (English edn. 62), *Le Plan au l'Anti-hasard* 65.
33 avenue du Maréchal-Lyautey, Paris 16e, France.

Massevitch, Alla Genrikhovna, D.SC.; Soviet astronomer; b. 9 Oct. 1918; ed. Moscow Industrial Pedagogical Inst.
Asst. Prof. of Astrophysics Moscow Univ. 46-48, Prof. 48-; Vice-Pres. Astronomical Council, Soviet Acad. of Sciences 52-; in charge of visual tracking of Soviet space vehicles; Chair. Working Group I, Cttee. for Space Research (COSPAR) 61-; Vice-Pres. Comm. 44 YAU (Extra-terrestrial Astronomy) 61-; Foreign mem. Royal Astronomical Soc. 62; mem. Int. Acad. of Astronautics 64.
Publs. 83 papers on internal structure of stars, stellar evolution and optical tracking of satellites, mainly in *Astronomical Journal of the U.S.S.R.*, *Publications of the Sternberg Astronomical Institute and Scientific Information of the Astronomical Council* 45-.
Vosstanya Ploshchad 1, kv. 403, Moscow; Astronomical Council of the U.S.S.R. Acad. of Sciences, Vavilova Street 20, Moscow V-312, U.S.S.R.

Massey, Sir Harrie Stewart Wilson, Kt., M.SC., PH.D., F.R.S.; British physicist; b. 08; ed. Melbourne Univ.
Aitchison Travelling Scholar Melbourne Univ. 29-31; research in atomic physics Cavendish Laboratory, Cambridge 29-33; Independent Lecturer in Mathematical Physics Queen's Univ., Belfast 33-38; Goldsmid Prof. of Mathematics Univ. Coll., Univ. of London 39-50; Quain Prof. of Physics, Univ. Coll. 50-; Vice-Dean of Faculty of Science Oct. 47-50; Fellow Royal Society 40; Chair. Atomic Scientists' Asscn. 46, Vice-Pres.47-53, Pres. 53-57; mem. Radio Research Board 46-50, 56-60; Scientific Adv. Panel, British Council 47-57; mem. Meteorological Research Cttee. 55-60; Vice-Pres. Royal Astronomical Soc. 50-52; Council Royal Soc. 50-52, 59-60; Council Physical Soc. (London) 49-54, Pres. 54-56;

Hughes Medallist, Royal Soc. 55, Royal Medallist 58; Pres. European Space Research Org. 59-64; Chair. British Nat. Cttee. for Space Research, Council for Scientific Policy 65-; mem. Governing Body, Rugby School 54-59, Chelsea Polytechnic 56-59, Nat. Inst. for Research in Nuclear Science 57-65, Advisory Council of Science Museum 59-61, Steering Group for Space Research 59-63, Bureau of Int. Cttee. on Space Research 59-, Central Advisory Council for Science and Technology 67-; Hon. D.Sc. (Belfast and Leicester) 64, Hon. LL.D. (Glasgow) 62.
Publs. *The Theory of Atomic Collisions* (with N. F. Mott) 33 (3rd edn. 65), *Negative Ions* 38 (2nd edn. 49), *Electronic and Ionic Impact Phenomena* (with E. H. S. Burhop) 51, *Atoms and Energy* 52, *The Upper Atmosphere* (with R. L. F. Boyd) 58, *Ancillary Mathematics* (with H. Kestleman) 58 (2nd edn. 64), *The New Age in Physics* 60 (2nd edn. 66), *Space Physics* 64.
Department of Physics, University College, London, W.C.1; Kalamunda, Pelhams Walk, Esher, Surrey, England.

Massigli, René; French diplomatist; b. 22 March 1888; ed. Ecole Normale Supérieure.
Mem. École Française de Rome 10-13; Lecturer, Lille Univ. 13-14; Sec. Conf. of Ambassadors 20; Asst. Sec. French Delegation to Washington 21; Sec. of Delegation to Genoa 21; Sec. Lausanne Conf. 22-23; mem. Council of State 24-28; Chief of L.N. Section, Ministry of Foreign Affairs 28-33; mem. French Delegation to Naval Conf., London 30; fmr. Deputy-Del. to Disarmament Conf. 32; Asst. Dir. of Political Section at Ministry of Foreign Affairs 33-37, Dir. 37-38; Ambassador to Turkey 38-40; arrived London, joined de Gaulle 43, Nat. Commr. for Foreign Affairs 43; Commr. for Foreign Affairs, French Cttee. for Nat. Liberation 43-44, mem. Advisory Council on Italy 43-44; Ambassador to Great Britain 44-55; Sec.-Gen. Ministry of Foreign Affairs 55-56; Pres. French Channel Tunnel Study Groups 57-; Grand Cross, Légion d'Honneur; Hon. G.C.V.O., C.H., K.B.E.
Publs. *Sur quelques maladies de l'Etat* 58, *La Turquie devant la Guerre* 64.
3 Avenue d'Orsay, Paris 7e, France.

Massine, Léonide; American choreographer; b. 9 Aug. 1896; ed. Imperial School of Opera, Moscow; studied under Domashoff, Enrico Cecchetti and Nicolas Legat.
Choreographer and principal dancer, Diaghileff Ballet, in Europe and America 14-20; first London appearance Drury Lane 14, New York Century Theatre 16; formed company to tour S. America 21; founded ballet school London 21-23; appeared Cochran's revues, London Pavilion, and produced ballets for Diaghileff 25-27; produced ballets Roxy Theatre, N.Y. 28-29, Opera House, Paris, and La Scala, Milan; produced dances and appeared in Cochran-Reinhardt production of *The Miracle*, Lyceum 32; producer and dancer, *Ballets Russes de Monte Carlo* 32-41, National Ballet Theatre, N.Y. 41-44; organised *Ballet Russe Highlights*, N.Y. 45-46; guest artiste and choreographer Sadler's Wells Ballet, Covent Garden 47-48; Royal Opera House, Copenhagen, La Scala, Milan, Opéra-Comique, Paris 49-52, Teatro dell'Opera, Rome, Rome Accad. di Danza 53-54.
Ballets include: *Good-Humoured Ladies, Parade, Boutique Fantasque, Tricorne, Beau Danube, Choreartium The School of Ballet, The Miracle, Gaité Parisienne, Seventh Symphony, Noble Vision, Sacré du Printemps, Rouge et Noir, Bacchanal, Labyrinth, Aleko, Les Saisons (Symphonie Allégorique), Clock Symphony, Donald of the Burthens, Laudes Evangelii* 52, *Resurrection and Life* 53, *Hymne à la Beauté* 56, etc.; Films (composed and danced his part): *Red Shoes* 48, *Tales of Hoffman* 51, *Carusello Napoletano* 53.
Publ. *My Life in Ballet* 68.
28 Forester Street, Long Beach, N.Y., U.S.A.

Massip, Roger; French journalist; b. 6 Nov. 1904; ed. Univ. of Paris.
Correspondent *Agence Havas* Bucharest 31-34, *Le Petit Parisien* Warsaw 34-37, Asst. Foreign Editor of latter 37-40; Editor underground newspaper *Libération* 42-44, Asst. Editor *Libération* 44-47; Foreign Editor *Le Figaro* 47-; Officier de la Légion d'Honneur, Officier de la Résistance.
Publs. *Que sera la nouvelle société des Nations?* 45, *Voici l'Europe* 58, *De Gaulle et l'Europe* 63.
c/o *Figaro*, 14 Rond Point des Champs Elysées, Paris 8e, France.

Massis, Henri, L. ès L. (*pseudonym* Agathon); French writer; b. 21 March 1886; ed. Lycée Condorcet, and the Sorbonne.
Editorial Sec. *L'Opinion* 11-14, Editor-in-Chief 20-36; Dir. *Revue Universelle* 36-44; served in both First and Second World Wars; mem. Académie Française 60-; Grand Prix de Littérature, Acad. Française 28; Grand Prix Osiris 66; Officier Légion d'Honneur, Croix de Guerre.
Publs. *Comment Emile Zola composait ses romans 06, La pensée de Maurice Barrès* 09, *L'Esprit de la Nouvelle Sorbonne* (with Alfred de Tarde) 11, *Les Jeunes Gens d'Aujourd'hui* (with Alfred de Tarde) 12, *Le Sacrifice* 15, *Jugements* 21-23, *Réflexions sur l'art du roman* 25, *Défense de l'Occident* 28, *Evocations* 31, *Debass* 32, *L'Honneur de Servir* 38, *La Guerre de Trente Ans* 40, *Les Idées Restent* 41, *Découverte de la Russie* 44, *D'André Gide à Marcel Proust* 48, *Charles Maurras et Notre Temps* 51, *L'Occident et son Destin* 56, *Visages des Idées* 58, *De l'Homme à Dieu* 59, *Salazar face à face* 61, *Barrès et nous* 62, *Au long d'une vie* 67.
14 rue du Pré-aux-Clercs, Paris 7e, France.
Telephone: BAB-00-08.

Masson, André; French artist; b. 4 Jan. 1896; ed. Académie Royale des Beaux-Arts, Brussels, and Ecole des Beaux-Arts, Paris.
Former mem. Cubist and Surrealist groups, Paris; illustrated many books; ballet sets *Les Présages* 33; U.S.A. 41-45; settled Aix-en-Provence 47; retrospective exhibitions Paris, London, New York, Hanover, Zurich, etc.; rep. at Dunn Int. Exhbn., London 63; Commissioned to paint ceiling of Théâtre de France 65; represented in principal galleries of contemporary art in Europe and America; Officier Légion d'Honneur, Commdr. des Arts et des Lettres; Grand Prix nat. des Arts 54, São Paulo Biennale Prize 63.
Publs. *Anatomie de mon Univers* 42, *La Pieuvre* 44, *La Rencontre de la Chimère* 44, *Mémorandum* 36-45, *Bestiaire* 45, *Métamorphoses* 46, etc.
26, rue de Sévigné, Paris 4e, France.

Masson, Marcel; French painter; b. 25 June 1911; ed. privately.
Began painting in cinemas and theatres, afterwards set up studio in Montmartre; one-man exhibitions in Paris, Canada, South America, Morocco, Tunisia, etc.; Médaille Ville de Paris, etc.
3 rue Alfred Stevens, Paris 9e, France.
Telephone: 828-42-39.

Masson, Paul Jean-Marie, L. en D.; French civil servant and diplomatist; b. 21 July 1920; ed. Ecole Nat. de la France d'Outre-Mer.
Career in West Africa 45-60; fmr. Sec. Gen. Guinea; High Commr. to Upper Volta 58-60; Dir.-Gen. Bureau pour le développement de la production agricole 61-; mem. French dels. to FAO Confs. 61, 63, 65; Préfet du Lot 67-; mem. Admin. Council Research Inst. for Tropical Agronomy, etc.; Chevalier Légion d'Honneur, Commdr. Etoile Noire du Bénin; Officier du Mérite Agricole.
Publ. *Bilateral assistance—help, trade or strategy*.
Préfecture du Lot, Cahors, France.
Telephone: 951.

Masson-Forestier, Henri; French newspaper director; b. 6 Sept. 1891; ed. Lycées in Rouen and Paris, Univ. of Paris, and Ecole Libre des Sciences Politiques.
Served 14-18 war; Dir. Société des Pétroles de Dabrowa (Poland) 19-22; on staff of *Figaro* 23-, now Admin.-Gen.; Vice-Pres. Syndicat de la Presse Parisienne; Pres. Union des Editeurs Exp. de Publications Françaises; Sec.-Gen. Féd. Nat. de la Presse Française; Pres. Caisse Générale Retraites de la Presse; Admin. Société Professionelle des Papiers de Presse; Conseiller du Commerce Extérieur; Croix de Guerre, Commdr. Légion d'Honneur.
24 rue Barbet-de-Jouy, Paris 7e, France.
Telephone: INV-37-13.

Massot, Henri Victor Joseph; French journalist; b. 25 April 1903; ed. Lycée Thiers, Marseille, and Faculté de Droit, Aix.
Journalist; with *Radical de Marseille* 22; *Petit Marseillais* 24; Editor *Marseille Matin* 32; Gen. Admin. *Paris Presse* 44, Dir.-Gen. 49-, *Paris Presse—France Soir* 65-; Pres. Syndicat de la Presse Parisienne and Conseil Superieur des Messageries; Vice-Pres. Féderation Nationale de la Presse Française; Pres. Conseil de Gérance des Nouvelles Messageries de la Presse Parisienne; Commdr. Légion d'Honneur.
2 bis rue Deleau, Neuilly-sur-Seine, France.
Telephone: 624-14-66.

Massoud-Ansari, Abdolhossein; Iranian diplomatist; b. 10; ed. school in Teheran, Imperial School of Law, Petrograd and Univ. of Moscow.
Directed various depts. in Ministry of Foreign Affairs; Consul-Gen. in India 37-40; Minister to the Scandinavian countries 40-44; Gov.-Gen. in Gilan 45-47, Ispahan 47-49, Fars 52; Ambassador to Afghanistan 49-51; Minister to Netherlands 52-54; Ambassador to Pakistan 55-56, to U.S.S.R. 56-61, to India 61-63, to Italy 65-; awards include Homayoun First Class (Iran) and many others.
Iranian Embassy, Via Bruxelles 57, Rome, Italy; also Khyaban Amol, Teheran, Iran.

Massu, Gen. Jacques; French army officer; b. 5 May 1908; ed. Ecole Spéciale Militaire de St. Cyr.
Joined Free French Forces Aug. 40; took part in all the campaigns of Gen. Leclerc's 2nd Armoured Div.; Cmmdr., Hanoi, Indochina 45-47, 1st Demibrigade, Colonial Parachute Commandos, 4th A.O.F. Brigade 51-54; Gen. of Brigade 55; as Commdr. 10th Parachute Div., directed airborne operation and landing at Port Said, Nov. 56; Mil. Commdr., Department of Algiers Jan. 57-60; headed the first Cttee. of Public Safety set up in Algiers and called upon Gen. de Gaulle to assume power May 58; Commdr. Algiers Army Corps Feb. 59-60, retd. 60; recalled to be Military Gov. of Metz Sept. 61-66; C.-in-C. French Troops in Germany 66-; Grand Officier de la Légion d'Honneur, Compagnon de la Libération, Croix de Guerre, D.S.O.
c/o Ministry of Defence, Paris, France.
Telephone: Baden 78-75-12.

Masterman, Sir John Cecil, Kt., O.B.E., M.A.; British educationist; b. 12 Jan. 1891; ed. Royal Naval Colls. Osborne and Dartmouth, Worcester Coll., Oxford and Freiburg Univ.
Midshipman 08; Student of Christ Church Oxford 19-46; Censor 20-26; Lieut. Intelligence Corps 40; Major (specially employed) 41-45; Provost of Worcester Coll. Oxford Jan. 47-61; Fellow of Eton Coll. 42-64; Governor Wellington Coll. 44-65; Vice-Chancellor, Univ. of Oxford 57-58; Hon. Student of Christ Church; Hon. Fellow St. Catharine's Coll., Cambridge, Hon. LL.D. Toronto Univ., Hon. D.C.L. King's Coll. Halifax, Nova Scotia, Hon. D.Litt. Heriot-Watt Univ.; Order of Crown of Yugoslavia (3rd Class).

Publs. *An Oxford Tragedy* 33, *Fate Cannot Harm Me* 35, *Marshal Ney* 37, *To Teach the Senators Wisdom* 52, *The Case of the Four Friends* 57, *Bits and Pieces* 61.
6 Beaumont Street, Oxford, England.
Telephone: 42133.

Mastroianni, Marcello; Italian film actor; b. 28 Sept. 1924; ed. Univ. of Rome.
Films include *Una Domenica d'Agosto* 49, *Le Notti Bianche* 57, *I Soliti Ignoti* 58, *Bell'Antonio* 60, *La Dolce Vita* 60, *La Notte* 61, *A Very Private Affair* 61, *Divorce —Italian Style* 61, 8½ 63, *Family Diary* 63, *Yesterday, Today and Tomorrow* 64, *Fantasmi a Roma* 64, *Casanova 70* 65, *Marriage—Italian Style* 65, *The Organizer* 65, *The 10th Victim* 65, *Ciao Rudy* 66, *Lo Straniero* 67, *Viaggiodi G. Mastorna* 67, *Shoot Louder, I Don't Understand, L'Etranger* 67.
c/o Titanus Films, Via Sommacampagna 28, Rome, Italy.

Masuda, Kaneshichi; Japanese politician; b. 4 Oct. 1898; ed. Law Dept., Kyoto Imperial Univ.
Administration Official, Ministry of Home Affairs 22, Chief of Archives and Documents Section 34; Gov. of Fukushima Prefecture 45; Gov.-Gen. of Hokkaido 46; Minister of Transportation 47; Chair. Political Affairs Research Cttee., Liberal Party 47; Minister of Labour 48; Minister of State, Dir. of Cabinet Secr. 49; Minister of Construction 50; Chief Sec. of Liberal Party 51; mem. House of Reps. 47-; Minister of State, Dir.-Gen. of Defense Agency 66-.
3-13-15, Minami-Aoyama, Minato-ku, Tokyo, Japan.
Telephone: 401-0956; 401-6509 (Tokyo).

Mata'afa Faumuina Mulin'u II, Hon. Fiame, C.B.E.; Samoan politician; b. 21; ed. Marist Brothers' School, Mulivai, and Malua Theological Coll., W. Samoa.
Elected to Legislative Assembly, W. Samoa 57; Minister of Agric. 57-59; Prime Minister and Minister of Police and Prisons, Immigration, External Affairs, District Affairs and Minister in Charge of Public Services 59-; Pres. Samoan Planters' Union 56-; Dir. W. Samoa Trust Estates Corpn.
Office of the Prime Minister, Apia, Western Samoa.

Matano, Kensuke, M.A., B.A.; Japanese business executive; b. 8 Jan. 1894; ed. Chuo, Columbia and Berlin Univs.
President, Iino Kaiun Kaisha, Ltd. 47-, Iino Sangyo Kaisha, Ltd. 47-; Adviser, Japan Air Lines 57-; Chair. Iino Air Service Co. Ltd. 62-; mem. Nippon Ship Owners' Asscn., Fed. of Econ. Orgs., Japan Fed. of Employers' Asscns., Japan ECAFE Asscn., Int. Chamber of Commerce; Medal of Honour with Blue Ribbon 59, with Dark Ribbon 60.
2-22, Uchisaiwai-cho, Chiyoda-ku, Tokyo, Japan.

Matanzima, Chief Kaiser; South African (Transkei) lawyer and politician; b. 15; ed. Lovedale Missionary Institution and Fort Hare Univ. Coll.
Chief, Amahale Clan of Tembus, St. Marks' District 40; mem. United Transkeian Gen. Council 42-56; Perm. Head Emigrant Tembuland Regional Authority and mem. Exec. Cttee. Transkeian Territorial Authority 56-58; Regional Chief of Emigrant Tembuland 58-61; Presiding Chief Transkeian Territorial Authority 61-63; Chief Minister of Transkei 63-.
Office of the Chief Minister, Umtata, Transkei, South Africa.

Matern, Hermann; German politician; b. 17 June 1892; ed. elementary school, Magdeburg.
Member Volkskammer 49-, Vice-Pres. 50-54, First Dep. Chair. 54-; mem. Political Bureau of Central Cttee. of Socialist Unity Party (S.E.D.).
Volkskammer, Berlin, Germany.

Mates, Leo; Yugoslav diplomatist; b. 11; ed. Univ. of Zagreb.
Chief Editor Tanjug Agency of Yugoslavia 45; entered

Foreign Service 45; Counsellor for Information, Yugoslav Embassy, London, and later Dir. U.N. Dept. Ministry of Foreign Affairs 47-48, Asst. Minister of Foreign Affairs 48-; Del. to U.N. Gen. Assembly 46-48 and 51-55, Permanent Rep. 53; Ambassador to U.S.A. 54-58; Sec.-Gen. to Pres. 58-61; Asst. to Sec. of State for Foreign Affairs 61-62; Dir. Inst. for Int. Politics and Economics, Belgrade 62-.
Institute for International Politics, Makedonska 25, Belgrade, Yugoslavia.

Mathé, Georges; French doctor; b. 9 July 1922; ed. Lycée Banville, Moulins, and Univ. de Paris à la Sorbonne.
Head of Clinic, Medical Faculty, Paris Univ. 52-53, Prof. 56-; Head, Service of Haematology, Inst. Gustave-Roussy 61-; Dir. Cancer Research Centre, Asscn. Claude-Bernard 61; Dir Cancer and Immunisation Inst., Hôpital Paul-Brousse 65-; Technical Counsellor, Ministry of Health 64-66; mem. Central Cttee. Union pour la Nouvelle République—Union Démocratique du Travail (UNR-UDT) 66-; Médaille d'or des Hôpitaux, Chevalier Légion d'Honneur.
Publs. *Physiologie Normale et Pathologique du Métabolisme de l'Eau* 52, *La Greffe* 62, *Aspects Histologiques et Cytologiques des Leucémies et Hématosarcomes* 63, *L'Aplasie Myéloïde et Lymphoïde de l'Irradiation Totale* 65.
Institut de Cancérologie et d'Immunogénétique, 14 avénue Paul-Vaillant-Couturier, Villejuif; and 11 *bis* rue Valentin-Haüy, Paris 15e, France.

Mather, Kenneth, C.B.E., D.SC., F.R.S.; British geneticist and university Vice-Chancellor; b. 22 June 1911; ed. Nantwich and Acton Grammar Schools and Univs. of Manchester and London.
Lecturer in Galton Laboratory, Univ. Coll. London 34-37; Rockefeller Research Fellow, California Inst. of Technology and Harvard Univ. 37-38; Head of Genetics Dept., John Innes Horticultural Inst. 38-48; Prof. of Genetics Univ. of Birmingham 48-65; Vice-Chancellor Univ. of Southampton Aug. 65-; mem. Agricultural Research Council 49-54, 55-60, Science Research Council 65-, Govt. Advisory Cttee. on Irradiation of Food 67-, Academic Advisory Cttee. Bath Univ. of Technology 67-; Darwin Medal, Royal Soc. 64.
Publs. *Measurement in Linkage in Heredity* 38, *Statistical Analysis in Biology* 43, *Biometrical Genetics* 49, *The Elements of Genetics* (with C. D. Darlington) 49, *Genes, Plants and People* (with C. D. Darlington) 50, *Human Diversity* 64, *Elements of Biometry* 67.
The University, Southampton, England.

Mather, Kirtley F., B.SC., PH.D.; American geologist; b. 13 Feb. 1888; ed. Denison and Chicago Univs.
Instructor Univ. of Arkansas 12-14; Fellow in Geology Univ. of Chicago 14-15; Associate Prof. of Geology Queen's Univ. Kingston, Canada 15-17 and Prof. of Palæontology 17-18; Prof. of Geology Denison Univ. 18-24; Associate Prof. of Physiography Harvard Univ. 24-27, Prof. of Geology 27-54 and Dir. Summer School of Arts and Sciences 34-43, Prof. Emeritus 54-; Geologist U.S. Geological Survey 17-45; Fellow Royal Geographical Soc.; Pres. American Asscn. Scientific Workers 42-46; Chair. editorial Cttee. Scientific Book Club 29-46; Pres. National Council Y.M.C.A. 46-48; Pres. American Asscn. for Advancement of Science 51, Foundation for Integrative Education 49-, Educational Research Corpn. 48-53; Pres. American Acad. of Arts and Sciences 57-61; Pres. Oliver Wendell Homes Asscn. 63-; Hon. Sc.D., Litt.D., L.H.D., LL.D.; Washburn Medal, Boston Museum of Science 64, Cullum Medal, American Geographical Soc. 65.
Publs. *Old Mother Earth* 28, *Science in Search of God* 28, *Sons of the Earth* 30, *Adult Education: A Dynamic for Democracy* (with Dorothy Hewitt) 37, *A Source Book of*

Geology (with S. P. Mason) 39, *Enough and to Spare* 44, *Crusade for Life* 49, *The World in Which we Live* 61, *The Earth Beneath Us* 64; Editor *Source Book in Geology 1900-1950* 67.
Geological Museum, Oxford Street, Cambridge, Mass. 02138; 3 Concord Avenue, Cambridge, Mass. 02138 (Residence), U.S.A.
Telephone: 864-4590.

Mathers, Fred Desbrisay, B.A.; Canadian businessman; b. 11 Jan. 1896; ed. Univ. of Edinburgh and McGill Univ.
Chair. Board of Dirs. Delnor Frozen Foods Ltd. 35-, Royal City Foods Ltd. 39-; Admin., Processed Fruits and Vegetables, Wartime Prices and Trade Board, Ottawa 42-45; Commr., Int. Pacific Salmon Fisheries Comm. 56-60; Pres. Canadian Manufacturers' Asscn. 61-62, Dir. British Columbia Hydro and Power Authority 62-; mem. Advisory Cttee. Guaranty Trust 57-.
P.O. Box 159, New Westminster, B.C., Canada.
Telephone: 604-522-0744.

Matheson, James Adam Louis, M.B.E., M.SC., PH.D., M.I.C.E., M.I.STRUCT.E., M.I.E.AUST.; British University Vice-Chancellor; b. 11 Feb. 1912; ed. Bootham School, York and Manchester Univ.
Lecturer, Birmingham Univ. 38-46; Prof. Civil Eng., Univ. of Melbourne 46-50; Beyer Prof. of Eng., Manchester Univ. 50-59; Vice-Chancellor, Monash Univ., Victoria, Australia 59-; mem. Mission on Technical Educ. to the W. Indies 57, Ramsay Cttee. on Devt. of Tertiary Educ. in Victoria 61-63, Commonwealth Scientific and Industrial Research Org. Advisory Council 62-, Royal Comm. into Failure of Kings Bridge 62-63; Trustee Inst. of Applied Science of Victoria 64-; mem. Council Inst. of Engineers, Australia 65, Council Inst. of Civil Engineers 66-68, Interim Council Univ. of Papua and New Guinea 65-; Chair. Papua and New Guinea Inst. of Higher Technical Educ. 66-, Australian Vice-Chancellors Cttee. 66-, Asscn. of Commonwealth Universities 67-68.
Publs. Papers on technical and educational subjects.
Monash University, Clayton, Victoria, Australia.
Telephone: 544-0611.

Mathews, Elbert George, A.B.; American diplomatist; b. 24 Nov. 1910; ed. Kidder Acad. and Jr. Coll. and Univ. of California.
Research Asst., Institute of Child Welfare, Univ. of Calif. 30-33; Accountant Golden State Co. Ltd. 33-35; joined Foreign Service, served Vancouver, Sydney, Managua, Washington, Kabul, Calcutta, Washington, Istanbul, Oslo 35-55; mem. Policy Planning Staff, State Dept. 55-59, Dep. Asst. Sec. Policy Planning 57-59; Ambassador to Liberia 59-62; Dir., Office of Eastern and Southern African Affairs, Dept. of State 62-64; Ambassador to Nigeria 64-.
American Embassy, Lagos, Nigeria.

Mathiassen, Therkel, M.A., PH.D.; Danish archaeologist; b. 5 Sept. 1892; ed. Copenhagen Univ.
Mem. Dr. Knud Rasmussen's 5th Thule expedition to Arctic America 21-24; leader archæological expeditions to Greenland 29, 30, 31-32, 33, 34 and 55; Curator Prehistoric Dept. of Nat. Museum 33, Head of Dept. 41, Chief Curator 46-62; Sec. of Society of Northern Antiquaries 45- 62; Fellow American Geographical Society; hon. mem. Prehistoric Society, London; mem. Royal Danish Acad. of Sciences and Letters and Archäologisches Institut des Deutschen Reiches.
Publs. *Archæology of the Central Eskimos* 27, *Material Culture of the Igulik Eskimos* 28, *Inugsuk, a medieval Eskimo settlement in North Greenland* 30, *Prehistory of the Angmagssalik Eskimos* 33, *Eskimo Archæology of Julianehaab District* 36, *Gudenaa Kulturen* 37,

Stenalderbopladser i Aamosen 43, *Danske Oldsager I* 48, *Studier over Vestjyllands Oldtidsbebyggelse* 48, *Vestsjaellands Oldtidsbebyggelse* 59; Editor, *Trap: Denmark* (5th edition).
[*Died* 14 *March* 1967]

Mathrani, Kewalram Pribhdas; Indian civil servant; b. 21 Aug. 1911; ed. Univ. of Edinburgh, Univ. Coll., London and School of Oriental Studies, London.
Indian Civil Service 36-; Sec. Finance Dept., Govt. of Saurashtra and Govt. of Bombay; Joint Sec. Ministry of Rehabilitation, Govt. of India 52-56; Sec. Ministry of Rehabilitation 64-65; Sec. Political and Services Dept., Bombay State 56-57; Sec. Industries and Co-operation Dept., Govt. of Bombay 58; Joint Sec. to Central Cabinet and Dir. Org. and Methods Div., Govt. of India 58-59; Sec. Ministry of Irrigation and Power, Govt. of India 65-; Chair. Industrial Finance Corpn. of India 61-64, Chair. Nat. Industrial Devt. Corpn. Ltd. 61-64; mem. Governing Body Indian Investment Centre.
11 Teen Murti Lane, New Delhi, India.

Mátrai, László, PH.D.; Hungarian librarian and writer; b. 17 Jan. 1909; ed. Budapest Univ.
Assistant 33, Librarian 35, Director-in-Chief of University Library, Budapest 45-; mem. I.I.P. (Inst. Int. Philosophy) 37-, Docent, Budapest Univ. 40-; Corresp. mem. Hungarian Acad. of Sciences 57-, regular mem. 62-; Prof. Univ. Budapest 64-.
Publs. *A jelenkori esztétika föirányai, Modern gondolkodás, Élmény és mü, Karakterológia, Haladás és fejlödés, Gondolat és szabadság, Régi magyar filozófusok XV-XVII.*
University Library, Károlyi-u. 10, Budapest, Hungary.
Telephone: 185-865.

Matsas, Alexander Anthony; Greek diplomatist; b. 3 May 1910; ed. Athens Univ. and Christ Church, Oxford.
Entered Greek Diplomatic Service 34; Vice-Consul in Egypt, Mansourah and Alexandria 37-41; went with Greek Govt. in exile to S. Africa, London and Cairo 41-44; First Sec. Embassy in Paris 47-50; Chargé d'Affaires a.i. The Hague 48 and 49; Counsellor to Embassy in Rome 53-57; Minister, Head of 1st Political Div., Athens 57-59; Ambassador to Turkey and Minister to Iran and Pakistan 59-62, Ambassador to U.S.A. 62-67.
Publs. Poems 37, 46, *Clytemnestra* (edited) 46, *Jocasta* (edited) 51, *Croesus* (edited) 59.
c/o Ministry of Foreign Affairs, Athens, Greece.

Matskevich, Vladimir Vladimirovich; Soviet agriculturist and politician; b. 09; ed. Kharkov Inst of Veterinary Science.
Dir. Kharkov Inst. of Veterinary Science 39; First Deputy Minister of Animal Husbandry of the Ukraine 46-47, Minister 49-53; First Dep. Minister of Agric. of U.S.S.R. 53-55, Minister 55-56, 58-60, 65-; Chair. Exec. Cttee. of Workers' Deputies, Tselinograd, Kazakh S.S.R. 60-65; mem. C.P.S.U. 39-, Central Cttee. C.P. 56-60, 66-; Vice-Chair. State Econ. Comm. 57-60; Leader, Soviet Agric. Del. to U.S.A. and Canada.
Ministry of Agriculture, Moscow, U.S.S.R.

Matsubara, Yosomatsu; Japanese shipbuilding executive; b. 15 Dec. 1895; ed. Nagasaki Higher Commercial School.
Kuhari Mining Co. until 34; Hitachi Seisaku (Mfg.) Co. 34-; Dir. Hitachi Shipbuilding and Eng. Co. 44-, Vice-Pres. 49-50, Pres. 50-67; Perm. Dir. Japan Fed. of Employers' Asscns.
Hitachi Shipbuilding and Engineering Co., 2-25 Nakanoshima, Kitaku, Osaka, Japan.

Matsuda, Isao; Japanese retail executive; b. 10 March 1886; ed. Keio Univ.
Mitsukoshi Ltd. (Department Store) 19-, Dir. 47-, Man. Dir. 49-63, Pres. 63-.
Mitsukoshi Ltd., Muromachi, Nihonbashi, Chuo-ku, Tokyo, Japan.

Matsuda, Tsuneji; Japanese business executive; b. 24 Nov. 1895; ed. Osaka Municipal Technical School.
Machine Industry, Osaka 15-26; Toyo Kogyo Co. Ltd. 27-, Dir. 38-, Pres. 51-; Man. Dir. Fed. of Econ. Orgs. 66-; Dir. Japan Automobile Manufacturers Asscn. 67-; Pres. Hiroshima Toyo Carp Co. Ltd. 68-; Medal of Honour with Blue Ribbon.
10-29 Banchi, Kami Nobori-cho, Hiroshima, Japan.
Telephone: Hiroshima 62-1111.

Matsui, Akira; Japanese diplomatist; b. 6 Jan. 1908; ed. Tokyo Imperial Univ.
Ministry of Foreign Affairs 31-, Dir. Research Bureau 50, Deputy Vice-Minister for Admin. 53; Minister to France 55-57; Perm. Rep. to UNESCO 55-57, mem. Exec. Board 56-62; Ambassador to Ceylon 57-59, to Sweden 59-62, concurrently to Iceland; Deputy Perm. Rep. to UN 62-63, Perm. Rep. 63-.
Permanent Mission of Japan to the United Nations, 866 United Nations Plaza, New York City, N.Y. 10017, U.S.A.
Telephone: 212-421-9580.

Matsui, Sashichiro; Japanese diplomatist; b. 13; ed. Tokyo Univ.
Entered Japanese Diplomatic Service 35 and worked in Washington and Rio de Janeiro; Chief, Third Section, Int. Co-operation Bureau, Ministry of Foreign Affairs 55-58; Chief Scientific section, UN Bureau 58; First Sec. Vienna 58-60, Bangkok 60-61; Dir. Colombo Plan Bureau 61-63; Counsellor, Ministry of Foreign Affairs (UN Bureau) 64-.
Ministry of Foreign Affairs, Tokyo, Japan.

Matsumoto, Shigeharu, B.A.; Japanese writer and executive; b. 2 Oct. 1899; ed. Faculty of Law, Univ. of Tokyo, Yale Univ., Univs. of Wisconsin, Geneva and Vienna.
Assistant, Faculty of Law, Univ. of Tokyo 28-30; Lecturer Chuo Univ., Hosei Univ., Japan Women's Univ. 29-33; Rep. Shanghai Branch Rengo News Service 33-34, Domei (now Kyodo) News Service 35-39; Editor-in-Chief Domei News Service 40-44, and Man. Dir. 44-45; mem. U.S. Educ. Comm. (Fulbright), Tokyo 54-57; Columnist Asahi Newspaper 56; Gen. Partner Matsumoto, Kojima and Matsukata (law office) 47-; Man. Dir. Int. House of Japan, Inc. 52-65, Chair. Board of Dirs. Int. House of Japan, Inc. 65-; Pres. Japanese Asscn. for American Studies 52-67, Man. Dir. 68-; Pres. Inst. of Nat. Econ. (Kokumin Keizai Kenkyu Kyokai) 51-61; Dir. Nippon Light Metal Co. 57-; Dentsu Advertising Ltd. 61-; Vice-Pres. Nat. Comm. of Japan for UNESCO 57-63; Counsellor, Inst. of Asian Econ. Affairs 60-; mem. Board of Govs. Japan Broadcasting Corpn. 61-65.
Publs. edited *Memoirs of Aisuke Kabayama* (in Japanese) 56; co-edited *A Documentary History of American People* 6 vols. (in Japanese) 50-58; translated: Albert Thomas's *Histoire Anecdotique du Travail* 28, Dr. S. Johnson's *Beikoku San-ijin no Shogai to sono Shiteki Haikei* (with Y. Takagi) 29, C. A. Beard's *The Republic* 2 vols. 48-49, *A Basic History of the United States* 2 vols. (with K. Kishimura) 54-56, *American Spirit* (with Y. Takagi) 54; edited: Arnold Toynbee's *Lessons of History* (lectures in Japan) 57, *A History of the World* 45-61 (in Japanese) 62, *The Mind of India* (lectures in Japan by J. Nehru and others) 61, *Lectures on Aspects of American Culture* (lectures in Japan by David

Riesman) 62, *Basic Problems of U.S. Foreign Policy* (lectures in Japan by George Kennan) 65.
The International House of Japan, Inc., 11-6, 5-chome, Roppongi, Minato-ku, Tokyo, Japan.

Matsuno, Raiszo; Japanese politician; b. 12 Feb. 1917; ed. Keio Univ.
Formerly with Hitachi Ltd.; Japanese Navy, Second World War; fmr. Pres. Johoku Brewing Co.; fmr. Private Sec. to Prime Minister (Mr. Yoshida); mem. House of Reps.; fmr. Parl. Vice-Minister, Ministry of Welfare; Dir.-Gen. Prime Minister's Office; Minister of Labour 59-60; Minister of State in charge of Defence Agency June 65-66; Minister of Agriculture 66-67; Liberal-Democrat.
84 Imazato Shirogane, Shiba, Minato-ku, Tokyo, Japan.

Matsuo, Shizuma, B.ENG., D.COM.; Japanese aviation executive; b. 03; ed. Kyushu Univ.
Communications Engineer, Japanese Civil Aviation Bureau, Korea 30-33, Aviation Officer 33, later Chief of Airfield, Ulsan and Taegu (Korea), and Osaka; Dir. Osaka Aeronautical Experimental Station; Dir.-Gen. Nat. Air Security Board 49-50, Kokucho 50-51; Senior Man. Dir. Japan Air Lines 51-57, Exec. Vice-Pres. 57-61, Pres. 61-.
Publ. *Air Transport Management* 60.
2558, 5-chome, Kamimeguro, Meguro-ku, Tokyo, Japan.

Matsushita, Konosuke; Japanese businessman; b. 27 Nov. 1894.
Founded Matsushita Electric Mfg. Co. 18, incorporated into Matsushita Electric Industrial Co. Ltd. 35, fmr. Pres., Chair. 61-; Pres. Matsushita Communication Industrial Co. Ltd. 58-66, Chair. 66-; Pres. Matsushita Real Estate Co. Ltd. 52-; Pres. Matsushita Electronics Corpn. 52-66, Chair. 66-; Chair. Kyushu Matsushita Electric Co. Ltd. 55-, Nakagawa Electric Co. Ltd. 53-, Matsushita Electric Works Ltd. 51-; Dir. Matsushita Electric Trading Co. Ltd.; Chair. Matsushita Electric Corpn. of America 59-; Chair. Victor Co. of Japan Ltd. 62-; Vice-Pres. Electronic Industries Asscn. of Japan 58-; Managing Dir. Fed. of Econ. Orgs. of Japan 56-; mem. Int. Chamber of Commerce 61-, Advisory Cttee. Japan Nat. Railway 62-; Blue Ribbon Medal 56; Commdr., Order of Orange Nassau (Netherlands) 58, Rising Sun 65; Hon. LL.D. (Waseda Univ.).
Publs. *What I do, and What I think, The Dream of My Work and the Dream of Our Life, The Words of Peace and Happiness through Prosperity, My View Towards Prosperity, Why?*.
Matsushita Electric Industrial Co. Ltd., 1006 Kadoma, Osaka, Japan.
Telephone: Osaka (991)-1121.

Matsushita, Masaharu, B.IUR.; Japanese businessman; b. 17 Sept. 1912; ed. Tokyo Imperial Univ.
Mitsui Bank 35-40; Matsushita Electric Industrial Co. Ltd. 40-, Auditor 44-49, Vice-Pres. 49-61, Pres. 61-; Auditor, Matsushita Real Estate Co. Ltd. 52-; Dir. Matsushita Communication Industrial Co. Ltd. 58-, Osaka Electric Industrial Co. Ltd. 56-, Kyushu Matsushita Electric Co. Ltd. 55-, Matsushita Electronics Corpn. 52-, Nakagawa Electric Inc. 55-.
2-banchi, 8-chome, Natsugi-cho, Nishinomiya City, Hyogo Prefecture, Japan.

Matsushita, Masatoshi, PH.D.; Japanese lawyer and university administrator; b. 01; ed. Rikkyo (St. Paul's) Univ., Tokyo, Carleton Coll. and Columbia Univ.
Prof. Rikkyo (St. Paul's) Univ. 29; Attorney for Gen. Tojo, Int. Military Court of the Far East; Pres. Rikkyo (St. Paul's) Univ. 55-; personal envoy of Prime Minister of Japan to Great Britain, requesting a suspension of nuclear tests 57.
Publs. *War Power of the United States, Fundamental Principles of American International Law*.
29 Shinano-machi, Shinjuku-ku, Tokyo, Japan.

Matta (R. A. S. Matta-Echaurren); Chilean artist; b. 11 Nov. 1911; ed. Catholic Univ., Santiago, Ecole d'Urbanisme et Architecture, Paris and Atelier Le Corbusier.

U.S.A. 39-; exhbns. at Julien Levy Gallery 40, Pierre Matisse Gallery 41, 43, 45, 47, Sidney Janis Gallery 49, 51, 54, Allen Frumkin Gallery (all in New York City) 54, Alexandre Idlas Gallery, N.Y. 64-, and other galleries in Paris 64-, Geneva 64-, Stockholm 59, Bologna 63, Amsterdam 64, Cuba 64, Lucerne 65; works permanently displayed at Museum of Modern Art, New York City, Harvard Athenaeum, St. Louis Museum, etc.

Boissy Sans Avoir, S.-et-O., France.

Mattarella, Bernardo; Italian lawyer and politician; b. 15 Sept. 1905; ed. Univ. of Palermo.

Under-Sec., Ministry of Education (Bonomi Cabinet) 44-45; Under-Sec. Ministry of Transport 48-53, Minister 53-55; Minister of Merchant Marine 53; Minister of Foreign Trade 55-57; Minister of Posts and Telecommunications 57-59; Minister of Transport 62, of Foreign Trade 63-65; Asst. Sec. of the Christian Democratic Party and Treas. of the Constituent Assembly; active in Italian Catholic orgs.

Publ. *Igino Giordani* 35.

Via Segesta 9, Palermo, Italy.

Matter, Jean; French businessman; b. 1 Jan. 1894; ed. Lycée Carnot and Ecole Polytechnique de Paris.

Vice-Pres. Seichimé; Vice-Pres. and Gen. Man. Centrale des Alliages; Dir. Aluminium Français, Compagnie Pechiney; Dir. Cie. Gén. d'Electro-Métallurgie, Cie. Métallurgique de Bonneville, and of several other concerns; Officier Légion d'Honneur, Order of St. Olaf, Croix de Guerre, Médaille de la Résistance.

Home: 1 rue de Beaune, Paris 7e; Office: 23 rue Balzac, Paris 8e, France.

Matthew, Sir Robert Hogg, Kt., C.B.E., M.A., P.P.R.I.B.A., F.R.A.I.S., F.R.S.E., M.T.P.I., A.R.S.A.; British architect; b. 12 Dec. 1906; ed. Melville Coll., Edinburgh.

Chief Architect and Planning Officer, Dept. of Health for Scotland 45; Architect to London County Council (designed Royal Festival Hall) 46-53; Prof. of Architecture, Edinburgh Univ. 53-; Pres. Int. Union of Architects 61-65; Pres. Royal Inst. of British Architects 62-64; Pres. Commonwealth Asscn. of Architects 65-; Hon. LL.D. (Sheffield).

Department of Architecture, The University, Edinburgh; Home: 31 Regent Terrace, Edinburgh 7, Scotland.

Telephone: WAVerley 5621 (Office).

Matthews, Sir Bryan Harold Cabot, Kt., C.B.E., F.R.S., SC.D.; British physiologist; b. 14 June 1906; ed. Clifton Coll. and King's Coll., Cambridge.

Beit Memorial Fellow for Medical Research 28-32; Fellow, King's Coll. 29-; Asst. Dir. Physiological Research, Cambridge 32-48; Reader in Experimental Physiology, Cambridge Univ. 48-52; Prof. of Physiology 52-; Consultant in Physiology to R.A.F. 41-; Head of R.A.F. Physiological Laboratory 40-44 and of the Inst. of Aviation Medicine from its foundation 44-46; Vice-Pres. Royal Soc. 57 and 58; Pres. Section I British Asscn. 61; Chair. Flying Personnel Research Cttee. R.A.F. 67-.

King's College, Cambridge, England.

Matthews, Denis; British pianist; b. 27 Feb. 1919; ed. Warwick School and Royal Acad. of Music, London.

First concerts, London 39; since then numerous recitals and tours in Great Britain, U.S.A., Canada, etc.; teaching, lecturing; numerous recordings.

Publ. *In Pursuit of Music* 66.

34 Warwick Avenue, London, W.9, England.

Telephone: 01-286-4376.

Matthews, Herbert Lionel; American newspaperman; b. 10 Jan. 1900; ed. Columbia Univ.

U.S. Army Service, First World War; *New York Times* 22-, successively Reporter, Foreign Editor and War Corresp., Paris Bureau 31-34, Abyssinian War 35-36, Spanish Civil War 36-39, Rome 39-42, India 42-43, Italian Campaign 43-45; Chief, London Bureau, *New York Times* 45-49, Editorial Staff, *New York Times*, New York 49-; numerous decorations.

Publs. *Eyewitness in Abyssinia* 37, *Two Wars and More to Come* 38, *The Fruits of Fascism* 43, *The Education of a Correspondent* 46, *Assignment to Austerity* (with Edith Matthews) 50, *The Yoke and the Arrows* 56, *The Cuban Story* 61, *Cuba* 64.

New York Times, 229 West 43rd Street, New York 36, N.Y., U.S.A.

Telephone: 556-1717.

Matthews, Very Rev. Walter Robert, C.H., K.C.V.O., M.A., D.D., D.LIT.; British ecclesiastic; b. 22 Sept. 1881; ed. Wilson's School, Camberwell, and King's Coll. London.

Fmr. Curate, St. Mary Abbot's, Kensington, and St. Peter, Regent Square, London, and Asst. Chaplain Magdalen Hospital; Lecturer in Philosophy, King's Coll. 08-18 and in Dogmatic Theology 09-18, Dean 18-32; Vicar of Christ Church, Crouch End, London 16-18; Chaplain, Gray's Inn 20, Preacher 29; Chaplain to the King 23-31; Dean of Exeter 31-34; Dean of St. Paul's Cathedral 34-67, Dean Emeritus 67-; Fellow, King's Coll., London; Freedom Cross of Haakon VII (Norway) 47; Order of White Lion (Class III) Czechoslovakia 47; Fellow Royal Society of Literature, Westfield Coll., Univ. of London 48; Pres. of the English Asscn. 55; D.D. h.c. (Cambridge) 58.

Publs. *Studies in Christian Philosophy* 21, *The Idea of Revelation* 24, *The Psychological Approach to Religion* 25, *God in Christian Thought and Experience* 30, *The Adventures of Gabriel in his Search for Mr. Shaw* 33, *Essays in Construction* 34, *The Purpose of God* 35, *Our Faith in God* 36, *Hope of Immortality* 37, *Signposts to God* 38, *Teaching of Christ* 39, *Moral Issues of the War* 40, *Following Christ* 40, *Foundations of Peace* 42, *Strangers and Pilgrims* 45, *St. Paul's in Wartime* 46, *The Problem of Christ in the 20th Century* 50, *Some Christian Words* 56, *The Search for Perfection* 57, *A History of St. Paul's Cathedral and the Men Associated With it* (Editor) 57, *The Lord's Prayer* 59, *The Thirty-Nine Articles* 61.

29 Buckingham Palace Mansions, London, S.W.1, England.

Mattila, Olavi Johannes; Finnish engineer, diplomatist and politician; b. 24 Oct. 1918; ed. Inst. of Technology and Helsinki School of Economics and Economic Sciences.

Commercial Rep., Finnish Embassy, Peking 52-56, Commercial Attaché, Buenos Aires 57-60; Chief of Bureau, Ministry of Foreign Affairs 60; Head of Commercial Div., Ministry of Trade and Industry 60-62; Head of Commercial Div., Ministry of Foreign Affairs 62-64; Second Minister for Foreign Affairs Nov.-Dec. 63-64; Minister of Trade and Industry Dec. 63-64; Pres. and Chair. Valmet Org. 65-; Commdr., Order of Lion of Finland, and other decorations.

Puistokatu 3.A.12, Helsinki, Finland.

Mattioli, Dr. Raffaele; Italian banker; b. 1895.

Chairman, Banca Commerciale Italiana; Vice-Pres. Banque Française et Italienne pour l'Amérique du Sud, Paris; Vice-Pres. Banca della Svizzera Italiana, Lugano; mem. Advisory Panel to Int. Finance Corpn. 63-; Chair. Italian Inst. for Historical Studies, Naples; mem. Riccardo Ricciardi, Publishers.

Banca Commerciale Italiana, 6 Piazza della Scala, Milan, Italy.

Matulis, Juozas Juozasovich; Soviet chemist; b. 1889; ed. Kaunus State Univ.
Teacher, Kaunas State Univ. 28-40, Vilnius State Univ. 40-45; mem. Lithuanian Acad. of Sciences 41-, Pres. 45-; Corresp. mem. U.S.S.R. Acad. of Sciences 46-; mem. C.P.S.U. 50-; Hero of Socialist Labour and other awards.
Presidium of Lithuanian Academy of Sciences, 3 Lenin Prospekt, Vilnius, U.S.S.R.

Matuschka-Greiffenclau, Graf Richard; German wine-grower; b. 11 May 1893; ed. Bonn and Berlin Univs.
Civil servant until 34; political and business activity 46-; mem. Hesse Landtag 48-50; Hon. Pres. Deutscher Weinbauverband 48; Vice-Pres. Int. Wine Bureau (Paris) 50-, Central Cttee. for German Agriculture 54-, Econ. and Social Cttee. of European Econ. Community 58-; Grosses Verdienstkreuz.
Schloss Vollrads, 6227 Winkel im Rheingau, German Federal Republic.
Telephone: 06723-3377.

Matute Ausejo, Ana Maria; Spanish writer; b. 26 July 1926; ed. "Damas Negras" French Nuns Coll.
Collaborated on literary magazine *Destino*; Visiting Lecturer, Indiana Univ. 65-66.
Publs. include *Los Abel* 47, *Fiesta Al Noroeste* (Café Gijon Prize) 52, *Pequeño Teatro* (Planeta Prize) 54, *Los Hijos Muertos* (Nat. Literary Prize and Critics Prize) 59, *Primera Memoria* (Nadal Prize) 59, *El Rio* 63, *El Tiempo* 63, *El Arrepentido y otras narraciones* 67.
Calle Platon 20-3-2, Barcelona 6, Spain.
Telephone: 228-30-78.

Matveyev, Alexei Nikolaevich; Soviet scientist; b. 22 March 1922; ed. Moscow State Univ.
Senior Scientific Worker, Moscow State Univ. 54-60; Prof. of Theoretical Physics, Moscow State Univ. 60-64; Head of Dept. of Univs., Ministry of Higher Educ., R.S.F.S.R. 60-62; Asst. Dir.-Gen. for Science, UNESCO 64-; Order of Red Banner (twice), Order of the Patriotic War, Order of Alexander Nevski, Order of Red Banner of Labour.
Publs. *Electrodynamics and Theory of Relativity* 64, *Quantum Mechanics and Structure of Atoms* 65.
UNESCO, Place de Fontenoy, Paris 7e, France.
Telephone: 566-57-57.

Matveyev, Leonid Mikhailovich; Soviet trade corporation official; b. 07; ed. Plekhanov Inst. of Nat. Econ., Moscow.
Consumer Co-operative orgs. 30-41; Soviet Army 41-48; Vice-Chair. Central Union of Consumers' Co-operatives of U.S.S.R. 48-49; Soviet orgs. in D.D.R. 49-54; Chair. *Exportkhleb* (cereals, pulses, oil-seeds, fodder) 54-; mem. Communist Party 30-; numerous decorations.
V/O Exportkhleb, Ministry of Foreign Trade, 32-34 Smolenskaya-Sennaya ploshchad, Moscow, U.S.S.R.

Matz, Friedrich; German archaeologist; b. 15 Aug. 1890; ed. Univs. of Tübingen and Göttingen.
Teacher Berlin 21; bibliographical work German Archæological Inst., Rome 25-29; Dozent Berlin Univ. 28; Asst. Dir. Archæological Inst. Berlin 29-34; Prof. Univ. of Muenster 34, Marburg Lahn Univ. 41; Prof. and Rector Philipps Univ. Marburg 46-47, Emeritus 58.
Publs. *Die Frühkretischen Siegel* 28, *Katalog der Bibliothek des Deutschen Archäologischen Instituts in Rom* 30-32, *Ein Zeuskopf in Villa Borghese* 31, *Kretisch-Mykenische Kunst, Antike* 36, *Wesen und Wirkung der Augusteischen Kunst* 38, *Geschichte der griechischen Kunst*, Vol. I 50, *Die Aegaeis* 50, *Der Gott auf dem Elefantenwagen* 52, *Kreta, Mykene, Troia* 56, *Götter-erscheinung und Kultbild im minoischen Kreta* 58, *Ein römisches Meisterwerk* 58, *Kreta und frühes Griechenland* 62.
Biegenstrasse 11, Marburg/Lahn, German Federal Republic; Home: Georg-Voigtstrasse 25, Marburg/Lahn.
Telephone: 2349.

Mauchly, John W(illiam), PH.D.; American physicist and research engineer; b. 30 Aug. 1907; ed. Johns Hopkins School of Engineering.
Research Asst., Johns Hopkins Univ. 32-33; Head, Dept. of Physics, Ursinus Coll., Pennsylvania 33-41; Assoc., Dept. of Terrestrial Magnetism, Carnegie Inst., Washington 36, 37, 38; Instructor, Electrical Engineering, Univ. of Pennsylvania 41-43, Asst. Prof. 43-46; Consultant, Naval Ordnance Laboratory, White Oaks, Maryland 44-45; Co-Founder, Electronic Control Co., for design and manufacture of electronic digital computing equipment, commercial and scientific applications 46; Pres. Eckert-Mauchly Computer Corpn. 47-51; Dir., Remington Rand Weather Project 51-53, Systems Studies Eckert-Mauchly Div. of Remington Rand 53, UNIVAC Applications Research Center and UNIVAC Div. of Sperry Rand Corpn. 54-59; Pres. Mauchly Assocs., Inc. 59-65, Chair. 65-; Dir. Pyrometer Corpn., Jonkers Business Machines, Inc., Data Systems Corpn.; Visiting Prof. of System Engineering, Carnegie Inst. of Technology, Pittsburgh 59-60; mem. American Physical Soc., Franklin Inst., American Astronomical Soc. and other learned socs.; Fellow, I.E.E.E. and American Statistical Asscn.; Howard Potts Medal of Franklin Inst. 49; John Scott Award 61.
Mauchly Associates, Inc., Fort Washington Industrial Park, Fort Washington, Pennsylvania; Home: Little Linden Farm, Ambler, Pennsylvania, U.S.A.

Maude, Angus Edmund Upton, M.A., M.P.; British politician and author; b. 8 Sept. 1912; ed. Rugby School and Oriel Coll., Oxford.
Financial journalist 33-39; war service (prisoner of war 3½ years) 39-45; Deputy Dir. Political and Economic Planning 49-50; Conservative Mem. of Parl. 50-59, 63-; Dir. Conservative Political Centre 51-55; Editor *The Sydney Morning Herald* 58-61.
Publs. *The English Middle Classes* (with Roy Lewis) 49, *Professional People* (with Roy Lewis) 52, *Biography of a Nation* (with Enoch Powell) 56, and editor of *One Nation* 50 and *Change is our Ally* 54 (booklets on social policy by nine M.P.s), *Good Learning* 64, *South Asia* 66.
House of Commons, London, S.W.1, England.
Telephone: 01-930-6240.

Maude, Evan Walter; British international bank official; b. 11 Feb. 1919; ed. Rugby School, and New Coll., Oxford.
R.N.V.R. (Fleet Air Arm) 40-45; H.M. Treasury 46; Asst. Private Sec. to Chancellor of Exchequer and Econ. Sec. 47-48; Private Sec. to Sec. of State for Co-ordination of Transport, Fuel and Power 51-53; Principal Private Sec. to Chancellor of Exchequer 56-58; Asst., then Deputy Under-Sec. of State, Dept. of Econ. Affairs 64-67; Exec. Dir., Int. Bank for Reconstruction and Devt., Int. Finance Corpn., and Int. Devt. Asscn. Aug. 67-.
International Bank for Reconstruction and Development, Washington, D.C. 20433, U.S.A.

Maudling, Rt. Hon. Reginald, P.C., M.P.; British politician; b. 7 March 1917; ed. Merton Coll., Oxford.
Called to Middle Temple Bar 40; served Royal Air Force and Air Ministry during 39-45 war; Conservative M.P. for Barnet Div. of Hertfordshire 50-; Parl. Sec. to Minister of Civil Aviation 52; Minister of Supply 55-57; Paymaster-General with seat in Cabinet 57-59; Pres. of Bd. of Trade 59-61; Sec. of State for the Colonies 61-62; Chancellor of the Exchequer 62-64; Exec. Dir. Kleinwort Benson Ltd. 64-; Dir. Dunlop Rubber Co. 64-, Associated Electrical Industries 64-; Vice-Chair. and Dir. Shipping and Industrial Trust 65-; Pres. Nat. Union of Conservative and Unionist Asscns. 67.
Bedwell Lodge, Essendon, Herts.; and **26 Chester** Square, London, S.W.1, England.

Maufe, Sir Edward, R.A., M.A., F.R.I.B.A.; British archi-tect; b. 12 Dec. 1883; ed. St. John's Coll. Oxford.
Architect, Guildford Cathedral, Runnymede Memorial, Kelling Hall, Norfolk, London Hospital Students' Hostel, St. Saviour's Church, Acton, St. Thomas's Church, Hanwell, Festival Theatre, Cambridge, Play-house, Oxford; additions to Trinity and St. John's Colls., Cambridge, and St. John's Coll., Oxford; Royal Gold Medal for Architecture 44; R.A. 47; architect for recon-struction Middle Temple, Gray's Inn, and St. Columba, Pont Street; Treas. Royal Acad. 54-58, Chief Architect, Commonwealth War Graves Comm.; mem. Royal Fine Art Comm. 47-53; Hon. Fellow, St. John's Coll., Ox-ford; Hon. LL.D. (Queen's Univ., Belfast); Hon. Master of the Bench, Gray's Inn.
139 Old Church Street, London, S.W.3, England.

Maulnier, Thierry (see Talagrand, J. L. A.).

Maurer, Friedrich, DR.PHIL.; German university pro-fessor; b. 5 Jan. 1898; ed. Univs. of Frankfurt, Heidel-berg and Giessen.
Lecturer Univ. of Giessen 25, Extra. Prof. 29, Prof. of Germanic Philology Erlangen 31, Freiburg 37-.
Publs. *Untersuchungen über die deutsche Verbstellung* 26, *Studien zur mitteldeutschen Bibelübersetzung* 29, *Die Sprache Goethes* 32, *Volkssprache* 33, 64, *Die Erlösung* (editor) 34, 64, *Das Rolandslied* (editor) 40, 64, *Nord-germanen und Alemannen* 42, 52, *Deutsche Wort-geschichte* Vols. I-III (with Stroh) 43, 59, *Leid* 51, 52, 64, *Die religiösen Dichtungen der 11 und 12 Jahrhunderten* Vols. I and II 65, *Die Pseudoreimare* 66, etc.
Schlossweg 18, 7802 Merzhausen bei Freiburg i. Br., German Federal Republic.
Telephone: Freiburg 34440.

Maurer, Georg, HON. C.B.E., M.D.; German surgeon; b. 29 May 1909; ed. Univ. of Munich.
Surgical Asst., later Chief Asst., Univ. Clinic of Surgery Munich 33-45; Surgeon-in-Chief Hospital Munich-Perlach 46-53, Medical Dir. 60-, and Surgeon-in-Chief, Hospital Rechts der Isar, Munich 53-; Prof. Extra-ordinary, Univ. of Munich 48; City Councillor, Munich; Second Sec. German Society of Surgery; Pres. Hospital Cttee. Bavarian Medical Asscn., Vice-Pres., Regional Pres. German Asscn. of Medical Directors.
Publs. *Morbus Fraenkel* 44, *Problem of salt-water balance in surgery* 58, *Tetanus prophylaxis* 59, *Staphylo-cocci hospitalism and "seesaw" medication* 59, *History of Surgery in Bavaria* 60, *Pancreatitis* 60, *Post-operation Treatment for Cancer* 60.
Munich 8, Ismaninger Strasse 22, German Federal Republic.

Maurer, Ion Gheorghe, D.IUR.; Romanian jurist and politician; b. 1902; ed. Craiova Military School and Bucharest Univ.
Joined Romanian Communist Party 36; imprisoned in concentration camp for political activities; Under Sec. of State for Transport 44-46, Ministry of Nat. Economy 46-47; mem. Grand Nat. Assembly 46-, Central Cttee. Romanian Workers' Party 46-, Exec. Cttee. and of the Perm. Presidium of the Central Cttee. of Romanian Communist Party 65-; Under-Sec. of State to Ministry of Communications and Public Works 45-46, Minister of Nat. Economy 46-47, Minister of Industry and Trade 47-48; active work for Workers' Party Cen. Org. 48-51, mem. Political Bureau 60-65; Minister for Foreign Affairs 57-58; Chair. Presidium Grand Nat. Assembly (Head of State) 58-61, Chair. Council of Ministers 61-; mem. Acad. of Romanian People's Republic, fmr. Dir. Inst. of Juridical Research; Order of the Star of the Republic, Order of Labour, Order "23 August", Hero of Socialist Labour, etc.
Council of Ministers, Bucharest, Romania.

Mauriac, Claude, D.IUR.; French writer; b. 25 April 1914; ed. Lycée Janson-de-Sailly.
Secretary to Gen. de Gaulle 44-49; Film Critic *Figaro Littéraire*; weekly literary column "La Vie des Lettres" in *Le Figaro*; Prix Sainte-Beuve for *André Breton* 49, Prix Médicis for *Le Dîner en Ville* 59.
Publs. Essays: *Aimer Balzac, Malraux ou le Mal du Héros, André Breton, Marcel Proust par Lui-Même, Conversation avec André Gide, Hommes et Idées d'Aujourd'hui, L'Alittérature Contemporaine*; Novels: *Toutes Les Femmes Sont Fatales* 57, *Le Dîner en Ville* 59, *La Marquise Sortit à Cinq Heures* 51, *L'Agrandisse-ment* 63; Plays: *La Conversation* 64, *Femmes Fatales* 66, *l'Oubli* 66.
24 Quai de Béthune, Paris 4e, France.

Mauriac, François; French novelist; b. 11 Oct. 1885; ed. Candéran Marian Coll., Lycée and Univ. of Bor-deaux.
Former Pres. Société des Gens de Lettres; Pres. Cttee. France-Maghreb until 66; Winner Grand Prix of Acad. Française 26; mem. Acad. Française; Nobel Prize in Literature 52; Grand Croix Légion d'Honneur.
Publs. include: *Les Mains jointes* 09, *Orages* 25 (verse); *Préséances, Le Baiser au Lépreux, Genitrix* 22, *Thérèse Desqueyroux* 27, *Le Noeud de Vipères* 32, *La Pharisienne* 41, *L'Agneau* 54 (novels); *Asmodée* 38, *Les Mals Aimés* 45 (plays); *Proust* 26, *La Vie de Jean Racine, La Vie de Jésus* 36, *Journal* 34-, *Bloc-Notes* 58, *Le Fils de l'Homme* 58, *Mémoires Intérieurs* 59 (essays, etc.), *Ce Que Je Crois* 62, *De Gaulle* 64, *Nouveaux Mémoires Intérieurs* 65, *Mémoires Politiques* 67.
38 avenue Théophile-Gautier, Paris 16e, France.

Maurice-Bokanowski, Michel; French politician; b. 6 Nov. 1912.
Former Sec.-Gen., Paris Region Rassemblement du Peuple Français (R.P.F.); Dep. from Seine (5th Div.) 51-58, elected U.N.R. Dep. from Bois-Colombes (Asni-ères) 58; Sec. of State for the Interior Jan. 59-Feb. 60; Minister of Posts and Telecommunications Feb. 60-April 62; Minister of Industry April 62-66; Mayor of Asnières 59; Commdr. Légion d'Honneur, Compagnon de la Libération, Croix de Guerre.
40 quai des Célestins, Paris 4e, France.

Maurstad, Toralv; Norwegian actor and theatre director; b. 24 Nov. 1926; ed. Universitet i Uppsala and Royal Acad. of Dramatic Art, London.
Début in Trondheim 47; Oslo Nye Teater 51; Oslo National Theatre 54; Managing Dir. Oslo Nye Teater (Oslo Municipal Theatre) 67-; Oslo Critics Award.
Plays acted in or directed include: *Young Woodley* 49, *Pal Joey* 52, *Peer Gynt* 54, *Long Day's Journey* 62, *Teenage Love* 63, *Hamlet* 64, *Arturo Ui* (in Bremen, Germany) 65, *Brand* (Ibsen) 66, *Of Love Remembered* (New York) 67; films: *Line* 60, *Kalde Spor* 62.
Oslo Nye Teater, Oslo, Norway.

Mavridoglu, Isidoros; Greek politician; b. 1912; ed. in England, and commercial and political sciences.
Former exporter; Liberal Deputy 52, Centre Union Deputy 64-; Minister of Mercantile Marine Sept. 65-66.
Chamber of Deputies, Athens, Greece.

Mavromihalis, Stylianos; Greek judge; b. 1900; ed. Univs. of Athens, Munich and Zürich.
Judge 23-, Pres. of the Areopagus (Supreme Court) 63-; Prime Minister Sept.-Nov. 63.
The Areopagus, Athens, Greece.

Mavros, George, LL.D.; Greek lawyer and politician; b. 09; ed. Athens and Berlin Univs.
Lawyer, Athens 32-; Asst. Prof. of Int. Law, Univ. of Athens 37-; M.P. 46-; Under-Sec. of State for Justice 45-46, Minister of Justice 46; Minister of National Econ. (Trade and Industry) 49-50; Minister of Finance 51, of Defence 52; Gov. for Greece to Int. Bank for

Reconstruction and Development 49-52; Minister of Co-ordination 63-64; Gov. Nat. Bank of Greece 64-66; Centre Union.
Publs. *Walker's Private International Law* 29, *Problems in the Differentiation of Real Property and Chattels in the International Law on Wills* 36, *Naval Privileges in International Law* 37.
8 Akadimias Street, Athens 134, Greece.

Maximova, Ekaterina Sergeyevna; Soviet ballet dancer; b. 1939; ed. Moscow School of Ballet.
Joined Bolshoi Theatre Ballet Co. 58; Honoured Artist of R.S.F.S.R.
Main roles: Masha (*Nutcracker*), Katerina (*Stone Flower*), Seventh Waltz, Prelude (*Chopiniana*), Maria (*Fountain of Bakhchisarai*), Giselle (*Giselle*), Mavka (*Song of the Forest* by Zhukovsky), Jeanne (*Flames of Paris*), the Muse (*Paganini* by Rachmaninov), Lizzie (*Thunder Road* by Karayev), Cinderella (*Cinderella*), Aurora (*Sleeping Beauty*), Kitri (*Don Quixote*).
State Academic Bolshoi Theatre of U.S.S.R., 1 Ploshchad Sverdlova, Moscow, U.S.S.R.

Maxwell, Gavin, M.A., F.R.S.L., F.R.G.S., F.A.G.S., F.I.A.L., F.Z.S.; British author; b. 15 July 1914; ed. Stowe and Hertford Coll., Oxford.
Army Service 39-44; commercial shark fishery 44-50; author 52-; Pres. Junior Exploration Soc. Cttee. World Wild Life Youth Fund; Heinemann Award, Royal Soc. of Literature.
Publs. *Harpoon at a Venture* 52, *God Protect Me from my Friends* 56, *A Reed Shaken by the Wind* 57, *The Ten Pains of Death* 59, *Ring of Bright Water* 60, *The Otter's Tale* 62, *The Rocks Remain* 63, *The House of Elrig* 65, *Lords of the Atlas* 66, *Raven Seek Thy Brother* 68.
Kyleakin Lighthouse, Wester Ross, Scotland; 11 The Boltons, London, S.W.10, England.

Maxwell, (Ian) Robert, M.C., M.P.; British publisher and politician; b. 10 June 1923; self-educated.
Served Second World War 40-45; German Section of Foreign Office (Head of Press Section, Berlin) 45-47; Chair. Robert Maxwell & Co. Ltd., 48-; Publisher and Chair. Board Pergamon Press, Oxford, London and New York 49-; Dir. Gauthier-Villars (Publishers), Paris 61-; Chair. Labour Nat. Fund Raising Foundation 60-; Chair. Labour Working Party on Science, Government and Industry 63-64; M.P. for Buckingham 64-; Treasurer Centre 42, 65-; Co-produced films *Don Giovanni* (Mozart), Salzburg Festival 54, *Bolshoi Ballet* 57; Editor *Information U.S.S.R.* 63, *The Economics of Nuclear Power* 65, Author *Public Sector Purchasing* (Report) 67.
4 Fitzroy Square, London, W.1; and Headington Hill Hall, Oxford, England.

Maxwell, William Donald; American newspaper editor; b. 12 Aug. 1900; ed. DePauw Univ., and Univ. of Chicago.
Reporter *Chicago Tribune* 20, Copywriter 21, Sports Editor 25, News Editor 30, City Editor 39, Asst. Man. Editor 42, Man. Editor 51, Editor 55-; Vice-Pres. and Dir. Tribune Co.; Dir. Associated Press, Ontario Paper Co. Ltd.; Trustee McCormick-Patterson Trust; Executor and Trustee R. R. McCormick Charitable Trust; Republican.
1427 Judson Avenue, Evanston, Ill., U.S.A.

Maxy, Max Herman; Romanian painter and graphic artist; b. 26 Oct. 1895; ed. Bucharest School of Fine Arts and in Berlin.
Teacher, N. Grigorescu Fine Arts Inst., Bucharest; Warden, Art Museum, Bucharest; works in the field of plastic arts since 17; one-man exhbns. in Romania, Berlin, Rome, Budapest, Venice, Prague, Belgrade, Sofia, Paris and Moscow; Merited Master of Art 65.

Major works: *Billiards, Abundance, Homage to Brancusi, Entering the Mine, The Thinker*.
c/o Art Museum of the Socialist Republic of Romania, Ştirbei Vodă 1, Bucharest; Home: G-ral Magheru 12-14, Bucharest, Romania.
Telephone: 12-90-78 (Home).

May, Ernst Georg; German architect and town planner; b. 27 July 1886; ed. Darmstadt Technische Hochschule, Univ. Coll., London, and Munich Technische Hochschule.
Rural housing in Silesia 19-24; City Engineer, Frankfurt am Main 25-30; town planning adviser, U.S.S.R. (master plans for Moscow, Magnitogorsk, Stalinsk, etc.) 30-33; private architectural practice in Tanganyika and Kenya (master plan for Kampala, house for Aga Khan, etc.) 33-53, in Hamburg (master plans for Neu-Altona, Mainz, Bremerhaven, Wiesbaden, etc.) 53-; hon. corresp. mem. R.I.B.A. and British Town Planning Inst.; Bundesverdienstkreuz First Class; Hamburg Schumacher Prize, Cornelius Gurlitt Medal (German Acad. of Town Planning); hon. degrees Hanover Technical High School, Freiburg Univ.
Hochrad 74, Hamburg-Gr. Flottbek, German Federal Republic.

May, Gerhard J. F.; Austrian ecclesiastic; b. 98; ed. Univs. of Vienna, Halle and Basle.
Vicar 20-25, Pastor in Celje, Yugoslavia 25-44; Bishop of the Lutheran Church in Austria 44-; Chair. Joint Council, Lutheran and Reformed Churches; Dr. Theol.
Schellinggasse 12, Vienna 1, Austria.

May, Mark Arthur, M.A., PH.D.; American psychologist; b. 12 Aug. 1891; ed. Maryville Coll., Columbia and Chicago Univs.
Served First World War 14-18; Prof. of Psychology Syracuse Univ. 19-24; Research Assoc., Teachers' Coll., Columbia Univ. 24-27; Prof. of Educational Psychology Yale Univ. 27-60, Emeritus 60-; Dir., Inst. of Human Relations, Yale Univ. 35-60; Scientific Consultant War Dept. 44; mem. of U.S. Advisory Comm. on Information 48-, Chair. 53-62; Chair. Board of Dirs. Teaching Films Custodians Inc.; Fellow, American Psychological Asscn., American Acad. Arts and Sciences; Hon. L.H.D. (Keuka Coll., Syracuse Univ., Maryville Coll.)
Publs. *The Education of American Ministers* (2 vols.) 34, *Studies in Character Formation* (3 vols., with H. Hartshorne) 28-30, *Co-operation and Competition* 37, *Education in a World of Fear* 41, *Social Psychology of War and Peace* 43, *Learning from Films* 57.
41 Brookside Drive, Hamden, Connecticut, U.S.A.

May, Morton D.; American retail business executive; b. 1914.
May Department Stores Inc., St. Louis 37-, Pres. and Dir. 51-62, Chair., Exec. Cttee., Pres. and Dir. 62-, also Chair. of Board 66-.
May Department Stores Inc., 6th and Olive Streets, St. Louis 1, Mo., U.S.A.

May, William Frederic, B.S., DR.ENG.; American business executive; b. 25 Oct. 1915; ed. Oak Park and River Forest High School, Oak Park, Illinois, Univ. of Rochester, N.Y., and Harvard Business School.
Executive Dept., American Can Co. 59, Corpn. Vice-Pres. and General Man. Canco Div. 59-62, Corpn. Vice-Pres. and Gen. Manager (Planning and Development) 62-64, Corpn. Exec. Vice-Pres. (Admin.) 64-65, Vice-Chair. 65, Chair. and Chief Exec. Officer 65-; Dir. Lincoln Center, Johns-Manville Corpn., Banker Trust, Great American Holding Co., N.A.M., C.E.D.; Trustee Univ. of Rochester, Polytechnic Inst. of Brooklyn.
Office: American Can Company, 100 Park Avenue, New York, N.Y. 10017; Home: 18 Ivy Hill Road, Chappaqua, N.Y. 10514, U.S.A.
Telephone: 212-972-4874 (Office); 914-666-7710 (Home).

Mayer, Albert, A.B., B.S. in C.E.; American architect and town planner; b. 29 Dec. 1897; ed. Columbia Univ. and Mass. Inst. of Technology.

Superintendent, Gen. Sup., Gen. Man. and Pres. J. H. Taylor Construction Co. Inc. 22-34; architectural and planning practice 34-, mem. of Mayer and Whittlesey and of Mayer, Whittlesey and Glass 37-59; Consultant U.S. Housing Admin., N.Y. State Housing Div. 35-38, United Provinces (Govt. of India) 46-60, U.S. Public Housing Admin. 62-; Fellow American Inst. of Architects, mem. American Inst. of Architects Cttee. on Urban Design; numerous awards and medals. Designs incl. New City of Kitimat (B.C.), New City of Ashdod Israel (consultant), New York City New School for Social Research, New Delhi Regional Plan, New City of Maumelle, Arkansas.

Publs. *Pilot Project India* 59, papers and lectures, incl. *Israel Plans* 59, *Some Implications of the Delhi Plan* 60, *Social Analysis and National Economic Planning in India* 61, *The Urgent Future* 66.

Office: 31 Union Square West, New York City 3; Home: 550 Park Avenue, New York City 21, N.Y., U.S.A. Telephone: 212-Algonquin-5-8700.

Mayer, Hans; German university professor; b. 19 March 1907; ed. Univs. of Cologne, Bonn, Berlin, and Graduate Inst. of Int. Studies, Geneva.

Emigrated from Germany 33-45; research at Int. Inst. of Social Research, New York, and Graduate Inst. of Int. Studies, Geneva 33-40; literary and dramatic critic in Switzerland 39-45; Chief Editor Frankfurt Radio 45-47; Lecturer in Sociology and the History of Culture, Akad. der Arbeit, Frankfurt 47-48; Prof. of History of Culture, Univ. of Leipzig 48-50, Prof. of the History of German Literature 50-64; Prof. History of German Literature, Technical High School, Hanover 65-; Prof. and Dir. of Inst. for the History of German Literature 55; mem. Exec. Deutsche Goethe-Gesellschaft, Deutsche Schillergesellschaft, Deutsche Schiller-Stiftung, P.E.N. Club; German Nat. Prize for Science 55; Literaturpreis der deutschen Kritiker 65.

Publs. *Von der dritten zur vierten Republik: Geistige Strömungen in Frankreich 1939-1945* 45, *Georg Büchner und seine Zeit* 46, *Thomas Mann, Werk und Entwicklung* 50, *Studien zur deutschen Literaturgeschichte* 54, *Schiller und die Nation* 54, *Deutsche Literatur und Weltliteratur: Reden und Aufsätze* 57, *Richard Wagner* 59, *Von Lessing bis Thomas Mann* 59, *Meisterwerke deutscher Literaturkritik*, Vol. I 54, Vol. II 56 (editor), *Bertolt Brecht und die Tradition* 61, *Aragon, Die Karwoche* (translation from the French), *Heinrich von Kleist, Der Geschichtliche Augenblick* 62, *Ansichten zur Literatur der Zeit* 62, *Dürrenmatt und Frisch, Anmerkungen* 63, *Zur deutschen Klassik und Romantik* 63, *Anmerkungen zu Brecht* 65, *Anmerkungen zu Richard Wagner* 66, *Grosse deutsche Verrisse* (editor) 67, *Zur deutschen Literatur der Zeit: Zusammenhänge, Schriftsteller, Bücher* 67.

Technische Hochschule, Hanover, German Federal Republic.

Mayer, John Anton, B.S., M.B.A.; American banker; b. 30 July 1909; ed. Univ. of Pennsylvania.

Joined Penn. Mutual Life Insurance Co. 33, Asst. to Vice-Pres. and Comptroller 34-35, Asst. Sec. 36-39, Asst. to Pres. 39-47, Sec. 47-49; Pres. and Dir. Reliance Life Insurance Co. 49-51; Vice-Pres. Mellon Nat. Bank and Trust Co. 51-57, Exec. Vice-Pres. 57-59, Pres. 59-67, Dir. 59-, Chief Exec. Officer 63-, Chair. of Board 67-; Dir. Bank of London and S. America Ltd., London 66-; official of other companies and orgs.

725 Devonshire Street, Pittsburgh 13, Pa., U.S.A.

Mayer, Joseph E. (husband of Maria Goeppert Mayer, *q.v.*), B.S., PH.D.; American chemical physicist; b. 5 Feb. 1904; ed. Calif. Inst. of Technology and Univ. of Calif.

Asst. Dept. of Chemistry Univ. of Calif. 27-28; Int. Educ. Board Fellow, Göttingen Germany 29-30; Assoc. Chemistry Johns Hopkins Univ. 30-34, Assoc. Prof. 34-39; Assoc. Prof. Chemistry, Columbia Univ. 39-45; Prof. of Chemistry, Inst. of Nuclear Studies, Univ. of Chicago 45-55; Consultant, Aberdeen Proving Ground, Ordnance Dept. U.S. Army 42-, Los Alamos Scientific Laboratory; Editor *Journal of Chemical Physics* 41-52; mem Nat. Acad. of Sciences and New York Acad. of Sciences; Corresp. mem. Heidelberg Akad. der Wissenschaften; mem. American Chemical Soc., American Physical Soc., Faraday Soc.; Chair. Comm. on Thermodynamic and Statistical Mechanics; Vice-Pres. Cttee. of Constants, Int. Union of Pure and Applied Physics, Scientific Cttee. Solvay Inst., Brussels; Carl William Eisendraht Prof. of Chemistry, Enrico Fermi Inst. of Nuclear Studies, Univ. of Chicago 55-60; Prof. Chemistry, Univ. of Calif. at La Jolla 60-; Dr. h.c. (Univ. Libre de Bruxelles); G. N. Lewis Medal and Peter Debye Prize (Amer. Chem. Soc.); Chandler Medal (Columbia Univ.); Kirkwood Medal (Yale Univ.).

Publs. *Statistical Mechanics* (with M. G. Mayer) 40; scientific articles.

2345 Via Siena, La Jolla, Calif., U.S.A. Telephone: 714-459-3030.

Mayer, Maria Goeppert (wife of Joseph E. Mayer, *q.v.*); American physicist; b. 28 June 1906; ed. Univ. of Göttingen, Germany.

Physics Asst., Johns Hopkins Univ. 30-32, Associate 32-36, Research Associate 36-39; Lecturer in Chemistry Columbia Univ. 41-45; Senior Scientist, Argonne National Laboratory 45-49; Volunteer Prof. of Physics, Univ. of Chicago 45-49; Prof. of Physics, Univ. of California, San Diego, La Jolla 60-; mem. Nat. Acad. of Sciences; mem. Akad. der Wissenschaften, Heidelberg; Nobel Prize in Physics 63; Hon. D.Sc., Russell Sage Coll., Mount Holyoke Coll. and Smith Coll.

Publs. *Statistical Mechanics* (with Joseph E. Mayer) 40, *Elementary Theory of Nuclear Shell Structure* (with J. H. D. Jensen) 55.

2345 Via Siena, La Jolla, California, U.S.A. Telephone: 714-459-3030.

Mayer, René; French politician; b. 4 May 1895; ed. Univ. of Paris.

Sec. of Communications Gen. Giraud Admin. Algiers; Commr. for Communications and Merchant Navy, French Cttee. for Nat. Liberation 43-44; Min. of Transport 44; High Commr. for German Affairs 45-46; Minister of Finance and Economic Affairs 47-48; Minister of Justice Bidault Cabinet 49-50, Pleven Cabinet 50-51, Queuille Cabinet 51; Vice-Pres. Council, Minister of Finance and Economic Affairs, Pleven Cabinet 51-52; Prime Minister Jan.-May 53; Chair. ECSC High Authority 55-57; Pres. and Dir.-Gen. Cie. de Recherches et d'Exploitation de Pétrole; Dir. Soc. Financière de Transports et d'Entreprises Industrielles, Soc. Le Nickel; Dir. Cie. d'Assurances La Union et le Phénix-espagnol, Le Phénix-espagnol Vie; Pres. Council Conservatoire Nat. des Arts et Métiers.

9 rue Vaneau, Paris 7e, France.

Mayer-Gunthof, Franz Josef, DR.JUR.; Austrian industrialist; b. 18 Aug. 1894; ed. Vienna and Oxford Univs.

War Service 14-18; took over firm V. Mayer & Söhne 20; Gen. Man. A. G. der Vöslauer Kammgarn-Fabrik Bad Vöslau 45-; Pres. Fed. of Austrian Industrialists 60, Textile Section, Fed. Chamber of Commerce 48; Vice-Pres. Wiener Börsekammer 49; Dir. Creditanstalt-bankverein 48, Gesellschaft der Musikfreunde und Konzerthausgesellschaft 47; Pres. Austrian U.N. Asscn. 56; mem. of Board, German Chamber of Commerce; Censor Oesterreichische Nationalbank; Hon. citizen

Technical Univ., Vienna; Hon. Dr. Comm. Sciences, Vienna.
Mozartgasse 4, Vienna IV, Austria.
Telephone: 65-32-25.

Mayhew, Christopher Paget, M.P., M.A.; British politician, writer and broadcaster; b. 12 June 1915; ed. Haileybury Coll. and Christ Church, Oxford.
M.P. for South Norfolk 45-50; Parl. Private Sec. to Lord Pres. of Council 45-46; Under-Sec. of State for Foreign Affairs Oct. 46-50; M.P. for Woolwich East 51-; Minister of Defence for the Navy 64-Feb. 66; Labour.
Publs. *Planned Investment* 39, *Those in Favour* 51, *Men Seeking God* 55, *Commercial Television: What is to be Done?* 59, *Co-existence Plus* 62, *Britain's Role To-morrow* 67.
House of Commons, London, S.W.1; Home: 39 Wool Road, Wimbledon, London, S.W.20, England.
Telephone: 01-946-3460 (Home).

Mayo, Charles William, A.B., M.D., M.S., F.R.C.S., F.A.C.S.; American surgeon; b. 28 July 1898; ed. Princeton Univ. and Univs. of Pennsylvania and Minnesota.
Intern Robert Packer Hospital, Sayre, Pa. 26-27; Fellow in Surgery, Mayo Foundation 27-31, Surgeon 31-64, Emeritus Surgeon; Consulting Surgeon and Head of Surgery Section, Mayo Foundation Graduate School, Univ. of Minnesota 32-35, Asst. Prof. of Surgery 35-40, Assoc. Prof. 40-47, Prof. 47-; Chair. Mayo Asscn.; mem. Board of Govs. Mayo Clinic; Editor *Post-Graduate Medicine;* mem. Editorial Boards *The American Surgeon, Surgery, Diseases of the Colon and Rectum;* mem. Advisory Council, Student American Medical Asscn., American Board of Surgery (Founder's Group); Trustee, Carleton Coll. Northfield, Minnesota 40-; Chair. Board of Regents, Univ. of Minnesota 61-; awards include Commdr. Order of the Crown (Italy), Order of Merit (Chile).
Publs. include: *Surgery of the Small and Large Intestine* 55.
Home: Mayowood, Rochester; Office: Mayo Clinic, Rochester, Minnesota, U.S.A.

Mayobre, José A., LL.D.; Venezuelan economist and diplomatist; b. 21 Aug. 1913; ed. Central Univ., Caracas, London School of Economics.
Chief, Dept. of Economic Research, Central Bank of Venezuela; Alternate Gov. for Venezuela, Int. Monetary Fund; Asst. Dir. Mexican Bureau, E.C.L.A.; Resident Rep. of TAB in Central America; Dir. Venezuelan Development Corpn.; Prof. of Economic Analysis 46-60; Minister of Finance 58-61; Ambassador to U.S.A., concurrently Rep. to OAS 60-62; Commr. for Industrial Development, UN Dept. of Econ. and Social Affairs 62-63; Exec. Sec. UN Economic Comm. for Latin America (ECLA) 63-67; Minister of Mines and Petroleum, Venezuela 67-; Rep. Sec.-Gen. of UN in Dominican Republic 65.
Publs. *The Parity of the Bolívar, Philosophy and Economic Science, The Economic Situation of Venezuela;* numerous UN publications.
Ministry of Mines and Petroleum, Caracas, Venezuela.

Maytag, Lewis B., Jr.; American airline executive; b. 1926; ed. Colorado College.
President and Dir. Nat. Airlines, Inc.; Dir. Maytag Co.
Office: P.O. Box 2055 AMF, Miami 59; Home: 3029 Brickell Street, Miami 36, Florida, U.S.A.

Mazar, Benjamin, D.PHIL.; Russian-born Israeli archaeologist; b. 28 June 1906; ed. Berlin and Giessen Univs.
Settled in Palestine 29; joined staff of Hebrew Univ. Jerusalem 43, Prof. of Biblical History and Archaeology of Palestine 51-, Rector 52-61, Pres. 53-61; Chair. Israel Exploration Soc.; Dir. excavations Ramat Rahel 32, Beth Shearim 36-40, 56, Beth Yerah 42-43, Tell

Qasile 48-50, 59, Ein Gedi 60, 62, 64, 65, Old City of Jerusalem 68; Hon. mem. British Soc. for Old Testament Study, American Soc. of Biblical Literature and Exegesis; mem. Admin. Council, Int. Asscn. of Univs.; Hon. D.H.L. Hebrew Union Coll. (Jewish Inst. of Religion, U.S.A.), Jewish Theological Seminary of America.
Publs. *Untersuchungen zur alten Geschichte Syriens und Palästinas* 30, *History of Archæological Research in Palestine* 36, *History of Palestine from the early days to the Israelite Kingdom* 38, *Beth Shearim Excavations 1936-40* 40 (2nd edn. 58), *Historical Atlas of Palestine: Israel in Biblical Times* 41, *Excavations at Tell Qasile* 51; Chair. Editorial Board *Encyclopaedia Biblica* 50, *Ein Jedi* 64, *The World History of the Jewish People* Vol. II 67.
Hebrew University of Jerusalem, Jerusalem; 9 Abarbanelst, Jerusalem, Israel.
Telephone: 39857.

Mazio, Aldo Maria; Italian diplomatist; b. 07; ed. Università degli Studi, Rome, and Yale Univ.
Research fellow, Yale Univ. 29-30, Asst. Prof. 30-31; joined Italian Foreign Service 32, early service Cairo, Ottawa, Washington, and Holy See; Consul-Gen., New York 49-52; Asst. Perm. Sec. Ministry of Foreign Affairs 52-55; Minister Dublin 55-58; Ambassador to Tunisia 58-62; Ambassador to the Netherlands 63-65; Ambassador to Belgium 65-.
Embassy of Italy, 43 Avenue Legrand, Brussels, Belgium.
Telephone: 48-78-78.

Maziol, Jacques; French lawyer and politician; b. 13 Jan. 1918.
Court of Appeal, Toulouse; Dep. 58-; Vice-Pres. Union pour la Nouvelle République 59, mem. Cen. Cttee.; Municipal Councillor, Toulouse 59; Gen. Councillor, Canton of Toulouse-Sud 59; Minister of Housing 62-66; Dir.-Gen. Radio Monte Carlo 66; Croix de Guerre (39-45).
21 boulevard Carnot, Toulouse, Haute-Garonne, France.

Mazovka, Vladimir Filippovich; Soviet politician; b. 1913; ed. Novocherkassk Polytechnical Inst.
Member C.P.S.U. 43-; teacher, chief of technical school Rostov 44-52; Second then First Sec. Andreyevsky District Cttee. of C.P. 52-54; Head of Section, Rostov City Cttee. of C.P. 54-61; Sec. Rostov City Cttee. of C.P. 61-63; First Sec. Rostov City Cttee. of C.P. 64-66; Chair. Exec. Cttee. Rostov Regional Soviet of Workers' Deputies 66-; Deputy to R.S.F.S.R. Supreme Soviet.
Rostov Regional Soviet of Workers' Deputies, Rostov-on-Don, U.S.S.R.

Mazoyer, Henri François, L. en D.; French diplomatist; b. 16 May 1906.
Director of Office, French High Comm. in Cameroon 47-49; Civil Controller and Chief of Staff and Information, Morocco 50-51; Chief of Office, Sec. of State for War 52-54; Counsellor for Foreign Affairs 57; Consul Gen. Léopoldville 57-60; Ambassador to Republic of Togo 60-64, to Repub. of Bulgaria 64-67; Officier, Légion d'Honneur.
c/o Ministry of Foreign Affairs, Paris, France.

Mazurov, Kiril Trofimovich; Soviet politician; b. 14; ed. Gomel Highway Technicum and Higher Party School.
Technician, road and bridge-building 33-36; served Soviet Army 36-39; engaged in Communist Youth League activities Gomel and Brest Oblasts 39-40; mem. C.P.S.U. 40-; served Army 41; resistance work 42; Sec. Byelorussian Communist Youth League 42-47; 1st Sec. Minsk City Party Cen. Cttee. 49-50, Regional Cttee. 50-53; Chair. Byelorussian Council of Ministers 53-56; First Sec. Byelorussian C.P. 56-65; First Deputy Chair.

U.S.S.R. Council of Ministers 65-; Candidate mem. Presidium of Cen. Cttee. of C.P.S.U., mem. 65-66, mem. Politburo 66-.
U.S.S.R. Council of Ministers, The Kremlin, Moscow, U.S.S.R.

Mbeka, Joseph, LIC. EN SC.ECON.; Congolese politician and diplomatist; b. 12 May 1932; ed. Univ. Lovanium de Kinshasa and Inst. National des Statistiques et Etudes Economiques, Paris.
Inspector of Econ. Affairs in Belgian Administration, Congo (Kinshasa); Chief of Cabinet at Ministry for the Plan and Econ. Co-ordination in first Congolese Govt. June-Sept. 60; Gen. Commr. for Plan and of Econ. Affairs 60-61; Sec.-Gen. at Ministry of Finance Feb.-July 61; Perm. Rep. of Congo to European Economic Community (EEC) 61-65; Dir. of Cabinet of President of Congo Dec. 65-66; Ambassador to France July 66-; Chief of Congolese Del. to UN 62; Leader, Del. of Congolese Experts at Congolese-Belgium financial settlement talks; Ordre National du Léopard.
Embassy of the Democratic Republic of the Congo, 20 rue Greuze, Paris 16e, France.

Mbekeani, Nyemba Wales; Malawi diplomatist; b. 15 June 1929; ed. Henry Henderson Inst. and London School of Economics.
Chief Clerk, Municipality of Blantyre and Limbe 45-58; Company Exec. 60-61; Asst. Town Clerk, Blantyre 63; High Commr. of Malawi in U.K. 64-67; Perm. Rep. to UN 67-.
Permanent Mission of Malawi to UN, 777 Third Avenue, New York, N.Y. 10017, U.S.A.

Mboya, Thomas Joseph (Tom); Kenyan politician; b. 15 Aug. 1930; ed. Roman Catholic School in Kenya, Ruskin Coll., Oxford.
Former Sanitary Health Inspector; fmr. Sec. Kenya Local Govt. Workers' Union; Gen. Sec. Kenya Fed. of Labour 53-62; Elected mem. Kenya Legislative Council 57; Sec. Gen. Kenya African Nat. Union (KANU) May 60-; Minister of Labour 62-63, of Justice and Constitutional Affairs 63-64, of Econ. Development and Planning 64-.
Publ. *Freedom and After* 63.
Ministry of Economic Development and Planning, Nairobi, Kenya, East Africa.

Mbu, Matthew Taiwo, LL.B., LL.M.; Nigerian politician and diplomatist; b. 20 Nov. 1927; ed. Univ. Coll. and Middle Temple, London.
Central Minister of Labour 54-55; Acting Fed. Minister of Trade and Industry 55; Fellow of Royal Economic Society 55; Fellow of Royal Society of Arts 58; Commr. for Nigeria in the U.K. 55-58; Chief Representative U.S.A. 59; Vice-Pres. Inter-Parliamentary Union 61-65; led Nigerian Del. to 18-Nation Conf. on Disarmament 62; Minister of State (Defence) 60-65; Chair. Eastern Nigeria Public Service Comm. 66-67; Commr. for Foreign Affairs, Biafra 67.
Foreign Affairs Commission, Enugu, Biafra.

Mead, Sir Cecil, Kt.; British business executive; b. 24 Dec. 1900.
With Guest, Keen & Nettlefolds Ltd. before First World War; R.N.V.R. in First World War; after First World War joined Technical Service org. of British Tabulating Machine Co. Ltd. (now Int. Computers and Tabulators Ltd.), later District Man., Birmingham, then Asst. Sales Man., Sales Man. 39, and Dir. Hollerith Machines (South Africa) (Pty.) Ltd. (now Int. Computers and Tabulators S.A. (Pty.) Ltd.) 39; Deputy Man. Dir. British Tabulating Machine Co. Ltd. 49-55, Man. Dir. 55-59; Man. Dir. Int. Computers and Tabulators Ltd. (merger of British Tabulating Machine Co. and Powers-Samas Accounting Machines Ltd.) 59-64, Deputy Chair. 60-65, Chair. and Chief Exec. 65-67; Chair. British Inst. of Management 63-64; Dir. Int.

Tutor Machines; Gov. Ashridge Management Coll.; mem. Council Foundation for Management Educ.
International Computers and Tabulators Ltd., I.C.T. House, London, S.W.15, England.

Mead, Margaret, M.A., PH.D., D.SC., LL.D.; American anthropologist; b. 16 Dec. 1901; ed. Barnard Coll. and Columbia Univ.
National Research Council Fellow (Study of Adolescent Girl in Samoa) 25-26; Asst. Curator of Ethnology, American Museum of Natural History 26-42; Assoc. Curator of Ethnology, American Museum of Natural History 42-67; Social Science Research Fellow (Study of Young Children in Admiralty Islands) 28-29; expeditions to New Guinea 31-33, to Bali 36-38, to Admiralty Islands 53, 64, 65, Bali 57-58; Visiting Lecturer in Child Study, Vassar Coll. 40-41; Exec. Sec. Cttee. on Food Habits, Nat. Research Council 42-45; Dir. Columbia Univ. Research in Contemporary Cultures 48-50; adjunct Prof. Columbia Univ. 54-; Visiting Prof. Univ. of Cincinnati 57-, Menninger Foundation 59-; Pres. World Fed. for Mental Health 56-57; Pres. Amer. Anthrop. Asscn. 60, Curator of Ethnology, American Museum of Natural History 64-69; Consultant, Div. Social Sciences, Fordham Univ. 68-69, Chair.-designate Social Sciences Div. and Prof. of Anthropology 69-.
Publs. *Coming of Age in Samoa* 28, *Growing Up in New Guinea* 30, *The Changing Culture of an Indian Tribe* 32, *Sex and Temperament in three Primitive Societies* 35, *Balinese Character: A Photographic Analysis* (with Gregory Bateson) 42, *And Keep Your Powder Dry* 42, *Male and Female* 49, *Soviet Attitudes towards Authority* 51, *Growth and Culture* (with Frances Cooke Macgregor) 51, *The Study of Culture at a distance* (ed. with Rhoda Metraux) 53, *Primitive Heritage* (ed. with Nicolas Calas) 53, *Themes in French Culture* (with Rhoda Metraux) 54, *Childhood in Contemporary Cultures* (ed. with Martha Wolfenstein) 55, *New Lives for Old* 56, *An Anthropologist at Work: The Writings of Ruth Benedict* 59, *People and Places* 59, *Continuities in Cultural Evolution* 64, *Family* (with Ken Heyman) 65, *Anthropologists and What They Do* 65, *American Women* (ed. with Frances B. Kaplan) 65.
American Museum of Natural History, Central Park West, at 79th Street, New York, N.Y. 10024; Home: 211 Central Park West, New York, N.Y. 10024, U.S.A.

Meade, James Edward, C.B., F.B.A., M.A.; British economist; b. 23 June 1907; ed. Malvern Coll., Oriel Coll., Oxford, and Trinity Coll., Cambridge.
Fellow and Lecturer in Economics, Hertford Coll., Oxford 30-37, Bursar 34-37; mem. Financial Section and Economic Intelligence Service, L.N.; Editor L.N. *World Economic Survey* 38-40; mem. Economic Section Cabinet Office 40-45, Dir. 46-47; Prof. of Commerce with special reference to Int. Trade, London School of Economics 47-57; Prof. of Political Economy, Univ. of Cambridge 57-; Visiting Prof. of Economics and Finance in Australian Nat. Univ. 56; Pres. Section F of British Asscn. for the Advancement of Science 57; Chair. Econ. Survey Mission to Mauritius 60, Pres. Royal Econ. Soc. 64-66.
Publs. *Public Works in their International Aspect* 33, *The Rate of Interest in a Progressive State* 33, *Economic Analysis and Policy* 36, *Consumers' Credits and Unemployment* 37, *The Economic Basis of a Durable Peace* 40, *Planning and the Price Mechanism* 48, *The Theory of International Economic Policy*, Vol. I 51, Vol. II 55, *A Geometry of International Trade* 52, *Problems of Economic Union* 53, *The Theory of Customs Unions* 55, *The Control of Inflation* 58, *A Neo-Classical Theory of Economic Growth* 61, *Efficiency, Equality, and the Ownership of Property* 64, *The Stationary Economy* 65.
Low Brooms, Little Shelford, Cambridge, England.

Meadows, Bernard William; British sculptor; b. 19 Feb. 1915; ed. City of Norwich School, Norwich School of Art and Royal Coll. of Art.
Exhibited Venice Biennale 52, 64, British Council Exhbns., N. and S. America, Germany, Canada, New Zealand, Australia, Scandinavia, Finland and France; open-air exhbns. of Sculpture, Battersea Park, London 52, 60, 63, 66, Holland Park 57, Antwerp 53, 59, Arnhem 58, British Pavilion, Brussels 58, São Paulo Bienal 58, Carnegie Int., Pittsburgh 59-61; one man exhibitions London and New York 57-; works in Tate Gallery, Victoria and Albert Museum and collections in Europe, America and Australia; Prof. of Sculpture, Royal Coll. of Art, London 60-.
34 Belsize Grove, London, N.W.3, England.
Telephone: 01-722-0772.

Meagher, Blanche Margaret, B.A., M.A.; Canadian diplomatist; b. 27 Jan. 1911; ed. St. Patrick's High School, Mount St. Vincent Coll., and Dalhousie Univ., Halifax, Nova Scotia.
Teacher, Halifax Public Schools 32-42; Dept. of External Affairs 42-, served Ottawa, Mexico, London, Tel Aviv, Vienna; Ambassador to Israel 58-61, concurrently High Commr. in Cyprus 61; Ambassador to Austria 62-66; Gov. from Canada, Int. Atomic Energy Agency 62-66; Chair. Board of Govs., Int. Atomic Energy Agency Sept. 64-65; High Commr. to Kenya Feb. 67-, to Uganda April 67-.
Office of the High Commissioner for Canada, P.O.B. 30481, Nairobi, Kenya.
Telephone: 27426.

Meany, George; American trade unionist; b. 16 Aug. 1894.
Plumber's apprentice 10, journeyman plumber 15; business rep. Plumbers' Local Union 463 N.Y.C. 22-34; Pres. N.Y. State Fed. of Labor 34-39; Sec.-Treas. American Fed. of Labor 40-52, Pres. 52-55; Pres. American Fed. of Labor and Congress of Industrial Organisations (AFL-CIO) (combined org.) 55-; Vice-Pres. and mem. Exec. Board I.C.F.T.U.; mem. Nat. Defense Mediation Board 41-42; War Labor Board 42-45, U.S. Del. UN 57, 59; Hon. Dr. Iur. (Seton Hall, Long Island Univ., Univ. of Pennsylvania, DePaul Univ., St. John's Univ., Boston Coll., Univ. of Mass., Fordham Univ., Catholic Univ., Georgetown Univ., Iona Coll.); Laetare Medallist 55; Americanism Gold Medal VFW 49; Presidential Medal of Freedom Award 64; Grand Official of Order of Merit of the Republic of Italy, and other honours; Democrat.
Home: 8819 Burdette Road, Bethesda, Md.; Office: AFL-CIO Building, Washington, D.C. 20006, U.S.A.

Meatchi, Antoine Idrissou; Togolese politician; b. 25; ed. Ecole Normale Fredéric Assomption, Karibougou (Mali), Ecoles Régionales d'Agriculture d'Ondes, and Montargis (France), Ecole Nationale d'Agriculture, Grigon, Ecole Supérieure d'Application d'Agriculture Tropicale, Nogent.
Deputy Chief of the Agricultural Service of Togo 53, Chief, Agricultural District of Klouto and Dir. Coll. Farm, Tové 53-55; mem. Council of Government 55; Minister of Agriculture 57-58; Minister of Finance, first Govt. of M. Gruniszky; Deputy 58, Pres. Union Démocratique des Populations Togolaises (U.D.P.T.) 58-63; Minister of Public Works, Posts and Telecommunications 63; Minister of Finance, Economy and the Plan 63-66; Vice-Pres. of the Republic of Togo 63-66; numerous decorations including Grand Officier Légion d'Honneur.
c/o Ministry of Finance, Lomé, Togo.

Méautis, Georges, PH.D.; Swiss Hellenist; b. 24 Oct. 1890; ed. Lausanne, Neuchâtel, Munich, and Paris Univs.
Lecturer 19 and Prof. of Greek Languages and Literature, Neuchâtel Univ. 20-61, Rector 39-41.

Publs. *Hermoupolis-la-Grande* 18, *Recherches sur le Pythagorisme* 22, *Aspects ignorés de la religion grecque* 25, *Aristocratie athénienne* 26, *Bronzes Antiques du Canton de Neuchâtel* 28, *L'âme hellénique d'après les vases grecs* 32, *The Eleusinian Mysteries* 32, *Maternité* 32, *Plutarque: Des délais de la justice divine* 35, *Eschyle et la Trilogie* 36, *Le Livre de la Sagesse pythagoricienne* 38, *Les chefs-d'oeuvre de la peinture grecque* 39, *Thucydide et l'Impérialisme athénien* 39, *Nicolas de Flue* 40, *L'Oedipe à Colone et le culte des héros* 40, *Pélerinages en Grèce* 41, *Philippe Etter: Sens et mission de la Suisse* 42, *Mythes inconnus de la Grèce antique* 44, *Dante, l'Anté-purgatoire* 44, *Tu l'emportes, Galiléen!* (novel) 47, *Platon vivant* 50, *L'Eternel Coriolan* 52, *Le crépuscule d'Athènes et Ménandre* 54, *Contes Neuchâtelois* 56, *Sophocle* 57, *Les pélerinages de l'âme* 59, *Les dieux de la Grèce et les Mystères d'Eleusis* 59, *Mythologie grecque* 59, *Philoctète* (translation of play by Sophocles) *L'authenticité et la date du Prométhée enchaîné d'Eschyle* 60, *Pindare le dorien* 62, *Thucydide et l'Impérialisme athénien* 64.
40 Crêt Taconnet, Neuchâtel, Switzerland.
Telephone: 53619.

Mechem, Edwin Leard, LL.B.; American lawyer and politician; b. 2 July 1912; ed. Univ. of Arkansas.
Land Surveyor, U.S. Reclamation Service, Las Cruces, N.M. 32-35; Agent, F.B.I., Tex., Ark. and Calif. 42-45; admitted to N.M. Bar 39, private law practice 39-50, 55-56, 58-61; Gov. of New Mexico 51-54, 57-58, 61-62; U.S. Senator from New Mexico 63-64; Republican.
Santa Fé, New Mexico, U.S.A.

Medaris, Major-Gen. John; American army officer; b. 12 May 1902; ed. Ohio State Univ.
U.S. Marine Corps in First World War 18-19; army service 21-27; management and business in S. America and U.S.A. 28-39; recalled to U.S. Army 39; served in France, Germany and Central Europe; Chief U.S. Army Mission to Argentina 48-52; Commdg. Gen., Army Ballistic Missile Agency, Redstone Arsenal 56-58; Commdg. Gen., U.S. Army Ordnance Missile Command 58-60; Pres. Lionel Corpn. 60-62, Vice-Chair. 62-63; Chair. Board Electronic Teaching Labs., Washington 60-61; Chair. Exec. Cttee. All-State Devt. Corpn., Miami 62-63; Pres. Medaris Management Inc.; Chair. Radio Free Europe; Board of Dirs. Pan American Mutual Funds; D.S.M., Soldiers Medal, Legion of Merit (Oak Leaf Cluster), Croix de Guerre with Palm.
Publ. *Count Down for Decision* 60.
Office: P.O.B. 10, Winter Park, Florida; Home: 910 S. Trotters Drive, Maitland, Florida 32751, U.S.A.

Medawar, Sir Peter Brian, Kt., C.B.E., M.A., D.SC., F.R.S.; British biological scientist; b. 28 Feb. 1915; ed. Marlborough Coll. and Magdalen Coll., Oxford.
Lecturer in Zoology, Oxford Univ. 38-47; Mason Prof. of Zoology, Birmingham Univ. 47-51; Jodrell Prof. of Zoology, Univ. Coll., London Univ. 51-62; Dir. Nat. Inst. for Medical Research 62-; Hon. Foreign Assoc. Nat. Acad. of Sciences, U.S.A., American Philosophical Soc., American Acad. Arts and Sciences; Royal Medallist, Royal Soc. 59, Nobel Prize in Medicine and Physiology 60.
Publs. *The Uniqueness of the Individual* 58, *The Future of Man* 60, *The Art of the Soluble* 67, scientific papers on growth, ageing, wound healing and transplantation.
Mount Vernon House, Holly Hill, London N.W.3, England.
Telephone: 01-435-0822.

Medi, Enrico, PH.D.; Italian physicist; b. 26 April 1911.
Former Titular Prof. of Experimental Physics, Univ. of Palermo; Titular Prof. of Geophysics Ateneo Romano 58; Dir. Nat. Inst. of Geophysics; mem. Constituent

Assembly and First Republican Legislature; fmr. Vice-Pres. Euratom Comm.
Istituto Nazionale di Geofisica, Città Universitaria, Rome, Italy.

Medici, Giuseppe; Italian agricultural economist and politician; b. 24 Oct. 1907; ed. Univs. of Milan and Bologna.
Prof. of Agricultural Economics, Univ. of Perugia 35, of Turin 36-47; Pres. Istituto Nazionale di Economia Agraria, Rome 47-62; mem. Italian dels. to ECA international confs.; Pres. Ente Maremma (Land Reform Agency) 51-53; Prof. Univ. of Naples 52, Univ. of Rome 60; mem. of the Senate (Christian Democrat); Minister of Agriculture 54-55, of the Treasury 56-June 58, of the Budget July 58-Jan. 59, of Education Feb. 59-July 60; Minister without Portfolio (with responsibilities for Administrative Reform) 62-63, Minister of the Budget June-Nov. 63, Minister of Industry and Commerce Dec. 63-March 65; Gov. European Investment Bank 58; Pres. Senate Comm. for Foreign Affairs 60-62.
Publs. include *Principii di Estimo* 48 (abridged edn. in English *Principles of Appraisal* 53); *Italy: Agricultural Aspects* 49, *I Tipi d'Impresa dell'Agricoltura* 51, *Agricoltura e Disoccupazione* Vol. I 52, *Land Property and Land Tenure in Italy* 52, *Lezioni di Politica Economica* 67.
The Senate, Rome, Italy.

Medvedev, Sergey Sergeyevich; Soviet chemist; b. 91; ed. Moscow Univ.
Karpov Physicochemical Inst. 22-; Instructor, later Prof., Moscow Inst. of Fine Chemical Technology 39-; Hon. Scientific and Technical Worker of R.S.F.S.R. 43-; Corresp. mem. U.S.S.R. Acad. of Sciences 43-58, acting mem. 58, now Academician and Head Laboratory of Polymerisation Processes, Karpov Physicochemical Inst., and Prof. of Polymer Synthesis, Inst. of Fine Chemical Technology; State Prize 46, Order of Lenin; Order of Red Banner of Labour (twice).
Publs. Papers on the polymerisation process.
Karpov Physicochemical Institute, Ul. Obucha 10, Moscow, U.S.S.R.

Meek, Theophile James, B.A., B.D., PH.D., D.D., F.R.S.C.; Canadian Semitic scholar; b. 81; ed. Univ. of Toronto, McCormick Theological Seminary, Marburg, Berlin and Chicago Univs., American School of Oriental Research, Jerusalem.
Prof. of Biblical History and Literature Millikin Univ. 09-18; Prof. of Old Testament and History of Religions Meadville Theological School 18-22; Prof. of Semitic Languages and History of Religions, Bryn Mawr Coll. 22-23; Prof. of Oriental Languages Univ. of Toronto 23-52, Prof. Emeritus 52-; Pres. American Oriental Society 42-43, and Society of Biblical Literature 43-44; Exec. Cttee. of the Humanities Research Council of Canada 43-48; hon. mem. Nat. Asscn. of Authors and Journalists; Assoc. Ed. *American Journal of Semitic Languages* 31-41; Hon. D.D. (Queen's Univ.).
Publs. *Cuneiform Bilingual Hymns, Prayers and Penitential Psalms* 12, *The Song of Songs: an American Translation* 27, *Old Akkadian, Sumerian and Cappadocian Texts from Nuzi* 35, *Hebrew Origins* (3rd edn. 60), *The Bible: An American Translation* (co-author) 31, (revising Editor 35-), *The Haverford Symposium on Archæology and the Bible* (co-author) 38, *Ancient Near Eastern Texts* (co-author) (2nd edn. 55), *Introduction and Exegesis of the Song of Songs,* and *Introduction and Exegesis of Lamentations,* Vols. V and VI, in *The Interpreter's Bible* 56; contributions in *The Encyclopædia Britannica, Encyclopædia Canadiana, Encyclopædia Americana, Twentieth Century Encyclopædia, The Ancient Near East* (co-author) 58.
52 Elgin Avenue, Toronto 5, Ont., Canada.

Meerbeke, René Louis Joseph Marie van; Belgian diplomatist; b. 95; ed. Univ. of Ghent.
Served Peru 21; Chargé d'Affaires Colombia 24, Envoy Extraordinary 45; Ambassador to Brazil 54-57, to U.K. 58-60; Grand Officier Ordre de la Couronne and Léopold II, Croix de Guerre 14-18 avec palmes, Officier Ordre de Léopold, Belgian and foreign decorations.
22 rue des Trevires, Brussels 4, Belgium.

Meester, Eibert; Netherlands politician; b. 19; ed. Technical Evening School.
Draughtsman and Asst. Managing Dir. Electrical Apparatus Works 35-43; Resistance Movement, Second World War; Second Sec. and District Official, Labour Party 46; Gen. Sec. Youth Section, Labour Party, Co-founder and Sec. Politieke Jongeren Contact-raad 46-52; Sec. Zuid-Holland District, Labour Party 52-59; Nat. Sec. and Treas., Labour Party 58-; M.P. 63-.
Tesselschadestraat 31, Amsterdam-West, Netherlands.

Mehdi, H.H. Prince Moulay Hassan Ben El; Moroccan diplomatist; b. 11.
Caliph Northern Zone of Morocco 25; Ambassador to Great Britain 57-64, to Italy 64-67; decorations include Ouissam Alaoui, Charles I Medal, Great Military Ouissam, Great Medal of Portugal, Great Dominican Medal, Great Naval Medal, Great Mahdaoui Medal, Great Houssni Medal.
Rabat, Morocco.

Mehnert, Klaus, PH.D.; German professor and journalist; b. 10 Oct. 1906; ed. Univs. of Tübingen, Munich, Berlin and California (Berkeley).
Secretary German Academic Exchange Service, Berlin 29-31, German Soc. for Study of Eastern Europe (also Editor *Osteuropa*) 31-33; newspaper corresp. in Moscow 34-36; Visiting Prof. Univ. of Calif. 36-37; Asst. Prof. of Modern History and Political Science, Univ. of Hawaii 37-41; Prof. German Medical Acad. and St. John's Univ.; Editor *The XXth Century,* Shanghai 41-45; in charge of Russian section, German Office for Peace Questions, Stuttgart 47-48; Editor-in-Chief *Christ und Welt* 49-54, *Osteuropa, Osteuropa-Recht, Osteuropa-Wirtschaft, Osteuropa-Naturwissenschaft* 51-; Radio and TV Commentator 50-; Prof. of Political Science, Aachen Inst. of Technology 61-; mem. Deutsche Akademie für Wissenschaft und Literatur, Mainz; Grand Cross of the Order of Merit.
Publs. *Youth in Soviet Russia* 32, *The Russians in Hawaii 1804-19* 39, *Stalin versus Marx* 51, *Asien, Moskau und Wir* 56, *Soviet Man and His World* 60, *Peking and Moscow* 63, *Mao's Zweite Revolution* 66, *Der Deutsche Standort* 67.
Templergraben 64, Aachen, German Federal Republic.
Telephone: 4222118.

Mehta, Asoka, B.A.; Indian politician; b. 24 Oct. 1911; ed. Wilson Coll., Bombay, and Bombay Univ. School of Economics.
Founder-mem. of former Socialist Party; imprisoned five times; Editor of official organ of former Socialist party 35-39; mem. Nat. Exec. of Socialist Party for 25 years; fmr. Chair. Praja Socialist Party; mem. Lok Sabha 54-57, 58-61, 67-; Deputy Chair. Indian Planning Comm. 63-66; Minister of Planning 66-67, of Petroleum, Chemicals and Social Welfare 67-.
Publs. *The Communal Triangle in India, Who Owns India, Political Mind of India, Democratic Socialism, Politics of Planned Economy, Socialism and Peasantry, Indian Shipping and The Plan: Perspective and Problems.*
5 Dadysett Road, Bombay, India.
Telephone: 35-77-36.

Mehta, Sir Chunilal B., Kt.; Indian industrialist; b. Jan. 1888.
Man. Dir. of several Joint Stock Companies; Pres. Indian Merchants' Chamber 40; Pres. Federation of

Indian Chambers of Commerce and Industry 41-42; Vice-Pres. Indian Central Cotton Cttee.; Editor *Financial News*, Bombay and *Indian Cotton Review*; Sheriff of Bombay 35-36.
Office: 43 Mahatma Gandhi Road, Bombay 1; Home: 52 Ridge Road, Malabar Hill, Bombay 6, India.
Telephone: 252933, 254857 (Office); 364783, 364922 (Home).

Mehta, Gaganvihari Lallubhai, M.A.; Indian diplomatist; b. 15 April 1900; ed. Univ. of Bombay and London School of Economics.
Asst. Editor, *Bombay Chronicle* 23-25; Man. Scindia Steam Navigation Co., Calcutta 28-47; Pres. Indian Chamber of Commerce 39-40, Fed. of Indian Chambers of Commerce and Industry 42-43; Commr. for Port of Calcutta 30-34, 40-42 and 46-47; mem. Inland Transport Cttee. of I.L.O. 47; mem. Constituent Assembly of India 47; Pres. Indian Tariff Board 47-50; mem. Planning Comm. 50-52; Chair. Import Control Enquiry Cttee. 50, Nuffield Foundation, Indian Advisory Cttee. 50-52, Tariff Comm. Jan.-Aug. 52; Indian Ambassador to U.S.A. and Mexico 52-58, and to Cuba 56-58; Chair. Hindustan Shipyard Ltd. 58-62, National Shipping Board 59-63, Indian Investment Centre, Industrial Credit Investment Corpn. of India Ltd.; mem. Air India 65-67, Indian Airlines Corpn. 65-67; Chair. Capital Issues Control Advisory Cttee.; Exec. Pres. Indo-American Soc.; Chair. Indian Inst. Technology 65-; Dir. of Board of Lube India Pvt. Ltd. 66-; Trustee of the *Statesman* 63-; Trustee of the Homi Bhabha Fellowship Council 66-; Hon. LL.D. (Rollins Coll. Florida, Simpson Coll. Iowa, Rhode Island); Hon. Fellow London School of Econs. 58; Padma Vibhushan 59.
Publs. *From Wrong Angles, Perversities, Conscience of a Nation, Understanding India.*
c/o The Industrial Credit and Investment Corporation of India Limited, ICICI Building, Third Road, 163 Backbay Reclamation, Bombay, India.
Telephone: 245081.

Mehta, Hansa; Indian educationist and social reformer; b. 3 July 1897; ed. Baroda Coll. and Bombay Univ.
President Gujerat Women's Co-operative Society, Bombay 28-48, The Bhagini Samej, Bombay 44-45; mem. Bombay Legislative Council 37-39, 41-52; Vice-Chancellor Indian Women's Univ. 46-48; Pres. All Indian Women's Conf. 45-46; Vice-Chair. Human Rights Comm., UN 50-52; mem. Constituent Assembly 47-50; Vice-Chancellor, Maharaja Sayajirao Univ. of Baroda 49-58; mem. Gen. Advisory Board of Education, Govt. of India; mem. Exec. Board UNESCO 58-60; Padma Bhushan 59; Hon. LL.D. (Leeds 64), Hon. D.Litt. (Allahabad 58, Baroda 59).
Publs. (Gujerati) *Balwartavali* 26, *Kishorvatavali* 28, *Tran Natako* 28, *Rukmini* 32, *Bavalana Parakrano* 34, *Golibarni Musafri* 34, *Arun nu Adbhut Swapnu* 34, *Himalaya Swarup ne Bija Natako* 41, Gujerati trans. *Hamlet* and *Merchant of Venice* 42, 44; (English) *Women under the Hindu Law of Marriage and Succession* 44, *Tract on Post-War Educational Reconstruction* 45, *Civil Liberties* 45, *Adventures of King Vikram* 48.
c/o Bank of Baroda, Bombay, India.

Mehta, Jivraj Narayan, L.M.S., F.C.P.S. (Bombay), M.D., M.R.C.P. (London); Indian politician, physician and diplomatist; b. 29 Aug. 1887; ed. Amreli High School, Grant Medical Coll., Bombay and The London Hospital, London.
Chief Medical Officer State of Baroda 23-25; Dean, Seth G.S. Medical Coll. and K.E.M. Hospital 25-42; Pres. India Medical Conf. 30-44, 47; Imprisoned for activities in "Quit India" Movement 32-34, 42-44; mem. Board of Scientific and Industrial Research India 44-63; Sec. and Dir.-Gen. Health Services Govt. of India 47-48; Dewan State of Baroda 48-49; Minister for Public Works, Govt.

of Bombay 49-51, Minister for Finance 52-60; Pres. Indian Conf. of Social Work 50, 52-54; mem. Atomic Research Cttee. 51-60; Vice-Chair. Gandhi Memorial Leprosy Foundation 52-; mem. Governing Body All India Inst. of Medical Sciences 57-63; Chair. Exec. Council Central Drug Research Inst., Lucknow 48-60; Chief Minister Gujerat 60-63; Indian High Commr. in U.K. 63-66.
Publs. *Presence of Glycogen in Suprarenal Bodies, The Height, Weight & Chest measurements enquiry relating to some School Children in Bombay.*
c/o Bank of Baroda Ltd., Bombay, India.

Mehta, Kanhaiya Lal, B.A.; Indian barrister and diplomatist; b. March 1913; ed. Maharana's Coll., Udaipur, Government Coll., Ajmer, and London School of Economics.
Called to Bar, Lincoln's Inn, London; Indian Civil Service 37-50; Chief Sec. Himachel Pradesh 52-53; Officer on Special Duty, Ministry of External Affairs 53-54; Adviser to Gov. of Assam, N.E. Frontier Agency, Shillong 54-59; Joint Sec. Ministry of External Affairs 59-62; Ambassador to Turkey 63-66.
c/o Ministry of Foreign Affairs, New Delhi, India.

Mehta, Mohan Sinha, M.A., LL.B., PH.D.; Indian diplomatist and educationist; b. 20 April 1895; ed. Agra Coll., Ewing Christian Coll., Univ. School of Law, Allahabad, and London School of Economics and Political Science.
Lecturer in Economics Agra Coll. 18-19, Government Coll., Ajmer 19-20; official in Mewar State Service 22-37; Dewan Banswara State 37-40; Revenue and Education Minister, Mewar State 41, Minister for Supplies 42-44; Chief Minister, Banswara State 44-47; Finance Minister, Mewar State 47-49; Indian Ambassador to the Netherlands 49-51; High Commissioner in Pakistan 51-55; Ambassador to Switzerland 55-58; mem. Indian Del. to UN Gen. Assembly 59; Vice-Chancellor, Rajasthan Univ. 60-66; Founder Pres. Vidya Bhawan Soc.; Pres. Indian Adult Educ. Asscn.; Pres. Seva Mandir Trust, Udaipur.
Publ. *Lord Hastings and the Indian States.*
Seva Mandir Vidya Bhawan, Udaipur (Rajasthan), India.

Mehta, Zubin (son of violinist Mehli Mehta); Indian conductor; b. 1936; ed. Vienna Acad. of Music.
First professional conducting in Belgium and Yugoslavia; Chief Conductor of Montreal Symphony and Los Angeles Philharmonic Orchestra; conductor at festivals of Holland, Prague, Vienna, Salzburg and Spoleto; debut at La Scala Milan 66; conducts regularly with the Vienna, Berlin and Israel Philharmonic Orchestras; winner of Liverpool Int. Conductors' Competition 58.
Office: 135 N. Grand, Los Angeles, Calif.; Home: 701 Stone Canyon Road, West Los Angeles, Calif., U.S.A.

Mei Yi; Chinese journalist and literary translator; b. 10.
During the civil war engaged on underground work for the C.C.P. in and around Shanghai; Dir. Broadcasting Admin. Bureau 52-; mem. Council of People's Asscn. for Cultural Relations with Foreign Countries 54; Vice-Pres. All-China Journalists' Asscn. 54-.
Publs. Many translations of Soviet literature, including Ostrovski's *How the Steel was Tempered.*
Broadcasting Administrative Bureau, Outside Fu Hsing Men, Peking, China.

Mein, John Gordon; American diplomatist; b. 10 Sept. 1913; ed. Georgetown Coll., Georgetown, Kentucky, George Washington Univ., Washington, D.C., American Univ., Washington, D.C., and National War Coll.
Department of State 41-42, 44-47, Rio de Janeiro 42-44; Second Sec., Rome 47-50; First Sec., Oslo 50-53; Counsellor, Djakarta 54-56; Dir. of Office of Southwest

Pacific Affairs, Dept. of State 57-60; Minister-Counsellor, Manila 60-62, Rio de Janeiro 63-65; Ambassador to Guatemala 65-; Meritorious Service Award, Dept. of State 59; Hon. LL.D. (Georgetown Coll.) 66.
American Embassy, 20 Calle 4-30, Zona 10, Guatemala City, Guatemala.

Meir, Golda; Israeli politician; b. Kiev 3 May 1898; ed. Teachers' Seminary, Milwaukee, U.S.A.
Teacher and leading mem. Zionist Labour Party, Milwaukee; Del. U.S. section World Jewish Congress until 21; immigrated Palestine 21; joined Merhavia collective farm village; with Solel Boneh, Histadruth Contracting and Public Works Enterprise 24-26; Sec. Women's Labour Council of Histadruth 28; mem. Exec. and Secretariat Fed. of Labour 29-46; Chair. Board of Dirs., Workers' Sick Fund 36; Head Political Dept., Fed. of Labour; Mapai Del., Actions Cttee., World Zionist Organisation; mem. War Economic Advisory Council of Palestine Govt. 39; Head Political Dept., Jewish Agency for Palestine, Jerusalem 46-48; Israel Minister to U.S.S.R. Aug. 48-April 49; Minister of Labour and Social Insurance 49-56; Minister of Foreign Affairs June 56-Jan. 66; Sec.-Gen. Mapai Feb. 66-.
8 Habaron Hirsch Street, Ramat Aviv, Israel.

Meissner, Wilhelm; German diplomatist; b. 1 April 1899.
Former mem. Sozialdemokratische Partei Deutschlands, later mem. Sozialistische Einheitspartei Deutschlands (S.E.D.); fmr. Personal adviser to Otto Grotewohl; later Ministry of External Affairs; Ambassador to Hungary 61-; Vaterländischer Verdienstorden in Bronze.
Embassy of the D.D.R., Benczur utja 31, Budapest, Hungary.

Meitus, Yuli Sergeyevich; Soviet composer; b. 1903; ed. Kharkov Inst. of Music and Drama.
Member Board, U.S.S.R. Composers' Union; Honoured Worker of the Arts of the Turkmen S.S.R. 44, and of the Ukrainian S.S.R. 48; State Prize 51, Order of Red Banner of Labour 60.
Principal compositions: First Symphonic Suite, on Ukrainian Themes 28, Second Symphonic Suite, *Dneprostroi* 28, Third Symphonic Suite, on the Liberation of West Ukraine 39, Fourth Symphonic Suite, for 25th Anniversary of October Revolution 42, Fifth Symphonic Suite, on Ukrainian Themes 44; Operas: *Perekop* 38, *Haidamaki* 41, *Abadan* 42, *Leili and Mezhnun* 45, *Young Guards* 46, *Dawn Over the River Dvina* 54, *Stolen Happiness* 57; other symphonic and choral works.
Composers' Union of the Ukraine, 3 Ulitsa Chekistov, Kiev, U.S.S.R.

Mejía-Palacio, Jorge; Colombian financial officer; b. 12; ed. Universidad del Cauca, Colombia.
Director La Patria, Manizales 41-46; mem. Municipal Council, Manizales 41-45; Dep. to Ass., Dept. of Caldas 43-45; Colombian Chargé d'Affaires, Sweden 47-48, Minister Counsellor, Colombian Embassy, Wash. 48-52; Rep. at Interamerican Economic and Social Council 49-52, Pres. 51; Exec. Dir. Banco Francés e Italiano of Latin America, Bogotá 53-54; Exec. Dir. La Nacional Insurance Co., Bogotá 53-54; Exec. Dir. for Brazil, Philippines, Colombia, Ecuador and Dominican Republic of Int. Bank for Reconstruction and Development 54-, Dir. Int. Finance Corpn. 56-, Dir. Int. Development Asscn. 60-; Minister of Finance, Colombia 62-63; Dir. Cen. Bank of Colombia 62-, Nat. Coffee Fed. of Colombia 62; del. to several Int. Confs.
Central Bank of Colombia, Apdo. 402, Bogotá, Colombia.

Melas, George; Greek diplomatist and politician; b. 1894; ed. Athens Univ. and Ecole des Sciences Politiques, Paris.

Attaché, Ministry of Foreign Affairs 15-21; First Sec., London 22-27; mem. Greek Del. to League of Nations 28-31; Dir. of Political Affairs, Ministry of Foreign Affairs 29-35; Liberal Deputy 36; Under-Sec. for Foreign Affairs and Minister of Foreign Affairs 45; Minister without Portfolio 47, of Justice 48-50, of Nat. Economy 48-49; Ambassador to U.S.A. 54-58, concurrently accred. to Cuba 55-58, to Haiti, Dominican Republic and Mexico 56-58; Centre Union Deputy 64-; Minister of Commerce 64-65, of Foreign Affairs July-Sept. 65; Minister without Portfolio and Commerce Sept. 65; Minister of Finance Oct. 65-67.
c/o Ministry of Finance, Athens, Greece.

Melchett, 3rd Baron, cr. 1928, of Landford; **Julian Edward Alfred Mond,** Bart.; British steel executive; b. 9 Jan. 1925; ed. Eton Coll.
Air Branch, R.N.V.R., Second World War; Dir. Guardian Assurance Co. Ltd., British Field Products Ltd.; Chair. Organising Cttee. for Nat. Steel Corpn. 66-April 67; Chair. Nat. (now British) Steel Corpn. April 67-.
16 Tite Street, London, S.W.3, England.

Melchior, Lauritz; American (b. Danish) opera singer; b. 20 March 1890; ed. Melchiors School, Copenhagen, and Royal Opera School, Copenhagen.
Début as baritone, Copenhagen 13, as tenor 18; appeared at Wagner Festival, Bayreuth, Covent Garden, London, Metropolitan Opera, New York, Berlin Opera, Hamburg Opera, Vienna, Paris, Barcelona, Buenos Aires, San Francisco, Chicago; numerous decorations.
136-71 Mulholland Drive, Beverly Hills, California, U.S.A.

Melchior, Mogens Gustav Ivar; Danish diplomatist; b. 14 July 1904; ed. Gl. Hellerup Gymnasium and Univ. of Copenhagen.
Foreign Service 30-; in Netherlands, China, Belgium, Switzerland, Finland, U.S.S.R., Norway, New Zealand and Ministry of Foreign Affairs, Copenhagen; Deputy Under-Sec. of State (Dir.-Gen. of Political Affairs) 57; Ambassador to Turkey 59-60, to Yugoslavia 60-; Commdr. Order of Dannebrog with Cross of Honour; Medal for Merit and foreign decorations.
Royal Danish Embassy, Užička 48, Belgrade, Yugoslavia.

Melentiev, Lev Alexandrovich; Soviet energy specialist; b. 1908; ed. Leningrad Polytechnical Inst.
Engineer, Leningrad Power System 29-33; Chief Designing Bureau, Leningrad Energy Cttee. 33-35; Senior Lecturer, Prof. Leningrad Engineering-Econ. Inst. 36-42; Senior Scientific Worker, U.S.S.R. Acad. of Sciences Inst. of Energy 42-60; Dept. Chief, Prof. Leningrad Engineering-Econ. Inst. 45-60; Pres. Board U.S.S.R. Acad. of Sciences Eastern Siberian Branch 60-65; Dir. U.S.S.R. Acad. of Sciences Siberian Dept. Inst. of Energetics 60-; mem. C.P.S.U. 47-; Corresp. mem. U.S.S.R. Acad. of Sciences 60-66, mem. 66-.
Publs. Works on general problems of energy development, energy systems and industrial heating.
U.S.S.R. Academy of Sciences, 14 Lenin Prospekt, Moscow, U.S.S.R.

Melikishvili, Georgy Alexandrovich; Soviet (Georgian) historian; b. 30 Dec. 1918; ed. Tbilisi Univ.
Works deal with the ancient history of the Near East and Transcaucasia; Prof. Tbilisi Univ.; Dir. of Historical Inst. of Georgian Acad. of Sciences; mem. Acad. of Sciences of Georgian S.S.R. 60-; Lenin Prize 57.
Publs. *Nairi-Urartu* 54, *Urartian Inscriptions in Cuneiform Characters* 60, *History of Ancient Georgia* 59.
Academy of Sciences, Tbilisi, Georgian S.S.R., U.S.S.R.

Melkumyan, Gurgen Allakhverdovich; Soviet politician; b. 1915; ed. C.P.S.U. Higher Party School.
Member C.P.S.U. 39-; Teacher and Journalist 35-39; Soviet Army service 39-45; Party Official in Azerbaijan

49-61; Second Sec., Nagorno-Karabakh Regional Cttee., C.P. of Azerbaijan 61-62, First Sec. 62-; mem. Central Cttee., C.P. of Azerbaijan; Deputy to U.S.S.R. Supreme Soviet.
Nagorno-Karabakh Regional Committee, Communist Party of Azerbaijan, Stepanakert, U.S.S.R.

Melkumyan, Suren Avvakovich; Soviet politician; b. 1908; ed. Transcaucasian Inst. of Railway Engineers. In charge of construction, chemical factory in Kirovokan 35-38, Dir. 38-48; mem. C.P.S.U. 41-; Head of Dept. Central Cttee. of the Communist Party of Armenia 48-54; Perm. Rep. of the Armenian S.S.R. Council of Ministers to the U.S.S.R. Council of Ministers 54-.
Permanent Representation of the Armenian S.S.R. Council of Ministers to the U.S.S.R. Council of Ministers, Armyansky pereulok 2, Moscow, U.S.S.R.

Mell, Max, PH.D.; Austrian dramatist and poet; b. 10 Nov. 1882.
Mem. Acads. of Poetry Mainz, Darmstadt, Munich, Berlin, Rumän. Akad. Gesellschaft; awarded Preis der Stadt Wien 24 and 27, Grillparzer Prize 29 and 40; Mozart Prize 37; Rosegger Prize 51; Österreichischer Staatspreis 54; mem. Öst. Kunstsenat, Öst. Kurie für Kunst; hon. mem. Austrian Acad. of Sciences 56.
Works include: *Gedichte* 19, *Das Apostelspiel* 23, *Das Schutzengelspiel* 23, *Das Nachfolge-Christi-Spiel* 27, *Gedichte* 29, *Die Sieben gegen Theben* 31, *Das Spiel von den deutschen Ahnen* 35, *Das Donauweibchen* 37, *Steirischer Lobgesang* 39, *Der Nibelunge Not* 43, *Gabe und Dank* 49, *Gedichte* 52, *Verheissungen* 54, *Die Osterfeier* 54, *Aufblick zum Genius* 56, *Jeanne d'Arc* 56, *Gesammelte Werke*, four vols. 62, *Paracelsus und der Lorbeer* 64.
Auhofstrasse 244, Vienna XIII, Austria.

Mellanby, Kenneth, C.B.E., B.A., PH.D., SC.D.; British entomologist and research worker; b. 26 March 1908; ed. Barnard Castle School, King's Coll., Cambridge, and London Univ.
Research work London School of Hygiene and Tropical Medicine 30-36, Wandsworth Fellowship 34; Sorby Research Fellow of the Royal Soc. 36; Univ. Lecturer Sheffield 36; Army Service (Major, R.A.M.C.) 42-45; Dep. Field Dir. M.R.C. Scrub Typhus Comm. in S.E. Asia; Univ. Reader in Medical Entomology, London School of Hygiene and Tropical Medicine 45-47; research worker 53-55; Principal Univ. Coll. Ibadan, Nigeria 47-53; Head of Dept. of Entomology, Rothamsted Experimental Station 55-61; Dir. Monks Wood Experimental Station, Huntingdon 61-; Hon. D.Sc. (Univ. Ibadan).
Publs. *Scabies* 43, *Human Guinea Pigs* 45, *The Birth of Nigeria's University* 58, *Pesticides and Pollutions* (New Naturalist) 67.
Barnes House, St. Ives, Hunts., England.
Telephone: St. Ives (Hunts.) 3413.

Mellink, Machteld Johanna, PH.D.; Netherlands archaeologist; b. 26 Oct. 1917; ed. Amsterdam and Utrecht Univs.
Field Asst. Tarsus excavations 47-49; Asst. Prof. of Classical Archaeology Bryn Mawr Coll. 49-53, Assoc. Prof., Chair. Dept. of Classical and Near Eastern Archaeology 53-62, Prof. 62-; staff mem. Gordion excavations organised by Pennsylvania Univ. Museum 50-, during which the putative tomb of King Midas was discovered 57; field dir. excavations at Karataş-Semayük in Lycia 63-.
Publs. *Hyakinthos* 43, *A Hittite Cemetery at Gordion* 56; *Archaeology in Asia Minor* (reports in *American Journal of Archaeology*) 55-; Editor *Dark Ages and Nomads* 64.
Bryn Mawr College, Bryn Mawr, Pa. 19010, U.S.A.
Telephone: 215-LA5-1000.

Mellish, Rt. Hon. Robert Joseph, P.C., M.P.; British politician; b. 3 March 1913; ed. elementary schools.
Army Service 39-45; Labour M.P. Rotherhithe Div. of Bermondsey 46-50; Parl. Private Sec. and Financial Sec. to Admiralty 46-49; M.P. for Bermondsey 50-; Parl. Private Sec. to Minister of Supply 50-51, to Minister of Pensions 51; Joint Parl. Sec. Minister of Housing and Local Govt. Oct. 64-Aug. 67; Minister of Public Building and Works Aug. 67-; Knight Commdr. of St. Gregory.
House of Commons, London, S.W.1; Ministry of Public Building and Works, Lambeth Bridge House, London, S.E.1, England.
Telephone: 01-930-6240, Extn. 213 (House of Commons); 01-735-7611, Extn. 1734 (Office).

Mellon, Paul, B.A., M.A.; American executive; b. 11 June 1907; ed. Choate School, Yale Univ. and Cambridge Univ.
Governor, T. Mellon and Sons, Pittsburgh; Pres. and Trustee Nat. Gallery of Art, Washington, Trustee Virginia Museum of Fine Arts, Richmond; Chair. of Board and Trustee, Bollingen Foundation and Old Dominion Foundation N.Y.C., A. W. Mellon Education and Charitable Trust, Pittsburgh; Trustee Avalon Foundation, N.Y.C.; Dir. Mellon Nat. Bank and Trust Co., Pittsburgh.
c/o Old Dominion Foundation, 1729 H Street, Washington, D.C., U.S.A.

Mellon, Richard King; American businessman; b. 19 June 1899; ed. Princeton Univ.
Messenger Mellon Nat. Bank 20, Asst. Cashier 24-28, Vice-Pres. 28-34, Pres. 34-46; Chair. of Board Mellon Nat. Bank and Trustee Co. 46-66, Hon. Chair. 67-; Gov. and Pres. T. Mellon & Sons; Dir. Aluminum Co. of America, Gen. Motors Corpn., Gulf Oil Corpn., Pennsylvania Co., Pa. R. R. Co.; Hon. LL.D., S.P.D., D.C.S., E.D.; decorated D.S.M.; Trustee American Museum of Natural History, Carnegie Inst., Carnegie Inst. of Technology, Mellon Inst. of Industrial Research, Univ. of Pittsburgh.
Home: Huntland Downs, Ligonier, Pa.; Office: Mellon Square, Pittsburgh, Pa., U.S.A.

Mellor, Sir John Serocold Paget, Bart.; British business executive; b. 6 July 1893; ed. Eton and New Coll., Oxford.
Barrister, Inner Temple; Army Service, First World War; Conservative M.P. 35-55; fmr. Deputy Chair. Prudential Assurance Co., Ltd., Chair. 65-; Dir. City of London Real Property Co. Ltd., London County Freehold and Leasehold Properties Ltd., City and Int. Trust Ltd., C.L.R.P. Investment Trust Ltd.
Binley House, nr. Andover, Hants., England.

Melnik, Ivan Alexandrovich; Soviet diplomatist; b. 1914; ed. C.P.S.U. High School.
Diplomatic Service 53-; Deputy Head 4th European Dept. 53-54; Counsellor, Soviet Embassy, Warsaw 54-56; Minister to Luxembourg 56-61; Counsellor 1st African Dept. 62; Ambassador to Mali 62-66; staff of Ministry of Foreign Affairs 66-.
Ministry of Foreign Affairs, 32-34 Smolenskaya-Sennaya ploshchad, Moscow, U.S.S.R.

Melnikov, Ivan Ivanovich; Soviet trade union official; b. 17 Dec. 1914; ed. forestry technical school.
Forestry worker, becoming Dir. of Forestry 43-45; mem. Communist Party of Soviet Union 41-; Sec. Central Cttee. Trade Union of Agricultural Workers and State Purchases 62-; Cand. mem. All-Union Council of Trade Unions.
Central Committee Trade Union of Agricultural Workers, 42 Leninsky Prospekt, Moscow, U.S.S.R.

Melnikov, Nikolai Ivanovich; Soviet foreign trade official; b. 1909; ed. Moscow Inst. of Mechanical Engineering.

Member C.P.S.U. 31-; Official, *Amtorg* Soviet Purchasing Comm. in U.S.A. 40-47; Chair. *Tekhnopromimport* Trust 47-50; Chief, Dept. of Reparations in German Democratic Republic 50-53; Chair. *Tekhnoexport* Trust 53-62; Official, State Planning Cttee. in German Democratic Republic 62-64; Chair *Prommashimport* Trust 64-; Order of Lenin. Order of Red Banner of Labour, Order of Red Star, Badge of Honour (twice). *Prommashimport* Trust, 32-34 Smolenskaya-Sennaya ploshchad, Moscow, U.S.S.R.

Melnikov, Nikolai Vasilievich; Soviet scientist; b. 1909; ed. Sverdlovsk Mining Inst.
Engineer and Administrator in mining and coal industries 34-45; Deputy Minister of Coal Industry in East Areas of U.S.S.R. 44-48; mem. U.S.S.R. Council of Ministers Bureau for Fuel and Coal Industries 44-54; Deputy Dir. Inst. of Mining U.S.S.R. Acad. of Sciences 55-60, Dir. 60-61; Corresp. mem. Acad. of Sciences of the U.S.S.R. 53-62, mem. 62-; Chair. State Cttee. for Fuel Industry, U.S.S.R. Gosplan 61-65; Head Laboratory of Open-Cast Mining, A. A. Skochinsky U.S.S.R. Acad. of Sciences 65-; Chair. of Council for Physical and Engineering Problems of Exploitation of Mineral Resources, U.S.S.R. Acad. of Sciences; joint State prizewinner for fundamental improvement in open-cast coalmining 46.
Publs. *Open-Cast Mineral Mining* 48, *Drilling Wells and Blast Holes at Open-Cast Workings* 53, *Mechanization of Works in Open-Cast Mining* 54, *Development of Science in the Field of Open-Cast Mining in the U.S.S.R.* 57, 61, *Reference Book for Engineers and Technicians on Open-Cast Mining Works* 50-62, *Fundamentals of Line Technology in Open-Cast Mining* 62, etc.
A. A. Skochinsky Mining Institute, U.S.S.R. Academy of Sciences, 4 Luybertsy, Moscow Region, U.S.S.R.

Melville, Sir Eugene, K.C.M.G.; British diplomatist; b. 15 Dec. 1911; ed. Queen's Park School, Glasgow, and St. Andrews Univ.
Colonial Office 36; Colonies Supply Mission, Washington 41-45; Private Sec. to Sec. of State for Colonies 45-46; Financial Adviser, Control Comm. for Germany 49-52; Asst. Under-Sec. of State, Colonial Office 52-61; Asst. Under-Sec. of State, Foreign Office 61-62; Minister (Econ.), British Embassy, Bonn 62-65; Perm. U.K. Del. to Council of European Free Trade Asscn. (EFTA) and to Gen. Agreement on Tariffs and Trade (GATT) 65-; Head of U.K. Mission to Office of UN and other Int. Orgs. in Geneva 65-.
Walford Cottage, High Street, Aldeburgh, Suffolk; Office: c/o Diplomatic Service Administrative Office, King Charles Street, London, S.W.1, England.

Melville, Sir Harry (Work), K.C.B., PH.D., D.SC., LL.D., F.R.I.C., F.R.S.; British chemist; b. 27 April 1908; ed. George Heriot's School, Edinburgh, Edinburgh Univ. and Trinity Coll., Cambridge.
Fellow Trinity Coll., Cambridge 33-43; Asst. Dir. Colloid Science Laboratory, Cambridge Univ. 38-40; Prof. of Chemistry, Aberdeen Univ. 40-48; Scientific Adviser to Chief Superintendent Chemical Defence, Min. of Supply 40-43; Superintendent Radar Research Station 43-45; Mason Prof. and Dir. of Chemistry Dept., Birmingham Univ. 48-56; mem. Advisory Council for Scientific and Industrial Research 46-51; mem. Scientific Advisory Council, Ministry of Supply 49-51, 53-56; Advisory Council on Scientific Research and Development 53-56; mem. Scientific Advisory Council, British Electricity Authority 49-56; mem. Scientific Advisory Council, Ministry of Power 54-60; mem. Advisory Council on Research and Development, Ministry of Power 60-; Sec. Dept. of Scientific and Industrial Research 56-65; Chair. Science Research Council 65-67; Principal Queen Mary Coll., London 67-.
Publ. *Experimental Methods in Gas Reactions* 38.

Norwood, Dodds Lane, Chalfont St. Giles, Bucks.; Office: Queen Mary College, Mile End Road, London, E.1, England.
Telephone: Chalfont St. Giles 2222.

Melville, Sir Leslie Galfreid, K.B.E., B.EC., F.I.A.; Australian economist; b. 26 March 1902; ed. Church of England Grammar School, Sydney, and St. Paul's Coll., Univ. of Sydney.
Public Actuary of South Australia 24-28; Prof. of Economics, Univ. of Adelaide 29-31; mem. of Cttees. on S. Australian Finances 27-30; mem. of Cttees. on Australian Finances and Unemployment 31 and 32; Financial Adviser to Australian Dels. at Imperial Economic Conf. 32, and to Australian Del. at World Economic Conf. 33; mem. Australian Financial and Economic Advisory Cttee. 39; Chair. Australian Del. to UN Monetary Conf., Bretton Woods 44; mem. Advisory Council of Commonwealth Bank 45-50; Chair. UN Sub-Comm. on Employment and Econ. Stability 47-50; Asst. Gov. (Central Banking) Commonwealth Bank of Australia; Exec. Dir. Int. Monetary Fund and Int. Bank for Reconstruction and Devt. Nov. 50-53; Vice-Chancellor, Australian Nat. Univ. Canberra 53-60; mem. Board, Reserve Bank 59-63, 65-; Chair. Commonwealth Grants Comm. 65-; Chair. Tariff Board 60-63; Devt. Advisory Service, Int. Bank for Reconstruction and Devt. 63-65.
71 Stonehaven Crescent, Canberra, Australia.
Telephone: 811838.

Memmi, Albert; Tunisian writer; b. 15 Dec. 1920; ed. Lycée Carnot, Tunis, Univ. of Algiers and Univ. de Paris à la Sorbonne.
Teacher of Philosophy in Tunis 55; Dir. Psychological Centre, Tunis 56; Researcher, Centre national de la recherche scientifique, Paris 59-; Asst. Prof. Ecole pratique des hautes études 59-66, Prof. 66-; Commdr. Ordre de Nichan Iftikhar.
Publs. include: *The Pillar of Salt* 53, *Strangers* 55, *Anthologie des écrivains nord-africains* 55, *Colonizer, Colonized* 57, *Portrait of a Jew* 62, *Le français et le racisme* 65, *The Liberation of the Jew* 66.
5 rue Saint Merri, Paris 4e, France.
Telephone: 887-02-63.

Mende, Erich, DR. IUR.; German politician; b. 28 Oct. 1916; ed. Gross-Strehlitz Coll. and Univs. of Cologne and Bonn.
Army service 36-45; studied law, Univs. of Cologne and Bonn 45-48, studied political science, Univ. of Cologne 48-49; co-founder of the Free Democratic Party F.D.P.), British Occupied Zone 45, mem. Exec. Cttee. Fed. Org. of F.D.P. 49-; mem. Bundestag 49-; Whip, Parl. Group of F.D.P. and mem. Exec. Cttee. 50-53; Deputy Chair. Parl. Group of F.D.P. 53-57, Chair. 57-63; Chair. F.D.P. 60-68; Chair. Investors Overseas Services in Deutschland G.m.b.H. 68-; Minister for All-German Affairs and Deputy Chancellor 63-Oct. 66; Knight of the Iron Cross.
Bundeshaus, Bonn, German Federal Republic.

Mendels, Morton M., M.A., B.C.L.; Canadian lawyer and administrator; b. 1 March 1908; ed. McGill Univ., Montreal.
Entered law practice 32 serving as legal Counsel to the Canadian Inst. of Plumbing and Heating and as Consultant Economist; served with Canadian Army 40-45 with final rank of Lt.-Col., Chief of Army Estimates, Finance, and Parl. liaison, Canadian Gen. Staff; Secretary International Bank 46-.
International Bank for Reconstruction and Development, 1818 H Street, N.W., Washington, D.C., U.S.A.

Mendes, Murilo; Brazilian poet; b. 01; ed. Rio de Janeiro; studied music, art and literature.
Civil servant; journalist; part of "Mouvement Moderniste" 22-; Prof. of Brazilian Literature, Rome Univ. 57-; Graça Aranha Prize (Brazil) 31; mem. Int. Asscn. of

Art Critics, European Soc. of Culture, European Community of Writers.

Publs. *Poemas* 30, *Tempo e Eternidade* 35, *A Poesia em Panico* 38, *O Visionário* 41, *As Metamorfoses* 44, *Mundo Enigma* 45, *O Discipulo de Emaús* 44, *Poesia Liberdade* 47, *Contemplação de Ouro Preto* 54, *Poesias Completas* 59, *Tempo Espanhol* 59, *Siciliana* 59, *Janela do Caos* 61, *Poesie* 61.

Via del Consolato 6, Rome, Italy.

Mendès-France, Pierre, LL.D.; French lawyer, economist and politician; b. 11 Jan. 1907.
Deputy 32-40, 45-58, 67-68; Professor Ecole Nationale d'Administration; Under-Sec. for the Treasury 38; tried by Vichy administration 40; escaped to serve with Fighting French Air Force; Finance Minister French Provisional Govt. 43-44; Head French Financial Missions Washington and Bretton Woods 44; Min. of Nat. Economy 44-45; Prime Minister and Minister of Foreign Affairs June 54-Feb. 55; Minister of State without Portfolio Feb.-May 56; Officier de la Légion d'Honneur, Croix de Guerre, Rosette de la Résistance, Médaille des Evadés, Grand Officier de l'Ordre de Léopold (Belgium); Parti Socialiste Unifié.
Publs. *L'oeuvre financière du gouvernement Poincaré, Histoire de la Stabilisation du Franc* 28, *Liberté, Liberté Chérie* 43, *Roissy en France* 49, *La Science Economique et l'Action* 54, *Gouverner c'est Choisir* 53, *7 mois et 7 jours* 55, *La Politique et la Vérité* 58, *Rencontres* 58 (with A. Bevan and P. Nenni), *La République Moderne* 62 (Trans. into English).
25 rue du Louvre, Paris, France.

Méndez Montenegro, Dr. Julio Cesar; Guatemalan law professor and politician.
Former Law Professor; brother of late Dr. Mario Méndez Montenegro, candidate for Pres. 65; Pres. of Guatemala July 66-; Partido Revolucionario.
Office of the President, Guatemala City, Guatemala.

Mendoza, Eugenio; Venezuelan business executive; b. 13 Nov. 1907.
Began career as office boy in hardware store 24; Head, Eugenio Mendoza y Cía. Sucrs. C.A. (cement, paper and paint); Head Mendoza Foundation 55, Poliomyelitis Foundation (philanthropic orgs.).
Eugenio Mendoza y Cía. Sucrs. C.A., Avenida Sucre, Catia, Caracas; P.O.B. 332, Caracas, Venezuela.

Mendume, Mikhail Klayevich; Soviet politician; b. 1922; ed. C.P.S.U. Higher Party School.
Member C.P.S.U. 41 ; Young Communist League Official 41-53; Party and Local Govt. Official 53-62; Chair. Council of Ministers Tuva Autonomous S.S.R. 62-; Deputy to Supreme Soviet of the U.S.S.R.
Council of Ministers, Tuva Autonomous S.S.R., Kyzyl, U.S.S.R.

Menemencioğlu, Turgut; Turkish diplomatist; b. 14; ed. Robert Coll., Istanbul.
Turkish Ministry of Foreign Affairs 39-; Perm. Del., European Office UN, Geneva 50-52; Counsellor, Turkish Embassy, Washington 52; Dir. Gen. Econ. Affairs, Ministry of Foreign Affairs 52-54; Dep. Perm. Rep. to UN 54-60; Ambassador to Canada 60; Perm. Rep. to UN 60-62; Ambassador to U.S.A. 62-67; Sec.-Gen. of CENTO (Central Treaty Org.) 67-.
Central Treaty Organisation, Eski Meklis, Ankara, Turkey.

Menen, (Salvator) Aubrey Clarence; British author; b. 22 April 1912; ed. Univ. Coll., London.
Dramatic Critic *The Bookman* 34; Dir. The Experimental Theatre, London 35-36; Dir. Personalities Press Service, London 37-39; Script Editor, Information Films, Govt. of India 43-45; Educ. Officer, Backward Tribes, Political Dept. of Govt. of India 46; fmr. Chief of Motion Picture Dept., J. Walter Thompson (Eastern) Ltd.

Publs. *The Prevalence of Witches* 49, *The Stumbling Stone* 49, *The Backward Bride* 40, *The Duke of Gallodoro* 52, *Dead Man in the Silver Market* 53, *The Ramayana* 54, *The Abode of Love* 56, *The Fig Tree* 59, *Rome for Ourselves* 60, *Speaking the Language Like a Native* 62, *SheLa* 62, *A Conspiracy of Women* 65.
c/o Helen Strauss, William Morris Agency Inc., 1740 Broadway, New York, N.Y., U.S.A.

Menéndez Pidal, Ramón; Spanish philologist; b. 69; ed. Madrid and Toulouse Univs.
Prof. Madrid Univ. 99; Visiting Prof. Johns Hopkins Univ. 99, Buenos Aires Univ. 14, Columbia Univ. N.Y. 38; Prof. Romance Philology Madrid Univ. 99-39; Dir. Royal Spanish Acad. 26-39 and 48-, Vice-Pres. Bd. of Extension Studies 10-30, Dir. Centre of Historical Studies; Dr. h.c. Univs. Toulouse, Hamburg, Oxford, Tübingen, Paris, Louvain, Brussels, Amsterdam, Bonn, Santiago de Chile, Havana, Bucharest, Genoa, Zürich, Palermo, Lisbon, Rio de Janeiro; mem. Madrid Acad. of History, Inst. de France, Hispanic Soc.; corresp. mem. British Acad.; Fellow, Accademia Nazionale dei Lincei, Rome; founder *Revista de Filología española.*
Publs. *Leyenda de los Infantes de Lara* 96, *Manual de Gramática Histórica Española* 04, *Cantar del mío Cid* 08-11, *L'Epopée Castillane à travers la littérature espagnole* 10, *Poesía juglaresca y juglares* 24, *Orígenes del Español* 26, *La España del Cid* 29, *Historia y Epopeya* 34, *El Imperio Hispánico y los Cinco Reinos* 50, *Reliquias de la poesía épica española* 51, *Los españoles en la historia y en la literatura* 57, *La Chanson de Roland y el neotradicionalismo* 58, *El Padre Las Casas, su Doble Personalidad* 63, etc.
Royal Spanish Academy, Calle de Felipe IV 4, Madrid, Spain.

Menéndez Tolosa, Lt.-Gen. D. Camilo; Spanish army officer and politician; b. 8 Feb. 1899; ed. Infantry Acad., Toledo.
Colonel, Immemorial Infantry Regt. 40-48; Dir.-Gen. of Supplies 48-50; Mil. Gov. of Santander 50-53; Gen. in command of Infantry, 11th Div. 54; Commdr. 62nd Div. and Mil. Gov. of Navarra 54; Dir.-Gen. of Services, Ministry of Army 54-57; Mil. Gov., Campo de Gibraltar 57-60; Capt.-Gen., 8th Mil. Region 60-62; Chief of Mil. Household of Head of State 62-64; Minister of the Army 64-.
Ministry of the Army, Madrid, Spain.

Menge, Walter Otto; American insurance executive; b. 11 Sept. 1904; ed. Wayne Univ. and Univ. of Mich.
Actuary, Grange Life Insurance Co., Lansing, Mich. 26-28; Assoc. Prof. Mathematics, Univ. of Mich. 28-37; Assoc. Actuary, Lincoln Nat. Life Insurance Co., Fort Wayne, Ind. 37-43, 2nd Vice-Pres. 43-45, Vice-Pres. 45-51, First Vice-Pres. 51-54, Pres. 54-64, Chair. 64-; Chair. of Board Lincoln Nat. Life Ins. Co. of N.Y.; Pres. Reliance Life Insurance Co., Pittsburgh 51-53; Dir. of several other companies and official of various professional and civic orgs.
Home: 331 River Drive, Jupiter, Florida 33458; Office: Lincoln National Life Insurance Co., Fort Wayne, Ind. 46801, U.S.A.

Menges, Dietrich Wilhelm von, D.IUR.; German business executive; b. 26 Oct. 1909; ed. Wilhelm Gymnasium, Königsberg, and Georg-August-Universität zu Göttingen.
In Export Dept., Ferrostaal AG, Essen 38; mem. Management Board, Ferrostaal AG 47-49, Chair. of Management Board 49-66; mem. Management Board Gutehoffnungshütte Aktienverein 61-66, Chair. Management Board 66-; Chair. Management Board Gutehoffnungshütte Sterkrade AG 66-; Chair. and mem. numerous Advisory Boards.
Office: Gutehoffnungshütte, 4200 Oberhausen (Rheinl.); Home: 43 Essen-Bredeney, Am Wiesental 16, German Federal Republic.

Menghin, Oswald Franz Ambrosius, DR. PHIL.; Austrian university professor (retd.); b. 19 April 1888; ed. Univ. of Vienna.

Archives, Library and Museum of Lower Austria 10-18; Prof. of Prehistory, Univ. of Vienna 18-45; Resident Prof. Univ. of Cairo 30-33; Rector of Univ. of Vienna 35-36; Minister of Education 38; Prof. at Univ. of Buenos Aires 48; Hon. Prof. La Plata Univ. 60; Editor *Acta Praehistorica*.

Publs. *Urgeschichte der bildenden Kunst* (with M. Hoernes) 25, *Weltgeschichte der Steinzeit* 31, *The Excavations of the Egyptian University in the Neolithic Site at Maadi*, I and II (with Mustapha Amer) 32, 36, *Geist und Blut* 34, *Migrationes Mediterraneae* 48, *Fundamentos cronológicos de la prehistoria de Patagonia* 52, *Vorgeschichte Amerikas* 57, *Origen y desarrollo racial de la especie humana* 58, 2nd edn. 65, *Vorgeschichte der Kanuindianer des südlischsten Amerika* 60, *Estudios de Prehistoria Araucana* 62.

Moreno 350 (Museo Etnográfico), Buenos Aires; Home: Corrientes 673, Buenos Aires, Argentina.

Telephone: 33-7788 (Office); 792-5562 (Home).

Menichella, Donato; Italian banker; b. 96; ed. Inst. Cesare Alfieri, Florence (Dr. of Social Science).

Employee of Bank of Italy 22-23, Banca Italiana di Sconto 23-28; Dir. of National Credit Bank 29-30; Dir.-Gen. of the Inst. for Industrial Reconstruction 33-43, of the Bank of Italy 48-60, Hon. Gov. 60-; Pres. of the Italian Foreign Exchange 48-60; Dir. Bank for Int. Settlements; Gov. for Italy, Int. Bank for Reconstruction and Development 48-60, alternate Gov. 61-.

Office: c/o Bank of Italy, Via Nazionale 91, Rome; Home: Via Merulana 247, Rome, Italy.

Menk, Louis W.; American railroad executive; b. 8 April 1918; ed. S. Denver High School and Denver Univ.

Telegrapher, Union Pacific Railroad 37-40; St. Louis-San Francisco Railroad, Tulsa 40, rising to Gen. Man. 56-58, Vice-Pres. and Gen. Man. 58-60, Vice-Pres. (Operation) 60-62, Pres. 62-64, Chair. and Pres. 64-65; Dir. and Pres. Burlington Lines (Chicago, Burlington and Quincy Railroad Co., The Colorado and Southern Railway Co., and Fort Worth and Railway Co.) Oct. 65-, now Pres. Northern Pacific Railway Co.; Dir. Asscn. of American Railroads, Chicago, Burlington & Quincy R.R. Co., Colorado & Southern Ry. Co., Northern Pacific Transport Co., Cuyuna Realty Co., Monad Co., Asscn. of American Railroads, St. Paul Metropolitan Improvement Comm., Greater St. Paul United Fund, Saint Paul Area Chamber of Commerce, First Nat. Bank of Chicago, American Invest. Co., Servomation Corpn., First Trust Co. of St. Paul, Hunt Foods and Industries, Inc., Gen. Mills, Inc., Brown Shoe Co., Upper Midwest Research and Devt. Council.

Northern Pacific Railway Company, Northern Pacific Building, St. Paul, Minn. 55101; Home: 5904 South Robert Trail, R.R.10, South St. Paul, Minn. 55075, U.S.A.

Menne, Bernhard; German journalist; b. 3 Sept. 1901.

Chief Editor *Prager Mittag* 37-38; Chief Editor *Welt am Sonntag* 48-.

Publs. *Krupp, Deutschlands Kanonenhönige* 36, *German Industry on the Warpath* 42, *The Case of Dr. Bruening* 43, *Armistice and Germany's Food Supply* 44.

Kaiser-Wilhelm-Strasse 1, 2 Hamburg 36, German Federal Republic.

Telephone: 34-10-10.

Menne, (Wilhelm) Alexander; German company director; b. 20 June 1904; ed. Bismarck Realgymnasium, Dortmund.

Trained at Dortmund Bank and Berlin Unilever Organisation; Man. Dir. Glasso Paint Production, London,

until 39; Dir. Glasurit Werke A.G., Hamburg, Hiltrup, until 51; Dir. Farbwerke Hoechst A.G., Frankfurt/M. 52-; Pres. Asscn. of the Chemical Industry, Frankfurt/M. 48; Vice-Pres. Fed. of German Industry 49; mem. of Board Industriekreditbank, Düsseldorf, Deutsche Südamerika Bank, Hamburg, Süddeutsche Kalkstickstoffwerke Trostberg; Chair. German-American Trade Promotion Office, Cologne and New York; mem. Atomic Energy Comm. 56-; German Foreign Trade Council 53-; Chair. Atomic Cttee. of Fed. of German Industry 56-; Grand Cross Order of Merit with Star (German).

Farbwerke Hoechst A.G., Frankfurt M-Hoechst, German Federal Republic.

Menner, Vladimir Vasilievich; Soviet geologist and paleontologist; b. 1905; ed. Moscow State Univ.

At staff Moscow section Geological Cttee. 27-29; Asst. Prof. Moscow Mining Acad. 29-30; Lecturer, Moscow Geology Investigating Inst. 30-65; scientific research work Petroleum Prospecting Inst. 32-34; U.S.S.R. Acad. of Sciences Paleontological Inst. 35-36; Senior Scientific Worker, Dept. Chief, Asst. Dir. U.S.S.R. Acad. of Sciences Geological Inst. 34-; Corresp. mem. U.S.S.R. Acad. of Sciences 63-66, mem. 66-.

U.S.S.R. Academy of Sciences, 14 Lenin Prospekt, Moscow, U.S.S.R.

Mennin, Peter, M.MUS., PH.D.; American composer; b. 17 May 1923; ed. Eastman School of Music and Rochester Univ.

Mem. Composition Faculty, Juilliard School of Music, New York City 47; Dir. Peabody Conservatory of Music, Baltimore 58-; Pres. Juilliard School of Music 62-; Nat. Music Council, Naumberg Music Foundation; Officer of Nat. Inst. of Arts and Letters; Board of Dirs. A.S.C.A.P., American Music Center; works commissioned by Koussevitsky Foundation, Coolidge Foundation, Library of Congress, Juilliard Music Foundation, etc.; works have been performed throughout U.S.A., and in Europe, South America and the Far East; American Acad. of Arts and Letters Award, first George Gershwin Memorial Award, two Guggenheim Awards, Columbia Records Chamber Music Award, Naumburg American Music Recording Award, Bearns Prize (Columbia Univ.).

Compositions include: seven symphonies, cello concerto, piano concerto and other orchestral works, *Sonata Concertante* for violin and piano, and other chamber and piano works, choral music.

Juilliard School of Music, 120 Claremont Avenue, New York, N.Y. 10027, U.S.A.

Telephone: MO3-7200.

Menninger, Karl; American psychiatrist; b. 22 July 1893; ed. Univ. of Wisconsin and Harvard Univ. Medical School.

Chief of Staff, Menninger Clinic 25-, Dir. Dept. of Education, Menninger Foundation 46-62, Dean, Menninger School of Psychiatry 46-, Chair. Menninger Foundation 54-; Pres. American Psychoanalytic Asscn. 41-43; Chair. Cttee. on Reorganisation, American Psychiatric Asscn. 44-49; Dir., Nat. Citizens Comm. for Public Schools 53-55; mem. Editorial Board, *Journal of American Psychoanalytic Asscn.* 54-56; Vice Pres. American Soc. of Criminology 60-62; Consultant, Bureau of Prisons, Dept. of Justice 56-, Forbes Air Force Base 60-; Chair. Education Cttee., Topeka Inst. for Psychoanalysis 60-; Senior Consultant Topeka State Hospital, Topeka Veterans Admin. Hospital; Prof. Univ. of Health Sciences, Chicago Medical School; Consultant for Illinois State Psychiatric Inst.; mem. Chicago Council on Foreign Relations; Hon. D.Sc. Washburn Univ., Univ. of Wisconsin 65, Hon. L.H.D. Park Coll., Hon. LL.D. Jefferson Medical Coll., Parsons Coll., Kansas State Univ. and Saint Benedict's Coll., Baker Univ., Kansas.

Publs. *Man Against Himself* 38, *Love Against Hate* 42,

The Human Mind 45, *A Guide to Psychiatric Books* 56, *A Manual for Psychiatric Case Study* 62, *Theory of Psychoanalytic Technique* 58, *A Psychiatrist's World* 59, *The Vital Balance* 63.
The Menninger Foundation, Box 829, Topeka, Kansas, U.S.A.

Menon, K. P. S.; Indian diplomatist; b. 18 Oct. 1898; ed. Madras Christian Coll. and Oxford Univ.
Joined I.C.S. 21; Deputy Sec. to Govt. of India in Foreign and Political Dept.; Agent to Govt. of India in Ceylon 29-33; fmr. Minister of Bharatpur State; Agent-Gen. in China 43; Alternate Rep. U.N. Gen. Assembly, N.Y. 46; Ambassador to China 47-48; Chair. U.N. Temporary Comm. on Korea 47; Sec. Ministry of Foreign Affairs 48-52; Ambassador to U.S.S.R. 52-61. Publs. *The Flying Troika* 63, *Many Worlds* (autobiog.) 66.
Palat House, Ottapalam, Kerala State, India.

Menon, Krishna (*see* Krishna Menon).

Menon, Mrs. Lakshmi N., M.A., L.T., T.DIP., LL.B.; Indian politician; b. 99; ed. H.H. Maharaja's School and Coll. for Women, H.H. Maharaja's Arts Coll., Trivandrum, Lady Willingdon Training Coll., New Delhi, and Maria Grey Training Coll., London.
Lecturer, Queen Mary's Coll., Madras 22-25, Gokhale Girls Schools, Calcutta 28-30, Isabella Theburn Coll., Lucknow 30-33; Alt. Del. to UN Gen. Ass. 48, 50, 53, 54, to UN Comm. on Status of Women, Beirut 49; Chief, Section on Status of Women, Human Rights Div., UN Secr., Lake Success 49-50; Principal, Women's Training Coll., Patna 51-53; Rep. Cttee. on Information from Non-Self Governing Territories 53; Parl. Sec. to the Prime Minister 52-57; Dep. Minister of External Affairs 57-62; Minister of State, Ministry of External Affairs 62-66; State Commr. for Guides, Bihar 52-; Pres. All India Women's Conf. 55-59; Pres. Indian Fed. of Univ. Women 61-67; mem. Rajya Sabha 52-66.
Publ. *The Position of Women.*
Plain View, Trivandrum, India.

Menon, Nedyam Balachandra, B.A.; Indian diplomatist; b. 18 March 1921; ed. Allahabad Univ.
Indian Navy 43-46; Indian Embassy, The Hague 49; Indian Mil. Mission, Berlin 51; Indian Embassy, Katmandu 54; High Comm. of India, Ottawa 57; Indian Embassy, Washington 59; Ministry of External Affairs Dir. (China Div.) 61; Nat. Defence Coll. 64; Indian Embassy, Bangkok and Perm. Del. to ECAFE 65; Deputy High Commr., Kuala Lumpur 66; Political Officer for Sikkim and Bhutan 67-.
c/o Ministry of External Affairs, New Delhi, India.

Menon, Panampilli Govinda, M.A., B.L.; Indian lawyer and politician; b. 1 Oct. 1908; ed. St. Thomas Coll., Trichur, St. Joseph's Coll., Trichinopoly, and Law College, Madras.
Set up legal practice 32; joined trade union and Labour movement 34; elected to State Legis. Assembly 35, 38, 45, 48, 52; Prime Minister, Cochin State 46-47; Minister of Education and Finance, Travancore-Cochin 48-54; Chief Minister, Travancore-Cochin 55-56; mem. Constituent Assembly of India 47, elected to Indian Parl. 62, 67; Chair. Parl. Cttee. on Public Undertakings 64; Minister of Food 66; Minister of Law 67-.
Office of the Law Minister, Shastri Bhavan No. 1, Dr. Rajendra Prasad Road, New Delhi, India.

Menon, Parakat Achutha, B.A.; Indian diplomatist; b. 2 Jan. 1905; ed. Presidency Coll., Madras, and New Coll., Oxford.
Joined I.C.S. 29, and held various appointments under Provincial Govt. of Madras and Central Govt. of India, including Under-Sec., Public Works Dept., Govt. of Madras 34-37; Under-Sec., Home Dept., Govt. of India 38-41; Collector and District Magistrate, Guntur, Madras 41-43; Deputy Sec. and Sec., India Supply

Mission, Washington, D.C. 43-47; adviser, Indian Del. to UN, San Francisco 45, N.Y. 46; served on Far East Comm., Washington, D.C. 46; Del. UNRRA Conf., Atlantic City 46; Jt. Sec. Ministry of External Affairs, Govt. of India 47-49; Minister to Portugal 49-51; Ambassador to Belgium and concurrently Minister to Luxembourg 51-54; Ambassador to Thailand 54-56, High Commr. in Australia and New Zealand 56-59; Ambassador to Argentina 59-60, to German Fed. Republic 60-64; Dir. State Bank of India; Chair. Fertilisers and Chemicals Travancore Ltd., etc.
c/o Ministry of External Affairs, New Delhi; 4A Tank Bund Road, Madras 34, India.

Menon, Vatakke Kurupath Narayana, M.A., PH.D.; Indian radio official; b. 27 June 1911; ed. Univ. of Madras and Edinburgh Univ.
Script Writer, Producer and Adviser for E. Services of B.B.C. during Second World War; returned to India 47; Dir. of Broadcasting, Baroda State 47-48; joined All-India Radio as Dir. of Staff Training 48, became Dir. of Delhi, Madras and Calcutta Stations, Dir. of External Services and Deputy Dir.-Gen.; Sec. Nat. Acad. of Music, Dance and Drama, India 63-65; Dir.-Gen. All-India Radio 65-; Pres. Int. Music Council (UNESCO); mem. Faculty of Music, Delhi Univ.; mem. Advisory Board Nat. Centre for the Performing Arts, Bombay; Vice-Chair. Int. Inst. for Comparative Music Studies, Berlin.
Publs. *Development of William Butler Yeats* 42, 60, *Kerala, a Profile* 61, *Balasaraswathi* 63.
All-India Radio, Broadcasting House, New Delhi; Home: 58 Wellesley Road, New Delhi, India.
Telephone: 382327 (Office); 384609 (Home).

Menotti, Gian Carlo; Italian composer; b. 7 July 1911; ed. Curtis Inst. of Music.
Went to U.S.A. 28; mem. teaching staff Curtis Inst. of Music 41-55; Guggenheim Award 46, 47; Pulitzer Prize 50, 55; Hon. Assoc. Nat. Inst. of Arts and Letters 53; Pres. Festival of Two Worlds, Spoleto, Italy; Hon. B.M. (Curtis Inst. of Music).
Compositions include: Operas: *Amelia Goes to the Ball, The Old Maid and the Thief, The Island God, The Telephone, The Medium, The Consul, Amahl and the Night Visitors, The Labyrinth* (own libretti), *The Saint Bleecker Street* 54, *The Last Savage* 63, *Martin's Lie* 64, Ballet: *Sebastian*; Film: *The Medium* (producer); *Vanessa* (libretto) 58, *The Unicorn, The Gorgon and The Manticore—a Madrigal Fable, Maria Golovin* 59, *The Last Superman* 61, *The Death of a Bishop of Brindisi* (cantata) 63; chamber music, songs, etc.
Capricorn, Mt. Kisco, N.Y., U.S.A.

Menshikov, Mikhail Alexeyevich, D.ECON.; Soviet diplomatist; b. 02; ed. Plekhanov Inst., Moscow.
Dir. Arkos Ltd., London 30-36; Dir. *Exportkhleb* (govt. agency for grain trade, etc.) 36-38; Chair. *Exportles* (govt. agency for timber trade) 38-43; del. first UNRRA Conf. Atlantic City, U.S.A. 43, apptd. Deputy to Dir.-Gen.; mem. UNRRA Del. to Poland 45; Deputy Minister of Foreign Trade 46, First Deputy Minister 47, Minister 49-51; mem. Econ. Co-operation Cttee., U.S.S.R. Council of Ministers 52; Ambassador to India 53-57, to U.S.A. 57-62; Minister of Foreign Affairs, R.S.F.S.R. 62-; Candidate mem. Central Cttee. C.P.S.U. 56-.
Ministry of Foreign Affairs of R.S.F.S.R., 79 Prospekt Mira, Moscow, U.S.S.R.

Menuhin, Yehudi; American violinist; b. 22 April 1916; ed. privately in America and Europe.
Studied with Sigmund Anker, Louis Persinger, Georges Enesco (in Romania) and with Adolph Busch in Basle; New York debut 25, Paris 27 and Berlin 29 (with Bruno Walter and the Berlin Philharmonic); first world tour 35, in retirement 35-37. subsequently appeared as soloist in orchestras under Toscanini, Furtwängler, Stokowski, Koussevitsky, Beecham, Paul Paray,

Walter, Mitropoulos, etc., etc.; has undertaken much research and restoration of neglected compositions; gave numerous benefit concerts during and after World War II; since 45 has toured extensively all over the world and has made documentary musical films in Europe and America; yearly festival at Gstaad 57-, Bath 59-; records for His Master's Voice; Hon. D.Mus. (Oxford, Belfast, Leicester), Hon. LL.D. (St. Andrews, Liverpool); Legion of Honour, France, Order of Leopold, Order of Crown, Belgium, Order of Merit, Germany, Hon. K.B.E. (U.K.); Mozart Medal 65.
Alma, California, U.S.A.

Menzel, Donald H., PH.D.; American astronomer; b. 11 April 1901; ed. Univ. of Denver and Princeton Univ. Instructor, Univ. of Iowa 24-25; Asst. Prof. Ohio State Univ. 25-26; Asst. Astronomer, Lick Observatory, Univ. of Calif. 26-32; Asst. Prof. Harvard Univ. 32-35, Assoc. Prof. 35-38, Prof. 38-, Chair. Dept. of Astronomy 46-49; Assoc. Dir. for Solar Research, Harvard Observatory 46-54; Dir. Sacramento Peak Station of Harvard Coll. Observatory 51-52; Acting Dir. Harvard Coll. Observatory 52-54, Dir. 54-66; Paine Prof. of Practical Astronomy 56-; Research Scientist, Smithsonian Astrophysical Observatory 66-; U.S. Navy Service 42-45; Pres. American Astronomical Society 54-56; Pres. Comm. on Solar Eclipses, Int. Astronomical Union 48-55; Pres. Comm. on Moon, Int. Astronomical Union 64-67; mem. Nat. Acad. of Sciences, American Acad. of Arts and Sciences; mem. American Philosophical Soc., Vice-Pres. 65-; Hon. D.Sc. Univ. of Denver 54.
Publs. *Stars and Planets* 31, 35, 38, *Elementary Manual of Radio Propagation* 48, *Our Sun* 49, 59, *Mathematical Physics* 53 (revised edn. 61), *Flying Saucers* 53, *The Story of the Starry Universe* 54, *Fundamental Formulas of Physics* 55, 60, *Writing a Technical Paper* 61, *Selected Papers on Physical Processes in Ionized Plasmas* 62, *The World of Flying Saucers* 63, *Stellar Interiors* 63, *Field Guide to the Stars and Planets* 64, *The Friendly Stars* 64, *Selected Papers on the Transfer of Radiation* 66, *Principles of Atomic Structure* 68.
Harvard College Observatory, 60 Garden Street, Cambridge, Mass. 02138, U.S.A.
Telephone: 868-7600, extension 2681.

Menzies, Arthur Redpath, B.A., M.A.; Canadian diplomatist; b. 29 Nov. 1916; ed. Canadian Acad., Kobe, Japan, Univ. of Toronto and Harvard Univ.
Department of External Affairs 40-, Second Sec., Havana 45-46; Head of American and Far East Div., Dept. of External Affairs, Ottawa 48-50; Head of Canadian Liaison Mission, Tokyo 50, later Chargé d'Affaires, Tokyo; Head, Far Eastern Div., Dept. of External Affairs 53-58; High Commr. in Malaya 58-61, concurrently Ambassador to Burma 58-61; Head of Defence Liaison (I) Div., Dept. of External Affairs 62-65; High Commr. in Australia 65-.
Canadian High Commission, Canberra, A.C.T., Australia.

Menzies, Peter Thomson, M.A., F.INST.P.; British business executive; b. 15 April 1912; ed. Musselburgh Grammar School and Univ. of Edinburgh.
Inland Revenue Department 33-39; Treasurer's Dept., Imperial Chemical Industries (I.C.I.) Ltd. 39-47, Asst. Treasurer 47-52, Deputy Treasurer 52-56; Finance Dir. I.C.I. Ltd. 56-67, Deputy Chair. 67-; Chair. Imperial Metal Industries Ltd. 64-; Dir. Westminster Bank Ltd. 61-, Commercial Union Assurance Co. 62-; Part-time mem. Central Electricity Generating Board 60-.
Imperial Chemical Industries Ltd., Imperial Chemical House, Millbank, London, S.W.1; Home: Kit's Corner, Harmer Green, Welwyn, Herts., England.

Menzies, Rt. Hon. Sir Robert Gordon, K.T., C.H., F.R.S., Q.C., LL.M.; former Australian politician; b. 20 Dec. 1894; ed. Melbourne Univ.
Mem. Victoria Legislative Council 28-29; mem. Victoria Legislative Assembly 29-34; Hon. Minister Victorian Govt. 28-29, Attorney-Gen. and Minister for Railways 32 and Deputy Premier 32-34; mem. Federal House of Representatives for Kooyong 34-66; Commonwealth Attorney-Gen. and Minister for Industry 34-39; Prime Minister 39-41; Treas. 39-40; Minister for Defence Coordination Nov. 39-41, for Trade and Customs Feb.-Mar. 40, for Information Mar.-Dec. 40, for Munitions June-Nov. 40; mem. United Australia Party, Deputy Leader 36-39, Leader 39-41 and 43; Opposition mem. Advisory War Council 41-44; Leader Fed. Opposition 43-49; Prime Minister 49-66; Lord Warden of Cinque Ports 65-; Chancellor, Univ. of Melbourne 67-; Leader of Mission to Pres. Nasser in Cairo on Suez Canal Aug./Sept. 56; numerous honorary degrees.
Publs. *The Rule of Law During War* 17, *Studies in the Australian Constitution* (joint author) 33, *To the People of Britain at War* (speeches) 41, *The Forgotten People* 43, *Speech is of Time* 58, *The Changing Commonwealth* 60, *Afternoon Light* (memoirs) 67, *Central Power in the Australian Commonwealth* 67.
Office: 95 Collins Street, Melbourne, 3000 Victoria; Home: 2 Haverbrack Avenue, Malvern, 3144 Victoria, Australia.

Meouchi, H.E. Cardinal Paul Pierre; Lebanese ecclesiastic; b. 94.
Ordained priest 17; fmr. pastor in New Bedford, Mass. and Los Angeles; Bishop of Tyre 34-55; Patriarch of the Maronites 55-; Asst. at the Papal Throne; created Cardinal 65.
Winter: Patriarcat Maronite, Bkerke, Lebanon; Summer: Patriarcat Maronite, Dimane, Lebanon.

Merchant, Livingston Tallmadge, B.A.; American diplomatist; b. 23 Nov. 1903; ed. Princeton Univ.
Assistant in investment firm 26-30, partner 30-42; Asst. Chief Div. of Defense Materials, Dept. of State 42, Chief Blockade and Supply Div. 43, Chief, War Areas Econ. Div. 44; U.S. Rep. Central Rhine Comm., Strasbourg 45; Econ. Counsellor, Paris 45; Chief, Aviation Div. Dept. of State 46; Foreign Service Officer 47; Counsellor, Nanking 47; Deputy Asst. Sec. of State for Far Eastern Affairs 49; Deputy to U.S. Special Rep. in Europe and Alt. Perm. Rep. NATO 52; Asst. Sec. of State 53, 58-59; Ambassador to Canada 56-58, 61-62; Under-Sec. of State (Political Affairs) 59-61; Special Rep. for Multilateral Force Negotiations 63-64; U.S. Exec. Dir. World Bank 65-; Trustee Princeton Univ. 62-66; Dir. Nat. Life Assurance Co. of Canada 63-; Hon. D.C.L.; Hon. LL.D.
4853 Loughboro Road, Washington, D.C. 20016, U.S.A.

Mercier, Pierre; French medical director; b. 6 Aug. 1910; ed. Lycée Auxerre and Univ. de Paris à la Sorbonne.
Assistant at Hôpital Raymond-Poincaré 38-51; successively research worker, laboratory head and section head, Institut Pasteur, Paris 38-51; Dir. Institut Pasteur, Athens 51-62; Asst. Sec.-Gen. Inst. Pasteur 63-66, Sec.-Gen. Jan.-June 66, Dir. 66-; Attaché French Embassy, Athens 51-62; Corresp. mem. Acad. de Médecine; Officier Légion d'Honneur, Officer Order of George I and Commdr. Order of Phoenix (Greece), Chevalier Ordre de Léopold.
Publs. over 140 works from 34-62.
28 rue du Docteur Roux, 75 Paris 15e; and 11 *bis* avenue Emile-Deschanel, 75 Paris 7e, France.

Mercouri, Melina; Greek film actress; b. 29.
Films include *Stella* 55, *He Who Must Die* 56, *Gipsy and the Gentleman*, *Never on Sunday* 59, *Phaedra* 61, *The Victors* 63, *Light of Day* 63, *Les Pianos Mécaniques* 64, *A Man Could Get Killed* 66, *10.30 p.m. Summer* 66; song and dance version of *Never on Sunday* called *Illya Darling*, Broadway 67.
c/o Jules Dassin, 25 rue du Montparnasse, Paris 6e, France.

Mercure, Jean; French actor and theatrical director; b. 27 March 1909; ed. Lycée Rollin, Paris.
Director Théâtre de la Ville, Paris; has directed or played leading roles in *The Flashing Stream, Skipper Next to God, Miss Mabel, Living Room, La Volupté de l'Honneur, Tea and Sympathy, The Caine Mutiny, Sur la Terre comme au Ciel, Sud, Cardinal d'Espagne, Vol de Nuit*; Grand Prix de la Mise en Scène 53, Prix de la meilleure réalisation lyrique for *Vol de Nuit* 60; Chevalier, Légion d'Honneur; Officier des Arts et Lettres.
Publs. French adaptations of *Skipper Next to God* (J. de Hartog), *Sur la Terre comme au Ciel* (with R. Thieberger) (Hochwälder), *Le Silence de la Mer* (Vercors), *Thunder Rock* (Ardrey), *The Living Room* and *The Potting Shed* (Greene).
12 Villa Léandre, Paris 18e, France.
Telephone: 076-21-14.

Méré, Charles; French dramatist; b. 29 Jan. 1883.
Hon. Pres. of Society of Authors and Dramatic Composers of France; Hon. Pres. of Int. Confederation of Authors' Societies; Commandeur Légion d'Honneur; Croix de Guerre (14-18).
Publs. Plays: *Les Trois Masques, La Flamme, Le Prince Jean, La Captive, La Femme masquée, Le Vertige, La Tentation, Music-Hall, La Chair, Le Lit Nuptial, Le Passage des Princes, Indiana, L'Affranchi, Le Pavillon d'Arnières*, etc.
27 rue La Bruyère, Paris 9e, France.
Telephone: 874-18-38.

Meretskov, Marshal Kirill Afanasyevich; Soviet army officer; b. 97; ed. Red Army Military Acad.
Soviet Army 18-; Commdr. and Chief of Staff of various Mil. Districts 21-41; Chief of Gen. Staff and Deputy People's Commissar of Defence of U.S.S.R. 40-41; C.-in-C. Volkhov, Karelian and First Far Eastern Fronts 41-45; C.-in-C. Primorye, Moscow and Northern Mil. Areas 45-55; Asst. Defence Minister of U.S.S.R. for Higher Mil. Educational Establishments 55-64, Gen. Inspector, Ministry of Defence 64-; mem. C.P.S.U.; Hero of the Soviet Union; Orders of Lenin (six times), Order of Victory, Order of Red Banner (four times), Order of Suvorov (twice), Order of Kutuzov, Sword of Honour with Coat of Arms in gold, and other awards.
Ministry of Defence, 37 Maurice Thorez Embankment, Moscow, U.S.S.R.

Merikoski, Veli Kaarlo, DR. IUR.; Finnish politician and university professor; b. 2 Jan. 1905; ed. Helsinki Univ.
Assistant teacher of Public Law, Helsinki Univ. 36, Prof. of Admin. Law 41-, Dean, Faculty of Law 47-51; mem. High Court of Impeachment 50-; Chair. Union of Finnish Lawyers 46-51, 56-58; Chair. Finnish People's Party 58-61; Minister of Foreign Affairs 62-63; mem. Finnish Acad. of Science and Letters; numerous awards and decorations.
Publs. *Freedom of Association* 35, *The Concept of Dispensation* 36, *The System of Government Grants* 38, *Textbook of Finnish Public Law*, Vol. I 44, Vol. II 46, *Lectures on the Legal Aspect of Social Welfare* 48, *The Rule of Law* 53, *Juridical Position of Universities and Student Organisations* 54, *Précis du Droit Public de la Finlande* 54, *The Citizen's ABC-book* 55, *Finnish Public Law*, Vol. I 52, Vol. II 62, *Le Pouvoir Discrétionnaire de l'Administration* 58, *The System of Legal Protection in Administration* 59, *University Autonomy* 66, *Public Administration under the Political Influence* 68.
Pohjoisranta 8 B, Helsinki, Finland.
Telephone: 666140.

Meritt, Benjamin Dean, A.B., A.M., LL.D., PH.D., D.LITT.; American philologist; b. 31 March 1899; ed. Hamilton Coll., American School of Classical Studies Athens, and Princeton Univ.
Instructor in Greek, Univ. of Vermont 23-24, Brown

Univ. 24-25; Asst. Prof. of Greek Princeton Univ. 25-26; Asst. Dir. American School of Classical Studies Athens 26-28; Associate Prof. of Greek and Latin Univ. of Michigan 28-29, Prof. 29-33; Visiting Prof. American School of Classical Studies Athens 32-33, Annual Prof. 36 and 54-55; Dir. Athens Coll. 32-33; Francis White Prof. of Greek Johns Hopkins Univ. 33-35; Prof. Inst. for Advanced Study, Princeton 35-; Fellow American Acad. of Arts and Sciences; hon. councillor, Greek Archaeological Society; mem. American Philological Asscn. 22-, Pres. 53; Eastman Prof. Oxford 45-46; Sather Prof. Univ. of Calif. 59; corresp. mem. Royal Flemish Acad.; mem. American Philosophical Soc.; corresp. mem. British Acad.; hon. mem. Soc. for the promotion of Hellenic Studies; Commdr. Royal Order of Phoenix (Greece).
Publs. *The Athenian Calendar in the Fifth Century* 28, *Supplementum Epigraphicum Graecum*, Vol. V (with Allen B. West) 31, *Corinth*, Vol. VIII, Part I, *Greek Inscriptions* 31, *Athenian Financial Documents* 32, *The Athenian Assessment of 425 B.C.* (with Allen B. West) 34, *Documents on Athenian Tribute* 37, *The Athenian Tribute Lists* (with H. T. Wade-Gery and M. F. McGregor), Vol. I 39, Vol. II 49, Vol. III 50, Vol. IV 53, *The Chronology of Hellenistic Athens* (with W. K. Pritchett) 40, *Epigraphica Attica* 40, *The Athenian Year* 61.
Institute for Advanced Study, Princeton, N.J., U.S.A.

Merkatz, Hans-Joachim von, DR.JUR.; German lawyer and politician; b. 7 July 1905; ed. Univs. of Jena and Munich.
On research staff Kaiser-Wilhelm-Inst. für Ausländisches Öffentliches Recht und Völkerrecht (now Max-Planck-Inst.) 35-38, Ibero-Amerika Inst. 38-45; legal adviser to Deutsche Partei 46; mem. Bundestag 49-; Dep. Chair. Deutsche Partei 53-55; Minister for Justice 56-57; Minister for Bundesrat and Länder Affairs 55-62; Minister for Refugees 60-61; mem. Christian Democratic Union 60-; mem. of Exec. Board of UNESCO 64; Prof. 66-; Hon. Knight Order of St. John; Commdr. Légion d'Honneur.
Publs. *Politische Entwicklung und rechtliche Gestaltung der Ministerverantwortlichkeit* 35, *Germany To-day* (co-Editor) 54, *Politik im Widerstreit* 57, *Die konservative Funktion* 57, *In der Mitte des Jahrhunderts* 63, *Besinnung auf Preussen* (Co-Editor) 64.
Wald-Strasse 62, 532 Bad Godesberg, German Federal Republic.
Telephone: 63332.

Merkulov, Vassily Yefimovich; Soviet foreign trade official; b. 1917; ed. Moscow Petroleum Inst. and Academy of Foreign Trade.
Member C.P.S.U. 44-; Dir. of Office, *Soyuzneftexport* Trust 50-51; Man. Dir., later, Gen. Dir. Joint-Stock Soc., Finland 51-56; Vice-Chair. *Soyuzneftexport* Trust 57-64; U.S.S.R. Commercial Rep. in U.A.R. 64-68; at Ministry of Foreign Trade 68-; Order of Lenin, Order of Patriotic War, Second Degree.
U.S.S.R. Ministry of Foreign Trade, 32-34 Smolenskaya-Sennaya ploshchad, Moscow, U.S.S.R.

Merlin, Jacques Joseph Alfred; French banker and insurance executive; b. 27 Aug. 1901; ed. Ecole Sainte-Croix, Neuilly.
Chairman Crédit Commercial de France, Union des Sociétés par Actions de Capitalisation du Secteur Privé; Chair. and Pres. Soc. Française d'Assurances pour Favoriser le Crédit; Vice-Chair. S.A. Française de Réassurances, Fédération Française des Sociétés d'Assurances; Dir. la Prévoyance R.D. & la Prévoyance Vie, Crédit Mobilier Industriel (SOVAC), Ciments Lafarge, Soc. de Produits Alimentaires et Diététiques (SOPAD), Lafarge Cement of N. America; mem. Office and Econ. Comm. of Conseil Nat. du Patronat Français; fmr.

Vice-Chair. Chambre de Commerce de Paris; Officier Légion d'Honneur.
Office: 1 rue Euler, Paris 8e; Home: 6 boulevard Suchet, Paris 16e, France.

Merrick, David; American theatrical producer; ed. St. Louis Univ.
Producer of numerous plays on Broadway, including *Fanny* 54, *The Matchmaker* 55, *Look Back in Anger*, *Romanoff and Juliet, Jamaica* 57, *The Entertainer, The World of Suzie Wong, La Plume de ma Tante, Epitaph for George Dillon, Maria Golovin* 58, *Destry Rides Again, Gypsy, Take Me Along* 59, *The Good Soup, Vintage '60', Irma la Douce, A Taste of Honey, Becket, Do Re Me* 60, *Carnival* 61, *Sunday in New York* 61, *Ross* 61, *I Can Get it for You Wholesale* 62, *Stop the World, I Want to Get Off* 62, *Tchin Tchin* 62, *Oliver!* 62, *Rehearsal* 63, *Hello Dolly* 64, *Pickwick* 65, *Inadmissible Evidence* 65, *Cactus Flower* 65, *Marat/Sade* 65, *Don't Drink the Water* 66, *I do! I do!* 66, *Philadelphia, Here I Come* 66, *Rosencrantz and Guildenstern Are Dead* 67, *How Now, Dow Jones* 67, *The Happy Time* 67.
246 West 44th Street, New York City, N.Y., U.S.A.

Merrill, John Ogden; American architect; b. 10 Aug. 1896; ed. Wisconsin Univ., Mass. Inst. of Technology.
Chief Architect, Mid-Western States Fed. Housing Admin. 39; in partnership with Skidmore and Owings 39-58, with whom he designed numerous govt. projects and private buildings including Oak Ridge, Tennessee, U.S. base at Okinawa, Lever House, New York, Terrace Plaza Hotel, Cincinnati, etc.; Fellow, American Inst. of Architects.
101 Gardner Place, Colorado Springs, Colo., U.S.A.

Merrill, Maurice Hitchcock, A.B., LL.B., S.J.D.; American lawyer and university teacher; b. 3 Oct. 1897; ed. Univ. of Oklahoma and Harvard Univ.
Served in U.S. Army 18; taught in Univ. of Okla. 19-22; practised law in Tulsa Okla. 22-24, 26; Assoc. Prof. of Law Univ. of Idaho 25-26; Asst. Prof. of Law Univ. of Nebraska 26-28, Prof. of Law 28-36; Prof. of Law Univ. of Okla. 36-50, Research Prof. of Law 50-68, Research Prof. Emeritus 68-; Act. Dean 45-46; mem. Judicial Council of Okla. 45-46, 47-65; Fellow, Inst. of Judicial Admin. 53-; Commr. from Okla. to Nat. Conf. of Commrs. on Uniform State Laws 44-, mem. Exec. Cttee. 61-, Vice-Pres. 63-67, Chair. Okla. del 49-; mem. Panel of Labor Arbitrators U.S. Conciliation Service 46-; mem. Nat. Acad. of Arbitrators; Fellow, American Bar Foundation 56-; Hatton W. Sumners Award 64; Distinguished Service Citation, Univ. of Okla. 68.
Publs. *Law of Covenants Implied in Gas and Oil Leases* 26, *Nebraska Annotations to Restatement of Contracts* (with William Sternberg and Lester B. Orfield) 32, *Nebraska Annotations to Restatement of Agency* 33, *Oklahoma Annotations to Restatement of Agency* 40; mem. of Board of Eds. and Ed. for Volume III (*The Nation and the States*), *Selected Essays on Constitutional Law* 38, *Cases and Materials on Administrative Law* 50, *Law of Notice* 52, *Administrative Law* (American Casebook Series) 54, *The Public's Concern with the Fuel Minerals* 60.
Home: 800 Elm Avenue, Norman, Oklahoma, U.S.A.; Office: 556 Monnet Hall, University of Oklahoma, Norman, Oklahoma, U.S.A.
Telephone: 321-6585 (Home); 325-5091 (Office).

Merry del Val y Alzola Alfonso (Marqués de Merry del Val); Spanish diplomatist; b. 1903; ed. Stonyhurst College and Deusto and Valladolid Univs.
Diplomatic Service 29-; Ambassador to the United States 64-.
Spanish Embassy, 2700 15th Street, N.W., Washington, D.C., U.S.A.

Mertens de Wilmars, Jacques E. M. J., DR. JUR., DR. POL. AND SOC. ECON., LIC. PHIL.; Belgian economist, univ. prof. and banker; b. 1 Feb. 1917; ed. Louvain Univ.
Barrister 39-45; Asst. Faculty of Economic and Social Sciences, Louvain Univ. 39-43, Lecturer 44, Asst. Prof. 45, Prof. 49, Dean 62-63; Chair. Inst. of Econ. Science 61-64; Econ. Adviser to Minister of Finance 45-46 and 47-48; Attaché, Nat. Bank Belgium 43, Sec. Gov. 46, Adviser 48, Chief Econ. Studies 53-58, Deputy Dir. 61-65, Adviser to the Board 65-; Chief of Cabinet to Prime Minister 58-61, Hon. Chief of Cabinet to Prime Minister 61-; mem. UN Population Comm. 51-64, Vice-Chair. 55-58, Chair. 59-63; mem. Belgian Del. ECOSOC (UN) 52, Special Financial Mission, UN Technical Assistance, Iran 52, Arbitration Comm. to Indonesia 53-56; Deputy mem. Monetary Cttee. EEC 58-, Chair. Deputies 68-; Vice-Chair. Comité de Politique Conjoncturelle EEC 60-; Officer Order of Léopold, Commdr. Order of Oranje-Nassau, Commdr. Order Merit (Austria), Commdr. Order Crown of Oak (Luxembourg), Commdr. Order St. Gregorius the Great (Holy See).
Publs. *La naissance et le développement de l'étalon-or 1696-1922* 44, *La politique du plein emploi et ses limites* 52, *Les objectifs de la politique économique sont-ils compatibles entre-eux?* 62, *The Economics of Aid to Less-Developed Countries* 63.
228 Avenue Winston Churchill, Brussels 18, Belgium. Telephone: 02/43-73-85.

Mertins, (Marshall) Louis, LL.D.; American poet; b. 7 Dec. 1885; ed. William Jewell Coll., Liberty (Mo.), Kansas City Seminary and Temple Univ.
Ordained Baptist Minister 06; Pastor and founder Swope Park Baptist Church, Kansas City 11-16; Chautauqua lecturer 16-26; Lecturer on World Literature, Valley Coll. 56-63; founder and Vice-Pres. California Writers' Guild; mem. Int. P.E.N. Club; Pres. of Exec. Board, Los Angeles Center.
Publs. Poems: *The Wishing Gate* 18, *The Sumac Trail* 19, *The Covered Wagon* 21, *The Mail Cart Man* 21, *A Voice Crying in the Wilderness* 23, *Tales of Kettle's Shop* 23, *The Baratarians* 24, *Chaucer: His Further Pilgrim* 41, *Three in Cornwall* 42, *Yule at Oxenforde* 43, *The Further Prologue* 44, *Sonnets I* 45, *II* 46, *Centennial Ode* (William Jewell College) 49; allegory: *This Way Out* 36; criticism: *The Intervals of Robert Frost* 47, *Robert Frost: Life and Talks Walking* 65.
"Far Hills", 554 Terracina Boulevard, Redlands, Calif., U.S.A.

Merton, Rev. Thomas James, O.C.S.O., B.A., M.A.; American ecclesiastic and author; b. 31 Jan. 1915; ed. Lycée de Montauban (France), Oakham School (England), Clare Coll., Cambridge, and Columbia Univ., New York.
Professor of English Literature, St. Bonaventure Univ. 40; entered Trappist (Cistercian) Order, at Monastery of Gethsemani 41, solemn vows 47, ordained priest 49, Master of Scholastics 51-55, of Novices 55-65, Prof. of Mystical Theology 61-65; Hon. LL.D. Univ. Kentucky 63.
Publs. *Seven Storey Mountain (Elected Silence)* 48, *Seeds of Contemplation* 49, *Ascent to Truth* 51, *Sign of Jonas* 52, *No Man is an Island* 55, *The Silent Life* 57, *Secular Journal* 58, *Selected Poems* 59, *Disputed Questions* 59, *The Behaviour of Titans* 60, *The Wisdom of the Desert* 61, *The New Man* 62, *New Seeds of Contemplation* 62, *Emblems of a Season of Fury* 63, *Life and Holiness* 63, *Seeds of Destruction* 64, *Gandhi on Non-Violence* 65, *Seasons of Celebration* 65, *The Way of Chuang Tzu* 65, *Conjectures of a Guilty Bystander* 66, *Mystics and Zen Masters* 67, *Cables to the Ace* 68, *Faith and Violence* 68.
Abbey of Gethsemani, Trappist P.O., Kentucky 40073, U.S.A.

Merz, Charles; American journalist; b. 23 Feb. 1893; ed. Yale Univ.

Manager Editor *Harper's Weekly* 15-16; Associate Editor *New Republic* 16-20; staff correspondent and Assoc. Editor *New York World* 21-30; mem. Editorial staff *New York Times* 31-38, Editor 38-61, Editor Emeritus 61-; Hon. Litt.D. (Yale, Columbia, Colgate, Wooster).

Publs. *The Great American Bandwagon* 28, *The Dry Decade* 31, *Days of Decision* 39.

10 Gracie Square, New York, N.Y., U.S.A.

Merzagora, Cesare; Italian industrialist and politician; b. 9 Nov. 1898.

Served in First World War 15-18; Dir. Banca Commerciale Italiana in Bulgaria 20-27; also Italian Consul at Philippopolis; founder of anti-fascist newspaper *La Voce d'Italia*, suppressed in 24; Dir. of banking institutes in foreign countries 27-38; Dir. of Pirelli and associated firms 38; mem. of Liberation Movement in Northern Italy; Pres. of its Central Economic Comm.; Minister of Foreign Trade in fourth and fifth De Gasperi Cabinets 47-49; Senator (Independent, Milan) 48-; Pres. of the Senate 53-Nov. 67, Life Senator 63-; Chair. Assicurazioni Generali April 68-.

1 Via di Villa Grazioli, Rome, Italy.

Meselson, Matthew Stanley, PH.B., PH.D.; American professor of biology; b. 24 May 1930; ed. Univ of Chicago and Calif. Inst. of Technology.

Research Fellow, Calif. Inst. of Technology 57-58, Asst. Prof. of Physical Chemistry 58-59, Senior Research Fellow in Chemical Biology 59-60; Assoc. Prof. of Biology, Harvard Univ. 60-64, Prof. of Biology 64-; Prize for Molecular Biology, Nat. Acad. of Sciences 63, Eli Lilly Award in Microbiology and Immunology 64.

Publs. numerous papers on the biochemistry and molecular biology of nucleic acids in various numbers of *Proceedings* of Nat. Acad. of Sciences and of *Journal of Molecular Biology*, etc.

The Biological Laboratories, 16 Divinity Avenue, Harvard University, Cambridge, Mass., U.S.A.

Meshcheryakov, Mikhail Vladimirovich; Soviet foreign trade official; b. 1911; ed. Inst. of Foreign Trade.

Member C.P.S.U. 39-; Official, People's Commissariat for Foreign Trade 31-41; Soviet Army 41-45; Official, Ministry of Foreign Trade 45-50, 56-60; Chief of Section, U.S.S.R. Trade Representation in China 50-52; U.S.S.R. Commercial Representative in Mongolia 52-56, 60-63; Specialist, *Soyuzpushnina* Trust 63-65; U.S.S.R. Commercial Rep. in Korean People's Democratic Republic 65-; Red Banner of Labour (twice), Order of Patriotic War, Second Degree (twice), Order of Red Star.

U.S.S.R. Trade Representation, Pyongyang, Korean People's Democratic Republic.

Mesnard, Pierre (Le Mega); French writer and university professor; b. 3 Nov. 1900; ed. Lycée de Poitiers, Ecole normale supérieure, Univ. de Paris à la Sorbonne, and Ecole nationale des langues orientales vivantes.

Former Maître de Conférences, Univ. of Jassy, Rumania; Prof. Univ. of Algiers and Dir. of Inst. of Philosophy 42-56; Founder of Centre for Higher Studies on the Renaissance, Tours 56-; Prof. of Renaissance Civilisation and Philosophy, Univ. of Poitiers 56-, Univ. of Orléans-Tours 66; mem. Acad. des sciences morales et politiques; Vice-Pres. Int. Centre for Humanism, Rome, Int. Soc. for Character Study; Past Pres. Int. Fed. Inst. of Renaissance; several decorations.

Publs. *L'Essor de la philosophie politique au XVIe siècle, Essai sur la morale de Descartes, Le Cas Diderot, Education et Caractère, Le Vrai Visage de Kierkegaard, Descartes ou le Combat pour la Verité.*

59 rue Néricault-Destouches, 37 Tours, Indre-et-Loire, France.

Telephone: 53-71-86.

Mesnil du Buisson, Robert Du, Count, D. ès L., D. en D.; French archaeologist; b. 19 April 1895.

Dir. French Archæological Missions in Syria, Egypt and France; Dir. Excavation at Palmyra 65-; Pres. Société Nat. des Antiquaires de France 46-47; Pres. Société Historique et Archéologique de l'Orne 47-55; Hon. Pres. 56-; Pres. Soc. du Manoir d'Argentelles; Dir. du Centre Culturel et Touristique de l'Orne; Vice-Pres. Soc. d'Ethnographie de Paris 60-; Commdr. Légion d'Honneur 46; Lauréat de l'Institut de France 40, 58, 63.

Publs. *Les Ruines d'El-Mishrifé au Nord-Est de Homs* 27, *La Technique des fouilles archéologiques* 33, *Le Site Archéologique de Mishrifé-Qatna* 35, *Les noms et signes égyptiens désignant des vases* 35, *Souran et Tell Masin* 35, *Le Site de Qadesh* 36, *Inscriptions juives de Doura-Europos* 37, *Inventaire des Inscriptions palmyréniennes de Doura-Europos* 39, *Les Peintures de la Synagogue de Doura* 245-246 *ap. J-C.* 39, *Tessères et Monnaies de Palmyre* 44, *Les Ouvrages du siège à Doura-Europos* 45, *Le Site archéologique d'Exmes (Uxoma)* 46, *Le Sautoir d'Atargatis et la chaîne d'amulettes* 47, *Baghouz, l'ancienne Corsôté* 48, *Une voie commerciale de haute antiquité dans l'Orne* 51, *Les Dieux et les Déesses en forme de vase dans L'Antiquité Orientale, La Palissade gauloise d'Alençon* 52, *L'Álcove royale dite "Lit de Justice d'Argentelles"* 53, *Un Constructeur du Château de La Celle-Saint-Cloud, Jacques Jérémie Roussel* 54, *Saint-Germain-en-Laye* 54, *Poissy* 55, *Chantilly* 57, *Une Famille de Chevaliers de Malte, les Costart* 60, *Plaques de Cheminées de l'Orne* 47-67, *Les Tessères et les Monnaies de Palmyre de la Bibliothèque Nationale* 62, *Inscriptions sur jarres de Doura-Europos* 59, *Origine et évolution du Panthéon de Tyr, Les Chausson de la Salle* 63, *Le dieu-Griffon à Palmyre et chez les Hittites* 63, *Les Origines du Panthéon Palmyrénien* 64, *Le dieu Ousô sur des monnaies de Tyr* 65, *Le drame des deux étoiles du matin et du soir dans l'antiquité orientale* 67.

63 rue de Varenne, Paris 7e, France, and Château de Champobert, par Exmes (Orne), France.

Telephone: (Paris) INValides 00-06.

Messer, Thomas M., B.A., M.A.; American museum director; b. 9 Feb. 1920; ed. Thiel Coll. (Greenville, Pa.), Boston, Paris and Harvard Univs.

With U.S. Office of War Information 42-43, U.S. Army 43-45, U.S. Mil. Govt. 45-46; studies at Sorbonne (Paris) 46-47; Dir., Roswell Museum, New Mexico 49-52; Asst. Dir. in charge of Nat. Exhibitions Programme, American Fed. of Arts 52-53, Dir. of Exhibitions 53-55, Dir. 55-56; Dir., Boston Inst. of Contemporary Art 56-61, Solomon R. Guggenheim Museum, New York 61-; Dr. of Fine Arts h.c. Univ. of Mass.; Adjunct Prof. of Art History, Barnard Coll. 65-66; Senior Fellow, Centre for Advanced Studies, Wesleyan Univ., Conn. Feb. 67-June 67; Knight First Class of the Royal Order of St. Olav.

Publ. *The Emergent Decade—Latin-American Painters and Painting in the 1960s.*

The Solomon R. Guggenheim Museum, 1071 Fifth Avenue, New York, N.Y. 10028; Home: 200 East 78th Street, New York, N.Y., U.S.A.

Telephone: EN9-5110.

Messerer, Asaf Mikhailovich; Soviet choreographer and dancer; b. 03; ed. Moscow School of Choreography.

Joined the Bolshoi Theatre Co. 21, *Premier Danseur* to 54; People's Artist of the R.S.F.S.R.; State prizewinner 41, 47.

Principal roles in: *Swan Lake, Casse Noisette* by Tchaikovsky, *Don Quixote* by Minkus, *Flames of Paris, Fountain of Bakhchisarai* by Asafiev, *Red Poppy* by Gliere, *Petrushka* by Stravinsky, etc.

State Academic Bolshoi Theatre, 1 Ploshchad Sverdlova, Moscow, U.S.S.R.

Messerschmitt, Willy, DR. ING.; German aviation engineer and businessman; b. 26 June 1898; ed. Technical Coll., Munich.

Designed gliders and sailplanes with engineer Harth 12-23; designed sporting and transport airplanes (single-spar wing), Bamberg, Germany 23-37; chief designer and Dir. Bayer. Flugzeugwerke, later called Messerschmitt A.G., Augsburg 27-45; Me 109 speed record for landplanes 37; world speed record 38; jet-propelled airplane Me 262; worked on reconstruction of industrial works, designing work in various engineering fields 45-54; Pres. Messerschmitt and Co. K.G. and Hon. Chair. of the Board, Messerschmitt A.G. (58); Nat. Prize for Art and Science; Knight's Cross; War Service Cross.

Mauerkircherstrasse 46, 8 Munich 27, German Federal Republic.

Telephone: 48-15-16.

Messiaen, Olivier; French organist and composer; b. 10 Dec. 1908; ed. Paris Conservatoire.

Organist, Trinité, Paris 31-; Co-founder *Jeune-France* movement 33; Prof. Ecole Normale and Schola Cantorum 36-39; Prof. of Harmony, Paris Conservatoire 42-47, of Analysis, Aesthetics and Rhythm 47-, of Composition 66-; Officier de la Légion d'Honneur, Grand Officier de l'Ordre national du Mérite, Commdr. des Arts et des Lettres.

Compositions include organ music: *La Nativité du Seigneur* 35, *Les Corps Glorieux* 39, *Messe Pentecôte* 49, *Livre d'Orgue* 59; vocal music: *Poèmes pour Mi* 36, *Chants de Terre et de Ciel* 38, *Harawi* (song cycle); chamber music: *Quatuor pour la Fin du Temps* 41, *Visions de l'Amen* 43, *Vingt Regards sur l'Enfant-Jésus* 44, *Trois Petites Liturgies de la Présence Divine* 44; orchestral: *Turangalila Symphonie* 46-48, *Couleurs de la cité céleste* 64, *Et Exspecto Resurectionem Mortuorum* 65; works based on bird-song: *Réveil des oiseaux* 53, *Oiseaux exotiques* 55, *Catalogue d'oiseaux* 58, *Chronochromie* 59, *Sept Haïkai* 63.

230 rue Marcadet, Paris 18e, France.

Messmer, Pierre A., LL.D.; French politician and overseas administrator; b. 20 March 1916.

Gov. Mauritania 52, Ivory Coast 54; High Commr. Cameroun 56; High Commr.-Gen. French Equatorial Africa 58, French West Africa July 58-60; Minister for the Armed Forces 60-; Commdr. Légion d'Honneur, Compagnon de la Libération, Croix de Guerre.

14 rue St. Dominique, Paris 7e, France.

Mestek, Karel; Czechoslovak politician; b. 1 Oct. 1907.

In underground movement in Second World War, imprisoned until 45; Deputy to Nat. Assembly 46-; Deputy Minister of Purchase of Agricultural Products 53-56; First Deputy Minister of Food Industry and Purchase of Agricultural Products 56-58; First Deputy Minister of Agriculture, Forestry and Water Resources 59-62; mem. Central Cttee. of C.P. of Czechoslovakia 62-; mem. Agriculture Comm. of Central Cttee. of C.P. of Czechoslovakia 63-; Chair. Central Admin. for Purchase of Agricultural Products 62-67; Minister of Agriculture and Food 67-; Order of the 25th February 48, 49; Order of Labour 65.

Ministry of Agriculture and Food, Těšnov 65, Prague 1, Czechoslovakia.

Mestiri, Mahmoud; Tunisian diplomatist; b. 25 Dec. 1929; ed. Inst. d'Etudes Politiques, Univ. de Lyons.

Served in several Tunisian Dels. to UN; Alt. Rep. to UN 58, 59; Head of Tunisian special Diplomatic Mission to Congo (Leopoldville) 60; Asst. to Personal Rep. of UN Sec.-Gen. to Govt. of Belgium 61; Deputy Perm. Rep. of Tunisia to UN 62-65; Sec.-Gen. for Foreign Affairs, Tunis 65-67; Perm. Rep. to UN 67-; Chair. UN Special Cttee. on the Situation with Regard to Implementation of Declaration on the Granting of Independence to Colonial Countries and Peoples 68-.

Permanent Mission of Tunisia to the United Nations, 40 East 71st Street, New York, N.Y. 10021, U.S.A.

Mesyatsev, Nikolai Nikolaevich; Soviet politician; b. 1920.

Member C.P.S.U. 41-; Soviet Army 41-45; mem. Cen. Cttee. Komsomol 46-52, Sec. 55-59; First Deputy Chair. All Union Soc. "Znanie" (Knowledge) 59-62; Diplomatic work and on staff of Cen. Cttee. of Communist Party of Soviet Union 62-64; Chair. State Cttee. on Broadcasting and TV, U.S.S.R. Council of Ministers Oct. 64-; Cand. mem. C.P.S.U. Central Cttee. 66-; mem. Cttee. U.S.S.R. Parl. Group; Deputy to U.S.S.R. Supreme Soviet.

Pyatnitskaya ul. 25, Moscow, U.S.S.R.

Metcalf, Keyes DeWitt, A.B., LITT.D., L.H.D., LL.D.; American librarian; b. 13 April 1889; ed. Oberlin Coll.

Exec. Asst. Oberlin Coll. Library 12, Acting Librarian 16-17; Chief of Stacks New York Public Library 13-16 and 17-18, Exec. Asst. 19-27, Chief of Reference Dept. 28-37; Librarian Harvard Coll., Dir. Harvard Univ. Library 37-55, Emeritus 55-; Pres. American Library Asscn. 42-43; Prof. of Bibliography Harvard Univ. 45-55; Prof. of Library Admin., Rutgers Univ. 55-58; library consultant 55-; Fulbright Lecturer, Nat. Commonwealth Library, Canberra, Australia 58-59; Consultant in over 300 libraries in 40 states and assignments in New Zealand, India, South Africa, Thailand, The Philippines, Ireland, Japan, Latin America, Costa Rica and Canada 58-66; Fulbright Distinguished Scholar, Queen's Univ. Belfast 66; Lecturer, York, England 66; mem. Bibliographical Socs., America and Great Britain; New York Public Library 50th Anniversary Award for services to research libraries.

Publs. *Planning Academic and Research Library Buildings* 65, and articles in professional periodicals.

68 Fairmont Street, Belmont, Mass. 02178, U.S.A.

Telephone: 484-3699.

Metcalf, Lee; American lawyer and politician; b. 28 Jan. 1911; ed. Montana State Univ.

Associate Justice Montana Supreme Court 46-52; mem. U.S. House of Representatives 52-60; Senator from Montana 61-; Democrat.

U.S. Senate, Washington, D.C., U.S.A.

Metcalfe, John Wallace, B.A., F.L.A.; Australian librarian; b. 1901; ed. Univ. of Sydney.

Library Asst., Univ. of Sydney 17-23, Public Library of N.S.W. 23-42, Principal Librarian 42-59; Librarian and Dir. School of Librarianship Univ. of N.S.W. 59-; Pres Library Asscn., Australia 56-59; mem. Australian del. UNESCO Conf. 47.

Publs. *Information Indexing and Subject Cataloging* 57, *Subject Classifying and Indexing of Libraries and Literature* 59.

School of Librarianship, University of New South Wales, Kensington, N.S.W., Australia.

Metz, Victor Raoul de; French industrialist; b. 28 April 1902; ed. Ecole Polytechnique, Ecole des Mines.

President and Director-General Compagnie Française des Pétroles; Pres. Compagnie Navale des Pétroles; Vice-Pres. Compagnie Française de Raffinage, Soc. Algérienne des Pétroles Mory, Compagnie Industrielle et Financière des Chantiers et Ateliers de Saint-Nazaire, Crédit National, Pechelbronn; Dir. Desmarais Frères; mem. Conseil d'Escompte, Banque de France; Officier Légion d'Honneur.

5 rue Michel-Ange, Paris 16e, France.

Meulemeester, Pierre M. V. de; Belgian United Nations official; b. 22 July 1908; ed. Lycée Français, London, Athénée Royal, Bruges, Univ. of Brussels and Catholic Univ., Louvain.

Private Sec. to Minister, Belgian Legation, Ottawa 37-38; Ministry of Econ. Affairs, N.Y. World Fair 38-39; Resistance Movement, Belgium 40-45; Belgian Ministry of Econ. Affairs 45-46; Dep. Chief of Protocol, Exec. Office of Sec. of UN 46-62, Chief of Protocol 62-; several decorations.
Executive Office of the Secretary-General, United Nations, New York City, N.Y.; Home: 37 Beekman Place, New York, N.Y. 10022, U.S.A.
Telephone: MU8-2985.

Mewis, Karl; German politician; b. 22 Nov. 1907.
Former fitter; joined Communist Party of Germany 24; mem. Cen. Cttee. and Cand. Mem. Political Bureau, Socialist Unity Party (S.E.D.); mem. Council of State 60-63; Chair. State Planning Comm. 61-63; Ambassador to Poland 63-.
Embassy of the German Democratic Republic, AI I Armii Wojska Polskiego 2-4, Warsaw, Poland.

Meyer, André Benoit Mathieu; banker; b. Paris, 3 Sept. 1898.
Senior Partner, Lazard Frères & Co., N.Y.C., Lazard Frères & Cie., Paris; Dir. Lazard Bros. & Co., Ltd., London, Soc. Financière de Transports et d'Entreprises Industrielles (Sofina), Brussels, Radio Corpn. of America, Chase Int. Investment Corpn., N.B.C., New-mont Mining Corpn., Allied Chemical Corpn., Monte-catini-Edison, Fiat; mem. Board of Trustees, Sloane-Kettering Inst., Memorial Hospital for Cancer Research, New York Univ.; Commdr. Légion d'Honneur.
Lazard Frères & Co., 44 Wall Street, New York City 5, N.Y., U.S.A.

Meyer, Armin Henry; American diplomatist; b. 19 Jan. 1914; ed. Lincoln Junior Coll., Capital Univ., Columbus, Ohio, Capital Univ. Theological Seminary and Ohio State Univ., Columbus, Ohio.
Asst. Prof. and Dean of Men, Capital Univ. 35-41; Radio Technician, Douglas Aircraft Co., Eritrea 42-43; News Editor, Office of War Information, Cairo 43-44; Public Affairs Officer, American Embassy, Baghdad 44-48; Public Affairs Adviser, Dept. of State 48-52; First Sec., Beirut 52-55, Counsellor, Kabul 55-57; Dep. Dir. Office of South Asian Affairs, Dept. of State 57-58, Office of Near Eastern Affairs 59-61, Dep. Asst. Sec. of State for Near Eastern and South Asian Affairs 61; Ambassador to Lebanon Oct. 61-April 65, to Iran April 65-.
American Embassy, Takhte Jamshid Avenue, Teheran, Iran.

Meyer, Augusto; Brazilian professor of literature, civil servant and writer; b. 24 Jan. 1902; ed. Colégio Bom Conselho, Ginásio Anchieta and Faculdade de Direito, Pôrto Alegre.
Professor of Theory of Literature, Faculty of Philosophy and Letters, Univ. of Brazil; Prof. of Brazilian Studies, Univ. of Hamburg 56-61; Dir. Public Library, Rio Grande do Sul 30-37, Nat. Book Inst. (organ of Ministry of Educ. and Culture) 37-54, 61-; mem. Historical and Geographical Inst. of Rio Grande do Sul, Brazilian Acad. of Philology, Brazilian Asscn. of Hygiene, Brazilian Acad. of Letters; Hon. mem. Brazilian Asscn. of Librarians.
Publs. Machado de Assis 35, 58, Prosa dos Pagos 43, A Sombra da estante 47, Cancioneiro Gaúcho 52, Guia do Folclore gaúcho 52, Prêto e Branco 56, Le Bateau Ivre 56, Poesias (collected poems) 57, Camões, o bruxo e outros estudos 60, A forma secreta 66, Segredos de Infância 66, No tempo da flor 66.
Avenida Rui Barbosa 624, Apto. 201, Botafogo, Rio de Janeiro, G.B., Brazil.

Meyer, Jean; French actor and theatrical director; b. 19 June 1914; ed. Conservatoire Nat. d'Art Drama-tique.
Former Sociétaire Comédie Française; Prof. Conser-vatoire Nat. d'Art Dramatique; Dir. Théâtre du

Palais Royal 60-, Centre d'Apprentissage d'Art Drama-tique, Théâtre Michel 64-; directed and acted in the films Le Bourgeois Gentilhomme 58, Le Mariage de Figaro 59; produced Trois Mariages de Mélanie 65; Chevalier Légion d'Honneur.
Publs. L'Age idiot (play) 63, Gilles Shakespeare ou les Aventures de Jean Perrin, Molière-Micmac (play), Le Vice dans La Peau (play).
5 rue Jacques Dulud, Neuilly-sur-Seine (Seine), France.

Meyer-Cording, Dr. Ulrich; German economist; b. 22 May 1911; ed. high school, Dresden, and Univs. of Grenoble, Berlin, Kiel, Exeter and Leipzig.
Lawyer, Stuttgart 48-50; Ministerial Adviser, Ministry of Justice, Bonn 50-57; Ministerial Man. in Ministry of Atomic Affairs 57-58; Ministerial Dir. and Head of European Dept., Ministry of Commerce 58-64; Prof. of Commercial and Business Law, Univ. of Cologne 58-64; Vice-Chair. European Investment Bank, Brussels 64-.
Publs. Das Recht der Banküberweisung 51, Monopol und Marktbeherrschung als Rechtsbegriffe 54, Die Vereins-strafe 57.
85 boulevard de Waterloo, Brussels 1, Belgium.
Telephone: 13-40-00.

Meyers, Franz, LL.D.; German lawyer and politician; b. 31 July 1908; ed. Freiburg and Cologne Univs.
Junior barrister 31; Asst. judge 34; lawyer 35; mem. Christian Democratic Union 48-; Minister of Interior, North Rhine-Westphalia 52-56; Minister Pres., North Rhine-Westphalia 58-66; mem. German Bundestag 57-58; mem. Landtag, North Rhine-Westphalia 50-; Pres. German Bundesrat 60-61, Vice-Pres. 61-62; Christian Democratic Union.
Mönchengladbach, Bergstrasse 137, German Federal Republic.

Meynell, Sir Francis, Kt., D.LITT., R.D.I.; British writer, publicist, book designer and publisher; b. 12 May 1891; ed. Downside and Trinity Coll., Dublin.
Dir. Daily Herald 18-20; founder and Dir. Nonesuch Press 23-; contrib. to Encyclopaedia Britannica, Man-chester Guardian, News Chronicle, etc.; Dir. Mather & Crowther Ltd. 37-61; Adviser on Consumer Needs, Board of Trade 41; mem. Council of Industrial Design 44; knighted 45; Typographic Adviser (unpaid) to H.M. Stationery Office 45-66; Dir. Cement and Concrete Asscn. 46-58; mem. Royal Mint Advisory Cttee. 54-; Advisory Council, Victoria and Albert Museum 46-58; Dir. The Bodley Head 56-.
Publs. The Typography of Advertisements 29, Seventeen Poems 45, English Printed Books 46, Poems and Pieces 61.
The Grey House, Lavenham, Suffolk, England.
Telephone: Lavenham 526.

Meynell, Laurence W.; English writer; b. 9 Aug. 1899; ed. St. Edmund's Coll., Ware.
Former schoolmaster, land agent; served with R.A.F.; Literary Editor Time and Tide 58-60.
Publs. Blue Feather 28, On the Night of the 18th 36, The Door in the Wall 36, The Dandy 38, The Hut 38, Dark Square 40, Strange Landing 46, The Evil Hour 47, The Bright Face of Danger 48, The Echo in the Cave 49, Party of Eight 50, Famous Cricket Grounds 51, The Man No One Knew 51, The Frightened Man 52, Too Clever by Half 53, Builder and Dreamer (life of I. K. Brunel) 53, Man of Speed (life of C. S. Rolls) 53, Give me the Knife 54, Under the Hollies 54, Policeman in the Family 54, Bridge under the water 55, Where is she now? 55, Great Men of Staffordshire 55, Life of James Brindley 56, Life of T. Telford, The Breaking Point 57, One Step from Murder 58, The Abandoned Doll 60, The House in Marsh Road 60, The Pit in the Garden 61, Virgin Luck 62, Sleep of the Just 63, More Deadly than the Male 64, Scoop 65, The Suspect Scientist 65, Die by the Book 66, The Mauve Front Door 67, Week End in the Scampi Belt 67; and under the pseudonym of Robert Eton: The

Pattern 34, *The Bus Leaves for the Village* 36, *Palace Pier* 38, *The Legacy* 39, *The Faithful Years, The Corner of Paradise Place, St. Lynn's Advertiser* 46, *The Dragon at the Gate* 48; as Stephen Tring (for Children): *The Old Gang* 51, *Barry Gets His Wish* 52, *Barry's Exciting Year* 52, *Penny Dreadful* 52, *Penny Penitent* 53, *Penny Triumphant* 54, *Penny Dramatic* 55, *Penny in Italy* 57, *Penny and the Pageant, Nurse Ross Takes Over* 58, *Nurse Ross Saves the Day* 60.
33 Park Crescent, Brighton 7, Sussex, England.
Telephone: Brighton 63706.

Meynen, Johannes, IUR.D.; Netherlands business executive; b. 13 April 1901; ed. Free Univ. of Amsterdam.
Assistant Sec., Arnhem Chamber of Commerce 25-26; Sales Man. European Office Hercules Powder Co. (U.S.A.), The Hague 27-40; N.V. Philips, Eindhoven 40-45; Major, Netherlands Army 44-45; Sec.-Gen. Netherlands War Office 45; Minister of War 45-46; Exec. Vice-Pres. Algemeene Kunstzijde Unie N.V. (A.K.U.) 47-62, Pres. 62-67, Deputy Chair. 67-; Vice-Chair. Nat. Bank of the Netherlands; Dir. Amsterdam-Rotterdam Bank, Overseas Gas and Electricity Works, and numerous other companies; Peter Stuyvesant Award; Knight, Netherlands Lion; Order of British Empire; Medal of Freedom (U.S.A.).
Pinkenbergseweg 33, Velp (Gld), Netherlands.

Meyner, Robert Baumle, A.B., LL.B.; American politician; b. 3 July 1908; ed. Lafayette Coll. and Columbia Univ. Law School.
State Senator (Dem.) from Warren Co., N.J. 48-52; Senate Minority Leader 50; Gov. of New Jersey 54-58, 58-62; Partner Meyner and Wiley (law firm) 62-; Admin., Cigarette Advertising Code, Inc.
24 Commerce Street, Newark, N.J. 07102; and 16 Olden Lane, Princeton, N.J. 08540, U.S.A.
Telephone: 201-624-2800.

Michalowski, Jerzy, LL.B.; Polish diplomatist; b. 26 May 1909; ed. Univ. of Warsaw.
Asst. in Polish Inst. of Social Affairs 33-36; Asst. Dir. of Polish Workers' Housing Organisation 36-39; Chief of Housing Dept. of Warsaw City Council 45; Counsellor of Polish Embassy in London Oct. 45-March 46; Deputy Del. of Poland to U.N. March to Nov. 46; Ambassador to Great Britain 46-53; Under-Sec. of State for Education 54-56; Polish rep. to Comm. of Supervision and Control in Vietnam 55-56; Permanent Rep. to the U.N. 56-60; Dir. Gen. Ministry of Foreign Affairs, Warsaw 60-67; Amb. to U.S.A. 67-; First Vice-Pres. ECOSOC 59, Pres. 62; mem. United Polish Workers' Party.
Publs. *Unemployment of Polish Peasants* 34, *Housing Problems in Poland* (published by L. N.) 35.
Polish Embassy, 2640 16th Street, N.W., Washington, D.C. 20009, U.S.A.

Michalowski, Kazimierz, DR. PHIL.; Polish archaeologist; b. 14 Dec. 1901.
Professor of Mediterranean Archaeology, Warsaw Univ.; mem. Presidium Polish Acad. of Sciences; Vice-Dir. Warsaw Nat. Museum, in charge of Franco-Polish excavations Egypt 37-39, Polish excavations Crimea 56-58, Egypt (Tell Atrib 57-, Alexandria 60-, Deir el Bahari 61-), Sudan (Faras 61-64, Dongola 65-), Syria (Palmyra 59-), Cyprus (Nea Paphos 65-); Chair. Int. Working Group of Archaeologists and Landscape Architects, Abu Simbel; Dir. of Polish Centre of Archaeology, Cairo; mem. and Hon. Prof. numerous foreign univs. and acads; Prix de l'Acad. des Inscriptions et Belles Lettres 33; State Prize 55, 66; Dr. h.c. (Strasbourg).
Publs. *Les portraits hellénistiques et romains* 32, *Fouilles Franco-Polonaises à Tell Edfou* 37-50, *Mirmeki* 56, *Palmyre-Fouilles Polonaises, Vols. I-V* 60-66, *Faras-*

Fouilles Polonaises, Vols. I-II 62-65, *Die Kathedrale aus dem Wüstensand* 67.
Sewerynów 6, Warsaw, Poland.
Telephone: 26-39-79.

Michelangeli (Arturo Benedetti Michelangeli); Italian concert pianist; b. 5 Jan. 1920; ed. privately and Conservatorio G. Verdi in Milan.
Taught by Paolo Chiuieri in Brescia, then by Giovanni Anfassi of Milan; studied violin, organ and composition at the Conservatoire in Milan; winner of Grand Prix of Geneva 39; given concerts throughout world; Academician of Accad. Sta. Cecilia, Rome, and Accad. Cherubini, Florence; Gold Medal of Italian Republic.
Via Marsala, 15 Brescia, Italy.

Michelet, Edmond; French politician; b. 8 Oct. 1899.
Served French Army 14-18; later became commercial agent; Pres. of Asscn. of French Commercial Agents; served in Resistance in Second World War; arrested and sent to Dachau; mem. Consultative Assembly; Minister for Armed Forces in De Gaulle Govt. 45, and Gouin and Bidault Govts. 46; Deputy for Corrèze (M.R.P.) 45-51; left M.R.P. and joined Gaullists 47; founded party of Républicains Populaires Indépendants, Senator; Minister for Ex-Servicemen's Affairs (de Gaulle Cabinet) June 58-Jan. 59; Minister of Justice (Debré Cabinet) Jan. 59-Aug. 61; mem. Comité Constitutionel Aug. 61-April 62; Minister of State for Civil Service 67-May 68; Minister of State May 68-; Pres. Anciens de Dachau; Commdr. de la Légion d'Honneur, Croix de Guerre.
Publs. *Rue de la Liberté, Contre la Guerre Civile, Le Gaullisme Passionnante Aventure.*
11 rue St. Dominique, Paris 7e, France.
Telephone: INV 96-40.

Micheli, Pierre; Swiss diplomatist; b. 4 Dec. 1905; ed. Univs. of Oxford, Berlin and Geneva.
Former Sec. to Pres. of Port and Waterways of Danzig; Swiss Fed. Political Dept. 33-, Paris, The Hague, Rio de Janeiro, Batavia, Tokyo 33-45; Chief of Div. of Int. Orgs. Berne 46, Minister Plenipotentiary 52; Minister to France 56-57, Ambassador to France 57-61; Sec.-Gen. Fed. Political Dept. of Switzerland 61-.
Junkerngasse 21, 3000 Berne, Switzerland.
Telephone: 031-22-16-65.

Michelin, François; French industrialist; b. 3 July 1926.
Manager Compagnie Générale des Etablissements Michelin, "Michelin & Cie." 59-.
Usines Michelin (Tyres), 63 Clermont-Ferrand, France.

Michelmore, Laurence, PH.D.; American United Nations official; b. 09; ed. Univ. of California and Harvard Univ.
Administrative Officer, Los Angeles Country Relief Admin. 34-35, Idaho Works Progress Admin. 35-36; Asst. Prof., Wayne Univ. 36-42; Research Dept. Detroit Bureau of Governmental Research 36-42; Staff, U.S. Budget Bureau 42-46; United Nations Secretariat 46-, Dep. Controller 52-55, Senior Dir. Technical Assistance Board 55-59, Dep. Dir. of Personnel 59-63, Personal Rep. of Sec.-Gen. on Malaysia 63; Commr. Gen. of UN Relief and Works Agency (UNRWA) 64-.
UNRWA Headquarters, Museitbeh Quarter, Beirut, Lebanon.
Telephone: 200968.

Michelsen, Hans Günter; German playwright; b. 1920.
Military Service and Prisoner-of-War 39-49; began to write 49; now freelance writer in Frankfurt/Main; Förderpreis des Niedersächsischen Kunstpreises, Hanover 63; Förderpreis des Gerhart-Hauptmann-Preises, Berlin 63; Gerhart-Hauptmann-Preis, Berlin 65; Literaturpreis der Freien Hansestadt Bremen 67.
Publs. plays: *Stienz* 63, *Feierabend 1* and *2* 63, *Lapp-*

schiess 64, *Drei Akte* 65, *Helm* 65, *Frau L* 66; radio play: *Episode* 64.
c/o Suhrkamp Verlag, 6 Frankfurt am Main, Grüneburgweg 69, German Federal Republic.

Michener, James Albert, A.B., A.M.; American writer; b. 13 Feb. 1907; ed. Swarthmore Coll., Colorado State Coll. of Education, Ohio State Univ., Univs. of Pennsylvania, Virginia, Harvard and St. Andrews (Scotland). Teacher 29-36; Prof. Colorado State Coll. of Educ. 36-41; Assoc. Ed., Macmillan Co. 41-49; U.S. Naval Reserve 44-45; mem. Advisory Cttee. on the Arts, U.S. State Dept. 57; Chair. Pres. Kennedy's Food for Peace Program 61; Pulitzer Prize for *Tales of the South Pacific* 47; Einstein Award 67.
Publs. *Unit in the Social Studies* 40, *Tales of the South Pacific* 47, *The Fires of Spring* 49, *Return to Paradise* 51, *The Voice of Asia* 51, *The Bridges at Toko-ri* 53, *Sayonara* 54, *Floating World* 55, *The Bridge at Andau* 57, *Rascals in Paradise* (with A. Grove Day) 57, *Selected Writings* 57, *The Hokusai Sketchbook* 58, *Japanese Prints* 59, *Hawaii* 59, *Report of the County Chairman* 61, *Caravans* 63, *The Source* 65, *Iberia* 68.
Box 125, Pipersville, Pa. 18947, U.S.A.

Michener, Rt. Hon. Roland, C.C., Q.C., P.C., B.C.L., M.A., Barrister-at-Law; Canadian Governor-General; b. 19 April 1900; ed. Univ. of Alberta and Oxford Univ.
Barrister, Middle Temple (England) 23, Ontario 24; Practising lawyer, Lang, Michener and Cranston, Toronto 24-57; mem. Ontario Legislature for St. David, Toronto 45-48, Provincial Sec. and Registrar for Toronto 46-48; Progressive Conservative mem. of House of Commons 53-62; Speaker of House of Commons 57-58, 58-62; High Commr. in India 64-67; Gov.-Gen. of Canada April 67-; Gen. Sec. for Canada for Rhodes Scholarships 36-64; fmr. Gov. Toronto Western Hospital; fmr. Pres. Lawyers Club, Empire Club, Board of Trade Club, Toronto; Hon. Vice-Pres. Canadian Inst. of Int. Affairs; Hon. Fellow Hertford Coll. Oxford 61; Hon. LL.D. Ottawa 48, Queen's 58, Laval 60.
Government House, Ottawa, Ontario, Canada.

Micklem, Nathaniel, M.A., D.D., LL.D.; British minister of religion, politician and professor; b. 10 April 1888; ed. Rugby School and Univ. of Oxford.
Prof. Old Testament, Selly Oak Colleges, Birmingham 21-27; Prof. New Testament, Queen's Theological Coll., Queen's Univ., Ontario 27-31; Principal Mansfield Coll. Oxford 32-53; Wilde Lecturer in Natural Theology and Comparative Religion, Oxford 49-50; Visiting Prof. and Cole Lecturer, Vanderbilt Univ., Tennessee 54; Pres. of the Liberal Party 57-58; Pres. Liberal Int. (British Group) 59-.
Publs. *National Socialism and the Roman Catholic Church* 39, *Religion* 48, *Law and the Laws* 52, *Faith and Reason: a Question from Duns Scotus* 53, *Ultimate Questions* 55, *The Abyss of Truth* 56, *The Idea of a Liberal Democracy* 57, *The Labyrinth Revisited* 60, *The Doctrine of Our Redemption* 61, *The Place of Understanding* 63, *A Religion for Agnostics* 65.
Monks Staithe, Princes Risborough, Bucks., England.

Micombero, Col. Michel; Burundian army officer and politician; b. 1940; ed. Catholic Colls. of St. Esprit, Bujumbura, and Military Acad., Brussels.
Recalled from Brussels Mil. Acad. when Burundi became independent 62; became Minister of Nat. Defence; Chief of Secs. of State 65-66; Prime Minister July 66-; Pres. Nov. 66-.
Office of the President, Bujumbura, Burundi.

Micunovic, Veljko; Yugoslav diplomatist; b. 16; ed. Belgrade Univ.
One of the organisers of National uprising in Montenegro; political leader in the territories of Montenegro, Bosnia, Serbia; Asst. Minister of the Interior; Asst.

Minister of Foreign Affairs 52; Ambassador to U.S.S.R. 55-58; Under-Sec. of State for Foreign Affairs 58-61, Dep. Sec. of State 61-62; Ambassador to U.S.A. 62-; mem. Cen. Cttee. of Yugoslav League of Communists; Order of Nat. Hero, Meritorious Services to the People, 1st Class, etc.
Yugoslav Embassy, 2410 California Street, Washington, D.C., U.S.A.

Middelburg, Duco G. E.; Netherlands diplomatist; b. 1907; ed. Rotterdam Inst. of Economics.
Netherlands Foreign Service 31-, served London, Hong Kong, Kobe, Paris 31-39; with Netherlands Govt. in exile in London during Second World War; Consul-Gen., Shanghai, Antwerp and Singapore after Second World War; Amb. to Poland 59-62, to Chile 62-67; Perm. Rep. to UN 67-.
Permanent Mission of Netherlands to UN, 711 Third Avenue, New York, N.Y. 10017, U.S.A.

Middelmann, Werner G.; German United Nations official; b. 10 Oct. 1909.
Electrical appliance and chemical industry, Germany 26-45, Exec. Dir. 35-45; in charge of Refugees and Expellees, Baden-Württemburg 45-46, U.S. Zone of Occupation 47, U.S. and British Zones of Occupation 47-49; Perm. Sec. Fed. Ministry for Expellees, Refugees, and War Victims, Bonn 49-61; Dir., E. Mediterranean Region, United Nations Children's Fund (UNICEF) 61-65; Comptroller, UNICEF New York 66-.
UNICEF, New York, United Nations, New York; 6600 Boulevard East, West New York, N.J. 07093, U.S.A.
Telephone: 201-868-4947.

Middleton, Drew, B.S.; American journalist; b. 14 Oct. 1914; ed. Syracuse Univ.
Sports editor Poughkeepsie (N.Y.) *Eagle News* 36; reporter Poughkeepsie *Evening Star* 36-37; sports writer N.Y. office Assoc. Press 39; war corresp. attached to B.E.F. France and Belgium 39-40, to R.A.F. 40-41, to U.S. Army and Navy, Iceland 41-42, Allied Forces, London 42; staff of *New York Times*, London 42; corresp. North Africa and Mediterranean area and Allied H.Q. Algiers 42-43; with U.S. Eighth Air Force and R.A.F. Bomber Commd. 43-44; U.S. First Army and SHAEF 44-45; Frankfurt, Berlin and Int. Mil. Trials, Nuremberg 45-46; Chief Corresp. *New York Times* in U.S.S.R. 46-47, Germany 47-53, London 53-62, Paris 62-65, U.N. (New York) 65-; U.S. Medal of Freedom 48; O.B.E. (Mil. Div.) 47; Hon. D.Litt. (Syracuse Univ.) 63.
Publs. *Our Share of Night* 46, *The Struggle for Germany* 49, *The Defence of Western Europe* 52, *The British* 57, *The Sky Suspended* 60, *The Supreme Choice: Britain and the European Community* 63, *The Crisis in the West* 65.
c/o The New York Times, 229 West 43 Street, New York City 36, N.Y., U.S.A.

Middleton, Sir George Humphrey, K.C.M.G.; British diplomatist; b. 21 Jan. 1910; ed. St. Lawrence Coll., Ramsgate, and Magdalen Coll., Oxford.
Entered Consular Service 33; Vice-Consul, Buenos Aires; Third Sec., Asunción 34, in charge of Legation 35, New York 36; Consul at Lemberg (Lwów) 39; in charge of Vice-Consulate, Cluj 39-40, Genoa 40, Madeira 40, Foreign Office 43; Second Sec., Washington 44; First Sec. 45; Foreign Office 47; Counsellor 49; Counsellor, British Embassy, Teheran 51; Chargé d'Affaires 51 and 52; Deputy High Commr. for U.K., Delhi 53-56; Ambassador to the Lebanon 56-58; Political Resident in Persian Gulf 58-61; Ambassador to Argentina 61-64, to United Arab Republic 64-65.
53 Albert Hall Mansions, London, S.W.7, England.

Middleton, William Shainline, M.D., F.R.C.P. (Lond.); American physician; b. 7 Jan. 1890; ed. Pennsylvania Univ.
Interne Philadelphia Gen. Hospital 11-12; Instructor

Clinical Medicine, Univ. of Wisconsin 12-15, Asst. Prof. Clinical Medicine 15-25, Assoc. Prof. Medicine 25-33, Prof. 33-60; Dean Medical School 35-55, Emer. Prof. Medicine, Emer. Dean Medical School 60-; Chief Medical Dir., Veterans Admin. 55-63; visiting Prof. Medicine, Univ. of Okla. 63-64; Master, American Coll. Physicians; mem. Asscn. American Physicians, American Clinical and Climatological Asscn.; foreign hon. mem. Asscn. Physicians, Great Britain and Ireland; Hon. Fellow, Royal Soc. Medicine; foreign corresp. mem. Sociedad de Medicina Interna de Buenos Aires; Lieut. and Capt. M.O.R.C., U.S. Army with B.E.F. and A.E.F. France 17-19; Lieut.-Col. and Col. Medical Corps, U.S. Army 42-45; Distinguished Service Medal; O.B.E.; Legion of Merit; Croix de Guerre; Hon. Sc.D. (Pennsylvania Univ. 46 and Univ. of Cambridge 50); LL.D. (Temple Univ. 56), L.H.D. (Franklin and Marshall 57), Litt.D. (Marquette Univ. 58); Outstanding Achievement Award, Veterans Admin. 60; Alfred Stengel Memorial Medal, American Coll. Physicians 62.
2114 Adams Street, Madison, Wisconsin, U.S.A.

Midence Soto, Ricardo Adolfo, LL.B.; Honduran business executive and diplomatist; b. 1929; ed. Instituto Central de Varones, Tegucigalpa, Colegio Inglés Americano, Guatemala City, Babson Inst. of Business Administration, U.S.A., and Universidad de Honduras, Tegucigalpa.
Former Gen. Manager, Herederos de Santos Soto; fmr. Manager and Sec. Admin. Council Soto Comercial S.A.; Dir. and Asst. Gen. Manager, Banco de Honduras; Ambassador to U.S.A. and Rep. to Org. of American States (OAS) 64-; Head, Honduran Mission to the 10th Foreign Ministers' Conf.; mem. of Honduran Del. to 19th UN Gen. Assembly.
Representation of Honduras to Organization of American States, 4715 Sixteenth Street, N.W., Washington, D.C. 20011, U.S.A.; Apdo. No. 6, Tegucigalpa, D.C., Honduras, Central America.

Mieghem, Jacques Van; Belgian meteorologist; b. 26 Oct. 1905; ed. Univ. of Brussels.
Head of Royal Meteorological Institute of Belgium 62-; Prof. Free University of Brussels 47-; mem. Royal Flemish Acad. of Belgium; Pres. of Aerological Comm. 51-57; mem. Special Cttee. Int. Geophysical Year 53-59, Int. Geophysical Cttee. 59-; Vice-Pres. Int. Asscn. of Meteorology 54-57; Pres. Int. Asscn. of Meteorology and Atmospheric Physics 57-60, Belgian Polar Inst. 58; Sec.-Gen. Int. Council of Scientific Unions 61-63; Chevalier Ordre de Léopold 43, Commdr. 57, Officier de l'Ordre de la Couronne 47.
Publs. *Etude sur la théorie des ondes* 34, *Prévision du temps par l'analyse des cartes météorologiques* 36, *Propagation des ondes électromagnétiques en milieu homogène* 44, *Thermodynamique de l'atmosphère* (with L. Dufour) 49.
1 Avenue Circulaire, Uccle, Brussels 18, Belgium.

Mielziner, Jo; American artist, designer and producer; b. France 19 March 1901; ed. Pennsylvania Acad. of Fine Arts.
Has designed settings and costumes for opera, ballet and numerous (254) productions, inc. *The Guardsman, Strange Interlude, Wild Duck, The Barretts of Wimpole Street, On Your Toes, Dodsworth, Winterset, I Married an Angel, Boys from Syracuse, Knickerbocker Holiday, High Tor, Abe Lincoln in Illinois, Annie Get Your Gun, Finian's Rainbow, Dream Girl, The Glass Menagerie, Happy Birthday, Carousel, Mister Roberts, A Streetcar Named Desire, Death of a Salesman, South Pacific, The Innocents, Guys and Dolls, The King and I, Can Can, Picnic, Tea and Sympathy, Fanny, Silk Stockings, The Lark, Pipe Dream, Middle of the Night, The Most Happy Fella, Look Homeward, Angel, Oh Captain!, The World of Suzie Wong, Sweet Bird of Youth, Gypsy, The Gang's All Here, Silent Night Lonely Night, The Best*

Man, Period of Adjustment, Little Moon of Alban, The Devil's Advocate, The Milk Train Doesn't Stop Here Any More, After the Fall, But for Whom Charlie, The Owl and the Pussycat; and designed and produced *Happy Hunting;* Hon. Doctorate of Fine Arts, Fordham Univ. 47; camouflage specialist; Major, U.S.A.A.F. 42-45; Collaborating designer for Lincoln Center Repertory Theatre and Univ. of Michigan Theatre; Consultant for Los Angeles Music Center and Krannert Center for the Performing Arts, Univ. of Illinois; designed setting for Michelangelo's *Pietà,* N.Y. World's Fair 64; Chair. American Theatre Planning Board; Acad. Award Oscar for Colour Art Direction on *Picnic.*
Publ. *Designing for the Theatre: Jo Mielziner.*
1 West 72nd Street, New York 23, N.Y., U.S.A.

Mies van der Rohe, Ludwig; German-born American architect; b. 27 March 1886; ed. Domschule and Gewerbeschule, Aachen, Kunstgewerbe Museum, Berlin. Professor of Architecture, Illinois Inst. of Technology 38-58, Prof. Emeritus 58-; private Architectural Practice, Chicago 58-; Gold Medal, American Inst. of Architects, Medal of Honor, Pan-American Architects Asscn., Award of Merit, Ruskin Soc. of America, Feltrinelli Prize; R.I.B.A. Gold Medal 59; Hon. mem. Royal Inst. of British Architects and many other academies; mem. Düsseldorf Acad., American Asscn. of Univ. Profs., American Acad. of Arts and Letters N.Y., etc.; Hon. D.Eng. Karlsruhe, Illinois and Brunswick Insts. of Technology; Hon. LL.D. Carolina; Hon. Dr. Fine Arts, Illinois and Northwestern Univs. and Carnegie Inst. of Technology; Hon. Dr. Humanities, Wayne Univ.; Orden Pour le Mérite (Cross of Commdr. 59) (German Federal Republic), numerous other awards.
Principal works include the German Pavilion, Barcelona Exhbn. 29, buildings for the Illinois Inst. of Technology since 41, Seagram Building (New York) 58, New Nat. Gallery, Berlin, office and apartment buildings in Chicago, Detroit, Newark, Des Moines, Baltimore, Toronto, Montreal, etc.
230 East Ohio Street, Chicago, Ill. 60611, U.S.A.
Telephone: WH3-0686.

Miettunen, Martti; Finnish politician; b. 17 April 1907.
Former Secretary Agrarian Party; fmr. Minister of Agriculture, Communications and Finance; Gov. of Lappland 58-61; Prime Minister of Finland July 61-62.
Helsinki, Finland.

Mifune, Toshiro; Japanese actor; b. 1920.
First screen apperance in *Shin Baka Jidai* (These Foolish Times) 47; played leading role in *Rashomon* 50; other films in which he has played important roles include *Yoidore Tenshi* (Drunken Angel) 48, *Shichinin no Samurai* (The Seven Samurai), *Miyamoto Musashi* (The Legend of Musashi) 54, *Kumonosu-Jo, Muhomatsu No Issho* (The Rickshawman) 58, *Kakushitoride No San Akunin* (The Hidden Fortress) 58, *Sengoku Guntoden* (Saga of the Vagabonds) 59, *Nippon Tanjo* (The Three Treasures) 59, *Ankokugai No Taiketsu* (The Last Gunfight) 60, *Taiheiyo No Arashi* (The Storm of the Pacific), *Yosimbo, Tsubaki Sanjuro, Osakajo Monogatari* (Daredevil in the Castle), *Grand Prix, Rebellion.*
c/o Toho Co. Ltd., 1-4 Yuraku-cho, Chiyoda-ku, Tokyo.

Migdal, Arkadiy Baynusovich; Soviet theoretical physicist; b. 1911; ed. Leningrad Univ.
Professor Moscow Engineering and Physics Inst. 44-; Corresp. mem. U.S.S.R. Acad. of Sciences 53-66, mem. 66-; Order of Lenin; Order of Red Banner of Labour.
U.S.S.R. Academy of Sciences, 14 Lenin Prospekt, Moscow, U.S.S.R.

Migone, Bartolomeo; Italian diplomatist; b. 2 June 1901; ed. Inst. of Social Sciences, Florence.
Entered Foreign Office 23; Sec. Italian Del. to League of Nations Assembly 28; Sec. Italian Legation Berne

30, Cairo 31; First Sec. Washington 33, Moscow 36; Counsellor of Embassy Santiago 40; Head of Press Bureau Foreign Office Rome 44; Counsellor Office of Italian Rep. London 44, Minister Counsellor, Chargé d'Affaires London 47; Minister Counsellor, Italian Embassy London 47-48; Minister to Sweden 48-51; Dir.-Gen. for Cultural Relations, Ministry of Foreign Affairs, Rome 52-55; Del. 7th Gen. Conf., UNESCO Paris 52, 8th Gen. Conf. Montevideo 54; mem. Cttee. of Cultural Experts, Council of Europe, Strasbourg 52-55; Chief of Foreign Minister's Cabinet, Ministry of Foreign Affairs 55-57; Ambassador to Holy See 58-64; Chair. Italian Nat. Freedom From Hunger Campaign Comm. Via Valdagno 8, Rome, Italy.

Migot, Georges; French musician; b. 27 Feb. 1891. Former Curator Instrumental Museum of Conservatoire Nat. de Musique; fmr. mem. Conseil Supérieur de l'Enseignement du Conservatoire and Comité de Propagande Nationale pour la Musique; Musical Dir. Int. Society of Friends of French Music; Pres.-Inspector Geneva Acad. of Music; mem. Jury of American Foundation of French Thought and Art; mem. Royal Acads. Bologna, Florence and Besançon; Grand Prix de la Musique française 58, Gold Medal "Arts et Sciences" 59, Grand Prix du disque for *Le Zodiaque Choréographielyrique*; Officier de la Légion d'Honneur, Croix de Guerre, Chevalier de l'Ordre des Arts et Lettres, Officier d'Académie, Officer of Orders of Polonia Restituta and of Crown of Italy.
Works: has published for theatre; orchestral, choral and religious music; symphonies, operas, ballets, oratorios; music for choir and strings, unaccompanied voices, wind instruments, piano, etc., a total of nearly 300 works; including *Le sermon sur la Montagne, La Passion, In memoriam pour les morts des deux guerres, Le Petit Evangéliaire, La Nuit Pascale et Résurrection, Requiem à Cappella, Le Rossignol en amour, Cantata de le Vie meilleure, Saint Germain d'Auxerre, Sinfonia da Chiesa* (for wind instruments), *Symphonie des Nombres, Symphonie Espace et Temps, L'Annonciation, Le Zodiaque Choréographielyrique, Cantate d'Amour;* thirteen Symphonies, four Concertos, two Suites, Sonatas, Duets, Trios, Quartets, many songs, and numerous other works.
Publs. *Lexique de Termes Musicaux, avec des Commentaires, J. P. Rameau et le Génie français dans la Musique, Collected Poems* (Prix de la Société des Gens de Lettres). 16 rue de Naples, Paris 8e, France.
Telephone: 522-66-97.

Migulin, Vladimir Vasilyevich; Soviet physicist; b. 10 July 1911; ed. Faculty of Physics and Mechanics of Polytechnical Inst. of Leningrad.
Engineer in Research Inst. of Leningrad 32-34; Senior Scientific Collaborator of the Physical Inst. of the Acad. of Sciences of the U.S.S.R., Moscow, and Chief of Div. 34-51; Asst. Lecturer 35-38, Lecturer 39-46, Prof. 47-54, 57-, Deputy Dean of the Faculty of Physics 54-57, Moscow Univ.; Dir. Inst. of Physical Research at Suchumi 51-54; Deputy Dir.-Gen. Int. Atomic Energy Agency for the Div. of Training and Technical Information 58-59; Editor *Moscow Univ. Bulletin*, Physics and Astronomy section 60-; Chief, Div. of Inst. of Radio-engineering and Electronics, Acad. of Sciences of U.S.S.R. 62-; State prizewinner (twice) for scientific works; several Orders of the Soviet Union.
Publs. include numerous articles in scientific journals on investigations on electrical oscillations in non-linear and parametric systems, investigations on the propagation of radio waves by interference methods and circuit theory and investigations on new methods of receiving of mm and sub-mm e-m waves.
Moscow University, Faculty of Physics, Moscow, U.S.S.R.

Mihailov, Gen. Ivan; Bulgarian lawyer, army officer and politician; b. 97; ed. Sofia Univ. and Moscow Mil. Acad.
Former solicitor; U.S.S.R. 23-44; Bulgarian Defence Ministry, Commdr. of Artillery 44-; Dep. Prime Minister 57-; Minister of Transport and Communications 57-58, of Defence 58-61; mem. Political Bureau of Cen. Cttee. of Communist Party, mem. Nat. Ass.; numerous awards.
Office of the Deputy Prime Ministers, Sofia, Bulgaria.

Mihalik, Sándor; Hungarian art-historian; b. 18 Feb. 1900; ed. Budapest, Rome, Paris, Berlin, London.
Editorial staff of Hungarian Information Office until 26; mem. of Hungarian Historical Inst. in Rome 26-30; mem. Acad. of Arts, Siena 28; Keeper of Hungarian Nat. Museum of Industrial Art 30-39, later Dir. 45-46; Dir. of Kassa Museum 40-45; Deputy Dir. of Hungarian National Museum 46-65.
Publs. *A rimaszombati ötvös céh, L'origine dello smalto filogranato, A kassai Miklós Börtön, Benczúr Kassán, Szentpeteri József, Old Hungarian Enamels.*
Nemzeti Muzeum, Muzeum krt, 14-16, Budapest VIII; Gorkij fasor 12, Budapest VI, Hungary.
Telephone: 224-527.

Mihály, András; Hungarian composer and professor of chamber music; b. 6 Nov. 1917; ed. Berzsenyi Gymnasium and F. Liszt Conservatoire of Music, Budapest.
First violoncello solo in orchestra of Budapest Opera House 46-47; Gen. Sec. of Budapest Opera 48-49; Prof. of Chamber Music, F. Liszt Conservatoire, Budapest 50-; Reader of Contemporary Music, Musical Dept., Hungarian Broadcasting Corpn. 59-; Kossuth Prize 55; Erkel Prize 50, 65.
Works include: Concerto for Violoncello and Orchestra 53, Concerto for Pianoforte and Orchestra 54, Fantasy for Wind Quintet and String Orchestra 55, Songs on the Poems of James Joyce 58, Concerto for Violin and Orchestra 59, String Quartet 60, Symphony 62, *Together and Alone* (opera in two acts) 65.
Vérhalom tér 9b, Budapest II, Hungary.
Telephone: 352-295.

Mihályfi, Erno; Hungarian journalist and politician; b. 3 Sept. 1898.
Editor *Független Magyarország* 39; founder mem. Smallholder's Party; Chair. Hungarian-Soviet Friendship Soc.; fmr. Minister of Information 47; commissioned Foreign Minister 47; Chair. Inst. for Cultural Relations 49-50; Chair. Asscn. of Hungarian Journalists 46-56; Deputy Minister of Educ. 51-58; mem. Nat. Presidium, Patriotic People's Front and the Presidential Council; Editor *Magyar Nemzet.*
Magyar Nemzet, Lenin krt. 9.11, Budapest VII, Hungary.
Telephone: 221-285.

Mikhailov, Alexander Alexandrovich; Soviet astronomer; b. 1888; ed. Moscow Univ.
Professor Moscow Univ. 18-50; Dir. Main Astronomical Observatory, U.S.S.R. Academy of Sciences, Pulkovo 47-65; Corresp. mem. U.S.S.R. Acad. of Sciences 43-64, mem. 64-; Chair. Astronomical Council, U.S.S.R. Acad. of Sciences 39-; mem. C.P.S.U. 56-; Vice-Pres. Int. Astronomical Union 46-48; Order of Lenin (twice).
U.S.S.R. Academy of Sciences, 14 Lenin Prospekt, Moscow, U.S.S.R.

Mikhailov, Nikolai Alexandrovich; Soviet politician; b. 1906.
Began work in Hammer & Sickle Works, Moscow; joined Communist Party 30; editor factory newspaper, Hammer & Sickle Works, and later Dynamo Works 32-37; worked for *Pravda* and *Komsomolskaya Pravda* 37-52; 1st Sec. Central Cttee. Young Communist League 38-52; Sec. Central Cttee. Communist Party 52-53; Sec. Moscow Regional Cttee. Communist Party 53-54;

Ambassador to Poland 54-55; Minister of Culture 55-60; Ambassador to Indonesia 60-65; Deputy to Supreme Soviet 46-; mem. Central Cttee. Communist Party 39-; Chair. Cttee. on Press under Council of Ministers of the U.S.S.R. 65-; three Orders of Lenin, Order of Patriotic War (1st Class).
State Committee for Press and Publishing, Moscow, U.S.S.R.

Mikhailov, Sergei Sergeyevich, M.SC.; Soviet diplomatist; b. 1912; ed. Univ. of Leningrad.
Diplomatic Service 40-; Counsellor, Turkey 45-46; Head of Sixth European Dept. of U.S.S.R. Ministry of Foreign Affairs 46-48; Deputy Head, First European Dept., U.S.S.R. Ministry of Foreign Affairs 48-49, 54-55; Counsellor, Rome 50-51; Minister to Uruguay 55-60; mem. staff Ministry of Foreign Affairs, later Dir. of Latin American Inst. of U.S.S.R. Acad. of Sciences 60-65; Ambassador to Brazil 65-.
U.S.S.R. Embassy, 175 Alice Street, Larangeiros, Rio de Janeiro, Brazil.

Mikhalkov, Sergei Vladimirovich; Soviet poet, playwright and children's writer; b. 1913.
Began writing 28, verses for children 35; joint author (with El-Registan) Soviet Anthem 43; mem. C.P. 50-; First Sec. Union of Moscow Soviet Writers 65-; Deputy of Supreme Soviet of R.S.F.S.R. 67-; Corresp. mem. Acad. of Pedagogical Sciences; two Orders of Lenin, three State Prizes.
Publs. *Dyadya Styopa* (Uncle Steve) 36 and *Collected Works* (poems, stories, plays) in two vols.; Film script: *Frontovye podrugi* (Frontline Friends) 41; Plays: *Tom Kenti* (after Mark Twain) 38, *Krasnyi galstuk* (Red Neckerchief) 47, *Ilya Golovin, Ya khochu domoi* (I Want to Go Home) 49, *Raki* (Lobsters) 52, *Zaika-Zaznaika* 55, *Basni Mikhalkova* 57, *Sombrero* 58, *Pamyatnik Sebe* (A Monument to Oneself) 58, *Dikari* (Campers) 59, *Collected Works* (4 Vols.) 64.
Union of Soviet Writers, ul. Vorovskogo 52, Moscow, U.S.S.R.

Mikheev, Mikhail Aleksandrovich; Soviet combustion engineer; b. 1902; ed. Leningrad Polytechnic Inst.
Leningrad Physicotechnical Inst., Cen. Steam Turbine Inst., and other Technical Research and Higher Educ. Insts., Leningrad and Moscow 25-33; Head, Heat Exchange Laboratory, Krzhizhanovsky Power Eng. Inst., U.S.S.R. Acad. of Sciences 33-; Prof. Moscow Power Eng. Inst. 36-; Corresp. mem. U.S.S.R. Acad. of Sciences 46-53, mem. 53-; State Prizes, Order of Lenin.
Publs. include: *Model Analysis of Heating Installations* 41, *Principles of Heat Transfer* 51.
U.S.S.R. Academy of Sciences, 14 Lenin Prospekt, Moscow, U.S.S.R.

Mikheyev, Pyotr Vasilyevich; Soviet foreign trade official; b. 1918; ed. Moscow Inst. of Chemical Engineering.
Academy of Foreign Trade 50-; posts at Ministry of Foreign Trade 50-58; Deputy Trade Rep. of U.S.S.R. in Finland 58-62; Vice-Chair. *Tekhmashimport* Asscn. 62-64, Chair. 64-; mem. C.P.S.U.; Order of Badge of Honour (twice).
Tekhmashimport Association, Ministry of Foreign Trade, 32-34 Smolenskaya-Sennaya ploshchad, Moscow, U.S.S.R.

Miki, Takeo, LL.M.; Japanese politician; b. 17 March 1907; ed. Meiji Univ., Tokyo.
Member House of Reps. 37-; Minister of Communications 47-48, of Transport 54-55, of Economic Planning 58-59; State Minister, Dir. of Science and Technology Agency, Chair. of Atomic Energy Comm. 61-62; Minister of International Trade and Industry 65-66; Minister of Foreign Affairs 66-; mem. Japanese Democratic Party.
185 Kichijoji, Musashino City, Tokyo-to; 29-7, 3-chome, Higashi-machi, Kichijoji, Musashino-shi, Tokyo, Japan.

Mikoyan, Anastas Ivanovich (brother of Artem Mikoyan, *q.v.*); Soviet politician; b. 25 Nov. 1895.
Mem. Communist Party 15-; a leading Party organiser in Baku Oct. 17; on Soviet defeat in 18 he was imprisoned, but freed 19; organised general strike in Baku; was jailed, escaped; was rearrested and deported to Georgia; escaped again and returned to Baku; after Soviet victory held various positions in the Caucasus; mem. Central Cttee. of Communist Party 23-; Candidate for Politburo 26-35, mem. 35-52; People's Commissar for Supplies 30-34 and for the Food Industry 34-Jan. 38; mem. Council of Labour and Defence; Vice-Chair. Council of People's Commissars 37-46; Minister for Foreign Trade until 49; participated British and American Missions, Moscow; mem. Cttee. of State Defence 42-45; former mem. Cttee. for Economic Rehabilitation of Liberated Areas; Vice-Chair. Council of Ministers and Minister of Home and Foreign Trade 53-55; First Deputy Chair. Council of Ministers 55-64; mem. Presidium Central Cttee., Communist Party 52-66; Chair. of Presidium of Supreme Soviet of U.S.S.R. July 64-Dec. 65, mem. 65-; awarded four Orders of Lenin, title Hero of Socialist Labour, and Hammer and Sickle Gold Medal 43.
Publ. autobiography 68.
Presidium of Supreme Soviet of U.S.S.R., Kremlin, Moscow, U.S.S.R.

Mikoyan, Artem Ivanovich (brother of Anastas Ivanovich Mikoyan, *q.v.*); Soviet aircraft designer; b. 1905; ed. Zhukovsky Air Force Acad.
Corresponding mem. Acad. of Sciences of the U.S.S.R. 58-; Lieut.-Gen. in the Engineering-Technical Service; Designer to U.S.S.R. Ministry of Aircraft Industry 56-; mem. C.P.S.U. 25-; State Prizewinner; Order of Lenin (five times); Hero of Socialist Labour (twice); Lenin Prize.
Principal work: joint design with M. Gurevich of the MiG-1 fighter 39-40, the MiG-3 40; the first Mikoyan design turbo-jet, MiG-9 46, the MiG-15, MiG-17, MiG-19, MiG-21.
Ministry of Aircraft Industry, Moscow, U.S.S.R.

Mikulich, Vladimir Andreyevich; Soviet party leader and politician; b. 1920; ed. C.P.S.U. Higher Party School.
Factory worker 37-40; with Soviet Army 40-45; mem. C.P.S.U. 43-; Young Communist League worker in Byelorussia 45-53; Sec. then First Sec. Minsk District Cttee., C.P. of Byelorussia 53-62; Second Sec. Brest Regional Cttee. C.P. of Byelorussia 62-Jan. 63, First Sec. 63-; mem. Central Auditing Comm. C.P.S.U.; Deputy to Supreme Soviet of the U.S.S.R.; Hero of Socialist Labour.
Brest Regional Committee, Communist Party of Byelorussia, Brest, U.S.S.R.

Mikulin, Alexandr Alexandrovich; Soviet aircraft engine designer; b. 95.
Constructor at the Scientific Inst. for Auto-Motors 23; Major-Gen. in the Engineering-Technical Service; Dip. of Dr. of Technological Science 38; mem. Acad. of Sciences of U.S.S.R. 54-; Hero of Socialist Labour; State Prizewinner (four times); Order of Lenin (three times), Order of Suvorov 1st and 2nd Class; many other decorations.
Principal designs: the AM-34 engine (first Polar Flight) 29, the AM-35, used in MiG planes 37, the AM-38f, for the IL-2 fighter 41-45; the AM-42; the first Soviet turbo-compressor and variable-pitch airscrew; also a number of jet engines.
Ministry of Aircraft Industry, Moscow, U.S.S.R.

Mil, Mikhail Leontyevich, D.TECH.S., Soviet aircraft designer; b. 1909; ed. Novocherkassk Aviation Inst.
Member C.P.S.U. 43-; Chief Designer, Helicopter Experimental Design Office 47; Designer-Gen., U.S.S.R. Ministry of Aircraft Industry 64; designed "Flying

Crane" helicopters: MI-1, MI-2, MI-4, MI-6, MI-8 and MI-10; Lenin Prize 62, Hero of Socialist Labour 66; Order of Lenin, Order of Red Banner of Labour, Order of Patriotic War 2nd Class, Order of Red Star, etc.
Ministry of Aircraft Engineering, Moscow, U.S.S.R.

Milani, Umberto; Italian artist; b. 1 Dec. 1912; ed. Scuola Superiore d'arte, Milan and Accad. di Brera, Milan.
Early career as painter, first one-man exhbn. 28, now mainly sculptor sometimes in the field of architecture; mem. Accad. di S. Luca 65; numerous nat. prizes and prizes at Milan Triennale 51 and 54, and Venice Biennale 62.
Major works: carvings for building of Milan Triennale.
Via Castelfidardo 11, Milan. Italy.

Milbank, Samuel Robbins, A.B.; American banker; b. 16 March 1906; ed. Princeton Univ.
With Brown Bros. & Co., New York 29-31; joined Wood, Struthers and Winthrop 31, Gen. Partner 36-; Pres. Milbank Memorial Fund, Pine Street Fund, Memton Fund; dir. numerous corpns.; Chair. Board of Trustees, Barnard Coll., N.Y.; Pres. American Numismatic Soc.; Fellow Royal Numismatic Soc. (Great Britain).
Office: 30 Wall Street, New York City 5; Home: 1 East End Avenue, New York 21, N.Y., U.S.A.

Miles, Bernard, C.B.E.; British actor and director; b. 27 Sept. 1907; ed. Uxbridge County School and Pembroke Coll., Oxford.
First stage appearance 30; written for, directed, and acted in films 37-; West End stage appearances 38-; music-hall stage appearances 50-; founded Mermaid Theatre, North London 50, formed Mermaid Theatre Trust, opened Mermaid Theatre, City of London (Puddle Dock) 59.
Mill Cottage, Little Bardfield, nr. Dunmow, Essex, England.

Miles, Josephine, M.A., PH.D.; American poet; b. 11 June 1911; ed. Univ. of California (Los Angeles and Berkeley).
Instructor in English, Univ. of California (Berkeley) 40, Prof. of English 52-; mem. American Acad. of Arts and Sciences 64; Shelley Award for Poetry 35, Nat. Inst. of Arts and Letters Award for Poetry 56.
Publs. Poetry: *Lines of Intersection* 39, *Poems on Several Occasions* 41, *Local Measures* 46, *Prefabrications* 55, *Poems 1930-60* 60, *Civil Poems* 66, *Kinds of Affection* 67; Prose: *Vocabulary of Poetry* 46, *Continuity of Poetic Language* 51, *Eras and Modes in English Poetry* 57 (revised edn. 64), *Emerson* 64, *Style and Proportion in the Language of Prose and Poetry* 67.
2275 Virginia Street, Berkeley, California 94709, U.S.A.

Mileykovsky, Abram Gerasimovich; Soviet economist; b. 1911; ed. Leningrad Univ.
Postgraduate, Asst. Prof. Leningrad Univ. 35-40; Service in the Army 40-56; mem. C.P.S.U. 40-; Head of Dept., Inst. of World Economy and Int. Relations, U.S.S.R. Acad. of Sciences 56; Corresp. mem. U.S.S.R. Acad. of Sciences 66-.
Publs. Works on economy and politics of Great Britain, state monopoly capitalism, analysis and criticism of Western economic theories, etc.
U.S.S.R. Academy of Sciences, 14 Lenin Prospekt, Moscow, U.S.S.R.

Milhaud, Darius; French composer; b. 4 Sept. 1892; ed Paris Conservatoire.
Honorary Prof. Conservatoire de Paris 47- also at Mills Coll., Oakland, Calif.; mem. "Group of Six"; Grand Officier Légion d'Honneur, Commdr. Ordre des Arts et Lettres.
Works include: *Le Boeuf sur le Toit* (ballet) 19, *L'Homme et son désir* (ballet), *La Brebis égarée* (opera) 15, *La Création du Monde* (ballet) 23, *Salade* (ballet), *Le Train*

Bleu (ballet) 24, *Les Malheurs d'Orphée, L'Enlèvement d'Europe, Le Pauvre Matelot, Maximilien, La Délivrance de Thésée, Christophe Colomb, Médée, Bolivar, David and Fiesta, La Mère Coupable* (operas), *L'Orestie d'Eschyle, Les poèmes juifs* 16, *Suites* for orchestra 18, *Ballade, Sérénade, Le Carnaval d'Aix, Saudades do Brazil, Printemps;* eighteen String Quartets, four Quintets, nine Sonatas, twelve Symphonies and 36 Concertos; *The Beloved Vagabond* (film), *Cortège Funèbre;* musical version of papal encyclical *Pacem in Terris* 63.
Publs. *Etudes, Notes sur Erik Satie, Notes sans Musique, Entretiens avec Claude Rostand; Correspondance Paul Claudel-Darius Milhaud.*
10 Boulevard de Clichy, Paris, France; and Mills College, Oakland, Calif., U.S.A.

Miljanić, Nikola, D.ECON.; Yugoslav economist; b. 5 Dec. 1921; ed. Faculty of Economics, Zagreb Univ.
Assistant Minister of Agriculture, Croatia 45-49; mem. Parl. of Croatia 46-54; Gen. Man. Nat. Bank of Yugoslavia 54-58; Alt. Exec. Dir. Int. Bank for Reconstruction and Devt. 58-60; Gen. Man. and Pres. Board of Yugoslav Investment Bank 60-62; Gov. Nat. Bank of Yugoslavia 62-; four Yugoslav decorations.
Publs. *Money and Credit* 62; and articles on monetary aspects of economic stability, financing of economic development, credit system of Yugoslavia, etc.
Narodni Banka, Bulevard revolucije 15, Belgrade; Home: Vasc Pelagića 46, Belgrade, Yugoslavia.
Telephone: 340353 (Office); 51504 (Home).

Miljević, Petar; Yugoslav diplomatist; b. 1914; ed. Law School in Zagreb.
Held various posts in Ministry of Foreign Trade, Belgrade after Second World War; entered Diplomatic Service 51; Econ. Counsellor, Bonn 51-54; Deputy Dir. for W. Europe, Office of Sec. of State for Foreign Affairs until 62; Minister Plenipotentiary, Head of Yugoslav Del. to OECD 62-.
Organization for Economic Co-operation and Development, 2 rue André Pascal, Paris 16e, France.

Millares, Manolo; Spanish artist; b. 1926.
Former Editor *Arqueros* (art review); Founder mem. El Paso Group; exhibited several int. exhbns. including Bienal, São Paulo 57, Biennale, Venice 58, Tokyo 58, 64, Minneapolis 59, Paris 60, 64, New York 60, Pittsburgh Int. 61, 64, 67, London 63, Venice 66-; Works in Tate Gallery, London, Nat. Gallery of Modern Art, Rome, Museum of Contemporary Art, Madrid, Museum of Modern Art, New York, Israel Museum, Moderna Museet, Stockholm, etc.
Hilarión Eslava 61, Madrid, Spain.
Telephone: 243-70-80.

Mille, Hervé; French journalist; b. 23 Sept. 1909.
Editor *Eclaireur de Nice* and *Paris Soir* 28-32; London correspondent of *Paris Soir* 33-35; editorial dir. *Paris Soir, Paris Midi, Marie Claire, Match* 36-42; Dir. *Paris Match* 49-, *Marie Claire* 54-, *Télé-sept-jours* 60-.
51 rue Pierre-Charron, Paris 8e, France.

Miller, Arjay Ray, B.S.; American business executive; b. 4 March 1916; ed. Univ. of California.
Teaching Asst. Univ. of Calif. Berkeley 37-40; Research Technician, Calif. State Planning Board 41; Economist, Fed. Reserve Bank of San Francisco 41-43; U.S.A.F. 43-46; Asst. Treas. Ford Motor Co. 47-53, Controller 53-57, Vice-Pres. and Controller 57-61, Vice-Pres. (Finance) 61-62, Vice-Pres. (Staff-Group) 62-63, Dir. 62-, Pres 63-68, Vice-Chair. Feb. 68-July 69; Dean Designate Graduate School of Business Admin., Stanford Univ.; Trustee of several insts. and mem. of various cttees.; Hon. D.Iur. (Calif., Nebraska Univs., Whitman Coll.).
Publ. *An Economic and Industrial Survey of the Los Angeles and San Diego Areas* (with Arthur G. Coons) 41.
2320 Devonshire Road, Ann Arbor, Michigan, U.S.A.

Miller, Arthur, A.B.; American playwright; b.17 Oct. 1915; ed. Univ. of Michigan.
Received Hopwood Award for play-writing, Univ. of Michigan 36 and 37; Theatre Guild Nat. Award 38; N.Y. Drama Critics Circle Award 47 and 49; Pulitzer Prize for Drama 49; Antoinette Perry Award 53; American Acad. of Arts and Letters Gold Medal for Drama 59; Pres. Int. PEN Clubs Org. 65-
Publs. *The Man Who Had All the Luck* 43, *Situation Normal* 44, *Focus* 45, *All My Sons* 47, *Death of a Salesman* 49, *The Crucible* 53, *A View From The Bridge* 55, *A Memory of Two Mondays* 55, *Collected Poems* 58, *After the Fall* 64, *Incident at Vichy* 64, *I Don't Need You Any More* (short stories) 67, *The Price* (play) 68; screenplay *The Misfits* 59.
c/o A.F.A. Inc., 1301 Avenue of the Americas, New York City, N.Y., U.S.A.

Miller, Frederick Robert, M.A., M.B., M.D., F.R.S., F.R.S.C., F.R.C.P.C., D.SC.; British physiologist; ed. Univs. Toronto, Cornell, Munich, Strasbourg, Liverpool, Oxford.
Asst. in Physiology, Cornell Univ. 03-05; Demonstrator of Physiology, Univ. of Toronto 07-10; Lecturer in Physiology, McGill Univ. 12-14; Prof. of Physiology, Univ. of Western Ontario 14-47, Research Prof. 47-50. Publs. Papers in physiological and neurological journals; subjects: nerve, muscle, salivary secretion, cardio-inhibitory centre, deglutition, vomiting mechanism, cerebellum, reflex physiology, electrophysiology, acetylcholine effects.
280 Carlton Street, Toronto 2, Canada.

Miller, George Paul; American politician; b. 15 Jan. 1891; ed. St. Mary's Coll., California.
Civil engineer, Calif. 12-; Exec. Sec., Calif. Div. of Fish and Game; mem. U.S. House of Reps. 45-, Chair. Cttee. on Science and Astronautics 61-; Democrat.
House of Representatives, Washington, D.C., U.S.A.

Miller, George William, B.S., J.D.; American business executive; b. 9 March 1925; ed. U.S. Coast Guard Acad., New London, Univ. of Calif. School of Law.
Lawyer with Cravath, Swaine & Moore, N.Y.C. 52-56; Vice-Pres., Textron Inc. 57-60, Pres. and Chief Admin. Officer 60-67, Chief Exec. Officer 68-; Pres. Textron Electronics, Inc. 59-60; mem. State Bar of Calif., Asscn. Bar City of N.Y.
165 Blackstone Boulevard, Providence 6, R.I., U.S.A.

Miller, Henry; American writer; b. 26 Dec. 1891; ed. City Coll., New York, and Cornell Univ.
Publs. include *The Air-Conditioned Nightmare, The Books in my Life, The Colossus of Maroussi, Remember to Remember, The Time of the Assassins, The Wisdom of the Heart, The Cosmological Eye, Big Sur and the Oranges of Hieronymus Bosch, Tropic of Cancer, Tropic of Capricorn, Plexus, Nexus, Sexus, Just Wild About Harry* (play), *Black Spring, Quiet Days in Clichy*.
Big Sur, nr. Monterey, Calif., U.S.A.

Miller, Jack Richard, A.B., M.A., LL.B.; American lawyer and politician; b. 6 June 1916; ed. Creighton Univ., Catholic Univ., Washington, D.C., Columbia Univ. and State Univ. of Iowa Coll. of Law.
Attorney, Office of Chief Counsel, Internal Revenue Service (Fed. Govt.) 47-48; Lecturer in Taxation, George Washington Univ. 48; Asst. Prof. of Law, Notre Dame Univ. Coll. of Law 48-49; mem. Iowa House of Reps. 55-56, Iowa State Senate 57-60, U.S. Senator from Iowa 61-; U.S.A.F. in Second World War; Col. U.S.A.F. Reserve; Republican.
Publs. *Farmers' Tax Saver* (annually revised), *Prentice-Hall Tax Ideas Service* (in co-operation).
5417 Kirkwood Drive, Washington 16, D.C., U.S.A.

Miller, James Roscoe, LL.D., M.D., M.S., D.SC.; American university president; b. 26 Oct. 1905; ed. Univ. of Utah and Northwestern Univ.

Asst. Prof. of Medicine Northwestern Univ. Med. School 39-41, Assoc. Prof. 41-49; Prof. 49-; Asst. Dean 33-41, Dean 41-49; Pres. Northwestern Univ. 49-; Dir. Sears Roebuck and Co., G. D. Searle and Co., American Hospital Supply Corpn., Museum of Science and Industry; Trustee, Wesley Memorial, Passavant Memorial and Evanston Hospitals, Sears Profit Sharing and Pension Fund, Chicago Natural History Museum Children's Memorial Hospital; fmr. mem. Hoover Comm. Medical Task Force.
Publs. on Internal Medicine and Medical Education.
619 Clark Street, Evanston, Ill., U.S.A.

Miller, John Duncan, C.M.G., British banker; b. 6 April 1902; ed. Wellington Coll. and Trinity Hall, Cambridge.
Army Service 40-45; Dir., British Information Services for Middle West, United States 45-47; Washington Correspondent, *The Times* 47-54; Special Rep. for Europe, Int. Bank for Reconstruction and Development (World Bank) 55-68; Rep. for Baring Bros. and Co. Ltd. on European Continent 68-.
8 Bishopsgate, London, E.C.2, England.

Miller, Otto Neil, PH.D.; American oil executive; b. 9 Jan. 1909; ed. Univ. of Michigan.
Researcher, Standard Oil Co. of Calif. 34, Gen. Man. Mfg. Dept. 46, Vice-Pres. 54, Dir. and Vice-Pres. 59, Pres. 61-66, Chair. 66-; Dir. American Petroleum Inst., Nat. Ind. Conf. Board, Calif. State Chamber of Commerce; mem. American Inst. of Chemical Engineers.
Standard Oil Co. of California, 225 Bush St., San Francisco 20, California, U.S.A.

Miller, Paul Lukens, A.B.; American investment banker; b. 6 Dec. 1919; ed. William Penn Charter School, Philadelphia, and Princeton Univ.
First Boston Corpn. 46-, Vice-Pres. 55-64, Dir. 59-, mem. Exec. Cttee. 63-, Pres. 64-; Dir. Aluminum Co. of America, Commonwealth Oil Refining Co., Inc., Cummins Engine Co., Inc.
First Boston Corporation, 20 Exchange Place, New York, N.Y. 10005, U.S.A.
Telephone: 212-344-1515.

Miller, Robert Watt; American businessman; b. 10 Oct. 1899; ed. Yale Univ.
Joined Pacific Lighting Corpn. 24, Exec. Vice-Pres. 29-41, Pres. 40-56, Chair. 56-; Chair. San Francisco Opera Asscn.; Dir. American Airlines, Caterpillar Tractors, Fibreboard Papers, Wells Fargo Bank; Legion of Merit, Star of Solidarity (Italy).
1021 California Street, San Francisco, Calif. 94108, U.S.A.
Telephone: GR4-4464.

Miller, William E., LL.B.; American lawyer and politician; b. 22 March 1914; ed. Notre Dame Univ., Albany Law School.
Private Law practice Lockport; U.S. Commr. for W. New York; U.S. Army 42-46; Asst. Prosecutor, Nürnberg War Crimes Trials; District Attorney, Niagara County 48; mem. U.S. House of Reps. 50-64; Chair. Republican Nat. Cttee. 61-64; nominated Republican candidate for Vice-Presidency of the U.S. July 64.
Lockwood Heights, Olcott, N.Y., U.S.A.

Millet, Pierre Georges Louis; French industrial official; b. 11 April 1922; ed. Ecole libre des Sciences Politiques, Univ. de Paris à la Sorbonne and Ecole Nationale d'administration.
Civil Administrator, Directorate of Budget, Ministry of Finance, Paris 47-51; Sub-Dir. Int. Inst. of Law, The Hague 52-54; Head of Office of Co-ordination of Nat. Accounts, Dept. of Econ. and Financial Studies, Ministry of Finance 55-57; Dir., Directorate-Gen. of Econ. and Financial Affairs, European Econ. Community (EEC), Brussels 61-65; Asst. Dir.-Gen. of Foreign Econ. Relations, Ministry of Finance, Paris

65-66; Vice-Pres. Union of Chemical Industries 66-;
Chevalier Légion d'Honneur.
69 Avenue Marceau, Paris, France.
Telephone: ELYsées 5603.

Millet, René Philippe Yves; French diplomatist; b.
15 Aug. 1910; ed. Ecole Fénelon, Lycées Condorcet et
Janson-de-Sailly, Paris, Ecole Libre des Sciences
Politiques, Paris.
Second Sec. French Embassy, Ankara 45, First Sec. 46;
Consul, Johannesburg 47-49, to Cen. Admin. 49-50;
Perm. Rep. to Econ. Comm. for Asia and Far East,
Second Counsellor, Bangkok 50-52; Second Counsellor,
Manila, and Chargé d'Affaires 52-54; Counsellor, High
Comm., Saigon 54-56; Consul Gen. Bizerta 56-60, Los
Angeles 60-62; Ambassador to Chad 62-65, to Burma
65-; Commdr. Légion d'Honneur.
French Embassy, Rangoon, Burma.

Milligan, Robert Lee; American oil executive; b.
11 Oct. 1900; ed. Ohio Wesleyan Univ.
Supt. The Fairbanks Co., Springfield, O. 22-24, Vice-
Pres., Gen. Man. 24-29; Treas. Indianapolis Switch &
Frog Co. 26-29; Asst. to Treas. The Pure Oil Co.
Chicago 29-33, Asst. Sec.-Treas. 33-47, Treas. 47-49,
Vice-Pres., Treas. 49-51, Exec. Vice-Pres. 51-54, Pres.
54-65, Chair. 65.
Home: 2440 Lincolnwood Drive, Evanston, Ill.; Office:
200 East Golf Road, Palatine, Ill., U.S.A.

Milliken, Frank Roscoe; American mining executive;
b. 25 Jan. 1914; ed. Massachusetts Inst. of Technology.
Chief Metallurgist, Gen. Eng. Co., Salt Lake City 36-41;
Asst. Manager Titanium Div. Nat. Lead Co. 41-52; Vice-
Pres. (Mining Operations), Kennecott Copper Corpn.
52-58, Exec. Vice-Pres. 58-61, Dir. 58-. Pres. 61-; Pres.
and Dir. Braden Copper Co.
Kennecott Copper Corporation, 161 East 42nd St., New
York City 17, N.Y., U.S.A.

Millin, Sarah Gertrude (Mrs.); South African novelist
and historian; Hon. D.Litt. (Univ. of the Witwaters-
rand).
Publs. include novels: *The Dark River* 20, *Middle Class*
21, *Adam's Rest* 22, *The Jordans* 23, *God's Stepchildren*
24, *Mary Glenn* 25, *An Artist in the Family* 27, *The
Coming of the Lord* 28, *The Fiddler* 29, *The Sons of
Mrs. Aab,* 31, *Three Men Die* 34, *What Hath a Man?* 38,
The Herr Witch Doctor 41, *King of the Bastards* 51, *The
Burning Man* 53, *The Wizard Bird* 62, *Goodbye Dear
England* 65; *The Night is Long* (Autobiography) 41;
biographies: *Rhodes* 33, *General Smuts* (2 vols.) 36;
sociology: *The South Africans* 26, *South Africa* 42; *The
People of South Africa* 51; essays: *Men on a Voyage* 30;
plays: *No Longer Mourn, General Smuts* (B.B.C. radio
play), 13 short plays and *General Smuts* produced
in U.S.A. (WOR), *War Diary: Vol. I World Blackout* 44,
Vol. II The Reeling Earth 45, *Vol. III The Pit of the
Abyss* 46, *Vol. IV The Sound of the Trumpet* 47, *Vol. V
Fire Out of Heaven* 47, *Vol. VI The Seven Thunders* 48,
The Measure of My Days (autobiography) 55, *Two
Bucks without Hair* (short stories) 57; compilation:
White Africans are also People.
34 Pallinghurst Road, Westcliff, Johannesburg, and
48 Leewenhof Road, Orangezicht, Cape Town, South
Africa.
Telephone: 41-26-17 (Johannesburg); 34-215 (Cape
Town).

Millionshchikov, Mikhail Dmitrievich; Soviet applied
physicist; b. 13; ed. Grozny Petroleum Inst.
Instructor, Grozny Petroleum Inst. 32-34, Instructor,
Moscow Aviation Inst. 34-43, Instructor, Moscow Eng.
and Physics Inst. 43-49, Prof. Moscow Eng. and Physics
Inst. 49-; Inst. of Mechanics, U.S.S.R. Acad. of Sciences
44-49; Corresp. mem. U.S.S.R. Acad. of Sciences 53-62,
mem. 62-, Vice-Pres. 62-; Chair. Dept. of Physical,
Technical and Mathematical Sciences, U.S.S.R. Acad.

of Sciences 60-66; Chief Editor *Atomic Energy*; mem.
C.P.S.U. 47-; Hero of Socialist Labour 67-; State Prize
(twice), Lenin Prize.
Publs. *The Decay of Homogenous Isotopic Turbulence
in a Viscous Incompressible Liquid* 39, *The Theory of
Homogenous Isotopic Turbulence* 41, co-author *Applied
Gas Dynamics* 48.
U.S.S.R. Academy of Sciences, 14 Lenin Prospekt,
Moscow, U.S.S.R.

Millot, Jacques, D. EN MED., D. en SC.; French museum
director; b. 9 July 1897; ed. Univ. de Paris à la Sor-
bonne and Muséum nat. d'Histoire naturelle.
Professor, Faculty of Medicine, Univ. of Paris 29-31;
Prof. Inst. of Ethnology 31-; Prof. Sorbonne 33-; Prof.
Muséum nat. d'Histoire naturelle 43-; Dir. of Scientific
Research, Madagascar 47-60; Pres. Acad. Malgache
48-58; Pres. Scientific Asscn. of Countries of Indian
Ocean 57-; Dir. Musée de l'Homme, Paris 60-; Pres.
Acad. des Sciences d'Outre-Mer 63; mem. Acad. des
Sciences (France) 63-; Hon. Dr. (Witwatersrand and
Perth).
Publs. *Cicatrication* 31, *Les races humaines* 36, *Traité
de Zoologie—Classe des Arachnides* 49, *Biologie des
races humaines* 51, *Le troisième coelacanthe* 54, *Les
crossoptérygiens actuels* 58, *Anatomie de Latimeria
Chalumnae I* 58, *II* 65.
14 bis Avénue du Président Wilson, Paris 16e, France.

Mills, Air Chief Marshal Sir George Holroyd, G.C.B.,
D.F.C.; British air force officer; b. 26 March 1902; ed.
Berkhamsted School and Royal Air Force Coll.,
Cranwell.
Served in Iraq 22-24, India 30-34, Staff Coll. 35; with
Air Ministry until 39; Bomber Squadron, Bomber
Command Staff Coll. and Air Ministry 40-44; Air Officer
Commanding Balkan Air Force 45; served Egypt 45-46;
Dir. of Plans, Air Ministry 46-48; Air Officer Commdg.
No. 1 Group 49-50; Head U.K. Mil. Del. to Western
Union Mil. Staff Cttee. 50-51; A.O.C. Malaya 52; Air
Officer Commdg.-in-Chief, Bomber Command 53-55;
Air A.D.C. to the Queen 56-62; Commdr. Allied Air
Forces Central Europe 56-59; Chair. British Defence
Staffs, concurrently U.K. Rep. Standing
Group NATO and Mil. Cttee. 59-62; Gentleman Usher
of the Black Rod, House of Lords 63-.
c/o Lloyds Bank Ltd., 6 Pall Mall, London, S.W.1.

Mills, Wilbur Daigh; American politician; b. 24 May
1909; ed. Hendrix Coll. and Harvard Law School.
Admitted to Ark. Bar 33, private legal practice, Searcy;
County and Probate Judge, White County 34-38;
Cashier, Bank of Kensett 34-35; mem. U.S. House of
Reps. 39-, Chair. Ways and Means Cttee. 63-; Democrat.
U.S. House of Representatives, Washington, D.C.,
U.S.A.

Millsaps, Knox, B.S., PH.D.; American mathematician;
b. 10 Sept. 1921; ed. Auburn Univ. and Calif. Inst. of
Technology.
Associate Prof. Ohio State Univ. 47-48; Physicist
Wright Air Devt. Center 48-49, Mathematician 50-51,
Chief Mathematician 52-55; Prof. of Physics, Auburn
Univ. 49-50, 51-52; Prof. of Mechanical Engineering,
Mass. Inst. of Technology 55-56; Chief Scientist, Air
Force Missile Devt. Center, U.S.A.F. 56-60; Exec. Dir.
Air Force Office of Scientific Research, U.S.A.F. 61-62;
Research Prof. of Aerospace Eng., Univ. of Florida
63-68; Head Prof. Mechanical Eng., Colorado State
Univ. 68-.
P.O. Box 1591, Fort Collins, Colorado 80521, U.S.A.
Telephone: 303-491-6558.

Milne-Watson, Michael, C.B.E.; British steel execu-
tive; b. 16 Feb. 1910; ed. Eton and Balliol Coll., Oxford.
Gas Light and Coke Co. 33-49, Gov. 46-49; Chair.
North Thames Gas Board 49-64; Chair. Richard
Thomas & Baldwins Ltd. 64-67; mem. Org. Cttee. Nat.

Steel Corpn. 66-67; Deputy Chair. Nat. (now British) Steel Corpn. 67-; R.N.V.R. 43-45; Dir. Northern and Employers Assurance Co. Ltd., Industrial and Commercial Finance Corpn. Ltd.

Office: British Steel Corpn., 22 Kingsway, London, W.C.2; Home: 57 Eaton Place, London, S.W.1, England.

Telephone: 01-242-1616.

Milstein, Nathan; American violinist; b. Odessa (Russia) 31 Dec. 1904; ed. St. Petersburg Conservatoire. Studied music under Stoliarsky and Leopold Auer; made extensive tours of Soviet Russia as soloist and in joint recitals with Vladimir Horowitz; left Russia 25; additional study with Eugène Ysaye in Brussels; from 20 until outbreak of Second World War made annual tours of all European capitals, also tours in South and Central America; first appearance in U.S.A. 29; since then annual extensive tours all over the world; Légion d'Honneur (France), Cross of Honour (Austria); mem. Acad. of Santa Cecilia (Italy).

c/o Hurok Concerts, Inc., 730 Fifth Avenue, New York City, N.Y., and 26 Cours Albert Ier, Paris 8e, France.

Telephone: ELYsées 24-25.

Milward, Sir Anthony Horace, Kt., C.B.E., B.A.; British airline executive; b. 2 March 1905; ed. Clare Coll., Cambridge.

Employed in the textile industry 26-40; with Fleet Air Arm 40-45; with British Overseas Airways Corpn. Jan.-April 46; with British European Airways April 46-, Chief Exec. 56-, Chair. 64-; mem. Air Registration Board 64-, Board of British Overseas Airways Corpn. 64-.

Tyler End, Penn, Bucks., England.

Milyutin, Yuri Sergeevich; Soviet composer; b. 1903; ed. Moscow Music Technicum.

Art Worker of Merit of the R.S.F.S.R.; People's Artist of R.S.F.S.R. 64; mem. C.P.S.U. 52-; State Prizewinner 49.

Principal works: operettas, *The Startled Maidens* 44, *Restless Happiness* 47, *Trembita* 49, *First Love* 53, *The Kiss of Chanita* 56, *Little Lamps* 58, *Tsirk Lights the Lamps* 60; also many popular songs.

[*Died June* 1968]

Mima, Yasuichi, B.COM.; Japanese mining executive; b. 3 Aug. 1903; ed. Tokyo Commercial Univ.

Kuhara Mining Co. (now Nippon Mining Co.) 28-, Dir. Nippon Mining Co. Ltd. 46-, Man. Dir. 47-57, Pres. 57-; Pres. Toho Titanium Co. 59-; Dir. Teikoku Oil Co. Ltd. 57-, Japan Petroleum Fed. 57-; Governing Dir., Japan Fed. of Employers' Asscns. 59-, Exec. Dir., Japan Fed. of Econ. Orgs. 59-, Dir. Japan Management Asscn. 59-, Pres. Japan Mining Industry Asscn. 62-; Order of Merit, Chile 62.

Nippon Mining Co., 3 Akasaka-Aoicho, Minatoku, Tokyo, Japan.

Mindszenty, H.E. Cardinal József; Hungarian ecclesiastic; b. 29 March 1892.

Ordained priest 15; Bishop of Veszprém 44; imprisoned 44-45; Archbishop of Esztergom and Primate of Hungary 45-; sentenced to life imprisonment 49, released 56; granted asylum in U.S. Legation, Budapest Nov. 56-; mem. Sacred Congregations of Sacraments, of Ceremonies and of Seminaries and Univs. of Study.

c/o The Legation of the United States, Budapest, Hungary.

Miner, Robert Graham, B.A., M.A.; American diplomatist; b. 16 Jan. 1911; ed. Hamilton Coll. and Yale Univ.

On staff of Athens Coll. 34-35, Robert Coll. Istanbul 35-37, Hamilton 37-41; Office of Strategic Services 42-43, U.S. Navy 42-46; joined Dept. of State as Section Chief 47; Sec. and Consul Athens 48, First Sec. 51; at Imperial Defence Coll. London 51; First Sec. Paris 52; Officer in

Charge Dominion Affairs 55; Consul Gen. Istanbul 56; Dir. Office of Greek, Turkish and Iranian Affairs 60; Amb. to Trinidad 62-67, to Sierra Leone 67-.

American Embassy, 14 Trelawney Street, Freetown, Sierra Leone.

Minkowski, Mieczyslaw, M.D.; Swiss neurologist of Polish origin; b. 15 April 1884 in Warsaw; ed. Warsaw, Munich and Breslau Univs.

Lecturer, Zürich Univ. 13 and Extra. Prof. 28; Hon. Prof. of Neurology 54-; Hon. Chair. Swiss Neurological Society, Zürich Society of Psychiatry and Neurology; Ed. *Schweizer Archiv für Neurologie und Psychiatrie*.

Publs. *Zum gegenwärtigen Stand der Lehre von den Reflexen* 25, *L'état actuel de l'étude des réflexes* 27, *Neurobiologische Studien am menschlichen Foetus* (in Abderhalden's *Handbuch der biologischen Arbeitsmethoden*) 28, *Pathologische Anatomie der Epilepsie* 36, *L'élaboration du Système nerveux* 38, *Zur Kenntnis der cerebralen Sehbahnen* 39, *Über metastatische Hirngeschwülste* 41, *Zum Problem der ersten Anfänge einer seelischen Entwicklung beim Foetus* 47, *Prenatal neuropathologic changes leading to neurologic or mental disorders* 52, *Sur les altérations de l'écorce cérébrale dans quelques cas de microcéphalie* 56, *I. P. Pavlov* 56, *Voyons-nous avec les yeux?* 56, *On neurological effects, immunological reactions and neuropathological findings in monkeys fed on or injected with calf brain* 57, *50 Jahre Schweizerische Neurologische Gesellschaft* 58, *Über einige Grenzprobleme der Neurobiologie* 61, *Neurobiologie, Moral und Religion* 63, *On Aphasia in polyglots* 64 (French trans. 65), *Schizophrénie et diaschisis* 66.

Freiestrasse 55, Zürich 8032, Switzerland.

Telephone: 057-325620.

Minnaert, Marcel Gilles Jozef, DR. PHIL.; Netherlands university professor; b. 12 Feb. 1893.

Lecturer, Univ. of Ghent 16-18; Observer, Univ. of Utrecht 20-37, Prof. of Astronomy and Dir. of Utrecht Observatory 37-63; mem. Royal Acad. Amsterdam; foreign mem. Royal Flemish Acad. Brussels, Leopoldina Acad., Halle, Uppsala Acad.; Foreign Assoc. Royal Astronomical Soc. London; corresp. mem. Inst. Coimbra; foreign hon. mem. American Acad. of Arts and Sciences; Foreign Assoc. Nat. Acad. of Sciences 64; Accad. Lincei Rome 66; Dr. h.c., Heidelberg 65, Moscow 66, Nice 68; Gold Medal of Royal Astronomical Soc. 47; Bruce Medal Astronomical Soc. of the Pacific 51, Prix Janssen 66.

Publs. *Natuurkunde in leerlingenproeven* 24, *de Natuurkunde van't vrije Veld* (3 vols.) 37-49, *Light and Colour in the Open Air* 40, *De Steerekunde en de Mensheid* 46, *Dichters over Sterren* 49, *Photometric Atlas of the Solar Spectrum* (with Mulders and Houtgast); contributions: *The Solar System*.

Zuilenstraat 25 bis, Utrecht; Sterrewacht "Sonnenborgh", Zonnenburg 2, Utrecht, Netherlands.

Telephone: 030-13008; 030-12841.

Minobe, Ryokichi, DR.POL.ECON.; Japanese district governor; b. 5 Feb. 1904; ed. Dept. of Econs., Tokyo Imperial Univ.

Professor, Hosei Univ. 35-38, Tokyo Univ. of Educ. 49-67; on Editorial Staff, *Mainichi Shimbun* 45-46; First Grade Official of the Cabinet 46; Chief of Statistic Datum Div., Administrative Control Agency 52, Dir. of Statistic Datum Bureau 57-59; Governor of Tokyo 67-.

No. 46, Nampeidai-machi, Shibuya-ku, Tokyo, Japan.

Minotis, Alexis (husband of Katina Paxinou, *q.v.*); American (Greek) theatre producer and actor; b. 1906. Acting on Greek stage since 25; mem. Nat. Theatre of Greece 30-; has played principal roles in and produced most classical plays from Aeschylus to Pirandello; has made many tours outside Greece with Nat. Theatre; produced Cherubini's opera *Medea*, with Callas in leading role, for Dallas (Texas) Civic Opera, at Covent

Garden, London and at La Scala, Milan; Ancient Greek Drama Festivals at Epidaurus and Athens 55-; produced *Oedipus Rex, Hecuba Medea* 55-58, *Oedipus at Colonus, Antigone* 62 at Théâtre des Nations, Paris; produced Friedrich Dürrenmatt's *Visit of an Elderly Woman*, Royal Theatre, Greece 61; played Oedipus in *Oedipus Rex*, London 66; several Greek and foreign decorations.
Lykiou 13, Athens, Greece.

Minow, Newton N.; American lawyer; b. 17 Jan. 1926; ed. Northwestern Law School.
Law Clerk to Supreme Court Chief Justice Vinson 51; Admin. Asst. to Governor of Illinois (Adlai Stevenson) 52, 53-54; served Stevenson's law firm 55-57, Partner 57-61; Chair. Fed. Communications Commission 61-63; Exec. Vice-Pres. General Counsel Encyclopaedia Britannica, Chicago 63-65; Dir. and Special Counsel, Curtis Publishing Co. 64-66; Dir. Rand Corpn. 65-; National Educational Television; Famous Artists Schools 67-; Partner, Leibman, Williams, Bennett, Baird & Minow 65-; Chair. and Dir. Chicago Educational Television Asscn.; Dir. Standard Computers Inc., Dynascan Corpn.; Board of Lay Trustees, Notre Dame Univ.; Democrat.
Home: 375 Palos Road, Glencoe, Ill.; Office: Leibman, Williams, Bennett, Baird & Minow, 208 South LaSalle Street, Chicago, Ill., U.S.A.
Telephone: 312-386-2200 (Office); 312-VE5-3118 (Home).

Mintoff, Dominic, B.SC., M.A.; Maltese politician; b. 16; ed. Univs. of Malta and Oxford.
Civil engineer in Great Britain 41-43; practised in Malta as architect 43-; rejoined and helped reorganise Maltese Labour Party 44; Elected to Council of Govt. and Executive Council 45; Mem. Legislative Assembly 47-; Deputy Leader of Labour Party, Deputy Prime Minister and Minister for Works and Reconstruction 47-49; resigned Ministry, Leader of Labour Party 49-; Prime Minister and Minister of Finance 55-58; Leader of the Opposition March 62-.
"The Olives", Tarxien, Malta.

Mints, Alexander Lvovich, D.SC.; Soviet (Russian) radio engineer; b. 8 Jan. 1895; ed. Moscow and Don Univs. and Inst. of Electrical Communication Engineers, Moscow.
Chief, U.S.S.R. Signal Corps Laboratories and Insts. 20-28; Laboratory Chief, Radio Engineering Insts. of U.S.S.R. State Industries 28-38; Asst. Prof. of Radio Engineering, Polytechnic Inst., Leningrad 29-30; Prof. of Radio Eng., Inst. of Electrical Communications Engineers, Leningrad 30-38; Chief Engineer, Design and Construction, High and Super High Power Broadcasting Stations of U.S.S.R. 24-43; Dir. Radiotechnical Inst., U.S.S.R. Acad. of Sciences, Moscow 46-, mem. U.S.S.R. Acad. of Sciences 58-; State Prizes 46, 51, A. S. Popov Gold Medal 50, Lenin Prize 59; Hero of Socialist Labour.
Publs. *Design Principles of Plate and Grid Modulation Systems* 26, 29, *High-Power Broadcasting Stations of W. Europe* 36, *Demountable High Power Valves* 35, 56, *Scientific and Design Problems of High Energy Heavy Particle Accelerators* 56, *New Design Principles of Super-High Energy Accelerators* 61, *Cybernetic Accelerator* 63, *1000 Ger proton Synchrotron design* 66.
Academy of Sciences of U.S.S.R., 14 Lenin Prospekt, Moscow, U.S.S.R.

Mints, Isaak Israilevich; Soviet historian; b. 96; ed. Inst. of Red Professors, Moscow.
Member U.S.S.R. Acad. of Sciences 46-; Chair. Scientific Council of U.S.S.R. Acad. of Sciences for Solution of problems in *History of Great October Socialist Revolution;* mem. C.P.S.U. 17-; State Prizes 43, 46.

Publs. Works on history of Octobe Revolution, Civil War and foreign military intervention.
Institute of History, U.S.S.R. Academy of Sciences, ulitsa D. Ulyanova 19, Moscow, U.S.S.R.

Mione, Auguste; French (b. Italy) building engineer; b. 24 Oct. 1898; ed. Lycée Belluno and Ecole supérieure du béton armé, Paris.
In Paris 23-; Founder, Pres., Dir.-Gen. La Construction Moderne Française; Dir. of SEDAC (Société d'équipement électrique et distribution d'appareils de chauffage), of AMME (Société auxiliaire de matériel moderne d'entreprise), of SAGE (Sociéré anonyme de gestion et d'exploitation); has constructed *Cité radieuse* of Le Corbusier, Marseilles, *La Citadelle*, Bagnols-sur-Cèze, Medical and Social Centre, Chamarande, etc.
Publ. *Le Dur Chemin de la liberté*.
Château de Chamarande, Chamarande (Essonne), France.

Mirambel, André; French higher education director; b. 1 Oct. 1900; ed. Univ. de Paris à la Sorbonne, and Ecole nationale des langues orientales vivantes.
Teacher in Lycées 24-29; Prof. Ecole des Langues orientales 29-, Dir. 58-; Lecturer Sorbonne and Dir. Neohellenic Inst. 38-; mem. Acad. des Inscriptions et Belles Lettres, Inst. de France 65-; Officier Légion d'Honneur; Commdr. Palmes académiques; Officer Order of King George I (Greece); Commdr. Order of Phoenix (Greece); Dr. h.c. Univ. of Salonica.
Publs. *Grammaire du grec moderne* 39, 49, 62, *Introduction au grec moderne* 48, 61, *Anthologie de la prose néohellénique 1884-1960* 50, *La Littérature grecque moderne* 53, *La Langue grecque moderne, description et analyse* 59, *Dictionnaire français-grec moderne et grec moderne-français* 62; numerous articles in Greek and French; has collaborated on encyclopedias and dictionaries.
2 rue de Lille, Paris 7e, France.
Telephone: BAB-09-91.

Mireaux, Emile; French economist and writer; b. 21 Aug. 1885.
Dir. Society for Economic Study and Information 24-31; Dir. of *Le Temps* (with Jacques Chastenet) Dec. 31-44; Senator for Hautes Pyrénées 35-40; Hon. Pres. Société d'Economie politique; Min. of Education and Arts in Pétain Cabinet July-Sept. 40; mem. Acad. des Sciences Morales et Politiques 40, Perm. Sec. 56-; Pres. Inst. de France 51.
Publs. *Les miracles du crédit* 32, *La Chanson de Roland et l'Histoire de France* 42, *Les Poèmes Homériques et l'Histoire Grecque—I Homère de Chios et les routes de l'étain* 48, *II L'Iliade, L'Odyssée et les rivalités coloniales* 49, *Philosophie du libéralisme* 49, *La Reine Bérénice* 51, *L'organisation du crédit dans les territoires d'outre-mer* 53, *La vie quotidienne au temps d'Homère* 54, *Problèmes Actuels de la Route Française* 56, *Le Moyen Age* (in *Neuf Siècles de Littérature Française*) 58, *Une province française au temps du Grand Roi: la Brie* 59, *Introduction sur Retif de la Bretonne* 63.
22 Avenue de Neuilly, Neuilly-sur-Seine, France.
Telephone: 624-80-92.

Miró, Joan; Spanish artist; b. 20 April 1893; ed. Barcelona Acad. of Fine Art.
Apart from painting, has executed ceramics, sculptures, engravings and lithographs; divides his time between Paris and Palma; Guggenheim Award for ceramic mural "Night and Day", UNESCO Building, Paris 58; exhibitions in New York, Paris, Zürich, London (Tate Gallery) 64, Tokyo and Kyoto 66.
c/o Galerie Maeght, 13 rue de Téhéran, Paris 8e, France.

Mironova, Zoya Vassilievna; Soviet chemical engineer and diplomatist; b. 1912; ed. Moscow Inst. of Chemical Technology.

Deputy Mayor of Moscow 51-59; then Deputy Perm. Soviet Rep. to UN and Soviet Rep. on UN Cttee. on Women's Rights; then at Ministry of Foreign Affairs, Moscow; Perm. Rep. of U.S.S.R. at UN European Office and other int. orgs. in Geneva 66-; rank of Amb.; State Prize (for work on producing a rare metal and its compounds) 50; Red Banner of Labour, Badge of Honour, etc.
European Office of the UN, Palais des Nations, Geneva, Switzerland.

Miroshnichenko, Nikolai Mikhailovich; Soviet politician; b. 1913; ed. Voronezh Veterinary Inst.
Veterinary worker 34-41; mem. C.P.S.U. 42-; Dir. Experimental Station, then Voronezh Trust of Cattle-Breeding State Farms 46-53; Deputy Chief, then Chief of Section Voronezh Regional Cttee. of C.P. 53-61; Sec. Regional Cttee. of C.P. on agriculture 61-62; Chair. Exec. Cttee. Voronezh Regional Soviet of Workers' Deputies 62-67; First Sec. Voronezh Regional Cttee. of C.P. 67-; Deputy to R.S.F.S.R. Supreme Soviet.
Voronezh Regional Committee of Communist Party, Voronezh, U.S.S.R.

Mirza, Maj.-Gen. Iskander, C.I.E., O.B.E.; Pakistani politician; b. 13 Nov. 1899; ed. Elphinstone Coll. and Sandhurst Acad.
Served in Army 21-26; joined Indian Political Service 26; Political Agent in Khyber 38-40; District Commr., Peshawar 40-45; Political Agent, Orissa States 45-46; Joint Sec. to Ministry of Defence, Govt. of India 46-47; Defence Sec., Govt. of Pakistan 47-54; Governor of East Bengal 54; Minister of Interior, States and Frontier Regions 54-55; Gov.-Gen. of Pakistan 55-56; Pres. 56-58.
40 Princes Gate, London, S.W.7, England.

Mischnick, Wolfgang; German politician; b. 29 Sept. 1921; ed. High School, Dresden.
Co-founder, Liberal Democratic Party, Dresden 45; town official, Dresden 46-48; mem. Central Cttee. of Liberal Democratic Party, Soviet Zone 46-48; fled to Fed. Germany 48; mem. Provincial Ass., Hesse, 54-57, Parl. Leader of F.D.P.; Fed. Chair. F.D.P. Youth Movement and Ed. *Stimmen der jungen Generation* 54-57; mem. Bundestag 57-; Dep. Chair. F.D.P., Hesse 57-; Fed. Minister for Refugees 61-63.
Kullmanstrasse 16, Frankfurt am Main, German Federal Republic.

Mises, Ludwig Edler von; American economist; b. 29 Sept. 1881; ed. Vienna Univ.
Prof. Vienna Univ. 13-38, Graduate Inst. of Int. Studies Geneva 34-40, Nat. Univ. Mexico 42; Economic Adviser to Austrian Chamber of Commerce and Industry 09-34; mem. Nat. Bureau Economic Research N.Y. 40-44; Visiting Prof. New York Univ. 45-; Citizen of U.S. 46.
Publs. *Liberalismus* 27, *Grundprobleme der National-ökonomie* 33, *The Theory of Money and Credit* 34, *Socialism: an Economic and Sociological Analysis* 36, *Nationalökonomie* 40, *Omnipotent Government* 44, *Bureaucracy* 44, *Planned Chaos* 47, *Human Action, a Treatise on Economics* 49, *Planning for Freedom* 52, *The Anticapitalistic Mentality* 56, *Theory and History* 57, *The Ultimate Foundation of Economic Science* 62.
777 West End Avenue, New York, N.Y. 10025, U.S.A. Telephone: MOnument 2-7877.

Mishima, Yukio; Japanese writer; b. 14 Jan. 1925; ed. Tokyo Univ.
Civil servant in Dept. of Finance 48-49; full-time writer 49-.
Publs. short stories: *The Blooming Forest* 44, *The Death in Midsummer, and other stories* (English version) 66; novels: *Confessions of a Mask, Thirst for Love, Sound of Waves, Temple of the Golden Pavilion, After the Banquet, The Sailor who fell from Grace with the Sea,*

Forbidden Colours; plays: *Five Modern Nô Plays, Madame de Sade.*
4-32-8, Minami-magome, Ota-ku, Tokyo, Japan. Telephone: 771-2975.

Mishin, Vasily Pavlovich; Soviet engineer; b. 1917; ed. Moscow Aviation Inst.
Specialist in applied mechanics; mem. C.P.S.U. 43-; Corresp. mem. U.S.S.R. Acad. of Sciences 58-66, mem. 66-.
U.S.S.R. Academy of Sciences, 14 Lenin Prospekt, Moscow, U.S.S.R.

Mishinkin, Vasily Kuzmich; Soviet trade union official; b. 09; ed. Leningrad Inst. of Civil Airfleet Engineers.
Central Admin. of Civil Airfleet 38-58; Chair. Cen. Cttee. of Aviation Workers' Trade Union 58-; mem. Auditing Comm. of All-Union Cen. Council of Trade Unions; mem. C.P.S.U. 39-; Order of Red Star, etc.
Central Committee of the Aviation Workers' Trade Union, 42 Leninsky Prospekt, Moscow, U.S.S.R.

Mishra, Dwarka Prasad; Indian journalist and politician; b. 5 Aug. 1901; ed. Raipur, Jabalpur and Allahabad.
Joined *Amrit Bazar Patrika* 20, Editor *Sharda* 22; mem. Indian Legislative Assembly 26; Editor *Lokmat* 30; Pres. Jabalpur Municipality 32; jailed 30, 32, 40, 42; Minister of Local Self-Govt., C.P. and Berar 37-39; Editor *Sarathi* 41-42; Minister of Home Affairs, Madhya Pradesh 46; Vice- Chancellor Saugor Univ. 56-61; mem. Madhya Pradesh Legis. Assembly 63; Chief Minister of Madhya Pradesh 63-July 67.
Nishat Manzil, Bhopal, Madhya Pradesh, India.

Mišković, Vojislav, D.SC.; Yugoslav university professor; b. 92.
Asst. Marseilles Observatory 19-22; Astronomer, Nice Observatory 22-25; Founder and Dir. Belgrade Observatory, 25-46; now Prof., Univ. of Belgrade; mem. Serbian Acad. of Sciences 39-, Gen. Sec. 45-48; Vice-Dir. of Mathematical Inst. of Acad. 48, Dir. Astronomical Inst. 48-54; Editor of bulletins of Belgrade Observatory.
Publs. *Etudes de Statistique stellaire* 24, *Nouvelles tables de précession* 35.
Serbian Academy of Sciences, Knez Mihailova 35/1, Belgrade, Yugoslavia.

Misra, Sirdar Iswary Raj, M.A., B.L.; Nepalese diplomat; b. 29 Oct. 1917; ed. St. Xavier's Coll., The Scottish Church Coll. and Univ. Law Coll., Calcutta, and Calcutta Univ.
Sectional Head, Dept. of Law, Katmandu 42; Head of Buying Agency to Govt. of Nepal, Calcutta 43-45; Dept. of Law, Katmandu 45-47; First Sec. Nepalese Embassy, London 47, later Counsellor; Deputy Sec. Ministry of Foreign Affairs 56-59; Registrar of Supreme Court, Katmandu 59-60; Judge of Western High Court 60-61; Judge of Supreme Court 61-65; Ambassador to France 65-67, to U.K. 65-, and concurrently to Italy and Greece 68-; Suprasidha Prabala Gorakha Dakshina Bahu (Nepal); Knight Commdr. Order of Orange Nassau (Netherlands); Grand Officier of Merit (France); Officier Légion d'Honneur.
Embassy of Nepal, 12A Kensington Palace Gardens, London, W.8, England.

Missiroli, Mario, PH.D.; Italian journalist; b. 25 Nov. 1886; ed. Bologna Univ.
Mem. of staff of *Don Chisciotte* and *Rinascenza* 1900, of *Gazzetta dell'Emilia* 06, of *Resto del Carlino* 09; correspondent of many dailies and co-Ed. *Tempo*, Rome 17-18; Ed. *Resto del Carlino* 18-21, *Secolo* 21-23; mem. of staff of *Messaggero* and contributor to *Illustrazione Italiana*; Ed. *Messaggero* 52; Ed. *Corriere della Sera*, Milan 58-61; Grand 'Ufficiale della Repubblica Italiana and Officier de la Légion d'Honneur.
Publs. *Critica negativa* 12, *La monarchia socialista* 13,

Satrapia 14, *Il papa in guerra* 17, *La repubblica degli accattoni* 17, *Polemica liberale* 18-54, *Opinioni* 21-56, *Amore e fame* 28, *Date a Cesare* 29, *L'Italia d'oggi* 42, *Da Tunisi a Versailles* 42, etc.
Via Solferino 28, Milan, Italy.

Missoffe, François; French industrialist and politician; b. 13 Oct. 1919; ed. Prytanée militaire de La Flèche.
Army service 40-46; U.N.R. (Union for the New Republic). Dep. to Nat. Ass. 58-; Gen. Treas. U.N.R. 59; Sec. of State for Domestic Trade April-Oct. 62, Minister of Repatriation 62-64; Ambassador to Japan 64-66; Minister for Youth and Sports 66-May 68; Chevalier, Légion d'Honneur.
Home: avenue Victor Hugo, Paris 16e, France.

Mistler, Jean; French writer; b. 1 Sept. 1897; ed. Lycées de Carassonne and Henri IV, Paris and Ecole normale supérieure.
Cultural Attaché, Budapest, and Priv. Dozent Univ. of Budapest; Head of Section, Ministry of Foreign Affairs 26; mem. Chamber of Deputies 28; Under-Sec. of State for Fine Arts 32; Minister of Posts, Telecommunications and Commerce 34; Pres. of Comm. for Foreign Affairs 36-40; Dir.-Gen. Maison du livre française 47-60; Dir. Dept. of Gen. Literature, Librarie Hachette 66-; mem. Acad. Française 66-; Dir. Accumulateur Fulmen and Cie. Industrielles des Téléphones.
Publs. include *Châteaux en Bavière, La Symphonie inachevée, Hoffmann le Fantastique, A Bayreuth avec Richard Wagner, Epinal et l'imagerie populaire, Le 14 Juillet, Le Bout du monde, Les Orgues de Saint Sauveur,* and numerous articles for *L'Aurore* 54-, and *Revue de Paris* 28-40.
11 rue de l'Université, Paris 7e, France.

Mitchell, Broadus, B.A., PH.D., L.H.D.; American economist; b. 27 Dec. 1892; ed. Johns Hopkins Univ.
Reporter 13-18; successively Instructor, Assoc. and Assoc.Prof. of Political Economy Johns Hopkins Univ. 19-39; Visiting Prof. Occidental Coll. 39-41; Candidate of Socialist Party for Governorship of Maryland 34; Consultant to Dir. N.R.A. Div. of Review Nov. 35-March 36; twice mem. Exec. Cttee. American Economic Asscn.; Act. Dir. of Research Int. Ladies' Garment Workers' Union 43-47; Lecturer in Economics Rutgers Univ. 47-49, Prof. 49-; Visiting Prof. Hofstra Univ. 58-67; Pres. Metropolitan Econ. Assocn. 50-51.
Publs. *The Rise of Cotton Mills in the South* 21, *General Economics* 37, *Depression Decade* 47, *American Adventure* 49, *Alexander Hamilton* (2 vols.) 57, 62, *Great Economists in their Times* 66, *Postscripts to Economic History* 67; in co-operation: *The Industrial Revolution in the South* 30, *Practical Problems in Economics* 38, *American Economic History* 47, *Economics, Experience and Analysis* 50, *A Bibliography of the Constitution of the U.S.* 64.
49 Barrow Street, New York, N.Y. 10014, U.S.A.
Telephone: CHelsea 2-8436.

Mitchell, Charles S(cott), B.S.; American business executive; b. 22 Sept. 1909; ed. North Carolina State Univ.
Cities Service Co. and subsidiaries 30-; Junior Engineer, Cities Service Oil Co. 30-31; Meter Dept., Cities Service Gas Co. 31-37; Asst. Superintendent, Panhandle Operations, and Sales Engineer 37-39; Buyer, Purchasing Dept., Cities Service Oil Co. (Del.) 39-43; Asst. Purchasing Agent 43-47; Engineer Marketing Div. 47-48; Manager Crude Oil Purchasing and Sales Div. 48-50; Manager Crude Oil Supply and Transport Div. 50-54; Staff Exec. Cities Service Co. 55-56, Dir. 55-, Vice-Pres. 56-59, Senior Vice-Pres. 59-64, Exec. Vice-Pres. 64-66, Pres. 66, 67, Chair. and Chief Exec. Officer 68-; official of subsidiary and other companies; mem. Board

of Dirs. American Petroleum Inst.; mem. Nat. Soc. of Professional Engineers; Vice-Pres. and mem. of Exec. Cttee. North Carolina Engineering Foundation.
Office: Cities Service Company, 70 Pine Street, New York, N.Y. 10005; Home: 785 Fifth Avenue, New York, N.Y. 10022, U.S.A.

Mitchell, Donald George; American industrialist; b. 26 April 1905; ed. Univ. of Cincinnati and Univ. of Florida.
Chief, Marketing Div. American Can Co. 33-37; Gen. Sales Man., Marshall Field and Co. 37-39; Vice-Pres. Pepsi-Cola Co. 39-42; Vice-Pres. (Sales) Sylvania Electric Products Inc. 42-46, Exec. Vice-Pres. 46, Pres. 46-53, Chair. 53-62; Pres. Gen. Telephone and Electronics Corpn. 59-61, Vice-Chair. 61-62; Chair. General Time Corpn. 64-; Chair. American Management Asscn.; Outstanding Civilian Service Award, U.S. Dept. of the Army 61; official of welfare orgs.
206 Oakridge Avenue, Summit, New Jersey, U.S.A.

Mitchell, George Wilder, B.A.; American economist; b. 23 Feb. 1904; ed. Wisconsin, Iowa and Chicago Univs.
Research Asst. Univs. of Wisconsin, Iowa and Chicago 25-33; Dir. of Research, Illinois Tax Comm. 33-39, 41-43, mem. of Comm. 39-40; Asst. to Dir., Dept. of Revenue, State of Illinois 43; Dir. Dept. of Finance, State of Illinois 49-51; Tax Economist, Federal Reserve Bank of Chicago 44-48, Vice-Pres. 51-61; mem. Bd. of Govs. of the Fed. Reserve System 61-; mem. Nat. Cttee. on Govt. Finance 61-65.
Publs. *Survey of Local Finance in Illinois* 39-40, *Assessment of Real Estate in Iowa and other Midwestern States* 31.
Federal Reserve System, Washington, D.C. 20551, U.S.A.

Mitchell, Sir Godfrey Way, Kt.; British company director; b. 31 Oct. 1891; ed. Aske's (Haberdashers' School).
With Rowe & Mitchell 08-14; served in Royal Engineers France, First World War 14-18; Man. Dir. George Wimpey & Co. Ltd. 19, Chair. 30-; Chair. Mono Containers Ltd. 47-61; mem. Restrictive Practices Court 57-63.
Office: George Wimpey & Co. Ltd., Hammersmith Grove, London, W.6; Home: Wilton Place, Ledborough Lane, Beaconsfield, England.
Telephone: 01-748-2000 (Office); 0494-6-3128 (Home).

Mitchell, Joseph Stanley, C.B.E., M.D., PH.D., F.R.S., F.R.C.P., F.F.R.; British radiotherapist; b. 22 July 1909; ed. Univ. of Birmingham, and St. John's Coll., Cambridge.
House Physician, Gen. Hospital, Birmingham 34; Fellow St. John's Coll., Cambridge 36-; Radiotherapist. Emergency Medical Service 39; Medical Officer in charge, later Dir., Radiotherapeutic Centre, Addenbrooke's Hospital, Cambridge 43; in charge of medical investigations, Montreal Laboratory, Nat. Research Council of Canada 44; Prof. of Radiotherapeutics, Univ. of Cambridge 46-57; Regius Prof. of Physic in the Univ. of Cambridge 57-; Pres. English Section Anglo-German Medical Society; Hon. Consultant, Atomic Energy Authority; Hon. D.Sc.; Pirogoff Medal 67; Hon. mem. German Roentgen Soc.
Publs. *Studies in Radiotherapeutics* 60, *The Cell Nucleus* 60, *Treatment of Cancer* 65.
Thorndyke, Huntingdon Road, Cambridge, England.

Mitchison, Baron (Life Peer) cr. 64, of Carradale in the County of Argyle; **Gilbert Richard Mitchison,** C.B.E., Q.C. (husband of Naomi Mitchison *q.v.*); British politician; b. 23 March 1890; ed. Eton Coll. and New Coll., Oxford.
Queen's Bays 14-18, finally Maj. G.S.O.2, British Mission to French Forces in Italy; Barrister, Inner Temple

17, Q.C. 46; M.P. 45-64; Parl. Sec. Ministry of Land and Natural Resources 64-66; Labour.
Publ. *First Workers' Government* 34.
Carradale House, Carradale, Argyll, Scotland.

Mitchison, Naomi (wife of Lord Mitchison, *q.v.*); British novelist and farmer; b. 1 Nov. 1897; ed. Dragon School, Oxford.
Editor *Outline for Boys and Girls* 32; Labour candidate for Scottish Univs. 35; Tribal Adviser to the Bakgatla (S.E. Bechuanaland).
Publs. *The Conquered* 23, *When the Bough Breaks* 24, *Cloud Cuckoo Land* 25, *Black Sparta* 28, *Anna Comnena* 28, *Nix-Nought-Nothing* 28, *Barbarian Stories* 29, *The Corn King and the Spring Queen* 31, *The Delicate Fire* 32, *We Have Been Warned* 35, *The Fourth Pig* 36, *Socrates* (with R. H. S. Crossman) 37, *Moral Basis of Politics* 38, *The Kingdom of Heaven* 39, *As it Was in the Beginning* (with L. E. Gielgud) 39, *The Blood of the Martyrs* 39, *Re-Educating Scotland* 45, *The Bull Calves* 47, *Men and Herring* (with D. Macintosh) 49, *The Big House* 50, *Lobsters on the Agenda* 52, *Travel Light* 52, *Swan's Road* 54, *Graeme and the Dragon* 54, *Land the Ravens Found* 55, *Chapel Perilous* 55, *Little Boxes* 56, *Behold Your King, The Far Harbour* 57, *Other People's Worlds, Five Men and a Swan* 58, *Judy and Lakshmi* 59, *Rib of the Green Umbrella* 60, *The Young Alexander* 60, *Karensgaard* 61, *Memoirs of a Spacewoman* 62, *The Fairy Who Couldn't Tell a Lie* 63, *When We Become Men* 64, *Return to the Fairy Hill* 66, *Friends and Enemies* 66, *African Heroes* 68.
Carradale House, Carradale, Argyll, Scotland.

Mitford, Jessica (sister of Hon. Nancy Mitford, *q.v.*); American (b. British) writer; b. 11 Sept. 1917.
Publs. *Hons and Rebels* (autobiography) 60, *The American Way of Death* 63.
6411 Regent Street, Oakland, California, U.S.A.

Mitford, The Hon. Nancy (sister of Jessica Mitford, *q.v.*); British writer; b. 28 Nov. 1904.
Publs. Novels: *Highland Fling, Christmas Pudding, Wigs on the Green, Pigeon Pie, Pursuit of Love* (musical 67), *Love in a Cold Climate, The Blessing, Don't Tell Alfred, Stanleys of Alderley, Ladies of Alderley* (family letters), *Madame de Pompadour* (biography), *Voltaire in Love* 57, *The Water Beetle* (essays) 62, *Louis XIV at Versailles* 64, *The Sun King* 66, *The Ladies of Alderley* 67.
7 rue Monsieur, Paris 7e, France.

Mitin, Mark Borisovich; Soviet philosopher; b. 5 July 1901; ed. Inst. of Red Professors, Moscow.
Party work 29-36; Scientific worker, Inst. of Philosophy 36-44; Lecturer, Higher Party School 45-50; mem. Central Cttee. of C.P.S.U. 39-56; mem. U.S.S.R. Acad. of Sciences 39-; Chief Editor *For a Lasting Peace, For a People's Democracy*, Prague 50-56; mem. staff All-Union Soc. *Znania* (Knowledge) 56-60; Chief Editor *Questions of Philosophy*; State Prize 43; Order of Lenin (twice); Order of Red Banner of Labour (twice) etc.
Ulitsa Frunze 10, Moscow; ul. Serafimovicha, 2/230, Moscow, J-72, U.S.S.R.

Mitra, Biren, Indian politician; b. 26 Nov. 1917; ed. Ravenshaw Coll., Cuttack.
Member Quit India movement 42; mem. Orissa Assembly 61-; Dep. Chief Minister, Orissa 61-63, Chief Minister (in charge of Finance, Industry, Planning and Co-ordination, Mining and Geology, Irrigation and Power, Cultural Affairs, Health and Commerce) Oct. 63-Jan. 65.
Katgorasahi, Cuttack, India.

Mitra, Sir Dhirendra Nath, Kt., C.B.E., B.A., B.L.; Indian lawyer; b. 18 April 1891; ed. St. Xavier's Coll., Presidency Coll., and Univ. Coll., Calcutta.

Fmrly. Solicitor for Govt. of India, New Delhi; Commr. of Oaths and Solicitor of Supreme Court of England; rep. at World Health Assembly, U.N. Conf. on Freedom of Information and Adviser, U.N. Conf. on Human Rights; Gov. League of Red Cross Societies; Leader of Indian Del. to Diplomatic Conf. for Establishment of Int. Conventions for the Protection of War Victims; mr. Legal Adviser and Solicitor to the High Commr. for India in the U.K.; personal rank of Minister on High Comm. for India 50; Sec. to Pres. of India 52; Chair. Banks Liquidation Proceedings Cttee. of India 52; Chief Adviser Hindusthan Co-operative Insurance Soc. Ltd. 52-54; Chair. Durgapur Projects Ltd., United Industrial Bank Ltd., Durgapur Chemicals Ltd., Clarion-McCann Advertising Services Ltd., etc.; Assoc. K.St.J. 49; M.D. h.c. Visva-Bharati Univ.
7 Ballgunge Circular Road, Calcutta 19, India.

Mitra, Sombhu; Indian actor and stage director; b. 22 Aug. 1915; ed. Ballygunge Govt. High School and St. Xavier's Coll., Calcutta.
Public Stage, Bengal 39-42; Producer-Dir.-Actor, Indian People's Theatre Asscn. 43-46; Producer-Dir.-Actor Bohurupee (non-commercial theatre) 48-; Fellow Sangeet Natak Akademie, New Delhi; Grand Prix Carlovy Vary Film Festival 57.
Productions include: *Four Chapters* (Tagore) 51, *An Enemy of the People* (Ibsen) 52, *Red Oleanders* (Tagore) 54, *The Doll's House* (Ibsen) 58, *Sacrifice* (Tagore) 61, *The King of the Dark Chamber* (Tagore) 64, *Oedipus Rex* (Sophocles) 64.
Publs. *Abhinay-Natak-Mancha* 57, *Putul Khela* 58, *Kanchanranga* 61, *Ghurnee* 67.
Bohurupee, 11a Nasiruddin Road, Park Circus, Calcutta 17, India.

Mitrany, David, PH.D., D.SC.; British political scientist; b. 1 Jan. 1888; ed. London School of Economics.
Member editorial staff *Manchester Guardian* 19-22; Asst. European Editor Carnegie Endowment's *Economic and Social History of the World War* 22-29; Visiting Prof. Harvard Univ. 31-33, Dodge Lecturer Yale Univ. 32, Prof. Inst. for Advanced Study, Princeton N.J. 33-, Adviser on Int. Problems Lever Bros. and Unilever Ltd. 43-.
Publs. *The Problems of International Sanctions* 25 (French edition 26), *The Land and the Peasant in Rumania* 28, *The Effect of the War in South-Eastern Europe* 37, *The Progress of International Government* 43, *A Working Peace System* 43 (Italian, Danish and Norwegian editions), *American Interpretations* 46, *Marx Against the Peasant* 51 (German, Italian, American, Portuguese, Chinese and Japanese edns., paperback 64), *A Working Peace System* (essays) 66.
Institute for Advanced Study, Princeton, N.J., U.S.A.; Lower Farm, Kingston Blount, Oxford, England.

Mitrega, Jan; Polish politician; b. 17; ed. Mining and Metallurgy Acad., Cracow.
Mineworker; fmr. mem. Communist Youth Movement; posts in Polish United Workers' Party 46-52; Vice-Minister of Mining and Power 52-59; Minister of Mining and Power 59-; mem. of Parl. 61-.
36 Krucza Street, Warsaw, Poland.

Mitry, Emmanuel Comte de, French industrialist; b. 21 June 1892.
President and Gen. Man. Soc. des Forges de Gueugnon; Pres. De. Wendel et Cie. until 67; Deputy Chair. De Wendel-Sidelor-Mosellane Jan. 68-; Vice-Pres. Etablissements Nozal; Dir. Anciens Etablissements Chavanne-Brun Frères, Distilleries de la Suze, Soc. Lorraine de Laminage Continu (SOLLAC); Officier Légion d'Honneur, Croix de Guerre.
10 rue de Clichy, Paris 9e; Château de Betange, Florange (Moselle), France.

Mitscherlich, Alexander, DR. MED.; German professor of medicine; b. 20 Sept. 1908; ed. Gymnasium, Hof, Bavaria, and Univs. of Munich, Prague, Berlin, Freiburg, Zürich and Heidelberg.
Director of Psychosomatic Clinic, Univ. of Heidelberg Medical School 48-67, Extraordinary Prof. of Psychosomatic Medicine 52-58, Prof. 58-; Prof. of Psychology, Univ. of Frankfurt; Dir. Sigmund Freud Inst. for Psychoanalysis and Psychosomatic Medicine, Frankfurt/Main 59-; Hon. mem. American Psychosomatic Soc. 52.
Publs. *Vom Ursprung der Sucht 47, Freiheit und Unfreiheit in der Krankheit 48, Medizin ohne Menschlichkeit 60, Auf dem Weg zur vaterlosen Gesellschaft 63, Die Unwirtlichkeit unserer Städte 65, Krankheit als Konflikt-Studien zur psychosomatischen Medizin I, II 66-67, Die Unfähigkeit zu trauern, Der Kranke in der modernen Gesellschaft* (editor, inter al.) 67.
Myliusstr. 20, Frankfurt, German Federal Republic.
Telephone: 729245.

Mitsotakis, Constantine; Greek politician; b. 18 Oct. 1918; ed. Univ. of Athens.
Lawyer Athens 41-, Crete 42-44; Publisher *Kiryx* 45; mem. Chamber of Deputies 46-, for Liberal Party 46-61, for Centre Union 61-; Minister of Finance, Transport and Public Works 51, of Finance 63-65; Minister of Co-ordination and *ad interim* of Mercantile Marine July 65-66.
1 Paravantinou Street, Athens 138, Greece.
Telephone: 724-997.

Mittag, Günter; German politician; b. 8 Oct. 1926; ed. secondary school, Stettin, and Transport Coll., Dresden.
Former Railway Inspector; mem. Socialist Unity Party (S.E.D.) 46-, Cand. mem. Central Cttee. 58-62, mem. 62-, Cand. mem. Politburo 63-66, mem. 66-; Sec. Econ. Comm. of Politburo (S.E.D.) 58-62, Sec. for Econs. 62, Head of Bureau for Industry and Building 63; mem. Volkskammer; mem. State Council 63-; Vaterländischer Verdienstorden in Silber 59, Gold 64; Order of Banner of Labour.
Sozialistische Einheitspartei Deutschlands, 102 Berlin, 2 Werderscher Markt, Germany.

Mitterrand, François Maurice Marie; French politician; b. 26 Oct. 1916; ed. Univ. of Paris.
Served 39-40; taken prisoner, escaped back to France where active in prisoner-of-war and resistance movements; missions to London and Algiers 43; Sec.-Gen. Organisation for Prisoners of War, War Victims and Refugees 44-46; Deputy 46-58, 62-; Minister for Ex-Service men 47-48; Sec. of State for Information attached Prime Minister's Office 48-49; Minister for Overseas Territories 50-51; Chair. U.D.S.R. 51-52; Minister of State Jan.-Feb. 52, Mar. 52-July 53; Del. to Council of Europe July-Sept. 53; Minister of the Interior June 54-Feb. 55; Minister of State 56-57; Senator 59-62; Candidate for Pres. of France 65; Pres. of Federation of Democratic and Socialist Left 65-; Pol. Dir. *Le Courrier de la Nièvre;* Officier Légion d'Honneur, Croix de Guerre, Rosette de la Résistance.
Publs. *Aux frontières de l'Union française, La Chine au défi* 61, *Le Coup d'Etat permanent* 64.
4 rue Guynemer, Paris 6e, France.

Mitterer, Otto; Austrian politician; b. 22 Oct. 1911; ed. grammar school and business college.
Family wholesale clock firm 32-40, 40-; mil. service 40-45; entered politics, mem. Austrian Econ. Union 47, Chair. Trade Section 55; Minister of Trade and Industry, mem. of the Nat. Council 68-; Kommerzialrat 56; Grosse Silberne Ehrenmedaille Vienna Chamber of Commerce 59; Grosses Silbernes Ehrenzeichen for Services to the Repub. of Austria 63.
Vienna 1, Goldschmiedgasse 10, Austria.

Miyamori, Kazuo; Japanese oil executive; b. 17 Sept. 1902; ed. Meiji Univ.
With Yamaguchi Bank Ltd. 25-33, joined Sanwa Bank Ltd. 33, Dir. 56, Deputy Pres. 64-66; Pres. and Chief Exec. Officer Maruzen Oil Co., Ltd. 64-; Pres. Maruzen Tanker Co., Ltd. and Maruzen Real Estate Co. 65-; Dir. Maruzen Petro Chemical Co., Ltd. 64-, Kansai Oil Co. and Kansai and Osaka Petro Chemical Cos., Ltd. 65-, Kanegabuchi Gosei Kagaku Kogyo Co., Ltd. 67-; Auditor, Palace Side Bldg. Co. 63-, Ohbayashi Road Construction Co. Ltd. and Japan Industrial Land Devt. Co. 64-.
261 Unoki-cho, Chyofu, Ohta-ku, Tokyo, Japan.

Miyamoto, Kenji; Japanese writer and politician; b. 17 Oct. 1908; ed. Tokyo Imperial Univ.
Member C.P. of Japan 31-, mem. Cen. Cttee. 33-, Gen. Sec. of Cen. Cttee. 58-; imprisoned 33-45.
Publs. *People's Literature 47, Problems of Democratic Revolution 47, Prospects of Our Revolution 48, Advance Towards Freedom and Independence 49, Reminiscences of Yuriko Miyamoto 54, Criticism of Critics 54, Prospects of Japanese Revolution 61, The Path of Our Party's Struggle 61, Actual Tasks and the Communist Party of Japan 66.*
Central Committee of the Communist Party of Japan, Sendagaya 4-chome 26, Shibuya-ku, Tokyo, Japan.

Miyazaki, Kagayaki; Japanese chemical executive; b. 19 April 1909; ed. Tokyo Univ.
Governing Dir. Japan Fed. of Employers Asscns. 49-; Man. Dir. Japan Chemical Industry Asscn. 50-; mem. Employers Cttee. of Central Labour Relations Board 53-62; Pres. Asahi Chemical Industry Co. Ltd. 61-; Councillor Asscn. Petrochemical Industries in Japan 61-; Dir. Japan Industrial Explosives Asscn. 61-; Exec. Dir. Fed. of Econ. Org. 66-; Pres. Japan Chemical Fibres Asscn. 67-; Chair. Cttee. for Econ. Devt. of KANSAI 67-; fmr. Pres. Electro-Chemical Soc. of Japan 67-68.
144 Funabashi-cho, Setagaya-ku, Tokyo, Japan.
Telephone: 429-2027.

Miyazawa, Kiichi; Japanese politician; b. 8 Oct. 1919; ed. Tokyo Univ.
Ministry of Finance 41-49; Private Sec. to Minister of Finance 49-51, to Minister of Int. Trade and Industry 51-52; mem. House of Councillors 53-65, Chair. Steering Cttee. 61-62; Minister of State in charge of Econ. Planning Agency 62-64, and 66-; mem. House of Representatives 67-.
1-34, 6-chome Jingu-mae, Shibuya-ku, Tokyo, Japan.

Mizener, Arthur, M.A., PH.D.; American university professor; b. 3 Sept. 1907; ed. Princeton and Harvard Univs.
Instructor in English, Yale Univ. 34-40; Asst. Prof. Wells Coll. 40-43, Assoc. Prof. 43-45; Prof. Carleton Coll. 45-51; Prof. Cornell Univ. 51-; Fulbright Lecturer in American Studies, Univ. of London 55-56; Guggenheim Fellow 65-66; Senior Fellow Nat Endowment for the Humanities 68.
Publs. *The Far Side of Paradise: A Biography of F. Scott Fitzgerald 51, Afternoon of an Author 57, The Sense of Life 64, Twelve Great American Novels 67.*
634 Highland Road, Ithaca, N.Y., U.S.A.
Telephone: 607-272-5551.

Mizukami, Tatsuzo, M.A.; Japanese business executive; b. 15 Oct. 1903; ed. Tokyo Commercial Coll.
Mitsui Bussan Kaisha 28-47; Exec. Man. Dir. Daiichi Bussan Kaisha Ltd. 47-57, Exec. Vice-Pres. 57-59; Exec. Vice-Pres. Mitsui and Co. 59-61, Pres. 61-; mem. Foreign Exchange Control Council 56-, Inquiry Comm. on Tax System 59-, Overseas Immigration Council 60-, Foreign Trade Transaction Control Council 61-; Dir. Japan Foreign Trade Council 60-; Exec. Dir. Fed. of

Econ. Orgs. 62-; Co-Chair. Japan Cttee. for Econ. Devt. 61-; Chair. Foreign Trade Div., Superior Export Council 62-.
300 Kakinokizaka, Meguro-ku, Tokyo, Japan.

Mizuno, Seiichi, B.LITT., D.LITT.; Japanese university professor; b. 24 March 1905; ed. Kyoto Univ.
Studied Chinese archæology in Peking 29-31; Research mem. of Research Inst. of Oriental Culture 31-48; Prof. of Research Inst. for Humanities, Kyoto Univ. 48-68, Prof. Emer. 68-; awards include Asahi-Sho and Onshi-Sho.
Publs. *Inner Mongolia and the Region of the Great Wall* (with N. Egami) 35, *Study of Cave-Temples at Lung-men, Honan* (with T. Nagahiro) 41, *Tsushima* (with others) 52, *Yun-kang* (with T. Nagahiro) (16 vols.) 50-55, *Bronze and Jades of Ancient China* 59, *Bronze and Stone Sculpture of China* 60, *Horyuji Monastery* 65.
91 Jodoji-Kamibabacho, Sakyo-ku, Kyoto, Japan.
Telephone: 771-6564.

Mizuta, Mikio; Japanese politician; b. 05; ed. Kyoto Univ.
Elected eight times as member of House of Reps. 46-; Parliamentary Vice-Minister of Finance 49-50; Dir. Economic Deliberation Board 53; Minister of International Trade and Industry 56-57; Minister of Finance 60-62, Dec. 66-; fmr. teacher, Senshu Univ., fmr. Dir. Tokyo Kohan Kogyo Co.; Liberal-Democratic Party.
2027, Hojo, Tateyama City, Chiba Prefecture, Japan.

Mjartan, Jozef; Czechoslovak politician; b. 22 Feb. 1900.
Farmer 25-52; mem. Unified Agricultural Co-operative 52-; Deputy to Nat. Assembly 45-54, 60-; Dep. Chair, Board Commrs. 48-53; Deputy and Deputy Chair. Slovak Nat. Council 53-60; mem. Presidium Central Cttee. Nat. Front, Prague 66-; mem. Presidium Slovak Reconstruction Party 48-, Deputy Chair. 50-66, Chair. 66-; Order of Slovak Nat. Rising First Class 46; Order of 25th February 1948 First Class 48; Order of Labour 60.
Slovak Reconstruction Party, Bratislava, Sedlárska 7, Czechoslovakia.

Mládek, Jan Victor, D.IUR.ET.RER.POL.; American (b. Czech) economist; b. 7 Dec. 1911; ed. Charles Univ., Prague, Paris Univ., Masaryk Univ., Brno.
Worked in Central Office, Brno 38-39; served with Czechoslovak Army in Exile, France, U.K. 39-42; Head of Monetary Dept., Ministry of Finance, Czechoslovak Govt. in Exile, London 42-45; Head of Currency and Banking Dept., Prague 45-46; Dir. Nat. Bank of Czechoslovakia 45-47; Gov. and Exec. Dir. Int. Monetary Fund (IMF) 46-48, Dep. Dir. of Operations 48-50, Dep. and Acting Dir. European and N. American Dept. 50-53, Dir. European Office (Paris) 53-61, work in underdeveloped countries 55-61, Dir. in charge of org. of African Dept. 61-64, now Dir. Central Banking Service.
Publ. *International Economic Institutions* 46.
3234 N. Street, N.W. Washington, D.C. 20007, U.S.A.
Telephone: 3331191.

Moberg, Vilhelm; Swedish author; b. 20 Aug. 1898; ed. public school.
Former farmhand and forest worker; later journalist for ten years; later freelance author.
Publs. 17 novels and 25 plays, including: *Ride this Night, The Earth is Ours, The Emigrants, Unto a Good Land, The Last Letter Home, When I Was a Child, A Time on Earth, The Peasant Year.*
Hagagatan 3, Stockholm, Sweden.
Telephone: 3763-38.

Mobutu, Lt.-Gen. Joseph-Désiré; Congolese politician; b. 14 Oct. 1930; ed. Léopoldville and Coquilhatville.
Sergeant-Major, Accountancy Dept., Force Publique, Belgian Congo 49-56; course at Institute of Social Studies, Brussels; journalist, Léopoldville; mem.

Mouvement National Congolaise; del. Brussels Round Table Conf. on Congo independence 59-60; Sec. of State for Nat. Defence, Lumumba cabinet, June 60; Chief of Staff, Congo Army, July 60; took over supreme power in name of army and suspended all political activity for three months Sept. 60; appointed a College of High Commrs. to take over govt.; Maj.-Gen. and C.-in-C. of Congolese Forces Jan. 61-65, Lt.-Gen. and Pres. of Congo Nov. 65-, also Pres. of Cabinet Oct. 66-.
Office of the President, Kinshasa, Congo (Kinshasa).

Moch, Jules; French politician; b. 15 March 1893; ed. Ecole Polytechnique.
Served Army 14-18 War; Dir. of Services for indus. and agric. restitution in Germany and ex-enemy countries 18-20; engineer 20-27; Dep. for Hérault 28-40; Sec.-Gen. in Prime Min. Blum's Office 36; Under-Sec. of State 37; Min. of Public Works 38; served in French Navy 39-40; imprisoned for anti-Pétain vote 40-41; active in resistance movement; later joined Gen. de Gaulle in London, rejoined Free French Naval Forces and Gen. Staff of Free French Armed Forces 43; sat in Consultative Assembly Algiers; took part in Mediterranean operations; Dep. to Nat. Constituent Assembly, Nat. Ass. 46-58, 62-; Min. of Public Works and Transport in four cabinets; Minister of Nat. Economy and Reconstruction Oct.-Nov. 47; Minister of the Interior and Vice Prime Minister 47-50, of Defence 50-51; Ministry of Interior 58; Perm. Del. to UN Disarmament Comm. 53-60; mem. Dir. Cttee., Socialist Party (S.F.I.O.); Croix de Guerre for both World Wars, Commdr. Légion d'Honneur, Médaille de la Résistance.
Publs. *Restitutions et Réparations* 21, *La Russie des Soviets* 25, *Socialisme et rationalisation* 27, *Jean Jaurès et les problèmes du temps présent* 27, *Le Parti Socialiste et la politique financière* 28, *Le rail et la Nation* 31, *Capitalisme et transports* 32, *Socialisme, crises, nationalisations* 32, *L'Espagne républicaine* (co-author) 33, *Pour marcher au pouvoir* 35, *Arguments et documents* 36, *Guerre aux trusts* 45, *Arguments socialistes* 45, *Confrontations* 52, *Yougoslavie, terre d'expériences* 53, *Alerte* 54, *La Folie des hommes* 54, *U.S.S.R., les yeux ouverts* 56, *Washington D. Smith, banquier de Wall Street* 57, *En retard d'une paix* 58, *Socialisme Vivant* 60, *Paix en Algérie* 61, *Le Pont sur la Manche* 62, *Non à la Force de Frappe* 64, *Histoire du réarmement allemand depuis 1950* 65.
45 allée de la Forêt, La Celle-Saint-Cloud (Yvelines), France.

Moch, Paul Albert; French mining executive; b. 8 Feb. 1908; ed. Collège Chaptal and Ecole nationale supérieure des mines de Paris.
Mining Engineer, Constantine; Vice-Pres., Admin. Council, Office of Petroleum Research; Pres. Régie autonome des pétroles; Pres. and Dir.-Gen., Soc. de gestion des participations de la Régie autonome des pétroles (SOGERAP), Cie. de recherche et d'exploitation de pétrole au Sahara (CREPS); Pres. Elf Union; Vice-Pres. Enterprise de Recherches et d'Activités Pétrolières (ERAP); Admin., Antarpétroles de l'Atlantique, Cie. des pétroles d'Algérie (C.P.A.), Soc. nationale des pétroles d'Aquitaine, Soc. des pétroles d'Afrique-équatoriale, Soc. nationale de matériel pour la recherche et l'exploitation de pétrole (SN MAREP), Sté. Elf pour la recherche et l'Exploitation des Hydrocarbures Elf R.E., Sté. Rhône Alpes Union pour le Raffinage et la Pétrochimie, Soc. pour la Valorisation des Pétroles bruts; mem. Econ. and Soc. Council 59-; Commdr. Légion d'Honneur, Officier du Mérite saharien; Commdr. Mérite Industriel et Commercial.
Office: 7 rue Nélaton, Paris 15e; Home: 12 rue Jean Nicot, Paris 7e, France.
Telephone: SOL 81-10; SEG 38-42.

Moczar, General Mieczyslav; Polish security official and politician; b. 13.

Polish communist guerilla activities, East and South-East Poland, Second World War; Head of Security Services, Łódź 45-56; Minister of State Farms 56; Vice-Minister of Interior and Chief of Polish Security Services 56-64; Minister of Interior Dec. 64-; Chair. of *Zbowid* (Ex-Servicemen's Org.).

Ministry of Interior, Warsaw, Poland.

Mód, Péter; Hungarian politician and diplomatist; b. 11; ed. Univ. of Paris.

Entered diplomatic service 47; Envoy to Greece 56-57; Head, Perm. Mission to the UN 57-61; First Deputy Foreign Minister 61-.

Ministry of Foreign Affairs, Budapest, Hungary.

Mödl, Martha; German singer; ed. Munich and Nuremberg Conservatoires.

Numerous appearances at German and foreign opera houses, and at Bayreuth Festivals 51-; mem. Staatsoper Stuttgart 53-.

Steindorfstrasse 6, Munich 22, German Federal Republic.

Modogoyev, Andrei Urupkheyevich; Soviet politician; b. 1915; ed. C.P.S.U. Higher Party School.

Member C.P.S.U. 40-; Teacher 32-39; Young Communist League Official 39-43; Party and Local Govt. Official 43-60; Chair. Council of Ministers, Buryat Autonomous S.S.R. 60-62; First Sec. Buryat Regional Cttee. C.P.S.U. June 62-; Alt. mem. C.P.S.U. Central Cttee.; Deputy to U.S.S.R. Supreme Soviet.

Buryat Regional Committee, Communist Party of the Soviet Union, Ulan-Ude, U.S.S.R.

Mody, Sir Hormasji Peroshaw, K.B.E., M.A., LL.B.; Indian administrator and company director; b. 23 Sept. 1881; ed. Bombay Univ.

Pres. Bombay Municipal Corpn. 23; Chair. Millowners' Assch. 27 and 29-34; Pres. Indian Merchants' Chamber 28; mem. Indian Legislative Assembly 29-43; mem. Constituent Assembly 48-49; mem. (Minister) for Supply, Viceroy's Exec. Council 41-43; Vice-Pres. Export Advisory Council 40, Board of Scientific and Industrial Research 40-41, War Resources Cttee. 41-43; mem. Indian Round Table Conf., London 30-31, and of Reserve Bank Cttee. of the Conf. 33-34; Employers del. Int. Labour Conf. Geneva 37; Dir. Tata Sons Ltd., and Allied Groups; Gov. of Bombay State 47; Gov. of Uttar Pradesh 49-52; Chair. Cen. Bank of India Ltd. 63-68; Chair. Indian Hotels Co. Ltd., Sir Dorabji Tata Trust; Patron-in-Chief, Cricket Club of India Ltd.; Life-Pres. Indo-American Soc., Indian Council of World Affairs, Bombay Branch; Hon. LL.D. (Banaras, Aligarh, Poona and Agra Univs.); Grand Cross Order of George I of Greece; Fellow, Royal Soc. of Arts.

Publs. *The Political Future of India* 08, *Biography of Sir Pherozeshah Mehta* 21, 64, *Reflections, Wise and Otherwise* 61.

Home: "Spirospero", 1 Carmichael Road, Bombay; Office: Bombay House, 24 Bruce Street, Fort, Bombay, India.

Moeneclaey, Etienne, B.LITT., B.SC.; French civil servant; b. 14 Feb. 1897.

Served in Army in First World War; Asst. to Insp. of Finances 20; Insp. of Finances 23; Asst. Sec. in Office of M. Tardieu, Min. of Public Works 26-28, Min. of the Interior 28-29, and Prime Min. 29-30; various other secretarial and financial posts 30-36; Directeur des Monnaies 34-46; Insp.-Gen. of Finances 46-; Commissaire de Gouvernement à l'Immobilière-constructeurs de Paris 47; Admin. of various insurance and shipping firms; served in French Army 39-40; Commandeur de la Légion d'Honneur; Croix de Guerre 14-18 and 39-45.

50 avenue Duquesne, Paris 7e, France.
Telephone: Segur 51-50.

Moens de Fernig, Count George; Belgian businessman; b. 99.

Chairman of Industrial Cos.; President Chamber of Commerce, Brussels 46-47; Minister of Food and Imports 47-48; Minister of Foreign Trade 49; Gen. Commr. for Int. Exhibition in Brussels 58; Grand Cross Orange Nassau (Neths.); Grand Cross, Crown of Luxembourg; Grand Cross, Légion d'Honneur (France); Commdr. of the Order of Léopold; Grand Cross of the Belgian Crown; Grand Cross, Order of Merit (Italy), etc.

66 rue Veydt, Brussels 5, and "Bleuterveld", Zelem (Limbourg), Belgium.

Moeschlin, Felix, Dr. h.c.; Swiss novelist and dramatist; b. 31 July 1882; ed. Realschule, Basle and Univs. of Basle and Zürich.

Editor *Schweizerland* 15-20; Journalist *Die Tat* 39-42. Publs. *Die Königschmieds* 09, *Hermann Hitz* 10, *Die vier Verliebten* 19, *Die Revolution des Herzens* (drama), *Meine Frau und ich* 25, *Die Vision auf dem Lofot* 26, *Wir wollen immer Kameraden sein* 26, *Barbar und Römer* 31, *Der Amerika-Johann* 32, *Südbrasilien* 36, *Der schöne Fersen* 37, *Wie ich meinen Weg fand* 53, *Wohin gehen wir?* 54, *Ich bin Dein und Du bist Mein* 55, *Wir durchbohren den Gotthard* 57, *Morgen geht die Sonne auf* 58, *Wunder in der Christnacht* 59, *Blumenwunder* 60.

Leimenstrasse 67, 4000 Basle, Switzerland.

Moffatt, Sir John; Zambian farmer and politician; b. April 1905; ed. Grey High School, Port Elizabeth, South Africa and Glasgow Univ.

Cadet, Colonial Service, Northern Rhodesia 27, District Officer 29; Commissioner for Nat. Development 45; retired from civil service 51; mem. Legislative Council N. Rhodesia 51-64; mem. Fed. Parl., Salisbury 54-62; Chair. Fed. African Affairs Board; leader Liberal Party, N. Rhodesia (disbanded Nov. 62).

Mkushi, Zambia.

Mogensen, Børge; Danish architect and furniture designer; b. 13 April 1914; ed. School of Craftsmanship, and Royal Acad. of Fine Arts, Copenhagen.

Head of Danish Co-operative Wholesale Society's furniture design office 42-50; teacher Royal Acad. of Fine Arts 45-47; private practice as furniture designer 50-; Eckersberg Medal for Fine Arts, Royal Acad. of Fine Arts; Silver Medal of Triennale, Italy 51.

Solosevej 37, 2820 Gentofte, Denmark.
Telephone: Gentofte 5729.

Moghioros, Alexandru; Rumanian politician; b. 11.

Member, Communist Party of Rumania, 29-; mem. Cen. Cttee. Union of Communist Youth 32; mem. Cen. Cttee. of Communist Party of Rumania 45-48, Cen. Cttee. and Political Bureau, Rumanian Workers' Party (now Communist Party) 48-, Sec. Cen. Cttee. 52-54, 65-; Deputy Chair. Council of Ministers 54-65.

Secretariat of Central Committee of Rumanian Communist Party, Bucharest, Rumania.

Mohale, A. S., M.A.; Lesotho diplomatist; b. 26 April 1928; ed. Pius XII Univ. Coll., South Africa, and Univ. of St. Francis Xavier, Canada.

Former teacher, Basutoland and South Africa; Lecturer and Deputy Dir. Extension Dept., Pius XII Univ. Coll. 60-61; Co-operative Training Officer, Basutoland 61, later Asst. Registrar of Co-operative Socs.; Supernumerary Head of Govt. Training Section 65; Amb. to U.S.A. and Perm. Rep. to the UN 66-, also High Commr. to Canada; Chair. Lesotho Del. to UNCTAD II, New Delhi 68.

Permanent Mission of the Kingdom of Lesotho to the United Nations, 866 United Nations Plaza, Suite 580, N.Y. 10017, U.S.A.

Mohammed, Brig. Jassim; Iraqi army officer and politician; b. 18; ed. Iraqi Mil. Coll., Iraqi Staff Coll., and British Staff Coll., Camberley.

Artillery Officer 38, rose to Director of Military Training,

Ministry of Defence 58; Dir. of Military Operations and Asst. Chief of Staff 58-59; Commandant, Iraqi Staff Coll. 59-64; Amb. of Iraq to Jordan 64, to Algeria 67-; Order of Rafidain.
Iraqi Embassy, Algiers, Algeria.

Mohammed Zahir Shah; King of Afghanistan; b. 30 Oct. 1914; ed. Habibia High School, Istiqlal Coll. (both in Kabul), Lycée Janson-de-Sailly and Univ. of Montpellier, France.
Graduated with highest honours; attended Infantry Officers' School, Kabul 32; married Lady Homira, November 4th 1931; children, Princess Bilqis, Prince Ahmad Shah Khan, Princess Maryam, Prince Mohammed Nadir Khan, Prince Shah Mahmoud Khan, Prince Mohammed Daoud Jan, Prince Mirvis Jan; Asst. Min. in Ministry of National Defence 32-33; acting Minister of Education 33; crowned King November 8th, 33.
Dilkusha, Royal Palace, Kabul, Afghanistan.

Mohn, Reinhard; German publisher; 29 June 1921; ed. high school.
Army Service 39-43; Prisoner of War in N. Africa and U.S.A. 43-46; Proprietor and Head, C. Bertelsmann Verlag 47-.
C. Bertelsmann Verlag, 4830 Gütersloh, Eickhoffstrasse 14/16, German Federal Republic.

Mohr, Ernst-Günther, DR.JUR.; German diplomatist; b. 9 Sept. 1904; ed. Univ. of Hamburg.
Entered Foreign Service 29; served Ministry of Foreign Affairs 29-32, Shanghai 32-33, Peking 33-36, Nanking 36-37, Memel 37-38; Ministry of Foreign Affairs 38-39, The Hague 39-40, Rio de Janeiro 40-41, Tangiers 42-44, Ministry of Foreign Affairs 44-45; Dept. Dir. Deutsches Büro für Friedensfragen Stuttgart 47-49; with Liaison Office to Allied High Comm. 49-51; Rep. to Council of Europe 51-52; Minister to Venezuela 52-55; Chief of Protocol, Ministry of Foreign Affairs 55-58; Ambassador to Switzerland 58-63, to Argentina 63-; Grand Cross with Star, Order of Merit.
Cerrito 550, Buenos Aires, Argentina.

Mohr, Otto Lous, M.D.; Norwegian anatomist and geneticist; b. 8 March 1886.
Professor Anatomy, Oslo Univ. 19-52; mem. Norwegian Acad. of Science 20- (Pres. 40-42), of Danish Acad. of Sciences 35- and Finnish Acad. of Science 37-; Royal Physiographical Soc., Lund, Sweden 40-, Societas Fauna et Flora fennica 46-, Belgian Acad. of Medicine 46-, American Philosophical Society 48-, Royal Society of Sciences, Trondheim 51-; hon. mem. Norwegian Medical Society 54-, Bergen Medical Society 56-, Nordic Genetics Society 60-; Chair. Board of Dirs. Norwegian State Broadcasting 45-57; Rector, Oslo Univ. 46-51; Chair. Int. Cttee. Genetics Congresses 33-39; Dunham Lecturer, Harvard Medical Coll. 33; LL.D. (Edinburgh Univ.) 47; Med.Dr. h.c. Kgl. Karolinska Medico-Chir. Inst., Stockholm; Fridtjof Nansen Prize, Norwegian Acad. of Science 30, Gunnerus Medal, Royal Society of Sciences, Trondheim 56.
Publs. on genetics, cytology, and birth control.
Thorsó herregaard pr. Fredrikstad, Norway.

Mohrt, Michel, L. en D.; French editor and writer; b. 21 April 1914; ed. Law School, Rennes.
Lawyer, Marseilles Bar until 52; Editor at Les Editions Gallimard 52-; Croix de Guerre; Grand Prix du roman de l'Académie française for *La Prison Maritime* 62.
Publs. Novels: *Mon Royaume pour un Cheval* 49, *La Prison Maritime* 61, *La Campagne d'Italie* 67; essay: *Le nouveau roman Americain* 56.
4 *bis* rue du Cherche-Midi, Paris 6e; Ker Velin, Locquirec, Finistère-Nord, France.
Telephone: BAB 42-12 (Paris).

Moi, Daniel Arap; Kenyan politician; b. 1924; ed. African Mission School, Kabartonjo, A.I.M. School and Govt. African School, Kapsabet.
Teacher 45-57; Head. Teacher, Govt. African School, Kabarnet 46-48, 55-57, Teacher Tambach Teacher Training School, Kabarnet 48-54; African Rep. mem., Legislative Council 57-63; Chair. Kenya African Democratic Union (KADU) 60-61; mem. House of Reps. 61-; Parl. Sec., Ministry of Educ. April-Dec. 61; Minister of Educ. Dec. 61-62, Local Govt. 62-64, Home Affairs 64-67; Pres. Kenya African Nat. Union (KANU) for Rift Valley Province 66-67; Vice Pres. of Kenya Jan. 67-.
Office of the Vice-President, Nairobi, Kenya.

Moinot, Pierre, L. ès L.; French civil servant; b. 29 March 1920; ed. Univs. de Paris, Caen and Grenoble.
Senior Civil Servant 46-; Technical Adviser, Private Office of André Malraux 59; Dir. Theatres and Cultural Action 60-62; French Del. to UNESCO 66; Dir.-Gen. of Arts and Letters 66-; Prix Int. roman langue française, Prix Sainte-Beuve, Prix des libraires de France.
Publs. *Armes et Bagages* 51, *La Chasse Royale* 54, *La Blessure* 56, *Le Sable Vif* 63.
51 avenue Raymond Poincaré, Paris 16e, France.

Moiseev, Igor Alexandrovich; Soviet choreographer; b. 21 Jan. 1906; ed. Bolshoi Theatre School of Choreography.
Artist and ballet master at the Bolshoi Theatre 24-39; Dir. of the Choreographic Dept. of the Theatre of People's Art 36; was one of the organisers of the U.S.S.R. Festival of Folk Dancing; Art Dir. of the Folk Dance Ensemble of the U.S.S.R. 37-; People's Artist of the U.S.S.R.; State Prizewinner 42, 47, 52; Lenin Prizewinner 67; two Orders of Red Banner of Labour; Order of Lenin.
State Folk Dance Company of the U.S.S.R., 20 Ploshchad Mayakovskogo, Moscow, U.S.S.R.

Mojsov, Lazar, D.IUR.; Yugoslav journalist, politician and diplomatist; b. 20; ed. Belgrade Univ.
Fmr. mem. Anti-Fascist Assembly for the Nat. Liberation of Macedonia; fmr. Public Prosecutor, Macedonia; Dir. *New Macedonia*; fmr. Head of Press Department, Fed. Govt. of Macedonia; mem. Yugoslav Fed. Parliament and Parliament of Macedonia; mem. Exec. Board, Socialist League of Working People of Yugoslavia; mem. Exec. Cttee. of Cen. Cttee., Macedonian League of Communists; mem. Central Cttee. League of Communists of Yugoslavia; Ambassador to U.S.S.R. 58-61; Dir. Inst. for Study of Workers' Movements 61-62; Dir. and Chief Editor *Borba* 62-64; Order of Merit for Exceptional Achievements First Class, Order of Merit for Services to the Nation, First and Third Class, Order of Brotherhood and Unity.
Publs. *The Bulgarian Working Party (Communist) and the Macedonian National Question* 48, *Vasil Glavinov: First Propagator of Socialism in Macedonia* 49, *Concerning the Question of the Macedonian National Minority in Greece* 54.
Borba, Moše Pijade 31, Belgrade, Yugoslavia.

Mokaddem, Sadok; Tunisian diplomatist; b. 14; ed. Lycée Carnot, Tunis, Faculty of Sciences, Montpellier and Faculty of Medicine, Paris.
Physician, Tunis; mem. Neo-Destour 34-, mem. Political Bureau 52-; Sec. of State for Justice 54-55, for Public Health 55; Dep. to Constituent Ass. 56-59; Ambassador to Egypt 56-57; Sec. of State for Foreign Affairs 57-62; Ambassador to France 62-64; Pres., Nat. Assembly 64-; Grand Cordon of Nat. Order of Independence and of the Republic; several foreign decorations.
National Assembly, Tunis, Tunisia.

Molchanov, Kirill Vladimirovich; Soviet composer; b. 1922; ed. Moscow Conservatoire.
Honoured Worker of the R.S.F.S.R. 63.

Principal compositions: Concerto No. 1 for Piano and Orchestra 45, Concerto No. 2 for Piano and Orchestra 47, Concerto No. 3 for Piano and Orchestra 53; Operas: *Stone Flower* 50, *Dawn* 56, *Del Carno Street* 60, *Romeo, Juliet and Gloom* 62, Incidental music for films: *It Happened in Penkovo* 50, *Vast is My Land* 58, *Stars of May* 59, *To the Seven Winds* 62, *Shore Leave* 62, Music for plays: *Griboyedov* 51, *Mary Stuart* 56, *Three Fat Men* 56, *Last Stop* 57, *Attacking the Storm* 65, Music for radio and television.
Composers' Union of the R.S.F.S.R., 8/10 Nezhdanova Street, Moscow, U.S.S.R.

Molchanov, Nikolai Semyonovich; Soviet internist and cardiologist; b. 1899; ed. Military Medical Acad.
Intern, Head of Dept., Moscow Mil. Hospital 23-31; Instructor, Mil. Medical Acad. 31-39; Deputy Supt. Mil. Medical Acad. 39-41; Chief Internist of Armies and Fronts 41-46; Deputy Head, Dept. of Internal Medicine, Head of Dept., Mil. Medical Acad. 46-65; mem. C.P.S.U. 51-; Corresp. mem. U.S.S.R. Acad. of Medical Sciences 53-60, mem, U.S.S.R. Acad. of Medical Sciences 60-; Head, Dept. of Postgraduate Training, Mil. Medical Acad. 65-; Deputy Chair. All-Union Soc. of Internists; mem. Presidium All-Russia Soc. of Internists and All-Union Soc. of Cardiologists; Order of Lenin 45, 46, Red Banner of Labour 43, Red Banner 44, Red Star 42, etc.
Publs. Over 150 works on toxic agents' influence on heart and that of heating procedures and ultra-high frequency currents on kidneys and stomach, on prophylaxis and treatment of stomach and duodenal ulcer, and burning lesions, on arterial hypotonia, etc.
Military Medical Academy, Lebedeva 6, Leningrad, U.S.S.R.

Moldovan, Roman; Rumanian politician and economist; b. 1911.
University Lecturer; Corresp. mem. Acad. of Socialist Republic of Rumania; Deputy to Grand Nat. Assembly; mem. Central Cttee. of Rumanian Communist Party 65-; Chair. State Planning Cttee. 65; Chair. Nat. Council of Scientific Research and Deputy Chair. Council of Ministers 65-67; Chair. State Cttee. for Price Fixing Dec. 67-.
Publs. include: *Formation and Movement of Capital in Rumania* 40, *Planned Management of National Economy in Rumanian People's Republic* 59; Co-author: *Rumania's Economic Development 1944-1964*, *Rumania's Industry 1944-1964*.
State Committee for Price Fixing, Bucharest, Romania.

Moldt, Ewald; German diplomatist; b. 1927; ed. Deutsche Akademie für Staats- und Rechtswissenschaften.
Former Counsellor, Poland; Ambassador of German Democratic Republic to Romania 65-; Vaterländischer Verdienstorden in Silber und Bronze.
Botschaft der Deutschen Demokratischen Republik, Str. Dumbrava Rosie 6-8, Bucharest, Romania.

Molina Silva, Sergio; Chilean economist and politician; b. 28.
Former Dir.-Gen. of Budget and Finances, Ministry of Finance; Del. several int. confs.; Minister of Finance Nov. 64-67; Pres. Banco Central de Chile; Independent.
Banco Central de Chile, Augustinas 1180, Santiago, Chile.

Molina Ureña, José Rafael, LL.B., BAR.-AT-LAW.; Dominican politician and diplomatist; b. 31 Jan. 1921; ed. Universidad de Santo Domingo.
Practised law 48-61; Founder and Vice-Pres. Inter-American Centre of Econ. and Social Studies (CIDES) 62; Pres. Nat. Fed. of Peasant Brotherhoods (FEN-HERCA); elected to Congress 62; Pres. Constituent Assembly 63, House of Deputies 63; Provisional Con-

stitutional Pres. of the Dominican Republic 65; Gen. Sec. Dominican Revolutionary Party and Pres. of its Political Comm. 66-67; Perm. Rep. of the Dominican Republic to UN Feb. 67-.
Dominican Mission to the United Nations, 7 East 63rd Street, New York 21, N.Y., U.S.A.

Molinari, Ricardo E.; Argentine writer; b. 20 March 1898; ed. secondary school.
Has received every poetry prize in Argentina.
Publs. include: *El Huésped y la Melancolía* 46, *Dias donde la Tarde es un Pájaro* 54, *Unida Noche* 57, *El Cielo de las Alondras y las Gaviotas* 63, *Una sombra antigua Canta* 66.
Martínez de Hoz S/N, Bella Vista, Prov. de Buenos Aires, Argentina.

Moll, Siegmund Bruno, PHIL.DR.; German economist; b. 10 Oct. 1885; ed. Heidelberg, Breslau, Leipzig, Göttingen and Berlin Univs.
Professor of Political Economy Kiel Univ. 11-20, Leipzig Univ. 20-34, Dean, Faculty of Philosophy 28; Pres. German Soc. for Protection of Monetary Standard 32; retd. 34; Prof. of Monetary Econs. and Finance, Univ. Mayor de San Marcos, Lima 36-59; Adviser, Ministry of Finance and Commerce (Peru) 48, Nat. Soc. of Industries 49-, Inst. of Econ. Research, San Marcos Univ. 62-; Hon. Dr. rer. pol. (Göttingen); Grosses Bundesverdienstkreuz.
Publs. *Zur Geschichte der Vermögenssteuern* 11, *Logik des Geldes* 16, *Die modernen Geldtheorien* 17, *Probleme der Finanzwissenschaft* 24, *Lehrbuch der Finanzwissenschaft* 30, *Die Finanzpolitik der Reichsbahn* 31, *Gerechtigkeit in der Wirtschaft* 32; edited *Probleme des Geld- und Finanzwesens* 24-34 and *Beiträge zur Finanzkunde* (with Felix Boesler) 28-34, *La Moneda* 38, *Finanzas y Guerra* 41, *El Sistema monetario del Perú* (with E. G. Barreto) 43, *El sistema tributario del Perú, El Futuro de las Finanzas* 50, *Problemas monetarios contemporáneos* 51, *Curso Superior de Finanzas* 55, *Hay justicia en la Economía?* 59, *Las tres Opiniones Sobre el Desarrollo Económico* 63, *Renta Nacional: Distribución y Desigualdad* 63, *El Problema Monetario Actual del Perú* 64, *El Destino del Oro* 65.
[*Died* 31 *Jan.* 1968]

Møller, Christian, D.PHIL.; Danish physicist; b. 22 Dec. 1904; ed. Univs. of Copenhagen, Rome and Cambridge.
Lecturer, Copenhagen Univ. 33-40, Dozent 40-43, Prof. of Mathematical Physics 43-, Dean of Faculty 47-48; Dir. Theoretical Study Group, CERN (European Centre for Nuclear Research) 54-57; mem. Scientific Policy Cttee. 59-; Dir. Nordita (Nordic Inst. for Theoretical Atomic Physics) 57-; mem. Royal Danish Acad. of Sciences, Royal Norwegian Acad. of Science, Kungl. Fys. Selsk, Swedish Acad. of Science; awarded Ole Romer Medal 66.
Publs. *The Theory of Relativity* 52; papers on atomic theory and relativity.
Frølichsvej 42a, Copenhagen, Denmark.
Telephone: Ordrup 4690.

Møller, Knud Ove, PH.D., M.D.; Danish pharmacologist; b. 21 June 1896; ed. Københavns Universitet.
Professor of Pharmacology 37-66; Chair. Danish Pharmacopœia Comm. 38-67; Chair. Danish Cttee. of Foreign Scientists in Danish Laboratories 46-51; mem. Nordic Pharmacopœia Council 48-67; Co-founder and Editor *Acta Pharmacologica et Toxicologica* 45-64; Co-founder and Chair. Nordic Soc. for Pharmacology; Co-founder and mem. Int. Council for Pharmacologists 53-62; mem. WHO Expert Advisory Panel of Int. Pharmacopœia 51-, WHO Sub-Cttee. on Int. Non-Proprietary Drug Names 59-; Danish, Norwegian and Swedish decorations.
Publs. *Pharmakologie für Zahnärzte* 34, *Stimulants* 45,

Manual in Pharmacology (6th Danish edn.) (5th Swiss edn.) 66.
Office: Department of Pharmacology, Juliane Mariesvej 20, 2100 Copenhagen Ø; Home: 8 Lundsgade, 2100 Copenhagen Ø, Denmark.
Telephone: ØB.1507.

Møller, Maersk Mc-Kinney; Danish shipowner; b. 13 July 1913.
Partner A. P. Møller 40-; Chair. Steamship Co. of 1912 Ltd., Steamship Co. Svendborg Ltd., Steamship Co. of 1960 Ltd., Maersk Line A/S, Odense Steel Shipyard Ltd., Danbritkem A/S, Roulunds Fabriker Ltd., The Tanganyika Planting Co. Ltd., Dansk Borelskab A/S, Dansk Industri Syndikat A/S; mem. Board Motorfabriken Bukh A/S, Det Danske Staalvalsevaerk A/S; Chair. Danish Shipping Board, Danish Nat. Cttee. of Int. Chamber of Commerce.
Kongens Nytorv 8, Copenhagen K, Denmark.
Telephone: 01-14 15 14.

Møller, Poul; Danish barrister and politician; b. 13 Oct. 1919; ed. Københavns Univ.
Civil Servant 39-52; Barrister 52-; Chief Editor *Dagens Nyheder* (Daily News) 53-58; Auditor of Public Accounts 61-68; Minister of Finance 68-; Chair. Nat. Youth Org. of Conservative People's Party 43-48; mem. Exec. Board of Conservative People's Party 43-48, 58-; mem. Folketing 50-, Finance Cttee. of Folketing 57-58, Nordic Council 58-68, Foreign Affairs Cttee. of Folketing 60-68, Youth Comm. 45-50, Council of Europe 64-68, Nat. Insurance Comm. 50-55, Tariff Comm. 53-59.
Publs. *Our Idea* 42, *Denmark—Socially* 46, *Political Reference Book* 50, *The Icelandic Manuscripts* 65.
Ministry of Finance, Christiansborg Slotsplads 1, 1218 Copenhagen K; Home: Grønningen 23, 1270 Copenhagen K, Denmark.

Møller-Christenson, Peter Vilhelm, M.D.; Danish professor of medical history; b. 28 June 1903; ed. Haslev Gymnasium and Københavns Universitet.
Medical practice 32-56; School Medical Officer 56-64; Fellow of Univ. of Copenhagen 63-, Prof. of Medical History and Dir. of Medical-Historical Museum 64-; numerous decorations.
Publs. *The History of the Forceps* (thesis) 38, *Ten Lepers from Naevsted in Denmark* 53, *Bone Changes in Leprosy* 61, *Osteo-archaeological Excavations in Medieval Danish Abbeys and Leprosy Hospital Cemeteries* 35-66.
Medical-Historical Museum of University of Copenhagen, 62 Bredgade, Copenhagen K; Office: Københavnsvej 27, Roskilde, Denmark.

Mollet, Guy; French politician; b. 31 Dec. 1905.
Taught in various lycées; served French Army 39-40; prisoner of war 40-42; joined Resistance; Sec. of Comité de Libération 44; mem. of both Constituent Assemblies 45 and 46; Pres. of Comm. on Constitution; Deputy for Arras (Socialist) 46-; Sec.-Gen. Socialist Party 46-; Min. of State in Blum Govt. 46; Vice-Premier March 51; French del. to Consultative Assembly of Council of Europe 49, Pres. 55, mem. of Permanent Comm. and of Cttee. of Ministers and Delegates; Prime Minister 56-57; Vice-Premier May 58; Minister of State (de Gaulle Cabinet) June 58-Jan. 59; Vice-Pres. Socialist Int.; Vice-Pres. Fédération de la Gauche Démocrate et Socialiste (F.G.D.S.); Mayor of Arras.
Publs. *Du français à l'anglais, Bilan et Perspectives Socialistes, 13 mai 1958-13 mai 1962.*
33 Place des Héros, Arras (Pas-de-Calais), France.

Molloy, John Gerald; Irish diplomatist; b. 30 March 1916; ed. Christian Brothers, Dublin, and Nat. Univ. of Ireland.
Executive Officer, Dept. of Industry and Commerce, Dublin 34-41; Admin. Officer, Dept. of Finance 41-44; Private Sec. to Sec., Dept. of Finance 44-46; First Sec. Dept. of External Affairs 46-49; Counsellor,

London 49-54; Counsellor, Dept. of External Affairs 54-57, Asst. Sec. 57-64; Ambassador to U.K. 64-.
Embassy of Ireland, 17 Grosvenor Place, London, S.W.1, England.

Molnár, Antal; Hungarian musician; b. 7 Jan. 1890; ed. Budapest High School of Music.
Mem. Waldbauer-Kerpely String Quartet 10-13; Teacher in Budapest 13-19; winner Francis Joseph Prize for composition 14; mem. Dohnányi-Hubay-Kerpely-Molnár Piano Quartet 16-18; Sec. Music Section of Art and Science Fed. 18; Prof. High School of Music Budapest 19-59; Dir. Pedagogic Society of Music 31-34; Leader-Dir. Syndicate of Musicians 46; Kossuth Prize 57; composer and critic.
Publs. *A zeneművészet könyve* 22, *Az új zene* 25, *A zenetörténet szociológiája* 23, *Bevezetés a zenekultúrába, Jazzband* 28, *Fizika és muzsika* 30, *Liszt esztétikája* 36, *A Ma zenéje* 37, *Zeneesztétika* 38, *Azene és az élet* 46, *Az új muzsika szelleme* 48, *Examples for Romantic Harmony* 53, *Schubert Emlékezete* 54, essays on Hungarian music 55-57, *Repertory of Baroque music* 58, *Brahms* 59, *Collection of Essays* 61, 63.
Karinthy-ut 14, Budapest XI, Hungary.

Molnár-C., Pál; Hungarian painter and engraver; b. 28 April 1894; ed. Ecole des Beaux Arts, Budapest.
Exhibited Lausanne 19, Budapest 27, Venice Biennale 30, 32, 34, etc.; awarded Prix de Rome 28, Gold Medal, Milan 32 and 35, Grand Prix and Gold Medal, Paris Int. Exhbn. 37, and many other prizes; represented in Nuremberg Municipal Museum, Rome, Venice, Chicago, New York, Edinburgh, Laing Art Gallery, Newcastle, Budapest, etc.; has illustrated many books, including *Angyali Udvözlet, The Little Flowers of St. Francis, Corialanus, Cyrano de Bergerac, Coriolan, Autobiography of Benvenuto Cellini* 57; executed decorative panels for Paris Universal Exposition, and monumental frescoes in various churches and buildings; hon. mem. Accademia Adriatica d'Italia, Österreichischer Künstler Bund.
Ménesi út. 63, Budapest XI, Hungary.
Telephone: 457-640.

Molochkov, Fyodor Fyodorovich; Soviet diplomatist; b. 1906; ed. Moscow Plekhanov Inst. of National Economy;
Member C.P. of Soviet Union 31-; entered Diplomatic Service 37; Asst. to Deputy People's Commissar for Foreign Affairs of U.S.S.R. 40; Deputy Head, Head of Protocol Dept., Ministry of Foreign Affairs 40-50; Minister to Switzerland 50-55; Head of Protocol Dept., Ministry of Foreign Affairs 55-; Red Banner of Labour, Great Patriotic War (2nd Class), Badge of Honour, etc.
Ministry of Foreign Affairs of the U.S.S.R., 32-34 Smolenskaya-Sennaya, Moscow, U.S.S.R.

Molotov, Vyacheslav Mikhailovich (*pseudonym* of Skryabin, V. M.); Soviet politician and diplomatist; b. 9 March 1890; ed. St. Petersburg (now Leningrad) Polytechnic.
Organised Bolshevik student groups and worked on *Zvezda* and *Pravda*; mem. Petrograd Soviet Exec. Cttee. Feb. 17; mem. Petrograd Military-Revolutionary Cttee. Oct. 17; held party posts in Petrograd, Nijni Novgorod, Donbass 18-20; Sec. Central Cttee. of Communist Party of the Ukraine 20; mem. Political Bureau of Party 21-53; mem. Presidium of Exec. Cttee. of the Communist Int. 28-34; Chair. Council of People's Commissars 30-41, Deputy Chair. Council of Ministers of U.S.S.R. 41-57; mem. Cttee. for drafting reforms to Constitution 35; Commissar, later Minister, for Foreign Affairs 39-49; mem. State Cttee. of Defence 41; Pres. Moscow Del. Anglo-Soviet Talks Sept. 41; First Vice-Chair. Council of Ministers and Minister for Foreign Affairs 53-56; Minister of State Control 56-57; mem. Presidium of Central Cttee. of Communist Party until 57; Ambassador to Mongolian People's Republic 57-60; Perm. Rep. U.S.S.R. Int. Atomic Energy Agency

Vienna Aug. 60-61; removed from C.P.S.U. 62; awarded Order of Lenin, Hammer and Sickle Gold Medal and title Hero of Socialist Labour; hon. mem. U.S.S.R. Acad. of Sciences.

Publs. (in Russian) *The Party's Policy in the Villages, Elections to the Soviets, Problems of the Working Class, On the Lessons of Trotskyism*, etc.

c/o Ministry of Social Security, 14 Shabolovka, Moscow, U.S.S.R.

Molstad, Melvin Carl, B.A., B.S., PH.D.; American university professor; b. 18 Nov. 1898; ed. Carleton Coll., Mass. Inst. of Technology and Yale Univ.

Jnr. Chemist, Dept. of Agriculture, Fixed Nitrogen Laboratory 20-21, Chemical Engineer 23-26; Instructor Yale Univ. 26-29; with Du Pont Co. 29-31; Asst. Prof. Yale Univ. 31-39; Assoc. Prof. Univ. of Pennsylvania 39-42, Prof. of Chemical Engineering 42-, Dept. Chair. 51-61; Consultant Atlantic Refining Co. 41, Davison Chemical Co. Baltimore 42-; Fulbright Prof., Trondheim Technical Univ. 54-55, Univ. of Tokyo 61-62; Ford Foundation Prof. Dartmouth Coll. 67; mem. American Soc. of Engineering Educ.; Hon. A.I.Ch.E., A.C.S.

University of Pennsylvania, Towne Building, Philadelphia 4, Pa. 19104; Home: 19 Shady Hill Road, Moylan, Pa. 19063, U.S.A.

Telephone: 215-594-8503 (Office); 215-565-0864 (Home).

Molyakov, Nikolai Ivanovich; Soviet diplomatist; b. 1910; ed. Leningrad Herzen Pedagogic Inst.

Member C.P. of Soviet Union 39-; First Sec., Soviet Embassy, Washington 44-46; First Sec., Soviet Mission to UN 46-48; First Sec., Asst. Deputy Head of U.S. Dept. of Min. of Foreign Affairs, Moscow 48-53; Counsellor, Embassy at Oslo 54-57; Deputy Head, Dept. for Int. Orgs. of Ministry of Foreign Affairs 57-61, Head of South East Asia Dept. 61-62; Perm. Soviet Rep. to UN and other Int. Orgs. in Geneva 62-66; Head, Consular Dept., Ministry of Foreign Affairs 66-; Order of Red Banner of Labour, etc.

Ministry of Foreign Affairs of the U.S.S.R., 32-34 Smolenskaya-Sennaya, Moscow, U.S.S.R.

Momigliano, Arnaldo Dante, D.LITT., F.B.A.; Italian historian; b. 5 Sept. 1908; ed. Univs. of Turin and Rome.

Professor Extraordinary Univ. of Rome 32-36; Prof. Univ. of Turin 36-39; research work, Univ. of Oxford 39-46; Supernumerary Prof. Univ. of Turin 45-64; Scuola Normale Superiore, Pisa 64-; Reader Univ. of Bristol 47-51; Prof. of Ancient History Univ. Coll., London 51-; Alexander White Visiting Prof. Univ. of Chicago 59; Sather Prof. in Classics, Univ. of Calif. 62, Gray Lecturer, Cambridge Univ. 63; Lauro de Bosis Lecturer and Visiting Prof., Harvard Univ. 65, Jackson Lecturer 68; Feltrinelli Prize Accad. Lincei 60; co-Editor *Rivista Storica Italiano* 48-; Socio Nazionale Accad. dei Lincei and Arcadia; Corresp. mem. Accad. Scienze Torino, German Archaeological Inst.; Foreign mem. Royal Dutch Acad.; Hon. mem. American Historical Asscn.; Hon. M.A. (Oxford), Hon. D.Litt. (Bristol, Edinburgh), etc.

Publs. *La composizione della storia di Tucidide* 29, *Prime linee di storia della tradizione maccabeica* 31, 68, *L'opera dell'imperatore Claudio* 32, 61, *Filippo il Macedone* 34, chapters in *Cambridge Ancient History X* 34, *Contributo alla Storia degli Studi Classici* 55, *Secondo Contributo alla Storia degli Studi Classici* 60, *The Conflict Between Paganism and Christianity in the Fourth century* (editor) 63, *Terzo Contributo alla Storia degli Classici* 66, *Studies in Historiography* 66.

University College, Gower Street, London, W.C.1, England.

Mommsen, Ernst Wolf; German business executive; b. 12 May 1910; ed. Ruprecht-Karl-Universität, Heidelberg, Christian-Albrechts-Universität, Kiel and Humboldt-Universität zu Berlin.

Management post, German Reich Industrial Asscn. 39; Ministry of Armament and War Production 40-45, finally Head of Central Div.; in Electrical Industry 46-48; mem. Board of Management Iron and Steel Fed. 48-53; Man. Klöckner-Drahtindustrie 53; mem. Management Board Klöckner-Werke A.G., Duisburg 53; mem. Management Board Rheinische Röhrenwerke A.G. 54, and Phoenix-Rheinrohr A.G. Vereinigte Hütten-und Röhrenwerke, Düsseldorf after merger of Hüttenwerke Phoenix A.G. with Rheinische Röhrenwerke A.G. 54-65, Pres. of Phoenix Rheinrohr Vereinigte Hütten-und Röhrenwerke 65-, now Pres. of Thyssen Röhrenwerke A.G.; Chair. of Board of Dirs. Thyssen Rohrleitungsbau G.m.b.H., Düsseldorf, Thyssenrohr Int. G.m.b.H., Düsseldorf, Deutsche Fina G.m.b.H., Frankfurt, Stahlform Berlin G.m.b.H., Berlin; Vice-Chair. Board of Dirs. Thyssen Steel and Pipe (Great Britain) Ltd., London, Blohm & Voss A.G., Hamburg, Handelsunion A.G., Düsseldorf; official of other companies; Dr. rer. pol. h.c. (Univ. of Munich).

Publs. *The Problem of Competition in the Steel Industry* (with von Grosse and Wessels) 54, *Creation of an Elite in the Economy* 55, *Planning without Planification* 62, *Structural Changes in the Raw Material Supply of the European Iron and Steel Industry* 62, *The Policy of Internal Management Development*.

Thyssen Röhrenwerke A.G., Düsseldorf, August-Thyssen-Strasse 1; Home: Düsseldorf, Orsoyer Strasse 58, German Federal Republic.

Monashev, Leonid Gavrilovich; Soviet politician; b. 1914; ed. Agricultural Inst., Stavropol.

Agronomist, Orlov Region 33-36; mem. C.P.S.U. 39-; Soviet Army 36-47; party work, Stavropol Region 48-54; Apparatus, Cen. Cttee. of C.P.S.U. 54-57; Second Sec. Kursk Rural Regional Cttee., C.P.S.U. 57-58, First Sec. 58-; mem. Central Cttee. of C.P.S.U. 61-; Deputy to U.S.S.R. Supreme Soviet.

Kursk Rural Regional Committee of the Communist Party of the Soviet Union, Kursk, U.S.S.R.

Mondadori, Alberto; Italian publisher; b. 8 Dec. 1914; ed. Verona, Milan and Univ. of Pavia.

At an early age Asst. Producer and Producer of motion pictures; founded *Tempo* magazine and directed it for four years; joined Mondadori Editore 45, Vice-Pres. until April 68; founded and directed *Epoca*, the first Italian magazine in colour 50; founded own publishing house Il Saggiatore di Alberto Mondadori Editore 58, Pres. 68-; Viareggio Prize for volume of poetry.

Il Saggiatore di Alberto Mondadori Editore, Corsa Europa 5/7, 20122 Milan, Italy.

Mondadori, Arnoldo; Italian publisher; b. 2 Nov. 1889.

Began his career as editor of the weekly *Luce!*; Pres. Arnoldo Mondadori Editore, Milan; Special Award from Nat. Educ. Board, Golden Book (Presidenza del Consiglio) 57; Cavaliere del Lavoro.

Casa Editrice Arnoldo Mondadori, Via Bianca di Savoia 20, Milan, Italy.

Mondale, Walter Frederick, LL.B.; American lawyer and politician; b. 5 Jan. 1928; ed. Minnesota public schools, Macalester Coll., Univ. of Minnesota and Univ. of Minnesota Law School.

Attorney-General, Minnesota 60-64; Senator from Minnesota 64-; fmr. mem. President's Consumer Advisory Council; fmr. mem. Exec. Board Nat. Asscn. of Attorneys General, and other legal orgs.; Democrat-Farmer-Labor.

U.S. Senate, Washington, D.C., U.S.A.

Monelli, Paolo, D.IUR.; Italian journalist and novelist; b. 15 July 1894; ed. Bologna Univ.

Officer of "Alpini" 15-21; prisoner of war 17-18; mem. of mil. missions 19-21; Vienna corresp. *Gazzetta del Popolo* 21-22; Berlin corresp. *La Stampa*, with special missions

to the Near East, Spitzbergen, etc. 22-26; Special corresp. *Corriere della Sera* 26-29, *La Stampa* 29-35; war corresp. Ethiopia 35-36; Dir. Paris office *Corriere della Sera* 36-39, war corresp. 40-43; imprisoned by Fascist govt. 43; Lieut.-Col. Corpo Italiano di Liberazione 44-45; special corresp. *La Stampa* 46-67; Editor and special corresp. *Corriere della Sera* 67-; contributor to *Il Mondo, Tempo, Espresso, France Soir*; Saint Vincent Great Prize for Journalism 60, Great Prize for Journalism, Accademia della Crusca, Florence 65; Gold Medal of Italia Nostra for defence of ancient monuments and landscape; four Medaglie al valore, Croix de Guerre Belge, etc.
Publs. *Le Scarpe al sole* 21, 55, 65 (English and American trans. *Toes Up*, French trans. *Les pieds devant*, also film), *Questo mestieraccio* 28, *La guerra i bella ma e scomoda* 29, 51, *Io e i tedeschi* 29, *Barbaro dominio* 33, *Il ghiottone errante* 35, 47, *Roma 1943* 45 (new edn. 63), *Naja parla* 47, *Mussolini piccolo borghese* 50 (English and American trans. *Mussolini: Intimate Life of a Dictator*, also Dutch trans.; new edn. 64), *Nessuna nuvola in cielo* 57, *Avventura nel primo secolo* 58, 64, *Il vero bevitore* 63, *Ombre Cinesi* 65, etc.
Via Venti Settembre 3, 00187 Rome, Italy.

Monési, Irène; French graphologist and novelist; b. 4 April 1923; ed. Coll. Saint-Marie à Neuilly, Coll. de Bouffémont, Inst. pédotechnique de Toulouse.
Taught maladjusted children for three years; Prix Femina 66.
Publs. *Althia* 57, *Cet acte tendre* 61, *Les Pères insolites* 62, *Le Faux Fuyant* 64, *Nature morte devant la fenêtre* 66.
16 rue Chanoinesse, Paris 4e, France.

Monicelli, Mario; Italian film director; b. 16 May 1915; ed. Università degli Studi, Pisa.
Former Asst. to Pietro Germi; writer of film *Riso Amaro*; film dir. 49-; Golden Lion, Venice Film Festival; Silver Medal, Berlin Film Festival; Silver Laurel Medal, San Francisco Film Festival.
Films include: *Guardie e Ladri* 48, *The Big Deal of Madonna Street* 55, *The Great War* 58, *The Organiser* 60, *Casanova '70* 63, *L'Armata Brancaleone* 65.
Piazza Teatro Pompeo 19, Rome, Italy.

Monk, Albert Ernest, C.M.G.; Australian trade unionist; b. 1900.
Has been employed in the Labour Movement since 19; Sec. Conference of Federated Unions 20-21; Clerk, Offices of Trades Hall Council 24-29, Asst. Sec. 29, Acting Sec. 33-34, Sec. 34-39; Sec. Australian Council of Trade Unions 45-49, Pres. 49-; mem. Governing Board, I.L.O.
Actu Building, 17-25 Lygon Street, Carlton, Victoria, Australia.

Monnerville, Gaston Charles François; French public servant; b. French Guiana 2 Jan. 1897; ed. Faculty of Law, Toulouse.
Admitted to Bar of Toulouse 18, Paris 21; Pres. of Union of Young Lawyers at the Paris Court 28; Dep. for Guiana 32-; Mayor of Cayenne 35; mem. of Radical and Radical-Socialist Party; Pres. of Party Colonial Comm.; Vice-Pres. of Party 38; Under-Sec. of State for Colonies 37, 38; served in Navy in Second World War; after Armistice was active in resistance movement 40-47; mem. of Consultative Assembly 44; Pres. of Comm. of Oversea France; re-elected for Guiana to Constituent Assembly Oct. 45 and June 46; Del. of France to U.N. Assembly; Councillor of the Republic Dec. 46; Senator for Lot 48, 55, 58; Pres. of Council of the Republic 47-58; Pres. Senate of the Republic and Senate of the Community 59-; Pres. Gen. Council of the Lot Dept. 51-; Croix de Guerre 40; Medal of the Resistance with Rosette; Chevalier de la Légion d'Honneur; Maire de Saint-Céré (Lot) 64.
Publ. *l'Enrichissement sans cause*.
Palais du Luxembourg, Paris 6e, France.

Monnet, Jean; French politician; b. 9 Nov. 1888.
French rep. on Inter-Allied Maritime Comm. First World War, awarded Hon. G.B.E.; fmr. 1st Deputy Sec.-Gen. L.N.; Chair. Franco-British Economic Coordination Cttee. 39; mem. British Supply Council in Washington 40-43; Algiers 43-44; Commr. for Armament, Supplies and Reconstruction, French Cttee. Nat. Liberation 43-44; Gen. Commr. for Modernisation Plan 47; Pres. E.C.S.C. High Authority 52-55; Chair. Action Cttee. for a United States of Europe 56; Wateler Peace Prize 51, Charlemagne Prize 53, U.S. Freedom Award 62; Freedom Medal 63; Family of Man Award for Peace; Robert Schuman Prize, Univ. of Bonn 66; Dr. h.c. Columbia, Glasgow and Princeton Univs., Hon. LL.D. (Cambridge, Yale, Oxford).
Publ. *Les Etats Unis d'Europe ont commencé* (extracts from speeches.)
Houjarray, par Montfort-l'Amaury (Seine-et-Oise); 83 avenue Foch, Paris 16e, France.

Monnington, Sir Walter Thomas, Kt., P.R.A.; British painter; b. 2 Oct. 1902; ed. Slade School of Fine Art, Univ. Coll., London.
Has taught at Royal Coll. of Art, Royal Acad. Schools of Fine Art, Camberwell Coll. of Art, Slade School of Fine Art; Trustee British Museum 63-; Chair. Faculty of Painting, British School of Rome until 67; Chair. Chichester Diocesan Art Council until 67; Pres. Royal Academy 67-; mem. Exec. Cttee. Nat. Art Collections Fund; Fellow Univ. Coll. London.
Works include: decorations and paintings, St. Stephen's Hall, Westminster and Bank of England; painted ceiling, Council Room, Council House, Bristol; painted ceiling, Univ. Chapel, Univ. of Exeter; decorations, Students' Union, Univ. Coll. London.
Office: Royal Academy of Arts, Burlington House, Piccadilly, London, W.1; Home: Leyswood, Groombridge, Tunbridge Wells, Kent, England.
Telephone: 01-734-7981 (Office); Groombridge 205 (Home).

Monod, André Théodore, D. ès sc.; French zoologist; b. 9 April 1902; ed. Ecole Alsacienne and Paris Univ.
Prof. Muséum Nat. d'Histoire Naturelle, Paris; fmr. Dir. Inst. Français d'Afrique Noire, Dakar; fmr. Dean, Faculty of Sciences, Dakar Univ.; mem. Inst. de France (Acad. des Sciences), Acad. des Sciences d'Outre-mer, Acad. de Marine; Officier Légion d'Honneur, Mérite Saharien, Commdr. Order of Christ, Gold Medal, Royal Geographical Soc. and American Geographical Soc.
Home: 14 quai d'Orléans, Paris 4e; Office: Muséum National d'Histoire Naturelle, 57 rue Cuvier, Paris 5e, France.
Telephone: 402-40-10 (Office); 326-79-50 (Home).

Monod, Jacques; French molecular biologist; b. 1910. Head of Dept. of Metabolic Chemistry, Pasteur Inst., Paris; Prof., Faculty of Science, Univ. of Paris; Vice-Pres. Molecular Biology Cttee., French Gen. Del. for Scientific Research; mem. Deutsche Akademie der Naturforscher Leopoldina 66-; Titular Prof. Coll. de France 67-; Foreign mem. Royal Soc. (U.K.), Czechoslovak Acad. of Sciences; Nobel Prize for Medicine 65.
Works include: research into physiology, kinetics and metabolism of growth of bacteria, the mechanism of the biosynthesis of enzymes and the regulation of cellular metabolism.
Institut Pasteur, 25-28 rue du Dr. Roux, Paris 15e, France.

Monrad, Carl Corydon, M.S.E., PH.D.; American chemical engineer; b. 15 Jan. 1905; ed. Univ. of Michigan.
Chemical engineer, Standard Oil Co. (Ind.) 30-37; Assoc. Prof. Carnegie Inst. of Technology 37-42, Prof. of Chemical Engineering 42-, Head of Dept. of Chemical Engineering 47-65; adviser and consultant to

many govt. depts. 40-45; Assoc. Dean Coll. of Engineering and Science 65-; mem. American Chemical Soc., American Inst. of Chemical Engineers, American Soc. for Engineering Educ.

Publs. Various publications on different aspects of chemical engineering.

Home: 339 Inglewood Drive, Pittsburgh, Pa. 15228; Office: Carnegie Institute of Technology, Pittsburgh, Pa., 15213, U.S.A.

Telephone: 621-2600 (Office).

Monroney, A. S. Mike; American politician; b. 2 March 1902; ed. Univ. of Oklahoma.

Political Reporter *Oklahoma News* 24-28; entered furniture business 28; Rep. for Oklahoma City 38-50; Senator from Oklahoma 50-; Democrat.

6205 Senate Office Building, Washington 25, D.C., U.S.A.

Mons, Jean; French civil servant; b. 25 Feb. 1906. Teacher and engineer for agricultural industries; Chief Controller of Indirect Contributions 24-26; served French Army 39-40; Prefect (First Class) 44; Sec.-Gen. of the Seine; Dir. Office of Prés. du Conseil 46; placed at disposal of Ministry of Foreign Affairs; Resident Gen. in Tunis 47-50; Perm. Sec.-Gen. for Nat. Defence 50-56; Conseiller Maître à la Cour des Comptes 56-; mem. Cttee. of Enquiry into Public Costs 60-, Nat. Conciliation Cttee. for Nat. Educ. 61-; Commdr. Légion d'Honneur, Croix de Guerre, Rosette de la Résistance, etc.

13 rue Cambon, Paris 1er, France.

Monsen, Per; Norwegian newspaper editor; b. 4 May 1913; ed. Hamar Kathedralskole.

Newspaper *Sörlandet* 32-37, *Bergens Arbeiderblad* 37-39, *Arbeiderbladet*, Oslo 39-, Editor 52-64; Norwegian Govt. Information Service, Stockholm 41-43, London 43-45; Press Attaché, Norwegian Military Mission, Berlin 48, 49; Dir. Int. Press Inst., Zürich 64-; Chair. Norwegian Press Federation 54-58.

International Press Institute, Münstergasse 9, Zürich 8001, Switzerland.

Monson, Sir William Bonnar Leslie, K.C.M.G., C.B.; British diplomatist; b. 28 May 1912; ed. Edinburgh Acad. and Hertford Coll., Oxford.

Dominions Office 35-39; Colonial Office 39-64; Chief Sec., West African Council 47-51; Asst. Under-Sec. of State Colonial Office 52-64; High Commr. in Zambia 64-66; Asst. Under-Sec. of State, Commonwealth Office 66-67; Deputy Under-Sec. of State Commonwealth Office 67-.

Commonwealth Office, Downing Street, S.W.1; and Golf House, Goffers Road, London, S.E.3, England.

Telephone: 01-852-7257.

Montagu, Hon. Ivor, M.A.; British film producer and journalist; b. 23 April 1904; ed. Westminster School, Royal Coll. of Science and Technology and King's Coll., Cambridge.

Research in Mammalian systematics 18-25; founded Film Society London 25; produced films 25-; directed *Bluebottles*, co-directed *Wings Over Everest, Man—One Family*; associate producer *The Man Who Knew Too Much, 39 Steps*; produced Spanish war films and *Peace and Plenty*; Technical Dir. Soviet Film Agency 41-42; leader-writer London *Daily Worker* 43-47; mem. World Peace Council; Lenin Peace Prize 59.

Publs. *On the Burrow of the Rodent Spalax* 24, *The Political Censorship of Films* 29, *The Traitor Class* 40, *The Red Army* 41, *Stalin* 42, *Soviet Soldier in Europe* 46, *Negotiation or War* 51, *Plot Against Peace* 52, *Land of Blue Sky* 56, *Film World* 64, *Vietnam* 66, *Germany's New Nazis* 67; co-author *Scott of the Antarctic* (screen play).

Old Timbers, Verdure Close, Garston, Watford, Herts., England.

Montan, Nils T., LL.B.; Swedish diplomatist; b. 23 Aug. 1916; ed. Univ. of Uppsala.

Joined Ministry for Foreign Affairs 39, served Budapest, Bucharest, Ministry for Foreign Affairs 39-46; Asst. Dir.-Gen. Export Asscn. of Sweden 46-48; served Frankfurt, Bonn, Ministry for Foreign Affairs 48-56; Counsellor, Washington 56-60; Ambassador and Perm. Rep. to European Free Trade Asscn., Geneva 60-64; Head Perm. Swedish Del. Geneva 64; Dep. Sec.-Gen. Ministry for Foreign Affairs, Stockholm 64-; Del. or Chair. numerous trade negotiations and conferences; numerous foreign decorations.

Ministry of Foreign Affairs, Stockholm, and Karlavägen 113, Stockholm No. Sweden.

Telephone: Stockholm 612922.

Montand, Yves (*pseudonym* of Yves Livi; husband of Simone Signoret, *q.v.*); French actor and singer; b. 13 Oct. 1921; ed. primary school, Marseilles.

Interpreter of numerous famous songs; stage performances in straight plays and variety; films include *Les Portes de la Nuit, Le Salaire de la Peur, Les Héros sont Fatigués, Marguerite de la Nuit, Hommes et Loups, Les Sorcières de Salem, Premier Mai, La Loi, Temps d'Aujourd'hui, Napoléon, Un Dénommé Squarcio, Aimez-vous Brahms, Ma Geisha, La Guerre est finie, Vivre pour vivre.*

Publ. *Du Soleil plein la tête* (memoirs) 55.

15 place Dauphine, Paris 1er, France.

Montanelli, Indro; Italian journalist and writer; b. 22 April 1909; ed. Univ. degli Studi, Florence and Univ. de Paris à la Sorbonne.

Special Correspondent *Corriere della Sera* 39-; War Corresp. in Finland, Norway, Spain, Albania and Greece; has won Bagutta and Marzotto Prizes.

Publs. *Storia di Roma* 57, *Storia dei Greci* 58, *Incontri* 61, *Garibaldi* 62, *Gente qualunque* 63, *Dante e il suo secolo* 64, *Italia dei secoli bui* 65; Plays: *I sogni muoiono all'alba* (also film), *Il Generale della Rovere* (also film), *Kibbutz.*

Piazza Navona 93, Rome, Italy.

Montanier, Francis; French painter; b. 18 Nov. 1895. Has participated in French official exhibitions in N.Y., Berne, Venice, Rome, Milan, Tokyo, Cairo, The Hague, Oslo, Helsinki, Oxford, Warsaw, Haiti, São Paulo, Australia, Prague, Bucharest; works exhibited in London, Edinburgh, Stockholm, Montreal, Rio de Janeiro, etc., and represented at the Musée d'Art Moderne, Paris, Collections de la Ville de Paris, in museums at Lyon, Nancy, Athens, Le Havre, Tourcoing, Grenoble, Luxembourg, Santiago (Chile), in many private collections, in Salon de Mai, Paris 49-60, and Ecole de Paris, Galerie Charpentier 56, 58; Officier des Arts et des Lettres.

5 rue du Douanier, Paris 14e, France.

Telephone: GOB 50-78.

Montgomery, Arthur, PH.D.; Swedish economic historian; b. 2 Sept. 1889; ed. Univs. of Uppsala and Stockholm.

Lecturer in Economic History, Univ. of Uppsala 21-24; Prof. of Economics, Swedish Univ. of Åbo, Finland 24-39; Prof. of Economic and Social History Univ. Coll. of Commerce, Stockholm 40-58; Hon. D. Pol. Sc. Univ. of Åbo 48.

Publs. In English: *How Sweden Overcame the Depression of 1930-33* 38, *The Rise of Modern Industry in Sweden* 39, *From a Northern Customs Union to EFTA* (Scandinavian Economic History Review) 60; in Swedish: *Swedish Social Policy in the Nineteenth Century* 34, *Swedish Economic History 1913-39* 46, *Russia and Our Foreign Policy* 49, *Stalinism* 53.

Karlavägen 72A, Stockholm Ö, Sweden.

Telephone: Stockholm 349560 (Office); Stockholm 606320 (Home).

Montgomery, Deane, PH.D.; American mathematician. b. 2 Sept. 1909; ed. Hamline Univ. and Univ. of Iowa; Assistant Prof. of Mathematics, Smith Coll. 35-38, Assoc. Prof. 38-42, Prof. 42-46; Assoc. Prof. Yale Univ. 46-48; Perm. mem. Inst. of Advanced Study, Princeton 48-51, Prof. of Mathematics 51-; Vice-Pres. Int. Mathematical Union 67-; Hon. Dr. (Hamline, Yeshiva and Tulane Univs.).

Publ. (with Leo Zippin) *Topological Transformation Groups* 55.

Office: Institute for Advanced Study, Princeton, N.J. 08540; Home: 55 Rollingmead, Princeton, N.J. 08540, U.S.A.

Montgomery of Alamein, 1st Viscount, cr. 46, of Hindhead in the County of Surrey, **Field-Marshal Bernard Law Montgomery,** K.G., G.C.B., D.S.O.; British army officer; b. 17 Nov. 1887.

Entered Army 08; served First World War; Lieut.-Col. 31; Commdr. 1st Bttn. Royal Warwickshire Regt. 31-34; Col. 34; Gen. Staff Officer, Staff Coll. Quetta 34-37; Commdr. 9th Infantry Brigade Portsmouth 37-38, 8th Div. 38-39; G.O.C.-in-C. Southeastern Commd. 41-42; G.O.C. 8th Army 42-43; promoted to Field Marshal 44; C.-in-C. British Group of Armies N.W. Europe 44-45; C.-in-C. British Forces of Occupation in Germany and British mem. Allied Control Council in Germany 45-46; Chief of Imperial Gen. Staff 46-48; Chair. of the Western Union Commanders-in-Chief 48-51; Deputy Supreme Allied Commdr. NATO 51-58; Col. Commdt. Parachute Regt. 44-56, Royal Tank Regt. 45, Army Physical Training Corps 46; Col. Royal Warwickshire Regt. 47; Order of Suvorov, Virtuti Militari 44, Order of King George of the Hellenes 44, Grand Cross of the Legion of Honour (France) 45, Distinguished Service Medal (U.S.A.) 45, Grand Cordon Order of Leopold 45, Médaille Militaire 58, etc.; Hon. LL.D. (St. Andrews, Glasgow, Toronto, Queen's, Belfast, McGill, British Columbia); Hon. Dr. Sc. (Louvain, Liège).

Publs. *Forward to Victory* 46, *Ten Chapters* 46, *Normandy to the Baltic* 47, *El Alamein to the River Sangro* 48, *Forward from Victory* 48, *Memoirs* 58, *An Approach to Sanity: a Study of East-West Relations* 59, *The Path to Leadership* 61, *Three Continents* 62, *History of Warfare* 67.

Isington Mill, Alton, Hampshire, England.

Montjoie, René; French government official; b. 29 Sept. 1926; ed. Ecole Polytechnique and Univ. of Chicago.

Assistant to Chief of Iron Metallurgy, Ministry of Industry 52-53, Asst. to Dir. of Mines 57-62; Mineral work, Metz 54-57; Prof. of Nat. Economy, Ecole nat. supérieure des mines, Nancy 57-62; Technical Adviser, Office of M. Pompidou 62-67; Commr.-Gen. of the Plan 67-.

19 rue de Civry, Paris 16e, France.

Montherlant, Henry de; French writer; b. 21 April 1896; ed. Lycée Janson-de-Sailly and Ecole Sainte-Croix Neuilly.

Served French Army First World War; awarded Grand Prix de Littérature of French Acad. 34; war corresp. in Second World War; his plays have been presented chiefly at Comédie Française; mem. Acad. Française 60-.

Publs. *La Relève du Matin* 20, *Le Songe* 22, *Les Olympiques* 24, *Chant Funèbre pour les Morts de Verdun* 24, *Les Bestiaires* 26, *Aux Fontaines du Désir* 27, *La Petite Infante de Castille* 29, *Mors et Vita* 32, *Encore un Instant de Bonheur* 34, *Les Célibataires* 34, *Service Inutile* 35, *Les Jeunes Filles, Pitié pour les Femmes* 36, *L'Equinoxe de Septembre* 38, *Les Lépreuses* 39, *Le Solstice de Juin* 41, *La Reine Morte* 42, *Fils de Personne* 43, *Malatesta* 46, *Le Maître de Santiago* 47, *Demain il fera Jour* 49, *Celles qu'on prend dans ses bras* 50, *La Ville dont le Prince est un Enfant* 51, *Port-Royal* 54, *Don Juan* 58, *Le Cardinal d'Espagne* 60, *Le Chaos et la*

Nuit 63, *La Guerre civile* 64, *Va jouer avec cette poussière* 66, *La Rose de sable* 67.

Société des Gens de Lettres, Hôtel de Massa, 38 rue du Faubourg-Saint-Jacques, Paris 14e, France.

Montini, H.E. Cardinal Giovanni Battista: (*see* Paul VI, Pope).

Montoya, Joseph M.; American lawyer and politician; b. 24 Sept. 1915; ed. Regis Coll., Denver, and Georgetown Univ.

Admitted to New Mexico Bar 39; owner Western Freight Lines 45-; mem. New Mexico State Legislature 37-40, Democratic Floor Leader 39-40; State Senator 40-46, 54-55; Lieut.-Gov. of New Mexico 47-51, 55-57; mem. U.S. Congress 56-64; Senator from New Mexico 65-.

209 Callecita Place, Santa Fe, New Mexico; and U.S. Senate, Washington, D.C., U.S.A.

Monzón, Gustavo Balcázar; Colombian politician; b. 27; ed. Colegio Berchmans de Cali, and Universidad Javeriana de Bogotá.

Magistrate Cali Municipality 49-51, Attorney 51-53; Manager, Mariano Ramos R. & Cía. Ltda., Cali; Del. Inter-American Econ. Conf., Buenos Aires 57; mem. Chamber of Reps. 58-62, Pres. Chamber of Reps. 60, Senator 62-; Gov. Valle del Cauca 62-64; Minister of Agriculture 64-65; Gran oficial Orden del Mérito Militar, Gen. José María Córdoba (Colombia); Liberal. 27-30 Apt. 201, Carrera 5a, Bogotá, Colombia.

Mookerjee, Sir Birendra Nath, Kt., M.A., M.I.E.; Indian businessman; b. 14 Feb. 1899; ed. Hastings House and Sibpur Engineering Coll., Calcutta, and Trinity Coll., Cambridge.

Asst. Martin & Co. 24; Partner, Burn & Co. 31- and Martin & Co. 34-, Governing Dir. Martin Burn Ltd. 58-; mem. Munitions Board and Defence Council, Second World War; Sheriff, Calcutta 40; Pres. Calcutta Board, fmr. Imperial Bank of India; mem. Governing Body, Sibpur Engineering Coll., Fellow Faculty of Engineering, Calcutta Univ.; Chair. Steel Corpn. of Bengal Ltd.; Dir. Darjeeling Himalayan Railway Co., and many others.

7 Harrington Street, Calcutta 16, India.

Moore, Daniel Killian, B.A.; American lawyer and politician; b. 2 April 1906; ed. Univ. of North Carolina.

Legal Practice, N. Carolina 28-41; mem. N.C. Gen. Assembly 41; U.S. Army 43-46; Solicitor 30th Judicial District of N.C. 46-48; Superior Court Judge 49-58; Counsellor and Asst. Sec. Champion Papers, Inc. 58-63; Gov. of North Carolina 65-; Democrat.

Executive Mansion, 200 N. Blount Street, Raleigh, North Carolina, U.S.A.

Moore, Douglas Stuart, A.B., MUS.B.; American composer, teacher and author; b. 10 Aug. 1893; ed. Yale Univ. and Schola Cantorum, Paris.

Curator Musical Arts, Cleveland Museum of Art 21-25; Assoc. in Music, Columbia Univ. 26, Asst. Prof. 27, Assoc. Prof. 28, Prof. 40, McDowell Prof. 45, Prof. Emer. 62, Columbia Univ.; Pres. Nat. Inst. of Arts and Letters 46-53; mem. American Acad. of Arts and Letters 51, Sec. 53-59, Pres. 59-62; Pulitzer Prize in Music 51; Hon. Mus.D. (Univ. of Rochester), Mus.D. (Yale) 55; New York Critics award in Opera for *The Ballad of Baby Doe* 58; Hon. L.H.D. Columbia Univ. 63.

Works include 2 symphonies 29, 45; operas: *White Wings, The Devil and Daniel Webster, Giants in the Earth, The Ballad of Baby Doe, Gallantry: a Soap Opera* 57, *The Wings of the Dove* 61, *Carry Nation* 65; chamber music, choral music, etc.

464 Riverside Drive, New York 27, N.Y., U.S.A.

Moore, George Stevens, B.S.; American banker; b. 1 April 1905; ed. Washington Univ., St. Louis, and Yale Univ.

Joined The Farmers Loan and Trust Co. (now First

Nat. City Trust Co.), Asst. Sec. 31; Asst. Vice-Pres. First Nat. City Bank of New York 34-39, Vice-Pres. 39-52, Exec. Vice-Pres. (Domestic Div.) 52-57, Exec. Vice-Pres. (Overseas Div.) 57-59, Pres. 59-67, Chair. 67-; Pres. Metropolitan Opera; Dir. of nine other companies.
National City Bank of New York, 55 Wall Street, New York City 15, N.Y., U.S.A.

Moore, Gerald, C.B.E.; British pianist; b. 30 July 1899; ed. Watford Grammar School, and Univ. of Toronto, Canada.
Studied piano with Prof. Michael Hambourg in Toronto 16; toured Canada as a boy pianist; returned to England 20; was accompanist and played chamber music; has accompanied most leading singers and instrumentalists and played at Festivals of Edinburgh, Salzburg, Holland, Granada, Seville, Besançon, Berlin, Vienna, etc.; also lectures and gives broadcast and television talks on music and the art of accompanying; lecture tours annually to the U.S.A.; Master Classes in Song Interpretation in U.S.A., Japan, Sweden, England; records; Pres. Inc. Soc. of Musicians 62; Cobbett Gold Medal for services to chamber music 51; Grand Prix du Disque for the recording of his farewell recital 67; D.Litt. h.c. Univ. of Sussex 68; Hon. R.A.M. Publs. *The Unashamed Accompanist* 43, *Singer and Accompanist* 53, *Am I Too Loud?* (Memoirs) 62.
Beechwood Cottage, Penn Bottom, Penn, Bucks., England.

Moore, Henry, O.M., C.H., F.B.A.; British sculptor; b. 30 July 1898; ed. Leeds School of Art and Royal Coll. of Art.
Trustee Tate Gallery 41-48, 49-56, Nat. Gallery 55-63, 64-; mem. Royal Fine Art Comm. 47-, Swedish Royal Acad. of Fine Arts; exhibited in London (Warren Gallery) 28, subsequently in Italy, Germany, Sweden, Switzerland, France, U.S.A. and Australia; retrospective exhibitions in Brussels, Paris 49, in Germany and Switzerland 50, London (Tate Gallery), Athens, New York 51, in South Africa and Sweden 52, Denmark, Norway, Holland, Germany, Brazil 53, Madrid 59, Hamburg, Essen, Zürich, London and Munich 60; works in Victoria and Albert Museum and Tate Gallery (London), Whitworth Inst. and Corpn. Gallery (Manchester), City Art Gallery (Wakefield and Leeds) Allbright Art Gallery (Buffalo), Museum of Modern Art (New York), Washington Univ. and museums in Tel-Aviv and St. Louis; awarded first prize for sculpture, Venice 48, São Paulo 53, Antonio Feltrinelli Prize for Sculpture, Rome; Hon. D.Litt. (London, Oxford, Reading, Hull and Leeds), Dr. h.c. (Cambridge, Harvard, Berlin, and Royal Coll. of Art London); foreign hon. mem. American Acad. of Arts and Sciences 55, Acad. des Lettres et des Beaux Arts de Belgique; Foreign mem. Swedish Royal Acad. of Fine Arts; foreign corresp. mem. Acad. Flamande des Sciences; Erasmus Prize 68.
Works include: *Mother and Child, Reclining Figure, Madonna and Child, Three Standing Figures, Family Group, King and Queen, Reclining Figure* (for Lincoln Center, New York), Sundial for *The Times* building, London.
Publs. *Heads, Figures and Ideas* 58, *Henry Moore on Sculpture* 66.
Hoglands, Perry Green, Much Hadham, Herts., England.

Moore, Marianne Craig, A.B.; American writer; b. 15 Nov. 1887; ed. Bryn Mawr Coll. and Carlisle Commercial Coll.
Teacher commercial dept. Carlisle (Pa.) U.S. Indian School 11-15; Asst. New York Public Library 21-25; acting editor *The Dial* 25-29; received Dial award 24, Helen Haire Levinson prize 35, Shelley Memorial prize 40, Harriet Monroe Poetry Award 44, John Simon Guggenheim Memorial Foundation Fellowship 45, Grant from American Acad. Arts and Letters 46; Nat. Book Award for Verse 52, Bollingen Prize in Poetry of Yale Univ. Library 52; Pulitzer Prize in Verse 52, etc.; mem. American Acad. of Arts and Letters; Hon. Litt.D. (Wilson Coll. 49, Mount Holyoke Coll. 50, Univ. of Rochester 51, Rutgers Univ. 55); Hon. L.H.D. (Smith Coll., Pratt Inst. 59), Hon. Litt.D. (Douglas Coll. and Washington Univ., St. Louis, Missouri); M. Carey Thomas Award 53; Edward MacDowell Medal 67; Chevalier of the Order "Arts et Lettres" 67.
Publs. *Poems* 21, *Observations* 24, *Selected Poems* 35, *What are Years?* 41, *Nevertheless* 44, *Collected Poems* 51, *The Fables of La Fontaine* (translation) 54, *Predilections* (prose) 55, *Like a Bulwark* 56, *O to be a Dragon* 59, *A Marianne Reader* 61, *Tell Me, Tell Me: Granite, Steel and Other Topics* 66 (poems), *Complete Poems* 67.
7B 35 West 9th Street, New York City, N.Y. 10011, U.S.A.

Moore, Robert Lee, B.S., M.A., PH.D.; American mathematician; b. 14 Nov. 1882; ed. Univs. of Texas and Chicago.
Asst. Prof. of Maths. Univ. of Tennessee 05-06; Instructor Princeton Univ. 06-08, Northwestern Univ. 08-11, Univ. of Pennsylvania 11-16, Asst. Prof. 16-20; Assoc. Prof. of Pure Maths. Univ. of Texas 20-23, Prof. 23-, Distinguished Prof. 37-53; mem. Nat. Acad. of Sciences, American Math. Soc., Assoc. Ed. of *Transactions* 13-26, mem. of Council 17-19, Vice-Pres. 23, Ed. of Colloquium Publications 29-36, Colloquium Lecturer 29, Visiting Lecturer 31-32, Pres. 36-38; Fellow of American Asscn. for the Advancement of Science, Vice-Pres. 47; Prof. Maths. and Astronomy 53-59, of Mathematics 59-.
Publs. *Foundations of Point Set Theory* (revised 62), *Fundamental Theorems Concerning Point Sets* 36.
Department of Mathematics, University of Texas, Austin, Texas, U.S.A.

Moore, William H., B.A.; American banker; b. 21 Nov. 1914; ed. Yale Univ.
Joined Bankers Trust Co., New York 38, Asst. Treas. 48, Asst. Vice-Pres. 49-51, Vice-Pres., Dir. and mem. Exec. Cttee. 56, Chair. of Board 57, Chair. 67-; Dir. American Can Co., Commonwealth Fund, Fairchild Hiller Corpn., The Hanna Mining Co., Int. Business Machines Corpn., Nat. Biscuit Co.; The Greater New York Fund, etc.; Trustee, The Vincent Astor Foundation; mem. Investment Cttee. Royal-Globe Insurance Companies; Hon. LL.D.
Banker Trust Company, 280 Park Avenue, New York, N.Y. 10017, U.S.A.

Moorehead, Alan, O.B.E.; Australian writer; b. 22 July 1910; ed. Scotch Coll. and Melbourne Univ.
Sunday Times Gold Medal 56; Duff Cooper Award 56.
Publs. *Mediterranean Front* 41, *A Year of Battle* 43, *The End in Africa* 43, *African Trilogy* 44, *Eclipse* 45, *Montgomery* 46, *The Rage of the Vulture* 48, *The Villa Diana* 51, *The Traitors* 52, *Rum Jungle* 53, *A Summer Night* 54, *Gallipoli* 56, *The Russian Revolution* 58, *No Room in the Ark* 59, *The White Nile* 60, *The Blue Nile* 62, *Coopers Creek* (Royal Soc. of Literature Award) 63, *The Desert War* 65, *The Fatal Impact* 66.
c/o National Bank of Australasia, Australia House, Strand, London, W.C.2, England.

Moorer, Admiral Thomas H., D.S.M., D.F.C.; American naval officer; b. 9 Feb. 1912; ed. U.S. Naval Acad.
Service in U.S. warships 33-41; Commdr. of bombing squadron 42-44; Gunnery and Tactical Officer, Staff of Commdr. Air Force, Atlantic 44-45; Strategic Bombing Survey, Japan 45-56; Naval Aviation Ordnance Test Station 46-48; Operations Officer on Staff of Commdr. Carrier Div. Four, Atlantic Fleet 49-50; Naval Ordnance Test Station, Inyokern 50-52; Staff of Commdr. of Air Force, Atlantic Fleet 53-55; Aide to

Asst. Sec. of Navy for Air 55-56; C.O. U.S. Navy 56-57; Special Asst., Strategic Plans Div., Office of Chief of Naval Operations, Navy Dept. 57; Commdr. Carrier Div. Six 59-60; Dir. Long Range Plans 60-62; Commdr. U.S. Seventh Fleet, W. Pacific 62-64; Commdr. in Chief U.S. Pacific Fleet 64-65; Commdr. in Chief U.S. Atlantic Fleet, Commdr. in Chief Atlantic and Supreme Allied Commdr. Atlantic (NATO Forces) 65-67; Chief of Naval Operations, U.S. 67-; Silver Star Medal 42; Legion of Merit 45.

c/o Department of the Navy, Washington 25, D.C.; Home: 402 Barbour Street, Eufaula, Alabama 36027, U.S.A.

Moores, John; British businessman; b. 96.
Member of Liverpool City Council 35-40; founder H. Littlewoods Ltd. (Multiple Stores), Littlewoods Pools, Littlewoods Mail Order Stores, John Moores Biennial Art Exhibition (Walker Art Gallery, Liverpool); Chair. Everton Football Club 60-.

c/o Littlewoods Mail Order Stores, Waterloo Building, Castle Street, Liverpool, England.

Moos, Ludwig von; Swiss federal councillor; b. 31 Jan. 1910; ed. Fribourg Univ.
Clerk, Commune of Sachseln 33-59; Editor *Obwaldner Volksfreund* 35-42; Pres. Commune of Sachseln 41-46; Judge Vice-Pres. Cantonal Tribunal 43-46; Councillor of States 43-59; Govt. Councillor 46-59; Fed. Councillor and Chief Fed. Dept. of Justice and Police 59-; Vice-Pres. Swiss Confederation 63, 68, Pres. 64; a Dir. Bank of Obwalden 46-59, Pres. 54-59; a Dir. Swiss Fed. Railways 54-59, Vice-Pres. 57-59; mem. Board of Swiss Fed. Inst. of Technology 57-59; Swiss Conservative Party.
Luternauweg 6, Berne, Switzerland.

Mora Becarra, Alberto; Cuban politician; b. 34; ed. Univ. of Havana.
Under-Sec. of Defence 59; Minister of Foreign Trade 60-64; mem. Partido Unido de la Revolución Socialista de Cuba.
c/o Ministry of Foreign Trade, Havana, Cuba.

Mora Otero, José Antonio; D.IUR.; Uruguayan diplomatist and international civil servant; b. 97; ed. Univ. of the Repub. (Montevideo).
Diplomatic posts Spain and Portugal 26-28, Brazil 28-30, U.S.A. 29-30; Chief, Int. Institutes Service, Ministry of Foreign Affairs 33-41, Dir. 45-46; Minister to Bolivia 42-45, to U.S.A. 46-51, Ambassador 51-56; Vice-Chair. Council of Org. of American States (OAS) 48-49, Chair. 54-55, Sec.-Gen. 56-May 68; Hon. D.H.L. (Rollins Coll.), D.C.L. (Pittsburgh), LL.D. (Colgate), Dr. h.c. (Univs. of Salamanca and Ceará 64).
Publs. *Sentido Internacional del Uruguay* 38, *La Organización Judicial en la Conferencia de San Francisco* 46.
Jaime Zudáñez 2866, Montevideo, Uruguay.
Telephone: 41-43-04.

Moraes, Dominic (son of Frank Moraes, *q.v.*); Indian writer and poet; b. 19 July 1938; ed. St. Mary's High School, Bombay, and Jesus Coll., Oxford.
Hawthornden Prize for *A Beginning* 57.
Publs. include: *A Beginning* 57, *Gone Away* 60, *My Son's Father* (autobiog.) 68; books of poems and travel books on India.
c/o Nova, Tower House, Southampton Street, London, W.C.1, England.

Moraes, Frank Robert (father of Dominic Moraes, *q.v.*), M.A., Barrister-at-Law; Indian journalist; b. 12 Nov. 1907; ed. St. Xavier's Coll., Bombay, Oxford Univ. and Lincoln's Inn.
Asst. Editor *The Times of India* 38-46, War Corresp. in Burma and China 43-46, Deputy Editor 49-50, Editor 50-57; Editor *The Times of Ceylon* 46-48, *The National Standard* 50; mem. Indian Cultural Del. to China 52; Editor *Evening News of India* and *The Times of India*

Annual; Editor-in-Chief *The Indian Express* 57-; Sheriff of Bombay 61-62.
Publs. *The Story of India, Report on Mao's China* 53, *Jawaharlal Nehru* 56, *Yonder One World* 58, *The Revolt in Tibet* 59, *India Today* 59, *Nehru: Sunlight and Shadow* 64, *The Importance of being Black* 65.
B-13, Maharani Bagh, New Delhi 14, India.

Moraes, Vinicius de, LL.B.; Brazilian writer and diplomatist; b. 13; ed. Nat. Faculty of Law, Colégio Santo Ignácio and Magdalen Coll., Oxford.
Ministry of Educ. 36-38; Ministry of Foreign Affairs 43; Film Critic 40-45; Sec. Embassy 44-47; Vice-Consul, Los Angeles 47-50; Consul, Montivedeo 58-60.
Publs. Poetry: *O Caminho para a Distância* 33, *Forma e Exegese* 46, *Ariana a Mulher* 36, *Novos Poemas* 38, 59, *Cinco Elegias* 43, *Poemas, Sonetas e Baladas* 46, *Patria Minha* 48, *Livro de Sonetos* 57, *Antologia Poética* 54, *Orfeu da Conceição* 56; Prose: *Procura-se uma Rosa* 61, *Para Viver um Grande Amor* 62; numerous translations.
Rua Paulo Cesar de Andrade n. 106 ap. 503, Parque Eduardo Guinle, Larangeiras, Rio de Janeiro, Brazil.

Morales, Armando; Nicaraguan artist; b. 15 Jan. 1927; ed. Instituto Pedagógico de Varones, Managua, Escuela de Bellas Artes, Managua and Pratt Graphic Art Center, New York.
First one-man exhbn. Lima 59, subsequently at Toronto, New York, Washington, D.C., Panama, Bogotá, Detroit, Caracas, Mexico City; Group exhbns. all over N. and S. America and in Europe; numerous awards for painting in the Americas including Carnegie Int. 64, and award at Arte de América y España Exhbn., Madrid.
32 West 82nd St. (3B), New York, N.Y. 10024, U.S.A.
Telephone: 799-2539.

Moran, 1st Baron, cr. 43, of Manton; **Charles McMoran Wilson,** Kt., M.C., M.D., F.R.C.P.; British physician.
Medical Officer 1st Battn. Royal Fusiliers 14-17; Medical Officer in charge Medical Side 7th Stationary Hospital Boulogne 17-18; Dean St. Mary's Hospital Medical School 20-45; Pres. Royal Coll. of Physicians 41-50; Consulting Physician St. Mary's Hospital; Fellow American Coll. of Physicians; Chair. Advisory Cttee. on Distinction Awards for Consultants; mem. Senate and Hon. Sec. Faculty of Medicine, Univ. of London.
Publs. *The Anatomy of Courage* 45, *Winston Churchill* 66.
25 Bryanston Square, London, W.1; Marshalls Manor, Maresfield, Sussex, England.

Morand, Paul; French diplomat and novelist; b. 13 March 1889; ed. Univs. of Paris and Oxford.
Fmr. Sec. of French Embassies in London 13, Rome 17 and Madrid 18; Chargé d'Affaires in Siam 25; fmr. Dir. of French Works Abroad at Ministry of Foreign Affairs; Liaison Officer British Ministry of Economic Warfare and French Ministry of Blockade 39-40; Minister Plen. in London July 40; Bucharest 43; Ambassador at Berne 44; Officier, Légion d'Honneur; Prix Combat 66.
Publs. Novels: *Green Shoots* 21, *Open All Night* 22, *Closed All Night, Lewis and Irene* 24, *L'Europe Galante* 25, *Rien que la terre, Living Buddha* 26, *Champions of the World* 28, *New York* 29, *"1900", Indian Air* 32, *France la Douce* 33, *Londres* 34, *Bucharest* 35, *L'homme pressé* 41, *Vie de Maupassant* 42, *Feu M. le Duc* 43, *Giraudoux, notre Jeunesse* 45, *Montociel* 46, *Journal d'un attaché d'Ambassade* 49, *Proust, le Visiteur du Soir* 50, *Le Flagellant de Séville* 51, *Théâtre* 59, *Bains de Mer* 60, *Fouquet* 61, *Le Prince de Ligne* 64, *Tais-toi* 65, *Nouvelles des yeux* 65, *Nouvelles du coeur* 65.
Château de l'Aile, Vevey, Switzerland.

Morandi, Luigi, B.SC.; Italian chemical executive; b. 1898.
Vice-Pres. Montecatini Co., Milan 49- (now Montecatini-Edison); Pres. Lombard Section, Italian Chemical Soc.

48; Pres. Board of Dirs. State Technical Inst. for Industrial Chemical Experts "Ettore Molinari", Milan 48-64; Pres. Fed. of Scientific and Technical Socs. of Milan 50; Vice-Pres. Gen. Council, Società Chimica Italiana (Pres. Lombard Section) 48; OECD Expert for Examination of Science Policy in France 64; mem. Lombard Inst., Acad. of Sciences and Arts 50; Nat. mem. Accademia Pugliese delle Scienze 64; Officier, Légion d'Honneur.
Publs. *I Funghi* (Mushrooms) 54, *Viaggio di un tecnico curioso nella civiltà sovietica* (Journey of an Interested Technologist to the Soviet Union) 61.
Montecatini-Edison S.p.a., Largo Donegani 1/2, Milan, Italy.

Morano, His Eminence Cardinal Francesco; Italian ecclesiastic; b. 8 June 1872; ed. Rome Univ., and Pontifical Roman Seminary.
Ordained priest 97; fmr. staff mem. Vatican Astronomical Observatory; with Supreme Sacred Congregation of the Holy Office 03-59, Consultant; fmr. Consultant Sacred Congregation of the Council, Pontifical Comm. for Authentic Interpretation of Canon Law; fmr. Sec. Supreme Tribunal of the Apostolic Signature; fmr. Papal Auditor; created Cardinal by Pope John XXIII 59.
Palazzo del S. Uffizio, Rome, Italy.

Moravia, Alberto; Italian writer and journalist; b. 28 Nov. 1907.
Pres. Int. P.E.N. 59.
Publs. Novels: *Gli indifferenti* 29, *Le Ambizioni Sbagliate* 35, *La Mascherata* 41, *Agostino* 44, *La Romana* 47, *La Disubbidienza* 48, *L'Amore Coniugale* 49, *Il Conformista* 51, *Il disprezzo* 54, *La Ciociara* 57, *La noia* 61, *L'Attenzione* 65; Plays: *Teatro* 58, *Beatrice Cenci* 65, *Il mondo è quello che è*; short stories: *La bella vita* 35, *L'Imbroglio* 37, *I Sogni del Pigro* 40, *L'Amante infelice* 43, *L'Epidemia* 45, *Due Cortigiane* 45, *Racconti Romani* 45, *I Racconti* 54, *Nuovi Racconti Romani* 59, *L'Automa* 63, *Una cosa è una cosa* 66; essays; *La speranza, L'Uomo, Come fine* 65.
Lungotevere della Vittoria 1, Rome, Italy.
Telephone: 378836.

Morawski, Jerzy; Polish politician and diplomatist; b. 11 Aug. 1919.
Active in revolutionary youth movement before, and in resistance during Second World War; mem. Polish Workers' Party; Sec. Cen. Cttee. Polish United Workers' Party 55-59; Editor-in-Chief *Trybuna Ludu* 56; mem. Political Bureau, Cen. Cttee. Polish United Workers' Party 56-59; Dep. Chair. Supreme Board of Control 59-64; Ambassador to U.K. 64-.
Polish Embassy, Portland Place, London W.1, England.

Moreau, Jeanne; French actress; b. 23 Jan. 1928; ed. Paris.
Stage actress with Comédie Française 48-52; Théâtre National Populaire 53; since 54 has appeared in *L'Heure éblouissante, La Machine Infernale, Pygmalion, La Chatte sur un toit brûlant, La Bonne Soupe*, etc.; since 48 has made more than 20 films incl.: *Touchez pas au grisbi, Le salaire du péché, Ascenseur pour l'Echafaud, Les Amants, Moderato Cantabile, Les Liaisons dangereuses, Dialogue des Carmélites, Jules et Jim, Eve, The Victors, La Baie Des Anges, Peau de Banane, The Train, Le Journal d'une Femme de Chambre, Mata Hari—H 21, Viva Maria, Mademoiselle* 66, *Chimes at Midnight* 66, *Great Catherine* 67, *l'Amour à travers les âges* 67, *The Sailor from Gibraltar* 67, *The Bride wore Black* 67.
9 rue du Cirque, Paris 8e, France.

Moreau de Melen, Jules; Belgian executive; b. 26 Aug. 1888; ed. Université Libre, Brussels, and Montefiore Electrical Inst.
Managing Dir. Petrofina 24-56, Vice-Chair. 56-61, Hon. Pres. 61-; Dir. Socotole; Hon. Vice-Chair. Fina; Hon.

Dir. Palmafina, Petrocom; Croix de Guerre with palms 18, Commdr. Order of Leopold II, and other decorations.
438 avenue Louise, Brussels 5, Belgium.

Moreau-Néret, Olivier, L. en D., L. es L.; French banker; b. 29 Jan. 1892.
Inspector of Finances 19; Deputy Dir. Treasury, Ministry of Finance, Head of Mission to London and Washington for discussion of Inter-allied debts 23-26; Hon. Dir. at Ministry of Finance 26; Sec.-Gen. then Dir. of Crédit Lyonnais 26-39; Sec.-Gen. Ministry of Finance 40; Dir.-Gen., later Pres., of Crédit Lyonnais 42-62; Prof. Inst. d'Etudes politiques; mem. of Acad. des Sciences morales et politiques; Grand Officier de la Légion d'Honneur 49; Commdr. Order of Leopold; Croix de Guerre.
Publs. *La Balance des Comptes* 36, *La Bourse* 38, *Les Valeurs Mobilières* 39, *Le Contrôle des Prix* 42, *Les Valeurs Etrangères* 56, *Les Valeurs Françaises depuis 1940* 57.
11 rue Dupont des Loges, Paris 7e, France.

Moreira, Adriano José Alves, LL.D.; Portuguese university professor and politician; b. 22; ed. Univ. of Lisbon.
Associate Prof., Higher Inst. for Social Sciences (ISOPO) 50-54, Prof. 54-58, Dir. 58-61; Under-Sec. of State for Overseas Affairs 60-61; Minister for Overseas Affairs 61-62; now Head of Lisbon Geographical Soc.; Hon. Pres. Int. Acad. Portuguese Culture, Lisbon; mem. Nat. Educ. Board; mem. Portuguese del. to UN Gen. Assembly 56-59; Plenipotentiary to Geneva Slavery Conf.; Consultative Cttee. of the Overseas Council 57-60; Military Order of Christ; Grand Officer, Order of Prince Henry; Grand Cross, Order of Saint Sylvester; Grand Cross of Catholic Queen; Grand Cross of Southern Cross of Brazil; Grand Cross of Order of Africa; Grand Cross of Order of Christ.
Publ. *The Prison Problem of the Overseas Provinces, Overseas Policy* 56, *Portugal and Article 73 of the United Nations Charter* 57, *International Jurisdiction and the Vote Problem in the United Nations* 58, *Juridical Studies* 60, *The Battle of Hope* 62, *Portuguese Party* 62, *Political Ideologies* 64.
Rua Vieira Lusitans, Lisbon, Portugal.

Morelli, Gaetano, LL.D.; Italian judge; b. 23 May 1900; ed. Univ. of Rome.
Lecturer in International Law, University of Urbino 27-32; Prof. Univ. of Modena 32-33, Univ. of Padua 33-35, Naples 35-51, Rome 51-; Judge, Int. Court of Justice 61-; mem. Institut de droit international 50-, First Vice-Pres. 61-63; mem. Perm. Conciliation Comm. between Luxembourg and Switzerland 50-, Higher Council of Public Educ. 51-58, Perm. Court of Arbitration 55-, Italian Nat. Comm. for UNESCO 56-61.
Publs. *La sentenza internazionale* 31, *Diritto processuale civile internazionale* (2nd edn.) 54, *La théorie générale du procès international* 37, *Lezioni di diritto internazionale privato* (2nd edn.) 43, *Nozioni di diritto internazionale* (7th edn.) 67, *Elementi di diritto internazionale privato italiano* (9th edn.) 68, *Studi di diritto processuale civile internazionale* 61, *Studi sul processo internazionale* 63, etc.
International Court of Justice, The Hague, Netherlands; and Via Lucrezio Caro 67, Rome, Italy.
Telephone: 354717.

Moreno Quintana, Lucio Manuel; Argentine lawyer, professor and diplomatist; b. 1898; graduated in law at Univ. of Buenos Aires.
Under-Sec. for Foreign Affairs 22-23, 45-46; Public Prosecutor, Civil and Commercial Court of La Plata 23-25, Judge 25-30; Legal Adviser, Buenos Aires Transport Control Comm. 38-43; mem. Permanent Court of Arbitration 45-55; headed Argentine Del. at 1st Session U.N. Gen. Assembly and 21st Session

League of Nations Assembly 46; Asst. Prof. of Int. Law 22-35; Prof. and Dir. Inst. of Economic Policy 35-47, Counsellor and Vice-Dean of Economics Faculty 36-40, of Law Faculty 48-52, Prof. and Dir. Inst. of Int. Law 47-55, Univ. of Buenos Aires; Prof. Int. Law School of Naval Warfare 50-54, of Army Warfare 52-54; Judge at the International Court of Justice 55-64.
Publs. *Inmigración* 20, *El sistema internacional americano* 25, *La diplomacia de Yrigoyen* 28, *Política Económica* 44, *Derecho Internacional Público* 50, *Derecho de Asilo* 52, *Preliminares del Derecho Internacional* 54, *Elementos de Política Internacional* 54, *Tratado de Derecho Internacional* 63.
José E. Uriburu 1568, Buenos Aires, Argentina.

Moreno Valle, Dr. Rafael; Mexican medical officer and politician; b. 23 Aug. 1917; ed. Escuela Médico Militar.
Postgraduate work in various North American hospitals; Prof. of Traumatology and Orthopaedics, Escuela Médico Militar 44-; Rep. for Military Health at national surgeons' assemblies 44-60; Brigadier-Gen. 52; Senator for Puebla State 58-64; Pres. of Senate twice; Pres. of Foreign Affairs Comm., Health Comm., and Perm. Comm., of Congress 62; Political Action Sec. of Nat. Exec. Cttee. of Partido Revolucionario Institutional 62-64; now Sec. of State for Health and Public Assistance; mem. Mexican Del. to Mexico-North America Inter-Parl. meetings; mem. Legislators' Comm. which travelled throughout world seeking disarmament and ban on nuclear weapons' tests; Founder-mem. Mexican Orthopaedics Soc.; mem. Latin American Orthopaedics and Traumotology Soc. and various North American acads. and asscns.
Secretaría de Salubridad y Asistencia, Mexico City, Mexico.

Moretti, Marino; Italian writer; b. 18 July 1885.
Novelist, short-story writer, poet; for many years connected with *Corriere della Sera*.
Publs. include *Poesie scritte col lapis* 10, *I Pesci fuor d'acqua* 14, *Il Sole del Sabato* 16, *Poesie scelte* 19, *La voce di Dio* 20, *I puri di cuore* 24, *Il segno della croce* 26, *L'Andreana* 35, *Scrivere non è necessario* 37, *La vedova Fioravanti* 40, *I coniugi Allori* 46, *Il fiocco verde* 48, *Il Pudore* 50, *I grilli di Pazzo Pazzi* 51, *Il Tempo Migliore* 52, *Uomini soli* 54, *1945* 56, *La camera degli Sposi* 58, *Tutte le Novelle* 59, *Il Libro dei Miei Amici* 60, *Romanzi della mia Terra* 61, *Tutti i ricordi* 62, *Anna degli Elefanti* 63, *Romanzi dal primo all'ultimo* 65, *Tutte le poesie* 66.
Cesenatico (Forlì), Italy.

Morgan, Sir Frank William, Kt., M.C.; British insurance executive; b. 23 June 1887; ed. Parmiter's School.
Prudential Assurance Co. 03-, Man. for India, Burma and Ceylon 28-33, for Near East 33-34, Gen. Man. 41-50, Dir. 50-53, Chair. 53-65, Pres. 65-; Army Service 14-18.
Hyde Heath Farm, nr. Amersham, Bucks., England.
Telephone: Chesham 3028.

Morgan, Graham James; American chemical and industrial executive; b. 19 Sept. 1917; ed. Carleton Coll.
U.S. Gypsum Co. 39-, Sales 39-45, management posts 45-49, Gen. Merchandise Dir. 51-53, Vice-Pres. (Merchandising) 53-54, Vice-Pres. and Asst. to Chair. of Board 54-59, Exec. Vice-Pres. 59, Pres. and mem. Exec. Cttee. 60-, Dir. 58-, Chief Exec. Officer 65-; Dir. of numerous other companies.
Home: 1500 North Lake Shore Drive, Chicago, Illinois 60610; Office: U.S. Gypsum Company, 101 S. Wacker Drive, Chicago 6, Illinois, U.S.A.

Morgan, Michèle (Simone Roussel); French actress; b. 29 Feb. 1920.
Studied with R. Simon (Paris); acted in a large number

of films including *Quai des Brumes, Symphonie Pastorale, Fabiola, Les Septs Péchés Capitaux, Les Orgueilleux, Obsession, Les Grandes Manoeuvres, Marguerite de la Nuit, Marie Antoinette, Si Paris Nous Etait Conté, Le Miroir à Deux Faces, Femmes d'un Eté, Pourquoi Viens-tu si Tard?, Les Scélérats, Fortunat, Le Puits aux Trois Vérités, Les Lions sont Lâches, Rencontres, Le Crime ne Paie Pas, Landru, Constance aux Enfers, Les Yeux cernés, Dis-moi qui tuer, Les Centurions;* Cannes Festival Prize for Best Actress 46; French "Victoire" for Best Actress 46, 48, 50, 52, 55.
Publ. *Mes Yeux ont vu* 65.
2 rue Saint Louis en l'Isle, Paris 4e, France.

Morgan, Thomas Ellsworth; American politician; b. 13 Oct. 1906; ed. Waynesburg Coll., Detroit Coll. of Medicine and Surgery and Wayne Univ., Detroit.
Intern, Grace Hospital, Detroit 33-34; Medical and surgical practice, Fredericktown, Pennsylvania 34-; mem. U.S. House of Reps. 45-49, 53-, Chair. Advisory Cttee. on Improving Govt. Org. 49, now Chair. Cttee. on Foreign Affairs; Democrat.
U.S. House of Representatives, Washington, D.C., U.S.A.

Morgan, Walter Thomas James, C.B.E., PH.D., D.SC., D.SC.TECH., F.R.I.C., F.R.S.; British biochemist; b. 5 Oct. 1900; ed. Univs. of London, Graz, and Zürich.
Grocers' Company Research Student 25-26; Beit Medical Research Fellow 26-28; Biochemist and First Asst. to Serum Dept., Lister Inst., Elstree 29-36; Rockefeller Research Fellow 36-37; mem. of staff of Lister Inst., London 28-; Deputy Dir., Prof. of Biochemistry and head of Div. of Biochemistry 41-; Hon. Sec. Biochemical Soc. 40-45, Biological Council 44-47; mem. Govt. Scientific Advisory Council 55-59; Croonian Lecturer Royal Soc. 59; Vice-Pres. Royal Soc. 61-64; Conway Evans Prize (Royal Soc. and Royal Coll. Physicians) 64, Karl Lansteiner Prize American Asscn. of Blood Banks 67, Paul Ehrlich Prize 68; M.D. h.c. (Basle), mem. Medical Research Council 66-.
57 Woodbury Drive, Sutton, Surrey, England.

Morgens, Howard J(oseph), A.B., M.B.; American businessman; b. 16 Oct. 1910; ed. Washington Univ. and Harvard Business School.
With Procter and Gamble Co. 33-, Advertising Man. 46, Vice-Pres. (Advertising) 48, Dir. 50-54, Exec. Vice-Pres. 54, Pres. 57-; Dir. Owens-Corning Fibreglass Corpn.; Dir. and fmr. Chair. Advertising Council; mem. Board of Govs. American Nat. Red Cross; Trustee The American Heritage Foundation; Hon. LL.D. Washington Univ. 58, Miami Univ. 59.
2347 Vista Place, Cincinnati 8, Ohio, U.S.A.

Morgenstern, Werner F. W. H.; German port authority official; b. 9 Feb. 1905; ed. Classical Secondary School of the Holy Cross.
Merchant Marine 27; in Canada 39-46; with Harrison Line 49-53; Head, Claims Assurance Dept., German-Africa Shipping Co. 53-56; Port Capt. Hamburg 56-; Commr. Ships' Reporting Office; Hon. Freeman, Nicaragua.
2 Hamburg 4, St. Pauli Landungsbrücken, Brücke 5, German Federal Republic.

en, Raffaello; Italian university professor and writer; b. 19 Sept. 1896; ed. Univ. degli Studi, Rome.
Teacher of History 23-30; Prof. Modern History, Univ. of Rome 30-33; Editor Modern History Section *Enciclopedia Italiana* 32-37; Prof. Medieval History Univ. of Palermo 38-41; Prof. Modern History Univ. of Perugia 42-48; Prof. Medieval History Univ. of Rome 48-; Chancellor Accad. dei Lincei 27-59; Pres. Italian Medieval Historical Inst. 53-; Foreign Assoc. Institut de France; mem. various academies including Accad. dei Lincei; several honours.
Publs. *Il Tramonto della potenza sveva in Italia* 36,

Gregorio VII 39, *Medioevo cristiano* 51 and 58, *La formazione degli Stati Europei* 59, *L'Idea d'Europa* 60, *Profilo storico della Civiltà Europea* 66.
Via della Lungara 10, Rome, Italy.
Telephone: 653-709.

Mori, Haruki; Japanese diplomatist; b. 11; ed. Univ. of Tokyo.
Ministry of Foreign Affairs, served U.S.A. and Philippines 35-41; Head of Econ. Section Dept. of Political Affairs 50-53; Counsellor Rome 53-55; Counsellor Asian Affairs, Tokyo 55-56; Sec. to Prime Minister 56-57; Counsellor Int. Co-operation 57; Dir. of American Affairs Bureau 57-60; Minister to U.K. 60-63, to France 63-64; Perm. Rep. to OECD 64-67; Deputy Vice-Minister at Ministry of Foreign Affairs 67-.
Ministry of Foreign Affairs, Tokyo, Japan.

Mori, Hisagoro, DR. ING.; Japanese business executive; b. 20 March 1891; ed. Tokyo Univ.
Ujigawa Electric Power Co. Inc. 19-51; Exec. Vice-Pres. Kansai Electric Power Co. Inc. 51-62, Adviser 62-63; Pres. Maruzen Oil Co. Ltd. 63-64, Maruzen Petro Chemical Co. Ltd. 63-64, Maruzen Tanker Co. Ltd. 63-65; Dir. Sakai Ironworks Ltd., Kansai Oil Co., Inc., Kansai Petro Chemical Co., Ltd.; Adviser, Kansai Electric Power Co., Ltd.; now Chair. of Board, Maruzen Oil Co., Ltd.; Blue Ribbon Medal for Industry.
32 Kawanishi-cho, Ashiya-shi, Hyogo-ken, Japan.

Möri, Jean; Swiss trade union official; b. 20 Aug. 1902.
Ed. *Gutenberg* 35-40; Sec. Swiss Federation of Typographers 39-46; Sec. Swiss Federation of Trade Unions 46-; ed. *Trade Unions Review;* mem. Swiss Socialist Party.
Union Syndicale Suisse, Monbijoustrasse 61, 3000 Berne, Switzerland.
Telephone: 45-56-66.

Mori, Yonejiro; Japanese business executive; b. 1 Jan. 1898; ed. Tokyo Commercial Coll.
Mitsubishi Shipbuilding and Eng. Co. 21-58, Man. Dir. 55-58; Pres. and Rep. Dir. Sasebo Ship Industry Co. Ltd. (now Sasebo Heavy Industries Co. Ltd.) 58-.
Sasebo Heavy Industries Co. Ltd., 5th Floor, New Ohtemachi Building, 4, 2-chome, Ohtemachi, Chiyoda-ku, Tokyo, Japan.

Morice, André; French politician; b. 11 Oct. 1900; ed. Nantes Lycée and Univ. of Paris.
In business 31-39; served army 39-44; Town Councillor for Nantes 45-, Asst. to Mayor 45-47; Deputy for Loire Inférieure 45-58; Under-Sec. for Technical Education, Schuman Govt. 47-48, Marie Govt. 48; Sec. of State for Technical Education and Sports in Queuille Govt. 49, Bidault Govt. 49-50, Pleven Govt. 50-51, Queuille Govt. 51; Minister of Nat. Education, Queuille Govt. July 51; Minister of the Merchant Marine, Pleven Govt. 51-52, Faure Govt. 52; Minister of Public Works, Travel and Tourism. Pinay Govt. 52 and Mayer Govt. 53; Dir. *Eclair de l'Ouest* 54; Minister of Industry and Commerce, Faure Govt. 55-56; Minister of Nat. Defence 57-58; Mayor of Nantes 65-; Senator for Loire-Atlantique 65-; Pres. Asscn. Française pour la Promotion du Travail, Mouvement Libéral pour l'Europe Unie; Croix de Guerre; Chevalier Légion d'Honneur.
13 boulevard Raspail, Paris 7e, France.

Morimoto, Kanzaburo; Japanese business executive; b. 13 Dec. 1892; ed. Kyoto Univ.
Takeda Chemical Industries Ltd. 19-, Statutory Auditor 25-33, Dir. 33-38, Man. Dir. 38-47, Senior Man. Dir. 47-60, Vice-Pres. 60-63, Chair. of Board of Dirs. 63-; Pres. Daiwa Real Estate Co. Ltd. 57-; Yellow Ribbon Medal 63.
Takeda Chemical Industries, 2-27 Doshomachi, Higashi-ku, Osaka, Japan.

Morin, Jean, L. en DR.; French civil servant; b. 23 June 1916; ed. Ecole Libre des Sciences Politiques.
Secretary General Inst. Scientifique des Recherches Economiques et Sociales 39; Auditeur, Cour des Comptes 41; Dir. of Personnel, Ministry of the Interior 44; Prefect, Manche 46; Dep. Dir. du Cabinet to Pres. of Provisional Govt. 46, to Minister of Foreign Affairs 47-48; Technical Adviser, Minister of the Interior 48-49; Prefect, Maine-et-Loire 49; Conseiller Référendaire, Cour des Comptes 49; Prefect, Haute-Garonne and Extraordinary Insp. Gen. of Admin. (5th Region) 58-60; Del.-Gen. in Algeria 60-62; Sec.-Gen. of Merchant Navy 62-; Commdr. Légion d'Honneur, Croix de Guerre, Médaille de la Résistance.
3 Place Fontenoy, Paris 7e, France.

Morinaga, Teiichiro; Japanese banker; b. 9 Sept. 1910; ed. The Fifth Higher School, Kumamoto and Tokyo Imperial Univ.
Ministry of Finance 32-59, Chief Sec. to Minister of Finance 47-53, Dir. Budget Bureau 53-57, Perm. Vice-Minister of Finance 57-59; Pres. Small Business Finance Corpn. 60-62; Pres. The Export-Import Bank of Japan 62-67; mem. The Export Council, Overseas Econ. Co-operation Council, Econ. Deliberation Council, Int. Trade Council (Japanese Govt. Orgs.).
c/o The Export-Import Bank of Japan, Ohte-machi, Chiyoda-ku, Tokyo, Japan.

Morinigo, Gen. Higinio; Paraguayan officer and politician; b. 97; ed. Nat. Coll. Asunción and Military School.
2nd Lieut. 19, served Northern Operational Dept. and 2nd and 3rd Infantry Regts. to 28; Capt. 27; War Coll., apptd. Staff Major; Battn. Commdt. Military School 32; Dir. Reserve School; served Chaco War; fmr. Chief of Staff to Commdr.-in-Chief, Ministry of War and Marine and Ministry of Interior; General 43; Pres. of Republic 40-June 48; exiled in Argentina 48-51, Brazil 51-56; returned to Paraguay 56, now living in Argentina; Cruz del Chaco, Cruz del Defensor and many other decorations; Dr. h.c. Fordham and Brazil Univs.
Calle General Urguiza 625-Acassuso, Buenos Aires, Argentina.

Morison, Samuel Eliot, D.LITT.; Rear Admiral U.S.N.R. (retd.); American historian; b. 9 July 1887; ed. Harvard Univ. and Ecole Libre des Sciences Politiques, Paris.
Harmsworth Prof. of American History, Oxford 22-25; Trumbull Prof. of American History, Harvard 25-55; served with U.S.N.R. during World War II; Fellow American Philosophical Society, British Academy; Legion of Merit with Combat Clasp, Balzan Award in History 63.
Publs. *Life of Harrison Gray Otis* 13, *Maritime History of Massachusetts* 21, *Oxford History of the U.S.* 27, *Builders of Bay Colony* 30, *Tercentennial History of Harvard Univ.* (5 vols.) 30-36, *Puritan Pronaos* 36, *Growth of the American Republic* (with Henry Steele Commager) 42, *Admiral of the Ocean Sea* 42, *History of U.S. Naval Operations in World War II* (15 vols.) 46-62, *By Land and Sea* 53, *Christopher Columbus, Mariner* 55, *Freedom in Contemporary Society* 56, *The Story of the "Old Colony" of New Plymouth* 56, *Strategy and Compromise* 58, *John Paul Jones: a Sailor's Biography* 59, *One Boy's Boston* 62, *Journals and Other Documents of Columbus* 63, *The Two-Ocean War* 63, *Vistas of History* 64, *The Caribbean as Columbus Saw It* 64, *The Oxford History of the American People* 65, *Spring Tides* 65, *Old Bruin: the life of Commodore Matthew C. Perry, U.S.N.* 67.
44 Brimmer Street, Boston, Mass. 02108, U.S.A.
Telephone: 227-5662.

Morley, Sir Alexander Francis, K.C.M.G., C.B.E.; former British diplomatist; b. 6 Jan. 1908; ed. Rugby School and Queen's Coll., Oxford.

India Office 30-38, 42-45; Private Sec. to Parl. Under-Sec. of State 33-36; Burma Office 38-40, 45-47; Ministry of Aircraft Production 40-42; Econ. Adviser to Lord Privy Seal 47-49; Dep. High Commr. in New Zealand 50-52; Asst. Under-Sec. of State for Commonwealth Relations 54; Dep. High Commr. in Calcutta 56-57; High Commr. in Ceylon 57-62; High Commr. in Jamaica 62-65; Amb. to Hungary 65-67.
47 Campden Hill Square, London, W.8, England.
Telephone: 01-727-9314.

Morley, Grace L. McCann, M.A., D. DE L'UNIV. DE PARIS; American art historian and museum director; b. 3 Nov. 1900; ed. Calif., Paris, Grenoble and Harvard Univs.
Instr. in French, later in History of Art Goucher Coll., Baltimore 27-30; Curator, Cincinnati Art Museum 30-33, Dir. San Francisco Museum of Art 35-60; Asst. Dir. Soloman R. Guggenheim Museum 59-60; Dir. Nat. Mus. of India 60-66, Educ. Fine Arts Building 39, Latin-American Painting Fine Arts Building 40, Pacific House Golden Gate Int. Exposition, San Francisco 40; Advisory Cttee. on Art, State Dept. Div of Cultural Relations 41-44; Pres. Western Asscn. of Art Museum Dirs. 39-40; mem. American Asscn. Art Museum Dirs., Vice-Pres. 52-53, Pres. 54-55; Trustee American Fed. of Arts, Vice-Pres. 39-51; Pres. Western Museums Conf. 46-48; mem. American Association of Museums, College Art Association, Int. Council Museums; Fellow Royal Soc. of Arts, Museums Asscn.; mem. U.S. Nat. Comm. for UNESCO 50-55; Editorial Board *UNESCO Museum;* Museums Consultant to UNESCO 46 and 52; Head of Museums UNESCO, Paris 47-49; Dir. UNESCO Int. Seminar on Museums and Education, Athens 54; Pres. Museums Asscn. of India 62-66; Vice-Chair. Govt. of India Central Advisory Board of Museums, Adviser on Museums, Ministry of Educ. (India) 66-; Watumull Award, India 62; Chevalier de la Légion d'Honneur 49; Hon. D.F.A., Hon. LL.D., Hon. Dr. of Humane Letters.
National Museum, Jan Path, New Delhi, India.

Morley, Robert, C.B.E.; British actor and dramatist; b. 26 May 1908; ed. Wellington Coll.
First London appearance in *Treasure Island,* Strand Theatre 29; first appearance in N.Y. 38; appeared in provinces and established repertory company with Peter Bull at Perranporth, Cornwall; has appeared in the plays *The Great Romancer, Pygmalion, The Man Who Came to Dinner, The First Gentleman, Edward My Son, The Little Hut, Hippo Dancing, A Likely Tale, Fanny, Halfway Up the Tree,* etc.; dir. *The Tunnel of Love* 57, *Once More with Feeling* 59; films since 37 include *Marie Antoinette, Major Barbara, Young Mr. Pitt, The Outcast of the Islands, The African Queen, Beat the Devil, Loser Takes All, Law and Disorder, The Journey, The Doctor's Dilemma, Libel, The Battle of the Sexes, Oscar Wilde, Those Magnificent Men in their Flying Machines, The Loved One, The Alphabet Murders, Sinful Davey, Hot Millions.*
Publs. *Goodness How Sad* 37, *Staff Dance* 44, *Edward My Son* (with Noel Langley) 48, *The Full Treatment* (with Ronald Gow) 52, *Hippo Dancing* 54, *Six Months Grace* (with D. Hamilton) 57, *Robert Morley: Responsible Gentleman* (with Sewell Stokes) 66.
Fairmans, Wargrave, Berkshire, England.

Moro, Aldo; Italian lawyer and politician; b. 16; ed. Bari Univ.
Former Pres. of Federazione Universitaria Cattolica Italiana and of Movement of Catholic Graduates; Mem. Constituent Assembly and of Co-ordination Cttee. of 18 for drafting of new Constitution; re-elected 48 and 53; Under-Sec. of State Foreign Affairs 49; Pres. Christian Democrat Parl. Group in the Chamber of Deputies 53-55; Minister of Justice 55-57, of Education 57-59;

Political Sec. Christian Democrat Party 59-63; Prime Minister Dec. 63-68, concurrently Minister of Foreign Affairs Dec. 65-Feb. 66.
Publs. *La capacità giuridica penale* 39, *Lo Stato* 43, *L'Antigiuridicità* 47, *Unità e pluralità di reati* 51.
Piazza del Gesù 46, Rome, Italy.

Morozov, Dmitry Ivanovich, M.SC.; Soviet trade corporation official; b. 02; ed. textile inst.
Assistant Prof. Textile Inst. and Industrial Acad., Moscow 32-39; in Foreign Trade missions 40, 41; Soviet Purchasing Comm., U.S. 43-45; in *Exportlen* (textile products), Deputy Chair. 41-43, 45-48, Chair. 48-51, 53-; Asst. Dir. U.S.S.R. Acad. of Foreign Trade 51-53; mem. C.P. 26-, Order of Red Banner of Labour, Order Badge of Honour, etc.
V/O *Exportlen,* Ul. Vlasova 33, Moscow, U.S.S.R.

Morozov, Ivan Pavlovich; Soviet politician; b. 1924; ed. Syktyvkar School of Medicine and C.P.S.U. Higher Party School.
Member C.P.S.U. 43-; Soviet Army service 42-44; Official, Young Communist League, Party, and Local Govt. 44-57; Chair. Inta City Soviet of Working People's Deputies 57-58; First Sec. Inta City Cttee. C.P.S.U. 58-63; Second Sec. Komi Regional Cttee. C.P.S.U. 63-65, First Sec. Oct. 65-; mem. Central Auditing Comm. of C.P.S.U.; Deputy to U.S.S.R. Supreme Soviet.
Komi Regional Committee, Communist Party of the Soviet Union, Syktyvkar, U.S.S.R.

Morrill, James Lewis, A.B.; American educator; b. 24 Sept. 1891; ed. Ohio State Univ.
Newspaperman 13-19; Exec. Sec. U.S. Food Admin. in Ohio and Ohio Branch, Council of Nat. Defence 17-19; Alumni Sec. and Ed. Ohio State Univ. 19-28; Instructor in Journalism and Educ. 25-29; Junior Dean Coll. of Educ. 28-32 and Vice-Pres. 32-41; Pres. Univ. of Wyoming 42-45, Univ. of Minnesota 45-60; Pres. Asscn. Land Grant Coll. and State Univs. 47-48, Chair. Nat. Defence Ctee. 52-54, mem. 55-57, mem. Cttee. on Govt. Controls of Higher Education 57-58, Chair. 59; Chair. American Council on Education 50-51, Chair. Cttee. on Relationships of Higher Education to Fed. Govt. 51-56; mem. Comm. on Education and Int. Affairs 57-59; Consultant Co-ordination of Exchange of Persons Programmes of Int. Educational Exchange Service and Int. Cooperation Administration, Dept. of State 55-56; Vice-Pres. Asscn. of American Univs. 52-54, Pres. 54-56; Pres. Nat. Asscn. of State Univs. 57-58; mem. Board of Trustees Inst. of Int. Education 57-60; mem. Board of Dirs. Educational Facilities Laboratory (Ford Foundation) 57-; Chair. Ford Foundation on the Univ. and World Affairs 59-60, Consultant, Ford Foundation 60-; Hon. LL.D. (Miami, Ohio State, Wyoming, Cincinnati and Northwestern Univs., Univs. of Exeter (England) and Calif. at Los Angeles, Carleton and Macalester Colls., Iowa State Coll., Michigan State Univ., Wisconsin, Minnesota and Hamline Univs.), L.H.D. (Muhlenburg Coll.); Commdr. Royal Order of North Star (Sweden) 56.
1752 Ardleigh Road, Columbus, Ohio 43221, U.S.A.
Telephone: 451-6749.

Morris, Benjamin Stephen, B.SC., ED.B.; British educationist and psychologist; b. 25 May 1910; ed. Rothesay Acad., Isle of Bute, and Univ. of Glasgow.
Asst. Master Glasgow schools 36-38; Lecturer in Psychology, Logic and Ethics, Jordanhill Training Coll. Glasgow 39-40, in Education, Univ. of Glasgow 40-46; Statistical and Intelligence Officer, Ministry of Food 41-42; Research Psychologist, War Office Selection Boards 42-45, Senior Psychologist (Lt.-Col.) 45; Senior Staff, Tavistock Inst. of Human Relations 46-50, and Chair. Management Cttee. 47-48; Dir. Nat. Foundation for Educational Research in England and Wales 50-56

Prof. of Education and Dir. Inst. of Education, Univ. of Bristol 56-.
Institute of Education, The University, Bristol 8; and Bracken Hill, Wrington, Somerset, England.
Telephone: Wrington 261.

Morris, Brewster Hillard, B.S., B.A., B.LITT.; American diplomatist; b. 7 Feb. 1909; ed. Haverford Coll. and Oxford Univ.
Vice-Consul Montreal 36, Vienna 38, Dresden 39, Berlin 40-41; Third Sec. Berlin 40-42; Third Sec. and Vice-Consul Stockholm 42-43, Second Sec. 44; Sec. Office of U.S. Political Adviser on German Affairs, Supreme H.Q., A.E.F. 44-48; First Sec. and Consul Moscow 48, Counsellor 49; attached to Nat. War Coll. 51; Dir. Office of German Political Affairs, State Dept. 52; in charge of political affairs, Office of German Affairs 53; Foreign Service Insp. 54-56, Senior Insp. 56; Political Counsellor London 57, Consul Gen. 58; Counsellor Bonn 60, Minister and Consul Gen. 61-63; Ambassador to Chad 63-67; Minister to Berlin 67-.
American Mission, Berlin, Germany.

Morris, James (Humphry), F.R.S.L.; British writer; b. 2 Oct. 1926; ed. Lancing and Christ Church, Oxford.
Army Service 43-48; Arab News Agency, Cairo 48-49; Editorial staff *The Times* 51-56, with British Mount Everest Expedition 53, Middle East Corresp. 55; Editorial staff *The Guardian* 57-62; Commonwealth Fellowship, U.S.A. 54; George Polk Memorial Award for Journalism (U.S.A.) 61; Heinemann Award for Literature 61.
Publs. *Coast to Coast* 56, *Sultan in Oman* 57, *The Market of Seleukia* 57, *Coronation Everest* 58, *South African Winter* 58, *The Hashemite Kings* 59, *Venice* 60, *The Upstairs Donkey* (for children) 62, *The Road to Huddersfield* 63, *Cities* 63, *The Presence of Spain* 64, *Oxford* 65, *Pax Britannica: The Climax of an Empire* 68.
Trefan, Llanystumdwy, Caernarvonshire, North Wales.
Telephone: Criccieth 2709.

Morris, John, C.B.E., M.A., M.SC.; British author and broadcaster; b. 27 Aug. 1895; ed. King's Coll., Cambridge.
Served in Regular Army (3rd Q.A.O. Gurkha Rifles) 15-33; William Wyse Student, Univ. of Cambridge 34-37; Prof. of English, Keio Univ., Tokyo 38-42; Talks Producer, B.B.C. Eastern Service 43, Head of B.B.C. Far Eastern Service 44-52; Controller, B.B.C. Third Programme Dec. 52-58; mem. Mount Everest Expeditions 22 and 36; Murchison Memorial Award, Royal Geographical Society, for explorations in Central Asia 29.
Publs. *Living with Lepchas* 38, *Traveller from Tokyo* 43, *The Phoenix Cup* 47, *From the Third Programme* (Editor) 56, *Hired to Kill* 60, *A Winter in Nepal* 63, *Eating the Indian Air* 68.
12 Clive House, 5 Connaught Place, London, W.2, England.
Telephone: 01-262-8628.

Morris, Sir Philip Robert, K.C.M.G., C.B.E., M.A., LL.D.; British educationist; b. 6 July 1901; ed. Tonbridge School, St. Peter's, York, and Trinity Coll., Oxford.
Lecturer in History and Classics Westminster Training Coll. 23-25; Admin. officer Kent Education Cttee., Asst. Dir. 32, Dir. 38-44; Educational Adviser H.M. Prisons 38-44; Dir.-Gen. of Army Education 44-46; Vice-Chancellor Univ. of Bristol 46-66; Vice-Chair. British Council 46-59; Chair. Secondary School Exams. Council 48-51; National Advisory Council on Training and Supply of Teachers 47-59; Life Trustee Carnegie U.K. Trust; Chair. B.B.C. West Regional Advisory Council 47-52, Vice-Chair. 61-; Gov. of B.B.C. 52-60 (Vice-Chair. 54-60); Chair. Management Cttee. Theatre Royal Bristol 46-63, Cttee. of Vice-Chancellors and Principals of the Univs. of the United Kingdom 55-58, Bristol Old Vic Trust Ltd. 63-; mem. Exec. Council Asscn.

of Commonwealth Univs., Vice-Chair. 51-55; Pres. Library Asscn. 55; Vice-Chair. United Bristol Hospital Board 48-66; Chair. Commonwealth Educ. Conf. 59, Commonwealth Educ. Liaison Cttee. 59-62; Hon. F.R.C.S., Hon. A.R.C.V.S.
Tanglewood, Townsend, Lower Almondsbury, Bristol, England.
Telephone: Almondsbury 2392.

Morris, Willie, B.A., M.A.; American editor and writer; b. 29 Nov. 1934; ed. Yazoo City High School, Mississippi, Univ. of Texas and New College, Oxford.
Editor-in-Chief *The Texas Observer* 60-62; Executive Editor *Harper's Magazine* 65-67, Editor-in-Chief 67-; Rhodes Scholarship 56; Houghton-Mifflin Literary Fellowship Award 67.
Publs. *The South Today, 100 Years After Appomatox* (Editor) 66, *North Toward Home* 67.
Harper's Magazine, 2 Park Avenue, New York City, N.Y., U.S.A.

Morris of Borth-y-Gest, Baron, cr. 59 (Life Peer); **John William Morris,** P.C., C.B.E., M.C., D.L., LL.D.; British judge; b. 11 Sept. 1896; ed. Liverpool Inst., Trinity Hall, Cambridge and Harvard Law School, U.S.A.
Called to the Bar 21; K.C. 35; Judge of Appeal, Isle of Man 38-45; Chair. Caernarvonshire Quarter Sessions; Judge of the High Court, King's Bench Div. 45-51; a Lord Justice of Appeal 51-60; Lord of Appeal in Ordinary 60-; hon. mem. Canadian and American Bar Asscns.; Pro-Chancellor, Univ. of Wales 56-.
Bryn Guallt, Portmadoc, North Wales.

Morrison-Scott, Sir Terence Charles Stuart, Kt., D.S.C., D.SC.; British museum director; b. 24 Oct. 1908; ed. Eton Coll., Christ Church, Oxford, and Royal Coll. of Science.
Assistant Master, Eton Coll. 35; joined staff British Museum (Natural History) 36; served World War II; Dir. Science Museum 56-60, British Museum (Natural History) 60-; Treas. Zoological Society of London 50-; Fellow Linnean Soc.; Gov. Imperial Coll. of Science and Technology.
Publs. *Checklist of Palaearctic and Indian Mammals* (with J. R. Ellerman) 51, *Southern African Mammals: A Reclassification* (with J. R. Ellerman and R. W. Hayman) 53.
British Museum (Natural History), London, S.W.7; Upperfold House, Fernhurst, Haslemere, Surrey, England.

Mors, Dr. Walter B., Brazilian chemist; b. 23 Nov. 1920; ed. Universidade de São Paulo.
Research Chemist, Northern Agricultural Inst., Belém 43-46; Research Chemist, Inst. of Agricultural Chemistry, Rio de Janeiro 47-62; Research Chemist, Inst. of Agricultural Technology, Ministry of Agriculture 63-, Dir. 66-; Prof. of Phytochemistry, Natural Products Research Center, Faculty of Pharmacy, Fed. Univ. of Rio de Janeiro (former Univ. of Brazil); mem. Brazilian Acad. of Sciences, Sec.-Gen. 65-; Sec. Brazilian Chemical Soc. 52-54.
Publs. include *Useful Plants of Brazil* (with Carlos Toledo Rizzini) 66.
Estrada de Jacarepaguá 6646, Rio de Janeiro ZC-89, Guanabara, Brazil.
Telephone: 92-0925.

Morse, David A., LITT.B., LL.B.; American lawyer; b. 31 May 1907; ed. Rutgers Univ. and Harvard Law School.
Admitted to N.J. Bar 32; U.S. Dept. of Interior, Solicitor's Staff 33-34; Chief Counsel, Petroleum Labour Policy Board 34-35; Special Asst. to U.S. Attorney-Gen. 34-35; Regional Attorney, Nat. Labour Relations Board 35-38; Partner, Law Firm of Coult, Satz, Tomlinson & Morse, Newark, N.J. 38-47; Lecturer on Labour

Relations, Labour Law and Administrative Law, various colls. and law schools 38-47; Dir. Labour Div., Allied Mil. Govt., Sicily and Italy 43-44; Dir. Manpower Div., U.S. Group Control Council (Germany) 44-45; Gen. Counsel Nat. Labour Relations Board, Washington 45-46; Asst. Sec. of Labour 46-47; Under-Sec. of Labour 47-48; Acting Sec. of Labour June-Aug. 48; fmr. U.S. Govt. mem. on the Governing Body of the I.L.O., and Govt. Del. to Int. Labour Confs.; Dir.-Gen. I.L.O. Sept. 48-; Dir. Franklin D. Roosevelt Foundation. Gustav Pollak Lecturer on Research in Govt., Harvard Univ. 55-56; Hon. LL.D. (Rutgers, Geneva). International Labour Office, Geneva, Switzerland. Telephone: Geneva 32-62-00.

Morse, Wayne Lyman, PH.B., M.A., LL.B., J.D.; American lawyer; b. 20 Oct. 1900; ed. Wisconsin, Minnesota and Columbia Univs. Instr. Wisconsin Univ. 24; Asst. Prof. Minnesota Univ. 24-28; Teaching Fellow, Columbia Univ. 28-29; Asst. Prof. of Law, Oregon Univ. 29-30, Associate Prof. 30-31, Dean and Prof. 31-44; Admin. Dir. U.S. Attorney-General's Survey of Release Procedures; Special Asst. to Attorney-Gen. 37; mem. Oregon State Crime Comm., etc.; Pacific Coast Arbitrator of Maritime Disputes 38-42; Chair. Pres. Railway Emergency Board 41; mem. War Labor Board 42-44; Senator from Oregon 45-; Democrat. Publs. *A Survey of the Grand Jury System* 31, *The Administration of Criminal Justice in Oregon* (with Ronald Beattie) 32, *Attorney-General's Survey of Release Procedures* 39. 417 Senate Office Building, Washington, D.C.; and 595 Crest Drive, Eugene, Ore., U.S.A.

Mortimer, Charles G.; American business executive; b. 26 July 1900; ed. East Orange High School and Stevens Inst. of Technology. Nat. Aniline & Chemical Co. 19-21, R. B. Davis Co. 21-24, Geo. Batten Co. 24-28; with Gen. Foods Corpn. 28-65, various marketing and operating positions 28-43; Vice-Pres. 43-52, Dir. 50-, Exec. Vice-Pres. 52-54, Pres. and Chief Exec. Officer 54-59, Chair. 59-65, Chief Exec. 59-65, Chair. Exec. Cttee. of the Board of Dirs. 65-; active in several areas of public service; Dir. First Nat. City Bank of N.Y., Ford Motor Co., Mobil Oil Corpn., The Second Federal Street Fund Inc., Boston, Bell and Howell Co.; Trustee, The Presbyterian Hospital of N.Y.C., Stevens Inst. of Technology, World Rehabilitation Fund, U.S. Churchill Foundation; hon. degrees Stevens Inst. of Technology, Hamilton Coll., Long Island and Jacksonville Univs.; Parlin Memorial Award 59. 17 Platt Place, White Plains, N.Y., U.S.A.

Mortimer, Raymond, C.B.E.; British writer; b. 25 April 1895; ed. Malvern and Balliol Coll., Oxford. Literary critic on the *Sunday Times*; Chevalier Légion d'Honneur. Publs. *Channel Packet* 42, *Manet's Bar aux Folies-Bergères* 44, *Duncan Grant* 44. 5 Canonbury Place, London, N.1, England.

Mortimer, Rt. Rev. Robert Cecil, D.D.; British ecclesiastic; b. 6 Dec. 1902; ed. Keble Coll., Oxford. Curate, St. Mary Redcliffe Bristol 26-29; Student and Tutor Christ Church Oxford 30-44; Regius Prof. of Moral and Pastoral Theology and Canon of Christ Church 44-49; Chancellor of Diocese of Blackburn 48-49; Bishop of Exeter 49-. Publs. *The Elements of Moral Theology, The Origins of Private Penance, Christian Ethics, The Duties of a Churchman, Western Canon Law.* The Palace, Exeter, Devon, England. Telephone: Exeter 72362.

Morton, Henry Vollam, F.R.S.L.; British author and journalist. Assistant Editor *Birmingham Express* 12; Sub-Editor

Daily Mail 13-14; mem. staff *Evening Standard* 19-21 and *Daily Express* 21-31; Special writer *Daily Herald* 31-40; Kt. Commdr. Order of Phoenix (Greece), Cavaliere Ufficiale, Ordine al Merito (Italy). Publs. include: *The Heart of London* 25, *In Search of England* 27, *In Search of Scotland* 29, *Blue Days at Sea* 32, *Scotland Again* 33, *In the Steps of the Master* 34, *In the Steps of St. Paul* 36, *Guide to London* 37, *Through the Lands of the Bible* 38, *Ghosts of London* 39, *Middle East* 41, *I Saw Two Englands* 42, *Atlantic Meeting* 43, *In Search of South Africa* 48, *In Search of London* 51, *In the Steps of Jesus* 54, *A Stranger in Spain* 55, *A Traveller in Rome* 57, *This is Rome* 60, *This is the Holy Land* 61, *A Traveller in Italy* 64, *The Waters of Rome* 66 (entitled *The Fountains of Rome* in America). Schapenberg, Somerset West, Cape Province, Republic of South Africa. Telephone: Somerset West 21203.

Morton, John C. A. B. M., C.B.E.; British journalist; b. 7 June 1893; ed. Harrow and Oxford. "Beachcomber" of the *Daily Express* 24-. Publs. include: *The Barber of Putney* 19, *Tally-Ho!* 22, *Mr. Thake* 29, *By the Way* 31, *Maladetta* 32, *Sobieski: King of Poland* 32, *St. Martin of Tours* 32, *Hag's Harvest* 33, *Morton's Folly* 33, *The Death of the Dragon* 34, *Skylighters* 34, *Vagabond* 35, *Stuff and Nonsense* 35, *The Bastille Falls* (Studies of French Revolution) 36, *The Dauphin* 37, *A Diet of Thistles* 38, *A Bonfire of Weeds* 39, *Saint-Just* 39, *I Do Not Think So* 40, *Fool's Paradise* 41, *Captain Foulenough and Company* 44, *The Gascon* 46, *The Tibetan Venus* 51, *Camille Desmoulins* 51, *Hilaire Belloc: A Memoir* 55, *Springtime: Tales of the Café Rieu* 56, *Marshal Ney* 58, *Merry-go-Round* 58, *The Best of Beachcomber* 63. Melleray, Sea Lane, Ferring, Sussex, England.

Morton, Thruston Ballard, A.B.; American politician; b. 19 Aug. 1907; ed. Yale Univ. Entered Ballard and Ballard Co. 29, and Pres. 46; fmr. Pres. of the Goodwill Industries of Kentucky, Inc.; served with U.S. Navy 41-45; mem. of U.S. Congress (Repub.) 46-52; managed the campaign of John Sherman Cooper 52; Asst. Sec. of State for Congressional Relations 53-56; U.S. Senator from Kentucky 57-; Chair. Republican Nat. Cttee. 59-61; Chair. Republican Senatorial Campaign 63. 437 Senate Office Building, Washington, D.C.; and 1415 Willow Avenue, Louisville, Kentucky, U.S.A.

Moruzzi, Giuseppe, M.D.; Italian physiologist; b. 30 July 1910; ed. Univ. of Parma. Assistant Prof., Dept. of Physiology, Univ. of Parma 33-36, Univ. of Bologna 36-42; Acting Prof. of Physiology, Univ. of Siena 42-43, Univ. of Parma 45-47; Prof. of Physiology, Univ. of Ferrara 47-48; Prof. of Physiology and Head of Inst. of Physiology, Univ. of Pisa 48-; Fellow, Rockefeller Foundation, Brussels 37-38, Cambridge Univ. 38-39; Visiting Prof., Northwestern Univ. 48-49; Hon. mem. American Physiological Soc., American Acad. of Arts and Sciences, American Neurological Asscn., E.E.G. Soc.; Foreign mem. American Philosophical Soc., Norske Videnskaps Akademi (Oslo), mem. Accad. Naz. dei Lincei; many hon. degrees. Publs. *L'epilessia sperimentale* 46 (French 50), *Problems in Cerebellar Physiology* 50, *The Physiology and Pathology of the Cerebellum* (with R. S. Dow) 58. Via S. Zeno 31, Pisa, Italy. Telephone: 23214.

Mosby, Håkon, DR. PHIL.; Norwegian university professor; b. 10 July 1903; ed. Univ. of Oslo. Assistant to Prof. Nansen, Univ. of Oslo 23; Amanuensis, Geofysisk Institutt, Bergen 27; Prof. of Physical Oceanography, Bergen Museum 47, Univ. of Bergen 48; Dir. of Geophysical Inst. 48-58, 63-; Dean of Faculty of Sciences, Univ. of Bergen 54-59, Rector 66-; Pres. Int. Asscn. of Physical Oceanography of the Int. Union of Geodesy and Geophysics 54-60; Chair. Norwegian Geophysical Comm. 48-58, 66-; Pres. NATO sub-cttee. on Oceanographic Research 60-65; mem. NATO Science Cttee. 65-; mem. Acad. of Sciences Oslo, Bergen, Gothenburg, Helsinki.

Geofysisk Institutt, Universitetet, Bergen, Norway.

Moscoso, Teodoro, B.S.; American diplomatist; b. 26 Nov. 1910; ed. Michigan Univ.
President Puerto Rican-American Drug Co. Inc. 36-39; Vice-Chair., Exec. Dir., Ponce (Puerto Rico) Housing Authority 38-42; Pres., Gen. Man., Puerto Rico Industrial Development Co. 42-50; Administrator, Econ. Development Admin., Puerto Rico 50-60; Ambassador to Venezuela 61; U.S. Co-ordinator, Alliance for Progress Dept. of State, Agency for Int. Development 61-64; Special Adviser to Asst. Sec. of State for Inter-American Affairs 64-.
c/o Department of State, Washington, D.C., U.S.A.

Moseley, Spencer Dumaresq, B.A., D.F.C.; American business executive; b. 21 Oct. 1919; ed. The Hill School, Cheshire Acad. and Yale Univ.
Assistant to Pres., Gen. American Transportation Corpn. 53-61, Dir. 55-, Pres. 61-67; Dir. Cherry Burrell Corpn., Container Corpn. of America, Archer Daniels Midland Co.; official of civic and educational orgs.
General American Transportation Corporation, 135 South La Salle Street, Chicago 3, Illinois, U.S.A.
Telephone: FI6-4100.

Moser, Hans Joachim, PH.D.; German musician; b. 25 May 1889; ed. Marburg, Berlin, Leipzig and Rostock Univs.
Lecturer in Music History and Theory Halle Univ. 19; Prof. Heidelberg Univ. 25 and Berlin Univ. since 27; Dir. State Acad. for Church and School Music Berlin and mem. Senate Acad. of Arts until 34; Playwright with Reichsstelle für Musikbearbeitungen 40-45; Lecturer in Music Reinickendorf Conservatoire 45-47; Prof. at Univ. of Jena and Musikhochschule Weimar 47; Dir. Conservatoire of Berlin 49-61.
Publs. *Geschichte der deutschen Musik* 20, *Die evangelische Kirchenmusik* 25, *Paul Hofhaimer* 29, *Die mehrstimmige Vertonung des Evangeliums* 31, *Musiklexikon* 33, 42, 51, 55, Suppl. 63, *Lehrbuch der Musikgeschichte* 34, *J. S. Bach* 35, *Luther* 36, 63, *Tönende Volksaltertümer* 35, *H. Schütz* 36, 54, *Die verborgene Symphonie* 36, *Ersungenes Traumland* 37, *Das deutsche Lied seit Mozart* 37, 65, *Musikfibel* 37, *Kleine deutsche Musikgeschichte* 38, *Kleines H. Schützbuch* 40, *Händel* 40, *C. M. von Weber* 40, *Goethe und die Musik* 49, *Bernhard Ziehn* 50, *Lebensvolle Musikerziehung* 52, *Musikgeschichte in 100 Lebensbildern* 52, *Musikaesthetik* 53, *Geschichte deutscher Tondenkmäler* 53, *Evangelische Kirchenmusik in Deutschland* 54, *Harmonielehre* I 54, II 64, *Die Musik der deutschen Stämme* 56, *Deutsches Sololied und Ballade, Buxtehude* 57, *Tonsprachen des Abendlandes* 58, *Musik in Zeit und Raum* 60, *Orgelromantik* 61, *Protestantenmusik in der Schule* 61, *Die Harfe mit 13 Saiten* 61, *Methodik der Musikgeschichtsforschung* 65, *Wartet noch des erscheinens, Liederbuch van Schöffer u. Apiarius van 1534* 65, *Deutsche Liedlein* 67.
Hessenallee 12, 1 Berlin 19, Germany.

Moses, Arthur; Brazilian biologist; b. 2 June 1886; ed. Rio de Janeiro Coll. and Univ.
Assistant, Oswaldo Cruz Inst. 09-17; Chief Veterinary Research Laboratory, Bureau of Animal Industry 17-21; Dir. Inst. for Experimental Veterinary Science 21-33; Asst. Chief Pathological Section, Inst. Animal Biology; Asst. Prof. Univ. of Brazil 12; Chair. Biological Cttee. of Nat. Research Council; Pres. Brazilian Acad. of Sciences 33, 41, 51-65, Nat. Research Council; mem. Nat. Cttee. Space Activities; now engaged on diagnosis and research work in private laboratory; Kuemmel

Prize, Hamburg Univ., German Red Cross medal, Légion d'Honneur.
Publs. *Dos metodos biologicos de diagnostico na cisticercose* 11, *O virus do mixoma dos coelhos* 11, *Sobre nova micose humana causada por cogumelo nao descrito proteomyces infestans* 13, *Fixação de complemento na blastomicose* 16, *Estudos sobre anafilaxia: Da anafilatoxina* 16, *Infectious Rabbit Myxomatosis, A review of recent observations* 39, *Especificidade antigenica e imunoquimica* 40.
Rua, Muniz Barreto 54, Rio de Janeiro, Brazil.

Moses, Sir Charles Joseph Alfred, Kt., C.B.E.; Australian broadcasting official; b. England 21 Jan. 1900; ed. Oswestry Grammar School, and Royal Mil. Coll., Sandhurst.
Lieut. in 2nd Border Regt. (British Regular Army) 18-22; fruit-grower, Bendigo, Australia 23-24; motor salesman and sales manager 24-30; announcer, Nat. Broadcasting Service 30-32; N.S.W. Sporting and Talks Ed., Australian Broadcasting Comm. 33-34; Fed. Talks Controller, A.B.C. 35; Gen. Man. A.B.C. 35-65; Sec.-Gen. Asian Broadcasting Union 65-; joined A.I.F. 40; rose to rank of Lt.-Col. 42; served in Malaya Feb. 41-Feb. 42, New Guinea Sept. 42-Feb. 43; mentioned in despatches Sept. 43; Commdr., Order of Merit (Austria); Dir. Australian Elizabethan Theatre Trust; Vice-Pres. Royal Agricultural Soc.; Pres. Amateur Athletic Asscn. of N.S.W.; Pres. Austrian-Australian Cultural Soc.; mem. Sydney Opera House Trust, etc.
Home: 78 Neco Beach Road, Darling Point, Sydney; Office: c/o Asian Broadcasting Union, 203 Castlereagh Street, Sydney, N.S.W., Australia.
Telephone: 617406 (Office); 324224 (Home).

Moses, David Gnanapragasam, M.A., PH.D.; Indian philosopher; b. 22 Jan. 1902; ed. Madras Christian Coll. Madras Univ., Union Theological Seminary, Columbia Univ.
Philosophy Lecturer, Noble Coll., Madras Univ. 24-26; Prof. Hislop Coll., Nagpur 26-40, Principal 40-, Dean, Faculty of Arts 58-61; Vice-Pres., Int. Missionary Council 47-61; Pres. Nat. Christian Council of India 59-63; mem. Presidium, World Council of Churches 61-. Publ. *Religious Truth and the Relation Between Religions.*
Hislop College, Nagpur, India.

Moses, Robert, B.A., M.A., PH.D.; American public official; b. 18 Dec. 1888; ed. Yale, Oxford and Columbia Univs.
Municipal Investigator, New York City 13; Chief of Staff, N.Y. State Reconstruction Comm. 19-21; Sec. N.Y. State Asscn. 21-26; Pres. L.I. State Park Comm. and Chair. State Council of Parks 24-63; Sec. of State, New York 27-28; Chair. Jones Beach State Parkway Authority and Bethpage Park Authority 33-63; Republican Candidate for Gov. of New York 34; New York City Park Commr. to consolidate City Park and Parkway system 34-60; sole mem. Henry Hudson Parkway Authority and Marine Parkway Authority 34-38, absorbed by New York City Parkway Authority 38; Chair. Triborough Bridge Authority 36; mem. New York City Planning Comm. 42-60; Chief Exec. Officer, New York City Tunnel Authority 45-46; Chair. Consolidated Triborough Bridge and New York City Tunnel Authority 46-68; New York City Construction Co-ordinator 46-60; Chair. Power Authority, State of N.Y. 54-63; Pres. New York World's Fair 1964-1965 Corpn. 60-68; Dir. Lincoln Center for Performing Arts 60-; mem. Nat. Cttee. for Immigration Reform 65; Lifetime mem. of New York Building Congress 66; Consultant and official on numerous urban reconstruction schemes; numerous awards and hon. degrees.
Office: Randall's Island, New York, N.Y. 10035; Homes: One Gracie Terrace, New York 10028; and Oak Beach, L.I., N.Y., U.S.A.

Moses, Siegfried, DR. JUR.; Israeli civil servant (retd.); b. 3 May 1887; ed. Univ. of Berlin.
Began law practice 12; organised food control, Danzig, during First World War; later Dep. Managing Dir. Deutscher Städtetag (organisation of German towns); Chair. Reichsstelle für Schuh-Versorgung (Controller of Footwear Supply); law practice 20-36; auditor 32-36; Dir. Schocken concern (chain stores) 23-29, mem. Board 30, Chair. 35; emigrated 36; Managing Dir. Haavara (organisation for transfer of Jewish property from Germany to Palestine) 37; expert on tax problems 41-49; Public Auditor, Tel-Aviv 38-49; State Comptroller of Israel 49-61; Pres. Zionist Organisation for Germany 33-37; Pres. Council of Jews from Germany and Leo Baeck Inst. for the history of Jews from Germany.
Publs. *Deutsches Kohlen-Wirtschaftsgesetz* 20, *Reform des Obligationen-Wesens* 33, *The Income Tax Ordinance of Palestine* 42, *Jewish Post-War Claims* 43, etc.
9 Shlomoh Molcho Street, Jerusalem, Israel.
Telephone: 33154.

Mosher, Samuel Barlow; American oil company executive; b. 1892; ed. Univ. of California.
Chairman Signal Oil and Gas Co.; mem. Nat. Petroleum War Council 40-47.
1010 Wilshire Boulevard, Los Angeles; and 5257 Austin Road, Santa Barbara, California 93105, U.S.A.

Moskalenko, Marshal Kiril Semyonovich; Soviet army officer; b. 02; ed. Dzerzhinski Artillery Academy.
Joined Soviet Army 20; Commdr. Rifle Corps, Voronezh Front 43; Commdr. 38th Army Group Kursk-Orel, commanded Dnieper battle 43-44; captured Vinnitsa and Zhmerinka 44; served Carpathia and Czechoslovakia 44-45; Commdr. Moscow Mil. District Anti-Aircraft Defence 45-53; Mil. Commdr., Moscow Mil. Region 53-60; Deputy Minister of Defence and C.-in-C. of Rocket Forces 60-62; Chief Insp., Ministry of Defence, Deputy Minister of Defence 62-; mem. Central Cttee. of C.P.S.U.; Deputy to U.S.S.R. Supreme Soviet; Hero of Soviet Union, Orders of Lenin (four times), October Revolution, Red Banner (five times), Suvorov (twice), Kutuzov (twice), and other awards.
Ministry of Defence, 34 Maurice Thorez Embankment, Moscow, U.S.S.R.

Moskalev, Vasily Nikitovich; Soviet trade union official; b. 09; ed. Higher Party School.
Worker in plant and Govt. Orgs. 24-41; Red Army 41-46; C.P.S.U. work 46-60, Instructor of Dept., Cen. Cttee. of C.P.S.U. 55-60; Chair. Cen. Cttee. of Trade Union of Local Industry and Public Services Workers 60-; mem. C.P.S.U. 32-; Order of Red Banner of Labour, etc.
Central Committee of the Trade Union of Local Industry and Public Services Workers, 42 Leninsky Prospekt, Moscow, U.S.S.R.

Moskovsky, Vasili Petrovich; Soviet journalist, politician and diplomatist; b. 04; ed. Lenin Military and Political Acad.
Member C.P.S.U. 28-; Soviet army service 27-53, 54-55; Editor Mil. Area Newspapers 39-41, of Army and Front Newspapers 41-45; Deputy Editor, then Editor, Soviet Army Newspaper *Krasnaya Zvezda* (Red Star) 45-53, 54-55; Apparatus Cen. Cttee. C.P.S.U. 53-54, 55-60; Dep. Chair. Council of Ministers R.S.F.S.R. 60-62; Ambassador to Korean People's Democratic Republic 62-65; Editor-in-Chief *Sovietskaya Rossiya* 65-; mem. Central Auditing Comm. of C.P.S.U. 52-.
Sovietskaya Rossiya, 24 ulitsa Pravdy, Moscow, U.S.S.R.

Moskwa, Zygmunt; Polish engineer and politician; b. 26 April 1908; ed. Warsaw Polytechnic School.
Member Democratic Party 45-; mem. Presidency of Cen. Cttee. Democratic Party 49-; Minister of Small

Industries and Handicrafts 56-58, of Posts and Telecommunications 58-.
Ministry of Posts and Telecommunications, Pl. Malachowskiego 2, Warsaw, Poland.
Telephone: 26-61-56.

Mosley, Sir Oswald Ernald, Bt.; British politician; b. 16 Nov. 1896; ed. Winchester and Sandhurst.
Conservative M.P. for Harrow 18-22; Independent M.P. 22-24; joined Labour Party 24; Labour M.P. for Smethwick 26-31; Chancellor of Duchy of Lancaster in Second Labour Govt. 29-30, when he resigned on question of unemployment policy; formed New Party 31; New Party Candidate for Stoke at General Election and was defeated; leader of British Fascist movement 32-40, when it was dissolved; detained under Defence Regulations 40, released 43; entered publishing business 46; founded Union Movement 48-.
Publs. *The Greater Britain* 32, *My Answer* 46, *The Alternative* 47, *Europe: Faith and Plan* 58, *300 Questions Answered* 61.
1 rue des Lacs, Orsay, Seine-et-Oise, France; 5 Lowndes Court, Lowndes Square, London, S.W.1, England.

Mosquera-Chaux, Victor, LL.D.; Colombian lawyer, politician and diplomatist; b. 1 Oct. 1919; ed. Seminario Conciliar de Popayán, Univ. del Cauca, Univ. de Leyes de Santiago, Chile.
Principal Deputy to Departmental Assembly of Cauca 42-47; Principal mem. Liberal Directorate, Cauca 42-60; M.P. for Cauca 47-49, 49-51; Senator of Republic for Cauca 58-62, 62-66, 66-70; Gov. Dept. of Cauca (Colombia) 59-60; Dir. Liberal Party, Cauca 60-62; Pres. Exec. Cttee. Nat. Liberal Party 60-62; Principal mem. Nat. Liberal Directorate 62-67; Amb. of Colombia to U.K. 67-.
Flat 3a, 3 Hans Crescent, London S.W.1., England; Calle 4a, P.O.-83, Popayán, Colombia.

Moss, Frank Edward, A.B., D.IUR.; American lawyer and politician; b. 23 Sept. 1911; ed. Utah and George Washington Univs.
Mem. legal staff, Securities and Exchange Comm., Washington 37-39; Law Clerk to Justice James H. Wolfe of Utah State Supreme Court 39; Judge, Salt Lake City Court 40-50; attached to U.S. Army Air Force Judge Advocate's Department during Second World War; Salt Lake County Attorney 50-58; Senator from Utah 58-; mem. Interior and Insular Affairs, Public Works, Nat. Water Resources and Small Business Senate Cttees.; fmr. Pres. Utah State Asscn. of County Officials, Nat. Asscn. of County and Prosecuting Attorneys; fmr. Dir. Utah U.N. Asscn.; Democrat.
Senate Office Building, Washington, D.C., U.S.A.

Mössbauer, Rudolf, PH.D.; German physicist; b. 31 Jan. 1929; ed. Technische Hochschule, Munich.
Research Asst. Max-Planck Inst., Heidelberg 55-57; Research Fellow, Technische Hochschule, Munich 58-60; Research Fellow, California Inst. of Technology 60, Senior Research Fellow 61, Prof. of Physics Dec. 61; Prof. of Physics Tech. Univ. of Munich 64-; Research Corpn. Award 60, Röntgen Prize, Univ. of Giessen 61, Elliot Cresson Medal of Franklin Inst., Philadelphia 61, Nobel Prize for Physics 61.
Publs. Papers on Recoilless Nuclear Resonance Absorption.
Department of Physics, California Institute of Technology, Pasadena, Calif., U.S.A. (March-May); and Physik Department, Technische Universität, Munich, Germany (June-Feb.).

Mossé, Robert; French economist; b. 20 Dec. 1906; ed. Univ. de Lyon and Paris à la Sorbonne.
Professor of Econs. (Int. Financial Relations), Univ. de Grenoble 35-; Labour arbitrator 36-38; Prof. New School for Social Research, New York 42-46; sometime

Prof. at Univs. of Washington and Illinois 42-44; Asst. Financial Attaché of French Republic, Washington, D.C. 44; French Del. to Bretton Woods, Econ. Officer, UN 46-48; Gen. Sec. European Communal Credit Community, Turin 57-67; specialist, Council of Europe and European Econ. Community 63-; Editor *Bilans de la Connaissance économique*, Paris 49-; mem. French UNESCO Cttee., Council Int. Econ. Asscn.; Officier Légion d'Honneur, Officier Palmes Académiques, Cavaliere della Repubblica Italiana; Hon. Dr. (Lisbon). Publs. *L'Economie collectiviste* 39, *Economie et Législation industrielle* 40, *Le système international de Bretton Woods* 48, *La Monnaie* 50, *Les Salaires* 53, *Bibliographie d'économie politique* 46-65 (with 2 supplements), *Problèmes monétaires internationales* 67, *L'Economie socialiste* 68, *Introduction à l'Economie* 68.
12 avenue Rochambeau, 38 Grenoble, France.
Telephone: 96-06-42.

Mostel, Zero (Sam Mostel), B.A.; American actor and painter; b. 28 Feb. 1915; ed. Coll. of the City of New York.
Artist W.P.A. Project 37-39; taught painting at Progressive Art Center; lecturer Museum of Modern Art, Frick Museum, Metropolitan Museum; started acting 42; appeared in several films, incl. *Dubarry was a Lady, Panic in the Streets, The Enforcer, Monsieur Lecoq*, etc.; theatre appearances on and off Broadway and also in Europe; *Beggar's Holiday* 46, *Good as Gold, Flight into Egypt, Ulysses in Nighttown, A Funny Thing Happened on the Way to the Forum* 61, *Fiddler on the Roof* 65; award for best male actor, Paris Festival 59; Antoinette Perry (Tony) Award Best Actor 62.
c/o Alvin Theatre, W. 52nd Street, New York City, N.Y., U.S.A.

Motherwell, Robert, A.B.; American painter; b. 24 Jan. 1915; ed. Stanford, Harvard, Grenoble and Columbia Univs.
A founder in New York of Abstract Expressionism (Tachisme); One-Man Shows Guggenheim Gallery 44, Kootz Gallery 46, 48, 49, 52, Janis Gallery 57, 59, 61, 62, Museum of Modern Art 65 (all New York), San Francisco Museum 47, Chicago Arts Club 47, Oberlin Coll. 53, Bennington Coll. 59, Berggruen Gallery, Paris 61, Odyssia Gallery, Rome 62, Der Spiegel Gallery, Cologne 62, The Phillips Collection, Washington 65; work has been exhibited at Tate Gallery (London), New York, Paris and Madrid Museums of Modern Art and at Brussels, Moscow, Venice, São Paulo, Amsterdam, West Berlin, Kassel and elsewhere; works in U.S. Pavilion, Venice 50, São Paulo 53, Brussels 58, Moscow 59, São Paulo 61.
173 East 94th Street, New York City 28, N.Y., U.S.A.

Mothes, Kurt, D.PHIL.; German plant biochemist; b. 3 Nov. 1900; ed. Univ. of Leipzig and Martin Luther Universität, Halle-Wittenberg.
Dozent in Botany and Pharmacognosy, Univ. of Halle 23-35; Prof. of Botany and Pharmacognosy, and Dir. of Botanical Inst., Univ. of Königsberg 35-45; Head, Dept. of Chemical Physiology, Inst. für Kulturpflanzenforschung, Gatersleben 49-57; Dir. Botanical Inst., Univ. of Halle 58-; Dir. of Botanical Studies, Univ. of Halle; Dir. of Plant Biochemistry Inst. of Acad. of Sciences, Berlin, at Halle; Prof. of Plant Biochemistry, Univ. of Halle; Pres. Deutsche Akademie der Naturforscher Leopoldina; Nat. Prize 53; Honoured People's Scientist; mem. numerous Acads.; Dr. med. h.c. (Halle), Dr. agr. h.c. (Kiel), Dr. phil. h.c. (Vienna), Dr. rer. nat. h.c. (Halle); Cothenius Medal (Leopoldina Acad.), Pazmany Medal (Univ. of Budapest), Gregor-Mendel Medal (Czech Acad. of Sciences), Otto Warburg Medal (Soc. for Physiological Chemistry), Carl-Mannich Medal (German Pharmaceutical Soc.), Hoest-Madsen Medal (Fed. Int. Pharm.).

Publs. *Stickstoff-Stoffwechsel, Physiologie und Biochemie der Alkaloide, Stoffregulation (Kinin)*.
Halle/Saale, Weinbergweg, German Democratic Republic.
Telephone: 38381.

Mott, Charles Stewart, M.E., E.D., LL.D.; American industrialist; b. 2 June 1875; ed. Stevens Inst. of Technology, Hoboken, N.J., Denmark and Germany.
Pres. and Gen. Manager Weston-Mott Co. 03-13; Pres. Union Industrial Trust and Savings Bank, Flint 09; Mayor of Flint (Michigan) 12, 13, 18; Dir. Gen. Motors Corpn. 13-; mem. Finance Cttee. 29-37, Audit Cttee. 41-, Vice-Pres. 16-37; Trustee Stevens Inst. of Technology 38-; mem. Advisory Council on Naval Affairs, Army Advisory Cttee. 47; Pres. Northern Illinois Water Co.; Dir. St. Louis County Water Co.; Long Island Water Co., Wayne Oakland Bank, U.S. Sugar Corpn.
1400 East Kearsley Street, Flint 3, Michigan, U.S.A.

Mott, Sir Nevill Francis, Kt., M.A., D.SC., F.R.S.; British physicist; b. 30 Sept. 1905; ed. Clifton Coll. and St. John's Coll., Cambridge.
Lecturer, Manchester Univ. 29-30; Fellow and Lecturer, Gonville and Caius Coll., Cambridge 30-33; Melville Wills Prof. of Theoretical Physics, Bristol Univ. 33-48; Dir. H. H. Wills Physics Laboratory and H. O. Wills Prof. of Physics, Bristol Univ. 48-54; Cavendish Prof. of Experimental Physics, Univ. of Cambridge 54-; Pres. Int. Union of Physics 51-57; mem. Inst. for Strategic Studies; Master, Gonville and Caius Coll., Cambridge 59-66; Hon. D.Sc. (London).
Publs. *An Outline of Wave Mechanics* 30, *The Theory of Atomic Collisions* (with H. S. W. Massey) 33, *The Theory of the Properties of Metals and Alloys* (with H. Jones) 36, *Electronic Processes in Ionic Crystals* (with R. W. Gurney) 40, *Wave Mechanics and its Applications* (with I. N. Sneddon) 48, *Elements of Wave Mechanics* 52, *Atomic Structure and the Strength of Metals* 56.
The Cavendish Laboratory, Cambridge, England.

Mottram, Ralph Hale, J.P., F.R.S.L.; British author; b. 30 Oct. 1883; ed. Norwich and Lausanne.
Barclay's Bank 00-27; Lieut. Norfolk Regiment, Flanders, First World War.
Publs. include: *The Spanish Farm* 24 (awarded Hawthornden Prize), *Sixty-Four, Ninety-Four* 25, *The Crime at Vanderlyndens* 26, *Our Mr. Dormer* 26, *The English Miss* 28, *The Boroughmonger* 29, *Europa's Beast* 30, *Castle Island* 31, *Home for the Holidays* 32, *Dazzle* 32, *The Lame Dog* 33, *Bumphrey's* 34, *Early Morning* 35, *Flower Pot End* 35, *Time to be Going* 37, *There was a Jolly Miller* 38, *You Can't Have It Back* 39, *Miss Lavington* 40, *The Ghost and the Maiden* 40, *The World Turns Slowly Round* 42, *The Corbells at War* 43, *Visit of the Princess* 45, *The Gentleman of Leisure* 48, *Come to the Bower* 49, *One Hundred and Twenty-eight Witnesses* 51, *The Part that is Missing* 52, *The Window Seat* 54, *Over the Wall* 55, *Scenes that are brightest* 56, *No one will ever know* 58, *Young Man's Fancy* 59, *Musetta* 60, *Time's Increase* 61, *To Hell, with Crabb Robinson* 62, *Happy Birds* 63, *Maggie Mackenzie* 65 (novels); *Ten Years Ago* 28, *The Headless Hound* 31 (essays); *Through the Menin Gate* 32, *Strawberry Time and the Banquet* 34 (stories); *A History of Financial Speculation* 29, *John Crome of Norwich* 31, *East Anglia* 33, *Journey to the Western Front* 36, *Portrait of an Unknown Victorian* 36, *Trader's Dream* 36, *Noah* 37, *Success to the Mayor* 38, *Old England* 38, *Autobiography with a Difference* 38, *Bowler Hat* 40, *Buxton the Liberator* 46, *The Glories of Norwich Cathedral* 47, *The Broads* 52, *If Stones could Speak* 53, *For Some we Loved; an intimate portrait of Ada and John Galsworthy* 56, *Another Window Seat* 57, *Vanities and Verities* 58.
4 Poplar Avenue, Eaton, Norwich, Norfolk, England.

Mouanza, Jonas; Congolese diplomatist; b. 2 Nov. 1926; ed. Teachers' Coll., Mouyondzi, and Teachers' Coll., Saint-Cloud, France.

Teacher, Pointe-Noire 48-50, Headmaster, schools at Pointe-Noire and Kinkala 50-60; Deputy School Insp., Boko 60-61; School Insp., Brazzaville 62-64; Perm. Rep. to UN 64-.

Permanent Mission of Congo (Brazzaville) to the United Nations, 444 Madison Avenue, New York, N.Y., U.S.A.

Moulins, Max; French government official; b. 2 Jan. 1914; ed. Faculty of Law, Paris.

Successively Sec.-Gen. of Hérault, Dep. Prefect of Aix-en-Provence, later of Cherbourg, Prefect of Rennes, Albi and Niort; Dir. of La Sûreté Nationale; Prefect of Haut-Rhin 55-58; Prefect, Regional Insp.-Gen. Algeria 59-60, Sec.-Gen. of Algeria 60-61; Sec.-Gen. Overseas Dept. 61-; Préfet de la Région Rhône-Alpes-Préfet du Rhône; Commdr. de la Légion d'Honneur, Croix de Guerre.

Préfecture du Rhône, Lyon, France.

Moulton, Alexander Eric, M.A., C.ENG., M.I.MECH.E., F.I.R.I., M.I.LOCO.E.; British engineer; b. 9 April 1920; ed. Marlborough Coll., King's Coll. Cambridge.

Worked in Engine Research Dept., Bristol Aeroplane Co. 39-44, Personal Asst. to Sir Roy Fedden 40-42; established Research Dept. of George Spencer, Moulton & Co. Ltd., originating work on rubber suspensions for vehicles and designing Flexitor, Works Man. then Tech. Dir. 45-56; formed Moulton Developments Ltd., development work on own designs of rubber suspensions for British Motor Corpn. including Hydroplastic 56, Chair. and Man. Dir. 56-67, Man. Dir. 67-; formed Moulton Bicycles Ltd. to produce own design Moulton Bicycle 62, Chair. and Man. Dir. 62-67, Dir. 67-; Dir. Moulton Consultants Ltd., Bicycle Consultants Ltd.; Design Centre Award 64, Amb. Award 64, Bidlake Memorial Plaque 64, Gold Medal Milan Triennale 64, Queens Award to Industry for Tech. Innovation (Moulton Developments Ltd.), Hon. Dr. Royal Coll. of Art.

Publs. Various papers on vehicle suspension.

The Hall, Bradford on Avon, Wiltshire, England.

Telephone: Bradford on Avon 2991.

Mountain, Sir Brian (Edward Stanley); British business executive; b. 22 Aug. 1899; ed. Charterhouse and Royal Military Coll., Sandhurst.

Army Service, First World War and Second World War; fmr. Gen. Manager Eagle Star Insurance Co. Ltd., now Chair.; numerous other directorships.

Eagle Star Insurance Co. Ltd., 1 Threadneedle Street, London, E.C.2, England.

Mountbatten of Burma, 1st Earl, cr. 47; **Admiral of the Fleet Louis (Francis Albert Victor Nicholas) Mountbatten,** K.G., P.C., O.M., G.C.B., G.C.S.I., G.C.I.E., G.C.V.O., D.S.O., F.R.S.; b. 25 June 1900; British naval officer and public servant; ed. Locker's Park, Osborne, Dartmouth, Christ's Coll., Cambridge.

Naval Cadet 13, Midshipman 16, Sub-Lieut. 18, Lieut. 20, Lieut.-Commdr. 28, Commdr. 32, Capt. 37, Commodore 41, Acting Vice-Admiral 41, Acting Admiral 43, substantive Rear-Admiral 46, Vice-Admiral 49, Admiral 53, Admiral of the Fleet 56; Col. of the Life Guards 65, Col.-Commdt. Royal Marines 65; served H.M.S. *Lion* 16, *Queen Elizabeth* 17, H.M. Submarine K6 18, H.M.S. P31 18, *Renown* 20, 21 (Prince of Wales tour to Australia and New Zealand 20, and India, Japan and the Far East 21), *Repulse* 21, *Revenge* 23; Signal School, Portsmouth 24, R.N. Coll., Greenwich 25; Asst. Fleet Wireless Signal Officer, Mediterranean Fleet 27-28, Senior Wireless Instr. 29-31; Fleet Wireless Officer 31-33; 2nd Destroyer Flotilla Signal and Wireless Officer 28-29; commanded

H.M.S. *Daring* 34, *Wishart* 35; Personal Naval A.D.C. to King Edward VIII 36, to King George VI 37-52; Capt. of *Kelly* and 5th Destroyer Flotilla 39-41; in command aircraft carrier *Illustrious* to Oct. 41; Adviser on Combined Operations 41-42, Chief of Combined Operations and mem. of Chiefs of Staff Cttee. 42-43; Supreme Allied Commdr. S.E. Asia 43-46; Viceroy of India March-Aug. 47; Gov.-Gen. of Dominion of India Aug. 47-June 48; Flag Officer Commanding First Cruiser Squadron, Mediterranean Fleet Oct. 48-50; 4th Sea Lord, and Chief of Supplies and Transport June 50-52; C.-in-C. Mediterranean 52-54; C.-in-C. Allied Forces, Mediterranean 53-54; First Sea Lord and Chief of Naval Staff 55-59; Chief of Defence Staff and Chair. Chiefs of Staff Cttee. 59-65; Gov. of Isle of Wight 65-; Chair. of Nat. Electronics Council; Personal A.D.C. to H.M. the Queen 53-; Legion of Merit and D.S.M. (U.S.A.); Grand Croix de la Légion d'Honneur and Croix de Guerre (France); Grand Cross of the Lion (Neths.), Grand Cross of Order of George I (Greece), Special Grand Cordon of the Cloud and Banner (China), Agga Maha Thiri Thudhamma (Burma), etc.; Hon. LL.D. (Cambridge, Leeds, Edinburgh, Southampton, London, Sussex), Hon. D.C.L. (Oxford), Hon. D.Sc. (Delhi and Patna); Hon. Lieut.-Gen., Hon. Air Marshal.

Broadlands, Romsey, Hants.; 2 Kinnerton Street, London, S.W.1; and Classiebawn Castle, Cliffoney, Co. Sligo, Ireland.

Telephone: 01-235-0081 (London) and Cliffoney 6.

Mountford, Charles Pearcy, O.B.E., M.A., DIP.ANTHRO.; British ethnologist and student of Australian primitive art; b. 9 May 1890; ed. Univs. of Adelaide and Cambridge.

Accompanied Univ. of Adelaide Expeditions as Ethnologist to Warburton Ranges, Western Australia 35, Granites, Central Australia 36, Nepabunna, South Australia 37, Yuendumu, Central Australia 51; and as Leader to Nepabunna, South Australia 38 and 39, Mann and Musgrave Ranges, Central Australia 40, Haaste Bluff, Central Australia 42, Western Arnhem Land 49, North-Eastern Arnhem Land 51, Ayers Rock, Central Australia 52, Central Mount Wedge, Central Australia 56, North-Western Central Australia 60, Ayers Rock 60, North-Western Australia 63, North-Eastern Australia 64; leader of Nat. Geographic Society of America Expeditions to Arnhem Land, Northern Australia 48, Melville Island, Northern Australia 54, North-western Australia 63, Cape York, N.E. Australia; Hon. Life Fellow Nat. Geographic Soc. of America, John Lewis Gold Medal, Royal Geographic Soc. (South Australian Branch), Founder's Gold Medal, Royal Geographic Soc. of Australia (Queensland Branch), Franklin Burr Award, Nat. Geographic Soc. of America; Nuffield Research Scholar 57-59; Natural History Medallion of Australia 49.

Publs. *The Art of Albert Namatjira* 44, *Brown Men and Red Sand* 48, *The Art, Myth and Symbolism of Arnhem Land* 56, *Australian Tree Portraits* 56, *The Tiwi, Their Art, Myth and Ceremony* 58, *Australian Aboriginal Art* 61, *Aboriginal Paintings from Australia* 65, *Ayers Rock—its People, their Beliefs and their Art* 65, *The Dreamtime: Aboriginal Mythology in the Art of Ainslie Roberts* 66, *Australian Aboriginal Portraits* 67, *Winbaraku and the Myth of Jarapiri* 67.

25 1st Avenue, St. Peters, South Australia.

Telephone: 63-1473.

Mountford, Sir James Frederick, Kt., M.A., D.LITT., D.C.L., LL.D.; British Latinist and educationist; b. 15 Sept. 1897; ed. West Bromwich Grammar School, Birmingham Univ., and Oriel Coll., Oxford.

Lecturer in Classics, King's Coll., Newcastle 18-19; Latin Lecturer Edinburgh Univ. 19-24; Prof. of Classics Cornell Univ. 24-27; Fereday Fellow St. John's Coll.

Oxford 24-27; Latin Prof. Univ. of Wales 28-32; Latin Prof. Liverpool Univ. 32-45; Chair. Joint Matriculation Board 47-49; Chair. of Cttee. of Vice-Chancellors 48; Pres. Classical Asscn. 63; Vice-Chancellor Liverpool Univ. 45-63.

Publs. *Quotations from Classical Authors in Medieval Latin Glossaries* 25, *Abavus Glossarium* 26, *Greek Music in Papyri and Inscriptions* (in New Chaps. in Greek Lit.) 29, edition of *Kennedy's Revised Latin Primer* 30, *The Scholia Bembina* 34, edition of *Arnold's Latin Prose Composition* (and Latin Versions) 38-40, *Outline of Latin Prose Composition* 42; Edition of *Sidgwick's Greek Prose Composition* 51, *Greek Verse Composition* 55, *British Universities* 66.

29 Aigburth Drive, Liverpool 17, England.
Telephone: Larklane 5817.

Moura, Decio de; Brazilian diplomatist; b. 25 June 1906; ed. Univ. of Rio de Janeiro and Brazilian War Coll.

Diplomatic Service 27-, Montevideo, London, Washington 27-41; later Consul-Gen., Lisbon; Minister, Teheran and Copenhagen; later Ambassador to Vatican and to Japan; Head Economic Dept., Ministry of Foreign Affairs 52-54, Under-Sec. of State 56-58; Ambassador to Argentina 64-.

Brazilian Embassy, Arroyo 1142, Buenos Aires, Argentina.

Moura de Brito, Dr. Raimundo; Brazilian physician and politician.

Former State Deputy, later State Sec. for Health, Guanabara; Fed. Minister of Health 64-67; Aliança Revovadora Nacional (ARENA).

c/o Ministry of Health, Brasilia, Brazil.

Moureu, Henri Bertrand Vincent; French engineer and research scientist; b. 2 Aug. 1899; ed. Ecole Supérieure de Physique et de Chimie, Paris, and Collège de France.

Assistant, then Deputy Dir., Collège de France 21-41; Dir. Municipal Laboratory of Paris 41-64; Dir. Ecole Pratique des Hautes Etudes 41-; Scientific Dir. Centre d'Etudes des Projectiles Autopropulsés, Ministry of Armed Forces 45-; Admin. Soc. l'Air Liquide 64-; Pres. Soc. Française d'Astronautique 64, 65; mem. Int. Acad. of Astronautics 65-; Pres. Soc. Chimique de France 65-66; Pres. Asscn. pour la Prévention de la Pollution atmosphérique 64-; mem. Acad. des Sciences 61-; Scientific Adviser to Paris Prefect of Police 64-; Dir. Maison de la Chimie, Inst. Pasteur, and Inst. océanographique de France 67-; mem. Comité National C.N.R.S. 67-; Co-editor *Annales de Chimie* 67; Pres. Asscn. Etude Problèmes Avancés 64-; Officier Légion d'Honneur, and other decorations.

Publs. include: *Notions fondamentales de Chimie organique* 46, *Astronautique et Recherche spatiale* 64.

18 rue Pierre Curie, Paris 5e, France.
Telephone: 033-12-59.

Moussa, Pierre L.; French civil servant; b. 5 March 1922; ed. Ecole Normale Supérieure.

Inspector of Finances 46-50; Technical Adviser to Sec. of State for Finance 50-51, Dept. of External Econ. Relations 51-54, Dir. Ministry for Overseas Territories 54-59; Dir. of Civil Aviation, Ministry of Public Works and Transport 59-62; Dir. Dept. of Operations for Africa, Int. Bank for Reconstruction and Development 62-64; Pres. French Fed. of Assurance Companies 65-; Chevalier, Légion d'Honneur.

Publs. *L'économie de la zone franc, Les Chances Economiques de la Communauté Franco-Africaine, Les nations prolétaires, L'économie de la zone franc, Les Etats-Unis et Les Nations Prolétaires.*

87 Quai d'Orsay, Paris 7e, France.
Telephone: TAItbout 96-12.

Moussatché, Haity; Brazilian physiologist and pharmacologist; b. 21 Feb. 1910; ed. Instituto Universario Fluminense and Universidade do Brasil.

Instructor in Physiology, Univ. de Rio de Janeiro (now Univ. do Brasil) 31-33, Asst. Prof. of Physiology 35; mem. staff Laboratory of Physiology, Instituto Oswaldo Cruz 34-35; Yellow Fever Lab., Rockefeller Foundation, Rio de Janeiro 35-37; mem. Div. of Physiology and Pharmacodynamics, Instituto Oswaldo Cruz 37-, Head of Dept. of Pharmacodynamics 54-, Dept. of Physiology 58-64; Prof. of Physiology, Rio de Janeiro 46-47; Private Docent, Univ. do Brasil 48-; mem. Brazilian Acad. of Sciences 52-; Vice-Pres. Brazilian Soc. for Advancement of Science 60-62.

Publs. include studies in experimental convulsions and studies on histamine release and cell metabolism in anaphylaxis pharmacology of natural products (animal venoms, plant products).

Division of Physiology and Pharmacodynamics, Instituto Oswaldo Cruz, Caixa Postal 926, Rio de Janeiro, Brazil.

Mowrer, Edgar A.; American journalist; b. 8 March 1892; ed. Chicago Univ., Univ. of Michigan and the Sorbonne.

War Correspondent *Chicago Daily News* in France and Belgium 14-15 and afterwards on Italian front; Chief Berlin Bureau of *Chicago Daily News* until 33, of Paris Bureau 34, later of Washington Bureau; with Office of Facts and Figures and Office of War Information 42-43; awarded Pulitzer Journalism Prize 33; syndicated columnist on world affairs 43-; also American Editor *Western World* 56-60.

Publs. *Immortal Italy* 22, *This American World* 28, *The Future of Politics* 30, *Germany Puts the Clock Back* 32, *Mowrer in China* 38, *Global Warfare* (with Marthe Rajchman) 42, *The Nightmare of American Foreign Policy* 48, *Challenge and Decision* 50, *A Good Time to be Alive* 59, *An End to Make-Believe* 61.

3301 Garfield Street, N.W., Washington 8, D.C., U.S.A.
Telephone: FE3-4166.

Mowrer, Paul Scott; American journalist and poet; b. 14 July 1887; ed. Univ. of Michigan.

Mem. staff *Chicago Daily News* since 05, Balkan War correspondent 12-13, Dir. of war news service in France 14-18, correspondent Peace and various Disarmament Confs., Dir. Foreign Service 22-24 and general European correspondent 24-34, Associate Editor and chief Editorial writer 34-36, Editor 36-44; Pulitzer Prize for best foreign corresp. 28; Dir. American Society Newspaper Editors 41; European Editor, *New York Post* 45-49.

Publs. *Balkanised Europe* 21, *Our Foreign Affairs* 24, *The Foreign Relations of the United States* 27, *House of Europe* 45; Poems: *Hours of France* 18, *The Good Comrade* 23, *And Let the Glory Go* 55, *Poems between Wars* 41, *On going to Live in New Hampshire* 53, *Fiji* 56, *Twenty-one and Sixty-five* 58, *The Mothering Land* 60, *High Mountain Pond* 62, *School for Diplomats* 64, *This Teeming Earth* 65, *The Island Ireland*.

Philbrick Road, Chocorua, N.H., U.S.A.
Telephone: 603-323-7767.

Moyers, Bill D.; American newspaper executive; b. 5 June 1934; ed. Univ. of Texas, Edinburgh Univ. and Southwestern Baptist Theological Seminary.

Executive Asst. to Senator Lyndon Johnson 59-60, Assoc. Dir. U.S. Peace Corps 61-63, Deputy Dir. 63; Special Asst. to Pres. Johnson 63-66, Press Sec. to Pres. July 65-66; Publisher of *Newsday*, Long Island, N.Y.

550 Stewart Avenue, Garden City, N.Y. 11530, U.S.A.
Telephone: PI1-1234 and PI1-1276.

Moyersoen, Ludovic Marie Odilon; Belgian lawyer and politician; b. 1 Aug. 1904; ed. Collège Saint Joseph, Alost, Collège Notre Dame de la Paix, Namur, and Université de Louvain.

Secretary of Union Catholique Belge 35-38; Asst. Chef de Cabinet to Prime Minister 44-45; Co-founder Social Christian Party 45, mem. Nat. Cttee. 45-47; Deputy for Alost 46-; Minister of Justice 50-52, of Interior 52-54; Vice-Pres. Chamber of Deputies 58-64, First Vice-Pres. 64; Sec. Comm. for Revision of Constitution 65; Minister of Nat. Defence 65-66; mem. Belgian Del. to UN 48; Alt. mem. Council of Europe 49-50, mem. 60; mem. Western European Union 60-63, Vice-Pres. 63-65; Pres. ITECO (Int. Technical Co-operation) and Nat. Cttee. for Voluntary Service Overseas 58-65; numerous decorations.
Publ. *Prosper Poullet en de politiek van zijn tijd.*
Chamber of Deputies, Brussels; and Hof "Ten Berg", Aelbrechtlaan, Aalst (Alost), Belgium.

Moyes, Rt. Rev. John Stoward, C.M.G., M.A., D.D., TH.D., D.LITT.; Australian ecclesiastic; b. 25 July 1884; ed. St. Peter's Coll., Adelaide, Univ. of Adelaide, and Australian Coll. of Theology.
Deacon 07; Asst. Curate, Port Pirie, S. Australia, Priest 08; Asst. Curate, St. Mary's, Lewisham, Diocese of Southwark, England 11-13; Rector of Prospect, S. Australia 13-19; Chaplain, Commonwealth Forces 17-19; Rector of Port Pirie 19-21, of Norwood 21-29; Archdeacon of Adelaide and Examining Chaplain 25-29; Bishop of Armidale, N.S.W. 29-64; Deputy Chancellor, Univ. of New England 60-; Episcopal Canon, St. George's Cathedral, Jerusalem 62-64; Australian del. to Princeton Peace Conf. 43, and to World Council of Churches Assembly, Amsterdam 48, Evanston 54; Hon. D.D. (Trinity Coll., Toronto); Hon. D.Litt. (New England Univ.); Freedom of Armidale and Tamworth. Publs. *Marriage and Sex* 31, *The Church and the Hour* 39, *Australia, the Church and the Future* 41, *American Journey* 44, *In Journeying Often* 49, *The Communist Way of Life and the Christian Answer* 51, *America Revisited* 55, *Third Time of Asking* 59, *Coventry Campaign* 60.
5 Laguna Street, Vaucluse, Sydney, N.S.W., Australia. Telephone: 37-2198.

Moyne, 2nd Baron, cr. 32, of Bury St. Edmunds; **Bryan Walter Guinness,** M.A., BAR. AT LAW, F.R.S.L.; British and Irish brewer and writer; b. 27 Oct. 1905; ed. Eton and Christ Church, Oxford.
Former Major, Royal Sussex Regiment; Vice-Chair. Arthur Guinness, Son and Co.; Chair. Iveagh (Housing) Trust, Dublin; Trustee Guinness (Housing) Trust, London; a Gov., Nat. Gallery of Ireland 55; Pro-Chancellor Trinity Coll., Dublin; Hon. LL.D. (Trinity Coll., Dublin) 58, (Nat. Univ. of Ireland) 61.
Publs. *23 Poems* 31, *Singing out of Tune* 33, *Landscape with Figures* 34, *Under the Eyelid* 35, *Johnny and Jemima* 36, *A Week by the Sea* 36, *Lady Crushwell's Companion* 38, *The Children in the Desert* 47, *Reflexions* 47, *The Animal's Breakfast* 50, *Story of a Nutcracker* 53, *Collected Poems* 56, *A Fugue of Cinderellas* 56, *Catriona and the Grasshopper* 57, *Priscilla and the Prawn* 60, *Leo and Rosabelle* 61, *The Giant's Eye* 64, *The Rose in the Tree* (verse) 64, *The Girl with the Flower* (short stories).
Biddesden House, Andover, Hants., England; Knockmaroon, Castleknock, Dublin, Ireland.

Moynet, André; French politician and business man; b. 19 July 1921; ed. Collège Saint-Michel, Lycée Voltaire, Paris.
With Free French Air Force, Cameroun, Gabon, Chad; with R.A.F., U.K.; with U.S.S.R. Air Force in Normandy; Commdr. Ecole des Moniteurs, Tours 45-46; Dep. to Nat. Ass. 46-, Sec. of State to President's Council 54-55; Pres. Nat. Ass. Cttee. of Nat. Defence and Armed Forces 62-; Test Pilot, Hurel-Dubois 32-01 and Caravelle; builder of Moynet Jupiter aircraft; Commandeur,

Légion d'Honneur, Médaille de l'Aéronautique, Compagnon de la Libération and several foreign decorations; Ind. Republican.
Publ. *Pilote de Combat.*
32 boulevard de la Saussaye, Neuilly-sur-Seine, France.

Moyniham, Maurice Gerard, B.COMM.; Irish banker; b. 19 Dec. 1902; ed. Univ. Coll., Cork.
Secretary Executive Council, Irish Free State 37; Sec., Govt. of Ireland 37-60; Civil Service Commr. 37-53; Dir. Central Bank of Ireland 53-60; Gov. 61-; mem. Commrs. of Charitable Donations and Bequests for Ireland 61-; D.Econ. Sc. h.c. (Nat. Univ. of Ireland) 55; Knight Commdr. of St. Gregory 59.
48 Castle Avenue, Clontarf, Dublin, Ireland. Telephone: 335220.

Moyzes, Alexander; Czechoslovak composer; b.4 Sept. 1906; ed. State Conservatoire, Prague.
Professor of Theory of Music and Composition, Acad. of Music and Dramatic Arts, Bratislava 28-48; Chief of Music Section, Czechoslovak Radio, Bratislava 37-48; Prof. Coll. of Music and Dramatic Arts, Bratislava 49-, Rector 67; mem. Central Cttee. Union of Czechoslovak Composers 50; one of founders of contemporary Slovak music; numerous prizes; Honoured Artist 61, Nat. Artist 66.
Compositions include: chamber: Sonata in E minor 25, *String Quartet* 39, *Wind Quartet* 33; vocal: *Colours on the Palette* 28, twelve folk songs from *Šariš* 29, *They are Singing in the Mountains* 33, *They are Singing, Playing, Dancing* 38, *Whose Organs are Playing* 47, *Ballad Cantata* 60, *In the Autumn* 61; orchestral: seven symphonies 29-55, *Jánošik, Nikola Suhaj* 34, *Down the River Váh* 35, *Concerto for Violin and Orchestra* 58, *Sonatina Giocosa* 62, *Concerto for Flute and Orchestra* 67; opera: *The Brave King* 62; music for theatre, radio plays and films.
College of Music and Dramatic Arts, Bratislava, Sturova 7, Czechoslovakia.

Mozgovoy, Ivan Alexeyevich; Soviet politician; b. 1927; ed. Kherson Inst. of Agriculture.
Member C.P.S.U. 51-; Sec. Kherson Regional Cttee. of Ukrainian Young Communist League, then of the Central Cttee. of Ukrainian Y.C.L. 53-62; Second Sec. Transcarpathian Regional C.P. of the Ukraine 62-66; First Sec. Rovno Regional Cttee., C.P. of the Ukraine 66-; mem. Central Cttee., C.P., Ukraine; Deputy to U.S.S.R. Supreme Soviet.
Rovno Regional Committee, Communist Party of the Ukraine, Rovno, U.S.S.R.

Mravinsky, Yevgeni Aleksandrovich; Soviet conductor; b. 03; ed. Leningrad Conservatoire.
Conductor Kirov State Acad. Opera and Ballet Theatre, Leningrad 32-38; Winner, All Union Conductors' Competition 38, Conductor Leningrad State Philharmonic Orchestra 38-; has toured England, Austria, German Fed. Republic, German Democratic Republic, Finland, Czechoslovakia, Switzerland, U.S.A., etc.; People's Artist U.S.S.R., Badge of Honour, State Prize, Lenin Prize 61.
Leningrad State Philharmonic Orchestra, 1 Ploshchad Iskusstv, Leningrad, U.S.S.R.

Mrozek, Slawomir; Polish writer; b. 30.
Former cartoonist and journalist.
Publs. include *The Elephant* 57, *The Rain* 62 (short stories), *The Ugupu Bird* (short stories) 68; Plays: *The Police* 58, *What a lovely Dream, Let's Have Fun, The Death of the Lieutenant* 63, *Striptease* 64, *Tango* 64, *On the High Seas.*
c/o Union of Polish writers, Krakowskie Prezedmieście 87; ul. Piekarska 4/5, Warsaw, Poland.

Mückenberger, Erich; German politician; b. 8 June 1910.
Former locksmith, Chemnitz; mem. Socialist Unity Party (S.E.D.) 46-, Sec. Cen. Cttee. 53-, mem. Politburo of Cen. Cttee. 54-; mem. Volkskammer 50-; several decorations.
Volkskammer, Berlin, Germany.

Mudaliar, Diwan Bahadur Sir A. Lakshamanaswami, M.D., LL.D., D.C.L., D.SC.; Indian doctor and educationist; b. 14 Oct. 1887; ed. Christian and Medical Colls., Madras.
Joined Madras Medical Service; Prof. of Obstetrics and Gynaecology, Medical Coll. 34-42; Superintendent Government Hospital for Women and Children, Egmore, and Principal Medical Coll. 39-42; mem. Syndicate, Madras Univ. 25-; Acting Vice-Chancellor 36 and 40 and Vice-Chancellor 42-; Chair. Inter-Univ. Board 48-49 and of its Standing Cttee. 49-51; mem. Indian Medical Council; mem. Exec. Board of W.H.O. 50-56, of UNESCO 50-56 (Chair. 55); Chair. Secondary Education Comm. 52-53; Padma Bhushan 54.
Publs. *Clinical Obstetrics, Ante-Natal and Neo-Natal Mortality of Infants, Casebook for Midwives.*
Kensington, Poonamallee High Road, Kilpauk, Madras, India.

Mudhaf, Muhalhel Mohamed Al-; Kuwaiti diplomatist; ed. in schools in Kuwait, Egypt and U.K.
Member staff Ministry of Education 53-61; Chargé d'Affaires, Lebanon 62-64, Syria 64-65; Amb. to Pakistan 65-67; Perm. Rep. to UN 67-.
Permanent Mission of Kuwait to the United Nations, 235 East 42nd Street, New York, N.Y. 10017, U.S.A.

Mudholkar, Janardan Ranganath, B.A., LL.B.; Indian judge; b. 02; ed. Elphinstone Coll., Bombay, Sidney Sussex Coll., Cambridge, and Lincoln's Inn, London.
Legal practice (barrister) Amraoti 25-29, Nagpur 30-41; Dist. and Sessions Judge 41-48; Judge Nagpur High Court 48-56; Act. Chief Justice, Bombay High Court Aug.-Sept. 60; Judge Supreme Court of India 60-66; Chair. Press Council of India July 66-.
Press Council of India, 31 Aurangzeb Road, New Delhi 11, India.

Mueller, George E.; American electrical engineer and missile scientist; b. 16 July 1918.
Vice-Pres. for Research and Devt., Space Technology Laboratories, Los Angeles until Aug. 63; Assoc. Admin. for Manned Space Flight, Nat. Aeronautics and Space Admin. (N.A.S.A.) Sept. 63-; Fellow A.I.A.A., I.E.E.E., Royal Aeronautical Soc.; mem. Nat. Acad. of Engineering, N.Y. Acad. of Sciences.
Publ. *Communications Satellites* (with E. Spangler), etc.
National Aeronautics and Space Administration, Washington, D.C. 20546; Home: 3043 West Lane Keys, Washington, D.C., U.S.A.
Telephone: 202-962-0224.

Mueller, Rt. Rev. Reuben Herbert; American ecclesiastic; b. 2 June 1897; ed. North Central Coll., and Evangelical Theological Seminary, Naperville, Illinois.
Minister of Evangelical United Brethren Church 20-; High School Teacher Wisconsin and Minnesota 19-24, Instructor North Cen. Coll. 24-26; Pastor at Minneapolis, South Bend and Indianapolis 21-37; District Supt. Indiana Conf. of Evangelical Church 37-42; Exec. Sec., Christian Educ. 42-56, Vice-Pres. of Board 57-; also on Board of World Council of Christian Educ.; Assoc. Sec. of Evangelism 46-54; Bishop 54-; Chair. Joint Comm. on Church Union (with Methodists) 54-; mem. Cen. Cttee. World Council of Churches 61-; Pres. Nat. Council of Churches of Christ 63-; mem. numerous Church Cttees.; many honorary degrees.
Publs. *Becoming a Christian, One Body, One Spirit,*
Motive in Christian Teaching, Renew My Church, The Living Word.
1401 Castle Avenue, Indianapolis, Indiana 46227, U.S.A.

Muetzelfeldt, Rev. Bruno, D.D.; Australian ecclesiastic; b. 7 Feb. 1918; ed. Immanuel Coll., Adelaide, and Lutheran Theological Seminary, Adelaide, S. Australia.
Minister of Lutheran Church, Albury, New South Wales 39-46; Exec. Sec. Lutheran Youth Dept. 46-51; Chaplain, Commonwealth Immigration Centre, Australia 47-51; Dir. Lutheran World Fed., Dept. of World Service in Australia and Exec. Sec. Board of Immigration, United Evangelical Lutheran Church in Australia 51-60; N.S.W. Pres. United Evangelical Lutheran Church in Australia 54-60; Sec. for Resettlement and Relief, Lutheran World Fed., Dept. of World Service, H.Q., Geneva 60-61; Dir. Lutheran World Fed., Dept. of World Service, Geneva 61-; mem. Int. World Refugee Year Cttee. 60-61; Chair. Int. Council of Voluntary Agencies 63-65; Consultant, Div. of Inter-Church Aid, Refugees and World Service 61-; Consultant, Dir. of Inter-Church Aid, Refugees and World Service, World Council of Churches 61-; Star of Jordan.
Lutheran World Federation, Ecumenical Centre, 150 Route de Ferney, 1211 Geneva 20, Switzerland.
Telephone: 33-34-00.

Müezzinoglu, Ziya; Turkish civil servant and diplomatist; b. 19; ed. Ankara Univ. and Germany and Switzerland.
Inspector of Finance, Turkish Ministry of Finance 42-53; Adviser to Treasury, Ministry of Finance 53-59; Dir.-Gen. of Treasury 59-60; Dir. Gen. of Treasury and Sec.-Gen. Org. for Int. Econ. Co-operation in Turkey 60; mem. Constituent Assembly 60; Chair. Interministerial Cttee. for Foreign Econ. Relations 62; Sec. of State of State Planning Org. 62-64; Ambassador to German Fed. Repub. 64-67; Amb., Perm. Delegate of Turkey to the European Communities 67-.
Délégation Permanente de Turquie auprès de la C.E.E., 479 avenue Louise, Brussels 5, Belgium.
Telephone: 49-34-44.

Muggeridge, Malcolm; British journalist; b. 24 March 1903; ed. Selhurst Grammar School and Selwyn Coll., Cambridge.
Lecturer, Egyptian Univ., Cairo 27-30; editorial staff, *Manchester Guardian* 30-32; *Manchester Guardian* corresp. in Moscow 32-33; Asst. Editor, *Calcutta Statesman* 34-35; editorial staff, *Evening Standard* 35-36, served in East and North Africa, Italy and France, Major, Intelligence Corps, in Second World War 39-45; *Daily Telegraph* Washington corresp. 46-47; Deputy Managing Editor, *Daily Telegraph* 50-52; Editor of *Punch* 53-57; Rector of Edinburgh Univ. 66-68; Légion d'Honneur, Croix de Guerre (with Palm), Médaille de la Résistance Française.
Publs. *Three Flats* (produced by Stage Society 31), *Autumnal Face* 31, *Winter in Moscow* 33, *The Earnest Atheist: a life of Samuel Butler* 36, *In a Valley of this Restless Mind* 38, *The Thirties* 40; edited English edition of *Ciano's Diary* 47, *Ciano's Papers* 48; *Affairs of the Heart* 49, *Tread Softly for you Tread on my Jokes* 66, *London à la Mode* (with Paul Hogarth) 66, *Muggeridge Through the Microphone* 68.
Park Cottage, Robertsbridge, Sussex, England.

Muhieddin, Zakaria; United Arab Republic (Egyptian) politician; b. 7 May 1918; ed. Military Coll., and Staff Officers' Coll., Cairo.
Former lecturer Mil. Coll. and Staff Officers' Coll., and Dir.-Gen. Intelligence; Minister of the Interior 53-58; Minister of Interior, United Arab Republic April 58-61; Vice-Pres. U.A.R. 61-; mem. Presidency Council 62-64; Deputy Pres. 64-65; Prime Minister 65-66; First Deputy Prime Minister June 67-March 68.
Cairo, U.A.R.

Mühlbock, Otto, PH.D., M.D.; Netherlands oncologist; b. 4 Jan. 1906; ed. Humboldt-Universität zu Berlin. Endocrinologist, Pharmacological Inst., Amsterdam 34-40; Head, Dept. of Biology, Netherlands Cancer Inst. 46-; Asst. Prof. of Oncology, Univ. of Amsterdam 54-58, Prof. 58-; De Snoo-Van't Hoogerhuis Award 58. Publs. scientific work on carcinogenesis.
Sarphatistraat 108, Amsterdam, Netherlands.

Muir, Sir David John, Kt., C.M.G., F.C.I.S., F.A.S.A., F.A.I.M., A.A.U.Q., J.P.; Australian civil servant; b. 20 June 1916; ed. Commercial High School, Brisbane. Clerk, Lands Dept. 33; Private Sec. to Queensland Premier 39; Investigations Officer, Sugar Cane Prices Board 43; Official Sec. to Premier 46; Permanent Under-Sec., Premier and Chief Sec.'s Dept., and Clerk, Exec. Council of Queensland 48; Agent-Gen. for Queensland in London 51-64; Dir. of Industrial Development, Queensland 64-; Australian rep. on Int. Sugar Council 51-64 (Chair. 58); Pres. Chartered Inst. of Secs. 64.
Home: 28 Buena Vista Avenue, Coorparoo, Brisbane; Office: Administration Building, Elizabeth Street, Brisbane, Queensland, Australia.
Telephone: 98-3012 (Home).

Muir, Malcolm; American publisher; b. 85; ed. public and private schools.
With McGraw-Hill Publishing Co. 05-37, Vice-Pres. 16-28, Pres. 28-37; Pres. and Publisher *Newsweek* 37-Feb. 59, Chair. Editorial Board 49-56, Chair. Board and Editor-in-Chief 59-61, Hon. Chair. Board *Newsweek* Inc.; Dep. Administrator N.R.A. 33; Dir. Nat. Asscn. of Manufacturers 35-43, Chair. War Cttee. 42-43; Past-Dir. American Arbitration Asscn.; Nat. Industrial Conf. Board; Labor-Management Council of War Production Board 43; N.Y. Chamber of Commerce; Citizens' Cttee. for Control of Crime in N.Y. City 40-43; Econ. Club of N.Y., Council on Foreign Relations; Past-Dir. Nat. Publishers' Asscn.; Board of Trustees of Cttee. for Econ. Development, Int. Press Institute, Foreign Policy Asscn., U.S. Council Int. Chamber of Commerce; Republican.
435 East 52nd Street, New York 22, N.Y.; and *Newsweek* Building, 444 Madison Avenue, New York, N.Y., U.S.A.

Muirshiel, 1st Viscount (cr. 64), of Kilmacolm; **John Scott Maclay,** P.C., C.H., C.M.G.; British shipowner and politician; b. 26 Oct. 1905; ed. Winchester and Trinity Coll., Cambridge.
M.P. for Montrose Burghs 40-50, for Renfrewshire West 50-64; Head British Merchant Shipping Mission to U.S.A. 44; Parl. Sec. Ministry of Production 45; Minister of Transport and Civil Aviation 51-52; Minister of State for Colonial Affairs 56-57; Sec. of State for Scotland 57-62; Pres. Assembly Western European Union 55-56; Pres. Nat. Liberal Council 57-.
Knapps, Kilmacolm, Renfrewshire, Scotland.

Mujeeb, Muhammad, B.A.; Indian educationist; b. 02; ed. Oxford Univ.
Joined Jamia Millia 26; Vice-Chancellor Jamia Millia 48-.
Publs. *History of Russian Literature, History of European Political Thought, Story of the World* (in Urdu), *A Glimpse of New China, World History—Our Heritage, Kimiyagar* (Urdu short stories), *Ordeal,* and four plays. Jamia Millia, Jamianagar, New Delhi, India.

Mujica Lainez, Manuel; Argentine writer and journalist; b. 11 Sept. 1910; ed. Colegio Lacordaire, Buenos Aires, Colegio Nacional de San Isidro, Ecole Descartes, Paris, and Faculty of Law, Univ. of Buenos Aires.
On staff of *La Nación* 32-, Art Critic; Sec. Nat. Museum of Decorative Arts 36-46; Gen. Dir. of Cultural Relations, Foreign Office 55-58; Nat. Prize for Letters; Grand Prix, Argentine Soc. of Writers; John F.

Kennedy Prize, and other awards; mem. Argentine Acad. of Letters, Nat. Acad. of Fine Arts.
Publs. *Glosas Castellanas* 36, *Don Galaz de Buenos Aires* 38, *Miguel Cane, padre* 42, *Vida de Aniceto el Gallo* 43, *Canto a Buenos Aires* 43, *Vida de Anastasio el Pollo* 47, *Aqui Vivieron* 49, *Misteriosa Buenos Aires* 51, *Los Idolos* 53, *La Casa* 54, *Los Viajeros* 55, *Héctor Basaldua* 56, *Invitados en el Paraíso* 57, *Bomarzo* 62, *El Unicornio* 65.
O'Higgins 2150, Buenos Aires, Argentina.

Mukanov, Sabit Mukanovich; Soviet (Kazakh) writer; b. 26 April 1900; ed. Literary Inst.
Member C.P.S.U. 20-; Orders of Red Banner of Labour 50, of Lenin 60.
Publs. Poems: *Farm Labourer, Ford into October* 27, *Sulushash* 28, *White Bear* (2 vols.), *Verses and Poems* 60, *Story of a Contemporary* 62; novels: *Son of the Bey* 31, *Temirtas* 35, *My Mekbety* (Kazakh for Universities) 39, *Botagoz* 46, *Herdsman's Son* 53, *A Bright Love* 59, *School of Life* (3 vols.) 38-65; history of literature: *The Kazakh literature of the XX century* 32, *The Roads of Our Development* 60, *Radiant Stars* 64; Plays: *Chokan Valikhanov* 57, *Saken Seifullin* 66.
Union of Soviet Kazakh Writers, Alma Ata, Kazakhstan, U.S.S.R.

Mukařovský, Jan, D.SC.; Czechoslovak philosopher; b. 11 Nov. 1891; ed. Charles Univ., Prague.
Lecturer in Aesthetics Charles Univ. Prague 29-37, Assoc. Prof., Comenius Univ., Bratislava 34; Assoc. Prof. Charles Univ. Prague 37, Prof. 38-, Rector 48-52; Dir. Inst. of Czech Literature, Czechoslovak Acad. of Sciences 52-61; co-founder and Vice-Chair. Prague Linguistic Circle; Academician, Czechoslovak Acad. of Sciences 52-; State Prize 49; Chair. Czechoslovak Peace Cttee. 55-66; Order of Republic 55, 61; Czechoslovak Peace Prize 66; Silver Plaque of Czechoslovak Acad. of Sciences 66.
Publs. *Příspěvek k estetice českého verše, O volném verši českém, Máchův Máj, Poldkova "Vznešenost přírody", Estetická funkce, norma a hodnota jako sociální fakty, Kapitoly z české poetiky,* etc.
Charles University, Prague 1, Czechoslovakia.

Mukesh; Indian singer and film producer; b. 23. Film producer 50-; owns the company Mukesh Films. Sagar Mandir, Shivaji Park Seaface, Mahim, Bombay, India.

Mukherjee, J. N., C.B.E., D.SC., F.N.I.; Indian research scientist; b. 93; ed. Univs. of Calcutta and London.
Asst. to Palit Prof. of Chemistry, Calcutta Univ. 15-19; Guruprasad Prof. of Chemistry 21-37, Ghose Prof. of Chemistry 37-45; fmr. Dir. Indian Agricultural Research Inst., New Delhi and Central Building Research Inst. Roorkee; fmr. Chair. Nat. Planning Cttee. of Indian Nat. Congress; Leader, Indian Del. 3rd Int. Congress of Soil Science 35; Convener and Pres. Indian Society of Soil Science 35; mem. India Scientific Mission to U.K. and U.S.A. 45; mem. Royal Society Empire Scientific Conf. and British Commonwealth Official Scientific Conf. 46; Leader, Indian Del. to Conf. on Tropical and Sub-Tropical Soil, U.K. 48; mem. U.N. Scientific Conf. on Conservation and Utilisation of Resources and Pres. of its Land Section Meeting U.S.A. 49; mem. Gen. Assembly Int. Council of Scientific Unions, London 46, Copenhagen 49; mem. Exec. Cttee. and Board Int. Council of Scientific Unions 47-52; Vice-Pres. Int. Soil Science Congress, Netherlands 50; Foreign Sec. Nat. Inst. of Sciences of India 52; Pres. Indian Science Congress Asscn. 52; Pres. Surendraneth Teaching Insts. 52-; mem. Central Tea Board 54; Scientific Adviser, Dept. of Agriculture and Forests, West Bengal 54-; Administrator, Board of Secondary Education, West Bengal 55-56; mem. Union Public

Service Comm. 56-58; Chair. Land Utilization Board, West Bengal 59-66; Padma Bhusan 64.
Publs. Over 250 papers on Physical Chemistry, Electro-Chemistry, Colloids, Soil Science, etc.
10 Puran Chand Nahar Avenue, Calcutta 13, India.

Mukherji, Ajoy Kumar; Indian politician; b. April 1901; ed. Hamilton School, Tamluk, Uttarpara Coll., Hooghly, and Presidency Coll., Calcutta.
Joined Non-Co-operation Movement 21; imprisoned several times during Civil Disobedience and Quit India Movements; mem. W. Bengal Legislative Assembly 52-; Minister of Irrigation, W. Bengal 52-63; Pres. W. Bengal Pradesh Cttee. 64-66; Founder-Pres. Bangla Congress 66-; Chief Minister of W. Bengal March 67-Nov. 67.
Writers' Building, Calcutta, India.

Mukhitdinov, Nuritdin Akhramovich; Soviet government official and diplomatist; b. 1917; ed. All-Union Extra-Mural Co-operative Inst.
Party and State activity, Uzbekistan 47-55; mem. Central Cttee. of the C.P.S.U. 52-61; First Sec. Central Cttee. of the Uzbek C.P. 55-57; alternative mem. Presidium of the Central Cttee. of the C.P.S.U. 56-57, mem. 57-61; mem. Cen. Cttee. of the C.P.S.U. 52-66; Deputy Chair. *Tsentrosoyuz* (Cen. Co-operative Alliance) 61-66; First Vice-Pres. Cttee. for Cultural Relations with Foreign Countries, U.S.S.R. Council of Ministers July 66-68; Amb. to Syrian Arab Repub. 68-; awarded Order of Lenin (twice).
U.S.S.R. Embassy, Damascus, Syrian Arab Republic.

Mukke, Mikhail Ivanovich; Soviet politician; b. 1907; ed. Plekhanov Inst. of National Economy.
With consumer co-operative orgs. and state reading system 27-41, 46-62; mem. C.P.S.U. 44-; with the Soviet Army 41-46; Perm. Rep. of Latvian S.S.R. Council of Ministers to U.S.S.R. Council of Ministers 62-; mem. Central Cttee. Latvian C.P.; Deputy to Latvian Supreme Soviet; Orders of the Red Banner of Labour, Red Star (twice), Badge of Honour (twice).
Permanent Representation of the Latvian S.S.R. Council of Ministers to the U.S.S.R. Council of Ministers, ulitsa Chaplygina 3, Moscow, U.S.S.R.

Mulamba, Gen. Leonard; Congolese army officer and politician; b. 1928; ed. Military School, Luluabourg.
Administrator of Re-occupied Areas in N.E. Congo 64-65; Prime Minister of Democratic Republic of Congo (Leopoldville) 65-Oct. 66; Amb. to India 67-.
Embassy of Democratic Republic of Congo, New Delhi, India.

Mulatier, Léon Frédéric; French telecommunications official; b. 26 May 1887; ed. Coll. classique, Montélimar, Ecole spéciale des Travaux publics and Ecole nat. supérieure des Postes et Télégraphes, Paris.
Joined Postal and Telegraph Service 06; Clerk, Ministry of Posts, Telegraphs and Telephones 19, Deputy Chief of Dept. 24, Chief of Dept. 33, Deputy Dir. of Personnel 34, Dir. of Personnel a.i. 34-35, Dir. of Telegraph and Radiocommunications Development 35; Vice-Dir. Int. Telecommunications Office, Berne 40, Dep. Sec.-Gen. 48, Sec.-Gen. 50-63 (now retd.); Prof. Ecole nat. supérieure des PTT 26-40; served in First World War 14-18; Dep. Chief, Posts and Telegraphs Service, Upper Silesia, Inter-Allied Govt. and Plebiscite Comm. 20; responsible for first radio-telephone link with U.S.A. 35, etc.; Head of French Del. at numerous int. telecommunications confs.; Sec.-Gen. of Telecommunications Confs., Atlantic City 47, Buenos Aires 52, Telegraph and Telephone Conf., Paris 49, Radiodiffusion Conf., Florence-Rapallo 50; Commdr. de la Légion d'Honneur (France), Grand Officer, Order of the Crown (Italy), Grand Officer Order of St. Sava (Yugoslavia),

Commdr. Order of St. Charles (Monaco), and other decorations.
55 Route de Chêne, Geneva, Switzerland.
Telephone: 36-33-92.

Muldoon, Hon. Robert David, M.P., F.P.A.N.Z., F.C.A.I., F.C.W.A., A.C.I.S., A.I.A.N.Z.; New Zealand politician and public accountant; b. 21 Sept. 1921; ed. Mount Albert Grammar School.
Senior Partner, Kendon Mills Muldoon and Browne, Auckland; Lecturer in Auditing 48-54; Pres. New Zealand Inst. of Cost Accountants 56, Auckland Horticultural Council 59-60; M.P. for Tamaki 60-; Parl. Under-Sec. to Minister of Finance 63-66; Minister of Tourism and Publicity 67, of Finance 67-; mem. Select Cttees., on Fishing Industry 63, Road Safety 65, Parl. Procedure 67; mem. Public Expenditure Cttee. 61-66, Chair. 63-66; Dominion Councillor, New Zealand Nat. Party 60-67; Lever Hulme Prize, Inst. of Cost and Works Accountants 47, Maxwell Award, New Zealand Inst. of Cost Accountants 56.
9 Beauchamp Street, Karori, Wellington, New Zealand.

Mulford, Raymon Howard; American business executive; b. 15 Sept. 1909; ed. Sequoia Union High School, San Francisco, Stanford Univ. and Harvard Business School.
Owens-Illinois Glass Co. 33-, Vice-Pres. (Personnel Admin.), Toledo, Ohio 49-53; Pres. and Gen. Manager, Kimble Glass Co. 53-60; Pres. Glass Container Div. Owens-Illinois Glass Co. 60-61; Pres. and Dir. Owens-Illinois Glass Co. (now Owens-Illinois Inc.) 61-; Dir. Nat. Petro Chemicals Corpn., Ohio Citizens Trust Co., Marathon Oil Co.
P.O. Box 1035, Toledo, Ohio 43601 and 3753 Edgevale Road, Toledo, Ohio 43606, U.S.A.
Telephone: 419-242-6543 (Office).

Mulgaokar, Shrikrishna; Indian journalist; b. 13; ed. Elphinstone School, Bombay.
Sub-Editor *Pioneer* 39; Asst. Ed. *Hindustan Times* 45-51 (Foreign Corresp., Paris 46-47); joined *Times of India* 51, Foreign Corresp., S.E. Asia and the Far East, the Middle East, London Ed. 53-57, Washington Corresp. 58; Ed. *Hindustan Times* 58-.
Connaught Circus, New Delhi, India.

Mulholland, R. D. Peter; Canadian banker; b. 28 Sept. 1904; ed. Peterborough Schools and Trinity Coll. School, Port Hope, Ontario.
Bank of Montreal 23-, served Hamilton, Ont., London, England, Paris, Montreal 23-41; Canadian Army 41-45; Head Office, Bank of Montreal 45-46, Asst. Man., Vancouver 46, Man., Victoria, B.C. 48, Ottawa 51, Montreal 53; Asst. Gen. Man. 58, Gen. Man. 59, Dir. and Vice-Pres. 60-64, Chief Gen. Man. 64-66, Exec. Vice-Pres. and Chief Gen. Man. 66-67, Pres. 67-; Chair. Bank of London and Montreal Ltd. 66-, Canadian Advisory Cttee., Royal Exchange Atlas Group of Insurance Companies 66-; Pres. Canadian Bankers' Asscn. 61-63, Hon. Pres. 65-67; Dir. Canadian Board, Standard Life Assurance Co. 66; Dir. Banque Transatlantique, Paris; official of numerous civic and educ. orgs.
Office: 129 St. James Street West, Montreal, P.Q.; Home: 3878 Ramezay Avenue, Montreal 6, P.Q., Canada.

Müller, Gebhard; German lawyer; b. 17 April 1900; ed. Univs. of Tübingen and Berlin.
Lawyer by profession; held several legal positions in Württemberg Courts 29-45; engaged in reconstruction of judicial system in Württemberg-Hohenzollern 45; Ministerial Dir. in Provincial Ministry of Justice Dec. 46; Provincial Pres. of C.D.U. March 47-57; Pres. of State, Minister of Finance and of Justice of Württemberg-

Hohenzollern 48-52, Prime Minister of Baden-Württemberg 53-58; Pres. of Constitutional Court, Karlsruhe 59-.
Friedrich Ebertstrasse 112, 7000 Stuttgart, German Federal Republic.

Müller, Heinrich, DIPL. ING.; German machinery executive; b. 2 May 1900; ed. Technical Univ., Hanover.
DEMAG A.G., Duisburg 27-, mem. Management Board 42-, Pres. 62-67; Senator h.c., Technical Univ., Hanover.
Wolfsberg 11, Mülheim/Ruhr-Speldorf, German Federal Republic.

Muller, Hilgard, D.LITT., LL.B., M.P.; South African politician and diplomatist; b. 4 May 1914; ed. Pretoria Univ., Oxford Univ., Univ. of South Africa.
University lecturer; elected mem. Pretoria City Council 51, Mayor 53-55; Nat. Party M.P. for Pretoria East 58-60; Amb. to the U.K. 61-64; Minister of Foreign Affairs 64-; Chancellor, Univ. of Pretoria 64; Dir. of various companies.
Publs. Books on Ancient History (Afrikaans, English).
Ministry of Foreign Affairs, Pretoria, South Africa.

Müller-Armack, Alfred, DR.RER.POL.; German economist; b. 28 June 1901; ed. Goethe-Gymnasium, Essen, Giessen, Freiburg, Munich and Cologne Univs.
Lecturer, Cologne Univ. 26; Extraordinary Prof. Cologne Univ. 34; Münster 38; Prof. Münster Univ. 40. Cologne 50-; Dir. Department of Economic Policy, Fed. Ministry of Economic Affairs 52-57, Sec. of State 57-63; Chair. Advisory Board Rheinische Stahlwerke 66-; Dr. iur. h.c., Vienna.
Publs. *Ökonomische Theorie der Konjunkturpolitik* 28, *Entwicklungsgesetze des Kapitalismus* 32, *Genealogie der Wirtschaftsstile* 44, *Wirtschaftslenkung und Marktwirtschaft* 47, *Das Jahrhundert ohne Gott* 48, *Diagnose unserer Gegenwart* 49, *Religion und Wirtschaft* 59, *Wirtschaftsordnung und Wirtschaftspolitik* 66.
Office: Institut für Wirtschaftspolitik, Universität zu Köln, Albertus-Magnus-Platz, 5000 Köln-Lindenthal; Home: Auf der Ruhr 11, 5039 Weiss (Kreis Cologne), Gemran Federal Republic.
Telephone: 20-2423-19 (Office).

Müller, Theodor; German business executive; b. 24 April 1911.
Representative for Maschinenwerkzenge in Spain 32-36; joined Ferrostaal A.G., Essen 37; Army service 42-45; returned to Ferrostaal A.G. 45; Deputy Gen. Man. Cia. Ferro e Aco, Vitoria, Brazil 59; Rep. for Ferrostaal in Spain 63; mem. Management Board Maschinenfabrik Esslingen, Esslingen 64; mem. Management Board Gutehoffnungshütte Sterkrade A.G. 66-; Chair. Supervisory Board Utkal Machinery Ltd., India.
43 Essen, Kantorie 43a, German Federal Republic.

Mulley, Rt. Hon. Frederick William, P.C., M.P.; British barrister, economist and politician; b. 3 July 1918; ed. Warwick School and Christ Church, Oxford.
Former clerk, Nat. Health Insurance Cttee., Warwickshire; Army Service 39-45, Prisoner-of-War 40-45; Adult Scholar, Christ Church, Oxford 45-47; Research Studentship, Nuffield Coll., Oxford 47-48; Fellow of St. Catharine's Coll., Cambridge 48-50; M.P. 50-; Parl. Private Sec. to Minister of Works 51; Called to Bar, Inner Temple 54; mem. Nat. Exec. Cttee. Labour Party 57-58, 60-; Deputy Sec. of State for Defence and Minister of Defence for the Army Oct. 64-65; Minister of Aviation Dec. 65-Jan. 67; Minister of State for Foreign Affairs Jan. 67-.
Publ. *The Politics of Western Defence* 62.
The Foreign Office, London, S.W.1, England.
Telephone: WHItehall 8440, Extension 520.

Mulli, Henry Nzioka, B.SC., DIP.ED.; Kenyan educationist, politician and diplomatist; b. 24 Sept. 1925; ed. Alliance High School, Kikuyu, Makerere Univ. Coll., Fort Hare Univ. Coll. and Oxford Univ.
Analytical Chemist, Govt. of Tanganyika 51-53; Head of Science Dept., Machakos High School 57-60; Parl. Sec. for Defence 62-63; Ambassador to People's Republic of China 64-65, to U.A.R. 65-.
Embassy of the Republic of Kenya, 7 Ahmed El Melehy Street, Bokki, Cairo, United Arab Republic.

Mulliken, Robert Sanderson, B.S., PH.D.; American professor of physics and chemistry; b. 7 June 1896; ed. Mass. Inst. of Technology and Univ. of Chicago.
Organic Chemical Research (mainly Chemical Warfare) 17-19; research on separation of isotopes 19-23; on isotope effect in diatomic spectra 23-26; on electronic spectra and electronic structure of diatomic and polyatomic molecules, and valence theory 25-; Nat. Research Fellow 21-25; Asst. Prof. of Physics, Washington Square Coll., New York Univ. 26-28; Assoc. Prof. of Physics, Univ. of Chicago 28-31, Prof. 31-61, Distinguished Service Prof. 61-; work on Plutonium Project at Chicago 42-45; Scientific Attaché, American Embassy, London 55; Ernest de Witt Burton Distinguished Service Prof. 56-61; mem. American Nat. Acad. of Sciences and American Philosophical Soc.; Baker Lecturer, Cornell Univ. 60, Indian Lecturer, Bombay 62, Visiting Prof. Amsterdam 65; Gilbert N. Lewis Gold Medal 60, Theodore W. Richards Gold Medal 60, Peter Debye Award 63, J. G. Kirkwood Medal 65, J. Willard Gibbs Medal 65, Nobel Prize in Chemistry 66; Hon. Fellow, Chemical Soc. (London); Foreign mem. Royal Soc. (U.K.) 67; mem. American Acad. of Arts and Sciences; Hon. mem. Société de Chimie Physique; Hon. Sc.D. (Columbia, Marquette), Hon. Ph.D. (Stockholm); Hon. Sc.D. (Cambridge) 67.
LMSS-Physics Department, University of Chicago, Chicago, Ill. 60637; and 5825 South Dorchester Avenue, Chicago, Ill. 60637, U.S.A.
Telephone: NO 7-4700 (Office); 493-0322 (Home).

Mumford, Lewis; American writer; b. 19 Oct. 1895; ed. New York City Coll., New York Univ., Columbia Univ.
Assoc. Editor *The Dial* 19; Acting Editor *Sociological Review* London 20; Lecturer Geneva School of Int. Studies 25 and 29; Guernsey Centre Moore Foundation Lecturer Dartmouth Coll. 29; Earle Lecturer Pacific School of Religion 47; Bampton Lecturer Columbia Univ. 51; co-Editor *The American Caravan* 26-36; mem. Board of Higher Education, City of New York 35-37; mem. Comm. on Teacher Education, American Council on Education 38-44; Consultant on Planning, City and County Park Board, Honolulu 38; Prof. of Humanities, Stanford Univ. 42-44; Prof. Univ. Pennsylvania 52-60; Hon. Assoc. Royal Inst. British Architects 42; Hon. mem. Town Planning Inst. (Gt. Britain) 46; Hon. Vice-Pres. Int. Housing and Town Planning Fed. 47; Bemis Prof. Massachusetts Inst. of Technology 57-60; Hon. Fellow Stanford Univ. 41; Fellow American Acad. of Arts and Sciences; mem. American Philosophical Soc.; mem. Nat. Inst. of Arts and Letters, Pres. American Acad. of Arts and Letters 63-66; Consultant on Planning, Christ Church, Oxford, England; hon. mem. American Inst. of Architects, American Inst. of Planners; Vice-Pres. Société Européenne de Culture; Co-Chair. Wenner-Gren Conf. on Man's Role in shaping the Face of the Earth 55; Gold Medal, Town Planning Inst. 57; Guggenheim Fellow 32, 38, 56; Ford Research Prof. Univ. of Pa. 59-61, Univ. of Calif. 61-62; Saposnekow lecturer, City Coll. of N.Y. 62; Gold Medal, Town Planning Inst. 57; Royal Gold Medal, R.I.B.A. 61, Presidential Medal of Freedom 64, Emerson-Thoreau Medal American Acad. of Arts and Sciences 65; Hon. LL.D., Edinburgh, Hon. D.Arch., Rome.
Publs. *Story of Utopias* 22, *Sticks and Stones* 24, *The Golden Day* 26, *Herman Melville* 29, *The Brown Decades* 31, *Technics and Civilisation* 34, *The Culture of Cities* 38, *Whither Honolulu?* 38, *Men Must Act* 39, *Faith for*

Living 40, *The South in Architecture* 41, *The Condition of Man* 44, *City Development* 45, *Values for Survival* 46, *Green Memories—The Story of Geddes Mumford* 47, *The Conduct of Life* 51, *Art and Technics* 52, *In the Name of Sanity* 54, *The Transformations of Man* 56, *The City in History* 61, *The Highway and the City* 63, *Herman Melville* 63, *The Myth of the Machine* 67.
Amenia, N.Y., U.S.A.

Mumford, L. Quincy, M.A.; American library administrator; b. 11 Dec. 1903; ed. Duke and Columbia Univs. Duke Univ. Library 22-28; Columbia Univ. Library 28-29; New York Public Library 29-45; Asst. Dir., Cleveland Public Library 45-50, Dir. 50-54; Librarian of Congress 54-; mem. for U.S. of UNESCO's Int. Advisory Cttee. on Bibliography, Documentation and Terminology; Benjamin Franklin Fellow of the Royal Soc. for the Encouragement of Arts, Manufactures and Commerce (London); Del. to Int. Fed. of Library Asscns.
3721 49th Street, N.W., Washington D.C. 20016, U.S.A.

Mumford, Milton Christopher, A.B.; American businessman; b. 14 April 1913; ed. Univ. of Illinois. Joined Marshall Field and Co., Chicago 35, Vice-Pres. 48-54, Gen. Man. Fieldcrest Mills Div. 50-53; Pres. Fieldcrest Mills Inc. 53-54; Vice-Pres. Lever Bros. Co. 54-55, Exec. Vice-Pres. 55-59, Pres. and Chief Exec. Officer 59-65, Chair. of Board 64-; Dir. Equitable Life Assurance Soc. of the U.S. 62-; Trustee, Educ. Facilities Laboratories Inc. (Ford Foundation) 58-65, Chair. 65-; Trustee, Nutrition Foundation 56, Consolidated Edison Co. of N.Y. 64-; Dir. Stamford Hospital, Stamford, Conn. 64-, Crown Zellerbach Corpn. 65-, Nat. Educational Television 65-, Unilever subsidiaries 65-, Fed. Reserve Bank of New York 66-; Nat. Volunteer Chair. United Community Campaigns of America 66-; mem. Nat. Industrial Conference Board 59-; Dir. Nat. Merit Scholar Scholarship Corpn. 65-; mem. American branch, Nat. Advisory Council of Int. Social Service 65, Corpn. Presbyterian Hospital (N.Y.) 66-, Nat. Council Foreign Policy Asscn. 67-; Board of Overseers of the Center for the Study of Violence, Brandeis Univ. 67-, Emergency Cttee. for American Trade 68-.
Lever Brothers Co., 390 Park Avenue, New York, N.Y. 10022, U.S.A.
Telephone: 212-688-6000.

Munch, Charles; French musician; b. 26 Sept. 1891; ed. Protestant Gymnasium, Strasbourg and Conservatoire of Music, Strasbourg.
Prof. of Violin, Strasbourg Conservatory and Concertmaster, Strasbourg Orchestra 19-25; Prof. of Violin, Leipzig Conservatory and Concertmaster, Leipzig Gewandhaus Orchestra 25-32; conducting debut, Paris, Straram Orchestra 32; Conductor, Paris Philharmonic Society Orchestra 35-38; Prof. of Violin, Ecole Normale, Paris 36-38; Prof. of Conducting Paris Conservatory and Conductor Orchestra of the Conservatory Concerts Society 38-46; American Tour, French Nat. Orchestra 48; Conductor and Music Dir., Boston Symphony Orchestra 49-62; Dir. Berkshire Music Center 51-62; Pres. Ecole normale de musique 63; Conductor Orchestre de Paris 67; Knight 40 and Commdr. 46 Legion of Honour; Commdr. Order of the Arts and Letters 57; Commdr. Order of the Cedar, Lebanon 57; Grand Prix du Disque, France 49, 51, 52, 54, 55, 56, 59, 61, Nat. Acad. of Recording Arts and Sciences Award 59, 62.
Publ. *Je suis chef d'orchestre* 54 (English edn. 56, German edn. 57, Russian edn. 61).
15 Place Dreux, "La Futaie", 78 Louveciennes, France.
Telephone: 969-0525.

Münchinger, Karl; German musician; b. 29 May 1915; ed. Staatliche Musikhochschule, Stuttgart and Konservatorium Leipzig.
Church organist in Stuttgart 37-41; Conductor Niedersachsenorchester Hanover 41-43; founded Stuttgart Chamber Orchestra 45 and its Conductor 45-, Klassische

Philharmonie Stuttgart 66 and its Conductor 66-; guest conductor of various symphony orchestras; Grosses Verdienstkreuz; Officier des Arts et des Lettres; Hon. Prof. Kultusministerium Baden-Württemberg.
Haus am Rebenhang, 7 Stuttgart-Rotenberg, German Federal Republic.
Telephone: Stuttgart 29-45-26.

Münchmeyer, Alwin; German merchant banker; b. 19 March 1908.
Partner Münchmeyer & Co. (Hamburg) 37-; Hon. Pres. Perm. Conf. of Chambers of Commerce and Industry of EEC countries; Pres. Bundesverband des privaten Bankgewerbes e.V., Ubersee-Club, Hamburg; Vice-Pres. Deutscher Industrie- und Handelstag, Hamburg Chamber of Commerce; mem. Council of Int. Chamber of Commerce; mem. Exec. Cttee. Verband des Privaten Bankgewerbes e.V.; Chair. Blohm & Voss A.G., Nord-Deutsche Versicherungs-Gesellschaft, Nord-Deutsche Lebensversicherungs-A.G., Hamburg-Bremer Feuer-Versicherungs-Gesellschaft, Vereinsbank in Hamburg, Niedersachsen Versicherungs-A.G., Allgemeine Kreditversicherung A.G., Mainz; Deputy Chair. Deutsche Philips G.m.b.H.; Trustee, Neue Sparcasse von 1864 (Hamburg); mem. Advisory Board Hermes Kreditversicherurgs A.G., Reemtsma Cigarettenfabriken G.m.b.H.; Chair. Foreign Trade Comm. of Ministry of Economy; mem. Govt. Devt. Policy Comm.
Münchmeyer & Co., Ballindamm 33, Hamburg 1, German Federal Republic.
Telephone: 33-92-81.

Munck, Niels; Danish civil engineer and industrialist; b. 31 Dec. 1902.
With ship builders Burmeister & Wain 27-65, sales engineer for Italy 33, Sec. to the Board 34, Man. Dir. Burwain Autodiesel A/S 38, Vice-Dir. Burmeister & Wain 43, Sales Dir. 48, Man. Dir. 52-; Dir. A/S Holeby Dieselmotor Fabrik, Nordisk Diesel A/S, A/S Nordisk Diesel's Financieringsselskab, Alpha-Diesel A/S, Burmeister & Wain American Corpn., etc.; mem. Cttee. Fed. of Danish Industries, Danish Acad. of Technical Sciences, Danish Cttee. Int. Chamber of Commerce, Cttee. for Atomic Energy.
Skovvangen 7, Charlottenlund, Copenhagen, Denmark.

Mundt, Karl Earl, A.M.; American educator and politician; b. 3 June 1900; ed. Carleton Coll. and Columbia Univ.
Teacher of Speech and Social Science High School Bryant, S.D. 23-24, Superintendent 24-27; Chair. Speech Dept. and Instructor in Social Sciences, Eastern State Teachers' Coll., Madison 27-36; part time devoted to insurance and loan business, Madison, S.D. 27-36; Sec.-Treas. Mundt Loan and Investment Co. Inc. Madison 36-48; mem. House of Reps. 38-48, Foreign Affairs Cttee. and Cttee. on Un-American Activities, Senate Cttee., Foreign Relations Cttee., Govt. Operations Cttee.; Senator from S. Dakota 48-; Pres. Nat. Forensic League 33-; Hon. Dr. Rider Coll. N.J., St. Johns Univ., N.Y., Huron Coll., S. Dakota; Editor of *The Rostrum* and Assoc. Editor of *The Speaker*; Republican.
Publs. Articles on soil, water conservation, public affairs and education.
Madison, S. Dakota, U.S.A.; and Senate Office Building, Washington, D.C., U.S.A.
Telephone: CL6-3031.

Münemann, Rudolf; German finance broker and banker; b. 8 Jan. 1908; ed. Wilhelmsgymnasium, Brunswick.
Owner of Münemann Group: Rudolf Münemann, Industriefinanzierungen, Munich (f. 28), Münemann Industrie-Handelsgesellschaft mbH (banking), Munich, Rudolf Münemann Finanzierungs-Anstalt, Liechtenstein, Rudolf Münemann (Great Britain) Ltd., Lon-

don; founded Münemann Industrie-Anlagen G.m.b.H., Munich (leasing of industrial properties) 63.
Rudolf Münemann Industriefinanzierungen, Über der Klause 12, Munich 90, German Federal Republic.
Telephone: Munich 49-49-21.

Munir, Mr. Justice Huhammad, N.Q.A., M.A., LL.B., LL.D. (Hon.); Pakistani lawyer; b. 3 May 1895; Practising lawyer in Amritsar 21, in Lahore 22-36; Pres. Income Tax Appellate Tribunal 40; High Court Judge 42; Chief Justice, Lahore High Court 49-54; Chief Justice of Pakistan 54-60; Minister of Law and Parl. Affairs 62; Acting Gov.-Gen. 54; represented Pakistan at conf. of Int. Comm. of Jurists, Athens 55; Vice-Chair. Int. Criminal Jurisdiction Cttee., UN.
Publs. *Principles and Digest of Law of Evidence, Constitution of the Islamic Republic of Pakistan.*
39 Gulberg V, Lahore, West Pakistan.
Telephone: 81673.

Muñiz, Carlos Manuel; Argentine diplomatist; b. 2 Feb. 1922; ed. Buenos Aires Univ.
Secretary of State 55-56; Amb. to Bolivia 55-59, to Brazil 59-62; Minister of Foreign Affairs 62-63; Int. and Const. Law Prof. Univ. of Buenos Aires; several decorations.
Publs. (Verse) *From this Land, They call it Life;* (Critical works), *Criminology and Literature, Questions on Realism-Truth and Censorship, Madrid and Barcelona-Spain's Two Extremes, Graham Greene.*
c/o Parera 117, Bue No. 5, Buenos Aires, Argentina.

Munk, Frank; American (fmr. Czechoslovak) economist and political scientist; b. 26 May 1901; ed. Prague, Columbia and Harvard Univs.
Student and youth leader Czechoslovakia; Fellow Rockefeller Foundation U.S. 31-33; Chair. Prague Univ. L.N. Fed. 34-36; Masaryk Acad. 31-38; with Social Inst. Min. of Welfare Prague 31-39; Lecturer Reed Coll. Portland, Oregon 39-41; Lecturer in Economics Univ. Calif., Berkeley, to 44; Dir. UNRRA Training Centre, Univ. Maryland 44-45; Chief Economic Adviser UNRRA 46; Prof. Reed Coll., Portland, Oregon 46-65; Dean Northwest Inst. Int. Relations 47-56; Visiting Prof. Univ. of Wash. 52; Public mem. Regional Wage Stabilisation Board 51-52; mem. Exec. Council, Pacific North-west Political Science Asscn. 52-55; Adviser on Intellectual Co-operation to the European Dir. Radio Free Europe, Munich 58-60; Research Fellow, Atlantic Inst. (Paris) 61-62; Visiting Prof. Political Science, Coll. of Europe (Brussels) 61-62; Research Consultant, Foreign Policy Research Inst., Univ. of Pennsylvania 63-65; Prof. of Political Science and Assoc. Dir. Central European Studies Center, Portland State Coll. 65-.
Publs. include *The Legacy of Nazism* 43, *Atlantic Dilemma* 63.
3808 S.W., Mt. Adams Drive, Portland, Oregon 97201, U.S.A.
Telephone: 503-228-5778.

Munongo, Godefroide; Congolese (Katanga) politician; b. *c.* 30; ed. Kisantu, Lower Congo.
Former Minister of Interior, Katanga; Minister of Health, South Katanga April-Aug. 63, East Katanga Aug. 63-July 64; Minister of Interior, Congo Republic July 64-65; Gov. of Katanga Oriental (now Sud-Katanga) June 65-66.
Lubumbashi (Elizabethville), Democratic Republic of Congo (Kinshasa).

Muñoz Grandes, Capt. Gen. Augustín; Spanish army officer and politician; b. 27 Jan. 1896; ed. Toledo Infantry Acad.
Commanded Army Spanish Corps. Spanish Civil War 36-39, Spanish Volunteer Blue Div., Soviet Front, Second World War; Chief of the Gen. Staff; Deputy Prime Minister July 62-July 67.
Supreme H.Q. of the Spanish Army, Madrid, Spain.

Muñoz Marín, Luis; Puerto Rican politician and journalist; b. 18 Feb. 1898; ed. Georgetown Univ., Washington.
Sec. to Puerto Rican Commr. Washington D.C. 16-18; Senator 32-; Founder Popular Democratic Party 38; Pres. Senate 41-48; Gov. of Puerto Rico 49-64; fmr. Editor *La Democracia,* Editor *La Revista de Indias;* founder and Editor of *El Batey.*
Publs. *Borrones* 17, *Madre haraposa* (in collaboration) 17, *These United States* 25.
Senate of Puerto Rico, San Juan, Puerto Rico.

Munro, Dana G.; American diplomatist and historian; b. 18 July 1892; ed. Wisconsin, Pennsylvania and Brown Univs.
Regional Economist Dept. of State 19-20; Economist Consul at Valparaiso 20-21; mem. Latin-American Div. of State Dept. 21-25; 1st Sec. Panama 25-27 and Nicaragua 27-29; Chief Latin-American Affairs Div. of State Dept. 29-30; Minister to Haiti 30-32; Prof. of Latin-American History and Affairs Princeton Univ. 32-61; Vice-Pres. Foreign Bondholders' Protective Council N.Y. 38-58, Pres. 58-67, Chair. Exec. Cttee. 67-; Dir. Woodrow Wilson School of Public and Int. Affairs, Princeton Univ. 39-58; mem. Nat. Advisory Cttee. on Inter-American Affairs 59-61.
Publs. *The Five Republics of Central America* 18, *The United States and the Caribbean Area* 34, *The Latin American Republics: A History* 42, *Intervention and Dollar Diplomacy in The Caribbean 1900-21* 64.
345 Harrison Street, Princeton, N.J. 08540, U.S.A.
Telephone: 609-924-1238.

Munro, Sir Leslie Knox, K.C.M.G., K.C.V.O., M.P., LL.M.; New Zealand lawyer and diplomatist; b. 26 Feb. 1901; ed. Auckland Univ. Coll.
Dean of Faculty of Law, Auckland Univ. Coll. 38; mem. Auckland Univ. Coll. Council 39-52; mem. Senate Univ. of N.Z. 47-52; Past Pres. Auckland Law Society; past mem. Council N.Z. Law Society; Del. Imperial Press Conf. 46; Editor *New Zealand Herald;* 42-52; Ambassador to U.S.A. and Permanent Rep. to U.N. 52-58, Pres. Trusteeship Council 53-54, N.Z. Rep. on Security Council 54-55, Pres. Gen. Ass. 57-58; UN Special Rep. on Question of Hungary 58-62; Sec.-Gen. of Int. Comm. of Jurists 61-63; Mem. of Parl. 63-; numerous honorary degrees; National Party.
Publ. *United Nations: Hope for a Divided World* 60.
24 Pollock Drive, Hamilton, New Zealand.
Telephone: 41307.

Munshi, Kanailal Maneklal, B.A., LL.B., D.LITT., LL.D.; Indian lawyer; b. 30 Dec. 1887; ed. Baroda Coll.
Joint-Ed. *Gujerat* 22-31; mem. Baroda Univ. Comm. 26; M.L.A. Bombay 27-46; mem. A.I.C.C. 30-36 and 47-50; imprisoned 30 and 32; Home Minister Government of Bombay 37-39; mem. Constituent Assembly and of its Drafting Cttee.; mem. Parliament 47-52; Agent-Gen. Government of India, Hyderabad 47-48; Minister of Food and Agriculture 50-52; Gov. Uttar Pradesh 52-57; Vice-Pres. Bar Asscn. of India 57-60; Chair. Sanskrit Visha Parishad 51-; Exec. Chair. Indian Law Inst. 57-60; Advocate Supreme Court of India and High Court of Bombay; Founder Pres. Bharatiya Vidya Bhavan; Trustee, Birla Educ. Trust; Chair. Bai Kabibai & Hansraj Morarji, Kanji Khetsey, Babulnath Temple Charity Trusts, Shree Somnath Trust.
Publs. *Gujerat and its literature, I follow the Mahatma, Glory that was Gurjaradesa, Bhagavad Gita and Modern Life, Creative Art of Life, The End of an Era, Saga of Indian Sculpture, Warnings of History, Reconstruction of Society through Trusteeship, Foundations of Indian Culture, Krishnavatara,* Parts I-V, and over 50 books in Gujerati.
Bharatiya Vidya Bhavan, Chaupatty Road, Bombay 7, India.

Munshi, Mrs. Lilavati Kanaiyalal; Indian politician; b. 99.
Joined Satyagraha movement 30; mem. All-India Congress Cttee. 31-34; arrested and sentenced to one year's imprisonment 32; mem. Bombay Municipal Corpn. 35-46; Chair. 39-40; Vice-Pres. Nat. Council of Women in India 53-58; Pres. Bombay Presidency Women's Council 50-51; Pres. All-India Women's Food Cen. Council 50-64; Chair. Delhi Conf. of Social Work; mem. Film Advisory Board and Cen. Board of Film Censors; mem. Indian Council of Agricultural Research 50-59; founder-mem. Gujerat Research Soc.; fmr. Editor *Pushpa* and *New Outlook;* Congress mem. Bombay Legislative Council 36-46; Chair. Rajkamal Publications Ltd.; Dir. Bombay Life Insurance Co., Oudh Sugar Mills and Lallubhai Shamaldas Co-operative Bank.
Publs. *Rekhachitro ane Bija Lekho, Jeevanmathi Judeli, Kumardevi, Rekha Chitro June ane Nava.*
Bharatiya Vidya Bhavan, Chowpatty Road, Bombay 7, India.

Munson, Charles Sherwood, B.A.; American industrialist; b. 14 Sept. 1888; ed. Yale Univ.
Joined Amoskeag Manufacturing Co. 12; Treas. Cuban Air Products 17, Pres. 19-42, Chair. 42-, Pres. Nat. Carbide Corpn. 19-41; Vice-Pres. Air Reduction Co. Inc. 24-37, Pres. 37-48, 49-64, Chair. Exec. Cttee. 64-, Chair. of Board 49; Pres. U.S. Industrial Chemicals 31-43, Chair. Exec. Cttee. 43-49; Dir. and mem. Advisory Council Morgan Guaranty Trust Co. of N.Y.; Dir. and mem. Finance Cttee. Nat. Distillers and Chemical Corpn., Dir. and mem. Exec. Cttee. Greyhound Corpn., Gen. Fire and Accident Insurance Co.; Dir. Baxter Laboratories, Warner Bros. Co., and numerous other companies.
Home: Sasco Hill, Southport, Conn. 06490; Office: 150 East 42nd Street, New York 10017, N.Y., U.S.A.

Muntasser, Mahmud; Libyan diplomatist; b. 03; ed. Rome Univ.
Former Vice-Chair. Admin. Council, of British Admin. of Tripoli; Prime Minister and Minister for Foreign Affairs 51-54; Ambassador to U.K. 54-57; Personal Adviser to King of Libya 57-58; Ambassador to Italy 58-62, and concurrently Minister to Greece March 59, and Yugoslavia May 61; Prime Minister 64-65; Chief of Royal Household 65-; Grand Cordon of Mohamed Ben Ali Senussi and decorations from many other countries.
Tripoli, Libya.

Muntasser, Dr. Omar Mahmud; Libyan politician and diplomatist; b. 28 July 1930; ed. Univs. of Florence and Oxford.
Member Libyan Del. to UN, New York 57; Minister, Washington 60-61; Minister, London 61-62; Minister of Justice 62, 63-64; Minister of Foreign Affairs March 63; Ambassador to U.K., concurrently accred. to Netherlands 64-, and Malta 66-.
Libyan Embassy, 58 Princes Gate, London, S.W.7, England.

Murad, Enver, M.SC.; Pakistani naval officer and diplomatist; b. 22 Feb. 1917; ed. Aligarh Muslim Univ.
Royal Indian Navy 42-47, Pakistan Navy 47-49, 52-57; Pakistan Foreign Service 49-52, 57-; Second Sec., Moscow 49-52; Deputy Sec., Ministry of Foreign Affairs 57-59; Counsellor, London 59; Chargé d'Affaires, later Minister, Morocco 59-63; High Commr. in Ceylon 63-67; Amb. to Austria 67-.
Embassy of Pakistan, P.O. Box 45, P.O. 49, Vienna 3, Austria; and Ministry of Foreign Affairs, Islamabad, Pakistan.

Muradov, Nuritdin Muradovich; Soviet politician; b. 1915; ed. Central Planning-Economic Inst.
Member C.P.S.U. 46-; Chair. District Planning Cttee., then Economist, Uzbek S.S.R. State Planning Cttee.,

later Chief of Section, Republican People's Commissariat for Trade, then Vice-Chair. Exec. Cttee. Regional Soviet of Working People's Deputies 33-51; First Sec. Namangansky District Cttee. of C.P. Uzbekistan, later Chair. Exec. Cttee. of Namangan, then of Khorezm, Regional Soviet of Working People's Deputies 51-65; First Sec. Surkhandaryinsk Regional Cttee. of C.P. Uzbekistan 65-; mem. Central Cttee. of C.P. Uzbekistan; Deputy to U.S.S.R. Supreme Soviet; Hero of Socialist Labour.
Surkhandaryinsk Regional Committee of Communist Party of Uzbekistan, Termez, U.S.S.R.

Muradyan, Badal Amayakovich; Soviet politician; b. 1915; ed. Erevan Polytechnic Inst.
Engineer 38-41; Soviet Army service 42-43; Geologist 43-53; mem. C.P.S.U. 51-; Party Official 53-61; First Sec. Erevan City Cttee. C.P. of Armenia 61-66; Chair. Armenian Council of Ministers 66-; mem. Central Cttee. C.P. of Armenia; Deputy to U.S.S.R. Supreme Soviet and to Armenian Supreme Soviet.
Council of Ministers, Armenian S.S.R., Erevan, U.S.S.R.

Muralt, Alexander von, M.D., PH.D.; Swiss physiologist; b. 19 Aug. 1903.
Research Fellow (Rockefeller Foundation) Harvard Univ. 29, Research Assoc. Harvard Univ. 30, Kaiser Wilhelm Inst. 30-35; Prof. of Physiology, Univ. of Berne 35-; Dir. Scientific Station, Jungfraujoch 37-; Pres. Swiss Acad. of Sciences 46-52; Pres. Th. Kocher Foundation 44-, Foundation for Fellowships in Medicine and Biology 42-48, Pres. 1.C.S.U. 49-52, Swiss Nat. Science Foundation 52-; Rector Berne Univ. 55-56; hon. degrees from Berne, Lausanne, Manchester, Geneva, Basle, Zürich, Cologne, Brussels and Rio de Janeiro Univs.
Publs. *Signalübermittlung im Nerven* 46, *Praktische Physiologie* 48, *Neue Ergebnisse der Nervenphysiologie* 58.
Physiological Institute, Bühlplatz 5, Berne, Switzerland.
Telephone: 23-07-84.

Muralt, Leonhard von; Swiss historian; b. 17 May 1900; ed. Univs. of Geneva and Zürich.
Lecturer in History, Univ. of Zürich 30-40; Ordinary Prof. for Modern General and Swiss History, Univ. of Zürich 40-; Hon. Dr. Theol. (Univ. of Berne).
Publs. *Die Badener Disputation 1526* 26, *Reformation und Gegenreformation* (in *Geschichte der Schweiz*) 32, *Huldrych Zwingli, Von göttlicher und menschlicher Gerechtigkeit* 34, *Das Zeitalter der Renaissance* (in *Die Neue Propyläen-Weltgeschichte* 41, *Machiavellis Staatsgedanke* 45, *Der Friede von Versailles und die Gegenwart* (trans. into English as *From Versailles to Potsdam* 48) 47, *Bismarcks Reichsgründung* 47, *Zürich im Schweizerbund* 51, *Quellen zur Geschichte der Täufer in der Schweiz I: Zürich* 52, *Bismarcks Verantwortlichkeit* 55, *Die Reformation* (in *Historia Mundi VII*) 57, *Der Historiker und die Geschichte, Ausgewählte Aufsätze und Vorträge* 60, Editor *Huldreich Zwinglis Sämtliche Werke* (*Corpus Reformatorum*) VI (I) 61, VI (II) 64, *Renaissance und Reformation* (in *Handbuch der Schweizergeschichte*) 67.
Wybüelstrasse 20, Zollikon bei Zürich, Switzerland.
Telephone: 051-658761.

Muramaya, Nagataka; Japanese newspaper proprietor; b. 94; ed. Kyoto Imperial Univ.
Director *Asahi Shimbun* 20-; Man. Dir. Asahi Welfare and Cultural Asscn. 52; Chair. of Board *Asahi Evening News* 53-; Dir. Asahi Broadcasting Corpn., Osaka 55; Pres. Japan Newspaper Publishers and Editors Asscn. 55; Vice-Pres. Fed. Int. des Editeurs de Journaux et Publications 58-; Pres. *Asahi Shimbun* 60-64; numerous decorations.
16 1-chome, Ichibeicho, Azabu, Minato-ku, Tokyo, Japan.

Murase, Itsuzo; Japanese insurance executive; b. 20 March 1902; ed. Kobe Univ.
Taisho Marine and Fire Insurance Co. Ltd. 26-, Manager, Tokyo Branch 46-54, Dir. and Manager Osaka Branch and Takamatsu Branch 54-58, Man. Dir. 58-60, Exec. Dir. 60-62, Pres. 62-; Pres. The Marine & Fire Insurance Asscn. of Japan 66-, Fire & Marine Insurance Rating Asscn. of Japan 62-66, Union of Machinery Insurers of Japan 63-65, The Japanese Hull Insurers' Union 63-65; Dir. Nippon Atomic Industry Group Companies Ltd. 63-, The Dominion Insurance Co. Ltd. 65-, Sena Co. Ltd. 66-67; mem. Insurance Council 65-; mem. other insurance asscns., Building Council 67.
No. 406, Shimoochiai 1-chome, Shinjuku-ku, Tokyo, Japan.

Murata, Masachika; Japanese architect; b. 6 Sept. 1906; ed. Tokyo Acad. of Fine Arts.
Designer, Shinichiro Okada Architect Office, Tokyo 29-30, Building Dept. of Ministry of Imperial Household, Tokyo 31-36; Researcher of facilities of Museums of Europe and America at request of Ministry of Educ. 37-39; Architect, Kameki Tuchiura Architect Office 40-46; Vice-Chief of Architectural Div., Conf. of Devt. of Kainan-tow (Hainan Island, China) 43; Pres. Masachika Murata Architect Office 46-; Dir. Board, Japan Architects Asscn. 54-; Dir. Sports and Recreation Facilities, Union of Int. Architects 59-.
Works include: Yokohama building of Yokohama Trading Building Co. Ltd. (Kanagawa Prefecture Architectural Prize) 51; Tokyo Metropolitan Indoor Pool, Tokyo 57; Exhbn. Halls of Tokyo Int. Trading Center, Tokyo 59; Miyazaki Kanko Hotel, Miyazaki Pref. 61; Tokyo Olympic Komazawa Stadium (Special Prize of Architectural Inst. of Japan and Building Contractors' Soc. of Japan) 62; Italian Embassy, Tokyo 63; Kyodo News Service Building, Tokyo 64; Y.M.C.A. Int. Youth Center, Shizuoka Pref. 64; Hotel Matsukura, Nagasaki Pref. 64; Hotel Hodaka, Nagano Pref. 64; Recreational facilities for IBM Japan, Tokyo and Kanagawa Pref. 65; Residence of Consul Gen. of South Africa, Tokyo 65; Mie Athletic Stadium 67, Mt. Tateyama Bus Terminal and Hotel 68; Police Headquarters, Aichi Pref. 68.
Office: Jingugaien Building, 2-7-25 Kita Aoyama, Minato-ku, Tokyo; Home: 2-14-4 Moto-Azabu, Minato-ku, Tokyo, Japan.
Telephone: 402-0016 (Office); 451-1672 (Home).

Murchison, Clinton Williams; American executive; b. 95; ed. Trinity Univ., San Antonio.
Pres. Delhi Oil 48-; owner First Nat. Bank of Athens, City Transportation, Dallas, Martha Washington Candy Co., Chicago, etc.; numerous other interests in the fields of railways, steamships, real estate, publishing, insurance, cinemas, etc.
1201 Main Street, Dallas, Texas, U.S.A.

Murdoch, (Jean) Iris (Mrs. J. O. Bayley); British writer and philosopher; b. 15 July 1919; ed. Froebel Educational Inst. (London), Badminton School (Bristol) and Somerville Coll., Oxford.
Worked at the Treasury 42-44, with UNRRA 44-46; Philosophy Studentship Newnham Coll. Cambridge 47-48; Fellow St. Anne's Coll. Oxford 48-63, Hon. Fellow 63-.
Publs. *Sartre: Romantic Rationalist* 53, *Under the Net* 54, *The Flight from the Enchanter* 55, *The Sandcastle* 57, *The Bell* 58, *A Severed Head* 61 (play 63), *An Unofficial Rose* 62, *The Unicorn* 63, *The Italian Girl* 64 (play 67), *The Red and the Green* 65, *The Time of the Angels* 66, *The Nice and the Good* 68.
Cedar Lodge, Steeple Aston, Oxfordshire, England.

Murdoch, Keith Rupert; Australian newspaper publisher; b. 31.
Chairman of Dirs., News Ltd., and assoc. Companies, publishers of *The Australian*, *The News* (Adelaide),

The Daily Mirror (Sydney), *Sunday Mirror* (Sydney), *Sunday Truth* (Brisbane), *Sunday Mail* (Adelaide), *Sunday Times* (Perth), *The News* (Darwin), *The New Idea*, etc.; Chair. Southern Television Corpn. Adelaide; Dir. Television Corpn. Sydney and Melbourne; Dir. Wellington Publishing Co. Ltd. (*The Dominion*).
92 Empire Circuit, Deakin, Canberra, A.C.T., Australia.

Murdock, Kenneth Ballard, A.M., PH.D.; American university professor; b. 22 June 1895; ed. Harvard Univ.
Asst. in English, Harvard Univ. 16-17, 19-20; Asst. Dean, Harvard 19-24; Instructor in English, Harvard 23-26, Sec. of English Dept. 24-28, Asst. Prof. 26-30, Assoc. Prof. 30-32, Prof. 32-64, Emer. 64-, Dean of Faculty of Arts and Sciences 31-36, Master of Leverett House 31-41; Chair. Cttee. on Gen. Educ. 55-60; mem. Board of Syndics. Harvard Univ. Press 54-58, 59-61; Dir. Harvard Center for Italian Renaissance Culture 61-64; Lecturer Scandinavian Univs. 46; Visiting Prof. Univs. of Oslo and Uppsala 49, Copenhagen 53; Lord Northcliffe Lecturer, London 51; Knight, Order of the North Star (Sweden); Hon. Litt.D. (Middlebury Coll.) 30, L.H.D. (Trinity Coll.) 32, LL.D. (Bucknell Univ.) 33, L.H.D. (Univ. of Vt.) 38, Fil.D. (Uppsala Univ.) 50, D.Litt. (Harvard) 60.
Publs. *Portraits of Increase Mather* 24, *Increase Mather, the Foremost American Puritan* 25, *The Sun at Noon* 39, *Literature and Theology in Colonial New England* 49; Part I of *The Literature of the American People* (editor A. H. Quinn) 51; Editor: *Selections from Cotton Mather* 26, *Handkerchiefs from Paul* 27, *A Leaf of Grass from Shady Hill* 28, *The Day of Doom* 29, *Manuductio ad Ministerium* 38, *Ett Kvinnoporträtt* 47, *The Notebooks of Henry James* (with F. O. Matthiessen) 47, *Literature and Theology in Colonial New England* 49, Part One of *The Literature of The American People* (ed. by A. H. Quinn) 51.
416 Widener Library, Cambridge, Massachusetts 02138; Home: Prince Street, Beverly, Mass., U.S.A.
Telephone: 922-5172.

Murena, H. A.; Argentine writer; b. 14 Feb. 1923.
Publs. *Primer testamento* (story) 46, *La vida nueva* (poetry) 51, *El juez* (play) 53, *El pecado original de América* (essay) 54, *La fatalidad de los cuerpos* (novel) 55, *El centro del infierno* (short stories) 56, *El círculo de los paraísos* (poetry) 58, *Las leyes de la noche* (novel) 58, *El escándalo y el fuego* 59, *Homo atomicus* 61, *Relámpago de la duración* 62, *Ensayos sobre subversión* 62, *El demonio de la armonía* 64, *Los herederos de la promesa* 65.
San José 910, Buenos Aires, Argentina.

Murgulescu, Ilie, D.SC.; Romanian chemist; b. 27 Jan. 1902; ed. Charles I High School, Craiova, and Univs. of Cluj and Leipzig.
Director of Studies and Prof. of Analytical and Physical Chemistry, Timişoara Polytechnical Inst. 34-49; Prof. of Physical Chemistry, Univ. of Bucharest 49-; mem. Grand Nat. Assembly 48-; Deputy Minister, later Minister of Educ. 50-56; Minister of Educ. and Culture 60-63; mem. Romanian Acad. of Sciences 48-, Pres. 63-66; Dir. Centre of Physical Chemistry 63-; Vice-Pres. Romanian Council of State 65-67; Vice-Pres. Grand Nat. Assembly 67-; Foreign mem. U.S.S.R. Acad. of Sciences, Czechoslovak Acad. of Sciences; Laureate, State Prize of Romania 62.
Publs. Over 150 papers in analytical and physical chemistry in Romanian and foreign scientific journals.
Chaussée Kiseleff 22, Bucharest, Romania.

Murnaghan, Francis Dominic, M.A., D.SC., PH.D.; American professor; b. 4 Aug. 1893; ed. Nat. Univ. of Ireland and Johns Hopkins Univ.
Instructor Rice Inst. 16; Assoc. Johns Hopkins Univ. 18, Assoc. Prof. 21, Prof. and Head of Dept. of Maths. 28-48; Prof. Instituto Técnico de Aeronáutica, Brazil

49-59; Consultant U.S. Navy, David Taylor Model Basin 55-63.

Publs. *Vector Analysis and the Theory of Relativity* 22, *Theoretical Mechanics* (with J. S. Ames) 29, *Hydrodynamics* (with H. Bateman and H. L. Dryden) 32, *The Theory of Group Representations* 38, *Analytic Geometry* 46, *Differential and Integral Calculus* 47, *Introduction to Applied Mathematics* 48, *Finite Deformation of an Elastic Solid* 51, *Calculo Avancado* 54, *Algebra Elementar e Trigonometria* 54, *Equações Diferenciais* 55, *The Laplace Transformation* 62, *The Calculus of Variations* 62, *The Unitary and Rotation Groups* 62.

6202 Sycamore Road, Baltimore 12, Md., U.S.A.

Murphy, Charles S.; American government official; b. 20 Aug. 1909; ed. Duke Univ., Durham, North Carolina.

Admitted to N. Carolina Bar 34; Office of Legislative Counsel, U.S. Senate 34-46; Admin. Asst. to Pres. of U.S. 47-50, Special Counsel 50-53; Partner, Morison, Murphy, Clapp and Abrams 53-61; Counsel to Dem. Nat. Advisory Council 57-60; Under-Sec. Dept. of Agriculture 60-65; Chair. Civil Aeronautics Board 65-68.

Greenbriar Lane, Annapolis, Md., U.S.A.

Telephone: 263-2463.

Murphy, Franklin David, A.B., M.D.; American educator; b. 29 Jan. 1916; ed. Univs. of Kansas and Göttingen and Univ. of Pennsylvania School of Medicine.

Dean of School of Medicine and Assoc. Prof. of Internal Medicine, Univ. of Kansas 48-51; Chancellor, Univ. of Kansas 51-60; Chancellor, Univ. of Calif. at Los Angeles 60-; Dir. Ford Motor Co., McCall Corpn., Times-Mirror Co., Hallmark Cards; mem. Board of Trustees, Kress Foundation; Hon. LL.D., Hon. L.H.D., Hon. D.Sc.

Publs. in field of chemotherapy, cardiovascular diseases, medical education and general education.

10570 Sunset Boulevard, Los Angeles, California 90024, U.S.A.

Murphy, George Arthur; American banker; b. 13 Dec. 1905; ed. Oglethorpe Univ., New York Univ. and Harvard Univ.

Joined Irving Trust Co., New York City 31, Vice-Pres. (Personal Trust Div.) 47-53, Senior Vice-Pres. (Loan Admin. Div.) and Senior Loaning Officer 54-57, Pres. 57-60, Chair. 60-, Dir. 56-; Chair. Charter New York Corpn. 66-.

Home: Washington, Conn. 06793; Office: 1 Wall Street, New York, N.Y. 10015, U.S.A.

Murphy, George Lloyd; American actor and politician; b. 4 July 1902; ed. Peddie Inst., Hightstown, N.J., Pawling School, N.Y., and Yale Univ.

Former actor and executive in motion picture industry; Chair. Republican State Cen. Cttee. of Calif. 53; fmr. Pres. Screen Actors Guild; Vice-Pres. Desilu Productions and Technicolor Corpn.; Senator from Calif. 65-; Republican.

452 Senate Office Building, Washington 25, D.C., U.S.A.

Murphy, Robert Cushman, PH.B., M.A., D.SC.; American ornithologist; b. 29 April 1887; ed. Brown and Columbia Univs.

Curator Brooklyn Museum 11-20; Associate Curator and Curator of Birds American Museum of Natural History 21-26, Curator of Oceanic Birds 26-42, Chair. Dept. of Birds 42-55, Lamont Curator of Birds 48-55, Emer. 55-; leader expeditions S. America, Antarctica, New Zealand, Pacific and Caribbean Islands; Contrib. Editor *Geographical Review*; mem. Antarctic Programs Cttee. Nat. Science Foundation 63-; mem. Exec. Council Long Island Univ. at Brookhaven 64-; mem. Asscn. of American Geographers, American Geophysical Union; Dir. and Past Pres. Nat. Audubon Soc.; Fellow American

Geographical Soc., New York Acad. of Sciences (Vice-Pres. 24), American Ornithologists' Union, American Phil. Soc., and American Asscn. for the Advancement of Science; Hon. Fellow Royal Hungarian Inst. and Royal Society of N.Z.; awarded Burroughs Medal 38, Brewster Medal 37, Cullum Medal American Geog. Soc. 40, Elliot Medal Nat. Acad. Sciences 43.

Publs. *Bird Islands of Peru* 25, *Wandering Among Forgotten Isles* (part author) 27, *Problems of Polar Research* (part author) 28, *Oceanic Birds of South America* (2 vols.) 36, *Logbook for Grace* 47, *American Land Birds* 53.

Briarlea, Old Field, Setauket, Long Island, N.Y., U.S.A.

Murphy, Robert Daniel, LL.M.; American diplomatist and businessman; b. 28 Oct. 1894; ed. Marquette Acad. and George Washington Univ.

Clerk Post Office Dept. 16-17, Legation Berne 17-19; Asst. to Chief, Treasury Dept. 19-20; Vice-Consul Zürich 21, Munich 21-24; Consul Seville 25-29; Consul Paris 30-41, Counsellor Embassy 39-41; American rep. Algiers 43-44; U.S. mem. Advisory Council for Italy 43-44; Political Adviser, with rank of Ambassador, to Gen. Eisenhower 44-45; Ambassador to Belgium 49-52, to Japan 52-53; Asst. Sec. of State 53-54; Deputy Under-Sec. of State 54-59; Under-Sec. of State (Political Affairs) June-Nov. 59; Chair. Corning Glass Works Int.

Publ. *Diplomat Among Warriors* 64.

717 5th Avenue, New York, N.Y. 10022; Home: 1701 Kalmia Road, N.W., Washington, D.C., U.S.A.

Murphy, William Beverly, B.S.; American business executive; b. 17 June 1907; ed. Univ. of Wisconsin.

Exec. Vice-Pres. A. C. Nielsen Co. 28-38; Campbell Soup Co. 38-42; War Production Board, Washington 42-45; Campbell Soup Co. 45-, Pres. 53-; Dir. American Telephone and Telegraph Co., Merck & Co. Inc.; Trustee Wisconsin Alumni Research Foundation, The Nutrition Foundation, Mass. Inst. of Technology; Chair. Business Council 65-66.

375 Memorial Avenue, Camden 1, N.J.; and 110 Maple Hill Road, Gladwyne, Pa., U.S.A.

Murphy, William Parry, A.B., M.D.; American physician; b. 6 Feb. 1892; ed. Univ. of Oregon and Harvard Univ. Medical School.

Intern, Rhode Island Hospital, Providence 20-22; Asst. Resident Physician Peter Bent Brigham Hospital, Boston 22-23, Junior Associate in Medicine 23-28, Associate in Medicine 28-35, Senior Associate in Medicine and Consultant in Hematology 35-58, Emeritus 58-; Asst. in Medicine Harvard Univ. Medical School 23-28, Instructor 28-35, Associate in Medicine 35-48; Lecturer on Medicine 48-58, Emer. 58-; discoverer (with Dr. George R. Minot) of liver treatment for pernicious anæmia; awarded Cameron Prize of Edinburgh Univ. 30, bronze medal American Medical Asscn. 34, Nobel Prize in Physiology and Medicine 34, Gold Medal Mass. Humane Society, Dip. in Internal Medicine 37, etc.; mem. Kaiserl. Leopold. Carolin. Deutsche Akad. der Naturforscher, American Society for Clinical Investigation, Asscn. of American Physicians, Society of Arts and Sciences, American Asscn. for the Advancement of Science, Fellow American Medical Asscn., Nat. Inst. of Social Sciences, Robert Kennedy Duncan Society of Mellon Inst.; Hon. mem. Society of Finnish Physicians for Internal Diseases, New York Acad. of Sciences, Univ. of Oregon Medical Alumni Asscn. 64; Commdr. Order of White Rose (Finland), Nat. Order of Merit, Carlos J. Finlay (Cuba); Hon. D.Sc. Gustavus Adolphus Coll, Distinguished Achievement Award, Boston 65.

Publ. *Anæmia in Practice: Pernicious Anæmia* 39.

Office: 1101 Beacon Street, Brookline, Mass.; 97 Sewall Avenue, Brookline 46, Mass., U.S.A.

Murray, George McIntosh, C.B.E.; British journalist; b. 16 Dec. 1900; ed. Archbishop Tenison's Grammar School.
Leader-writer *Daily Mail* 33-39, Chief Leader-writer 39-; Dir. Associated Newspapers 55; mem. Press Council 53, Vice-Chair. 57, Chair. 59-63; mem. Commonwealth Press Union 64.
Publs. *The Life of King George V* 35, *His Majesty King Edward VIII* 36, *King George VI and the Coronation* 37, *The Impatient Horse* 52.
45 Grove Way, Esher, Surrey, England.

Murray, Jack Keith, O.B.E., E.D., B.A., B.SC.AGR., N.D.D., F.A.I.A.S.; Australian agriculturalist; b. 8 Feb. 1889; ed. Univ. of Sydney.
Served in A.I.F. in both World Wars; retired with rank of Colonel; Lecturer in Bacteriology and Dairy Technology, Hawkesbury Agric. Coll., N.S.W. 20-23; Principal, Queensland Agric. Coll. 23-45; Prof. of Agric., Univ. of Queensland 27-45; Admin. of Territory of Papua and New Guinea Oct. 45-52; Pres. Exec. and Legislative Councils of the Territory; Macrossan Lecturer, Univ. of Queensland 46; Australian Del., S. Pacific Region Conf. 47; Fellow Australian Nat. Research Council; Pres. Section K (Agric. and Forestry), Australian and New Zealand Assen. for the Advancement of Science 35; Pres. Queensland Royal Soc. 36, Hon. Life mem. 68; mem. Senate, Univ. of Queensland 53-55, 57-; Gov. Cromwell Coll., Univ. of Queensland 53-55, 57-; mem. Council of Univ. Women's Coll. 53-55, 57-, Nat. Council; Colombo Plan Adviser on Agricultural Educ. 56-57; Acting Warden Int. House, Univ. of Melbourne 60; D.Sc. h.c. (Queensland) 68.
49 Dell Road, St. Lucia, Brisbane S.W.6, Queensland, Australia.
Telephone: Brisbane 70-2382.

Murray, James Dalton, C.M.G.; British diplomatist; b. 6 March 1911; ed. Stowe School and Magdalene Coll., Cambridge.
Joined Consular Service 33, Vice-Consul, San Francisco 33-36, Mexico City 36-39; Second Sec. Washington 39-43; First Sec. and Consul La Paz 43-45; First Sec. Prague 45; Foreign Office 45-48; Office Commr.-Gen. for S.E. Asia 48-50; Counsellor, Foreign Office 50-52; Deputy High Commr. in Pakistan 52-55; Foreign Office 55-59; Counsellor Lisbon 59-61; Minister Romania 61-63, Amb. 63-65; High Commr. in Jamaica 65-; non-res. Amb. to Haiti 66-.
British High Commission, Kingston, Jamaica.

Murray, Sir (Francis) Ralph (Hay), K.C.M.G.; British diplomatist; b. 3 March 1908; ed. Brentwood School and St. Edmund Hall, Oxford.
British Broadcasting Corpn. 34-39; Foreign Office 39-45; Allied Comm. for Austria 45-46; Special Commr.'s Staff, S. E. Asia 46-47; Foreign Office 47-51; Counsellor, Madrid 51-54; Minister, Cairo 54-56; Asst. Under-Sec. of State Foreign Office 57-61; Dep. Under-Sec. of State, Foreign Office 61-62; Amb. to Greece 62-67; Gov. of B.B.C. 67-.
The Old Rectory, Stoke Hammond, Bletchley, Bucks., England.

Murray of Newhaven, Baron (Life Peer) cr. 64, of Newhaven; **Keith (Anderson Hope) Murray,** K.C.B., B.SC., PH.D., B.LITT., M.A.; British university administrator; b. 28 July 1903; ed. Edinburgh Acad., Edinburgh Univ., Cornell Univ., N.Y. and Oxford Univ.
Ministry of Agriculture 25-26; Commonwealth Fund Fellow 26-29; Agricultural Econs. Research Inst., Oxford 29-32, Research Officer 32-39; Ministry of Food 39-40; R.A.F.V.R. 41-42; Dir. of Food and Agriculture, Middle East Supply Centre 42-45; Fellow and Bursar, Lincoln Coll., Oxford 37-53, Rector 44-53; Chair. Univ. Grants Cttee. 53-63; Chancellor, Southampton Univ. 64-; Dir. Bristol Aeroplane Co. 64-, Metal Box Co. 64-, Leverhulme Trust 65-; Trustee,

Wellcome Trust 65-; Hon. Fellow Oriel and Lincoln Colls., Oxford and Downing Coll., Cambridge; Hon. LL.D., Hon. D.C.L.
The Leverhulme Trust, 21-23 New Fetter Lane, London, E.C.4, England.

Murtazayev, Kayum Murtazayevich; Soviet politician; b. 1926; ed. Fergana Pedagogical Inst.
Member C.P.S.U. 48-; industrial worker 42-48; Sec. of City Cttee., then of Regional Cttee., later First Sec. Central Cttee. of Young Communist League, Uzbekistan 48-58; Sec. Central Cttee. of Y.C.L., U.S.S.R. 58-60; First Sec. Tashkent City Cttee. of C.P. Uzbekistan 60-65; First Sec. Bokhara Regional Cttee. of C.P. Uzbekistan 65-; mem. Central Cttee. C.P. Uzbekistan; Deputy to U.S.S.R. Supreme Soviet; mem. Cttee. U.S.S.R. Parliamentary Group.
Bokhara Regional Committee of Communist Party of Uzbekistan, Bokhara, U.S.S.R.

Murthy, B. S., B.A., B.ED.; Indian politician; b. 07; ed. Government Arts Coll. Rajahmundry, Training Coll. Rajahmundry, Madras Christian Coll. and Madras Law Coll.
Parliamentary Sec. for Labour and Industry, Madras 37-39, 46-47; Chief Whip, Madras Legislative Congress Party 46-47; Pres. Andhra Pradesh Agricultural Labour Congress 46-, Andhra Provincial Harijan Sewak Sangh 40-49; fmr. Editor *Navjiwan* (Teluga weekly); mem. Lok Sabha 52-; Dep. Minister of Community Devt and Co-operation April 62-67; Deputy Minister of Health and Family Planning 67, of Health, Family Planning and Urban Devt. Nov. 67-.
Publs. *Revolt of Six Cross, Agony, Andhra Virakumar.*
5 Ashoka Road, New Delhi, India.

Murumbi, Joseph; Kenyan politician; b. 18 June 1911; ed. Bangalore and Bellary, S. India.
Staff of Admin. of Somalia 41-51; Asst. Sec. Movement for Colonial Freedom 51-57; Press and Tourist Officer, Moroccan Embassy, London 57-62; Treas. Kenyan African Nat. Union (KANU) 62; mem. Kenya House of Reps. 63-; Minister of State in Prime Minister's Office 63-64; Minister of External Affairs 64-66; Vice-Pres. of Kenya 66-Dec. 66; Chair. Rothmans of Pall Mall (Kenya) Ltd. Sept. 66-; Dir. of other Kenya companies.
P.O. Box 1730, Nairobi, Kenya.
Telephone: Nairobi 61397.

Muryavyev, Nikolai Ivanovich; Soviet trade corporation official; b. 07; ed. Inst. of Foreign Trade.
Worked in trade orgs. 24-39; trade missions to Germany 39-41, U.K. 42; Asst. Dir. (Fur Dept.) *Amtorg* Stock Co., U.S. 42-48, Chair. 52-58; Dir. Karakul and Fur Office *Sojuzpushnina* (furs, etc.) 48-52, Vice-Chair. 58-62, Chair. 62-; mem. Communist Party; Order of Badge of Honour (twice), etc.
V/O *Sojuzpushnina,* ul. Kuibysheva 6, Moscow, U.S.S.R.

Musa, Gen. Mohammad, M.B.E.; Pakistani army officer and politician; b. 20 Oct. 1908; ed. Univ. of the Punjab, Indian Military Acad., Dehradun, Staff Coll., Quetta (Pakistan) and Imperial Defence Coll. (London).
Army officer 34; active service in North Africa, Second World War; Asst. Dir. of Intelligence, Home Dept., Govt. of India 44; Staff Officer Armed Forces Nationalization Cttee. India 46; Brig. 48; Maj.-Gen., commanded garrison E. Pakistan 51; Deputy Chief of Staff 57; C.-in-C. 58-66; Gov. of W. Pakistan Sept. 66-; Hilal-i-Pakistan, Hilal-i-Quaid-e-Azam, Hilal-i-Jurrat.
Residence of the Governor, Lahore, West Pakistan.

Musafir, Giani Gurmukh Singh; Indian writer and politician; b. 15 Jan. 1899; ed. Rawalpindi and Training Coll., Lahore.
Joined Congress 23; mem. All-India Congress Cttee. 30-; mem. Constituent Assembly 47-52; mem. Parl. 52-66; mem. Exec. Congress Party in Parl. 52-66; mem.

Working Cttee. of All-India Congress Cttee. 52-57; Pres. Punjab Pradesh Congress Cttee. 47-59; Chief Minister of Punjab 66-67; mem. Legislative Council, Punjab 66-; Chair. Jallianwala Bag Memorial Trust Man. Cttee.; took active part in Akali movement; Gen. Sec. Shri Gurudwara Prabandhak Cttee. and Shiromani Akali Dal; Leader and Del. to numerous int. conferences.

Publs. Short Stories: *Vakhri Duniya, Sasta Tamasha, Alne de Bot, Kandhan Bol Pahiyan, 27 January, Sab Achha, Gutar, Allah Wale*; Poetry: *Sabar de Ban, Prem Ban, Jivan Pandh, Toote Khamb, Musafirian, Kav Saneh, Sahaj Seti*; General: *Gandhi Gita, Anand Marg, Bagi Jernel, Vinvi Sadi de Shahid*.

21 Feroz Shah Road, New Delhi, India.

Telephone: 48191.

Musakhanov, Mirzamakhmud Mirzarakhmanovich; Soviet (Uzbek) politician; b. 1912; ed. Moscow Textile Inst.

Textile Industry worker 37-48; mem. C.P.S.U. 43-; Dep. Minister, Light Industry, Uzbekistan 48-53; Minister Light and Food Industries 53; Ministerial Sec. Council of Ministers, Uzbekistan 53-55; Sec. Tashkent Regional Cttee. C.P. Ukraine 55-56, 58; Chair. *Gosplan*, Dep. Chair. Council of Ministers, Uzbekistan 56-58; Chair. Uzbekistan Trade Union Council 58-59; Sec. All-Union Central Council of Trade Unions 59-61; First Deputy Chair. Council of Ministers, Uzbekistan 65-; Candidate mem. Cen. Cttee. C.P.S.U. 61-; Deputy to Uzbek S.S.R. and U.S.S.R. Supreme Soviets.

Council of Ministers of Uzbekistan, Tashkent, Uzbek S.S.R., U.S.S.R.

Musatov, Leonid Nikolayevich; Soviet diplomatist; b. 1921; ed. Ulyanovsk Pedagogic Inst.

Member C.P. of Soviet Union 40-; worked for Young Communist League 39-40; Army service 40-46; Party official 46-62; Sec. Ulyanovsk Regional Cttee., C.P. of Soviet Union 57-62; Counsellor, Second African Dept., Ministry of Foreign Affairs 64; Counsellor-Minister, Soviet Embassy, Conakry 64-65; Amb. to Mali 65-; Red Banner of Labour, Badge of Honour, etc.

U.S.S.R. Embassy, Bamako, Mali.

Musgrave, Sir Cyril, K.C.B.; British administrator; b. 21 June 1900; ed. St. George's Coll., London.

With Inland Revenue 20-37, Air Ministry 37-40, Ministry of Aircraft Production 40-46; Under-Sec. (Air), Ministry of Supply 46-51, Deputy Sec. 51-53, Second Permanent Sec. 53-56, Permanent Sec. 56-59; Chair. Iron and Steel Board 59-67; dir. various companies; mem. Organizing Cttee. for Steel Nationalization 66-67, part-time mem. 67-.

Cornerfield, Stock, Essex, England.

Telephone: Stock 214.

Muskhelishvili, Nikolai Ivanovich; Soviet mathematician; b. 1891; ed. St. Petersburg Univ.

Professor at the Tbilisi Polytechnical Inst. and Univ. 22-; his main research concerns the theory of elasticity, integral equations, problems of the theory of functions; Pres. of Acad. of Sciences of Georgian S.S.R. 41-; mem. U.S.S.R. Acad. of Sciences; Chair. U.S.S.R. Nat. Cttee. of Pure and Applied Mechanics; mem. Exec. Board, Int. Union of Pure and Applied Mechanics; State Prize 41, 47; Hero of Socialist Labour 45; awarded Order of Lenin (four times), Order of the Red Banner of Labour. Publs. *Singular Integral Equations* 46, *Analytical Geometry Course* 47, *Certain Fundamental Problems of the Mathematical Theory of Elasticity* 49.

Academy of Sciences of Georgian S.S.R., Tbilisi, Georgian S.S.R., U.S.S.R.

Muskie, Edmund Sixtus, A.B., LL.B.; American lawyer and politician; b. 28 March 1914; ed. Bates Coll., Maine and Cornell Law School, Ithaca, New York.

Admitted to Massachusetts Bar 39, Maine Bar 40, Federal District Court 41; practised as lawyer, Waterville Maine 40-; served U.S. Navy 42-45; mem. Maine House of Reps. 47-51; Democratic Floor leader 49-51; District Dir. for Maine, Office of Price Stabilisation 51-52; City Solicitor Waterville, Maine 54-55; Governor of the State of Maine 55-59; Senator from Maine 59-; Senate Asst. Majority Whip 66-; Chair. Senate Sub-Cttees. on Air and Water Pollution, Intergovernmental relations, and Int. Finance; Chair. Dem. Senatorial Campaign Cttee. 67-; mem. Exec. Cttee. Nat. Governors' Conf.; Hon. LL.D. (Bates, Lafayette, Bowdoin and Colby Colls., Maine, Portland and Suffolk Univs.); Democrat.

Senate Office Building, Washington 25, D.C.; 5409 Albia Road, Washington, D.C., U.S.A.

Telephone: 202-225-5344.

Mustapha, A. T. M., M.A., LL.B.; Pakistani lawyer and politician; b. 25; ed. Islamia Coll., Calcutta, Muslim Univ., Aligarh, and Lincoln's Inn, London.

Barrister, Dacca High Court 50-57, Supreme Court 57-61; mem. Pakistan Del. to UN 60-61; Minister of Law and Information, East Pakistan June 62; Leader People's Democratic Group, East Pakistan Assembly, later Leader Muslim League Party; fmr. Leader of House, E. Pakistan Assembly; Minister of Education, Pakistan Sept. 63-65.

8-A, Satellite Town, Rawalpindi, Pakistan.

Mutesa II, Sir Edward Frederick William Walugembe Mutebi Luwangula, K.B.E. (**Kabaka of Buganda**); Ugandan former ruler; b. 19 Nov. 1924; ed. King's Coll., Budo, Makerere Coll., and Magdalene Coll., Cambridge.

Succeeded as Kabaka of Buganda 39, crowned 42, married 48, deposed 53, reinstated 55, deposed 66; Pres. and Commdr.-in-Chief of Uganda 63-66; holds Hon. Comm. in Grenadier Guards; Ugandan, Greek and Ethiopian decorations; living in England 66-.

Publ. *Desecration of my Kingdom* 67.

Muto, Itoji; Japanese business executive; b. 24 Feb. 1892; ed. Fernley School, England.

Kanegafuchi Spinning Co. Ltd. 30-, Pres. 47-; Pres. Kanegafuchi Silk Co. Ltd. 58-, Kanegafuchi Weaving Co. Ltd. 60-, Kanegafuchi Real Estate Co. Ltd. 62-; Head, Economic Mission to Iran 60; mem. Exec. Cttee. All-Japan Spinners Asscn., Japan Chemical Fibres Asscn.; Managing Dir. Fed. of Japan Employers' Asscns.; Dir. and Councillor, All-Japan Silk Yarn Asscn.

Publs. (essays in Japanese) *Random Notes of a Spinning Wheel* 53, *An Eye of a Needle* 61.

35 Nango-cho, Nishinomiya-shi, Hyogo Prefecture, Japan.

Muttukumaru, Anton Marian, O.B.E., E.D., I.D.C., B.A., Barrister-at-Law (Gray's Inn); Ceylonese army officer; b. 08; ed. St. Joseph's Coll., Colombo, and Jesus Coll., Oxford.

Advocate of Supreme Court in Ceylon 34-39 and 46-48; served in Ceylon Defence Force 34-49, Regular Force 49-59; Military A.D.C. to the Queen 54-59; Commdr. of the Army 55-59; High Commr. in Pakistan 60-63, Minister to Afghanistan 60-61, Ambassador to Iraq 61-62, Ambassador to Iran 62, High Commr. Australia and New Zealand 63-67.

c/o Ministry of External Affairs, Colombo, Ceylon.

Müürisepp, Alexei Alexandrovich; Soviet (Estonian) politician; b. 17 July 1902; ed. Tomsk Railway Inst., Higher Party School Moscow.

Member C.P.S.U. 26-; railway engineer 37-45; Head of the Power Dept. of the Cen. Cttee. of the Estonian C.P. 46; Head of the Light Industry Dept. of the Cen. Cttee. of the Estonian C.P. 48; mem. and Sec. of the Cen. Cttee. of the Estonian C.P. 49-; Vice-Chair. Council of Ministers of the Estonian S.S.R. 50, Chair. 51-61; Chair. of Presidium of Supreme Soviet of Estonian S.S.R. 61-, and Vice-Chair. Presidium of the Supreme Soviet of the U.S.S.R. 61-; candidate mem. Cen. Cttee. C.P. of the Soviet Union 52-66, mem. C.P.S.U. Cen. Auditing Comm. 66-; Deputy to U.S.S.R. and Estonian S.S.R. Supreme Soviets; awarded four Orders of Lenin, Order of Red Banner of Labour, Order of Red Star. Presidium of Supreme Soviet of the Estonian S.S.R., Tallinn, Estonia, U.S.S.R.

Muzhitsky, Alexander Mikhailovich; Soviet politician; b. 1912; ed. Lipatov Agricultural Technical School and Higher Party School.
Member C.P.S.U. 32-; worker and teacher 27-31; Soviet Army 31-33 and 41-42; Komsomol and Party Leader 34-41, 42-44; Sec. Ternopol Regional Cttee. of C.P. of Ukraine 44-45; First Deputy Chair. Exec. Cttee. Kharkov Regional Soviet of Working People's Deputies 53-58; Chair. Exec. Cttee. Poltava Regional Soviet of Working People's Deputies 59-62; First Sec. Poltava Regional Cttee. of C.P. of Ukraine 62-; mem. Central Cttee. of C.P. of Ukraine; Candidate mem. Central Cttee. of C.P.S.U. 66-; Deputy to U.S.S.R. Supreme Soviet.
Poltava Regional Committee of C.P. of Ukraine, Poltava, U.S.S.R.

Mwaanga, Vernon Johnson; Zambian diplomatist; b. 1939; ed. Hodgson Technical Coll., Lusaka, Stanford Univ., U.S.A. and Oxford Univ., U.K.
Joined Zambian independence movement 60; mem. United Nat. Independence Party 61-, later Regional Party Sec., Monze and Come Areas; Deputy High Commr. for Zambia in U.K. 64-65; Ambassador to U.S.S.R. 65-.
Embassy of Zambia, Moscow, U.S.S.R.

Mwemba, Joseph Ben; Zambian teacher and diplomatist; b. 28 July 1917; ed. Univ. Coll., Fort Hare, South Africa, and Teachers' Coll., Munsie, Indiana, U.S.A.
Primary school teacher 45-48, secondary school teacher 52-60; Educ. Officer 61-63; Admin. Officer, Ministry of Finance 64-65; Perm. Sec. Ministry of Educ. 65-66; Perm. Rep. to UN 66-; Pres. N. Rhodesia Teachers' Asscn. 53-60.
Permanent Mission of Republic of Zambia to the United Nations, 641 Lexington Avenue, New York, 10022, U.S.A.

Mycielski, Zygmunt; Polish composer and music critic; b. 07; ed. in Cracow and Paris.
Prisoner of war in Germany; Pres. Union of Polish Composers 49-50; State Prize 52 for *Polish Symphony*, Union of Polish Composers Prize 54; Ed. *Ruch muzyczny* (musical bimonthly).
Compositions, orchestral: *Polish Symphony, Piano Concerto, Nowy lirnik Mazowiecki* (Cantata), *Ouverture Silesienne*, Second Symphony, Third Symphony; *String Trio, 5 Preludes for Piano* 57; ballet: *Narcyz, Zabawa w Lipinach*; and choral music, etc.
Publs. *Ucieczki z Pieciolinii* (musical essays), *Notatki o muzyce* 61.
Rynek Starego Miasta 27, Warsaw, Poland.

Myers, Charles Franklin, Jr.; American industrial executive; b. 17 July 1911; ed. Davidson Coll. and Harvard Univ.
Bank of New York 35-39; Vice-Pres. and Dir. Wachovia Bank and Trust Co. 39-47; Dir. and Treas. Burlington Industries Inc. 47-, Exec. Vice-Pres. 61-62, Pres. 62-; Dir. Chase Manhattan Bank and other companies.
Burlington Industries Inc., 301 N. Eugene St., Greenboro, N. Carolina, U.S.A.

Myers, William Irving, B.S., PH.D.; American agriculturalist; b. 18 Dec. 1891; ed. Cornell Univ.
Instructor in Farm Management, Cornell Univ. 14-18; Asst. Prof. of Farm Management 18-20; Prof. of Farm Finance 20-59, Emer. 59-; Head Dept. of Agricultural Econs. 38-43; Dean N.Y. State Coll. of Agricul-

ture 43-59; Asst. to Chair. Federal Farm Board 33; Dep. Gov. Farm Credit Admin. 33, Gov. 33-38; Pres. Federal Farm Mortgage Corpn. 34-38; Dir. Federal Surplus Relief Corpn. and Commodity Credit Corpn. 34-38; Chair. Land Cttee. of Nat. Resources Planning Board 38-43; mem. N.Y. State War Council 43-46, Research Advisory Board of Cttee. for Econ. Development 42-45; Dep. Chair. and Dir. Federal Reserve Bank N.Y. 42-54; Dir. several companies; mem. President's Famine Cttee. 46; N.Y. State Comm. on Agriculture; President's Cttee. on Foreign Aid 47; Agricultural Cttee. U.S. Chamber of Commerce 51-54; Trustee, Twentieth Century Fund 41-47; Rockefeller Foundation, Gen. Educ. Board 41-57; Mutual Life Insur. Co. N.Y. 43-; Trustee of American Inst. of Co-operation 44-59, Chair. of Board 44-48; Trustee Carnegie Inst. of Washington.; Chair. Nat. Agricultural Advisory Comm. 52-60; Consultant for Agricultural Sciences Rockefeller Foundation 59-66; Trustee, Agricultural Devt. Council; mem. Int. Devt. Advisory Board, Int. Co-operation Admin. 53-57; Trustee, Vassar Coll. 55-63; Dir. N.Y. State Science and Technology Foundation 64-; Dir. and Chair. Exec. Cttee. Marine Midland Trust Co. of Southern N.Y.
1483 East Shore Drive, R.D.1, Ithaca, N.Y., U.S.A.

Mykle, Agnar; Norwegian writer; b. 8 Aug. 1915; ed. Univ. of Economical and Political Sciences, Bergen.
Sec. A.O.F. Oslo (Workers' Educational Asscn.), head of Drama Dept.; worked for newspaper and founded Norwegian Puppet Theatre; writes novels and short stories.
Publs. *Taustigen* (The Rope Ladder) 47, *Tyven, tyven skal du hete* (*The Hotel Room* in U.K. and U.S.A.) 51, *Jeg er like glad, sa gutten* (It's all the same to me, said the boy) 53, *Lasso rundt fru Luna* (Lasso round the Moon) 55, *Puppet theatre* (a manual), *Sangen om den røde ruben* (The Song of the Red Ruby) 56, *Kors på halsen* (Cross my Heart) 58, *Rubicon* 65.
Asker, Norway.

Myklebust, Oddmund; Norwegian politician; b. 21 April 1915.
Chairman fishermen's org., Sunnmöre 54-57, 59-; sat on various govt. fishery comms.; Council mem. Fish Sales Co-operative for Sunnmöre and Romsdal and Herring Sales Co-operative; Minister of Fisheries 65-; Centre Party.
Ministry of Fisheries, Oslo, Norway.

Mynors, Sir Humphrey (Charles Baskerville), Bt.; British banker; b. 28 July 1903; ed. Marlborough and Corpus Christi Coll., Cambridge.
Fellow Corpus Christi Coll. Cambridge 26-33; with Bank of England 33-64, Dir. 49-54, Deputy Gov. 54-64; Chair. Finance Corpn. for Industry Ltd.
Whitmoor House, Sutton Green, Guildford, Surrey, England.

Mynors, Sir Roger (Aubrey Baskerville), Kt., M.A.; British university professor; b. 28 July 1903; ed. Eton Coll. and Balliol Coll., Oxford.
Fellow Balliol Coll., Oxford 26-44 (now Hon. Fellow); Prof. of Latin and Fellow of Pembroke Coll., Cambridge 44-53; Prof. of Latin and Fellow of Corpus Christi Coll., Oxford 53-; Fellow British Acad. 44; Hon. D.Litt. Cambridge and Durham; Hon. mem. American Acad. of Arts and Sciences; fmr. Pres. Union Académique Internationale.
Publs. *Cassiodorus* 37, *Durham MSS* 39, *Catullus* 60, *Pliny's Letters* 63, *Balliol MSS* 63, *Panegyrici* 64.
Corpus Christi College, Oxford, England.

Myrberg, Pekka Juhana, PH.D.; Finnish mathematician; b. 30 Dec. 1892; ed. Univ. of Helsinki.
University Lecturer 19-26; Prof. of Mathematics, Finland Inst. of Technology 26-38; Univ. of Helsinki

38-59; Chancellor Univ. of Helsinki 52-62; Pres. State Cttee. for Scientific Research 49-64.

Publs. Several works on mathematical subjects, especially the theory of functions.

Mannerheimintie 75A, Helsinki 27, Finland.

Myrdal, Alva (wife of Karl Gunnar Myrdal, *q.v.*); Swedish cabinet minister, diplomatist, sociologist and writer; b. 31 Jan. 1902; ed. Stockholm and Uppsala Univs., U.S.A. and Geneva.

Director, Training Coll. Stockholm 36-48; Principal Dir. UN Dept. of Social Affairs 49-50; Dir. UNESCO Dept. of Social Sciences 51-55; Minister to India, Burma and Ceylon 55-56, Amb. 56-61; Swedish Foreign Office 61; Senator 62, Minister without Portfolio 66-; Sec. Govt. Comm. on Women's Work 35-38; mem. Royal Comm. on the Handicapped 43-47, on Educ. Reform 46-50, etc.; Del. to ILO Conf., Paris 45, Geneva 47, and to UNESCO Confs., Paris 46, New Delhi 56; Leader, Swedish Del. to 18-Nation Disarmament Cttee., Geneva 62-; mem. UN Cttee. to examine methods of resolving situation in S. Africa 64; Chair. Swedish Fed. of Business and Professional Women 35-38 and 40-42; Vice-Chair. Int. Fed. Business and Professional Women 38-47, Swedish Inst. 61-64; Chair. World Council on Pre-School Educ. 47-49, Cttee. Int. Peace Research Inst. 64-66, etc.; exec. mem. World Fed. of UN Asscns. 48-50; Hon. LL.D. (Mount Holyoke Coll., Leeds, Edinburgh and Columbia Univs.).

Publs. *Crisis in the Population Question, City Children, Nation and Family, Comments on World Affairs, Post War Planning, Are we too many?, Women's Two Roles* (with Viola Klein); Editor *Via Suecia* (multilingual refugee magazine) 45-47 and *Round Table on Social Problems* (for the Co-op Movement) 46-48.

Ministry of Foreign Affairs, Stockholm, Sweden.

Myrdal, Karl Gunnar (husband of Alva Myrdal, *q.v.*), LL.D.; Swedish economist and politician; b. 6 Dec. 1898; ed. Stockholm Univ.

Lecturer in Political Economy, Stockholm Univ. 27; Asst. Prof. Geneva Institut Universitaire de Hautes Etudes Internationales 30; Prof. Political Economy and Financial Science, Stockholm Univ. 33-50; Govt. Adviser on financial, economic and social questions 33; conducted investigation on American Negroes for Carnegie Corpn. 38-43; Minister of Trade and Commerce 45-47; Exec. Sec. U.N. Economic Comm. for Europe, Geneva April 47-57; Prof. of Int. Economy, Stockholm Univ. 60-; Senator; Hon. LL.D. (Harvard, Yale, Birmingham, Brandeis, Leeds, Edinburgh, Swarthmore, Sir George Williams, Michigan and Howard Univs.); Hon. Dr. Lit. (Fisk), Hon. L.H.D. (Columbia), Dr. Humane Letters (New School of Social Research); Hon. D.D. (Lincoln), Hon. Ph.D. (Stockholm); Hon. J.D. (Nancy).

Publs. *Prisbildningsproblemet och föränderligheten* 27, *Sveriges väg genom penningkrisen* 31, *Das politische Element in der nationalökonomischen Doktrinbilaung* 32, *The Cost of Living in Sweden 1830-1930* 33, *Kris i befolkningsfrågan* 34, *Finanspolitikens ekonomiska verkningar* 34, *Monetary Equilibrium* 39, *Population, A Problem for Democracy* 40, *An American Dilemma: The Negro Problem and Modern Democracy* 44, *Warnung gegen Friedensoptimismus* 45, *The Political Element in the Development of Economic Theory* 53, *An International Economy, Problems and Prospects* 56, *Economic Theory and Under-developed Regions* 57, *Value in Social Theory* 58, *Beyond the Welfare State* 60, *Challenge to Affluence* 63, *Asian Drama* 68.

Västerlånggatan 31, Stockholm C; and Stockholm University, Inst. for Int. Econ. Studies, Sveav. 166, Stockholm Va, Sweden.

Telephone 37-08-60, Extension 713 (Office); 21-36-71 (Home).

Myres, John Nowell Linton, M.A., F.B.A., F.S.A.; British librarian; b. 27 Dec. 1902; ed. Winchester Coll., New Coll., Oxford.

Lecturer, Tutor, Christ Church, Oxford 28-48, Librarian 38-48; Ministry of Food 40-45; Librarian, Bodleian Library, Oxford Univ. 48-65; Pres. Council for British Archaeology 58-61; Vice-Pres. Soc. of Antiquaries 59-63, Dir. 66-; Chair. Standing Conf. of Nat. and Univ. Libraries 59-61; Ford's Lecturer, Oxford 58-59; Pres. Library Asscn. 63; Pres. Soc. for Mediaeval Archaeology 63-66; Fellow Winchester Coll. 50-; Hon. LL.D. (Toronto); Hon. D.Litt. (Reading); Hon. D.Lit. (Belfast).

Publs. *St. Catharine's Hill, Winchester* (with others) 30, *Roman Britain and the English Settlements* 36.

Manor House, Kennington, Oxford, England.

Telephone: Oxford 35353.

Myrvoll, Ole; Norwegian economist and politician; b. 18 May 1911; ed. Univ. of Oslo, School of Banking, and Univ. of Virginia, U.S.A.

Teacher, Univ. School of Econs. and Business Admin., Bergen 42-, Prof. of Theoretical Social Econs. 57-; Visiting Prof. Colgate Univ., U.S.A. 58-59; Visiting Tallman Prof., Bowdoin Coll., Maine 62; mem. State Banks Comm. 55, Monetary and Credit Political Comm. 60-63; mem. Council Bergens Privatbank 60; mem. Bergen City Council 48-55; Alt. mem. Storting 58-; Minister of Wages and Prices 63; Minister of Finance 65-; Liberal.

Ministry of Finance, Oslo, Norway.

Mysore, H.H. Maharaja Sri Jaya Chamaraja Wadiyar Bahadur, G.C.B., G.C.S.I., B.A.; Indian governor; b. July 1919; ed. privately Trinity Coll. of Music, London and Univ. of Mysore.

Governor of Mysore State; Chancellor of Mysore, Madras, Annamalai and Karnatak Univs.; Gov. Madras State; Chair. The Indian Board for Wild Life; Hon. LL.D. (Benares Hindu Univ.) 42; Hon. D.Litt. (Univs. of Queensland and Annamalai); Hon. LL.D. (Univ. of Annamalai); Hon. Fellow Trinity Coll. of Music, London.

Publs. many books on Indian philosophy and aesthetics.

The Palace, Bangalore, Mysore, India.

Mzhavanadze, Vasili Pavlovich; Soviet (Georgian) politician; b. 1902; ed. V. I. Lenin Military Political Acad.

Served Red Army 26-53; Regimental Commissar, Soviet-Finnish War 39-40; Army Staff Commissar, Army Mil. Council, Leningrad and Ukrainian front 41-45; 1st Sec. Georgian Communist Party 53-; Deputy U.S.S.R. Supreme Soviet and Georgian S.S.R.; mem. Presidium Supreme Soviet, Georgian S.S.R. 55; mem. Central Cttee. Communist Party Soviet Union 56-; Candidate mem. Presidium of Cen. Cttee. of C.P.S.U. until 66, Alt. mem. Politburo 66-; Order of Lenin, 3 Orders of the Red Banner, Order of Kutuzov, Order of Suvorov.

Central Committee of Communist Party of Georgian S.S.R., Tbilisi, Georgian S.S.R., U.S.S.R.

N

Na Champassak, Sisouk; Laotian government official and diplomatist; b. 28; ed. Univ. of Paris and Acad. of Int. Law, The Hague.

Former Head, Political Dept., Board of Council of Ministers, later Head, Perm. Secr. of Political Affairs, Board of Council of Ministers; Dir., Secr.-Gen. of Council of Ministers 55-56; Dep. Perm. Rep. to UN 56-58; Sec. of State for Information and Youth 58-61; Perm. Rep. to UN 61-63; Ambassador to India 63-64; Minister of Finance 64-.

Ministry of Finance, Vientiane, Laos.

Nabeshima, Tsunatoshi; Japanese business executive; b. 14 April 1910; ed. Univ. of Tokyo.

Entered Sumitomo Electric Industries 33, Dir. 56-, Man. Dir. 58-61, Senior Man. Dir. 61-66, Pres. 66-; Dir. Tokai Rubber Industries 64-, Meidensha Electric Mfg. 66-; mem. Rotary Club of Osaka, Kansai Econ. Fed., Japan Fed. of Employers, Fed. of Econ. Orgs.

Sumitomo Electric Industries, Kitahama, Higashiku, Osaka; Home: 9-28 Aioi-cho, Nishinomiya City, Hyogo Prefecture, Japan.

Nabokov, Vladimir; American (b. Russian) author and lepidopterist; b. 23 April 1899; ed. St. Petersburg and Cambridge Univ., England.

Left Russia 19, studied England, lived Germany and France, in U.S.A. 40-; Lecturer, Wellesley Coll. 40-41, 42-48; Research Fellow in Lepidoptera, Harvard Univ. Museum of Comparative Zoology 42-48; Prof. of Russian and European Literature, Cornell Univ. 48-59; Guggenheim Awards 43 and 53, American Acad. of Arts and Letters Award, Brandeis Univ. Award 64.

Publs. include verse and novels in Russian and in English. Biography: *Nikolai Gogol*; Treatise on butterflies: *The Nearctic Members of the Genus Lycaeides*; Translations: *Three Russian Poets* 45, *The Song of Prince Igor's Campaign* 60, *Eugene Onegin* (with commentary) 64; Short stories: *Nine Stories, Nabokov's Dozen, Nabokov's Quartet;* Play: *The Waltz Invention;* Memoirs: *Conclusive Evidence* 51, *Speak, Memory* 66; Novels: *The Real Life of Sebastian Knight* 41, *Bend Sinister* 47, *Lolita* 55, *Pnin* 57, *Invitation to a Beheading* 59, *Pale Fire* 62, *The Gift* 63, *The Defence* 64, *The Eye* 65, *Despair* 65, *King, Queen, Knave* 68.

c/o McGraw-Hill Book Co., Trade Dept., 330 West 42nd Street, New York, N.Y. 10036, U.S.A.

Nabrit, James Madison, Jr., A.B., J.D.; American university president; b. 4 Sept. 1900; ed. Morehouse Coll., Atlanta and Northwestern Univ.

Teacher, Leland Coll., Baker, Louisiana; Dean, Arkansas State Coll.; Teacher, Law School, Howard Univ. 36-56, Admin. Asst. to Pres., Sec. 39-55, Dir., Public Relations 40-50, 55-58, Sec. of Univ. 39-60, Dean of Law School 58-60, Pres. of Univ. 61-July 67; Deputy U.S. Rep. to UN 66-67; Adviser, U.S. Del. to ILO Conf., Geneva 59, 60; mem. Board of Trustees, Howard Univ.; Hon. LL.D., Morehouse 55, Lincoln Univ. 61, Georgetown Univ. 63, Johnson C. Smith Univ. 64, Catholic Univ. of America 64, West Virginia State Univ. 66, Tuskegee Inst. 66, Virginia State Coll. 66, St. Lawrence Univ. 66, Morgan State Coll. 66, Northwestern Univ. 66; Hon. D.C.L. Bates Coll. 63.

7211 Sixteenth Street, N.W., Washington, D.C., U.S.A.

Nabrit, Samuel Milton, M.S., PH.D.; American foundation executive; b. 21 Feb. 1905; ed. Morehouse Coll. and Brown Univ.

Prof. of Biology, Morehouse Coll. 25-31; Prof., Chair. of Dept. of Biology, Atlanta Univ. 32-55, Dean, Graduate School 47-55; Pres., Texas Southern Univ., Houston 55-66; Commr. U.S. Atomic Energy Comm. 66-67; Co-ordinator, Carnegie Grants-in-Aid Program 48-; mem. Nat. Cttee. on Research Science Education 36-, mem. Nat. Scientific Board 56-, etc.; Exec. Dir. The Southern Fellowships Fund 67-; Hon. LL.D. (Morehouse Coll.); D.Sc. (Brown, Howard and Atlanta Univs.), Hon. LL.D. (Morgan and Bethune-Cookman Colls.).

The Southern Fellowships Fund, 795 Peachtree Street, N.E., Suite 484, Atlanta, Georgia 30308, U.S.A. Telephone: 404-879-4891.

Nabwera, Burudi; Kenyan politician and diplomatist; b. 27; ed. London School of Economics and Political Science.

Teacher 54-56; Research Asst., Kenya Ministry of Home Affairs 57-58; London School of Economics 58-61; Organiser Kenya African Nat. Union (K.A.N.U.) 61-63, K.A.N.U. Nat. Headquarters Official 63; Perm. Rep. of Kenya to the United Nations 63-; Ambassador to U.S.A. 64-.

866 United Nations Plaza, Room 486, New York, N.Y. 10017, U.S.A.; Shivagala School, Kabras, P.O. Box 274, Kakamega, Kenya.

Naccache, George; Lebanese newspaper executive, politician and diplomatist; b. 20 Nov. 1904; ed. Jesuit Coll., Alexandria, and Univ. Saint-Joseph, Beirut.

Owner and Editor of dailies *L'Orient* and *Al-Jaryda*; Pres. Beirut Exec. Council of Major Projects 63-64; Minister of Public Works and Minister of Information and Tourism 60, 64; Minister of Public Works 65; Pres. Libano-Arab Centre of Public Relations 65; Ambassador to France 66-.

Embassy of the Lebanon, rue Copernic 42, Paris 16e, France; and P.O.Box 688, Beirut, Lebanon.

Nadao, Hirokichi; Japanese politician; b. 99; ed. Tokyo Univ.

Entered Home Ministry 24; Gov. Oita Prefecture 41; Chief, Livelihood Bureau and Sanitation Bureau, Home Ministry 44; Vice-Minister of Home Affairs 45; mem. House of Reps. 45-; Minister of Education 56-57, 58-59, 63-64, Nov. 67-; fmr. mem. House of Reps. Standing Cttees. for the Budget and Local Education; fmr. Vice-Chair. Political Affairs Investigation Cttee. of Liberal Party; mem. Local Admin. System Research Council; Dir. Paper Bag Mfg. Co.; Liberal Democratic Party.

House of Representatives, Tokyo, Japan.

Nadezhdina, Nadezhda Sergeyevna; Soviet ballet master; b. 1908; ed. Second Petrograd Ballet School.

Ballerina at Bolshoi Theatre 25-34; Ballet Master, Moscow Variety Soc. 35-48; Organizer, Leader and Ballet Master Beriozka Dance Ensemble; People's Artist of U.S.S.R. 66; State Prize; Gold Medal of World Peace Council.

Moscow Philharmonic Society, 19 Gorky Street, Moscow, U.S.S.R.

Nadjakov, Georgi; Bulgarian scientist; b. 8 Jan. 1897; ed. Univ. of Sofia.

Research worker in Paris 25-26; Prof. Experimental Physics, Sofia 32; Vice-Pres. Bulgarian Acad. of Sciences 45-48; Foreign mem. Acad. of Sciences of U.S.S.R. 58-; Rector of Univ. of Sofia 47-52; Vice-Pres. Cttee. for the Peaceful use of Atomic Energy at the Council of Ministers; Dir. Inst. of Physics and Atomic Research

Centre, Sofia since its foundation 46-; corresp. mem. Göttingen Acad. of Sciences 40-.
Bulgarian Academy of Sciences, Sofia; and 1 T. Strashimirov Str., Sofia, Bulgaria.

Nagano, Shigeo; Japanese business executive; b. 15 July 1900; ed. Tokyo Imperial Univ.
Gen. Man. Fuji Steel Works, Japan Iron and Steel Co. Ltd. 34-46, Man. Dir. Japan Iron and Steel Co. Ltd. 46-47, 48-50; Dep. Dir.-Gen. Govt. Economic Stabilization Board 47-48; Pres. Fuji Iron and Steel Co. Ltd. 50-; Vice-Pres. Tokyo Chamber of Commerce and Industry 52-; Exec. Dir. Fed. of Econ. Orgs. 54-; Exec. Dir. Fed. of Employers' Asscns. 54-; Hon. Pres. Japan Iron and Steel Fed. 65-; Pres. Pacific Basin Econ. Co-operation Cttee. 67-.
Office: Fuji Iron and Steel Co. Ltd., 10, 3-Chome, Marunouchi, Chiyoda-ku, Tokyo; Home: 34-4, 4-Chome, Matsubara, Setagaya-ku, Tokyo, Japan.
Telephone: 212-2111 (Office); 321-0141 (Home)

Nagayama, Tadanori, Japanese politician; b. 97; ed. Chuo Univ.
Former Mayor of Shikishin-mura, Hiba-gun, Hiroshima Prefecture; mem. Hiroshima Prefectural Assembly 30-36; mem. House of Reps. 36-46, 52-; Parl. Councillor of Welfare 39; Mayor of Shobara City, Hiroshima Prefecture 54; Minister of Home Affairs June 65-66; Chair. Hiroshima Prefecture Nat. Health Insurance Fed.; Vice-Chair. Central Cttee. All-Japan Nat. Health Insurance Asscn.; Dir. Japan Small and Medium Enterprises Fed.; Liberal Democrat.
House of Representatives, Tokyo, Japan.

Nagel, Louis; French publisher; b. 08; ed. Univs. of Vienna and Prague.
Founder of Nagel Publications; publisher of Nagel Travel Guides and trans. of French drama; Pres. of Int. Acad. of Tourism and mem. of P.E.N. Club, and several professional asscns.; Gold Medal of City of Rome, Silver Medal of City of Rome, Silver Medal of Paris, Officer of Order of the Phoenix (Greece), Hon. G.C.M.G., Grand Officer of Order of Malta, Ordine al Merito della Repubblica Italiana, Diploma "Prestige de la France"; Consul-Gen. of Cyprus in Switzerland.
Publs. Works on philosophy, including *La Paix éternelle, est-elle une utopie?* 46.
7 rue de Savoie, Paris 6e, France, and Chemin Puthou 5, Grange Canal, Geneva, Switzerland.
Telephone: Geneva 34-17-30.

Naggar, Abd El Moneim El; United Arab Republic (Egyptian) army officer and diplomatist; b. 20; ed. Cairo Mil. Acad., Cairo Staff Acad., Cairo Univ. and Inst. des Hautes Etudes, Univ. de Paris.
Egyptian Army 39-57; Mil. Attaché, Paris 53-54, Madrid 55-57; Head of East European Dept., Ministry of Foreign Affairs, Cairo 58; U.A.R. Consul-Gen., Bombay 59-62, Hong Kong 62-63; Ambassador to Greece 63-64, to France 64-; numerous decorations.
Embassy of the United Arab Republic, avenue d'Iéna 56, Paris 16e, France.

Nagy, Mrs. József; Hungarian politician; b. 1921.
Textile worker; Dir. textile factory 48-; Deputy Minister of Light Industry 51; Deputy Pres. Nat. Planning Office 52-55; Minister of Light Industry 55-; mem. Central Cttee. Hungarian Socialist Workers' Party.
Ministry of Light Industry, Budapest; Budapest, II. Fö u 68, Hungary.
Telephone: 154-090.

Nahmias, Joseph Jacques; French petroleum executive; b. 14 May 1901.
Founded Société France-Pétrole (later called Pétrofrance) 34, founded Société Pétrotankers 37, Pres./Dir.-Gen. Pétrofrance and Pétrotankers; Pres. Pétrofrance

Inc., New York; Dir., Pétrotransport, Pétrorep, Pétrosarep, Propétrol, Texaco-S.M.P.P., Casablanca, Cofimap, Pres. Asscn. of Petroleum Producers.
42 avenue Raymond-Poincaré, Paris 16e, France.

Naicker, Gangathura Mohambry; South African doctor; b. 10; ed. Edinburgh Univ.
President, Natal Indian Congress 45-63; Pres. South African Indian Congress 54-63; arrested five times 46-60 for opposing measures discriminating against Indian community and non-European Community; arrested during 1961 emergency and placed under banning order 61-.
Publ. *Historical Synopsis of Anti-Indian Legislation in South Africa* 45.
26 Short Street, Durban, Natal, South Africa.

Naik, Vasantrao Phulsing; Indian politician; b. 1 July 1913; ed. Neil City High School, Nagpur, Morris Coll., and Univ. Coll. of Law, Nagpur.
Director Madhya Pradesh Co-operative Central Bank 51-52; mem. Legislative Assembly, Madhya Pradesh 52; Dep. Minister for Revenue, Madhya Pradesh; Minister for Co-operation, Bombay 56-57, for Agriculture and Aarey Milk Colony, Bombay 57-60; Minister for Revenue, Maharashtra 60-63, Chief Minister 63-.
Office of the Chief Minister, Bombay, Maharashtra, India.

Naim, H.R.H. Mohammad; Afghan diplomatist and politician; b. 11; ed. Istiqlal Coll. Kabul.
Entered Political Section, Ministry of Foreign Affairs 30, Dir. 33; Minister to Italy 34; Under-Sec. Ministry of Foreign Affairs 36; Minister of Public Instruction 39; Minister to Great Britain 46; Ambassador to U.S.A. 48; Dep. Prime Minister and Minister of Foreign Affairs 53-63.
c/o Ministry of Foreign Affairs, Kabul, Afghanistan.

Naipaul, V. S., B.A.; Trinidadian writer; b. 17 Aug. 1932; ed. Queen's Royal Coll., Port-of-Spain and Univ. Coll., Oxford.
For two years freelance broadcaster with the B.B.C., producing programmes for the Caribbean area; reviewer on *New Statesman*; grant from Trinidad Govt. to travel in Caribbean 61, in India 62-63, in Uganda 66; Somerset Maugham Award 61; Phoenix Trust Award 62; Hawthornden Prize 64.
Publs. *The Suffrage of Elvira, The Mystic Masseur, Miguel Street, A House for Mr. Biswas, The Middle Passage, Mr. Stone and the Knights Companion, An Area of Darkness, The Mimic Men 67, A Flag on the Island* 67.
c/o André Deutsch Ltd., 105 Great Russell Street, London, W.C.1, England.

Nair, Vallillath Madhathil Madhavan, M.A., BAR.-AT-LAW; Indian diplomatist; b. 8 Oct. 1919; ed. Presidency Coll., Madras, Brasenose Coll., Oxford, Gonville and Caius Coll., Cambridge, and Inner Temple, London.
Entered Indian Civil Service 42; Sub-Divisional Officer, Sitamarhi (Bihar) 44-46; Under Sec. Ministry of External Affairs, New Delhi 46-49; First Sec. Cairo 50-53; Deputy Sec. Ministry of External Affairs 53-55; Deputy High Commr. for India, Ceylon 55-56, Acting High Commr. Ceylon 56-57; Commr. for India, Malaya and Singapore 57, High Commr. for India, Malaya 57-58; Ambassador to Cambodia 58-60, to Norway 60-63; Joint Sec. Ministry of External Affairs 64-67; Amb. to Poland 67-.
Embassy of India, 3 Aleja Roz, Warsaw, Poland; c/o Ministry of External Affairs, New Delhi, India.
Telephone: Warsaw 332514 (Office); 212251 (residence).

Najar, Amiel Emile, LIC. en DR.; Israeli diplomatist; b. 6 Sept. 1912; ed. Univ. of Paris.
Pres. of Exec., Zionist Fed. of Egypt 43-47; Dir. Western European Div., Ministry of Foreign Affairs 52-57, Asst. Dir.-Gen. Ministry of Foreign Affairs 57-58; Minister to

Japan 58-60; Ambassador to Belgium and Luxembourg, Chief of Mission to the European Econ. Community, the European Atomic Energy Comm. and the High Authority of Coal and Steel 60-; mem. Israeli Del. to UN 48, 51-57, 64; Observer, Suez Conf., London 56. Embassy of Israel, 35 rue Washington, Brussels; Residence: 81 avenue du Pérou, Brussels, Belgium.

Nakabe, Kenkichi; Japanese business executive; b. 25 March 1896.
Hayashikane Store 10-, Exec. Dir. 24-42; Trustee, later Dir., Great Japan Fisheries Asscn.; Dir., Taiyo Fisheries Co. 35, now Pres.; Exec. Dir., Taiyo Whaling Industry Co. 36-; Dir. Asia Oil, Miyoshi Oil & Fats, Taiyo Pearl, Taiyo Mink and other companies; Japanese Govt. Rep. Int. N. Pacific Fisheries Comm. 56-, Japan-Soviet Comm. on Fisheries 56-, Japan-Korea Comm. on Fisheries 65-, Int. Whaling Comm. 59-; Medal of Honour with Blue Ribbon, 2nd Class Order of the Rising Sun.
1-4-1 Marunouchi, Chiyoda-ku, Tokyo, and 1-2 Sadoharu-cho, Ichigaya, Shinyuku-ku, Japan.

Nakagaki, Kunio; Japanese politician; b. 11.
Director, Kagome Tomato Produce Co., Aichi Marine Product K.K.; Aichi Construction and Eng. K.K.; mem. Lower House of Parl. 47-; Chair. Lower House Audit Cttee.; Parl. Vice-Minister of Health and Welfare; Dep. Sec.-Gen. Dem. Liberal Party; Minister of Justice 62-63. 25 Aza-Kurayashiki Oaza-Kamiyokosuka, Yokosuka-Mura, Hanzu-Gun, Aichi Pref., Japan.

Nakagawa, Fukio; Japanese automobile executive; b. 24 Dec. 1899; ed. Kobe Commercial Senior High School.
Senior Man. Dir. Toyota Motor Co. Ltd. 50-53, Vice-Pres. 53-61, Dir. Toyota Motor Sales U.S.A. Inc. 57-, Pres. Toyota Motor Co. Ltd. 61-, Vice-Pres. Japan Automobile Manufacturers Asscn. Inc. 67-.
13-4 Nanzan-cho, Showa-ku, Nagoya, Japan.
Telephone: 052-841-1283.

Nakagawa, Toru; Japanese diplomatist; b. 30 March 1911; ed. Tokyo Univ.
Foreign Service 33-, served New York, and Ministry of Foreign Affairs 33-39; Sec. to Premier 39; Sec. China, concurrently Consul, Shanghai 42; Dir. Japanese Overseas Office, Philippines 52-53; Head, Asia Bureau, Ministry of Foreign Affairs 53-57; Minister, U.K. 57-60; Head, Treaty Dept., Ministry of Foreign Affairs 60-64; Ambassador to Italy 64-65, to U.S.S.R. 65-.
Japanese Embassy, Kalashny per. 12, Moscow, U.S.S.R., and 6448 Omiyamae, Suginamiku, Tokyo.
Telephone: 391-3492.

Nakamura, Torata; Japanese politician; b. 3 Aug. 1902; ed. Itoshima Agricultural School.
Former Dir. Fukuoka Prefectural Agricultural Asscn.; Organiser, Fukuoka Prefectural Farm Youths' League; mem. House of Reps.; Minister of Transport June 65-66; Liberal Democrat.
House of Representatives, Tokyo, Japan.

Nakamura, Umekichi; Japanese politician; b. 01; ed. Hosei Univ.
Worked in law office of *Bukichi Miki*; elected House of Reps. 46; Chair. Steering Cttee. of House of Reps. 55; Minister of Justice 56-57; Minister of Construction 60-62, of Educ. 65-66; Liberal Democrat.
2-1480 Takad-honcho, Toshima-ku, Tokyo, Japan.

Nakashima, Masayoshi; Japanese brewing executive; b. 29 July 1909; ed. Keio Univ.
President Asahi Breweries Ltd. 66-, Hokkaido Asahi Breweries Ltd. 66-; Dir. Imperial Hotel 66-, Hotel New Osaka 66-, Nippon Research Center 66-.
Asahi Breweries Ltd., 3-1 Kyobashi, Chuo-ku, Tokyo, Japan.

Nakasone, Yasuhiro; Japanese politician; b. 27 May 1918; ed. Tokyo Imperial Univ.
Member House of Reps.; fmr. Minister of State, Dir.-Gen. of Science & Technology Agency; Chair. Nat. Org. Liberal-Democratic Party, Joint Cttee. on Atomic Energy, Special Cttee. on Scientific Technology; Pres. Takushoku Univ; Minister of Transport Nov. 67-.
Publs: *Ideal of Youth, South Pole—Human & Science, Frontier in Japan.*
Office: 2-1-3, Kasumigaseki, Chiyoda-ku, Tokyo; Home: 2-18-6, Takada, Toshima-ku, Tokyo, Japan.
Telephone: 982-7896 (Home); 580-4272 (Office).

Nakayama, Ichiro, D.ECON.; Japanese university professor; b. 98; ed. Hitotsubashi and Bonn Univs.
Professor of Economics, Hitotsubashi Univ. 37-62, Pres. 49-55, Prof. Emeritus 62-; mem. Central Labour Relations Comm. 46-, Chair. 50-60; Pres. Japanese Inst. of Labour 61-; mem. Exec. Cttee. Int. Economic Asscn. 56-62; mem. Japan Acad. 63-.
Publs. *Pure Economics* 33, *Equilibrium Analysis of Economic Development* 39, *General Theory of Economics* 44, *The Accumulation of Capital* 53.
861 Komaba-cho, Meguro-ku, Tokyo, Japan.

Nakayama, Komei; Japanese surgeon; b. 25 Sept. 1910; ed. Chiba Univ.
Assistant Prof. of Surgery, Chiba Univ. 41-47, Prof. of Surgery 47-63; Prof. of Surgery, Tokyo Women's Medical Coll. 64-; Visiting Prof. St. Vincent Hospital, Sydney, Australia 61; Vice-Pres. Medical Div., Japanese Science Council; Pres. Int. Coll. of Surgeons; numerous Japanese and foreign awards.
Azuba Daiichi Mansions, 50-2-4 Roppongi Minataku, Tokyo, Japan.

Nakayama, Sohei, M.COM.; Japanese banker; b. 5 March 1906; ed. Tokyo Coll. of Commerce.
Nippon Kogyo Ginko (Industrial Bank of Japan Ltd.) 29-, Dir. 47-50, Man. Dir. 50-51; Dir. Japan Devt. Bank 51-54; Deputy Pres. Industrial Bank of Japan 54-61, Pres. 61-; Chair. Financial Policy Cttee. Tokyo Chamber of Commerce and Industry 64-; mem. Exec. Cttee. Japan Cttee. for Econ. Devt. 64-; Vice-Chair. Tokyo Bankers' Asscn. Inc. 63-; Exec. Dir. Fed. of Econ. Orgs. 62-.
Office: Nippon Kogyo Ginko, 1-1, 5-chome, Yaesuchuo-ko, Tokyo; Home: No. 10, 10, 6-chome, Zushi, Zushi-City, Kanagawa Prefecture, Japan.

Nakayasu, Kanichi; Japanese industrialist; b. 5 April 1895; ed. Mechanical Department, Tokyo Higher Engineering School.
Kobe Shipyard, Mitsubishi Shipbuilding Co. 18-23; Ube Cement Mfg. Co. 23, later Dir., Eng. Dept., Chief Engineer, Dir. 34, Vice-Pres. Ube Industries Ltd. 52-58, Pres. 58-; Dir. Korea Cement Mfg. Co.; Dir., Federation of Japanese Employers' Asscns.
1976-1 Kogushi, Ube City, Yamaguchi Prefecture, Japan.

Nakhai, Hossein Ghods, G.C.V.O.; Iranian diplomatist; ed. Coll. of Political Sciences, Teheran.
Counsellor, Iranian Embassy, Washington 34, London 42, Dir.-Gen. Ministry of Foreign Affairs 50; Deputy Minister and Acting Minister of Foreign Affairs 50; Iranian Ambassador to Iraq 51 and 53, to Japan 56-58, to Great Britain 58-61; Minister of Foreign Affairs 61; Minister of Finance May 61-July 62; Ambassador to U.S.A. 62-63; Minister of the Imperial Court 63-67; Amb. to Vatican 67-; Homayoun Order (1st Class).
Publs. *Rubaiyat* (in Persian and English), *God and Man, The Development of Personality, The Shahsavan's Daughter, Paradise, Lady of the Isles* (in English).
Imperial Iranian Embassy, Via Antonio Gramsci, Rome, Italy.

Nalivkin, Dmitry Vasilievich; Soviet geologist and palaeontologist; b. 89; ed. Petrograd (now Leningrad) Mining Inst.

Professor at the Petrograd Mining Inst. 20; on the Geological Cttee. Trust 17-49; Pres. Sub Cttee. on Tectonic Maps, Int. Geological Cong. Stratigraphy Cttee. of U.S.S.R.; principal work devoted to the stratigraphy and palaeontology of the Palaeozoic in Central Asia and the Russian Platform; in Laboratory of Pre-Cambrian Geology, U.S.S.R. Acad. of Sciences 56-; State prize-winner 46; awarded Karpinsky Gold Medal of the Acad. of Sciences of the U.S.S.R. 49, Lenin Prize for directing the compilation of the geological map of the U.S.S.R. 57; mem. U.S.S.R. Acad. of Sciences 46.
Publs. *Outline of Geology of Turkestan* 26, *Brakhiopods of Late and Middle Devon in Turkestan* 30, *Semiluk and Voronezh Layers* 30, *Geological Structure of the Pamirs* 32, *Don and Elets Layer* 34, *Brakhiopods of Late and Middle Devon and Early Carbon in North Eastern Kazakhstan* 38, *Second Baku Oil Deposits Between the Volga and the Urals* 39, *Brakhiopods of the Main Devon Field* 41, *Geological History of the Urals* 43, *Devon Sedimentations in the U.S.S.R.* 47, *Atlas of Main Forms of Fossils in the U.S.S.R.* 47, *Theory of Faces: Geographical Conditions of Sedimentation Formation* 55-56, *Short History of Geology in the U.S.S.R.* 57, *Geology in the U.S.S.R.* 62, *Problems of Global Geology: Some General Causes of Tectogenesis and Regularities of Location of Mineral Resources* 63.
Laboratory of Pre-Cambrian Geology, U.S.S.R. Academy of Sciences, Naberezhnaya Makarova 2, Leningrad, U.S.S.R.

Namboodiripad, E. M. Sankaran; Indian politician; b. 14 June 1909; ed. Board High School, Perintalmanna, Victoria Coll., Palghat, St. Thomas Coll., Trichur.
Chief Minister, Kerala 57-59, 67-; Acting Gen. Sec., Indian C.P. 62-63, now Leader Marxist-Communist Party of India.
Publs. *The National Question in Kerala, Mahatma and the Ism* (both in English).
Plot 10, Nandavaram Housing Colony, Trivandrum, Kerala State, India.

Namgyal, His Highness Maharaj Kumar Palden Thondup, O.B.E.; The Chogyal of Sikkim; b. 1923; ed. St. Joseph's Coll., Darjeeling and Bishop Cotton School, Simla.
Attended Indian Civil Service Training Course, Dehradun; Pres. Sikkim State Council 43-49; Pres. Maha Bodhi Soc. of India 53; Founder-Pres. Namgyal Inst. of Tibetology, Gangtok, Sikkim; succeeded his father as Chogyal of Sikkim Dec. 63; married Sangey Deki (died 57), daughter of Theiji Tsewang Rinzing Namgyal of Lhasa 50; two sons and a daughter; married Miss Hope Cooke 63; one son; O.B.E. 47; Padma Vibhushan 54; Commdr. Ordre de l'Etoile Noire 56, Hon. Maj.-Gen. of Indian Army 65.
The Palace, Gangtok, Sikkim.

Namy, Louis Lucien; French painter and politician; b. 14 June 1908.
Senator from Seine-et-Oise 51-; Conseiller-Gen. from Arpajon 45-; Chevalier des Palmes Académiques; Communist.
Palais du Luxembourg, Paris 6e; 18 rue du 22-Août 1944, Arpajon (S. et O.), France.

Nanda, Guizarilal, B.A., M.A., LL.B.; Indian politician; b. 4 July 1898; ed. Forman Christian Coll., Lahore, Agra Coll. and Allahabad Univ.
Prof. of Economics, Bombay National Coll. and Sec., Textile Labour Asscn. 22-46; imprisoned 32 and 42-44; Parl. Sec. Govt. of Bombay 37-39; Chair. Standing Cttee. of Ahmedabad Municipality 40-42; Del. to I.L.O. Conf. 47, Asian Regional Conf. 47; organiser of Indian T.U. Conf. 47; Minister for Labour, Govt. of Bombay 48-50; Deputy Chair. National Planning Comm. 50-51; Minister for Planning 51-52; Minister for Planning,

Irrigation and Power 52-57; Minister for Labour, Employment and Planning 57-63; Minister for Home Affairs 63-Nov. 66; Acting Prime Minister May-June 64, 66.
Publs. *Some Aspects of Khadi, Approach to the Second Five Year Plan,* etc.
6 Hastings Road, New Delhi, India.

Nannen, Henri; German editor; b. 25 Dec. 1913; ed. Ludwig-Maximilians-Univ., Munich (art history).
Art Editor for Bruckmann Verlag, Munich 37-39; served in Second World War; Publisher and Editor *Hannoversche Neueste Nachrichten* 46-47, *Abendpost* Hanover 47-48; Publisher and Editor-in-Chief *Der Stern* (magazine), Hamburg 48-; Hon. Citizen of Volkach 62.
Publs. *Glanz von Innen* 43, *Kleines Musikbrevier* 43.
Hamburg-Wellingsbüttel, Wellingsbütteler Weg 92, German Federal Republic.

Napier, Hon. Sir John Mellis, K.C.M.G., K.ST.J.; British jurist; b. 24 Oct. 1882; ed. City of London School and Adelaide Univ.
Called to S. Australian Bar 03; K.C. 22; Puisne Judge of S. Australia 24-42, Chief Justice 42-67; Lieut.-Gov. S. Australia 42-; Chancellor of Univ. of Adelaide 48-61.
Glenwood, Stirling East, South Australia.

Napoli, Jacopo; Italian composer; b. 26 Aug. 1911; ed. S. Pietro a Majella Conservatoire of Music, Naples.
Obtained diplomas in Composition, Organ and Piano; held Chair of Counterpoint and Fugue at Cagliari Conservatoire, and at Naples Conservatoire; Dir., S. Pietro a Majella Conservatoire of Music, Naples 55-62; Dir. Giuseppe Verdi Conservatoire of Music, Milan; Dir., Scarlatti Arts Soc. 55-; his works have been presented in Germany and Spain and broadcast by Italian Radio Network.
Works: (Operas) *Il Malato Immaginario* 39, *Miseria e Nobiltà* 46, *Un curioso accidente* 50, *Masaniello* 53, *I Pescatori* 54, *Il Tesoro* 58, (oratorio) *The Passion of Christ, Il Rosario* 62, *Il Povero Diavolo* 63, *Piccola Cantata del Venerdì Santo* 64, (orchestral works) *Overture to Love's Labours Lost* 35, *Preludio di Caccia* 35, *La Festa di Anacapri* 40,
55 Via Andrea da Isernia, Naples, Italy.

Narain, Govind, B.SC., M.SC.; Indian civil servant and business administrator; b. 5 May 1917; ed. Allahabad Univ. and Balliol Coll., Oxford.
District Magistrate 45-47; Home Sec. Uttar Pradesh 48-51; Adviser-Sec. to King of Nepal 51-54; Sec. to Uttar Pradesh Public Works Dept., Power and Information Depts. 54-55; Development Commr. to Uttar Pradesh Govt.; Sec. Depts. of Planning, Econs., Statistics and Information 55-58, Chief Sec. Uttar Pradesh Govt. 58-61; Managing Dir. The State Trading Corpn. of India Ltd. 61-63, Chair. May-Sept. 63; Chair. Minerals and Metals Trading Corpn. of India Ltd. Oct. 63-; Adviser to Gov. of Kerala 65; Resumed as Chair. Minerals and Metals Trading Corpn., New Delhi April 65 on termination of Kerala assignment; Sec. Dept. of Family Planning, Govt. of India, Mar.-Dec. 66; Sec., Ministry of Health & Family Planning, Govt. of India Jan. 67-.
AB/2, Wellesley Road, New Delhi, India.
Telephone: 40875.

Narasimhan, Chakravarthi Vijayaraghava, M.B.E., M.A.; Indian civil servant; b. 21 May 1915; ed. Madras and Oxford Univs.
Entered Indian Civil Service 36, appointed to Madras Cadre 37, District Officer Madras 37-42, Madras Govt. Secretariat (successively Under Sec., Deputy Sec. and Sec., Food Department and Board of Revenue) 42-50; successively Deputy Sec. and Joint Sec. Ministry of Food and Agriculture, Ministry of Finance, Govt. of India 50-56; Exec. Sec. U.N. Economic Comm. for Asia and the Far East 56-59; Under Sec. for Special

Political Affairs, UN 59-61, Chef de Cabinet 61-; Under Sec. for Gen. Assembly Affairs 62-.
130 East 40th Street, Apt. 20-D, New York, N.Y. 10016, U.S.A.

Narayan, Jayaprakash; Indian politician; b. 11 Oct. 1902; ed. Bihar and U.S.A.
Member Working Cttee. Indian Nat. Congress 31, Act. Sec.-Gen. 31-32; founded Congress Socialist Party 34, Sec.-Gen. 34-50; founded Socialist Party 48; merged with Kisan Mazdoor Sabha Praja Party to form Praja Socialist Party, leader 52-57; a leader of Quit India Movement 42-43; imprisoned several times; Pres. Indian Railwaymen's Fed., All India Post and Telegraph Employees Union and Defence Employees Fed. 46-52; engaged in Bhoodan (Land Gift Movement) 57-; Pres. All India Panchayat Parishad, All India Asscn. of Voluntary Agencies for Rural Development 59-63; Chair. All India Peace Brigade, Afro-Asian Council, India-Pakistan Reconciliation Group, Co-Chair. World Peace Brigade.
Kadam Kuan, Patna 3, Bihar, India.

Narayan, Rasipuram Krishnaswamy; Indian writer; b. 10 Oct. 1906.
Publs. (all in English), novels: *Swami and Friends* 35, *The Bachelor of Arts, The Dark Room, The English Teacher, Mr. Sampath, The Financial Expert, Waiting ,or the Mahatma, The Guide* 58, *The Man-Eater of Malgudi* 61, *Gods, Demons and Others* 64, *The Sweet-Vendor* 67; short stories: *An Astrologer's Day, The Lawley Road.*
Yadavagiri, Mysore 2, India; c/o David Higham Associates, 76 Dean Street, London, W.1, England.

Narayan, Shriman; Indian civil servant and diplomatist; b. 5 June 1912; ed. A.P. Mission High School, Mainpuri, Agra Coll., Agra, and Univ. of Allahabad.
General Sec. Indian Nat. Congress and Chief Editor All-India Congress Cttee. Econ. Review 52-58; mem. Indian Planning Comm. 58-64; Chair. Indian Planning Comm. Prohibition Enquiry Cttee. 54-55, Standing Cttee. on Basic Educ. 57-60; Amb. to Nepal 64-67; Gov. of Gujerat 67-.
Publs. *Gandhian Plan of Economic Development for India, Gandhian Constitution for Free India, One Week with Vinoba, Gandhian Plan Reaffirmed, England through Indian Eyes, Constructive Programme for Students, Towards a Socialistic Economy, Socialist Pattern of Society, India and China, India's Current Problems, Principles of Gandhian Planning, Trends in Indian Planning, Tragedy of a Wall, On Education;* several poems and essays in Hindi.
Office of the Governor, Ahmedabad, India.

Narita, Tomomi; Japanese politician; b. 12; ed. Tokyo Univ.
Former Pres. Kagawa Prefectural Fed. of Socialist Party; mem. House of Reps.; successively, mem. Central Exec. Cttee. of Socialist Party, Chair., Control Cttee., Left Wing Socialist Party, Chair., Policy Board, Socialist Party 61-62, Sec.-Gen. 62-67.
Socialist Party of Japan, 1, 1-chome, Nagata-cho, Chiyoda-ku, Tokyo, Japan.

Narlikar, Jayant Vishnu, F.R.A.S., M.A., PH.D.; Indian scientist; b. 19 July 1938; ed. Banaras Hindu Univ. and King's Coll. Cambridge.
Berry Ramsey Fellow, King's Coll. Cambridge 63-69; Graduate Staff Mem ., Inst. of Theoretical Astronomy, Cambridge 66-; awarded Padmabhushan by the Indian Govt. Jan. 65.
Publs. Articles on cosmology, general relativity and gravitation, quantum theory, astrophysics etc. in the *Proceedings of the Royal Society*, London, *The Monthly Notices of the Royal Astronomical Society*, London, *The*

Astrophysical Journal, Nature, Observatory, and scientific articles in various magazines.
King's College, Cambridge, England.
Telephone: Cambridge 62551.

Nash, John Northcote, C.B.E., R.A.; British artist; b. 11 April 1893; ed. Wellington Coll.
Artists Rifles 16, served France until 18 when commissioned paint war pictures for Imperial War Museum; mem. Society of Wood Engravers and of London Group; Asst. Teacher of Design, Royal Coll. of Art 34; represented in Tate Gallery, Victoria and Albert Museum, Manchester, Leeds, Sheffield, Bath, Dublin, Brighton, Rochdale, Newport, Aberdeen, Durban (S.A.); A.R.A. 40; Official War Artist to Admiralty 40-41; Capt. Royal Marines 41; Acting Major 43-44; R.A. 51; Hon. Fellow Royal Coll. of Art; Dr. h.c. Univ. of Essex.
Bottengom's Farm, Wormingford, nr. Colchester, Essex, England.
Telephone: Great Horkesley 308.

Nash, Ogden; American writer; b. 19 Aug. 1902; ed. St. George's School, Newport, R.I., and Harvard Univ.
Publs. *Hard Lines* (poems) 31, *Free Wheeling* 31, *Happy Days* 33, *The Primrose Path* (poems) 35, *The Bad Parent's Garden of Verse* 36, *I'm a Stranger Here Myself* 38, *The Face is Familiar* 41, *Good Intentions* 42, *One Touch of Venus* (musical comedy) 43, *Many Long Years Ago* (poems) 45, *Versus* 49, *Parents Keep Out* 51, *The Private Dining Room* 53, *You Can't Get There from Here* 57, *The Christmas that Almost Wasn't* 57, *Everyone but Thee and Me* 63, *Marriage Lines* 64, *The Untold Adventures of Santa Claus* 65.
333 E. 57th Street, New York City 22, N.Y., U.S.A.

Nash, Philleo; American anthropologist; b. 25 Oct. 1909; ed. Univs. of Wisconsin and Chicago.
Lecturer in Anthropology, Univ. of Toronto 37-41; Man. Biron Cranberry Co. 41-42, Pres. 46-; Special Asst. to Dir., White House liaison, Office of War Information 42-46; Special Asst., The White House 46-52; Admin. Asst. to Pres. of U.S. 52-53; Lieut.-Gov. of Wis. 59-61; Asst. to Asst. Sec. for Public Land Management, Dept. of Interior 61-62, U.S. Commr. of Indian Affairs 61-66; Consulting Anthropologist 66-; Dir. Asscn. American Indian Affairs 43-61.
1028 Connecticut Avenue, N.W., Washington, D.C. 20036; and 540 N. Street, S.W., Washington, D.C. 20024, U.S.A.
Telephone: 554-3775.

Nash, Rt. Hon. Sir Walter, P.C., C.H., G.C.M.G., M.P.; New Zealand politician; b. 12 Feb. 1882; ed. Kidderminster, England.
N.Z. Del. to 2nd Int. Labour Conf. 20; mem. Nat. Exec. Labour Party 19-37, 50-; Sec. 22-32; Nat. Pres. 35-36; mem. N.Z. Parl. 29-; mem. Wellington Harbour Board 33-38; Minister of Finance, Customs, etc. 35-49; Minister of Social Security 38-40, of Marketing 36-41; Minister of N.Z. in U.S.A. 42-44; mem. Pacific War Council, Washington 42-44; mem. N.Z. War Cabinet 39-45; Deputy Prime Minister of N.Z. 40-49; Leader of the Opposition 50-57, 60-63; Prime Minister, Minister of External Affairs, Minister of Maori Affairs 57-60; N.Z. rep. Imperial Conf. 37; leader of N.Z. Del. Int. Monetary Conf., Bretton Woods 44; del. to British Commonwealth P.M.s' Conf., London 46, 60; leader of N.Z. Del. to Confs. on Trade and Employment, Geneva 47, Havana 47-48; leader N.Z. del. ECAFE Conf. 58, SEATO Council of Ministers 58, UN 58, 60, Colombo Plan Consultative Cttee. 58; Chair. SEATO Council of Ministers 59; Leader N.Z. del. Antarctic Conf. 59, Anzus Council 59, U.N. 59, Colombo Plan Consultative Cttee. 59; leader N.Z. Labour Party; Vice-Pres. N.Z. Inst. of Int. Affairs; Hon. LL.D. (Cambridge, England,

Tufts Coll., Mass., and Temple Univ., Philadelphia). 14 St. Albans Grove, Lower Hutt, New Zealand; and [*Died 4 June* 1968.]

Nashashibi, Nasser Eddin; United Arab Republic journalist and politician; b. 1924; ed. American Univ. of Beirut.
Acting Chief Adviser, King Abdullah of Jordan 50, Acting Chief Chamberlain 51; fmr. Chief Controller and Dir. Hashemite Broadcasting; fmr. Head Press Dept., Foreign Office, Amman; Roving Editor *Akhbar El Yom*, Cairo; Chief Editor of daily *Al-Goumhouria*, Cairo 59-64; Special Diplomatic Envoy of daily *Al-Ahram* in Europe; Roving Amb. of the Arab League 65-67.
Publs. twelve books.
38 Rue Athenée, Geneva, Switzerland.
Telephone: Geneva 463763.

Nasi, Giovanni, D.ING.; Italian industrialist; b. 1918; ed. Politechnico di Torino.
Grandson of Giovanni Agnelli (founder of FIAT); Vice-Chair. of FIAT (manufacturers of land, sea and air vehicles and engines); Pres. UNACOMA (Italian Asscn. of Farm Machinery Manufacturers), Turin Agency for Int. Exhbns., Centre for Winter Road Transit; Mayor of Sestriere; Commendatore della Repubblica Italiana.
10 Corso Marconi, Turin, Italy.

Nasir, Mohammed; Iraqi diplomatist; b. 11; ed· American Univ. of Beirut and Columbia Univ. New York· Professor, later Dean, Coll. of Educ., Univ. of Baghdad to 64; Dir.-Gen. Ministry of Educ. 57; Minister of Educ. 64; Amb. to U.S.S.R. 65-66; Minister of Culture and Nat. Orientation 66; attended numerous int. and political confs.
Publs. *Readings in Arabic Literature* (2 vols.) 41, *A Guide to Study in the U.S.A.* 57, joint author *Civic Education* 39.
c/o Ministry of Culture, Baghdad, Iraq.

Nasir, Sharif Husain bin; Jordanian politician.
Former Minister of Royal Court; Prime Minister April 63-July 64; Great Uncle of King Hussein.
Amman, Jordan.

Nason, John William, A.M.; American educator; b. 9 Feb. 1905; ed. Chicago Latin School, Phillips Exeter Acad., Carleton Coll., Yale Divinity School, Harvard Graduate School, Oxford Univ.
Instructor in Philosophy Swarthmore Coll. 31-34, Asst. Prof. 34-40, Pres. 40-53; Pres. Foreign Policy Asscn. 53-62; Pres. Carleton Coll. 62-; Asst. to American Sec. Rhodes Trust 34-40; Pres. United Nations Council Philadelphia 42-45, Vice-Pres. 45-47; Pres. World Affairs Council of Philadelphia 49-51, 52-53; Fellow and mem. Board of Dirs. Soc. for Religion in Higher Educ.; Trustee, Edward W. Hazen Foundation, Eisenhower Exchange Fellowships 53-65, Danforth Foundation; Educators' Advisory Comm. Esso Educ. Foundation; Hon. LL.D. (Pennsylvania, Carleton, Swarthmore, Hamilton, Brandeis, Johns Hopkins); Litt.D. (Mühlenberg Coll., Hahnemann Medical School and Coll.); L.H.D. (Dropsie Coll., and Coll. of Wooster).
Publs. *American Higher Education in 1980—Some Basic Issues* 66.
Carleton College, Northfield, Minnesota 55057, U.S.A.
Telephone: 507-645-4431.

Nasriddinova, Yadgar Sadikovna; Soviet civil engineer and politician; b. 1920; ed. Inst. of Railway Transport Engineering, Tashkent.
Works Supt. Great Ferghana Canal, and the Construction of the Railway Line at "Angrenugol" Coalmines; later Sec. Cen. Cttee. Young Communist League of Uzbekistan 42-50; mem. C.P.S.U. 42-; Party work 50-52; Minister of Building Materials, Uzbek S.S.R. 52-55, Vice-Chair. Council of Ministers 55-59; Pres. Presidium,

Supreme Soviet of the Uzbek S.S.R. 59-; Deputy Chair. Presidium of Supreme Soviet of U.S.S.R. 60-; mem. Central Cttee. of C.P.S.U. 56-; mem. Presidium of Central Cttee. of C.P. of Uzbekistan.
Presidium of Supreme Soviet of Uzbek S.S.R., Tashkent, Uzbek S.S.R., U.S.S.R.

Nasser, Col. Gamal Abdel; United Arab Republic (Egyptian) army officer and political leader; b. 5 Jan. 1918; ed. El Masria Secondary School, Cairo, and Military Acad., Cairo.
Serving army officer until 52; posted to Mil. Acad. 42, graduated with distinction; fought in the Palestine war; led the coup d'état of July 23rd, 1952; Deputy Prime Minister and Minister of the Interior 52-54; Prime Minister and Military Governor of Egypt 54-56; Pres. of Egypt 56-58; Pres. of United Arab Republic 58-, also Prime Minister and Head of Arab Socialist Union June 67-; Hero of the Soviet Union.
The Presidency, Cairo, U.A.R.

Nasution, Gen. Abdul Haris; Indonesian officer; b. 3 Dec. 1918; ed. Netherlands Military Acad., Bandung.
Sub-Lieut. Netherlands Indies Army 41; Col. 45; suppressed Indonesian Communist Party's rebellion (Madiun revolt) 48; Army Chief of Staff 50-52, re-appointed 55-62; Chair. of Jt. Chiefs of Staff and mem. Nat. Council 57; Lieut.-Gen. 58; planned campaign against rebellion in Sumatra and Sulawesi 58; Minister of Defence and People's Security 59-66; Chair. People's Consultative Congress 66-; apptd. Gen. 60; Dep. C.-in-C. West Irian (W. New Guinea) Command 62.
Publs. *Principles of Guerilla Warfare, The Indonesian National Army, Notes on the Army Policy of the Republic of Indonesia*.
People's Consultative Congress, Djakarta, Indonesia.

Nasyrova, Halima; Soviet singer; b. 1913; ed. the Uzbek Opera Studio of the Moscow Conservatoire.
Soloist (soprano), Uzbek Navoi State Theatre of Opera and Ballet 39-; Deputy, Uzbek Supreme Soviet 37-58, to Supreme Soviet of U.S.S.R. 58; People's Artist of U.S.S.R. 37; State prizewinner 42, 51; awarded Order of Lenin (twice), Order of Honour (twice), Red Banner of Labour (twice).
Principal roles: Carmen, Leili (*Leili and Mejnun*), Gyulsara (*Gyulsara*), Zukhra (*Takhiz and Zukhra*), Zainab (*Zainab and Omon*), Akjunus, (*Yertargin*), Anorgul (*Buron*), Nodira (*The Great Canal*), Maisara (*Maisara's Pranks*), Nagriz (*Nagriz*), Perikolla (*Perikolla*), etc.
Uzbek Navoi State Theatre of Opera and Ballet, Tashkent, Uzbek S.S.R., U.S.S.R.

Naszkowski, Marian, M.A.; Polish politician; b. 15 Aug. 1912; ed. Lwów Univ.
Active in revolutionary youth movement and later in Communist Party before World War; imprisoned for political activities; during war took part in formation of Polish Army in U.S.S.R.; Chief Polish Mil. Mission, Paris 45-47; Amb. to U.S.S.R. 47-50; Vice-Minister of Defence 50-52, of Foreign Affairs 52-; mem. Cen. Cttee. Polish United Workers' Party 50; Chair. of Polish Del. Eighteen Nations Cttee. on Disarmament, Geneva 62.
Publs. *Niespokojne dni* (Unrestful Days) and *Lata Próby* (The Years of Test) memoirs.
23 Aleja I Armii WP, Warsaw, Poland.

Natali, Lorenzo; Italian lawyer and politician; b. 2 Oct. 1922; ed. Collegio d'Abruzzo dei Padri Gesuiti and Univ. di Firenze.
Deputy to Parl.; Under-sec. of State for the Press and Information 55-57; Under-sec. of State in Ministry of Finance 57-59, in Ministry of Treasury 60-64; Minister for the Merchant Marine Feb. 66-68, of Public Works 68-; Christian Democrat.
Ministry of Public Works, Rome; Home: Via Nibby 18, Rome, Italy.

Nathan, Otto, PH.D.; American economist; b. Germany 15 July 1893; ed. Würzburg, Freiburg and Munich Univs.

Statistical and Economic Adviser to Reich Dept. of Economics 20-33; Dir. Dept. for Research on Int. Economic Problems, Inst. for Business Cycle Research; Co-Editor *Vierteljahrshefte für Konjunkturforschung* 26-30; mem. German Del. to World Econ. Conf., Geneva 27; Lecturer Hochschule für Politik Berlin 28-33; Economic Adviser to Pres. Hoover's Emergency Cttee. on Employment 31; Visiting Lecturer Princeton Univ. 33-35; Associate Prof. of Economics N.Y. Univ. 35-58; Prof. of Economics Vassar Coll. 42-44; Chief Economic Analyst U.S. Treasury Dept. 44-45; Visiting Prof. of Econs., Howard Univ. 46-52; Consultant on Econ. Literature, Library of Congress 46-52.

Publs. *Some Considerations of Unemployment Insurance in the Light of German Experience, The N.I.R.A. and Stabilisation, Cartels and the State in the Light of German Experience, International Economic Action and Peace, Consumption in Germany during the Period of Rearmament, The Nazi Economic System* 44, *Nazi War Finance and Banking* 44, *Private Enterprise and Full Employment, Development of Underdeveloped Countries and the Development of Poland since 1945*; edited *Die Wirtschaft des Auslandes, 1900-07* 28, co-ed. *Einstein on Peace* 60, *Economics of Permanent Peace.*

55 East 10th Street, New York City 3, N.Y., U.S.A. Telephone: 477-2948.

Nathan, Robert; American novelist; b. 2 Jan. 1894; ed. Exeter Acad. and Harvard Univ.

Lecturer in Poetry, New York Univ. 24-25; mem. Exec. Cttee. U.S. P.E.N. Club (Pres. 40-42); mem. and Vice-Pres. Nat. Inst. of Arts and Letters; Chancellor, Acad. of American Poets; mem. Acad. Motion Picture Arts and Sciences.

Publs. *Autumn* 21, *Jonah* 25, *Fiddler in Barly* 26, *The Woodcutter's House* 27, *The Bishop's Wife* 28, *There is Another Heaven* 29, *The Orchid* 30, *One More Spring* 33, *Road of Ages* 35, *Selected Poems* 35, *The Enchanted Voyage* 36, *Winter in April* 37, *The Barly Field* 38, *Music at Evening* (play) 38, *A Winter Tide* 39, *Portrait of Jennie* 39, *Dunkirk* 40, *They Went on Together* 41, *Tapiola's Brave Regiment* 41, *The Sea Gull Cry* 41, *Journal for Josephine* 42, *But Gently Day* 43, *Morning in Iowa* 44, *The Darkening Meadows* 45, *Mr. Whittle and the Morning Star* 47, *Long After Summer* 49, *The River Journey* 49, *The Green Leaf* 50, *Married Look* 50, *The Sleeping Beauty* (play) 50, *The Innocent Eve* 51, *Jezebel's Husband* (play) 51, *Sir Henry* 55, *The Rancho of the Little Loves* 56, *So Love Returns* 58, *The Snowflake and the Starfish* 59, *The Weans* 60, *The Color of Evening* 60, *The Wilderness Stone* 61, *A Star in the Wind* 62, *The Married Man* 62, *The Devil with Love* 63, *The Fair* 64, *The Mallot Diaries* 65, *Juliet in Mantua* (play) 66, *Stonecliff* 67.

1240 N. Doheny Drive, Hollywood 69, Calif., U.S.A.

Natta, Giulio, DR. ING.; Italian chemist; b. 26 Feb. 1903; ed. Polytechnic Inst. of Milan.

Former Prof., Univs. of Pavia, Rome and Turin; Prof. and Dir., Dept of Industrial Chemistry, Polytechnic Inst. of Milan 38-; Nobel Prize for Chemistry 63; Dr. h.c. (Turin, Mainz, Genoa, Brooklyn Polytechnic, Catholic Univ. of Louvain); numerous Italian and foreign awards.

Publs. About 450 scientific articles.

Via Mario Pagano 54, Milan, Italy.

Naudé, Jozua Francois (Tom), J.P.; South African politician; b. 15 April 1889.

Practised law, Pietersburg 10, and mem. its Town Council and various public bodies until 20; mem. Parl. for Pietersburg 20-; former Speaker Union Parl. and Minister of Posts and Telegraphs; Minister of Health

56, of Finance 56-58, of Interior 58-60; Pres. of Senate 60-; Acting State Pres. of South Africa June 67-68.

The Senate, Cape Town, Republic of South Africa.

Naudé, Stefan Meiring, M.SC., PH.D.; South African physicist; b. 31 Dec. 1904; ed. Univs. of Stellenbosch, Berlin and Chicago.

Instructor Univ. of Chicago 29-30, Research Fellow 31; Senior Lecturer in Physics, Univ. of Cape Town 31-33; Prof. of Experimental Physics, Univ. of Stellenbosch 34-45; Dir. Nat. Physical Laboratory, Pretoria 46-50; Vice-Pres. Council of Scientific and Industrial Research 50-52, Pres. 52-; Fellow Royal Soc. of South Africa; Chair. Suid Afrikaanse Akademie vir Wetenskap en Kuns, Foundation for Education and Science; mem. American Physical Soc., Deutsche Physikalische Gesellschaft, South African Asscn. for the Advancement of Science, Advisory Scientific Council Atomic Energy Board, Univs. Advisory Cttee., Defence Council, Fuel Research Inst., Council Univ. of Pretoria, Int. Rotary, Associated Scientific and Technical Socs.; Nat. Chair. Simon van der Stel Foundation, Trustee, South African Foundation; Hon. D.Sc., Hon. LL.D.

Home: 420 Friesland Avenue, Lynnwood, Pretoria; Office: Council for Scientific and Industrial Research, P.O. Box 395, Pretoria, Republic of South Africa.

Naudé, William Christiaan, D.COMM.; South African diplomatist; b. 5 May 1909; ed. Boys High School, Stellenbosch and Stellenbosch and London Univs.

Diplomatic service in London, Geneva, Washington; Consul-Gen. Lourenço Marques 51-54; Del. to UN 53, 59, 63, 65; Leader, South African Dels. to GATT, Geneva, 54-57, 66, to ICEM 56-57; Minister Switzerland 56-57; Under-Sec. for External Affairs 57-59, Deputy Sec. 59-60; Amb. to United States 60-65; Principal Deputy Sec. for Foreign Affairs 65-66; Amb. Perm. Rep. Geneva 66-.

114 Rue du Rhône, Geneva, Switzerland.

Naumenko, Pyotr Vasilievich; Soviet politician; b. 05; ed. Kharkov Inst. of Chemical Technology.

Worker, Naftaleum Plant, Kharkov 17-21; Trudovai Khimik Factory, Kharkov 22-30; Production Manager, Chief Engineer, Uritski First State Soap Works, Kharkov 35-37; People's Commissariat for Food Industry, U.S.S.R. Ministry of Food Industry 37-57; Chair. Technico-Econ. Council, Moscow City Econ. Council 57-58; Deputy Chair. State Scientific Technical Cttee. R.S.F.S.R. 58-61; Deputy Chair. State Cttee. for Co-ordination of Research under Council of Ministers, R.S.F.S.R. 61-62; Chair. State Cttee. for Food Industry under U.S.S.R. Planning Cttee. 62-65; Deputy Minister of Food Industry 65-; State Prize (twice); two orders of Red Banner of Labour, and other awards.

U.S.S.R. Ministry of Food Industry, 5 Ul. Dzerzhinskogo, Moscow, U.S.S.R.

Nauta, Walle Jetze Harinx, M.D., D.SC.; American anatomist; b. 8 June 1916; ed. Univ. of Leiden.

Lecturer, Univ. of Utrecht 41-46; Assoc. Prof. Univ. of Leiden 46-47; Assoc. Prof. Univ. of Zürich 47-51; Neurophysiologist, Walter Reed Army Inst. of Research 51-; Prof. of Anatomy, Univ. of Maryland 55-64; Mass. Inst. of Technology 64-.

Publs. *Hypothalamic Regulation of Sleep in Rats* 46, *Silver Impregnation of Degenerating Axons* 54, *Ascending Pathways in the Brain Stem Reticular Formation* 58, *Hippocampal Projections* 58.

Department of Psychology, Massachusetts Institute of Technology, Cambridge, Mass. 02139, U.S.A.

Navarre, Général Henri; French army officer; b. 31 July 1898; ed. Ecole Spéciale Militaire, St. Cyr.

Joined 2nd Régiment de Hussards 17, served through all ranks to Brigadier 45, Divisional Gen. 50 and Gén. de Corps d'Armée 52; served in the Levant (Spahis) 20-22, in Germany 22-26; Cours des Hautes Etudes

Germaniques 25; Cours d'Auto-mitrailleuses 26; Ecole de Guerre 28-30; in Morocco 31-36; Chief of German Section, General Staff of Army 38-40; Chief of Staff to Gen. Weygand and to Gen. Juin in Algiers 40-42; recalled to France by Admiral Darlan 42; Resistance leader 43-45; brigade command during advance into Germany; Dir. of the Council of the Gen. C.-in-C. Germany 45-48; Commdr. Constantine Div. 48-49; Inst. des Hautes Etudes de la Défense Nationale 49-50; in command 5th Armoured Division 50-52; Dep. C.-in-C. French Forces in Germany 52, Chief of Staff of the C.-in-C. Central Europe 52-53; C.-in-C. (Combined Forces) Indo-China 53-54; mem. Conseil Supérieur de Guerre 56; retd. 56; awards include Grand-Officier Légion d'Honneur.
Publ. *Agonie de l'Indo-chine* 56.
Bastide du Malvan, "L'Ara", Vence (A.-M.), France.
Telephone: 32-04-05.

Navarro Rubio, Mariano; Spanish lawyer and politician; b. 14 Nov. 1913; ed. Univ. of Zaragoza.
Colonel in legal dept. of the army; Under-Sec. of Public Works April 55-Feb. 57; Minister of Finance Feb. 57-65; Governor, Bank of Spain 65-: Cruz de guerra con palmas, Great Cross of Carlos III, Légion d'Honneur, and several other decorations.
Calle de Alcalá No. 50, Madrid 14, Spain.
Telephone: 221-11-10.

Navasqués y Ruiz de Velasco, Emilio de, Conde de Navasqués, D. EN D., LIC. EN FIL.; Spanish diplomatist; b. 23 March 1904; ed. Univ. de Madrid and Ecole Libre des Sciences Politiques, Paris.
Secretary of Spanish Comm. of League of Nations 33-34; First Sec., Lisbon 43; Dir.-Gen. (Political and Econ.), Ministry of Foreign Affairs 44-47; Under-Sec. for Foreign Econs. and Trade 47; Minister, The Hague 48-50; Amb. to Argentina 50-51; Under-Sec. for Foreign Affairs 51-55; Insp.-Gen., Ministry of Foreign Affairs 55-56; Amb. to Italy 56-59; Dir. of Escuela Diplomática 59-; Pres. Council of Admin. of IBERIA (Spanish Airlines) 65-; Pres. Calatrava (oil firm) 65-; Vice-Pres. Empresa Nacional Siderúrgica 65-; Gran Cruz de Isabel la Católica, and orders from Portugal, Argentina, Peru, Egypt, Lebanon, etc.
Avenida Miraflores 31, Madrid (20), Spain.

Navrátil, Jan, M.D., D.SC.; Czechoslovak surgeon; b. 26 Jan. 1909; ed. Medical Faculty, Masaryk Univ., Brno.
Assistant Prof. of Surgery Purkyně Univ., Brno 46-53, Head of Second Surgical Clinic, Medical Faculty 53-; Prof. of Surgery 54-; Corresp. mem. Czechoslovak Acad. of Sciences 65-; mem. Czechoslovak Surgical Soc., Deutsche Akad. der Naturforscher Leopoldina, Halle, Soc. Int. Cardio-Vasculaire, Soc. Int. de Chirurgie, Brussels, American Heart Asscn., New York, American Coll. of Chest Physicians, Chicago, Int. Coll. of Surgeons, Chicago; Czechoslovakia Peace Prize 59, J. E. Purkyně Medal 60, Order of Republic 62.
Publs. *Repair of Heart Defects by Open Chest Surgery* 63; and papers in Czechoslovak and foreign medical journals.
Brno, Pekarská 48, Czechoslovakia.

Navrotsky, Vasily Korneyevich; Soviet hygiene specialist; b. 1897; ed. Kharkov Medical Inst.
Physician in Byelorussia and Ukraine 21-27; Head of Dept., Dir., Ukrainian Inst. of Occupational Hygiene and Occupational Diseases 27-49; Corresp. mem. U.S.S.R. Acad. of Medical Sciences 48-60, mem. U.S.S.R. Acad. of Medical Sciences 60-; Head of Dept. Kharkov Inst. for Postgraduate Medical Training 49-; mem. Board All-Union and Ukrainian Socs. of Hygienists; Badge of Honour 45, and other decorations.
Publs. Over 100 works on occupational hygiene in chemical, coal and iron ore industries, and industrial toxicology.

Kharkov Institute for Postgraduate Medical Training, Prospekt Pravdy 15, Kharkov, U.S.S.R.

Nawng, Sama Duwa Sinwa; Burmese politician; b. 15; ed. Buddhist Monastery, Mogaung.
Began political career 35; active in movement for Burmese independence 37-47; worked in co-operation with Bogyoke Aung San; Minister for Kachin State 48-55, for Nat. Solidarity 55-56 and 57-58; mem. Burmese Parl. for Myitkyina West 51-58; Minister for Kachin State 60-62; Ambassador to People's Republic of China 64-.
Burmese Embassy, Peking, People's Republic of China.

Nay, Ernst Wilhelm; German painter; b. 11 June 1902; ed. Berlin Acad. of Fine Art.
Studied for several years with Karl Hofer; began to paint in an expressionistic and neo-realist style, but gradually evolved towards an abstract position; went to Norway by invitation of Edvard Munch 37-38; rep. at numerous exhibitions, including the Brussels Int. Exhibition 58; numerous one-man exhibitions.
Lortzingstrasse 9, Köln-Lindenthal, German Federal Republic.

Nayar, Sushila, M.B., B.S., M.D., D.P.H.; Indian doctor; ed. Lahore Coll. for Women, Lady Hardinge Medical Coll., Delhi, Johns Hopkins Univ., U.S.A.
Medical attendant to Mahatma Gandhi and his Ashram; rural and communal medical work at Sevagram and Noakhali, W. Punjab and Delhi; Chief Medical Officer Faridabad; Sec. Medical Board of Kasturba Trust; Sec. Leprosy Board of Gandhi Memorial Trust; fmr. Minister of Health, Rehabilitation and Transport, Delhi State; fmr. Speaker Delhi Legislative Assembly; Minister of Health, Govt. of India 62-67.
Publs. *Kasturba, Karavas ki Kahari*, etc.
1 Curzon Lane, New Delhi, India.

Nazarkin, Konstantin Ivanovich; Soviet banker and politician; b. 06; ed. Tashkent Finance and Econs. Inst.
Began work in Gosbank system 25; Manager Uzbek Repub. Board of U.S.S.R. Gosbank 44-49; mem. Board of U.S.S.R. Gosbank 49-57; Deputy Chair. Board of External Trade Bank of U.S.S.R. 61-63; Chair. Board of Int. Bank for Econ. Co-operation Oct. 63-.
International Bank for Economic Co-operation, Kuznetsky most 15, Moscow, U.S.S.R.

Nazarshoyev, Moyensho Nazarshoyevich; Soviet politician; b. 1929; ed. Dushanbe Pedagogical Inst.
Member C.P.S.U. 53-; Teacher, Tadjik Univ., later Deputy Chief of Section; mem. Central Cttee. of C.P. of Tadjikstan 63-; First Sec. Gorno-Badakhshansky Regional Cttee. of C.P. of Tadjikstan 63-; Deputy to U.S.S.R. Supreme Soviet.
Gorno-Badakhshansky Regional Committee of Communist Party of Tadjikstan, Khorog, U.S.S.R.

Ne Win, General (Maung Shu Maung); Burmese army officer and politician; b. 11; ed. Govt. High School, Prome and Rangoon Univ.
Joined Allied Forces 45; Vice-Chief of Gen. Staff and Major-Gen. 48; Deputy Prime Minister 49-50; Gen. 56; Prime Minister and Minister of Defence Oct. 58-60; Chief of Gen. Staff 60-; Prime Minister, Minister of Defence, Finance, and Revenue, Nat. Planning and Justice 62-63, Prime Minister, Minister of Nat. Planning and Defence 63; Prime Minister and Minister of Defence, also Chair. of Revolutionary Council 65-; Legion of Merit (U.S.A.).
Office of the Prime Minister, Rangoon, Burma.

Neale, Sir John Ernest, M.A., F.B.A.; British historian; b. 7 Dec. 1890; ed. Liverpool and London Univs.
Professor of Modern History Manchester Univ. 25-27; Astor Prof. of English History London Univ. 27-56; Trustee London Museum 45-; foreign mem. American Acad. of Arts and Sciences 50-; mem. Editorial Board

History of Parl. Trust 51-; Hon. mem. American Historical Asscn. 68-; Hon. D.Litt. (Wales, Birmingham and Leeds), Hon. Litt.D. (Liverpool, Cambridge), Hon. D.Lit. (London); Hon. L.H.D. (Amherst). Publs. *Queen Elizabeth* 34 (awarded James Tait Black Memorial Prize); *The Age of Catherine de Medici* 43, *The Elizabethan House of Commons* 49, *Elizabeth I and Her Parliaments 1559-1561* 53, *Elizabeth I and Her Parliaments 1584-1601* 57, *Essays in Elizabethan History* 58.

Adare, 57 Penn Road, Beaconsfield, Bucks., England.
Telephone: Beaconsfield 4466.

Neckermann, Josef; German businessman; b. 5 June 1912; ed. grammar school, Würzburg.

Joined his father's business 33; in charge of a Würzburg store 34-38; Head of mail order house Berlin 38; State Commr. for Clothing 39-45; Head, Zentrallagergemeinschaft m.b.H., Berlin 39-45; Founder textile wholesale business Frankfurt am Main 48; Owner and Manager Neckermann Versand KGaA 50, Mail Order Houses, Frankfurt am Main; founded Neckermann Eigenheit G.m.b.H. 63, Neckura Neckermann Versicherungs A.G. 65, N.U.R. Neckermann und Reisen G.m.b.H. & Co. K.G. 64, Neckermann Anlagen-Beratung Gesellschaft zur Vermittlung von Kapitalanlagen m.b.H. 67, Neckermann-Fonds Verwaltungsgesellschaft 68; Bronze Medal, Olympic Games 60; World Championship of dressage 66.

Neckermann Versand KGaA, 6000 Frankfurt/Main, German Federal Republic.
Telephone: 410001.

Needham, Joseph, M.A., PH.D., SC.D., F.R.S.; British biochemist, historian of science and orientalist; b. 1900; ed. Oundle School and Cambridge Univ.

Fellow Caius Coll. 24-, Pres. 59-66, Master 66-; Univ. Demonstrator in Biochemistry, Cambridge 28-33; Visiting Prof. of Biochemistry, Stanford Univ., Calif. 29; Dunn Reader in Biochemistry, Cambridge 33-66; Lecturer Yale Univ., Cornell Univ., Oberlin Coll. 35; Oliver Sharpey Lecturer, Royal Coll. Physicians 35-36, Herbert Spencer Lecturer, Oxford 36-37; lectured Warsaw, Lwów, Cracow and Wilno Univs. 37; Head of Sino-British Science Co-operation Office and Counsellor British Embassy, Chungking 42-46; Head of Div. of Natural Sciences UNESCO 46-48; now Honorary Counsellor to UNESCO; Chair. Ceylon Govt. Comm. on Univ. Education 58; Hitchcock Prof. Univ. of Calif., Noguchi Lecturer, Johns Hopkins Univ. 50; Hobhouse Lecturer, London Univ. 50; Visiting Prof. Univ. of Lyon 51; Dickinson Lecturer, Newcomen Soc., London 56; Wilkins Lecturer, Royal Soc. London 58; lectured Colombo, Singapore, Peking, Jaipur Univs. 58; Grey Lecturer, Newcastle 61; lectured Bucharest, Iaşi, Cluj, Timişoara Univs. 62; Peking, Kyoto, Osaka Univs. 64; Myers Lecturer Royal Anthropological Inst. 64; foreign mem. Nat. Acad. of China (Academia Sinica); mem. Int. Acads. of the History of Science, of the Philosophy of Science and the History of Medicine; Order of Brilliant Star (China), Hon. D.Sc. (Brussels), Sir Wm. Jones Medallist, Asiatic Soc. of Bengal; George Sarton Medallist, Historical Science Soc.

Publs. *Man a Machine* 27, *The Sceptical Biologist* 29, *Chemical Embryology* (3 vols.) 31, *The Great Amphibium* 32, *A History of Embryology* 35, *Order and Life* 35, *Adventures before Birth* (trans.) 35, *Biochemistry and Morphogenesis* 42, *Time, the Refreshing River* 42, *History is on Our Side* 44, *Chinese Science* 45, *Science Outpost* 48, *Science and Civilisation in China* (6 vols.) 54-, *The Development of Iron and Steel Technology in China* 58, *Heavenly Clockwork* 60, *Time and Eastern Man* 65, *Clerks and Craftsmen in China and the West* 68, *The Grand Titration, Science and Society in China and the West* 68, *Within the Four Seas* 68; Editor: *Science, Religion and Reality* 25, *Christianity and Social*

Revolution 35, *Perpectives in Biochemistry* 36, *Background to Modern Science* 38, *Science in the Soviet Union* 42, *The Teacher of Nations* 42, *Hopkins and Biochemistry* 49.

The Master's Lodge, Gonville and Caius College, Cambridge, England.
Telephone: Cambridge 52183 and 53275, extension 301.

Neel, Louis Boyd, C.B.E., M.A., M.R.C.S., L.R.C.P., HON. R.A.M.; British musician; b. 19 July 1905; ed. R.N. Coll., Dartmouth, and Caius Coll., Cambridge.

Qualified and practised as doctor; forsook medicine for music and founded the Boyd Neel Orchestra (of which he is Conductor) 33; the orchestra appeared at the Salzburg Festival 37; toured Portugal 39; during Second World War returned to medical work; the orchestra toured France, Australia and N.Z. 47, Germany, Holland, Portugal 48-49; France, Denmark, Norway, Sweden and Finland 50; Italy, Germany, France 51; Canada, America 52; conducted first performance Glyndebourne 34; conductor, Sadler's Wells Opera 45; D'Oyly Carte London Seasons 48-49; Edinburgh Festival 48, 51; Mayer Children's Concerts, London; Dean, Royal Conservatory of Music, Toronto Sept. 53-; formed Hart House Orchestra 54, performed at Stratford, Ontario, Festival 55, Brussels World Fair with Hart House Orchestra 58, toured Canada with Hart House Orchestra 58-60, conducted orchestras in New Zealand and Australia for ABC 64; toured Sweden, Finland, Norway (Bergen Festival), Belgium and England with Hart House Orchestra, playing at Aldeburgh Festival 66, and at EXPO 67 Montreal 67.

Publ. *The Story of an Orchestra* 50.

Edward Johnson Building, University of Toronto, Toronto 5, Ont., Canada.

Néel, Louis Eugène Félix; French scientist; b. 22 Nov. 1904; ed. Lycée du Parc, Lyon, Lycée Saint-Louis, Paris, and Ecole Normale Supérieure, Paris.

Professor, Univ. of Strasbourg 37-45, Grenoble 45-; Scientific Adviser to Navy 52-; French Rep. to Scientific and Org. Cttee. of NATO; Pres. French Physical Soc. 57; Pres. Int. Union of Pure and Applied Physics 63-; mem. Directorate of Nat. Centre for Scientific Research 49-; Dir. of Inst. Polytechnique 54-, Centre of Nuclear Studies, Grenoble 56-; Foreign mem. U.S.S.R. Acad. of Sciences, Royal Netherlands Acad., German Leopoldina Acad., Rumanian Acad. of Sciences, Royal Soc. (U.K.); Croix de Guerre 40; Commandeur des Palmes Académiques; Commandeur Légion d'Honneur; Prix Holweck 52, Gold Medal (Centre Nat. de la Recherche Scientifique) 65.

Publs. over 200 works on various aspects of magnetism.
41 avenue du Maréchal Randon, Grenoble, France.

Nef, John Ulric, S.B., PH.D.; American historian; b. 13 July 1899; ed. Harvard Univ.

Asst. Prof. of Economics, Swarthmore Coll. 27-28, Asst. Prof. of Economics, Chicago Univ. 29-31, Associate Prof. 31-35, Associate Prof. of Economic History 35-36, Prof. 36-50; Chair. Cttee. Social Thought 45-64; Visiting Prof. Inst. d'Etudes Politiques, Paris 49; temporary Prof. Coll. de France, Paris 53; Wiles Lecturer, Univ. of Belfast 56; Smith Lecturer, Univ. of St. Thomas 61; Vice-Chair. American Council of Learned Societies 52-53; Chair. Center for Human Understanding 62-; Dr. h.c. (Paris); Officier Légion d'Honneur, Order of the Phoenix (Greece).

Publs. *The Rise of the British Coal Industry* (2 vols.) 32, *Industry and Government in France and England, 1540-1640* 40, *The United States and Civilization* 42 (2nd edn. 67), *The Universities Look for Unity* 43, *La route de la guerre totale* 49, *War and Human Progress* 50, *Letters and Notes of Elinor Castle Nef*, Vol. I 53, *La Naissance de la Civilisation industrielle et le Monde contemporain* 54, *Cultural Foundations of Industrial Civilisation* 58, *Religion and the Study of Man* 61, *A la Recherche de la*

Civilisation 62, *Bridges of Human Understanding* 64, *Conquest of the Material World* 64.
2726 N Street, N.W., Washington, D.C. 20007, U.S.A.
Telephone: 333-2983.

Negahban, Ezatollah, B.A., M.A., PH.D.; Iranian archaeologist; b. 1 March 1925; ed. Teheran and Chicago Univs. Associate Prof., Univ. of Teheran 56-62, Prof. 62-, Dir. Univ. Inst. of Archaeology 58-; Technical Dir. Iranian Archaeological Service 60-65; Technical Adviser to Ministry of Culture 65-; Hon. mem. German Archaeological Inst.; mem. Perm. Council, Congress of Pre- and Proto-historic Archaeology; excavated at Marlik 61-62, Haft Tepe 66; Dir. Iranian Archeological (Iran Bastan) Museum 66-.
Publs. *The Gold Treasures of Marlik* 62, *Preliminary Report on Marlik Excavation* 64.
Box 319, Teheran, Iran.
Telephone: 83856.

Negrão de Lima, Francisco, LL.B.; Brazilian diplomatist and politician; ed. Belo Horizonte and Rio de Janeiro.
Former Deputy from Minas Gerais in the Senate and Chamber of Deputies; Chief of Staff, Ministry of Justice and Interim Minister of Justice 38-41; Amb. in Bolivia 53; Mayor of Rio de Janeiro 55; at Foreign Office until 59; at Lisbon Embassy 59-65; Gov. of Guanabara State 65-; Founder Paraguayan-Brazilian Inst., Asunción; Leader of Special Mission to Pres. of Uruguay 51.
Office of the Governor, Rio de Janeiro, Guanabara State, Brazil.

Nègre, Maurice; French journalist; b. 20 April 1901. On editorial staff of *Eclair, Journal, Matin, Ami du Peuple*, successively 21-31; Dir. Warsaw Office of Havas Agency 31-34; Budapest Office 34-38; Bucharest Office 38-39; Dir. Information Service, French Embassy, Bucharest 40; worked for Allies in Balkans 40-42; played prominent part in French Resistance, founding clandestine news service "Supernap" 42-44; arrested and sent to Buchenwald 44, liberated 45; Dir.-Gen. Agence France-Presse 45-47 and 49-54; foreign affairs commentator, Radiodiffusion Française 47-49; Public Relations Consultant 55-; Technical Adviser, Société Ediradio 64; Commdr. de la Légion d'Honneur, Médaille de la Résistance, Croix de Guerre (Belgium), and Officier de la Couronne de Belgique.
14 avenue du Général Claverie, Paris 16e, France.

Nehru, Braj Kumar, B.SC., B.SC.(ECON.); Indian civil servant and Barrister-at-Law; b. 4 Sept. 1909; ed. Allahabad Univ., London School of Economics, Balliol Coll., Oxford, Inner Temple, London.
Joined Indian Civil Service 34; Asst. Commr. 34-39; Under Sec., Dept. of Education, Health and Lands, Govt. of India 39; Officer on special duty, Reserve Bank of India, Under Sec., Finance Dept., Govt. of India 40, Joint Sec. 47; Exec. Dir. Int. Bank for Reconstruction and Development and Minister, Indian Embassy, Washington 49-54; Sec., Dept. of Economic Affairs, Ministry of Finance 57-58, Commr. Gen. for Economic Affairs 58-61; Ambassador to U.S.A. 61-67; rep. Reparations Conf. 45, Commonwealth Finance Ministers Conf., UN Gen. Assembly 49-52, 60, FAO Confs. 49-50, Sterling Balances Confs. 47-49, Bandung Conf. 55; deputed to enquire into Australian Fed. Finance 46; mem. UN Advisory Cttee. on Admin. and Budgetary Questions 51-53; Adviser to Sudan Govt. 55; mem. UN Investments Cttee 62-.
c/o Ministry of External Affairs, New Delhi, India.

Nehru, Ratan Kumar; Indian civil servant and diplomatist; b. 10 Oct. 1902; ed. Allahabad and Oxford Univs.
Joined Indian Civil Service 25; served Madhya Pradesh

25-33; joined Central Govt. Admin., successively held posts of Collector of Customs, Bombay and later Madras, Commr. of Northern India Salt Revenue, Deputy and Joint Sec. in various Govt. depts. and Chair. Central Board of Revenue; Sec. to Ministry of Communications 47; Minister in Washington 48; Minister to Sweden, Denmark and Finland 49-51; Special Sec. for U.N. Affairs and later Commonwealth Sec. in Ministry of External Affairs 51-52; Foreign Sec. in Ministry of External Affairs 52-55; Ambassador to China 55-58; Ambassador to U.A.R. concurrently accred. to Lebanon and Libya 58-60; Sec.-Gen. Ministry of External Affairs 60-65, Chair. Preparatory Cttees. of Govt. of India for Conf. on Disarmament, and the UN Trade and Development Conf. 63-65; mem. Board of Trade and Nat. Defence Council; Vice Chancellor, Allahabad Univ. 65-.
Senate House, Allahabad, India.

Neidlinger, Gustav; German baritone singer; b. 21 March 1912; ed. Humanistisches Gymnasium, Mainz, and Opernschule, Frankfurt/Main.
Has performed at Stadttheater, Mainz, Stadttheater, Plauen, Staatsoper, Hamburg, Staatsoper, Stuttgart, Bayreuth Festival, Deutsche Oper, Berlin, La Scala, Milan, Covent Garden, London, Grand Opera, Paris, Teatro La Fenice, Venice, Rome Opera and Opera S. Carlo, Naples; currently with Staatsoper, Stuttgart.
7 Stuttgart, Traubergst. 3, German Federal Republic.

Neihardt, John Gneisenau, LITT.D., LL.D.; American author; b. 8 Jan. 1881; ed. Nebraska Normal Coll.
Literary Editor *St. Louis Post-Dispatch* 26-38; Dir. of Information Office of Indian Affairs U.S.A. 44; Field Rep. of the Commr. of Indian Affairs 46-48; Lecturer in English, Univ. of Missouri 48-; Chancellor, Acad. of American Poets, New York 52; Nat. Inst. of Arts and Letters, New York; Hon. Litt.D. (Nebraska, Missouri), Hon. LL.D. (Creighton), Fulbright Award 64.
Publs. *The Lonesome Trail* 07, *Poetic Values* 25, *The Stranger at the Gate* 12, *Life's Lure* 14, *Collected Poems* 26, *Black Elk Speaks* 32, 62, *A Cycle of the West* (5 book-length narrative poems) 41, in one volume 49, 62, *When the Tree Flowered* 51, *Eagle Voice* (London) 53, *Ich rufe mein Volk* (Germany) 55, *Zwarte Eland Spreekt* (Holland) 64, *Lyric and Dramatic Poems* 65.
Skyrim Farm, Route 7, Columbia, Mo., U.S.A.; and University of Missouri, Columbia, Mo., U.S.A.

Neilan, Edwin Peter; American banker; b. 24 Oct. 1905; ed. Omaha Univ., Rice Univ., Texas Univ., Rutgers Graduate School of Banking, South Texas School of Law.
Securities Analyst, Houston Bank & Trust Co. 28-33; Chief Trust Examiner Federal Reserve Bank of Dallas 33-36, New York 36-37, Philadelphia 37-40; Assoc. Trust Officer, Bank of Delaware 40-42; U.S. Naval Reserve 42-46; Vice-Pres. and Sec. Bank of Delaware 46-52, Exec. Vice-Pres. 52-56, Pres. 56-59, Chair. of Board 59-; Pres. Delaware Bankers 52; Chair. Board Greater Wilmington Development Council 61-63; Pres. United Fund Northern Delaware 61-63; Vice-Pres. Chamber of Commerce of U.S. 62-63, Pres. 63-64; Chair. of Board 64-65; Vice-Pres. State Bank Div., American Bankers Asscn. 62-64, Pres. 64-65; American Employer Del. Int. Labour Org.
Bank of Delaware, 901 Market Street, Wilmington, Delaware, U.S.A.

Neild, Robert Ralph; British economist; b. 10 Sept. 1924; ed. Charterhouse, and Trinity Coll., Cambridge.
Royal Air Force 43-44, Operational Research, R.A.F., 44-45; Secr., UN Econ. Comm. for Europe, Geneva 47-51; Econ. Section, Cabinet Office (later Treasury) 51-56; Lecturer in Econs. and Fellow of Trinity Coll., Cambridge 56-58; Nat. Inst. of Econ. and Social Research 58-64; Econ. Adviser to Treasury 64-67; Dir.

Int. Inst. for Peace and Conflict Research, Stockholm, May 67-.

Publ. *Pricing and Employment in the Trade Cycle* 64.
18 Chepstow Place, London W.2, England.

Neill, Alexander Sutherland, M.A.; Scottish educationist; b. 17 Oct. 1883; ed. village school and Edinburgh Univ.
Joint Founder Neue Schule, Hellerau, Dresden 21-23, Sonntagsberg 23 and Lyme Regis 24; Principal Summerhill School.
Publs. *A Dominie's Log* 15, *The Problem Child* 26, *The Problem Parent* 31, *Is Scotland Educated?* 36, *That Dreadful School* 37, *The Last Man Alive* 38, *The Problem Teacher* 39, *Hearts not Heads in the School* 45, *The Problem Family* 48, *The Free Child* 54, *Summerhill* 62, *Freedom, not Licence* 66, *Talking of Summerhill* 67.
Summerhill School, Leiston, Suffolk, England.

Neill, Rt. Rev. Stephen Charles, M.A.; British ecclesiastic; b. 31 Dec. 1900; ed. Dean Close School, and Trinity Coll., Cambridge.
Fellow, Trinity Coll., Cambridge 24-28; Missionary in Diocese of Tinnevelly 24-27 and 28-30; Warden, Bishop's Theological Coll., Nazareth, S. India 30-39; Examining Chaplain to Bishop of Tinnevelly 29-39; Bishop of Tinnevelly 39-45; Chaplain, Trinity Coll. Cambridge, and Lecturer in Theology 45-47; Select Preacher, Univ. of Oxford 45, Univ. of Cambridge 48; Hulsean Lecturer, Cambridge 46-47; Asst. Bishop to the Archbishop of Canterbury 47-50; Co-Dir. Study Dept. World Council of Churches; Assoc. Gen Sec. 48-51; Gen. Editor, World Christian Books, 52-62; Visiting Prof. of Missions, Univ. of Hamburg 56-57, 62-67; Dir. World Christian Books 62-; Bampton Lecturer, Univ. of Oxford 64; Hon. D.D. (Trinity Coll., Toronto, Culver-Stockton and Glasgow); Hon. Th.D. (Hamburg and Uppsala); Hon. Litt.D. (St. Paul's Univ., Tokyo).
Publs. *How Readest Thou?* 25, *Out of Bondage* 28, *Builders of the Indian Church* 34, *Beliefs* 38, *Foundation Beliefs* 42, *The Challenge of Jesus Christ* 44, *Christ, His Church and His World* 48, *The Cross over Asia* 48, *Fulfil Thy Ministry* 52, *The Christian Society* 53, *Christian Partnership* 53, *Towards Church Union 37-52*, 53, *Under Three Flags* 54, *The Christian's God* 54, *Christian Faith Today* 55, *The Christian Character* 55, *Who is Jesus Christ?* 56, *The Unfinished Task* 57, *Anglicanism* 58, *Paul to the Galatians* 58, *A Genuinely Human Existence* 59, *Christian Holiness* 60, *Brothers of the Faith: the Ecumenical Movement 1919-1960* 60, *What is Man?* 60, *Christian Faith and Other Faiths* 61, *The Eternal Dimension* 63, *Christian Missions* 64, *The Interpretation of the New Testament* 64, *Colonialism and Christian Missions* 66, *The Church and Christian Union* 67.
Hofweg 89, 2 Hamburg 22, German Federal Republic.
Telephone: Hamburg 22-21-17.

Neirinck, José D., DR. SOC. SC.; Belgian international civil servant; b. 1920; ed. Univ. of Ghent.
Social-Econ. Adviser at the Planning and Documentation Office, Nat. Sec., Gen. Belgian Fed. of Labour 47-54; Deputy Exec. Asst., later Exec. Asst. to Minister of Labour and Social Welfare 54-58; Deputy Gov., Dir.-Gen. Belgian Nat. Social Security Service 58-63; Vice-Pres. Nat. Pension Fund for Employees 58-63; Dir.-Gen. of Social Affairs, European Econ. Community (EEC) 63-; Officer Order of Crown, commemoration medals Armed Resistance and World War II.
Publs. on social-economic matters.
European Economic Community, 170 rue de la Loi, Brussels 4; and Maarschalklaan 16, Ukkel (B.-18), Belgium.

Neizvestny, Ernst Iosifovich; Soviet artist and sculptor; b. 1925; ed. V. I. Surikov State Inst. of Arts (M. G. Manizer's studio).
Soviet Army 42-45; sculptor at studios of U.S.S.R.

Agricultural Exhbn. (now Econ. Achievements of U.S.S.R. Exhbn.) 53-54; mem. Artists' Union of U.S.S.R. 55-.
Main works: *Kremlin Builder, First Wings, The Youth, Mother,* series: *War—is . . .; Robots and Semi-robots, Great Mistakes,* etc.
U.S.S.R. Artists' Union, 25/9 Ulitsa Gorkogo, Moscow, U.S.S.R.
Telephone: B-1-10-21.

Neklyudov, Alexei Ivanovich; Soviet politician; b. 1906; ed. Higher Party School.
Member C.P.S.U. 29-; Soviet Army 28-32; Deputy Chief, Section of Research Inst. 32-39; official, Central Cttee. of C.P. of Kazakhstan, later First Sec., City Cttee., then Sec. Regional Cttee. of C.P. of Uzbekistan 39-59; First Sec. East Kazakhstan Regional Cttee. of C.P. 59-; mem. Central Cttee. of C.P. of Kazakhstan; Deputy to U.S.S.R. Supreme Soviet.
East Kazakhstan Regional Committee of Communist Party of Kazakhstan, Ust-Kamenogorsk, U.S.S.R.

Nekrasov, Victor Platonovich; Soviet writer; b. 1911; ed. Inst. of Engineering and Architecture, Kiev.
Former architectural student; Actor and Set Designer, Kiev, Vladivostok, Kirov, Rostov-on-Don 37-41; Army Officer (Engineers) 41-44; journalist; writer 47-; State Prize 47; Badge of Honour 60.
Publs. *In the Trenches of Stalingrad* (novel) 46, *The Native Town* (novel) 54, *First Journey* (essays on a visit to Italy) 58, *Vassia Konakoff* (short stories) 60, *Kira Georgievna* (novel) 62, *Both Sides of the Ocean* (essays on a visit to Italy and U.S.A.) 62, *A Month in France* 65, *Distance of 12,000 Kilometres* (Stories about Kamchatka) 65, *Travels in Different Measurements* 67.
Union of Soviet Writers, Ulitsa Vorovskogo 52, Moscow, U.S.S.R.

Nellemose, Knud; Danish sculptor; b. 12 March 1908; ed. Royal Acad. of Art, Copenhagen.
First exhbn. of sculpture 31; mem. State Art Foundation 58-64; awarded Eckersberg Medal 44, Kai Nielsen Bequest 47, Carlsberg Travelling Scholarship 47-48; Knight of the Order Dannebrog; busts of Their Majesties the King and Queen of Denmark; works represented in the State Gallery of Copenhagen and in other Danish Museums, Nat. Museums of Stockholm and Oslo, and include *Group of Wrestlers* and *Young Men with Discus* and a marble bust of Hans Andersen for his 150th anniversary celebrations; represented at Venice Biennale 50, and other int. exhbns.
Mathilde Fibigersvej 3, Copenhagen F, Denmark.

Nelson, Gaylord Anton, LL.B.; American lawyer and politician; b. 4 June 1916; ed. Clear Lake High School (Polk County, Wis.), San José State Coll., Calif., and Wisconsin Univ. Law School.
Practising Attorney, Madison, Wis. 46-58; Wisconsin State Senator 48-58; Gov. of Wisconsin 58-62; U.S. Senator from Wisconsin 63-; army service 42-46; Democrat.
3812 Kenilworth Drive, Chevy Chase, Maryland; and 5750 Bittersweet Place, Madison, Wisconsin, U.S.A.
Telephone: Maryland 225-5323.

Nelson of Stafford, Baron, succeeded to title 62; **Henry George Nelson,** M.A., C.ENG., M.I.C.E., M.I.MECH.E., F.I.E.E., F.R.Ae.S.; British industrialist; b. 2 Jan. 1917; ed. Oundle and King's Coll., Cambridge.
With English Electric Co. Ltd. 39-42; Man. Dir. D. Napier & Son Ltd. 42-49; Exec. Dir. Marconi's Wireless Telegraph Co. Ltd. 46-58; Dep. Man. Dir. English Electric Co. Ltd. 49-56, Man. Dir. 56-62, Chairman and Chief Executive 62-; Director The Marconi Co. Ltd., Marconi Int. Marine Co., English Electric Co. Ltd., John Inglis Co. (Toronto), Canadian Marconi (Montreal), London Board of Advice, Nat. Bank of Australasia; Joint Chair. Babcock & Wilcox & Taylor Woodrow

Atomic Power Construction Co. Ltd.; Dir. Bank of England 61-; Joint Deputy Chair. British Aircraft Corpn.; Minister of Technology's Advisory Council 64-; Chair. Int. Electric Asscn. 55; mem. many other councils and cttees.; Hon. D.Sc., C.Eng.

19 Acacia Road, St. John's Wood, London, N.W.8; The English Electric Co. Ltd., English Electric House, Strand, London, W.C.2, England.

Telephone: 01-240-1234 (Office).

Nemerov, Howard; American writer and teacher; b. 1 March 1920; ed. Fieldston School and Harvard Coll.
Royal Canadian Air Force, U.S. Army Air Force, attached R.A.F. Coastal Command 41-45; Instructor in English, Hamilton Coll., Clinton, N.Y. 46-48; mem. Faculty of Literature, Bennington Coll. 48-66, at Brandeis Univ. 66-; mem. Nat. Inst. of Arts and Letters; Visiting lecturer, Univ. of Minnesota 58-59; Writer in residence, Hollins Coll. 62-63; Consultant in Poetry, Library of Congress, Washington, D.C. 63-64; Head of Directorate, Inst. for Research of Party History 65-66; Head of Directorate, Acad. of Party 67-; Fellow, American Acad. of Arts and Sciences; Hon. degree Lawrence Univ. 64; several awards.
Publs. *The Image and the Law* 47, *The Melodramatists* 49, *Guide to the Ruins* 50, *Federigo* 54, *The Salt Garden* 55, *The Homecoming Game* 57, *Mirrors and Windows* 58, *A Commodity of Dreams and Other Stories* 59, *New and Selected Poems* 60, *The Next Room of the Dream* 62, *Essays on Poetry and Fiction* 63, *Journal of the Fictive Life* 65, *The Blue Swallows* 67.
Brandeis University, Waltham, Mass.; Home: 40 Parker Street, Lexington, Mass., U.S.A.

Nemes, Dezsö; Hungarian politician and historian; b. 6 Sept. 1908; ed. University.
Joined the Communist Party 26; imprisoned 28-31; Sec. Hungarian Trades Union Council 45-48; Dept. Head, Ministry of Culture 50-53; Dir. *Szikra* (publishers) 53-56; Ed.-in-Chief *Népszabadság* (daily newspaper) 57-61; mem. Central Cttee., Hungarian Socialist Workers' Party, Alt. mem., Political Cttee. 57-59, mem. Political Cttee. 59-, Sec. Central Cttee. 59-65; Head of Directorate, Inst. for the Research of Party History, Hungarian Acad. of Sciences 65-; Kossuth Prize; Decoration of Liberty (silver); People's Econ. Decoration (4th degree); Order of Labour Medal.
Publs. *International Labour Movement* 49, *History of the General Worker Society 1868-1873* 52, *Documents of the History of the Counter-Revolution 1-3*, 53-59, *Liberation of Hungary* 55, *History of the Counter-Revolution in Hungary in 1919-1921* 62, *The Foreign Policy of the Bethlen Government* 64.
Széchenyi rakpart 19, Budapest V, Hungary.

Németh, Julius; Hungarian university professor, emer. since 65; b. 2 Nov. 1890; ed. József Eötvös Coll., Budapest.
Studied Turkish Languages in Turkey, U.S.S.R., Bulgaria, Albania, Yugoslavia, 07-66; reader in Turkish Philology, Univ. of Budapest 15, Prof. 16-, Dean of Faculty of Arts 32-33, 35, Rector of Univ. 47-49; Dir. of Inst. of Linguistics of the Hungarian Acad. 51-65; mem. Hungarian, Bulgarian, German, Saxon Acads. of Sciences; Hon. mem. Societas Uralo-Altaica, Göttingen, Finno-Ugrian Soc. Helsinki, Royal Asiatic Soc. London, Turkish Linguistic Soc. Ankara, Turkish History Soc. Ankara; Kossuth Prize; Indiana Univ. prize for Altaic Studies 67.
Publs. *Turkische Grammatik* 16, *A honfoglaló magyarság kialakulása* 30, *Die Inschriften des Schatzes von Nagy-Szent-Miklós* 32 (re-edited 64), *Zur Einteilung der türkischen Mundarten Bulgariens* 56, *Eine Wörterliste der Jassen, der ungarländischen Alanen* 59, *Turkish Grammar* 62, *Die Türken von Vidin—Sprache, Folklore, Religion* 65, *Turkish Reader for Beginners* 66.
Karinthy ut. 24. III. 1, Budapest XI, Hungary.

Németh, László; Hungarian writer; b. 18 April 1901; ed. Medical University.
Founder-Manager of paper, *Tanu* 32; Chief Critic and Leader of Folk Writers' Movement 34; Dir. Hungarian Radio Dept. of Literature 34-35; Auxiliary Teacher 45-50; literary translator 45-; Kossuth Prize.
Publs. *Gydsz* (Sorrow) 35, *Bun* (Guilt) 36 (novels), *Berzsenyi* 37 (critical essay), *Utolsó Kisérlet* (The Last Try) 37-41, *Készülodés* (Preparation), *A minöség forradalma* (The Revolution of Quality), *Kisebbségben* (In Minority) (all essays), *Széchenyi* 42, *Zsigmond Móricz* 43 (novels), *Az értelmiség hivatása* (The Intellectuals' Vocation) 43 (essays), *Iszony* (Repulsion) 47, *Égetö Eszter* 56 (novels), *The Two Bólyais* (play); translations of Shakespeare, Tolstoy, Jirasek, etc.
c/o Association of Hungarian Writers, Bajza u. 18, Budapest VI; Home: Aszófó, Sajkod, Hungary.
Telephone: 229-073.

Nenni, Pietro; Italian journalist and politician; b. 9 Feb. 1891.
Socialist; imprisoned (with Mussolini) 11 for participating in riots against Italo-Turkish war; Co-editor with Carlo Rosselli *Il quarto stato*; Paris Corresp., later Editor *Avanti* until its suppression 26; emigrated to France 26; with Randolfo Pacciardi, Political Commissar of Garibaldi Brigade in Spain; arrested in Vichy France and sent to Italy, where imprisoned; released Aug. 43; Sec.-Gen. Italian Socialist Party Aug. 44-63; Vice-Pres. Council of Ministers in Parri Cabt. 45; Vice-Premier and Minister of Constituent Assembly in De Gasperi Cabt. 45-46; Minister of Foreign Affairs 46-Jan. 47; Deputy Prime Minister Dec. 63-68; Pres. Partito Socialista Italiano.
Palazza Montecitorio, Rome, Italy.

Neporozhny, Pyotr Stepanovich, D.SC.(ENG.); Soviet engineer and politician; b. 1910; ed. Leningrad Water Transport Engineering Inst.
Power engineer 35-; fmr. engineer on hydro-technical projects, Northern U.S.S.R., construction of hydroelectric stations, Ukraine; fmr. Vice-Chair. Council of Ministers of Ukrainian S.S.R., Chair. Ukraine Building Cttee.; First Dep. Minister of Electric Power Station Construction (U.S.S.R.) 59-62, Minister of Power Eng. and Electrification 62-63, 65-; Chair. State Cttee. for Power Eng. and Electrification 63-65; Candidate mem. Central Cttee. of C.P.S.U.; Deputy to U.S.S.R. Supreme Soviet.
Ministry of Power Engineering and Electrification of the U.S.S.R., 7 Kitaisky proezd, Moscow, U.S.S.R.

Nepote, Jean; French police official; b. 24 Jan. 1915; ed. Lycée Corneille, Rouen, and Univ. de Lyon.
Public service 35-; Commr. of Police, Sûreté Nationale 41; Asst. to Sec.-Gen., INTERPOL (Int. Police Org.) 46-63, Sec.-Gen. of INTERPOL 63-; Chevalier Légion d'Honneur, Croix de Guerre (39-45).
26 rue Armengaud, 92 Saint-Cloud, Hauts de Seine, France.

Nerée tot Babberich, Marie Frederik Frans Antoon de, DR.IUR.; Netherlands and international civil servant; b. 8 Jan. 1915; ed. Klein Coll., Groot Coll. (Roermond), Leiden Univ.
Official at Cour des Comptes 38, Ministry of Econ. Affairs 40; Joint Sec.-Gen., States Gen. (Second Chamber), The Hague 45; Sec.-Gen. E.C.S.C. Common Assembly 52-58, European Parliament 58-61; political prisoner 42-44; military service (major of reserve) 44-45; lecturer at Saarbrücken Univ. 54; Deputy Commr.-Gen. Int. Exhbn., Montreal; Commdr. Order of Merit of Italian Republic, Ordre de Léopold II, Ordre de la Couronne de Chêne.
Publs. On Netherlands public law.
"Camphuysen", Babberich, Netherlands.

Neri, Italo; Italian broadcasting executive; b. 10; ed. Univ. of Florence.

Former Prof. of Political Sciences, Univ. of Rome; Radiotelevisione Italiana (R.A.I.) 54-, fmr. Chief Editor *Giornale Radio*, fmr. London Corresp.; Founder and Chief Editor Radio Sera (2nd Programme); responsible for radio and visual services for Central and S. Europe at UN, New York 56-58; Dir. Centro Olimpico (broadcasting services to Rome Olympic Games) 58-60; Dir. Telescuola Centre (Italian Educational TV) 60-.

Publs. *La questione del Nilo* 37, *Lineamenti della colonizzazione spagnola* 39, *Il terribile Everest* 52.

67 via Italio Panattoni, Rome, Italy.

Nerman, Birger, DR. PHIL.; Swedish archaeologist and historian; b. 6 Oct. 1888; ed. Uppsala Univ.

Asst. Prof. of Archæology Uppsala Univ. 19; Prof. of Archaeology Tartu Univ. 23-25; Dir. State Historical Museum 38-54; Vice-Pres. Swedish-Latvian Society, Stockholm; Pres. Swedish Antiquarian Society; Hon. Sec. for Sweden, Viking Society, London; Hon. mem. Permanent Council Int. Archaeological Congress; mem. Swedish Acad. of Literature, History and Antiquities; mem. Acad. of Science of Finland; hon. and corresp. mem. various European literary and scientific societies; excavated in Sweden, Estonia, Latvia, Lithuania, Germany, etc.; Pres. Baltic Cttee., Stockholm 43.

Publs. About 250 works on archæology, ancient history, philology and politics.

St. Rosenvik 3B, Djurgården, Stockholm, Sweden.

Nerman, Einar; Swedish artist; b. 6 Oct. 1888; ed. Norrköping, Stockholm, and under Matisse, Paris.

Cartoonist various European and American journals, including *The Tatler, The Sketch, Die Dame, Strix, Thalia, The New Yorker, Vogue, La Vie Parisienne*; portrait painter and decorative artist; composer music for Swedish nursery rhymes, children's songs and Swedish songs; exhibited London 25 and 27, New York 28; went to New York 39; working there as a portrait painter, cartoonist, illustrator of children's papers; illustrated *The Goose Girl*, New York 29, Selma Lagerlöf's *Jerusalem* 30, *En saga om en saga* 35, *A Child's First Book* 45, *Let's Play* 46, *Fairy Tales from the North* 46, *Carikature* for *The Studio*, New York 46, *Celibriteter och lackerheter* 53, *100 gubbar* 58, *Darling of the Gods* (autobiography) 63.

Hersbyholms Gård, Lidingö, Sweden.

Neruda, Pablo; Chilean poet; b. 04; ed. Univ. of Chile.

Consul Rangoon 27, Colombo 29, Batavia (Djakarta) 30, Buenos Aires 33, Madrid 36; refugee resettlement work in Paris 38-39; Sec. Chilean Embassy Mexico 39, Ambassador 40-42; Senator 45; lived abroad 48-52; returned to Chile 52; mem. World Peace Council 50-; Pres. Chilean Writers' Union 59-; Int. Peace Prize 50, mem. Lenin Peace Prize Cttee.; Lenin Peace Prize 53; Hon. mem. Chile and Harvard Univs.; Hon. D.Litt. (Oxford) 65.

Publs. *Crepusculario* 23, *Veinte Poemas de Amor y una Canción Desesperada* 24, *Residencia en la Tierra* 25-35, *Tercera Residencia* 43, *Canto General* 50, *Las Uvas y el Viento* 54, *Memorial de Isla Negra* 54, *Odas Elementales* 34-60, *Estravagario* 59, *Piedras de Chile* 61, *Canción de Gesta* 61, *Cantos Ceremoniales* 62, *The Heights of Macchu Picchu* 67; Films: *The Fame and Death of Joaquin Murientanz, The Life of Pablo Neruda.*

Unión de Escritores Chilenos, Santiago, Chile.

Nervi, Pier Luigi; Italian architect; b. 21 June 1891; ed. Bologna Univ.

Pioneer in the use of reinforced concrete in architecture; has designed and constructed numerous stadiums, dockyards, aerodromes, oil storage plants, etc.; Partner Nervi and Nebbiosi 23-32, Nervi and Bartoli 32-; Prof. Rome Univ.; mem. Int. Conf. of Modern Architecture 47, Accad. S. Luca 60-, Bayrischer Akad. 60-; Hon.

mem. American Acad. of Arts and Letters, American Acad. Arts and Sciences; Foreign mem. Swedish Royal Acad. of Fine Arts; Grand Cross, Italian Order of Merit, Pubblica Istruzione Gold Medal, "Frank P. Brown Medal" (Franklin Inst. Philadelphia) 57, Österreichischer Gewerbeverein "Exner Medal" 58, R.I.B.A., Royal Gold Medal 60, Premio A.I.T.E.C., Rome 62, American Concrete Industry Board Award 63, Deutscher Beton Verein E.V. "Emil Mörsch" Medal 63; Hon. Degrees Edinburgh Univ., Technische Hochschule Munich, Warsaw Univ., Harvard Univ., Dartmouth Coll. N.H., Cavaliere del Lavoro, Rome; Gold Medal of the American Inst. of Architects 64; Gold Medal, Inst. of Structural Engineers, U.K. 68.

Publs. *New Structures* 63, *Aesthetics and Technology in Building* 65.

Lungotevere A. da Brescia 9, Rome, Italy.

Nesmeyanov, Alexander Nikolaevich, DR. CHEM. SCI.; Soviet organic chemist; b. 9 Sept. 1899; ed. Moscow Univ.

Research Asst. 22, Professor 35, Rector of Moscow Univ. 48-51; elected corresp. mem. U.S.S.R. Acad. of Sciences 39, full mem. 43-, Pres. 51-61; Dir. Inst. of Organic Chemistry 39-54, and Inst. of Elemento-Organic Chemistry 54-; Deputy to the Supreme Soviet of the U.S.S.R. 51-61, Supreme Soviet R.S.F.S.R. 47-50; fmr. Chair. Lenin Prize Cttee. (Science and Inventions), hon. mem. Acads. of Science of Germany, New York, Bulgaria, Rumania, Hungary, Czechoslovakia, Poland; Scottish Royal Soc., foreign mem. Royal Soc. 61, New York Acad. of Arts and Sciences; Dr. h.c., Univs. of Paris, Jena, Calcutta; awarded State Prize, First Class, four Orders of Lenin and the Order of the Red Banner of Labour.

Institute of Elemental Organic Compounds, Academy of Sciences of U.S.S.R., Vavilova 14, Moscow, U.S.S.R.

Nesterenko, Alexey Efremovich; Soviet diplomatist; b. 1915; ed. Leningrad Engineering Inst.

Ambassador of the U.S.S.R. to Pakistan 61-65; Under-Sec. for Political and Security Council Affairs, UN Sept. 65-.

UN Secretariat, New York, N.Y., U.S.A.

Nesterov, Anatoly Innokentievich; Soviet internist and rheumatologist; b. 1895; ed. Tomsk Univ.

Intern, Asst., Lecturer, Prof., Tomsk Univ. 20-35; Dir., Sochi Inst. of Clinical Medicine 35-39; Dir., Moscow Inst. of Health Resort Treatment 39-41; Prof., Novosibirsk Medical Inst. 41-43; Deputy Dir. Moscow Inst. of Physiotherapy 43-44; Dir. Moscow Inst. of Physiotherapy 44-51; mem. C.P.S.U. 46-; Corresp. mem. U.S.S.R. Acad. of Medical Sciences 45-50, mem. 50-; Head of Dept., Second Moscow Medical Inst. 47-; Academician-Sec., U.S.S.R. Acad. of Medical Sciences 53-57; Dir. Inst. of Rheumatism, U.S.S.R. Acad. of Medical Sciences 58-; Chair. All-Union Soc. of Internists; mem. Board All-Russian and Moscow Socs. of Internists; Deputy Chair. Medical Comm. and mem. Lenin Prizes Cttee.; Chair. Problem Comm. on Rheumatism, U.S.S.R. Acad. of Medical Sciences; Editor *Problems of Rheumatism;* Vice-Pres. League Against Rheumatism; Hon. mem. Rheumatological Socs. of Poland, U.S.A., Italy, Sweden, Netherlands and Turkey, and Purkyně Medical Soc. (Czechoslovakia).

Publs. Over 120 works on rheumatism and joint troubles, complex treatment of war trauma and diseases, and climic of collagenous diseases.

Second Moscow Medical Institute, Moscow, U.S.S.R.

Nesterov, Mikhail Vasilyevich; Soviet economist and foreign trade official; b. 1892; ed. Moscow Commercial Inst.

Chairman, Presidium of the U.S.S.R. Chamber of Commerce 44-; Chair. Special Cttee. on Foreign Trade Arbitration of the UN Econ. Comm. for Europe; Chair. U.S.S.R.-Japan Business Co-operation Cttee. U.S.S.R.-

Japan Friendship Soc. 58; mem. of councils of several Soviet and int. social orgs.; Order of Lenin, Order of Red Banner of Labour (twice) and other awards.
U.S.S.R. Chamber of Commerce, 6 Ulitsa Kuibysheva, Moscow, U.S.S.R.

Nestingen, Ivan Arnold; American government official; b. 23 Sept. 1921; ed. Univ. of Wisconsin.
Admitted to Wis. Bar 49, practice in Madison 49-56; Mayor of Madison 56-61; Under-Sec. U.S. Dept. of Health, Educ. and Welfare 61-65.
4281 Potomac Avenue, N.W., Washington, D.C. 20007, U.S.A.

Netchkina, Militsa Vasilyevna; Soviet historian; b. 25 Feb. 1901; ed. Kazan Univ.
Lecturer, Workers Faculty, Kazan Univ. 23-24; Research Worker, Russian Asscn. of Research Insts. of Social Sciences 25-28; Research Worker, Inst. of History, U.S.S.R. Acad. of Sciences 28-; Prof. of Russian History, Moscow Univ. 34-48; Prof. of Russian History, U.S.S.R. Acad. of Sciences 48-57; Head of Chair of Russian History 58-60; mem. U.S.S.R. Acad. of Sciences; Chair. Scientific Council on the History of History 60-; Chief, Research Group in the History of the Revolutionary Situation of 1859-61 in Russia, Inst. of History, U.S.S.R. Acad. of Sciences 58-; U.S.S.R. State Prize 48, Prize of U.S.S.R. Acad. of Sciences 56; Order of Lenin, Order of Red Banner of Labour.
Publs. *The Society of United Slavs* 27, *V. O. Klyuchevsky* 30, *Literary form of Karl Marx's "Capital"* 32, *Pushkin and Decembrists* 37, *History of the U.S.S.R. (Russia in the XIX century)* 40, *Chernyshevisky in the years of revolutionary situation* 41, *Griboyedov and Decembrists, Ogaryov in the years of revolutionary situation* 47, *Voltaire and Russian Society, Moscow at the beginning of XIX century* 49, *Sophia Kovalevskaya—her literary and social work* 50, *Decembrists' Movement, Relations between the St. Petersburg and the London centres of Russian revolutionary Movement* 55, *On the "Ascending" and the "Descending" stages of the feudal system in Russia* 58, *"Semlya i Volya" of the 1860's* 60, *Periodization of the Soviet historical science* 61, *History of Historical Science* 65, *Lenin as Historian of the Revolutionary Movement in Russia* 65.
Dm. Ulianov Street 19, Institute of History, Moscow, U.S.S.R.

Netherlands, Queen Juliana of (*see* Juliana).

Netherthorpe, Baron, cr. 59, of Anston; **James Turner,** Kt., B.SC. (AGRIC.); British agriculturist; b. 6 Jan. 1908; ed. Leeds Univ.
Engaged in farming since 28; Chair. Notts. County Branch Nat. Farmers' Union 39, 40 and 41; Notts. del. to Nat. Farmers' Union Council 42-44; Pres. Nat. Farmers' Union 45-60; leader U.K. delegation to Dominions and U.S.A. 44 and 45; Dir. Abbey Nat. Building Soc., The Steetley Co. Ltd.; Pres. Int. Fed. of Agricultural Producers 46-48; mem. Council of Royal Agricultural Soc. of England; Pres. Royal Agricultural Soc. 65-; Deputy Chair. British Nat. Exports Council; mem. British Productivity Council; Dir. Lloyd's Bank Ltd.; Chair. Fisons Ltd.; Joint Deputy Chair. Richard Costain Ltd.; Hon. LL.D.
Hadley Hurst, Monken Hadley, Barnet, Herts., England.

Neto, Antonio Agostinho, M.D.; Angolan physician, poet and politician; b. 22; ed. protestant school, Luanda, and Univ. of Coimbra, Lisbon.
Colonial Health Service; imprisoned three times 52-60; mem. Movimento Popular de Libertação de Angola (M.P.L.A.) 57-, Head 60-; qualified as Doctor 59; imprisoned Cape Verde Islands, later Portugal 60-62, escaped July 62.
B.P. 2353, Brazzaville, Republic of the Congo.

Neuberger, Mrs. Maurine Brown; American politician; b. 9 Jan. 1907; ed. Univ. of Oregon.
Former teacher Milton-Freewater, Newberg, Portland (Oregon); mem. Oregon House of Reps. 51-55; Senator from Oregon 60-67; Chair. President's Advisory Council on Status of Women; mem. Gen. Advisory Cttee. of U.S. Arms Control and Disarmament Agency; Lecturer in American Govt., Boston Univ. and Radcliffe Inst.; Democrat.
Department of Labor Building, Washington, D.C. 20210, U.S.A.
Telephone: 202-961-3777.

Neuman, Alois, LL.D.; Czechoslovak politician; b. 12 March 1901; ed. Charles Univ., Prague.
Member Nat. Assembly 35; Burgomaster of České Budějovice 37-39; mem. Int. Illegal Cttee. of Political Prisoners, Buchenwald Concentration Camp 43; mem. Provisional Nat. Assembly 45, Constituent Nat. Assembly 46; Vice-Chair. Central Cttee. Czechoslovak Socialist Party 48; Vice-Chair. Central Action Cttee. of Nat. Front 48; Minister of Posts 48-60; Chair. Czechoslovak Socialist Party 60-68, Hon. Chair. 68-, Govt. Comm. for Legislature 66; Minister of Justice 60-68; Order of Republic 55; Klement Gottwald Order 61; Czechoslovak Peace Prize 66; numerous decorations.
Publs. *Sickness, Invalidity and Old Age Insurance* 28, *Communities and Social Insurance* 34, *Workers Social Insurance* 34, *Soviet Man and his Country* 51, *German People on New Roads* 52, *In the Great Chinese Country* 53, *Peoples Democratic Legal Order in the Service of the Working People* 55, *German Democratic Republic—New State, New People, New Life* 56.
Prague 2, Vyšehradská 16, Czechoslovakia.
Telephone: 234-555.

Neuman, Tony, D.IUR.; Luxembourg lawyer and business executive; b. 20 June 1902.
Public notary 29-57; Auditor, Aciéries Réunies de Burbach-Eich-Dudelange (ARBED) 36, Dir. 46-, Second Vice-Pres. 57-60, First Vice-Pres. 60-61, Pres. 61-; Pres. Société des Participations des Aciéries Réunies de Burbach-Eich-Dudelange (ARBED-Participations), S.A. des Ciments Luxembourgeois, Luxembourg, Columeta, Comptoir Metallurgique Luxembourgeois, Luxembourg; S.A. des Anciens Etablissements Paul Wurth, Luxembourg; Luxembourg Chamber of Commerce; Dir. several Luxembourg and other companies; numerous decorations.
Administration Centrale de l'ARBED, avenue de la Liberté; and 179 avenue de la Faïencerie, Luxembourg.
Telephone: 278-37 (Home).

Neumann, Alfred; German politician; b. 15 Dec. 1909; ed. elementary school.
Carpenter by trade; active mem. labour movement since 28; mem. Int. Brigade in Spain; 1st Sec. Greater Berlin District of Socialist Unity Party (S.E.D.) until 57; mem. Politbüro S.E.D. 57-61; Pres. Econ. Council until 65; Minister of Materials and Deputy Prime Minister 65-; mem. Volkskammer; Hans Beimler Medal; Vaterländischer Verdienstorden (gold).
Ministry of Materials, Berlin, Germany.

Neumann, Robert; British (b. Austrian) author; b. 22 May 1897; ed. Maximilian-Gymnasium, Vienna, and Universität Wien.
Emigrated to England 34, took British nationality 47; alternative Swiss domicile 58-; Hon. Pres. Austrian P.E.N. Club, Int. Vice-Pres. P.E.N.; mem. Free Acad. of Arts, Hamburg, Deutsche Akademie für Sprache und Dichtung, Darmstadt, etc.; Austrian Grand Cross for Arts and Sciences.
Publs. (in German, trans. into English) *Flood* 30, *Passion* 31, *Ship in the Night* 32, *On the Make* 32, *Mammon* 33, *The Queen's Doctor* 35, *Zaharoff* 35, *A Woman Screamed* 38, *By the Waters of Babylon* 39, *Festival* 63; (in English) *Scene in Passing* 42, *The*

Inquest 44, *Children of Vienna* 46, *Blind Man's Buff* 49, *Insurrection in Poshansk* 52, *The Dark Side of the Moon* 61, *The Pictorial History of the Third Reich* 62; (in German) *Mit fremden Federn* 30, *Unter falschen Flagge* 32; (Parodies) *Die Pest von Lianora* 27, *Der Tatbestand* 65, *Kauieren* 66, etc.; (autobiography) *The Plague House* 59, *Ein Leichtes Leben* 63, *Vielleicht das Heitere* 68; Complete Edition (trans. 28 languages) 59
La Giorgica, Locarno-Monti, Switzerland.
Telephone: Locarno 7-47-79.

Neumann, Václav; Czechoslovak conductor; b. 29 Sept. 1920; ed. Prague Conservatoire.
Former viola player, Smetana Quartet; mem. Czech Philharmonic Orchestra; deputised for Rafael Kubelik 48; later conducted orchestras in Karlovy Vary and Brno; Conductor Prague Symphony Orchestra 56-63, Prague Philharmonic 63-64; Chief Conductor Komische Oper, Berlin 57-60, conducted first performance of *The Cunning Little Vixen* (Janacek); Conductor Leipzig Gewandhaus Orchestra and Gen. Music Dir. Leipzig Opera House 64-67; conductor Czech Philharmonic Orchestra 67-; has toured Austria, England, France, Switzerland and German Fed. Repub. 64-; also visited U.S.A. with Czech Philharmonic Orchestra; Nat. Prize of German Dem. Repub. 66; Honoured Artist 67.
Prague 1-Staré Město, Široká 10, Czechoslovakia.

Neumeyer, Fritz; German professor of music, harpsichordist and composer; b. 2 July 1900; studied under F. Bölsche, A. von Fielitz, J. Kwast and W. Klatte, and at Univs. of Cologne and Berlin.
Orchestra Conductor, Saarbrücken Municipal Theatre 24-27; Leader Saarbrücken Asscn. for Early Music, and harpsichordist 27; Chamber Trio for Early Music (with Scheck and Wenzinger) 35-; Lecturer, Hochschule für Musik, Berlin 39-44; Prof. of Historical Keyboard instruments, Hochschule für Musik, Freiburg/Breisgau 46-; concert harpsichordist with *Capella Coloniensis* and Wiener Solisten; has considerable collection of old keyboard instruments; Johann-Stamitz Prize.
Works include: ballads, songs, choral works, Four Meditations for String Trio.
78 Freiburg/Breisgau, Silberbachstrasse 21, German Federal Republic.

Neunylov, Boris Alexandrovich; Soviet agrochemist; b. 1908; ed. Far Eastern Agricultural Inst.
Agronomist 27-30; Senior Research Assoc. Head of Dept., Deputy Dir. Far Eastern Rice Experimental Station 40-63; Chief Agronomist of Rice Farm 40-46; Postgraduate Dokuchayev Soil Inst. U.S.S.R. Acad. of Sciences 53-55; Chair. Presidium Far Eastern Section, Siberian Branch U.S.S.R. Acad. of Sciences 64-; mem. U.S.S.R. Acad. of Agricultural Sciences 66-; Hero of Socialist Labour.
Publs. Works on selection of high-yield rice varieties in Soviet Far East.
U.S.S.R. Academy of Sciences, 14 Lenin Prospekt, Moscow, U.S.S.R.

Neustadt, Richard Elliott; American political scientist; b. 27 June 1919; ed. Univ. of California (Berkeley) and Harvard Univ.
Economist, Office of Price Admin. 42; Staff mem., Bureau of Budget 46-50; White House 50-53; Prof. of Public Admin. Cornell Univ. 53-54, of Govt., Columbia Univ. 54-65, Harvard Univ. 65-; Assoc. Dean, Kennedy School of Govt. and Dir. Inst. of Politics, Harvard 65-; mem. Inst. for Strategic Studies 63-; Fellow American Acad. of Arts and Sciences 64-; Visitor Nuffield Coll., Oxford 61-62, Assoc. mem. 65-; Special Consultant, Sub-Cttee. on Nat. Policy Machinery, U.S. Senate 59-61; mem. Advisory Board on Comm. on Money and Credit 60-61; Special Consultant to Pres.-Elect Kennedy 60-61, to Pres. Kennedy 61-63, to Bureau of Budget 61-, to Dept. of State 63-; mem. Council on Foreign Relations 63-; Consultant to Pres. Johnson 64; Democrat.
Publ. *Presidential Power* 60.
Bureau of Budget, Washington, D.C. 20025; Littauer Center 127, Harvard University, Cambridge, Mass. 02135; and 10 Traill Street, Cambridge, Mass. 02138, U.S.A.
Telephone: 617-491-6127 (Home).

Neustupný, Jiří, PH.D., D.SC.; Czechoslovak archaeologist and museologist; b. 22 Sept. 1905; ed. Charles Univ., Prague.
Keeper, Nat. Museum Prague 25-; Lecturer, Charles Univ. 50-; mem. Council Int. Congress of Prehistoric Sciences 48-65, Vice-Chair. 66-; rep. Czechoslovak museums, UNESCO Confs. Mexico City 47, Paris 48, U.S.A. 65; Head of Center for Museological Education 67; Prof. of Prehistory and Museology 68; Dir. many excavations in Czechoslovakia.
Publs. *Prehistory of Mankind* 47, *Questions de muséologie moderne* 50, *Vorgeschichte der Lausitz* 51, *Studies on the Eneolithic Plastic Arts* 56, *Czechoslovakia before the Slavs* 61, *Museum and Research* 68; Editor *Fontes Archaeologici Pragenses* 58.
Národní Museum, Václavské nám. 68, Prague I, Czechoslovakia.
Telephone: 23-35-41.

Neutra, Richard Joseph; American architect and city planner; b. 8 April 1892; ed. Inst. of Technology of Vienna Univ., and Univ. of Zürich.
Adviser on school planning to Dept. of Education; Pres. Calif. State Planning Board; mem. Board of Architectural Examiners; Channel Heights Housing Project voted best in ten-year period by Museum of Modern Art, N.Y. 42; has won numerous nat. and int. awards; hon. mem. R.I.B.A., Asscn. of Architects of Mexico, Cuba, Bolivia; Accad. di Venezia, Acad. d'Architecture, France; Hon. Dr. Univ. of Graz, Rome, Berlin Technische Hochschule and Adelphi Univ.; buildings he has designed in U.S.A. include univs., schools, churches and theatres, the Lincoln Memorial Museum, Gettysburg and the Hall of Records, Los Angeles.
Publs. *How America Builds* 26, *America New Building in the World* 29, *Architecture of Social Concern* 38; *Circle* 39, *Preface to a Master Plan* 42, *Mystery and Realities of the Site* 54, *Survival through Design* 54, *Life and Human Habitat, Progettare per sopravvivere* (Italy), *Wenn wir weiter leben wollen* (Germany) 56, *Planificar para sobrevivir* (Mexico) 57, *Realismo biológico* (Buenos Aires), *Human Setting in an Industrialized civilization* 59, *Richard Neutra*, Vol. I: *Building and Projects—1950*; Vol. II: *1950-1960* 61; Vol. III: *1960-1966* 67, *Mensch und Wohnen* 61, *World and Dwelling* 62, *Life and Shape* 62, *Auftrag für Morgen* (Germany) 62.
2300 Silverlace Boulevard, Los Angeles 39, Calif.; also 2379 Glendale Boulevard, Los Angeles, Calif. 90039, U.S.A.
Telephone: 666-1806.

Nevanlinna, Rolf Herman, D.PHIL.; Finnish mathematician; b. 22 Oct. 1895; ed. Helsinki Univ.
Dozent of Mathematics, Helsinki Univ. 22-26, Prof. 26-47, Dean of the Faculty of Sciences 33-36, 38-39, Rector 41-45; Prof. of Mathematics, Zürich Univ. 47-48; mem. Acad. of Finland 48-; Pres. Int. Mathematical Union 59, now mem. Exec. Cttee.; Hon. Prof. Zürich Univ.; Hon. Fellow Georg-August-Univ., Göttingen; Hon. mem., Foreign mem., Corresp. mem. several acads.; Wihuri Int. Mathematical Prize 58.
Publs. *Le théorème de Picard-Borel et la théorie des fonctions méromorphes* 29, *Eindeutige analytische Funktionen* 36, 53, *Uniformisierung* 53, *Absolute Analysis* (with F. Nevanlinna) 59; *Raum, Zeit und Relativität* 64; *Einführung in die Funktionentheorie* (with V. Paatero) 65; numerous mathematical papers

and articles on philosophy, pedagogy, the arts, etc.
Department of Mathematics, University of Helsinki,
Aurorankatu 16-20 C, Helsinki, Finland.

Neville, John, O.B.E.; British actor and theatre
director; b. 2 May 1925; ed. Chiswick County Grammar
School and Royal Acad. of Dramatic Art, London.
With Bristol Old Vic Co., Old Vic Co. London 53,
played Othello, Iago, Hamlet, Aguecheek and Richard
II; mem. Chichester Theatre Co. 62; created part of
Alfie (*Alfie* by Bill Naughton), London 63; Dir. Notting-
ham Playhouse 63-68, Newcastle Playhouse 67.
Films acted in include: *Mr. Topaz, Oscar Wilde, Billy
Budd, A Study in Terror.*
c/o Peter Crouch Ltd., 12 Orange Street, London,
W.C.2, England.

Nevins, Allan, M.A., LL.D., LITT.D.; American journal-
ist and historian; b. 20 May 1890; ed. Illinois and
Columbia Univs.
Mem. staff *New York Nation* 13-20 and *Evening Post*
13-23; Literary Editor *New York Sun* 23-25; mem. staff
New York World 24-31; Prof. in American History
Cornell Univ. 27-28; Prof. of American History Colum-
bia Univ. 31-58; Sir George Watson Prof. of American
History, Literature and Insts. Great Britain 34-35;
Harmsworth Prof. Oxford Univ. 40-41, 65-66; Rep.
O.W.I. Australia and New Zealand 43-44; Dir. of U.S.
Information Service in Great Britain, and Chief Public
Affairs Officer, U.S. Embassy 46-47; Visiting Prof. Univ.
of Jerusalem 52; Pres. American Acad. of Arts and
Letters 66-68; Senior Research Scholar of Huntington
Library, San Marino, Calif. 58; Chair. U.S. Civil War
Centennial Comm. 61-; Prof. Univ. of Birmingham 66.
Publs. *Life of Robert Rogers* 14, *American Social
History Recorded by British Travellers* 23, *The American
States During and After the Revolution* 24, *The Emergence
of Modern America* 27, *Frémont: Pathmarker of the West*
27, *Henry White: Thirty Years of American Diplomacy*
30, *Grover Cleveland: A Study in Courage* 32 (Pulitzer
Prize for biography), *Hamilton Fish: The Inner History
of the Grand Administration* 36 (Pulitzer Prize for
biography), *The Gateway to History* 38, *John D.
Rockefeller: The Heroic Age of American Business* 40,
America in World Affairs 41, *This is England Today*
41, *America, The Story of a Free People* 42, *The Ordeal
of the Union* (Scribner Centenary Prize, Bancroft Prize)
46, *The Emergence of Lincoln* 50, *The World of Eli
Whitney* 52, *Ford: The Times, The Man, The Company*
(Vol. I) 53, (Vol. II) 57, (Vol. III) 62, *The War for the
Union: The Improvised War 1861-62* 59, *War Becomes
Revolution 1862-63* 60, *The State Universities and
Democracy* 62, *Life of Herbert H. Lehman* 62.
c/o Huntington Library, San Marino, Calif., U.S.A.

Newbigin, Rt. Rev. Lesslie, M.A., D.D.; British mission-
ary; b. 8 Dec. 1909; ed. Leighton Park School, Queens'
Coll., Cambridge, and Westminster Coll., Cambridge.
Secretary, Student Christian Movement, Glasgow 31-
33; ordained to Ministry, Church of Scotland 36; with
Mission, Madras, S. India 36-39; Missionary in charge,
Kancheepuram 39-46; Bishop in Madura, Church of
South India 47-59; Gen. Sec. Int. Missionary Council
59-61; Assoc. Gen. Sec. World Council of Churches, and
Dir. Div. of World Mission and Evangelism 61-65; Bishop
of Madras 65-.
Publs. *Christian Freedom in the Modern World* 37, *The
Reunion of the Church* 48, *South India Diary* 51, *The
Household of God* 53, *Sin and Salvation* 55, *One Body,
One Gospel, One World* 58, *A Faith for this One World?*
61, *Trinitarian Faith for Today's Mission* 64, *Honest
Religion for Secular Man* 66.
P.O.B. 702, Cathedral, Madras 6, India.
Telephone: 85804.

Newburn, Harry K., B.E., A.M., PH.D.; American
educator; b. 1 Jan. 1906; ed. Western Illinois State
Univ. and State Univ. of Iowa.

Teacher, High School Principal and Superintendent
in Illinois Public Schools 25-27 and 28-31; Principal
Univ. High School, State Univ. of Iowa 31-38, Dir. 38-
41; concurrently Asst. Prof. Education 34-36; Associate
Prof. 36-41, Prof. and Dean Coll. of Liberal Arts 41-45;
Pres. Univ. of Oregon 45-53; Pres. Educational Tele-
vision and Radio Center 53-58; Consultant Ford Founda-
tion 58-59; Pres. Montana State Univ. 59-63; Prof. of
Education, Arizona State Univ. 63-; Acting Pres. (on
leave) Cleveland State Univ. 65-66.
Home: 324E. Concorda Drive, Tempe, Arizona 85281:
Office; 404 Education Building, Arizona State
University, Tempe, Arizona 85281 U.S.A.
Telephone: Office: 602-961-3510; Home: 602-967-7988.

Newby, Percy Howard; British author; b. 25 June
1918; ed. St. Paul's Coll., Cheltenham.
Served in Army (R.A.M.C.) 39-42; Lecturer in English
Literature Fouad I Univ., Cairo 42-46; mem. B.B.C.
Talks Dept. 49-58, Controller Third Programme 58-;
Atlantic Award for Literature 46; Somerset Maugham
Prize 48.
Publs. *A Journey to the Interior* 45, *Agents and Witnesses*
47, *Mariner Dances* 48, *The Snow Pasture* 49, *Maria
Edgeworth* 50, *The Young May Moon* 50, *The Novel
45-50, A Season in England* 51, *The Retreat* 53, *The
Picnic at Sakkara* 55, *Revolution and Roses* 57, *Ten
Miles from Anywhere* 58, *A Guest and his Going* 59,
The Barbary Light 62, *One of the Founders* 65, *Something
to Answer For* 68.
Upton House, Cokes Lane, Chalfont St. Giles, Bucks.,
England.
Telephone: Little Chalfont 2079.

Newell, Homer Edward; American physicist; b.
11 March 1915; ed. Harvard Univ. and Univ. of Wisconsin.
Graduate Asst. Mathematics Dept. Univ. of Wisconsin
37-40; Instructor, Asst. Prof., Mathematics Dept.
Univ. of Maryland 40-44; Theoretical Physicist,
Naval Research Laboratory, Head, Rocket-Sonde Research Branch; Act. Supt. Atmosphere and Astrophysics Div., Naval Research Lab. 55-58; also Science
Program Co-ordinator for Project Vanguard; Asst. Dir.
for Space Sciences, Nat. Aeronautics and Space Admin.
(N.A.S.A.) 58-60, Dep. Dir. Space Flight Programs
60-61, Dir. Office of Space Sciences 61-63, Assoc. Admin.
for Space Science and Applications, 63-67, Assoc.
Admin. N.A.S.A. 67-; mem. American Geophysical
Union (Fellow, Vice-Pres. 68-), American Asscn.
for the Advancement of Science (Fellow), American
Inst. of Aeronautics and Astronautics (Fellow), Re-
search Soc. of America; Hon. D.Sc. (Central Methodist
College); awarded American Rocket Soc. Pendray
Award 58, American Astronautical Asscn. Space Flight
Award 60, AMVETS Civil Servant of the Year Award
61, President's Award for Distinguished Fed. Civil
Service for 65; Career Service Award of Nat. Civil
Service League 65; N.A.S.A. Distinguished Service 67.
Publs. *High Altitude Rocket Research* 53, *Vector Analysis*
55, *Space Book for Young People* 58, *Guide to Rockets,
Missiles and Satellites* 58, *Sounding Rockets* 59, *Window
in the Sky* 59, *Express to the Stars* 61.
Office of Associate Administrator, National Aero-
nautics and Space Administration, 400 Maryland
Avenue, S.W., Washington D.C. 20546; 3704 33rd
Place, Washington D.C. 20008, U.S.A.
Telephone: 202-962-6602 (Office); 202-966-3234 (Home).

Newhouse, Samuel Irving; American newspaperman;
b. 96.
Pres. numerous newspapers, including *Long Island
Daily Press, Syracuse Herald-Journal, Syracuse Post-
Standard, Harrisburg Patriot-News, Portland-Oregonian,
St. Louis Globe-Democrat, Birmingham News, Times-
Picayune, States-Item.*
Newark, N.J., U.S.A.

Newley, Anthony; British actor, writer and composer; b. 24 Sept. 1931; ed. Italia Conti School of Drama.
Films include *Above us the Waves, Cockleshell Heroes, Battle of the River Plate, Port Afrique, Idle on Parade, Fire Down Below, Good Companions, How to Murder a Rich Uncle, No Time to Die, The Man Inside, The Bandit of Zhobe, Killers of Kilimanjaro, The Heart of a Man, The Small World of Sammy Lee, The Lady is a Square, Sweet November, Doctor Dolittle, Can Heironymus Merkin Ever Forget Mercy Humppe and Find True Happiness.*
Stage appearances include *Cranks* 55, and two musicals written in collaboration with Leslie Bricusse, *Stop the World I Want to Get Off, The Roar of the Greasepaint— the Smell of the Crowd.*
Televison series include *The Strange World of Gurney Slade, The Johnny Darling Show.*
c/o Essex Music, 68 Oxford Street, London, W.1; c/o Theo Cowan Ltd., 45 Clarges Street, London W.1, England.
Telephone: 01-499-8573.

Newman, Barnett; American painter; b. 29 Jan. 1905; ed. Coll. of City of New York, Cornell Univ. and Art Students' League, New York, under Duncan Smith, William von Schlegel and John Sloan.
Has exhibited in U.S.A., Europe, South America and Japan 47-; pictures in Museum of Modern Art and Whitney Museum, New York, Kunst Museum, Basle, Nationalmuseum, Stockholm, Stedelijk Museum, Amssterdam, and private collections in London, Paris, Boston, Los Angeles, etc.
Publs. *The Ideographic Picture* 47, *The First Man was an Artist* 47, *The Object and the Image* 48, *The Sublime is Now* 48.
685 West End Avenue, New York, N.Y. 10025, U.S.A.

Newman, Paul; American actor; b. 26 Jan. 1925; ed. Kenyon Coll. and Yale Univ. School of Drama.
Military service 43-46; Best Actor, Acad. of Motion Pictures, Arts and Sciences 59, 62, 64.
Stage appearances include: *Picnic* 53-54, *Desperate Hours* 55, *Sweet Bird of Youth* 59, *Baby Want a Kiss* 64.
Films include: *The Rack* 55, *Somebody Up There Likes Me* 56, *Cat on a Hot Tin Roof* 58, *Rally Round the Flag, Boys* 58, *The Young Philadelphians* 58, *From the Terrace* 60, *Exodus* 60, *The Hustler* 62, *Hud* 63, *The Prize* 63, *The Outrage* 64, *What a Way to Go* 64, *Lady L* 65, *Torn Curtain* 66, *Hombre* 67, *Cool Hand Luke* 67, *The Secret War of Harry Frigg* 68.
c/o Charles H. Renthal, 1501 Broadway, New York City 36, N.Y., U.S.A.

Newsom, David Dunlop, A.B., M.S.; American diplomatist; b. 6 Jan. 1918; ed. Richmond Union High School and Calif. and Columbia Univs.
Reporter, *San Francisco Chronicle* 40-41; U.S. Navy 41-45; Newspaper publisher 45-47; Information Officer, U.S. Embassy, Karachi 47-50; Consul, Oslo 50-51; Public Affairs Officer, U.S. Embassy, Baghdad 51-55; Dept. of State 55-59; U.S. Nat. War Coll. 59-60; First Sec. U.S. Embassy, London 60-62; Dir. Office of Northern African Affairs, State Dept. 62-65; Amb. to Libya 65-; Dept. of State Meritorious Service Award 58.
American Embassy, Sharia Malika Fatma, Tripoli, Libya.

Newsom, Sir John Hubert, Kt., C.B.E., LL.D.; British publisher; b. 8 June 1910; ed. Imperial Service Coll. and The Queen's Coll., Oxford.
County Education Officer, Hertfordshire 40-57; Jt. Managing Dir., Longmans, Green & Co. Ltd.; Chair. Central Advisory Council for Education (England) 61-63, Vice-Chair. 63-; Chair. Education Advisory Council, Independent Television Authority 64-, Public Schools Comm. 66-68, Harlow Devt. Corpn. 66-.

Publs. *Education of Girls* 48, *The Child at School* 50, *Galloway Gamble* 51, *Rogues Yarn* 53, *The Intelligent Teachers' Guide to Preferment* 54.
Corner House, Fair Green, Sawbridgeworth, Herts., England.

Newstetter, Wilber Irvin, M.A.; American dean and professor of social administration; b. 30 Nov. 1896; ed. Univ. of Pennsylvania and Western Reserve Univ.
Assistant Purchasing Agent The Glidden Co. 19-20; Social worker and Dir. Woodland Center Cleveland 20-26; Asst. Prof. of Group Work Western Reserve Univ. 26-30, Assoc. Prof. 30-34, Prof. 34-38, Act. Dean 37-38; Dir. Univ. Centers Cleveland 26-38, Harkness and Wawokiye Camps 20-33, Camp Northland 34-44; Dean Graduate School of Social Work, Univ. of Pittsburgh, and Prof. of Social Admin. 38-; Pres. American Asscn. Schools of Social Work 38-40; Board of Dirs. and mem. Exec. Cttee., Community Chest of Pittsburgh; Exec. Cttee. Nat. Conf. of Social Work 49-51; Treas. Council on Social Work Education; A.B. (Univ. of Penn.), A.M. (Western Reserve Univ.); Centennial Award in Social Work, Michigan State Univ. 55.
Publs. *Wawokiye Camp: A Research Project in Group Work, Group Adjustment: A Study in Experimental Sociology* (co-author and ed.).
Star Route, Box 144, Sheffield, Pa., U.S.A.

Newton, Sir Leslie Gordon, Kt., B.A. (Cantab.); British journalist; b. 16 Sept. 1907; ed. Blundell's School and Sidney Sussex Coll., Cambridge.
Entered journalism 35; Army Service 39-45; joined *Financial Times* 46, Features Editor, Leader Writer and Columnist 46-50, Editor 50-; Int. Publishing Corpn. Hannen Swaffer Award as Journalist of the Year for 1966 67.
10 Princes Gate Mews, London, S.W.7, England.

Nezeritis, Andreas; Greek composer; b. 97; ed. Conservatoire of Athens, and studies under Denis Lavrangas.
President League of Greek Composers 57; awarded First Prize, Acad. of Athens 52; Gold Cross, Order of King George 65; works performed in Greece, Germany, Netherlands, France, Italy, U.S.S.R., Czechoslovakia and U.S.A.; Fellow Int. Inst. of Arts and Letters 58-.
Works include: two operas *The King Aniliagos* and *Hero and Leander*; three symphonies, No. 1 in G minor, No. 2 in C minor and No. 3 in D minor; Concerto for Violin and Orchestra; Concertino for Piano and Orchestra; Five Psalms of David for four Soloists, Mixed Chorus and Full Orchestra; Concerto for String Orchestra; two Greek Rhapsodies; five Symphonic dances; also ballet and vocal music and piano music.
54 Eptanissou Street, Athens (807), Greece.
Telephone: 873-239.

Nezu, Kaichiro; Japanese business executive; b. 29 Sept. 1913; ed. Economics Department, Tokyo Univ.
Director, Fukotu Life Insurance Co. 40-, Tokyo Gas Co. Ltd., Yokohama Warehouse Co. 40-; Pres. Tobu Railway Co. 41-; Vice-Pres. All-Japan Private Railways Asscn.; Dir. Fed. of Econ. Orgs. 41-; Councillor, Japan Central Cultural League, Chamber of Commerce and and Industry, Tokyo.
2-1, 1 Chome, Oshiage, Sumida-ku, Tokyo, Japan.

Nezvál, Ferenc; Hungarian politician; b. 09; ed. Univ. of Economics and Political Sciences.
Shoemaker; Dep. Mayor of Budapest; First Dep. Minister, Town and Rural Development 54; Minister of Justice 56-66.
XI Solomi ut 42, Budapest, Hungary.

Ngaiza, Christopher Pastor; Tanzanian diplomatist; b. 29 March 1930; ed. Nyakato Secondary School, Tabora Secondary School, Makerere Univ. Coll. and Loughborough Co-operative Coll., England.
Local Courts Magistrate 52; private business 53-54; Sec.-Manager Bukoba District Bahaya Co-operative

Store Ltd. 55-57; student Loughborough Co-operative Coll. 57-59; Rep. and Coffee Auctioneer, Bukoba Native Co-operative Union Ltd. 59-61; Counsellor for Tanganyika, Perm. Mission to UN, New York 61-62; Counsellor, Tanganyika High Comm., London 62-64; High Commr. of Tanzania in U.K. 64-65 (relations broken off 65).
Ministry of Foreign Affairs, Dar es Salaam, Tanzania.

Ngala, Ronald; Kenyan politician; b. 1923; ed. Makerere Coll., Uganda.
Teacher, then Headmaster various Schools 46-55; Sec. Kenya Nat. Party 59-60; mem. cttee. of newly-formed Kenya African Nat. Union Mar. 60; Leader Coast African Political Union May 60; founder mem. and Leader Kenya African Democratic Union 60-64; Vice-Pres. Kenya African Nat. Union 66-; Minister of Labour and Social Security 60; resigned March 61; Minister of Educ. and Leader of Government Business May 61-Nov. 61; Minister of State for Constitutional Affairs and Admin. April 62-63; Pres. Coast Regional Assembly, Mombasa, Kenya 63-66; Chair. Maize Marketing Board 65-66; Minister of Co-operatives and Social Services 66-; Chair. African elected mems. del., Kenya Conf., London 60.
Ministry of Co-operatives and Social Services, Nairobi, Kenya.

Ngapo Ngawang Jigme; Chinese (Tibetan) politician. Former Vice-Chair. Preparatory Cttee. Tibet Autonomous Region, later Acting Chair.; Vice-Chair. Nat. People's Congress Standing Cttee.; Chair. Chinese C.P. Tibet Autonomous Region 65-.
Office of the Chairman for Tibet Autonomous Region, Lhasa, Tibet.

Ngo Dinh Nhu, Madame; Viet-Namese politician.
Widow of Ngo Dinh Nhu, brother and Adviser to the late President Ngo Dinh Diem; arrested by Viet Minh, later escaped 46; organised first popular demonstration in support of Govt. of Prime Minister Ngo Dinh Diem 54; Official Hostess for Pres. Ngo Dinh Diem 55-63; fmr. Dep., Nat. Ass., author of "Family Bill"; founder of programme of paramilitary service for women Oct. 61; Founder-Pres. Vietnamese Women's Solidarity Movement.
Paris, France.

Ngo Dinh Thuc, Most Rev. Pierre Martin; Viet-Namese ecclesiastic; b. 97.
Ordained priest 25, Church of Sesina 38-60, Archbishop of Hué 60-, but without power over his See 64-; mem. Comm. *De Missionibus,* Second Vatican Oecumenical Council 62-65; brother of the late Pres. Ngo Dinh Diem.
c/o The Vatican, Rome, Italy.

Ngom Jua, Augustine; Cameroonian politician; b. Nov. 1924; ed. St. Anthony's School, Njinikom, Elementary Training Centre, Kake-Kumba, and Govt. Teacher Training Coll., Kumba.
Teacher, Bafut Catholic School 40-42; Headmaster, Muyuka Catholic School 46-47, Catholic School, Dikome 49-50, Catholic School, Njinikom 51; Sec. Kom Improvement Asscn. 52; Chair. Regional Consultative Cttee., Enugu 53; mem. House of Assembly 54-57; Minister of Educ. and Social Services 59; Sec. of State for Finance and Deputy Minister of Health 61-62; Prime Minister of West Cameroon May 65-67; Grand Order of Valour (Cameroon), Knight Commdr. Humane Order of African Redemption (Liberia), Great Cross Second Class of the Order of Merit of the Fed. Repub. of Germany, Order of Commdr. (Tunisia), Grand Officer of the Nat. Order of Senegal.
Buea, West Cameroon, Federal Republic of Cameroon.

Ngoyi, Mrs. Lilian; African politician; b. 24 Sept. 1911; ed. in Transvaal.
Machinist in clothing factory; mem. African Nat. Congress 52-, Nat. Exec. 54, Head of A.N.C. Women's

League; mem. Nat. Exec. Fed. of South African Women 54-, Nat. Pres. 56-; on trial for treason 56-61 (acquitted 61); banned from attending gatherings 62-; confined to Orlando for five years 63; arrested 64.
9870B Nkungu Street, Orlando West 2, P.O. Phirima, South Africa.

Nguyen Khanh, Brig.-General; Viet-Namese army officer and politician; b. 27; ed. Viet-Nam Military Acad., Dalat, Army Staff Schools, Hanoi and France, and U.S. Command and General Staff Coll., Fort Leavenworth.
French Colonial Army 54, Viet-Namese Army 54-; Chief of Staff to Gen. Duong Van Minh 55; took part in coup against Pres. Diem Nov. 63; Prime Minister Jan. 64-Oct. 64; regained control Jan.-Feb. 65; Roving Ambassador 65-.
c/o Ministry of Foreign Affairs, Saigon, Republic of Viet-Nam.

Nhu, Madame (*see* Ngo Dinh Nhu).

Niarchos, Stavros Spyros, LL.D.; Greek shipowner; b. 3 July 1909; ed. Athens Univ.
Joined family grain and shipping business; started independent shipping concern 39; served in R.H.N.V.R. 41-45; Hon. Naval Attaché, Greek Legation, Washington 44-48; returned to shipping business; pioneered supertankers; head of Niarchos group of companies; Grand Cross, Order of the Phoenix, Commdr. of Order of George I, Commdr. Order of St. George and St. Constantine.
c/o Niarchos (London) Ltd., 41-43 Park Street, London, W.I, England.

Nichkov, Vlas Nikiforovich; Soviet politician; b. 02; ed. Kirov Forestry Acad., Leningrad.
Director, lumber harbour Leningrad sea port 29-37; Dean of Faculty Kirov Forestry Acad., Leningrad 37-39; Asst. Dir. Inst. of Foreign Trade, Leningrad 39-41; Soviet Army 41-43; Dept. Chief, People's Commissariat of Forestry Industry of the U.S.S.R. 43-44; employee of Amtorg in U.S.; Chair. V/O *Exportles* (export and import timber, paper, pulp) 48-67; mem. Communist Party; Order of Lenin; two Orders of Red Banner of Labour and other decorations.
V/O Exportles, Smolenskaya-Sennaya pl. 32/34, Moscow K-3, U.S.S.R.

Nicholls, Sir John Walter, K.C.M.G., O.B.E.; British diplomatist; b. 4 Oct. 1909; ed. Malvern Coll. and Pembroke Coll., Cambridge.
Entered Foreign Office 32; served Athens 34-36, Foreign Office 36-39; Asst. Sec. Ministry of Economic Warfare 39-43; Counsellor, Lisbon 43-44; served Austria 44-46, Foreign Office 46-49; Minister in Moscow 49-51; Asst. Under-Sec. of State 51-54; Ambassador to Israel 54-57, to Yugoslavia 57-60, Belgium 60-63; Dep. Under Sec. of State, Foreign Office 63-66; Ambassador to S. Africa 66-.
Thorpes, Felsted, Essex, England; and Foreign Office, London, S.W.I, England.

Nichols, Beverley; British writer; ed. Marlborough and Balliol Coll., Oxford.
Editor *The American Sketch,* New York 28-29; contrib. feature *Sunday Chronicle.*
Publs. *Prelude, Patchwork, Self, Crazy Pavements, Are They the Same at Home? Twenty-Five, The Star-Spangled Manner, Women and Children Last, Evensong, Down the Garden Path, For Adults Only, A Thatched Roof, Failures, Cry Havoc!, A Village in a Valley, The Fool Hath Said . . . , No Place Like Home, News of England, Revue, Green Grows the City, Men do not Weep, Verdict on India, The Tree That Sat Down, The Stream That Stood Still 47, All I Could Never Be 49, Uncle Samson 50, The Magic Mountain 50, Merry Hall 51, A Pilgrim's Progress 52, Laughter on the Stairs 53, No Man's Street 54, The Moonflower 55, Sunlight on the Lawn 56, Death to Slow Music 57, The Rich Die Hard,*

The Sweet and Twenties 58, *Murder by Request* 60, *Cats A.B.C., X.Y.Z., A Case of Human Bondage* 66, *The Art of Flower Arrangement* 67; plays: *The Stag, Cochran's 1930 Revue, Avalanche, Evensong* (with Edward Knoblock), *When the Crash Comes, Messmer, Floodlight, Song on the Wind* (operetta), *Shadow of the Vine, Lady's Guide.*
c/o Jonathan Cape Ltd., 30 Bedford Square, London, W.C.1, England.

Nichols, Leslie Edwin, B.SC. (AGR); Australian diary executive; b. 4 July 1912; ed. Univ. of Sydney.
Assistant Dir., Senior Dairy Technologist and Dir. of Research Queensland Dept. of Primary Industries 37-65; Commonwealth Dairy Expert 65-.
Department of Primary Industry, New Customs House, 11 William Street, Melbourne, Victoria, Australia.
Telephone: 620341.

Nichols, Thomas S.; American businessman; b. 8 May 1909; ed. Univ. of Pennsylvania.
With E. I. du Pont de Nemours & Co. 26-37; Vice-Pres. and Dir. Prior Chemical Corpn. 37-48; Pres. Chair. and Dir. Mathieson Chemical Corpn., N.Y. 48-54, merged with Olin Industries Inc., forming Olin Mathieson Chemical Corpn., Pres. 54-57, Chair. of Board 57-63, Chair. of Exec. Cttee. 63-; Dir. of other companies and official of numerous educational and business orgs.
Home: 680 Madison Avenue, New York City 10021; Office: 460 Park Avenue, New York City 22, N.Y., U.S.A.

Nicholson, Ben, O.M.; British artist; b. 10 April 1894.
Works in Tate Gallery, Victoria and Albert Museum, Arts and British Council collections, galleries in Europe, U.S.A., Canada, Australia, S. America, Japan, etc.; retrospective exhbns. at Temple, Newsam, Leeds 44, Venice Biennale 54, Stedelijk Museum, Amsterdam 54, Musée d'Art Moderne, Paris 55, Palais des Beaux Arts, Brussels 55, Kunsthalle, Zürich 55, Tate Gallery 55, São Paulo 57, Rio de Janeiro 58, Buenos Aires 58, Kunsthaus, Berne, Galerie Beyeler, Basle 68; First Prize 39th Carnegie Int. Exhibition 52, Ulissi Prize XXVII Venice Biennale 54, Gov. of Tokyo Award, 3rd Int. Exhibition, Tokyo 55, Grand Prix, 4th Int. Exhibition, Lugano 56; U.S.A. Guggenheim Int. Award 56, Int. Prize for painting, IVth Bienal, São Paulo, Brazil 57.
Publs. *Lund Humphries* (*Monograph* Ben Nicholson), *Paintings, Reliefs and Drawings*, Vol. 1, 48, Vol. 2, 56 (introduction by Sir Herbert Read); *Monograph BN— The meaning of his art* (introduction by Dr. J. P. Hodin) 57; *Monograph BN* (introduction by Sir John Summerson) 48, *Monograph BN* (introduction by David Baxandall) 62, *Monograph BN* (introduction by Sir Herbert Read) 62, *Monograph BN* (introduction by Ronald Alley) 63.
Gimpel-Hanover Galerie, Zürich, Switzerland.

Nicholson, Sir John (Norris), Bt., C.I.E., J.P.; British shipping executive; b. 19 Feb. 1911; ed. Winchester Coll. and Trinity Coll. Cambridge.
Captain 4th Cheshires (T.A.) 39-41; Ministry of War Translator, India and South East Asia 42-46; Chair. Liverpool Port Employers' Asscn. 57-61, Martins Bank Ltd. 62-64 (Deputy Chair. 59-62), Cttee. of European Nat. Shipowners' Asscns., Management Cttee. *H.M.S. Conway* 58-65, Ocean Steam Ship Co. Ltd. 65-; Dir. Royal Insurance Co. Ltd., Martins Bank Ltd.; mem. Shipping Advisory Panel 62.
Ocean Steam Ship Co., India Buildings, Water Street, Liverpool 2; Homes: Brooke House, Parkgate, Cheshire; and Mottistone Manor, Isle of Wight, England.

Nicholson, Hon. John Robert, P.C., O.B.E., Q.C., M.P.; Canadian businessman and politician; b. 1 Dec. 1901; ed. Harkins Acad. and Dalhousie Univ., Halifax.
Called to the Bar 23, fmr. partner Locke, Lane, Nichol-

son and Shepherd, Vancouver; Dep. Controller of Supplies, Dept. of Munitions and Supply, Ottawa 41-42; Gen. Man. Polymer Corpn. Ltd., Ontario 42-43, Man. Dir. 43-47, Exec. Vice-Pres. 47-51; Chief in Brazil of Brazilian Traction Light and Power Co. Ltd. 51-57; Pres. Council of Forest Industries of British Columbia 60-61; M.P. 62-; Minister of Forestry 63-64; Postmaster Gen. 64-65; Minister of Citizenship and Immigration 65; Minister of Labour Dec. 65-April 68; Liberal.
1101-235 Somerset Street West, Ottawa 4, Ontario, Canada.

Nicholson, Ralph, M.A., B.A., HON. LL.D.; American newspaper publisher; b. 12 Feb. 1899; ed. Earlham Coll. and Harvard Univ.
Air Corps U.S.N.R. 18-19; began as carrier boy 12-16; part-time reporter 16-20; European Corresp. Phila. *Public Ledger* 20-21; Vice-Pres. and Treas. Editorial Research Asscn. 23-25; Production Man. *New York Evening Post* 25-27; Gen. Manager *Japan Advertiser* and Trans-Pacific Advertising Agency Tokyo 27-28; Production Manager *New York Telegram* 28-29; Asst. business Manager Pittsburgh Press 29-30; Manager Dept. Public Relations General Motors Corpn. 30-31. General Manager McFadden Newspapers 32; Asst. Publisher *New York Daily Mirror* 32-33; General Manager, Vice-Pres., and Treas. Tampa Times Co. 33-41, Vice-Pres., Dir. 33-51; Pres., Treas., Dir. The Item Co. Inc. 41-49; Dir. Office of Public Affairs, U.S. High Commr. for Germany 49-50; Dir. Pullman Co. 47-50; Vice-Pres. 36-37 and Pres. 37-38 Assoc. Dailies of Florida; Vestryman, Trinity Church, New Orleans 47-49; Trustee, Earlham Coll. 48-50, etc.; mem. Judicial Council of Florida 55-61, Vice-Chair. 57-60; Owner-Publisher *Dothan* (Ala.) *Eagle* 56-66, *The Troy* (Ala.) *Messenger* 61-66, *The Brundidge* (Ala.) *Banner* 61-66, *The Chronicle* (Pascagoula, Miss.) 63-66; Dir. Tallahassee Bank and Trust Co. 59-64; mem. Nat. Defense Exec. Reserve 59-; Democrat.
Residence and Office: Rose Hill Plantation, Route 1, Box 221, Tallahassee, Fla. 32301, U.S.A.
Telephone: 385-3143.

Nickerson, Albert L., B.SC.; American business executive; b. 17 Jan. 1911; ed. Harvard Univ.
Began as service station attendant, Socony Mobil Oil Co. Inc. 33; elected to Board of Dirs., Mobil Oil Co. Ltd., London 45, Chair. 46; Dir. Socony Mobil Oil Co. Inc. (now called Mobil Oil Corpn.) 46, Vice-Pres., Dir. 51, Pres. 55, Chair. Exec. Cttee. and Chief Exec. Officer 58-, Chair. of the Board 61-; Dir. and Treas. American Petroleum Inst. 65-66, Treas. 66-68; Dir. Fed. Reserve Bank of N.Y. 64-67; Trustee Rockefeller Univ.; Fellow of Harvard Coll.; Chair. Balance of Payments Advisory Cttee. of U.S. Dept. of Commerce; Chair. the Business Council 66-68; Dir. Metropolitan Life Insurance Co., Transportation Asscn. of America; mem. Exec. Board of Nat. Alliance of Businessmen.
431 Grace Church Street, Rye, New York 10580, U.S.A.

Nicodim (*see* Rotov, Most Rev. Boris Georgievich).

Nicol, Davidson S. H., C.M.G., M.A., M.D., PH.D. (CANTAB.); Sierra Leonean doctor and educationist; b. 14 Sept. 1924; ed. Prince of Wales School, Freetown, Cambridge Univ., London Hospital.
Research Asst. and Demonstrator in Physiology, London 50-52; lecturer in Physiology and Biochemistry, Ibadan 52-54; medical research and teaching, Cambridge 54-59; Fellow, Christ's Coll., Cambridge; Senior Pathologist, Sierra Leone Govt. 58-60; guest lecturer numerous American univs.; Principal, Fourah Bay Coll., The Univ. Coll. of Sierra Leone, Freetown 60-67; Vice-Chancellor, Univ. Sierra Leone 66-68; Chair. Conf. on Inter-Univ. Co-op. in W. Africa 61, Needs and Priorities Cttee., Univ. of E. Africa 63, Sierra Leone Nat. Library Board; Pres. Sierra Leone Nat. Red Cross

Soc. 63-65, West African Science Asscn. 63-65; Dir. Central Bank Sierra Leone 63-; Hon. D.Sc. (Newcastle upon Tyne, and Kalamazoo Coll., Michigan, U.S.A.). Publs. *The Structure of Human Insulin* 60, *Africa, A Subjective View* 64.
Christ's College, Cambridge, England.

Nicolareisis, Demetrios J.; Greek diplomatist; b. 13 Oct. 1908; ed. Florence and Univ. of Athens.
Diplomatic Service 36-; Vice-Consul and Political Counsellor to Mil. Gov. of N. Epirus, Argyrocastro 40-41; Crete, London and Cairo 41-44; Head of Mission for Repatriation of Prisoners of War, Rome 44-46; Head, First Political Section, Ministry for Foreign Affairs 46-47; Consul, Hamburg, and Chargé d'Affaires, Bonn 48-52; Head NATO Dept., Ministry of Foreign Affairs 52-53; Asst. Greek Del. to NATO, Paris 53-56; Chargé d'Affaires and Counsellor, London 56-58; Asst. Chair. Greek-Yugoslav Comm. 59; Ambassador to Yugoslavia 60-64, to U.K. 64-67.
Publs. Collected critical essays.
Royal Ministry of Foreign Affairs, 2 Zalokosta Street; 12 Solonos Street, Athens, Greece.

Nicolin, Curt René; Swedish executive; b. 10 March 1921; ed. Royal Inst. of Technology, Stockholm.
President, Svenska Turbin AB Ljungström, Finspong 55-59, Turbin AB de Laval Ljungström, Finspong 59-61; Interim Pres. Scandinavian Airlines System (S.A.S.) 61-62; Pres. A.S.E.A., Västerås 61-.
Villa Asea, Villagatan 1, Västerås, Sweden.

Nicoll, (John Ramsay) Allardyce; British literary historian; b. 28 June 1894; ed. Glasgow Univ.
Prof. English Language and Literature London Univ. 24-34; Prof. of History of Drama and Dramatic Criticism and Chair. Drama Dept. Yale Univ. 34-45; Prof. English Language and Literature Univ. of Birmingham 45-61, Emeritus Prof.; Dir. Shakespeare Inst. Stratford-upon-Avon 51-61; Visiting Prof., Univ. of Pittsburgh, U.S.A. 63-64, 65 and 67; Editor *Shakespeare Survey* 48-68.
Publs. *The Development of the Theatre, Masks, Mimes and Miracles, British Drama, History of English Drama 1660-1900, Theory of Drama, Film and Theatre, The English Stage, Stuart Masques and the Renaissance Stage, World Drama, The Elizabethans, The World of Harlequin, The Theatre and Dramatic Theory.*
Wind's Acre, Colwall, nr. Malvern, Worcs., England.
Telephone: Colwall 310.

Niebuhr, Reinhold, M.A., D.D.; American theologian; b. 21 June 1892; ed. Elmhurst Coll. and Yale Univ.
Minister Bethel Evangelical Church Detroit, Mich. 15-28; Assoc. Prof. of Ethics Union Theological Seminary New York City 28-30, Prof. 30-60; Editor *Christianity and Crisis*; Hon. D.D. Oxford, Glasgow, Manchester, Yale, Harvard, Columbia, Pennsylvania and Amherst Univs.
Publs. *Does Civilization Need Religion?* 28, *Moral Man and Immoral Society* 32, *Reflections on the End of an Era* 34, *An Interpretation of Christian Ethics* 35, *Beyond Tragedy* 37, *Christianity and Power Politics* 40, *The Nature and Destiny of Man* Vol. I 41, Vol. II 43, *The Children of Light and The Children of Darkness* 45, *Discerning the Signs of the Times* 46, *Faith and History* 49, *The Irony of American History* 52, *Christian Realism* 53, *The Self and the Dramas of History* 55, *Nations and Empires* 60, *A Nation so Conceived* (with A. Heimert) 63, *Man's Nature and his Communities* 65.
404 Riverside Drive, New York City, N.Y. 10025; and Yale Hill, Stockbridge, Mass. 01262, U.S.A.
Telephone: (New York) 212-666-8534 and (Stockbridge) 413-298-3192.

Niederalt, Alois; German lawyer and politician; b. 10 April 1911; ed. Univ. of Munich.
Former barrister; posts in Bavarian Govt. 47-62; mem.

Bundestag 53-; Minister for Upper House and Fed. States Affairs 61-66; Christian Dem. Union (C.D.U.)/C.S.U.).
c/o Bundestag, Bonn, German Federal Republic.

Nieh Jung-chen; Marshal of the Chinese Army; b. 99; ed. France, Moscow Mil. Acad.
Took part in the May 4th movement; lectured at Whampoa Mil. Acad.; in North Expedition, later joined Red Army; campaigns against Japanese in Hopei; in 8th Route Army 37; central cttee. mem C.C.P. 45; on North China Government Council 48; commanded 5th Field Force of P.L.A. 49; rep. northern mil. command in 1st N.P.C. and on standing cttee 54; Vice-Chair. Council of National Defence; decorated for war services; Vice-Premier State Council 56-; Chair. Scientific and Technological Comm. 58-.
State Council, Peking, China.

Niehans, Paul, D.MED., L. en THEOL.; Swiss surgeon; b. 21 Nov. 1882; ed. Univs. of Berne, Neuchâtel, Oxford, Berlin.
Surgeon, First World War; Surgeon to four hospitals, Switzerland (50,000 operations); Head of Research Centre for Cellular Therapy; performed first operation injecting fresh cells 31, first operation injecting preserved cells 49; mem. Pontifical Acad. of Sciences, Rome; Senator, Tübingen Univ.; Hon. Pres. Soc. Int. de Recherche pour Thérapie cellulaire; Grande Croix de Mérite de l'Allemagne; Chevalier de Saint Save.
Publs. over 60 articles on cellular therapy.
Burier, La Tour de Peilz, près Vevey, Switzerland.

Niekerk, Hon. Christiaan Van, D.T.D., LL.D.; South African politician; b. 74; ed. Victoria Coll. Stellenbosch.
A Commdt. Republican Forces under Gen. de Wet 1900-02; Del. Peace Conf. Vereeniging 02; Principal Cyfergat Govt. School 04; Vice-Principal Boshof Govt. School 05-07; mem. Legislative Assembly for Kroonstad West 07-10; M.P. for Boshof 10-24; Senator 24, 29, 40; Pres. Senate 30-40; Leader of Opposition in Senate 40-48; re-elected Senator 48 and 55; Pres. of Senate 48, 56-60; Nationalist.
Market Square, Boshof, Orange Free State, South Africa.

Nielsen, Knud Axel; Danish lawyer and politician; b. 10 Feb. 1904; ed. Univ. of Copenhagen.
Lawyer 32-; mem. Parl. 53-; Minister of Justice 64-68; Social Democrat.
Munksvej 4, Hadsund; Strandvejen 30, Copenhagen, Denmark.
Telephone: Copenhagen 29-15-35; Hadsund (08)-57-12-00.

Nielsen, Morris; American businessman; b. 4 Aug. 1904; ed. schools in Nebraska.
Joined The Babcock and Wilcox Co., New York City 24, rose to Vice-Pres. Boiler Div. 54-55, Exec. Vice-Pres. 55-57, Pres. 57-65, Dir. 54-, Chair. and Chief Exec. Officer 65-; Life Trustee, Carnegie Inst. of Technology; Dir. and Trustee of several companies and orgs.
Home: 1035 Fifth Avenue, New York City 28; Office: 161 E. 42nd Street, N.Y.C. 17, N.Y., U.S.A.

Nielsen, Niels, DR.PHIL.; Danish geographer; b. 3 Oct. 1893; ed. Copenhagen Univ. and Sorbonne, Paris.
Geographical investigations Iceland 23, 24, and 27; expeditions to Vatnajökull Iceland 34 and 36; Head Skalling Laboratory (Inst. for research on tides, dunes and salt marshes) 30; Vice-Pres. Royal Danish Geographical Soc. 31, Vice-Pres.; Danish Sec. Union Int. de Géographie 34; Prof. Geography Univ. of Copenhagen 39-64; Editor *Geografisk Tidsskrift, Meddelelser fra Skalling Laboratoriet, Folia Geographica Danica, Kulturgeografiske Skrifter*; Chief Editor *Meddelelser om Grønland.*
Publs. *La production du fer en Jutland* 26, *Evidence of*

the Extraction of Iron in Greenland by the Norsemen 29, *Contributions to the Physiography of Iceland* 32, *Eine Methode zur exakten Sedimentationsmessung* 35, *Vatnajökull* 37, *Atlas of Denmark*, Vol. I 49.
Strandboulevarden 32, Copenhagen Ø, Denmark.

Nielsen, Sivert Andreas; Norwegian diplomatist; b. 24 Nov. 1916; ed. Oslo Univ.
Worked Bank of Norway 40-41; political prisoner 41-45; Dep. Attorney Oslo Police 45-46; UN Secr. 46-48; Sec. Norwegian Embassy, Washington 48-50; Section Chief, Ministry of Defence 50-51; Dir. NATO Interim staff 50-51; Div. Chief, Under-Sec., Minister of Defence 52-58; Permanent Del. to UN 58-66; participated in preparatory work NATO and ministerial confs. NATO 49-58; rep. Advisory Cttee. to Sec.-Gen. UNEF 58-; Norwegian Rep. on UN Security Council 63-64,Chair. or Vice-Chair. Norwegian Del. to 13th-21st Sessions of Gen. Assembly of UN; Dir. Bergens Privatbank, Oslo, 66.
Bergens Privatbank, Kirkegaten 23, Oslo, Norway. Telephone 20-70-90 (Oslo).

Nielsen, Sven Aage; Danish diplomatist; b. 23 June 1921; ed. Aarhus Univ.
Danish Foreign Service 47-, served Bucharest, Belgrade, Athens, Buenos Aires 47-62; Deputy Head of Secr. for Technical Co-operation with the Developing Countries, Copenhagen 62-63; Deputy Head Danish Del. to Org. for Econ. Co-operation and Development (OECD) 63-65, Head 65-.
Danish Delegation to the OECD, 6 rue Jean Richepin, Paris 16e, France.

Niemeyer, Gerhart, DR.JUR.; American political scientist; b. 07; ed. Cambridge, Munich and Kiel Univs. Lecturer Law Faculty Madrid Univ. 33; Research Associate Inst. of Int. and Economic Studies Madrid 34; Prof. Fed. Spanish Asscns. Int. Studies 34; Lecturer in Politics Princeton Univ. 37, Asst. Prof. 40-44; Visiting Lecturer Yale Univ. 42; Prof. of Political Science Oglethorpe Univ. 44-50; Assoc. Prof. Yale Univ. Summer 46; Visiting Prof. Columbia Univ. Summer 52; U.S. Dept. of State 50-53; Council on Foreign Relations 53-55; Yale Univ. 54-55, Univ. of Notre-Dame 55-, The Nat. War Coll. 58-59; Fulbright Prof. Univ. of Munich 62-63, Co.-Dir. Inst. of Communism and Constitutional Democracy, Vanderbilt 62-66, Foreign Policy Task Force, Republican Party 65-68.
Publs. *Einstweilige Verfügungen des Weltgerichtshofs* 32, *Vom Wesen der gesellschaftlichen Sicherheit* 35, *The Significance of Function in Legal Theory* 40, *Law Without Force* 41, *An Inquiry into Soviet Mentality* 56, *Facts on Communism: 1, The Communist Ideology* 59; co-author *The Second Chance* 44; Editor *Hermann Heller: Staatslehre* 34; co-editor *Handbuch des Weltkommunismus* 58, *Handbook on Communism* 62 (English Edition), *Communists in Coalition Governments* 63, *Outline of Communism* 66.
806 East Angela Boulevard, South Bend, Ind., U.S.A.

Niemeyer, Oscar; Brazilian architect; b. 07; ed. Escola Nacional de Beles Artes, Rio de Janeiro.
Designed Ministry of Education and Health Building, Rio de Janeiro 37-43, Brazilian Pavilion, New York World Fair 39, with others designed U.N. building New York City 47; Dir. of Architecture for new capital of Brasilia and given a free hand in design of public and other buildings 57-; Designer of Bienal Exhbn. Hall, São Paulo, urban area of Grasse (near Nice) 66, French C.P. bldg., Paris 66; Lenin Peace Prize 63, Prix Int. de *l'Architecture d'aujourd'hui* 66.
Rua Carvalho Azevedo 96, Rio de Janeiro, Brazil.

Niemeyer, Sir Otto Ernst, G.B.E., K.C.B.; British financier; b. 23 Nov. 1883; ed. St. Paul's School and Balliol Coll., Oxford.

Mem. Treasury Staff 06-27; Controller of Finance in the Treasury 22-27; fmr. Dir. Bank of England; mem. Financial Cttee. of L.N. 22-37; mem. Joint Exchequer Board of Gt. Britain and N. Ireland 29-49, mem. Council Foreign Householders; fmr. Dir. Barlow and Jones, Bank for Int. Settlements (Vice-Chair.), Pres. 56-65; Dir. Nat. Bank of Egypt 28-50; Dir. Banque des Pays de l'Europe Centrale (Paris) 28-57, Central Mining Investment Corpn., Int. Nickel Co. of Canada; financial mission to Australia and New Zealand 30, Brazil 31, Argentina 33, India 36, China 41-42; Gov. London School of Econs.; Gov. Marlborough Coll., St. Paul's School; High Sheriff County of London 45.
Nash House, Lindfield, Haywards Heath, Sussex, England.

Niemöller, (Friedrich Gustav Emil) Martin; German theologian; b. 14 Jan. 1892; ed. Elberfeld Gymnasium and Univ. of Münster.
Served in German Navy 10-18, becoming submarine commdr.; Ordained 24; Man. Provinzialverband der Inneren Mission, Westfalen 24-31; Pastor Berlin-Dahlem 31-37; founder and Pres. Pfarrer-Notbund (Pastors' Union) and Die Bekennende Kirche (Confessing Church); imprisoned Sachsenhausen and Dachau concentration camps 37-45; Pres. Kirchliches Aussenamt (Office for External Relations of Evangelical Church in Germany) 45-56; Pres. Evangelical Church in Hesse and Nassau 47-64; Pres. World Council of Churches 61-; Lenin Peace Prize 67; Hon. D.D. (Göttingen, St. Louis, Halifax, Delhi, Chicago, Bethany Biblical Seminary, Budapest, Bratislava, London, Ontario), Hon. Dr. of Letters (New Delhi).
Publs. *Vom U-Boot zur Kanzel* 34; sermons: . . . *dass wir an Ihm bleiben* 38, *Alles und in allen Christus!* 35, *Dennoch getrost* 39, *Ach Gott vom Himmel sieh darein* 46, . . . *zu verkündigen ein gnädiges Jahr des Herrnl* 46, *Herr ist Jesus Christus* 46, *Herr, wohin sollen wir gehen?* 57, *Reden* (1945-1954) 58, *Reden* (1955-57) 58, *Reden* (1958-61) 61, *Reden* (1961-63).
Brentanostrasse 3, Wiesbaden, German Federal Republic. Telephone: 44-28-18.

Nier, Alfred O(tto) C(arl), M.S.E.E., PH.D.; American physicist; b. 28 May 1911; ed. Univ. of Minnesota.
Nat. Research Fellow, Harvard Univ. 36-38; Asst. Prof. Univ. of Minnesota 38-40, Assoc. Prof. 40-44, Prof. of Physics 44- (on leave for war work 43-45); first to separate rare isotope of uranium U-235, 40.
Department of Physics, University of Minnesota, Minneapolis 14, Minn., U.S.A.

Nieto Antúnez, Admiral Pedro; Spanish naval officer and politician; b. 1898; ed. Escuela Naval Militar.
Commdt.-Dir. Escuela Naval Militar 38-44; Adjutant to Chief of State 46-50; Sub-Chief of Staff 50-52, 54-57; Commdt.-Gen. of the Navy 57-58; Admiral, Chief of Central Staff and Sec.-Gen. Ministry for the Navy 58-61; Under-Sec. for Merchant Navy 61-62; Minister for the Navy 62-; numerous decorations.
Ministerio de Marina, Montalban 2, Madrid, Spain.

Nieto Caballero, Agustín, LL.B.; Colombian educationist; b. 1889; ed. Colombia and U.S. Univs., Univ. of Paris, and Coll. de France.
Studied in U.S.A. and Europe 04-14; co-founder and Rector Gimnasio Moderno, Bogotá, principal modern school of S. America 14-; initiator of many educational reforms and founder of students' organisations and institutions; Dir.-Gen. of Primary and Secondary Education in Ministry of Education and responsible for reform of primary and secondary schools 32-36; Del. to L.N. 31 and 34; guest of honour World Education Congress, Cheltenham 36; Pres. 5th Int. Conf. of Public Instruction, Geneva 36; Rector Nat. Univ. of Colombia 38-41; Pres. Colombian Del. to 8th American Scientific Congress 40; Ambassador to Chile 41-43; mem. Nat. Council of Education; Head of Colombian Del. to World

UNESCO Conf. Nov. 47 and many other Int. Confs. on Education to date; Pres. World Education Conf., Geneva 59; Pres. Int. Cttee. of ten for curriculum Studies UNESCO; corresp. mem. Colombian Acad., Inst. de France; Gran Oficial Cruz de Boyacá, Order of the Alliance for Progress (Pan American Union), Medalla de Oro (Spain) 64, and other decorations.
Publs. *Rumbos de la Cultura, Los Maestros, La Segunda Enseñanza y Reformas de la Educación, Crónicas de Viaje, Crónicas Ligeras, Una Escuela*.
Gimnasio Moderno, Cra. 9 No. 74-99, Bogotá, Colombia.
Telephone: 494526.

Niewodniczanski, Henryk, PH.D., D.SC.; Polish physicist; b. 10 Dec. 1900; ed. Vilno, Tübingen and Cambridge Univs.
Rockefeller Foundation Scholar; Asst. Vilno Univ. 21-32, Prof. of Experimental Physics Poznan 37-39; Prof. of Physics, Vilno Univ. 39 and Jagellonian Univ., Cracow 45-, Dir. Dept. of Physics 48-; has also lectured at Lublin and Wroclaw Univs.; Dir. Dept. of Nuclear Physics, Inst. of Physics (Polish Acad. of Sciences) 52-, Cracow Inst. of Nuclear Physics 55-; Vice-Chair. Peaceful Uses of Nuclear Energy Cttee., mem. Physics and Astronomy Cttees., Chair. Int. Geophysical Co-operation Cttee. 59-61, Polish Acad. of Sciences; mem. Polish Acad. Sciences and Letters, Cracow 47, Polish Acad. Sciences 52-, Scientific Council Joint Inst. of Nuclear Research, Dubna (U.S.S.R.) 56, Int. Cttee. Weights and Measures, Sèvres (France) 66-.
Publs. works in Polish, English, French, German, Russian.
13 Al. Mickiewicza, Cracow, Poland.
Telephone: Cracow 348-11.

Nigrelli, Ross F., B.S., M.S., PH.D.; American pathologist; b. 12 Dec. 1903; ed. Pennsylvania State Univ. and New York Univ.
U.S. Dept. of Agric. 27; Teaching Fellow Biology N.Y. Univ. 27-29, Inst. 29-31; Research Fellow N.Y. Zoological Soc. (N.Y. Aquarium) 31-32, Parasitologist 32-34; Instr. Biology Coll. City of N.Y. (Evening and Summer session) 36-43; Instr. Biology N.Y. Univ. 43-45; Pathologist, Aquarium, N.Y. Zoological Society 34-; Adjunct Assoc. Prof. New York Univ. 49-58; Consultant U.S. Dept. Interior 43-48; Consultant Bingham Oceanographic Lab. Yale Univ. 43-60; Fed. Security Agency Food and Drug Admin. 45-; Tech. Advis. Cttee. Atlantic States Marine Fisheries' Comm. 46-56; Dept. Marine and Aviation N.Y.C. 46-; Vice-Pres. of N.Y. Acad. Sciences and Chair. Biology Section 45-47, Record Sec. 54; Adjunct Prof. of N.Y. Univ. Grad. School Arts and Sciences 58-; Dir. Laboratory of Marine Biochemistry and Ecology, N.Y. Zoological Soc. 58-63, Dir. of Research 63-65; Dir. Osborn Laboratories of Marine Sciences, N.Y. Aquarium 66-, N.Y. Zoological Soc. 65-; mem. American Socs. of Zoologists, Parasitologists, Tropical Medicine, Protozoologists (Pres. 48-49), President's Advisory Cttee., Subpanel on Biological Oceanography 65-; Fellow American Asscn. for Advancement of Science, N.Y. Zoological Soc., N.Y. Acad. of Sciences (Vice-Pres. 55-57, Pres. 57), American Acad. of Microbiology 57-; Hon. Fellow, Consular Law Soc., Affiliate Royal Soc. of Medicine; Trustee, N.Y. Acad. of Sciences 59; Order of Merit, Soc. d'Encouragement pour la Recherche et l'Invention (France) 64.
Office: New York Aquarium, West 8th Street, Brooklyn, N.Y. 11224; Home: 27 Barracuda Road, East Quoque, Long Island, New York, U.S.A.
Telephone: 212-266-8500.

Niizeki, Yasutaro; Japanese business executive; b. 2 April 1897; ed. Tokyo Higher Commercial School.
Managing Dir. Mitsui Bassan Kaisha Ltd. 47; Pres. Daiichi Bussan Kaisha Ltd. 47-59; Pres. Mitsui and Co. 59-61, Chair. of Board of Dirs. 61-; mem. Int. Trade Council of Ministry of Int. Trade and Industry 56-;

Councillor, Japan External Trade Org. 58-; Dir. Japan Foreign Trade Council Inc. 61-, United Nations Assocn. of Japan 62-; Medal of Honour with Blue Ribbon 58.
100 Tokiwamatsucho, Shibuya-ku, Tokyo, Japan.

Nijalingappa, Siddavanahalli; Indian lawyer and politician; b. 10 Dec. 1902; ed. Bangalore and Poona Univ.
Advocate in Mysore High Court 26-37; convicted for political reasons 39, disbarred 40, imprisoned 42-44, 47; mem. Mysore Congress Working Cttee. 39-51; Pres. State Congress 45-46, Karnataka Provincial Congress Cttee. 46-54; mem. Indian Constitutent Ass. 46-47, of Lok Sabha 52-56; Chief Minister of Mysore and leader Mysore Congress Legislative Party 56-58, 62-68; Pres. Indian Nat. Congress 67-; Chair. Indian Oil Co. 60-62.
Office of the Chief Minister, Bangalore, Mysore, India.

Nikezic, Marko; Yugoslav diplomatist; b. 21.
Yugoslav Ambassador to Egypt 53-56, to Czechoslovakia 56-58, to U.S.A. 58-62; Under-Sec. of State, Ministry of Foreign Affairs, Belgrade 62-65; Sec. of State for Foreign Affairs 65-; Order of Meritorious Services to the People, etc.
Ministry of Foreign Affairs, Belgrade, Yugoslavia.

Nikiforov, Dmitry Semenovich; Soviet diplomatist; b. 1917; ed. Leningrad Shipbuilding Inst.
Diplomatic Service 46-; at staff of Ministry of Foreign Affairs 46-51, 56-58; First Sec. 52-56; Deputy Chief of Protocol, Ministry of Foreign Affairs 58-62, 66-68; Amb. to Lebanon 62-66, to Senegal 68-.
U.S.S.R. Embassy, Dakar, Senegal.

Nikoi, Amon, B.A., PH.D.; Ghanaian economist; b. 19 Jan. 1930; ed. Amherst Coll. and Harvard Univ., Mass.
Trade and Econ. Section, Embassy of Ghana, Washington 57-58; Perm. Del. of Ghana to UN 58-60; Alt. Dir. Int. Monetary Fund (IMF) 60-65, Exec. Dir. 65-.
International Monetary Fund, Washington, D.C. 20431, U.S.A.

Nikolayenko, Boris Zinovyevich; Soviet foreign trade official; b. 1914; ed. Moscow Power Inst.
Academy of Foreign Trade 48-; Senior Engineer for Soviet Trade Representation in Hungary 48-55; Vice-Chair. *Soyuzpromexport* 57-64, Chair. 64-; mem. C.P.S.U.; Red Banner of Labour.
Soyuzpromexport, Ministry of Foreign Trade, Smolenskaya-Sennaya ploshchad 32-34, Moscow, U.S.S.R.

Nikolayev, Anatoly Nikolayevich, M.SC.; Soviet diplomatist; b. 1915.
Diplomatic Service 48-; Deputy Head Treaty Legal Dept., U.S.S.R. Ministry of Foreign Affairs 53-55, 57-60; Counsellor, Soviet Representation to UN 55-57; Ambassador to Thailand 60-65; mem. Staff Ministry of Foreign Affairs 65-.
Ministry of Foreign Affairs, Smolenskaya Sennaya ploshchad 32-34, Moscow, U.S.S.R.

Nikolayev, Anatoly Petrovich; Soviet obstetrician; b. 1896; ed. Kiev Univ.
Physician in the Ukraine 17-22; Intern, Asst. Lecturer, Kiev Inst. for Postgraduate Medical Training 22-33; Head of Dept. Poltava Inst. of Obstetrics and Gynecology 33-36; Deputy Dir. Donetsk Inst. of Maternal and Child Health 36-41; Soviet Army Medical Officer 41-44; Corresp. mem. U.S.S.R. Acad. of Medical Sciences 46-51, mem. 52-; Head of Clinic and Deputy Dir. Moscow Inst. of Obstetrics and Gynecology 44-48; Head of Clinic and Deputy Dir. Leningrad Inst. of Obstetrics and Gynecology 50-54, Kiev Inst. of Pediatrics, Obstetrics and Gynecology 54-; mem. C.P.S.U. 55-; Chair. Ukrainian Scientific Soc. of Obstetricians and Gynecologists; Order of Lenin 52, etc.
Publs. Over 200 works on prophylaxis and therapy of foetal asphyxia, painless birth, etc.
Institute of Pediatrics, Obstetrics and Gynecology, Khutor Otradny, Kiev, U.S.S.R.

Nikolayev, Anatoly Vasilevich; Soviet chemist; b. 1902; ed. Leningrad Univ.
Head, Pavlodar Salt Expedition, U.S.S.R. Acad. of Sciences 27-31, Head, Combined Kulunda Expedition 31-35; at Inst. of Gen. and Inorganic Chemistry, U.S.S.R. Acad. of Sciences 34-57; Instructor, Moscow, Polygraphic Inst. 36-41; Instructor, later Prof., Moscow Inst. of Non-Ferrous Metals and Gold 46-57; Dir. Inst. of Inorganic Chemistry, Siberian Dept., U.S.S.R. Acad. of Sciences 57-; Corresp. mem. and Presidium mem. Siberian Dept., U.S.S.R. Acad. of Sciences 58-66, mem. 66-.
Institute of Inorganic Chemistry, Siberian Dept., U.S.S.R. Academy of Sciences, Novosibirsk, U.S.S.R.

Nikolayev, Col. Andriyan (husband of Valentina Vladimirovna Tereshkova, *q.v.*); Soviet (Chuvash) cosmonaut; b. 5 Sept. 1929; ed. Forestry Coll. and Zhukovsky Air Force Engineering Acad.
Former lumberjack; Army 50-; Air Force Fighter Pilot, later Test Pilot; cosmonaut training 60-, stand-in for Maj. Herman Titov 61; launched into orbit around Earth August 11th 62, returned Aug. 15th after completing 64 orbits; Commdr. Soviet Astronauts' Detachment 64-; mem. Communist Party 57-; Deputy Supreme Soviet R.S.F.S.R.; Order of the Red Star Order of Lenin, Hero of Soviet Union.
Zvendry Gorodok, Moscow, U.S.S.R.

Nikolayev, Grigory Iosifovich; Soviet politician and foreign trade official; b. 1918; ed. Inst. of Foreign Trade. Soviet Army 36-38 and 41-43; various posts in Ministry of Foreign Trade; Vice-Chair. *Sovfrakht* (State ship chartering and insurance agency) 55-56, Chair. 56-63; in Council of Mutual Econ. Aid 63-65; U.S.S.R. Commercial Rep. in Romania 65-; mem. C.P.S.U; Order of the Red Banner, Order of the Red Star and other decorations.
U.S.S.R. Trade Representation, Bucharest, Romania.

Nikolayev, Konstantin Kuzmich; Soviet politician; b. 1910; ed. Urals Industrial Inst.
Assistant, Deputy Dean, then Deputy Chief of Section, Urals Industrial Inst. 36-41; mem. C.P.S.U. 40-; Party leader Sverdlovsk 41-46; First Vice-Chair. later Chair. Exec. Cttee. Sverdlovsk Regional Soviet of Working People's Deputies 48-62; First Sec. Sverdlovsk Regional Cttee. of C.P. 62-; Candidate mem. Central Cttee. C.P.S.U. 61-66; mem. Central Cttee. C.P.S.U. 66-; Deputy to Supreme Soviet of U.S.S.R.
Sverdlovsk Regional Committee of Communist Party of U.S.S.R., Sverdlovsk, U.S.S.R.

Nikolayev, Vasili Fyodorovich; Soviet diplomatist; b. 1910; ed. Sverdlov All-Union Communist Univ. and Acad. of Social Sciences of C.P.S.U. Central Cttee.
Member C.P. of Soviet Union 31-; Party official 36-48; First Sec. North Kazakhstan Regional Cttee., Kazakh C.P. 40-44; Sec. Water Transport District Cttee., C.P. of Ukraine 44-45; Sec. Odessa City Cttee., C.P. of Ukraine 45-48; in Teaching Service 48-54; Deputy Head Fourth European Dept., Ministry of Foreign Affairs 54-56; Counsellor Soviet Embassy, Romania 56-60; Deputy Head, Fifth European Dept., Ministry of Foreign Affairs 60-62; Counsellor-Minister, Prague 62-65; Amb. to Iraq 65-; Red Banner of Labour, Badge of Honour and other decorations.
U.S.S.R. Embassy, Baghdad, Iraq.

Nikolayeva, Tatyana Nikolayevna; Soviet trade union official; b. 1919; ed. Ivanovo Pedagogical Inst.
Assistant Head, later Head, Propaganda and Agitation Dept. of Ivanovo City Cttee. of Communist Party 48-50; Sec., later First Sec. Ivanovo City Cttee. of C.P.S.U. 50-59; Sec. All-Union Cen. Council of Trade Unions 59-; mem. Central Cttee. of C.P.S.U.; Dep. to U.S.S.R. Supreme Soviet; Perm. Rep. of U.S.S.R. in UN Comm. on the Status of Women; mem. Exec. Cttee. of World Fed. of Trade Unions, Presidium of Soviet Peace Cttee.; Vice-Pres. Soviet-Polish Friendship Soc.; Order of Lenin and other decorations.
All-Union Central Council of Trade Unions, 42 Leninsky Prospekt, Moscow, U.S.S.R.

Nikula, Karl Oscar, DR. PHIL.; Finnish historian; b. 31 May 1907.
Schoolteacher in Jakobstad and Helsinki 32-45; Dir. of Historical Museum of Turku/Åbo 45-52; Lecturer, Åbo Acad. 45-51; Prof. Åbo Acad. 51-, Rector 62-66.
Publs. *Åbo sjöfarts historia* 30, *Svenska skärgårdsflottan 1756-91* 33, *Tenala och Bromarf socknars historia* I-II 38; *Boktryckarna Frenckell och deras föregångare vid Åbo akademi* 42, *Malmska handelshuset i Jakobstad* 48, *Jakobstad 1652-1952* 52, *W. Rosenlew & Co. Aktiebolag 1853-1953* 53, *La Flotte suédoise de l'archipel au XVIIIème siècle (Revue int. d'histoire militaire)* 55, *The Castle of Turku* 55, *Augustin Ehrensvard 1710-1772* 60, *Les troupes légères de l'armée suède* 61, *The Story of the Tobacco Factory in Jakobstad* 62, *Finnlands Ostgrenze* 63.
Slottsgatan 28A, Åbo, Finland.
Telephone: 17-494.

Nilsson, Birgit (Frau Bertil Niklasson); Swedish opera singer (soprano); b. 17 May 1918; ed. Stockholm Royal Acad. of Music.
With Stockholm Opera 47-51; sang at Glyndebourne (England) 51, Bayreuth 54, Munich 55, Hollywood Bowl, Buenos Aires and Florence 56, Bayreuth and London (Covent Garden) 57, Milan (La Scala), Naples, Vienna, Chicago and San Francisco 58, New York (Metropolitan) 59, Bayreuth 60, Covent Garden 62 and 63; sang in *Turandot*, Paris 68; particularly well known for her Wagnerian roles; Medal for Promotion of Art of Music, Royal Acad. of Music, Stockholm 68.
Box 522, Stockholm C, Sweden.

Nilsson, Fritiof, B.L. (*pseudonym* Fritiof Nilsson Piraten); Swedish writer; b. 4 Dec. 1895; ed. Univ. of Lund.
Mem. Swedish Law Society and Bar Council; gave up practice 31 to devote himself to writing; one of foremost Swedish humorists; authority on South Swedish folklore.
Publs. *Bombi Bitt* 32 (translated into English 33), *Bock i Örtagård* 33, *Småländsk tragedi* 36, *Bokhandlaren som slutade bada* 37, *Historier från Färs* 40, *Tre Terminer* 43, *Bombi Bitt och Nick Carter* 46, *Vänner Emellan* 55; *Flickan m. Bibelspråken* 59, *Vers på Växel* 64, *Millionären* 65, plays and numerous short stories (many appearing in trans. in English periodicals).
Kivik, Sweden.

Nilsson, Gösta; Swedish engineer and business executive; b. 18 Feb. 1912.
High Tension and Lighting Research Inst., Uppsala 36-37; Admin. Investigator, Swedish State Power Board 37-44, Head of Operations and Planning Dept. 44-46, Head of Älvkarleby Power Station 46-48, Dir.-Gen. and Vice-Chief, Swedish State Power Board 48-53; Man. Dir. AB Scania-Vabis (manufacturers of trucks, buses, diesel engines) 53-; Deputy Chair. Linjeflyg AB 59-65, Swedish Metal Trades Employers Asscn. 58-63; Dir. AB Statsgruvor (State Mines Co.) 50-65, Swedish Asscn. of Automotive Industries and Wholesale Merchants 53-, Stockholm Chamber of Commerce 56-, Gen. Asscn. of Swedish Exporters 63-, Swedish Road Asscn. 64-.
AB Scania-Vabis, Södertälje, Sweden.

Nilsson, Karl N. A.; Swedish business executive; b. 28 Aug. 1907; ed. Royal Inst. of Technology, Stockholm.
With Swedish Fan Manufacturing Co. 32-33, 43-49, Exec. Vice-Pres. 53; A.S.E.A. Rep. in India 33-43, Exec. Vice-Pres. 59, Acting Pres. 61; Sales Manager

Svenska Fläktfabriken 49, Exec. Vice-Pres. 53; Pres. Scandinavian Airlines System 62-. Ysätervägen, Djursholm, Sweden.
Telephone: 7-551700.

Nilsson, Torsten; Swedish politician; b. 1 April 1905; ed. in Sweden and Germany.
Began career as bricklayer 22-29; Sec. Social Dem. Youth Organization, Skåne 27-30, Chair. 30-34, Chair. Soc. Dem. Youth Org. of Sweden 34-40, Sec., Social Dem. Party 40-48; mem. of Parl. 41-; Minister of Communications 45-51, of Defence 51-57; Minister of Social Welfare 57-62; Minister for Foreign Affairs 62-.
Ministry for Foreign Affairs, Stockholm 16, Sweden.

Nimmanheminda, Sukich, M.SC.; Thai government official and diplomatist; b. 25 Nov. 1906; ed. Assumption Coll. Bangkok and London Univ.
Lecturer in Mathematics Chulalongkorn Univ. 32, Sec.-Gen. 34, Head Dept. of Mathematics 35; Dir.-Gen. Vocational Education Dept., Ministry of Education 39; Senator 46-47; M.P. 47-59; Dep. Minister of Education 47; Minister of Industries 48; Minister of Economic Affairs 57-59; Dep. Prime Minister 58-59; Ambassador to India Nov. 59-63, concurrently Minister to Nepal, Ceylon and Afghanistan; Ambassador to U.S.A. 63-; fmr. Leader Sahabhumi Unionist Party; Grand Cordon Order of the Crown of Thailand, Grand Cordon Order of the White Elephant, etc.
Royal Thai Embassy, 2300 Kalorama Road, N.W., Washington, D.C., U.S.A.

Nin-Culmell, Joaquin Maria; American musician; b. 5 Sept. 1908; ed. Schola Cantorum and Nat. Conservatoire, Paris.
Studied privately with Manuel de Falla; Instructor, Middlebury Coll., Vermont 38, 39, 40, Williams Coll. 40-50; Prof. of Music, Univ. of Calif. 49-, Inst. of Creative Arts 65-66; has appeared as pianist and conductor with the San Francisco Symphony and other orchestras in the United States and Europe; Corresp. mem. Royal Acad. of Fine Arts of San Fernando (Madrid 1962).
Compositions: Piano Concerto, *El burlador de Sevilla* (ballet), Piano Quintet, *Sonata Breve, Tonadas* (piano), *Three Old Spanish Pieces* (orchestra), *Diferencias* (orchestra), Concerto for cello and orchestra (after Padre Anselmo Viola), *Mass in English* (for mixed chorus and organ), *La Celestina* (opera), Cantata for voice and harpsichord or piano and strings (after Padre Jose Pradas), songs, choral pieces, etc.
Department of Music, University of California, Berkeley 4, Calif., U.S.A.

Ningkan, Dato Stephen Kalong, P.N.B.S., P.D.K.; Sarawak politician; b. 20 Aug. 1920; ed. St. Augustine's School, Betong, Sarawak.
Schoolmaster, St. Augustine's School, Betong 47-49; Hospital Asst., Shell Hospital, Kuala Belait, Brunei 50-60; Sec. Shell Dayak Club, Seria, Brunei 55-56, 58-60; Founder-Pres. Brunei Dayak Asscn.; Co-founder Sarawak Nat. Party, Sec.-Gen. 61-64, Chair. 64-; responsible for Sarawak United Front 62, later Sarawak Alliance, Sec.-Gen. 62-; Chief Minister, Sarawak 63-66, Sarawak National Party, 289 Jalan Dato Wee Kheng Chiang, Kuching, Sarawak, Malaysia.

Nininger, Harvey Harlow, A.M., SC.D.; American meteorite expert; b. 17 Jan. 1887; ed. Northwestern State Normal School, Okla., McPherson Coll., Kansas, Pomona Coll., Calif., and Univ. of California.
Substitute Prof. of Biology, State Teachers Coll., Alva, Okla. 12-13, Prof. of Biology, La Verne Coll., Calif. 14-18; Instr. Pomona Coll. 16; Laboratory Asst. Univ. of California 18; Special Field Agent, U.S. Bureau Entomology 18-19; Extension Entomologist, Kansas State Agricultural Coll. 19; Prof. of Biology, Southwestern Coll. 19-20, McPherson Coll. 20-30; Pres. Kansas Acad. of Science 24-25; organized Nininger Laboratory 30 (became

American Meteorite Laboratory 37); Curator of Meteorites Colorado Museum of Natural History 30-46; Dir. American Meteorite Laboratory Denver; Instr. in Meteoritics Denver Univ.; Pres. Society for Research on Meteorites 37-41; Fellow, American Asscn. for Advancement of Science, Arizona Acad. of Science; began study of meteorites 23; has discovered more than 255 different meteorite falls; possessed the largest private collection of meteorites in the world; Founder and Dir. American Meteorite Museum 46-60; mem. and fmr. Pres. Kansas Acad. Sciences; expeditions to tektite fields, Philippines, Vietnam, Thailand, Australia, Czechoslovakia, Germany, Australian meteorite craters, European meteorite collections 58-60; meteorite consultant, Arizona State Univ. 60-.
Publs. *A Field Guide, Birds of Central Kansas* 27, *Our Stone-Pelted Planet* 33, *A Comet Strikes the Earth* 42, *Chips from the Moon* 47, *The Nininger Collection of Meteorites* 50, *Out of the Sky* 52, *Arizona's Meteorite Crater—Present, Past and Future* 56, *Ask a Question about Meteorites* 62.
P.O. Box 420, Sedona, Arizona 86336, U.S.A.
Telephone: 282-3613.

Nipperdey, Hans Carl, DR.JUR.; German jurist; b. 21 Jan. 1895; ed. Jena, Leipzig and Heidelberg Univs.
Extra. Prof. Jena Univ. 24; Prof. of Civil and Commercial Law and Labour Legislation, Dir. Inst. of Labour Legislation and Economic Law Cologne Univ. 25-, Dean Faculty of law 53; Pres. of Fed. Court of Labour Legislation, Kassel 54-63; Hon. Pres. German Labour Court Soc.; Corresp. mem. Accad. Nazionale dei Lincei, Instituto de Derecho del Trabajo Universidad Estatal Santa Fe, Centro de Estudios Jurídicos Universidad Cuzco, American Acad. of Political and Social Sciences; Hon. mem. Acad. of Human Rights; Hon. Pres. Int. Soc. of Social Law, Geneva; Grosses Bundesverdienstkreuz, Richard Strauss Medal; Dr. rer.pol. h.c., Dr.jur. h.c.
Publs. *Kontrahierungszwang und diktierter Vertrag* 20, *Tarifrecht* 24, *Stromsperre* 29, *Wettbewerb und Existenzvernichtung* 30, *Grundrechte der Reichsverfassung* 29, *Europäisches Arbeitsvertragsrecht* 30, *Lehrbuch des Bürgerlichen Rechts* 59-60, *Grundrechte und Privatrecht* 61, *Die Frage der tarifl. Regelung der Einziehung von Gewerkschaftsbeiträgen* 63, *Die Neuregelung des Rechts der privaten Tonbandaufnahme* 64, *Kommentar zum Tarifvertragsgesetz* 64, *Grundriss des Arbeitsrechts* 65, *Soziale Marktwirtschaft und Grundgesetz* 65, *Risikoverteilung in mittelbar von rechtmässigen Arbeitskämpfen betroffenen Betrieben* 65, etc.
Wolfgang Müllerstrasse 13/15, 5 Köln-Marienburg, German Federal Republic.
Telephone: 38-16-18.

Nishimura, Eiichi; Japanese politician; b. 04.
Former Man. Wakayama and Osaka Branches, Showa Life Insurance Co.; mem. Municipal Ass. Sakai City; mem. House of Reps. 45-, Minister of Health and Welfare 62-63; mem. Central Exec. Cttee. Democratic Socialist Party, now Sec.-Gen.
Shiba Sakuragawa-cho, Minato-ku, Tokyo, Japan.

Nishimura, Naomi; Japanese politician; b. 05; ed. Tokyo Univ.
Chief Sec. to Prime Minister 48; Parliamentary Vice-Minister (Ministry of Finance) 51; Minister of State and Dir.-Gen. of Defence Agency 60-61; Chair. Liberal-Democrat Party Policy Board Dec. 66-.
Publ. *Stranger in Moscow*.
14 Akasaka Shinsaka-machi, Minato-ku, Tokyo, Japan.

Nishio, Suehiro; Japanese politician; b. 91; ed. Primary School.
Factory apprentice 05; mem. Yuaikai (Workers' Friendship Soc., first Japanese trade union) 15, Sec. 19; founded Preparatory Cttee. for Trade Unions 16; arrested 20, 21, 22; del. to ILO Confs. 24, 32; Sec.-Gen.

Sodomei (Gen. Fed. of Trade Unions) 25-40 (suppressed); founder mem. Exec. Shakai Minshu (Socialist People's) Party 25; mem. House of Reps. 28-38 (expelled) 39-; formed Kinro Kokumin To (Nat. Workers' Party) of expelled mems. of Shakai Taishu (Socialist Mass) Party 40, party banned; founded Social Democratic Party of Japan 45; re-established Sodomei 46; Dep. Prime Minister May 47-Feb. 48; resigned from Social Democratic Party 59; Founder Chair. Japan Democratic Socialist Party Jan. 61-.
Publs. *With People* (autobiography) 50, *Road to the New Party* 59.
1 Shiba Sakuragawa-cho, Minato-ku, Tokyo, Japan.

Nishiyama, Yataro, B.TH.; Japanese steel executive; b. 5 Aug. 1893; ed. Tokyo Imperial Univ.
Kawasaki Dockyard Co. 19-, Chief, Steel Sheet Plant 38, Dir. 42; Pres. Kawasaki Steel Corpn. 50-; Insp. Kawasaki Dockyard Co. 61-; Dir. Japanese Iron and Steel Fed., Fed. of Econ. Orgs., Kansai Econ. Fed.; Councillor, Iron and Steel Inst. of Japan; Gov. Dir., Japan Fed. of Employers Asscns.; Exec. Councillor, Kobe Chamber of Commerce and Industry; Chair. and Pres. Kawasaki Steel Corpn. 65-; Hattori Prize 33, Ranjuhosho Prize 61, Watanabe Gisuke Prize 62.
7 Hiratamachi, Ashiya City, Hyogo Prefecture, Japan.

Nisot, Joseph, D. en D.; Belgian lawyer and diplomatist; b. 94; ed. Univs. of Ghent, Cambridge, Geneva, Freiburg, and Harvard.
Legal adviser, Ministry of Foreign Affairs, Brussels 19-22, to League of Nations, Geneva 22-44; rapporteur in *Research in Int. Law*, Harvard Law School 40-42; fmr. legal adviser to Belgian Embassy, Washington, D.C.; Belgian rep., UNRRA Confs. 43, 44, 46, and at ILO Conf., Philadelphia, World Monetary Conf., Bretton Woods, and Civil Aviation Conf., Chicago 44; FAO Conf., Quebec, and Conf. of Jurists for Preparation of Statute of Int. Court of Justice, Washington 45; rep. of Belgium on UN Atomic Energy Comm., and Security Council's Cttee. of Experts; Vice-Chair. UN Special Collective Measures Cttee.; Perm. Belgian rep. to UN 57-59; mem. Permanent Court of Arbitration (The Hague).
13 Avenue de Champel, Geneva, Switzerland.

Nissim, Isaac; Israeli Rabbi; b. 96.
In Israel 25-; Chief Rabbi of Israel and Pres. Rabbinical High Court 55-; Pres. Rabbinical Seminary, Jerusalem 57-; Chair. Gt. Rabbinical Court; Head of Sephardic Community.
Publs. *Yen Hatov, Canogah Zidkah.*
Office of The Chief Rabbi of Israel, Balfour Street 7, Jerusalem, Israel.

Nitze, Paul Henry; American administrator; b. 16 Jan. 1907; ed. Harvard Univ.
New York Investment Banker 29-40; State Dept. 40-44; Vice-Chair., Strategic Bombing Survey 44-46; Dep. Dir., Office of International Trade Policy, 46-48; Dep. to Asst. Sec. of State for Economic Affairs 48-49; Dir., Policy Planning Staff 50; Pres., Foreign Service Education Foundation; Chair., Cttee. on National Security Organization; Asst. Sec. of Defense for International Security Affairs 60-63; Deputy Sec. of Defense 63, 67-; Sec. of the Navy Oct. 63-67.
Publ. *U.S. Foreign Policy 1945-1955.*
3120 Woodley Road, Washington; The Pentagon, Washington, D.C. 20350, U.S.A.

Niven, (James) David Graham; British actor; b. 1 March 1910; ed. Stowe and Royal Mil. Coll., Sandhurst.
Officer in British Army 29-32, 39-46; various occupations 32-35; film extra, Hollywood 35-38; starring roles since 38 in the films *Bachelor Mother, Wuthering Heights, Raffles, The First of the Few, The Way Ahead, A Matter of Life and Death, The Elusive Pimpernel, The Moon is*

Blue, Carrington V.C., Around the World in Eighty Days, The Little Hut, Bonjour Tristesse, My Man Godfrey, Separate Tables, Ask Any Girl, Happy Anniversary, Please Don't Eat the Daisies, The Guns of Navarone, The Best of Enemies, The Pink Panther, 55 Days at Peking, Bedtime Story, Lady L, Where the Spies Are, Eye of the Devil, Casino Royale, Extraordinary Seaman, Prudence and the Pill, and many others; American Motion Picture Acad. Award, Best Actor of the Year for *Separate Tables;* American Legion of Merit and British medals.
Publ. *Round the Rugged Rocks.*
Château D'Oex, Vaud, Switzerland; c/o Coutts & Co., 440 Strand, London, W.C.2, England.

Nixon, Peter James; Australian politician and farmer; b. 28 March 1928; ed. Wesley Coll. Melbourne.
Elected to House of Representatives 61; mem. Joint Cttee. Public Accounts 64; mem. Joint Cttee. Foreign Affairs 67; Minister for the Interior Oct. 67-; Country Party.
Parliament House, Canberra, Australia.
Telephone: Canberra 71556.

Nixon, Richard Milhous, A.B., LL.B.; American lawyer and politician; b. 9 Jan. 1913; ed. Whittier Coll. and Duke Univ. Law School.
Practised law in Whittier 37-42; Attorney with Office of Emergency Management, Washington, D.C. 42; served with U.S. Navy 42-46; attained rank of Lieut.-Commdr.; mem. Congress for 12th Calif. District 47-51; Senator from Calif. 51-53; Vice-Pres. of U.S.A. Jan. 53-61; Republican candidate for Presidency 60; affiliated with law firm Adams, Duque and Hazeltine 61-63; Republican Candidate for Governor, Calif. 62; partner, Nixon, Mudge, Rose, Guthrie, Alexander & Mitchell Dec. 63-.
Publ. *Six Crises* 62.
Office: 20 Broad Street, New York 5, N.Y.; Home: 810 Fifth Avenue, New York 21, N.Y., U.S.A.
Telephone: HAnover 2-6767 (Office).

Niyazbekov, Sabir Bilyalovich; Soviet politician; b. 1912; ed. Higher Party School of C.P.S.U. Central Cttee.
Secretary Village Soviet, District Soviet 28-32; Komsomol work 31-35; Army Service 35-38; Govt. and Party work 38-56; First Sec., West Kazakhstan, Tselinograd, South Kazakhstan, Alma-Ata, Regional Cttees. Communist Party of Kazakhstan; Chair. Presidium, Supreme Soviet, Kazakh S.S.R.; Deputy Chair. Presidium, U.S.S.R. Supreme Soviet 65-; Alt. mem. C.P.S.U. Central Cttee.; mem. Central Cttee. Communist Party of Kazakhstan; Deputy to U.S.S.R. Supreme Soviet.
Presidium Supreme Soviet of the Kazakh S.S.R. Alma-Ata, U.S.S.R.

Nizsalovszky, Endre, LL.D.; Hungarian jurist; b. 25 Sept. 1894; ed. Debrecen and Berlin Univs.
Mem. Law Court 16-20; mem. Codification Section of Ministry of Justice 20-30; Prof. of Commercial Law, Debrecen Univ. 30-34 and of Civil and Commercial Law, Royal Hungarian Palatine-Joseph Univ. of Technical and Economic Sciences 34-38; Prof. of Juridical Procedure, Péter Pázmány Univ. Budapest 38-43; Prof. of Civil Law, Lorand Eötvös (fmrly. Péter Pázmány) Univ., Budapest 43-57; corresp. mem. Hungarian Acad. of Sciences 39-54, full mem. 54-; mem. St. Stephen Acad. 41-51; mem. Permanent Court of Arbitration, The Hague 55-61.
Publs. *A jelzáloglog jogszabályai* 29, *Az érdekkutató jogtudomány (Interessenjurisprudenz)* 33, *A korlátolt dologi jogok* 39, *Az alanyi magánjog és a perjog* 42, *Magyar családi jog* 49, *Kötelmi jog I, Általános tanok* 49, *Aktuelle Fragen der Lieferverträge* 55, *A szellemi alkotások joga* 55, *A Család Jogi Rendjének Alapjai* 63, *Szalay László kodifikációs kapcsolatai és a sioni epizód*

64, *Les relations de László Szalay avec certains travaux de codification a l'étranger* 64, *La Protection des Artistes Exécutants* 64, *Az Öröklési Viszonosság és a Devizayog* (*La réciprocité en matière de succession et la legislation sur le contrôle des changes*) 66, *Eötvös József életmüvének ismeretlen elemei* 66, *Eötvös József levelei Szalay Lászlóhoz* 67, *Eötvös József ésa notaperek* 67, *Order of the Family: Legal Analysis of Basic Concepts* 68.
Borbolya utca 5, Budapest II, Hungary.
Telephone: Budapest 154-985.

N'Jie, Alhaji Alieu Badara, M.B.E., J.P.; Gambian politician; b. 1904; ed. Wesleyan Boy's High School, Bathurst, Gambia.
Gambian Civil Service 25-59, ultimately first Registrar Supreme Court; mem. Bathurst Town Council (now City Council) 47-, Chair. General Purposes Cttee. 59-61; Minister of Works and Services 62, of Works and Communications 62-65; Minister of Foreign Affairs and High Commr. in Senegal 65-67; Chair. Gambia Tourist Board 67; Minister for Local Govt., Lands and Mines 68.
Ministry of Foreign Affairs, Bathurst, Gambia.

Njine, Michel; Cameroon diplomatist; b. 1 Jan. 1918. Cameroon Admin. Service 37; Counsellor of Territorial Assembly of Cameroon 52; Deputy of Legis. Assembly 56; Minister of Public Works, Transportation and Mines 57-58; Deputy Prime Minister in Charge of Nat. Educ., Youth and Sports 58-60; Dir. Cameroon Nat. Office of Tourism 60-62; Amb. to Ivory Coast 62-65, to German Fed. Repub. 65-67; Perm. Rep. to UN 67-.
Permanent Mission of Cameroon to the United Nations, 866 United Nations Plaza, New York, N.Y. 10017, U.S.A.

Njoku, Raymond Amanze; Former Nigerian politician, barrister and solicitor; b. Aug. 1916; ed. St. Charles Coll., Onitsha and King's Coll., Univ. of London.
Teacher 33-42; Law practice 47-54; mem. Eastern House of Assembly 53-54; mem. House of Reps. 53-66; Fed. Minister of Trade and Industry 54-57; Minister of Transport 57-59, of Transport and Aviation 57-64, of Communications 65-66; mem. Gov. Privy Council 54-60, Gov.-Gen. Privy Council 55-60; Pres. Eastern Region Cttee., Nat. Convention of Nigerian Citizens (N.C.N.C.) 51-53, Second Nat. Vice-Pres. 57-64; Chair. Gen. Council Commonwealth Parl. Asscn. 61-62; Knight of the Great Cross of Equestrian Order of St. Gregory the Great.
Providence Villa, 14-16 Mere Street, P.O. Box 150, Owerri, Nigeria.

Nkomo, Joshua; Rhodesian politician; b. 17; ed. Adam's Coll., Natal, Univ. of S. Africa, Johannesburg. Welfare Officer, Rhodesia Railways, Bulawayo, then Organising Sec., Rhodesian African Railway Workers' Union 45-50; Pres. African Congress; employed in insurance and real estate; Pres.-Gen. African National Congress 57; lived abroad when African National Congress banned 59; elected Pres. Nat. Dem. Party, Aug. 60; returned to S. Rhodesia; Pres. Zimbabwe African Peoples' Union (ZAPU) 61-; imprisoned 63-64; banished to Nuanetsi area April 64, to Gonakudzingula Restriction Camp, near Mozambique border Nov. 64-.

Nkrumah, Kwame, B.D., M.A., M.SC., LL.D.; Ghanaian politician; b. 21 Sept. 1909; ed. Teacher Training Coll., Achimota, Ghana, Lincoln and Pennsylvania Univs., London School of Economics and Gray's Inn, London. Schoolmaster, primary schools, Elmina and Axim 31-34, Roman Catholic Seminary, Amisano 34-35; Student in U.S.A. 35-45 and in England 45-47 (Gray's Inn); Gen. Sec., W. African Nat. Secretariat, London 45-47; Joint Sec. Pan-African Congress, Manchester 45, and Editor *New African*, London 45-47; former mem. and first Gen. Sec. United Gold Coast Convention 47-49; left U.G.C.C. and formed Convention People's Party demanding immediate self-govt. 49; imprisoned for inciting illegal strikes 50, elected Municipal mem. for Accra, first Gen. Election under new constitution Feb. 51 and released from prison to become Leader Govt. Business in Assembly; Prime Minister of Gold Coast 52-57, of Ghana 57-60, Pres. 60-66, in charge of Armed Forces, Police and Budget Bureau 61-66, Volta River Project 62-66, Finance 64-66, Foreign Trade 65-66; Minister of External Affairs 57-58, of the Interior 58-59; Life Chair. Convention People's Party, Sec.-Gen. 60-66; Chancellor, Univ. of Ghana 61-66, Kwame Nkrumah Univ. of Science and Technology 61-66; P.C. (U.K.) 59, Lenin Peace Prize 61.
Publs. *Towards Colonial Freedom* 46, *What I Mean by Positive Action* 50, *Education and Nationalism in West Africa, Education in the Colonial Liberation Movement, Ghana* 57, *I Speak of Freedom* 61, *Africa Must Unite* 63, *Consciencism* 64, *Neo-Colonialism, The Last Stage of Imperialism* 65, *Challenge of the Congo* 67, *Axioms of Kwame Nkrumah* 67.
Conakry, Guinea.

Nkweta, Lucas Zaa; Cameroonian agronomist and diplomatist; b. 17 Jan. 1929; ed. Umuahia Coll., E. Nigeria, School of Agriculture, Ibadan, and Univ. Coll., Ibadan.
Former agronomist, Cameroon Devt. Corpn., and fmr. Principal Agricultural Officer, W. Cameroon Govt.; First Sec., Cameroon Embassy, London 63; Consul-Gen., Lagos 64-65; Amb. to U.K. 65-; Chevalier de l'Ordre de la valeur.
Embassy of Cameroon, 84 Holland Park, London, W.11, England.
Telephone: 01-727-0771.

Noble, Rt. Hon. Michael Antony Cristobal, P.C., M.P.; British politician; b. 19 March 1913; ed. Eton Coll. and Magdalen Coll., Oxford.
Served with R.A.F.V.R. 41-45; M.P. 58-; Scottish Whip 60-62; Sec. of State for Scotland 62-64; Conservative. Strone, Cairndow, Argyll, Scotland.

Noble, Sir Peter (Scott), Kt., M.A., LL.D.; British classical scholar; b. 17 Oct. 1899; ed. Aberdeen and Cambridge Univs.
Lecturer in Latin Liverpool Univ. 26-30; Fellow St. John's Coll. Cambridge 28-31; Prof. of Latin Language and Literature Leeds Univ. 30-38; Regius Prof. of Humanity Univ. of Aberdeen 38-52; mem. Univ. Grants Cttee. 43-53; Principal King's Coll. London 52-67; mem. Gen. Dental Council 56-; Vice-Chancellor, Univ. of London 61-64.
48 Aubrey Walk, London, W.8, England.

Noble, Robert Laing, M.D., PH.D., D.SC., F.R.S.C.; Canadian university professor; b. 3 Feb. 1910; ed. Univs. of Toronto and Aberdeen.
Asst. Editor *Journal of Endocrinology*, London 38; Sec. of Canadian *Physiological* Society 45-49; fmr. Prof. and Assoc. Dir. The Collip Medical Research Laboratory, Univ. of Western Ontario; Ellen Mickle Fellowship 34; Leverhulme Fellowship of Coll. of Physicians 35-37; Pres. Canadian Physiological Soc. 59; Dir. Brit. Columbia Cancer Research Centre, Univ. of Brit. Columbia, Vancouver, Canada, and Prof. of Physiology 60-; over 100 written works, especially on endocrinology and cancer.
Cancer Research Centre, University of British Columbia, Vancouver 8; 4746 West 2nd Avenue, Vancouver, B.C., Canada.
Telephone: 224-0818.

Noble, Roberto Jorge; Argentine lawyer and journalist; b. 9 Sept. 1902; ed. Univ. of Buenos Aires.
Mem. Parl. 30 and 31-35; Vice-Pres. of Chamber of Deputies 33-35; promoter of many legal reforms; Sec. of

State for Province of Buenos Aires 36-39; founder and Dir. of daily newspaper *Clarín* 45-; Grand Cross, Knights of Malta, Grand Cross of Saint Lazarus, Commdr. of the Order Isabel the Catholic, Knight of Legion of Honour, Cross of Merit (Italy), Order of the White Rose (Finland), Commdr. Order of the Southern Cross (Brazil), Grand Cross Order of Merit (Spain), and other awards.

Piedras 1743, Buenos Aires, Argentina.

Noel-Baker, Rt. Hon. Philip J., P.C., M.P.; British politician; b. Nov. 1889; ed. Bootham School, York, Haverford Coll., Pennsylvania, Cambridge and Munich Univs., and the Sorbonne.

Fellow of King's Coll., Cambridge; Cassell Prof. of Int. Relations, London Univ. 24-29; Labour M.P. for Coventry 29-31 and for Derby South 36-; Parl. Private Sec. to Sec. of State for Foreign Affairs 29-31; Dodge Lecturer, Yale Univ. 34; mem. Foreign Office Advisory Council on Aliens 40-42; Parl. Sec. to Ministry of War Transport 42-45; Minister of State 45-Oct. 46; Sec. of State for Air Oct. 46-47; Sec. of State for Commonwealth Relations Oct. 47-50; Minister of Fuel and Power 50-51; Pres. Int. Council of Sport and Physical Educ. (UNESCO) 60-; Chair. Parl. Labour Party Foreign Affairs Group 64-; Nobel Peace Prize 59, Albert Schweitzer Book Prize 60.

Publs. *Disarmament, The League of Nations at Work, The Juridical Status of the British Dominions in International Law, The Private Manufacture of Armaments, The Arms Race: a Programme for World Disarmament* 58, *World Disarmament Now* 64, etc.

16 South Eaton Place, London, S.W.1, England.

Nofal, Sayed, DR. ARTS; United Arab Republic (Egyptian) international civil servant; b. 10; ed. Cairo Univ.

Head of Literary Dept. *Al Siyassa* 35-38; Teacher, Cairo Univ. 38; later Dir. of Technical Secr., Ministry of Educ. and Ministry of Social Affairs; later Dir. of Legislative Dept., Upper House of Egyptian Parl.; later Dir. Political Dept., League of Arab States, Asst. Sec.-Gen. 60-.

Publs. include *Poetry of Nature in Arabic and Western Literature* 44, *Egypt in the United Nations* 47, *The Egyptian Parliament in a Quarter of a Century* 51, *The Political Status of the Emirates of the Arab Gulf and Southern Arabia* 59, *History of Arabic Literature* 60.

League of Arab States, Midan Al Tahrir, Cairo, United Arab Republic.

Noguchi, Isamu; American sculptor and landscape designer; b. 7 Nov. 1904; ed. High Schools, Rolling Prairie and La Port, and Columbia and New York Univs.

Apprentice to Onorio Ruotolo 23, to Brancusi, Paris 27; First Exhibition, N.Y. 28; works include sculpture and gardens for Connecticut Gen. Life Insurance Co., The First Nat. Bank of Fort Worth, Chase Manhattan Bank, Yale Library of Precious Books, UNESCO Building, Paris and The John Hancock Building; Billy Rose Art Garden at Israel Museum, Jerusalem; ballet and stage sets; exhibits in many perm. collections.

Publ. *A Sculptor's World* 67.

33-38 10th Street, Long Island City, New York, U.S.A.

Nogueira, Alberto Franco; Portuguese diplomatist and politician; b. 18; ed. Lisbon Univ.

Third Sec., Ministry of Foreign Affairs 43-45, Second Sec. 45-51; Second Sec. and Chargé d'Affaires, Portuguese Embassy, Tokyo 46-50; First Sec., Ministry of Foreign Affairs 51-54; Head of Political Affairs 54; Consul-Gen., London 55-58; Portuguese Rep., C.C.T.A. 55-60; Dir.-Gen. Political Affairs 60-61; Minister of Foreign Affairs 61-.

Publs. *Journal of Literary Critic* 53, *Struggle for the East* 57, *United Nations and Portugal* 63, *The Third World* 67.

Ministry of Foreign Affairs, **Lisbon**, Portugal.

Nogueira, Dênio Chagas; Brazilian economist; b. 12 Dec. 1920; ed. Universidade do Brazil and Univ. of Michigan.

Head, Finance Dept. Nat. Econ. Council 51-64; Editor-in-Chief *Conjuntura Econômica* 53-; Econ. Consultant to Econ. Comm. for Latin America and OAS on Foreign Investments in Latin American Free Trade Asscn. 60, to OAS on the Treaty of Montevideo (LAFTA) 61; Exec. Dir. Superintendency of Money and Credit, Brazil (SUMOC) 64-65; fmr. Pres. Central Bank of Brazil; Pres. Banco Geral do Brazil.

Publs. *Joint International Business Ventures in Brazil* 59, *Foreign Private Investments in LAFTA* 60, *Reforma Agraria, Problemas e Soluções* 64.

Rua da Alfandega 27, Rio de Janeiro, G.B., Brazil.

Nojiri, Kiyohiko (*pseudonym* Jiro Osaragi); Japanese writer; b. 11 Oct. 1897; ed. Tokyo Univ.

Joined Diplomatic Service; later schoolteacher; mem. Japan Art Acad.; Japan Art Acad. Award 50.

Publs. include *Hayabusa-no-Ginji* 24, *Kurama Tengu, Kitkyo* (Homecoming) 50.

c/o Japan Art Academy, Tokyo, Japan.

Nokin, Max; Belgian businessman; b. 10 Dec. 1907; ed. Liège Univ.

Société Générale de Belgique 49-61, Gov. 62-; Chair. Usines de la Vieille Montagne, S.I.D.M.A.R.; Chair. and Man. Dir. Cimenteries C.B.R. Cementbedrijven; Vice-Chair. A.R.B.E.D., Cockerill-Ougrée-Providence; Dir. Sogemines Ltd. (Montreal), Compagnie Miron Ltée. (Montreal); Croix de Guerre avec palme, Commdr. Ordre Léopold II, Officier Ordre de la Couronne, numerous decorations.

3 Montagne du Parc, Brussels 1, Belgium.

Nol, Lt.-Gen. Lon; Cambodian politician; b. 13 Nov. 1913; ed. Khmer Royal Military Acad.

Positions until 55 include: Gov. of Kratie and Battambang provinces, Army Area Commdr., Chief of Nat. Police, Dir. of Customs and Gen. Commr. for Sports; Minister of Nat. Defence and Chief of Gen. Staff 55-66; C.-in-C. of the Khmer Royal Armed Forces 60; Deputy Prime Minister of Cambodia 63; Prime Minister 66-67.

Phnom-Penh, Cambodia.

Nolan, Sidney Robert, C.B.E.; British (Australian) artist; b. 22 April 1917; ed. Melbourne State and Technical schools, Melbourne Nat. Gallery.

One-Man Shows Paris, London, New York, Rome, Venice and capital cities of Australia; Arts Council Travelling Exhibition, Great Britain; also exhibited at Pittsburgh Int. Exhibition 53, 54, 55, 64, New Delhi Int. Exhbn. 53, Pacific Loan Exhbn., Australia and U.S.A. 56, Brussels Int. Exhibition 58, Dunn Int. Exhibition London 63; set designs for the *Rite of Spring*, Covent Garden 62, *The Display*, Canberra 65; Commr. for Australia and Del. for Australian Documentary Films, Venice Biennale 54; Italian Govt. Scholarship 56; Commonwealth Fund Fellowship for travel in U.S.A. 59-61; Nat. Univ., Canberra Fellowship 65.

Principal works in Tate Gallery (London), Museum of Modern Art (New York), Nat. Galleries of Australia, Tom Collins Memorial (Perth Univ.), Contemporary Art Soc. and Arts Council of Great Britain (London).

Publ. *Ned Kelly* 64.

c/o Bank of New South Wales, 47 Berkeley Square, London, W.1, England.

Nolde, O. Frederick, PH.D., LL.D., L.H.D., LITT.D.; American professor; b. 30 June 1899; ed. Muhlenberg Coll., Lutheran Theological Seminary at Philadelphia and Univ. of Pennsylvania.

Fellow, Instructor and Asst. Prof. Lutheran Theological Seminary 23-31, Prof. 31, Dean of Graduate School 43-62; Instructor, Asst. Prof., Lecturer, Univ. of Pennsylvania 25-43; Assoc. Gen. Sec. (Int. Affairs), World

Council of Churches 48-; Dir. Comm. of the Churches on Int. Affairs 46-; Vice-Chair. Carnegie Endowment for Int. Peace; Hon. D.D.
Publs. *Guidebook in Catechetical Instruction* 32, *Yesterday, Today and Tomorrow* 33, *The Church Worker* (with Paul J. Hoh) 34, *Truth and Life* 37, *Christian World Action* 42, *Christian Messages to the Peoples of the World* 43, *Power for Peace* 46.
Home: 7602 East Lane, Philadelphia, Pa. 19118; Office: 297 Park Avenue South, New York 10, N.Y., U.S.A.
Telephone: CHestnut Hill 7-3328.

Nolen, Herman Christian, A.B., M.A., PH.D.; American business executive; b. 14 July 1902; ed. Univ. of Wisconsin, Univ. of North Carolina and Ohio State Univ.
With Continental Motors, Muskegon, Mich. 22-25; Sales Dept., Shaw Taylor Co., Muskegon 25-27; Salesman, Store Designer, Grand Rapids Store Equipment Co. 27-32; Ohio State Univ., rising to Prof. of Marketing 34-47; Vice-Pres. (Drug Buying), McKesson and Robbins 47-50, Vice-Pres. (Drug Merchandising) 50-53, Dir. 53-, Exec. Vice-Pres. 53-56, Pres. 56-61, Chief Exec. Officer 61-, Chair. of Board 62-; Dir. B. F. Goodrich Co., Owens-Corning Fiberglas Corpn., American Optical Co., Dollar Savings Bank, Fed. Street Fund; mem. other business orgs.
Publs. Co-author *The Chain Store Problem* 38, *Drug Store Management* 41, *Sales Management* 50.
80 Wrexham Road, Bronxville, N.Y., U.S.A.

Nolting, Frederick Ernest, Jr., M.A., PH.D.; American diplomatist and banker; b. 24 Aug. 1911; ed. St. Christopher's School, Richmond, Virginia, Univ. of Virginia and Harvard Univ.
Investment Firm, Richmond 34-39; Lecturing Fellowship in Philosophy, Univ. of Va. 41-42; U.S. Navy 42-46; Dept. of State 46-64, Asst. to Deputy Under-Sec. of State 50-53, Special Asst. to Sec. of State for Mutual Security Affairs 53-55; Dir. Office of Political Affairs, U.S. Del. to NATO 55-57; Dep. Chief of Mission, U.S. Del. to NATO and European Regional Orgs. (USRO), Alt. U.S. Rep. on North Atlantic Council 57-61; Ambassador to Viet-Nam 61-63; Vice-Pres. European Offices Morgan Guaranty Trust Co. of New York 64-.
58 avenue Foch, Paris 16e, France.
Telephone: OPéra 2420 (Office); PAssy 8544 (Home).

Nono, Luigi; Italian composer; b. 29 Jan. 1924.
Studied with Bruno Maderna and Hermann Scherchen; teacher New Music Summer School, Kranichsteiner Musikinstitut, Darmstadt 57-, Dartington Hall Music Summer School, Devon (England) 59, 60.
Compositions. *Variazioni canoniche sulla serie dell' op. 41 di A. Schoenberg* 50, *Polifonica-Monodia-Ritmica* 51, *Composizione per Orchestra, I Epitafio per F. Garcia-Lorca, II Epitafio per F. Garcia-Lorca* 52, *III Epitafio per F. Garcia-Lorca, Due Espressioni per Orchestra* 53, *La Victoire de Guernica* (poem by P. Eluard), *Liebeslied, Der Rote Mantel* (ballet) 54, *Canti per 13, Incontri* 55, *Il Canto Sospeso* 56, *Varianti* 57, *La Terra e la Campagna* (words by C. Pavese), *Cori di Didone* (words by G. Ungaretti) 58, *Composizione per Orchestra N. 2—Diario Polacco '58* 59, *Ha Venido* (words by A. Machado) 60, *Sarà dolce tacere* (words by C. Pavese) 60, *Omaggio a Emilio Vedova* (electronic music) 60, *Intolleranza 1960* 61 (words by A. M. Ripellino, V. Mayakovsky, P. Elvard, H. Alleg, J.-P. Sartre, B. Brecht, I. Fucik), *Sul Ponte di Hiroshima* 62 (words by G. Anders, J. L. Pacheco and C. Pavese), *Canciones A Guiomar* 63 (words by A. Machado), *Dal Diario Italiano* 64, *A Floresta é Jorem e Cheja de vida* 66, *La Fabrica illuminata* (words by G. Scabia) 66, *Ricorda Cosa ti Hanno Fatto in Auschwitz* 66, *Per bastiana tai-yangcheng* 67.
Giudecca 882, Venice, Italy.
Telephone: Venice 28368.

Noon, Sir Firoz Khan, K.C.I.E., K.C.S.I., HON. LL.D. (Toronto), M.A.; Pakistani lawyer and politician; b. 7 May 1893; ed. Chief's Coll., Lahore, and Wadham Coll., Oxford.
Advocate Lahore High Court 17-26; mem. Punjab Legislature 20-36; Min. for Local Self-Govt. Punjab Govt. 27-30; Education Min. 31-36; High Commr. for India in Great Britain 36-41; Punjab Nat. Unionist and mem. Moslem League; mem. Governing Body of I.L.O. Geneva, Permanent Cttee. Int. Inst. of Agriculture Rome, Int. Rubber Regulation Cttee.; Int. Tea Cttee., Imperial Economic Cttee., Int. Sugar Council London, Imperial Communications Advisory Council, Imperial Shipping Cttee.; Hon. Fellow Wadham Coll. Oxford; Labour mem. Viceroy's Exec. Council 41-42, Defence mem. 42-45; Indian Rep. British War Cabt. 44-45; Indian Del. to San Francisco Conf. April 45; mem. of Provincial Legislature and All-Pakistan Constituent Assembly and Legislature 47-56; Gov. of E. Pakistan April 50-53; Chief Minister of Punjab 53-55; Mem. of Parl. for Karachi; Foreign Minister Sept. 56-57; Prime Minister, Minister for Foreign Affairs, Commonwealth Relations, States and Frontier Regions, Defence and Kashmir Affairs 57-58; Leader of Republican Party 58-.
Publs. *Canada and India* 39, *Wisdom from Fools* 40, *Illustrated India* 40, *Scented Dust* 41.
Al-Viqar, Noon Avenue, Lahore, Pakistan.

Nord, F(riedrich) F(ranz), D.SC.; American university professor; b. 89; ed. Technische Hochschule (Berlin and Karlsruhe) and Univ. of Berlin.
Instructor, Inst. of Technology, Karlsruhe 12-13; Asst. Prof. Kaiser Wilhelm Inst., Berlin-Dahlem 14-20, Univ. of Berlin 21-38, Chief of Research 33-38; Rockefeller Foundation travelling fellow, U.S.A. 25-27; Prof. of Organic Chemistry and Enzymology, Fordham Univ., N.Y. 38-; Chief Investigator, U.S. Atomic Energy Comm., Office of Naval Research, U.S. Public Health Service, and Nat. Science Foundation, Washington, D.C.; Fellow N.Y. Acad. of Sciences; Carl Neuberg Medallist 49; Medallist Soc. de Chimie Biologique de France 59; Dr. Agr. Sc. h.c., Univ. of Pisa 55, Hon. D.Sc. Fordham Univ. 67; Hon. mem. Acad. of Sciences, Ferrara, Italy 61; foreign mem. Bavarian Acad. of Sciences, Munich, Germany 68; Editor *Advances in Enzymology* 41-, *Archives of Biochemistry and Biophysics* 42-.
Publs. *Mechanism of Enzyme Action and Associated Cell Phenomena* 29, *Zum Mechanismus der Enzymwirkung unter besonderer Beruecksichtigung der Kryolyse* 33, *Handbuch der Enzymologie* 40.
Laboratory of Organic Chemistry and Enzymology, Fordham University, Bronx, New York, N.Y. 10458; Home: 333 Westchester Avenue, Fleetwood, Mount Vernon, N.Y. 10552, U.S.A.
Telephone: 667-8687.

Nord, Hans Robert, D.IUR.; Netherlands lawyer and international civil servant; b. 11 Oct. 1919; ed. Gymnasium, The Hague, and Leiden Univ.
Barrister, The Hague 43-45; Legal Adviser 45-61; Pres. European Movement in the Netherlands 58-61; Chair. Netherlands Atlantic Cttee. 54-61; Sec.-Gen. European Parl. 61-; Officer, Order of Orange Nassau, Commdr. Order of Merit of Italy.
Publs. *The Idea of Representation in Constitutional Law* 45, *Problems of International Government* 48, *International and Supra-National Co-operation* 52, *In Search of a Political Framework for a United Europe* 56, *NATO* 61.
15 Rue Conrad I, Luxembourg-ville, Luxembourg.
Telephone: 22703.

Norden, Albert; German politician and professor; b. 4 Dec. 1904; ed. Wuppertal-Elberfeld.
Joined German Communist Party 20; wood-work instructor, Elberfeld 21-23; imprisoned for anti-fascist

activity 23-24, 27, 39-40; Ed. *Deutschlands Stimme* 45; Man. Press Dep., Ministry of Information 46; Prof. Humboldt Univ., Berlin 46; mem. Social Dem. Party 46-; mem. Cen. Cttee., Social Dem. Party 55-, Politburo of the Cen. Cttee. 58-; mem. Presidium of Nat. Council, Nat. Front of Dem. Germany 54-; mem. Presidium, German Peace Council 58-; mem. Bureau, World Council for Peace 58-; fmr. mem. of Board German Press Asscn.; Nat Prize for Art and Literature (2nd Class) 51; Order of Merit of the Fatherland (Silver) 58, etc.
Central Committee of the Social Democratic Party, 102 Berlin, 2 Werderscher Markt, Germany.

Nordenfalk, Carl (Adam Johan), FIL.DR.; Swedish museum official; b. 13 Dec. 1907; ed. Univs. of Uppsala, Stockholm, Gothenburg.
Asst. Curator, Gothenburg Art Museum 35-44; Curator, Nat. Museum of Arts, Stockholm 44-58, Dir. Gen. 58-; mem. Royal Soc. of Sciences (Uppsala), Royal Swedish Acad. of Letters, Int. Cttee. on History of Art, Council of Europe Exhibition cttee.; Prof. h.c.; Corresp. Fellow British Acad. 67-, Bavarian Acad. of Sciences (Munich), German Archaeological Inst. etc.; Hon. mem. Swedish Royal Acad. of Fine Arts.
Publs. *Die spätantiken Kanontafeln* 38, *Vincent van Gogh* 43, *Kung Praktiks och Drottning Teoris jaktbok* 55; also co-author of several books: (with A. Grabar) *Le Haut Moyen-Age* 57, *La peinture romaine* 58, *Treasures of Swedish Art* 65.
Nationalmuseum, 10324 Stockholm 16; and Vapnargatan 1, Stockholm Ø, Sweden.
Telephone: 24-42-00 (Office).

Nordenson, Harald, PH.D.; Swedish industrialist; b. 10 Aug. 1886; ed. Uppsala Univ.
Lecturer physical chemistry Uppsala Univ. 14-19; Technical Dir. Liljeholmens Stearin A.B. Stockholm 17-29, Man. Dir. 29-50, Chair. 50-63; Chair. *Svenska Dagbladet*, Stockholm, 40-62, Stockholms Superfosfat Fabriks AB 31-60, Nitroglycerin A.B. 38-60, A.B. Stockholms Bryggerier 50-63, The Royal Dramatic Theatre 33-38; Pres. Chamber of Commerce, Stockholm 39-53; Cons. mem. of First Chamber of the Riksdag 38-53; mem. Swedish Acad. of Sciences, Soc. of Sciences Uppsala, Swedish Acad. of Eng. Sciences.
Danviksgatan 10, Stockholm, Sweden.
Telephone: 770140.

Nordman, Carl Axel, DR. PHIL., HON. F.S.A.; Finnish archaeologist; b. 28 Jan. 1892; ed. Univ. of Helsinki.
Asst., Danish Nat. Museum, Copenhagen 12-14, 15-19, Nat. Museum of Finland, Helsinki 19-21; Keeper, Cabinet of Coins and Medals, Nat. Museum of Finland 21-30, Historical Dept. 30-36; Lecturer in Prehistory, Helsinki Univ. 21-36; State Archæologist (Chief Inspector of Monuments and Dir. of Nat. Museum) 36-59; Pres. Swedish Literary Society of Finland 47-53, Finnish Museums Asscn. 40-60, Societas Scientiarum Fennica 54-55; Dep. Chair. Finnish Archaeological Soc. 37-60; Ed. *Finska Fornminnesföreningens Tidskrift* (Journal of Finnish Archæological Society) 26-53, etc.
Publs. *Studier öfver gånggriftkulturen i Danmark* 18, *Anglo-Saxon Coins found in Finland* 21, *Karelska järnåldersstudier* 24, *Den yngre stenåldern i Mellan-, Väst- och Nordeuropa* 27, *The Megalithic Culture of Northern Europe* 35, *Vapnen i Nordens forntid* 43, *Medelti da Skulptur i Finland* 65, etc.
Boulevard en 10, Helsinki, Finland.
Telephone: 640046.

Nordmeyer, Hon. Arnold Henry; New Zealand politician; b. 7 Feb. 1901; ed. Otago Univ.
Member House of Reps. for Oamaru 35-49; mem. for Brooklyn 51-54, for Island Bay 54-; Minister of Health 41-47, of Industries and Commerce May 47-49; Nat.

Pres. N.Z. Labour Party 50-55; Minister of Finance 57-60; Leader, Parl. Labour Party 63-65.
Kellsmere Crescent, Island Bay, Wellington, S.2., New Zealand.

Nordoff, Paul; American musician; b. 6 June 1909; ed. Philadelphia Musical Acad., Juilliard School, New York City.
Teacher Philadelphia Conservatoire; Asst. Prof. Mich. State Coll.; won two Guggenheim Fellowships, Ford Foundation Faculty Fellowship 54-55; Pulitzer award 40; Prof. Bard Coll. 49-59; music therapy for handicapped children, England 59, autistic children, U.S.A. 61-65, Inst. of Logopedics, Kansas 62, Teacher Consultant, Board of Public Educ., Philadelphia, Pennsylvania 62-, Chief Music Therapist, Univ. of Pennsylvania, Dept. of Child Psychiatry 62-; now travelling on a Music Therapy Demonstration and Training Project for Handicapped Children in Scandinavia 67-69; Dr. Mus. h.c. (Combs Coll. of Music).
Compositions include two piano concertos, opera, *Secular Mass*, music for Katharine Cornell's production *Romeo and Juliet*, *The Masterpiece* (opera) 41, *Tallyho* (ballet, with Agnes de Mille), *Salem Shore*, *Every Soul is a Circus* (dances for Martha Graham), *The Sea Change*, *Mr. Fortune* (operas); (with Ralph Knight) *Robert Burns: Poems and Songs*, *Music Therapy for Handicapped Children: Investigations and Experiences*, *Pif-Paf-Poltrie*, *Children's Play-Songs* Vol. I and II, *The Story of Artaban*, *The Three Bears*, *The Children's Christmas Play*, *Fun for Four Drums* (all with Clive Robbins).
c/o RFD 1, Chester Springs, Pa. 19425, U.S.A.

Norfolk, The Duke of, Bernard Marmaduke FitzAlan-Howard, K.G., P.C., G.C.V.O., G.B.E.; British peer; b. 30 May 1908.
Mayor of Arundel 35-36; Joint Parliamentary Sec. to Ministry of Agriculture 41-45; Earl Marshal and Hereditary Marshal and Chief Butler of England; Premier Duke and Earl; Lord Lieutenant of Sussex 49-; Reserve of Officers, late 2nd Light Royal Horse Guards; Major Royal Sussex Regiment; M.C.C. Team Manager, Australia 62-63; Vice-Chair. Turf Board 65-; Pres. Council for Preservation of Rural England 45-; Elder Brother, Trinity House 65; Royal Victorian Chain 53.
Arundel Park House, Arundel, Sussex, England.

Nørgaard, Ivar, B.SC. (ECON.); Danish politician; b. 26 July 1922; ed. Københavns Universitet.
Secretary, Econ. Board, Danish Labour Movement 48-55; Principal, Esbjerg Folk High School 55-61; Chief Editor *Aktuelt* 61-65; Minister of Econ. Affairs 65-68, also Minister of European Market Relations 67-68; mem. Parl. 66-.
Publs. Economic articles.
Nydamsvej 15, Bagsvaerd, Denmark.

Noriega-Morales, Manuel, DR. ECON. SC.; Guatemalan international civil servant; b. 15 Sept. 1907; ed. National School of Commercial Sciences, Guatemala, Univ. of San Carlos, Guatemala and Harvard Univ., U.S.A.
Auditor, Court of Accounts, Guatemalan Govt. 32-34; Dir., Bureau of Budget, Ministry of Finance 35-38; Dir.-Gen. Accounting Office, Ministry of Finance 39-43; Minister of Economic Affairs 45-46; Pres. Central Bank of Guatemala 46-54; Gov. for Guatemala of Int. Monetary Fund and Int. Bank for Reconstruction and Development 46-54; Minister of Economy and Labour 50-51; Economic Consultant, UN Econ. Comm. for Latin America 55; Deputy Dir., Cen. American Research Inst. for Industry, Guatemala 56-60, Dir. 64-; Dir. Technical Assistance Div. Inter American Devt. Bank Washington 60-61; mem. Cttee. of Development Experts, Alliance for Progress Program, Organization

of American States, Washington 62-; Del. to numerous Inter-American Confs.; Order of Quetzal.

Instituto Centroamericano de Investigación y Tecnología Industrial (ICAITI), Avenida La Reforma 4-47, Zona 10, Guatemala.

Norlund, Niels Erik, PH.D.; Danish mathematician; b. 26 Oct. 1885; ed. Copenhagen, Paris and Göttingen Univs.

Former Prof. of Mathematics Copenhagen Univ.; former Dir. Danish Geodetic Inst.; Pres. Rask-Örsted Foundation 28-64; Pres. Royal Danish Acad. of Science 27-33; Vice-Pres. Int. Council of Scientific Unions 31, Pres. 34; Foreign mem. Royal Society and Royal Astronomical Society; mem. Acads. of Science in Paris, Rome, Stockholm, Oslo, Uppsala, Naples and Helsinki; Editor *Acta mathematica;* Hon. D.Sc. (London and Dijon); Hon. D.Eng. (Darmstadt); Hon. Ph.D. (Lund and Oslo).

Publs. *Vorlesungen über Differenzenrechnung* 24, *Leçons sur les séries d'interpolation* 26, *Leçons sur les équations aux différences finies* 29, *The Map of Denmark* 42, *The Map of Iceland* 44.

Malmøgade 6, Copenhagen, Denmark.

Telephone: Øbro 3046.

Norman, Arthur Gordon, C.B.E., D.F.C.; British business executive; b. 18 Feb. 1917; ed. Blundell's School.

Thomas De La Rue and Co. 34-, Asst. Gen. Man. 47, Dir. 51, Man. Dir. 53, Chair. 64-; R.A.F. 41-46; Deputy Chair. Export Council for Europe; Deputy Pres. Confederation of British Industry 66-; mem. Overseas Resettlement Bureau Advisory Council; mem. Council British Inst. of Management, Council of Industrial Design; part-time Dir. of B.O.A.C.

33 Bryanston Square, London W.1., England.

Norman, Mark Richard, O.B.E.; British business executive; b. 3 April 1910; ed. Eton Coll. and Magdalen Coll., Oxford.

Joined Gallaher Ltd. 30; Lazard Bros. and Co. Ltd. 32-39; Dir. Gallaher Ltd. 48-, Chair. 63-; Managing Dir. Lazard Bros. and Co. Ltd. 60-; Partner Edward de Stein and Co. 46-60; Chair. Wiggins Teape 66-; Dir. other public companies.

Moor Place, Much Hadham, Herts., England.

Norman, Willoughby Rollo; British business executive; b. 12 Oct. 1909; ed. Eton Coll. and Magdalen Coll., Oxford.

Army Service 39-45; Vice-Chair. Boots Pure Drug Co. Ltd. 54-61, Chair. 61-; Chair. Atlas Assurance Co. Ltd. 64-; Underwriting mem. of Lloyds; Dir. Nat. Provincial Bank Ltd., Royal Exchange Assurance, Sheepbridge Engineering Ltd., English China Clays Ltd.

Pickwell Manor, Melton Mowbray, Leics., England.

Telephone: Somerby 215.

Normann, A. Christian; Danish merchant and politician; b. 23 March 1904; ed. agricultural school.

Journalist 23-33; Purchasing and Sales Man. Haustrup Fabriker Ltd., Odense 34-46, Dir. 34-; mem. Odense Town Council 43-46; f. Normann Publishing Office, Odense; Part-owner *Helsinger Dagblad* 58-; M.P. 50-; Minister of Fisheries 60; Dir. The Danish Nat. Bank 57-, Danish Milk Co. 67; mem. Nordic Council 57-60, European Council 64-, Danish Defence Cttee.; Man. Dir. machinery firm, Copenhagen; Liberal.

Bergmannsdal, Sdr. Strandvej 54, Elsinore, Denmark.

Telephone: Copenhagen 143210 (Office); Elsinore 214063 (Home).

Normann, Leif Otto; Danish shipowner; b. 1 Oct. 1890; ed. Public High School and Naval Coll., Copenhagen.

Royal Danish Navy 06-10; joined shipping firm 10; N.Y. 12-15, South America 21-22; Man. United Steamship Co. Ltd. 23, Managing Dir. 34-64; Chair. Danish Shipowners' Asscn. 53-59, Maritime Council 53-59, Titan Motor Works, Hotel Codan and Baltica Insurance Co

47-64; Vice-Chair. Elsinore Shipbuilding & Engineering Co. Ltd., Frederikshavns Shipbuilding Yard Ltd., Aarhus Shipbuilding and Engineering Co. Ltd. 36-65, Private Insurers Ltd., etc.; Dir. War Risk Insurance Inst. for Danish Ships, Copenhagen Free Port Co. Ltd. 48-56, etc.; mem. Council of Tourist Asscn., Int. Chamber of Commerce (Danish Cttee.), Ice-Breaking Council, Danish Shipping Board 39-49 and 52-61; Vice-Pres. Int. Chamber of Shipping 54-56; Judge, Maritime and Mercantile Court 37-41; Knight Commdr. 1st Class and Silver Cross of Order of Dannebrog; Knight Commdr. of Norwegian Order of St. Olav, Knight Commdr. Swedish Order of Vasa, Greek Order of George I.

5 Kvaesthusgade, Copenhagen, Denmark.

Norodom Sihanouk; former King of Cambodia; b. 31 Oct. 1922; ed. in Saigon and Paris.

Elected King April 26th 41, abdicated March 2nd 55; Prime Minister and Minister of Foreign Affairs Oct. 55, March 56, Sept. 56, April 57; Permanent rep. to U.N. Feb. 56-Sept. 56; elected Head of State after death of his father 60-, has taken oath of fidelity to vacant throne; head of the Popular Socialist Community; musician and composer.

Royal Palace, Phnom Penh, Cambodia.

Norrish, Ronald George Wreyford, SC.D., F.R.S.; British chemist; b. 9 Nov. 1897; ed. Perse School, Cambridge, and Emmanuel Coll., Cambridge.

Served in France, First World War 16-19; Fellow of Emmanuel Coll., Cambridge 25-; Lecturer 30-36, Prof. of Physical Chemistry, Univ. of Cambridge 37-65, Prof. Emer. 65-; Pres. Faraday Soc. 53-55; Vice-Pres. Royal Inst. of Chemistry 57-59; Liversidge and Faraday Lecturer, Chemical Soc. 58, 65; Pres. British Asscn., Section B 60-61; Bakerian Lecturer, Royal Soc. 66; Hon. mem. Polish Chemical Soc. Corresp. mem. Acad. of Sciences, Göttingen, Royal Soc. of Sciences, Liège; Foreign mem. Polish Acad. of Sciences; Hon. mem. Royal Soc. of Science, Uppsala; Meldola Medal, Royal Inst. of Chemistry 26, Davy Medal, Royal Soc., London 58, Lewis (Combustion Inst.) Medal 64, Faraday Medal, Chemical Soc. 65; Nobel Prize for Chemistry 67; Hon. D. de. l'Univ. (Paris); Hon. D.Sc. (Sheffield, Leeds).

Department of Physical Chemistry, Univ. of Cambridge; Home: 7 Park Terrace, Cambridge, England.

Telephone: Cambridge 55147.

Norstad, Gen. Lauris; American air force officer; b. 24 March 1907; ed. U.S. Military Acad.

Commissioned Cavalry 30; attended Air Corps Flying Schools 30-31; Air Corps Service 31-36; Adjutant 61st School Squadron, G.H.Q., Long Island 36, 9th Bombardment Group 37; entered Air Corps Tactical School, Alabama 39; Officer-in-Charge 9th Bombardment Group Navigation School 40; Adjutant 25th Bombardment Group 40; Asst. Chief of Staff in Intelligence, G.H.Q., Virginia 40-42; Asst. Chief of Staff (Operations) Twelfth Air Force, in England and N. Africa, 42; Dir. of Operations, Mediterranean Allied Air Forces 43-44; Chief of Staff Twentieth Air Force, Washington 44-45; Asst. Chief of Air Staff (Plans) 45; Dir. of Plans and Operations, War Dept. 46-47; Lieut.-Gen. 47; Deputy Chief of Staff (Operations) 47-50; Acting Vice-Chief of Staff 50; C.-in-C. U.S. Air Forces in Europe 51-56; Supreme Allied Commdr. in Europe 56-62; Pres. Owens-Corning Fiberglas Corpn. 63-; Dir. United Air Lines, McKesson and Robbins Inc., English-Speaking Union of U.S.A. 64; Trustee Rand Corpn.; D.S.M. with two Oak Leaf Clusters, Silver Star, Legion of Merit with Cluster, Air Medal; Hon. O.B.E., Légion d'Honneur, Croix de Guerre, Ordre du Ouissam Alaouit Cherifien (Morocco), Dr. of Mil. Science (Maryland), Diploma for the Royal Order of King George I (Greece), Grand Cross Order of Avis (Portugal).

Office: 717 Fifth Avenue, New York 22, N.Y., U.S.A.

Northrop, John Howard, B.S., A.M., PH.D.; American chemist; b. 5 July 1891; ed. Columbia Univ.
W. B. Cutting Travelling Fellow, Columbia Univ.; working in Jacques Loeb's Laboratory, Rockefeller Inst. 15; apptd. to staff of Rockefeller Inst. 16, mem. 24-61, Emer. 61-; Visiting Prof. Univ. of Calif. 49-58, Emer. 62-; Stevens Prize, Coll. of Physicians and Surgeons Columbia Univ. 31; Capt. Chemical Warfare Service 17-18; discovered and worked on fermentation process for manufacturing acetone; Sc.D. Harvard Univ. 36, Columbia Univ. 37, Yale Univ. 37, Princeton Univ. 40, Rutgers 41; LL.D. Calif. 39; De Lamar Lecturer, School of Hygiene and Public Health, Johns Hopkins Univ. 37; Jessup Lecturer Columbia Univ. 38; Hitchcock Lecturer Calif. 39; Thayer Lecturer Johns Hopkins Univ. 40; Chandler Medal, Columbia Univ. 37; Daniel Giraud Elliot Medal for 1939, Nat. Acad. of Sciences; shared Nobel Prize in Chemistry 46; Alex. Hamilton Award, Columbia Univ. 61; mem. Nat. Acad. of Sciences, Halle Akademie der Naturforscher, etc.; Cert. of Merit U.S.A. 48; Hon. mem. Chemical Society, London.
Publ. *Crystalline Enzymes* 39.
Department of Medical Microbiology and Immunology, School of Public Health, Berkeley, Calif., U.S.A.

Nosaka, Sanzo; Japanese politician; b. 92; ed. Keio Univ.
Secretary Brotherhood Asscn. (later called Japanese Fed. of Labour) 17; visited U.K. and joined Communist Party of Great Britain 19-20; founder mem. Communist Party of Japan 22; arrested for first time 23; mem. Cen. Cttee. Communist Party of Japan 31; in Moscow as mem. Presidium Com. Cttee. Communist International 35-43; in Yenan (China) 40-45; returned to Japan and elected mem. Cen. Cttee. and Politburo Communist Party of Japan 46; mem. House of Reps. and Chair. Communist Group in Diet 46-50; underground activity 50-55; First Sec. Cen. Cttee. Communist Party of Japan 55-58, Chair. 58-; mem. House of Councillors 56-.
Publs. *Selected Works*, 2 vols.
26, 4-chome, Sendagaya, Shibuya-ku, Tokyo, Japan.

Nosavan, General Phoumi; Laotian army officer and politician.
Secretary of State for Defence 59; promoted to Gen. 60; Minister of Defence 60, and Sports, Youth and Ex-Servicemen 60; Dep. Premier, Minister of the Interior, Culture and Social Welfare (Prince Souvanna Phouma Cabinet) 60; Dep. Premier and Minister of Defence (Prince Boun Oum Cabinet) 61; Vice-Premier and Minister of Finance (Provisional Nat. Union Govt. Cabinet) July 62-65; exiled 65; Leader of Social Democratic Party.

Nosek, Jiří; Czechoslovak international administrator; b. 29 Aug. 1911; ed. School of Economic Science, Prague.
Acting Perm. Rep. of Czechoslovakia to UN 50-53; First Vice-Pres. ECOSOC 51, 52, Second Vice-Pres. 54; Perm. Rep./Ambassador to UN 53-54; Vice-Minister of Foreign Affairs 55-56; Ambassador to India and Ceylon 56-59; Vice-Minister of Foreign Affairs 59-62; Under-Sec., Office of Conf. Services, UN 61-62; Chair. Econ. and Financial Cttee. UN 52, 57, of Social, Humanitarian and Cultural Cttee. 54, of Admin. and Budgetary Cttee. 59; Order of Labour 58.
United Nations, New York City, N.Y., U.S.A.

Nossack, Hans Erich; German writer; b. 30 Jan. 1901; ed. Jena Univ.
Factory worker 19-22; employed by commercial firms 25-33; in business of his own 33-56; full time writer 56-; Guest Prof. of Poetry, Frankfurt Univ. 68, mem. Akademie der Wissenschaften und der Literatur, Mainz, Deutsche Akademie für Sprache und Dichtung, Darmstadt; George Büchner-Preis 61, Wilhelm Raabe-Preis 63.

Publs. *Gedichte* (poems) 47, *Nekyia* (novel) 47, *Interview mit dem Tode* 48, *Die Rotte Kain* (play) 49, *Der Neugierige* (story) 55, *Die Begnadigung* (story) 55, *Spätestens im November* (novel), *Die Hauptprobe* (play) 56, *Spirale* (novel) 56, *Über den Einsatz* (essay) 56, *Begegnung im Vorraum* (stories) 58, *Der Juengere Bruder* (novel) 58, *Unmögliche Beweisaufnahme* (novel) 59, *Freizeitliteratur* (essay) 59, *Nach dem letzten Aufstand* (novel) 61, *Ein Sonderfall* (play) 63, *Sechs Etüden* (stories) 64, *Das kennt man* (novel) 64, *Das Testament des Lucius Eurinus* (story) 65, *Die Schwache Position der Literatur* (essays) 66.
Goethestr. 21, 6 Frankfurt/Main, German Federal Republic.

Notestein, Wallace, M.A., PH.D.; American historian; b. 16 Dec. 1878; ed. Coll. of Wooster and Yale Univ.
Assistant Prof. of History Kansas Univ. 05-07; Instr. in History 08; Asst. Prof. 10, Prof. 17-20 Minnesota Univ.; research asst. to American Peace Comm. 19; Prof. English History Cornell Univ. 20-28, Sterling Prof. Yale Univ. 28-47, Prof. Emeritus 47-; mem. British Prime Minister's Cttee. of House of Commons Records 29-32; corresp. Fellow British Acad., Assoc. Phil. Soc.; Hon. Litt.D. (Harvard, Birmingham, Yale), Hon. D.Litt. (Oxford), Hon. LL.D. (Glasgow).
Publs. *History of English Witchcraft* 13, *Source Problems in English History* (with A. B. White) 15, *Commons Debates 1629* (with F. H. Relf), *D'Ewes' Journal of the Long Parliament* 23, *Winning of Initiative by House of Commons* (Raleigh Lecture British Acad.) 24, *Commons Debates 1621* (7 vols. with F. H. Relf and H. Simpson) 35, *English Folk* 38, *The Scot in History* 46, *The English People on the Eve of Colonisation* 54, *Four Worthies* 56.
236 Edwards Street, New Haven, Connecticut, U.S.A.
Telephone: 562-6746.

Noth, Gottfried, D.D.; German ecclesiastic; b. 26 Jan. 1905; ed. Univs. of Leipzig and Erlangen.
Curate in Dresden 30, Pastor in Zethau/Erzgeb 32-42; Pastor of Holy Trinity Church, Dresden 42-53; mem. Evangelical-Lutheran Church Council for Saxony 45-; Bishop of Saxony 53-.
Tauscherstrasse 44, 8021 Dresden 21, German Democratic Republic.
Telephone: Dresden 31804.

Notowidigdo, Mukarto; Indonesian civil servant; b. 1 Nov. 1911; ed. Law School, Djakarta.
Served with Finance Dept., Netherlands East Indies Govt. 35; during that period organised a nationalist group; Sec. Indonesian Study Club during Japanese occupation; twice imprisoned by Japanese; mem. Exec. Cttee., Vice-Chair. Int. Affairs Cttee., Indonesian Nat. Party 45; Inspector-Gen. Indonesian Foreign Service; Deputy Chief Del. to U.N. 50-52; Minister for Foreign Affairs, Wilopo Cabinet 52; Ambassador to U.S.A. 53-60, to India 60-64, to Canada 64-65.
Department of Foreign Affairs, Taman Redjambon 6, Djakarta, Indonesia.

Noüe, Count Jehan de; French United Nations official; b. 17 June 1907; ed. Ecole des Roches, Ecole des Sciences Politiques, Sorbonne.
Lecturer, U.S.A. 37-39; French Liaison Officer, B.E.F. 39-40, in Italy and Tunisia 43-44; Lecturer and Prof. U.S.A. and Canada 40-42; Allied Control Comm., Rome 44-45, Berlin 45; Preparatory Comm. and 1st UN Gen. Ass., London 46; Chief of Protocol UN, New York 46-62, Geneva 62-; Knight, Sovereign Order of Malta, Croix de Guerre, Bronze Star.
8 rue Robert de Traz, Geneva, Switzerland.
Telephone: 35-20-21.

Nourissier, François; French writer and journalist; b. 18 May 1927; ed. Lycée Saint Louis, Lycée Louis-le-Grand, Paris, Ecole libre des Sciences politiques, Paris, and Faculté de Droit, Paris.

On staff of Secours Catholique Int., and work with Int. Refugee Org. 49-51; Dir. Chalet Int. des Etudiants, Combloux (World Univ. Service) 51-52; Sec.-Gen. Editions Denoël 52-56; Editor-in-Chief *La Parisienne* (review) 56-58; Literary Adviser to Editions Grasset 58-; Literary Dir. *Vogue* (French) 64-66, Contributing Editor *Vogue* (American) 64-; Literary Critic *Les Nouvelles littéraires* 63-; Prix Félix Fénéon 52, Grand Prix de la Guilde du Livre 65 (Swiss), Grand Prix du Roman de l'Académie française 66.
Publs. *L'Eau grise* (novel) 51, *Lorca* (essay) 55, *Les Orphelins d'Auteuil* (novel) 56, *Le Corps de Diane* (novel) 57, *Portrait d'un indifférent* 57, *Bleu comme la nuit* 58, *Un petit bourgeois* 64, *Une Histoire française* 66, *Les Français* (essay) 67.
11 *bis* rue Jean-Goujon, Paris 8e, France; Caux, 1824, Canton de Vaud, Switzerland; Château d'Arpaillargues, par Uzès 30 (Gard), France.

Nourse, Edwin Griswold, PH.D.; American economist; b. 20 May 1883; ed. Cornell and Chicago Univs.
Instructor in Finance Wharton School of Finance and Commerce, Univ. of Pennsylvania 09-10; Prof. of Economics Univ. of S. Dakota 10-12, Univ. of Arkansas 15-18; Prof. of Agricultural Economics Iowa State Coll. 18-23; Chief Agric. Div. Inst. of Economics, Brookings Institution 23-29; Dir. Inst. of Economics, Brookings Institution 29-42; Vice-Pres. Brookings Institution 42-46; Chair. Social Science Research Council 42-45; Pres. American Economic Asscn. 42; Chair. Council of Economic Advisers, Exec. Office of the President 46-Oct. 49; Vice-Chair. Joint Council on Economic Education 51-63; Fellow American Farm Econ. Asscn. 57-; Visiting Distinguished Prof. of Econ., Pennsylvania State Univ. 59; Guest Scholar, Brookings Inst. 62-; Distinguished Fellow, American Econ. Asscn. 65; Converse Award, American Marketing Asscn. 55, Freedoms Foundation Award 50, Rosenberger Gold Medal, Chicago Univ. 59; Fellow, American Acad. Arts and Sciences, American Philosophical Soc.; Hon. LL.D., Hon. D.Sc.
Publs. *Agricultural Economics* 16, *American Agriculture and the European Market* 24, *The Legal Status of Agricultural Co-operation* 27, *America's Capacity to Produce* 34, *Marketing Agreements under the Agricultural Adjustment Act* 35, *Three Years of Agricultural Adjustment Administration* (with J. S. Davis and J. D. Black) 36, *Industrial Price Policies and Economic Progress* (with Horace B. Drury) 38, *Price Making in a Democracy* 44, *The 1950's Come First* 51, *Economics in the Public Service* 53.
3802 Jocelyn Street, N.W., Washington, D.C., U.S.A.

Novák, Josef, DR.RER.NAT., DR.SC.; Czechoslovak university professor; b. 19 April 1905.
Asst. Univ. of Brno 35-45, Prof. Mathematics 45-48; Czech Technical Univ., Prague 48-50; Mathematics Inst. of the Czechoslovak Acad. of Sciences 50; Academician, Czechoslovak Acad. of Sciences 52-; Chair. of Mathematics and Physics Section of the Czechoslovak Acad. of Sciences 55-61; Order of Labour 65.
Žitná 25, Prague I, Czechoslovakia.

Novella, Agostino; Italian trade unionist; b. 28 Sept. 1905.
Sec. Gen. Confederazione Generale Italiana di Lavoro (CGIL); fmr. Pres. World Fed. of Trade Unions (WFTU) 59.
Confederazione Generale Italiana di Lavoro, Corso d'Italia 25, Rome, Italy.

Novikov, Anatoly Grigorievich; Soviet composer; b. 96; ed. Moscow Conservatoire.
Has composed many popular songs and choral songs to words by Pushkin; won first prize at the Prague International Festival of Democratic Youth for his *Hymn of the Democratic Youth* 47; Chair. Organising Cttee.,

Union of Composers of R.S.F.S.R. 57-, Sec. of Union 60-; he won two prizes at the Berlin Festival 51, and Budapest Festival 49; Art Worker of Merit of the R.S.F.S.R.; State prizewinner 46, 48; Order of Red Banner of Labour 56, of Lenin 66; People's Artist of R.S.F.S.R.
Work: *When You are with Me* 62.
Union of Soviet Composers, 8/10 Nezhdanova Street, Moscow, U.S.S.R.

Novikov, Ignaty Trofimovich; Soviet administrator; b. 1906; ed. Dneprodzerzhinsk Metallurgical Inst.
Director of power station 33-37; mem. C.P.S.U. 26-; Chief Engineer and subsequently Dir. of factory Saratov 37-41; Sec. Saratov District Cttee. C.P. 41-43, Chief *Glavenergozapchast* (Soviet area electricity authority) 43-50; Deputy Head of Construction Gorky Power Station 50-54; Head of Construction Kremenchug Power Station 54-58; Minister of Power Station Construction 58-62; Dep. Chair. Council of Ministers 60-; Chair. State Cttee. for Construction 62-; mem. Central Cttee. C.P.S.U.; Deputy to U.S.S.R. Supreme Soviet.
State Committee for Construction, U.S.S.R. Council of Ministers, 4 Prospekt Marxa, Moscow, U.S.S.R.

Novikov, Ilya Alexandrovich; Soviet trade union official; b. 11; ed. secondary school.
Young Communist League 30-37, Party work 38-50; Vice-Chair. Moscow City Trade Union Council 50-54; Chair. Cen. Cttee. of Trade Union of the Workers of the Timber, Paper and Woodworking Industries 54-63; mem. All-Union Central Council of Trade Unions 64-68; Chair. Auditing Comm., All-Union Central Council of Trade Unions 63-; mem. C.P.S.U., Order of Lenin; Order of Red Banner of Labour (twice), etc.
All-Union Central Council of Trade Unions, 42 Lenin Prospekt, Moscow, U.S.S.R.

Novikov, Kirill Vasilyevich; Soviet diplomatist; b. 1905; ed. Leningrad Polytechnic Inst.
Member C.P. of Soviet Union 25-; Asst. Head, Second Western Dept., Ministry of Foreign Affairs 40; Counsellor, Soviet Embassy, London 40-42; Head, Second European Dept., Ministry of Foreign Affairs 42-47; Amb. to India 47-52; Head of South East Asia Dept., Ministry of Foreign Affairs 53-55; Deputy Head, Head of Dept. of Int. Relations, Ministry of Foreign Affairs and mem. of Collegium of the Ministry 56-; Order of Lenin, of Red Banner of Labour and other awards.
Ministry of Foreign Affairs, 32-34 Smolenskaya-Sennaya ploshchad, Moscow, U.S.S.R.

Novikov, Pyotr Sergeyevich; Soviet mathematician, b. 01; ed. Moscow Univ.
Lecturer Moscow Mendeleyev Inst. 29-34; Senior Lecturer Steklov Mathematical Inst. 34-57, Head of Mathematical Logic Dept. 57-; mem. U.S.S.R. Acad. of Sciences 60-; Lenin Prize 57; Order of Lenin, Order of Red Banner of Labour.
Publs. works in field of theory of pluralities and mathematical logic.
U.S.S.R. Academy of Sciences, 14 Lenin Prospekt, Moscow, U.S.S.R.

Novikov, Vladimir Nikolaevich; Soviet politician; b. 1907; ed. Technical Inst., Leningrad.
Technician, Designer, Engineer and Dir. Izhevsk Armaments Plant; mem. C.P.S.U. 36-; Deputy Commissar for Armaments 41-48; mem. staff Ministry of Defence Industry 48-54, Deputy Minister of Defence Industry 54-55; First Deputy Minister of Machine Building 55-57; Chair. Leningrad Regional Econ. Council 57-58; Chair. R.S.F.S.R. Planning Cttee. and First Deputy Chair. R.S.F.S.R. Council of Ministers 58-60; Chair. U.S.S.R. Planning Cttee. (GOSPLAN) 60-62; Perm. Soviet Rep. to Exec. Cttee. of Council for Mutual Econ. Aid (COMECON) July 62-; Chair. U.S.S.R. Council of Ministers Comm. for Foreign Econ.

Affairs 62-; Vice-Chair. U.S.S.R. Council of Ministers 65-; mem. C.P.S.U. Central Cttee. 61-; Deputy to U.S.S.R. and R.S.F.S.R. Supreme Soviets; Hero of Socialist Labour; Order of Lenin, etc.
U.S.S.R. Council of Ministers, The Kremlin, Moscow, U.S.S.R.

Novo, Salvador, PH.D.; Mexican author and educationist; b. 30 July 1904; ed. Nat. Univ.
Professor of Italian Literature Nat. Univ. 22 and of Spanish Literature 23; Dir. Editorial Dept. Min. of Educ. 24-32; Editor *Resumen* and *La Razón* 30-; fmr. Dir. Press Dept. Foreign Office; Associate Producer Cinematográfica Internacional S.A. Mexico 38-; winner of Premio Ciudad de México (Mexico City Award) Mexican Book Fair 46; Head of Theatre Dept., Inst. of Fine Arts; Pres. of Television Comm. 47; Pres. Mexican Theatre Centre, Int. Theatre Inst. 49-51; Fellow Mexican Acad. 52; founded Teatro de la Capilla 52; Dir. School of Dramatic Arts 56; Historian of Mexico City 65.
Publs. *Ensayos* 25, *Return Ticket* 28, *Nuevo Amor* 33, *Seamen Rhymes* 33, *Le Troisième Faust* 34, *Continente Vacío* 35, *En Defensa de lo Usado* 38, *Poesías Escogidas* 38, *Nueva Grandeza Mexicana* 46, *Florido Laude* 46, *Este y otros Viajes* 51, *Las Aves en la Poesía Castellana* 53, *Poesías Completas (1915-1955)* 55, *Sátira* 55, *Diálogos* 57, *Actuación y Dirección teatral* 59, *Poesías Completas* 61, *Letras Vencidas* 62, *Breve Historia de Coyoacán* 62, *1001 Sonetos Mexicanos* 63, *Joyas de la Amistad* 63, *Sonetos* 64, *Historia y Antología de la Fiebre Amarilla* 64, *Toda la Prosa* 64, *La Vida en México durante el período Presidencial de Lázaro Cárdenas* 64, *La Vida de México durante Avila Camacho* 65, *La Vida en México durante Miguel Alemán* 66, *101 Poemas Norteamericanos Modernos (Antología Bilingüe)* 66, *D. Juan Tenorio (Antología)* 66, *(poesia, prosa, teatro)* 66, *Hist. Gastronómica de la Ciudad de México* 67.
Films: *Perjura, El Capitán Aventurero, El Signo de la Muerte, Bajos Fondos, Los que Volvieron, El Abrigo Delator, Isaura;* Plays: *Don Quixote* 47, *Astucia* 48, *La Culta Dama* 51, *El Joven II* 51, *A 8 Columnas* 56, *Yocasta, o Casi* 61, *Ha Vuelto Ulises* 62, *Cuauhtémoc* 62, *La Guerra de las Gordas* 63, *El Sofá* 63, *El Espejo Encantado* 66.
Francisco Sosa 138, Coyoacán, Mexico 21, D.F., Mexico. Telephone: 24-90-02.

Novobátzky, Károly; Hungarian physicist; b. 3 May 1884.
Member Hungarian Working People's Party 48, now mem. Cen. Cttee. Hungarian Socialist Workers' Party; now Vice-Pres. Hungarian Acad. of Sciences; Hon. Pres. Lóránd Eötvös Physical Soc.; research into Theory of Relativity, Quantum Electrodynamics, Electrodynamics of Insulating Materials; twice awarded Kossuth Prize; Acad. Gold Medal.
Hungarian Academy of Sciences, Akadémia-utca 2, Budapest V; also Budapest XIV, Hejó-u. 20, Hungary. Telephone: 833-645.

Novomesky, Ladislav; Czechoslovak writer; b. 27 Dec. 1904; ed. Teachers Coll., Modra.
Teacher in Bratislava 23-25; Editor of dailies *Pravda chudoby, Rudé právo, Haló-noviny, Ludovy denník, Slov-zvesti,* periodicals *Tvorba, DAV, Budovatel* 25-44; Deputy Chair. Slovak Nat. Council 44; Commr. of Slovak Nat. Council for Educ. and Culture 45-50; political imprisonment 51-63; professional writer 63-; mem. Cen. Cttee. of C.P. of Slovakia 44-50; mem. Slovak Nat, Council 44-45; Deputy to Nat. Assembly and Slovak Nat. Council 45-50; Chair. Asscn. of Slovak Writers 46; mem. Cen. Cttee. of C.P. of Czechoslovakia 49-50; Order of Slovak Nat. Rising First Class, Klement Gottwald State Prize 64, Nat. Artist 64, L Štúr Prize 67.
Publs. Collections of poems: *Sunday* 27, *Rhomboid* 32, *The Open Window* 35, *Saints Behind the Village* 39,

Villa Theresa (poem) 63, *30 Minutes to Town* (poem) 63, *The Unexplored World* 64.
Bratislava, Martinčekova 32, Czechoslovakia.

Novosyolov, Efim Stepanovich; Soviet politician; b. 1906; ed. Kharkov Engineering Inst.
Worker, later engineer, Staro Kramatorsk Engineering Factory (Donets Basin) 22-29, 33-38; mem. C.P.S.U. 25-; engineer, People's Commissariat of Heavy Engineering 38-39; Chief Engineer, Dir. of Central Research Inst. for Engineering Technology 39-42; Dir. of Novo-Kramatorsk Engineering Factory, Elektostal (Moscow Region) 42-49; Deputy Minister for Building and Road Building Engineering 49-53; Head of Central Heavy Engineering Div. of Ministry for Heavy and Transport Engineering 53-54; Minister for Engineering for the Building and Road Building Industries 54-57; Head of Dept., State Planning Cttee. of U.S.S.R. 57-60; Vice-Chair. State Econ. Council of U.S.S.R. 60-62; Chair. State Cttee. for Engineering for Building, Road Building and Municipal Industries (U.S.S.R. State Cttee. for Construction) 62-65; Minister for Engineering for Building, Road Building and Municipal Industries 65-; mem. Central Auditing Cttee. C.P.S.U.; Deputy to U.S.S.R. Supreme Soviet.
Ministry for Engineering for the Building, Road Building and Municipal Industries, Maly Cherkassky pereulok 1/3, Moscow, U.S.S.R.

Novotný, Antonín; Czechoslovak politician; b. 10 Dec. 1904.
Joined C.P. 21; Chair. Pragu ♭ Karlín District of C.P. 30-35, and also factory worker; mem. Regional Cttee. for Prague 35; Del. to 7th Congress of the Comintern in Moscow 35; Sec. Prague Region of C.P. 37; Regional Sec. C.P., Hodonín 37-38; active in underground movement during Nazi occupation of Czechoslovakia and jailed in Nazi prisons and Mauthausen Concentration Camp 41-45; Leading Sec. Prague Regional Cttee. of C.P. 45-51; mem. Cen. Cttee. 46-May 68; Sec. Cen. Cttee. and mem. of the Presidium of Cen. Cttee. 51-68; Deputy Prime Minister Jan.-Sept. 53; First Sec. Central Cttee. Sept. 53-68; Pres. of the Czechoslovak Repub. and C.in-C. of the Czechoslovak Armed Forces 57-68; Chair. Cen. Cttee. of Nat. Front 59-68; Klement Gottwald Order 63, Hero of Socialist Labour 64, Czechoslovak Peace Prize 66; Soviet, Korean, Ethiopian, Cambodian, Indonesian, Yugoslav, Bulgarian and U.A.R. decorations.
Prague, Czechoslovakia.

Novozhilov, Valentin Valentinovich; Soviet mechanical engineer; b. 1910; ed. Leningrad Physico-mechanical Inst.
Leningrad Research Insts. 31-46; Instructor, Leningrad Univ. 46-49, Prof. 49-; Assoc. Laboratory of Mathematical and Econ. Problems, Eng. Econ. Inst. 62-; Corresp. mem. U.S.S.R. Acad. of Sciences 58-66, mem. 66-.
Leningrad University, Leningrad, U.S.S.R.

Nowak, Roman; Polish politician; b. 21 July 1900.
Participated in Silesian uprisings 20, 21; imprisoned for revolutionary activity 27-31; in Soviet Union 33-34; Chair. Cen. Trade Union Dept. of the C.P. of Poland (K.P.P.) Cen. Cttee. 34-36; mem. Nat. Secretariat of C.P. of Czechoslovakia 37-39; Vice-Chair. of Union of Poles & Slavs, Bolivia 39-46; Second Sec. Polish Workers Party (P.P.R.) Voivodship Cttee., Katowice 46-48; Second Sec. Polish United Workers Party (P.Z.P.R.) Voivodship Cttee., Katowice 48-50; Sec. P.Z.P.R. Voivodship Cttee., Opole 50-56; mem. Communist Parties of Germany, Upper Silesia and Poland 21-; mem. P.P.R. 46-48, P.Z.P.R. 48-, P.Z.P.R. Cen. Cttee. 48-, Political Bureau of Cen. Cttee. 56, Chair. Cen. Party Control Commission 56-; mem. Seym, mem.

Council of State 57-; Order of the Banner of Labour, First Class 64 and others.
Polska Zjednoczona Partia Robotnicza, Nowy Świat 6, Warsaw, Poland.

Nowacki, Pawel Jan, D.SC., A.M.I.E.E.; Polish university professor and nuclear physicist; b. 05; ed. Jahn Realschule, Berlin, High School, Poznań, Technical Univ., Lwów.
Lecturer, Technical Univ., Lwów 29, 31-36; Design Engineer, Siemens Co., Germany and Poland 30-37; Senior Scientific Officer, Royal Aircraft Establishment, Farnborough, during War to 46; Chief Engineer, Study Office, Polish Central Electricity Bd. 47-52; Prof. Chair of Electrical Machinery, Technical Univ., Warsaw 47-53, Electrical Instruments 53-59, Nuclear Engineering 59-; Dir.-Gen. Inst. of Nuclear Research, Warsaw 58-; Corresp. mem. Polish Acad. of Sciences 56-61, mem. 61-; Corresp. mem. Royal Swedish Acad. of Technical Sciences 58-, Schweizerische Gesellschaft für Automatik 59, mem. Polish State Council for the Utilisation of Atomic Energy 56-; mem. Exec. Council, Int. Fed. of Automatic Control (IFAC) 57-61, Vice-Pres. 61-; has received a number of awards.
Publs. *Long Transmission Lines* 53, *The Calculation of Short-Circuit Currents in Electrical Networks* 55, *Symmetric Components* 54, *Theory of Automatic Control*, Vol. 1 58, Vol. 2 62, *The Polish Power Programme* 47, (with other) *The Polish Nuclear Power Programme* (Second Geneva Conference) 58, *Theory of the Magnetohydrodynamic Generator* 61, *The Programming and Utilisation of Research Reactors* (IAEA Symposium, Vienna) 61, *Théorie et Applications de la Physique des Plasmas à Basses Températures* 65.
Ulisa Walowa 4 m. 34, Warsaw, Poland.
Telephone: 314373.

Nowacki, Witold, DR. ING.; Polish university professor; b. 20 July 1911.
Dozent Warsaw Polytechnic 45; Prof. Gdańsk Polytechnic 46-52; Prof. Warsaw Polytechnic 52-54; Prof. Warsaw Univ. 55-; mem. Polish Acad. of Sciences 52, Deputy Gen. Sec. 57-65, Gen. Sec. 65-; Foreign mem. Czechoslovak Acad. of Sciences; Polish State Prizes 49, 55 and 65.
Publs. *Mechanics of Structural Analysis, Thermoelasticity, Dynamics of Elastic Systems*, papers on applied mechanics, especially theories of structure and elasticity.
Polska Akademia Nauk, Palac Kultury Nauki, Warsaw, Poland.
Telephone: 20-33-80.

Nowak, Zenon; Polish politician; b. 05.
Member Polish Communist Party 24, mem. Cen. Cttee. 32; mem. Cen. Cttee. Polish Workers' Party, later Polish United Workers' Party 45-, mem. Political Bureau 48-56; Dep. Chair. Council of Ministers 54-.
Council of Ministers, Warsaw, Poland.

Noyes, Albert (*see* Noyes, (William) Albert).

Noyes, Eliot Fette, B.A., M.ARCH.; American architect and industrial designer; b. 12 Aug. 1910; ed. Phillips Acad., Andover, Harvard Coll. and Harvard Graduate School of Architecture.
Worked in office of Gropius and Breuer, Cambridge, Mass.; fmr. Dir. of Dept. of Industrial Design, Museum of Modern Art, New York; U.S. Air Force, Second World War; Design Dir., Norman Bel Geddes & Co. 46-47; Eliot Noyes and Assocs. (architecture and industrial design) 48-; Assoc. Prof. (critic in architectural design) Yale Univ. 48-51; Consultant Dir. of Design for Int. Business Machines (IBM) and Westinghouse; Pres. Int. Design Conf. in Aspen; Fellow American Inst. of Architects, Industrial Designers Soc. of America, Fellow Royal Soc. of Arts.
Principal works: Bubble Houses of Concrete, Florida;

own house, New Canaan, IBM Typewriter, IBM Executary Dictating Machine, office buildings, schools, exhbns. at World's Fairs, etc.
Eliot Noyes and Associates, 96 Main Street, New Canaan, and 210 Country Club Road, New Canaan, Connecticut, U.S.A.
Telephone: 203-966-0752 (Home).

Noyes, (William) Albert, Jr., B.A., D. ès S.; American chemist; b. 18 April 1898; ed. Grinnell Coll., Univ. of Paris, Univs. of Geneva, Illinois and Calif.
Instr., Univ. of Calif. 21-22, Univ. of Chicago 22-23, Asst. Prof. 23-29; Assoc. Prof. Brown Univ. 29-35, Prof. 35-38; Prof. Univ. of Rochester 38-63, Emer. 63-; Chair. Chemistry Dept. 39-55, Dean, Graduate School 52-56; Act. Dean and Dean Coll. of Arts and Science 56-58, Univ. Distinguished Prof. 61-63; Ashbel Smith Prof. of Chemistry, Univ. of Texas 63-; Section Chair. Nat. Defence Research Cttee. 40-42, Div. Chief 42-46; Staff, Chief Chemical Warfare Service, U.S. Army 42-46; Adviser Dept. Army and Dept. of State; Chair. Div. of Chemistry and Chemical Technology, Nat. Research Council 47-53; mem. Board of Trustees, Sloan-Kettering Inst. for Cancer Research 50-63; mem. Executive Cttee. Int. Union of Pure and Applied Chemistry 55-59, Pres. 59-63; Pres. American Chemical Society 47; mem. Nat. Acad. of Sciences, American Philosophical Society; Hon. mem. Société Chimique de France; Royal Soc. of Physics and Chemistry (Spain), Soc. of Chemistry (Belgium); foreign hon. mem. Acad. of Sciences, Lisbon; King's Medal for Service in Cause of Freedom (British), Medal of Merit (U.S.A.), Officier, Légion d'Honneur, Priestley Medal, Willard Gibbs Medal; Hon. D.Sc. (Grinnell Coll., Rhode Island, Paris, Indiana Univs., Univ. of Ottawa, Univ. of Montreal, Univ. of Illinois, Univ. of Rochester, Carleton Univ. (Ottawa); Editor *Journal of American Chemical Society* 50-62, *Journal of Physical Chemistry* 52-64.
Publs. *Photochemistry of Gases* (with P. A. Leighton) 41, *Modern Alchemy* (with W. A. Noyes) 32, *Traité de Chimie Physique* (with H. Weiss); translation into French of book by E. W. Washburn 25; (Ed.) *Chemistry in World War II* 48, *Photochimie et Spectroscopie* 37, *Advances in Photochemistry* Vols. 1-5 (with G. S. Hammond, J. N. Pitts).
5109 Lucas Lane, Austin, Texas 78731, U.S.A.
Telephone: 512-GL2-5571.

Ntiro, Sam; Tanzanian artist and diplomatist; b. 1923; ed. Makerere Coll., Kampala, and Slade School of Fine Art, London.
Lecturer, Dept. of Fine Art, Makerere Coll., Kampala, Uganda 55-61; Tanganyika Foreign Service 61-64, Acting High Commr. in London 62-63, High Commr. 63-64; on special duty, Ministry of External Affairs, Dar es Salaam March-Oct. 64; Head of Art Dept., Nat. Teachers' Coll., Kyambogo, Kampala, Uganda March 65-June 66; Warden, Livingstone Hall, Makerere Univ. Coll., Kampala, Uganda June 66-67; Commr. for Culture in Tanzania 67-; exhibition of paintings, London 67.
P.O.B. 521, Moshi, Tanzania.

Nu, U, B.A.; Burmese politician and writer; b. 1907; ed. Rangoon Univ.
For some years headmaster Nat. High School, Pantanaw; joined Dobhama Asiayone (Our Burma) Organisation; sentenced to term of imprisonment at outbreak of Second World War; released after Japanese occupation; organised Dobhama Asiayone and later joined wartime Govt. as Minister of Foreign Affairs in Dr. Ba Maw's Cabinet 43-44; Minister for Publicity and Propaganda 44-45; elected Vice-Pres. Anti-Fascist People's Freedom League (Nationalist Coalition) after Allied re-occupation; elected Speaker Constituent Assembly 47; Deputy Chair. Gov.'s Exec. Council July

47; signatory Anglo-Burmese Treaty, London, preliminary to Burmese Independence and first Prime Minister of Burmese Republic 48-56; resigned to devote himself to the reorganisation of Anti-Fascist People's Freedom League; Prime Minister 57-58; Prime Minister, Minister of Home Affairs, Relief and Resettlement, Democratisation of Local Administration, Information, Transport, Posts and Telegraphs, Shipping and Aviation, Housing and Rehabilitation 60-62; in custody 62-Oct. 66.
Publs. Plays and stories.
Rangoon, Burma.

Nucker, Delmas Henry; American administrator; b. 12 April 1907; ed. Indiana public schools.
With U.S. Office of Price Admin., Washington 42-44, UNRRA 44-46; Asst. to Gen. Man., Alaska Railroad 47-50; Exec. Officer, U.S. Dept. of Interior Office of Territories 50-54; Deputy High Commr., U.S. Trust Territory of the Pacific Islands 54, Acting High Commr. 54-56, High Commr. 56-61; Special Rep. of U.S., UN Trusteeship Council 55-61, Chief, Insular Affairs, Dept. of Interior 61-62; Dir. Agency for Int. Development Mission, Afghanistan 63-; Dept. of Interior Distinguished Service Award 55.
U.S. Agency for International Development Mission, Kabul, Afghanistan.

Nugawela, Edward Alexande; Ceylonese government official; b. 21 Sept. 1898; ed. Royal Coll., Colombo.
Former advocate; fmr. Major, Ceylon Light Infantry; Minister of Educ. 47-52, of Health 52-56; now Chair. Public Service Comm. of Ceylon.
2 Paget Road, Colombo 5, Ceylon.

Nunes, H.E. Cardinal José da Costa; Portuguese ecclesiastic; b. 15 March 1880.
Ordained 03; appointed Priest at Macão 20, consecrated 21; Archbishop of Goa and Damão 40-53; Titular Patriarch of Odessa 53-62; created Cardinal by Pope John XXIII 62; mem. of the Council, Propaganda Fide, Rites; Vice-Chamberlain of the Holy Roman Church.
Palazzo Apostolico, Vatican City, Italy.

Núñez-Jiménez, Capt. Antonio; Cuban scientist and politician; b. 23; ed. Havana Univ.
Professor at Central Univ., Las Villas 55; fought under Major Che Guevara with Castro's guerillas; Exec. Dir. Agrarian Reform Inst. (I.N.R.A.) 60-62; Pres. Comisión Nacional de la Academia de Ciencias de la Républica de Cuba 62-.
Publs. *Geography of Cuba*, etc.
Capitolio Nacional, Havana, Cuba.

Nungesser, Roland; French politician; b. 9 Oct. 1925; ed. Ecole Libre des Sciences Politiques.
Commissaire-général du Salon nautique international; Vice-Prés. Chambre syndicale des industries nautiques; Prés. du Conseil national de la navigation de plaisance; Mayor of Nogent-sur-Marne 59; mem. Chamber of Deputies 58-, Sec. of State for Housing 66-67; Sec. of State at Ministry of Economy and Finance 67-68; Minister of Youth and Sports May 68-; Union pour la nouvelle République.
Assemblée Nationale, Paris 7e, France.

Nuorvala, Aarne Johannes; Finnish lawyer; b. 18 April 1912; ed. Helsinki Secondary School and Univ. of Helsinki.
Civil Servant, Ministry of Finance 44; Junior Cabinet Sec. 45, Senior 46-50; Junior mem. Comm. for Drafting Legislation 50-55, Senior mem. 55; Extra Justice of Supreme Admin. Court 55-57, Justice 57-63; Sec.-Gen., Deputy Prime Minister and mem. Cabinet 63-64; Chancellor of Justice 64, Pres. Supreme Admin. Court 65.
Korkeavuorenkatu 13A 2, Helsinki 13, Finland.

Nur, Abdul Mohsen; United Arab Republic (Egyptian) politician.
Minister of State for Land Reform 62-63, for Agrarian Reform and Land Reclamation 63; Deputy Prime Minister for Agriculture and Irrigation 64-68; Minister of Local Government 68-.
Ministry of Local Government, Cairo, United Arab Republic.

Nureyev, Rudolf; Ballet dancer (b. U.S.S.R.); b. 1939; ed. Kirov Ballet School, Leningrad.
Formerly with Kirov Ballet; sought political asylum, Paris 61; joined Le Grand Ballet du Marquis de Cuevas; appeared in Australia 64; frequent guest star at Royal Opera House, Covent Garden; appears frequently with Dame Margot Fonteyn; Choreographer and Dir. *Raymonda* 65, *Tancredi* 66, *Don Quixote* (Vienna) 66; appeared in *Jazz Calendar* 68, produced *The Nutcracker* 68; films include *Swan Lake* 66; Gold Star, Paris 63.
Publ. *Nureyev* 62.
Villa La Turbie, Monte Carlo, Monaco.

Nuriev, Ziya Nurievich; Soviet politician; b. 15; ed. C.P.S.U. High School.
In education system 33-38, 40-42; Soviet Army 38-40; Party work 42-52; Second Sec. 53-57; First Sec. Bashkir Oblast Party Cttee. 57-; Deputy and mem. Presidium U.S.S.R. Supreme Soviet 54-; mem. Central Cttee. of C.P.S.U. 61-.
Bashkir District Committee of C.P.S.U., Ufa, Bashkir A.S.S.R., U.S.S.R.

Nurock, Mordechai; Israeli rabbi and politician; b. 28 April 1884.
Mem. Latvian Parl. 22-34, leader of democratic minority faction comprising Russians, Jews and Poles; Chief Rabbi of Kurland before First World War; Vice-Pres. Democratic Community in Moscow during First World War; one of founders and Exec. Leader World Jewish Congress; one of founders and leaders of Nat. Minorities in Europe 25; since 24 mem. Zionist Action Cttee.; leader religious Zionist Movement, Mizrachi; mem. Exec. Keren Hayesod; Minister for Posts, Telegraphs and Telephones, Govt. of Israel 52; mem. Knesset.
The Knesset, Jerusalem, Israel.

Nuseibeh, Anwar Zaki, M.A.; Jordanian diplomatist; b. 20 Jan. 1913; ed. Govt. Arab Coll., Jerusalem, and Queens' Coll., Cambridge.
Land Officer, Palestine 36, Magistrate 37-42; Lecturer in Constitutional Law, Jerusalem Law Classes 36-48; fmr. mem. Jordan Parl. and Senator; Chief Arab Del., Jordan and Israel Mixed Armistice Comm. 51; Minister of Defence 53, of Educ. 54-55, of Reconstruction and Devt. 54-55; Gov. of Jerusalem, Jordan 61-62; Ambassador to U.K. 65-66; Order of El Kawkab (1st Class); Assoc. Knight Order of St. John of Jerusalem; Knight of Order of Holy Sepulchre.
c/o Ministry of Foreign Affairs, Amman, Jordan.

Nuseibeh, Dr. Hasem; Jordanian politician.
Deputy Chair. of Devt. Board 58-60; Under-Sec. Ministry of Nat. Economy 59-60; Sec.-Gen. of Devt. Board 61-62; Minister of Foreign Affairs 62-63, 65-66.
c/o Ministry of Foreign Affairs, Amman, Jordan.

Nussbaumer, Albert Charles; Swiss banker; b. 93.
Dir. Swiss Bank Corpn., Basle; Chair. S. A. Adolphe Saurer, Textile Machines and Lorries, Arbon; Chair. Société Internationale Pirelli S.A., Basle; Dir. Pirelli Società p.a., Milan; Dir. Montecatini, Milan, Dir. Banca Unione, Milan; Chair. Nitrochemie S.A., Basle; Vice-Chair. Cie. Néerlandaise de l'Azote S.A., Brussels; Dir. S. A. Danzas and Cie., Basle, Transports Internationaux; Chair. Société Financière Italo-Suisse, Geneva; Dir. Swiss Fed Cross Soc., Berne.
Villa Yasmin, Lugano-Montagnola, Switzerland.

Nyamweya, James; Kenyan politician; b. 28 Dec. 1927; ed. King's Coll., London and Lincoln's Inn, London.
Legal Assistant in Ministry of Legal Affairs, Kenya 58-59; Advocate, Private Legal Practitioner, Supreme Court of Kenya 59-63; Founder-mem. and mem. Central Exec. Cttee. Kenya African Nat. Union (KANU) 59-63, Chair. Kisii 62-64; Parl. Sec. to Ministry of Justice and Constitutional Affairs 63, and in the Office of the Prime Minister 64-65; Minister of State, Provincial Admin. Civil Service, Office of the Pres. 65-66; Leader of Govt. Business in the House of Representatives May-Dec. 66; Minister of State, Foreign Affairs, Office of the Pres. and Leader of Govt. Business in Nat. Assembly Jan. 67, now Minister of Power and Communications; Hon. LL.B., London.
Ministry of Power, P.O.B. 30582, Nairobi, Kenya.

Nyberg, Alf Erik Gunnar, FIL.DR.; Swedish meteorologist; b. 19 June 1911; ed. Universitet i Uppsala, Stockholms Universitet and Univ. of Chicago.
First State Meteorologist, Swedish Meteorological and Hydrological Inst. 45-52, Chief of Div. 52-55, Dir.-Gen. 55-; Asst. Prof. Stockholm Univ. 47; mem. Exec. Cttee. World Meteorological Org. (WMO) 55, Pres. European Regional Asscn. 56-63, Pres. WMO 63-; UN Technical Evaporation Missions: Syria 54, East Africa 62.
Publs. *A Synoptic-aerological Investigation* 45, *Meridional Heat Transport* 54, *An Experimental Study of the Field Variation of the Eddy Conductivity* 56, *A Study of the Evaporation and the Condensation at a Snow Surface* 65, *The Evaporation in Southern Sweden* 66.
Sveriges meteorologiska och hydrologiska institut, Fridhemsgatan 9, Box 12 108, Stockholm 12, Sweden.

Nyein, U Kyaw, B.A., B.L.; Burmese banker; b. 12; ed. Univ. Coll., Rangoon.
Chairman, Union Bank of Burma 54-58, 60; Dir. State Commercial Bank 54, Dep. Chair. 63; Chair. State Agricultural Bank 63-; Gov. Int. Monetary Fund 54, Int. Bank for Reconstruction and Development (World Bank), Int. Finance Corpn. and Int. Devt. Asscn. 62; Minister of Finance 58-60.
15 Gyatawya Road, Bahan, Rangoon, Burma.

Nyerere, Julius Kambarage, M.A.; Tanzanian politician; b. 1922; ed. Musoma Native Authority Primary School, Tabora Govt. Senior Secondary School, Makerere Coll., Uganda and Edinburgh Univ.
Teacher, St. Mary's Roman Catholic School, Tabora 46-49; student at Edinburgh Univ. 49-52; teacher, St. Francis' Roman Catholic Coll. 53-55; Founder-Pres. Tanganyika African Nat. Union (T.A.N.U.) 54-, Elected mem. Tanganyika Legislative Council 58, leader Elected Members Org. 58-60; Chief Minister 60-61; Prime Minister May 61-Jan. 62; Pres. of Tanganyika Dec. 62-64, of Tanzania 64-; Minister of External Affairs Dec. 62-March 63, Sept. 65-; Chancellor, Univ. of East Africa June 63-.
Publ. *Freedom and Unity—Uhuru na Umoja* 67.
State House, Dar es Salaam, Tanzania.

Nyers, Rezső; Hungarian politician; b. 23.
Printer until 45; now economist; Vice-Pres., Nat. Asscn. of Co-operatives 54-56; Minister of Food Industry 56-57; Pres. Nat. Asscn. of Co-operatives 57-60; Minister of Finance 60-62; Sec. Central Cttee. Hungarian Socialist Workers' Party 62-; Pres. State Econ. Cttee. 62-; mem. Political Cttee. Hungarian Socialist Workers' Party 66-.
Hungarian Socialist Workers' Party, Budapest, Hungary.

Nykopp, Johan Albert, M.A.; Finnish diplomatist and businessman; b. 27 May 1906; ed. Univ. of Helsinki.
Entered Foreign Service 30; Attaché, Moscow 31-35; Vice-Consul, Leningrad 35-37; Sec., Foreign Ministry 37-39, Head of Section 39-40; Sec. and later Counsellor, Moscow 40-41; Deputy Dir., Commercial Div., Foreign Ministry 45-47, Dir. 47-51; Minister to U.S.A. 51-55, Ambassador 55-58, Minister to Mexico and Cuba 51-58, to Colombia and Venezuela 54-58; Pres. Export and Import Licence Board of Finland 49-51; Gov. for Finland, Int. Bank for Reconstruction and Development 50-51; Man. Dir. of Finnish Employers' Confederation 58-61; Man. Dir., Tampella Ltd., Tampere 62-; Commdr. Order of the Lion; Knight, Order of White Rose (Finland); Commdr. Order of St. Olav (Norway); Commdr. Polonia Restituta (Poland); Commdr. de la Légion d'Honneur (France); Grand Officer Order of Orange Nassau (Neths.).
Tampella, Tampere, Finland.
Telephone: 21400.

Nylander, C. T.; Ghanaian educationalist and politician; b. 30 Sept. 1905; ed. Accra Methodist and Govt. Schools in Kumasi, and Accra Govt. Training Coll.
Govt. schoolteacher 26; Asst. Education Officer 52; elected to Legislative Assembly as mem. for Dangbe-Shai 54 and for Ga 56; Parliamentary Sec. Ministry of the Interior 56; Minister of Educ. 57-59; Minister of Health and Social Welfare 59; Minister of State for Defence 59-60; Chair. of Library Services, Ghana 60-61; High Commr. in Canada 61-64; Ambassador to Yugoslavia 64-66, to Liberia 66-.
Embassy of Ghana, Monrovia, Liberia; Home: Wetse Kojo Str. Korle Gonnio, P.O. Box 1260, Accra, Ghana.

Nyman, Olle; Swedish painter; b. 24 Dec. 1909; ed. Decorative School Philip Månsson and Royal Acad. Art School, Stockholm.
Professor Royal Acad. of Arts 53-63; mem. Arts Council of Govt. 56-58; mem. Swedish Royal Acad. 53; first one-man exhbn. Stockholm 50; represented in Museum of Modern Art, Stockholm and Museum of Art, Malmö; mem. Art Cttee. School of Stockholm 58-62, and Cttee. Thiel Gallery Stockholm.
Major works include: monumental wall decorations in Stockholm at Bromma Airport 36 and 55, City Hospital of Medicine 51, High School of Medicine 55, roof painting for Olaus Petri Church 58, tapestry for Handelsbanken 59, Skandinaviska banken 64.
Strandpromenaden 61, Saltsjö-Duynäs, Stockholm, Sweden.

Nypels, Leopold August, LL.D.; Netherlands judge; b. 29 Dec. 1888; ed. Univ. of Leiden.
Barrister Supreme Court 11; Judge Supreme Court 31; Vice-Pres. Supreme Court 50-58; Pres. Benelux Comm. for uniform law 58-66; Vice-Pres. State Comm. for int. private law 58-66; Vice-Pres. Council for Election 58-63, Pres. 63-66.
Vroenhof Warmond, Netherlands.
Telephone: Warmond 205.

Nyun, U; Burmese civil servant; b. 11; ed. Rangoon Univ., London School of Economics, London Univ. School of Oriental Studies.
Joined Indian Civil Service 31; after Burmese independence Under Sec. and later Sec., Ministry of Commerce and Industry 48-50; Chief, Industry and Trade Div., U.N. Econ. Comm. for Asia and the Far East (E.C.A.F.E.) 51-57, Dep. Exec. Sec. E.C.A.F.E. 57-59, Exec. Sec. Feb. 59-.
Economic Commission for Asia and the Far East, Sala Santitham, Bangkok, Thailand.

O

Oakes, John Bertram, A.M., LL.D.; American journalist; b. 23 April 1913; ed. Princeton Univ., and The Queen's Coll., Oxford.

Reporter *Trenton Times* 36-37; Political Reporter *Washington Post* 37-41; served U.S. Army 41-46; Editor, Review of the Week, Sunday *New York Times* 46-49, mem. Editorial Board 49-61, Editorial Page Editor 61-; Carnegie Foundation Travel Award, Europe and Africa 59; Columbia-Catherwood Award (for int. journalism) 61, George Polk Memorial Award 66 (as editor).

Publ. *The Edge of Freedom* 61.

New York Times, 229 West 43rd Street, New York 36, N.Y.; and 1120 Fifth Avenue, New York City, N.Y., U.S.A.

Telephone: TE1-4583 (Home).

Oakeshott, Michael Joseph, M.A.; British political scientist; b. 11 Dec. 1901; ed. Caius Coll., Cambridge.

Fellow of Caius Coll. 25-; Univ. Lecturer in History, Cambridge 29-49; Fellow of Nuffield Coll., Oxford 49-50; Prof. of Political Science, Univ. of London (London School of Economics) 50-; Muirhead Lecturer, Birmingham Univ. 53; Ludwig Mond Lecturer, Univ. of Manchester 59.

Publs. *Experience and its Modes* 33, 66, *A Guide to the Classics* 36, *Social and Political Doctrines of Contemporary Europe* 37, *Hobbes's Leviathan* (editor) 46, *The Voice of Poetry in the Conversation of Mankind* 59, *Rationalism and Politics* 62.

London School of Economics, Houghton Street, Aldwych, London, W.C.2, England.

Oakeshott, Walter Fraser, M.A.; British university official; b. 11 Nov. 1903; ed. Balliol Coll., Oxford.

Schoolmaster, Bec School 26-27, Merchant Taylors School 27-30, Winchester Coll. 30-38; High Master, St. Paul's School, London 38-46; Headmaster, Winchester Coll. 46-54; Rector of Lincoln Coll., Oxford 54-; Vice-Chancellor, Oxford Univ. 62-64; Rhind Lecturer, Edinburgh Univ. 56; Master, Skinners Co. 60-61; Trustee Pilgrim Trust and Vice-Pres. Bibliographical Soc., London, Pres. 66-.

Publs. *Men Without Work* (co-author) 38, *Artists of the Winchester Bible* 45, *Sequence of Medieval Art* 50, *Classical Tradition in Medieval Art* 59, *The Queen and the Poet* 60, *The Mosaics of Rome from the Third to the Fourteenth Centuries* 68.

Rector's Lodgings, Lincoln College, Oxford, England; Via della Mercede 21, Rome, Italy.

Oates, James Franklin, Jr., B.A., J.D.; American lawyer and insurance executive; b. 11 Nov. 1899; ed. Phillips Exeter Acad., and Princeton and Northwestern Univs.

Mem. law firm of Cutting, Moore & Sidley (Chicago) and its successor Sidley, Austin, Burgess & Harper 24-48; Chief Purchase Policy, Office of the Chief of Ordnance, Washington 42-44; Chair. and Chief Exec. Officer People's Gas, Light and Coke Co., Chicago 48-57; Pres. and Chair. Equitable Life Assurance Soc. of the U.S. 57-64, Chair. and Chief Exec. Officer 64-; Dir. Chase Manhattan Bank, First Nat. Bank of Chicago, Brooklyn Union Gas Co., New York Telephone Co., Colgate-Palmolive Co.; Trustee Princeton Univ., Northwestern Univ., George Williams Coll.

1285 Avenue of the Americas, New York 10019; Home: 201 East 62nd Street, New York, N.Y. 10021, U.S.A.

Obanye, Benedict Cyril Ikem, M.A., LL.B., D.P.A.; Nigerian lawyer and diplomatist; b. 20; ed. Christ the King Coll. Onitsha, Nigeria and Trinity Coll., Dublin, Ireland.

Chairman, Onitsha Urban County Council 58-61; Legal Adviser, E. Nigeria Local Govt. Asscn. 58-61; mem. E. Nigeria Legislature 60-61; law practice, Onitsha 52-62; High Commr. for Fed. of Nigeria in India 62-66.

c/o Ministry for Foreign Affairs, Lagos, Nigeria.

Obbink, Hendrik Willem, D.D.; Netherlands university professor; b. 20 March 1898; ed. Univs. of Utrecht and Groningen.

Minister of Dutch Reformed Church 23-39, serving at Ootmarsum, Geldermalsen, Middelburg and Utrecht; Hon. Lecturer Hebrew and Aramaic Univ. of Utrecht 32-39, Prof. of History of Religions and Egyptian Language 39-; Pres. Theological Section, Academic Council of the Netherlands; Knight Order of the Netherlands Lion.

Publs. *The Magic Significance of the Name, Especially in Egypt* 25, *The Book of Daniel* 32, *History of the Ancient Near East* 39 and 51, *Theological Considerations on the Old Testament* 38, *Cybele, Isis, Mithras, Oriental Religions in the Roman Empire* 65.

Dillenburgstraat 29, Utrecht, Netherlands.

Telephone: 030-17188.

Oberhammer, Vinzenz; Austrian museum director; b. 23 Nov. 1901; ed. Innsbruck Univ.

Asst. Tyrolean Folk Art Inst., Innsbruck 28; Asst. Innsbruck Inst. of Art History 29, Lecturer 36, Prof. 49, Vienna 63; Curator Ferdinandeum Museum, Innsbruck 38; First Dir. and Dir. of Pictures Gallery, Kunsthistorisches Museum, Vienna 55-66.

Publs. *Die Bronzestandbilder des Maximilian grabmales in der Hofkirche zu Innsbruck* 35, *Das Alter von Schloss Tirol* 48, *The Vienna Gallery* 64.

Kunsthistorisches Museum, Vienna I; and Anzenal Obj. 3/16, Vienna III, Austria.

Telephone: 6580615.

Oberth, Hermann Julius; German physicist and rocket pioneer; b. 25 June 1894; ed. Munich, Göttingen, Heidelberg and Klausenburg Univs.

Prof. S.L. Roth College, Mediasch 25-38; experiments with gasoline and liquid air rockets; further research on rockets for army and air force Vienna Technical Univ. 38-40, Dresden 40-41; Advisory Engineer Peenemünde rocket base 41-43, Westfälisch-Anhaltische Sprengstoff A.G. 43-45; further experiments on the Brienzersee (Switzerland) 49, for Italian Navy La Spezia 50-53, for U.S. Army Redstone Arsenal (Huntsville, Ala.) 55-58; R.E.P.-Hirsch Prize (French Astronautical Soc.) 29, Medal of German Soc. for Space Research 50, Diesel Medal (Asscn. of German Inventors) 54, American Astronautical Soc. Award 55, Edward Pendray Award 56, Bundesverdienstkreuz (I Klasse) of the German Federal Republic 61, and other decorations.

Publs. *Die Rakete zu den Planetenräumen* 23, *Wege zur Raumschiffahrt* 29, *Forschung und Jenseits* 32, *Menschen im Weltraum* 55, *Das Mondauto* 58, *Stoff und Leben* 59, *Katechismus der Uraniden* 66.

8501 Feucht bei Nürnberg, Untere Kellerstrasse 13, German Federal Republic.

Obote, (Apollo) Milton; Ugandan politician; b. 1924. Labourer, clerk, salesman, Kenya 50-55; founder-mem. Kenya African Union; mem. Uganda Nat. Congress 52-60; mem. Uganda Legislative Council 57-; formed and mem. of Uganda People's Congress 60-; Leader of the Opposition 61-62; Prime Minister 62-66; Minister of Defence and Foreign Affairs 63-65; assumed full powers of Govt. Feb. 66-; Pres. of Uganda April 66-.

Office of the President, Entebbe, Uganda.

O'Boyle, H.E. Cardinal Patrick A.; American ecclesiastic; b. 1896.
Ordained Priest 21; Archbishop of Washington 48-; created Cardinal by Pope Paul VI 67.
Archbishop's House, 1721 Rhode Island Avenue, Washington, D.C. 20036, U.S.A.

Obraztsov, Sergei Vladimirovich; Soviet puppet theatre artist; b. 5 July 1901; trained as an artist.
Acted in Music Studies Co., Moscow Arts Theatre; started puppet variety theatre 23, Head, Central Puppet Theatre 31-; numerous tours abroad; Vice-Pres. Union Int. des Marionnettistes (U.N.I.M.A.) 57-, Pres. Soviet Section 58-; People's Artist of U.S.S.R.; State Prize 46; Orders of Red Banner of Labour 46, 61.
Principal works include: *Kashtanka* (Chekhov) 35, *By a Wave of the Hand* (Tarakhovokaya) 36, *Aladdin's Magic Lamp* 40, *Night Before Christmas* (Gogol) 41, *King Deer* (Gozz) 43, *Merry Bear-Cubs* (Polivanova) 45, *Mowgli* (Kipling) 45, *Unusual Concert* 46, *Devil's Mill* (Drda) 53, *Divine Comedy* (Shtock) 61, *I-go-go* (Speransky) 64. Publ. *My Profession.*
Central Puppet Theatre, 32A Gorky Street, Moscow, U.S.S.R.

Obregón, Alejandro; Colombian painter; b. 4 June 1920; ed. Stonyhurst Coll., England, Middlesex School, Concord, and Museum School of Fine Arts, Boston.
Director, School of Fine Arts, Bogotá 49-51; one-man exhbns. Bogotá, Barranquilla, Cali, Paris, Milan, Washington, New York, Lima, Madrid, Barcelona, Munich, São Paulo and Rio de Janeiro; numerous prizes include 1st Nat. Prize, Guggenheim International 59; represented in numerous galleries including: Museum of Modern Art, New York, Phillips Gallery, Washington, Museo Nacional, Bogotá, Instituto Arte Contemporáneo, Lima, Museo de Arte Moderno, Bogotá, Museo Nacional, La Paz, Galerie Creuze, Paris, Galerie Buchholz, Munich, Galeria Profili, Milan and Instituto Cultura Hispánica, Madrid.
Apartado Aéreo 37, Barranquilla, Colombia.

Obreimov, Ivan Vasilevich; Soviet physicist; b. 94; ed. Petrograd Univ.
State Optical Inst. 19-24; Leningrad Physicotechnical Inst. 24-29; Ukrainian Physicotechnical Inst. 24-29, Dir. Ukrainian Physicotechnical Inst. 29-37; Corresp. mem. U.S.S.R. Acad. of Sciences 33-58, mem 58-; in Inst. of Elementary Organic Compounds, U.S.S.R. Acad. of Sciences 44-65; at Inst. of Gen. and Inorganic Chemistry 65-; State Prize 46, Vavilov Gold Prize, U.S.S.R. Acad. of Sciences 59.
Publs. *Application of Fresnel Diffraction in Physical and Technical Measurements* 45, *Identification of Hydro Carbons by Dispersion Curves* 55, *Double Refraction in Organic Crystals* 57, *Formation of Ultramicroscopic Heterogenity during Plastic Deformation of Rock Salt* 56, *On Digital Coding of Scientific Concepts* 61.
Institute of General and Inorganic Chemistry, Academy of Sciences, Lenin Prospekt 31, Moscow, U.S.S.R.

O'Brien, Conor Cruise, B.A., PH.D.; Irish writer and diplomatist; b. 3 Nov. 1917; ed. Trinity Coll., Dublin.
Entered Dept. of External Affairs of Ireland 44, Counsellor, Paris 55-56, Head UN Section and mem. Irish Del. to UN 56-60, Asst. Sec.-Gen., Dept. of External Affairs of Ireland 60; Rep. of Sec.-Gen. of UN in Katanga, May-Dec. 61; Vice-Chancellor, Univ. of Ghana 62-65; Regent's Prof. and Holder of Albert Schweitzer Chair. in Humanities, New York Univ. 65-.
Publs. *Maria Cross* (under pseud. Donat O'Donnell) 52, *Parnell and his Party* 57, *The Shaping of Modern Ireland* (ed.) 59, *To Katanga and Back* 62, *Conflicting Concepts of the United Nations* 64, *Writers and Politics* 65, *The United Nations: Sacred Drama* 67, *Murderous Angels* (play) 68.

New York University, Washington Square, New York, N.Y., U.S.A.; and Whitewater, Howth Summit, Dublin, Ireland.
Telephone: Dublin 322474.

O'Brien, Kate; Irish novelist and playwright; b. 3 Dec. 1897; ed. Univ. Coll., Dublin.
Publs. *Distinguished Villa, The Bridge, The Schoolroom Window* (plays); *Without My Cloak* (Hawthornden and James Tait Black prizes), *The Ante-Room, Mary Lavelle, Pray for the Wanderer, The Land of Spices, The Last of Summer, That Lady, The Flower of May, As Music and Splendour* (novels); *Farewell Spain* (travel); *Teresa of Avila* (biography); *English Diaries and Journals, My Ireland* 62, *Presentation Parlour* 63.
177 The Street, Boughton, Faversham, Kent, England.

O'Brien, Lawrence Francis, LL.B.; American government official; b. 7 July 1917; ed. Cathedral Grade and High Schools, Springfield, Mass., Northeastern Univ.
United States Army 43-45; O'Brien Realty Co. (family business), Springfield, Mass. 42-52; Board Pres. and Business Man. Western Mass. Hotel and Restaurant Health Fund 52-58; State Dir. of Org. for campaigns of John F. Kennedy for Senate of U.S., Mass. 52, 58; Public Relations work, Springfield 58-60; Nat. Dir. of Org. for Democratic Nat. Cttee. and for Kennedy-Johnson campaign 60; Special Asst. to Pres. of U.S. for Congressional Relations 61-65; Postmaster-Gen. 65-68; Hon. Doctorates from Western New England Coll., Northeastern Univ., Villanova Univ., St. Anselm's Coll.
c/o Post Office Department, 12th and Pennsylvania Avenue, Washington, D.C. 20260, U.S.A.

O'Brien, Sir Leslie Kenneth, G.B.E.; British banker; b. 8 Feb. 1908.
Entered Bank of England 27, apptd. Deputy Chief Cashier 51, Chief Cashier 55-62, Dir. 62-64, Deputy Gov. 64-66, Gov. 66-; Fellow and Vice-Pres. Inst. of Bankers 64.
35 Cheapside, London, E.C.2, England.
Telephone: 01-606-6666.

Ö Buachalla, Liam, M.COMM.; Irish Senator and university professor; b. 99; ed. St. Vincent's and St. Patrick's Schools, Drogheda, the Nat. Univ. of Ireland.
Former Pres. Gaelic League and Irish Technical Assen.; mem. Senate, Nat. Univ. of Ireland, and fmr. mem. Board, School of Celtic, The Dublin Institute for Advanced Studies; mem. Senate 39-, Chair. 58-; Prof. of Economics, Commerce and Accountancy, Univ. Coll., Galway (Nat. Univ. of Ireland), Dean, Faculty of Commerce; sometime Editor *Ar Aghaidh.*
Publs. *Bunādhas ne Trāchtala, Cuntais agus Cunta-saíocht, Bunādhas an Gheilleagair, Ard-Chuntasaíocht, Fordś Teoíriciulacht an Gheilleagair.*
Inis Ealga, Galway, Ireland.

Ocampo, Victoria, C.B.E., Argentine writer and publisher; ed. privately.
Founder Editor *Sur* (literary magazine) 31-; Head of Management, Teatro Colón, Buenos Aires 33; Founder, Argentine Women's Union 36, Pres. 36 and 38; Vice-Pres. PEN Int.; Pres. Comm. of Letters of Nat. Foundation for the Arts in Argentina; Palmes Académiques, Officier Légion d'Honneur, Commdr. des Arts et Lettres.
Publs. *De Francesca a Beatrice* 24, *La Laguna de los nenufares* 26, *Testimonios* (series I-VI) 35-47, *Domingos en Hyde Park* 36, *San Isidro* 41, *338.171 TE* 42, *Soledad sonora* 50, *El viajero y una de sus sombras* 51, *Lawrence de Arabia y otros ensayos* 51, *Virginia Woolf en su diario* 54, *Habla el algarrobo* 59, *Tagore en las barrancas de San Isidro* 61, *Antología de Jawaharlal Nehru: Seleccion y Prologo* 66; trans. Camus, Colette, William Faulkner,

Graham Greene, T. E. Lawrence, Dylan Thomas, John Osborne, Lanza del Vasto.
Revista Sur Viamonte 494 and Elortondo 1811, San Isidro, Buenos Aires, Argentina.
Telephone: (Office) 32-5148; 31-3220.

Ochab, Edward; Polish politician; b. 06; ed. Cracow School of Commerce and Jagiellonian Univ.
Joined Polish Communist Party 29; frequently imprisoned· co-organiser of Union of Polish Patriots and Polish Army in the Soviet Union 39-45; Minister of Public Admin. 45; Chair. Central Cttee. of Trade Unions 48-49; mem. Politburo, Central Cttee. Polish United Workers' Party 54-, First Sec. Central Cttee. 56; Minister of Agriculture 56-59; Sec. Central Cttee. Polish United Worker's Party 59-; Vice-Pres. Council of State 61-64, Pres. Aug. 64-April 68.
Polish United Workers Party, Warsaw, Poland.

Ochel, Willy, DIPL. ING.; German business executive; b. 27 Jan. 1903.
Chairman of Management Board, Hoesch A.G. (Dortmund); Pres. Dortmund Chamber of Commerce and Industry; Vice-Pres. Assen. of German Chambers of Industry and Commerce; Hon. Dr. Ing.
Karl-Trimerstrasse 12, Dortmund, German Federal Republic.

Ochiai, Eiichi, B.SC.; Japanese trade unionist; b. 15 Jan. 1916; ed. Yokohama Nat. Univ.
Mitsui Metal Mine Co. Ltd. 36-41, Toshiba Electric Co. 43-46; Adviser, Japan Assen. of Science and Technology 44-47; Pres. All-Japan Electric Industry Workers Unions 46-48; mem. Exec. Board Congress of Industrial Labour Union 46-49; Gen. Sec. Nat. Fed. of Industrial Orgs. 49-64; mem. Labour Problems Cttee. 61-64, Small and Medium Enterprise Retirement Counter-measure Cttee. 60-64; Dir. Tokyo Office, Int. Confederation of Free Trade Unions (ICFTU) and Special Rep. in Japan 64-; Trustee, Japan ILO Assen. 62-.
Publs. *Import of Foreign Capital and Production Struggle 49, Directory of Trade Union Administration 49, Earth of North America and Blood of Great Britain 59.*
Kuzumaki-machi, Iwate-gun, Iwate Prefecture, Japan.

Ochoa, Severo, M.D.; Spanish-born American biochemist; b. 24 Sept. 1905; ed. Madrid, Glasgow, Berlin, Heidelberg and London Univs.
Lecturer Univs. of Madrid, Heidelberg, Plymouth and Oxford 31-41; Instructor and Research Assoc. Washington Univ. St. Louis 41-42; Research Assoc. New York Univ. 42, Chair. Dept. of Biochemistry 54-; U.S. citizen 56-; Visiting Prof. Univ. of Calif. 49, Univ. of Brazil 56; Foreign mem. Royal Soc. (U.K.) 65; Nobel Prize in Medicine (with Kornberg) 59; Pres. Int. Union of Biochemistry 61-; numerous hon. degrees.
New York University School of Medicine, 550 First Avenue, New York, N.Y. 10016, U.S.A.

Ockrent, Roger Albert; Belgian diplomatist; b. 20 March 1914; ed. Brussels Univ., and Ecole Libre des Sciences Politiques, Paris.
Professor, Université Libre de Bruxelles; Director of Commission Bancaire 44-47; Sec. to the Prime Minister and Sec. of the Council of Ministers 47-48; Sec.-Gen. Administration Belge de Coopération Economique (Plan Marshall et Coopération Economique Européenne) 48-53; Permanent Rep., Head of Belgian Delegation and Vice-Chair. of the Council, OEEC 53-57; Chair. Exec. Cttee. of OEEC 57-61 and OECD 61-; Amb. 59-; Grand Officer of Leopold II, Commdr. de l'Ordre de la Couronne, Officier Ordre de Léopold, Chevalier Ordre de Léopold II avec palmes, Croix de Guerre 1940 avec palmes, Médaille de la Résistance, and several foreign decorations.
4 Square du Ranelagh, Paris 16e, France; and Club de la Fondation Universitaire, 11 Rue d'Egmont, Brussels, Belgium.

O'Connor, Basil, A.B., LL.B.; American lawyer; b. 8 Jan. 1892; ed. Dartmouth Coll., and Harvard Law School.
Admitted to Massachusetts Bar 15, New York Bar 16; practising lawyer since 15; with Cravath and Henderson, N.Y. 15-16; with Streeter and Holmes, Boston 16-19; practised in New York 19-25; partner in Roosevelt and O'Connor, New York 25-33; Senior member of law firm O'Connor and Farber 34-; Pres. American Nat. Red Cross 44-49, Pres. Nat. Health Council 57-58; Pres. Int. Medical Congress, Int. Poliomyelitis Congress, The Nat. Foundation, Georgia Warm Springs Foundation; Chair. Board of Trustees, Tuskegee Inst.; Trustee and Senior Vice-Pres. Salk Inst. for Biological Studies; also Dir. or Trustee of numerous business and philanthropic companies and asscns.; Medal for Merit (U.S.A.); Commdr. Nat. Order of Legion of Honour; Assoc. Knight Order of St. John of Jerusalem; many Red Cross medals and 16 foreign decorations; Hon. LL.D. (9 Univs.); Dr. Hum. Coll. of Wooster, Tuskegee Inst.
O'Connor and Farber, 120 Broadway, New York, N.Y. 10005, U.S.A.; and 35 East 76 Street, New York, N.Y. 10021, U.S.A.

O'Connor, Mgr. Martin John, A.B., S.T.D., J.C.D.; American ecclesiastic; b. 18 May 1900; ed. St. Thomas Coll., Scranton, Pa., American Coll., and Urban Coll. of Propaganda, Rome.
Served in U.S. Army 18; ordained priest 24; Asst. Pastor Scranton Cathedral 25-27, Sec. to Bishop and Chancellor of the Diocese 29-35, Diocesan Consultor 32-46, Pastor 34-43, Officialis 37-46, Vicar-Gen. 38-46; Titular Bishop of Thespiae and Auxiliary Bishop of Scranton 43; Pastor, St. Mary's Church, Wilkes Barre, Pa. 43; Rector, North American Coll., Rome 46-65; Pres. Pontifical Comm. for Motion Pictures 52-64, Cttee. for Press Relations for Vatican Council 63-, Pontifical Comm. for Communications Media 64-; mem Int. Holy Year Cttee. 50, Central Marian Year Cttee 56, Int. Marian Acad. 58; Asst. Pontifical Throne 53-; Titular Archbishop of Laodicea in Syria 59-; Consultor, Sacred Congregation for Seminaries and Universities 54-, Consultor, Sacred Propaganda Fide 60-; Apostolic Nuncio to Malta 65-; Vice-Pres. Post Conciliar Comm. for Apostolate of the Laity 66-; Chaplain *in gremio religionis* of the Sovereign Order of Malta 47, Kt. Commdr. with Star, Knights of the Holy Sepulchre 51, Grand Officer, Italian Order of Merit 57.
Apostolic Nunciature, Valletta, Malta.

Oda, Takio; Japanese diplomatist; b. 16 March 1907; ed. Tokyo Univ.
Successively Sec., Japanese Embassy, Wash.; Chief Econs. Dept., Cen. Post-War Liaison Office 46; Dir. Gen. Affairs, Commercial and Research Depts.; Dir. Int. Trade and Industry Bureau 50-52; Dir. Econs. Bureau of Foreign Ministry 52-54; Minister Plenipotentiary in Britain 54-57, Minister to Denmark 57-58, Amb. to Indonesia 58-62; Vice Foreign Minister 63-64; Chair. Board Int. Public Relations Co. 66-; Pres. Japan-Denmark Soc. 66.
Central Co-operative House, Apt. 410, 15 Ageba-cho, Shinjuku-ku, Tokyo, Japan.
Telephone: 260-5041 (Home); 501-7571 (Office).

Odawara, Daizo; Japanese iron executive; b. 10 Nov. 1892; ed. Onomichi Commercial School, Hiroshima Prefecture.
Kubota Iron Works 17-, Man. Dir. 45-50, Pres. Kubota Iron and Machinery Works Ltd. 50-; Pres. Osaka Chamber of Commerce and Industry 60-; Vice-Pres. Fed. of Econ. Orgs. of Japan.
1-517, 5-cho Uenoshiba-cho, Sakai, Osaka, Japan.

Oddi, Mgr. Silvio; Vatican diplomatist; b. 1910.
Ordained 33; Titular Archbishop of Mesembria 53; Apostolic Delegate in Palestine, Jerusalem and Cyprus 53-56; Apostolic Internuncio in Egypt and U.A.R.

56-62; Apostolic Nuncio in Belgium and Luxembourg 62-.
72 avenue de Tervueren, Brussels 4, Belgium.
Telephone: 34-20-31.

Odegaard, Charles (Edwin), PH.D.; American university president; b. 10 Jan. 1911; ed. Dartmouth Coll., and Harvard Univ.
Travelling Fellowship for study in France 34-35; Asst. in History, Radcliffe Coll. 35-37; Instructor to Prof. in History, Univ. of Illinois 37-48, Asst. for Humanities to Dean of Graduate Coll. 48; Exec. Dir. American Council of Learned Socs. 48-52; Prof. of History, Dean of Coll. of Literature, Science and Arts, Univ. of Michigan 52-58; Pres. Univ. of Washington, Seattle 58-; mem. U.S. Nat. Comm. UNESCO 49-55; Pres. Int. Council of Philosophy and Humanistic Studies 59-; U.S. Naval Reserve 42-46; mem. American Council on Educ. (fmr. Chair.), American Historical Asscn.
Publ. *Fideles and Vassi in the Carolingian Empire* 45.
806 36th Avenue E., Seattle 2, Washington, U.S.A.

Odelola, Amos Oyetunji, B.SC., M.A.; Nigerian economist; b. 4 March 1927; ed. Oduduwa Coll., Ife, Univ. of Hull, England, and Yale Univ., U.S.A.
Agricultural Asst., Dept. of Agriculture, Nigeria, then Statistical Asst., Dept. of Statistics; then Admin. Officer, W. Nigerian Govt.; Special Asst. to Sec.-Gen., Comm. for Technical Cooperation in Africa (CCTA) 63-64, Acting Sec.-Gen. 64-65; Exec. Sec. Scientific, Technical and Research Comm. of Org. for African Unity (OAU) (successor to CCTA) 65-.
Scientific, Technical and Research Commission of Organisation for African Unity, Nigerian Ports Authority Building, P.M.B. 2359, Marina, Lagos, Nigeria.

Odinga, A. Oginga; Kenyan politician; b. 11; ed. Alliance High School, Kikuyu, and Makerere Coll.
Former teacher; mem. Cen. Nyanza African District Council, Sakwa Location Advisory Council 47-49; mem. Legislative Council 57-; Vice-Pres. Kenya African Nat. Union (KANU) 60-66, founded Kenya People's Union 66; Minister for Home Affairs 63-64; Vice-Pres. of Kenya Dec. 64-April 66.
Publ. *Not Yet Uhuru* 67.
Kenya People's Union, Nairobi, Kenya.

Odlum, Floyd B., A.B., LL.B., M.B.A.; American foundation trustee; b. 30 March 1892; ed. Univ. of Colorado.
Chair. Atlas Corpn. 29-60; Chair. of Board R.K.O. Radio Pictures 37-48, Consolidated Vultee Aircraft Corpn. 47-53; Chair. Board of Trustees Lovelace Foundation for Medical Educ. and Research; Trustee Air Force Aid Soc.
80 Pine Street, New York City 5, N.Y., U.S.A.

O'Donnell, Phillip Kenneth, A.B.; American lawyer; b. 4 March 1924; ed. Harvard Univ. and Boston Coll. Law School.
Assistant Counsel, Senate Select Cttee. to Investigate Improper Activities in Labor-Management Relations 57-59; Special Asst. to Pres. of the U.S. 61-65; mem., Democratic Party.
5720 Massachusetts Avenue, N.W., Washington, D.C., U.S.A.

Odria, Gen. Manuel Arturo; Peruvian army officer and politician; b. 97; ed. Mil. Coll. Chorillos.
Commissioned 19; Instructor, Mil. Coll., Chorillos 19-27; Captain 27; Instructor, Staff Coll. 27-30, School of Naval Warfare 30; Major 30, commanded Infantry Battalion, Chorillos Mil. Coll.; Lieut. Colonel 36, later Colonel; Deputy Controller and later Controller, Staff Coll. 41; Brigadier Gen. and Chief of Army General Staff 46-47; Minister of Home Affairs 47; commanded revolutionary army in coup d'état and assumed leadership 48; Pres. Mil. Junta of Govt.; Constitutional Pres. 50-56; leader of Unión Nacional Odriísta (U.N.O.) and the Party's Presidential candidate at elections 62, 63.
Unión Nacional Ordriísta, Jirón Callao 535, Lima, Peru.

O'Driscoll, Timothy Joseph, B.A.; Irish tourist official; b. 6 July 1908; ed. Presentation Coll., Cork, and Trinity Coll., Dublin.
Irish Civil Service 28-56; Irish Rep. to Int. Civil Aviation Org. 46-48, Org. for European Econ. Co-operation (OEEC) 48-50; Chair. Irish Export Board 51-55; Amb. to Netherlands 55-56; Dir.-Gen. Irish Tourist Board; mem. Board Irish Airlines; Pres. Int. Union of Official Tourist Orgs. 61-63; Pres. European Travel Comm. 65-; Consultant on Tourism to UN 67-68; Chair. OECD Tourism Cttee. 64-66; Order of Prince Henry the Navigator (Portugal); Commdr. Order of George I (Greece).
Bord Failte (Irish Tourist Board), Baggot Street Bridge, Dublin; Home: Evergreen Lodge, Ballybrack, Co. Dublin, Ireland.
Telephone: Dublin 65871 (Office); Dublin 803459 (Home).

Oduber, Daniel; Costa Rican diplomatist and politician; b. 21; ed. Colegio Seminario, San José, Liceo de Costa Rica, Universidad de Costa Rica, McGill Univ. and Univ. of Paris.
Secretary-Gen. of Junta 48-49; Special Rep. to UN 49; Chief of Propaganda, Nat. Liberation Party 51-53, Sec.-Gen. 56-58; mem. Legislative Assembly, Head of Parl. Group of Nat. Liberation Party 58-62; Candidate for Pres. of Republic 61; Minister of Foreign Affairs May 62-Feb. 66.
c/o Ministry of Foreign Affairs, San José, Costa Rica, Central America.

Oehlert, Benjamin Hilborn, B.S., LL.B.; American diplomatist; b. 13 Sept. 1909; ed. Univ. of Pennsylvania.
Attorney, Mexican Claims Div., Dept. of State 35-38; Asst. Counsel, Coca Cola Co. 38-42, Asst. to Pres., Vice-Pres. 42-48, 53-65, Senior Vice-Pres. 65-67; Pres. Minute Maid Co. 61-65; Vice-Pres. W. R. Grace & Co. 48-53; Amb. to Pakistan 67-.
Publ. *The Restatement in the Courts Eminent Domain in Pennsylvania.*
American Embassy, Rawalpindi, Pakistan.
Telephone: 64975.

Öellers, Fritz, DR.JUR.; German lawyer and diplomatist; b. 25 July 1903; ed. Univs. of Halle and Marburg.
Practised law and served as Dir. on several industrial enterprises 30-51; mem. Economic Council, Frankfurt 48; mem. Bundestag 49-51; Ambassador to Brazil 51-56; Ambassador to Turkey 56-59; co-founder Freie Demokratische Partei.
Frundsbergstrasse 36, Strasslach (OBB), German Federal Republic.
Telephone: 08170/627.

Oelman, Robert Schantz, A.B.; American business executive; b. 9 June 1909; ed. Dartmouth Coll., and Univ. of Vienna.
With Nat. Cash Register Co., Dayton, Ohio 33-, Asst. to Pres. 42-45, Asst. Vice-Pres. 45-46, Vice-Pres. 46-50, Exec. Vice-Pres. 50-57, Pres. 57, Chair. and Pres. 62, Chair. and Chief Exec. Officer 64-, Dir. 48-; Dir. Koppers Co. Inc., Ohio Bell Telephone Co., Procter & Gamble Co., Winters Nat. Bank & Trust Co., First Nat. City Bank, New York, etc.; fmr. Vice-Pres. and Dir. Nat. Asscn. of Manufacturers; fmr. Pres. and Dir. Business Equipment Manufacturers Asscn.; Trustee Dartmouth Coll.; mem. Nat. Industrial Conf. Board; Hon. H.H.D. Univ. of Dayton; Hon. LL.D. Miami Univ., Hon. M.A. Dartmouth Coll., Hon. L.H.D. Wilmington Coll.
235 Park Road, Dayton, Ohio 45419, U.S.A.

Oelssner, Fred; German social scientist; b. 27 Feb. 1903; ed. elementary school; studied social sciences in Moscow.
Member C.P. 20; imprisoned for political reasons 23-25; emigrated to France and U.S.S.R. during Nat. Socialist

regime; mem. Deutsche Akad. der Wissenschaften, Dir. Inst. for Econ. Sciences; Vaterländischer Verdienstorden (gold), Nat. Prizewinner.
Leipsiger Strasse 3/4, 108 Berlin, Germany.
Telephone: 22-04-41.

O'Faoláin, Seán, M.A., A.M., D.LITT.; Irish writer; b. 1900; ed. Nat. Univ. of Ireland, Univ. of Dublin (Trinity College) and Harvard Univ.
Commonwealth Fellow 26-28; John Harvard Fellow 28-29; Lecturer in English Boston Coll. 29, St. Mary's Coll. Strawberry Hill 29-33; Dir. Arts Council of Ireland 57-59.
Publs. *Lyrics and Satires from Tom Moore* 29, *Midsummer Night Madness* 32, *Life Story of De Valera* 33, *A Nest of Simple Folk* 33, *Constance Markievicz: a Biography* 34, *There's a Birdie in the Cage* 35, *A Born Genius* 36, *Bird Alone* 36, *The Autobiography of Wolfe Tone* 37, *A Purse of Coppers* 37, *The Silver Branch* (translations) 37, *King of the Beggars* (biography) 38, *She Had to Do Something* (play) 38, *An Irish Journey* 39, *Come Back to Erin* 40, *The Great O'Neill* (biography) 42, *Story of Ireland* 43, *Teresa* 47, *The Irish* 48, *The Short Story* 48, *Summer in Italy* 49, *Newman's Way* (biography) 52, *South to Sicily* 53, *The Vanishing Hero* 56, *The Stories of Seán O'Faoláin* 58, *I Remember, I Remember* 62, *Vive Moi* 65, *The Heat of the Sun* (short stories) 66.
Knockaderry, Killiney, Co. Dublin, Ireland.

Offelen, Jacques Van; Belgian politician; b. 18 Oct. 1916.
Professor at Inst. Supérieur de Commerce, Antwerp; mem. Chamber of Representatives 58-; Minister for External Trade 58-61; Minister for Econ. Affairs 66-; Parti pour la liberté et le progrès.
Publs. *La lutte d'Anvers pour la liberté du commerce des céréales* 45, *Chronique du plan Marshall* 49, *Deux Ans de politique économique* 56, *Pouvoir et Liberté* 62.
Ministry for Economic Affairs, Brussels; and Rue Roberts Jones 64, Brussels 18, Belgium.

Offroy, Raymond, LL.D.; French diplomatist; b. 3 May 1909.
Attaché Bucharest 37, Sec. 38; Sec. Athens 40, Acting Consul-Gen. Salonika 41; Head of Admin. Services Free French Foreign Office, French Nat. Cttee.'s rep. to Inter-Allied War Crimes Comm. 41 and to Netherlands Govt. 42; Acting Counsellor of Embassy 42; Diplomatic Asst. to Gen. Catroux mission to Gen. Giraud, Algiers 43; Deputy Sec. to French Provisional Govt., Gen. Sec. to Economic Cttee. 44; Head of Information and Press Section, Ministry of Foreign Affairs 45-49; Consul-Gen. Milan 49-52; Diplomatic Adviser to High Commr. in Indo-China 51, Deputy Commr.-Gen. 53; Asst. Del. to Geneva Conf. 54; Ambassador to Thailand 54-57; French Rep. to S.E.A.T.O. 55-57; Dir. of Central Information Office, Paris 57-59; Head, Franco-African Community Dept., Ministry of Foreign Affairs, Chair. Franco-African Community, Cttee. of Foreign Affairs 59-60; Ambassador to Nigeria 60-61, to Mexico 61-65; Député de la Seine Maritime 67; Officier Légion d'Honneur.
18 avenue Friedland, Paris 8e, France.
Telephone: Wagram 18-11.

O'Flaherty, Liam; Irish novelist; b. 96 in the Aran Islands; ed. Rockwell Coll., Blackrock Coll., and Nat. Univ.
Publs. *Thy Neighbour's Wife, The Black Soul, The Informer, The Tent and other stories* 26, *Mr. Gilhooley* 26, *The Life of Tim Healy* 27, *The Assassin* 28, *The Mountain Tavern and other stories* 29, *A Tourist's Guide to Ireland* 29, *The House of Gold* 29, *Two Years* 30, *I Went to Russia* 31, *The Puritan* 32, *Skerrett* 32, *Shame the Devil* 34, *Hollywood Cemetery* 35, *Famine* 37, *Short Stories of Liam O'Flaherty* 37, *Land* 46, *Two Lovely Beasts* (short stories) 48.
c/o A. D. Peters, 10 Buckingham Street, London, W.C.2, England.

Ofori-Atta, Aaron Eugene Asante; Ghanaian teacher, lawyer and politician; b. 5 Dec. 1912; ed. Mfantsipim School, Achimota School, Trinity Coll., Dublin, and Middle Temple, London.
Vice-Principal, Akim Abuakwa State Coll. 36-39, Principal 39-45; mem. Middle Temple, London 47, called to Bar 51; fmr. Minister of Communications and Minister of Local Govt., Ghana; Minister of Justice 61-65; Speaker of Nat. Assembly 65-66.
Parliament House, Accra, Ghana.

Öftering, Heinz Maria, DR. JUR., DR.-ING; German businessman; b. 1903; ed. Univs. of Munich, Heidelberg and Paris.
Regierungsrat in German Ministry of Finance 35-45; Pres. Court of Accounts, Rheinland-Pfalz 45-50; Ministerial Dir. German Federal Finance Ministry 50-57; Pres. and Chair. of Board of German Federal Railways 57-60; co-publisher *Deutsche Steuerzeitung* and *Steuer und Wirtschaft*; Hon. Prof. Univ. of Mainz.
Publ. *Grosser Lohnsteuerkommentar* 40.
Bernusstrasse 22, Frankfurt-am-Main, German Federal Republic.

Ogawa, Masaru, B.A., M.A.; Japanese journalist; b. 1915; ed. Univ. of California at Los Angeles, Tokyo Imperial, Columbia Univs.
Domei News Agency 41-46; Kyodo News Service 46-48; *The Japan Times* 48-, Chief, political section 49, Asst. Managing Editor 50, Chief Editor 52, Managing Editor 58-64, Dir. 59-, Exec. Editor 64-; Lecturer, Tokyo Univ. 54-58.
2, 14-banchi, 5-chome, Mejiro, Toshima-ku, Tokyo, Japan.

Ogbu, Edwin Ogebe; Nigerian diplomatist; b. 28 Dec. 1926; ed. Bethune-Cockman Coll., Florida, and Stanford Univ., California, U.S.A.
Assistant Sec. Ministry of Finance, Kaduna 57; Sec. Students Affairs, Nigerian High Comm., London 60; Sec. Fed. Public Service Comm. 60-62; Perm. Sec. Fed. Ministry of Works 62-63, Fed. Ministry of Finance 63-66, Fed. Ministry of External Affairs 66-68; Perm. Rep. to UN 68-.
Permanent Mission of Nigeria to the United Nations, 757 Third Avenue, New York, N.Y. 10017, U.S.A.

Ogdon, John (Andrew Howard); British concert pianist; b. 27 Jan. 1937; ed. Manchester Grammar School and Royal Manchester Coll. of Music.
Concert appearances in London, Spoleto, Edinburgh, Moscow, Milan, Antwerp; Michaelangeli Festival, Brescia 66; Liszt Prize, London 61, Tchaikovsky Award, Moscow 62; Harriet Cohen Int. Award.
8 Highfield Gardens, London, N.W.11, England.

Ogg, Sir William Gammie, M.A., B.SC., B.SC. (Agric.), LL.D., PH.D., F.R.S.E.; British chemist; b. 2 Nov. 1891; ed. Aberdeen Univ., and Christ's Coll., Cambridge.
Research Officer Aberdeen Univ. Agricultural Dept. 14; Chemist H.M. Explosives Factory Oldbury 14-16; Chief Chemist and Works Man. Explosives Factory Greetland 16-18; Research Fellow Board of Agriculture for Scotland 19-20, working in U.S. and Canada; Research worker Christ's Coll., Cambridge 20-24; Advisory Officer in Soils, Edinburgh and East of Scotland Coll. of Agriculture 24-30; First Dir. Macaulay Inst. for Soil Research and Research Lecturer in Soil Science, Aberdeen Univ. 30-43; Dir. Rothamsted Experimental Station and Consultant Dir. Commonwealth Bureau of Soil Science 43-58; Foreign corresp. French Acad. of Agriculture, foreign mem. Royal Acad. of Agriculture of Sweden; Corresp. mem. All-Union Acad. of Agri-

cultural Sciences of the U.S.S.R.; Hon. Fellow Royal Agricultural Soc. of England.
Arnhall by Edzell, Angus, Scotland.
Telephone: Edzell 400.

Ogilvie, Sir William Heneage, K.B.E., M.A., M.D., M.CH.; F.R.C.S.; HON. F.A.C.S., HON. F.R.C.S.(C.), HON. F.R.A.C.S.; British surgeon; b. 14 July 1887; ed. Clifton Coll., New Coll. Oxford, and Guy's Hospital.
Surgeon Urgency Cases Hospital France 15-17, Royal Army Medical Corps 17-20; Surgical Registrar Guy's Hospital 20, Senior Demonstrator of Anatomy 22, Asst. Surgeon 25, Surgeon and Teacher Clinical Surgery 32-52, consulting Surgeon 52-; Hunterian Prof. Royal Coll. Surgeons 24, Vice-Pres. 45; Consulting Surgeon to Guy's Hospital and Royal Masonic Hospital; Examiner in Surgery, Oxford and Cambridge Univs.; Col. Army Medical Service 40, Brig. 42, Major-Gen. 43; Consulting Surgeon E. Africa Force, Middle East Force, Eastern Command; Editor *The Practitioner* March 46-; Hon. M.S. (Fouad I), Hon. LL.D. (Witwatersrand).
Publs. *Recent Advances in Surgery, Treatment of Fractures, Forward Surgery in Modern War* 44, *Surgery, Orthodox and Heterodox* 49, *Hernia* 59, *No Miracles Among Friends* 59, *Fifty* 62, *The Tired Business Man* 62.
18 Clifton Road, London S.W.19, England.

Ogilvy, David Mackenzie, C.B.E.; British advertising executive; b. 23 June 1911; ed. Fettes Coll., Edinburgh, and Oxford Univ.
Associate Director Audience Research Inst., Princeton 39; Second Sec. British Embassy, Washington 42; founder 48, since Pres., Ogilvy, Benson and Mather, New York; Chair. Ogilvy & Mather, London, March 65-; Dir. New York Philharmonic Symphony Society.
Publ. *Confessions of an Advertising Man* 64.
521 East 84th Street, New York, N.Y. 10028, U.S.A.

Ogmore, 1st Baron, cr. 50, of Bridgend; **Lieut.-Col. David Rees-Williams,** P.C., T.D., J.P.; British lawyer and politician; b. 22 Nov. 1903; ed. Mill Hill School, Univ. of Wales.
Qualified as solicitor with honours 29; fmrly. practised in Straits Settlements as mem. Bar; Lieut.-Colonel R.A. Staff Officer 1st Grade; M.P. for South Croydon 45-50; mem. Govt. Mission to Sarawak 46 on cession of Sarawak to H.M. the King; Chair. Burma Frontier Areas Cttee. of Enquiry 47; Parl. Under-Sec. of State, Colonial Office 47-50; Parl. Under-Sec. of State for Commonwealth Relations 50-51; mem. U.K. Del. to UN Assembly 50; Privy Counsellor 51; Minister of Civil Aviation 51; Chair. African Defence Facilities Conf., Nairobi 51; mem. Nigerian Bar 56; Order of Agga Maha Thray Sithu (Burma) 56, Panglima Mangku Negara (Malaya) 59; Justice of the Peace for London; Pres. of the Liberal Party 63-64; Dir. Property Owners Building Soc., and other companies; Chair. South of England Housing Soc. Ltd.
47 Abingdon Court, Kensington, London, W.8, England.
Telephone: WEStern 4963.

O'Gorman, Juan; Mexican architect and artist; b. 6 July 1905; ed. National Univ. of Mexico.
With C. Obregon Santacilia and J. Villagran, Architects 26-29; private architectural practice 29-32; Prof. Polytechnic Inst., Mexico City 32-46; Head, Dept. of Architecture, Secr. of Public Educ. 32-35; Visiting critic School of Architecture, Yale Univ. 66; Works include: murals for Mexico City Airport, Patzcuaro (Mich.) Library; mosaics for Library of Univ. of City of Mexico, Secr. of Public Works and Communications buildings; stone mosaics, mural of Cuauhtemoc in the Hôtel Posada de la Misión, in Taxco Guerrero; and murals in Castle of Chapultepec, Mexico City, Mexican Inst. of Social Security, Mexico City and Banco Internacional, Mexico City; paintings in Museum of Modern Art, New York City, Palace of Fine Arts, Mexico City; Elias Sourasky Nat. Art Award 67.
Calzado San Jeronimo 162, San Angel, Mexico 20, D.F., Mexico.
Telephone: 48-32-90.

Ogundipe, Brig. Babafemi Olatunde; Nigerian diplomatist; b. 6 Sept. 1924; ed. Wesley and Banham Memorial Schools, Port Harcourt and Imperial Defence Coll., London.
Joined the army 43, service in Burma and India until 46; commissioned 53; served Germany 53-54; Brigade Maj. in Congo 60-63, Chief of Staff of UN Forces May-Dec. 63; Mil. Adviser, London 66; Chief of Staff, Nigerian Mil. Forces 66; High Commr. in U.K. 66-; River Benue Star.
Nigeria High Commission, 9 Northumberland Avenue, London, W.C.2, England.

Ohara, Soichiro, PH.D.; Japanese business executive; b. 29 June 1909; ed. Tokyo Univ.
President, Kurashiki Rayon Co. 39-47, 48-; Vice Dir.-Gen., Price Board 47-48; Pres. Kurashiki Cotton Spinning Co. 41-47, Dir. 53-; Dir. Kei-Han-Shin Kyuko Railway Co. 50-, Daimaru Department Store Inc. 55-, Asahi Broadcasting Co. 59-; mem. Cttee. Econ. Council 55-; Chair. Livelihood Study Council 64-; mem. Cttee. Social Devt. Council 65-, Agricultural Policy Council 63-, Employment Policy Council 65-; Chair. Ohara Art Gallery 64-, Japan Austria Soc. 57-, Japan Folkscraft Asscn.
Publ. *Man-Made Fibre Industry* 61.
Shinhankyu Building, 8 Umeda, Kita-ku, Osaka, Japan.

Ohashi, Takeo, LL.B.; Japanese lawyer and politician; b. 04; ed. Tokyo Imperial Univ.
House of Reps. 43-; Minister of State in charge of Nat. Police Reserve and Nat. Rural Police 50-53; concurrently Attorney-Gen. 50-51; Adviser, Japanese Del. Int. Labour Conf., Geneva 37; mem. Educational Area Planning Cttee., Sec. Local Govt. System Investigation Council and mem. Public Works Cttee. 46; law practice 48-62; Minister of Labour 62-64, of Transport 66-67; mem. Jiyuto (Liberal) Party.
c/o Ministry of Transport, Tokyo, Japan.

Ohira, Masayoshi; Japanese politician; b. 12 March 1910; ed. Tokyo Commercial Coll.
Ministry of Finance 36, Supt. Yokohama Revenue Office 37-38, Private Sec. to Minister of Finance 49; mem. House of Reps. 52-; Chief Cabinet Sec. 60-62; Minister for Foreign Affairs 62-64; Chair. Policy Board, Liberal Democratic Party Nov. 67-.
Publs. Essays: *Sugao no Daigishi* (A Parliamentarian As He Is) 54, *Random Thoughts on Public Finance* 56.
105 Komagome Hayashi-cho, Bunkyo-ku, Tokyo, Japan.

Ohkami, Hajime; Japanese investment executive; b. 97; ed. Tokyo Univ.
Yamaichi Securities Co. Ltd. 21-, Dir. 35-, Man. Dir. 38-43, Senior Man. Dir. 43-47, Exec. Vice-Pres. 47-54, Pres. 54-.
1-3 Kabuto-cho, Nihonbashi, Chuo-ku, Tokyo, Japan.

Ohno, Katsumi; Japanese diplomatist; b. 05; ed. Kyoto Imperial University.
Chief Japanese diplomatic mission to the Philippines 53; Min. to Austria 55-56; Ambassador to Germany 56-57; Vice-Min. of Foreign Affairs 57-58; Ambassador to Great Britain 58-64.
c/o Ministry of Foreign Affairs, Tokyo, Japan.

Ohta, Kaoru, B.ENG.; Japanese chemical engineer and trade unionist; b. 12; ed. Osaka Imperial Univ.
Dai-Nippon Patent Fertilizer Co. Ltd. 35-39; Nitrogen Factory, Ube Kosan Co. Ltd. 39-; Chair. Ube Nitrogen Workers' Union 46-49; Vice-Pres. Nat. Federation of Chemical Industry Workers' Unions 49-50; Pres. Nat.

Confederation of Ammonium Sulphate Industry Workers' Unions; Pres. Confederation of Synthetic Chemical Industrial Workers' Unions 50-; Vice-Pres. Gen. Council of Trade Unions of Japan (SOHYO) 52-53, 55-58, Pres. 58-66.
Publs. *On Trade Unions, Today's Labour Movement, On Administration of Trade Unions, Industrial Security Wage, Labour Movement in Japan.*
c/o Sohyo Kaikan, Shiba Park, Minato-ku, Tokyo, Japan.

Ohtaka, Masato, B.ARCH.; Japanese architect; b. 8 Sept. 1923; ed. Tokyo Univ.
At Maekawa-Kunio Architecture Design Office 49-61; established Ohtaka Architecture Design Office 62; also Lecturer Tokyo and Waseda Univs.
Works include Plan for new town at Tama, Tokyo, Chiba Public Hall and Agricultural Co-operative Asscns.
Yoyogi Building, 5-18 Sendagaya, Shibuya-ku, Tokyo, Japan.

Ohya, Kazuo, LL.B.; Japanese business executive; b. 8 Sept. 1902; ed. Kyoto Univ.
Sumitomo Ltd. Partnership Co. 28; Man. Dir. Nissin Chemical Co. Ltd. (later Sumitomo Chemical Co. Ltd.) 47-56, Senior Man. Dir. Sumitomo Chemical Co. 56-63, Pres. 63-65, Counsellor 65-; Dir. Japan Exlan Co. Ltd. 63-, Chair. of Board 65-; Pres. Japan Lactam Ltd. 63-; Pres. Osaka Labour Standard Asscn. 63; Perm. Dir. Japan Fed. of Employers' Asscn. 63; Blue Ribbon Medal.
Office: Japan Exlan Co. Ltd., 1-25 Dojima Hamadori 1-chome Kita-ku, Osaka; Home: 1478-1 Furushinden, Sumiyoshi-cho, Higashinada-ku, Kobe, Japan.
Telephone: Osaka (06)-344-1451 (Office); Kobe (078)-85-5864 (Home).

Ohya, Shinzo; Japanese executive; b. 5 July 1894; ed. Tokyo Coll. of Commerce.
President Teikoku Rayon Co. Ltd. 45-48, 56-, name changed to Teijin Ltd. 62-; mem. House of Councillors 47-56; Minister of Int. Trade and Industry 48-49; Minister of Finance 48-49; Minister of Transportation 49-50; Pres. Japan Chemical Fibres Asscn. 48; Counsellor Osaka Chamber of Commerce and Industry 57-; Dir. of Fed. of Econ. Orgs. 58-, Japan Fed. of Employers' Asscns. 58-, Japanese Nat. Cttee. of Int. Chamber of Commerce 59-; Vice-Chair. Int. Protection Cttee. of Int. Law, Int. Chamber of Commerce 61-; Counsellor Italy-Japan Soc. 63-; Vice-Pres. France-Japan Soc. 64-; several decorations.
1-71, 1-chome, Tamagawa Todoroki-cho, Setagaya-ku, Tokyo, Japan.

Oistrakh, David Fyodorovich (father of Igor Oistrakh, q.v.); Soviet violinist; b. 1908; ed. Odessa Musical-Dramatic Inst.
Lecturer Moscow Conservatoire 34-39, Prof. 39-; 1st prize All-Ukraine competition 30, 1st prize Leningrad All-Union competition, 2nd prize Wienawski Int. competition 35, 1st prize Ysaye Int. competition 37; People's Artist of U.S.S.R.; awards include State Prize, Lenin Prize and Order of Lenin; Commdr. of Lion of Finland.
State Conservatoire, 13 Herzen Street, Moscow, U.S.S.R.

Oistrakh, Igor Davidovich (son of David Oistrakh, q.v.); Soviet violinist; b. 1931; ed. Music School and State Conservatoire, Moscow.
Student State Conservatoire 49-55; many foreign tours, several concerts with father David Oistrakh; 1st prize, Violin competition, Budapest 52, Wieniawski competition, Poznań; Honoured Artist of R.S.F.S.R.
State Conservatoire, 13 Herzen Street, Moscow, U.S.S.R.

Oittinen, Reino Henrik, M.A.; Finnish politician and civil servant; b. 26 July 1912.
Principal of Workers' Acad. 45-50; Minister of Educ. 48-50, 51-53, 57-58, 63-64, 66-68; Dir.-Gen. Nat. Board of Schools 50-; Deputy Prime Minister 57-58, 64, 66-68; Chair. Finnish Nat. Comm. for UNESCO 57-65, mem. 66-; prominent in workers' educational activities; mem. of numerous state and municipal cttees.; mem. Social Democratic Party; Hon. Dr. Pedagogics.
Kouluhallitus, Etelä Esplanadik. 16, Helsinki 13, Finland.

Oizerman, Teodor Ilyich; Soviet philosopher; b. 1914; ed. Chernyshevsky Inst. of History, Philosophy and Literature.
Industrial worker 30-33; Postgraduate 38-41; Army Service 41-46; Asst. Prof. Moscow Inst. of Econs. 46-47; Asst. Prof., Prof. Moscow Univ. 47-, Head of Chair. 54-; Corresp. mem. U.S.S.R. Acad. of Sciences 66-.
Publs. Works on German classical philosophy, history of Marxist philosophy, modern Western philosophy, methodological problems of history and philosophy.
U.S.S.R. Academy of Sciences, 14 Lenin Prospekt, Moscow, U.S.S.R.

Ojima, Arakaku; Japanese business executive; b. 9 Feb. 1893; ed. Tokyo Univ.
With Ministry of Commerce and Industry; fmr. Dir. Japan Steel Works; now Chair., Yawata Iron and Steel Co.; Counsellor, Bank of Japan; mem. Econ. Council of Japan.
24 Hachiyamamachi, Shibuya-ku, Tokyo, Japan.

Ojukwu, Lieut.-Col. Chukwuemeka Odumegwu, M.A.; Nigerian army officer and politician; b. 4 Nov. 1933; ed. C.M.S. Grammar School and King's Coll., Lagos, Epsom Coll., U.K., Lincoln Coll., Oxford, Eaton Hall Officer Cadet School, U.K. and Joint Services Staff Coll., U.K.
Administrative Officer, Nigerian Public Service 56-57; joined Nigerian Army 57; at Nigerian Army Depot, Zaria 57; army training in U.K. 57-58; joined 5th Battalion Nigerian Army 58; Instructor, Royal West African Frontier Force Training School, Teshie 58-61; returned to 5th Battalion Nigerian Army 61; Maj. Army H.Q. 61; Deputy Asst. Adjutant and Quartermaster-Gen. Kaduna Brigade H.Q. 61; Congo Emergency Force 62; Lieut.-Col. and Quartermaster-Gen. 63-64; Commdr. 5th Battalion, Kano 64-66; Mil. Gov. of E. Nigeria 66-67; proclaimed Head of State of Republic of Biafra (E. Region of Nigeria) May 67-.
P.O. Box 1088, Enugu, Eastern Nigeria.

Okada, Kenzo; Japanese artist; b. 28 Sept. 1902; ed. Tokyo Fine Arts Univ.
Works in Guggenheim Museum, Museum of Modern Art (both in New York City); in Dunn Int. Exhibition, Tate Gallery, London 63; Campana Memorial Prize, Art Inst. of Chicago 54, Logan Prize 55.
51 West 11th Street, New York City 11, N.Y., U.S.A.

Okada, Toshio; Japanese business executive; b. 9 Feb. 1896; ed. Tokyo Univ. of Mercantile Marine.
President, Osaka Shosen Kaisha (Osaka Mercantile Steamship Co.).
1 Sozec-ho, Kitaku, Osaka; 167 Hase, Kamakura City, Kanagawa, Japan.

Okasha, Sarwat, D. ès L.; United Arab Republic (Egyptian) diplomatist, politician and banker; b. 21; ed. Military Coll. and Cairo Univ.
Cavalry Officer 39; took part in Palestine war 48-49; Mil. Attaché, Berne 53-54, Paris 54-56; Counsellor in Presidency of Repub. 56-57; Egyptian Ambassador to Italy 57-58; U.A.R. Minister of Culture and Nat. Guidance 58-62; Chair. and Man. Dir. Nat. Bank 62-66; Deputy Prime Minister and Minister of Culture 66-67; Minister of Culture 67-; Pres. of Supreme Council for

Literature, Art and Social Sciences; numerous awards and foreign decorations.
Publs. Nineteen works (including translations) 42-62.
Ministry of Culture, Cairo, United Arab Republic.

O'Keeffe, Adrian Francis; American business executive; b. 09; ed. Roxbury Latin School and Dartmouth Coll.
Employed by First National Stores 30-, elected Pres. 48-67, Chair. of the Board 67-; Dir. New England Mutual Life Assurance Co., First Nat. Bank of Boston, The Gillette Co.
Home: 1415 Commonwealth Ave., West Newton, Mass.; Office: 5 Middlesex Ave., Somerville, Mass., U.S.A.

Okita, Saburo; Japanese economist; b. 3 Nov. 1914; ed. Tokyo Univ.
Served in Ministry of Posts 37-39, Ministry of Greater East Asia 39-45, Ministry of Foreign Affairs 45-47, Econ. Stabilization Board, Chief Research Section 47; UN Econ. Comm. for Asia and the Far East 52; Chief, Econ. Co-op. Unit, Econ. Planning Agency 53, Dir. Planning Bureau 57-, Dir. Devt. Bureau 62-63; Pres Japan Econ. Research Centre and Special Adviser to the Minister of Econ. Planning Agency 64-; Hon. Dr. Econ. (Nagoya Univ.).
Publs. *The Future of Japan's Economy* 60, *Japan's Post-War Economic Policy* 61, *Economic Planning* 62, *Conditions for a Developed Nation* 65, *Japanese Economy in the Asian Setting* 66, *Future Vision for Japanese Economy* 68.
5-13-12 Koishikawa, Bunkyo-ku, Tokyo, Japan.
Telephone: 03-811-0742.

Okoshi, Arata; Japanese business executive; b. 16 Feb. 1898; ed. Mining and Metallurgy Dept., Ryojun Inst. of Technology.
Trustee, Japan Coal Asscn. 48-; Vice-Pres. Tobu Coal Asscn. 49-51; Pres. Joban Coal Mining Co. 48-.
Higashi 5-4, Ginza, Chuoka, Tokyo; 44 Takanawa-Minamicho, Minato-ku, Tokyo, Japan.

Okun, Arthur M., A.B., PH.D.; American economist; b. 28 Nov. 1928; ed. Public Schools, Passaic, N.J., and Columbia Univ.
Instructor, Yale Univ. 52-56, Asst. Prof. 56-60, Assoc. Prof. 60-62, Prof. and Dir. of Graduate Studies in Econs., Yale Univ. 63-64; Editor *Yale Economic Essays* 63-64; Staff mem. Cowles Foundation for Research in Econs., Yale Univ. 56-64; Staff Economist, Council of Econ. Advisers 61-62, mem. Council of Econ. Advisers 64-68, Chair. 68-.
Publs. Editor *The Battle Against Unemployment, An Introduction to a Current Issue of Public Policy;* articles on economic forecasting, inflation, monetary and fiscal policy, potential GNP.
Council of Economic Advisers, Washington, D.C. 20506; Home: 5035 Macomb Street, N.W., Washington, D.C. 20016, U.S.A.
Telephone: 203-395-5036 (Office); 203-363-7845 (Home).

Okpara, Michael Iheonukara; Nigerian doctor and politician; b. Dec. 1920; ed. Methodist School (Umuegwu), Methodist Coll. (Uzuakoli), Higher Coll. and Nigerian School of Medicine (Lagos).
Asst. Medical Officer 47-48, resigned and entered private practice; Hon. Surgeon Methodist Hospital, Amachara 48-51; Chair. Umuahia branch Nat. Council of Nigerian Citizens 50-52, mem. Nat. Exec. Cttee. 51-, Nat. Pres. 60; Chair. Eastern Nigeria Working Cttee. 54-57; Pres. Gen. Bende Divisional Union 50-59; mem. Eastern Nigeria House of Assembly 52-; Minister without Portfolio, Eastern Nigeria 52-53, Minister of Health 54-57, Minister of Production 57-58, Minister of Agriculture 58-59, Premier 59-66; Commr. for Health and Educ., Biafra 67-; mem. Nat. Defence Council 54-59, Nat. Police Advisory Council 56-59; Grand Commdr.

Order of the Niger; Leader United Progressive Grand Alliance (U.P.G.A.) 64.
Enugu, Eastern Region, Nigeria, West Africa.

Okumura, Tsunao, B. ECON.; Japanese investment executive; b. 5 March 1903; ed. Kyoto Imperial Univ.
Nomura Securities Co. Ltd. 26-, Dir. 45-, Pres. 48-59, Chair. 59-; mem. Overseas Emigration Deliberation Council 59-, Econ. Council 62-, Taxation System Research Cttee. 59-62; Exec. Councillor, Tokyo Chamber of Commerce and Industry 61-; Exec. Dir., Fed. of Econ. Orgs. 62-; Governor, Tokyo Stock Exchange 58-62; Chair. Bond Underwriters Asscn. 59-60; Dir. Tokyo Securities Dealers Asscn. 48-62, Asahi Fire and Marine Insurance Co., Nippon Glass Co., Nippon Television Broadcasting Co., Nippon Yakin Kogyo Co. Ltd.; Auditor, Tokyo Life Insurance Co., Teikoku Oil Co. Ltd.
1, 1-chome, Nihonbashi-Tori, Tokyo; 14 Hiroocho, Azabu, Minato-ku, Tokyo, Japan.

Olah, Franz; Austrian trade union official; b. 10; ed. High School.
Piano maker; imprisoned four times for political reasons 33-45; mem., Vienna Town Council and Vienna Diet 45-48, Austrian Nat. Council 48; Chair., Building and Wood Workers Trade Union 49-57; Vice-Pres., Federation of Austrian Trade Unions 55; Pres., Austrian Federation of Trade Unions 59-61; Second Pres. Austrian Nat. Council 59-63; Minister for the Interior 63-64.
Seemullergasse 38, Vienna XVII, Austria.

Olav V; King of Norway; b. 2 July 1903; ed. secondary school, Oslo, Norwegian Military Acad., and Balliol Coll., Oxford.
Studied political history and political science; married 29 Princess Märtha of Sweden (died 54); Commdr.-in-Chief, Norwegian Forces, Second World War; succeeded his father, King Haakon VII, Sept. 21, 57.
Royal Palace, Oslo, Norway.
Telephone: 44-19-20.

Oldenbourg, Zoé; French (born Russian) writer; b. 31 March 1916; ed. Lycée Molière and Sorbonne, Paris. In France 25-; studied theology, Great Britain 38; mem. Jury of Prix Femina 61-; Prix Femina for *La Pierre Angulaire* (*The Cornerstone*) 53.
Publs. *Argile et Cendres* 46, *La Pierre angulaire* 53, *Bûcher de Montségur* 59, *Les Brûlées* 61, *Les Cités charnelles* 61, *Essai historique sur les Croisades* 63, *Catherine de Russie* 65.
35 rue Poussin, Paris 16e, France.

O'Leary, Paul Martin, M.A., PH.D.; American university professor and administrator; b. 29 Nov. 1901; ed. Univ. of Kansas, Harvard Univ., and Cornell Univ.
Instructor in Economics Cornell Univ. 24; Asst. Prof. 29, Prof. 36-; Dean School of Business and Public Admin. Cornell Univ. 45-52, Coll. of Arts and Sciences 52-57; Dep. Admin. in charge of Rationing Office of Price Admin. during Second World War; mem. Dodge Financial Mission to Occupied Japan 49.
Publs. *Questions and Problems in Economics* (with S. H. Slichter) 31, *Corporate Enterprise in Modern Economic Life* 33, *An Introduction to Money, Banking and Corporations* (with John H. Patterson) 37.
Cornell University, Ithaca, N.Y., U.S.A.

Olewiński, Marian, M.S. (ENG.); Polish engineer and politician; b. 15 Sept. 1912; ed. Warsaw Polytechnic School.
Building trade until 39; posts in Polish Workers' Party and Polish United Workers' Party 45-51; Ministry of Transport and Communications 51-60; Minister of Building and Building Materials 60-.
3/5 Zurawia Street, Warsaw, Poland.

Olin, John Merrill, B.S.; American businessman; b. 10 Nov. 1892; ed. Cornell Univ.
Chemical engineer, Equitable Powder Manufacturing Co. 13; chemical engineer, Western Cartridge Co. 13, Asst. to Pres. 14-18, First Vice-Pres. and Dir. 18-44, and Pres. and Dir. Olin Industries Inc. (consolidation of Western Cartridge Co., Winchester Repeating Arms Co., Olin Corpn., etc.) 44-54; Chair. of Board, Olin Mathieson Chemical Corpn. (merger of Olin Industries Inc. and Mathieson Chemical Corpn.) 54-57, Chair. Financial and Operating Policy and Exec. Cttees. 57-62; Chair. Exec. Cttee. and Dir. Olin Mathieson Chemical Corpn. 62-63; Pres. and Dir. Illinois State Bank, East Alton; Dir. St. Louis Union Trust Co., First Nat. Bank and Trust Co., Alton; Trustee Wash. Univ. Corpn., St. Louis, Cornell Univ., American Museum of Natural History, Johns Hopkins Univ., Midwest Research Inst.; Dir. World Wildlife Fund; Hon. Chair. and Dir. Olin Mathieson Chemical Corpn. 63-.
Home: Box 373, Alton, Ill.; Office: Olin Mathieson Chemical Corporation, East Alton, Ill., U.S.A.

Oliphant, Sir Mark Laurence Elwin, K.B.E., F.R.S.; British physicist; b. Australia 8 Oct. 1901; ed. Adelaide Univ., and Trinity Coll., Cambridge.
Messel Research Fellow, Royal Society 31; Lecturer and Fellow, St. John's Coll. 34; Asst. Dir. Research, Cavendish Lab., Cambridge 35; Prof. and Dir. of Dept. of Physics Birmingham Univ. 37-50; Vice-Principal Sept. 48-49; Dir. of post-graduate Research School of Physical Sciences, Australian Nat. Univ. 50-63; Prof. of Particle Physics 50-64; Pres. Australian Acad. of Sciences 54-57; Hon. Fellow, St. John's Coll., Cambridge 52.
Australian National University, Box 4 G.P.O., Canberra, A.C.T., Australia.

Olivecrona, Herbert, M.D.; Swedish surgeon; b. 11 July 1891; ed. Uppsala and Stockholm Univs.
Asst. Surgical Clinics of Leipzig, Baltimore and Stockholm 18-25; Asst. Surgeon-in-Chief, Serafimerlasarettet, Stockholm 25-35, Dir. 35-60; Associate Prof. of Surgery 24-35; Prof. of Neurological Surgery, Royal Caroline Inst. 35-60; set up clinic in Egypt at request of U.A.R. Govt. 61; Hon. M.D. (Athens and Cologne), D.S. (Gustavus Adolphus Coll., St. Peter, Minn.).
Publs. *Die chirurgische Behandlung der Gehirntumoren* 27, *On changes of the optic canals in cases of intracranial tumours* 32, *On suprasellar cholesteatomas* 32, *Die parasagittalen Meningeome* 34, *Gefässgeschwülste und Gefässmissbildungen des Gehirns* 36, *Chirurgie der Hirntumoren* 40, *Tractotomy* 42, *Parasagittal meningiomas* 47, *Surgical treatment of angina pectoris* 47, *Arteriovenous aneurysm of the brain* 48, *Hypophysectomy in cancer of the breast* 53, *Surgical treatment of intracranial tumours*, Vol. 4, *Handbuch der Neurochirurgie*.
Karolinska Sjukhuset, Stockholm 60; and Strandvägen 49, Stockholm Ö, Sweden.
Telephone: 340500/2049 (Office); 671545 (Home).

Oliveira Santos, João, LL.D.; Brazilian international civil servant; b. 26 Oct. 1914; ed. Universidade do Brazil and American Univ., Washington, D.C.
At Ministry of Labour, Industry and Commerce, Brazil 35-52, 50-54; on active service in Brazilian Air Force 43-45; Lecturer American Univ., Washington 45-46; Deputy Dir. and Acting Dir. Dept. of Econ. and Social Affairs, Gen. Secr. of Org. of American States (OAS), Washington, D.C. 55-58; Sec.-Gen. Latin American Coffee Agreement 58-59, Coffee Study Group, Wash. 58-, Int. Coffee Agreement 59-63; Exec. Dir. Int. Coffee Org., London 63-68; Operations Man., Inter-American Devt. Bank, Washington D.C. 68-; Consultant on Commodities for UN 62; Order of the Sun of Peru (twice), Order of Honour and Merit of Haiti and Order of Ruben Dario of Nicaragua.
Publs. *Analysis of the Trends of the International Coffee Market* (in Portuguese; 3rd edn.) 63, and numerous articles on trade and economics.
7214 Park Terrace Drive, Alexandra, Virginia 22307, U.S.A.

Oliver, Roland, M.A., PH.D.; British Africanist; b. 30 March 1923; ed. Cambridge Univ.
Lecturer, School of Oriental and African Studies, Univ. of London 48-49, 50-57, Reader 58-63, Prof. of African History 63-; organised first confs. on history and archaeology of Africa, London Univ. 53, 57, 61; founded and edited *Journal of African History* 60-.
Publs. *The Missionary Factor in East Africa* 52, *Sir Harry Johnston and the Scramble for East Africa* 57, *The Dawn of African History* 61, *Short History of Africa* (with J. D. Fage) 62, *History of East Africa* (with G. Mathew) 63, *Africa since 1800* (with A. Atmore) 67.
c/o School of Oriental and African Studies, University of London, London W.C.1; 38 Newton Road, London W.2, England.
Telephone: 01-229-4873.

Oliver, William F(rederick); American sugar refining executive; b. 23 Sept. 1914; ed. Princeton Univ.
American Sugar Refining Co., New York City 35-, Exec. Vice-Pres 53-54, Pres. and Dir. 54-, Chief Exec. Officer 55-; Dir. City Bank Farmers Trust Co., American Enka Corpn.
American Sugar Refining Co., 120 Wall Street, New York City 5, N.Y., U.S.A.

Oliver, Lieut.-Gen. Sir William Pasfield, G.B.E., K.C.B., K.C.M.G.; British army officer; b. 8 Sept. 1901; ed. King's Coll. School, Cambridge, Radley Coll. and Royal Military Coll., Sandhurst.
Commissioned in The Queen's Own Royal West Kent Regiment 20, Adjutant 27, Captain 30; Staff Coll. Camberley 34-35; Staff Captain A.H.Q. India 35-37, G.S.O. II India 37-39; G.S.O. I 40-41; Battn. Comdr. 41-42; Dep. Dir. Mil. Operations, War Office 42; Dir. of Mil. Operations Middle East 43-44, Chief of Staff 45-46; Student Imperial Defence Coll. 47, Brigade Commdr. 48, Instructor 49-50; Chief of Staff, Eastern Command 51-52; Staff Officer to High Commr., Malaya 53; G.O.C. Berlin 54-55; Vice-Chief Imperial Gen. Staff 55-57; P.S.O. to Sec. of State for Commonwealth Relations 57-59; U.K. High Commr. in Australia Oct. 59-65; Commr.-Gen. for 1967 Montreal Exhbn. (Expo 67) 65-68; Deputy Lieut. of Kent 58; Col., Queen's Own Royal West Kent Regiment 49-59; Legion of Merit, Grand Cross Order of Phoenix (Greece).
Little Crofts, Sweetpaws, Crowborough, Sussex, England.
Telephone: Warren 5411.

Olivetti, Arrigo, D.IUR.; Italian business executive; b. 89; ed. Univ. of Turin.
Former Sales Manager, Sec.-Gen., Vice-Chair. and Managing Dir. Ing. C. Olivetti & Co., S.p.A., Hon. Chair. 63-; Chair. O.S.I. (Mechanical); Dir. Fergat S.p.A. (Mechanical), Soc. Autostrada Torino Ivrea Valle d'Aosta (A.T.I.V.A.), Inst. of European Studies, Turin; Pres. Piero Martinetti Foundation for Studies in Philosophy, Religion and History; mem. Central Cttee. Centre Int. Formation Européenne (CIFE), Paris; War Cross, Cavaliere del Lavoro.
Via Montenavale 24, 10015 Ivrea, Italy.
Telephone: Ivrea 22-20 and 24-80.

Olivier, Sir Laurence Kerr, Kt.; British actor manager; b. 22 May 1907; ed. St. Edward's School, Oxford.
First appearance, Shakespearian play, Stratford 22; Birmingham Repertory Company 25-28; subsequent appearances in London, New York, Paris and Denmark; Old Vic Theatre Company 44-45, 49, toured Australia and New Zealand 48; Actor-Manager, St. James's Theatre, London 50-51; Shakespeare Memorial Theatre, Stratford-on-Avon 55; Dir. Chichester Festival Theatre

62-65, The National Theatre 62-; Hon. D.Litt. (Oxon.), Hon. LL.D. (Edin.), Hon. M.A. (Tuft's); Chevalier, Légion d'Honneur; Commdr. Order of Dannebrog (Denmark) and Grand Officer, Ordine al Merito della Repubblica (Italy); Sonning Prize (Denmark) 66.

Stage appearances include many Shakespearian and classical plays, *The Entertainer, Rhinoceros, Becket,* etc.; produced and appeared in *Venus Observed, Caesar and Cleopatra, The Broken Heart, Uncle Vanya,* etc. Films include *Wuthering Heights, Rebecca, Pride and Prejudice, 49th Parallel, Carrie, Beggar's Opera, The Prince and the Showgirl, The Devil's Disciple, Spartacus, The Entertainer, Term of Trial, Khartoum, Othello;* produced, directed and played in *Henry V, Hamlet* and *Richard III;* National Theatre appearances include *Uncle Vanya, Othello, Master Builder, Love for Love, The Dance of Death, A Flea in Her Ear.* Television appearances include *John Gabriel Borkman, The Moon and Sixpence, The Power and The Glory.*

4 Royal Crescent, Brighton, Sussex, England.

Olpin, A. Ray, A.B., PH.D.; American physicist; b. 1 June 1898; ed. Brigham Young Univ. Provo, Utah, and Columbia Univ.

Instructor, Mathematics and Physics, Brigham Young Univ. 22-24; Asst. in Physics Columbia Univ. 24-25; mem. Technical Staff, Bell Telephone Laboratories N.Y. City 25-33; Lecturer Brooklyn Polytechnic Inst. 31-33; Dir. of Research, Kendall Mills, Charlotte, N.C. 33-39; Prof. and Dir. of Industrial Research, Field Dir. Engineering Experiment Station, and Exec. Dir. Research Foundation, Ohio State Univ. 39-46; Consultant Anthony Wayne Research Foundation 44-45; Pres. Univ. of Utah 46-64, and of Carbon Coll., Price, Utah 59-64; Assoc. Ed. *Journal of Applied Physics* 37-38; Man. Ed. *Science and Appliance* 39-45.

Business Office Bldg., 102 University of Utah, Salt Lake City, Utah 84112; 2431 Beacon Drive, Salt Lake City, Utah 84108, U.S.A.

Olshansky, Mikhail Alexandrovich; Soviet agronomist politician; b. 1908; ed. Maslovsky Inst. of Selection and Seed Production.

Scientist at All-Union Plant Selection and Genetic Research Inst., Odessa 28-41, Asst. Dir. 45-51; Rector Kuibyshev Agricultural Inst. 42-45; Academician, All-Union Acad. of Agricultural Sciences 48-, Vice-Pres. 51-61, Pres. 62-64; Minister of Agriculture, U.S.S.R. 60-61; Cand. mem. Central Cttee. C.P.S.U. 61-66; Deputy to U.S.S.R. Supreme Soviet; Order of Lenin, Order of Red Banner of Labour, State Prize Laureate.

All-Union Academy of Agricultural Sciences, 7 Bolshoi Kharitonyevsky pereulok, Moscow, U.S.S.R.

Olszak, Wacław, D.SC.(TECH.), D.ENG.; Polish university professor; b. 24 Oct. 1902; ed. Warsaw, Vienna and Paris Univs.

Dozent Mining Coll., Cracow 37; Prof. Applied Mechanics, Cracow 46, at Warsaw Tech. Univ. 52; Head of Dept. of Mechanics of Continuous Media, Polish Acad. of Sciences 52; mem. Polish Acad. of Sciences 54, mem. Presidium 60; Vice-Pres. Int. Asscn. for Shell Structures (I.A.S.S.)57; Pres. Int. Union of Testing and Research Laboratories (R.I.L.E.M.) 62; prizes for bridge and engineering structures 35, 37, 48, 53, Polish Nat. Prizes 50, 55, 66; Dr. h.c. Univs. of Toulouse and Liège and Technical Univ. of Vienna; Foreign mem. Acad. of Sciences, Belgrade, Toulouse, Budapest, Halle, Royal Swedish Acad. of Technical Sciences and Finnish Acad. of Technical Sciences.

Publs. Research in Applied Mechanics, especially theory of plasticity and theory of structures; *Plane Elastic Problems* 34, *Prestressed Structures* 55, *Non-Homogeneity in Elasticity and Plasticity* (Editor) 59, *Recent Trends in the Development of the Theory of Plasticity* (with others) 62, *Theory of Prestressed Structures* (with others) 62; *Non-Classical Shell Problems* (Editor,

with A. Sawczuk) 64, *Theory of Plasticity* (with others) 65; Editor *Archives of Applied Mechanics.*

Polish Academy of Sciences, ul. Swietokrzyska 21, Warsaw, Poland.

Telephone: 268911 (Office).

Öman, Ivar, PH.D.; Swedish politician; b. 18 April 1900; ed. Uppsala Univ.

Political Editor *Nya Dagligt Allehanda* 25-40; Conservative mem. Stockholm Town Council 31-47; M.P. 38-40; Civic Counsellor Stockholm 40-46; Pres. Stockholm Building Comm. 47; Dir. Statistical Office City of Stockholm 47-65; Gov. Rotary Int. District 134 59-60. Publs. *Men of the Great War* 20, *The Ministry of Karl Staaff* 23, *English Newspaper Trusts* 30, *Statistical Office, City of Stockholm 1905-55* 55, *Great Cities and their Surroundings* 57.

De Geersgatan 10, Stockholm, Sweden.

Omar Ali Saifuddin, His Highness the Former Sultan of Brunei, D.K., P.S.P.N.B., P.S.N.B., S.P.M.B., D.M.N., D.K. (Kel), D.K. (J), D.K. (Sel.), K.C.M.G.; former ruler of Brunei; b. 1916; ed. Malay Coll., Kuala Kangsar, Perak, Malaya.

Served as a Govt. official in various depts. in Brunei; First Minister or Grand Vizier and mem. of State Council 57-50; Sovereign Monarch of Brunei 50-Oct. 67; visited U.K. and Europe 52, 53, 57, 59, 63, U.K. and America 65; on homage to Mecca 53 and 62, trip round the world 65.

Istana Darul Hana, Brunei, South-East Asia.

Omari, Dunstan Alfred, M.B.E., B.A., DIP. ED.; Tanzanian civil servant; b. 22; ed. St. Joseph's Secondary School, Chidya, St. Andrew's Secondary School, Minaki, Makerere Univ. Coll. and Univ. of Wales (Aberystwyth).

Education Officer (Broadcasting Duties) 53-54; District Officer 55-58, District Commr. 58-61; Tanganyika High Commr. in the U.K. 61-62; Perm. Sec., Prime Minister's Office, and Sec. to the Cabinet, Tanganyika 62; Perm. Sec., President's Office, and Sec. to the Cabinet, Tanganyika 62-63; Sec.-Gen. East African Common Services Org. 64- (now called East African Community); Chair. East African Currency Board 64-.

Publ. *Talks on Citizenship* 54.

East African Community Central Secretariat, Arusha, Tanzania.

Ommeren, Philippus van; Netherlands shipowner; b. 4 Dec. 1900; ed. High School.

Started with Phs. van Ommeren's Scheepvaartbedrijf N.V. 19 (now called Phs. van Ommeren N.V.); mem. Board Netherlands Shipping and Trading Cttee. Ltd., London, during Second World War; Pres. Board of Dirs. N.V. Assurantie Mij. "De Zeven Provincien", The Hague, retd.; Officer Order of Orange Nassau, Knight Order of Netherlands Lion, Commdr. Order of Merit (Italy).

Office: Westerlaan 10, Rotterdam, Netherlands; Home: "Le Cret", 1068 Montbesson (VD), Switzerland.

Telephone: 021-328664.

Ó'Móráin, Dónall; Irish public official; b. 6 Sept. 1923; ed. Coláiste Muire, Dublin, Univ. Coll., Dublin, and King's Inns, Dublin.

Called to the Bar 46; Managing Editor of Retail Food Trade Journal 46-50; Gen. Manager, printing and publishing firm 51-63; Founder, Gael-Linn (voluntary nat. cultural and social asscn.) 53, Chair. 53-63, Dir.-Gen. 63-; Chair. Convocation of Nat. Univ. of Ireland 55-; Chair. Irlandia-Crannae Furniture Group 66-; Chair. Inisfree Handknits Group 65-; mem. Radio Telefis Éireann Authority 65-, Consultative Council, Dept. of Finance 65-; Dir. Glens of Antrim Tweed Co. Ltd. 67-; mem. Irish. Film Industry Comm. 67-.

32 Sydney Avenue, Blackrock, Dublin, Ireland.

Telephone: Dublin 880541.

Onana-Awana, Charles; Cameroonian politician; b. c. 1923; ed. Ecole Supérieure, Yaoundé and Ecole nationale de la France d'Outre-Mer, Paris.
With the Ministry of Finance 43-57; Head, Office of Deputy Prime Minister for the Interior 57-58; Asst.-Dir. Office of Prime Minister Feb.-Oct. 58; Perm. Sec. French Cameroons, Paris 58-59; Minister of Finance 60-61; Del. to the Presidency in charge of Finance, the Plan and Territorial Admin. 61-65; Sec.-Gen. Union Douanière et Economique de l'Afrique Centrale 65-; fmr. Dir. Banque Centrale de l'Afrique Equatoriale et du Cameroun; fmr. Gov. Int. Monetary Fund; Officier Ordre de la Valeur, Cameroon, Commdr. Légion d'Honneur, Ordre de la Rédemption Africaine, Ordre Tchadien.
Secrétaire Général de l'U.D.E.A.C., Boîte Postale 946, Bangui, Central African Republic.

Onar, Siddik Sami; Turkish law professor; b. 97; ed. Istanbul Law School and Paris Univ.
Practised law and served as judge 22-33; Prof., Admin. Law, Istanbul Univ. 33-; Pres., Istanbul Univ. 46-48 and 59-64; Dean, Faculty of Law 33-37, 43-46.
Publs. *Administrative Law* 44, *General Principles of Administrative Law I* 52, *II* 60; many articles on law.
Istanbul University, Istanbul, Turkey.

Onassis, Aristotle Socrates; Argentine (formerly Greek) shipowner and business executive; b. 06 in Turkey; ed. Evangeliki Scholi, Smyrna.
Went as refugee to Greece and from there migrated to Argentina 23, where he revived family tobacco merchants' business; later Greek Consul in Buenos Aires; purchased ships in Canada 32-33, first tanker the *Ariston* in Sweden 36; since 45 has built super-tankers in U.S.A., France, Germany, Japan, whaling fleet sold to Japan 56; interest in Société des Bains de Mer (controlling Monte Carlo Casino) (now sold); founded Olympic Airways S.A. 57; founder of Olympic Cruises (now sold).
1668 Alvear Av., Buenos Aires, Argentina; or c/o Olympic Maritime, S.A., 17 ave. d'Ostende, Monte Carlo, Monaco.

Ondo, Jean-François; Gabon politician; b. 16; ed. Oyem Regional School and Libreville Town School.
Former civil servant, Gabon; Minister of Nat. Educ., Youth and Sports 58-60, Nat. Defence 60-61, Cultural and Social Affairs, Youth and Sports 61-62; Minister of State for Justice 62-63; Minister of State for Labour Jan.-Feb. 63; Minister of State for Foreign Affairs 63; numerous decorations; Bloc Démocratique Gabonais.
c/o Ministry of Foreign Affairs, P.O. Box 389, Libreville, Gabon.

O'Neal, Edward A.; American business executive; b. 9 Sept. 1905; ed. Davidson College.
Joined Swann Corpn., Anniston, Alabama 26 (acquired by Monsanto Co.) 35; Plant Man., Anniston 39-41, Plant Man. Monsanto Phosphate Div., Trenton, Mich. 41-44, Production Man. Phosphate Div. 44-46; Man. Dir. Monsanto Chemicals Ltd., London 47-52, Chair. 49-55, Dir. 64-; Gen. Man. Monsanto Overseas Div. 53-55, Vice-Pres. 54-56, Dir. Monsanto 55-56, 61-, Vice-Pres. 62-64, mem. Exec. Cttee. 64-, mem. Finance Cttée. 64-68 and Chair. Board of Dirs. 65-; mem. Monsanto Corporate Devt. Cttee. 67-; Pres. Chemstrand Corp. 54-64; Dir. Monsanto Europe, S.A., Brussels, St. Louis Union Trust Co.; Dir. Monsanto Textiles Div., London; mem. Board of Trustees Washington Univ. and Polytechnic Inst. of Brooklyn; Dir. Foreign Policy Asscn.
Monsanto Company, 800 North Lindbergh Boulevard, St. Louis, Mo. 63166; and 59 Briarcliff, St. Louis, Mo. 63124, U.S.A.
Telephone: OX4-1000 (Office); WY3-4525 (Home).

O'Neil, Michael Gerald, A.B.; American rubber executive; b. 29 Jan. 1922; ed. Coll. of Holy Cross, and Harvard Univ.
Director, The General Tire and Rubber Co. 50-, Asst. to Pres. 51-57, Vice-Pres. and Exec. Asst. to Pres. 57-60, Pres. 60-; served Second World War; official of numerous business and philanthropic orgs.
The General Tire and Rubber Co., 1708 Englewood Avenue, Akron 9, Ohio, U.S.A.

O'Neil, Thomas Francis, A.B.; American rubber executive; b. 18 April 1915; ed. Coll. of Holy Cross and Harvard Graduate Business School.
Director, The General Tire and Rubber Co. 48-, Vice-Pres. 50-60, Vice-Chair. Board 60-61, Chair. 61-; Pres. RKO-General Inc. 55-62, Chair. of Board 62-; served Second World War.
The General Tire and Rubber Co., 1440 Broadway, New York 18, N.Y., U.S.A.

O'Neill, C. William, B.A., LL.B.; American politician and lawyer; b. 14 Feb. 1916; ed. Marietta Coll., and Ohio State Univ. Law School.
Mem. Ohio Legislature 38-50; served with U.S. Army 43-46; Speaker of Ohio House of Reps. 47-48 and Minority Leader 49-50; Attorney-Gen. of Ohio 51-56; Gov. of Ohio 57-58; private law practice 59-60; Judge, Supreme Court of Ohio 60-; LL.D. h.c. from seven univs.
1560 London Drive, Columbus 21, Ohio, U.S.A.
Telephone: 451-8828.

O'Neill, The Hon. Sir Con Douglas Walter, K.C.M.G., M.A.; British diplomatist; b. 3 June 1912; ed. Eton Coll., and Balliol Coll., Oxford.
Fellow All Souls Coll., Oxford 35-45; called to the Bar 36; entered Diplomatic Service 36; served Berlin 38; resigned from Service 38; served army 40-43; with Foreign Office 43-46; on staff of *The Times* 46-47; rejoined Foreign Office 47; served Frankfurt and Bonn 48-52; Imperial Defence Coll. 53; Head News Dept., Foreign Office 54-55; Chargé d'Affaires, Peking 55-57; Asst. Under-Sec. Foreign Office 57-60; Ambassador to Finland 61-63, to European Econ. Community 63-65; Deputy Under-Sec. in charge of Econ. Affairs, Foreign Office 65-68; Dir. Hill, Samuel June 68-.
c/o Foreign Office, London, S.W.1, England.

O'Neill, Rt. Hon. Terence Marne; British (N. Ireland) politician; b. 10 Sept. 1914; ed. Eton Coll.
Irish Guards 39-45; M.P. (N. Ireland) 46-, Parl. Sec. Ministry of Health 48-53; Deputy Speaker and Chair. Ways and Means Cttee. 53-55; Joint Parl. Sec. Home Affairs and Health 55; Minister of Home Affairs, April-Oct. 56, of Finance Sept. 56-63; Prime Minister (N. Ireland) 63-; Unionist Party.
Office of The Prime Minister, Stormont Castle, Belfast 4, Northern Ireland; and Glebe House, Ahoghill, County Antrim, Northern Ireland.
Telephone: Ahoghill 246.

Onetti, Juan Carlos; Uruguayan writer; b. 1 July 1909; ed. High School.
Editor *Marcha* (weekly newspaper), Montevideo 39-42; Editor Reuter Agency, Montevideo 42-43, Buenos Aires 43-46; Editor *Vea y Lea* (magazine), Buenos Aires 46-55; Man. of advertising firm in Montevideo 55-57; Dir. of Municipal Libraries, Montevideo 57-; Nat. Literature Prize of Uruguay 63.
Publs. novels: *El pozo* 39, *Tierra de nadie* 41, *Para esta noche* 43, *La vida breve* 50, *Un sueño realizado y otros cuentos* (stories) 51, *Una tumba sin nombre* 59, *Los adioses* 54, *La cara de la desgracia* 60, *Jacob y el otro* (story) 61, *El Astillero* 61, *El infierno tan temido* 62, *Tan triste como ella* 63, *Juntacadaveres* 65.
Gonzalo Ramirez 1497, Montevideo, Uruguay.

Ong, Yoke Lin; Malaysian politician and diplomatist; b. 1917.
Member Kuala Lumpur Municipal Council 52-; co-founder Alliance Party; mem. Fed. Legislative Council 54-; Malayan Minister of Posts and Telecommunications 55-56, of Transport 56-57, of Labour and Social Welfare 57-59, of Health and Social Welfare 59-62; M.P. 59-62; Vice-Pres. Commonwealth Parl. Asscn. 61; Ambassador to U.S.A. and UN 62-64; Ambassador to U.S.A and Minister without Portfolio, Malaysia 64-.
c/o Cabinet Office, Kuala Lumpur, Malaya, Malaysia.

Onganía, Gen. Juan Carlos; Argentine army officer and politician; b. 1914; ed. School of War.
Army career in cavalry and armoured corps; C.-in-C. of Army 63-Nov. 65; President of Argentina June 66-.
Office of the President of Argentina, Buenos Aires, Argentina.

Onnes, Nicolaas Ernst Rost (see Rost Onnes, N. E.).

Onsager, Lars, CH.E., PH.D., SC.D., DR. TECH.; American (b. Norwegian) chemist; ed. Norges Tekniske höyskole, Trondheim, and Yale Univ.
Associate in Chemistry, Johns Hopkins Univ. 28; Instructor of Chemistry, Brown Univ. (Providence, R.I.) 28-33; Sterling Fellow, Yale Univ. 33-34, Asst. Prof. 34-40, Assoc. Prof. 40-45, J. Willard Gibbs Prof. of Theoretical Chemistry 45-; Fulbright Scholar, Mond Laboratory, Cambridge 51-52; mem. Nat. Acad. of Sciences and other Acads. in U.S.A., Norway and Sweden; mem. Neuroscience Associates 62-; Rumford Medal (American Acad.) 53, Lorentz Medal 58, G. N. Lewis Medal, J. G. Kirkwood Medal, Willard Gibbs Medal 62, T. W. Richards Medal 64, Debye Award 65.
Publs. articles on theory of electrolytes, reciprocal relations in irreversible processes, dipole moments in liquids, crystal statistics, interpretation of the de Haas-van Alphen effect, and electrical properties of ice.
Sterling Chemistry Laboratory, Yale University, New Haven, Conn. 06520; Home: 841 Whitney Avenue, New Haven, Conn. 06511, U.S.A.

Onyeama, Charles D., LL.B.; Nigerian judge; b. 5 Aug. 1917; ed. King's Coll., Lagos, Achimota Coll., Gold Coast, Univ. Coll., London and Brasenose Coll., Oxford.
Cadet Admin. Officer, Nigeria 44; mem. Legislative Council of Nigeria and Eastern House of Assembly 46-51; mem. Nigerianization Comm. and mem. Gen. Conf. and Constitutional Drafting Cttee. 48-50; Chief Magistrate, Nigeria 52-56; Acting High Court Judge, W. Nigeria 56-57; High Court Judge, Lagos 57-64; Acting Chief Justice, Lagos High Court 61 and 63; Justice of Supreme Court of Nigeria 64-66; Judge Int. Court of Justice, The Hague 66-.
International Court of Justice, Peace Palace, The Hague, Netherlands.
Telephone: 39-23-44.

Ooka, Shohei; Japanese writer; b. 09; ed. Univ. of Kyoto.
Translator of French literature, especially Stendhal; soldier and prisoner of war in the Philippines 44-45; novelist and critic 48-; Teacher at Meiji Univ. 52-55; visited U.S.A., England and France as Creative Fellow, Rockefeller Foundation 53-54; Yokomitsu Prize 40, Yomiuri Prize 52.
Publs. Translated Alain's *Stendhal* 40, Stendhal's *Chartreuse de Parme* 49, etc.; novels: *Furyoki* (Memories of a Prisoner of War) 49, *Musashino Fujin* (A Woman of Musashino Plain) 50, *Nobi* (Fires of the Plain) 51, *Sanso* (Oxygen) 53, *Hamlet Nikki* (Diary of Hamlet) 55, etc.
1-19 Higashi-machi, Oiso, Kanagawa-ken, Japan.

Oorschot, Wilhelmus Petrus Hubertus van, LL.D.; Netherlands official; b. 30 April 1910; ed. Univ. of Utrecht.
Dir.-Gen. Foreign Economic Relations to the Ministry of Econ. Affairs, The Hague 57-; Chair. of GATT 61, 63; Kt. Order Netherlands Lion; Officer Order of Orange Nassau; Commdr. Order of the Oak Crown of Luxemburg; Grand Officer of the Order of Léopold II of Belgium; Commdr. of the Order of Merit of Italy; Commdr. of the Legion of Honour, France; Grand Officer of the Order of the Southern Cross of Brazil; Norwegian, Spanish, Tunisian, Austrian and Honduran awards.
Sniplaan 10, The Hague, Netherlands.
Telephone: 322602.

Oort, Jan Hendrik; Netherlands astronomer; b. 28 April 1900; ed. Univ. of Groningen.
Asst. Astronomical Laboratory, Groningen 21; Research Asst. Yale Univ. Observatory, U.S.A. 22-24; Astronomer Leiden Observatory 24; Prof. of Astronomy and Dir. of Observatory, Univ. of Leiden 45-; Gen. Sec. Int. Astronomical Union 35-48; Pres. 59-61; Foreign mem. of various Academies of Arts and Sciences; Vetlesen Prize, Columbia Univ. 66; Hon. Dr. Univs. of Copenhagen, Glasgow, Oxford, Louvain, Harvard, Brussels, Cambridge, Bordeaux, Canberra.
Publs. Numerous contributions to learned journals.
Sterrewacht 5, Leiden, Netherlands.
Telephone: 21315.

Oparin, Alexander Ivanovich; Soviet biochemist; b. 2 March 1894; ed. Moscow Univ.
Lecturer, later Prof., Univ. of Moscow 20-; founder with A. N. Bach of Biochemical Inst. U.S.S.R. Acad. of Sciences 35, Dir. of the Inst. 46-; mem. Acad. of Sciences 39-; mem. U.S.S.R. Peace Cttee., Cttee. on Space Research (COSPAR) 64; Vice-Pres. World Fed. of Scientific Workers 52; mem. Bulgarian Acad. of Sciences 52; Leopoldina Acad. of Scientific Research 56; Gen Assembly Int. Union of Biochemistry 53, Vice-Pres. 61; hon mem. Japanese Biochemical Soc. 55; corresp. mem. Suomalaisten Kemistien Seura (Finnish Chemical Soc.) 59; Hon. Dr. Nat. Sc. Friedrich Schiller Univ. Jena 58, Hon. Dr. Univ. of Poitiers 63, Hon. Dr. Univ. of Warsaw; Hon. mem. German Acad. of Science (Berlin); Hon. mem. Acad. of Science of Cuba; Orders of Lenin and of the Red Banner of Labour.
Publs. include *Proizkhoshdenie zhizni* (Origin of Life) 24, *Vozniknovenie zhizni na Zemle* (Origin of Life on Earth) 36, 57, *Zhin ee pzizoda proizkhoshednie i razvitie* (Life: Its Nature, Origin and Development) 60, *The Chemical Origin of Life* 65.
Bach Institute of Biochemistry, U.S.S.R. Academy of Sciences, Leninsky Prospekt 33, Moscow, U.S.S.R.

Openg, Datu Abang Haji, O.B.E.; Sarawak administrator; b. 05; ed. English and Malay Schools.
Clerk, Sarawak Govt. Service 24-32, Native Officer Magistrate 32-37, Senior Native Officer 37-40, Senior Native Officer, Special Grade 40, 46-49, District Officer, Limbang 49-51, Senior Service Admin. Officer 51-58; mem. Council Negri 40-; mem. Supreme Council 51-; mem. Kuching Municipal Council 53-; Pres. Majlis Islam 55-; Gov. of Sarawak Sept. 63-.
The Governor's Residence, Kuching, Sarawak, Malaysia.

Opie, Eugene Lindsay, A.B., M.D., D.SC., LL.D.; American pathologist; b. 5 July 1873; ed. Johns Hopkins Univ. Medical School.
Asst. Associate in Pathology Johns Hopkins Univ. 98-04; mem. Rockefeller Inst. for Medical Research 04-10; Prof. of Pathology, Washington Univ. 10-23 and Univ. of Pennsylvania 23-32; Dir. Henry Phipps Laboratories 23-32; Prof. of Pathology, Cornell Medical Coll. 32-41; Research Guest, Rockefeller Inst. Medical Research 41-53, affil. Rockefeller Univ. 53-; mem. Nat. Acad. of Sciences, Asscn. of American Physicians; Fellow, American Asscn. for the Advancement of Science; mem. Board of Scientific Dirs. Rockefeller

Inst. for Medical Research 28-32; Scientific Dir. Int. Health Div. Rockefeller Foundation 35-38; Visiting Prof. Peiping Union Medical Coll. 39; awarded Trudeau Medal 29, Weber-Parkes Prize 45, Banting Medal 46, Kovalenko Medal of Nat. Acad. of Sciences 59, New York Acad. of Medicine Medal 60, Duckett Jones Memorial Award 65; D.Sc. Rockefeller Univ. 66.
Publs. *Diseases of the Pancreas* 02, *Epidemic Respiratory Disease* 21, *Tuberculosis in School children* 29, *The Relation of inflamation to the colligative properties of solutions* 66.
Rockefeller Institute, 66th Street and York Avenue, New York 21, N.Y., U.S.A.
Telephone: 360-1000.

Oppenheim, Tan Sri Sir Alexander, S.M.N., Kt., O.B.E., M.A., PH.D., D.SC.; British mathematician; b. 4 Feb. 1903; ed. Manchester Grammar School, and Balliol Coll., Oxford.
Commonwealth Fund Fellow Chicago 27-30; Lecturer Edinburgh Univ. 30-31; Prof. of Mathematics Raffles Coll. Singapore 31-42, 45-49, Dep. Principal 47 and 49; Prof. of Mathematics Univ. of Malaya 49-57, Dean Faculty of Arts 49, 51 and 53, Acting Vice-Chancellor 55, Vice-Chancellor 57-65; Visiting Prof. of Mathematics, Reading Univ. 65-68, Univ. of Ghana 68-; prisoner of war in Singapore and Thailand 42-45; Dean Prisoner of War Univ. 42; Pres. Malayan Mathematical Soc. 51-55, 57, Singapore Chess Club 56, American Univ. Club 56, Oxford and Cambridge Soc. 52, 57, Assoc. of Southeast Asian Insts. of Higher Learning 59-61; Fellow Royal Soc. of Edinburgh, World Acad. of Art and Science.
Department of Mathematics, University of Ghana; and c/o 664 Finchley Road, London, N.W.11; and Matson House, Remenham, Nr. Henley-on-Thames, Oxon., England.
Telephone: Henley 2049.

Oppenheim, Sir Duncan Morris, Kt.; British tobacco manufacturer and solicitor; b. 6 Aug. 1904; ed. Repton School.
Asst. Solicitor, Messrs. Linklaters & Paines, London 29; Solicitor to, and Dir. of, China Assoc. Co. of British-American Tobacco Co. Ltd. 34; Asst. Solicitor to British-American Tobacco Co. London 35, Solicitor 36-49, Dir. 43-, Deputy Chair. 47-49, Vice-Chair. 49-53, Chair. 53-66, Pres. 66-; Chair. Royal Coll. of Art Council 56, Pro-Provost 67; Chair. Council of Industrial Design 60; Dir. Lloyds Bank Ltd. 56; Chair British Nat. Cttee. of Int. Chamber of Commerce 63, Court of Govs., Admin. Staff Coll., Henley 63; Chair. Royal Inst. of Int. Affairs 66, Asscn. of Societies of Art and Design 66, British Chamber of Commerce in Netherlands; mem. Advisory Cttee. Victoria and Albert Museum, London.
43 Edwardes Square, London, W.8, England.

Oppenheimer, Harry Frederick, M.A.; South African industrialist; b. 28 Oct. 1908; ed. Charterhouse and Christ Church, Oxford.
Chairman, Anglo-American Corpn. of South Africa Ltd., De Beers Consolidated Mines Ltd.; Chair. or Dir. of 68 or more subsidiary and other companies; M.P. 47-58; Chancellor, Cape Town Univ. 67-; mem. United Party until 59; Hon. D.Econ., Univ. of Natal; Hon. LL.D., Univ. of Leeds.
Brenthurst, Federation Road, Parktown, Johannesburg, South Africa.

Oppler, Kurt; German diplomatist; b. 24 Nov. 1902; ed. High School, Breslau, Breslau Univ.
In commercial position 21-27; legal practice 32-37; in Netherlands and Belgium 38-44; Chief, Dept. Hessian Ministry of Justice 46-47; Dir. Bipartite Personnel Office, Econ. Council, Frankfurt 47-52; Joined Foreign Office 52, Envoy and Minister to Iceland 52-56; Ambassador to Iceland 56, to Norway 56-59, to Belgium 59-63, to Canada 63-67; Grand Cross, Order of

Icelandic Falcon, St. Olav Order (Norway), Order of Merit (Germany), Order of the Crown (Belgium), Grand Cross of the Order of Leopold (Belgium).
Alwinenstrasse 24, Wiesbaden, German Fed. Republic.

Oprecht, Hans Wilhelm, DR. PHIL.; Swiss publisher, broadcasting official and politician; b. 19 July 1894; ed. Univ. of Zürich.
State Guardian 18; Nat. Councillor 25-63; Pres. of Swiss Socialist Party 36-53; Dir. Büchergilde Gutenberg Zürich 47-53; Pres. Swiss T.V. Corpn. for Publicity 60-64, Swiss Broadcasting Corpn. 60-64.
Rämistrasse 18, Zürich 1, Switzerland.

Ore, Oystein, PH.D., HON.M.A.; American mathematician; b. 7 Oct. 1899 in Norway; ed. Univs. of Oslo, Göttingen and Paris.
Fellow, Mittag-Leffler Inst., Stockholm 23-24; Fellow, Rockefeller Int. Education Board 24-26; mem. Norwegian Acad. of Science 26; Research Associate, Oslo Univ. 25-28; Asst. Prof. of Mathematics, Yale Univ. 27, Associate Prof. 28, Prof. 29-; Fellow, Branford Coll. 33-; mem. Editorial Board *Annals of Mathematics* 30-40, *Duke Mathematical Journal* 36-40, *Transactions* of American Mathematical Society 37-45; *American Journal of Mathematics* 38-41; mem. Council American Mathematical Society 34-37, Nat. Research Council 39-42, Dir. American Relief for Norway 42-47; Relief Mission Norway 45; Guggenheim Fellow, Rome 54; mem. American Acad. of Arts and Sciences 65-; Kt. Norwegian Order of St. Olav 47.
Publs. *Les corps algébriques et la théorie des idéaux* 35, *L'algèbre abstraite* 36, *Number Theory and its History* 48, *Cardano, the gambling scholar* 53, *Niels Henrik Abel* 54, *Niels Henrik Abel, Mathematician Extraordinary* 57, *Theory of Graphs* 62, *Graphs and Their Uses* 63, *The Four Colour Problem* 67, *Invitation to Number Theory* 68; Joint Editor of R. Dedekind's *Gesammelte Werke* I-III 30-32.
326 Yale University, New Haven, Conn.; Home: 26 Hall Street, Hamden, Conn., U.S.A.

O'Regan, (Andrew) Brendan; Irish business executive; b. 15 May 1917; ed. Blackrock Coll., Dublin.
Comptroller, Sales and Catering Dept., Shannon Airport 44-; Chair. Irish Tourist Board 57-; Chair. Shannon Free Airport Devt. Co. Ltd. 59-.
Shannon International Free Airport, Co. Clare; Home: "Coraveen", Lifford, Ennis, Co. Clare, Ireland.

Orff, Carl; German composer; b. 10 July 1895; ed. Akademie der Tonkunst, Munich.
Prof. and Head of Master Class of Musical Composition, Hochschule für Musik, Munich, until 60; Head of Orff Inst. at Mozarteum Academy, Salzburg 61-; mem. Bavarian Acad. of Fine Arts; mem. Swedish Acad., etc.; Dr. h.c.; Orden Pour le Mérite (German Fed. Repub.).
Compositions: *Carmina Burana, Catulli Carmina, Trionfo di Afrodite, Die Kluge, Der Mond, Antigone, Die Bernauerin, Ödipus der Tyrann, Astutuli, Comoedia de Christi Resurrectione, Ludus de nato Infante mirificus, Prometheus, Schulwerk.*
St. Georgen 134, Diessen-am-Ammersee, German Federal Republic.

Organov, Nikolai Nikolayevich; Soviet diplomatist; b. 1901; ed. Higher Party School, Moscow.
Full-time Party duties 23-43; Third Sec., later First Sec., Primorsk Territorial Cttee. of C.P.S.U. 47-52; First Sec. Krasnoyarsk Territorial Cttee. of C.P.S.U. 52-58; Deputy Chair. Council of Ministers Russian Fed. Republic 58-59; Chair. Presidium Supreme Soviet Russian Fed. Republic and Deputy Chair. U.S.S.R. Supreme Soviet Presidium 59-62; mem. Central Cttee. of C.P.S.U. 52-; Amb. to Bulgaria 62-67; Head of Dept., Cen. Cttee. of C.P.S.U. 67-; Order of Lenin (twice).
C.P.S.U. Central Committee, 4 Staraya ploshchad, Moscow, U.S.S.R.

Orekhovich, Vasily Nikolayevich; Soviet biologist; b. 1905; ed. North Caucasus Univ.
School teacher 27-30; Postgraduate (Moscow) 30-32; Asst. Lecturer, Moscow Communist Univ. 31-35; Senior Research Worker, Moscow Inst. of Morphogenesis 33-36; mem. C.P.S.U. 39-; Head of Lab. and Deputy Dir. Moscow Inst. of Biological and Medical Chemistry, 41-48; Dir. Inst. of Medical and Biological Chemistry, U.S.S.R. Acad. of Medical Sciences 50-53, mem. 53-; mem. Presidium 53-57; Academician-Sec. Dept. of Medico-Biological Sciences, Vice-Pres. U.S.S.R. Acad. of Medical Sciences 60-63; Head of Lab. Inst. of Natural Products Chemistry, U.S.S.R. Acad. of Sciences 59-; Vice-Pres. All-Union Biochemical Soc. and Int. Biochemistry Cttee.; mem. Presidium Moscow Biochemical Soc.; mem. Exec. Cttee. Int. Fed. for Clinical Chemistry, mem. Scientific Cttee. Perm. Int. Symposium on Proteins; Order of Red Banner of Labour 52, 61, Badge of Honour 45, 51, and other Soviet decorations; Pasteur Medal 57; French Biochemical Soc. Medal 58, Second Int. Biochemistry Congress Medal 52.
Institute of Medical and Biological Chemistry, Pogodinskaya 10, Moscow, U.S.S.R.

Orel, Admiral Alexander Yevstafievich; Soviet naval officer; b. 1908; ed. General Staff Acad.
Merchant marine sailor, secondary technical school student, captain's mate 24-29; Naval Service 29-; Commdr. of ships and formations 41-59; Commdr. Baltic Fleet 59-; mem. C.P.S.U. 37-; Deputy to U.S.S.R. Supreme Soviet.
Ministry of Defence, 34 Maurice Thorez Embankment, Moscow, U.S.S.R.

Oribe, Emilio N., LL.D.; Uruguayan lawyer and diplomatist; b. 21; ed. Liceo Francés, Montevideo, Universidad de la República, Montevideo, and Université de Paris à la Sorbonne.
Foreign Service and studies, Paris 46-49; Sec.-Gen. Uruguay Mission to UN 49-51; First Sec. Washington 51-52; First Sec. and Chargé d'Affaires, Netherlands 52-60; Uruguayan Embassy, Washington, and Del. to Org. of American States (OAS) 60, Deputy Rep. of Uruguay to OAS 61; Chargé d'Affaires *a.i.*, Havana 61-62; Acting Rep. of Uruguay on Council of OAS 62, later Perm. Rep.; Chair. Council of OAS 67-68.
Publs. *La Comité de Défense politique et l'Evolution du Système interaméricain* 48, *La Conférence de Genève et le Statut juridique du Plateau continental* 60, *El Plan Kennedy y la Planificación para el Económico y Social en América Latina* 61.
Representation of Uruguay to Organization of American States, 2632 Massachusetts Avenue, N.W., Washington, D.C. 20008, U.S.A.

Orieux, Jean, D. ès L.; French inspector of education and writer; b. 20 May 1907; ed. Collège Commandant Arnould, Bordeaux, Ecole Normale de la Gironde, Ecole Normale Supérieure de Saint-Cloud and Univ. de Paris à la Sorbonne.
Professor of Literature, Bourges 31-36, Beauvais 36-37, Marrakesh, Morocco 51-55; Insp. of Educ., St. Yrieix 37-41, Oran, Algeria 41-44, Rabat, Morocco 44-46, Grenoble 55, Nantes 57, Paris 57-58, Libourne 65-66; Hon. Insp. of Educ.; Officier d'Académie, Chevalier Légion d'Honneur; Grand Prix du Roman, Acad. française 46, Prix du Maroc 53, Prix au Service de la pensée française 54, Grand Prix de la critique littéraire 66.
Publs. *Fontagre* 45, *Menus Plaisirs* 45, *Un Déjeuner de Soleil* 46, *Les Ciseaux d'Argent* 47, *L'Aigle de Fer* 49, *La Mal Mariée* 51, *Cinq Filles et une Fusil* 53, *Les Bonnes Fortunes* 54 (novels); *Kasbahs en plein Ciel* 52 (travel); *Bussy Rabutin* 58, *Voltaire* 66 (biography).
Place du Temple, 24 Le Bugue (Dordogne), France.

Oriol y Urquijo, Antonio María; Spanish judge.
Lawyer; fmr. Dir.-Gen. of Welfare and Social Works; Minister of Justice 66-; Pres. Supreme Assembly of the Spanish Red Cross; Nat. Del. Auxilio Social (Social Help); Individual Mil. Medal.
Plaza Independencia 6, Madrid, Spain.

Orive Alba, Adolfo; Mexican civil engineer; b. 07; ed. Nat. Engineering Faculty, Nat. Univ. of Mexico.
Specialised in construction of irrigation projects, Bureau of Reclamation 28; Engineer and Chief Engineer Hydraulic Works Div., Ministry of Communications and Public Works 29-31; Chief Engineer, Nat. Irrigation Comm. 32-35, in charge of completion of "Rodriguez" dam, Lower Calif. 36-37; Engineer Mexican Section of Int. Water Boundary Comm. 38-40; Exec. Commr. Nat. Irrigation Comm. 40-46; Sec. of Hydraulic Resources 47-52, Consulting Engineer 53-; study of Hydraulic Resources of Cuba 54.
Rio Atoyac 110-302, Mexico City, D.F., Mexico.

Orlich, José Francisco; Costa Rican businessman and politician; b. 08.
Has interests in coffee, sugar-cane, rice, livestock, gold mining, shoe factories, grocery stores; Presidential candidate 58; Pres. of Costa Rica 62-66; Nat. Liberation Party.
c/o National Liberation Party, P.O.B. 2244, San José, Costa Rica.

Orlov, Aleksandr Leonidovich; Soviet diplomatist; b. 1907.
Deputy U.S.S.R. High Commr. in Germany, Counsellor Minister to Soviet Embassy in the German Democratic Republic 52-56; Deputy Minister of Foreign Affairs 59-.
Ministry of Foreign Affairs, 32-34 Smolenskaya-Sennaya ploshchad, Moscow, U.S.S.R.

Orlov, Georgi Mikhailovich; Soviet architect; b. 8 April 1901; ed. Moscow Higher Technical Schools.
Director of architectural group of Dnieper Hydro-Electric Power Station 27-32; Asst. Chief Architect, Central Volga Building Org. 32-35; Chief Architect, Chirchik Hydro Electric Power Station (Uzbekistan) 33-36; Chief Architect, No. 1 Architecture Studio 38-42; Chief Architect, restoration work at Dnieper Hydro-Electric Power Station 44-51; Chief Architect *Gidroenergoproject* (Hydro-power designing) Research and Designing Inst. 51-61; Exec. mem. Moscow Branch, Soviet Architects' Union 51-55, mem. Presidium Soviet Architect's Union 55-63; Vice-Pres. U.S.S.R. Acad. of Construction and Architecture 61-63; Pres. of U.S.S.R. Union of Architects 63-; First Sec. Soviet Architects' Union 63-; State Prize 51; Order of Lenin, Order of the Red Banner of Labour, Order of the Badge of Honour, and various medals.
Chief projects include: series of constructions for Dnieper Hydro-Electric Power Station; construction of amenities of housing estate for builders of Chirchik Hydro-Electric Power Station (Uzbekistan); design for main construction of Kakhova Hydro-Electric Project (power station, dam, locks); design for building of Kremenchug Hydro-Electric Power Station.
Union of Architects of U.S.S.R., ulitsa Shchuseva 3, Moscow, U.S.S.R.

Orlov, Georgi Mikhailovich; Soviet politician; b. 03; ed. Leningrad Timber Acad.
Former engineer, cellulose and paper industry; mem. C.P.S.U. 40-; Minister of Timber Industry of U.S.S.R. 44-57, of R.S.F.S.R. 57-58; Dep. Chair. *Gosplan,* R.S.F.S.R. 58-60, First Dep. Chair. 60-62; Chair. State Cttee. for Gosplan for Timber, Pulp and Paper Industries, U.S.S.R. 62-65; Deputy Chair. U.S.S.R. Council of Ministers State Cttee. for Material and Equipment Supply 65-; Candidate mem. Central Cttee. of C.P.S.U. 52-66; Order of Lenin, Order of Red Banner of Labour.
State Committee for Material and Equipment Supply of U.S.S.R. Council of Ministers, Moscow, U.S.S.R.

Orlov, Mikhail Anatolyevich; Soviet politician; b. 1912; ed. Higher Party School.

Member C.P.S.U. 40-; Komsomol worker 32-43; Sec. Kamchatka Regional Cttee. of C.P. 44-49; First Sec. Khabarovsk City Cttee. of C.P., later Sec. Khabarovsk Territorial Cttee. of C.P. 50-56; First Sec. Kamchatka Regional Cttee. of C.P. 56-; mem. Central Auditing Comm. of C.P.S.U. 56-; Deputy to U.S.S.R. Supreme Soviet.

Kamchatka Regional Committee of C.P.S.U., Petropavlovsk-Kamchatsky, U.S.S.R.

Orlov, Vladimir Pavlovich; Soviet politician; b. 1921; ed. Ivanovo Textile Inst.

Shop supt. 43-45; mem. C.P.S.U. 48-; successively Sec. Young Communist League (Y.C.L.) Cttee. Chapayevsk, Sec. City Y.C.L. Cttee., Sec. Chapayevsk City Cttee. of C.P., Chair. Exec. Cttee. City Soviet of Working People's Deputies, Sec. City then Regional Cttee. of C.P., later Chair. Exec. Cttee. Kuibyshev Regional/Industrial Soviet of Working People's Deputies 45-64; Sec. Kuibyshev Regional Cttee. of C.P. 64-65; Chair. Exec. Cttee. Kuibyshev Regional Soviet of Working People's Deputies 65-67; First Sec. Kuibyshev Regional Cttee. of C.P. 67-; Deputy to Supreme Soviet of U.S.S.R. Kuibyshev Regional Committee of Communist Party, Kuibyshev, U.S.S.R.

Orlova, Lyubov Petrovna; Soviet actress; b. 02; ed. Moscow Conservatoire and Moscow Ballet School.

Acted at the Nemirovich-Danchenko Musical Theatre, Moscow 26-33; appeared in cinema 26-, in Mossoviet Theatre 55-; People's Artist of the U.S.S.R.; State prizewinner 41, 50; awarded Order of Lenin, Order of the Red Banner of Labour.

Principal film roles: Anyuta (*Jolly Fellows* 34), Marion Dickson (*Circus* 36), Dunya (*Volga-Volga* 38), Tanya (*Bright Path* 40), scientist Nikitina and singer Shatrova (*Spring* 47), Janet Sherwood (*Meeting on the Elbe*), (*Russian Souvenir* 60); several theatre roles including Nora (*A Doll's House* 59).

Mossoviet Theatre, 16 Bolshaya Sadovaya ulitsa, Moscow, U.S.S.R.

Orlowski, Witold; Polish physician; b. 24 Jan. 1874; ed. St. Petersburg Medical School.

Professor of Internal Medicine, Kazan 07-19, Cracow 19-25, Warsaw Univ. 25-50, Warsaw Acad. of Medicine 50; Hon. Prof. Warsaw Univ. and Acad. of Medicine; Editor *Polskie Archiwum Medycyny Wewnetrznej* (Polish Archives of Internal Medicine) 28-48, *Rozprawy Wydzialu Medycznego Polskiej Akademii Nauk* (Treatises of the Dept. of Medical Science); author of *Internal Medicine* (in 8 vols.); mem. Polish Acad. of Sciences, Cracow Acad. of Sciences, New York Acad. of Sciences and various Polish and foreign socs.; State Prize 1st Class; Hon. M.D. Łódź, Dr. h.c. Łódź Acad. of Medicine, Cracow Acad. of Medicine.

54 Polna, Warsaw 1, Poland.

Ormandy, Eugene, B.A., MUS.D.; American musician; b. Hungary 18 Nov. 1899; ed. Royal State Acad. of Music, Gymnasium and Univ., Budapest.

Student of the Royal State Acad. at the age of 5; toured Hungary and later Central Europe, as child prodigy; Head of Master Classes, State Conservatorium of Music, Budapest 19; went to U.S.A. 21, naturalised 27; substituted for Toscanini as Conductor of the Philadelphia Orchestra; Conductor, Minneapolis Symphony Orchestra 31-36; Music Dir. and Conductor, Philadelphia Orchestra 36-; Commdr. de la Légion d'Honneur (France); Knight, Order of Dannebrog (Denmark); Knight of the Order White Rose (Finland); Order of Merit, Juan Pablo Duarte Dominican Republic); Commdr., Order of Dannebrog, Commdr., Order of the Lion of Finland; Hon. Cross for Arts and Sciences

(Austria); Sibelius Medal and many hon. doctorates and awards from various acads. and univs. in the U.S.A.

c/o Philadelphia Orchestra, 230 South 15th Street, Philadelphia, Pa. 19102, U.S.A.
Telephone: 215-KI5-3830.

Ormesson, Comte Wladimir d'; French diplomatist; b. 2 Aug. 1888; ed. Lycée Janson-de-Sailly, Paris, and Ecole libre des sciences politiques.

Journalist on *Temps, Journal de Genève* 24-34; Editorial Staff of *Figaro* 34-40, 44-, Dir. Société fermière d'édition du *Figaro* and *Figaro Littéraire* until 64; Ambassador to the Vatican May-October 40, to Argentina 45-48, to the Vatican 48-56; mem. Académie Française 56-; Pres. Admin. Council of Radiodiffusion-Télévision Française (O.R.T.F.) 64-; Grand-Croix Légion d'Honneur and numerous other decorations, including Dag Hammarskjöld Prize 65.

Publs. *Nos illusions sur l'Europe centrale* 22, *La Confiance en l'Allemagne* 28, *La Paix religieuse* 29, *Enfances diplomatiques* 31, *Qu'est-ce qu'un Français: Clemenceau, Poincaré, Briand* 35, *La Papauté, La Présence française dans la Rome des Papes, La Ville et les Champs, Les Vraies Confidences, Auprès de Lyautey* 64, *Le Clergé et l'Académie* 65, etc.

Château d'Ormesson, Ormesson-sur-Marne, S.-et-O., France.

Ornano, Comte Michel d'; French politician and administrator; b. 12 July 1924; ed. Lycée Carnot, Univ. of Paris.

Mayor of Deauville 62-; mem. Council on Foreign Trade 56-, mem. Directing Council 63-; mem. Council of Ministers 67-; Sec. Comm. of Foreign Affairs to Nat. Assembly.

Villa Mirasol, 88 rue du Général Leclerc, Deauville, (Calvados); Assemblée Nationale, Place du Palais Bourbon, Paris 7ème, France.

O'Rourke, Dennis; American sugar executive; b. 31 Oct. 1914; ed. Nebraska State Teachers Coll. and George Washington Univ. Law School, Washington, D.C.

Attorney, Office of Gen. Counsel, U.S. Dept. of Agriculture, Washington 39, rising to Chief, Basic Commodity Div.; Gen. Counsel, Holly Sugar Corpn. 45-53, Vice-Pres. 53-63, Pres. and Chief Exec. Officer 63-67, Chair. of Board and Chief Exec. Officer 67-, Dir. 56-; Trustee U.S. Beet Sugar Asscn.; Dir. The Sugar Asscn. Inc., First Nat. Bank of Colorado Springs; mem. Mexico-U.S. Cttee. of U.S. Chamber of Commerce; Adviser to U.S. Del. to Int. Sugar Council, Mexico City 60, Int. Sugar Conf., Geneva 65.

Holly Sugar Corporation, Colorado Springs, Colorado; Home: 8 Heather Drive, Colorado Springs, Colorado, U.S.A.

Orrick, William Horsley, Jr.; American government official; b. 10 Oct. 1915; ed. Hotchkiss School, Yale and Univ. of California (Berkeley).

Admitted to Calif. Bar 41; Partner, Orrick, Dahlquist, Herrington and Sutcliffe, San Francisco 41-61; Asst. Attorney Gen. Dept. of Justice 61-62; Dep. Under Sec. for Admin., Dept. of State 62-63; Asst. Attorney Gen. Dept. of Justice 63-65; Chair. U.S. Del. to OECD Cttee. on Restrictive Business Practices 63; Partner, Orrick, Dahlquist, Herrington and Sutcliffe 65-.

405 Montgomery Street, San Francisco, Calif. 94104, U.S.A.

Országh, László, PH.D., B.A.; Hungarian philologist; b. 25 Oct. 1907; ed. Budapest and Rollins Coll., Florida.

Lecturer in English, Budapest Univ. 42-47; Prof. of English, Debrecen Univ. 47-50, 57-; Head, Lexicographical Dept., Linguistic Inst. of Hungarian Acad. of Sciences, and Ed. of the Dictionary of the Hungarian Language 50-62.

Publs. *History of American Literary History Writing,*

The Rise of the English Novel, Shakespeare, English-Hungarian Hungarian-English Dictionary, History of American Literature.
Balaton u. 12, Budapest V, Hungary.
Telephone: Budapest 327-828.

Ortiz Mena, Antonio, LL.L.; Mexican lawyer and politician; b. 1908; ed. Escuela Nacional de Jurisprudencia.
Leading legal positions, Dept. of Fed. District and office of Attorney-Gen.; Dir.-Gen. of Professions at the Secr. of Public Educ.; during Second World War, mem. of Cttee. for Political Defence of the American Continent and Adviser to Mexican Del. at the Chapultepec Conf.; on Editorial Comms. for the Fed. Law of Civil Procedure, to reform certain Articles of the Constitution; Deputy Dir. Banco Hipotecario Urbano y de Obras Públicas, S.A. 48-52; Dir.-Gen. Inst. of Social Insurance 52; Vice-Pres. Admin. Council, Int. Asscn. of Social Insurance 53; Alt. Del. to Conf. of Ministers of Finance and Economy, Rio de Janeiro 54, Inter-American Conf. of Insurance, Caracas 55; Pres. Inter-American Perm. Cttee. of Social Insurance 55; Sec. for the Treasury and Public Credit 58-.
Secretaría de Hacienda, Mexico, D.F., Mexico.

Ortiz-Monasterio, Juan Manuel; Mexican banker; b. 7 March 1898; ed. Scientific Inst., Military Acad., and Nat. Univ., Mexico City, Tulane Univ. of New Orleans, and American Inst. of Banking.
Vice-President Hibernia Nat. Bank, New Orleans 20-38, Mercantile Trust Co. St. Louis 39-46; Chair. Exec. Cttee. Banco Comercial Mexicano, Mexico City 47-57; Pres. Mexican Nat. Cttee. of Int. Chamber of Commerce 56-63, now Hon. Pres.; Chair. Int. Cttee. of Board of Dirs. of Banco Comercial Mexicano 63-; Chair. Rivetex S.A.; Dir. E. R. Squibb & Sons de Mexico, KLM Royal Dutch Airlines of Mexico, Consorcio Industrial, Industrias Lubrizol de Mexico, Financiera Comermex, Inversora Mexicana, The Texas & Pacific Railway Co., Electronica S.A., American-British Cowdray Hospital; numerous decorations.
Sierra Madre 415, Lomas; and Isabel La Catòlica 55, Mexico City, Mexico.
Telephone: 20-84-36 (Home); 18-02-40 (Office).

Ortiz Sanz, Fernando; Bolivian journalist and diplomatist; b. 27 Dec. 1914; ed. Univ. of Chuquisaca.
Deputy for Sucre, Bolivian Parl. 44-46; Minister to Vatican 46-49; Under-Sec. for Foreign Affairs 51-52; later Prof. of History of Culture, Univ. of Chuquisaca; on staff of Bolivian newspapers *La Razón, El Diario* and *La Noche* for 10 years; Perm. Rep. to UN 65-; mem. Bolivian Acad. of Spanish Language 58-; Bolivian Nat. Award for Literature 63.
Bolivian Mission to the United Nations, 211 East 43rd Street, New York, N.Y. 10017, U.S.A.

Ortoli, François-Xavier; French economist; b. 16 Feb. 1925; ed. Hanoi Faculty of Law, and Ecole Nationale d'Administration, Paris.
Inspector of Finances 48-51; Technical Adviser to the Office of the Minister of Economic Affairs and Information 51-53; Technical Adviser, Office of the Minister of Finances 54; Asst. Dir. to the Sec. of State for Economic Affairs and Sec.-Gen. Franco-Italian Cttee. of EEC 55; Head, Commercial Politics Service of Sec. of State for Economic Affairs 57; Dir.-Gen. of the Internal Market Div. of EEC 58; Sec.-Gen. Inter-Ministerial Cttee. for Questions of European Econ. Co-operation, Paris 61-; Dir. of Cabinet to Prime Minister 62-66; Commr.-Gen. of the Plan 66-67; Minister of Works 67-68, of Education 68-; Légion d'Honneur, Médaille Militaire, Croix de Guerre 45; Médaille de la Résistance, etc. 92 boulevard Malesherbes, Paris 8e; and 2 rue de Bagatelle, Neuilly-sur-Seine, France.

Ortona, Egidio; Italian diplomatist; b. 16 Sept. 1910; ed. Univs. of Turin and Poitiers, London School of Economics.
Entered diplomatic service 32; mem. Italian Del. to World Economic Conf., London 33; Consul, Cairo and Johannesburg; Sec. of Embassy, London, Chief of Office of Minister of Foreign Affairs 43; mem. Economic Mission to U.S.A. 44; Counsellor, later Minister, Italian Embassy, Washington 45-58; Permanent Rep. of Italy to UN with Ambassador's rank 58-61; Pres. UN Security Council 59-60; Dir.-Gen. of Econ. Affairs, Italian Ministry of Foreign Affairs 61-66; Sec.-Gen. Ministry of Foreign Affairs 66-67; Amb. to U.S.A. 67-; Pres. XIV Assembly of ICAO 62, European Conf. on Satellite Communication 63-64.
Italian Embassy, Washington, D.C., U.S.A.

Ortutay, Gyula, PH.D.; Hungarian politician and ethnographer; b. 24 March 1910; ed. Szeged Univ.
On staff of Hungarian Nat. Museum and Hungarian Radio 35-; mem. of resistance movement and Hungarian Nat. Independence Front; after Liberation became Pres. of Hungarian Radio and mem. of Parl.; Prof. of Folklore, Budapest Univ. 46-; Minister of Education 47-50; Rector of the Eötvös Loránd Univ. 57-63; Gen. Sec. People's Patriotic Front 57-64, Vice-Pres. 64-; mem. Pres. Council Hungarian People's Republic; mem. Hungarian Acad.; Hon. mem. Finnish Ugrian Soc.; Editor *Magyarságtudomány, Ethnographia, Acta Ethnographica;* on Editorial Board of *Fabula.*
Publs. *Székely-népballadák, Nyiri és rétközi parasztmesék, Magyar népismeret, Parasztságunk élete, Fedics Mihály mesél, Kis magyar néprajz, Magyar népmüvészet, Ungarische Volksmärchen.*
Pasaréti ut. 83, Budapest II, Hungary.
Telephone: 341-135.

Osadebay, Dennis Chukude; Nigerian politician; b. 29 June 1911; ed. Hope Waddell Institute, Calabar, Lincoln's Inn, London, and London Univ.
Law practice, Aba and Benin; Jt. Founder Nat. Council of Nigeria and the Cameroons (N.C.N.C.) 44; mem. Federal House of Reps. 52-54; Ldr. Opposition, W. Nigeria Assembly 54-56, 58-60; Pres. Federal Senate 60-64; Admin. Mid-West Region, Nigeria Aug. 63-Feb. 64; Premier, Mid-West Region of Nigeria 64-66; Vice-Pres. Nat. Council of Nigerian Citizens 64; Acting Gov.-Gen. of the Fed. of Nigeria, June-August 61.
Publ. *Africa Sings* (poems) 52.
c/o Premier's Lodge, Benin; P.O.B. 7, Asaba, Nigeria.

Osborne, John James; British playwright, actor and producer; b. 12 Dec. 1929; ed. state schools and privately.
Journalist 47-48; tour *No Room at the Inn* 48-49; actor-manager, Ilfracombe 51; repertory Leicester, Camberwell, Kidderminster, Derby, Bridgewater, etc.; also appeared London; Dir. Woodfall Film Productions Ltd.; Dir. John Osborne Productions Ltd.
Plays: *Look Back in Anger* 56, *The Entertainer* 57, *Epitaph for George Dillon* (with Anthony Creighton) 58, *The World of Paul Slickey* 59, *A Subject of Scandal and Concern* 60, *Luther* 61, *Plays for England* 62, *Inadmissible Evidence* 64, *A Patriot for Me* 64, *A Bond Honoured* (trans. of Lope de Vega's *La Fianza Satisfecha*) 66, *The Hotel in Amsterdam* 68, *Time Present* 68; screen play for *Tom Jones* 63.
11A Curzon Street, London, W.1, England.

Osborne, Stanley de Jongh; American businessman; b. 27 March 1905; ed. Phillips Acad., Andover, and Harvard Univ.
Dir. Publicity Harvard Athletic Asscn. 27-28; with Old Colony Fisheries Co. 29-30; Asst. to Pres. Atlantic Coast Fisheries Co. 29-30, Treas. 30-36, 39-43, Sec. 32-42, Vice-Pres. 36-43; Vice-Pres. Eastern Airlines Inc. 44-50; Financial Vice-Pres. Mathieson Chem. Corpn.,

Baltimore 50-54; Exec. Vice-Pres. Olin Mathieson Chemical Corpn. 54-57, Dir. 57-, Pres. 57-63, Chair. of Board and Chair. Exec. Cttee. 63-64; Gen. Partner Lazard Frères & Co. 64-; Special Advisor to the Pres. of the U.S. 63-64; mem. President's Advisory Cttee. (Supersonic Aircraft) 64-; Trustee, Cttee. for Econ. Devt.; Special Consultant to the Nat. Aeronautics and Space Admin.; Dir. of several companies.
44 Wall Street; and I East End Avenue, New York City, N.Y., U.S.A.
Telephone: HA2-1200 (Office).

Osborne, W. Irving, Jr., PH.B.; American business executive; b. 19 Nov. 1904; ed. Evanston High School, and Yale Coll.
D. H. Burnham & Co., Architects, Chicago 26-29; Cornell Wood Products Co. (later Cornell Paperboard Products Co.) 29-61, Pres. Cornell Paperboard Products Co. 33-57, Chair. of Board, Cornell Paperboard Products Co. 57-59, Chair. Cornell Paperboard Products Co. Div. of St. Regis Paper Co. 59-61; Pres. Pullman Inc. 61-66, Pres. and Chair. 66-.
Pullman Inc., 200 S. Michigan Avenue, Chicago, U.S.A.

Osipov, Georgi Ivanovich; Soviet politician; b. 1906; ed. Higher Party School of Central Cttee. of C.P.S.U. Soviet Army 20-28; Communist Party official 31-; Second Sec. Ussuri Regional Cttee. of C.P.S.U. 39-42; mem. staff Central Cttee. of C.P.S.U. 43-47; Second Sec. then First Sec. Komi Regional Cttee. and Syktyvkar City Cttee. of C.P.S.U. 47-56; First Sec. Mordovian Regional Cttee. of C.P.S.U. 58-; Cand. mem. Central Cttee. of C.P.S.U.; Deputy to U.S.S.R. Supreme Soviet; several decorations.
Mordovian Regional Committee of the C.P.S.U., Saransk, Mordovian A.S.S.R., U.S.S.R.

Osma, Şinasi; Turkish army officer and politician; b. 1913; ed. Military War Coll. and Gen. Staff Coll.
In various units and branches of the Armed Forces 42-50; Mil. Attaché at Amman and Baghdad 55-58; retd. from Army 60; co-founder, Justice Party 61, then Gen. Sec. for three years, now Pres. of its Central Cttee. of Arbitration and mem. of Central Exec. Cttee.; mem. for Izmir, Nat. Assembly 61-, also mem. Foreign Affairs and Defence Cttees., Nat. Assembly.
Yenişehir Ferzi, Çakmak Sokak 10/12, Ankara, Turkey.

Osman, Hassan Mutwakil Mohamed; Sudanese cotton executive; b. Jan. 1918; ed. Coll. of Agriculture, Sudan.
Agriculturalist with Sudanese Dept. of Agriculture 42-48; Senior Officer Atbara Dairy 48-50; Insp. of Mechanized Crop Production 50-51; Insp. of Agriculture, Sennor and Fung Districts 51-54; Govt. Soil Conservation Officer 54-57; Asst. Dir. of Agriculture, Dept. of Agriculture 59-62, Deputy Dir. 63-65, Dir. 66; Man. Dir. Sudan Gezira Board 66-; mem. Council, Univ. of Khartoum, Board of Faculty of Agriculture, and Khartoum Technical Inst.
Sudan Gezira Board, Barakat, Blue Nile Province, Sudan.

Osman, Osman Ahmed, B.SC.; United Arab Republic (Egyptian) civil engineer; b. 1917; ed. Cairo Univ.
Chairman The Arab Contractors (Osman Ahmed Osman & Co) 52-, and of its assoc. companies, Saudi Enterprises, Kuwaiti Engineering Co., The Arab Contractors (Libya), The Libyan Co. for Contracting and Devt.; Republic Medal (First Class), Russian Hero of Labour Medal.
Chief works undertaken include: (in Egypt) Aswan High Dam, Suez Canal deepening and widening, Port Said Shipyard, Cairo Int. Airport, Salhia reclamation project, High Dam Electric Power Transmission Lines; (in Saudi Arabia) Dhahran Airport, Riyadh Mil. Coll., Dammam Mil. Barracks; (in Kuwait) Municipality Centre, Kuwait drainage system; (in Libya) Benghazi

drainage system, Benghazi Stadium; (in Iraq) Kirkuk Feeder Canal No. 2 and 3; (in Jordan) Khaled Ibn El-Walid Dam and Tunnels.
Publ. *The High Dam* (lecture) 66.
The Arab Contractors, 34 Adly Street, Cairo, U.A.R.
Telephone: 49988.

Osman, Yacoub, LL.B.; Sudanese diplomatist; b. 12; ed. Gordon Coll., Khartoum, Secondary School, Cairo and Leeds Univ.
Worked in aircraft factory in London in Second World War, also Arabic translator in British Broadcasting Corporation; returned to Sudan 45; joined independence movement, became Editor of *El-Nil* (daily of independence movement) and Asst. Gen. Sec. of Umma (Independence) Party; rep. independence movement in London; resigned from Umma Party 55; Perm. Rep. to UN 56-59; Ambassador to U.S.S.R. 59-64, to Ethiopia 64-, also accred. to Czechoslovakia 64.
Embassy of Sudan, Box 1110, Kirkos Kebelie, Addis Ababa, Ethiopia.

Osman Daar, Aden Abdulla; Somali businessman and politician; b. 08; ed. Government School, Somalia.
Member Somalia Territorial Council 51-55, Vice-Pres. 53-55; Pres. Somali Youth League 54-56, 58-59; Pres. Legislative Assembly 56-60, Constituent Assembly 60; Pres. of the Somali Republic 61-67.
Mogadishu, Somalia.

Osmanczyk, Edmund Jan; Polish journalist and author; b. 10 Aug. 1913; ed. in Warsaw, Berlin and France.
Editor of Press Centre, Union of Poles in Germany 32-39; War corresp. Radio Warsaw 39; Warsaw underground 39-44; War corresp. 45; Corresp. Potsdam Conf., Nuremberg Trials; Permanent Corresp., *Czytelnik* in Berlin 46-50; Corresp. Polish Radio Moscow 56, 59-60, Diplomatic Corresp. P.A.P. and Polish Radio Washington 57-58; Dep. to Seym 52-56, 57-61; Diplomatic Correspondent for Latin America, Polish Press Agency and Polish Radio and T.V. 61-; mem. Polish PEN Club.
Publs. *Walka jest zwycieska* (The Struggle is Victorious) (verse) 45, *Sprawy Polaków* (Polish Affairs) 46, *Dokumenty pruskie* (Prussian Documents) 47, *Niemcy 1945-1950* (Germany 1945-1950) 51, *Wspolczesna Ameryka* (The Contemporary America) 60, *Ciekawa Historia ONZ 1945-1965* (The Interesting History of UN 1945-1965) 65.
Rio Amazonas 57-503, Mexico 5, D.F., Mexico.
Telephone: 461892.

Osorio-Tafall, Bibiano F.; Mexican (b. Spain) United Nations official; b. 1903; ed. Universidades de Santiago y de Madrid and Biologische Anstalt, Dahlen.
Government posts in Spain and prof. of several academic insts. in Spain and Mexico until 49; Fisheries Regional Officer for Latin America, Food and Agriculture Org. (FAO) 49-51, Dir. Regional Office for Western Latin America, Santiago, Chile 51-55, Chief, Technical Assistance Mission in Chile 55-56; Resident Rep. in Chile, UN Technical Assistance Board (now UN Devt. Programme—UNDP) 56-59, in Indonesia 59-61, in U.A.R. 61-64; Resident Rep. UNDP, Dem. Repub. of Congo 64-66; Special Rep. of the Sec.-Gen. of UN in Cyprus Feb. 67-.
Office of UN Special Representative in Cyprus, P.O. Box 1642, Nicosia, Cyprus.

Ossiannilsson, Karl Gustav, F.F.R.S.L.; Swedish writer; b. 30 July 1875; ed. Univ. of Lund.
Teacher 97-1900; since 1900 has written many novels, short stories, plays, lyrics, films, radio-plays; trans. works of Corneille, Pepys, Addison and Steele, Robert Browning, Swinburne, A. Bennett, Verhaeren, Kropotkin; King Albert Medal (Belgium).
Publs. Poetry, including: *Collected Poems* 20, *Choice of Poems* 34, *Den gamle och den unge* (Poetry) 50; Novels:

Barbarskogen, Lille Benjamin, Smeden Bång, En ung mans väg, Slätten, Grevarna Andersson, Lasse i Gatan, Drottingens Kurir 51, *Rättskaffens Folk* (Play), *Dröttmen och verkligheten* 53, *Kärlekens strider* 54, *Poems* 54, *Nils Dacke* 56, *En Amazon på äventyr* 57, *Bland tsarer och bojarer* 58, *Stora Mogul* 59, *Riddarkedjan* 59, *Ulla-Britas kung* 59, *Segernamnet* 60, *Studenterna* 60, *Drabanterna* 61, *Kung Gåtfull* 61, *Hertig Hårdhänt* 63, *En projke med flax* 65; many translated into other languages.
Linghem, P.O.B. 10, Sweden.

Östbye, Rolf; Norwegian industrialist; b. 17 April 1898; ed. Oslo, Trondheim Technical Coll., and Scandinavian Brewing Coll., Copenhagen.
Manager and Dir. of breweries and flour mills 21-47; Dir. Standard Telephone and Cable Co. 47-53; Dir. Norsk Hydro 53, Pres. Norsk Hydro 56-66; Chair. of Board Norsk Hydro, Norsk Spraengstofindustri A/S, A/S Atlas Copco Norway, ASEA-Per Kure and Alnor A/S; Chair. Board of Reps. Den norske Creditbank and Det Norske Luftfartselskap A/S; Deputy Chair. Board of Reps. Forsikrings A/S Norden; mem. Board of Reps. DE-NO-FA og Lilleborg Fabriker A/S and Wilh. Wilhelmsen; Chair. Norwegian Export Council; mem. of Exec. Cttee. Norwegian Technical Scientific Board; Hon. mem. Royal Norwegian Scientific Soc.; Consul-Gen. for Denmark.
Norsk Hydro, Bygdøy Allé 2, Oslo; Hoffsjef Lövenskiolds vei 55, Ö. Ullern, Norway.

Osterling, Anders Johan, PH.D.; Swedish author and critic; b. 13 April 1884; ed. Lund Univ.
Librarian Lund Univ. 09-19; Literary Critic *Svenska Dagbladet* 19-35, and of *Stockholms-Tidningen* 36-; mem. Swedish Acad. 19-; Pres. Swedish PEN Club 23-36; Perm. Sec. Swedish Acad. 41-64; Pres. Nobel Foundation 47; Chair. Nobel Literature Prize Cttee.
Publs. *Preludier* 04, *Arets visor* 07, *Bäckahästen* 09, *Facklor i stormen* 13, *Idyllernas bok* 17, *De sju strängarna* 22, *Jordens heder* 27, *Tonen från havet* 33, *Skånska utflykter* 34, *Dagens gärning I-III* 21-26-31, *Horisonter* 39, etc.
Blockhusringen 39, Stockholm, Sweden.

Osterrieth, Frederick; Belgian merchant and company director; b. 03.
Hon. Pres. of Antwerp Chamber of Commerce; Pres. Anglo-Belgian Ferry Boats; Vice-Pres. Belgian Railways; Dir. Banque de Bruxelles and Banque Belge d'Afrique; Pres. Office de Récupération Economique (O.R.E.); Del. to Int. Chamber of Commerce; fmr. Vice-Pres. Office Belge du Commerce Extérieur.
Markgravestraat 12, Antwerp, Belgium.

Ostrovitianov, Konstantin Vasilyevich; Soviet economist; b. 1892; ed. Moscow Commercial Inst.
Member of Communist Party since 14 (candidate for Cen. Cttee. 52, 56); Dean of Workers Faculty of Plekhanov Inst. of Nat. Economy and Prof. Political Economy 22-25; Vice-Rector Plekhanov Inst. 25-29; Fellow Communist Acad. 30, and mem. Presidium 30-36; Prof. Moscow Univ. 38-; corresp. mem. U.S.S.R. Acad. of Sciences 39, full mem. 53, Dir. Inst. of Econs. 46-53, Editor *Voprosy Economiki* 47-52, Vice-Pres. of the Acad. 53-62; Editor *Vestnik* (Acad. of Sciences) 53-62, in Inst. of Econ., Acad. of Sciences of U.S.S.R. 62-; mem. Czechoslovak Acad. of Sciences; Chair. Soviet-Czechoslovakia Soc. of Friendship 58-; two Orders of Lenin, of the Red Banner of Labour, of the Red Star.
Publs. *Political Economy* (with Lapidus) (2 vols.), *Studies in the Economics of Pre-Capitalist formations, Zemelnaya Renta i Razvitiye Kapitalizma v Selskom Obshchestve, O Kharaktere Ekonomicheskikh Zakonov Sotsializma, O Roli Sovietskovo Gosudarstva v Razvitii Sotsialisticheskoi Ekonomiki, O Zakone Stoimosti pri Sotsializme, Stroitelstvo Communisma i Tovarno—*

denejnie otnosheniya 62, *Dumi o prosholm* 67, etc., co-author of textbook *Politicheskaya Ekonomiya*, 54, 58 and 62 edns.
Institute of Economics of the Academy of Sciences of the U.S.S.R., Volkhonka 14, Moscow, U.S.S.R.

Ostrower, Fayga; Brazilian (b. Polish) painter and engraver; b. 14 Sept. 1920; ed. Fundação Getúlio Vargas, Rio de Janeiro.
Lecturer in Theory of Composition and Analysis, Museum of Modern Art, Rio de Janeiro 54-65, Fed. Univ. of Minas Gerais 66-; John Hay Whitney Lecturer, Spelman Coll. Atlanta 64; mem. Jury for Bienal of São Paulo and Nat. Show of Fine Arts, Rio de Janeiro; Vice-Pres. Brazilian Cttee., Int. Asscn. of Plastic Arts; numerous one-man exhbns. and works in collections in the Americas and Europe; Hon. mem. Accademia delle Arti del Disegno, Florence; numerous prizes including awards at São Paulo Bienal in 55, 57, 61, 63, Venice Bienale 58, 62, Venezuela Bienale 67.
Rua do Russell 426, Apto. 302, Rio de Janeiro, Brazil. Telephone: 25-1709.

Otani, Sachio, B.ARCH.; Japanese architect; b. 20 Feb. 1924; ed. Univ. of Tokyo.
Architectural designer under Dr. Kenzo Tange 46-60; Lecturer in Architecture, Univ. of Tokyo 55-64; Assoc. Prof. of Urban Engineering, Univ. of Tokyo 64-; works include Kojimachi area (of Tokyo) redevelopment plan 60-64, Tokyo children's cultural centre 61-63 and Kyoto Int. Conf. Hall 63-66.
Department of Urban Engineering, Faculty of Engineering, University of Tokyo, 1-3-7 Hongo, Bunkyo-ku, Tokyo; Home: 111 Shoan Kita-machi, Suginami-ku, Tokyo, Japan.

Otero, Alejandro; Venezuelan artist; b. 7 March 1921; ed. School of Fine Arts, Caracas.
Early portraits in expressionist impasto, then landscapes in yellow, ochre and blue until shared a studio with Pascual Navarro in Paris 45-48; transition from figurative to abstract art through still lifes 45-48; participated in exhbn. *Les Mains Eblouies*, Galerie Maeght 47; returned to Venezuela and presented one-man exhbns. at Museum of Fine Arts, Caracas 49; Editor *Los Disidentes* after return to Paris 50; turned to optical art and collages 51; executed monumental comms. for Univ. City of Caracas 52-55; series of abstract paintings *Colour-Rhythms* 55-60; returned to Paris 60-64; Vice-Pres. Inst. of Culture and Fine Arts, Caracas 64-; collages from newspaper cuttings, in gay colours 64-; Retrospective Exhbn. Signals, London 66; other one-man exhbns. in Washington, D.C., Caracas, Venezuela, and Klagenfurt, Austria; numerous awards and honours.
Institute of Culture and Fine Arts, Caracas, Venezuela.

Otero De Navascués, Marqués de Hermosilla, **José María;** Spanish scientist; b. 07; ed. San Fernando Navy Ordnance School, Madrid Univ., Eidgenössische Technische Hochschule, Zürich, Technische Hochschule, Berlin.
Head, Navy Optical Laboratory 34-36, Optics Div., Nat. Physical Laboratory 40-46; Assoc. Dir., Naval Research Laboratory 42-47, Dir. 45-55; Prof. Navy Ordnance Graduate School 47-55; Pres. Real Sociedad Española Física y Química 54-58; Vice-Pres. Spanish UNESCO Cttee. 53-57, Int. Comm. of Optics 53-59; Vice-Pres. Nuclear Energy Bd. 51-58; Pres. and Chair., Spanish Nuclear Energy Comm. 58-; Dir. Inst. of Optics "Daza de Valdés" 46-; mem. Exec. Cttee. Spanish Nat. Council for Scientific Research 47-; Chair. Spanish Nat. Council of Physics 50; Pres. European Nuclear Energy Agency (OECD) 61-; Exec. Vice-Pres. European Atomic Energy Soc. 60-62; Fellow, Spanish Royal Acad. of Sciences 45-; mem. of Board Centre Européen de

Recherches Nucléaires; many Spanish and foreign awards.
Publs. Research papers on Physics (optics) and Nuclear Energy.
Alfonso XII 32, Madrid, Spain.

Otero Monsegur, Luis María; Argentine lawyer and banker; b. 9 Feb. 1914; ed. Univ. Nacional de Buenos Aires.
Former posts include Pres. Asscn. Argentina de Estudios del Derecho Fiscal, Inst. Nacional de Reaseguros; fmr. Vice Pres. Banco Cen. de la República Argentina, now Pres.; Alt. Gov. Int. Monetary Fund; Titular Gov. Int. Bank for Reconstruction and Development, Int. Finance Corpn., Int. Development Asscn., and Inter-American Development Bank.
Publs. *El Requisito de Duración Determinada en las Sociedades de Responsibilidad Limitada, La Compraventa de Acciones frente a nuestra Ley de Impuesto a los Réditos, El Conjunto Económico en nuestro Sistema Impositivo Nacional, La Prima de Emisión de Acciones y el Impuesto a las Ganancias Eventuales, Informe presentado sobre el Instituto Nacional de Reaseguros al Superior Gobierno de la Nación*, etc.
Lavalle 556, Buenos Aires, Argentina.

Othman, Mohamed Ben; Libyan politician; b. Oct. 1922; ed. Libyan religious and Arabic schools.
Teacher 42-43; in Liberation Movement; Head of Fezzan Del. in Legislative Assembly 50-51; Rep. for Fezzan, U.N. Council for Libya 51; Minister of Health, Fed. Govt. 51-58, of Econ. Affairs Feb.-Oct. 60; Prime Minister Oct. 60-63; Order of Independence (First Class).
Geraba Street 6, Tripoli, Libya.

Othmer, Donald Frederick, B.SC., M.S., PH.D.; American chemical engineer; b. 11 May 1904; ed. Armour Inst., Chicago, and Univs. of Nebraska and Michigan.
Development Engineer Eastman Kodak Co. and Tennessee Eastman Corpn. 27-32; Prof. Polytechnic Inst. of Brooklyn 32, Head Dept. of Chemical Engineering 37-61, Distinguished Prof. 61; consulting chemical engineer to numerous companies and govt. depts. in U.S. and abroad incl. U.S. Army, U.S. Navy, Depts. of State and Interior, Office of Saline Water, UN World Health Org., U.S. Dept. of Health, Educ. and Welfare, etc.; Fellow, American Asscn. for Advancement of Science, New York Acad. of Sciences, American Insts. of Chemists (Dir. 50-) and Consulting Engineers; mem. American Inst. of Chemical Engineers (Dir. 56-59), American Chemical Soc., Japan Soc. of Chemical Engineers, American Soc. of Mechanical Engineers Arbitration Asscn., Soc. de Chimie Industrielle, Soc. Chemical Industry, American Soc. of Eng. Educ., Newcomen Soc., etc.; Dir. Engineers' Joint Council 56-59, Chemurgic Council; inventor and licensor (about 80 U.S. and many foreign patents) on methods, processes and equipment in manufacture of chemicals, solvents, synthetic fibres, acetylene, wallboard, petroleum refining, fermentation, desalination of seawater, plastics, refrigeration, wood utilization, acetic acid, evaporation, heat transfer, petrochemicals, pigments, engineering equipment, salt, pharmaceuticals, distillation, sugar refining, synthetic rubber, pulping liquor recovery, zinc smelting, etc.; Lecturer in Swiss Univs. 48, Canadian 50, Indian 52, Japanese 55; European Congress of Chemical Engineers 58, 61, 62-65, and other int. congresses; Hon. Del. ACHEMA 58, 61, 64, 67; Hon. Prof. Concepción Univ. 51; Hon. Dr. Eng. Univ. of Nebraska 62; Hon. mem. Deutsche Gesellschaft für Chemisches Apparatewesen, Barber-Coleman Award 58, Tyler Award 58.
Publs. Over 250 articles in technical press; Editor *Fluidization*, co-Editor *Kirk-Othmer Encyclopædia of Chemical Technology* (17 vols. 47-60; Vols. 1-15, 2nd edn. 63-68), Co-author *Fluidization and Fluid Particle Systems*

60; Adviser, Perry's *Chemical Engineer's Handbook* 3rd edn., Technical Editor UN Report, *Technology of Water Desalination* 64.
333 Jay Street, Brooklyn, New York 11201; 140 Columbia Heights, Brooklyn, N.Y. 11201, U.S.A.
Telephone: MA5-1845 and 643-5120.

Ötker, Rudolf-August; German industrialist and shipowner; b. 20 Sept. 1916; ed. Univs. of Hamburg and Vienna.
Owner August Ötker Nahrmittelfabrik, Bielefeld, Westphalia, Hamburg-Südamerikanische Dampfschiffahrtsgesellschaft Eggert & Amsinck, Bankhaus Hermann Lampe KG, Bielefeld, Bankhaus Erich Sültz, Hamburg; holder of controlling interest of Condor Versicherungsgesellschaften, Hamburg, Deutscher Ring Versicherungsgesellschaften, Hamburg, Bank für Brau-Industrie, Frankfurt; numerous other business interests.
Lutterstrasse 14, 48 Bielefeld, German Federal Republic.
Telephone: 63-063.

Ottaviani, H.E. Cardinal Alfredo, D.IUR.UTR., TH.D., PH.D.; Vatican ecclesiastic; b. 29 Oct. 1890; ed. Pontifical Roman Seminary and Pontifical Inst. of Canon and Civil Law, Rome.
Ordained priest 16; created Cardinal by Pope Pius XII 53; Pro-Sec. Sacred Congregation of the Holy Office 53-59, Sec. 59-68, Bishop 62; mem. Sacred Congregation de Propaganda Fide, of the Consistory and of Extraordinary Ecclesiastical Affairs; mem. Supreme Tribunal of the Apostolic Segnatura, Pontifical Comm. for the Authentic interpretation of the Code of Canon Law; Pres. Pontifical Comm. "de Doctrina fidei et morum" 62.
Publs. *Compendium Iuris Publici Ecclesiastici* (4th edn.) 56, *Institutiones Iuris Publici Ecclesiastici* (6th edn.) 58, *Il Baluardo*.
Palazzo del Santo Uffizio, Vatican City, Rome, Italy.

Otten, Pieter Franziskus Sylvester; Netherlands businessman; b. 95; ed. Technical Univ. of Delft.
Joined Philips' Gloeilampenfabrieken 24, Asst. Gen. Man. 27, Chair. of the Council of Asst. Gen. Mans. and Secs. 34, Gen. Man. 36, Pres. 39; in U.S.A. 40-44; Chair. of the Presidium of the Board of Management N. V. Philip's Gloeilampenfabrieken 46-61, Chair. and Del. Dir. of the Board of Dirs. 61-; Adviser Amrobank; Grand Officer Orders Orange Nassau and House Order of Orange, and Orders of Greece, Argentina, Thailand, Japan and Spain; Commdr. Legion of Honour (France, Austria and Belgium), Commdr. of Merit (Italy), Southern Cross (Brazil); Companion of the Order of the Netherlands Lion 36; Hon. Citizen of Eindhoven, Valkenswaard and Schenectady.
't Heihuis, Valkenswaard, Netherlands.
Telephone: Eindhoven 60000.

Ötüken, Adnan; Turkish librarian; b. 11; ed. Lycée and Univ. of Istanbul, and Staatsbibliothek, Berlin.
Asst. Turkish Language and Literature Dept., Univ. of Istanbul 40; Dir. of Publications, Acting Asst. Dir.-Gen. of Higher Education, and Asst. Dir.-Gen. of Fine Arts, Ministry of Education 52-54; Lecturer in Library Science, Univ. of Ankara; mem. Executive Cttee. Turkish Nat. Comm. of UNESCO, and Executive Board Turkish Librarians Asscn.; Dir. Turkish Nat. Library 60-65; Under-Sec. for Cultural Affairs, Ministry of Educ. 65-67; Lecturer of Turkish Language and Lit., Lycée Teachers' Training Coll., Ankara, 67-; Gen. Sec. Turkish-Iraqi Standing Cttee. of Cultural Agreement; fmr. Turkish Cultural Attaché in Germany.
Publs. *Bibliyotek bilgisi ve bibliyografi* (Library Science and Bibliography) 40, *Istanbul Üniversitesi Yayimlari Bibliyografyasi* (Bibliography of the Publications of the University of Istanbul) 41, *Seçme eserler bibliyo-*

grafyası. 1. *cilt* (Selected Bibliography, Vol. 1) 46, *Millî Kütüphane kurulurken* (Establishing the National Library) 46, *Istanbul Universitesi Yayimlari Bibliyografyasi, 1933-45* (Bibliography of the Publications of the University of Istanbul, 1933-45, with Acaroğlu) 47, *Dünya edebiyatından tercümeler. Klâsikler Bibliyografyasi, 1940-48* (Bibliography of classical and modern works translated and published by Turkish Ministry of Education, 1940-48) 47, 2nd edn. *1940-50* 52, *Millî Kütüphane Nasil Kuruldu* (How the Turkish National Library was founded) 55.
Lycée Teachers' Training College, Ankara, Turkey.
Telephone: 126234.

Otuko, Fanuel Adala; Kenyan diplomatist; b. 20; ed. Ex-Servicemen's Coll., Kabete.
Post Office telegraphist 38-39; King's African Rifles 39-46; Community Development Officer, Kisuma 50-54; later Sec.-Gen., Luo Union of East Africa, mem. Nyanza Regional Assembly, Chair. Nyanza Region Law and Order Cttee.; Ambassador to U.S.S.R. 63-.
Embassy of Kenya, Moscow, U.S.S.R.

Ouimet, J. Alphonse, B.A., B.ENG.; Canadian radio engineer and administrator; b. 12 June 1908; ed. St. Mary's Coll., Montreal and McGill Univ.
Research Engineer Canadian Television Ltd. 32-33; Research Engineer and Dir. Canadian Electronics Co. 33-34; Research Engineer Canadian Broadcasting Corpn. (C.B.C.), Ottawa 35-36, Operations Engineer, Montreal 37-39, Gen. Supervisor of Engineering 39-40, Asst. and later Chief Engineer 41-51, Asst. Gen. Man. 51-52, Gen. Man. 53-58, Pres. 58-68; Fellow Inst. of Radio Engineers; mem. Engineering Inst. of Canada, Int. Television Cttee.
c/o Canadian Broadcasting Corporation, 1500 Bronson Avenue, Ottawa, Canada.

Ould Ahmedou, Bakar; Mauritanian diplomatist; b. 30; ed. Collège de Rosse, Mauritania.
Deputy to Nat. Assembly 59-; Amb. to Tunisia 61-62, to France, Great Britain, Italy and Switzerland 62-65; Itinerant Amb. accred. to Ghana, Ivory Coast, Liberia and Mali 65-; mem. Mauritanian del. to UN 60, 61, 62; Admin. Sec. and Sec.-Gen. of Mauritanian Section, AIDBA (Int. Asscn. for the Devt. of Libraries in Africa); Commandeur du Mérite National Mauritanien.
c/o Ministry of Foreign Affairs, Nouakchott, Mauritania.

Ould Cheikh, Mohamed; Mauritanian politician; b. 1930; ed. Ecole Primaire Bontilmih, Collège Rosso, and Lycée Dakar.
Schoolteacher 49-60; Commdr. of Cercle de l'Assaba 60-61; Sec.-Gen. for Nat. Defence 61-65; Minister of Foreign Affairs and Nat. Defence July 65-Feb. 66.
Ministère des Affaires Etrangères et de la Défense Nationale, Nouakchott, Mauritania.

Ould Daddah, Abdallahi; Mauritanian diplomatist; b. 25 April 1935; ed. Lycée Wan Wollenhoven and Université de Paris.
Former Directeur de Cabinet, Ministry of Foreign Affairs; Sec.-Gen., Ministry of Foreign Affairs 62-64; Ambassador to France, concurrently accred. to U.K., Italy and Switzerland 65-66; Perm. Rep. to UN and Amb. to U.S.A. 66-; Commandeur du Mérite Nat. Mauritanien.
Permanent Mission of the Islamic Republic of Mauritania to the United Nations, 150 East 52nd Street, New York, N.Y. 10022, U.S.A.

Ousmane, Sembene; Senegalese writer; b. 23; ed. Primary School.
Plumber, bricklayer, apprentice mechanic; served in Europe in Second World War; docker in Marseille; studied film production in U.S.S.R.; first prize for novelists at World Festival of Negro Arts, Dakar 67.

Publs. *Le Docker Noir* 56, *O pays, mon beau peuple* 57, *Les Bouts de Bois de Dieu* 60, *Vehi Ciosare* 65.
c/o Institut Français d'Afrique Noire, University of Dakar, Dakar, Senegal.

Outze, Børge; Danish editor; b. 18 March 1912.
Journalist in Odense 28-36, for *Nationaltidende*, Copenhagen 36-43; chief of Danish underground movement News Service; Editor *Information* (daily newspaper) 45-; awarded Croix de Guerre with Star, for services in underground movement; mem. Danish PEN Club.
Publs. *Denmark during the German Occupation* 45, *Danmarks Frihedskamp* (with Ebbe Munck) 46, *Spidser* (with Erik Seidenfaden) 48, *Danmark under den anden Verdenskrig* I-IV 62, and translations.
Amager Strandvej 164, Copenhagen, Denmark.

Overbeck, Egon, DR. RER. POL.; German business executive; b. 11 Jan. 1918; ed. Reform-Realgymnasium Rendsburg/Holstein, and Johann Wolfgang Goethe Univesitätr, Frankfurt am Main.
Army Service, Lt. 38, Major on Gen. Staff 44; university studies after Second World War; Dept. Dir. Metallgesellschaft, Frankfurt am Main 54; Dir. Allianz A.G., Munich, Siemens A.G., Munich, Algama Steel Corpn. Ltd., Sault Ste. Marie/Canada; mem. Exec. Board Vereinigte Deutsche Metallwerke, Frankfurt am Main 56, Advisory Council, Deutsche Bank A.G.; Chair. of Management Board Mannesmann A.G., Düsseldorf (pipes, machinery and steel) 62-; several war decorations.
Publ. *Possibilities of Maintaining and Increasing West German Lead-Zinc Production* 51.
Mannesmann A.G., Mannesmann- Ufer 2, 4, Düsseldorf, German Federal Republic.
Telephone: 82-01.

Overby, Andrew Norris, M.S.; American banker; b. 27 March 1909; ed. Univ. of Minnesota and Columbia Univ.
With Irving Trust Co. New York 30-41; Asst. to Vice-Pres. 36-41; Special Asst. to Vice-Pres. Fed. Reserve Bank of N.Y. 42; U.S. Army 42-46; Chief, Int. Div., Reciprocal Aid Branch 42-45; Exec. Officer to Dir. of Material, H.Q. Army Service Forces 45-46; Asst. Vice-Pres. Fed. Reserve Bank of N.Y. 46; Special Asst. to Sec. of the Treasury 46-47; U.S. Exec.-Dir. Int. Monetary Fund, and Special Asst. to the Sec., U.S. Treasury Dept. 47-49; Deputy Man. Dir. Int. Monetary Fund 49-52; Asst. Sec. Treasury Dept. 52-57; U.S. Exec.-Dir. Int. Bank for Reconstruction and Development 52-57; mem. Nat. Security Council Planning Board 52-57; Vice-Pres. and Dir. The First Boston Corpn., New York City 57-64, Vice-Chair. and Dir. 64-; Dir. Handelsfinanz A.G. Zürich 58-, Commonwealth Oil Refining Co., Inc. 62-, Grangesberg American Corpn. 65-, Liberian Iron Ore Ltd. 65-, Int. Exec. Service Corps. 65-; Legion of Merit, Alexander Hamilton Award (Treasury Dept.), Army Commendation Ribbon, etc.
Home: Manhattan House, 200 East 66th Street, New York 21, N.Y.; Office: 20 Exchange Place, New York 5, N.Y., U.S.A.

Overstreet, Harry Allen, B.A., B.SC.; American philosopher; b. 25 Oct. 1875; ed. California and Oxford Univs.
Instructor and Associate Prof. of Philosophy, Univ. of California 01-11; Prof. of Philosophy, Coll. of City of New York 11-39, Emeritus; Lecturer, New York New School for Social Research 24-28.
Publs. *Influencing Human Behaviour* 24, *About Ourselves* 27, *The Enduring Quest* 31, *We Move in New Directions* 33 *A Guide to Civilized Leisure* 34, *A Declaration of Interdependence* 37, *Town Meeting Comes to Town* (with B. W. Overstreet) 38, *Let Me Think* 39,

Leaders for Adult Education (with B. W. Overstreet) 41, *Our Free Minds* 41, *The Mature Mind* 49, *Where Children Come First* (with B. W. Overstreet) 49, *The Great Enterprise: Relating Ourselves to Our World* 52, *The Mind Alive* (with B. W. Overstreet) 54, *The Mind Goes Forth* (with B. W. Overstreet) 56, *What We Must Know About Communism* (with B. W. Overstreet) 58, *The War Called Peace* (with B. W. Overstreet) 61, *The Iron Curtain* (with B. W. Overstreet) 63, *The Strange Tactics of Extremism* (with B. W. Overstreet) 64.
3409 Fiddler's Green, Falls Church, Virginia, U.S.A.

Overton, William Ward, Jr.; American banker; b. 30 April 1897; ed. Kansas City Business Coll., and Texas Univ.
President, W. W. Overton and Co. 13-61, Chair. of Board 61-, Chair. of Board Texas Bank and Trust Co. of Dallas 47-, Pres. 61-65; Dir. Dallas Texas Corpn., Southland Corpn., Southwestern Life Insurance Co., Beaver, Meade & Englewood Railroad Co., Texas Research League, Dallas Metropolitan Opera, Dallas Zoological Soc., Dallas Museum for Contemporary Arts; Trustee Nat. Industrial Conf. Board, Texas Research Foundation, Southwestern Medical Foundation; mem. Cen. Business District Asscn., Texas Mid-Continent Oil and Gas Asscn., Newcomen Soc., American Bankers' Asscn., American Red Cross, Columbia Univ., Dallas Chamber of Commerce, and many other Dallas and charitable orgs.; Distinguished Service Plaque, etc.
Home: 4830 Cedar Springs, Dallas, Texas; Office: Texas Bank and Trust Co., P.O.B. 5267, Dallas 22, Texas, U.S.A.
Telephone: LA1-5877.

Ovezov, Balysh; Soviet politician; b. 1915; ed. Teachers' Training School, Tashauz, Ashkhabad Pedagogical Inst.
Held Exec. posts in the Young Communist League 31-39; Sec. Central Cttee. of the Turkmenian Young Communist League 39; Deputy People's Commissar of Education of Turkmenia 40; Sec. Central Cttee. of the Turkmenian C.P. 45-50; mem. Central Auditing Cttee. of the Central Cttee. of the C.P.S.U. 52-61, mem. C.P.S.U. Central Cttee. 61-; Chair. of the Council of Ministers of Turkmen S.S.R. 51-60; 1st Sec. Central Cttee. C.P. of Turkmen S.S.R. 60-; Deputy to U.S.S.R. and Turkmenian S.S.R. Supreme Soviets; awarded two Orders of Lenin, Order of the Red Banner of Labour, Badge of Honour (twice).
Central Committee of Communist Party of Turkmen S.S.R., Ashkhabad, Turkmen S.S.R., U.S.S.R.

Owe, Aage Willand; Norwegian chemical engineer; b. 9 Oct. 1894; ed. Univ. of Oslo and Technical Univ., Trondheim.
Asst. Prof. Technical Univ. Trondheim 20-23; research chemist, O. Mustad & Son, Oslo 23-27, Chief Chemist 27-35; Technical Dir. A/S Margarincentralen 35-47; Dir. of Industrial Supply, Ministry of Supply 45; Chair. A/S Nordisk Lettmetall 45-47; Chair. Govt. Fuel Comm. 40-42 and 45-50; Chair. Norsk Brenselimport A/S Oslo 40-59; Man. Dir. and Vice-Chair. A/S Ardal og Sunndal Verk, Oslo 47-64; mem. of Board O. Mustad and Son, Oslo 57-59; mem. Norwegian Energy Commission 58-; Chair. Cttee. of Industrial-Educational Relations of the Technical Univ., Trondheim 59-67; Pres. Asscn. of Norwegian Engineers 37-46, hon. mem.; Pres. Norwegian Chemical Soc. 50-54, Hon. mem.; Chair. Royal Norwegian Council for Scientific and Industrial Research 64-67; Chair. Norwegian Devt. Foundation 65-67; Norway-Netherlands Asscn. 66-; mem. Royal Norwegian Soc. of Science (Trondheim), Norwegian Acad. of Science and Letters (Oslo), Norwegian Acad. of Technical Science; Orders of the North Star (Sweden), White Rose (Finland) and St. Olav (Norway) (Com-mander); H.M.'s Gold Medal for scientific work; The Norsk Hydro Prize of the Asscn. of Norwegian Engineers.
Øvre Ullern Terrasse 25, Øvre Ullern, Oslo 3, Norway. Telephone: 245760.

Oweini, Hussein; Lebanese business executive and politician; b. 1900.
Prime Minister of Lebanon 51; Foreign Minister 59-60; private business 60-64: Prime Minister, Minister of Interior and Defence Feb. 64-July 65, also Minister of Foreign Affairs June-July 65.
Beirut, Lebanon.

Owen, Arthur David Kemp; British economist and UN administrator; b. 26 Nov. 1904; ed. Leeds Grammar School, and Leeds Univ.
Fmr. Dir. Sheffield Social Survey; Co-Dir. Pilgrim Trust Unemployment Enquiry 36; Stevenson Lecturer in Citizenship, Glasgow Univ. 37; Dir. of Political and Economic Planning (P.E.P.) 40; Personal Asst. to Sir Stafford Cripps 41-43; mem. Foreign Office Reconstruction Dept. 43-45; Foreign Office Observer, I.L.O. Conf., Philadelphia 44; mem. British Del., U.N. Conf., San Francisco April 45; Deputy Exec. Sec. Preparatory Comm. of U.N. 45; Asst. Sec.-Gen. in charge of Economic Affairs 46-49; Chair. UN Technical Assistance Board 49-52, Exec. Chair. 52-65; Co-Administrator, UN Devt. Programme 66-.
UN Development Programme, United Nations, New York, N.Y., U.S.A.

Owen, Frank, O.B.E., B.A.; British journalist, author and broadcaster; b. 1905; ed. Monmouth School and Sidney Sussex Coll. Cambridge.
Journalist *South Wales Argus* 28-29; mem. Lloyd George's Political Staff 29; Liberal M.P. for Hereford 29-31; mem. staff *Daily Express* 31-38; Editor *Evening Standard* 38-41; Chair. Press Freedom Cttee., Council for Civil Liberties; Trooper Royal Armoured Corps 42; cadet Sandhurst 43; Capt., producing S.E.A.C. daily newspaper S.E. Asia Command and *Phoenix Weekly* 44-46; Lt.-Col.; Dir. of Information S.E.A.C. Forces 45-46; with *Daily Mail* 46-50, Editor March 47-50; with *Daily Express* 50-55.
Publs. *Red Rainbow* (novel, with Sir Wynne Cemlyn-Jones) 31, *His Was the Kingdom* (with R. J. Thompson) 37, *Three Dictators* 39, *Guilty Men* (with Michael Foot) 40, *China, Our Unknown Ally* 41, *The Campaign in Burma* 46, *Tempestuous Journey, The Life and Times of David Lloyd George* 54, *Peron, his Rise and Fall* 57, *Fall of Singapore* 60.
26 Palace Chambers, Bridge Street, London, S.W.1, England.
Telephone: 01-839-5312.

Owen, Sir (William) Leonard, Kt., C.B.E., M.ENG., M.I.C.E., M.I.MECH.E., M.I.CHEM.E.; British engineer; b. 3 May 1897; ed. Liverpool Univ.
Designer of chemical plant Brunner, Mond and Co. (later I.C.I. (Alkali) Ltd.) 22; Engineering Dir. of the Royal Filling Factories, Ministry of Supply 40-45; Dir. of Engineering, Dept. of Atomic Energy Production, Ministry of Supply 46 and Asst. Controller 47; Dir. of Engineering and Deputy Man. Dir. U.K. Atomic Energy Authority, Industrial Group 54-57, and Man. Dir. 57-64, mem. for Production, and Executive head of Risley Production Group 59-61, mem. for Production and Engineering 61-63; part-time mem. U.K. Atomic Energy Authority 63-64; Dir. United Gas Industries 61-, Cammell Laird and Co. Ltd. 63-, Hagley Trust Ltd. 64-, Clutsom and Kemp Ltd. 65-, Talson Construction Ltd. 65-; Chair. Scottish Aviation Ltd., Ross Ltd. 64-, Jarvis Robinson Transport Ltd. 65-; Hon. D.Sc. Univ. of Manchester 62.
Eyarth, Rosemary Lane, Beaumaris, Anglesey, Wales.

Owings, Nathaniel Alexander, B.S.; American architect; b. 5 Feb. 1903; ed. Univ. of Illinois, Cornell Coll. of Architecture.

Research in Egypt, India and the Far East 35-36; in partnership with Skidmore and Merrill 39-, with whom he designed numerous Govt. projects and private buildings including Oak Ridge, Tennessee, U.S. Base at Okinawa, Lever House, New York, Terrace Plaza Hotel, Cincinnati, Air Force Acad., Colorado, Chase Manhatten Bank, N.Y.C., John Hancock Western Home Office, San Francisco, Crown Zellerbach Building, San Francisco, etc.; Fellow American Inst. of Architects; Trustee, American Acad. in Rome, Cttee. for Econ. Development (C.E.D.); Dir. Standard Insurance Co., Portland, Ore.; Assoc. Nat. Acad. of Design.
1 Bush Street, San Francisco 4, California, U.S.A.

Owono, Joseph N.; Cameroon diplomatist; b. 17 Dec. 1921; ed. Agricultural Coll. of Cameroon.
Agricultural Officer 43-57; Chef de Cabinet, Ministry of Finance 58-60; Chargé d'Affaires, Washington 60-61; Amb. to Liberia 61-62, to U.A.R. 62-65, to U.S.A. and Canada 65-; Perm. Rep. to UN 66-.
Permanent Mission of Federal Republic of Cameroon to the United Nations, 757 Third Avenue, New York, N.Y. 10017, U.S.A.

Owusu-Afriyie, Osei Hyiaman, B.COM., LL.B.; Ghanaian politician; b. 23; ed. Achimota Secondary School, Gold Coast, Fourah Bay Coll., Sierra Leone, King's Coll., London, London School of Economics, Lincoln's Inn, London.
Worked on *Hampshire Chronicle, Northern Echo* and *West Africa,* London; State Council Sec., Offinso Native Authority Admin. 50-52; Convention People's Party M.P. for Kumasi South 59-; Regional Commr. 60-61; Minister of Labour and Social Welfare 61-64; Minister of Health 64-66.
c/o Ministry of Health, Accra, Ghana.

Öz, Tahsin Şukru; Turkish antiquarian; b. 88; ed. Istanbul Univ.
Dir. Nat. Museum 07-28; Dir. Topkapi Palace Museum 28-52: mem. High Cttee. of Turkish Monuments.
Publs. *Guide Book to the Palace of Topkapi* 33, *Zwei Stiftungsurkunden des Sultan Mehmet II Fatih* 35, *Arşiv Kilavuzu,* Vol. I 38, II 40, *Risalei Mimariye* 44, *Türk kumasve kadifeleri Fask* (Turkish Woven Fabrics and Velvets), Vol. I 46, Vol. II 51, *Topkapi Sarayinda Fatih Sultan Mehmet II* 53, *Emanati Mukaddese* (Holy Relics) 54, *Türk Cinileri* 54, *The Topkapi Suray Museum* 50, *Masterpiece* 52, *Turkish Ceramics* 54, *Istanbul Camileri (The Mosques of Constantinople)* Vols. I, II 62, etc.
Cağaloğlu Mollafenari sok, 36, Istanbul, Turkey.

Özel, Ahmet; Turkish engineer and politician; b. 12 Nov. 1910; ed. Technical Univ. of Istanbul, and Paris Ecole Nat. Supérieure de Télécommunications.
Dozent Technical Univ. of Istanbul and Factory Engineer 39, Prof. 49, Dir. Civil Aeronautical Inst. and Dean Electrical Faculty 52, Pres. 53-54; Dep. from Sivas to Grand Nat. Ass. 54-57; Minister of Educ. 55-57; Pres. Atatürk Univ. 57-58; Prof. Mathematics and Physics Atatürk Univ. 58-67; Pres. Black Sea Tech. Univ., Trabzon 67-.
Publs. *Courses on Radio-Electricity, The Role of the Atmosphere in the Propagation of Electro-Magnetic Waves, The Application of Heaviside's Symbolic Computations of Electrotechnics, Electro-magnetic theory and Radiation,* general mathematics courses, etc.
K.T.Ü. Rektörü Trabzon, Turkey.
Telephone: 2232.

Ozga-Michalski, Jozef; Polish politician; b. 8 March 1919.
During occupation, mem. of the leadership of the Peasant Battalions and editor of underground peasant periodicals 40-44; Organizer of Peasant Party (S.L.) and co-organizer of the Voivodship People's Council (V.P.C.), Kielce 44; after the liberation, first Chair. of V.P.C. Kielce 45-47; Chair. Central Board of Peasant Self-Aid Union 49-53; Chair. Central Union of Agricultural Circles 59-62; Vice-Chair. Polish Cttee. of Peace Defenders 50-; mem. World Peace Council 52-; Chair. Central Board of the Lay Schools Soc. 59-62, Polish-Italian Group of the Interparliamentary Union 61-, Polish-Brazilian Friendship Soc. 62-; mem. S.L. 44-49, United Peasant Party (Z.S.L.) 49-; Sec. of S.L. Central Cttee. 49- and Z.S.L. Central Cttee. 49-55, Vice-Chair. Z.S.L. Central Cttee. 55-; mem. Home Nat. Council (K.R.N.) and Seym 47-; Vice-Marshal of Seym 52-56; mem. Council of State 57-; mem. Polish Writers Union 45-; Commdrs. Cross with the Star of the Polonia Restituta Order 64.
Zjednoczono Stronnictwo Ludowe, 4/8 Grzybowska, Warsaw, Poland.

P

Paar, Jack; American television performer; b. 1 May 1918.
Radio announcer, Indianapolis, Youngstown, Pittsburgh, Cleveland, Buffalo; appeared in films: *Walk Softly Stranger* 50, *Love Nest* 51, *Down Among the Sheltering Palms* 53; TV programme *Up to Paar* 52, TV *Morning Show* 55, *Tonight Show* 57-58, *Jack Paar Show* 58-62, *The Jack Paar Program* 62-65.
c/o NBC-TV, 30 Rockefeller Plaza, New York City 20, N.Y., U.S.A.

Paasio, Kustaa Rafael; Finnish politician; b. 6 June 1903.
Early career as typographer, later as journalist; Editor-in-Chief *Turun Päivälehti* 42-66; mem. municipal council Turku 45-; mem. Parl. 48-; Pres. Comm. for Foreign Affairs 49-66; Candidate for Presidency 62; Pres. Social Democratic Party 63-; Prime Minister 66-March 68.
Home: Puutarhakatu 11, Turku, Finland.

Pace, Frank, Jr., M.A., LL.D.; American business executive; b. 5 July 1912; ed. Princeton and Harvard Univs.
Asst. District Attorney in Arkansas 36-38; Gen. Attorney for the Revenue Dept., State of Arkansas 38-41; mem. of firm Pace, Davis & Pace 41-42; served U.S. Army Air Forces 42-46; now Lieut.-Col., Air Force Reserve; Special Asst. to Attorney Gen. of the U.S. 46; Exec. Asst. to the Postmaster-Gen. 46-48; Vice-Pres. Universal Postal Union 47, Rep. at U.N. 47-48; Chief U.S. Del. to the 12th Universal Postal Congress, Paris 47; Asst. Dir. Bureau of the Budget 48-49, Dir. 49-50; mem. Cttee. on Contributions, U.N. 49-50, President's Advisory Cttees. on Management Improvement and on Int. Economic Growth; Defence Adviser; Chair. NATO Defence Ministers' Confs., Brussels 50, Del. Canada and Italy 51; U.S. Sec. of the Army 50-53; Exec. Vice-Pres. Gen. Dynamics Corpn., N.Y. 53-57, Dir. 53-, Pres. 57-59, Chair. and Chief Exec. Officer 59-62; Chair. Canadair Ltd. 57-62; Pres. Int. Exec. Service Corps 64-, Public Broadcasting Corpn. 68-; Dir. numerous other companies; Pres. Nat. Inst. of Social Sciences 56-; Hon. M.A. (Princeton), Hon. LL.D. (Louisville, Syracuse, Arkansas, Temple Univs., Dartmouth, Northland, Adelphi Colls.), Hon. Sc.D. (Lafayette, Clarkson Colls.), Hon. L.H.D. (Washington Coll.).
720 Fifth Avenue, New York, N.Y. 10019, U.S.A.

Pachachi, Adnan al, PH.D.; Iraqi diplomatist; b. 14 May 1923; ed. American Univ. of Beirut.
Joined Foreign Service 44, served Washington, Alexandria; Dir.-Gen. Ministry of Foreign Affairs 58-59; Perm. Rep. of Iraq to United Nations 61-65; Minister of Foreign Affairs 66-.
Ministry of Foreign Affairs, Baghdad, Iraq.

Pacheco Areco, Jorge; Uruguayan newspaper editor and politician; b. 1921.
Assistant Editor *El Día* (Montevideo daily) until 61, Editor 61-65; Vice-Pres. of Uruguay 67; Pres. of Uruguay Dec. 67-.
Casa Presidencial, Avenida Suárez, Montevideo, Uruguay.

Packard, Vance, A.B., M.S.; American author and teacher; b. 22 May 1914; ed. Pennsylvania State Univ. and Columbia Univ.
Reporter for Boston *Record* 37; worked for four years in New York for Associated Press; editorial staff of *American Magazine* 42-56, *Collier's* Magazine 56.

Publs. *The Hidden Persuaders* 57, *The Status Seekers* 59, *The Waste Makers* 60, *The Pyramid Climbers* 62, *The Naked Society* 64.
87 Mill Road, New Canaan, Conn., U.S.A.

Paço D'Arcos, Joaquim; Portuguese writer; b. 08.
Director Trans-Zambesia Railway Co. Ltd.; novelist, playwright, essayist, poet; awarded many literary prizes; work translated into various languages; Chair. Portuguese Soc. of Writers 60-62, 65-.
Publs. *The Last Hero, Ana Paula, Diary of an Emigrant, Anxiety, Loves and Voyages of Pedro Manuel, Snow over the Sea, The Accomplice, The Absent, Pathology of Dignity, United States 1942, The Novel and the Novelist, The Road to Sin, Triple Mirror, Imperfect Poems, Churchill—The Statesman and the Writer, The Forest of Concrete—Lights and Shadows of the United States, The Captive Doe, Carnival and Other Tales, Memoirs of a Banknote, Cela 27,* etc.
Avenida A.A. Aguiar 38, Lisbon, Portugal.

Padilla Nervo, Luis; Mexican judge, diplomatist and politician; b. 98; ed. Nat. Univ. of Mexico, Washington Univ. and London School of Economics and Political Science.
Entered Diplomatic Service 20; held various posts including Minister successively to Costa Rica, Denmark, El Salvador, Netherlands, Panama, Paraguay, Uruguay and United States; represented Mexico at the UN 45-53; Pres. Gen. Ass. of UN 51-52; Mexican Sec. of State for Foreign Affairs 52-58; Perm. Rep. of Mexico to UN 59-64; Judge, Int. Court of Justice 64-; Chair. UN Disarmament Comm. 59.
International Court of Justice, The Hague, Netherlands.

Padilla Segura, Ing. J.; Mexican electrical engineer and politician; b. 12 March 1922; ed. Escuela Superior de Ingeniería Mecánica y Electrica del Instituto Politécnico Nacional.
Former Dir.-Gen. Instituto Politecnico Nacional, fmr. Vice-Pres. of Centre for Research and Advanced Studies, Factory Inspectorate, and Nat. Centre for Technical and Industrial Educ.; mem. Natural Sciences Cttee. (Mexico), UNESCO; mem. Managing Cttee. Nat. Technical Council for Educ.; mem. U.S.A.-Mexico Comm. for Space Research; Sec. for Communications 64-; Vice-Pres. Nat. Asscn. of Univs. and Insts. of Higher Educ.; mem. Mexican Asscn. of Mechanical and Electrical Engineers, Mexican Coll. of Mechanical and Electrical Engineers, Mexican Physical Soc., Franco-Mexican Asscn. of Engineers; Ordre des Palmes Académiques; Hon. D.Sc. (Univs. of Yucatán and Sinaloa.)
Secretaría de Comunicaciones y Transportes, Mexico D.F., Mexico.

Padley, Walter Ernest, M.P.; British trade unionist and politician; b. 24 July 1916; ed. Chipping Norton Grammar School and Ruskin Coll., Oxford.
President, Union of Shop, Distributive and Allied Workers 48-64; M.P. 50-; mem. Nat. Exec. Cttee. of Labour Party 56-, Chair. Overseas Sub-Cttee. 63-, Chair. Labour Party 65-66; Rep. of Labour Party at Socialist Int. 63-; Minister of State for Foreign Affairs Oct. 64-67.
Publs. *The Economic Problem of the Peace* 44, *Am I My Brother's Keeper?* 45, *Britain: Pawn or Power?* 47, *Soviet Russia: Empire or Free Union?* 47.
73 Priory Gardens, Highgate, London, N.6, England.
Telephone: 01-347-2969.

Pafford, John Henry Pyle, M.A., D.LIT., F.S.A., F.L.A.; British librarian; b. 6 March 1900; ed. Trowbridge High School and Univ. Coll., London.
Library Asst., Univ. Coll., London 23-25; Librarian and Tutor, Selly Oak Colleges, Birmingham 25-31; Sub-librarian, Nat. Central Library, London 31-45; Lecturer, Univ. of London School of Librarianship 37-61; War Office, Books and Libraries for Army Education 44-45; Goldsmiths' Librarian, Univ. of London 45-67; Library Adviser, Inter-Univ. Council for Higher Educ. Overseas 60-68; Fellow, Univ. Coll. London.
Publs. Bale's *King Johan* 31, *Library Co-operation in Europe* 35, *The Sodder'd Citizen* (Malone Soc.) 36, *Books and Army Education* 46, *American and Canadian Libraries* 49, *W. P. Ker: A Bibliography* 50, *The Winter's Tale* (Arden Shakespeare) 63.
202 Somerset Road, London S.W.19, England.
Telephone: 01-946 0115.

Paganelli, Arrigo, D.IUR.; Italian business executive; b. 31 May 1899; ed. Università degli Studi, Urbino.
Deputy to Legislative Chamber; fmr. Nat. Commissar of Italian Youth; fmr. Pres of Italian Tourism Co.; in STET (Società Finanziaria Telefonica) group 58-; Chair. of Board Tirrena Telephone Co. (TETI) 58-64; Chair. of Board of STET (telephone holding company of Inst. for Industrial Reconstruction) 64-; Dir. Società Italiana per l'Esercizio Telefonico (SIP).
Office: Via Arcangelo Corelli 10, Rome; Home: Via dei Pecori 3, Florence, Italy.
Telephone: 85-89.

Page, Denys Lionel, LITT.D.; British classical scholar; b. 08; ed. Christ Church, Oxford and Vienna Univ.
Lecturer, Christ Church, Oxford 31-32, Student and Tutor 32-50; Regius Prof. of Greek, Cambridge Univ. 50-; Master of Jesus Coll. Cambridge 59-; attached to Foreign Office 39-45, H.Q. Supreme Allied Command, South East Asia 45-46; lecture tours in U.S.A. 39, 54, 57-58.
Publs. *Actors' Interpolations in Greek Tragedy* 34, *Euripides' Medea* 38, *Greek Literary Papyri* 41, *Alcman* 51, *Corinna* 53, *Sappho and Alcaeus* 55, *The Homeric Odyssey* 55, *Aeschylus' Agamemnon* (co-ed.) 57, *History and the Homeric Iliad* 59, *Poetae Melici Graeci* 62, *The Oxyrhynchus Papyri* Vol. XXIX 64, *The Greek Anthology: Hellenistic Epigrams* (co-editor) 65, *The Garland of Philip* 68, *Melica Graeca Selecta* 68.
The Master's Lodge, Jesus College, Cambridge, England.
Telephone: Cambridge 53310.

Page, Harold James, C.M.G., O.B.E., B.SC., F.R.I.C.; British agricultural chemist; b. 29 May 1890; ed. Univ. Coll. London, Berlin, Paris.
Lecturer in Biochemistry London Univ. 10-12; war service 14-19; Chief of Royal Horticultural Society's Chemistry Dept. 19-20; Chief Chemist and Head Chemistry Dept. Rothamsted Experimental Station 20-27; Head Imperial Chemical Industries Agricultural Laboratories 27-32, Controller of Agricultural Research I.C.I. 32-36; Dir. Rubber Research Inst. of Malaya 36-46; civilian prisoner of war in Japanese hands 42-45; Principal, Imperial Coll. of Tropical Agriculture, Trinidad, B.W.I. 47-52; Agricultural Officer, Soil Improvement and Management, FAO 52-55; Editor *Empire Journal of Experimental Agriculture* 55-64; Fellow Univ. Coll., London; mem. of various scientific societies.
Brackens, West Lavington, Midhurst, Sussex, England.

Page, Robert Guthrie, A.B., LL.B.; American lawyer and business executive; b. 7 July 1901; ed. Phillips Academy, Andover, Yale Univ. and Harvard Law School.
Secretary to Mr. Justice Louis D. Brandeis, Washington 26-27; Root, Clark, Buckner & Ballantine, New York City (law firm) 27-34; Regional Admin., Securities and Exchange Comm., New York City 35; Debevoise, Stevenson, Plimpton & Page, New York City (law firm) 36-47; Pres. Phelps Dodge Corpn. 47-66, Chair. Board, Chief Exec. Officer 66-; Dir. Chrysler Corpn. 59-, Bigelow-Sanford Inc. 49-, Manufacturers Hanover Trust Co. 55-.
Phelps Dodge Corporation, 300 Park Avenue, New York 22, N.Y., U.S.A.

Page, Robert Morris; American physicist and research director; b. 2 June 1903; ed. Hamline Univ. and George Washington Univ.
Physicist, U.S. Naval Research Laboratory 27-; developed first pulse radar 34, Head Radar Research Section of Laboratory 38-45, Supt. Radio Div. III 45-52, Assoc. to Dir. of Research 52-54, Assoc. Dir. of Research 54-57, Dir. of Research 57-66; Inventor Monopulse Tracking Radar 44, MADRE over-the-horizon Radar 49; Fellow of various American scientific associations, and numerous awards.
Publ. *The Origin of Radar* 62.
U.S. Naval Research Laboratory, Washington, D.C. 20390, U.S.A.

Pagnol, Marcel (Paul); French author and film producer; b. 25 Feb. 1895; ed. Lycée de Marseille, Montpellier Univ.
Former schoolmaster; scenario and dialogue for the films *Marius* 31, *Fanny* 32, *Topaze;* dir., produced and wrote dialogue for the films *Le Gendre de Monsieur Poirier* 33, *Le Voyage de Monsieur Perrichon, Joffroi, Angèle* 34, *Merlusse* 35, *Cigalon* 35, *Regain* 36, *Le Schpountz* 37, *La Femme du Boulanger* 38, *La Fille du Puisatier* 40, *Naïs* 46, *La Belle Meunière* 47, *Le Rosier de Madame Husson* 49, *Manon des Sources* 52, *Carnaval* 53, *Les Lettres de mon Moulin* 54, *Fanny* (2nd edition) 61; mem. Acad. Française 47-; Hon. Pres. Syndicat Autonome du Cinéma Française; Commdr. Légion d'Honneur, Commdr. Arts et Lettres.
Publs. Literary: *La Petite Fille aux Yeux sombres, Pirouettes, Critiques des Critiques, Notes sur le Rire, Les Lettres de mon Moulin, Le Château de ma Mère, La Gloire de mon Père, The Time of Secrets;* translations: *Hamlet, A Midsummer Night's Dream* (Shakespeare), *Bucolics* (Virgil); plays: *Les Marchands de Gloire* 25, *Jazz* 26, *Topaze* 28, *Marius* 29, *Fanny* 32, *César* 46, *Judas* 55, *Fabien* 56.
Villa la Lestra, 12 boulevard des Moulins, Monte Carlo, Monaco; 16 square du Bois-de-Boulogne, Paris 16e, France.

Pahang, H.H. The Sultan of, Sultan Sir Abu Bakar Ri'ayatud'din Almuadzam Shah ibni Al-marhum Al-Mu'ta-sim Billah Sultan Abdullah, G.C.M.G.; Malayan ruler; b. 04; ed. Malay Coll., Kuala Kangsar.
Succeeded his father June 32; married Raja Fatimah, daughter of the late Sultan Iskandar Shah of Perak; patron of Red Cross Society, Pahang, of Malayan Anti-Tuberculosis Asscn., etc.
Pekan Lama, Kuantan, Pahang, Malaya, Malaysia.

Pahlavi, Mohammad-Reza; His Imperial Majesty the Shahanshah Aryamehr, Emperor of Iran; b. 26 Oct. 1919.
Succeeded to throne on the abdication of his father, Reza Shah the Great, Sept. 16th, 41; personally led the Imperial Iranian Army in liberation of province of Azarbaijan 46; married (1) Princess Fawzia, sister of King Farouk of Egypt; divorced Nov. 48; daughter, Princess Shahnaz Pahlavi; (2) Soraya Esfandiari, Feb. 12th, 51; divorced March 58; (3) Farah Diba, Dec. 21st, 59; sons, Reza Kurush Pahlavi and Ali Reza Pahlavi, daughter, Maasoumeh Farahnaz; Dr. h.c. (Michigan, Columbia, Pennsylvania, California (Berkeley), New York and Washington Univs., U.S.A. and Univs. of Punjab, Agra, Beirut, Rio de Janeiro, Bucharest, Sofia, Peshawar, Istanbul and Teheran).
Publs. *Mission for My Country* 61, *The White Revolution* 67.
The Imperial Palace, Teheran, Iran.

Pai, Ei Whan, B.S., M.B.A.; Korean diplomatist and economist; b. 1907; ed. in Korea and Business Admin. Colleges in U.S.A.
With Straw Brokerage Co., U.S.A. 38-42; Dept. of Justice, U.S.A. 42; Far Eastern Div., Office of Censorship, Washington, D.C. 43; Far Eastern Div., Foreign Econ. Admin., Washington, D.C. 44; Financial Advisor to Mil. Govt. Coll., Virginia; Asst. Dir. Dept. of Finance, Mil. Govt., Korea 46-49, Pres. of Fed. of Financial Asscns., Korea, Financial Advisor to Nat. Econ. Board, Mil. Govt. Korea; Pres. of Korean Chamber of Commerce, Hawaii, and Pres. of Far Eastern Trading Co., Hawaii 50; Gov. of Bank of Korea 60; Amb. to Japan 61, to Argentina, Chile, Paraguay, Uruguay and Bolivia 65, to U.K. 67-.
Embassy of Republic of Korea, 36 Cadogan Square, London, S.W.1, England.
Telephone: 01-489 7698/8025/0690.

Paik, General Sun Yup; Korean army officer and diplomatist; b. 20; ed. Pyongyang Normal School and Mukden Mil. Acad., Manchuria.
Korean Constabulary 46-48; Repub. of Korea Army 48-60, Chief of Staff 52-54, 57-59, Gen. 53, Chair. Joint Chiefs of Staff 59-60; Ambassador to Repub. of China 60-61, to France 61-65, to Canada 65-; Korean, French and U.S. decorations.
Suite 608, 151 Slater Street, Ottawa, Canada.

Paish, Frank Walter, M.C., M.A.; British university professor (retd.); b. 15 Jan. 1898; ed. Winchester Coll., and Trinity Coll., Cambridge.
Served in First World War 16-19; employed in Standard Bank of S. Africa, Ltd., in London and S. Africa 21-32; Lecturer in Commerce, London School of Economics 32-38, Reader 38-49, Prof. 49-65, Prof. Emer. of London Univ. 65-; Deputy Dir. of Programmes, Ministry of Aircraft Production 41-45; Prof. of Econs (with special reference to Business Finance) in the Univ. of London 49-65.
Publs. *Insurance Funds and their Investment* (with G. L. Schwartz) 34, *The Post-war Financial Problem and Other Essays* 50, *Business Finance* 53, *Studies in an Inflationary Economy* 62, *Long-term and Short-term Interest Rates* 66, and many articles in journals.
Shorey's, Ewhurst, Cranleigh, Surrey, England.
Telephone: Ewhurst 520.

Pal, Benjamin Peary, M.SC., PH.D.; Indian agricultural scientist; b. 26 May 1906; ed. Rangoon and Cambridge Univs.
Second Econ. Botanist, Imperial Agricultural Research Inst., 33-37, Imperial Econ. Botanist 37-50; Designated as Head, Div. of Botany, Indian Agricultural Research Inst. then Dir. 50-65; Dir.-Gen. Indian Council of Agricultural Research 65-; fmr. Chair. Special Advisory Cttee. on Food and Agriculture, Dept. of Atomic Energy; fmr. Pres. Botany and Agriculture Sections, Indian Science Congress and of many botanical and agricultural socs.; has served on Govt. Educ. Comm., heading its Task Force on Agricultural Educ.; Vice-Chair. All India Fine Arts and Crafts Soc.; helped to establish Post-graduate School at Indian Agricultural Research Inst.; research in wheat breeding and genetics; revision work on Int. Code of Nomenclature of Agricultural and Horticultural Plants; mem. Linnean Soc. of London, Indian Botanical Soc., Royal Horticultural Soc. of London, All Union Lenin Acad. of Agricultural Sciences; Fellow Nat. Inst. of Sciences of India; Awards include Padma Shri 58, Rafi Ahmed Kidwai Memorial Prize of the Indian Council of Agricultural Research 60, and Srinivisa Ramanujam Medal, Nat. Inst. of Sciences of India 64.
Publs. *Beautiful Climbers of India, Charophyta, The Rose in India, Wheat;* and over 120 scientific papers.
Indian Council of Agricultural Research, Krishi Bhavan, New Delhi 12, India.

Paladino, Morris; American international trade union official; b. 1920; ed. City Coll. New York, Harvard Univ., U.S.A.
Representative, later Asst. Man. local brs., Int. Ladies' Garment Workers' Union 41-61; Dir. of Educ., later Dir. of Org. and Asst. Gen. Sec. Inter-American Regional Org. of Workers (ORIT) (affiliated to Int. Confed. of Free Trade Unions—ICFTU) 61-64, helped to found ORIT Labour Coll. 62; Deputy Exec. Dir. American Inst. for Free Labour Devt. (AIFLD) June 64-67; Asst. Gen. Sec. ICFTU Feb. 67-.
International Confederation of Free Trade Unions, 37-39 rue Montagne aux Herbes Potagères, Brussels 1, Belgium.

Palamarchuk, Luka Fomich; Soviet journalist and diplomatist; b. 1906; ed. Kiev Univ.
Member C.P.S.U. 28-; Dir. of a School 28-29; Head of Dept., Editorial Offices *Chervony Krai* (newspaper), Vinnitsa 29-30; Deputy Editor and Editor, regional newspapers 30-37; Deputy Editor *Perets* (Kiev satirical journal) 37-41; Chair. Radio Cttee., Ukrainian Council of People's Commissars 41-42; Editor *Radyanska Ukraina* (newspaper) 42-48, 49-52; Diplomatic Service 52-; Deputy Foreign Minister of Ukrainian S.S.R. 52-54; Minister of Foreign Affairs of Ukrainian S.S.R. 54-65; Amb. to Morocco 65-; Orders and medals of U.S.S.R.
U.S.S.R. Embassy, Rabat, Morocco.

Palar, Lambertus Nicodemus; Indonesian diplomatist; b. 5 June 1902; ed. Djakarta and Amsterdam.
Netherlands Labour Movement 29-47; mem. Exec. Board Netherlands Labour Party 45-47; mem. Netherlands Parl. 45-47; went to Indonesia 47, Perm. Rep. of Indonesia to UN 50-53, 62-65; Ambassador to India 53-56, to German Fed. Repub., later U.S.S.R. 56, to Canada 57-62, to U.S.A. 65-66.
c/o Ministry of Foreign Affairs, Djakarta, Indonesia.

Palasi, Villar; Spanish university professor and politician; b. 1923; ed. Faculty of Philosophy and Literature, Univ. of Valencia.
Professor of Admin. Law, Madrid Univ. 65-; fmr. Under-Sec. of Information and Tourism, later Under-Sec. for Commerce; Minister of Educ. 68-.
Ministry of Education, Madrid, Spain.

Paleckis, Iustas Igno; Soviet politician; b. 22 Jan. 1899; ed. Kaunas Univ.
Worker in printing works 15-22; teacher 22-26; Dir. of Lithuanian News Agency *Elta* 26-27; Corresp. of Riga papers and journals 27-39; sent to a concentration camp for opposing the Smetona dictatorship 39; Pres. of the Presidium of the Supreme Soviet of Lithuania and Vice-Pres. of the Supreme Soviet of the U.S.S.R. 40-67; Chair. of Soviet of Nationalities of the Supreme Soviet of the U.S.S.R. 67-; Alt. mem. Central Cttee. of the C.P.S.U. 52-; awarded Order of Lenin (five times), Order of the Patriotic War, 1st Class.
Presidium of the Supreme Soviet, Kremlin, Moscow, U.S.S.R.

Palencia, Benjamín; Spanish painter; b. 03; ed. primary schools at Barrax (La Mancha), private schools in Madrid.
Taught himself to paint; first One-Man Show Madrid Museum of Modern Art 23; yearly exhibitions since that year in Madrid, other Spanish cities and in America; rep. at Biennales of Venice and São Paulo; Exhbns. Paris (Galerie Pierre) 33, New York (Harriman Gallery) 34, Munich (Kunstverein), Düsseldorf (Malcasten) 58, Paris 59; Primera Medalla de Bellas Artes, Gran Premio 1st Hispano-American Art Biennale.
Publs. *Niños, Niños de mi molino, Italia con B. Palencia, Giotto, raiz viva de la Pintura (Cruz y Raya); Pintores Modernos: Pinturas de B. Palencia.*
Sagasta 19, Madrid, Spain.

Palewski, Gaston; French politician and diplomatist; b. 20 March 1901; ed. Univs. of Paris and Oxford.
On staff of Resident Gen. in Morocco 24-25; successively Chef du Cabinet of Min. for Colonies and Justice; Dir. du Cabinet Min. of Finance 29-39; Dir. Political Affairs, Free France 40; Commdt. Free French Forces in Ethiopia and E. Africa 41-42; Dir. du Cabinet to Gen. de Gaulle 42-46; Foreign Affairs specialist, Exec. Cttee. Rassemblement du Peuple Français 47; Deputy (Seine) 51-56; Vice-Pres. R.P.F. Parl. group; formerly 1st Deputy Pres. Nat. Assembly; Minister. Deputy to the Prime Minister 55-56; Ambassador to Italy 57-62; Minister of State for Science, Atomic Questions and Space 62-65; Pres. and mem. Constitutional Council 65-; Grand Officier Légion d'Honneur, Croix de Guerre, Compagnon de la Libération.
1-2 rue de Montpensier, Paris 1er, France.

Palewski, Jean-Paul; French lawyer and politician; b. 19 July 1898; ed. Univ. of Paris and St. Cyr Mil. Acad. Lawyer, Paris Law Courts; Dep. to Nat. Ass. 46-55, 58-, mem. Cttee. on Justice 51-55, Vice-Pres. Finance Cttee. 51-55, Pres. Nat. Assembly Cttee. on Finance, General Economy and Planning 62-; Pres. of High Council for Industrial Property 58-62; mem. Council of Libraries of France 64-; Commdr. Légion d'Honneur, Croix de Guerre, Médaille de la Résistance.
Publs. *Le Rôle de chef d'entreprise dans la grande industrie, L'Organisation scientifique du travail, Vies polonaises, Pensées d'un otage, L'Ame polonaise, Stanislas Auguste Poniatowski, Louveciennes.*
National Assembly, Paris 7e, France, and 27 route de Versailles, Louveciennes, S.-et-O., France.

Paley, William S., B.S.; American broadcasting executive; b. 28 Sept. 1901; ed. Univ. of Chicago, Univ. of Pennsylvania.
Chairman, Columbia Broadcasting System Inc.; Life Trustee, Columbia Univ.; Trustee Museum of Modern Art; Dir. N.Y. World's Fair 39; Pres. and Dir. William S. Paley Foundation Inc.; Joint Chair. and Trustee North Shore Hospital; Dir. Resources for the Future Inc.
485 Madison Avenue, New York 22, N.Y., U.S.A.

Palfrey, John Gorham; American government official; b. 12 March 1919; ed. Milton Acad. and Harvard Univ. Admitted to D.C. Bar 48; Office of Gen. Counsel, Atomic Energy Commission 47-50; mem. Inst. Advanced Study, Princeton 50-52; Lecturer, Columbia School of Law 52-54, Assoc. Prof. 54-56, Prof. 56-62, Dean Columbia Coll. 58-62; mem. U.S. Atomic Energy Comm. 62-66; Fellow, Inst. of Politics, Harvard Univ. 66-67; Prof. of Law and History, Columbia Univ. 67-.
Home: 1165 Fifth Avenue, New York 27, N.Y., U.S.A.

Palgen, Rudolf, PH.D.; Luxembourg university professor; b. 23 April 1895; ed. Echternach (Gymnasium), Univs. of Munich, Heidelberg, Marburg-Lahn, Montpellier, and Paris.
Lecturer in French Univ. of Breslau 19-40; Prof. of Romance Philology Tübingen Univ. 40-41; Prof. at Graz, Austria 41-; also Head of Dept. of Romance Philology and of Dept. of Italian Language and Literature; hon. mem. Inst. Grand-Ducal Luxembourg; Officier Couronne de Chêne; Commdr. Ordre du Mérite, Luxembourg, Ufficiale al Merito, Repubblica Italiana.
Publs. include *Der Stein der Weisen* 22, *Villiers de l'Isle Adam* 25, *Die Weltanschauung H. Bergsons* 29, *Das mittelalterliche Gesicht der Goettlichen Komoedie* 35, *Dantes Sternglaube* 40, *Italienische Literaturgeschichte* 49, *Ursprung und Aufbau der Komödie Dantes* 54, *Werden und Wesen der Komödie Dantes* 55, *L'Origine del Purgatorio* 67.
Koerblergasse 83, A-8010 Graz, Austria.
Telephone: 32350.

Palladin, Alexandr Vladimirovich; Soviet biochemist; b. 85; ed. St. Petersburg Univ.
Prof. at the Kharkov Inst. of Forestry and Afforestation 16; Prof. at the Kharkov Medical Inst. 21; Dir. of the Ukrainian Inst. of Biochemistry 25; Prof. at the Univ. of Kiev 34; Pres. of the Acad. of Sciences of the Ukraine 46-; mem. U.S.S.R. Acad. of Sciences; awarded Order of Lenin (five times).
Principal Publs. *Text Book of Biological Chemistry, The Chemical Nature of Vitamins, Cerebral Metabolism in Different Functional States.*
Academy of Sciences of the Ukraine, 54 Vladimirskaya Street, Kiev, Ukrainian S.S.R., U.S.S.R.

Pallottino, Massimo, D.LITT.; Italian university professor; b. 9 Nov. 1909; ed. Univ. of Rome.
Inspector, Dept. of Antiquities of Rome 33; Dir. Museo Nazionale di Villa Giulia, Rome and excavations of Cerveteri 37; Lecturer and later Acting Prof. Univ. of Rome 38; Prof. of Classical Archæology Univ. of Cagliari 40; Prof. of Etruscology and Italic Antiquities, Univ. of Rome 45-; Vice-Pres. Inst. of Etruscan Studies, Italian Inst. of Prehistory; mem. Directorate Int. Asscn. for Classical Archæology, Accademia Nazionale dei Lincei, Pontificia Accademia di Archeologia, Deutsches Archäologisches Institut, Soc. Antiquaries of London, Prehistoric Soc., London; Dir. *Encyclopaedia of World Art; Archeologia Classica.*
Publs. *Elementi di Lingua Etrusca* 36, *Tarquinia* 37, *Etruscologia* 42, 47, 55, 68, *L'Arco degli Argentari* 46, *L'Origine degli Etruschi* 47, *La Civilisation Etrusque* 50, *La Sardegna Nuragica* 50, *Etruscan Painting* 52, *Testimonia Linguae Etruscae* 54, 68, *The Etruscans* 56, *Che cos' è l'Archeologia* 63.
9 Via dei Redentoristi, Rome, Italy.
Telephone: 6569364.

Palm, Franklin Charles, A.B., M.A., PH.D.; American historian; b. 16 Aug. 1890; ed. Oberlin Coll. and Univ. of Illinois.
Prof. of History, Colorado Coll. 18-21; Asst. Prof. of Modern European History, Univ. of California 21-29, Assoc. Prof. 29-39, Prof. 39-57, Prof. Emeritus 57-.
Publs. *The Economic Policies of Richelieu* 20, *Politics and Religion in 16th Century France* 27, *A Syllabus of the History of Western Europe* 27, *The Establishment of French Absolutism* 28, *Calvinism and the Religious Wars* 32, *Europe since Napoleon* 34, *The Middle Classes: Then and Now* 36, *European Civilization: a Political, Economic and Cultural History* (with J. W. Thompson and J. J. van Nostrand) 39, *England and Napoleon III: A Study of the Rise of a Utopian Dictator* 48, *Western Civilization Since 1660*, Vol. II, 49, *Western Civilisation from the XVIII Century*, Vol. II (with Charles R. Webb, Jr.) 58.
2414 Telegraph Avenue, Berkeley, Calif. 94704, U.S.A.
Telephone: 848-3154.

Palme, Sven Olof Joachim, B.A., LL.B.; Swedish politician; b. 30 Jan. 1927; ed. Kenyon Coll., Ohio, and Univ. of Stockholm.
Special Counsel to Swedish Prime Minister 53-63; mem. of Parl. 58-; mem. Exec. Swedish Social Democratic Youth and Workers Educational Asscn. 55-61; Minister without Portfolio 63-65; Minister of Communications 65-67, of Educ. and Ecclesiastical Affairs 67-; mem. Exec. Swedish Social Democratic Party 64-; mem. Swedish Del. to UN 61; Chair. Comms. on Student Welfare 60-63.
Tornedalsgatan 18, Vällingby, Sweden.

Palmén, Erik Herbert, M.SC., D.PHIL.; Finnish meteorologist and oceanographer; b. 31 Aug. 1898; ed. Univ. of Helsinki.
Asst. Finnish Inst. of Marine Research 22, Dir. 39; Prof. of Meteorology, Univ. of Helsinki 47; Prof. and mem. Acad. of Finland 48-; Visiting Prof. Univ. of Chicago 46-48, 49-50, 52 and 56, Univ. of Calif. 54; main

fields of research include tropical and extra-tropical cyclones, jet steam, structure of atmospheric fronts, general atmospheric circulation, interaction between atmosphere and oceans, and ocean currents; Pres. Finnish Scientific Society 58; Symons Memorial Gold Medal, Royal Meteorological Society 57, Carl-Gustaf Rossby award, American Meteorological Soc. 60, Buys-Ballot Gold Medal, Royal Netherlands Academy of Sciences and Letters 64; Rossby Prize, Swedish Geophysical Soc. 66.

Institute of Meteorology, University of Helsinki, Helsinki, Finland.

Palmer, H(arold) Bruce; American public official; b. 16 Nov. 1908; ed. Culver Mil. Acad. and Univ. of Michigan.

Mutual Benefit Life Insurance Co. 31-62, Vice-Pres. (Agencies) 47-48, Admin. Vice-Pres. 49-50, Exec. Vice-Pres. 51-53, Pres. 53-62; Pres. Nat. Industrial Conf. Board 63-; mem. Exec. Int. Exec. Service Corps 64-; mem. Board of Dirs. New York World's Fair 61-65; Vice-Pres. and mem. Exec. Cttee. Boys' Club of America 64-; Chair. Board for Fundamental Educ. 64-; Vice-Pres. Nat. Fund for Graduate Nursing Educ. 61-; mem. Exec. Cttee. Nat. Board of Dirs. of Junior Achievement 63-67, Chair. 67-; several awards and hon. degrees.

National Industrial Conference Board, 845 Third Avenue, New York 10022, N.Y., U.S.A.

Palmer, James Lindley; A.M., C.P.A.; American retailer and museum executive; b. 12 March 1899; ed. Brown Univ., Univ. of Chicago.

Spent two years in small manufacturing business 19-21; mem. of Faculty, Univ. of Chicago School of Business 22-36; Business Consultant with various Corpns. 22-36; with Marshall Field & Co. in various exec. capacities 36-, Pres. 49-64; Pres. Chicago Natural History Museum 64-; varied experience with several welfare organizations, incl. Community Fund of Chicago Inc., Pres. 46-49; various cttee. and advisory assignments with Federal, State and City Govts. 40-; Dir. Marshall Field, Harris Trust and Savings Bank, Int. Harvester Co., Chicago Lighthouse for the Blind, Community Fund of Chicago Inc., Gen. Candy Corpn.; Fellow Brown Univ.

921 N. Hawthorne Place, Lake Forest, Illinois, U.S.A.

Palmer, Joseph, II, B.S.; American diplomatist; b. 16 June 1914; ed. Phillips Exeter Acad., Harvard Univ. and Georgetown Univ. School of Foreign Service.

Federal Bureau of Investigation 38-39; Foreign Service Officer 39, served Mexico City, Nairobi 40-45; Asst. Chief, Div. of African Affairs, Dept. of State 45-49; London 49-53, Dept. of State 54-56; Dep. Asst. Sec. of State for African Affairs 56-58; Consul-Gen. Rhodesia and Nyasaland 58-60; Ambassador to Nigeria 60-63; Dir.-Gen. of Foreign Service, Dept. of State 64-66; Asst. Sec. of State for African Affairs 66-.

Department of State, Washington, D.C., U.S.A.

Palmer, Leonard Robert, M.A., D.PHIL., PH.D.; British philologist; b. 5 June 1906; ed. Canton High School and Univ. Coll., Cardiff, Trinity Coll., Cambridge and Vienna Univ.

Assistant Lecturer in Classics, Manchester Univ. 31-35, Lecturer 35-41; attached to Foreign Office 41-45; Prof. of Greek, Head, Department of Classics, King's Coll., London Univ. 45-52; Fellow of Worcester Coll. and Prof. of Comparative Philology, Oxford Univ. 52-; Hon. Sec. Philological Soc. 47-51, Pres. 57-60; Corresp. mem. Deutsches Archäologisches Inst.

Publs. Translation of E. Zeller's *Outlines of the History of Greek Philosophy* 31; *Introduction to Modern Linguistics* 36, *A Grammar of the Post-Ptolemaic Papyri*, Vol. I (Publications of the Philological Soc.) 45, *The Latin Language* 54, *Mycenaeans and Minoans* 61, *The Interpretation of Mycenaean Texts* 63, *Homer: Language and*

Dialect (in *A Homeric Companion*) 62, *The Find Places of the Knossos Tablets* 63; numerous articles in British and foreign learned periodicals.

1 Oriel Square, Oxford, England.

Palmero, Juan S.; Argentine lawyer and politician; b. 03.

Legal Practice, Córdoba; Provincial Senator 38-40; Provincial Minister of Govt. 56-58; Minister of Interior Oct. 63-66; Unión Cívica Radical del Pueblo.

c/o Ministry of the Interior, Buenos Aires, Argentina.

Palthey, Georges Louis Claude, D.IUR.; French United Nations official; b. 26 Aug. 1910; ed. Univs. of Lyon and Paris.

Finance Officer, Control of Expenditure Commitments, French Ministry of Finance 34-42; Chief Secretariat, Gen. Dept. of Economic Control 42-45; Dep. Financial Comptroller, French Missions in Great Britain 45-47; Deputy Dir., Personnel United Nations 47, Dir. 48-54; Deputy Dir., European Office of UN, Geneva 54-65; Deputy Dir.-Gen. UN Office, Geneva 65-; Croix de Guerre.

Publ. *Le Contrôle préalable des Finances publiques.*

2 rue des Granges, Geneva, Switzerland.

Telephone: 26-16-13.

Pamplin, Robert Boisseau; American business executive; b. 25 Nov. 1911; ed. Virginia Polytechnic Inst. and Northwestern Univ.

Georgia-Pacific Corpn. (forest products) 34-, Sec. and Treas. 36-48, Financial Vice-Pres. 48-52, Admin. Vice-Pres. 52-56, Exec. Vice-Pres. 56-69, Pres. 59-; Chair. Trustees Lewis and Clark Coll.

Georgia-Pacific Corporation, Commonwealth Building, P.O.B. 311, Portland, Oregon 97207; Home: 404 S.W. Edgecliff Road, Portland, Oregon 97129, U.S.A.

Pan Tse-li; Chinese diplomatist.

Chair. Ninghsia Provincial People's Govt. 49; Sec. Ninghsia Provincial Cttee. of C.C.P. 49; head of the political dept. of an army corps. of the People's Liberation Army 49; Vice-Chair. Shensi Provincial People's Govt. 51; mem. North-west Admin. Council 53; Sec. Shensi Provincial Cttee. of C.C.P. 53; Assoc. mem. Cen. Cttee. of C.C.P.; Ambassador to North Korea 54; Ambassador to India 54-62, to U.S.S.R. 62-.

Embassy of the People's Republic of China, Moscow, U.S.S.R.

Panard, Pierre Marie Maurice; French public servant; b. 1 Nov. 1916; ed. Univ. de Paris à la Faculté de Droit and Ecole Libre des Sciences Politiques.

Clerk, Ministry of Finance 41-46, Civil Admin. 46-47; transferred to Finance Comm. of Nat. Assembly 47-49, Chief, Technical Services 61-62; Chief, Office Sec. of State for Marine 49-50; Financial Comptroller 56-61; Dir. Office Minister of Public Works and Transport 62-64; Chief, Central Bureau of Finance 64; Dir.-Gen. Compagnie Générale Transatlantique 64-; Chevalier Légion d'Honneur, Croix de Guerre.

7 rue de Colonel-Moll, Paris 17e, France.

Telephone: ETOile 0235.

Panchen Lama; Tibetan religious and political leader; b. 38.

Vice-Chair. Preparatory Cttee. for Tibetan Autonomous Region 56-59; Provisional Chair. Preparatory Cttee. for Tibetan Autonomous Region on flight of Dalai Lama to India March 59-65; del. Second Chinese Nat. People's Congress April 59; Hon. Chair. Chinese Buddhist Asscn.

Lhasa, Autonomous Region of Tibet, China.

Pandit, Vijaya Lakshmi; Indian politician and diplomatist; b. 18 Aug. 1900; ed. privately.

Joined Non-Co-operation Movement, imprisoned for one year 31; mem. Allahabad Municipal Board 36, Chair. Education Cttee. Municipal Board; Minister of Local Self-Govt. and Public Health, Uttar Pradesh Govt.

37-39, 46-47 (1st woman minister); mem. Congress Party; sentenced to three terms of imprisonment 32, 41 and 42; detained under Defence Regulations Aug. 42-June 43; sister of late Pandit Nehru; Leader of Indian Del. to UN 46-51, 63; Ambassador to U.S.S.R. 47-49, to U.S.A. 49-51; mem. Indian Parl. 52-54; Pres. UN Assembly 53-54; High Commr. for India in United Kingdom and Ambassador to Ireland 55-Aug. 61, concurrently Ambassador to Spain 58-Aug. 61; Gov. of Maharashtra 62-64; mem. Lok Sabha Nov. 64-; Hon. D.C.L.(Oxford). E.8, Mafatlal Park, B. Desai Road, Bombay, India.

Pannwitz, Rudolf; German writer; b. 27 May 1881; ed. Univ. of Berlin.
Lived in Germany 81-15, in Austria 15-21, in Dalmatia 21-48 and in Switzerland 48-; Grosses Verdienstkreuz and Schillerpreis.
Publs. *Dionysische Tragödien* 13, *Die Krisis der europäischen Kultur* 17, *Mythen* 19-21, *Kosmos Atheos* 26, *Das Neue Leben* (novel) 27, *Der Friede* 50, *Der Nihilismus und die werdende Welt* 51, *Beiträge zu einer europäischen Kultur* 54, *Landschaftgedichte* 54, *König Laurin* (epic poem) 56, *Der Übergang von heute zu morgen* 58, *Hermann Hesses Westöstliche Dichtung* 57, *Der Aufbau der Natur* 61, *Wasser wird sich ballen* (poems) 63, *Thebais* (epic poem) 65, *George und Verwey* 65, *Gilgamesch-Sokrates, Titanentum und Humanismus* 66.
Ciona-Carona (Lugano), Ticino, Switzerland.

Panofsky, Wolfgang Kurt Hermann, A.B., PH.D.; American (born German) scientist; b. 24 April 1919; ed. Princeton Univ. and California Inst. of Technology. In U.S.A. 34-; mem. of staff Radiation Laboratory, Calif. Univ. 45-51; Asst. Prof. 47-48, Assoc. Prof. 48-51; Prof. Stanford Univ. 51-63, Dir. High Energy Physics Laboratory 53-61, now Dir. Linear Accelerator Center; mem. President's Science Advisory Cttee. 60-64; Hon. D.Sc. (Case Inst. of Technology and Univ. of Sasketchewan); Lawrence Prize, U.S. Atomic Energy Comm. 61. Stanford Linear Accelerator Center, Stanford University, P.O. Box 4349, Stanford, Calif. 94305; Home: 25671 Chapin Avenue, Los Altos Hills, Calif., U.S.A. Telephone: 948-6286.

Panova, Vera Fyodorovna; Soviet writer; b. 20 March 1905.
Journalist 22-45; State prizewinner 47, 48, 50; Order of Red Banner of Labour 65.
Publs. novels: *The Train* 46, *Companions* 46, *The Factory* 47, *Bright Shore* 49, *Span of the Year* 53, *Time Walked* 55, *Sezegea* 56, *A Sentimental Novel* 58, *Walja, Wolodja* (short stories) 59, *Plays* 58, *Seeing off White Nights* (play) 61, *How are you Lad* (play), *Boy and Girl* 62, *Who is Dying?* 65, *Sisters* 65 (short stories), *Theses of a Novel* 65, *It's Not the Dusk Yet* (play) 65, *It's Ages Since We Met* (play) 65, *Loyalty* (play) 67.
Union of Writers of the R.S.F.S.R., Moscow, U.S.S.R.

Pant, Apasaheb Balasaheb; Indian politician and diplomatist; b. 11 Sept. 1912; ed. Univs. of Bombay and Oxford, and Lincoln's Inn, London.
Former Minister of Educ., Aundh State, Prime Minister 38-44, Minister 44-48; mem. All-India Congress Cttee. 48; Commr. for Govt. of India, British East Africa 48-54, concurrently Consul-Gen. in Belgian Congo and Ruanda Urundi 48-54, concurrently Commr. in Central Africa and Nyasaland 50-54; Ministry of External Affairs, New Delhi 54-55; Political Officer, Sikkim and Bhutan 55-61; Ambassador to Indonesia 61-64, to Norway 64-66, to U.A.R. 66-; Del. to UN Gen. Assembly 65; Padma Shri 54.
Embassy of India, 19 Mohamed Mazhar, Zamalek, Cairo, United Arab Republic; Home: 893-895 Bhandarkar Inst. Road, Deccan Gymkhana, Poona 4, India.

Pant, Sumitranandan; Indian writer; b. 1900.
Member Sahitya Acad.
Publs. *Pallav* 26, *Vina-Gramthi* 30, *Birth of Poetry,*

Jyotsna (drama) 34, *Panch Kahaniyan* (short stories) 36, *Uppara* (poetry) 49, *Gradya-Path* (essays) 53, etc. c/o All-India Radio, Allahabad; 18-B7 K. G. Marg, Allahabad, U.P., India.

Panton, Verner; Danish architect and designer; b. 26; ed. Odense Technical School, Copenhagen Royal Acad. of Fine Arts.
In collaboration as architect with Arne Jacobsen 50-52; study in European countries 53-55; independent designer and architect 55-; has designed furniture, carpets, curtains, lamps, wall decorations and upholstery fabrics for France and Son, Fritz Hansen, Pluslinje A/S, Louis Poulsen and Unika Vaev (Denmark), and for Dux, Kaufeld, Kill G.m.b.H., Pausa, Thonet and Vereinigte Werkstätten (Germany); buildings include cardboard house 57, inn at Fyn 58, spherical house 60, plastic house 60, hotel at Trondheim (Norway) 60, project for exhibition halls at North Zealand (Denmark) 60; designed Dansk Kobestævne Exhibition 58; furniture exhibitions Brussels, Frankfurt, Stuttgart, Amsterdam, Paris, Cologne, Copenhagen, Sydney, Oslo, Stavanger, Gothenburg, Stockholm, London, Basle, Hamburg, Muncih, Zurich and in U.S.A.
Office: Hasenrainstrasse 61, 4102 Binningen, Switzerland.

Panufnik, Andrzej; British (b. Polish) composer and conductor; b. 24 Sept. 1914; ed. Warsaw State Conservatoire and the State Acad. of Music, Vienna.
Conductor Cracow Philharmonic Orchestra 45-46; Dir. Warsaw Philharmonic Orchestra 46-47; Vice-Pres. Polish Composers' Union 48-54; Vice-Chair. Int. Music Council of UNESCO 50-53; settled in England 54; Musical Dir. City of Birmingham Symphony Orchestra 57-59; visiting conductor leading European and South American orchestras 47-; mainly composer since 59; First Prize Chopin Competition 49; Banner of Labour 1st Class 49; State Prizewinner 51 and 52; Pre-Olympic Competition First Prize 52; Prix de Composition Musicale Prince Rainier III de Monaco 63, Sibelius Centenary Medal 65; Knight of Mark Twain (U.S.A.) 66.
Compositions: *Trio* 34, *Five Polish Peasant Songs* 40, *Tragic Overture* 42, *Nocturne* 47, *Lullaby* 47, *Twelve Miniature Studies* 47, *Sinfonia Rustica* 48, *Hommage à Chopin* 49, *Old Polish Suite* 50, *Concerto in Modo Antico* 51, *Heroic Overture* 52, *Rhapsody* 56, *Sinfonia Elegiaca* 57, *Polonia—Suite* 59, *Concerto for Piano and Orchestra* 62, *Landscape* 62, *Sinfonia Sacra* 63, *Two Lyric Pieces* 63, *Song to the Virgin Mary* 64, *Autumn Music* 65, *Jagiellonian Triptych* 66, *Epitaph* 67, *Reflections* 67.
Riverside House, Twickenham, Middlesex, England.
Telephone: 01-892 1470.

Panya, Khamphan; Laotian diplomatist; b. 17; ed. Lycée Sisowath, Pnom Penh, Faculty of Medicine and Pharmacy, Hanoi and Faculty of Law, Univ. of Paris.
Ministry of Foreign Affairs 53-; Dep. Sec.-Gen. High Council of French Union 54-55; Rep. of Laos, Saigon 56; Ambassador to India 56-58; Minister of Foreign Affairs 58-60, of Public Works 61-62; Ambassador to U.S.S.R. 63-.
Embassy of Laos, 18 ulitsa Katchalova, Moscow, U.S.S.R.

Panyushkin, Alexandr Semyonovich; Soviet politician and diplomatist; b. 05; ed. Frunze Military Acad.
Soviet army service 20-21; railway worker 22-24; mem. C.P.S.U. 27-; Soviet Frontier Defence Forces 24-39; Ambassador to China 39-44; Apparatus, Cen. Cttee. C.P.S.U. 44-47; Ambassador to U.S.A. 47-52, to Chinese People's Repub. 52-53; with Ministry of Internal Affairs 53; on staff of Central Cttee. C.P.S.U. 54-, mem. Central Auditing Cttee.
Central Committee of the Communist Party of the Soviet Union, Moscow, U.S.S.R.

Papadopoulos, George; Greek army officer (retd.) and politician; b. 1919; ed. War Acad., Artillery School, and Officers Training School in Middle East.

Second Lieut. 40, Lieut. 43, Capt. 46, Major 49, Lieut.-Col. 56, Col. 60, Brig. and retd. Dec. 67; served on Albanian front in Greek-Italian war 40; joined nat. resistance units during German occupation; Staff Officer 44-45, Intelligence Officer 45-46; Commdr. Artillery Battery 46; Training Officer, Artillery School 46-48; Commdr. 131st Mountain Artillery Unit 48, 144th Mountain Artillery Unit 48-49; then Artillery Instructor and Unit Commdr. 49-54; Intelligence Bureau, Army Gen. Staff 54; Chief of Staff, Artillery Div. 55-57; Central Intelligence Service 59-64; Commdr. 117th Field Artillery Unit 64-65, First Army Force 65-66; at Third Staff Bureau, Army Gen. Staff 66-April 67; Minister to Prime Minister's Office April-Dec. 67; Prime Minister, Minister of Defence and Minister to Prime Minister's Office Dec. 67-; Commdr. Royal Order of Phoenix; Medal of Mil. Merit and numerous other medals.
Office of the Prime Minister, Athens, Greece.

Papaligouras, Panayis, M.C., D.S.O., LL.D.; Greek politician and lawyer; b. 6 June 1917; ed. Univs. of Athens and Geneva.

Lecturer sociology Univ. of Geneva 41; with Greek Forces in the Middle East 42-44, secret mission to occupied Greece 44; Sec.-Gen. Ministry of Supply 45, later Under-Sec. of State; Under-Sec. of State Ministry of Commerce 52, Minister 53; Minister of Agriculture 53; Minister of Co-ordination 54-55, 61-63, of Trade and Industry 56-58; Mem. Parl., Nat. Radical Union Party; Mil. Cross of George I, and other decorations.
Publ. *Théorie de la Société Internationale* 41.
4 Pindarou Street, Athens, Greece.
Telephone: 629-750.

Papandreou, Andreas George (son of George Papandreou, *q.v.*), PH.D.; Greek educationist and politician; b. 5 Feb. 1919; ed. Athens Coll., Athens Univ. Law School and Harvard Univ.

Associate Prof., Univ. of Minnesota 47-50, Northwestern Univ. 50-51; Prof. Univ. of Minnesota 51-55; Prof., Chair. Economics Dept., Univ. of California 55-59; Dir. Centre of Economic Research, Athens, Greece 61-64; Economic Adviser, Bank of Greece 61-62; Minister to Prime Minister, Greece 64- Nov. 64; Minister of Econ. Co-ordination 65; Deputy from Ahaia 65-67; in prison 67.
Publs. *Economics as a Science* 58, *A Strategy for Greek Economic Development* 62, *Fundamentals of Model Construction in Macroeconomics* 62.
Guizi 58, Psychico, Athens, Greece.

Papandreou, George (father of Andreas Papandreou, *q.v.*); Greek politician; b. 88; ed. Athens and Berlin Univs.

Prefect of Lesbos 15; Gov.-Gen. of Aegean Islands 16-20; Minister of Interior 23; M.P. 23; Minister of Nat. Economy 25, of Education 30, of Communications 33; Leader Socialist Democratic Party 35; arrived Cairo April 44; Prime Minister April 44; returned Athens Oct. 44 as Prime Minister, Cabinet of Nat. Union; Minister of the Interior Jan.-Sept. 47; Deputy Premier and Minister of Co-ordination 50-51; Prime Minister and Minister of Education Nov. 63-65; Leader of Centre Union Party 61-; under house arrest April-Oct. 67; Grand Cross of the Order of King George I (Greece), Grand Cross of Germany, Egypt, etc.
Publs. *Greek Future, Political Themes* (4 vols.), *Liberation of Greece.*
Kastri, Kifissias, Athens, Greece.

Papanin, Ivan Dmitrievich; Soviet polar explorer; b. 26 Nov. 1894.

Head of Polar stations at Tixi Bay on Franz Josef Land 32-33, on Cape Chelyuskin 34-35; in charge of the first Soviet drifting station in the Central Arctic 37-38; Head of the Central Northern Sea Route Admin. 38-46; Rear-Admiral; mem. Board of the U.S.S.R. I.G.Y. Cttee.; Head of Dept. of Marine Explorations and Dir. Research Inst. of Biology of Inland Waters (U.S.S.R. Acad. of Sciences); Chair. Moscow Branch of U.S.S.R. Geographical Soc., Hero of the Soviet Union 37, 40; awarded Order of Lenin (seven times), Order of the Red Banner (twice), Order of the Red Star, Order of Nakhimov, Order of the Red Banner of Labour.
Department of Marine Explorations of U.S.S.R. Acad. of Sciences, 14 Lenin Prospekt, Moscow B-71, U.S.S.R.

Papaspyrou, Dimitrios; Greek lawyer and politician; b. 2 Nov. 1902; ed. Univ. of Athens.

Lawyer; Deputy for EPEK-Liberal Party 50-61, Centre Union Deputy 61-; Minister of Justice 51-52, 63-64, 65; Minister of Agriculture 51-52; Minister of Prime Minister's Office 64; mem. of F.D.K. (Liberal Democratic Centre) 65-; Speaker of Chamber of Deputies Nov. 65-67.
79 Léoforos Vassilissis Sophias, Athens, Greece.
Telephone: 712-155.

Papathanassiou, Aspassia; Greek actress; ed. Dramatic Art School of National Theatre of Greece.

Played a variety of leading roles with various Greek theatrical groups; founder-mem. Piraikon Theatre; has toured extensively in Europe and N. and S. America; appeared at Int. Festivals in Berlin, Paris, Florence and Vienna; appeared on T.V. in London, Moscow and U.S.A.; has given over 450 performances of ancient tragedy; toured U.S.S.R. 67; in U.K. 67-.
c/o Lom Associates Ltd., 6a Maddox Street, London, W.1, England.

Papen, Franz von; German politician; b. 29 Oct. 1879; ed. Mil. School.

Military Attaché in Mexico and in Washington 14-16; Lieut.-Col. and Chief of Staff 4th Turkish Army 18; mem. Zentrum Party in Prussian Diet 21-31; resigned from Zentrum and was commissioned by Pres. Hindenburg to form a non-Party Cabinet 32; while Chancellor he dismissed the Socialist Cabinet of Prussia and became Reich Commr. for Prussia 32; negotiated Lausanne Conf. for Abolition of Reparations 32; Vice-Chancellor in Hitler Cabinet Jan. 33 and Commr. for Prussia Jan.-April 33; negotiated Concordat with Vatican July 33; Plenipotentiary of Reich Govt. in questions relating to Saar Nov. 33; relieved of Vice-Chancellorship June, appointed Special Min. to Austria July 34, Ambassador with special mission 36-38; Ambassador-at-large; Ambassador to Turkey 39-44.
Publs. *Memoirs* 52, *Europa was nun?* 54, *Marginal Notes about the Yazrs 1926-33* 67, *Vom Scheitern einer Demokratie* 68.
Erlenhaus, Obersasbach/Baden, German Federal Republic.
Telephone: Achern 2460.

Papi, Giuseppe Ugo; Italian economist; b. 19 Feb. 1893.

Professor of Economics, Messina Univ. 27, Pavia Univ. 31, Naples Univ. 35, Rome Univ. 38-, Rector 53-66; Gen. Sec. Int. Inst. of Agriculture 39-48; Vice-Pres. and Pres. Food and Agriculture Cttee., OEEC; Pres. Int. Econ. Asscn. 62; Hon. LL.D. (Grenoble 55, Salonika 57, Bordeaux 58, Frankfurt 58, Paris 58, Aix-Marseille 60, Glasgow 61, Lille 65); Légion d'Honneur; Grosses Verdienstkreuz, Cavaliere di Gran Croce al Merito della Repubblica.
Publs. *Cost Variations and Business Cycles* 29, *The Colonial Problem; an Economic Analysis* 38, *Elements and Directive Principles of Economic Planning* 42, *Uniformities in a Consumer's Plan* 42, *Theory of the Economic Behaviour of the Government* 56, *Principles of Economics* (3 vols.) 53-61, *International Economics* 60,

Some Problems of Italian Economy 63, *Dictionary of Economics* 67.
7 Plinio Street, Rome, Italy.
Telephone: 351-080.

Papon, Maurice Arthur Jean, L.EN D.; French aviation executive; b. 3 Sept. 1910; ed. Lycée Louis-le-Grand and Facultés de Droit et de Lettres, Paris.
Editor, Ministry of Interior 35-36; Attaché, Cabinet of the Under-Sec. of State 36, Foreign Affairs 37-39; Sec.-Gen. Gironde 42-44; Prefect of Lands 44-45; Deputy Dir. for Algeria at Ministry of Interior 46-47; Prefect of Corsica 47-49, Constantine, Algeria 49-51; Sec.-Gen., Prefecture of Police 51-54; Protectorate of Morocco 54-55; Technical Adviser, Cabinet of Sec. of State for Interior 56; Insp.-Gen. for Admin., East Algeria 56-58; Prefect of Police, Paris 58-67; Pres., Dir.-Gen. Sud-Aviation Jan. 67-; Commdr. Légion d'Honneur, Commdr. de l'Ordre du Mérite Civil and mil. awards.
Publs. *L'Ere des responsables* 54, *Vers un nouveau discours de la méthode* 65.
Office: 37 boulevard de Montmorency, Paris 16e; Home: "La Noualla", Gretz-Armainvilliers (Seine-et-Marne), France.

Papp, János; Hungarian politician; b. 25; ed. chemical industry secondary school, Szeged, Communist Party Univ.
Chemical technician, Ajka Power Station 46-49; Head, Industrial and Transport Dept., Veszprém County Party Cttee. 49-56; First Sec. Veszprém County Party Cttee. 56-; Del. to the Nat. Ass. 58-; Minister of the Interior 61-63; Deputy Chair. Council of Ministers 63-65; mem. Central Cttee. Hungarian Socialist Workers' Party.
Veszprém County Party Committee, Veszprém, Hungary.

Paradjanov, Sergei Iosifovich; Soviet film director; b. 1924; ed. U.S.S.R. State Inst. of Cinematography.
Director at Kiev Dovzhenko Studios 52-; Mar del Plata Film Festival Award, Argentina, for *Shades of Forgotten Ancestors* 65.
Films include *First Lad* 56, *Ukrainian Rhapsody* 58, *Flower on the Stone* 59, *Shades of Forgotten Ancestors* 64.
Kiev A. Dovzhenko Film Studios, Brest Litovskoye Chaussee 110, Kiev, U.S.S.R.

Paraense, Wladimir Lobato, M.D.; Brazilian scientist; b. 16 Nov. 1914; ed. Colégio Estadual Pais de Carvalho, Pará, and Univ. do Recife.
Scientific Investigator, Ministry of Health, Brazil 40-; Prof. of Protozoology, Instituto Oswaldo Cruz 51, Instituto Nacional de Endemias Rurais 60; Research Assoc., Serviço Especial de Saúde Pública 54-56; mem. Pan American Health Org./WHO Working Group for Devt. of Guidance for Identification of American Planorbidae 61-; Dir. Inst. Nacional de Endemias Rurais 61-63; Active mem. Inst. of Malacology, Mich., U.S.A. 63-; mem. WHO Board of Experts in Parasitic Diseases 64-; Chief, Schistosomiasis Snail Identification Center for the Americas, Pan American Health Org. and Ministry of Health of Brazil 64-; mem. Sociedade de Biologia do Rio de Janeiro, Soc. Brasileira para o Progresso da Ciência (Counsellor 59-), American Asscn. for Advancement of Science, Royal Soc. of Tropical Medicine and Hygiene (U.K.), Academia Brasileira de Ciências, Int. Soc. of Hematology 54, Soc. of Protozoologists, U.S.A., Soc. Brasileira de Genética, Soc. de Biologia de Minas Gerais (Pres. 61-63), Conchological Soc. of Great Britain and Ireland, Int. Acad. of Zoology, India, Soc. Brasileira de Medicina Tropical, Soc. Brasileira de Parasitologia (Pres. 65-67), American Microscopical Soc., several medals.
Publs. 97 papers on zoological, parasitological and pathological aspects of tropical medicine, chiefly malaria, piroplamosis, leishmaniasis and bilharziasis (especially molluscan intermediate hosts.).
Rua Araguari 1670/101, Belo Horizonte, Minas Gerais, Brazil.
Telephone: 4-4807.

Parain, Brice; French writer; b. 10 March 1897; ed. Ecole Normale Supérieure and Ecole des Langues Orientales.
Cultural Attaché U.S.S.R. 25-26; Sec. of Literary Dir. of Librairie Gallimard 27-61; Officier Légion d'Honneur, and Croix de Guerre; Grand Prix Littéraire de la Ville de Paris 67.
Publs. *Essai sur la Misère Humaine* 34, *Recherches sur la Nature et les Fonctions du Langage* 43, *La Mort de Jean Madec* 45, *L'Embarras du Choix* 47, *La Mort de Socrate* 50, *Sur la Dialectique* 53, *De Fil en Aiguille* 60, *Noir sur Blanc* 62, *Joseph* 64, *France, marchande d'églises* 66, *Entretiens avec B. Pinçaud* 66, and others.
72 rue des Cheneaux, Sceaux 92, France.
Telephone: ROB 17-72.

Parandowski, Jan; Polish writer; b. 95; ed. Lwów Univ.
Chair. Polish P.E.N. Club; Int. Vice-Pres. P.E.N.; Prof. of Comparative Literature, Univ. of Lublin 44-52.
Publs. *Aspasie* 25, *Deux Printemps* 27, *Le roi de la vie (Oscar Wilde)* 29, *Le Disque Olympique* 32, *Visites et Rencontres* 34, *Ciel en flammes* 36, *Trois signes du Zodiaque* 38, *L'heure méditerranéenne* 49, *Voyages littéraires* 49, *Alchimie des Mots* 50, *Cadran solaire* 52, *Essais* 53, *Pétrarque, Odyssée* (translation) 59, *Souvenirs et Silhouettes* 60, *Medea* (play) 61, *Retour à la Vie* 61, *Nuit de Septembre* 62, *Quand j'etais critique théâtral* 63, *Feuillets épars* 65, *Acacia* 67, *Esquisses* 68.
Zimorowicza 4, Warsaw, Poland.

Paraskevopoulos, Ioannis; Greek economist and banker; ed. in Greece and at Albert-Ludwigs-Universität, Freiburg, Ludwig-Maximilians-Univ., Munich, and Univ. Leipzig.
Started with Deutsche Bank, Germany, then joined Midland Bank, England; with Nat. Bank of Greece 30-, helped organize its Industrial Credit Dept., Man., then Econ. Adviser, later Deputy Gov. 54-66, Gov. July 66-67; Prof. at Panteios School of Political and Econ. Science; fmr. Prime Minister, Minister of Supply, Nat. Economy, Commerce, Industry, Labour, Interior, Foreign Affairs, Co-ordination; Acting Prime Minister Dec. 66.
c/o National Bank of Greece, 86 Eolou Street, Athens 121, Greece.

Pardee, Arthur Beck, PH.D.; American biochemist; b. 13 July 1921; ed. Univ. of California (Berkeley) and California Inst. of Technology.
Postdoctoral Fellow, Univ. of Wisconsin 47-49; Instructor, Asst. and Assoc. Prof. Univ. of Calif. (Berkeley) 49-61; Senior Postdoctoral Fellow, Pasteur Inst. 57-58; Prof. and Chair. Biochemical Sciences, Princeton Univ. 61-67, Prof. of Biology 67-; mem. Editorial Board *Biochimica Biophysica Acta* 62-; Trustee Cold Spring Harbor Lab. 63-; mem. American Acad. of Arts and Sciences 63-; Paul Lewis Award, American Chemical Soc. 60.
Publs. Articles on a binding site for sulphate and its relation to sulphate transport into salmonella typhimurium, enzyme synthesis in synchronous cultures of bacteria, cell division and a hypothesis of cancer; *Experiments in Biochemical Research Techniques* 57.
Moffett Laboratories, Princeton University, Princeton, N.J. 08540; Home: 291 Russell Road, Princeton, N.J. 08540, U.S.A.

Párdi, Imre; Hungarian politician; b. 1922.
Former machine fitter; worked as Party official 45-, fmr. Sec. Tatabánya Town, Komárom County and Veszprém County Cttees., Hungarian Socialist Workers

Party; mem. Central Cttee. Hungarian Socialist Workers Party 62-; Chair. Nat. Planning Office 67-.
National Planning Office, Budapest, Hungary.

Pardo, Arvid; Maltese diplomatist; b. 14; ed. Università degli Studi, Rome, and Université de Tours.
Officer-in-Charge, United Nations Archives 45-46; Dept. of Trusteeship and Information for Non-Self-Governing Territories, United Nations 46-60; Secr., Technical Assistance Board, UN, later Deputy Resident Rep. in Nigeria and Ecuador 60-64; Perm. Rep. of Malta to the United Nations 65-.
Permanent Mission of Malta to the United Nations, 155 East 44th Street, 22nd Floor, New York City, N.Y., U.S.A.

Parente, H.E. Cardinal Pietro; Italian ecclesiastic; b. 16 Feb. 1891.
Ordained Priest 16; Archbishop of Perugia 55-59; Titular Archbishop of Ptolemais in Thebaide 59-; Assessor, Sacred Congregations for Doctrine and Faith; created Cardinal by Pope Paul VI 67.
Piazza S. Uffizio 11, Rome, Italy.
Telephone: 698-3493 (Vatican).

Parin, Vasily Vasilyevich; Soviet physiologist; b. 1903; ed. Perm Univ.
Laboratory Asst., Perm Pedagogical Inst. 21-25, Asst. and Lecturer, Dept. of Physiology 25-32, Head and Prof. of Physiology 30-33; Head and Prof. of Physiology, First Moscow Medical Inst. 33-41, Dir. 41-42; U.S.S.R. Deputy People's Commissar of Health 42-45; Head, Dept. of Physiology, Moscow Medical Inst. 43-47; imprisoned 47-53; Head, Physiology Lab., Inst. of Therapy, U.S.S.R. Acad. of Medical Sciences 54-56; Head, Chair. of Clinical and Experimental Physiology, Central Postgraduate Medical Inst., Moscow 56-; mem. U.S.S.R. Acad. of Medical Sciences; mem. U.S.S.R. Acad. of Sciences 66-; Order of Lenin; Order of Red Banner of Labour (thrice).
U.S.S.R. Academy of Sciences, 14 Lenin Prospekt, Moscow, U.S.S.R.

Paris, Jacques Emile, LL.D.; French diplomatist; b. 13 Jan. 1905; ed. Coll. Fénelon, La Rochelle, Ecole Libres des Sciences Politiques.
Attaché Brussels 29; Sec. Rio de Janeiro 31, Madrid 33, Oslo 38; Chargé d'Affaires to Norwegian Govt. in London 41; Head of Protocol and Europe Service, Nat. Commissariat for Foreign Affairs, London 42; Counsellor French Mission to Allied Governments, London 44; Minister to Bulgaria 45-50; Minister to Syria 50-52, Ambassador 52-55; Ambassador to Iran 55-57; Minister to Rumania 58-60, Ambassador to Ireland 60-64; Ambassador to Luxembourg 64-.
French Embassy, 19-21 rue Notre-Dame, Luxembourg; 12 avenue Paul-Doumer, Paris 16e, France.
Telephone: 727-7606.

Park Chung Hee, General; Korean army officer and politician; b. 30 Sept. 1917; ed. Taegu Normal School, Japanese Mil. Acad., Artillery School (U.S.A.) and Mil. Command and Gen. Staff Coll., Korea.
Teacher 37-40; Japanese Army 40-45; Korean Army 45-63; Deputy Chair. Supreme Council for Nat. Reconstruction May-July 61, Chair. July 61-Nov. 63; Acting Pres. of Repub. of Korea March 61-Nov. 63, Pres. Dec. 63-.
Publs. *Leadership*: *In the Midst of the Revolutionary Process* 61, *People's Path to the Fulfilment of Revolutionary Tasks*: *Direction for National Movement* 61, *Our Nation's Path* 62, *The State, the Revolution and I* 63.
The Blue House (Presidential Mansion), Seoul, Korea.

Parker, Sir Karl Theodore, Kt., c.b.e., m.a., ph.d., f.b.a.; British art historian; studied Continental art centres and British Museum.
Editor *Old Master Drawings* since inception 26; fmr. Asst. Keeper Dept. of Prints and Drawings, British Museum; Keeper Dept. of Fine Art, Ashmolean Museum Oxford 34-45; Keeper of the Ashmolean Museum 45-62; Trustee, Nat. Gallery 62-.
Publs. *North Italian Drawings of the Quattrocento, Drawings of the Early German Schools, Alsatian Drawings of the XV and XVI Centuries, Drawings of Antoine Watteau, Catalogue of Drawings in the Ashmolean Museums* (Vol. I, 38), *Holbein's Drawings at Windsor Castle* 45, *The Drawings of Antonio Canaletto in Windsor Castle* 48, *Antoine Watteau: Catalogue Complet de son Oeuvre dessiné* Vol. I (with J. Mathey) 57, Vol. II 58.
4 Saffrons Court, Compton Place Road, Eastbourne, Sussex, England.

Parker of Waddington, Baron (Life Peer), cr. 58, of Lincoln's Inn; **Hubert Lister Parker,** Kt., p.c.; British judge; b. 28 May 1900; ed. Rugby School and Trinity Coll., Cambridge.
Called to the Bar 24; Junior Counsel in Common Law to Admiralty 34, to Treasury 45-50; Bencher of Lincoln's Inn 45; Judge of the High Court of Justice, Queen's Bench Div. 50-54; knighted 50; Lord Justice of Appeal 54-58; Lord Chief Justice of England 58-.
Royal Courts of Justice, Strand, London, W.C.2; and Pile Oak Lodge, Shaftesbury, Dorset, England.

Parkes, Ed.; American business executive; b. 22 Nov. 1904; ed. Univ. of Arkansas.
Design Engineer Ark. Power & Light Co. 26-28; Engineer United Gas Pipe Line Co. 28-29, Dist. Supt. 29-30, Asst. Gen. Supt. 30-37, Gen. Supt. Field Lines 37-47, Vice-Pres. and Dir. 47-55, Pres. 56; Exec. Vice-Pres., Dir. United Gas Corpn. 55, and Pres. 58-67, and Chair. 67-; Dir. American Petroleum Inst. 56-.
Home: 5815 Creswell Road, Shreveport 71106; Office: 1525 Fairfield Avenue, Shreveport, La., U.S.A.
Telephone: 318-868-1370.

Parkes, Sir Roderick Wallis, K.C.M.G., O.B.E.; British civil servant and diplomatist; b. 2 April 1909; ed. St. Paul's School and Magdalen Coll., Oxford.
Entered Indian Civil Service 32; served in Punjab until 35; Indian Political Service 35-47; Asst. Political Agent, South Waziristan 35; Sec. and later Counsellor, British Legation, Kabul 36-39; Political Agent, Eastern Kathiawar 41-42; served in Rajputana and Baroda 43, Kolhapur 44, Punjab States 45; Liaison Comm., Govt. of India Food Dept. 46-47; retired from Indian Political Service and entered H.M. Foreign Service 48; with Western Dept. 48; Counsellor in Cairo 49; Head Information Div., British Middle East Office, Beirut 52; Head Information Services Dept., Foreign Office 53; Counsellor and later Chargé d'Affaires, Djakarta 54; Ambassador to Saudi Arabia 55-56, to Viet-Nam 57-61, to Sudan 61; Group Chair. Civil Service Selection Board; Amb. to Jordan 62-66; Dir. National and Grindlays Bank 67; Order of the Star of Jordan 1st Class.
The Old House, Castletown, Isle of Man; 48 Lamb's Conduit Street, London, W.C.1, England.
Telephone: Castletown 2384; 01-242-8060.

Parkinson, Charles Jay; American lawyer and business executive; b. 30 April 1909; ed. Univ. of Utah and Oxford Univ.
Partner in law firms, Salt Lake City, Utah; Counsel, Basic Magnesium Inc., Henderson, Nevada 41-45; Counsel, The Anaconda Co. and affiliated companies, and Int. Smelting and Refining Co., Salt Lake City, Utah 45-55; Vice-Pres. Anaconda Aluminium Co., New York 55-57; Gen. Counsel, The Anaconda Co., New York 57-60, Exec. Vice-Pres. 60-64, Pres. 64-; Dir. The

Anaconda Co., Fansteel Metallurgical Corpn., Chase Manhattan Bank.
The Anaconda Company, 25 Broadway, New York, N.Y. 10004, U.S.A.

Parkinson, Cyril Northcote, M.A., PH.D.; British historian and author; b. 30 July 1909; ed. St. Peter's School, York, Emmanuel Coll., Cambridge Univ. and King's Coll., London Univ.
Following a period of research in London, was elected Fellow of Emmanuel Coll., Cambridge; Senior History Master, Blundell's School, Tiverton, Devon 37-39; Master, Royal Naval Coll., Dartmouth 39-40; commissioned in Queen's Royal Regt. 40 and served as O.C.T.U. instructor, instructor and staff officer attached to R.A.F. and on Gen. Staff; Lecturer, Liverpool Univ. 46; Raffles Prof. of History, Univ. of Malaya 50-58; Visiting Prof., Illinois Univ. 59, Visiting Prof. Univ. of Calif. 60; Fellow of the Royal Historical Soc.; Julian Corbett Prize, London Univ.
Publs. *Edward Pellew, Viscount Exmouth* 34, *Trade in the Eastern Seas 1793-1813* 37, *Always a Fusilier* 49, *War in the Eastern Seas 1793-1815* 54, *Parkinson's Law: The Pursuit of Progress* 57, *The Evolution of Political Thought* 58, *The Law and the Profits* 60, *British Intervention in Malaya 1867-77* 60, *In-laws and Outlaws* 62, *East and West* 64, *Ponies Plot* 65, *A Law unto Themselves* 66, *Left Luggage* 67.
Les Câches House, St. Martins, Guernsey, Channel Islands, United Kingdom.
Telephone: Guernsey 37449.

Parks, Robert Joseph; American electrical engineer; b. 1 April 1922; ed. California Inst. of Technology.
U.S. Army 45, later Hughes Aircraft, Culver City, later Calif. Inst. of Technology; Surveyor Project Man. 65-66; Asst. Laboratory Dir. for Flight Projects, Jet Propulsion Laboratory, Calif. Inst. of Technology (responsible for Ranger, Surveyor and Mariner Projects 60-).
Jet Propulsion Laboratory, California Institute of Technology, 4800 Oak Grove Drive, Pasadena, California 91103, U.S.A.
Telephone: 213-354-3442.

Parlin, Charles C(oolidge), B.S., LL.B.; American lawyer; b. 22 July 1898; ed. Univ. of Pennsylvania and Harvard Univ.
Admitted to New York Bar 23; Senior Partner, Shearman and Sterling, New York City 45-; Dir. numerous companies; fmr. Lay Rep. World Council of Churches, Pres. World Council of Churches 61-.
123 Hillside Avenue, Englewood, N.J., U.S.A.

Parmar, Y. S., B.A., M.A., LL.B., PH.D.; Indian lawyer, agriculturalist and politician; b. 4 Aug. 1906; ed. Shamsher High School, Nahan, Forman Christian Coll. (Punjan Univ.), Lahore, Canning Coll. (Lucknow Univ.), Lucknow.
Sub-judge and Magistrate, Sirmur State 30-37; District and Sessions Judge, Sirmur State 37-41; Pres. Himalayan Hill States Regional Council 47; mem. Chief Commr.'s (Himachal Pradesh) Advisory Council 48-50; mem. Constituent Assembly of India 49, Provincial Parl. 50-51; Pres. Himachal Pradesh Congress Cttee. 48-50, 60-64; Standing Council for Himachal Pradesh in Supreme Court of India 60-63; mem. Himachal Pradesh Legislative Assembly and Himachal Pradesh Chief Minister 52-56, 63-67, 67-.
Publs. *Social and Economic Background of Himalayan Polyandry, Himachal Pradesh—Its Future and Status.*
Office of the Chief Minister, Simla; and Village Bharyog, P.O. Bagthan, District Sirmur, Himachal Pradesh, India.

Parnas, Józef, DR. MED. VET.; Polish microbiologist; b. 09; ed. Univ. of Lwów.
Former Asst. Prof. of Scientific Inst., Puławy; served Second World War; Prof. Acad. of Medicine, Lublin;

Chief, Dept. of Microbiology; Founder, Chodźko Inst. of Rural Medicine; fmr. Rector, Marie Curie Univ., Lublin; Hon. Pres. Int. Asscn. of Rural Medicine, Tours, France, Polish Soc. for Microbiology, Lublin; Fellow of Royal Soc. of Medicine, Royal Soc. of Tropical Medicine and Hygiene, London; mem. American Soc. for Microbiology, Soc. of Tropical Medicine in Antwerp, Půrkyně Medical Soc., Prague, Argentine Medical Soc.; adviser to the WHO; Dr.med.h.c. Půrkyně Univ.; D.Agri.h.c. Brno, Czechoslovakia, Charles Darwin Medal, U.S.S.R. Acad. of Sciences; mem. Brucellosis Cttee. Int. Asscn. of Microbiological Socs.
Publs. include *Anthropozoonoses Brucellosis, Tularemia, Leptospirosis, Brucellaphages, Rural Medicine and Hygiene.*
Academy of Medicine, Chopin Street 17/6, Lublin, Poland.
Telephone: 2-25-73.

Parodi, Alexandre; French politician; b. 17 June 1901.
Mem. Council of State 26; Deputy Sec.-Gen. Nat. Economic Council 29-38; Technical Counsellor Ministry of Labour 38; Dir.-Gen. of Labour, Ministry of Labour 39-40; relieved of post by Vichy; Del.-Gen. of Provisional Govt. of Republic for Occupied France 44; Minister of Labour 44-45; Ambassador of Provisional Govt. to Rome; Permanent Rep. of France, Security Council, U.N. 46-49; Sec.-Gen. Ministry of Foreign Affairs 49-55; Ambassador and Permanent Rep. to N.A.T.O. 55-57; Ambassador to Morocco 57-60; Vice-Pres. Council of State 60-.
191 Boulevard St. Germain, Paris 7e, France.

Parodi, Anton Gaetano; Italian journalist and playwright; b. 19 May 1923; ed. Università degli Studi, Turin and Genoa.
Journalist 45-; professional journalist 47-; Corresp. of *Unità*, Budapest 64-; Premio nazionale di teatro Riccione 59, 65, Premio nazionale di teatro dei giovani 47.
Plays include: *Il gatto, Il nostro scandalo quotidiano, L'ex maggiore Hermann Grotz, Adolfo o della magia, Filippo l'Impostore, Una corda per il figlio di Abele, Quel pomeriggio di domenica, Dialoghi intorno ad un uova, Una storia della notte, Pioggia d'estate, Cielo di pietra, I giorni dell'Arca, Quello che dicono.*
Via Benevenuto Cellini 34/7, Genoa, Italy.

Parr, Albert Eide; American (b. Norwegian) oceanographer; b. 15 Aug. 1900; ed. Oslo Univ.
Asst. in Zoology Bergen Museum 18-19; Asst. Norwegian Bureau of Fisheries 24-26; Asst. N.Y. Aquarium 26; Curator Bingham Oceanographic Collection Yale Univ. 27-42, Asst. Prof. of Zoology 31-37, Assoc. Prof. 37-38, Prof. of Oceanography 38-42, Dir. Marine Research 37-42, Dir. Peabody Museum 38-42, Research Assoc. and Trustee Oceanographic Inst. Woods Hole 38-; Dir. American Museum Natural History 42-59, Trustee 53-58, Senior Scientist 59-.
The American Museum of Natural History, Central Park West, New York 24, N.Y., U.S.A.

Parra, Nicanor; Chilean poet; b. 5 Sept. 1914; ed. Universidad de Chile, Brown Univ., U.S.A., and Oxford.
Prof. of Theoretical Mechanics, Univ. of Chile 64-; has given poetry readings in Los Angeles, Moscow, Leningrad, Havana, Lima, Ayacucho, Cuzco; Premio Municipal de Poesia, Santiago 37, 54.
Publs. Poetry: *Cancionero sin nombre* 37, *Poemas y antipoemas* 54, *La cueca larga* 58, *Antipoems* 58, *Versos de salon* 62, *Discursos* (with Pablo Neruda) 62, *Deux Poèmes* (bi-lingual) 64, *Antologia* (also in Russian) 65, *Antologia de la Poesia Sovietica Rusa* (bi-lingual) 65, *Canciones Rusas* 67, *Defensa de Violeta Parra* 67;

Scientific Works: *La Evolucion del Concepto de Masa* 58, *Fundamentos de la Fisica* (trans. of Foundation of Physics by Profs. Lindsay and Margenau) 67.
Instituto Pedagogico, avenida Macul 774, Santiago, Chile.

Parri, Feruccio; Italian politician; b. 19 Jan. 1890. School teacher; war service 15-18; imprisoned by Special Tribunal 27-33; founded Giustizia e Libertà, during Second World War, Action Party; Dep. Commdr. Partisan Mil. Courts; Pres. Council of Ministers 45; Senator for Socialist Party 58-63, Life Senator 63-.
The Senate, Rome, Italy.

Parrot, André; French archaeologist; b. 15 Feb. 1901; ed. Univ. de Paris à la Sorbonne, Ecole du Louvre and Ecole archéologique française de Jerusalem.
Professor, Faculty of Protestant Theology, Univ. of Paris 37-55, Ecole du Louvre 37-; Dir. Louvre Museum 68-; Head Keeper of Nat. Museums 46-65, Insp.-Gen. 65-; Dir. of French archaeological expeditions to Mari (Syrian Repub.) and Larsa (Iraq); mem. Institut de France (Académie des inscriptions et belles-lettres); Corresp. Fellow of the British Acad.; Assoc. mem. Belgian Acad.; mem. Institutum archaeologicum germanicum; Commandeur Légion d'Honneur, des Arts et des Lettres; Croix de Guerre 39-45.
Publs. *Mari, une ville perdue* 36, *Archéologie mésopotamienne* 46-53, *Tello-vingt campagnes de fouilles* 48, *Ziggurats et Tour de Babel* 48, *Découverte des Mondes ensevelis* 52, *Mari—le temple d'Ishtar* 56, *Mari—le Palais* (3 vols.) 58-59, *Sumer* 60, *Assur* 61, *Abraham et son temps* 62, *Terre du Christ* 65.
11 rue du Val Grâce, Paris 5e, France.
Telephone: ODEon 75-83.

Parrott, Sir Cecil Cuthbert, K.C.M.G., O.B.E., M.A.; British diplomatist; b. 29 Jan. 1909; ed. Berkhamsted School and Peterhouse, Cambridge.
Head, UN Dept., Foreign Office 50-52; Principal Political Adviser to U.K. Del. to UN 52; Counsellor, Brussels 52-54; Minister, Moscow 54-57; Librarian, Dir. of Research and Keeper of the Papers at the Foreign Office 57-60; Ambassador to Czechoslovakia 60-66; Prof. of Russian and Soviet Studies, Lancaster Univ. 66-; Hon. Fellow Inst. of Linguists.
Publs. Various articles in academic and literary journals on Russian and Slavic subjects.
Lonsdale College, University of Lancaster, Bailrigg, Lancaster, England.
Telephone: Lancaster 65201.

Parry, Sir David Hughes, Q.C., M.A., LL.D., D.C.L.; British barrister; b. 3 Jan. 1893; ed. Pwllheli County School, Univ. Coll. of Wales, Aberystwyth, and Peterhouse, Cambridge.
Served in First World War 15-19; called to Bar (Inner Temple) 22; Lecturer in Law, Aberystwyth 20-24, London School of Economics 24-28; Reader in English Law, Univ. of London 28-30; Prof. English Law 30-59; Vice-Chancellor Univ. of London 45-48; Chair. Cttee. of Vice-Chancellors and Principals 47-48; Pres. Society of Public Readers of Law 48-49; Dir. Inst. of Advanced Legal Studies 47-59; Hon. Bencher, Inner Temple; Dep. Chair. Caernarvonshire Quarter Sessions 50-66; Vice-Pres. Nat. Council of Social Service; mem. War Works Comm., Univ. Grants Cttee. 48-54, Colonial Univ. Grants Cttee. 46-50; Chair. Colonial Social Service Research Council 51-55, Court of Univ. of London 62-; Pres. Univ. Coll. of Wales, Aberystwyth 54-64; Hon. Fellow Peterhouse, Cambridge; Chair. Cttee. on N.Z. Univs. 59, Cttee. on Legal Status of the Welsh Language; mem. Royal Comm. of Remunerations of Doctors and Dentists, Inter-Dept. Cttee. on Business of Criminal Courts; Hon. LL.D. (Wales, Birmingham, Western Ontario, British Columbia, New Brunswick, Cambridge, Hull, Exeter and London), D.C.L. (McGill); Cymmrodorion Medal 59; Fellow London School of Econs.

Publs. *Law of Succession* 37, 46, 53, 61, 66, 11th and 12th editions of *Wolstenholme and Cherry Conveyancing Statutes* (joint); 12th and 13th editions of *Williams on Executors* (joint), *Sanctity of Contracts in English Law* 59 (Hamlyn Lectures).
Neuadd Wen, Llanuwchllyn, Bala, Merioneth, Wales.
Telephone: Llanuwchllyn 255.

Parry, John Horace, C.M.G., M.B.E.; British historian; b. 26 April 1914; ed. King Edward's School, Birmingham, and Clare Coll, Cambridge.
Royal Navy 40-45; Tutor, Clare Coll., Cambridge and Univ. Lecturer in History 45-49; Prof. of Modern History, Univ. Coll. of W. Indies 49-56; Principal of Univ. of Ibadan, Nigeria 56-60, Univ. Coll. of Swansea 60-65; Vice-Chancellor, Univ. of Wales 63-65; Gardiner Prof. of Oceanic History and Affairs, Harvard Univ. Oct. 65-.
Publs. *The Spanish Theory of Empire* 40, *The Audiencia of New Galicia* 48, *Europe and a Wider World* 49, *The Sale of Public Office in the Spanish Indies* 53, *A Short History of the West Indies* 56, *The Age of Reconnaissance* 63, *The Spanish Seaborne Empire* 64.
Widener 45, Harvard University, Cambridge, Mass. 02138, U.S.A.

Parry, Thomas, D.LITT., F.B.A.; British university principal; b. 14 Aug. 1904; ed. Univ. Coll. of North Wales, Bangor.
Asst. Lecturer in Welsh and Latin, Univ. Coll., Cardiff 26-29; Lecturer in Welsh Univ. Coll., Bangor 29-47; Prof. of Welsh 47-53; Librarian of the Nat. Library of Wales, Aberystwyth 53-58; Principal Univ. Coll. of Wales, Aberystwyth 58-; Vice-Chancellor Univ. of Wales 61-63, 67-69; Hon. D.Litt. Celt.
Publs. *Hanes Llenyddiaeth Gymraeg* (History of Welsh Literature) 45, *Lladd wrth yr Allor* (Eliot's *Murder in the Cathedral*), *Gwaith Dafydd ap Gwilym* 52, *Llywelyn Fawr* (a play) 54, *Oxford Book of Welsh Verse* 62.
Plas Penglais, Aberystwyth, Cardiganshire, Wales.
Telephone: Aberystwyth 3583.

Parsloe, Guy; British author and administrator; b. 5 Nov. 1900; ed. London Univ.
Sec. and Librarian Inst. of Historical Research 27-43; Sec. Inst. of Welding 43-67; First Sec.-Gen. Int. Inst. of Welding 48-66, Vice-Pres. 66-; Sec. O.E.E.C. Welding Techniques Mission to U.S.A. 53; Editor-in-Chief *British Welding Journal* 54-67; Sec. British Commonwealth Welding Confs. 57, 65.
Publs. *The English Country Town, ca.* 400 bibliographies in *Cambridge Bibliography of English Literature*; Editor *Guide to the Historical Publications of the Societies of England and Wales* 29-43, *Minute Book of the Corporation of Bedford 1647-1664, Wimbledon Village Club and Lecture Hall: 1858-1958—A Centenary Record, Wardens' Accounts of the Worshipful Company of Founders of the City of London 1497-1681*.
1 Leopold Avenue, London, S.W.19, England.
Telephone: 01-946-0764.

Parsons, Sir Maurice Henry, Kt.; British banker; b. 19 May 1910; ed. Univ. Coll. School, London.
Entered Bank of England 28, Private Sec. to Gov. (Lord Norman) 39-43; Alt. Exec. Dir. for U.K. on Int. Monetary Fund 46-47; Int. Bank for Reconstruction and Devt. 47, Dir. of Operations, Int. Monetary Fund 47-50; Deputy Chief Cashier, Bank of England 50-55, Asst. to Govs. 55-57, Exec. Dir. 57-66, Deputy Gov. July 66-; Alt. Gov. for U.K. on Int. Monetary Fund 57-66.
Clifford House, Shalford, Nr. Guildford, Surrey, England.
Telephone: Guildford 61523.

Parsons, Talcott, DR. PHIL., L.H.D.; American university teacher; b. 13 Dec. 1902; ed. Amherst Coll., London School of Econs., Univ. of Heidelberg.
Instructor in Econs. Amherst Coll. 26-27, Harvard

Univ. 27-31, Asst. and Assoc. Prof., Harvard Univ 31-44, Prof. of Sociology 44-; Visiting Prof. of Social Theory, Univ. of Cambridge 53-54; Fellow, Center for Advanced Study in the Behavioral Sciences 57-58; Pres. American Sociological Asscn. 49, Editor *The American Sociologist* 65-67, Sec. 60-; Fellow American Acad. of Arts and Sciences, Pres. 67-; mem. American Philosophical Soc.; Hon. Dr.rer.pol. (Cologne) 63; Hon. LL.D. (Chicago) 67.

Publs. *The Structure of Social Action* 37, *Essays in Sociological Theory* 49, *The Social System* 51, *Structure and Process in Modern Societies* 60, *Societies: Evolutionary and Comparative Perspectives* 66, *Sociological Theory and Modern Society* 67, *American Society: Perspectives, Problems, Methods* 68; with others *Toward a General Theory of Action* 51, *Working Papers in the Theory of Action* 53, *Family, Socialization and Interaction Process* 60, *Theories of Society*, 2 vols. 61, *The Negro American* 66.

330 William James Hall, Harvard University, Cambridge, Mass. 02138; 62 Fairmont Street, Belmont, Mass., U.S.A.

Telephone: 868-7600 (Office); 484-5610 (Home).

Part, Sir Antony Alexander, K.C.B., M.B.E., B.A.; British civil servant; b. 28 June 1916; ed. Harrow School and Trinity Coll., Cambridge.

Assistant Principal, Board of Educ. 37-39; Asst. Private Sec. to successive Ministers of Supply 39-40; Army 40-44; Private Sec. to successive Ministers of Educ. 45-46; Head of Bldg. Branch, Ministry of Educ. 46-52; Commonwealth Fund Fellowship, U.S.A. 50-51, Under-Sec., Ministry of Educ. 54-60, Head of Further Educ. Branch 56-60, Deputy Sec. 60-63; Deputy Sec., Ministry of Public Bldg. and Works 63-65, Perm. Sec. 65-68; Perm. Sec. Board of Trade 68-; Hon. D.Tech. (Brunel) 66.

c/o Board of Trade, 1 Victoria Street, London, S.W.1, England.

Parthasarathi, Gopalaswami, B.A., M.A.; Indian diplomatist; b. 7 July 1912; ed. Univ. of Madras and Oxford Univ.

Assistant Editor *The Hindu* 36-49; Chief Rep. Press Trust of India, London 49-52, Chief Ed. Press Trust of India 51-53; Chair. Int. Comm. for Cambodia 54-55; Int. Supervisory Comm. for Viet-Nam 55-56; Ambassador to Indonesia 57-58, to People's Republic of China 58-61; Chair. Int. Comm. for Supervision and Control, Viet-Nam 61-62; High Commr. in Pakistan 62-65, Perm. Rep. of India to UN Aug. 65-.

Office: 3 East 64th Street, New York, N.Y. 10021, U.S.A.; Home: 49 St. Mary's Road, Madras, India.

Partridge, Eric Honeywood, M.A., B.LITT.; British writer; b. New Zealand 6 Feb. 1894; ed. Queensland and Oxford Univs.

Served with Australian Forces 15-18; Lecturer in English Literature Manchester and London Univs. 25-27; founder and Man. Dir. Scholartis Press 27-31; served Army 40-42, R.A.F. 42-45; now engaged in revision of various works; Hon. D.Litt., Queensland.

Publs. *Eighteenth Century English Romantic Poetry* 24, *Three Personal Records of the War* (with R. H. Mottram and John Easton) 29, *Songs and Slang of the British Soldier* (with John Brophy) 30, *Slang To-day and Yesterday: A History and a Study* 33, *Name this Child* (a dictionary of Christian names) 36, 59, *A Dictionary of Slang and Unconventional English* 37, 16th and enlarged edn. 67, *The World of Words: A General Introduction to Language* 38, *A Dictionary of Clichés* 39, *A Dictionary of Abbreviations* 43, *Journey to the Edge of Morning* 46, *Usage and Abusage: A Guide to Good English* 47, *Words at War: Words at Peace* 48, *Forces' Slang: 1939-1945* (with Wilfred Granville and Frank Roberts) 48, *English: A Course for Human Beings* 49, *Name into Word* 49, *A Dictionary of the Underworld* 50, *Here, There and Everywhere* (Essays upon Language) 50, *A History of English since 1900* (with John W. Clark) 51, *From Sanskrit to Brazil* (Essays upon Language) 52, *The "Shaggy Dog" Story* 53, *You Have a Point There* 54, *The Concise Usage and Abusage* 55, *What's the Meaning?* 56, *English Gone Wrong* 57, *Origins: An Etymological Dictionary* 58, *A Charm of Words* (essays on language) 60, *Adventuring Among Words* 61, *The Gentle Art of Lexicography* 63, *The Long Trail* (with John Brophy) 65.

15 The Woodlands, Southgate, London, N.14, England.

Partridge, Ernest John; British tobacco executive; b. 18 July 1908; ed. Queen Elizabeth's Hospital, Bristol. Assistant Sec., Imperial Tobacco Co. 44-46, Sec. 46-57, Dir. 49-, mem. Exec. Cttee. 57-60, Deputy Chair. 60-64, Chair. 64-; Dir. British-American Tobacco Co. Ltd. 63-, Nat. Provincial Bank 68-; Chair. Industrial Management Research Asscn., Council of Industry for Management Educ.; mem. Nat. Econ. Devt. Council.

Imperial Tobacco Co. Ltd., East Street, Bedminster, Bristol 3; Bourton House, Flax Bourton, Nr. Bristol; and Flat 5, 5 Grosvenor Square, London, W.1, England.

Partridge, John Walters, B.S.; American utility executive; b. 24 July 1910; ed. Lafayette Coll.

Engineer, Columbia Gas System 31; Pres. Charleston Group Companies 51-61; Pres. and Dir. Columbia Gas System Inc. 61-.

120 East 41st Street, New York, N.Y. 10017, U.S.A. Telephone: OR9-4500.

Pascal, Paul Victor Henri, SC.D.; French chemist; b. 4 July 1880.

Prof. of Chemistry Lille Univ. 08-28; Prof. of Chemistry Univ. of Paris 28-50, at Ecole Normale Supérieure 28-62; and at Ecole Centrale des Arts et Manufactures; corresp. Acad. of Sciences 26, mem. 45-; Grand Officier Légion d'Honneur, Commdr. Palmes Académiques.

Publs. include *Poudres, explosifs et gaz de combat, Synthèses et catalyses industrielles, Métallurgie, Traité de chimie minérale* (12 vols., 2nd edn. 32 vols.), *Liaisons interatomiques, interioniques et intermoléculaires, Chimie générale* (6 vols.), *Etudes magnétochimiques et chimie générale.*

6 place du Panthéon, Paris 5e; Château du Mesnil-Soleil, Damblainville 14, Morteaux, France. Telephone: DANton 7758 (Paris).

Pashchenko, Grigory Stepanovich; Soviet diplomatist; b. 1913; ed. Krupsky Pedagogical Inst., Leningrad. Diplomatic Service 42-, Ministry of Foreign Affairs, later Australia and Czechoslovakia 42-55; Ministry of Foreign Affairs 55-59; Minister-Counsellor, Warsaw 59-62; Amb. to Sierra Leone 62-66; on staff of Ministry of Foreign Affairs 66-.

Ministry of Foreign Affairs, 32-34 Smolenskaya-Sennaya ploshchad, Moscow, U.S.S.R.

Pashev, Apostol Pavlov; Bulgarian politician; b. 14; ed. Civil Engineering Inst., Czechoslovakia.

Member Young Communist League 32-34, Communist Party 34-; fmr. Dir. of Dams "Vecha" and "Vassil Kolarov"; fmr. Chief Engineer, later Dir. State Enterprise "Hidrostroy"; Dep. Minister of Electrification 52-59; Head Dept. of Building, Transport and Communications, Cen. Cttee. of Communist Party 53-61; Dep. Chair. State Cttee. for Building, later Dep. Chair. State Cttee. for Planning 61-62, Chair. 62-.

State Committee for Planning, Sofia, Bulgaria.

Pashkov, Mikhail Vasilyevich; Soviet trade union official; b. 1914; ed. Ukrainian Polygraphic Inst. and Higher Party School.

Komsomol official, Volchansk, Kharkovsky Region 30-34; Student, Ukrainian Polygraphic Inst.; Engineer, Printing works, Kharkov 39-40; C.P. official, Moscow 40-52; Deputy Chief of Gen. Man. Dept. of Printing and Publishing Industries, Council of Ministers of U.S.S.R.

52-53; Deputy Minister of Culture of R.S.F.S.R. 53-61; Rector, Moscow Polygraphic Inst., Chair. Scientific Technical Soc. of Printing and Publishing Industry of U.S.S.R., mem. Central Cttee. of Cultural Workers' Union 61-66, Chair. 66-; mem. All-Union Council of Trade Unions 68-.
Central Committee of Cultural Workers' Union, 42 Leninsky Prospekt, Moscow, U.S.S.R.

Pasmore, (Edwin John) Victor, C.B.E., M.A.; British artist; b. 3 Dec. 1908; ed. Harrow School and L.C.C. Central School of Arts and Crafts (evening classes).
Local Govt. service, L.C.C. County Hall 27-37; associated with "Euston Road" school of painting 37-39; Visiting Teacher Camberwell School of Art 45-49, Cen. School of Arts and Crafts 49-53; Master of Painting, Durham Univ. 54-61; Consultant Architectural Designer Peterlee New Town 55; retrospective exhibitions Venice Biennale 60, Musée des Arts Décoratifs, Paris 61, Stedelijk Museum, Amsterdam 61, Palais des Beaux Arts, Brussels 61, Louisiana Museum, Copenhagen 62, Kestner Gesellschaft, Hanover 62, Kunsthalle, Berne 63, Tate Gallery, London 65, etc.; Carnegie Prize for Painting 64-.
Principal works include *The Gardens of Hammersmith* (Nat. Gallery of Canada), *The Thames at Chiswick* (Melbourne Nat. Gallery), *The Snow Storm* (Arts Council of Great Britain), *The Inland Sea, Abstract Relief* (Tate Gallery), *Abstract Mural Painting* (Barnsbury School, London).
12 St. German's Place, Blackheath, London, S.E.3, England.
Telephone: 01-858-0369.

Pasolini, Pier Paolo; Italian poet, writer and film director; b. 22.
Publs. *Poesie a Casarsa* 42, *I Diari* 45, *Dov'è la mia Patria* 49, *Poesia dialettale del '900* 52, *La meglio Gioventù* 54, *Dal Diario* 54, *Ragazzi di Vita* 55, *Canzoniere italiano* 55, *Le Ceneri di Gramsci* 57, *L'Usignolo della Chiesa cattolica* 58, *Una Vita violenta* 59, *Sonetto primaverile* 60, *La Poesia popolare italiana* 60, *Orestiade di Eschilo* 60, *Passione e Ideologia* 60, *Roma 1950* 60; Films: *Accattone* 61, *Mamma Roma* 62, *Il Vangelo Secondo Matteo, Uccelacci e uccellini, Requiescant* 67, *Oedipus Rex.*
Via Carini 45, Rome, Italy.

Passos, John Dos (*see* Dos Passos, John).

Passuth, László, LL.D.; Hungarian writer; b. 15 July 1900; ed. Kolozsvár, Cluj and Szeged Univ.
First novel 36; mem. Cttee. for Foreign Affairs, Asscn. of Hungarian Writers, European Community of Writers; Vice-Pres. Hungarian PEN Club.
Publs. include: *The Rain-God Mourns for Mexico* 39, *Joanna of Naples* 40, *A Castle in Lombardy* 41, *Born in Purple* 43, *In Black Velvet* 47, *The Musician of the Duke of Mantua* 57, *Lagunes* 58, *The Gods Shiver in Golden Mist* 64.
Rózsahegy utca 1, Budapest II, Hungary.
Telephone: 355-825.

Pasteur Vallery-Radot, Louis, M.D.; French physician; b. 13 May 1886; ed. Univ. de Paris.
Doctor of Medicine 18; Doctor Paris hospitals 20; lecturer Paris Univ. 27; Professor of Clinical Medicine; Faculty of Medicine, Paris 39-59, Hon. Pres. Sept. 59; Grand Croix de la Légion d'Honneur, Croix de Guerre, Rosette de la Résistance, etc.; hon. degrees from many foreign univs., incl. Athens, Rio de Janeiro, São Paulo, Santiago de Chile, Buenos Aires, Montreal, Munich; Co-président d'honneur de la Maison de l'Amérique Latine; mem. Constitutional Council 59-65; mem. Royal Soc. of Medicine, London; mem. Asscn. of American Physicians, Acad. nat. de Médecine, Acad. Française, Conseil de l'Ordre de la Légion d'Honneur, etc.

Publs. *Les Grands Problèmes de la Médecine* 36, *l'Anaphylaxie Expérimentale et Humaine* 37, *Publication des Oeuvres Complètes de Pasteur* 39, *Traité des Maladies des Reins* 49, *Publication de la Correspondance de Pasteur* 51, *Héros de l'Esprit Français* 51, *Comment traiter l'Asthme de l'Adulte* 53, *Pasteur Inconnu* 54, *Science et Humanisme* 56, *Images de la Vie et de l'oeuvre de Pasteur* 57, *Lettres de Claude Debussy à sa femme Emma* 57, *Tel était Claude Debussy* 58, *Médecine à l'échelle humaine* 59, *Précis des Maladies des reins* 60, *Médecine d'hier et d'aujourd'hui, Mémoires d'un non-conformiste* 66, etc.
24 avenue Gabriel, Paris 8e, France.

Pastor, Antonio Ricardo; Spanish scholar, university professor, banker and diplomat; b. 14 Sept. 1894; ed. Balliol Coll., Oxford, Univ. of Madrid, Univ. of Munich.
Spanish Govt. Scholar Balliol Oxford 16-20; Taylorian Asst. Lecturer Oxford 20-21; Cervantes Reader King's Coll. Univ. of London 21-30; Cervantes Prof. Univ. of London 30-45; now Fellow King's Coll. London; Inspector of L.C.C. Evening Institutes 22-36; Cultural Attaché, Spanish Embassy 44-46; corresp. mem of Spanish Royal Acad. of History, Hispanic Society of America; mem. Higher Council for Scientific Research, Madrid; founded Inst. of Spain in London and Fundación Pastor de Estudios Clásicos in Madrid; Dir. Banco Pastor, Fenosa (hydro-electric construction company), etc.; Légion d'Honneur, Grand Cross, Order of Republic (Spain); Knight Commdr. Order of Isabella the Catholic; Knight Commdr. Order of the Phoenix (Greece), etc.
Publs. *Un Embajador de España en la Escena Inglesa* (Count Gondomar) 25, *Spanish Chivalry* 28, *The Idea of Robinson Crusoe* 29, *Aspects of the Spanish Renaissance* 32, *Breve Historia del Hispanismo Inglés* 48, *Introducción a Toynbee* 52, *Cicerón Persgeuido* 61.
Fundación Pastor de Estudios Clásicos, Serrano 107, Madrid 6, Spain; and The Athenæum, London, S.W.1, England.

Pastor de la Torre, Celso; Peruvian lawyer and diplomatist; b. 14; ed. Germany and Catholic Univ., Lima.
Law Practice for 23 years; fmr. Prof. of Logic and Law; mem. Consultative Comm. of Ministry of Foreign Affairs, Peru; Gov. of Peru to Int. Bank for Reconstruction and Devt. and Int. Monetary Fund; Founder Partido Acción Popular and fmr. Sec.-Gen. and mem. Political Cttee.; Ambassador to United States 63-.
Embassy of Peru, 1320 16th Street, N.W., Washington, D.C., U.S.A.

Pastore, Giulio; Italian politician; b. 17 Aug. 1902; self-educated.
Former journalist and trade union organiser; Founder and first Sec. Italian Workers' Christian Action; fmr. mem. Secr. Gen. Confederation of Labour; Sec. Italian Fed. of Free Trade Unions 51; mem. Exec. Council Int. Confederation of Free Trade Unions 59; mem. Constituent Ass. 48-; Minister without Portfolio and Comptroller of Southern Italy Development Fund and the Under-developed Areas of Central and S. Italy 58-63, Dec. 63-; Christian Democrat.
Via Nemorense 132, Rome, Italy.

Pastore, John O., LL.B.; American lawyer and politician; b. 17 March 1907; ed. Providence Classical High School and Northeastern Univ.
Admitted to Rhode Island Bar 32; mem. House of Reps., Rhode Island Gen. Assembly 34-38; Asst. Attorney Gen., Rhode Island 37-38, 40-41; Lieut. Gov. Rhode Island 44-45, Gov. 45-50; U.S. Senator from Rhode Island 50-; mem. Joint Cttee. on Atomic Energy, Commerce and Appropriations Senate Committees; mem. U.S. Delegation to UN 55, Congressional Adviser with reference to Int. Atomic Energy Agency (I.A.E.A.); Senator-Designee, first Conf. on Peaceful Uses of Atomic Energy, Geneva 55, initiation of I.A.E.A., Vienna 57; Hon. LL.D. Providence Coll.,

Rhode Island Univ., Brown Univ.; Hon. Ed.D. Rhode Island Coll. of Education; Hon. Sc.D. Rhode Island Coll. of Pharmacy, Bryant Coll., Northeastern Univ.; Democrat.
Senate Office Building, Washington 25, D.C., U.S.A.; 91 Mountain Laurel Drive, Garden Hills, Cranston, Rhode Island, U.S.A.

Pastori, Aurelio; Uruguayan diplomatist and lawyer; b. 24 Dec. 1906; ed. Univ. of Montevideo.
Former Prof. Univ. of Montevideo 36-58; Legal Practice 31-; Dir. Govt. Oceanographic and Fishery Service 51-58; Perm. Rep. Latin American Free Trade Asscn. 61-63; Rep. Econ. and Social Council of UN 61-62, Chief Rep. 62-63; mem. numerous other UN Cttees.; Ambassador to France 64-; mem. various commercial and industrial societies.
Publs. *El Control de la Ejecución del Presupuesto, Sociedades Cooperativas, El Movimiento Cooperativista en el Uruguay*, and legal publications.
Embassy of Uruguay, 33 rue Jean Giraudoux, Paris 16e, France; Home: Treinta y Tres 1383 (2nd Floor), Montevideo, Uruguay.

Pastyřík, Miroslav; Czechoslovak trade unionist and politician; b. 16 Aug. 1912.
Chairman Břeclav District Cttee. of Communist Youth 30-38; mem. C.P. of Czechoslovakia 33-; Chief Sec. Hodonín District Cttee., C.P. of Czechoslovakia 45-46; Deputy and Sec. of Communist Deputies Club in Provincial Nat. Cttee. 46-49; Sec. Gottwaldov Regional Cttee. of C.P. of Czechoslovakia 46-48, Chief Sec. 48-50; mem. Central Cttee. of C.P. of Czechoslovakia 49-, Head of Dept. 50-63; mem. and Vice-Pres. Central Council of Trade Unions 63-65, Pres. 65-68; Deputy to Nat. Assembly 64-; mem. Gen. Council, and Vice-Pres., World Fed. of Trade Unions (WFTU) 65-.
National Assembly, Czechoslovakia.

Patcèvitch, Iva; American publisher; b. 19 Nov. 1900; ed. Russian Imperial Naval Acad.
Came to U.S. 23; associated with Hemphill Noyes & Co. Jan. 24-Dec. 28; personal asst. to Pres. and Budget Dir. Condé Nast Publs. Inc. 28-32; Man. Dir. Les Editions Condé Nast Paris 32-36; Exec. Asst. to Pres. Condé Nast Publs. Inc. 36-42, Dir. 35-, mem. Exec. Cttee. 36-, Pres. and Chair. Board of Dirs. 42-; Liaison Officer between Russian and British troops in Persia, Turkestan and Caucasus June 18-Nov. 19; Légion d'Honneur 50.
420 Lexington Avenue, New York 17, N.Y., U.S.A.

Patel, Baburao; Indian writer, editor and film producer; b. 4 April 1904.
Began free-lance journalism 22; wrote, directed and produced motion pictures, founder and Editor *Filmindia* 35-; lectured in U.S. and Europe on India's ancient culture and civilization; set up a production code and fought for revision of film censorship; Ed. *Mother India*; Man. Dir. Sumati Publications Pvt. Ltd. 58; Mem. Parl.
Publs. *Grey Dust, Burning Words, The Sermon of the Lord, Prayer Book, Rosary and the Lamp, Homœopathic Lifesavers for Home and Community*; Films: (wrote and produced) *Kismet, Mahananda, Bala Joban, My Darling, Maharanee, Draupadi, Gvalan*.
Girnar, Pali Hill, Bombay 50, India.
Telephone: 533414.

Patel, Bhagvatprasad Raojibhai, M.A., A.I.A.; Indian civil servant; b. 12; ed. Proprietary High School, Ahmedabad, Gujerat and Baroda Colls., and Bombay Univ.
Indian Civil Service 36-, Ministry of Food, Govt. of India 47-48; Chief Sec. State of Pepsu 48-50, Saurashtra 50-54; Dir.-Gen. of Shipping 54-55; Vice-Chair., Dir. and Gen. Man. Air-India 55-66; Sec. Dept. of Defence Supply, Govt. of India 66-; Chair. Export-Credit and Guarantee Corpn. 64-; mem. Indian Airlines Corpn.

Board 58-; mem. Exec. Council, Nat. Aeronautical Laboratory.
Publ. *Land Reforms in Saurashtra* 53.
Ministry of Defence, South Block, New Delhi, India.

Patel, Bhogilal Prabhudas; Indian civil servant; b. 16 Oct. 1912; ed. Baroda Coll., Royal Inst. of Science, Bombay, London School of Econs., and Middle Temple, London.
Indian Civil Service 36-; Registrar of Co-operative Socs. and Dir. of Agricultural Marketing and Rural Finance, Bombay State; Registrar-Gen. of Money Lenders, Bombay State 46-50; Commr., Ahmedabad Municipal Corpn. 50-54; Gen. Man., Bombay Electric Supply and Transport Undertaking 54-56; Man. Dir. State Bank of India 56-60; Adviser (Programme Admin.) to Indian Planning Comm. 60-63; Chair. State Trading Corpn. of India Ltd. 63-.
Express Building, Mathura Road, New Delhi, India.

Patel, Indraprasad Gordhanbhai, B.A., PH.D.; Indian economist; b. 24; ed. Baroda Coll., Bombay Univ., King's Coll., Cambrdige and Harvard Univ.
Professor of Econs., Maharaja Sayajirao Univ., Baroda 49-50; Economist and Asst. Chief, Financial Problems and Policies Div., Int. Monetary Fund 50-54; Dep. Econ. Adviser, Indian Ministry of Finance 54-58; Alt. Exec. Dir. for India, Int. Monetary Fund 58-61; Chief Econ. Adviser, Ministry of Finance, India 61-63; Econ. Adviser Planning Comm. 61-63; visiting Prof., Delhi School of Economics, Delhi Univ. 64.
c/o Delhi School of Economics, Delhi University, New Delhi 6, India.

Patel, Jeram; Indian painter and graphic designer; b. 20 June 1930; ed. Sir J. J. School of Art, Bombay, Central School of Arts and Crafts, London.
Reader in Applied Arts, M.S. Univ., Baroda 60-61; Reader in Visual Design, School of Architecture, Ahmedabad 61-62; Deputy Dir. All India Handloom Board 63-66; Reader in Applied Arts, M.S. Univ. Baroda 66-; mem. *Group 1890* (avant-garde group of Indian artists), Lalit Kala Akademi; one man exhbns. in London 59, New Delhi 60, 62-65, in Calcutta 66; in Tokyo Biennale 57-63, São Paulo Biennale 63; represented in Nat. Gallery of Modern Art, New Delhi, Art Soc. of India, Bombay, Sir J. J. Inst. of Applied Art, Bombay, and in private collections in U.S.A., London, Paris and Tokyo; Lalit Kala Akademi Nat. Awards 57, 64; Bombay State Award 57; Silver Medal, Bombay Art Soc. 61, Gold Medal Rajkot Exhbn.
Faculty of Fine Arts, M.S. University, Baroda 2, India.

Pathak, Gopal Swarup; Indian lawyer and politician; Member Lok Sabha for Uttar Pradesh; fmr. Judge.
Allahabad High Court; Pres. Indian Soc. of Int. Law, mem. Indian Comm. of Jurists; Minister of Law 66-67; Gov. of Mysore 67-.
Raj Bhavan, Bangalore, Mysore, India.

Patil, Sadashiv Kanoji; Indian politician; b. 14 Aug. 1900; ed. St. Xavier's Coll., Bombay, London School of Economics and University Coll., London Univ.
Joined the Indian Nat. Congress 20 and was imprisoned eight times; Gen.-Sec. Bombay Provincial Congress Cttee. 29-45 and Pres. 46-57; mem. A.I.C.C. 30-64 and mem. of its Working Cttee. 45-51, 56-57, Treas. 60-64; mem. Congress Working Cttee. 65-; mem. Bombay Legislative Assembly 37-46; mem. of the Bombay Municipal Corpn. 35-52; Mayor of Bombay three terms 49-52; mem. Constituent Assembly 47-50; mem. Provisional Parl. 50-52; mem. of Lok Sabha 52-; Minister for Irrigation and Power 57-58; Minister for Transport and Communications 58-59, for Food and Agriculture 59-Aug. 63; mem. Congress Party Parl. Board Aug. 63-; Minister of Railways June 64-67.
Publ. *Indian National Congress: A Case for Reorganisation.*
Home: Shanti Kutir, Marine Drive, Bombay 1, India.

Patiño, Antenor; Bolivian diplomat and businessman; b. 12 Oct. 1894; ed. Paris Univ. Law Faculty.
Formerly Sec. Bolivian Legation, Paris, Chargé d'Affaires, Madrid and mem. Bolivian del. to L.N.; Minister to U.K. 41-44; Pres. Patiño Tin Mining Enterprises; Chair. British-American Tin Mines and Tahiland Tin Mines; Dir. British Tin Investment Corpn., Arnhem Smelting Co., Gen. Tin Investment Corpn.; Grand Officer Condor of the Andes, Chevalier Légion d'Honneur.
Home: 9 rue d'Andigne, Paris 16e; Office: 45 avenue Foch, Paris 16e, France.

Patnaik, Bijoyanand; Indian politician; b. 5 March 1916.
Active in Orissa politics 47-; Chair. Orissa Congress Party; Chief Minister of Orissa 61-Aug. 63.
Bhuvaneshwar, Orissa, India.

Patolichev, Nikolai Semyonovich; Soviet politician; b. 08; ed. Mil. Acad.
Member C.P.S.U. 28-; held exec. posts for Young Communist League in Gorky and Chelyabinsk regions 28-31; at Head Office of Central Cttee. of C.P.S.U. 37-39; First Sec. of the Yaroslavl Regional Cttee. of the Party 39-41, of the Chelyabinsk Regional Cttee. 41-46; mem. Organisational Bureau and Sec. of the Central Cttee. of the Party 46-47; Vice-Chair. of the Council for Collective Farms of the Soviet Govt. 46; Sec. Ukrainian Communist Party Central Cttee. 47; First Sec. Rostov Regional Cttee. of C.P. 47-50; First Sec. Central Cttee. of Byelorussian C.P. 50-56; mem. Central Cttee. of C.P.S.U. 41-; First Deputy Minister of Foreign Affairs of U.S.S.R. 56-58; Minister of Foreign Trade 58-; Deputy to U.S.S.R. Supreme Soviet; Order of Lenin (six times), Order of the Red Banner of Labour.
Ministry of Foreign Trade, 32-34 Smolenskaya-Sennaya ploshchad, Moscow, U.S.S.R.

Paton, Alan Stewart, B.ED., B.SC.; South African writer and politician; b. 11 Jan. 1903; ed. Pietermaritzburg Coll. and Natal Univ.
Teacher 24-36; Principal Diepkloof Reformatory for African Juvenile Delinquents, Johannesburg 36-48; Pres. Liberal Party of South Africa till 68; Hon. L.H.D. (Yale Univ.); Hon. D.Litt. Kenyon Coll. and Univ. of Natal; Freedom Award 60; Award from Free Acad. of Art, Hamburg 61.
Publs. *Cry, The Beloved Country* 48, *Too Late the Phalarope* 53, *The Land and People of South Africa* 55, *South Africa in Transition* 56, *Hope for South Africa* 58, *Debbie Go Home* (short stories) 61, *Hofmeyr* 65, musical *Mkhumbane* (Village in the Gulley).
23 Lynton Road, Kloof, Natal, Republic of South Africa.
Telephone: Durban (Natal) 77423.

Paton, Boris Evgenyevitch; Soviet metallurgist; b. 18; ed. Kiev Polytechnic Inst.
Institute of Electro Welding, Ukrainian S.S.R. Acad. of Sciences, Dir. 53-; mem. C.P.S.U. 52-; Corresp. mem. Ukrainian S.S.R. Acad. of Sciences 51-58, mem. 58-, Pres. 62-; mem. U.S.S.R. Acad. of Sciences 62-, mem. Presidium 62-; Cand. mem. C.P.S.U. Central Cttee. 61-66, mem. 66-; Deputy to U.S.S.R. Supreme Soviet 66-; Deputy Chair. Union Soviet U.S.S.R. Supreme Soviet 66-; State Prize 50, Lenin Prize 57, Red Banner of Labour and other decorations.
E. O. Paton Institute of Electro Welding, Ulitsa Gorkogo 69, Kiev, Ukrainian S.S.R., U.S.S.R.

Paton, Sir George Whitecross, Kt., LL.D., M.A., D.C.L.; British educationist; b. 16 Aug. 1902; ed. Univ. of Melbourne and Magdalen Coll., Oxford.
Asst. Lecturer London School of Economics 30-31; Prof. Jurisprudence Univ. of Melbourne 31-51, Vice-Chancellor 51-68; Chair. Royal Comm. on Television (Aust.) 53; Chair. Australian Vice-Chancellor's Cttee. 57-60.

Publs. *A Text Book of Jurisprudence, Bailment in the Common Law* 52.
7 Dunraven Avenue, Toorak, Victoria, Australia.
Telephone: 24-1034.

Paton, Herbert James, M.A., D.LITT., LL.D., F.B.A.; British philosopher; b. 30 March 1887; ed. Glasgow, Oxford and Tübingen Univs.
Fellow Queen's Coll. Oxford 11-27; Dean 17-22; Junior Proctor 20-21; Admiralty Naval Intelligence Div. 15-19; Sub-Comm. on Polish Affairs Paris 19; Rockefeller Research Fellow Univ. of California 25-26; Prof. of Logic and Rhetoric Glasgow 27-37, Dean Faculty of Arts 35-37; White's Prof. of Moral Philosophy and Fellow Corpus Christi Coll. Oxford Univ. 37-52; mem. Royal Inst. Int. Affairs since foundation; Curator Bodleian Library 38-52; with Foreign Press and Research Service (Foreign Office Research Dept.) 39-44; mem. L.N. Union Exec. Cttee. 39-48; Gifford Lecturer, St. Andrews Univ. 49-51; Crown Assessor, St. Andrews Univ. Court 53-60; Visiting Prof., Univ. of Toronto 55; Hon. Fellow Queen's Coll. Oxford; Hon. Fellow Corpus Christi Coll. Oxford; Emeritus Prof. Univ. of Oxford.
Publs. *The Good Will, Kant's Metaphysic of Experience, The Categorical Imperative, The Moral Law, In Defence of Reason, The Modern Predicament.*
Nether Pitcaithly, Bridge of Earn, Perthshire, Scotland.
Telephone: Bridge of Earn 248.

Paton, Thomas Angus Lyall, C.M.G., B.SC., M.I.C.E., M.I.STRUCT.E.; British civil engineer; b. 10 May 1905; ed. Cheltenham Coll. and Univ. Coll., London.
With Sir Alexander Gibb and Partners 25-, Partner 38-, Senior Partner 55-; mem. U.K. Trade Mission to Arab States 53, to Egypt, Sudan and Ethiopia 55; Fellow Univ. Coll. London, American Soc. of Civil Engineers; Telford Prize, Inst. of Civil Engineers; responsible for design and supervision of many large factories for textile and heavy engineering industries and major hydro-electric projects, including Kariba Dam Scheme (Rhodesia) and Owen Falls Scheme (Uganda).
15 Hillbrow, Richmond-on-Thames, Surrey, England.
Telephone: 930-1907.

Patrick, John; American dramatist; b. 17 May 1905; ed. Holy Cross Coll.
Radio writer, San Francisco 32-35, film writer, Hollywood 36-37, free-lance dramatist, London and New York 40-; served American Field Service 42-44; Pulitzer Prize 54, Drama Critics Circle Award, Tony Award and Donelson Award 54, Screen Writers Guild Award 57, Foreign Correspondent Award 57.
Publs. Plays: *The Willow and I* 42, *The Hasty Heart* 45, *The Story of Mary Surratt* 47, *The Curious Savage* 50, *Lo and Behold* 51, *The Teahouse of the August Moon* 53, *Good as Gold* 57, *Everybody Loves Opal* 62, *It's Been Wonderful* 65, *Everybody's Girl* 66, *Scandal Point* 67; films: *Enchantment* 48, *The President's Lady* 52, *Three Coins in the Fountain* 54, *Mister Roberts* 54, *A Many Splendoured Thing* 55, *High Society* 56, *Les Girls* 57, *Some Came Running* 58, *The World of Suzie Wong* 60, *Gigot* 61, *Main Attraction* 63.
Hasty Hill Farm, Haverstraw Road, Suffern, N.Y., U.S.A.

Pattakos, Stylianos; Greek army officer and politician; b. 1912; ed. Cadet School, Higher War Coll. and Nat. Defence School.
Second Lieut. 37, Lieut. 40, Capt. 45, Major 48, Lieut.-Col. 52, Col. 62, Brig.-Gen. 67; Minister of Interior April 67-Dec. 67; Deputy Premier and Minister of Interior Dec. 67-June 68; First Dep. Premier and Minister of Interior June 68-; Major-Gen. (retd.) Dec. 67; Gold Medal for Gallantry (twice); War Cross, Third Class (thrice); War Cross, Second Class.
Ministry of Interior, Athens, Greece.

Patten, Bradley M., A.B., M.A., PH.D.; American anatomist; b. 14 June 1889; ed. Dartmouth Coll. and Harvard Univ.
Instructor, Associate Prof. of Histology and Embryology Western Reserve Univ. 14-34; Asst. Dir. for Medical Sciences Rockefeller Foundation 34-36; Prof. and Dir. of Anatomical Dept. Univ. of Michigan Medical School 36-59, Emeritus 59-; 2nd Vice-Pres. American Asscn. of Anatomists 34-36; Associate Editor *American Journal of Anatomy* 41-58; Consultant on Embryology, Stedman's Medical Dictionary 59-; Hon. Life mem. Michigan State Medical Soc. 60-.
Publs. *The Early Embryology of the Chick* 20, *The Embryology of the Pig* 27, *The Cardiovascular System, Morris Anatomy* 42, *Human Embryology* 46, *The Development of the Heart* in Gould's *Pathology of the Heart* 53, *Foundations of Embryology* 58.
2126 Highland Road, Ann Arbor, Mich., U.S.A.

Patterson, Most Rev. Cecil John, C.M.G., C.B.E., D.D., M.A.; British ecclesiastic; b. 9 Jan. 1908; ed. St. Paul's School and St. Catharine's Coll., Cambridge.
Deacon 31, Priest 32; London curacy 31-34; Missionary, Nigeria 34-; Asst. Bishop 42-45, Bishop on the Niger 45-, Archbishop of West Africa 61-.
Bishopscourt, P.O. Box 42, Onitsha, Nigeria.

Patterson, Ernest Minor, M.A., PH.D., LL.D.; American economist; b. 79; ed. Park Coll. and Univs. of Chicago and Pennsylvania.
Prof. of Latin, Henry Kendall Coll., Muskogee, Okla. 02-05; Prin. Wasatch Acad. Mt. Pleasant Utah 05-08; Dean Washington Coll. Tenn. 08-09; Instr. in Finance Univ. of Pennsylvania 10-15, Asst. Prof. of Economics 15-19, Prof. of Economics 19-50, Emeritus 50-, Chair. Dept. of Economics 19-32, Chair. Graduate Group Cttee. in Econs. 19-36; Pres. American Acad. of Political and Social Science 30-53, Emeritus 53-; mem. American Philosophical Soc. 32- (Sec. 43-48); Vice-Pres. Tax Policy League 33-41; Vice-Pres. American Econ. Asscn. 36; mem. Polish Inst. Arts and Sciences 43-, etc.
Publs. *The Operation of the New Bank Act* (with Thomas Conway, Jnr.) 14, *Western Europe and the United States* 22, *Europe in 1927: An Economic Survey* 27, *The World's Economic Dilemma* 30, *America, World Leader or World Led* 32, *Consumer Credit and Its Uses* (co-author) 38, *The Economic Bases of Peace* 39, *Planning for America* (co-author) 41, *Economic Problems of War* (co-author) 41, *An Introduction to World Economics* 47.
Garden Court Apartments, 47th and Pine Streets, Philadelphia 43, Pa., U.S.A.

Patterson, Gardner, M.A., PH.D.; American economist; b. 13 May 1916; ed. Univ. of Michigan and Harvard Univ.
U.S. Treasury Rep. Africa and Middle East 41-44; U.S. Navy 44-46; U.S. mem. Greek Currency Cttee., Athens 46-48; Asst. Prof. of Econs. Univ. of Michigan 48-49; Prof. of Econs. and Dir. of Int. Finance Section, Princeton Univ. 49-57; Prof. of Econs. and Dir. of Woodrow Wilson School of Public and Int. Affairs, Princeton Univ. 57-64, Prof. of Econs. and Acting Chair. Dept. of Econs. 65-66; Asst. Dir.-Gen., General Agreement on Tariffs and Trade (GATT) 66-68; Prof. of Econs. 68-; Econ. Adviser, U.S. Embassy, Israel 53-54, U.S. Embassy, Ankara 55-56; Head, U.S. Econ. Survey Mission to Tunisia 61; Ford Foundation Research Fellow, Geneva 63-64; Dir. Foreign Bondholders Protective Council (U.S.A.) 64-.
Publ. *Survey of United States International Finance 1949-54* 50-55, *Discrimination in International Trade, The Policy Issues* 66.
Department of Economics, Princeton University, New Jersey; 128 Fitz Randolph Road, Princeton, New Jersey, U.S.A.
Telephone: 924-3403 (Home).

Pattinson, John Mellor, C.B.E.; British oil executive; b. 21 April 1899; ed. Rugby School, Cambridge Univ. and Royal Mil. Acad., Woolwich.
Royal Field Artillery 18-19; Anglo-Iranian Oil Co., S. Iran 22-45, Gen. Man. 37-45; Man. Dir. British Petroleum Co. Ltd. 52-65, Deputy Chair. 60-65; Dir. other oil and chemical companies; Dir. Chartered Bank.
Oakhurst, Oakcroft Road, West Byfleet, Surrey, England.

Patton, James George, LL.D.; American agriculturist; b. 8 Nov. 1902; ed. Western State Coll. of Colo.
Athletic Dir., Instructor in Physical Education, Colo. 27-29; Gen. Agent Life Insurance Co. 31; Organiser Co-operative Insurance, Colo. Farmers' Union 32-34; Sec. Colo. Farmers' Union 34-37, Pres. 38-41; Dir. Nat. Farmers' Union 37-40, Pres. 40-66; Pres. James G. Patton & Assocs., Tucson 66-; Pres. Nat. Farmers' Union Life Insurance Co., Nat. Farmers' Union Service Corpn., Nat. Farmers' Union Auto Property and Casualty Co.; mem. Economic Stabilisation Board 42-43; mem. Nat. Labour Management Policy Comm.; fmr. mem. Advisory Board War Mobilisation and Reconversion Admin.; mem. Nat. Advisory Board Agricultural Marketing 46-53; U.S. Consultant, UN Conf., San Francisco 45, U.S. Adviser, F.A.O. Confs., Quebec 45, Copenhagen 46, Geneva 47, Washington 48; Del. Int. Fed. Agricultural Producers 46- (Vice-Pres. 56, Pres. 58-59).
7090 Circolo Place, Tucson, Arizona 85705, U.S.A.

Patton, Thomas F.; American executive; b. 6 Dec. 1903; ed. Ohio State Univ.
Admitted to Ohio bar 26; mem. law firm Andrews & Belden 26-32, partner in succeeding firm Belden, Young & Veach 32-36; Gen. Counsel, Republic Steel Corpn. 36-44, Vice-Pres. and Gen. Counsel 44-53, Dir. 43-; Asst. Pres., 1st Vice-Pres. 53-56, Pres. 56-, Chief Exec. Officer 60-, Chair. 63-.
Home: 2711 Landon Road, Shaker Heights 22; Office: 1707 Republic Building, Cleveland 1, Ohio, U.S.A.

Pátzay, Pál; Hungarian sculptor; b. 17 Sept. 1896; ed. Budapest and Collegium Hungaricum, Rome.
Professor Budapest Coll. of Fine Arts; early work tends towards Expressionism, becoming more classical in later periods; Franz Joseph Award of Distinction, Budapest, Kossuth Prize 50, 65; Eminent Artist of Hungarian People's Repub.
Works include: *Boy Carrying Fruit* 15, *Veiled Female Head* 16, *Grief, Wind on the Danube, Female Combing Hair,* Hussar Monument at Székesfehérvár and equestrian statue of Hunyadi at Pécs.
Budapest II, Gábor Áron-u. 16, Hungary.
Telephone: 364-752.

Pauk, György; British (b. Hungarian) violinist; b. 26 Oct. 1936; ed. Franz Liszt Acad. of Music, Budapest under Zathureczky, Leo Weiner and Zoltan Kodàly.
Concerts all over East Europe 52-58, and over the rest of the world; settled in Western Europe 58, Holland 58-61, England 61-; has recorded all Mozart Violin Sonatas and Schubert Violin and Piano Music, etc.; Paganini Prize 56, Sonata Competition Prize, Munich 57, Jacques Thibaud Prize 59.
22 Hillside Grove, London, N.W.7, England.
Telephone: 01-959-1939.

Paul VI, His Holiness Pope (Giovanni Battista Montini); Vatican ecclesiastic; b. 26 Sept. 1897; ed. Collegio Cesare Arici, Brescia, Liceo Arnaldo da Brescia, Seminary at Brescia, Pontifical Ecclesiastical Seminary, Milan, Pontificia Universitas Gregoriana and Università degli Studi, Rome.
Ordained, Brescia 20; attaché Apostolic Nunciature, Warsaw 23-24; Sec. of State, Vatican 24-37; Chaplain to students Rome Univ.; Nat. Spiritual Dir. Italian Fed. of Catholic Univ. Students (FUCI); lecturer on the diplomatic history of the Holy See at the Ecclesiastical

Acad. 31-36; Substitute Sec. of State to Cardinal Pacelli (later Pius XII) 37-39, to Pius XII 39-52, Pro.-Sec. of State 52-54; Archbishop of Milan 54-63; created Cardinal by Pope John XXIII 58; elected Pope June 63.
Apostolic Palace, Vatican City, Rome, Italy.

Paul, John Rodman, A.B., M.D., SC.D., F.R.C.P.; American physician and teacher; b. 18 April 1893; ed. St. George's School, Princeton Univ. and Johns Hopkins Univ.
Asst. in Pathology Johns Hopkins Univ. 19-20; Intern, Pennsylvania Hospital, Phil. 20-22; Dir. Ayer Clinical Laboratory, Pennsylvania Hospital 22-28; Asst.-Assoc. Prof. of Internal Medicine 28-40, and Prof. Preventive Medicine Yale Univ. School of Medicine 40-62, Emer. 62-; Dir. Viral Infections Comm., Armed Forces Epidemiological Board 41-56, WHO Regional Serum Bank 61-66; Chair. Virus and Rickettsial Study Section, U.S. Public Health Service 46-51; Consultant to the Sec. of the U.S. Army and to U.S. Public Health Service; mem. Expert Cttee. on Viruses, WHO 52-57; mem. Nat. Acad. Sciences, American Acad. of Arts and Sciences, Asscn. American Physicians; hon. mem. Royal Soc. of Medicine; Fellow Royal Coll. Physicians, London, American Coll. of Physicians; U.S. Medal of Freedom; Hon. M.A., Sc.D.
Publs. *The Epidemiology of Rheumatic Fever* 31, 3rd edn. 57, *Clinical Epidemiology* 58, 2nd edn. 66.
Office: 333 Cedar Street, New Haven, Conn. 06510, U.S.A.
Telephone: LO2-1161, Extension 659.

Paul, Sir John Warburton, G.C.M.G., O.B.E., M.C., K.St.J.; British colonial governor; b. 29 March 1916; ed. Weymouth Coll., and Selwyn Coll., Cambridge.
Royal Tank Regiment 37-45; Colonial Service, Sierra Leone 45-62, Dist. Commr. 52-56; Perm. Sec. 56-59; Provincial Commr. 59-60; Sec. to the Cabinet 60-62; Gov. of the Gambia 62-65, Gov.-Gen. 65-66; Gov. of British Honduras 66-.
Office of the Governor, Belize City, British Honduras; Home: Sherrens Mead, Sherfield-on-Loddon, Hants., England.

Paul-Boncour, Jean, L. en D.; French diplomatist; b. 30 July 1898.
Ministry of Foreign Affairs Paris 22; Third Sec. Washington 23-24; Sec. French Del. to Conf. on Arms Traffic Geneva 25; mem. French Information Mission to Naval Conf. Geneva 27; Sec.-Gen. of French Dels. to Naval Conf. London 30 and Disarmament Conf. 32-35; Sec.-Gen. to French Del. London Naval Conf. 35-36; Chargé d'Affaires Romania 36-38; Sec.-Gen. Inter-Govt. Comm. for Refugees, Evian 38; French Observer Pan-American Conf. Lima 38; Head of Press and Information Service, Quai d'Orsay 39-40; Press Counsellor Washington 40; First Counsellor, Peking, Chungking 40-43; joined Free French 43; Head, Anglo-American Section, Commissariat of Foreign Affairs, Algiers 44; Minister to Romania 45-47; del. to U.N. Enquiry Comm. in Korea 48; Ambassador to Thailand 51-54; Sec.-Gen. Geneva Conf. on Indo-China 54; Minister to Hungary 56-62; Ambassador to Argentina 62-64; Commdr. Légion d'Honneur.
2 avenue de Ségur, Paris 7e; Les Roches, Vailly-sur-Sauldre 18, France.
Telephone: Vailly 29; INValides 32-42.

Paul-Boncour, Joseph, LL.D.; French politician; b. 4 Aug. 1873.
Barrister; Dir. Waldeck-Rousseau and Vivian Cabinets 99 and 06-09; Republican Socialist Deputy 09 and Socialist 11; Min. of Labour in Monis Cabinet 11; Senator for Loir-et-Cher 31; resigned from Socialist Party 31; Min. of War in Herriot Cabinet 32; Prime Min. and Min. of Foreign Affairs Dec. 32-Jan. 33; Min. of Foreign Affairs in Daladier, Sarraut, Chautemps and

Daladier Cabinets Jan. 33-Feb. 34; mem. L.N. Del. 24-26, Permanent Del. 32-36; Min. of State in charge L.N. affairs Jan.-June 36; mem. Council 33-34; fmr. Pres. Foreign Affairs Comm. of Chamber; headed French Del. to U.N. Assembly 44; Conseiller de la République 46-48; Officier de la Légion d'Honneur.
Publs. *Le Fédéralisme économique, La République et la décentralisation, Les Syndicats de fonctionnaires, Art et démocratie, Trois Plaidoiries, Entre deux Guerres: Souvenirs sur la IIIe République,* etc.
17 rue de Téhéran, Paris 8e, France.

Pauley, Edwin W., M.S.; American industrialist; b. 7 Jan. 1903; ed. Georgia Mil. Acad. and Univ. of Calif.
Pres. Independent Petroleum Association 34-38; Special Rep. of California Govt. on Natural Resources Comm. 39 and Interstate Oil and Compact Comm. 40; Organiser of State of Calif. Defence Council 41; Treasurer Democratic Nat. Cttee., Sec. 41-43; Petroleum Co-ordinator for European War on Petroleum Lend-Lease Supplies for Russia and the U.K. 41; U.S. Industrial and Commercial Adviser Potsdam Conference; U.S. Rep. on Allied Comm. on Reparations (with Rank of Ambassador) 45-46; Special Adviser on Reparations to Sec. of State 47-48; Special Asst. Sec. of Army 47; Regent, Univ. of California since 39; Founder, Petrol Corpn., Los Angeles; Int. Independent Oil Producer (U.S.A., Mexico); Chair. of Board Pauley Petroleum Inc.
Home: 9521 Sunset Blvd., Beverly Hills, Calif., U.S.A.; Office: 10,000 Santa Monica Boulevard, Los Angeles 67, Calif., U.S.A.

Paulhan, Jean, L. ès L.; French writer; b. 2 Dec. 1884; ed. Lycée Louis-le-Grand and Sorbonne.
Held teaching and other posts 07-14; served French Army 14-18; Sec. *Nouvelle Revue Française* 20-25; Dir. 25-40; active in Resistance; founded *Les Lettres Françaises* 41; received Grand Prix of French Acad. for his works 45; mem. Académie Française 63-; Grand Officier de la Légion d'Honneur, Croix de Guerre.
Publs. *Les Hain-Tenys Merinas* 13, *Le Guerrier Appliqué* 15, *Le Pont Traversé* 20, *Jacob Cow le Pirate* 21, *La Guérison Sévère* 27, *Les Fleurs de Tarbes* 41, *Fautrier l'Enragé* 44, *Clef de la Poésie* 44, *F.F. ou le Critique* 45, *Braque le Patron* 45, *Entretiens sur des Faits-Divers* 45, *Guide d'un Petit Voyage en Suisse* 47, *De la Paille et du Grain* 48, *Les Causes Célèbres* 50, *L'Aveuglette* 52, *La Peinture moderne, ou l'espace d'avant les raisons* 55, *Les Douleurs imaginaires* 56, *Le clair et l'obscur* 58, *Une curieuse société secrète, ou la conscience en plein jour, Oevres complètes* (Vol. I, *Récits,* Vol. II, *Grammaire des idées,* Vol. III, *Don des Langues*) 66, 68.
5 rue des Arènes, Paris 5e, France.
Telephone: POR-28-15.

Pauling, Linus Carl, PH.D., SC.D., L.H.D., U.J.D., D.H.C.; American university professor; b. 28 Feb. 1901; ed. Oregon State Coll., Calif. Inst. of Technology and Univs. of Munich, Copenhagen and Zürich.
Full-time Asst. in Quantitative Analysis, Oregon State Coll. 19-20; part-time Asst. Chemistry, Mechanics and Materials, Oregon State Coll. 20-22; Graduate Asst., Calif. Inst. of Technology 22-23, Teaching Fellow 23-25, Research Assoc. 25-26, Nat. Research Fellow, Chemistry 25-26; Fellow John Simon Guggenheim Memorial Foundation 26-27; Asst. Prof. of Chemistry, Calif. Inst. of Technology 27-29, Assoc. Prof. 29-31, Prof. 31-64; Prof. of Chemistry, Univ. of California, at San Diego 67-; Chair. Div. of Chemistry and Chemical Engineering, Calif. Inst. of Technology, Dir. of the Gates and Crellin Laboratories 36-58; George Fisher Baker Lecturer in Chemistry, Cornell Univ. 37-38; Eastman Prof. Oxford Univ. 48; Research Prof. Center for Study of Democratic Insts. 63-; awards include: Langmuir Prize 31, William H. Nichols Medal 41, Willard Gibbs Medal 46, Theodore William Richards Medal 47, Davy Medal 47, Medal for Merit 48, Gilbert Newton Lewis

Medal 51, Nobel Prize for Chemistry 54, for Peace 62, Thomas Addis Medal 55, John Phillips Memorial Award, Avogadro Medal 56, Pierre Fermat Medal, Paul Sabatier Medal 57; mem. Nat. Acad. of Sciences, American Acad. of Arts and Sciences, Deutsche Akad. der Naturforscher Leopoldina; hon. mem. or Fellow Chemical Soc. of London, Acad. of Sciences of Liège, Royal Inst., Swiss Chemical Soc.; Chemical Soc. of Japan, Nat. Inst. Sciences India, Royal Norwegian Scientific Society, Trondheim; foreign mem. Royal Society, Norwegian Acad. Science and Letters; Acad. of Sciences U.S.S.R.; corresp. foreign mem. Accad. della Scienze, Lisbon Acad. Science; Foreign Assoc. Acad. des Sciences (France); Hon. Fellow, Indian Acad. Sciences, Austrian Acad. of Science, European Soc. of Haematology, etc.; hon. degrees from numerous univs.
Publs. *The Structure of Line Spectra* (with S. Goudsmit) 30, *Introduction to Quantum Mechanics, with Applications to Chemistry* (with E. Bright Wilson, Jr.) 35, *The Nature of the Chemical Bond* 39 (2nd edn. 40, 3rd edn. 60), *General Chemistry* 47 (2nd edn. 53), *College Chemistry* 50 (3rd edn. 64), *No More War!* 58, 62, *The Architecture of Molecules* (with R. Hayward) 65.
P.O. Box 109, La Jolla, California 92037, U.S.A.

Paulo Couto, Carlos de; Brazilian geologist; b. 30 Aug. 1910; ed. Colégio Militar de Porto Alegre.
In Brazilian Treasury Dept. 36-44; Researcher in Geology and Paleontology, Museu Nacional, Rio de Janeiro 44-60, geologist 60-, Dir. Dept. of Geology 60-66; Chief Researcher, Nat. Research Council, Brazil; mem. Univ. Fed. do Rio de Janeiro; mem. Acad. Brasileira de Geologia, Soc. Brasileira de Paleontologia; Corresp. mem. Acad. Colombiana de Ciencias Exactas, Físicas y Naturales, Soc. of Vertebrate Paleontology (U.S.A.); mem. Editorial Board *Evolution* 53-55; Fellow, John Simon Guggenheim Memorial Foundation, New York 51-52; Lecturer in numerous Univs. and Colls.; Prize and José Bonifácio de Andrada e Silva Gold Medal, Soc. de Brasileira de Geologia 64.
Publs. *Paleontologia Brasileira (Mamiferos)* 53, and over 150 papers on vertebrate paleontology and geology.
Museu Nacional, Quinta de Boa Vista, Rio de Janeiro, Guanabara, ZC-08, Brazil.

Pauls, Dr. Rolf Friedemann; German diplomatist; b. 26 Aug. 1915; ed. Naumburg Domgymnasium and Universität Hamburg.
Major in German Army 36-45; Sec. to Parl. Council, Bonn 48-49; Foreign Service 50-; Personal Asst. to Sec. of State for Foreign Affairs (Prof. Hallstein) 52-55; Counsellor for Political Affairs, Washington 56-60; Counsellor and Deputy Ambassador, Athens 60-63; Deputy Dir.-Gen. of Dept. for Econ. Affairs, Foreign Office, Bonn 63-65; Ambassador to Israel 65-68.
c/o Ministry of Foreign Affairs, Bonn, German Federal Republic.

Paulssen, Hans Constantin, DR. IUR.; German business executive; b. 1892; ed. Univs. of Freiburg, Munich and Jena.
General Man. Aluminium-Industrie-Gemeinschaft Konstanz G.m.b.H.; Chair. of Board Martinswerk G.m.b.H., Bergheim, Aluminium-Hütte Rheinfelden G.m.b.H., Aluminium-Walzwerke Singen G.m.b.H., Singen, Aluminium-Giesserei Villingen G.m.b.H., Villingen, Gothaer Feuerversicherung A.G., Cologne, Gothaer Transport-u. Rückversicherungs A.G., Cologne, Gothaer Lebensversicherung A.G., Göttingen; Hon. Senator, Univ. of Freiburg; Hon Pres. Fed. of German Employers Asscns., Cologne; Pres. Chamber of Industry and Commerce, Constance, Rheinschiffahrtsverband Konstanz e.V., Constance, Employers Asscn. of Iron and Metal Industries of Baden, Freiburg, Board of Trustees Ifo-Institut für Wirtschaftsforschung, Munich; mem.

many other Boards, Councils, etc.; Order of Merit of German Fed. Repub. with Star and Sash.
D Constance 7750, Hebelstrasse 4, German Federal Republic.
Telephone: Constance 62101.

Paumgartner, Bernhard; Austrian conductor, musicologist and composer; b. 14 Nov. 1887; ed. Universität Wien, and musical studies under Bruno Walter.
Music Coach, Vienna State Opera; Dir., Vienna Tonkünstler Orchestra, Lecturer, Acad. of Music, Vienna 17; Dir. of Mozarteum, Salzburg; Conductor, Salzburg Festivals; Pres. and Prof., Acad. of Music and Dramatic Art, Salzburg 49-; Pres. Salzburg Festivals 60-; Guest Conductor in London, Paris, Moscow, Budapest, Prague, Brussels, Germany, U.S.A., Japan and Switzerland; Austrian and foreign decorations.
Publs. *Das Taghorn* 23, *Mozart* 27, *Schubert* 45, *J. S. Bach* 50.
Compositions: operas *Das heisse Eisen* 22, *Die Höhle von Salamanca* 23, *Rossini in Neapel* 35, also ballets, stage music, choral music, songs and orchestral music.
Girardistrasse 38, A-5020 Salzburg, Austria.
Telephone: Salzburg 74649

Paustovsky, Konstantin Georgievich; Soviet writer; b. 1892; ed. Moscow Univ.
Order of Lenin 67; Order of Red Banner of Labour (twice).
Publs. *Kara Bugaz* 32, *Kolchida* 34, *The Romantics* 35, *Black Sea* 36, *Northern Tales* 39, *Distant Years* 46, *Tale of the Forests* 48, *Birth of the Sea* 52, *Restless Youth* 55, *The Golden Rose* 56, *The Beginning of the Unknown Age* 58, *A Time of Great Expectations* 59, *Throw To The South* (play) 61, *Simple Hearts* (play) 63, *Smoke of the Fatherland* (novel) 64, *Book of Wandering* (stories) 64, *Selected Prose* 65, *Slow Approach of Thunder* 65, *Story of a Life* (Vol. II) 66, Vols. III and IV 66-67.
Union of Writers of the U.S.S.R., Ul. Voroskogo 52, Moscow, U.S.S.R.

Pauwels, François Désiré, LL.D.; Netherlands jurist and writer; b. 88; ed. Amsterdam and Utrecht Univ.
Solicitor in Amsterdam; poet and novelist.
Publs. Poems: *Enkele versen* 16, *Fantomen* 19, *Tziganen* 24, *Verzamelde gedichten* 28, *Het boek "Morgen"* 31, *Het boek "Strijd"* 40, *Klinkende Boeien* 45, *Dag van Leugen* 48; Novels: *Boeven en Burgers* 26, *Ambtsgeheim* 28, *Tine Kipra's Echtscheiding* 29, *De Lachende beklaagde* 30, *De Vrouw met de twee Gezichten* 31, *De Madonna van Juan-les-Pins* 34, *Het Kartonnen Dorp* 36, *Rechter Thomas* 37, *Het Duel* 39, *Griffioen* 46, *Maria Dolorosa* 47, *De Serafijn* 48, *De Zaak Tom X, Crimineel Commentaar* 53, *Het Recht viert feest* 55, *Tijgers* 56, *'n Hond huilt in de nacht* 57, *Slachtoffer zonder Keus* 58, *Als het niet waar is* 61.
P.C. Hooftstraat 22, Amsterdam, Netherlands.

Pavate, Dadasaheb Chintamani; Indian mathematician and government official; b. 2 Aug. 1899; ed. Karnatak Coll., Dharwar, and Sidney Sussex Coll., Cambridge.
Professor of Mathematics, Banaras Hindu Univ. 28-30; entered Bombay Educ. Service 30; Dir. of Public Instruction, Bombay State 47-54; Vice-Chancellor Karnatak Univ. 54-67; Gov. of Punjab 67-; mem. Official Language Comm. 55-56; Leader Indian Del. to 19th Int. Educ. Conf., Geneva 56; Padma Bhushan 67.
Publs. include *Elements of Calculus, Modern College Algebra, Memoirs of an Educational Administrator*.
Office of the Governor, Chandigarh, Punjab, India.

Pavicevic, Miso; Yugoslav diplomatist; b. 21 April 1915.
Permanent Representative of Federal People's Republic of Yugoslavia to the UN until 64; Asst. State Sec. for Foreign Affairs 64-.
Secretariat for Foreign Affairs, Belgrade, Yugoslavia.

Pavlov, Dmitri Vasilievich; Soviet politician; b. 05; ed. Acad. of Foreign Trade.

Mem. Communist Party of the Soviet Union 26-; various exec. posts in the economic field 37-49; Minister of Food Industry 49-51; Chair. State Cttee. on Supply of Foodstuffs and Consumer Goods, U.S.S.R. Council of Ministers 51-52; Minister of Fish Industry 52-53; First Deputy Minister of Trade 53-54, Minister of Trade 55-59; Minister of Trade of R.S.F.S.R. 59-; Deputy to R.S.F.S.R. Supreme Soviet.

Ministry of Trade of R.S.F.S.R., 47 Kirov Street, Moscow, U.S.S.R.

Pavlov, Georgi Sergeyevich; Soviet politician; b. 10; ed. Dnieprodzerzhinsk Metallurgical Inst.

Second, later First Sec. Dnieprodzerzhinsk City Cttee. of C.P.S.U. 43-47; mem. staff, Central Cttee. of C.P.S.U. 47-49, 57; First Sec. Magnitogorsk City Cttee. of C.P.S.U. 49-50, of Chelyabinsk Regional Cttee. 50-51; Deputy Chair. Exec. Cttee. Kostroma Regional Soviet of Workers' Deputies 51-54; Sec., First Sec., later Second Sec. Kostroma Regional Cttee. of C.P.S.U. 54-57; First Sec. Mari Regional Cttee. of C.P.S.U. 57-63; Exec. Party and State Control Cttee. of Central Cttee. of C.P.S.U. and U.S.S.R. Council of Ministers 63-65; Head of Dept. C.P.S.U. Central Cttee. 65-; Cand. mem. C.P.S.U. Central Cttee. 61-; Deputy to U.S.S.R. Supreme Soviet; several decorations.

C.P.S.U. Central Committee, 4 Staraya ploshchad, Moscow, U.S.S.R.

Pavlov, Grigory Petrovich; Soviet politician; b. 1913; ed. Voronezh Agricultural Inst.

Member C.P.S.U. 40-; trade union and Komsomol leader, later First Sec. District Cttee. of C.P., Ryazan and Lipetsk Region 36-47; First Sec. Lipetsk District, later Regional Cttee. of C.P. 47-56; Vice-Chair., later Chair. Exec. Cttee. Lipetsk Regional Soviet of Working People's Deputies 56-63; Sec., later First Sec. Lipetsk Regional Cttee. of C.P. 61-; Candiate mem. Central Cttee. of C.P.S.U. 66-; Deputy to U.S.S.R. Supreme Soviet.

Lipetsk Regional Committee of C.P.S.U., Lipetsk, U.S.S.R.

Pavlov, Sergei Pavlovich; Soviet politician; b. 19 Jan. 1929; ed. Technical Inst., and Moscow Inst. of Physical Culture.

Komsomol work 52-56; mem. C.P.S.U. 54-; Sec., Second Sec., First Sec., Moscow City Cttee., Komsomol 56-58; Sec. Central Cttee. Komsomol 58-59, First Sec. 59-68; Chair. Central Council of Sports Socs. June 68-; mem. Central Cttee. C.P.S.U. 61-; Deputy to U.S.S.R. Supreme Soviet.

Central Council of Sports Societies, Moscow, U.S.S.R.

Pavlov, Todor Dimitrov; Bulgarian scientist; b. 90; ed. Sofia State Univ.

Teacher 10-21; Publicist 22-32; Prof. Dialectical Materialism, Moscow 32-36; mem. Regents' Council, Bulgaria 44-46; Prof. Philosophy, Sofia State Univ. 45-47; Pres. Bulgarian Acad. of Sciences 47-62, Hon. Pres. 62-; Head Inst. of Philosophy 45-; Editor-in-Chief of journal *Philosophical Thought* 45-; mem. Presidium of Nat. Assembly 62; Dep. Grand Nat. Assembly and First and Second Nat. Assemblies 46-63; mem. Politbureau of the Central Cttee. of the Bulgarian C.P. 66-; Serbian Acad. of Sciences, Belgrade, Polish Acad. of Sciences, Czechoslovak Acad. of Sciences; Hon. or foreign mem. several Acads.; mem. European Community of Writers 62, European Soc. of Culture in Venice; hon. doctor Sofia, Moscow, Prague, Berlin; Hero of Socialist Labour (twice) and many other honours.

Publs. *Theory of Reflection* 36, *General Theory of Art* 38, *Fundamental Problems of Aesthetics* 49, *Literary Science and Criticism* 54-55, *The Philosophy of Dialecti-*

cal Materialism and the particular Sciences 56, *Selected Works* 57-60, *Zur Geschichte der Ästhetik, Grundgesetze der Kunst, Informatzia, otrajenie, tvortchestvo.*

12 Dobrudja Street, Sofia, Bulgaria.

Paxinou, Katina (wife of Alexis Minotis q.v.); Greek-born American actress; b. 1904; studied music and singing at Conservatoire, Geneva.

Made debut on Greek stage 29; leading lady of Nat. Theatre of Greece 32-68; has interpreted many classical roles, both in Greece and abroad, incl. Clytemnestra, Elektra, Medea and Hecuba, played Gertrude in *Hamlet* in London and Berlin 39, Hedda Gabler in New York, *House of Bernarda Abba* 51, *Blood Wedding* 59, Madam Zachanasian in *The Visit* 61; played Hecuba, World Theatre Season, London 66, Jocasta (*Oedipus Rex*), London 66; played Pilar in film *For Whom the Bell Tolls* (Hemingway), Roseria Peowndi in *Rocco and His Brothers* 60, and made other films; returned from U.S.A. to Greece 50; played classical roles both in Athens and abroad; awards incl. Oscar for *For Whom the Bell Tolls*, Prix Cocteau for part of Christine in O'Neill's *Mourning Becomes Electra*; also the Highest Decoration for Valour by Greek King.

13 Lykioy Street, Athens, Greece.

Paye, Lucien; French educationist and diplomatist; b. 28 June 1907; ed. Lycée David d'Angers, Lycée Louis-le-Grand, Ecole Normale Supérieure.

Former teacher, Morocco; served with Moroccan units in French Army; Second World War; fmr. Dir. of Reforms and Dir. of Planning, Algeria 45-48; Dir. of Education, Tunisia 48-55; later Dir. of Political Affairs and the Public Service, Algeria; Rector, Univ. of Dakar, Senegal 57-60, Dir.-Gen. 60-61; Minister of Educ. (France) 61-62; Ambassador to Senegal 62-64, to People's Repub. of China 64-; Commdr. Légion d'Honneur, Croix de Guerre.

French Embassy, Peking, People's Republic of China.

Payne, Anthony Monck-Mason, M.D., F.R.C.P.; British medical officer; b. 10 Aug. 1911; ed. Trinity Coll. Cambridge and St. Bartholomew's Hospital, London.

Senior Epidemiologist, Medical Research Council's Public Health Laboratory, Oxford 48-52; Chief Medical Officer, Endemo-epidemic Diseases and Virus Diseases, World Health Org. (WHO) 52-60, Sec., Expert Cttees. on Hepatitis, Influenza, Poliomyelitis and Respiratory Virus Diseases, Asst. Dir.-Gen. of WHO 66-; Anna M. R. Lauder Prof. of Epidemiology and Public Health and Chair. of Dept., Yale Univ. 60-67; Vice-Chair. Advisory Cttee. on Medical Research, Pan-American Health Org. (PAHO); mem. Technical Board, Milbank Memorial Fund; mem. numerous acads. and socs. including Int. Epidemiological Asscn., Royal Soc. of Health, American Epidemiological Soc. and New York Acad. of Sciences, and of many cttees. of U.S. Public Health Service and Nat. Acad. of Sciences; Fellow Royal Coll. of Physicians, London and Brandford Coll., Yale Univ.

Publs. over sixty papers on biological and social aspects of epidemiology.

World Health Organization, avenue Appia, 1211 Geneva, Switzerland.

Telephone: 34-60-61.

Payne, Rev. Ernest Alexander, C.H., D.D., LL.D.; British Minister of Religion; b. 19 Feb. 1902; ed. King's Coll., London, Regent's Park Coll., London, Mansfield Coll., Oxford and Marburg Univ., Germany.

Pastor Bugbrooke Baptist Church, Northampton 28-32; Baptist Missionary Soc. 32-40; Senior Tutor, Regent's Park Coll., Oxford 40-51, Lecturer in Comparative Religion and History of Modern Missions, Oxford Univ. 46-51; Gen.-Sec. Baptist Union of Great Britain and Ireland 51-67; Vice-Chair. Cen. Cttee. World Council of Churches 54-; mem. Free Church Fed. Council, Moderator 58-59; Vice-Pres. British Council of Churches 60-62,

Chair. Exec. Cttee. 62-; Vice-Pres. Baptist World Alliance.
Publs. *The Saktas* 33, *The Free Church Tradition in the Life of England* 44, *H. Wheeler Robinson: A Memoir* 46, *The Baptists of Berkshire* 51, *The Fellowship of Believers* 44, 52, *James Henry Rushbrooke—A Baptist Greatheart* 54, *The Growth of the World Church* 55, *The Baptist Union—A Short History* 59, *Free Churchmen—Unrepentant and Repentant* 65.
Elm Cottage, Manor Road, Pitsford, Northants., England.
Telephone: ONO-18-519.

Paynter, Richard K., Jr.; American insurance official; b. 29 Oct. 1904; ed. Barnard School for Boys and Princeton Univ.
Investment Banking 26-33; Railroad Statistician, New York Life Insurance Co. 34-37, Asst. Treas. 37-43, Asst. Vice-Pres. 43-44, Treas. 44-46, Vice-Pres. and Treas. 46-49, Financial Vice-Pres. 49-54, Exec. Vice-Pres. 54-59, Chair. of Finance Cttee. and Exec. Vice-Pres. 59-62, Chair. of Board 62-; Dir. New York Life Insurance Co., The Chemical Bank New York Trust Co., Otis Elevator Co., Gen. Cable Corpn. etc.; official of numerous civic and religious orgs.
"Westmoreland", Province Line Road, Princeton, New Jersey, U.S.A.

Paynter, William; British trade unionist; b. 6 Dec. 1903; ed. Elementary Schools.
Executive, South Wales Miners' Fed. 36, South Wales Agent 39, South Wales Pres. 51; Nat. Sec., Nat. Union of Mineworkers 59-; mem. Gen. Council T.U.C. 60-61; Communist.
National Union of Mineworkers, 222 Euston Road, London, N.W.1, England.

Paz, Octavio; Mexican writer and diplomatist; b. 31 March 1914; ed. Univ. of Mexico.
Founder, dir. or editor several Mexican literary reviews, including *Barandal* 31, *Taller* 39, *El Hijo Pródigo* 43; Guggenheim Fellowship (U.S.A.) 44; fmr. Sec. Mexican Embassy, Paris; Chargé d'Affaires a.i., to Japan 51; posted to Secr. for External Affairs; Ambassador to India 62-; Int. Poetry Grand Prix 63.
Publs. Poetry: *Luna Silvestre* 33, *Raíz del Hombre* 37, *Entre la Piedra y la Flor* 40, *A la Orilla del Mundo* 42, *Libertad bajo Palabra* 49, *Piedra de Sol* 57, *La Estación Violenta* 58; prose: *El Laberinto de la Soledad* 50 (*Labyrinth of Solitude* 61), *Aguila o Solé* 51, *El Arco y la Lira* 56, *Las Peras del Olmo* 57, etc.
Mexican Embassy, 136 Golf Links, New Delhi, India.

Paz Estenssoro, Victor; Bolivian politician; b. 2 Oct. 1907; ed. Univ. Mayor de "San Andrés".
Finance official 32-33; Deputy Tarija 38-39 and 40-41; Pres. Banco Minero 39; Prof. Economic History, Univ. of La Paz 39-41; Minister of Finance 41-44; Leader of Nat. Revolutionary Movement; Pres. of Republic 52-56; Ambassador to the U.K. 56-59; Pres. of Republic 60-64.
Publs. *Esquema de la Organización Política y Administrativa de Bolivia, Aspecto de la Economía Boliviana, Revolución y Contrarrevolución, Proceso y Sentencia de la Oligarquía Boliviana, La Revolución Boliviana.*
Lima, Peru.

Pazhwak, Abdurrahman; Afghan civil servant; b. 7 March 1919.
Has been successively mem. Historical Section of Afghan Acad.; Dir. Foreign Publications Section of Afghan Press Dept.; Editor daily *Islah* and acting Dir.-Gen. of Bakhtar News Agency; Pres. Pashto-Tolana; Dir.-Gen. Publs. Section, Afghan Press Dept.; Sec. and Press and Cultural Attaché, Afghan Embassy, London; mem. of Section of Information Dept. of ILO.; Press and Cultural Attaché, Afghan Embassy, Washington; Dir. Section for East Asia and Dir. a.i., Section for UN, and Int. Confs., Afghan Ministry for Foreign

Affairs; Dir.-Gen. Political Affairs in Ministry of Foreign Affairs 56; Perm. Rep. to UN 58-; Pres. UN Human Rights Comm. 63, 21st Session of UN Gen. Assembly 66, 5th Special Session 66 and of Emergency Session of General Assembly on Middle East 66.
Publs. *Aryana or Ancient Afghanistan, Pakhtunistan* (both in English), *Tales of the People* 58 (in Persian), and many other works.
Afghan Mission to the United Nations, 200 East 42nd Street, New York City, N.Y., U.S.A.
Telephone: MU8-8280.

Pazos, Dr. Felipe; Cuban lawyer and economist; b. 12; ed. Havana Univ. and Columbia Univ., New York.
Assistant to Minister of Finance, Cuba 41-42; Commercial Counsellor, Cuban Embassy, Washington 42-46; Dir. Div. of Latin American Affairs and fmr. Dep. Dir., Dept. of Economic Studies, Int. Monetary Fund 46-49; Pres. Banco Nacional, Cuba 49-52, 59; fmr. Research Dir. Center for Latin American Monetary Studies, Mexico; Econ. Counsellor, Govt. of Puerto Rico's Development Bank 64; mem. Cttee. of Nine, Alliance for Progress 64.
Government Development Bank for Puerto Rico, P.O. Box 4591, San Juan, Puerto Rico.

Peacock, Sir Kenneth Swift, Kt.; British industrialist; b. 19 Feb. 1902; ed. Oundle School.
Has served with Guest, Keen & Nettlefolds Ltd. in varying capacities, Man. Dir. 36, Chair. and Man. Dir. 53-63, Chair. 64-65, Pres. 65-.
Lower Coscombe, Temple Guiting, Glos., England.
Telephone: Stanton 221.

Peacock, Ronald, M.A., D.PHIL., LITT.D.; British university professor; b. 22 Nov. 1907; ed. Leeds Modern School, Univs. of Leeds, Berlin, Innsbruck and Marburg.
Asst. Lecturer in German Univ. of Leeds 31-38, Lecturer 38-39, Prof. 39-45; Prof. of German Language and Literature Univ. of Manchester 45-62, Pro-Vice-Chancellor 58-62; Visiting Prof. of German Literature, Cornell Univ. 49; Visiting Prof. Univ. of Heidelberg 60-61; Prof. German, Bedford Coll., Univ. of London 62-; Prof. Univ. of Freiburg 65, 67-68.
Publs. *The Great War in German Lyrical Poetry* 34, *Das Leitmotiv bei Thomas Mann* 34, *Hölderlin* 38, *The Poet in the Theatre* 46, *The Art of Drama* 57, *Goethe's Major Plays* 59.
Greenshade, Woodhill Avenue, Gerrard's Cross, Bucks., England.
Telephone: 49-84886.

Peake, Harald, M.A.; British banker; b. 28 Oct. 1899; ed. Eton and Trinity Coll., Cambridge.
Served in Coldstream Guards in First World War, subsequently Yorkshire Dragoons Yeomanry; raised and commanded No. 609 (W. Riding) Squadron, R. Aux. A.F. 36; Dir. Aux. A.F., Air Ministry 38; Dir. of Public Relations, Air Ministry 40-42; Dir. of Air Force Welfare 42-43, Special Duty List Air Ministry 43-45, retd. with rank of Air Commodore; pupil in coal mining industry 23; Rolls Royce Ltd. 37-; Dir. Lloyds Bank Ltd. 43-, Vice-Chair. 47-62, Chair. 62-; fmr. Chair. London Board, Nat. Bank of Australasia; fmr. Dir. Bank of London and South America Ltd., fmr. Dir. Nat. Commercial Bank of Scotland; Sub-Gov. of London Assurance Co. 54, Gov. 59-64; Chair. Steel Co. of Wales Ltd. 55-62, Dir. 62-67; Dir. Lloyds and Scottish Ltd. 63-, Lloyds Bank, Europe, Ltd. 63-, Lloyds Bank Unit Trust Managers Ltd., Nat. Bank of New Zealand Ltd.; Dir. Intercontinental Banking Services Ltd. 67-.
2 Shepherds Close, Lees Place, North Audley Street, London, W.1, England.
Telephone: 01-629-1264.

Peal, Samuel Edward; Liberian diplomatist; b. 3 Feb. 1923; ed. Central Nat. School, White Plains, and Liberia Coll.
Former Town Clerk, Millsburg; Foreign Service, Paris,

London, Hamburg; fmr. Ambassador to Netherlands, to Guinea; now Ambassador to U.S.A.; numerous decorations.

Embassy of the Republic of Liberia, Washington D.C., U.S.A.

Peale, Mundy I., PH.B.; American executive; b. 15 June 1906; ed. Chicago Univ.

With Repub. Aviation Corpn. 39-, Dir. 44-, Pres. 47-64; Chair. Repub. Aviation Int., Lugano, Switzerland, now Dir.; Chair. Aircraft Industries Asscn. 53; Dir. American Can Co., ACF Industries Inc., Royal Netherlands Aircraft Factories, New York Telephone Co.; mem. Hoover Comm. Task Force, Procurement and Production Advisory Cttee., U.S. Defense Dept.; Officier, Légion d'Honneur, Commdr., Italian Order of Merit; Hon. Dr. Eng. (Clarkson Coll. of Technology), Hon. LL.D. (Hofstra Coll.).

Publs. *What is the Truth About Buying Air Power?* 52, *What the Aircraft Industry Means to Every American, Just How Strong is the U.S. Air Force?* 53, *The Economics of Defense Production* 58.

150 E. 69th Street, New York City, N.Y. 10021, U.S.A.

Pearkes, Major-Gen. George Randolph, V.C., P.C., C.B., D.S.O., M.C.; Canadian army officer (retd.) and politician; b. Watford, England 26 Feb. 1888; ed. Berkhamsted School.

Emigrated to Canada 06; joined Royal North-West Mounted Police 11; served Canadian Army in France in First World War, winning V.C. and other decorations; Staff Coll., Camberley 19; army service 15-45; G.O.C. 1st Canadian Div. 40, G.O.C. in C. Pacific Command, Canada 42-45, retd.; mem. of Parl. 45-60; Minister of Defence and mem. Privy Council 57-60; Lieut.-Gov. Province of British Columbia 60-; Hon. LL.D. Univ. British Columbia; Progressive Conservative.

Government House, Victoria, British Columbia, Canada.

Pears, Peter, C.B.E.; British tenor; b. 22 June 1910; ed. Lancing Coll. and Univ. of Oxford.

With B.B.C. Singers 34-37, New English Singers 36-38; tours abroad with Benjamin Britten since 39; Sadler's Wells Opera 43-46; first performance of many new works by Benjamin Britten, Tippett and Berkeley; soloist at Lucerne Festival, Edinburgh Festivals, Holland Festival, and all Aldeburgh Festivals 47-; co-founder Aldeburgh Festival.

Important roles include Peter Grimes (*Peter Grimes*) 45, 53, Male Chorus (*The Rape of Lucretia*) 46, 51, The Evangelist (*St. Matthew Passion*) annually 47-, The Captain (*Billy Budd*) 51, Tamino (*Magic Flute*), Essex (*Gloriana*) 53, Vashek (*The Bartered Bride*) 55, Pandarus (*Troilus and Cressida*) 56, David (*Die Meistersinger*) 57, Flute (*Midsummer Night's Dream*) 60, The Mad Woman (*Curlew River*) 64, 65, Nebuchadnezzar (*Burning Fiery Furnace*) 66.

Publ. (with Benjamin Britten) *Purcell Edition* 48-.

c/o Mrs. Susan Phipps, 101 Offord Road, London, N.1, England.

Pearson, Charles Chester; American executive; b. 15 July 1906; ed. Whittier Coll. Calif. (degree in aeronautical engineering).

Joined Landing-Gear Section of Engineering Dept. of Douglas Aircraft Co., Santa Monica, as engineering draughtsman 30; served as project engineer on a succession of important mil. aircraft during 30's, becoming Asst. to Chief Engineer at Santa Monica 39, and placed in charge of Master Schedules for all seven Douglas plants 40; Gen. Man. Douglas plant Oklahoma City 42; Eastern Man. and Asst. to Pres. Douglas Aircraft Co. 46; joined Curtiss-Wright Corpn. as Gen. Man. Airplane Div., Columbus, Ohio Jan. 47, Vice-Pres. Curtiss-Wright Corpn. N.Y. 48; Pres., Gen. Man. and Dir. Glenn L. Martin Co. July 49-52, Vice-Pres. 52-53; Vice-Pres. Beech Aircraft Corpn. 53-58; Asst. Dir.

Lockheed Missile Systems Div. 58-59, Man. Polaris Mfg. 59-60, Asst. Manager Polaris Missile System 60-61, Asst. Gen. Manager Missile System Div. 62-; mem. Inst. of Aeronautical Sciences and Soc. of Automotive Engineers; awarded President's Certificate of Merit 48.

Lockheed Missiles and Space Co., Sunnyvale, California, U.S.A.

Pearson, Sir (James) Denning, Kt., J.P., B.SC., C.ENG.; British engineer and business executive; b. 8 Aug. 1908; ed. Canton Secondary School, Cardiff Technical Coll. and London Univ.

Rolls Royce 32-, established Rolls-Royce Technical Office, Montreal (later Rolls-Royce of Canada) 45, Gen. Sales and Service Man. Aero Engine Div. 46-49, Dir. 49-, Chief Exec. Aero Engine Div. 52-54, Man. Dir. Aero Engine Div. 54-, Chief Exec. and Dep. Chair. Rolls-Royce Ltd. 57-; Pres. of SBAC 63-64; Chair. Rolls-Royce and Assocs. Ltd., Bristol Siddeley Engines Ltd.; mem. Nat. Econ. Devt. Council (N.E.D.C.) 64-66; Chair. of Govs. Derby Coll. of Technology 67-; Hon. Fellow of Royal Aeronautical Soc., Hon. Dr. Ing. (Brunswick Univ.), and other hon. degrees.

Green Acres, 255 Duffield Road, Allestree, Derbyshire, England.

Telephone: Derby 58451.

Pearson, Drew (Andrew Russell), A.B.; American columnist; b. 13 Dec. 1897; ed. Swarthmore Coll.

Dir. American Friends' Service Cttee., Serbia, Montenegro and Albania 19-21; Instructor in Industrial Geography, Univ. of Pa. 21-22; lecturer and reporter 23-26; staff *United States Daily* 26-33, *Baltimore Sun* 29-32; newspaper column *Daily Washington Merry-Go-Round* 32-; reported London Naval Conf. 30, U.N. Conf. San Francisco 45, Paris Peace Conf. 46, etc.; Hon. LL.D. (Harding Coll. 45, William Jewell Coll. 48).

Publs. Co-author: *Washington Merry-Go-Round, More Merry-Go-Round, The American Diplomatic Game, The Nine Old Men, U.S.A. Second Class Power?, Will Khrushchev Bury Us?*

1313 29th Street, N.W., Washington, D.C., U.S.A.

Pearson, Egon Sharpe, C.B.E., M.A., D.SC., F.R.S.; British statistician; b. 11 Aug. 1895; ed. Winchester and Trinity Coll., Cambridge.

Lecturer Univ. Coll. 21; Prof. of Statistics London Univ. and Head of Statistics Dept. at Univ. Coll. 33-60, Prof. Emeritus 60-; Man. Editor *Biometrika* 36-66, Man. and Tables Editor 66-; mem. Int. Statistical Inst.; Assoc. mem. Ordnance Board, Ministry of Supply 43-; Pres. Royal Statistical Soc. 55; Hon. mem. Inst. of Actuaries 56.

2820 Dumbarton Avenue, N.W., Washington, D.C., U.S.A.

Pearson, James B.; American lawyer and politician; b. 7 May 1920.

Local Government posts, Kansas City suburbs; fmr. State Senator, Kansas; fmr. State Chair. Republican Party; U.S. Senator from Kansas 62-.

U.S. Senate, Washington 25, D.C., U.S.A.

Pearson, Rt. Hon. Lester Bowles, P.C., O.B.E., M.A., LL.D.; Canadian politician; b. 23 April 1897; ed. Toronto and Oxford Univs.

Served in First World War; employed by Armour & Co., Chicago 19-21; Lecturer, Univ. of Toronto 23-26, Asst. Prof. 26-28; First Sec. Dept. of External Affairs, Ottawa 28-35; Office of the High Commr. for Canada, London 35-38, Counsellor 38-41; Asst. Under-Sec. of State for External Affairs 41-42; Minister-Counsellor, Washington 42; Minister to U.S.A. 44, Ambassador 45; Under-Sec. of State for External Affairs 46; Sec. of State for External Affairs 48-57; Leader, Liberal Party, Leader of the Opposition 58-63; Prime Minister 63-68; Liberal M.P., Ont. 48-April 68; Hot Springs Food Conf. 43; Chair. UN Interim Comm. on Food and Agriculture 43, FAO Conf., Quebec 45, Cttee. on Supplies, UNRRA

43; rep. Canada UNRRA meetings 44, 45, 46; Senior Adviser Canadian Del. San Francisco Conf. 45, and Canadian rep. subsequent meetings of UN Gen. Ass.; Chair. UN Political and Security Cttee. 47; Chair. Canadian dels. to 3rd-11th Gen. Ass. 48-56; Chair. Political and Security Cttee. 49; Pres. 7th Session Gen. Ass. 52; Canadian rep. signing of N. Atlantic Treaty, Washington 49, and head Canadian del. to subsequent NATO meetings; Chair. N. Atlantic Council 51-52; Del. to Japanese Peace Treaty Conf., San Francisco 51, to Geneva Conf. 54; Chancellor, Victoria Univ., Toronto 51-58; B.B.C. Reith Lecturer 68; Hon. Fellow, St. John's Coll., Oxford; hon. degrees from Univs. of Toronto, Yale, N.Y., Rochester, Princeton, Clark, McMaster, Syracuse, Ceylon, Oxford, Columbia, Laval, Maine, Harvard, Manchester, British Columbia, Johns Hopkins, Victoria, Bishops' New School for Social Research, and Dartmouth, Rollins and Bates Colls. etc.; Nobel Peace Prize 57, Family of Man Award 65.
Publs. *Democracy in World Politics* 55, *Diplomacy in the Nuclear Age* 59.
c/o Liberal Party, 251 Cooper Street, Ottawa, Canada.

Peart, Rt. Hon. (Thomas) Frederick, P.C., M.P.; British politician; b. 30 April 1914; ed. Wolsingham Grammar School, Henry Smith Secondary School, Hartlepool, Bede Coll., Durham Univ. and Inner Temple.
Councillor, Easington Rural District Council 37-40; Army Service 39-45; M.P. 45-, Parliamentary Private Sec., Ministry of Agriculture and Fisheries 45-51; British Del. and Rep. Agriculture Cttee., Vice-Pres., Cttee. for Culture and Science, Council of Europe; Chair. Council of Europe's Special Cttee. dealing with Agricultural Refugees 54; Minister of Agriculture, Fisheries and Food 64-68; Lord Privy Seal and Leader of House of Commons April 68-; Labour.
House of Commons, London, S.W.1, England.

Peccei, Aurelio, M.A., D.ECON.; Italian business executive; b. 4 July 1908; ed. Higher Commercial School "Quintino Sella", Turin, and Univ. of Turin.
Fiat Co., Turin 30-, Divisional Manager 46-, mem. Steering Cttee.; Founder Fiat industries in Argentina 53, Chair. of Board Fiat Concord, Buenos Aires 53-; Man. Dir. Italconsult, Rome 57-; Man. Dir. Ing. C. Olivetti & Co. S.p.A., Ivrea 64-67, Vice-Chair. 67-; Chair. Cttee. for Atlantic Economic Co-operation, Paris.
Ing. C. Olivetti & Co. S.p.A., Via Jervis, Ivrea, Italy.
Telephone: 525.

Peck, Sir Edward Heywood, K.C.M.G.; British diplomatist; b. 5 Oct. 1915; ed. Clifton Coll. and Queen's Coll., Oxford.
Probationer Vice-Consul, Barcelona 38-39; Foreign Office 39-40; Consulate, Sofia 40, Ankara 40-44; Consul, Adana 44, Iskenderun 44-45; Consulate-Gen., Salonica 46; transferred to Foreign Office 47; seconded to C.R.O. for service at New Delhi 50-52; Counsellor, Foreign Office 52-54, Berlin 55-58, Singapore 59-60; Asst. Under Sec. of State, Foreign Office 61-66; High Commr. of U.K. in Kenya 66-68; Deputy Under-Sec. of State Foreign Office 68-.
c/o Foreign Office, London, S.W.1; 19 The Rise, Sevenoaks, Kent, England.

Peck, Gregory, B.A.; American actor; b. 5 April 1916; ed. California Univ.
Films include: *Days of Glory* 43, *Keys of the Kingdom* 44, *Spellbound* 45, *The Valley of Decision* 45, *Duel in the Sun* 46, *The Macomber Affair* 47, *Gentleman's Agreement* 48, *Twelve O'Clock High, The Great Sinner* 49, *Captain Horatio Hornblower, David and Bathsheba* 51, *The Snows of Kilimanjaro* 52, *Roman Holiday* 53, *The Purple Plain* 54, *The Man in the Grey Flannel Suit, Moby Dick* 56, *Designing Woman* 57, *The Big Country,*

The Bravados 58, *Pork Chop Hill* 59, *On the Beach* 59, *Beloved Infidel* 59, *Guns of Navarone* 60, *Cape Fear* 61, *How the West Was Won* 61, *To Kill a Mocking Bird* 62, *Captain Newman, M.D.* 63, *Behold a Pale Horse* 63, *Mirage* 64, *Arabesque* 65.
Anthony Productions Inc., Universal City, Calif. 91608, U.S.A.

Pecker, Jean-Claude; French astronomer; b. 10 May 1923; ed. Lycée de Bordeaux, Univs. de Bordeaux, Grenoble and Paris à la Sorbonne, and Ecole Normale Supérieure.
Research Asst. Centre National de la Recherche scientifique (C.N.R.S.) 46-52; Asst. Prof. Univ. of Clermont-Ferrand 52-55; Asst. Astronomer Paris Observatory 55-62, Astronomer 62-65; Dir. Nice Observatory 62-; Prof. Collège de France 63-; Asst. Gen. Sec. Int. Astronomical Union 61-63, Gen. Sec. 64-67; Officier Palmes Académiques; Chevalier Légion d'Honneur; Prix Forthuny, Inst. de France; Prix Stroobant Acad. des Sciences de Belgique 65; Prix Manley-Bendall de l'Acad. de Bordeaux 66; Assoc. Royal Astronomical Soc. 68.
Publs. include *L'Astronomie au jour le jour* (with P. Couderc and E. Schatzman) 54, *Astrophysique générale* 59, *Le Ciel* 59.
2 rue Pierre Semard, 92 Bagneux, France.
Telephone: 735-40-21.

Pecora, William T(homas), B.S., PH.D.; American geologist and government official; b. 1 Feb. 1913; ed. Princeton and Harvard Univs.
Instructor in Geology, Harvard Univ. 37-39; U.S. Geological Survey 39-, Research Geologist 39, Chief, Branch of Geochemistry and Petrology 57-64, Chief Geologist 64-65, Dir. 65-; mem. Nat. Acad. of Sciences; Fellow American Acad. of Arts and Sciences; Fellow and Councilor, Geological Soc. of America, Mineralogical Soc. of America; Pres. Geological Soc. of Washington 64.
4572 Indian Rock Terrace, N.W., Washington, D.C. 20007, U.S.A.

Pedersen, Helga, CAND.IUR.; Danish judge; b. 24 June 1911; ed. Københavns Universitet and Columbia Univ., New York.
Danish Dept. of Justice 36-46; Judge, District Court of Copenhagen 48-50, 53-56; Minister of Justice 50-53; Judge, Court of Appeal, Copenhagen 56-64; Judge of Supreme Court, Copenhagen 64-; mem. Danish Parl. (Liberal Party) 53-64; Del. to UN and UNESCO conferences on several occasions; mem. Nat. Comm. of UNESCO, Danish Council for Planning of Higher Educ., Danish Council on Copyright; Chair. Representatives of Danish State Art Foundation; Commdr. Order of Dannebrog (Denmark); Grand Cross Order of Orange Nassau (Netherlands).
Statholdervej 19, Copenhagen N.V., Denmark.
Telephone: Ægir 3220.

Pedersen, Johannes, PH.D., D.D.; Danish orientalist; b. 7 Nov. 1883; ed. Univ. of Copenhagen.
Studied theology and semitic languages, Copenhagen 02-08; worked on trans. of Bible into Danish 08-09; continued studies 09-12; Collaborator, Arabic Dictionary, Leipzig 13-19; studied in Egypt, Palestine, Syria 20-21; Prof. of Semitic Philology, Copenhagen 22-50; mem. Royal Danish Acad. 24-, Chair. History and Philosophy Section 42-63, Pres. of the Acad. 63-; Dir. Carlsberg Foundation 26-55, Chair. 33-55; mem. Rask-Örsted 50-55; mem. numerous Danish and foreign academic orgs.; Grand Cross of Dannebrog 55.
Publs. *Der Eid bei den Semiten* 14, *Israel* Vols. I, II, (Danish 20, 34, 58, English 26, 46, 54, 59) Vols. III, IV (Danish 34, 60, English 40, 47, 53, 57, 59); Danish *al-Azhar* 22, *Muhammedansk Mystik* 23, 52, *Hebrew Grammar* 26, *Islams Kultur* 28, *Den Arabiske Bog* 46,

Sulami: Tabaqat Al-Sufiyya 60 (Arabic edn. with French introduction).
Bjerregaardsvej 13, Copenhagen/Valby, Denmark.
Telephone Valby 9150.

Peech, Alan James, B.A., LL.D.; British steel executive; b. 24 Aug. 1905; ed. Wellington Coll. and Magdalen Coll., Oxford.
Director numerous companies including Steel, Peech and Tozer, Stewarts and Lloyds Ltd., Steel Peech (Canada) Ltd. and Iron and Steel Investments Ltd.; Gov. Wellington Coll.; Pres. British Iron and Steel Fed. 67-; Dir., Chair. and fmr. Joint Gen. Man. Dir. United Steel Companies Ltd.; Deputy Chair. British Steel Corpn. July 67-; Hon. LL.D., Sheffield Univ.
Home: High House, Blyth, Nr. Worksop, Notts., England.

Peeters, Flor; Belgian composer and organist; b. 4 July 1903; ed. Lemmens Inst., Mechelen.
Organist, Metropolitan Cathedral of Belgium, Mechelen 23-; Prof. of Organ, Lemmens Inst., Mechelen 23-52, Royal Conservatory of Ghent 31-48; Prof. of Organ and Composition, Conservatory of Tilburg (Netherlands) 35-48; Prof. of Organ and Composition, Royal Flemish Conservatory, Antwerp 48-68; Dir. of Royal Flemish Conservatory 52-68; world-wide recitals; mem. Royal Flemish Acad. for Fine Arts; Hon. mem. Royal Acad. of Music, London; Hon. D.Mus. (Catholic Univ. of America); Prix Lemmens-Tinel; Commdr. Order of Gregory the Great; Grand Officier de l'Ordre de la Couronne.
Compositions: (organ) Sinfonia, Lied-Symphony, Passacaglia and Fugue, 3 preludes and fugues, 300 chorale preludes, concerto for piano and organ, concerto for organ and orchestra, concerto for piano and orchestra, chamber music, piano music and lieder.
Publs. *Ars Organi* (3 vols.), *Old Netherlands Masters for the Organ* (3 vols.), *Anthologia pro organo* (4 vols.).
Villa Adagio, Stuivenbergbaan 123, Mechelen, Belgium.

Pegov, Nikolai Mikhailovich; Soviet politician and diplomatist; b. 05; ed. Industrial Acad., Moscow.
Sec. Far Eastern Territory Cttee. of the Party 38; First Sec. Maritime Territory Cttee.; held exec. post in the Central Cttee. of the C.P.S.U. 47; Sec. Central Cttee. of the C.P.S.U. 52; Sec. Presidium of the Supreme Soviet of the U.S.S.R. 53-56; Soviet Ambassador to Iran 56-63, to Algeria 63-67, to India 67-; mem. C.P.S.U. Cen. Cttee. 39-; awarded Order of Lenin (twice), Order of the Red Banner of Labour, Order of the Patriotic War, 1st Class and other decorations.
U.S.S.R. Embassy, New Delhi, India.

Pehrsson, C. J. Hjalmar; Swedish publisher; b. 16 Oct. 1900; ed. High School.
Independent owner of firm Importbokhandeln, Stockholm 36-50; Dir. Continental Book and Publications Distributing Co., Stockholm 43-; Adviser to Centre for European Culture on question of founding a European Library and producing a European Bibliography 52-; Dir. of Collection "Petite Bibliothèque Payot", Edns. Payot, Paris 62-; Sec.-Gen., Int. Publishers Asscn. (Union internationale des Editeurs) 64-.
Union internationale des Editeurs, avenue Miremont 3, Geneva; Home: avenue Krieg 13, Geneva, Switzerland. Telephone: 463018 (Office); 311823 (Home).

Pei, Ieoh Ming, M.ARCH., A.I.A.; Chinese-born American architect; b. 26 April 1917; ed. Shanghai, Massachusetts Inst. of Technology and Harvard Univ.
In U.S.A. 35-; naturalised citizen 54-; architectural practice 39-, I.M. Pei & Assocs. 55-; Asst. Prof. Harvard Graduate School of Design 45-48; Wheelwright Fellow, Harvard Univ. 51; M.I.T. Traveling Fellowship 40; inventor of the Helix system for apartment houses; mem. Council of Harvard Foundation for Advanced Study and Research 63-, Advisory Cttee. on Arts and Architecture, John F. Kennedy Memorial Library 64-; Trustee American Fed. of Arts 64-; Brunner Award of Nat. Inst. of Arts and Letters 61.
Projects include Mile High Center (Denver), Tunghai Univ. (Formosa), M.I.T. Earth Science Building (Cambridge, Mass.), U.S. Embassy Building (Montevideo); East-West Center, Univ. of Hawaii; redevelopment projects in New York, Philadelphia, Washington, Chicago and Pittsburgh; Laboratories of Nat. Center for Atmospheric Research, Boulder, Colorado.
600 Madison Avenue, New York City, N.Y. 10022, U.S.A.

Pei Wen-chung; Chinese archæologist; b. 04; ed. Peking Univ., Paris Univ., London Univ.
Thesis on 4th Quaternary Period in Far East; geological work in Shansi, Shensi, Shantung, etc.; discovered the Peking man; mem. of Geological Survey and Dir. of Chou-k'ou-tien Institute; worked in Peiping Research Institute, Central Research Institute, London Univ. 34; after 49 on East China Higher Education Cttee., etc.; cttee. of the Chiu San Society and delegate for it to 2nd Session C.P.P.C.C. 54; cttee. of Dept. of Physics and Geology, Acad. Sinica 55; Prof. in Inst. of Palaeontology Acad. Sinica 56; Central Cttee. of Chiu San Society; Hon. Fellow of Royal Anthropological Inst. London 58.
Inst. of Palaeontology, Chinese Academy of Sciences, Peking, People's Republic of China.

Peierls, Sir Rudolf Ernst, Kt., C.B.E., PH.D., M.A., SC., F.R.S.; British scientist; b. Germany 5 June 1907; ed. Berlin, Munich, Leipzig, and Zürich Univs.
Asst. Federal Technical High School, Zürich 29; Rockefeller Fellow 32; Hon. Research Fellow Manchester Univ. 33-35; Research Asst. Royal Society Mond Laboratory Cambridge Univ. 35-37; Prof. of Applied Mathematics Birmingham Univ. 37-46; work on atomic energy, Birmingham, New York, Los Alamos 40-45; Prof. of Mathematical Physics, Birmingham Univ. 46-63; Wykeham Prof. Univ. of Oxford 63-; Fellow New Coll., Oxford 63; Lorentz Medal Royal Netherlands Acad. of Sciences 62; Council of Royal Soc., London 58; Royal Medal of Royal Soc. 59, Max Planck Medal, Asscn. of German Physical Socs. 63; Guthrie Medal, Inst. of Physics and Physical Soc. 68.
Publs. *Quantum Theory of Solids* 55, *The Laws of Nature* 55.
Department of Theoretical Physics, University of Oxford, 12 Parks Road, Oxford, England.
Telephone: Oxford 59291.

Peive, Ian Woldemarovich; Soviet scientist; b. 06; ed. Moscow Timiryazev Acad. of Agriculture.
Expert on agro-chemistry and plant breeding; at the U.S.S.R. Flax Research Inst. 30-44; Rector of the Latvian Acad. of Agriculture 44-50; Pres. of the Acad. of Sciences of Latvia 51-59; Chair. of the Soviet of Nationalities of the Supreme Soviet of the U.S.S.R. 58-66; Chief Sec. U.S.S.R. Acad. of Sciences 66-; Chair. Council of Ministers of Latvia 59-62; Dep. Chair. Parliament Group U.S.S.R.; mem. Central Cttee. of C.P.S.U.; mem. U.S.S.R. and Latvian S.S.R. Acads. of Sciences; Lenin Prize.
Principal publs. (in Latvian): *Linkoptba* 48, *Augsnes pētisanas agrokimiskās metōdes* 49, *Mikroelementu mēslojums lauksaimniecibā* 49; (in Russian) *The Use of Trace Elements in Agriculture of the Non-chernosem Zone of the U.S.S.R.* 54, *Trace Elements in Plant Breeding* 58, *Content of forms of Trace Elements that are available to Plants in the Soils of the U.S.S.R.* 59, *Trace Elements and Enzymes* 60, *Biochemistry of Soils* 61.
U.S.S.R. Academy of Sciences, 14 Lenin Prospekt, Moscow, U.S.S.R.

Pelaez, Emmanuel; Philippine lawyer and politician; b. 30 Nov. 1915; ed. Univ. of Manila and Univ. of the Philippines.
Special Prosecutor, People's Court 45-46; mem. House

of Reps. 50-53; mem. Senate 54-59; Vice-Pres. of Philippines 62-65; Sec. of Foreign Affairs 62-63.
Manila, Philippines.

Pelényi, John; American university official (formerly Hungarian diplomatist); b. 15 Feb. 1885; ed. Vienna Consular Acad.
Consular Attaché Pittsburgh 08; Vice-Consul Chicago 09, Cleveland 15; Counsellor Washington Legation 20-30; Resident Min. and Head of Permanent Del. to L.N. 30-31; Min. Plenipotentiary and Head of Del. 31-33; Min. to U.S. 33-40, also accred. to Cuba and Mexico 34-40; resgnd. Nov. 40 when Hungary joined the Axis; Prof. of Political Science Dartmouth Coll. 41-53, Emeritus 54-; Pres. Free Europe Univ. in Exile, Strasbourg 53-57, Emeritus 57-; Hon. Pres. of Hungarian Library and Historical Soc., New York 59.
11 River Ridge Road, Hanover, N.H., U.S.A.

Pelikán, Jiří; Czechoslovak television official; b. 7 Feb. 1923; ed. Charles Univ., Prague.
In illegal movement, Second World War, imprisoned 40; worked at Prague Regional Cttee., C.P. of Czechoslovakia 47-49, 52-53, at Central Cttee., C.P. of Czechoslovakia 49-52; Central Cttee. of Czechoslovak Youth Union 54-63; Deputy to Nat. Assembly 48-53, 64-; Chair. Int. Union of Students 53-63; Gen. Dir. Czechoslovak Television 63-; mem. Ideological Comm. of Central Cttee. of C.P. of Czechoslovakia 63-.
Husova 23, Prague 2, Czechoslovakia.
Telephone: 248250 and 232405.

Pell, Claiborne de Borda, A.M.; American politician; b. 22 Nov. 1918; ed. Princeton and Columbia Univs.
Limited Partner, Auchinloss, Parker and Redpath; U.S. Coastguard 41-45; now, Capt. U.S.C.G.R.; United States Foreign Service Officer; Instructor and Lecturer, Naval and Mil. Govt. Schools 44-45; served State Dept., Czechoslovakia, Italy, Wash. 45-52; company dir. and trustee 52-60; Consultant, Dem. Nat. Cttee. 53-60; U.S. Del. to Inter-Govtl. Maritime Consultative Org. (IMCO) London 59; Senator from Rhode Island 61-; Legion of Honour (France), Crown of Italy, etc.; Democrat.
Publ. *Rochambeau and Rhode Island* 54.
U.S. Senate, Washington, D.C., U.S.A.

Pella, Giuseppe; Italian economist and politician; b. 18 April 1902; ed. Univs. of Rome and Turin.
Founder and 1st Pres. of Catholic Organisation for Secondary School Students 19; active in commercial finance until 39; participated in Int. Wool Conf. 32-39; Christian Democrat Deputy 46-; Under-Sec. of Finance 46-47, Minister 47-48; Minister of Treasury and *ad interim* Minister of Budget 48-51, of Budget 51-52, of Budget and Treasury 52-54; Prime Minister, Minister for Foreign Affairs and Budget 53-54; Deputy Prime Minister, Minister of Foreign Affairs 57-58; a Governor of Int. Monetary Fund and Rep. on O.E.E.C.; Pres. Common Assembly, European Coal and Steel Community 54-56; Minister of Foreign Affairs Feb. 59-Feb. 60; Minister of Budget July 60-62; Pres. Int. Centre of Studies and Documentation, European Communities, Nat. Inst. of Accounting; Dir. of newspaper *Stato Sociale*.
Camera dei Deputati, Palazzo Montecitorio, Rome; Via Ludovisi 35, Rome, Italy.

Pellegrino, H.E. Cardinal Michele; Italian ecclesiastic; b. 25 April 1903.
Ordained Priest 25; Archbishop of Turin 65-; created Cardinal by Pope Paul VI 67.
Arcivescovado 12, Turin, Italy.

Pelser, Petrus Cornelius, B.A., LL.B.; South African politician; b. 28 Feb. 1907; ed. Paarl Gimnasium, Univ. of South Africa (private study) and Univ. of the Witwatersrand.
Joined Public Service 25; Dept. of Mines 25-37, Dept. of Commerce and Industry 37-43; Attorney, Klerksdorp 43; mem. Provincial Council, Klerksdorp 50; mem. Parl. 53-, Deputy Chair. of Cttees., House of Assembly 62-66, Deputy Speaker and Chair. of Cttees. 66; Minister of Justice and Prisons Sept. 66-; Nat. Party.
Ministry of Justice, Union Buildings, Pretoria, South Africa.

Pelshe, Arvid Yanovich; Soviet politician; b. 99; ed. Institute of Red Professors.
Elected to Petrograd Soviet 17; Party duties Archangel 17-19; served in Red Army and Navy 19-29; Party duties Kazakhstan 33; Teacher at Higher Educational Insts. Moscow 37-40; mem. Central Cttee. Latvian Communist Party 40-41, Sec. 41-59, First Sec. 59-66; mem. Politburo of Central Cttee. of C.P.S.U. April 66-; Chair. Party Control Cttee. of C.P.S.U. Central Cttee. 66-; Deputy to U.S.S.R. Supreme Soviet.
Central Committee of C.P.S.U., 4 Staraya ploshchad, Moscow, U.S.S.R.

Pelt, Adrian; Netherlands international official; b. 8 May 1892; ed. Ecole des Sciences politiques, Paris.
London corresp. 15-16, and Paris corresp. 16-19, mem. editorial staff of various Dutch newspapers; entered Information Section of League of Nations 20, becoming Dir. of this Section 34; during Second World War, organised and directed Netherlands Govt. Information Bureau, London; mem. Netherlands del. to San Francisco Conf. 45, UN Preparatory Comm., and First Session of Gen. Assembly; appointed Asst. Sec.-Gen. in charge of Dept. of Conference and Gen. Services 46; UN Commr. for Libya 49-52; Dir. UN European Office, Geneva, Sept. 52-57; Sec.-Gen. World Fed. of UN Asscns. 58-63, Pres. 63-66, Hon. Pres. 66; Wateler Peace Prize; Dr. h.c. Univ. of Amsterdam; Knight Order of the Lion; Grand Cordon of the Order of the Senussi (Libya).
Le Mestral, Hermance, Geneva, Switzerland.

Pemán, José Maria; Spanish author; b. 97; ed. Coll. San Felipe Neri and Univs. of Seville and Madrid.
Dir. of Real Academia Española 39-42 and 47-50; mem. Acad. Argentina de Letras, Lisbon Acad. of Sciences; Hispanic Soc. of America, Acad. de Cuba, Acad. de Puerto Rico; Dr. h.c. (Univ. of Santo Domingo); Juan March Prize 57; Gran Cruz Orden Alfonso X, Gran Cruz de Carlos III, Gran Cruz Orden del Mérito (Ecuador), Gran Cruz Orden del Sol (Peru), Gran Cruz del Mérito (Peru).
Publs. include essays, poems, novels and plays, in particular: *Elegía de la Tradición de España* 31, *El Divino Impaciente* (Real Academia Española Award, 1933) and his essay *Nieve en Cádiz* (Mariano de Cávia Award, 1935), *Edipo, Antigona, Hombre Nuevo*.
Felipe IV, No. 4, Madrid, and Plaza de San Antonio, Cadiz, Spain.

Penderecki, Krzysztof; Polish composer; b. 23 Nov. 1933; ed. Uniwersytet Jagiellonski, Cracow.
Studied composition first with Skolyszewski, later with Malawski and Wiechowicz, Cracow; graduated from Univ. of Cracow 58; Prof. of Composition, Univ. of Cracow 58-66; Prof. of Composition, Folkwang Hochschule für Musik, Essen 66-; Fitelberg Prize for *Threnody for the Victims of Hiroshima* 60, also UNESCO award 61, Polish Ministry of Culture Award 61; Cracow Composition Prize for *Canon* 62; North Rhine-Westphalia Grand Prize for *St. Luke Passion* 66, also Pax Prize (Poland) 66; Jurzykowski Prize, Polish Inst. of Arts and Sciences 66.
Works include: *Psalms of David* (for choir and percussion) 58, *Strophes* (for soprano speaker and ten instruments) 59, *Anaklasis* (for strings and percussion) 60, *Dimensions of time and silence* (for 40 singers and chamber ensemble) 60, *String Quartet* 60, *Threnody for the Victims of Hiroshima* (for 52 strings) 60, *Polymorphia* (for 48 strings) 61, *Fluorescences* (for large orchestra) 62, *Sonata for 'cello and orchestra* 64, *Passio*

et mors domini nostri Jesu Christi secundum (for soprano, baritone, bass, boys' choir, mixed chorus and large orchestra) 63-65, *De natura sonoris* (for large orchestra) 66, *Dies irae* (for soprano, tenor, bass, chorus and large orchestra) 67.
43 Essen, Olbrichstrasse 38, German Federal Republic.

Pendergrass, Eugene Percival, M.D.; American doctor; b. 6 Oct. 1895; ed. Wofford Coll., Univs. of N. Carolina and Pennsylvania.
Director Dept. of Radiology, Univ. of Pa. Hospital 39-61; Dir. Dept. of Radiology Jeanes Hosp., Philadelphia 48-61; Pres. Medical Staff, Univ. of Pa. Hospital 49-53; Prof. of Radiology, School of Medicine and Graduate School of Medicine Univ. of Pa. 36-61, Emeritus Prof. of Radiology 61-; Dir. Bicentennial Observance School of Medicine 62-65, Wilson Prof. of Research Radiology 64-66; mem. Nat. Research Council (Cttee. on Radiology), American Coll. of Radiology and Pres. 48-49; mem. American Roentgen Ray Society, Radiological Soc. of N. America; Chair. of Board of Dirs. 52 and Pres. 54; Sec.-Gen. Fifth Inter-American Congress on Radiology 55; mem. Operation Crossroads (Bikini) 46; Consultant to Atomic Bomb Casualty Comm. 48-49, 68-; Chair. Cttee. on Cancer Control, Nat. Cancer Inst. 60; mem. Board Scientific Counsellors, Nat. Cancer Inst. 57-59, Pneumoconiosis Comm. 59-; mem. Pneumoconiosis Panel U.S. Public Health Service; del. Section in Radiology A.M.A. 57-65, Diagnostic Research Panel N.C.I. 61-62; mem. Special Medical Advisory Group, Veterans' Admin. 57-62; Pres. American Cancer Soc. 58-59, mem. of Board 60-65; Pres. Board of Trustees Picker Foundation: Trustee Presbyterian Hospital, American Oncologic Hospital, Philadelphia; Hon. Dr.Sc. Wofford Coll. 59; Gold Medal American Medical Asscn. 29, award American Roentgen Ray Soc. 44, Radiological Soc. of N. America 46, 57, and of American Coll. of Radiology 56, Strittmatter Award, Philadelphia Coll. Physicians 65; American Cancer Soc. Annual Nat. Award 66.
Publs. *The Head and Neck in Roentgen Diagnosis* (with Pancoast and Schaeffer) 40, *The Pneumoconiosis Problem* 58, and many medical publications.
428 Owen Road, Wynnewood, Pa. 19096, U.S.A.
Telephone: MI2-2760 (Home); EV2-4300 (Office).

Penfield, James Kedzie, A.B.; American diplomatist; b. 19 April 1908; ed. Stanford Univ.
Joined Foreign Service 30, Mexico, China, Greenland, Czechoslovakia, U.K., Austria, Greece, Washington; fmr. Dep. Asst. Sec. of State for African Affairs; Amb. to Iceland 61-67; Foreign Service Insp., Dept. of State 67-.
Longbranch, Washington; c/o Department of State (O/FI), Washington, D.C. 20520, U.S.A.

Penfield, Wilder Graves, C.C., O.M., C.M.G., M.D., B.LITT., M.A., D.SC., F.R.S., F.R.C.S., F.R.C.P., F.R.S.M.; Canadian neuro-surgeon and writer; b. 26 Jan. 1891; ed. Princeton, Johns Hopkins and Oxford Univs.
Surgeon, Red Cross Hospital, Paris 17; Associate Prof. of Surgery, Columbia Univ., New York 21-28; Asst. Surgeon, Presbyterian Hospital and New York Neurological Inst. 21-28; founded laboratory of Neuro-Cytology 24; Neuro-Surgeon, Royal Victoria and Montreal Gen. Hospitals 28-60; fmr. Chair. Neurology and Neuro-Surgery Dept., McGill Univ.; Dir. Montreal Neurological Inst. 34-60, Hon. Consultant 60-; Pres. American Neurological Asscn. 51; mem. American Philosophical Soc., Polish Acad. of Sciences and Letters, Acad. Nat. de Médecine, France, Deutsche Gesellschaft für Neurologie, Nat. Acad. of Sciences, U.S.A., Acad. of Sciences, U.S.S.R., Polish Acad. of Sciences, Chinese Medical Asscn., American Acad. Arts and Sciences, etc.; U.S. Medal of Freedom; Chevalier Légion d'Honneur; Order of Merit; many hon. degrees; Médaille Lannelongue 58; Lister Medal 61; The Royal Bank Centennial

Award 67; Gold Medal of Royal Soc. of Medicine 68, and numerous other awards.
Publs. *Cytology and Cellular Pathology of the Nervous System* (Editor), *Epilepsy and Cerebral Localization* 41, *Manual of Military Neurosurgery* 41, *The Cerebral Cortex of Man* 50, *Epileptic Seizure Patterns* 50, *Epilepsy and the Functional Anatomy of the Human Brain* 54, *No Other Gods* 54, *The Excitable Cortex in Conscious Man* 58, *Speech and Brain Mechanisms* 59, *The Torch* 60, *Second Career* 63, *The Difficult Art of Giving, The Epic of Alan Gregg* 67, *Man and his Family* 67.
Montreal Neurological Institute, 3801 University Street, Montreal, Canada.
Telephone: 842-1251-292.

Peng Chen; Chinese politician and administrator.
At 21 joined Communist Youth League; prominent in student and trade union activity; six years in prison; during the war Sec. of Northern Bureau of Central Cttee. of C.C.P.; from 49 he was on Peking municipal govt., various admin. posts and cttees.; Sec.-Gen. and Vice-Chair. of Standing Cttee. of N.P.C. 54; Vice-Chair. and Sec.-Gen. of Second Nat. Cttee. of C.P.P.C.C. 54; mem. Eighth Central Cttee. of Chinese Communist Party; mem. Political Bureau of C.C.P. 45; Sec.-Gen. Standing Cttee., Nat. People's Congress 61; First Sec. Peking C.P. 51-66; Dep. Leader Chinese Del. to Communist Party Ideological Talks, Moscow July 63; reported shot Jan. 67.
Political Bureau, Chinese Communist Party, Peking, People's Republic of China.

Peng Teh-huai; Chinese politician; b. 1900; ed. Hunan Mil. School.
Joined Red Army 18, Communist Party 27; commanded 3rd Red Army Corps 30; C.-in-C. all North-East Red Armies 36; Deputy Commdr. 8th Route Army 37; Vice-Chair. People's Revolutionary Mil. Council 52; mem. Politburo, Chinese C.P. 45; Minister of Defence 53-59; Vice-Premier 59-65.
Political Bureau of Chinese Communist Party, Peking, People's Republic of China.

Pengel, Johan Adolf; Surinam politician; b. 20 Jan. 1916; ed. Graaf Von Zinzendorf High School of the Moravian Brethren.
Civil servant, Record Office of Second and Third Cantonal Courts 38; Mem. of Parl. 49-54, 55-, Speaker 54-55; Leader, Nat. Party 58-, Chair. Exec. Board 62-; Prime Minister, Minister of Gen. Affairs and of Home Affairs, Temporary Minister of Finance 63-67, 67-; inaugurated Surinam Labour Fed. 50; Officier, Order of Orange-Nassau; Commdr. Order of House of Orange.
Office of the Prime Minister, Paramaribo, Netherlands Surinam.

Penney, Baron (Life Peer), cr. 67, of East Hendred; **William George Penney,** K.B.E., M.A., PH.D., D.SC., F.R.S.; British scientist; b. 24 June 1909; ed. Sheerness Technical School and Royal Coll. of Science, London Univ.
Commonwealth Fund Fellow, Univ. of Wis., U.S.A.; Senior Student of 1851 Exhibition, Trinity Coll., Cambridge 33-36; Asst. Prof. Mathematics, Imperial Coll., London Univ. 36-45; Principal Scientific Officer, Dept. Scientific and Industrial Research 44-45; Chief Supt. Armaments Research, Ministry of Supply 46-52; Dir. Atomic Weapons Research Establishment, Aldermaston 53-58; mem. for Weapons Research and Devt., U.K. Atomic Energy Authority 54-59, for Research 59-61, Dep. Chair. 61-64, Chair. 64-67; Dir. Tube Investments 68-; Treas. Royal Soc. 56-60; Rumford Medal, Royal Soc. 66; Rector, Imperial Coll. of Science and Technology 67-; Hon. D.Sc. (Univs. of Oxford and Durham and Bath Univ. of Technology).
Orchard House, East Hendred, Wantage, Berks., England.

Penn-Nouth, Samdech; Cambodian politician; b. 06; ed. Cambodian School of Administration.
Ministry of Colonies, Paris 38; Assistant to Minister of Palace 40; Acting Minister of Finance 45; Gov. of Pnom-Penh 46-48; Minister of State 46; Minister of State without Portfolio 47; Prime Minister Sept. 48-Jan. 49, 52-55, 58; Ambassador to France 58-60; Prime Minister, Minister of the Interior and Minister of Religious Affairs Jan.-Nov. 61; Prime Minister and Minister of Religious Affairs 61-62; Adviser to the Govt. 67; Prime Minister 67-; numerous decorations.
Pnom-Penh, Cambodia.

Penrose, Sir Roland Algernon, C.B.E.; British artist and art critic; b. 14 Oct. 1900; ed. Leighton Park School, Reading and Queens' Coll., Cambridge.
Studied and painted in France 22-34; with Surrealist Group 35-39; army 40-45; Founder, Inst. of Contemporary Arts (I.C.A.) Chair. 47-; Fine Arts Officer, British Council, Paris 56-59, mem. Fine Arts Panel 55-; mem. Arts Council 57-; Trustee, Tate Gallery 59-66.
Publs. *The Road is Wider than Long* 39, *In the Service of the People* 45, *Picasso, His Life and Work* 58, *The Sculpture of Picasso* 67.
Farley Farm, Chiddingly, nr. Lewes, Sussex, England. Telephone: Chiddingly 308.

Pepin, Jean-Luc, B.A., L.PH., LL.L.; Canadian politician; b. 1 Nov. 1924; ed. Univ. of Ottawa and Institut d'Etudes politiques, Paris.
Professor, Univ. of Ottawa 51-56, 58-63; Rep., Nat. Film Board, London (U.K.) 56-58; Parl. Sec. to Minister of Trade and Commerce 63; Minister without Portfolio 65; Minister of Mines and Technical Surveys (later Minister of Energy, Mines and Resources) Dec. 65-.
Office: House of Commons, Ottawa; Home: 16 Rothwell Drive, R.R.1, Ottawa, Ontario, Canada.

Pepler, L. A.; South African administrator.
Civil Service 31-; Dept. of Native Affairs 49-; Dir., Bantu Agriculture 56; Dir. Bantu Devt. 61-66, Bantu and Physical Devt. of Bantu Homelands 66-.
Department of Bantu Administration and Development, Pretoria, South Africa.

Pepper, Claude Denson; American politician; b. 8 Sept. 1900; ed. Univ. of Alabama and Harvard Univ.
Instructor in Law, Univ. of Ark. 24-25; private legal practice 25-36; mem. U.S. Senate 36-51, House of Reps. 62-; Chair. Florida Del., Dem. Nat. Convention 40-44; Dir. Wash. Fed. Savings & Loan Asscn., Miami, Wash. Security Co., Miami, Investment Mortgage Co. of Florida.
U.S. House of Representatives, Washington D.C.; 2121 North Bayshore Drive, Miami, Flor., U.S.A.

Pepper, Stephen Coburn, M.A., PH.D.; American professor of philosophy; b. 29 April 1891; ed. Concord High School, Browne and Nichols Schools, Harvard Univ.
Instr. in Philosophy and Psychology, Wellesley 16-17; Asst. in Philosophy, Univ. of Calif. 19-20, Instr. 20-23, Asst. Prof. 23-27, Assoc. Prof. 27-30, Prof. 30-58; Chair. Art Dept. 38-52, Philosophy Dept. 53-58, Emer. 58-; Asst. Dean, Coll. of Letters and Science 40-47; Mills Prof. of Intellectual and Moral Philosophy and Civil Polity 53-; Visiting Prof. Macalester Coll. and Hamlin Univ. 58, Colby Col. 59, Tulane Univ. 61, Williams Coll. 64, Carlton Coll. 67; mem. American Acad. Arts and Sciences, Int. Inst. of Philosophy; Hon. L.H.D. (Colby Coll.) 50, L.L.D. Univ. of Calif.) 60, L.H.D. (Tulane Univ.) 61.
Publs. *Modern Colour* (with C. G. Cutler) 19, *Aesthetic Quality* 38, *World Hypotheses* 42, *The Basis of Criticism in the Arts* 45, *A Digest of Purposive Values* 47, *Principles of Art Appreciation* 49, *The Work of Art* 56, *The Sources of Value* 58, *Ethics* 60, *Concept and Quality* 67.
2718 Buena Vista Way, Berkeley, Calif. 94708, U.S.A. Telephone: 845-2508.

Pepping, Ernst; German composer; b. 12 Sept. 1901; ed. Hochschule für Musik, Berlin.
Teacher at Berlin Kirchenmusikschule 34; Prof. Berlin Musikhochschule 53-; mem. Akad. der Künste, Berlin and Munich; numerous prizes include Mendelssohn Prize 26, Düsseldorf Robert Schumann Prize 55, Bremen Philharmonische Gesellschaft 62; hon. Dr. Phil. Berlin Free Univ. 61.
Compositions include three symphonies, piano concerto, *Te Deum,* string quartet, four piano sonatas, organ concertos and partitas, *Passionsbericht des Matthäus, Deutsche Messe, Missa Dona nobis pacem* and other church music.
Publ. *Der Polyphone Satz.*
Johannesstift, Berlin-Spandau, Germany.
Telephone: 361-1274.

Peralta Azurdia, Enrique; Guatemalan politician and army officer; b. 08; ed. Polytechnic School, Guatemala City.
Guatemalan army 26-, rose from Lieut. to Col.; fmr. Dir. Polytechnic School; Mil. Attaché, Mexico, Chile, Costa Rica, El Salvador and U.S.A., fmr. Ambassador to Cuba, El Salvador and Costa Rica; Dir.-Gen. Agrarian Affairs 58-59, Minister of Agriculture 59-60, of Defence 61-63, Chief of State and Minister of Defence 63-July 66.
Guatemala City, Guatemala.

Peralta Paez, Benjamin; Ecuadorean diplomatist and politician; b. 08;
Legation Sec. Rio de Janeiro 35-38; First Sec. Legation, La Paz 38, Buenos Aires 38-39, Santiago 39-40; Head of Chancery Information Dept. 40-44; First Sec. Legation Lima 44-46; Counsellor, Embassy, Lima 46-47; Minister to Guatemala (also accred. to El Salvador, Honduras and Nicaragua) 49-50, to Dominican Repub. 50-52; Envoy Extraordinary to U.S.A. 52-53, Ambassador 53, Alt. Ambassador to Org. of American States (O.A.S.) 53-57; Ambassador to Dominican Repub. 57-58; Technical Assessor on Frontier Demarcation, Min. of Foreign Affairs 58-60; Under-Sec. for Foreign Affairs 61-62; Minister of Foreign Affairs 62-63.
c/o Ministry of Foreign Affairs, Quito, Ecuador.

Percy, Charles Harting; American business executive and politician; b. 27 Sept. 1919; ed. Univ. of Chicago.
Sales trainee, apprentice, Bell & Howell 38, Man., War Co-ordinating Dept. 41-43, Asst. Sec. 43-46, Corpn. Sec. 48-49, Pres. 49-61, Chief Exec. Officer 61-63, Chair. Board 61-66; Senator from Illinois 67-; U.S. Naval Reserve 43-45; Republican.
U.S. Senate, Washington 25, D.C., U.S.A.

Perdigão, José de Azeredo, LL.D.; Portuguese lawyer and foundation official; b. 96; ed. Lisbon and Coimbra Univ.
Lawyer, Lisbon 19-26; Keeper of Registered Buildings Dept., Lisbon 26-58; Chair. Bd. of Administrators Calouste Gulbenkian Foundation 56-; fmr. Pres. Conf. of Inst. of Portuguese Lawyers; fmr. Dir. Nat. Overseas Bank; Dr. h.c. Science, Bahia Univ. 59 and other decorations.
Calouste Gulbenkian Foundation, Parque de Santa Gertrudes, Avenida de Berne, Lisbon, Portugal.
Telephone: 762146.

Perdomo Paredes, Roberto, LL.D.; Honduran diplomatist and politician; b. 22; ed. Universidad Nacional de Nicaragua and Universidad Nacional de España.
Secretary Honduran Embassy, Netherlands 58-59; Honduran Del. to Int. Court of Justice 58-59; Under-Sec. of Foreign Affairs 59-62, Minister of Foreign Affairs 62-63, Prof. Juridical and Social Law, Nat. Univ. of Honduras; Pres. Society of Lawyers of Honduras; numerous decorations.
Despacho de Abogados, Tegucigalpa, D.C., Honduras.

Pereira, William Leonard; American architect and planner; b. 25 April 1909; ed. Univ. of Illinois School of Architecture.

Associate Holabird & Root, architects, Chicago 30-32; private architectural practice, Chicago 32-38, Los Angeles 38-50; partnership, Pereira & Luckman, architects and engineers 50-58; Principal, William L. Pereira and Assocs. 58-; mem. Nat. Council on the Arts; Fellow American Inst. of Architects; numerous awards.

Principal works: design of Los Angeles County Museum of Art, Occidental Center, CBS Television City, Marineland of Pacific, Los Angeles Int. Airport (in association), research and development centres for Lockheed, Hoffman, Gen. Telephone, Astropower; campus buildings for Univ. of Calif., Los Angeles, Brigham Young Univ. and Univ. of Southern Calif.; master plans for 93,000 acre Irvine Ranch, Santa Catalina Island, 10,700 acre Mountain Park, Univ. of Calif., Irvine, Univ. of S. Calif., Occidental Coll., Hawaii Loa Coll. and Central Univ. Library, Univ. of Calif. (San Diego).

William L. Pereira and Associates, 5657 Wilshire Boulevard, Los Angeles, Calif. 90036, U.S.A.

Perek, Luboš, DR.RER.NAT.; Czechoslovak astronomer; b. 26 July 1919; ed. Masaryk Univ., Brno, and Charles Univ., Prague.

Assistant, Astronomical Inst., Masaryk Univ., Brno 46, Head 53; Head, Stellar Dept., Astronomical Inst. of Czechoslovak Acad. of Sciences, Prague 56, Dir. Astronomical Inst. 68-; Vice-Pres. Comm. of the Galactic Structure and Dynamics, Int. Astronomical Union 61-64, Asst. Gen. Sec., Int. Astronomical Union 64-67, Gen. Sec. 67-70; Visiting Prof., Dearborn Observatory, Evanston, Ill. 64; Corresp. mem. Czechoslovak Acad. of Sciences 65-; mem. Czechoslovak Astronomical Soc., Astronomische Gesellschaft, Astronomical Soc. of the Pacific, Exec. Cttee. Int. Council of Scientific Unions 67-70.

Publs. include *Catalogue of Galactic Planetary Nebulae* (with L. Kohoutek) 67.

Astronomical Institute of Czechoslovak Academy of Sciences, Budečská 6, Prague 2, Czechoslovakia. Telephone: 258757.

Perelman, Sidney Joseph; American writer; b. 1 Feb. 1904; ed. Brown Univ.

Film script writer; articles for *New Yorker* 35-; Best Screen Writer Award 56; mem. Screen Writers' Guild, Dramatists' Guild.

Publs. *Dawn Ginsbergh's Revenge* 29, *Parlor, Bedlam and Bath* 30, *Strictly from Hunger* 37, *Look Who's Talking* 40, *The Dream Department* 43, *Crazy Like a Fox* 44, *Keep it Crisp* 46, *Westward Ha* 48, *Chicken Inspector No. 23* 67; Plays: *All Good Americans* 34, *The Night Before Christmas* 41 (both with Laura Perelman), *One Touch of Venus* 43 (with Ogden Nash), *The Beauty Part* 63.

Erwinna, Bucks County, Pa., U.S.A.

Perera, Liyanagé Henry Horace, B.A.; Ceylonese international official; b. 9 May 1915; ed. St. Benedict's Coll., Colombo, Univ. Coll. London, Univ. of Ceylon.

Senior Master in Govt. and History, Ceylon 36-59; Asst. Registrar, Aquinas Univ. Coll., Colombo 60-61; Educ. Dir. World Fed. of UN Asscns. 61-63, Deputy Sec.-Gen. and Educ. Dir. 63-66, Sec.-Gen. 66-; mem. Int. Cttee. on Adult Educ. (UNESCO) 63.

Publs. *Ceylon and Indian History (Early Times to 1500), Ceylon Under Western Rule (1500-1948), Groundwork of Ceylon and World History (Early Times to 1500).*

World Federation of United Nations Associations, 65 rue de Lausanne, 1202 Geneva; Home: 22 avenue Luserna, 1203 Geneva, Switzerland.

Telephone: 31-89-44 (Office); 33-07-98 (Home).

Perera, Nanayakkarapathirage Martin, PH.D.; Ceylonese politician; b. 6 June 1905; ed. Ceylon Univ. Coll., and London School of Economics.

Lecturer, Ceylon Univ. 35-36, 45-46; Founder-mem. Lanka Sama Samaj Party 35, now Pres.; mem. Ceylon State Council 36; imprisoned 40-42, 43-45; mem. Ceylon House of Representatives 47-, Leader of the Opposition 47-52, 56-60; Minister of Finance June 64-65; Mayor of Colombo 55; Pres. Ceylon Fed. of Labour; Hon. D.Sc. (Ceylon).

Ceylon Federation of Labour, 47 Driebergs Avenue, Colombo 10; (Home) 106 Cotta Road, Colombo, Ceylon. Telephone: 91891 (Home).

Peressutti, Enrico, DR.ARCH.PROF.; Italian architect; b. 28 Aug. 1908; ed. School of Architecture, Milan.

Architect 32; Visiting Prof. Architectural Association School, London 50-51, M.I.T. Cambridge, Mass. 52, Princeton, N.J. 53, 54-56, 57-59, Yale 57, 62; private practice with Belgiojoso and Rogers in town planning, architecture, interior decoration and industrial design; works incl. Italian Merchant Navy Pavilion at Int. Exhibition, Paris 37; houses, factories, pavilions, health resort for children, Legnano 39; Post Office, Rome 39; monument in Milan cemetery 46; U.S. Pavilion at Triennale 51; Olivetti showroom, N.Y. 54; Labyrinth for Young People at Triennale 54; restoration and arrangement Castello Sforzesco Museums, Milan 56; Torre Velasca (Milan) 58; Canadian Pavilion (Venice Biennale); Italian Pavilion (Brussels World Exhibition) (in collaboration) 58, Hispano Olivetti Building, Barcelona.

Publs. *Stile* (in collab.) 36, *Piano Regolatore della Val d'Aosta* (in collab.) 43, *Piano A.R.* 45.

Studio Architetti B.B.P.R., Via dei Chiostri 2, Milan, Italy.

Perette, Carlos Humberto; Argentine lawyer and politician; b. 12 Dec. 1915; ed. Univ. Nac. del Litoral.

Former Counsel to Provincial Legislature of Entre Rios, Deputy 52-55, 58-62; mem. Chamber of Deputies of Argentina; Vice-Pres. of Argentina Oct. 63-June 66.

Paraná, Entre Rios, Argentina.

Pérez Godoy, Gen. Ricardo Pio; Peruvian army officer and politician; b. 9 June 1905; ed. Colegio Santo Tomas de Aquino and Escuela de Oficiales del Ejército.

Director-Gen. of Training, Peruvian Army 56-57; Controller-Gen. of Army 58-59; Chief of Staff of Joint Command of Armed Forces 60-62; Prefect of Dept. of Arequipa 52-53, 55-56; Pres. of Mil. Junta of Govt. of Peru 62-63; mem. Centro de Altos Estudios Historicos del Perú; now Gen. of a Division; numerous decorations.

Publs. include *Teoría de la Guerra y Doctrina de Guerra, La Maniobra y la Batalla.*

Blasco Nuñez de Balboa 225, Miraflores, Lima, Peru.

Pérez-Guerrero, Manuel, LL.D.; Venezuelan politician; b. 18 Sept. 1911; ed. Univ. of Paris and Ecole des Sciences Politiques, Paris.

Member, Economics Dept., League of Nations 37-40; Sec. Import Control Comm., Ministry of Finance, Venezuela 40-42; mem. Economics and Statistics Section, Int. Labor Org. 42-43; Ministry of Foreign Relations, Venezuela 43-44; Dir. Div. of Coordination and Liaison, UN 46-47; Minister of Finance, Venezuela 47-48; Exec. Sec. Technical Assistance Board, UN 49-53, Resident Rep., Technical Assistance Board, Egypt 53-57, Special Rep., Tunisia and Morocco 57-58; Dir. Non Self-Governing Territories, UN 58-59; Chief, Office of Co-ordination and Planning, Venezuela 59-62; mem. Board of Dirs. Central Bank 59-63; Resident Rep., Technical Assistance Board, UN, Algeria 63; Minister of Mines and Hydrocarbons Dec. 63-67; Perm. Rep. of Venezuela to UN 67-; Leader of UN Mission to Aden 67.

Permanent Mission of Venezuela to the United Nations, 521 Park Avenue, New York, N.Y. 10021, U.S.A.; and Avenida Principal de La Castellana 67, Caracas, Venezuela.

Pérez Jiménez, Col. Marcos; Venezuelan officer and politician; b. 14; ed. Caracas Mil. School and Lima War Coll.

Army Chief of Staff in Acción Democrática Govt.; mem. of subsequent three-man Junta and Minister of Defence; Pres. of Venezuela Dec. 52-58; extradited from U.S.A. to Venezuela Aug. 63.

Caracas, Venezuela.

Perham, Dame Margery, D.C.M.G., C.B.E., D.LITT., F.B.A.; British scholar of colonial affairs; b. 6 Sept. 1895; ed. St. Hugh's Coll., Oxford.

Asst. Lecturer in History Sheffield Univ.; in Somaliland 22-23; Fellow and Tutor, St. Hugh's Coll., Oxford 24-29; Rhodes Travelling Fellowship in N. America, Polynesia, Australia and Africa 29-31, and in West Africa 31-32; Research Fellow, St. Hugh's Coll. 31-39; Reader in Colonial Admin. Oxford Univ. 39-48; Dir. Oxford Univ. Inst. of Colonial Studies 45-48; Official Fellow Nuffield Coll., Oxford 39-; Rockefeller Travelling Fellowship of Int. Inst. of African Languages and Culture in E. Africa and Sudan 32; Research Lecturer in Colonial Admin., Oxford 35-39; mem. Advisory Cttee. on Education in the Colonies 39-45, of Higher Education Comm. and West Indies Higher Education Cttee. 44, of Inter-Univ. Council on Higher Education Overseas 46-; Reith Lecturer 61; Pres. Univs. Mission to Central Africa 63-64; Pres. The African Studies Asscn. of Britain 63-64; Editor *Colonial and Comparative Series* (formerly *Colonial Research Publs.*) 41-; Hon. LL.D. (St. Andrews), Hon. D.Litt. (Southampton, London and Cambridge); Fellow British Acad. 61; Hon. Fellow, Nuffield and St. Hugh's Colls. and School of Oriental and African Studies.

Publs. *Major Dane's Garden* 24, *Josie Vine* 26, *The Protectorates of South Africa* (with Lionel Curtis) 35, *Ten Africans* (Ed.) 36, *Native Administration in Nigeria* 37, *Africans and British Rule* 41, *African Discovery* (with J. Simmons) 43, *Race and Politics in Kenya* (with E. Huxley) 44, *Studies in Colonial Legislatures* (Ed.) 46-, *The Economics of a Tropical Dependency* (Ed.) 46-48, *The Government of Ethiopia* 48, *Lugard, The Years of Adventure* 56, ed. with Mary Bull *The Diaries of Lord Lugard 1889-1892* 59, *1894-5, 1898* 63, *Lugard, The Years of Authority* 60, *The Colonial Reckoning* 62, *African Outline* 66, *The Colonial Sequence 1930-1949* 67.

5 Rawlinson Road, Oxford, England.

Pericot García, Luis, DR.HIST.; Spanish university professor; b. 5 Sept. 1899; ed. Univs. of Barcelona and Madrid.

Asst. Faculty of Philosophy and Letters, Univ. of Barcelona 20, Asst. Prof. 23; Prof. Univ. of Santiago de Compostela 25, Univ. of Valencia 27; Prof. of Ancient Spanish History, Univ. of Barcelona 34-55, of Prehistory 55-, Sec. Faculty of Philosophy and Letters 34; Vice-Dean 51-54; mem. Higher Council of Scientific Research; Regional del. Archæological Excavations, Barcelona; Hon. Dir. Prehistoric Research Service, Province of Valencia; Hon. Fellow Royal Anthropological Inst. of Great Britain; Corresp. Fellow British Acad.; Pres. 4th Int. Congress of Prehistoric and Protohistoric Sciences; Martorell, Duque de Loubat and Dusseigneur Prizes; Gran Cruz Alfonso X El Sabio; Stella della Solidarietà Italiana; Chevalier Légion d'Honneur.

Publs. *La Civilización Megalítica Catalana y la Cultura Pirenaica* 25, *España Primitiva y Romana* 34, 58, *La América Indígena I* 36, 62, *La Cueva del Parpalló* 42, *Arte Rupestre* 50, *La España Primitiva* 50, *Las Raíces de España* 52, *Prehistoria de Marruecos* 53.

Rambla de Cataluña 89-3°-2ª, Barcelona, Spain.

Telephone: 215-1760.

Perier, François; *pseudonym* of François Pillu; French actor; b. 10 Nov. 1919; ed. Conservatoire Nat. d'Art Dramatique, Paris.

Co-Dir. Théâtre de la Michodière, Paris 51-65; has appeared in numerous plays including *Les Jours Heureux, Les J 3, Les Mains Sales, Bobosse, Le Ciel de Lit, Gog et Magog, La Preuve par Quatre*; films include: *Premier Bal* 41, *Lettres d'Amour* 42, *Un Revenant, Le Silence est d'Or* 46, *Orphée* 49, *Souvenirs Perdus* 50, *Les Evadés* 54, *Gervaise* 55, *Le Notti di Cabiria* 56, *Bobosse* 58, *Le Testament d'Orphée* 60, *L'Aimant de Cinq Jours* 61, *La Vista* 63; British Film Acad. Award 56, Victoire du Cinéma Française 57; Officier, Ordre des Arts et Lettres.

c/o Lebovici, 55 avenue George V, Paris 8e, France.

Perkins, Dexter, PH.D., M.A.; American university professor; b. 20 June 1889; ed. Boston Latin School, Harvard Univ., and Ecole des Sciences politiques.

Instructor, Univ. of Cincinnati 14-15; on teaching staff, Univ. of Rochester 15-54; Prof. and Chair. of Dept. of History 25-54; City Historian of City of Rochester 36-47; Sec. American Historical Asscn. 28-39; Pitt Chair in American History and Insts. Cambridge Univ. 45-46; Pres. Salzburg Seminar in American Studies 50-61; Moderator, American Unitarian Asscn. 52-53; John L. Senior Prof. American Civilisation, Cornell 53-59; Prof. Emer. 59-; Lecturer, Nat. War Coll., Washington, D.C., 47-61; Official Historian, OWI, San Francisco Conf. 45; Pres. American Historical Asscn. 56.

Publs. *The Monroe Doctrine 1823-26, 1826-67, 1876-1907* (3 separate vols.), *Hands Off! A History of the Monroe Doctrine 1823-1940, America and Two Wars, The U.S. and the Caribbean, The Evolution of American Foreign Policy, The American Approach to Foreign Policy, Charles Evans Hughes and American Democratic Statesmanship, The New Age of Franklin Roosevelt, The American Way, America's Quest for Peace, The United States and Latin America.*

316 Oxford Street, Rochester 7, N.Y., U.S.A.

Perkins, Dudley, M.A., M.INST.T.; British lawyer and port authority official; ed. Clifton Coll. Bristol and King's Coll., Cambridge.

Solicitor 37; Asst. Legal Adviser, British Broadcasting Corpn. 45-48, Nat. Coal Board 48-51; Legal Adviser Port of London Authority 52, Deputy Gen. Man. 62-64, Dir.-Gen. April 64-; mem. Council of the Law Soc. 54-62, Central Transport Consultative Cttee. 62-, South East Econ. Planning Council 66-; Deputy Chair. London Port Employers 64-; Hon. Treas. Nat. Asscn. of Port Employers 64-.

Port of London Authority, P.O. Box 242, Trinity Square, London, E.C.3, England.

Perkins, James Alfred, A.B., M.A., PH.D.; American scientist; b. 11 Oct. 1911; ed. Swarthmore Coll. and Princeton Univ.

Instructor in political science, Princeton Univ. 37-39; Asst. Dir. School of Public and Int. Affairs 39-41; Dir. Pulp and Paper Div., O.P.A. 41-43; Asst. to Administrator, Foreign Econ. Admin. 43-45; Vice-Pres. Swarthmore Coll. 45-50; Exec. Assoc., Carnegie Corpn. 50-51, Vice-Pres. 51-63; Sec. Carnegie Foundation for Advancement of Teaching 54-55, Vice-Pres. 55-63; Pres. Cornell Univ. 63-; Deputy Chair. Research and Development Board, Dept. of Defense 51-52; consultant Rand Corpn. 58-62, Trustee 61-; Vice-Pres. and Board mem. Home Trust Co. 55-; Trustee Memorial Sloan-Kettering Cancer Center 63-, trustee and dir. of other orgs.; Chair. Board of Trustees United Negro Coll. Fund 65; mem. various Govt. cttees. including Carnegie Comm. for Study of Future Structure and Financing of Higher Education in U.S. 67.

Office: 300 Day Hall, Cornell University, Ithaca, N.Y.; Home: 511 Cayuga Heights Road, Ithaca, N.Y., U.S.A.

Perkins, Richard Sturgis; American banker; b. 27 June 1910; ed. Hamilton Tutoring and Berkshire Preparatory Schools.

Thompson Fenn & Co. 29-32; Wood, Struthers & Co.

32-36; Harris, Upham & Co. 36-51; First Nat. City Bank 51-, Chair. Exec. Cttee. 59-; official of other companies.
First National City Bank of New York, 399 Park Avenue, New York City, N.Y. 10022, U.S.A.

Perkins, Thomas L.; American lawyer and businessman; b. 9 Nov. 1905; ed. Phillips Andover Acad. and Univ. of Virginia.
Broker, New York City 30-40; admitted to New York bar 40, in practice in New York City 40-; Chair. American Cyanamid Co. 58-61, The Duke Endowment 60, Duke Power Co. 61-; official of other companies and professional orgs.
Home: 603 Purchase Street, Rye, N.Y. 10580; Office: 30 Rockefeller Plaza, New York City 20, N.Y., U.S.A.

Perkinson, Jesse Dean, B.S., M.S., PH.D.; American science administrator and biochemist; b. 24 Oct. 1914; ed. Univ. of Tennessee and Univ. of Rochester.
Fellow Univ. of Rochester 39-43; U.S. Navy Reserve 44-46; Research Associate, Univ. of Georgia 46-49; Senior Scientist, Oak Ridge Inst. of Nuclear Studies 49-52; Assoc. Prof. of Biochemistry, Univ. of Tenn. 52-57; Chief of Training and Educ. U.S. Atomic Energy Comm. 57-58; Exec. Sec. Inter-American Nuclear Energy Comm. (IANEC) 58-; Dir. Dept. of Scientific Affairs, Pan American Union, Org. of American States 58-; Fellow American Asscn. for the Advancement of Science.
Department of Scientific Affairs, Pan American Union, Washington, D.C. 20006; 4510 Drummond Avenue, Chevy Chase, Maryland 20015, U.S.A.
Telephone: DUI-8733 (Office).

Perlis, H.H. The Raja of; Tunku, Syed Putra ibni Al-marhum Syed Hassan Jamalullail, D.M.N., S.M.N., D.K. (Brunei), K.C.M.G.; Malaysian ruler; b. 1920.
Appointed Bakal Raja (Heir-Presumptive) of Perlis April 38; attached to Courts in Kangar 40; worked for a year in the Land Office, Kuala Lumpur, and for a year in the Magistrates' Court, Kuala Lumpur; in private business during Japanese occupation; Timbalan Yang di-Pertuan Agong (Dep. Paramount Ruler) of Malaya April-Sept. 60, Yang di-Pertuan Agong (H.M. the Paramount Ruler) Sept. 60-Sept. 63, of Malaysia Sept. 63-66.
Istana Arau, Perlis, Malaya, Malaysia.

Perlman, Alfred Edward; American railway executive; b. 22 Nov. 1902; ed. Mass. Inst. Technology.
With Northern Pacific Railway, Forsyth, Mont. 23-34; Railway Div., Reconstruction Finance Corpn. 34-35; with Chicago, Burlington and Quincy Railroad 35-36; Engineer (Maintenance of Way) Denver and Rio Grande Western Railroad Co. 36-41, Chief Engineer 41-47, Gen. Man. 47-52, Exec. Vice-Pres. 52-54; Pres. Dir. New York Central System 54-66; Pres. and Chief Operating Officer Pennsylvania New York Central Transportation Co. 66-.
Home: Premium Point, New Rochelle, N.Y.; Office: 230 Park Avenue, New York City 17, N.Y., U.S.A.

Perloff, Harvey (Stephen), PH.D.; American economist and planner; b. 8 June 1915; ed. Univ. of Pennsylvania, London School of Econs. and Harvard Univ.
Economist Fed. Reserve Board 41-43; Consultant, Govt. of Puerto Rico 46-47, 50-51; Prof. of Social Science, Univ. of Chicago 47-55, Head Planning School 51-55; Consultant Presidents' Water Resources Policy Comm. 50, Tenn. Valley Authority 53-54; UN Missions to Turkey and Israel 54; Dir. Program of Regional Studies, Resources for the Future 55-61, 65-; Consultant, State Dept. 63-65; mem. Cttee. of Nine, Alliance for Progress 61-64; mem. Comm. on the Year 2000, American Acad. of Arts and Science 65-; mem. several planning cttees. and organizations; Chair. Advisory Cttee. on Urban Planning and Development, Organization of American

States; Consultant, Dept. of Housing and Urban Devt., Dept. of Health, Educ. and Welfare.
Publs. *State and Local Finance in the National Economy* 44, *Puerto Rico's Economic Future* 50, *Education for Planning—City, State and Regional* 57, *Regions, Resources and Economic Growth* 60, *Planning and the Urban Community* 61, *How a Region Grows* 63, *Regional Economic Integration in the Development of Latin America* 63, *Design for a Worldwide Study of Regional Development* 66, *Issues in Urban Economics* (ed. with L. Wingo) 68.
3809 Raymond Street, Chevy Chase, Maryland; Office: Resources for the Future Inc., 1755 Massachusetts Avenue, N.W., Washington, D.C. 20036, U.S.A.
Telephone: 202-462-4400; and 301-OL-6-8127.

Perón, General Juan Domingo; Argentine politician; b. 95; ed. Colegio Internacional de Olivos, Colegio Internacional Politécnico, and Colegio Militar de la Nación.
Commissioned Lieut. Infantry 13, advancing through grades to General of the Army 50; Private Sec. Minister of War 30; Prof. Mil. History Escuela Superior de Guerra 30-36; A.D.C to Minister of War 36; Mil. Attaché, Argentine Embassy, Chile 36; Head of Mission visiting Europe 39-41; Dir. Centro de Instrucción de Montaña 41-43; Chief of Staff 1st Army Div. 43; Head Secr., Ministry of War 43, later Sec. of Labour and Welfare; Vice-Pres. 44; Pres. of Argentina 46-55; in exile following overthrow of regime Sept. 55.
Publs. *El Frente Oriental de la Guerra Mundial de 1914 28, Apuntes de Historia Militar 29, Las Operaciones de la Guerra Franco-prusiana 1870 39, La Comunidad Organizada 48, Conducción Política 50, La Fuerza es el Derecho de las Bestias 56, Vende-Patrias 58.*
Quinta 17 de Octubre, Ciudad Puerta de Hierro, Madrid, Spain.

Perowne, Stewart Henry, O.B.E., K.ST.J., M.A., F.S.A.; British historian and orientalist; b. 17 June 1901; ed. Haileybury Coll., Corpus Christi Coll., Cambridge, Harvard Univ.
English Lecturer, Govt. Arab Coll., Jerusalem 27-30; Asst. Sec. Palestine Govt. 30-32, Asst. District Commr. 32-34; Asst. Sec., Malta 34-37; Political Officer, Aden 37; Arabic Programme Organiser, B.B.C. 38; Information Officer, Aden 39-41; Public Relations Attaché, British Embassy, Baghdad 41-44, Oriental Counsellor 44-47; Colonial Sec. Barbados 47-50; Acting Gov. Mar.-Oct. 49; Adviser, Ministry of Interior, Cyrenaica 50-51; Adviser on Arab Affairs, U.K. Del. U.N. Gen. Assembly 51; discovered ancient Aziris 51; Hon. Asst. Jerusalem Diocesan Refugee Organisation 52; designed and supervised building of seven Arab refugee villages 52-56; mem. Church of England Council on Foreign Relations 65.
Publs. *The One Remains 54, Herod the Great 56, The Later Herods 58, Hadrian 60, Caesars and Saints 62, The Pilgrim's Companion in Jerusalem and Bethlehem 64, The Pilgrim's Companion in Roman Rome 64, The Pilgrim's Companion in Athens 64, Jerusalem* (Famous Cities Series) *65, The End of the Roman World 66.*
44 Arminger Road, London, W.12, England.

Perret, Roland Paul, DIP.ING.; Swiss physicist and consulting engineer; b. 23 Nov. 1931; ed. Ecole Polytechnique de l'Univ. de Lausanne.
Began career as Asst. to Prof. of Nuclear Physics, Lausanne Univ.; Chief Physicist, D. Bonnard and A. Gardel (Consulting Engineers), Lausanne 55-57; consultant OEEC 55-60; Scientific Adviser, Head of the Scientific Div. of the European Nuclear Energy Agency (ENEA) of OECD 60-.
Publs. Studies and patents on semi-conductors in nuclear electronics, articles and surveys; unpublished studies on diffusion chambers, nuclear ship propulsion,

production of energy from radio-isotopes, and on world-wide resources of uranium and thorium.
European Nuclear Energy Agency, 38 Bd. Suchet, Paris 16e, France.
Telephone: TRO-3220, Extension 2044.

Perrin, Francis Henri Jean Siegfried, D. ès sc.; French scientist; b. 17 Aug. 1901; ed. Lycée Henri IV, Paris, Ecole Normale Supérieure, Univ. of Paris.
Assistant Univ. of Paris 23, Lecturer 33, Prof. 35-; Visiting Prof. Columbia Univ., New York 41-44; Rep. to Consultative Assembly Algiers, later Paris 44-45; Titular Prof. of Atomic Physics, Coll. de France 46-; High Commr. for Atomic Energy 51-; mem. Institut de France 53-, Acad. des Sciences, Acad. d'Agriculture, Scientific Action Cttee. for Nat. Defence 57-; mem. Euratom Scientific and Technical Cttee.; Grand Officier Légion d'Honneur, Grand Croix Mérite National, Commandeur, Palmes Académiques, Economie Nationale.
4 rue Froidevaux, Paris 14e, France.

Perrin, René Jean Louis; French marine engineer and business executive; b. 22 Aug. 1897; ed. Ecole Polytechnique.
Former Marine Engineer and Chief Marine Engineer; Prés. d'Honneur, Compagnie Française de Raffinage; Vice-Pres. Compagnie Française des Pétroles; Admin. Soc. Nat. d'Investissement, S.A. des Pétroles Mory, Soc. d'Hydrocarbures de Saint-Denis, Lille-Bonnières et Colombes, Compagnie Auxiliaire de Navigation; Commandeur, Légion d'Honneur.
86 avenue Raymond-Poincaré, Paris, 16e, France.

Perrin, René Marie Victor; French industrial executive; b. 7 June 1893; ed. Ecole Polytechnique.
Président-Directeur Gén. Soc. d'électrochimie d'Ugine; Hon. Pres. Comptoir Industriel d'Etirage des Métaux; Pres. Papeteries de Vizille; official of other companies; Commandeur, Légion d'Honneur.
39 avenue Franklin-Roosevelt, Paris 8e, France.

Perrone, João Consani, B.SC., M.A., D.CHEM.; Brazilian protein chemist; b. 22 Jan. 1922; ed. Universidade do Brasil, Rio de Janeiro, and Univ. of Calif. (Berkeley).
Head of Research, Nat. Council of Research 52-60; Assoc. Prof. of Organic and Biological Chemistry, Univ. of Brazil 51-; Head, Laboratory of Protein Chemistry, Instituto Nacional de Tecnologia 52-; Prof. of Protein Chemistry and Gen. Enzymology, Instituto de Química 62-; mem. Brazilian Acad. of Sciences.
Rua Marquês de Pinedo, 45 Apdo. 401, Laranjeiras, Rio de Janeiro, GB, Brazil.
Telephone: 25-1617.

Perroux, Prof. François, L. ès L., AGRÉGÉ DES SC. ECONS.; French professor; b. 19 Dec. 1903; Coll. des Maristes, Lyons, Univ. de Lyon and Univ. de Paris à la Sorbonne.
Rockefeller Fellow 34; Prof. Collège de France 55-; Dir. of Studies, Ecole Pratique des Hautes Etudes 55-; Founder-Dir. Inst. of Applied Econ. Science 44-; Dir. Inst. of Study of Econ. and Social Devt.; mem. Exec. Cttee. for Nat. Revenue, Exec. Council for Accountancy, Statistical Soc. of Paris, Econ. and Social Council, Nat. Cttee. of Scientific Research, etc.; mem. Acad. des Sciences d'Outre-Mer, Paris, Accad. Pugliese delle Scienze, Bari, Accad. Nazionale dei Lincei, Rome, Società nazionale di Lettere e belle arti, Naples, British Acad.; Foreign mem. Accad. delle scienze, Turin; Hon. mem. American Econ. Asscn.; Officier Légion d'Honneur, Commdr. Ordre des Palmes Académiques, Grand Officier Ordre Nat. du Mérite, Officier Ordre de la Couronne (Belgium), Grand Officier Ordre Nat. du Sénégal, Commendatore Ordine al Merito (Italy); Dr. h.c. São Paulo, Coimbra, Liège, Frankfurt-am-Main, Lisbon, Cordoba, Georgetown (Washington), Montevideo.
Publs. include Les Mythes hitlériens 36, Capitalisme et Communauté du Travail 38, Des Mythes hitlériens à l'Europe allemande 40, Communauté 40, La Valeur 43, Le Revenu National, son calcul et sa signification 47, Les Comptes de la Nation 49, L'Europe sans rivages 54, La Capitalisme 48, 6th edn. 65, La Coexistence pacifique 58, Economie et Société 61, Le IVe Plan français 62, L'Economie des jeunes nations 62, Industrie et Création Collective 64, Les Techniques Quantitatives de la Planification 65.
Institut de Science Economique Appliqué, 11 boulevard Sébastapol, Paris 1er, France.
Telephone: Louvre 91-87/91-99/93-70 (Office).

Perse, Saint-John, (see Leger, Alexis).

Persianinov, Leonid Semenovich; Soviet gynecologist; b. 1908; ed. Second Leningrad Medical Inst.
Physician, Kostroma Region; Post-graduate, Research Assoc. Asst. Prof. Inst. of Post-graduate Medical Training, Kazan; Army Surgeon 41-45; Head of Chair, Moscow Medical Inst. 51-58; Head of Chair Second Moscow Medical Inst. 58; Chief Obstetrician-Gynecologist U.S.S.R. Ministry of Public Health 59-; Corresp. mem. U.S.S.R. Acad. of Medical Sciences 60-65, mem. 65-; Chair. Board U.S.S.R. Soc. of Obstetricians-Gynecologists; WHO Expert on Obstetrics and Gynecology; mem. Editorial Board magazine Obstetrics and Gynecology; mem. Int. Fed. of Obstetricians and Gynecologists; Hon. mem. Purkiněŷ Soc. Czechoslovakia, Union of Obstetricians-Gynecologists, Yugoslavia; Order of Lenin, Red Star, etc.; Merited Scientist Byelorussian S.S.R. Snegirev Prize.
Publs. Over 150 works on regulation of birth, mother's traumatism in childbirth, anaesthesia in obstetric and gynecological operations.
Second Medical Institute, 1 Malaya Pirogovskaya Street, Moscow, U.S.S.R.

Perutz, Max Ferdinand, PH.D., F.R.S.; British biochemist and crystallographer; b. 19 May 1914; ed. Theresianum, Vienna, and Univs. of Vienna and Cambridge.
Director Medical Research Council Unit for Molecular Biology, Cavendish Laboratory, Univ. of Cambridge 47-62; Chair. Medical Research Council Laboratory of Molecular Biology, Univ. Postgraduate Medical School, Cambridge 62-; Reader Davy Faraday Research Laboratory, Royal Inst. 54-: Chair. European Molecular Biology Org.; Hon. Dr. Phil. (Vienna and Edinburgh); Nobel Prize for Chemistry 62.
Publs. Proteins and Nucleic Acids: Structure and Function 62, various papers on the structure of proteins.
42 Sedley Taylor Road, Cambridge, England.

Pescatore, Gabriele; Italian university professor and civil servant; b. 21 Oct. 1916; ed. Univ. of Naples.
Appointed Counsellor of State 50; Prof. of Admiralty Law, Univ. of Rome; Pres. of the Cassa del Mezzogiorno (Southern Italy Development Fund) 54-; Vice-Pres. Int. Council of Regional Economies, Mediterranean Council of Regional Economies; Knight-Commdr. of the Pius Order; Grand Cross, Knight of the Republic's Order of Merit; Gold Medal Award for Sciences and Art.
Cassa del Mezzogiorno, Piazzale Kennedy, Eur, Rome; Via A. Stoppani 34, Rome, Italy.

Pescatore, Pierre, D.IUR.; Luxembourg diplomatist and professor of law; b. 20 Nov. 1919.
Ministry of Foreign Affairs 46-, Sec., later mem., Del. to UN Gen. Ass. 46-52; Legal Adviser, Min. of Foreign Affairs 50-58; Dir. for Political Affairs, Min. of Foreign Affairs 58-; Min. Plenipotentiary 59; Sec.-Gen. Ministry of Foreign Affairs 64-67; Judge, Court of Justice of the European Communities 67-; Prof. Law Faculty and Inst. for European Legal Studies, Univ. of Liège; Lectured Hague Acad. of Int. Law 61; Assoc. Inst. de Droit Internationale 65-.

Publs. *Essai sur la notion de la loi* 57, co-author *Aspects juridiques du Marché commun* 58, *Introduction à la Science du droit* 60, *Relations extérieures des Communautés européennes* 62, *Conclusion et effet des traités internationaux selon le droit constitutionnel du G.-D. de Luxembourg* 64, *La Fusion des Communautés européennes* 65, *L'Union économique belgo-luxembourgeoise* 65, *La Fusion des Communautés européennes au lendemain des Accords de Luxembourg* 67, *Distribucion de competencias y de poderes entre los Estados miembros y las Communidas Europeas* 68, *Personnalité internationale et politique commerciale des communautés européennes* 68.
16 rue de la Fontaine, Luxembourg.
Telephone: Luxembourg 215-21.

Pesenti, Antonio; Italian economist and politician; b. 15 Oct. 1910; ed. Univs. of Pavia, Vienna, Berne, Paris, London School of Economics.
Lecturer Sassari Univ. 35; active in underground anti-Fascist movement 30-35; took part in Italian anti-Fascist Congress in Brussels 35; arrested and sentenced to 24 years' imprisonment by special tribunal; released Sept. 43; Under-Sec., later Min. of Finance April 44-June 45; Lecturer on Finance, Univ. of Rome 45; Prof. Univ. of Parma 48, of Pisa 60; Ed. *Critica Economica*; mem. Italian Constituent Assembly; Pres. Economic Centre for Reconstruction; mem. of Parliament 48, of Senate 53-; Communist.
Publs. *Politica finanziaria e monetaria dell' Inghilterra* 34, *La politica monetaria delle Devisenverordnungen* 33, *I soggetti passivi dell'obbligazione doganale* 34, *Ricostruire dalle rovine* 45, *Economia politica*, Vol. I 54, Vol. II. 58, *Scienza delle Finanze e diritto finanziario* 61.
Via Nomentana 372, Rome; Istituto di Economica e finanza, Università-Pisa, Italy.
Telephone: Rome 897530; Pisa 29537.

Pesmazoglu, John Stevens, PH.D.; Greek economist; b. 18; ed. Varvakion High School, Athens, Univ. of Athens, and St. John's Coll., Cambridge.
Served in Greek Albanian campaign 40-41 and in liberation of Greece 44-45; research student, Cambridge 45-49; Lecturer in Political Economy, Univ. of Athens 50-67, Prof. 67-; Dir.-Gen. Greek Ministry of Co-ordination in charge of econ. devt. and external financial relations 51-55; Econ. Adviser Bank of Greece 55-60; Alt. Gov. for Greece, Int. Monetary Fund (IMF) 55-67; Deputy Gov. Bank of Greece 60-67; Leader of Greek mission to negotiations for European Free Trade Area and asscn. of Greece with Common Market 57-61; Chair. Interdepartmental Cttee. for European Co-operation 62-65; Trustee Royal Hellenic Research Foundation; Grand Commdr. Royal Order of George I, Commdr. of the Phoenix; Commdr. Légion d'Honneur, Grand Commdr. of the Yugoslav Standard with Gold Crown.
Publs. Studies and articles on devt. and monetary policies and on European integration.
6 Neophytou Vamva Street, Athens (138), Greece.
Telephone: 712-458.

Petäjäniemi, (Armas) Eero (Emil); Finnish newspaper editor; b. 2 May 1907; ed. Univ. of Helsinki.
London corresp. *Helsingin Sanomat* 36-39, 46-49, Berlin corresp. (also for *Berlingske Tidende* and *Dagens Nyheter*) 39-44; Editor *Valitut Palat* (Readers Digest) 45; Helsinki corresp. *New York Times* 49-57; Editor-in-Chief *Iltasanomat* 49-56, *Uusi Suomi* 56-; Chief of Press and Information, Olympic Games, Helsinki 51-52; Chair. Helsinki Press. Asscn. and Board mem. Finnish Press Asscn. 50-57; Pres. Foreign Press Asscn., Berlin 44-45; mem. State Film Board 54-, Finnish News Bureau 56-; Perm. mem. Int. Press Inst. 53-; Pres. Int. Press Inst. Finnish Cttee. 63; White Rose (Knight), Olympic Cross of Merit I, Officer, French Black Star, Commdr. Icelandic Falcon, Medal of Merit, Finnish Press Asscn., etc.

Uusi Suomi, Lönnrotinkatu 4, Helsinki; Home: Mariankatu 8, Helsinki 17, Finland.
Telephone: 14696 (Home).

Péter, János; Hungarian ecclesiastic and politician; b. 10; ed. Budapest, Protestant Theological Faculty, Paris and Trinity Coll., Glasgow.
Bishop Transtibiscan Synod of the Reformed Church 49-56; Pres. Inst. of Cultural Relations 57-58; mem. of Nat. Assembly 53-; First Deputy Foreign Minister 58-61; mem. Presidential Council 57-61; Foreign Minister 61-; mem. Central Cttee. Hungarian Socialist Workers' Party 66-.
Foreign Ministry, Bem József Rakpart 47, Budapest, Hungary.

Peters, Sir Rudolph (Albert), Kt., M.C. (with Bar), M.D., F.R.S., F.R.C.P.; British university professor; b. 13 April 1889; ed. Wellington Coll., Berks., King's Coll. London, and Caius Coll., Cambridge, and St. Bartholomew's Hospital, London.
Benn W. Levy Student of Biochemistry Cambridge 12-13; served R.A.M.C. in First World War; fmr. Dunn Lecturer and Senior Demonstrator in Biochemistry, Cambridge; Whitley Prof., Oxford 23-54, Emeritus 54-; mem. Scientific Staff, Agricultural Research Council 54-59; Hon. Fellow of Trinity Coll. Oxford; Hon. Fellow Gonville and Caius Coll. Cambridge; Pres. Int. Council of Scientific Unions 58-61; Pres. Cambridge Philosophical Soc. 65-67; Assoc. Sciences Naturelles, Acad. Royale Belgique 48; hon. mem. Biochemical Soc., Royal Soc. Medicine, Nutrition Soc.; Foreign mem. Royal Neths. Acad. 50; Foreign hon. mem. American Acad. of Arts and Sciences 50, Soc. of Biochemistry, Biophysics and Microbiology, Helsinki; Foreign mem. Accad. Lincei, Rome; Hon. Fellow, Royal Soc. of Medicine 59; Royal Medal of Royal Soc. 49; Cameron Prize, Edinburgh 49; Hopkins Medal 59; Hon. Fellow, Royal Soc. of Edinburgh; U.S. Medal of Freedom (with Silver Palm) 47; Hon. M.D. (Liège) 50; F.R.S.E. (Hon.); Doctor h.c. (Paris); Hon. D.Sc. (Cincinnati, London, Leeds); Hon. D.M. (Amsterdam); Hon. D.Sc. (Aust. Nat. Univ.) 61; Hon. LL.D. (Glasgow Univ.) 63, Hon. mem. Physiological Soc. 65, American Inst. of Nutrition 67; Hon. Fellow Coll. of Pathology 67.
Publs. *Biochemical Lesions and Lethal Synthesis* 63, contribs. to scientific journals.
3 Newnham Walk, Cambridge; Department of Biochemistry, Tennis Court Road, Cambridge, England.
Telephone: 50819.

Petersen, Everett Newton, B.A., B.S.; American librarian and international civil servant; b. 15 Feb. 1909; ed. Wayne Univ., Univ. of Michigan, Columbia Univ. and Western Reserve Univ.
Director of Public Relations, Director of Extension Activities, Detroit Public Library 39-47; UNESCO 47-, Head, Public Library Development Section 48-57, Head, Division of Libraries, Documentation and Archives 57-64, Chief, UNESCO Library Service 64-.
UNESCO, Place de Fontenoy, Paris 7e, France.

Petersen, Harald; Danish editor and politician; b. 27 Oct. 1893; ed. Magleby Realskole and Gjedved Seminarium.
Studied languages and economics until 16; journalist with the *Ringsted Folketidende* 16; Parl. reporter for *Venstres Generalkorrespondance* 18-19; with Venstre Party Press Agency 19-; Head of Venstre Parl. Secretariat 20; Sec. of Venstre Parl. Group 25; Sec. of Venstre nat. org. 29-45; mem. of Lower House 43-50; Vice-Pres. of Venstre Parl. Group 45-; Minister of Defence 45-47; Man. Dir. Mortgage Bank of Kingdom of Denmark 48-50 and 53-64; Minister of Defence 50-53; mem. Venstre (Danish Liberal Party).
Strandvej 223, Charlottenlund, Denmark.

Petersen, Howard C., B.A., J.D., LL.D.; American lawyer and banker; b. 7 May 1910; ed. De Pauw Univ., Univ. of Michigan Law School.

Admitted to N.Y. Bar 35; Assoc. of Cravath, de Gersdorff, Swaine & Wood (Law firm) 33-41; mem. of Nat. Emergency Cttee. of Mil. Training Camps Asscn. 40; one of principal drafters of Burke-Wadsworth Bill; Counsel Cttee. for drafting regulations under Selective Service Act 40; Asst. to Under-Sec. of War 41, Exec. Asst. to Under-Sec. of War, Special Asst. to Sec. of War 45, Asst. Sec. of War 46-47; Exec. Vice-Pres. and Dir. Fidelity-Philadelphia Trust Co. Pa. (now The Fidelity Bank) 47-50, Pres. 50-66, Chair. 66-; Nat. Finance Chair. Citizens Cttee. for Eisenhower 52; Chair. Board of Managers Univ. of Pa. Museum, Advisory Cttee. of Export-Import Bank; Trustee, Cttee. for Econ. Devt., Int. Legal Center; Carnegie Endowment for Int. Peace; mem. President's Cttee. on Educ. Beyond the High School 57; Special Asst. to Pres. for Trade Policy 61-62; Formulation and promotion of Trade Expansion Act 62; Negotiated conclusion of GATT tariff negotiations with EEC 60-62; Rep. on Fed. Advisory Council 60-63; Pres. Pa. Bankers' Asscn. 63-64; mem. American Philosophical Soc., Council on Foreign Relations; Dir. and Vice-Chair. Adela Investment Co. S.A.; Dir. American Acad. Political and Social Science, Panama Canal Co., Insurance Co. of N. America, Fed. Reserve Bank of Philadelphia, Commonwealth Land Title Insurance Co.; Co-Chair. Greater Philadelphia Movement; Medal for Merit 45, Exceptional Civilian Service Award 45, Selective Service Medal 46; LL.D. St. Joseph's Coll. 62; D.Sc. Drexel Inst. 62.

Radnor, Pennsylvania; The Fidelity Bank, Broad and Walnut Streets, Philadelphia, Pa. 19109, U.S.A.

Petersen, Kristen Helveg; Danish politician; b. 29 Nov. 1909; ed. Skaarup Teachers Training Coll.

Inspector of Schools 53-57; State Adviser, Ministry of Educ. 57-61, Minister 61-64, Dir. of Educ. 64-65; Chair. Co-ordinating Cttee. for Educ. 64; Chair. Planning Cttee. for Higher Educ. 65-; Amb. in disarmament question 66; mem. of Folketing; text-books and articles on education.

Skindergade 28, Copenhagen K, Denmark.

Petersen, William E., A.B., B.S.; American banker; b. 20 Sept. 1906; ed. Columbia Coll. and Columbia School of Business.

Joined Irving Trust Co., N.Y.C. 28, Vice-Pres. 47-57, Senior Vice-Pres. 57-60, Dir. 59-, Pres. 60-; Pres. and Dir. Irving Int. Banking Corp., Irving Int. Finance Corpn.; Dir. Charter New York Corpn.; Chair. Board of Trustees, Columbia Univ.; Trustee Clarkson Coll. of Technology; Dir. West Virginia Pulp & Paper Co.; mem. Asscn. of Reserve City Bankers; Hon. D.H.L. (Clarkson Coll. of Technology, N.Y.).

Irving Trust Company, One Wall Street, New York 10015; Home: 18 Dellwood Circle, Bronxville, New York 10708, N.Y., U.S.A.

Telephone: 212-553-2743 (Office).

Peterson, Roger Tory; American ornithologist; b. 28 Aug. 1908; ed. Nat. Acad. of Design.

Decorative artist 26; Science and Art Instructor, Brookline, Mass. 31-34; engaged in bird painting and illustration of bird books 34-; on admin. staff of Nat. Audubon Soc., Sec. 60-; U.S. Army 43-45; Ed. Houghton Mifflin Co. Field Guide Series 46-, Naturalist Series 65-; Art Dir. Nat. Wildlife Fed.; Hon. D.Sc. (Franklin and Marshall Coll., Ohio State Univ., Allegheny Coll.); numerous medals.

Publs. *Field Guide to the Birds* 34, *Junior Book of Birds* 39, *A Field Guide to Western Birds* 41, *Birds over America* 48, *How to Know the Birds* 49, *Wildlife in Color* 51, *A Field Guide to the Birds of Britain and Europe* (with Guy Mountfort and P. A. D. Hollom) 54,

Wild America (with James Fisher) 55, *The Bird Watcher's Anthology* 57, *Field Guide to Birds of Texas* 60, *The Wonderful World of Birds* (with James Fisher) 64, *The Birds* 63, *Field Guide to Wildflowers* 68; co-author: *The Audubon Guide to Attracting Birds;* Illustrator: *Birds of South Carolina, Birds of Newfoundland, Arizona and its Birdlife, Birds of Nova Scotia, Birds of Colorado.*

Neck Road, Old Lyme, Connecticut, U.S.A.

Telephone: 434-7800.

Peterson, Rudolph A.; American (born Sweden) banker; b. 6 Dec. 1904; ed. Univ. of Calif. Coll. of Commerce.

Field Rep., successively Vice-Pres. and Gen. Man. Mexico City, Div. Operations Man., Chicago, Commercial Credit Co. 25-36; Dist. Man. Fresno, later Vice-Pres. San Francisco, Bank of America Nat. Trust and Savings Asscn. 36-46; Pres. Allied Building Credits 46-52; Vice-Pres. Transamerica Corpn. 52-55; Pres. Man. Exec. Officer, Bank of Hawaii, Honolulu 56-61; Vice-Chair. of Board of Dirs. Bank of America Nat. Trust and Savings Asscn. 61-63, Pres. 63-; Dir. Dillingham Corpn., Asscn. of Reserve City Bankers, Fireman's Fund Insurance Co., Fund American Companies, Int. Executive Service Corps, Swedish Chamber of Commerce of U.S.A.

Bank of America National Trust and Savings Association, 300 Montgomery Street, San Francisco, California; Home: 11 Glen Alpine Road, Piedmont, Calif., U.S.A. Telephone: 658-4261 (Home).

Pétin, Jean; French manufacturer; b. 4 Feb. 1903. Chair. Ets. J. J. Carnaud & Forges de Basse-Indre 45-; Vice-Chair. Soc. Nantaise des Chargeurs de l'Ouest. Office: 37 rue de Surène, Paris 8e; Home: 56 rue de Varenne, Paris 7e, France.

Petit, Daniel; French financial official; b. 4 March 1918; ed. Lycée de Rheims and Faculty of Law, Univ. of Paris.

Auditor, Court of Accounts 45; Chef de Cabinet of Min. of Armed Forces 48, Vice-Pres. of Council 48; Referendary Councillor 50; Technical Councillor to Cabinet 53-54, to Min. of Finance 54-55; Gen. Sec. La Bourse de Paris (Stock Exchange) 62-.

4 place de la Bourse, Paris 2e, France and 11 rue Marbeau, Paris 16e, France.

Petit, Eugène Pierre (pseudonym **Claudius**)**;** French politician and town planner; b. 22 May 1907; ed. Ecole Nationale Supérieure des Arts Décoratifs.

Former cabinet-maker and teacher; mem. Chamber of Deputies 46-55, 58-62; Minister of Reconstruction and Town Planning 48-53; Mayor of Firminy 53-; Minister of Labour 54; Vice-Pres. Nat. Assembly 59-60, 61-62; Pres. Entente démocratique Group, Nat. Assembly 62; Officier Légion d'Honneur, Compagnon de la Libération, Croix de Guerre (39-45).

17 rue des Barres, Paris 4e, France.

Petit, Pierre; French composer; b. 21 April 1922; ed. Lycée Louis-le-Grand, Université de Paris à la Sorbonne and Conservatoire de Paris.

Head of Course, Conservatoire de Paris 50; Dir. of Light Music, Office de Radiodiffusion et Télévision Française (ORTF) 60-64, Dir. of Musical Productions, ORTF 64-; Dir.-Gen. Ecole Normale de Musique de Paris 63-; Music Critic of *Parisien-Liberé;* mem. Gov. Council Conservatoire de Paris; Officier des Arts et Lettres; Officier de l'Ordre du Cèdre du Liban; Premier Grand Prix de Rome 46.

Compositions include: Suite for four 'cellos 45, *Zadig* (ballet) 48, *Ciné-Bijou* (ballet) 52, *Feu Rouge, Feu Vert* 54, Concerto for piano and orchestra 56, Concerto for organ and orchestra 60, *Furia Italiana* 60, Concerto for two guitars and orchestra 65.

Publ. *Verdi* 57.

2 rue de l'Amiral-Cloué, Paris 16e, France.

Petit, Roland (husband of Zizi Jeanmaire, *q.v.*); French dancer and choreographer; b. 13 Jan. 1924; ed. Paris Opera Ballet School.

Premier Danseur Paris Opera 40-44; founded Les Vendredis de la Danse 44, Les Ballets de Champs-Elysées 45, Les Ballets de Paris 48; Chevalier des Arts et des Lettres.

Works include *Le Rossignol et la Rose, Le Jeune Homme et la Mort, Les Demoiselles de la Nuit, Deuil en Vingt-quatre Heures, Le Loup, Cyrano de Bergerac, Carmen, Les Forains, La Belle au Bois Dormant, Hans Christian Andersen, Folies Bergères, L'Eloge de la Folie, Paradise Lost.*

12 rue de la Paix, Paris 2e, France.

Petit de Murat-Regunaga, Ulyses Raúl; Argentine writer; b. 28 Jan. 1907; ed. Colegio Nacional de San Isidro.

Former journalist; Nat. Prize for Literature 42, 43, 44; Nat. Prize for Cinematography 43, 44; Fellow Int. Inst. of Arts and Letters, Lindau; Vice-Pres. Argentine Soc. of Writers; Pres. Consejo Cine de la Sociedad General de Autores de la Argentina.

Works: Poetry: *Las Islas* (Civic Prize of Buenos Aires) 35, *Conmemoraciones* 29, *Rostros* 31, *Marea de Lágrimas* 37, *Aprendizaje de la Soledad* 42, *Las Manos Separadas* 51, *Ultimo Lugar* 65; Plays: *La Novia de Arena* 45, *Un Espejo para la Santa, Un Patricio del 80X, Ultimo Lugar* 64, *Estampas de la Tierra Purpúrea* 66; Films: *Prisioneros de la Tierra* 40, *La Guerra Gaucha* 42, *Todo un Hombre* 43, *Donde Mueren las Palabras* 46, *Su Mejor Alumno* (First Prize, Argentine Acad. of Cinematography) 44, *Tierra del Fuego* (First Prize, Argentine Acad. of Cinematography) 49, *Suburbio* 50, *La Orquidea* 51, *Reto a la Vida* 53, *Mulata* 53, *La Entrega* 54, *La Duda* 54, *En Cuerpo y Alma* 54, *Juventud Desenfrenada* 56, *Esposas Infieles* 57, *Magia Negra, Manicomio, La Rebelión de los Adolescentes* 58, *El Dinero de Dios* 59, *El Romance de un Gaucho* (Prize, Best Script, Instituto Nacional de Cine) 62, *El Perseguidor* 65, *Al Diablo con este Cura* 67; Novels: *El Balcón Hacia La Muerte, La Vida Fanática, El Miserable Amor, La Noche de Buenos Aires* 63; Essays: *Genio y Figura de Benito Lynch* 68.

O'Higgins 1399, Buenos Aires, Argentina.

Telephone: 73-2879.

Petitpierre, Max, Docteur en droit; Swiss barrister and notary; b. 26 Feb. 1899; ed. Univ. of Neuchâtel, Zürich and Munich.

Barrister 22; Doctor of Law 24; Notary 25; Prof. of Private Int. Law and of Comparative Civil Law in Law Faculty of Univ. of Neuchâtel 26-31 and 38-44; Pres. of the Swiss Chamber of Watchmakers 43-44; Deputy to the Council of States 42-44; mem. of Federal Council 45-61; fmr. Chief of Fed. Political Dept.; Chair. Nestlé Alimentana Co.; Pres. Swiss Confederation 50, 55 and 60; Radical.

Publs. *Les Conventions conclues par la Suisse avec l'Allemagne, l'Autriche et la Tchécoslovaquie concernant la reconnaissance et l'exécution des jugements civils* 33, *Le droit applicable à la succession des étrangers domiciliés en Suisse* 29, *La reconnaissance et l'exécution des jugements civils étrangers en Suisse* 25, *Droit international privé de la Suisse.*

Port-Roulant 3a, Neuchâtel, Switzerland.

Petrassi, Goffredo; Italian composer; b. 16 July 1904; ed. Conservatorio S. Cecilia, Rome.

Superintendent Teatro Fenice, Venice 37-40; Pres. Int. Society for Contemporary Music 54-56; now Prof. of Composition, Conservatorio S. Cecilia.

Works include: orchestral: *Partita* 32, *First Concerto* 33, *Second Concerto* 51, *Récréation Concertante* (Third Concerto) 53, *Fourth Concerto* 54, *Fifth Concerto* 55, *Invenzione Concertata* 57, *Quartet* 57; operas and ballets: *Follia di Orlando* 43, *Ritratto di don Chisciotte* 45, *Il Cordovano* 48, *Morte dell'Aria* 50; choral works:

Salmo IX 36, *Magnificat* 40, *Coro di Morti* 41, *Noche Oscura* 51, *Mottetti* 65; voice and orchestra *Quattro Inni Sacre* 42; chamber music: *Serenata* 58, *Trio* 59, *Suoni Notturni* 59, *Propos d'Alain* 60, *Concerto Flauto* 60, *Seconda Serenata-Trio* 62, *Settimo Concerto* 64.

Via Flaminia 43, Rome, Italy.

Telephone: 378264.

Petrén, Bror Arvid Sture; Swedish lawyer; b. 3 Oct. 1908; ed. Lund Univ., Kungliga Univ. of Uppsala, and Albert-Ludwigs-Univ., Freiburg im Breisgau.

Judge Svea Court of Appeal 43; Head Legal Dept. Ministry of Foreign Affairs 49-63; Legal Adviser, Swedish Del. to UN 48-60; Deputy Vice-Pres. Labour Court of Sweden 51-63; Pres. Svea Court of Appeal 63-67; mem. European Comm. of Human Rights 54-66, Pres. 62-66; Judge, Int. Court of Justice 66-; mem. Perm. Court of Arbitration 55-; Grand Cross Order of Polar Star and other decorations.

Publs. *La confiscation des biens étrangères et les réclamations internationales auxquelles elle peut donner lieu, History of the Svea Court of Appeal 1614-1654* 64.

International Court of Justice, The Hague, Netherlands.

Petrén, (Bror Erik) Gustaf, D.IUR.; Swedish judge; b. 5 Dec. 1917; ed. Lund Cathedral School and Univ. of Lund.

Assistant Judge, Town Court of Stockholm 45-51, Asst. Judge, Court of Appeal (Stockholm) 52-60, Ordinary Judge 61-; Asst. Prof. Stockholm Univ. 49-; Chair. Swedish Section, Int. Comm. of Jurists 59-; Sec.-Gen. Nordic Council (Swedish Section) 52-; Knight Commdr. Order of Polar Star 61, and of Icelandic Falcon 65.

Publs. *Compulsion in Public Law* 49, Ed. *Press Legislation* 65, *Basic Laws of Sweden* 68.

Styrmansgatan 5, Stockholm, Sweden.

Telephone: 08-673301.

Petridis, Peto; Greek composer; b. 92; ed. American Robert Coll.

Corresp. *The Musical Times,* London 15, *The Christian Science Monitor* 26-28, *Vimo, Proia, Kathimerini,* Athens; Ed. *Combat* 25-28; mem. Acad. of Athens.

Compositions include: *Le Clavier Modal, Greek and Ionic Suites,* piano suites, three piano concertos, *Digenis Akritas* 37-39, five symphonies, violin and cello concertos, oratorio *St. Paul, Byzantine Requiem,* opera *Zefyra,* ballet *The Pedlar,* symphonic music for *Sound and Light on the Acropolis,* etc.

90 Queen Sophia Avenue, Athens, Greece.

Petrie, Sir Charles, Bt., C.B.E., M.A., F.R.HIST.S.; British writer; b. 28 Sept. 1895; ed. privately and Corpus Christi Coll., Oxford.

Royal Artillery 14-19; attached Secretariat War Cabinet 18-19; mem. staff *Outlook* 25-28; Foreign Editor *English Review* 31-37; corresp. mem. Royal Spanish Acad. of History, Inst. Fernando El Católico, Saragossa; Pres. Military History Soc. of Ireland; Assoc. Editor *Empire Review* 40-41, Editor 41-43; Managing Editor *New English Review* 45-50; Editor *Household Brigade Magazine* 44-; on staff of *Illustrated London News* 58-; Hon. D.Phil. (Valladolid).

Publs. *History of Government* 29, *George Canning* 30, revised 46, *Mussolini* 31, *The Jacobite Movement* 32, 59, *Monarchy* 33, *History of Spain* (with Louis Bertrand) 34, *Spain* 34, *Letters of King Charles I* 35, *William Pitt* 35, *The Four Georges* 35, *Walter Long and His Times* 36, *Bolingbroke* 37, *Lords of the Inland Sea* 37, *The Chamberlain Tradition* 38, *Louis XIV* 38, *The Life and Letters of Austen Chamberlain* 39, 40, *Twenty Years' Armistice—and After* 40, *When Britain Saved Europe* 41, *Diplomatic History 1713-1933* 46, *Earlier Diplomatic History 1492-1713* 49, *Chapters of Life* 50, *The Marshal Duke of Berwick* 53, *Lord Liverpool and His Times* 55, *Wellington: A Reassessment* 56, *The Spanish Royal House* 58, *The Victorians* 60, *The Modern British Monarchy* 61,

Philip II of Spain 63, *King Alfonso XIII and His Age* 63, *Scenes of Edwardian Life* 65, *Don John of Austria* 67. 190 Coleherne Court, London, S.W.5, England.

Petrie, Joseph Richards, M.A., PH.D.; Canadian economist; b. 12 April 1908; ed. New Brunswick, Chicago and McGill Univs.
Deputy Assessor Chicago 32-35; Prof. Economics and Politics New Brunswick Univ. 40-50; Sec. New Brunswick Advisory Board Economic Development 40-45; Asst. Co-ordinator of Production Dept. of Munitions and Supply 42-43; Asst. Dir. Canadian Mutual Aid Board 43; Sec. New Brunswick Cttee. of Reconstruction 43-45; Vice-Pres. Khaki Univ. of Canada in the U.K. 45-46; Pres. Maritime Intercollegiate Athletic Union 47-50; Associated Alumni Univ. of New Brunswick 47-50; Chair. Fredericton Tax Comm. 47; Dir. of Research Canadian Tax Foundation 50-52; Dir. of Research, Jones Heward & Co. 52-56; Pres. Montreal Inst. of Investment Analysts 55-56; Gov. Sir George Williams Univ. 56-; Consulting Economist 57; mem. Federal Cttee. on Unemployment Insurance 62-63; Pres. Canadian Caribbean Corp. Ltd., Barbados, W.I. 64-; Econ. Adviser to West Indies Stock Exchange, Trinidad 65-.
Publs. *The Regional Economy of New Brunswick* 44, *The Taxation of Corporate Income in Canada* 52, *The Beverage Distilling Industry in Canada* 57, *Some Economic Facts About the Beverage Distilling Industry in Canada* 61, *Fiscal Policy and the Development of the Canadian Tax System* 64, *The Capital Market in Canada* 65, *A Review of Some Critical Issues in the Report of the Royal Commission on Taxation* 67.
1408 Laird Boulevard, Montreal 16, Canada.
Telephone: 874-3656; and 737-6089.

Petrilli, Giuseppe; Italian administrator; b. 24 March 1913; ed. Univ. of Rome.
Pres. Inst. Nat. d'Assurances contre les maladies; Pres. Nat. Organisation of Ecoles des Services Sociaux; mem. Council of Economy and Work; mem. E.E.C. Commission, Pres. Social Affairs Section 58-60; Pres. Inst. for Industrial Reconstruction (IRI) 60-; Pres. Italian Council of European Movement 64-; Vanoni Prize 64.
Istituto per la Ricostruzione Industriale, Via Vittorio Veneto 89, Rome, Italy.

Petrosian, Tigran Vartanovich; Soviet chess-player; b. 1929; ed. Teachers' Coll., Erevan.
Chess Champion of Tiflis 47, later Champion of Georgia and Armenia; Moscow City Champion 51; Grand Master 52, later Int. Grand Master; World Chess Champion 63; Post-graduate Student in Philosophy, Teachers' Coll. Erevan 62-.
Central Council of Union of Sport Societies and Organizations, Skaterny pereulok 4, Moscow, U.S.S.R.

Petrosyants, Andronik Melikonovich; Soviet politician; b. 06; ed. Urals Engineering Mechanical Inst.
Engineer Ural Machine Works 33-39; Deputy People's Commissar for Heavy Machine Building 39-41; First Deputy to People's Commissariat of Machine Tool Industry 39-41; People's Commissar of the Tank Industry 41-45; Staff of Ministry of Medium Machine Building 45-55, Deputy Minister 55-62; Chair. State Cttee. for Use of Atomic Energy 62-; Order of Lenin.
State Committee for Use of Atomic Energy, Moscow, U.S.S.R.

Petrov, Boris Nikolaevich; Soviet power engineer; b. 13; ed. Moscow Power Engineering Inst.
Associate, Inst. of Automation and Telemechanics, U.S.S.R. Acad. of Sciences 39-; Instructor Moscow Aviation Inst. 44-, Prof. 48-; corresp. mem. U.S.S.R. Acad. of Sciences 53-60, mem. 60-; Dept. Head Inst. of Automation and Telemechanics, U.S.S.R. Acad. of Sciences 60-; Chief Editor *Technical Cybernetics Series*, U.S.S.R. Acad. of Sciences Bulletin.

Publs. *The Construction and Conversion of Structural Systems* 45, *The Principle of Invariance and Conditions for its Application in Calculating Linear and Non-Linear Systems* 60, *On Evaluation of Oscillation Processes in Complex Non-Linear Systems with Different Original Deviations* 64.
Institute of Automation and Telemechanics, U.S.S.R. Academy of Sciences, 15a Kalanchouskaya, Moscow, U.S.S.R.

Petrov, Georgy Ivanovich; Soviet hydro-aeromechanic; b. 12; ed. Moscow Univ.
Research Insts. 35-; Prof. Moscow Univ. 53-; corresp. mem. U.S.S.R. Acad. of Sciences 53-58, mem. 58-; Bureau mem. Dept. of Technical Science, U.S.S.R. Acad. of Sciences 60-; Editor-in-Chief *Izvestiya Akademsi Nauk S.S.S.R., Seriya Mekhanika* (Bulletin of the U.S.S.R. Acad. of Sciences, Mechanics Series); State Prize 49.
Publs. *The Propagation of Oscillations in a Viscous Liquid, and the Inception of Turbulence* 38, *The Application of Galerkin's Method to the Problem of Flow Stability in a Viscous Liquid* 40, *Estimation of Accuracy of Approximate Calculation of Proper Value by Galerkin's Method* 57.
State University, Lenin Hills, Moscow, U.S.S.R.

Petrov, Ioakim Romanovich; Soviet physiopathologist; b. 1893; ed. Military Medical Acad.
Assistant Military Doctor 12-20; Asst. Lecturer, Doctor, Junior Lecturer Military Medical Acad. 22-37; Head of Lab. Inst. of Hygiene of Labour and Safety Engineering 26-36; Senior Lecturer, Head of Chair, Consulting Prof. Military Medical Acad. 37-; Corresp. mem. U.S.S.R. Acad. of Medical Sciences 53-60, mem. 60-; Head of Lab. Inst. of Blood Transfusion, Leningrad 32-62; Head of Chair, First Leningrad Medical Inst. 39-40; Scientific Consultant, Leningrad Inst. of Blood Transfusion 62-; Deputy Chair. U.S.S.R. Soc. of Physiopathologists, mem. Int. Soc. of Blood Transfusion; Order of Lenin, Red Banner of Labour, Red Banner, etc.
Publs. Over 250 works on problems of pathological physiology, electric traumas, shock, oxygen hunger, loss of blood, blood substituting solutions, restoration of the function of brain after clinical death.
Kirov Military Medical Academy, 6 Lebedev Street, Leningrad, U.S.S.R.

Petrov, Vladimir Mikhailovich; Soviet trade corporation official; b. 22; ed. Industrial Inst. of the Urals and Acad. of Foreign Trade.
Soviet Baltic Fleet 39-42; foundry worker 40-42; Asst. Dir., later Dir., Electrical Engineering Office, *Mashinoimport* (mining, electrical, railway goods, etc.) 49-51; other posts, *Mashinoimport*, then *Mashinoexport* 51-55; Asst. Soviet Trade Rep. in Yugoslavia 56-59; Soviet Trade Rep. in Iraq 59-61; Chair. *Autoexport* (automobiles) 61-; mem. C.P.S.U.; several decorations.
V/O Autoexport, Ministry of Foreign Trade, 32-34 Smolenskaya-Sennaya Square, Moscow, U.S.S.R.

Petrovsky, Boris Vasilyevich; Soviet surgeon; b. 1908; ed. First Moscow Univ.
Physician at various hospitals 30-50; mem. C.P.S.U. 42-; Head of Chair of Surgery, Second Moscow Inst. of Medicine 51-56; Head of Chair of Hospital Surgery, First Moscow Medical Inst., and Dir. Inst. of Clinical and Experimental Surgery 56-65; Minister of Health of U.S.S.R. 65-; Candidate mem. Central Cttee. C.P.S.U.; Deputy to U.S.S.R. Supreme Soviet; mem. U.S.S.R. Acad. of Medical Sciences 57-; mem. U.S.S.R. Acad. of Sciences; Honoured Scientific Worker of R.S.F.S.R.
Main works: has studied problems of blood transfusion, oncology, surgery of vessels and organs of thoracic cavity, surgical treatment of congenital and acquired heart diseases.
Publs. *Drip Transfusion of Blood and Blood-Substitute*

Compounds 48, *Surgical Treatment of Vascular Wounds* 49, *Surgical Treatment of Carcinoma of the Oesophagus and Cardia* 50, *Blood Transfusion in Surgery* 54.
U.S.S.R. Ministry of Health, Rakhmanovsky pereulok 3, Moscow, U.S.S.R.

Petrovsky, Ivan Georgievich; Soviet mathematician; b. 18 Jan. 1901; ed. Moscow Univ.
Prof. of Mathematics 33; mem. U.S.S.R. Acad. of Sciences 46-; mem. Presidium 48-; Rector of Moscow Univ. 51-; mem. Presidium of U.S.S.R. Supreme Soviet; State prizewinner 46, 52; awarded Order of Lenin.
Principal Publs. *On the Topology of Real Plane Algebraic Curves* (*Annals of Mathematics, Princeton, N.Y. 1938*) 38, *Lectures on Partial Differential Equations* 55, *On the number of the limit cycles of the equation* $\frac{dy}{dx} = \frac{P(x,y)}{Q(x,y)}$, *where* $P(x,y)$ *and* $Q(x,y)$ *are polynomials* (with E. M. Landis) 55, 57, *Lecture on the Theory of the Properties of Differential Equations* 64.
Moscow University, Lenin Hills, Moscow B-234, U.S.S.R.

Petryanov-Sokolov, Igor Vasilevich; Soviet physical chemist; b. 1907; ed. Moscow Univ.
Professor Moscow Chemical Technological Inst. 47-; Assoc. Karpov Physico-chemical Inst., U.S.S.R. Acad. of Sciences; Corresp. mem. U.S.S.R. Acad. of Sciences 53-66, mem. 66-; Chief Editor *Khimiya i zhizn* 64-; Order of Lenin; State Prize.
U.S.S.R. Academy of Sciences, 14 Lenin Prospekt, Moscow, U.S.S.R.

Petrželka, Karel, LL.D.; Czechoslovak lawyer; b. 2 April 1907; ed. Brno Univ.
Several years service as judge before Second World War; Chair. Cttee. of New Codification of Czechoslovak Law 48-50 (Ministry of Justice); Lecturer in Int. Law Charles Univ., Prague; Dir. Legal Dept. Min. of Foreign Affairs 50-52; Ambassador to U.S.A. 52-59; Czechoslovak Rep. (Vice-Chair.) IAEA 59-60; mem. Del. VI-XII Sessions UN Gen. Assembly; Chair. Legal Cttee. XI UN Gen. Assembly; Chair. Czechoslovak Del. UN Conf. on Consular Relations; Chair. Czechoslovak Del. III, IV and VI Gen. Conf. IAEA; Minister to Austria 62-66; Chief of the Office of the Nat. Assembly 66-67; mem. Legal Comm. Central Cttee., C.P. of Czechoslovakia 66; Amb. to Cambodia and Laos 67-.
Ministry of Foreign Affairs, Prague 1, Černínský palác, Czechoslovakia.

Petterssen, Sverre, PH.D., C.B.E.; American meteorologist; b. 19 Feb. 1898.
Chief of Met. Office Bergen 31-39; Prof. and Head of Met. Dept. Mass. Inst. of Technology 39-42; served with Met. Office British Air Ministry 42-45; Chief of Norwegian Weather Forecasting Service 45-48; Dir. Scientific Services U.S. Air Force, Weather Service 48-52; Prof. of Meteorology, Univ. of Chicago 52-63, Chair. Dept. of Meteorology 60-61; Chair. Dept. of Geophysical Sciences, Univ. of Chicago 61-63; Pres. of Comm. on Maritime Met. 39-46 and of Aerological Comm. of Int. Met. Org. 46-51; Pres. Met. Div. of ICAO 46, and of Tech. Comm. of Conf. of North Atlantic States 46; mem. Norwegian Acad. of Science and Letters; Pres. American Meteorological Soc. 58-60; Hon. mem. Royal Meteorological Soc., Peruvian Meteorological Soc.; Foreign mem. Finnish Acad.; Buys Ballot Gold Medal, Netherlands Acad. of Science 48; N.Y. Board of Trade Gold Award; U.S.A.F. Distinguished Service Award and of Chicago Council of Scientific Societies; Charles Franklin Brooks Award, American Meteor Soc.; Cross of Liberation; Commdr. Order of St. Olav.
Publs. *Weather Analysis and Forecasting, Introduction to Meteorology.*
5700 Blackstone Avenue, Chicago, Ill., U.S.A.

Petukhov, Boris Fyodorovich; Soviet politician; b. 1913; ed. Rostov-on-Don Inst. of Agricultural Engineering.

Engineer 36-50; mem. C.P.S.U. 40-; First Sec. Armavir City Cttee. of C.P. 50-51; First Vice-Chair. Exec. Cttee. Krasnodar Territorial Soviet of Working People's Deputies 51-52, Chair. Exec. Cttee. 54-60; Second Sec. Krasnodar Territorial Cttee. of C.P. 52-54; Second Sec. North Ossetia Regional Cttee. of C.P. 60-61; First Sec. Kirov Regional Cttee. of C.P. 61-; Candidate mem. Central Cttee. of C.P.S.U. 61-; Deputy to Supreme Soviet of U.S.S.R.; mem. Budget Cttee. of Soviet Union.
Kirov Regional Committee of C.P.S.U., Kirov, U.S.S.R.

Petukhov, Valentin Afanasevich; Soviet nuclear physicist; b. 07; ed. Leningrad Polytechnic Inst.
Teacher of Physics Kharkov Physical Inst. 34-54; Dep. Dir. High Energy Lab. United Inst. Nuclear Research Dubna 54-; has worked in cosmology and on accelerators; Lenin Prize for his part in creating 10,000 million electron volt syncrophasotron.
United Institute of Nuclear Research, Dubna, Moscow Region, U.S.S.R.

Peugeot, Rodolphe; French businessman; b. 2 April 1902.
Pres. and Man. Dir. Société Peugeot et Cie., Société Comtoise de Participation; Dir. Soc. des Automobiles Peugeot, Ets. Peugeot Frères and of a number of other concerns; Officier Légion d'Honneur, Croix de Guerre, Médaille de la Résistance.
Home: 47 rue Spontini, Paris 16e; Office: 102 rue Danton, Levallois (Seine), France.

Peugeot, Roland; French motor-car executive; b. 20 March 1926; ed. Lycées Janson-de-Sailly and Saint-Louis Paris and Harvard Business School, Mass., U.S.A.
President Etablissements Peugeot Frères; Vice-Pres. and Gen. Man. Peugeot S.A.; Vice-Pres. Automobiles Peugeot; Dir. of subsidiaries and other companies.
170 avenue Victor-Hugo, Paris 16e, France.

Pevler, Herman H., B.S., C.E.; American transportation executive; b. 20 April 1903; ed. Purdue Univ.
Engineer, Supervisor of Tracks, Pennsylvania Railroad Co. 27-35, Div. Engineer, Supt. 35-42, Gen. Supt. E.-Pennsylvania Div. 42-46, Gen. Man. W. Region 46, Central Region 46-48, Vice-Pres. New York Zone 48-51, Vice-Pres. W. Region 51-55, Vice-Pres. and Regional Man. N.W. Region 55-59; Pres. Wabash Railroad System 59-63; Pres. and Dir. Norfolk and Western Railway Co. and wholly-owned subsidiaries 63-; official of business, civic and educational orgs.
Office: 8 N. Jefferson Street, Roanoke, Va. 24011; Home: 15 Cardinal Road, S.W., Roanoke, Va. 24014, U.S.A.
Telephone: 344-9863 (Office); 342-7407 (Home).

Pevsner, Nikolaus, C.B.E., M.A., PH.D., F.S.A., F.R.I.B.A., F.B.A.; British university teacher and art historian; b. 30 Jan. 1902; ed. St. Thomas's School, Leipzig and Univs. of Leipzig, Berlin, Munich and Frankfurt.
Asst. Keeper, Dresden Art Gallery 24-28; Lecturer, Göttingen Univ. 28-33; Prof. of Art History, Birkbeck Coll. Univ. of London 44-; Slade Prof. of Fine Art, Univ. of Cambridge 49-55; Fellow of St. John's Coll. 49-55; Art Editor Penguin Books and Joint Editor *The Architectural Review*; Henry Elias Howland Memorial Prize, Yale Univ. 63; Royal Gold Medal for Architecture 67.
Publs. *The Baroque Architecture of Leipzig* (in German) 28, *Italian Painting from the End of the Renaissance to the End of the Rococo* (in German) 27-30, *Pioneers of Modern Design* 36 (revised and enlarged 60), *An Enquiry into Industrial Art in England* 37, *Academies of Art, Past and Present* 40, *German Baroque Sculpture* (with S. Sitwell and A. Ayscough) 38, *An Outline of European Architecture* 43, 63, *Matthew Digby Watt* 50, *High Victorian Design* 51, *The Buildings of England* 51, etc. (34 vols. to date), *The Englishness of English Art* 56, *The Planning of the Elizabethan Country House* 61, etc.
2 Wildwood Terrace, North End, London, N.W.3.

Pew, J(ohn) Howard; American businessman; b. 27 Jan. 1882; ed. Grove City Coll., Pa., and Mass. Inst. of Technology.
Engineer, Marcus Hook Refinery, Sun Oil Co. 01, Asst. Supt., Supt., Vice-Pres. and Pres. 12-47, Chair. of Board 63-; Dir. Sun Oil Co., Sun Shipbuilding and Dry Dock Co., Pres. Board of Trustees, Grove City Coll.
Home: Knollbrook, Mill Creek Road, Ardmore, Pa., Office: 1608 Walnut Street, Philadelphia 3, Pa., U.S.A.

Peyrefitte, Alain Antoine; French diplomatist, politician and writer; b. 26 Aug. 1925; ed. Lycée de Montpellier, Ecole Normale Supérieure, Univs. de Montpellier et de Paris à la Sorbonne.
Secretary, Bonn 47; Dep. Dir. of European Orgs. 56-58; Counsellor of Foreign Affairs 58; Dep. 58-; Rep. Assembly European Parliament and UN Gen. Assembly 59-62; Sec. of State to Prime Minister (Information) 62, (Repatriates) 62; Minister of Information Dec. 62-66; Minister-Del. for Scientific Research and Atomic Questions 66-67; Minister of Educ. 67-May 68; Union pour la Nouvelle République (UNR).
Publs. *Rue d'Ulm, les Roseaux froissés, le Mythe de Pénélope, le Sentiment de Confiance, Faut-il partager l'Algérie?*
Home: Les Uzelles Chartrettes, S.-et-M., France.

Peyrefitte, (Pierre) Roger, B.A.; French author; b. 17 Aug. 1907; ed. Coll. d'Ardouane (Hérault), du Caousou (Toulouse), Lycée (Foix), Toulouse Univ., Ecole des Sciences Politiques, Paris.
Joined Diplomatic Service 31; Attaché, Ministry of Foreign Affairs 31-33, 38-40; Sec. Athens 33-38; resigned 40; re-instated 43, mem. del. of French Govt. in occupied France 43-45; dismissed 45; re-instated by judgement of Council of State 62.
Publs. *Les Amitiés Particulières* (Prix Théophraste Renaudot) 44-45, *Mademoiselle de Murville* 46, *Le Prince des Neiges* 47, *L'Oracle* 48, *Les Amours singulières* 49, *La Mort d'une Mère* 50, *Les Ambassades* 51, *Du Vésuve à l'Etna* 52, *La Fin des Ambassades* 53, *Les Clés de St. Pierre* 55, *Jeunes Proies* 56, *Chevaliers de Malte* 57, *L'Exilé de Capri* 59, *Le Spectateur Nocturne* 60, *Les fils de la Lumière* 61, *La Nature du Prince* 63, *Les Juifs* 65, *Notre Amour* 67.
9 avenue du Maréchal Maunoury, Paris 16e, France.

Pfleiderer, Otto, DR. SC. POL.; German banker; b. 17 Jan. 1904; ed. Univs. of Tübingen, Hamburg and Kiel.
Ministry of Finance, Württemberg-Baden, Stuttgart 45-48, Pres. Landeszentralbank von Württemberg-Baden 48-52, von Baden-Württemberg 53-57, in Baden-Württemberg, Stuttgart 57-; mem. Board of Dirs. Bank deutscher Länder 48-57, Deutsche Bundesbank 57-; Prof., Univ. of Heidelberg 47-; Exec. Dir. Int. Monetary Fund, Washington 52-53.
Publs. *Die Staatswirtschaft und das Sozialprodukt* 30, *Pfund, Yen und Dollar in der Weltwirtschaftskrise* 37, *Währungsordnung und europäische Integration* 64.
Marstallstrasse 3, Stuttgart, German Federal Republic.

Pflimlin, Pierre, DR. en D.; French politician; b. 5 Feb. 1907; ed. Lycée de Mulhouse, Institut Catholique, Paris, and Strasbourg Univ.
Member of Bar, Strasbourg 33-64; served French Army 39-40; Deputy for Bas-Rhin 46-67; Under-Sec. for Nat. Economy 46; Minister of Agriculture 47-49 and 50-51; Minister for Foreign Economic Relations 51-52; Minister for Overseas Territories 52-53, of Finance 55-56 and 57-58; Prime Minister May 58; Minister of State, de Gaulle Cabinet, June 58-Jan. 59; Pres. Mouvement Républicain Populaire 56-59; Co-Pres. "Centre Démocratique" Group, Nat. Ass. 62-63; Mayor of Strasbourg 59-; Minister of Co-operation, April-May 62; Pres. of Assembly of Council of Europe 63-66.
Publs. *Perspectives sur notre Economie, L'Industrie de*

Mulhouse, La Structure économique du IIIe Reich, L'Alsace—Destin et volonté (with René Uhrich), *L'Europe communautaire* (with Raymond Legrand-Lane).
Mairie de Strasbourg, 9 rue Brulée, Strasbourg, France.
Telephone: 32-99-03.

Pham van Dong; Viet-Namese political leader; b. 06.
Close collaborator of Ho Chi Minh; underground communist worker since 25; imprisoned by French authorities for seven years; upon release in 36, resumed revolutionary activities; became one of the founders of Viet Minh; Prime Minister 54-, concurrently Minister of Foreign Affairs 54-61.
Office of the Prime Minister, Hanoi, Democratic Republic of Viet-Nam.

Pham Van Ky; Viet-Namese writer; b. 16; ed. Secondary School, Hanoi, and Univ. of Paris.
Went to France 39; prepared thesis on religion for the Institut des Hautes Etudes Chinoises; Grand Prix du Roman, Académie Française 61.
Publs. *Fleurs de jade* (poems), *L'homme de nulle part* (short stories) 46, *Frères de sang* (novel) 47, *Celui qui régnera* (novel) 54, *Les yeux courroucés* (novel) 58, *Les contemporains* (novel) 59, *Perdre la demeure* (novel) 61, *Poème sur Soie* (poems) 61, *Des Femmes Assises Çà et La* (novel) 64, *Mémoires d'un Eunuque* (novel) 66.
62 avenue du Général de Gaulle, Maisons-Alfort 94, France.
Telephone: 368-22-94.

Philip, Kjeld, DR. ECON.; Danish economist and politician; b. 3 April 1912; ed. Copenhagen Univ.
Instructor Aarhus Univ. 37-43 and Prof. of Social Politics and Public Finance 43-49, Prof. of Econs. and Social Politics, Stockholm Univ. 49-51; Prof. of Economics, Univ. of Copenhagen 51-57, 64, 66-; Minister of Commerce 57-60; Minister of Finance 60-61; Minister of Econ. Affairs 61-64; Chair. Co-ordination Cttee. 55; Dir. Inst. of History and Econs. 56-60; UN Senior Econ. Adviser to Prime Minister of Somalia 65; Chair. Comm. on East African Cooperation 65-67.
Publs. *En fremstilling og analyse af Den danske Kriselovgivning* 31-38, 39, *Bidrag til Laeren om Forbindelsen mellem, det offentliges Finanspolitik og den økonomiske Aktivitet* 42, *Staten og Fattigdommen* 47, *Division of Work between the Central and Local Governments in Norway, Sweden, England and Wales, and Holland* 48, *La Política Financiera y la Actividad Económica, Madrid* 49, *Inter-governmental Fiscal Relations* 53, *Skattepolitik* 55, second edn. 65.
Rungstedvej 91, Rungsted Kyst, Denmark.
Telephone: 01-863848.

Philips, Frederik Jacques; Netherlands engineer, businessman and welfare worker; b. 05; ed. Technical Univ. of Delft.
Joined N. V. Philips' Gloeilampenfabrieken as Works Engineer 30; Man. 31, in control of mechanical workshops; Dep. Dir. 36 and Dir. 39, Vice Pres. of the Board of Management 46-61, Pres. March 61-; Companion of the Order of the Dutch Lion; Commdr. of the Order of Saint Gregory the Great, Cedar of Lebanon; Officer Cross of the French Legion of Honour; Commdr. of the Dannebrog Order; Grand Officer, Order of Merit (Argentine), Japanese, Thai and Belgian honours.
N. V. Philips' Gloeilampenfabrieken, Philips' Industries, Eindhoven, Netherlands; and De Wielewaal, Eindhoven, Netherlands.

Phillippe, Gerald Lloyd; American electrical industry executive; b. 27 Sept. 1909; ed. Univ. of Nebraska.
General Electric Co. 33-, Comptroller, Apparatus Dept. 50-51, Man. Finance, Apparatus Sales Div. 51-53, Comptroller 53-61, Pres. 61-63, Chair. of Board 63-.
General Electric Co., 570 Lexington Avenue, New York City 22, N.Y., U.S.A.

Phillips, Rev. Canon John Bertram, M.A.; British writer and broadcaster; b. 16 Sept. 1906; ed. Emanuel School, London, and Emmanuel Coll. and Ridley Hall, Cambridge.

Assistant Master, Sherborne Prep. School for Boys 27-28; Curate St. John's, Penge, London 30-33; Freelance journalist and Editor Sec. Pathfinder Press 34-36; Curate St. Margaret's, Lee, London 36-40, Vicar of Good Shepherd, Lee 40-44; Vicar of St. John's Redhill 45-55; trans., writer, lecturer, broadcaster and preacher 55-; Wiccamical Prebendary of Exceit, Chichester Cathedral 57-60; Canon of Salisbury Cathedral 64-; D.D. (Lambeth) 66.

Publs. *Letters to Young Churches* 47, *Your God is too Small* 52, *The Gospels in Modern English* 52, *Making Men Whole* 52, *Plain Christianity* 54, *When God Was Man* 54, *Appointment with God* 54, *The Young Church in Action* 55, *New Testament Christianity* 56, *The Church under the Cross* 56, *St. Luke's Life of Christ* 56, *The Book of Revelation* 57, *Is God at Home?* 57, *The New Testament in Modern English* 58, *A Man Called Jesus* 59, *God our Contemporary* 60, *Good News* 63, *Four Prophets* 63, *Ring of Truth* 67.

Golden Cap, 17 Gannetts Park, Swanage, Dorset, England.

Phillips, John Frederick Vicars, D.SC., F.R.S.E., F.R.S.S.AFR.; South African ecologist, conservationist and agriculturist; b. 15 Feb. 1899; ed. Dale Coll., King William's Town, South Africa, and Univ. of Edinburgh.

Initiated research into indigenous forests, Knysna, S. Africa 22-27; ecologist and later Dep. Dir. Tsetse Research, Tanganyika Territory; Prof. of Botany, Univ. of Witwatersrand, Johannesburg 31; Gen. Man., later Joint Gen. Man. and Chief Agricultural Adviser to Overseas Food Corpn. (East African Groundnuts Scheme) 48; Consultant in Agriculture to FAO and Int. Bank of Reconstruction and Development; British Gov. Econ. Survey Mission of High Comm. Territories, Southern Africa 59; Chair. Cttee. of Enquiry into African Educ., Nyasaland 61; Prof. of Agriculture, Univ. Coll., Ghana and Adviser in Agricultural Educ. to Ghana Ministry of Education 52-60; Chair. Cttee. reporting on development of economic resources in Southern Rhodesia 60-62; co-ordinating agro-economic aspects of the Tugela Basin 63-; Visiting Prof. Univ. of Pa. 66; Leader of UN Survey Team, Socio-economy of Hill Tribes, Thailand 67.

Publs. *The Forests of George, Knysna and the Zitzikama: A Brief History of their Management, 1778-1939, Agriculture and Ecology in Africa* 59, *Kwame Nkrumah and the Future of Africa* 60, *Development of Agriculture and Forestry in the Tropics: Patterns, Problems and Promise* 61 (2nd edn. 66).

c/o University of Natal, P.O. Box 375, Pietermaritzburg, Natal; Home: 'Green Shadows', P.O. Sweetwaters, Natal, South Africa.

Phillips, Hon. Sir Rowland Ricketts, Kt.; Jamaican judge; b. 30 Sept. 1904; ed. Cornwall Coll., Jamaica.

Called to Bar 41; Crown Counsel, Jamaica 43; Resident Magistrate, Jamaica 46; Puisne Judge, British Guiana 54-59, Jamaica 59-62; Chief Justice of Jamaica 62-.

Supreme Court, Kingston, Jamaica.

Phillips, Wendell, A.B., F.R.G.S., F.R.A.I., F.A.G.S., F.R.C.A.S., F.R.A.S.; American explorer and archaeologist; b. 25 Sept. 1921; ed. Univ. of Calif., Berkeley.

President and Dir. Philpryor Corpn. 51-58; Pres. Middle East American Oil Co. 55-56; Chair. P.T.P. Corpn., Reno, Nev. 62-, Phillips Pacific, Sacramento, Calif. 60-; Pres. American Foundation for Study of Man, Washington 49-; Dir.-Gen. Antiquities, Oman 53; Econ. Adviser and Rep. of H.M. Sultan of Oman 56-; mem. many scientific expeditions; Dir. African expedition 47-49, Sinai Expedition 50, Oman Geographical Expedition 61; excavations in Yemen 51-52, Sumhuram, Dhofar

52-53, Sohar, Oman 58; mem. several learned socs.; Hon. Dr. Univs. of Redlands, Colorado, Trinity, Pacific, Marietta, and Kyungpook Nat. Univ., Calvin Coolidge, Emporia, Sterling, and Whitworth Colls.

Publs. *Qataban and Sheba* 55, *Unknown Oman* 66, *Oman, a History* 67.

International Market Place, Suite 207, Halau Building, Honolulu, Hawaii 96815; and Diamond Head Apartments, 2969 Kalakaua Avenue, Honolulu, Hawaii 96815, U.S.A.

Phinitakson, Luang, Barrister at Law; Thai diplomatist; b. 11; ed. Assumption Coll., Bangkok, Middle Temple, London, and National Defence Coll., Bangkok.

Director of Econ. Dept., Min. of Foreign Affairs 43-47; Counsellor Thai Embassy, London 47-49; Min. to India 49-52; Dir.-Gen. Econ. Dept. Min. of Foreign Affairs 52-53. UN Dept. 53; Ambassador to Japan 54-57; Ambassador attached to Min. of Foreign Affairs 58-59; Ambassador to Indonesia 59-; several decorations.

Publ. *Diplomatic Practice and Thailand's Diplomacy.*

Royal Thai Embassy, 23 Djalan Diponegoro, Djakarta, Indonesia.

Phocas, Eugène; Greek university professor; b. 03; ed. Univs. of Athens, Paris and Berlin.

Assistant Prof. Univ. of Athens 24-26, Prof. 36-41, Doyen of Medical School 52-53, mem. Senate 59, Rector 61-62; Prof. of First Medical Clinic 62-; Scientific Counsellor to Ministry of Tourism; mem. Supreme Council of Health; Dr. h.c. Univ. de Paris à la Sorbonne; Officier Légion d'Honneur and other foreign decorations.

Publs. *Traité d'Hydrotherapie et Climatologie Médicale* 58, *Maladies du Rhumatisme* 62, *Clinique Médicale* (3 vols.) 64.

150 avenue du 28 octobre (Patission), Athens, Greece.

Phurissara, Prince Norodom; Cambodian lawyer and politician; b. 1919.

Government Service 44-; Deputy Provincial Gov., later in Ministry of Foreign Affairs and Ministry of Planning; Deputy State Sec. of Interior 61, State Sec. 62-64; Dir. of Admin. of Council of Ministers 64-66; Dean of Faculty of Law, Royal Univ., Pnom Penh 64-66; Minister of Foreign Affairs Nov. 66-.

Ministry of Foreign Affairs, Pnom Penh, Cambodia.

Piaget, Jean, D. ès SC., DR.H.C. (Harvard); Swiss psychologist; b. 9 Aug. 1896; ed. Neuchâtel, Zürich and Paris Univs.

Private Docent 21; Prof. of Philosophy, Neuchâtel Univ. 26; Prof. of Child Psychology and History of Scientific Thought, Geneva Univ. 29-; Prof. of Gen. Psychology, Lausanne Univ. 37-54; Dir. Int. Bureau of Education 29-; co-Dir. Inst. for Scientific Education 33; Hon. Sc.D. (Cambridge).

Publs. include *Le langage et la pensée chez l'Enfant, Le Jugement et le Raisonnement chez l'Enfant, La Représentation du Monde chez l'Enfant, La Causalité physique chez l'Enfant, Le Jugement moral chez l'Enfant, La Construction du Réel chez l'Enfant, La Naissance de l'Intelligence chez l'Enfant, Le Développement des Quantités chez l'Enfant, Les Mécanismes Perceptifs, Biologie et Connaissance.*

Institut des Sciences de l'Education, L'Université, Geneva, Switzerland.

Piatier, André (Sylvain); French economist; b. 25 June 1914; ed. Univ. of Paris, London School of Econs., Inst. für Konjunkturforschung, Berlin, Hague Acad., etc.

Rockefeller Fellow and Asst., Faculté de Droit, Paris, and Sec. Inst. Int. de Finances Publique 36-39; war and resistance, lecturer Univ. of Strasbourg, Centre d'Etudes Economiques de la Marine 39-45; Dir. Economic Studies and Research, Inst. Nat. de la Statistique, Paris 46-56; Prof. of Economic Sciences, Cairo 55-56; Pres. of Experts, Int. Travel Inst. 48-57, Prof. Ecole

Pratique des Hautes Etudes (Sorbonne), Inst. d'Etudes Politiques, Ecole Nat. d'Admin., Ecole d'Application de la Statistique, Inst. d'Etudes de Développement Economique et Social, Paris, etc.; Pres. Cttee. for Econ. Science and Devt. 60-66, Délégation gén. à la Recherche Scientifique; Officier Légion d'Honneur, Médaille de la Résistance; Dir. Centre d'Etude des Techniques Economiques Modernes (CETEM).

Publ. Several works in field of economics; Dir. of collections *Observation Economique, Développement Economique* (25 vols.), *Techniques Economiques Modernes, Rhythmes Economiques.*

11 *bis*, rue Vauquelin, Paris 5e, France.
Telephone: POR 2704.

Picart le Doux, Jean; French painter, tapestry designer and book illustrator; b. 31 Jan. 1902; ed. Lycée Condorcet and private Acads. of Art.

Career devoted to graphic art and since 43 to tapestry designing; Prof. Ecole nationale supérieure des arts décoratifs, Paris; Co-founder Assoc. des Peintres-Cartonniers de tapisserie 45; one-man exhibitions since 50 in Paris, Lucerne, Geneva, Berlin, Zürich, Copenhagen, The Hague etc.; has participated in over 700 group exhibitions in France and abroad including Bienal of São Paulo 58, Decorative Art Exhibition, Tokyo 60, Int. Biennale of Tapestry, Lausanne; represented in Musées Nat. d'Art Moderne, Paris and Warsaw, Univ. of Kansas, Kultusministerium Stuttgart, etc.

Major Works: over 200 patterns for tapestries; Murals: painting Polytechnic Toulouse, mosaic *Groupe Scolaire* Choisy-le-Roi; Book Illustrations: *Paris ma rose* (Nazim Hikmet), *Le Bestiaire* (Apollinaire).

Studio: 163 avenue Victor Hugo, 75 Paris 16e; Home: 91 rue Boileau, Paris 16e, France.
Telephone: 727-93-71.

Picasso, Pablo Ruiz; Spanish painter; b. 25 Oct. 1881; ed. Barcelona.

Worked in Paris since 01; founder and leader of the cubist school; designer for Diaghilev Ballet 17-27; Dir. Prado Gallery Madrid 36-39; painted murals for Spanish Pavilion, Paris Exhibition 37, for UNESCO Building, Paris 58.

Many hundreds of his works are in museums, galleries and private collections throughout the world; although his most important work is in the field of painting, he has also executed a large number of drawings, sculptures, lithographs, ceramics and theatrical décors; he has also appeared in two films illustrating his work and techniques; Major Exhbn. Paris 66; Sculpture Exhbn., London 67; Lenin Peace Prize 62.

Publs. Engravings: *The Dream and Life of General Franco* 37; plays: *Le Désir attrapé par la Queue* 45, *Les Quatres Petites Filles* 65.

Villa Californie, Cannes (A.-M.); and Mas Notre-Dame-de-Vic, par Mougins (A.-M.), France.

Piccard, Jacques Ernest Jean; Swiss scientist; b. 28 July 1922; ed. Univ. of Geneva and Inst. Universitaire de Hautes Etudes Internationales, Geneva.

Asst. Prof. of Economics, Geneva 46-48; consultant scientist to several American orgs. for deep sea research; collaborated with father, Prof. Auguste Piccard, in construction of bathyscaph *Trieste*; built first tourist submarine *Auguste Piccard*; has made more than 60 dives in Mediterranean and Pacific, one to 35,800 feet (deepest ever dive) in Jan. 1960; Prof. of Oceanic Engineering at Stevens Inst. of Technology, Hoboken, New Jersey; Croix de Guerre (France), U.S. Distinguished Public Service award 60, Hon. D.Sc., American Int. Coll.

19 avenue de l'Avenir, 1012 Lausanne, Switzerland.
Telephone: 021-28-80-83.

Picchia, Menotti Del, D.LITT., LL.D.; Brazilian journalist, author and civil servant; b. 92; ed. Porto Alegre and S. Paulo.

Fmr. Dir. journals *Mandú, Cidade de Itapira, Tribuna de Santos, A Gazeta, O Correio Paulistano, O Anhanguera,* reviews *Nossa Revista, S. Paulo* and *A. Cigarra,* and Union of Brazilian Journalists; fmr. Dir. State of S. Paulo Credit Bank; Dir. Dept. of Propaganda and Publicity of S. Paulo State; a leader, with Graça Aranha and Ronald de Carvalho, of the "Semana de Arte Moderna" with Cassiano Ricardo and Plinio Salgado of nationalist literary movement "Verdeamarelo."

Publs. of which some are translated into other languages: *Poemas do Vicio e da Virtude, Juca Mulato, Mascaras, Angustia de D. João, Chuva de Pedra, República dos Estados Unidos do Brasil, Poemas de Amor;* ballads: *Lais, Tragedia de Zilda, A Tormenta, O Homem e a Morte, O Misterio do Sertão, Cummunkú; Salomé;* novels and stories: *A Mulher que Pecou, O Crime daquela Noite, Toda Núa, O Despertar de S. Paulo;* essays and monographs: *A Crise da Democracia, Pelo Divorcio, O Momento Literario Brasileiro;* plays: *Jesus, Suprema Conquista, Mascaras;* historical works: *Pão de Moloch, Nariz de Cleopatra;* children's books.

A Noite, São Paulo, Brazil.

Piccinato, Luigi, DR. ARCHIT.; Italian architect and town planner; b. 30 Oct. 1899; ed. Architecture High School, Padua, and Univ. of Rome.

Assistant Prof. of Town Planning, Rome 23-30; Lecturer Town Planning, Naples Univ. 27-50, Tucuman and Buenos Aires Univ. 49-50; Prof. of Town Planning Univ. of Venice 50-64, Univ. of Rome 64-; mem. Consiglio Superiore, Ministry of Works and Buildings 64; mem. numerous architectural socs.; Olivetti First Prize for Town Planning, Golden Medal of Merit, Italian Repub.; Vice-Pres. Istituto Nazionale di Urbanistica.

Major works: town plans at Sabaudia, Padua, Matera, Pescara, Siena, L'Aquila, Catania, Bolzano, Naples, Rome 61, Venice 61, Orvieto, Macerata, Carrara and other Italian towns; Istanbul, Atakoy, Bursa (Turkey), Ezeiza (Buenos Aires), Regional Plans of Venice, Bolzano, Campania, houses at Rome, Ivrea and Venice; Eliseo Theatre, Rome; Mediterraneo Theatre, Naples; Stadium, Pescara.

Piazza Stefano Jacini 23, Rome, Italy.
Telephone: 32-03-74.

Piccioni, Attilio; Italian politician; b. 14 June 1892; ed. Univs. of Rome and Turin.

Municipal Councillor Turin 20-23; retired from public life during fascist régime; organised Christian Democrat Party in Tuscany 43; formerly Min. of Justice, Min. for Foreign Affairs; Vice-Pres. Council of Ministers July 60-62; Minister of Foreign Affairs 62-63; Minister without Portfolio 63-; Pres. Christian Democrat Party.

Presidency of the Council of Ministers, Palazzo Chigi, Rome, Italy.

Pickard, Sir Cyril Stanley, K.C.M.G.; British diplomatist; b. 18 Sept. 1917; ed. Alleyn's School, Dulwich, and New Coll., Oxford.

Ministry of Home Security 39; Royal Artillery 40-41; Office of Minister of State, Cairo 41-45; UNRRA Balkan Mission 44, later with UNRRA in Germany; Home Office 45-48; Commonwealth Relations Office (C.R.O.) 48-; Office of U.K. High Commr. in India 50-52; Official Sec. to Office of U.K. High Commr. in Australia 52-55; Head, S. Asia and Middle East Dept., C.R.O. 55-57; Deputy High Commr. in New Zealand 58-61; Asst. Under Sec. of State, C.R.O. 62-66; Acting High Commr., Cyprus 64; High Commr. in Pakistan 66-.

British High Commission, Islamabad, Pakistan.

Pickavance, Thomas Gerald, C.B.E., PH.D.; British physicist; b. 19 Oct. 1915; ed. Univ. of Liverpool.

Research on Atomic Bomb Project, Directorate of Tube Alloys, Liverpool 40-46; Lecturer in Physics, Liverpool Univ. 42-46; Head of Cyclotron Group A.E.R.E.,

Harwell 46; Principal Scientific Officer 47 and Senior Principal Scientific Officer 50; Deputy Head of Gen. Physics Division A.E.R.E. 55; Dir. Rutherford High Energy Laboratory, Nat. Inst. for Research in Nuclear Science 57-65, Science Research Council 65-.
Craigellachie, Hinksey Hill Top, Oxford, England.
Telephone: 35243.

Pickens, Russell Marion, B.S., M.S., PH.D.; American executive; b. 17 April 1898; ed. Montana State Coll. and Iowa State Coll.
Research Chemist to Chemical Dir., Pont Rayon and Du Pont Cellophane Co. at Buffalo, N.Y. 25-30; Technical Dir. Ravonier Inc. 30-44, Technical Sales Dir. 44-49, Vice-Pres. (Sales) 49-58; mem. New York Acad. of Sciences; Consultant, Rayonier 58-; Hon. D.Sc.
1223 Spring Street, Seattle, Washington 98104, U.S.A.
Telephone: Main 4-6648.

Pickering, Edward Davies; British journalist; b. 4 May 1912; ed. Middlesbrough High School.
Chief Sub-Editor *Daily Mail* 39; Royal Artillery 40-44; Staff of Supreme Headquarters Allied Expeditionary Force 44-45; Managing Editor *Daily Mail* 47-49, *Daily Express* 51-57, Editor *Daily Express* 57-62; Managing Dir. Beaverbrook Publications 62-63; Dir. Beaverbrook Newspapers 56-63; Editorial Dir. and Dir. The Daily Mirror Newspapers Ltd. 64-68; Editorial Dir. Int. Publishing Corpn. Chair. I.P.C. Newpaper Div. and Chair. Daily Mirror Newspapers Ltd. 68-; mem. Press Council 64; Dir. Int. Publishing Corpn. 66.
Daily Mirror Newspapers Ltd., Holborn Circus, London E.C.1; 5 Eldon Road, London, W.8, England.
Telephone: 01-937-4414.(Home).

Pickering, William Hayward, M.S., PH.D.; American scientist; b. 24 Dec. 1910; ed. Calif. Inst. of Technology.
California Inst. of Technology 36-, Prof. of Electrical Eng. 46-, Dir. Jet Propulsion Laboratory 54-; mem. Scientific Advisory Board U.S.A.F. 45-48; Chair. Panel on Test Range Instrumentation Research and Development Board 48-49; Directed devt. of Army Corporal and Sergeant missiles 50-55, and many spacecraft, including Explorer I; mem. U.S. Technical Panel on Earth Satellite Programs IGY 56-58, Army Scientific Advisory Panel 63-65; Pres. A.I.A.A. 63; Fellow I.E.E.E.; Hon. Fellow A.I.A.A.; mem. Nat. Acad. of Sciences, American Asscn. Univ. Profs., American Geophysical Union, Nat. Acad. of Engineering, American Asscn. for Advancement of Science, Royal Soc. of New Zealand, Int. Acad. of Astronautics (Vice-Pres. 62); mem. Int. Astronautics Fed., Pres. 65-66; hon. mem. New Zealand Inst. of Eng., and Aerospace Medical Asscn.; Fellow American Acad. of Arts and Sciences; Hon. D.Sc. (Occidental Coll., Clark Univ.); Italian Order of Merit 66, etc.
Jet Propulsion Laboratory, California Institute of Technology, 4800 Oak Grove Drive, Pasadena, Calif. 91103; Home: 292 St. Katherine Drive, Pasadena, Calif. 91103, U.S.A.
Telephone: 213-354-3405 (Office).

Pickersgill, John Whitney, P.C., B.LITT.; Canadian politician; b. 23 June 1905; ed. Univ. of Manitoba and Oxford Univ.
Lecturer in History, Wesley Coll., Univ. of Manitoba 29-37; entered Dept. of External Affairs 37, Private Sec. to Sec. for External Affairs 42-45; Special Asst. to Prime Minister 45-52; Clerk of Privy Council and Sec. to Cabinet 52-54; M.P. for Bonavista-Twillingate 53-67; Federal Sec. of State 53-54; Minister of Citizenship and Immigration 54-57; mem. Official Opposition 57-63; Sec. of State 63-64; Minister of Transport 64-67; Pres. Canadian Transport Comm. 67-; Liberal.
Publs. *The Mackenzie King Record* 60, *The Liberal Party* 62, *Le Parti Libéral* 63.
550 Maple Lane East, Rockcliffe Park, Ottawa, Ontario, Canada.

Pickford, Mary; American actress; b. 9 April 1894.
Stage debut at age of 5; fmr. organiser Pickford-Lasky Productions Inc.; Head of Mary Pickford Co., Hollywood; mem. Nat. Advisory Cttee., White House Conf. on Ageing 59; Dir. American Soc. for the Aged, Inc.
Silent films include *Hearts Adrift, Tess of the Storm Country, Stella Maris, Daddy Long Legs, Pollyanna, Rebecca of Sunny Brook Farm, Poor Little Rich Girl, Little Lord Fauntleroy*; talking films include *Coquette, The Taming of the Shrew, Kiki.*
Publs. *Why not try God?* 34, *The Demi-Widow* 35, *My Rendezvous with Life* 35, *Sunshine and Shadow* 55.
Pickfair, Beverly Hills, Calif., U.S.A.

Pieraccini, Giovanni; Italian journalist and politician; b. 25 Nov. 1918; ed. Univ. of Pisa.
Organiser, Young Socialist Federation; mem. Editorial Staff *La Nazione del Popolo* 44-46, Jt. Editor *Nuovo Corriere* 46-48; Editor *Avanti* 59-63; M.P. 48-; fmr. mem. Finance and Treasury Comms. and Foreign Affairs Cttee.; Minister of Public Works 63-64, of Budget 64-68; Socialist Party.
Chamber of Deputies, Rome, Italy.

Pierce, John Robinson, B.S., M.S., PH.D.; American electrical engineer; b. 27 March 1910; ed. Calif. Inst. of Technology.
Bell Telephone Laboratories 36-, Dir. of Electronics Research 52-, Dir. of Research, Electrical Communications 55-, Communications Principles 58-61; Exec. Dir. Research-Communications Principles and Systems Div. 61-65, Research-Communications Sciences Div. 65-; mem. Nat. Acad. of Science, Nat. Acad. of Engineering; Fellow Acoustical Soc. of America, American Physical Soc., Inst. of Electrical and Electronics Engineers, American Acad. of Arts and Sciences; Stuart Ballantine Medal 60, Air Force Asscn. H. H. Arnold Trophy 62, and many other medals and trophies.
Publs. *Theory and Design of Electron Beams* 54, *Traveling Wave Tubes* 50, *Electrons, Waves and Messages* 56, *Man's World of Sound* 58, *Symbols, Signals and Noise* 61, *The Research State: A History of Science in New Jersey* 64, *Electrons and Waves* 64, *Quantum Electronics* 66, *Waves and Messages* 67.
Bell Telephone Laboratories, Murray Hill, New Jersey 07971; 16 Roberts Road, Warren, New Jersey 07060, U.S.A.
Telephone: 201-647-3859.

Pierce, Sydney David, O.B.E., B.A., B.C.L., LL.D.; Canadian diplomatist; b. 30 March 1901; ed. Lower Canada Coll., McGill Univ.
Lecturer, Dalhousie Univ. 26; Canadian Dept. of Munitions and Supply, Washington 40-44, Dir.-Gen.44; Ambassador to Mexico 47-49, to OEEC 50-51; Minister and Dir. Washington Office, Dept. of Defence Production 51-53; Ambassador to Brazil 53-58; Deputy High Commr., London 58-59; Ambassador to Belgium, Luxembourg and the European Communities 59-66; Ambassador and Chief Negotiator GATT Conf., Geneva 66-67.
174 Duffesir Road, Ottawa, Canada.

Pierre, Abbé; (see Grouès, Henri).

Pierrot, George Francis, A.B.; American writer; b. 11 Jan. 1898; ed. Univ. of Washington.
Reporter 19; editor *University of Washington Daily, Canning Age* 20; reporter *Seattle Times* 20-21; Lecturer in Journalism Univ. of Washington 21; Publicity Sec. Seattle Chamber of Commerce; Associate Editor *Business Magazine* Detroit 22; Asst. Managing Editor *American Boy Magazine* 22-24; Editor *American Boy-Youth's Companion* 24-36, staff writer 31, travelled round world; Pres. and Dir. World Adventure Series Lectures 33-; Dir. World Adventure Series, Junior Adventurers, Round-the-World; corresp. World Letters Inc. 38-39; Press Dir. Ford Motor Co., New York

World's Fair 39-40; Pres. Sprague Publications Inc. 40-41; Managing Dir. Metropolitan Detroit U.S.O. 42-43; co-leader Mexican expedition 44; Exec. Sec. Medical Science Centre of Wayne Univ. 43-47; Pres. George F. Pierrot Productions 59-; television producer: *World Adventure* series 48-, *George Pierrot Show* 53-; *George Pierrot Presents* (daily) 58-; Distinguished Service Award, Wayne State Univ. 61; Stenius Award 62.

Publs. *Yea, Sheriton* 25, *The Vagabond Trail* 35.

2224 Burns Avenue, Detroit 4, Mich., U.S.A.

Pierson, Marc-Antoine; Belgian lawyer and politician; b. 26 March 1908; ed. Univ. Libre de Bruxelles. Former lawyer Court of Appeal, Brussels and Town Councillor; Deputy and Pres. Socialist Party; Minister of Econ. Affairs 65-66; Del. Council of Europe and Western European Union; fmr. Pres. and mem. Interparliamentary Council of Benelux; Commdr. Ordre de Léopold, Officier Légion d'Honneur, Grand Croix Orange-Nassau.

Publs. *Histoire du Socialisme en Belgique, Belgique, Terre d'Exil, Traité de Procédure civile.*

107 boulevard de Waterloo, Brussels, Belgium.

Pierson, Warren Lee, A.B., LL.B.; American banker and lawyer; b. 29 Aug. 1896; ed. Univ. of Calif. and Harvard Univ.

Served in French Army First World War; Pres. American Cable and Radio Corpn., All-America Cables and Radio Inc., and The Commercial Cable Co. 45-47; Chair. Board of Dirs. Trans World Airlines Inc. 47-61, Chair. Exec. Cttee. 61-; Chair. Bd. of Dirs. Great Western Financial Corpn. 55-; Dir. Int. Telephone and Telegraph Corpn., American Cable and Radio Corpn., All-American Cables and Radio Inc., Commercial Cable Co., Mackay Radio and Telegraph Co., Vertientes-Camaguey Sugar Co. of Cuba, Wah Chang Corpn., West Coast Savings and Loan Asscn. 57-; Pres. IATA 50-51; Dir. Fruehauf Trailer Co. 53-, etc.; mem. Exec. Council U.S. Int. Chamber of Commerce; Dir. Molybdenum Corpn. of America 60-; Pres. Int. Chamber of Commerce 55-57; Commdr. Légion d'Honneur (France), Order of the White Rose (Finland); Commdr. Order of Southern Cross (Brazil), Order Aztec Eagle (Mexico), Order of the Star of Italian Solidarity (Italy), Commdr. Order of Christ (Portugal), Grand Officer Order of Merit (Italy), Commdr. Order of Merit (German Fed. Repub.).

Home: 655 Park Avenue, New York, N.Y.; Office: 320 Park Avenue, New York, N.Y., U.S.A.

Pieyre de Mandiargues, André; French writer; b. 14 March 1909.

Prix des Critiques for *Soleil des loups* 51; Prix Goncourt for *La Marge* 67.

Publs. *Dans les années sordides* (poems and prose) 43, *Hereda ou la persistance de l'amour pendant une rêverie* (poem) 45, *L'Etudiante* 46, *Le Musée noir* 46, *Les Incongruités monumentales* 48, *Les Sept Périls spectraux* 50, *Les Masques de Léonor Fini* 51, *Soleil des loups* 51, *Marbre* 53, *Astyanax* 56, *Les Monstres de Bomarzo* (essays) 57, *Le Belvédère* (essays) 58, *Feu de braise* 59, *La Marée* 59, *Cartolines et dédicaces* 60, *Sugai* 60, *L'Age de craie* 61, *Deuxième belvédère* 62, *La Motocyclette* (novel) 63, *Saint-John Perse, A l'honneur de la chair* 63, *Sabine* 64, *Le Point où j'en suis* 64, *Beylamour* 65, *Les Corps illuminés* 65, *Larmes de généraux* 65, *Porte dévergondée* 65, *La Marge* (novel) 67.

11 rue Payenne, Paris 3e, France.

Piffl-Perčević, Theodor, DR. IUR.; Austrian politician; b. 11; ed. Humanistisches Gymnasium Kollegium Kalksburg, and Universität Graz.

Former lawyer and in private business; political prisoner 38, 39-40; war service 42-45; Deputy Dir. and Head of Legal Dept. of Chamber of Agriculture and Forestry, Styria 45-64; mem. Austrian Nat. Council 60-; Fed. Minister of Educ. 64-.

Prinz Eugenstrasse 12, Vienna IV, Austria.

Piganiol, André Félix Guy; French historian; b. 17 Jan. 1883; ed. Ecole Normale Supérieure, and Ecole française de Rome.

Prof. of Roman History, Univ. of Strasbourg 19-28; Prof. of Ancient History at the Sorbonne 28-42; Prof. (Chair. of Roman Civilisation), Collège de France 42-54; Dir. Circonscription des Antiquités Historiques de Paris-Nord 53-64; mem. Acad. des Inscriptions et Belles-Lettres; Corresp. Fellow British Acad. 67.

Publs. *Essai sur les origines de Rome* 16, *Recherches sur les jeux romains* 23, *Conquête romaine* 27, 67, *L'Empereur Constantin* 32, *Histoire de Rome* 39 (5th edn. 62), *L'Empire chrétien* 47, *Les documents cadastraux de la colonie romaine d'Orange* 63, *Le sac de Rome* 64.

40 rue du Père Corentin, Paris 14e, France.

Telephone: POR-84-79.

Piggott, Stuart, B.LITT., F.B.A., F.S.A.; British university professor; b. 28 May 1910; ed. Churchers' Coll., Petersfield, and St. John's Coll., Oxford.

Investigator, Royal Comm. on Ancient Monuments (Wales) 28-33; Asst. Dir. Avebury Excavations (Wilts.) 34-38, war service, Lieut.-Col., Intelligence Corps. 39-45; Abercromby Prof. of Prehistoric Archaeology, Univ. of Edinburgh 46-; Commr. Royal Comms. on Ancient Monuments (Scotland 46, England 49); mem. German Archaeological Inst. 53; foreign hon. mem. American Acad. of Arts and Sciences 60; Hon. D. Litt. Hum. Columbia Univ.

Publs. *Fire among the Ruins* (poems) 48, *British prehistory* 49, *Prehistoric India* 50, *William Stukeley* 50, *Neolithic Cultures of the British Isles* 54, *Scotland Before History* 58, *Approach to Archæology* 59, *Ancient Europe* 65, *Prehistoric Societies* (with J. G. D. Clark) 65; Editor *The Dawn of Civilization* 61.

Department of Archaeology, The University, Edinburgh, Scotland.

Pignon, Edouard; French painter; b. 12 Feb. 1905.

Came to Paris from Marles les Mines (Pas de Calais) 27; pupil of the painter Auclair 28, of the sculptors Wlerick and Arnold 30-34; devoted himself exclusively to painting 36-; Salon des Indépendants 32-38, des Surindépendants 38, des Tuileries and d'Automne 43, de Mai (founding mem.) 44-; decorative panel at Int. Exhibition, Paris 37; rep. at Paris Exhbns. 41, 42, 43, 54, 55, 56, 57; One-Man Shows Paris 46, 49, 52-56, 58, 59; Retrospective Exhbn., Musée d'Art Moderne, Paris 67; many foreign exhibitions, inc. Dunn Int. Exhibition, London 63; mural *Récréations* for Girls School at Creil 39; costumes and décor for *Scheherazade* 48, *Mère Courage* (Théâtre Nat. Populaire) 52, *Mandragore* 53, *Ce Fou de Platonov, Le Malade Imaginaire* 56, *On ne badine pas avec l'amour* (Théâtre Nat. Populaire) 59; works in museums at Paris (Art Moderne), Amsterdam, Brussels, Liège, London (Tate Gallery), New York (Modern Art), São Paulo, Stockholm, Gothenburg; contract with Galerie de France; principal periods; *Les Maternités* 42-43; *Les Poissons, Femmes Assises* 44, *Les Catalanes* 45-46, *Le Port d'Ostende* 47, *Les Mineurs* 49, *Les Oliviers* 50, *Les Vendanges, Cueillettes de Jasmins* 53, *Les Electriciens* 55, *Les Paysages de Bandol* 58, *Les Combats de Coqs* 59-60; Grand Prize for Painting, São Paulo Bienal 51.

Publs. Illustrations for *Les Blasons* (poem by Maurice Sceve), *Arbres et Voiles* (Veridet), *Dialogue de l'Arbre* (Valéry) 57, etc.

c/o Galerie de France, 3 rue du Faubourg-Saint-Honoré, Paris 8e, France.

Pignon, Léon, L. en D.; French government official; b. 19 April 1908; ed. Ecole Coloniale.

Pupil-Administrator Tonkin 32; Ministry for the Colonies, Paris; served French Army 39-40; prisoner of war; released 42; attached to Bureau for the Colonies Algiers; attached to State Secretariat for the Colonies after creation of French Nat. Liberation Cttee.; Minis-

try of French Overseas Territories, Paris; political counsellor to Commr. in Indo-China with rank of Administrator First Class; Federal Commr. for Foreign Affairs 46-47; Commr. of the Republic in Cambodia 47-48; High Commr. in Indo-China 48-50; del. U.N. Trusteeship Council 50-54; Dir. Political Affairs, Ministry of French Overseas Territories 54-59; Judge French Community Court of Arbitration 59-60; Counsellor of State Jan. 62-; Pres. Central Cttee. of Overseas Territories for 5th Plan 64; Commdr. de la Légion d'Honneur; Commdr. of the Order of Leopold.
16 rue du Ranelagh, Paris 16e, France.

Pigoń, Stanisław; Polish critic and historian; b. 85; ed. Cracow.
Assistant Prof. Poznań 19-21; Prof. of History of Literature, Wilno Univ. 21, Rector of Univ. 27-28; mem. Acad. of Sciences 29-; Prof. Cracow Univ. 31; prisoner in German Concentration Camp (Oranienburg) 39-40; Editor of *Brodziński's, Fredro's, Żeromski's, Orkan's Complete Works*; Editor-in-Chief Nat. Edition of *Mickiewicz' Works*.
Al. Słowackiego 52, Cracow, Poland.
Telephone: 342-20.

Pike, Rt. Rev. James A., D.D., L.H.D., D.LITT., J.U.D., LL.D.; American ecclesiastic; b. 14 Feb. 1913; ed. Hollywood High School, Univ. of Santa Clara, Univ. of Calif. (Los Angeles), Yale Univ., Cambridge Univ., Virginia Theol. Seminary, Gen. Theological Seminary and Union Theological Seminary.
Member of Calif. Bar and Bar U.S. Supreme Court; Attorney, U.S. Securities and Exchange Comm. and War Shipping Admin., Second World War; Chair. Calif. Advisory Cttee., U.S. Comm. on Civil Rights; ordained Priest, Episcopal Church 46, served St. John's Lafayette, Wash.; Tutor Gen. Theological Seminary; Rector, Christ Church, Poughkeepsie 47-49; Chaplain and Chair. Dept. of Religion, Columbia Univ. 49-52; Adjunct Prof. of Religion, Columbia Univ. 52-58; Lecturer in Law, Univ. of Calif. 66-67; Adjunct Prof., Graduate Theological Union 66-67; Dean, Cathedral of St. John the Divine, N.Y.C. 52-58; Bishop Coadjutor of Calif. May 58, Bishop of Calif. Sept. 58-66; Medallion of Valour, Israel.
Publs. *Cases and Other Materials on the New Federal and Code Procedure* 38, *Beyond Anxiety* 53, *If You Marry Outside Your Faith* 54, *Doing the Truth* 56, *The Next Day* 57, *Our Christmas Challenge* 61, *A New Look at Preaching* 61, *Beyond the Law* 63, *A Time for Christian Candor* 64, *Teen-Agers and Sex* 65, *What is This Treasure?* 66, *You and the New Morality—74 Cases* 67, *If This be Heresy* 67.
Center for the Study of Democratic Institutions, Box 4068, Santa Barbara, Calif. 93103, U.S.A.
Telephone: 805-969-3281.

Pike, Marshal of the Royal Air Force, Sir Thomas Geoffrey, G.C.B., C.B.E., D.F.C.; British air force officer; b. 29 June 1906; ed. Bedford School and R.A.F. Coll., Cranwell.
Joined R.A.F. 23, Squadron-Leader 37, Group Captain 41, Air Commodore 44, Air Vice-Marshal 50; Marshal of the Royal Air Force 62-; served Second World War 39-45; A.O.C. No. 11 Group, Fighter Command 50-51; D.C.S. H.Q. Air Forces, Central Europe 51-53; Dep. Chief of Air Staff 53-56; Air Officer C.-in-C. Fighter Command 56-59; Chief of Air Staff 60-63; Deputy Supreme Commdr., Allied Forces, Europe 64-67; Legion of Merit, U.S.A.
Little Wynters, Hastingwood, Harlow, Essex, England.

Pilcher, Sir John (Arthur), K.C.M.G.; British diplomatist; b. 16 May 1912; ed. Shrewsbury and Clare Coll., Cambridge.
Served Japan 36-39, China 39-41; Ministry of Information and Foreign Office 41-48; Press Attaché, Rome

48-51; Foreign Office 51-54; Counsellor, Madrid 54-59; Ambassador to Philippines 59-63; Asst. Under-Sec. of State, Foreign Office 63-65; Amb. to Austria 65-67, to Japan 67-.
British Embassy, Tokyo, Japan; 22 Cheyne Row, London, S.W.3, England.

Pilkington, Baron (Life Peer), cr. 68, of St. Helens in the County Palatine of Lancashire; **Harry Pilkington;** British businessman; b. 19 April 1905; ed. Rugby and Magdalene Coll., Cambridge.
Director Pilkington Brothers Ltd. 34-, Chair. 49-; Dir. Bank of England 55-; Pres. Fed. of British Industries 53-55; Pres. Council of European Industrial Feds. 54-57; Chair. Nat. Advisory Council for Education for Industry and Commerce 56-67; Chair. Royal Comm. on Doctors, and Dentists' Pay 57-60, Cttee. of Inquiry into the Future of Sound and Television Broadcasting 60-62; Chancellor, Loughborough Univ. of Technology 66-.
Windle Hall, St. Helens, Lancashire, England.
Telephone: 23423.

Pillai, Narayana Raghavan, K.C.I.E., C.B.E., M.A., LL.B.; Indian civil servant; b. 24 July 1898; ed. Christian Coll., Madras, and Trinity Hall, Cambridge.
Secretary, Dept. of Commerce 42; Commr.-Gen. for Economic and Commercial Affairs in Europe, Paris 48; Sec. to Cabinet 50; Sec.-Gen., Ministry of External Affairs 52-60; Chair. Guest, Keen, Williams Ltd.; Hon. D.Litt. (Travancore).
Guest, Keen, Williams Ltd., Jeevan Vihar, Parliament Street, New Delhi, India.

Pillai, Pattom A. Thanu; Indian politician; b. 85.
Former teacher and lawyer; organised Travancore State Congress Party 38; Chief Minister (Congress) Travancore State 46; resgnd. and joined Indian Socialist Party (later merged with Praja Socialist Party) 46; Chief Minister Travancore-Cochin State 54-55, 60-62; Gov. Punjab 62-64, Andhra Pradesh 64-.
Raj Bhavan, Hyderabad, Andhra Pradesh, India.

Pillsbury, Philip Winston; American executive; b. 16 April 1903; ed. Blake School, Hotchkiss and Yale Univ. Joined The Pillsbury Co. 24, Dir. 28-, Treas. 40, Pres. and Dir. 40-52, Chair. 52-65, Chair. Finance Cttee., Exec. Cttee. 65-; official of other companies; LL.D. (Grinnell).
330 West Ferndale Road, Wayzata, Minn., U.S.A.
Telephone: 612-473-8682.

Pilyugin, Nikolai Alekseevich; Soviet scientist in automation and telemechanics; b. 1908; ed. Bauman Higher Technical School, Moscow.
Worker 26-35; engineer, Dir. several research Insts. 35-; Corresp. mem. U.S.S.R. Acad. of Sciences 58-66, mem. 66-; mem. C.P.S.U. 40-; Deputy to U.S.S.R. Supreme Soviet; mem. Comm. of Council of Nationalities for Industry, Transport and Communications; Hero of Socialist Labour (twice); Lenin Prize Winner.
Publs. Works on problems of automatic control.
U.S.S.R. Academy of Sciences, 14 Lenin Prospekt, Moscow, U.S.S.R.

Pimenov, Mikhail Alexandrovich; Soviet politician; b. 1914; ed. Higher Party School.
Wood-cutter 29-30; Exec. in timber industry 30-37; in coal mining 37-39; Party work 39-52; mem. C.P.S.U. 40-; Perm. Staff, Central Cttee. C.P.S.U. 52-60; Second Sec. Central Cttee. C.P. Turkmenistan 60-63; State Cttee. for Food Industry, U.S.S.R. Gosplan 63-65; Chief Inspector, Cttee. for Party-State Control, Central Cttee. of C.P.S.U. and U.S.S.R. Council of Ministers (later U.S.S.R. People's Control Cttee.) 65-; Cand. mem. Central Cttee. C.P.S.U. 61-66.
U.S.S.R. People's Control Committee, Ulitsa Kuibysheva 21, Moscow, U.S.S.R.

Pinard, Roch, B.L.; Canadian lawyer and politician; b. 10; ed. Univ. of Montreal.
Admitted to Bar 32; joined legal firm Mercier, Blain, Bissonnette and Fauteux; founded legal firm Bissonnette, Pinard and Perreault 35, changed to Bertrand, Pinard, Pigeon, Paré and Ozère and finally to Pinard, Pigeon, Paré and D'Amour 49-; M.P. for Chambly-Rouville 45-57; mem. External Affairs Cttee. 45-57; mem. Canadian Del. to U.N. 53; Parliamentary Asst. to Sec. of State for External Affairs 53-54, Sec. of State 54-57; Vice-Pres. Canadian Del. to U.N. 55.
Messrs. Pinard, Pigeon, Paré et D'Amour, Montreal, Quebec, Canada.

Pinay, Antoine; French industrialist and politician; b. 30 Dec. 1891.
Served First World War 14-18; engaged in leather industry; Deputy from Saint Etienne (Saint Chamond) 36; Senator from Loire 38; elected to Constituent Assembly 45, to Nat. Assembly 46-58; Sec. of State for Economic Affairs, first Queuille Cabinet 48-49; Minister of Public Works and Transport in first Pleven Cabinet and subsequent cabinets 50-52; Prime Minister March-Dec. 52; Minister of Foreign Affairs Feb. 55-56; Minister of Finance and Economic Affairs, de Gaulle Cabinet, June 58-Jan. 59, Debré Cabinet Jan. 59-Jan. 60; Pres. Cie. française pour la diffusion des techniques 60-; Adviser Soc. pour l'expansion industrielle française à l'étranger 62-; Mayor of Saint Chamond; Pres. of Regional Econ. Devt. for Rhône-Alpes 64-; Dir. Caisse d'aide à l'équipement des collectivités locales 66-.
Saint-Chamond, Loire, France.

Pincus, Arye Louis, B.A., LL.B.; Israeli lawyer; b. 21 May 1912; ed. Witwatersrand Univ., Johannesburg.
Practising lawyer in S. Africa 34-48; founder Habonim Labour Zionist Movement; Chair. S. African Labour Zionist Movement 39-48; Vice-Chair. S. African Zionist Fed. 40-48; settled in Israel 48; Man. Dir. El Al Israel Airlines 49-57; practising lawyer 57-; mem. Exec' and Treas. Jewish Agency 61-65, Chair. 65-; Chair. Board of Govs. Tel-Aviv Univ. 62-; mem. Central Cttee. Mapai, Histadrut; mem. Exec. Poalei Zion World Union.
Derech Ganim, Kfar Shmaryahu, Israel.

Pindborg, Jens Jørgen, D.D.S.; Danish oral pathologist; b. 17 Aug. 1921; ed. Royal Dental Coll., Copenhagen, and Univ. of Illinois.
Instructor, Research Assoc. and Assoc. Prof., Royal Dental Coll., Copenhagen 43-59, Prof. and Chair. Dept. of Oral Pathology 59-; Head, Dental Dept., Univ. Hospital, Copenhagen 53-; Consultant, Danish Nat. Health Service 58-66; Chief, Dental Corps, Royal Danish Navy 46-59; Perm. Guest Lecturer, Royal Dental Coll., Malmö, Sweden; Visiting Prof. Univ. of Illinois 58, 61, Hebrew Univ. Jerusalem 60, WHO Visiting Prof. in India 63-64; Head, Collaborating Center under WHO Int. Reference Center for Oropharyngeal tumours, Agra, India 64-; Consultant for Ministry of Health Uganda 66; Research expert for WHO to New Guinea and Fiji 66; Dir. WHO Int. Reference Centre on Odontogenic Tumours 66-; Consultant, WHO in Brazil and Colombia 67; Dir. WHO Int. Reference Centre on Oral Precancerous Conditions 67-; Editor-in-Chief, Danish Dental Journal 62-; Pres. Asscn. of Hospital Dentists 54-66, Danish-Israeli Asscn. 64-; Founding mem. Int. Acad of. Oral Pathology; Fellow American Asscn. for Advancement of Science.
Publs. *The Dentist in Art* 60, *Syndromes of Head and Neck* (with R. J. Gorlin) 64, *Atlas of Diseases of the Oral Mucosa* 68, and six books in Danish and 150 papers on oral pathology, oral medicine and cancer research.
4 Universitetsparken, Copenhagen Ø, Denmark.
Telephone: 371700.

Pindling, Hon. Lynden Oscar; Bahamas politician; b. 22 March 1930; ed. Govt. High School, Bahamas, and London Univ.
Lawyer 52-67; Leader of Progressive Liberal Party; Premier of Bahamas Jan. 67-.
Office of the Prime Minister, Nassau, Bahamas.

Pineau, Christian; French politician; b. 14 Oct. 1904.
Assistant Sec.-Gen. Conf. Gen. du Travail; editorial staff *Le Peuple*; founder clandestine "Libération Nord"; escaped to London, returned to France, arrested, again escaped to London, returned a second time, arrested and sent to Buchenwald; released 45; Deputy to Constituent Assemblies 45-46, Nat. Assembly 46-58; Minister of Food 45, of Public Works 48 and 49, of Finance 48, of Foreign Affairs 56-58; Dir.-Gen. and Pres. *France-Villages, France-Môtels*.
Publs. Books for Children include: *Contes de je ne sais quand, Plume et le Saumon, L'Ourse aux pattens verts, Comerouse le Mystérieux, Histoires de la Forêt de Bercé.*
55 rue Vaneau, Paris 7e, France.

Piñera Carvallo, José; Chilean diplomatist; b. 10 Aug. 1917; ed. Univ. de Paris à la Sorbonne and Univ. Católica de Chile.
Former Prof. of Econ. Geography, Catholic Univ. of Chile; fmr. Head of Dept. of Planning and Technical Assistance and Dept. of Investments and External Credits, Chilean Devt. Corpn.; fmr. Exec. Sec. Chilean Foreign Investments Cttee.; fmr. Pres. Inst. for Research on Natural Resources; fmr. Vice-Pres. Chilean Inst. for Rational Management of Enterprises; represented Chile at numerous int. confs.; Amb. to Belgium and Luxembourg and EEC and Rep. to ECSC until 66; Perm. Rep. of Chile to UN 66-; Pres. Trade and Devt. Board of UN Conf. on Trade and Devt. (UNCTAD) 66.
Permanent Mission of Chile to the United Nations, 211 East 43rd Street, New York, N.Y. 10017, U.S.A.

Ping Chieh-Son; Chinese politician.
Secretary-General Chinese People's Political Consultative Conf. 65-.
Office of the Secretary-General of C.P.P.C.C., Peking, People's Republic of China.

Pinget, Robert; French writer; b. 19 July 1919; ed. legal studies at univ.
Former barrister, later painter; taught French in England; literary career 51-; Prix des Critiques 63, Prix Femina 65.
Publs. *Fantoine et Agapa* 51, *Mahu ou le Matériau* 52, *Le Renard et la Boussole* 55, *Graal Flibuste* 57, *Baga* 58, *Le Fiston* 59, *Lettre morte* 59, *La Manivelle* (play) 60, *Clope au dossier* 61, *Architruc* (play) 61, *L'Hypothèse* (play) 61, *L'Inquisitoire* 62, *Quelqu'un* 65, *Autour de Mortin* (dialogue) 65, *Le Libera* 68.
4 rue de l'Université, Paris 7e, France.

Pinheiro, Israel; Brazilian engineer and politician; b. 4 Jan. 1896; ed. Anchieta Jesuit Coll., Nova Friburgo, and Ouro Preto School of Mines.
President Companhia Cerâmica João Pinheiro 22; local politics Caeté 22-31; mem. later Pres. Minas Gerais State Consultative Council 31-33, Sec. for Transport and Works 33, later Sec. for Agriculture; mem. Washington Agreements Comm. during Second World War; Pres. Companhia Vale do Rio Doce 42-46; Fed. Deputy 46-56, mem. numerous comms., including special comm. for moving Fed. Capital; Pres. company for new capital 56-61; First Mayor of Brasilia 60-61; private engineer 61-65; Gov. State of Minas Gerais 65-; Founder-mem. fmr. Partido Social Democrático.
Govêrno do Estado de Minas Gerais, Palácio da Liberdade, Belo Horizonte, Minas Gerais, Brazil.

Pinter, Harold, C.B.E.; British playwright; b. 10 Oct. 1930; ed. Hackney Downs Grammar School, London.
Actor, mainly in English and Irish provincial repertory 49-58; playwright 57-.

Plays: *The Room* 57, *The Dumb Waiter* 57, *The Birthday Party* 57, *A Slight Ache* 58, *The Caretaker* 59, *A Night Out* 59, *Night School* 60, *The Dwarfs* 61, *The Collection* 62, *The Lover* 62, *The Tea Party* (T.V. play) 64, *The Homecoming* 65, *The Basement* (T.V. play) 67, *Landscape* 68; screen-play for *The Servant* 63, *The Pumpkin Eater* 64, *The Quiller Memorandum* 66, and *Accident* 67; Dir. *The Man in the Glass Booth* (London) 67.
7 Hanover Terrace, London, N.W.1, England.

Pinto, Dr. Carlos Alberta de Carvalho; Brazilian politician; b. 10.
Minister of Tribunal de Contas, State of São Paulo; Prof. of Law, Catholic Univ.; mem. Acad. de Ciencas Econômicas, São Paulo; then Sec. of Finance, Municipal State Govts.; Gov. of São Paulo 59-63; Brazilian Minister of Finance June 63-64; Christian Democrat.
c/o Ministry of Finance, Rio de Janeiro, Brazil.

Pinto Barbosa, António Manuel; Portuguese economist and diplomatist; b. 31 July 1917; ed. Universidade Técnica de Lisboa.
Teacher 41-50; Prof., Inst. of Higher Econ. and Financial Sciences 51-; Pres. Comm. for Reorganisation of Industrial Resources 51-54; Under-Sec. of State at Treasury 51-54; Minister of Finance and Gov. of Int. Bank for Reconstruction and Devt. 55-65; Gov. Bank of Portugal (Banco de Portugal) and Gov. Int. Monetary Fund 66-; Grand Cross, Order of Christ, Order of Prince Henry and of Isabella the Catholic.
Publs. *L'Industrie des Conserves au Portugal* 41, *L'Economie, aspects positifs et aspects théologiques* 43, *L'Economie du Café* 45, *La crise des exportations métropolitaines pour l'étranger* 50, *La tâche du Ministre des Finances* 55, *Banco de Fomento Nacional* 59, *L'Activité du Ministre des Finances* 60, *La Défense de la Stabilité Financière* 62, *Communication du Ministre des Finances sur le crédit extérieur* 62, *La phase actuelle des finances portugaises* 64, *La Dévaluation de 1949 et le Commerce Extérieur Portugais* 66.
Rua Almirante António Saldanha 3, Bairro do Restelo, Lisbon, Portugal.

Pinto-Coelho, Luis da Camara; Portuguese lawyer and diplomatist; b. 12; ed. Liceu Pedro Nuñes, Univ. of Lisbon and Univ. of Rome.
Civil Governor, District of Castelo Branco 34-36; Gen. Sec. Portuguese Youth Org. 36-37; lawyer 39-61; Prof. Univ. of Lisbon 40-; Legal Adviser, Ministry of Economy 42-60; Deputy at Nat. Assembly 45-49; Nat. Commissary, Portuguese Youth Org. 46-52; Ambassador to Spain 61-; several decorations.
Publ. *The Co-Proprietor and the Portuguese Law* 39, 42.
Portuguese Embassy, Pinar 1, Madrid, Spain.

Piontek, Heinz; German writer; b. 15 Nov. 1925; ed. Theologisch-Philosophische Hochschule, Dillingen.
Berlin Prize for Literature 57, East German Writers' Prize, Esslingen 57; mem. Bavarian Acad. of Fine Arts 60-; Rom-Preis, *Villa Massimo* 60.
Publs. *Die Furt* (poems) 52, *Die Rauchfahne* (poems) 53, *Vor Augen* (stories) 55, *Wassermarken* (poems) 57, *Buchstab-Zauberstab* (essays) 59, *Aus meines Herzens Grunde* (anthology) 59, *John Keats: Poems* 60, *Weisser Panther* (radio play) 62, *Mit einer Kranichfeder* (poetry) 62, *Kastanien aus dem Ferer* (stories) 63, *Windrichtungen* (journey reports) 63, *Neue deutsche Erzählgedichte* (anthology) 64, *Klartext* (poetry) 66, *Die mittleren Jahre* (novel) 67.
Winzererstrasse 49, 8000 Munich 13, German Federal Republic.

Piore, Emanuel Ruben, B.A., PH.D.; American physicist; b. 19 July 1908; ed. Univ. of Wisconsin.
Chief Scientist, U.S. Navy Office of Naval Research 51-55; Vice-Pres. for Research, Avco Corpn. 55-56; Dir. of Research, Int. Business Machines Corpn., York 56-60, Vice-Pres. for Research and Engineering 60-63, Vice-

Pres. and Group Exec. 63-65, Vice-Pres. and Chief Scientist 65-, mem. Board of Dirs.; Fellow, American Physical Soc., Inst. of Electrical and Electronics Engineers, American Acad. of Arts and Sciences; mem. Nat. Acad. of Sciences, Nat. Science Board, Nat. Acad. of Eng.; consultant to President's Science Advisory Cttee.
115 Central Park West, New York 23, N.Y., U.S.A.
Telephone: 212-ENdicott 2-1772.

Piotrovsky, Boris Borisovich; Soviet historian; b. 1908; ed. Leningrad State Univ.
Scientific worker, Head of Section, State Acad. of Material Culture (now Inst. of Archaeology), U.S.S.R. Acad. of Sciences 29-53; Dir., Leningrad Branch, Inst. of Archaeology, U.S.S.R. Acad. of Sciences 53-54; Scientific Collaborator, Scientific Dir. of Eastern Dept., and Deputy Dir. for Scientific Matters, State Hermitage Museum, Leningrad 31-61, Dir. 61-; mem. C.P.S.U. 45-; Corresp. mem. Armenian Acad. of Sciences; Honoured Art Worker of Armenia 61; Hon. mem. Prehistory and Protohistory Soc. of Florence; Corresp. mem. British Acad. 67; Red Banner of Labour (three times), Dr. h.c. (Univ. of Delhi).
Main works: history and archaeology of Ancient East and Caucasus; in charge of excavations at Urart Fortress, Erevan (Armenia) 39-; directed U.S.S.R. Acad. of Sciences archaeological expedition in Nubia (United Arab Republ) 60-62; over 120 scientific works, incl. *History and Culture of Uraratu* (State Prize) 46.
State Hermitage, Dvortsovaya naberezhnaya 34, Leningrad, U.S.S.R.

Piovene, Guido; Italian writer and journalist; b. 27 July 1907.
Correspondent for Germany on *Ambrosiano* 30-33, with *Pan* 33-35, with *Corriere della Sera* from 35, then joined *La Stampa*, Turin; has contributed articles for numerous cultural and literary magazines.
Publs. *La Vedova allegra* 31, *Lettere di una Novizia* 42, *La Gazzetta nera* 43, *Pietà contro pietà* 46, *I falsi Redentori* 49, *De America* 53, *Viaggio in Italia* 57, *Processo dell'-Islam all Civiltà occidentale* 57, *Le Furie* 63, *Madame La France* 66, *La gente che perdé Jerusalemme* 67.
Piazza Belgioioso 2, Milan, Italy.
Telephone: 791345.

Piper, David Towry, M.A., F.S.A.; British museum director and writer; b. 21 July 1918; ed. Clifton Coll. and St. Catharine's Coll., Cambridge.
Served in Indian Army 40-45, Japanese Prisoner-of-War 42-45; Asst. Keeper Nat. Portrait Gallery, London 46-64, Dir. 64-67; Slade Prof. of Fine Art, Oxford Univ. 66-67; Dir. Fitzwilliam Museum, Cambridge 67-.
Publs. *It's Warm Inside* 53, *The English Face* 57, *Trial by Battle* 59, *Catalogue of 17th Century Portraits in the National Portrait Gallery* 63, *Companion Guide to London* 64; Editor: *Enjoying Paintings* 64, *Painting in England, 1500-1880* 65.
Fitzwilliam Museum, Trumpington Street, Cambridge, England.

Piper, John; British painter and author; b. 13 Dec. 1903; ed. Epsom Coll. and Royal Coll. of Art.
Exhibited London 25-; paintings bought by Tate Gallery, Victoria and Albert Museum, Contemporary Art Society, etc.; war artist, commissioned to paint ruins of House of Commons 41, and two series of water-colours for H.M. The Queen 42-43; Trustee of Tate Gallery 46-53, 54-61, 68-; mem. Royal Fine Art Comm. 59-; Trustee, Nat. Gallery 67-; designer of opera and ballet (London, Milan and Venice), of stained glass (Oundle Coll. Chapel, Coventry Cathedral, St. Andrew's, Plymouth, Eton Coll. Chapel, etc.) Retrospective Exhbn., Cologne 65; Hon. D.Litt. (Oxford and Leicester Univs.); Hon. A.R.C.A.; Hon. A.R.I.B.A.

Publs. *Shell Guide to Oxfordshire* 38, *Brighton Aquatints* 39, *British Romantic Painters* 42, *Buildings and Prospects*; *Romney Marsh* (King Penguin series, with own water-colours); and with John Betjeman: *Architectural Guide to Buckinghamshire, Architectural Guide to Berkshire.*
Fawley Bottom Farmhouse, nr. Henley-on-Thames, Oxon., England.

Piper, Klaus; German publisher; b. 27 March 1911; ed. Maximilians-Gymnasium, Munich, and bookselling schools.
With R. Piper & Co., Munich (book publishers) 32-, Partner 41-53, sole Managing Dir. 53-; mem. Finance Cttee. of German Booksellers Asscn., Central PEN of German Fed. Repub., German UNESCO Comm., Rotary Club, Asscn. of Literary Publishers; Golden Cultural Medal, Italian Ministry of Foreign Affairs 63.
Publs. *Offener Horizont* 53, *Nach 50 Jahren* 54, *Stationen —Piper-Almanach 1904-1964* 64; Editor: Reinhard Piper *Mein Leben als Verleger* 64.
Piper & Co., K.G., Georgenstrasse 4, Munich 13, German Federal Republic.

Pipinelis, Panayotis; Greek diplomatist and politician; b. 99; ed. Commercial College, Neuchâtel and Univ. of Freiburg.
Minister of Govt.-in-Exile to Govts. of Poland, Belgium and Luxembourg, in London 42; Chief of Household of King of Greece 42-46; Minister of Foreign Affairs 50; Perm. Del. to NATO 52; Minister of Commerce 61-63; Prime Minister June 63-Sept. 63; Minister of Econ. Co-ordination April 67; Minister of Foreign Affairs Nov. 67-; many decorations, including Grand Cross of the Royal Order of George I (Greece), Order of the Nile (Egypt), Leopold II (Belgium); Nat. Radical Union.
Publs. include: *Die Sozialpolitische und Staatsrechtliche Stellung des Königturus in Griechenland, Humanisme et Politique, Greece's International Position and Social Problems* (in Greek), *Memoirs* (in Greek), *More Light on Our National Policy in World War II* (in Greek).
King George II Square, Athens, Greece.

Pipping, Hugo Edvard, DR. PHIL.; Finnish economist; b. 12 June 1895; ed. Univ. of Helsinki.
Assistant Librarian, Univ. Library, Helsinki 19-28; Prof. of Econ. and Statistics, Swedish Commercial Univ., Helsinki 28-41; Prof. of Econ., Univ. of Helsinki 41-58; Dean Faculty of Political and Social Science 45-50, Vice-Rector 50-58; Chancellor Åbo Acad. 58-67; Sec. Economic Soc. Finland 24-41, mem. of Board 41-68; Editor of Society's journal *Ekonomiska Samfundets Tidskrift* 48-67; mem. of Scientific Soc. Finland, Finnish Historical Soc., Royal Soc. of Arts and Sciences, Gothenburg and Scientific Soc. of Lund, Sweden; Sec.-Gen. Finnish Production Cttee. 40-42; Vice-Chair. Swedish Literary Soc. of Finland 47-66; visited U.S.A. on Rockefeller Grant 48; Grand Cross of Finnish Lion; Commdr. of White Rose 51, of Swedish Order of North Star 48; Hon. Dr. rer. pol. (Helsinki), Ph.D. (Uppsala).
Publs. *Myntreformen dr 1865* 28, *Jean Cronstedt* 32, *Behov och levnadsstandard* 35, *Finlands näringsliv* 36, *Landsbygdens sociala problem i Finland* 40, *Ekonomiska Samfundet i Finland 1894-1944* 44, *Standard of Living* 53, *Från pappersrubel till guldmark. Finlands Bank 1811-1961* 61, *Bankliv genom hundra år* 62.
7A6 Kronbergsgatan, Helsinki 16, Finland.
Telephone: 634935.

Pirasteh, Said Mehdi, PH.D.; Iranian lawyer and politician; b. 19; ed. Teheran Univ.
Successively clerk, Ministry of Justice, Public Prosecutor, Rep. of Public Prosecutor at Judicial Court, Asst. to Public Prosecutor of Supreme Court, Under-Sec. Ministry of Interior, Gov.-Gen. of Fars and Southern Ports, Gov.-Gen. of Khusistan; mem. Chamber of

Deputies 52-64; Minister of Interior 63-64; Amb. to Iraq 64-.
Imperial Iranian Embassy, Karradet Mariam, Baghdad, Iraq.

Piraten (*see* Nilsson, F.)

Pirbhai, Count Sir Eboo, Kt., O.B.E.; Kenyan company director; b. 25 July 1905; ed. Duke of Gloucester School, Nairobi.
Representative of Aga Khan in Africa; mem. Nairobi City Council 38-43; mem. Legislative Council 52-60; Pres. Central Muslim Asscn.; Pres. Aga Khan Supreme Council, Africa; Brilliant Star of Zanzibar.
P.O. Box 898, Nairobi, Kenya.

Pire, R.P. Dominique-Georges, TH.D., O.P.; Belgian ecclesiastic and social worker; b. 10 Feb. 1910; ed. Coll. de Bellevue (Dinant), Studium de la Sarte-Huy, Angelicum Univ., Rome and Louvain Univ.
Lecturer in Moral Philosophy, Studium de la Sarte-Huy 37-47; founded various charitable organisations, including Les Stations de Plein-Air de Huy (for poor children) 38 and Le Service d'Entr'Aide Familiale (for poor families) 40; active in the Resistance 40-45; founded Aide aux Personnes Déplacées (Aid to Displaced Persons) 49, an international refugee relief organisation; four homes for old refugees have been set up in Belgium, seven European Villages for refugees have been founded, five in Germany and one each in Belgium and Austria; founded "The Heart Open to the World" Asscn. 59, Fraternal Dialogue between Black, White and Yellow 59, Peace Univ. 60, First Island of Peace in Pakistan 62, second in India 67; Nobel Peace Prize 58; Sonning Prize 64; Chevalier, Légion d'Honneur, Croix de Guerre avec Palmes, Médaille de la Résistance, Médaille de la Guerre 40-45, Médaille de la Reconnaissance Nationale, Croix d'Honneur du Mérite Civique Française, Orden Pour le Mérite, Federal Republic of Germany.
Publs. *Building Peace* 67, and numerous articles.
Office: 35 rue du Marché, Huy, Belgium; Home: 28 Plaine de la Sarte, Huy, Belgium.

Pirelli, Alberto; Italian industrial ist; b. 28 April 1882.
Honorary Chair. Pirelli, S.p.A., Milan; Managing Dir. Pirelli and Co., Milan; Dir. Société Int. Pirelli, Basle; mem. Int. Chamber of Commerce, Pres. 28-29; Hon. Pres. Istituto degli Studi della Politica Int. of Milan; Hon. Plenipotentiary Minister; Minister of State 38.
"Centro Pirelli", Piazza Duca d'Aosta 3, Milan, Italy.

Pirelli, Leopoldo; Italian businessman; b. 27 Aug. 1925.
Chairman, Pirelli S.p.A., Milan; Managing Dir. Pirelli and Co., Milan; Dir. Société Int. Pirelli, Basle, Montecatini-Edison S.p.A. Milan, Generale Industrie Metallurgiche, Firenze, La Centrale, Milan, Riunione Adriatica di Sicurtà, Milan, Mediobanca, Milan, FIDIA (Finanziaria Italiana di Investimenti Azionari), Milan, Rome, Italconsult, Automobile Club of Milan.
"Centro Pirelli", Piazza Duca d'Aosta 3, Milan, Italy.

Pirenne, Jacques, Comte, LL.D., PH.D.; Belgian historian; b. 91; ed. Ghent Univ.
Tutor to Prince Leopold (now ex-King Leopold III) 20-24; Chargé de Cours Univ. of Brussels 21, Prof. 24-54; Sec. Oriental Inst. 30-; scientific mem. Oriental Inst. of Prague 33; Michonis Prof. Coll. de France 35; awarded Quinquennial Prize for Historical Sciences for work 30-35; Lecturer Univ. of Cairo 39; Prof. Univ. of Grenoble 40, Univ. of Geneva 41-44; Head King Leopold's Secretariat with title "Secretary to the King" Aug. 45; Editor *Archives d'Histoire du Droit Oriental* 35-; mem. Académie Royale de Belgique 45-, Acad. Septentrionale (Paris) 60; Grand Croix Ordre de

la Couronne, Grand Officier Ordre de Léopold, Officier Légion d'Honneur, etc.

Publs. *Histoire des Institutions et du Droit Privé de l'Ancienne Egypte* (3 vols.) 32-35, *La civilisation sumérienne* 44, *La civilisation babylonienne* 45, *Les Grands Courants de l'Histoire Universelle* (7 vols., many trans.) 44-56, *La Belgique devant le nouvel équilibre du monde* 45, *Civilisations Antiques* 50, *Histoire de l'Europe de 1500 à 1955* (3 vols.) 60-62, *Histoire de la civilisation de l'ancienne Egypte* (3 vols.) 60-63, *La Religion et le Morale de l'Egypte antique* 64, *La Société hebräique, d'après le Bible* 64.

15 rue Buchholtz, Brussels, Belgium; Château de Hierges, Ardennes, France.

Pirzada, Sharifuddin, LL.B., S.PK.; Pakistani lawyer and politician; b. 12 June 1923; ed. Univ. of Bombay. Secretary Muslim Students' Fed. 43-45; Sec. Provincial Muslim League 46; Man. Editor *Morning Herald* 46; Prof., Sind Muslim Law Coll., Karachi 47-55; Adviser to Constitution Comm. of Pakistan 60; Chair. Pakistan Company Law Comm. and mem. Int. Rivers Cttee. 60; Pres. Pakistan Branch Int. Law Asscn. and Pres. Legal Aid Soc.; Pres. Karachi Bar Asscn.; Senior Advocate, Supreme Court of Pakistan; Attorney-Gen. of Pakistan 64-66, 68-; Minister of Foreign Affairs 66-68.

Publs. include: *Evolution of Pakistan, Fundamental Rights and Constitutional Remedies in Pakistan.*

C-37, K.D.A. Scheme No. 1, Habib Ibrahim Rahimtoola Road, Karachi, Pakistan.

Pisani, Edgar; French politician; b. 9 Oct. 1918; ed. in Tunisia and Paris.

Resistance 44-45; Dir. Ministry of the Interior Office 46-47; Prefect, Upper Loire 46-47; Prefect, Upper Marne 48-54; Senator, Upper Marne 54-; Minister of Agriculture 61-66, of Equipment 66-67, also Minister of Housing 67; Mayor of Montreuil-Bellay 65; mem. Chamber of Deputies 67-; Movement for Reform.

1 rue Bayard, Paris 8e; Mairie de Montreuil-Bellay 49, France.

Telephone: ELY-21-42; and 52-30-12.

Pisson, Paul; French industrialist; b. 26 Jan. 1891. President, General Confederation of Small and Medium Enterprises and Fed. of Music Industries; Vice-Pres. Nat. Council of French Employers; mem. Nat. Credit Council, Higher Council for Electricity and Gas; Vice-Pres. Econ. Council 47-59; mem. Econ. and Social Council, representing Private Industrial Enterprises, Vice-Pres. 59-67; Pres. de la Caisse de garantie des sociétés de caution mutuelle; Officier, Légion d'Honneur, Commandeur du Mérite commercial et de L'Economie nationale.

47 rue de Babylone, Paris 7e, France.

Pistarini, Pascual Angel; Argentine army officer and politician; b. 6 Oct. 1915; ed. Colegio Militar de la Nación, Escuela Superior de Guerra and Escuela Nacional de Guerra.

Commissioned 48; Cavalry Chief of Staff 59; Brig.-Gen. 60; Commdr. 4th Cavalry Div. 61-62; Commdt. of Cavalry 62-63; Commdr. 1st Army Corps 63-65; Maj.-Gen. 63, Lieut.-Gen. 65; Commdr.-in-Chief of the Army 66-Dec. 66; Argentine record holder for equestrian high jump 46-; Commdr. Orden Militar de Ayacucho (Peru); Grand Officer Orden al Mérito Militar (Brazil). Billingshurst 1558, Piso 8 Dto. 15, Buenos Aires, Argentina.

Piston, Walter, A.B., MUS.D.; American musician; b. 20 Jan. 1894; ed. Harvard Univ. and in Paris. Member Harvard Music Faculty 26-60; Walter W. Naumburg Prof. of Music 48-60, Emer. 60-; Mus.D. h.c. from four univs.; mem. American Acad. of Arts and Letters; mem. American Acad. of Arts and Sciences;

New York Critics' Circle Award 43; Pulitzer Prize in Music 48, 61.

Works: Eight symphonies, concertos for violin, and many other compositions.

Publs. *Harmonic Analysis* 33, *Harmony* 41, *Counterpoint* 47, *Orchestration* 55.

127 Somerset Street, Belmont, Mass., U.S.A.

Pisula, Feliks; Polish politician; b. 08; ed. Poznań University.

Member People's youth organisations until 39; mem. Resistance Movement 39-44; Ministry of Agriculture 44-57; Minister of Food and Purchases 57-; mem. Central Cttee. United People's Party 62-.

20 Swietkrzyska Street, Warsaw, Poland.

Pitblado, Sir David B., K.C.B., C.V.O.; British government official; b. 18 Aug. 1912; ed. Strand School, London, Emmanuel Coll., Cambridge and Middle Temple.

Dominions Office 35-39, Asst. Private Sec. to Sec. of State for Dominions Affairs 37-39; N. American Secr. War Cabinet Office 42; Treasury 42-, Under-Sec. Econ. Planning Staff, Treasury 49-51; Principal Private Sec. to Prime Minister (Lord Attlee, Sir Winston Churchill, Lord Avon) 51-56; Financial Attaché, British Embassy, Wash.; Alt. Exec. Dir. Int. Bank for Reconstruction and Devt. 56-58; Vice-Chair. Management Board of European Payments Union and Monetary Agreement 58-60; Third Sec. Treasury 60; Exec. Dir. for U.K. of Int. Bank and Affiliates, and of Int. Monetary Fund; Head of U.K. Treasury and Supply Del., and Econ. Minister, British Embassy, Washington 61-63; Deputy-Sec., Ministry of Power 65-66; Perm. Sec. Ministry of Power 66-.

23 Cadogan Street, London, S.W.3, England.

Pithart, Vilém, LL.D.; Czechoslovak diplomatist; b. 28 May 1911; ed. Universita Karlova, Prague.

Head of Cabinet of Ministry of Industry 48; Deputy Minister of Industry, Deputy Minister of Heavy Industry, Deputy Minister of Heavy Eng., Deputy Minister of Eng. 48-54; Amb. to Yugoslavia 54-60; Dept. Head, Ministry of Foreign Affairs 60; Deputy Minister of Foreign Affairs 62-64; Deputy Minister and Sec.-Gen. Ministry of Foreign Affairs 64-66; Amb. to France 66-; Order of Labour 61.

Ambassade de la République Socialiste Tchécoslovaque, 15 avenue Charles Floquet, Paris 8e, France.

Pitman, Sir (Isaac) James, K.B.E., M.A.; British publisher and politician; b. 14 Aug. 1901; ed. Eton and Christ Church, Oxford.

Joined Sir Isaac Pitman & Sons Ltd. 23, Chair. and Managing Dir. 34-; served R.A.F. 40-43, admin. duties, Air Ministry; Dir. Bank of England 41-45; Dir. of Organisation, Treasury 43-45; Conservative M.P. for Bath 45-64; Pro-Chancellor of Bath Univ. 66-; Dir. Boots Pure Drug Co. Ltd., Bovril Ltd.; invented and introduced the Initial Teaching Alphabet.

Holme Wood, Chisbridge Cross, nr. Marlow, Bucks.; and 58 Chelsea Park Gardens, London S.W.3, England.

Pitter, Ruth; British poetess; b. 7 Nov. 1897; ed. Coborn School, London.

Junior clerk, War Office 17-18; painter of furniture, etc. Suffolk and London 18-30; own business in partnership with Kathleen O'Hara 30-43; war-work at The Morgan Crucible Co., Battersea, London 43-45; worked at home 45-; Hawthornden Prize 37; Heinemann Award 54; Queen's Medal for Poetry 55.

Publs. *First Poems* 20, *First and Second Poems* 27, *Persephone in Hades* (privately printed) 31, *A Mad Lady's Garland* 34, *The Rude Potato* 41, *The Bridge* 45, *Pitter on Cats* 46, *Urania* 51, *The Ermine* 53, *Still by Choice* 66, *Poems 1926-1946* 68.

Office: c/o Cresset Press, Barrie Books Ltd., 2 Clements Inn, London, W.C.2; Home: The Hawthorns, Chilton Road, Long Crendon, Aylesbury, Bucks., England. Telephone: Long Crendon 373.

Pittermann, Bruno, PH.D., LL.D.; Austrian politician; b. 3 Sept. 1905; ed. Vienna Univ.
Sec. of Chamber of Labour, Klagenfurt, Carinthia 29-34, when dismissed for political reasons; Sec. Dept. of Social Welfare and Admin., later Head of Dept.; Sec.-Gen. Vienna Chamber of Labour; Parly. Deputy; Vice-Chancellor (Deputy Prime Minister) 57-66; Chair. Socialist Party until 67; mem. Consultative Vice-Pres. Assembly, Council of Europe; Pres. Socialist Int.
Ballhausplatz 2, Vienna I, Austria.

Pizzardo, H.E. Cardinal Giuseppe; Italian ecclesiastic; b. 13 July 1877.
Priest 03; Under-Sec. of State 21; Titular Archbishop of Nicea 30; Sec. for Extraordinary Ecclesiastical Affairs to the Pope 29; Cardinal 37; Bishop of Albano 48-66, Hon. Bishop of Albano 66-; Prefect, Sacred Congregation of Seminaries and Univs. of Study; mem. Sacred Congregations of the Holy Office of the Consistory, of Religious, of Ceremonies, De Propaganda Fide and of Extraordinary Ecclesiastical Affairs; Vice-Dean Sacred Coll. of Cardinals 65-; mem. Pontifical Comms. for Biblical Studies and for Vatican City State, Cardinalicial Comms. for the Admin. of the Properties of the Holy See, of the Inst. of Works of Religion; Grand Chancellor, Gregorian Pontifical Univ.
Via della Conciliazione 10, Rome, Italy.

Plá y Deniel, H.E. Cardinal Enrique; Spanish ecclesiastic; b. 19 Dec. 1876.
Ordained 1900; Bishop of Avila 18-35, of Salamanca 35-41; Archbishop of Toledo and Primate of Spain 41-; created Cardinal 46; mem. Sacred Congregations for the Oriental Church, of Religions and of Rites.
[Died 5 July 1968].

Planchon, Roger; French theatrical director and playwright; b. 12 Sept. 1931.
Founder Théâtre de la Comédie, Lyons; Dir. Théâtre de la Cité, Villeurbanne 57-; Croix de Guerre.
Publs. Plays: *La Remise* 61, *Pattes blanches* 64, *Bleus, Blancs, Rouges ou les Libertins* 67, *Dans le Vent* 68.
Théâtre de la Cité, 8 place de la Libération, Villeurbanne (Rhône), France.

Plant, Sir Arnold, Kt., B.COM., B.SC. (ECON.); British university professor; b. 29 April 1898; ed. London School of Econs. Univ. of London.
Professor and Dean of the Faculty of Commerce, Univ. of Capetown, S. Africa 24-30; Prof. in the Univ. of London 30-65, Prof. Emer. 65-; Temporary British Civil Servant 40-46; mem. Govt. Cttees. of Enquiry and formerly of the Monopolies and Restrictive Practices Comm.; Chair. Industrial Injuries Advisory Council, Chair. Advertising Standards Authority 62-65; Hon. Fellow, London School of Econs.
19 Wildwood Road, London, N.W.11, England.

Plantey, Alain Gilles; French government official; b. 19 July 1924; ed. Univs. de Bordeaux and Paris à la Sorbonne.
Staff of Council of State 49; French del. to UN 51-52; Master of Requests Council of State 56-; Legal Adviser Org. for European Econ. Co-operation (OEEC) 56-57; Prof. Ecole Royale d'Administration Cambodia 57; Gen. Sec. *Agence France-Presse* 58; Asst. Sec.-Gen. for the Community and African and Madagascan Affairs at the Presidency 61-; French Amb. in Madagascar 66-; Council mem. Ecole Nationale d'Administration and Museum Nationale d'Histoire naturelle; numerous decorations.
Publs. *La Réforme de la Justice marocaine* 49, *La Justice Répressive et le Droit Pénal Chérifien* 50; *Au Coeur du*

Problème Berbère 52, *Traité Pratique de la Fonction Publique* 56 and 63; *La Formation et le Perfectionnement des Fonctionnaires* 57, *La Communauté* 59.
51 rue Geoffroy Saint-Hilaire, Paris 5e, France.

Plaskett, Harry, F.R.S., M.A.; British astronomer; b. 5 July 1893; ed. Toronto Univ.
Astronomer Victoria Astrophysical Observatory 19-27; Lecturer, Associate Prof. and Prof. of Astrophysics Harvard Univ. 28-32; Savilian Prof. of Astronomy Oxford Univ. and Fellow New Coll 32-60, Emer. Prof. 60-; Pres. Royal Astronomical Soc. 45-47, Gold Medal 63.
48 Blenheim Drive, Oxford, England.
Telephone: Oxford 58109.

Plate, Juan, LL.D.; Paraguayan lawyer, economist and diplomatist; b. 8 April 1918; ed. Universidad Nacional del Paraguay.
Under-Sec. of State 40-41; mem. Civil and Commercial Court of Appeal 41-43; Minister of Agriculture and Finance 43-45; Prof. of Political Econs. and Finance, Nat. War Coll. of Paraguay 45-52; mem. Board of Dirs. Bank of Paraguay and Cen. Bank of Paraguay 46-50; mem. Council of State 51-55; Ambassador of Paraguay to Argentina 56-58; Ambassador to United States and to Org. of American States (OAS) 58-.
Pan American Union, Washington 6, D.C., U.S.A.

Platen, Baron Carl Henrik G:son von, B.A., M.POL.SC.; Swedish diplomatist; b. 14 Dec. 1913; ed. Lunds Universitet, London School of Econs. and Université de Paris à la Sorbonne.
Entered Foreign Service 39, served Moscow, Rome, Ankara, Washington, Geneva, Paris; Envoy and Perm. Rep. to UN and other int. orgs., Geneva 59, Ambassador 60-63; Ambassador at Large and Negotiator, UN Disarmament Conf. 63; Swedish Rep. to OECD, Paris 64-, to UNESCO 65-; Chair. OECD Industry Cttee.
Publ. *Diplomatikoch politik* 66.
Délégation de Suède, 48 avenue Montaigne, Paris 8e, France.
Telephone: 359-86-22.

Plath, Werner, DR.JURIS. UTR.; German insurance executive; b. 10 Dec. 1902; ed. Univs. of Tübingen and Kiel.
General Man. National Allgemeine Versicherungs-AG, National Lebensversicherungs-AG, Stettiner Rückversicherungs-A.G. 47-; Vice-Chair. Board of Dirs. Concordia Lebensvers.-A.G., Kölnische Rückvers.-G; Board of Dirs. Colonia Köln. Vers.-A.G., Union Krankenvers. A.G.; Dir. Westdeutsche Finanzierungs-G.m.b.H., Westdeutsche Kreditbank für Baufinanzierung A.G., Dresdner Bank, L. Possehl & Co. m.b.H., Nordstern Rückversicherungs A.G., Roland Rechtsschutz-Versicherungs A.G.; Grosses Verdienstkreutz.
Elsässer Strasse 36-38, 24 Lübeck, German Federal Republic.
Telephone: 3101201.

Platon, Dr. Nicolas; Greek archaeologist; b. 1909; ed. Univ. of Athens and Ecole des Hautes Etudes pratiques supérieurs, Paris.
Assistant at Heraklion Museum, Crete 30-35; Ephor of Antiquities in Beotia, etc. 35-38; Ephor of Antiquities in Crete and Dir. Heraklion Museum 38-62; Ephor of Antiquities and Dir. of Acropolis in Athens 61-65; Gen. Ephor of Antiquities 65-; Prof. at Univ. of Salonika 66-; Knight Order of Phoenix, Greece; Commendatore al Merito della Repubblica Italiana; Major works include: excavations in Crete, Beotia, Euboea, Skopelos and the great excavation of the Minoan Palace, Zakros, East Crete; Hon. mem. German and Austrian Inst., of Soc. for Promotion of Hellenic Studies; mem. Greek Archaeological Soc., Soc. of Cretan Studies.

Publs. *Crete* in *Archaeologia Mundi*, Geneva and many scientific monographs.
Faculty of Philosophy, Univ. of Salonika and Léof. Alexandras 126, Athens, Greece.
Telephone: 63529 (Salonika); 669092 (Athens).

Platt, Baron (Life Peer), cr. 67, of Grindleford; **Robert Platt,** Bt., M.D., F.R.C.P.; b. 16 April 1900; ed. Univ. of Sheffield.
Physician, Royal Infirmary, Sheffield 31-45; Lieut.-Col., later Brig., Royal Army Medical Corps 41-45; Prof. of Medicine, Manchester Univ. 46-65, Emer. 65-; Physician, Manchester Royal Infirmary 46-65; mem. Medical Research Council 53-57; Pres. Royal Coll. of Physicians, London 57-62; Chair. Clinical Research Board, Medical Research Council 64-67; Chair. Manchester Chamber Concerts Soc. 52-65; Pres. Eugenics Soc. 66-68; Chair. Advisory Cttee. on Distinction Awards, Ministry of Health 67-; mem. Asscn. of American Physicians; Hon. LL.D. (Sheffield and Belfast); Hon. M.D. (Bristol); Hon. F.R.A.C.P., Hon. F.A.C.P., Hon. F.C.G.P.
24 Topcliffe Way, Cambridge, England.

Platt, Benjamin Stanley, C.M.G., M.SC., PH.D., M.B., CH.B.; British nutritionist; b. 5 June 1903; ed. Leeds Univ.
Research Board 23-25; Beit Memorial Research Fellow, Bacteriology Dept., Univ. of Leeds 26-27, 31-32; House Physician, General Infirmary, Leeds 27-31; First House Physician 31; Assoc. in Medicine Div. of Clinical Research, Henry Lester Inst. of Medical Research, Shanghai 32-38; Dir. Medical Research Council's Human Nutrition Research Unit 44-67, Prof. of Human Nutrition, Univ. of London, and Head of Dept. of Human Nutrition, London School of Hygiene and Tropical Medicine; hon. mem. American Inst. of Nutrition 66.
Nutrition Building, National Institute for Medical Research, The Ridgeway, Mill Hill, London, N.W.7, England.

Platt, Sir Harry, Bt., M.D., M.S., F.R.C.S.; British surgeon; b. 7 Oct. 1886; ed. Manchester Univ. and U.S.A. Capt. Royal Army Medical Corps (T.F.) 15-19; Emeritus Prof. of Orthopaedic Surgery, Univ. of Manchester; Consultant Adviser in Orthopaedics, Ministry of Health 40-63; Pres. Royal Coll. of Surgeons of England 54-57; Pres. Société Int. de Chirurgie Orthopédique et de Traumatologie; Pres. Int. Fed. of Surgical Colls. 58-66; mem. American, French, Scandinavian, Italian, Neths., Australian, Argentine and Belgian Orthopædic Societies; Hon. Fellow, Royal Coll. of Surgeons and American, Royal Edinburgh, Royal Canadian, Royal Australasian and South African Colls. of Surgeons; Hon. LL.D. (Manchester, Liverpool and Belfast Univs.); Hon. M.D. (Berne), Docteur Honoris Causa (Univ. Paris) 66.
Publs. on orthopædic surgery and medical education.
11 Lorne Street, Manchester 13, Lancs., England.
Telephone: 061-273-3433.

Platteel, Pieter Johannes, PH.D.; Netherlands colonial administrator; b. 14 Aug. 1911; ed. Utrecht Univ.
Entered Netherlands Indies Civil Service 37; war service as reserve officer 40-45; Commr., Netherlands Indies Civil Service 48; Dir. Social Welfare Department, The Hague 54; Gov. Netherlands New Guinea 58-62; Burgomaster of Ede 62-; Knight, Order of Orange Nassau; Knight, Order of Netherlands Lion; Anti-Revolutionary Party.
Publs. *Grondslagen der Constitutie van Nederlandsch-Indië* 36; numerous articles on political and social science in periodicals.
c/o Town Hall, Ede; and Oude Arnhemseweg 19, Ede, Netherlands.
Telephone: 08380-13446.

Plattner, Karl; Italian painter; b. 13 Feb. 1919; ed. Acad. of Florence, Brera Acad. Milan and Art Acad. Paris.

Has lived in Brazil and France, now resident in Italy; One-man exhibitions at Merano, Bolzano, Verona, Innsbruck, Stuttgart, Munich, São Paulo, Rio de Janeiro, Chicago, Paris, Rome, Milan and Vienna 51-66 and other European cities; Group shows in Germany, Italy, Brazil, France, Uruguay and Sicily, including Biennali at Venice and São Paulo; numerous prizes.
Major Works: Fresco for War Memorial, Naturno, Italy 51; Fresco for Provincial Council Building, Bolzano 54-55; Panel for *Folhas* Newspaper building São Paulo and for Air France São Paulo 55-56; Panel for new Festival Hall Salzburg 60-61; Fresco for Europa Chapel, near Innsbruck 63-64; Panel for Austria A.G. Building, Vienna 65.
Piazza Borromeo 8, Milan, Italy.
Telephone: 875927.

Platzer, Wilfried; Austrian diplomatist; b. 5 April 1909; ed. Foreign Service School Vienna and Univ. of Vienna.
Diplomatic Service 33, Austrian Legation, Berlin 34, Foreign Office, Vienna 35-38, Counsellor Econ. Section 46-49, Political Section 49; Counsellor, Austrian Embassy, Wash. 50-54, Minister, Chief Econ. Section 54-58, Ambassador to United States 58-65; Under-Sec. for Econ. Affairs (with rank of Ambassador), Ministry for Foreign Affairs 66-; Sec.-Gen. for Foreign Affairs 67-.
Ballhausplatz 2, Vienna, Austria.
Telephone: 36-33-20.

Plaude, Karl Karlovich; Soviet thermal physicist; b. 1897; ed. Inst. of Civil Engineering.
Teacher, Inst. of Civil Eng., Riga 32-38, Inst. of Industrial Bldg. 32-38, Latvian State Univ. 45-53; Dir. Inst. of Energetics and Electrical Eng., Latvian Acad. of Sciences 47-; mem. Latvian Acad. of Sciences 51-, Pres. 60-; Corresp. mem. U.S.S.R. Acad. of Sciences 60-; mem. C.P.S.U. 46-; Orders and medals of U.S.S.R. Presidium of Latvian Academy of Sciences, 19 Turgenev Street, Riga 6, U.S.S.R.

Playfair, Sir Edward Wilder, K.C.B.; British company director and former government official; b. 17 May 1909; ed. Eton and King's Coll., Cambridge.
Inland Revenue 31-34; Treasury 34-46, 47-56 (Control Office for Germany and Austria 46-47); Perm. Under-Sec. of State for War 56-59; Perm. Sec. Ministry of Defence 60-61; Chair. Int. Computers and Tabulators Ltd. 61-65; Dir. Westminster Bank, Glaxo Group, Tunnel Portland Cement; Trustee *The Observer*.
12 The Vale, London, S.W.3, England.
Telephone: 01-352-4671.

Playford, Hon. Sir Thomas, G.C.M.G., M.P.; Australian politician; b. 5 July 1896; ed. Norton Summit Public School.
Served Australian Imperial Forces First World War; M.P. for Murray District 33, for Gumeracha District 38-66; Commr. for Crown Lands and Minister of Irrigation and Repatriation, S. Australian Govt. April-Nov. 38, Premier, Treas. and Minister of Immigration, S. Australian Govt. Nov. 38-March 65; Leader of Opposition 65-66; Leader Liberal Country League.
Norton Summit, South Australia.

Plaza (Lasso), Galo; Ecuadorean politician; b. 06; ed. Colegio Nacional Mejia, Univs. of Calif. and Maryland and Georgetown Univ. Foreign Service School.
Attaché Washington 30-31; mem. Municipal Council Quito 37-38, Pres. 38; Minister of Nat. Defence 38-40; Ambassador to U.S.A. 44-46; Senator 47; Pres. of Republic of Ecuador 48-52; mem. Special Policy Cttee. on Technical Assistance 53; Vice-Chair. Interamerican Research Cttee. 57; Chair. U.N. Observatory Group in Lebanon 58, UN "BASIC" Cttee. in the Congo 60, E.C.L.A. Latin American Common Market Cttee. 58-59; Vice-Chair. Oxford Conference 61; UN Sec.-Gen. Rep.

in Cyprus 64; UN Mediator in Cyprus 64-66; Sec.-Gen. of Org. of American States 68-; hon. degrees from Univ. of Maryland and New School for Social Research, New York, Columbia Univ., New York, Washington and Harvard Univs.; decorations from U.S.A., Mexico, Venezuela, Guatemala, Colombia, Chile, Costa Rica, Cuba, Bolivia, China.
Organisation of American States, Pan American Union, Washington 6, D.C., U.S.A.; Home: Avenida 6 de Diciembre 1300, Quito, Ecuador.

Pleasence, Donald; British actor and producer; b. 5 Oct. 1919; ed. Ecclesfield Grammar School, Yorkshire, England.
Made first stage appearance 39; first London appearance in *Twelfth Night* at Arts Theatre 42; R.A.F. 42-46 (prisoner-of-war 44-46); returned to stage in *The Brothers Karamazov* 46, *Peter Pan* 47; Perth Repertory Theatre 47; Birmingham Repertory Theatre 48-50; Bristol Old Vic Co. 50-51; *Right Side Up* and *Saints' Day* London 51; appeared in New York with Laurence Olivier's Co. 51-52; *Hobson's Choice* Arts Theatre 52; played in own play *Ebb Tide* at Edinburgh Festival and Royal Court Theatre, London 52; Stratford-on-Avon season 53; *Antony and Cleopatra* London 53; *The Rules of the Game* 55, *The Lark* 55, *Misalliance* 56, *Restless Heart* 57, *The Caretaker* (London and New York) 60-, *Poor Bitos* (co-producer), *The Man in the Glass Booth* (co-producer) 67; numerous film appearances include *The Beachcomber, Manuela, Heart of a Child, The Caretaker, The Greatest Story Ever Told, Fantastic Voyage, The Hallelujah Trail, The Great Escape, Doctor Crippen, Cul-de-Sac, Will Penny*; numerous television appearances in Britain and America; Television Actor of the Year Award 58; London Critics Best Stage Performance Award 60; Variety Club Award: Stage Actor of 1967.
Willows, Datchet, Bucks, England.
Telephone: Slough 43615.

Plenderleith, Harold James, C.B.E., M.C., B.SC., PH.D., F.R.S.E., F.S.A., F.M.S.; British chemist; b. 19 Sept. 1898; ed St. Andrews Univ.
Keeper, Research Laboratory, British Museum 24-59; Prof. of Chemistry, Royal Acad. 36-58; Chair. Hon. Scientific Advisory Cttee. Nat. Gallery 44-58; Hon. Treas. Int. Inst. for the Conservation of Museum Objects 50-58, Vice-Pres. 59-65, Pres. 65-68; mem. ex-officio ICOM Directory Board on Conservation; Dir. Int. Centre for Study of Preservation and Restoration of Cultural Property, Rome 59-; Hon. LL.D. (St. Andrews); Gold Medal Soc. Antiquaries of London 64.
Publs. *The Preservation of Antiquities, The Conservation of Prints, Drawings and Manuscripts, The Preservation of Leather Bookbinding, The Conservation of Antiquities and Works of Art* 56.
Palazzo Lancellotti, Via Lancellotti, Rome, Italy.
Telephone: 653427.

Plescoff, Georges; French financial adviser and international bank official; b. 9 March 1918; ed. Univ. de Paris and Ecole Nat. d'Administration.
Teacher 37; mem. staff Council of State 45; Insp. of Finances 47; Special Asst. to Sec. of State for Finance and Econ. Affairs 51; with Econ. Comm. for Europe 52-54; Ministry of Finance 55; Tech. Adviser to Minister of Econ. Affairs 56; Dir. Caisse des Dépôts et Consignations 57-67; mem. Board Agence France-Presse 57-67; Vice-Pres. Soc. d'Etudes pour le Développement Economique et Social (SEDES) 58-67; mem. French Antitrust Comm. 60-67; mem. Board Banque Française du Commerce Extérieur, Soc. Nat. des Pétroles, and Pres. France-Obligations (investment trust) 61-67; mem. Stock Market Cttee. 62-67; mem. Board Soc. Nat. d'Investissements Tunisienne 65-67; mem. Finance, Credit and Tax Section, Econ. and Social Council (France) 65-66; Financial Counsellor French Embassy,

Washington, and Exec. Dir. Int. Monetary Fund, Int. Bank for Reconstruction and Devt. and affiliates 67-.
French Embassy, 2535 Belmont Road, N.W., Washington, D.C., U.S.A.

Pleskot, Václav; Czechoslovak diplomatist; b. 1 Jan. 1921; ed. Lycée and Univ. of Prague and Advanced School of Econs., Prague.
Director of Nat. Bank of Czechoslovakia 48-52; Vice-Pres. of State Cttee. for Physical Culture and Sport 52-55, Pres. 55-57; Dir. at Ministry of Finance 58; Dir. of Dept. for Western Europe, Ministry of Foreign Affairs 59-60; Ambassador to France 60-66; Vice-Minister and Sec.-Gen. Ministry of Foreign Affairs 66-; Order of Labour 55.
Ministry of Foreign Affairs, Prague 1, Černínský palác, Czechoslovakia.
Telephone: 093.

Pleven, René, D. en D.; French politician; b. 15 April 1901; ed. Ecole des Sciences Politiques, Paris.
Asst. Head French Air Mission in U.S.A. 39; mem. Franco-British Co-ordination Cttee. 40; Sec.-Gen. Govt. of French Equatorial Africa 40; negotiated agreement for dispatch of war material to Free French, Washington 41; Nat. Commr. for Economy, Finance and Colonies 41-42, for Foreign Affairs and Colonies 42-43, for Colonies 43; Commr. for Colonies French Cttee. for Nat. Liberation 43-44; Minister for Colonies, French Provisional Govt. Sept.-Nov. 44; Minister of Finance 44-46; Minister of Nat. Defence Bidault Cabinet 49-50, Queuille Cabinet July 50; Prime Minister July 50-March 51; Vice-Premier Mar.-Aug. 51; Prime Minister Aug. 51-Jan. 52; Minister of Nat. Defence, Pinay Cabinet Mar.-Dec. 52, Mayer Cabinet Jan.-May 53, and Laniel Cabinet 54; Minister of Foreign Affairs May 58; Deputy (Côtes-du-Nord) 45-; Pres. Comm. for Econ. Devt. of Brittany 64-, Breton Centre Ltd. 65-; mem. European Parl. Assembly; Dr. h.c. Columbia Univ.
Publ. *Avenir de la Bretagne.*
7 rue d'Uzès, Paris 12e; 12 rue Châteaubriand, Dinan (Côtes du Nord), France.

Plimpton, Francis T. P., A.B., LL.B.; American lawyer and government official; b. 7 Dec. 1900; ed. Amherst Coll. and Harvard Univ.
Admitted to Bar 26; law practice 26-31, 33-61, 65-; Gen. Solicitor, Reconstruction Finance Corpn. 32-33; Partner, Debevoise, Plimpton, Lyons and Gates (and predecessor firms) 33-61, 65-; Deputy Rep. of U.S.A. to UN with rank of Ambassador 61-65, Acting Rep. July 65-; Del. 15-19th UN Gen. Assemblies; Dir. of numerous financial, educational, legal and cultural orgs.; Fellow, American Acad. of Arts and Sciences; Hon. LL.D.
320 Park Avenue, New York City, N.Y. 10022; Home: 131 East 66th Street, New York City, N.Y. 10021; also Chichester Road, West Hills, Huntingdon, L.I., N.Y. 11743, U.S.A.
Telephone: PL2-6400.

Plimsoll, Sir James, C.B.E.; Australian diplomatist; b. 25 April 1917; ed. Sydney High School and Univ. of Sydney.
With Economic Department, Bank of New South Wales, Sydney 38-42; served in Australian Army 42-47; mem. Australian Del., Far Eastern Comm. 45-48; Rep. UN Comm. for Unification and Rehabilitation of Korea 50-52; Asst. Sec., Department of External Affairs 53-59; Perm. Rep. to UN 59-63; High Commr. in India and Ambassador to Nepal 63-65; Sec. Dept. of External Affairs 65-.
Department of External Affairs, Canberra, A.C.T., Australia.

Plisetskaya, Maiya Mikhailovna; Soviet ballerina; b. 20 Nov. 1925; ed. Moscow Choreographical School.
Soloist, Bolshoi Ballet 43, now a Principal Dancer; First Prize, Budapest Int. Competition 49; People's

Artist of the R.S.F.S.R. 51; People's Artist of the U.S.S.R. 56, Lenin Prize 64.
Main ballet roles: Odette-Odile (*Swan Lake*, Tchaikovsky), Raimonda (*Raimonda*, Glazunov), Zaryema (*The Fountain of Bakhchisarai*, Asafiev), Kitri (*Don Quixote*, Minkus), Juliet (*Romeo and Juliet*, Prokofiev), Girl-Bird, Syunmbike (*Shuralye*, Yarullin), Laurencia (*Laurencia*, Krein), Yegina (*Spartak*, Khachaturian). State Academic Bolshoi Theatre, 1 Sverdlov Square, Moscow, U.S.S.R.

Plojhar, Josef; Czechoslovak politician; b. 2 March 1902; ed. theological studies.
Arrested by the Gestapo and imprisoned in Buchenwald concentration camp 39 and later in Dachau; Chair. of the organisation of the Czechoslovak People's Party in České Budějovice district 45; Deputy to Nat. Assembly 45-; Minister of Health 48-68; Chair. of the Czechoslovak People's Party 51-68; mem. Presidium of Central Cttee. of Nat. Front 55-; Czechoslovak Peace Prize 66, and other decorations; Dr. Theol. h.c.
c/o Ministry of Health, Prague, Czechoslovakia.

Plomer, William, C.B.E., F.R.S.L.; British author; b. 10 Dec. 1903.
Member staff Admiralty 40-45; Hon. D.Litt. (Durham); Queen's Gold Medal for Poetry 63.
Publs. *Turbott Wolfe, Sado, I Speak of Africa, The Invaders, Paper Houses, The Family Tree, The Fivefold Screen, The Case is Altered, The Child of Queen Victoria, Cecil Rhodes, Visiting the Caves, Ali the Lion, Kilvert's Diary* (Ed.), *Selected Poems, Double Lives, The Dorking Thigh, Curious Relations* (Ed.), *Four Countries, Museum Pieces, Gloriana, A Shot in the Park, At Home, Collected Poems, Message in Code* (Ed.), *Curlew River, Taste and Remember, The Burning Fiery Furnace, The Prodigal Son.*
c/o Jonathan Cape Ltd., 30 Bedford Square, London, W.C.1, England.

Plowden, Baron, cr. 59 (Life Peer); **Edwin Noel Plowden,** K.C.B., K.B.E.; British administrator; b. 6 Jan. 1907; ed. Switzerland and Pembroke Coll., Cambridge.
Temporary Civil Servant Ministry of Economic Warfare 39-40; Ministry of Aircraft Production 40-46; mem. Aircraft Supply Council, Chief Exec. 45-46; Chief Planning Officer and Chair. Econ. Planning Bd. 47-53, mem. 53-59; Vice-Chair. Temporary Council Cttee. of NATO 51-52; Chair. Designate U.K. Atomic Energy Authority 53-54, Chair. 54-59; Chair. Cttee. of Enquiry into Treasury Control of Public Expenditure 59-61; Chair. Cttee. of Enquiry into Org. of Representational Service Overseas 62-63; Chair. Cttee. of Enquiry into Aircraft Industry 64-65; Visiting Fellow Nuffield Coll., Oxford 56-64; Hon. Fellow Pembroke Coll., Cambridge 58; Chair. Tube Investments Ltd. 60-; Dir. Nat. Provincial Bank Ltd., and Commercial Union Assurance Co. Ltd.
Martels Manor, Dunmow, Essex; and 7 Cottesmore Gardens, London W.8, England.

Plowright, Joan Anne (Lady Olivier); British actress; b. 28 Oct. 1929; ed. Scunthorpe Grammar School and Old Vic Theatre School.
Member Old Vic Company, toured South Africa 52-53; first leading rôle in *The Country Wife*, London 56; mem. English Stage Company 56; best actress (Tony) Award for *A Taste of Honey*, N.Y. 60.
Principal plays acted in: *The Chairs* 57, *The Entertainer* 58, *Major Barbara* and *Roots* 59, *A Taste of Honey* 60, *Uncle Vanya* 62, 63, 64, *St. Joan* 63, *Hobson's Choice* 64, *The Master Builder* 65, *Much Ado About Nothing* 67, *Tartuffe* 67.
c/o L.O.P. Ltd., 8 Norfolk Street, London, W.C.2, England.
Telephone: 01-836-2033.

Plumptre, Arthur Fitzwalter Wynne, C.B.E., M.A.; Canadian economist and international banking official; b. 5 June 1907; ed. Appleby School, Oakville, Ontario, Upper Canada Coll., Univ. of Toronto and Cambridge Univ.
Assistant Prof. of Political Economy, Univ. of Toronto 30-41; Financial Attaché, Canadian Legation, Washington, and Washington Rep., Wartime Prices and Trade Board 42-45; Sec., Wartime Prices and Trade Board, Ottawa 45-47; Assoc. Editor *Saturday Night*, Toronto 47-49; Head of Economic Div., Dept. of External Affairs, Ottawa 49-52; Minister and Dep. Head Canadian Del. to NATO Council and OEEC, Paris 52-54; Dir. Int. Economic Relations Div., Dept. of Finance, Ottawa 54; Asst. Dep. Minister, Dept. of Finance, Ottawa 55-65; Exec. Dir. for Canada, Ireland and Jamaica Int. Bank for Reconstruction and Devt. (World Bank) and Int. Monetary Fund (IMF) 62-65; Principal, Scarborough Coll., Univ. of Toronto 65-.
Publs. *Central Banking in the British Dominions* 40, *Mobilizing Canada's Resources for War* 41.
130 Old Kingston Road, West Hill, Ontario, Canada. Telephone: 416-284-6227.

Po I-po; Chinese politician; ed. Taiyuan Normal School.
Mem. Chinese Communist Party; arrested 31, released 36; fought in Sino-Japanese War; Vice-Chair. North China People's Govt. 48-49; Vice-Chair. Cttee. of Financial and Economic Affairs; Minister of Finance 49-53; Chair. National Construction Comm. 54-56; Chair. State Econ. Comm. 56-; Vice-Premier State Council; Dir., General Office of Industry and Communications, State Council 61-; Dep. Chair. State Planning Comm. 62-; Alt. mem. Politburo of Chinese C.P.
State Council, Peking, China.

Pode, Sir Julian, Kt., F.C.A., F.C.I.S., J.DIP.M.A.; British accountant and executive; b. 26 June 1902; ed. H.M.S. *Conway.*
District Accountant, Guest Keen & Nettlefolds Ltd., Dowlais 26; Man. Dir. The Steel Co. of Wales Ltd. 47-62, Chair. 62-67; Vice-Chair. Hodge Group 63-; Dir. The Steetley Co. Ltd., The Nat. Industrial Fuel Efficiency Service (and Chair.), Lloyds Bank Ltd. (and Chair. South Wales Cttee.), Iron and Steel Investments Ltd. (and Chair.); Pres. British Iron and Steel Fed. 62, 63, and 64; Vice-Pres. Iron and Steel Inst.; Chair. Wm. France, Fenwick and Co., Ltd.; Prince of Wales Dry Dock Co., Swansea, Ltd., North Sea Marine Eng. Construction Co. Ltd.; mem. Industrial Coal Consumers' Council; High Sheriff, Glamorgan 48; Hon. Freeman, Port Talbot.
[*Died* 11 *June* 1968].

Podedworny, Boleslaw; Polish politician; b. 7 Jan. 1898.
Worked on own small-holding as farmer; served in war of 18-21; participated in Silesian Rising; active in politics in peasants' organisations 23-; in hiding during German occupation 39-44; Chair. Council Peasants' Party (SL), and Vice-Chair. Nat. Council, Bialystok 44-45; Vice-Chair. Exec. Council Peasants' Party 45-49; Dep. to Nat. Council of the Homeland (KRN); Vice-Minister of Agriculture 46; Minister of Forestry 47-54; Vice-Pres. Council of Productive Co-operation 54-56; mem. State Council 56-57, Vice-Chair. 57-; mem. Parl. 49-; Vice-Chair. Exec. Council United Peasants' Party (ZSL) 57-; Chair. ZSL group in Parl. 57-.
United Peasants' Party Headquarters, 4/8 Grzybowska, Warsaw, Poland.

Podgayev, Grigory Efimovich; Soviet politician; b. 1920; ed. Tomsk Industrial Inst. and Higher Party School.
Member C.P.S.U. 40-; Engineer 40-42; with Soviet Army 42-45; Instructor, Territorial Cttee. of C.P. then

First Sec. Vyazma District Cttee. of C.P. 45-58; Chief of Section Khabarovsk Territorial Cttee. of C.P., then First Sec. Khabarovsk City Cttee. of C.P. 58-61; Chair. Exec. Cttee. Regional Soviet of Jewish Autonomous Region 61-62; First Sec. Regional Cttee. of C.P. of Jewish Autonomous Region 62-; Deputy to Supreme Soviet of U.S.S.R.

Regional Committee of U.S.S.R. Communist Party of Jewish Autonomous Region, Birobidjan, U.S.S.R.

Podgorny, Nikolai Viktorovich; Soviet politician; b. 1903; ed. Mikoyan Technological Inst. of Food Industry, Kiev.

Member Communist Party 30-; Engineer, later Chief Engineer of sugar factories and sugar trusts 31-39; Deputy People's Commissar of Ukrainian Food Industry 39-40, 44-46; Deputy People's Commissar of U.S.S.R. Food Industry 40-42; Dir. Moscow Technological Inst. of Food Industry 42-44; Perm. Rep. of Ukrainian S.S.R. Council of Ministers to U.S.S.R. Council of Ministers 46-50; First Sec. Kharkov District 50-53; Second Sec. Ukraine C.P. 53-57; full mem. Presidium of Central Cttee. of Communist Party of Ukrainian S.S.R. 57-63; C.P.S.U. Sec. 63-; Cand. mem. Presidium of C.P.S.U. Central Cttee. 58-60, mem. 60-66, mem. Politburo 66-; mem. Central Auditing Comm. C.P.S.U. Central Cttee. 52-56; Deputy to U.S.S.R. and Ukrainian S.S.R. Supreme Soviets; Chair. Presidium U.S.S.R. Supreme Soviet 65-; Hero of Socialist Labour.

The Kremlin, Moscow, U.S.S.R.

Podtserob, Boris Fyodorovich; Soviet diplomatist; b. 1910; ed. Leningrad Flistor Language Inst.

Diplomatic Service 37-; Asst. and later Senior Asst., U.S.S.R. Ministry of Foreign Affairs 42-49; Sec.-Gen., mem. Collegium of Ministry of Foreign Affairs 49-52, 57-65; Deputy Foreign Minister of U.S.S.R. 52-53; Head, First European Dept., U.S.S.R. Ministry of Foreign Affairs 53-54; Ambassador to Turkey 54-57, to Austria 65-.

U.S.S.R. Embassy, 3rd Raisnerstrasse 45-47, Vienna, Austria.

Podzerko, Viktor Andreyevich; Soviet trade union official; b. 12; ed. Dneprodzerzhinsk Metallurgical Inst.

Steel Plant 30-52; Sec. Cen. Cttee. of Trade Union of Workers of Metallurgical Industry 52-55, Chair. 55-64; Chair. Central Cttee. of Trade Union of Workers of Metallurgical Industry 55-64; Vice-Chair. Int. Amalgamation of Workers of Metallurgical and Machine-Building Industries 55-65; mem. All-Union Central Council of Trade Unions; Sec. World Fed. of Trade Unions 64-; Candidate mem. Central Cttee. C.P.S.U.; two Orders of Red Banner of Labour; Badge of Honour, etc.

Nám. Curieovych 1, Prague 1, Czechoslovakia.

Pogrebnyak, Yakov Petrovich; Soviet politician; b. 1928; ed. Donetsk Industrial Inst.

Member C.P.S.U. 53-; Foreman 54-57; Sec., later First Sec. Kramatorsk City Cttee. of C.P., later Second Sec. of Donetsk Regional Cttee. of C.P., Ukraine, then Second Sec. Poltava Regional Cttee. of C.P. Ukraine 57-66; First Sec. Ivano Frankovsk Regional Cttee. of C.P. Ukraine 66-; mem. Central Cttee. of C.P. Ukraine; Deputy to U.S.S.R. Supreme Soviet.

Ivano-Frankovsk Regional Committee of C.P.S.U., Ivano-Frankovsk, U.S.S.R.

Pogue, Lloyd Welch, A.B., LL.B., S.J.D.; American lawyer; b. 21 Oct. 1899; ed. Grinnell Coll., Univs. Nebraska, Michigan, Harvard.

Admitted Mass. Bar 27, N.Y. Bar 34; U.S. District Court Mass. 31, Southern District N.Y. 34, Supreme Court of U.S. 40; U.S. Court of Appeals for D.C. 41; District Court of U.S. for D.C. 46; with firm Ropes, Gray, Boyden & Perkins Boston 27-33 (including Paris

office 30); partner in firm Searle, James & Crawford N.Y. 33-38; Asst. Gen. Counsel in charge economic regulatory work Civil Aeronautics Authority from inception to 39, Gen. Counsel 39-41, Chair. Civil Aeronautics Board 42-46; mem. U.S. dels. to following confs.: Chicago Int. Civil Aviation 44, Bermuda UK-US (Vice-Chair.), Interim Assembly PICAO 46 (Vice-Chair.) and First Assembly ICAO 47; Vice-Chair. Industry Panel, Air Co-ordinating Cttee. 48; fmr. mem. Travel Advisory Cttee. Dept. of Commerce; Chair. of Board Nat. Aeronautics Asscn. 48; mem. Advisory Cttee. Aero Law, American Bar Asscn., Council on Foreign Relations; practising attorney Washington, D.C.

1001 Connecticut Avenue, N.W. Washington 36, D.C., U.S.A.

Telephone: 202-393-5333.

Pohl, Otakar, IUR.D.; Czechoslovak banker; b. 11 Oct. 1914; ed. Charles Univ. and Free School of Political Sciences, Prague.

Former Deputy Man., firm of Chartered Accountants; imprisoned for anti-Nazi activity 43-45; various political and econ. posts 45-48; Deputy Chief of Econ. Section, Pres. of Republic's Office 48-50; Gen. Man., Czechoslovak State Bank 50-53, 57-, Deputy Gen. Man. 56-57; mem. Econ. Comm. of Central Cttee. of C.P. of Czechoslovakia 63-; mem. State Planning Comm. 64-65; mem. State Comm. for Finance, Prices and Wages 65-.

Státní banka československá, Na příkopě 28, Prague 1, Czechoslovakia.

Pohle, Wolfgang, LL.D.; German lawyer; b. 28 Nov. 1903; ed. Univs. of Göttingen, Leipzig and Heidelberg.

Assistant judge 29; legal adviser Mining Union 29; Man. Dir. Friedrich Flick KG, Düsseldorf, Chamber of German Commerce and Industry, Düsseldorf, and Chamber of German-Spanish Commerce and Industry, Madrid; Pres. Legal Cttee. Fed. of German Industries; mem. Supervisory Board Allgemeine Transportmittel AG; Chair. Supervisory Board Int. Computers and Tabulators G.m.b.H., Düsseldorf; mem. Bundestag.

Friedrich Flick KG, Friedrichstrasse 62-68, Düsseldorf; Home: Ahornstrasse 8a, 4005 Büderich-Meererbusch, German Federal Republic.

Poisson, Emile; Dahomeyan diplomatist; b. 25 May 1905; ed. Lycées in Sénégal and Aix-en-Provence and various Insts. in Paris.

Teacher in Dahomey and France 25-33; founded primary and secondary schools at Porto-Novo 36, and Ouidah 58; founded first Union of Dahomeyan Businessmen 45; mem. Gen. Council of Dahomey; Senator Conseil de la République Paris 47-55; mem. M.R.P., successively Vice-Pres. Comm. Territoires d'Outre-Mer, Sec. Comm. for Educ., mem. Comm. for Foreign Affairs and of Senatorial Sub-Comm. before foundation of OECD; Rep. Consultative Assembly Council of Europe 52-55; Mayor of Ouidah 56-61; Deputy Nat. Assembly of Dahomey 59-60, Minister of Justice and Public Employment 59-60; Rep. to EEC 62-, Ambassador to France and U.K. 64-67, concurrently to the Netherlands, Belgium and Italy 65-67; Chevalier de l'Etoile Noire, Bénin, and Officier Order National Dahomey.

c/o Ministry of Foreign Affairs, Cotonou, Dahomey.

Poitier, Sidney; American actor; b. 20 Feb. 1924; ed. Western Senior High School, Nassau, Governors High School, Nassau.

Army Service 41-45; acted with American Negro Theatre 46; appeared in *Anna Lucasta* 48, *A Raisin in the Sun* 59; Silver Bear Award, Berlin Film Festival 58; New York Film Critics Award 58; Academy Award (Oscar) Best Actor of 63; has appeared in the following films: *Cry the Beloved Country* 52, *Red Ball Express* 52, *Go, Man, Go* 54, *Blackboard Jungle* 55, *Goodbye My Lady* 56, *Edge of the City* 57, *Something of Value* 57, *The Mark of the Hawk* 58, *The Defiant Ones* 58, *Porgy and*

Bess 59, *A Raisin in the Sun* 60, *Paris Blues* 60, *Lilies of the Field* 63, *The Long Ships* 64, *The Bedford Incident* 65, *The Slender Thread* 66, *A Patch of Blue* 66, *Duel at Diablo* 66, *To Sir with Love* 67, *In the Heat of the Night* 67, *Guess Who's Coming to Dinner* 68.
c/o General Artists Corporation, 640 5th Avenue, New York City 19, N.Y., U.S.A.

Pokrovsky, Boris Alexandrovich; Soviet opera producer; b. 12; ed. Lunachursky Inst. of Theatrical Arts. Producer of opera and ballet, Gorki Theatre 37-43; Producer Bolshoi Theatre 43-52, Chief Producer 52-63; Prof. Lunacharsky Inst. 54-; People's Artist of the U.S.S.R.; State Prize 47, 48, 49, 50.
Productions include: *Carmen* (Bizet), *Judith* (Serov), *Eugene Onegin* (Tchaikovsky), *The Snow Maiden, Sadko* (Rimsky-Korsakov), *The Bartered Bride* (Smetana), *War and Peace* (Prokofiev), *Khovanschchina* (Mussorgsky), *Midsummer Night's Dream* (Britten).
State Academic Bolshoi Theatre, 1 Ploshchad Sverdlova, Moscow K, U.S.S.R.

Poku, Bediako; Ghanaian diplomatist; b. 1918; ed. Methodist School and Kumasi Teachers' Coll.
Former teacher of history and geography; mem. Convention People's Party 49-, Sec.-Gen. 59; Amb. to Israel 59-63; High Commr. in Uganda 64-65; Amb. to People's Repub. of China 65-66, to U.S.S.R. 66-.
Embassy of Ghana, Ul. Pogodinskaya 12, Moscow, U.S.S.R.

Poláček, Karel; Czechoslovak politician; b. 7 July 1913.
Held a number of official positions and mem. of the Nat. Assembly; Minister of Heavy Eng. 53; Eng. 53-55; Deputy Prime Minister 55-58; Minister of Gen. Eng. 58-65; Minister 65-67; Chair. Perm. Eng. Comm., Council of Mutual Econ. Assistance 56-; mem. Central Cttee. C.P. of Czechoslovakia 52-62; Chair. Metal Workers' Trade Union 66-; Deputy Chair. Central Council of Trade Unions 67-68, Chair. 68-, mem. Presidium 67-.
Central Council of Trade Unions, Prague, Czechoslovakia.

Polak, Carel Hendrik Frederik; Netherlands law professor and politician; b. 2 Sept. 1909; ed. Rijksuniversiteit te Leiden.
Civil servant 34; Prof. of Agricultural Law, Agricultural Coll., Wageningen 46; Prof. of Admin. Law, Univ. of Leiden 51; Minister of Justice 67-.
Prins Hendriklaan 22, Oegstgeest, Netherlands.

Polanski, Roman; Polish film director; b. 18 Aug. 1933; ed. Polish Film School, Łódź.
Films include: *Two Men and a Wardrobe* 58, *When Angels Fall, Le Gros et Le Maigre, Knife in the Water* (prize at Venice Film Festival 62), *The Mammals* (prize at Tours Film Festival 63), *Repulsion* (prize at Berlin Film Festival 65), *Cul de Sac.*
Films acted in include: *A Generation, The End of the Night, See You Tomorrow, The Innocent Sorcerers, Two Men and a Wardrobe, The Fearless Vampires.*
c/o Cadre Film Ltd., 140 Park Lane, London, W.1, England.

Polanyi, Michael, F.R.S.; Hungarian-born British physical chemist and philosopher; b. 12 March 1891.
Member Kaiser Wilhelm Inst. of Physical Chemistry 22-33, resigned; Prof. of Physical Chemistry Manchester Univ. 33-48; Prof. of Social Studies 48-58; Senior Research Fellow, Merton Coll. Oxford 59-61; Riddell Lecturer, Durham 46; mem. Max Planck Gesellschaft 48; Alexander White Visiting Prof. Chicago 49, 54; Gifford Lecturer, Aberdeen 51-52; Lindsay Lecturer, Keele 58; Eddington Lecturer, Cambridge 60; F. C. Bose Lecturer, Calcutta 61; May Lecturer, Inst. of Metals 61; Distinguished Visiting Scholar, Univ. of Virginia 61; McEnnerney Lecturer, Berkeley 62;

Terry Lecturer, Yale 62; Fellow Center Behavioral Studies, Palo Alto 62-63, Fellow, Center of Advanced Studies, Wesleyan Univ. 65-66; Distinguished Prof. of Religion Duke Univ. 64; Hon. foreign mem. American Acad. 61; mem. Int. Acad. Philosophical Sciences 62; Hon. D.Sc. (Princeton 36, Leeds 47, Notre Dame 65, Toronto 67), Hon. LL.D. (Aberdeen 59, Wesleyan 65, Manchester 66).
Publs. *Atomic Reactions* 32, *U.S.S.R. Economics* 35, *Money and Unemployment* (diagrammatic film) 39, *The Contempt of Freedom* 41, *Full Employment and Free Trade* 45, *Science, Faith and Society* 46, *Logic of Liberty* 51, *Personal Knowledge* 58, *The Study of Man* 59, *Beyond Nihilism* 60, *The Tacit Dimension* 66.
22 Upland Park Road, Oxford, England.

Polevoi (Kampov), Boris Nikolaevich; Soviet writer and journalist; b. 08.
Technologist in Proletarska Factory, Kalinin 28; became professional journalist 28; war correspondent for *Pravda,* Finnish War 39-40, and World War 41-45; mem. C.P.S.U. 40-; Col. in Soviet Army; Deputy to Supreme Soviet R.S.F.S.R. 51-66; mem. Board Union of Soviet Writers 46-; mem. Board Union of Soviet Journalists 59-; Editor *Yunost* (Youth) magazine; awarded two State Prizes; two Orders of the Red Banner (Military Division), two Orders of the Patriotic War (1st degree), Order of the Red Star, Order of the Red Banner (Civilian Division), Order of Lenin, a number of medals and five foreign orders.
Publs. *Goryachii tsekh* (*The Hot Shop*) 39, *Okrovavlennye kamni* (*Blood-stained Stone*) 42, *Do poslednego dykhaniya* (*Till their Last Breath*) 43, *Ot Belgoroda do Karpat* (*From Belgorod to the Carpathians*) 44, *Povest o Nastoyashchem cheloveke* (*Story of a Real Man*) 46, *My-sovetskie lyudi* (*We Are Soviet People*) 48, *Vernulsya* (*He Came Back*) 49, *Zoloto* (*Gold*) 50, *Sovremenniki* (*Contemporaries*) 52, *Amerikanskiye Dnevniki* (*American Diaries*) 56, *Za tridevyat zemel* (*In the Far-away Lands*) 56, *30 tyssyach li po novomu Kitayu* (*Three hundred thousand li across the New China*) 57, *Glubokyi Till* (*Far Behind the Lines*) 58, *Chelovek Cheloveku Brat* (*All Men are Brothers*) 60, *Blizko y Daleko* (*From Near and Far*) 60, *Vstrechi na perekrjestkah* (*Meetings on the Cross-Roads*) 61, *Nash Lenin* (*Our Lenin*) 62, *Na dikom brege* (*On the Wild Shore*) 63, *Doctor Vera* (*Doctor Vera*) 66, *V bolshom nastuplenii* (*In Great Offensive*) 66.
Union of Soviet Writers, ul. Vorovskogo 52, Moscow, U.S.S.R.

Polunin, Nicholas, M.S., M.A., D.PHIL., D.SC., F.L.S., F.R.G.S., F.R.H.S.; British biologist and author; b. 26 June 1909; ed. Oxford, Yale and Harvard Univs.
Botanical, etc., exploring expdns. Spitsbergen, Lapland, Greenland, Iceland, Labrador, Hudson Bay and Strait, Baffin, Southampton, Devon and Ellesmere Islands 30-38 (collections chiefly in Nat. Museum of Canada, Gray Herbarium Harvard Univ., British Museum, Fielding Herbarium Oxford); explorations in Canadian Northwest Territories, Alaska, Ungava-Labrador, and Arctic Archipelago 46-49; visited vicinity of magnetic North Pole 47 and flew over geographical North Pole summer 48 and winter 49; field work in Middle East 56-59, and in West Africa 62-65; U.S. Order of Polaris; Botanical Tutor various Oxford Colls. 32-47; Henry Fellow, Yale Univ. 33-34; Dept. of Scientific and Industrial Research, Senior Research Award 35-38; Research Assoc. Harvard Univ. 36-37; Foreign Research Assoc. 38-50, Research Fellow 50-53; Fielding Curator and Keeper, Univ. Herbaria, Oxford, Univ. Demonstrator and Lecturer in Botany 39-47, Univ. Moderator 41-45; Lecturer (and latterly Senior Research Fellow) New Coll., Oxford 42-47; Haley Lecturer, Acadia Univ. 50; Macdonald Prof. of Botany, McGill Univ., Montreal 47-52; Guggenheim Memorial Fellow 50-52; Lecturer in Plant Geography, Yale Univ. 53-

55 while Project Dir. U.S. Air Force; Prof. of Plant Ecology and Taxonomy and Head Dept. of Botany, Dir. Univ. Herbarium, Faculty of Sciences, Baghdad 55-59; Guest Prof. Univ. of Geneva 59-; Prof. of Botany Univ. of Ife, Ibadan 62-66; Fellow, American Inst. for Advancement of Sciences and mem. of other learned societies; Editor *International Industry* 43-46, *World Crops Books* 54-68 and *Plant Science Monographs* 54-67.
Publs. *Russian Waters* 31, *The Isle of Auks* 32, *Botany of the Canadian Eastern Arctic* (3 vols.) 40-48, *Arctic Unfolding* 49, *Circumpolar Arctic Flora* 59, *Introduction to Plant Geography and some related sciences* 60, *Eléments de Géographie botanique* 67.
c/o New College, Oxford, England; 1249 Avusy, Geneva, Switzerland.
Telephone: 56-17-07.

Polvani, Giovanni; Italian physicist; b. 17 Dec. 1892. Teacher, Experimental Physics, Univ. of Bari, later of Technical Physics, Univ. of Pisa; fmr. Dir. Inst. of Physics, Univ. of Milan; mem. Nat. Council for Research 60, Pres. 62-65; Dir. of Nuovo Cimento; Pres. Italian Physics Soc. 65, Hon. Pres. 65-.
Publs. include: *A. Pacinotti: La Vita e l'opera* (3 vols.) 34, *L'opera scientifica di A. Volta* 45, *Elementi di termodinamica teoretica* 46, *Elementi di metrologia teoretica* 47, *Termodinamica del calore raggiante* 50, *L'uomo dinnanzi alla natura* 50.
Presso 7 Piazzale delle Scienze, Rome, Italy.

Polwarth, 10th Baron, Henry Alexander Hepburne-Scott, M.A., LL.D.; British chartered accountant; b. 17 Nov. 1916; ed. Eton Coll. and King's Coll., Cambridge. Deputy Gov., Bank of Scotland 60-66, Gov. 66-; mem. Western Hemisphere Exports Council 58-64; Partner Chiene and Tait, Edinburgh 50-66, Pres. 66-; Chancellor Univ. of Aberdeen 66-; Deputy Chair. Gen. Accident, Fire and Life Assurance Co.; Chair. Exec. Cttee. Scottish Council 55-; Dir. several companies; mem. Historic Buildings Council for Scotland 53-66; Hon. LL.D. St. Andrews Univ, Univ. of Aberdeen.
13 Ainslie Place, Edinburgh; and Harden, Hawick, Roxburghshire, Scotland.
Telephone: Hawick 2069.

Polyakov, Ivan Evteyevich; Soviet politician; b. 1914; ed. Higher Party School.
Electric welder 31-36; Soviet Army Service 36-38; Komsomol leader 39-46; Sec. Underground Gomel Regional Cttee. of Young Communist League, Byelorussian S.S.R. and Commissar, First Gomel Partisan Brigade 42-44; Second, then First, Sec. Vitebsk City Cttee. of C.P. of Byelorussia 57-; Candidate mem. of Central Cttee. C.P.S.U. 61-66, mem. 66-; Bureau of Central Cttee. of C.P. of Byelorussia; Deputy to U.S.S.R. Supreme Soviet; mem. C.P.S.U. 40-.
Minsk Regional Committee of Communist Party of Byelorussia, Minsk, U.S.S.R.

Polyakov, Vasily Ivanovich; Soviet agricultural journalist and politician; b. 1913; ed. Agricultural Technical School, Voronezh, and Inst. of Journalism, Leningrad.
Agronomist 33-38; mem. C.P.S.U. 39-; Head of Dept. and Exec. Sec. Editorial Board *Sotsialisticheskoe Zemldelie* 38-41; Red Army, Second World War; *Pravda* 46-60; later Editor Agricultural Dept. and mem. Editorial Board; Editor *Rural Life* 60-62; Head Agriculture Dept., Central Cttee. of C.P.S.U. March-Nov. 62, Chair. U.S.S.R. Bureau of Agriculture (C.P.S.U.) 62-64; Sec. Central Cttee. of C.P.S.U. 62-64; Deputy Chief Editor *Ekonomicheskaya Gazeta* 64-; Deputy to U.S.S.R. Supreme Soviet.
Ekonomicheskaya Gazeta, ulitsa Pravdy 24, Moscow, U.S.S.R.

Polyansky, Dmitri Stepanovich; Soviet politician; b. 17; ed. Kharkov Inst. of Agriculture and Higher Party School of Central Cttee. of C.P.S.U.
Exec. work in Young Communist League, service in Soviet army and study at Higher Party School 39-42; Party work in Siberia 42-45; exec. in Central Cttee. of Party 45-49; Second Sec. Crimea regional Cttee. of Party, and Chair. Exec. Cttee. Crimea regional Soviet of Working People's Deputies 49-52; First Sec. Crimea regional Cttee. of Party 54-55; First Sec. of Chkalovsk (now Orenburg) regional Cttee. then First Sec. of Krasnodar territorial Party Cttee. 55-58; Chair. Council of Ministers of R.S.F.S.R. 58-62; Dep. Premier U.S.S.R. 62-65, First Deputy Premier 65-; Deputy Supreme Soviet of the U.S.S.R. and R.S.F.S.R.; alt. mem. Presidium of Central Cttee. of C.P.S.U. 58-60, mem. 60-66, mem. Politburo 66-; Order of Lenin (twice), etc.
Publs. *Pearl of Russia* 58, *Great Plans for the Economic and Cultural Progress of the Russian Federation* 59.
Council of Ministers of the U.S.S.R., Kremlin, Moscow, U.S.S.R.

Pomfret, John Edwin, A.M., PH.D.; American educator; b. 21 Sept. 1898; ed. Univ. of Pennsylvania.
Assoc. Prof. of History, Univ. of South Carolina 24-25; Instr., Asst. Prof., and Assoc. Prof. of History Princeton Univ. 25-37, also Asst. Dean 34-36; Dean of Senior Coll. and Graduate School, Vanderbilt Univ. 37-42; Pres. of the Coll. of William and Mary 42-51; Dir. H. E. Huntington Library and Art Gallery 51-66; Hon. LL.D. Univ. of Pa., Univ. of Chattanooga, Mills Coll., Hon. D.Litt., Univ. of Southern Calif., Claremont Graduate School, Claremont Colls.
Publs. *The Struggle for Land in Ireland* 30, *The Geographic Pattern of Mankind* 35, *California Gold Rush* 54, *Twelve Americans Speak* 54, *Province of West New Jersey* 56, *Province of East Jersey* 62, *New Jersey Proprietors and Their Lands* 65.
Route 2, Box 324, Carmel, Calif., U.S.A.
Telephone: 408-624-6666.

Pompidou, Georges Jean Raymond; French administrator and politician; b. 5 July 1911; ed. Ecole Normale Supérieure, Ecole Libre des Sciences Politiques.
Schoolmaster, Marseilles and Paris; on de Gaulle's personal staff 45-46; Dep. Dir.-Gen., Tourism 46-49; fmr. Dir.-Gen. Rothschild's Bank; Head, French Cabinet 58-59; mem., Constitutional Council 59-62; Prime Minister 62-July 68; Maître des Requêtes honoraire Council of State; Officier de la Légion d'Honneur; Democratic Union for 5th. Republic.
Publs. studies of *Britannicus, Taine* 54, *Malraux* 55, *Anthologie de la poésie française* 61.
24 quai de Béthune, Paris 4e, France.

Ponce Enriquez, Camilo; Ecuadorean politician and university professor; b. 12; ed. Univs. of Quito and Chile.
Vice-Pres. Quito Municipal Council 43; mem. Junta Govt. 44; as Minister of Foreign Relations led Ecuadorean Dels. to San Francisco and Chapultec Confs. 45; Vice Pres. Nat. Assembly 46; Prof. of Constitutional Law, Catholic Univ. of Ecuador 50-; Del. to UNESCO 52; Senator 52; Minister of Government and Justice 53-56; Pres. of Ecuador 56-60; founder and leader Christian Social Movement.
Publs. *Ideas Constitucionales de Bolívar* 35, *Génesis y Ocaso de un Régimen* 42, *Parliamentary Speeches* 53-54.
Bolívar 343, Apdo. 2184, Quito, Ecuador.

Ponce Miranda, Neftali; Ecuadorean diplomatist; b. 5 Feb. 1908; ed. Univ. of Quito.
Held various posts in diplomatic service 34-; First Sec. Wash. 41-43; Dir. of Protocol Ministry of Foreign Relations 43; Counsellor Caracas 43, Bogotá 44; Minester-Counsellor Wash. 44-46; Rep. of Ecuador to Chapultec and San Francisco Confs. 45, to UN Gen. Ass. 46;

Ambassador to U.S.A. 47; Minister of Foreign Affairs 48-52; Prof. of Private Int. Law, Catholic Univ. of Quito 52-54; Ambassador to Brazil 56-60, to UN 60-61, to U.S.A. 61-63; Minister of Foreign Affairs 63-64.
c/o Ministry of Foreign Affairs, Quito, Ecuador.

Ponomarev, Boris Nikolayevich; Soviet historian and politician; b. 05; ed. Moscow State Univ. and Red Professors' Inst.
Red Army 19, Mil. Revolutionary Cttee. Zaraisk 19-20; Young Communist League, Moscow Region 20-22; Sec. *Krasny Vostok* Factory Party Org., Moscow Region 22-23; mem. Propagandist Group, Cen. Cttee. of C.P.S.U. 26-28; Asst. Dir. Red Professors' Inst. 33-36; Exec. Cttee. Communist Int. 36-39; Asst. Dir. Marx-Engels-Lenin Inst. 43-45; Cen. Cttee. C.P.S.U. 44-46; First Dep. Chief Soviet Information Bureau, U.S.S.R. Council of Ministers 46-49; Head of Dept., Central Cttee. C.P.S.U. 49-61, mem. of Central Cttee. 56-, Sec. 61-; Deputy to U.S.S.R. Supreme Soviet; corresp. mem. Acad. of Sciences of U.S.S.R. 58, mem. 62-; Order of Lenin (twice); Order of Red Banner of Labour (twice), etc.
Publs. Works on history of C.P.S.U. and int. workers' movements.
Central Committee of Communist Party of Soviet Union, 4 Staraya Ploshchad, Moscow, U.S.S.R.

Ponomaryeov, Mikhail Alexandrovich; Soviet politician; b. 1918; ed. Perm State Univ.
Member C.P.S.U. 39-; Chief of Section, machine and tractor station, later Deputy Chief of Section, Perm Regional Cttee. of C.P. 41-44, First Sec. Perm Regional Cttee. of Young Communist League, then Insp., Central Cttee. of Y.C.L. 44-46; Chief of Section, Perm Regional Cttee. of C.P. 46-51; Official, Central Cttee. C.P.S.U. 55-59; First Sec. Kalmyk Regional Cttee. of C.P. 59-61; First Sec. Vladimir Regional Cttee. of C.P. 61-; Candidate mem. Central Cttee. C.P.S.U. 61-; Deputy to U.S.S.R. Supreme Soviet.
Vladimir Regional Committee of Communist Party, Vladimir, U.S.S.R.

Pons, Louis Marie; French diplomatist; b. 13 March 1909; ed. Institution de Caoucou, Toulouse and Faculty of Law, Toulouse.
Residency Gen., Morocco 33-42; Tunis 43; Ministry of the Interior 45; Sub-Prefect, Bône (Algeria) 45-47; Morocco 47-54; with Cen. Admin. (Conf. Secr.) 54-55; Counsellor, Ministry of Foreign Affairs 57-61; Ambassador to Guinea 61-64; Ambassador to Rumania 64-; Officier de la Légion d'Honneur, Bronze Star Medal.
French Embassy, Str. Biserica Amzei 15, Bucharest, Romania.

Ponte, Maurice Jules Henry; French scientist and business executive; b. 5 April 1902; ed. Prytanée militaire, La Flèche and Ecole normale supérieure.
Research with Henri Abraham, Sir William Bragg and Prince Louis de Broglie 24-29; with Compagnie Générale de T.S.F. (Radio) 29-, now Pres. and Dir.-Gen.; Pres. of French Soc. of Electricians 48, of Radioelectricians 49, Vice-Pres. Inst. of Radio-Engineers 54, Pres., Dir.-Gen. French Television Co., la Société Mistral, Milan, La Société Ducati, Bologna; mem. Scientific Council of High Comm. for Atomic Energy; fmr. Pres. of Consultative Cttee. on Scientific Research of Asscn. for Advancement of Science; mem. Académie des Sciences, Institut de France 63-; Commandeur Légion d'Honneur, Commandeur de L'Education nationale.
Publs. Papers on X-rays, Electronics and Radio-Electricity.
47 rue Dumont d'Urville, Paris 16e; and 7 rue Le Sueur, Paris 16e, France.

Pontecorvo, Bruno Maksimovich (brother of Guido Pontecorvo, *q.v.*, and Gillo Pontecorvo); Soviet (b. Italy) physicist; b. 1913; ed. Pisa and Rome Univs.
Instructor, Rome Univ. 33-36; at scientific institutions in France 36-40; in U.S.A. 40-43; research at Chalk River, Canada, under E. Fermi, leading to devt. of neutron physics 43-48; Assoc. Harwell Laboratory, U.K. 48-50; went to U.S.S.R. 50; mem. C.P.S.U. 55-; Corresp. mem. U.S.S.R. Acad. of Sciences 58-64; mem. 64-; in charge of team at Joint Nuclear Research Inst., Dubna; Order of Lenin 63; Lenin Prize 63.
Joint Nuclear Research Institute, Dubna, nr. Moscow, U.S.S.R.

Pontecorvo, Guido, DR.AGR., PH.D., F.R.S. (brother of Bruno Pontecorvo, *q.v.*, and Gillo Pontecorvo); British (b. Italian) scientist and university professor; b. 29 Nov. 1907; ed. Università degli Studi, Pisa and Univ. of Edinburgh.
Assistant and later Regent of Section, Ispettorato Compartimentale Agrario, Florence 30-38; Research Student, Inst. of Animal Genetics, Edinburgh 38-40, Dept. of Zoology, Univ. of Glasgow 41-43; Lecturer, Inst. of Animal Genetics, Univ. of Edinburgh 43-45; Lecturer, Senior Lecturer, Reader, Dept. of Genetics, Univ. of Glasgow, Prof. 45-68; Hon. Dir. Medical Research Council Unit for Cell Genetics 64-68; mem. staff, Imperial Cancer Research Fund 68-; Jesup Lecturer, Columbia Univ. 56, Messenger Lecturer, Cornell Univ. 57, Leeuwenhoek Lecturer 62; Visiting Prof. Albert Einstein Coll. of Medicine, New York 64, 65, Washington State Univ. 67; Sec., Genetical Soc. 46-52, mem. of Council 53-54, Vice-Pres. 54-57, Pres. 64-65; fmr. mem. of Council, Inst. of Biology; mem. Council, Soc. for Gen. Microbiology 56-60; Fellow Royal Soc. of Edinburgh (mem. Council 58-61), of London (mem. Council 58-59); Foreign mem. Danish Royal Soc., Hon. Foreign mem. American Acad. of Arts and Sciences; Hansen Prize 61.
Imperial Cancer Research Fund, Lincoln's Inn Fields, London, W.C.2; Home: Flat 25, Cranfield House, 97-107 Southampton Row, London, W.C.1, England.

Ponti, Carlo, LL.D. (husband of Sophia Loren, *q.v.*); French (b. Italian) film producer; b. 11 Dec. 1913; ed. Università degli Studi, Milan.
Legal practice in office of Milan barrister 35-38; film producer 38-.
Major films produced: *Roma Città Aperta* 45 (New York Critics Prize 47), *To Live in Peace* 45, *Attila* 53, *Ulysses* 53, *La Strada* 54 (Oscar), *War and Peace* 55, *Two Women* (Oscar Award for best foreign actress) 60, *Boccaccio '70* 61, *Yesterday, Today, Tomorrow* 63 (Oscar), *Marriage, Italian Style* 64, *Casanova '70* 64, *Lady L* 65, *Dr. Zhivago* 65 (six Oscars), *The 25th Hour* 66, *Blow Up* 66 (Cannes Film Festival Award), *The Girl and the General* 66, *More than a Miracle* 66, *Ghosts, Italian Style* 67, *Smashing Time* 67, *Diamonds for Breakfast* 67.
Bürgenstock, Nidwalden, Switzerland; 32 Avenue George V, Paris 8e, France; 1 Piazza d'Ara Coeli 1, Rome, Italy.

Ponti, Gio(vanni); Italian architect and designer; b. 18 Nov. 1891; ed. Milan Polytechnic.
Designed and planned buildings in Milan, Padua, São Paulo, Buenos Aires, Baghdad, Stockholm, Caracas, Teheran, New York, Islamabad, Rome, Taranto, Beirut; with others designed Pirelli skyscraper, Milan; Consultant Architect in Paris, Lourdes, Rhodesia, Canada and Spain; worked on interior design of Italian liners (inc. *Andrea Doria*); designed costumes and settings for the La Scala Theatre, Milan, murals for Padua Univ.; contributed to the Triennale; organised Exhibitions overseas; designed furniture; Prof. of Architecture, Milan School of Architecture; mem. Nat. Acad. of St. Luke; founded and edits *Domus* (architectural magazine); Dr. h.c. (Royal Coll. of Art, U.K.).
Via Dezza 49, Milan, Italy.

Pontryagin, Lev Semyonovich; Soviet mathematician; b. 08; ed. Moscow Univ.

Has been blind 22-; Prof. of Mathematics at Moscow Univ. 35-; discovered the general law of duality 32, constructed the general theory of topological commutative groups; Corresp. mem. Acad. of Sciences of the U.S.S.R. 39, mem. 58; State prizewinner for his monograph *Continuous Groups* 38; shared Lenin Prize for monograph *Theory of Optimum Processes* 62; awarded Order of Lenin.

Publs. *The General Topological Theorem of Duality for Closed Sets* 34, *Fundamentals of Combinational Topology* 47, *Characteristic Cycles of Differential Manifolds* 47, *Vector Fields in Manifolds* 49, *Continuous Groups* 54, *Smooth Manifolds and their Application in Homotopy* 55, *Mathematical Theory of Optimum Processes* (with others) 61, *Ordinary Differential Equations* (textbook) 61, *One Probability Problem of Optimal Control* 62, *On Some Differential Games* 64.

V.I. Steklov Mathematical Institute of the Academy of Sciences of the U.S.S.R., 28 Vavilov Street, Moscow, U.S.S.R.

Poole, 1st Baron, cr. 58, of Aldgate; **Oliver Brian Sanderson Poole,** P.C., C.B.E.; British politician; b. 11 Aug. 1911; ed. Eton Coll. and Christ Church, Oxford.

Served 39-45 war; M.P. for Oswestry Division of Salop 45-50; mem. Lloyds; Joint Treasurer Conservative Party Organisation 52-55, Chair. 55-57, Deputy Chair. 57-59, Jt. Chair. April-Oct. 63, Vice-Chair. Oct. 63- Oct. 64; Chair., Thomas Stephens, Poole (Holdings); Dir. Whitehall Securities Corpn. Ltd.; Exec. Deputy Chair. Lazard Brothers Jan. 65-Oct. 65, Chair. Oct. 65-; Dir. Reserve Bank of Rhodesia Dec. 65-.

12 Egerton Terrace, London, S.W.3, England.

Poonacha, Cheppudira Muthana; Indian politician; b. 1910; ed. St. Aloysius Coll., Mangalore.

Joined Satyagraha Movement 30, imprisoned for Satyagraha activities; Sec. District Congress Cttee., Coorg 33; mem. Exec. Cttees., Karnatak and All India Congress Cttees. and Coorg District Board 38, Pres., Coorg District Board 41; mem. Exec. Cttee. Coorg Legislative Council and Leader, Congress Legislative Party in the Council 45-46; mem. Constituent Assembly and Provisional Parl. 47-51; Chief Minister of Coorg 52-56; Minister for Industries and Commerce 57, and later for Home and Industries at Mysore; Chair. State Trading Corpn. of India 59-63; Leader of Trade Dels. to various countries 61, 63; mem. Rajya Sabha 64; Minister for Revenue and Expenditure 2 Jan.-24 Jan. 66; Minister of State in Ministry of Transport and Aviation Jan. 66-March 67; Minister of Railways 67-. Ministry of Railways, New Delhi, India.

Popal, Ali Ahmad, PH.D.; Afghan educationist; b. 22 Feb. 1916; ed. Nedjat Secondary School, Kabul, and Univ. of Jena.

Teacher and Dir., Nedjat School, Kabul 42-46; Dir. of Teachers Training Coll. 46-47; Head of Primary Educ. Dept., Ministry of Educ. 47-49, also Teacher and Dean in Faculty of Women, Kabul Univ. 47-49; Head of Gen. Educ. Dept., Ministry of Educ. 49-51, Deputy Minister of Educ. 52-56, Minister of Educ. 56-64, Second Vice-Premier 62-64; Amb. to German Fed. Repub., also accred. to Sweden and Switzerland 64-66; Amb. to Turkey 66-67; First Deputy Prime Minister and Minister of Educ. Nov. 67-; Order of Maaref, 3rd Class 46, 1st Class 64; Order of Sardarie-Ahlie 58, and orders from U.A.R., Yugoslavia and German Fed. Repub. Ministry of Education, Kabul, Afghanistan.
Telephone: 20666.

Pope, Arthur Upham, A.B., M.A.; American art expert; b. 7 Feb. 1881; ed. Harvard, Brown and Cornell Univs. Former Instr. Brown Univ., Asst. Prof. Univ. Calif., Acting Assoc. Prof. Amherst Coll.; with Personnel Div., Gen. Staff U.S. Army 18-19; Dir. Legion of Honor

Museum, San Francisco 23; research Iran 25-; sixteen subsequent expeditions; organised 1st Int. Exhbn. Persian Art, Philadelphia 26, and joint organiser First Int. Congress Persian Art; Founder Dir. American Inst. Persian Art and Archæology (now Asia Inst.) 28; Int. Exhbn. Persian Art (with Sir Arnold Wilson) London 31; Dir. Second Int. Congress Persian Art with Sir Denison Ross 31; exhbns. Photographic Survey Persian Architecture, Paris, Berlin, Warsaw, Moscow, Copenhagen, Vienna, London, Stockholm, American Museums and Univs.; Joint Dir. 3rd Int. Congress, Leningrad-Moscow 35, Assoc. Dir. 3rd Int. Exhbn., Persian Art, Leningrad 35; Harvard Lecturer to French Univs. 35, Chancellor Asia Inst., N.Y., Chancellor Emeritus 55-; Advisory Curator, Muhammadan Art Inst. Chicago 25-35; Adviser, Persian Art, Pa. Museum; Adviser on Art to Iranian Govt. 25-; Organiser and Chair. Cttee. for Nat. Morale 40-45; lectured in principal Indian Univs. 48; Dir. Int. Exhbn. Persian Art, N.Y. 39, 50, 4th Int. Congress Persian Art, N.Y., Washington and Ed. in Chief *Proceedings* 60-62; Pres. Int. Asscn. Persian Art 60; Dir. Asia Inst. of Pahlavi Univ., Shiraz; Pres. 5th Int. Congress of Persian Art, Teheran, Shiraz, April 68; mem. various Oriental Societies; Hon. Ph.D. (Teheran), Order Houmayoun (1st Class), Commdr. Order of the Crown, Iran; Order Elmi (1st Class), Iranian Acad.

Publs. *Early Oriental Rugs* 26, *An Introduction to Persian Art* 31, *Survey of Persian Art* (Editor) 12 vols. 38 (re-issued 65), *Biography of Maxim Litvinov* 43, *Masterpieces of Persian Art* 46, *Persian Architecture* 64. Asia Institute, Pahlavi University, Shiraz, Iran.

Pope, J(ack) M(iltz), A.B.; American business executive; b. 24 June 1913; ed. Stanford Univ.

Staff Accountant, Price, Waterhouse and Co., San Francisco 36-42; with Food Machinery and Chemical Corpn., San José, Calif. 42-; successively Asst. Man., Procurement and Eng. Div., Staff Asst. to Controller, Asst. Controller, then Vice-Pres. 54-59, Exec. Vice-Pres. 60-66, Pres. of Food Machinery and Chemical Corpn. 66-; Dir. Philadelphia Nat. Bank; mem. American Inst. of Certified Public Accountants.

FMC Corporation, 1105 Coleman Avenue, San José 10, Calif., U.S.A.

Pope-Hennessy, John Wyndham, C.B.E., F.B.A., F.S.A., F.R.S.L.; British civil servant and art historian; b. 13 Dec. 1913; ed. Balliol Coll., Oxford.

Joined staff Victoria and Albert Museum 38, Keeper Dept. of Architecture and Sculpture 54-66; Slade Prof. of Fine Art, Oxford Univ. 56-57; Robert Sterling Clark Prof. of Art, Williams Coll., Williamstown, U.S.A. 61-62; Slade Prof. of Fine Art, Cambridge Univ. 64-65; Dir. Victoria and Albert Museum 67-.

Publs. *Giovanni di Paolo* 37, *Sassetta* 39, *Sienese Quattrocento Painting* 47, *A Sienese Codex of the Divine Comedy* 47, *The Drawings of Domenichino at Windsor Castle* 48, *A Lecture on Nicholas Hilliard* 49, *Paolo Uccello* 50, *Fra Angelico* 52, *Italian Gothic Sculpture* 55, *Italian Renaissance Sculpture* 58, *Italian High Renaissance and Baroque Sculpture* 63, *Catalogue of Italian Sculpture in the Victoria and Albert Museum* 64, *Italian Bronzes in the Kress Collection* 65, *The Portrait in the Renaissance* 67, *Essays on Italian Sculpture* 68.
41 Bedford Gardens, London, W.8, England.

Popják, George Joseph, M.D., D.SC., F.R.I.C., F.R.S.; British (b. Hungary) biochemist; b. 5 May 1914; ed. Royal Hungarian Francis Joseph Univ., Szeged, Hungary, and Postgraduate Medical School, Univ. of London.

Demonstrator, Dept. of Pathology, St. Thomas' Hospital, London 41-47; mem. Scientific Staff, Nat. Inst. for Medical Research, London 47-53; Dir. Medical Research Council Experimental Radio-pathology Research Unit, Hammersmith Hospital, London 53-62; Visiting Scientist, Nat. Heart Inst., Nat. Insts. of

Health, Bethesda, Md., U.S.A. 60-61; Joint Dir., Chemical Enzymology Laboratory, "Shell" Research Ltd. 62-68; Assoc. Prof. in Molecular Sciences, Warwick Univ. 65-68; Prof. of Biochemistry, Univ. of Calif. at Los Angeles Oct. 68-; Foreign mem. Royal Flemish Acad. of Sciences and Fine Arts, Belgium; Ciba Medal, Biochem. Soc. 65; Stouffer Prize 67.
Publs. Numerous articles in scientific journals, mainly on problems of lipid metabolism; monograph *Chemistry, Biochemistry and Isotopic Trace Technique* 55.
Department of Biochemistry, University of California, Los Angeles, Calif. 90024, U.S.A.

Popkov, Valery Ivanovich; Soviet electrical engineer; b. 1908; ed. Moscow Power Engineering Inst.
At All-Union Electrotechnical Inst. 32-36; Assoc., Power Eng. Inst., U.S.S.R. Acad. of Sciences 43-; Corresp. mem. U.S.S.R. Acad. of Sciences 53-66, mem. 66-; Order of Red Banner of Labour.
U.S.S.R. Academy of Sciences, 14 Lenin Prospekt, Moscow, U.S.S.R.

Popov, Boris Veniaminovich; Soviet politician; ed. Higher Party School.
Member C.P.S.U. 31-; Party worker 33-43; Official of Central Cttee. of C.P. for Ryazan Region 43-47; Second Sec. Tashkent Regional Cttee. of C.P. of Uzbekistan 50-58; in Central Cttee. C.P.S.U. 58-61; Second Sec. Central Cttee. of C.P. of Latvia 61-67; First Sec. Archangelsk Regional Cttee. of C.P. 67-; mem. Central Revision Comm. of C.P.S.U. 66; Deputy to U.S.S.R. Supreme Soviet.
Archangelsk Regional Committee of Communist Party, Archangelsk, U.S.S.R.

Popov, Georgi Ivanovich; Soviet engineer and politician; b. 12; ed. Leningrad Inst. of Railway Transport Engineers.
Worker in Red Triangle Factory, Leningrad 36-41, 45-52; Soviet Army 41-45; mem. C.P.S.U. 42-; political and party work, Leningrad 52-56; First Sec. Viborg Town Cttee., C.P.S.U. 56-57; Second Sec. Leningrad District City Cttee., C.P.S.U. 57-60; First Sec. Leningrad City Cttee. C.P.S.U. 60-; mem. Central Cttee. of C.P.S.U. 64-; Deputy to U.S.S.R. Supreme Soviet.
Leningrad City Committee of Communist Party of Soviet Union, Leningrad, U.S.S.R.

Popov, Oleg Konstantinovich; Soviet actor; b. 1930; ed. Moscow State Circus School.
Clown on slack wire at Tbilisi Circus 50; clown at Saratov Circus 51; appeared in France, Britain, Poland, etc.; clown at Moscow Circus 55-; People's Artist of R.S.F.S.R.; Winner of Warsaw Int. Festival of Circus Art 56, Oscar Prize, Brussels 58.
All Union Organisation of State Circuses, 15 Neglinnaya Street, Moscow, U.S.S.R.

Popova, Nina Vasilievna; Soviet politician; b. 08; ed. Chernyskevsky Inst. of History, Philosophy and Literature.
Member C.P.S.U. 32-; party work 38-45; Sec. Cen. Council of Trade Unions 45-47; Chair. Cttee. of Soviet Women, Vice-Pres. Int. Dem. Fed. of Women 45-; Chair. All-Union Soc. for Foreign Cultural Relations, then Chair. Presidium of Union of Soviet Socs. of Friendship and Cultural Relations with Foreign Countries 58-; Cand. mem. Central Cttee. C.P.S.U. 56-61, mem. 61-; Deputy to U.S.S.R. Supreme Soviet, mem. Cttee. for Int. Affairs, Soviet of Nationalities; Int. Lenin Prize 63.
Union of Soviet Societies for Friendship and Cultural Relations with Foreign Countries, Prospekt Kalinina 14, Moscow, U.S.S.R.

Popovic, Koca; Yugoslav soldier and politician; b. 14 March 1908; ed. Univ. of Belgrade and in Switzerland and France.
Fmr. student of literature and mem. group of pro-gressive Yugoslav writers; volunteer in Spanish Republican Army 36; early organiser Yugoslav Liberation Army during 41-45 war; later Divisional, Corps and Army Commdr.; Chief of the Gen. Staff 46-53; Sec. of State for Foreign Affairs 53-65; Head, Comm. for Int. Econ. and Political Relations, Yugoslav C.P. 65-66; Vice-Pres. of Yugoslavia July 66-; decorations include Order of Freedom, Spomenica 1941, etc.
Kneca Miloša 24, Belgrade, Yugoslavia.

Popović, Milentije; Yugoslav politician; b. 1913; ed. Belgrade Technical Faculty.
Member Communist Party of Yugoslavia 39-, Instructor 39-41; in Nat. Liberation Army; Minister of Interior, Minister of Trade and Supplies, and Pres. of Planning Comm., Serbia 45-47; Minister in Federal Govt., later mem. Federal Exec. Council, Minister of Foreign Trade, Minister of Finance and Pres. Federal Cttee. for Scientific Work; fmr. mem. Exec. Cttee. Federal Board of Yugoslav Socialist Alliance, fmr. Pres. Political and Ideological Comm., later Sec.-Gen. Fed. Board of Yugoslav Socialist Alliance; now Pres. Federal Assembly; mem. Central Cttee. League of Communists of Yugoslavia; Order of Nat. Hero.
Federal Assembly, Belgrade, Yugoslavia.

Popovic, Vladimir; Yugoslav diplomatist; b. 27 Jan. 1914; ed. Medical Faculty, Univ. of Belgrade.
Served with Republican Army of Spain during Spanish Civil War 37-39; as leader of People's Liberation Movement in Croatia, mem. Supreme H.Q. People's Liberation Army and Partisans' Units of Yugoslavia 41-45; Commdr. Third Army Corps, People's Liberation Army, rank of Major-Gen., Bosnia 44; Political and Mil. Rep. of Yugoslavia to Bulgaria 45; Yugoslav Ambassador to U.S.S.R. 45-48; First Deputy Foreign Minister, Belgrade 48-50; Ambassador to U.S.A. 50-54; Chair. Foreign Affairs Cttee., Nat. Assembly 54-55; Ambassador to China 55-58; mem. Fed. Exec. Council, Chair. Org. and Admin. Cttee., Chair. Foreign Economic Relations Cttee., mem. Co-ordinating Cttee., mem. Cabinet 58-62; Chair. Foreign Affairs Cttee., Fed. Assembly 63-; del. to Paris Peace Conf. 46, to regular sessions UN Gen. Assembly 46-50 (head of del. 50); Head of del. to the Conf. on the Problems of Econ. Devt., Cairo 62, to the UN Conf. on Trade and Devt., Geneva 63; mem. Yugoslav del. to the second Conf. of Heads of State of the Unaligned Countries, Cairo 64; Order of Nat. Liberation First Class, Order of Partisan Star First Class, Order of Merit to the People First Class, Order of Brotherhood and Unity First Class, Order of Valour First Class, Order of the Nat. Hero, etc.
Foreign Affairs and International Relations Committee, Federal Assembly, Belgrade, Yugoslavia.
Telephone: 331-377.

Popovich, Col. Pavel Romanovich; Soviet (Ukrainian) cosmonaut; b. 5 Oct. 1930; ed. Industrial Technical School, Magnitogorsk and Zhukovsky Air Force Engineering Acad.
Joined Army 51; transferred to Air Force; Fighter Pilot; first to join cosmonaut training unit; launched into orbit around earth Aug. 12th 62, returned Aug. 15th after completing 48 orbits in space ship *Vostok 4*; mem. Communist Party; Deputy Supreme Soviet Ukrainian S.S.R.; Eng. Pilot Cosmonaut of the U.S.S.R.
Zvezdny Gorodok, Moscow, U.S.S.R.

Popper, Sir Karl Raimund, Kt., M.A., PH.D., D.LITT., F.B.A.; Austrian-born British philosopher; b. 28 July 1902; ed. Vienna Univ.
Senior Lecturer in Philosophy, Canterbury Univ. Coll., Christchurch, New Zealand 37-45; Reader in Logic, London Univ. 45-48; Prof. of Logic and Scientific Method 49-; Head, Dept. Philosophy, Logic and Scientific Method, London School of Econs. 45-66; William James Lecturer, Harvard Univ. 50; Fellow, Stanford Center for Advanced Study in the Behavioral Sciences

56-57; Annual Philosophical Lecturer, British Acad. 60; Shearman Lecturer, Univ. Coll. London 61; Herbert Spencer Lecturer, Oxford Univ. 61; Visiting Prof. Calif. and Minn. Univs. 62, Indiana 63, Univ. of Denver 66; Farnum Lecturer, Princeton Univ. 63, Arthur Holly Compton Memorial Lecturer, Washington Univ. 65; Visiting Fellow Salk Inst. for Biological Studies 66-67; mem. Council Asscn. for Symbolic Logic 51-55, Int. Acad. for Philosophy of Science 48-; Fellow, British Acad. 58-; Foreign Hon. Mem. American Acad. Arts and Sciences 66-; Hon. mem. Harvard Chapter of Phi Beta Kappa 64-; Pres. Aristotelian Soc. 58-59, British Soc. for the Philosophy of Science 59-61; Hon. LL.D. Chicago, Denver.
Publs. *Logik der Forschung, The Open Society and Its Enemies, Misère de l'Historicisme, The Poverty of Historicism, The Logic of Scientific Discovery, On the Sources of Knowledge and of Ignorance, Conjectures and Refutations: The Growth of Scientific Knowledge, Of Clouds and Clocks: An Approach to the Problem of Rationality and the Freedom of Man, In Search of Enlightenment,* over 100 papers for periodicals and journals of learned societies.
Fallowfield, Manor Road, Penn, Bucks., England.
Telephone: Penn 2126.

Porché, Wladimir; French radio and television official; b. 9 June 1910.
Joined state broadcasting service 35; organised early television programmes 35-36; television research during the occupation; Dir.-Gen. Radiodiffusion-Télévision Française 46-57, Hon. Dir.-Gen. 57-; Conseiller d'Etat 56-; Légion d'Honneur.
Publ. *Amours en Valespir.*
46 rue du Bac, Paris 7e, France.

Porritt, Sir Arthur, Bt., G.C.M.G., K.C.V.O., C.B.E.; British (b. New Zealand) Gov.-Gen. of New Zealand; b. 10 Aug. 1900; ed. Wanganui Collegiate School and Otago Univ., New Zealand, Oxford Univ. and St. Mary's Medical School, London.
St. Mary's Hospital Surgical Staff 36-65; War Service with R.A.M.C. Second World War; mem. Royal Medical Household 36-; Surgeon to Duke of York 36, to Household 37-46, to King George VI 46-52, Sergeant-Surgeon to Queen Elizabeth 53-67; Consulting Surgeon to the Army; Pres. Royal Coll. of Surgeons of England 60-63; Pres. B.M.A. 60-61; mem. Int. Olympic Cttee. 34-67; Chair. British Empire and Commonwealth Games 48-67; Gov.-Gen. of New Zealand 67-; Hon. Fellow Royal Coll. of Surgeons of Edinburgh, Glasgow, Ireland, Australasia and Canada, and American and South African Coll. of Surgeons; Gold Medal B.M.A.; Bronze Medal, 100 metres, Olympic Games 24, Hon. LL.D. St. Andrews, Otago and New Zealand, Hon. D.Sc. Oxford, Hon. M.D. Bristol.
Publs. *Athletics* (with D. G. A. Lowe) 29, *Essentials of Modern Surgery* (with R. M. Handfield-Jones) 39, and numerous articles in medical journals.
Government House, Wellington, New Zealand.

Porritt, R. V., B.SC.; Canadian mining executive; b. 14 Feb. 1901; ed. Royal Military Coll. and McGill Univ.
Worked in various mines until 26; with Noranda Mines 26-; Man. Waite Amulet Mines (subsidiary of Noranda) 32; at Horne Mine, Noranda, as Surveyor, Underground Foreman, Asst. Man. and Man. until 51; since then, at Head Office, Toronto, as Gen. Man., then Exec. Vice-Pres., later Pres. 64-; Pres. 15 subsidiary cos. of Noranda Mines Ltd., Chair. of Board 1 subsidiary co. and Dir. of 29 subsidiary cos.
Noranda Mines Limited, Suite 1700, 44 King Street West, Toronto 1, Ont., Canada.
Telephone: 362-7111.

Porsild, (Alf) Erling, M.B.E., PH.D., F.R.S.C.; Canadian (b. Danish) botanist; b. 17 Jan. 1901; ed. Sorø Acad. and Copenhagen Univ.
Botanical Asst. Danish Arctic Research Station, Disko, Greenland 22-25; botanist in charge of grazing studies and introduction of domesticated reindeer from Alaska to Canada 26-35; Curator and Head of Div. of Botany, Nat. Museum of Canada, Ottawa 36-45, Chief Curator 45-; Canadian Consul to Greenland 41-44; has done extensive field work or led botanical expeditions to Alaska, Yukon, Arctic and Subarctic Canada, Rocky Mountains and Arctic and Alpine parts of Europe; Foreign Hon. mem. American Acad. of Arts and Sciences, and Botanical Socs. in Norway, Sweden and Finland; Massey Medal 66.
Publs. *Botany of Southeastern Yukon* 51, *Vascular Plants of the Western Canadian Arctic Archipelago* 55, *Illustrated Flora of the Canadian Archipelago* 57, 63; and over 200 scientific and popular papers and articles, mainly on the taxonomy and distribution of plants.
45 Leonard Avenue, Ottawa 1, Ontario, Canada.

Portal of Hungerford, 1st Viscount, cr. 46, of Hungerford; 1st Baron, cr. 45; Marshal of the Royal Air Force Charles Frederick Algernon Portal, K.G., G.C.B., O.M., D.S.O., M.C., HON. LL.D. Manchester, Belfast, Birmingham, Bristol, and Cambridge, HON. D.C.L. Oxford and Durham; British officer; b. 21 May 1893; ed. Winchester and Christ Church, Oxford.
Served First World War 14-18; Officer Commanding Aden 34-35; Instructor Imperial Defence Coll. 36-37; Dir. Organisation Air Min. 37-39; Air mem. for Personnel Air Council 39; Commander-in-Chief, Bomber Command Mar.-Oct. 40; Chief of Air Staff 40-45; Pres. M.C.C. 58-59, Chair. British Aircraft Corpn. 60-, British Match Corpn. 59-64, now Dir.; Dir. Barclays Bank, Portal's Ltd., Whitbread Investment Trust.
West Ashling House, Chichester, Sussex, England.

Porter, George, F.R.S., SC.D., PH.D., M.A.; British professor of chemistry; b. 6 Dec. 1920; ed. Thorne Grammar School, Leeds Univ. and Emmanuel Coll., Cambridge.
War Service in R.N.V.R.; Demonstrator Physical Chemistry, Univ. of Cambridge 49-52, Asst. Dir. of Research 52-54; Asst. Dir. British Rayon Research Asscn. 54-55; Prof. of Physical Chemistry, Univ. of Sheffield 55-63, Firth Prof. and Head of Dept. of Chemistry 63-66; Prof. of Chemistry, The Royal Institution, London 63-66; Dir. and Fullerian Prof. of Chemistry, The Royal Inst. 66-; Hon. Fellow Emmanuel Coll., Cambridge; Hon. Prof. Univ. of Kent; visiting Prof., Univ. Coll., London; Corday-Morgan Medal Chemical Soc. 55; Nobel Prize in Chemistry 67.
Publs. *Chemistry for the Modern World* 62, *Progress in Reaction Kinetics* (Editor), and numerous scientific papers.
The Royal Institution, 21 Albemarle Street, London, W.1, England.
Telephone: 01-493 0669.

Porter, Katherine Anne; American writer; b. 15 May 1890; ed. private schools and convents in southern U.S.A.
Guggenheim Fellowship for work in fiction 31-32, renewed 38-39; Fellow of Library of Congress (Fellow of Regional American Literature) 44; Vice-Pres. Nat. Inst. of Arts and Letters New York 50-52; Fulbright Lecturer, Univ. of Liège 54-55; elected mem. Nat. Acad. Arts and Letters 67; awarded Gold Medal of Soc. for the Libraries of New York Univ. 40; two-year Ford Foundation Grant 60-62; Hon. D.Litt. (Univ. of N. Carolina, Women's Coll., Smith Coll., La Salle Coll., Rutgers Univ.); Hon. D.H.L. (Univs. of Michigan and Maryland), Emerson-Thoreau Medal (American Acad. of Arts and Sciences); Nat. Book Award 66; Pulitzer

Prize 66; Gold Medal for Fiction (Nat. Inst. of Arts and Letters) 67; Gold Medal for Services to Literature (Collins Coll.) 67.

Publs. *Flowering Judas* (short stories) 30, *Pale Horse, Pale Rider* (3 short novels) 39, *The Leaning Tower* (short stories) 44, *The Days Before* (collected essays) 52; *K.A.P.'s French Song Book* (trans. from French) 33; *The Itching Parrot* (novel, trans. from Spanish) 42, *Ship of Fools* (novel) 62, *Collected Stories of Katherine Anne Porter* 65.

3601 49th Street, N.W., Washington, D.C. 20016, U.S.A.

Porter, L(ester) G(ilbert); American business executive; b. 19 Feb. 1903; ed. Univ. of Illinois.

Borg-Warner Corpn. Chicago 34-, Treas. 51, later Dir., Exec. Vice-Pres., Pres. 61-; Chair. Borg-Warner Ltd., Australia; Dir. La Salle Nat. Bank, Illinois Power Co.

Borg-Warner Corporation, 200 S. Michigan Avenue, Chicago 4; 229 East Lake Shore Drive, Chicago 11, Illinois, U.S.A.

Porter, Richard William; American electrical and technological executive; b. 24 March 1913; ed. Univ. of Kansas and Yale Univ.

General Electric Co. 37-50, originated first mil. and commercial applications of amplidyne generators 37-45, responsible for aircraft automatic tracking equipment for first fire control radar 40-41; Manager Guided Missiles Dept. 50-55, Consultant Engineering Services 55-63, General Electric Co., Special Assignment 63-; Advisory Cttee. U.S. Dept. of Defense 55-56; Scientific Advisory Board U.S. Air Force 48-51, 60-; mem. Space Science Board, Nat. Acad. of Sciences 58, Chair. Int. Relations Cttee. 59-, Adviser U.S. Del. to UN 62-; Vice-Pres. Cttee. on Space Research, Int. Council of Scientific Unions 59-; numerous awards.

Publs. *Das Amerikanische Erdsatellitenprogram* 56, *Recovery of Data in Physical Form* 56, *What the Future Holds* 58, *Preview of Scientific Progress* 59, *Weather Modification and Space Exploration* 59, *Adventures in Energy Conversion* 60.

Cat Rock Road, Cos Cob, Connecticut, U.S.A.

Portman, Eric, British actor; b. 13 July 1903; ed. Rishworth School, Yorks.

Plays include: *The Comedy of Errors* 24, *Hamlet* 27, *Major Barbara* 29, *The Beaux' Stratagem* 30, *Desire Under the Elms* 31, *The Master Builder* 31, *Caste* 32, *The Rivals* 33, *Diplomacy* 33, *Bitter Harvest* 36, *Julius Caesar* 37, *Madame Bovary* 37, *I Have Been Here Before* 38, *Julius Caesar* (modern dress) 39, *Jeannie* 40, *Playbill* 48, *His Excellency* 50, *The Moment of Truth* 51, *The Living Room* 53, *Separate Tables* 54-56, *A Touch of the Poet* 58, *A Passage to India* 62, *The Claimant* 64, *The Creeper* 65, *Justice* 68; films inc.: *49th Parallel, One of Our Aircraft is Missing, We Dive at Dawn, Millions Like Us, A Canterbury Tale, Men of Two Worlds, Wanted for Murder, Dear Murderer, Cairo Road, His Excellency, The Colditz Story, The Good Companions, Freud, West Eleven, The Whisperers.*

Lower Penpol, St. Veep, Cornwall, England.

Portmann, Adolf, DR. PHIL.; Swiss professor; b. 27 May 1897; ed. Univs. of Basle, Paris, Munich, Berlin and Geneva.

Privat Dozent Univ. of Basle 26-31, Prof. of Zoology and Dir. of the Zoological Laboratory 31-, Rector of the Univ. 47; Pres. Int. Asscn. Univ. Profs. 48-51, Pres. Rectors' Conf. (Swiss Univs.) 62-64.

Publs. *Biologische Fragmente zu einer Lehre vom Menschen* 51, *Einführung in die vergleichende Morphologie der Wirbeltiere* 59, *Die Tiergestalt* 60, *Das Tier als soziales Wesen* 56, *Biologie und Geist* 56, *Neue Wege der Biologie* 61.

Zoolog. Anstalt, Rheinsprung 9, Basle, Switzerland.

Poskonov, Alexei Andreevich; Soviet government financial official; b. 04; ed. Leningrad Inst. of Finance and Economics.

Worked in finance orgs. 23-; mem. Communist Party of Soviet Union 28-; People's Commissar of Finance, R.S.F.S.R. 40-45; Dep. Finance Minister of U.S.S.R. 45-60, First Dep. Finance Minister 60-63; Chair. State Bank of U.S.S.R.; Deputy to U.S.S.R. Supreme Soviet, mem. Central Auditing Cttee.

State Bank of the U.S.S.R., Neglinnaya 12, Moscow, U.S.S.R.

Pospelov, Pyotr Nikolaevich; Soviet politician; b. 98; ed. Moscow Inst. of Red Professors.

Joined Communist Party 16; worked at H.Q., Central Cttee. of Party 24-26; mem. Central Control Comm. 30, and mem. Editorial Boards of *Pravda* and of the magazine *Communist*; Asst. Head, Dept. of Propaganda, Central Cttee. of Party 37; mem. Central Cttee. 39; Editor *Pravda* 40; Dir. Marxism-Leninism Inst. of Central Cttee. 49-52, 61-; mem. and Chief, Editorial Board of Soviet Encyclopaedia 49-52; mem. Central Cttee. of C.P.S.U. 52-60; Sec. Central Cttee. 53-60; Candidate mem. Presidium, Central Cttee. of C.P.S.U. 57-61; mem. U.S.S.R. Acad. of Sciences; awarded Order of Lenin (twice), Order of the Patriotic War (1st Class), State Prize, Hero of Socialist Labour, etc.

Institute of Marxism-Leninism of Central Committee of C.P.S.U., Trety Celskokhozyaistvenny proezd 4, Moscow, U.S.S.R.

Post, Mrs. Marjorie Merriweather; American philanthropist and business executive; b. 15 March 1887; ed. Battle Creek, Michigan, public school, and Mount Vernon Seminary and Junior Coll.

Daughter of Charles William Post; has married four times; maiden name restored 64; Owner and Operator, Postum Cereal Co. Ltd. 14-22; mem. Board of Dirs. Gen. Foods Corpn. 36-58, Dir. Emeritus 58-; First Alumna Trustee, First Life Trustee of Board, Mount Vernon Seminary; mem. Board of Exec. Cttee. and mem. Board of Dirs., Nat. Symphony, Washington D.C.; mem. Board of Exec. Cttee., Washington Chapter, American Red Cross; mem. Board Nat. War Funds Inc. 43-46; Chair. Nat. Women's Council U.S. Flag Asscn. 33; mem. Board of Dirs. Nat. Savings & Trust, Washington, D.C. 59; mem. Advisory Cttee. Nat. Cultural Center 59; mem. numerous other philanthropic orgs. and recipient of many citations and decorations from foreign govts.

Philanthropic works include: equipped No. 8 Base Hospital Savenay, France, First World War; maintained food kitchens in slums of New York (operated by Salvation Army) 29-35; Hon. Chair. Parcels for Belgian Prisoners and Parcels for Belgium 40-44; Benefactress, C.W. Post Coll., Long Island Univ.

4155 Linnean Avenue, N.W., Washington, D.C. 20008, U.S.A.

Postel-Vinay, André; French civil servant; b. 4 June 1911; ed. Univ. of Paris.

Financial Inspector 38; General Man. Caisse Centrale de Coopération Economique 44-; mem. Board of Dirs. Banque Centrale des Etats de l'Afrique équatoriale et du Cameroun, Banque Centrale des Etats de l'Afrique de l'Ouest; Officier Légion d'Honneur, Compagnon de la Libération, Membre du Conseil de l'Ordre de la Libération, Grand Officier de l'Ordre National du Mérite.

233 boulevard Saint-Germain, Paris 7e, France.
Telephone: 468-62-83.

Postgate, Raymond William, O.B.E.; British historian, novelist, journalist and gastronome; b. 6 Nov. 1896; ed. Perse School, Cambridge, Liverpool Coll. and St. John's Coll., Oxford.

Former Dep. Ed. XIVth edn. *Encyclopaedia Britannica;*

European rep. Alfred A. Knopf Inc., New York 30-50; Pres. Good Food Club 50-.
Publs. *The International During the War* 18, *The Bolshevik Theory* 20, *Revolution from 1789 to 1906* 20, *The Workers' International* 20, *The Builders' History* 23, *Out of the Past* 22, *Murder, Piracy and Treason* 25, *History of the British Workers* 26, *That Devil Wilkes* 30, *The Conversations of Dr. Johnson* 30, *Robert Emmet* 31, *No Epitaph* 32, *Karl Marx* 33, *How to Make a Revolution* 34, *What to Do with the B.B.C.* 35, (with G. A. Vallance) *Those Foreigners* 37, *Verdict of Twelve* 40, *Somebody at the Door* 43, (with G. D. H. Cole) *The Common People 1746-1946* 46, *Life of George Lansbury* 51, *Good Food Guide* 51-, *Plain Man's Guide to Wine* 51-, *The Ledger is Kept* 53, *The Story of a Year, 1848* 55, *An Alphabet of Wine* 55, *Every Man is God* 59, *Home Wine Cellar* 60.
45 Hendon Lane, London, N.3; and Red Lion Cottage, Blean, Kent, England.
Telephone: 01-346-0688 (London); Blean 474.

Poswick, Charles, LL.D.; Belgian lawyer and politician; b. 6 Oct. 1924.
Counsellor, Cabinet of Prime Minister Eyskens (58-61), later, Asst. Chief of Cabinet, Ministry of Justice; mem. Parl. for Namur 65-; Minister of Nat. Defence 66-; Parti de la Liberté et du Progrès (P.L.P.), Partij voor Vrijheid en Voornitgang (P.V.V.).
Ministry of National Defence, rue de la Loi 2, Brussels 1, Belgium.

Potez, Henry Charles Alexandre; French construction engineer; b. 30 Sept. 1891; ed. Ecole Nationale Supérieure Aéronautique.
Founded Société des Aéroplanes Henry Potez 19; Pres. Chamber of Aeronautical Industries 31-35; Man. Dir. Ets. Henry Potez (planes, heating); Pres. Potez-Industries; Pres. Société de Gestion Immobilière; Gov. Dir. Potez Industries of Ireland Ltd., Potez Aerospace Ltd.; Vice-Pres. de la Soc. Gaumont; Dir. various cos.; Pres. Asscn. Française des Ingénieurs et Techniciens de l'Aéronautique; Pres. Amis du Musée de l'Air; Hon. Pres. fmr. Students of Ecole Nat. Supérieure de l'Aéronautique, Union Syndicale des Industries Aéronautiques et Spatiales; Grand Officier Légion d'Honneur; Croix de l'Ordre National du Mérite; Commdr. l'Economie Nationale; several foreign orders.
46 avenue Kléber, Paris 16e, France.
Telephone: Passy 01-95.

Poto Ndamase, Paramount Chief Victor; South African (Transkei) politician; b. 98; ed. Buntingdale Inst., Mission Schools at Clarkebury, Queenstown and Leribe and Fort Hare Univ. Coll.
Paramount Chief of West Pondoland 18-; fmr. mem. Pondoland Gen. Council, United Transkeian Gen. Council, Bantu Representation Council, Transkeian Territorial Authority; defeated candidate in elections for Chief Minister of Transkei 63.
Office of the Paramount Chief of the West Pondos, Nyandeni, Transkei, South Africa.

Potter, David Morris, M.A., PH.D.; American university professor; b. 6 Dec. 1910; ed. Emory and Yale Univs.
Instructor in History, Univ. of Mississippi 36-38, Rice Institute 38-42; Asst. Prof. Dept. of History, Yale Univ. 42-47, Assoc. Prof. 47-49, Prof. 49-50, Coe Prof. of American History 50-61; Coe Prof. of American History, Stanford Univ. 61-; Commonwealth Fund Lecturer, Univ. Coll., London 63; Harold Vyvyan Harmsworth Prof. of American History, Oxford 47-48; Hon. LL.D., D.Litt.
Publs. *Lincoln and His Party in the Secession Crisis* 42, *Trail to California: The Overland Journal of Vincent Geiger and Wakeman Bryarly* 45, *A Union Officer in the Reconstruction* (with J. H. Croushore) 48, *Nationalism and Sectionalism in America* (with T. G. Manning)

49, *Government and the American Economy* (with T. G. Manning) 49, *People of Plenty* 54.
Department of History, Stanford University, Stanford, Calif., U.S.A.

Potter, Stephen; British writer; b. 1 Feb. 1900; ed. Westminster School and Merton Coll., Oxford.
Lecturer in English Literature, London Univ. 26; Writer-Producer B.B.C. 38, Ed. of Literary Features and Poetry 42, Chair. Literary Cttee. 43; Dramatic Critic *New Statesman* 45-46; Book Critic *News Chronicle* 46-47; Editor *Leader* Magazine 49-51.
Publs. *The Young Man* (novel) 29, *D. H. Lawrence: A First Study* 30, *The Nonesuch Coleridge* 34, *Minnow Among Tritons, Letters of Mrs. S. T. Coleridge* 34, *Coleridge and S.T.C.* 35, *The Muse in Chains—A Study in Education* 37, *Gamesmanship* 47, *Lifemanship* 50, *One Upmanship* 52, *Humour Anthology* 54, *Potter on America* 56, *Supermanship* 58, *The Magic Number* 59, *Steps to Immaturity* 59, *Squawkey* 65, *Anti-Woo* 65, *The Complete Golf Gamesmanship*.
23 Hamilton Terrace, London, N.W.8, England.

Potter, Major-Gen. William Everett, B.S.; American army officer (retd.) and business executive; b. 17 July 1905; ed. West Point, M.I.T., Command and Gen. Staff School, and Nat. War Coll.
Joined Corps of Engineers 28; with U.S. Army in Europe in Second World War as chief of Troops section, exec. of Propaganda and Psychological Warfare Div., Chief of Planning Branch, G-4 Section, Chief of Plans and Operations Branch G-4 Section; Asst. Chief of Engineers for Civil Works, Wash. 49-51; Nat. War Coll. 51; Div. Engineer, Missouri River Div. 52-56; Gov. Canal Zone and *ex officio* Pres. Panama Canal Co. 56-60; Exec. Vice-Pres. New York World's Fair 1964-65 Corpn. 60-65; Vice-Pres. Admin. Florida Project, Walt Disney World Co., EPCOT Planning.
Walt Disney World Co., 100 S. Orange Avenue, Florida 32801, U.S.A.

Pöttgen, Ernst Ludwig; German theatre director; b. 1925; ed. Staatliche Hochschule für Musik, Berlin-Charlottenburg and Munich, Universität München and Universität Mainz.
Naval Officer, Second World War; Asst. Dir. Landestheater, Darmstadt 48, Bayerische Staatsoper, Munich 51, Stadttheater, Frankfurt/Main 55, Hamburgische Staatsoper 56; Dir. Hamburgische Staatsoper 56; Chief Dir. and Deputy Man. Nat. Theater Mannheim 58; Chief Dir. of Opera, Württembergisches Staatstheater, Stuttgart 61-; Dir. Teatro Colón, Buenos Aires 60, Deutsche Oper am Rhein, Düsseldorf 64, Salzburg Festival 65-, Florence Maggio Musicale Festival 65-.
Burgstrasse 59b, Stuttgart-Kaltental, German Federal Republic.

Pottle, Frederick Albert, M.A., PH.D.; American university professor; b. 3 Aug. 1897; ed. Colby Coll. and Yale Univ.
Served in American Expeditionary Force First World War 18-19; Asst. Prof. of English, Univ. of New Hampshire 21-23; Instructor in English, Yale Univ. 25-26, Assistant Professor 26-30, Professor 30-66, Sterling Professor of English 44-66, Professor Emeritus 66-; Fellow Davenport Coll., Yale Univ., American Acad. of Arts and Sciences, American Philosophical Soc., Provinciaal Utrechtsch Genootschap van Kunsten en Wetenschappen; Editor *The Private Papers of James Boswell* 30-37; Chair. Editorial Cttee. Yale Editions of the *Private Papers of James Boswell* 49-; Trustee Colby Coll. 32-59, and Gen. Theological Seminary; Messenger Lecturer Cornell Univ. 41; Guggenheim Fellow 45-46, 52-53; Fellow Int. Inst. Arts and Letters; Hon. Litt.D. (Colby Coll.) 41, (Rutgers Univ.) 51, LL.D. (Glasgow Univ.) 36.
Publs. *The Literary Career of James Boswell* 29, *Stret-*

chers, the Story of a Hospital on the Western Front 29, Vols. 7-18 of *The Private Papers of James Boswell* 30-34, *Boswell's Journal of a Tour to the Hebrides* (with C. H. Bennett) 36, 62, *The Idiom of Poetry* 41, rev. and enlarged 46; *Boswell's London Journal, 1762-63* 50, *Boswell in Holland, 1763-64* 52, *Boswell on the Grand Tour: Germany and Switzerland, 1764* 53, *Boswell on the Grand Tour: Italy, Corsica and France 1765-66* (with Frank Brady) 55, *Boswell in Search of a Wife, 1766-69* (with Frank Brady) 56, *Boswell for the Defence, 1769-74* (with W. K. Wimsatt) 59, *Boswell, the Ominous Years 1774-76* (with Charles Ryskamp) 63, *James Boswell, The Earlier Years, 1740-1769* 66.
Department of English, Yale University, New Haven, Conn. 06520; Home: 35 Edgehill Road, New Haven, Conn. 06511, U.S.A.

Potts, Frederic Augustus; American banker; b. 6 May 1904; ed. Yale Univ.
With Dominick & Dominick, Investment Bankers, New York City 26-28; Gen. Partner J. W. Davis & Co., mems. New York Stock Exchange 28-40; Vice-Pres. Philadelphia Nat. Bank 42-47, Pres. 47-64, Chair. 64-; Dir. of several other companies.
Home: Spruce Road, Ambler, Pa.; Office: Broad and Chestnut Streets, Philadelphia 1, Pa., U.S.A.
Telephone: 215-M16-1384 (Home); 215-LO9-2100 (Office).

Poujade, Pierre; French politician; b. 1 Dec. 1920.
Served 39-45 war; after 45 became publisher and bookseller, also active in politics; mem. Saint Céré Municipal Council 51; Founder Pres. Union de Défense de Commerçants et Artisans; Founder Union et Fraternité Française; Founder Dir. *Union et Défense* (daily), *Fraternité Française* (weekly).
Publ. *J'ai Choisi le Combat* 56.
49 rue Emile-Zola, Limoges, France.

Poukka, (Kalle) Pentti, M.A.; Finnish newspaper editor; b. 13 Sept. 1919; ed. Univ. of Helsinki.
Public Relations Officer Yhtyneet Paperitehtaat 49-52; Research Worker, Taloudellinen Tutkimuskeskus; mem. Helsinki City Council 65-; Editor-in-Chief *Talouselämä* 54-55; Leader-writer and Economic Editor *Uusi Suomi* 55-57; Editor-in-Chief *Kauppalehti* 57-63, *Uusi Suomi* 64-.
Publs. *Teollisuuden rahoitus vv 1947-1952* (Financing Industry 1947-1952), *Huomispäivän suomalainen* (The Finn of Tomorrow).
c/o *Uusi Suomi*, Helsinki; Armas Lindgrenintie 7a, Helsinki 57, Finland.
Telephone: 688949 (Home).

Poumpouras, Anthony; Greek lawyer and diplomatist; b. 06; ed. Univs. of Athens, Univ. of Paris and Inst. of Higher International Studies. Paris.
Foreign Service 31-, served Santi-Quarante (Albanie), Alexandria, Chicago, Washington, New York 35-52; Dir. of Foreign Minister's Private Office 52; Counsellor, London 52-53, Bonn 53-55; Perm. Rep. of Greece to Int. Orgs., Geneva 55-57; Ambassador to Romania 57-60; Dir. Fourth Political Dept., Ministry of Foreign Affairs 60-62; Amb. to Turkey 62-66; Amb. to Italy 66-.
Royal Greek Embassy, Viale Gioacchino Rossini 4, Rome, Italy.

Pound, Ezra, PH.D., M.A.; American poet and composer; b. 30 Oct. 1885; ed. Univ. of Pennsylvania and Hamilton Coll.
Began publishing 08; London Editor *Little Review* 17-19; contrib. to *Action, British Union Quarterly, Criterion, Townsman, Rassegna Monetaria*; Editor *The Exile*; indicted for treason by American Govt. July 43; Speaker on Rome Radio 43-44, captured in Northern Italy by 5th Army May 45, detained in U.S.A. until April 58; Bollingen Prize for 1948; Fellow Acad. of American Poets 63.

Publs. 41 vols. *Personae* (collected shorter poems), *XXX Cantos, Cantos 31/41, Fifth Decade of Cantos, Cantos LII/LXXI*; prose: *Make It New, A B C of Reading, A B C of Economics, Social Credit an Impact, Jefferson and/or Mussolini, Polite Essays, Guide to Kulchur*; translations and studies from the Fenollosa MSS. (including *Certain Noble Plays of Japan and Cathay), Ta Hio, Guido Cavalcanti, Letters* 51, *Translations* 53, *Literary Essays* 54; musical compositions: *Le Testament,* an opera or song drama, *Cavalcanti.*
Brunnenburg, Tirolo Merano, Italy; c/o Messrs. Horne & Birkett, 19 Cowley Street, Westminster, London, S.W.1, England.

Powdermaker, Hortense, PH.D.; American anthropologist; b. 24 Dec. 1900; ed. Goucher Coll. and London School of Econs., Univ. of London.
Research Assoc., Inst. of Human Relations, Yale Univ. 34-37; Faculty, Queens Coll. of the City Univ. of New York 38-67, Prof. of Anthropology 54-67; fieldwork in New Ireland 29-30; rural community in Mississippi 33-34, Hollywood 47-48, N. Rhodesia 53-54; Pres. New York Acad. of Sciences 44-46, Chair. Anthropology Section; Pres. American Ethnological Soc. 46-47; Research Assoc. Dept. of Anthropology, Univ. of California (Berkeley); Vice-Pres. New York Acad. of Sciences; Fellow American Anthropological Soc.
Publs. *Life in Lesu, The Study of a Melanesian Society in New Ireland* 33, *After Freedom, A Cultural Study in the Deep South* 39, *Probing our Prejudices* 44, *Hollywood, the Dream Factory* 50, *Copper Town: Changing Africa—The Human Situation on the Rhodesian Copperbelt* 62, *Stranger and Friend, The Way of an Anthropologist* 66.
1321 Arch Street, Berkeley, Calif. 94708, U.S.A.
Telephone: 415-849-2294.

Powell, Adam Clayton, Jr.; American clergyman and politician; b. 29 Nov. 1908; ed. Colgate Univ., Columbia Univ. and Shaw Univ.
Minister, Abyssinian Baptist Church 37-60; Founder, Co-Publisher, Editor-in-Chief *People's Voice* 42; mem. U.S. House of Reps. 45-67, fmr. Chair. Cttee. on Educ. and Labour; Delegate to Parl. World Govt. Conf., London 51-52, to ILO Conf., Geneva 61; Knight of Golden Cross, Ethiopia; Democrat.
Publs. *Is This A White Man's War?* 42, *Stage Door Canteen* 44, *Adam Clayton Powell* 60.
132 West 138th Street, New York City 31, N.Y., U.S.A.

Powell, Anthony Dymoke, C.B.E.; British writer; b. 21 Dec. 1905; ed. Eton and Balliol Coll., Oxford.
Served Second World War in Welch Regiment and Intelligence Corps; Orders of White Lion (Czechoslovakia), Leopold II (Belgium), Oaken Crown and Croix de Guerre (Luxembourg); James Tait Black Prize (for *At Lady Molly's*); Trustee of Nat. Portrait Gallery.
Publs. *Afternoon Men* 31 (performed as a play 63), *Venusberg* 32, *From a View to a Death* 33, *Agents and Patients* 36, *What's Become of Waring* 39, *John Aubrey and His Friends* 48, *Selections from John Aubrey* 49, the *Music of Time* series: *A Question of Upbringing* 51, *A Buyer's Market* 52, *The Acceptance World* 55, *At Lady Molly's* 57, *Casanova's Chinese Restaurant* 60, *The Kindly Ones* 62, *The Valley of Bones* 64, *The Soldier's Art* 66, *The Military Philosophers* 68.
The Chantry, near Frome, Somerset, England.

Powell, Cecil Frank, F.R.S., M.A., PH.D.; British university professor; b. 5 Dec. 1903; ed. Judd School, Tonbridge, and Sidney Sussex Coll., Cambridge.
Research Asst. to Prof. A. M. Tyndall, Bristol 28; mem. joint Royal Society and Colonial Office Expedition to investigate seismic and volcanic activities in Montserrat, B.W.I. 35; Melville Wills Prof. of Physics, Univ. of Bristol 48-63; Dir. H. H. Wills Physics Laboratory 64-; Pro-Vice-Chancellor, Univ. of Bristol 64-; Dir. high-altitude balloon experiments, Mediterranean (51, 53 and 61) and Po Valley (54, 55, 57); Chair. Scientific

Policy Cttee. C.E.R.N. 61-63; Pres. Cosmic-Ray Comm. of I.U.P.A.P. 59-63; mem. Science Research Council, Chair. its Nuclear Physics Board 65-; Vernon Boys Prizeman, Physical Soc. 47; Hughes Medal of Royal Soc. 49; Nobel Prize for Physics 50; Royal Medal of Royal Soc. 61; Lomonossov Gold Medal of U.S.S.R. Acad. of Sciences 67; Hon. Fellow Inst. of Physics; Hon. mem. Royal Irish Acad.; Foreign mem. Acad .of Sciences of the U.S.S.R.; Hon. Fellow, Sidney Sussex Coll., Univ. of Cambridge 68-; Hon. Sc.D. Univs. of Bordeaux, Berlin, Dublin, Warsaw, Padua, Moscow.
Publs. *Nuclear Physics in Photographs* (with G. P. S Occhialini) 47, *The Study of Elementary Particles by the Photographic Method* (with P. Fowler and D. Perkins) 59.
12 Goldney Avenue, Bristol 8; and The H. H. Wills Physical Laboratory, Royal Fort, Bristol, England. Telephone: 37196.

Powell, Rt. Hon. Enoch (*see* Powell, Rt. Hon. (John) Enoch.)

Powell, Herbert Butler; American diplomatist; b. 13 July 1903; ed. Univ. of Oregon and National War Coll., Washington.
U.S. Army 26-63, General 60; Chief of Staff, Infantry Div., Europe 44-45; Commanding Officer, 17th Infantry Combat Team, Korea 50-51; Gen. Staff, Dept. of the Army, Washington 51-54; Commd. Gen., 25th Infantry Div., Hawaii 54-56; U.S. Army Pacific 56; Army Infantry Center, Fort Benning 56-58; Third U.S. Army 60; Continental Army Commd., Fort Monroe 60-63, also Commdr.-in-Chief, U.S. Army Strike Commd. and U.S. Army Atlantic; Amb. to New Zealand 63-67; Lecturer, U.S. War Colls., Ecole Supérieure de Guerre, British School of Infantry and Canadian School of Infantry; D.S.C., D.S.M., L.M., B.S.M. and many other decorations.
c/o Army National Bank, Fort Leavenworth, Kan., U.S.A.

Powell, Rt. Hon. (John) Enoch, P.C., M.B.E., M.P.; British politician; b. 16 June 1912; ed. King Edward's School, Birmingham and Trinity Coll., Cambridge.
Fellow Trinity Coll. Cambridge 34-38; Prof. of Greek, Univ. of Sydney, N.S.W. 37-39; army service rising to rank of Brig. 39-44; Conservative M.P. Wolverhampton S.W. 50-; Parl. Sec. Ministry of Housing and Local Govt. 55-57; Financial Sec. to Treasury 57-58; Minister of Health 60-63; Dir. Nat. Discount Co. Feb. 64-.
Publs. *The Rendel Harris Papyri* 36, *First Poems* 37, *A Lexicon to Herodotus* 38, *The History of Herodotus* 39, *Casting-off, and other poems* 39, *Herodotus, Book VIII* 39, *Llyfr Blegywryd* 42, *Thucydidis Historia* 42, *Herodotus* (transl.) 49, *Dancer's End and The Wedding Gift* (poems) 51, *The Social Services, Needs and Means* 52, (jointly) *One Nation* 50, *Change is our Ally* 54, *Biography of a Nation* 55, *Saving in a Free Society* 60, *Great Parliamentary Occasions* 60, *A Nation Not Afraid* 65, *A New Look at Medicine and Politics* 66; *The House of Lords in the Middle Ages* (with Keith Wallis) 68.
33 South Eaton Place, London, S.W.1, England.

Powell, Sir Richard Royle, G.C.B., K.B.E., C.M.G., B.A.; British civil servant; b. 30 July 1909; ed. Sidney Sussex Coll., Cambridge.
Served Admiralty 31-46; Under-Sec. Ministry of Defence 46-48; Deputy Sec. Admiralty 48-50; Deputy Sec. Ministry of Defence 50-56, Permanent Sec. 56-59; Permanent Sec. Board of Trade 60-68.
56 Montagu Square, London, W.1, England.

Power, Donald Clinton, B.S., LL.B., M.A.; American lawyer and business executive; b. 25 Dec. 1899; ed. Ohio State Univ.
Chairman of Board, Gen. Telephone & Electronics Corpn., New York 66-, Chair. of Board and Chief Exec. Officer 51-66; Dir. American Manufacturers Mutual Insurance Co. (N.Y.), Canada Dry Corpn., Gen. Public Services Corpn., Gen. Tel. & Elec. Corpn., G.T. & E. Service Corpn., Irving Trust Co., Curtiss-Wright Corpn., Sylvania Electric Products, Inc., Charter New York Corpn.; Copper Range Co., Boston, Mass.; Automatic Electric Co. (of Chicago); Gen. Tel. Directory Co., Des Plaines, Ill.; Brown Steel Co. (of Columbus, Ohio); Gen. Tel. Co. of Ohio, Marion, Ohio; Gen. Tel. Co. of Florida, Tampa, Fla; Compagnia Dominicana de Telefonos C.p.A., Santo Domingo, Dominican Republic; Anglo-Canadian Tel. Co. Montreal; British Columbia Tel. Co., Vancouver, Hunt Foods and Industries Inc., Fullerton, Calif.; Jeffrey Co., Ohio State Life Ins. Co.; Trustee Cttee. for Econ. Development; mem. Nat. Industrial Conf. Board, Pres. U.S. Independent Telephone Asscn. 56-57, and many other positions in the field of public service; many awards for distinguished service; Hon. LL.D. Uppsala Coll.; Hon. D.B.A. Rio Grande Coll.; Republican.
General Telephone & Electronics Corpn., 730 Third Avenue, New York City 17, N.Y., U.S.A.

Power, Gen. Thomas Sarsfield; American Air Force officer; b. 18 June 1905; ed. Barnard Preparatory School, N.Y., Air Corps Primary Flying School, etc.
Construction Engineer 24-28; Commissioned Air Reserve, U.S. Army, 28; advanced through grades to Gen. 57; served with Bombardment Units 29-43; Deputy Chief of Staff (Operations), H.Q. 2nd Air Force, Colorado Springs 43-44; Exec. and Deputy Wing Commdr. 304th Bomb Wing, 15th Air Force, Italy, 44; Commdr. 314 Bomb Wing, Colorado Springs-Guam 45; Staff Joint Task Force I (Bikini Bomb Test) 46; Deputy Asst. Chief of Air Staff 46-48; Air Attaché, London 48; Deputy Commdr. H.Q. Strategic Air Command 48-54; Commdr. Air Research and Development Command 54-57; Commdr.-in-Chief, U.S. Strategic Air Command 57-64; Dir. Joint Strategic Target Planning Staff 60-64; Vice-Chair. of Board Eversharp Inc.; Board of Dirs. Bucyrus-Eric Co., Hedge Fund of America Inc.; Silver Star, Legion of Merit, Bronze Star Medal, Air Medal with Oak Leaf Cluster, D.S.M., D.F.C., Croix de Guerre (with palm); Hon. LL.D. (Creighton Univ., Univ. of Akron, St. Mary's Coll.).
c/o The Pentagon, Washington, D.C.; and Thunderbird Country Club, Palm Springs, Calif., U.S.A.
Telephone: 714-328-3362.

Powles, Sir Guy Richardson, K.B.E., C.M.G., E.D., LL.B.; New Zealand public servant; b. 5 April 1905; ed. Wellington Coll., Victoria Univ. Coll.
Barrister, Supreme Court of New Zealand 27-40; War Service, to rank of Col. 40-46; Counsellor, Washington; High Commr., Western Samoa 49-60; High Commr. India 60-62, Ceylon 61-62, Ambassador to Nepal 61-62; Ombudsman, New Zealand 62-.
Office of the Ombudsman, Wellington; Home: 34A Wesley Road, Wellington C.1, New Zealand.
Telephone: 49-491.

Pozderac, Hakija; Yugoslav politician; b. 19; ed. secondary technical school.
Former Sec.-Gen. of Govt. of People's Repub. of Bosnia and Herzegovina, State Under-Sec. in State Secr. for Econ. Affairs, State Sec. for Gen. Admin. and Budget, Bosnia and Herzegovina; Dir.-Gen. Yugoslav Nat. Bank; Dir. of Inst. of Econ. Planning, Bosnia and Herzegovina; Under-Sec., Fed. Sec., for Gen. Econ. Affairs until 65; Minister for Industry and Commerce 65-; mem. Yugoslav Fed. Exec Council.
Ministry for Industry and Commerce, Belgrade, Yugoslavia.

Pozhidayev, Dmitri Petrovich; Soviet diplomatist; b. 1913; ed. Zaporozhye Machine Building Inst.
Electrical fitter, Dnieper Hydro-Electric Power Station 31-32; student 32-37; engineer, Urals Wagon-Building

Factory 37-38; Diplomatic Service 39-; Vice-Consul, Maku (Iran) 42-43; Asst. to Deputy Minister of Foreign Affairs of U.S.S.R. 44-46; Deputy Head, Head, First European Dept., U.S.S.R. Foreign Ministry 46-48; Counsellor, Brussels 48-53; Counsellor, Counsellor-Minister, Rome 55-57; Amb. to Switzerland 57-58, to Morocco 58-62; Head of First African Dept., U.S.S.R. Foreign Ministry 62-65; Amb. to United Arab Repub. 65-67; on staff at Ministry of Foreign Affairs 67-; mem. C.P.S.U. 39-; Order of Red Star, Red Banner of Labour and other medals of U.S.S.R.
Ministry of Foreign Affairs, 32-34 Smolenskaya-Sennaya ploshchad, Moscow, U.S.S.R.

Prabhjot Kaur; Indian poet and politician; b. 6 July 1927; ed. Khalso Coll. for Women, Lahore and Punjab Univ.
First collected poems published 43 (aged sixteen); represented India at numerous int. literary confs. 56-; mem. Legislative Council, Punjab 66-; mem. Central Comm. of United Nations Educational, Scientific and Cultural Org. (UNESCO); received honours of Sahitya Shrimati 64 and Padma Shri 67; title of Rajya Kavi (Poet Laureate) by Punjab Govt. 64 and the Sahitya Akademi Award 65.
Publs. 35 books, including: Poems: *Supne Sadhran* 49, *Do Rang* 51, *Pankheru* 56, *Lala* (in Persian) 58, *Benkapani* 58, *Pabbi* 62; Short Stories: *Kinke* 52, *Aman de Na* 56.
D-203 Defence Colony, New Delhi, India.

Prader, Georg, LL.D.; Austrian politician; b. 15 June 1917; ed. Seitenstetten Hochschule and Universität Wien.
Army Service, Second World War; with Provincial Govt. of Lower Austria 46-49; with Lower Austrian Employees Section, Fed. of Austrian Workers and Employees (ÖAAB) 49, mem. Governing Body ÖAAB 53-, Chair. Lower Austrian Employees Section 56-, Deputy Provincial Chair. Lower Austrian Section 56-; mem. Bundesrat 54-59, Nationalrat 59-; Minister of Defence 64-; People's Party.
Ministry of Defence, Vienna, Austria.

Prado Vallejo, Julio; Ecuadorean lawyer, diplomatist and politician; b. 3 July 1924; ed. Univ. Central del Ecuador.
Chargé d'Affaires, Brazil 53-54, U.S.A. 54-57; Pres. Inter-American Comm. for Econ. Co-operation 56; Legal Adviser on Int. Agreements at Ministry of Finance 58; Prof. at Central Univ. of Ecuador 58-; Minister of Foreign Affairs 67-68; Gran Oficial Cruzeiro do Sul (Brazil); Gran Cruz Al Mérito (Ecuador).
Publs. *Réplica a al peruanidad de Túmbez, Jaen y Mainas* 45, *Demarcación de Fronteras – Ejecución del Protocolo de Río de Janeiro de Enero 29 de 1942* 50.
Calle Tamayo 1313 y Colón, Quito, Ecuador.
Telephone: 238-375.

Prado Ugarteche, Manuel; Peruvian banker and politician; b. 89; ed. School of Engineering and San Marcos Univ., Lima, Peru.
Professor higher mathematics Faculty of Science San Marcos Univ. 15-19; Deputy Peruvian Congress 19-21; Pres. Central Reserve Bank, Lima 34-39; Pres. of Repub. 39-45 and 56-62; exiled in Paris 62; Hon. G.B.E.
Publs. Several works on engineering and teaching: *Presiones hidrostáticas* 12, *La enseñanza profesional* 18, *El régimen metereológico* 19, etc.
[*Died* 14 *August* 1967.]

Prain, Sir Ronald Lindsay, Kt., O.B.E.; British company director; b. 3 Sept. 1907; ed. Cheltenham Coll.
Controller Die and Tool Control (Ministry of Supply) 40-45, Quartz Crystal Control 43-45; Chair. Roan Selection Trust group of companies, Merchant Bank, Zambia Ltd.; Dir. Barclays Bank D.C.O. (Zambian Local Board), Int. Nickel Co. of Canada Ltd., Minerals Separation Ltd., Pan Holding S.A., San Francisco Mines of Mexico Ltd., Selection Trust Ltd., and other companies; Pres. British Overseas Mining Asscn. 52, Inst. of Metals 60-61; Chair. Agricultural Research Council of Rhodesia and Nyasaland 59-63, Commonwealth Council of Mining and Metallurgical Insts.
Publ. *Selected Papers* (4 vols.).
Waverley, St. George's Hill, Weybridge, Surrey; 43 Cadogan Square, London, S.W.1, England; Kafne House, Cairo Road, P.O. Box 851, Lusaka, Zambia.
Telephone: Weybridge 42776; also 01-235-4900.

Prakasa, Sri, B.A., LL.B., Barr.-at-Law; Indian politician; b. 3 Aug. 1890; ed. Allahabad and Cambridge Univs.
Connected with *Leader*, Allahabad 17-18, *Independent*, Allahabad 19, *Aj*, Banaras 20-43, *National Herald*, Lucknow 38-48, *Sansar*, Banaras 43-49; mem. A.I.C.C. 18-45; founder mem. Kashi Vidyapith 21; mem. Banaras Municipal Board 21-25; Gen. Sec. United Provinces Congress Cttee. 28-34, and Indian Nat. Congress 29-31; Pres. U.P. Political Conf. 34 and Pres. United Provinces Congress Cttee. 34-35; M.L.A. Central 34 and 45; Chair. Reception Cttee. Indian Nat. Congress 36; imprisoned for Congress activities 30, 32, 41 and 42; mem. Constituent Assembly for U.P. 46; High Commr. for India in Pakistan 47-49; Gov. of Assam 49-50; Federal Minister of Commerce 50-51, for Natural Resources and Scientific Research 51-52; Gov. of Madras 52-56; Gov. of Bombay 56-60, of Maharashtra 60-62; mem. of Lok Sabha 50-52 (resgnd.); Padma Vibushan 57.
Publs. *Annie Besant, As Woman and as Leader, Pakistan: Birth and Early Days* (in English), *Grihast Gita, Sphut Vichar, Hamari antarik Gatha, Nagarik Shastra* (in Hindi).
Sevashrama Sigra, Varanasi (Banaras) 1, U.P.; and Vishtrani Kutir, Rajpur (Dehra Dun), India.

Prasad, Baleshwar, I.A.S., M.A.; Indian civil servant; b. 1 Jan. 1914; ed. Patna Univ.
Asst. Magistrate 50; Dep. Commr. 52; Political Adviser to Indian del. to Viet-Nam Int. Supervision and Control Comm. 56-59; Dewan (Prime Minster) of Sikkim 59-63; Chief Commr., Manipur 63-.
Chief Commissioner's House, Imphal, Manipur, India.

Prasad, P. S. Narayan; Indian economist; b. 24 Sept. 1910; ed. Andhra, Benares Univs.
Lecturer Andhra Univ. 34-36; Prof. of Economics, Wadia Coll., Poona 37-40; Head, Economics Dept., Maharajah's Coll., Jaipur 40-45; Reserve Bank of India 46-53; Exec. Dir. for India on Int. Monetary Fund 53-57; Asst. Dir. Economic Staff, World Bank 57-; Chair. World Bank's Mission to Libya 58-60; Economic Adviser to Nigeria 61-63; Dir. Asian Inst. for Econ. Devt. and Planning, Bangkok 63-; mem. Advisory Board of the Mekong Co-ordination Cttee.
U.N. Asian Institute for Economic Development and Planning, Henri Dunant Street, Bangkok, Thailand.
Telephone: 54051-5.

Prate, Alain; French civil servant and international official; b. 5 June 1928; ed. Ecole Nationale d'Administration.
Assistant Insp. of Finances 53-55, Insp. 55-58; Del. to conf. on EEC 57; Sec. of Monetary Cttee., European Econ. Community (EEC) 58-61; Dir. for Econ. Structure and Devt., Directorate-Gen. for Econ. and Financial Affairs, EEC 61-65; Dir.-Gen. of Internal Market, EEC 65-.
European Economic Community, 23 avenue de la Joyeuse Entrée, Brussels 4; Home: 42 rue des Astronomes, Brussels 18, Belgium.
Telephone: 74-10-67.

Prato, Eugenio; Italian diplomatist; b. 4 Dec. 1903; ed. Liceo Gioberti and Università degli Studi, Turin.
Foreign Service 28-; Vice-Consul in Switzerland,

Yugoslavia and Morocco 28-36; Third Sec., Albania 36-40; First Sec. Greece 41-43; concentration camp 43-44; First Sec. U.S.S.R. 45-47; Ministry of Foreign Affairs 47-49; Consul-Gen. Tunis 49-52; Vice Dir.-Gen. Dept. of Econ. Affairs, Ministry of Foreign Affairs 52-55; Ambassador to Libya 55-58, to Australia 58-62; Ministry of Foreign Affairs 62-64; Ambassador to Brazil 64-; Knight, Sovereign Mil. Order of Malta.
Italian Embassy, 154 rua Larangeiras, Rio de Janeiro, Brazil.

Pratolini, Vasco; Italian writer; b. 19 Oct. 1913.
Lugano prize 47; Viareggio prize 55; Feltrinelli prize 57, Marzotto prize 63.
Publs. Novels and stories: *Via de' Magazzini* 42, *Cronaca familiare* 47, *Cronache di poveri amanti* 47, *Le ragazze di San Frediano* 50, *Metello* 55, *Lo scialo* 60, *La constanza della ragione* 63, *Allegoria e Derisione* 66.
Via Tolmino 12, Rome, Italy.
Telephone: 858435.

Pratt, James Davidson, C.B.E., M.A., B.SC., F.R.I.C., C.ENG., M.I.CHEM.E.; British chemist; b. 13 Aug. 1891; ed. Gordon's Coll., and Aberdeen Univ.
Assistant to Prof. of Chemistry, Aberdeen Univ. 13-14; served in Army 14-21; Controller, Chemical Warfare Research, War Office 23-28; Gen. Man. (later Dir.) and Sec. Asscn. of British Chemical Manufacturers 28-57; Controller Chemical Defence Research and Development Min. of Supply 40-45; Pres. of Chemical Defence Board 40-49; lent to Ministry of Supply to assist in organisation of explosives and chemical production for rearmament and forward planning 51-53; Chair. British Road Tar Asscn. 37-40, 44-60; Past Vice-Pres. of Inst. of Chem. Engineers, Chemical Society and Society of Chemical Industry; past mem. of Road Research Board and Chair. Road Tar Research Cttee. of Dept. of Scientific and Industrial Research 46-65; awarded American Medal of Freedom with Silver Palms.
138 Earls Court Road, London, W.8, England.

Praz, Mario, K.B.E., DR. JURIS., D.LITT.; Italian university professor; b. 6 Sept. 1896; ed. Rome and Florence Univs.
Came to England 23; Senior Lecturer in Italian, Liverpool Univ. 24-32; Prof. of Italian Studies, Manchester Univ. 32-34; now Prof. of English Language and Literature, Univ. of Rome; mem. Standing Cttee. Int. Conf. of Univ. Profs. of English; Editor *English Miscellany* (Rome); British Acad. Gold Medallist for Anglo-Italian Studies 35; mem. Accad. dei Lincei 52-, and hon. mem. Modern Language Asscn. of America 54; Hon. D.Litt. (Cambridge, Sorbonne and Aix-Marseille).
Publs. *Secentismo e marinismo in Inghilterra* 25, *Penisola Pentagonale* 28, *La carne, la morte e il diavolo nella letteratura romantica* (*The Romantic Agony*) 30, *Studi sul concettismo* 34, *Storia della letteratura inglese* 37, *Studi e svaghi inglesi* 37, *Studies in 17th-Century Imagery* Vol. I 39, Vol. II 48, *Gusto neoclassico* 40, *Machiavelli in Inghilterra ed altri saggi* 42, *Fiori freschi* 43, *Ricerche anglo-italiane* 44, *La filosofia dell' arredamento* 45, *Motivi e figure* 45, *Cronache letterarie anglosassoni* Vols. I, II 51, Vols. III, IV 66, *La Casa della Fama* 52, *Lettrice notturna* 52, *La crisi dell'eroe nel romanzo vittoriano* 52, *Viaggi in Occidente* 55, *The Flaming Heart* 58, *La Casa della Vita* 58; *Bellezza e bizzarria* 60, *I volti del tempo* 64, *An Illustrated History of Interior Decoration* 64, *Panopticon Romano* 67; translations from Shakespeare, Jane Austen, Lamb, Pater, G. Moore, XIXth-Century Poets; Editor new Italian trans. of Shakespeare's plays, vol. of trans. from Elizabethan dramas, etc.
Palazzo Ricci, Via Giulia 146, Rome, Italy.
Telephone: 657759.

Prebisch, Raúl; Argentinian economist; b. 17 April 1901; ed. Buenos Aires Univ.
Prof. of Political Economy, Buenos Aires Univ. 25-48

(retd.), Hon. Prof. 55-; Deputy Dir., Argentinian Dept. of Statistics 25-27; Dir. of Economic Research, Nat. Bank of Argentina 27-30; Under Sec. for Finance 30-32; Adviser to Ministries of Finance and Agriculture 33-35; Organiser and first Dir.-Gen., Central Bank of the Republic of Argentina 35-43; Exec. Sec. UN Economic Comm. for Latin America 48-62; Dir.-Gen. of Latin American Inst. for Econ. and Social Planning 62-; Sec.-Gen. UN Conf. on Trade and Development, Geneva 64-; Hon. mem. Faculty of Econs., Univ. of Chile 56; Dr. h.c. Columbia and Los Andes (Colombia) Univs.
UNCTAD, c/o Palais des Nations, 1211 Geneva, Switzerland.

Prelog, Vladimir, DR. ING.; Swiss (b. Yugoslav) chemist; b. 23 July 1906; ed. Inst. of Technology and School of Chemistry, Prague.
Chemist, G. J. Driza Laboratories, Prague 29-35; Lecturer (Dozent), Univ. of Zagreb 35-40, Assoc. Prof. 40-41; Privatdozent Eidgenössische Technische Hochschule 42, Assoc. Prof. 47-50, Prof. of Organic Chemistry 50-, Head of Laboratory of Organic Chemistry 57-; Foreign mem. Royal Soc. (U.K.), Acad. of Sciences of U.S.S.R., Nat. Acad. of Sciences, U.S.A., American Acad. of Arts and Sciences, etc.; Werner Prize, Marcel Benoist Prize, Stas Medal, Medal of Honour, Rice Univ. and other prizes; Dr. h.c. (Zagreb, Liverpool and Paris).
Office: Universitätsstrasse 6, 8006 Zürich; Home: Bellariastrasse 41, 8038 Zürich, Switzerland
Telephone: 457802.

Preminger, Otto Ludwig, D.IUR.; Austrian-born American film and theatre director and producer; b. 5 Dec. 1906; ed. Vienna Univ.
Actor in Max Reinhardt's company 23; f. Comedie Theatre, Vienna 26, producer at Schauspielhaus 27, producer-dir. for Reinhardt's theatre, Josefstadt 28; dir. *Libel*, N.Y. 35, successive Broadway plays produced and directed incl. *In Time to Come, Outward Bound, My Dear Children, Margin for Error*; Assoc. Prof. Yale Univ. 39-41; producer and dir. for 20th Century Fox 41-51, films incl. *Margin for Error* and *Laura*; producer-dir. of *The Moon is Blue* on Broadway 50; ind. film producer-director 51-, films incl. *The Moon is Blue* 51, *Carmen Jones* 54, *The Man with the Golden Arm* 55, *St. Joan* 56, *Bonjour Tristesse* 57, *Porgy and Bess* 58, *Anatomy of a Murder* 59, *Exodus* 60, *Advise and Consent* 62, *The Cardinal* 63, *In Harm's Way* 64; produced and directed *Critic's Choice* on Broadway 60, *Bunny Lake is Missing* 65, *Hurry Sundown* 66, *Too Far to Walk* 68.
711 Fifth Avenue, New York 22, N.Y., U.S.A.
Telephone: PL5-8700.

Prempeh II, Otumfuo Sir Osei Agyeman, K.B.E.; King of Ashanti; Ghanaian Ruler; b. 92.
Nephew and successor of late King Prempeh; recognised by British Govt. as King of Ashanti Jan. 35; direct descendant of Ossei Tutu, first occupier of the Golden Stool.
Asantehene's Office, Manhyia, Kumasi, Ashanti, Ghana.

Prentice, Reginald Ernest, M.P., J.P.; British politician; b. 16 July 1923; ed. Whitgift School and London School of Econs.
Temporary civil servant 40-42; Royal Artillery 42-46; student at London School of Econs. 46-49; mem. staff Transport and Gen. Workers Union, Asst. to Legal Sec., in charge of Union's Advice and Service Bureau 50-57; M.P. for East Ham (North) 57-; Minister of State, Dept. of Educ. and Science Oct. 64-66; Minister of Public Building and Works 66-67, of Overseas Devt. 67-; Labour.
House of Commons, London, S.W.1; and 5 Hollingsworth Road, Croydon, Surrey, England.
Telephone: 01-657-0988.

Prentzel, Felix Alexander, DR. IUR., DIPL.-ING.; German business executive; b. 19 March 1905; ed. Technische Hochschule, Berlin-Charlottenburg, and Univ. of Erlangen.

IG.-Farbenindustrie A.G., Berlin 34-47; Fed. Ministry of Commerce 47-55; mem. Management Board DEGUSSA (Deutsche Gold-und Silber-Scheideanstalt, formerly Roessler) 55-59, Chair. of the Management Board 59-; mem. Advisory Board Farbwerke Hoechst A.G., Frankfurt, Metallgesellschaft A.G., Frankfurt, Norddeutsche Affinerie, Hamburg, Frankfurter Versicherungs-A.G., Frankfurt, Didier-Werke A.G., Wiesbaden, NSU Motorenwerke A.G., Neckarsulm, Schilde A.G., Bad Hersfeld.

DEGUSSA, Weissfrauenstrasse 9, (Postfach 3993), 6 Frankfurt/Main, German Federal Republic.

Preobrazhensky, Boris Sergeyevich; Soviet otolaryngologist; b. 1892; ed. Moscow Univ.

Army Surgeon 14-18; Head of Hospital Dept., Intern 18-32; Lecturer Inst. of Defectology 22-24; Asst. Lecturer Second Moscow Univ. 25-38; Head of Chair, Moscow Evening Medical Inst. 32-36; Dir. Semashko Clinic 35-41; Head of Chair, Second Moscow Medical Inst. 41; Corresp. mem. U.S.S.R. Acad. of Medical Sciences 45-50, mem. 50-; Hon. mem. Púrkinyě Medical Soc., Czechoslovakia, mem. Organizing Cttee. of Int. Congresses of Otolaryngologists 61-; Chair. R.S.F.S.R. and Moscow Socs. of Otolaryngologists; Order of Lenin (five times), Bulgarian Order for Civic Services, Hero of Socialist Labour, Merited Scientist of R.S.F.S.R.

Over 150 works on various problems of otolaryngology.

Second Medical Institute, 1 Malaya Pirogovskaya Street, Moscow, U.S.S.R.

Press, Frank American geophysicist; b. 4 Dec. 1924; ed. Coll. of City of New York and Columbia Univ.

Research Associate, Columbia Univ. 46-49, Instructor, Geology 49-51, Asst. Prof. of Geology 51-52, Assoc. Prof. 52-55; Prof. Geophysics, Calif. Inst. of Technology 55-65, Dir. Seismological Laboratory 57-65; Prof. of Geophysics and Chair. of Dept. of Geology and Geophysics, Mass. Inst. of Technology 65-; Pres. Science Advisory Cttee. 61-64; Consultant to U.S. Navy 57-.

Massachusetts Institute of Technology, Department of Geology and Geophysics, Cambridge, Mass., U.S.A. Telephone: 617-864-6900.

Preti, Luigi; Italian politician; b. 23 Oct. 1914. Former lawyer and Prof. of Philosophy and Pedagogy; mem. Constituent Assembly 46-; Under-Sec. to State to Treasury (War Pensions Dept.) 54; Minister for Finance 58-59, 66-68; Minister of Foreign Trade 62-63; Minister without Portfolio Dec. 63-66; Social Democrat.

Chamber of Deputies, Rome, Italy.

Prêtre, Georges; French conductor; b. 14 Aug. 1924; ed. Lycée and Conservatoire de Douai, Conservatoire national supérieure de musique de Paris and Ecole des chefs d'orchestre.

Director of Music, Opera Houses of Marseille, Lille and Toulouse 46-55, Dir. of music Opéra-comique, Paris, 55-59, at l'Opéra 59-; conductor of the symphonic asscns. of Paris and of principal festivals throughout the world; also conducted at La Scala, Milan and major American orchestras; Conductor Metropolitan Opera House, New York 64-65, La Scala, Milan 65-66, Salzburg 66.

19 rue de Montbuisson, Louveciennes, S.-et-O., France.

Prica, Srdja, Yugoslav diplomatist; b. 20 Sept. 1905; ed. Zagreb Univ.

Journalist in Yugoslavia 30-35, in U.S.A. 38-45; Editor *Rad*, trade-union paper in Belgrade 46; Dir. in Ministry of Foreign Affairs 46-49, Dep. Minister 49-51; Ambassador to France 51-55; Under-Sec. of State for Foreign Affairs 55-60; Ambassador to Great Britain 60-65; now Amb. to Italy; Del. to UN Gen. Assembly

48, 50, 51, 57, 59; mem. Central Cttee. Communist League of Yugoslavia.

Yugoslav Embassy, Via dei Monti Parioli 20, Rome, Italy.

Price, Byron, A.B., A.M., LL.D.; American journalist and public servant; b. 25 March 1891; ed. Wabash Coll. Reporter and editor United Press Asscn. Chicago and Omaha 12; with Associated Press 12-41, News Editor Washington Bureau 22-27, Chief 27-37, Exec. News Editor 37-41; Dir. of Censorship U.S. 41-45; personal rep. Pres. Truman on special mission to Germany 45; Vice-Pres. Motion Picture Asscn. of America; Chair. Asscn. of Motion Picture Producers 46-47; awarded Pres. Medal for Merit 46; Hon. K.B.E. 48; Asst. Sec.-Gen. for Admin. and Financial Services, United Nations 47-54; Dir. Gen. Press Congress of the World 59.

Chesterton, Maryland, U.S.A.

Telephone: 778-3588.

Price, Don Krasher, A.B., B.A., B.LITT., LL.D., L.H.D.; American Professor of Government; b. 23 Jan. 1910; ed. Vanderbilt and Oxford Univs.

Reporter *Nashville Evening Tennessean* 30-32; mem. staff Home Owners' Loan Corpn. 35-37, Social Science Research Council 37-39, Public Admin. Clearing House 39-53, U.S. Bureau of the Budget 45-46, Hoover Comm. on Org. of Exec. Branch of Govt. 47-48; Deputy Chair. Research and Devt. Board, U.S. Dept. of Defense 52-53; Assoc. Dir. The Ford Foundation 53-54, Vice-Pres. 54-58; Dean, John Fitzgerald Kennedy School of Govt. (fmrly. Graduate School of Public Admin.), Harvard Univ. and Prof. of Govt., Harvard Univ. 58-; mem. President's Advisory Cttee. on Govt. Org. 59-61; Consultant to Exec. Office of the Pres. 61-; Trustee, The RAND Corpn., Vanderbilt Univ., Twentieth Century Fund; mem. Board of Dirs. Social Science Research Council, American Asscn. for the Advancement of Science (Pres. 67, Chair. of Board 68); Hon. A.M.; Faculty Prize of Harvard Univ. Press for *The Scientific Estate* 65.

Publs. *City Manager Government in the United States* (with Harold and Kaahryn Stone) 40, *Organization and Control* (with W. Y. Elliott and others) 52, *Government and Science* 54, *The Political Economy of American Foreign Policy* 55, *The Secretary of State* (Editor) 60, *The Scientific Estate* 65.

Littauer Center 121, Harvard University, Cambridge, Mass. 02138, U.S.A.

Price, George Cadle; British Honduran politician; b. 19; ed. St. John's Coll., Belize and St. Augustin Seminary, Mississippi.

City Councillor 47-; founder-mem. People's United Party (P.U.P.) 50; Sec. P.U.P. 50-56; Pres. Gen. Workers Union 47-52; mem. Legislative Council 54-; mem. Exec. Council 54-57; fmr. mem. for Nat. Resources; First Minister 61-63, leader of del. to London for self-Govt. constitutional talks, Premier 64-, Minister of Finance and Development 65-; Chair. Reconstruction and Development Corpn.

Office of the Premier, Belize City, British Honduras.

Price, Leontyne; American soprano singer; b. 10 Feb. 1927; ed. Central State Coll., Wilberforce, Ohio and Juilliard School of Music.

Appeared as Bess (*Porgy and Bess*), Vienna, Berlin, Paris, London, New York 52-54; recitalist, soloist 54-; soloist Hollywood Bowl 55-59; opera singer NBC-TV 55-58, San Francisco Opera Co. 57-59, 60-61, Vienna Staatsoper 58, 59-60, 61; recording artist RCA-Victor 58-; appeared Covent Garden 58-59, Chicago 59, 60, Milan 60-61, Metropolitan Opera, New York 61-62, 66, Paris Opéra as Aida 68.

1133 Broadway (Suite 603), New York City, N.Y. 10010, U.S.A.

Price, Willard DeMille, B.A., M.A., LITT.D.; American writer; b. 28 July 1887; ed. Western Reserve and Columbia Univs.

Editor various magazines; directed N. African expdn. to make films of Arab life 19-20; toured Indian, Burmese, Egyptian, Japanese and Philippine Univs. 30; ethnographic studies Battaks (Sumatra) 30, Bagobos (Philippines) 35; expeditions for Nat. Geographic Soc., Micronesia, Egypt, Japan, etc. 36-66; foreign corresp. for American and British publs., China, Manchuria, Mongolia, Japan, Latin America and Africa 33-68.

Publs. *Ancient Peoples at New Tasks, The Negro Around the World, Study of American influence in the Orient, Pacific Adventure, Riptide in the South Seas, Japan Reaches Out, Children of the Rising Sun, Where are you going, Japan?, Barbarian, Japan Rides the Tiger, Japan's Islands of Mystery, The Son of Heaven, Key to Japan, Roving South, Rio Grande to Patagonia, Tropic Adventure, Amazon Adventure, I Cannot Rest from Travel, South Sea Adventure, The Amazing Amazon, Journey by Junk, Underwater Adventure, Adventures in Paradise, Volcano Adventure, Roaming Britain, Whale Adventure, Incredible Africa, The Amazing Mississippi, African Adventure, Elephant Adventure, Rivers I Have Known, America's Paradise Lost, Safari Adventure, Lion Adventure, Gorilla Adventure.*

625 Verbena Lane, Cathedral City, Calif., U.S.A.

Price Thomas, Sir Clement, K.C.V.O., F.R.C.S., F.R.C.P.; British surgeon; b. 22 Nov. 1893; ed. Caterham School, Univ. Coll. Cardiff, and Westminster Hospital London.

Asst. Surgeon, Westminster Hospital, London 27, and Brompton Hospital London 33; Surgeon Westminster Hospital 41-59, Brompton Hospital 46-59; Consulting Surgeon, King Edward VII Sanatorium, Midhurst; Civilian Consultant in Thoracic Surgery to the R.A.F.; fmr. consultant to the Army; fmr. Adviser in Thoracic Surgery to Ministry of Health; Hon. Consulting Surgeon to Westminster and Brompton Hospitals 59; Vice-Pres. and fmr. mem. Court of Examiners, Royal Coll. of Surgeons until 64; Pres. Welsh Nat. School of Medicine; fmr. Pres. Royal Soc. of Medicine; Pres. World Medical Asscn. 65-66, British Medical Asscn. 65-66; mem. numerous foreign medical socs.; Hon. Fellow, American Coll. of Surgeons 54, American Asscn. for Thoracic Surgery, Int. Soc. of Surgeons; Hon. F.R.C.S.I.; Hon. F.R.C.S. (Edinburgh) 59; Hon. M.D. (Paris and Lisbon); Hon. LL.D. (Wales and Queen's Univ., Belfast).

28 Blenheim Road, London, N.W.8, England.

Priestley, John Boynton (husband of Jacquetta Hawkes, *q.v.*), M.A., LL.D., D.LITT.; British writer; b. 13 Sept. 1894; ed. Bradford and Trinity Hall Cambridge.

Pres. London P.E.N. Club 36-37; Chair. 1941 Cttee. (on War Aims); contrib. to many periodicals, "Postscripts"; B.B.C.; Chair. UNESCO Int. Theatre Conf. Paris 47, and Prague 48; Chair. British Theatre Conf. 48; Pres. Int. Theatre Inst. 49; mem. Nat. Theatre Board 65-67.

Publs. Criticism: *English Comic Characters, The English Novel, Meredith, Peacock, The Art of the Dramatist* 57, *Literature and Western Man* 60; Novels: *Adam in Moonshine, Benighted, The Good Companions, Angel Pavement, Faraway, Wonder Hero, They Walk in the City, The Doomsday Men, Let the People Sing, Blackout in Gretley, Daylight on Saturday, Three Men in New Suits, Bright Day, Festival at Farbridge, The Magicians, Low Notes on a High Level, Saturn over the Water, The Thirty-First of June, The Shapes of Sleep, Sir Michael and Sir George* 64, *Lost Empires* 65, *Salt is Leaving* 66, *It's an Old Country* 67, *The Image Men* (Vol. I: *Out of Town*; Vol. II: *London End*) 68; Essays: *English Journey, Midnight on the Desert, Rain upon Godshill, Thoughts in the Wilderness, Delight, Charles Dickens; A Pictorial Biography, Man and Time* 64; Plays: *Dan-*

gerous Corner, Eden End, Cornelius, Laburnum Grove, Bees on the Boat Deck, Time and the Conways, I Have Been Here Before, Music at Night, When We are Married, Johnson Over Jordan, Goodnight Children, They Came to a City, How are They at Home?, Desert Highway, An Inspector Calls, Ever Since Paradise, The Linden Tree, Home is To-morrow, Summer Day's Dream, Dragon's Mouth and *The White Countess* (both with Jacquetta Hawkes), *Mr. Kettle and Mrs. Moon, Take the Fool Away, The Glass Cage;* assisted in dramatisation of Iris Murdoch's *A Severed Head* 63; *The Pavilion of Masks* (play) 63; libretto for *The Olympians* (opera); Television plays: *Now Let Him Go, The Stone Faces, Doomsday for Dyson;* Radio talks: *Postscripts 1940;* Reminiscences: *Margin Released, Trumpets over the Sea* 68.

B3 & 4 Albany, Piccadilly, London, W.1; Home: Kissing Tree House, Alveston, Stratford-on-Avon, Warwickshire, England.

Priestley, Sir Raymond Edward, M.C., M.A., D.LITT., D.SC., LL.D.; British educationist; b. 20 July 1886; ed. Tewkesbury Grammar School and Bristol, Sydney and Cambridge Univs.

Geologist Shackleton Antarctic Expedition 07-09; Scientist Northern Party Scott Antarctic Expedition 10-13; war service 14-19; Fellow Clare Coll. Cambridge 23-34; Sec. Board of Research Studies Cambridge Univ. 23-34 and of Gen. Board 26-34; Sec.-Gen. of Faculties Cambridge Univ. 34; Vice-Chancellor Melbourne Univ. 35-38; Vice-Chancellor and Principal Birmingham Univ. 38-52; Chair. Royal Comm. on Civil Service 53-55; Dir. Falkland Islands Rear Base 55-59; Pres. British Asscn. for the Advancement of Science 56; Hon. Fellow, Clare Coll., Cambridge; Founder's Medal, Royal Geographical Soc. 59; Pres. Royal Geog. Soc. 61-63.

Publs. *Antarctic Adventure, Scott's Northern Party, Breaking the Hindenburg Line, History of Signal Service in France,* etc.

Barn Hill, Bredon's Norton, Tewkesbury, Glos., England. Telephone: Bredon 209.

Prieto, Justo Pastor, Dr. h.c. (Rio de Janeiro); Paraguayan lawyer, educationist and politician; b. 97; ed. Asunción Univ.

Secretary and legal adviser Police Dept. 22; Pres. Municipal Council 23; Nat. Dep. and Pres. Exec. Board Liberal Party 24; Prof. of Law Military School, Superior School of War and Escuela Normal de Profesores 24; Prof. and Dean Faculty of Law and Social Sciences Asunción 28, Rector of Univ. 29; Minister of Justice and Educ. 32; Dir. *El Liberal;* Prof. of Sociology Faculty of Econ. Science Buenos Aires; Pres. of Senate 39; Minister of Foreign Affairs 39; Pres. of Comm. on Continental Defence at Panama Conf. 39; Prof. of Industrial Sociology, Argentine Business Coll. 66-; Extra. Prof. Sociology Univ. Mayor de San Andrés, Bolivia; Pres. Cttee. for Self-Determination of the People; mem. Academia Ciencias Políticas, Buenos Aires, Académie Internationale des Sciences Politiques, Geneva, Institut International de Sociologie, Societé des Americanistes de Paris, del Instituto Latino Americano de Sociología.

Publs. *Efectos jurídicos de las obligaciones naturales* 19, *La sociología: su historia y estado actual* 27, *El tratado de Rio de Janeiro* 29, *La universidad y la solución de los problemas económicos, políticos y sociales* 31, *Misión social del profesor de Enseñanza secundaria* 34, *Síntesis sociológica* 37, *18 meses de regresión política* 37, *Ideas para la concepción de la juventud universitaria como poder espiritual* 38, *Dos Vidas Ejemplares* 39, *Valor Social de la Salud* 39, *Sentido Social de la Cultura Universitaria* 42, *El Paraguay en la empresa emancipadora* 42, *Los problemas generales de la Sociología* 43, *La Vida indómita de Augusto Comte* 44, *Estudiantes hoy, dirigentes mañana* 45, *El Problema del Paraguay Mediterráneo* 46, *Eusebio Ayala, Presidente de la*

Victoria 50, *Paraguay, la Provincia Gigante de las Indias* 51, *Manual del Ciudadano Liberal Paraguayo* 53, *Los Partidos politicos en la Constitución Social* 60, *Sociología Industrial* 67, *Sociólogos argentinos en la tradicion continental* 67.
Lima 131, Buenos Aires, Argentina.

Prigogine, Ilya, PH.D.; Belgian university Professor; b. 25 Jan. 1917; ed. Univ. Libre de Bruxelles.
Professor at Univ. of Brussels 47-; Dir. Instituts Internationaux de Physique et de Chimie 62-; Dir. Center for Statistical Mechanics and Thermodynamics, Univ. of Texas; mem. Académie Royale de Belgique 53; Foreign Hon. mem. American Acad. of Sciences and Arts 60; Fellow Acad. of Sciences of New York 62; mem. Romanian Acad. of Science 65; mem. Royal Soc. of Sciences Sweden 67; Foreign Assoc. Nat. Acad. of Sciences U.S. 67; mem. Corres. de la Soc. Royale des Sciences, Liège 67; Prix Francqui 55, Prix Solvay 65.
Publs. *Traité de Thermodynamique, conformément aux méthodes de Gibbs et de De Donder* (with R. Defay) 44, 50, *Etude Thermodynamique des Phénomènes Irréversibles* 47, *Introduction to Thermodynamics of Irreversible Processes* 62, *The Molecular Theory of Solutions* (with A. Bellemans and V. Mathot) 57, *Statistical Mechanics of Irreversible Processes* 62.
6 avenue de la Forêt, Brussels 5, Belgium.
Telephone: 731646.

Prikhodov, Yuri Kondratyevich; Soviet diplomatist and foreign trade official; b. 1906; ed. Lenin Military and Political Acad.
Factory-worker 19-28; trade union organiser 25-28; Soviet Navy 28-35; C.P.S.U. posts 38-39; Counsellor, Soviet Mission, Mongolia 40-46, Envoy to Mongolian People's Repub. 48-50; Ministry of Foreign Affairs 46-48, 51-54, 60-61; Ambassador to Bulgaria 54-60; Senior Vice-Pres. of Chair. of Presidium of U.S.S.R. Chamber of Commerce 60-; Order of Lenin, Order of Red Banner of Labour, and other decorations.
Chamber of Commerce, 6 Kuibyshev Street, Moscow, U.S.S.R.

Prince, William Henry Wood; American businessman; b. 7 Feb. 1914; ed. Groton School for Boys and Princeton Univ.
With First Nat. Bank of Chicago 36-42, 45-47; Sec.-Treas. Sherman Hotel, College Inn Food Products Co. Chicago 39-42; with Union Stock Yard & Transit Co. 48-57, Pres. 49-57; Dir. Armour & Co. 50-, Vice-Chair. 57, Pres. 57-61, 67-, Chair. 61-68; Dir. of other companies.
Armour & Company, 401 N. Wabash Avenue, Chicago, Ill. 60611, U.S.A.

Pringle, George H.; American (b. Canadian) business executive; b. 1 July 1903; ed. Pictou Acad., Dalhousie Univ., Halifax, Nova Scotia, and McGill Univ., Montreal.
Canada Paper Co. 26-27; Mead Pulp and Paper Co., Chillicothe, Ohio 27-, Div. Engineer, Chillicothe Div. 44-48; Asst. Chief Engineer, The Mead Corpn. 48-51, Chief Engineer 51-52, Vice-Pres. (White Paper Operations) 52-57, Exec. Vice-Pres. (Manufacturing) 57-58, Exec. Vice-Pres. 58-63, Pres. 63-; official of civic orgs.
The Mead Corporation, Talbott Tower, Dayton, Ohio 45402, U.S.A.

Pringle, John Martin Douglas, M.A.; British journalist; b. 28 June 1912; ed. Shrewsbury School, and Lincoln Coll., Oxford.
Member staff of *Manchester Guardian* 34-39; served in Army 40-44; Asst. Editor *Manchester Guardian* 44; joined staff *The Times* 48; Editor *Sydney Morning Herald* 52-57, 65-; Deputy Editor *The Observer* 58-63; Public Affairs Div., Television Station ATN7, Sydney, Australia 63-64; Managing Editor *Canberra Times* 64-65.

Publs. *China Struggles for Unity* 38, *Australian Accent* 58, *Australian Painting Today* 63.
27 Bayview Street, McMahon's Point, North Sydney, N.S.W., Australia.
Telephone: 92-7560.

Pritchard, Sir Derek Wilbraham, Kt.; British business executive; b. 8 June 1910; ed. Clifton Coll., Bristol.
Took over family business of E. Halliday and Son Ltd., Manchester; Army Service, Second World War 39-46; Dir. E. K. Cole Ltd. 46-; joined Ind. Coope Ltd. as Man. Dir. Grants of St. James's Ltd. 49-, Dir. Ind. Coope Ltd. 51-61, Ind. Coope Tetley Ansell Ltd. 61-63, Vice-Chair. Allied Breweries Ltd. 63-; Chair. Skol Int. Ltd. 63-, E. Halliday and Son Ltd., Grants of St. James's Ltd.; Dir. Pye of Cambridge Ltd., Guardian Assurance Co. Ltd., Allied Brewing Investments Ltd., and other companies; Deputy Chair. British Nat. Export Council 65-66, Chair. 66-; Deputy Chair. Allied Breweries 67-.
Office: 156 St. John Street, London, E.C.1; Home: West Haddon Hall, nr. Rugby, Warwicks., England.

Pritchard, John Michael, C.B.E.; British conductor; b. 5 Feb. 1921; ed. Sir George Monoux School, London.
Conductor, Derby String Orchestra 43-51, Jacques Orchestra 50-52, Glyndebourne Festivals 52-; Conductor and Musical Dir. Royal Liverpool Philharmonic Orchestra 57-61; Principal Conductor and Artistic Dir. London Philharmonic Orchestra 62-66; Co-Dir. Opéra de Marseille 66-; Principal Conductor and Music Counsellor Glyndebourne Opera 63-; visiting conductor with principal orchestras throughout the world.
Carters Corner Place, Nr. Hailsham, Sussex, England.
Telephone: Herstmonceux 2360.

Pritchard, Sir Neil, K.C.M.G.; British diplomatist; b. 14 Jan. 1911; ed. Liverpool Coll. and Worcester Coll., Oxford.
Dominions Office 33, Private Sec. to Perm. Under-Sec. 36-38; Asst. Sec. Rhodesia and Nyasaland Royal Comm. 38; Sec. Office of U.K. High Commr. Pretoria 41-45; Principal Sec. Office of U.K. Rep., Dublin 48-49; Asst. Under-Sec. of State, Commonwealth Relations Office (C.R.O.) 51-54; Dep. U.K. High Commr., Canada 54-57, Australia 57-60; Act. Dep. Under-Sec. of State, C.R.O. 61; High Commr. of U.K. in Tanganyika 61-63; Dep. Under-Sec. of State, C.R.O. (now Commonwealth Office) 63-67; Amb. to Thailand 67-.
British Embassy, Bangkok, Thailand; Home: 13 Denbigh Gardens, Richmond, Surrey, England.

Pritchett, Victor Sawdon, C.B.E.; British author and critic; b. 16 Dec. 1900; ed. Alleyn's School.
Director of *New Statesman*; has lectured in four univs. in U.S.A. including Brandeis Univ., Cambridge, Mass. 68.
Publs. *Marching Spain, Clare Drummer, The Spanish Virgin, Shirley Sanz, Nothing Like Leather, Dead Man Leading, You Make Your Own Life, In My Good Books, It May Never Happen, Why Do I Write?* (with Elizabeth Bowen and Graham Greene), *The Living Novel, Mr. Beluncle, Books in General, The Spanish Temper, Collected Short Stories, When My Girl Comes Home, London Perceived, The Key to My Heart, Foreign Faces, New York Proclaimed, The Living Novel and Later Appreciations, Dublin, A Cab at the Door* (autobiog.) 68.
12 Regent's Park Terrace, London, N.W.1, England.

Pritt, Denis Nowell, Q.C.; British lawyer and politician; b. 22 Sept. 1887; ed. Winchester, London Univ., Germany, Switzerland, Spain.
Barrister 09; K.C. 27; Chair. Int. Cttee. for Investigation of the Reichstag Fire Sept. 33; Pres. Soc. for Cultural Relations with the U.S.S.R. 33-; Labour M.P. for N. Hammersmith 35-40, Labour (Independent) 40-50; mem. Exec. Labour Party 37-Mar. 40, expelled; Pres. Student Labour Fed. 39; Prof. of Law, Univ. of Ghana 65-66; Hon. Pres. Int. Asscn. of Democratic

Lawyers; mem. World Peace Council Bureau, Pres. British Peace Cttee. 51-; Pres. British-Rumanian Friendship Soc. 50-; Joint-Pres. Soc. for Friendship with Bulgaria; Lenin Int. Peace Prize 54; Star of Int. Friendship 66; Hon. Dr.Iur. (Charles Univ., Prague, State Univ., Sofia, Humboldt Univ., Berlin, Lomonosov Univ., Moscow).
Publs. *Twelve Studies in Soviet Russia* (in collaboration), *Light on Moscow, Must the War Spread?, The Zinoviev Trial, Federal Illusion, Choose Your Future, U.S.S.R. Our Ally, The Fall of the French Republic, India Our Ally?, Revolt in Europe, A New World Grows, The Mosley Case, War Criminals, The Star-Spangled Shadow, The State Department and the Cold War, The Truth about the U.S.S.R., Light on Korea, New Light on Korea, Russia is for Peace, Spies and Informers in the Witness Box, The Law Versus the Trade Unions* (jointly), *The Labour Government 1945-51, From Right to Left* (autobiog.), *Brasshats and Bureaucrats* (autobiog.), *The Defence Accuses* (autobiog.).
Barn End, Pamber Heath, Basingstoke, England.
Telephone: Silchester 319.

Pritytsky, Sergei Osipovich; Soviet politician; b. 18 Feb. 1913; ed. Higher Party School, Moscow.
Farm labourer 25-32; mem. C.P.S.U. 32-; Komsomol, W. Byelorussia 32-39; Soviet work 39-41; partisan movement, Byelorussia 41-45; First Sec. Grodno Regional Cttee. of Communist Party of Byelorussia 48-52; Central Cttee. C.P. of Byelorussia 52-54; First Sec. Molodechno Regional Cttee. 54-60, Minsk Regional Cttee., Byelorussian C.P. 60-62; Sec. Central Cttee. C.P. of Byelorussia 62-67; Deputy to U.S.S.R. and Byelorussian S.S.R. Supreme Soviets; Chair. Presidium of Supreme Soviet of Byelorussian S.S.R.; mem. Central Cttee. of C.P.S.U. 61-.
Presidium of Supreme Soviet of the Byelorussian S.S.R., Minsk, Byelorussian S.S.R., U.S.S.R.

Procházka, Vladimir, LL.D., DR.SC.; Czechoslovak politician, diplomatist and professor; b. 12 Sept. 1895.
Member Parl. 46-54; Rapporteur-Gen. and mem. Parl. Cttee. drafting the Constitution of May 9th, 48; Ambassador to U.S. 51-52; Prof. of Soviet Economy and Law 45, of Czechoslovak Law and Government, Charles Univ., Prague 49; Academician 52-, mem. Presidium Czechoslovak Acad. of Sciences 55-65, Chair. Section of Economics, Law and Philosophy, 55-61; Editor-in-Chief *Czechoslovak Encyclopædia* 58-; mem. Comm. of Nat. Front drafting new Constitution of July 11th, 60; Order of the Republic 55, 65, Order of 25 Feb. 1948, 49.
Antonínská 6, Prague 7, Czechoslovakia.
Telephone: 37-37-72.

Prochnow, Herbert Victor, B.A., M.A., PH.D.; American banker and writer; b. 19 May 1897; ed. Wisconsin State Univ., Univ. of Wisconsin and Northwestern Univ.
Principal, Kendall (Wisconsin) High School 17; Union Trust Co., Chicago 23-29; The First Nat. Bank of Chicago 29-, Dir. 60-, Pres. 62-; Dir. First Chicago Int. Finance Corpn., First Chicago Int. Banking Corpn., First Chicago Corpn.; Sec. Fed. Advisory Council of Fed. Reserve System 45-; Consultant to Sec. of State 55, 57; Dep. Under-Sec. of State for Economic Affairs 55-56; Alt. Gov. for U.S. of Int. Bank and Int. Monetary Fund 55-56; Pres. Chicago Asscn. of Commerce and Industry 64, 65; several hon. degrees.
Publs. *The Public Speaker's Treasure Chest* 42, 64, *Great Stories from Great Lives* 44, *Meditations on the Ten Commandments* 46, *The Toastmaster's Handbook* 49, *Term Loans and Theories of Bank Liquidity* 49, *The Successful Speaker's Handbook* 51, *1001 Ways to Improve your Conversation and Speeches* 52, *Meditations on the Beatitudes* 52, *The Speaker's Treasury of Stories for all Occasions* 53, *Speaker's Handbook of Epigrams and Witticisms* 55, *Speaker's Treasury for Sunday School Teachers* 55, *The Toastmasters and Speaker's Handbook* 55, *A Treasury of Stories, Illustrations, Epigrams and Quotations for Ministers and Teachers* 57, *The New Guide for Toastmasters and Speakers* 56, *A Family Treasury of Inspiration and Faith* 58, *The New Speaker's Treasury of Wit and Wisdom* 58, *The Complete Toastmaster* 60, *Effective Public Speaking* 60, *A Dictionary of Wit, Wisdom and Satire* 62, *1000 Tips and Quips for Speakers and Toastmasters* 62, *Practical Bank Credit* 63, *World Economic Problems and Policies* 65.
First National Bank of Chicago, 38 S. Dearborn Street, Chicago 90, Illinois; Home: 2950 Harrison Street, Evanston, Ill. 60201, U.S.A.

Prohaska, Carl Wilhelm, D.SC.; Danish naval architect; b. 15 Feb. 1903; ed. Technical Univ. of Denmark.
Naval Architect at shipyards in Denmark and France 28-36; Prof. Technical Univ. of Denmark 37-; Dir. Hydro-Aerodynamics Laboratory, Lyngby 57-; Dir. Danish Ship Research Inst. (incorporating Danish Shipbuilders Computing Office) 61-; consulting Naval Architect; Chair. FAO Fishing Boat Conf. 63, and Int. Load-Line Conf. Technical Cttee. London 66; Vice-Pres. Danish Soc. of Nat. Sciences; Chair. of Cttee. Int. Towing Tank Conf., and Inter-Govt. Maritime Consultative Org.; mem. Danish Eng. Inst. and Acad. of Technical Sciences, Swedish Eng. Acad. and numerous other Int. Eng. Socs.; Commdr. Order of Dannebrog, and Ordre Nat. du Mérite (France); William Froude Gold Medal of Royal Inst. Naval Architects.
Publs. include *Two-Nodal Ship Vibrations* 41, *Residuary Stability* 47, *Comparative Calculus in Naval Architecture* 59, *Trial Trip Analysis* 62.
Juul Steens Alle 9, Hellerup, Denmark.

Prokhorov, Alexandr Mikhailovich; Soviet physicist; b. 1916; ed. Leningrad State Univ.
Physicist, P.N. Lebedev Inst. of Physics, U.S.S.R. Acad. of Sciences 39-; Corresp. mem. U.S.S.R. Acad. of Sciences (Dept. of Pure and Applied Physics) 60-66; mem. 66-; mem. C.P.S.U. 50-; Lenin Prize 59; Nobel Prize for Physics for work in field of quantum electronics 64; Chair. Soviet Nat. Cttee. U.R.S.I.
P.N. Lebedev Institute of Physics, U.S.S.R. Academy of Sciences, 53 Lenin Prospekt, Moscow, U.S.S.R.

Prokhorov, Vasili Ilich; Soviet trade union official; b. 1906; ed. Moscow Higher Technical School.
Designing Engineer 30-40; Soviet Army Service 40-41; Sec. Zhdanov District Cttee. of C.P.S.U. 41-46; Deputy U.S.S.R. Supreme Soviet; Sec. All-Union Central Council of Trade Unions 55-; Order of the Patriotic War 1st class, Order of Red Banner of Labour, etc.
All-Union Central Council of Trade Unions, Leninsky prospekt 42, Moscow, U.S.S.R.

Prokofiev, Alexander Andreevich; Soviet poet; b. 2 Dec. 1900.
Poems deal with N. Russian folklore; translator of Ukrainian, Byelorussian and Estonian poetry; mem. C.P.S.U. 19-; State Prize 46, Lenin Prize 61, Order of Lenin (thrice).
Publs. Collected poems 27-47, 50, 54; *Russia* 46, *Appletree above the Sea* 58, *Invitation for Travel* 60, *Road Poetry* 63, *My Everyday Bread* 64, *The Golden Gates* 64, *The Wonderful Alarm* 65, *The Arc* 66, *Things I Like* 67.
Union of Soviet Writers, 52 Vorovsky Street, Moscow, U.S.S.R.

Prokofiev, Mikhail Alexeevich; Soviet chemist and government official; b. 18 Nov. 1910; ed. Moscow State Univ.
Member C.P.S.U. 41-; First Deputy Minister of Higher and Specialized Secondary Educ. of U.S.S.R. 59-66; Minister of Educ. of R.S.F.S.R. 66-; Deputy to R.S.F.S.R. Supreme Soviet; mem. Acad. of Pedagogical Sciences.
Ministry of Education of U.S.S.R., Moscow, U.S.S.R.

Prokosch, Frederic, PH.D.; American writer; b. 17 May 1908; ed. Yale Univ. and King's Coll. Cambridge. Publs. Novels: *The Asiatics* 35, *The Seven Who Fled* 37, *Night of the Poor* 39, *The Skies of Europe* 41, *The Conspirators* 43, *Age of Thunder* 45, *The Idols of the Cave* 46, *Storm and Echo* 48, *Nine Days to Mukalla* 53, *A Tale for Midnight* 55, *A Ballad of Love* 60, *The Seven Sisters* 63, *The Dark Dancer* 65, *The Wreck of the Cassandra* 66, *The Missolonghi Manuscript* 67; poems: *The Assassins* 36, *The Carnival* 38, *Death at Sea* 40, *Chosen Poems* 44, *Some Poems of Hoelderlin* (Trans.) 44. c/o Secker and Warburg, 14 Carlisle Street, Soho Square, London, W.1, England; 44 avenue de New York, Paris 16e, France.

Proksch, Anton; Austrian composer, trade union official and politician; b. 97; ed. School of Printing. Active service 15-18; employed by Austrian Trade Union Comm. 19-24; Youth Sec. in Federation of Free Trade Unions 24-34 when he was dismissed and was unemployed; arrested for political reasons 35-36; compositor 36-44; mil. service 44-45; mem. Parl. 45-66; Gen. Sec. Austrian Trade Union Congress 45-66; given leave from this post to become Federal Minister of Social Admin. 55-66. Publs. *Handbuch des Österreichischen Gewerkschaftsbundes, Probleme der Österreichischen Sozialpolitik, Vollbeschäftigung Entwicklungsgebiete Dauerarbeitsplätze, Die sozialen Lasten.* Home: Haubenbiglstrasse 8-5, Vienna 19, Austria.

Promyslov, Vladimir Fedorovich; Soviet construction engineer and politician; b. 15 July 1908; ed. Moscow Construction Engineering Institute. Member C.P.S.U. 28-; fmr. Deputy Chair. Council of Ministers, R.S.F.S.R. and Minister of Construction, R.S.F.S.R. 59-63; Chair. Exec. Cttee., Moscow City Soviet of Working People's Deputies 63-; mem. Central Cttee. C.P.S.U. 61-; Deputy U.S.S.R. Supreme Soviet. 13 Gorky Street, Moscow City Soviet, Moscow, U.S.S.R.

Prorokov, Boris Ivanovich; Soviet artist; b. 1911; ed. Higher Artist-Technical Inst. Member of Communist Party 45-; Corresp. mem. U.S.S.R. Acad. of Arts 54-; Honoured Artist of R.S.F.S.R. 55-; People's Artist of R.S.F.S.R. 63; Lenin Prize 61; works include *This Must Not Happen Again* (Second World War). U.S.S.R. Academy of Arts, Kropotkinskaya ulitsa 21, Moscow, U.S.S.R.

Protich, Dragoslav, LL.B., D.SC.; Yugoslav diplomat and UN official; b. 15 July 1902; ed. Belgrade Univ. and Brussels Free Univ. Financial Attaché, Yugoslav Legation, Brussels 23-26; Attaché Ministry of Foreign Affairs, Belgrade 26-28. Sec. to Yugoslav Legation, Vienna 28-29; Second Sec; Yugoslav Legation, London 29-33; First Sec. Ministry of Foreign Affairs, Belgrade 33-35; Dir. of Cabinet of Minister of Foreign Affairs, Belgrade 35-38; Counsellor, Foreign Ministry, Belgrade 38-40; Counsellor Yugoslav Legation, Athens 40-41; Counsellor Yugoslav Legation, Cairo 41-42; Counsellor, Yugoslav Embassy London and Chargé d'Affaires of Yugoslavia to the Netherlands 42-46; Under-Sec. for Political and Security Council Affairs, UN 46-58; Under-Sec. for Trusteeship and Information from Non-Self Governing Territories 58-63; Under-Sec. for Special Political Affairs 63-64; Dir. UN Training Programme for Foreign Service Officers 62-Dec. 67. 345 East 56th Street, New York, N.Y.; Pleasant Valley Road, Wolfeboro, New Hampshire, U.S.A.

Proudman, Joseph, C.B.E., M.A., D.SC., LL.D., F.R.S.; British university professor; b. 30 Dec. 1888; ed. Widnes, Univ. of Liverpool and Trinity Coll., Cambridge. Lecturer in Mathematics Liverpool 13-19; Smith's Prize, Cambridge 15; Fellow, Trinity Coll., Cambridge 15-21; Prof. of Applied Mathematics, Liverpool 19-33; Dir. of Tidal Inst., Liverpool 19-45; Adams Prize, Cambridge 23; Prof. of Oceanography, Univ. of Liverpool 33-54, Pro-Vice-Chancellor 40-46, Emeritus 54-; Gen. Sec. Int. Asscn. of Physical Oceanography 33-48; Agassiz Medal, U.S. Acad. of Sciences; Hughes Medal, Royal Soc.; mem. Norwegian Acad. of Science and Letters; Pres. Int. Asscn. of Physical Oceanography 51-54; Chair. Advisory Cttee. on Research in connection with Coastal Flooding, Ministry of Agriculture, Fisheries and Food 54-66; Corresp. Bureau des Longitudes, Paris. Publ. *Dynamical Oceanography* 53. "Edgemoor", Verwood, Dorset, England. Telephone: Verwood 2285.

Prouty, Winston Lewis; American politician; b. 1 Sept. 1906; ed. Newport public schools and Lafayette Coll. Mayor of Newport 38-41; mem. Vermont House of Reps. 41, 45, 47, Speaker 47; Chair. Vermont State Water Conservation Board 48-50; mem. U.S. House of Reps. 50-58; Senator from Vermont 59-; Pres. Prouty & Miller Lumber Co.; Vice-Pres. Taunton Lumber Co.; Republican. Senate Office Building, Washington 25, D.C., U.S.A.

Prouvost, Jean; French business executive and editor; b. 24 April 1885; ed. Collège de Boulogne-sur-Mer and Beaumont Coll., England. Director, Peignage Amédée Prouvost and Co., Filatures Prouvost Masurel and Co., La Lainière de Roubaix; Dir.-Gen. of *Paris-Midi* and *Paris-Soir* 32-39; Minister of Information 40; now Pres., Dir.-Gen., Chief Editor of *Marie-Claire, La Maison de Marie-Claire* and *Paris-Match*; Admin. S.A. *Figaro*; Dir. *Télé 7 Jours*; Admin. Délégué de Radio Télé Luxembourg; Mayor of Yvoyle-Marron. 216 rue de Rivoli, Paris; *Paris Match*, 51 rue Pierre Charron, Paris 8e; and Domaine Saint-Jean, 41 Yvoyle-Marron, France. Telephone: 225-00-24.

Provenchères, Monsignor Charles de, L. ès L., L. en THÉOLOGIE; French ecclesiastic; b. 3 Sept. 1904; ed. Institut du Sacré-Coeur, Moulins, and Institut Catholique, Paris. Ordained Priest 28; Curate at Cusset 28-31; Spiritual Dir. at Institut du Sacré-Coeur Moulins 31-38; Dir. Petit Séminaire Moulins 38-45; served French Army 39-40; Archbishop of Aix, Arles and Embrun 45-; Légion d'Honneur, Croix de Guerre, Hon. Dr. (Laval). L'Archevêché, 12 rue Marie et Pierre Curie, Aix-en-Provence, France. Telephone: 91-26-04-59.

Proxmire, William, M.A.; American politician; b. 11 Nov. 1915; ed. Yale and Harvard Univs. U.S. Army Intelligence Service 41-46; State Assemblyman (Dem.) for Wisconsin 51-52; U.S. Senator from Wisconsin 57-; Pres. Artcraft Press, Waterloo, Wisconsin 54-57; Democrat. Senate Office Building, Washington 25, D.C., U.S.A.

Průšek, Jaroslav, PH.D., DR. SC.; Czechoslovak university professor; b. 14 Sept. 1906; ed. Oriental studies at Prague, Gothenburg, Halle, Leipzig, and in China and Japan. Studied Chinese linguistics, literature and history; Prof of Chinese and Japanese Literature, Charles Univ., Prague 47-; corresp. mem. Czechoslovak Acad. of Sciences 52-; Academician 55, and Chair. of Linguistics and Literature Section 55-61; Dir. Oriental Inst. of Czechoslovak Acad. of Sciences 53-; Laureate of the State Prize 52 and 54; Hon. Ph.D. Humboldt Univ. Berlin 60; Hon. mem. German Acad. of Sciences; Silver Plaque of Czechoslovak Acad. of Sciences; mem. Saxon Acad. of Sciences 65, Order of Labour 66.

Publs. *History of Chinese Literature* 55, *Studies in Modern Chinese Literature* 64, *The Origins and the Authors of hua-pen* 68.

Gogolova 2, Prague 1; and Oriental Institute, Lázeňská 4, Prague 1, Czechoslovakia.

Pryce, Maurice Henry Lecorney, M.A., PH.D., F.R.S.; British university professor; b. 24 Jan. 1913; ed. Royal Grammar School, Guildford, Trinity Coll., Cambridge, and Princeton Univ., U.S.A.

Fellow Trinity Coll. and Faculty Asst. Lecturer Cambridge 37; Reader in Theoretical Physics Liverpool Univ. 39; Admiralty Signal Establishment 41; Nat. Research Council of Canada (Atomic Energy) 44; University Lecturer and Fellow of Trinity Coll. Cambridge 45; Visiting Prof. Princeton Univ. 50-51; Wykeham Prof. of Physics, Oxford 46-54; Henry Overton Wills Prof. of Physics, Bristol 54-64; Prof. Univ. of Southern California 64-68; Prof. Univ. of British Columbia 68-.

Physics Dept., Univ. of British Columbia, Vancouver 8; 4754 W. 6th Avenue, Vancouver 8, Canada.

Pryce-Jones, Alan Payan, T.D.; British writer and editor; b. 18 Nov. 1908; ed. Eton Coll. and Magdalen Coll., Oxford.

Asst. Editor *The London Mercury* 28-32; Editor *The Times Literary Supplement* 48-59; served in France, Austria, Italy, Second World War 39-45, Lieut.-Col. 45; Trustee Nat. Portrait Gallery 50-61; Dir. The Old Vic Trust 50-61; mem. Council of Royal Coll. of Music 56-61; Program Assoc. (Humanities and Arts) Ford Foundation 61-63; Book Critic *New York Herald-Tribune* 63-67; Theatre Critic *Theatre Arts* 63-.

Publs. *The Spring Journey* 31, *People in the South* 32, *27 Poems* 35, *Private Opinion* 36, *Prose Literature 1945-50*; libretto for Berkeley's opera *Nelson* 54; *The American Imagination* (edited) 60, *Vanity Fair* (libretto) 62.

19 East 55th Street, New York 22, N.Y., U.S.A.

Przybos, Julian; Polish poet and essayist; b. 5 March 1901.

Ambassador to Switzerland 47-51; Dir. Jagiellonian Univ., Cracow 51-55.

Publs. Verse: *Sruby* (Screws), *Oburacz* (With Both Hands), *W glab las* (In the Depths of the Forest), *Rownanie serca* (Equation of the Heart), *Miejsce na Ziemi* (Place on Earth), *Najmniej słów* (The Least of Words), *Narzedzie ze Swiatla* (Tool of Light) 58, *Poezje Zebrane* (Collected Poems) 59, *Proba Calosci* (Essays on Totality) 61, *Wiecej o Manifest* (More than a Manifesto) 62, *Na Znak* 64, *Kwiat Nieznany* (The Unknown Flower) 68; Essays: *Czytajac Mickiewicza* (Reading Mickiewicz), *Linia I Gwar* (Line and Murmur) 2 vols. 59, *Sens Poetycki* (Poetic Sense) 63; Folk Verse Anthology: *Jabloneczka* (The Little Apple Tree).

Piaseczynska 122 m. 57, Warsaw 36, Poland.

Telephone: 41-11-92.

Psurtsev, Nikolai Demyanovich; Soviet politician; b. 1900; ed. Higher Communications School and Military Electro-Technical Acad.

Member C.P.S.U. 19-; served Red Army, Chief of Communications, Soviet-Finnish War 39-40; Col.-Gen. in Second World War; Minister of Communications 48-; Order of Lenin; Four Orders of the Red Banner, Order of Kutuzov, Order of Suvorov; Cand. mem. C.P.S.U. Central Cttee. 61-; Deputy to U.S.S.R. Supreme Soviet. Ministry of Communications, 7 Gorki Street, Moscow, U.S.S.R.

Ptasinski, Jan; Polish politician and diplomatist. First Sec. Gdańsk Cttee. of Polish United Workers' Party until Dec. 67; Amb. to U.S.S.R. Dec. 67-.

Polish Embassy, Ul. A. Mickiewicz 2, Moscow, U.S.S.R.

Pucar, Djuro Stari; Yugoslav metal worker and politician; b. 99.

Member Communist Party of Yugoslavia 22-; Trade Union and Party posts 22-29; political imprisonment 29-39; mem. Central Cttee. Yugoslav Communist Party 40-; organising revolution, Bosnia 41-45; Sec. Central Cttee. of League of Communists of Bosnia and Herzegovina 48-; mem. Exec. Cttee. of Central Cttee. of League of Communists of Yugoslavia 52-; Pres. Republican Assembly, Bosnia and Herzegovina 53-63; Sec. Central Cttee. of League of Communists of Bosnia and Herzegovina; mem. Council of Federation; Dep. of Council of Nationalities, Fed. Assembly; National Hero.

43 Djure Djakovića, Sarajevo, Yugoslavia.

Pucci, Emilio, Marchese di Barsento, M.A., DR.SOC.SC.; Italian couturier; b. 20 Nov. 1914; ed. Reed Coll., Portland (Oregon) and Florence Univ.

Air Force torpedo-bomber pilot 38-52; started his own fashion house 50; Neiman Marcus Fashion Award 54, Burdine Fashion Award 55; *Sports Illustrated* "Sporting Look" Designer's Award 61; Vice-Pres. of Formfit Int. 61; Man. Dir. Antico Setificio Fiorentino; works under the name "Emilio Pucci"; mem. Chamber of Deputies; Liberal.

Palazzo Pucci, 6 Via dei Pucci, Florence, Italy.

Púčik, Jozef; Czechoslovak economist, politician and diplomatist; b. 9 March 1912; ed. Commercial Coll., Prague.

Minister of Chemical Industry 54-65; Minister-Chair. State Planning Office 51-54; Deputy to Nat. Assembly 56-64; mem. Econ. Comm., Central Cttee., C.P. of Czechoslovakia 63-66; Amb. to Hungary 66-; Order of Labour 62 and other awards.

Embassy of the Czechoslovak Socialist Republic, Népstadion utja 22, Budapest XIV, Hungary.

Telephone: 297-800; and 297-808.

Pudney, John Sleigh; British poet, novelist and publisher; b. 19 Jan. 1909; ed. Gresham's School, Holt.

B.B.C. writer and feature programmes producer 33; columnist *News Chronicle* 30; joined R.A.F. 40; *Daily Express* book critic 47; Literary Editor *News Review* 48-50; Editor *Pick of To-day's Short Stories* (annual).

Publs. Poetry: *Collected Poems* 57, *Sixpenny Songs*, *The Trampoline* 59, *Spill Out* 67; prose: *The Green Grass Grew All Round* 42, *Who Only England Know* 43, *Air Battle of Malta* 44, *Atlantic Bridge* 45, *Laboratory of the Air* 48, *King George VI* 52, *The Queen's People* 53, *The Smallest Room* 54, *Six Great Aviators* 55, *The Seven Skies* 59, *Home and Away* 60, *The Camel Fighter* 64, *Bristol Fashion* 60, *A Pride of Unicorns* 60, *The Golden Age of Steam* 67, *De Lesseps' Canal* 68; novels: *Estuary* 48, *Shuffley Wanderers* 49, *The Accomplice* 50, *Hero of a Summer's Day* 57, *Thin Air* 61; collections of short stories: *It Breathed Down My Neck* 46, *The Europeans* 48; children's books: the "*Fred and I*" series 50-65, *The Grandfather Clock* 57, *Crossing the Road* 58, "*The Hartwarp*" series 62-67, *For Johnny* (radio documentary) 65, *The Concorde* (film script) 65, *Le Festin des Morts* (English film script) 67.

May Cottage, Fairwarp, Uckfield, Sussex, England.

Telephone: Nutley 2323.

Puget, Gen. André Jean Baptiste Marie Gabriel; French air force officer; b. 29 Jan. 1911; ed. Ecole Spéciale Militaire de Saint-Cyr.

Free French Forces in U.K. 43-45; Air Attaché, London 54-57; Major-Gen., Air Force 57-60; Gen. of Air Div. 60-61; Chief of Gen. Staff for French Nat. Defence 61-; Pres. Sud Aviation 62-66; Amb. to Sweden 67-; Grand Officier, Légion d'Honneur.

French Embassy, Stockholm, Sweden; and 25 avenue Maréchal-Lyautey, Paris 16e, France.

Pugliese, Dr. Juan Carlos; Argentine politician and lawyer; b. 17 Feb. 1915; ed. Escuela Normal, Tandil. Magistrate, 33-40; later Universidad Nacional de La Plata; Provincial Senator (Tandil) 54; mem. later Pres. Tandil Town Council 60-62; mem. Chamber of Deputies

63-; Vice-Chair. Govt. Party, Minister of Econs. 64-66; Unión Cívica Radical del Pueblo.
c/o Ministerio de Economía, Buenos Aires, Argentina.

Pugsley, Chester DeWitt, A.B.; American lawyer; b. 29 March 1887; ed. Harvard Univ.
Admitted N.Y. Bar 13; mem. firm Rabenold & Scribner N.Y. 17-27; Dir. Westchester County Nat. Bank Peekskill 15-33, Vice-Pres. 18-30, Vice-Chair. and Counsel 30-33; served U.S. Field Artillery First World War; mem. Chamber of Commerce of State of N.Y., etc.; made gift to Govt. of Greece for establishment of Nat. Park on Mount Olympus; gifts to New York Univ.; Coll. of City of N.Y., Harvard Univ., American Scenic and Historic Preservation Society, Vassar Coll., Carmel Library, Rollins Coll. Library, Duke Univ., Univ. of Virginia, Columbia Univ., Earlham Coll. Princeton, William and Mary Coll., Yale, Brown and Syracuse Univs., etc.; founded, with govt. co-operation, insts. of int. affairs several countries including Bulgaria, Greece, Lithuania, Denmark, Spain and Finland; resettled trust for int. scholarships to provide course and seminar at Harvard Law School on World Organisations (U.N. Law) 50.
400 Washington Street, Peekskill, N.Y. 10566, U.S.A.
Telephone: 914-737-1105.

Puiseux, Robert; French industrialist; b. 1 March 1892; ed. Lycée Henri IV and Lycée Saint Louis, Paris.
Former President, Soc. Anonyme André Citroën, Hon. Pres. 58-; fmr. Co-Gérant Compagnie Générale des Etablissements Michelin (until 59), Manufacture Française des Pneumatiques (until 59); Officier Légion d'Honneur, Croix de Guerre (1914-18), Commdr. de l'Economie Nat.
4 Cité Chabrol, Clermont-Ferrand, France.

Pulinckx, Raymond; Belgian business administrator; b. 24; ed. Inst. supérieur de Commerce de l'Etat, Anvers.
Chef de Cabinet, Ministry of Econ. Affairs 58-61; Dir.-Gen., Fed. of Belgian Industries 61-62, Dir.-Gen. and Administrator 62-; Chevalier de l'Ordre de Léopold, Commdr. de l'Ordre de la Couronne de Chêne, Officier de l'Ordre de la Couronne.
4 rue Ravenstein, Brussels 1, Belgium.

Pulitzer, Joseph, Jr., A.B.; American newspaper editor and publisher; b. 13 May 1913; ed. Harvard Univ.
Reporter *San Francisco News* 35; mem. staff *St. Louis Post-Dispatch* 36-48, Assoc. Editor 48-55, Editor and Publr. 55-; Vice-Pres. Pulitzer Pub. Co. 40-55, Pres. 55-; served U.S. Navy 42-45.
Home: 4903 Pershing Avenue, St. Louis 8; Office: *St. Louis Post-Dispatch*, St. Louis 1, Mo., U.S.A.

Pullai, Árpád; Hungarian politician; b. 25.
Former County Sec., Hungarian Fed. of Democratic Youth; Hungarian Working People's Party 48, fmr. First Sec. Debrecen Municipal Party Cttee., fmr. Editor *Party Life*; Sec. Central Cttee. Hungarian Communist Youth Union 58-61, First Sec. 61-64; mem. Central Cttee. Hungarian Socialist Workers' Party 62-; Chief of Party and Mass Org. Dept. of Central Cttee. of Hungarian Socialist Workers Party 64-66.
Hungarian Socialist Workers Party, Széchény Rakpart 19, Budapest V, Hungary.

Pulliam, Eugene Collins; American newspaper publisher; b. 3 May 1889; ed. Graduate Prep. School, Baker Univ. Kansas, and DePauw Univ. Ind.
Began as a reporter Kansas City (Mo.) *Star* 10-12; Editor Atchison (Kan.) *Champion* 12-15, Franklin (Ind.) *Star* 15-23; Publ. Lebanon (Ind.) *Reporter* 23; Pres. Central Newspapers Inc., Indianapolis Newspapers Inc., Muncie Newspapers Inc., Phoenix Newspapers Inc., Phoenix, Ariz.; Dir. New York Central

Railroad, Associated Press, American Inst. for Foreign Trade.
307 North Pennsylvania Street, Indianapolis, Indiana, U.S.A.

Pünder, Herman (Joseph), JUR.D.; German lawyer; b. 1 April 1888; studied law in Freiburg, London, Berlin.
Gerichtsassessor in Prussian Ministry of Justice 19; Referent in Reich Ministry of Finance 19-25; Ministerial Dir. at Reich Chancellery 25-26; State Sec. and Head of Reich Chancellery 26-32; Regional Pres. in Münster 32-33; arrested by Gestapo 44; inmate of concentration camps until liberated by U.S. Army 45; Lord Mayor of Cologne Nov. 45-May 48; Chair. of Bizonal Exec. Cttee., Frankfurt 48-49; mem. of North Rhine/Westphalia Diet 46-49; mem. Cologne City Council 45-48; mem. Centre Party 22 until dissolution by Hitler; co-founder of Christian Democratic Union in Westphalia 45; Hon. mem. Management of German Municipal League, Hon. Pres. German-Belgian-Luxembourg Chamber of Commerce Cologne; mem. Bundestag 49-57; fmr. Vice-Pres. E.C.S.C .Common Assembly, mem. Consultative Assembly, Council of Europe; Grosses Bundesverdienstkreuz mit Stern und Schulterband.
Marienburger Strasse 42, Köln-Marienburg, German Federal Republic.

Pungan, Vasile; Romanian university professor and diplomatist; b. 2 Nov. 1926; ed. Inst. of Economics, Bucharest.
Dean of Faculty, Agronomical Inst. "Nicolae Bălcescu", Bucharest 54; Gen. Dir., Ministry of Agriculture and Forestry 55-58; Counsellor, Romanian Embassy, Washington 59-62; Dir. and mem. Foreign Office Coll. 63-66; Amb. to U.K. 66-; Romanian decorations.
Embassy of Romania, 4 Palace Green, London, W.8, England.
Telephone: 01-937-9666.

Purcell, Edward Mills, PH.D.; American physicist; b. 30 Aug. 1912; ed. Purdue Univ., Technische Hochschule, Karlsruhe, and Harvard Univ.
Instructor in Physics, Harvard 38-40; Radiation Laboratory, Mass. Inst. of Technology 40-46 (Faculty Instructor on leave of absence, Harvard 41-45); Assoc. Prof. of Physics, Harvard 45-49, Prof. of Physics 49-58, Donner Prof. of Science 58-60; Gerhard Gade Univ. Prof. 60-; Senior Fellow, Society of Fellows, Harvard Univ. 50-; mem. Nat. Acad. of Sciences of U.S.A., American Acad. of Arts and Sciences, American Philosophical Soc.; co-winner Nobel Prize in Physics 52.
5 Wright Street, Cambridge, Mass. 02138, U.S.A.

Purdy, James; American writer; b. 23; ed. Chicago and Spain.
Interpreter, editor and other posts in Cuba, Mexico, Washington, D.C.
Publs. Novels: *Don't Call Me by My Right Name* 56, *63 Dream Palace* 56, *Color of Darkness* 57, *Malcolm* 59, *The Nephew* 60, *Cabot Wright Begins* 63, *Eustace Chisholm and the Works* 67; Play: *Children is All* 62; *An Oyster is a Wealthy Beast* (Story and Poems) 67.
c/o Jonathan Cape Ltd., 30 Bedford Square, London, W.C.1, England.

Puri, Yogendra Krishna; Indian diplomatist; b. 25 July 1916; ed. Government Coll., Lahore, and Univ. Coll., London.
Indian Civil Service, Assam 38-46; Dep. Sec., Ministry of Finance 47; Minister without Portfolio 47; Dir.-Gen. Ministry of Rehabilitation 48; Dep. High Commr. in Pakistan 48-51; Dep. Sec. Ministry of External Affairs 51-53; Indian Embassy, Paris 53-55; Counsellor Indian High Comm., London 55; Jt. Sec. Ministry of External Affairs 55-60; High Commr. in Malaya 60-63, in Malaysia 63-64, Amb. to Morocco and Tunisia 64-67, to Sweden 68-.
Indian Embassy, Stockholm, Sweden.

Purtell, William Arthur; American politician and industrialist; b. 6 May 1897.
Pres., Treasurer and Gen. Man. Billings & Spencer Co, Hartford 37-44, Dir. and Chair. Exec. Cttee. 44-47; Pres., Treasurer and Gen. Man. Dir. Holo-Krome Screw Corpn., Hartford 29-52; Vice-Pres., Treasurer and Gen. Man. Sparmal Engineering Corpn. 38-52, fmr. Dir. Colts Manufacturing Co., Hartford Conn. Trust Co. Billings and Spencer, Veeder-Root Inc., Hartford Gas Co., Nat. Fire Insurance Co.; Senator from Conn. 52-58; Republican; fmr. Chair. Board of Trustees Hillyer Coll.; now Dir. American Supply and Machinery Manufacturers Asscn. and mem. Board of Trustees, Robinson School; Hon. LL.D. Trinity Coll., Hillyer Coll.
514 Maple Avenue, Old Saybrook, Conn. 06475, U.S.A. Telephone: 388-3204.

Puryear, Vernon John, A.M., PH.D.; American educationist; b. 31 March 1901; ed. Baylor Univ. and Univ. of Missouri.
Instructor in History Univ. of Missouri 26-28; Teaching Fellow in European History Univ. of California 28-29; Prof. of History and Political Science Albany Coll. 29-33; Associate Prof. of Social Science Humboldt State Coll. 33-34, Prof. 34-37; Asst. Prof. of History Univ. of California 37-42, Assoc. Prof. 42-48, Prof. 48-52; Prof. of Political Science 52-68; mem. American Historical Asscn., American Acad. of Political and Social Science, American Political Science Asscn., Foreign Policy Asscn., Acad. of Political Science.
Publs. *England, Russia and the Straits Question 1844-56* (awarded H. B. Adams Prize of American Historical Asscn.) 31, *International Economics and Diplomacy in the Near East* 35, *France and the Levant* 41, *Napoleon and the Dardanelles* 50.
P.O. Box 158, Davis, Calif. 96516, U.S.A. Telephone: 753-2956.

Pusey, Nathan M., A.M., PH.D.; American university president; b. 4 April 1907; ed. Harvard Univ.
Asst. Harvard Univ. 33-34; Sophomore Tutor, Lawrence Coll. 35-38; Asst. Prof. History and Literature; Scripps Coll., Claremont, Calif. 38-40; Asst. Prof. Classics, Wesleyan Univ. 40-43, Assoc. Prof. 43-44; Pres. Lawrence Coll., Appleton, Wis. 44-53; Pres. Harvard Univ. 53-; mem. Central Cttee. World Council of Churches, mem. American Council on Educ., American Acad. of Arts and Sciences; Vice-Chair., Board of Trustees, Woodrow Wilson Nat. Fellow Foundation; Trustee, Carnegie Foundation for Advancement of Teaching; Chair. Board of Dirs., Fund for Theological Education Inc.; Hon. LL.D. (Wesleyan Univ., Ripon Coll., Yale Univ., Columbia Univ., Brown Univ., Princeton Univ., Boston Univ., Northeastern Univ., Williams Coll., Jewish Theological Seminary, Tufts Univ., Univ. of Pennsylvania, Johns Hopkins Univ., Northwestern, Calif. Univs., Rockefeller Inst., St. Louis Univ., Univ. of North Carolina, Oberlin Coll., Seoul Nat. Univ., Korea, Marquette Univ., Dickinson Coll., Wheaton Coll. and Lehigh Univ.); Hon. L.H.D. (Coe and Lawrence Colls., Colgate Univ. and Boston Coll.); D. de l'Université (Montreal); D.Litt. (Univ. of Delhi); Litt.D.

(Morehouse Coll. and Univ. of Wisconsin); D.D. (Pacific School of Religion).
Publ. *The Age of the Scholar* 63.
Massachusetts Hall, Harvard University, Cambridge, Mass. 02138, U.S.A.

Pushkin, Boris Konstantinovich; Soviet foreign trade official; ed. Moscow Technical Inst. of Fisheries and the Fish Industry.
Member C.P.S.U. 40-; Official, U.S.S.R. Trade Representation in Hungary 45-47; Dir. of Office, *Tekhnoexport* Trust 47-55; Vice-Chair. *Mashinoexport* Trust 55-63; Dir. of Office, *Tekhsnabexport* 63-64; U.S.S.R. Commercial Rep. in Hungary 64-; Order of Red Banner of Labour (twice), Order of Patriotic War, Second Degree.
U.S.S.R. Trade Representation, Budapest, Hungary.

Pustovoit, Vasiliy Stepanovich; Soviet geneticist and selectionist; b. 1886; ed. Kuban Agricultural Institute.
Department Chief, Kuban Agric. Inst. 26-30; Dir. Experimental Selection Station "Kruglik", Krasnodar, later reorganized into the U.S.S.R. Research Inst. of Oil-Plants 12-30; Dept. Man. Inst. of Oil-Plants 35-; Prof., mem. U.S.S.R. Lenin Acad. of Agric. Sciences 56-; mem. U.S.S.R. Acad. of Sciences 64-; Merited Agriculturist of U.S.S.R.; Hero of Socialist Labour (twice); State and Lenin Prize Winner.
Publs. Basic works on methods of selection of rich oily sunflower.
U.S.S.R. Academy of Sciences, 14 Lenin Prospekt, Moscow, U.S.S.R.

Putrament, Jerzy; Polish writer and journalist; b. 10; ed. Univ. of Vilno.
Ambassador to Switzerland 45-47, to France 48-50; Gen. Sec. Union of Polish Writers 50-54; State Prize, Second Class.
Publs. Verse: *Wojna i wiosna* (War and Spring) 44, *Wiersze wybrane* (Selected Verse) 51; Novels: *Rzeczywistość* (Reality) 48, *Wrzesień* (September) 52, *Rozstaje* (Crossroads) 54, *Pasierbowie* 65.
Krakowskie Przedmieście 87/89, Warsaw, Poland.

Puzanov, Alexandr Mikhailovich; Soviet diplomatist; b. 1906; ed. Plesski Agricultural Technicum.
State and Econ. activity 37-52; Chair. Council of Ministers of R.S.F.S.R. 52-56; Ambassador to Dem. People's Repub. of Korea 57-62, to Yugoslavia 62-67, to Bulgaria 67-; mem. C.P.S.U. Central Cttee. 52-.
U.S.S.R. Embassy, Sofia, Bulgaria.

Pysin, Konstantin Georgievich; Soviet politician; b. 1910; ed. Perm Agricultural Inst.
Member C.P.S.U. 39-; Chair. Exec. Cttee. Perm Regional (47-49) and Altai Territorial Soviets of Working People's Deps. 49-55; First Sec. Altai Territorial Cttee. of C.P.S.U. 55-61; Deputy Minister of Agriculture of U.S.S.R. 61-62, Minister 62-63; on staff of Central Cttee. of C.P.S.U. 63-64; First Deputy Chair. Council of Ministers of R.S.F.S.R. 64-; mem. Central Cttee. C.P.S.U.; Deputy to U.S.S.R. Supreme Soviet; Order of Lenin (twice), Order of Red Banner of Labour.
Council of Ministers of R.S.F.S.R., ulitsa Delegetskaya 3, Moscow, U.S.S.R.

Q

Qavam, Mohammed; Iranian diplomatist; b. 22; ed. Univ. of Teheran.

Formerly with Ministry of Finance; Chef de Cabinet to Prime Minister 47; Ministry of Foreign Affairs 47-, Ambassador to Kuwait 63-64, to Ethiopia 64-.

Publ. *Evolution of Government Institutions in Iran.*

Imperial Iranian Embassy, Ras Desta Damtew Avenue, P.O. Box 528, Addis Ababa, Ethiopia.

Quadros, Janio; Brazilian politician; b. 17; ed. São Paulo School of Law.

Part-time high school teacher; practised law; mem. São Paulo City Council 47-59; State Deputy 50; Mayor, São Paulo City 52-55; Gov. São Paulo State 55-59; Federal Deputy 59-60; Pres. of Brazil Jan.-Aug. 61 (resigned); political rights suspended for 10 years, April 64.

São Paulo, Brazil.

Quaison-Sackey, Alexander, M.A.; Ghanaian diplomatist; b. 9 Aug. 1924; ed. Mfantsipim School, Exeter Coll. Oxford, London School of Economics and Lincoln's Inn, London.

Former teacher at Mfantsipim School and with Gold Coast Secretariat; Labour Officer Gold Coast 52-55; Attaché British Embassy, Rio de Janeiro 56; Head of Chancery and Official Sec. Ghana High Commission, London 57-59; Perm. Rep. of Ghana to UN 59-65; Minister of Foreign Affairs 65-66; mem. Convention People's Party; Vice-Pres. UN Gen. Assembly 61-62, 64; Ambassador to Cuba 61, to Mexico 62; under house arrest 66, released June 66.

Publ. *Africa Unbound* 63.

c/o Ministry of Foreign Affairs, Accra, Ghana.

Quandt, Herbert; German industrial executive; b. 22 June 1910.

Chairman of Management Board of Varta AG, Hagen; Managing Dir. Allgemeine Gesellschaft für Industrie-beteiligungen, Stuttgart, Draeger-Werker G.m.b.H.; Hon. D.Phil.

Seedammweg 55, 638 Bad Homburg v.d.H., German Federal Republic.

Telephone: 06172-20091.

Quaroni, Pietro, DR. IUR.; Italian diplomatist; b. 3 Oct. 1898.

Attaché, Constantinople 20; Third Sec. 21; Second Sec. 23; Buenos Aires 23, Moscow 25; First Sec. 26; Tirana 28; Ministry of Foreign Affairs 31, Counsellor 32; Consul-Gen., Salonika 35; Minister to Afghanistan 36; Minister to U.S.S.R. 45-46; Ambassador to France 47-58; Ambassador to Germany 58-61, to U.K. 61-64; Chair. Italian State Radio and TV 64-; Hammarskjöld Prize 66; numerous decorations.

Publs. *Memoirs of an Ambassador, Diplomatic Bags* 66.

Radiotelevisione Italiana, Via del Babuino 9, Rome, Italy.

Quasimodo, Salvatore; Italian poet and critic; b. 20 Aug. 1901; ed. Rome Polytechnic.

First published poems in *Solaria* (Florence); contributor to principal Italian (including *Circoli, L'Italia Letteraria, Il Frontespizio, Letteratura, Primato, Gazzetta del Popolo*) and numerous foreign reviews; Asst. Editor *Tempo* 38-40, now Dramatic Critic; Prof. of Italian Literature, Giuseppe Verdi Conservatory, Milan 41-; awarded (with Dylan Thomas) Etna-Taormina Int. Prize 53; translations of his verse have appeared in Argentina, Australia, Belgium, Brazil, Czechoslovakia, France, Germany, Great Britain, Romania, Spain, Sweden, U.S.A., U.S.S.R., and Yugoslavia; mem. dell' Accademia dei Cherubini, Accademia del Parnaso; Premio Viareggio

58; Nobel Prize for Literature 59; Hon. D.Litt. (Oxford) 67.

Publs. Verse: *Acque e terre* 30, *Oboe Sommerso* 32, *Odore di Eucalyptus ed altri versi* 33, *Erato e Apollion* 36, *Poesie* 38, *Ed è subito sera* 42, *Giorno dopo giorno* 46, *La vita non è sogno* 49, *Billy Budd* (libretto) 49, *Il falso e vero verde* 53, *La terra impareggiabile* (collected verse) 58; *Tutte le Poesie, Il poeta e il politico e altri saggi, Dare e avere* (poems since 66); translations: *Romeo and Juliet, Macbeth, Othello, Richard III, The Tempest* (Shakespeare), of Greek lyric poets, *Il fiore della Antologia Palatina, Poesie scelte di E. E. Cummings, Edipo Re, Elettra* (Sophocles), *Le Coefore* (Aeschylus), *Carmina* (Catullus), *Il Tartufo* (Molière), *Il Vangelo secondo Giovanni, Poesie* (Verude).

[*Died* 14 *June* 1968.]

Quastel, J. Hirsch, D.SC., PH.D., A.R.C.S., F.R.I.C., F.R.S.C., F.R.S.; British biochemist; b. 2 Oct. 1899; ed. Sheffield Central Secondary School, Imperial Coll. of Science, London, and Trinity Coll., Cambridge.

Served First World War; Fellow Trinity Coll. 24; Dir. of Research Cardiff City Mental Hospital 29-41; Fellow Royal Soc. London 40, Royal Soc. of Canada 52; Dir. Unit of Soil Metabolism, Agricultural Research Council 41-47; Prof. of Biochemistry McGill Univ. Montreal, Canada 47-66; Dir. McGill Unit of Cell Metabolism 65-66; Prof. of Neurochemistry and Hon. Prof. of Biochemistry, Univ. of British Columbia 66-; Pres. Montreal Physiological Soc. 50; Fellow New York Acad. of Sciences; Hon. Fellow Japanese Pharmacological Soc., Canadian Soc. of Microbiologists, Indian Brain Research Asscn.; Hon. Consultant Montreal Gen. Hospital; Pres. Canadian Biochemical Soc. 63; Royal Soc. Leverhulme Visiting Prof. India 66.

Publs. *Neurochemistry, Metabolic Inhibitors, Chemistry of Brain Metabolism in Health and Disease, Methods in Medical Research* Vol. 9.

Neurochemistry Department, Faculty of Medicine, Univ. of British Columbia, Vancouver 8, B.C., Canada. Telephone: 228-2202.

Quat, Phan Huy; Viet-Namese physician and politician; b. 08; ed. Hanoi Medical School.

Minister of Educ., later of Defence 49-53; Sec.-Gen. Nat. Popular Front 52; Acting Premier 54; imprisoned 60-63; Minister of Foreign Affairs 64; Prime Minister of Repub. of Viet-Nam 65.

c/o Office of the Prime Minister, Saigon, Republic of Viet-Nam.

Quayle, Anthony, C.B.E.; British theatre director, producer and actor; b. 7 Sept. 1913; ed. Rugby and Royal Acad. of Dramatic Art.

First stage appearance at Q Theatre 31; joined the Old Vic Company 32; first appearance in New York at Henry Miller Theatre 36; with Old Vic at Elsinore 37, and on tour of Continent and Egypt 39; served in Royal Artillery 39-45; reappeared at the Criterion Theatre in *The Rivals* 45; produced *Crime and Punishment* at the New Theatre 46; produced and acted in Shakespeare's plays at Shakespeare Memorial Theatre, Stratford-on-Avon Feb. 48-56; Dir. Shakespeare Memorial Theatre 49-56; produced *Harvey* at Prince of Wales's Theatre, London Dec. 48; produced Terence Rattigan's *Who is Sylvia*, Criterion Theatre, London Oct. 50; toured Australia with Shakespeare Memorial Theatre Company 49-50 and Jan.-Oct. 53; acted name part in *Tamburlaine*, New York Jan. 56; acted in *A View From The Bridge*, London 56; European tour of *Titus Andronicus* 57; dir. and acted in *The Firstborn*, New York, acted in

Long Day's Journey into Night, Edinburgh and London, 58, Look After Lulu, Chin-Chin 60, The Right Honourable Gentleman 64, Incident at Vichy 66, Dir. Lady Windermere's Fan, London 66, Galileo, New York 67; films: Woman in a Dressing Gown, The Man Who Wouldn't Talk, Ice Cold in Alex, Serious Charge, Tarzan's Greatest Adventure, The Challenge, The Guns of Navarone, H.M.S. Defiant 61, Lawrence of Arabia 62, The Fall of the Roman Empire 64, Operation Crossbow, A Study in Terror; also radio and TV plays; directed colour production Ceasar and Cleopatra for Nat. Broadcasting Co. Television.
Publs. Eight Hours from England, On Such a Night.
22, Pelham Crescent, London, S.W.7, England.

Queen, Ellery (see Dannay, Frederic, and Lee, Manfred)·

Queeny, Edgar Monsanto, A.B.; American businessman; b. 29 Sept. 1897; ed. St. Louis public schools, Pawling School (N.Y.) and Cornell Univ.
With Monsanto Chemical Co. 19-, Sales Man. 24, Pres. 28-43, Chair. 43-60, Chair. Finance Cttee. 60-65, now Dir.; Dir. American-Korean Foundation, Herbert Hoover Foundation, World Rehabilitation Fund; hon. mem. Business Council (Wash.); Trustee Ducks Unlimited Inc., Ducks Unlimited, Canada; Councillor and Senior mem. Nat. Industrial Conf. Board (fmr. Vice-Chair.); Chair. of Trustees, Barnes Hospital (St. Louis); Hon. Vice-Pres. St. Louis Syuphony Soc.; Hon. life mem. East African Natural History Asscn. and White Hunters Asscn. of Kenya; Hon. Trustee, American Museum of Natural History.
Publs. Cheechako 41, The Spirit of Enterprise 43, Prairie Wings 46.
[Died 7 July 1968]

Queneau, Raymond; French writer; b. 21 Feb. 1903; ed. Univ. of Paris.
Director and Editor Encyclopédie de la Pléiade; mem. Acad. Goncourt.
Publs. include Le Chiendent 33, Un rude hiver 40, Pierrot, mon ami 42, Exercises de style 47, L'instant fatal 48, Petite Cosmogonie Portative 50, Le dimanche de la vie 52, Zazie dans le Métro 59, Les Oeuvres Complètes de Sally Mara 62, Le Chien à la Mandoline 65, Les Fleurs bleues 65, Une histoire modèle 66.
c/o Gallimard, 5 rue Sebastien-Bottin, Paris, France.

Quennell, Peter; British writer; b. 9 March 1905; ed. Berkhamsted Grammar School and Balliol Coll., Oxford.
Former Prof. of English Literature, Tokyo Bunrika Daigaku 30; Editor Cornhill Magazine 44-51, History Today 51-.
Publs. Baudelaire and the Symbolists, A Superficial Journey, Byron: The Years of Fame, Byron in Italy 41, Caroline of England, Four Portraits, Ruskin: The Portrait of a Prophet 52, Spring in Sicily, The Singular Preference, Hogarth's Progress 54, The Sign of the Fish 60, Shakespeare: the poet and his background 63, Aspects of 17th Century Verse, Memoirs of the Comte de Gramont (trans.), Letters of Madame de Lieven; Editor: Memoirs of William Hickey, Byron: A Self Portrait (1798-1824), Mayhew's London Labour and the London Poor (3 vols.).
Bracken House, 10 Cannon Street, London, E.C.4, England.

Quenum, Dr. Alfred Auguste; Dahomeyan physician; b. 26; ed. African School of Medicine and Pharmacy, Dakar, and Faculty of Medicine, Univ. of Bordeaux.
Formerly at Centre d'Etudes Nucléaires, Saclay; later Dakar Faculty of Medicine; Prof. of Histology and Embryology, Dakar Faculty of Medicine 62-64; Regional Dir. for Africa, World Health Org. 65-.
World Health Organization Regional Office for Africa, P.O. Box 6, Brazzaville, Congo.

Querejazu Calvo, Roberto; Bolivian diplomatist and writer; b. 24 Nov. 1913; ed. Sucre.
Director of Minister's Cabinet, Legal and Political Depts., Bolivian Foreign Service 39-42; First Sec. Embassy, Brazil 43; Counsellor, London 47-48, Chargé d'Affaires 48-52, Amb. (concurrently to the Netherlands) 66-; Under-Sec. of State for Foreign Affairs, Bolivia 66; Sec.-Gen. Bolivian Del. to UN 46; Bolivian Rep. to UN Conf. on Tin 51, to Interamerican Conf. for De-Nuclearization of Latin America, Mexico 64; Del. to UN Gen. Assembly 65, Second Interamerican Conf. Extraordinary, Rio de Janeiro 65; Cross of the Chaco and Award of Mil. Merit, Bolivia and several foreign awards.
Publs. Masamaclay—History of the Chaco War 65; Bolivia 68; many articles in Bolivian newspapers.
Bolivian Embassy, London, S.W.1, England.

Queuille, Henri, M.D.; French politician; b. 31 March 1884.
Radical-Socialist Deputy for Corréze 14-35; Pres. Gen. Council of Corrèze 21-40; Under-Sec. of State for Agriculture in Millerand and Leygues Cabinets 20; Minister of Agriculture 25-27, of Posts, Telegraphs and Telephones in Herriot Cabinet June-Dec. 32, of Agriculture 32-34, and of Health 34; Minister of Public Works, Chautemps Cabinet June 37-Mar. 38; Minister of Agriculture, Daladier Cabinet April 38-March 40, of Food in Reynaud Cabinet Mar.-June 40; joined Gen. de Gaulle 43; Commr. without Portfolio, French Cttee. of Nat. Liberation, Algiers 43-44; mem. of Nat. Assembly 46-58; Prime Minister Sept. 48-Oct. 49; Vice-Premier Oct. 49-Feb. 50; Minister of the Interior Feb.-June 50; Prime Minister July 50; Minister of the Interior July 50-Mar. 51; Prime Minister Mar.-Aug. 51; Minister of State Aug. 51-Jan. 52; Deputy Prime Minister and Minister of State Jan.-Dec. 52; Deputy Prime Minister Jan.-May 53 and June 53-54.
100 rue du Cherche-Midi, Paris 6e, France.

Quine, Willard Van Orman, M.A., PH.D.; American philosophy professor; b. 25 June 1908; ed. Oberlin Coll. and Harvard Univ.
Sheldon Travelling Fellow (Harvard) to Vienna, Prague and Warsaw 32-33; Junior Fellow, Soc. of Fellows, Harvard 33-36, Faculty Instructor in Philosophy 36-41, Assoc. Prof. 41-48, Prof. of Philosophy 48-56, Edgar Pierce Prof. of Philosophy, Harvard Univ. 56-; U.S. Naval Reserve 42-46; Visiting Prof. Univ. of São Paulo, Brazil 42, George Eastman Visiting Prof., Oxford Univ. 53-54; Pres. Asscn. for Symbolic Logic 53-55; mem. Inst. for Advanced Study, Princeton 56-57; Fellow, Center for Advanced Study in Behavioral Sciences, Stanford 58-59; Gavin David Young Lecturer, Adelaide Univ., Australia 59; Visiting Prof. Tokyo Univ. 59; Fellow, Wesleyan Univ. Center for Advanced Study 65; Fellow, American Acad. of Arts and Sciences, American Philosophical Soc.; Corresp. Fellow British Acad.; Visiting Prof. Rockefeller Univ. 68; Pres. American Philosophical Asscn. 58; mem. Institut Int. de Philosophie, Académie Int. de Philosophie des Sciences, Instituto Brasileiro de Filosofia; several hon. degrees.
Publs. A System of Logistic 34, Mathematical Logic 40, Elementary Logic 41, O Sentido da Nova Lógica 44, Methods of Logic 50, From a Logical Point of View 53, Word and Object 60, Set Theory and its Logic 63, The Ways of Paradox 66, Selected Logic Papers 66.
38 Chestnut Street, Boston 8, Mass., U.S.A.
Telephone: 742-2813.

Quinn, Anthony Rudolph Oaxaca; American actor-director of Irish and Mexican descent; b. 21 April 1916; ed. Los Angeles.
First appeared on stage 36; has appeared in the films Viva Zapata, Lust for Life, La Strada, Man from Del Rio, The Black Orchid, Warlock, Last Train from Gun

Hill, Heller in Pink Tights, Savage Innocents, Guns of Navarone, Barabas, Lawrence of Arabia, The Visit, Zorba the Greek, The Twenty-Fifth Hour, Guns for San Sebastian; Dir. *The Bucaneer* 58; Venice Film Festival Award for *La Strada* 54, American Motion Picture Acad. Awards for Best Supporting Actor for *Viva Zapata* 52, and *Lust for Life* 56.

333 Las Casa Avenue, Pacific Palisades, Calif., U.S.A.

Quinn, William Francis, LL.B.; American politician; b. 13 July 1919; ed. St. Louis Univ. and Harvard Law School.

Served in U.S. Navy 42-46; worked with Honolulu law firm of Robertson, Castle and Anthony 47-57 and partner 50-57; admitted to practice in Territorial and Fed. Courts 48; mem. Exec. Cttee. of the Bar Asscn. of Hawaii and Advisory membership Cttee. of the American Bar Asscn.; mem. Hawaii Statehood Comm. 57; Territorial Gov. of Hawaii 57-59; first Gov. of State of Hawaii July 59-62; mem. Exec. Cttee. Nat. Govs. Conf. 59-60; Pres. Pacific Area Travel Asscn. 60-61; Partner, Quinn and Moore 62-64; Exec. Vice-Pres. Dole Co., Honolulu 64-65, Pres. 65-; Republican.

Office: 650 Iwilei Road, Honolulu, 96817; Home: 1365 Laukahi Street, Honolulu, Hawaii 96821, U.S.A.

Telephone: 563-411 (Office).

Quinn, William John, B.A., LL.B.; American lawyer and railway executive; b. 8 May 1911; ed. St. Thomas Coll. St. Paul (Minn.) and Univ. of Minnesota Law School.

Law practice St. Paul (Minn.) 35-37, Asst. District Attorney 37-40; Attorney Soo Line Railroad 40-42; Special Agent Fed. Bureau of Investigation 42-45; Asst. Commercial Counsel Soo Line Railroad 45, Commercial Counsel 46-52, Asst. Gen. Counsel 52, Gen. Counsel 52-53, Vice-Pres. and Gen. Counsel 53-54; Gen. Solicitor Chicago, Milwaukee, St. Paul and Pacific Railroad 54-55, Vice-Pres. and Gen. Counsel 55-58, Pres. 58-66; Pres. Chicago Burlington & Quincy RR Co. 66-; Dir. Asscn. of American Railroads, Skil Corpn., James B. Clow and Sons, Continental Illinois Nat. Bank & Trust Co. of Chicago, Universal Oil Products Co.; Hon. LL.D. St. Thomas Coll. (St. Paul, Minn.).

Office: 848 Union Station, Chicago 6, Ill.; Home: 1201 Chatfield Road, Winnetka, Ill., U.S.A.

Telephone: 312-446-5007.

Quintana, Carlos, M.SC., M.B.A.; Mexican engineer; b. 1912; ed. Instituto Politécnico Nacional, Mexico, and Columbia and Harvard Univs., U.S.

Former Prof. of Engineering, Nat. Polytechnic Inst., Mexico City; in Dept. of Industrial Research, Bank of Mexico 44-50; Dir. Industrial Devt. Div., Econ. Comm. for Latin America (ECLA) 50-60, Exec. Sec. ECLA Feb. 67-; Manager Industrial Programming, Nacional Financiera 60-67; mem. Governing Council, Mexican Inst. for Technological Research 61-67; mem. Govt. Econ. Missions to Yugoslavia, Czechoslovakia, U.S.S.R. and Poland.

Economic Commission for Latin America, Casilla 179 D, Santiago, Chile.

Quintanilla, Luis, B.S., L.ès L., PH.D.; Mexican diplomatist; b. 1900; ed. Sorbonne and Johns Hopkins Univ.

Entered diplomatic service 21, Protocol Div. 22; 3rd Sec. Washington 23, and Sec. Guatemala 26, Washington 29; 1st Sec. Paris 30; Sec.-Gen. Del. to League of Nations 32; Counsellor, Washington 35, Minister-Res. 29, Minister 38, Ambassador 42-45; adviser to Mexican Del., at U.N. Conf., San Francisco 45; Ambassador to Colombia 45, to Organisation of American States, Washington, D.C. 45; Rep. Inter-American Peace Comm. 48-; Chair. of Council 49-50; Chair. Inter-American Peace Commission, Washington, D.C. 48; Mexican del. to Second Gen. Assembly, U.N., New York 47, and 9th Int. Conf. of American States, Bogotá, Colombia 48; Dir. Inst. Nacional de la Vivienda 59.

Publs. *Avión* 23, *Radio* 24, *Teatro Mexicano del Murciélago* 24, *The Other Side of the Mexican Church Question* 35, *A Latin American Speaks* 43, 46, *Pan Americanism and Democracy* 52, *Democracia y Panamericanismo* 52, *Bergsonismo y Política* 53, *The Caribbean: Contemporary Trends* 53, *The Control of Foreign Relations in Modern Nations* 57, *The Greatness of Woodrow Wilson* 57.

Reyna 87, San Angel Inn, Mexico 20, D.F., Mexico.

Quintero, H.E. Cardinal José Humberto; Venezuelan ecclesiastic; b. 22 Sept. 1902.

Ordained priest 26; Archbishop of Acrida 53-60; Archbishop of Caracas 60-; created Cardinal and titular priest of St. Andrew and St. Gregory at Monte Celio 61; mem. Sacred Congregations of Sacraments, of Rites and of Seminaries and Univs. of Study.

Palacio Arzobispal, Apartado 954, Caracas, Venezuela.

Quinton, Harold; American executive; b. 20 Jan. 1899; ed. Washburn Acad. and Northwestern Univ.

Sec. Precision Machine Co., Washington 20-21; Auditor, Income Tax Unit, Treasury Dept. 21-23, Tech. Adviser 24-25; Tax Specialist Arthur Andersen & Co., C.P.A., Chicago 25-27, Man. Partner, Los Angeles office 28-42; Vice-Pres. Southern Calif. Edison Co., Los Angeles 42, Exec. Vice-Pres. 48-54, mem. Board of Dirs. 45-, mem. Exec. Cttee. 45, Pres. 54-59, Chair., Chief Exec. Officer 59-65, Chair. Board and Exec. Cttee. 66-; mem. Advisory Cttee. Edison Electric Inst. 58-, mem. Cttee. of Past Presidents 61-; Dir. Kaiser Steel Corpn., Kaiser Industries Corpn., Buffum's, Long Beach, Western Bancorporation; Dir. and mem. Los Angeles Admin. Cttee. United Calif. Bank; Trustee Univ. of S. Calif., Vice-Chair. of Board and Treas. 65-; mem. Exec. Cttee. Nat. Asscn. of Electric Companies, Chair. of Board 64; mem. Board Stanford Research Inst. 65-.

Home: 1736 Mandeville Lane, Los Angeles, Calif. 90049; Office: 601 West 5th Street, P.O. Box 351, Los Angeles, Calif. 90053, U.S.A.

Quiroga, Elena; Spanish writer.

Publs. *Viento del Norte* 51, *La Sangre* 52, *Algo Pasa en la Calle* 54, *La Enferma*, *La Careta* 55, *Placida*, *La Joven* 56, *La Ultima Corrida* 58.

c/o Editorial Noguer, S.A., Paseo Gracia 98, Barcelona; Home: Ferraz 39, Madrid 8, Spain.

Quiroga y Palacios, H.E. Cardinal Fernando, DR. THEOL.; Spanish ecclesiastic; b. 21 Jan. 1900; ed. Pontifical Univ. of Santiago de Compostela and Pontifical Biblical Inst., Rome.

Priest, Campobecerros 22; Coadjutor of Sta. Eufemia, Orense 23; Prof. Orense Seminary 28, Spiritual Dir. and Prof. 30; Priest, Sta. Eufemia and Administrator of Diocesan Funds 35; Canon of Valladolid and Prof. at Valladolid Seminary 42; Bishop of Mondoñedo 45; Archbishop of Santiago de Compostela 49-; created Cardinal by Pope Pius XII 53; mem. Sacred Congregations of the Council, of Rites, and of Ceremonies.

Palacio Arzobispal, Plaza de la Inmaculada 1, Santiago de Compostela, Spain.

Quizpez Asin-Mas, Carlos; Peruvian painter; b. 06; ed. National School of Fine Arts, Lima, and San Fernando School of Fine Arts, Madrid.

Federal Art Project, Calif.; Prof. School of Fine Arts, Lima 43; Prof. of Mural Painting and Principal Teacher of Drawing and Painting; many mural paintings in public buildings in Peru; Gold Medal of Municipality of Lima for murals in Chamber of Deputies 41.

854 Los Eucaliptos, Chaclacayo, Lima, Peru.

Qureshi, Anwar Iqbal, B.A., M.A., M.SC., PH.D.; Pakistani economist; b. 10 April 1910; ed. Foreman Christian Coll., Lahore, London School of Economics, Trinity Coll., Dublin.

Professor, Head Econs. Dept., Osmania Univ. 37-47; Econ. Adviser, Govt. of Hyderabad 44-47; Dep. Econ.

Adviser Govt. of Pakistan 47-51; Adviser, Int. Monetary Fund (Latin America, Middle and Far Eastern Dept.) 51-55; Financial and Econ. Adviser, Saudi Arabia 55-59; Econ. Adviser, Govt. of Pakistan 61-; Pres. Pakistan Econ. Asscn.; mem. Preparatory Cttee. Asian Devt. Bank; Pakistani Rep. at numerous int. econ. confs; Satara-i-Quaiz Azam 65.

Publs. *The Farmer and His Debt* 34, *Agricultural Credit* 36, *The State and Economic Life* 37, *State Banks for India* 39, *Islam and the Theory of Interest* 46, *The Future of Co-operative Movement in India* 47, *Economic Development of Hyderabad* 48, *Development in Pakistan's Economy since the Revolution* 60, *Pakistan's March on Road to Prosperity* 65.

c/o Ministry of Finance, Islamabad, West Pakistan, Pakistan.

Telephone: 63429; 20812.

Qureshi, Ishtiaq Husain, M.A., PH.D.; Pakistani scholar and politician; b. 20 Nov. 1903; ed. St. Stephen's Coll. (Univ. of Delhi), and Sidney Sussex Coll., Cambridge.

Lecturer in History, St. Stephens Coll. 28; Reader in History Univ. of Delhi 40, Prof. and Head of Dept. of History 44, Dean of Faculty of Arts 45; mem. for Bengal, Constituent Assembly of India 47; Prof. of History and Head of Dept. of History, Punjab Univ. 48; Deputy Minister of the Interior, Information and Broadcasting, Refugees and Rehabilitation, Govt. of Pakistan 49, Minister of State 50, Minister for Refugees and Rehabilitation, Information and Broadcasting 51-53; Minister of Education 53-55; mem. Advisory Council of Islamic Ideology 62-63; Visiting Prof. Columbia Univ., New York 55-60; Dir. Central Inst. of Islamic Research, Karachi 60-62; Vice-Chancellor Univ. of Karachi 62-; Star of Pakistan 64.

Publs. *The Administration of the Sultanate of Delhi* 41, *The Pakistani Way of Life* 56, *The Muslim Community in the Indo-Pakistan Sub-Continent* 62, *The Struggle for Pakistan* 65, *The Administration of the Moghul Empire* 67. Zeba Manzar, 1 Sharafabad, Shahid-i-Millat Road, Karachi 5, Pakistan.

Telephone: 41339.

Qvist, Søren Peter; Danish editor; b. 23 Dec. 1882. Began career as journalist 02; Editor-in-Chief *Fyns Tidende* 22-62; mem. Lower House, Danish Parl. 20-22; Chair. Radio News Cttee. of Danish Press; fmr. Chair. Liberal Party; Dir. Fyens Landmandsbank and Fyens Konservesfabrik; Commdr. Order of Dannebrog (Denmark); Knight of Order of North Star (Sweden). Korsdalsgaard, Børkop, Denmark.

R

Rabaeus, Bengt, M.A.; Swedish international official; b. 4 May 1917; ed. Kungliga Universitet i Uppsala.
Entered Foreign Service 46, served Prague, Paris, Swedish Del. to UN (New York); Counsellor, Swedish Del. to OEEC, Paris 57-59; Head of Political Div., Foreign Office, Stockholm 59-61; First Counsellor, Paris 61-62; Amb. to Algeria 63-66; Deputy Sec.-Gen. European Free Trade Asscn. (EFTA) 66-.
EFTA Secretariat, 35 Avenue de Budé, 1211 Geneva 12; Home: 89 route de Chêne, Geneva, Switzerland.
Telephone: 34-90-00 (Office); 36-35-76 (Home).

Rabemananjara, Jacques; Madagascan politician; b. 23 June 1913.
Joined French Admin. 39; in France during Second World War, became known as novelist and poet; Deputy for Madagascar in French Nat. Assembly 46; later Sec.-Gen. Democratic Movement for Malagasy Renovation (M.D.R.M.); detained in France after Madagascar uprising 47; Minister of Econ. Affairs, Madagascar 60-65, of Agric., Land and Food 65-67, of Foreign Affairs 67-; mem. Exec. Cttee. Soc. Africaine de Culture.
Publs. include Plays: *Les Dieux Malgaches* 47, *Les Boutriers de l'Aurore* 57 *Agape des Dieux-Tritiva* 62; poems: *Sur les Marches du Soir* 42, *Antsa* 56.
Ministry of Foreign Affairs, Tananarive, Madagascar.

Rabi, Isidor Isaac, B.CHEM., PH.D.; American professor of physics; b. 29 July 1898; ed. Cornell and Columbia Univs.
Tutor in Physics Coll. City of N.Y. 24-27; Barnard Fellow Columbia 27-28; Int. Educ. Board Fellow Munich, Copenhagen, Hamburg, Leipzig, and Zürich 28-29; Ernest Kempton Adams Fellow 35; Lecturer Physics Columbia Univ. 29-30; Asst. Prof. Colombia Univ. 30-35, Assoc. Prof. 35-37, Prof. 37-; Higgins Prof. of Physics 51-64; Exec. Officer Dept. of Physics 45-49; Scientific Advisory Cttee. Ballistic Research Laboratory Aberdeen 39-65; Assoc. Dir. Radiation Laboratory M.I.T. 40-45; Chair. Vacuum Tube Devt. Cttee. (NDRC) 42-45; Consultant Los Alamos 43-45, 56-; Council American Physical Soc. 45-, Pres. 50-51; Council Nat. Acad. 46-49; Consultant Joint Research and Devt. Board 46-48; Gen. Advisory Cttee. Atomic Energy Comm. 46-56, Chair. 52-56, Consultant 56-; Trustee, Associated Universities, Inc. 46-, Pres. 61-62, Chair. 62-63; Prize, American Asscn. for Advancement of Sciences 39; Elliot Cresson Medal, Franklin Inst. 42; Nobel Prize in Physics 44; Barnard Medal 60; Editor Board *Physical Review* 35-38; mem. American Acad. of Sciences, Nat. Acad. 40-; del. UNESCO Conf. 50; Vice-Pres. Int. Conf. on the Peaceful Uses of Atomic Energy 55-58; mem. Presidential Science Advisory Cttee., N.A.T.O. Science Advisory Cttee., I.A.E.A. Scientific Advisory Cttee., Adviser to UN Science Cttee.; Atoms for Peace Award (U.S.) 67; Hon. D.Sc. Princeton, Harvard, Birmingham, Clark, Technion, Brandeis and Coimbra Univs., and Adelphi and Franklin Marshall Colls., LL.D. Dropsie Coll., Sc.D. Williams Coll., L.H.D. Hebrew Union Coll. and Oklahoma City Univ., Litt.D. Jewish Theological Seminary of America.
Work in the field of nuclear physics, quantum mechanics, and molecular beams.
Publ. *My Life and Times as a Physicist* 60, *Man and Science* 68.
450 Riverside Drive, New York 27, N.Y., U.S.A.
Telephone: 662-3129.

Rabibhadana, H.S.H. Prince Plerng Nobadol; Thai lawyer and diplomatist; b. 30 Dec. 1906; ed. Assumption Coll., and Debsirindr School, Bangkok, and Middle Temple, London.

Called to English bar 29; Judge, Ministry of Justice, Thailand 29-42; private legal practice 42-53; Chief, Int. Agreement Div., Ministry of Foreign Affairs 53-56; First Sec. Wash. 56-60; Dir.-Gen. Treaty and Legal Dept. Ministry of Foreign Affairs 60-63; Ambassador to U.K. 63-68; Commdr. Crown of Thailand; other decorations.
c/o Ministry of Foreign Affairs, Bangkok, Thailand.

Rabin, Maj.-Gen. Itzhak; Israeli army officer and diplomatist; b. 1922; ed. Agricultural School, Kfar Tabor, and Staff Coll., England.
Palmach commands 43-48, including War of Independence; represented Israel Defence Forces (I.D.F.) at Rhodes armistice negotiations; fmr. Head of Training Dept. I.D.F.; C.-in-C. Northern Command 56-59; Head, Manpower Branch 59-60; Deputy Chief of Staff and Head, Gen. Staff Branch 60-64, Chief of Staff I.D.F. 64-68; Amb. to U.S. Jan. 68-; Dr. Phil., Univ. of Jerusalem 67.
Israeli Embassy, 1621 22nd Avenue, N.W., Washington, D.C., U.S.A.

Rabinowitch, Eugene, PH.D.; Russian-born American chemist; b. 27 April 1901; ed. Berlin Univ.
Research Assoc. Göttingen Univ. 29-33, Univ. Coll. London 34-38, Massachusetts Inst. of Technology 39-44, Manhattan Project 44-46; Research Prof. Illinois Univ. 47-; Editor *Bulletin of Atomic Scientists*; mem. American Chemical Soc., American Physical Soc., American Biophysical Soc., etc.; Kalinga Prize 66.
Publs. *Rare Gases* 28, *The Periodic System* 30, *Photosynthesis*, Vol. I 46, Vol. II 1 51, Vol. II 2 58, *Dawn of a New Age* 63.
University of Illinois, Urbana, Ill., U.S.A.

Raborn, Vice-Admiral William Francis, Jr.; American naval officer (retd.); b. 8 June 1905; ed. U.S. Naval Acad.
Ensign U.S. Navy 28; Dep. Dir. Guided Missile Div., Office Chief Naval Operations 52-54; Commanding Officer U.S.S. *Bennington* 54-55; Asst. Chief Staff Commdr. Atlantic Fleet 55; Dir. Special Projects, Fleet Ballistic Missile System (*Polaris*) 55-62; Dep. Chief of Naval Operations (Devt.) 62-63; Vice-Pres. Program Management Aerojet Gen. Corpn. 63-65; Vice-Pres. Gen. Rep. Aerojet Gen. Corpn. 66-.
Office: 1120 Connecticut Avenue, N.W., Washington, D.C. 20036; Home: 1606 Crestwood Lane, McLean, Virginia 22101, U.S.A.
Telephone: 202-337-5800, Extension 209 or 210 (Office).

Rabotnov, Yury Nikolaevich; Soviet mechanical engineer; b. 1914; ed. Moscow Univ.
Instructor, Moscow Inst. of Power Eng. 35-46; Head, Strength Laboratory, Inst. of Mechanics, U.S.S.R. Acad. of Sciences 46-58; Prof. Moscow Univ. 47-; corresp. mem. U.S.S.R. Acad. of Sciences 53-58, mem. 58-; Deputy Dir. Inst. of Hydrodynamics, Siberian Dept., U.S.S.R. Acad. of Sciences 58-; Chief Editor *Journal of Applied Mechanics and Technical Physics* 58-65; at Moscow State Univ. 65-.
Publs. *The Local Stability of Shells* 46, *The Equilibrium of an Elastic Medium with After-effects* 48, *The Technical Theory of Approximation of Elasto-Plastic Shells* 51, *Some Problems of Theory of Creep* 48, *Modelling of Creep* 61, *Unclassified Problems of Theory of Shells* 64, *Symmetric Problems of Creep of Circular Cylindrical Shells* 64.
Moscow State University, Moscow, Lenin Hills, U.S.S.R.

Rad, Gerhard von, D.THEOL.; German theologian; b. 21 Oct. 1901; ed. Gymnasium Nürnberg, Gymnasium Coburg, Friedrich-Alexander-Universität zu Erlangen-Nürnberg and Eberhard-Karls-Universität, Tübingen. Privat Dozent, Leipzig 30; Prof., Friedrich-Schiller-Universität, Jena 34-45, Georg-August-Universität zu Göttingen 45-50, Prof. of Old Testament Studies, Ruprecht-Karl-Universität, Heidelberg 50-; mem. Akad. der Wissenschaften, Heidelberg 55-; Orden Pour le Mérite.
Publs. include: *Gesammelte Studien zum Alten Testament* 58, *Das Erste Buch Mose* (6th edn.) 61, *Theologie des Alten Testaments*, Vol. I (4th edn.) 62, Vol. II (4th edn.) 65, *Das fünfte Buch Mose* 64.
Amselgasse 15 (69), Heidelberg, German Federal Republic.

Radcliffe, 1st Viscount, cr. 62, of Hampton Lucy in the County of Warwick; **Cyril John Radcliffe,** P.C., G.B.E., Q.C.; British lawyer; b. 30 March 1899; ed. Haileybury and New Coll., Oxford.
Fellow of All Souls' Coll. Oxford 22-37; called to Bar Inner Temple 24; K.C. 35; Asst. Dir.-Gen. Press and Censorship Bureau 40; Controller Press and Censorship Div., Ministry of Information 41, Deputy Dir.-Gen. of Ministry 41, Dir.-Gen. 41-45; Vice-Chair. Gen. Council of the Bar 46-49; Chair. Punjab and Bengal Boundary Comm. 47; Bencher Inner Temple 43; Lord of Appeal in Ordinary 49-64; Chair. Royal Comm. on Taxation of Profits and Income 52-55; Chair. B.B.C. Gen. Advisory Council 52-55; Constitutional Commr. for Cyprus 56; Chair. Treasury Cttee. on Monetary and Credit Policy 57-59; Chair. Inquiry into Security Services 61; Chair. Vassall Tribunal 62; Chair. School of Oriental and African Studies 59-; Reith Lecturer, B.B.C. 51, Montague Burton Lecturer, Glasgow Univ. 53; Lloyd Roberts Lecturer, Royal Soc. of Medicine 55; Rede Lecturer, Cambridge Univ. 61; Romanes Lecturer, Oxford Univ. 62; Oration at London School of Econs. 65; Hon. Fellow New Coll., Oxford 49; Trustee, British Museum, Chair. of Trustees 63-68; Chair. of Trustees British Commonwealth Int. News Agency 59-; Chancellor, Univ. of Warwick 65-; mem. Court of Univ. of London 58-63; Hon. LL.D. (Univs. of Wales, Manchester and Sussex, St. Andrews Univ., Northwestern Univ., Ill.); Hon. D.C.L. (Oxford Univ.); Life Trustee Shakespeare Birthplace Trust, Sir John Soane's Museum; Gov. Royal Shakespeare Theatre.
Publs. *The Problem of Power, The Law and its Compass* 61, *Censors* 61, *Mounstuart Elphinstone* 62.
5 Campden Hill Gate, London, W.8; and Hampton Lucy House, Warwick, England.

Radford, Courtenay Arthur Ralegh, M.A., D.LITT., F.S.A., F.B.A., F.R.HIST.S.; British archaeologist; b. 7 Nov. 1900; ed. St. George's School, Harpenden and Exeter Coll., Oxford.
Inspector of Ancient Monuments for Wales and Monmouthshire under Office of Works 29-34; Dir. British School of Rome 36-40; corresp. mem. German Archæological Inst.; mem. Royal Comm. on Ancient Monuments in Wales and Monmouthshire 35-46; mem. Royal Comm. on Historical Monuments in England 54; Pres. Prehistoric Society 54-58, Royal Archaeological Inst. 60-63.
Culmcott, Uffculme, Devon, England.
Telephone: Craddock 251.

Radhakrishnan, Sir Sarvepalli, Kt., M.A., D.LITT., LITT.D., D.C.L., LL.D., F.B.A.; Indian leader, educationist and philosopher; b. 5 Sept. 1888; ed. Madras Christian Coll.
Upton Lecturer Manchester Coll. Oxford 26; Hibbert Lecturer 29-30; Haskell Lecturer in Comparative Religion Chicago Univ. 26; Vice-Chancellor Andhra Univ. Waltair 31-36; Spalding Prof. of Eastern Religions and Ethics Oxford Univ. 36-52; Vice-Chancellor

Benares Hindu Univ. 39-48; mem. Int. Cttee. of Intellectual Co-operation of L.N. 31-39; Leader Indian del. UNESCO 46-47; Chair. Exec. Board UNESCO 47, Pres. 52; Chair. Univ. Education Comm. 48-49; Ambassador to U.S.S.R. 49-52; Vice-Pres. Republic of India 52-62, Pres. 62-May 67; Chancellor Delhi Univ. 53-62; Chair. Indian P.E.N., Vice-Pres. Int. P.E.N.; Pres. and First Fellow, Sahitya Akademi; Fed. German Order of Merit; Goethe Medal 59; Hon. O.M.; Hon. Fellow British Acad., All Souls Coll., Oxford.
Publs. *The Philosophy of Rabindranath Tagore* 18, *The Reign of Religion in Contemporary Philosophy* 20, *The Philosophy of the Upanishads* 24, 35, *Indian Philosophy* (2 vols.), 23, 26, *The Hindu View of Life* 27, *An Idealist View of Life* 32, *East and West in Religion* 33; Editor *Contemporary Indian Philosophy* 36, *Mahatma Gandhi* 39; *Eastern Religions and Western Thought* 39, *India and China* 44, *Education, Politics and War* 44, *Religion and Society* 47, *Is This Peace?* 45, *Bhagavadgita* 48, *Dhammapada* 50, *The Principal Upanishads* 53, *East and West* 56, *Recovery of Faith* 56, *Brahma Sutra* 60, *Fellowship of the Spirit* 62, *Religion in a Changing World* 67.
"Girija," 30 Edward Elliot Road, Mylapore, Madras, India.

Radliński, Antoni; Polish chemical engineer and politician; b. 10; ed. Lwów Polytechnic School.
Assistant, Lwów Univ. until 35; chemical industry 35-39, 45-56; Minister of Chemical Industry 57-; mem. Polish Workers' Party 45-48, Polish United Workers' Party 48-.
4 Wspólna Street, Warsaw 63, Poland.

Rado, Sandor, M.D., DR.POL.; American (b. Hungarian) psychiatrist; b. 8 Jan. 1890; ed. Budapest, Berlin, Vienna and Bonn. Univs.
Asst. Clinic of Psychiatry in Budapest 16-19; Lecturer Psychoanalytical Inst. Berlin, 22-31; Editor *Internationale Zeitschrift für Psychoanalyse* and *Imago* 25-31; Educational Dir. New York Psychoanalytical Inst. 31-41; Clinical Prof. of Psychiatry and Dir. Psychoanalytic Clinic for Training and Research, Dept. of Psychiatry, Coll. of Physicians and Surgeons, Columbia Univ. 44-55; Prof. of Psychiatry, N.Y. State Univ. 56-58; Pres. and Dean, N.Y. School of Psychiatry 58-67; Consulting Psychoanalyst, Manhattan State Hospital; Visiting Prof. Tulane Univ. School of Medicine; Consultant, Army Medical Center, Walter Reed Hospital, Washington 47-52.
25 East 86th Street, New York, N.Y. 10028, U.S.A.

Radok, Alfréd; Czechoslovak theatre and film director; b. 17 Dec. 1914; ed. Faculty of Philosophy, Charles Univ., Prague.
Imprisoned during Second World War; Dir. at various theatres in Prague and of Czechoslovak Films; Dir. at Prague Nat. Theatre 54, 66-; Artistic Dir. *Laterna Magica* (programme for Brussels Exhbn.) 58; later at Prague Municipal Theatres; directed plays *Swedish Match* (Chekhov), Vienna 65, *The Last Ones* (Gorky), Munich 65, *Donna Benarda's House* (Lorca), Berlin 67, *A Play About Love and Death* (Romain Rolland) 67, *Mr. Pimpian's Funny Adventures* (Children's musical); State Prize 59; Honoured Artist 64.
U nemocenské pojištovry 4, Prague 1, Czechoslovakia.
Telephone: 65518.

Radwan, Abbas; United Arab Republic (Egyptian) politician.
Minister of Interior, Exec. Council, Egyptian Region of United Arab Repub. 59; Minister of State, U.A.R. 62, of Local Govt. 63; Deputy Prime Minister for Local Admin. Services 64-65; mem. Supreme Exec. Cttee. Arab Socialist Union 65-67.
c/o Arab Socialist Union, Cairo, United Arab Republic.

Radwan, Ahmed Fathi; United Arab Republic (Egyptian) diplomatist.
Diplomatic service 40-; Minister of Information 52, later Minister of Nat. Directions; Minister of State 52-54; Minister of Communications 54-56, of Nat. Guidance 56-58; U.A.R. Amb. to Jordan 59-61, to Tunisia 61-.
Embassy of the United Arab Republic, 88 Avenue Mohamed V, Tunis, Tunisia.

Radzinowicz, Leon, M.A., LL.D.; Polish-born British lawyer and penologist; b. 15 Aug. 1906; ed. Cracow, Geneva, Paris and Rome Univs.
Lecturer, Geneva Univ. 28-31; reported on Belgian penal system 30; Lecturer, Warsaw Free Univ. 32-36, Asst. Prof. 36-39; visited England to report on English penal system for Polish Ministry of Justice 38; Asst. Dir. of Research, Cambridge Univ. 46-49, Fellow of Trinity Coll. 48-, Dir. Dept. of Criminal Science 49-59, Wolfson Prof. and Dir. of Inst. of Criminology 59-; mem. Gov. Body, Int. Soc. for Social Defence; Vice-Pres. Assoc. Int. de Droit Pénal, Paris 47-; Head UN Social Defence Section 47-48; mem. Royal Comm. on Capital Punishment 49-53, Home Office Advisory Council on Treatment of Offenders 50-, Royal Comm. on English Penal System 64-; First Pres. British Acad. of Forensic Sciences; Chair. Scientific Council, European Problems of Crime, Council of Europe 63-; Assoc. Fellow, Silliman Coll., Yale Univ. 66-; Adjunct Prof. of Law and Criminology, Columbia Law School 66-; J. B. Ames Prize and Medal, Harvard Law School 50; Chevalier, Ordre de Léopold 30, Coronation Medal 53; Walter E. Meyer Visiting Research Fellow, Yale Law School 62-63.
Publs. Numerous books and articles in Polish, French, Italian and English on Criminology and Penology; *History of English Criminal Law and Its Administration from 1750* Vol. I 48, Vols. II and III 56, Vol. IV 68; *In Search of Criminology* 61, *The Need for Criminology* 65, *Ideology and Crime* 66, Editor *Cambridge Studies in Criminology* (twenty-one vols.).
21 Cranmer Road, Cambridge, England.

Rafael, Gideon; Israeli diplomatist; b. Germany 5 March 1913; ed. Univ. of Berlin.
Immigrated 34; mem. Kibbutz 34-43; active in Haganah and war services 39-42; Jewish Agency, Political Dept. 43; in charge of preparation of Jewish case for Jewish Agency, Political Dept., Nuremberg War Crimes Trial 45-46; mem. of Jewish Agency Comm. to Anglo-American Comm. of Enquiry 46, and of Jewish Agency mission to UN Special Comm. for Palestine 47; mem. Israel Perm. Del. to UN 51-52; alt. rep. to UN 53; rep. at UN Gen. Assemblies 47-66; Counsellor in charge of Middle East and UN Affairs, Ministry for Foreign Affairs 53-57; Amb. to Belgium and Luxembourg 57-60, to the European Econ. Community 59; Deputy Dir.-Gen. Ministry of Foreign Affairs 60; Head of Israel Del. Int. Conf. Law of the Sea, Geneva 60; Deputy Dir.-Gen. Ministry for Foreign Affairs 60-65; Perm. Rep. to UN, Geneva 65-66; Special Amb. and Adviser to Foreign Minister May 66-67; Perm. Rep. of Israel to UN 67; Dir.-Gen., Ministry for Foreign Affairs 67-.
Kiryath Yovel, Jerusalem, Israel.

Ragab, Major-Gen. Hassan F., B.SC.; United Arab Republic (Egyptian) army officer and diplomatist; b. 11; ed. Cairo Univ., Ecole Supérieure d'Electricité, Paris, and Egyptian Staff Coll., Cairo.
Electrical Engineer, Ramleh Electric Railway, Alexandria 35-39; joined Egyptian Army 39, Gen. Staff Coll., Cairo 43; Dir. Topographic Service, G.H.Q., Egyptian Army 44; Military Attaché, Washington 45; Under-Sec. of State for Armament Factories, Ministry of War 52; Head, Military Mission to Turkey 53, Economic Mission to U.S.S.R. 54; Ambassador to China 56-58; Ambassador for U.A.R. in China 58-59, to Italy 59-61, to Yugoslavia 61-Mar. 62; Ministry of Foreign Affairs,

Cairo 62-; Grand Order of Republic of Egypt, Order of the Nile, Order of Bravery, Order of Merit (U.S.A.).
Publs. *Diesel Engines* 38, *Ragab Sun Compass* 44, *Electrification of Helwan Line* 45, *Establishment of National Planning Board and 5-Year Plan for Egypt* 55.
Ministry of Foreign Affairs, Cairo, U.A.R.

Ragghianti, Carlo Ludovico, D.LITT.; Italian art historian and critic; b. 18 March 1910; ed. Univ. of Pisa.
Founder and Dir. *La Critica d'Arte* 35-; Prof. of History of Medieval and Modern Art, Univ. of Pisa 39-; Dir. Univ. Inst. of History of Art; Founder and Dir. Studio Italiano di Storia dell' Arte, Florence 45-; Under-Sec. of State for Educ. and the Fine Arts 45; Nat. Adviser 46; mem. various Int. Acads.
Publs. include *Le Vite del Vasari* 43-47, *Impressionismo* 44, *Commenti di critica d'arte* 45, *Miscellanea di critica d'arte* 46, *Ponte a Santa Trinità* 48, *Profilo della critica d'arte* 48, *Cinema arte figurativa* 51, *L'arte e la critica* 51, *La Pittura fiorentina del Dugento* 52, *Una Lotta nel suo corso* 52, *Frank Lloyd Wright* 52, *Il mito dell'impressionismo* 52, *Disegno della liberazione italiana* 54, *Il pungolo dell'arte* 56, *Manzu* 56, *Mondrian e l'arte del XX secolo* 62, *Pittori di Pompei* 63, *Michelangelo* 65.
Villa La Costa, Florence, Italy.

Raghavan, Venkatarama, M.A., PH.D.; Indian Sanskrit scholar; b. 22 Aug. 1908; ed. Tiruvarur High School and Madras Univ.
Superintendent Sarasvati Mahal Manuscript Library, Tanjore 30; successively Research Scholar, Research Asst., Lecturer, Reader, Prof. and Head of Dept., Madras Univ. Dept. of Sanskrit 31-; mem. Govt. of India Sanskrit Comm. and Cen. Sanskrit Board, Indian Acad. of Letters, Fellow, Acad. of Music, Dance and Drama; Hon. corresp. mem. Ecole Française d'Extrème Orient, Austrian Acad. of Sciences; Pres. All-India Oriental Conf.; Kane Gold Medal (Bombay Asiatic Soc.) 53; awarded title of "Kavikokila" by Sankaracharya 53; "Padma-bhushan" by Govt. of India 63; Indian Acad. of Letters, Award for best book on Sanskrit research 66; Editor *Journal of Oriental Research, Madras Music Academy Journal, Sanskrita-Pratibha, Madras University Sanskrit Series.*
Publs. include: English: *Some Concepts of Alankara Sastra* 42, *Bhoja's Sringara Prakasa* 43, *New Catalogus Catalogorum* 49, *The Indian Heritage, Sanskrit and Allied Indological Studies in Europe, Yantras or Mechanical Contrivances in Ancient India* 56; Tamil: *Varalakshmivratam* (short stories) 50, *Bharata Natya* 59, *Kadaikkadal* 59, *Nataka Lakshanaratnakosa* 61; Patel Lectures: *The Great Integrators—Saint-Singers of India* 66; Sanskrit: *Rasalila, Kamasuddhi, Manunitichola, Davabandi Varadaraja, Prekshanakatrayi, Vimukti, Valmiki pratibha, Nativpuja* (poems and plays).
Department of Sanskrit, University of Madras, Madras 5; Home: 7 Sritrishnapuram Street, Royapettah, Madras 14, India.
Telephone: 85091 (Home).

Raghuramaiah, Kotha, M.A., LL.B., BARR.-AT-LAW; Indian lawyer and politician; b. 12; ed. Lucknow Univ. and the Middle Temple.
Legal practice 37-41; Provincial Judicial Service 41-51; mem. Lok Sabha 52-; Dep. Minister of Defence 57-62; Minister of State in the Ministry of Defence 62-63; Minister of Defence Production 62-64, of Supply 64-65, of Technical Devt., Supply and Social Security 65-67; Minister of State for Law 67, Minister of State in Ministry of Petroleum and Chemicals and of Social Welfare Sept. 67-; mem. Railway Corruption Enquiry Cttee. 54; Chair. Petitions Cttee., Lok Sabha 55-57; Congress Party.
14 Asoka Road, New Delhi, India; Ministry of Petroleum and Chemicals, New Delhi, India.

Rahi, Michel, LL.D.; United Arab Republic international civil servant; b. 22 Nov. 1912; ed. Jesuit Coll., Cairo, Cairo Univ., Univ. de Paris à la Sorbonne, and Inst. des Hautes Etudes Internationales, Paris.
On admin. staff, Egyptian Postal Admin. 34-50; First Sec. Int. Bureau, Universal Postal Union (UPU) 50-56, Counsellor, Int. Bureau, UPU 56-64, Asst. Dir.-Gen. Int. Bureau, UPU 64-66, Dir.-Gen. 66-.
Gantrischstrasse 43, 3000 Berne, Switzerland.

Rahimtoola, Sir Fazal Ibrahim, Kt., C.I.E., J.P.; Indian industrialist; b. 21 Oct. 1895; ed. St. Xavier's High School and Coll., Bombay, and Poona Law Coll.
Chairman Bharat Line Ltd.; Dir. Ahmedabad Advance Mills Ltd., Tata Power Co. Ltd., Tata Iron and Steel Co. Ltd., Swadeshi Mills Ltd., Overseas Communications Service (Government of India), New Swadeshi Sugar Mills Ltd., Sultania Cotton Mfg. Co. Ltd., Fazalbhai Ibrahim and Co. Prvt. Ltd.; mem. Central Legislative Assembly 25-30, Legislative Assembly 37, Bombay Legislative Council 48, Indian Tariff Board 30, Acting Pres. 32, Pres. 35; Sheriff of Bombay 50; Chair. Indian Fisheries Cttee. and Deep-Sea Fisheries Station, Govt. of India; Dir. Nat. War Front; mem. War Risk Insurance Claims Cttee. of Govt. of India, Central Food Council and its Standing Cttee., Post-War Reconstruction Cttee. for Agricultural Research, Govt. Price-Fixation Cttee. (Planning Dept.), All-Indian Council for Technical Educ., UNESCO Nat. Comm. for India and its Science Sub-Comm., East India Asscn., London, etc.; Del. to UNESCO Conf., Florence 50; Econ. Adviser to Junagadh State (Saurashtra); Hon. Consul-Gen. for Thailand in Bombay; F.R.S.A.
Ismail Building, 381 Dr. Dadabhoy Naoroji Road, Fort, Bombay 1, B.R., India.
Telephone: 255046 (Office); 364031 (Home).

Rahimtoola, Habib Ibrahim, B.A., LL.B., F.R.P.S.; Pakistani diplomatist and politician; b. 10 March 1912; ed. St. Xavier's School and Coll., and Government Law Coll., Bombay.
Was Dir. over 15 joint stock companies in India; Pres. Fed. of Muslim Chambers of Commerce and Industry, New Delhi 47-48; Bombay Provincial Muslim Chamber of Commerce 44-47; Bombay Provincial Muslim League Parl. Bd. for Local Bodies 45-47; Del. Prime Ministers' Confs. London 48, 49, 51, Commonwealth Conf., S.E. Asia, London 50, Afro-Asian Conf. Bandung 55; Leader Pakistan Trade Del. to British East Africa 56; High Commr. for Pakistan in Great Britain 47-52; Ambassador to France 52-53; Gov. Sind 53, Punjab 54; Minister for Commerce, Central Govt. 54-55, for Commerce and Industries 55-56; Chair. Karachi Development Authority 58-60, Water Co-ordination Council 58-60, Pakistan Govt. Shipping Rates Advisory Bd. 59-, Bandenawaz Ltd., Pakistan Oxygen Ltd., United Bank Ltd., Pakistan Chemicals Ltd., Int. Industries Ltd., Pakistan Cables Ltd., Chambon (Pakistan) Ltd., Pakistan-Japan Cultural Asscn., Royal Commonwealth Soc., Pakistan; Pakistan-Ceylon Asscn., Photographic Soc. of Pakistan.
"Kulib", B/59, K.D.A. No. 1, Habib I. Rahimtoola Road, Karachi-8, Pakistan.

Rahman, Habibur; Pakistani diplomatist; b. 09; ed. Univs. of Dacca and Calcutta.
Called to the Bar 32; Public Prosecutor 40-50; Dir. Bengal Co-operative Bank 32-41; Chair. Co-operative Bank, Bogra 34-38; Dir. Reserve Bank of India, Eastern Area, Calcutta 38-47; Adviser Pakistan del. to UN Economic and Social Council 50; Pres. District Muslim League and mem. Working Cttee. East Pakistan Muslim League 48-50; Minister to Italy 50-53; High Commr. in Australia and New Zealand 53-56; Ambassador to Belgium 56-58; Minister for Education, Information and Broadcasting and Minority Affairs 58-60,

of Educ. 60-61; Ambassador to Switzerland, Austria, Yugoslavia and the Vatican 62-64; mem. Nat. Assembly 63-; Leader Pakistan del. to ILO conf., to Vienna Consular Relations Convention 63; Chair. Tripartite Int. Labour Org. Conf. on food products and drink industry 63.
Satani House, Bogra, East Pakistan.

Rahman, Shaikh Abdur, B.A., M.A.; Pakistani judge; b. 4 June 1903; ed. Islamia Coll. Lahore, Govt. Coll. Lahore, and Exeter Coll., Oxford.
Joined Indian Civil Service as Asst. Commr. 28, later District and Sessions Judge and Legal Remembrancer, Punjab; Acting Judge, Lahore High Court 46; mem. Bengal Boundary Comm. 47; Custodian Evacuee Property 48; Additional Judge, Lahore High Court 48, Permanent Judge 48; Vice-Chancellor Punjab Univ. 50; Acting Chief Justice, Lahore High Court 54, Chief Justice 54-55; Permanent Chief Justice of Western Pakistan High Court 55-58; Judge, Supreme Court of Pakistan 58-, Chief Justice, Supreme Court of Pakistan 68-; Chair. Central Urdu Devt. Board, Lahore 64-; Pres. Pakistan Art Council; Hon. LL.D. (Cairo Univ., Punjab Univ.).
Publs. *Tarjuman-i-Asrar* (Urdu translation), *Hadis-i Dil* (Speeches and lectures in Urdu) 63, *Safar* (Urdu poetry) 64.
65 Gulberg, Lahore, West Pakistan.
Telephone: 80109.

Rahman, Tunku Abdul (*see* Abdul Rahman, Tunku).

Raikin, Arkady Isaakovich; Soviet actor-producer; b. 1911; ed. Leningrad Ostrovsky Dramatic Inst.
Actor Leningrad Komsomol Theatre 35-37; Leningrad Novy Theatre 37-39; Founded Leningrad Miniature Theatre 39; People's Artist of the R.S.F.S.R.; Order of Patriotic War.
Leningrad State Theatre of Miniatures, Leningrad, U.S.S.R.

Raimondi, Most Rev. Luigi, J.C.D.; Vatican diplomatist; b. 25 Oct. 1912; ed. Diocesan Seminary, Acqui, Italy.
Pontificium Institutum Utriusque Juris S. Appollinaris, Rome, and Pontificia Accademia Ecclesiastica, Rome.
Ordained priest 36; Nunciature of Guatemala 38-42; Apostolic Delegation, Washington 42-49; Apostolic Internunciature, New Delhi 49-53; Titular Archbishop of Tarsus 54-; Apostolic Nuncio to Haiti 54-57; Apostolic Del. to Mexico 57-67, to U.S.A. 67-.
3339 Massachusetts Avenue, N.W., Washington, D.C., U.S.A.

Rain, Pierre; French university professor and librarian; b. 1 Jan. 1881.
Dir. *Revue des Etudes Historiques* 10-20; Vice-Pres. later Pres., Société des Etudes Historiques 21, 22, and 47-48, 63; Sec.-Gen. Bibliothèque et Musée de la Guerre 19; Dir. Bibliothèque Ecole des Sciences Politiques 19-49; Pres. Société d'Histoire de la III République 50-51; Prof. of Diplomatic History, Institut d'Etudes Politiques 29-62; Grand Prix Gobert de l'Académie Française 52; Officier Légion d'Honneur.
Publs. *L'Europe et la Restauration des Bourbons* 08, *Le Tsar idéologue: Alexandre I* 13, *La Révolution, l'Empire, la Restauration* (in *Histoire générale des peuples*) 23, *Chronique des Châteaux de la Loire* 23, *L'Europe de Versailles (1919-39)* 45, *La diplomatie française d'Henri IV à Vergennes* 45, *L'organisation de la paix, des origines à l'O.N.U.* 46, *La diplomatie révolutionnaire* 49; collaborated in: *La Revue des Deux Mondes, la Revue politique et parlementaire, la Revue d'histoire diplomatique,* etc.
43 rue de l'Université, Paris 7e, France.

Raine, Kathleen Jessie (Mrs. Charles Madge), M.A., British poet; b. 08; ed. Girton Coll., Cambridge.
Fellow, Girton Coll., Cambridge 56-; various English

and American poetry prizes and awards; Blake scholar.
Publs. *Stone and Flower* 43, *Living in Time* 46, *Collected
Poems* 46, *The Pythoness* 49, *The Year One* 52, *Collected
Poems* 56, *Blake and Traditional Mythology* 62, *The
Hollow Hill* 65, *Defending Ancient Springs* 67.
47 Paultons Square, London, S.W.3; and Girton College,
Cambridge, England.

**Rainier III, His Serene Highness Prince, Louis Henri
Maxence Bertrand;** Prince of Monaco; b. 31 May 1923;
ed. Summerfields School, Hastings (England), Mont-
pellier Univ., and Ecole Libre des Sciences Politiques,
Paris.
Hereditary Prince of Monaco 44; succeeded his grand-
father Prince Louis II 49; founded Monaco Red Cross
48, American Friends of Monaco 52, Prix Rainier 55;
Grand Master Ordre de St. Charles de Monaco, Grand
Cross Légion d'Honneur, Belgian, Swedish, Greek,
Lebanese, Italian, Netherlands and San Marino orders;
served in French army as Lieut. and Col. 44-45; married
Grace Kelly 56.
Palais de Monaco, Monte Carlo, Principality of Monaco.

Rais, Mohsen; Iranian diplomatist; b. 96; ed. Iran
and Univ. of Geneva.
Chargé d'Affaires, Paris 31; Dir. Dept. of L.N. and
Treaties, Teheran; Minister to Germany and Nether-
lands 35-38; Political Dir.-Gen., Ministry for Foreign
Affairs and Acting Minister of Foreign Affairs 38;
Minister to Balkan countries 39, to French Govt.,
Vichy 41; Minister of Posts, Telegraphs and Telephones
42; Minister to Iraq 43-47; Ambassador to Great Britain
47-50; Minister of Foreign Affairs 50; Ambassador to
France 58; Gov.-Gen. of Azerbaijan 58-60; Ambassador
to Netherlands 60-61, to U.K. 61-62, to France 62-63;
Senator 64-; Gov.-Gen. of Teheran 64-.
The Senate, Teheran, Iran.

Raiser, Ludwig, D.IUR.; German university professor;
b. 27 Oct. 1904; ed. Eberhard-Ludwigs-Gymnasium,
Stuttgart, and Univs. of Munich, Geneva and Berlin.
Member Management Board of insurance firm in
Magdeburg 37-43; Mil. Service 43-45; Prof. Univ. of
Göttingen 45-51, Rector, Univ. of Göttingen 48-50;
Pres. German Research Asscn., Bad Godesberg 51-55;
Prof. of Urban Trade and Business Law, Univ. of
Tübingen 55-; mem. German Science Council 58-65,
Chair. 61-65; mem. Synod Protestant Church; Grosses
Bundesverdienstkreuz mit Stern.
Publs. *Die Wirkungen der Wechselerklärungen im
Internationalen Privatrecht* 31, *Das Recht der Allge-
meinen Geschäftsbedingungen* 35, *Lehrbuch des Sachen-
rechts* (with M. Wolff) 10th edn. 57, *Die Universität im
Staat* 58, *Dingliche Anwartschaften* 61, *Das Bildungsziel
der heutigen Universität* 65, *Deutsche Hochschulprobleme
im Lichte amerikanischer Erfahrungen* 66, *Grundgesetz
und Privatrechtsordnung* 67.
Tübingen, Rappenberghalde 16, German Federal
Republic.

Raisman, Sir (Abraham) Jeremy, G.C.M.G., G.C.I.E.,
K.C.S.I., M.A.; British civil servant and banker; b. 19
March 1892; ed. Leeds High School and Univ., and
Pembroke Coll., Oxford.
Joined Indian Civil Service 16; Asst. Magistrate and
Under-Sec. Bihar and Orissa 16-22; Customs Dept.
Bombay and Calcutta 22-28; Commr. Income Tax,
Punjab and N.W. Frontier Province 28-31; Joint Sec.
Commerce Dept. Govt. of India 31-34; mem. Central
Board of Revenue 34; Dir. Reserve Bank of India 38;
Sec. 38-39; Finance mem. Govt. of India 39-45; Vice-
Pres. Gov.-Gen's Exec. Council; Hon. Fellow Pembroke
Coll. 45; mem. Industrial Advisory Panel 46-; Chair.
Fiscal Comm. for Fed. of Rhodesia and Nyasaland 52,
Nigeria Fiscal Comm. 57-58, Econ. and Fiscal Comm.
for East Africa 60-61; Dir. Lloyds Bank Ltd. 46, Vice-
Chair. 48-53, Deputy Chair. 53-; Lloyds and Scottish

Finance Ltd. 58-; Chair. Public Works Loans Board,
Commonwealth Trust Ltd.
Fieldhead, Shamley Green, nr. Guildford, Surrey,
England.

Raj, James S.; Indian international civil servant; b.
7 Nov. 1913; ed. Madras Christian Coll., and Univ.
Coll., London.
Former Lecturer in Econs., Univ. of Rangoon; Indian
civil service, Ministries of Food and Agriculture 42-53;
Chief of Multiple Currency Practices Div., Int. Monetary
Fund (IMF) 53-56; Alt. Exec. Dir. for India, IMF and
World Bank 56; Dir. Asian Dept., IMF 56-59; Con-
troller of Stock Exchanges, India 59-60; Deputy Gen.
Man. of Industrial Credit and Investment Corpn.
of India 60-64; Gen. Man. Nigerian Industrial Devt.
Bank, Lagos 64-66; Deputy Exec. Vice-Pres. Int.
Finance Corpn. 66-67, Vice-Pres. 67-.
International Finance Corporation, 1818 H Street,
N.W., Washington, D.C. 20433; Home: 2475 Virginia
Avenue, N.W., Washington, D.C. 20037, U.S.A.
Telephone: 337-7568 (Home); DU1-4122 (Office).

Rajagopalachari, Chakravarti; Indian politician; b.
78; ed. Central Coll., Bangalore, Presidency Coll. and
Law Coll., Madras.
Joined Bar 1900; practised at Salem, India 00-19;
joined Mahatma Gandhi's Satyagraha campaign and
non-co-operation movement 19-20; Gen. Sec. Indian
Nat. Congress 21-22 (mem. working cttee. 22-42,
46-47, 51-54); Sec. Prohibition League of India 30; Prime
Minister, Madras 37-39; associated with Indian freedom movement since 06; induced All-India Congress
Cttee. to offer co-operation in war effort 40; imprisoned
in connection with Indian freedom movement 5 times
21-42; assisted Mahatma Gandhi in Gandhi-Jinnah
talks 44; mem. Interim Govt. of India 46-47; Gov. West
Bengal Aug. 47-June 48; acted as Gov.-Gen. India
Nov. 47; Gov.-Gen. India June 48-Jan. 50; Minister
without Portfolio July-Dec. 50; Minister of Home Affairs
50-51; Chief Minister Govt. of Madras 52-54; Bharat-
Ratna Award 55; Founder, Swatantra Party 59; Chief
Writer for journal *Swarajya*.
Publs. *Fatal Cart and Other Stories, Prohibition Manual*
35, *Marcus Aurelius and Socrates in Tamil, Tamil
Essays, Mahabharat, Ramayama, Upanishads for Lay
Readers, Bhagavat Gita Selections and Notes, Hinduism,
Doctrine and Way of Life*; Edited Mahatma Gandhi's
Young India during Gandhi's incarceration.
Naoroji Road, Kilpauk, Madras 10, India.

Rajah, Arumugam Ponnu; Singapore lawyer and
diplomatist; b. 23 July 1911; ed. St. Paul's Inst.,
Serenban, Raffles Inst., Singapore, and Oxford Univ.,
England.
Singapore City Councillor 47-49, 51-57; mem. Singapore
Legislative Assembly 59-, Speaker 64-66; High Commr.
in U.K. 66-.
High Commission of Singapore, 8 Knightsbridge Court,
Sloane Street, London, S.W.1, England.

Rajakapse, Sir Lalita, Kt., Q.C., B.A., LL.D.; Ceylonese
lawyer, politician and diplomatist; b. 3 May 1900; ed.
St. Joseph's Coll., Colombo and University Coll.,
London.
Called to English Bar 24, Ceylon Bar 25; Lecturer,
Ceylon Law Coll. 26, Examiner 27; Commr. of Assize,
Supreme Court, Ceylon 47; mem., then Leader, Senate
47; Minister of Justice 47-53; Amb. to France 65-67;
High Commr. in U.K. 67-; Founded Revata Coll.,
Balapitiya 33; mem. Council of Legal Educ., Ceylon 39,
Councils, Univ. of Ceylon 46, and Vidyodaya and
Vidyalankara Univs. 59; mem. Ceylon Del. to Com-
monwealth Conf. on Foreign Affairs 50; Chair. Gal Oya
Comm. 56; Fellow Univ. Coll. London 68.
Ceylon High Commission, 13 Hyde Park Gardens,
London, W.2; 21 Addison Road, London, W.14, Eng-
land; and Lumbini, Horton Place, Colombo, Ceylon.

Rajapatirana, Don William, O.B.E.; Ceylonese banker; b. 01; ed. Ananda Coll., Colombo, London School of Economics and Columbia Univ.
Commissioner of Income Tax, Estate Duty and Stamps 48-50; Alt. Exec. Dir. Int. Monetary Fund 50-53; Dep. Gov. Cen. Bank of Ceylon 53-59, Gov. 59-67; Chair. Nat. Wage Policy Comm. 59-60.
206 Bullers Road, Colombo 7, Ceylon.

Rakhimov, Kasym Rakhimovich; Soviet politician; b. 1902; ed. Moscow Timiryazev Agricultural Acad.
Head of Agriculture Dept., Fergana Region 23-46; mem. C.P.S.U. 25-; Deputy Minister of Agriculture, Uzbek S.S.R. 30-32, Minister 39-50; Dir. cotton-growing state farms trust Uzbek S.S.R. 33-38; Deputy Minister for Cotton Growing of the U.S.S.R. 50-53; Vice-Chair. Uzbek S.S.R. Council of Ministers 54-56; Perm. Rep. of Uzbek S.S.R. Council of Ministers to U.S.S.R. Council of Ministers 56-.
Permanent Representation of the Uzbek S.S.R. Council of Ministers to the U.S.S.R. Council of Ministers, Kursovoi pereulok 17, Moscow, U.S.S.R.

Rakhmatov, Mirzo; Soviet politician and diplomatist; b. 1914; ed. All-Union Party School.
Komsomol work 34-40; mem. C.P.S.U. 40-; party work 40-48; Dep. Chair. Council of Ministers, Tadjik S.S.R. 51-56; Sec. Cen. Cttee. C.P. of Tadjik S.S.R. 56; Chair. Presidium of Supreme Soviet of Tadjik S.S.R. 56-63; Minister of Culture of Tadjik S.S.R. 63-66; Amb. to Yemen Arab Republic 66-; Deputy Chair. Presidium of Supreme Soviet of U.S.S.R. 58-64; mem. Central Auditing Comm. of C.P.S.U. 61; Deputy to Supreme Soviets of U.S.S.R. and Tadjik S.S.R.
U.S.S.R. Embassy, Sana'a, Yemen Arab Republic.

Rakotomalala, Louis; Malagasy diplomatist; b. 11 Sept. 1901.
Former Minister for Foreign Affairs; fmr. Dir., Madagascar Bank; Ambassador to U.S.A. and Perm. Rep. to UN 60-; mem. Malagasy (Madagascar) Academy.
[Died 1 July 1968].

Rallis, George (see Rhallys, George).

Ralph, Henry A. J.; American banker; b. 01; ed. Public Schools, Alameda, California, and American Inst. of Banking.
Vice-President and New York Rep., Bank of America NT & SA 45, Vice-Pres. and Manager, Bank of America, New York 50, Exec. Officer and Dir. 58; Vice-Pres. and Dir. Bamerical Int. Financial Corporation 61; Pres., Chief Exec. Officer and Dir., World Banking Corpn. 64-67; adviser in banking to U.S. and other orgs. 67-; numerous decorations.
Sulgrave Manor, Cable Beach, P.O. Box 100, Nassau, Bahamas.

Ram, Hon. Jagjivan, B.SC.; Indian politician; b. April 1908; ed. Benares Hindu Univ. and Calcutta Univ.
Gen. Sec. All-India Depressed Classes League until 36, Pres. 36-46; M.L.C., Bihar 36, Parl. Sec. 37-39; Sec. Bihar Provincial Congress Cttee. 40-46; Vice-Pres. Bihar Branch All India Trade Union Congress 40-46; imprisoned for political activities 40, released on medical grounds 43; Head, Del., I.L.O. Conf., Geneva, Chair. 33rd Session of Conf. 50; Chair. Preparatory Asian Regional Conf., I.L.O., New Delhi 47; Minister of Labour 46-52 (in Interim Govt. and first Indian Govt.), Minister of Communications 52-Dec. 56, 62-Aug. 63; Minister for Railways and Transport Dec. 56-April 57; Minister for Railways April 57-62, Minister of Transport 63-64; Minister of Labour and Employment Jan. 66-March 67, of Food and Agriculture March 67-; mem.

Working Cttee. and Central Parl. Board, All-India Congress Cttee. 48-.
Ministry of Food and Agriculture, New Delhi, India.

Rama, Carlos M.; Uruguayan writer, lawyer, professor and editor; b. 26 Oct. 1921; ed. Univs. of Montevideo and Paris.
Journalist 40-48; Exec. Sec. of Uruguayan Bar Asscn. 48-49; Prof. of Universal History in secondary schools 44-48; Editor Nuestro Tiempo 54-56, Gacetilla Austral 61-; Pres. Ateneo del Uruguay, and El Siglo Ilustrado S.A.; Prof. of Sociology and Social Research, Prof. of Contemporary History, Prof. of Theory and Methodology of History, Univ of Montevideo; Commdr. Order of Liberation (Spain).
Publs. La Historia y la Novela 47, Las ideas socialistas en el siglo XIX 47, 49, 63, 67, Ensayo de Sociología Uruguaya 56, The History of ideas in contemporary historiography 58, Teoría de la Historia 59, L'Amérique Latine 59, 67, Las clases sociales en el Uruguay 60, La Crisis española del siglo XX 60, 62, Itinerario español 61, Revolución social y fascismo en el siglo XX 62, La religión en el Uruguay 64, Sociología del Uruguay 65, Historia del movimiento obrero y social latino americano Contemporáneo 67, Los afro-uruguayos 67.
Coronel Alegre 1340, Montevideo, Uruguay.
Telephone: 70562.

Rama Rau (see Rau).

Ramachandran, Gopalasamudram Narayana, M.A., M.SC., D.SC., PH.D.; Indian scientist and university professor; b. 8 Oct. 1922; ed. Maharaja's Coll., Ernakulam (Cochin), Indian Inst. of Science, Univs. of Madras and Cambridge.
Lecturer in Physics, Indian Inst. of Science 46-47, Asst. Prof. 49-52; 1851 Exhbn. Scholar, Univ. of Cambridge 47-49; Prof. Univ. of Madras 52-, and Head, Dept. of Physics 52-; Dean, Faculty of Science 64-; part-time Prof. of Biophysics, Univ. of Chicago 67-; Editor Current Science 50-58; mem. Editorial Board J. Molecular Biology 59-66, Biochimica et Biophysica Acta 65-, Indian Journal of Pure and Applied Physics 63-; Fellow, Indian Acad. of Sciences 50-, mem. Council 53-, Sec. 56-58, Vice-Pres. 62-64; Dir. U.G.C. Centre of Advanced Study in Physics 62-; mem. Physical Research Cttee. 59-; mem. Nat. Cttee. for Biophysics 61-; Fellow Nat. Inst. of Sciences 63-; mem. Board of Scientific and Industrial Research, India; Chair. Nat. Cttee. for Crystallography 63-; Senior Visiting Prof. Univ. of Michigan 65-66; Hon. mem. American Soc. of Biological Chemistry 65-; specialist in optics, crystal physics, X-ray crystallography and biophysics; Bhatnagar Memorial Prize, Watumull Prize, John Arthur Wilson Award 67.
Publ. Crystal Optics (in Handbuch der Physik, vol. 24, Berlin), Molecular Structure of Collagen (in International Review of Connective Tissue Research, Vol. I, New York), Advanced Methods of Crystallography (Editor), Aspects of Protein Structure, London (Editor), Treatise on Collagen (Editor) 67.
Centre of Advanced Study in Physics, University of Madras, A. C. College Buildings, Madras 25, India.
Telephone: 441678.

Ramachandran, T. N.; Indian archaeologist; b. 16 March 1903; ed. Presidency Coll., Madras Univ. and London Univ. Inst. of Archaeology.
Curator Archæological Section, Madras Govt. Museum 25-35; Asst. Superintendent Archæological Survey of India, Calcutta 35-38, Superintendent 38-52, Dep. Dir. Gen. Delhi 52-53, Joint Dir. Gen. 53-58; Special Officer Nagarjunakonda Excavations, Govt. of India Dept. of Archæology 58-61; Special Officer for Archæology, Govt. of Madras 61-, for Publications, H.R. & C.E. Dept. 66-; Pres. Asiatic Sec. I.C.O.M.; Fellow Asiatic Soc. Narasimhacharya Prizeman, Bysany Madhava

Gold Medal (Madras Univ.), Lokavedasamanvayakalpataru 63, Padma Bhushan 64.

Publs. include *Buddhist Sculptures from Goli* 29, *South Indian Metal Images* 32, *The Golden Age of Indo-Javanese Art* 33, *The Royal Artist Mahendra Varman I* 33, *Three Styles of Temple Architecture* 34, *Tiruparuttikuwram and its temples* 34, *Nagarjunakonda* 38, *Jaina Monuments of India* 44, *Khandagiri and Udayagiri Caves* 50, *Nagapattinam Buddhist Bronzes* 54, *Archaeological Reconnaissance in Afghanistan* 56, *New Light on Indus Culture* 58, *Historic India and her temples* 58, *Preservation of Monuments* 55, *The Great Temple of Tanjore*, *The Sittannavasal Cave* 62, *Is the World Morally Progressing?*, *Buddhist India and the World*, *Homage to Vaisali*, *Asvamedha Sites Near Kalsi*, *Kiratarjuniya in Indian Art.*

8 Kapalinagar, Madras 4, India.

Telephone: 84260.

Raman, Sir Chandrasekhara Venkata, Kt.; Indian physicist; b. 7 Nov. 1888; ed. Presidency Coll., Madras. Indian Finance Dept. 07-17; Prof. of Physics Calcutta Univ. 17-33; Prof. Indian Inst. of Science, Bangalore 33-48; Nobel Prizeman for Physics 30; Pres. Indian Acad. of Sciences 34-; Dir. Raman Research Inst.; Nat. Research Prof. of Physics 48-; awarded Mateucci Medal, Rome 29, Hughes Medal of Royal Society 30, Franklin Medal, Philadelphia Inst. 41; Foreign mem. Inst. de France 49, Zürich Physics Society, Acad. of Sciences of U.S.S.R., Czechoslovakia, Hungary and Romania, Royal Irish Acad., Royal Soc. of New Zealand, Optical Soc., America, etc; many honorary degrees.

Publs. *Molecular Diffraction of Light, Mechanical Theory of Bowed Strings and Violin Tone, Diffraction of X-rays, Theory of Musical Instruments, Diamond and Crystal Physics, Physiology of Vision.*

Raman Research Inst., Hebbal Post, Bangalore 6, India.

Ramanathan, Kalpathi Ramakrishna, M.A., D.SC.; Indian scientist; b. 1893; ed. Victoria Coll., Palghat and Presidency Coll., Madras.

Demonstrator in Physics, Trivandrum Coll. 14-21; Hon. Dir. Trivandrum Observatory; Madras Univ. Research Scholar under Prof. C. V. Raman 21-22; Lecturer in Physics, Univ. Coll., Rangoon 22-25; joined Indian Meteorological Dept. 25-48; Dir. Kodaikanal and Bombay Observatories; Superintending Meteorologist, Poona 39; Deputy Dir.-Gen. of Observatories until 48; Dir. Physical Research Laboratory Ahmedabad 48-; Pres. Indian Science Congress, Mathematics and Physics Section, Lahore 39; Founder Fellow of Indian Acad. of Sciences and of Nat. Inst. of Sciences of India; Pres. Int. Asscn. of Meteorology 51-54, Union of Geodesy and Geophysics 54-57; Chair. Radio Research Cttee, India 61-, Cloud and Rain Physics and Cosmic Ray Research Cttee. 56-; Chair. Cen. Board of Geophysics 59-; Pres. Int. Ozone Comm. 59-; Chair. Board of Research in Nuclear Science, Dept. of Atomic Energy, India 61-; Pres. Indian Nat. Cttee. for IQSY (Int. Year of the Quiet Sun); main fields of research: problems of molecular scattering of light in fluids, anisotropy of molecules, atmospheric and solar radiation, study of the Indian monsoon, general circulation of the atmosphere, atmospheric ozone, physics of the ionosphere and aeronomy; Padma Bhushan 65.

Physical Research Laboratory, Ahmedabad 9, Gujerat, India.

Ramani, Radhakrishna; Malaysian lawyer and diplomatist; b. 21 Oct. 1901 in India; ed. Univ. of Madras, India, and Middle Temple, London.

Lawyer, Kuala Lumpur 30-42, 45-63, Madras 42-45; mem. Legislative Council, Fed. of Malaya 48-54; Deputy Rep. of Malaya to UN 63, of Malaysia 63-65, Perm. Rep. of Malaysia to UN 64-.

Permanent Mission of Malaysia to the United Nations, 845 Third Avenue, New York 22, N.Y., U.S.A.

Ramanujam, G.; Indian trade unionist; b. 2 Feb. 1916.

Founder-Sec. Tamilnad Indian Nat. Trade Union Congress; Pres. Indian Nat. Textile Workers Fed. 56, Indian Nat. Plantation Workers Fed. 60; Pres. Indian Nat. Trade Union Congress 58, 59, Gen. Sec. 65-.

Indian National Trade Union Congress, 17 Janpath, New Delhi, India.

Rambert, Charles Jean Julien; French architect; b. 23 March 1924; ed. Lycée Pierre-Corneille Rouen, Inst. Saint-Aspais Melun and Ecole nationale supérieure des beaux-arts.

Architect 52-, Govt. registered architect 53; Technical Counsellor, Centre d'information et de documentation du bâtiment 55-61, Editor-in-Chief *Revêtements sols et murs* 57-64; Prof. of Construction and History of Art, Ecole de secrétariat technique du bâtiment 57-; Arbitrator-expert, Tribunal de Commerce 60, and de Grande Instance, Versailles 63; Sec. Soc. of Registered Architects 54-57, Sec.-Gen. 57-; Editor-in-Chief *L'Architecture française* 64-; Counsellor, Ordre des Architectes de Paris 64; Asst. Dir. of Studies, Ecole Nationale Supérieure des Beaux Arts 65; several awards.

Publs. *Constructions scolaires et universitaires* 55, *L'Habitat collectif, Problème urbain* 57, *Maisons familiales de plaisance* 59, *Magasins* 61, *Histoire de l'architecture civile en France* 63, French adaptation of *World Architecture* 64, *Architecture* 68.

35 avenue de Ségur, Paris 7e; and 48 rue Saint-Didier, Paris 16e, France.

Telephone: 783-35-51.

Rambert, Dame Marie, D.B.E. (Mrs. Ashley Dukes); Founder and Director of Ballet Rambert; b. 20 Feb. 1888; ed. Warsaw, Poland and Russia.

Member Diaghilev Company 12-13; opened Rambert Ballet School 20; founded the first English Ballet Company 26; owner-director Mercury Theatre; has presented Ballet Rambert for 41 years in Britain, the Commonwealth, Europe, China and America; teacher of Frederick Ashton, Antony Tudor, Andrée Howard and other well-known choreographers; Royal Acad. of Dancing Award 56, Légion d'Honneur; D.Litt. (Sussex Univ.).

Publs. Transl. *Ulanova: Her Childhood and Schooldays* 62, co-author: *Dancers of Mercury: The Story of Ballet Rambert* 60.

19 Campden Hill Gardens, London, W.8, England.

Telephone: 01-727-5946.

Rambin, J. Howard, Jr.; American oil executive; b. 2 June 1911; ed. Louisiana State Univ.

Vice-Pres. (Domestic Producing Dept.) Texaco Inc. 57-58, Senior Vice-Pres. (Worldwide Producing Activities) 58-62, Exec. Vice-Pres. (Southern Operations) 62-64, Pres. 64-65, Dir. 64-, Chair. and Chief Exec. Officer 65-; Dir. Freeport Sulphur Co. 64-, American Petroleum Inst. 64-, Lincoln Center for the Performing Arts 66-; Mid-Continent Oil and Gas Asscn.

Texaco Inc., 135 East 42nd Street, New York, N.Y. 10017, U.S.A.

Ramey, James Thomas, A.B., LL.B.; American government official; b. 5 Dec. 1914; ed. Amherst Coll., and Columbia University School of Law.

Tennessee Valley Authority 41-47; Asst. Gen. Counsel, Atomic Energy Comm. 47-52, Asst. Manager, Chicago Operations Office, AEC 52-56; Exec. Dir., Joint Congressional Cttee. on Atomic Energy 56-62; Commr. U.S. Atomic Energy Comm. 62-.

6817 Hillmead Road, Bethesda, Maryland, U.S.A.

Ramgoolam, Sir Seewoosagur, Kt., L.R.C.P., M.R.C.S.; British (Mauritius) physician and administrator; b. 1900; ed. Royal Coll., Mauritius and Univ. Coll., London.

Municipal Councillor 40-53, 56; Dep. Mayor of Port Louis 56, Mayor 58; mem. Legislative Council 48-;

mem. Exec. Council 48-; Liaison Officer for Educ. 51-56; Ministerial Sec. to the Treasury 58-60; Minister of Finance 60-61, Leader of the House 60-, Chief Minister and Minister of Finance 61-, Premier and Minister of Finance 64-; Chair. Board of Dirs. *Advance* (daily); Pres. Indian Cultural Asscn.; Editor *Indian Cultural Review.*
85 Desforges Street, Port Louis, Mauritius.
Telephone: 2-0460.

Ramírez-Pane, Ruben, M.D.; Paraguayan physician and diplomatist; b. 3 June 1920; ed. German Coll., Asunción, National Univ. of Paraguay, Columbia and Harvard Univs.
Director-Gen. of Social Security 48-49; Prof. of Preventive Medicine and Assoc. Prof of Endocrinology, Nat. Univ. of Paraguay; mem. Exec. Cttee. of Republican Nat. Asscn. Party, Paraguay; mem. Parl. 60-63; Perm. Rep. of Paraguay to UN April 62-65; Orden Cruzeiro do Sul (Brazil); Orden del Mérito Civil (Spain). Publs. *Clínica de las Enfermedades Profesionales, Los sindromes de la Corteza Suprarenal, Capítulos de Medicina Preventiva,* etc.
c/o Ministry of Foreign Affairs, Asunción, Paraguay.

Ramírez Vazquez, Pedro; Mexican architect; b. 16 April 1919; ed. Univ. Nacional Autónoma de Mexico. Professor of Design and City Planning, Nat. School of Architecture, Univ. of Mexico; Past Pres. Soc. of Mexican Architects and Nat. Coll. of Architects of Mexico; Chair. Organizing Cttee., Games of XIX Olympiad; Grand Prix of Twelfth Milan Triennial for prefabricated rural school project; Gold Medal, Eighth São Paulo Biennial for Nat. Museum of Anthropology, Mexico City.
Major works include: co-author of design for Nat. School of Medicine, University City; plans for several cities in Mexico; numerous prefabricated schools in Mexico (also used in S. America, Europe and Asia); buildings in Mexico City of Ministry of Labour, Nat. Labour Conciliation Board, Nat. Inst. for Protection of Infancy, Ministry of Foreign Affairs, and Aztec Stadium; Mexican pavilions at Brussels, Seattle and New York World Fairs; museums of Ciudad Juarez and Mexico City; Nat. Gallery of History and Nat. Gallery of Modern Art, Mexico City; Nat. Museum of Anthropology, Mexico City; 1968 Olympic Games Stadium, Mexico City.
Avenida de las Fuentes 170, Mexico, D.F., Mexico.

Ramkumar, Ramkumar, M.A.; Indian artist; b. 23 Sept. 1924; ed. Delhi Univ., Académie André Lhote, Paris, and Acad. Montmartre, Paris (with Fernand Léger).
Worked in bank for one year; French Govt. scholarship, Paris 50-52; returned to India 52; exhbns. in Europe 55, 58; travelled in Europe, Afghanistan, Ceylon, Turkey and Egypt; mem. Lalit Kala Akademi, Sahitya Akademi; Nat. Award, Nat. Art Exhbn., India 56, 58; one-man exhbns. in Delhi, Bombay, Calcutta, Paris, Prague, Warsaw, Colombo 50-65; Group exhbns. with other Indian artists in London, New York, Tokyo, etc.; exhibited at Int. exhbns., Venice, São Paulo, Tokyo. Publs. two novels, two collections of stories, and one travel book.
14 A/20 W.E. Area, New Delhi 5, India.

Rammler, Erich, DR.ING.; German mining engineer; b. 9 July 1901; ed. Bergakad., Freiberg.
Assistant in Staatliche Hütten- und Blaufarbenwerke 25-28; on staff of Laboratory for Fuel Technology 28-36; Hon. Dir. of div. of Brown Coal Research Inst. 33-38; in practice as Technical Consultant 36-45; research activity 45-49; Prof. of Fuel Technology, Thermal Econs., etc. Bergakad., Freiberg 49-66; Emeritus 66-; mem. Deutsche Akad. der Wissenschaften 53, Sächsische Akad. der Wissenschaften 59; Nat. Prize 51; Dr. Ing. h.c., Aachen 58.

Richard-Wagner-Strasse 12, Freiberg/Sa., German Democratic Republic.
Telephone: 3388 (Home); 512379 (Office).

Ramo, Simon; American engineering executive; b. 7 May 1913; ed. Univ. of Utah and California Inst. of Technology.
With General Electric Co., Schenectady 36-46; Lecturer, Union Coll. 41-46; Dir., Research Electronics Dept., Dir., Guided Missiles Research and Development, Vice-Pres. and Dir. of Operations, Hughes Aircraft Co., Culver City 46-53; Exec. Vice-Pres., Dir., The Ramo-Wooldridge Corpn., Los Angeles 53-58; Pres., Space Technology Laboratories Div. of Ramo-Wooldridge Corpn. 57-58; Scientific Dir., U.S.A.F. Ballistic Missiles Programmes *Thor, Atlas, Titan* 54-58; Exec. Vice-Pres. Thompson Ramo Wooldridge Inc. 58-61, Vice-Chair. 61-64; Research Assoc. Calif. Inst. of Technology 46-; Pres. Bunker-Ramo Corpn. 64-67, Dir. 64-; Dir. Semi-conductors Inc., Union Bank; mem. Pres.'s Science Advisory Cttee. 59-; mem. Editorial Board, McGraw-Hill Electronics Science Series 60-.
Publs. *Fields and Waves in Modern Radio* (with J. R. Whinnery) 44, 53; *Introduction to Microwaves* 45.
Office: 8433 Fallbrook Avenue, Canoga Park, California; Home: 276 Tavistock Avenue, Los Angeles, Calif. 90049, U.S.A.

Ramonet, Edouard Jean; French politician; b. 14 June 1909; ed. Lycée Louis-le-Grand, Paris, and Florence Univs.
Attached to Ministry of Foreign Affairs 37; Dir. Inst. Français, Porto 42; Deputy to both Constituent Assemblies 45-46, Deputy from Indre 46-58; Sec. Nat. Assembly 46; Mayor of Châteauroux 47-59; Pres. Economic Affairs Comm. 51; resigned from Parti Républicain Radical et Radical-Socialiste and joined new Parti Radical-Socialiste 56; Minister for Industry, de Gaulle Cabinet June 58-Jan. 59; mem. Comm. Nat. des Musées de Province, Conseil de l'Ordre de l'Economie Nat.; Commdr. Ordre de l'Economie Nationale.
Rue Catherine-Lamamy, Châteauroux (Indre), France.

Ramos, Celso; Brazilian industrialist and politician; ed. Colégio Catarinense.
Founded Fed. of Industries, Santa Catarina 50, Pres. 50-61; founded Dept. of Social Service in Industry, Santa Catarina 51; founded Dept. of Nat. Service and Industrial Apprenticeship, Santa Catarina 53; Gov. of the State of Santa Catarina 62-65; Pres. (founder), Faculty of Social Service 58-; mem. Nat. Council of the Nat. Confederation of Industry.
Avenida Trompowsky 19, Florianópolis, Santa Catarina, Brazil.

Ramos, João Baptista; Brazilian lawyer and politician; b. 7 May 1910; ed. Rio Branco High School and Univ. of São Paulo.
Member Chamber of Deputies 54-; Leader of fmr. Labour Party 57; Minister of Labour 60; Parl. Observer to Int. Labour Org. Conf., Geneva 64; First Vice-Pres. Chamber of Deputies 65, 66, Pres. 66-.
Publ. *Organic Law on Social Welfare* 60.
Chamber of Deputies, Brasilia, D.F., Brazil.

Ramos, João de Deus Battaglia, LL.D.; Portuguese diplomatist; b. 25 Aug. 1902; ed. Univ. de Lisboa.
Entered diplomatic service 24; Sec. Washington Embassy 34; Counsellor, London Embassy 45; Minister, Oslo 48-50, Stockholm 50-56, Helsinki 56-58, Karachi 58-61; Amb. Rio de Janeiro 61-67; Portuguese Rep. at Org. for Econ. Co-operation and Devt. (OECD) 67-; Head, Portuguese Del. to Conf. of Int. Tourist Orgs. 46, to Anglo-Portuguese trade talks 48, to Inter-American Conf. of Org. of American States (OAS) 65; Chair. Ceremonial and Exec. Cttees. for Rio de Janeiro 4th Century Celebrations 65.
Organization for Economic Co-operation and Development, 2 rue André-Pascal, Paris 16e, France.

Ramos, Narciso, LL.B.; Philippine politician; b. 11 Nov. 1919; ed. Univ. of the Philippines, Rizal and National Univ., Manila.

Legal practice, Manila and Pangasinan 25-34; mem. House of Reps. and Nat. Assembly 34-46; Counsellor, then Minister-Counsellor, Washington Embassy 46-49; Philippine Alt. Gov. of Int. Monetary Fund (IMF) and World Bank for Reconstruction and Devt. (IBRD-World Bank) 47-49; Minister, Buenos Aires 49-52, New Delhi 52-56; Amb. Taipei 56-65; Sec. of Foreign Affairs 65-; Leader Philippine Dels. to Int. Telecommunication Union (ITU) Conf., Atlantic City 47, Colombo Plan Consultative Cttee. meeting, Singapore 55; Commdr. Legion of Honour 59.

Secretariat for Foreign Affairs, Manila, Philippines.

Rampal, Jean-Pierre Louis; French flautist; b. 7 Jan. 1922; ed. Univ. de Marseille.

World-wide tours 45-; participant in major festivals in Rio de Janeiro, Aix, Menton, Salzburg, Edinburgh, Prague, Athens, Zagreb, Granada, Tokyo, etc.; Editor for Ancient and Classical Music, Int. Music Co., New York City 58-; mem. French Musicological Soc.; Chevalier de l'Ordre des Arts et Lettres de France; Grand Prix du Disque 54, 56, 59, 60, 61, 63, 64; Oscar du Premier Virtuose Français 56.

Home: 15 Avenue Mozart, Paris 16e, France; Office: c/o Colbert Management, 850 7th Avenue, New York City 10019, N.Y., U.S.A.

Rampton, Calvin L., LL.B.; American lawyer and politician; b. 6 Nov. 1913; ed. Davis High School, Univ. of Utah, and George Washington Univ., Washington, D.C. Administrative Asst. to Congressman J. W. Robinson 36-38; County Attorney, Davis County, Utah 39-40; Asst. Attorney-Gen. of Utah 41, 46-48; U.S. Army, Second World War; U.S. Supreme Court 46-; Gov. of Utah 65-; Democrat.

State Capitol, Salt Lake City, Utah, U.S.A.

Ramsey, Most Rev. Arthur Michael, D.D.; British ecclesiastic; b. 14 Nov. 1904; ed. Repton School, Magdalene Coll., Cambridge, and Cuddesdon Theological Coll.

Curate, Liverpool Parish Church 28-30; sub-Warden of Lincoln Theological Coll. 30-36; Lecturer, Boston Parish Church 36-38; Vicar, St. Benedict, Cambridge 39-40; Canon, Durham Cathedral, and Van Mildert Prof. of Divinity, Univ. of Durham 40-50; Regius Prof. of Divinity, Univ. of Cambridge 50-52; Lord Bishop of Durham 52-56; Archbishop of York 56-61, of Canterbury 61-; Pres. World Council of Churches 61-; Hon. Fellow Magdalene Coll., Cambridge; Hon. D.C.L. (Oxford and Kent); Hon. S.T.D. (New York and Columbia); Hon. LL.D. (Univ. of Canterbury, New Zealand); Hon. D.D. (Edinburgh, Durham, Leeds, Hull, Manchester, London, Huron Coll., Trinity Coll., Toronto and Virginia Theological Seminary); Hon. Dr. of Laws (Los Angeles Occidental Coll.); Dr. h.c. (Inst. Catholique, Paris) and other honorary degrees.

Publs. *The Gospel and the Catholic Church* 36, *The Resurrection of Christ* 45, *The Glory of God and the Transfiguration of Christ* 49, *F. D. Maurice and the Conflicts of Modern Theology* 51, *Durham Essays and Addresses* 56, *From Gore to Temple* 60, *Introducing the Christian Faith* 61, *Canterbury Essays and Addresses* 64, *Sacred and Secular* 65.

Lambeth Palace, London, S.E.1, and Old Palace, Canterbury, Kent, England.

Ramsey, Rt. Rev. Ian Thomas, M.A., D.D.; British ecclesiastic; b. 31 Jan. 1915; ed. Christ's Coll., Cambridge and Ripon Hall, Oxford.

Chaplain, Fellow and Tutor Christ's Coll. Cambridge 43-51; Canon Theologian of St. Alban in Leicester Cathedral 44-46; Nolloth Prof. of Philosophy of the Christian Religion and Fellow of Oriel Coll. Oxford 51-66; Bishop of Durham 66-; Lecturer at various colleges in Britain, Canada and the U.S.A.; Burney Prize 38; Hon. D.D. Oxford, Durham and Glasgow Univs.

Publs. *Miracles: An Exercise in Logical Mapwork* 52, *Religious Language* 57, *Freedom and Immortality* 60, *On Being Sure in Religion* 63, *Models and Mystery* 64, *Science and Religion* 64, *Christian Discourse* 65; Ed.: *Reasonableness of Christianity* (John Locke) 58, *Prospect for Metaphysics* 61, *Biology and Personality* 65, *Christian Ethics and Contemporary Philosophy* 66.

Auckland Castle, Bishop Auckland, Co. Durham, England.

Telephone: Bishop Auckland 2576.

Ramsey, Norman Foster, Jr., M.A., PH.D., D.SC.; American scientist; b. 27 Aug. 1915; ed. Columbia, Harvard and Cambridge Univs.

Assoc. Univ. of Illinois 40-42; Asst. Prof. Columbia Univ. 42-46; Research Assoc. Massachusetts Inst. of Technology Radiation Laboratory 40-43; Expert Consultant to Sec. of War 42-45; Group Leader and Asscn. Division Head, Los Alamos Laboratory of Atomic Energy Project 43-45; Chief Scientist of Atomic Energy Laboratory, Tinian 45; Assoc. Prof. Columbia Univ. 45-47; Head Physics Dept., Brookhaven Nat. Laboratory 46-47; Assoc. Prof. Harvard Univ. 47-50; Dir. Harvard Nuclear Laboratory 48-50 and 52-53; Air Force Scientific Advisory Cttee. 47-55; Dept. Defence Panel on Atomic Energy 53-58; Prof. of Physics, Harvard Univ. 50-; Higgins Prof. of Physics, Harvard Univ. 66-; Scientific Adviser NATO 58-59; Gen. Advisory Cttee., Atomic Energy Comm. 60-; Dir. Varian Associates 63-66; Pres. Univs. Research Asscn. 66-; mem. Nat. Acad. of Sciences, American Acad. of Arts and Sciences, American Philosophical Soc.; Trustee, Carnegie Endowment for Int. Peace 62-; Presidential Order of Merit; Lawrence Award 60.

Publs. *Nuclear Moments* 53, *Nuclear Two-Body Problems* 53, *Molecular Beams* 55, *Quick Calculus* 65; and numerous articles in the *Physical Review*.

55 Scott Road, Belmont 02178, Massachusetts, U.S.A.

Rana, Damodar Shumshere Jung Bahadur, B.A.; Nepalese social worker and politician; b. 28; ed. Missionary School Darjeeling, Central Hindu School, Banaras and Banaras Hindu Univ.

Executive mem. social orgs. in Nepal 54-60; Chief Admin. Morang District 61; Chair. Special Comm. Kosi Zone 61, Commr. 62-64; mem. Nat. Panchayat, mem. Exec. Cttee. and Foreign Affairs Cttee.; Ambassador to the U.S.S.R. 64-67, concurrently to Poland, Hungary and Czechoslovakia; awarded Prabala Gorkha Dakchina Bahu.

Phora Darbar, Katmandu, Nepal.

Ranasinha, Sir Arthur Godwin, C.M.G., C.B.E.; Ceylonese banker; b. 24 June 1898; ed. St. Thomas' Coll., Colombo and Trinity Coll., Cambridge.

Magistrate, Point Pedro, Balapitiya, Jaffna 23-28; District Judge, Avissawella 28-30, Badulla 30-32; Sec. to Minister of Agriculture and Lands 33-36; Public Trustee 36-44; Custodian of Enemy Property 39-44; Superintendent of Census 44-46; Sec. to Vice-Chair. Board of Ministers on his political Mission to London 45; Land Commr. 46-47; Permanent Sec. Ministry of Agriculture and Lands 47-50; Sec. to Cabinet and Deputy Sec. to the Treasury 50; Chair. and Leader of Ceylon Del. to Commonwealth Consultative Cttee. on Colombo Plan 50-51; Permanent Sec. Ministry of Finance, Sec. to the Treasury and Sec. to the Cabinet 50-54; Gov. Central Bank 54-59; Ambassador to Italy, and concurrently Greece and Israel 59-61; Chair. People's Bank Comm. 65-66, Taxation Enquiry Comm. 66-67, Tea Comm. 67; Pres. Ceylon Political Science Asscn.

Publ. *General Report on the Census of Ceylon* 46.

Rangiri, Lady McCallum's Drive, Kandy, Ceylon.

Telephone: Kandy 7283.

Randall, Sir John Turton, Kt., D.SC., F.R.S.; British biophysicist; b. 23 March 1905; ed. Univ. of Manchester. Research Staff of G.E.C. Ltd. Wembley 26-37; Warren Research Fellow of Royal Society in Univ. of Birmingham 37-43; Temporary Lecturer Cavendish Laboratory Cambridge 43-44; Prof. of Natural Philosophy in Univ. of St. Andrews 44-46. Wheatstone Prof. of Physics in Univ. of London (King's Coll.) 46-61, Prof. of Biophysics 61-; Dir. Medical Research Council, Biophysics Research Unit, King's Coll. 47-, Chair. School of Biological Science 63-.
Publs. *The Diffraction of X-rays by Amorphous Solids and Liquids* 34, *The Nature and Structure of Collagen* (Editor) 53.
King's College, Department of Biophysics, 26-29 Drury Lane, London, W.C.2, England.
Telephone: 01-836-8851.

Randall, Michael Bennett; British journalist; b. 12 Aug. 1919; ed. St. Peter's School, Seaford, and Canford School.
Assistant Editor, *Sunday Chronicle* 52-53; Editor *Sunday Graphic* 53; Asst. Editor *Daily Mirror* 53-56; Asst. Editor *News Chronicle* 56-57; Asst. Editor *Daily Mail* 57, Deputy Editor 61-63, Editor 63-66; Man. Editor (News) *Sunday Times* 67-; Hannen Swaffer Award as Journalist of 1965 66.
Gate House, 180 Kew Road, Richmond, Surrey, England.
Telephone: 01-940-3564.

Randers, Gunnar, M.SC.; Norwegian physicist; b. 28 April 1914; ed. Oslo Univ.
Research Fellow, Mount Wilson Observatory, California 39-40; Instructor, Univ. of Chicago 40-42; Captain, Norwegian Army and Scientific Officer, British Ministry of Supply 42-45; Dir. Astrophysics Inst., Oslo Univ. 46-47; chief scientist, Norwegian Defence Research Establishment 47-51; Dir. Dutch-Norwegian Joint Establishment for Nuclear Energy Research 51-59; exec. Vice-Pres. European Atomic Energy Society 54-56; Chair. Norwegian Atomic Energy Council 55-; Man. Dir. Inst. for Atomenergi, Kjeller 48-; special adviser on atomic energy matters to the Sec.-Gen. of the U.N. 54; Scientific Adviser to Dir.-Gen. Int. Atomic Energy Agency, Vienna 58, Gov. 60; Dir. American Nuclear Society 55-57; Chair. Norwegian Agency for Int. Devt. 63-; Pres. European Atomic Energy Soc. 66-67; mem. Royal Astronomical Soc., Norwegian Acad. of Science; Commdr. Norwegian Order of St. Olav, and Netherlands Orders of Orange-Nassau and House of Orange, Commdr. Finland's White Rose, and Sweden's Vasa Order, Commdr. Yugoslav Flag Order.
Publs. *Atom Energy* 46, *Atoms and Common Sense* 50.
Kjeller, Lilleström, Norway; and Trosterudstien 4, Slemdal, Oslo, Norway.
Telephone: 71-25-60.

Randolph, Jennings, A.B.; American educator, executive and politician; b. 8 March 1902; ed. Salem Coll.
Assoc. Editor *West Virginia Review* 25; Dir. Dept. of Public Speaking and Journalism, Davis and Elkins Coll. 26-32; Prof. of Public Speaking, Southeastern Univ. 36; mem. U.S. House of Reps. 33-47; Asst. to Pres. and Dir. of Public Relations, Capital Airlines; Dean, Coll. of Business Admin., Southeastern Univ.; U.S. Senator from West Virginia 58-; several honorary degrees; Democrat.
Senate Office Building, Washington 25, D.C., U.S.A.

Randolph, (Asa) Philip; American labour leader; b. 15 April 1889; ed. Coll. of City of New York.
Organiser and Pres., Brotherhood of Sleeping Car Porters 25-; Pres. Negro-American Labor Council 60-; Vice-Pres. A.F.L.-C.I.O. 57-; Organiser and Dir. March on Washington Movement 41; Organiser and Dir. Washington Freedom March Aug. 63.
230 W. 150th Street, New York City, N.Y., U.S.A.

Ranganathan, Padma Sri Shiyali Ramamrita, M.A., D.LITT., L.T., F.L.A.; Indian university professor; b. 9 Aug. 1892; ed. Madras Christian Coll., Teachers' Coll., Saidapet, and Univ. Coll., London.
Lecturer in Mathematics Govt. Colls. of Madras 17-20; Asst. Prof. of Maths., Presidency Coll., Madras 21-24; Univ. Librarian Madras 24-44; Univ. Librarian and Prof. of Library Science, Benares Hindu Univ. 45-47; Prof. of Library Science, Univ. of Delhi 47-55; Chair. Libraries Cttee., Univ. Grants Comm. 58, working party Science Planning Comm. 59; Dir. Seminars on Work-Flow in Univ. Libraries 59; Social Service Documentation 59; Visiting Prof. of Library Science, Vikram Univ. 57-59; Prof. Documentation Research and Training Centre, Bangalore 62-64; Nat. Research Prof. in Library Science 65-; founded Sarada Ranganathan Chair of Library Science, Madras Univ. 57; Established Sarada Ranganathan Endowment for Library Science 63.
Publs. *Classification and International Documentation* 48, *Preface to Library Science* 48, *Rural Adult Education* 49, *Library Tour* 50, *Library Development Plan for India* 50, *Classification and Communication* 51, *Philosophy of Classification* 51, *Five Laws of Library Science* 57, *Library Administration* 59, *Library Manual* 60, *Education for Leisure* 61, *Social Science Research and Libraries* 61, *Documentation and its Facets* 63, *Colon Classification* 63, *Classified Catalogue Code* 64, *Library Book Selection* 66, *Prolegomena to Library Classification* 67, *Ramanujan—the Man and the Mathematician* 67, *Physical Bibliography* 68.
Documentation Research and Training Centre, 112 Eleventh Cross Road, Bangalore 3, India.
Telephone: 3657.

Ranieri Mazzilli, Paschoal; Brazilian civil servant and politician; b. 10; ed. Caconde Public School, São Paulo State Univ. and School of Advanced Military Studies, Rio de Janeiro.
Federal Tax Collector 32, Dir. of Treasurer's Office, Fed. District 40-45, Dir. of Income Tax Dept. 45-46, Sec.-Gen. Finances of Federal District City Hall 46-47; Dir. Fed. Savings Bank of Rio de Janeiro 47-48; Head, Finance Minister's Office 48-50; Fed. Dep. 51-, Pres., Chamber of Deputies 58-65; Pres. of Republic *pro tem.* April 60, August-September 61, April 62, April 64; Pres. Inter-Parl. Council of Inter-Parl. Union; Cavaliere di Gran Croce, Italy, Commdr., Légion d'Honneur, Grand Cross of the Nat. Order of Merit, Paraguay, etc.
Publs. *Problems in Tax-Collection* 42, *The Reorganisation of the Federal Treasurer's Office, The National Treasury during the New State.*
Super Quadra 107, bloco 5, Apto. 504, Brasilia, Brazil.

Rank, 1st Baron, cr. 57, of Sutton Scotney; **Joseph Arthur Rank,** J.P.; British industrialist; b. 22 Dec. 1888; ed. Leys School.
Director of some 44 companies including: Gaumont British Ltd., Odeon Cinema Holdings Ltd., Odeon Properties Ltd., Ranks (Ireland) Ltd., Ranks Pensions Ltd., The Riverside Milling Co. Ltd., Rank Television and Gen. Trust Ltd., Odeon Associated Theatres Ltd.; Pres. Rank Organisation Ltd.; Chair. Religious Films Ltd., Ranks Hovis McDougall Ltd.
Sutton Manor, Sutton Scotney, near Winchester, Hampshire; and 38 South Street, London, W.1, England.
Telephone: 01-629-7454.

Rank, Joseph McArthur; British business executive; b. 24 April 1918; ed. Loretto School.
Joined Mark Mayhew Ltd., Flour Millers 36; Royal Air Force 40-46; Joint Managing Dir. Joseph Rank Ltd.

55-; Deputy Chair. Ranks Hovis McDougall Ltd. 65-; Pres. Nat. Asscn. of British and Irish Millers 57-58. Landhurst, Hartfield, Sussex, England.

Ránki, György; Hungarian composer; b. 30 Oct. 1907; ed. Budapest and Paris.
Erkel Prize; Kossuth Prize 54; Merited Artist of the Hungarian People's Republic.
Works include *On the Outskirts of Town* (cantata) 47, *1848* (folk-song cantata) 48, *Sword Dance* 49, *Song of Freedom* 51, *King Pomade's New Clothes* (opera, 1st and 2nd Suite for Orchestra), *Two Wonder Oxen* 56, *Pentaevophonia* (quintet for woodwind) 58, *Winner Unknown* (children's opera) 60, *Three Nights* (drama with music) 61, *1514* (fantasy for piano and orchestra) 61, *Ladies at Choice* (operetta) 61, *A Streetcar Named Desire* (incidental music) 62; *Peter in Musicland* (children's opera) 62, *A Midsummer Night's Dream* (incidental music) 64, *The Circus* (ballet) 65, *1944* (oratorio) 66, *Aurora Tempestuosa* 67, *Panic* (musical comedy) 67; film and stage music 30-67.
Gülbaba-utca 36, Budapest II, Hungary.
Telephone: 359-407.

Rankl, Karl; British (naturalised) composer and conductor; b. 1 Oct. 1898.
Conductor Volksoper Vienna 21-25, Stadt Theater Reichenberg 25-27, Königsberg 27-28, Berlin State Opera 28-31, Wiesbaden State Opera 31-32, Graz Opera House 33-37, German Opera Prague 37-38; in England 39-; Musical Dir. Covent Garden Opera Company 46-51; permanent conductor Scottish Nat. Orchestra Oct. 52-57; Musical Dir. Elizabethan Trust Opera, Sydney, Australia 58-60.
Works include 8 symphonies, string quartet, many songs, Violin Concerto, *Suite for Strings*, *Suite for Orchestra* from "*Deirdre*"; an opera, *Deirdre of the Sorrows*, Variations on *Waltzing Matilda* (for orchestra), Suite for Orchestra, Sinfonietta Nos. 1 and 2, Theme and Variations, *Der Mensch* (oratorio), 60 songs.
25 Acacia Road, St. John's Wood, London N.W.8, England.
Telephone: 01-722 5293.

Ranković, Aleksandar; Yugoslav politician; b. 28 Nov. 1909.
Active in trade union movements and illegal Communist Party; arrested and imprisoned for political activites 29-35; after release was in military service and active in workers' movement; arrested by Gestapo 41, but released by Partisans; mem. Supreme Staff Nat. Liberation Army and collaborator of Marshal Tito 41-45; Minister of the Interior 46; Vice-President and Minister of the Interior 48; Vice-Pres. Fed. Exec. Council 53-63; Vice-Pres. of Yugoslavia June 63-66; Sec. C.P. Secr. until 66; Pres. Cen. Cttee. Union of Veterans of Nat. Liberation War; several decorations.
Andre Nikolića No. 5, Belgrade, Yugoslavia.
Telephone: 51-882.

Rannat, Mohamed Ahmed Abu; Sudanese judge; b. 05; ed. Gordon Coll., Khartoum and School of Law, Khartoum.
Translator 25-33; Clerk 33-36; went to School of Law 36-38; District Judge (2nd Grade) 38-44; District Judge (1st Grade) and Dep. Asst. Legal Sec. and Inspector of Native Courts 44-49; studied in England 49-50; Judge of High Court attached to Court of Appeal 50-55; Chief Justice of Sudan 55-64; mem. U.N. Sub-Comm. on Prevention of Discrimination and Protection of Minorities 64-; mem. Constitutional Comm. for S. Arabia 65.
c/o United Nations, New York City, U.S.A.

Ransom, John Crowe, B.A.; American writer and university professor; b. 30 April 1888; ed. Vanderbilt Univ., and Christ Church, Oxford.
Prof. of English, Vanderbilt Univ. 27-37, Carnegie Prof.

of Poetry, Kenyon Coll. 37-58; Editor *Kenyon Review*, Guggenheim Fellowship 31-32; Bollingen Award 51, Russell Loines Award (Nat. Acad. of Arts and Letters) 51.
Publs. *Poems About God* 19, *Grace after Meat* 24, *Chills and Fever* (poems) 24, *Two Gentlemen in Bonds* (poems) 27, *God without Thunder* 30, *World's Body* 38, *New Criticism* 41, *Poetics* 42, *College Prima of Writing* 43, *Selected Poems* 45, Editor: *Topics for Freshmen Writing* 35, *Kenyon Critic: Studies in Modern Literature* 51.
Box 48, Gambier, Ohio, U.S.A.

Rantanen, Vihtori; Finnish trade union leader; b. 30 March 1917.
Former official, Paper Workers' Union; Exec. Confederation of Finnish Trade Unions, mem. of Exec. Cttee., Vice-Pres., Pres. 61-.
Mäntyviita 7 I, Tapiola, Finland.

Rao, Calyampudi Radhakrishna, M.A., SC.D., F.N.I., F.R.S.; Indian statistician; b. 10 Sept. 1920; ed. Andhra and Calcutta Univs.
Research at Indian Statistical Inst. 43-46, Cambridge Univ. 46-48; Prof. and Head of Div. of Theoretical Research and Training 49-64; Dir. Research and Training School, Indian Statistical Inst. 64-; Fellow Inst. of Math. Statistics; Treas. 61-65, now mem. Int. Statistical Inst.; Co-editor of *Sankhye* (Indian Journal of Statistics); Bhatnagar Memorial Award for Scientific Research; Padma Bhusan; Gay Silver Medal Royal Statistical Soc.; Hon. D.Sc. (Andhra).
Publs. include: *Advanced Statistical Methods in Biometric Research*, *Linear Statistical Inference and its Application;* over one hundred research papers in mathematical statistics.
Indian Statistical Institute, 203 B.T. Road, Calcutta 35, India.
Telephone: 56-3220 and 56-3222.

Rao, Kanuru Lakshmana, PH.D., M.I.C.E., M.I.STRUCT.E., M.I.E.; Indian engineer and politician; b. 15 July 1902; ed. Univ. of Madras and Univ. of Birmingham.
Former Chief Engineer (Floods), Indian Central Govt.; fmr. mem. (Design and Research), Central Water and Power Comm., Govt. of India, and Pres. Central Board of Irrigation and Power; mem. Parl. 62-; Minister of State for Irrigation and Power 63-; Pres. Int. Soc. on Soil Mechanics and Foundation Engineering; Pres. Inst. of Engineers 59-61; conferred Padma Bhushan 63 by Pres. of Indian Republic.
Publ. *Calculations, Designs and Testing of Reinforced Concrete.*
9 Janpath, New Delhi, India.

Rao, Raja; Indian writer; b. 21 July 1909; ed. Nizam Coll., Hyderabad, Univs. of Montpellier and Paris.
Publs. *Kanthapura, Cow of the Barricades, The Serpent and The Rope*; short stories in French and English.
c/o Oxford Univ. Press, Apollo Bunder, Bombay 1, India.

Rao, Vijayendra Kasturi Ranga Varadaraja, M.A., B.A., PH.D.; Indian economist and government official; b. 8 July 1908; ed. Wilson Coll., Bombay, and Gonville and Caius Coll., Cambridge.
Principal and Prof. of Econs., L.D. Arts Coll., Ahmedabad 37-42; Prof. and Head of Dept. of Econs., Delhi Univ. 42-57; Dir. of Statistics, Govt. of India 44-45; Planning Adviser, Govt. of India 45-46; Food and Econ. Adviser, Embassy of India, Washington 46-47; Founder and Dir. Delhi School of Econs., Delhi Univ. 49-57, Vice-Chancellor, Delhi Univ. 57-60; Founder and Dir. Inst. of Econ. Growth 60-63; mem. Indian Planning Comm. 63-66; Chair. UN Sub-Comm. on Econ. Devt. 47-50; Union Minister for Transport and Shipping 66-.
Publs. *Taxation of Income in India* 31, *An Essay on*

India's National Income, 1925-29 39, *The National Income of British India, 1931-32* 40, *War and Indian Economy* 43, *India and International Currency Plans* 46, *Post-war Rupee* 48, *Foreign Aid and India's Economic Development* 62, *Essays on Economic Development* 63, *Greater Delhi—A Study in Urbanisation 1947-57* 65, *Education and Human Resource Development* 66.
Union Ministry for Transport and Shipping, Transport Bhawan, Parliament Street, New Delhi, India.

Raoul-Duval, Gérard; French diplomatist; b. 3 March 1908; ed. Lycée Janson-de-Sailly, Paris.
Ministry of Foreign Affairs 34-, French Embassy, Bucharest 34, Consulate, Los Angeles 36, Hong Kong 41, Sec. of Embassy, Ottawa 44, Consul-Gen. Salonika 45, Minister-Resident, Rangoon 48, Counsellor of Embassy, Warsaw 50, Buenos Aires 52, Minister in Charge of Consulate-Gen. Hong Kong 56-59, Counsellor, Tunis 59, Ambassador to Pakistan 62-64, to Chile 65-; Officier, Légion d'Honneur.
French Embassy, Santiago, Chile; "le Mas Saint-Pierre," Chemin de Bibenas, Aix-en-Provence (Bouches-du-Rhone), France.

Rapacki, Adam; Polish politician; b. 24 Dec. 1909; ed. Higher School of Economics and Commerce, Warsaw.
Active in revolutionary youth movement until 39; prisoner-of-war 39-45; mem. Exec. Cttee. Polish Socialist Party 46-48; mem. of Seym 47-; mem. Central Cttee. of Polish United Workers Party 48-; Deputy Chair. Polish Peace Cttee. 49; Minister of Shipping 47-50, of Higher Education 50-56, of Foreign Affairs 56-; mem. Political Bureau of Central Cttee. of Polish United Workers Party 48-54, 56-; proposed atom-free zone (Rapacki Plan) UN 57, 62.
Ministry of Foreign Affairs, Warsaw, Poland.

Raphaël-Leygues, Jacques; French diplomatist and former politician; b. 13 Dec. 1913.
Head Commr. Nat. Marine; with Office of Pres. of Council 38-39; Army service 39-45, in Indochina 45-50; Councillor for French Union 50-58; Peace Missions to Far East 52-54; Dep. to Nat. Ass. 58-62, Vice-Pres. of Cttee. for Foreign Affairs 59-62, Vice-Pres. of Nat. Assembly 62; Mayor and Gen. Councillor Villeneuve-sur-Lot; Ambassador to Ivory Coast 63-; Commdr. Légion d'Honneur; Lauréat de l'Académie Française.
Publs. Plays: *Saigon* 46, *Grand Chef Blanc*; Poetry: *Retour de Mer, Mers indiennes, Minuit à quatre*.
Ambassade de France, B.P. 1393, Abidjan, Ivory Coast; 6, avenue Frédéric-Le-Play, Paris 7e, France.

Rappleye, Willard Cole, A.B., M.D.; American university professor and administrator; b. 11 Feb. 1892; ed. Univ. of Ill., and Harvard Medical School.
Worked with manufacturing companies 09-11; Instructor in Comparative Anatomy, Univ. of Ill. 13-14, in Biology 13-14; Tutor in Economics 13-14; John Harvard Hon. Scholarship 15-18; with Harvard Dental School 15-17; Asst. Physician, Foxboro State Hospital, Mass. 17-18; Mass. General Hospital, Boston 18-19; Dir. Clinical Laboratories, Univ. of Calif. 19-20, Dir. of Hospitals and Prof. of Hospital Admin. 20-22; Medical Adviser, Calif. State Board of Control 20-22; Act. Supt. Pacific Colony for Feeble-minded, Calif. 20-22; Supt., New Haven Hospital 22-26; Prof. Hospital Admin., Yale Univ. 22-26; Dir. of Study, Comm. on Medical Educ. 25-32; Dean Faculty of Med. 31-58, Emer. 58-, Prof. of Medical Economics, Columbia Univ. 31-60, Vice-Pres. in charge of Medical Affairs 49-58; Dir. N.Y. Post Graduate School 33-47; Dean School of Dental and Oral Surgery 33-45; mem. Advisory Board for Medical Specialities 33-44, Pres. 37-44, Chair. Comm. on Graduate Medical Education 37-39; Pres. Advisory Council on Medical Education 39-44; Pres. Asscn. of American Medical Colls. 38-39; Chair. Exec. Council 42-44; Commr. of Hospitals, N.Y. City 40-42; Chair. Board of Dirs., Health Insurance Plan of Greater New

York 44-48; Pres. Josiah Macy Jr. Foundation 41-; Chair. William J. Matheson Comm. 31-54; Pres. William J. Matheson Foundation 54-64; Fellow N.Y. Acad. of Medicine; Hon. A.M. (Yale), Hon. Sc.D. (Trinity Coll. and Rutgers Univ.), Hon. Med.ScD. (Women's Medical Coll. of Pa.); Hon. L.H.D. (N.Y. Medical Coll.).
31 East 79th Street, New York City 21, N.Y., U.S.A.

Rapson, Ralph, B.ARCH.; American architect; b. 13 Sept. 1914; ed. Alma (Mich.) Coll., Univ. of Mich. Coll. of Architecture, and Cranbrook Acad. of Art.
Practising architect 41-; Head Dept. of Architecture Chicago Inst. of Design 42-46; Assoc. Prof. of Architecture M.I.T. School of Architecture 46-54 (leave of absence to execute designs in Europe for State Dept. 51-53); Prof. and Head of School of Architecture, Univ. of Minnesota 54-; mem. American Inst. of Architects, Int. Congress of Modern Architecture; Dir. Walker Art Gallery; fmr. Chair. Editorial Board *Northwest Architect*; numerous awards include Parker Medal 51, American Inst. of Architects Honor Award for U.S. Embassy, Stockholm 54, two Merit Awards 55, Honour Award 58.
Designs include projects for U.S. Government, several churches and schools, commercial, industrial and residential buildings, particularly U.S. Embassy, Stockholm, U.S. Embassy, Copenhagen, U.S. Consulate, Le Havre, St. Peter's Lutheran Church (Edina, Minn.), Fargo (N.D.) Civic Center, St. Paul (Minn.) Arts and Science Center, American Embassy, Beirut, Dr. William G. Shepherd House, St. Paul, Tyrone Guthrie Repertory Theatre, Minn. (Designs also executed for Embassies at Athens, The Hague and Oslo.)
720 Washington Avenue, S.E., Minneapolis 14, Minn., U.S.A.

Raschid, M. A., B.SC., B.L.; Burmese politician; b. 12; ed. Rangoon Univ.
Prior to Second World War was active in trade union movement, especially in B.O.C. Refinery Workers' Union and Shop Assistants' Welfare Society, of which he was Pres.; enrolled as Advocate of High Court 40; co-opted mem. Main Drafting Cttee. of Constitution of Union of Burma, Minorities Cttee., Citizenship Cttee. and English Drafting Cttee.; Chair. Court of Industrial Arbitration; Chair. Labour Legislation Cttee. 47-52; Chair. Dock Labour Board; President Union of Burma Labour Organisation, All-Burma Burman Muslim Org.; fmr. Pres. Int. Labour Org. 61; Del. to African-Asian Conf.; Sec. Burmese Del. Asian Relations Conf., New Delhi 47; mem. Dels. to I.L.O. Confs. 48 and 50; leader Dels. to I.L.O. Petroleum Cttee. 50 and I.L.O. Conf. 51-56, Pres. 61; mem. Burmese Parl. for Rangoon (East) 51; Minister for Housing and Labour 52-54, for Trade Development and Labour 54-56, for Mines 56-58, for Education 58, for National Planning 58, for Industry, Mines and Labour 60-62, mem. Advisory Cttee. Int. Inst. for Labour Studies, Geneva 61-; Pres. All-Burma Burman Muslim Org. 60-.
16 Golden Valley Road, Rangoon, Burma.

Rashid, Rashid Al-; Kuwaiti civil servant and diplomatist; ed. Claremont Men's Coll., California, U.S.A., and Claremont Graduate School.
Assistant Technical Dir., Public Works Dept., Kuwait 59-61; Asst. Sec. for Kuwait Govt. Secretariat 61; Dir. of Political Dept., Ministry of Foreign Affairs, Kuwait 62-63; Perm. Rep. of Kuwait to UN Sept. 63-67; Under-Sec. Ministry of Foreign Affairs 67-.
Ministry of Foreign Affairs, Kuwait.

Rashidov, Sharaf Rashidovich; Soviet politician; b. 1917; ed. Zhizak Teachers' Training Coll., Uzbek State Univ.
Teacher 36-37; Sec. and Asst. Ed. 38-41, Ed. of the newspaper *Lenin-Yuly* 41, 43; School Dir. 42; cadres Sec. of the Samarkand Regional Cttee. of the Party 44-47; Chief Ed. of the republican newspaper *Kzyl*

Uzbekistan, Pres. of the Presidium of the Uzbek Union of Soviet Writers 47-50; Pres. of the Presidium of the Supreme Soviet of Uzbekistan, Vice-Pres. of the Presidium of the Supreme Soviet of the U.S.S.R. 50-59; **one of the chief organisers of the Afro-Asian Solidarity Cttee., Cairo 57; 1st Sec. Uzbek Communist Party 59-;** Candidate mem. Presidium of Cen. Cttee. of C.P.S.U. 61-66, Alt. mem. Politburo 66-; awarded Order of Lenin, Order of the Red Banner of Labour, Order of the Red Star, Badge of Honour.
Central Committee of Communist Party of Uzbekistan, Tashkent, Uzbek S.S.R., U.S.S.R.

Rasminsky, Louis, C.B.E., LL.D., D.H.L.; Canadian banker; b. 1 Feb. 1908; ed. Univ. of Toronto and London School of Economics.
League of Nations official 30-39; Dir. Research and Statistical Section, Foreign Exchange Control Board of Canada 40-42; Alternate Chair. and Chief Exec. Officer of Board 42-51; Exec. Asst. to Govs. of Bank of Canada 43-54; Deputy Gov. Bank of Canada 55-61, Gov. 61-; mem. Canadian Del. to Bretton Woods Conf. 44, and to San Francisco Conf. of U.N. 45; Exec. Dir. of Int. Monetary Fund 46-62, Int. Bank 50-62, Int. Finance Corpn. 57-62; Exec. Dir. Int. Development Asscn. 60-62.
Bank of Canada, Ottawa, Canada.

Rasmussen, Steen Eiler; Danish architect and town planner; b. 9 Feb. 1898.
Member Copenhagen Acad. of Fine Arts 22; Prof. of Architecture, Royal Acad. of Fine Arts, Copenhagen 38-68; Pres. Danish Town Planning Inst. 42-48; Pres. Copenhagen Regional Planning Cttee. 44-58.
Publs. *London, The Unique City* 37, *Towns and Buildings* 51, *Experiencing Architecture* 59; and books in Danish, Swedish and German on architecture, town planning, industrial art.
Dreyersvej 9, Rungsted Kyst, Denmark.
Telephone: 863510.

Rasmussen, Viggo F.; Danish business executive; b. 20 Jan. 1915; ed. Copenhagen School of Business Science.
Danish Air Lines 32-, Vice-Pres. 47, Exec. Vice-Pres. Scandinavian Airlines System 50; Pres. and Managing Dir. United Breweries (Tuborg Breweries and Kings Brewhouse) 62-; Vice-Chair. Brewers' Asscn.; mem. Board of Reps. of Privatbanken, Copenhagen; mem. Acad. of Technical Sciences; Knight First Degree, Order of Dannebrog, Knight Order of Vasa, Commdr. Order of Merit of the Italian Republic.
Tuborg Breweries Ltd., Strandvejen 50, 2900 Hellerup; Home: 23 Lundegaardsvej, 2900 Hellerup, Denmark.
Telephone: 29-3311 (Office); HE 4822 (Home).

Rasschaert, Théo; Belgian trade unionist; b. 22 Jan. 1927; ed. Athenée, Antwerp, and Inst. supérieur de Commerce de l'Etat, Antwerp.
Studies Dept., Féd. du Travail de Belgique 51-59; mem. Belgian Del. to negotiations for Treaty of Rome 57-58; Sec. responsible for econ. questions and problems of collective negotiation, Secrétariat Syndical Européen (European Trade Union Secr.—CISL) 59-67, Sec.-Gen. of European Trade Union Secretariat 67-.
Publs. Articles on labour problems and European questions.
Secrétariat Syndical Européen, 110 rue des Palais, Brussels 3, Belgium.
Telephone: 16-81-05.

Rasulov, Jabar; Soviet politician; b. 1913; ed. Mid-Asian Cotton Inst.
Member of Communist Party 39-; People's Commissar for Agriculture, Tadzhik 45; Chair. Tadzhik Council of Ministers 46-55; Dep. U.S.S.R. Supreme Soviet 46, 50, 54, 58, 62, 66; Deputy Chair. Soviet of Union; mem. Cen. Revision Comm., C.P.S.U. 52-56; mem. Bureau

Cen. Cttee. C.P., Tadzhik S.S.R. 54; mem. Econ. Comm., Council of Nationalities, U.S.S.R. Supreme Soviet 54-58; Deputy Minister of Agriculture U.S.S.R. 55; Sec. Cen. Cttee. Tadzhik C.P. 58-60; Amb. to Togo 60-61; First Sec. Cen. Cttee. of C.P. of Tadzhik S.S.R. 61-; mem. Cen. Cttee. C.P.S.U. 56-; Order of Lenin (five times); Order of the Red Banner of Labour.
Central Committee of Communist Party of Tadzhik S.S.R., Dushambe, Tadzhik S.S.R., U.S.S.R.

Ratanov, Anatoli Petrovich; Soviet diplomatist; b. 1921.
Member C.P. of Soviet Union 43-; worked for Young Communist League 43-54; Editor journal, *Molodoi Kommunist* (Young Communist) 54-58; Perm. Rep. of U.S.S.R. Cttee. of Youth Orgs. to World Fed. of Democratic Youth 58-60; First Sec., Phnom-Penh, Cambodia 60-62, Counsellor 62-63; Amb. to Cambodia 65-68; on staff at Ministry of Foreign Affairs 68-; Order of Lenin, Red Banner of Labour, Badge of Honour, etc.
Ministry of Foreign Affairs, 32-34 Smolenskaya-Sennaya ploshchad, Moscow, U.S.S.R.

Ratcliffe, John Henry, C.B.E.; Canadian industrialist; b. 2 Aug. 1894; ed. Listowel High School and Toronto Univ.
With A. E. Ames & Co. Ltd., Toronto 18-21, McLeod, Young, Weir & Co. Ltd. 21-; Dir. Hayes Steel Products Ltd., Photo Engravers and Electrotypers Ltd., Standard Radio Ltd., C.F.R.B. Ltd., Great Lake Power Co. Ltd., Winnipeg Central Heating Co. Ltd., British Northwestern Insurance Co., Security Nat. Insurance Co., Canadian Gen. Securities Ltd., and Traders Finance Corpn. Ltd.; Chair. and Dir. McLeod, Young, Weir & Co. Ltd.
McLeod, Young, Weir & Company Limited, 50 King Street West, Toronto 1; Home: 76 Glenview Avenue, Toronto 12, Ont., Canada.

Rathbone, Perry Townsend; American museum director; b. 3 July 1911; ed. Harvard Univ.
Curator Detroit Inst. of Arts 36-40; Dir. City Art Museum, St. Louis 40-55; Dir. Museum of Fine Arts, Boston 55-; Chevalier Légion d'Honneur and several hon. degrees.
Publs. *Charles Wimar: Painter of the Indian Frontier* 46, *Max Beckmann* 48, *Mississippi Panorama* 49, *Westward the Way* 54, *Lee Gatch* 60.
Museum of Fine Arts, Boston 02115, Mass.; Home: 151 Coolidge Hill, Cambridge 02138, Mass., U.S.A.

Ratnayake, Abhayratne, B.A.; Ceylonese lawyer and politician; b. 7 Jan. 1900; ed. Dhamaraja Coll., Kandy, and Royal Coll., Colombo.
Member State Council 31-47; Acting Minister of Educ. 43; Minister of Food, later Minister of Home Affairs 48; now Pres. of Ceylon Senate.
7 Jayaratne Avenue, Colombo 5, Ceylon.

Ratsimamanga, Albert Rakota, D.SC., D.MED.; Madagascan diplomatist; b. 28 Dec. 1907; ed. Univ. of Paris.
Research Dir. Centre Nat. de la Recherche Scientifique; Dir. Ecole Pratique des Hautes Etudes; Ambassador of Malagasy Repub. to France 60-, to German Fed. Repub. 61-; mem. Exec. Council, UNESCO 60, Vice-Chair. 62; corresp. mem. of l'Académie des Sciences de Paris 66; Grand Officier, Légion d'Honneur, etc.
Major works: Thèse sur l'Anthropologie de Madagascar, Travaux sur la Biochimie de la Surrénale, Hormones Steroidiques et Vitamines Hydrosolubles, Etudes Expérimentales sur l'Action antituberculeuse et anti-lépreuse des phtalydrazides.
Embassy of the Malagasy Republic (Madagascar), 1 boulevard Suchet, Paris 16e, France.

Rattigan, Terence Mervyn, C.B.E.; British dramatist; b. 10 June 1911; ed. Harrow and Trinity Coll., Oxford.
Publs. Plays: *First Episode* 34, *French Without Tears*

36, *After the Dance* 39, *Flare Path* 42, *While the Sun Shines* 43, *Love in Idleness* 44, *O, Mistress Mine* (N.Y. 45), *The Winslow Boy* 46 (N.Y. 47), *Playbill* 48 (N.Y. 49), *Adventure Story* 49, *Who is Sylvia?* 50, *The Deep Blue Sea* 52 (N.Y. 52), *The Sleeping Prince* 53 (N.Y. 56), *Separate Tables* 54 (N.Y. 56), *Variation on a Theme* 58, *Ross* 60 (N.Y. 61), *Man and Boy* 63; films: *Quiet Wedding* 40, *French Without Tears* 39, *Journey Together* 45, *The Way to the Stars* 46, *While the Sun Shines* 47, *The Winslow Boy* 48, *The Browning Version* 51, *The Sound Barrier* 52, *The Final Test, The Man Who Loved Redheads, The Deep Blue Sea* 55, *The Prince and the Showgirl* 57, *Separate Tables* 59, *The V.I.P.s* 63, *The Yellow Rolls-Royce* 64.
c/o Dr. Jan Van Loewen, 81 Shaftesbury Avenue, London, W.1, England.

Rau, Sir Benegal Rama, (married to Lady Dhanvanthi Rama Rau, *q.v.*), C.I.E., M.A.; Indian diplomatist and banker; b. 10 Jan. 1889; ed. Presidency Coll., Madras and King's Coll., Cambridge.
Entered Indian Civil Service 13; Deputy High Commr. in London 34-38; Agent-Gen. and High Commr. in Union of South Africa 38-41; Chair. Bombay Port Trust 41-46; Ambassador to Japan 47-48; leader of Del. to Commonwealth Conf. Canberra 47; Ambassador to U.S. 48-49; Gov. Reserve Bank of India 49-57.
Mafatlal Park, Bombay, India.

Rau, Chalapathi M.; Indian newspaper editor.
Asst. Ed. *National Herald*, Lucknow 38-42, when the paper closed; Asst. Ed. *Hindustan Times*, New Delhi 43-45; Asst. Ed. *National Herald* 45-46, and Ed. 46-; Alternate rep. UNESCO Gen. Conf. New Delhi 56, Paris 60; Rep. U.N. Gen. Assembly 58; Pres. Indian Fed. of Working Journalists; mem. Indian Press Comm. Publ. *Fragments of a Revolution* 65.
National Herald, 1 Bhisheshwar Nath Road, P.O. Box 122, Lucknow, India.

Rau, Lady Dhanvanthi Rama (wife of Sir Benegal Rama Rau, *q.v.*,), M.A.; Indian social worker; b. 10 May 1893; ed. St. Mary's High School, Hubli, and Presidency Coll., Univ. of Madras.
Lecturer in English, Queen Mary's Coll., Univ. of Madras 17-19; Sec. All India Child Marriage Abolition League, Simla 27-28; mem. Board, Int. Alliance of Women for Suffrage and Equal Citizenship 32-38; Pres. Bombay Branch, All India Women's Conf. (A.I.W.C.) 46, Pres. A.I.W.C. 46-47; Pres. Family Planning Asscn. of India 49-63; mem. Family Planning Programmes and Research Cttee., Ministry of Health, Govt. of India 53, Chair. Social and Moral Hygiene Enquiry Cttee. 55; mem. Central Social Welfare Board 56-61; mem. Consultative Cttee. of Planning Comm. for Third Five Year Plan (Health) 61; Pres. Int. Planned Parenthood Fed. 63-; Kaiser-I-Hind Gold Medal (U.K.) 38; Lasker Award (U.S.A.) 55; Padma Bhusan 59.
D/10, Mafatlal Park, Bhulabai Desai Road, Bombay 26, India.

Rau, Santha Rama (daughter of Sir Benegal Rama Rau, *q.v.*, and Lady Rama Rau, *q.v.*), (Mrs. Faubion Bowers); Indian writer; b. 24 Jan. 1923; ed. St. Paul's Girls' School, London, and Wellesley Coll., U.S.A.
Numerous journeys in Europe, India, America, Southeast Asia, Japan and Russia; fmr. teacher Hani Freedom School, Tokyo.
Publs. *Home to India, East of Home, Remember the House, View to the South-East, My Russian Journey*; dramatised version of E. M. Forster's *A Passage to India*; *Gifts of Passage* (autobiog.).
10D Mafatlal Park, Bhulabhai Desai Road, Bombay, India.

Rau, Walter Franz, DR. RER. POL.; German international civil servant; b. 1 Sept. 1907; ed. Friedrich-Wilhelm Univ., Berlin, and Christian Albrecht Univ., Kiel.
Scientific Research Dept., Inst. für Weltwirtschaft und Seeverkehr, Univ. of Kiel 32-33; Financial Editor *Kreutz Zeitung* 33-36; Deputy Dir. Econ. Research Dept., Gemeinschaftsgruppe Deutscher Hypothekenbanken 36-38; Econ. Research Dept., I.G. Farben Industry A.G. 38-45; in President's Office, Govt. of Schleswig-Holstein 46-51; Econ. Adviser, Ministry of Econs., Bonn 51-64; Deputy Sec., Ministry for Econ. Co-operation 64-67; Deputy Sec.-Gen. Org. for Co-operation and Econ. Devt. (OECD) 67-.
Organisation de Co-opération et de Développement Economiques, 2 rue André-Pascal, Paris 16e, France.

Rauch, Henry E.; American textile executive; b. 21 Sept. 1902; ed. Bentley School of Accounting and Finance, Boston.
Controller, American Thread Co., New York City 38-42, Exec. Vice-Pres. 42-50, Dir. 51-52; Pres., Peterzell and Gelles Inc. 50-51, Management Consultant 51; Burlington Industries Inc. 52-, Senior Vice- Pres., Comptroller 61-62, Chair. 62-.
504 Country Club Drive, Greensboro, North Carolina, U.S.A.

Rauchfuss, Wolfgang; German politician; b. 27 Nov. 1911.
Former business official; Deputy Minister of Foreign and Inner German Trade 62-65; Vice-Chair. Council of Ministers Dec. 65-; Sozialistische Einheitspartei Deutschlands.
Ministerrat, Berlin, Germany.

Rauchhaupt, Friedrich Wilhelm von, LL.D., PH.D., L. en D.; German jurist; b. 13 Aug. 1881.
Lecturer in Law, Heidelberg Univ. 22; Visiting Prof. Buenos Aires Univ. 26, 67 and Santiago de Chile 26; Extraordinary Prof. Heidelberg since 29 (retd. 46, reinstated 56); hon. mem. of Reales Academias de Jurisprudencia y Legislación and de Ciencias Morales y Politicas, of Instituto de Estudios Políticos, Madrid, of the Facultad de Leyes y Ciencias Políticas, Santiago de Chile, Int. Inst. of Space Law in the Int. Astronautical Fed., of the Scientific Soc. for Air and Space Legal Questions, Int. Law Asscn., Hermann Oberth-Gessellschaft, Hanover. Publs. *Eigentümergrunddienstbarkeit* 06, *Depositenrecht* 07, *The Prize Court Rules* 14, *Handbuch der deutschen Wahlgesetze und Geschäftsordnungen* 16, *Geschichte der spanischen Gesetzesquellen* 23, *Estudio comparativo entre el desarrollo del derecho español y el alemán* 23, *Völkerrechtliche Eigentümlichkeiten Amerikas, insbes. Hispanoamerikas* 24, *Correlaciones en el desarrollo de los derechos de Europa y de América* 28, *Rechte Europas* (2 vols.) 31-32, *Völkerrecht* 36, *Über die Christlichen Ritterorden* 53, 56, 58, 60, *Zur Geschichte der Familie v. R.* 55, *Vergleich und Angleichbarkeit der Rechte Süd- und Mittel-Amerikas* 55, *Der Aufbau des englischen Rechts*, 5th edn. 65, *Über die Atomenergie und Atomenergierecht* 57, *Die Geschichte der spanischen Gesetzgebung seit 1923* 58, *Die Hauptgebote des Neuen Testamentes: Gottesliebe, Nächstenliebe, Feindesliebe im geltenden Recht* 59, 61, *Überblick der Geschichte des Völkerrechts in den spanischsprachigen Staaten von Europa und Amerika* 59, *Die Zurückkehr zur Rechten Gotteserkenntnis* 60, *Die Wiederentdeckung des Völkerrechts durch Hugo Grotius* 61, *Über Weltraumrecht* 62, *El Derecho divino y el Derecho natural en el Derecho rigente* 62, etc.; contributions to the First to Eleventh Colloquium on the Law of Outer Space 58-68, *Dir Weltraumflüge und die Rechtwissenschaft* 63 (also in English), and journal articles.
Plöck 45-49, Heidelberg, German Federal Republic.
Telephone: 28-2-67.

Raunio, Eino Albin; Finnish politician; b. 18 Jan. 1909; ed. elementary school and Workers Academy. Began as lecturer; office manager of newspaper in Forssa 36-40; mem. of Parliament 39-; Chair. Forssa City Council 64-; Minister of Finance Jan. 68-.
Helsinki, Gyldenintie 5B, Finland.
Telephone: 677197.

Rauschenberg, Robert; American artist; b. 22 Oct. 1925; ed. Kansas City Art Inst., Acad. Julien, Paris, Black Mountain Coll., North Carolina and Art Students League, New York.
Travel in Italy and North Africa 52-53; Designer of Stage-Sets and Costumes for Merce Cunningham Dance Company 55-65, Lighting for Cunningham Co. 61-65; Costumes and Sets for Paul Taylor Dance Co. 57-59; Choreography in America 62-; affiliated with Leo Castelli Gallery, New York City 57-; works in Tate Gallery, London, Albright-Knox Gallery, Buffalo, Whitney Museum of American Art, New York City, Andrew Dickson White Museum, Cornell Univ., Museum of Modern Art, N.Y., Goucher Coll. Collection, Towson, Maryland, etc., numerous one-man shows in U.S.A. and Europe; Exhbn. at Stedelijk Museum, Amsterdam 68; First Prize, Venice Biennale 64.
Leo Castelli Gallery, 4 East 77th Street, New York City 21, New York, U.S.A.

Ravanel, Jean, D. en D.; French civil servant; b. 2 May 1920; ed. Faculty of Law, Grenoble Univ.
Entered Civil Service 45; Technical Adviser, Ministry of Public Works and Transport 54-55; Dir. Cabinet of Minister of Agriculture 58-62, and of Minister of Public Works and Transport 62; Chair. Gen. Commissariat for Tourism 63-; Chevalier Légion d'Honneur; Aeronautical Medal.
Commissariat Général au Tourisme, 8 avenue de l'Opéra, Paris 1er; Home: 87 avenue Kléber, Paris 16e, France.

Ravegnani, Giuseppe; Italian critic, journalist and author; b. 13 Oct. 1895.
Successively Literary Critic *Il Resto del Carlino*, Editor *Il Corriere Italiano*, Chief Reporter *Il Regno*, Editor *La Fiera Letteraria*, Literary Critic *La Stampa*, contributor to *Corriere della Sera* and numerous other papers; Dir. *Il Corriere Padano*, *Il Gazzettino*, *La Gazzetta di Venezia*, Chief Editor and now Literary Editor *Epoca*; Dir. Biblioteca Ariostea, Ferrara; Premio Viareggio for *Uomini Visti* 55, Premio Marzotto 56.
Publs. *Antologia di Novelle Catalane* (translation), *Uomini Visti* (2 vols.); numerous critical works on Ariosto and XIX century Italian literature.
Piazza Morbegno 5, Milan, Italy.

Ravila, Paavo Ilmari, PH.D.; Finnish professor; b. 5 July 1902; ed. Turku and Helsinki.
Prof. of Finnish Language Univ. of Turku 34-49; Prof. of Finno-Ugric Linguistics Univ. of Helsinki 49-56, Rector 53-56; Pres. Finno-Ugric Society; mem. Acad. of Finland 56-, Pres. 61-63; Chancellor Univ. of Helsinki 63-.
Publs. *Das Quantitätssystem des Seelappischen Dialektes von Maattivuono* 32, *Mordwinische Volksdichtung* (Vols. I-IV) 39-45.
Ritokalliont 1, Helsinki, Finland.

Rawlings, General Edwin William, B.A., M.B.A.; American corporation executive; b. 9 Nov. 1904; ed. Hamline Univ., Harvard Univ. Graduate School of Business Administration.
Entered the Army 29, progressed from flying cadet to four star Gen. 54, Head, Air Material Command, Wright-Patterson A.F.B., Dayton 51-59, retd. 59; Financial Vice-Pres. Gen. Mills, Inc. 59-60, Exec. Vice-Pres. 60-61, Pres. 61-; D.F.C., D.S.M. with Oak Leaf Cluster, Air Force Asscn.'s Citation of Honor; Hon. O.B.E.;

Hon. Dr. of Business Admin. (Hamline, Tufts Univs.), Hon. D.Hum. (Dayton Univ.), Hon. LL.D. (Ohio Wesleyan, Miami Univs., Hendrix Coll.).
9200 Wayzata Blvd., Minneapolis, Minn. 55440, U.S.A.

Rawlinson, Rt. Hon. Sir Peter Anthony Grayson, P.C., Q.C., M.P.; British lawyer and politician; b. 26 June 1919; ed. Downside and Christ's Coll., Cambridge.
Served in Irish Guards 39-46; called to the Bar, Inner Temple 46; Mem. of Parl. 55-; Recorder of Salisbury 61-62; Solicitor-Gen. 62-64; mem. Bar Council 66; Conservative.
55 Chelsea Square, London, S.W.3, England.

Rawsthorne, Alan, C.B.E., F.R.M.C.M.; British composer; b. 2 May 1905; ed. Royal Manchester Coll. of Music.
Taught at Dartington Hall 32-34; served in Army Second World War; Hon. R.A.M.
Compositions include Variations for two Violins 38, Symphonic Studies 39, two Piano Concertos, *Cortèges* (Fantasy Overture) 45, Overture *Street Corner* 45, two Violin Concertos, Quartet for Clarinet and Strings, Sonata for 'Cello and Piano, Concerto for String Orchestra, Concerto for Oboe and String Orchestra, three String Quartets, *Madame Chrysanthème* (ballet), 3 symphonies, Sonata for Violin and Piano, *A Canticle of Man* (chamber cantata), *Practical Cats* (for speaker and orch.), Improvisations on a Theme by Constant Lambert 61, Concerto for 10 Instruments 61; Divertimento for Chamber Orchestra 62, Piano Trio, Quintet for Wind and Piano 62, *Carmen Vitale* 63, *Elegiac Fragments* 64, Chamber Cantata 65, Cello Concerto 66; *Ballade* (for piano) 67; songs and piano music.
Sudbury Cottage, Little Sampford, Saffron Walden, Essex, England.

Ray, Satyajit; Indian film director; b. 2 May 1921; ed. Ballygunge Govt. School, Presidency Coll., Calcutta.
Commercial artist in Calcutta before beginning his career in films; directed *Pather Panchali* (Cannes Int. Film Festival Award for " the most human document" 56, Golden Laurel Award, Edinburgh Film Festival 57), *Aparajito* (sequel to *Pather Panchali*, Grand Prix, Venice Film Festival 57), *The Philosopher's Stone*, *Dzhalsagar* (The Music Room), *Apur Sansar* (The World of Apu), *The Goddess* 61, *Three Daughters* 61, *Abhijan* 62, *Kanchanjangha* 62, *Mahanagar* 64, *Charulata* 65, *Kapurush-o-Mahapurush* 65, *Nayak* 66; composed the music for all his films since *Three Daughters*; Editor *Sandesh*, children's magazine; Magsaysay Award for Journalism and Literature 67.
3 Lake Temple Road, Calcutta 29, India.

Raymond, Ernest; British novelist; b. 31 Dec. 1888; ed. St. Paul's School.
Ordained 14; Chaplain to the Forces in First World War; resgnd. Orders 23; Fellow Royal Soc. of Literature 47, Knight Order of Merit of Italian Republic 56.
Publs. *Tell England, Damascus Gate, Wanderlight, The Old Tree Blossomed, Through Literature to Life, The Berg* (play), *The Jesting Army, Once in England, Newtimber Lane, Child of Norman's End, We, the Accused* (Gold Medal, Book Guild 36), *A Family That Was, The Marsh, In the Steps of St. Francis, The Multabello Road* (play), *The Miracle of Brean, A Song of the Tide, The Last to Rest, Was There Love Once? The Corporal of the Guard, For Them That Trespass, The Five Sons of Le Faber, The Kilburn Tale, In the Steps of the Brontës, Gentle Greaves, The Witness of Canon Welcome, A Chorus Ending, Two Gentlemen of Rome, The Chalice and the Sword, To The Wood No More, The Nameless Places* 55, *The Lord of Wensley* 56, *The Old June Weather* 57, *The City and the Dream, The Quiet Shore* 58, *The Visit of Brother Ives* 60, *Paris, City of Enchantment, Mr. Olim* 61, *The Chatelaine* 62, *One of Our Brethren* 63,

Late in the Day 64, *The Tree of Heaven* 65, *The Mountain Farm* 66, *The Bethany Road* 67, *The Story of My Days* 68.
22 The Pryors, East Heath Road, Hampstead, London, N.W.3, England.
Telephone: 01-435-3716.

Raymond, Sir Stanley Edward, Kt., M.INST.T.; British transport official; b. 10 Aug. 1913; ed. Orphanage and Grammar School, Hampton, Middlesex.
Tax Officer, Civil Service 30; Asst. Sec. Soc. of Civil Servants 39-45; Royal Artillery 42-45; joined London Passenger Transport Board 46; Chief Staff and Welfare Officer, British Road Services 47-55, Chief Officer (Org.) 52-55; Asst. Manpower Adviser, British Transport Comm. 55-56, Dir. of Establishment and Staff 56-57; Chief Commercial Manager, Scottish Region, British Railways 57-59, Asst. Gen. Manager 59-61; Traffic Adviser, British Transport Comm. 61-62; Gen. Manager, Western Region of British Railways 62-63, Chair. Western Railways Board 63; mem. British Railways Board Oct. 63-64, Vice-Chair. 64-65, Chair. 65-67.
124 Chiltern Court, Baker Street, London, N.W.1; 26 Cavendish House, Kings Road, Brighton, Sussex, England.
Telephone: 01-935-4503; and 0273-23084.

Rayne, Max; British company director; b. 8 Feb. 1918; ed. Central Foundation School and Univ. Coll., London.
Royal Air Force 40-45; Founder Dir. British Commercial Property Investment Trust Ltd. 48; Chair. London Merchant Securities Ltd. 60-; Dir. Sanitas Trust Ltd. 48-, New River Co. Ltd. 62-, Hazell Sun Ltd. 63-, British Printing Corpn. Ltd. 64-; Gov. St. Thomas's Hospital 62-; mem. Council St. Thomas's Hospital Medical School 65-; mem. Estates Sub-Cttee. King Edward's Hospital Fund for London 60-, Finance Cttee. 64-, Gen. Council 66-; Gov. Royal Ballet School 66-, Yehudi Menuhin School 66-, Malvern Coll. 66-; mem. Jewish Welfare Board 66-; Hon. Fellow, Univ. Coll., London 66-; Founder and Patron Max Rayne Foundation, created 62, to continue philanthropic work of Max Rayne Charitable Trust in fields of education, research, medical and general welfare, the arts, etc.
33 Duke Street, London, W.1, England.

Razafimbahiny, Jules Alphonse; Malagasy (Madagascar) economist; b. 19 April 1922; ed. Institut des Sciences Juridiques et Financières, Faculté de Droit, Paris, and Institut des Hautes Etudes Politiques, Paris.
President of Comm. of Overseas Countries associated with Econ. and Social Council of Common Market and EURATOM, Brussels 58-59; Technical Counsellor to Minister of State for Nat. Economy, Madagascar 60-61; First Sec.-Gen. OAMCE (Org. Africaine et Malgache de Co-opération Economique) 61-64; Ambassador to U.K., Italy, Greece and Israel 65-; Sec. of Foreign Affairs 67-; Pres. Admin. Council Société d'Energie, Madagascar, Pan-African Inst. of Devt.; Commdr. Ordre Nat. (Chad, Mauritania), Officier Ordre Nat. (Madasgacar and Upper Volta), Grand Croix de l'Ordre de Saint Sylvestre (Vatican), Grand Croix de l'Ordre National de la République Italienne.
Ministry of Foreign Affairs, Tananarive, Malagasy Republic.
Telephone: 211-98 and 211-99.

Razak bin Hussain, Tun Abdul; Malaysian lawyer and politician; b. 22; ed. Malay School, Pekan, Malay Coll., Kuala Kangsar and Lincoln's Inn, London.
Joined Malay Admin. Service 39, Malayan Civil Service 50; State Sec., Pahang 52; Mentri Besar, Pahang 55; Minister of Education (Fed. Govt.) 55-57; Deputy Prime Minister and Minister of Defence 57-59, Prime Minister Feb.-Aug. 59; Deputy Prime Minister, Minister

of Defence and Rural Development, Malaya 59-63, Malaysia 63-, now also Minister of Home Affairs; Leader of Youth Section, United Malays Nat. Org. 50, Deputy Pres. 51-; Orang Kaya Indra Shahbandar (Major Chief of State of Pahang); Hon. LL.D. (Univ. of Malaysia) and other awards.
Deputy Prime Minister's Office, Jalan Dato' Onn, Kuala Lumpur, Malaya, Malaysia.
Telephone: 88350.

Razif, Mohammed; Indonesian diplomatist; b. 10; ed. Djakarta Law Faculty.
Private legal practice, Sumatra 39; Official, Dept. of Justice, Djakarta 41; Dist. Judge, Djakarta 42; Magistrate of Semarang 43; Head Diplomatic and Consular Section, Ministry of Foreign Affairs 46; Chief Econ. and Financial Section, Indonesian High Comm. The Hague 50; Consul-Gen. Singapore, Malaya, Sarawak, Brunei and British North Borneo 50-54; Minister to Belgium and Luxembourg 54-56; Dir. Afro-Asian Affairs Dept., Ministry of Foreign Affairs 56-57; Ambassador to Malaya 57-63; Head of Western Europe Directorate, Foreign Office, Djakarta 63-.
Foreign Office, Djakarta, Indonesia.

Razik, Sir Fareed, Kt., O.B.E.; Ceylonese politician; b. 29 Dec. 1893; ed. Zahira Coll., Colombo, and Royal Coll., Colombo.
Member State Council 31-48; mem. Senate 48-52, House of Reps. 52-; Leader of Ceylon Moor Community; founder of first Muslim Ladies' Coll. in Ceylon; founder and Pres. Moors' Islamic Cultural Home.
Hajara Villa, 27 Fareed Place, Colombo 4, Ceylon.

Razin, Leonid Alexeyevich; Soviet foreign trade official; b. 1908; ed. Gorky Mechanical Engineering Inst.
Work in foreign trade system 38-; Official of Soviet Purchasing Comm. in the U.S.A. 41-45; with Soviet Trade Mission in Japan 46-49; Chair. Transport Machinery Import Asscn. 51-55; Soviet Trade Rep. in Belgium 55-57; with Ministry of Foreign Trade 58-63; Chair. Sudoimport (Ship Imports) Asscn. 63-.
Sudoimport, Ministry of Foreign Trade, Smolenskaya-Sennaya ploshchad 32-34, Moscow, U.S.S.R.

Razuvayev, Grigory Alexeevich; Soviet organic chemist; b. 1895; ed. Leningrad Univ.
Instructor, Red Army Engineering Acad. 25-27; Laboratory Head, Inst. of High Pressure, U.S.S.R. Acad. of Sciences 29-34; Instructor, Gorky Univ. 46-, Dir. Chemical Research Inst., Gorky Univ. 56-; Corresp. mem. U.S.S.R. Acad. of Sciences 58-66, mem. 66-; Lenin Prize 58.
U.S.S.R. Academy of Sciences, 14 Lenin Prospekt, Moscow, U.S.S.R.

Razzaz, Ahmed Munif, M.B., B.CH.; Jordanian physician and politician; b. 19; ed. Amman Secondary School, American Univ. of Beirut and Cairo.
Teacher 39-41; mem. Baath Party 49-, Jordan Regional Leadership 56-, Sec. 60-, Nat. Leadership 59-, Sec.-Gen. Baath Party 65-; exiled to Syria 52-53; imprisoned 57-59, 61, 63-64; arrested 66.
Publs. *Features of New Arab Life* (in Arabic) 53, *Evolution of the Meaning of Nationalism* (in Arabic) 60, (English trans.) 63, *Freedom and its Problems in Underdeveloped Countries* 65.
National Baath Party, rue Abdul Aziz No. 66, Damascus, Syrian Arab Republic.

Rea, 2nd Baron, cr. 35, of Eskdale, **Philip Russell Rea,** P.C., O.B.E., M.A., D.L., J.P.; British politician; b. 7 Feb. 1900; ed. Westminster School, Christ Church, Oxford, and Grenoble Univ.
Underwriting mem. of Lloyds; Dir. Rea Brothers Ltd., Scottish & Mercantile Investment Co. Ltd., Rea Ltd., and R. and J. H. Rea Ltd.; served army 14-18 and 39-45 war; with Foreign Office 46-50; Vice-Chair. Liberal Party Exec. 51-54, Pres. Liberal Party 55,

Liberal Leader, House of Lords 55-67; Deputy Speaker, House of Lords; Chevalier Légion d'Honneur; Officer Belgian Order of the Crown; Croix de Guerre with Palm. 5 St. John's House, 30 Smith Square, London, S.W.1, England.

Read, Sir Herbert, Kt., D.S.O., M.C.; British poet and critic; b. 4 Dec. 1893; ed. Univ. of Leeds.
Asst. Principal, Treasury 19-22; Asst. Keeper Victoria and Albert Museum 22-31; Prof. of Fine Art Univ. of Edinburgh 31-33; Editor *Burlington Magazine* 33-39; Pres. Inst. of Contemporary Arts, London, Brit. Soc. of Aesthetics; Trustee, Tate Gallery, London 65-; Erasmus Prize 66; Hon. Litt. D. (Leeds, York, Buffalo Boston).
Publs. *English Prose Style* 28, *Art Now* 33, *Collected Poems* 35, *Art and Society* 36, *Collected Essays in Literary Criticism* 38, *Annals of Innocence and Experience* 40, *Thirty-Five Poems* 40, *The Politics of the Unpolitical* 43, *Education Through Art* 43, *Art and Industry* 44, *A World Within a War* (poems) 44, *A Coat of Many Colours, Art and Society* 45, *The Grass Roots of Art* 47, *Education for Peace* 49, *The Philosophy of Modern Art* 52, *The True Voice of Feeling* 53, *Icon and Idea* 55, *The Art of Sculpture* 56, *Moon's Farm and Other Poems* 56, *The Tenth Muse* (essays) 57, *Concise History of Modern Painting* 59, *The Forms of Things Unknown* 60, *Letter to a Young Painter* 62, *To Hell with Culture, The Contrary Experience* 63, *A Concise History of Modern Sculpture* 64, *Contemporary British Art* 64, *The Origins of Form in Art, Henry Moore: Life and Work* 65, *Collected Poems, Poetry and Experience* 67, *Art and Alienation* 67, *Hans Arp, Life and Work* 68.
[*Died* 12 *June* 1968].

Read, John Erskine, S.M., Q.C., B.A., LL.D., D.C.L.; Canadian barrister; b. 5 July 1888; ed. Dalhousie, Columbia and Oxford Univs.
Admitted to Bar of Nova Scotia 13; served Canadian Army (Major, despatches, wounded) 14-17; Prof. of Law and Dean of Faculty of Law, Dalhousie Univ. 20-29; Legal Adviser, Dept. of External Affairs, Ottawa 29-46; Judge of Int. Court of Justice 46-58; mem. Appeals Cttee. Opium Protocol 63-; has represented Canadian Govt. at various Imperial and Int. Confs.; Counsel for Canadian Govt. in proceedings before Supreme Court of Canada, Supreme Court of U.S.A., Judicial Cttee. of Privy Council, Int. Joint Comm: and Special Int. Tribunals; Hon. Fellow Univ. Coll., Oxford; Hon. Master of the Bench, Gray's Inn 53, Hon. LL.D. (Dalhousie and McMaster) 46; D.C.L. (Oxford) 52, (Acadia) 61.
35 Wilton Crescent, Ottawa 1, Canada.
Telephone: 1-613-234-0721.

Reagan, Ronald; American actor and politician; b. 1911; ed. public schools at Tampico, Monmouth, Galesburg and Dixon, Illinois, and Eureka Coll.
Former radio sports announcer and editor, Central Broadcasting Co.; appeared in more than fifty films; appeared on *Death Valley Days* TV series; operated horse-breeding and cattle ranch; mem. Board of Dirs. Int. Holding Co. and Coastal Life Insurance Co.; Player and Production Supervisor, Gen. Electric Theater TV for eight years; fmr. Pres. Screen Actors Guild, Motion Picture Industry Council; mem. Board of Dirs. Cttee. on Fundamental Educ., St. John's Hospital; U.S. Air Force 42-46; Gov. of Calif. 67-; numerous awards; Republican.
State Capitol, Sacramento, Calif., U.S.A.

Reale, Oronzo; Italian lawyer and politician; b. 24 Oct. 1902; ed. Univ. degli Studi, Rome.
Secretary, Young Republican Fed. 20-24; Founder-mem. and Exec. Partito d'Azione 42; mem. Cttee. for Nat. Liberation; mem. Exec. Cttee. Italian Republican Party (P.R.I.) 48-; mem. Chamber of Deputies 58-;

Political Sec. P.R.I. 49-64; Minister of Justice 64-68; mem. Nat. Consultative Assembly 45-46.
c/o Ministerio di Grazia e Giustizia, 1 Via del Pollaiolo 5, Rome, Italy.

Reardon, Timothy James, Jr.; American government official; b. 18 May 1915; ed. Phillips Exeter Acad. Harvard Coll.
Worked in Boston Advertising Agency 38-41; Nat. Advertising Man., Lowell Sun Newspaper 41-42; service in U.S.A.F. attaining rank of Captain 42-46; Admin. Asst. to Senator John F. Kennedy 47-60; Special Asst. to the Pres. for Cabinet Affairs 61-64; Special Asst. to Chair. Federal Deposit Insurance Corpn. 64-65, Exec. Asst. to Board of Dirs., F.D.I.C. 65-.
Federal Deposit Insurance Corporation, Washington 25, D.C.; Home: 3134 Dumbarton Avenue, N.W., Washington, D.C., U.S.A.

Rebbeck, Denis, C.B.E., M.A., M.SC., PH.D.; British shipbuilder; b. 22 Jan. 1914; ed. Campbell Coll., Belfast and Pembroke Coll., Cambridge.
Assistant Man. Harland and Wolff Ltd., Belfast 39, Dir. 46, Deputy Man. Dir. 53-62, Man. Dir. 62-, Deputy Chair. 63-; Dir. D. and W. Henderson Ltd. and A. and J. Inglis Ltd. 48-68, Chair. 57-68; Dir. Iron Trades Employers Insurance Asscn. Ltd. and Iron Trades Mutual Insurance Co. Ltd. 50-; Belfast Harbour Commr. 62; Exec. Council, Shipbuilders' and Repairers' Nat. Asscn.; Pres. Shipbuilding Employers' Fed. 62-63; Dir. Colvilles Ltd., Glasgow 63-67; Shipbuilding Corpn. Ltd., London 63, Nat. Commercial Bank of Scotland Ltd. 65-; mem. Management Board, Engineering Employers Fed. 63, Gen. and Technical Cttees., Lloyd's Register of Shipping; Akroyd Stuart Award, Inst. of Marine Engineers 43.
The White House, Craigavad, Co. Down, N. Ireland.
Telephone: Holywood 2294.

Rebeyrolle, Paul; French artist; b. 3 Nov. 1926; ed. Lycée Gay-Lussac, Limoges.
Exhibitions at Salon des Indépendants, Salon d'Automne, Salon de Mai, Salon de la Jeune Peinture (France); Dir. Salon de Mai; works in collections in England, Sweden, Belgium, U.S.A., Poland, Italy, Japan, etc.; rep. at Dunn Int. Exhbition, London 63; First Prize, la Jeune Peinture 50, Fénéon Prize 51, First Prize at French Section, Paris Biennale 59.
25 rue Victor Basch, Montrouge, France.

Rebinder, Pyotr Aleksandrovich; Soviet physical chemist; b. 98; ed. Moscow Univ.
Associate Moscow Inst. of Physics and Bio-Physics 23-34; Prof. of Physics, Moscow Pedagogic Inst. 29-; corresp. mem. U.S.S.R. Acad. of Sciences 33-46, mem. 46-; Head Dept. of Dispersed Systems, Inst. of Physical Chemistry, U.S.S.R. Acad. of Sciences 35-; Prof. Moscow Univ. 42-; State Prize, Order of Red Banner of Labour, Order of Lenin, etc.
Publs. Co-author *Research on the Applied Physical Chemistry of Surface Phenomena* 36, co-author *The Physical Chemistry of Flotation Processes* 33, co-author *The Physical Chemistry of Detergent Action* 35, *New Trends in the Development of Colloidal Chemistry* 59.
U.S.S.R. Academy of Sciences, 14 Lenin Prospekt, Moscow, U.S.S.R.

Rebling, Eberhard; German pianist and musicologist; b. 4 Dec. 1911; ed. Berlin Univ.
Emigrated to Holland 36; with resistance movement in Holland 41-45; Music Critic and Pianist, Amsterdam 45-51; Chief Editor periodical *Musik und Gesellschaft*, Berlin 52-59; Rector and Prof. Deutsche Hochschule für Musik Hanns Eisler, Berlin 59-; Nat. Prize 54, Peace Medal 64.
Publs. *Een eeuw Nederlandse Danskunst* 50, *Den Lustelijcken Mey* 50, *Johann Sebastian Bach* 51, *Ballett*

gestern und heute 56, *Ballett sein Wesen und Werden* 64, *Ballett von A-Z* 66.
1603 Eichwalde near Berlin, Pushkinallee 41, D.D.R.
Telephone: Berlin 675047.

Rebocho Vaz, Lieut.-Col. Camilo Augusto de Miranda;
Portuguese army officer and administrator; b. 7 Oct.
1929; ed. Univ. de Coimbra, Escola do Exército,
Lisbon and Inst. de Altos Estudo Militares, Lisbon.
Military service in Portugal, Azores and Angola; 2nd
Commdt., Infantry Regt., Luanda, Angola 60; Commdr.
of anti-terrorist activities 61; Gov. District of Uige,
Angola 61-66; Gov. of Angola 66-; numerous military
decorations.
Governo-Geral de Angola, Luanda, Angola.

Reckitt, Basil Norman, M.A., T.D., D.L.; British
business executive; b. 12 Aug. 1905; ed. Uppingham
and King's Coll., Cambridge.
Joined Reckitt & Sons Ltd., Hull 27, Dir. 37-, later
Chair; Dir. Reckitt & Colman Holdings Ltd. 53-, Vice-
Chair. 53-65, Deputy Chair. 65-66, Chair. June 66-;
Royal Artillery 38-44; Mil. Govt., Germany 44-45; Hon.
LL.D. (Hull) 67.
Publs. *History of Reckitt & Sons Limited, Charles I and
Hull.*
Reckitt & Colman Holdings Ltd., Hull, Yorks.,
England.

Redcliffe-Maud, Baron (Life Peer) cr. 67, of City and
County of Bristol; **John Primatt Redcliffe Maud,** G.C.B.,
C.B.E., M.A., A.B.; British diplomatist and college
principal; b. 3 Feb. 1906; ed. New Coll., Oxford, and
Harvard Coll.
Fellow, Univ. Coll., Oxford 29-39, Dean 32-39, Univ.
Lecturer in Politics, Oxford Univ. 38-39; Councillor,
Oxford City 30-35; Master, Birkbeck Coll., Univ. of
London 39-43; Second Sec. Ministry of Food 43-44;
Second Sec. Ministry of Reconstruction 44, Sec. 45;
Permanent Sec. Ministry of Education 45-52, Ministry
of Fuel and Power 52-57, Ministry of Power 57-58;
mem. Economic Planning Board 52-58; First Council
Meeting, UNRRA 43; Gen. Conf. UNESCO 46, 47,
48, 49, 50, 51; Exec. Board, UNESCO 46-50; Pres.
Exec. Board 49-50; High Commr. in Union of South
Africa and for Basutoland, Bechuanaland Protectorate
and Swaziland, Jan. 59-61, for Basutoland, Bechuana-
land and Swaziland 61-63; Ambassador to South
Africa 61-63; Master of University Coll., Oxford 63-
Chair. Royal Comm. on Local Govt. for England 66-67;
High Bailiff of Westminster 67-; Hon. Fellow New Coll.
64-; Hon. LL.D. (Witwatersrand Univ. 60, Natal Univ.
63, Leeds Univ. 67).
Publs. *City Government: the Johannesburg Experiment*
38; contrib. to *Oxford and the Groups* 34, *Personal
Ethics* 35, *Man's Dilemma and God's Answer* 44, *Educa-
tion in a Changing World* 51, *The British Tradition* 51,
etc.
The Master's Lodgings, University College, Oxford,
England.
Telephone: Oxford 44395.

Reddaway, William Brian, M.A., F.B.A.; British
economist; b. 8 Jan. 1913; ed. Oundle School, and
King's Coll., Cambridge.
Assistant, Bank of England 34-35; Research Fellow in
Econs. Univ. of Melbourne 36-37; Fellow of Clare Coll.,
Cambridge 38-; Board of Trade 40-47; Lecturer,
Cambridge Univ. 47-55, Dir. Dept. of Applied Econs.
55-, Reader in Applied Econs. 57-65; Econ. Adviser, Org.
for European Econ. Co-operation (OEEC) 51-52;
Research Assoc. Center for Int. Studies, New Delhi
59-60; Visiting Lecturer Econ. Devt. Inst., Washington
66-67; mem. Royal Comm. on the Press 61-62; mem.
Nat. Board for Prices and Incomes 67; Editor *London
and Cambridge Economic Bulletin* 51-; Adam Smith
Prize, Cambridge 34.

Publs. *The Russian Financial System* 35, *The Economics of a Declining Population* 39, *The Measurement of
Production Movements* 48, *The Development of the
Indian Economy* 62, *The Effects of U.K. Direct Investment Overseas* 67.
4 Adams Road, Cambridge, England.
Telephone: Cambridge 50041.

Reddi, Bezwada Gopala; Indian politician; b. 07; ed.
Visva Bharathi, Santiniketan.
Served in Govt. of Madras successively as Minister of
Local Administration, Leader of House and Minister for
Finance, Commercial Taxes, Elections, Agencies, Motor
Transport and Registration; Pro-Chancellor of Andhra
Pradesh Univ. 51-55; head of United Congress Legisla-
tive Party, Andhra Pradesh Assembly 55-; Chief
Minister and Minister of Finance, Education, Press,
Stationery and Home Dept., Andhra Pradesh 55-56,
Home Minister 56-57, Finance Minister 57-58; Minister
for Economic Affairs Govt. of India April-May 58,
Minister Revenue and Civil Expenditure May 58-61, of
Housing, Works and Supply 61-62; Minister of Infor-
mation and Broadcasting 62-Aug. 63; Gov. of Uttar
Pradesh 67-; elected to Rajya Sabha 58; mem. Indian
Congress Party, Pres. Andhra Pradesh Congress Cttee.
53; Hon. D.Litt.
Governor's Camp, Raj Bhavan, Uttar Pradesh, Luck-
now Naini Tal, India.

Reddish, Sir Halford (Walter Lupton) Kt., F.C.A.;
British chartered accountant and company director; b.
15 Aug. 1898; ed. Rugby School.
Chairman and Managing Dir., The Rugby Portland
Cement Co. Ltd.; Dir. Hawker Siddeley Group Ltd.,
Alfred Herbert Ltd., Granada Group Ltd., Norwich
Union Socs., Scottish Union and Nat. Insurance Co.
(London Boards) and of other companies; mem. Board
of Referees (Inland Revenue); mem. Council, Inst. of
Dirs., Econ. League, Cement Makers Fed., Cement and
Concrete Asscn.; Underwriting mem. of Lloyd's.
Crown House, Rugby, Warwickshire, England.
Telephone: Rugby 2244.

Reddy, Kasu Brahmananda, B.A., B.L.; Indian
politician; b. 09.
President Guntur District Board 36; mem. Madras
Assembly 46-52; Gen. Sec. Andhra Pradesh Congress
Cttee. 55; Minister of Finance and Planning, Andhra
Pradesh 60-62, of Finance and Co-operation 62-64,
Chief Minister 64-.
Office of the Chief Minister, Hyderabad, Andhra
Pradesh, India.

Reddy, Kolli Venkata Raghunatha, M.A., LL.B.; Indian
lawyer and politician; b. 4 Sept. 1924; ed. V. R. Coll.,
Nellore, and Annamalai Univ. and Lucknow Univ.
Member Senate Annamalai Univ. 47-59; Advocate,
Madras High Court 50, Supreme Court 58, also Andhra
Pradesh High Court; mem. Rajya Sabha 62; Union
Minister of State for Industrial Devt. and Company
Affairs 67-.
Publ. *Criminal Law—Procedural and Substantial.*
Ministry of Industrial Development, New Delhi, India.

Reddy, Kysasambally Chengalaraya, B.A., B.L.; Indian
politician; b. 02; ed. Pachaiyappa's Coll. and Law Coll.,
Madras, Univ. of Madras.
Mem. Mysore Legislature 30-52; Pres. Kolar District
Board 33-37; former Ed. *Janavani;* Pres. Mysore
Peoples' Federation 35-37; effected coalition of Peoples'
Fed. with Mysore Congress 37; mem. Working Cttee.,
Mysore Congress 37-52, Leader Parliamentary Party
37-52, Pres. 37-38 and 46-47; mem. Exec. Council,
All-India States Peoples' Conf. 44-45, Rep. to U.K. and
Continent 45-46; mem. Constituent Assembly of India
47-50; launched Satyagraha for the establishment of
responsible govt. in Mysore State 47; Leader Mysore
Legislative Ass. (three times) and Chief Minister, Mysore

State 47-52; mem. Council of States 52-57; M.P. (Lok Sabha) 57, 62-65; Gov. of Madhya Pradesh Feb. 65-; Central Minister of Production 52-57; Minister of Works, Housing and Supply 57-61, of Commerce and Industry 61-64; LL.D. (h.c.).

Raj Bhavan, Bhopal, Madhya Pradesh, India.

Reddy, Marri Channa, M.B., B.S.; Indian agriculturalist and politician; b. 13 Jan. 1919; ed. Chadarghat High School and Osmania Univ.

Left medical practice to devote himself to politics in Hyderabad; held organisational posts in Indian Nat. Congress Party; leader in Hyderabad Congress; mem. Rajya Sabha 50-51; Minister of Agriculture, Andhra Pradesh 52, later Minister of Planning, Rehabilitation, Panchyat Raj, Industry and Commerce, Commercial Taxes, Education and Finance, Andhra Pradesh; Union Minister of Steel, Mines and Metals March 67-68.

3 Janpath, New Delhi; Vijaya Villa Lalaguda, Secunderabad, India.

Telephone: 36120 and 618649 (New Delhi); 71313 (Secunderabad).

Reddy, Neelam Sanjiva; Indian politician; b. 13; ed. Adyar Arts Coll., Anantapur.

Sec. Andhra P.C.C. 36-46; active in Satyagraha movement; mem. and Sec. Madras Legislative Assembly 46; mem. Indian Constituent Assembly 47; Minister for Prohibition, Housing and Forests, Madras Govt. 49-51; Pres. Andhra P.C.C. 51-; mem. Rajya Sabha 52-53; mem. Andhra Pradesh Legislative Assembly 53-; Deputy Chief Minister, Andhra Pradesh 53-56, Chief Minister 56-57; Leader, Andhra Congress Legislature Party 53-; Pres. All-India Congress Party 60-62; Chief Minister, Andhra Pradesh 62-64; Minister of Steel and Mines, India 64-65, of Transport, Aviation, Shipping and Tourism 65-67; Speaker of Lok Sabha 67-.

The Lok Sabha, New Delhi, India.

Redgrave, Sir Michael (Scudamore), Kt., C.B.E., M.A., D.LITT. (father of Vanessa Redgrave, q.v.); British actor; b. 20 March 1908; ed. Clifton Coll., and Magdalene Coll., Cambridge.

Liverpool Repertory Theatre 34-36; Old Vic 36-37, John Gielgud's Company 37-38; Michel St. Denis's Company 38-39, Old Vic 49-50, Stratford-on-Avon Company 51, 53, 58; appeared in *Beggar's Opera* and *Thunder Rock* 40; served in Royal Navy 41-42; appeared in *A Month in the Country* 43, *Uncle Harry* 44, *Macbeth* (London and New York) 47, *Hamlet* (London, Zürich, Elsinore and Holland Festivals) 50, *Winter Journey* (*Country Girl*) 52, *Merchant of Venice, King Lear* (Stratford-on-Avon), *Anthony and Cleopatra* (London, Stratford-on-Avon, Belgium, Paris) 53-54, *A Touch of the Sun, Hamlet* (Stratford-on-Avon) 58, *The Aspern Papers* 59-60, *The Tiger and the Horse* 60-61; toured Russia playing *Hamlet* 58-59, *The Complaisant Lover* 61-62, *Out of Bounds* 62; films include *The Lady Vanishes, The Stars Look Down, Thunder Rock, The Way to the Stars, Dead of Night, Fame is the Spur, The Browning Version, The Importance of Being Earnest, The Dam Busters, The Innocents, The Loneliness of the Long Distance Runner, The Heroes of Telemark*; joined Nat. Theatre 63; Dir. Opening Season of Yvonne Arnaud Theatre, Guildford 65; produced *A Month in the Country*, London 65; Dir. *Werther* 66, *La Bohème*, Glyndebourne 67; Commdr. Order of Dannenbrog.

Publs. *The Seventh Man* (play) 36, *Actor's Ways and Means* 53, *Mask or Face* 55, *The Mountebank's Tale* (novel), *The Aspern Papers* (play) 59, *Circus Boy* (play) 63.

3 Hans Crescent, London, S.W.1, England.

Redgrave, Vanessa, C.B.E. (daughter of Sir Michael Redgrave, q.v.); British actress; b. 30 Jan. 1937; ed. Queensgate School, London, and Central School of Speech and Drama.

Evening Standard Award, Best Actress 61, and Variety Club Award 61; Award for Best Actress, Cannes Film Festival 66 for *Morgan—A Suitable Case for Treatment*. Principal roles: Helena, *A Midsummer Night's Dream* 59, Stella, *The Tiger and the Horse* by Robert Bolt 60, Katerina, *The Taming of the Shrew* 61, Rosalind, *As you Like It* 61, Imogen, *Cymbeline* 62, Nina, *The Seagull* by Chekhov 64, Miss Jean Brodie, *The Prime of Miss Jean Brodie* 66, film roles include: Leonie, *Morgan—A Suitable Case for Treatment* 65, Sheila, *Sailor from Gibraltar* 65, Guinevere, *Camelot* 67, *Blow Up* 67, Clarissa *Charge of the Light Brigade* 68, Isadora *Isadora Duncan* 68.

30 St. Peter's Square, London, W.6, England.

Redman, Roderick Oliver, M.A., PH.D., F.R.S.; British astronomer; b. 17 July 1905; ed. Marling School, Stroud, and St. John's Coll., Cambridge.

Asst. Astronomer, Dominion Astrophysical Observatory, Victoria, B.C. 28-31; Asst. Dir., Solar Physics Observatory, Cambridge 31-37; Univ. Lecturer in Astrophysics 33-37; Fellow of St. John's Coll., Cambridge 32-39 and 47-; Chief Asst., Radcliffe Observatory, Pretoria, S. Africa 37-47; Prof. of Astrophysics and Dir. of the Observatories, Cambridge Univ. 47-; Pres. Royal Astronomical Soc. 59-61.

The Observatory, Madingley Road, Cambridge, England.

Telephone: 52413.

Reece, Hon. Eric Elliott; Australian trade unionist and politician; b. 6 July 1910.

Former Organiser, Australian Workers' Union; Federal President, Australian Labour Party 52-55; mem. Tasmanian Parliament 46-; Minister of Housing 46-47, of Lands, Works, Mines and Local Govt. 47-58; Deputy Premier of Tasmania Aug. 58, Premier Aug. 58-.

Premier's Office, Hobart, Tasmania, Australia.

Reed, Sir Carol, Kt.; British film producer; b. 30 Dec. 1906; ed. King's School, Canterbury.

First appeared on stage at Empire Theatre, London 24; acted small parts 24-27; joined Edgar Wallace as actor and producer 27; left theatre for film production 30; since then has directed *Midshipman Easy, Laburnum Grove, A Girl in the News, Bank Holiday, Penny Paradise, Who's Your Lady Friend, Talk of the Devil, Climbing High, A Girl Must Live, The Stars Look Down, Night Train to Munich, Kipps, The Young Mr. Pitt, The Way Ahead, A Letter from Home, The New Lot, Odd Man Out, The Fallen Idol, The Third Man, Outcast of the Islands, The Man Between, Kid for two Farthings, Trapeze, The Key, Our Man in Havana, Running Man, The Agony and the Ecstasy, Oliver*; served in army in Second World War and directed war film called *The True Glory*; Golden Thistle Award 67.

213 King's Road, Chelsea, London, S.W.3, England.

Reed, Philip Dunham, B.S. in E.E., LL.B.; American corporation executive; b. 16 Nov. 1899; ed. Univ. of Wisconsin and Fordham Univ.

With law firm 21-; Vice-Pres. and Patent Counsel Van Heusen Products Inc. 22-26; with Gen. Electric Co. 26-42 and 45-59, mem. Law Dept., Asst. to Pres. and Dir. 37-39, Chair. 40-42, 45-58, Chair. of Finance Cttee. 46-59; Chair. Int. Gen. Electric Co. until merger with parent company 45-52; Chief, Bureau of Industries, War Production Board 42-; Deputy Chief U.S. Mission for Econ. Affairs, London 42-43, Chief 43-45; Consultant to U.S. Del. to San Francisco Conf. 45; Chair. U.S. Del. Anglo-American Council on Productivity 48-52; mem. Comm. on Inf. of U.S., Inf. Agency 48-61; Pres. Int. Chamber of Commerce 49-51, now Hon. Pres.; mem. The Business Council 40-, Vice-Chair. 51-52; Trustee and mem. Research and Policy Cttee. of Cttee. for Econ. Devt. 46-, Chair. 48-49; Dir. Fed. Reserve Bank of N.Y. 59-65, Chair. 60-65; Dir. of numerous companies;

President's Certificate of Merit Award; Commdr. de la Légion d'Honneur; Hon. LL.D. (Union Coll., Brooklyn Polytechnic Inst., Univ. of Wisconsin, Swarthmore Coll.); Hon. D.Eng. (Rensselaer Polytechnic Inst.); Hon. Dr.Comm.Sc. (N.Y. Univ.); Republican.
Home: Rye, N.Y.; Office: 375 Park Avenue, New York City 22, N.Y., U.S.A.

Reedy, George Edward, Jr.; American government official; b. 5 Aug. 1917; ed. Univ. of Chicago.
Congressional Correspondent, United Press, Washington D.C. 38-41, 46-51; U.S. Army Air Corps 42-45; Staff Consultant, Senate Armed Services Preparedness Subcttee. 51-52; Staff Dir., U.S. Senate Minority Policy Cttee. 53-54, Majority Policy Cttee. 55-60; Special Asst. to Vice-Pres. Lyndon B. Johnson 61-63; Press Sec. to the Pres. 64-65; Aide to Pres. Johnson 65-66; Vice-Pres. (Planning), Struthers Wells Corpn. 66-; Special Consultant to President 68-.
The White House, Washington D.C., U.S.A.
Telephone: 456-1414.

Rees, Elfan, M.A., D.D.; British congregational clergyman; b. 26 Feb. 1906; ed. Jesus Coll., Oxford and Mansfield Coll., Oxford.
Director, South Wales Council of Social Service 34-44; Chair. Welsh Cttee. for Care of Refugees 38; Senior Welfare Specialist Balkan Div., UNRRA 44, later Dir., Displaced Persons Div., UNRRA Mission to Czechoslovakia; Dir., Refugee Div., World Council of Churches 47-, Perm. Rep. in Europe of Comm. of Churches on Int. Affairs, Geneva 48-.
Publs. *The Problem of Leisure* 37, *The Refugee and the United Nations* 55, *The Century of the Homeless Man* 57, *We Strangers and Afraid.*
World Council of Churches, 150 Route de Ferney, 1211 Geneva 20, Switzerland.
Telephone: Geneva 33-34-00.

Rees, John Rawlings, C.B.E., M.A., M.D., F.R.C.P., D.P.H.; British physician; b. 25 June 1890; ed. Bradford Grammar School, King's Coll., Cambridge, and London Hospital.
Capt. R.A.M.C. 14-19; Resident appts. London Hospital 14, 19-20, Bowden House (Medical Supt.) 20-27, Tavistock Clinic 20-46 (Medical Dir. 32-46); Consulting Psychiatrist to British Army (Brigadier) 39-55; Dir. World Fed. for Mental Health 49-61; Pres. Int. Cttee. for Mental Hygiene; mem. Expert Panel WHO, Standing Cttee. on Mental Health, Ministry of Health; Pres. 3rd Int. Conf. on Mental Health London 48; First Pres. World Fed. for Mental Health 48-49, Hon. Pres. 62-; Hon. Fellow or mem. Psychiatric Socs. in U.S., France, Switzerland, Germany, Austria, Peru, India, etc.; Vice-Pres. Nat. Asscn. for Mental Health, London.
Publs. *The Health of the Mind* 29, *Shaping of Psychiatry by War* 45, *Reflections* 66, *The Case of Rudolf Hess* (ed.) 47, *Modern Practice in Psychological Medicine* (ed.) 49; with others: *Introduction to Psychological Medicine* 36.
116 Bickenhall Mansions, Baker Street, London, W.1, England.
Telephone: 01-935-8872.

Rees-Mogg, William; British journalist; b. 14 July 1928; ed. Charterhouse and Balliol Coll., Oxford.
President Oxford Union 51; *Financial Times* 52-60, Chief Leader Writer 55-60, Asst. Editor 57-60; City Editor *Sunday Times* 60-61, Political and Econ. Editor 61-63, Deputy Editor 64-67; Editor of *The Times* 67-.
Office: The Times, Printing House Square, London, E.C.4; Homes: 13 Cowley Street, London, S.W.1; and Ston Easton Park, nr. Bath, Somerset, England.

Reeves, Rt. Rev. Richard Ambrose, M.A.; British ecclesiastic; b. 6 Dec. 1899; ed. Sidney Sussex Coll., Cambridge, Coll. of the Resurrection, Mirfield, and General Theological Seminary, New York.

Sec. Theological Coll. Dept. of Student Christian Movement and Curate of St. Alban's, Golders Green, London 26-31; Rector, St. Margaret's Church Leven, Fife 31-35; Sec. World's Student Christian Fed. Geneva 35-37; Vicar St. James Church Haydock 37-42; Rector of Liverpool 42-49; Bishop of Johannesburg 49-61; deported from South Africa Sept. 12th, 60; Prelate Order of St. John of Jerusalem 53; S.T.D. (General Theological Seminary, New York); Fellow, Ancient Monuments Society; Hon. Fellow, Sidney Sussex Coll., Cambridge 60; Sec. Student Christian Movement 62-65; Asst. Bishop of London 62-66; St. Michael's Church, Lewes, and Asst. Bishop of Chichester 66-.
Publs. *Shooting at Sharpeville: the Agony of South Africa* 60, *South Africa—Yesterday and Tomorrow* 62, *Let the Facts Speak* 62, *Calvary Now* 65.
St. Michael's Rectory, St. Andrew's Lane, Lewes, Sussex, England.
Telephone: Lewes 4723.

Reggiani, Serge; Italian-born French actor; b. 2 May 1922; ed. Conservatoire Nat. d'Art Dramatique.
Notable theatrical roles in *Britannicus, Les Parents Terribles, Un Homme comme les Autres, Les Trois Mousquetaires, Les Sequestrés d'Altona,* etc.; films include: *Le Carrefour des Enfants Perdus, Les Portes de la Nuit, Manon, Les Amants de Vérone, La Ronde, Casque d'Or, Napoléon, Les Salauds vont en Enfer, Les Misérables, Marie Octobre, la Grande Pagaille, la Guerre Continue, Tutti a casa, le Doulos, le Guépard.*
6 rue de Savoie, Paris 6e, France.

Regnier, Charles; German actor and theatrical director; b. 15; ed. school of dramatic art.
Acted in Vienna, Zürich, Hamburg, Cologne, Munich, Düsseldorf, Bochum and Wuppertal; appeared in many films; trans. works of Giraudoux, Cocteau, Maugham, Feydeau, Labiche, Mauriac, Colette; German Critics' Prize 55.
8194 Ambach/Starnbergersee, German Federal Republic.
Telephone: 08177-532; and 08151-4466.

Rehberg, Poul Kristian Brandt, M.S.C., D.PHIL.; Danish zoologist; b. 29 March 1895.
Asst. University Zoophysiological Lab., Univ. of Copenhagen 21; Reader 36; Prof. of Zoophysiology, Univ. of Copenhagen 45-65; mem. Videnskabernes Selskab 44; Defence Research Cttee. 52-60; Chair. of Danish Cttee. Int. Union of Biological Sciences 47-64; mem. Danish State Research Foundation 52-61, Chair. Nat. Science section 59-61; Chief Adviser, Civil Defence Research 50-60; mem. Board and Exec. *Politiken;* Exec. mem. Danish Atomic Energy Comm. 56, Chair. 62; Vice-Pres. World Asscn. of World Federalists 56, Acad. of Technical Science, Copenhagen 57; mem. NATO Science Cttee. 57-60, Danish Science Advisory Council 66; Board of Carlsberg Foundation 60; Chair. Research Fund for Congenital Diseases 64; Hon. M.D. (Lund) 50, Hon. M.V.D. (Copenhagen) 58.
Publs. *Studies on Kidney Function* 26; various textbooks on physiology.
Grünersvei 19B, 2840 Holte, Denmark.
Telephone: 01-42-33-19.

Rehwinkel, Edmund; German administrative official; b. 28 Jan. 1899.
President Farmers' Asscn., Celle; Pres. State Farmers' Asscn. of Lower Saxony; Pres. German Farmers' Confederation, Bonn; Vice-Pres. European Conference of Agriculture, Brugg, Switzerland; mem. Economic and Social Board of E.E.C.
Publs. anthologies: *Zwischen Gestern und Heute* 54, *Mosaik* 56.
24 Lindenstrasse, Westercelle bei Celle, German Federal Republic.

Reich, John Theodore, PH.D.; Austrian-born American theatrical director; b. 30 Sept. 1906; ed. Realgymnasium I, and Max Reinhardt School, Vienna, Vienna and Cornell Univs.
Dramaturgist and Asst. Producer, Burgtheater, Vienna 31-32; Dramaturgist and Producer, Max Reinhardt Theatres, Vienna 32-38; Asst. Producer, later Producer, Salzburg Festivals 34-37; Asst., later Assoc. Prof. of Drama, Ithaca Coll., N.Y. 38-45; Drama Dir. CBS Television, New York 45-46; Assoc. Prof. of Theatre, Smith Coll., Barnard Coll. 47-51; Asst., later Assoc. Prof. of Theatre, Columbia Univ., Supervisor of Production Training, New York TV Workshop and also independent producer 51-57; Head, Goodman Theatre and School of Drama, Chicago Art Inst. 57-; Treas. Ford Foundation's Theatre Communications Group 65-; Producing Dir. Professional Theatre Program, Univ. of Chicago 66-; Ford Foundation Award 59; Chevalier, Ordre des Arts et Lettres 64.
Publs. *Mary Stuart* (adaptation of Schiller's play, with Jean Goldstone) 58; numerous other adaptations and articles.
Goodman Theatre, Art Institute of Chicago, Chicago 60603; 2052 Lincoln Park West, Chicago 60614, Ill., U.S.A.
Telephone: 236-7080 (Office); 348-0112 (Home).

Reichelderfer, Francis W., A.B.; American meteorologist; b. 6 Aug. 1895; ed. Northwestern Univ., Evanston, Ill., Harvard Univ., and Geophysical Inst., Bergen, Norway.
Appointed Naval meteorological officer 18; Dir. Naval Meteorological Organisation 22-28; qualified Airplane Pilot 19 and Airship Pilot 31; Meteorologist, First Transatlantic Flight; Int. Aviation Races, and other special assignments, and organisation new services; promoted Commdr. U.S.N. 38; Chief, United States Weather Bureau 38-63; Hon. D.Sc. Northwestern Univ.; mem. American Asscn. Advancement of Science, American Geophysical Union (Vice-Pres. 49-53), Nat. Advisory Cttee. for Aeronautics (Vice-Chair. 45-55), Int. Union Geodesy and Geophysics, Nat. Acad. of Sciences, American Meteorological Society (Pres. 40-41), Inst. of Aeronautical Sciences (mem. and Hon. Fellow, Robert M. Losey award 42, Pres. Washington Section 45-46); Cleveland Abbe award 63; mem. Int. Meteorological Organization 39-51 (Vice-Pres. Exec. Cttee. 46-51); Pres. World Meteorological Org. 51-55; mem. U.S. Exec. Cttee. Int. Geophysical Year 53-59, Exec. Cttee. 54-59; Consultant, World Meteorological Org. 64-; Award for role in meteorological co-operation among nations, Chile 43, Cuba 45, Japan 60 and others; Hon. Fellow American Asscn. for Advancement of Science, American Meteorological Soc., Royal Meteorological Soc., London.
3031 Sedgwick Street, N.W., Washington, D.C. 20008, U.S.A.
Telephone: EM-35142.

Reichstein, Tadeus, DR. ING. CHEM.; Swiss chemist; b. 20 July 1897; ed. Eidgenössische Technische Hochschule, Zürich.
Assistant Eidgenössische Technische Hochschule Zürich 22-30, Prof. of Organic Chemistry 30-38; Prof. of Pharmacy Univ. of Basle 38-46, Prof. of Organic Chemistry 46-; awarded Nobel Prize for Medicine and Physiology 50; Dr. h.c. (Sorbonne, Geneva, Zürich, Abidjan and Basle).
Institut für Organische Chemie, St. Johanns-Ring 19, CH-4000, Basle, Switzerland.

Reid, Baron (Life Peer), cr. 48, of Drem; **James Scott Cumberland Reid,** P.C., C.H.; British lawyer and politician; b. 1890; ed. Cambridge Univ.
Advocate; admitted to Scottish Bar 14; Conservative M.P. for Stirling and Falkirk Burghs 31-35, for Hillhead Div. of Glasgow 37-48; Solicitor-Gen. for Scotland 36-41,

Lord Advocate 41-45; Lord of Appeal in Ordinary 48-; Chair. Malaya Constitutional Comm. 56-57.
Danefold, West Grinstead, Sussex, England.

Reid, Escott Meredith; Canadian university principal; b. 21 Jan. 1905; ed. Toronto and Oxford Univs.
Rockefeller Foundation Fellow 30-32; Nat. Sec. of Canadian Inst. of Int. Affairs 32-38; Acting Prof. of Govt. and Political Science, Dalhousie Univ., Halifax 37-38; apptd. to Dept. of External Affairs 39; served Ottawa, Washington, London; Asst. Under-Sec. of State for External Affairs 47-48; Deputy Under-Sec. 48-52; Acting Under-Sec. 48-49; High Commr. in India 52-57; Ambassador to German Fed. Repub. 58-62; Dir. S. Asia and Middle East Dept. of Int. Bank for Reconstruction and Development 62-65; Principal, Glendon Coll. and Prof. of Political Science, York Univ., Toronto 65-; mem. Canadian Del. Int. Civil Aviation Conf. Chicago 44, San Francisco 45; Exec. Cttee. and Prep. Comm. of UN, London 45; First, Second and Twelfth Sessions UN Gen. Assembly; Chair. Assembly Cttee. on Procedure and Organisation 47.
Glendon College, York Univ., 2275 Bayview Avenue, Toronto 12, Ontario, Canada.

Reid, Helen Rogers (mother of Ogden Rogers Reid, q.v.), B.A.; American newspaper woman; b. 23 Nov. 1882; ed. Grafton Hall, Wis., and Barnard Coll.
New York Herald Tribune since 18, Vice-Pres. 22-47, Pres. 47-53, Chair. of Board 53-55, Dir. European Edn.; Hon. Litt.D. (Miami Univ. Columbia Univ. Bates Coll., Manhattan Coll. of Sacred Heart), Hon. Dr. Humanities (Rollins Coll.); Hon. LL.D. (Oglethorpe Univ., Univ. of Toronto, Smith Coll., Univ. of Wisconsin, Temple Univ., Mount Holyoke Coll.), Hon. L.H.D. (New York, Yale, Long Island, Lafayette, Syracuse Univs.); Republican.
834 Fifth Avenue, New York City, N.Y., U.S.A.

Reid, Norman Robert, D.A., F.M.A., F.I.I.C.; British art gallery director; b. 27 Dec. 1915; ed. Wilson's Grammar School, London, and Edinburgh Coll. of Art.
Army Service 39-46; Tate Gallery 46-, Deputy Keeper 48-54, Deputy Dir. 54-59, Keeper 59-64, Dir. 64-; Fellow, Int. Inst. for Conservation of Historic and Artistic Works, Sec.-Gen. 63-65, Vice-Chair. 66-; Officer, Order of Aztec Eagle (Mexico); mem. many cttees.
The Tate Gallery, Millbank, London, S.W.1; Home: 50 Brabourne Rise, Park Langley, Beckenham, Kent, England.

Reid, Ogden Rogers (son of Helen Rogers Reid, q.v.), A.B.; American journalist and diplomatist; b. 24 June 1925; ed. Yale Univ.
Reporter *New York Herald Tribune* 50-51 various depts. 52-53; Pres. and Editor New York Herald Tribune S.A., Paris 53-59, Dir. 53-; Vice-Pres. New York Herald Tribune Inc. 54-55; Pres. and Editor New York Herald Tribune Inc. 55-58, Dir. 50; Ambassador to Israel 59-61; Chair. New York State Comm. Against Discrimination 61-62, Dir. Panama Canal Co. 56-59, Mass. Mutual Life Insurance Co. 57-60; Congressman for Westchester County, N.Y. 62-; Nacional do Cruzeiro do Sul, Brazil 56; Chevalier of the Legion of Honour 57; Hon. LL.D. Adelphi Coll. (N.Y.); Hon. Fellow Bar-Ilan Univ., Israel 59; Republican.
Publs. *How Strong is America? The Score on National Defense* (with Robert S. Bird) 50.
Ophir Hill, Purchase, New York, N.Y.; Home: 2901 Garfield Terrace, N.W., Washington, D.C. 20008, U.S.A.
Telephone: 202-225-6506 (Office); 202-265-8257 (Home).

Reid Cabral, Dr. Donald J.; Dominican politician, lawyer and businessman; b. 9 June 1923; ed. Universidad de Santo Domingo.
Former automobile dealer; Pres. Reid & Pellerano C.A. 51-; Pres. Automobile Dealers' Asscn. 55-62; Vice-Pres.

Council of State 62-63; Minister of Foreign Affairs Sept.-Dec. 63; Amb. to UN 63; Amb. to Israel 63; Pres. Triumvirate which ruled Dominican Republic 63-65; Minister of Foreign Affairs 64; Minister of Armed Forces 64-65.
Calle Cervantes 8, Santo Domingo, Dominican Republic. Telephone: 5-3641/2; 5-2597; 9-3389.

Reifenberg, Benno Carl; German journalist; b. 16 July 1892; ed. Geneva, Munich and Berlin Univs.
On staff of *Frankfurter Zeitung* 21-43; Paris corresp. 30-31; *Die Gegenwart* 45-58; contrib. *Frankfurter Allgemeine Zeitung*; mem. Bavarian Acad. of Fine Art, German Acad. of Language and Literature, PEN Club; Goethe Medal, Grand Cross of Merit of the German Federal Republic, Goethe Prize (Frankfurt), Hon. Dr. h.c. (Frankfurt).
Publs. *Max Beckmann* 51, *Das Abendland Gemalt* 52, *Lichte Schatten* 53, *In den Tag gesprochen* 62, *Die Grossen Deutschen.*
Schönbergerfeld 3, (6242) Kronberg/Taunus, German Federal Republic.
Telephone: 06173-2372.

Reilly, Sir (D'Arcy) Patrick, G.C.M.G., O.B.E., M.A.; British diplomatist; b. 17 March 1909; ed. Winchester Coll., and New Coll., Oxford.
Fellow of All Souls Coll. Oxford 32-39; entered Diplomatic Service 33; served Teheran 35-38, Foreign Office 38, Algiers 43, Paris 44, Athens 45; Counsellor, Athens 47; Imperial Defence Coll. 49; Asst. Under-Sec. of State, Foreign Office 50-53; Minister in Paris 53-56; Deputy Under-Sec., Foreign Office 56; Ambassador to U.S.S.R. 57-60; Deputy Under-Sec. Foreign Office 60-64; Official Head U.K. Del. to UN Conf. on Trade and Devt.; Amb. to France 65-68.
Hampden Cottage, Ramsden, Oxford, England.

Reines, Frederick, M.E., M.S., PH.D.; American physicist; b. 16 March 1918; ed. Stevens Inst. of Technology and New York Univ.
Staff mem. and Group Leader, Theoretical Div., Los Alamos Scientific Laboratory 44-59; Prof. and Head, Dept. of Physics, Case Inst. of Technology 59-66; Prof. of Physics and Dean of Physical Sciences, Univ. of Calif., Irvine 66-; Fellow, American Asscn. for Advancement of Science, American Physical Soc., American Acad. of Arts and Sciences; Hon. D.Sc. (Witwatersrand).
Publs. Papers on detection of free neutrino 53-57, observation of high energy neutrinos in the cosmic radiation 65, effects of nuclear explosions 50, whole body counting of natural radioactivity in humans 53, liquid scintillation counters 52-66.
2655 Basswood Street, Newport Beach, Calif. 92660, U.S.A.

Reinhardt, G. Frederick, M.A.; American diplomatist (retired); b. 21 Oct. 1011; ed. Univ. of California, Cornell Univ. and Alfieri Inst., Florence.
With Int. Boundary Comm. U.S. and Mexico 35-36; entered Foreign Service 37; served Vienna 37-38, Dept. of State 39, Tallinn 39, Riga 40, Moscow 40-42, Dept. of State 43, Algiers 43-44, Caserta 44, Paris 45, Frankfurt 45, Moscow 46-48, Dept. of State 48-51, Paris 51-55; Ambassador to Republic of Viet-Nam 55-57; Counsellor of Dept. of State 57-60; Amb. to U.A.R., concurrently Minister to the Yemen 60-61; Amb. to Italy 61-68; Hon. LL.D. Univ. of Calif., Mills Coll. and Gonzaga Univ.
Stanford Research Institute, Pelikanstrasse 37, 8001 Zürich, Switzerland.

Reischauer, Edwin Oldfather, A.M., PH.D.; American historian and diplomatist; b. 15 Oct. 1910; ed. Oberlin Coll., Harvard Univ., and Univ. of Paris.
Studied in France, Japan, China 33-38; Instructor, Harvard 38-42; Military Intelligence, Second World

War; Special Asst. to Dir. Office of Far Eastern Affairs, Dept. of State 45-46; Assoc. Prof. Far Eastern Languages 46-50, Prof. 50-61; Dir. Harvard-Yenching Inst. 56-61; Amb. to Japan 61-66; Prof. Harvard Univ. 66-; Legion of Merit.
Publs. *Selected Japanese Texts for University Students* (3 vols.-compiler, with S. Elisseeff) 42-47, *Japan Past and Present* 46, 63, 64 (new edn.), *Translations from Early Japanese Literature* (with Joseph Yamagiwa) 51, *Wanted: An Asian Policy* 55, *Ennin's Diary: The Record of a Pilgrimage to China in Search of the Law* 55, *Ennin's Travels in T'ang China* 55, *The United States and Japan* (rev. edn.) 50, 65, *East Asia: The Great Tradition* (with John K. Fairbank) 60, *East Asia: The Modern Transformation* (with Fairbank and Craig) 65, *Beyond Vietnam: The United States and Asia* 67.
1737 Cambridge Street, Cambridge, Mass. 02138, U.S.A. Telephone: 868-7600, Extension 3220.

Reiss, Sir John Anthony Ewart, Kt.; British cement executive; b. 8 April 1909; ed. Eton Coll.
Associated Portland Cement Manufacturers 34-, Dir. 47, Man. Dir. 50, Chair. 56-; Chair. British Portland Cement Manufacturers 56-.
23 Chester Square, London, S.W.1, England.

Reith, 1st Baron, cr. 40, of Stonehaven; **John Charles Walsham Reith,** P.C., G.C.V.O., G.B.E., C.B., T.D., M.I.C.E.; British engineer; b. 20 July 1889; ed. Glasgow Acad., Gresham's School, Holt, Royal Technical Coll., Glasgow. Engineer with S. Pearson & Son Ltd. 13; served R.E. 14-15; in charge munitions contracts for Great Britain-America 16-17; served Admiralty 18, Ministry of Munitions 19; Gen. Man. Wm. Beardmore & Co. Ltd., Coatbridge 20; first Gen. Man. British Broadcasting Co. Ltd. 22, Man. Dir. 23, Dir.-Gen. British Broadcasting Corpn. 27-38; Chair. Imperial Airways Ltd. 38-39, First Chair. British Overseas Airways Corpn. 39-40; Minister of Information Jan.-May 40; National M.P. for Southampton 40; Minister of Transport May-Oct. 40, of Works and Buildings (later Works and Planning) 40-42; Lt. Commdr. R.N.V.R. Coastal Forces 42-43; Extra Naval Asst. to 3rd Sea Lord 43; Dir. Combined Operations Material Dept., Admiralty 43-45; 45,000-miles air tour of Commonwealth; Chair. Commonwealth Telecommunications Conf. 45, New Towns Cttee. 46, Commonwealth Telecommunications Board 46-50, Hemel Hempstead Development Corpn. 47-50, National Film Finance Corpn. 48-51, Colonial Development Corpn. 50-59, State Building Soc. 60-64; Vice-Chair. British Oxygen Co. Ltd. 54-66; Dir. Phoenix Assurance Co. Ltd.; Lord Rector, Univ. of Glasgow 65-; Lord High Commr. to the Gen. Assembly of the Church of Scotland 67; Hon. D.C.L. (Oxford); LL.D. (Aberdeen, Manchester, Glasgow); Hon. M.Sc. (Lafayette); Hon. Fellow Worcester Coll., Oxford; Hon. F.R.I.B.A.; mem. Queen's Bodyguard for Scotland (The Royal Company of Archers).
Publs. *Into the Wind* 49, *Wearing Spurs* 66.
The Athenaeum, Pall Mall, London, S.W.1, England. Telephone: 01-930-4843.

Rekola, Esko Johannes; Finnish lawyer and civil servant; b. 10 June 1919; ed. Helsinki Univ.
Chief of Taxation Dept., Ministry of Finance 57-59, Chief of Budget Dept. 59-63, 64-65; Alt. Gov. Int. Bank for Reconstruction and Devt. 62-66; Minister of Finance 63-64; Chief of the Prime Minister's Office 65-66; Gen. Man. Finnish State Railways 66-.
Kuusiniementie 12B, Helsinki 34, Finland.
Telephone: 486260.

Remarque, Erich Maria; American writer; b. Germany 22 June 1898; ed. Univ. of Münster.
Served First World War; after war was teacher, race driver, sports editor, dramatic critic and writer.
Publs. *Im Westen nichts Neues* (*All Quiet on the Western*

Front) 29, *The Road Back* 31, *Three Comrades* 37, *Flotsam* 41, *Arch of Triumph* 46, *Spark of Life* 51, *A Time to Live and Time to Die* 54, *The Black Obelisk* 57, *Heaven has no Favourites* 61, *The Night in Lisbon* 64; film script *The Last Act* 55; play *Berlin 1945*.
Porto-Ronco, Ticino, Switzerland.

Remez, Brig.-Gen. Aharon; Israeli air force officer and diplomatist; b. 8 May 1919; ed. Herzlieh Grammar School, Tel Aviv.
Agricultural training in kibbutz, Givat Haim 37-39; Emissary to Zionist Youth Movement, U.S.A. 39-41; Royal Air Force 41-47; mem. kibbutz Kfar Blum 47-; Dir. of Planning and Operations, later Chief of Staff, Israel Air Force 48; Commdr.-in-Chief Israel Air Force 48-51; Head, Ministry of Defence Purchasing Mission, U.S.A. 51-53; Aviation Adviser to Minister of Defence 53-54; mem. Board of Dirs. Solel Boneh Ltd., Exec. Dir. Koor Industries Ltd. 54-59; Admin. Dir. Weizmann Inst. of Science, Rehovot 59-60; Dir. Int. Co-operation Div., Ministry for Foreign Affairs 60-64, Adviser on Int. Co-operation to Minister for Foreign Affairs 64-65; Ambassador to U.K. 65-.
Embassy of Israel, 2 Palace Green, London, W.8, England.
Telephone: 01-937-8091.

Renard, H.E. Cardinal Alexandre, D. ès L.; French ecclesiastic; b. 7 June 1906; ed. Coll. Jeanne d'Arc, Grand Séminaire and Univ. catholique de Lille.
Ordained Priest 31; Prof., college at Marcq 33-36, seminary at Haubourdin 36-38, Catholic Univ. of Lille 38-43; Chaplain to Women Students, Lille diocese 38; Diocesan Dir. of Works 47; Bishop of Versailles 53-67; Archbishop of Lyons and Primate of France 67-; created Cardinal 67; Officier Légion d'Honneur.
Publs. include *Philosophie et Pédagogie de l'école nouvelle, Possibilité de la philosophie chrétienne, Exigences spirituelles du christianisme, En équipe dans le Christ, Fidélité au Christ et présence au monde, Pour une évangélisation et une catéchèse d'Eglise, Vie Spirituelle de la religieuse aujourd'hui, Situation actuelle de l'Eglise, Prêtres Diocésains aujourd'hui.*
Archevêché, 1 place de Fourvière, Lyons Ve, Rhône, France.

Renaud, Madeleine (wife of Jean-Louis Barrault, *q.v.*); French actress and author; b. 21 Feb. 1903; ed. Lycée Racine and Paris Conservatoire.
Pensionnaire, Comédie Française 21-47; co-Dir. Compagnie Madeleine Renaud—Jean-Louis Barrault 47-; plays in which she has played important roles include *Le Soulier de Satin, Occupe-toi d'Amélie, Les Nuits de Colère, Christophe Colomb, La Dame aux Camélias*; films include *Jean de la Lune, La Maternelle, Remorques, Le Ciel est à nous, Le Plaisir, Dialogue des Carmélites, Le Jour le plus long*; Chevalier, Légion d'Honneur, Commdr. des Arts et des Lettres.
Publs. A number of plays and novels.
18 avenue du Président-Wilson, Paris 16e, France.

Renault, Mary (*pseudonym* of Mary Challans); British writer; b. 4 Sept. 1905; ed. Clifton High School, Bristol, St. Hugh's Coll., Oxford, and Radcliffe Infirmary, Oxford.
Nurse during Second World War; resident in South Africa 48-; Fellow of Royal Soc. of Literature 59, Nat. Pres. P.E.N. Club of South Africa 61.
Publs. *Purposes of Love* 39, *Kind are Her Answers* 40, *The Friendly Young Ladies* 44, *Return to Night* 46, *North Face* 48, *The Charioteer* 53, *The Last of the Wine* 56, *The King Must Die* 58, *The Bull from the Sea* 62, *The Lion in the Gateway* 64, *The Mask of Apollo* 66.
Delos, Glen Beach, Camps Bay, Cape, South Africa.

Renchard, William S(hryock), A.B.; American banker; b. 1 Jan. 1908; ed. Princeton Univ.
With the Nat. Bank of Commerce, N.Y.C. 28-29, the Guaranty Trust Co., N.Y.C. 29-30; Joined the Chemical Bank New York Trust Co. 30, Pres. and Dir. 60-66, Chair. and Chief Exec. Officer, the Chemical Bank New York Trust Co. 66-; mem. American Bankers' Asscn. Govt. Borrowing Cttee.; official of many business and public bodies.
Chemical Bank New York Trust Company, 20 Pine Street, New York City, N.Y., U.S.A.

Rendahl, Hialmar, PH.D.; Swedish zoologist; b. 26 Dec. 1891.
Lecturer in Zoology, Stockholm Univ. 24; Prof. and Keeper of Vertebrate Zoology Dept., Swedish Museum of Natural History, Stockholm 33-57, Prof. Emeritus 58-; hon. foreign mem. American Society Ichthyology and Herpetology.
Publs. *A List of the Birds of the Pearl Islands* 20, *The Fishes of Juan Fernandez and Easter Islands* 21, *Om flyttfåglar* 25, *Studien über innerasiatische Fische* 33, *Fagel boken, Sveriges fåglar i ord och bild* 35, 6th edn. 57, *Giftormar och ormgifter* 36, *Die Welt der Tiere, Säugetiere* 38, *Die Zugverhältnisse der schwedischen Rabenvögel* 60, *Die Zugverhältnisse der schwedischen Lerchen* 64, *Zur Frage von der Frühlingsankunft des Kuckucks in Frankreich* 65, *Die Zugverhältnisse der schwedischen Bachstelzen* 67, and other works on brain anatomy, ichthyology, herpetology and ornithology.
Naturhistoriska Riksmuseet, Stockholm 50, Sweden.

Rendel, Sir George William, K.C.M.G., M.A.; British diplomatist; b. 23 Feb. 1889; ed. Downside and Queen's Coll., Oxford.
Entered Diplomatic Service 13; served Berlin, Athens, Rome, Lisbon, Madrid, and in Foreign Office 20-38; Head Eastern Dept. Foreign Office 30-38; Minister to Bulgaria 38-41, to Yugoslav Govt. in London 41-42, Ambassador 42-43; Ambassador to Belgium 48-50; Foreign Office 44-47; Chief U.K. del. for negotiations of Treaty of Brussels Feb.-Mar. 48; U.K. mem. (and Chair.) of the Tripartite Comm. on German Debts 51-53; Chair. Singapore Constitutional Comm. 53-54; U.K. Rep., Saar Referendum Comm. 55; re-employed by Foreign Office on Anglo-Egyptian Financial Agreement 59-64; Vice-Pres. Catholic Union of Great Britain 51-67; Dir. and Chair. Singer & Friedlander Ltd. 53-68; Dir. Int. Aeradio Ltd. 52-60.
Publ. *The Sword and the Olive* 57.
48 Lowndes Square, London, S.W.1, England.
Telephone: 01-235-5110

Reneker, Robert William, PH.B.; American business executive; b. 1912; ed. Calumet High School, and Univ. of Chicago School of Business.
Purchasing Dept., Swift and Co. 33-34, Office of Vice-Pres. 44, later in office of Pres.; Vice-Pres. Swift and Co. 55-64, Pres. 64-, Dir. 59-; official of numerous civic orgs.
Office: Swift & Co., 115 W. Jackson Boulevard, Chicago 60604; Home: 10158 South Leavitt Avenue, Chicago, Ill., U.S.A.

Renn, Ludwig (*pseudonym* of Arnold Vieth von Golssenau); German author; b. 22 April 1889.
Army officer until 20; converted to Communism 27; sentenced to 2½ years imprisonment after Reichstag fire 33; emigrated to Switzerland, commanded Thälmann battalion in Spain; emigrated to Mexico; returned to Germany 47; Prof. of Anthropology 47; mem. of German Acad. of Arts; Nationalpreise 55, 61, Kinderbuchpreise 54, 55, 56, 58, 61; Dr. h.c. 49.
Publs. *Krieg* 28, *Nachkrieg* 30, *Russlandfahrten* 32, *Vor grossen Wandlungen* 36, *Kriegführung und Propaganda* 39, *Adel im Untergang* 44, *Movelia* 50, *Vom alten und neuen Rumänien* 52, *Trini* 54, *Im Spanischen Krieg* 55, *Nobi* 55, *Herniu und der blinde Asni* 56, *Meine Kindheit und Jugend* 57, *Krieg ohne Schlacht* 57, *Herniu und Armin* 58, *Auftraggeber: Arbeiterklasse* 60, *Auf den*

Trümmern des Kaiserreichs 61, *Camilo, Inflation* 63, *Zu Fuss zum Orient* 66, *Answeg* 67; translated into many languages.
Am Kornfeld 78, Berlin/Kaulsdorf, Germany.
Telephone: Berlin 59-77-98.

Rennell, 2nd Baron, cr. 33, of Rodd; **Francis James Rennell Rodd,** K.B.E., C.B., M.A. (Oxon.); British banker; b. 1895; ed. Eton and Balliol Coll., Oxford.
Served First World War, France 14-15, Italy 16, Middle East 17-19; entered Diplomatic Service 19; Rome and Sofia; served Foreign Office 23-24, resgnd.; mem. Stock Exchange 26-28; mem. staff Bank of England 29-32; Man. Bank for Int. Settlements 30-31; partner in Morgan, Grenfell & Co. 31-; Min. Econ. Warfare 39-40; served British Army 40-45; Major-Gen. in charge Military admin. Italian Colonies and Chief Allied Military Govt. in Italy 43; explored Southern Sahara 22, 27. awarded Royal Geographical Society's Founder's Medal 29; Pres. Royal Geographical Soc. 45-48, Hon. Vice-Pres. 48-; Visiting Fellow Nuffield Coll. Oxford 47-59; mem. Board B.O.A.C. 54-59; Dir. Morgan Grenfell & Co., and other companies; Trustee, London Museum 54-; Hon. LL.D. Manchester.
Publs. *People of the Veil, General William Eaton, British Military Administration in Africa 1940-45, Valley on the March,* and many other publs.
23 Great Winchester Street, London, E.C.2, England; The Rodd, near Presteigne, Radnorshire, Wales.
Telephone: 01-588-6565 (Office); Presteigne 362 (Home).

Rennert, Günther, DR.JUR.; German opera and theatre producer; b. 1 April 1911; ed. law, Jura, theatrical science, Munich and Berlin.
Asst. producer films, operas and plays 33-35; producer in Frankfurt 35-37, Wuppertal 37-39, Mainz and Königsberg 39-42; head producer Charlottenburg Opera House 42-45, Munich 45-46; Opera Dir. and Dir. State Opera House, Hamburg 46-56; free-lance producer of opera and plays in Hamburg, Berlin, Stuttgart, Vienna, Frankfurt, Munich and abroad, including the Edinburgh Festival 52 and 55, 56, 58, Salzburg Festival 49-, Dublin, Naples, London, Milan, Paris, Buenos Aires, Metropolitan Opera, New York, Canada, San Francisco; Dir. State Opera House, Munich 67-; mem. Akademie der Künste. Berlin; Art Counsellor and Head of Production, Glyndebourne Festival Opera 60-; Johannes-Brahms-Médaille 58.
Publs. stage versions of Handel, Gluck, Rossini, Monteverdi and Prokofiev operas.
Schwalbenweg 11a, Krailling/Starnberg, German Federal Republic.

Rennie, Sir John Shaw, G.C.M.G., O.B.E.; Governor-General of Mauritius; b. 12 Jan. 1917; ed. Hillhead High School, Glasgow Univ., and Balliol Coll., Oxford.
District Officer, Tanganyika 40-51; Dep. Colonial Sec. Mauritius 51-55; British Resident Commr. New Hebrides, Western Pacific 55-62; Gov. and C.-in-C. Mauritius 62-68; Gov.-Gen. and C.-in-C. Mauritius 68-.
Government House, Le Réduit, Mauritius.

Renoir, Jean (son of late Auguste Renoir); French film producer and writer; b. 15 Sept. 1894; ed. Univ. d'Aix-en-Provence.
Served French Army 14-18; professional playwright 24-; Prof. of Dramatic Art Univ. of Calif. 60; Vice-Pres. Cinémathèque Française; Louis Delluc Prize 37, Venice Biennale 37, 46, 51; Grand Prix de l'Acad. du Cinéma 56; mem. American Acad. of Arts and Sciences 64; Chevalier Légion d'Honneur, Croix de Guerre, Commandeur de l'Ordre des Arts et des Lettres; has produced, written and directed many films, including *Nana, Tire-au-Flanc, La Chienne, Madame Bovary, La Grande Illusion, Le Crime de Monsieur Lange, La Bête Humaine, La Règle du Jeu, The River, The Golden Coach, Eléna et les Hommes, French Can-Can,*

Le Déjeuner sur l'Herbe, Le Testament de Docteur Cordellier 59, *Le Caporal Epinglé* 61, etc.; stage plays: *Orvet, Carola, Mise en Scène Théâtrale, Jules César.*
Publs. *Orvet* 53, *Renoir, my Father* 62, *The Notebooks of Captain Georges* 66.
7 avenue Frochot, Paris 9e, France.

Renshaw, John Brophy; Australian politician; b. 8 Aug. 1909; ed. Binnaway School and Holy Cross Coll., Ryde, Sydney.
Farmer; mem. Binnaway-Coonabarabran Shire Council 37, Shire Pres. 39; mem. New South Wales legislature 41-, Minister for Lands, N.S.W. Govt. 50-52, for Public Works and Local Govt. 52-59, Deputy Premier and Treas. 59-64, Minister for Industrial Development and Decentralisation 62-64, Premier, Treas., Minister for Industrial Devt. and Decentralization 64-65, Leader of Opposition in Legislative Assembly 65-; Australian Labour Party.
Parliament House, Sydney, New South Wales, Australia.
Telephone: 20351.

Renzetti, Giuseppe, DR. ECON.; Italian railway executive; b. 20 March 1906; ed. Univ. of Rome.
Commercial Dept. Italian State Railways 33-47; Gen. Agent of Italian State Railways in Switzerland 47-48, Commercial Man. Milan 49-54, Rome 55-58; Dir.-Gen. for Transport, European Econ. Community, Brussels 58-62; Gen. Man. Italian State Railways, Rome 62-65; Councillor of State 66-.
Via Aquileia 22, Rome, Italy.
Telephone: 841552.

Reshetnikov, Fyodor Pavlovich; Soviet painter; b. 06; ed. Moscow Arts Inst.
Took part in the Sibiryakov, Chelyuskin Arctic Expeditions 32-34; war artist in Sebastopol and Kerch 41-42; mem. Acad. of Arts of the U.S.S.R. 53; State prize-winner 49, 51; Order of the Red Banner of Labour, Order of the Red Star.
Principal works: *Germans in Kerch (Bagerovo)* 42, *Armoured Train Zheleznvak* 43, *Home for the Holidays* 48, *First Match* 52, *Another Bad Mark* 52; series of caricatures 61-62.
Academy of Arts of the U.S.S.R., 21 Kropotkinskaya ulitsa, Moscow, U.S.S.R.

Reshtya, S. K. (*see* Rishtya).

Resnais, Alain; French film director; b. 3 June 1922; ed. Institut des Hautes Etudes Cinématographiques, Paris.
Short films directed (48-59) include *Van Gogh* 48, *Guernica* (with Robert Hessens) 50, *Les statues meurent aussi* (with C. Marker) 52, *Nuit et brouillard* 55; Long films include *Hiroshima mon amour* 59, *L'année dernière à Marienbad* 61, *Muriel* 63, *La Guerre est finie* 66.
70 rue des Plantes, Paris 14e, France.

Resor, Stanley Rogers, B.A., LL.B.; American lawyer and government official; b. 5 Dec. 1917; ed. Groton, Yale Univ., and Yale Univ. Law School.
U.S. Army Service, Second World War; legal practice 46-65, Partner law firm Debevoise, Plimpton, Lyons and Gates 46-65; Under-Sec. of the Army April-July 65, Sec. of the Army July 65-; mem. American Bar Asscn., numerous cttees., etc.; Silver Star, Bronze Star, Purple Heart, Distinguished Unit Citation.
Office: Room 3E 718, The Pentagon, Washington, D.C. 20301; Home: 4959 Hillbrook Lane, Washington, D.C. 20016, U.S.A.

Restivo, Franco; Italian politician; b. 25 May 1911.
Professor, Univ. of Palermo 43-; Pres. Sicilian Regional Parliament 49-55; mem. Chamber of Deputies 58-, Vice-Pres. Chamber of Deputies 63-66; Minister of Agriculture 66-68, of Interior 68-; Christian Democrat.
Ministry of Interior, Rome, Italy.

Reston, James; Scottish-born American journalist; b. 3 Nov. 1909; ed. Dayton, Ohio public schools and Illinois Univ.

First brought to U.S.A. 10, permanently settled 20-; began his career on *Springfield* (Ohio) *Daily News* and as sports publicity dir. for Ohio State Univ.; travelling Sec., Cincinnati Baseball Club; Sports Writer, Associated Press, New York 34-37; Assoc. Press Corresp., London 37-39; *New York Times* London Bureau 39-41, Washington Bureau 41; Dir. Office of War Intelligence Information Service, U.S. Embassy, London 42; Asst. to Publisher, *New York Times* 43, Acting Head, London Bureau 43-45, Nat. Corresp. 45, Diplomatic Corresp. 46, Head of Washington Bureau 53-64, Assoc. Editor 64-68, Exec. Editor 68-; Pulitzer Awards 44 and 57, George Polk Memorial Award 54, Raymond Clapper Award 55, etc.; Chevalier, Légion d'Honneur; Hon. D.Litt., Colgate and Rutgers Univs.; Hon. LL.D. (New York).

Publ. *The Artillery of the Press* 67, *Sketches in the Sand* 67.

The New York Times, 229 West 43rd Street, New York 10036, U.S.A.

Retivol, Vsevolod Sergeyevich; Soviet trade union official and economist; b. 10; ed. Bauman Mechanical Machine-Building Inst.

Worked in various enterprises 27-32; State Ball-Bearing Plant No. 1, fitter, foreman, engineer, shop supt., chief engineer of shop, Sec. of Party Cttee. 32-51; leading Party posts 51-54; Dir. State Ball-Bearing Plant No. 1 54-56; Chair. Central Cttee. of the Machine-Building Workers' Union 56-63; staff of Council of Mutual Econ. Aid (COMECON) 63-; mem. of C.P.S.U.; Order of Lenin, Badge of Honour (twice), 2 State medals.

Council of Mutual Economic Aid, 14 Petrovka, Moscow, U.S.S.R.

Rétoré, Guy; French theatre director; b. 7 April 1924; ed. Univ. of Paris.

Public Relations Dept., S.N.C.F. until 55; Actor and Producer, Théâtre de Boulevard until 55; formed "La Guilde" (theatrical company), Menilmontant, East Paris 55; opened Théâtre de Menilmontant 57; Dir. Maison de la Culture, Menilmontant 62-; Dir. Théâtre de l'Est Parisien (also gives concerts, ballets, films and conferences).

Plays produced include: *La Fille du Roi* (Cosmos) 55, *Life and Death of King John* 56, *Grenadiers de la Reine* (Farquhar, adapted by Cosmos) 57, *L'Avare* (Molière), *Macbeth* (Shakespeare), *Les Caprices de Marianne* (Musset), *La fleur à la bouche* (Pirandello), *Le Médecin malgré lui* (Molière), *Le Manteau* (Gogol, adapted by Cosmos) 63, *La Locandiera* (Goldoni), *Arden of Faversham* 64, *Monsieur Alexandre* (Cosmos) 64, *Macbeth* (Shakespeare) 64, *Turcaret* (Lesage) 65, *Measure for Measure* (Shakespeare) 65, *Le Voyage de Monsieur Perrichon* (Labiche) 65, *Live Like Pigs* (Arden), *The Silver Tassie* (O'Casey) 66-67, *Les 13 Soleils de la Rue St. Blaise* (A. Gatti).

Théâtre de l'Est Parisien, 17 rue Malte Brun, Paris 20e, France.

Telephone: PYR 94-58; and MEN-79-09.

Retta, Ato Abbebe, G.C.V.O.; Ethiopian diplomatist and politician; b. 27 Sept. 1909; ed. Ethiopian schools and colls. in various monasteries, Ethiopia and abroad. Principal Private Sec. to Gov.-Gen. of Wag 29-32; joined Emperor's entourage in Great Britain during Italian occupation; after restoration, was for four years Counsellor of Ethiopian Legation, London; returned to Ethiopia, becoming mem. Govt. as Head of Ministry of Public Health; Minister to Great Britain 48-49, Ambassador 49-56, concurrently Minister to Norway, Sweden, Denmark and Neths.; Minister of Commerce 56-58; Minister of Public Health 58-66; Minister of Commerce and Industry 66-.

Ministry of Commerce and Industry, Addis Ababa, Ethiopia.

Reusch, Hermann, DR. PHIL., DR. ING.; German business executive; b. 2 Aug. 1896; ed. Univs. of Tübingen and Giessen, and Berlin and Aachen Technical Colls.

Military Service 14-18; Mine Dir. Hervest-Dorsten and Hamm 27-35; mem. Board Gutehoffnungshütte Oberhausen AG, and Gutehoffnungshütte Co. for Mines and Foundries 35-42; South West Commercial Management, Serbia 42-45; fmr. Chair. Board Gutehoffnungshütte Sterkrade Co. and Gutehoffnungshütte Sterkrade AG 47; mem. Presidium Fed. Asscn. of German Industry, Int. Chamber of Commerce, Max Planck Soc., etc.; Grosses Bundesverdienstkreuz mit Stern.

7157 Oppenweiler, Würtemberg, Postfach 15, German Federal Republic.

Telephone: 07-191/8-205.

Reuter, Paul; Luxembourg diplomatist; b. 20.

Department of Foreign Affairs 48-; Perm. Del. to Council of Europe 56-59; Perm. Del. to NATO 59-67, to OEEC 59-61, to OECD 61-67; Amb. to Netherlands 67-.

Embassy of Luxembourg, Tolweg 7, The Hague, Netherlands.

Reuter, Richard Ward, B.A., L.H.D.; American international relief administrator; b. 17 Jan. 1918; ed. Amherst Coll.

Administrative positions merchandising and insurance 38-41; served (civilian) with American Friends Service Cttee. 41-45; with CARE Inc. 46-49, 51-62, Exec. Dir. 55-62; Special Asst. to Pres., Dir. U.S. "Food for Peace" Programme 62-66; now with Int. Div. of Kraft Foods; several orders and decorations.

International Division, Kraft Foods, 500 Peshtigo Court, Chicago, Ill. 60690, U.S.A.

Reuther, Victor G.; American labour union executive; b. 1 Jan. 1912; ed. Univ. of W. Virginia, Wayne Univ.

Travelled abroad 35; assembly-line worker Kelsey-Hayes Wheel Co., Detroit 35; Dir. United Automobile Workers (U.A.W.), Indiana 37, Int. Rep. 37, later Asst. Dir. War Policy Div., Dir. Educ. Programme in U.S. and Canada 51, European Rep. 51; fmr. Asst. to Pres. Congress of Industrial Orgs. (C.I.O.); Admin. Asst. to Pres. U.A.W., Dir. Int. Affairs Dept.; mem. State and Nat. Cttees. War Manpower Comm. and War Productivity Board, U.S. Govt., World War II; Co-Chair. Anglo American Council on Productivity 49; lost an eye when shot in the face by gangsters 49; mem. Commerce Technical Advisory Board; Democrat.

United Automobile Workers (U.A.W.), 1126 16th Street, N.W. Washington 20036, D.C., U.S.A.

Reuther, Walter Philip; American labour leader; b. 1 Sept. 1907; ed. Wayne Univ.

Apprenticed as a tool and die maker 24; employed by various motor makers 27-32; began to organise workers in automobile industry 35; Dir., Gen. Motors Dept. of United Automobile Workers 39; Vice-Pres. Int. Union of United Automobile, Aerospace and Agricultural Implement Workers of America 42-46, Pres. 46-; Vice-Pres. C.I.O. 46, Pres. 52-56; Vice-Pres. combined A.F.L.-C.I.O. 56-67; mem. Advisory Cttee. on defense mobilisation, President's Advisory Cttee. on Labor-Management Relations 61-, and of numerous other Govt. Cttees. and Comms.; Dir. or Trustee of many civic, cultural, educational and health orgs. including UN Asscn. of U.S.A. and American Cancer Soc.; Hon. Dr. Legal Letters (Boston Univ., St. Mary's Coll. of the Pacific, St. Francis Xavier Univ. Canada, Univ. of Michigan) Hon. Dr. Humanities (West Virginia State Coll., Iowa, Rhode Island, Wayne State and Wilberforce Univs.); Dr. of Laws (Roosevelt Univ.).

8000E Jefferson Street, Detroit, Mich. 48214, U.S.A.

Reutov, Oleg Alexandrovich; Soviet organic chemist; b. 1920; ed. Moscow Univ.
Soviet Army 41-45; Instructor, Moscow Univ. 45-54, Prof. 54-; Corresp. mem. U.S.S.R. Acad. of Sciences 58-64, mem. 64-; mem. C.P.S.U. 42-.
U.S.S.R. Academy of Sciences, 14 Lenin Prospekt, Moscow, U.S.S.R.

Reutter, Hermann; German pianist and composer; b. 17 June 1900; studied music at Munich.
Director Staatliche Hochschule für Musik und Darstellende Kunst, Stuttgart 56-66; Prof. Musik-Hochschule, Munich.
Published works include choral music, cantatas, song cycles, orchestral and solo works; operas: *Odysseus, Dr. Johannes Faust, Don Juan, Faust;* five one-act pieces: *Saul, Ballade der Landstrasse, Lübecker Totentanz, Witwe von Ephesus, Brücke von San Luis Rey, Tod des Empirokles;* ballet: *Kirmes von Delft, Notturno Montmartre.*
Elfenstrasse 107, 7 Stuttgart-Möhringen, German Federal Republic.
Telephone: 711597.

Revel, Jean-François; French writer; b. 19 Jan. 1924; ed. Univ. de Paris à la Sorbonne.
Teacher of French Literature, Institut Français, Mexico, later Florence 52-56; Teacher of Philosophy, Lille and Paris 56-61; Literary Adviser Editions Julliard and Pauvert 61-66, Editions Laffons 66-.
Publs. novel: *Histoire de Flore* 57; essays: *Pourquoi des Philosophes?* 57, *Pour l'Italie* 58, *Le Style du Général* 59, *Sur Proust* 60, *La Cabale des Dévots* 62, *En France* 65, *Contrecensures* 66.
55 quai de Bourbon, Paris 4e, France.
Telephone: ODEon 65-87.

Reverdin, Oliver, D. ès L.; Swiss professor, politician and editor; b. 15 July 1913; ed. Univs. of Geneva and Paris, and Ecole Française d'Athènes.
School teaching, Geneva and France 38-41; Attaché Swiss Legation, Rome 41-44; Lecturer and Asst. Prof. Ancient Greek Literature, Univ. of Geneva 45-58, Ordinary Prof. 58-; Parly. Ed. *Journal de Genève,* Berne 45-54, and Man. Editor 55-59, Man. 59-67; Deputy (Liberal) of Geneva at the Conseil National; Chair. Soc. Suisse des Sciences Humaines 60-68; mem. Nat. Council for Scientific Research 63-, Chair. 68-; rep. Consultative Assembly, Council of Europe 64-, Chair. of the Cultural and Scientific Cttee. 66-, of the Cttee. for Science and Technology 67-.
Publs. *La Religion de la Cité platonicienne* 45, *La Guerre du Sonderbund vue par le Général Dufour* 48, *Quatorze calvinistes chez les Topinambous* 57, *La Crète, Berceau de la Civilisation Occidentale* 60, *Connaissance de la Suisse* 64.
8 rue des Granges, 1204 Geneva, Switzerland.
Telephone: 022-243126.

Rexroth, Kenneth; American author; b. 22 Dec. 1905; ed. High School in Chicago.
Independent lecturer, weekly columnist for San Francisco *Examiner,* contributor and reviewer *New York Times, Nation,* etc.; two Guggenheim Fellowships, two Commonwealth Club medals, Eunice Tietjens Poetry Magazine Award, Shelley Memorial Award, Longview Foundation Award, Nat. Acad. of Arts and Letters Grant, Rockefeller Grant, Deutsche Akademischer Austauschdienst Grant.
Publs. *In What Hour* 40, *Phoenix and Tortoise* 44, *Signature of All Things* 49, *Art of Worldly Wisdom* 49, *Dragon and Unicorn* 52, *In Defense of the Earth* 56 (verse); *Beyond the Mountains* 51 (play); *Poems of Milczy* 52, *100 Poems from the Japanese* 55, *100 Poems from the Chinese* 56, *30 Spanish Poems* 57 (translations); *A Bird in the Bush* 59 (essays); *The Homestead Called*

Damascus 62, *An Autobiographical Novel* 66, *Complete Shorter Poems* 67.
250 Scott Street, San Francisco, Calif., U.S.A.
Telephone: UN3-6754.

Rey, Henri François, LIC. de PHIL.; French writer; b. 31 July 1919; ed. Lycée de Perpignan, Univ. of Montpellier.
Former journalist, broadcaster and scriptwriter.
Publs. *La Fête Espagnole* 58 (Prix des Deux Magots), *La Comédie* 60, *Les Pianos Mécaniques* 62 (Prix Interallié), *Les Chevaux Masqués* 65, *Le Rachdingue* 67.
44 rue Boissonade, Paris 14e, France.

Rey, Jean, D. en D.; Belgian lawyer and politician; b. 15 July 1902; ed. Athénée Royal, Liège and Univ. of Liège.
Advocate, Liège Court of Appeal 26-; Communal Councillor, Liège 35-58; Deputy for Liège 39, 46-58; Captain of Reserves 40; prisoner of war in Germany 40-45; founder mem. Entente Libérale Wallone; Vice-Pres. Conseil Supérieur de la Famille 47; Alternative Del. U.N. 3rd Gen. Assembly, Paris 48, Consultative Assembly, Council of Europe, 1st Session 49, 5th Session 53; Minister of Reconstruction (Eyskens Coalition Govt.) 49-50, of Econ. Affairs 54-58; mem. and Sectional Pres. for External Relations European Econ. Community Comm. 58-67; Pres. of combined Exec. of EEC, ECSC and Euratom July 67-; Grand Officier, Ordre de Léopold, Grand Croix Order of Orange Nassau, Grand Cordon Order of the Lion of Finland, Commdr. Ordre de la Couronne de Chêne (Luxembourg), Croix de Guerre, etc.
235 rue de la Loi, Brussels, Belgium.

Reyes, Narciso G., A.B.; Philippine journalist; b. 6 Feb. 1914; ed. Univ. of Santo Tomas.
Associate Editor *Philippines Commonweal,* Manila 35-41; at Nat. Language Faculty, Ateneo de Manila 39-41; Assoc. Editor *Manila Post* 45-47; Assoc. News Editor *Evening News,* Manila 47-48; Man. Editor Philippine Newspaper Guild's organ 47-48; Adviser to Philippine Mission to UN and Alt. Rep. of the Philippines to numerous ECOSOC sessions and UN Gen. Assemblies, and many other UN activities 48-; Philippine Amb. to U.K. 67-; Chair. 19th Session UN Social Development Comm. 68-.
Philippine Embassy, 9A Palace Green, London, W.8, England.
Telephone: 01-937-4723 (Residence); 01-937-3646/7/8 and 01-937-9158 (Office).

Reyes Heroles, Jesús; Mexican public administrator; b. 3 April 1921; ed. Univ. Nacional Autónoma de México, Univs. of Buenos Aires and La Plata.
Adviser Secretariat of Works and Social Security 44; Asst. Prof. of Law, Univ. Nacional Autónoma Mexico 44-45, Prof. 46-; mem. Inst. of Econ., Political and Social Studies of Partido Revolucionario Institucional (P.R.I.) 49-51, 60, Counsellor Pres. of Nat. Exec. Cttee. P.R.I. 52; Counsellor Presidency of the Republic 52-58; Chief Economist Nat. Railways of Mexico 53-58; Asst. Technical Dir.-Gen. Instituto Mexicano del Seguro Social 58-64; Nat. Deputy 61-64; Dir.-Gen. Petróleos Mexicanos 64-; numerous conferences and essays on labour law, economics and social problems.
Petróleos Mexicanos, Avenida Juárez 92, Mexico 1 D.F., Mexico.

Reynaud, Roger; French trade unionist and civil servant; b. 19 May 1916.
Former Inspector, Ministry of Finance, mem. Conseil Economique, mem. Finance Comm., Modernisation and Re-equipment Plan; Sec.-Gen. French Christian Trade Union Fed. 45; Vice-Pres. Gen. Fed. of Govt. Employees; fmr. mem. Council, Int. Confed. of Christian Trade Unions; mem. ECSC High Authority 58-67.
c/o European Coal and Steel Community, 2 Place de Metz, Luxembourg, Grand Duchy of Luxembourg.

Reynolds, David Parham; American industrial metals executive; b. 16 June 1915; ed. Princeton Univ.
Reynolds Metals Co., Louisville 37-, Salesman 37-41, Asst. Man. Aircraft Parts Div. 41-44, Asst. Vice-Pres. 44-46, Vice-Pres. 46-58, Exec. Vice-Pres. 58-; Dir. other cos.
Reynolds Metals Co., 6601 Broad Street, Richmond 18; 8905 Tresco Road, Richmond, Virginia, U.S.A.
Telephone: AT2-2311 (Office); AT2-2226 (Home).

Reynolds, Rt. Hon. Gerald William, P.C., M.P.; British politician; b. 17 July 1927; ed. Acton County School, and Ealing Technical Coll.
Councillor, Acton Borough Council 49-65; Alderman, London Borough of Ealing 64-66; Mayor of Acton 60-61; Local Govt. Adviser to British Labour Party 52-58; M.P. 58-; Parl. Under-Sec. of State for Defence for the Army 64-65, Minister of Defence for the Army 66-67, Minister of Defence for Administration 57-; Labour.
House of Commons, London, S.W.1, England.

Reynolds, Richard Samuel, Jr., B.S.; American industrialist; b. 27 May 1908; ed. Davidson Coll., N.C., and Wharton School of Finance, Univ. of Pennsylvania.
Fmr. mem. N.Y. Stock Exchange; with two partners formed banking firm of Reynolds & Co. 30; became associated with Reynolds Metals Co. as Asst. to Pres. 38, Treas. 38-48, Vice-Pres. 33-38, Pres. Aug. 48-, now Chair.; fmr. Pres. Aluminum Asscn.; Chair. of Board Robertshaw Controls Co.; mem. President's Advisory Cttee. on Labor Management Policy, Nat. Export Advisory Council.
Home: 4509 Sulgrave Road, Richmond, Va.; Office: Reynolds Metals Co., Richmond, Va., U.S.A.

Reyre, Jean André Marie; Franch banker, b. 9 Dec. 1899; ed. Faculté de Droit de Paris and Ecole Libre des Sciences Politiques.
Entered Banque de Paris et des Pays-Bas 24, Asst. Man. 41, Man. 45, Dir.-Gen. 48, Dir. 55, Vice-Pres. Dir. Gen. 62-67, Pres. Dir. Gen. 67-; Pres. Dir. Gen. Soc. d'Investissements de Paris et des Pays-Bas; Chair. Paribas Corpn.; Pres. Compagnie Centrale de Financement; Vice-Pres. Cie. Générale de Participations et d'Entreprises, C.S.F., Soc. Belge COPEBA; Dir. several other companies; Officier Légion d'Honneur; Croix de Guerre (First World War).
96 avenue de Suffren, Paris 15e, France.

Rhallys, George J., LL.D.; Greek lawyer; b. 18; ed. Athens Univ.
Served Reconnaissance Groups 40-41 and Tank Corps 45-48; elected Deputy for Athens 50, 51, 52, 56, 61, 63, 64; regular mem. Greek Del. to European Council, Strasbourg 53-58; mem. Greek parliamentary Del. visiting British House of Commons 53; Minister to Prime Minister's Office 54-56; Minister of Public Works and Communications 56-58; Minister of the Interior 61-63; Minister of Public Order April 67; Greek Rally Party; Medal of Valour, War Cross with two bars, D.S.M., and several foreign awards.
Publs. *John Rhallys, The Possibility of Increasing the Yield of Greek Agriculture, Democracy and Communism* (in Greek).
Kanari 4, Athens, Greece.

Rham, Georges-William de, D. ès SC. MATH.; Swiss mathematician; b. 10 Sept. 1903; ed. Collège d'Aigle, Gymnase classique de Lausanne, and Univs. de Lausanne et Paris.
Privat-Docent, Univ. of Lausanne 32, Extraordinary Prof. 36-43, Full Prof. 43-; Extraordinary Prof. Univ. of Geneva 36-53, Full Prof. 53-; mem. Swiss Nat. Council for Scientific Research 56-; Visiting Prof. Harvard Univ. 49-50; temporary mem. Inst. for Advanced Study, Princeton 50, 57-58; Pres. Int. Mathematical Union 62-66; Foreign mem. Accad. dei Lincei; Dr. h.c. (Univs. of Strasbourg, Grenoble, Lyon and Swiss Fed. Polytechnical Inst.).
Publs. include: *Variétés différentiables, Formes, Courants, Formes harmoniques* 55 (2nd edn. 60).
7 avenue des Bergières, Lausanne, Switzerland.

Rhijn, Arie Adriaan van, J.D., D.SC., LL.D., PH.D.; Netherlands civil servant; b. 92; ed. Groningen and Utrecht Univs.
Dep. Sec. Court of Arbitration for Railway Personnel 17-18; Sec. Master Printers' Union 19-27; Chief of a Dept. in the Min. of Social Affairs 28-32; Sec.-Gen. of the Min. of Econ. Affairs 33-39; Min. of Agric. and Fisheries 40-41; Chair. Netherlands Financial Control Board 41-45; Sec.-Gen. of the Min. of Social Affairs 45-50; Secretary of State for Social Affairs 50-58; mem. Council of State 60-67; Knight of the Order of the Netherlands Lion; Commdr. Order of Orange Nassau; Great Commdr. Star of Rumania; Knight Commdr. Order of Crown of Belgium 49.
Publs. *Free Competition and Collective Labour Agreement* 24, *Planning* 46, *Social Security* 46.
Wassenaarscheweg 69, The Hague, Netherlands.
Telephone: 070-248856.

Rho, Paolo; Italian railway executive and international civil servant; b. 29 June 1916; ed. Università degli Studi, Florence.
Army Service 40-43; Sec.-Gen., then Dir. provincial labour office, Ministry of Labour and Nat. Service 44-47; Inspector, Turin Commercial Div., Italian State Railways 47-48; Asst. Gen. Rep., Italian State Railways, Berne, Switzerland 48-50; Head, Int. Freight Rates Dept., later Head of Secr. of Asst. Dir.-Gen., Directorate-Gen. of Italian State Railways, Rome 50-58; Head of Div., Directorate-Gen. for Transport, EEC Comm., Brussels 58-63; Hon. Dir. EEC Comm. 58-63; Special duties with Dir.-Gen., Italian State Railways 63-65; Dir.-Gen. for Transport, EEC Comm. 65-.
European Economic Community, 23 avenue de la Joyeuse Entrée, Brussels 4, Belgium.

Rhoades, Donald Arthur; American business executive; b. 4 Jan. 1903; ed. Fresno High School, and Univ. of California, Berkeley, California.
Kaiser Org. 27-; Kaiser Paving Co. 27-39; Project Man. Columbia Construction Co. (Kaiser) 39-42; Operations Man. Perm. Cement Co. and Perm. Metals Corpn. (predecessor of Kaiser Aluminum and Chemical Corpn.) 43-46, Vice-Pres. and Gen. Man. 46, Dir. 48-; Pres. and Chief Exec. Kaiser Aluminum and Chemical Corpn. 58-63, Management Assoc. 63-; Pres. The Aluminum Asscn. 54-55, Dir.-at-Large 61-63, Hon. Dir. 64; Vice-Pres. Kaiser Industries Corpn. 64-; Dir. Kaiser Cement and Gypsum Corpn. 65-.
Kaiser Center, 300 Lakeside Drive, Oakland 12, Calif., U.S.A.

Riad, Mahmoud; United Arab Republic (Egyptian) diplomatist; b. 17; ed. Military Acad. and General Staff Coll.
Egyptian Rep. to Mixed Armistice Comm. 49-52; Dir. Dept. of Arab Affairs, Ministry of Foreign Affairs 54-55; Ambassador to Syria 55-58; President's Counsellor on Foreign Affairs 58-62; Chair. U.A.R. Del. to UN Econ. Comm. for Africa 61, Perm. Rep. to UN 62-64; Minister of Foreign Affairs under Dep. Prime Minister for Foreign Affairs 64-.
Ministry of Foreign Affairs, Cairo, U.A.R.

Riazanov, Vladimir Alexandrovich; Soviet hygienist; b. 1903; ed. Voronezh Univ.
Physician, Voronezh 26-31; Head of Dept. Inst. of Occupational Disease 31-33; Physician, Sanitation Inspector, Deputy Chief, Perm Regional Health Dept. 33-45; Deputy Chief Sanitation Inspector, R.S.F.S.R. Commissariat of Public Health 45-46; Deputy R.S.F.S.R. Minister of Public Health 46-52; Head of Chair,

Central Inst. of Post-graduate Medical Training 52-62; Dir. Inst. of General and Communal Hygiene 62-; Corresp. mem. U.S.S.R. Acad. of Medical Sciences 61-65, mem. 65-; Academic Sec. Dept. of Hygiene, Microbiology and Epidemiology 64-66; WHO expert; mem. several scientific socs; Order of Red Star, Badge of Honour, Red Banner of Labour (twice), Merited Doctor of R.S.F.S.R., Erisman Prize of U.S.S.R. Acad. of Medical Sciences.

Publs. Over 60 works on communal hygiene.

Institute of General and Communal Hygiene, 10 Pogodinskaya Street, Moscow, U.S.S.R.

Ribeyre, Paul; French businessman and politician; b. 11 Dec. 1906.

Dir. La Reine Mineral Water Co.; Deputy from Ardèche to the two Constituent Nat. Assemblies 45-46; Deputy to Nat. Assembly 46-58; Senator for Ardèche 58-; Under-Sec. of State for Public Health and Population 49, Minister of Public Health 51-52, of Commerce 53, of Justice 53-54, of Industry May 58; fmr. Pres. Conseil Gén. de l'Ardèche, Asscn. Parlementaire pour la Liberté de l'Enseignement; Chevalier de la Légion d'Honneur; mem. Directing Cttee. of Centre Democrat Party 66-.

31 rue La Pérouse, Paris 16e, France.

Ribicoff, Abraham A. (Abe), LL.B.; American lawyer and politician; b. 9 April 1910; ed. Univ. of Chicago.

Admitted to Connecticut Bar 33; served on Conn. Legislature 39-43; Judge Hartford Municipal Court 41-43 and 45-47; mem. House of Reps. 49-53; Gov. of the State of Conn. 55-61; Sec. of Health, Education and Welfare 61-July 62; U.S. Senator from Conn. 63-; Democrat; Order of Merit (Italy).

3402 Que Street, N.W., Washington, D.C., U.S.A.

Ricardo, Sir Harry (Ralph), Kt., LL.D., F.R.S.; British engineer; b. 26 Jan. 1885; ed. Rugby School and Trinity Coll., Cambridge.

Mechanical engineer with Rendel, Palmer and Tritton, Consulting Engineers 07-15; Consulting engineer to Mechanical Warfare Dept., designed petrol engines for tanks 16; consulting engineer to Air Ministry on aero engines 18, mem. Advisory Cttee. on Aero Engine Research and Devt. 18-43; research work on design of high-speed internal combustion engines; Technical Dir. Ricardo & Co. Ltd. 19-64; mem. War Cabinet Engineering Cttee. 42-45; Vice-Pres. Inst. Mechanical Engineers 42, Pres. 44-45; mem. Scientific Advisory Council, Ministry of Fuel and Power 48; awarded Royal Soc. Rumford Medal 44.

Publs. *The Internal Combustion Engine,* 2 vols., *Engine of High Output.*

Woodside, Graffham, Petworth, Sussex, England.

Richard, René; French engineer; b. 10 April 1904.

Engineer, Etablissements Japy; Gen. Sec. Nat. Fed. of Engineers and Higher Staff; Econ. Councillor 51-59; Vice-Pres. Econ. Council 55-59; Vice-Pres. Econ. and Social Council, representing CGT-FO 59-67; mem. Confederate Bureau, Confédération Générale de Travail-Force Ouvrière (CGT-FO); mem. Nat. Council on Productivity; mem. Econ. High Council of Org. for Saharan Regions; mem. numerous Cttees.; Commissariat-Gen. of the Plan; Officier Légion d'Honneur, Officier du Mérite économique.

1 place Edouard-Renard, Paris 12e, France.

Richards, Arthur L.; American diplomatist; b. 21 June 1907; ed. Pasadena Jr. Coll., George Washington Univ. and Nat. War Coll.

Joined Foreign Service 30, Mexico, Washington, Teheran, Jerusalem, Cairo, Cape Town, Pretoria, Washington, Teheran 30-52; Dir. Office of Greek, Turkish and Iranian Affairs, Dept. of State 52-54; Consul-Gen. Istanbul 54-56; Operations Co-ordinator, Dept. of State 56-58; Special Asst. to Under-Sec. of State for Law of Sea 58-60; Ambassador to Ethiopia 60-

62; Dep. Rep. of U.S. to 18-Nation Disarmament Cttee., Geneva 63-65; now Dir. Washington Int. Centre.

Meridian House, 1630 Crescent Place, N.W. Washington, D.C. 20009, U.S.A.

Telephone: 202-332-1030.

Richards, Audrey Isabel, C.B.E., M.A., PH.D., F.B.A.; British university teacher; b. 8 July 1899; ed. Cambridge and London Univs.

Field research Bemba tribe, N.E. Rhodesia 30-34; Lecturer in Social Anthropology, London School of Economics 35-38, Sen. Lecturer, Univ. of the Witwatersrand, Johannesburg 38-41; Principal, Colonial Office 41-45; Reader in Social Anthropology London, Univ. 46-50; Dir. East African Inst. of Social Research, Makerere Coll., Uganda 50-56; Smuts Reader in Commonwealth Affairs, Univ. of Cambridge 61-66; Pres. Royal Anthropological Inst. 59-61; Dir. Anglia Television Co. 59-63; Pres. African Studies Asscn. 63-66; Fellow Newnham Coll. 56-; Rivers Memorial Medal, Wellcome Medal.

Publs. *Hunger and Work in a Savage Tribe* 33, *Land, Labour and Diet in N. Rhodesia* 39, *Chisungu, a study of girls' initiation ceremonies in N. Rhodesia* 56, *The Changing Structure of a Ganda Village* 66; Editor: *Economic Development and Tribal Change* 54, *East African Chiefs* 60.

Crawley House, Elmdon, Saffron Walden, Essex.

Telephone: Chrishall 362.

Richards, Ceri Giraldus, C.B.E.; British painter; b. 6 June 1903; ed. Royal Coll. of Art, London.

Many one-man exhibitions, London; works in Nat. Collections in Britain and other countries; one-man exhibition, London 60; rep. at Dunn Int. Exhibition, London 63; reredos for Liverpool Cathedral; Trustee, Tate Gallery 58-65; prize at Venice Biennale 62; Hon. D.Litt.

12 Edith Grove, Chelsea, London, S.W.10, England.

Richards, Dickinson W., A.M., M.D.; American physician; b. 30 Oct. 1895; ed. Yale and Columbia Univs.

Research Fellow, Nat. Inst. for Medical Research, London 27-28, research at College of Physicians and Surgeons, Columbia Univ. 28-; Prof. of Medicine, Columbia Univ. 47-61, Emer. 61-; Nobel Prize in Physiology and Medicine 56; Hon. D.Sc. (Yale) 57; Editor *Circulation of the Blood, Men and Ideas.*

320 Oakwood Road, Englewood, N.J., U.S.A.

Richards, Ivor Armstrong, C.H., M.A., LITT.D., F.B.A.; British literary critic; b. 26 Feb. 1893; ed. Clifton and Magdalene Coll., Cambridge.

Lecturer in English and Moral Sciences 22. Fellow Magdalene Coll. 26; Charles Kingsley By-Fellowship 35; Visiting Prof. Tsing Hua Univ. Peking 29-30, Harvard 31; mem. Cttee., King's Medal for Poetry 33; Dir. Orthological Inst. (Basic English), China 36-38; Univ. Lecturer, Harvard 39-44, Prof. 44-63, Emer. 63; Loines Award for Poetry 62; Hon. Litt.D. (Harvard); Hon. Fellow, Magdalene Coll., Cambridge 64.

Publs. *Foundations of Aesthetics* (with C. K. Ogden and James Wood) 21, *The Meaning of Meaning* (with C. K. Ogden) 23, *Principles of Literary Criticism* 24, *Science and Poetry* 25, *Practical Criticism* 29, *Mencius on the Mind* 31, *Basic Rules of Reason* 33, *Coleridge on Imagination* 34, *Interpretation in Teaching* 38, *How to Read a Page* 42, *Basic English and its Uses* 43, *Nations and Peace* 47, *The Portable Coleridge* 50, *The Wrath of Achilles* 50, *Speculative Instruments* 55, *Goodbye Earth and other Poems* 58, *The Screens and other Poems* 60, *Tomorrow Morning, Faustus!* 62, *Why so, Socrates?* 63, abridged version *Plato's Republic* 65, *So Much Nearer* (essays) 68.

1000 Memorial Drive, Cambridge, Mass. 02138, U.S.A.

Telephone: Kirkland 7-4848.

Richardson, Burton Taylor, M.A.; Canadian journalist; b. 29 Jan. 1906; ed. Manitoba, Syracuse (U.S.A.), and London School of Economics.
Staff writer of *Winnipeg Free Press*; correspondent in Ottawa 40-44, in Washington, D.C. 45, in London, England 46: Ed. of Saskatoon *Star-Phoenix* 46-48, *Winnipeg Citizen* 48; Assoc. Ed. *Ottawa Citizen* 49-51; Sec. to Royal Comm. on S. Saskatchewan River 51-53; Editor *The Telegram* (Toronto) 53-62, Special Corresp. in Washington D.C. 62-63; Special Asst. to Prime Minister Diefenbaker (later Leader of Opposition) 63-65; Consultant, Ontario Econ. Council 66-; Consulting Assoc. P. S. Ross and Partners 61-.
Publ. *Canada and Mr. Diefenbaker* 62.
Apt. 705, 581 Avenue Road, Toronto, Canada.
Telephone: 416-481-8959.

Richardson, Sir Egerton Rudolf, Kt., C.M.G.; Jamaican government official and diplomatist; b. 15 Aug. 1912; ed. Calabar High School, Kingston, Balliol Coll., Oxford.
Jamaican civil service 33-, Asst. Treas. 44, Asst. Colonial Sec. 47, Perm. Sec. Ministry of Agriculture 52-53, Under-Sec. Ministry of Finance 53-56, Financial Sec. of Jamaica 56-62; Perm. Rep. of Jamaica to the UN 62-66; Amb. to U.S.A. and Mexico 67-.
Jamaican Embassy, 1666 Connecticut Avenue, N.W. Washington, D.C. 20009; 1645 Myrtle Street, N.W. Washington, D.C. 20012. U.S.A.
Telephone: 387-1010; and 723-6222.

Richardson, Gordon Dalyell, M.A., F.L.A.A.; Australian librarian; b. 23 Nov. 1917; ed. Sydney Univ.
Assistant, Public Library, New South Wales 34-40; Infantry Officer, Australian Imperial Force 40-45; Dep. Principal Librarian, N.S.W. 54-56; Acting Principal Librarian 56-57; Mitchell Librarian 58-; Principal Librarian and Sec. Public Library, N.S.W. 59-; Exec. mem. Library Board of N.S.W. 59-; Principal Archivist, N.S.W. 61-; Vice-Pres. Library Asscn. of Australia 64-66, Pres. 67-68; Fellow Royal Inst. of Public Admin.
10 Ayres Road East, St. Ives, N.S.W., Australia.
Telephone: 44-3559.

Richardson, Gordon William Humphreys, M.B.E., B.A., LL.B.; British merchant banker; b. 25 Nov. 1915; ed. Nottingham High School, and Gonville and Caius Coll., Cambridge.
South Notts. Hussars Yeomanry 39, Staff Coll., Camberley 41; Called to the Bar, Gray's Inn 47; mem. Bar Council 51-55; Industrial and Commercial Finance Corpn. Ltd. 55-57; Dir. J. Henry Schroder and Co. 57-; Chair. J. Henry Schroder Wagg and Co. Ltd. 62-; Chair. Schroders 65-, J. Henry Schroder Banking Corpn. (U.S.A.) 67-, Schroders AG (Switzerland) 67; Dir. Bank of England 67-; Vice-Chair. Legal and Gen. Assurance Soc. Ltd. 60-, Lloyds Bank Ltd. 62-66; mem. Company Law Amendment Cttee. 59-62; Chair. Cttee. on Turnover Taxation 63-64; mem. Court, London Univ. 62-65.
120 Cheapside, London, E.C.2; and 64 Chelsea Square, London, S.W.3, England.
Telephone: 01-352-1308 (Home); 01-588-4000 (Office).

Richardson, Sir Ralph David, Kt.; British actor; b. 02; ed. Xavierian Coll. Brighton.
First appeared on stage Brighton 21; acted in *Eden End* and *Cornelius* London 35; *Romeo and Juliet* U.S.A. 35-36; *Promise, Bees on the Boat Deck,* and *The Amazing Dr. Clitterhouse* London 36-37; *Johnson over Jordan* London 38; *A Midsummer Night's Dream* and *Othello* Old Vic 38; served in Fleet Air Arm 39-44; acted at Old Vic Seasons 44-45, 45-46, 46-47 (also producing *Richard II*); toured France, Belgium and Germany with Old Vic 45, and appeared with the Company in N.Y. 46; acted

and produced *Royal Circle*, Wyndham's Theatre, London 48; acted in *The Heiress* Haymarket Theatre 49, *Home at Seven* Wyndham's Theatre 50, *The Three Sisters* Aldwych Theatre 51; Stratford Memorial Theatre season 52; *The White Carnation* Globe Theatre 53, *A Day by The Sea* 54; tour of Australia and New Zealand 56; *Timon of Athens* Old Vic, *Waltz of the Toreadors* New York 57; *Flowering Cherry* Haymarket Theatre 58; *The Complaisant Lover* Globe Theatre 59; *The Last Joke* 60; *School for Scandal* Haymarket Theatre 62, Broadway 63; *Six Characters in Search of an Author* Mayfair Theatre, London 63; South American tour 64; *Carving a Statue* 64, *You Never Can Tell* 66, *The Rivals* Haymarket Theatre 67, *The Merchant of Venice* Haymarket Theatre 67; first appeared in films in *The Ghoul* 33; since then films include: *Things to Come, The Man Who Could Work Miracles, Bulldog Drummond, South Riding, Divorce of Lady X, The Citadel, Four Feathers, Q Planes, Night of the Fire, The Silver Fleet* 42, *The Volunteer* 43, *School for Secrets* 47, *Anna Karenina* 47, *The Fallen Idol* 48, *The Heiress* (Hollywood) 48, *Outcast of the Islands* and *Home at Seven* 51, *The Sound Barrier* 52, *The Holly and the Ivy* 52, *Richard III* 55, *Smiley* 56, *The Passionate Stranger* 57, *Our Man in Havana* 59, *Exodus* 60, *Lion of Sparta* 60, *Long Day's Journey into Night* 62, *Woman of Straw* 63, *Dr. Zhivago* 65, *Khartoum* 66, *The Wrong Box* 66.
1 Chester Terrace, Regent's Park, London, N.W.1, England.

Richardson, Tony; British stage and film producer; b. 5 June 1928; ed. Wadham Coll., Oxford.
Artistic Dir. Royal Court Theatre 56-; Dir. Woodfall Film Productions Ltd. 58-.
Plays produced or directed include: *Look Back In Anger, The Chairs, Pericles* and *Othello* (Stratford), *The Entertainer, Luther, The Seagull, St. Joan of the Stockyards.*
Films (produced or directed): *Look back In Anger* 58, *The Entertainer* 59, *Saturday Night and Sunday Morning* 60, *A Taste of Honey* 61, *The Loneliness of the Long Distance Runner* 62, *Tom Jones* 63, *The Loved One* 64, *Summer Fires* 65, *The Sailor from Gibraltar* 66, *Mademoiselle* 66, *Red and Blue* 66, *The Charge of the Light Brigade* 68.
11A Curzon Street, London, W.1, England.
Telephone: 493-7613.

Riches, Sir Derek (Martin Hurry), K.C.M.G., British diplomatist; b. 26 July 1912; ed. Univ. Coll. School, and Univ. Coll., London.
Entered Foreign Service 34, served Beirut, Ethiopia, Cairo, Kabul 34-49, Jedda 51-52, Khartoum 53; Head of Eastern Dept., Foreign Office 55-59; Ambassador to Libya 59-61, to Congo 61-63, to Lebanon 63-67.
8 Voltaire, Ennerdale Road, Kew Gardens, Surrey, England.

Riches, Edward John, M.A.; New Zealand international civil servant; b. 30 July 1905; ed. Univ. of New Zealand and Univ. of Michigan.
Joined Research Div. of Int. Labour Office 27, Asst. Econ. Adviser 41, Acting Chief, Econ. and Statistical Section 41-46, Econ. Adviser 46-60, Treasurer and Financial Comptroller (Asst. Dir.-Gen.) 61-.
c/o International Labour Office, Geneva; and 22 Avenue Krieg, 1208 Geneva, Switzerland.
Telephone: 32-62-00 (Office); 36-02-37 (Home).

Richler, Mordecai; Canadian writer; b. 31; ed. Montreal Hebrew Acad., Baron Byng High School and Sir George Williams Univ.
Canada Council Junior Arts Fellowship 59, 60; Fellowship in Creative Writing, Guggenheim Foundation, New York 61.
Publs. (novels) *The Acrobats* 54, *Son of a Smaller Hero* 55, *A Choice of Enemies* 57, *The Apprenticeship of*

Duddy Kravitz 59, *The Incomparable Atuk* 63, *Cocksure* 68; (film scripts) *No Love for Johnnie*, etc.; (TV Plays) *The Trouble with Benny*, etc.

11b Parkhill Road, London N.W.3, England.

Richmond, Sir John Christopher Blake, K.C.M.G.; British diplomatist; b. 7 Sept. 1909; ed. Lancing Coll., Hertford Coll., Oxford, and Univ. Coll., London.
On archæological expeditions, Beisan, Jericho, Tel El Duweir, Ithaca 31-36; H.M. Office of Works 37-39; served in Middle East in Second World War 39-46; Dept. of Antiquities, Palestine Govt. 46-47; British Foreign Service, Oriental Sec., Baghdad 47-51; Foreign Office 51-53; Counsellor, Amman 53-55; Consul-Gen. Houston, Texas 55-58; British Property Comm., Cairo 59; Political Agent, Kuwait Oct. 59-61, Ambassador to Kuwait 61-63; Supernumerary Fellow, St. Antony's Coll., Oxford 63-64; Ambassador to Sudan 65-66; Lecturer in Modern Near East History, Durham Univ. 66-.
20 The Avenue, Durham, England.

Richter, Conrad Michael; American novelist and short story writer; b. 13 Oct. 1890; ed. High School.
Began as reporter on Pittsburg and Johnstown Pa. newspapers; Editor *Weekly Courier*, Patton, Pa. 09; N.Y. Univ. Gold Medal for distinguished writing 42; mem. Nat. Inst. of Arts and Letters; Ohioana Library Medal 47; Pulitzer Prize (for trilogy *The Trees*, *The Fields* and *The Town*) 51; Nat. Book Award for fiction (for *The Waters of Kronos* 68) 61; Hon. Litt.D. (Susquehanna Univ., Univ. of New Mexico, Lafayette Univ.), Hon. LL.D. (Temple Univ.), Hon. L.H.D. (Lebanon Valley College).
Publs. *Brothers of No Kin and Other Stories* 24, *Early Americana and Other Stories* 36, *The Sea of Grass* 37, *The Trees* 40, *Tracey Cromwell* 42, *The Free Man* 44, *The Fields* 46, *Always Young and Fair* 47, *The Town* 50, *The Light in the Forest* 53, *The Mountain on the Desert* 55, *The Lady* 57, *The Waters of Kronos* 60, *A Simple Honorable Man* 62, *The Grandfathers* 64, *Individualists Under the Shade Trees in a Vanishing America* 65, *A Country of Strangers* 66, *The Awakening Land* 66, *Over the Blue Mountain* 67, *Death of the Aristocrat* 68.
11 Maple Street, Pine Grove, Pennsylvania, U.S.A.
Telephone: 717-345-3472.

Richter, Gisela M. A., M.A., LITT.D.; American archaeologist; b. 15 Aug. 1882; ed. Girton Coll., Cambridge, and British School of Archaeology, Athens.
Assistant in Dept. of Greek and Roman Art New York Metropolitan Museum of Art 06, Asst. Curator 10, Assoc. Curator 22, Curator 25-48; Hon. Curator 48-; Life Fellow, Metropolitan Museum of Art; Assoc. Editor *The American Journal of Archæology*; Hon. Fellow Somerville Coll., Oxford, Girton Coll., Cambridge; American Asscn. of Univ. Women Achievement Award 44; mem. Accad. Pontificia di Archeologia, Rome, Soc. of Antiquaries (London), American Philosophical Soc. (Philadelphia), Accad. di Archeologia Naples, Accad. Nazionale dei Lincei, British Acad.; Hon. D.Litt. (Oxford), L.H.D. (Smith Coll.), D.F.A. (Rochester Univ.), Ph.D. (Basle), Litt.D. (Cambridge and Dublin).
Publs. *Greek, Etruscan and Roman Bronzes in the Metropolitan Museum* 15, *Handbook of the Classical Collection* 17 (6th edn. 30), *Catalogue of Engraved Gems of the Classical Style in the Metropolitan Museum* 20, *The Craft of Athenian Pottery* 23, *Ancient Furniture* 26, *The Sculpture and Sculptors of the Greeks* 29 (2nd edn. 30, revised edn. 50), *Animals in Greek Sculpture* 30, *Handbook of the Etruscan Collection in the Metropolitan Museum* 40, *Kouroi* 42, 60, *Archaic Attic Gravestones* 44, *Greek Painting* 44 (2nd edn. 49), *Attic Red-Figured Vases: A Survey* 46, 58, *Roman Portraits* 49, *Archaic Greek Art* 49, *Three Critical Periods in Greek Sculpture* 52, *Attic Black-Figured Kylikes in the Metropolitan Museum* 53, *Catalogue of Greek Sculptures in the Metropolitan Museum* 54, *Greek Portraits I* 55, *Ancient Italy* 55,

Catalogue of the Engraved Gems, Greek, Etruscan and Roman, in the Metropolitan Museum 56, *Catalogue of Greek and Roman Antiquities, Dumbarton Oaks* 56, *Handbook of Greek Art* 59, 5th edn. 67, *Greek Portraits II* 59, *Greek Portraits III* 60, *The Archaic Gravestones of Attica* 61, *Greek Portraits IV* 62, *Greek Portraits V* 64, *The Portraits of the Greeks* (3 vols.) 65, *The Furniture of the Greeks, Etruscans and Romans* 66, *Korai, Archaic Greek Maidens* 68, *The Engraved Gems of the Greeks, Etruscans and Romans* Part One, 68.
81 Viale delle Mura Gianicolensi, Rome, Italy.
Telephone: 501514.

Richter, Hans Werner; German writer; b. 12 Nov. 1908.
Prisoner-of-war in U.S.A., Second World War; free-lance writer 46-; Founder and founder mem. Group 47.
Publs. *Die Geschlagenen* 49, *Sie fielen aus Gottes Hand* 51, *Spuren im Sand* 53, *Du Sollst nicht töten* 55, *Linus oder Der Verlust der Würde* 58, *Almanach der Gruppe 47 1947-1962* 62, *Bestandsaufnahme—Eine deutsche Bilanz* 62, *Walther Rathenau—Reden und Schriften* 64, *Plaedoyer fur eine neue Regierung oder Keine Alternative* 65, *Menschen in freundlicher Umgebung* 65, *Doda* 66.
7 Rembrandtstrasse, München-Pasing, German Federal Republic.
Telephone: Munich 880486.

Richter, Hermann, DR. RER. POL.; German business executive; b. 29 Jan. 1903; ed. Freiburg, Bonn and Cologne Univs.
Chairman, Gold-u. Silberscheideanstalt (Degussa), Frankfurt/M., Farbwerke Hoechst A.G., Frankfurt/M., Hoechst-Metalgesellschaft A.G., Frankfurt/M., NSU Motorenwerke A.G., Neckarsulm; Vice-Chair. Dresdner Bank A.G., Brown Boveri & Cie. A.G., Mannheim, Norddeutscher Lloyd, Bremen; mem. Advisory Board Volkswagenwerk A.G., Wolfsburg.
Düsseldorf, Fahneburgstrasse 21, German Federal Republic.
Telephone: 62-63-67.

Richter, Svyatoslav Theofilovich; Soviet pianist; b. 20 March 1915; ed. Moscow Conservatoire.
Won First Prize at the Third U.S.S.R. Competition of Executant Musicians 45; extensive tours all over the world; State and Lenin prizewinner; People's Artist of U.S.S.R.; Order of Lenin.
Repertoire includes works by Bach (cycle of 48 Preludes and Fugues), Beethoven, Schubert, Rachmaninov, Scriabin, Prokofiev, Ravel, Debussy, Mozart, Schumann, Rubinstein, Myaskovsky, Shostakovich, etc.
Moscow State Philharmonic Society, 20 Mayakovsky Square, Moscow, U.S.S.R.

Richter, Willi; German trade union leader; b. 1 Oct. 1894; ed. village school.
Vice-President International Confederation of Free Trade Unions (ICFTU) 56-; fmr. Pres. Fed. of German Trade Unions (D.G.B.).
Stockheimerstrasse 32, Frankfurt am Main, German Federal Republic.

Richthofen, Oswald Freiherr von; German diplomatist; b. 10 Nov. 1908; ed. Univs. of Leipzig and Berlin.
Foreign Service 35-, Copenhagen, Budapest, Vienna 35-38, Calcutta 38-40, Budapest 40-43; Military Service 43-45; private business 45-51; Head, German Legation, Dublin 51; Minister to Saudi Arabia 57-59, Amb. 59-63, concurrently Minister to Yemen 59-63; Amb. to Sudan 63-65; Ministry of Foreign Affairs 65-66; Amb. to Singapore Nov. 66-.
c/o German Embassy, 6th Floor, International Building, Box 1697, Singapore.
Telephone: 361355-7.

Rickett, Sir Denis Hubert Fletcher, K.C.M.G., C.B.; British civil servant; b. 27 July 1907; ed. Rugby and Balliol Coll., Oxford.

Joined staff of Economic Advisory Council 31; Offices of the War Cabinet 39; Private Sec. to Minister of Production 43-45; Asst. (for work on atomic energy) to Chancellor of the Exchequer 45-47; transferred to Treasury 47; Principal Private Sec. to the Prime Minister 50-51; Minister (economic) to U.S.A. and Head of U.K. Treasury and Supply Del. 51-54; Third Sec., Treasury 54-60, Second Sec. 60-68; Vice-Pres. World Bank 68-; Fellow of All Souls Coll., Oxford 29-49.
International Bank for Reconstruction and Development (World Bank), 1818 H Street, N.W., Washington, D.C. 20433, U.S.A.

Rickover, Rear Admiral Hyman George; American naval officer; b. 1900; ed. U.S. Naval Acad.
Commissioned 22; in charge of atomic submarine project, Atomic Energy Comm. 46-47, Navy Department 47-; responsible for the programme for designing and building the world's first atomic ship U.S.S. *Nautilus*; Special Gold Congressional Medal 59; Enrico Fermi Award 64.
Publs. *Education and Freedom* 58, *Swiss Schools and Ours* 61.
c/o Bureau of Ships, Department of the Navy, Washington, D.C., U.S.A.

Riddick, Gerard Galloway; British business executive; b. 2 Sept. 1921; ed. Stowe School and Clare Coll., Cambridge.
Army Service 40-45; Thomas De La Rue and Co. Ltd. 45-, Personal Asst. to Chair. 45, Branch Manager, Bombay Factory 47-48, Acting Works Manager (England) 48, Man. Dir. Karachi Factory 49-51; Asst. to Gen. Man., Plastics Div. Thomas De La Rue and Co. 51, Sales Man. (Industrial Laminates) 52, Gen. Sales Man., Plastics Div. 53; Gen. Man., Plastics Div. 54; Dir. Thomas De La Rue and Co. 56; Man. Dir. Formica Ltd. 57, Formica Int. 59, Chair. Formica Ltd. 60-63; Dir. Thomas De La Rue Int. and Chair. Formica Int. Ltd. 63-; Deputy Chair. The De La Rue Co. Ltd. and Chair. Thomas De La Rue Int. Ltd., Potterton Int. Ltd., De La Rue Bull Machines Ltd. 64-66, Thomas Potterton Ltd. 67-; Deputy Chair. De La Rue Bull Machines Ltd. 66-.
The Knoll, Penn, Buckinghamshire, England.

Riddle, Oscar, PH.D., LL.D., D.H.C.; American biologist; b. 27 Sept. 1877; ed. Univs. of Indiana and Chicago.
Research Assoc. Station for Experimental Evolution Carnegie Inst. 12-14, mem. research staff 14-45; Lecturer S. America, India, and Mexico 45-47; Fellow American Acad. of Arts and Sciences; mem. American Philosophical Society, Nat. Acad. of Sciences, American Society of Zoologists and American Physiological Society; Gold Medal American Inst. of City of New York 34; Humanist of 1958, American Humanist Asscn.; Scroll of Honor 64, Nat. Inst. of Social Sciences.
Publs. *Carbohydrate and Fat Metabolism in Pigeons, Endocrines and Constitution, The Unleashing of Evolutionary Thought*, etc.
Route 4, Box 576, Plant City, Florida, U.S.A.
Telephone: 752-4532.

Riddleberger, James Williams, A.B., A.M.; American diplomat; b. 21 Sept. 1904; ed. Randolph Macon Coll., Georgetown, and American Univs.
Research Asst. Library of Congress 24-27; Special Expert U.S. Tariff Commission 27-29; entered Foreign Service 29; Vice-Consul and Consul Geneva 30-35; Sec. at Berlin Embassy 36-41; German Desk, State Department 41-42; First Sec., Embassy, London 42-44; Chief, Central European Div., State Dept. 44-47; Dir. of Political Affairs, U.S. Mil. Govt., Berlin 47-49; Political Adviser to U.S. High Commr., Berlin and Bonn 49-50, and to E.C.A., Paris 50-52; Dir. German Bureau, Dept. of State 52-53; Ambassador to Yugoslavia 53-58; Ambassador to Greece 58-59; Dir. Int. Co-operation Admin. 59-61; Chair. Development Assistance Cttee., OECD.

Paris 61-62; Amb. to Austria 62-67; John Carroll Award (Georgetown Univ.).
Woodstock, Virginia, U.S.A.

Ride, Sir Lindsay Tasman, Kt., C.B.E.; British (b. Australian) educationalist; b. 10 Oct. 1898; ed. Scotch Coll., Melbourne, Melbourne Univ., New Coll., Oxford, and Guy's Hospital Medical School, London.
Former Demonstrator in Physiology and Pharmacology, Guy's Hospital, London; Prof. of Physiology, Univ. of Hong Kong 28-52, Dean of Medical Faculty and Vice-Chancellor 49-64, Dir. of Inst. of Modern Asian Studies 60-64, Prof. Emer. 65-; Chair. Asscn. of Univs. of British Commonwealth 60-61; Vice-Pres. Asscn. of S.E. Asian Institutions of Higher Learning 63-64; Research Assoc., Inst. of Social Studies, Chinese Univ. of Hong Kong 65-; Hon. LL.D. (Toronto, Melbourne and London).
Publs. *Genetics and the Clinician* 40, *Morrison, The Scholar and the Man* 58, *Biographical Note on James Legge* 61, *The Old Protestant Cemetery, Macao* 63.
Newhaven, Taipo Kau, New Territories, Hong Kong.

Rideal, Sir Eric Keightley, Kt., M.B.E., F.R.S., D.SC., M.A., PH.D., F.R.I.C., M.R.I.; British chemist; b. 11 April 1890; ed. Oundle School, Trinity Hall, Cambridge, and Bonn Univ.
Capt. First World War; Prof. Physical Chemistry Illinois Univ. 20; Lecturer and Prof. Cambridge Univ. 21; Prof. Colloid Science Cambridge Univ. 30-46; Fullerian Prof. Royal Inst. London; Dir. Davy Faraday Laboratories 46-50; Prof. King's Coll. London 50-55; Chair. Advisory Council to Minister of Supply on Scientific Research and Technical Development 53-58; former Pres. Chemical Society, Faraday Society, Society of Chemical Industry; Hon. D.Sc. (Dublin, Belfast, Turin, Bonn and Birmingham); Hon. Fellow, Trinity Hall, Cambridge and King's Coll., London; Hon. D.Tech.(Brunel).
Publs. *Recent Developments in Catalytic Chemistry* 21, *Colloid Chemistry* 24, *Disinfection and Disinfectants* (with S. Rideal), *Electrometallurgy, Ozone, Catalysis in Theory and Practice* (with H. S. Taylor), *An Introduction to Surface Chemistry, Interfacial Phenomena* (with J. T. Davies), *Concepts in Catalysis* 68.
22 Westbourne Park Road, London, W.2; The Spinney, West Runton, Cromer, Norfolk, England.
Telephone: 01-229-5595; and West Runton 423.

Ridgway, General Matthew B., D.S.C. (with O.L.C.), D.S.M. (with 3rd O.L.C.); American army officer; b. 3 March 1895; ed. U.S. Military Acad.
Commissioned Lieut. U.S. Army 17 and advanced through grades to Lieut.-Gen. 45, Gen. 51; technical adviser to Gov.-Gen. of Philippines 32-33; Asst. Chief of Staff 6th Corps Area 35-36, Deputy Chief of Staff Second Army 36; Asst. Chief of Staff Fourth Army 37-39; accompanied Gen. Marshall to Brazil 39; War Plans Div., War Dept. Gen. Staff 39-42; Asst. Div. Commdr. 82nd Infantry Div. 42, Div. Commdr. 42; Commdg. Gen. 82nd Airborne Div., Sicily, Italy, Normandy 42-44; Commd. 18th Airborne Corps, Belgium, France, Germany 44-45; Commdr. Luzon Area 45; Commdr. Mediterranean Theatre of Operations and Deputy Supreme Allied Commdr. Mediterranean Sept. 45-Jan. 46; senior U.S. Army mem. Mil. Staff Cttee., U.N. 46-48; Chair. Inter-American Defence Board 46-48; C.-in-C. Caribbean Commd. 48-49; Deputy Army Chief of Staff for Admin. 49-50; Commdr. Eighth Army in Korea 50-51; Commdr. U.N. Command in Far East, C.-in-C. Far East and Supreme Commdr. Allied Powers in Japan 51-52; Supreme Allied Commdr., Europe 52-53; Chief of Staff U.S. Army 53-55; Chair. Board of Trustees, Mellon Inst. of Industrial Research 55-60.
Publ. *The Korean War* 67.
Home: 918 West Waldheim Road, Fox Chapel, Pittsburgh, Pa. 15215, U.S.A.

Riding, Laura, C.I.A.L. (Mrs. Schuyler B. Jackson); American writer; b. 01; ed. Cornell Univ.
Honorary mem. of The Fugitives (Southern U.S. poets) 24; in England and abroad 26-39.
Publs. include: *The Close Chaplet* (first of nine volumes of poems) 26, *Contemporaries and Snobs* 27, *Survey of Modernist Poetry* (with Robert Graves) 27, *Anarchism is not Enough* 28, *Experts are Puzzled* 30, *Progress of Stories* 35, *A Trojan Ending* 37, *Collected Poems* 38, *The Left Heresy* (with Harry Kemp) 39, *Lives of Wives* 39; edited *Epilogue* 35-37, *The World and Ourselves* 38; contributor to *Chelsea* 62, 64, *Civiltà Delle Macchine* 63, *Art and Literature* 65, *The Telling* (complete book *Chelsea*) 67.
Box 35, Wabasso, Florida 32970, U.S.A.

Rieber, Torkild; Norwegian-born American oil executive; b. 13 March 1882; ed. High School, and Nautical Acad. in Norway.
Came to U.S. 98; naturalized citizen of U.S. 04; went to sea 97, serving in various capacities on sailing and steam vessels; finally as master of one of first tankers under American flag 05, later bought by The Texas Co.; served in Terminal and Refining Depts. of The Texas Co. 09-19; Vice-Pres. and Dir. American Republics Corpn. interests 19-27; Vice-Pres. in charge Export and Marine Depts., Dir. and mem. Exec. Cttee., the Texas Co. 28, chair. of Board 35-40; Pres. Barber Oil Corpn. and its predecessor Barber Asphalt Corpn. and subsidiaries 42-56, Chair. of Board 56; Chair. of Board American Gilsonite Co., Salt Lake City 46-; Dir. Hotel Waldorf-Astoria Corpn., N.Y., American Steamship Owners Mutual Protection & Indemnity Asscn. Inc., United States Lines Co., American Petroleum Inst.
Home: 812 Fifth Avenue, New York City, N.Y. 10021; Office: 30 Rockefeller Plaza, New York, N.Y. 10020, U.S.A.

Riefler, Winfield W(illiam), B.A., PH.D.; American economist; b. 9 Feb. 1897; ed. Amherst Coll., and Robert Brookings Graduate School.
Served in France First World War 17-19; Foreign Trade Official Dept. of Commerce, Buenos Aires 21-23; Div. of Research and Statistics, Fed. Reserve Board 23-33; Exec. Sec. Cttee. on Bank Reserves 30-32; Chair. Central Statistical Board 33-35; Economic Adviser to Exec. Council 33-34; to Nat. Emergency Council 34-35; Prof. of School of Economics and Politics of Inst. for advanced Study, Princeton 35-48; Asst. to Sec. of Treasury 39; on leave of absence to act as Minister to London (Special Asst. to Ambassador) in charge of Economic Warfare 42-44; Asst. to Chair. Board of Govs. Fed. Reserve System 48-59; Dir. Nat. Bureau of Econ. Research 36-42, 45-48; Dir. Foreign Policy Asscn. 38-40; Dir. Fed. Reserve Bank of Phila. 41-42; Chair. Cttee. on Social and Econ. Aspects of Atomic Energy 45; Dir. Council on Foreign Relations 45-50; Sec. Fed. Open Market Cttee. 52-60; Trustee Foreign Service Educational Foundation 48-60; Fellow American Statistical Asscn. (Pres. 41), Royal Econ. Soc., London; Hon. L.H.D. (Amherst Coll.) 44; Croix de Guerre.
Publ. *Money Rates and Money Markets in the United States* 30.
430 Island Circle, Sarasota, Florida 33581, U.S.A.
Telephone: 924-3105.

Riemens, Hendrik, DR.ECON.SC.; Netherlands author and diplomatist; b. 08; ed. Univ. of Amsterdam.
Various diplomatic posts in Berlin 34-35, Shanghai 35, Batavia 35; Dept. of Economic Affairs 35, Shanghai 36-37, Hong Kong 37, Shanghai 38, London 38, Dublin 38-39, Washington 40-43, New York 43-46; Dept. of Foreign Affairs 46, London 47-49, New York (UN) 49-50; Minister to Venezuela 50-54; Minister-at-Large, Latin America, concurrently Dir. for Economic Relations 54-56; Minister and Special Ambassador, Monrovia 56; Adviser on atomic affairs 57-59; Board mem. and Sec., Study Centre for Latin America, Univ. of Amsterdam.
Publs. *The Amortisation Syndicate* 35, *Les Pays-Bas dans le monde* 39, *The Netherlands Story of a Free People* 44, *Les Pays-Bas* 45, *The Financial Development of the Netherlands* 49, *Perspectives in the Netherlands* 58, *L'Europe devant l'Amérique latine* 62, *Latin America* 63, *Mexico* 64, *Belgium, Country of Contrasts*.
Julianalaan 84, Overveen, Netherlands.

Rienäcker, Günther, DR.PHIL.; German chemist; b. 13 May 1904; ed. Univ. of Munich.
Prof. Univ. of Göttingen 37; Prof. and Dir. Inst. of Inorganic Chemistry, Univ. of Rostock 42; Prof. of Inorganic Chemistry, Univ. of Berlin 54-, Dir. 1st Chemical Inst. 54-62; mem. and Gen. Sec. Deutsche Akad. der Wissenschaften, Dir. of its Inst. for Research into Catalysts; mem. Exec. Council, Deutscher Kulturbund, Deutsche Akad. der Naturforscher (Leopoldina); Hon. mem. Hungarian Acad. of Sciences; Foreign mem. Acad. of Sciences, U.S.S.R.; mem. Inst. d'Egypte, Cairo; Nat. Prize 55.
Tschaikowskistrasse 40-42, 111 Berlin-Niederschönhausen, Germany.
Telephone: 489741.

Riese, Otto, LL.D.; German judge; b. 27 Oct. 1894; ed. Lausanne, Leipzig and Frankfurt Univs.
Attached to Frankfurt-am-Main Court 23, Ministry of Justice 25; Prof. of Law, Lausanne Univ. 35, Dean, Faculty of Law 50; Senatspräsident, High Court of Justice, Karlsruhe 51; Judge, E.C.S.C. Court 52-58, Vice-Pres. 53 and 56; Judge, Court of the European Communities 58-63; Vice-Pres. 58, 62-63; Dir. Inst. of Comparative Law, Lausanne Univ. (retd. Oct. 66).
Publs. *Das internationale Recht der Zivilen Luftfahrt unter besonderer Berücksichtung des Schweizerischen Rechts* 49, *Der Entwurf zur internationalen Vereinheitlichung des Kaufrechts* 56, *Une juridiction supranationale pour l'interprétation du droit unifié?* 61.
61 *bis* ave. des Cerisiers, 1009 Pully (VD), Lausanne, Switzerland.
Telephone: (021) 28-11-32.

Riesman, David, A.B., LL.B., LL.D., D.LIT., ED.D.; American social scientist; b. 09; ed. Harvard Univ. and Harvard Law School.
Law clerk to Mr. Justice Brandeis, Supreme Court 35-36; Practised law 36-37; Prof. of Law, Buffalo Univ. 37-41; Dep. Asst. Dist. Attorney, New York County 42-43; Asst. Treasurer, Sperry Gyroscope Co. 43-46; Prof. Social Sciences, Chicago Univ. 46-58; Prof. Social Sciences, Harvard 58-; mem. Carnegie Comm. on Future of Higher Education 67-; on board of editors, *American Journal of Sociology;* contributor to *Journal of Nervous and Mental Diseases*; Nat. Sponsor, Cttee. for a Sane Nuclear Policy.
Publs. *The Lonely Crowd* 50, *Faces in the Crowd* 52, *Thorstein Veblen: A Critical Interpretation* 53, *Individualism Reconsidered* 54, *Constraint and Variety in American Education* 56, *Abundance for what?* 64.
49, Linnaean Street, Cambridge 38, Mass., U.S.A.

Rietz, Hans; German politician; b. 14; ed. secondary school, Bitterfeld.
Former locksmith; I. G. Farben 32-39; Mil. Service, Second World War; mem. Dem. Peasants' Party (D.B.D.) 49-; mem. Volkskammer 54-; now Vice-Chair. Council of State.
Volkskammer, Berlin, Germany.

Rifaat, Kameleddin; United Arab Republic (Egyptian) politician.
Minister of Labour, United Arab Repub. 61-62; mem. Presidency Council 62-64; Dep. Prime Minister for Scientific Affairs 64-65; mem. Supreme Exec. Arab Socialist Union 65-; Minister of Labour June 67-.
Ministry of Labour, Cairo, U.A.R.

Rifa'i, Abdul Monem; Jordanian diplomatist; b. 17; ed. American Univ. of Beirut.

In Service of King Abdullah 38; Chief Sec. of Govt. and Chief Censor 40; Asst. Chief of Royal Court 41-42; Consul-Gen. in Cairo, Lebanon and Syria 43-44; Del. to Treaty Conf. with Great Britain 46; Counsellor in Washington, and Del. to U.N. 49; Minister to Iran and Pakistan 49; Ambassador to United States 53-57, to Lebanon 57-58, to Great Britain 58; Dir. of Radio, Press and Tourism 58-59; Rep. to UN 59-65; Ambassador to United Arab Republic 66-67 (withdrawn Feb. 67); Minister of Foreign Affairs 67-.
Ministry of Foreign Affairs, Amman, Jordan.

Riisager, Knudåge; Danish composer; b. 97; ed. Univ. of Copenhagen.

Sec. Ministry of Finance 26, Chief of section 39-50; Chair. Soc. of Young Musicians 22-24; musical adviser Danish State Radio 42-56; Dir. Royal Danish Conservatoire of Music 56-67; mem. Board, Asscn. of European Conservatory Dirs. 56-63, Pres. 63-66; works performed throughout Europe, U.S.A., etc.; Wilhelm Hansen Memorial Award 25, Ancker Award 31, Danish States Cultural Foundation Award 42; Walther Gieseking Medal 64; Commdr. of the Order of Dannebrog; also several foreign orders.

Works include three symphonies 25, 27, 35, overture *Erasmus Montanus* 20, Suite *Dionysiaque* 24, variations on a theme by Mezangeau 26, *Jabiru* 26, overture *Klods Hans* 29, *Trumpet Concertino*, *Divertimento* 25, *Sinfonietta* 24, two quintets 21, 27, four string quartets 18, 20, 22, 25, sonatas 23, 27, etc.; ballets: *Etudes, Qarrtsiluni, Moonrendeer, The Lady from the Sea*.
Glahns Allé 43, Copenhagen, Denmark.
Telephone: 307332.

Rikhye, Maj.-Gen. Indar Jit; Indian army officer and United Nations official; b. 30 July 1920; ed. Indian Military Acad.

Served 6 DCO Lancers, Iraq, Iran, Syria, Lebanon, Palestine, Italy 39-45, North-West Frontier (India) 45-47; fmr. Commdr. Royal Deccan Horse, Jammu and Kashmir; Commdr. Indian Contingent, UN Force, Gaza 57-58, Chief of Staff UN Emergency Force 58-60; Commdr. Infantry Brigade, Indian Army 60; Mil. Adviser to Sec.-Gen. of UN 60-; with UN Force in Congo, West Irian, Yemen and Cyprus, established a UN Military Training Team in Ruanda-Urundi 60-61; UN Supervisor in Netherlands New Guinea 62, Adviser to Sec.-Gen. of UN on Cuba 62, Palestine 65, and Dominican Repub. 65-66; Commdr. UNEF Gaza Feb. 66-Dec. 67; Mil. Adviser to Sec. Gen. of UN 68-.
United Nations, New York City, N.Y., U.S.A.

Riklis, Meshulam; American (b. Turkish) business executive; b. 23; ed. High School, Israel, Univ. of Mexico and Ohio State Univ.

Co-Director Youth Activities and Military Training, Hertzlia High School, Tel Aviv 42; went to U.S. 47, naturalised 55; Teacher of Hebrew, Talmud Torah School, Minneapolis 51; Research Dept., Piper, Jaffray and Hopwood 51-53, Sales Rep. 53-56; Chair., Chief Exec. Officer Rapid Electrotype Co., American Colortype Co. 56-57, Pres. Rapid-American Corpn. 57-58, Pres. and Chair. 58-65; Chair. McCrory Corpn., Glen Alden Corpn. 65-.
7 Shelter Bay Drive, Kings Point, Long Island, N.Y., U.S.A.

Riley, Vice-Admiral Herbert Douglas, D.S.M., D.F.C., B.S.M., C.M., C.B.E.; American naval officer; b. 24 Dec. 1904; ed. Baltimore Polytechnic Inst., U.S. Naval Acad. and Nat. War Coll.

U.S. Navy 27-64, Vice-Admiral 58-64; aviation squadrons 29-41, Operations Officer, *Patrol Wings Pacific* 42, Commdg. Officer U.S.S. *Makassar Strait* 44-45; strategic planner, Office of Chief of Naval Operations, Navy Dept. 46-47; Asst. Chief of Staff, Plans,

Atlantic Fleet 50-51; Deputy Chief of Staff, Supreme Allied Command Atlantic, NATO 51-52; Commdg. Officer U.S.S. *Coral Sea* 52-53; Chief of Staff, Attack Carrier Task Force, 6th Fleet 54; Dir. Politico-Military Policy Office, Chief of Naval Operations 55-56; Commdr. Div. 1, also Attack Carrier Task Force, 7th Fleet 57; Chief of Staff U.S. Pacific Command 58; Deputy Chief of Naval Operations 61; Dir. Joint Staff, Joint Chiefs of Staff 62-64; Consultant to Keep Films Ltd., London. Queen Anne Colony, Stevensville, Maryland 21666, U.S.A.
Telephone: 301-643-5903.

Riley, Lieut.-Gen. William Edward, D.S.M.; American officer (retd.); b. 97; ed. Coll. of St. Thomas, Infantry School, Fort Benning, Ga., Command and Staff School, Fort Leavenworth, Kan., and Naval War Coll., Newport, R.I.

Entered U.S. Marine Corps as Second-Lieut. 17; advanced through various grades to Major-Gen.; retd. with rank of Lieut.-Gen. June 51; Chief of Staff U.N. Truce Supervision Organisation, Palestine 48-53; Deputy Dir. for Management Int. Co-operation Admin., Washington 53-55; Dir. of Mission to Turkey (with rank of Minister) 55-59; Dir. U.S. Operations Mission to Chile (U.S.O.M.) 60-62; Silver Star Citation; Croix de Guerre; Philippine Island Medal; Hon. LL.D. (Coll. of St. Thomas, St. Paul, Minn.).
4050 N. Ocean Drive (501), Lauderdale-by-Sea, Florida 33308, U.S.A.

Rimington, Claude, M.A., PH.D., D.SC., F.R.S.; British university professor; b. 17 Nov. 1902; ed. Cambridge and London Univs.

Biochemist, Woollen Industries' Research Asscn., Leeds 28-31; Empire Marketing Board Research Fellow at Onderstepoort Veterinary Research Laboratory, Pretoria, South Africa 31-36; Scientific Research Officer, Div. of Veterinary Services, Govt. of Union of S. Africa 36-37; Biochemist on staff of Nat. Inst. for Medical Research of Medical Research Council of Great Britain 37-45; Prof. of Chemical Pathology, Univ. of London, and Head of Dept. of Chemical Pathology, Univ. Coll. Hospital Medical School 45-67, Emeritus Prof. Univ. of London; Hon. F.R.C.P.(E).
Department of Chemical Pathology, University College Hospital Medical School, London, W.C.1; Home: Warwick Close, 62 Deansway, London, N.2, England.

Rinkel, Andreas, HON. D.TH.; Netherlands ecclesiastic; b. 10 Jan. 1889; ed. Old Catholic Seminary, Amersfoort.

Ordained Priest 14; Vicar, Enkhuizen 14-20, Amersfoort 20-37; Prof. of Theology, Ethics and Liturgy 20-48; Canon of the Metropolitan Chapter of Utrecht 26; Archbishop of Utrecht 37-; Editor of *Geloof en Leven* 15-20, ot *De Oud-Katholiek* 20-36, of *Internationale Kirchliche Zeitschrift* 20-37.

Publs. *Handboek voor geloofs—en Zedeleer* 30, *Die Heilige Eucharistie*; Sermons: *Van heerlijkheid tot heerlijkheid* 23, *Uit den rijkdom zijner genade* (3 vols.) 25, *De moeilijke weg* 30, *De gave Gods* 30; Essays: *Psalter* (2 vols.) 37, *Dogmatic Lectures* 56; composer of liturgical church music, masses and hymns.
Emmalaan 8, Utrecht, Netherlands.
Telephone: 030-19989.

Rios, Juan; Peruvian poet, dramatist and dramatic critic; b. 28 Sept. 1914.

National Prize for Playwriting 46, 50, 52, 54, 60; Nat. Poetry Prize 48, 53; Writers' Fellowship, UNESCO, Europe and Egypt 60-61; Dramatic Critic of *Expreso;* writer for *Oiga*.
Publs. *Teatro* (I) 61, *Ayar Manko* 63.
Dos de Mayo 657, Miraflores, Lima, Peru.

Ripman, Hugh Brockwell; British World Bank official; b. 16 April 1909; ed. Westminster School and London School of Econ.
Baring Bros. & Co. Ltd., London 28-41; Inspector of

Establishments, War Office, London 41-45; Control Comm. for Germany and Austria 45-46; First Sec., British Embassy, Washington 46-47; Chief, End Use Supervision, World Bank 47-52, Asst. to Dir of Technical Operations, World Bank 52-56, Chief, Industry Div., Projects Dept. 56-62, Asst. Dir. Projects Dept. 62-65, Deputy Dir. Projects Dept. 65-67; Dir. of Administration, World Bank June 67-.
International Bank for Reconstruction and Development (World Bank), 1818 H Street, N.W. Washington, D.C. 20433; Home: 4825 Bending Lane, N.W., Washington, D.C. 20017, U.S.A.
Telephone: DUdley 1-2011 (Office); FEderal 7-2846 (Home).

Rippon, Rt. Hon. Geoffrey, P.C., Q.C., M.A., M.P.; British barrister and politician; b. 28 May 1924; ed. King's Coll., Taunton, and Brasenose Coll., Oxford.
Called to Bar, Middle Temple 48; mem. Surbiton Borough Council 45-54, Mayor 51-52; mem. London County Council 52-61; Mem. of Parl. for Norwich 55-64, for Hexham 66-; Parl. Sec. Ministry of Aviation 59-61; Joint Parl. Sec. Ministry of Housing and Local Govt. 61-62; Minister of Public Building and Works 62-64; Dir. Fairey Co. Ltd.; Dir. Holland and Hannen & Cubitts 64-, Chair. 67-; mem. Court, Univ. of London 58-; Conservative.
Publs. *Forward from Victory* (co-author) 43, *The Rent Act* 57.
39 Cadogan Square, London, S.W.1, England.
Telephone: 01-235-5204.

Risgaard Knudsen, Jens; Danish trade unionist and politician; b. 14 April 1925; ed. elementary school.
Chairman, Social Democratic Youth Asscn., Thisted 45-49; mem. Cttee. of Horticultural Trade Union, Thisted 46-49; Chair. Joint Council of Youth Orgs., Thisted 48-49; Sec. Danish Horticultural Trade Union 49-59; Sec. Danish Fed. of Trade Unions 59-64; Minister of Fisheries 64-68; mem. Parl. 64-.
Vadbro 40, So'borg, Copenhagen, Denmark.
Telephone: SØ.8233.

Rishtya, Kassim; Afghan civil servant and diplomatist; b. 13; ed. Istiqlal High School, Kabul.
Clerk in Press Section, Ministry of Foreign Affairs 32; Chief Clerk Foreign Relations Section, Ministry of Communications 32; trans. at Afghan Acad. of Literature 33, mem. 34, Dir. Publs. Div. 36, Vice-Pres. 38; Dir.-Gen. of Publs. Press. Dept. 40-44, Pres. 48; Pres. Govt. Econ. Planning Board 49, Govt. Co-operative Org. 52, Bakhtar News Agency 54; Minister of Information 56-60; Afghan Del. to UN 10th Gen. Ass.; headed Press Del. to U.S.S.R. 56; Ambassador to Czechoslovakia, Poland and Hungary 60-62, to United Arab Republic 62-67; Editor *Kabul Almanach* and *Kabul Magazine* 36-38.
Publs. *Afghanistan in the 19th Century, Jawani Afghan*, and several novels.
c/o Ministry of Foreign Affairs, Kabul, Afghanistan.

Risseeuw, Col. Jan Adriaan; Netherlands army officer and civil servant; b. 14; ed. military colleges in the Netherlands and the U.K.
Officer, Royal Netherlands Army 35-61; Dir.-Gen. Netherlands Nat. Tourist Office 61-; M.B.E.
De Eerensplein 42, The Hague, Netherlands.

Rist, Léonard B.; French economist; b. 27 April 1905; ed. Univ. of Paris and Paris School for Oriental Languages.
Attaché, French Embassy, Moscow 27-28; entered private banking and Vice-Pres. Morgan et Cie. 28-45; Chief of the Finance Division of the Allied Comm. on Austria (French element) 45-46; temporary French Alt. Exec. Dir. of Int. Bank 46; Dir. Economic Dept. Int. Bank for Reconstruction and Development 46-60; Special Rep. of Int. Bank for Africa April 61-, Special Adviser, Int. Bank for Reconstruction and Development 63-; Chevalier Légion d'Honneur.
3130 Ordway Street, Washington 8, D.C., U.S.A.; and 18 *bis*, rue du Parc de Clagny, Versailles, Seine et Oise, France.

Risterucci, Jean, L. en D.; French civil servant and diplomatist; b. 11 April 1911; ed. Ecole Nat. de la France d'Outre-Mer.
Official in Indochina Civil Service 35-52; Political Advisor to High Commr. 50-52; High Commr. in Cambodia 52-54; Dir. du Cabinet to Sec. of State for Armed Forces (Air); Inspector-Gen. (Admin. Affairs), French West Africa; High Commr. in Gabon 59-60, High Rep. 60-62; Dir. of Overseas Territories 63; High Commr. in Pacific and New Hebrides and Gov. of New Caledonia 65-; Officier Légion d'Honneur, Croix de Guerre, Médaille de l'Aéronautique; Commdr. or Grand Officier in Cambodian, Vietnamese and Laotian orders; Grand Officier of the Equatorial Star (Gabon).
Office of the Governor, Nouméa, New Caledonia.

Ritchie, Albert Edgar, B.A.; Canadian diplomatist; b. 20 Dec. 1916; ed. Mount Allison Univ. and Oxford Univ.
Deputy Under-Sec. of State for External Affairs 64-66; Amb. to U.S.A. July 66-; Hon. LL.D. (Mount Allison Univ.) 66.
Embassy of Canada, 1746 Massachusetts Avenue, N.W., Washington, D.C. 20036, U.S.A.

Ritchie, Charles Stewart Almon; Canadian diplomatist; b. 23 Sept. 1906; ed. Halifax, Oxford, Harvard and Paris Univs.
Third Sec., Dept. of External Affairs 34-36, Washington 36-39; Second Sec., London 39-43; First Sec., London 43-45, Ottawa 45-47; Counsellor, Paris 47-50; Assistant Under-Sec., Ottawa 50-52; Dep. Under-Sec. 52-54; Ambassador to German Fed. Republic and Head of Military Mission, Berlin 54-58; Perm. Rep. United Nations 58-62; Ambassador to U.S.A. 62-66; Perm. Rep. to NATO 66-67; Canadian High Commr. in U.K. 67-.
Canadian High Commission, 12 Upper Brook Street, London, W.1, England.

Ritchie, Robert James; Australian airline executive; b. 5 Nov. 1915; ed. Cleveland Street High School, Sydney.
Joined Amalgamated Wireless Australia Ltd. 29, later flew with Kingsford Smith Aerial Services Ltd., Sydney, and Mandated Airlines Ltd., New Guinea; Pilot, W. R. Carpenter & Co. 38; First Officer, Quantas Empire Airways Ltd. 43, Captain 44, Flight Captain 46; Flight Captain (Constellations) 47-48; Flight Superintendent, Kangaroo Service 47-48; Asst. Operations Manager, Quantas 49-55, Technical Manager 55-59, Dir. of Technical Services 59-61, Deputy Chief Exec. and Deputy General Manager 61-67, General Manager 67-.
Office: Quantas House, 70 Hunter Street, Sydney, New South Wales; Home: 4 Waterloo Road, North Ryde, N.S.W., Australia.

Ritchie-Calder, Baron (Life Peer), cr. 66, of Balmashannar; (**Peter**) **Ritchie Calder,** C.B.E., M.A.; British writer and university professor; b. 1 July 1906; ed. Forfar Acad., Scotland.
Police Court Reporter, *Dundee Courier* 22, *Daily News* (London) 26-30, *Daily Chronicle* 30, *Daily Herald* 30-41; Dir. of Plans of Political Welfare, Foreign Office 41-45; Special Adviser, Supreme H.Q. 45; Science Editor *News Chronicle* 45-47; Editorial Staff, *New Statesman* 45-47; mem. Council, British Asscn. 45-60, U.K. Del UNESCO 46, 47, 66, 68; Special Adviser, FAO Famine Conf. 46, UN and Specialized Agencies Missions for Deserts 49-50, S.E. Asia 51-52, Arctic 55, Congo 60; UN Sec. Atoms for Peace Conf. 55, 58; Prof. of Int. Relations, Edin-

burgh Univ. 60-66; Chair. Edinburgh Univ. Settlement; Founder-mem. and fmr. Chair. Asscn. British Science Writers; UNESCO Kalinga Prize 60.

Publs. *The Birth of the Future* 34, *Conquest of Suffering* 35, *Roving Commission* 35, *The Lesson of London* 41, *Carry on London* 41, *Start Planning Britain Now* 41, *Profile of Science* 51, *Men Against the Desert* 51, *The Lamp is Lit* 51, *Men Against Ignorance* 53, *Men Against the Jungle* 54, *Science Makes Sense* 55, *Medicine and Man* 57, *Men Against the Frozen North* 58, *Ten Steps Forward* 58, *The Hand of Life* 59, *From Magic to Medicine* 59, *The Inheritors* 61, *Agony of the Congo* 61, *Living With the Atom* 62, *The Life Savers* 62, *Commonsense about a Starving World* 62, *Two-Way Passage* 64, *Man in the Cosmos* 68, *Evolution of the Machine* 68.
1 Randolph Place, Edinburgh 3, Scotland; 10 Denny Crescent, London, S.E.11, England.
Telephone: 031-225-5565; and 01-735-8969.

Ritchie of Dundee, 3rd Baron (cr. 05); **John Kenneth Ritchie**, P.C.; British businessman; b. 02; ed. Royal Naval Coll. Osborne, Winchester Coll. and Magdalen Coll., Oxford.
Deputy Chair. London Stock Exchange 54-59, 65-, Chair. 59-65; Chair. Bow Group of Hospitals 48-58, English Asscn. of American Bond and Shareholders Ltd.; Dir. Anglo-Portuguese Telephone Co. Ltd., Hutchinsons Ltd.
40 Thurloe Square, London, S.W.7, England.

Ritter, Kurt, DR.AGR.; German university professor; b. 13 April 1894.
Prof. of Constitutional Law, Univ. of Berlin 28-34; independent activities 35-45; administrative activities 45-51; Prof. and Dir. of Inst. for Agricultural Policy and Agricultural History, Humboldt Univ. Berlin 51-57; Dir. of Inst. for Agricultural History of Deutsche Akad. der Landwirtschaftswissenschaften, Berlin 57-61; mem. Deutsche Akad. der Landwirtschaftswissenschaften, Berlin; Nat. Prize.
Publs. *Die Einwirkung des weltwirtschaftlichen Verkehrs auf die Entwicklung und den Betrieb der Landwirtschaft, insbesondere in Deutschland* 21, *Deutschlands Wirtschaftslage und die Produktionssteigerung der Landwirtschaft* 22, *Agrarzölle* 24, *Weltproduktion und Welthandel der Molkereierzeugnisse* 30, *Svetová Krise Zemedelská* 30, *Die Krise der deutschen Agrarpolitik* 31, *Die Schweinehaltung der Welt und der Handel mit ihren Erzeugnissen* 31, *Die Produktion und Aussenhandel der Vereinigten Staaten von Amerika an Gartenbauerzeugnissen* 31, *Die Standardisierung landwirtschaftlicher und gartenbaulicher Erzeugnisse in den Vereinigten Staaten von Amerika* 31, *Weltproduktion und Welthandel an frischen Südfrüchten* 33, *Agrarpolitische Aufsätze und Vorträge* (18 vols.) 24-33, *Muss ein grosser Teil der Menscheit weiter hungern?* 56, *Agrarwirtschaft und Agrarpolitik im Kapitalismus* Vol. I (2nd edn.) 56, Vol. II 59, *Zu einigen aktuellen Tendenzen und Widersprüchen in der kapitalistischen Landwirtschaft* 59.
Dorfstrasse 29, Altenhof via Eberswalde, German Democratic Republic.

Ritz, Charles C.; Swiss hotel executive; b. 91; ed. Univ. of Commerce, Geneva.
Chairman, Ritz Hotel, Paris; Dir. Ritz Hotel, London, Ritz Hotel, Lisbon, Ritz Carlton, Boston; manufacturer of fishing tackle.
Publ. *A Fly Fisher's Life.*
Hotel Ritz, 15 place Vendôme, Paris 1er, France.
Telephone: OPEra 28-30.

Rivera Carballo, Lt.-Col. Julio Adalberto; El Salvadorean army officer and politician; b. 21; ed. mil. schools in El Salvador and Italy.
Held various command positions in armed forces; Chief Dept. of Public Security; Dir. Manuel Enrique Araujo Mil. School; mem. Civilian Mil. Directorate 61-62;

Leader, Party of Nat. Conciliation; Pres. of El Salvador July 62-67.
San Salvador, El Salvador.

Rivett, Rohan Deakin, B.A.; Australian journalist; b. 17; ed. Wesley Coll., Melbourne, Queen's Coll., Melbourne Univ. and Balliol Coll., Oxford.
Reporter, *Melbourne Argus* 39-40; War Corresp. Radio Singapore 41-42; Prisoner of War 42-45; Reporter, *Melbourne Herald* 46-48, Melbourne Herald Cable Service, Britain and Europe 48-51; Ed. *Adelaide News* 51-60; Dir. News Ltd. of Australia 52-60; News Commentator, B.B.C. and A.B.C. 48-61; Chair. Australian Cttee., Int. Press Inst. (IPI) 54-62, Dir. IPI 62-64; Coronation Medal.
Publs. *Behind Bamboo* 46, *Near North* 48, Three Cricket Booklets 47-51, *Australia and the Migrant* 57, *Australia Looks Ahead* (co-author) 61.
c/o International Press Institute, Munstergasse 9, Zürich, Switzerland.

Rivette, Jacques; French film director; b. 1 March 1928; ed. Lycée Corneille, Rouen.
Journalist and Critic on *Cahiers du Cinéma* 53-; Asst. to Jacques Becker and Jean Renoir 54; Director of Films 56-.
Films: *Le coup du berger* (director) 56, *Paris nous appartient* (author and director) 58-60, *La Religieuse* (director) 66.
19 rue Michel le Comte, Paris 3e, France.

Rivière, Georges Henri; French ethnographer; b. 97.
Chief Keeper of Musée National des Arts et Traditions Populaires; Gen. Sec. Société d'ethnographie française; Permanent Adviser of Int. Council of Museums; Officer, Legion of Honour.
Palais de Chaillot, Paris 16e, France.

Rizzoli, Angelo; Italian publisher; b. 31 Oct. 1889.
President of Rizzoli Editore S.p.A., Milan, publishing series *Grandi Monografie d'Arte Rizzoli*, *Classici Rizzoli* and *Biblioteca Universale Rizzoli*, and periodicals including *Oggi*, *L'Europeo*, *Annabella*, *Bella*, *Novella 2000*, *Sogno*; Chair. Board of Dirs. Rizzoli Film, Rome and Rizzoli Film Distributors, New York; Cavaliere del Lavoro 36; Chevalier Légion d'Honneur 53 and other awards.
Via Civitavecchia 102, Milan, Italy.
Telephone: 2588.

Roa Bastos, Augusto; Paraguayan writer and journalist; b. 17; ed. Asunción.
Publs. Poetry: *Poemas*, *El Naranjal Ardiente*; novels: *El Trueno entre las Hojas*, *Hijo de hombre*, *Los inocentes*; Screen plays: *El Trueno entre las Hojas*, *Sabaleros*, *La Sed*, *Shunko*.
Berutti 2828, Martínez, Buenos Aires, Argentina.

Roa García, Dr. Raúl; Cuban author, professor and politician.
Lecturer in Law and Social Sciences, then Prof. Univ. of Havana; Dean of Social Sciences 48-59; Cuban Rep., Org. of American States 56-58; Minister of Foreign Affairs 59-; Guggenheim Fellow 45-46; Nat. journalism award Justo de Lara 54.
Publs. *Historia de las Doctrinas Sociales* 48, *Quince Años Despues* 50, *Viento Sur* 53, *Retorno a la Alborada* 64.
Ministry of Foreign Affairs, Havana, Cuba.

Rob, John Vernon, C.M.G.; British diplomatist; b. 17 Dec. 1915; ed. Oundle School, and St. John's Coll., Cambridge.
Entered Foreign Service 39; served in British Army 40-45; Counsellor, U.K. High Commission, New Delhi 55-58, British Embassy, Warsaw 59-60; Ambassador to Congo Republic (Brazzaville), Central African Republic, Gabon and Republic of Chad 60-62; Inspector

of Foreign Service Establishments, Foreign Office 62-65; High Commr. in Singapore 65-.
c/o H.M. Diplomatic Service Administration Office, King Charles Street, London, S.W.1, England.

Robarts, David John; British banker; b. 06; ed. Eton and Magdalen Coll. Oxford.
Chairman National Provincial Bank Ltd.; Dir. Robert Fleming and Co. Ltd., Union Discount Co. of London Ltd. and other companies; Chair., Cttee. of London Clearing Bankers.
7 Smith Square, London, S.W.1, England.

Robarts, E. K.; British dairy executive; b. 1908; ed. Bishops Stortford College and Hertfordshire Inst. of Agriculture, St. Albans.
Producer-retailer with C. M. Robarts & Son., which was acquired by Express Dairy 42; Dir. Express Dairy 47, Managing Dir. 60, Deputy Chair. 66-67, Chair. 67-; fmr. Chair. Middlesex Agricultural Exec. Cttee.
Express Dairy Co. Ltd., Tavistock Place, London, W.C.1, England.

Robarts, John Parmenter, Q.C., P.C.; Canadian politician; b. 1917; ed. Univ. of Western Ontario and Osgoode Hall Law School.
Naval service 40-45; Called to the Bar of Ontario 47, Q.C. 54; mem. London Ontario City Council 50; mem. Ontario Legislature 51, 55, 59; Minister of Educ. 59-62; Prime Minister of Ontario 61-; Hon. LL.D. Univ. of Toronto, Univ. of Ottawa.
Parliament Buildings, Toronto, Ontario, Canada.

Robbe-Grillet, Alain; French writer and agronomist; b. 18 Aug. 1922; ed. Lycée Buffon, Lycée St. Louis and Inst. Nat. Agronomique, Paris.
Chargé de Mission, Inst. Nat. de la Statistique 45-48; Engineer Inst. des Fruits Tropicaux (Guinea, Morocco, Martinique and Guadeloupe) 49-51; Literary Adviser Editions de Minuit.
Publs. Novels: *Les Gommes* 53, *Le Voyeur* 55, *La Jalousie* 57, *Dans le Labyrinthe* 59, *La Maison de Rendez-vous* 65; essay: *Pour un Nouveau Roman* 64; films: *L'Année Dernière à Marienbad* 61, *L'Immortelle* 63, *Trans-Europ Express* 66; short stories: *Instantanés* 62.
18 boulevard Maillot, Neuilly-sur-Seine, France.
Telephone: SAB.31-22.

Robbins, Baron (Life Peer), cr. 59, of Clare Market, **Lionel Charles Robbins,** C.B., C.H., B.SC. (Econ.), M.A. F.B.A.; British economist; b. 22 Nov. 1898; ed. Univ. Coll., London, and London School of Economics.
Served First World War 16-19; Lecturer, New Coll., Oxford 24, London School of Economics 25-27; Fellow and Lecturer. New Coll., Oxford 27-29; Prof. of Economics in Univ. of London 29-61; Hon. Fellow Univ. Coll., London, London School of Econs., London Graduate School of Business Studies, Manchester Coll. of Science and Technology; Dir. Econ. Section Offices of the War Cabinet 41-45; mem. Council Royal Econ. Soc., Board of Trustees, Nat. Gallery 52-59, 60-; Tate Gallery 53-59, 62-67; Dir. Royal Opera House, Covent Garden 56-; Chair. *Financial Times* 61-; Pres. British Acad. 62-67; Chair. Prime Minister's Cttee. on Higher Educ. 61-63; Chancellor, Univ. of Stirling 68-; mem. Accad. dei Lincei, American Philosophical Soc., American Acad. of Arts and Science; Hon. L.H.D. (Columbia); Hon. D.Litt. (Durham, Exeter, Strathclyde, Sheffield, Heriot Watt); Hon. LL.D. (Strasbourg, Exeter, Leicester and Cambridge Univs. and Univ. of Calif.); Doutor en Ciências Económicas e Financeiras (Tech. Univ., Lisbon); Hon. D.Sc. (Econ.) London.
Publs. *An Essay on the Nature and Significance of Economic Science, The Great Depression, Economic Planning and International Order, The Economic Basis of Class Conflict and Other Essays in Political Economy, The Economic Causes of War, The Economic Problem in Peace and War, The Theory of Economic Policy in*

English Classical Political Economy, The Economist in the Twentieth Century, Robert Torrens and the Evolution of Classical Economics, Politics and Economics, The University in the Modern World.
Financial Times, Bracken House, Cannon Street, London, E.C.4 England.
Telephone: 01-248-8000.

Robbins, Frederick Chapman, A.B. B.S., M.D.; American scientist and university professor; b. 25 Aug. 1916; ed. Univ. of Missouri and Harvard Medical School.
Served U.S. Army 42-46; Senior Fellow, Nat. Research Council 48-50; Research Fellow, Harvard Medical School 48-50; Instructor, Harvard Medical School 50-51, Assoc. (Pediatrics) 51-52; Assoc., Research Div. of Infectious Disease, Children's Medical Center, Boston 50-52; Assoc. Physician and Assoc. Dir. of Isolation Services, Children's Hospital, Boston 50-52; Research Fellow, Boston Lying-in Hospital 50-52; Asst. Children's Medical Service, Mass. Gen. Hospital, Boston 50-52; Dir. Dept. of Pediatrics and Contagious Diseases, Cleveland Metropolitan Gen. Hospital 52-66; Prof. of Pediatrics, Case Western Reserve Univ. School of Medicine, Cleveland 52-, Dean 66-; Assoc. Pediatrician Univ. Hospitals, Cleveland 52-; Bronze Star 45; First Mead Johnson Award (jointly) 53; Noble Prize (jointly) 54; Hon. D.Sc. (John Carrol and Mo. Univs.).
Publs. various scientific papers related to virus and rickettsial diseases, especially "Q" fever in the Mediterranean area and cultivation of poliomyelitis viruses in tissue culture.
Case Western Reserve University, 2019 Adelbert Road, Cleveland, Ohio 44106; and 2467 Guilford Road, Cleveland Heights, Ohio 44118, U.S.A.
Telephone: 216-368-2820.

Robbins, Jerome; American choreographer and director; b. 18; ed. New York Univ.
Dancer in Broadway choruses 38-40; American Ballet Theatre soloist 41-46; Assoc. Artistic Dir., New York City Ballet 49-; formed Ballets: U.S.A.; touring U.S. and Europe 58-; Antoinette Perry (Tony) Award for *Fiddler on the Roof* 65.
Choreographed: Ballets: *Fancy Free* 44, *Interplay* 45, *Facsimile* 47, *Pas de Trois* 47, *The Cage* 51, *Fanfare* 53, *Afternoon of a Faun* 53, *The Concert* 56, *N.Y. Export op. Jazz* 58, *Moves* 61, *Events* 61, *Les Noces* 65, and many others; Musicals include: *On the Town* 45, *High Button Shoes* 47, *Call Me Madam* 50, *The King and I* 51 (film 56), *The Pajama Game* (co-dir.) 54, *Bells are Ringing* (dir.) 56, *West Side Story* (dir. and choreographer) 57, (film 60), *Gypsy* (dir. and choreographer) 59, *Oh Dad, Poor Dad* (dir.) 62, *Fiddler on the Roof* (dir. and choreographer) 64; Opera: *The Tender Land* 54.
17 51st Street, Weehawken, New Jersey, U.S.A.

Robbins, William Jacob, A.B. (Lehigh), HON. SC.D., PH.D. (Cornell), SC.D. (Fordham); American botanist, b. 22 Feb. 1890; ed. Lehigh and Cornell Univs.
Instructor in Biology Lehigh Univ. 10-11; Summers Asst. Marine Biology Laboratory Woods Hole 12-14; Instructor Plant Physiology Cornell Univ. 12-16; Prof. Botany Alabama Polytechnic Inst. and Plant Physiologist Agricultural Experiment Station 16-17; Soil Biochemist Bureau Plant Industry U.S. Dept. of Agriculture 19; Prof. Botany Missouri Univ. 19-37; Dean Graduate Faculty 30-37; Prof. Botany, Columbia 37-58, Dir. N.Y. Botanical Garden 37-58, Prof. and Dir. Emeritus 58-; mem. Nat. Acad. of Science and Nat. Research Council 48-, Treas. 48-60; mem. American Philosophical Soc. of Philadelphia 41; Trustee Rockefeller Univ.; Pres. American Philosophical Soc. 56-59, Exec. Officer 59; Assoc. Dir. Nat. Science Foundation 62-63; Pres. Fairchild Tropical Garden 62-.
Publ. *General Botany.*
Rockefeller University, 66th Street and York Avenue, New York, N.Y., U.S.A.

Robens of Woldingham, Baron, cr. 61 (Life Peer), of Woldingham in the County of Surrey; **Alfred Robens,** P.C.; British politician; b. 18 Dec. 1910; ed. Council School.

Official of Union of Distributive and Allied Workers 35-; Manchester City Councillor 42-45; Labour M.P. for Wansbeck Div. of Northumberland 45-50, Blyth 50-60; Parl. Private Sec. to Minister of Transport 45-47; Parl. Sec. Minister of Fuel and Power 47-51; Minister of Labour April-Oct. 51; Labour Relations Consultant, Atomic Power Construction Ltd. 60; Dep. Chair. Nat. Coal Board 60-61, Chair. 61-; mem. Nat. Econ. Development Council (N.E.D.C.) 62-, Royal Comm. on Trade Unions and Employers' Asscns. 65-; Chair. of Govs. Guy's Hospital June 65; Dir. Bank of England 66-; Chancellor Univ. of Surrey 66-; Hon. D. Civil Law (Newcastle Univ.); Hon. LL.D. (Leicester Univ.); Dir. of *The Times*; Chair. Joint Econ. Mission to Malta 67.
Walton Manor, Walton-on-the-Hill, Surrey, England.

Robert, Louis; French archaeologist; b. 15 Feb. 1904; ed. Paris Univ., Ecole Normale Supérieure.
Member French School, Athens 27-32; Dir. of Studies, Ecole des Hautes Etudes 32-; Prof. of Greek Epigraphy and Antiquities Coll. de France 39-; dir. excavations at Amyzon 49 and Claros (Temple of Apollo) 50-61; mem. Acad. des Inscriptions et Belles Lettres (Pres. 66) and of numerous foreign socs.; Officier Légion d'Honneur.
Publs. *Villes d'Asie Mineure, Etudes Anatoliennes, Les Gladiateurs dans l'Orient Grec, Etudes de Numismatique Grecque, Hellenica* (13 vols.), *Noms Indigènes dans l'Asie Mineure* 57, *La Carie* (with his wife, Jeanne Robert), *Monnaies antiques en Troade,* etc.
31 avenue du Parc Montsouris, Paris 14e, France.

Roberti, H.E. Cardinal Francesco; Vatican ecclesiastic; b. 89.
Ordained priest 13; created Cardinal by Pope John XXIII 58; mem. Sacred Congregations of Sacraments, of the Council, De Propaganda Fide; Prefect Supreme Tribunal of the Apostolic Signature 59-; mem. Comm. for the Interpretation of Canon Law; Pres. Court of Cassation.
Piazza San Callisto 16, Rome, Italy.

Roberts, Chalmers McGeagh; American journalist; b. 18 Nov. 1910; ed. Amherst Coll.
Reporter *Washington Post,* D.C. 33-34, Associated Press, Pittsburgh Bureau 34-35, *Toledo News-Bee* 36-38, *Japan Times,* Tokyo 38-39; Asst. Managing Editor *Washington Daily News* 39-41; Sunday Editor *Washington Times-Herald* 41; Office of War Information, London and Washington 41-43; *Life* magazine 46-47; *Washington Star* 47-49; *Washington Post* 49-, Chief National News Bureau 59-.
Publs. *Washington Past and Present* 50, *Can We Meet the Russians Half Way?* 58.
Washington Post, 1515 L. Street, N.W., Washington D.C.; Home: 6699 Macarthur Boulevard, Washington 16, D.C., U.S.A.

Roberts, Sir Frank Kenyon, G.C.M.G., G.C.V.O., M.A.; British diplomatist (retired); b. 27 Oct. 1907; ed. Bedales and Rugby Schools and Trinity Coll., Cambridge.
Third Sec. Foreign Office 30-32, British Embassy Paris 32-35; Second Sec. Cairo 35-37, Foreign Office 37-45 (First Sec. 41, Head of Central Dept. 41-45, Acting Counsellor 43); Chargé d'Affaires to Czechoslovak Govt. in London 43; Minister to U.S.S.R. 45-47; Private Sec. to Foreign Sec. 47-49; mission to Moscow 48; Deputy High Commr. in India 49-51; Deputy Under-Sec. of State, Foreign Office 51-54; Ambassador to Yugoslavia 54-57; U.K. Permanent Rep. on N. Atlantic Council Feb. 57-60; Ambassador to U.S.S.R. 60-62, to German Fed. Repub. 63-68; Adviser on Int. Affairs to Unilever and Lloyds.
25 Kensington Court Gardens, London, W.8, England.
Telephone: 01-937-1140.

Roberts, Rt. Hon. Goronwy Owen, P.C., M.P.; British politician; b. 20 Sept. 1913; ed. Ogwen Grammar School, Univ. Coll. of N. Wales, Bangor, and Univ. of London.
Infantry, Army Reserve 41; Youth Education Officer, Caerns. Education Authority 41-44; M.P. 45-; Minister of State, Welsh Office 64-66, Dept. of Education and Science 66-67, Foreign Office 67-; mem. House of Commons Panel of Chairmen 63-64; Chair. Regional Econ. Cttee. for Wales 65; fmr. Chair. Hughes & Son Ltd., Publishers, Wrexham; fmr. Lecturer in Education, Univ. Coll., Swansea; mem. Court of Govs., Univ. Coll. of Wales, Nat. Museum of Wales; mem. Fabian Soc.; Trustee, Oppenheimer Trust for Ex-Servicemen; Labour.
House of Commons, London, S.W.1; Homes: Plas Newydd, Pwllheli, Caernarvons., Wales; 5 Okeover Manor, North Side, London, S.W.4, England.

Roberts, Henry Reginald, B.A.; Canadian life insurance executive; b. 2 June 1916; ed. Univ. of Toronto.
Group Pension Dept., Connecticut General Life Insurance Co. 45-48, Asst. Sec. Group Pension Dept. 48-50, Accident Dept. 50-58, Second Vice-Pres. Conn. Gen. Life Insurance Co. 58-60, Exec. Vice-Pres. and Dir. March 60-March 61, Pres. March 61-; Dir. Aetna (Fire) Insurance Co. 62-, Chair. of the Board 66-; Fellow, Soc. of Actuaries; official of business orgs.
171 Bloomfield Avenue, Hartford, Connecticut, U.S.A.

Roberts, James A., D.S.O., E.D.; Canadian government official; b. 19 Aug. 1907; ed. Univ. of Toronto Schools, and Jarvis Coll. Inst., Toronto.
Canadian Army Service, Second World War; fmr. business executive; Dep. Minister, Dept. of Trade and Commerce, Ottawa 60-64; Dep. Sec.-Gen. North Atlantic Treaty Organisation (NATO) 64-.
OTAN/NATO, Brussels 39, Belgium.
Telephone: 41-00-40.

Roberts, Sir Stephen Henry, Kt., C.M.G., M.A., D.SC., LITT.D., LL.D., D.C.L.; Australian historian; b. 16 Feb. 1901; ed. Melbourne Univ., London and Paris.
Lecturer and Research Fellow Melbourne Univ. 20-25; research London and Paris 25-29, Germany 35-36; Challis Prof. of History Sydney Univ. 29-46; Dean Faculty of Arts 42-47; mem. of Senate 42-; Chair. Professorial Board 44-45, 46-47; Vice-Chancellor and Principal 47-67, Prof. Emeritus 49; Chair. Australian Vice-Chancellor's Cttee. 52-53; Chair. State Cancer Council; Hon. D.Litt. (Sydney); Commdr., Royal Danish Order of Dannebrog 60, Commdr. Order of Cedars of Lebanon 62, Commdr. Royal Order of Phoenix (Greece), Italian Order of Merit; Officier, Légion d'Honneur.
Publs. *History of Australian Land Settlement* 23, *Population Problems of the Pacific* 25, *French Colonial Policy 1870-1925* 18, *The Squatting Age in Australia* 32, *History of Modern Europe* 33, *The House that Hitler Built* 37.
Wyuna Road, Point Piper, Sydney, N.S.W., Australia.

Roberts, Walter Orr, PH.D.; American solar astronomer; b. 20 Aug. 1915; ed. public schools, Brockton, Mass., Amherst Coll. and Harvard Univ.
Established and directed solar coronagraph station of Harvard Coll. Observatory, Climax, Colorado 40-46; Dir. High Altitude Observatory, Boulder, Colorado 46-60; Dir. Nat. Center for Atmospheric Research, Boulder 60-; Pres. Univ. Corpn. for Atmospheric Research, Boulder 67-; Pres. American Asscn. for Advancement of Science 68; Trustee The MITRE Corpn., Amherst Coll., Kettering Foundation, Max C. Fleischmann Foundation; mem. Advisory Cttee. World Meteorological Org., Editorial Board *Journal of Planetary and Space Science,* Geophysics Board of Nat. Acad. of Sciences; Hon. D.Sc. (Ripon Coll., Amherst Coll., The Colorado Coll., C.W. Post Coll. of L.I. Univ., Carleton Coll.).
National Center for Atmospheric Research, Boulder, Colorado 80302, U.S.A.
Telephone: 303-444-5151.

Robertson, Alexander, M.A., B.SC., PH.D. LL.D., F.R.S.; British chemist; ed. Aberdeen, Glasgow, Manchester and Graz Univs.
Rockefeller Int. Fellow Manchester and Graz Univs. 24-26; Junior Lecturer in Chemistry Manchester Univ. 26-28; Reader in Chemistry London Univ. 28-30; Reader in Biochemistry 30-33; Prof. of Organic Chemistry Liverpool Univ. 33-57, now Prof. Emer.; mem. Univ. Grants Cttee. 55-59; mem. Agricultural Research Council 60-65; Treas. Lawes Agricultural Trust, Rothamsted Experimental Station; Davy Medal of Royal Soc. 52.
Roxholme Estates, Sleaford, Lincolnshire, England.

Robertson, James Louis; American government official; b. 31 Oct. 1907; ed. Grinnell Coll., Iowa, George Washington Univ., and Harvard Law School.
U.S. Senate Post Office 27; later Special Agent, Fed. Bureau of Investigation; admitted to Court of Appeals Bar, D.C. 31, to Supreme Court of United States 35; Office of Comptroller of Currency 33-43; U.S. Naval Reserve 43-44; Dep. Comptroller of Currency 44-52; mem. Board of Govs. Fed. Reserve System 52-, Vice-Chair. 66-.
5114 Brookview Drive, Westhaven, Maryland, U.S.A.

Robertson, Sir James Wilson, K.T., G.C.M.G., G.C.V.O., K.B.E., M.A.; British overseas administrator; b. 27 Oct. 1899; ed. Merchiston Castle School, Edinburgh and Balliol Coll., Oxford.
Asst. District Commr. Sudan Political Service 22; District Commr. 33; Compensation Commr. Jebel Aulia Dam 36; Dep. Gov. White Nile Province 37; Deputy Gov. Gezira Province 39, Acting Gov. 40-41; Asst. Civil Sec. 41-42; Deputy Civil Sec. 42-45, Civil Sec. 45-53 (periodically Acting Gov.-Gen. of the Sudan); Chair. British Guiana Constitutional Comm. 54; Dir. Uganda Co. Ltd. 54-55, 61-; Hon. Fellow, Balliol Coll. 53-; Gov.-Gen. and C.-in-C. Nigeria 55-Nov. 60; Chair. Commonwealth Inst. 61-68; Dir. Barclays Bank D.C.O. 61-; Commr. Kenya Coastal Strip Inquiry 61, Chair. Royal Overseas League 62-68; Deputy Chair. Nat. Cttee for Commonwealth Immigrants 65-; Hon. LL.D. (Leeds).
The Old Bakehouse, Cholsey, Berkshire, England; Douglas Cottage, Killichonan, Rannoch Station, Perthshire, Scotland.
Telephone: Cholsey 234; Bridge of Gaur, 242.

Robertson, John Monteath, C.B.E., M.A., PH.D., D.SC., LL.D., F.R.I.C., F.INST.P., F.R.S., F.R.S.E.; British university professor; b. 24 July 1900; ed. Perth Acad., and Glasgow Univ.
Commonwealth Fellow, U.S.A. 28-30; mem. of staff, Davy Faraday Research Laboratory, The Royal Institution, London 30-39; Senior Lecturer in Physical Chemistry, Univ. of Sheffield 39-41; Scientific Adviser (Chemical) H.Q. Bomber Command, R.A.F. 41-42; Gardiner Prof. of Chemistry and Dir. of the Chemical Laboratories, Univ. of Glasgow 42-; mem. Univ. Grants Cttee. 60-64; mem. Turin Acad. of Sciences; Davy Medal, Royal Soc. 60, Longstaff Medal, Chemical Soc. 66; Pres. Chemical Soc. 62-64.
42 Bailie Drive, Bearsden, Glasgow; and The University, Glasgow. Scotland.
Telephone: Western 8855, Extension 419 (Office).

Robertson, Norman Alexander; Canadian university official; b. 4 March 1904; ed. Univ. of British Columbia, Balliol Coll., Oxford, and Brookings Graduate School, Washington.
Third Sec. Dept. of External Affairs, Ottawa, Canada 29; Lecturer in Govt., Harvard 33-34; Under-Sec. of State for External Affairs 41-46; High Commr. for Canada in the U.K. 46-49 and 52-57; Amb. to U.S.A. 57-58; Under-Sec. of State for External Affairs 58-64; Dir. Graduate School of Int. Affairs, Carlton Univ., Ottawa 65-; Clerk of Privy Council and Sec. to Cabinet March 49-52; Hon. LL.D. (British Columbia, Queen's and Toronto Univs.); Hon. D.C.L. (Cambridge, Acadia and Bishop's Univs.); Hon. Fellow, Balliol Coll., Oxford.
541 Manor Avenue, Rockcliffe Park, Ottawa 2, Canada.

Robertson, Reuben Buck, A.B.; American industrialist; b. 11 June 1879; ed. Yale Univ. and Cincinnati School of Law.
Admitted to bar 03; with Robertson and Buchwalter, Cincinnati 03-06; legal work in industry 07-12; Gen. Man. Champion Fibre Co. 12-18, Vice-Pres. 18-25, Pres. 25-35, Exec. Vice-Pres. 35-45; Champion Paper and Fibre Co. Pres. 45-50, 55-62, Chair. of Board 50-60, Hon. Chair. 62-; mem. Nat. War Labor Board 39-45 war; mem. President's Labor Industry Conf. 41; fmr. Chair. of Southern Conf. on Human Relations in Industry; fmr. Pres. American Paper and Pulp Asscn.; fmr. Dir. Nat. Asscn. of Manufacturers; Hon. D.Sc. North Carolina State Coll.), Hon. LL.D. (West Carolina Coll.).
820 Town Mountain Road, Asheville, N.C., U.S.A.
Telephone: 252-2474.

Robertson, Rutherford Ness, D.SC., PH.D., F.R.S.; Australian botanist; b. 29 Sept. 1913; ed. St. Andrew's Coll., Christchurch, New Zealand, Sydney Univ., and St. John's Coll., Cambridge.
Assistant Lecturer, later Lecturer in Botany, Sydney Univ. 39-46; Senior Research Officer, later Chief Research Officer, Commonwealth Scientific and Industrial Research Org. (C.S.I.R.O.), Div. of Food Preservation 46-59, mem. Exec. of C.S.I.R.O. 59-62; Visiting Prof. Univ. of California 58-59; Prof. of Botany, Univ. of Adelaide 62-; Chair. Australian Research Grants Cttee. 65-; Fellow Australian Acad. of Science 54; Foreign Assoc. U.S. Acad. of Sciences 62; Pres. Australian and New Zealand Asscn. for the Advancement of Science 65; Clarke Memorial Medal, Royal Soc. of New South Wales 54; Farrer Memorial Medal 63; A.N.Z.A.A.S. Medal 68.
Publ. *Electrolytes in Plant Cells* (co-author) 61, *Protons, Electrons Phosphorylation and Active Transport* 68.
Botany Department, University of Adelaide, Adelaide. Australia.
Telephone: 23-4333.

Robertson of Oakridge, Baron, cr. 61, of Oakridge in the County of Gloucester; **Gen. Brian Hubert Robertson,** Bt., G.C.B., G.B.E., K.C.M.G., K.C.V.O., D.S.O., M.C.; British army officer and transport administrator; b. 96; ed. Charterhouse School and Royal Mil. Acad. Woolwich.
Served First World War (despatches, D.S.O., M.C.) 15-19; Waziristan Expedition (despatches, Brevet Major) 22-23; retired pay 33; S. Africa 34-39; served Middle East (C.B.E., C.B.) 41-43; Chief Admin. Officer to Field Marshal Alexander in Italy 43-45 (K.C.V.O.); Dep. Mil. Gov., British Zone of Occupation in Germany 45-47; Mil. Gov. of British Zone of Germany, C.-in-C. of British Forces in Germany, and British mem. of Allied Control Council for Germany Nov. 47; High Commr. for GermanySept. 49-50; C.-in-C. Middle East Land Forces 50-53; Chair. British Transport Comm. 53-61; Chair. Advisory Council, Independent Television Authority 65-; Dir. Dunlop Rubber Co. Ltd., Int. Sleeping Cars; A.D.C. Gen. to King 49-52, to Queen 52; Hon. LL.D.
Isle Green, Far Oakridge, Gloucestershire, England.

Robeson, Paul, LL.B., B.A.; American singer and actor; b. 9 April 1898; ed. Columbia Univ., Rutgers, Hamilton, and Morehouse Colls.
Vice-Pres. British Soviet Friendship Soc.; Hon. L.H.D. Appeared in *Voodoo* 23, *All God's Chillun, Porgy, Black Boy* 25, *Othello* 30, *The Hairy Ape* 31, *Stevedore* 33; *Othello* (Stratford-on-Avon) 59; films: *Sanders of the River, Emperor Jones, Showboat, King Solomon's Mines, Jericho*; awarded State Peace Prize (U.S.S.R.) 52.
Publ. *Here I Stand* 60.
c/o H. Lee Lurie, 10 East 40th Street, New York City, N.Y., U.S.A.

Robichaud, Hedard J., M.P.; Canadian politician; b. 11; ed. Académie Sainte-Famille, Tracadie, Sacred Heart Coll. and Saint Joseph Univ.
Inspector of Fisheries, Dominion Govt. 39-46; Dir. of Fisheries, New Brunswick 46-52; M.P. 53-, Minister of Fisheries 63-; Liberal.
Ministry of Fisheries, Ottawa, Ontario, Canada.

Robichaud, Louis Joseph, Q.C.; Canadian politician; b. 21 Oct. 1925; ed. Sacred Heart and Laval Univs.
Private law practice 51-60; mem. New Brunswick Legislature 52-, Leader of Opposition 58-60; Prime Minister, New Brunswick 60-; Hon. Dr. of Commerce (Univ. of Moncton); Liberal.
Prime Minister's Residence, Fredericton, New Brunswick, Canada.

Robinson, Sir Albert Edward Phineas, Kt., M.A.; British (Rhodesian) business executive; b. 15; ed. Durban High School and Stellenbosch, London, Cambridge and Leiden Univs.
Barrister-at-Law, Lincoln's Inn; Imperial Light Horse, N. Africa 40-43; mem. Johannesburg City Council and Leader United Party 45-48; United Party M.P., South African Parl. 47-53; perm. resident in S. Rhodesia 53-; Dir. Banks, Building Socs., several financial and industrial cos. 53-61; Chair. Central African Airways Corpn. 57-61; mem. Monckton Comm. 60; High Commr., Fed. of Rhodesia and Nyasaland in the U.K. 61-63; Dir. Anglo-American Corpn. of South Africa Ltd., Anglo-American Corpn. Rhodesia Ltd., Zambian Anglo-American Ltd.; Deputy Chair. Gen. Mining and Finance Corpn. Ltd., Highveld Steel and Vanadium Corpn. Ltd., and other companies in Rhodesia and South Africa.
P.O.B. 2341, Salisbury, Rhodesia; P.O.B. 4587, Johannesburg, South Africa.

Robinson, Edward Austin Gossage (husband of Prof. Joan Robinson, q.v.), C.M.G., O.B.E., F.B.A., M.A.; British economist; b. 20 Nov. 1897; ed. Marlborough Coll. and Christ's Coll., Cambridge.
Fellow of Corpus Christi Coll. Cambridge 23-26; Tutor to H.H. the Maharajah of Gwalior 26-28; Univ. Lecturer Cambridge 29; Fellow of Sidney Sussex Coll Cambridge 31-; mem. Econ. Section War Cabt. 39-42; Chief Econ. Adviser and Head of Programmes Div., Ministry of Production 42-45; mem. Reparations Mission, Moscow and Berlin 45; Econ. Adviser, Board of Trade 45-46; Cen. Econ. Planing Staff 47-48; mem. U.K. Del. to OEEC 48; Reader in Econs. Univ. of Cambridge 49, Prof. of Econs. 50-65, now Emer.; Sec. Royal Econ. Soc. 46-; Treas. Int. Econ. Asscn. 50-59, Pres. 59-62; mem. Exec. Council Dept. Scientific and Industrial Research 54-59; OEEC Adviser on Italian Development 54-58; Chair. OEEC Energy Advisory Comm. 57-60; Joint Editor *The Economic Journal* 44-.
Publs. *The Structure of Competitive Industry* 32, *Monopoly* 40; Editor or Joint Editor: *Economic Consequences of the size of Nations* 60, *Economic Development of Africa South of the Sahara* 63, *Problems in Economic Development* 65, *The Economics of Education* (with J. E. Vaizey) 66.
Sidney Sussex College, Cambridge, England.
Telephone: Cambridge 57815.

Robinson, Edward G.; Romanian-born American actor; b. 12 Dec. 1893; ed. Columbia Univ. and American Acad. of Dramatic Arts.
Began stage career 13; Chevalier de la Légion d'Honneur. Appearance include *Darkness at Noon* (U.S. tour) 51-52, *The Middle of the Night* (New York) 56-58; a very large number of films including: *A Slight Case of Murder, The Amazing Dr. Clitterhouse, Blackmail, The Sea Wolf, Double Indemnity, Mr. Winkle Goes to War, The Stranger, All My Sons, Key Largo, House of Strangers, Operation X, The Glass Web, Black Tuesday,*

The Darkest Hour, The Ten Commandments, Nightmare, Hell on Frisco Bay, A Hole in the Head, Seven Thieves, Pepe, My Geisha, Sammy Going South, The Prize, The Cincinnati Kid, The Biggest Bundle of them all, Grand Slam, Never a Dull Moment.
910 Rexford Drive, Beverly Hills, Calif., U.S.A.

Robinson, Forbes; British opera singer; b. 21 May 1926; ed. Kings School, Macclesfield, St. Pauls Coll., Cheltenham, and Loughborough Coll.
Trained in Leicester, Manchester and at La Scala, Milan 52-53; Debut, Covent Garden 54, and Promenade Concerts 57; Principal Bass, Royal Opera House, Covent Garden 54-; has sung in opera and concerts in Europe, Argentina and the U.S.A. and many festivals in Europe, also in four television operas and own radio series; created title role *King Priam* (Tippett) and was the first to play the speaking role of Moses in *Moses and Aaron* (Schönberg) in English; won Great Caruso Voice Contest 52, Opera Medal 63.
225 Princes Gardens, London, W.3, England.
Telephone: 01-992-5498.

Robinson, Mrs. Joan Violet (wife of Prof. E. A. G. Robinson, q.v.); British economist; b. 31 Oct. 1903; ed. St. Paul's Girls' School, London and Girton Coll., Cambridge.
Assistant Lecturer in Economics, Cambridge Univ. 31, Lecturer 37-49, Reader 49-Oct. 65, Prof. Oct. 65-; Fellow of the British Acad.
Publs. *Economics of Imperfect Competition* 33, *Essays in the Theory of Employment* 37, *Introduction to the Theory of Employment* 37, *Essay on Marxian Economics* 42, *Collected Economic Papers* 51, *The Rate of Interest and Other Essays* 52, *The Accumulation of Capital* 56, *Essays in the Theory of Economic Growth* 62, *Economic Philosophy* 63, *Collected Economic Papers,* Vol. III 65, *Economics: An Awkward Corner* 66.
62 Grange Road, Cambridge, England.

Robinson, Rt. Rev. John Arthur Thomas, M.A., PH.D., B.D.; British ecclesiastic and writer; b. 15 June 1919; ed. Marlborough Coll., Jesus and Trinity Colls., Cambridge, and Westcott House, Cambridge.
Curate, St. Matthew, Moorfields, Bristol 45-48; Chaplain, Wells Theological Coll. 48-51; Fellow and Dean, Clare Coll., Cambridge 51-59; Lecturer in Divinity, Cambridge Univ. 53-59; Examining Chaplain to Archbishop of Canterbury 53-59; Six Preacher, Canterbury Cathedral 58-; Bishop Suffragan of Woolwich 59-; Proctor in Convocation, Diocese of Southwark 60-.
Publs. *In the End, God* . . . . 50, *The Body* 52, *Jesus and His Coming* 57, *On Being the Church in the World* 60, *Christ Comes in* 60, *Liturgy Coming to Life* 60, *Twelve New Testament Studies* 62, *Honest to God* 63, *The Honest to God Debate* 63, *Christian Morals Today* 64, *The New Reformation?* 65, *But that I can't Believe* 67, *Exploration into God* 67.
17 Manor Way, Blackheath, London, S.E.3, England.
Telephone: 01-852-4145.

Robinson, John Foster, C.B.E.; British business executive; b. 2 Feb. 1909; ed. Harrow, and Christ Church, Oxford.
Director, E. S. and A. Robinson Ltd. 43-48, Managing Dir. 48-58, Dep. Chair. 58-61, Chair., E. S. and A. Robinson (Holdings) Ltd. 61-; Deputy Chair. Dickinson Robinson Group Ltd.
St. George's Hill, Easton-in-Gordano, near Bristol, England.

Robinson, Rt. Hon. Kenneth, P.C., M.P.; British politician; b. 19 March 1911; ed. Oundle School.
Insurance Broker, Lloyds' 27-40; Naval service 41-46; Company Sec. 46-49; M.P. 49-, Asst. Whip 50-51, Opposition Whip 51-54; Minister of Health Oct. 64-; Vice-Pres. Asscn. for Mental Health 58-, mem. Exec. Cttee. The Nat. Trust 51-; Labour.

Publs. *Wilkie Collins, a Biography* 51, *Policy for Mental Health* 58, *Patterns of Care* 61, *Look at Parliament* 62. 12 Grove Terrace, London N.W.5, England.

Robinson, Kenneth Ernest, J.P., M.A., F.R.HIST.S.; British University Vice-Chancellor; b. 9 March 1914; ed. Monoux Grammar School, Walthamstow, and Hertford Coll., Oxford, and London School of Economics.
Entered Colonial Office 36; Asst. Sec. 46-48, resgnd.; Fellow of Nuffield Coll. 48-57, Librarian 51-57; Reader in Commonwealth Govt., Oxford 48-57; Leverhulme Research Fellow 52-53; Visiting Lecturer, School of Advanced Int. Studies, Johns Hopkins Univ. 54, Duke Univ. 63, Acadia Univ. 63; part-time mem., Directing Staff, Civil Service Selection Board 51-56; Prof. of Commonwealth Affairs and Dir. of Inst. of Commonwealth Studies, Univ. of London 57-65; mem. Colonial Econ. Research Cttee. 49-62; Colonial Social Science Research Council 58-62; Council of Overseas Devt. Inst. 60-65; Royal Inst. of Int. Affairs 62-65; Int. African Inst. 60-65; African Studies Asscn. of U.K. 63-65; Gov. London School of Econs. 59-65; Vice-Chancellor, Univ. of Hong Kong 65-; corresp. mem. Acad. des Sciences d'Outre-Mer, Paris; Editor *Journal of Commonwealth Political Studies* 61-65; Special Commonwealth Award, Ministry of Overseas Devt. 65.
Publs. *Africa Today* (co-author) 55, *Africa in the Modern World* (co-author) 55, *Five Elections in Africa* (with W. J. M. Mackenzie) 60, *Essays in Imperial Government* (with A. F. Madden) 63, *The Dilemmas of Trusteeship* 65, *A Decade of the Commonwealth* (with W. B. Hamilton and C. Goodwin) 66, *University Co-operation and Asian Development* (co-author) 67, *L'Europe au XIXe et XXe siècles*, Vol. VII (co-author) 68.
The Lodge, 1 University Drive, Hong Kong; and The Old Rectory, Church Westcote, Gloucestershire, England.
Telephone: 433697.

Robinson, Raymond, M.A., LL.B., M.P.; Trinidadian politician; b. 11 Dec. 1926; ed. Bishop's High School, Tobago, St. John's Coll., Oxford, and Inner Temple, London.
M.P. West Indies 58-61; Rep. of Trinidad and Tobago Council of Univ. of West Indies 59-61; Minister of Finance and Governor for Trinidad Board of Govs. of Int. Monetary Fund and Int. Bank for Reconstruction and Development 61-67; Deputy Leader, Peoples National Movement Jan. 67-; Minister of External Affairs April 67-; Studentship Prize, Inner Temple.
Publs. *The New Frontier and the New Africa* 61, *Fiscal Reform in Trinidad and Tobago* 66, *The Path of Progress* 67, *The Teacher and Nationalism* 67.
21 Ellerslie Park, Maraval, Trinidad, Trinidad and Tobago.

Robinson, Sir Robert, Kt., O.M., D.SC., F.R.I.C., F.R.S.; British scientist; b. 13 Sept. 1886; ed. Manchester Univ. Prof. of Organic Chemistry Sydney Univ. 12; Heath Harrison Prof. of Organic Chemistry Liverpool Univ. 15; Prof. of Chemistry St. Andrews Univ. 21; Prof. of Organic Chemistry Manchester Univ. 22, Univ. of London 27; Waynflete Prof. of Chemistry Oxford Univ. 30-55; Pres. Chemical Society 40-41; Dir. Shell Chemical Co. 55-; Pres. B.A.A.S. 55, Soc. of Chemical Industry 58-59; Foreign mem. U.S.S.R. Acad. of Sciences 66-; Swiss Society of Chemistry Paracelsus Gold Medal 39, Davy, Royal and Copley Medallist of Royal Society; Gold Medal of Franklin Inst. 47; Albert Gold Medal Royal Society of Arts 47; Nobel Prize for Chemistry 47; Longstaff, Faraday and Flintoff Medals, Chemical Soc.; Priestley Medal 53; mem. Colonial Products Research Council 43-46; P.R.S. 45-50; Commdr. Légion d'Honneur; Hon. D.Sc. (London, Durham, Wales, Liverpool, Cambridge, Sheffield, Nottingham, Bristol,

Oxford, Zagreb, Delhi, Strathclyde, and Hokkaido), Hon. LL.D. (Edinburgh, Birmingham, St. Andrews, Belfast, Glasgow, Manchester, Liverpool), Hon. D. Pharm. (Madrid, Paris), Hon. M.I.C.E.; Hon. Fellow Magdalen Coll. Oxford; hon. mem. Parl. Scientific Cttee.
Grimm's Hill Lodge, Great Missenden, Bucks., England.
Telephone: Gt. Missenden 2465.

Robinson, William Edward; American business executive; b. 27 June 1900; ed. LaSalle Acad., Providence, and New York Univ.
New York World-Telegram 31-33; Hearst Gen. Management staff 33-36; *New York Herald Tribune* 36-54; Chair. and Chief Exec. Officer, Robinson-Hannagan Associates 54-55; Coca-Cola Co. 55-, Pres., Dir., Chair. of Board up to 61, Chair. Exec. Cttee. 61-.
c/o The Coca-Cola Company, 515 Madison Avenue, New York 22, N.Y.; Home: Quaker Lane, Greenwich, Conn., U.S.A.

Robles, Marco Aurelio; Panamanian politician; b. 06. Former government official; Minister of Govt. and Justice 60-64; Pres. of Panama Oct. 64-; Partido Liberal. Palacio del Gobierno, Panama City, Panama.

Roblin, Hon. Dufferin; Canadian politician; b. 17 June 1917; ed. St. John's Coll. School, Winnipeg; Manitoba and Chicago Univs.
Canadian Air Force, attaining rank of Wing Commdr. 39-45; Manitoba Legislature 49-; Ldr. Manitoba Progressive Conservatives 54-; Premier, Manitoba 58-; mem. Privy Council of Canada July 67-.
96 Kingsway, Winnipeg 9, Manitoba, Canada.
Telephone: GLobe 3-06-58.

Robson, Dame Flora McKenzie, D.B.E.; British actress; b. 28 March 1902; ed. Palmers Green High School, London.
D.Litt. h.c. (Durham Univ. and Univ. of Wales); Orders of White Lion and White Rose, Finland.
Appearances include *Will Shakespeare* 21, *Desire Under the Elms* 31, *Dangerous Corner* 32, *For Services Rendered* 32, *All God's Chillun* 32, Shakespeare productions at the Old Vic 32-33; plays: *Ladies in Retirement, Black Chiffon* and *Macbeth* in New York; *The House by the Lake* 56-58, Ibsen's *Ghosts* 58-59, *The Aspern Papers* 59-60, *Time and Yellow Roses* 61, *The Corn is Green* 61, *Close Quarters* 63, *John Gabriel Borkman* 63, *Importance of Being Earnest* 68 in London; *Brother and Sister* 67 on tour; also films in London and Hollywood.
Marine House, 14 Marine Gardens, Brighton 7, Sussex, England.

Robson, William Alexander, PH.D., LL.M., B.SC. (ECON.); British jurist and political scientist; b. 14 July 1895; ed. London School of Economics and Political Science.
Barrister; Prof. of Public Admin. London School of Econs. 47-62; Principal, Mines Dept. 40-42, Ministry of Fuel and Power 42-43; Asst. Sec. Air Ministry 43, Civil Aviation 45; mem. Council Town and Country Planning Asscn., Vice-Pres. Inst. of Public Admin., Dept. Cttee. Greater London Planning Admin., Cttee. on training in Public Admin. for Overseas Countries; Pres. Int. Political Science Asscn. 52-55; Chair. Greater London Group; Hon. Fellow London School of Economics; Dr. h.c. (Paris, Lille, Grenoble, Algiers); Hon. D.Litt. (Durham and Manchester Univs.).
Publs. *The Town Councillor* (with Rt. Hon. C. R. Attlee), *Justice and Administrative Law, The Development of Local Government, The Relation of Wealth to Welfare, The Law of Local Government Audit, A Century of Municipal Progress, Civilisation and the Growth of Law, the British Civil Servant, Public Enterprise, The Government and Misgovernment of London, Social Security, The British System of Government, Planning and Performance, The War and the Planning Outlook, Population and the People, British Government since*

1918, Problems of Nationalised Industry, The University Teaching of Political Science, Great Cities of the World, The Civil Service in Britain and France, Nationalised Industry and Public Ownership, The Governors and the Governed, Local Government in Crisis, Politics and Government at Home and Abroad; Joint Editor *The Political Quarterly*.
48 Lanchester Road, London, N.6, England.
Telephone: 01-883-1331.

Roca, Blas; Cuban politician; b. 08; ed. Grammar School.
Former cobbler; official Cuban Shoe Workers'; Union 29-30; fmr. Leader, Oriente Communist Party Cttee. mem., Cuban Communist Party; Sec. Gen. Partido Unido de la Revolución Socialista Cubana (P.U.R.S.C.) 62-65, mem. Secr. Partido Comunista (formerly P.U.R.S.C.) 65-; Editor *Hoy* 62-65.
Publ. *The Foundations of Socialism in Cuba* 61.
Prado y Teniente Rey, Havana, Cuba.

Rocaut-Quillet, Jean; French publisher; b. 6 May 1898.
Sec.-Gen. Publishing Co., Aristide Quillet 31-50, Dep. Dir. 50, Pres., Dir.-Gen. 55-; Pres., Dir.-Gen. *Les Dernières Nouvelles de Strasbourg* 61-; Vice-Pres. Syndicat des Quotidiens Régionaux; Deputy Treasurer, Fédération Nationale de la Presse Française; Commdr. Légion d'Honneur, Croix de Guerre.
Home: 4 rue André-Colledeboeuf, Paris 16e; Office: 278 Boulevard St. Germain, Paris, 7e, France.

Rocha, Antonio; Mexican politician; b. 1912; ed. Univ. Autónoma de San Luis Potosí.
Lawyer 35-; Justice Attorney for State of San Luis Potosí; Sec.-Gen. Govt. of State of Tamaulipas; Deputy to Union Congress; Senator; Pres. of Senate and Senate Comms. on Legislative and Constitutional Matters; Prof. of Penal Law and Procedure; now Attorney-Gen. of Mexico; Rep. of Mexican Govt. at various int. confs. in Latin America; mem. Mexican Acad. of Penal Sciences, Int. Asscn. of Penal Law and Mexican Soc. of Geography and Statistics.
Secretaría de la Procuraduría General, Mexico City, Mexico.

Rocha-e-Silva, Mauricio, DR. MED.; Brazilian pharmacologist and biochemist; b. 10; ed. Univ. of Rio de Janeiro.
Research Asst., Faculty of Sciences of São Paulo Univ. 35-37; Asst. Instituto Biologico, São Paulo 37-42, Head of Dept. of Biochemistry and Pharmacodynamics 42-; Lecturer, Univs. of Brazil and São Paulo 52; Prof. Pharmacology, Univ. of São Paulo 57-; Co-founder and Pres. Brazilian Asscn. for Advancement of Science; Fellow of Guggenheim Foundation, N.Y. for research work in U.S.A. 40-42; Fellow of British Council for research work in London 46-47; full mem. Brazilian Acad. of Sciences; Hon. mem. American Acad. of Allergy.
Publs. *Histamine and Anaphylaxis* 46, *Bradykinin* 49, *Histamine, its Role in Anaphylaxis and Allergy* 55, *Histamine and Antihistaminics* (section of book) 66, *Foundations of Pharmacology* 61, 68.
Department of Pharmacology, University of São Paulo, Riberião Prêto, São Paulo, Brazil.

Rochdale, Viscount, cr. 60, 2nd Baron, cr. 13; **John Durival Kemp,** O.B.E., T.D., D.L., B.A.; British industrialist; b. 5 June 1906; ed. Eton Coll., and Trinity Coll., Cambridge.
Man. and later Dir., Kelsall & Kemp Ltd., Rochdale 28-39; served with British Expeditionary Force in France 39-40; attached to U.S. Forces in Pacific with rank of Colonel 44; later with Combined Operations Command, India; Brigadier 45; mem. Cen. Transport Consultative Cttee. 52-57; Pres. Nat. Union of Manufacturers 53-56; Vice-Pres. British Productivity Council 55-56; Gov. B.B.C. 54-59; Dir. Consett Iron Co. 56-67; Chair. The Cotton Board 57-62; Chair. Kelsall & Kemp Ltd., Rochdale; Chair. Cttee. of Enquiry into the Major Docks of Great Britain 61-62; Dir. Williams Deacon's Bank Ltd.; Pres. British Legion (North Western Area) 54-61, Econ. League 63-; Vice-Pres. Lancashire and Merseyside Industrial Development Asscn.; mem. Western Hemisphere Exports Council 53-64; mem. Past Upper Baliff, Worshipful Company of Weavers; Chair. Nat. Ports Council 63-67, Cttee. of Inquiry into Shipping Industry 67-.
Lingholm, Keswick, Cumberland, England.

Roche, Emile; French international civil servant; b. 24 Sept. 1893.
Journalist, Editor of *Cri des Flandres* 27, Dir. of *La République* 29-39, *La Semaine Economique et Financière* 48-50; Pres. Radical-Socialist Fed. of the North 32-56; mem. of Econ. Council 51-, Pres. 54-59; mem. French Econ. and Social Council 59, Pres. 59-; Pres. Econ. and Social Cttee. of European Econ. Community (EEC) and of Euratom 62-64; Grand Officier, Légion d'Honneur.
Publs. *Caillaux que j'ai connu, L'or n'est plus roi, On a voté.... et maintenant, Perspectives franco-marocaines, L'Ere des métamorphoses.*
Office of the President of The Economic and Social Council, 1 avenue d'Iéna, Paris 16e, France.
Telephone: BAL.35-85.

Roche, James M.; American motor executive; b. 16 Dec. 1906; ed. LaSalle Univ., Chicago.
General Motors 27-; Statistician, Cadillac Sales and Service Branch, Chicago 27; Head of Business Management Dept., Cadillac Motor Car Div., Detroit 35; Gen. Sales Manager, Cadillac Motor Car Div., 50-57, Gen. Manager 57-60; Vice-Pres. Gen. Motors 57-60, Vice-Pres. (Gen. Motors Marketing Staff) 60-62, Exec. Vice-Pres. and Dir. 62-65; Pres., Chief Operating Officer, Chair. Exec. Cttee., Dir. and mem. Finance Cttee. Gen. Motors June 65-Oct. 67, Chair. Oct. 67-.
General Motors Corporation, General Motors Building, Detroit 2, Michigan, U.S.A.

Roche, Jean Casimir Henri Hilaire, D. en MED., D. ès S.; French university professor; b. 14 Feb. 1901.
Asst. in Physiology, Montpellier Univ. 20-23; Lecturer in Biochemistry, Univ. of Strasbourg 25-30; Prof. of Biochemistry, Univ. of Lyon 30-31, Marseilles Univ. 31-47; Hon. Prof. 48-; Dir. of Laboratory Comparative Biochemistry, Ecole des Hautes Etudes, Paris 41-; Prof. of Biochemistry, Collège de France, Paris 47-; Rector Univ. of Paris 61-; Dir. of Laboratoire Maritime du Collège de France, Concarneau, Brittany and Pres. Inst. des Hautes Etudes, Tunis (Univ. of Paris); mem. Acad. des Sciences, Acad. de Médicine; Hon. mem. Romanian Acad.; Hon. D.C.L. (Oxford), Hon. D.Sc. (London, Frankfurt, New York, Bucharest, Montreal, Southampton, Pamplona), D.Med. (Naples, Liège).
Publs. *Essai sur la Biochimie générale et comparée des pigments respiratoires* 36, *Précis de Chimie* 34.
Office: 47 rue des Ecoles, Paris 5e; Home: 5 rue de la Sorbonne, Paris 5e, France.

Roche, John P., A.B., A.M., PH.D.; American professor of politics; b. 7 May 1923; ed. Hofstra Coll. and Cornell Univ.
Instructor, then Assoc. Prof. of Political Science, Haverford Coll. 49-56; Prof. of Politics and History, Brandeis Univ. 56-, Chair. Dept. of Politics 56-59, 61-65, Dean, Faculty of Arts and Sciences 58-60; Visiting appts.: Swarthmore Coll., Cornell and Columbia Univs. and Mass. Inst. of Technology and Lecturer, Univ. of Aix-en-Provence; Fellow, Fund for the Advancement of Educ. 54-55, Rockefeller Foundation 61-62, 65-66; Nat. Chair. Americans for Democratic Action 62-65; Consultant, Vice-Pres. Hubert H. Humphrey and U.S. Dept. of State 64-66; Special Consultant to the Pres. of the U.S. 66-.

Publs. *The Dynamics of Democratic Government* (with Murray S. Stedman, Jr.) 54, *Aspects of Liberty* 58, *Courts and Rights* 61, revised edn. 66, *The American Image: the Political Process* (with Leonard W. Levy) 63, *The Quest for the Dream: The Development of Civil Liberties and Human Relations in Modern America* 63, *Shadow and Substance: Essays on the Theory and Structure of Politics* 64, *The Crossroad Papers* 65, *The Dynamics of Modern Government* (with Meehan and Stedman) 66, *John Marshall: Major Opinions and Other Writings* (Editor) 67; numerous articles on law and politics.
The White House, Washington, D.C., U.S.A.

Roche, Josephine, A.M.; American industrialist; b. 2 Dec. 1886; ed. Vassar Coll., and Columbia Univ.
Exec. Sec. Colorado Progressive Service 13-15; Special Agent England and U.S., Comm. for Relief in Belgium 15; Dir. Girls' Dept. Juvenile Court, Denver 15-18, Referee 25-27; Investigator Nat. Consumers' League 18, Pres. 39-; Dir. Foreign Language Information Service 18-23, New York and Washington; Dir. Editorial Div. U.S. Children's Bureau 23-25; with Rocky Mountain Fuel Co. 27-50; Vice-Pres. 28-29, Pres. 29-34, Pres. and Gen. Man. 37-50; mem. Nat. Board Dirs. Federal Re-employment Service 33; Asst. Sec. U.S. Treas. 34-37, Rep. Pres. Cabinet Cttee. on Economic Security; Chair. Interdeptl. Cttee. to Co-ordinate Health and Welfare Activities, Fed. Govt. 34-40; Chair. Nat. Health Conf. 38; Dir. United Mine Workers of America Welfare and Retirement Fund 48-, Trustee 50-; Hon. D.Litt., etc.
907 15th Street, N.W., Washington, D.C., U.S.A.

Roché, Louis; French diplomatist; b. 16 Oct. 1903; ed. Ecole Libre des Sciences Politiques, and Trinity Coll., Cambridge.
Diplomatic Service, Warsaw 31-32, Brussels 32-34, Vienna 34-37, London 37-40, Dublin 40-41; B.B.C. London 42-43; in London 43-45; Political Observer, Bavaria 49-52; Amb. to Australia 52-55, to Lebanon 56-60; Dir. of American Affairs, Ministry of Foreign Affairs 60-63; Amb. to Austria 63-; Commdr. Légion d'Honneur.
Publs. *Si proche et lointaine, le Solitaire de Castille*.
Ambassade de France, 2 Technikerstrasse, Vienna, Austria; and 4 Quai des Celestins, Paris IV, France.

Roche, Marcel, M.D., B.S.; Venezuelan parasitologist; b. 15 Aug. 1920; ed. Coll. Sainte Croix de Neuilly, St. Joseph's Coll., Philadelphia, Johns Hopkins Univ., Baltimore, and Harvard School of Medicine, Boston.
Intern, Johns Hopkins Hospital, Baltimore 46-47; Asst. Resident, Peter Bent Brigham Hospital, Boston 47-48; Research Fellow, Harvard School of Medicine, Boston 48-50; Research work, New York Public Health Research Inst. 50-51; Dir. Luis Roche Inst. for Medical Research 52-58; Dir. Venezuelan Inst. for Scientific Research 58-, Chief of Dept. of Physiopathology 58-.
Instituto Venezolano de Investigaciones Científicas, Apartado 1827, Caracas, Venezuela.
Telephone: 691941-51.

Rochereau, Henri R. M. V.; French politician; b. 25 March 1908.
Senator from Vendée 46-59; Pres. Economic and Planning Comm. 59; Minister of Agriculture 59-61; mem. European Parl. 56-59; mem. Comm. of European Econ. Community 61-67; mem. Combined Comm. of EEC, ECSC and Euratom 67-.
European Economic Community, 23-27 Avenue de la Joyeuse Entrée, Brussels 4, Belgium.

Rochereau de La Sablière, Bertrand; French diploma-tist; b. 9 July 1903; ed. Ecole Fontanes, Ecole Libre des Sciences Politiques, and Univ. de Paris à la Sorbonne.
Press and Information Service, Central Admin. of Ministry of Foreign Affairs 30-37; served Brussels, Kaunus and Middle East 37-45; Counsellor, Greece

45-47, Turkey 47-52; Consul-Gen., Jerusalem 52-54; Asst. Dir. UNRWA, Beirut 55-57; Ambassador to Paraguay 57-59, to Colombia 59-65, to Israel 65-; Officier Légion d'Honneur, Commandeur du Merit National and other decorations.
Ambassade de France, 112 Tayeleth Herbert Samuel, Tel-Aviv, Israel; Home: 2 rue de Villiers, Levallois-Perret, France.

Rochet, Waldeck; French agriculturist and politician; b. 5 April 1905.
Market gardener; Dep. to Nat. Ass. 36-40, 54-; Del. to Provisional Consultative Ass. 44; Pres. Agricultural Cttee., Nat. Ass. 46-47; Dir. of *La Terre*; Pres. Commu-nist Party in Nat. Ass. 58-59, 62-64; Dep. Sec.-Gen. of Communist Party until 64, Sec.-Gen. 64-.
National Assembly, Paris 7e, France, and 14 rue Jules-Gauthier, Nanterre, Seine, France.

Rocheta, Manuel Farrajota; Portuguese diplomatist; b. 06; ed. Lisbon Univ.
Diplomatic posts Hamburg 31-34, Copenhagen 34-39, Bucharest 43-45, Dublin 45; First Sec., Washington 46-50, Minister-Counsellor 50; Asst. Dir.-Gen. Political Dept. Foreign Ministry, Lisbon 51-54, Dir.-Gen. 54-55; Envoy, Bonn 55-56, Ambassador 56-58; Ambassador to Brazil 58-61, to U.K. 61-; foreign honours.
Portuguese Embassy, 11 Belgrave Square, London, S.W.1, England.

Rock, John; American physician; b. 24 March 1890; ed. Harvard Coll., and Harvard Medical School.
Practised obstetrics at Boston and Brookline, Mass. 21-44, Gynecology 21-; Surgeon, Free Hospital for Women, Brookline 24-56, Consulting Gynecologist 56-; Dir. Fertility and Endocrine Clinic 26-56; Clinical Prof. of Gynecology, Harvard Medical School, Boston 47-56, Emeritus Prof. 56-; mem. Board of Consultation, Massachusetts Gen. Hospital, Boston 45-60, Hon. Surgeon 60-; Dir. Rock Reproductive Clinic, Inc. (fmrly. Rock Reproductive Study Center) 56-; Lasker Award of Planned Parenthood Fed. of America, Ortho Award of American Soc. for the Study of Sterility; Oliver Bird Medal 63, Modern Medicine Award 66; Hon. Sc.D. Amherst Coll.; Dr. h.c. Univ. of San Marcos, Lima; Hon. LL.D. Harvard Univ.
Publs. *The Time Has Come, A Catholic Doctor's Pro-posals to End the Battle Over Birth Control* 63, Co-author *Voluntary Parenthood* 49, and numerous articles.
77 Glen Road, Brookline, Mass., U.S.A.
Telephone: BE-2-8490.

Rockefeller, David (son of John D. Rockefeller, Jr.), B.S., PH.D.; American banker; b. 12 June 1915; ed. Harvard Univ., and Univ. of Chicago.
Sec. Mayor Fiorello H. LaGuardia, N.Y.C. 40-41; Asst. Regional Dir. U.S. Office of Defence 41-42; served in U.S. Army 42-45; Asst. Man. Foreign Dept. Chase Nat. Bank 46; Vice-Pres. 49, Senior Vice-Pres. 52, Exec. Vice-Pres. 57, Pres. and Chair. Exec. Cttee. of Board of Dirs., Dir. Chase Manhattan Bank 61-; Chair. and Dir. Chase Int. Investment Corpn.; Chair. Museum of Modern Art, Rockefeller Univ., Center for Inter-American Relations, and other chairmanships; Dir. and Vice-Pres. Council on Foreign Relations, Inc.; Dir. Rockefeller Brothers Inc., Rockefeller Center Inc., Morningside Heights, Inc.; Trustee Univ. of Chicago., Hon. Trustee Int. House, New York; Hon. LL.D. (Columbia Univ.); French Legion of Honour, Grande Médaille d'Honneur, Legion of Merit, etc.
Room 5600, 30 Rockefeller Plaza, New York 20, U.S.A.

Rockefeller, James S.; American businessman; b. 8 June 1902; ed. Yale Univ.
Worked with Brown Brothers & Co. 24-30; joined Nat. City Bank of New York 30; Asst. Cashier 31, Asst. Vice-Pres. 33, Vice-Pres. 40, Senior Vice-Pres. 48, Exec. Vice-Pres. 52, Pres. and Dir. 52-59, Chair. and Dir. 59-67,

Nat. City Bank of New York, now First Nat. City Bank; served with U.S. Army 42-46; Dir. First Nat. City Trust Co. (Bahamas) Ltd., Kimberly-Clark Corpn., Northern Pacific Railway Co., The Nat. Cash Register Co., Pan American World Airways, Cranston Print Works Co., Anaconda Co.; Vice-Pres. and Dir. Indian Spring Land Co.; Pres. and Dir. Nat. Realty Corpn.; mem. Board of Managers of the Memorial Hospital for Cancer and Allied Diseases, New York; Trustee of Estate of William Rockefeller, Amer. Museum of Natural History.
c/o First National City Bank, 399 Park Avenue, New York 10022, N.Y., U.S.A.
Telephone: 212-559-4444.

Rockefeller, John Davison, 3rd (son of John D. Rockefeller, Jr.), B.S.; American executive; b. 21 March 1906; ed. Princeton Univ.
Chairman, Board of Trustees, Rockefeller Foundation; Chair. Asia Soc. Inc.; Trustee Emer. Princeton Univ., Trustee Rockefeller Bros. Fund; Pres. Japan Soc. Inc., The Agricultural Devt. Council Inc., J.D.R. 3rd Fund, Inc.; Chair. Board, Population Council Inc., Lincoln Center for the Performing Arts Inc.; Consultant, Dulles Mission to Japan on Peace Settlement 51; Adviser, U.S. del. Japanese Peace Treaty Conf., San Francisco 51; served in U.S.N.R. 42-45; Special Asst. to Under-Sec. of Navy 45; Hon. Chair. United Negro Coll. Fund; numerous foreign decorations (U.K., Republic of China, Ethiopia, Japan, Thailand, Laos).
Home: 1 Beekman Place, New York City 22; Office: 30 Rockefeller Plaza, New York City, N.Y. 10020, U.S.A.

Rockefeller, Laurance Spelman (son of John D. Rockefeller, Jr.), B.A.; American financier; b. 26 May 1910; ed. Princeton Univ.
Vice-Pres. Air Youth of America 38-42; Dir. Nat. Aeronautics Asscn. 42-44, Creole Petroleum Corpn. 41-43, McDonnell Aircraft Corpn. 41-42, 45-50; U.S.N.R. Bureau of Aeronautics 42-45; Chair. Rockefeller Brothers Inc., Rockefeller Center Inc., Estate Good Hope Corpn., Dorado Beach Hotel Corpn., Caneel Bay Plantation Inc., Memorial Sloan-Kettering Cancer Center, Advisory Council, Dept. of Philosophy, Princeton Univ.; Dir. Resources for the Future; Trustee, Alfred P. Sloan Foundation Inc., Nat. Geographic Soc., Nat. Board of Y.W.C.A. of U.S.A.; Dir. American Cttee. Int. Wildlife Protection; Pres. American Conservation Asscn., Rockefeller Brothers Fund Inc., Nat. Recreation and Park Asscn.; Trustee and Vice-Pres. New York Zoological Soc.; Trustee and Pres. Jackson Hole Preserve Inc.; Trustee, founder and Vice-Pres. Conservation Foundation; Commr. and Senior Vice-Pres. Palisades Interstate Park Comm.; Life mem. of the Corpn., Mass. Inst. of Technology; Public mem. Public Land Law Review Comm.; Commdr. Royal Order of the Lion (Belgium) 50.
Room 5600, 30 Rockefeller Plaza, New York, N.Y. 10020; Home: 834 Fifth Avenue, New York, N.Y., U.S.A.

Rockefeller, Nelson Aldrich (son of John D. Rockefeller, Jr.), A.B.; American public servant and politician; b. 8 July 1908; ed. Lincoln School, New York City, and Dartmouth Coll.
Clerk, N.Y., London and Paris branches, Chase Nat. Bank 31; Dir. Rockefeller Center, Inc. 31-58, Pres. 38-45, 48-51, Chair. of Board 45-53, 56-58; Co-ordinator of Inter-American Affairs 40-44; Asst. Sec. of State 44, 45; Founder and Pres. American Int. Asscn. for Economic and Social Development 46-53, 57-58, Dir. 46-53, 56-; Founder and Pres. Int. Basic Economy Corpn. 47-53, 56-58, Chair. 58, Dir. 47-53, 56-58; Chair. Int. Development Advisory Board 50, 51; Chair. President's Advisory Cttee. on Govt. Organisation 52-58; Under-Sec. of Health, Education and Welfare 53-54; Special Asst. to Pres. 54-55; Pres. Museum of Modern Art, N.Y.

39-41, 46-53, Chair. 57-58, Trustee 32-; Founder, Pres. Museum of Primitive Art, N.Y. 54-; Pres. Rockefeller Bros. Fund Inc. 56-58, Trustee 40-; Founder and Chair. Govt. Affairs Foundation Inc. 53-58; Trustee, Inst. for Int. Social Research 57-; Dir. Ibec Housing Corpn. 56-58; Gov. New York State 59-; Order of Merit (Chile) 45; Nat. Order of Southern Cross (Brazil) 46; Order of Aztec Eagle (Mexico) 49; Grande Croix de l'Ordre de Léopold II (Belgium) 59; Hon. LL.D. (Fordham Univ., Jewish Theological Seminary, Mich. State Coll., etc.), Hon. L.H.D. (Hamilton Coll.); Republican.
Pocantico Hills, North Tarrytown, New York, U.S.A.

Rockefeller, Winthrop (son of John D. Rockefeller, Jr.); American businessman and politician; b. 1 May 1912; ed. Lincoln School, New York City, Loomis School, Windsor, Connecticut and Yale Univ.
Humble Oil and Refining Co. (Texas) 34-37; Chase Nat. Bank 37-38; Exec. Vice-Pres. Greater New York Fund 38; foreign dept. Socony-Vacuum Oil Co. 39-51; served in U.S. Army 41-46, rising to Lieut.-Col. 77th Infantry Regt.; Chair. of the Board Colonial Williamsburg Inc., Williamsburg Restoration; Pres. Santa Gertrudis Breeders Int.; Chair. Arkansas Industrial Devt. Comm. 55-64; Rep. Nat. Ctteeman. Arkansas 61-; Dir. Rockefeller Center Inc., Rockefeller Brothers Inc.; Founding Trustee Rockefeller Brothers Inc., Trustee Vanderbilt Univ. Southwest Center for Advanced Studies, Dallas, Loomis School; fmr. Trustee Nat. Urban League; Gov. of Arkansas 66-; Hon. LL.D. Coll. of William and Mary, Hendrix Coll., Ark. and Univ. of Arkansas, Hon. L.H.D. New York Univ and Univ. of San Francis Xavier (Bolivia); Bronze Star with two Oak Leaf Clusters, Purple Heart.
Winrock Farms, Route 3, Morrilton, Ark., U.S.A.
Telephone: Park 7-5481.

Rockwell, Willard Frederick, Jr., B.S.; American industrialist; b. 3 March 1914; ed. Pennsylvania State Univ.
Cost Accountant, Pittsburgh Equitable Meter Co. 35-36, Accountant 37-39, Vice-Pres., Controller 39-43, Vice-Pres., Gen. Manager 45-47; Asst. to Controller, Timken-Detroit Axle Co. 33-37; Pres., Rockwell-Standard Corpn. 63-; Rockwell Manufacturing Co. 47-64, Vice-Chair. May 64-; Dir., Allegheny Airlines Inc., National Union Insurance Cos., Real Estate Co. of Pittsburgh, United Engineering and Foundry Co., etc.; Dir. and mem. of Exec. Cttee. of Pennysylvania Chamber of Commerce; mem.American Inst.of Industrial Engineers, American Petroleum Inst., etc., Hon LL.D. (Grove City Coll.), Hon. D.Eng. (Tufts Univ., Washington and Jefferson Coll.).
400 N. Lexington Avenue, Pittsburgh, Pennsylvania, U.S.A.

Rode, Ebbe; Danish actor; b. 10 May 1910.
Member staff Dagmarteatret 31, Royal Theatre, Copenhagen 32-57, 65-; guest actor at theatres in Aarhus, Aalborg, Odense and Copenhagen; Knight of the Order of Dannebrog.
Leading roles in plays including: *Etienne*, *Topaze*, *Winterset*, *Ah! Wilderness*, *Waterloo-Bridge, Caesar and Cleopatra, Dolls House, Pygmalion, Otto Frank, The School for Scandal*; has acted in numerous films and on television and radio.
Publ. *My Meeting with Albert Schweitzer in His Hospital*.
Solbakken 28, Virum, Denmark.

Rodenstock, Rudolf (Rolf), DR.RER.POL.; German manufacturer; b. 1 July 1917; ed. Technical Univ., Munich.
Prof. with special duties, Univ. of Munich 56; proprietor of Optische Werke G. Rodenstock, Munich; Pres. Landesverband der Bayerischen Industrie, Munich; mem. Presidency, Bundesvereinigung der Deutschen

Arbeitgeberverbände, Cologne; Vice-Pres. Bundesverband der Deutschen Industrie, Cologne; mem. Board Deutsche Allgemeine Spiegelglas A.G., Münchener Rückversicherungs-Ges., Bayernwerk A.G., Messe- u. Austellungs A.G., Industriekreditbank A.G., Gesellschaft der Freunde der Bayerischen Akad. der Wissenschaften, Munich, Deutsches Industrieinstitut, Cologne. Romanstrasse 32, Munich 19; and c/o Optische Werke G. Rodenstock, Isartalstrasse 39-43, Munich 5, German Federal Republic.

Röder, Franz-Josef, DR.PHIL.; German politician; b. 22 July 1909; ed. Univs. of Freiburg i. Breisgau, Innsbruck and Münster.
Schoolteacher abroad 37-45; Chief Interpreter German Fed. Railways 46-48, later Dir. Dillingen Gymnasium; mem. Saar Landtag (Land Parliament) 55-; Minister of Education, Culture, Saar Land Govt. 57-65, Minister Pres. 59-; mem. Bundestag Jan.-Sept. 57; Pres. Bundesrat 59-60; Chair. Saar Christian Democratic Union.
Am Ludwigsplatz 14, 66 Saarbrücken, German Federal Republic.
Telephone: 2-14-01.

Rodgers, Sir John (Charles), Bart., M.A., F.S.S., M.P.; British administrator and politician; b. 5 Oct. 1906; ed. St. Peter's, York, Ecole des Roches, France, and Keble Coll., Oxford.
Sub-Warden, Mary Ward Settlement, London 29; Lecturer and Admin. Asst. Hull Univ. 30; Deputy Chair. J. Walter Thompson Co. Ltd.; Chair. New English Library (Holdings) Ltd., etc.; Foreign Office 39, 44 and 45; Special Mission to Portugal Dec. 45; Ministry of Information 39-41; Dept. of Overseas Trade 41-42; Minister of Production 42-43; Gov. Admin. Staff Coll. 46-; B.B.C. Gen. Advisory Council, 46-52; M.P. 50-; Parl. Private Sec. to Sir David (now Viscount) Eccles 51-57; Parl. Sec. to Board of Trade 58-60; mem. Exec. Cttee. British Council 57-58, Tucker Cttee. on Evidence before Examining Justices 57; mem. of Council and leader Parl. Panel Inst. of Dirs. 55-58; Dir. British Film Inst. 58-59; Int. Pres. Centre Européen de Documentation et Information; Vice-Pres. INFRA (Int. Freedom Acad.) 66-68; mem. Foundation for Management Educ. 60-, Council British Inst. of Management 65-; Vice-Chair. Exec. Cttee. PEP (Political and Econ. Planning) 62-; Knight Grand Cross of Civil Merit, Spain; Conservative.
Publs. *Mary Ward Settlement: a History* 30, *Marketing Survey of the United Kingdom* (joint) 36-38, *The Old Public Schools of England* 38, *The English Woodland* 42, *Industry Looks at the New Order* (joint) 42, *English Rivers* 48, *Tobias and Raphael* 48, *York* 51, *One Nation* (joint) 51; Editor: *Poems of Thomas Gray* 53, *Change is our Ally* 55, *Automation and the Consumer* (joint) 57, *Monopolies and the Consumers Interests* (joint) 63.
The Dower House, Groombridge, Kent, England.
Telephone: Groombridge 213.

Rodgers, Richard; American composer; b. 28 June 1902; ed. Columbia Univ., and New York Inst. of Musical Art.
Produced various shows; Pres. Dramatists' Guild 43-47; mem. Authors League of America; Pres. and Producing Dir., Lincoln Center for the Performing Arts Music Theatre.
First score *Lido Lady* 26; later shows include *Pal Joey* 40, *Oklahoma* (Pulitzer Award) 43, *Carousel* 45, *Allegro* 47, *South Pacific* (Pulitzer Prize) 49, *The King and I* 51, *Me and Juliet* 53, *Pipe Dream* 55, *Cinderella* (TV) 57, *Flower Drum Song* 58, *The Sound of Music* 59, *No Strings* 63, *Do I Hear a Waltz?* 65, *Androcles and the Lion* (TV) 67; scores for films *Love Me Tonight, State Fair* and others; scores for TV series *Victory at Sea, The Valiant Years.*
c/o Rodgers and Hammerstein, 598 Madison Avenue, New York 22, N.Y., U.S.A.

Rodinò di Miglione, Marcello; Italian broadcasting official; b. 17 April 1906; ed. Univ. of Naples.
Former Dir.-Gen. Southern Italy Power Co. (S.M.E.); fmr. Treas. Nat. Asscn. of Electrical Companies; Del.-Manager Radiotelevisione Italiana (R.A.I.); Del. Man. S.I.P.R.A. (advertising agency), M.C.M. (Southern Cotton Mfg.); Pres. Telespazio; fmr. Pres. European Broadcasting Union; Cavaliere del Lavoro and other decorations.
Telespazio, Via del Babuino 51, Rome; and M.C.M., Via G. S. Felice 8, Naples, Italy.

Rodionov, Alexei Alexeyevich; Soviet diplomatist; b. 1922; ed. U.S.S.R. Finance and Economics (Correspondence) Inst.
Young Communist League and C.P. work 40-64; First Sec. Omsk City Cttee., C.P.S.U. 53-60; Sec. Omsk Regional Cttee., C.P.S.U. 60-62; Diplomatic Service 64-; Counsellor-Minister, New Delhi 64-66; Amb. to Burma 66-; Orders of Red Banner (thrice).
U.S.S.R. Embassy, Rangoon, Burma.

Rodionov, Georgi Michailovich; Soviet (Russian) diplomatist; b. 15; ed. Moscow Inst. of Economic Planning.
U.S.S.R. Ministry of Foreign Affairs 46-50; First Sec. U.S.S.R. Embassy, U.K. 50-54; Asst. Dep. Minister of Foreign Affairs, U.S.S.R. 54-55, 60-61; Counsellor, U.S.S.R. Mission, New Zealand 56-60; Dep. Minister of Foreign Affairs, R.S.F.S.R. 61-62; Ambassador to Ghana Nov. 62-Jan. 68; several decorations.
c/o Ministry of Foreign Affairs, Moscow, U.S.S.R.

Rodionov, Nikolai Nikolayevich; Soviet politician; b. 15; ed. Moscow Steel Inst.
Engineer, Magnitogorsk and Leningrad 41-48; mem. C.P.S.U. 44-; party work, Leningrad 48-54; Second Sec. Leningrad City Cttee. C.P.S.U. 54-56, First Sec. 56-60; Second Sec. Central Cttee. C.P. Kazakhstan 60-62; Dep. Chair. Council of National Economy, Leningrad Econ. Region 62-65; First Sec. Chelyabinsk Regional Cttee. of the C.P.S.U. 65-; Candidate mem. Central Cttee. C.P.S.U. 61-66, mem. 66-; Deputy to U.S.S.R. Supreme Soviet.
Chelyabinsk Regional Cttee. of C.P.S.U., Chelyabinsk, U.S.S.R.

Rodopoulos, Constantine, LL.D.; Greek politician; b. 96; ed. Univs. of Athens, Paris and Vienna.
Secretary-General, Ministry of Nat. Economy 24-27; mem. of Chamber of Deps. 32-; Under-Sec. of State for War 34-35; Minister/Gov.-Gen. of N. Greece 46-47; Minister of War 48-49, of Public Health 49-50, of Press and Information 50-53, of Public Works April 67; Pres. Chamber of Deputies 53-65; Pres. Hellenic Group, Interparliamentary Union; mem. NATO Parliamentarians' Conf.; Repr. Consultative Assembly, Council of Europe; Pres. Hellenic Citizens' Comm. on NATO; numerous Greek and foreign decorations; Nat. Radical Union.
17 Vyron Street, Psychico, Athens, Greece.

Rodríguez, Carlos Rafael; Cuban journalist, writer and politician.
Member Communist Party 32-, Exec. Cttee. 40-; Dir. Havana Univ. Econ. School; Editor *Hoy* 59-62; Pres. Nat. Land Reform Inst. 62-65.
c/o National Land Reform Institute, Havana, Cuba.

Rodríguez Monegal, Emir; Uruguayan writer; b. 28 July 1921; ed. Lycée Français, Montevideo, and Univ. of Montevideo.
Teacher of general literature, secondary schools,

Montevideo 45-52; Prof. of English Literature, Instituto de Profesores, Montevideo 52-62; Visiting Prof. of Latin American Literature, El Colegio de México, Mexico 64; Visiting Prof. Harvard Univ. 65; Editor *Mundo Nuevo* (literary magazine), Paris 65-.
Publs. *El juicio de los parricidas* 56, *Obras completas de José Enrique Rodó* (Editor) 57, *Las raíces de Horacio Quiroga* 60, *Literatura uruguaya del medio siglo* 66, *El viajero inmóvil: Introducción a Pablo Neruda* 66.
Mundo Nuevo, 97 rue Saint Lazare, Paris 9e, France.

Rodríguez Ramos, Manuel, A.B., LL.B., M.C.L.; American lawyer and law professor; b. 08; ed. Univ. of Puerto Rico and Tulane Univ. of Louisiana.
Private law practice 32-36; Asst. Attorney-Gen. of Puerto Rico 36-44; law lecturer (*ad honorem*) Coll. of Law, Univ. of Puerto Rico; Visiting Prof. Coll. of Law, Tulane Univ. 46-47; Visiting Prof. Luxembourg Univ.; Dean, Faculty of Law, Univ. of Puerto Rico 44-60, Dean Emer. 61-; Dir. Legal Aid Soc. of Puerto Rico; fmr. Gov. Puerto Rico Rotary Int.; Chief Editor *Revista Jurídica de la Universidad de Puerto Rico* 32, and Faculty Adviser 44-; Order of the Coif.
Publs. *Ley Municipal* 40, *Interaction of Civil Law and Anglo-American Law in Puerto Rico* 48, *In Rem Actions in Puerto Rico* 55, *Casos y Notas de Derechos Reales* 56 (2nd edn. 63), *A Glimpse at Latin-American Law.*
P.O. Box 1175, Hato Rey, Puerto Rico 00919.

Rodzinski, Witold, PH.D.; Polish diplomatist and historian; b. 18; ed. Columbia Univ., U.S.A. and Warsaw Inst. of Social Sciences.
Social Affairs Dept., U.N. Secretariat 46-48; Counsellor, Press and Information Dept., Polish Ministry of Foreign Affairs 48-49; Research Fellow, Warsaw Inst. of Social Sciences 50-56; Prof. of World History, Warsaw Teachers' Training Coll. 51-54; Lecturer, Polish Acad. Inst. of Oriental Studies 54-56; Counsellor, Polish Embassy, Peking 56-57; Head of Afro-Asian Dept., Ministry of Foreign Affairs and Lecturer in World History, Univ. of Warsaw 58-60, 64-66; Amb. to U.K. 60-64, to People's Republic of China 66-.
Polish Embassy, Peking, People's Republic of China.

Roem, Mohammad; Indonesian politician; b. 08; ed. Law School, Djakarta.
Solicitor in private practice, Djakarta 39-45; fmr. leader of Islamic Youth Movement; Indonesian Minister of the Interior 46-48; Del. to Round Table Conf. with Netherlands Govt. 49; first High Commr. of Indonesia to the Netherlands 50; Minister of Foreign Affairs 50-51, of Home Affairs 52-53; First Vice-Premier 56-57; mem. Exec. Cttee. Masjumi Party 57-59, 3rd Deputy Chair. 59; Pres. Islamic Univ., Medan; detained Jan. 62-.
c/o Djalan Tjhik Ditiro 58, Djakarta, Indonesia.

Roemer, Karl Josef; German lawyer; b. 30 Dec. 1899; ed. Cologne, Munich, Freiburg i. B. and Bonn Univs.
Worked for a private bank 21-24, later Assessor and Judge, Cologne; Chief of External Relations Dept., official banking inst. in Berlin 32-48; Advocate, Berlin 36-46; Advocate, Courts of First Instance and Appeal, Saarbrücken 47-53; attached to Govt. Services for study of problems of economic re-organisation, mem. Sonderstelle Geld und Kredit (monetary reform), Counsellor to Govt. on int. law and foreign jurisdiction 47-53, on judicial missions abroad for Fed. Govt. 50-52; Advocate Gen. E.C.S.C. Court 52-58, Court of the European Communities 58-.
26 rue Frantz Clément, Luxembourg.
Telephone: Luxembourg 29793.

Roemers, D., D.ECON.; Netherlands politician; b. 1915; ed. Amsterdam Univ.
Formerly in Price-Control Dept. of State Textile Office; Economic Adviser Industrial Tobacco Group 45-47; Dir. Scientific Research Bureau, Netherlands Fed. of Trade Unions (N.V.V.) 47-52, Sec. 52-56, Vice-

Pres. 56-59, Pres. 59-65; mem. Netherlands Social Econ. Council 50-59, Vice-Pres. 59-65; M.P. 52-67; Burgomaster of Vlissingen (Flushing) 67-; Labour.
Sint Maartenlaan 13, Vlissingen, Netherlands.

Rogers, Benjamin, B.A., M.SC.(ECON); Canadian diplomatist; b. 3 Aug. 1911; ed. Dalhousie Univ., and Univ. of London.
With Royal Inst. of Int. Affairs, London 35-36; Acting Nat. Sec. Canadian Inst. of Int. Affairs 37-38; entered Dept. of External Affairs 38; served Australia 39-43, U.S.A. 43-44, Brazil 44-48, Dept. of External Affairs 48-50; Chargé d'Affaires, Prague 50-52; Dept. of External Affairs 52-55; Ambassador to Peru 55-58, Ambassador to Turkey 58-60; Dep. High Commr. to U.K. 60-64; Ambassador to Spain and Morocco 64-.
Publ. *Canada Looks Ahead* (with R. A. MacKay) 38.
The Canadian Embassy, Apartado 587, Madrid; Residence: Zurbano 36, Madrid, Spain.
Telephone: 247-54-00 (Office); 223-48-21 (Residence).

Rogers, (N.) Ernesto, DR. ARCH.; Italian architect; b. 16 March 1909; ed. School of Architecture, Milan.
Prof. of Theory of Architecture at Milan Polytechnic; Private practice with others in Town Planning, Architecture, Interior Decoration and Industrial Design, Milan; works include houses, factories, pavilions, health resort for children at Legnano 39; Post Office, Rome 39; monument to the dead in German concentration camps at Milan Cemetery 46; Olivetti Showroom, Fifth Ave., N.Y.; Italian Merchant Navy Pavilion at Int. Exhibition, Paris 37, U.S. Pavilion at Triennale 51; restoration of Sforza Castle Museums 56; Torre Velasca, Milan; Canadian Pavilion, Venice Biennale; Italian Pavilion (in collaboration), Brussels Int. Exhibition 58; town planning studies (in collaboration): Pavia 33, Milan 45, regional plan for Valle d'Aosta 36-37, Elba Island 40; Consultant for Town Planning, Buenos Aires 48; Adviser for Town Planning, Lima 48; Visiting Prof. Lausanne Univ. 44-45, Geneva Univ. 45, Tucuman Univ. 48, Architectural Asscn. School, London 49; Prof. Italian Culture Univ. of Calif. 59; lecturer other univs. and cultural centres, Europe, America and Asia; mem. Council CIAM (Congrès int. d'Architecture Moderne); mem. Cttee. of Five Architects, UNESCO; Accademia di S. Luca, Rome, World Acad. of Art and Science; Editor *Domus* magazine 46-47, *Casabella-Continuita* magazine 54-.
Publs. *Stile* (with Banfi, Belgiojoso, Peressutti) 36; in collaboration: *Piano regionale della Valle d'Aosta* 43, *Piano A.R.* 45, *The Heart of the City* 52, *Auguste Perret* 55, *Esperienza dell'Architettura* 58, *Utopia della Realtà* 65 (with others).
Studio Architetti B.B.P.R., Via dei Chiostri 2, Milan, Italy.

Rogers, Lindsay, B.A., PH.D., LL.D.; American political scientist; b. 23 May 1891; ed. Baltimore City Coll., Univ. of Maryland, and Johns Hopkins Univ.
Teacher Baltimore City Coll. 10-15; admitted to Maryland Bar 15 and to U.S. Supreme Court 50; Asst. Prof. of Political Science Univ. of Virginia 15-18, and Associate Prof. 18-21; Lecturer on Govt. Harvard 20-21; Lecturer on Public Law, Columbia Univ. 20-21, Associate Prof. of Govt. 21-27; Prof. of Public Law 27-29 and Burgess Prof. 29-59; Assoc. Editor *American Political Science Review* 23-28 and of *Political Science Quarterly* 21-59; Asst. Dir. I.L.O. 42-47; Consultant U.S. Senate Cttee. on Foreign Relations 52-53 and 56-66.
Publs. *The Postal Power of Congress* 16, *America's Case Against Germany* 17, *The American Senate* 26, *Crisis Government* 34, *The Pollsters* 49, *Expectations of Politics* 53.
175 Riverside Drive, New York City, N.Y., U.S.A.

Rogers, William P., LL.B.; American lawyer; b. 23 June 1913; ed. Canton High School, New York, Colgate Univ., and Cornell Univ. Law School.

Joined law firm of Cadwalader, Wickersham and Taft, New York 37; Asst. District Attorney, New York County 38-42, 46-47; officer in U.S. Navy 42-46; Chief Counsel, Senate War Investigating Cttee. 47-49, Senate Permanent Investigating Cttee. 49-50; mem. law firm of Dwight, Royall, Harris, Koegel and Caskey 50-52; Deputy Attorney Gen. of the U.S. 53-57, Attorney Gen. 57-61; U.S. Rep., Gen. Assembly UN 65; U.S. Rep., UN *Ad Hoc* Cttee. on S.W. Africa 67; mem. Pres. Comm. on Law Enforcement and Admin. of Justice 65-67; with Royall, Koegel and Rogers 61-. 200 Park Avenue, New York 17, N.Y., U.S.A.

Rohe, Ludwig Mies van der (*see* Mies van der Rohe, Ludwig).

Rohrer, Herbert, DR.RER.POL.; German businessman; b. 3 June 1901; ed. Univs. of Munich and Erlangen. Mem. of the Board of Execs. Schering A.G., Berlin 34-39; Pres. Osram G.m.b.H. 39-45; Pres. Feldmühle A.G. 57-63, mem. of the Board 64-, Vice-Chair. 65-; Vice-Chair. Dynamit Nobel A.G., Troisdorf/Köln, Krauss-Maffei A.G., Munich 67-, Board of Trustees of Int. Foundation HUMANUM, Lugano; mem. Board Rothesay Paper Corpn., St. John, Intercontinental Pulp Co. Ltd., Vancouver. 81 Garmisch-Partenkirchen, Gsteig 46, German Federal Republic. Telephone: 3417.

Roijen, J. H. van, PH.D.; Netherlands diplomatist; b. 10 April 1905; ed. Univ. of Utrecht. Attaché Netherlands Legation in Washington 30-33; mem. Netherlands Foreign Office 33; First Sec. at Tokyo 36; head Political Div. in Netherlands Foreign Office 39; imprisoned three times for activities in Resistance Movement 40-44; Asst. del. U.N. Gen. Assembly, San Francisco, London, New York 45-48, U.N. Econ. and Soc. Council 47; Minister without Portfolio June 45-46; Minister of Foreign Affairs Mar.-June 46; Ambassador to Canada Mar. 47-50, to U.S.A. Sept. 50-64, to U.K. and Iceland Mar. 64-; Commdr. Order of Netherlands Lion, Order of British Empire, Order of Sacred Treasure (Japan); Grand Cross, Order of Oak Crown (Luxembourg). Netherlands Embassy, 38 Hyde Park Gate, London, S.W.7, England. Telephone: 01-584-5040.

Roiseland, Bent; Norwegian farmer and politician; b. 11 Oct. 1902. Member of the Storting (Parl.) 45-; Pres. of the Lagting (Upper House) 54-58, 61-62, 65-; mem. Nordic Council; Chair. of Norges Venstrelag (Liberal Party) 52-64; Chair. of the Liberal group in the Storting; mem. Board of Auditors for State Accounts. Mandal, Norway.

Rokossovsky, Marshal Konstantin Konstantinovich, K.C.B.; Soviet army officer; b. in Poland 96; ed. Military Acad., Frunze. Major Tzarist Army, First World War; joined Red Army 17; Major-Gen. 40, Lt.-Gen. 41, Col.-Gen. Jan. 43, Gen. of Army May 43; served Central Front Aug.-Sept. 41, Mozhaisk Sector Oct. 41; Commander-in-Chief Don Front Nov. 42-Jan. 43, led Lower Don offensive and encirclement operations Stalingrad area; Commdr. Central Front and Byelorussian Front Troops Oct. 43; awarded Orders of Suvorov and Kutuzov 43, Order of Lenin (seven times), Virtuti Militari (first class), Hero of Soviet Union (twice), Order of Victory, Red Banner (six times), Legion of Merit, Order of Lenin and other honours; Marshal of Poland, Defence Minister and Chief of Polish Armed Forces Nov. 49-56, Deputy Prime Minister 52-56; Deputy Minister of Defence, U.S.S.R. 56-62; Chief Inspector, Ministry of Defence 57-62; General Inspector, Ministry of Defence 62-;

Deputy to U.S.S.R. Supreme Soviet; Cand. mem. C.P.S.U. Central Cttee. 61-. Ministry of Defence, 34 Maurice Thorez Embankment, Moscow, U.S.S.R.

Roll, Sir Eric, K.C.M.G., C.B., PH.D., B.COM.; British banker and former civil servant; b. 1 Dec. 1907; ed. Univ. of Birmingham. Assistant Lecturer, Univ. Coll., Hull 30, Prof. of Econs. and Commerce 35-39; Special Fellow, Rockefeller Foundation 39-41; Dep. mem., Combined Food Bd. 41-46; Asst. Sec. Ministry of Food 46-47, The Treasury 47, Under-Sec. 48-53; Chair. Econ. Cttee., OEEC 48-53; Minister, U.K. Del. to NATO 52-53; Under-Sec. Ministry of Agriculture, Fisheries and Food 53-57; Exec. Dir. Int. Sugar Council 57-59; Dep. Sec. Ministry of Agriculture, Fisheries and Food 60-62; Dep. Leader, U.K. Del. to EEC Brussels Conf. 62-63; Econ. Minister and Head of U.K. Treasury Del., Washington 63-65; Exec. Dir. for U.K., Int. Monetary Fund (I.M.F.), Perm. Under-Sec. of State, Dept. of Econ. Affairs 64-66; Exec. Dir. S. G. Warburg & Co. Ltd.; Dir. Bank of London and South America, Times Newspapers Ltd., Rootes Motors Ltd., Dominion, Lincoln Insurance Co. Ltd., Bunzl Pulp & Paper Ltd., Bank of England; Chair. Book Devt. Council. Publs. *An Early Experiment in Industrial Organization* 30, *Spotlight on Germany* 33, *About Money* 34, *Elements of Economic Theory* 35, *Organized Labour* (co-author) 38, *The British Commonwealth at War* (co-author) 43, *A History of Economic Thought* 54, *The Combined Food Board* 57, *The World after Keynes* 68. D2 Albany, Piccadilly, London, W.1, England. Telephone: 01-734-1997.

Roll, Lyle Charles; American business executive; b. 13 Sept. 1907; ed. Illinois Wesleyan Univ. Kellogg Co. 27-, Sales Manager, Kellogg Co. of Canada 47-49, Asst. to Pres. Kellogg Co. 49-52, Vice-Pres. 52, Exec. Vice-Pres. 53-57, Pres. Gen. Manager 57-, now also Chair.; Dir. Consumers Power Co., Grocery Mfrs. of America, Smucker Co.; Vice-Chair. and Trustee of the Nutrition Foundation; Trustee, W. K. Kellogg Foundation. Kellogg Company, Battle Creek, Michigan, U.S.A.

Rollefson, Ragnar, M.A., PH.D.; American physicist; b. 23 Aug. 1906; ed. Univ. of Wisconsin. Instructor in Physics, Univ. of Wisconsin 30-36, Asst. Prof. 36-42, Assoc. Prof. 42-46, Prof. 46-, Chair. Physics Dept. 47-51, 52-56, 57-61; with Radar Laboratory, Mass. Inst. of Technology (M.I.T.) 42-45; Chief Scientist, Naval Research Laboratory Field Station 46, Dept. of Army 56-57; Act. Dir. Univ. Research Asscn. Devt. Laboratory 57-60; Dir. Int. Scientific Affairs Dept., State Dept. 62-64. Department of Physics, University of Wisconsin, Madison, Wis.; Home: 4206 Wanetah Trail, Madison, Wis., U.S.A. Telephone: 233-7892.

Rolshoven, Hubertus, DR. ING.; German mining executive; b. 15 Feb. 1913; ed. Technische Hochschule, Berlin. Engineer, Bochum 45-46; Works Manager, Consolidation Colliery, Gelsenkirchen 47-53; Manager, Mining Works, Essen 53-56; Managing Dir., Management Board, Hansa Bergbau, A.G. Dortmund 56-57; Chair. of Management Board Saarbergwerke A.G., Saarbrücken 57-; Vice-Pres. Saar-Lorraine Coal Union, Saarbrücken; Dir. other mining and business firms. Publs. *Beobachtungen über die Geologie des Kunnitales und des oberen Ramistales im Cercergebirge* 39, *Der Steinkohlenbergbau an der Saar* 60. Haus Blauberg, Saargemünder Strasse 226a, Saarbrücken-St. Arnual, German Federal Republic.

Rolz-Bennett, José; Guatemalan United Nations official; b. 9 Aug. 1918; ed. Univ. of San Carlos, Guatemala.
Dean of Faculty of Humanities and Prof. Faculty of Law, Univ. of San Carlos, Guatemala 45-55; Pres. of Board of Dirs. Guatemalan Social Security Inst. 46-48; mem. Guatemalan Del. to UN Gen. Assembly 55-57; Perm. Rep. of Guatemala to UN 58; Acting Dir. Trusteeship Div., UN Secretariat 58-62; Chief UN Rep. in Katanga Jan.-June 62; Deputy Chief of Cabinet, UN Secretariat June 62-64; Personal Rep. of UN Sec.-Gen. and temporary Administrator in West New Guinea 62; Personal Rep. of UN Sec.-Gen. for Cyprus discussions 64; Under-Sec. for Special Political Affairs, UN Secretariat 65-; in charge of Office of Public Information June 65-.
United Nations Secretariat, New York City, N.Y.; 1355 Roosevelt Avenue, Pelham Manor, New York, N.Y., U.S.A.

Romains, Jules; French writer; b. 26 Aug. 1885.
Mem. French Acad.; Grand Officier de la Légion d'Honneur; Int. Pres. P.E.N. 36-41; went to U.S.A. after capitulation of France 40; returned to France 45.
Publs. Poems: *La Vie unanime* 08, *Odes et prières* 13, *Europe* 16, *Chants des dix années* 23, *L'Homme Blanc* 37, and other vols.; novels: *Mort de quelqu'un* 11, *Les Copains* 13, *Lucienne* 22, *Le Dieu des corps* 28, *Quand le navire* 29, *Les Hommes de Bonne Volonté: Le 6 octobre, Crime de Quinette, Les amours enfantines, Eros de Paris, Les Superbes, Les Humbles, Recherche d'une Église, Province, Montée des Périls, Les Pouvoirs, Recours à l'Abîme, Les Créateurs, Mission à Rome, Le Drapeau noir, Prélude à Verdun, Verdun, Vorge contre Quinette, La Douceur de la Vie, Cette grande Lueur à l'Est, Le Monde est ton aventure, Journées dans la Montagne, Les Travaux et les Joies, Naissance de la Bande, Comparutions, Le Tapis magique, Françoise, Le 7 octobre, 1932-1946, Salsette découvre l'Amérique* 42, *Bertrand de Ganges* 47, *Le Moulin et l'Hospice* 49, *Violation de Frontières* 51, *Saints de notre calendrier* 52, *Examen de Conscience des Français* 54, *Passagers de cette Planète* 55, *Le Fils de Jerphanion* 56, *Une Femme Singulière* 57, *Le Besoin de voir clair* 58, *Situation de la Terre* 58, *Les Mémoires de Mme. Chauverel* 59-60, *Pour Raison Garder* 60, 63, 67, *Un Grand Honnête Homme* 61, *As it is on Earth* 62, *Portraits d'Inconnus* 62, *Napoléon par lui-même* 63, *Ai-je fait ce que j'ai voulu?* 64, *Lettres à un ami* 64, 65; plays: *Cromedeyre le Vieil* 29, *M. le Trouhadec* 23, *Knock* 23, *Le Dictateur* 26, *Jean le Maufranc* 27, *Donogoo* 30, *Musse* 30, *Boen* 31, *Grace encore pour la Terre* 40, etc.; numerous essays and short stories.
6 rue de Solférino, Paris 7e, France.

Román y Vega, Albino, B.SC., B.A., B.PHIL.; Nicaraguan lawyer and international official; b. 8 March 1922; ed. Colegio Centroamérica Granada, Nicaragua and City Coll., New York.
Secretary, Tribunal, León 41, Judge in Civil Law, Leon 42; Sec. Honorable Municipal Corpn., León 44; Deputy Dir. Nat. Inst.; Prof. of Civil and Comparative Law, Nat. Univ. of Nicaragua 47-48, mem. Examining Cttee. of Faculty of Law and Notarial Law, mem. of the Faculty 47-48; Lawyer and Notary, Nat. Bank of Nicaragua 47-57; Legal Assessor and Dir. of Legal Dept., Gen. Secr., Org. of Central American States (ODECA) 57-64, Sec.-Gen. ODECA Feb. 64-; Perm. Sec. Central American Comm. of Jurists 57-64; Gran Cruz, Rubén Darío and Placa de Plata (Nicaragua), Ordén del Sol (Peru), Aguila Azteca (Mexico).
Organization of Central American States—ODECA, San Salvador; and 83 Avenida Norte 635, San Salvador, El Salvador.

Romanov, Alexandr Iosifovich; Soviet diplomatist; b. 18 Oct. 1912; ed. Higher Engineering and education in the Humanities.

Former Engineer; Foreign Service 46-, Ministry of Foreign Affairs, and Minister-Counsellor, London 60-64; Amb. to Nigeria 64-.
U.S.S.R. Embassy, Lagos; and 15 Alexander Avenue, Ivaji, Lagos, Nigeria.
Telephone: 23730.

Romanov, Alexei Vladimirovich; Soviet journalist and politician; b. 1908; ed. Higher Literary Courses and Higher Party School.
Member C.P.S.U. 39-; successively journalist, Sec. *Pravda*, Editor *Gorkovskaya Kommuna*, and *Sovietskaya Byelorussia* 29-55; Dep. Chief Editor *For A Lasting Peace, For a People's Democracy* 53-55; on staff of Central Cttee. C.P.S.U. 55-61; mem. Bureau Central Cttee. of R.S.F.S.R. 61-62; Chair. State Cttee. on Cinematography 63-; Cand. mem. Central Cttee. C.P.S.U. 61-; Deputy to U.S.S.R. Supreme Soviet.
State Committee of U.S.S.R. Council of Ministers for Cinematography, 7 Maly Gnezdnikovsky pereulok, Moscow, U.S.S.R.

Romanov, Grigory Vassilyevich; Soviet politician; b. 1923; ed. Leningrad Shipbuilding Inst.
Member 44-; Soviet Army service 41-45; Party worker 46-57; Sec. Kirovsky District Cttee. of C.P., Leningrad; Sec. Leningrad Regional Cttee. of C.P. 57-63, Second Sec. 63-; mem. Central Cttee. C.P.S.U. 66; Deputy to U.S.S.R. Supreme Soviet.
Leningrad Regional Committee of Communist Party, Leningrad, U.S.S.R.

Romanov, Pavel Konstantinovich; Soviet publishing official; b. 1913; ed. Leningrad Inst. of Transport Engineering, and Higher Party School, Moscow.
With Soviet Army 41-45; Staff of C.P.S.U. Central Cttee. 45-57; fmr. Head of *Glavlit* (censorship org.) until 63; Chair. State Cttee. on the Press and Publishing Aug. 63-65, First Deputy Chair. 65-.
State Committee on the Press and Publishing, 26 Petrovka, Moscow, U.S.S.R.

Romanovsky, Sergei Kalistratovich; Soviet politician; b. 1923.
Deputy Chair. U.S.S.R. Cttee. for Youth Orgs. 48-57; Secretary of *Komsomol* (Young Communist League) 57-59; Dep. Minister of Culture, U.S.S.R. 59-60; Dep. Chair. Cttee. for Cultural Relations with Foreign Countries 60-62, Chair. 62-Dec. 67; Chair. U.S.S.R. Comm. for UNESCO 62-68; Amb. to Norway 68-; Deputy to U.S.S.R. Supreme Soviet.
U.S.S.R. Embassy, Oslo, Norway.

Romanówna, Janina; Polish actress and theatrical director; b. 06; ed. Lwów.
First stage appearance, Teatr Narodowy, Warsaw 24; since then has played and directed at the Boguslawski and Polski Theatres; Prof., Higher Theatre School; major roles include Eliza Doolittle (Shaw's *Pygmalion*), The Countess (Beaumarchais' *The Marriage of Figaro*), title role in Giraudoux' *La Folle de Chaillot*.
Teatr Polski, Warsaw, Poland.

Romeo Goria, Jesús; Spanish politician; b. 16.
Former executive, Peñarroya steel works and mining co.; Minister of Labour 62-; Falangist.
Ministry of Labour, Madrid, Spain.

Romer, Alfred Sherwood, A.B., PH.D.; American university professor and museum director; b. 28 Dec. 1894; ed. Amherst Coll., and Columbia Univ.
Instructor Anatomy, N.Y. Univ. 21-23; Assoc. Prof. Vertebrate Paleontology, Univ. of Chicago 23-31, Prof. 31-34; Prof. Zoology, Harvard Univ. 34-65, Alexander Agassiz Prof. 47-65, Prof. Emer. 65-; Dir. Museum of Comparative Zoology, Harvard Univ. 46-61; Curator of Vertebrate Paleontology 34-65; Pres. 16th Int. Congress of Zoology (Washington 63); Pres. American Asscn. for Advancement of Science 65-66, Chair. of Board 67-; mem. Nat. Acad. Sciences U.S.A., American Philo-

sophical Soc. and other U.S. and foreign socs.; medals include Elliot and Thompson Medals (Nat. Acad. of Sciences), Penrose Medal (Geological Soc. America), Hayden Medal (Philadelphia Acad. Nat. Sciences), Paleontological Soc. Medal; Hon. S.D. (Harvard, Amherst, Dartmouth, Buffalo, Lehigh).
Publs. *Man and the Vertebrates* 33, *Vertebrate Paleontology* 33, *Vertebrate Body* 49, *Osteology of Reptiles* 56, *The Vertebrate Story* 59, *Notes and Comments on Vertebrate Paleontology* 68, *The Procession of Life* 68.
Home: 38 Avon Street, Cambridge, Mass. 02138, U.S.A. Telephone: 617-547-3045.

Romero, José E., A.B., LL.B.; Philippine diplomatist and attorney-at-law; b. 97; ed. Univ. of the Philippines. Elected mem. of Provincial Board of Oriental Negros 25-31; House of Reps. and Nat. Assembly 31-46; Chair. of Cttee. on Public Instruction, House of Reps., and *ex-officio* mem. Board of Regents, Univ. of the Philippines 34-36; elected to Constitutional Convention and Chair. of Cttee. on Rules and Floor Leader 34-35; Floor Leader of Nat. Assembly 36-38; Chair. Cttee. on Economic Readjustment 38-41; Chair. Cttee. on Foreign Relations and of Joint Congressional Cttee. on Rehabilitation and Reconstruction 45-46; elected to Philippine Senate 46; Minister to Great Britain and concurrently to Norway, Sweden and Denmark 49-54; Rep. Philippines Sugar Asscn., Washington, D.C. 54-57; Sec.-Treas. Philippine Sugar Asscn. 57-59; Sec. of Educ. 59-61; Sec.-Treas. Philippine Sugar Asscn. 61-; mem. American Soc. of Int. Law; Patron Int. Bar Asscn.
15 Galaxy Street, Bel-Air III, Makati, Rizal, Philippines.

Romero, José Luis; Argentine historian; b. 24 March 1909; ed. Univ. de la Plata, Argentina.
Former Prof. of History, Univs. of La Plata, Buenos Aires and Montevideo; Founder-Dir. of review *Imago Mundi*; Founder and Dir. Centre for Study of Social History, Univ. of Buenos Aires until 65; Hon. Prof. Univs. of Buenos Aires and Montevideo 65-, Dir. of Seminars of Urban Studies; Rector of Univ. of Buenos Aires 55-56, Dean of Faculty of Philosophy and Letters 62-65; Visiting Lecturer, Univs. of Chile, San Marcos de Lima, Toulouse, Caen, Poitiers, Ecole des Hautes Etudes (Paris), and Columbia Univ., New York; fmr. Pres. Argentine Soc. of Writers; fmr. mem. Exec. Cttee. Socialist Party; Dr. h.c. Univ. of Montevideo; Officier des Palmes Académiques (France).
Publs. *La Cultura occidental, La historia y la vida, Sobre la biografía y la historia, La Edad Media, Ensayos sobre la burguesía, Maquiavelo historiador, Las ideas políticas en Argentina, Argentina imágenes y perspectivas, El desarrollo de las ideas en la sociedad argentina del siglo XX, La revolución burguesa en el mundo feudal.*
Cerreti 928, Adrogué (B.A.), Argentina.

Romm, Mikhail Ilyich; Soviet film director; b. 01; ed. Faculty of Sculpture, State Higher Art-Technical Inst. Scenario writer 29-30, film producer 31-; Artistic Dir. Theatrical Studio of Film Actors 54-; Prof., All-Union State Inst. of Cinematography 57-; Managing Creative Dir. Mosfilm Studio; State prizewinner; awarded Order of Lenin; People's Artist of the U.S.S.R.
Principal films: (silent) *Dumpling* (based on the short story *Boule de Suif* by De Maupassant and commended at the Int. Film Festival in Venice) 34; *13* (medal at world Exhbn. in Paris) 36, *Lenin in October, Lenin in 1918* 37-39, *Dream* 41, *No. 217* (commended at the Int. Film Festival in Cannes) 45, *Secret Mission* 50, *Admiral Ushakov, Ships Storm the Bastions* 53, *Murder in Dante Street* 56, *Nine Days of One Year* (first prize at festival at Karlovy Vari) 61, *Common Fascism* (first prize at Leipzig Festival) 65.
Mosfilm Studio, 1 Mosfilmovskaya ulitsa, Moscow, U.S.S.R.

Romnes, Haakon Ingolf, B.S.; American executive; b. 2 March 1907; ed. Univ. of Wisconsin.
Engineer with Bell Telephone Laboratories, New York 28-35, American Telephone and Telegraph Co. 35-50, Gen. Man. (Long Lines Dept.) 50-52, Chief Engineer 52-55, Vice-Pres. 55-59; Pres. Western Electric Company 59-63; Vice-Chair. of the Board, American Telephone and Telegraph Co. 64-Jan. 65, Pres. Jan. 65-Feb. 67, Chair. of the Board Feb. 67-; Hon. LL.D. (Wisconsin).
195 Broadway, New York City, N.Y. 10007, U.S.A. Telephone: 212-393-1000.

Romney, George Wilcken; American businessman and politician; b. 8 July 1907; ed. Latter-Day Saints Univ., and Univ. of Utah.
Mormon missionary in U.K. 27-29; Tariff Specialist to U.S. Senator David I. Walsh 29; joined Aluminium Co. of America 29, later its Rep. and also of Aluminium Wares Asscn., Washington, D.C.; Detroit Man. Automobile Manufacturers' Asscn. 39, Gen. Man. 42-48; Man. Dir. Automotive Council for War Production 41, also connected with Automotive Council for Air Defense; U.S. Employer Del. to ILO Metal Trades Industries Confs. Toledo (Ohio), Stockholm and Geneva 46-49; Asst. to Pres. Nash-Kelvinator Corpn. 48-50, Vice-Pres. 50-54, Exec. Vice-Pres. and Dir. 54; Pres. and Chair. American Motors Corpn. (successor co. to Nash-Kelvinator Corpn.) 54-62; Gov. of Michigan 63-; fmr. Chair. Redisco Inc.; Dir. Redisco of Canada Ltd., Kelvinator Ltd. (Great Britain), Kelvinator of Canada Ltd., American Motors of Canada Ltd., Douglas Aircraft Corpn.; numerous awards include Vermilye Medal (Franklin Inst. of Philadelphia) 59; Pres. Detroit Stake, Church of Jesus Christ of Latter Day Saints (Mormon); Hon. LL.D. Wayne State Univ. and Brigham Young Univ.; Industry's "Man of the Year", Associated Press 58, 59, 60; Republican.
State Capitol, Lansing, Michigan, U.S.A. Telephone: 517-373-3400.

Rompe, Robert, DR.PHIL.; German physicist; b. 10 Sept. 1905; ed. Technical Univ., Berlin-Charlottenburg. On staff of Inst. Buch 45; Prof. of Physics and Dir. II Physical Inst. of Humboldt Univ., Berlin 46-; mem. Deutsche Akad. der Wissenschaften and Dir. of its Inst. für Strahlungsquellen 49-; mem. Exec. Cttee. Forschungsgemeinschaft der naturwissenschaftlichen, technischen und medizinischen Institut der Deutsche Akad. der Wissenschaften; mem. Research Council of DDR; Deputy Pres. Council for Peaceful Use of Atomic Energy; Foreign mem. Czechoslovak Acad. of Sciences; Nat. Prize 51; Vaterländischer Verdienstorden (silver); Euler Medal of U.S.S.R. Acad. of Sciences 57.
Ekhoffstrasse 27, Berlin-Köpenick, Germany.

Romulo, Carlos; Philippine writer, educator and diplomatist; b. 14 Jan. 1899; ed. Univ. of the Philippines and Columbia Univ.
Associate Prof. of English, Univ. of the Philippines 26-30, mem. Board of Regents 31-41; Editor-in-Chief TVT Publications 31, Publisher DMHM Newspapers 37-41; Staff of Gen. MacArthur and Sec. of Information and Public Relations, Philippine War Cabinet in U.S.A. 43-44, Brigadier Gen. 44; Acting-Sec. of Public Instruction 44-45, Chief Del. to UN 45-55, Pres. 49-50, Security Council 57; Sec. of Foreign Affairs 50-52; Ambassador to the U.S.A. 52-53, 55-62, Special Envoy 54-55, concurrently Minister to Cuba 59; Pres. Univ. of the Philippines 62-, Philippine Acad. of Sciences and Humanities; Presidential Adviser on Foreign Affairs; Sec. Dept. of Educ. 66-; numerous decorations, honours, hon. degrees and awards.
Publs. *I saw the Fall of the Philippines* 42, *Mother America* 43, *My Brother Americans* 45, *Crusade in Asia* 55, *The Meaning of Bandung* 56, *The Magsaysay Story* 56, *Friend to Friend* 58, *I Walked with Heroes*

(An Autobiography) 61, *Contemporary Nationalism and World Order* 64, *Mission to Asia* 64, *Identity and Change* 65, *Evasions and Response* 66.
Quezon Hall, University of the Philippines, Diliman, Quezon City; and 74 McKinley Road, Forbes Park, Makati, Rizal, Philippines.

Ronchi, Vasco; Italian professor of physics; b. 19 Dec. 1897; ed. Univs. of Pisa and Florence and Scuola Normale Superiore, Pisa.
Army service 15-19; Reader, Inst. of Physics, Florence Univ. 20-27; Founder-Dir. Istituto Nazionale di Ottica di Firenze-Arcetri 27-; Pres. of Council, Int. Union of History and Philosophy of Science of ICSU 57-; Pres. Italian Ophthalmological Asscn. 39-, Asscn. of Astronautical Sciences 56-, Italian Group of Scientific History, Giorgio Ronchi Foundation 45-, Industrial School Benvenuto Cellini 43-; mem. of numerous cttees. of Consiglio Nazionale delle Ricerche and int. comms.; mem. numerous Nat. and Int. Acads.; Fellow, Optical Soc. of America; numerous medals.
Major work: Inventor of Ronchi test for testing interference in optical instruments.
Publs. *Lezioni di Ottica Ondulatoria, Storia della luce, Optics, the Science of Vision, Critica dei fondamenti dell'acustica e dell' ottica, Sul modo di sperimentare, Galileo e il suo cannocchiale.*
Largo E. Fermi 1, Florence, Italy.
Telephone: 22-11-63.

Rønne, Torben; Danish diplomatist; b. 14 April 1919; ed. Copenhagen Univ.
Foreign Service 45-; Attaché Paris 47-49; Ministry of Foreign Affairs 49-54; Private Sec. Minister of Foreign Affairs 50-53; First Sec. Rome 54-57; Chief Sec. Foreign Policy Cttee. in Folketing 58-59; Head, NATO Dept., Ministry of Foreign Affairs 59-62; Ambassador to Norway 62-65, to the U.S.A. 65-; numerous decorations.
Danish Embassy, 3200 Whitehaven Street, N.W., Washington 8, D.C., U.S.A.

Rood, Johannes (Jon) Joseph Van, PH.D., M.D.; Netherlands immunologist; b. 7 April 1926; ed. Univ. of Leiden.
Worked in bloodbanking 52-; in charge of Bloodbank and foundation of Dept. of Immunohaematology, Univ. Hospital, Leiden 57; work in tissue typing 58-; worked on antibody synthesis in Public Health Research Inst., New York 62; Lecturer in Immunohaematology, Univ. of Leiden 65-.
Publs. *Leukocyte Antibodies in Sera of Pregnant Women* 58, *Leukocyte Grouping, a Method and its Application* 62, *Leukocyte Groups, the Normal Lymphocyte Transfer Test and Homograft Sensitivity* 65, *The Relevance of Leukocyte Antigens* 67, *A Proposal for International Co-operation: EUROTRANSPLANT* 67.
Department of Immunohaematology, University Hospital, Leiden, Holland.
Telephone: 01710-47222-2091.

Roolvink, Bauke; Netherlands trade union official and politician; b. 31 Jan. 1912; ed. Trade Unions Training Coll. of the Protestant National Federation of Trade Unions.
Bench fitter; Second Chair. Protestant Trade Union for the Metal Industry 46-52; Sec. Protestant Nat. Fed. of Trade Unions 52-59; State Sec. for Social Affairs and Public Health 59-63; mem. Second Chamber of the States-Gen. July 63-67; Minister of Social Affairs and Public Health April 67-; Knight, Order of Netherlands Lion, Grand Cross, Order of Leopold II of Belgium.
Ministry of Social Affairs and Public Health, 73 Zeestraat, The Hague; Home: 85 Johan Gerardtsweg, Hilversum, Netherlands.
Telephone: 070-18-32-20.

Room, Thomas Gerald, SC.D., F.R.S.; British mathematician; b. 10 Nov. 1902; ed. Alleyn's School, London, St. John's Coll., Cambridge.
Lecturer in Mathematics Liverpool Univ. 25-27; Fellow St. John's Coll. Cambridge 26-29; Lecturer in Mathematics Cambridge Univ. 27-35; Prof. of Mathematics Sydney Univ. 35-, Dean Faculty of Science 52-56, 60-65; Visiting Prof. of Mathematics, Univ. of Washington 48, Univ. of Tennessee 49, Univ. of Sussex 66; mem. Princeton Inst. of Advanced Study 48 and 57.
Publs. *Geometry of Determinantal Loci* 39, *The Sorting Process* 66, *A Background to Geometry* 67.
High Walden, St. Ives, N.S.W., Australia.
Telephone: (Sydney) 44-2798.

Roos, Joseph Marie-Philippe; French public servant; b. 13 March 1906; ed. Ecole Polytechnique, and Ecole Supérieure Aéronautique.
Dir. of Air Transport, Min. of Public Works 46-47; Gen. Man. Société des Usines Chausson 47-55, Chair. 55-61; Pres. Air France 61-67; Pres. Inst. of Air Transport 60-; Commdr. Légion d'Honneur, Croix de Guerre.
55 boulevard Lannes, Paris 16e, France.

Roosa, Robert V., A.B., M.A., PH.D.; American banker and government official; b. 21 June 1918; ed. Univ. of Michigan.
Teacher of Economics, Michigan, Harvard, Mass. Inst. of Tech. 39-43; Fed. Reserve Bank of New York 46-60, Vice-Pres. Research Dept. 56-60; Under-Sec. for Monetary Affairs, U.S. Treasury 61-64; with Brown Bros. Harriman and Co. 65-; Dir. Prudential Insurance Co. of America 65, American Express Co. 66, Anaconda Co. 67; mem. American Acad. of Arts and Sciences, American Philosophical Soc.; Independent.
Publs. *Money, Trade and Economic Growth* (Editor) 51, *Federal Reserve Operations in the Money and Government Securities Markets* 56, *Monetary Reform for the World Economy* 65, *The Dollar and World Liquidity* 67, *The Balance of Payments: Free Versus Fixed Exchange Rates* (with Milton Friedman) 67.
Woodlands Road, Harrison, N.Y. 10528; and 59 Wall Street, New York City, N.Y., U.S.A.
Telephone: 914-967-7646.

Roosevelt, Franklin Delano, Jr.; American lawyer and politician; b. 17 Aug. 1914; ed. Harvard, and Univ. of Virginia.
United States Naval service 41-45; mem. U.S. House of Reps. 49-53; Pres., Roosevelt Automobile Co. 58-63; Under-Sec. of Commerce 63-65; Chair. Equal Employment Opportunity Comm. 65-66; Cand. for Gov. of New York 66; Democrat.
45 E. 66th Street, New York, N.Y., U.S.A.

Roosjen, Anton Bernard; Netherlands broadcasting official; b. 94; ed. Vrije Univ., Amsterdam.
President, Netherlands Christian Soc. of Broadcasters; Pres. Nederlandsche Radio Unie (co-operative body of Netherlands Broadcasting Socs.); Vice-Pres. Nederlandse Televisie Stichting; mem. Parl.
Zach. Jansenstraat 21, Amsterdam, Netherlands.

Rootes, 2nd Baron, of Ramsbury; William Geoffrey Rootes; British car manufacturer; b. 14 June 1917; ed. Harrow and Christ Church, Oxford.
Army service 39-45; Rootes Group 46-; Chair. Rootes Motors Ltd. and Dir. of assoc. companies.
Rootes Motors Ltd., Devonshire House, Piccadilly, London, W.1, England.
Telephone: 01-499-3401.

Rootes, Sir Reginald Claud, Kt.; British engineer and business executive; b. 20 Oct. 1896; ed. Cranbrook School, Kent.
President Soc. of Motor Manufacturers and Traders 45-46, Deputy Pres. 46-50; Pres. Motor Industry Research Asscn. 52-53; Vice-Pres. Engineering Employers'

Fed.; Chair. Rootes Motors Ltd. 65-67; retd.; Gov. Coll. of Aeronautics.
Polla House, Hothfield, Ashford, Kent, England.

Roper, Elmo; American marketing consultant; b. 31 July 1900; ed. Univs. of Minnesota and Edinburgh. Marketing consultant 33-; mem. Advisory Cttee. Purchases Div., Office of Production Management, Dep. Co-ordinator of Information; mem. Board Office of Facts and Figures, 41-42; Dep. Dir. Office of Strategic Services 42-45; Consultant, U.S.N. and U.S.A.F. 44-45; Research Dir. *Fortune* Survey of Public Opinion 35-50; Dir. Home Life Insurance, Int. Research Assocs. Inc., Tiffany and Co., Audits and Survey, Thomas Y. Crowell Co.; mem. Market Research Council; fmr. Chair. Connecticut Civil Rights Comm.; fmr. Co-Chair. of Board Fund for the Republic; radio commentator 48-54; newspaper columnist; mem. Editorial Board *Saturday Review;* Dir. Atlantic Council of the U.S.; mem. of Board Freedom House, Nat. Planning Asscn.; American Univ. in Cairo; Founder Roper Public Opinion Center; Hon. A.M. (Williams Coll.), Hon. LL.D. (Univ. of Louisville), Hon. L.H.D. (Univ. of N. Dakota, and Williams Coll.), Hon. D.Sc. (Univ. of Nebraska).
Home: West Redding, Conn., U.S.A.; Office: 111 West 50th Street, New York City 20, N.Y., U.S.A.

Ropner, Sir William Guy, Kt.; British shipowner; b. 14 June 1896; ed. Harrow School.
Served in France in First World War; joined firm of Sir R. Ropner & Co. Ltd. 19; served in Ministry of Shipping in Second World War; Dir. Sir R. Ropner & Co. Ltd., Consett Iron Co., and other companies.
Hillside, Patrick Brompton, Bedale, Yorks., England.

Rosa, João Guimarães; Brazilian diplomatist and writer; b. 08; ed. Univ. of Minas Gerais.
Former doctor in Brazilian hinterland; entered Ministry of Foreign Affairs 34, served in Europe and South America, Consul-Gen. Hamburg 38-42; Head of Frontiers Service, Ministry of Foreign Affairs; mem. Brazilian Acad. of Letters.
Publs. *Sagarana* 46, *Corpo de Baile* (2 Vols.) 56, *Grande Sertão: Veredas* 56, *Primeiras Extórias* 62.
Frontiers Department, Ministry of Foreign Affairs, Rio de Janeiro, Brazil.

Rosay, Françoise (Françoise Bandy de Nalèche); French actress; b. 19 April 1891; ed. Lycée de Versailles, and Paris Conservatoire d'Art Dramatique.
Dramatic performances in France and European countries; has appeared in a very large number of films, including *Le Grand Jeu, La Kermesse Héroïque, Drôle de Drame, Les Gens du Voyage, Le Mystère Barton, Maria Chapdelaine, L'Auberge Rouge, Les Septs Péchés Capitaux, La Reine Margot, Le Long des Trottoirs, Les Amants de Salzbourg, Les yeux de l'amour, Le Bois des amants, Le Cave se Rebiffe, Sans Tambour ni Trompette, The Longest Day;* Chevalier Légion d'Honneur.
195 rue de l'Université, Paris 7e, France.

Rösch, Jean; French astronomer; b. 5 Jan. 1915; ed. Lycée in Algiers and Ecole Normale Supérieure, Paris.
Astronomical Asst. Observatory of Bordeaux 40-43, Asst.-Astronomer 43-47, Dir. Pic du Midi Observatory 47-; Lecturer, Univ. of Bordeaux 43-63; Prof. of Astronomy, Univ. de Paris à la Sorbonne 64-; Research on astronomical subjects including binocular vision, the solar system and telescopic images, and choice of sites for observatories; Pres. and mem. numerous astronomical Comms.; Pres. Soc. Astronomique de France; Chevalier Légion d'Honneur; Prix Benjamin Valz 42, and Médaille Janssen of Académie des Sciences 44.
Publs. Numerous works on astronomy.
Observatoire du Pic du Midi, 65 Bagnères-de-Bigorre; and Institut d'Astrophysique, 98 bis boulevard Arago, Paris, France.
Telephone: 62-95-00-69.

Rose, Hon. Sir Alan Edward Percival, K.C.M.G., Q.C. (Ceylon), LL.B., M.A.; British barrister-at-law; b. 8 Oct. 1899; ed. Aldenham School, and Trinity Coll., Cambridge.
Served in British Expeditionary Force, First World War 18-19; called to Bar (Inner Temple) 23; entered Colonial Legal Service 29; Chief Police Magistrate Fiji 29; Crown Counsel Northern Rhodesia 31; Solicitor-Gen. Palestine 36, Chair. Comms. of Inquiry into loss of S.S. *Patria* 40, and into corruption in Customs Dept. 42; acted as Chief Justice Palestine 44; Judge of Supreme Court of Ceylon 45; acted as Legal Sec. 46; Attorney-Gen. of Dominion of Ceylon 47-51; Chief Justice 51-55; Officer Administering the Govt. of Ceylon March-May 52 and June-Aug. 53; Chair. Supreme Court Reconstitution Comm. 52; Comm. of Inquiry into affairs of Nairobi City Council 56; Medical Appeal Tribunal (Midland Region) 57-58; Chief Justice of Singapore 58-63.
9 Hove Place, Hove, Sussex, England.
Telephone: Brighton 733666.

Rose, Bram, M.D., PH.D., F.R.S.(C); Canadian physician; b. 21 April 1907; ed. Westmount High School and McGill Univ.
Research Asst. McGill Univ. Clinic 36-39, Research Assoc. 39-40; Asst. Physician, Royal Victoria Hospital, Montreal 42; Asst. Prof. of Medicine, McGill Univ. Clinic 50; Assoc. Physician Royal Victoria Hospital 51; Assoc. Prof. of Medicine, McGill Univ. Clinic 55; Physician, Royal Victoria Hospital 61; Prof. of Experimental Medicine, McGill Univ. Clinic 63-; Consultant in Allergy and Dir. of Allergy Laboratory, Queen Mary Veterans Hospital 49-; Hon. Consultant in Medicine, Jewish Gen. Hospital, Montreal 57-; Regional Cons., Jewish Nat. Home for Asthmatic Children, Denver 59-; Dir. Div. of Immunochemistry and Allergy, Univ. Clinic, Royal Victoria Hospital 55-; Pres. Int. Asscn. of Allergology; Past Pres. of Canadian and American Acads. of Allergy; mem. Training Grant Cttee., Nat. Inst. of Allergy and Immunology, Nat. Inst. of Health, Bethesda, Maryland.
Publs. Over 150 works, on histamine, cardiac catheterization, metabolism, shock, (blackout) acceleration in aircraft, ACTH, cortisone, immunoglobulins, and immune mechanisms in disease; Section Editor of *Immunological Diseases* 66.
Division of Immunochemistry and Allergy, 11th Floor Medical Wing, Royal Victoria Hospital, Montreal 2, Quebec, Canada.

Rose, Eliot Joseph Benn; British journalist; b. 7 June 1909; ed. Rugby, and New Coll., Oxford.
Served R.A.F. 39-45; Literary Editor *The Observer* 48-51; Dir. International Press Institute, Zürich 52-62; Dir. Survey of Race Relations in Britain 63-.
37 Pembroke Square, London, W.8, England.

Rose, Wilfrid Andrew; Trinidadian diplomatist; b. 4 Oct. 1916; ed. Tranquility Boys' Intermediate School, Queen's Royal Coll., Imperial Coll. of Tropical Agriculture, Trinidad, Coll. of Estate Management, London, and London Univ.
Agricultural Technologist, Food Control Dept., Trinidad, Second World War; later Estate Manager and Housing Manager, Planning and Housing Comm., Trinidad and Tobago; Dir. Colonial Development Syndicate Ltd., Trinidad Industries Ltd. 43-48; mem. West Indies Nat. Party 44; Foundation mem. People's Nat. Movement 56; Minister of Communications and Works, Fed. Govt. of West Indies 58-62; High Commr. of Trinidad and Tobago in Canada 62-64, in U.K. 64-; concurrently Amb. to E.E.C., Amb. and Perm. Rep. to UN European Office and to GATT 65-.
High Commission of Trinidad and Tobago, 51 South Audley Street, London W.1, England.

Roseman, Alvin, A.B., M.A., LL.B.; American university professor; b. 31 March 1910; ed. Western Reserve Univ., and Univ. of Chicago.
Staff Consultant, Public Welfare Asscn. 33-35; Exec. Officer, Social Security Board 35-39; Asst. to Fed. Security Administrator 39-41; Asst. Dir., U.S. War Manpower Comm. 41-43; Dep. Chief of Mission to Middle East (UNRRA) and Balkans 43-45; Chief, International Activities, U.S. Bureau of the Budget 45-49; U.S. Rep. to U.N. agencies at Geneva 49-51; Dep. Chief, U.S. Econ. Mission to Greece 51-53; Dir., Public Services, International Co-operation Admin. 53-57; Dir., U.S. Econ. Mission to Cambodia 57-59; Regional Dir. for the Far East, International Co-operation Admin. 59-60; Asst. Dir.-Gen., UNESCO 60-63; Assoc. Dean and Prof. of Int. Affairs, Univ. of Pittsburgh Graduate School of Public and International Affairs 63-; Outstanding Public Service Citation 57; Distinguished Career Award 59.
Publs. *Shelter Care and the Homeless Local Man* 35, *International Professional Education for Business and Public Administration* (co-author) 67, *American Universities and Development Assistance* (co-author) 67, and numerous articles in professional journals.
University of Pittsburgh, Pittsburgh, Pa. 15213; Home: 148 Maple Heights Drive, Pittsburgh 32, Pa., U.S.A.
Telephone: 683-2230 (Home).

Rosen, Martin M., M.A.; American economist; b. 7 Aug. 1919; ed. Univs. of Cincinnati and Minnesota.
Economist, U.S. Treasury Dept. 41-42; served with U.S. Army 42-46; Deputy Chief, Finance Division U.S. Element, Allied Comm. for Austria 45-46; mem. of Economic Staff, Int. Bank 46; on leave to be Consultant to W. A. Harriman, U.S. Special Rep. in Europe 48-Acting Chief Economist 48, Chief Economist 50, Asst. to Dir. Economic Staff 51, Asst. Dir. Dept. of Operations, Europe, Africa and Australasia 52, Asst. Dir. Dept. of Technical Operations 55, Dir. Dept. of Operations, Far East, Int. Bank for Reconstruction and Development 57-61; Dir. Dept. of Operations, Far East, Int. Development Asscn. (IDA) 60-61; Exec. Vice Pres. Int. Finance Corpn. 61-.
International Finance Corporation, 1818 H Street, N.W., Washington, D.C.; Home: 2115 Paul Spring Road, Alexandria, Va., U.S.A.
Telephone: DU 1-2281 (Office); 768-7751 (Home).

Rosen, Milton William, B.S.; American engineer and physicist; b. 25 July 1915; ed. Univ. of Pennsylvania, Univ. of Pittsburgh, and California Inst. of Technology.
Engineer Westinghouse Electric and Mfg. Co. 37-38; Engineer-physicist Naval Research Laboratory, Wash. 40-58, Scientific Officer Viking Rocket 47-55, Head Rocket Development Branch 53-55, Technical Dir. Project Vanguard (earth satellite) 55-58; Engineer Nat. Aeronautics and Space Admin. (NASA) 58-; Chief Rocket Vehicle Development Programs 58-59, Dep. Dir. Launch Vehicle Programs 60-61, Dir. Launch Vehicles and Propulsion 61-63; Senior Scientist, Office of DOD and Interagency Affairs, Nat. Aeronautics and Space Admin. 63-.
Publ. *The Viking Rocket Story* 55.
National Aeronautics and Space Administration, Washington, D.C. 20546, U.S.A.

Rosenberg, Ludwig; German trade union official; b. 29 June 1903; ed. State Coll. of Economics and Admin., Düsseldorf.
Secretary, Clerical Workers' Union 28-33; political refugee in Great Britain 33-46; Trades Union Liaison Office, Bielefeld 46-47; Trades Union Council, Frankfurt/Main 48-50; Exec. Cttee. DGB (German Fed. of Trade Unions), Chief, Foreign Relations Dept. 50-53, Vice-Pres. Exec. Cttee. 59-62, Chair. 62-; Pres. Econ. and Social Cttee., EEC and Euratom 60-62, Vice-Pres. 58-60, 62-63; Senator of Max-Planck-Soc.; mem. of Monnet Cttee., United States of Europe; mem. various nat. and int. insts.; German and Italian decorations; Social Democratic Party.
DGB (Deutscher Gewerkschaftsbund), Kennedy-Damm, Stromstrasse 8, Düsseldorf, German Federal Republic.

Rosenblith, Walter Alter; American scientist and university professor; b. 13; ed. Berlin, Lausanne, Paris, Bordeaux Univs.
Research, Paris 38-39, N.Y. Univ. 39-40, Univ. Calif. (Los Angeles) Grad. Scholar and Asst. in Physics 40-43; Asst. Prof., Assoc. Prof., Acting Head, Dept. of Physics, South Dakota School of Mines and Technology 43-47; Research Fellow, Harvard Univ., Psycho-Acoustic Laboratory 47-51; Assoc. Prof., Communications Biophysics, Massachusetts Inst. of Technology (M.I.T.) 51-57, Prof. 57-; Research Assoc. in Otology, Harvard Medical School and Massachusetts Eye and Ear Infirmary 57-; Fellow, American Acad. of Arts and Sciences, Acoustical Soc. of America, World Acad. of Art and Science, New York Acad. of Sciences; mem. Council Int. Union for Pure and Applied Biophysics, Central Council, Exec. Cttee. and Hon. Treas. Int. Brain Research Org. (UNESCO); Inaugural Lecturer Tata Inst. for Fundamental Research 62; Weizmann Memorial Lectures 62; Consultant, WHO 65-.
Publ. *Noise and Man* (with K. N. Stevens) 53, *Processing Neuroelectric Data* (Editor) 59, *Sensory Communication* (Editor) 61.
Massachusetts Institute of Technology, Room 20B-221, Cambridge, Mass. 02139; 164 Mason Terrace, Brookline 02146, Mass., U.S.A.
Telephone: 617-734-1110 (Home).

Rosenblueth, Arturo Stearns, M.D.; Mexican physiologist; b. 2 Oct. 1900; ed. Monterrey, and School of Medicine, Paris.
Instructor, University of Mexico 28, Assoc. Prof. 29-30; Guggenheim Memorial Foundation Fellow, Harvard Univ. 30-31, Fellow 32, Instructor and Tutor in Physiology, Harvard Medical School 33-34, Asst. Prof. and Tutor 35-43; Head of Dept. of Physiology, Nat. Inst. of Cardiology, Mexico 44-60; Dir. Research Center I.P.N., Mexico 60-; mem. Colegio Nacional de México.
Publs. *The Transmission of Nerve Impulses at Neuroeffector Junctions and Peripheral Synapses* 50; with W. B. Cannon: *Autonomic Neuro-Effector Systems* 37, *The Supersensitivity of Denervated Structures* 49.
Apartado Postal 14-740, Mexico 14, D.F., Mexico.
Telephone: 67-42-00; 67-44-75.

Rosenheim, Sir Max Leonard, K.B.E., M.A., M.D., P.R.C.P.; British physician; b. 15 March 1908; ed. Shrewsbury School, St. John's Coll., Cambridge, and Univ. Coll. Hospital Medical School.
Junior hospital posts, Univ. Coll. Hospital (UCH) and Westminster Hospital 32-38; Bilton Pollard Travelling Fellowship, Research Asst. Mass. Gen. Hospital, Boston 39; First Asst., Research Unit, UCH Medical School 39; Army service 41-46; on Staff, UCH 46-, Prof. of Medicine London Univ. and Dir. Medical Unit UCH Medical School 50-; mem. Council, Royal Coll. of Physicians 54-56, Pres. 66-; mem. Medical Research Council 61-65; Hon. mem. Asscn. of American Physicians, Hon. Foreign mem. American Acad. of Arts and Sciences, Hon. Fellow, Univ. Coll., London.
University College Hospital Medical School, University Street, London, W.C.1; Home: 39 Eton Avenue, London, N.W.3, England.

Rosenko, Pyotr Akimovich; Soviet politician; b. 1907; ed. Donetsk Mining Inst.
Mining Engineer 31-54; mem. C.P.S.U. 43-; Dep. Minister of Coal Industry, Ukraine 54; Dep. Chair. Council of Ministers, Ukraine 54-57, 59-; First Dep. Chair. State Planning Comm. of Ukraine 57-59, Chair. 59-63; First Deputy Chair. Ukrainian S.S.R. Council of

Ministers 63-; mem. Central Cttee. of C.P.S.U. 61-66, cand. mem. 66-; Deputy to U.S.S.R. Supreme Soviet. Council of Ministers of the Ukrainian S.S.R., Kiev, Ukrainian S.S.R., U.S.S.R.

Rosenman, Samuel Irving, A.B., LL.B.; American lawyer; b. 13 Feb. 1896; ed. Columbia Univ.
1st Lieut. U.S. Army 18; mem. N.Y. State Legislature 22-26; N.Y. State Bill Drafting Commr. 26-28; Counsel to Gov. Roosevelt 29-32; Justice N.Y. Supreme Court 32-43; Special Counsel to Pres. Franklin D. Roosevelt 43-45; personal rep. of Pres. Roosevelt with rank of Minister to make an econ. survey of Britain, France, Belgium, and Holland 45; Special Counsel to Pres. Truman 45-46; mem. Steel Industry fact-finding Board 49; Chair. Railway Labor Emergency Board 63-; mem. Presidential Maritime Industry Board 61, Exec. Cttee. of Lawyers Cttee. for Civil Rights; Pres. Asscn. of the Bar of New York 64-66; awarded Medal for Merit 46; Officier Légion d'Honneur (France) 47; Democrat.
Publs. *Working with Roosevelt* 52; compiler and editor, *Public Papers and Addresses of Franklin D. Roosevelt 1928-1945* (13 vols.).
575 Madison Avenue, New York 22, N.Y., U.S.A.

Rosenstein-Rodan, Paul N., DR.RER.POL., B.COMM.; British economist and university professor; b. 19 April 1902; ed. Vienna Univ.
Assistant Vienna Univ. 26-29; Editor *Zeitschrift f. Natoek.*, Vienna 28-32; Library of Economics, Allen and Unwin, London 36-56; Lecturer, Reader, Head of Dept. of Political Economy Univ. Coll., Univ. of London 31-47; Asst. Dir. Economics Dept. and Head Economics Advisory Staff, Int. Bank for Reconstruction and Development, Washington, D.C. 47-53; Prof. of Economics, Mass. Inst. of Technology and Center for Int. Studies, Cambridge (Mass.) 53-; Consultant, U.N. Comms. for Latin America, Asia and the Far East and for FAO; mem. Panel of Experts, Alliance for Progress; Fellow American Acad. of Arts and Sciences; Italian Order of Merit.
Publs. *Marginal Utility* 26, *The Role of Time in Economic Theory* 34, *Complementarietà . . .* 34, *Problems of Industrialization of Eastern and Southeastern Europe* 43, *Notes on the Theory of the Big Push* 55, *International Aid for Underdeveloped Countries* 61.
Massachusetts Institute of Technology, Cambridge 39, Mass.; and 10 Emerson Place, Boston, Mass. 02114, U.S.A.
Telephone: 227-7730 (Home).

Rosenstock-Huessy, Eugen F. M., LL.D., PH.D.; American jurist and sociologist; b. 6 July 1888; ed. Zürich, Berlin and Heidelberg Univs.
Lecturer Leipzig Univ. 12-21; army officer 14-18; Dir. Acad. of Labour, Frankfurt 21; Prof. of History of Law and of Sociology, Breslau Univ. 23-34, Harvard Univ. 33-36; at Dartmouth Coll. 35-57, Emer. 57-; founder German School for Adult Education 27; Vice-Chair. World Asscn. for Adult Education; research, Egypt 50; Guest Prof. Göttingen 50, Berlin 52, Münster 57 and 58, Los Angeles 59, Cologne 61-62, Univ. of Calif. (Santa Cruz) 65, 66, 67, Univ. of Connecticut 68; Eugen Rosenstock-Huessy Gesellschaft founded Germany 63; Hon. Dr. Theol., Hon. D. Phil., Hon. LL.D.
Publs. *Königshaus und Stämme* 14, *Das Alter der Kirche* 27, *Die Europäischen Revolutionen* 31 (third edn. 61), *Faraday and Paracelsus* 37, *Out of Revolution, Autobiography of Western Man* 38, *The Christian Future* 46 (enlarged English edn. 47), *The Multiformity of Man* 48, *Der Atem des Geistes* 51, *Heilkraft und Wahrheit* 52, *Magna Charta Latina* 55, *Der unbezahlbare Mensch* 55, *Soziologie I* 56, *II* 58, *Das Geheimnis der Universität* 59, *Biblionomics* 59, *The Generations of The Faith, Die*

Sprache des Menschengeschlechts, 2 Vols. 63, *Die Interim des Rechts* 64, *Judaism despite Christianity* 68.
"Four Wells", Norwich, Vt., U.S.A.
Telephone: 649-1861.

Rosenthal, Abraham Michael; American (born Canadian) newspaperman; b. 2 May 1922.
New York Times 44-, U.N. Bureau 46-54, New Delhi 54-58, Warsaw 58-59, Geneva 59-61, Tokyo 61-63, Metropolitan Editor 63-66, Asst. Man. Dir. 66-; Pulitzer Prize 60.
Publs. *38 Witnesses, One More Victim* (co-author).
New York Times, 229 West 43rd Street, New York City 36, N.Y., U.S.A.
Telephone: 556-1234.

Rosenthal, Philip, M.A.; German ceramics executive; b. 23 Oct. 1916; ed. Wittelsbacher Gymnasium, Munich, St. Laurence Coll., Ramsgate, and Exeter Coll., Oxford.
Chairman, Management Board Rosenthal A.G., Selb; Chair. Advisory Board Rosenthal Isolatoren G.m.b.H., Selb; mem. Advisory Board Messe und Ausstellungs G.m.b.H., Hanover; Chair. Asscn. of Ceramics Industry; Deputy Chair. Design Council of Fed. of German Industries; mem. Management Board Deutsche Keramische Gesellschaft, Bad Honnef; Chair. of Presidium of Labour Council of Ceramics Industry; Pres. Féd. Européenne des Industries de Porcelaine et le Faïence de Table et d'Ornamentation, Brussels.
8672 Selb/Ofr., Schloss Erkersreuth, German Federal Republic.
Telephone: 2551 (Office); 2549 (Home).

Roser, Rev. Francisco Xavier, S.J., DR.PHIL.; Brazilian (b. Austrian) physicist; b. 04; ed. Colegio Anchieta (Nova Friburgo, Brazil), Vienna and Innsbruck Univs.
Professor of Physics and Mathematics, Colegio Anchieta, Nova Friburgo 40-46; Prof. of Physics Colegio S. Ignacio, Rio de Janeiro 46-49; Prof. of Physics Rio de Janeiro Catholic Univ. 49-, Dir. Physical Inst. 56-; Founder-mem. Rio de Janeiro Physical Research Centre 48-; Del. UN Scientific Cttee. on Radiation 56-; mem. American Physical Soc., Brazilian Acad. of Sciences, Co-operative Research Foundation; Austrian Cross of Merit for Science and Arts 63.
[*Died 12 Feb. 1967*]

Roseveare, Rt. Rev. Reginald Richard, C.B.E.; British ecclesiastic; b. 18 May 1902; ed. Sedbergh School, and Kelham Theological Coll., Newark.
Professed mem. Society of the Sacred Mission (Kelham) 28; Deacon 29; Priest 30; Asst. Curate, St. George, Nottingham 29-34; Tutor, Kelham Theological Coll. 34-37; Vicar, Parson Cross 37-52; Rural Dean, Ecclesfield 42-52; Residentiary Canon, Sheffield Cathedral 45-52; Proctor in Convocation 50-52; Provincial of the Soc. of the Sacred Mission in S. Africa 52-56; Lord Bishop of Accra 56-67; expelled from Ghana Aug.-Nov. 62.
Publs. *A Parish Communion Book* 38, *Getting Married in Church* 44.
Kelham, Newark, Notts., England.

Roshchin, Alexei Alexandrovich; Soviet diplomatist; b. 1905; ed. Leningrad Inst. of National Economy.
Member C.P.S.U. 28-; Diplomatic Service 36-; Asst. Head, later Head, Third Western Dept., U.S.S.R. Foreign Ministry 38-39; Counsellor to Chief Soviet Rep. on European Consultative Comm., London 44-46; Deputy Head, later Head, U.S.S.R. Foreign Ministry UN Dept. 46-52; Senior Counsellor Soviet Mission to UN 52-53; Deputy Head U.S.S.R. Foreign Ministry UN Dept. 53-54, Deputy Head, Int. Orgs. Dept. 54-56; Counsellor-Minister, London 56-59; Counsellor, Office of U.S.S.R. Foreign Minister 59-64; Head of Second European Dept., U.S.S.R. Foreign Ministry 64-66;

Soviet Rep. on Eighteen-Nations Disarmament Cttee., Geneva 66-; Orders and medals of U.S.S.R.
Eighteen-Nations Disarmament Committee, Geneva, Switzerland.

Rosini, Giuseppe; Italian shipping executive; b. 01. Engineer, later Deputy Manager Soc. Grandi Fucine Italiane Gio'Fossati & Co. 27; later Manager Stabilimento Fossati, and Fonderie Ghisa e Metalli, of Ansaldo Co.; Consultant Cantieri Riuniti Dell' Adriatico, Cantieri del Quarnaro, Motomeccanica, Stabilimento di S. Eustacchio 45-46; Gen. Man. Soc. Industriale S. Giorgio-Genoa 48; Man. Dir. and Gen. Man. Ansaldo Co. 49-59; Pres. FINMARE 59-; numerous decorations.
c/o FINMARE, Via Barberini n. 22, Rome, Italy.

Ross, Alan Strode Campbell, M.A.; British philologist; b. 1 Feb. 1907; ed. Malvern Coll., and Balliol Coll., Oxford.
Won Henry Skynner Scholarship in Astronomy to Balliol Coll. Oxford 24; Asst. Lecturer in English Language Leeds Univ. 29-36, Lecturer 36-39; seconded to Foreign Office 40-45; Lecturer in English Language Birmingham Univ. 46, Reader 47, Prof. 48-51, Prof. of Linguistics 51-; Corresp. mem. Société Finno-ougrienne. Publs. *The Dream of the Rood* (with B. Dickins) 34, *Studies in the Accidence of the Lindisfarne Gospels* 37, *The 'Numeral-signs' of the Mohenjo-daro Script* 38, *The 'Terfinnas' and the 'Beormas' of Ohthere* 40, *Essentials of Anglo-Saxon Grammar* 48, *Tables for Old English Sound-changes* 51, *Ginger* 52, *Noblesse Oblige* (with Nancy Mitford and others) 56, *Lindisfarne Gospels,* Urs Graf Edition (with several others) 57, 61, *Etymology* 58, *Essentials of German Grammar* 63, *Essentials of English* 64, *The Pitcairnese Language* (with A. W. Moverley) 64, I. I. Revzin's *Models of Language* (trans. with N. F. C. Owen) 66, *Arts v. Science* (Editor) 67.
Dept. of Linguistics, Birmingham University, Birmingham; c/o Union Club, Colmore Row. Birmingham 3, England.

Ross, Sir Archibald David Manisty, K.C.M.G., M.A.; British diplomatist; b. 12 Oct. 1911; ed. Winchester, and New Coll., Oxford.
Diplomatic Service 36-; Minister, Rome 53-56; Asst. Under-Sec. of State 56-60; Ambassador to Portugal 61-66, to Sweden 66-.
British Embassy, Stockholm, Sweden.
Telephone: 670140.

Ross, Colonel The Hon. Frank Mackenzie, C.M.G., M.C., K.ST.J., LL.D.; Scottish-born Canadian businessman; b. 14 April 1891; ed. Royal Acad., Tain, Scotland. Served with Canadian Army First World War; Chair. Int. Paints (Canada) Ltd., Grosvenor-Laing (B.C.) Ltd., Lafarge Cement of N. America Ltd., Deeks McBride Ltd., Canadian Allied Property Investments Ltd., McCord Street Sites Ltd., Guildford Devt. Corpn. Ltd., Mayfair Shopping Centre Ltd., Third Properties Ltd.; Pres. T. C. Gorman Construction Co. Ltd., Vancouver Iron & Engineering Works Ltd., West Coast Shipbuilders Ltd.; Dir. Inter City Papers Ltd.; Vice-Pres. and Dir. Canadian Imperial Bank of Commerce, Toronto; Dir. R.C.A. Victor Co. Ltd. (Montreal), Canada Trust Co. Ltd., and many other companies; Lieut.-Gov. of British Columbia 55-60; Hon. degrees: Univs. of New Brunswick, British Columbia, Aberdeen and St. Francis Xavier Univ. (Nova Scotia).
Home: 4899 Belmont Avenue, Vancouver 8, B.C.; Office: 1101 West 6th Avenue, Vancouver 9, B.C., Canada.
Telephone: 224-1212 (Home); 731-1112 (Office).

Ross, John Carl; British company director; b. 29 July 1901; ed. Culford School, Bury St. Edmunds.
Joined family business and assumed control 29; Chair. Ross Group Ltd. 45-, Orbit Holdings Ltd. 62-; Chair.

Great Grimsby Coal, Salt and Tanning Co. Ltd. 61-; mem. Lloyd's, London; Chair. Lincolnshire Branch, Inst. of Dirs. 58-60.
Ross House, Grimsby, Lincolnshire; and Tudor Court, Humberston Avenue, New Waltham, Grimsby, Lincolnshire, England.

Ross, Rt. Hon. William, P.C., M.B.E., M.P.; British politician; b. 7 April 1911; ed. Ayr Acad., and Glasgow Univ.
Former schoolmaster; Army Service, Second World War; M.P. 46-; Sec. of State for Scotland Oct. 64-; Chair. Regional Econ. Advisory Council for Scotland 65-; Labour.
10 Chapelpark Road, Ayr, Scotland.

Ross, Sir William David, K.B.E., M.A., D.LITT., LL.D., LITT.D., L.H.D., F.B.A.; British philosophical scholar; b. 15 April 1877; ed. Edinburgh Univ., and Balliol Coll., Oxford.
Fellow and Tutor Oriel Coll. Oxford 02 and Provost 29-47; Univ. Dep. Prof. of Moral Philosophy 23-28, Vice-Chancellor 41-44; Pres. British Acad. 36-40; Visiting Prof. of Philosophy Columbia Univ. 39; Pres. Aristotelian Soc. 39-40; Chair. Council Royal Inst. of Philosophy 40-; mem. Nat. Arbitration Tribunal 41-52; Chair. Civil Service Arbitration Tribunal 42-52; Chair. Royal Comm. on the Press 47-49; Hon. Fellow Merton, Balliol and Oriel Colls., Oxford, Trinity Coll., Dublin; Commdr. First Class, Order of St. Olav (Norway), Grand Officer, Order of Polonia Restituta (Poland); numerous hon. degrees.
Publs. Editions of Aristotle and Theophrastus; *The Right and the Good* 30, *Foundations of Ethics* 39, *Plato's Theory of Ideas* 51, *Kant's Ethical Theory* 54.
17 Bradmore Road, Oxford, England.

Rössel, Mrs. Agda; Swedish diplomatist; b. 4 Nov. 1910; ed. Swedish Inst. Social Politics.
Secretary, Union of Women Employees, Nat. Telephone Co. 39-41; various advisory posts 41-50; mem. Int. Fed. of Business and Professional Women 47-, Vice-Pres. 50-52; mem. Swedish del. to U.N. 52-58, Perm. Rep. 58-64; Amb. to Yugoslavia 64-.
Swedish Embassy, Pariska 7, Belgrade, Yugoslavia.

Rossel, Marie-Thérèse; Belgian newspaper director; b. 10.
Director, *Le Soir;* Officier de l'Ordre de Léopold; Officier de l'Ordre de la Couronne; Chevalier de la Légion d'Honneur; Officier de l'Ordre au Merite d'Italie.
21 place de Louvain, Brussels, Belgium.

Rosseland, Svein; Norwegian astronomer; b. 31 March 1894; ed. Oslo Univ.
Prof. of Astronomy, Oslo Univ. 28-64, Dir. and Founder, Univ. Inst. of Theoretical Astrophysics 34; Visiting Prof. Harvard Univ. 29-30; Prof. of Astronomy Princeton Univ. 41-46; Exec. Cttee. mem. Royal Norwegian Council of Scientific and Industrial Research 46-53, Vice-Pres. 47-51; Chair. Research Cttee., Central Inst. of Industrial Research 50-56, Vice-Chair. of Board 56-; mem. Norwegian Acad. of Sciences and Letters, Pres. 48-60, and Vice-Pres. 49-59, Dean Faculty of Science 51-53; founded Oslo Solar Observatory 54; founded *Astrophysica Norvegica* 34; Dir. and Founder Oslo Space Track Facility 60; contrib. to *Handbuch der Astrophysik;* mem. NATO Science Cttee. 58-65; mem. scientific societies in Sweden, Denmark, Belgium and England; Commdr. with Star Royal Order of St. Olaf; Hon. D.Sc. (Copenhagen and Stockholm).
Publs. *Astrophysik auf atomtheoretischer Grundlage* 31, *Theoretical Astrophysics* 36, *The Pulsation Theory of Variable Stars* 49.
Institute of Theoretical Astrophysics, Box 1029, Blindern, Oslo 3; Home: Ovenbakken 18C, Oslo 7, Norway.
Telephone: Oslo 244760 (Home).

Rossellini, Renzo; Italian composer and musical critic; b. 2 Feb. 1908; ed. Conservatorio di Musica di S. Cecilia, Rome.

Director, Musical Inst. G. B. Pergolesi, Varese 33-40; then Vice-Dir. and Prof. of Composition Conservatorio G. Rossini, Pesaro; Music Critic *Il Messaggero*, Rome; mem. Nat. Council of UNESCO 58-; mem. Management Cttee., Nat. Orchestra of Monte Carlo 65-, Italian Authors and Writers Soc. 66-; mem. Accad. Nazionale di S. Cecilia, Accad. Cherubini, Florence, Accad. Filarmonica, Bologna.

Compositions: Lyric operas: *La Guerra* 56, *Il Vortrice* 58, *Le Campane* 59, *Uno Squardo dal Ponte* 61, *Il Linguaggio dei Fiori* 63, *La Leggenda del Ritorno* 66, *L'Avventuriero* 67.

Publs. *Polemica Musicale* 62, *Pagine di un Musicista* 64.

Palais Héraclès, Monte Carlo, Monaco; and 12 Via Lisbona, Rome, Italy.

Rossellini, Roberto; Italian film and operatic director; b. 8 May 1906.

Sound effects technician for films 34-; Operatic productions include *Jeanne d'Arc au Bûcher* (Honegger) 53, *La Figlia di Jorio* (Pizzetti) 54; films directed include *Prélude à l'Après-midi d'un Faune* 38, *Il Tacchino Prepotente*, *La Vispa Teresa* 39, *La Nave Bianca* 41, *L'Uomo della Croce* 42, *Desiderio* 43, *Roma Città Aperta* 45, *Paisà* 46, *Germania Anno Zero* 48, *Stromboli* 50, *Dov'è la Libertà?* 52, *Viaggio in Italia* 54, *Joan of Arc at the Stake* 55, *Il Generale della Rovere* 59, *Vanina Vanini* 61, *Anima Nera* 62, *La Prise de Pouvoir par Louis XIV* 66.

Viale B. Buozzi 49, Rome, Italy.

Rossem, Arnold van, DR. TECH. SC.; Netherlands rubber technologist; b. 14 Sept. 1887; ed. Technical Univ., Delft.

Director of the Netherlands Govt. Rubber Inst. 16-41, of Rubber Research Inst. T.N.O. 41-53; Dir. of Research Dept. of Rubber Foundation 36-50; Extraordinary Prof. in Rubber Technology, Technical Univ., Delft 39-58; Officer of Order of Orange Nassau; Knight of Order of Netherlands Lion.

Publs. *Bijdrage tot de kennis van het vulcanisatieproces* 16, *The American Rubber Industry and its scientific information* 27, *Vijfentwintig jaar Rijksrubberdienst* 35, *Van Empirie tot Wetenschap in de Rubberindustrie* 40, *De Rubberindustrie in de Vereenigde Staten van Amerika* 53, *Rubber: Winning, Eigenschappen en Verwerking* 58, *Opmars der Techniek* 62, *Lever in een Riskante "Technische Wonder" Wereld* 62.

10 Kanaalweg, Delft, Netherlands.

Telephone: 01730-24488.

Rossi, H.E. Cardinal Agnelo; Brazilian ecclesiastic; b. 4 May 1913.

Ordained priest 37; Bishop of Barra do Pirai 56; Archbishop of São Paulo 64-; created Cardinal 65.

Palácio Pio XII, Rua Pio XII 279, São Paulo, Brazil.

Rossides, Zenon George; Cypriot diplomatist; b. 8 Feb. 1895; ed. Limassol Coll., and Middle Temple, London.

Called to Bar 23; law practice in Cyprus 25-54; mem. Nat. Delegation to London 29-31; mem., Ethnarchy Council 46-48 and 58-59; mem. Exec. 50-59; Ambassador to U.S.A. and Perm. Rep. of Cyprus to UN 60-.

Publs. *The Island of Cyprus and Union with Greece* 51, *The Problem of Cyprus* 58.

Embassy of Cyprus, 2211 R. St., N.W., Washington, D.C.; 165 East 72nd, New York City 21, N.Y., U.S.A.

Rossini, Frederick Dominic, M.S., PH.D., D.SC., D.ENG.SC., LITT.D.; American chemist; b. 18 July 1899; ed. Carnegie Inst. of Technology, and Univ. of Calif.

Asst. in Physics, Carnegie Inst. of Technology 23-24, Asst. in Mathematics 24-26; Teaching Fellow in Chemistry, Univ. of Calif. 26-28; Physical Chemist, Nat.

Bureau of Standards 28-50, Chief of Section on Thermochemistry and Hydrocarbons 36-50; Silliman Prof., Head Dept. of Chemistry, Dir. Chemical and Petroleum Research Lab., Carnegie Inst. of Technology 50-60; Dir. American Petroleum Inst. Research Projects 35-60; Lecturer in Chemical Thermodynamics, Graduate School Nat. Bureau of Standards 34-50; Dean, Coll. of Science and Assoc. Dean, Graduate School, Univ. of Notre Dame 60-67, Vice-Pres. for Research 67-; Board of Editors *Journal of American Chemical Society* 46-56; Comm. on Thermochemistry, Int. Union of Pure and Applied Chemistry 34-61; Pres. Comm. on Chemical Thermodynamics 52-61; Consultant Nat. Science Foundation 52-62; Chair. Div. of Petroleum Chemistry, American Chemical Soc. 54; mem. Nat. Acad. of Science; received Hillebrand Award of Chemical Soc. of Wash. 34 and U.S. Dept. of Commerce Gold Medal for Exceptional Service 50; Pittsburgh Award, American Chemical Soc. 59; Laetare Medal (Univ. of Notre Dame) 65, John Price Wetherill Medal (Franklin Inst.) 65, William H. Nichols Medal (American Chemical Soc.) 66, and other awards; Marburg Lecturer, American Soc. for Testing Materials 53; Chair. Div. Chemistry and Chemical Tech., Nat. Research Council 55-58; Pres. Albertus Magnus Guild 61-65.

411 North Ironwood Drive, South Bend, Indiana 46615, U.S.A.

Rossiter, Roger James, B.SC., M.A., D.PHIL., B.M., B.CH., F.R.S.C., F.R.I.C.; British biochemist; b. 13; ed. Univs. of Western Australia and Oxford.

Demonstrator in Biochemistry and Tutor in Physiology, Oxford Univ. 38-46; Carnegie Research Scholar 41; served in R.A.M.C. 43-46; now Prof. of Biochemistry and fmr. Dean, Faculty of Graduate Studies, Univ. of Western Ontario, and Consultant in Biochemistry, Westminster, Victoria and St. Joseph's Hospitals, London, Ont.; mem. Biochemical Soc., American Soc. of Biological Chemists, Canadian Physiological Soc., Soc. for Experimental Biology and Medicine, Canadian Biochemical Soc., Canadian Soc. for Clinical Chemistry; Fellow Royal Soc. of Medicine, Royal Soc. of Canada and Chemical Inst. of Canada.

Department of Biochemistry, University of Western Ontario, London, Ont., Canada.

Rost Onnes, Nicolaas Ernst, LL.D.; Netherlands banker; b. 92; ed. Utrecht Univ.

Chairman and del. mem. Board of Dirs. Hollandsche Bank-Unie N.V.; Chair. Board of Dirs. N.V. Administratie en Trustkantoor voor Handel en Industrie, N.V. Administratiekantoor voor Handel en Nijverheid, Boom-Ruygrok N.V., N.V. Koninklijke Pharmaceutische Fabrieken v/h Brocades-Stheeman & Pharmacia, Merrem & La Porte N.V., Blydenstein Willink N.V.; Dir. Friesch-Gröningsche Hypotheekbank N.V., Gröninger Industriele Crediet Bank N.V., De Nederlandsche Fondsen Maatschappij "NEFO" N.V.; Nederlandse Overzeese Financierings-Maatschappij N.V., N.V. Overslagbedrijf (Amsterdam); mem. Board Inst. de Estudios Hispánicos, Portugueses e Ibero-americanos, Inst. for Netherlands American Industrial Co-operation; Knight, Order of Neths. Lion, Comendador de la Orden del Mérito Civil (Spain), Comendador Ordem do Cruzeiro do Sol (Brazil), Commdr. de la Orden de Mayo al Mérito (Argentina).

Amsteldijk 194, Amsterdam Z, Netherlands.

Rostand, Jean; French writer and biologist; b. 30 Oct. 1894.

Mem. Acad. Française 59-; Kalinga Prize (UNESCO) 59.

Author of *La loi des riches, Les Familiotes, Deux Angoisses, Le Mariage, Valère ou l'Exaspéré, Julien ou une Conscience, De la Vanité, Hommes de vérité, Journal d'un caractère, Ignace ou l'Écrivain, Les Chromosomes, L'Aventure humaine, La Vie des Crapauds, La Vie des*

Libellules, La Vie des Vers à soie, La Vie et ses pro-blèmes, La Parthénogenèse des Vertébrés, La Nouvelle Biologie, L'Homme, Pensées d'un biologiste, Les Idées nouvelles de la génétique, La Formation de l'être, L'Evo-lution des espèces, La genèse de la Vie, L'Avenir de la Biologie, Science et Génération, Esquisse d'une histoire de la biologie, Ce que je crois, etc.
29 rue Pradier, Ville d'Avray (Seine-et-Oise), France. Telephone: 926-4331.

Rostoft, Sverre Walter; Norwegian business executive and politician; b. 12 Dec. 1912; ed. Univ. of Oslo. Managing Dir. Kristiansands Mekaniske Verksted (shipyard), Kristiansand 45-65; mem. Oddernes Munici-pal Council 52-55; mem. Storting 54-57, 65-; fmr. Dir. several industrial concerns in Norway and Sweden; Minister of Industries 65-; Past Pres. Norwegian Asscn. of Industries; Conservative.
Ministry of Industries, Oslo, Norway.

Rostow, Eugene Victor, LL.B. (brother of Walt Whitman Rostow, *q.v.*); American lawyer, economist and government official; b. 25 Aug. 1913; ed. Yale Coll., King's Coll., Cambridge, and Yale Law School. Admitted to N.Y. Bar 38, practised in New York City 37-38; mem. Faculty, Law School, Yale 38-, Prof. of Law 44-, Dean 55- (on leave 66-); Visiting Prof., Univ. of Chicago 41; Pitt Prof. of American History and Insts., Professorial Fellow, King's Coll., Cambridge 59-60; Guggenheim Fellow 59-60; Adviser to Dept. of State 42-44, 61-66; Asst. Exec. Sec. Econ. Comm. for Europe, UN 49-50; Under-Sec. of State for Political Affairs, Dept. of State 66-; Fellow, American Acad. of Arts and Sciences; Hon. LL.D. (Cambridge).
Publs. *Planning for Freedom* 59, *The Sovereign Preroga-tive* 62.
1913 23rd Street, N.W., Washington, D.C.; and (summer) Peru, Vermont, U.S.A.

Rostow, Walt Whitman, PH.D. (brother of Eugene Rostow, *q.v.*); American economist; b. 7 Oct. 1916; ed. Yale and Oxford Univs.
Instructor in Economics Columbia Univ. 40-41; served as Major, 42-45; Asst. Chief German-Austrian Econ. Div. State Dept. 45-46; Harmsworth Prof. of American History, Oxford Univ. 46-47; Asst. to Exec. Sec. UN Econ. Comm. for Europe 47-49; Pitt Prof. of American History Cambridge Univ. 49-50; Prof. of Econ. History M.I.T. and Staff mem. M.I.T. Center for Int. Studies 51-60; Dep. Special Asst. to the President for Nat. Security Affairs Jan.-Nov. 61; Counsellor and Chair. Policy Planning Council, Dept. of State Dec. 61-66; Special Asst., The White House April 66-; Legion of Merit, Hon. O.B.E. (U.K.).
Publs. *The American Diplomatic Revolution* 47, *Essays on the British Economy of the XIX Century* 48, *The Process of Economic Growth* 52, *The Growth and Fluctua-tion of the British Economy 1790-1850* (with A. D. Gayer and A. J. Schwartz) 53, *The Dynamics of Soviet Society* (with A. Levin and others) 53, *The Prospects for Com-munist China* (with others) 54, *An American Policy in Asia* (with R. W. Hatch) 55, *A Proposal: Key to an Effective Foreign Policy* (with Max F. Millikan) 57, *The United States in the World Arena* 60, *The Stages of Economic Growth* 60, *View from the Seventh Floor* 64, *A Design for Asian Development* 65.
c/o The White House, Washington, D.C.; Home: 3414 Lowell Street, N.W., Washington 16, D.C., U.S.A.

Rostropovich, Mstislav Leopoldovich; Soviet 'cellist; b. 1927; ed. Moscow Conservatoire.
First Concert 42; First Prize, All-Union Concourse of Musicians 45; First Prize, International Cellists Competition, Prague; numerous concert tours in U.S.S.R. and abroad, particularly as cellist in trio with Emil Gilels and Leonid Kogan; Prof. Moscow and

Leningrad Conservatoires 60-; State Prize 51; People's Artist of R.S.F.S.R. 64; Lenin Prize 64.
Tchaikovsky Conservatoire, 13 Ulitsa Herzena, Mos-cow, U.S.S.R.

Rotblat, Joseph, C.B.E., M.A., D.SC., PH.D.; British (b. Polish) physicist; b. 4 Nov. 1908; ed. Univ. of Warsaw. Research Fellow, Radiological Laboratory of Scientific Soc. of Warsaw 33-39; Asst. Dir. of Atomic Physics, Inst. of Free Univ. of Poland 37-39; Oliver Lodge Fellow, Univ. of Liverpool 39-40; Lecturer, later Senior Lecturer, Dept. of Physics, Univ. of Liverpool 40-49, Dir. of Research in Nuclear Physics, Univ. of Liverpool 45-49; Prof. of Physics in Univ. of London, at St. Bartholomew's Hospital Medical Coll. 50-; mem. Polish Acad. of Sciences; Sec.-Gen. the Pugwash Confs.; Editor *Physics in Medicine and Biology.*
Publs. *Atomic Energy, a Survey* 54, *Atoms and the Universe* 56, *Science and World Affairs* 62, *Aspects of Medical Physics* 66, *Pugwash* 67.
8 Asmara Road, London, N.W.2, England.
Telephone: 01-435-1471.

Roth, Cecil, B.LITT., M.A., D.PHIL., F.R.HIST.S., F.R.S.L.; British historian; b. 5 March 1899; ed. London and Oxford.
Served First World War 17-19; Leverhulme Research Fellow 35-36; Pres. Jewish Historical Soc. of England 36-45, 56-57; corresp. mem. Accad. Colombaria Florence, Deputazione di Storia Patria, Venice, etc.; lectured S. Africa, America, Israel, Brazil; Reader in Jewish Studies, Oxford 38-64; Visiting Prof. Columbia Univ. 58, Bar Ilan Univ., Israel 65-66, Queen's Coll. and City Univ., New York 66-; Editor *Encyclopedia Judaica.*
Publs. *The Last Florentine Republic* 25, *History of the Marranos* 32, *A Short History of the Jewish People* 36, *The Spanish Inquisition* 37, *The Jewish Contribution to Civilisation* 38, *The Magnificent Rothschilds* 39, *History of Jews in England* 41, *The Sassoon Dynasty* 41, *History of Jews in Italy* 46, *The House of Nasi* 47-48, *The Intellectual Activities of Medieval English Jewry* 49, *The Jews of Medieval Oxford* 51, *Life of Benjamin Disraeli* 52, *Personalities and Events* 53, *The Aberdeen Codex of the Hebrew Bible, The Dead Sea Scrolls* 58, *The Jews in the Italian Renaissance* 59, *A History of the Jews in England* 64, *Gleanings* 67, Editor *Jewish Art: an Illustrated History* 61, *Essays and Portraits* 62, *The Sarajevo Haggadah* 63.
21 Rehov Balfour, Jerusalem, Israel; c/o Lloyds Bank, 263 Tottenham Court Road, London, W.1, England.
Telephone: 30716 (Home).

Roth, Rupert, D.IUR.; Austrian business executive; b. 19 Sept. 1903; ed. Humanistisches Gymnasium, Graz, and Konsular Akademie, Vienna.
Civil Servant 34-38; served Eastern Front, Second World War 42-45; Pres. of Chamber of Commerce, Steiermark 46-; Österreichisch-Alpine Montangesell-schaft (mining) 46-, Gen. Dir. 64-; Grosses Goldenes Ehrenzeichen für Verdienste um die Republik Öster-reich.
Österreichisch-Alpine Montangesellschaft, 1010 Vienna 1, Friedrichstrasse 4, Austria.

Rotha, Paul; British film producer, writer and journalist; b. 3 June 1907; ed. Highgate School and Slade School of Art, London.
Painter and designer; art critic, *The Connoisseur* 27-28; produced documentary films for Empire Marketing Board, *The Times,* Shell-Mex, etc.; formed own cos. 41 and 44; awarded gold medals Venice Film Festival 34; Brussels Film Festival 35; British Film Acad. award 48, UN award 53; mem. Council British Film Acad. 47-51, Fellow 51, Chair. of Council 51; Head of Television Documentary B.B.C. 53-55.
Productions include: *The World is Rich, World of Plenty, Land of Promise, Total War in Britain, A City Speaks,*

Contact, To-day We Live, Cover to Cover, The Future's in the Air, The Face of Britain, New Worlds for Old, The Fourth Estate, World Without End (with Basil Wright); *No Resting Place* 50, *Cat and Mouse* (features) 57, *Cradle of Genius* 59, *The Life of Adolf Hitler* 60, 61, *De Overval (Silent Raid)* (Dutch Feature) 62.
Publs. *The Film Till Now* 30, 49, 60, 63, 64, 67, *Celluloid: The Film Today* 31, *Documentary Film* 35, 39, 52, 64, *Movie Parade* 36, 50, *Portrait of a Flying Yorkshireman* 52, *Television in the Making* 56, *Rotha on the Film* 58, *The Innocent Eye*, biography of Robert J. Flaherty (with Basil Wright and A. Calder-Marshall) 63, *History of the British Documentary Film* 68.
c/o John Farquharson Ltd., 15 Red Lion Square, London, W.C.1, England.

Rothé, Jean-Pierre-Edmond, D. ès s.; French university professor; b. 16 Nov. 1906.
Asst. Faculty of Sciences, Strasbourg Univ. 28; Asst. Prof. 37, Prof. 45-; Dir. Inst. de Physique du Globe de Strasbourg 46-; Sec.-Gen. Int. Asscn. of Seismology of Int. Union of Geodesy and Geophysics; Dir. Int. Bureau of Seismology; Chevalier Légion d'Honneur.
Publs. *Contribution à l'étude des anomalies de champ magnétique terrestre* 37, *Séismes et Volcans* 46, 58, 62, *Prospection géophysique*, Vol. I 49, Vol. II 51, *La radioactivité des vosges hercyniennes* 57.
77 rue du Général Conrad, 67 Strasbourg, France.
Telephone: 353305.

Rothenberger, Anneliese; German opera singer (soprano); b. 19 June 1926; ed. Real and Musikhochschule, Mannheim.
Debut, Coblenz Theatre 47; Hamburg Opera House 48; Vienna State Opera 57-; has sung at La Scala, Milan, Metropolitan Opera, New York, Salzburg Festival, etc. Films *Die Fledermaus* 55, *Der Rosenkavalier.*
Vienna State Opera, Vienna, Austria.

Rothenstein, Sir John Knewstub Maurice, Kt., C.B.E., M.A., PH.D., LL.D., F.M.A.; British writer and art director; b. 11 July 1901; ed. Bedales School, Worcester Coll., Oxford, and Univ. Coll., London.
Assistant Prof. of Art History Univ. of Kentucky 27-28, Univ. of Pittsburgh 28-29; Dir. of City Art Galleries Leeds 32-34, Sheffield 33-38; Dir. and Keeper Tate Gallery 38-64; mem. British Council 38-64; mem. Exec. Cttee. Contemporary Art Soc. 38-64; mem. Art Panel, Arts Council Great Britain 42-52, 54-56; mem. Advisory Cttee. on decoration of Westminster Cathedral 53-; mem. Council Friends of the Tate Gallery 58-; Hon. Fellow, Worcester Coll., Oxford 63-; Rector Univ. of St. Andrews 64-67; mem. Advisory Council, Oxford Museum of Modern Art 66-; Prof. of Art History, Fordham Univ., New York 67-; Editor *The Masters* 65-67; Kt. Commdr., Order of Aztec Eagle (Mexico) 53.
Publs. *The Portrait Drawings of William Rothenstein 1889-1925* 26, *Eric Gill* 27, *The Artists of the 1890's* 28, *Morning Sorrow* (novel) 30, *Sixteen Letters from Oscar Wilde* (editor) 30, *British Artists and the War* 31, *Nineteenth Century Painting* 32, *An Introduction to English Painting* 33, *The Life and Death of Conder* 38, *Augustus John* 44, *Edward Burra* 45, *Manet* 45, *Foreign Pictures in the Tate Gallery* 49, *Turner* 49, 60, *London's River, an Anthology* (with Father Vincent Turner, S.J.) 51, *Modern English Painters*, Vol. I. *Sickert to Smith* 52, Vol. II, *Lewis to Moore* 56, *The Moderns and their World* (introduction) 57, *The Tate Gallery* 58, 62, *British Art since 1900: an Anthology* 62, *Matthew Smith* 62, *Paul Nash* 62, *Augustus John* 63, *Sickert* 63, *Turner* (with Martin Butlin) 64, *Francis Bacon* (with Ronald Alley) 64, *Summer's Lease* (autobiography I) 65, *Brave Day, Hideous Night* (II) 66.
Beauforest House, Newington, Warborough, Oxfordshire; and 8 Tryon Street, London, S.W.3, England.
Telephone 0096-32-482 and 01-584-7849.

Rothermere, 2nd Viscount, cr. 19, of Hemsted; **Esmond Cecil Harmsworth;** British newspaper proprietor; b. 29 May 1898; ed. Eton.
Conservative M.P. for the Isle of Thanet 19-29; Chair. Associated Newspapers Ltd.; Chair. Newspaper Proprietors Asscn. Ltd. 34-61; for a short time Dir. of Press Relations, Min. of Information 39, resgnd.; mem. Ministry Advisory Council; succeeded to title 40; Dir. Reuters 45-; Chancellor Newfoundland Memorial Univ. 52-61.
Warwick House, St. James's, London, S.W.1, England.

Rothfels, Hans, PH.D.; German historian; b. 12 April 1891; ed. Freiburg, Munich, Berlin and Heidelberg Univs.
Lecturer Berlin Univ. 24-26; Prof. of Modern History Koenigsberg Univ. 26-34; Research Fellow St. John's Coll., Oxford 39-40; Visiting Prof. Brown Univ., Providence (U.S.A.) 40-46; Prof. of Modern European History, Univ. of Chicago 46-56, of Modern History Tübingen Univ. 51-59, Prof. Emer. 59-; Chair. German Historical Asscn. 58-62; Editor *Vierteljahrshefte für Zeitgeschichte* 53-, *Akten zur deutschen aussen Politik* 61-; mem. Heidelberg Akad., Corresp. mem. Göttingen Akad., Grosses Bundesverdienstkreuz (with Star); mem. Order "Pour le Mérite" in Sciences and Arts.
Publs. *C. von Clausewitz: Politik und Krieg* 20, *Bismarck und der Staat* 25, *Th. Lohmann und die Kampfjahre der staatlichen Sozialpolitik* 26, *Prinzipienfragen der Bismarckschen Sozialpolitik* 29, *Ideengeschichte und Parteigeschichte* 30, *Bismarck und der Osten* 34, *Th. von Schön, Friedrich Wilhelm IV und der Revolution von 1848* 36, *The German Opposition to Hitler* 48 (German edn. 49, new Eng. Edn. 62), *Gesellschaftsform u. Ausw. Politik* 53, *Bismarck-Briefe* 55, *Zeitgeschichtliche Betrachtungen* 59, *Bismarck der Osten und das Reich* 60.
18 Waldhäuserstr., 74 Tübingen, German Federal Republic.

Rothko, Mark; American artist; b. 25 Sept. 1903; ed. Yale Univ. and Art Students League.
Full-time painter 26-; numerous exhbns. in American museums; exhibited at Venice Biennale 58; mem. Fed. of Modern Painters and Sculptors.
118 East 95th Street, New York City, N.Y., U.S.A.

Rothschild, 3rd Baron, cr. 85; **Nathaniel Mayer Victor Rothschild,** G.M., F.R.S., PH.D., SC.D.; British scientist; b. 31 Oct. 1910; ed. Harrow and Trinity Coll., Cambridge.
Fellow of Trinity Coll., Cambridge 35-39; Mil. Intelligence 39-45; Chair. Agric. Research Council 48-58; mem. B.B.C. Gen. Advisory Council 52-56; Asst. Dir. of Research, Dept. of Zoology, Cambridge Univ.; Research Co-ordinator of Royal Dutch Shell Group of Companies 65-; Vice-Chair. "Shell" Research Ltd. 61-63, Chair. 63-; Dir. Shell Int. Research Mij., Shell Chemicals U.K. Ltd.; Shell Research N.V.; Hon. Fellow Trinity Coll., Cambridge, Weizmann Inst. of Science, Israel, Bellairs Research Inst. of McGill Univ., Barbados, Univ. Coll., Cambridge; Hon. D.Sc., Newcastle and Manchester; American Legion of Merit, American Bronze Star.
Publs. *A Classification of Living Animals, Fertilization,* and a number of scientific papers.
11 Herschel Road, Cambridge, England.
Telephone: 50488.

Rothschild, Baron Alain James Gustave Jules de; French banker; b. 7 Jan. 1910; ed. Univ. de Paris.
Partner in Banque de Rothschild Frères; Dir. Soc. d'investissement du Nord; fmr. Mayor of Chamant; Chevalier Légion d'Honneur, Croix de Guerre.
21 rue Laffitte, Paris 9e, France.

Rothschild, Edmund Leopold de; British merchant banker; b. 2 Jan. 1916; ed. Harrow and Trinity Coll., Cambridge.

Royal Artillery 39-46; N. M. Rothschild & Sons 46-, Senior Partner 60-; Deputy Chair. British Newfoundland Corpn. Ltd., Churchill Falls (Labrador) Corpn. Ltd.; Dir. Alliance Assurance Co. Ltd., Sun Alliance and London Insurance Ltd., Sun Insurance Office Ltd., Anglo-Israel Securities Ltd., Carreras Ltd., Alfred Dunhill Ltd., Five Arrows Securities Co. Ltd., Sun Alliance and London Assurance Co. Ltd.; mem. Council Royal Nat. Pension Fund for Nurses; Trustee, Queen's Inst. of District Nursing, British Freedom from Hunger Campaign; Joint Treas. Council of Christians and Jews and Friends of Hebrew Univ.
Publ. *Window on the World.*
Home: Inchmery House, Exbury, nr. Southampton, Hants. SO4 1AE; Office: New Court, St. Swithins Lane, London, E.C.4, England.
Telephone: 01-626-4356 (Office).

Rothschild, Baron Elie Robert de; French banker; b. 29 May 1917; ed. Lycée Louis le Grand, Faculty of Law, Univ. de Paris.
President and Dir.-Gen. Cie. des chemins de fer du P.L.M., des Chemins de Fer "Paris-Orleans"; Dir. Franco-Britannique de Participations, New Court Securities Corpn., Five Arrows Security Co. Ltd., Canada, Assicurazioni Generali Trieste, Cie. du Nord; Vice-Pres. Cie. d'assurances "La Concorde", Banque Rothschild; Chevalier Légion d'Honneur, Croix de Guerre.
21 rue Laffitte, Paris 9e; Home: 11 rue Masseran, Paris 7e, France.
Telephone: 824-97-40 (Office); FON 90-90 (Home).

Rothschild, Baron Guy Edouard Alphonse Paul de; French banker; b. 21 May 1909; ed. Lycées Condorcet and Louis le Grand, Faculty of Law and Arts, Univ. de Paris.
Chairman Banque Rothschild, Société Minière et Métallurgique de Peñarroya; Dir. and Chair. Exec. Cttee. Compagnie du Nord; Dir. Sté. Le Nickel, The Rio-Tinto-Zinc Co. Ltd. (London), S.A. de Gérance et d'Armement (Saga), Cie. franco-africaine de recherches pétrolières (Francarep), S.A. Femmes d'Aujourd'hui (Brussels), Nat. Provincial & Rothschild (International) Ltd., New Court Securities Corpn., European Property Co. Ltd. (London); Chair. Board Five Arrows Security Co. Ltd., Canada; Officier Légion d'Honneur, Croix de Guerre.
10 rue de Courcelles, Paris 8e, France.

Rothschild, Robert, DR. RER. POL.; Belgian diplomatist; b. 11; ed. Univ. of Brussels and Acad. of Int. Law, The Hague.
Entered Foreign Office 37; served Lisbon 41, Chungking 44, Shanghai 46, Washington, D.C. 50; Deputy Permanent Rep. to NATO 52; Chef de Cabinet, Foreign Office 54-58; Ambassador to Yugoslavia 58-60; Dep. Chief of Diplomatic Mission to the Republic of Congo 60; Chef de Cabinet, Foreign Office 61-64; Ambassador to Switzerland 64-66, to France 66-; awards include Commdr. Order of Leopold (Belgium).
Belgian Embassy, rue de Tilsitt 9, Paris 17e, France; 57 Avenue de Général de Gaulle, Brussels, Belgium.

Rotov, Boris Georgievich (Most Rev. Nikodim); Soviet ecclesiastic; b. 16 Oct. 1929; ed. Ryazan Pedagogic Inst. and Leningrad Theological Seminary and Theological Acad.
Ordained monk and deacon 47, hierodeacon 47; worked in Yaroslavl and Uglich 49-52; priest, Yaroslavl Cathedral and Sec. to Archbishop 52-54, Dean 54-56; Russian Orthodox Mission in Jerusalem 56-59; Chief, Moscow Patriarchate Chancellery, Deputy Chair. Dept. for Foreign Ecclesiastical Relations 59-60, Chair. 60-; Bishop of Podolsk, Vicar of Moscow Eparchy 60-, Archbishop 61-; mem. Comm. for Inter-Christian Relations 60-; Head Moscow Patriarchate Publishing

House 60-; perm. mem. Holy Synod 61-; Metropolitan of Minsk and Byelorussia 63-, of Leningrad and Ladoga 63-; mem. Central Cttee. and Exec. Cttee. of World Council of Churches; Vice-Pres. Christian Peace Conf.; Orders of Eastern Patriarchs.
Publs. *History of the Russian Orthodox Mission in Jerusalem, Christian Liturgy and Churches at the time of St. John Chrysostom.*
Moscow Patriarchate, 18 Ryleev Street, Moscow, U.S.S.R.

Rottier, Antoine Cyrille Julien; Netherlands business executive; b. 13 March 1910; ed. Univ. of Economic Science, Tilburg.
With Ministry of Econ. Affairs; DSM (Staatsmijnen) Limburg 36-, Man. Dir. 49-62, Chair. 62-; Knight, Order of Netherlands Lion.
Publ. *De beambte in onderneming en maatschappij.*
DSM (Staatsmijnen), 2 Van der Maesenstraat, Heerlen; 31 Valkenburgerweg, Heerlen, Netherlands.
Telephone: 0440-08111-2535.

Rötzsch, Helmut; German librarian; b. 23; ed. Buchhändler-Lehranstalt, Leipzig, and Karl-Marx Univ., Leipzig.
Director of Acquisition Dept., Deutsche Bücherei 55-58, Dep. Director, Deutsche Bücherei 59-61, Gen. Dir. 61-; Town Councillor, Leipzig 61-; Vice-Pres. Beirat für das wissenschaftliche Bibliothekswesen der D.D.R. 62-; Service Medal of German Democratic Republic 59, 64.
Publs. *Der Börsenverein der deutschen Buchhändler zu Leipzig und die Deutsche Bücherei* 62, *Die Deutsche Bücherei—die deutsche Nationalbibliothek* 62, Editor: *Deutsche Bücherei 1912-62.*
Karl-Rothe-Strasse 15, Leipzig, German Democratic Republic.

Rouamba, Tensoré Paul; Upper Voltan diplomatist; b. 28 March 1933; ed. Univs. of Bordeaux, Grenoble and Paris.
Former mem. Constitutional Chamber of Supreme Court of Upper Volta; fmr. Asst. Prof., Centre of Tropical Geography, Univ. of Abidjan; Prof. at Normal School, Ouagadougou 63-65; Perm. Rep. of Upper Volta to UN 66-.
Permanent Mission of Upper Volta to the United Nations, 236 East 46th Street, New York, N.Y. 10017, U.S.A.

Rougemont, Denis de, L. ès L.; Swiss author; b. 8 Sept. 1906.
Lecturer, Univ. of Frankfurt-on-Main 35-36; Prof. Ecole Libre des Hautes Etudes, New York 41; one of the founders of the Personalist Movement in Paris 33; contrib. to leading periodicals in Europe, North and South America; Dir. Centre Européen de la Culture; Chair. Exec. Cttee. Congress for Cultural Freedom 51-66; Chair. Round Table Council of Europe 53, 55; Chair. European Asscn. of Music Festivals, Prof. Inst. Univ. d'Etudes Européennes, Geneva; Corresp. mem. Acad. des Sciences morales et politiques, Paris.
Publs. *Politique de la Personne, Penser avec les Mains, Journal d'un Intellectuel en Chômage, Journal d'Allemagne, L'Amour et L'Occident* (new version 56), *Nicolas de Flue, Mission ou Démission de la Suisse, The Heart of Europe, La Part du Diable, Les Personnes du Drame, Lettres sur la Bombe Atomique, Vivre en Amérique, Journal des Deux-Mondes, L'Europe en Jeu, Doctrine fabuleuse, Suite Neuchâteloise, Lettres aux Députés Européens, La Confédération Helvétique, L'Aventure Occidentale de l'homme, Comme toi-même, Vingt-huit siècles d'Europe, Les Chances de l'Europe, The Christian Opportunity, La Suisse ou l'histoire d'un peuple heureux, Journal d'une époque (1926-1946).*
01 Ferney-Voltaire, Ain, France.
Telephone: Ferney 30-44.

Roughton, Francis John Worsley, F.R.S., PH.D., M.A.; British physiologist; b. 6 June 1899; ed. Winchester Coll., and Trinity Coll., Cambridge.
Awarded Gedge Prize 22 and Rolleston Prize 24; Dunn Lecturer in Biochemistry Cambridge Univ. 23; Rockefeller Fellow U.S.A. 29; Fellow Trinity Coll. Cambridge 23- and Univ. Lecturer in Physico-Chemical Physiology 27-46; Sec. Physiology Section British Asscn. 31-34; Dir. Hopkinson House and Vincent House 34-; Co-Ed. *Biochemical Journal* 35-41; Prof. of Colloid Science, Cambridge Univ. 47-66.
Ellerslie, 9 Adams Road, Cambridge, England.

Rouhani, Fuad, LL.M.; Iranian lawyer and executive; b. 23 Oct. 1907; ed. Teheran, London Univ.
Anglo-Iranian Oil Co., Legal and Admin. Branches 26-51; Chief Legal Adviser, Nat. Iranian Oil Co. 51-54, Dir. 54-, Man. Dir., Dep. Chair. 56-; Sec.-Gen. and Chair. Board of Govs., Org. of Petroleum Exporting Countries (OPEC) 61-64; Prof. of Iranian Studies at Columbia Univ. 64-65; Sec.-Gen., Org. of Regional Co-operation for Devt. between Iran, Pakistan and Turkey 65-; Amb. 65; Adviser to Prime Minister of Iran.
Regional Co-operation for Development, 5 Vassal Shirazi, North of Boulevard, P.O. Box 3273, Teheran; and 16 Kh. Rasht (Behjatabad), Teheran, Iran.
Telephone: 43807.

Rouleau, Joseph-Alfred; Canadian bass singer; b. 20 Feb. 1929; ed. Coll. Jean De Brebeuf, Montreal, Univ. of Montreal, Conservatoire of Music, Province of Quebec.
Three years in Milan for singing studies; debut in Montreal 55, at Royal Opera House, Covent Garden 57-, has sung over 30 roles at Covent Garden; guest artist at principal Opera Houses all over the world; tour of Canada 60, tour of Australia with Joan Sutherland 65, second tour of Russia 66, tour of Romania; recordings for E.M.I. include: Scenes from *Anna Bolena, Ruddigore, Romeo et Juliett* (Gounod); for L'oiseau lyre: *l'enfance du Christ* (Berlioz); for Decca: *Semiramide, Boris Godunov,* and *Renard* (Stravinsky); several awards including Prix Calixa-Lavallée 67 (La Société St. Jean Baptiste, Montreal).
Major roles include: Boris Godunov (*Boris Godunov*), Philip II (*Don Carlo*), Basilio (*Barber of Seville*), Mephisto (*Faust*), Dosifei (*Khovanschina*), Don Quixote (*Don Quixote*).
Royal Opera House, London, W.C.2, England.

Roullier, Jean Georges; French civil servant; b. 10 Dec. 1898; ed. Faculté des Lettres et de Droit, Paris.
Secretary-Gen. Dept. of Shipping 39-40; Asst. Dir. Econ. and Supply Dept. 44-48; Asst. Dir. of Maritime Transport 48-50; Dir. of Depts. of Gen. Admin. and of Seafarers, Ministry of Merchant Marine 50-63; Chair. Cen. Cttee. for Maritime Safety 50-63; Vice-Chair. Higher Council of the Merchant Marine; Sec.-Gen. UN Inter-Governmental Maritime Consultative Org. (IMCO) 63-Dec. 67; Commdr. Legion of Honour.
Publ. *Les transports maritimes de la France en guerre* 46.
c/o Inter-Governmental Maritime Consultative Organization, 22 Berners Street, London, W.1, England.
Telephone: 01-580-6141.

Roumajon, Yves Pierre Jean; French psychiatrist; b. 13 Dec. 1914; ed. Lycée Champollion, Grenoble, Collège Municipal de Chalons-sur-Marne, Lycée Faidherbe, Lille, and Lycée Louis-le-Grand, Paris.
Former Intern, Hôpitaux Psychiatriques de la Seine; Medical Head of Psychiatric Service, Choquan Hospital, S. Viet-Nam 50-52; Head of Clinic, Faculty of Medicine 53; Doctor, Seine Centre for Educational Guidance for Children and Adolescents 53-60; Psychiatrist, Educ. Service for Young Prisoners, Fresnes Prison 58-; Expert at Paris Court of Appeal 58-, and Court of Cassation 63-; mem. Board of Dirs. Int. Soc. of Criminology 63; Vice-Pres. Société Générale de Prison et de Législation

Criminelle 64; Chevalier Légion d'Honneur, Croix de Guerre 39-45, etc.
15 rue Nélaton, Paris 15e, France.
Telephone: 783-16-19.

Rountree, William Manning, LL.B.; American diplomatist; b. 28 March 1917; ed. Atlanta (Ga.) Technological High School, and Columbus Univ., Washington, D.C.
Accountant and Auditor U.S. Treasury Dept. 35-41; Budget Officer and Dep. to Asst. Admin. Lend Lease Admin. 41-42; Gen. Asst. to Dir. U.S. Economic Operations in Middle East 42-45; Special Asst. and Economic Adviser to Head of Near Eastern, South Asian and African Div., State Dept. 46-48; Special Asst. U.S. Ambassador to Greece 48-49; Dep., later Dir. Office of Greek, Turkish and Iranian Affairs 49-52; Counsellor of Embassy, Ankara 52-53; Minister Counsellor Teheran 53-55; Dep. Asst. Sec. of State for Near Eastern, South Asian and African Affairs 55-56, Asst. Sec. 56-59; Ambassador to Pakistan 59-62, to the Sudan 62-65, to the Republic of South Africa 65-.
American Embassy, Pretoria, South Africa.

Rous, (Francis) Peyton, B.A., M.D., SC.D.; American pathologist; b. 5 Oct. 1879; ed. Johns Hopkins Univ.
Instructor in Pathology Michigan Univ. 06-08; Asst. Associate and Mem. in Pathology Rockefeller Inst. for Medical Research 09-45, Mem. Emer. 45; Linacre Lecturer, Cambridge Univ. 29; Hon. Fellow Trinity Hall, Cambridge, Weizmann Inst. of Science, Israel; Scientific Consultant, Sloan-Kettering Inst. for Cancer Research; mem. Nat. Acad. of Sciences, American Philosophical Society, Royal Danish Acad. of Sciences, Asscn. American Physicians, Norwegian Acad. of Science and Letters; foreign mem. Royal Society, London; hon. mem. British Physiological Society, Pathological Society of Great Britain and Ireland, N.Y. Pathological Society; Hon. Fellow Royal Society of Medicine, London; foreign corresp. Acad. of Medicine Paris, and B.M.A.; awarded John Scott Medal 27, Royal Coll. of Surgeons of England Walker Prize for Cancer Research 41; Anna Fuller Memorial Award 52; Asscn. American Physicians Kober Medal 53; Univ. of Texas Bertner Medal and Award 54, Kovalenko Medal, Nat. Acad. of Science 56; Distinguished Service Award, U.S. Cancer Society 57; Lasker Award American Public Health Asscn.; Landsteiner Award, American Asscn. of Blood Banks 58; N.Y. Acad. Medicine Medal 59, Judd Award, Memorial Center for Cancer N.Y. 59, Gold Medal, Royal Soc. of Medicine (London), UN Award for Cancer Research 62, Nat. Medal for Science (U.S.A.) 66, Paul Ehrlich Prize (German Fed. Repub.) 66, Nobel Prize for Medicine 66, and other awards; Editor *Journal of Experimental Medicine;* Hon. Sc.D. (Yale, Cambridge Eng., Michigan, McGill, Chicago, Rockefeller Inst., Birmingham Eng., Hartford U.S.A.), Hon. M.D. (Zürich), Hon. LL.D. (St. Lawrence).
Publs. Research on pathology and bacteriology, especially cancer.
Rockefeller University, 66th Street and York Avenue, New York 21, N.Y., U.S.A.

Rous, Sir Stanley Ford, Kt., C.B.E., J.P.; British sports administrator; b. 25 April 1895; ed. St. Luke's Coll., Exeter.
Served European War 14-18; Asst. Master Watford Grammar School 21-34; Sec. of the Football Asscn. 34-61; Vice-Pres. European Football Fed. 60; Chair. The Central Council of Physical Recreation; mem. Int. Fed. of Football Asscns., Pres. 61-; Chair. Arts Educational Trust; Chevalier Couronne de Chêne, Luxembourg; Chevalier de la Légion d'Honneur, France; Commendatore dell'Ordine al merito della Repubblica Italiana.
115 Ladbroke Road, London, W.11, England.
Telephone: 01-727-4113.

Rousseau, Jacques, D.SC., F.R.S.C.; Canadian botanist and ethnographer; b. 5 Oct. 1905; ed. Univ. of Montreal, and Cornell Univ.

Lecturer, Institut Botanique, Montreal Univ. 28-35; Prof. 35-44; Asst. Dir., Montreal Botanical Garden 38-44; Dir. 44-57; Dir. Canadian Museum of Human History 57-59; Assoc. Prof., Sorbonne 59-62; Research Prof. Centre d'Études Nordiques, Univ. Laval, Quebec 62-.

Publs. Books, pamphlets and articles on geography, flora and ethnology of Quebec-Labrador Peninsula, etc.

5208 Côte St. Antoine, Montreal 28, Canada.

Telephone: 482-4230.

Rousseaux, André; French author and critic; b. 23 March 1896.

Author of numerous works of criticism; literary critic of *Le Figaro*; mem. P.E.N. Club; Commdr. Légion d'Honneur.

Publs. *Littérature du XX siècle* (6 vols.) 38-58, *Le Monde Classique* (7 vols.) 42-56, *Le Prophète Péguy* (2 vols.) 46.

5 rue d'Assas, Paris 6e, France.

Telephone: Littré 71-83.

Rousselet, Marcel, D. en D., D. ès L.; French lawyer; b. 6 Dec. 1893; ed. Nancy and Paris Univs.

Entered Magistracy 20; Dep. at Tribunal de la Seine 32; Pres. Tribunal de la Seine 44-50; Pres. Paris Court of Appeal 50-62, First Hon. Pres. Sept. 62-; mem. l'Institut de France, Acad. des Sciences Morales et Politiques 59-; Commdr. de la Légion d'Honneur.

Publs. *Les Livres fonciers en Alsace Lorraine* 20, *La Magistrature sous la Monarchie de Juillet* 37, *L'Affaire du Duc de Praslin et la Magistrature* 37, *Histoire de la Justice* 43, *Les Souverains devant la Justice* 46, *Histoire de la Magistrature Française des Origines à nos Jours* 57, *Berryer devant la Cour d'Assises* 65, *Les cas de Conscience du Magistrat* 67.

52 rue des Ecoles, Paris 5e, France.

Roussin, André Jean Paul, B. ès L.; French playwright; b. 22 Jan. 1911; ed. Inst. Mélizan, Marseilles.

Left journalism to found "*Le Rideau Gris*" with Louis Ducreux; Officier de Mérite National; Commdr. des Arts et Lettres; Chevalier de la Légion d'Honneur.

Plays include: *Am-Stram-Gram, Une grande fille toute simple, Jean- Baptiste le Mal-Aimé, Le Tombeau d'Achille, La Sainte Famille, La Petite Hutte, Les Oeufs d'Austriche, Nina, Bobosse, Lorsque l'enfant paraît, La Main de César, Le Mari, la Femme et la Mort, L'Amour Fou, La Mamma, Une femme qui dit la verité, Les Glorieuses, L'Ecole des Autres, Un amour qui ne finit pas, La Voyante, La Locomotive.*

7 rue Gutenberg, Boulogne-sur-Seine (Seine), France.

Roux, Abraham Johannes Andries, D.SC., B.SC.; South African nuclear scientist; b. 18 Oct. 1914; ed. Univ. of the Witwatersrand.

Lecturer, Dept. of Mechanical Engineering, Witwatersrand Univ. 39-44; Senior Lecturer, Stellenbosch Univ. 44-46; Principal Research Officer, Nat. Building Research Inst., Council for Scientific and Industrial Research (C.S.I.R.) 46-52, Officer in Charge C.S.I.R. Mech. Engineering Research Unit 52, Nat. Physical Research Lab. 52-55, Dir. Nat. Mech. Engineering Research Inst., C.S.I.R. 55-57, Vice-Pres. C.S.I.R. 57-60; Part-time Dir. Atomic Energy Research Programme 56-59, Dir. of Research, Atomic Energy Board 59-60, Dir. Atomic Energy Board 60-64, Dir.-Gen. June 64-Oct. 67, Chair. Nov. 67-; Chair. Nat. Inst. for Metallurgy 67-; D.Sc. h.c.

Publs. *Mechanical Engineering Research in South Africa* 52, *Mechanical Engineering in Relation to Industry* 55-57, *Developments in the Field of Nuclear Power and their Impact on South Africa* 58, *The Atomic Energy Research and Development Programme of South Africa* 59, *Science, Industry and the Professional Society* 60, *The First Reactor Installation of the Republic of South Africa* 62, *South Africa's Programme of Nuclear Research* 62, *The Scope of Research and Development in the Field of Radioisotopes and Nuclear Radiation in South Africa* 64, *Nuclear Engineering in South Africa* 64, *Power Generation in South Africa with Special Reference to the Introduction of Nuclear Power* (Co-author) 66.

Atomic Energy Board, Private Bag 256, Pretoria, South Africa.

Telephone: 79-4441.

Roux, Ambroise; French business executive; b. 26 June 1921; ed. Collège Stanislas, Paris, and Ecole Polytechnique.

Chief Engineer, First Electrical Area 49; Asst. Govt. Rep., Electricité de France 50; Technical Adviser, later Private Sec. to Minister of Industry and Commerce 52-54; Dir. Electricité de France 52-55, Soc. de transports pétroliers par pipe-lines 52-55; Asst. Dir.-Gen. Cie. générale d'électricité 55-63, Dir.-Gen. 63-66, Admin. Dir. Gen. 66-; Pres. Dir.-Gen. Cie. continentale Edison 56-, Cie. industrielle des télécommunications 66-; Vice-Pres. Patronat Français 66-; official of numerous other companies and orgs.; Officier Légion d'Honneur; Commandeur du Mérite Commercial.

Office: 54 rue La Boëtie, Paris 8e; Home: 17 Place des Etats-Unis, Paris 16e, France.

Telephone: 359-48-01.

Roux, Jacques; French diplomatist; b. 1 March 1907; ed. Collège Saint-Joseph, Avignon, Facultés de droit d'Aix en Provence et de Paris.

Diplomatic Service, London 34-37; Ministry of Foreign Affairs 37; Sec. Chungking 45, Counsellor Nanking 46; Dir. of Asian Dept., Ministry of Foreign Affairs 52-56, Asst. Dir.-Gen. of Political Affairs 56, 57-63, Asst. Dir. Office of Minister 56-57; Amb. to United Arab Republic 63-; Commdr. Légion d'Honneur.

Ambassade de France, 29 Sharia Giza, Cairo, United Arab Republic.

Rovensky, John Edward; American banker, economist and industrialist.

Began banking career with First Nat. Bank Pittsburgh, later with Nat. Bank of Commerce, N.Y. City, Vice-Pres. 20-26; First Vice-Pres., later Vice-Chair. Bank of America 26-31; Vice-Pres. Nat. City Bank of N.Y. 32-44; Chair. of Board, A.C.F. Industries Inc. (retd. 55); mem. Acad. of Political Science, American Economic Assccn.; Fellow Royal Economic Society (London), Economic Society of S. Africa.

Clarendon Court, Bellevue and Rovensky Aves., Newport, R.I.; 750 Third Avenue, N.Y.C. 17, N.Y., U.S.A.

Rowan, Carl Thomas, B.A., M.A.; American diplomatist; b. 11 Aug. 1925; ed. Oberlin Coll., and Univ. of Minnesota.

Served U.S. Navy 43-46; journalist 48-61; Dep. Asst. Sec. of State for Public Affairs 61-63; Ambassador to Finland 63-64; Dir. U.S. Information Agency 64-65; Columnist, *Chicago Daily News* 65-; numerous hon. degrees.

2832 Elicott Street, N.W., Washington, D.C., U.S.A.

Rowan, Sir (Thomas) Leslie, K.C.B., C.V.O.; British industrialist; b. 22 Feb. 1908; ed. Queens' Coll., Cambridge.

Entered Colonial Office 30; Treasury 33; Asst. and later Principal Private Sec. to Prime Minister (Mr. Churchill) 41-45; (Mr. Attlee) 45-47; Permanent Sec. Office of Minister for Economic Affairs 47; Second Sec. H.M. Treasury 47-49; Econ. Minister, British Embassy, Washington 49-51; Second Sec. H.M. Treasury 51-58; Man. Dir. Vickers Ltd. 62-; Dep. Chair. British Nat. Export Council 65; Deputy Chair. Vickers Ltd. 66-67, Chair. 67-.

16 The Vale, Chelsea, London, S.W.3, England.

Rowicki, Witold; Polish conductor and composer; b. 14; ed. Cracow Conservatoire.

Debut as conductor 32; appearances as soloist and in chamber ensembles 32-45; Prof., Cracow Conservatoire 38; violinist and violist in Cracow Philharmonic Orchestra 40-45; Founder, Musical Dir. and Chief Conductor Radio Symphony Orchestra, Katowice 45-50, State Higher School of Music, Warsaw 52-54; organiser, Musical Dir. and Chief conductor Warsaw Philharmonic Orchestra, now Nat. Philharmonic Orchestra 50-; Dir. Teatr Wielki Opera Centre 65-; conducted in many European, African, Asian, North and South American countries.

Chocimska 35, m. 12, Warsaw, Poland.

Rowland, John Russell; Australian diplomatist; b. 10 Feb. 1925; ed. Cranbrook School, Sydney, and Univ. of Sydney.

Department of External Affairs 44-, served Moscow 46-48, Saigon 52, 54-55, Washington 55-56, London 57-59; Asst. Sec., Dept. of External Affairs 61-65; Ambassador to U.S.S.R. 65-.

Publ. *The Feast of Ancestors* (poetry).

Australian Embassy, Moscow, U.S.S.R.

Rowland, Raymond Edgar, B.S. (Agriculture); American businessman; b. 8 Dec. 1902; ed. Univs. of Illinois and Wisconsin.

Joined Ralston Purina Co. as Junior Salesman 26, later various sales and production positions, Asst. Vice-Pres. 40-43, Vice-Pres. 43-56, Dir. 51-, Pres. 56-64, Chair. of Board 64-68; Dir. Ralston Purina Co. and subsidiaries; Dir. Union Electric Co., Norfolk and Western Railway, Mercantile Trust Co. (St. Louis), Transit Casualty Co., St. Louis Chamber of Commerce, Lindenwood Coll. (St. Charles, Mo.); Dir. Granite City Steel Corpn.; mem. Chicago Board of Trade, Univ. of Wis. Foundation; Trustee Central Presbyterian Church, Barnes Hospital, Wisconsin Alumni Research Foundation; David Ranken Jr. School of Mechanical Trades.

Ralston Purina Co., 835 South 8th Street, St. Louis, Mo. 63199, U.S.A.

Telephone: CH1-3600.

Rowley, Rev. Harold Henry, M.A., D.D., B.LITT., F.B.A.; British ecclesiastic and Semitic scholar; b. 24 March 1890; ed. Baptist Coll., Bristol, St. Catherine's Society, and Mansfield Coll., Oxford.

Min. of United Church, Wells (Som.) 17-22; Missionary in China 22-30; Associate Prof. Old Testament, Cheeloo Univ. Tsinanfu 24-29; Asst. Lecturer in Semitic Languages, Univ. Coll., Cardiff 30-34; Prof. of Semitic Languages, Univ. Coll. of N. Wales 35-45; Dean of Bangor School of Theology 36-45; Vice-Principal Univ. Coll. Bangor 40-45; Lecturer in History of Religions, Univ. Coll. of N. Wales 40-44; Prof. Semitic Languages and Literatures, Univ. of Manchester 45-49; Prof. Hebrew Language and Literature, Univ. of Manchester 49-59; Emeritus 59-; Pres. Baptist Union of U.K. 57-58; Hon. D.D. (Oxford, Durham, Wales, Edinburgh and Manchester), Hon. Theol.D. (Uppsala, Marburg and Zürich), Hon. LL.D. (McMaster), Hon. Dr. (Strasbourg).

Publs. *The Aramaic of the Old Testament* 29, *Darius the Mede* 35, *The Relevance of the Bible* 41, *The Relevance of Apocalyptic* 44, *The Missionary Message of the Old Testament* 45, *The Rediscovery of the Old Testament* 46, *The Growth of the Old Testament* 50, *The Biblical Doctrine of Election* 50, *From Joseph to Joshua* 50, *Submission in Suffering and other Essays* 51, *The Servant of the Lord and other Essays* 52, *The Zadokite Fragments and the Dead Sea Scrolls* 52, *The Unity of the Bible* 53, *Prophecy and Religion in Ancient China and Israel* 56, *The Faith of Israel* 56, *From Moses to Qumran* 63, *Men of God* 63, *Worship in Ancient Israel* 67; Editor *Studies in the Old Testament Prophecy* 50, *The Old Testament and Modern Study* 51, *Journal of Semitic Studies* 56-60, Peake's *Commentary on the Bible*, New Edn. 62, Hasting's *Dictionary of the Bible*, New Edn. 63, Manson's *Companion to the Bible*, New Edn. 63.

The Field, Cowle Road, Stroud, Glos., England.

Telephone: Stroud 3888.

Rowse, Alfred Leslie, D.LITT., F.R.S.L.; British writer; b. 4 Dec. 1903; ed. in Cornwall, and Christ Church, Oxford. Fellow British Acad., All Souls Coll. Oxford.

Publs. *Mr. Keynes and the Labour Movement* 36, *Sir Richard Grenville of the Revenge* 37, *Tudor Cornwall* 41, *Poems of a Decade 31-41*, *A Cornish Childhood* 42, *The Spirit of English History* 43, *Poems Chiefly Cornish* 44, *The English Spirit* 44, *West Country Stories* 45, *The Use of History* 46, *Poems of Deliverance* 46, *The End of an Epoch* 47, *The England of Elizabeth* 50, *The English Past* 51 (revised edition entitled *Times, Persons, Places* 65), Lucien Romier's *History of France* trans. and completed 53, *The Expansion of Elizabethan England* 55, *The Early Churchills* 56, *The Later Churchills, Poems Partly American* 59, *The Elizabethans and America* 59, *St. Austell: Church, Town, Parish* 60, *Appeasement: A Study in Political Decline* 61, *Ralegh and the Throckmortons* 62, *William Shakespeare: A Biography* 63, *Shakespeare's Sonnets* 64, *Christopher Marlowe: A Biography* 64, *A Cornishman at Oxford* 65, *Shakespeare's Southampton* 65, *Bosworth Field and the Wars of the Roses* 66, *Poems of Cornwall and America* 67, *Cornish Stories* 67.

All Souls College, Oxford, England.

Roy, Sir Asoka Kumar, Kt., M.A., B.L.; Indian lawyer; b. 9 Sept. 1886; ed. Doveton, Presidency and Ripon Colls., Calcutta.

Called to Bar Middle Temple 12; Standing Counsel Bengal 29, fmr. Act. Judge High Court, Calcutta 32 and 33-34; Kt. 37; Advocate-Gen. Bengal 34-43; Law mem. Viceroy's Exec. Council 43-46; Dir. Jardine Henderson Ltd., The Titaghur Paper Mills Co. Ltd., Bengal Coal Co. Ltd., Indian Copper Corpn. Ltd., Anglo India Jute Mills Co. Ltd. and 12 other companies.

3 Upper Wood Street, Calcutta 16, India.

Telephone: 44-5440.

Roy, Bhabesh Chandra, D.I.C., M.SC., DR.ING.; Indian geologist; b. 1 Aug. 1907; ed. Imperial Coll., London, Univ. of Nancy, and Univ. of Freiberg, Germany.

Joined Geological Survey of India 37, Dir. 58-61, Dir.-Gen. 61-65; UN Fellow in U.S.A. and Canada 57; mem. Oil and Natural Gas Comm. 64-; Del. to ECAFE Mineral Confs. in Tokyo 55, Kuala Lumpur 58, U.S.S.R., U.K., France and Germany 55, Rome and Bandung 63, Vienna 64, Antwerp 66, Mexico City 67; Leader Del. Int. Geological Congress, Copenhagen 60; and numerous other int. geological meetings; Pres. Geological, Mining and Metallurgical Inst. of India 58-59; Co-ordinator Geological Map for Asia and Far East 58-68; Vice-Pres. Int. Union of Geological Sciences 61-68; Sec.-Gen. Int. Geol. Congress, New Delhi 64; Chair. Dept. of Geology, Univ. of Nigeria 66-67, U.G.C. Prof., Presidency Coll., Calcutta 68-; Editor *Journal of Mines, Metals and Fuels* 68-; Vice-Pres. I.G.C. Comm., History of Geol. Sciences 68-; Fellow, Nat. Inst. of Sciences of India.

Publs. include: *Mineral Resources of Bombay* 51, *Economic Geology and Mineral Resources of Saurashtra* 53, *The Nellore Mica Belt* 56, *The Economic Geology and Mineral Resources of Rajasthan and Ajmer* 57; numerous articles on Geology and Mineral Resources.

37/3, Southend Park, Calcutta 29, India.

Telephone: 46-3189.

Roy, Claude; French writer; b. 28 Aug. 1915; ed. Univ. of Paris.

War service 39-40; imprisoned and escaped 40; in the Free Zone of France 40-43; contributed to the review *Poésie* 40, 41, etc., and to the review *Fontaine*; mem. Resistance in Southern Zone, Les Etoiles movement;

contributed to the clandestine Press *Les Lettres Fran-çaises*; War Corresp. after the Liberation; Croix de Guerre; mem. Exec. Cttee. Société Européenne de Culture.
Publs. *L'Enfance de l'Art* 41, *Clefs pour l'Amerique, Clefs pour la Chine, Descriptions Critiques, La Nuit est le manteau des pauvres, Le Soleil sur la Terre, Le Malheur d'Aimer, Le journal des Voyages, L'Homme en Question, De la Sagesse des Nations, Gérard Philipe* (with Anne Philipe), *Léone et les Siens, L'Amour du théâtre, La Derobée.*
c/o Editions Gallimard, 5 rue Sébastien-Bottin, Paris 7e, France.

Roy, Jamini; Indian painter; b. 87; ed. Calcutta School of Art.
Abandoned European style and evolved a personal idiom based on Bengali folk-art; has worked both in oils and brush drawings, in which medium his *Studies of Christ* are particularly well known; exhbns. in India and abroad.
18 Dehi Serampore Lane, Calcutta 19, West Bengal, India.

Roy, H.E. Cardinal Maurice, D.D., D.PH.; French Canadian ecclesiastic; b. 25 Jan. 1905; ed. Laval Univ., Quebec, Inst. Angelicum, Rome, and Inst. Catholique and Sorbonne, Paris.
Ordained Priest 27; Prof. of Theology, Laval Univ. 30-46; Army Chaplain (Canadian Army Overseas) 39, 45; Rector of Grand Seminary (School of Theology). Laval Univ. 46; Bishop of Trois Rivières, Quebec 46-47; Archbishop (R.C.) of Quebec 47-; Bishop Ordinary to Canadian Armed Forces; Primate of Canada 56-; cr. Cardinal by Pope Paul VI 65.
Archevêché, C.P. 459, Quebec 4, Quebec, Canada.

Roy, Maurice; French engineer; b. 7 Nov. 1899; ed. Ecole Polytechnique, and Ecole Nat. Supérieure des Mines.
Engineer Corps des Mines 22; Prof. Ecole Nat. des Ponts et Chaussées 26-50, concurrently Prof. Ecole Nat. supérieure de l'Aéronautique; Dir. *La Science Aérienne* 30-35; Prof. Ecole Polytechnique 47-; Dir. Office Nat. d'Etudes et de Recherches Aéronautiques 49-62; Chair. Exec. Cttee. Int. Council of Aeronautical Sciences; Pres. Int. Union of Theoretical and Applied Mechanics; Pres. Cttee. on Space Research; fmr. Pres. French Mathematical Soc.; mem. Acad. des Sciences; Commdr. Légion d'Honneur; F.I.Ae.S. (U.S.), F.R.Ae.S. (U.K.).
Publs. include papers on jet propulsion and theory of flight.
86 avenue Niel, Paris 17e, France.
Telephone: 924-01-02.

Roy Chowdhury, Devi Prasad, M.B.E.; Indian sculptor and painter; b. 15 June 1899.
Principal Govt. Coll. of Arts and Crafts, Madras 29-57; fmr. Chair. Lalita Kala Akad., New Delhi; Dir. and Pres. Art Seminar of UNESCO, Tokyo 55; many prizes in Nat. Modern Sculpture exhbns., Govt. of India; Hon. LL.D. (Rabindra Bharati Univ., Calcutta) 68.
Sculptures include: *Martyrs Memorial* in Bronze at Bihar, *Triumph of Labour* at Madras and New Delhi, *Mahatma Gandhi* at Madras and Calcutta, *Rhythm*, Nat. Museum, New Delhi.
Publs. Eight books of short stories and novels, and novels and articles on art.
63 Shambhu Nath Pandit Street, Calcutta 25, India.
Telephone: 47-2921.

Royère, Jean André; French diplomatist; b. 2 Jan. 1909; ed. Lycée Janson-de-Sailly, and Univ. of Paris.
Vice-Consul, Consul and Consul-Gen. in China and Japan 32-52; Consul-Gen. in Singapore 55, Tunis 58-63; Ambassador to Sudan 63-; Officier, Légion d'Honneur.
French Embassy, Block 6H, East Plot 2, Khartoum, Republic of the Sudan.

Royle, Sir Lancelot Carrington, K.B.E.; British company director; b. 31 May 1898; ed. Harrow School and Royal Military Acad., Woolwich.
Served in France First World War 18; resgnd. commission 21; took up appt. with Van den Berghs Ltd., subsequently by amalgamation Lever & Unilever Ltd., recalled to Army Second World War 39-45; appt. mem. of Macharg/Royle Cttee. by Treasury 40; Chair. Navy, Army and Air Force Insts. 41-53; Chair. and Managing Dir. Home and Colonial Stores Ltd. 47-58; Chair. Lipton Ltd. 52-58, Liptons Overseas Ltd. 59-63; Dir. Allied Suppliers Ltd. 47-62, Liptons Ltd. 52-63, Clowes Walker Ltd. 59-65, U.P.M. Ltd. 60-65, Malgavita Ltd. 65-68, British Match Corpn. 60-68, Oxo Ltd. 60-68, Bryant and May Ltd. 60-, Liebigs Extract of Meat Co. Ltd. 60-; Pres. Multiple Shops Fed. 60-63; Gov. of Harrow School 47-62.
31 Elsworthy Road, London, N.W.3, England.

Royster, Vermont Connecticut, A.B., LL.D.; American journalist; b. 30 April 1914; ed. Univ. of North Carolina.
Reporter New York City News Bureau 36, *Wall Street Journal* 36; Washington corresp. *Wall Street Journal* 36-41, 45-46, Chief Washington corresp. 46-48, Editorial Writer and Columnist 46-48, Assoc. Editor 48-51, Senior Assoc. Editor 51-58, Editor 58-; Vice-Pres. Dow Jones & Co. Inc. 65; Pres. American Soc. of Newspaper Editors 65-66; served U.S. Navy 41-45; mem. Pulitzer Board for Prizes in Journalism and Letters; Hon. Litt.D. (Philadelphia), Hon. L.H.D. (Elon Coll., N.C.); Pulitzer prize for editorial writing 53.
Publs. *Journey through the Soviet Union* 64, *A Pride of Prejudices* 67.
Wall Street Journal, 30 Broad Street, New York City, N.Y., U.S.A.

Rozewicz, Tadeusz; Polish poet and playwright; b. 21; ed. Univ. of Cracow.
Former factory-worker and teacher; State Prize for Poetry 55; Literary Prize, City of Cracow 59.
Publs. 12 vols. of poetry, two prose collections and several plays including *He Left Home.*
c/o Union of Polish Writers, Krakowskie Prezedmiescie 87, Warsaw, Poland.

Rozhdestvensky, Gennadi Nikolaevich; Soviet conductor; b. 1931; ed. Moscow State Conservatoire.
Assistant Conductor, Bolshoi Theatre 51, Conductor 56-60; Chief Conductor of U.S.S.R. Radio and TV Symphony Orchestra 60-65; Principal Conductor Bolshoi Theatre 65-; has been guest conductor for numerous orchestras throughout Europe, America and Asia; Merited and People's Artist of the R.S.F.S.R.
State Academic Bolshoi Theatre, 1 ploshchad Sverdlova, Moscow, U.S.S.R.

Ruark, Arthur Edward, M.A., PH.D.; American physicist; b. 9 Nov. 1899; ed. Johns Hopkins Univ.
Worked at Bureau of Standards 21-26; Asst. Prof. Yale Univ. 26-27; Mellon Inst. of Industrial Research 27-29; Head of Physics Division, Gulf Research Laboratory 29; Prof. of Physics, Univ. of Pittsburgh 30-34; Head of Physics Dept. and Kenan Research Prof. Univ. of North Carolina 34-44; Consultant, Naval Research Laboratory 44-46; Head Research Division, Applied Physics Laboratory of Johns Hopkins Univ. 46-47; Asst. Dir. Inst. for Co-operative Research, Johns Hopkins Univ. 48-49; Head Navy Research Project, Johns Hopkins Univ. 49-52; Temerson Prof. of Physics, Univ. of Alabama 52-56; Chief, Controlled Thermonuclear Branch, U.S. Atomic Energy Comm. 57-60; Asst. Dir. of Research, U.S. Atomic Energy Comm. 61-65, Senior Assoc. Dir. of Research 66-.
Publs. *Atoms, Molecules and Quanta* (with Harold C. Urey), *Atomic Physics* (with mems. of the Pittsburgh Physics Staff) and articles on Atomic Physics.
4101 Byeforde Court, Kensington, Md., U.S.A.

Rubbra, Edmund, C.B.E., M.A., D.MUS., LL.D.; British composer; b. 23 May 1901; ed. Reading Univ., and Royal Coll. of Music.
Lecturer in Music, Oxford Univ.; Fellow, Worcester Coll., Oxford; Prof. of Composition, Guildhall School of Music and Drama, London; Orchestral works include: eight symphonies, *Festival Overture* and *Farnaby Improvisations*; Concertos for piano, violin and viola; vocal works include: sets of songs for tenor and baritone (with strings) and Ode for Contralto and Orchestra; motets, madrigals and masses for unaccompanied voices; seven works for chorus and orchestra; chamber music includes: sonatas for violin, cello and oboe with piano, three string quartets, piano quintet, piano trio, and works with recorder; songs with string quartet, harp or piano; Preludes for piano.
Publ. *Counterpoint* 60.
Lindens, Bull Lane, Gerrard's Cross, Bucks., England.
Telephone: Gerrard's Cross 84650.

Rubel, John H.; American business executive; b. 27 April 1920; ed. California Inst. of Technology.
Research Laboratory, Gen. Electric Co. 42-45, Lockheed Aircraft Corpn. 45-46, Hughes Aircraft Co. (and Dir. Airborne Systems Laboratories) 46-59; Dept. of Defense 59-, Asst. Dir. Defense Research and Engineering for Strategic Weapons 59-, Asst. Dir. of Defense, Research and Engineering and Act. Dir. 60-, Asst. Sec. Defense, Research and Engineering 61-63; Vice-Pres. and Dir. Technical Planning, Litton Industries Inc. 63-65. Vice-Pres. and Dir. Fast Deployment Logistic Ship Project 66-; Vice-Pres. and Dir. Advanced Marine Technology Div. 67-68, Senior Vice-Pres. 68-.
Litton Industries Inc., 9370 Santa Monica Boulevard, Beverly Hills, Calif.; Home: 416 S. Bristol Avenue, Los Angeles, Calif. 90049, U.S.A.

Ruben, Vitali Petrovitch; Soviet politician; b. 1914; ed. Yaroslav Agricultural Coll., Higher Party School.
Worked as agronomist and teacher until 41; party work 41-44; worked with Central Cttee. Latvian C.P. 44-47; Second Sec. Daugavpils Regional Cttee. Latvian C.P. 47-48; attended C.P.S.U. School 48-51; Central Cttee. Latvian C.P., Councils of Agric. and Gosplan of Latvia 51-61; Dep. Chair. Council of Ministers, Latvian S.S.R. 61-62, Chair. 62-; Candidate mem. Central Cttee. C.P.S.U.; Deputy to U.S.S.R. Supreme Soviet.
Council of Ministers of Latvian S.S.R., Riga, Latvian S.S.R., U.S.S.R.

Rubin, Reuven; Israeli artist; b. 13 Nov. 1893; ed. Ecole des Beaux Arts, Paris, and Acad. Colorossi.
Israeli Minister to Rumania 48-50; first one-man exhibition, Anderson Galleries, N.Y. 20; since 20 numerous one-man exhibitions in Jerusalem, Tel-Aviv, Paris, London, New York, Los Angeles, San Francisco, Geneva; exhibited at Venice Biennale 48, 50, 52, Metropolitan Museum, N.Y. 53, etc.; works in Modern Art Museum, Paris, Museum of Modern Art, N.Y., Brooklyn Museum, Brandeis Univ. Museum, San Antonio, Los Angeles, Sarasota, Detroit Museum, Norton Gallery, Palm Beach and other U.S. museums, Manchester (England), Melbourne (Australia), Tel-Aviv and Jerusalem Museums and in private collections in Europe and America; décor for Habimah and Ohel Theatres, Israel; mural for Supreme Religious Centre, Jerusalem 57-58; mem. The Hebrew Inst. of Religion N.Y. 45-, Provisional Council for UNESCO in Israel; mem. Art Council of Israel; awarded Prize of Honour for artistic achievement, Tel-Aviv 64.
Publs. *Visages d'Israel, God Seekers*.
14 Bialik Street, Tel-Aviv, Caesarea-by-the-Sea, Israel.
Telephone: 61-5581.

Rubinacci, Leopoldo; Italian politician; b. 13 Sept. 1903.
Lawyer; Regional Sec. Italian Catholic Youth Movement 22-27; Dep. from Naples 43-45; fmr. Dir. Cttee. of Confederazione Generale Italiana del Lavoro (CGIL); fmr. Vice-Pres. Senate Cttee. on Labour and Social Security; Minister of Labour 51-54; later Vice-Pres European Parl., European Communities (EEC, ECSC, EURATOM); Minister without Portfolio 66-; Christian Democrat.
c/o Chamber of Deputies, Rome, Italy.

Rubinowicz, Wojciech, PH.D.; Polish physicist; b. 22 Feb. 1889; ed. Czerniowce Univ.
Asst. Czerniowce Univ. 12-19, Docent 19-20; Prof., Ljubljana Univ. 20-22, Lwów Polytechnic 22-37, Lwów Univ. 37-41, 44-45, Warsaw Univ. 46-60; fmr. mem. Soc. Scientiarum Leopoliensis, Soc. Scientiarum Varsaviensis, fmr. Polish Acad. of Learning, Polish Acad. of Sciences; Dr.rer.nat. h.c. (Humboldt Univ.), Dr.rer. phys. h.c. (Jagellonian Univ., Cracow).
Publs. Numerous works in the field of theoretical physics, including *Wektory i tensory* (Vectors and Tensors) 50, *Kwantowa teoria atomu* (Quantum Theory of the Atom) 54, 57, 59 (German edn.), *Mechanika teoretyczna* (Theoretical Mechanics) (with Krolikowski) 55, 64, 67, *Die Beugungswelle in der Kirchoffschen Theorie der Beugung* 57, 66, *Quantum Mechanics* 68.
Hoża 74, Warsaw, Poland.
Telephone: 285393.

Rubinstein, Arthur; Polish pianist; b. 28 Jan. 1889; ed. Warsaw and Berlin Acad. Music.
First concert Warsaw 95, debut with Berlin Symphony Orchestra 02; first U.S. tour 06; toured Europe, South America, Australia, Africa, China, Japan, U.S., etc.; Commdr. de la Légion d'Honneur (France); Commdr. Order of the Crown (Belgium), Italian, Spanish, Polish and other decorations; Hon. Dr. Mus. (Northwestern, Yale, Brown, Rutgers Univs.).
80 avenue Foch, Paris, France.

Rubottom, Roy Richard, Jr.; American diplomatist; b. 13 Feb. 1912; ed. Southern Methodist and Texas Univs.
In commerce 35-37; Asst. Dean, Student Life Texas Univ. 37-41; served in U.S. Navy (Commander) 41-46; Naval liaison officer, Mexico 43-45; Naval Attaché, Paraguay 45-46; Appointed Foreign Service Officer 47; Embassy Sec. and Consul Bogotá 47-49; in charge Mexican Affairs, State Dept. 50-52; Dir. Mid-American Affairs 52-53; 1st Sec., Madrid Embassy 53-54; Dir. Operations Mission, Madrid 54-56; Dep. Asst. Sec. and Acting Asst. Sec., of State for Inter-American Affairs 56; Asst. Sec. 57-60; Ambassador to Argentina 60-61; faculty adviser for State Dept., Naval War Coll. 61-64; Vice-Pres. Southern Methodist Univ., Texas 64-.
c/o Southern Methodist Univ., SMU Box 102, Dallas, Texas, U.S.A.
Telephone: EMerson-3-5611, Extension 248.

Rubtsov, Vasily Ivanovich; Soviet politician; b. 1913; ed. Leningrad Forestry Technical Acad.
Chief of Forestry Department, fmr. State Cttee. for Timber, Paper and Pulp Woodworking Industries 63-66; Chair. U.S.S.R. State Cttee. for Forestry 66-; mem. C.P.S.U. 43-; Orders of Red Star, Badge of Honour, etc.
Publs. 55 scientific papers on forestry and forest improvement.
U.S.S.R. State Committee for Forestry, 4-a Khavsko-Shabolovsky pereulok, Moscow, U.S.S.R.

Ruchkin, Mikhail Ivanovich; Soviet trade union official; b. 10; ed. Higher Party School of the C.P.S.U. Central Committee.
Soviet Army 32-34; Y.C.L. work 34-38; leading Party and trade union work 38-52; instructor of a dept. of the C.P.S.U. Cen. Cttee. 52-57; Chair. Cen. Cttee. of the Trade Union of Co-operative and State Trade Workers 57-63; on staff of All-Union Central Council of Trade Unions 63-; mem. of C.P.S.U.; mem. of All-Union

Central Council of Trade Unions; Badge of Honour (twice) and two State medals.

All-Union Central Council of Trade Unions, 42 Leninsky Prospekt, Moscow, U.S.S.R.

Rucinski, Joseph; Polish-born American economist; b. 13 Aug. 1907; ed. Inst. Supérieur de Commerce, Antwerp, and Univ. of Geneva.

Mem. of the Money and Credit Dept. of the Polish Ministry of Finance 32-39; Financial Counsellor of the Polish Embassy, London 39-42; Economic Adviser to the Polish Foreign Office in London 42; went to the U.S. 45; joined staff of the Int. Bank 46; Asst. Dir. of the Dept. of Operations for Asia and the Middle East 52 and Dir. 55; Dir. of the Dept. of Operations for South Asia and the Middle East 57-61; Vice-Pres. Kaiser Industries Dec. 61-67; Vice-Pres. Allied Chemical Corpn. 67-.

Allied Chemical Corporation, 61 Broadway, New York, N.Y. 10006, U.S.A.

Rud, Gerasim Yakovlevich; Soviet (Moldavian) politician; b. 1907; ed. Rybnitsa Coll. of Horticulture and Viticulture, Moscow Timiryazev Acad. of Agriculture.

Lecturer and Head of Dept. at the Moldavian Higher Communist Agricultural School in Tiraspol 33-37, Dir. 37-40; mem. Central Cttee. of the Moldavian C.P. 40-62; first Vice-Chair. of the Council of People's Commissars of Moldavia 40-44; People's Commissar for Foreign Affairs of Moldavia 44-46; mem. Bureau of the Central Cttee. of the Moldavian C.P. 46-58; Chair. of the Council of Ministers of Moldavia 46-58; Dir. Scientific Research Inst. for Food Industry, Moldavian S.S.R. 58-62; Rector, Agricultural Inst., Kishinev 62-; awarded Order of Lenin.

Agricultural Institute, Kishinev, Moldavia, U.S.S.R.

Ruda, José Maria, LL.D.; Argentine lawyer and diplomatist; b. 9 Aug. 1924; ed. Univ. de Buenos Aires and New York Univ.

Office of Legal Affairs, UN Secr. 51-55; Sec. of State, Salta Province, Argentina 56-57; Counsellor, La Paz 57-60; mem. Argentine Del. to UN 59-, Chair. Argentine Del. 65, Perm. Rep. to UN 66-; Assoc. Prof. of Int. Law, Univ. of Buenos Aires 59-, later Prof. of Int. Law, Nat. War Coll.; Visiting Prof. Colegio de Mexico 63; Del. to numerous int. confs.

Publs. include *The Powers of the General Assembly of the UN in Political and Security Matters* 56, *Jurisdiction of the International Court* 59, *Relations Between the United Nations and the Organization of American States in Connexion with International Peace and Security* 59, *A Study in Politics and Law: The United Nations* 62, *The Evolution of International Law.*

Permanent Mission of Argentina to the United Nations, 300 East 42nd Street, New York, N.Y. 10017, U.S.A.

Rudenko, Roman Andreevich; Soviet lawyer; b. 07.

At the Procurator's Office 29-; Chief Soviet Prosecutor at the Nuremberg Trials 45-46; Procurator of the Ukraine 44-53; State Judiciary Counsellor, Procurator-Gen. of the U.S.S.R. 53-; Cand. mem. C.P.S.U. Central Cttee. 56-61, mem. 61-; Deputy to U.S.S.R. Supreme Soviet; has attended Confs. of the Int. Asscn. of Democratic Lawyers; awarded Order of Lenin (four times), Order of the Red Banner of Labour.

Office of the Procurator-General of the U.S.S.R., 15a Pushkinskaya Street, Moscow, U.S.S.R.

Rudenko, Marshal Sergei Ignatievich; Soviet Air Force officer; b. 1904; ed. Zhukovsky Air Force Acad.

Commdr. of an air army, taking part in the fighting at Stalingrad, Kursk, Berlin, in Byelorussia 41-49; Chief of Staff of Air Force 49-58, First Dep. C.-in-C. Soviet Air Force 58-; Marshal of Aviation 55-; Hero of the Soviet Union; awarded Order of Lenin (four times),

Suvorov (three times), Red Banner (four times), Kutuzov, also Polish honours.

Ministry of Defence, 34 Maurice Thorez Embankment, Moscow, U.S.S.R.

Rudhart, Hans Wilhelm, DR. RER. POL.; German business executive; b. 30 Sept. 1902.

Vice-Pres. Gutehoffnungshütte Aktienverein and Gutehoffnungshütte Sterkrade AG; Pres. Employers' Feds.; mem. of management of German Industry Inst., Fed. Asscn. of German Industry, Trade Asscn. of Iron and Steel Industry, etc.; mem. or Pres. of Board of Dirs. Schwäbische Hüttenwerke G.m.b.H., Zahnräderfabrik Augsburg Renk AG, Eisenwerk Nürnberg AG, Vereinigte Aluminiumwerke AG, Bonn Gutehoffnungshütte Schwerte G.m.b.H., UTMAL, India, The Libyan Drilling and Servicing Co. Ltd., Associated Tunnelling Co. Ltd., London.

Publs. *Die preussische Staatsbank mit besonderer Berücksichtigung der letzten zwei Jahrzehnte.*

43 Essen-Bredeney, Am Tann 7, German Federal Republic.

Rudnev, Konstantin Nikolaevich; Soviet politician; b. 1911; ed. Tula Engineering Inst.

Chairman State Cttee. of Defence Technology 58-61; Chair. State Cttee. for Co-ordination of Scientific Research Work 61-65; Deputy Chair. U.S.S.R. Council of Ministers 61-65; Minister of Instrument Making, Automation and Control Devices Industry 65-; mem. C.P.S.U. Central Cttee. 61-; Deputy, U.S.S.R. Supreme Soviet; Hero of Socialist Labour.

Ministry of Instrument Making, Automation and Control Devices Industry, Moscow, U.S.S.R.

Rudnicki, Adolf; Polish writer; b. 12.

Awarded State Prize, Class II 55.

Publs. *Szczury* (Rats), *Zołnierze* (Soldiers), *Niekochana* (The Unloved One), *Lato* (Summer), *Ucieczka z Jasnej Polany* (Flight from Yasna Polyana), *Zywe i martwe morze* (Living and Dead Seas), *Pateczka czyli kazdemu to na czym mu mniej zalezy* (The Baton, or To Each What He Least Cares For), *Niebieskie karthi* (Blue Pages, 8 vols. of Short stories and Essays), *Krowa* (The Cow).

Kanonia 18, Warsaw, Poland.

Telephone: 31-36-09.

Rudolph, Paul Marvin, M.ARCH.; American architect; b. 23 Oct. 1918; ed. Alabama Polytechnic Inst., and Harvard Univ.

Fellow in Architecture, Harvard Univ. 41-42; Officer in Charge, Ship Construction, U.S. Naval Reserve, Brooklyn Navy Yard 43-46; partner, architectural firm of Twitchell & Rudolph, Sarasota (Florida) 47-51; architectural practice at Sarasota and Cambridge, Mass. 52-; Chair. Dept. of Architecture, Yale Univ. 58-65; numerous honours and awards including Best House of the Year Award, America Inst. of Architects 49, Outstanding Young Architects Award, São Paulo Int. Competition 54, House chosen by *Architectural Record* as one of fifty most significant buildings completed since 1900 56, Arnold Brunner Prize in Architecture, American Acad. of Arts and Letters 58, Boston Arts Festival Award for Commercial Building; Award of Merit A.I.A. Honors Award 62, 64, First Honor Award A.I.A. Honors Award 64, *Architectural Record* Award of Excellence for House Design 63.

Important projects include Good Design Exhibition (Chicago Merchandise Mart and New York Museum of Modern Art) 51, U.S. Embassy, Amman, Jordan 54, Art, Music and Drama Building, Wellesly Coll., Mass., Junior-Senior High School, Sarasota, Blue Cross-Blue Shield Inc. Headquarters Building, Boston, Greeley Memorial Laboratory, Yale Forestry School 57, Arts and Architecture Building, Yale Univ., Church Street Redevelopment Project, New Haven, Conn., Tuskegee Inst., Montgomery, Ala. 58, work at Yale 60, Auburn

61, and Endo Laboratories, Garden City, N.Y., Parking Garage, New Haven, Conn., I.B.M. Components Div. Facilities, East Fishkill, N.Y., Elderby Housing, New Haven, Creative Arts Center for Colgate Univ., N.Y. 31 High Street, New Haven, Conn., U.S.A.

Rudziński, Witold; Polish musicologist and composer; b. 14 March 1913; ed. Vilno and Paris.
Prof. Łódź Conservatoire 45-47; Dir. Dept. of Music, Ministry of Culture 47-48, in Superior School of Music, Warsaw; Dir. State Philharmonic and Warsaw Opera; Editor *Muzyka*.
Works include Piano Concerto, two Symphonies, Symphonic Suite, two String Quartets, two Sonatas for piano and violin, cantata, flute quartet, song cycle, chamber works for piano, flute, 'cello and woodwind instruments, Operas *Janko Muzykant*, *Commandant de Paris*, *Le Renvoi des Ambassadeurs grecs*, *Sulamith*; works for choir and orchestra, etc.
Publs. Musical encyclopedia, monographs on Moniuszko and Bartok.
c/o Union of Polish Composers, Rynek Starego Miasta 27, Warsaw; ul. Narbutta 50/6, Warsaw 12, Poland. Telephone: 4514-95.

Rueff, Jacques Léon; French economist; b. 23 Aug. 1896; ed. Ecole Polytechnique, Paris.
Inspector of Finance 23; mem. of Economic and Financial Section, L.N. Secretariat 27; Financial attaché to French Embassy, London 30; Prof. of Economics, Ecole libre des Sciences politiques, Paris 31; Asst. Dir. Mouvement Général des Fonds 34, Dir. 36; Vice-Gov. Bank of France 39-40; Pres. of Economic and Financial Del. to Mil. Mission for German and Austrian Affairs Dec. 44; economic adviser to C.-in-C., Germany 45; French Del. to Reparations Comm., Moscow July 45; Pres. of Paris Conf. on Reparations Dec. 45; Pres. of Inter-allied Reparations Agency in Brussels Jan. 46; Del. to Peace Conf. in Paris and to second Assembly of U.N.; mem. of U.N. Economic and Employment Comm.; Judge Court of Justice of European Steel and Coal Community 52-58; Judge, Court of European Communities 58-62; Pres. Cttee. for Reform of French Financial Situation 58, Cttee. for Suppression of Obstacles to Econ. Expansion 59; mem. Econ. and Social Council 62; Hon. Pres. Société d'Economie Politique de Paris; Prof. of Econs., Institut des Sciences politiques, Paris; Hon. Vice-Gov. Bank of France; mem. Académie Française, Acad. des Sciences morales et politiques, Chancelier de l'Institut de France; Grand Officer Legion of Honour; Croix de Guerre (3 citations).
Publs. include: *Des Sciences physiques aux Sciences morales* 22 (translated into English), *Théorie des Phénomènes monétaires* 27, *L'Assurance-chômage* 31, *L'Ordre social* 45, *Epître aux dirigistes* 49, *Une cause du désordre mondial: l'état actuel du système des paiements internationaux*, *La régulation monétaire et le problème institutionnel de la monnaie* 53, *Discours sur le Crédit*, *L'Age de l'inflation* 63, *Le lancinant problème de la balance des paiements* 65, *Discours de receptions à l'Académie française*, *Les fondements philosophiques des systèmes économiques* 67, *Les Dieux et les Rois* 67.
51 rue de Varenne, Paris 7e, France.

Ruehmann, Heinz; German actor and stage director; b. 7 March 1902; ed. Secondary Modern School.
Stage actor, Breslau, Hanover, Berlin and Munich 22-60; with Theatre of Vienna 60-; acted in films: *Der Mann der nicht nein sagen konnte*, *Der eiserne Gustav*, *Die Pauker*, *Menschen im Hotel*, *Ein Mann geht durch der Wand*, *Der Jugendrichter*, *Mein Schulfreund*, *Der brave Soldat Schwejk*, *Das schwarze Schaf*, *Der Lugner*, *Max der Taschendieb*, *Regie: Lauter Lugen*, *Lauter Liebe*, *Sophienlund*, *Der Engel mit dem Saitenspiel*, *Die kupferne Hochzeit*, *Hauptmann von Koepenick*; Hon. mem. Inst. Artists' Lodge; Grosse Verdienstkreuz; Kunstpreis of Berlin 57, Ernst-Lubitsch Prize of

Screenwriters Club 59, German Film Critics' Prize for *Der brave Soldat Schwejk* 61, Filmband in Gold Prize of the Film Fed. for *Das Schwarze Schaf*.
8 München-Geiselgasteig, Robert Kochstr. 20, German Federal Republic.

Ruf, Sep; German architect; b. 9 March 1908; ed. Technische Hochschule, Munich.
Freelance architect 31-; Prof., Acad. of Fine Arts, Nuremberg 47, Acad. of Fine Arts, Munich 53-; Cultural Prize of City of Nuremberg.
Major works include: branches of Bayerische Staatsbank, Nuremberg and Erlangen; new buildings for Acad. of Fine Arts, Nuremberg; Maxburg Admin. Buildings (with Prof. Theo Pabst), Munich; German Pavilion, Brussels World Fair (with Prof. Egon Eiermann); new building for Church of St. John of Capistran, Munich; Max-Planck-Institut für Physik und Astrophysik (Heisenberg Inst.), Munich.
Munich 13, Franz-Joseph Strasse 26, German Federal Republic.

Rugambwa, H.E. Cardinal Laurian; Tanzanian ecclesiastic; b. 12 July 1912; ed. Katigondo Seminary, De Propaganda Fide Univ., Rome.
Ordained priest 43; missionary work in East Africa; studied canon law in Rome; Bishop of Rutabo 53; created Cardinal by Pope John XXIII 60; transferred to Bukoba Diocese 60.
Cardinal's Residence, Private Bag, Bukoba, Tanzania, East Africa.
Telephone: Bukoba 446.

Ruhemann, Helmut; British picture restorer, lecturer and author; b. 91; ed. Art Acads. of Munich and Karlsruhe, and Acad. Julien, Paris.
Artist 11-20; free-lance picture restorer 20-29; Curator and Chief Restorer to the State Galleries, Berlin 29-33; emigrated to England 33; free-lance restoring for the Nat. Gallery, London, and other museums; lecturer on the technique of the Old Masters and on technical examination of paintings at Art Colls. and Courtauld Inst. of Art, London Univ., of which appointed Technical Consultant 35; Lecturer-in-charge of its Technology Dept. 46-51; Consultant Restorer to the Nat. Gallery 46-53; training restorers at the Nat. Gallery 46-; Lecturer in Europe and U.S.A. on art restoration and techniques, and on detection of forgeries; UNESCO Mission to Guatemala 56; Founding Fellow, Int. Inst. for Conservation of Historic and Artistic Works.
Publs. *Artist and Craftsman* 48, *The Artist at Work* 51, joint author and Ed. *La Conservation des Peintures* 38, *The Cleaning of Paintings: Problems of Potentialities* 68.
National Gallery, London, W.C.2; 63 Blenheim Terrace, London, N.W.8, England.
Telephone: 01-930-7618 (Office); MAIda Vale 6931 (Home).

Ruini, Meuccio; Italian politician; b. 14 Dec. 1877.
Civil Service 1900; Dir.-Gen. for South Italy 12-13; Councillor of State 13; fmr. Dep. to Parl.; Under-Minister, Ministry of Labour 19; Minister for Colonies 20; Pres. E.N.I.T., and Export Inst.; Organiser, Nat. Union of New Democracy 23; Minister without Portfolio 44; for Public Works 44; Pres. Inter-Ministerial Cttee. for Reconstruction 44-45; Pres. Council of State 45; Pres. of Senate 53; Pres. Nat. Council of Economy 57-59; Life Senator 63-.
Publs. *Le opere pubbliche in Calabria* 13, *La questione meridionale e l'ora presente* 14, *Il pensiero di Wilson* 18, *La montagna italiana in guerra e dopo la guerra* 19, *Le possibilità economiche d'Italia* 22, *La democrazia italiana e l'unione nazionale* 25, *L. Corvetto genovese, ministro e restauratore delle finanze di Francia* 29, *Le quattro vite di P.Rossi* 29, *La Signora di Stael* 31, *Verso la Costituente* 45, *Storia della Svizzera come nazione e come società di nazioni* 47, *Il Parlamento e la sua riforma* 52, *Il diritto di stampa nella Costituzione* 52, *La funzione*

legislativa 53, *Il referendum popolare e la revisione della Costituzione* 53, *L'Organizzazione Sindacale e lo sciopero nella Costituzione* 53, *Profili storici di Amendola, Sacchi, Bissolati, Bonomi, Giuffrida, Orlando, Croce* 53, *Opera Omnia* (7 vols.).
Via Giuseppe Ferrari 12, Rome, Italy.

Ruiz Cortines, Adolfo; Mexican politician; b. 90; ed. Instituto Veracruzano.
Took part in Mexican Revolution 12; served Mexican army 12-26; mem. Comm. for Reorganisation of Mexican Railroads 22; Dir. Social Statistics Dept. 26; Gen.-Sec. Govt. of Federal District 35, of Veracruz 40; of Ministry of Interior 41; mem. Parl. 37-, Gov. State of Veracruz 44; Sec. of State for Interior 48-51; Pres. of Mexico 52-58; Partido Revolucionario Institucional (PRI).
V. Carranza 25, Mexico City, Mexico.

Rukmini, Devi; Indian dancer and arts patron; b. 04.
Started dancing under Anna Pavlova; extensive tours throughout India with dance recitals and lectures; also lectures and writes on Theosophy, Religion, Art, Culture, Education, etc.; Pres. World Federation Young Theosophists; Dir. The Besant Theosophical High School, Adyar, Dr. V. Swaminatha Iyer Tamil Library; Head Int. Theosophical Centre, Huizen, Holland; Pres. The Bharata Samaj, Indian Vegetarian Congress; Chair. Animal Welfare Board; Dir. Arundale Training Centre for Teachers, Adyar; mem. Indian Nat. Comm. for Co-operation with UNESCO, Gov. Body Indian Council for Cultural Relations, Cen. Advisory Board of Educ., Senate Annamalai Univ.; Pres. Kalakshetra Int. Arts Centre; Productions include *The Light of Asia, Incidents from the Life of Bishma, Karaikal Ammayar* (Tamil), *Rukmini Swayamvaran* (Kathakali), *Kutvala Kuravanji* (temple drama), *Kumara Sambhavm, Ramayana* (dance drama), *Usha Parinayam* (Telegu); Padma Bhushan 56, *Gita Govindam, Andal Charitram, Kannappar Kuravanji.* Publs. *Yoga: Art or Science, Message of Beauty to Civilisation, Women as Artists, Dance and Music, The Creative Spirit, Art and Education.*
Adyar, Madras 20, India.

Rulon, Phillip Justin, A.M., PH.D.; American university professor; b. 11 March 1900; ed. Stanford and Minnesota Univs.
Instructor in Mathematics and Gen. Science, Peninsula School, Calif. 25-28; Instructor in Educational Psychology, Univ. of Minnesota 28-30; Instructor in Education, Harvard Univ. 30-34, Asst. Prof. 34-40, Assoc. Prof. 40-44, Prof. of Education 44- and Acting Dean 43-48; Pres. Educational Research Corpn. 54-58, Treas. 58-; Hon. A.M. (Harvard).
Publs. *The Earth and its Life* (with E. E. Cureton) 32, *The Sound Motion Picture in Science Teaching* 33, *Measurement and Observational Techniques in Educational Evaluation and Guidance* 40, *An Experimental Comparison of Two Shorthand Systems* (with W. L. Deemer, Jr.) 42, *Multivariate Statistics for Personnel Classification* 67.
13 Kirkland Street, Cambridge 38; Home: 10 Craigie Street, Cambridge, Mass., U.S.A.

Rumbold, Sir Anthony, Bart., K.C.M.G., C.B.; British diplomatist; b. 7 March 1911; ed. Eton and Magdalen Coll., Oxford.
Laming Fellow, Queen's Coll., Oxford 33; Foreign Office 35-, Washington, Allied Headquarters (Mediterranean), Prague, Paris; Principal Private Sec. to Sir Anthony Eden 54, to Mr. Macmillan 55; Asst. Under-Sec. of State, Foreign Office 58-60; Minister in Paris 60-63; Amb. to Thailand 65-67, to Austria 67-.
British Embassy, Metternichgasse 6, Vienna, Austria; Home: Hatch House, Tisbury, Wiltshire, England.

Rumbold, Sir (Horace) Algernon (Fraser), K.C.M.G., C.I.E.; British government official (retd.); b. 1906; ed. Wellington Coll., and Christ Church, Oxford.

Assistant Principal, India Office 29, Private Sec. to Parl. Under-Sec. of State for India 30-33, to Perm. Under-Sec. of State 33-34, Principal 34, Asst. Sec. 43; Commonwealth Relations Office 47-; Dep. High Commr. in South Africa 49-53; Asst. Under-Sec. of State, Commonwealth Relations Office 54-58, Dep. Under-Sec. of State 58-66; Chair. Cttee. on Inter-Territorial Questions, Central Africa 63.
Shortwoods, West Clandon, Surrey, England.

Rumiantsev, Alexei Matveyevich; Soviet journalist and politician; b. 05; ed. Kharkov Economics Inst.
Commissariat of Agriculture, later Justice, Ukraine 26-30; Dir. Inst. of Econs., U.S.S.R. Acad. of Sciences, Head Social Science Dept., Ukrainian Acad. of Sciences 30-43; mem. C.P.S.U. 40-; party work, Kharkov Regional Cttee., Communist Party of Ukraine 43-52; on staff of Central Cttee. of C.P.S.U. 52-56; Editor-in-Chief *Kommunist* 56-58, *Problemy Mira i Sotsialisma* (Problems of Peace and Socialism) 58-64, *Pravda* Nov. 64-66; Sec. Econ. Branch of the U.S.S.R. Acad. of Sciences 66-; mem. Central Cttee. of C.P.S.U. 52-; corresp. mem. U.S.S.R. Acad. of Sciences 60-66, mem. 66-, Vice-Pres. 66-.
U.S.S.R. Academy of Sciences, 14 Lenin Prospekt, Moscow, U.S.S.R.

Rumor, Mariano; Italian politician; b. 16 June 1915.
Member of Parl. 48-; Deputy Sec. Christian Democrat Party 54-64, Sec.-Gen. 64-65, now Political Sec.; fmr. Under-Sec. for Agriculture, fmr. Under-Sec. to the Presidency; Minister of Agriculture 59-63, of Interior 63; Pres. European Union of Christian Democrats 65-.
Chamber of Deputies, Rome, Italy.

Runciman, The Hon. Sir Steven (James Cochran Stevenson), Kt., M.A., F.B.A.; British historian; b. 7 July 1903; ed. Eton Coll., and Trinity Coll., Cambridge.
Fellow Trinity Coll., Cambridge 27-38; Lecturer Cambridge Univ. 31-38; Press Attaché, British Legation, Sofia 40-41; Prof. of Byzantine Studies, Istanbul Univ. 42-45; Rep. of British Council, Greece 45-47; Chair. Anglo-Hellenic League 51-67; Trustee, British Museum 60-67; Pres. British Inst. of Archaeology at Ankara 62-; Fellow British Acad. 57; Hon. Fellow Trinity Coll., Cambridge; Foreign mem. American Philosophical Soc. 65; Kt. Commdr. Order of the Phoenix (Greece); Hon. Litt.D. (Cambridge, Chicago, Durham and London); Hon. LL.D. (Glasgow); Hon. D.Phil. (Salonika); Hon. D.D. (Wabash, U.S.A.).
Publs. *The Emperor Romanus Lecapenus* 29, *The First Bulgarian Empire* 30, *Byzantine Civilisation* 33, *The Medieval Manichee* 47, *History of the Crusades* (3 vols.) 51-54, *The Eastern Schism* 55, *The Sicilian Vespers* 58, *The White Rajahs* 60, *The Fall of Constantinople 1453* 65, *The Great Church in Captivity* 68.
Elshieshields, Lockerbie, Dumfriesshire, Scotland.
Telephone: Lochmaben 280.

Runciman of Doxford, 2nd Viscount, cr. 37; **Walter Leslie Runciman,** Bt., A.F.C., O.B.E., M.A.; British shipowner and industrialist; b. 26 Aug. 1900; ed. Eton and Trinity Coll., Cambridge.
Chairman, Walter Runciman & Co. Ltd., Moor Line Ltd., Anchor Line Ltd., Lloyds Bank Europe Ltd.; Deputy Chair. Lloyds Bank Ltd.; Chair. Trustees Nat. Maritime Museum; Pres. Royal Inst. of Naval Architects 51-61; Chair. North of England Shipowners' Asscn. 31-32; Chair. Council, Armstrong Coll., Durham Univ. 35-37; Dir.-Gen. British Overseas Airways Corpn. 40-43; Air Attaché, Teheran 43-46; Pres. Chamber of Shipping of the U.K. 52, Chair. Gen. Council of British Shipping 52; Hon. D.C.L. (Durham).
10 Southwick Place, London, W.2, England.
Telephone: 01-723-6882.

Rundall, Sir Francis (Brian Anthony), G.C.M.G., O.B.E.; British diplomatist; b. 11 Sept. 1908; ed. Marlborough Coll., and Peterhouse, Cambridge.

Entered Gen. Consular Service 30; served in Antwerp, Colón, Panama, Boston, Barcelona, Piraeus; Consul in New York 44-46: transferred to Foreign Office 46; H.M. Inspector of Foreign Service Establishments 49-53; Chief Admin. Officer, U.K. High Comm. in Germany 53; H.M. Consul Gen. in New York 53-57; Ambassador to Israel 57-59; Deputy Under-Sec. of State for Admin., Foreign Office 59-63; Amb. to Japan 63-67.
Lime Tree Cottage, Church Oakley, Basingstoke, Hants., England.
Telephone: Oakley 217.

Runge, Sir Peter Francis, Kt.; British sugar refiner; b. 11 May 1909; ed. Charterhouse and Trinity Coll., Oxford.
Tate & Lyle Ltd. 31, Dir. 35-, Joint Vice-Chair. 58-; Dir. Vickers Ltd. 65-; Chair. Tate & Lyle Refineries Ltd. 65-; mem. Exec. Cttee. Industrial Welfare Soc. 50-56, mem. Council 50-; Chair. London and South-East Region, Fed. of British Industries 58-60, Pres. Fed. of British Industries 63-65, Vice-Pres. Confed. of British Industry 65-; Chair. Royal Commonwealth Soc. for the Blind 65-; mem. Nat. Econ. Devt. Council 64-66; Chair. The Industrial Soc. 66-; Commdr. of Order of Duarte Sanchez y Mella (Dominican Repub.).
Finings, Lane End, Buckinghamshire, England.
Telephone: Lane End 241.

Rupert, Anthony Edward, M.SC.; South African business executive; b. 4 Oct. 1916; ed. Volks High School, Graaf Reinet, and Univs. of Pretoria and South Africa.
Lecturer in Chemistry, Pretoria Univ. 39-41; Founder, Chair. and Managing Dir. Rembrandt Group of Companies (tobacco) 48-; Dir. Carreras Ltd., London, Rothmans Tobacco Holdings Ltd., London 50-; Chair. Technical and Industrial Investments Ltd. 50-; Technical Adviser to Tobacco Industry Control Board 50-; mem. South African Chemical Inst., Board of Trustees of Nat. Devt. and Management Foundation, South African Inst. of Management, Council of Univ. of Stellenbosch, Board of Trustees of South African Foundation, South African Acad. for Arts and Science; Hon. Industrial Adviser to the Govt. of Lesotho; Hon. Prof. Univ. of Pretoria 64-; Hon. D.Sc. (Pretoria); Hon. D.Comm. (Stellenbosch).
Office: Alexander Street, Stellenbosch; Home: 13 Thibault Street, Mostertsdrift, Stellenbosch, South Africa.
Telephone: Stellenbosch 2331.

Ruppel, Aloys (Leonhard), DR.PHIL.; German professor; b. 21 June 1882; ed. Univs. of Würzburg, Marburg, Berlin, Münster and Strasbourg.
Scholarship, Prussian Historical Inst., Rome, 09-10; Asst. and Dir. State Archives for Lorraine, Metz 11-19; Dir. Country Library Fulda 19-20; Dir. City Library and Archives, Mainz 20-34, and 44-50; Dir. Gutenberg Museum 20-62; Man. Int. Gutenberg-Gesellschaft 20-; Prof. Univ. of Mainz 47-; Great Gold Medal, Ibero-American Exhibition, Seville 30; Grand Prix Int. Exhibition Paris 37; Gutenberg Medal City of Mainz 47; O.M. German Fed. Repub. 52; mem. Acad. at Erfurt; Hon. Fellow, Pierpont Morgan Library, N.Y.; Hon. Citizen of Mainz; Goldener Ehrenring, Int. Gutenberg-Gesellschaft; Bundesverdienstorden; Chevalier, Légion d'Honneur, Officier de l'Ordre de la Couronne de Belgique; Chevalier, Ordre National de la République du Sénégal; Commdr., Ordre du Cèdre du Liban.
Publs. include: *Johannes Gutenberg, sein Leben und sein Werk* 47, *Grosse Drucker* 53, *Haben die Chinesen und Koreaner die Buchdruckerkunst erfunden?* 55, *Druckte Gutenberg vor seiner Bibel ein grösseres Werk?* 55, *The Wandering Legend of the Theft of the Art of Printing, Rettet das Grab Gutenbergs* 56, *Gutenberg—Kleine Biographie* 57, *Die Technik Gutenbergs und ihre Vorstufen* 62, *Gutenberg und Columbus, die Väter der Neuzeit* 64,

Die Stadt Mainz und ihr grosser John Gutenberg 64, *Wer war der wirkliche Erfinder der Druckkunst* 64, *40 Jahre Gutenberg—Jahrbuch* 65; Editor *Int. Gutenberg Jahrbuch* 26-.
Fischtorplatz 15, 65 Mainz; and Gutenberg Gesellschaft, Liebfrauenplatz 5, Mainz, German Federal Republic.
Telephone: 26278 (Home).

Rurik, Josef; German engineer and business executive; b. 19 Sept. 1922; ed. Prague, and Technische Hochschule, Munich.
Head of a devt. group for comparative steam turbines 51; joined Gutehoffnungshütte Sterkrade A.G. 55, Dir. Dept. of Machine Construction 63, mem. Management Board July 66-.
42 Oberhausen, Otto-Weddingen-Strasse 28, German Federal Republic.

Rusakov, Konstantin Victorovich; Soviet politician and diplomatist; b. 1909.
Former Engineer; fmr. U.S.S.R. Minister of Fisheries; fmrly. on staff of Central Cttee. of Communist Party of Soviet Union; Counsellor, Warsaw 58-60; Ambassador to Mongolian People's Republic 62-63; Deputy Head of Dept., Central Cttee. of C.P.S.U. 63-65; First Deputy Head of Dept. 65-; mem. Central Auditing Comm. C.P.S.U.
Central Committee of C.P.S.U., 4 Staraya ploshchad, Moscow, U.S.S.R.

Rush, Kenneth, A.B., LL.B.; American lawyer and businessman; b. 17 Jan. 1910; ed. Univ. of Tennessee, and Yale Univ. Law School.
Joined Union Carbide Corpn. 36, Dir. 48, Vice-Pres. 49-61, Exec. Vice-Pres. 61-66, Pres. 66-, mem. Exec. Cttee. 66-; Dir. Union Carbide Group 58; Dir. U.S. Council Int. Chamber of Commerce 55-, American Sugar Co. 62-, Foreign Policy Asscn. 64-; Dir. and mem. of Exec. Cttee., Manufacturing Chemists Asscn. 65-67, Chair. 66-67; Dir. Bankers Trust Co. 66-, Bankers Trust New York Corpn. 66-; Gov. The Pinnacle Club 66-; Sec.-Treas. and Trustee Grand Central Art Galleries Inc.; mem. American Bar Asscn., Devt. Council, Univ. of Tennessee, Council on Foreign Relations, Industries Advisory Cttee. of the Advertising Council Inc. 66-.
270 Park Avenue, New York, N.Y. 10017; North Manursing Island, Rye, N.Y. 10580, U.S.A.
Telephone: 914-WO7-0857.

Rushton, William Albert Hugh, F.R.S., M.R.C.S.; British physiologist; b. 8 Dec. 1901; ed. Gresham's School, Holt, Emmanuel Coll., Cambridge, and Univ. Coll. Hospital, London.
Stokes Student, Pembroke Coll., Cambridge 27-29; Johnson Foundation Fellow, Univ. of Pennsylvania 29-31; Research Fellow, Emmanuel Coll., Cambridge 30-32, 35-37, Lecturer in Physiology, Univ. of Cambridge 35-53, Dir. of Medical Studies, Trinity Coll., Cambridge 36-53, Fellow of Trinity 38-; Reader in Physiology, Univ. of Cambridge 53-65, Prof. of Visual Physiology 66-; Fellow of the Royal Soc. 48; Foreign Hon. mem. American Acad. of Arts and Sciences; awarded Prentice Medal of American Acad. of Optometry 63, Feldberg Prize 67; Silliman Lecturer, Yale Univ. 66, Waynflete Lecturer, Oxford 68.
Publs. include numerous papers in *Journal of Physiology* on nerve excitation and conduction 27-51, visual pigments and mechanism of vision 51-.
Trinity College, Cambridge, England.
Telephone: Cambridge 58201.

Rusinek, Michal; Polish writer; b. 29 Sept. 1904; ed. Cracow Univ.
Dir. Acad. of Letters, Warsaw 34-39; prisoner at Mauthausen concentration camp during the war; Head of Dept. Ministry of Fine Arts; Sec.-Gen. of Polish P.E.N. Club 46; Vice-Pres. Polish Writers Union, Warsaw; Vice-Pres. Union of Polish Authors and Composers; Hon.

Chair. Int. Writers' Fund, London PEN Club; Man. Dir. Authors Agency; Editor-in-Chief *Littérature Polonaise*-(Polish Literature).
Publs. *Burza nad brukiem, Czlowiek z bramy, Ziemia miodem plynaca, Pluton z dzikiej Łaki, Z barykady w doline glodu, Wiosna admirala, Muszkieter z Itamariki, Królestwo pychy, Niebieskie ptaki, Zielone zloto, Kolorowe podróze, Dwie Ewy, Prawo Jesieni, Igraszki Nieba, Malowane zycie, Opowieści niezmyślone.*
Odolańska ul. 30, Warsaw, Poland.

Rusk, Dean, M.A.; American Secretary of State; b. 9 Feb. 1909; ed. Davidson Coll., N.C., St. John's Coll., Oxford, and Univ. of Calif. Law School.
Associate Prof. of Govt., Mills Coll. Calif. 34-38, Dean of Faculty 38-40, mil. service 40-46; Asst. Chief Div. of Int. Security Affairs, U.S. Dept. of State 46; Special Asst. to Sec. of War 46-47; Dir. of Office of UN Affairs 47-49, Asst. Sec. of State 49, Deputy Under-Sec. of State 49-50, Asst. Sec. of State for Far Eastern Affairs 50-52; Pres. The Rockefeller Foundation 52-61; Sec. of State 61-; Pres. Gen. Education Board 52-61; mem. Asscn. of American Rhodes Scholars, American Soc. of Int. Law, Council on Foreign Relations; awards include Legion of Merit with Oak Leaf Cluster and Cecil Peace Prize 33; Hon. LL.D. (18 univs. and colls.); Hon. L.H.D. (3 univs. and colls.); Hon. D.C.L. Oxon. 62, Hon. Fellow, St. John's Coll., Oxford; Democrat.
Department of State, Washington 25, D.C., U.S.A.

Russell, 3rd Earl, cr. 1861; **Bertrand Arthur William Russell,** O.M., M.A., F.R.S.; British philosopher, mathematician and educationist; b. 18 May 1872; ed. Trinity Coll., Cambridge.
Fellow Trinity Coll. Cambridge 95 and 44-, Lecturer 10-16; Chair. No Conscription Fellowship 16; imprisoned for pacifist propaganda; former Lecturer Univ. of California; appointed Lecturer in Mathematics, New York City Coll. 40, appt. revoked; Prof. of Philosophy, Barnes Foundation 40-43; Nobel Prize for Literature 50, UNESCO Kalinga Prize 57, Sonning Prize 60.
Publs. *German Social Democracy* 96, *Essay on the Foundations of Geometry* 97, *Philosophy of Leibniz* 1900, *Principles of Mathematics* 03, *Principia Mathematica* (with Prof. A. N. Whitehead) 10-13, *Philosophical Essays* 10, *Problems of Philosophy* 11, *Our Knowledge of the External World as a Field for Scientific Method in Philosophy* 14, *Principles of Social Reconstruction* 17, *Mysticism and Logic* 18, *Roads to Freedom* 18, *Introduction to Mathematical Philosophy* 19, *The Practice and Theory of Bolshevism* 20, *The Analysis of Mind* 21, *The Problem of China* 22, *The ABC of Atoms* 23, (with Dora Russell) *The Prospects of Industrial Civilization* 23, *Icarus* 24, *The ABC of Relativity* 25, *What I Believe* 25, *On Education* 26, *Analysis of Matter* 27, *An Outline of Philosophy* 27, *Sceptical Essays* 28, *Marriage and Morals* 29, *The Conquest of Happiness* 30, *The Scientific Outlook* 31, *Education and the Social Order* 32, *Freedom and Organisation 1814-1914* 34, *In Praise of Idleness* 35, *Which Way to Peace?* 36, *The Amberley Papers* (with Patricia Russell) 37, *Power: A New Social Analysis* 38, *Let the People Think* 40, *An Inquiry into Meaning and Truth* 41, *A History of Western Philosophy* 46, *Human Knowledge* 48, *Authority and the Individual* 49, *Unpopular Essays* 50, *New Hopes for a Changing World* 51, *The Impact of Science upon Society* 52, *Satan in the Suburbs* (fiction) 53, *Nightmares of Eminent Persons* 54, *Human Society in Ethics and Politics* 54, *Portraits from Memory* 56, *Why I am not a Christian* 57, *My Philosophical Development* 59, *Wisdom of the West* 59, *Has Man a Future?* 61, *Fact and Fiction* 61, *Unarmed Victory* 62, *The Autobiography of Bertrand Russell, 1872-1914* 67, *War Crimes in Vietnam* 67, *The Autobiography of Bertrand Russell 1914-1938* 68.
Plas Penrhyn, Penrhyndeudraeth, Merionethshire, Wales.

Russell, Donald Joseph; American businessman; b. 3 Jan. 1900; ed. Stanford Univ.
With Southern Pacific Co. 20-41, Asst. to Pres. 41, Vice-Pres. 41-51, Exec. Vice-Pres. 51, Pres. 52-64, Chair. 64- also Dir. and mem. Exec. Cttee.
65 Market Street, San Francisco, Calif. 94105, U.S.A.

Russell, Donald Stuart; American lawyer and politician; b. 22 Feb. 1906; ed. Univ. of Michigan.
Admitted to S. Carolina Bar 28; legal practice 30-42; mem. Price Adjustment Board, War Dept., Wash. 42; Asst. to Dir. Econ. Stabilisation 42, Asst. to Dir. War Mobilisation 43; U.S. Army 44; Dep. Dir. Office of War Mobilisation Reconversion 45; Asst. Sec. of State 45-47; Pres. Univ. of S. Carolina 52-57; legal practice 57-62; Gov. of S. Carolina 62-65; Senator from S. Carolina 65-66; Fed. Judge 66-; Democrat.
716 Otis Boulevard, Spartanburg, South Carolina, U.S.A.

Russell, Francis Henry, A.B., LL.B., LL.D.; American lawyer and foreign service officer; b. 1 Oct. 1904; ed. Tufts Coll., and Harvard Law School.
Private Law practice 29-41; Chief Div. of World Trade Intelligence, Dept. of State 41-45; Dir. Office of Public Affairs 45-52, and Chair. Nat. Conf. on American Foreign Policy Dept. of State 49-50-51; Counsellor, Embassy, Tel-Aviv 52-53, Chargé d'Affaires 53-54; Special Asst. to the Sec. of State 55-56; Ambassador to New Zealand 57-61, to Ghana 61-62, to Tunisia 62-; U.S. del. Colombo Plan Ministerial Conf. 59.
American Embassy, Tunis, Tunisia.

Russell, George, B.S.; American automobile executive; b. 15 March 1905; ed. Univ. of Minnesota.
Treasurer, Gen. Motors Corpn. 51-56, Vice-Pres. (Finance) and Dir. 56, Exec. Vice-Pres. and Dir. 58, Vice-Chair. of Board and Chair. Finance Cttee. 67-; Dir. Automobile Manufacturers Asscn.; Trustee, Automotive Safety Foundation, Cttee. for Econ. Devt., Urban America Inc.; Dir. ADELA Investment Co. S.A.; Dir. Cttee., Int. Asscn. for the Promotion and Protection of Private Foreign Investments (APPI).
Business: 3044 West Grand Boulevard, Detroit, Michigan 48202; 1775 Broadway, New York, N.Y. 10019, U.S.A.
Telephone: TR3-7200, Ext. 8863 (Detroit); PL7-4000, Ext. 424 (New York).

Russell, Admiral James Sargent; American naval officer; b. 22 March 1903; ed. Naval Acad., Annapolis and Calif. Inst. of Technology.
Merchant Marine 18-22; U.S. Navy 26-65, Naval Aviator 29-65, Admiral 58-65; Aircraft Carrier Desk, Bureau of Aeronautics 39-41, Dir. of Military Requirements 43-44; Commdng. Officer, Aircraft Squadron 42; Chief of Staff to Commdr. Carrier Div. 2, Pacific Campaigns 44-45; Commdng. Officer *U.S.S. Bairoko* 46-47, *U.S.S. Coral Sea* 51-52; Dep. Dir., Military Application, Atomic Energy Comm. 47-51; Office of Chief of Naval Operations 52-54; Commdr. Carrier Div. 17 and 5, Pacific Fleet 54-55; Chief, Bureau of Aeronautics 55-57; Dep. Commdr. Atlantic Fleet 57-58; Vice-Chief of Naval Operations 58-61; C.-in-C. NATO Forces in Southern Europe 62-65; recalled to active duty to direct review of safety in aircraft-carrier operations 67; Consultant to Boeing Co. 65-; Dir. Alaska Airlines 65-, Airtronics Inc. 65-; Collier Trophy 56; D.F.C., D.S.M., and numerous other decorations.
7734 Walnut Avenue, S.W., Tacoma, Washington, D.C. 98498, U.S.A.
Telephone: 206-588-9356.

Russell, Sir John Wriothesley, K.C.V.O., C.M.G.; British diplomatist; b. 23 Aug. 1914; ed. Eton Coll., and Trinity Coll., Cambridge.
Foreign Service 36-, served Foreign Office, Moscow, Washington, Warsaw, Rome 36-53; Counsellor 53,

Dir.-Gen. British Information Services, New York 53-56; Counsellor, Teheran 56-59; Foreign Office Spokesman (Head of News Dept., Foreign Office) 59-62; Amb. to Ethiopia 62-66, to Brazil 66-.
British Embassy, Rio de Janeiro, Brazil.

Russell, Richard Brevard, LL.B.; American politician; b. 2 Nov. 1897; ed. Georgia Univ.
Mem. Georgia Legislature 21-31, Speaker 23-26, 27-28, 29-31; Governor of Georgia 31-33; U.S. Senator from Georgia 33-; Democrat.
Winder, Ga., U.S.A.

Russell, Sir (Sydney) Gordon, C.B.E., M.C., R.D.I., F.S.I.A.; British industrial designer; b. 20 May 1892; ed. Campden Grammar School.
Served with Worcestershire Regt. 14-19; partner Russell & Sons 19; Dir. Gordon Russell Ltd., The Lygon Arms Ltd.; mem. Art Workers' Guild 26-, Master 62; elected Royal Designer for Industry 40, Master of Faculty 47-49; mem. Utility Furniture Cttee. and Furniture Production Cttee., Board of Trade 43-47; original mem. Council of Industrial Design 44, Dir. of Council of Industrial Design 47-59, mem. 60-; mem. Design Panel, British Railways Board 56-66; Pres. Design and Industries Asscn. 59-62; mem. Bank Note Design Cttee. of Bank of England, Arts Advisory Cttee. of UNESCO Nat. Comm., U.K. 60-66, Nat. Council for Diplomas in Arts and Design 61-; Albert Medal of Royal Soc. of Arts 62; Hon. F.R.I.B.A., Hon. Designer R.C.A.; Hon. A.I.L.A.; Hon. LL.D. Birmingham Univ. 60; Officer Order of Vasa (Sweden); Commdr. Order of St. Olav (Norway).
Kingcomb, Chipping Campden, Gloucestershire, England.
Telephone: Campden 253.

Russell of Liverpool, 2nd Baron (cr. 1919); **Edward Frederick Langley Russell,** C.B.E., M.C.; British author; b. 10 April 1895; ed. Liverpool Coll., and St. John's Coll., Oxford.
Served in British Army in France 14-18, later with Indian Cavalry; served in office of Judge Advocate-Gen. 34-54; during Second World War Dep. Judge Advocate-Gen. to B.E.F., First Army, Allied Force H.Q. and British Army of the Rhine; responsible for all War Crimes trials in British Zone of Germany 46-51; awarded Mil. Cross (2 bars).
Publs. *The Scourge of the Swastika* 54, *Though the Heavens Fall* 56, *The Knights of Bushido* 58, *That Reminds Me* 59, *If I Forget Thee* 60, *The Royal Conscience* 61, *The Trial of Adolf Eichmann* 62, *The Tragedy of the Congo* 62, *South Africa, Today and Tomorrow* 63, *Knight of the Sword* 64, *Deadman's Hill: Was Hanratty Guilty?* 65, *Caroline the Unhappy Queen* 67, *Return of the Swastika* 68.
105 Highlands Heath, Portsmouth Road, London, S.W.15, England.

Russo, Alfio; Italian journalist; b. 13 March 1902.
Special correspondent in the Balkans for *La Stampa*, Turin; fmr. Ed. *La Sicilia*; fmr. Editor-in-Chief *Il Risorgimento Liberale*; fmr. Special Corresp. *Corriere della Sera*, Paris; Ed.-in-Chief *La Nazione* and *La Nazione Sera*, Florence 53-61; Editor *Corriere della Sera*, Milan 61-68.
c/o *Corriere della Sera*, Milan, Italy.

Russo, Carlo; Italian politician; b. 19 March 1920.
Former mem. Nat. Cttee. of Liberation, Savona; mem. Chamber of Deputies 48-; Under-Sec. to Presidency of Council of Ministers 54, 55-57, 59-60; Under-Sec. for Defence 58-59; Under-Sec. for Foreign Affairs 60-62; Minister of Posts and Telecommunications 62-65, of Foreign Trade June 68-; Christian Democrat.
Ministry of Foreign Trade, Rome, Italy.

Rustomji, Nari Kaikhosru, M.A.; Indian civil servant; b. 16 May 1919; ed. Bedford School and Christ's Coll., Cambridge, England.
Joined Indian Civil Service 41; Under-Sec. Assam Home and Political Dept. 44; Adviser to Gov. of Assam 48; Dewan (Prime Minister) of Sikkim, Speaker, Sikkim Council, Pres. Sikkim Exec. Council 54-59; Adviser to Governor of Assam for North East Frontier Agency and Nagaland 59; Adviser to Govt. of Bhutan 63-66; Chief Sec. to Gov. of Assam 66-.
"Lumpyngad", Shillong, Assam, India.
Telephone: Shillong 83.

Rusznyák, István, DR. MED.; Hungarian physician; b. 22 Jan. 1889; ed. Univs. of Budapest and Berlin.
Professor at Szeged Univ. 31-46, at Budapest Univ. 46-63; Dir. Inst. Experimental Medicine 60-; mem. of Parl. 45-67; Kossuth Prize 49, 56; Pres. Acad. of Sciences 49-; mem. Acads. Soviet Union, Bulgaria, Czechoslovakia and Poland, and Yugoslav Acad. of Sciences and Arts; Corresp. mem. German Acad., Medical Acad. Switzerland, British Medical Asscn.; Hon. mem. Acad. of Romania.
Roosevelt tér 9, Budapest V, Hungary.
Telephone: 119-812.

Rutten, Franciscus Josephus Theodorus, DR. PSYCH., DR. LIT.; Netherlands psychologist; b. 15 Sept. 1899; ed. Univs. of Utrecht and Louvain, Sorbonne, Leipzig and Vienna Univs.
Teacher, St. Ignatius Coll., Amsterdam; Asst. Psychological Laboratory, Univ. of Nijmegen; Extra. Prof. Univ. of Nijmegen 30, Ord. Prof. 33-, Rector Magnificus 40, Dir. of Psychological Laboratory; arrested by Germans 44; Minister of Education, Arts and Sciences 48-52; Catholic Party; mem. New York Acad. of Sciences; Commdr. Order of Orange Nassau; Grand Cross Order of the Crown (Belgium); Grand Cross Order of Phoenix (Greece); Oak Crown (Luxembourg); Dr. h.c. Univ. of Athens.
Publs. *Felix Timmermans* 28, *Psychologie der waarneming* (Psychology of Perception) 30, *Symposion over het probleem der psychologie* (Symposium of Psychological Problems) 39, *Training en opleiding tot vakman* (Training and Instruction for Craftsmen) 47, *De overgang van het agrarische volkstype in het industriele type* (The transition of an agricultural worker into an industrial worker) 47, *Persoonlijkheid in de spiegel der samenleving* (Personality reflected in the Community) 47, *Menselijke Verhoudingen* (Human Relations) 55, *Analyse gebarental doofstommen* 57, *De geschiedkundige ontwikkeling der Sociale psychologie in Nederland* 58, *Inter-human relations: How do they stand today?* 60.
Pater Brugmanstraat 1, Nijmegen, Netherlands.

Ruud, Johan T., M.SC., PH.D.; Norwegian marine biologist and university administrator; b. 27 June 1903; ed. Oslo Univ.
Asst. Prof. of Marine Biology Oslo Univ. 24-36, Assoc. Prof. 36-39, Prof. 39-, Rector of Oslo Univ. 58-63; Chair. Sealing Board, Central Cttee. for Norwegian Research; Vice-Pres. Int. Council for the Exploration of the Sea; mem. Norwegian Acad. of Science in Oslo 40-; mem. Det Kgl. Norske Vidensk. Selskab 61, Det Kgl. Danske Vidensk. Selskab 62, Linnean Soc. of London 64, Kungliga Vetenskaps och Vitterhetssamhället Göteborg 65; Hon. mem. Royal Irish Acad. 67.
Publs. *On the Biology of Southern Euphausiidae* 32, *Euphausiacea* 36, *The Surface Structure of the Baleen Plates as a Possible Clue to Age in Whales* 40, *Further Studies on Baleen Plates and their Application to Age Determination* 45, *Modern Whaling and its Prospects* 52, *Vertebrates without Erythrocytes and Blood Pigment* 54, *International Regulation of Whaling* 56.
Frederiksgt. 3, Oslo 1, Norway.
Telephone: 33-07-34.

Růžek, Miloslav, PH.D.; Czechoslovak diplomatist; b. 25 Jan. 1923; ed. Charles Univ., Prague.
Ministry of Culture 49-50, Foreign Trade 50-53, of State Control 53-54, of Foreign Affairs 54-; Counsellor, London 54-57; Amb. to U.S.A. 59-63, to U.K. 66-; Section Head, Ministry of Foreign Affairs 64-66.
6-7 Kensington Palace Gardens, London, W.8, England.

Ruzicka, Leopold; Croatian-born Swiss chemist; b. 87; ed. Inst. of Technology, Karlsruhe.
Former Professor of Organic Chemistry Zürich Fed. Inst. of Technology; awarded Nobel Chemistry Prize (with Adolph Butenandt) 39, for work on polymetylenes and the higher terpen compounds; foreign mem. Royal Society London 42-.
Freudenbergstr. 101, Zürich 44, Switzerland.

Ryabikov, Vasily Mikhailovich; Soviet politician; b. 1907; ed. Leningrad Naval Acad.
Worked in textile mill, Ivanovo 24; designing engineer, Communist Party organiser Bolshevik Plant Leningrad 37-39; Dep. People's Commissar for Armaments 39-40; First Dep. Minister for Armaments 40-51; Dep. Minister of Medium Machine-Building 53-55, Minister 55-57; Dep. Chair. of the R.S.F.S.R. Council of Ministers 58-61; Chair. of the Supreme Council of Nat. Economy 60-61; First Dep. Chair. of the U.S.S.R. State Planning Cttee. and Minister of the U.S.S.R. 61-63, 65-; First Deputy Chair. U.S.S.R. Council of Nat. Economy and Minister of U.S.S.R. 63-65; mem. C.P.S.U. Central Cttee.; Deputy U.S.S.R. Supreme Soviet; State Prizes 51, 53; Hero of Socialist Labour; Orders of Lenin and other awards.
U.S.S.R. State Planning Committee, 12 Marx prospekt, Moscow, U.S.S.R.

Ryabinkina, Elena Lvovna; Soviet ballet dancer; b. 1941; ed. Bolshoi Theatre Ballet School.
Joined Bolshoi Theatre Ballet Company 59.
Principal roles: Odette-Odille (*Swan Lake*), Raimonde (*Raimonde*), Mirta (*Giselle*), Kitri (*Don Quixote*), Vanina Vanini (*Vanina Vanini*), Persian Dance (*Khovanshchina*), Zarema (*Fountain of Bakhchisarai*), etc.
State Academic Bolshoi Theatre of the U.S.S.R., ploshchad Sverdlova, Moscow, U.S.S.R.

Ryan, James, M.B., B.CH., B.A.O., D.P.H.; Irish physician and politician; b. 6 Dec. 1892; ed. St. Peter's Coll., Wexford, Ring Irish Coll., and National Univ., Dublin.
Junior physician City Skin and Cancer Hospital 21-26; imprisoned Easter 16; M.P. for South Wexford 18; imprisoned on Spike Island 20-21; Vice-Chair. Wexford County Council 19-22; elected Dáil mem. for County Wexford 21-65; Minister for Agriculture 32-37; mem. Irish Del. to Econ. Conf., Ottawa 32; mem. Del. British-Irish negotiations 38; Minister for Health and Minister for Social Welfare 47-48 and 51-54; Dir. New Ireland Assurance Co., Irish Nat. Assurance Co., Nat. Tanners and Burnhohse (Ireland) Ltd. 54-57; Minister for Finance 57-65; mem. Senate 65-.
Kindlestown House, Delgany, Co. Wicklow, Ireland.

Ryan, Gen. John Dale; American air force officer; b. 10 Dec. 1915; ed. U.S. Military Acad., West Point.
Served Second World War; Dir. of Training, Advanced Bombardment School, Midland Field, Tex. 42-Aug. 43; Operations Officer H.Q. Second Air Force, Colorado Springs Aug. 43-Jan. 44; Commdr. Second Bombardment Group and Operations Officer, 5th Bombardment Wing, 15th Air Force in Italy Jan. 44-Feb. 45; Air Training Command at Carswell, Tex. and participation in Bikini Atoll nuclear weapons tests April 45-Sept. 46; Eighth Air Force Dir. of Operations and commdr. at various U.S. bases Sept. 46-June 56; with Strategic Air Command June 56-67; Vice C.-in-C. Aug. 64-Nov. 64, C.-in-C. Dec. 64-67; C.-in-C. Pacific Air Force 67-; U.S.A.F. Insp.-Gen. Aug. 63-Aug. 64; numerous decor-ations, including D.S.M., Legion of Merit and Croix de Guerre avec palme; Hon. LL.D., Creighton Univ., Omaha 66.
H.Q. Pacific Air Command, CMR I, Box I, APO San Francisco, Calif. 96553; Home: 225 Skyview Drive E., San Antonio, Tex., U.S.A.

Ryan, Peter Allen, B.A., M.M.; Australian publisher; b. 4 Sept. 1923; ed. Malvern Grammar School, Melbourne and Univ. of Melbourne.
Military Service 42-45; Dir. United Service Publicity Pty. Ltd. 53-57; Public Relations Manager, Imperial Chemical Industries of Australia and New Zealand Ltd. 57-61; Asst. to Vice-Chancellor, Univ. of Melbourne 62; Dir. Melbourne Univ. Press 62-.
Publs. *Fear Drive My Feet* 59, *The Preparation of Manuscripts*.
103 Kooyong Road, Armadale, Melbourne, Australia.

Ryan, Robert Joseph; American diplomatist; b. 14; ed. Massachusetts State Coll. and Columbus Univ.
Member D.C. Bar; Dep. of State 37-; Exec. Dir. Bureau of Near Eastern, South Asian and African Affairs 55-58; Nat. War Coll. 58; Admin. Counselor, Paris 59-64; Ambassador to Niger 64-.
American Embassy, Niamey, Niger.

Ryan, Sylvester James American judge; b. 10 Sept. 1896; ed. City of New York Coll., and Fordham Univ.
Admitted to New York State Bar 18, private practice in New York City 18-47; Chief Asst. and Act. Dist. Attorney, Bronx County, New York 24-47; U.S. Dist. Judge for Southern Dist. of New York 47-60, Chief Judge 60-.
U.S. Court House, Foley Square, New York City 7, N.Y., U.S.A.

Rybakov, Boris Aleksandrovitch; Soviet historian and archaeologist; b. 08; ed. Moscow Univ.
Director archaeological expeditions at Vshchizh, Vyshgorod, Moscow, Zvenigorod, Chernigov, etc. 32-; Assoc. Inst. of History of Material Culture, U.S.S.R. Acad. of Sciences 36-39; Lecturer, Moscow Univ. 38-43, Prof. 43-; Dir. Inst. of History of Material Culture, now Inst. of Archaeology, U.S.S.R. Acad. of Sciences 43-; corresp. mem. U.S.S.R. Acad. of Sciences 53-58, mem. 58-; Bureau mem. Dept. of Historical Science, U.S.S.R. Acad. of Sciences 57-; Bureau mem. Nat. Cttee. of Soviet Historians 57-; Foreign mem. Czechoslovak Acad. of Sciences; State Prize 49, 52.
Publs. include *The Radimichians* 32, *Chernigov Antiquities* 49, *Russian Systems of Linear Measurements from 11th-15th Century* 49, *Handicraft of Ancient Rus* 48.
State University, Lenin Hills, Moscow, U.S.S.R.

Rybicki, Marian; Polish lawyer and politician; b. 15; ed. Univ. of Warsaw.
Assistant Counsel for Prosecution, Dist. Court, Warsaw 45-47; Head Legal Bureau of The Seym 47-48; Dir. Educational Section, Cen. Exec. Cttee., Polish Socialist Party and Sec. Cen. Exec. Cttee. 48-49; First Sec. Vojvodship Cttee. of Polish United Workers' Party, Cracow 49-50; Head of Chancellory of State Council 50-52, Sec. to State Council 52-56; Chief Public Prosecutor 56-57; Minister of Justice 57-65; Prof. of Law, Inst. of Legal Sciences, Polish Acad. of Sciences 65-; Sec. All-Polish Cttee. of the Nat. Unity Front 67-.
Instytut Nauk Prawnych P.A.N., Warsaw, Ul. Nowy Świat 72, Pałac Staszica, Poland.
Telephone: 26-78-53.

Ryckmans, Rev. Gonzague, C.L.M., D.PHIL.; Belgian philologist; b. 10 Dec. 1887; ed. St. Jan Berchmans Coll., Antwerp, Université Catholique de Louvain, Theological Seminary, Malines, Ecole biblique et archéologique française, Jerusalem, and Ecole des Hautes Etudes, Paris.
Army Chaplain 14-18; Prof. at Theological Seminary, Malines 20-30; Prof. of Semitic Philology and Epi-

graphy, Univ. of Louvain 30-58, Emeritus 58-; mem. Royal Flemish Acad. of Belgium, Inst. de France, Accad. Naz. dei Lincei, Rome, Royal Acad. of Sciences, Amsterdam; Grand Officier Ordre de Léopold, Commandeur Ordre de la Couronne; Decennal Prize for Classical and Oriental Philology 59.
Publs. *Répertoire d'Epigraphie sémitique, Corpus inscriptionum semiticarum vol. V, Les noms propres sud-sémitiques* (3 vols.), *Les religions arabes préislamiques, Grammaire accadienne, L'Arabie antique et la Bible, Inscriptions sud-arabes* (séries 1-22).
Sint-Antoniusberg 5, Louvain, Belgium.
Telephone: 016-237-99.

Rydbeck, Olof, B.A., B.L.; Swedish diplomatist and radio administrator; b. 15 April 1913; ed. Djursholm Secondary School, Uppsala Univ.
Attaché Ministry for Foreign Affairs 39, Berlin 40, Ankara 41; Second Sec. Ministry for Foreign Affairs 43-45, Washington 45-46; First Sec. Washington 46-50, Bonn 50-53; Head of Press Section Ministry for Foreign Affairs 53-55; Dir. Swedish Broadcasting Corpn. 55-; mem. Board for Psychological Defence Preparedness 54-, Board of Dirs. Stockholm Concert Soc. 55-62, Cen. Cttee. Swedish Red Cross 55-, Council Swedish Inst. 56-, Royal Acad. of Music 62-; Dir. T.T. (Swedish Central News Agency) 67-, Inst. of Int. Affairs 67-; Pres. European Broadcasting Union 61-64, Hon. Chair. 64-; Amb.-at-Large 65-.
Swedish Broadcasting Corporation, 105 10 Stockholm, Sweden.
Telephone: 670865.

Ryelandt, Daniel-Benoit, D. en D.; Belgian barrister; b. 03; ed. Univ. of Louvain.
Barrister, Brussels Court of Appeal 27; Sec. to Prime Minister 32; Head of Secretariat of Ministries of Interior and Agriculture 34-38; Gen. Manager of Agence-Télégraphique Belge de Presse (Belga) 38-; mem. of Cttee. of *Revue Générale Belge* (monthly).
6 rue de la Science, Brussels, Belgium.

Ryerson, Knowles Augustus, M.S., LL.D.; American horticulturalist and educationist; b. 17 Oct. 1892; ed. Univ. of Calif.
Agricultural damage investigator, American Peace Comm. 19; mem. staff Univ. of California Agricultural Extension Service 19-25; Horticulturalist Haiti Agricultural Experimental Station 25-27; Horticultural Survey of Palestine 27; Dir. Div. of Foreign Plant Introduction U.S. Dept. of Agriculture 28-34; Chief Bureau of Plant Industry 34; fmrly in charge Tropical and Sub-Tropical Fruit Investigations U.S. Dept. of Agriculture 35-37; Dir. and Prof. of Horticulture Coll. of Agriculture Univ. of California; Davis Campus 37-52; Dean Coll. of Agriculture, Berkeley Campus 52-60; on leave, serving as Special Rep. Pacific Ocean Area, Board of Economic Warfare, Foreign Economic Admin. 42-44; Chair. Pacific Science Board, Nat. Research Council (U.S.) 46-53; mem. Hopkins Comm. Civil Govt., Guam and Samoa 47; mem. Research Council, South Pacific Comm. 48-53, 63-, Commr. 53-56, Senior Commr. 56-63; Rep. Pacific Science Council 50-63; Admin. Board, Inter-American Inst. of Agricultural Sciences, Costa Rica 45-54, Chair. 50-54.
15 Arlmonte Drive, Berkeley, California 94707, U.S.A.

Ryland, John Peter, C.B.E., D.F.C., B.AGR.SC.; Australian airline executive; b. 11; ed. Xavier Coll., Melbourne, and Univ. of Melbourne.
Commercial airline pilot prior to Second World War; R.A.A.F. 39-45; mem. Ansett Airways Ltd. 46; joined Trans-Australia Airlines as Man. Airline School 46,

Asst. Gen. Man. (Operational) 47, Asst. Gen. Man. 49, Gen. Man. 55-.
26 Embling Road, Malvern, Victoria, Australia.

Ryle, Gilbert, M.A.; British philosopher; b. 19 Aug. 1900; ed. Brighton Coll., and Queen's Coll., Oxford.
Philosophy Tutor, Christ Church, Oxford 24; officer in Welsh Guards during Second World War; Waynflete Prof. of Metaphysical Philosophy and Fellow of Magdalen Coll., Oxford 45-; Editor *Mind* 47-.
Publs. *The Concept of Mind* 49, *Dilemmas* 54, *Plato's Progress* 66.
Magdalen College, Oxford; and Yarm, Chilswell Lane, Hinksey Hill, Oxford, England.

Ryle, Sir Martin, Kt. M.A., F.R.S.; British physicist; b. 27 Sept. 1918; ed. Bradfield Coll., and Christ Church, Oxford.
Worked at Telecommunications Research Estab. 39-45; ICI Fellowship, Cambridge 45; Univ. Lecturer 48; Fellow of Trinity Coll., Cambridge 49-; Reader in Physics, Cambridge Univ. 57-59, Prof. Radio Astronomy 59-; Dir. Mullard Radio Astronomy Observatory 58-; Henry Draper Medal, U.S. Nat. Acad. of Sciences 65.
5A Herschel Road, Cambridge, England.

Rypka, Jan, PH.D., DR.SC.; Czechoslovak philologist; b. 28 May 1886.
Professor of Turkish and New Persian Philology, Charles Univ., Prague 27-; mem. Czechoslovak Acad. of Sciences 52; Corresp. mem. Iranian Acad. of Sciences; Hon. mem. Türk Tarih Kurumu 63; Officier Légion d'Honneur, Order of Dannish (Iran); Dr. h.c. Warsaw, Paris and Teheran Univs.; Order of the Republic 56, State Prize 57, Gold Plaque of Czechoslovak Acad. of Sciences 66.
Publs. Numerous works including *History of Iranian Literature* 68.
Prague 5, Smichov, Holečkova 17, Czechoslovakia.
Telephone: 54-68-36.

Rysanek, Leonie; Austrian soprano; b. 14 Nov. 1928; ed. Vienna Conservatoire.
Appearances in Innsbruck, Bayreuth, Vienna, Berlin, London, Paris, Milan, Rome; with Munich State Opera, Metropolitan Opera, New York; recordings RCA Victor; Chappel Gold Medal, London 56; Silver Rose, Vienna Philharmonic 56.
Alterbeuern über Rosenheim, Upper Bavaria, German Federal Republic.

Rytkheu, Yuri Sergeevich; Soviet writer; b. 1930; ed. Leningrad Univ.
Foremost Chukchi writer; works have been translated into Russian; started writing for the newspaper *Soviet Chukotka* 47.
Publs. Short stories: *Friends and Comrades, People of our Coast* 53, *When the Snow Melts* (novel) 60, *The Sorceress of Konerga* 60, *The Saga of Chukotka* 60, *Farewell to the Gods* 61 (short stories), *Nunivak* (tales) 63, *The Magic Gauntlet* (novel) 63, *In the Vale of the Little Sunbeams* (novel) 63, *The Walrus of Dissent* (stories) 64, *Blue Peppers* (stories) 64, *Wings Are Becoming Stronger in Flight* (novel) 64, *Bear Stew* (verses) 65, *Time of Snow Melting*.
Union of Writers of the U.S.S.R., Ul. Vorovskogo 52, Moscow, U.S.S.R.

Ryzhov, Nikita Semionovich; Soviet diplomatist; b. 1907; ed. Moscow Industrial Acad.
Former U.S.S.R. Minister of Textile Light Industry; Diplomatic Service 57-; Amb. to Turkey 57-66, to Italy 66-; mem. Central Auditing Comm. of C.P.S.U. 66-.
U.S.S.R. Embassy, Rome, Italy.

S

Saad, Dr. Ahmed Bey Saad; United Arab Republic (Egyptian) lawyer and politician; b. 21 Feb. 1900; ed. Univ. de Paris à la Sorbonne.

Public Attorney, Court of Appeals, Ministry of Justice, Cairo 22-29; Consul, Genoa 29-31; Consul-Gen. Hamburg 31-33, Liverpool 33-37; Chargé d'Affaires Baghdad 37-38; Dir. Section for Eastern Affairs, Ministry of Foreign Affairs Cairo 38; Dir. of Passports and Nationality, Ministry of Interior 38-44; Postmaster-Gen. 44; Under-Sec. of State, Ministry of Finance 45-51; Gov. Nat. Bank of Egypt 51-52, 55-57; Gov. for Egypt of IBRD 46-52, 55-58; Gov. for Egypt of IMF 46-52, for U.A.R. 58-59; Gov. for Saudi Arabia of IBRD and IMF 58-.

International Monetary Fund, 19th and H Streets, N.W., Washington, D.C. 20431, U.S.A.

Saari, Eino Armas; Finnish forestry expert and politician; b. 7 Oct. 1894; ed. Helsinki, Oxford and Yale Univs.

Prof. of Forestry Helsinki Univ. 25-63; mem. of national and international forestry organisations; cttee. Chair. Third World Forestry Congress 47-49 (Pres. 49); Vice-Chair. European Forestry Commission of F.A.O. 50, Chair. 51; Chair. Nat. F.A.O. Comm. of Finland; Chair. Finnish People's Party 51-58; mem. of Parl. 54-58; Minister of Social Affairs 56-57; Chancellor School of Social Sciences, Kalevontie 57-.

School of Social Sciences, Tampere, Kalevontie 4, Finland.

Saarinen, Aarne; Finnish politician; b. 5 Dec. 1913.
Former mason; fmr. mem. Social-Democratic Party; Joined Finland-U.S.S.R. Soc. 40; mem. Finnish Communist Party 44, mem. Central Cttee. 57-, mem. Political Bureau 64-, Chair. Finnish Communist Party 66-; Officer Building Workers' Union 45, Sec. for Educ. 47-50, Pres. 54-66; mem. Gen. Council of World Fed. of Trade Unions 61-; mem. Diet 62-; Vice-Pres. Finnish Peace Supporters' Org.

The Communist Party of Finland, Sturenkatu 4, Helsinki, Finland.

Saba, Hanna, D. en. D.; United Arab Republic (Egyptian) jurist and diplomatist; b. 23 July 1909; ed. Coll. of Jesuit Fathers, Cairo, Faculté de Droit, Paris, and Ecole libre des Sciences politiques, Paris.

Ministry of Foreign Affairs, Cairo 42, Counsellor 46, Minister 52; Dir. of Treaties Div., UN Secr. 46-50; Juridical Adviser, UNESCO 50-62; Asst. Dir.-Gen. of UNESCO 67-; Grand Officier du Mérite d'Egypte; Officier du Nil.

Publs. *L'Islam et la nationalité* 32, *L'évolution dans la technique des traités, Les droits économiques et sociaux dans le projet de pacte des droits de l'homme, Les ententes et accords régionaux dans la Charte des Nations Unies* (Course at Acad. of Int. Law, The Hague 52), *L'Activité quasi-législative des Institutions spécialisées des Nations Unies* (Course at Acad. of Int. Law, The Hague 64).

UNESCO, Place de Fontenoy, Paris, 7e; Home: 3 boulevard de la Sassaye, Neuilly (Hauts de Seine), France.

Sabah, Sheikh Jabir al-Ahmed al-Jabir al-; Kuwaiti politician; b. 1928.
Former Head of Dept. of Finance and Economy; Minister of Finance and Industry Jan. 62-65; Prime Minister 65-; appointed Crown Prince 60.
Office of the Prime Minister, Kuwait.

Sabah, Sheikh Sabah al-Ahmed al-Jabir al; Kuwaiti politician; b. 1929; ed. Mubarakiyyah National School, Kuwait and privately.

Member Supreme Cttee. 55-62; Minister of Public Information and Guidance and of Social Affairs 62-63; Minister of Foreign Affairs 63-, acting Minister of Finance and Oil 65.
Ministry of Foreign Affairs, Kuwait.

Sabah, Sheikh Sabah al-Salim al-; Amir of Kuwait; b. 1913.
Member Supreme Exec Cttee. 55-62; Deputy Prime Minister and Minister of Foreign Affairs 62-63; Prime Minister 63-65; succeeded his brother Sheikh Abdullah al-Salim al-Sabah as Amir of Kuwait Nov. 65.
Office of the Amir of Kuwait, Kuwait.

Sabah, Sheikh Salem S. al- (son of Sheikh Sabah al-Salem al-Sabah, Amir of Kuwait); Kuwaiti diplomatist; b. 18 June 1937; ed. Secondary School, Kuwait, Gray's Inn, London, and Christ Church, Oxford.

Joined Foreign Service 63; fmr. Head Political Dept. Ministry of Foreign Affairs; Ambassador to the U.K. 65-; rep. of Kuwait to confs. in Middle East and Africa, including Arab Summit Conf., Casablanca Oct. 65.
Embassy of Kuwait, 40 Devonshire Street, London, W.1; and 11A Belgrave Square, London, S.W.1, England.

Sabato, Ernesto; Argentine writer; b. 24 June 1911; ed. Universidad Nacional de la Plata.
Former Dir. of Cultural Relations, Argentina; has lectured in following Univs.: Paris, Columbia, Calif., Buenos Aires, Santiago de Chile, Montevideo, Madrid, Warsaw; First Prize for Prose, Buenos Aires 45; Ribbon of Honour, Argentine Soc. of Letters; Chevalier, Ordre des Arts et des Lettres (France).

Publs. *Uno y el Universo* 45, *Heterodoxia* 51, *Hombres y Engranajes* 52, *El Túnel* (novel) 48, *Héroes y Tumbas* (novel) 62, *El escritor y sus fantasmas* 64, *Alejandra* (novel) 67.
Bonifacini 1147, Santos Lugares, Argentina.

Sabin, Albert B(ruce), B.S., M.D.; American virologist; b. 26 Aug. 1906; ed. New York Univ.
Research Assoc. in bacteriology, New York Univ. Coll. of Medicine 26-32; House Physician, Bellevue Hospital, New York City 32-34; Fellow in Medicine, Nat. Research Council, Lister Inst. (England) 34; Asst., Rockefeller Inst., N.Y.C. 35-37, Assoc. 37-39; Assoc. Prof. of Research Pediatrics, Univ. of Cincinnati Coll. of Medicine 39-46, Prof. 46-60, Distinguished Service Prof. 60-; developer of oral polio vaccine; Medical Corps. U.S. Army, Second World War; mem. Nat. Acad. of Sciences (U.S.A.); Hon. Sc.D., L.H.D., Litt.H.D., Ph.D., F.R.S.H.; Int. Antonio Feltrinelli Prize, Rome, and numerous awards for work in medical research.

The Children's Hospital Research Foundation, Elland and Bethesda Avenue, Cincinnati, Ohio 45229; and 400 Rawson Woods Lane, Cincinnati, Ohio 45220, U.S.A. Telephone: 751-0794.

Sabri, Ali; United Arab Republic (Egyptian) politician; b. 30 Aug. 1920.
Fought in Palestine War 48; Minister for Presidential Affairs, Egypt 57-58, U.A.R. 58-62; Pres. Exec. Council 62-64, Prime Minister 64-65; Vice-Pres. of Republic Oct. 65-67; Sec.-Gen. Arab Socialist Union Oct. 65-67, 68-; Deputy Prime Minister and Minister of Local Govt. 67-Oct. 67; Resident Minister for Suez Canal Zone Oct. 67-68.
Arab Socialist Union, Cairo, U.A.R.

Sachar, Bhim Sen, B.A., LL.B.; Indian politician; b. 1 Dec. 1893; ed. Punjab Univ.
Joined Bar 18; joined Non-co-operation Movement 21;

Sec. Punjab Provincial Congress Cttee. 21; Registrar National Univ., Lahore; Sec. Municipal Cttee., Gujranwala 22-24; Municipal Commr. Gujranwala 24-33; founded Sunlight of India Insurance Co., Ltd.; Dir. Gujranwala Electric Supply Co. Ltd.; Local Dir. Punjab Nat. Bank Ltd.; mem. Punjab Legislative Assembly 36-56; leader Congress Party, Punjab Legislative Assembly 40; Finance Minister, Punjab Government 46-47; Dep. Leader Congress Party, Pakistan Constituent Assembly 47; Leader Congress Legislature Party, Punjab 49; Chief Minister, Punjab 49, 52-56; Gov. Orissa 56-57; Gov. Andhra Pradesh 57-62; High Commr. in Ceylon 64-67, concurrently Amb. to Maldive Islands 66-67.
No. 47, Sector 4, Chandigarh, Punjab, India.

Sacher, Paul; Swiss musician; b. 28 April 1906; ed. Univ. and Conservatoire of Basle.
Founder of Basle Chamber Orchestra 26, with Chamber Choir 28; founder of Schola Cantorum Basiliensis 33; conductor of Collegium Musicum Zürich 41-; Dir. Basle Acad. of Music 54-; has conducted in almost all European countries; Hon. Pres. Asscn. of Swiss Musicians; Dr. Phil. h.c. of Basle Univ.; Schönberg Medal 53; Mozart Medal 56.
Publs. Articles in reports of Basle Chamber Orchestra, and book on *Adolf Hamm* (organist).
Schönenberg, 4133 Pratteln, Basle, Switzerland.

Sachs, Nelly; German-born poet and dramatist; b. 10 Dec. 1891; ed. Berlin.
Refugee in Sweden since 40; Swedish Lyric Prize, Jahresring Literature Prize, Annette Droste Prize, Dortmund Prize, Friedenspreis des Deutschen Buchhandels 65, Nobel Prize in Literature 66.
Publs. *In den Wohnungen des Todes* 47, *Sternverdunkelung* 49, *Und Niemand weiss weiter* 57, *Flucht und Verwandlung* 59, *Gesammelte Lyrik* 61, *Gesammelte Dramatik* 62, *Ausgewählte Gedichte* 63, *Vom Leiden Israels* 64, *Guhende Rütsel* 64, *Späte Gedichte* 65, *Die Suchende* 66; translations of Swedish poetry: *Von Welle und Granit* 47, *Aber auch diese Sonne ist heimatlos* 58.
Bergsundsstrand 23, Stockholm, Sweden.

Sadat, Col. Anwar es-; United Arab Republic (Egyptian) officer and politician.
President of Egyptian Nat. Union 57-61, of Nat. Assembly of U.A.R. 61-; mem. Presidency Council 62-64, Pres. Afro-Asian Conf. Cairo 58.
The National Assembly, Cairo, United Arab Republic.

Sadiq, Ghulam Muhammad, B.A., LL.B.; Indian politician; b. 12; ed. C.M.S. High School, Srinagar, S.P. Coll., Srinagar, Islamia Coll., Lahore, and Muslim Univ., Aligarh.
Member Jammu and Kashmir State Legislature 34; Chair. Muslim Conf., Jammu and Kashmir 39; Minister of Development, Jammu and Kashmir 48-51; Pres. Jammu and Kashmir Constituent Assembly 51-53; Minister of Health and Educ. 53-57; Leader Democratic Nat. Conf. 57-61; Prime Minister of Jammu and Kashmir 64-.
Office of the Prime Minister, Srinagar, Jammu and Kashmir, India.

Sadiq, Issa, PH.D.; Iranian educationist; b. 94; ed. Univs. of Paris, Cambridge (England), and Columbia (New York).
Directed various depts. Ministry of Education 19-30; mem. Nat. Constituent Assembly 25, 49; Pres. and Prof. Nat. Teachers' Coll.; Dean of Faculties of Arts and Science Teheran Univ. 32-41, Prof. 32-; Chancellor of Univ. 41; Minister of Educ. 41, 43-45, 47, 60-61; Vice-Pres. Persian Acad. 37-; mem. Board of Governors, Nat. Bank of Persia 37-52; Senator for Teheran 49-52, 54-60, 63, 67, 67-; Pres. Persia-America Relations Soc. 49-53; mem. Royal Cultural Council 62-.
Publs. *Principles of Education, New Methods in Educa-*

tion, *History of Education, Modern Persia and her Educational System* (in English), *A Year in America, The March of Education in Persia and the West, A Brief Course in the History of Education in Iran, A History of Education in Europe, History of Education in Persia from the Earliest Time till Today, Memoirs* (Autobiography), etc.
316 Avenue Hedayat, Valiabad, Teheran; and The University, Avenue Shah Reza, Teheran, Iran.

Sadler, Donald Harry, O.B.E., M.A.; British astronomer; b. 22 Aug. 1908; ed. Trinity Coll. Cambridge.
Entered H.M. Nautical Almanac Office 30, Deputy Superintendent 33, Superintendent 36-; Sec. Royal Astronomical Society 39-47; Pres. Inst. of Navigation 53-55; Gen. Sec. Int. Astronomical Union 58-64; Vice-Pres. Council of Fed. of Astronomical and Geophysical Services 66-; Pres. Royal Astronomical Soc. 67-.
c/o H.M. Nautical Almanac Office, Royal Greenwich Observatory, Herstmonceux Castle, Hailsham, Sussex; Home: 21 Brookfield Court, Bexhill-on-Sea, Sussex, England.
Telephone: Bexhill 3780 (Home).

Sadler, Marion, A.B., M.A.; American airline executive; b. 7 Feb. 1911; ed. Baylor Preparatory School, Chattanooga, Tenn., Vanderbilt Univ. and Duke Univ.
Public school teacher, Tennessee 32-41; with American Airlines 41-, Pres. and Dir. 63-68; Dir. Marine Midland Grace Trust Co., George W. Helme Co., Marine Midland Corpn.
c/o American Airlines Inc., 633 Third Avenue, New York, N.Y. 10017, U.S.A.

Sadovsky, Mikhail Alexandrovich; Soviet physicist; b. 1904; ed. Leningrad Polytechnical Inst.
Scientific Worker, U.S.S.R. Acad. of Sciences Seismological Inst. 30-41; mem. staff Presidium U.S.S.R. Acad. of Sciences 41-46; Deputy Dir. U.S.S.R. Acad. of Sciences Inst. of Chemical Physics 46-60; Dir. U.S.S.R. Acad. of Sciences Schmidt Inst. of Earth Physics 60-; Corresp. mem. U.S.S.R. Acad. of Sciences 58-66, mem. 66-; mem. C.P.S.U. 41-; Hero of Socialist Labour; State Prize (4 times); Academician-Sec. U.S.S.R. Acad. of Sciences Section of Earth-Science 66-.
U.S.S.R. Academy of Sciences, 14 Lenin Prospekt, Moscow, U.S.S.R.

Sádovský, Štefan; Czechoslovak politician; b. 13 Oct. 1928; ed. Coll. of Economy, Bratislava.
Secretary West Slovak Regional Cttee., C.P. of Slovakia 62-66; Chair. West Slovak Regional Nat. Cttee. 66-67; Deputy, Slovak Nat. Council 66-; mem. Central Cttee. C.P. of Slovakia 66-; mem. Central Cttee. C.P. of Czechoslovakia 66-; Candidate mem. Presidium Central Cttee. of C.P. of Czechoslovakia 66-; Sec. Central Cttee. C.P. of Czechoslovakia 67-; Chair. Agricultural Comm., Central Cttee. C.P. of Czechoslovakia 67-.
Central Committee of Communist Party of Czechoslovakia, nábř. Kyjevské brigády 12, Prague 1, Czechoslovakia.

Sadr, Javad, PH.D.; Iranian diplomatist and politician; b. 12; ed. Univ. de Paris à la Sorbonne.
Ministry of Interior 39, Ministry of Foreign Affairs 41; fmr. mem. Information and Legal Affairs Div., Ministry of Foreign Affairs, later First Sec. and Consul, Palestine; fmr. Private Sec. to Minister of Foreign Affairs; fmr. Minister in Yugoslavia; fmr. Deputy Minister of Interior; fmr. Ambassador to Japan; Minister of Interior 64-66, of Justice 66-.
Ministry of Justice, Teheran, Iran.

Sadron, Charles Louis; French research scientist; b. 12 May 1902; ed. Lycée de Chateauroux and Univs. of Poitiers and Strasbourg.
Professor at Lycées of Troyes 27-28 and Strasbourg 28-31; engaged on aeronautical research 31-33; Rockefeller Scholar (Inst. of Technology Pasadena) 33-34;

research sponsored by Nat. Research Fund 34-37; Prof., Univ. of Strasbourg, 37-62, Museum Nat. d'Histoire Naturelle, Paris 62-; Scientific Adviser to UNESCO 46-47; Dir. Centre de Recherches sur les Macromolécules, Strasbourg 47-67; Dir. Centre de Biophysique Moléculaire, Orléans 67-; Sec. Int. Comm. on Macromolecular Chemistry 52-57; mem. Consultative Cttee. of Scientific and Technical Research 58-60; Titular Prof., Nat. Museum of Natural History in the Chair. of Biophysics 61-; Lauréat de l'Institut; Fellow, New York Acad. of Science; Officier de la Légion d'Honneur, Croix de Guerre, Commdr. des Palmes Académiques.
Publs. About 150 publications on magnetism, mechanics of fluids, physical chemistry of macromolecules, particularly biological macromolecules, biophysics.
Centre de Biophysique Moléculaire, La Source, 45-Orléans, France.
Telephone: 87-02-03.

Sadykov, Abid Sadykovich; Soviet chemist; b. 1913; ed. Central Asia State Univ.
Teacher, Uzbek State Univ. 39-41, Central Asia State Univ. 41-46; Dir. Inst. of Chemistry, Uzbek Acad. of Sciences 46-50; Rector, Tashkent State Univ. 58-66; mem. Uzbek Acad. of Sciences 47-, Pres. 66-; Corresp. mem. U.S.S.R. Acad. of Sciences 66-; mem. C.P.S.U. 46-; Orders and medals of U.S.S.R.
Publs. *The Chemistry of Alkaloids, Cotton Leaves as Valuable Chemical Raw Material.*
Presidium of Uzbek Academy of Sciences, 70 Gogol Street, Tashkent, U.S.S.R.

Saeland, Einar; Norwegian scientist; b. 3 April 1915; ed. Oslo Univ. and Coll. de France.
Research Chemist, Norsk Hydro 39-42; Research Scientist, Norwegian Defence Research Establishment 47-50; Research Scientist and Head of Isotope Dept., Netherlands-Norwegian Joint Establishment for Nuclear Energy Research 51-57; Dep. Dir. OECD European Nuclear Energy Agency (ENEA) 58-62, Deputy Dir.-Gen. 62-64, Dir.-Gen. 64-; mem. Editorial Board *Nukleonik* (atomic energy journal published in Berlin).
Publs. A number of scientific works on nuclear chemistry, radiation chemistry and application of radioactive isotopes.
European Nuclear Energy Agency, 38 boulevard Suchet, Paris 16e, France.
Telephone: TRO 46-10.

Saenz, Abelardo, M.D.; Uruguayan bacteriologist and diplomatist; b. 14 Sept. 1895.
Mem. staff, Faculty of Medicine, Univ. of Montevideo 18-27; Asst. Inst. Pasteur, Paris 28, Head of Laboratory 32; Technical Sec., Int. Comm. of Experts, L.N. 33; in charge of practical work on bacteriology of tuberculosis, Faculty of Medicine, Univ. of Paris 33-39; in charge of practical work in microbiology, Inst. Pasteur 34, 35, 38; Departmental Head, Inst. Pasteur 38; Hon. Prof. Faculty of Medicine, Montevideo 38; awarded Gold Medal, Faculty of Medicine, Montevideo 23, Boggio Prize, Acad. de Médecine, Paris 33, Pasteur Gold Medal of Inst. Pasteur 39, Henriette Regnier Prize of Acad. des Sciences, Inst. de France 39, Médaille des Epidémies 40 and Audiffret Prize 41, both of Acad. de Médecine, Paris; mem. numerous learned societies; del. to many int. confs. on medicine and public health; mem. Exec. Council Int. Union against Tuberculosis 52; Counsellor, Uruguayan Legation, Paris 30-44; Minister to France 44, Ambassador 50-63, to Belgium 63-65; Chief of Perm. Del. to UNESCO; Commdr. de la Légion d'Honneur (France), Commdr. Nat. Order of Southern Cross (Brazil), etc.
Publ. *De la Science à la Diplomatie* 61.
185 rue de Vaugirard, Paris 15e, France.

Saez, Raúl; Chilean civil engineer; b. 13; ed. Deutsche Schule, Santiago, Lycée Janson-de-Sailly, Paris, and Univ. of Chile, Santiago.
Engineering work 37-41; Asst. Prof. and Prof., Eng. School, Univ. of Chile 34-44; Engineer, Empresa Nacional de Electricidad (ENDESA), Chile 40-45, Chief Engineer 45-51, Admin. Dir. 51-55, Dir. 55-61, Gen. Dir. 61-64; Planning Dir. Nat. Devt. Corpn. 50-52; mem. and Co-ordinator of Cttee. of Nine, Alliance for Progress 62-64; Exec. Vice-Pres. Devt. Corpn. of Chile 65-; mem. Int. Acad. Management; several Chilean awards.
Publs. *Atomos para la Paz* 56, *Casas yara Chile* 60, *Criterios Económicos para la Selección y Desarrollo de Centrales y Sistemas Eléctricos* 63.
c/o Ministry of Foreign Affairs, Santiago, Chile.

Safonov, Dmitry Fyodorovich, M.SC.; Soviet diplomatist; b. 1909; ed. Bauman Higher Technical School, Moscow.
Foreign Service 45-; Counsellor, Soviet Embassy, London 59-60; Counsellor, Second European Dept., U.S.S.R. Ministry of Foreign Affairs 60-63; Amb. to Uganda 63-.
U.S.S.R. Embassy, P.O.Box 3222, Kampala, Uganda.

Safronchuk, Vasily Stepanovich; Soviet diplomatist; b. 1925; ed. Moscow Inst. of International Relations.
Lecturer, researcher at Moscow Inst. of Int. Relations 55-59; First Sec. Counsellor at Soviet Embassy in U.K.; Deputy Chief Second European Dept. Foreign Ministry; Amb. to Ghana 67-.
U.S.S.R. Embassy, Accra, Ghana.

Sagan, Françoise; pseudonym of Françoise Quoirez; French writer; b. 21 June 1935; ed. Couvent des Oiseaux and Couvent du Sacré Coeur, Paris.
Prix des Critiques for *Bonjour Tristesse* 54.
Publs. *Bonjour Tristesse, Un Certain Sourire, Dans un Mois, dans un An, Aimez-vous Brahms . . . ?, Les merveilleux Nuages, La Chamade, Le Garde du Coeur* 68 (novels), *Toxique* (autobiographical fragment); scenario for the ballet *Le Rendez-vous Manqué* (with Michel Magne); own film adaptation of *Dans un Mois, dans un An;* plays: *Un Château en Suède, Les Violons, Parfois . . . , a Robe Mauve de Valentine, L'Echarde, Le Cheval Evanoui.*
c/o M. René Julliard, 30 rue de l'Université, Paris 7e, France.

Saget, Louis Joseph Edouard; French government official; b. 27 April 1915; ed. Univ. de Paris.
Mayor of Tananarive 54-56; First Counsellor, French Embassy, Madagascar 59-60; High Commr. in Comoro Islands 60-62; Commissaire aux Comptes, European Launcher Devt. Org. 63-66; Gov. of French Somaliland 66-; High Commr. in Djibuoti 67; Officier Légion d'Honneur, Croix de Guerre, Commandeur de l'Etoile Noire, Chevalier de l'Ordre Nat. Malgache.
1 rue de Laborde, Mereville (Essonne), France.

Sahay, Bhagwan, B.SC.; Indian civil servant and diplomatist; b. 15 Feb. 1905; ed. Univ. of Allahabad and School of Oriental Studies, London.
Joined Indian Civil Service 29; District Magistrate 35-37; Deputy Sec. Industries Dept., United Provinces 37-39, Commr. Census Operations 39-41; Sec. Indian Council of Agricultural Research, New Delhi 41-43; Joint Sec. Dept. of Agriculture, Govt. of India 44-45 ; Commr. of Food and Civil Supplies 46-49; Chief Sec., United Provinces 49-51; Chief Commr. of Himachal Pradesh 51-52, of Bhopal State 52-54; Ambassador to Nepal 54-59; Chief Commr. of Delhi 59-63; Lieut.-Gov. of Himachal Pradesh 63, then Kerala; Gov. of Jammu and Kashmir 67- Padma Bhushan 61.
Office of the Governor, Srinagar, Jammu and Kashmir, India.

Sahay, Krishna Ballabh, B.A.; Indian politician; b. 31 Dec. 1898; ed. Zila School, Hazaribagh, and St. Columba's Coll., Hazaribagh.
Joined non-Cooperation Movement 20; mem. Bihar Legislative Council 23; political imprisonment 30, 32, 33, 40, 42; Editor *Mother India* 30-31, *Chotanagpur Darpan* 41-45; mem. Bihar Legislative Assembly and Parl. Sec. Bihar Govt. 37-40, 62-; Minister for Land Revenue, Bihar Govt. 46-57; Cabinet Minister, Bihar 62-63; Chief Minister of Bihar 63-67.
Patna, Bihar, India.

Sahay, Vishnu, B.SC.; Indian civil servant; b. 22 Nov. 1901; ed. Univ. of Allahabad and Lincoln Coll., Oxford. Indian Civil Service 25-, Sec. to Govt. of India, Ministries of Food, Agriculture, Labour, Kashmir Affairs, and to Cabinet 47-62; mem. Indian Planning Comm. 62; Governor of Assam 62-.
Government House, Shillong, Assam, India.

Saheki, Isamu, LL.B.; Japanese transport executive; b. 25 March 1903; ed. Tokyo Imperial Univ.
Kinki Nippon Railway Co. 26-, Exec. Vice-Pres. 47-51, Pres. 51-; Chair. Miyako Hotel Ltd., Shima Kanko Hotel Ltd., Nagoya Miyako Hotel Ltd.; Dir. of air and motor transport cos.; Vice-Pres. Osaka Chamber of Commerce and Industry; fmr. Exec. Dir. Japan Fed. of Employers' Asscn.; Exec. Dir. Private Railway Asscn.; Director, Japan Tourist Asscn.; Adviser to Japan Air Lines Co.; Founder, Yamato Bunka Kan Museum 60; Blue Ribbon Medal.
6-1-1 Uehonmachi, Tennoji-ku, Osaka, Japan.

Sahgal, Mrs. Nayantara; Indian writer; b. 10 May 1927; ed. Wellesley Coll., U.S.A.
Publs. *Prison and Chocolate Cake, A Time to be Happy, From Fear Set Free* 62, *This Time of Morning*.
34 Raja Gardens, New Delhi 15, India.

Sahl, Mort(on) Lyon; American entertainer; b. 11 May 1927; ed. Compton Coll., Univ. of S. Calif.
U.S. Air Force, Alaska; night club entertainer and satirist 50-, at Hungary I, San Francisco 53-; has appeared on numerous TV shows; appeared in revue *The Next President* 58; in films *In Love and War* 58, *All the Young Men* 60.
c/o Verve Records, Beverly Hills, Calif., U.S.A.

Said, El-Said Mostafa El-, LL.B., LL.D.; United Arab Republic (Egyptian) laywer and professor; b. 08; ed. Mansourah Secondary School and Cairo Univ.
Public Prosecutor 29-38; Lecturer and Asst. Prof. of Criminal Law, Cairo Univ. 32-42; Prof. of Criminal Law, Alexandria Univ. 42; Dean of Faculty of Law, Alexandria Univ. 46; Attorney-Gen., Alexandria Court of Appeal 49; Prof. of Criminal Law, Cairo Univ. 50, Dean of Faculty of Law, Cairo Univ. 52; Rector of Alexandria Univ. 54-58; Rector of Cairo Univ. 58-61; Ambassador to Portugal 62-64, to Somalia 64-; Chair. of Supreme Council of the Univs.
Publs. *On the Scope and Exercise of Marital Rights* 36, *The Egyptian Penal Code Annotated,* 3rd edition 37, *Crimes of Forgery Under the Egyptian Law,* 4th edition 53, *Principles of Criminal Law,* 3rd edition 47, *The Expansion of Higher Education in the United Arab Republic* 60.
Embassy of the United Arab Republic, Via Agostino Franzoi, Mogadishu, Somalia.

Said, Mohammed; Algerian politician.
Member Front de Libération Nationale (F.L.N.); fmr. Minister of State, Algerian Provisional Govt., Tunis, later Algiers; mem. Political Bureau (in charge of Educ. and Public Health) July 62-Sept. 62; Minister for Ex-Servicemen and War Victims Sept. 62-63, Second Vice-Pres. 63-65; mem. Revolutionary Council 65-.
Office of the Revolutionary Council, Algiers, Algeria.

Said Bin Taimur, His Highness Sir, G.C.I.E.; Sultan of Muscat and Oman; b. 10; ed. India and Iraq.
Pres. Council of Ministers 29-32; succeeded his father Sayyid Sir Taimur Bin Feisal as the 13th ruling member of his dynasty.
Muscat, Oman.

Saif al-Islam Mohamed al-Badr, H.R.H.; Imam of the Yemen; b. 27; ed. Coll. for Higher Education, Sana'a (Yemen).
Minister for Foreign Affairs 55-61, and Minister of Defence and C.-in-C. 55-62; succeeded to Imamate on the death of his father, Imam Ahmed Sept. 62; in hills, Yemen, leading Royalist Forces in civil war 62-.
Yemen, Arabia.

Saifudin; Chinese (Uighur) administrator.
Took part in people's revolutionary rising in Sinkiang Province in 32, and in 44 in revolutionary risings in Ili, Tacheng, Ashan, etc.; Vice-Chair. Nationalities Affairs Commission 49; Vice-Chair. Sinkiang Provincial People's Govt. 49; joined C.C.P. in 50; Deputy Chair. Sinkiang Democratic League for Peace 50, and Chair. of same 53; Vice-Chair. North-west Administrative Council 53; Sec. Sinkiang Office of Central Cttee. of C.C.P. 53-55; Vice-Chair. Standing Cttee. N.P.C. 54-; Chair. Sinkiang Uighur Autonomous Region 55-.
Urumchi, Sinkiang Uighur Autonomous Region, China.

Saillant, Louis; French trade unionist; b. 27 Nov. 1910.
Member Admin. Cttee. Confédération Gén. du Travail 38; organised clandestine C.G.T. meetings 40-44; rep. C.G.T. on Conseil Nat. de la Résistance 43-44; Pres. 45; mem. Del. of C.G.T. to Moscow 45; Pres. French Del. World T.U.C. 45; Sec. C.G.T. 45; Gen. Sec. W.F.T.U. 45-; Chevalier de la Légion d'Honneur; Croix de Guerre; Médaille de la Résistance; Lenin Int. Peace Prize 57; Hon. doctorate Patrice Lumumba Univ. Moscow 67.
World Federation of Trade Unions, nám. Curieovych 1, Prague 1, Czechoslovakia.

Sainsbury, Baron (Life Peer), cr. 62, of Drury Lane; **Alan John Sainsbury;** British retail executive; b. 13 Aug. 1902; ed. Haileybury School.
J. Sainsbury Ltd. (grocery and provision firm) 21-, Pres. 67-; mem. Williams' Cttee. on Milk Distribution 47-48; mem. Food Research Advisory Cttee. 60-, Chair. 65-; mem. Nat. Econ. Devt. Council (N.E.D.C.) Cttee. for the Distributive Trades 64-; Vice-Pres. Royal Soc. for Encouragement of Arts, Manufactures and Commerce 62-66, The Asscn. of Agriculture 65-; Pres. The Grocers' Inst. 63-66, Pestalozzi Children's Village Trust 63-, Multiple Shops Fed. 63-65, Royal Inst. Public Health and Hygiene 65-; Chair. Cttee. of Inquiry into relationship of pharmaceutical industry with Nat. Health Service 65-67; mem. Labour Party 45-; mem. Court of Univ. of Essex 66-; Gov. City Literary Inst. 67-.
Stamford House, Blackfriars, London, S.E.1, England.
Telephone: 01-928-3355.

Saint-Denis, Michel Jacques; French drama director and teacher; b. 13 Sept. 1897; ed. Coll. Rollin, Paris, and Lycée de Versailles.
First theatre work at the Vieux Colombier; founded La Compagnie des Quinze 30 producing and acting; founded the London Theatre Studio 35; Head of French Section B.B.C. (under pseudonym Jaques Duchesne) 40-44; founded English Service of Radio-Diffusion Française 44; Co-founder Old Vic Theatre Centre and Old Vic School (Dir.-Gen. 46-52); Dir. Centre National Dramatique de l'Est and founder Ecole Supérieure d'Art Dramatique, Strasbourg (Dir.-Gen. 52-57); advised on the foundation of the Nat. Theatre School of Canada, Montreal; Consultant, Drama Div. of Juilliard School at Lincoln Center, New York 59; Insp.-Gen. of Theatre (attached to the Ministry of Cultural Affairs, Paris) 59-; Gen. Artistic Adviser to the Royal Shakespeare

Theatre, Stratford-on-Avon and London 62-; Co-Dir. Royal Shakespeare Theatre 65-; Officier Légion d'Honneur; Hon. C.B.E. (U.K.).
Productions include: *The Witch of Edmonton* 37, *Three Sisters* 38, *Twelfth Night* 39, *Oedipus* (play) 45, *Oedipus Rex* (opera), *The Cherry Orchard* 62.
Publ. *The Rediscovery of Style* 60.
Royal Shakespeare Theatre, Stratford-on-Avon, Warwickshire; and 2 Bloomfield Terrace, London, S.W.1. England.

Sainteny, Jean; French banker and politician; b. 29 May 1907.
Banking career in Indochina 29-31, and Paris 32-39; Resistance Movement 39-45; French Commr. to China 45, to Tonkin and Annam 45-47; Gov. of the Colonies 46; Del.-Gen. to N. Viet-Nam 54-58; Commr.Gen. for Tourism 59-62; Minister for Ex-Service Men 62-66; Dir. Air France 67-.
Publ. *Histoire d'Une Paix Manquée; Indochine 1945-47* 53.
204 rue de Rivoli, Paris 1er, France.

St. John-Stevas, Norman Antony Francis, M.P.; British barrister, author and journalist; b. 18 May 1929; ed. Ratcliffe, Cambridge, Christ Church, Oxford and Yale.
Barrister, Middle Temple 52; Lecturer, King's Coll., London 53-56; Tutor in Jurisprudence, Christ Church, Oxford 53-55, Merton Coll., Oxford 55-57; Founder mem. Inst. of Higher European Studies, Bolzano 55; Legal Adviser to Sir Alan Herbert's Cttee. on Book Censorship 54-59; Legal and Political Corresp., *The Economist* 59-64; Conservative M.P. 64-.
Publs. *Obscenity and the Law* 56, *Walter Bagehot* 59, *Life, Death and the Law* 61, *The Right to Life* 63, *Law and Morals* 64, *The Literary Essays of Walter Bagehot* 65, *The Historical Essays of Walter Bagehot* 68.
1 Hampstead Square, London, N.W.3, England.

St. Laurent, Rt. Hon. Louis Stephen, P.C., Q.C., LL.D., D.C.L.; Canadian barrister and politician; b. 1 Feb. 1882; ed. Laval Univ.
Sworn of Privy Council and appointed Minister of Justice and Attorney-Gen. for Canada 41-46, 48; M.P. 42-58; Privy Council of U.K. 46; Sec. of State for External Affairs 46-48; Dep. Chair. Canadian Del. to U.N. Conf., San Francisco 45, Chair. Del. 1st Session U.N. Gen. Assembly 46, 2nd Session 47; nat. leader of Liberal Party 48-58; Prime Minister 48-57; Leader of the Opposition 57-58; Liberal; retd. from Parl. and politics and resumed law practice, Quebec 58; Hon. LL.D. (Queen's, Manitoba, Montreal, Bishop's, Dalhousie, Ottawa, Dartmouth, McGill, St. Louis, St. Lawrence, Toronto, W. Ontario, Northwestern, B.C., McMaster, Sherbrooke, London Univs., and Rensselaer Polytechnic Inst., St. Francis Xavier Univ., Antigonish, N.S., Peshawar Univ., Delhi Univ., Saskatchewan Univ., Royal Mil. Coll., Kingston); Special LL.D. (Laval Univ.); Hon. D.C.L. (Mt. Allison Univ., Oxford Univ.); Freedom of City of London; Hon. Life Pres. Canadian Bar Asscn.
201 East Grand Allée, Quebec, P.Q., Canada.

Saito, Kiyoshi; Japanese wood print artist; b. 1907.
First specialized in oil painting and held many exhbns. in Japan; later turned to wood printing, often using Haniwa (Ancient Clay Image) as material; one-man exhbn. in U.S.; awarded Prize for Japanese Artists at Int. Arts Exhbn., Brazil.
156 Moro, Itabashi-ku, Tokyo, Japan.

Saito, Nobufusa, D.SC.; Japanese atomic scientist; b. 28 Sept. 1916; ed. Tokyo Imperial Univ.
Former Asst. Prof., Kyushu and Seoul Univs., Prof. of Inorganic Chemistry, Tokyo Univ. 56-; fmr. Consultant to Int. Atomic Energy Agency (I.A.E.A.), Dir. of Isotopes Div. 63-65; Prof. Inorganic and Nuclear Chemistry, Tokyo Univ. 65-; Dir. Japan Radioisotopes Asscn.

67-; Technical Adviser, Japan Atomic Energy Research Inst. 66-; mem. Chemical Soc. of Japan, American Chemical Soc., Atomic Energy Soc. of Japan.
Department of Chemistry, Faculty of Science, University of Tokyo, Bunkyo-ku, Tokyo, Japan.
Telephone: Tokyo 812-2111, Extn. 3292.

Saito, Shizuo; Japanese diplomatist; b. 14; ed. Tokyo Imperial University.
Counsellor, London 59-62; Minister in Bangkok 62-63; Dir. UN Bureau 63-64; Ambassador to Indonesia 64-.
Japanese Embassy, 82-84 Djl. Daska V, Blok 1/III, Kebajoran, Djakarta, Indonesia.

Saiyidain, Khwaja Ghulam, B.A., M.ED.; Indian educationist; b. 14 Feb. 1904; ed. Univs. of Aligarh and Leeds.
Prof. of Education Aligarh Muslim Univ. 26-39; Dir. of Education Jammu and Kashmir State 39-46; Educational Adviser to Rampur Government 46-47; Educational Adviser to Bombay Government 47-50; joint Educational Adviser to Government of India 51-54; Additional Sec. Min. of Education 54-55; Sec. and Education Adviser to the Government of India, Ministry of Education 56-60, on special duty 60-61; Visiting Prof. Columbia Univ. 58; Educational Adviser to Jammu and Kashmir Govt. 62; mem. Educ. Comm. 64-66; D.Litt. h.c.
Publs. *The School of the Future, Principles of Education, Iqbal's Educational Philosophy, Problems of Educational Reconstruction*, etc.
New Delhi, India.

Sakata, Eiichi; Japanese politician; b. 97; ed. Agricultural Coll. of Tokyo Univ.
Director Japan Plants Fibre Asscn.; fmr. Chair. House of Reps. Agriculture-Forestry Cttee.; fmr. Pres. Food Org.; mem. House of Reps.; Minister of Agriculture and Forestry June 65-66; Liberal Democrat.
4-40-4 Daizawa, Setagaya-ku, Chiyoda-ku, Tokyo, Japan.
Telephone: 414-9264.

Sakharov, Andrei Dimitrievich; Soviet physicist; b. 24; ed. Moscow State Univ.
Physicist, P.N. Lebedev Physics Inst., Acad. of Sciences 45-; mem. Acad. of Sciences of U.S.S.R. (Dept. of Nuclear Physics) 53-; basic works on problems of theoretical physics.
U.S.S.R. Acad. of Sciences, Leninsky prospekt 14, Moscow, U.S.S.R.

Sakomizu, Hisamitu; Japanese politician; b. 02; ed. Tokyo Imperial Univ.
Ministry of Finance 26-42; Dir., General Affairs 42-45; mem., House of Peers 45-52; elected mem., House of Reps. 52, 53, House of Councillors 56; Minister of State, Dir. Gen., Economic Planning Agency 60-61; Minister of Postal Service 61-62; Chair. 12th Session, Colombo Plan Conference 60; 3rd Order of Merit (Order of Sacred Treasure) 45; Liberal Democratic Party.
Publs. *The Life of Kantaro Susuki, True Facts of the Termination of the War.*
c/o Ministry of Postal Service, Tokyo, Japan.

Sakurada Takeshi; Japanese textile executive; b. 17 March 1904; ed. Tokyo University.
Nisshin Spinning Co. Ltd. 43-, Man. Dir. 44-45, Pres. 45-64, Chair. of Board 64-; Rep. Governing Dir. Japan Fed. of Employers Asscns.
3 Yokoyamacho, Nihonbashi Chuo-ku, Tokyo, Japan.

Sakurai, Toshiki, B.ENG.; Japanese business executive; b. 1 April 1893; ed. Tokyo Imperial Univ.
With Mitsubishi Shipbuilding & Engineering Co. Ltd. 19-43; Gen. Man. Nagoya Engine Works, Mitsubishi Heavy Industries Ltd. 43-45, Gen. Man. Fourth Engineering Works 45, Gen. Man. Kyoto Engineering Works 45-46, Dir. and Gen. Man. Kyoto 46-49, Man.

Dir. and Gen. Man. 49; Man. Dir. Mitsubishi Heavy Industries 49-50; Exec. Vice-Pres. Mitsubishi Nippon Heavy Industries Ltd. 50-52, Pres. 52-61, Chair. Board of Dirs. 61-64; Counsellor, Mitsubishi Heavy Industries Ltd. 64-; Adviser, The Shipbuilders' Asscn. of Japan; Blue Ribbon Medal; Second Order of Merit.
Mitsubishi Heavy Industries Ltd., 10, 2-chome, Marunouchi, Chiyoda-ku, Tokyo, Japan.

Sakurauchi, Yoshio; Japanese politician; b. 12; ed. Keio Univ.
President Japan Electrochemical Asscn.; mem. House of Reps.; Minister of Int. Trade July 64-66; Liberal Democrat.
c/o Ministry of International Trade, Tokyo, Japan.

Sala, Admiral Antoine; French naval officer; b. 8 Oct. 1897; ed. Naval Coll., Brest.
Various appointments at sea and in naval air bases (pilot) 16-28; Asst. Naval Attaché and Air Attaché French Embassy, London 28-32; commanded cruisers and light cruisers; Naval Attaché, London 45-49; C.-in-C. French Naval Forces in the Mediterranean 51-55; Full Admiral 55; Naval Deputy to the Supreme Allied Commdr., Europe, at SHAPE, Paris 56-58, retd.; mem. Acad. de Marine; Grand Officer Legion of Honour, Croix de Guerre, Hon. C.B.E., D.S.O. (U.K.), etc.
22 rue Barbet de Jouy, Paris 7e, France.
Telephone: INValides 58-26.

Salacrou, Armand Camille; French playwright; b. 9 Aug. 1899; ed. Faculty of Medicine, Faculty of Letters, Faculty of Law, Paris.
Thirty plays produced in Paris, first performance in Théâtre de l'Oeuvre 25, first included in repertoire of Comédie-Française 44; Pres. Société des Auteurs et Compositeurs Dramatiques; fmr. Pres. of Int. Theatre Inst. (UNESCO); mem. Acad. Goncourt; Commandeur de la Légion d'Honneur.
Plays. *Le Pont de l'Europe* 27, *Atlas-Hotel* 31, *Une femme libre* 34, *L'Inconnue d'Arras* 35, *La Terre est ronde* 38, *Histoire de rive* 39, *Les Fiancés du Havre* 44, *Les Nuits de la colère* 46, *L'Archipel Lenoir* 47, *Les Invités du Bon Dieu, Sans Interdit* 53, *Le Miroir, Une Femme trop honnête* 56, *Boulevard Durand* 60, *Comme les Chardons* 64, etc.
1 bis avenue Foch, Paris 16e, France.

Salah, Abdullah A.; Jordanian diplomatist; b. 31 Dec. 1922; ed. Bishop Gobat's School, Jerusalem, and American Univ. of Beirut.
Field Educ. Officer, United Nation Relief and Works Agency (UNRWA), Jordan 52-62; Ambassador to Kuwait 62-63, to India 63-64, to France 64-Dec. 66; Minister of Foreign Affairs Dec. 66-67; several decorations.
c/o Ministry of Foreign Affairs, Amman, Jordan.

Salam, Abdus, M.A., PH.D., D.SC., F.R.S.; Pakistani university professor; b. 29 Jan. 1926; ed. St. John's Coll., Cambridge.
Professor of Mathematics, Govt. Coll., Lahore 51-54; Head, Mathematics Dept., Panjab Univ., Lahore 52-54; Lecturer, Univ. of Cambridge 54-56; Prof. of Theoretical Physics, Imperial Coll. of Science and Technology, Univ. of London 57-; mem. Pakistan Atomic Energy Comm. 59-; Pakistan Science Council 62-, Chief Scientific Adviser to Pres. 61-; Gov., Int. Atomic Energy Agency 62-63; Dir. Int. Centre for Theoretical Physics 64-; mem. UN Advisory Cttee. on Science and Technology 64-; mem. London and American Physical Socs.; many awards.
Department of Physics, Imperial College of Science and Technology, London, S.W.7, England and International Centre for Theoretical Physics, Piazza Oberdan 6, Trieste, Italy.
Telephone: 01-589-5111, ext. 723; and Trieste 69161.

Salam, Saeb; Lebanese politician; b. 05; ed. American Univ. of Beirut.
Elected Provisional Head, Lebanese Govt. 43, Deputy 43-47, 51, Minister of Interior 46, 60-61, of Foreign Affairs 46, Prime Minister 52, 53, 60-61, concurrently Minister of Defence 61; pioneer Lebanese civil aviation 45; Pres. Middle East Airlines Co., Beirut 45-56; Pres. National Fats and Oil Co. Ltd., Beirut.
c/o Office of the Prime Minister, Beirut, Lebanon.

Salan, Raoul Albin Louis; French army officer; b. 99; ed. Coll. de St Cyr.
2nd Lieut. 19, Lieut. 21, Capt. 30, Commandant 38, Lieut. Col. 41; Head, Deuxième Bureau, French West Africa 41-43; Col. 43; Gén. de Brigade, commanding 9th Division of Colonial Infantry, later 14th Div. of Infantry 44; Commdr. French troops in China and at Tongkin 45-46; Gén. de Division, commanding Tongkin troops 47; Commandant Supérieur, French troops in Far East 48; Gén. de Corps d'Armée, C.-in-C. Indochina 52-53; Inspector Gen., Land Defence 53; mem. Conseil Supérieur de la Guerre et des Forces Armées 55; Commdr. 10th Army District, Supreme Commdr., Algeria 56-May 58; Del. Gen. of French Govt., C.-in C., Algeria May-Dec. 58; Military Gov. of Paris 59-60; in exile 60-61; implicated in Algiers revolt April 61, sentenced to death *in absentia* July 61, captured in Algiers April 62; sentenced to life imprisonment and stripped of military honours May 62; granted pardon June 68; Médaille Militaire, Grand Croix de la Légion d'Honneur, Croix de Guerre (14-18 and 39-45), C.B.E., D.S.C. (U.S.A.).
Publ. *Etude sur les langues "Lu" du Haut-Laos.*
c/o Ministry of Justice, Paris, France.

Salazar, António de Oliveira, LL.D.; Portuguese economist and statesman; b. 28 April 1889; ed. Coimbra Univ.
Professor of Econ. Sciences, Coimbra Univ. 18; mem. of Portuguese Parl. 21; Minister of Finance 26 and 28-40; Minister for the Colonies *ad interim* 30; Pres. of the Council of Ministers 32-; Minister of War *ad interim* 36-44, Minister of Foreign Affairs 36-47, Minister of Defence 61-62; ex-officio mem. Council of State; Pres. Nat. Union; Hon. D.C.L. Oxford; Hon. LL.D. Fordham; Grand Cross of many Portuguese and foreign Orders.
Publs. *O Ágio do Ouro* 16, *Questão cerealífera do Trigo* 16, *Alguns aspectos de Crise das Subsistências* 18, *A minha Resposta no processo de sindicância da Universidade de Coimbra* 19, *O Centro Católico Português* 22, *Reducão dos Gastos Públicos* 23, *Discursos e Notas Politicas* (Vol. I 28-34, II 35-37, III 38-43, IV 44-50, V 51-58, VI 59-66), *The Road for the Future* 63, *Dictionnaire Politique de Salazar* 64.
Presidência do Conselho, Palácio de S. Bento, Lisbon, Portugal.

Salcedo-Bastardo, José Luis; Venezuelan writer and diplomatist; b. 26; ed. Universidad Central de Venezuela, Univ. of Paris and London School of Economics.
Teacher of Social Sciences 45; Chief Ed. *Revista Nacional de Cultura* 48-50; Asst. Lecturer, Universidad Central de Venezuela 49; Founder Rector, Univ. of Santa Maria, Caracas 53; Senator for Estado Suore, mem. Senate Foreign Relations Cttee. 58; Ambassador to Ecuador 59-61, to Brazil 61-63; Pres. Nat. Inst. of Culture and Fine Arts; numerous awards.
Publs. *Por el Mundo Sociológico de Cecilio Acosta* 45, *En Fuga hacia la Gloria* 47, *Visión y Revisión de Bolivar* 57, *Biografía de Don Egidio Montesinos* 57.
Apartado Postal 2777, Caracas, Venezuela.

Sale, Rhys Manly; Canadian motor car executive; b. 97.
First Nat. Bank, Detroit 14-15; Imperial Bank of Canada 15; Ford Motor Co. of Canada Ltd. 15-16, Ford Motor Co. of Australia Pty. Ltd. 25-26; Ford Motor Co. of Canada Ltd. 27-, rose to Exec. Vice-Pres.,

Pres. 56-60, Chair. 60-; Dir. of other companies and official of civic orgs.

Ford Motor Co. of Canada Ltd., P.O. Box 20, Oakville, Ontario, Canada.

Saleh, Jehanshah, M.D.; Iranian surgeon, gynæcologist and politician; b. 20 April 1905; ed. Syracuse Univ. N.Y.

Intern, St. Joseph's Hospital, Syracuse, N.Y. 33, Orange Memorial Hospital, N.J. 34, Resident Surgeon 35; Prof. of Anatomy, Teheran Univ. Faculty of Medicine 36-41, Prof. of Gynaecology 40-47, Dean 47-54; Dir. and Chief of Gynaecological and Obstetrical Service, Vaziri Hospital, Teheran 36-37; Dir. and Chief Surgeon, Women's Hospital, Teheran 37; Minister of Public Health 50, 53, 54, 55, 56 and 60-61; Minister of Education March-May 61; Dean Faculty of Medicine Teheran Univ. 63, Chancellor Teheran Univ. 62-, mem. Board of Dirs. and Chief of Public Health Section, Red Lion and Sun (analogous to the Red Cross) 38-; Fellow, Int. Coll. of Surgeons; Pres. Iranian Asscn. of Obstetricians and Gynæcologists, and of Iran-America Medical Soc.; mem. American Medical Asscn., Iranian Central Council of Sanitation, Central Council for Education and Teheran Univ. Council; WHO expert adviser in medical education and auxiliary branches 52-.

Publs. *The Relation of Diet to the Preservation of Teeth* 31, *Morphine Addiction and its Treatment* 32, *Diseases of Women* 41, *Normal and Abnormal Obstetrics* 42, *Recent Advances in Gynaecology* 60, *Text Book of Gynaecology* 64, etc.

Takhte Jamshid Avenue No. 10, Teheran, Iran.

Salgado Gama, Clovis; Brazilian surgeon and politician; b. 06; ed. Faculty of Medicine, Univ. of Brazil.

Professor, Univ. of Brazil 35, Univ. of Minas Gerais 36; Gov. Province of Minas Gerais 55; Minister of Education 56-60; mem. Brazilian and Int. Colls. of Surgery; hon. mem. Societies of Gynæcology, Brazil, Buenos Aires, Rosario and Santiago de Chile; Commdr. Légion d'Honneur; mem. Republican Party.

Publs. *Do tratamento das afecções cirúrgicas do colon, Elementos de diagnóstico ginecologico, Sei criar e educar meu filho.*

Avenida Pasteur 368, Rio de Janeiro, Brazil.

Salibayev, Khatam Khakimovich; Soviet politician; b. 1910; ed. Central Asian Cotton Irrigation Polytechnic Inst. and Higher Party School.

Director of Leninabad Agricultural Technical Coll. 31-35; Dir. Teachers' Training Coll. 35-37; Vice-Chair. Leninabad Regional Soviet of Working People's Deputies 39-40; Chair. State Planning Comm. Tadjik S.S.R. Council of People's Commissars 40-42, People's Commissar for Educ. 42-43; Vice-Chair. Tadjik Council of People's Commissars 43-45; Chair. Kurgan-Tyube City Soviet of Working People's Deputies 47-51; Minister of Municipal Economy of Tadjik S.S.R. 51-53; Chair. Dushanbe City Soviet of Working People's Deputies 56-57; Rector Dushanbe Shevchenko State Inst. of Pedagogical Sciences 57-61; Perm. Rep. of Tadjik S.S.R. Council of Ministers to U.S.S.R. Council of Ministers 61-; mem. Central Cttee. Tadjik C.P. 61-; Deputy to Tadjik Supreme Soviet; Order of Lenin, Red Banner of Labour (twice), Badge of Honour (twice), etc. Permanent Representation of Tadjik S.S.R. Council of Ministers to U.S.S.R. Council of Ministers, Skatertny pereulok 19, Moscow, U.S.S.R.

Salim, Khalil; Jordanian politician and banker; b. 1921; ed. American Univ. of Beirut, Inst. of Education, London and Columbia Univ.

Teacher in Secondary Schools 41-49; Lecturer Teachers Coll. 50; Dir. Cultural Affairs 52; Sec. Jordan Nat. Comm. for UNESCO 50-58; Asst. Under-Sec. of Educ. 55-62; Minister of Social Affairs 62; Minister of State, Prime Minister's Office 62-63; Chair. Authority for Tourism and Antiquities 62-63, Minister of Nat. Economy 62-63; Gov. Central Bank of Jordan 63-; Chair. Board of Jordan Co-operation Union; mem. Jordan Devt. Board and mem. Board of Trustees Univ. of Jordan.

Publs. *Re-organization of Educational Administration in Jordan* 60, 15 textbooks on Mathematics and numerous articles on Mathematics, Popular Science, Education, Economics and Banking.

Central Bank of Jordan, P.O.B. 37, Amman, Jordan.

Salimei, Jorge Néstor, D.ECON.; Argentine business executive; b. 3 Aug. 1926; ed. Coll. De La Salle and Univ. de Buenos Aires.

Oil manufacturer and Dir. of companies in flour milling, food products, and basic cereals for export; Pres. Banco de Boulogne S.A.; Minister of Economy and Labour June-Dec. 66.

Publs. Works on Argentine social and econ. problems.

Corrientes 1145, Buenos Aires, Argentina.

Salinger, J(erome) D(avid); American author; b. 19; ed. Manhattan public schools and a military coll.

Travelled in Europe 37-38; army service with 4th Infantry Division (Staff Sergeant) 42-46.

Publs. *The Catcher in the Rye, Franny and Zooey, Raise High the Roof Beam, Carpenters* 63 (novels), *For Esmé with Love and Squalor* (stories); numerous stories, mostly in the *New Yorker*, 48-.

c/o Harold Ober Associates Inc., 40 E. 49th Street, N.Y.17, U.S.A.

Salinger, Pierre Emil George, B.S.; American journalist and politician; b. 14 June 1925; ed. Univ. of San Francisco.

San Francisco Chronicle 42-55; U.S. Navy Second World War; Press Officer, Calif., Stevenson for Pres. Campaign 52, Richard Graves for Gov. (Calif.) 54; West Coast Ed., Contributing Ed. *Collier's Magazine* 55-56; Investigator, Senate Labor Rackets Cttee. 57-59; Press Sec. to Senator John F. Kennedy Sept. 59-Jan. 61, to Pres. John F. Kennedy Jan. 61-Nov. 63, to Pres. Lyndon Johnson Nov. 63-March 64; U.S. Senator from California Aug. 4, 64-Jan. 65; Vice-Pres. National General Corpn. 65-, Continental Airlines 65-; Democrat.

Publ. *With Kennedy* 66.

1438 North Kings Road, Los Angeles, Calif., U.S.A.

Salis, Jean Rodolphe de, D. ès L.; Swiss professor; b. 12 Dec. 1901; ed. Gymnase de Berne and Univs. of Montpellier, Berne, Berlin and Paris.

Corresp. of *Der Bund* in Paris 30-35; syndic of the foreign press in Paris 31-35; Prof. of History, Swiss Inst. of Technology, Zürich 35-; commentator of Radio Beromuenster ("Weltchronik") 40-47; observer at First Gen. Assembly of UNESCO 46; Prof. Univ. of Vienna, Summer 47; mem. of University Comm. (Germany, British Zone) 48; Del. to UNESCO Gen. Conf. 54, 60; Pres. Pro Helvetia Foundation 52-64; Dr. h.c. Univ. Geneva 59.

Publs. *Sismondi, La vie et l'oeuvre d'un Cosmopolite philosophe* (2 vols.) 32, *Rainer Maria Rilkes Schweizer Jahre* 36, *Giuseppe Motta, Dreissig Jahre Eidgenössische Politik* 41, *Fritz Wotruba* 47, *Weltgeschichte der Neuesten Zeit,* Vol. I 51, Vol. II 55, Vol. III 60, *Im Lauf der Jahre* 62.

Swiss Institute of Technology, Zürich, Switzerland.

Salisbury, 5th Marquess of; **Robert Arthur James Gascoyne-Cecil,** K.G., P.C., F.R.S.; British politician; b. 27 Aug. 1893; ed. Eton and Christ Church Oxford.

Conservative M.P. for Southern Div. of Dorset 29-41; Parl. Under-Sec. of State for Foreign Affairs 35-38; resigned; Paymaster-Gen. May-Dec. 40; Pres. British Group Inter-Parl. Union; P.C. 40; Sec. of State for Dominion Affairs 40-42, for Colonies 42-43; Lord Privy Seal 42-43; Sec. of State for Dominion Affairs 43-July 45; Leader House of Lords 42-45, 51-57; Chancellor

Liverpool Univ. 51-; Lord Privy Seal 51-52; Sec. of State for Commonwealth Relations 52; Lord Pres. of the Council 52-57; Dir. Westminster Bank Ltd. 57-; Chair. Royal Comm. on Historical Monuments 57-; Trustee, Nat. Gallery 59-66.
Hatfield House, Hatfield, Hertfordshire, England.

Salisbury, Sir Edward James, Kt., C.B.E., D.SC., LL.D., F.R.S., F.L.S., V.M.H., V.P.R.H.S.; British botanist; b. 16 April 1886; ed. Univ. Coll. School and Univ. Coll. London.
Senior Lecturer East London Coll. 14-18; Lecturer Univ. Coll. 18, Fellow 20, Reader in Plant Ecology 24, Quain Prof. of Botany 28; Hon. Fellow Botanical Society of Edinburgh 38; Fellow Queen Mary's Coll. 38; Fellow Wye Coll.; Governor Royal Holloway Coll., Queen Mary Coll., East Malling Research Station; Trustee Rothamsted Experimental Station; Vice-Pres. Royal Society 42-55; Dir. Royal Botanic Gardens, Kew 43-56; mem. Senate Univ. of London 34-44; Sec. Royal Soc. 45-55; Chair. Joint Comm. of Agricultural Research Council and Agricultural Improvement Council 45-56; Percy Sladen Trustee; Chair. Commonwealth Bursaries Comm. 53-65; Fullerton Prof. of Physiology, Royal Inst. 47-52; Hon. LL.D. (Edinburgh and Glasgow); Hon. Fellow Inst. of Biology.
Publs. *An introduction to the Study of Plants* 14-38, *Botany for Medical Students* 21, *The East Anglian Flora* 33, *The Living Garden* 35, *Plant Form and Function* 38, *The Reproductive Capacity of Plants* 42, *Downs and Dunes* 52, *Weeds and Aliens* 60, *The Biology of Garden Weeds* 62, etc.
Croindene, Strandway, Felpham, Sussex, England.

Salisbury, Harrison Evans, B.A.; American journalist; b. 14 Nov. 1908; ed. Univ. of Minnesota.
United Press Int. 30-48; Moscow Corresp., *New York Times* 49-54, Nat. Affairs Editor 61-63, Asst. Man. Editor 64-; Pulitzer Prize for Int. Correspondence 55; George Polk Memorial Journalism Award 67.
Publs. *Russia on the Way* 46, *American in Russia* 55, *The Shook-Up Generation* 59, *To Moscow—and Beyond* 60, *Moscow Journal* 61, *A New Russia?* 62, *The Northern Palmyra Affair* 62, *Orbit of China* 67, *Behind the Lines—Hanoi* 67, *The Soviet Union: The 50 Years* 67.
The New York Times, 229 W. 43rd Street, New York 36; Home: 349 E. 84th Street, New York City, N.Y., U.S.A.

Salk, Jonas Edward, B.SC., M.D.; American scientist; b. 28 Oct. 1914; ed. New York Univ. Coll. of Medicine and Coll. of New York City.
Fellow in Chemistry, N.Y. Univ. Coll. of Medicine 35-36, Christian A. Herter Fellow 37-38, Fellow in Bacteriology 39-40; at Mt. Sinai Hospital, New York 40-42; Nat. Research Council Fellow, School of Public Health, Univ. of Michigan 42-43, Research Fellow in Epidemiology 43-44, Research Assoc. in Epidemiology 44-46, Asst. Prof. 46-47; Assoc. Prof. of Bacteriology and Dir. of Virus Research, School of Medicine, Univ. of Pittsburgh 47-49, Research Prof. 49-55; Prof. Preventive Medicine 55-56; Commonwealth Prof. Preventive Medicine 56-57; Commonwealth Prof. Experimental Medicine 57-63, Prof. at Large 63-; Dir. and Fellow, Salk Inst. for Biological Studies 62-; Consultant to Sec. of Army in Epidemic Diseases 47-54; on Consulting Staff, Municipal Hospital for Contagious Diseases 48-56; specialist polio research; mem. American Epidemiological Society, Society of American Bacteriologists, American Asscn. of Immunologists, American Society for Clinical Investigation, Society for Experimental Biology and Medicine; Fellow of American Public Health Asscn., American Asscn. for the Advancement of Science, Asscn. American Physicians.
The Salk Institute for Biological Studies, P.O.Box 1809, San Diego, Calif. 92112, U.S.A.
Telephone: 714-453-4100.

Sallal, Marshal Abdullah; Yemeni army officer and politician; b. 17; ed. in Iraq.
Returned to Yemen from Iraq 39; imprisoned 39; Army Service 40-48, 55-; imprisoned 48-55; Gov. of Hodeida 59-62; Chief of Staff to Imam Mohammed 62; Pres. of the Revolutionary Council, Commdr.-in-Chief of the Republican forces, Yemeni Civil War Sept. 62-Nov. 67, concurrently Prime Minister Sept. 66-Nov. 67.
Sana'a, Yemen Arab Republic.

Sallinger, Rudolf; Austrian building contractor; b. 3 Sept. 1916; ed. Technische Hochschule, Vienna.
Proprietor of stonemason's firm, Vienna 43-; Head of Guild of Stone-Masons, Vienna 50, later Deputy Head of Fed. of Guilds; Chair. Trade Section, Chamber of Commerce, Vienna; Pres. Chamber of Commerce, Vienna 60-64; Pres. Fed. of Chambers of Commerce 64-; Pres. Austrian Nat. Cttee. for Int. Trade; mem. Nationalrat 66-; Pres. Fed. Econ. Chamber 66-; numerous decorations.
1050 Vienna, Nikolsdorfergasse 37, Austria.

Salman, Fadhil; Iraqi diplomatist; b. 23; ed. Law Coll., Baghdad, Faculty of Law, Univ. of Paris.
Lecturer, Law Coll., Baghdad Univ. 55-56, at Coll. of Commerce and Econs. 56-59; Dir. Arab League Section, Foreign Ministry, Baghdad 59-60; Dir.-Gen., United Nations Dept. 60-62; Counsellor, Iraqi Embassy, Iran 62, Chargé d'Affaires, Iraqi Embassy, Iran April 62-Feb. 64; Minister, Perm. Rep. to UN Geneva 64-.
Publ. *L'Action publique* 56.
Permanent Mission of Iraq, 72 rue de Lausanne, Geneva, Switzerland; Adamya, Haibat Khatoon, Baghdad, Iraq.

Salman, Mohamed; Iraqi politician; b. 08; ed. Baghdad Military Acad.
Commissioned 28; sent to England on military course 31-38; in Iraq 38-46; imprisoned by British 45; in Egypt 46-49; Military Adviser to Arab League 49-51; Organiser of Arab League anti-Israel Boycott Bureau, Damascus 53; Head of Dept. of Oil Affairs, Arab League 54-60; Minister of Oil, Iraqi Government, December 60-63.
Baghdad, Iraq.

Salmon, Robert; French journalist; b. 6 April 1918; ed. Lycée Louis le Grand, Ecole Normale Supérieure and at the Sorbonne.
Mem. Provisional Consultative Assembly 44, First Constituent Assembly 45; Founder Pres. and Dir. Gen. *France-Soir* 44-; Pres. Soc. France-Editions (*Elle*, *Le Journal de Dimanche*, *Paris-Presse*, etc.); Pres. Soc. de Publications Economiques (*Réalités*, *Connaissance des Arts*, *Entreprise*, etc.); Sec. Gen. Féd. Nat. de la Presse; Pres. French Cttee. Int. Press Inst., etc.
Publs. *Le sentiment de l'existence chez Maine de Biran* 43, *Notions élémentaires de psychologie* 47, *L'organisation actuelle de la presse française* 55, *Information et Publicité* 56, *L'Information économique, clé de la prosperité* 63.
100 rue Réaumur, 75 Paris 2e, France.

Salmon, Sir Samuel Isidore, Kt., M.A.; British company executive; b. 18 Oct. 1900; ed. Bedales School and Jesus Coll., Cambridge.
J. Lyons & Co. Ltd. (catering and food manufacturing business) 22-, Dir. 33-, Man. Dir. 49-65, Chair. 65-68; mem. London County Council 49-65, Greater London Council 65-67.
12 Hyde Park Place, London, W.2, England.
Telephone: 01-603-2040.

Salomies, Ilmari Johannes, M.A., D.THEOL.; Finnish ecclesiastic; b. 24 April 1893; ed. Helsinki Univ.
Ordained 20; Prof. of Church History, Helsinki Univ. 38; Bishop of (Viipuri-) St. Michael's 43, Archbishop of Finland 51-64.
Publs. *Henrik Renqvist I-II* (Studies in the History of

Religious Movements in Finland) 30-31; *Der Hallesche Pietismus in Russland zur Zeit Peters des Grossen* 36, *The History of the Church of Finland* I 44, II 49, III 62. Runebergink 35B, Helsinki 10, Finland.

Salonen, Olavi Oskar, M.A.; Finnish business executive; b. 28 Aug. 1914.
Entered Co-operative Soc. service 34, Head of Dept. 47-57, Asst. Man. 57-58, Man. Food Dept. 59; Chair. Board of Dirs. Oil Refinery Ltd. 58, Renlund Ltd. 59, Food Stuffs Industry 62; mem. Parl. Cttee., Bank of Finland 66-; Minister of Trade and Industry 66-68; Alt. mem. Board of Admin. Int. Bank for Reconstruction and Devt. 66-; Minister of Co-operation for Nordic Countries 66-68; mem. State Council for Science 66-68; mem. Defence Council 66-68; Chair. Econ. Council 68; Chair. GATT 67-; Chair. UNCTAD II, New Delhi 68; Vice-Chair. Outokumpu Ltd. 66-.
Puistokatu 3-A-13, Helsinki 14, Finland.

Salter, 1st Baron, cr. 53; **James Arthur Salter,** P.C., G.B.E., K.C.B.; British economist; b. 15 March 1881; ed. Oxford High School and Brasenose Coll., Oxford.
Entered Admiralty 04; Asst. Sec. National Health Insurance Comm. 13; Asst. Dir. of Transport at the Admiralty 16; Dir. of Ship Requisitioning 17; Sec. Allied Maritime Transport Council 18; Sec. British Dept. of Supreme Economic Council 19; Dir. Economic and Financial Section of the L.N. 22-30; Gladstone Prof. of Political Theory and Institutions Oxford Univ. 34-44; Independent M.P. for Oxford Univ. 37-50; Parl. Sec. to Ministry of Shipping 39-41, to Ministry of War Transport 41-44; Senior Deputy Dir.-Gen. UNRRA 44; Chancellor of Duchy of Lancaster 45; Conservative M.P. for Ormskirk April 51-Sept. 53; Minister of State for Economic Affairs 51-52; Minister of Materials 52-53; Officier de la Couronne Belgique: Commandeur Légion d'Honneur; Commendatore Order of the Crown of Italy; Brilliant Jade (China); Hon. Fellow, Brasenose, Fellow All Souls Coll Oxford; Hon. D.C.L. (Oxford), Dr. h.c. (Manchester, Vienna, Harvard, Columbia, McGill, Univ. of California, Amherst).
Publs. *Allied Shipping Control* 21, *Recovery* 32, *The Framework of an Ordered Society* 33, *The United States of Europe* 33, *World Trade* 39, *Security* 39, *Personality in Politics* 47, *Memoirs of a Public Servant* 61, *Slave of the Lamp* 67.
West House, 35 Glebe Place, London, S.W.3, England. Telephone: 01-352-7091.

Saltonstall, Leverett, A.B., LL.D.; American lawyer and politician; b. 1 Sept. 1892; ed. Harvard Univ.
Admitted to Massachusetts Bar 19; mem. law firm Gaston, Snow, Saltonstall and Hunt 26-28; Asst. District Attorney Middlesex County (Mass.) 21-22; mem. Massachusetts House of Reps. 23-36; Speaker 29-36; Gov. of Massachusetts 38-44; Senator from Massachusetts 44-67; Asst. Floor Leader 55; fmr. Chair. Republican Conf. of Senators; Republican.
Dover, Mass., U.S.A.

Saltzman, Charles Eskridge, B.S., B.A., M.A.; American investment banker; b. 19 Sept. 1903; ed. Cornell Univ., U.S. Military Acad., and Oxford Univ.
With N.Y. Telephone Co., successively Commercial Engineer, Commercial Asst. Man., Commercial Man., Directory Production Man. 30-35; with N.Y. Stock Exchange 35-49, beginning as Asst. to Exec. Vice-Pres., later Sec. and Vice-Pres.; on mil. leave of absence 40-46; served as 2nd Lieut. Corps of Engineers, U.S. Army 25-30; Commissioned 1st Lieut. N.Y. Nat. Guard 30, advanced to Lieut.-Col. 40, on active duty in U.S. Army 40-46; serving overseas 42-46, Brig.-Gen. 45; Major-General U.S. Army, retd.; on leave of absence from N.Y. Stock Exchange for govt. service 47-49; Special Asst. to Sec. of State 47; Asst. Sec. of State in charge of occupied areas 47-49; Gen. Partner, Henry

Sears & Co. June 49-56 (on leave of absence for govt. service June 54-Jan. 55); Under-Sec. of State for Admin. June 54-Jan. 55; partner Goldman Sachs & Co. 56-; Dir. Continental Can Co. Inc., A. H. Robins Co., Inc.; Nat. Pres. English-Speaking Union of United States 61-; awarded D.S.M. (U.S.), L.M. (U.S.), O.B.E. (U.K.), Croix de Guerre (France), Bronze Medal (Italy), Ouissam Alouitte (Morocco), Cross of Merit (Poland), The War Medal (Brazil); Grand Officer, Order of the Crown of Italy.
55 Broad Street, New York, N.Y. 10005; and 1021 Park Avenue, New York, N.Y. 10028, U.S.A.

Salvat, Augustín, LIC. EN DERECHO; Mexican government official; b. 23 Oct. 1908; ed. Escuela Benito Juárez, Salina Cruz, Oaxaca and Univ. Nacional Autónoma de México.
With Compañía Mexicana de Luz y Motriz 24-39; Sec. Mexican Electrical Workers' Union 35; qualified in law 44; directed youth org. in Manuel Avila Camacho's Campaign; later held various admin. posts in Govt. of Fed. District; Treas., later Sec. of Finance for twelve years, Partido Revolucionario Institucional (PRI); Sec. for Tourism 66-.
Publs. include *Industria Eléctrica, Desarrolo Industrial y el Ahorro Popular, Justicia Social y Revolución Mexicana, Israel, Breve relato de un Gran Pueblo.*
Secretaría de Turismo, Mexico D.F., Mexico.

Salvatorelli, Luigi, D. ès L.; Italian historian and journalist; b. 11 March 1886; ed. Univ. of Rome.
Sec. Ministry of Education 09-16; Prof. Univ. of Naples 16-21; political co-Dir. *La Stampa,* Turin 21-25; mem. Liberation Cttee. and Partito d'Azione 42-46; Political leader writer *La Stampa* 48-; mem. Central Board of Historical Studies 45-; mem. Accad. Nazionale dei Lincei 47-; Officier de la Légion d'Honneur; Cavaliere di Gr. Croce al merito della Repubblica Italiana.
Publs. *Il significato di Nazareno* 11, *Vita di San Francesco d'Assisi* 26, *Il Pensiero politico italiano dal 1700 al 1870* 35, *L'Italia Comunale* 40, *Pensiero e Azione del Risorgimento* 43, *Chiesa e Stato dalla Rivoluzione francese ad oggi* 55, *Spiriti e figure del Risorgimento* 61, *Miti e Storia* 64; with Giovanni Mira: *Storia d'Italia nel periodo fascista* 56, 64, *Storia del Novecento* 51, 64.
Via Bartolomeo Gosio 85, 00191 Rome, Italy.

Salvetti, Carlo; Italian physicist; b. 30 Dec. 1918; ed. Univ. of Milan.
Former Prof. of Theoretical Physics, Univ. of Bari; fmr. Dir.-Gen. Nuclear Study Centre, Ispra; fmr. Dir. Int. Atomic Energy Agency (IAEA) Div. of Research; Head, Dept. of Gen. Physics, Univ. of Milan; fmr. Gov. for Italy to IAEA, Chair. Board of Govs. IAEA 63-64; Chair. European Atomic Energy Soc. 67-68; Chair. Consorzio Italiano ROVI 68; Vice-Pres. and mem. Steering Commission, Italian Nat. Cttee. for Nuclear Energy (C.N.E.N.).
c/o C.N.E.N., via Belisario 15, 00187 Rome, Italy. Telephone: Rome 4682.

Salzman, Pnina; Israeli pianist; b. 23; ed. Ecole normale de musique and Conservatoire national de musique, Paris.
Gave first concert in Paris at age of twelve; since then has given concerts in Israel, Egypt, Lebanon, S. Africa, Rhodesia, Mozambique, Australia, New Zealand, France, Britain, Belgium, Denmark, Sweden, Norway, Finland and U.S.A., under baton of Sir Malcolm Sargent, Charles Munch, Koussevitsky, etc.; over 200 concerts with Israeli orchestras.
4 Dizengof Street, Tel-Aviv, Israel.

Samaniego, Gen. Marcial; Paraguayan soldier and politician; b. 10; ed. mil. schools.
Sometime Commdr. Engineer Battalion; previous posts include Army Dir. of Engineering; Commdr. Army Air

Force; Under-Man. Ferrocarril del Norte; Dir. Civil Aviation; Under-Sec. of Defence; Dir. Paraguayan Mil. Coll.; Minister of Public Works and Communications 54, of Defence 56-62, of Public Works and Communications 62-65; Cruz del Chaco, Cruz del Defensor, Medalla de Boquerón.
Calle Paris 423, Asunción, Paraguay.

Samaran, Charles, LITT.D.; French historian and paleographer; b. 28 Oct. 1879; ed. Ecole des Chartes and Ecole des Hautes Etudes.
Fmr. mem. French School in Rome; mem. Société Nationale des Antiquaires since 30; mem. Cttee. of Historical Works 28-; Prof. of Latin and French Paleography Ecole des Hautes Etudes 27-; Prof. of Bibliography and Archive Administration, Ecole des Chartes 33-52; Dir. Archives de France 41-48, Hon. Dir. 48-; Pres. Int. Council of Archives 48; mem. Acad. des Inscriptions et Belles-Lettres 41; Pres. Int. Coll. of Paleography 52; Pres. Comm. Supérieure des Archives 58, History and Philology Sec., Comité des Travaux historiques et scientifiques 59, Conseil de perfectionnement de l'Ecole des Chartes 61; Editor *Histoire Littéraire de la France* 61.
Publs. *La Fiscalité pontificale en France au XIVe siècle* (Bordin Prize 05), *La Maison d'Armagnac au XVe siècle* (Gobert Prize 07), *Les Diplômes originaux des Mérovingiens* 08, *D'Artagnan, capitaine des mousquetaires du roi* 12 (Montyon Prize of Acad. Française), *Jacques Casanova, Vénitien* 14, *Jean de Bilhères-Lagraulas, cardinal de Saint-Denis* 21, *Chronique latine inédite de Jean Chartier* 28, *Thomas Basin, Histoire de Charles VII et de Louis XI* 33, 44, 66, *Auctarium Chartularii Universitatis Parisiensis* (Estrade-Delcros Prize) (4 vols.) 35, 37, 38, 42, *Etudes Sandionysiennes* 44, *Aspects de l'Université de Paris* 48, *Balzac Livre du Centenaire* 52, *Alexandre Dumas, Trois Mousquetaires* 56, *Les Institutions féodales en Gascogne au moyen âge* 57, *Manuscrits latins datés* (5 vols.) 59, 62, 65, *L'Histoire et ses méthodes* (with others) 61, *Pierre Bersuire* 62, *Vocation Universitaire de Paris* 62, *Alexandre Dumas: Vingt Ans Après* 62, *Thomas Basin, Histoire de Louis XI* 63, 66, *De Rousseau à Nerval* 64, *Chartes de Gascogne* 66.
8 avenue Gourgaud, Paris 17e, France.
Telephone: GAL 90-23.

Samarin, Alexander Mikhailivich; Soviet metallurgist; b. 1902; ed. Moscow Institute of Steel.
Scientific and lecturing work Moscow Inst. of Steel 30-61; mem. Comm. on Higher Educ. to U.S.S.R. Cen. Exec. Cttee. 32-34; Deputy U.S.S.R. Minister for Higher Educ. 46-51; Acting Dir. of U.S.S.R. Acad. of Sciences Inst. of History of Natural Science and Engineering 53-55; Deputy Dir. U.S.S.R. Acad. of Sciences Inst. of Metallurgy 55-61; Deputy Chair. State Cttee. on Co-ordination of Scientific Research of U.S.S.R. Council of Ministers 61-66; Head of Laboratory, U.S.S.R. Acad. of Sciences Inst. of Metallurgy 66-67, Dir. 67-; Corresp. mem. U.S.S.R. Acad. of Sciences 46-66, mem. 66-.
Publs. Works on electrometallurgy of steel and ferroalloys.
U.S.S.R. Academy of Sciences, 14 Lenin Prospekt, Moscow, U.S.S.R.

Samayoa Chinchilla, Carlos; Guatemalan writer; b. 10 Dec. 1898; ed. Instituto Nacional de Varones and Escuela Politécnica.
Editor *Diario de Centro América* 22-28; Secr. of Presidency 32; Under-Sec. of the Presidency 44; Minister of Guatemala to Colombia 44-46; Dir. Nat. Library 47-48; Ambassador to Venezuela 48; Dir. *Diario del Pueblo* 50; voluntary exile in El Salvador 50-54, Co-founder Gen. Directorate of Fine Arts of El Salvador; Dir. Guatemala Inst. of Anthropology and History 54-; Founder "Santiago" Museum, "Libro Antiguo"

Museum, and Museum of Arts and Crafts; numerous medals.
Publs. *Madre Milpa* 34, *Cuatro Suertes* 36, *La Casa de la Muerta* 41, *El Dictador y Yo* 50, *Estampas de la Costa Grande* 54, *El Quetzal no es Rojo* 56, *Chapines de Ayer* 57, *The Art of the Ancient Maya* 59, *Aproximación al Arte Maya* 64.
Instituto de Antropología e Historia, Edificio No. 5 La Aurora, Zona 13, Guatemala City, Guatemala.

Sambasivan, Dr. G.; Indian malariologist.
Malariologist, Travancore 35; World Health Organization 49-, Senior Malaria Adviser, South East Asia Regional Office of W.H.O., New Delhi 61-64; Dir. W.H.O. Malaria Eradication Activities 64-.
World Health Organization, Palais des Nations, Geneva, Switzerland.

Sambath, Huot; Cambodian diplomatist; b. 29 Jan. 1928; ed. Cambodia and France.
Chairman Cttee. for Foreign Affairs, Cambodian Parl. 58-62; Head Cambodian Dels. to UN 62, 63, 64; First Sec. of State and later Minister for Foreign Affairs 62-64; Perm. Rep. of Cambodia to UN 65; Amb. to Cuba 65-.
Permanent Mission of Cambodia to the United Nations, 845 Third Avenue, New York 22, N.Y., U.S.A.

Sambu Zhamsarangin, *see* Zhamsarangin, Sambu.

Samii, Mohammed Mehdi; Iranian banker; b. 24 July 1918; ed. Inst. of Chartered Accountants in England and Wales.
Bank Melli Iran 45-51; National Iranian Oil Co. 51-53; Bank Melli Iran 53-59; Industrial and Mining Development Bank of Iran 59-63; Gov. Bank Markazi Iran (Central Bank of Iran) 63-.
Bank Markazi Iran, Teheran, Iran.
Telephone: 68761.

Samkalden, Ivo; Netherlands civil servant and university professor; b. 10 Aug. 1912; ed. Univ. of Leiden.
Sec. Comm.-Gen. for Neths. E. Indies 46; Asst. Prof. of Public Law, Leiden Univ. 47-48; Head of Legislative and Juridical Dept., Ministry of Agriculture, Fisheries and Food 48-52; Prof. of Law and Political Science, Agricultural Univ., Wageningen 52-56; Minister of Justice of the Netherlands 56-58, 65-66; Prof. Int. Law, Leiden Univ. 58-65, 67; Mayor of Amsterdam Aug. 67-; mem. Partij van de Arbeid (Labour Party).
Herengracht 502, Amsterdam C, Netherlands.
Telephone: 220200.

Samoré, Mgr. Antonio; Vatican ecclesiastic; b. 4 Dec. 1905.
Ordained 28; Titular Archbishop of Tirnovo 50-; Cardinal 67; Pres. Pontifical Comm. on Latin America.
Office: Pontifical Commission for Latin America, Piazza Pio XII 3, Rome; Home: Palazzo del Tribunale, Vatican City, Rome, Italy.
Telephone: Vatican 698, ext. 3311 (Office), ext. 3164 (Home).

Sampaio, Paulo, Dr.; Brazilian aviation executive; b. 07; ed. Polytechnic High School, Rio de Janeiro.
Naval Air Reserve; Engineer, Civil Aeronautics Dept.; Pres. Aero Brasil; Pres. Panair do Brasil 43-55, 61-65.
Rua da Assembleia 104, Rio de Janeiro, Brazil.

Sampedro, José Luis; Spanish economist and novelist; b. 1 Feb. 1917; ed. Madrid Univ.
Civil Service, Ministry of Finance 35-50, 57-62; Asst. Prof. of Econ. Structure, Madrid Univ. 47-55, Prof. 55-; Economist, Ministry of Commerce 51-57; Adviser to Spanish Del. to UN 56-58; Special Prof. of Econ. Sociology, Madrid Univ. 62-65; Asst. Gen. Dir. Banco Exterior de España 62-; Spanish Nat. Award for new playwrights 50.
Publs. Economics: *Principles of Industrial Location*

54, *Effects of European Economic Integration* 57, *Economic Reality and Structural Analysis* 58, *The European Future of Spain* 60, *Regional Profiles of Spain* 64, *Decisive Forces in World Economics* 67; Fiction: *Congreso en Estocolmo* (Congress in Stockholm) 52, *El Río que nos lleva* (The River which Carries Us) 62; plays: *La Paloma de Cartón* (The Paper Dove) 50, *Un sitio para vivir* (A Place to Live in) 56.
Carretera de Húmera 1, Aravaca (Madrid), Spain.
Telephone: 2070286.

Samper, Armando; Colombian agricultural economist; b. 20; ed. Cornell Univ.
Research and teaching posts in agricultural econs., Colombia 43-49; Inter-American Inst. of Agricultural Sciences of Org. of American States (O.A.S.), Turrialba, Costa Rica 49-, Head of Scientific Communications Service 49-54, Dir. of Regional Services 55-60, Dir. of Inst. 60-; Visiting Prof. Univ. of Chicago 54-55; mem. Research Cttee. FAO Freedom from Hunger Campaign, Soc. for Int. Devt., Int. Asscn. of Agricultural Econs.
Publs. *Importancia del Café en el Comercio Exterior de Colombia* 48, *A Case Study of Cooperation in Secondary Education in Chile* 57.
Inter-American Institute of Agricultural Sciences of the Organisation of American States, Apartado 4359, San José, Costa Rica.

Sampurnanand, Dr., B.SC., L.T., D.LITT.; Indian educator and politician; b. 1 Jan. 1891; ed. Queen's Coll., Benares and Teaching Coll., Allahabad.
Teacher, Prem Mahavidyalava, Brindaban and Harish-chandra High School, Benares; lecturer, Daly (Rajkumar) College, Indore; Headmaster, Dungar Coll., Bikaner 18-21; Editor *Today* (English daily) and *Maryada* (Hindi monthly); mem. All-India Congress Cttee. 22-; Sec. United Provinces Provincial Congress Cttee.; Pres. Second All-India Socialist Conf., Bombay; Minister of Education, United Provinces Govt. 38-39; Pres. 29th Hindi Sahitya Sammelan, Poona Session 40; Minister for Education, Finance and Labour, Uttar Pradesh Govt. 46-51, Home and Labour Minister 51-54, Chief Minister 55-61; Gov. of Rajasthan 62-67; Chancellor, Kashi Vidyapitha; Mangala Prasad Prize for *Samajavada*; All-India Nat. Congress.
Jalipa Devi, Varanasi (U.P.), India.
Publs. Several books in Sanskrit, Hindu and English.
Telephone: 2760.

Samuel, 2nd Viscount, cr. 37, of Mount Carmel and of Toxteth, Liverpool, **Edwin Herbert Samuel,** C.M.G.; British lecturer and author; b. 98; ed. Westminister School, Balliol Coll., Oxford Univ., and Columbia Univ., New York.
Second Lieut. Royal Field Artillery 17; Palestine Civil Service 20-48; Visiting Prof., Dropsie Coll., Philadelphia 48-49, State Univ., New York 63; Principal, Israel Inst. of Public Admin. 49-; Senior Lecturer on British Institutions, Hebrew Univ. of Jerusalem 52-; Lecturer Witwatersrand Univ. 55; European Dir., "Conquest of the Desert" Exhibition, Jerusalem 51-53; Dir., *Jewish Chronicle* (London) 51-, Vallentine Mitchell (publishers), London 65-; Adviser, Magen David Adom (Israeli Red Cross) 57-; Dir. Ellern Investment Corpn., Tel Aviv 64-, Moller Textile Corpn., Nahariya 65.
Publs. *A Primer of Palestine* 32, *Handbook of the Jewish Communal Villages in Palestine* 38, 45, *The Theory of Administration* 47, *Problems of Government in the State of Israel* 56, *British Traditions in the State of Israel* 60; short stories: *A Cottage in Galilee* 57, *A Coat of Many Colours* 60, *My Friend Musa* 63, *The Cucumber King* 65, *His Celestial Highness* 68; for children: *Capt. Noah and His Ark.*
House of Lords, London, S.W.1, England; 15 Rashba Road, Jerusalem, Israel.
Telephone: LO 33871 (Israel).

Samuelson, Paul Anthony, PH.D., LL.D., D.LITT.; American economist; b. 15 May 1915; ed. Univ. of Chicago and Harvard Univ.
Prof. of Economics at Massachusetts Inst. of Technology 40-; Consultant, Nat. Resources Planning Board 41-43, to War Production Board 45, to U.S. Treasury 45-53; mem. Radiation Laboratory Staff 44-45; Guggenheim Fellow 48-49; Vice-Pres. Econometric Soc. 49-50, Pres. 51; Vice-Pres. American Economic Asscn. 55, Pres. 60-61; on Editorial Board of *Econometrica;* Pres. Int. Econ. Asscn. 65-68; consultant to Rand Corpn. 49-; Research Advisory Board Cttee. for Economic Devt. 60, Advisory Board to Pres. Eisenhower's Comm. on Nat. Goals 60, Nat. Task Force on Economic Educ. 60-61, Comm. on Social Sciences 68-; Comm. on Money and Credit, Economic Adviser to Pres. Kennedy during election campaign; author of report to Pres. Kennedy on State of American Economy 61; Hon. LL.D. (Chicago, Oberlin, Boston); Hon. D.Litt. (Ripon); Hon. D.Sc. (E. Anglia); mem. American Acad. of Arts and Sciences, American Philosophical Soc.; Corresp. Fellow, British Acad.
Publs. *Foundations of Economic Analysis* 47 (2nd Edn. 61), *Economics: An Introductory Analysis* 48, 52, 55, 58, 61, 64, 67 (many foreign edns.), *Readings in Economics* (with R. L. Bishop and J. R. Coleman) 52, 55, 58, 67, *Linear Programming and Economic Analysis* 58; joint author of other books and articles on economics.
75 Clairemont Road, Belmont 78, Massachusetts, U.S.A.

San Miguel, Manuel; Argentine administrator and former World Bank official; b. 21 Jan. 1922; ed. Univ. of Rosario.
Under-Secretary for Commerce 56-57; Vice-Pres. Nat. Inst. of Grains and Elevators 56; Vice-Pres. Commerce Cttee. Econ. Comm. for Latin America (ECLA) 56, Del. for ECLA 61-63; Rep. for Inter-American Econ. and Social Council, Latin-American Free Trade Asscn. (LAFTA) 59-63; Dir. Dept. of Econs., Univ. of Buenos Aires 61-63, Prof. 64; Alt. Gov. World Bank 64, Exec. Dir. 64; Vice-Pres. Nat. Devt. Council 64, and Soc. for Int. Devt. 65-.
Consejo Nacional de Desarrollo, Buenos Aires, Argentina.

Sananikone, Phoui, Laotian politician; b. 03.
Head of Province 41-46; Pres. Chamber of Deputies 48-50, 60-; Prime Minister and Pres of the Council of Ministers Feb. 50-Nov. 51, 58-Dec. 59; Minister of Foreign Affairs 53-54, 54-56, 57-58, 59; Vice-Pres. Council of Ministers 53-56; numerous other cabinet posts; Pres. Nationalist group, Rassemblement du Peuple Lao 62-; Grand Croix Ordre Royal du Million d'Eléphants et du Parasol Blanc; Commdr. Légion d'Honneur; Croix de Guerre avec palme.
National Assembly, Vientiane, Laos.

Sánchez, Luis Alberto, PH.D., LIT.D., HIST.D.; Peruvian university professor and politician; b. 1900; ed. Sacré Coeur, Universidad Mayor de San Marcos.
Assistant Director, Nat. Library of Peru 28-30; Dean, Faculty of Philosophy, History and Literature, Univ. Mayor de San Marcos, Lima 46, 61, Rector 46-48, 61-64; mem. of the Chamber of Deps. 31-36, 45-48, Pres. 45; Special Ambassador to Colombia 46, Mexico 60-61; Dir. Editorial Ercilla, Santiago, Chile 35-45; mem. Exec. Nat. Cttee. of the Partido Aprista Peruano (APRA Party) 31-34, 45-49, 56-; mem. Board of Trustees, American Inst. for Free Labor Development, Washington 62-; exiled 32-33, 34-45, 48-56; Nat. Culture Prize 59, 60; Peruvian and foreign honours.
Publs. *La Literatura Peruana* (6 vols.) 51, *Historia General de América* (2 vols.) 42, 6th edn. 58, *Proceso y Contenido de la Novela Hispano-Americana* 53, *Historia de la Literatura Americana* 51, *Escritores Representativos*

de América (2 vols.) 57, *Examen Espectral de América Latina* 62.

P.O. Box 673, Lima, Peru.

Sánchez-Bella, Alfredo; Spanish diplomatist; b. 2 Oct. 1916; ed. Universidad de Madrid.

Director newspaper *Avance* of Valencia; Under-Sec. Consejo Superior de Investigaciones Científicas 40-41; Dir. Jiménez de Cisneros Coll. Madrid Univ. 41-45; Dir. Instituto de Cultura Hispánica 46-56; Dir. *Mundo Hispánico* and founder of historical *Cuadernos Hispanoamericanos;* Ambassador to Dominican Republic 57-59, to Colombia 59-62, to Italy 62-; numerous awards and honours.

Publs. *El Marqués de Valparaiso, vida y ventura de un hispanoamericano del siglo XVII, El Conde-Duque de Olivares, La investigación científica en el mundo, Problemas Universitarios y otros ensayos, La problemática hispanoamericana en la hora presente.*

Embassy of Spain, Largo Fontanella Borghese 19, Rome; and Via Garibaldi 35, Rome, Italy.

Sánchez Cantón, Francisco Javier, DR. en FIL. y LETRAS; Spanish art historian; b. 91; ed. Madrid Univ. Joined Prado Museum 19, Dep. Dir. 22-60, Dir. 60-; Prof. of Art History, Madrid Univ. 22-, Dean of Faculty of Philosophy and Letters 50, Vice-Rector 58-; Dir. Real Acad. de la Historia 57-; mem. Real Acad. Española, Real Acad. de Bellas Artes. Real Acad. Española de la Lengua; Gran Cruz de Alfonso X el Sabio, Gran Oficial de Santiago da Espada (Portugal), Officier de la Légion d'Honneur, Commdr. Ordre de la Couronne (Belgium), Order of Polar Star (Sweden); Dr. h.c. Lund Univ.

Publs. *Fuentes Literarias para la Historia del Arte Español* (five vols.) 23-43, *Dibujos españoles* (five vols.) 30, *Retratos de los Reyes de España* 45, *Vida y obras de Goya* 51, *Los Dibujos de Goya* (two vols.) 52.

Real Academia de la Historia, Léon 21, Madrid XIV, Spain.

Sánchez-Gavito, Vicente, A.B., LL.B.; Mexican diplomatist; b. 25 May 1910; ed. Univ. Nacional Autónoma de México and Escuela Libre de Derecho.

Entered Diplomatic Service of Mexico 35-; Counsellor, Embassy in Washington 43-47; Dir.-Gen. Diplomatic Service, Foreign Office 47-51; Minister, Washington 56-58, Amb. 59-65; Amb. to Brazil 65-; mem. UN Tribunals in Libya and Ethiopia 51-55; Mexican Rep., Council of Org. of American States (OAS) 59-65, Chair. of Council 60, Chair. Interamerican Peace Cttee. 61, Honduras-Nicaragua Mixed Comm. 61, mem. Mexican Dels. to numerous Foreign Ministers' Meetings and Extraordinary Interamerican Confs. of OAS (Pres. of Mexican Dels. to 9th Foreign Ministers' Meeting and to 1st Extraordinary Interamerican Conf.); Orders of the: Southern Cross (Brazil), Liberator (Venezuela), Ethiopian Star, Cedar of Lebanon, Orange-Nassau (Netherlands).

Praia do Flamengo 344, Rio de Janeiro, Brazil.

Sánchez Hernández, Col. Fidel; Salvadorean politician. Former Mil. Attaché, Washington; Minister of Interior until 67; Pres. of El Salvador July 67-; Leader of Partido de Conciliación Nacional (P.C.N.).

Office of the President, San Salvador, El Salvador.

Sánchez Quell, H., LL.D.; Paraguayan politician and diplomatist; b. 07; ed. Univ. of Asunción.

Mem. Colorado Party 30; former Editor *Patria, La Unión, Rumbos, La Prensa, Jornada;* fmr. posts incl. Prof. Univ. of Asunción, Dir.-Gen. of Nat. Archives, Vice-Pres. Chamber of Reps., Ambassador to Mexico; Paraguayan Rep. to U.N. until 54; Minister of Foreign Affairs 54-57; Ambassador to Brazil 57-59, to France 59-62; mem. Permanent Arbitration Court of The Hague, Pan American Inst. of Geography and History, Paraguayan Inst. of Historical Research, Argentine Inst. of Law, Argentine Acad. of Sociology, Historical and Geographical Inst. of Uruguay, Mexican Athenaeum of Sciences and Arts.

c/o Ministry of Foreign Affairs, Asunción, Paraguay.

Sánchez-Vilella, Roberto; Puerto Rican politician; b. 13; ed. High School, Ponce, Puerto Rico and Ohio State Univ.

Engineer 34-41; Asst. Commr. of the Interior 41-42; Gen. Man. Puerto Rico Transport Authority 42-45; City Man. San Juan 45-46; Special Asst. to Pres. of Senate 46-47; Resident Engineer, Caribe Hilton Hotel 47-48; Exec. Sec. of Puerto Rico 49-51; Sec. of Public Works, Commr. of Puerto Rico 51-59; Sec. of State 52-65; Gov. 65-.

Office of the Governor, San Juan, Puerto Rico, Caribbean.

Sandage, Allan Rex, PH.D., D.SC.; American astronomer; b. 18 June 1926; ed. Univ. of Illinois and California Inst. of Technology.

Staff mem. Mount Wilson and Palomar Observatories 52-; Visiting Lecturer, Harvard Univ. 57; Consultant, Nat. Science Foundation 61-63; mem. Cttee. on Science and Public Policy 65; Philips Lecturer, Haverford Coll. 68; Research Assoc. Australian Nat. Univ. 68-69; Helen Warner Prize of American Astronomical Soc. 60; Eddington Medal, Royal Astronomical Soc. (U.K.) 63; Pope Pius XI Gold Medal, Pontifical Acad. of Sciences 66; Gold Medal, Royal Astronomical Soc. (U.K.) 67, Rittenhouse Medal 68.

Publs. Numerous scientific papers and *Hubble Atlas of Galaxies.*

701 Santa Barbara Street, Pasadena, Calif., U.S.A.

Sandberg, Willem; Netherlands museum director; b. 24 Oct. 1897; ed. Acad. of Fine Arts, Amsterdam, Univs. of Vienna and Utrecht.

Designer in Amsterdam 28-38; Asst. Dir. Municipal Museum, Amsterdam 38-45, Dir. 45-62; Head, Int. Section "Art since 1950" U.S. World's Fair 62-64; Chair. Exec. Cttee. Israel Museum, Jerusalem 64-68; Co-founder Fed. of Professional Artists in the Netherlands 45, Pres. 47-51; Vice-Pres. Netherlands Arts Council 48-60; Hon. degree Univ. of Buffalo, N.Y. 62; Gold Medallist American Inst. of Graphic Arts, City of Amsterdam; many foreign decorations.

Publs. many articles on art and museum building; Co-editor *Pioneers of Modern Art.*

Keizersgracht 640, Amsterdam, Netherlands.

Telephone: 231876 and 725385.

Sandblom, (John) Philip, M.D., M.S.; Swedish professor of surgery and university administrator; b. 29 Oct. 1903; ed. Northwestern Univ. and Karolinska Institutet, Stockholm.

Assoc. Prof. of Surgery Karolinska Institutet, Stockholm 44; Surgeon in Chief Crown Princess Louise's Children's Hospital 45-50; Prof. of Surgery and Head of Dept. of Surgery, Lund Univ. 50-, Chancellor of Lund Univ. 57-; mem. of Board Soc. for Modern Art 36-46, Gen. Art Soc. 43-, Asscn. for Pictorial Art 43-48; Treas. Swedish Surgical Soc. 46-52, Pres. 57-58; mem. Insurance Advisory Board 47-50; Assoc. mem. Asscn. Française de Chirurgie, corresp. mem. Deutsche Gesellschaft für Chirurgie, and Norwegian and Finnish Surgical Socs.; Pres. elect Soc. Int. de Chirurgie; Hon. Fellow American Coll. of Surgeons; Hon. mem. Amer. Surgical Asscn. and Danish Surgical Soc.; an Editor of *Acta Chirurgica Scandinavica.*

Publs. Papers on Wound Healing, Gall bladder, Heart, Vascular and Child Surgery.

Östervångsvägen 42, Lund, Sweden.

Sander, Bruno Hermann Max; Austrian geologist; b. 23 Feb. 1884; ed. Gymnasium Innsbruck and Leopold-Franzens Universität, Innsbruck.

Assistant, Technische Hochschule of Vienna 09-; Lecturer

in Geology, Univ. of Innsbruck 12-14, Univ. of Vienna 14-22; Geologist, Geological Inst., Vienna 13-22; Prof. of Mineralogy and Petrography, Univ. of Innsbruck 22-55, Emeritus 55-; mem. Acads. of Vienna, Bologna, Modena, Uppsala, Berlin, Halle, Nat. Acad. of Sciences, Washington; Corresp. mem. Geol. Soc. of America, American Asscn. for the Advancement of Science, Geol. Soc. of Finland, Geological Soc. of London; Int. Prize of Accad. dei Lincei, Rome; numerous medals; Dr. h.c. Göttingen 37, Vienna 65.
Publs. *Gefügekunde der Gestine* 30, *Einführung in die Gefügenkunde der Geologischen Körper* (2 vols.) 48-50; geological maps and treatises on geology and petrography; other books and treatises under pseudonym *Santer*.
Mineralogisches Institut, 6020 Innsbruck, Austria.
Telephone: 25476.

Sanders, Carl Edward; American lawyer and politician; b. 15 May 1925; ed. Richmond Acad. and Univ. of Georgia Law School.
U.S. Air Corps 42-45; legal practice 47-63; mem. Georgia House of Reps. 54-56, Georgia Senate 56-62, Floor Leader 59, Pres. 60-62; Governor of Georgia 63-67; official of numerous civic orgs.; Democrat.
205 The Prado, N.E., Atlanta, Georgia, U.S.A.

Sanders, William; American lawyer and diplomatist; b. 14 April 1903; ed. Stanford, George Washington, Columbus and Oxford Univs.
International Telephone and Telegraph Corpn., New York 29-32; admitted to D.C. Bar 35, legal practice 35-36; Chief, Juridical Div., Pan-American Union 36-41; Principal Attorney, Co-ordinator of Inter-American Affairs 42; Alt. mem. Emergency Advisory Cttee. for Political Defense, Montevideo 42-43, mem. 44-45; Assoc. Chief, Div. of Int. Org. Affairs, Office of Special Political Affairs, Dept. of State 45-48; Special Asst. Bureau of UN Affairs, Dept. of State 48-52, Acting Deputy Asst. Sec. of State 50-52; U.S. del. conferences Inter-American system, NATO and UN 45-58; U.S. rep. I.A. Council of Jurists 48-58; Counsellor and Deputy Chief Mission, Chile 53-56; Asst. Sec.-Gen. Org. of American States 58-; Pres. Pan American Devt. Foundation 63-;
Publs. *Improvement and Co-ordination of Inter-American Peace Instruments* 40, *Sovereignty and Interdependence in the New World* 48.
Pan American Union, 17th Street and Constitution Avenue, Washington, D.C., 20006, U.S.A.
Telephone: DU 1-8205.

Sanderson, 1st Baron, cr. 60, of Ayot; **Basil Sanderson,** M.C.; British shipowner; b. 19 June 1894; ed. Rugby and Trinity Coll. Oxford.
Director Shaw Savill & Albion Co. Ltd. 36-, Chair. 47-63; fmr. Dir. Furness Withy & Co. Ltd., Ford Motor Co. Ltd.; Dir. Bank of England 46-65, Finance Corpn. for Industry 53-66; Dir. British Maritime Trust Ltd.; Chair., London Gen. Shipowners' Soc. 33-34; Chair., Nat. Council of Port Labour Employers 34-40; Chair. Shipping Fed. 34-50, Pres. 50-63; Pres. Int. Shipping Fed. 34-51; Pres. British Employers Confederation 38-39; Dir. of Shipping in Port, Ministry of Shipping 39-41; Head of Port and Transit Control, Ministry of War Transport 41-45; Chair. Shipowners' side of Nat. Maritime Board 46-51; High Sheriff, County of London 48-49; mem. Econ. Planning Board 57-62; mem. Council of Chamber of Shipping.
Publ. *Ships and Sealing Wax* 68.
Ayot Bury, Welwyn, Herts.; and Lloyds' Building, 14/19 Leadenhall Street, London, E.C.3, England.

Sandoungout, Marcel; Gabon trade unionist and diplomatist; b. 25 Oct. 1927.
Former trade unionist, Gabon; fmr. Chef de Cabinet to Minister of Planning for Agriculture; Chief, Div. for

Int. Orgs., Ministry of Foreign Affairs 60; mem. Nat. Assembly 61, Chair. Cttee. for Foreign Affairs and Defence, 61, 62; Del. to Defence Council of African and Malagasy Union 61, 62; Minister of Health and Social Affairs May-Dec. 62, for Public Works, Tourism and Posts and Telecommunications 63-64; Amb. to German Fed. Repub., Belgium, Netherlands, Norway, Denmark, Sweden and Luxembourg 64-66; Perm. Rep. to GATT and EEC 64-66; Perm. Rep. to UN 67-.
Permanent Mission of Gabon to the United Nations, 866 UN Plaza, Room 536, New York, N.Y. 10017, U.S.A.

Sandys, Rt. Hon. Duncan Edwin, P.C., M.P.; British politician; b. 24 Jan. 1908; ed. Eton and Magdalen Coll. Oxford.
Diplomatic Service 30-33; served at Foreign Office and British Embassy, Berlin; M.P. (Cons.) for Norwood Div. of Lambeth 35-45, for Streatham Div. of Wandsworth 50-; Lieut. Territorial Army 37; mem Conservative Party Nat. Exec. 38-40; served in Norway 40; Lieut.-Col. 41; disabled on active service 41; Finance mem. of Army Council 41-43; Parl. Sec. to Ministry of Supply 43-44; Chair. of Cabinet Cttee. for defence against German "V" weapons 43-45; Minister of Works 44-45; founded European Movement 47, Chair. Int. Exec. 47-50; mem Consultative Assembly of Council of Europe 50-51; Minister of Supply 51-54; Minister of Housing and Local Govt. 54-57; Minister of Defence 57-59; Minister of Aviation 59-60; Sec. of State for Commonwealth Relations 60-62, Sec. of State for Commonwealth Relations and Sec. of State for Colonies 62-64; Founder Civic Trust, Pres. 56-.
86 Vincent Square, London, S.W.1, England.

Sanger, Frederick, C.B.E., B.A., PH.D., F.R.S.; British research biochemist; b. 13 Aug. 1918; ed. Bryanston School and St. John's Coll., Cambridge.
Biochemical research at Cambridge 40-; Beit Memorial Fellowship 44-51; mem. External Staff, Medical Research Council 51-; Fellow, King's Coll., Cambridge 54-; Hon. Foreign mem. American Acad. of Arts and Sciences 58-; hon. mem. American Soc. of Biological Chemists, Japanese Biochemical Soc.; corresp. mem. Association Quimica de Argentina; mem. Acad. of Science of Argentina and Brazil, World Acad. of Arts and Science; Corday-Morgan Medal and Prize, Chemical Soc. 51, Nobel Prize for Chemistry 58, Alfred Benzon Prize 66.
Publs. Various papers on protein structure and metabolism in scientific journals.
Medical Research Council Laboratory of Molecular Biology, Cambridge Univ., and 252 Hills Road, Cambridge, England.
Telephone: Cambridge 48011.

Sänger, Fritz Paul; German journalist; b. 24 Dec. 1901; ed. Univ. of Berlin.
Sub-editor *General Anzeiger* (Stettin) 21; with Pressestelle Deutscher Beamtenbund 23-27; editor *Preussische Lehrerzeitung* 27-33, dismissed by Hitler; with the *Frankfurter Zeitung* 35-43 and *Neues Wiener Tagblatt* 43-44; Editor *Braunschweiger Neue Presse/Braunschweiger Zeitung* 45-46; Editor and founder *Sozialdemokratischer Pressedienst* 46-47; Editor-in-Chief *Deutscher Presse-Dienst* (D.P.D.), later merged in the *Deutsche Presse-Agentur* (D.P.A.) 47-59; mem. Board of Dirs. Deutschlandfunk; mem. Deutscher Presserat, mem. Sozialdemokratische Partei Deutschlands (S.P.D.) since 20; mem. Bundestag 61-.
Publs. *Handbuch des Deutschen Bundestages* 49, 52, 54 and 58; "*Soziale Demokratie*", *Bemerkungen zum Grundsatzprogramm der SPD* 60, 62, 64, *Erich Ollenhauer, Reden und Aufsätze* 64.
Erlenweg 28, 2000 Wedel, German Federal Republic.
Telephone: 04103-3716.

Sangster, John Young; British industrialist; b. 29 May 1896; ed. Hurstpierpoint Coll.
Practical experience in German and French cycle and motor car factories 13-14; war service 14-18; produced prototype 8 h.p. air-cooled car which, sold to the Rover Co., became the famous Rover-8 19; Asst. to Works Man., Rover Co. 20-21; joined Ariel Works 23, Joint Man. Dir. 26; acquired Ariel Motor Cycle Co. and set up Ariel Motors Ltd. 32; acquired Triumph Motor Cycle Co. and set up Triumph Engineering Co. Ltd. 36; Triumph factory, Coventry, completely destroyed in air raids 40, rebuilt at Allesley, near Coventry; sold Ariel Motors Ltd. to Birmingham Small Arms Co. Ltd. 45, Triumph Engineering Co. Ltd. 51; Dir. Birmingham Small Arms Co. Ltd. 51-; Chair. Birmingham Small Arms Co. Ltd. 56-61; Pres. British Cycle and Motor Cycle Industries Asscn. 53-54; Liveryman, Coachmakers and Coach Harness Makers Co.
51 South Street, London, W.1, England.
Telephone: 01-499-7594.

Sanguineti, Edoardo; Italian writer; b. 9 Dec. 1930; ed. Univ. degli Studi, Turin.
Former Prof. of Modern and Contemporary Italian Literature Univ. of Turin.
Publs. *Laborintus* 56, *Opus metricum* 60, *Interpretazione di Malebolge* 61, *Tre studi danteschi* 61, *Tra liberty e crepuscolarismo* 61 and 65, *Alberto Moravia* 62, *K. e altre cose* 62, *Passaggio* 63, *Capriccio italiano* 63, *Triperuno* 64, *Ideologia e linguaggio* 65, *Il realismo di Dante* 66, *Guido Gozzano* 66, *Il Giuoco dell' Oca* 67.
Via Amerigo Vespucci 25, Turin, Italy.
Telephone: 585026.

Sanguinetti, Alexandre; French politician; b. 27 March 1913; ed. Coll. Stanislas, Paris and Ecole de Droit, Cairo.
War service, Second World War; Head of Office, Ministry of Information 59-61, Ministry of the Interior 61-62; mem. Chamber of Deputies 62-; Minister for Veterans 66-67; Vice-Pres. Comm. for Nat. Defence; Chevalier Légion d'Honneur, Médaille Militaire, Croix de Guerre.
Publ. *La France et l'Arme atomique.*
Home: 12 rue de Rémusat, Paris 16e, France.

Sani'i, Gen. Asadollah; Iranian army officer and politician; b. 04; ed. Officers' Training Coll.
Special Adjutant to Shahanshah; Deputy Minister of War 61, 62, Minister of War 63-; Third, Second and First Order of Merit; Third, Second and First Order of Honour; Second and First Order of Homayoun; First Order of Service.
Ministry of War, Teheran, Iran.

Sanjines Goytia, Col. Julio; Bolivian army officer and politician; b. 6 Oct. 1924; ed. West Point Military Acad., U.S.A., Escuela de Oficiales, Peru, Fort Belvoir, U.S.A., and State Univ. of Iowa.
Instructor and Prof. Bolivian Mil. Acad. 46-48; Bolivian Army 50-52; in exile (Peru) 53-60; Man. of industrial and construction firm; First Dir. and Founder UN Andean Indian Mission in Ecuador; returned to Bolivia 60; Head of Civic Action Div., U.S.A.I.D./Bolivia; Pres. Board of Dirs. *El Diario* (newspaper); Minister of Nat. Economy 64-65; Amb. to U.S.A. and Canada 65.
Publs. *Evolution of the Military Engineers* 53, *Civic Action* 63.
2914 Avenida Ecuador, La Paz, Bolivia.
Telephone: 23729.

Sanjivayya, D., B.A., B.L.; Indian politician; b. 14 Feb. 1922; ed. Govt. Arts Coll., Anantapur and Madras Law Coll.
Advocate 50; elected to Madras Legislature as Congress nominee from Kurnool 52; Minister of Co-operatives and Housing (Madras) 52-54, Local Admin. and Labour (Andhra Pradesh) 54-60, Chief Minister of Andhra Pradesh 60-62; Pres. of Indian Nat. Congress 62-64; Minister of Labour and Employment 64-66; Minister of Industry 66-67.
c/o Ministry of Industry, New Delhi, India.

Sankar, R.; Indian politician; b. 08; ed. Science and Law Coll., Trivandrum.
Lawyer, Quilon Dist. Court; Gen. Sec. State Congress 40-44; elected to Travancore Legislative Ass. 48, Indian Constituent Ass. 48; Dep. Chief Minister of Kerala 60-62, Chief Minister, Kerala State 62-64.
Lakshminivas, Kunnukuzhi, Trivandrum, Kerala, India.

Sanminiatelli, Bino; Italian artist and writer; b. 7 May 1896; ed. Univs. of Padua, Rome and Siena.
Member Futurist and Dada movements, Dir. with painter Prampolini of avant-garde magazine *Noi*; represented with etchings in important int. and nat. exhbns. in Venice and Rome; works hung in Galleria Nazionale d'Arte Moderna Rome, Florence and Turin; etchings published by Ceschina; Vice-Pres. Dante Alighieri Soc.; Pres. Cento Amici del Libro; Viareggio Prize 33, Encomio della Reale Accad. d'Italia 35, Rustichello Prize 61, Marzotto Prize 63.
Publs. *Fiamme a Monteluce* 38, *L'Omnibus del Corso* 40, *Cervo in Maremma* 42, *Gente in Famiglia* 51, *Le Proibizioni* 54, *Il Viaggiatore sedentario* 53, *Mi dico addio* 59, *La Mora* 61, *Il Permesso di Vivere* 63, *Vita di Michelangelo* 64.
Vignamaggio, Greve in Chianti, Florence, Italy.

Sansbury, Rt. Rev. Cyril Kenneth, D.D.; British ecclesiastic; b. 21 Jan. 1905; ed. St. Paul's School, London, Peterhouse, Cambridge, and Westcott House, Cambridge.
Ordained Deacon 28, Priest 29; Curate, Diocese of Southwark 28-32; Missionary in Japan 32-41; Prof. Central Theological Coll., Tokyo, and Chaplain, St. Andrew's Church, Tokyo 34-41; Chaplain, Royal Canadian Air Force 41-45; Warden, Lincoln Theological Coll. 45-52; Canon and Prebendary, Lincoln Cathedral 48-53; Warden, St. Augustine's Coll., Canterbury 52-61; Hon. Canon of Canterbury 53-61; Bishop of Singapore and Malaya 61-66; Gen. Sec. British Council of Churches 66-; Asst. Bishop, Diocese of London 66-.
Publ. *Truth, Unity and Concord, Anglican Faith in an Ecumenical Setting* 67.
British Council of Churches, 10 Eaton Gate, London, S.W.1, England.
Telephone: 01-730-9611.

Santa Cruz, Marquis de; José Fernández Villaverde y Roca de Togores, LL.D.; Spanish diplomatist; b. 4 April 1902; ed. Univ. of Madrid and New Coll. Oxford.
Entered Diplomatic Service 21; First Sec. London 39, Minister 44; Minister, Copenhagen 48-50, The Hague 50-53; Ambassador to Egypt 53-55; Under-Sec. of State for Foreign Affairs 55-58; Ambassador to U.K. 58-; Sec.-Gen. of Ibero-American Aeronautical Conf. Madrid 26; Hon. Fellow, New Coll., Oxford.
Spanish Embassy, 24 Belgrave Square, London, S.W.1, England.

Santa Cruz, Domingo Santa María; Chilean civil engineer and politician; b. 20.
Former Prof. of Physics, Universidad Católica, Santiago; Minister of Econ. Nov. 64-67; Christian Democrat.
Ministry of Economy, Santiago, Chile.

Santa Cruz, Victor; Chilean lawyer and diplomatist; b. 13; ed. Stonyhurst Coll., Instituto Nacional and Univ. de Chile.
Professor of Civil Law, Univ. of Chile 41; mem. Chilean Parl. 45; Ambassador to U.K. 59-; mem. Anglo-Chilean Soc.
Chilean Embassy, 3 Hamilton Place, London, W.1, England.

Santaella, Dr. Héctor; Venezuelan economist, banker and diplomatist; b. 19 May 1920; ed. Colegio La Salle, Caracas, Liceo Andrés Bello, Caracas, and Universidad Central de Venezuela, Caracas.
Chief of Econ. Section, Directorate of Econ. Policy, Venezuelan Foreign Service 43; later Head of Dept. of Econ. Information, Ministry of Foreign Affairs; fmr. Venezuelan Gov. Int. Bank for Reconstruction and Devt.; fmr. Alt. Dir. Int. Monetary Fund; Ambassador to U.S.A. 58; Sec. of Govt. Junta, Republic of Venezuela 58-59; mem. Nat. Congress 64-; Pres. Chamber of Deputies 64-65; Amb. to U.K. 65-66; Minister of Communications 66-67; fmr. Chair. Inveco, Bank of Repub., Bank of S. America; fmr. Sec. Nat. Banking Council; Dir. Venezuelan Fed. of Chambers and Asscns. of Commerce and Production; fmr. Pres. Asscn. of Venezuelan Exporters; fmr. Prof. of Econ. Theory, Venezuelan Central Univ.; numerous decorations.
Home: Transversal 5, No. 10-Sebucán, Caracas, Venezuela.

Santorini, Paul E.; DR.SC.PHYS. ET MATH., DIPL.-ING.; Greek engineer and physicist; b. 8 June 1893; ed. Univ. of Zürich and Eidgenössische Technische Hochschule, Zürich.
Engineer, Löntschwerk 11 Hydro-electric Plant, Glarus, Switzerland 18-19; Engineer, Ministry of Communications 19-22; Dir., Athens Construction Co. 22-30; Dir., Dept. of Hydrometry, Ministry of Agriculture 30-46; Extra. Prof. of Applied Physics, Athens Univ. 35; High-frequency Absorbomicrometer 29; discovered "Elastic Inertia Effect" in concrete mass under deformation 30; Electronic Weapons Research, G.H.Q. Athens 36-40; built Greece's radar, the first centimetric wavelength radar 34-36, and the first proximity fuse 36; established means for propagation of centimetric electro-magnetic waves beyond optical line of sight 37; holds the two basic patents for the "Electronic Brain H" for automatic guidance of missiles 42; established lowest duration limit of observable physical phenomena in nature 58; Ord. Prof. of Experimental Physics and Dir. of Experimental Physics Laboratory, Nat. Technical Univ. of Athens 46-64, Emeritus 64-; Chief Greek Govt. Del. to 35 Int. Scientific Congresses 31-; Fellow, N.Y. Acad. of Sciences 65; mem. or corresp. mem. many foreign Acads. of Sciences; various hon. degrees and awards; medals include Vermeil Medal for Research and Invention (Paris), Fermat Medal Acad. of Sciences of Toulouse, King George II Gold Medal of Royal Inst. of Agronomic Sciences, etc.; Commdr. Royal Order of George I and Commdr. Royal Order of Phoenix (Greece) and many foreign decorations.
Publs. about 230 papers in French, German, etc., Proceedings of Academies and Congresses and scientific journals.
P.O. Box 49, Athens, Greece.
Telephone: 631-046.

Santos, H.E. Cardinal Rufino J.; Philippine ecclesiastic; b. 26 Aug. 1908.
Ordained priest 31; Titular Bishop of Barca 47; Archbishop of Manila 53-; created Cardinal by Pope John XXIII 60; Vicar Castrense for the Philippines 51-.
Arzobispado de Manila, 1000 General Solano, P.O. Box 132, Manila, Philippines.

Sanz de Santamaría, Carlos; Colombian civil engineer and economist.
Former Minister of Economy, Minister of Finance, Minister of Foreign Affairs; Colombian Ambassador to Brazil and twice Colombian Ambassador to the U.S.; Chair. Inter-American Cttee. on the Alliance for Progress (CIAP) 64-.
Inter-American Committee on the Alliance for Progress, 1725 Eye Street, N.W., Washington, D.C. 20006, U.S.A.

Sao Hkun Hkio; Burmese politician; ed. Cambridge Univ.
Former Deputy Prime Minister; Minister of Foreign Affairs and Minister for Shan State Affairs 60-62; detained after *coup d'état* March 62 until Feb. 68.
Rangoon, Burma.

Sapena Pastor, Raúl, B.SC., B.LITT., LL.D.; Paraguayan university professor and politician; b. 9 Oct. 1908; ed. Univ. of Paraguay.
Former mem. Supreme Court of Justice of Paraguay, Pres. Civil and Commercial Court of Appeals, Attorney-Gen., Judge Civil and Criminal Courts; Minister to Bolivia 41, to Uruguay 42-44; Ambassador to Argentina 48-49; Del. to numerous Inter-American and Int. Confs.; fmr. Prof. of Public Int. Law and Prof. of Political Economy, School of Law and Social Sciences and Dean of the School, Prof. of Private Int. Law at School of Econ. Sciences, Univ. of Paraguay; Rector Nat. Univ. of Paraguay 54-55; Counsellor of State 47-48, 56-; fmr. Pres. Bank of Paraguay, Dir. Bank of Republic of Paraguay, Sec. to Ministry of Economy, Legal Adviser to Foreign Ministry; Minister of Foreign Affairs 56-; mem. Perm. Court of Arbitration, The Hague 54-; Paraguayan Rep. Inter-American Council of Jurisprudence since its inception; Pres. Nat. Comm. for Codification of Int. Law, Nat. Council Foreign Trade; Prof. Private Int. Law, School of Law and Social Sciences; Vice-Pres. Paraguayan Acad. Law and Social Sciences; mem. American Soc. Int. Law; hon. mem. Inst. Spanish Culture, Madrid; numerous foreign decorations.
Publs. include *Derecho Internacional Privado*, Vol. I 44.
Ministry of Foreign Affairs, Venezuela 157, Asunción, Paraguay.

Sapir, Pinchas; Israeli politician; b. Lithuania 09.
Emigrated to Palestine 29; employed as agricultural labourer; Asst. Dir. Mekorot (Israel's major water development Co.) 37-47, after establishment of State of Israel, became Dir.-Gen. Ministry of Defence and subsequently Dir.-Gen. of Treasury; Minister of Commerce and Industry 55-63, of Finance, Commerce and Industry 63-65, of Finance 65-.
Ministry of Finance, Jerusalem, Israel.

Saporta, Marc, B.A., PH.M., LL.D.; French writer; b. 20 March 1923; ed. Univs. of Paris and Madrid.
Worked in the Dept. of Cultural Activities UNESCO 48-53, Asst. Editor *Informations et Documents* 54-; Literary Critic *l'Express* 54-, *La Quinzaine Littéraire* 66-.
Publs. *Les Lois de l'Air* 53, *La convention universelle du droit d'auteur de l'UNESCO* 52; (novels): *Le Furet* 59, *La Distribution* 61, *La Quête* 61, *Composition Numéro Un* 62, *Les invités* 64.
41 Boulevard Lannes, Paris 16e, France.

Sarabhai, Vikram Ambalal, M.A., PH.D.; Indian scientist; b. 12 Aug. 1919; ed. Gujerat Coll., Ahmedabad and St. John's Coll., Cambridge.
Research worker on cosmic radiation under Sir C. V. Raman, Indian Inst. of Science, Bangalore for five years and on nuclear physics, Cavendish Laboratory; research on cosmic radiation, Physical Research Laboratory, Ahmedabad, now Prof. of Cosmic Ray Physics; Chair. Indian Nat. Cttee. for Space Research; Chair. COSPAR Consultative Group on Potentially Harmful Effects of Space Experiments; Chair. Suhrid Geigy Ltd., Sarabhai Merck Ltd., Sarabhai Chemicals, Standard Pharmaceuticals Ltd.; Chair. Indian Atomic Energy Comm. 66-; Vice-Pres. and Scientific Chair. of UN Conf. on Exploration and Peaceful Uses of Outer Space, Vienna Aug. 68; Dir. numerous other companies; mem. Board of Scientific and Industrial Research for Indian Govt., Govt. Nat. Planning.

Council, Pugwash Continuing Cttee. and Convenor of Indian Pugwash Cttee.; S.S. Bhatnagar Memorial Award in Physics 62.
Chidambaram, Ahmedabad 13, Gujerat, India.

Saraceno, Pasquale, PH.D.; Italian economist; b. 14 June 1903; ed. Milan Univ.
Joined Istituto per la Ricostruzione Industriale (I.R.I.) 33, now General Economic Adviser; Prof. of Industrial Econs., Univ. Inst. of Venice 59-; Vice-Pres. SVIMEZ (Southern Italy Industrial Development Asscn.); Gold Medal Benemeriti Scuola, Cultura ed Arte, Gran Croce al merito della Repubblica Italiana.
Publs. *Elementi per un piano economico 1949-52* 48, *Lo sviluppo economico dei paesi sovrapopolati* 52, *L'IRI-Origini, ordinamente e attività* 56, *Iniziativa privata e azione pubblica nei piani di sviluppo economico* 59, *Lo Stato e l'Economia* 63, *La produzione industriale* 67.
Via Fratelli Ruspoli 8, Rome, Italy.
Telephone: 4677 (Office).

Sarafoff, Dimiter, DOZENT, DR.MED.HABIL., LIC.JUR. et RER. POL.; Bulgarian surgeon; b. 96; ed. Univs. of Sofia and Leipzig.
Lecturer in surgery, attached to Leipzig Univ. 39-43, to Univ. of Berlin 43; practising specialist in Surgery and Urology in Sofia.
Publs. *Untersuchungen über den Bau und die postmortale Reaktionsfähigkeit der Milz* 28, *Das Gewebsbild des fieberhaften Rheumatismus X* 32, *Zur Technik der Künstlichen Darmfistel mit Hinblick auf ihren späteren Spontanverschluss* 33, *Ein einfaches und ungefährliches Verfahren zur operativen Behandlung des Mastdarmvorfalles* 37, *Über die Aetiologie der Wanderniere sowie ein einfaches Verfahren zu ihrer operativen Befestigung* 42, *Neuere Gesichtspunkte bei der operativen Behandlung des Mastdarmvorfalles* 51, *Über den diagnostischen Wert der Pyelographie bei entzündlichen Prozessen in den Fetthüllen der Niere* 52, *Über mikroskopische Veränderungen an der Fettkapsel der Wanderniere* 53, *Die Leitungsanaesthesie bei Oberbauchoperationen mittels der Blutplombe als Depotanaestheticum* 54, *Neuere Gesichtspunkte bei der operativen Behandlung des Kryptorchismus* 54, *Über chirurgische Behandlung mancher Blasendivertikel von der eröffneten Blase aus* 54, *Über der Leistungsfähigkeit der Divertikelhalsplastik* 57, *Operative Behandlung der Wanderniere—Bericht über die Dauerergebnisse bei 71 operierten Kranken* 58, *Über Diverticulosis der Harnblase und ihre Behandlung mittels Divertikelhalsplastik von der eröffneten Blase aus* 62.
Ul. Asparuch 52, Sofia, Bulgaria.

Saragat, Giuseppe; Italian politician; b. 19 Sept. 1898; ed. Università degli Studi, Turin.
Bank Clerk 19-26; joined Socialist Party 22; Sec. Turin Branch 22, associated with party magazine *Rivoluzione Liberale*; lived in exile first in Vienna 26-35, then Paris 35-43; associated with Italian Socialist weeklies *Rinascità* and *Libertà*; returned to Italy 43; mem. executive of Socialist Party; Minister without Portfolio 44; Pres. Constituent Assembly 46; Ambassador to France 45-47; Sec. Italian Socialist Labour Party 47-64; Deputy Prime Minister 47-49, 54-57; Minister of Merchant Marine 47-49; Minister of Foreign Affairs 63-64; fmr. mem. of the Senate; Pres. of Italian Republic 64-.
Publs. *L'humanisme marxiste, Socialismo e libertà* 44, *Quaranta anni di lotta per la democrazia, scritti e discorsi 1925-1965* 66.
Palazzo del Quirinale, Rome, Italy.

Sarasin, Pote; Thai lawyer, politician and international administrator; b. 06; ed. Wilbraham Acad., Mass., and Middle Temple, London.
Practised law in Thailand 33-45; mem. Senate 48-50;

Deputy Minister of Foreign Affairs 48, Minister of Foreign Affairs 49-50, Prime Minister 57; represented Thailand on U.N. Korea Comm. 50; Ambassador to U.S.A. 52-57; Del. to U.N. 52-55; Prime Minister Sept. 57-Jan. 58; Sec.-Gen. SEATO 57-63; Minister of Econ. Affairs and Nat. Devt., Thailand 63-; mem. Thai Bar Asscn.
Ministry of National Development, Bangkok, Thailand.

Sarc, Omer Celâl, DR.RER.POL.; Turkish professor and administrator; b. 01; ed. Robert Coll., Istanbul, Handelshochschule, Berlin, and Univ. of Berlin.
Asst. Prof. of Economics, Univ. of Istanbul 26, Assoc. Prof. of Applied Economics and Statistics 33, Prof. of Applied Economics and Statistics 38-55, 57-, Dean of Faculty of Economics 36-48, Rector of the Univ. 49-51, 63-, Pro-Rector 51-53; Visiting Prof. Columbia Univ., School of Int. Affairs 54-55; Chief, Middle East Unit, Dept. of Economic Affairs, United Nations, New York 55-56; Dir. Econ. and Social Affairs, Council of Europe 59-61; Hon. Dr. Jur. (Fouad I Univ., Cairo).
Publs. *Agricultural and Industrial Policy* 34, *Theory of Statistics* 35, *The Foundations of Turkish Economy* 50.
University of Istanbul, Istanbul, Turkey.

Sarell, Roderick Francis Gisbert, C.M.G.; British diplomatist; b. 23 Jan. 1913; ed. Radley and Magdalen Coll., Oxford.
Consular Service 36-46, Vice-Consul, Persia 37, Italian E. Africa 39, Iraq 40-42, Second Sec. Addis Ababa 42-46; Foreign Service 46-, Rome, Bucharest, Foreign Office, Rangoon 46-56; Consul-Gen. Algiers 56-59; Counsellor, Foreign Office 59-63; Ambassador to Libya 64-.
British Embassy, Tripoli, Libya; Home: The Littens, Hampstead Norris, Newbury, Berks., England.
Telephone: Yattendon 274 (Home).

Sargant, William Walters, M.A., M.B., F.R.C.P., D.P.M.; British psychiatrist; b. 1907; ed. Leys School, St. John's Coll., Cambridge and Geraldine Harmsworth School, St. Mary's Hospital, Paddington.
Assistant to Medical Professorial Unit, St. Mary's Hospital 32-34; Medical Officer and Physician Maudsley Hospital, London 35-49; Asst. Clinical Dir. Sutton Emergency Hospital 39-47; Physician in Charge of Dept. of Psychological Medicine, St. Thomas's Hospital, London 48-; Rockefeller Travelling Fellow and Research Fellow, Harvard Medical School, U.S. 38-39; Visiting Prof. of Neuropsychiatry, Duke Univ. Medical School, U.S. 47-48; Registrar Royal Medico-Psychological Asscn.; Pres. Section of Psychiatry, Royal Soc. of Medicine 56-57; Examiner in Psychological Medicine, Conjoint Board of England 60-63; Assoc. Sec. World Psychiatric Asscn. 61-66; Lecturer American Soc. of Biological Psychiatry and New York Coll. of Medicine 64.
Publs. Psychiatric papers in medical journals; *Physical Methods of Treatment in Psychiatry* 44, 4th edn. 63, *Battle for the Mind* 57, *The Unquiet Mind* 67.
Department of Psychological Medicine, St. Thomas's Hospital, London, S.E.1; and 23 Harley Street, London, W.1, England.

Sargent, John Turner; American publisher; b. 26 June 1924.
Doubleday and Co. Inc., Editor 49-50, Advertising and Publicity, Trade Sales Manager 50-60, Vice-Pres. and Dir. 60-61, Pres. 61-; Trustee East River Savings Bank.
Doubleday and Co. Inc., 227 Park Avenue, New York City, N.Y. 10017; and 535 East 72nd Street, New York City, N.Y., U.S.A.
Telephone: 212-826-2000 (Office).

Sarkar, Amal Kumar; Indian judge; b. 29 June 1901; ed. Univ. of Calcutta and Lincoln's Inn, London.
Practised as Advocate of the High Court, Calcutta

30-48; Judge of the High Court, Calcutta 49-57; Judge of the Supreme Court of India 57-66, Chief Justice 66. 55 Baghbazar Street, Calcutta 3, India. Telephone: 55-2477.

Sarkisov, Semjon Alexandrovich; Soviet scientist; b. 1895; ed. Moscow Univ.
Co-founder of Moscow Brain Inst. 26, now Dir.; mem. U.S.S.R. Acad. of Medical Sciences 45 , mem. of its Presiding Council 47-53, 57-60, 62-; Pres. Medical Section, Union of Soviet Socs. for Cultural Relations with Foreign Countries; mem. Council, Soviet Soc. of Neuropathologists and Psychiatric Council, Int. Fed. of Electroencephalography and Clinical Neurophysiology 57-61, Royal Soc. of Medicine (U.K.); Bulgarian Soc. Neuropathologists and Psychiatrists, Scientific Council of Rumanian Acad. of Sciences, French Soc. of Neurologists; Order of Sign of Honour 42, Order of Lenin 51, Order of Red Banner of Labour 61, 65.
Publs. Over 100 works on scientific subjects.
Moscow Brain Institute, 5 Ulitsa Obukha, Moscow, U.S.S.R.

Sarlós, Istvan; Hungarian politician; b. 1921; ed. Budapest Univ.
Joined Working-Class Movement and the Social Democrat Party 39; held various mass organizational and Party positions 45-59; First Sec. of 6th District Cttee. Hungarian Socialist Workers' Party 59-63, mem. Central Cttee. 66-; Chair. Budapest Metropolitan Council Exec. Cttee. 63-.
Budapest Föváros Tanácsa Végrehajtö-bizottsága, Városház u. 9-11, Budapest V, Hungary.

Sarmento, Major-Gen. Syseno; Brazilian army officer and United Nations official; b. 07; ed. Brazilian Mil. Acad., Realengo, and Brazilian War Coll.
Infantry Officer 28; Commdr. Infantry Battalion, Brazilian Expeditionary Force, Second World War; Brig.-Gen. 60; Commdr. 2nd Mixed Brigade and Chef de Cabinet to Minister of War; Major-Gen. 64; Gen. Officer Commanding 4th Infantry Div. 64-65; Commdr. UN Emergency Force (UNEF), Gaza 64-66; in India engaged on India-Pakistan dispute Oct. 65-; numerous decorations.
c/o United Nations, New York City, N.Y., U.S.A.

Sarmento Rodrigues, Rear-Admiral Manoel Maria, K.C.V.O.; Portuguese naval officer and overseas administrator; b. 20 June 1899; ed. Univ. of Coimbra and Naval School, Lisbon.
Lieut. 22; Commdg. Officer torpedo boat *Lis* 24; A.D.C. to Gov.-Gen. of Portuguese India 25; Commdg. Officer gunboat *Faro* 29; Port Capt., Chinde, Portuguese East Africa 31; Commdg. Officer river gunboat *Tete* 32; Port Capt. Quelimane, Portuguese East Africa 35; Naval Staff 38; Chief of Staff, Light Flotilla 39, Home Fleet 40; Commdg. Officer destroyer *Lima* 41; Gov. of Portuguese Guinea 45; Prof. Colonial School, Lisbon 49-; Deputy for Mozambique, Nat. Assembly 49-57; Portuguese Del. Comm. of Technical Co-operation in Africa South of the Sahara 49, 50; Commdg. Officer Fleet Air Arm 50; Minister for Overseas Provinces 50-55; Pres. I.N.C.I.D.I. 55-57; Commdg. Officer Portuguese Naval Squadron 55-; Commdr. Portuguese Naval Group, Supt. Naval Acad. 57-61; Pres. African Advisory Cttee. ILO 59; Advisory Cttee. Bilderberg Meetings 59; Gov.-Gen. and C.-in-C. Armed Forces, Mozambique 61-64; Grand Cross Portuguese Orders of Christ, Empire, Avis and Prince Henry and several foreign decorations; mem. Acad. des Sciences d'Outre Mer, Paris, Acad. Marine, Paris and Acad. of Sciences, Lisbon.
Publs. *The Heroic Life of Nelson* 41, *The Battle of the Atlantic* 42, *Anchorages of the Azores Islands* 43, *The Government of Guinea* 49, *Unity of the Portuguese Nation* 56, *The Presence of Mozambique in the Life of the Nation* 65, and several other books and articles.
R. Jorge Alvares, 3-5° Lisbon 3, Portugal. Telephone: 512381.

Sarmiento, Dr. Emilio; Bolivian diplomatist; b. 13; ed. Instituto Andres Bello, Santiago de Chile, Colegio Nacional Sucre de Cochabamba, Bolivia, and Universidad Mayor de San Andrés, La Paz.
Head of Consular Dept., Ministry of Foreign Affairs 37-38; Asst. Dir., Legal Dept. 38-39, Dir. of Dept. of Intellectual Co-operation 39-40; First Sec., Peru 40-41, Argentina 42-43, Mexico 44-45, U.S. 45-46; Minister-Counsellor, Argentina 52-54; Adviser, Ministry of Foreign Affairs and temp. Under-Sec. 54-56; Dir. Inst. of Int. Studies, Ministry of Foreign Affairs 54-56; Ambassador to Vatican 56-58; Alt. Rep., later Ambassador to Organization of American States (OAS) 60-64.
c/o Ministry of Foreign Affairs, La Paz, Bolivia.

Sarnoff, General David (father of Robert W. Sarnoff, *q.v.*); American radio, television and electronics pioneer and executive; b. Russia 27 Feb. 1891; ed. New York public school and Pratt Inst.
Came to U.S.A. 1900; messenger boy Commercial Cable Co. 06; office boy Marconi Wireless Telegraph Co. 06; Wireless Operator on Ship and Shore 08-12; Radio Inspector Marconi Co. and Instructor Marconi Inst. 12; Chief Radio Inspector and Asst. Chief Engineer 13; Contract Man. 14; Asst. Traffic Man. 15-16; Commercial Man. 17-19; Commercial Man. Radio Corpn. of America (absorbed Marconi Co.) 19-20, Gen. Man. 21, Vice-Pres. and Gen. Man. 22, Exec. Vice-Pres. 29, Pres. 30-49, Chair. of Board and Chief Exec. Officer of RCA 47-, resigned as Chief Exec. Officer, continued as Chair. of Board 66-; Dir. RCA, RCA Communications Inc., Nat. Broadcasting Co. Inc.; during First World War played important part in equipping U.S. troops with wireless; apptd. Lieut.-Col. U.S. Army 24, Colonel 31, Brig.-Gen. 44; mem. Econ. Club of New York, Armed Forces Communications and Electronics Asscn., Veteran Wireless Operators Asscn., and many other societies; Fellow, Inst. of Electrical and Electronics Engineers and Royal Soc. of Arts (London); Hon. Fellow Weizmann Inst. of Science; over 26 hon. degrees; U.S. Medal for Merit and Legion of Merit; James Forrestal Memorial Award 56, and other awards of merit; Commdr. French Legion of Honour, etc.
RCA Building, 30 Rockefeller Plaza, New York, N.Y. 10020, U.S.A.

Sarnoff, Robert W. (son of Gen. David Sarnoff, *q.v.*); American communications executive; b. 2 July 1918; ed. Harvard Univ. and Columbia Univ. Law School.
With Radio Division, New York World's Fair 39; Office of the Co-ordinator of Information 41; served in U.S. Navy, including duty in South Pacific 42-45; executive in Cowles publications and broadcasting enterprises in Des Moines and N.Y. 45-48; with Nat. Broadcasting Co. 48-, Vice-Pres. 51, mem. Board of Dirs. 53, Exec. Vice-Pres. 53, Pres. 55-58, Chair. and Chief Exec. Officer 58-66; Dir. Radio Corpn. of America 57-, Pres. and Chief Exec. Officer 66-; Dir. Random House Inc.; Trustee John Fitzgerald Kennedy Library Corpn.; Dir. American Arbitration Asscn.; Chair. Board of Trustees Franklin and Marshall Coll.; Trustee Whitney Museum of American Art; mem. Board of Govs., American Red Cross; Officer of French Order of Arts and Letters 66; hon. doctorates from 10 American colls. and univs.; Commdr. Order of Merit (Italy) 68.
30 Rockefeller Plaza, 885 Park Avenue, New York, N.Y., U.S.A.

Saroyan, William; American writer; b. 31 Aug. 1908.
Publs. short stories: *The Daring Young Man on the Flying Trapeze* 34, *Inhale and Exhale, Three Times Three, The Gay and Melancholy Flux* 36, *Little Children*

37, *Love, Here is My Hat, The Trouble with Tigers* 38, *Peace, It's Wonderful* 39, *Saroyan's Fables, My Name is Aram* 40, *Dear Baby* 44, *The Assyrian* 50, *The Whole Voyald* 57; plays: *My Heart's in the Highlands, The Time of Your Life* (Pulitzer Prize) 39 (film 47), *Love's Old Sweet Song* 40, *The Beautiful People* 41, *Sweeney in the Trees, Across the Board on Tomorrow Morning* 41, *Razzle Dazzle* (16 plays) 42, *Get Away, Old Man* 46, *Jim Dandy, Fat Man in a Famine* 47, *The Slaughter of the Innocents* 52, *The Cave Dwellers* 56, *Sam, The Highest Jumper of Them All* (or *The London Comedy*) 60, *Here Comes There Goes You Know Who* (autobiography) 62, *Not Dying* 66; novels: *The Human Comedy* 43 (film 44), *The Adventures of Wesley Jackson* 46, *Rock Wagram* 51, *Tracy's Tiger* 52, *The Laughing Matter* 55, *Papa, You're Crazy* 57, *Boys and Girls Together* 63, *One Day in the Afternoon of the World* 64, *Not Dying* 66.
2729 W. Griffith Way, Fresno, Calif. 93705, U.S.A.

Sarpaneva, Timo Tapani; Finnish designer; b. 31 Oct. 1926; ed. Industrial Art Inst., Helsinki.
Designed for A. Ahlström Oy, Iittala Glassworks 50-; Teacher in Textile Printing and Design, Industrial Art Inst., Helsinki 53-57; Design Consultant, Porin Puuvilla Cotton Mill 55-66; Design Consultant, AB Kinnasand Textile Mill, Sweden 64-; invited by Brazilian Govt. to Lecture on and exhibit Finnish art glass 58; Exhbn. architect for Finnish industrial art exhbns. in most European countries, Japan and U.S.A.; architect for Finnish Section, Expo 67, Montreal; private exhbns. in Helsinki, Stockholm, Copenhagen, London, Paris, New York, Amsterdam, Reykjavik; numerous awards, including three Grand Prix at Milan Triennali; Hon. Dr. of Design, Royal Coll. of Art, London 67.
Vuorimihenkatu 5a, Helsinki 14, Finland.
Telephone: 657-113; 659-313.

Sarper, Selim; Turkish diplomatist; b. 99; ed. Univ. of Ankara.
Entered Ministry of Foreign Affairs 27; served in various diplomatic positions in Odessa, Moscow, Komotini, Berlin, and Bucharest, as asst. private Sec. to Minister of Foreign Affairs, and as head of a political section of Ministry of Foreign Affairs 27-39; Sec.-Gen. to Bureau of Press, attached to Prime Ministry 39, Dir.-Gen. of Press Dept. 40-44; promoted to rank of Minister 44; Ambassador to Moscow Sept. 44-46; Ambassador to Rome 46-47; permanent rep. of Turkey to U.N. with rank of Ambassador 47-57, to NATO Council, Paris 57-59; Sec.-Gen. Ministry of Foreign Affairs 59-May 60; Minister of Foreign Affairs May 60-March 62; fmr. Chair. UN Special Collective Measures Cttee.; fmr. Chair. Disarmament Comm.
c/o Ministry of Foreign Affairs, Ankara, Turkey.

Sarraute, Nathalie, L. ès L., L. en D.; French authoress; b. 18 July 1902; ed. Univs. of Paris and Oxford.
Prix International 64.
Publs. *Tropismes* 39, *Portrait d'un Inconnu* 48, *Martereau* 53, *L'Ere du Soupçon* 56, *Le Planétarium* 59, *Les Fruits d'Or* 63, *Le Silence et le Mensonge* 67.
12 avenue Pierre I de Serbie, Paris 16e, France.

Sartre, Jean-Paul; French writer; b. 5 June 1905; ed. Lycée Henri IV and Ecole Normale Supérieure, Paris.
Taught at Lycée du Havre, and later travelled in Egypt, Greece and Italy 29-34; at Inst. Français, Berlin 34; taught philosophy at Lycée Condorcet 35-42; served in army 39-41 (prisoner of war 40-41); active in resistance movement 41-44; resgnd. from teaching 44; Founder Dir. *Les Temps Modernes;* was offered, but declined, Nobel Prize for Literature 64.
Publs. Philosophy: *L'Etre et le Néant* 43, *L'Existentialisme est un humanisme* 46, *Réflexions sur la question juive* 47, *Sur l'Amour, L'Idiot de la famille, Question de Méthode, Critique de la Raison Dialectique;* Novels: *La Nausée* 38, *Le Mur* 39, *Les Chemins de la Liberté*

Vol. I (*L'Age de Raison*), Vol. II (*Le Sursis*) 45, Vol. III (*La mort dans l'âme*) 49; Plays: *Les Mouches* 42, *Huis-Clos* 44, *La Putain respectueuse* 46, *Morts sans sépulture* 47, *Les Mains sales* 48, *Le Diable et le Bon Dieu* 51, *Nekrassov* 53, *Les Sequestrés d'Altona* 59; Screenplay: *Les Sorcières de Salem* (from Arthur Miller's *The Crucible*); *Saint-Genet* (literary criticism) 63; *Les Mots* (memoirs) 64, *Baudelaire* 64, *Situations* 65, *The Ghost of Stalin* 67 (literary criticism), *The Communists and the Peace* 68.
42 rue Bonaparte, Paris 6e, France.

Saryan, Martiros Sergeevich; Soviet painter; b. 1880; ed. Moscow School of Painting.
Mem. Acad. of Arts of the U.S.S.R. 47-; Pres. of the Armenian Soviet Artists' Union 38-51; People's Artist of the Armenian S.S.R.; State prizewinner 41; awarded Order of Lenin (twice); Hero of Socialist Labour 65; Golden Star, Hammer and Sickle Medal; Gold Medal (Brussels) for *Armenia* and *Flowers of Erevan* 58; People's Artist of the U.S.S.R. 60; Lenin Prize for *My Homeland* 61.
Works: portraits of E. Charents 23, V. Papazyan 24, A. Tamanyan 33, G. Ulanova, A. Isaakian 40, self-portrait 42, A. Iohannessian 58, Anna Aghmatova, Levon Ogan, *My Contemporaries* (series of portraits); *My Homeland* (series of landscapes); *Ararat Valley, In the Tumanyan Mountains* 52, *Biurakan* (series) 57, *The Ararat Mountains* 57-58, etc.
41 Moscovskaya ulitsa, Erevan, Armenian S.S.R., U.S.S.R.

Sasabe, Kureo; Japanese business executive; b. 26 March 1893; ed. Kyoto Univ.
Bank of Japan 18, Asst. Man. London Branch 26, Insp., later Researcher, Stocks and Business Bureaux; Vice-Pres., Ito Bank 36; now Chair., Nagoya Shipbuilding, and Matsuzakaya Department Store; Pres., Central Japan Broadcasting Co.
13 Showa-cho, Minato-ku, Nagoya, Japan.

Sassen, Emmanuel Marie Joseph Antony, DR. JUR.; Netherlands politician and international administrator; b. 8 Sept. 1911; ed. Roman Catholic Univ., Nijmegen.
Lawyer at 's-Hertogenbosch; mem. of Provincial Govt. of Noord-Brabant; mem. of Second Chamber; Vice-Pres. of Roman Catholic Democratic Party 46-48; Minister for Overseas Territories 48-49; Senator 52-58; rep. Joint Assembly of European Coal and Steel Community 52-58; mem. Euratom Comm. 58-67; mem. Combined Exec. of EEC, ECSC and Euratom 67-.
c/o European Communities, 23-27 avenue de la Joyeuse Entrée, Brussels 4, Belgium.
Telephone: 35-00-40.

Sasson, Eliahu (Elias); Israeli diplomatist and politician; b. 2 Feb. 1902; ed. St. Joseph Coll., Beirut.
Owner and Editor of Arab newspaper *El Hayyat,* Damascus 19-21; corresp. and editor of various Hebrew and Arab newspapers, Jerusalem, Damascus, Beirut, Baghdad, Cairo and Tel-Aviv 24-31; Head of Div. for Arab Affairs, Political Dept., Jewish Agency 32-47; Head of Middle Eastern Dept., Israeli Ministry of Foreign Affairs 47-50; Minister to Turkey 50-52; Minister to Italy Jan. 53-57, Ambassador 57-60, to Switzerland 57-60; Minister of Posts Nov. 61-66; Min. of Police 67; mem. Israeli del. at Israel-Egyptian Armistice negotiations, Rhodes, and signatory of the Armistice Treaty 48-49; Jt. Head of Israel del. at Lausanne Conf. of Palestine Conciliation Comm. 49; mem. Israeli del. at UN 47-48; numerous foreign awards and honours.
Ministry of Police, Hakirya-Tel Aviv, Israel.
Telephone: Tel Aviv 25-53-56.

Sastroamidjojo, Ali, DR. JUR.; Indonesian diplomatist and politician; b. 03; ed. High School, Djakarta, and Leiden Univ.
Law practice Djakarta 28, Surakarta 29; active in nationalist political parties 28-, and co-founder Gerindo

Party (Indonesian Movement) 37; Deputy Minister for Information, Cabinet of Republic of Indonesia 45; later Sec.-Gen. Nat. Defence Council, Jogjakarta; mem. Indonesian del., Inter-Asian Relations Conf., New Delhi 47; Minister of Education and Culture 47; Deputy Chair. Indonesian del. which agreed to Renville Truce Agreement and spokesman for Indonesia U.N. Security Council 48; Deputy Chair. Republican del. for negotiations with Dutch to implement truce; interned by Dutch authorities Dec. 48; Deputy Chair. del. for renewed truce negotiations 49; resgnd. July 49 to attend Hague Conf. to settle Indonesian question; Indonesian Ambassador to U.S.A. Jan. 50 and 53; Rep. Indonesian Del. to U.N. General Assembly; Leader, Partai Nasional Indonesia until 66; Prime Minister 53-55 and 56-57; Perm. Rep. to UN 57-60; Perm. Deputy Chair. Provisional People's Consultative Assembly 60-66; arrested Aug. 67.
Djalan Drawang 4, Djakarta, Indonesia.

Sathe, Ramchandra, M.D., F.R.C.P., M.R.C.P.; Indian physician; b. 28 Nov. 1905; ed. Elphinstone High School, Elphinstone Coll., Grant Medical Coll., Bombay, and St. Bartholomew's Hospital, London.
Emeritus Prof. of Medicine, Grant Medical Coll., Bombay; Hon. Dir. of Postgraduate Studies in Medicine, Grant Medical Coll., Bombay; Pres. Asscn. of Physicians of India 60, Indian Medical Asscn. 62, World Medical Asscn. 62-63; Vice-Chancellor Bombay Univ. 63-66; Deputy Pres. Elect, World Conf. on Medical Educ. 66; Pres. Diabetic Asscn. of India; mem. Health Survey and Planning Cttee., Drugs and Equipment Standards Cttee., Indian Pharmacopea Cttee., Nat. Formulary Cttee., Govt. of India; J. J. Gold Medal for Clinical Medicine; Howlett Prize for Hygiene.
Publs. include: articles on nutritional oedema, cirrhosis of liver, treatment of hypertension, diabetes, jaundice, etc.
Nagindas Mansion, Girgaum Road, near Opera House, Bombay 4, India.

Sato, Eisaku, LL.B.; Japanese politician; b. 01; ed. Tokyo Univ.
Vice-Minister of Transportation 47-48; Chief Cabinet Sec. 48-49; Minister of Postal Service 51, of Telecommunications 51, of Posts and Telecommunications 51-52; Minister of Construction 52-53; Minister of Finance 58-60; Minister of Int. Trade and Industry 61-62, of State, Dir. of Science and Technology Agency and Hokkaido Development Agency, Chair. Atomic Energy Comm., and in charge of Olympic Affairs 63-64; Prime Minister Nov. 64-.
193 Kitazawa 2-chome, Setagaya-ku, Tokyo, Japan.

Sato, Hisashi; Japanese business executive; b. 97; ed. Faculty of Engineering, Tokyo Univ.
Joined Mitsubishi Shipbuilding and Engineering Co. Ltd. 21; Vice-Gen. Manager Hiroshima Shipyard and Engine Works, Mitsubishi Heavy Industries Ltd. 45, Gen.-Manager 47, Gen.-Manager Nagasaki Shipyard and Engine Works 49; Senior Managing Dir. Mitsubishi Shipbuilding and Engineeering Co. Ltd. 57, Pres. 59-; Exec. Vice-Pres. Mitsubishi Heavy Industries Ltd.; Pres. Shipbuilders' Asscn. of Japan.
40-4, 6-chome, Denenchofu, Ota-ku, Tokyo, Japan.

Sato, Misugi, B.SC., M.SC.; Japanese dairy executive; b. 14 Feb. 1898; ed. Colls. of Agriculture, Hokkaido Imperial Univ. and Ohio State Univ.
Managed dairy plant, Dept. of Dairying, Ohio State Univ. 22; Plant Man. and Technical Chief, Fed. of Hokkaido Co-op Creamery Asscns. 25-37, Senior Exec. Dir. Hokkaido Kono-Kosha 41-45; Staff mem. and Adviser Econ. Stabilization Board 47-50; Area Dir. Dairy Soc. Int. 49-57, Vice-Pres. 58-67; Pres. Hokkaido Co-op Dairy Co. 49; Pres. Snow Brand Milk Products Co. 50-63, Chair. 63-; Dir. Hokkaido Broadcasting Co. 51-67, Sapporo Co-op Bank 51-67, Chair. 57-58; mem.

Exec. Cttee. Fed. of Japan Employers' Asscn. and Sapporo Chamber of Commerce 61-67; Pres. Rakuno Gakuen Coll. of Dairying 66-; past official various Hokkaido asscns.; Del. int. dairy asscns.; awards include Ranju Decoration 60 and Dairy Soc. Int. Certificate of Honour as "Herald" 1965.
Publs. *What We Should Eat* 29, *Dairy Industry in New Zealand and Australia* 42.
Snow Brand Milk Products Co. Ltd., 36 Naebo-Cho, Sapporo; Home: 580 Nishi 8, Minami 16, Sapporo, Japan.

Satre, Pierre Henri; French aeronautical engineer; b. 4 May 1909; ed. Lycée Thiers Marseille.
Engineer, Centre d'essais du matériel aérien, Villacoublay 34-36, service technique aéronautique 36-41; Chief Engineer Toulouse engineering office of Soc. Sud-Aviation 41-58, Technical Dir. 59-; research on the following aeroplanes Armagnac 49, Grognard 50, Caravelle 55, Durandal 56; Laureate Acad. des Sciences; Officier Légion d'Honneur, Médaille de l'Aéronautique, Commandeur de l'Ordre Nat. du Mérite.
Sud-Aviation, 37 boulevard de Montmorency, Paris 16e; 1 boulevard de la République, Chaton, S.-et-O., France.

Sattar, Abdul; Maldive Islands diplomatist; b. 18 June 1936; ed. St. Peter's Coll., Colombo, Ceylon.
Under-Sec., Dept. of External Affairs, Maldive Islands 58-59; Deputy to Minister of External Affairs and Minister of Educ. 59-60; Maldive Islands Rep. in Ceylon 60-66, Amb. to Ceylon 66-67; Perm. Rep. to UN and Amb. to U.S.A. 67-.
Permanent Mission of Maldive Islands to the United Nations, The Maldivian Philatelic Agency, Pennsylvania Building, 225 West 34th Street, New York, N.Y. 10001, U.S.A.

Satterthwaite, Joseph Charles, A.M.; American diplomatist; b. 4 March 1900; ed. Univ. of Michigan.
Entered U.S. Foreign Service 24, first post at Stuttgart; Dept. of State, Washington 26-27; Guadalajara, Mexico 27-29; Mexico City 29-53; Buenos Aires 34-37; Baghdad 37-40; Ankara 40-44; Chargé d'Affaires, Damascus 44-45; Office of Near Eastern and African Affairs, Dept. of State 45; Sec. U.S. Dels., North and Central American Regional Radio Conf., Mexico City 33, and Inter-American Conf. for the Maintenance of Peace, Buenos Aires 36; Sec.-Gen., U.S. Del., Int. Telecommunications Conf., Cairo 38; Minister and Chief of U.S. Special Diplomatic Mission to the Kingdom of Nepal 47; Dir. Office of Near Eastern and African Affairs 48-49; Ambassador to Ceylon 49-53; Diplomatic Agent at Tangier, Morocco (with Rank of Minister) 53-55; Ambassador to Burma 55-57; Dir.-Gen. of Foreign Service 57-58; Asst. Sec. of State for African Affairs 58-61; Amb. to South Africa 61-65; Consultant to the Administrator of N.A.S.A. (Nat. Aeronautics and Space Admin.) 66-; Hon. LL.D. Univ. of Michigan 58.
Tecumseh, Michigan; Home: 5120 Upton Street, N.W., Washington, D.C. 20016, U.S.A.
Telephone: 362-7260 (Home).

Satyukov, Pavel Alexeevich; Soviet journalist; b. 1911; ed. Gorky Teacher Training Inst., and C.P.S.U. Higher Party School.
Began career on Gorky youth newspaper 30-; later contributor to *Komsomolskaya Pravda*; served in Air Force during Second World War and edited an Air Force paper; worked in Press Dept. of Central Cttee. C.P.S.U., Asst. Editor and later Editor *Kultura i Zhizn* (Culture and Life) 46-49; Chief Sec. *Pravda* 49-55, Asst. Editor 55, Editor-in-Chief 56-64; mem. Editorial Board *Party Life* (organ of C.P.S.U.) 64-; mem. C.P.S.U. 39-, mem. Central Cttee. 61-66; Order of Lenin, Order of Red Banner of Labour; Lenin Prize.
Partiinaya Zhizn (Party Life), 5 ulitsa Marxa-Engelsa, Moscow, U.S.S.R.

Saud, H.M. Ex-King Saud ibn Abdul Aziz, G.B.E.; Ex-King of Saudi Arabia; Viceroy of Nejd; b. 15 Jan. 1901; ed. Kuwait (Nejd).
Fought against Kharras 19; C.-in-C. of all troops of the Kingdom of Saudi Arabia; succeeded to throne 53; relinquished throne to brother, Faisal, Nov. 64; Prime Minister 61-62.
Hilton Hotel, Cairo, United Arab Republic.

Sauer, Richard C.; American petroleum executive; b. 28 Feb. 1906; ed. Cleveland public schools and Cleveland Coll.
Joined Standard Oil Co. (Ohio) 22, Head of Refined Products Distribution Dept. 30-38, Man. Supply and Distribution Dept. 38-47, Vice-Pres., Supply and Distribution Dept. 47-59, Senior Vice-Pres., Supply and Transportation 59-60, Exec. Vice-Pres. 60-, Dir. 58-.
The Standard Oil Company (Ohio), Midland Building, Cleveland 15, Ohio, U.S.A.

Saul, Ralph Southey, B.A., LL.B.; American lawyer and stock exchange official; b. 21 May 1922; ed. Univ. of Chicago and Yale Law School.
War Service, U.S. Naval Reserve 43-46; Attached to American Embassy, Prague 47-48; Admitted to District of Columbia Bar 51, to New York Bar 52; Assoc., firm of Lyeth and Voorhees, New York City 51-52; Asst. Counsel to Gov. of New York State 52-54; Staff Attorney, Radio Corpn. of America 54-58; with Securities and Exchange Comm. 58-65, Dir. Div. of Trading and Markets 63-65; Vice-Pres. for Corporate Devt., Investors Diversified Services, Inc. 65-66; Pres. American Stock Exchange 66-.
American Stock Exchange, 86 Trinity Place, New York 6, N.Y.; Home: 275 Manor Road, Ridgewood, New Jersey, U.S.A.
Telephone: 212-964-3200.

Saunders, John Anthony Holt, D.S.O., M.C.; British banker; b. 1917.
British Army 40-45; rejoined Hong Kong and Shanghai Banking Corpn. 45, Chief Man. 62-, Chair. 64-; Chair. Mercantile Bank Ltd., Hongkong & Shanghai Banking Corpn. of Calif.; Justice of the Peace, Hong Kong; mem. Hong Kong Exec. Council 66-; Chair. of Stewards, Royal Hong Kong Jockey Club; Treas. Univ. of Hong Kong.
37 Plantation Road, The Peak; Office: The Hongkong and Shanghai Banking Corpn., P.O. Box 64, Hong Kong.
Telephone: 222011 (Office).

Saunders, Stuart Thomas, A.B., LL.B.; American lawyer and transport executive; b. 16 July 1909; ed. Roanoke Coll. and Harvard Univ. Law School.
Law practice, Washington, D.C. 34-39; mem. firm Douglas, Obear and Campbell 36-39; Asst. Gen. Solicitor Norfolk & Western Railway Co. 39-54, Gen. Counsel 54-56, Exec. Vice-Pres. 56-58, Pres. 58-63; Chair. Board and Chief Exec. Officer Pa. Railroad Co. 63-; Dir. Chase Manhattan Bank, U.S. Steel Corpn., Equitable Life Assurance Soc., Georgia-Pacific Corpn., First Pa. Banking and Trust Co., Bell Telephone Co. of Pa., First Nat. Exchange Bank of Va., Philadelphia Saving Fund Soc., Virginia Hot Springs Inc., Philadelphia Orchestra Asscn.; Trustee several educational orgs.; mem. President's Advisory Cttee. on Labour-Management Policy.
Office: 6 Penn Plaza, Philadelphia, Pa.; Home: Cobble Court, 40 West Ardmore Avenue, Ardmore, Pa., U.S.A.

Sauser, Gustav, PH.D., M.D.; Austrian physician and anatomist; b. 99; ed. Univs. of Innsbruck, Erlangen, Tübingen, and Basle, Chemical School of Wiesbaden, Fresenius.
Began as Asst. Chemist to industrial firm; Dir. First Anatomy Dept. Univ. of Vienna 36-38; Dir. Inst. for Anatomy, Histology, and Embryology State Univ. of Innsbruck, Tyrol 45-; Dean, Medical Faculty,

State Univ. of Innsbruck 46-48, Rector 48-49; Senator 50-51, 56-60, 63-66.
Publs. *Manifestation of the Occipital Plate* 33, *Anatomical Modulation* 34, *The Structure of the Spongiosa in the Pirogow-Guenther-stump* 35, *Im Ötztaler* 38, *The Problem of Structures in Morphology and Chemistry* 45-, *Bioquantums* 46, *Paries elastico-musc. tracheae* 57, etc.
A-6020 Müllerstrasse 59, Innsbruck; and Universität Innsbruck, Tyrol, Austria.

Sauvagnargues, Jean; French diplomatist; b. 2 April 1915; ed. Ecole Normale Supérieure.
Ministry of Foreign Affairs 41-, attached to French Embassy Bucharest later on staff of Gen. de Gaulle 45-46; Head of Political Service for German Affairs 46-49, Deputy Dir. for Central Europe 49-54; Minister, Pinay Cabinet 55-56; Dir.-Gen. for Moroccan and Tunisian Affairs Jan.-March 56; Ambassador to Ethiopia 56-60; Dir. for Middle Eastern Affairs and African Affairs; Ambassador to Tunisia 62-; Officier, Légion d'Honneur.
French Embassy, Place de L'Indépendance, Tunis, Tunisia.

Sauvé, Maurice; Canadian politician; b. 20 Sept. 1923; ed. London School of Economics and Univ. of Paris.
Former Adviser to Quebec Liberal Leader, Jean Lesage; Minister of Forestry 64-65, of Rural Devt. and Forestry 65-; Liberal.
Ministry of Rural Development and Forestry, Ottawa, Canada.

Sauvy, Alfred; French economist, sociologist and demographer; b. 31 Oct. 1898; ed. Ecole Polytechnique.
Director Institut de Conjoncture 37-45; Sec.-Gen. for Family and Population 45; Dir. Institut National d'Etudes Démographiques 45-62; mem. UN Statistical Comm. 46; Pres. UN Population Comm. 50-53; Pres. Société de Statistique de Paris 47; mem. Nat. Social and Econ. Council; Prof. of Econs. and Opinion, Inst. of Political Studies 42-58; mem. Int. Statistical Inst.; Pres. Int. Population Union 61-63; Dr. h.c. Geneva, Brussels, Liège and Utrecht Univs.; fmr. Pres. Union Internationale pour l'Etude Scientifique de la Population; Prof. Social Demography (Life of Populations), Collège de France; Dir. Institut de Démographie de l'Université de Paris; Commandeur de la Légion d'Honneur.
Publs. Principal works: *Essai sur la conjoncture et la prévision économique* 38, *Richesse et population* 43, *Le pouvoir et l'opinion* 49, *Théorie Générale de la Population* 52, 54, 56, 63, 66, *L'Opinion Publique* 56, *La Bureaucratie* 56, *La Nature Sociale* 57, *La Montée des Jeunes* 59, *Le plan Sauvy* 60, *Les Limites de la Vie Humaine* 61, *Fertility and Survival* 61, *Population Explosion* 61, *La Prévention des Naissances* 62, 67, *Marx contre Malthus* 63, 66, *Mythologie de notre temps* 65, *Histoire économique de la France entre les deux guerres* Vol. I (*1918-1931*) 65, Vol. II *De Pierre Laval à Paul Reynard* 67.
76 rue Lepic, Paris 18e, France.

Savang Vatthana, H.M. Boroma-setha Khatya Sourya Vongsa Phra Maha Sri, L. en D.; King of Laos; b. 07; ed. Paris Univ.
Took active part in politics during the lifetime of his father; Chief Del. Arbitration Comm. Washington 47, Japanese Peace Treaty Conf. San Francisco 51; appointed Regent August 59; succeeded his father King Sisavong Vong Oct. 59.
Palais Royal, Luang Prabang, Laos.

Savic, Pavle; Yugoslav physical chemist; b. 10 Jan. 1909.
Lecturer Univ. of Belgrade 32-34; worked with Mme. Curie in Paris 35-39; Prof. of Univ. of Belgrade 39-41; with Supreme H.Q. of Nat. Liberation Army 41-45; Prof. of Physical Chemistry, Faculty of Sciences, Univ. of Belgrade 45-, head of Physio-Chemical Inst. Faculty

of Sciences; mem. Serbian Acad. of Sciences and Arts, Acad. of Sciences of U.S.S.R.; Hon. Dr. of Chemistry; Orders of Nat. Liberation, Meritorious Services to the People; Yugoslav Government award for work on low temperatures 49; Order of the Repub. (Yugoslavia) 66, Officier de la Légion d'Honneur 66, etc.

Publs. include many scientific papers on nuclear physics.

Physico-Chemical Institute of Faculty of Sciences, Studenski trg 16, Belgrade; and Kičevska 22, Belgrade, Yugoslavia.

Savkar, Dattatraya Sitaram, B.A., M.COM.; Indian economist and international civil servant; b. 17 Jan. 1909; ed. Bombay Univ.

Professor, H.L. Coll. of Commerce, Ahmedabad 36-45; Reserve Bank of India 45-67; Deputy Dir. of Research 45-51, Dir. of Research 51-59, Econ. Adviser 59-67; Alt. Exec. Dir. for India, Int. Monetary Fund 48-51, Dir. Asian Dept., Int. Monetary Fund 59-; mem. Economist Panel, Planning Comm. Govt. of India 54-59.

Publs. *Joint Stock Banking in India* 38, *Modern Economic Development of Great Powers* 43.

4437 45th Street N.W., Washington, D.C. 20016, U.S.A. Telephone: EM2-5920.

Savvopoulos, Evangelos; Greek politician; b. 29 March 1916; ed. Athens Univ. Law School and Athens Graduate School of Economic and Commercial Science.

Assistant, later Fellow, Athens Graduate School of Econs. and Business Science 36-43; Dir. *Arezap* and *Taegetus* companies (family business) 36-; Greek Rally Deputy 51-56, Nat. Radical Union Deputy 56-58, Progressive Party Deputy 58-61, Centre Union Deputy 61-67; Minister of Commerce and Educ. 65; Minister to Prime Minister's Office Oct. 65-66; numerous decorations.

Publs. include: *Logical Organisation* 38, *Geo-economic Studies in Greek Territory* 39, *A Policy of Economic Self-Sufficiency* 41, *Christianity and Labour* 58, *An Introduction to Applied Sociology, G. Gemistos Plithon.*

Athens, Greece.

Saw, Ba; Burmese politician; b. 17 Nov. 1914; ed. Govt. High School, Kyaukpyu, and Ananda Coll., Colombo, Ceylon.

Joint Editor Burma Propaganda Office, British Ministry of Information (Far-Eastern Bureau), New Delhi 43; guerrilla warfare training in India and Ceylon 44; parachuted to Kyaukpyu District as leader of Resistance campaign in Southern Arakan 45; after British re-occupation was foreign news corresp. in Calcutta; formed Kyaukpyu District Anti-Fascist People's Freedom League and People's Volunteer Organisation (Pres. and mem. Exec. both organisations); mem. Constituent Assembly for Kyaukpyu North 48-50; Special District Commr. Kyaukpyu 50-51; elected to Union Parl. for Kyaukpyu (South) 51-62; Minister for Minorities and Refugee Welfare 52-53, for Relief Resettlement and Social Welfare 53-56, for Religious Affairs and Social Welfare 56-58, for Social Welfare and Religious Affairs, Union Culture, Health, Immigration and Nat. Registration 60-62; Ambassador to Thailand and the Philippines 62-64, to U.S.S.R., Rumania, Poland, Czechoslovakia and Hungary 64-.

Burmese Embassy, Gertsena 41, Moscow, U.S.S.R.; and Kyaukpyu, Burma.

Sawada, Setsuzo, LL.B.; Japanese diplomatist and administrator; b. 84; ed. Tokyo Imperial Univ.

Foreign Service 09-; Sec. Japanese Embassy, London 11-18; Councillor, Washington 25-29; Consul Gen. N.Y. 29-31; Minister to League of Nations 31-34; Ambassador to Brazil 35-38; Diplomatic Adviser to Prime Minister Suzuki 45; Pres. Govt. Univ. for Foreign Service 49-56; Vice-Pres. Nat. Comm. for UNESCO 52-59; Pres. Govt.

Council for Overseas Emigration 59-, Inst. of World Economy 39-, Nat. Fed. of Scientific Research Asscns. 54-.

545 Gokurakuji, Kamakura, Japan.

Sawallisch, Wolfgang; German conductor; b. 26 Aug. 1923; ed. Wittelsbacher Gymnasium, Munich.

Studied under Profs. Ruoff, Haas and Sachsse; mil. service 42-46, prisoner of war in Italy; conductor Augsburg 47-53; Musical Dir. Aachen 53-58, Wiesbaden 58-60, Cologne Opera 60-63; Conductor Hamburg Philharmonic Orchestra 60-; Principal Conductor Vienna Symphony Orchestra 60-; Prof. Staatliche Hochschule für Musik, Cologne 60-63; Conducted at many Festivals; Recordings in U.S.A. and Britain; Hon. Conductor NHK Symphony Orchestra, Tokyo; Österreichisches Ehrenkreuz für Kunst und Wissenschaft.

Wiener Symphoniker, Vienna III, Lothringerstrasse 20, Austria; Home: 8211 Grassau, German Federal Republic.

Telephone: 08641-2315 (Home).

Sawaya, Paulo; Brazilian scientist; b. 03; ed. Faculty of Medicine, Univ. of São Paulo.

Asst. Prof. of Zoology, Univ. of São Paulo 37, Assoc. Prof. 38, Prof. of Gen. and Animal Physiology 39-, Head of Dept., Dean Faculty Science, Philosophy and Letters; Consultant Nat. Research Council, Rio de Janeiro 56 and Brasilia Univ.; Pres. Technical Council of Education, São Paulo; Dir. Marine Biological Inst., Univ. of São Paulo; main fields of research: colour changes in animal neurosecretion, muscular physiology of invertebrates.

Universidade de São Paulo, Cidade Universitária "Armando de Salles Oliveira", Caixa Postal 11230, São Paulo 9, Brazil.

Sawyer, Grant, LL.B.; American lawyer and politician; b. 14 Dec. 1918; ed. Twin Falls public schools, Nevada Univ. and Georgetown Univ. Law School.

Private, U.S. Infantry 42, commissioned 44; law practice in Elko, Nevada 48-; District Attorney, Elko County 50-58; fmr. Democratic Chair., Elko County; Chair. Democratic State Convention, Wells 52, Boulder City 54; State Chair., Democratic Party 55; Nevada Rep., Resolutions and Byelaws Cttee., Democratic Nat. Convention, Chicago 56; Gov. of Nevada 58-67; mem. Exec. Cttee. Nat. Govs. Conf. 60, Chair. Cttee. on State Planning 62; Chair. Nat. Govs. Conf. 64-65; Pres. Council State Govts. 64-65; Chair. Western Govs. Conf. 65-66; mem. American Bar Asscn., American Judicature Soc., etc.; Democrat.

Carson City, Nevada, U.S.A.

Sawyer, Ralph Alanson, A.B., PH.D.; American professor of physics; b. 5 Jan. 1895; ed. Dartmouth Coll. and Univ. of Chicago.

Fellow and Asst in Physics, Univ. of Chicago 17-18; Served Signal Corps. 18; Ensign U.S.N.R.F., engaged in design of optical instruments for the Bureau of Ordnance 18-19; Instr. in Physics, Univ. of Michigan 19, Asst. Prof. of Physics 22-27, Assoc. Prof. 27-30, Prof. 30-46; on leave from Univ. of Mich. to serve in the U.S.N.R. as Lieut.-Commdr. in Charge of the Armour and Projectile Laboratory at the Naval Proving Ground, Dahlgren, Va. 41-45; Commdr. U.S.N.R. and Experimental Laboratories Officer 43-45; Technical Dir. of Joint Task Force One, engaged in carrying out the "Crossroads" Atomic Bomb Test at Bikini Atoll 46; Dean. Horace H. Rackham School of Graduate Studies. Univ. of Mich. 46-64; mem. Nat. Research Council 49-52, 59-; Capt. U.S.N.R. 50; Dir. Michigan Memorial-Phoenix Project 51-59; Dir. Optical Society of America 41-45, Vice-Pres. 53-55, Pres. 55-57; Pres. Asscn. of Graduate Schools in the Asscn. of American Universities 57; mem. of Gov. Board of American Inst. of Physics 54-59, Chair. 59-,

Acting Dir. 64-65, 66; Vice-Pres. for Research Univ. of Michigan 59-64; Consultant Goddard Space Flight Center, Nat. Aeronautics and Space Admin. 64-65; Executive Secretary National Academy of Sciences Advisory Panels to National Bureau of Standards; mem. American Asscn. for the Advancement of Science; Navy Commendation Ribbon; Frederic Ives Medal, Optical Soc. of America; Hon. Sc.D. (Dartmouth Coll. and Michigan Coll. of Mining and Tech.), Hon. LL.D. (Wayne Univ.); Spectroscopy Soc. of Pittsburgh Award 61, Medal Soc. of Applied Spectroscopy, New York Section 66.

Publ. *Experimental Spectroscopy* 44, 3rd. edn. 63.
Home: 1208 Wells Street, Ann Arbor, Mich., 48104; Office: University of Michigan, Ann Arbor, Mich., U.S.A. Telephone: 313-662-1248.

Saxild, Jorgen, M.SC.; Danish civil engineer; b. 6 June 1891.
Employed by various English and French engineering firms 14-17; Man.-Dir. Kampmann, Kierulff & Saxild A/S (Kampsax), civil engineers and contractors, Copenhagen 17-; Man.-Dir. Saxild & Partners, London 23-26; Dir. Peter Lind Holding Co. Ltd. London 35-; Man. Dir. Danish-Swedish Consortium for construction of railways in Turkey and Iran 27-39; Dir. Kampsax-Invest A/S, Copenhagen 41; Dir. East Asiatic Co. Ltd., Copenhagen, and other companies 48-; Chair. Danish Govt. Cttee. for Technical Assistance (UN) 51-62; Managing Dir. Kampsax Holding A/S 57-; Pres. Danish Soc. for Civil Engineers 48-52; mem. Acad. for Technical Sciences 41, Council mem. 57-61; Chair. Danish Council for Technical Co-operation with Developing Countries 62-66; Kt. Commdr. of the Order of Dannebrog, and holder of several other Scandinavian and foreign decorations.
Granhøjen 1, Hellerup, Denmark.
Telephone: Gentofte 5101.

Say, Rt. Rev. Richard David, D.D.; British ecclesiastic; b. 4 Oct. 1914; ed. Univ. Coll. School, Christ's Coll., Cambridge and Ridley Hall, Cambridge.
Curate of St. Martin-in-the-Fields 43-50, Gen. Sec., Church of England Youth Council 44-47; Gen. Sec., British Council of Churches 47-55; Rector of Hatfield and Domestic Chaplain to Marquess of Salisbury, K.G. 55-61; Hon. Canon of St. Albans 57-61; Bishop of Rochester 61-; Church of England del. to World Council of Churches 48, 54, and 61; Sub-Prelate of the Order of St. John of Jerusalem.
Bishopscourt, Rochester, Kent, England.

Sayenko, Georgy Alexandrovich; Soviet trade union official; b. 23 April 1906; ed. Higher Party School of the C.P.S.U. Central Committee.
Party work 31-49; Ministry of the Merchant Marine 52-60; Chair. Central Cttee. of Sea and River Workers' Trade Union 60-; mem. C.P.S.U.; mem. All-Union Central Council of Trade Unions 68-; Order of Lenin, Order of the Red Banner of Labour (twice), Badge of Honour (twice), four State medals.
Central Committee of the Sea and River Workers' Trade Union, 42 Leninsky Prospekt, Moscow, U.S.S.R.

Sayushev, Vadim Arkadievich; Soviet politician; b. 30; ed. Leningrad Mining Inst.
Member C.P.S.U. 52-; Sec., Sverdlovsk Dist. (Leningrad) Cttee. Komsomol 54-58, Leningrad Regional Cttee. 55-58; Second Sec., then First Sec., Leningrad Regional Cttee., Komsomol 58-61; Sec., Cen. Cttee. Komsomol 61-; Cand. mem. Cen. Cttee. C.P.S.U. 61-.
Central Committee of the Communist Party of the Soviet Union, Moscow, U.S.S.R.

Sazhin, Nikolai Petrovich; Soviet metallurgist; b. 1897; ed. Moscow Mendeleev Institute of Chemistry and Technology.
At staff of Chemical-Analytical Lab., Volshsky-

Kamsky Bank, Sverdlovsk 18-20; in Red Army 20; pharmacy worker in Far East 20-26; worker in chemical plant, Chita 26-32; Scientific worker State Inst. of Rare Metals 33, Deputy Dir. 41-; Corresp. mem. U.S.S.R. Acad. of Sciences 53-64, mem. 64-; State Prize (twice); Hero of Socialist Labour.
Publs. Works on metallurgy of rare elements.
U.S.S.R. Academy of Sciences, 14 Leninsky Prospekt, Moscow, U.S.S.R.

Scaglia, Giovanni Battista; Italian journalist and politician; b. 20 Sept. 1910; ed. Collegio Ghislieri and Università di Pavia.
President of Catholic Action 45-49; Editor *Studium* (magazine) 49-; mem. Chamber of Deputies 48-; Under-Sec. of Educ. 54-59; Deputy Sec. of Christian Democrat Party 59-64; Minister without Portfolio for Parl. Liaison 64-.
3 Via Antonio Rosmini, Bergamo, Italy.

Scalfaro, Oscar Luigi; Italian lawyer and politician; b. 9 Sept. 1918; ed. Università Cattolica del Sacro Cuore, Milan.
Christian Democrat mem. Chamber of Deputies 48-; Under-Sec., Ministry of Works and Social Security 54, at the Presidency of the Council of Ministers 55, Ministry of Justice 55-58, Minister of the Interior 59-62; fmr. Sec. then Vice-Pres. of Christian Democrats in Chamber of Deputies, Vice Political Sec. 65-66; Minister of Transport and Civil Aviation 66-.
Ministero dei Trasporti, Rome, Italy.

Scammon, Richard M.; American psephologist; b. 17 July 1915; ed. Univ. of Minnesota, London School of Economics, Univ. of London and Univ. of Michigan.
Research Sec., Radio Office, Univ. of Chicago 39-41; Army Service 41-46; Chief, Political Activities Branch, Civil Admin. Div., Office of Military Govt. United States (Germany) 46-48; Chief, Div. of Research for Western Europe, Dept. of State 48-55; Dir. Elections Research Center, Governmental Affairs Inst., Washington 55-61, 65-; Dir. of the Census 61-65; Chair. U.S. Del. to Observe Elections in U.S.S.R. 58, Chair. President's Comm. on Registration and Voting Participation 63, OAS Electoral Mission to the Dominican Repub. 66; Chair. Select Comm. on Western Hemisphere Immigration 66-68; Editor, *America Votes* Vol. 1 56, Vol. 2 58, Vol. 3 60, Vol. 4 62, Vol. 5 64, Vol. 6 66, Vol. 7 68; Editor, *America at the Polls* 65.
5508 Greystone Street, Chevy Chase, Maryland 20015, U.S.A.
Telephone: 202-387-6066.

Scarbrough, 11th Earl of, cr. 1690; **(Lawrence) Roger Lumley,** K.G., P.C., G.C.S.I., G.C.I.E., G.C.V.O.; British politician and administrator; b. 27 July 1896; ed. Eton, Sandhurst and Oxford Univ.
Served First World War 16-18; Conservative M.P. for E. Hull 22-29, for York 31-37; Parl. Private Sec. to Under-Sec. of State for Colonies 23-24, to Sir A. Chamberlain 24-26, to Mr. A. Eden 35-37; Gov. of Bombay 37-43; Act. Major-Gen. 43-44; Parl. Under-Sec. of State for India and Burma May-July 45; Pres. Royal Asiatic Society 46-49, East India Asscn. 46-51; Chair. Inter-Departmental Comm. on Oriental, Slavonic, East European and African Studies 45-46; Chair. of Govs. School of Oriental and African Studies 51-59; Lord Lieut. W. Riding, Yorks.; Lord Chamberlain of the Household Oct. 52-63; Grandmaster of English Freemasons 51-67, Pro Grand Master 67-; Chair. Commonwealth Scholarship Comm. 60-63; Pres. Royal Central Asian Soc. 54-60; Chancellor Univ. of Durham 58-; High Steward of York Minister 67-; Hon. D.C.L. (Durham) 49; Hon. LL.D. (Sheffield, Leeds, London); Royal Victorian Chain.
Sandbeck Park, Rotherham, Yorks., England.

Scelba, Mario, D.JUR.; Italian politician; b. 5 Sept. 1901; ed. Rome Univ.

Founder mem. Italian People's Party 19; practised as lawyer after suppression of People's Party 26-; re-entered politics 41 and became one of founders of Christian Democrat Party and newspaper *Il Popolo;* Minister for Posts and Telecommunications 45-47; Minister of the Interior 47-53, 60-62; Prime Minister and Minister of the Interior 54-55; mem. Chamber of Deputies; Deputy to the European Parliamentary Assembly 58-; Pres. Nat. Council of the Christian Democrat Party 66-; hon. degrees Univ. of Ottawa, Columbia Univ. (Washington), Fordham Univ. and St. John's Univ. (New York).

Chamber of Deputies, Rome, Italy.

Schaaf, C(arl) Hart, A.B., PH.D.; American United Nations official; b. 14 Jan. 1912; ed. Univ. of Michigan, Montpelier, Stockholm.

Associate Professor of Administration, Coll. of William and Mary (Richmond Div.) 40-42; State Rationing Admin., Virginia 42-43; Asst. Dep. Dir.-Gen. and Chief, Supply for Europe, UN Relief and Rehabilitation Admin. 44-47; Assoc. Prof. of Admin., School of Business and Public Admin., Cornell Univ. 47-49; Exec. Dir., United World Federalists 49; Dep. Exec. Sec. UN/ECAFE 49-54; Resident Rep. in Israel for UN/TAB 54-57, in the Philippines 57-59; Exec. Agent, Cttee. for Coordination of Investigations of the Lower Mekong Basin. 59-.

Publs. *Fiscal Planning at the State Level* 41, *Economic Cooperation in Asia* 50, *The United Nations Economic Commission for Asia and the Far East* 53, *The Lower Mekong* (with Russell Fifield) 62, *Burke's Idea, Partition* (plays) 48.

Economic Commission for Asia and the Far East, Sala Santitham, Bangkok, Thailand.

Schacht, Hjalmar Horace Greely; German financial specialist; b. 22 Jan. 1877; ed. Univs. of Kiel, Berlin, Munich and Leipzig.

Managing Sec. Soc. for Commercial Treaties 01-03; Archivist 03-08, Asst. Manager 08-15 Dresdner Bank; Managing Partner of Nationalbank and (after amalgamation 22) of Darmstädter und Nationalbank; Reich Currency Commr. 23; played leading role in stabilisation of German currency; Pres. of the Reichsbank 24-30; mem. Comm. for reorganization of Reichsbank under Dawes Plan 24; Del. to Young Conf.; Del. Conf. for Int. Bank; opposed Young Plan and resigned from Reichsbank 30, but was reappointed Pres. March 33, resigned 39; Acting Minister of Nat. Economy 34-37; Minister without Portfolio; arrested June 44; indicted as major Nazi war criminal Oct. 45; acquitted by Int. Mil. Tribunal at Nuremberg Oct. 46; sentenced by denazification court to 8 years detention in labour camp May 47; sentence quashed Jan. 49; Pres. banking firm Schacht & Co. 53-63; retd.

Publs. *The Stabilization of the Mark* 27, *The End of Reparations* 31, *Abrechnung mit Hitler* 48, *Mehr Geld, Mehr Kapital, Mehr Arbeit* 49, *76 Years of My Life* 53, *Kreditpolitik und Exportfinanzierung von morgen* 56, *Kapitalmarktpolitik* 57, *Schluss mit der Inflation* 60, *Magie des Geldes* 66.

Kufsteinerplatz 2, Munich, German Federal Republic.

Schadewaldt, Wolfgang Otto Bernhard, DR. PHIL.; German classicist; b. 15 March 1900; ed. Humboldt-Universität zu Berlin.

Private Lecturer Berlin 27; Prof., Königsberg 28, Freiburg i. Br. 29, Leipzig 34, Berlin 41; Prof. of Classics, Eberhard-Karls-Universität, Tübingen 50-; mem. PEN Club, Acad. for German Language and Poetry, Acads. of Leipzig, Berlin, Heidelberg and Vienna; hon. mem. Greek Humanistic Soc.; mem. Cen. Directorate German Archaeological Inst.; Knight Order

Pour le Mérite for Sciences and Arts 62, Reuchlin Prize of Pforzheim 63, Grand Cross of Merit with Star (German Fed. Repub.) 64, Translator Prize, Acad. for German Language and Poetry, Darmstadt 65.

Publs. *Ilias-Studien* 38, *Von Homers Welt und Werk* (4th edition) 65, *Sappho* 50, *Griechische Sternsagen* 57, *Homer, Odyssee* (trans. into German prose) 58, *Hellas und Hesperien* 60, *Goethe-Studien, Natur und Altertum* 63, *Griechisches Theater* (trans. of Aeschylus, Sophocles, Aristophanes, Menander) 64.

19 Nägelstrasse, 74 Tübingen, German Federal Republic.

Telephone: 07122-22230.

Schaefer, Clemens, PH.D.; German physicist; b. 24 March 1878; ed. Bonn and Berlin Univs.

Asst. Berlin Technical High School 00; Lecturer in Physics Breslau Univ. 03; Asst. Prof. 10; Prof. of Natural Philosophy Breslau Univ. 17; Prof. of Experimental Physics Marburg Univ. 20; Prof. and Dir. Physical Inst. Breslau Univ. 26; Prof. of Gen. Physics, Cologne Univ. 46-.

Publs. *Principles of Dynamics* 19, *Letters between C. F. Gauss and C. L. Gerling* 27, *Introduction to Maxwell's Theory of Electricity and Magnetism* 29, *Introduction to Theoretical Physics* (4 vols.) 29, *The Physical Work of C. F. Gauss* 29, *Infra-red Spectrum* (with Matossi) 30, *Practical Physics* (with Bergmann and Kliefoth) 43, *Text-Book of Experimental Physics* (with Bergmann), Vol. I 43, Vol. II 50, Vol. III 56.

Mehlemerstr. 21, Cologne, German Federal Republic.

Schaeffer, Claude Frédéric Armand, M.A.; French archæologist; b. 6 March 1898; ed. Strasbourg and Paris Univs.

Curator Prehistoric, Roman and Early Medieval Museum, Palais Rohan, Strasbourg 21-32; Curator Coins and Medals Dept. Strasbourg Univ. 26-32; Curator French Nat. Museums 33-; Dir. of Research at Nat. Centre of Scientific Research, Paris, 46-54; Prof. Collège de France 54-; Vice-Pres. Comm. des Fouilles, Direction des Relations Culturelles, Ministry of Foreign Affairs; Dir. expedition Ras Shamra, Syria 29- (discovered Canaanite alphabetic cuneiform records); Cyprus 32, 34, 35, 46, 47, 49-, Malatya, Turkey 46, 47, 48, 50; mem. Archæological Cttee. Min. of Education; Hon. Fellow St. John's Coll., Oxford; mem. Académie des Inscriptions, Inst. de France, Nat. Society of Antiquaries France, Royal Acad. Denmark; corresp. mem. Belgian Royal Acad.; corresp. Fellow of British Acad.; Hon. Fellow Royal Anthropological Inst. of Great Britain and Ireland, Royal Asian Soc., etc.; hon. mem. Deutsche Morgenländische Gesellschaft; served as Capt. Corvette with Free French Naval Forces 40-45; D.Litt. h.c. (Oxon.), D.C.L. h.c. (Glasgow), Hon. F.S.A., Gold Medal, Soc. of Antiquaries 58, Scientific and Philological Soc., Famagusta, Cyprus 65.

Publs. *Haches néolitiques* 24, *Tertres funéraires préhistoriques dans la forêt de Haguenau* (2 vols.) 26, 30, *Missions en Chypre* 36, *Ugaritica I* 39, *Cuneiform Texts of Ras Shamra-Ugarit* 39, *Stratigraphie comparée et Chronologie de l'Asie occidentale* 48, *Ugaritica II* 49, *Enkomi-Alasia* 52, *Ugaritica III* 56, *IV* 61, *V* 66.

Le Castel Blanc, 14 rue Turgot, St. Germain-en-Laye, Seine-et-Oise, France.

Schaeffer, Pierre; French engineer, writer and composer; b. 14 Aug. 1910; ed. Ecole Polytechnique.

Director of Research, Radiodiffusion-Télévision Française 59-; a leader of movement for development of musique concrète (works include *Symphonie pour un Homme Seul* and music for films); mem. Centre Nat. de la Recherche Scientifique; Chevalier Légion d'Honneur, Chevalier des Palmes Académiques.

Publs. *Amérique, nous t'ignorons* (essay) 46, *les Enfants de coeur* (novel) 49, *A la Recherche d'une Musique*

Concrète 52, Traité des Objets musicaux 66, La Musique concrète 67.
R.T.F. Research Dept., 5 avenue du Recteur Poincaré, Paris 16e; Home: 13 rue des Petits-Champs, Paris 1er, France.

Schaetzel, John Robert; American diplomatist; b. 28 Jan. 1917; ed. Pomona Coll., California, Univ. of Mexico and Harvard Univ.
Administrative Asst., Bureau of the Budget 42; Special Asst. to Dir. of Office of Int. Trade Policy, Dept. of State 45-50; Special Asst. to Asst. Sec. of State for Econ. Affairs 50-54; Nat. War Coll. 54-55; Officer in charge of peaceful uses of atomic energy, Office of Special Asst. to Sec. for Disarmament and Atomic Energy 55-59; mem. Presidential Task Force 60-61; Special Asst. to Under Sec. of State for Econ. Affairs 61, to Under Sec. of State 61-62; Deputy Asst. Sec. of State for Atlantic Affairs 62-66; Rep. to European Communities 66-; Rockefeller Public Service Award 59. U.S. Mission to the European Communities, 23 avenue des Arts, Brussels 4, Belgium.

Schäfer, Walter Erich, DR. PHIL.; German theatre director and playwright; b. 16 March 1901; ed. Karlsgymnasium, Stuttgart, and Eberhard-Karls-Universität, Tübingen.
Writer, Lecturer at Stuttgarter Musikhochschule; Dramatic Producer, Stuttgart 29-33, Mannheim 34-48; Dir. and Chief Dramatic Producer, Kassel 39-45, Augsburg 48-49; Supt. then Gen. Supt. Württembergische Staatstheater, Stuttgart 49-; Dir. Wiener Staatsoper 62-63; Grosses Verdienstkreuz 59; Officier de l'Ordre des Arts et des Lettres 65.
Publs. novels: *Die 12 Stunden Gottes 26, Die letzte Wandlung 28;* theatre: *Günther Rennert—Regisseur in dieser Zeit 62;* plays: *Richter Feuerbach 30 Der 18 Oktober 32, Schwarzmann und die Magd 33, Die Reise nach Paris 36, Theres und die Hoheit 40, Das Feuer 41, Die Verschwörung 49, Aus Abend und Morgen (Hora Mortis) 52;* radio plays: *Malmgren 29, Dir fünf Sekunden des Mahatma Gandhi 49, Der Staatssekretär 49, Spiel der Gedanken 50, Konferenz in Cristobal 52, Die Himmelfahrt des Physikers M.N. 58.*
Württembergische Staatstheater Stuttgart, 7000 Stuttgart-Sonnenberg, Feuerreiterweg 32, German Federal Republic.
Telephone: 763673.

Schaff, Adam, PH.D.; Polish sociologist and philosopher; b. 13; ed. Lwów Univ. and Ecole des Sciences Politiques et Economiques, Paris.
Scientific work in U.S.S.R. 40-45; Prof. Łódź Univ. 45-48; Prof. of Philosophy, Warsaw Univ. 48-; Dir. Polish United Workers' Party Inst. of Social Sciences 50-57; mem. Polish Acad. of Sciences (Chair. Philosophy Cttee. 51-, Dir. Inst. of Philosophy and Sociology 57-68), Bulgarian Acad. of Sciences; mem. Cen. Cttee. Polish United Workers' Party 59-; mem. Exec. Cttee. Int. Fed. of Philosophical Asscns.; Pres. Board of Dirs. of the European Centre for Social Sciences in Vienna; Editor *Myśl Współczesna* (Contemporary Thought) 46-51, *Myśl Filozoficzna* (Philosophical Thought) 51-56.
Publs. *Pojęcie i słowo* (Concept and Word) 46, *Wstęp do Teorii Marksizmu* (Introduction to the Theory of Marxism) 47, *Narodziny i rozwój filozofii marksistowskiej* (Birth and Development of Marxist Philosophy) 49, *Z zagadnień marksistowskiej Teorii Prawdy* (Some Problems of the Marxist Theory of Truth) 51, *Obiektywny Charakter Praw Historii* (The Objective Character of Historical Laws) 55, *Wstęp do Semantyki* (Introduction to Semantics) 60, *Filozofia Człowieka* (A Philosophy of Man) 62, *Język i poznanie* (Language and Cognition) 63, *Marksizm a jednostka ludzka* (Marxism and the Human Individual) 65.
Aleja I Armii 2/4, Warsaw, Poland.
Telephone: 28-18-32.

Schaffner, Hans; Swiss lawyer and politician; b. 16 Dec. 1908; ed. Universität Bern.
Advocate 34; Sec. High Court of Berne 38-41; Lawyer to Directorate of Fed. Industry, Trade and Labour Office 38-41; Head of Cen. Office for War Econ. 41-45; Del. of Fed. Council for Trade Agreements 45-61; Dir. Div. of Commerce of Fed. Dept. for Public Econ. 54-61; mem. Steering Board for Trade of O.E.E.C. 53-61; Fed. Councillor, Head of Fed. Dept. for Public Economy 61-; Pres. of Swiss Fed. Council 66; Pres. Ministerial Council of Org. for European Co-operation and Development (O.E.C.D.) 65; Dr. h.c. (Berne) 59.
Federal Department of Public Economy, Bundeshaus, Berne, Switzerland.

Schaper, Lieut.-Gen. Heye; Netherlands air force officer; b. 8 Sept. 1906.
Sub-Lieut. Netherlands Naval Reserve 30; served with submarine and later naval aviation Holland and Dutch East Indies 38; Flying Instructor and Test Pilot, Holland 40; evacuated to England and served as pilot in R.A.F. 40-42; prisoner of war 42-45; Commanding Officer, Netherlands Naval Air Service, Dutch East Indies 45-46; Head of naval aviation, Ministry of Navy, Holland 46-49; Rear-Adml. and Flag Officer Air. Royal Netherlands Navy 49; transferred to Royal Netherlands Air Force as Deputy Chief of Staff, in rank of Major-Gen. 54; Chief of Staff, Royal Netherlands Air Force Lieut.-Gen. 56-61; Chair. Joint Chiefs of Staff 57-59; Chief of the Mil. House of H.M. Queen Juliana 62; Sec. of State for Air 66-67; Chief of the Mil. House of H.M. Queen Juliana 67-; awarded Willemsorde and D.F.C.; Chancellor, Netherlands Order of Knighthood.
Noordeinde 68, The Hague, Netherlands.
Telephone: 070-630206.

Scharf, Kurt Franz Wilhelm, TH.D. D.D.; German ecclesiastic; b. 21 Oct. 1902; ed. Tübingen, Jena and Halle/Saale Univs.
Pastor Friesack 28, Sachsenhausen 33; Präses Brotherhood of Brandenburg Confessional Churches 35; Chair. Conf. of Brotherhoods of Confessional Churches in Germany 37; several times arrested and forbidden to preach and publish by Nazi régime; Präses Brandenburg Confessional Synod 35; Provost Berlin-Brandenburg Province 45; Chair. Utd. Evangelical Church 55, Dep. Chair. 61-; Chair. Evangelical Church in Germany 61-67; Bishop of Berlin-Brandenburg (Evangelical Church) 66-; Publisher *Rundbriefe der Bekennenden Kirche* 33-45 (illegal 35-45); Hon. Th.D. Humboldt Univ. Berlin; Hon. D.D. Eden Seminary Webster Groves (Mass.).
Jebensstrasse 3, Berlin 12, Germany.
Telephone: 31-02-01.

Scharoun, Hans, DR. ING.; German architect; b. 20 Sept. 1883; ed. Technische Hochschule, Berlin.
Professor, Acad. of Fine Arts, Breslau until 32; work for Greater Berlin Council 45-46; later Head of Inst. for Town Planning, Technical Univ., Berlin; Pres. Acad. of Fine Arts, Berlin; touring exhbn. *Hans Scharoun's Buildings and Designs 67*; numerous prizes and decorations.
Major works include design of new Berlin Opera House, State Library, Berlin, Philharmonic Hall, Berlin.
Berlin 13, Heilmannsring 66a, Germany.

Schaufelberger, William; French industrialist; b. 23 Aug. 1902; ed. Ecole Polytechnique.
Chair. Cie. Gén. d'Electrolyse des Palais; Vice-Chair. Cie. Gén. du Duralumin et du Cuivre Cégédur; Dir. Compagnie Gén. d'Entreprises Electriques, Soc. des Procédés Sauter, Electro-Crédit, Etablissements Charpentier, Vogt et Goguel, Seichimé, Rhénalu; Chevalier Légion d'Honneur.
9 Avenue Frédéric-Le-Play, Paris 7e, France.

Schaus, Eugène, DR.JUR.; Luxembourg lawyer and politician; b. 11 May 1901; ed. Univs. of Brussels, Berlin, and Paris.

Lawyer 25-; Pres. Corpn. of Barristers; Minister of the Interior, of Justice and of Physical Education 45-51, Dep. Prime Minister and Minister of Foreign Affairs and Defence 59-66; mem. Council of Europe 51-; mem. Assembly Coal and Steel Community 51-58, of European Parliament 58-.

Grande rue 56, Luxembourg.

Schaus, Lambert, D. en D.; Luxembourg lawyer and politician; b. 08.

Legal practice in Luxembourg 32-52; mem. Luxembourg City Council 36-40; deported by occupying power to Germany 40-45; mem. Constituent Assembly, Chief Alderman, City of Luxembourg 46; Sec. Christian Social Party 46; Minister of Supply and Economic Affairs 46-48, of Armed Forces 47-48; mem. Council of State 48-53; Minister to Belgium 52-55, Ambassador 55-58; mem. European Economic Community Comm. 58-67; Perm Rep. to NATO Council 67-.

c/o Office: NATO, Brussels 39; Home: 21 avenue Jeanne, Brussels 5, Belgium.

Telephone: 49-31-07.

Schetinin, Semyon Nikolayevich; Soviet politician; b. 1910; ed. Mines Technical School and Higher Party School.

Member C.P.S.U. 32-; Mechanic 28-38; Party Leader of Mine 38-41; Sec. Gorlovka Underground City Cttee. of C.P. 41-43; Second, then First Sec., Donetsk City Cttee. of C.P. Ukraine 48-51; Second Sec. Irkutsk Regional Cttee. of C.P. 51-55; Chair. Exec. Cttee. Irkutsk Regional Soviet of Working People's Deputies 56-57; First Sec. Irkutsk Regional Cttee. of C.P. 57-; mem. Central Cttee. C.P.S.U. 61-; Deputy to U.S.S.R. Supreme Soviet.

Irkutsk Regional Committee of Communist Party of U.S.S.R., Irkutsk, U.S.S.R.

Scheel, Walter; German politician; b. 8 July 1919; ed. Reform-Gymnasium, Solingen.

Served German Air Force, World War II; fmr. head of market research org.; fmr. mem. Landtag North Rhine-Westphalia; mem. Bundestag 53-, Vice-Pres. 67-; Fed. Minister for Econ. Co-operation 61-Oct. 66; Chair. of Free Democrats Sept. 67-.

Publ. *Konturen einer neuen Welt* 65.

Düsseldorf-Benrath, Meliesallee 5A, German Federal Republic.

Scheele, Leonard Andrew, A.B., M.D.; American physician; b. 25 July 1907; ed. Michigan and Wayne Univs.

Various appointments in United States Public Health Service, Surgeon-General 48-56; Pres. Warner Chilcott Laboratories 56-60; Senior Vice-Pres. Warner-Lambert Pharmaceutical Co. 60-, Dir. 57-62, 63-68; Pres. Warner-Lambert Research Inst. 65-68; served in Second World War, holding assignments in military govt. and civil affairs in Africa, Italy, and later in N.W. Europe 43-45.

2510 Virginia Avenue N.W., Washington, D.C. 20037, U.S.A.

Telephone: 202-338-2273.

Schell, Maximilian; Swiss actor; b. 8 Dec. 1930; ed. Humanistiches Gymnasium, Basle, Freies Gymnasium, Zürich, and Univs. of Zürich, Basle and Munich.

Corporal, Swiss Army 48-49; various appearances on stage in Switzerland and Germany 52-55; German debut in *Children, Mothers and the General* 55; American film debut in *Young Lions* 57, on Broadway stage in *Interlock* 58; Critics Award (Broadway) 58; New York Critics Award 61; Golden Globe Award 61; Acad. Award 61.

Principal films acted in: *Judgment at Nuremberg* 61,

Five Finger Exercise 61, *Reluctant Saint* 62, *Condemned of Altona* 62, *Topkapi* 63, *Return from the Ashes* 65, *Beyond the Mountains* 66, *The Deadly Affair* 66, *Battle Horns* 66.

Principal plays acted in: *Hamlet, Prince of Homburg, Mannerhouse, Don Carlos, Sappho* (Durrell), *A Patriot for Me, The Twins of Venice;* Dir. *All for the Best* (Vienna).

Office: c/o William Morris Agency, New York City, U.S.A.; Home: Culmanstrasse 49, Zürich, Switzerland.

Schelling, Friedrich Wilhelm Eugen Eberhard von; German banker; b. 3 May 1906; ed. Kaiserin Augusta Gymnasium, Berlin and Univs. of Heidelberg and Berlin.

Judge, Berlin 31-32; Reichsbank, Berlin 32-45; Reichsbankdirektor, Hamburg 46-48; Bank deutscher Länder, Frankfurt (Main) 48-57; Pres. of Landeszentralbank of Free and Hanseatic City of Hamburg 57-.

Office: Landeszentralbank in der Freien und Hansestadt Hamburg, Alter Wall 2-8, 2 Hamburg 11; Home: Kaspar-Ohm-Weg 16, 2 Hamburg-Wellingsbüttel, German Federal Republic.

Telephone: 36-13-01 (Office); 5-26-11-90 (Home).

Schelsky, Helmut, DR. PHIL.; German sociologist; b. 14 Oct. 1912; ed. Univs. of Königsberg and Leipzig. Privatdozent of Philosophy and Sociology, Univ. of Königsberg; Assoc. Prof., Univ. of Strasbourg 43-44; German Red Cross and journalism 44-48; Prof. of Sociology, Akademie für Gemeinwirtschaft, Hamburg 48-53; Prof. of Sociology, Univ. of Muenster and Dir. Sozialforschungstelle, Dortmund.

Publs. *Arbeitslosigkeit und Berufsnot der Jugend* (2 vols.) 53, *Wandlungen der deutschen Familie in der Gegenwart, Aufgaben und Grenzen der Betriebssoziologie* 54, *Arbeiterjugend gestern und heute* 55, *Soziologie der Sexualität* 55, *Die sozialen Folgen der Automatisierung* 57, *Schule und Erziehung in der industriellen Gesellschaft* 57, *Die skeptische Generation* 57, *Ortsbestimmung der deutschen Soziologie* 59, *Die soziale Idee der deutschen Universität* 60, *Anpassung oder Widerstand?* 61, *Der Mensch in der wissenschaftlichen Zivilisation* 61, *Einsamkeit und Freiheit, Idee und Gestalt der deutschen Universität und ihrer Reformen* 63, *Auf der Suche nach Wirklichkeit* 65. Pleistermühlenweg 101, St. Mauritz, Muenster/Westf. 44, German Federal Republic.

Schendel, Arthur F. E. Van, PH.D.; Netherlands museum director; b. 18 May 1910; ed. High School, Florence, Italy, and Univ. of Paris.

Assistant, Dept. of Paintings, Rijksmuseum, Amsterdam 35, later Curator and Dir. of Dept., Gen. Dir. Rijksmuseum 59-; Pres. Int. Inst. for the Conservation of Historic and Artistic Works 61-64; Pres. Int. Council of Museums 65; has published articles on Rembrandt in *Oud-Holland*, etc.

Publs. *Le Dessin en Lombardie jusqu'au 15ème siècle* 38, *G. H. Breitner* 39, *The Rijksmuseum* 66.

Rijksmuseum, Stadhouderskade 42, Amsterdam, Netherlands.

Scherger, Air Chief Marshal Sir Frederick Rudolph William, K.B.E., C.B., D.S.O., A.F.C.; Australian air force officer; b. 18 May 1904; ed. Royal Mil. Coll., Duntroon.

Transferred to R.A.A.F. 24; Flying Instructor 25-34 and Chief Flying Instructor 34-39, Point Cook; R.A.A.F. Chief Test Pilot 39; Dir. of Training 38-40; A.O.C. New Guinea 43-44; Task Force Commdr. Allied Air Forces in attacks and landings at Aitape and Noemfoor; A.O.C. First Tactical Air Force, New Guinea 45; attended Imperial Defence Coll. 46; Deputy Chief of Air Staff 47-51; Head, Australian Joint Services Staff, Washington 51-52; loaned to R.A.F. as A.O.C. Malaya 52-54; Air mem. for Personnel 54-57; Chief of Air Staff, R.A.A.F. 57-60; Chair. Chiefs of Staff Cttee. 60-66; Chair. Australian Nat. Airlines Comm. 66-.

37 Kensington Road, South Yana, Victoria, Australia.

Schermerhorn, W.; Netherlands politician; b. 17 Dec. 1894; ed. Delft Technical Univ.

Assistant Prof. Heuvelink until 26; Prof. in Surveying, Levelling and Geodesy at Delft Univ. 26; instituted the "Geodetisch Bureau" (Inst. of Geodesy) 23; surveying-Adviser to Public Works and management of "Meetkundige Dienst" (Surveying Service) 31; consultant to K.L.M. (Royal Dutch Airlines); introduced aerial photogrammetry into Holland; Sec. of State Committee of Geodesy; Chair. Int. Society for Photogrammetry 38-48; Chair. anti-Fascist Organisation E.D.D. (Eenheid door Democratie) until May 10th 40; during German occupation spent considerable time in hostage camp; played important part in Netherlands Resistance Movement; Chair. "Nederlandsche Volksbeweging"; Prime Minister and Min. for the Co-ordination of the War Effort June 45-46; Chair. Gen. Comm. for the Netherlands Indies Sept. 46-Nov. 47; mem. of Parliament 48-51; mem. of the Senate 51-63; Dean, Int. Training Centre for Aerial Survey, Delft 51-63; Dr. h.c. (Ghent) 46, (Zürich) 63, (Milan) 64, (Glasgow) 65, (Hanover) 67.

Zandvoorter Allee 304, Haarlem, Post Heemstede, Netherlands.

Telephone: 023-87259.

Scherrer-Bylund, Paul, PH.D.; Swiss librarian; b. 18 Aug. 1900; ed. Univs. of Munich, Berlin and Glasgow.

Asst. Librarian, Univ. Library of Basle 28-31, Librarian 31-47; Chief Librarian, Library of Swiss Fed. Inst. of Technology, Zürich 47-52, Dir. 53-62; Dir. Central Library, Zürich Univ. 63-; Vice-Pres. Swiss Asscn. of Librarians; Pres. Swiss Soc. of Bibliophiles; hon. mem. Int. Asscn. Bibliophily.

Publs. include *Thomas Murners Verhältnis zum Humanismus, untersucht auf Grund seiner "Reformatio poetarum"* 29, *Zwei neue Schriften Thomas Murners* 29, *Zum Kampfmotiv bei Thomas Murner* 35, *Erasmus im Spiegel von Thomas Murners Reformationspublizistik* 36, *Die Toten im deutschen Lyrik zweier Weltkriege* 44, *Sub aeternitatis specie* 53, *Vom Werden und von den Aufgaben der Bibliotheken technischer Hochschulen* 55, *Die Gründung des Eidg. Polytechnicums und das schweizerische Nationalbewusstsein* 55, *Bibliotheken und Bibliothekare als Träger kultureller Aufgaben* 56, *Epigonen-Angst* 57, *Vornehmheit, Illusion und Wirklichkeit als Grundmotive des "Felix Krull"* 58, *Bruchstücke der Buddenbrooks-Urhandschrift* 58, *Die Bibliothek des deutschen Patentamtes und die kulturellen Aufgaben technischer Bibliotheken* 59, *Aus Thomas Manns Vorarbeiten zu den Buddenbrooks* 59, *Thomas Manns Mutter liefert Rezepte für die Buddenbrooks* 59, *Thomas Mann und die Wirklichkeit* 60, *Ueber den Sinn des Thomas Mann Archivs* 61, *Von der Macht und der Sendung des Buchdrucks* 61, *Die Zeit im Bibliothekarischen Beruf* 65.

Home: Beckhammer 32, Zürich 8057; Office: Zentralbibliothek, Zähringerplatz 6, Zürich, Switzerland.

Scheyven, Baron Louis Maurice Emile Marie; Belgian diplomatist; b. 13 Dec. 1904; ed. Louvain Univ.

Held diplomatic posts in Cairo 31-34, Berlin 35, Peking 37, Cairo 42-44, Counsellor in Paris 44; Belgian rep. on Allied High Comm., Bonn; Head of Belgian Mil. Mission, Berlin 49-51; Head Political Dept. Ministry Foreign Affairs 51-53, Sec.-Gen. with rank of Ambassador 53-59; Ambassador to U.S.A. 59-; Grand Officier Ordre de Léopold II, Ordre de la Couronne, Grand Officer, Order of the Nile, of the Légion d'Honneur, of the Couronne de Chêne (Luxembourg), and of the Order of Orange-Nassau; Grand Commdr., Order of the Aztec Eagle (2nd Class) (Mexico); Grand Cross, 2nd Class, Order of Merit of the German Federal Republic, Grand Cross Nat. Order of Southern Cross (Brazil), etc.

Belgian Embassy, 3330 Garfield Street, N.W., Washington, D.C., U.S.A.

Schiff, Dorothy; American newspaper publisher; b. 11 March 1903; ed. Bryn Mawr Coll.

Dir., Vice-Pres. and publisher *New York Post* 39-42, owner and publisher 43-.

New York Post, 75 West Street, New York 6, N.Y., U.S.A.

Schiff, Emile Louis Constant; Netherlands diplomatist; b. 2 March 1918; ed. Rijksuniversiteit, Leiden.

Second Sec., Washington 45-49; Second, later First Sec., Madrid 49-52; Private Sec. to Ministers of Foreign Affairs, The Hague 52-54; Counsellor, Perm. Mission to UN 55-59; Minister, Washington 59-64; Ambassador to Indonesia 64-; Officer, Order of Orange Nassau, War Commemoration Cross (Netherlands); Commdr. Order of Civil Merit (Spain); Officer Order of Dannebrog (Denmark); Chevalier, Légion d'Honneur (France).

Royal Netherlands Embassy, Djakarta, Indonesia.

Schiller, Karl, DR. RER. POL.; German economist and politician; b. 24 April 1911; ed. Univs. of Kiel, Frankfurt/M., Berlin and Heidelberg.

University Asst., Heidelberg 34-35; Head of Research Group, Inst. for World Econs., Kiel 35-41; Army Service 41-45; Asst. Prof. Univ. of Rostock 44, Visiting Prof. Univ. of Kiel 45-46; Prof. of Econs., Dir. of Social Econ. Seminars and Inst. for Foreign Trade and Overseas Commerce, Univ. of Hamburg 47-, Rector, Univ. of Hamburg 56-58; mem. Council of Scientific Advisers, Fed. Ministry of Econs. 47-; mem. Council of Scientific Advisers, Fed. Ministry of Econ. Co-operation; Senator for Econs., Hamburg 48-53, Berlin 61-64; mem. Bundesrat 49-53; Deputy Chair. Econ. Cttee., Exec. Cttee. of Social Democrat Party (S.P.D.) 62-64, Chair. 64-, mem. Exec. Cttee. S.P.D. 64-, mem. Presidium 66-; mem. Bundestag, Deputy Chair. and Econ. Spokesman of S.P.D. Parl. Group 65-; Fed. Minister of Econs. Dec. 66-.

Publs. *Aufgaben und Versuche: Zur neuen Ordnung von Wirtschaft und Gesellschaft* 53, *Der Ökonom und die Gesellschaft: Das freiheitliche und soziale Element in der Wirtschaftspolitik* 64, *Berliner Wirtschaft und deutsche Politik, Reden und Aufsätze 1961-1964* 64; numerous economic and political articles.

Bundesministerium für Wirtschaft, 53 Bonn, German Federal Republic.

Schilpp, Paul Arthur, M.A., B.D., PH.D., American (German-born) university professor, philosopher and writer; b. 1897; ed. Bayreuth Gymnasium, Baldwin-Wallace Coll. (Ohio), Northwestern Univ., Garrett Theol. Seminary, Evanston, and Stanford Univ.

Professor of Psychology and Religious Education, Coll. of Puget Sound 22-23, Prof. of Philosophy, Coll. of the Pacific 23-34; Lecturer, Associate Prof. and (since 50) Prof. of Philosophy, Northwestern Univ. 36-65, Emeritus 65-; Visiting Distinguished Prof. of Philosophy, Southern Ill. Univ. 65-; Visiting Professor, Ohio State Univ. 31, Univ. of Munich 48, Pacific Philosophy Inst. 54; Founder, Pres. and Editor Library of Living Philosophers; Watumull Foundation Research Fellowship for India 50-51; Pres. American Philosophical Asscn. (Western Div.) 58-59; Hon. Litt.D. (Baldwin-Wallace Coll.); Hon. L.H.D. (Springfield Coll.).

Publs. *Do We Need a New Religion?* 28, *Kant's Pre-Critical Ethics* 38, *The Quest for Religious Realism* 38, *Lamentations on Christmas* 45, *Human Nature and Progress* 54, *The Crisis in Science and Education* 63; Editor and Contributor *Higher Education Faces the Future* 30, *Theology and Modern Life* 40, *Library of Living Philosophers* (12 vols. so far published), *The Student Seeks an Answer* 60, *New Frontiers of Christianity* 62, *In Albert Schweitzer's Realms* 62, *Religion Ponders Science* 64, *The World of Philosophy* (Pakistan) 66.

9 Hillcrest Drive, Carbondale, Ill.; and Department of Philosophy, Southern Illinois University, Carbondale, Ill. 62901, U.S.A.
Telephone: 618-453-2769 (Office); 618-549-6335 (Home).

Schiotz, Fredrik Axel, TH.M., TH.D., D.D., LL.D., LITT.D., L.H.D.; American ecclesiastic; b. 15 June 1901; ed. St. Olaf Coll., Northfield, Minnesota, and Luther Theological Seminary, St. Paul, Minnesota.
Pastor Lutheran congregations 30-38, 45-48; Exec. Sec. Student Service Comm. of American Lutheran Conf. 38-45; Exec. Sec. Comm. on Younger Churches and Orphaned Missions of Nat. Lutheran Council 48-54; Pres. Evangelical Lutheran Church 54-60; Chair. Comm. on World Mission of Lutheran World Fed. 49-57, Vice-Chair. 57-63; Chair. Board for Lutheran World Fed. Broadcasting Service 60-64; Pres. American Lutheran Church 61-, Lutheran World Fed. 63-; mem. Nat. Lutheran Council Exec. Cttee. 55-67; mem. Lutheran Council, U.S.A., Exec. Cttee. 67-; mem. World Council of Churches Cen. Cttee. 61-; Commdr., with star, Order of St. Olav.
Publ. *Release* 35.
Home: 7001 Wooddale Ave. South, Minneapolis, Minn. 55424; Office: The American Lutheran Church, 422 South Fifth Street, Minneapolis, Minnesota 55415, U.S.A.
Telephone: 336-0970 (Office); 927-7833 (Home).

Schippers, Thomas; American conductor; b. 9 March 1930; ed. Curtis Inst. Philadelphia, Juilliard School of Music and Yale Univ.
Has conducted orchestras in many American cities and Europe; resident conductor New York City Opera Company 51-54, Metropolitan Opera 55-; guest conductor principal orchestras and opera houses Europe, U.S., Asia; Dir. Spoleto Int. Festival, Italy 58-.
c/o Columbia Artists Management Inc., 113 West 57th Street, New York City, N.Y., U.S.A.

Schirra, Captain Walter Marty, Jr.; American astronaut; b. 12 March 1923; ed. Newark Coll. of Engineering and Naval Academy, Annapolis.
Military Flight Training 45; fighter-pilot, Korea; Project Mercury, National Aeronautics and Space Admin. 59-, made six orbital flights of the earth in spaceship *Sigma VII* Oct. 3, 62; in charge of Operations and Training, Astronaut Office 63-; flew in Gemini VI and made contact with Gemini VII Dec. 65.
National Aeronautics and Space Administration, Manned Spacecraft Center, Houston 1, Texas, U.S.A.

Schjelderup, Gunnar; Norwegian engineer; b. 5 April 1895; ed. Technische Hochschule, Dresden.
Asst. Engineer, Kristiansand Nikkelverk 18; Metallurgical Engineer, British American Nickel, Canada, and American and German steelworks 19-20; Metallurgical Engineer, Christiania Spigerverk steelworks, Supt., and later Vice-Pres., Manager 26-61, now Tech.); Commdr. Order of St. Olav (Norway), of Vasa (Sweden); mem. Det Norske Videnskapsakademi, Oslo, Ingeniörsvetenskapsakademien, Stockholm.
Office: Christiania Spigerverk, Postboks 4224, Oslo; Home: Trosterudveien 7, Slemdal, Oslo, Norway.

Schjelderup, Harald Krabbe, PH.D.; Norwegian psychologist; b. 21 May 1895; ed. Oslo, Copenhagen, Berlin, Freiburg and Vienna Univs.
Professor of Psychology and Dir. Psychological Inst. Oslo Univ. 22-65; Dean of Faculty of Humanities 45-49; Gold Medallist Oslo Univ. 16; Kt. Order of St. Olav.
Publs. *Til sansefornemmelsernes psykofysiologi* 19, *Hauptlinien der Entwicklung der Philosophie von Mitte des 19. Jahrhunderts bis zur Gegenwart* 20, *Filosofiens historie* 24, *Psykologi* 27, *Über drei Haupttypen der religiösen Erlebnisformen und ihre psychologische Grundlage* 32, *Nevrose og oppdragelse* 37, *Nevrosene og*

den nevrotiske Karakter 40, *Nevrose eller Sunnhet* 48, *Innføring i Psykologi* 57, *Det skjulte Menneske* 61.
Psykologist Inst., Universitetet, Oslo; and Kilenveien 4, Lysaker, Oslo, Norway.

Schjelderup, Kristian Vilhelm Koren, B.D., D.D.; Norwegian ecclesiastic; b. 18 Jan. 1894; ed. Univs. of Oslo, Marburg, Berlin and Strasbourg.
Assoc. Prof. of Theology, Univ. of Oslo 21-27; mem. The Christian Michelsen Inst. for Science and Spiritual Freedom, Bergen 30-35; Founder and first Pres. the Norwegian Academy of Humanism (Nansen-skolen) 38-45; ordained Minister of Norwegian Church 45; Bishop of Hamar 47-64; mem. Int. Psychoanalytical Asscn. 28-; Pres. Norwegian Polio Asscn.; Commdr. Order of St. Olav.
Publs. *Religionens sandhet i lys av den relativitetsteoretiske virkelighetsopfatning* 21, *Der mennesker blir guder* 23, *Hvem Jesus var og hvad kirken har gjort ham til* 24, *Religion og religioner* 26, *Die Askese* 28, *Über drei Haupttypen der religiösen Erlebnisformen* 32, *Toleransens og fordragelighetens problem* 34, *På vei mot hedenskapet* 35, *Guds hus i fangeleiren* 45, *Oppgjør med nazismens ideologi* 45, *Tiden kaller på kirken* 48, *Den grunn hvor på jeg bygger* 57, *Ved Dören* 60, *Veien jeg måtte gå* 62, *Lys i mörket* 65.
Peder Claussönsgt. 19, Kristiansand 5, Norway.
Telephone: 26336.

Schlaginhaufen, Otto, PH.D.; Swiss anthropologist; b. 8 Nov. 1879; ed. Zürich Univ.
Asst. Anthropological Inst., Zürich Univ. 02-05, Berlin Ethnographical Museum 05-06, Dresden Museum 06-11; mem. scientific expedition to Melanesia 07-10; Extra. Prof. of Anthropology, Zürich Univ. 11; Prof. Zürich Univ. 17-50, Dir. Anthropological Inst., Hon. Prof. 50-; Pres. Julius Klaus-Foundation for Heredity, Social Anthropology and Racial Hygiene, Zürich.
Publs. *Das Hautleistensystem der Primatenplanta* 05, *Anthropometrische Untersuchungen an Eingeborenen in Deutsch-Neuguinea* 14, *Die menschlichen Skelettreste aus der Steinzeit des Wauwilersees* 25, *Zur Anthropologie der mikronesischen Inselgruppe Kapingamarangi* 29, *Beobachtungen über die Handform bei Schweizern* 32, *Die Vierlingsgeschwister Gehri und ihr Verwandtschaftskreis* 40, *Anthropologia Helvetica I* 46, *II* 59, *Muliama, Zwei Jahre unter Südsee-Insulanern* 59, *Anthropologie von Neuirland* 65.
Schlimbergstrasse 40, 8802 Kilchberg bei Zürich, Switzerland.
Telephone: (051) 91-43-48.

Schlauch, Margaret, A.B., M.A., PH.D.; Polish (b. American) philologist; b. 25 Sept. 1898; ed. Barnard Coll. and Columbia Univ., New York.
Assistant Prof., New York Univ. 27-31, Assoc. Prof. 31-40, Full Prof. 40-51; Prof. of English Philology, Warsaw Univ., Poland 51-, Chair. of Dept. 53-65; Visiting Prof., Univ. of Connecticut 66, 67-68; Corresp. mem. Polish Acad. of Sciences; Officer, Order of Polonia Restituta.
Publs. *Chaucer's Constance* 27, *Medieval Narrative* 28, *The Saga of the Volsungs* 30, *The Gift of Tongues* 42, *English Medieval Literature and its Social Foundations* 56, *Modern English and American Poetry* 56, *Zarys Wersy fikacji Angielskiej* (Outline of English Versification) 58, *The English Language in Modern Times* 59, *Antecedents of the English Novel* 63, *Language and the Study of Languages Today* 67, Polish trans. 67.
Brzozowa 10 m. 12, Warsaw, Poland.
Telephone: 31-78-12.

Schleinzer, Dr. Karl; Austrian agriculturalist and politician; b. 8 Jan. 1924; ed. Stuttgart, Königsberg, and Vienna Coll. of Agriculture.
Lieutenant, Alpine Regt., Second World War; Chair.

Carinthian Branch, People's Party; Deputy Chair. Carinthian Farmers' Fed.; mem. Agricultural Dept., Property Valuation Sub-Cttee., Ministry of Finance; Minister of Defence 61-64, of Agriculture and Forestry 64-.
Ministry of Agriculture and Forestry, Vienna, Austria.

Schlenker, Rudolf; German tobacco executive; b. 18 June 1915; ed. business management studies, Cologne.
Adviser, Provincial Economy Office, Württemberg/Baden, and in Provincial Parl. after Second World War, later in Econ. Admin. Office, Frankfurt; in Fed. Ministry of Economy, Bonn 49-51, in Washington, D.C. 51-53; mem. Management Board H. F. and Ph. F. Reemtsma 53-, Spokesman of Management Board 58, Chair of Management Board 62-; Chair. Cigarette Industry Asscn.; Vice-Pres. Hamburg Chamber of Commerce; mem. Advisory Board Deutsche Bank A.G., Nordd.-Lloyd Bremen; mem. Advisory Council Aachener und Münchener Feuer-Versicherungs-Gesellschaft, Gerling-Konzern.
H. F. and Ph. F. Reemtsma, Hamburg-Gr. Flottbek, Parkstrasse 51, German Federal Republic.

Schlesinger, Arthur, Jr., A.B.; American writer and educator; b. 15 Oct. 1917; ed. Phillips Exeter Acad., Harvard Univ. and Peterhouse, Cambridge, England. Society of Fellows, Harvard 39-42; with Office of War Information 42-43; Office of Strategic Services 43-45; U.S. Army 45; Assoc. Prof. of History, Harvard Univ. 47-54, Prof. 54-62; Special Asst. to Pres. of U.S.A. 61-64; Schweitzer Prof. of the Humanities, City Univ. of N.Y. 66-; Consultant, Econ. Co-operation Admin. 48, Mutual Security Admin. 51-52; mem. Adlai Stevenson campaign staff 52 and 56; Pulitzer Prize for History 45, for Biography 66, Bancroft and Parkman Prizes 58; Nat. Book Award 66; Gold Medal, Nat. Inst. of Arts and Letters 67; Hon. Litt.D. (Muhlenberg) 50, Hon. LL.D. (Bethany) 56, (New School for Social Research) 66; Hon. D.C.L. (New Brunswick) 60; Hon. L.H.D. (Tusculum Coll.) 66.
Publs. *Orestes A. Brownson: A Pilgrim's Progress* 39, *The Age of Jackson* 45, *The Vital Center* (English title *The Politics of Freedom*) 49, *The General and the President* (with R. H. Rovere) 51, *The Age of Roosevelt:* Vol. I *The Crises of the Old Order* 57, Vol. II *The Coming of the New Deal* 59, Vol. III *The Politics of Upheaval* 60, *The Politics of Hope* 63, *A Thousand Days* 65, *The Bitter Heritage: Vietnam and American Democracy 1941-1966* 67.
Office: City University of New York, 33 West 42nd Street, New York, N.Y. 10036; Home: 166 East 61st Street, New York, N.Y., U.S.A.
Telephone: 790-4261.

Schlesinger, John Richard; British film director; b. 26; ed. Uppingham School and Balliol Coll. Oxford. Early career as actor on television and in films *Single-handed, Battle of the River Plate, Brothers in Law* and numerous others; directed shorts for *Tonight* and *Monitor;* made films for B.B.C. Television including part of *The Valiant Years;* joined Sapphire Films for *Four Just Men.*
Chief films: *Terminus* (Venice Golden Lion 62) 61, *A Kind of Loving* (Berlin Golden Bear) 62, *Billy Liar* 63, *Darling* (New York Film Critics' Award) 65; *Far From the Madding Crowd* 67, *Midnight Cowboy* 68; plays: *No Why* (John Whiting), Aldwych Theatre 64, *Timon of Athens* Royal Shakespeare Theatre, Stratford 65, *Days in the Trees* (London) 66.
c/o London International, Park House, Park Street, London, W.1, England.

Schlesinger, John Samuel; South African business executive; b. 23; ed. Michaelhouse and Harvard Univ. United States Army Air Corps, Second World War; Pres. Schlesinger Org. (real estate) 49-, developments in

Johannesburg, Durban, Cape Town and Port Elizabeth; Chair. and Man. Dir. African Life Assurance Soc. Ltd., African Guarantee and Indemnity Co. Ltd., African Consolidated Investments Corpn. Ltd., African Amalgamated Advertising Ltd., African Realty Trust Ltd., African Caterers Ltd.
Schlesinger Organisation, P.O. Box 1182, Johannesburg, South Africa.

Schlesinger, Theodore; American retail executive; b. 27 Oct. 1908; ed. City Coll. of New York and Fordham Univ.
Allied Stores Corpn. 29-, Asst. to Pres. 39-45, Vice-Pres. 45-59, Pres. and Chief Exec. Officer 59-, Dir. 55-.
Allied Stores Corporation, 401 Fifth Avenue, New York City, N.Y., U.S.A.

Schlieker, Willy Hermann; German industrialist; b. 14; ed. Elementary and High School in Hamburg. Sales Rep. German export firm in Haiti 36-38; Export Man. Ruhr steel construction firm 39; with raw material dept. Vereinigte Stahlwerke, Düsseldorf 40-42; Steel Controller, Ministry of War Production 43-45; industrial adviser 46-47; since 48 built up the Schlieker Group, comprising Schlieker Yard (shipbuilding), Schlieker Kessel-u. Maschinenbau (engines and boilers), Reederei Willy H. Schlieker & Co. (shipping) (all Hamburg), Walzwerk Neviges (electrical sheet-mill), Metall- und Kaltwalzwerk Langenberg (strip mill), Schlieker Eisenhandel G.m.b.H. (steel), Schrottverwertung Niederrhein G.m.b.H. (scrap), Schlieker Anlagen-Export G.m.b.H., Düsseldorf.
Fischers Allee 97, Hamburg-Altona, German Federal Republic.

Schlier, Heinrich; German university professor; b. 1900; ed. Univs. of Leipzig and Marburg.
Pastor 27; Reader, Jena 28; Marburg Univ. 30; Lecturer, Theological School, Elberfeld 35; Pastor, Lutheran Church, Elberfeld 37; Prof. of the New Testament and Church History Bonn Univ. 45, Hon. Prof. 52.
Publs. *Religionsgeschichtliche Untersuchungen zu den Ignatiusbriefen* 29, *Christus und die Kirche im Epheserbrief* 30, *Der Brief an die Galater* 51, 62, 65, *Die Zeit der Kirche* 56, 58, 65, *Der Brief an die Epheser* 57, 58, 62, 63, 65, *Besinnung auf das NT* 64, 68.
Wegelerstrasse 2, Bonn, German Federal Republic.
Telephone: 53416.

Schlitter, Oskar; German diplomatist; b. 04. Ministry of Foreign Affairs 29-45; Diplomatic Service 52-; Ambassador to U.K. 53-54; in Ministry of Foreign Affairs 58-65; Ambassador to Greece 65-.
Embassy of the German Federal Republic, 3 rue Caraoli et Dimitriou, Athens, Greece.

Schlosser, Hermann; German business executive; b. 8 Oct. 1889; ed. Landgraf-Ludwigs-Gymnasium, Giessen.
Commercial studies, Hamburg 08-10; commercial posts, Calcutta and New Delhi 10-14; joined Deutsche Gold- und Silber-Scheidenanstalt (Degussa) 15; Military Service 15-18; Degussa 18-, mem. Board of Dirs. 26-39, Chair. Board of Dirs. 39-, Chair. Supervisory Board 59-, Hon. Chair. 65-; Hon. mem. Asscn. of the Chemical Industry.
6461 Hof Eich, Gelnhausen-Land, German Federal Republic.

Schlumberger, Jean, L. ès L.; French writer; b. 26 May 1877; ed. Paris Univ.
Founder (with Gide) of the *Nouvelle Revue Française;* co-operated with Jacques Copeau in founding the Vieux Colombier theatre; regular contributor to *Le Figaro;* awarded literature prize by Académie Française 43; Croix de Guerre; Commdr. Légion d'Honneur; Dr. h.c. (Univ. of Leiden) 55; Goethe Plakette 59.
Publs. Novels: *L'Inquiète Paternité* 11, *Un Homme Heureux* 21, *Le Camarade Infidèle* 22, *Le Lion devenu*

Vieux 24, *Les Yeux de 18 Ans* 28, *Saint-Saturnin* 31, *Histoire de 4 Potiers* 35, *Stéphane le Glorieux* 40; Criticism: *Plaisir à Corneille* 36, *Essais et Dialogues* 37, *Jalons* 42, *Théâtre* 43, *Le Procès Pétain* 49, *Eveils* 50, *Passion* 56, *Madeleine et André Gide* 56, *Œuvres*, 7 vols. 62.
78 rue d'Assas, Paris 6e, France.
Telephone: 326-68-48.

Schmaus, Michael, DR. THEOL.; German theologian and university professor; b. 17 July 1897; ed. Gymnasium Rosenheim and Univ. Munich.
Ordained 22; Lecturer Philosophische-theologische Hochschule und Seminar Freising 24-29; Lecturer Munich Univ. 27-29; Prof. of Dogmatic Theology, German Univ. in Prague 29-33; Prof. Univ. Münster 33-46, Munich 46-65, Emer. 65-; Rector Munich Univ. 51-52; mem. Bavarian Acad. of Sciences; Commdr. of Greek Order of Phoenix; Commdr. Spanish Order of Civil Merit; Bayerischer Verdienstorden; Grosses Bundesverdienstkreuz.
Publs. *Die psychologische Trinitätslehre des Heiligen Augustinus* 27, *Der Liber propugnatorius des Thomas Anglicus* 30, *Katholische Dogmatik*, 8 Vols. 38-64, *Handbuch der Katholischen Dogmatik* 68, *Die Druckform Augustins in seinem Werk "De Trinitate"* 62, articles, translations and several series.
8035 Gauting bei München, Junkerstrasse 5, German Federal Republic.
Telephone: Munich 862800.

Schmeisser, Kurt; German foreign trade official; b. 21 May 1909.
Head of China and Glass, and Machine Export Trade Corpns. 50-58; Foreign Trade Rep. of German Democratic Republic (D.D.R.) in Iraq and Sweden 58-62; Gen. Dir. of Int. Leipzig Trade Fair 62-.
Leipziger Messeamt, Markt 11/15, 701 Leipzig, German Democratic Republic.
Telephone: 2030.

Schmid, Erich, DR. PHIL.; Austrian scientist; b. 4 May 1896; ed. Univ. Wien.
Member staff Kaiser Wilhelm-Inst. für Faserstoffchemie 22-24; metallurgist, Metalgesellschaft A.G., Frankfurt 24-28; Head of Physics Dept., Kaiser-Wilhelm Inst. für Metallforschung, Berlin-Dahlem 28-32; Teacher at Technische Hochschule, Berlin 32; Prof. and Head of Physics Inst., Univ. of Fribourg (Switzerland) 32-36; Head of Metal Laboratories, Metalgesellschaft A.G., Frankfurt 36-45; Head of Laboratories of Vacuumschmelze A.G., Hanau am Main 46-51; Prof. of Physics and Head of Second Physics Inst., Univ. of Vienna 51-67, Emer. 67-; Pres. Austrian Acad. of Sciences 63-; mem. Deutsche Akad. der Naturforscher Leopoldina, New York Acad. of Sciences; Hon. mem. Japanese Soc. of Metallurgy; Foreign mem. Max Planck Inst. für Metallforschung, Stuttgart; numerous medals and decorations.
Publs. *Kristallplastizität* (with W. Boas) 35, *Gleitlager* (with R. Weber) 53, *Texturen in Metallen und Legierungen* (6th edition) 57, *Bedeutung von Korpuskularbestrahlung für die Eigenschaften von Festkörpern* (with K. Lintner) 55, *Werkstoffe des Reaktorbaues* (with K. Lintner) 62.
A 1090 Vienna, Universitätstrasse 10, Austria.
Telephone: 42-40-062.

Schmid, Karl (Carlo), DR. JUR.; German lawyer, writer and politician; 3 Dec. 1896; ed. Univ. of Tübingen and Kaiser Wilhelm Inst. of Foreign Public and Int. Law.
Lawyer 24, Judge 25; Dozent Univ. of Tübingen 29; Prof. of Public Law 45-50; Pres. of Social Democratic Party in Württemberg 46-; mem. Central Cttee. of SPD 47-; Minister of State in Württemberg 45-52; mem. of Diet 46-; mem. of Parl. Council in Bonn 48-49; mem. and Vice-Pres. Fed. Parl. 49-; Prof. of Political

Science Univ. of Frankfurt 53-; Minister for Bundesrat and the Länder 66-; mem. Council of Europe; mem. PEN; Presidential candidate 59; Goethepreis der Stadt Frankfurt/Main 67.
Publs. *Machiavelli* 56, *Politik und Geist* 62; trans. of Baudelaire and Calderón.
Johann-Klotzstrasse 15, Frankfurt-am-Main, German Federal Republic.

Schmidheiny, Ernst; Swiss airline executive; b. 02.
Director, Swissair 47-, mem. Exec. Cttee. 53-, Chair. 58-66; Chair. Swiss Holdebank-Willdegg Cement Co. Swissair, Balsberg-Kloten, Zürich, Switzerland.

Schmidheiny, Max, DIPL.ENG.; Swiss engineer and industrialist; b. 3 April 1908; ed. Gymnasium Trogen and Eidgenössische Technische Hochschule, Zürich.
President and Dir. of many companies in Switzerland and abroad, incl. Chair. of Brown, Boveri, Baden; mem. Swiss Chamber of Commerce; Hon. Freeman of Pagig/Gr.; Dr. h.c. Univ. of Basle, High Commercial School, St. Gall.
CH-94 Heerbrugg, Switzerland.

Schmidt, Arno Otto; German novelist; b. 18 Jan. 1914; ed. Univ. of Breslau.
Employed 34-39; Soldier and Prisoner of War 39-45; Writer 46-; Grand Prize for Literature, Akademie für Wissenschaft und Literatur, Mainz 50; Fontanepreis 64, Grand Award for Literature, Fed. German Industries 65.
Publs. *Leviathan* 49, *Brands Haide* 51, *Aus dem Leben eines Fauns* 53, *Das steinerne Herz* 56, *Die Gelehrtenrepublik* 57, *Dya na sore* 58, *Rosen und Porree* 59, *Kaff* 60, *Belphegor* 61, *Kühe in Halbtrauer* 64, *Die Ritter vom Geist* 65, *Trommler beim Zaren* 66; Biography: *Fouqué und einige seiner Zeitgenossen* 58, *Sitara und der Weg dorthin* (Karl May) 63; translations from English (Hunter, Ellin, Faulkner, Poe, Cooper, Collins, Joyce, etc.).
3101 Bargfeld Krs. Celle Nr. 37, German Federal Republic.
Telephone: Steinhorst 500.

Schmidt, Helmut H. W.; German economist and politician; b. 23 Dec. 1918; ed. Univ. Hamburg.
Manager of Transport Admin. of State of Hamburg 50-53; mem. Bundestag 53-62, 65-; Chair. Social Democrat (S.P.D.) Parl. Party in Bundestag 67-; Vice-Chair. Social Democratic Party (S.P.D.) 68-; Senator (Minister) for Domestic Affairs in Hamburg 62-65.
Publ. *Defence or Retaliation* 62, *Beiträge* 67.
Bundeshaus, 53 Bonn, German Federal Republic.
Telephone: Bonn 16-2418.

Schmidt, Maarten, PH.D., SC.D.; Netherlands astronomer; b. 28 Dec. 1929; ed. Univs. of Groningen and Leiden.
Scientific Officer, Univ. of Leiden Observatory 49-59; Carnegie Fellow Mt. Wilson Observatory, Pasadena 56-58; Assoc. Prof. Calif. Inst. of Technology 59-64; Prof. of Astronomy 64-; discovered large red shifts in spectra of quasi-stella radio sources (quasars).
California Institute of Technology, Pasadena, California, U.S.A.
Telephone: 213-795-6841.

Schmidt, Orvis Adrian, M.A.; American economist; b. 28 Jan. 1912; ed. Lawrence Coll., Wis., Tufts Coll., Mass., and Univ. of Chicago.
Served with U.S. Treasury Dept. 36-47; Asst. Dir. Dept. of Operations, Western Hemisphere, Int. Bank for Reconstruction and Development 52-56, Dir. 56-64; Special Adviser to the President 64-.
International Bank for Reconstruction and Development, 1818 H Street, N.W., Washington, D.C.; Home: 3414 Cummings Lane, Chevy Chase, Maryland, U.S.A.
Telephone: OLiver 2-7828.

Schmidt-Clausen, Kurt Hermann, DR.THEOL.; German international church official; b. 1 Oct. 1920; ed. Hanover Gymnasium, Univs. of Vienna and Göttingen, Christ Church Coll., Oxford, and Loccum Preachers' Seminary.

Pastor, City Parish, Hanover 51-52; mem. Admin. Staff Evangelical Lutheran Church of Hanover 52-55; Pastor, Wunstorf Suburban Parish (near Hanover) 55-60; Asst. Exec. Sec., later Acting Exec. Sec., Lutheran World Fed. 60-61, Exec. Sec. 61-64, Gen. Sec. 64-65; Chair. Ecumenical Comm., Evangelical Lutheran Church of Hanover; Chair. Ecumenical Comm., United Evangelical Lutheran Church of Germany; Editor *Lutheran World* (quarterly).

Publ. *Vorweggenommene Einheit* 64.

Evangelical-Lutheran Church of Hanover, Rote Rebhe 6, 3000 Hanover, German Federal Republic.

Schmidt-Isserstedt, Hans, DR.PHIL.; German musical director; b. 5 May 1900; ed. Hochschule für Musik, Berlin and Univs. of Berlin, Heidelberg, Münster.

Senior conductor Rostock, Darmstadt, Hamburg; Opera Dir. German Opera House, Berlin; Chief Conductor, North German Radio 45-; Chief Conductor Stockholm Philharmonic Orchestra 55-64; guest conductor all important orchestral socs. of Old and New World.

Works: *Hassan gewinnt* (three-act opera), orchestral music, chamber music, vocal music, etc.

Norddeutscher Rundfunk, Rothenbaumchaussee 132, Hamburg 13, German Federal Republic.

Schmit, André, L. en DR.; French civil servant; b. 12 Feb. 1915; ed. Ecole des Sciences Politiques, Ecole Nat. de la France d'Outre-Mer (Indo-China) and Cambridge Univ.

Colonial Administration (Indo-China) 41-45; Asst. Dir. Press Relations, Ministry of Information 46, Inspector Gen. 46; Dir. Press Council 47; Dir. Nouvelles Messageries de la Presse Parisienne 49-; Chef de Cabinet, Ministry of Public Works and Reconstruction 54-55; Chef de Cabinet, Ministry of State 56-57, Ministry of Defence 57; Chef de Cabinet of Pres. of Nat. Assembly 58-; Officier, Légion d'Honneur.

48 avenue de New York, Paris 16e, France.

Schmitt, Bernadotte Everly, M.A., PH.D., LL.D., LITT.D.; American historian; b. 19 May 1886; ed. Tennessee, Wisconsin and Oxford Univs.

Instructor History, Western Reserve Univ. 10-14, Asst. Prof. 14-17, Assoc. Prof. 17-24, Prof. 24-25; Prof. Mod. History, Chicago Univ. 23-39; MacLeigh Prof. 39-46, Emeritus 46-; Editor *Journal of Modern History* 29-46; Co-Editor *Cambridge Modern History* 35-49; Pulitzer Prize for History 31, edited *Some Historians of Modern Europe* 42; *Poland* (United Nations Series) 45; Special Adviser Historical Div., Dept. of State, Washington, D.C. 46-49; Chief German War Documents Project of same, and U.S. Editor-in-Chief of *Documents on German Foreign Policy 1918-1945* 49-52; Vice-Pres. American Historical Ass. 59-, Pres. 60; Hon. mem. Historical Asscn. (Great Britain) 59; Hon. Fellow Merton Coll., Oxford 66; Hon. D.Litt. (Oxford).

Publs. *England and Germany, 1740-1914* 16, *The Coming of the War, 1914-30, Triple Alliance and Triple Entente* 34, *The Annexation of Bosnia, 1908-09* 37, *From Versailles to Munich* 39, *What Shall We Do With Germany?* 43, *The Origins of the First World War* 58, *The Fashion and Future of History* 60.

P.O. Box 324, Alexandria, Va. 22313, U.S.A.

Telephone: Temple 6-2981.

Schmitthenner, Paul; German architect; b. 15 Dec. 1884; ed. Karlsruhe and Munich Univs.

Head of Architectural Office Kolmar 08; Chief Architect of German Building Soc. Breslau 12; attached to Reich Minister of the Interior 17; Prof. Stuttgart Technical High School 18; mem. Prussian Acad. of Arts and of Building; hon. mem. Acad. of Arts, Munich; Knight Orders of Merit; Dr. Ing. h.c.

Buildings include Gartenstadt (Staaken) 14, Haus des Deutschtums (Stuttgart) 24, Sammelschule (Zuffenhausen) 30, Königin-Olga-Bau (Stuttgart) 50, Dresdner Bank (Heilbronn) 55, Frankona-Versicherung Office Building (Munich) 57, Rathaus (Hechingen) 58.

Publs. *Das Deutsche Wohnhaus* 32, *Die Baukunst im neuen Reich* 34, *Das sanfte Gesetz in der Kunst* 40.

7401 Schloss, Kilchberg Krs., Tübingen, German Federal Republic.

Telephone: Tübingen 33777.

Schmitz, Wolfgang, DR. IUR.; Austrian commercial official and politician; b. 28 May 1923; ed. High School, Vienna and Vienna and Fribourg (Switzerland) Univs.

Legal practice 49-50; Austrian Fed. Econ. Chamber 50-64, Sec. Econ. Policy Dept. and Sec. Austrian Nat. Cttee. of Int. Chamber of Commerce 50-64, Head of Econ. Policy Dept. Jan.-April 64; Fed. Minister of Finance 64-68; Pres. Austrian Nat. Bank 68-, Inst. for Advanced Studies 68-; Gov. of IMF for Austria 68-; Dir. Austrian Inst. for Econ. Research 68-; Hon. LL.D. (St. John's Univ., New York).

Publs. *Die Wirtschaftliche Integration Europas, Stand und Möglichkeiten im Spiegel des Wiener Kongresses der Internationalen Handelskammer* 53, *Der Ausgleich-der Familienlasten-Allgemeine Theorie und praktische Verwirklichung in Österreich* 55, *Der Welthandel geht jeden an* 55, *Die Österreichische Wirtschaftspolitik im Zeichen der Europäischen Integration* 60, *Die Österreichische Wirtschafts- und Sozialpolitik, Würdigung, Kritik, Ansatzpunkte* 61, *Budget und Konjunktur* 66, and numerous articles.

Österreichische Nationalbank, Otto Wagner Platz 3, A 1090 Vienna, Austria.

Telephone: 42-56-11.

Schmücker, Kurt; German politician; b. 10 Nov. 1919; ed. Secondary School and Trade School.

Apprentice to printing and journalism; military service 39-46; printing works, Oldenburg 46-, owner 54-; mem. Bundestag 49-, Chair. Econ. Policy Cttee; Minister of Econs. 63-66, for Fed. Property 66-; Christian Democrat.

Bundestag, Bonn, German Federal Republic.

Schneider, Alan Leo (Abram Leopoldovitch); American (b. Russian) theatre director and lecturer; b. 12 Dec. 1917; ed. Forest Park High School, Baltimore, Maryland, Maryland Inst. of Art, Baltimore, Johns Hopkins Univ., Univs. of Maryland and Wisconsin and Cornell Univ.

Office of War Information 43-44; Instructor, Speech and Drama Dept., The Catholic Univ. of America 41-47, Asst. Prof. 49-52; Artistic Dir. Arena Stage, Washington, D.C. 52-53, Assoc. Dir. 61-63; Drama Critic *The New Leader* 62-63; Assoc. Dir. Tyrone Guthrie Theatre 64; Artistic Dir. Ithaca Festival Theater 63-, Actors Studio Theatre 62-; mem. Board of Dirs. Theatre Communications Group 63-; mem. Advisory Board New Dramatists Cttee. 55-, *Tulane Drama Review* 62-, N.Y. State Council on the Arts 65-, Nat. Theatre Conf. 65; Lecturer at major univs. in U.S. 45-; recent awards include Prix Filmcritica, Venice 65, Prix Special du Jury, Tours 66, Preis der Kurzfilmtage, Oberhausen 66.

Plays directed include: (U.S.A.) *Jim Dandy* 42, *Waiting for Godot* 56, *Endgame* 58, *Krapp's Last Tape* 60, *Happy Days* 61, *The Caucasian Chalk Circle* 61, *The Dumb Waiter* and *The Collection* 62, *Who's Afraid of Virginia Woolf?* 62, *The Ballad of the Sad Café* 63, *Tiny Alice* 64, *Herakles* 65, *Slapstick Tragedy* 66, *A Delicate Balance* 66, *You Know I Can't Hear You When the Water's Running* 67, *I Never Sang for My Father* 67, *Box-Mao-Box* 68; (Israel) *The Cherry Orchard* 66; (England) *The Trip to Bountiful* 56, *Who's Afraid of Virginia Woolf?* 64; (France) *The Skin of Our Teeth* 55.

Films and TV: *Oedipus the King* 56, *The Life of Samuel Johnson* 57, *The Years Between* 58, *The Secret of Freedom* 59, *Waiting for Godot* 60, *Act Without Words, II* 65, *Film* 65, *Eh, Joe?* 66.
30 Scenic Drive, Hastings-on-Hudson, New York, U.S.A.

Schneider, Ernst Georg, DIPL. KFM., DR. RER. POL.; German business executive; b. 6 Oct. 1900; ed. Univ. of Frankfurt/Main.
Kohlensäure Industrie 22-, Pres. 32-; Pres. of banking, coalmining, steel construction and chemical firms 46-; Pres. Deutscher Industrie und Handelstag, Bonn; Dr. med. h.c. (Medical Acad., Düsseldorf).
Berliner Allee 57, 4000 Düsseldorf, German Federal Republic.
Telephone: 834-281.

Schneider, Erwin Eugen, D.PHIL.; Austrian theologian and painter; b. 92; ed. Vienna, Marburg and Halle Univs.
Lutheran Evangelical church service (Minister at Ljubljana, Belgrade and Vienna, Oberkirchenrat in Vienna) 18-47; Prof. of Theology Vienna Univ. 47-, Rector 58-59, Pro-Rector 60; Pres., Johannes Mathesius-Gesellschaft 61; Grosses Silbernes Ehrenzeichen; Hon. D.D. Heidelberg 58.
Publs. Numerous works on dogmatics, ethics, religious philosophy and ecclesiastical art.
Paintings in various Austrian Protestant churches and in Vienna Univ.
Dannebergplatz 16, 1030 Vienna, Austria.
Telephone: 7350762.

Schneider, Liliane Louise Hélène; French company executive; b. 26 Sept. 1902.
Cinematographer 31; Dir. of Schneider and Co. 60-; Dir. of Usines Schneider 60-; Dir. and Hon. Pres. Schneider S.A. 66-; Chevalier Légion d'Honneur.
42 rue d'Anjou, Paris 8e, France.

Schneiderhan, Wolfgang (husband of Irmgard Seefried *q.v.*); Austrian violinist; b. 28 May 1915; studied under Prof. Julius Winkler and Prof. Ottokar Sevcik.
Professor at Mozarteum, Salzburg 36-56, at Musikhochschule, Vienna 39-50, at Conservatoire, Lucerne 49-; leader of master classes; Beethoven Plakat 60.
Reckenbühlstrasse 20, Lucerne, Switzerland.

Schnippenkoetter, Swidbert, D.IUR.; German diplomatist; b. 9 Aug. 1915; ed. Rheinische Friedrich Wilhelms-Universität, Bonn, Ludwig-Maximilians Universität, Munich, Law Society's School of Law London, Univ. of Virginia, Charlottesville.
Entered German Foreign Service 50; Embassy in Mexico 52-55; Ministry of Foreign Affairs, Bonn 55-57; Comm. of European Econ. Community, Brussels 58-60; Embassy in Wash. 60-63; Planning Council, Ministry Foreign Affairs, Bonn 63-65; Amb. and Plenipotentiary of the German Fed. Govt. for Disarmament and Arms Control 65-.
Auswärtiges Amt., 53 Bonn; and Reitersdorferstrasse 6, 534 Rhoendorf, German Federal Republic.

Schnitzler, William F.; American trade unionist; b. 21 Jan. 1904.
Worked in Newark, N.J., ammunition factories during First World War; baker's asst. 20; mem. Local 84, Bakery and Confectionary Workers Int. Union of America 24, Business Agent 34, Int. Rep. 37, later Gen. Rep., Second Vice-Pres., Financial Sec., Gen. Sec.-Treas. 46, Pres. 50-52; Sec.-Treas. American Fed. of Labor (A.F.L.) 52-55; mem. Joint Unity Sub-cttee. which brought about merger between A.F.L. and Congress of Industrial Organisations (C.I.O.) 54-55; Sec.-Treas. A.F.L.-C.I.O. 55-.
Office: A.F.L.-C.I.O., 815 16th Street, N.W., Washington, D.C. 20006; Home: Bethesda, Md., U.S.A.
Telephone: 202-628-3870.

Schnurre, Wolfdietrich; German writer; b. 22 Aug. 1920; ed. Humanistisches Gymnasium.
Army Service 39-45; Freelance writer 45-; Founder-mem. "Group 47" 47; mem. Akademie für Sprache und Dichtung 59, West German PEN 58-61; Young Generation Prize, Culture Prize of Berlin 58, Immermann Prize, Düsseldorf 59, George Mackensen Literature Prize 62.
Publs. *Aufzeichnungen des Pudels Ali* (satire) 51, 62, *Kassiber* (poems) 56, 64, *Abendländler* (satirical poems) 57, *Protest im Parterre* (fables) 57, *Eine Rechnung, die Nicht Aufgeht* (short stories) 58, *Als Vaters Bart noch Rot War* (novel) 58, *Das Los Unserer Stadt* (novel) 59, *Man Sollte Dagegen Sein* (short stories) 60, *Die Mauer des 13 August* (documentary) 61, *Berlin—eine Stadt Wird Geteilt* (documentary) 62, *Funke im Reisig* (short stories) 63, *Schreibtisch unter freiem Himmel* (essays) 64, *Ohne Einsatz kein Spiel* (short stories) 64, *Die Erzählungen* (stories) 66, *Spreezimmer möbliert* 67, *Die Zwengel* (for children) 67, *Hand-und Fussroten, Der Gipsengel* (novel), *Was ich für mein Leben gern tue* (collection of prose pieces) 68.
Goethestrasse 29, Berlin 37, Germany.
Telephone: 84-05-63.

Schnyder, Felix; Swiss diplomatist; b. 5 March 1910; ed. Berne Univ.
Served in Swiss Foreign Service, Berne, Moscow, Berlin, Washington 40-57; Swiss Minister to Israel 57-58; Perm. Swiss observer at UN 58-60; Chair., Exec. Cttee. UNICEF 60; UN High Commnr. for Refugees 61-65; Ambassador to U.S.A. 66-.
Embassy of Switzerland, 2900 Cathedral Avenue N.W., Washington, D.C. 20008, U.S.A.
Telephone: HO2-1811.

Schocken, Gershom Gustav; Israeli editor and publisher; b. Sept. 1912; ed. Univ. of Heidelberg and London School of Economics.
Joined staff of *Haaretz* (daily newspaper) 37; publisher and editor 39-; Dir. Schocken Publishing House Ltd.; mem. Knesset (Parliament) 55-59.
Haaretz Building, P.O. Box 233, Tel-Aviv, Israel.
Telephone: Tel-Aviv 623311.

Schoeller, Gerhard; German businessman; b. 26 June 1886; ed. Munich Univ. (law) and Univs. of Freiburg and Darmstadt (chemistry).
Sec. Feinpapierfabrik Felix Schoeller jr., Burg Gretesch, 10, Co-owner 11, and Gen. Man. 58; Hon. Pres. Trust Organisation of the Cellulose and Paper Industry, Bonn; Hon. Senator Technical Univ. Darmstadt 50-.
Burg Gretesch, Post Lüstringen bei Osnabrück, German Federal Republic.

Schoemann, Barend Jacobus, M.INST.T.; South African politician; b. 19 Jan. 1905.
Leader Witwatersrand National Party 40-; fmr. Minister of Labour, Minister of Public Works, Minister of Forestry; Minister of Transport 54-; M.P. for Maraisburg.
Ministry of Transport, Pretoria, Republic of South Africa.

Schoenhofen, Leo H., Jr.; American business executive; b. 8 Aug. 1915; ed. Univ. of Wisconsin and Northwestern Univ.
Oklahoma Gas and Electric Co., Oklahoma City 36-38; Container Corpn. of America, Chicago 40-, Vice-Pres. 52-54, Senior Vice-Pres. 56-61, Pres. and mem. Exec. Cttee. 61-64, Pres. and Chief Exec. Officer 64-; U.S. Naval Reserve 43-46.
Container Corporation of America, 38 S. Dearborn Street, Chicago, Illinois, U.S.A.

Scholz, Ernst; German architect and diplomatist; b. 19 July 1913; ed. Technische Hochschule, Berlin, and Bauhaus, Berlin, and Universität Rostock.
Former architect, Berlin; fmr. mem. Kommunistische Partei Deutschlands; fought in Spanish Civil War

37-39; mem. French Resistance 40-45; posts in commerce and building industry, German Democratic Republic (D.D.R.) 46-56; Ambassador of D.D.R. to Arab States 56-58; Minister of Building, D.D.R. 58-63; Minister to United Arab Republic (U.A.R.) 63-; mem. Sozialistische Einheits Partei Deutschlands (S.E.D.). Legation of the German Democratic Republic, 13 Sh. Hussein Wassef (Doqqi), Cairo, United Arab Republic.

Scholz, Paul; German politician; b. 2 Oct. 1902. Former agricultural worker; fmr. Dep. Chief Editor *Der Freie Bauer* (The Free Peasant); founder-mem. Dem. Peasants Party of Germany, later Gen. Sec. and Dep. Chair.; mem. People's Chamber (D.D.R.) 50-; Minister of Agriculture and Forestry 50-52; Dep. Chair. Council of Ministers 52-; Chair. Central Advisory Council for Agricultural Production Co-operatives, Council of Ministers 56-.
Council of Ministers of the German Democratic Republic, Berlin, Germany.

Scholz, Wilhelm von, PH.D.; German writer; b. 15 July 1874; ed. Berlin, Lausanne, Kiel and Munich Univs.
Producer Stuttgart Provincial Theatre 16-22; First Chair. Poetry Section of Prussian Acad. of Arts 26-28; **Pres. of the Union of German Dramatists; Dr. h.c. (Heidelberg).**
Publs. Plays: *Der Jude von Konstanz* 05, *Der Wettlauf mit dem Schatten* 22, *Die gläserne Frau* 24, *Vertauschte Seelen*, *Die Frankfurter Weihnacht* 38; *Ewige Jugend* (fairy tale) 48, etc.; novels: *Perpetua* 26, *Weg nach Ilok* 28, *Unrecht der Liebe* 31, *Berlin und Bodensee* (autobiography) 34, *Der Zufall und das Schicksal* (essays) 35, *Eine Jahrhundertwende* (2 vols. of autobiography) 36, *Die Gefährten* 37, *An Ilm und Isar* (autobiographical) 39; poems: *Lebensjahre* 39, *Die Gedichte* (complete edn.) 44, *Raum über uns* 54, *Unter den Sternen* (selection) 63, 66; aphorisms: *Irrtum und Wahrheit* 50, *Die ausgewählten Gedichte* 53; *Das Säckinger Trompeterspiel*, *Die Marquise von Rovergue* (plays) 55, *Friedrich Schiller* (biography) 56, *Das Drama* (essays) 56, *Bilder und Gestalten* 56, *Goethe in der Schweiz* (essay) 56, *Das Inwendige* (short stories) 58, *Nur Zufälle* (short story) 59, *Spanisches Welttheater* (4 plays after Calderón) 61, *Zwischenreich* (short stories) 62, *Bodensee-Dreiländersee* (travel) 63; *Mein Theater* (autobiography) 64, *Ausgewählte Schauspiele* (plays) 64, *Der Kopf im Fenster* (novel) 65, *Theodor Dorn* (novel) 67.
Villa Seeheim, Constance (Bodensee), Federal Germany. Telephone: 65429.

Schomburg, Lieut.-Gen. August, M.S. (Mechanical Engineering); American engineer and army officer; b. 3 July 1908; ed. U.S. Military Acad. and Mass. Inst. of Technology.
Six years service with Infantry after graduation; later at Aberdeen Proving Ground, Md. until 44; assigned to War Dept. Gen. Staff 44-46; Asst. Mil. Attaché, OMA, Ottawa 46-49; Dir. of Research, Development and Engineering, Watertown Arsenal, Mass. 49-52; course at Industrial Coll. of the Armed Forces 52-53; attached to G-4, H.Q., USAREUR 53-56; Asst. Chief of Ordnance, Research and Development, later Deputy Chief of Ordnance 56-59; Commanding Gen. U.S. Army Missile Command, Redstone Arsenal, Ala. 60-62; Commanding Gen. U.S. Army Supply and Maintenance Command, Washington D.C. 62-64; Commandant Industrial Coll. of the Armed Forces, Washington D.C. 63-67, Consultant 67-; Chair. Advisory Council to School of Govt. and Business, George Washington Univ., Washington D.C. 67-; Legion of Merit, Commendation Ribbon (both with Oak Leaf Cluster), Distinguished Service Medal.
1600 South Eads Street, No. 1222 South Arlington, Virginia 22202, U.S.A.
Telephone: 703-521-2454.

Schonberg, Harold C.; American music critic; b. 29 Nov. 1915; ed. Brooklyn Coll. and New York Univ. Associate Editor *American Music Lover* 46-48; Music critic *New York Sun* 46-50; Contributing Editor and Record Columnist *Musical Courier* 48-52; Music and Record Critic *New York Times* 50-60, Senior Music Critic 60-; columnist for *The Gramophone* (London) 48-60; U.S. Army service 42-46.
Publs. *The Guide to Long-Playing Records: Chamber and Solo Instrument Music* 55, *The Collector's Chopin and Schumann* 59, *The Great Pianists* 63, *The Great Conductors* 67, contributing Editor *International Cyclopedia of Music and Musicians*.
New York Times, Times Square, New York City, N.Y., U.S.A.

Schönberg, Mario; Brazilian university professor; b. 2 July 1916; ed. Univ. de São Paulo and Escola Politecnica of Univ. de São Paulo.
Instructor in Physics, Polytechnic, São Paulo 36; Asst. Prof. Theoretical Physics, Univ. of São Paulo 37; worked in Rome, Zürich, Coll. de France, Paris, Washington D.C., Princeton Univ., and Yerkes Observatory 38-42; returned to Brazil 42-48, 53-; Prof. of Pure, Celestial and Higher Mechanics, Univ. of São Paulo 44-, Prof. of Quantum Mechanics 44-62, Dir. Dept. of Physics 53-61; with Free Univ. of Brussels 48-53; mem. Brazilian Acad. of Sciences 42.
Publs. 80 papers on theoretical, mathematical and experimental physics and astrophysics, and pure mathematics; articles on art criticism.
Universidade de São Paulo, Caixa Postal 9105, São Paulo; Home: Rua São Vicente de Paulo 501, Apto. 105, São Paulo, Brazil.

Schonell, Sir Fred Joyce, Kt., PH.D., D.LIT.; Australian educationist; b. 3 Aug. 1900; ed. Perth Modern School, Univ. of Western Australia.
Research, Educ. Psychology, King's Coll., London and Inst. of Educ., London 28-31; Lecturer, Educ. Psychology, Goldsmith's Coll., London 31-42; Sessional Lecturer, Comparative Educ., Inst. of Educ. 40-45; Prof. of Educ., Univ. Coll. Swansea 42; Prof. of Educ., Univ. of Birmingham 46-50, Univ. of Queensland 50-59, Pres. of Professional Board 56-59, Vice-Chancellor 60-; Hon. D.Litt. (Univ. of Western Australia) 63; Hon. LL.D. (Univ. of Sydney) 65; Hon. F.B.Ps.S., F.A.C.E.
Publs. *Essentials in Teaching and Testing Spelling* 32, *Education of the 'C' Child (Year Book of Education)*, 35, *Diagnostic Tests* 36, *Diagnostic Arithmetic Tests* 37, *Essential Intelligence Test* 40, *Backwardness in the Basic Subjects* 42, *The Psychology and Teaching of Reading* 45, *Diagnostic and Attainment Testing* 49, *Essential Arithmetic Tests* 49, *Practice in Basic Arithmetic* 54, *Diagnosis and Remedial Teaching in Arithmetic* 57, *The Subnormal Child at Home* 59, *Happy Venture Teacher's Manual* 60, *Promise and Performance —Student Progress at University Level* (with others) 62, *The Slow Learner* (with others) 62, *Failure in School* (with others) 62.
University of Queensland, Brisbane, Australia.

Schöner, Josef Andreas Carl, LL.D., DR. RER.POL.; Austrian diplomatist; b. 18 Feb. 1904; ed. Vienna Univ. Service in Austrian law courts; Foreign Service 33-; Attaché, Washington 34; Ministry of Foreign Affairs 34-38; dismissed 38; worked for private firms 38-41; war service 41-45; returned to Foreign Service 45; Counsellor, London 47-48, Washington 48-50; Chief, Austrian Liason Offices, Bonn 50-52; Minister, Bonn 52-53; Dir., Political Affairs Dept., Foreign Office 53-55; Sec.-Gen. Foreign Affairs 55-58; Ambassador to Fed. German Repub. 58-66; Amb. to U.K. 66-; Grosses Silbernes Ehrenzeichen mit Stern; Grand Officer Legion of

Honour; Grand Crosses, Germany; Hon. G.C.V.O. 66; Order Knights of Malta, etc.
Austrian Embassy, 18 Belgrave Square, London, S.W.1, England.
Telephone: 01-235-3731.

Schonland, Sir Basil Ferdinand Jamieson, Kt., M.A., PH.D., F.R.S., C.B.E.; South African physicist; b. 5 Feb. 1896; ed. St. Andrews Coll. and Rhodes Univ. Coll. Grahamstown and Gonville and Caius Coll. Cambridge. Lecturer, later Prof. of Physics Univ. of Cape Town 22-37; Dir. Bernard Price Inst. of Geophysics and Carnegie Price Prof. of Geophysics Witwatersrand Univ. 37-54; Dep. Dir. Atomic Energy Research Establishment, Harwell 54-58, Dir. 58-60; Dir. of Research Group of which Harwell forms a part 60-61 (retd.); Halley Lecturer Oxford 37; Supt. Army Operation Research Group, Ministry of Supply 41-44; Brigadier (Scientific Adviser) to C.-in-C. 21st Army Group B.L.A. 44; Pres. S.A. Council Scientific and Industrial Research 45-50; Chree Lecturer Physical Society of London 43; F.R.S. South Africa; Hughes Medal 45; Elliott-Cresson Medal Franklin Inst. of Philadelphia 50; Faraday Medal of Inst. of Electrical Engineers 62; Chancellor Rhodes Univ. 51-63, Pro-Chancellor Univ. of Southampton 60; Hon. Sc.D. (Cambridge, Cape Town, Rhodes, Southampton); Hon. LL.D. (Natal); Hon. Fellow Gonville and Caius Coll. 59.
Publs. *Atmospheric Electricity* 32, *The Lightning Discharge* (Halley Lecture) 37, *The Flight of Thunderbolts* 50, *The Atomists 1805-1933* 68.
The Down House, Shawford, near Winchester, Hants, England.
Telephone: Twyford 2221.

Schorer, Mark, PH.D., LL.D.; American writer and teacher; b. 17 May 1908; ed. Univ. of Wisconsin and Harvard Univ.
Briggs-Copeland Faculty Instructor, Harvard Univ. 40-45; Assoc. Prof. of English Univ. of Calif., Berkeley 45-47, Prof. of English 47-, Chair. Dept. of English 60-65; Fulbright Lecturer, Univ. of Pisa 52-53, Univ. of Rome 63.
Publs. *William Blake: The Politics of Vision* 46, *The State of Mind: Thirty-Two Stories* 47, *The Wars of Love* (novel) 54, *Sinclair Lewis: An American Life* 61, *The World We Imagine: Selected Essays* 68.
68 Tamalpais Road, Berkeley 94708, Calif., U.S.A.
Telephone: 415-848-8789.

Schotman, Johan Wilhelm, M.D.; Netherlands psychiatrist, philosopher, poet and writer; b. 10 March 1892; ed. Leyden Univ.
Practised as Physician 19-21; Hydrographic Expedition to Lunghai Railroad, China 21-27; Asst. Psychiatrist, Santpoort Mental Hospital 27-28: Psychiatrist, Maasoord Mental Hospital, near Rotterdam 28-37; Practice as Consultant Psychiatrist Gouda 37-39, Bussum 39-48; retd.; Pres. Nederlandsche Vertalingen Society 31-; Dir. Zwolle Historical Museum 54-62; mem. Neths. Soc. of Literature, P.E.N. Club; Pres. Zwolle Branch Dickens Fellowship; Dir. Art School "Gerard Terborch", retd.
Publs. Poetry: *Der Geesten Gemoeting* 27, *Cloisonné* 36, *Hellevaart* 47; Philosophy and Psychology: *De schone gave* 27, *Naar open water* 36, *Jodulphus en de Kater* 39, *De macht tot Vrijheid* 46, *China Ongereed* 41; Prose: *Het Vermolmde Boeddhabeeld* I 27, II 28, III 29, *Wind in Bamboestengels* 46, *Arcadië en Asfalt*; Essays: *Analysen en Retouches* 53; and several other works; transalations of about 38 works from English, French and German.
Willemskade 11, Zwolle, Netherlands.

Schöttle, Erwin; German politician; b. 18 Oct. 1899.
Former employee in printing trade; later became a journalist; emigrated to Switzerland 33, later to U.K.; in German Service of B.B.C. 41-46; later became a leading member of Social Democratic Party, Württemberg; mem. Bundestag 49-, Vice-Pres. 61-.
Bundestag, Bonn, German Federal Republic.

Schoutheete de Tervarent, Guy A. W. M. J. de; DR. JUR.; Belgian diplomatist; b. 25 April 1891.
Various foreign service appointments in The Hague 19, Tokyo 21, Peking 23, Vienna 25, Rome 26, Bucharest 28, Berlin 28, Budapest 33, Cairo 38; Minister to Denmark 45-52; Ambassador to Japan 52-56; mem. Belgian Acad.
Publs. *La Légende de Ste. Ursule dans la littérature et l'art du Moyen Age* 31, *Le diptyque de St. Bertin au Musée de Dijon* 31, *Les énigmes de l'art* (4 vols.) 36-52, *Attributs et symboles dans l'art profane 1450-1600* (2 vols.) 58-59, *De la Méthode Iconologique* 61.
12 rue Emile Claus, Brussels, Belgium.

Schouwenaar-Franssen, Johanna Frederika; Netherlands teacher and politician; b. 3 May 1909; ed. Univ. of Leyden.
Teacher of classics; mem. Rotterdam Town Council, Benelux Parl. Conf., European Parl.; mem. Parl. (First Chamber); Minister of Social Welfare 63-65; Liberal; Knight Order of Neths. Lion.
24 Beethovenlaan, Bilthoven, Netherlands.
Telephone: 03402-3623.

Schramm, Percy Ernst, DR.PHIL.; German historian; b. 14 Oct. 1894; ed. Realgymnasium, Hamburg, and Univs. of Marburg, Heidelberg, etc.
Privatdozent, Heidelberg 24; Prof. of Medieval and Modern History, Univ. of Göttingen 29-64; mem. Acads. of Göttingen, Munich, Vienna, Stockholm, Spoleto and Medieval Acad. of America; Chancellor Chapter "Pour le Mérite".
Publs. *Kaiser, Rom und Renovatio* 29, *Geschichte des englischen Königtums* 37, *Der König von Frankreich* 39, *Hamburg, Deutschland und die Welt* 52, *Herrschaftzeichen und Staatssymbolik* (3 vols.) 54-56, *Sphaira, Globus, Reichsapfel* 58, *Denkmale der deutschen Könige und Kaiser* 62, *Neun Generationen* 63-64 (2 vols.).
Herzberger Landstrasse 66, 34 Göttingen, German Federal Republic.
Telephone: 0551-57113.

Schramm, Wilbur, A.M., PH.D., LITT.D.; American educationist; b. 5 Aug. 1907; ed. Marietta Coll., and Harvard and Iowa Univs.
Newspaper reporter and desk editor, corresp. of Associated Press 24-30; Asst. Prof., Assoc. Prof. and later Prof. of English, Univ. of Iowa 35-41; Editor, Harcourt, Brace & Co. (publishers) 41; Dir. of educational services, U.S. Office of War Information 42-43; Educational Consultant to Navy Dept. 43; Educational Adviser to War Department 43-46; Dir. School of Journalism, Univ. of Iowa 43-47; Asst. to the Pres. Dir. Inst. of Communications Research, Dir. Univ. Press, and Prof. of Communications, Univ. of Ill. 47-55, Dean, Div. of Communications 50-55; Prof. Communications Stanford Univ. 55-, Dir. Inst. for Communication Research 58-; Janet M. Peck Prof. of Int. Communications 62, Prof. of Educ. 67-; Chair. U.S. Nat. Council on Research in Journalism; Fellow Center for Advanced Study in the Behavioral Sciences 59-60; mem. Editorial Board *Public Opinion Quarterly, Journalism Quarterly* and *Communications Review*.
Publs. *Approaches to a Science of English Verse* 35, *American Medley* (stories) 37, *Francis Parkman* 38, *Literary Scholarship* 41, *Windwagon Smith and Other Yarns* 47, *The Lost Train* 48, *The Reds Take a City* 51; Editor: *The Story Workshop* 39, *Two Creative Traditions* 40, *American Literature* 46, *Iowa Studies in Newspaper Reading* 46-47, *Communications in Modern Society* 48, *Process and Effects of Mass Communication* 54, *Four Theories of The Press* 56, *Responsibility in Mass Communications* 57, *One day in the World's Press* 59, *The Impact of Educational Television* 60, *Television in*

the Lives of our Children 61, *The Science of Human Communication* 63, *The People Look at Educational Television* 63, *Mass Media and National Development* 64, *Communication and Change in the Developing Countries* 66, *The New Media: Memo to Educational Planners* 67. 1518 Hamilton, Palo Alto, Calif. 94303; Office: Institute for Communication Research, Stanford University, Stanford, Calif. 94305, U.S.A.
Telephone: 415-325-7373 (Home); 415-321-2300 (Office).

Schram-Nielsen, Erik, PH.D.; Danish diplomatist; b. 6 June 1911; ed. Metropolitan School, Copenhagen and Univ. of Copenhagen.
Entered Foreign Service 36; studied in the Middle East 37-38; Deputy Under-Sec. of State, Ministry of Foreign Affairs 59-61; Perm. Rep. to NATO 61-66; Ambassador to France 66-.
Publ. *System of Damages in Islamic Law* 45.
Danish Embassy, Avenue Marceau 77, Paris 16e, France.

Schröder, Dr. Gerhard; German lawyer and politician; b. 11 Sept. 1910; ed. Kaiser-Wilhelm-Gymnasium in Trier and Univs. of Königsberg, Edinburgh, Berlin and Bonn.
Asst. Law Faculty Bonn Univ. and Kaiser-Wilhelm Inst. for Int. Private Law, Berlin 33-36; practice in Berlin 36-39; served 39-45 war; served *Land* Govt. Nordrhein-Westfalen 45-47; mem. post-war Comm. on Electoral Law; practice in Düsseldorf since 47; concerned with reorganisation of mining and iron and steel industries 47-53; mem. (Christian Democratic Union) Federal Parl. 49-; mem. Central Exec. Cttee. CDU; Chair. Protestant Working Group CDU/CSU; Minister of the Interior 53-61, of Foreign Affairs 61-66, of Defence 66-.
Publ. *Decision for Europe* 64.
Hardthöhe, Bonn, German Federal Republic.
Telephone: 20161.

Schröder, Gerhard, German public servant; b. 3 March 1921; ed. Marburg Univ.
Officer, Radio, Film and Press Affairs, Ministry of Education, Lower Saxony 52-59; Head of Arts Dept., Ministry of Education, Lower Saxony 60-61; mem. Admin. Council, North German Radio 55-61; Vice-Chair. Board of Governors, Norddeutsches Werbefernsehen G.m.b.H. 58-64; Dir. Gen. Norddeutscher Rundfunk (North German Radio) 61-.
Rothenbaumchausse 132-134, 2 Hamburg 13, German Federal Republic.
Telephone: 44-19-31.

Schroder, Helmut William Bruno; British banker; b. 18 Jan. 1901; ed. Eton and Corpus Christi Coll., Oxford.
Partner, J. Henry Schroder and Co., Merchant Bankers 26-57; Chair. J. Henry Schroder and Co. Ltd. 57-62; Chair. Schroders Ltd. 59-65; Dir. J. Henry Schroder Wagg and Co. Ltd. 62-65; Pres. Schroders Ltd. 66-.
120 Cheapside, London, E.C.2; Home: Flat 23, 51 South Street, London, W.1, England.
Telephone: 01-588-4000.

Schröder, Kurt, DR. PHIL.; German mathematician; b. 31 July 1909; ed. Friedrich-Wilhelms Universität, Berlin.
Lecturer, Berlin 40; Prof. of Applied Mathematics and Dir. Mathematical Inst., Humboldt Universität zu Berlin 46-, Pro-Rector for Research 51, Rector of Univ. 59-65; mem. E. Berlin Acad. of Sciences 52-; mem. Research Council of Council of Ministers of D.D.R. 57-; Pres. Mathematical Soc. of D.D.R. 63-; Vaterländischer Verdienstorden in Gold.
Humboldt-Universität zu Berlin, Unter den Linden 6, Berlin, Germany.

Schroeder, Hermann; German composer; b. 26 March 1904; ed. Universität Innsbruck and Musikhochschule Köln.
Teacher, Rheinische Musikschule, Cologne 30-38; Organist, Trier Cathedral 38, Head of City Music Acad., Trier 40-46; Teacher, Musikhochschule, Cologne 46-48, Prof. 48-; Lecturer, Univ. of Bonn 46-, Univ. of Cologne 56-61; Acting Dir. of Musikhochschule, Cologne 58-61; Leader, Cologne Bach Soc. 47-61; Robert Schumann Prize (City of Düsseldorf) 52; Arts Prize (Rheinland-Pfalz. Province) 56; Order of Gregory the Great.
Compositions include: organ music, operatic and orchestral music.
5 Köln-Bayenthal, Bernhardstrasse 145, German Federal Republic.
Telephone: 0221-386338.

Schryver, August-Edmond de; Belgian lawyer and politician; b. 16 May 1898; ed. Ghent Univ.
Advocate Ghent Court of Appeal 21; mem. of Parl. 28-65; Minister of Agriculture 35, of the Interior 36, of Justice 39, of Econ. Affairs 40; mem. Belgian Govt. in Exile, London 42-44; Deputy Prime Minister 44; Acting Chair. Belgian Del. San Francisco Conf. 45; Founder and First Pres. Christian Social Party 45-49; Chair. European Union Christian Democrats (N.E.I.) 49-59; Minister for African Affairs 59-60; Minister of State; Chair. Belgian Cttee. Volunteers Overseas.
Kwaadham 36, Ghent, Belgium.

Schuh, Oscar Fritz; German theatre director; b. 15 Jan. 1904.
Theatrical work, Augsburg, Oldenburg, Osnabrück, Darmstadt, Gera, Prague; Staatsoper, Hamburg, later Vienna; Dir. Theater am Kurfürstendamm, Berlin 53-58; Dir. City Theatres, Cologne 59-63; Dir. Deutsches Schauspielhaus Hamburg 63-68.
Harvesthuderweg 19, Hamburg 13, German Federal Republic.

Schultz, Adolph H., PH.D.; Swiss university professor; b. 14 Nov. 1891; ed. Univ. of Zürich.
Research Assoc. of Carnegie Inst. of Washington, Dept. of Embryology 16-25; Assoc. Prof. of Physical Anthropology, Johns Hopkins Univ. 25-50; Prof. of Anthropology and Dir. of Anthropological Inst., Univ. of Zürich 51-62, Prof. Emer. 62-; mem. Nat. Acad. of Sciences (U.S.A.), American Philosophical Soc.; Foreign Fellow, Zoological Society of London; Hon. mem. Anatomical Soc. of Great Britain and Ireland, Soc. d'Anthropologie de Paris, New York Acad. of Sciences, Soc. for Study of Human Biology, corresp. mem. German and Italian Anthropological Socs., Austrian Acad. of Sciences; Dr. h.c. Univ. of Basle.
Publs. *The Life of Primates* 68, *Handbook of Primatology* 56-68 (co-editor).
Anthropologisches Institut, Sempersteig 3, Zürich; Home: Dolderstrasse 81, Zürich 7, Switzerland.

Schultze, Charles Louis, PH.D.; American economist and government official; b. 12 Dec. 1924; ed. Georgetown Univ. and Univ. of Maryland.
U.S. Army 43-46; Admin. Asst. Democratic Nat. Cttee. 48; Research Specialist, Army Security Agency 48-49; Instructor, Coll. of St. Thomas (St. Paul, Minn.) 49-51; Economist, Office of Price Stabilization 51-52, Council of Econ. Advisers 52-53, 55-59, Machine and Allied Products Inst. 53-54; Assoc. Prof. of Econs., Indiana Univ. 59-61; Prof. of Econs., Univ. of Maryland 61-62, 68-; Asst. Dir., Bureau of the Budget 62-65, Dir. 65-Jan. 68.
Publs. *Recent Inflation in the United States* 59, *Prices, Costs and Output for the Postwar Decade* 59, *National Income Analysis* 64.
Home: 5826 Nevada Avenue, N.W., Washington, D.C. 20015, U.S.A.

Schuman, Frederick Lewis, PH.D.; American political scientist; b. 22 Feb. 1904; ed. Chicago Univ.
Instructor in Political Science, Chicago Univ. 27-32; Fellow Acad. Political and Social Science Berlin 33; Prof. Williams Coll. 36-, Woodrow Wilson Prof. of Govt. 38-; Fellow Social Science Research Council 29-30, American Acad. Political and Social Science 33; mem. American Political Science Asscn., American Society Int. Law; Principal Political Analyst, Foreign Broadcast Intelligence Service, Fed. Communications Comm. 42-43; Visiting Lecturer in Int. Relations, Harvard 38, California 39 and 55. Cornell 44, Columbia 46, Chicago 56, Central Wash. Coll. 59, Portland State Coll. 61, Stanford 63, Hawaii 63.
Publs. *American Policy toward Russia since 1917* 28, *War and Diplomacy in the French Republic* 31, *International Politics* 33, *Conduct of German Foreign Affairs* 34, *Rotary?* 34, *Hitler and the Nazi Dictatorship* 35, *Germany since 1918* 37, *Europe on the Eve* 39, *Night Over Europe* 41, *Design for Power* 42, *Soviet Politics* 46, *The Commonwealth of Man* 52, *Russia since 1917* 57, *International Politics* 58, *Government in the Soviet Union* 61, *The Cold War: Retrospect and Prospect* 62.
Williams College, Williamstown, Mass., U.S.A.

Schuman, William Howard; B.S., M.A.; American musician; b. 4 Aug. 1910; ed. Columbia Univ. and privately.
Lecturer and Dir. of Chorus, Sarah Lawrence Coll., Bronxville 35-45; Dir. of Publications, G. Schirmer Inc. 45-51; Pres. Juilliard School of Music 45-61; Pres. Lincoln Center for the Performing Arts 62-; Honorary doctorates from Chicago Musical Coll., Univ. of Wisconsin, Philadelphia Conservatory of Music, Cincinnati Coll. of Music, Columbia Univ., Hartt Coll. of Music, Colgate Univ., Allegheny Coll., New York Univ., Brandeis Univ., Oberlin Coll., Adelphi Coll., Northwestern Univ., Bates Coll. and others; Hon. mem. Royal Acad. of Music; Pulitzer Prize for Music, Guggenheim Fellowships, Award of Nat. Inst. of Arts and Letters, League of Composers Award, New York Critics Circle Award and Award of Merit of Nat. Assscn. of American Composers and Conductors.
Compositions include: nine symphonies, four string quartets, *"Amaryllis" Variation for String Trio, American Festival Overture, Credendum, New England Triptych, Circus Overture, Concerto for Piano and Orchestra, Concerto for Violin and Orchestra, A Song of Orpheus* fantasy for 'cello and orchestra, *The Witch of Endor,* secular cantatas and music for ballets, band works and piano music.
Lincoln Center for the Performing Arts Inc., 1865 Broadway, New York City 23, N.Y., U.S.A.

Schumann, Horst, German politician; b. 6 Feb. 1924; ed. elementary school.
Former piano-maker, fmr. mem. Kommunistische Partei Deutschlands; mem. Sozialistische Einheitspartei Deutschlands; (S.E.D.) 45-; District Sec. Freie Deutsche Jugend (F.D.J.), Leipzig 47-48; Sec. for Pioneer Questions in Saxon F.D.J. 49-50; First Sec. Saxon F.D.J. 50-52; First Sec. F.D.J. District Headquarters 52-55; mem. Bureau of Cen. Cttee. of F.D.J. 55-, Cen. Cttee. S.E.D. 59-; First Sec. Cen. Cttee. F.D.J. 59-; mem. State Council 60-, Volkskammer 63-; Freie Deutsche Jugend, Unter den Linden 36-38, Berlin W.8, Germany.

Schumann, Maurice; French writer and politician; b. 10 April 1911.
With Havas News Agency 32-40; Chief Official Broadcaster, B.B.C. French Service 40-44; Liaison Officer with Allied Expeditionary Forces from D-Day until liberation of Paris; mem. of French Provisional Consultative Assembly Nov. 44-July 45; mem. of both Constituent Assemblies Oct. 45-May 46 and June-Nov. 46; Chair. of Popular Republican Movement (M.R.P.)

45-49; Deputy for Nord 45-; Sec. of State for Foreign Affairs 51-54; Pres. Foreign Affairs Comm. of Nat. Assembly 59; Minister of State attached to the Prime Minister's Office (Territorial Planning) April-May 62; Minister of State for Scientific Research April 67-May 68; Minister of Social Affairs May 68-; chief contrib. (as editorial writer) to *L'Aube* (Paris daily paper); Compagnon de la Libération; Chevalier Légion d'Honneur, Order of Léopold; Croix de Guerre.
Publs. *Le germanisme en marche* 38, *Mussolini* 39, *Les problèmes ukrainiens et la paix européenne* 39, *Honneur et Patrie* 46, *Le vrai malaise des intellectuels de gauche* 57, *Le Rendezvous avec quelqu'un* (novel) 61; *La voix du couvre-feu* (novel) 64.
53 avenue Maréchal-Lyautey, Paris 16e, France.

Schürer, Gerhard; German politician; b. 1921.
Former machine fitter; mem. Sozialistische Einheitspartei Deutschlands (S.E.D.) 48-; Dept. Head for Planning, Dept. of Planning and Finance, Central Cttee. of S.E.D. 55-61, Head of Dept. of Planning and Finance 61-62; Deputy Chair. State Planning Comm. 62-63, First Deputy Chair. 63-65, Chair. 65-; mem. Council of Ministers 63-; mem. Central Cttee. of S.E.D. 63-.
State Planning Commission, Berlin, Germany.

Schürmann, Carl Willem Alwin, LL.M.; Netherlands lawyer and diplomatist; b. 6 Jan. 1903; ed. Leiden Univ. and Lincoln's Inn, London.
Barrister-at-Law, Rotterdam 24-40; Head Legal Dept., Netherlands Shipping and Trading Cttee., London 40-44; Prosecutor Netherlands Maritime Court, London 41-44; Mil. Gov. Province of Limburg 44-45, Province of North Holland 45; Head Legal Dept., Netherlands Mil. Mission to Germany 45-46; Counsellor of Legation, Warsaw 46-48; Minister to Thailand 48-50; Deputy High Commr., Indonesia 50-52; Dir.-Gen. Indonesian Affairs, Ministry of Foreign Affairs 52-55; Permanent Rep. to UN 55-64; Pres. Int. Conf. on Protection of Cultural Property in the Event of Armed Conflict 54, Int. Trade Arbitration Conf. of U.N. 58; Vice-Pres. Gen. Assembly UN 58, 61; Chair. Cttee. on Revision of Admin. Tribunal Judgements of UN 59; UN Cttee. on Information from Non-Self-Governing Territories 61; Pres. Econ. and Social Council of the UN 60, UN Conf. for the adoption of a Single Convention on Narcotic Drugs 61; Pres. Political and Security Cttee., 18th Assembly 63; Pres. Int. Conf. on Uniform Law of Sale 64; Ambassador to U.S.A. 64-; Knight, Order of the Lion, Commdr. Order of Orange Nassau (Netherlands), Officer Legion of Merit (U.S.A.), etc.
Publs. Books and articles on Netherlands and International Law.
2347 S. Street, N.W., Washington, D.C., U.S.A.

Schuschnigg, Kurt von; Austrian politician and professor; b. 14 Dec. 1897; ed. Fribourg and Innsbruck.
Attorney at Law; Deputy 27; Founder and Chief of *Ostmärkische Sturmscharen,* patriotic organisation for defence of Austrian independence; Min. of Justice in Buresch Cabinet Jan. May 32 and in Dollfuss Cabinet May 32-July 34, also of Education Sept. 33-July 34; Federal Chancellor after assassination of Dollfuss July 34; Chancellor, Min. of Defence and Foreign Affairs 36-38; Min. for Public Security 37; fmr. mem. Christian Social Party; Leader of Patriotic Front May 36-38; arrested after Nazi Putsch Mar. 38; imprisoned; liberated by Allied Advance May 45; Prof. Political Science, St. Louis Univ., Mo. 48-68.
Publs. *Farewell Austria* 38, *Austrian Requiem* 47.
Mutters, near Innsbruck, Austria.

Schut, Willem Frederik; Netherlands civil engineer and politician; b. 21 Aug. 1920; ed. Secondary School, Amsterdam and Technological Inst., Delft.
Planner, Inst. for Town and Country Planning, South Holland 43, Deputy Dir. 45-46, Dir. Jan. 46-67; Private

Planning Consultant, Middleburg 56-67; Minister of Housing and Physical Planning April 67-; Bronze Cross 46; Grand Cross in Order of Merit of Luxembourg 67.
Ministry of Housing and Physical Planning, Van Alkemadelaan 85, The Hague; Home: Adrianalaan 161, Rotterdam, Netherlands.

Schütz, Klaus; German politician; b. 17 Sept. 1926; ed. Paulsen-Real-Gymnasium, Humboldt Univ. zu Berlin and Harvard Univ., U.S.A.
War service, seriously wounded 44-45; Asst., Inst. für Politische Wissenschaften, Freie Univ., Berlin 51; mem. City Assembly 54-57; mem. Bundestag 57-61; Liaison Senator between Berlin Senate and Bonn Govt. 61-66; mem. Bundesrat 61-, Pres. 67-; Under-Sec. Ministry of Foreign Affairs 66-67; Governing Mayor of West Berlin 67-; Chair. Berlin Social Democratic Party 68-.
Berlin 31, Johannisberger Strasse 34, Germany.
Telephone: 7801-3300.

Schütz, Paul, DR. RER. POL.; German banker; b. 27 June 1910; ed. Univs. of Würzburg, Berlin and Freiburg im Breisgau.
Industrial posts 36-46; Chair. of Management Board of a credit house 47-61; Pres. of Saarland Asscn. of Savings and Deposit Banks 55-61; Pres. of Landes-zentralbank im Saarland 61-; mem. of Board of Deutsche Bundesbank, Frankfurt.
Willi-Graf-Strasse 30, 66 Saarbrücken 3, German Federal Republic.

Schuurmans, Constant; Belgian diplomatist; b. 8 Dec. 1914; ed. St. Thomas School, Louvain.
Foreign Service 46-; Second Sec., later First Sec., Paris 48-52; Sec. to Sec.-Gen. of Ministry of Foreign Affairs 52-58; Chef de Cabinet, Ministry of Foreign Affairs 58-61; Minister to Greece 61-62, Ambassador to Greece 62-65; Perm. Rep. to UN 65-.
Permanent Mission of Belgium to the United Nations, 809 United Nations Plaza, New York, N.Y. 10017, U.S.A.

Schuyler, Gen. Cortlandt Van Rennsselaer; American army officer; b. 22 Dec. 1900; ed. U.S. Mil. Acad. and Command and Gen. Staff School.
Served Coast Artillery 22-27; Instructor in Maths. U.S. Mil. Acad. 27; retd. Coast Artillery 31; Prov. Marshal Chesapeake Bay 34; Grad. Coast Artillery School 36, Command and Staff School 37; office of Chief Coast Artillery 39; Exec. Officer, later Asst. Chief of Staff, H.Q. Anti-Aircraft Comm. 42; Chief of Staff 43; C.O. Anti-Aircraft Artillery Training Centre 43; Chief U.S. Mil. Rep. Control Comm. for Romania 44; U.S. Gen. Staff Appts. 47-51; assigned to SHAPE 51; C.G. 28th Infantry Div. 53; Chief of Staff SHAPE 53-59 (retd.); Exec. Asst. to Gov. of N.Y. State 59-63; Commr. of Gen. Services 60-; Distinguished Service Medal, Legion of Merit, Commdr. Légion d'Honneur.
143 Washington Avenue, Albany, N.Y., U.S.A.
Telephone: 518-GRidley 4-5982.

Schwab, J(acob) W(alter); American executive; b. March 1892.
Stock clerk Sol Friedman & Co. 08-12; clerk Cohen-Hall-Marx & Co. New York City 12-23, Sec. 23-27, Dir. 27-, Treas. and Dir. 27-38, Pres. and Dir. 38-46, Chair. and Dir. 46-65; Pres. Leonard Securities Corpn.; Pres. United Merchants and Manufacturers Inc. 39-59, Chair. 59-; Pres. Montefiore Hospital and Medical Center 63-66.
Home: 930 Fifth Avenue; Office: 1407 Broadway, New York City, N.Y., U.S.A.

Schwabe, Kurt, DR. ING. HABIL.; German engineer; b. 29 May 1905.
Teacher, Technische Hochschule Dresden 33-, Prof. of Physical and Electrical Chemistry 49-, Rector (now Technische Universität Dresden) 61-65; mem. German Acad. of Sciences, E. Berlin, Saxon Acad. of Sciences,

Leipzig (now Pres.); Nat. Prize (First Class), Order of Banner of Labour, Hero of Labour; Dr. rer. nat. h.c.
Technische Universität Dresden, Mommsenstrasse 13, 8027 Dresden, German Democratic Republic.

Schwalb López Aldana, Fernando; Peruvian politician; b. 26 Aug. 1916.
Minister of Foreign Affairs July 63-Sept. 65, Prime Minister Jan. 64-Sept. 65; Pres. Banco Central de Reserva del Peru 66-Sept. 67; Partido Acción Popular.
Jirón Carabaya 940- Of. 201, Lima, Peru.
Telephone: 81-0-20.

Schwartz, Abba Philip, B.S., LL.B.; American lawyer and government official; b. 17 April 1916; ed. George-town and Harvard Univs.
Member, law firm; mem. District of Columbia Bar 40-; fmr. Dir. of Reparations, UN Int. Refugee Org.; Administrator Bureau of Security and Consular Affairs State Dept. 62-66; Gov. American Red Cross 63-.
c/o Department of State, Washington, D.C., U.S.A.

Schwartz, Sven Gustav, M.SC., PH.D.; Swedish mining engineer; b. 25 Oct. 1891; ed. Royal Inst. of Technology.
Mining engineer in Swedish and American enterprises 16-28; Man. Mining Dept. Compagnie Franco-Malgache d'Entreprises, Madagascar 28-32; Man. Skånska Cementaktiebolaget 33-36, Bolidens Gruvaktiebolag 36-41; Man. Dir. AB Stockholms Bryggerier 41-49; Managing Director, Bolidens Gruvaktiebolag 49-59, Chair. Board of Dirs. 59-; Pres. State Industrial Comm. 42-46; Pres. Royal Swedish Acad. of Engineering Sciences 53-55; Chair. Swedish Employers' Fed. 47-51 and 54-; Chair. Swedish Brewers' Asscn. 48-; mem. Board Fed. of Swedish Industries 43-, Skandinaviska Banken 43-63, Skånska Cement AB 47-, AB Iföverken 47-, Uddeholms AB 49-; mem. Royal Swedish Acad. of Mil. Sciences; Grand Cross North Star, etc.
c/o Bolidens Gruvaktiebolag, Sturegatan 22, Stockholm; Home: Strandvägen 19, Djursholm, Sweden.

Schwarz, Rudolf; British conductor; b. 29 April 1905; ed. in Vienna.
Conductor, Opera House, Düsseldorf 23-27, Opera House, Karlsruhe 27-33; worked for Jewish Cultural Organisation in Berlin 36-41; Conductor, Bournemouth Municipal Orchestra 47-51, City of Birmingham Symphony Orchestra 51-57; Conductor-in-Chief B.B.C. Symphony Orchestra 57-62; Conductor "Harmonien's" Symphony Orchestra, Bergen and Northern Sinfonia Orchestra, Newcastle-upon-Tyne 64-.
24 Wildcroft Manor, London, S.W.15, England.

Schwarz, Štefan, Dr. rer. Nat., D.SC.; Czechoslovak mathematician; b. 18 May 1914; ed. Universita Karlova, Prague.
Assistant, Charles Univ., Prague 37; Docent, Univ. of Bratislava 45; Professor, Technical Univ., Bratislava 47-; mem. Czechoslovak Acad. of Sciences 60-, Vice-Pres. 65-; mem. Slovak Acad. of Sciences 53-, Vice-Pres. 58-65, Pres. 65-; Dir. Mathematical Inst. 63-; mem. Central Cttee. of C.P. of Czechoslovakia and of Slovakia 66-; State Prize 55; Order of Labour 64.
Publs. Three books and about 75 papers, mostly in algebra and number theory, in particular on theory of semi-groups.
Porubského 10, Bratislava, Czechoslovakia.

Schwarz-Bart, André; French writer; b. 28; ed. Sorbonne.
In Resistance Movement, Second World War; worked as factory hand and porter at Les Halles; Prix Gon-court 59; Jerusalem Prize 67.
Publs. *Le Dernier des Justes* 59, *Un plat de porc aux bananes vertes* (with Simone Schwarz-Bart) 67.
c/o Editions du Seuil, 27 rue Jacob, Paris 16e, France.

Schwarzenberg, Johannes Erkinger, G.C.V.O., DR. JUR.; Austrian diplomatist; b. 31 Jan. 1903; ed. Univ. of Vienna.

Joined Civil Service 27, and later Diplomatic Service; Attaché Rome 33, Berlin 36; left Diplomatic Service 38; Del. and Dir. Int. Cttee. of the Red Cross Geneva 40-46; re-entered Austrian Diplomatic Service 46; Counsellor Paris 46; Political Rep. and Minister to Italy 47-52, Ambassador 52-55; Ambassador to Great Britain 55-65, to the Vatican 65-.
Austrian Embassy, Via Reno 9, Rome, Italy.

Schwarzenstein, Franz F.; German travel executive; b. o6; ed. private study.
Chief, Press Dept. of Reichbahnzentrale für den Deutschen Reiseverkehr (German Central Office for Tourism), Berlin 28-45; Army Service 39-45; Editor-in-Chief, Radio Station Südwestfunk, Baden-Baden 46-49; Chief of Press and Public Relations Dept. Deutsche Zentrale für Fremdenverkehr (German Central Tourist Asscn.) 49-, Deputy Exec. Dir. 55-; Editor-in-Chief *Deutschland Revue* (quarterly), *Der Fremdenverkehr* (monthly); Pres. German Comm. of Int. Acad. of Tourism.
Deutsche Zentrale für Fremdenverkehr, Beethovenstrasse 69, Frankfurt/Main, German Federal Republic.

Schwarzhaupt, Elisabeth, D.IUR.; German politician; b. 7 Jan. 1901; ed. Frankfurt and Berlin Univ.
Judge, Frankfurt and Dortmund, dismissed by Nazis 33; Legal Adviser, German Fed. of Pensioners 34-36; Legal Adviser, Central Board of Evangelical Church in Germany 36-; Legal Adviser, Foreign Office, Evangelical Church 48-; mem. Bundestag 53-; Minister of Public Health 61-66; mem. Comm. of Laity, World Council of Churches; Christian Democrat.
Home: Ziegenhainer Strasse 19, 6 Frankfurt/Main-Eschersheim, German Federal Republic.
Telephone: Frankfurt/M. 522891.

Schwarzkopf, Elisabeth (wife of Walter Legge); German singer; b. 9 Dec. 1915; ed. Berlin Conservatoire and in England.
Played in *Parsifal* 38, as Zerbinetta in *Ariadne auf Naxos* 41; sang at inauguration of post-war Bayreuth Festival; since 47 principal soprano at Vienna State Opera, La Scala Milan, Covent Garden, San Francisco; Metropolitan Opera, N.Y. 64-66; regular guest singer, Salzburg Festival; created Anne Trulove in Stravinsky's *Rake's Progress*; principal roles include Contessa, *Le nozze di Figaro*, Marschallin, *Rosenkavalier*, Fiordiligi, *Cosi fan Tutte*, Eva, *Meistersinger*, Donna Elvira, *Don Giovanni*, Gräfin, *Capriccio*, etc.
c/o International Music Establishment, Vaduz, Liechtenstein.

Schwedhelm, Karl; German writer and broadcasting official; b. 14 Aug. 1915; ed. Universität Berlin.
Former librarian; with Süddeutscher Rundfunk 47-, now Dir. of Dept. of Literature; mem. P.E.N.
Publs. *Dichtungen der Marceline Desbordes-Valmore* 47, *Fährte der Fische* 55, *E. Glissant: Carthago* 59, *Nelly Sachs* 68.
7057 Winnenden, Bachstrasse 10, German Federal Republic.
Telephone: 07195-3115.

Schweikart, Hans; German theatre manager, director and actor; b. 1 Oct. 1895; ed. Schiller-Realgymnasium, Charlottenburg, and Marie Seebachschule, Royal Theatre, Berlin.
Actor, Wiesbaden, Görlitz, Magdeburg, Cologne 15-18; Actor, Max Reinhardt's Deutsches Theater, Berlin 18-23; Actor, Dir. and Second Man. Otto Falckenberg's Theater, Munich 23-29; Actor, Dir. Theater am Schiffbauerdamm (Berlin), Volkstheater (Vienna), Kammerspiele (Munich) 29-34; First Dir., Residenztheater, Munich 34-38; Chief Producer, Bavaria Film Co. 38-42; play and film dir. 42-47; Man. Dir., Kammerspiele, Munich 47-63; German Order of Merit, Bavarian Order of Merit.
Friedrich-Herschel-Strasse 3, Munich 27, German Federal Republic.

Schweikher, Paul, B.F.A., M.A.; American architect; b. 28 July 1903; ed. Colorado and Yale Univs.
Private architectural practice 33-; co-founder, Chicago Workshops 33-35; Lieut. Commdr. in U.S. Naval Reserve 41-45; Partner, Schweikher and Elting 45-53; Visiting Critic in Architecture, Yale Univ. 47-51, Prof. of Architecture, Chair. Dept. of Architecture 53-56; Prof. of Architecture, Head, Dept. of Architecture, Carnegie Mellon Univ. 56-; lecturer, panellist and juror at numerous educational and professional insts. 46-; mem. Fulbright Fellowships in Architecture selection cttee. 53-55, interviewing cttee. for American Acad. in Rome fellowships 55; Adviser, Memphis (Tenn.) Arts Center Competition 56; Consultant on master planning, Yale Univ. 53-56, Maryville Coll., Tenn. 54-58; Buffalo Univ. 55-57; mem. Arts Club of Chicago (Board of Dirs. 39-56), Pittsburgh Plan for Art 57-59, Pittsburgh Planning Comm. 61-63; mem. Advisory Council, Princeton Univ. School of Architecture 60-; Adviser, Allegheny Square Competition, Pittsburgh 64; Visiting Prof. Princeton 60-61; Ford Foundation research grant for theatre design 60-61; life mem. Chicago Art Inst. 46-; Fellow, Silliman Coll., Yale 54-55; architectural work at exhbns. New York Museum of Modern Art and several other museums and insts. 33-; work chosen for American Architecture Exhbn., Moscow 59; Progressive Architecture Awards 56, 57, 60, Distinguished Citizen Award, Denver 58, Architect of the Year, Pittsburgh 66, Artist of the Year, Pittsburgh 68, and other awards.
5935 Fifth Avenue, Pittsburgh, Pa. 15232, U.S.A.
Telephone: 412-362-1438.

Schweitzer, Pierre-Paul; French official of Monetary Fund; b. 29 May 1912; ed. Univs. of Strasbourg and Paris and Ecole Libre des Sciences Politiques, Paris.
Assistant Insp. of Finances 36-39, Insp. of Finances 39-46; Deputy Dir. of External Finance 46-47; Alt. Exec. Dir. for France, IMF 47-48; Sec.-Gen. Inter-ministerial Cttee. for European Econ. Co-operation 48-49; Financial Counsellor, French Embassy, Washington 49-53; Dir. of Treasury, Ministry of Finance 53-60; Deputy Gov. Banque de France 60-63; Man. Dir. Int. Monetary Fund (IMF) 63-; Commdr. Légion d'Honneur, and many other awards.
Home: 1717 Foxhall Road, N.W., Washington 20007; Office: International Monetary Fund, 19th and H Streets, Washington, D.C. 20431, U.S.A.

Schweizer, Samuel; Swiss banker; b. 2 March 1903; ed. Univs. of Basle and Geneva.
Private practice, Geneva 26-29; Swiss Bank Corpn. London Office 29-33, Basle Office 34-, Sub-Man. attached to Gen. Management 39-48, Manager, attached to General Management 48-50, Man. Basle Office 50-52, Gen. Man. 52-61, Chair. of Board 62-; Vice-Chair. CIBA Ltd.; Dir. Brown, Boveri & Co. Ltd., Société Anonyme des Câbleries et Tréfileries de Cossonay, Metal Works Ltd., Nestlé Alimentana Co., Société Int. Pirelli S.A., Sulzer Brothers Ltd., Crédit Commercial de France; mem. Bankrat of Swiss Nat. Bank, Int. Chamber of Commerce (Rep. of Swiss Nat. Cttee. in Comm. on Int. Monetary Relations); Vice-Chair. Comité de Direction de l'Inst. Suisse à Rome; Hon. Treas. Int. World Wildlife Fund.
Home: Landskronstrasse 5, Arlesheim (BL), Switzerland; Office: Aeschenvorstadt 1, Basle, Switzerland.

Schwinger, Julian Seymour, PH.D.; American physicist; b. 12 Feb. 1918; ed. Columbia Univ.
National Research Council Fellow 39-40; Research Assoc. Univ. of Calif. (Berkeley) 40-41; Instructor, later Asst. Prof. Purdue Univ. 41-43; staff mem. Radiation Lab., Mass. Inst. of Technology 43-46; mem. staff Metallurgy Lab., Univ. of Chicago 43; Assoc. Prof. Harvard Univ. 45-47, Prof. 47-; mem. Nat. Acad. of Sciences, American Acad. of Arts and Sciences, American Physical Soc., Civil Liberties Union; Editor *Quantum*

Electrodynamics 58; Nobel Prize for Physics (with R. Feynman and S. Tomonaga) 65, and other awards. Harvard University, Cambridge, Mass. 02138, U.S.A.

Schwippert, Hans, DR. ING.; German architect; b. 25 June 1899; ed. Realgymnasium and Technischen Hochschulen, Hanover, Darmstadt and Stuttgart.
Teacher at Aachen Coll. of Architecture, Interior Building and Planning 27; Dozent, Technische Hochschule, Aachen 35, Prof. of Domestic Architecture 46-61, Prof. Emeritus 61-; Head of Building Dept., Province of North Rhine-Westphalia 45-46; Prof. of Architecture, Staatliche Kunstakademie für Bildende Künste, Düsseldorf 46-58, Dir. 58-; mem. Acad. of Arts, Berlin 55-; Architecture Prize of Province of North Rhine-Westphalia 57; Officer Order of Crown (Belgium); Grosses Bundesverdienstkreuz.
Buildings include: Bundeshaus, Bonn 49, "Interbau" block of flats, Berlin 57, St. Hedwig's Cathedral, Berlin 56-63, House of Science, Düsseldorf 61.
4 Düsseldorf, Leo-Statz-Strasse 14, German Federal Republic.
Telephone: 432321.

Sciascia, Leonardo; Italian writer; b. 8 Jan. 1921; ed. Istituto Magistrale Caltanissetta.
Has won many prizes including Premio Crotone, Premio Libera Stampa Lugano, and Premio Prato.
Publs. *Le parrocchie di Regalpetra* 56, *Gli zii di Sicilia* 58, *Il giorno della civetta* 61, *Pirandello e la Sicilia* 61, *Il consiglio d'Egitto* 63, *Morte dell'inquisitore* 64, *Feste religiose in Sicilia* 65, *A ciascuno il suo* (novel).
Via Redentore 131, Caltanissetta, Italy.

Scoccimarro, Mauro; Italian journalist and politician; b. 30 Oct. 1895; studied economics.
Mem. Socialist Party 17-21, Communist Party 21-; imprisoned during Fascist régime; Minister for Occupied Territories under Bonomi 44; Minister of Finance 45-47; Vice-Pres. Senato della Repubblica 48-; Vice-Pres. Comm. on Foreign Affairs; Pres. Group of Communist Senators.
Palazzo Madama, Rome, and Via Botteghe Oscure 4, Rome, Italy.

Scofield, Paul, C.B.E.; British actor; b. 21 Jan. 1922; trained London Mask Theatre Drama School.
Birmingham Repertory Theatre 41 and 43-46; Stratford-on-Avon Shakespeare Memorial Theatre 46-48; Arts Theatre 46; Phoenix Theatre 47; with H. M. Tennent 49-56; Chekhov's *Seagull*, Anouilh's *Ring Round the Moon*, Charles Morgan's *The River Line*, *Richard II*, *Time Remembered*, *A Question of Fact*, *Hamlet* (also in Moscow), *Power and the Glory*, *Family Reunion*, *A Dead Secret*, *Expresso Bongo*, *The Complaisant Lover*, *A Man for all Seasons*, Stratford Festival, Ont., Canada 61, *Coriolanus*, *Don Armado* New York 61-62, *A Man for All Seasons* London 62-63, *King Lear* 63, *Timon of Athens* 65, *The Government Inspector* London 66, *Staircase* 67, *Macbeth* 68; Films: *The Train* 63, *A Man for All Seasons* 67 (Oscar and New York Film Critics Award, Moscow Film Festival and British Film Acad. Awards).
The Gables, Balcombe, Sussex, England.

Scott, David Aubrey, C.M.G.; British diplomatist; b. 3 Aug. 1919; ed. Charterhouse and Birmingham Univ.
Royal Artillery 39-47; Chief Radar Adviser, British Mil. Mission to Egyptian Army 45-47; Commonwealth Relations Office 48-, South Africa 51-53; Cabinet Office 54-56; Singapore 56-58; British Deputy High Commr. in Fed. of Rhodesia and Nyasaland 61-63; Imperial Defence Coll. 64; Deputy High Commr. in India 65-67; High Commr. in Uganda 67-; Amb. to Rwanda (non-resident) 67-.
Brunswood, Manor Way, Guildford, Surrey, England.

Scott, Rev. G(uthrie) Michael; British ecclesiastic; b. 30 July 1907; ed. King's Coll., Taunton, St. Paul's Coll., Grahamstown, South Africa, and Chichester Theological Coll.
Curate of Slaugham 30-32, St. Stephen's, Kensington 32-34; Domestic Chaplain to Bishop of Bombay 35-37; Chaplain to St. Paul's Cathedral, Calcutta 37-38, Kasauli 38-39; Curate to St. Alban's Coloured Mission, Johannesburg 43-46; Rep. of Herero, Berg, Damara and Nama Tribes of South-West Africa at UN 48-; Hon. Dir. Africa Bureau, London 52-; mem. Nagaland Peace Mission 64-66, expelled by India 66; special licence to officiate in the Diocese of Chichester 49-.
Publs. *Shadow over Africa* 50, *Attitude to Africa* 51, *The Orphans' Heritage* 58, *A Time to Speak* 58, *The Nagas: India's Problem or the World's*.
Africa Bureau, 38 Great Smith Street, London, S.W.1; and c/o Lloyds Bank, 6 Pall Mall, London, S.W.1, England.
Telephone: 01-799-5808.

Scott, Hugh, A.B., LL.B.; American lawyer and politician; b. 11 Nov. 1900; ed. Pennsylvania Univ., Randolph-Macon Coll. and Virginia Univ.
Asst. District Attorney, Philadelphia 26-41; mem. U.S. House of Reps. (6th Pa. District) 40-42, 44-58; served in U.S. Merchant Marine and Navy (Commdr.) in Second World War and in Navy in Korean War; fmr. Gen. Counsel, Republican Nat. Cttee.; Nat. Chair., Republican Nat. Cttee. 48-49; Chair. of Regional Organization, Eisenhower campaign and on personal staff, Chair. Eisenhower Headquarters Cttee. 52; U.S. Senator from Pennsylvania 59-; mem. Judiciary and Rules Cttees.; del. by Presidential designated at numerous int. confs.; mem. Board of Visitors, U.S. Naval Acad. 48; mem. Philadelphia and American Bar Asscns., Pennsylvania Bar Asscn. (fmr. Chair. Criminal Law Cttee.), American Soc. of Int. Law, etc.; Hon. LL.D. Randolph-Macon Coll., Temple Univ.; Hon. L.H.D. La Salle Coll. 55; Republican.
Publs. *Scott on Bailments* 31, *How to Go into Politics* 49, *Politics, U.S.A.* (co-author) 60, *The Golden Age of Chinese Art* 67, *Come to the Party* 68, *How to Run for Public Office and Win* 68.
Senate Office Building, Washington 25, D.C., U.S.A.
Telephone: 225-6324.

Scott, Sir Ian Dixon, K.C.M.G., K.C.V.O., C.I.E.; British diplomatist; b. 6 March 1909; ed. Queen's Royal Coll., Trinidad, Balliol Coll., Oxford, London School of Econs.
Entered Indian Civil Service 32; joined Indian Political Service 35; Asst. Dir. of Intelligence, Peshawar 41; Deputy Private Sec. to the Viceroy 45-47; Foreign Service, London 50, First Sec., Foreign Office 50-51; British Legation, Helsinki 52; First Sec. and Head of Chancery, Lebanon 54, Counsellor 56, Chargé d'Affaires 56-58; Amb. to Congo 60-61, to Sudan 61-65, to Norway 65-68.
British Embassy, Oslo, Norway.

Scott, Karl Edwin, B.A., J.D., LL.D.; American (b. Canadian) lawyer and business executive; b. 06; ed. Fort William, Aurora and Toronto Elementary and Secondary Schools, Eastern Michigan Univ. and Detroit Coll. of Law.
Teacher of English, Detroit 28-34; Law Practice, Detroit 34-43; Admin. of War Contracts, Fisher Body Div., Gen. Motors Corpn., Detroit 43-46; joined Ford Motor Co., Dearborn, Mich. 46, Dir. of Org. Planning 46-59, Exec. Vice-Pres. Ford Motor Co. of Canada Ltd. 59-60, Pres. Ford Motor Co. of Canada Ltd. 60-.
R.R.1 Caledon East, Ontario, Canada.

Scott, Peter Markham, C.B.E., D.S.C., M.A., (son of late Captain Robert Falcon Scott); British artist and ornithologist; b. 14 Sept. 1909; ed. Oundle, Trinity Coll., Cambridge, Munich State Acad., and Royal Acad., London.

Founded, now Hon. Dir., The Wildfowl Trust 46; rep. Great Britain in Olympic Games, in single handed sailing (bronze medal) 36; served in Navy during 39-45 War; Pres. Int. Yacht Racing Union; Chair. Olympic Int. Yacht Racing Jury, Melbourne 56, Naples 60, Tokyo 64; 1st Vice-Pres. and Chair. World Wildlife Fund; Vice-Pres. Inland Waterways Asscn., Royal Yachting Asscn.; mem. Council of London Zoological Soc.; Pres. Wildlife Youth Service; Chair. Survival Service Comm. of Int. Union for the Conservation of Nature and Natural Resources, British Gliding Asscn.; Hon. LL.D. (Aberdeen and Exeter).
Publs. *Morning Flight* 35, *Wild Chorus* 38, *The Battle of the Narrow Seas* 45, *Portrait Drawings* 49, *Key to the Wild Fowl of the World* 49, *Wild Geese and Eskimos* 51, *A Thousand Geese* (with James Fisher) 53, *The Eye of the Wind* 61; illustrated many books incl. *Bird in the Bush* (Lord Kennet), *Grey Goose*, and *Through the Air* (Michael Bratby), *The Snow Goose* (Paul Gallico), etc.; Joint Ed. and Illustrator of Wildfowl Trust Annual Reports 48-.
The New Grounds, Slimbridge, Glos., England.
Telephone: Cambridge (Glos.) 333.

Scott, William George, C.B.E.; British artist; b. 15 Feb. 1913; ed. Enniskillen, Belfast School of Art and Royal Acad. Schools, London.
Exhibitions at Leger Gallery 42, 44, 46, Leicester Gallery 48, 51, Hanover Gallery 53, 56, 61, 65, Tate Gallery 63 (all in London); Martha Jackson Gallery, New York 54, 58; Venice Biennale 58; São Paulo, Brazil 53, 61.
13 Edith Terrace, Chelsea, London, S.W.10, England.
Telephone: 01-352-8044.

Scott Fox, Sir (Robert) David (John), K.C.M.G.; British diplomatist; b. 20 June 1910; ed. Eton and Christ Church, Oxford.
Diplomatic Service 34-, served Berlin 37, Prague 37-39, Rio de Janeiro 40-44, Foreign Office 44-49; Counsellor, Jeddah 49-51, Chargé d'Affaires 49, 50; Counsellor, Ankara 51, Chargé d'Affaires 51, 52, 53, 54; Minister (Econ. and Social Affairs) to U.K. Del. to UN 55-58; Minister to Romania 59-61; Amb. to Chile 61-66, to Finland 66-.
British Embassy, Helsinki, Finland.

Scotto, Renata; Italian soprano; b. 34; ed. under Ghirardini at Milan.
Joined La Scala Opera Company after debut in *La Traviata* at Teatro Nuovo, Milan 53; then studied under Merlino and Mercedes Llopart; known for roles in *La Sonnambula*, *I Puritani*, *L'Elisir d'amore*, *Lucia di Lammermoor*, *Falstaff*, *La Bohème*, *Turandot*, *I Capuleti*, etc.
presso Il Teatro alla Scala, via Filodrammatici 2, Milan, Italy.

Scranton, William W., A.B., LL.B.; American lawyer and politician; b. 19 July 1917; ed. Hotchkiss School, Yale Univ. and Yale Univ. Law School.
U.S. Army Air Force 41-45; Pennsylvania bar 46; Assoc. O'Malley, Harris, Harris and Warren 46-47; Vice-Pres. Int. Textbook Co., Scranton, Pa. 47-52, later Dir. and mem. Exec. Cttee.; Pres. Scranton-Lackawanna Trust Co. 54-56; Chair. Board and Dir. Northeastern Pennsylvania Broadcasting Co. 57-61; Special Asst. to U.S. Sec. of State 59-60; mem. U.S. House of Reps. 60-62; Gov. of Pennsylvania 63-67; Dir. Scott Paper Co., I.B.M. World Trade Corpn., Fidelity Bank, American Int. Bank, McCall Corpn.; numerous honorary degrees; Republican.
Box 116, Dalton, Pennsylvania; Office: 704 Northeastern Bank Building, Scranton, Pennsylvania, U.S.A.

Scribner, Charles, Jr., A.B.; American publisher; b. 13 July 1921; ed. St. Paul's School and Princeton Univ. In U.S. Navy 43-46, 50-52; Advertising Man., Charles

Scribner's Sons 46-48, Production Man. 48-50, Pres. 52-; Pres. Princeton Univ. Press 57-, American Book Publisher's Council 66-; hon. M.A.
791 Park Avenue, New York, N.Y. 10021, U.S.A.

Scripps, Charles Edward; American newspaper publisher; b. 27 Jan. 1920; ed. William and Mary Coll. and Pomona Coll.
Reporter, Cleveland Press, Ohio 41; Successor-Trustee, Edward W. Scripps Trust 45, Chair., Board of Trustees 48-, Vice-Pres., Dir., E. W. Scripps Co. 46-, Chair. of Board 53-; Dir. various Scripps-Howard newspapers.
Union Central Building, Cincinnati 2, Ohio, U.S.A.

Scully, Vincent William Thomas, C.M.G., F.C.A.; Canadian company executive; b. 9 Jan. 1900; ed. Christian Brothers School, New Ross (Ireland), and Trinity Coll., Dublin.
Practised as chartered accountant with Clarkson, Gordon, Dilworth and Nash, Toronto 25-32; chartered accountant Ontario 29; Dir. and Sec.-Treas. J. D. Woods & Co. Ltd. 32-45; Comptroller and Sec.-Treas., York Knitting Mills Ltd. 32-45; Sec.-Treas. Plateau Co. Ltd. (Crown Co.) 40-41; Treas. and subsequently Pres., War Supplies Ltd. (Crown Co.) 41-44; Pres. Victory Aircraft Ltd. (Crown Co.) 44-45; Deputy Minister of Reconstruction and Supply and Vice-Pres. Nat. Research Council 45-47; Deputy Minister of Nat. Revenue for Taxation, Canada 48-51; Comptroller The Steel Co., Canada Ltd. 51, Pres. 57-, Chair. of Board 66-; Dir. Sun Life Assurance Co. of Canada, British-American Oil Co. Ltd., Bank of Montreal, Royal Canadian Geographical Soc.; Gov. McMaster Univ., Hamilton, Camrose Tubes Ltd., Welland Tubes Ltd., Wabush Lake Railway Co. Ltd.; awarded United States Medal of Freedom (Bronze Palm).
28 Aberdeen Avenue, Hamilton, Ontario, Canada.

Sculthorpe, Peter Joshua; Australian composer; b. 29 April 1929; ed. Launceston Grammar School, Univ. of Melbourne and Wadham Coll., Oxford.
Senior Lecturer in Music, Univ. of Sydney 63-; Visiting Fellow, Yale Univ. 65-67; comms. from bodies including Australian Broadcasting Comm., Birmingham Chamber Music Soc., American Wind Symphony Orchestra, Australian Elizabethan Theatre Trust and Australian Ballet; working on *The Convict and Mrs. Fraser* for Sydney Opera House 69.
Compositions published include: *The Lonelinessof Bunjil* 53, *Piano Sonatina* 54, *Violin Sonata* 55, *Irkanda* I 55, II 59, III 60, IV 61, *Ulterior Motifs*, a musical farce and music for various revues 57-9, *Sonata for Viola and Percussion* 60, *Orchestral Suite* (from film *They Found a Cave*) 62, *Sonata for Piano* 63, *The Fifth Continent* 63, *Three Haiku* 64, *String Quartet No. 6* 64, *South by Five* 65, *Sun Music* 65, II 66, III (*Anniversary Music*) 67, IV 67, *Morning Song for the Christ Child* 66, *Tabuh-tabuhan* 67, *Autumn Song* 68, *Orchestral Suite* from film *The Age of Consent* 68, Sun Music Ballet 68, various works for radio, television, theatre & film.
147B Queen Street, Woollahra, Sydney, New South Wales 2025, Australia.
Telephone: 32-4701.

Seaborg, Glenn T(heodore), B.A., PH.D.; American chemist; b. 19 April 1912; ed. Univ. of California.
Research Assoc., Univ. of Calif. 37-39, Instructor 39-41, Asst. Prof. 41-45, Prof. of Chemistry 45-, Dir. Nuclear Chemical Research, Lawrence Radiation Laboratory 46-58, Assoc. Dir. Lawrence Radiation Laboratory 54-61, Chancellor, Univ. of Calif., Berkeley 58-61; on leave of absence to head plutonium work of Manhattan Project at Univ. of Chicago Metallurgical Laboratory 42-46; on leave of absence to serve as Chair. U.S. Atomic Energy Comm. 61-; Chair. Steering Cttee., Chemical Educ. Material Study (CHEM Study), Nat. Science Foundation 59-; Pres. Board of Trustees, Science Service 66-; co-

discoverer of elements 94 (plutonium), 95 (americium), 96 (curium), 97 (berkelium), 98 (californium), 99 (einsteinium), 100 (fermium), 101 (mendelevium), and element 102 (nobelium); author of actinide concept of heavy element electronic structure; Nobel Prize in Chemistry 51; Enrico Fermi Award 59; Franklin Medal 63; other awards include more than 30 hon. degrees.

Publs. *The Transuranium Elements: Research Papers* (ed. with J. J. Katz and W. M. Manning) 49, *Production and Separation of U²³³* (ed. with L. I. Katzin) 51, *The Actinide Elements* (ed. with J. J. Katz) 54; *Comprehensive Inorganic Chemistry* Vol. I (with others) 53, *The Chemistry of the Actinide Elements* (with J. J. Katz) 57, *The Transuranium Elements* 58, *Elements of the Universe* (with E. G. Valens) 58, *Man-made Transuranium Elements* 63; *Education and the Atom* (with D. M. Wilkes) 64, *The Nuclear Properties of the Heavy Elements*, Vol. I: *Systematics of Nuclear Structure and Radioactivity*, and Vol. II: *Detailed Radioactivity Properties* (with E. K. Hyde and I. Perlman) 64; about 200 papers on nuclear chemistry and physics, etc. United States Atomic Energy Commission, Washington D.C., 20545, U.S.A.
Telephone: 301-973-6111.

Seago, Edward Brian, R.B.A., R.W.S.; British artist; b. 31 March 1910.
Exhibited Royal Academy, R.B.A., R.O.I., New English Art Club, Royal Society of Portrait Painters; one-man exhibitions in London, Brussels, Oslo, Bergen, Toronto, New York, Los Angeles, Montreal, Chicago, San Francisco, Melbourne and Johannesburg; loan exhbns. Norwich, Bristol, King's Lynn, St. James' Palace (pictures painted on Duke of Edinburgh's World Tour 56/57); work mostly landscape, some portraits, still-life; served R.E. 39-44; series of paintings of Italian Campaign 44; official portrait of King George VI and Queen Elizabeth (the Queen Mother) for R.A.F. Coll., Cranwell 48; equestrian portrait of H.M. the Queen for Coldstream Guards 56.
Publs. *Circus Company, Caravan, Peace in War, High Endeavour, With the Allied Armies in Italy, A Canvas to Cover, Tideline, With Capricorn to Paris*; with John Masefield: *Country Scene, A Tribute to Ballet, A Generation Risen.*
The Dutch House, Ludham, Norfolk, England.

Seamans, Robert Channing, Jr.; American scientist and government official; b. 30 Oct. 1918; ed. Harvard and Mass. Inst. of Technology.
Massachusetts Inst. of Technology 41-55, teaching and project management positions, successively Assoc. Prof. Dept. of Aeronautical Engineering, Chief Engineer Project Meteor, Dir. Flight Control Laboratory; Radio Corpn. of America 45-60, successively Man. Airborne Systems Lab., Chief Systems Engineer Airborne Systems Dept., Chief Engineer Missile Electronics and Control Div.; Assoc. Administrator and later Deputy Administrator Nat. Aeronautics and Space Admin. (N.A.S.A.) 60-68; Consultant to Admin. (N.A.S.A.) 68-; Visiting Prof. of Aeronautics and Astronautics and of Management, Mass. Inst. of Technology 68-; mem. Scientific Advisory Board, U.S. Air Force 57-62, Assoc. Adviser 63-67; Nat. del. to AGARD.
190 Brattle Street, Cambridge, Massachusetts 02138, U.S.A.

Searight, Rodney Gerald; British company director; b. 1909.
Gen. Man. Shell Co. of Egypt Ltd. 47-52; Chair. Anglo-Egyptian Oilfields 51-52; Dir. Iranian Oil Participants' Ltd. 54-58; Chief Rep., Baghdad, Iraq Petroleum Co. Ltd. 58-60; Dir. Shell Int. Petroleum Co. 63-.
129 Oakwood Court, London, W.14, England.

Searle, Humphrey, B.A.; British composer; b. 26 Aug. 1915; ed. Winchester Coll., New Coll., Oxford, and Royal Coll. of Music.

Studied privately with Anton Webern; mem. B.B.C. Music Dept. 38-40; army service 40-46; Producer B.B.C. Music Dept. 46-48; Gen. Sec. Int. Soc. for Contemporary Music 47-49; mem. Sadler's Wells Ballet Advisory Panel 51-57; Hon. Sec. Liszt Soc. 50-62; Resident Composer, Stanford Univ., Calif., U.S.A. 64-65; Prof. of Composition, Royal Coll. of Music, London 65-; Guest Composer Aspen Music Festival, Colorado, U.S.A. 67.
Compositions include First Piano Concerto 44, *Trilogy* on Texts of Edith Sitwell and James Joyce 49-52, *Poem for 22 Strings* 50, Piano Sonata 51, First Symphony 53, Second Piano Concerto 55, *Noctambules* (ballet) 56, *The Great Peacock* (ballet) 58, *The Diary of a Madman* (opera) 58, Second Symphony 58, Third Symphony 60, Fourth Symphony 62, *Dualities* (ballet) 63, *The Photo of the Colonel* (opera) 64, Fifth Symphony 64, Scherzi for Orchestra 64, *The Canticle of the Rose* 65, *Oxus* scena 67; *Hamlet* (opera) 68, *Progressions for 9 instruments* 68; music for stage, radio, TV and films.
Publs. *The Music of Liszt* 54, *Twentieth Century Counterpoint* 54, *Ballet Music: An Introduction* 58.
44 Ordnance Hill, London, N.W.8, England.
Telephone: 01-722-5182.

Searle, Ronald, A.G.I., F.S.I.A.; British artist; b. 3 March 1920; ed. Central School, Cambridge and Cambridge School of Art.
First drawings published 35-39; served with Royal Engineers 39-46; prisoner-of-war in Japanese camps 42-45; contributor to nat. publs. 46-; mem. *Punch* 'Table' 56-; special features artist *Life* magazine 55-, *Holiday* 57, *The New Yorker* 66-; One-Man Exhbns. Leicester Galleries (London) 50, 54, 57, Kraushaar Gallery (New York) 59, Bianchini Gallery (New York) 63, Kunsthalle (Bremen) 65, in Paris 66, 67, 68, in Munich 67, 68, in London 68, etc.; work rep. in Victoria and Albert Museum and British Museum (London), Bibliothèque Nationale, Paris and in several German and American museums; designer of several films including *John Gilpin, On the Twelfth Day, Energetically Yours* (awards at Venice, Edinburgh, San Francisco and other film festivals), *Germany 1960, Toulouse-Lautrec;* Los Angeles Art Dirs. Club Medal 59, Philadelphia Art Dirs. Club Medal 59, Nat. Cartoonists' Soc. Award 59, 60, Gold Medal, III Biennale, Tolentino, Italy 65.
Publs. *Forty Drawings* 46, *John Gilpin* 52, *Souls in Torment* 53, *Rake's Progress* 55, *Merry England* 56, *Paris Sketchbook* 57, *The St. Trinian's Story* (with Kaye Webb) 59, *U.S.A. For Beginners* 59, *Russia for Beginners* 60, *The Big City* 58 (all with Alex Atkinson) *Refugees 1960* 60, *Which Way did he Go?* 61, *Escape from the Amazon* 63, *From Frozen North to Filthy Lucre* 64, *Those Magnificent Men in their Flying Machines* 65, *Haven't We Met Before Somewhere?* (with Heinz Huber) 66, *Searle's Cats* 67, *The Square Egg* 68, etc.
c/o Hope Leresche and Steele, 11 Jubilee Place, London, S.W.3, England.
Telephone: 01-352-4311.

Sears, Paul Bigelow, B.SC., B.A., M.A., PH.D.; American ecologist; b. 17 Dec. 1891; ed. Ohio Wesleyan Univ., Univ. of Nebraska, and Univ. of Chicago.
Instructor in Botany, Ohio State Univ. 15-19; Asst. Prof. Univ. of Nebraska 19-25, Assoc. Prof. 25-27; Prof. and Head of Dept. of Botany, Univ. of Oklahoma 27-38, Oberlin Coll. 38-50; Dir. of Conservation, Yale Univ. 50-60; Chair. Botany Dept., Yale 53-55; Pres. American Asscn. for the Advancement of Science 56, Chair. of Board of Dirs. 57; Trustee, Pacific Tropical Botanical Garden 63-; Hon. D.Sc. (Ohio Wesleyan); Hon. Litt.D. (Marietta Coll.); Hon. LL.D. (Arkansas, Nebraska and Wayne State Univs.); Hon. D.Sc. (Oberlin Coll. and Bowling Green State Univ.).

Publs. *Deserts on the March* 35, *This is Our World* 37, *Life and Environment* 39, *Charles Darwin* 50, *Where There is Life* 62, *The Living Landscape* 66.
4 North Forest Circle, New Haven, Conn., U.S.A.
Telephone: 387-4807.

Seaton, Frederick Andrew; American newspaper publisher; b. 11 Dec. 1909; ed. Kansas State Coll.
Radio sports announcer 29-37; Asst. Dept. of Public Speaking, Kan. State Coll. 29-30; Business Man. Manhattan (Kan.) Little Theatre 30-31; Wire News Editor *Manhattan Morning Chronicle* 32; City Editor *Manhattan Evening Mercury* 33; Assoc. Editor Seaton Publs., Manhattan 33-37; Pres. Seaton Publ. Co., Neb. Broadcasting Co., Neb. Television Corpn., Manhattan (Kan.) Broadcasting Co., Winfield (Kan.) Publ. Co., Alliance (Neb.) Publ. Co., Sheridan (Wyo.) Newspapers Inc., Farm Life Publ. Co., Denver; Vice-Pres. Seaton Publ. Co., Manhattan, Kan., Coffeyville (Kan.) Publ. Co., Midwest Broadcasting Co., Coffeyville, Kan.; active for many years in Young Republican Club of Kan.; Vice-Chair. Kan. Republican State Cttee. 34-37; State Senator, Neb. 45-49; Chair. Neb. Legislative Council 47-49; U.S. Senator for Neb. 51-52; Political Adviser to Dwight D. Eisenhower 52; Asst. Sec. of Defense for Legislative, Liaison and Public Relations 53-55; Admin. Asst. to Pres. 55-56; Sec. of the Interior 56-61; Dir. First Nat. Bank, Hastings 61-; mem. Nat. Editorial Asscn., Inland Daily Press Asscn., American Acad. Political and Social Science, Newcomen Soc., etc.; Hon. Dr. Jur. (Kansas State Coll.), Hon. D.Litt. (Maryville Coll.).
908 West Second Street, Hastings, Neb., U.S.A.

Sebald, William Joseph, B.S., LL.B., LL.D.; American diplomatist; b. 5 Nov. 1901; ed. U.S. Naval Acad. and Univ. of Maryland.
Naval Officer 22-30; practised Law 33-41; served on H.Q. Staff, C.-in-C. U.S. Fleet, Second World War 41-45; joined Staff of U.S. Political Adviser for Japan Jan. 46, Counsellor of Mission U.S. Polad Tokyo; apptd. Deputy for Supreme Commdr. for the Allied Powers, Chair. and mem. for the U.S., Allied Council for Japan Sept. 47; Chief Diplomatic Section G.H.Q., S.C.A.P. 47; Minister Plenipotentiary 48, U.S. Political Adviser for Japan with personal rank of Ambassador 50-52; Ambassador to Burma 52-54; Deputy Asst. Sec. Far Eastern Affairs 54-57; Ambassador to Australia 57-61; Legion of Merit; First Class Order with Grand Cordon of the Rising Sun (Japan).
Publs. *Civil Code of Japan, Annotated* 34, *Criminal Code of Japan, Annotated* 36, *A Selection of Japan's Emergency Legislation* 37, *Principal Tax Laws of Japan* 38, *Commercial Code of Japan* 45, *With MacArthur in Japan* 65, *Japan: Prospects, Options, and Opportunities* (with C. Nelson Spinks) 67.
245 Spring Line Drive, Naples, Florida 33940, U.S.A.
Telephone: MI2-7795.

Sebilleau, Pierre; French diplomatist; b. 16 Sept. 1912; ed. Lycée de Nantes, Univ. de Paris à la Sorbonne and Ecole Libre des Sciences Politiques.
Embassy, Warsaw 38; Counsellor, Rome 45-55; Minister Plenipotentiary, Head of Service of Bilateral Agreements, Econ. Dept., Ministry of Foreign Affairs 55, later Dir. of East Africa Dept.; Ambassador to Libya 60-62, Syria 62-64, Brazil 64-65, Denmark 66-; Officier Légion d'Honneur.
French Embassy, Copenhagen K, Denmark.

Sedov, Leonid Ivanovich; Soviet foreign trade corporation official; b. 1917; ed. Moscow Mining Inst.
Mineworker, Khabarovsk Territory 40-41; Red Army 41-44; *Soyuzpromexport* 44-46; Soviet Trade Mission in Britain 46-51; U.S.S.R. Ministry to Foreign Trade 51-55; Trade Counsellor, Soviet Embassy, Indonesia 55-56, Trade Rep. in Indonesia 56-60; Chair. *Soyuzpromexport* (coal and mineral) 60-64; Head

of Dept. U.S.S.R. Ministry of Foreign Trade 64-; mem. C.P.S.U.; Badge of Honour, etc.
U.S.S.R. Ministry of Foreign Trade, 32/34 Smolenskaya-Sennaya ploshchad, Moscow, U.S.S.R.

Sedov, Leonid Ivanovich; Soviet scientist; b. 14 Nov. 1907; ed. Moscow Univ.
At the Aero-hydro-dynamics Inst. 31-; Prof. at Moscow Univ. 37-; at the Central Aircraft Engine Designing Inst. 47-; mem. U.S.S.R. Acad. of Sciences 53-; Chief Editor *Cosmic Research*; Chair. Int. Astronautic Fed. 59-63; awarded two Orders of Lenin, two Orders of Red Banner, Chaplygin Prize 46, State Prize 52, Lomonosov Prize 54, Hero of Socialist Labour 67; hon. mem. of a number of foreign acads. and univs.
Publs. *Extension of Powerful Blasts, Some Unsteady Movements in Compressible Liquid* 45, *Plane Problems in Hydro-dynamics and Aerodynamics, Methods of Similarity and Scale in Mechanics* 51, *Nonlinear Mechanics of Continuous Media* 62.
Academy of Sciences of U.S.S.R., Leninsky Prospekt 14, Moscow; Home: Kwartira 84, MGY Zona U, Moscow B-234, U.S.S.R.

Sedoy, Pavel Anisimovich; Soviet foreign trade official; b. 1913; ed. Dniepropetrovsk Inst. of Metallurgy.
Served with Soviet Army 41-45; metallurgical engineer 46-60; with Ministry of Foreign Trade 60-; Vice-Chair. *Promsyryeimport* (imports of industrial raw materials) Asscn. 60-66, acting Chair. 66-67, Chair. 67-; mem. C.P.; several decorations.
Promsyryeimport, Ministry of Foreign Trade, 32-34 Smolenskaya-Sennaya ploshchad, Moscow, U.S.S.R.

Sedwitz, Walter J., M.A., PH.D.; American economist; b. 14 April 1925; ed. Univ. de Paris à la Sorbonne and Columbia Univ.
Former Dir. of Latin American Studies, Council on Foreign Relations; Economist, UN 49, U.S. Dept. of Commerce 51-53; Research Fellow, Council on Foreign Relations 53-54; Dir. of Research Dept., Fed. Reserve Bank of New York 53-59; Adviser to several Latin American countries in econ. and financial sphere 53-59; Prof. of Econs., Queens Coll., New York City Coll.; Dir. Dept. of Econs., Pan American Union, Org. of American States (OAS) Washington 61-63; Asst. Sec. for Econ. and Social Affairs, OAS 63-; Exec. Sec. Inter-American Econ. and Social Council, OAS 53-; Exec. Sec. Inter-American Cttee. on Alliance for Progress, Inter-American Econ. and Social Council of OAS 63-; Co-ordinator of Alliance for Progress in Econ. and Social fields 63-.
Office: Pan American Union, Washington, D.C.; Home: 6704 Tulip Hill Terrace, Bethesda, Maryland, U.S.A.

Seebohm, Frederic; British banker; b. 18 Jan. 1909; ed. Leighton Park School, Reading, and Trinity Coll., Cambridge.
Barclays Bank Ltd. 29-, Sheffield, York and Birmingham, Dir. 47-; Dir. Barclays Bank D.C.O. 51-55, Vice-Chair. 55-59, Deputy Chair. and Chair. London Cttee. 59-65, Chair. Jan. 65-; Chair. Friends' Provident and Century Life Office, Century Insurance Co. Ltd., Century Insurance Trust Ltd. till 68, Dir. 68-; Pres. Inst. of Bankers 66-68; Chair. Export Guarantees Advisory Council 67-; Dir. other companies; Gov. London School of Econs. and Political Science; official of commercial, social and educational orgs.
Barclays Bank D.C.O., 54 Lombard Street, London, E.C.3; Home: Gannet House, Chapmore End, Near Ware, Hertfordshire, England.
Telephone: 01-626-5656 (Office); Ware 3453 (Home).

Seefried, Irmgard (wife of Wolfgang Schneiderhan *q.v.*); Austrian singer; ed. Augsburg Conservatoire.
Aachen 40-43; Vienna State Opera House 43-; numerous concert tours, incl. Scala Milan, Covent Garden London, Metropolitan New York, Salzburg, Lucerne and Edin-

burgh Festivals; numerous recordings; Mozart Ring 48, Mozart Medal, Lehmann Medal, Österreichisches Ehrenkreuz für Wissenschaft und Kunst, Officer's Cross of Royal Danish Dannebrog Order.
State Opera House, Vienna, Austria.

Seeger, Arno; German business executive; b. 14; ed. Humanistisches Gymnasium, Wuppertal, and Univs. of Cologne, Bonn, Berlin and Jena.
Deutsche Bank and Deutsche Überseeische Bank 32-38; Dir. Chamber of Commerce, Düsseldorf 38-45; private consultant 47-62; mem. Board of Dirs., Fried. Krupp, Essen 62-67, private consultant 68-; Advisory Board, Gerling-Konzern, Cologne; J. Vaillant K.G., Remscheid Riloga-Werk, Remscheid; Roisdorfer Brunnen, Roisdorf.
Freiligrathstrasse 13, Düsseldorf, German Federal Republic.
Telephone: 48-50-88.

Seeiso, Constantine Bereng; Lesotho (Basutoland) ruler; b. 2 May 1938; ed. Roma Coll., Basutoland, Ampleforth Coll., and Corpus Christi Coll., Oxford Univ.
Paramount Chief Basutoland 60-66, with title of Motlotlehi Moshoeshoe II; King of Lesotho 66-, with title of Moshoeshoe II.
The Royal Palace, Maseru, Lesotho, Southern Africa.

Seferiades, George; Greek diplomatist and writer; b. 29 Feb. 1900; ed. Smyrna, Athens and Paris.
Entered Foreign Service 26; Vice-Consul in London 31-34; Consul in Albania 36; Head Foreign Press Service, Athens 38-41; worked for Greek Foreign Office in Egypt, S. Africa 41-44; Chef de Cabinet to the Regent 45-46; Ankara 48-50; London 51-52; Ambassador to Lebanon, Minister to Syria, Iraq and Jordan until August 56; Ambassador to Great Britian 57-62; Hon. Litt.D. (Oxford and Cambridge), Hon. D.Phil. (Salonika); Nobel Prize for Literature 63; numerous decorations.
Publs. Several literary works under the name of George Seferis: *The Turning Point* 31, *Mythistorema* 35, *Gymnopedia* 36, *Essays* 62, *Poems* 62, *Cyprus* 53, *On the Greek Style* 66, etc.; and in English trans. *The King of Asine and Other Poems* 48, *Poems* 60, *Dikter* 63, etc.
Agras 20, Athens 501, Greece.

Sefrin, Max; German politician; b. 21 Nov. 1913; ed. Oberrealschule.
Served as pilot, Second World War; prisoner of war in U.S.S.R.; on return worked as man. of private firm; Hon. Councillor for Trade and Supply, City Council of Jueterborg 46-; mem. Volkskammer 52-; mem. Christian Dem. Union (C.D.U.), Deputy Gen. Sec. and Pres. of its Parl. group in Volkskammer; Deputy Chair. Council of Ministers and Minister of Health 58-; Vaterländischer Verdienstorden (bronze).
Christian Democratic Union, Otto-Nuschke-Strasse 59-60, Berlin, W.8, Germany.

Segal, Ronald Michael, B.A.; South African author b.; 14 July 1932; ed. Univ. of Cape Town and Trinity Coll., Cambridge.
Dir. Faculty and Cultural Studies Nat. Union of South African Students 51-52; Pres. Univ. of Cape Town Council of Univ. Socs. 51; won Philip Francis du Pont Fellowship to Univ. of Virginia (U.S.A.) 55 but returned to South Africa to found *Africa South* (quarterly) 56; helped launch economic boycott April 59; banned by South African Govt. from all meetings July 59; in England with *Africa South in Exile*, April 60-61; Gen. Ed. Penguin African Library 61-; Hon. Sec. South African Freedom Asscn. 60-61; Convenor, Int. Conf. on Econ. Sanctions against South Africa 64, Int. Conf. on S.W. Africa 66.
Publs. *The Tokolosh* (a fantasy) 60, *Political Africa: A Who's Who of Personalities and Parties* 61, *African Profiles* 62, *Into Exile* 63, *Sanctions Against South Africa* (Editor) 64, *The Crisis of India* 65, *The Race War* 66, *South West Africa: Travesty of Trust* (Editor) 67, *America's Receding Future* 68.
The Old Manor House, Manor Road, Walton-on-Thames, Surrey, England.
Telephone: Walton-on-Thames 27766.

Ségalat, André; French executive; b. 10 Aug. 1910; ed. Ecole des Sciences Politiques.
Conseiller d'Etat; Sec.-Gen. of the Govt. 46-58; Pres. of the Admin. Council of the Société Nat. des Chemins de Fer Français 58-; Commdr. de la Légion d'Honneur.
88 rue Saint Lazare, Paris 9e, France.

Segawa, Minoru; Japanese investment executive; b. 31 March 1906; ed. Osaka Commercial Univ.
Nomura Securities Ltd. 29-, Dir. 46-, Man. Dir. 48-52, Exec. Vice-Pres. 52-59, Pres. 59-; Dir. Tokyo Securities Dealers Asscn. 62-, Tokyo Stock Exchange 62- (now Chair.), Mainichi Broadcasting Co. Ltd. 58-, Nippon Koka Railway Co. Ltd. 61-; Auditor, Toho Distiller Co. Ltd. 53-, Tokyo Koku Precision Instrument Co. 57-.
1-55 Minamicho, Aoyama, Minato-ku, Tokyo, Japan.

Segers, Paul Willem; Belgian politician; b. 21 Dec. 1900; ed. Catholic Univ. of Louvain.
Secretary, General Federation of Christian Workers 27-47, Pres. 47; mem. City Council of Antwerp 32-; Senator 49-; Minister of Communications 49-54, 58-61; Minister of Nat. Defence 61-65, Vice-Pres. of Council and Minister in charge of Co-ordination of Social Policies 65-66; Minister of State 67, of Nat. Defence June 68-; Christian Socialist Party; seven Belgian and foreign awards.
Avenue Rubens 1, Antwerp, Belgium.

Segerstedt, Torgny, D.PHIL.; Swedish university administrator; b. 11 Aug. 1908; ed. Lund Univ.
Asst. Prof. in Moral Philosophy, Lund Univ. 34-38; Prof. of Moral Philosophy, Uppsala Univ. 38, of Sociology 47, Dean of Faculty of Philosophy 47-54, and Rector 55-; Chair. Social Science Research Council; Chair. Univ. Comm. 57-63; Chair. Bank of Sweden Research Council 65-; Commdr. Order of Northern Star; Commdr. of the Order of Finnish White Rose; Officer French Legion of Honour; Dr. h.c. (Univ. of Helsinki).
Publs. *Value and Reality in Bradley's Philosophy* 34, *The Problem of Knowledge in Scottish Philosophy* 35, *Common-Sense-Skolan* 37, *Värde och Verklighet* (*Value and Reality*) 38, *Democratins Problem* 39, *Ordens Makt* 44, *Människan i industrisamhället* 52, 55, *The Nature of Social Reality* 66.
Kyrkogårdsgatan 5A, Uppsala, Sweden.

Seghers, Anna; German author; b. 19 Nov. 1900.
Mem. Deutsche Akad. der Künste; Pres. German Writers' Asscn.; Kleist Prize 28; Nat. Prize 51, 59; mem. Lenin Peace Prize Cttee.; Lenin Peace Prize.
Publs. *Der Aufstand der Fischer von Sankt Barbara* 28, *Die Gefährten* 32, *Das siebte Kreuz* 42, *Transit* 48, *Die Toten bleiben jung* 49, *Der Mann und sein Name* 52, *Der Bienenstock* 53, *Brot und Salz* 58, *Die Entscheidung* (novel) 59, *Das Licht auf dem Galgen* (story) 61, *Karibische Geschichten* (stories) 62, *Über Tolstoi—Über Dostojewski* (essays) 63, *Die Kraft der Schwachen* (novel) 65, *Das wirkliche Blau* (stories) 67, *Das Vertrauen* (novel) 68, etc.
Aufbau Verlag, Französischestrasse 32, Berlin, W.8, Germany.

Seghers, Pierre; French writer, poet and literary editor; b. 5 Jan. 1906; ed. Coll. de Carpentras (Vaucluse).
While serving with the army (39) founded magazine *Poètes Casqués* published yearly as *Poésie* 40, 41, etc. until 48; active in production and distribution of clandestine publications 40-44, founder mem. Comité National des Ecrivains; early collaborator on *Parisien Libéré*; fmr. Vice-Pres. Syndicat de la Presse Périodique Française; f. *Autour du Monde* (anthology of foreign

poets) 52; Chevalier de la Légion d'Honneur; Chevalier des Arts et des Lettres.

Publs. *Bonne Espérance* 39, *L'Homme du Commun* 44, *Considérations ou Histoires sous la Langue* 44, *Le Domaine Public* 45, *Le Futur Antérieur* 47, *Jeune Fille* 49, *Six Poèmes pour Véronique* 50, *Poèmes Choisis* 52, *Le Coeur-Volant* 54, *Racines* 57, *Les Pierres* 58, *Chansons et Complaintes* 59, *Piranèse* 60, *Le Livre d'or de la Poésie Française* 62.

118 Rue de Vaugirard, Paris 6e, France.

Segni, Antonio; Italian university professor and politician; b. 2 Feb. 1891; ed. Univ. of Rome.

Began career as lawyer; Prof. of Civil Procedure, Univ. of Perugia; later Prof. and Pres. Law Faculty, Univ. of Cagliari; Prof. Univ. of Pavia; Prof. of Commercial Law and fmr. Dean, Univ. of Sassari; at present Prof. of Civil Procedure, Univ. of Rome; mem. Sardinian Clandestine Cttee. for Liberation, First Regional Council for Sardinia; Constituent Assembly; mem. for Sardinia, Italian Parl.; Under-Sec. of Agriculture and Forestry 44; Minister of Agriculture and Forestry 46; Minister of Public Instruction 51-54; Prime Minister 55-57; Deputy Prime Minister and Minister of Defence July 58-Jan. 59; Prime Minister and Minister of the Interior Feb. 59-Feb. 60; Minister of Foreign Affairs March 60-62; Pres. of the Italian Republic 62-Dec. 64; Senator-for-Life 64-; Dir. *Studi Sassaresi* 21-; Commdr. Order of St. Gregory the Great (Holy See); Charlemagne Prize 64; Christian Democrat.

Publs. *L'Intervento Adesivo, L'Intervento in Appello, Il Processo Monitorio, La Sentenza dichiarativa di Fallimento, La Cosa giudicata.*

26 viale Esperanto, Eur, Rome, Italy.

Segovia, Andrés; Spanish guitarist; b. 18 Feb. 1894. Concerts throughout the world 14-; author of numerous arrangements of classical pieces for guitar; numerous recordings.

c/o Ibbs and Tillett Ltd., 124 Wigmore Street, London, W.1, England.

Segrè, Emilio, PH.D.; Italian-born American physicist; b. 1 Feb. 1905; ed. Univ. of Rome.

Asst. Prof. Univ. of Rome 28-35; Prof. of Physics and Dir. Physics Laboratory Palermo Univ. 36-38; Research Asst. and Lecturer Univ. of Calif., Berkeley 38-42; Group Leader Los Alamos Scientific Laboratory 42-46; naturalised U.S. citizen 44; Prof. of Physics Univ. of Calif. Berkeley 46-; mem. Nat. Acad. of Sciences, American Philosophical Soc., Accad. dei Lincei, Heidelberg Acad. of Sciences, etc.; Hoffman Medal (German Chemical Soc.), Cannizzaro Medal (Accad. dei Lincei), Nobel Prize in Physics (with Owen Chamberlain) 59; Hon. D.Sc. Palermo Univ., Gustavus Adolphus Coll., S. Marcos Univ., Lima etc.; Commdr. Merito della Repubblica (Italy); co-discoverer of the elements Technetium, Astatine and Plutonium, of the slow neutrons and the anti-proton.

Publs. Numerous papers on atomic and nuclear physics in *Physical Review, Proceedings of the Royal Society* (London), *Nature, Nuovo Cimento,* etc.

Department of Physics, University of California, Berkeley, California 94720; Home: 36 Crest Road, Lafayette, Calif. 94549, U.S.A.

Telephone: 254-5231 (Home).

Séguy, Georges; French trade unionist; b. 16 March 1927.

Apprentice typographer 42; mem. French C.P. 42-; arrested by Gestapo and deported to Mauthausen Concentration Camp 44; electrician, S.N.C.F. (French Railways) 45; Sec. of Confédération Général du Travail des Cheminots 49-65, Sec. Gen. 65-67; Sec. Gen. of Confédération Général du Travail (C.G.T.) 67-.

Confédération Général du Travail, 213 rue Lafayette, Paris 10e, France.

Telephone: BOT 86-50 (Office).

Sehgal, Amar Nath, B.SC., M.A.; Indian sculptor; b. 5 Feb. 1922; ed. Punjab Univ., Govt. Coll., Lahore, and New York Univ.

One man exhibitions New York 50-51, Paris 52, East Africa and India; Hon. Art Consultant to Ministry of Community Development, Govt. of India 55-; organised sculpture exhibition, Belgrade 64, Musée d'Art Moderne, Paris 65; Sculpture Award, Lalit Kala Akademy; President's Award, Lalit Kala Akademy 58. Major works: *Voice of Africa* (Ghana) 59, *A Cricketer* 61, Mahatma Gandhi, Amritsar, *To Space Unknown* (bronze, Moscow) 63; commissioned to decorate Vigyan Bhawan (India's Int. Conferences Building) with bronze sculptural mural depicting rural life of India; works in Jerusalem, Vienna, Paris, West Berlin.

Publs. *Arts and Aesthetics, Organising Exhibitions in Rural Areas.*

J-23 Jangpura Extension, New Delhi, India.

Seidenfaden, Erik; Danish writer and college warden; b. 24 April 1910; university education.

With *Nationaltidende,* Copenhagen 31-34; London corresp. of *Berlingske Tidende* 35-37; city editor of *Politiken* 37, Rome corresp. 40; during German occupation of Denmark was head of Free Danish information services in Stockholm; Editor-in-Chief of independent daily *Information* and monthly review of foreign affairs *Fremtiden* 46-66; Warden Danish Students' Coll., La Cité Int. de l'Université, Paris 66-; contributor on foreign affairs to Scandinavian, English and American newspapers and periodicals including *Berlingske Tidende* 67-; Copenhagen Corresp., *The Times,* London; mem. Council of the Inst. for Strategic Studies, London; Pres. Students Asscn., Copenhagen Univ. 64-65; Hon. M.B.E. (U.K.).

Publs. *Borgerkrig i Spanien* (Civil War in Spain) 36, *Hitler beskyddar Danmark* (Hitler Protects Denmark) 43 (published in Stockholm), *Spidser* 48, *Den hellige krig om det hellige land* 56, *Nuclear Arms and Foreign Policy* 60, *Disengagement* 61, *Disarmament* 62.

La Fondation Danoise, 9 boulevard Jourdain, Paris 14e, France.

Seidenfaden, Gunnar, D.SC.; Danish scientist and diplomatist; b. 24 Feb. 1908; ed. Copenhagen Univ.

Expeditions to Greenland 28-34, Thailand 34-35, Spitzbergen 38; U.S.A., Canada, Alaska 47-49, South America 50, Far East 55-57, China and Japan 58, Thailand 64, 66 and 68; Danish Foreign Service 40-, Wash. 45-50, Ministry of Foreign Affairs, Copenhagen 50-55, Amb. S.E. Asia 55-59, to U.S.S.R. 59-61; Deputy Under-Sec. of State 61-; Danish and foreign awards.

Publs. *Modern Arctic Exploration* 38, *The Orchids of Thailand* (with Tem Smitinand) 59-65.

Ministry of Foreign Affairs, Copenhagen; Home: Borsholmgård pr. Saunte, Denmark.

Seidler, Harry, M.ARCH., F.R.A.I.A., M.R.A.I.C.; Australian (b. Austrian) architect; b. 25 June 1923; ed. Wasagymnasium, Vienna, Austria, Cambridge Technical School, U.K., Univ. of Manitoba, Canada, Harvard Univ., U.S.A., and Black Mountain Coll., U.S.A.

Post graduate work under Walter Gropius, Harvard Univ. 46; study with painter Josef Albers, Black Mountain Coll. 46; Chief Asst. with Marcel Breuer, New York 46-48; Principal Architect, Harry Seidler and Assocs., Sydney, Australia 48-; Sir John Sulman Medal 51; Architecture and Arts Building of the Year Award 60. Major Works: flats and housing units in Australia, CIBA Co. Headquarters, Lane Cove, New South Wales 61; urban redevelopment projects for McMahons Point 57, The Rocks, Sydney Cove 62; city centre redevelopment "Australia Square", Sydney 62-66; Hon. Fellow American Inst. of Architects 66; R.A.I.A. Wilkinson Award 65 and 66.

Publs. *Houses, Interiors and Projects 1949-1954, Harry Seidler 1955-63.*

Office: 47-53 Macquarie Street, Sydney, New South Wales 2000; Home: 13 Kalang Avenue, Killara, N.S.W. 2071, Australia.
Telephone: 271739 (Office); 495986 (Home).

Seifert, Jaroslav; Czechoslovak poet; b. 23 Sept. 1901; ed. secondary school, Prague.
Writer and journalist for various Prague dailies and periodicals; co-founder Devětsil Art Asscn. 20; Editor *Rovnost*, Brno 22, *Sršatec* (periodical) 22-25; Editor in Chief *Nová scéna* (theatre monthly) 30; Editor *Pestré Květy* (weekly) 31-33, *Ranní noviny* (daily) 33-39, *Národní práce* (daily) 45-49; State Prizes 36, 55; Nat. Artist 66.
Publs. include: *Ruce Venušiny* (Venus' Hands—State Prize) 36, *Maminka* (Mother—State Prize) 54, *Koncert na ostrově* (Concert at the Island—State Prize) 68.
Union of Czechoslovak Writers, Národní třída 11, Prague 1, Czechoslovakia.

Seifert, Robin (Richard), F.R.I.B.A., DIP.ARCH.; British architect; b. 25 Nov. 1910; ed. Central Foundation School London and Univ. Coll. London.
Commenced architectural practice 34; Corps of Royal Engineers 40-44; Indian Army 44-46; Hon. Lt. Col. 46; private practice 48-; Principal of R. Seifert and Partners, formed April 58; Liveryman, City of London; mem. Nat. Road Safety Advisory Council, Home Office Cttee. of Management for Homeless Discharged Prisoners.
Principal works include: Centre Point, St. Giles Circus; Drapers Gardens; Nat. Provincial Bank H.Q.; Royal Garden Hotel, Kensington; Tolworth Towers, Surbiton; Woolworth House, Marylebone Rd.; I.C.T. H.Q., Putney; Kellogg House, Baker Street (all in London area).
Office: 34 Red Lion Square, London, W.C.1; Home: Eleventrees, Milespit Hill, Mill Hill, London, N.W.7.
Telephone: 01-242-1644 (Office); 01-959-3397 (Home).

Seigner, Louis; French actor; b. 23 June 1903; ed. Lycée de Lyon and Conservatoires d'Art dramatique de Lyon et de Paris.
Actor, Théâtre des Celestins, Lyon 19-23, Théâtre de l'Odéon, Paris 23-39; Pensionnaire, Comédie Française 39-43, Sociétaire 43-, Doyen 60-; Prof. Conservatoire National d'Art Dramatique 62-; Officier Légion d'Honneur, Commandeur des Arts et des Lettres.
Plays acted in include: *Le Roi soleil, Madame Sans-Gêne, Cyrano de Bergerac, Pelléas et Mélisande, Le Chevalier Canepin, Le Dindon.*
Films acted in include: *La Symphonie fantastique, Nous sommes tous des assassins, La Belle Otéro, Marguerite de la nuit, Le Bourgeois gentilhomme, La Verité, L'Eclipse, Les Amitiés particulières, Le Soleil Noir.*
12 rue Pierre-Curie, Paris 5e, France.

Seip, Helge Lunde; Norwegian journalist and politician; b. 5 March 1919; ed. Oslo, Harvard (U.S.A.) and Cambridge (England) Univs.
Asst. Oslo Univ. 39; Statistical Sec. Norwegian Leather Board 41; Consultant Rieber A/S 42, Ministry of Finance 45; Div. Head Ministry of Commerce 48, Cen. Bureau of Statistics 52; Chief Political Editor *Dagbladet* (Oslo daily) 54, Editor-in-Chief 54-; mem. Norwegian Parliament 53-, 61 and 65-; mem. Nordic Cultural Comm. 55-, Nordic Council 58-62; Minister of Labour and Local Affairs Oct. 65-67; Liberal.
Publ. *Kommunenes Ökonomi* 49.
Gl. Drammensveg 146, Blommenholm, Norway.

Seitz, Frederick, A.B., PH.D.; American physicist; b. 4 July 1911; ed. Stanford and Princeton Univs.
Instructor of Physics, Univ. of Rochester 35-36, Asst. Prof. 36-37; on staff of Research Laboratory of Gen. Electric Co. 37-39; Asst. Prof., Univ. of Pa. 39-41; Assoc. Prof. 41-42, Prof. and Head of Dept. of Physics, Carnegie Inst. of Technology 42-49, Univ. of Ill. 49-; NATO Science Adviser 59-; mem. American Philo-

sophical Soc., Pres. Nat. Acad. of Sciences 62, American Physics Soc. 61; mem. American Acad. of Arts and Sciences, President's Science Advisory Cttee., Naval Research Advisory Cttee., and numerous other advisory cttees.; mem. Board of Trustees, Rockefeller Univ. etc.; co-editor *Solid State Physics* (series); several honorary degrees.
Publs. *The Modern Theory of Solids* 40, *The Physics of Metals* 43.
Home: 3025 Whitehaven Street, N.W., Washington, D.C.; Office: National Academy of Sciences, Washington, D.C. 20418, U.S.A.

Seitz, Gustav; German sculptor; b. 11 Sept. 1906; ed. Hochschule für bildende Künste, Berlin.
Master's studio, Prussian Acad. of Arts, Berlin 33-38; Prof. Hochschule für bildende Künste, Berlin 46-50; Prof. and Head of Master's Studio, Deutsche Akad. der Künste, Berlin 50-58, Hochschule der Bildenden Künste, Hamburg 58-; sculptures and drawings in several German and foreign museums.
Hochschule der Bildenden Künste, Lerchenfeld 2, Hamburg 24, German Federal Republic.
Telephone: 2281497

Sekers, Sir Nicholas Thomas, Kt., M.B.E., F.R.S.A.; British silk manufacturer; b. 15 Dec. 1910; ed. Marko Real School, Budapest, Acad. of Commerce, Budapest, and Textile Technological Coll., Krefeld, Germany.
Director, Adria Silk Mills Ltd., Budapest, Hungary 31-37; Man. Dir. West Cumberland Silk Mills Ltd., Whitehaven, U.K. 38-; Trustee Glyndebourne Arts Trust Ltd. 54-, Rosehill Arts Trust Ltd. 59-, Chichester Festival Theatre 62-; Dir. Meadow Players Ltd., Oxford 62-65; Chair. Sekers Fabriks Ltd.; Dir. Sekers Mills Ltd.; Chair. London Mozart Players 62-67, Vice-Chair. 67-; London Philharmonic Orchestra Council 65-; Gov. The Yehudi Menuhin School 65-67, Vice Chair. 67-; Hon. Assoc. Manchester Coll. of Art 63; Fellow, Soc. of Industrial Artists 65-; mem. Council of Industrial Design 66-; Freeman of Worshipful Co. of Musicians 66-; Fellow, Royal Soc. of Arts 67-; mem. Council of the Shakespeare Theatre Trust 67-; Duke of Edinburgh's Prize for Elegant Design 62; Hon. M.A. Univ. of Manchester 63.
Rosehill, Moresby, Whitehaven, Cumberland; and 1 Harriet Walk, Lowndes Square, London, S.W.1, England.
Telephone: Whitehaven 2673; 01-235-3410.

Seki, Yoshinaga, M.SC.; Japanese business executive; b. 20 June 1892; ed. Tokyo Imperial Univ.
Mitsubishi Holding Co., Shipbuilding Dept. 15-23, Mitsubishi Electric Mfg. Co. 23-, Dir. 43-45, Man. Dir. 45-49, Vice-Pres. 49-56, Pres. 56-64, Chair. 64-; Chair. Mitsubishi Atomic Power Industries Inc. May 65-; official of numerous Japanese electrical and business orgs.; Medal with Blue Ribbon 60.
Mitsubishi Electric Corpn., 12, 2-chome, Marunouchi, Chiyoda-ku, Tokyo, Japan.

Seldes, Gilbert (Vivian); American writer; b. 3 Jan. 1893; ed. Harvard Univ.
Newspaper correspondent abroad during First World War; Washington correspondent *L'Echo de Paris* 18; Man. Editor *The Dial* 20-23; special writer *New York Journal* 32-37; Dir. of Television Programmes, Columbia Broadcasting System 37-45; Dean Annenberg School of Communications, Univ. of Pennsylvania 59-63; Programme Consultant, Nat. Educ. Television 64.
Publs. *The United States and the War* 17, *The Seven Lively Arts* 24, 58, *The Stammering Century* 28, *Lysistrata* (play) 30, *The Years of the Locust* 32, *Mainland* 36, *Movies for the Millions* 37, *Your Money and Your Life* 37, *Proclaim Liberty!* 42, *The Great Audience* 50, *The Public Arts* 56.
125 East 57th Street, New York, N.Y. 10022, U.S.A.
Telephone: PL3-9509.

Seligman, Henry, o.b.e., ph.d.; British scientist; b. 25 Feb. 1909; ed. Liebigschule, Frankfurt am Main, Univs. of Lausanne, Paris and Zürich.
Joined Atomic Energy Team, Cavendish Laboratory, Cambridge 41; worked on atomic research with N.R.C., Canada 43-46; founded Isotope Div., Harwell 47, Deputy Dir.-Gen. of Research and Isotopes at the Int. Atomic Energy Agency, Vienna 58-; Pres. Joint Cttee. on Applied Radioactivity, Int. Council of Scientific Unions (ICSU) 57-.
International Atomic Energy Agency, Kaerntnerring 11, 1010 Vienna, Austria.
Telephone: 52-45-25.

Selkirk, Earl of; George Nigel Douglas-Hamilton, p.c., g.c.m.g., g.b.e., a.f.c., q.c.; Scottish advocate and politician; b. 4 Jan. 1906; ed. Eton, Balliol Coll., Oxford, and Univs. of Edinburgh, Bonn, Vienna and Paris.
Admitted to Faculty of Advocates 35; commanded 603 Squadron A.A.F. 34-38; mem. King's Bodyguard for Scotland 35-39 and of Edinburgh Town Council 35-40; Commr. for Gen. Board of Control (Scotland) 36-39 and for Special Areas (Scotland) 35-39; served R.A.F. 39-45; elected a Scots Representative Peer 45-63; Lord-in-Waiting 51-53; Paymaster Gen. 53-55; Chancellor of the Duchy of Lancaster 55-57; First Lord of the Admiralty 57-59; U.K. Commr. for Singapore and Commr.-Gen. for S.E. Asia, Singapore 59-63; U.K. Council Rep. to South-East Asia Treaty Org. 60-63; Pres. Building Socs. Asscn., Nat. Ski Fed. of Great Britain, Royal Central Asian Soc.; Freeman of Hamilton 37.
60 Eaton Place, London, S.W.1, England.
Telephone: 01-235-6926.

Sellers, Rt. Hon. Sir Frederic Aked, Kt., p.c., m.c.; British judge; b. 14 Jan. 1893; ed. Liverpool Univ.
Served with the King's Regt., First World War 14-18; called to the Bar (Gray's Inn), Northern Circuit 19; K.C. 35; Bencher of Gray's Inn 38; Treas. of Gray's Inn 52; Recorder of Bolton 38-46; Judge of the High Court (Queen's Bench Div.) 46-57; Lord Justice of Appeal 57-68; Chair. of Govs., Mill Hill School; Chair. Standing Cttee. on Criminal Law Revision 59-; Hon. LL.D.
Highwood Lodge, Mill Hill, London, N.W.7, England.

Sellers, Peter Richard Henry, c.b.e.; British actor; b. 8 Sept. 1925; ed. St. Aloysius Coll., Highgate.
Debut at Windmill Theatre 48; toured 49-54; radio shows include *Ray's a Laugh, The Goon Show;* television shows *Idiots Weekly, A Show Called Fred, Son of Fred;* films *The Ladykillers, The Smallest Show on Earth, The Naked Truth, Tom Thumb, Carleton Browne of the F.O., The Mouse that Roared, I'm Alright Jack, Up the Creek, Two Way Stretch, Battle of the Sexes, Never Let Go, The Millionairess, Mr. Topaze, The Running, Jumping and Standing Still Film, Only Two Can Play, The Waltz of the Toreadors, Lolita, The Wrong Arm of the Law, Heavens Above!, Dr. Strangelove, The Pink Panther, The World of Henry Orient, What's New, Pussycat? A Shot in the Dark, After the Fox, Casino Royale, The Bobo, The Party, I Love You, Alice B. Toklas;* British Film Acad. Award 59, Golden Gate Trophy 59, San Sebastian 62.
c/o C.M.A. Ltd., 22 Grafton Street, London, W.1, England.

Sellin, (Johan) Thorsten, a.m., ph.d., ll.d.; American (b. Swedish) sociologist; b. 26 Oct. 1896; ed. primary and secondary schools in Sweden, Augustana Coll., Rock Island, Illinois and Univs. of Pennsylvania, Minnesota and Paris.
Assistant Prof., Univ. of Pa. 22-30, Prof. of Sociology 30-; Lecturer, Columbia Univ. 35-46; Visiting Prof. Univs. of Uppsala, Stockholm and Lund 46-47, Princeton Univ. 49, Univ. of Calif. 58; Fulbright Lecturer, Cambridge Univ. 59-60; Sec.-Gen. Int. Penal and Penitentiary Comm. 50-51, 12th Int. Penal and Penitentiary Congress 50; Consultant, Swedish Penal Code Comm. 46-47, American Law Inst. Youth Correction and Model Penal Code projects; Official, UN Comms. of Experts on Prevention of Crime and Treatment of Offenders 49-56; Pres. Int. Soc. of Criminology 56-66, Int. Penal and Penitentiary Foundation 65-; Pres. Fourth Int. Congress of Criminology 60 (Hon. Pres. Fifth Congress 65); Gen. Rapporteur First UN World Congress on Prevention of Crime and Treatment of Offenders; Editor *Annals* of the American Acad. of Political and Social Science 29-; mem. American Philosophical Soc., Social Science Research Council, Royal Soc. of Humanistic Knowledge (Lund), History of Law Soc. (Paris), Mexican Acad. of Penal Sciences; Grand Officer Order of North Star (Sweden); Penitentiary Medal (France); Gold Medal German Criminological Soc.; Hon. Dr. Augustan Coll. and Univs. of Uppsala, Pennsylvania and Leiden.
Publs. *Crime in the Depression 37, Culture Conflict and Crime 38, The Criminality of Youth 40, Pioneering in Penology 44, The Death Penalty 59, The Measurement of Delinquency* (co-author) 64; Editor: *Capital Punishment 67.*
4106 Locust Street, Philadelphia, Pa. 19104, U.S.A.

Sellner, Gustav Rudolf; German theatre director; b. 25 May 1905; ed. Gymnasium, Univ. of Munich, and drama training at Kammerspiele, Munich.
Actor, Producer, Stage Dir. and Dir., Oldenburg, Göttingen, Hanover 24-38; Producer at Kiel, Essen and Hamburg 45-51; Dir. Hessisches Landestheater, Darmstadt 51-, Deutsche Oper, Berlin 61-; numerous awards and prizes.
First performances include *Alkmeme* (Giselher Klebe) Berlin 61, *Dir Orestie* (Darius Milhaud) Berlin 63, *Montezuma* (Roger Sessions) Berlin 64, *Der Junge Lord* (Hans Werner Henze) Berlin 65, *Die Bassariden* (Henze) Salzburg 66, *Zwischenfälle bei einer Notlandung* (Boris Blacher) Hamburg 66, *Prometheus* (Carl Orff) Stuttgart 68.
Publs. include *Theatralische Landschaft* (with Werner Wien) 62.
Deutsche Oper Berlin, 1 Berlin 10, Richard-Wagner-Strasse 10, Germany.
Telephone: 34-01-81.

Selmer, Mrs. Ragnhild Elisabeth Schweigaard; Norwegian judge and politician; b. 1923; ed. Univ. of Oslo.
Assistant Judge, Municipal Court of Asker and Baerum 50; mem. Oslo City Council 51-55; Law Section, Ministry of Justice 55-65; Judge, Court of Probate, Oslo 65; Minister of Justice 65-; mem. Nat. Consumer Council; Rep. Nat. Council of Norwegian Women; Conservative.
Ministry of Justice, Oslo, Norway.

Selwyn-Clarke, Sir Selwyn, k.b.e., c.m.g., m.c., c.st.j., m.d., b.s., f.r.c.p., m.r.c.s., d.p.h., d.t.m. & h., b.l.; British doctor; b. 17 Dec. 1893; ed. Bedales and London Univ.
Resident Medical Officer and Asst. Anaesthetist, St. Bartholomew's Hospital 16; Medical Officer, 285 Brigade R.F.A. and Queen Victoria Rifles, B.E.F. 16-18; M.O.H. Gold Coast, Colonial Medical Service 19; Chief Health Officer, Federated Malay States 30; Dir. of Medical Services Hong Kong 38; Gov. and C.-in-C. of the Seychelles 47-51; Principal Medical Officer, Ministry of Health 51-56; Medical Sec. Society of Medical Officers of Health 56-61; C.M.O. The King's Troop, R.H.A. 62-; Fellow Royal Soc. of Medicine, Life Fellow Royal Soc. of Hygiene and Tropical Medicine; Hon. Life Fellow British Red Cross Soc., Ghana Red Cross Soc.; Fellow Royal Soc. of Arts; Médaille en Argent des Epidémies 28; Langley Memorial Prizeman 24.
Publs. *Smallpox in Negro and Negroid Tribes of the Gold Coast 21, Vaccination and Smallpox 21, Exhibition of Acetylarsinic Acid in Treatment of Framboesia 26,*

Influence of Rainfall on Incidence of Malaria in the Federated Malay States 31, *Hong Kong Medical History of the Pacific War* 52, *The Bight of Benin and Beyond* 53, *Make your Home Safer* 54, *Housing and Health* 55, *Family Doctor and Health Visitor* 55, *An ABC of Housing* 55, *The Old Folks at Home* 56, *The British Rehabilitation Service* 56, *The Child as a Hospital Patient* 57, *Children in Hospitals* 58, *Family Housing and Health in Tropical Countries* 58, *Seychelles* (Encyclopaedia Britannica) 59, *Personal Health in the Tropics* 60, *Multiple Sclerosis* 60, *Commonwealth Opportunities* 61, *Team Work* 61, *Round the World in Twenty-Eight Days* 61, *Seychelles* 62, *Report on the Health Services of Ghana* 62, *The Sainsbury Report and the General Practitioner* 68. 3 Stirling Mansions, Canfield Gardens, London, N.W.6, England.

Selye, Hans, PH.D., D.SC., M.D., F.R.S.C.; Canadian university professor; b. 26 Jan. 1907; ed. Prague, Paris, Rome and McGill Univs.
Asst. in Experimental Pathology at Univ. of Prague 29-31; Rockefeller Research Fellow in Biochemical Hygiene, Johns Hopkins Univ. 31; Rockefeller Research Fellow in Biochemistry, McGill Univ. 32-33, Lecturer 33-34, Asst. Prof. 34-37; Asst. Prof. of Histology, McGill Univ. 37-41, Assoc. Prof. 41-45; Prof. and Dir. of Institute of Experimental Medicine and Surgery, Univ. of Montreal 45-; Guest Lecturer U.S.A. and Canada 50-; consultant to Surgeon-Gen., U.S. Army 47-57; Hon. Prof. Guatemala, Univ. of San Carlos; Fellow, N.Y. Acad. of Sciences, Royal Soc. of Canada and American Asscn. for the Advancement of Science, American Geriatrics Soc., Int. Coll. of Surgeons (Hon.), and numerous other North and South American and European Acads. and Socs.; numerous honorary degrees; awards include: Casgrain and Charbonneau prize; Gordon Wilson medal; Heberden Research Medal; Medal of Accad. Medico Fisica of Florence; Semmelweiss Medal (New York), Henderson Gold Medal, American Coll. of Angiology Award 59, Western Soc. of Periodontology Award 60, Samuel Charles Miller Memorial Award 60, B'nai B'rith Humanitarian Award 61; Hon. Citizen of Verona 55.
Publs. *The Steroids* 43, *Ovarian Tumors* 46, *Textbook of Endocrinology* 49, *Stress* 50, *On the Experimental Morphology of the Adrenal Cortex* 50, *First Annual Report on Stress* 51, *Second Annual Report on Stress* 52, *The Story of the Adaptation Syndrome* 52, *Third Annual Report on Stress* 53, *Fourth Annual Report on Stress* 54, *Fifth Annual Report on Stress* 55, *The Stress of Life* 56, *The Chemical Prevention of Cardiac Necroses* 58, *The Pluricausal Cardiopathies* 61, *Calciphylaxis* 62, *From Dream to Discovery* 64, *The Mast Cells* 65, *Thrombohemorrhagic Phenomena* 66, many scientific papers.
Institut de Médecine et de Chirurgie Expérimentales, Université de Montréal, P.O. Box 6128, Montreal; and 659 Milton Street, Montreal, Quebec, Canada. Telephone: 343-6378/9.

Semichastnov, Ivan Fyodorovich; Soviet foreign trade official; b. 1905.
Member C.P.S.U. 29-; Deputy People's Commissar for Foreign Trade 46-49; First Vice-Chair. Soviet Control Comm. in Germany 49-53; Rep. Ministry of Foreign Trade, in German Dem. Repub. 53-54; Deputy Minister of Foreign Trade 65-; Order of Lenin (twice), Order of Red Banner of Labour (three times), Order of Red Banner, Order of Red Star (twice).
Ministry of Foreign Trade, 32-34 Smolenskaya-Sennaya ploshchad, Moscow, U.S.S.R.

Semichastny, Vladimir Efimovich; Soviet politician; b. 1924; ed. Kemerovo Chemical Technological Inst.
Former First Sec., Communist League of Youth; fmr. senior official, Soviet Communist Party, Moscow; fmr. Sec., Communist Party of Azerbaijan; Chair. State Security Cttee. of Council of Ministers of U.S.S.R. 61-67;

First Vice-Chair. Ukrainian Council of Ministers June 67-; Cand. mem. Central Cttee. C.P.S.U. 56-64, mem. 64-.
Council of Ministers of Ukrainian S.S.R., Kiev, U.S.S.R.

Semyonov, Nikolai Nikolaevich, D.SC.; Soviet scientist; b. 15 April 1896; ed. Leningrad State Univ.
Asst. Dir. and Laboratory Man. Physico-Technical Inst., Leningrad 20-30; Asst. Prof. 20-, later Prof. Leningrad Polytechnic Inst.; Dir. Inst. of Chemical Physics, Leningrad 31-; Prof. Moscow State Univ. 44-; Deputy to U.S.S.R. Supreme Soviet; mem. U.S.S.R. Acad. of Sciences 32-, Vice-Pres. 63-, Academician, Sec. Dept. of Chemical Sciences 57-; mem. Chemical Soc. of England 43-; foreign mem. Royal Soc. of England 58; hon. mem. Indian Acad. of Sciences 59; mem. German Acad. of Naturalists (Leopoldina) 59; hon. mem. Hungarian Acad. of Sciences 61; hon. life mem. New York Acad. of Sciences 62; Foreign associate, Nat. Acad. of Sciences, U.S.A. 63; Hon. mem. Czech. and Romanian Acads. of Sciences 65; Corresp. mem. German Acad. of Sciences Berlin; Hon. Fellow Royal Soc. of Edinburgh 66; Dr. h.c. Oxford 60, Brussels 62, Milan 64, Budapest, Prague, London 65; Orders of Lenin (five); Order of Red Banner of Labour; Nobel Prize 56; State Prize 41; Hero of Socialist Labour.
Publs. *Chain Reactions* 34, *Some Problems of Chemical Kinetics and Reactivity* 54 (2nd edn. revised and translated into English) 58, and over 200 articles in the field of chemical physics.
U.S.S.R. Academy of Sciences, 14 Leninsky Prospekt, Moscow; Home: Vorobyevskoye chaussée 2-b, Flat 1-a, Moscow V-334, U.S.S.R.

Semyonov, Vladimir Semyonovich; Soviet diplomatist and politician; b. 11; ed. Moscow Inst. of Philosophy, History and Literature.
Counsellor in Kaunas 39-40, Berlin 40-41, Stockholm 42-45; Political Adviser Berlin 45-53; rank of Minister 45, of Amb. 49; High Commr. in Germany 53-54; Deputy Foreign Minister 55-; mem. Central Auditing Comm. C.P.S.U. 61-66; Cand. mem. C.P.S.U. Central Cttee. 66-.
Ministry of Foreign Affairs, 32-34 Smolenskaya-Sennaya ploshchad, Moscow, U.S.S.R.

Sen, Asoke-Kumar, M.A., M.SC.; Indian lawyer and politician; b. 10 Oct. 1913; ed. Jagannath Intermediate Coll., Dacca, Presidency Coll., Calcutta, Dacca Univ. and London School of Economics.
Called to Calcutta Bar 41; Prof. City Coll. 41-43; Junior Standing Counsel, West Bengal Govt. 50-56; Law Minister and mem. of the Indian Cabinet 57-66, of Social Security 64-66, and of Posts and Telegraphs 63-64; Editor *Calcutta Law Journal;* mem. Indian Nat. Congress Party.
Publ. *Handbook of Commercial Law.*
9 Raisina Road, New Delhi, India.

Sen, Dr. Binay Ranjan; Indian diplomatist and international administrator; b. 1 Jan. 1898; ed. Calcutta and Oxford Univs.
District Magistrate, Midnapore 37-40; Revenue Sec., Govt. of Bengal 40-43, Dir. of Civil Evacuation 42-43; Relief Commr. 42-43; Dir.-Gen. of Food, Govt. of India 43-46, Sec., Dept. of Food 46-47; Minister in Washington 47-48; Sec. Ministry of Agriculture 48; Chargéd'Affaires and Minister in Washington 48-50; Indian Ambassador to Italy and Yugoslavia 50-51 and 52-55, to U.S.A. 51-52; Ambassador to Japan 55-56; Dir.-Gen. Food and Agriculture Org. of UN (FAO) 56-67.
c/o Food and Agriculture Organization of the United Nations, Viale delle Terme di Caracalla, Rome, Italy.

Sen, Prafulla Chandra; Indian politician; b. 97; ed. Scottish Church Coll. and Calcutta Univ.
Imprisoned in cause of Indian independence 30, 40,

42; mem. All-India Congress Cttee. 30-; Minister, W. Bengal 48-62, Chief Minister 62-67.
c/o Mantri Niwas, Raj Bhavan, Calcutta 1, India.

Sen, Sukumar, M.A., PH.D.; Indian philologist; b. 4 March 1900; ed. Raj Coll. Burdwan, Sanskrit Coll. and Univ. of Calcutta.
Research Student Univ. of Calcutta 24-26, Khaira Research Scholar 27-29, Lecturer 30-54, Khaira Prof. of Indian Linguistics and Phonetics and Head of Dept. of Comparative Philology 54-64; Pres. Linguistic Soc. of India 54; Fellow Asiatic Soc.
Publs. English: *History of Brajabuli Literature* 35, *Old Persian Inscriptions of the Akhaemenian Emperors* 41, *History and Prehistory of Sanskrit* 57, *History of Bengali Literature* 59, etc.; Bengali: *History of Bengali Literature*, 4 vols. 41-58.
403 Grand Trunk Road, Burdwan, India.

Sen, Triguna, D.ING.; Indian university official and politician; b. 14 Dec. 1905; ed. Calcutta and Germany.
Special Admin. Officer, Coll. of Eng. and Technology, Bengal 43-44, Principal 44-53; Vice-Chancellor of Jadavpur Univ. 56-66; Vice-Chancellor Banaras Hindu Univ. 66-67; fmr. mem. Indian Planning Comm. (Educ.); Minister of Educ. 67-; Mayor of Calcutta 58, 59; Padma Bhusan 65.
Ministry of Education, New Delhi, India.

Senanayake, Dudley Shelton, B.A.; Ceylonese barrister and politician; b. 19 June 1911; ed. Corpus Christi Coll., Cambridge.
Barrister of Middle Temple; elected to State Council (Legislative Assembly) 36, to House of Representatives 47; Minister of Agriculture and Lands 47; Prime Minister, Minister of Defence and Minister of External Affairs Mar. 52-53; Pres. United Nat. Party 58-; Prime Minister, Minister of External Affairs and Defence March 60-July 60; Leader of the Opposition 61-65; Prime Minister and Minister of Defence, External Affairs and Planning and Econ. Affairs 65-, also of Information and Broadcasting.
Woodlands, Kanatta Road, Colombo 8, Ceylon.

Senanayake, Maithripala; Ceylonese politician; b. 16; ed. St. Joseph's Coll., Anuradhapura, St. John's Coll., Jaffna, and Nalanda Vidyalaya, Colombo.
Joined Govt. Service 40, Cultivation Officer 40-47; mem. Parl. 47-; Minister of Transport and Works 56-Dec. 59; Minister of Industries, Home Affairs and Cultural Affairs July 60-July 63; Minister of Commerce and Industries July 63-June 64, of Rural and Industrial Development 64-65; Sri Lanka Freedom Party.
121 MacCarthy Road, Colombo 7, Ceylon.

Senda, Kenzo; Japanese business executive; b. 90; ed. Waseda Univ.
Successively, Man. Dir. Teninami Railway Ltd., Toyokawa Railway Co., Nagoya Railroad; Vice-Pres., now Chair., Nagoya Railroad; also Pres., Aichi Shipbuilding Industry Co.
1-223 Sasashimacho, Nakumaraku, Nagoya, Japan.

Sender, Ramón José, LIC. EN FIL. Y LET.; Spanishborn American author and educator; b. 3 Feb. 1901; ed. Colegio de la Sagrada Familia, Reus (Catalonia), Inst. de Zaragoza, Inst. de Teruel and Madrid Univ.
Infantry Officer, Morocco 23-24; Editor *El Sol*, Madrid 24-31; free-lance writer 31-36; Major on Gen. Staff, Spanish Republican Army 36-39; Prof. of Spanish Literature, Amherst Coll., Mass. 43-44, Denver Univ. 44; Prof. of Spanish Literature, New Mexico Univ. 47-63, Prof. Emer. 63; Visiting Prof. Ohio State Univ. 51, Univ. of Calif. 62; Medal of Morocco, Spanish Mil. Cross of Merit.
Publs. in English: *Pro Patria* 34, *Seven Red Sundays* 35, *Mr. Witt among the Rebels* 36, *Counter-attack in Spain* 38, *A Man's Place* 40, *Dark Wedding* 43, *Chronicle of Dawn* 44, *The King and the Queen* 48, *The Sphere* 49,

The Affable Hangman 54, *Before Noon* 57, *Requiem for a Spanish Peasant* 60, *Exemplary Novels of Cibola* 63.
American Literary Agency, 11 Riverside Drive, New York 23, N.Y., U.S.A.

Senghor, Léopold Sédar; Senegalese writer and politician; b. 9 Oct. 1906; ed. Lycée de Dakar, Lycée Louis le Grand, Paris and Paris Univ.
Teacher, Lycée, Tours 35-44, Lycée Marcelin Berthelot, Paris 44-48; mem. Constituent Assemblies 45-46; Deputy from Senegal to Nat. Assembly 46-58; Prof., Ecole Nat. de la France d'Outre-Mer 48-58; Sec. of State, Présidence du Conseil 55-56; mem. Consultative Assembly, Council of Europe; Pres. Fed. Assembly, Mali Fed. of Senegal and Sudan 59-60, Pres. Senegal Republic 60-, also Minister of Defence 68-; leader, Union Progressiste Sénégalaise, nat. party of Parti Fédéraliste Africain (P.F.A.); Dag Hammarskjöld Prize 65; Peace Prize of German Book Trade, Frankfurt.
Publs. *Ethiopiques, Chants d'Ombre, Hosties Noires, Nocturnes, On African Socialism.*
Office of the President, Dakar, Senegal, West Africa.

Senkin, Ivan Ilyich; Soviet politician; b. 15; ed. Moscow Timiryazev Agricultural Acad.
Agronomist, Karelian-Finnish S.S.R. 39-41; Soviet Army 41-46; Communist Party official, Sverdlovsk Region 46-55; Dep. Chair. Council of Ministers, later Second Sec. of Central Cttee. of Communist Party of Karelian-Finnish S.S.R. 55-56; Second Sec. Karelian Regional Cttee. of C.P.S.U. 56-58, First Sec. 58-; mem. Central Auditing Comm. of C.P.S.U. 61-66; Cand. mem. C.P.S.U. Central Cttee. 66-; Deputy to U.S.S.R. Supreme Soviet; several decorations.
Regional Committee of Karelian C.P.S.U., Petrozavodsk, Karelian A.S.S.R., U.S.S.R.

Senn, Alfred, PH.D.; American philologist; b. 19 March 1899; ed. Univ. of Fribourg.
Teacher Univ. of Lithuania, Kaunas 22-30; Sterling Research Fellow Yale Univ. 30-31; Prof. of Germanic and Indo-European Philology, Univ. of Wisconsin 31-38; Prof. of Germanic Philology Univ. of Pa. 38-48, Prof. of Germanic and Balto-Slavic Studies 48-, Chair. Dept. of Slavic and Baltic Studies 47-65; Pres. American Asscn. of Teachers of German 56-59, Asscn. Internationale des Langues et Littératures Slaves 60-63.
Publs. *Anthologia Latina* 23, *Germanische Lehnwortstudien* 25, *Kleine litauische Sprachlehre* 29, *An Introduction to Middle High German* 37, *Word-Index to Wolfram's Parzival* 38, *The Lithuanian Language* 42, *Lithuanian Dialectology* 45, *A Russian Grammar* 51, *Wörterbuch der litauischen Schriftsprache* Vol. I (with Max Niedermann and Franz Brender) 32, Vol. II (with Max Niedermann and Anton Salys) 51, Vol. III (with Anton Salys) 57, Vol. IV (with Anton Salys) 63, Vol. V 67, *Handbuch der litauischen Sprache* Vol. I 57, Vol. II 64, *Storia della letteratura lituana* 57 (2nd Edn. 64).
207 Cynwyd Road, Bala-Cynwyd, Pa., U.S.A.

Sennikov, Arkady Andreyevich; Soviet trade union official; b. 08; ed. Higher Party School of the C.P.S.U. Central Committee.
Young Communist League and Party work 25-39; Vice-Chair. Council of People's Commissars of the Turkmen S.S.R.; Party work 45-60; Chair. Central Cttee. of Trade Union Workers of State Insts. 60-; mem. All-Union Central Council of Trade Unions 68-; mem. C.P.S.U.; Order of Lenin and other decorations.
Central Committee of the Trade Union of Workers of State Institutions, 42 Leninsky Prospekt, Moscow, U.S.S.R.

Sentís, Carlos; Spanish lawyer and journalist; b. 11; ed. Real Colegio Escuelas Pias, Barcelona and Barcelona Univ.
London corresp. for Silver Jubilee 35, in Italy 36, later France; National Journalism Prize "Mariano de Cavia"

May 46; Special corresp. U.S. and Canada for *ABC*
Madrid and *La Vanguardia* Barcelona May 46, Carib-
bean countries 49; special corresp. U.N. Gen. Assem-
blies N.Y. and Paris 47, 48; former attaché, Spanish
Embassy, Brussels and Paris; special correspondent in
Paris for *Informaciones* Madrid, *La Vanguardia*
Barcelona, *Clarín* Buenos Aires 56-; Hon. Attaché
Paris 58-62; Gen. Dir. News Agency *Efe*, Madrid
Feb. 63-.
Publs. *La Europa que he visto morir* 42, *Africa en blanco
y negro* (*Del Congo a Argel con el General de Gaulle*) 45,
La paz vista desde Londres 46.
c/o *Efe*, Ayala 5; and Princesa 22, Madrid, Spain.

Seper, H.E. Cardinal Franjo, PH.D., TH.D.; Yugoslav
ecclesiastic; b. 2 Oct. 1905; ed. Gregorian Univ., Rome.
Sec. to Archbishop of Zagreb 34-41; Rector Zagreb
Major Seminary 41-51, Church of Christ the King,
Zagreb 51-54; Archbishop Coadjutor to Cardinal
Stepinac 54-60; Archbishop of Zagreb 60-, cr. Cardinal
65; Prefect of the Sacred Congregation for the Doctrine
of the Faith, Rome 68; Hon. LL.D.
Piazza St. Uffizio 11, Rome, Italy.
Telephone: Vatican 3296.

Sépinski, Augustin Joseph Antoine, Lic. in Canon
Law, D.TH.; French ecclesiastic; b. 26 July 1900; ed.
Franciscan Studium (Metz) and Strasbourg Univ.
Entered Order of Friars Minor (Franciscans) 19,
ordained priest 24; Dir. Coll. St. Antoine, Metz 29-33,
Phalsbourg 33-38; Minister Provincial, Metz 38-45;
Del. Gen. for Southern France 43-45; Definitor Gen.,
Rome 45-51; Minister Gen. of the Order 51- (re-elected
57); Titular Archbishop of Assura 66-; Apostolic Del.
of Jerusalem, Palestine, Cyprus 66-; Chevalier Légion
d'Honneur; Dr. h.c. Univs. of St. Bonaventure (New
York) and Dublin and Quincy Coll. (Ill.).
Publ. *La Psychologie du Christ chez Saint Bonaventure*
48; trans. *Cristo Interiore secondo San Bonaventura* 64.
Apostolic Delegation, P.O. Box 19199, Jerusalem, Israel.
Telephone: 82298.

Seppala, Richard Rafael, Barrister-at-Law; Finnish
diplomatist; b. 15 Jan. 1905; ed. Turku Lyceum,
Hamina Reserve Officers' School, Helsinki Univ.
Entered Foreign Service 30; served in Riga, Rio de
Janeiro and London; Chief of Bureau, Ministry of
Foreign Affairs 42-43, Asst. Dir. and Dir. Political
Dept. 43-48; Consul Gen. and Permanent Observer,
U.N. 48-53; Sec. Gen., Ministry of Foreign Affairs 53,
Sec. of State 54-56; Ambassador to France 56-58, 65-,
to U.S.A. 58-65; Grand Commdr. White Rose of
Finland, Crown of Belgium, French Legion of Honour,
Icelandic, Netherlands, Polish, Brazilian, Mexican and
British decorations.
Finnish Embassy, 2 rue Fabert, Paris 7e, France.

Sereni, Emilio; Italian agronomist and politician;
b. 13 Aug. 1907; ed. Rome and Univ. of Naples.
Graduated in agricultural science at Portici Univ. 27;
Dir. of the Observatory for Rural Economics, Portici 28;
joined Communist Party 28; sentenced to 15 years'
imprisonment by Fascist Special Court 30, released 36;
Editor of Italian daily paper *La Voce degli Italiani*,
Paris 37-43; re-arrested 43-44; mem. Nat. Liberation
Cttee. for Northern Italy 44-45; Commr. for Home
Ministry in Northern Italy 45; mem. of Constituent
Assembly 46; Ministry of Post-War Assistance 46-47;
Minister for Public Works 47; Senator 48; Gen. Sec.
Italian Movement of Partisans of Peace 50; mem.
Bureau, World Peace Council 51; mem. Central Cttee.
and of Directorate of Italian Communist Party;
Senator 53-63; Pres. Nat. Peasant Alliance 55; Prof. of
History of Agriculture, Rome Univ. 60; mem. Chamber
of Deputies 63-; Editor *Critica marxista* 66.
Publs. *I Comitati di Liberazione Nazionale nella cos-
pirazione, nell'insurrezione, nella ricostruzione* 45, *La
questione agraria nella rinascita nazionale italiana* 46,
Il capitalismo nelle campagne 47, *Il Mezzogiorno all'opposizione* 48, *Scienza marxismo cultura* 49, *Comunità
rurali nell'Italia antica* 56, *Vecchio e nuovo nelle campagne italiane* 57, *Storia del paesaggio agrario italiano*
61, *Due linee di politica agraria* 62, *Per la storia delle
più antiche tecniche e della nomenclatura della vite e del
vino* 65, *Capitalismo e mercato nazionale in Italia* 66.
Camera dei Deputati, Rome, Italy.

Sergent, Jean; French author; b. 12 July 1897; legal
and literary education.
Asst. Curator, Maison de Victor Hugo 34; Asst. Curator,
Musée Galliéra 36; Curator, Maison de V. Hugo and
Hauteville House (Guernsey) 43-61, Hon. Curator 61-.
Publs. *Les Marches du Ciel* (novel) 46, *Les Dessins de
V. Hugo* 50, *L'Hôtel Lauzun* 54.
3 rue de l'Etang, La Verrière (Yvelines), France.
Telephone: 952-86-85.

Sergent, René Edmond; French civil servant; b.
16 Jan. 1904; ed. Ecole Polytechnique.
With Ministry of Finance 29-37; Financial Dir. Nat.
Societies for Aeronautical Construction 37-40; mem. and
later Dir. Foreign Trade Dept., Ministry of Finance
40-44; Chair. French Economic and Financial Dept.,
Berlin Control Comm. 45-47; Financial Attaché, French
Embassy, London 47; Asst. Sec.-Gen. (Economics and
Finance), N.A.T.O. 52-55; Sec.-Gen. Organisation for
European Economic Co-operation 55-60; Vice-Pres.
Syndicat Gén. de la Construction Electrique 60-; Officier
Légion d'Honneur.
1 boulevard de Beauséjour, Paris 16e, France.
Telephone: 288-30-31.

Sergi, Sergio, M.D.; Italian anthropologist; b. 13
March 1878.
Physician to a mental asylum 02-24; Asst. in Anthro-
pology Rome Univ. 07 and Prof. since 16; Technical
Dir. Istituto Italiano di Antropologia; Dir. *Rivista di
Antropologia;* Dir. *Archivio di Antropologia Criminale*
39-49.
Publs. *Cerebra Hererica* 09, *Crania Habessinica* 12, *Über
die Morphologie des Lobus frontalis beim Menschen* 14,
Discovery of Neanderthal Man in Italy 29, *Discovery of
the Garamantes of Libya* 34, *Il cranio neandertaliano del
Monte Circeo* 39, *Craniometria e craniografia del primo
paleantropo di Saccopastore* 44, *Il Cranio del secondo
paleantropo di Saccopastore* 48, *Pantogoniostato-cranio-
steophorus and axidiatheter* 50, *L'homme du paléolithique
supérieur dans la grotte des Arene Candide* 52, *Morphological Position of the Prophaneranthropi* 55, *Die
Neandertalischen Palaeanthropen in Italien* 56, *Capelli
di Tasmaniano e di Boscimano* 57, *Röntgenographische
Darstellung morphologischer Merkmale am Neandertaler
Schädel Circeo* 60, *Saggio radiografico di caratteristiche
morfologiche del cranio neandertaliano del Monte Circeo*
60, *The Genetic Independence in Human Hair of the
Degree of Curvature and the Shape of the Transverse
Section* 61, *I tipi umani più antichi, Preominidi e
ominidi fossili* 66, etc.
Piazza Crati 11, 00199 Rome, Italy.
Telephone: 8380032.

Sergiev, Pyotr Grigorievich; Soviet parasitologist and
epidemiologist; b. 10 July 1893; ed. Univ. of Kazan.
Dir. of the Inst. of Malaria, Medical Parasitology and
Helminthology (later Martinovsky Inst. of Medical
Parasitology and Tropical Medicine) 34-, also Chief of
the Laboratory of Measles, Inst. of Virology of the
Acad. of Medical Sciences of the U.S.S.R.; mem.
C.P.S.U.; has carried out research on septic angina,
Japanese encephalitis, malaria, etc.; mem. Acad. of
Medical Sciences of the U.S.S.R. 44, Vice-Pres. 57-60;
State prizewinner 46, 52; awarded Order of Lenin
(three times), Hero of Socialist Labour.
Martinovsky Institute of Medical Parasitology and
Tropical Medicine, Ministry of Health of the U.S.S.R.,
Moscow, U.S.S.R.

Serisawa, Kojiro; Japanese author; b. 97; ed. Tokyo and Paris Univs.
Administrative Official Ministry of Agriculture 22-25; Prof. at Chuo Univ. 30-32; Vice-Pres. Japanese PEN Club 48-; awarded Prix des Amitiés Françaises 59.
Publs. *Death in Paris* 40, *One World* 54, *Mrs. Aida* 57, *Under the Shadow of Love and Death* 53, *House on the Hill* 59, *Parting* 61, *Love, Intelligence and Sadness* 62.
52 Otaki-machi, Nakamo-ku, Tokyo, Japan.

Serkin, Rudolf; American pianist; b. 28 March 1903.
Début with the Vienna Symphony Orchestra 15; with Adolf Busch in a series of sonatas for violin and piano; American début 33; appeared with Toscanini 34, with Nat. Orchestral Asscn. 37; annual tours of the U.S.A. 34-; Head Piano Dept., Curtis Inst. of Music; Dr. h.c. Curtis Inst., Temple Univ., Univ. of Vermont.
Curtis Institute of Music, Philadelphia, Pa.; R.F.D.3, Brattleboro, Vermont, U.S.A.

Serlachius, Ralph Erik; Finnish industrialist; b. 24 Jan. 1901; ed. Dresden Technical Univ. and Ecole des Hautes Etudes Commerciales, Paris.
Chair. and Man. Dir. G. A. Serlachius Ltd. 42-; Chair. Tammer Tehtaat Ltd., Central Industrial Laboratory, Forest Extension Bureau, Mänttä Savings Bank; Chair. The Art Foundation of Gösta Serlachius, Guarantee Asscn. for Care of Disabled Ex-Servicemen; Deputy Chair. Osakeyhtiö Toppila; Chair., Deputy Chair. or Dir. many other companies and asscns.; Counsellor of Mines 48; Minister of Communications and Public Works 53-54; Dr. Tech. h.c. (Åbo Acad.); Cross of Liberty, 3rd and 4th class; mem. Chapter Orders White Rose and Finnish Lion; Commdr. with Grand Cross of Finnish Lion; Commdr. Legion of Honour, and other foreign decorations.
Mänttä, Finland.

Serocki, Kazimierz; Polish composer; b. 3 March 1922; ed. Warsaw, Łódź and Paris.
State Prize for music 52 and 63, many other international and national prizes.
Compositions include two symphonies (one choral), Sinfonietta for two string orchestras, Musica concertante for chamber orchestra, Episodes for strings and three groups of percussion, Segments for seven instrumental groups, Symphonic frescos, *Niobe* for two voices, choir and orchestra, Continuum for percussion, *Forte e Piano* (for 2 pianos and orchestra), *Heart of the Night*, *Eyes of Air* song cycles, chamber and piano music.
Piwarskiego 16, Warsaw 36, Poland.
Telephone: 410796.

Serpa, Ivan Ferreira; Brazilian artist; b. 6 April 1923; ed. under Axel Leskochesk.
Professor of Painting, Museum of Modern Art, Rio de Janeiro 52-; one-man and group exhbns. all over the world including São Paulo Bienales 51-; Retrospective exhbns. at Museum of Modern Art, Rio de Janeiro 61, 65, Museum of Contemporary Art, São Paulo 65, and Museum of Art, Belo Horizonte 65.
Works include: collages 53-55, abstract paintings 61-62, concrete paintings 51-57; women 63 and 65, black series 64-65, twilight scenes 64-65, scenes of everyday life 66.
Rua Juruviara 104, Meyer, Guanabara, Brazil.

Serpan, Iaroslav, D. ès sc.; French artist and biologist; b. 4 June 1922; ed. Lycée de Versailles, and Univ. of Paris.
Studied biology and mathematics at Paris Univ.; research in biology; began painting 40; active mem. of Paris surrealist group 46-48; since leaving this group in 48, one of representatives of earlier "informal cut"; now one of leaders of avant-garde trends in modern European painting; paintings in main European and American collections; group exhibitions in Europe, South America, Japan and the U.S.A.; one-man

exhibitions in Paris, Brussels, Milan, Venice, Rome, New York, Tokyo, Copenhagen and in Germany 51-; Mural decoration for Besançon Univ. (enamelled lava); Marzotto Prize 63.
45 avenue d'Aligre, 78-Le Pecq, France.
Telephone: 966-63-37.

Serraj, Lieut.-Col. Abdel Hamid; Syrian army officer and politician; ed. Mil. Acad. Homs.
Further military training in France 52; Asst. Mil. Attaché, Paris 54; Mil. Intelligence Commdr. 55-58; leader Arab Socialist Resurrectionist Party April 55-58; Minister of the Interior, Syrian Region U.A.R. 58; Chair. of Exec. Council of Syrian Region and Minister of State for United Arab Republic 60-61; Dep. Pres. of U.A.R. (Internal Affairs) 61-Sept. 61 resigned; Sec.-Gen. of Nat. Union in Syrian Region 60-61; detained by Syrians after *coup d'état* Oct. 61, escaped and fled to U.A.R. May 62.
c/o Council of Ministers, Cairo, United Arab Republic.

Serrano, Hector Escobar; Salvadorean jurist; b. 1904; ed. Mexican Nat. Law School and Salvador Law School.
Prof. of Political Rights San Salvador Univ. 27; attached Berlin Legation 28-29; Prof. of Int. Law San Salvador Univ. 31-34; Del. to Central American Conf. in Guatemala 34; Criminal Court Judge 32-34; Min. to Honduras July 34; Min. of Finance, Public Credit, Industry and Commerce 44-46; Minister to Spain 53-60; Minister of Foreign Affairs 62-65; Perm. Rep. to UN 65-.
Publ. *The Paulian Action in Mexican Civil Law* 26.
Permanent Mission of El Salvador to the United Nations, 211 East 43rd Street, New York 17, N.Y., U.S.A.

Serrano-Camargo, Gabriel; Colombian architect; b. 24 March 1909; ed. Univ. Nacional de Colombia.
Founder and for 33 years collaborator and Dir. of Dept. of Architecture Cuellar Serrano Gómez Arq.; Pres. Colombian Del. to congresses in Mexico, Moscow, London and Washington, D.C.; Counsellor and Prof. Nat. Univ. of Colombia; mem. Comm. for Regulatory Plan of Bogotá; Pres. Board of Dirs. Museum of Modern Art, Bogotá; Pres. Soc. of Architects; Pres. Pan-American Fed. of Architectural Socs.; Hon. Pres. Colombian Soc. of Architects; Nat. Engineering Prize 48, Nat. Architects Prize 62.
Edif. Seguros Bolívar, Carrera 10A 16-39, piso 15, Bogotá, Colombia.
Telephone: 410-612.

Sert, José Luis, M.ARCH.; Spanish-born American architect; b. 1 July 1902; ed. Barcelona Escuela Superior de Arquitectura.
Worked with Le Corbusier, Paris 29-30; private practice in Barcelona 29-38; settled in U.S. 39; co-Founder and Partner Town Planning Associates, New York 41-56; naturalized U.S. citizen 51; Co-Founder and Partner, Sert, Jackson and Associates (fmrly. Sert, Jackson and Gourley) 57-; Dean and Prof. Harvard Univ. Graduate School of Design 53-; mem. Int. Congress of Modern Architecture (Pres. 47-56); Fellow American Inst. of Architects; mem. American Inst. of Planners, American Acad. Arts and Sciences, Nat. Inst. Arts and Letters; hon. mem. R.I.B.A. Peruvian Inst. of Urbanism, Soc. Colombiana de Arquitectos; Hon. M.A. Harvard Univ.; Hon. Litt.D. Boston Coll.; Projects include: U.S. Embassy, Baghdad, Harvard Univ. Holyoke Center, Boston Univ. Student Union and Law and Educ. Buildings, Musée Fondation Maeght (France), Center for Study of World Religions, Harvard Univ., Negea Service Corpn., Cambridge, Mass., Mugar Library, Boston Univ.; Design Consultant Dormitory, Liberal Arts Building, Library, Univ. of Guelph, Ont.; Master Plans for Havana, Bogotá, etc.
Publs. *Can Our Cities Survive?* 47, *The Heart of the City*

(with Rogers and Tyrwhitt) 52, *Antoni Gaudi* (with Sweeney) 60.
Home: 64 Francis Avenue, Cambridge, Mass.; Office: 26 Church Street, Cambridge, Mass. 02138, U.S.A.

Sertoli, Giandomenico, IUR.D.; Italian international civil servant; b. 26 Sept. 1922; ed. Univs. of Padua and Institut des Hautes Etudes Internationales, Geneva.
Assistant to the Pres. and Sec. Bd. of Dirs., ARAR, Rome 46-54; mem. Finance Dept., European Coal and Steel Community, Luxembourg 54-58; Dep. Manager Finance and Treasury Dept., European Investment Bank 58-60, Manager 60-.
c/o European Investment Bank, 85 boulevard de Waterloo, Brussels 1, Belgium.
Telephone: 13-40-00.

Servais, Léon; Belgian trade unionist and politician; b. 7 Nov. 1907.
Member Confédération des Syndicats Chrétiens 28-; Pres. Mouvement Ouvrier Chrétien 47-50; mem. Senate 50-; Minister for Social Security 58-61, of Labour and Employment 61-; Christian Socialist.
Ministère de l'Emploi et du Travail, rue Lambermont 2, Brussels, Belgium.

Servan-Schreiber, Jean-Claude, L. en DR.; French newspaperman; b. 11 April 1918; ed. Oxford and Sorbonne Univs.
Served World War II in Flanders 40, in Resistance 41-42, in North Africa 43, France 44, Germany 45; with *Les Echos* 46-, Gen. Man. 57, Dir. 63-65; Deputy for Paris 65-; Asst. Sec.-Gen. U.N.R.-U.D.T.; mem. Board Jacques de Saint Phalle et Cie. (advertising agency), Paris; Officier de la Légion d'Honneur, Mil. Medal, Croix de Guerre, Croix du Combattant Volontaire de la Résistance, Legion of Merit (U.S.A.).
Assemblée Nationale, Paris 7e, France.

Servan-Schreiber, Jean-Jacques; French journalist and writer; b. 13 Feb. 1924; ed. Ecole Polytechnique, Paris.
Joined as a volunteer the Free French Army of General de Gaulle as fighter pilot 43 (U.S. Air Force); diplomatic editor of *Le Monde* 48-51; founder and Dir. of *L'Express* 53-; Croix de la Valeur Militaire.
Publs. *Lieutenant en Algérie* 57, *Le Défi Americain* 67.
L'Express, 25 rue de Berri, Paris 8e, France.

Servolini, Luigi, D.LIT., D.F.A.; Italian xylographer, writer and art critic; b. 1 March 1906; ed. Pisa Univ., Acad. of Fine Arts, Carrara.
Professor of Xylography and Lithography, R. Istituto del Libro di Urbino, and Dir. of Library, Urbino Univ. 30-39; Dir. artistic and cultural insts. at Forli 39-53; Dir. Istituto Poligrafico Rizzoli, Milan 53-56; Gen. Sec. Nat. Asscn. of Artists-Engravers of Italy; Prof. History of Art; Headmaster; also painter and lithographer and has since 26 taken part in many important exhbns.; works represented in 55 European and American Public Galleries; has won several prizes; Hon. mem. Accademia della Poesia, Rome; Accademico Disegno, Florence; Fellow Royal Soc. of Arts, London; Editor "Comanducci" Dictionary; mem. Ordine dei Giornalisti (Rome) 35, Asscn. Lombarda de Giornalisti (Milan); Editor *La Voce degli IDIT* (fortnightly), *Incisione* (quarterly); Kt. Commdr. Italian Repub.
Publs. *Ugo da Carpi* 29, *La Xilografia a chiaroscuro italiana nei secoli XVI, XVII e XVIII* 30, *Tecnica della Xilografia* 35, *A. Bosse* 37, *Problemi e aspetti dell'Incisione* 39, *J. de' Barbari* 43, *Pittura gotica romagnola* 44, *Xilografia giapponese* 49, *La Xilografia* 50, *Incisione italiana di cinque secoli* 51, *Incidere* 52, 61, *Dizionario Incisori ital. moderni e contemporanei* 55, *Mosaico di Romagna* 57, *Autobiografia di Bodoni* 58, *I procedimenti artistici e industriali della Grafica* 59-63, *Gli Incisori d'Italia* 60, *Il Comanducci: Dizionario dei*

Pittori 3rd edn. 62, *Acqueforti di Giovanni Fattori* 66, *Athena: Storia dell' Arte classica e italiana* (3 vols.) 66-68, *Dalla pietra litografica alla stampa offset* 68.
Via Coccoluto-Ferrigni 101, Leghorn; Via Carlo Forlanini 17, Milan, Italy.
Telephone: Leghorn 31940.

Sessions, Roger Huntington, A.B., B.M.; American composer and teacher; b. 28 Dec. 1896; ed. Harvard Coll., Yale Univ. School of Music and private studies with Ernest Bloch.
Asst. and later Instructor, Smith Coll. 17-21; Teacher and Asst. to Dir., Cleveland Inst. of Music 21-25; Guggenheim Fellowship, Florence 26-28, Walter Damrosch Fellowship, American Acad. in Rome 28-31, Carnegie Foundation Fellowship, Berlin 31-33; Lecturer, New School for Social Research, N.Y., and Teacher, Malkin Conservatory, Boston 33-34; Lecturer, Boston Univ. Coll. of Music, and Teacher, Dalcroze School of Music, N.Y. 34-35; private teaching, musical composition, N.Y. 35-45; Instructor, Asst. Prof. and Assoc. Prof., Princeton Univ. 35-45; Prof. of Music, Univ. of Calif., Berkeley 45 (sabbatical leave, Fulbright Award, Florence 51-52); William Shubael Conant Prof. Music Princeton Univ. 53-65; mem. faculty Juilliard School of Music 65-; mem. Int. Soc. for Contemporary Music, Pres. U.S. Section 34-42; Nat. Inst. of Arts and Letters 38-, American Acad. of Arts and Letters 53-, Akad. der Künste, Berlin 60-, American Acad. of Arts and Sciences 61-; Hon. D. Mus. (Wesleyan, Rutgers, Harvard Univs.).
Compositions include *Concerto for Violin and Orchestra* 37, *String Quartet No. 1 in E Minor* 38, *Duo for Violin and Piano* 48, *String Quartet No. 2, Sonata No. 2 for Pianoforte* 48, *Symphony No. 2* 49, *Symphony No. 3* 57, *No. 4* 58, *String Quintet* 58, *Divertimento for Orchestra* 60, *Montezuma* (opera) 63, *Symphony No. 5* 64, *No. 6* 66, *Six Pieces for Violin Solo* 66.
Publs. *The Intent of the Artist* 41, *The Musical Experience of Composer, Performer, and Listener* 50, *Harmonic Practice* 51.
63 Stanworth Lane, Princeton, N.J., U.S.A.

Setalvad, Motilal Chimanlal, B.A., LL.B.; Indian lawyer; b. 12 Nov. 1884; ed. Elphinstone Coll., and Government Law Coll.
Advocate Bombay High Court 11; Advocate-Gen., Bombay 37; resigned 42; mem. Indian del. to the Gen. Assembly of the UN 47, 48, 49 (Leader); Principal Rep. of India for the Kashmir question at the Security Council Session 52; Attorney-Gen. of India 50-62; Chair. Law Comm. 55; mem. All-India Bar Cttee.; Vice-Pres. Indian Branch Int. Law Asscn.; Pres. Supreme Court Bar Asscn., Bar Asscn. of India, India Comm. of Jurists; Leader Indian Del. Asian-African Legal Consultative Cttee. 57, 58, 60, 61, 62; Presented Indian case (v. Portugal) Int. Court of Justice 58-60; Commonwealth mem. British Inst. of Int. and Comparative Law; mem. Rajya Sabha 66-; Hon. LL.D. Banaras Hindu Univ. 67; Padma Vibhushan.
Publs. *Civil Liberties, Common Law in India* (Hamlyn Lectures 60).
Office: 1 Jantar Mantar Road, New Delhi 1; Home: Nirant, Juhu, Bombay 54, India.
Telephone: 45442, 45071 (New Delhi); 532119 (Bombay).

Sethna, Homi Nusserwanji, B.SC., M.SE.; Indian scientist; b. 24 Aug. 1923; ed. St. Xavier's School and Coll., Bombay, and Michigan Univ.
Works Man. Indian Rare Earths Ltd. (Govt. co.) 49-59; Chief Scientific Officer, Atomic Energy Establishment, Trombay (now Bhabha Atomic Research Centre) 59, Dir. of its Eng. Group until 66, Dir. Bhabha Atomic Research Centre Feb. 66-; constructed Monazite Plant, Alwaye, Kerala, Thorium and Uranium Metal Plants and Plutonium Plant, Trombay, Bombay and Uranium Mill, Jagugoda, Bihar; Deputy Sec.-Gen. of UN Conf.

on Peaceful Uses of Atomic Energy, Geneva 58; Dir. Fertilizer Corpn. of India Ltd., Rare Earths Ltd.; mem. Scientific Advisory Cttee., to the Cabinet 61-, and of the Int. Atomic Energy Agency (IAEA) 66-; mem. for Research and Devt., Atomic Energy Comm. Feb. 66-; Padma Shri award 59, Shanti Swarup Bhatnagar Memorial Award 60, Padma Bhushan 66.
Bhabha Atomic Research Centre, Old Yacht Club Bldg., Apollo Pier Road, Bombay 1-BR., India.

Setoh, Shoji; Japanese electrical engineer; b. 18 March 1891; ed. Imperial Univ., Tokyo.
Asst. Prof., Tokyo Imperial Univ. 18-23; sent abroad by Japanese Govt. to study electrical engineering in Germany, Switzerland, U.K., and U.S.A. 23-25; Prof., Tokyo Imperial Univ. 25-51, Prof. Emeritus 51-, Dean of Engineering 42-45, 48-51; with Inst. of Physical and Chemical Research Tokyo 25-47; Pres. Inst. of Electrical Engineers of Japan 41-42; Vice-Pres. Nat. Research Council of Japan 47-49; Pres. Japanese Electrotechnical Cttee. 47-51; Dir. Electric Power Engineering Research Inst., Japan Electric Power Generation and Transmission Co. 47-49; Pres. Japan Society of Electronmicroscopy 48-54; Managing Dir. Tokyo Shibaura Electric Co. 51-62; Counsellor, Atomic Energy Comm. of Japan 56- and Japan Atomic Energy Research Inst. 57-; Vice-Pres. Japan Radio-Isotope Asscn. 55-; Pres. Nippon Atomic Industry Group Co. Ltd. 58-; Chair. Tokyo Electrical Engineering Coll. 59-; Managing Dir. Japan Atomic Industrial Forum 62-; Pres. Atomic Energy Soc. of Japan 63-65.
Kitasawa 1-24-15, Setagaya-ku, Tokyo, Japan.

Setoyama, Mitsuo; Japanese politician; b. 04; ed. Meiji Univ.
Served District Courts, Miyazaki and Yamaguchi; Asst. Mayor, later Mayor of Niyakanojo City; fmr. Pres. River Conservation Asscn.; fmr. Dir. Hyuga Firewood and Charcoal Production Co.; mem. House of Reps. 49-, fmr. Chair. Standing Cttee. for Construction; Deputy Minister of Agriculture 57; Minister of Construction June 65-67; Liberal Democrat.
c/o Ministry of Construction, 1-2 Kasumingaseki, Chiyoda-ku, Tokyo, Japan.

Sette Camara, José; Brazilian diplomatist; b. 20; ed. Univ. of Minas Gerais and McGill Univ., Canada.
Brazilian Diplomatic Service 45-; Third Sec. Washington 47; Vice-Consul, Montreal 47-50; Third Sec. UN, New York 50-52; Sec. to Civil Household of Pres. of Brazil 52-55, Deputy Head of Civil Household 56-59, Head 59-60; Consul, Florence 55-56; Provisional Gov., State of Guanabara 60; Head Perm. Del. of Brazil to UN, Geneva 60-61; Ambassador to Canada 61-62; Mayor of Brasilia 62-63; Ambassador to Switzerland 63-64; Perm. Rep. to UN 64-.
Brazilian Mission to the United Nations, 605 Third Avenue, New York City, N.Y. 10016, U.S.A.

Severyns, Albert, D.PHIL.; Belgian professor; b. 4 Oct. 1900; ed. Paris, Liège Univs., Ecole Pratique des Hautes Etudes, Paris, Ecole Française d'Athènes.
Joined staff of Liège Univ. 28, Ordinary Prof. (Greek Literature and Philology) 31-67, Emer. 67; Exchange Prof. Paris 49, Strasbourg 53, 61, Oslo 54, Bergen 54, Leeds 56, London 56, Lyon 57, Poznań 60, Catania 65; Pres. Royal Acad. of Belgium 61; Vice-Pres. Nat. Foundation of Scientific Research 55-60; mem. of various foundations of learning and cultural cttees.; many Belgian decorations and awards from national and foreign acads.
Publs. Studies of Greek writers.
45 rue Justin Lenders, Liège, Belgium.
Telephone: 04-436466.

Sevilla Sacasa, Guillermo; Nicaraguan diplomatist; b. 08; ed. Universidad Centenaria de León.
Judge in district civil and criminal law courts 27-34;

deputy to Congress 34, Pres. Chamber of Deputies 35-36; Pres. Nat. Congress 36, 37, 40; fmr. Prof. of Civil and Int. Law, Univ. Nacional de Nicaragua; Ambassador to U.S.A. 43- (concurrently to Canada); also Perm. Rep. to UN 47-; Del. to Org. of American States; Chief of Nicaraguan del. to UN conf., San Francisco 55; Gov. for Nicaragua IMF and World Bank; numerous foreign decorations.
Nicaraguan Embassy, 1627 New Hampshire Avenue, N.W., Washington, D.C., U.S.A.

Seydewitz, Max; German politician; b. 19 Dec. 1892. In youth apprenticed to printing trade; Ed. of Social Democratic newspaper in Halle 18; Chief Ed. *Sächsisches Volksblatt*, Zwickau 20; elected to Reichstag 24; co-publisher and Ed. *Der Klassenkampf* (fortnightly) 27; left Social Democratic Party (SPD) and helped to found Socialist Workers' Party (SAP) 31; emigrated to Czechoslovakia 33, Norway 38, Sweden 40; returned to Germany 45; Editor of periodical *Einheit*; Dir. Berlin Radio 46; Prime Minister of Saxony 47; mem. Volkskammer 49, Pres. of Economic and Financial Cttee.; Dir.-Gen. State Art Collection 55-; mem. Socialist Unity Party (SED); Nat. Prize.
Publs. *Todesstrahlen und andere Kriegswaffen* 34, *Stalin oder Trotzki?* 36, *Hakenkreuz über Europa* 38, *Den tyska hemmafronten* 43, *Civil Life in Wartime Germany* 44, *Es geht um Deutschland* 49, *Jde o Nemecko* 50, *Wo blieben unsere Männer?* 54, *Dresden mahnt Europa* 55, *Niemiecka Republika Demokratyczna* 55, *Die Unbesiegbare Stadt* 55, *Der Antisemitismus in Westdeutschland* (with Ruth Seydewitz) 56, *Mezi Odrou a Rynem* 57, *Das Dresdener Galeriebuch* and *Die Dresdener Kunstschätze* (with Ruth Seydewitz) 57, *Deutschland-Zwischen Oder und Rhein* 58, *Die grosse Kraft* 61, *Goethe und der General Winter* 62, *Germania meschdu Odrom i Rejnom, Moskau* 60, *Die Dame mit dem Hermelin* (with Ruth Seydewitz, trans. into 5 languages) 63, *Die Dresdener Gemäldegalerie Alte und Neue Meister.*
Albertinum, Georg-Treu-Platz, 8051 Dresden, German Democratic Republic.

Seydou, Amadou; Niger diplomatist; b. c. 28; ed. Dakar, Algiers, Cairo and Univ. of Paris.
Former teacher; Chargé d'Affaires, Niger Embassy, Paris 60-61, Amb. to France 61; Commdr. Légion d'Honneur.
c/o Ministry of Foreign Affairs, Niamey, Niger.

Seydoux Fornier de Clausonne, François (brother of Roger Seydoux Fornier de Clausonne, q.v.), L. ès L., L. en D.; French diplomatist; b. 15 Feb. 1905; ed. Ecole Libre des Sciences Politiques, Paris Univ. Law Faculty.
Sec. Berlin 33, Counsellor 38; mem. Bureau d'Etudes Clandestin, Ministry of Foreign Affairs 43; First Counsellor, Brussels 45; Sec. Gen. French del. to U.N. Gen. Assembly, Paris 46; Dir. European Affairs, Ministry of Foreign Affairs 49-55; Ambassador to Austria 55-58, to German Fed. Repub. 58-62, to NATO 62-64, to German Fed. Repub. Feb. 65-; Ambassadeur de France 65; Grand Officier Légion d'Honneur.
French Embassy, Rheinaustrasse, Bad Godesberg, German Federal Republic.

Seydoux Fornier de Clausonne, Roger (brother of François Seydoux Fornier de Clausonne, q.v.), L. en D.; French diplomatist; b. 28 March 1908.
Asst. to Financial Attaché, French Embassy, London 31-32; Asst., Office of French Resident-Gen., Morocco 33; Sec.-Gen. Ecole des Sciences Politiques, Paris 34-45, Dir. 42; Dir. Inst. d'Etudes Politiques de l'Université de Paris 47; Head of Cultural Relations, French Foreign Office 47-50; Vice-Pres. UNESCO 48; Consul-Gen. New York 50-52; Minister in Washington 52-54; Minister in Tunisia 54-56; High Commr. in Tunisia 55-56, Ambassador 56-57; Dir.-Gen. of Culture and Technical Affairs, Ministry of Foreign Affairs 56; Ambassador to Morocco 60-62; Ambassador and Perm. Rep. to UN,

New York 62-67; Perm. Rep. to NATO 67-; Administrator, Fondation Nationale des Sciences Politiques; Commdr. Légion d'Honneur; Croix de Guerre.
60 rue de Varenne, Paris 7e, France.

Seynes, Philippe de; French United Nations official; b. 4 Jan. 1910; ed. Ecole Libre des Sciences Politiques.
Ministry of Finance 35-45; mem. French Mission in Germany, later Dep. Sec.-Gen. Allied Reparations Agency Brussels 45-49; Financial Adviser to French Del. to U.N. 49-54, on staff of Minister of Foreign Affairs 54, (Adviser to M. Mendès-France); Under-Sec. for Econ. and Social Affairs, United Nations 55-, Principal Adviser to Sec.-Gen. 62; Chevalier, Légion d'Honneur, Croix de Guerre.
United Nations, New York City, N.Y., U.S.A.

Seyrig, Henri Arnold; French archaeologist; b. 10 Nov. 1895; ed. Univ. of Paris.
Member and Sec. French School at Athens 22-29; Dir. of Antiquities, Syria and Lebanon 29-41; Dir. French Inst. of Archaeology, Istanbul 41; Cultural Adviser Free French Del. in U.S.A. 42-45; Dir. French Inst. of Archaeology Beirut 46-60, 62-66; Dir. Musées de France 60-62; Corres. F.B.A., Hon. F.S.A., Hon. LL.D.
81 rue des Saars, 2000-Neuchâtel, Switzerland.
Telephone: 038-4-10-30.

Sferza, Dr. Gino; Italian business executive; b. 6 Feb. 1911; ed. Univ. of Bologna.
Ente Addestramento Lavoratori (Workers' Training Org.) 38; Gen. Vice-Sec. Confederazione Unitaria dei Lavoratori (Workers' Union) 46-47; Personnel Man. Terni Co. 47, Montecatini Co. 50-, now Man. Dir. and Gen. Man.; Man. Dir. Monteshell Petrochimica Co.; Pres. Società ACNA, Milan; Vice-Pres. Soc. Cokitalia, Milan, Soc. Polymer-Milano; mem. Admin. Council Soc. Vetrobel-Trieste.
Montecatini, Largo G. Donegani 1-2, Milan, Italy.

Sha Chien-li; Chinese jurist and politician; b. 03.
Jointly responsible for the formation of the national united front against the Japanese in 37; Vice-Minister of Trade 49; Asst. Sec.-Gen. Shanghai Municipal People's Govt. 49; Vice-Chair. All-China Federation of Democratic Youth 49; Vice-Minister of Commerce 53; Sec.-Gen. All-China Fed. of Industry and Commerce 53; Minister of Local Industry 54; on board of dirs. of Bank of China 54; mem. Central Cttee. of China Dem. League 56; Minister of Light Industry 56-58, of Food 58-.
Ministry of Food, Peking, China.

Shaabi, Qahtan Muhammed as-; Southern Yemen politician; b. 1920; ed. school in Aden, and studied agricultural engineering, Khartoum Univ.
Director of Agriculture, Lahej State 55-58; joined South Arabian League 58, Public Relations Officer 59-60; Adviser to Ministry of South Yemen Affairs, Govt. of Yemen People's Repub. 63; founder-mem. Nat. Liberation Front (N.L.F.) 63, later Sec.-Gen.; mem. N.L.F. Del. to Geneva talks on independence of S. Arabia Nov. 67; Pres. of People's Repub. of Southern Yemen, also Prime Minister and Supreme Commdr. of Armed Forces Nov. 67-.
Office of the President, Aden, People's Republic of Southern Yemen.

Shackleton, Baron (Life Peer, cr. 58); **Edward Arthur Alexander Shackleton**, P.C., O.B.E., M.A.; British politician; b. 15 July 1911; ed. Radley Coll. and Magdalen Coll., Oxford.
Surveyor, Oxford Univ. Expedition to Sarawak 32; Organiser and Surveyor, Oxford Univ. Expedition to Ellesmereland 34-35; Royal Air Force 40-45; M.P. 46-55; Parl. Private Sec. to Minister of Supply 45-50, to Lord Pres. of Council 50-51, to Foreign Sec. 51; Minister of Defence for the Royal Air Force 64-67; Minister without Portfolio and Deputy Leader House of Lords 67-68; mem. Cabinet Jan. 68-; Leader, House of Lords Jan. 68-; Lord Privy Seal Jan.-April 68; Paymaster-Gen. April 68-; Pres. Asscn. of Special Libraries and Information Bureaux (A.S.L.I.B.); Vice-Pres. Royal Geographical Soc.; Pres. Arctic Club 60; Cuthbert Peek Award, Royal Geographical Soc. 33, Ludwig Medallist, Munich Geog. Soc. 38; Labour.
Publs. *Arctic Journeys, Nansen the Explorer, Borneo Jungle* (part author).
Long Coppice, Canford Magna, Wimborne, Dorset, England.
Telephone: Broadstone 3635.

Shadman, Seyed Fakhraddin, DR.JUR., D.PHIL.; Iranian writer, politician and diplomatist; b. 08; ed. Teheran, London and Paris Univs.
Deputy Public Prosecutor Teheran 28; Lecturer School of Oriental Studies 34; 1st Hon. Sec. Persian Legation, London; Vice-Del. of Persian Govt. to Anglo-Iranian Oil Co. 34-47; Chair. Nat. Iran Insurance Co. (Bimeh Iran) 47; Minister of Nat. Economy 48, 53-55; Chair. Supreme Council Seven Year Plan Organisation 53; Minister of Justice 54; Prof. History Teheran Univ.
Publs. *Dar Rahe Hind* (On the Way to India), *Ketabe Binam* (The Nameless Book), *Modern History* (transl. from French), *Taskhire Tammadone Faranghi* (The Conquest of Western Civilization), *Tariki va Roshanai* (Darkness and Light).
22 Koocheye Dey Ave., Vessale Shirazi, Teheran, Iran.

Shafei, Col. Hussain; United Arab Republic (Egyptian) army officer and politician; b. 18; ed. Mil. Coll., Cairo.
Commissioned as 2nd Lieut. 38; took part in Palestine hostilities 48; graduated from Staff Officers' Coll. 53 and apptd. Officer-in-Charge Cavalry Corps; Minister of War and Marine 54, of Social Affairs (Egypt) 54-58; Minister of Labour and Social Affairs, U.A.R. 58-61; Dep. Pres. of U.A.R. and Minister of Social Affairs and Waqfs 61-62; mem. Presidency Council 62-64; Deputy Prime Minister and Minister for Waqfs 67-.
Ministry for Waqfs, Cairo, U.A.R.

Shaffer, George Wilson, A.B., PH.D.; American psychologist; b. 23 Nov. 1901; ed. Johns Hopkins Univ.
Dir. Physical Educ., Playground Athletic League, Baltimore, Md. 17-28; Prof. of Psychology, Univ. of Baltimore 28-34; Lecturer Psychology and Dir. of Health of Physical Educ., Johns Hopkins Univ. 34-; Dean, Coll. of Arts and Sciences 42-; Prof. of Psychology 41-, Dean of Univ. 47; Chief Psychologist Sheppard Pratt Mental Hospital 28-; Visiting Prof. of Psychology, William and Mary Coll. (Summers) 33 and 34, Goucher Coll. 44, Univ. of Calif. 54; Board of Examiners Nat. Comm. of Clinical and Experimental Hypnosis; Editor *International Journal of Clinical and Experimental Hypnosis;* Fellow American Psychological Asscn. American Psychopathological Asscn., etc.; Diploma Abnormal and Clinical Psychology.
Publs. *Textbook of Abnormal Psychology* 34, *Case Histories in Clinical and Abnormal Psychology* 47, *Fundamental Concepts in Clinical Psychology* 52, etc.
Home: De Sota Apartments, Baltimore, Md., U.S.A.; Office: Johns Hopkins University, Baltimore, Md., U.S.A.

Shaffer, Peter Levin; British playwright; b. 15 May 1926; ed. St. Paul's School, London, and Trinity Coll., Cambridge.
Evening Standard Drama Award 58; New York Drama Critics Circle Award 59-60.
Plays: *Five Finger Exercise* 58, *The Private Ear* and *The Public Eye* 62, *The Royal Hunt of the Sun* 64, *Black Comedy* 65, *White Liars* 67; also TV Plays.
18 Earls Terrace, Kensington High Street, London, W.8, England.
Telephone: 01-937-7972.

Shafik, Doria (Ahmed); United Arab Republic (Egyptian) journalist and feminist; b. 19; ed. Univ. of Paris.

Studied abroad; on return became Ed. *La Femme Nouvelle* 44, *Bent el Nil* (in Arabic) 46-, *Katkout* and *Doria Shafik Magazine*; organised Bent el Nil Union (feminist movement) 48.

Publs. *La Bonne Aventure, L'Esclave Sultane, L'Amour Perdu, L'Art pour l'Art dans L'Egypte Antique, La Femme et l'Islam, La Femme Egyptienne, Voyage autour du Monde.*

6 Salah el Din, Zamalek, Cairo, U.A.R.

Shaginyan, Marietta Sergeevna, D.PHILOG.; Armenian-born Soviet writer; b. 21 March 1888; ed. Classical Gymnasium and Faculty of History and Philology of the Moscow Higher Courses for Women.

Corresponding mem. Acad. Sciences of Armenia 50; State prizewinner 51; awarded Order of Lenin 67, Order of the Red Banner of Labour (three times); Order of the Red Star, Order of the Sign of Honour.

Publs. totalling 79 books include; novels: *Your Own Destiny* 16, *Transformation* 22-23, *Adventures of a Society Lady* 23, *Mess-Mend* 24-25, *Hydro Centre* 30-31, *The Ulyanov Family* 57; sketches: *The Five-Year Plans* 47, *Travels through Soviet Armenia* 50; literary studies: *Taras Shevchenko* 46, *Goethe* 50, *Nizami Studies* 55, *Sergei Rachmaninoff, Resuscitation (Josef Myslivecek)* 64, etc.; *Selected Works* (7 vols.), *First All-Russian ...* (Chronicle novel) 65, *Travels through Europe: Holland, Great Britain, France* 66, *Three Days on the Fiat* 67.

U.S.S.R. Writer's Union, 52 Ulitsa Vorovskogo, Moscow; Home: Arbat 45, flat 9, Moscow, U.S.S.R. Telephone: 1-34-17 (Home).

Shah, Jayantilal Chhotalal; Indian judge; b. 29 Sept. 1906; ed. R.C. High School, Ahmedabad, Gujerat Coll. and Elphinstone Coll., Bombay.

Legal practice, Ahmedabad Dist. Court, and Bombay High Court; Judge, Bombay High Court until 59, Judge, Supreme Court 59-.

11 Tuglak Road, New Delhi, India.

Shah, Kodardas Kalidas, B.A., LL.B.; Indian lawyer and politician; b. 15 Oct. 1908; ed. Gujerat Coll. and New Poona Coll.

Joined Nat. Movement 30, in custody 32, detained for participation in "Quit India" Campaign 42; Fellow S.P. Coll., Poona; Teacher, Poddar High School, Santa Cruz, Bombay; started legal practice, Bombay 34; Legal Adviser to Maharajah of Baroda 48-67; mem. Bombay Legislative Assembly 52, Rajya Sabha (Upper House of Parl.) 60-; Gen. Sec. Bombay Pradesh Cttee., Vice-Pres. 55-57, Pres. 57-60; Gen. Sec. All-India Congress Cttee. 62-63; Union Minister of Information and Broadcasting 67-; Sec. Bombay Famine Relief Cttee.; Leader Indian Del. to Apartheid Conf. London 64.

Ministry of Information and Broadcasting, New Delhi; Home: 8 Dr. Rajendra Prasad Road, New Delhi 1, India.

Shah, Manubhai, B.SC.; Indian politician; b. 1 Nov. 1915; ed. Baroda Coll. and Univ. of Bombay.

Technical and Admin. Posts, Delhi Cloth and Gen. Mills 37-48; mem. Saurashtra Legislative Ass. 48, Minister of Finance, Industries and Planning, Govt. of Saurashtra 48-56; Union Minister of Industry 56-62; Minister of Int. Trade 62-64, Minister of State for Commerce 64-65, Minister for Commerce 65-67.

1 Tuglak Road, New Delhi, India.

Shah, Rishikesh; Nepali politician and diplomatist; b. 25; ed. Patna Univ. and Allahabad Univ., India.

Lecturer in English and Nepali Literature, Tri-Chandra Coll. 45-48; Opposition Leader, First Advisory Ass. 52; Gen. Sec., Nepali Congress 53-55; Permanent Rep. (with rank of Ambassador) to United Nations

56-61, Ambassador to U.S.A. 58-61; Minister of Finance, Planning and Econ. Affairs 61-62; Minister of Foreign Affairs July-Sept. 62; Ambassador-at-Large 62, now Visiting Prof. East-West Center, Hawaii.

c/o Ministry of Foreign Affairs, Katmandu, Nepal.

Shaha, Agha, M.A., LL.B.; Pakistani diplomatist; b. 25 Aug. 1920; ed. Madras Univ. and Allahabad Univ.

Indian Civil Service 43; Pakistan Foreign Service 51-; Deputy Sec., Ministry of Foreign Affairs, in charge of UN and Int. Confs. Branch 51-55; First Counsellor and Minister, Wash. 55-58; Deputy Perm. Rep. to UN 58-61; Dir.-Gen. in charge Divs. of UN and Int. Conf. Affairs, Soviet, Chinese and Arab Affairs, Ministry of Foreign Affairs 61-64; Additional Foreign Sec. 64-67; Perm. Rep. to UN 67-.

Pakistan Mission to the United Nations, Pakistan House, 8 East 65th Street, New York, N.Y. 10021, U.S.A.

Shahabuddin, Khwaja; Pakistani politician.

Former Minister of Interior and Information; later Gov. of North-west Frontier Province; later Ambassador to Saudi Arabia and United Arab Republic; Minister of Information and Broadcasting March 65-.

Ministry of Information and Broadcasting, Karachi, Pakistan.

Shahn, Ben; Lithuanian-born American painter; b. 12 Sept. 1898; ed. New York Univ.

Worked in a lithographic studio 13-18; executed lithographs and paintings 18-30; Dir. Graphics U.S. Resettlement Admin. 34-37, Office of War Information 41-44; commissioned to carry out murals for public buildings in the U.S., including Social Security Building (Washington, D.C.), Bronx (N.Y.) Post Office, Hightstown (N.J.) School; mosaic murals: Grady High School (Brooklyn, N.Y.), Nashville (Tenn.) and New Haven (Conn.) Synagogues; Lecturer, Brooklyn Museum Art School 50-51, Harvard Univ., etc.; collection of works exhibited in U.S. Pavilion, Venice Biennale 54; rep. at Brussels Int. Exhbn. 58, Dunn Int. Exhbn. London 63; retrospective Exhbn., Amsterdam 61, Santa Barbara Museum of Art, Calif. 67; numerous awards including Temple Gold Medal, Pa. Acad. Exhbn. 56.

Publs. *The Shape of Content, The Alphabet of Creation.*

Roosevelt, New Jersey, U.S.A.

Shakhbut bin Sultan al Nihaiyan, H.H. Sheikh; Former Ruler of Abu Dhabi; b. 1905; brother of Zaid bin Sultan bin Zaid, *q.v.*

Succeeded to Sheikhdom 28; son Saied, b. 30; son Sultan, b. 36; deposed Aug. 66.

Manama, Bahrain.

Shalchian, Hassan; Iranian civil engineer and politician; b. 13; ed. State Univ. of Belgium.

Ministry of Roads 39-, successively Dir. of Technical Dept., Dir. Chalus Road Dept., Dir. Dept. of Technical Inspection, Dir.-Gen. of Roads, mem. Supervisory Board of Ministry of Roads; fmr. Head of Construction Dept.; fmr. Exec. for Implementation of Third Plan Projects, Ministry of Roads; Perm. Under-Sec. (Admin.) Ministry of Roads 62, Technical Under-Sec. 63; Minister of Roads and Communications Oct. 63; Man. Dir. Water and Power Authority, Azerbaijan Province April 64; again Minister of Roads and Communications Dec. 64-.

Ministry of Roads and Communications, Maidan Ark, Teheran, Iran.

Shaltiel, Gen. David; Israeli diplomatist and officer; b. 16 Jan. 1903; ed. Univ. of Hamburg.

Went to Israel 23; worked in orange groves; later officer in Hagana; commdr. Jerusalem region during war for independence of Israel; Col. 48; Inspector-Gen. Israeli Army; Brig.-Gen. 50; Mil. Attaché for Western Europe 50-52; Israel Minister to Brazil 52-55, concurrently Minister to Venezuela; Minister to Mexico, Cuba,

Dominican and all Central American Republics 56-59; Head of Division of Economic Co-ordination, Ministry of Foreign Affairs 60-63; Ambassador to the Netherlands 63-66; Israeli, French, Spanish, Mexican, Guatemalan and Brazilian decorations.
c/o Ministry of Foreign Affairs, Jerusalem, Israel.

Shammas, Saeed Yacoob; Kuwaiti administrator and diplomatist; b. 27 July 1927; ed. Mobarakiyya School, Kuwait, Bristol Coll. of Commerce, U.K., London School of Economics and Oxford Univ.
Manager, Municipality Dept., Kuwait 54-55; Admin. Asst., Civil Service Comm., Kuwait 55-57, Dep. Dir.-Gen. 58-60; Consul-Gen. and Chargé d'Affaires, Kuwait Mission to UN 62-63; Amb. of Kuwait to U.S.S.R. 64-67, also to Poland, Czechoslovakia, Hungary and Romania 65-67, Amb. to France 67-.
Office: 25 avenue Paul Doumer, Paris 16e, France; Home: P.O. Box 547, Kuwait.
Telephone: MOL-27-77 (Office).

Shand, Thomas Philip, M.P.; New Zealand politician; b. 11; ed. Christ's Coll. and Univ. of New Zealand.
Pilot in World War II; sheep farmer; mem. of Parl. 46-; Postmaster-Gen. and Minister of Civil Aviation 54-57, of Labour, Immigration, Electricity and Mines 60-; National Party.
121 Upland Road, Wellington, N.I., New Zealand.

Shane, Charles Donald, A.B., PH.D.; American astronomer; b. 6 Sept. 1895; ed. Univ. of California.
Instructor, Univ. of Calif. 20-24, Asst. Prof. 24-29, Assoc. Prof. 29-35, Prof. 35-45; Astronomer, Lick Observatory, Univ. of Calif. 45-63, Dir. 45-58; Asst. Dir. Radiation Laboratory, Univ. of Calif. 42-44; Dir. of Personnel Los Alamos 44-45; Pres. Asscn. of Univs. for Research in Astronomy Inc. 57-62; Hon. LL.D.
P.O. Box 582, Santa Cruz, Calif., U.S.A.
Telephone: 408-438-1142.

Shankar (Shankar Pillai, K.); Indian newspaper cartoonist; b. 31 July 1902.
Former cartoonist for *Hindustan Times*, New Delhi; founded *Indian News Chronicle*, Delhi 47; Founder and Editor *Shankar's Weekly* 48-; initiated Shankar's Int. Children's Art Competition 49; founded Children's Book Trust 57 of which he is now Exec. Trustee; founder and Ed. Children's World Magazine 68.
9 Purana Kila Road, New Delhi 1, India.

Shankar, Ravi; Indian sitar player and composer; b. 7 April 1920; ed. under Ustad Allauddin, Khan of Maihar.
Trained in the *Guru-Shishya* tradition; pupil of Ustad Allauddin Khan 38; solo sitar player; fmr. Dir. of Music All-India Radio and founder of the Nat. Orchestra; Founder-Dir. Kinnara School of Music, Bombay 62-; many recordings of traditional and experimental variety in India, U.K. and the U.S.A.; Concert tours in Europe, U.S.A. and the East; Visiting Lecturer Univ. of Calif. 65; Silver Bear of Berlin; Award of Indian Nat. Acad. for Music, Dance and Drama 62; award of Padma Bhushan 67.
Film Scores: *Pather Panchali, The Flute and the Arrow, Nava Rasa Ranga,* etc. and many musical compositions.
6 Pavlova, Little Gibbs Road, Bombay 6, India.

Shankar, Uday, A.R.C.A.; Indian dancer and artist.
Joined Anna Pavlova's Company, London 22, touring America, Canada and Mexico; formed own troupe, numerous tours of America and Europe; founded Uday Shankar India Culture Centre for dance, drama and music, Admora, closed during Second World War, reopened Calcutta 65; composed ballets; produced and directed film *Kalpana* (Imagination); created innumerable dance dramas and two shadow plays, *Ramleela* and *Lord Buddha;* Fellow, Sangeet Natak Akad.; Nat. Award as Creative Artist; Hon. D.Lit., Rabindra Bharati Univ.
38 Golf Club Road, Calcutta 33, India.

Shankiti, Sheikh Mohammed Amin; Jordanian politician and diplomatist.
Former Minister of Education; Ambassador to Saudi Arabia and the Sudan July 63-.
Embassy of the Hashemite Kingdom of Jordan, Jeddah, Saudi Arabia.

Shanks, Carrol Meteer, LL.B., B.A.; American lawyer and insurance executive; b. 14 Oct. 1898; ed. Univ. of Washington and Columbia Univ. School of Law.
Lecturer Columbia Univ. School of Law 25-27; with law firm of Root, Clark, Buckner and Ballantine (New York) 25-29, 31-32; Assoc. Prof. of Law Yale Univ. 29-30; Asst. Solicitor Prudential Insurance Co. of America 32, Gen. Solicitor 38, Vice-Pres. and Gen. Solicitor 39, Exec. Vice-Pres. 44, Pres. 46-60; Pres. Universal Controls, Inc. 62-67; Partner Shanks, Davis and Remer.
Publs. *Cases on Corporate Reorganization* 31, *Cases and Materials on Business Units,* 3 vols. 31-32 (both with William O. Douglas).
575 Park Avenue, New York, N.Y. 10021, U.S.A.
Telephone: 838-4900.

Shann, Keith Charles Owen, C.B.E., B.A.; Australian diplomatist; b. 22 Nov. 1917; ed. Trinity Grammar School, Kew, and Trinity Coll., Melbourne Univ., Australia.
United Nations Div., Dept. of External Affairs 46-49; Australian Mission to UN, New York 49-52; Head, UN Branch, Dept. of External Affairs 52-55; Australian Minister to the Philippines 55-56, Ambassador 56-59; Australian External Affairs Officer, London 59-62; Amb. to Indonesia 62-66; First Asst. Sec. Dept. of External Affairs 66-.
11 Grey Street, Deakin, Canberra, Australia.
Telephone: 7-1042.

Shannon, Claude Elwood, PH.D.; American applied mathematician; b. 30 April 1916; ed. Univ. of Michigan and Massachusetts Inst. of Technology.
Research mathematician Bell Telephone Laboratories 41-56, Consultant 57-; Visiting Prof. of Communication Sciences Massachusetts Inst. of Technology 56, Prof. of Communication Sciences and Mathematics 57-58, Donner Prof. of Science 58-; Fellow Center for Advanced Study in the Behavioral Sciences, Stanford, Calif. 57-58, Inst. of Radio Engineers; mem. Nat. Acad. of Sciences, American Acad. of Arts and Sciences, I.R.E., American Mathematical Soc.; Alfred Noble Prize A.I.E.E., Morris Liebman Award I.R.E., Stuart Ballantine Medal, Franklin Soc., Research Corpn. Award.
Publs. *Mathematical Theory of Communication* 49; numerous technical papers; Editor (with J. McCarthy) *Automata Studies* 56.
5 Cambridge Street, Winchester, Mass., U.S.A.

Shannon, James Augustine, A.B., M.D., PH.D.; American medical research administrator; b. 9 Aug. 1904; ed. Coll. of Holy Cross, Worcester, Mass. and New York Univ. Coll. of Medicine and Graduate School.
Assistant Prof. of Physiology, New York Univ. 35-41, Asst. Prof. of Medicine 41-42, Assoc. Prof. of Medicine 42-46; Consulting Physician N.Y. hospitals 38-44; Dir. Squibb Inst. for Medical Research, New Brunswick, New Jersey 46-49; Chair. Malaria Study Section, Nat. Insts. of Health, Bethesda, Maryland 46-47, Assoc. Dir. Nat. Heart Inst., Nat. Insts. of Health 49-52, Assoc. Dir. Intramural Affairs 52-55, Dir. 55-; Special Consultant to Surgeon-Gen., U.S. Public Health Service 46-49; mem. WHO Adv. Comm. on Med. Research 59-63; Consultant, President's Science Advisory Comm. 59-65, Advisory Comm. on Research to A.I.D. 63-; PAHO Advisory Comm. on Med. Research 62-; mem. U.S. Nat. Acad. of Sciences 65-; mem. American Acad. of Arts and Sciences 65-; Presidential Medal for Merit 48, Nat. Acad. of Science Public Welfare Medal

62; Rockefeller Public Service Award 64, Presidential Distinguished Fed. Civilian Service Award 66; several hon. degrees; chair. and mem. of numerous cttees. of Nat. Research Council.

National Institutes of Health, Bethesda, Md. 20014, U.S.A.

Shantaram, V(ankudre); Indian film director, producer and actor; b. 18 Nov. 1901; ed. Kolhapur High School.

Worked in film industry 20-; Founder mem. Prabhat Film Co., Poona; fmr. Chief Producer Govt. of India Films Div., mem. Censor Board, Film Advisory Board, Film Enquiry Cttee.: has directed and produced over 60 films 26-, including *King of Ayodhya, Chandrasena, Duniya-na-mane, Shakuntala* (first Indian film released in U.S.A.), *Ramjoshi, Amar Bhoopali, Jhanak Jhanak Payal Baaje* and *Do Ankhen Barah Haath* (11 awards incl. Berlin Gold Bear, Int. Catholic Award and Hollywood Foreign Press Award).

Rajkamal Kalamandir Private Ltd., Parel, Bombay 12, India.

Shapiro, Haim Moshe; Israeli politician; b. 02; ed. Theological Seminary, Berlin.

Head, Educational and Cultural Dept., Kovno, Lithuania 19; mem. Zionist Admin. Board 25; emigrated to Palestine 25; deputy mem., then full mem., Zionist Exec. of Jewish Agency 35; also Head of Immigration Dept. of Jewish Agency; Minister of Immigration and Health 48-49, of the Interior, Immigration and Health 49-51, of the Interior and Religious Affairs 51-52, of Social Welfare and Religious Affairs 52-58; mem. Knesset 49-; Chair Religious Nat. Party; Minister of Interior 59-; Religious Nat. Party.

Ministry of the Interior, Jerusalem, Israel.

Shapiro, Jacob Shimshon, LL.B.; Israeli lawyer and politician; b. 1902; ed. Kharkov Univ. and Law School, Jerusalem.

Came to Palestine 24; Co-founder Kibbutz Givat Hashlosha; Attorney-Gen., Govt. of Israel 48-49; Minister of Justice 66-; Israeli Labour Party.

Ministry of Justice, Jerusalem, Israel.

Shapiro, Karl Jay; American poet; b. 10 Nov. 1913; ed. Johns Hopkins Univ.

Served with U.S. Army 41-45; Consultant in poetry, Library of Congress 46-47; Assoc. Prof. of Writing, Johns Hopkins Univ. 47-50; Ed. *Poetry* 50-55; Prof. of Writing, Univ. of Nebraska 56-66; Prof. of English, Univ. of Illinois at Chicago Circle 66-; Ed. *Prairie Schooner* 56-63; Jeanette S. Davis Prize 42; Levinson Prize 43; Contemporary Poetry Prize 43; American Acad. of Arts and Letters Grant 44; Pulitzer Prize (Poetry) 45; Shelley Memorial Prize 45; Guggenheim Fellowship 45-46, 53-54; Fellow in American Letters, Library of Congress; mem. Nat. Inst. of Arts and Letters; Hon. D.H.L. Wayne State Univ. 60.

Publs. *Poems* 35, *Person, Place and Thing* 42, *The Place of Love* 42, *V-Letter and Other Poems* 44, *Essay on Rime* 45, *Trial of a Poet* 47, *Bibliography of Modern Prosody* 48, *Poems 42-53* 53, *Beyond Criticism* 53, *Poems of a Jew* 58; Ed. *Newberry Library Bulletin* 53-, *In Defence of Ignorance* 60, *American Poetry Anthology* 60, *The Bourgeois Poet* 64, *A Prosody Handbook* (with Robert Beum) 65.

305 W. Fullerton Parkway, Chicago, Illinois 60614, U.S.A.

Shapley, Harlow, M.A., PH.D., LL.D., D.SC., D.LITT.; American astronomer; b. 2 Nov. 1885; ed. Missouri and Princeton Univs.

Astronomer Mount Wilson Observatory 14-21; Dir. Harvard Observatory 21-52, Emer. 52-; Exchange Lecturer Belgium 26; Halley Lecturer Oxford 28; Darwinian Lecturer Royal Astronomical Society 34; Pres. Variable Star Comm. of Int. Astronomical Union 25-32; Pres. Nebular Comm. 32-46; Pres. International Observatories Comm. 46-55; Pres. American Acad. Arts and Sciences 39-44; American Astronomical Society 43-46; Pres. American Asscn. for Advancement of Science 47; Nat. Research Society 43-47; Pres. Science Service and Science Clubs of America 40-55; mem. American Comm. on UNESCO 46-50; Vice-Pres. Amer. Philosophical Soc. 44-46, Sec. 59-; Trustee, Mass. Inst. of Technology, Worcester Foundation for Experimental Biology, Woods-Hole Oceanographic Inst., etc.; fmr. Trustee Institut de Recherche Scientifique en Afrique Centrale; research worker in photometry and cosmogony; hon. degrees from many Univs. including Delhi, Copenhagen, Harvard and Mexico; hon. foreign mem. of Italian, Austrian, Indian, Belgian and French Nat. Acads., etc.; has also been awarded many medals and prizes incl. Pope Pius XI prize Vatican Acad.

Publs. *Source Book in Astronomy* 29, *Star Clusters* 30, *Flights from Chaos* 30, *Galaxies* 43, *A Treasury of Science* 43, *Readings in Physical Sciences* 48, *Climatic Second Source Book in Astronomy* 61, *Science Ponders Changes* 54, *Inner Metagalaxy* 57, *Of Stars and Men* 58, *Science Ponders Religion* 60, *Second Source Book in Astronomy* 61, *The View from a Distant Star* 64, *Beyond the Observatory* 67.

Sharon Cross Road, Peterboro, New Hampshire, U.S.A. Telephone: 617-876-7360.

Shaposhnikov, Vladimir Nikolaevich; Soviet microbiologist; b. 84; ed. Physico-Mathematical Faculty, Moscow Univ.

Moscow Chemical and Pharmaceutical Inst. 21-35; Dir., Dept. of Industrial Microbiology, Inst. of Microbiology, U.S.S.R. Acad. of Sciences 35-; Dir., Dept. of Technical Microbiology, Inst. of Microbiology, U.S.S.R. Acad. of Sciences 35-, Head, Chair of Microbiology, Moscow Univ. 38-; mem. U.S.S.R. Acad. of Sciences 53-; State Prize 49.

Publs. Co-author *New Developments in Pine Tapping* 37, *The Significance of Physiological Symptoms in the System of Micro-organisms* 42, *Industrial Microbiology* 48, *Physiology of Metabolism in Micro-organisms in Connection with Function Evolution* 60, *Destruction of Wool by Micro-organisms* 64.

Moscow State University, Leninsky Gory, Moscow, U.S.S.R.

Sharaf, Abdul Hamid; Jordanian diplomatist.

Former Head, Arab and Palestine Affairs, Ministry of Foreign Affairs; Dir. Broadcasting Service 63-64; Dir., Political Dept., Ministry of Foreign Affairs; Asst. Chief of Royal Cabinet 64-65; Minister of Information 65-67; Amb. to U.S.A. Aug. 67-.

Embassy of Jordan, 2319 Wyoming Avenue, N.W., Washington, D.C., U.S.A.

Sharif-Emami, Jaffar, G.C.M.G.; Iranian engineer and politician; b. 8 Sept. 1910; ed. German Central Railway School and Boras Technical School, Sweden.

Joined Iranian Civil Service 30; Technical Asst. Iranian Railways 43-46; Chair. and Man. Dir. Irrigation Authority 46-50; Under-Sec. of State to Ministry of Roads, Minister of Roads 50-51; mem. High Council, Plan Org. 51, Man. Dir. 51-52; Chair. High Council, Plan Org. 53-54; Senator 55, 63-; Minister of Industry and Mines 57-60; Prime Minister Aug. 60-May 61; Dep. Trustee Pahlavi Foundation 61-; Pres. Chamber of Industry and Mines 62-67; Chair. Industrial and Mining Devt. Bank 63-; Pres. of the Senate 63-; Pres. Iranian Asscn. of World Federalists 64-; Pres. Iranian Engineers Asscn. 66-; Pres. Third Constituent Assembly 67-; Hon. Pres. Chamber of Industries 67-; Order of Homayoun (3rd and 1st Class), Order of Tadj (1st Class) and many foreign decorations.

Darrooss, Ehteshamieh 48, Teheran, Iran.

Sharp, Dale E(lbert), A.B., M.B.A.; American banker; b. 3 Oct. 1903; ed. Washburn Coll. (Topeka, Kansas) and New York Univ. Graduate School of Business Administration.
With Nat. Bank of Commerce N.Y. 24-28, John Nickerson & Co. N.Y. 28-30; Instructor Bucknell Univ. 30-31, N.Y. Univ. 28-30; joined Guaranty Trust Co. of N.Y. 31, Vice-Pres. 42-55, Exec. Vice-Pres. 55-57, Pres. 57-59; Pres. Morgan Guaranty Trust Co. of N.Y. 59-61, Vice-Chair. 62-; Dir. and Chair. Exec. Cttee. Yorkshire Insurance Co. of N.Y., Seaboard Fire and Marine Insurance Co.; Dir. numerous concerns including Wilson & Co., Morgan Guaranty Int. Banking Corpn., Morgan Guaranty Int. Finance Corpn., American Smelting and Refining Co., Commerce and Industry Asscn. of N.Y. Inc., N.Y. Univ., Putnam Foundation; Hon. LL.D.; Republican.
Cove Neck Road, Oyster Bay, N.Y., U.S.A.

Sharp, Margery, B.A.; British writer; ed. London Univ.
Publs. *The Flowering Thorn, Four Gardens* 35, *The Nutmeg Tree* 37 (play, U.S.A. 40, England 41), *Cluny Brown* 44, *Britannia Mews* 46, *The Foolish Gentlewoman* 48 (play, England 49), *Lise Lillywhite* 51, *The Gypsy in the Parlour* 54, *The Eye of Love* 57, *The Rescuers* 59, *Something Light* 60, *Martha in Paris* 62, *Miss Bianca* 62, *The Turret* 63, *Martha, Eric and George* 64, *The Sun in Scorpio* 65, *Miss Bianca in the Salt Mines* (for children) 66, *Lost at the Fair* (for children) 67.
c/o Westminster Bank, St. James's Square, London, S.W.1, England.

Sharp, Hon. (William) Mitchell, B.A., M.P.; Canadian economist and politician; b. 11 May 1911.
Director Econ. Policy Div. of Dept. of Finance 47; fmr. Dep. Minister of Trade and Commerce; fmr. Vice-Pres. Brazilian Traction Co.; Chair. UN Int. Coffee Conf. 62; Minister of Trade and Commerce 63-65; Minister of Finance 65-68; Sec. of State for External Affairs 68-; Liberal.
Department of External Affairs, East Block, Parliament Buildings, Ottawa, Canada.
Telephone: 992-5074.

Shashin, Valentin Dmitrievich; Soviet oil executive and politician; b. 1916; ed. Moscow Petroleum Inst.
Worked at oilfields in Bashkiria 31-61; mem. C.P.S.U. 45-; Head of Chief Admin. of Oil and Gas Industry of Econ. Council of R.S.F.S.R. 60-65; Minister of Oil Industry, U.S.S.R. 65-; mem. Central Auditing Cttee. C.P.S.U. 66-; Deputy to U.S.S.R. Supreme Soviet 66-; Order of Lenin, Order of Red Banner of Labour and other decorations.
U.S.S.R. Ministry of Oil Industry, 26/1 Maurice Thorez Embankment, Moscow, U.S.S.R.

Shaw, Byron Thomas; American government official; b. 7 Sept. 1907; ed. Utah State Agricultural Coll., Univ. S. California, Ohio State Univ.
Teacher High Schools, Driggs and Sugar City, Idaho 30-37; Graduate Asst. in Agronomy, Ohio State Univ. 38-39, Instructor 39-40; Instructor, Univ. of Calif. 40; Assoc. Prof. of Agronomy, Ohio State Univ. 40-43; Agronomist, Soil and Fertiliser Div., Bureau of Plant Industry, Soils and Agricultural Eng., U.S. Dept. of Agriculture 43-45, Head Soil Management and Irrigation Investigations 45-47; Asst. Research Admin., Agricultural Research Service, U.S. Dept. of Agriculture 48-52, Research Admin. 52-65, Asst. to Admin. 65-; mem. Gen. Admin. Board, Graduate School, U.S. Dept. of Agriculture 55-63; Distinguished Service Award, U.S. Dept. of Agriculture 55; Editor *Soil Physical Conditions and Plant Growth.*
U.S. Department of Agriculture, Washington 25, D.C., U.S.A.

Shaw, Irwin, B.A.; American writer; b. 27 Feb. 1913; ed. Brooklyn Coll.
Formerly worked on radio; served in U.S. Army in Europe and Africa during Second World War; contributor to *The New Yorker, Esquire,* etc.
Publs. Plays: *Bury the Dead, Siege, The Gentle People, Retreat to Pleasure, Sons and Soldiers, The Assassin, The Survivors, Children from their Games;* Short Stories: *Sailor off the Bremen, Welcome to the City, Act of Faith, Mixed Company, Tip on a Dead Jockey;* Novels: *The Young Lions, The Troubled Air, Lucy Crown, Two Weeks in Another Town, Voices of a Summer Day, Love on a Dark Street.*
c/o Weidenfeld and Nicolson, 20 New Bond Street, London, W.1, England.

Shaw, Patrick, C.B.E.; Australian diplomatist; b. 13; ed. Ballarat Coll., Scotch Coll., Melbourne, and Univ. of Melbourne.
Served Tokyo 40-42, New Zealand 43-45, Chungking and Nanking 45-47; British Commonwealth Rep. on Allied Council for Japan and Head of Australian Mission in Japan 47-49; Counsellor, Head of Pacific Division, Dept. of External Affairs 50-51; Permanent Del. to U.N., Geneva 51-53; Asst. Sec. Dept. of External Affairs 53-56; Ambassador to Fed. Republic of Germany 56-60; Head Australian Military Mission, Berlin; Australian Govt. Rep. on Governing Board of I.L.O.; Ambassador to Indonesia 60-62; First Asst. Sec. Dept. of External Affairs, Canberra 63, Deputy Sec. 64; Perm. Rep. of Australia to UN, New York 65-.
Australian Mission to the United Nations, 750 Third Avenue, New York 17, N.Y., U.S.A.; and 8 Hotham Crescent, Deakin, Canberra, A.C.T., Australia.

Shaw, Thomas Richard, C.M.G.; British diplomatist; b. 5 Sept. 1912; ed. Repton and Clare Coll., Cambridge.
Probationary Vice-Consul, Istanbul 34-37, Bushire 37; Act. Consul, Tientsin 38-39, Trieste 40, Léopoldville 40, Elisabethville 42; Vice-Consul, Rabat 43; Vice-Consul at the Foreign Office 44-45, Consul 45-49; Consul, Bremen 49-53; Act. Consul Gen., N.Y. 53; Consul Gen., Izmir 55-57; Foreign Service Insp. 57-61, Senior Insp. of Foreign Service Establishments 61-63; Ambassador to Upper Volta, Niger and Ivory Coast 64-67, and to Dahomey 64-65; Minister, Tokyo 67-.
British Embassy, Tokyo, Japan; Home: Upton, Harrow Road West, Dorking, Surrey, England.
Telephone: Dorking 2685 (Home).

Shaw, Hon. Walter Russell, B.SC.; Canadian politician; b. 20 Dec. 1888; ed. St. Catherines Public School, Prince of Wales Coll., Toronto Univ.
Joined Prince Edward Island Govt. 16; Dep. Minister of Agriculture 34; Leader Conservative Party 58-; Premier and Minister of Agriculture 59-62, Premier and Pres. of the Council 62-67; served World War II; founder Prince Edward Island Fed. of Agriculture, Prince Edward Island Agricultural Council; Pres. Agricultural Science Soc., Canadian Horticultural Council.
Clyde River P.C., St. Catherines, Prince Edward Island, Canada.

Shawcross, Baron (Life Peer), cr. 59, of Friston; **Hartley Shawcross,** Kt., P.C., Q.C., LL.M.; British jurist; b. 4 Feb. 1902; ed. Dulwich Coll. and abroad.
Called to Bar 25; Senior Law Lecturer Liverpool Univ. 27-34; Deputy Regional Commr. S.E. Region 41; Regional Commr. N.W. Region 42-45; Recorder of Salford 41-45; Chair. Catering Wages Comm. 43-45; Asst. Chair. East Sussex Quarter Sessions 41; Labour M.P. for St. Helens 45-58; Attorney-General 45-51; Pres. Board of Trade April-Nov. 51; Judge of Int. Court of Arbitration, The Hague; Legal Consultant to The Shell Petroleum Co., Dir. 58-; Chair. Royal Comm. on the Press 61-62; Chair. British Medical Research Council 62-65; Chair. "Justice" (British branch of Int. Comm. of Jurists); Chief Prosecutor, Nuremberg Trials 45-46.

U.K. del. UN 45-49; withdrew from Labour Party 58; mem. Monckton Comm. 59-June 60 (resigned); Pres. Rainer Foundation; Chair. Dominion Lincoln Assurance Co. Ltd., Morgan Guaranty Trust Int. Advisory Council; Dir. Shell Transport and Trading Co. Ltd., E.M.I. Ltd., A.E.I. Ltd., Times Newspapers Ltd., Ranks, Hovis Macdougall Ltd., Caffyns Ltd., Morgan et Cie. S.A., Morgan et Cie. International S.A.; Special Adviser to Morgan Guaranty Trust Co. of N.Y.; mem. Court of London Univ.; Sussex Univ. Exec. Council, Pro-Chancellor 62-65, Chancellor 65-; mem. Int. Cttee. of Jurists, Board of Trustees, American Univ. of Beirut, Council of Int. Chambers of Commerce; Hon. mem. New York and American Bar Asscns.; Hon. LL.D. (Columbia, Bristol, Michigan, Lehigh Univs.). Friston Place, Sussex; 12 Grays Inn Square, London, W.C.1, England.
Telephone: East Dean 2206; and 01-242-5500.

Shawn, William; American editor; b. 31 Aug. 1907; ed. Univ. of Michigan.
Reporter, Las Vegas (N.M.) *Optic* 28; Midwest Editor *Int. Illustrated News*, Chicago 29; reporter *The New Yorker* 33-35, Assoc. Editor 35-39, Man. Editor 39-52, Editor *The New Yorker* 52-.
Home: 1150 Fifth Avenue, New York 28, N.Y.; Office: 25 West 43rd Street, New York 36, N.Y., U.S.A.

Shazar, Zalman (Schneor Zalman Rubashov); Israeli (b. Russian) Jewish historian and head of state; b. 6 Oct. 1889; ed. St. Petersburg Acad. of Jewish Studies and Univs. of Freiburg, Strasbourg and Berlin.
Delegate to Labour Zionist Conf., Minsk, Russia 06; settled in Palestine 24; Editorial staff *Davar* (Histadrut daily), later Editor 25-49; Minister of Educ., Israel 49-50; mem. Exec. Jewish Agency (in charge of Information Dept.) 52, Acting Chair. 56; Head, Zionist Organisation Dept. for Educ. and Culture in the Dispersion 54-63; Pres. of Israel 63-; Mapai.
Publs. *Kochvei Boker* (autobiographical sketches) 50 (English trans. 67), *Or Ishim* (biographical and historical studies) 55.
The President's House, Jerusalem, Israel.

Shchelokov, Nikolai Anisimovich, M.SC.; Soviet politician; b. 1910; ed. Dnepropetrovsk Metallurgical Inst.
Member C.P. of Soviet Union 31-; Miner 26-32; Engineer 33-38; Local Govt. and Party work 38-41; Army service 41-46; Head of Dept., Central Cttee. of C.P. of Ukraine 47-51; First Vice-Chair., Council of Ministers of Moldavian S.S.R. 51-62; Chair. Moldavian Council of Nat. Econ. 62-65; Second Sec., Central Cttee. of Moldavian C.P. 65-66; U.S.S.R. Minister of Public Order 66-; mem. C.P.S.U. Central Cttee. 66-; Deputy to U.S.S.R. Supreme Soviet; Soviet orders and medals.
Ministry of Public Order, Moscow, U.S.S.R.

Shcherbakov, Ilya Sergeyevich; Soviet diplomatist; b. 1912; ed. Chelyabinsk Teachers' Training Inst.
Teacher in secondary school 30-40; Soviet Army service 41-49; at offices of Central Cttee. of C.P.S.U. 52-63; joined Diplomatic Service 63; Minister-Counsellor, Peking 63-64; Amb. to Dem. Repub. of Viet-Nam 64-; mem. Central Auditing Comm. of C.P.S.U. 66-.
U.S.S.R. Embassy, 58 Chan-Fu Street, Hanoi, Democratic Republic of Viet-Nam.

Shcherbitsky, Vladimir Wasiljewich; Soviet politician; b. 1918; ed. Dnepropetrovsk Chemical Engineering Inst.
Instructor, Young Communist League District Cttee. 34; served Soviet Army Second World War; joined Communist Party 41; Candidate mem. Central Cttee., Ukraine Supreme Soviet 35; mem. Presidium Ukraine Communist Party 56, Sec. Central Cttee. 57-61; Prime Minister of Ukraine 61-63 and Oct. 65-; alternate mem. of Presidium of the Central Cttee. of C.P.S.U. 61-63, Alt. mem. Politburo 66-; First Sec.

Dnepropetrovsk Industrial District Cttee. of Ukraine Communist Party 63-64; First Sec. Dnepropetrovsk District Cttee. Ukraine C.P. 64-65; mem. Central Cttee. of C.P.S.U. 61-; Deputy to U.S.S.R. Supreme Soviet.
Ukrainian S.S.R. Council of Ministers, Kiev, U.S.S.R.

Shchetinin, Semyon Nikolayevich; Soviet politician and diplomatist; b. 1910; ed. Mining School and C.P.S.U. Central Cttee. Higher Party School.
Member C.P.S.U. 32-; Teacher, Party Organiser in mining industry 35-41; Sec. Goslovka Underground Cttee. C.P.S.U. 41-43; Sec. Donets Regional and City Cttees., C.P. Ukraine Party Coll. 43-51; Chair. Exec. Cttee. Irkutsk Regional Soviet of Workers Deputies 56-57, First Sec. Irkutsk Regional Cttee. C.P.S.U. 51-55, 57-68; Amb. to Mongolian People's Repub. 68-; mem. Central Cttee. of C.P.S.U. 61-; mem. Mandate Comm. of Soviet of Union, U.S.S.R. Supreme Soviet, Deputy to U.S.S.R. Supreme Soviet.
U.S.S.R. Embassy, Ulan-Bator, Mongolian People's Republic.

Shchukin, Aleksandr Nikolaevich; Soviet radio engineer; b. 1900; ed. Leningrad Electrotechnical Inst.
Instructor, Leningrad Electrotechnical Inst. 29-39, Prof. 33-; Leningrad Naval Acad. 33-45; Corresp. mem., U.S.S.R. Acad. of Sciences 46-53, mem. 53-; mem. Communist Party 44-; Presidium mem. Lenin Prize Cttee. for Science and Technology 60-; Order of Lenin.
Publs. numerous works on radio engineering.
U.S.S.R. Academy of Sciences, 14 Leninsky Prospekt, Moscow, U.S.S.R.

Shea, Joseph Francis; American scientist; b. 5 Sept. 1926; ed. Univ. of Michigan.
Instructor, Eng. Mechanics, Univ. of Mich. 48-50, 53-55; Research Mathematician, Bell Telephone Laboratory 50-53, Development Engineer 55-59; Dir., Advanced System R. and D., and Man. Titan Inertial Guidance Program, A.C. Spark Plug 59-61; Space Program Dir., Space Technology Lab. 61-62; Deputy Dir., Manned Space Flight (Systems), Nat. Aeronautics and Space Admin. 62-63, Program Manager Apollo Spacecraft, Manned Spacecraft Center 63-67, Deputy Assoc. Man. for Manned Space Flight April-July 67; Vice Pres. Polaroid Corpn. 67-.
Polaroid Corpn., Cambridge, Mass., U.S.A.

Shearer, The Hon. Hugh Lawson; Jamaican politician; b. 18 May 1923; ed. St. Simon's Coll.
Member Kingston and St. Andrew Corpn. 47-51; mem. House of Reps. 55-59; mem. Legislative Council (now Senate) 61-; Minister without Portfolio and Leader of Government Business in the Senate 62-67; mem. Cen. Exec., Jamaica Labour Party; Chair. Jamaican del. to UN 62-; Minister of External Affairs Feb. 67-; Prime Minister and Minister of Defence April 67-.
Office of the Prime Minister, Kingston, Jamaica.

Sheean, (James) Vincent; American journalist and writer; b. 5 Dec. 1899; ed. Univ. of Chicago.
Foreign corresp. 22-27 and since then at intervals in Europe and Asia; contrib. to magazines and reviews in England and America; Editorial Adviser review *Decision*; Officer, U.S. Air Corps.
Publs. *An American Among the Riffi* 26, *The Anatomy of Virtue* 27, *The New Persia* 27, *Gog and Magog* 29, *The Tide* 33, *Personal History* 35, *Sanfelice* 37, *A Day of Battle* 38, *The Pieces of a Fan* 37, *The Eleventh Hour* 39 (in America, *Not Peace but a Sword*), *Bird of the Wilderness* 41, *Between the Thunder and the Sun* 43, *This House Against This House* 46, *Lead Kindly Light* 49, *The Indigo Bunting, Rage of the Soul* 52, *Lily* 54, *Mahatma Gandhi* 55, *First and Last Love* 57, *Orpheus at Eighty* 59, *Nehru: Ten Years of Power* 59, *Dorothy and Red* 63, *The Arabian Destiny* 67.
Twin Farms, South Pomfret, Vt., U.S.A.

Sheen, Most Rev. Fulton John, J.C.B., PH.D., S.T.D.; American Roman Catholic bishop; b. 8 May 1895; ed. St. Viator Coll., Catholic Univ. of America, Anglicum Coll., Rome, and Louvain Univ., Belgium (Agregé en Philosophie).

Ordained 19; Papal Chamberlain 34; Domestic Prelate 35; Nat. Dir. Society for the Propagation of the Faith 50-66; Prof. of Philosophy, Catholic Univ. of America 26-50; Auxiliary Bishop of New York 51-66; Bishop of Rochester 66-; Titular Bishop of Caesariana 51-; radio and television series for many years; editor *World-mission* and *Mission*; Hon. LL.D., Hon. Litt.D., Hon. L.H.D., Cardinal Mazella Philosophy Medal Georgetown Univ.

Publs. *God and Intelligence* 25, *Life of All Living* 29, *Divine Romance* 30, *Eternal Galilean* 34, *Moral Universe* 36, *Cross and Beatitudes* 37, *God and Country* 41, *Declaration of Dependence* 41, *God and War and Peace* 42, *Love One Another* 44, *Communism and the Conscience of the West* 48, *Lift Up Your Heart* 50, *Way to Happiness* 54, *God Love You* 55, *Life is Worth Living*, IV and V, 56 and 57, *Life of Christ* 58, *This is the Mass* 58, *This is Rome* 60, *Go to Heaven* 60, *This is the Holy Land* 61, *These are the Sacraments* 62, *The Priest is not his own* 63, *Missions and the World Crisis* 63, *The Power of Love* 64, *Christmas Inspirations* 66, *Lenten and Easter Inspirations, Guide to Contententment, The Quotable Bishop Sheen, Footprints in a Darkened Forest* 67, etc.

50 Chestnut Street, Rochester, N.Y. 14604, U.S.A.

Shehan, H.E. Cardinal Lawrence Joseph; American ecclesiastic; b. 18 March 1898; ed. St. Charles Coll. Catonsville, St. Mary's Seminary, Baltimore and North American Coll., Rome.

Ordained priest 22; Asst. St. Patrick's Church, Washington, D.C. 22-45, parish priest 41-45; named Titular Bishop of Lydda and Auxiliary to the Archbishop of Baltimore and Washington 45; Pastor of St. Philip and St. James Church, Baltimore 45-53; first Bishop of Bridgeport, Connecticut 53-61; Co-adjutor Archbishop of Baltimore 61, Archbishop 61-; created Cardinal 65; mem. Secretariat for Promotion of Christian Unity 63-; Consultor, Comm. for Revision of Code of Canon Law 64-; Chair. Bishops' Comm. for Ecumenical Affairs 64-; Press Dept. Nat. Catholic Welfare Conf. 64-.

408 North Charles Street, Baltimore, Md. 21201, U.S.A.

Sheibani, Tala'at A. Al-, PH.D.; Iraqi lawyer and politician; b. 17; ed. Coll. of Law, Baghdad, Cairo Univ., Indiana Univ., U.S.A.

Lawyer 41-43; Teacher, Coll. of Commerce and Economics, Baghdad 51-53; Dir. Economic Bureau, Ministry of Development 54; Dir.-Gen. Fed. of Industries 57-58; Acting Minister of Oil 59-60; Minister of Planning 59-63.

Publs. *Influencing Powers on Constitutions* 54, *The Reality of Agricultural Property in Iraq* 58.

Al-Khansa Street, Najib Pasha, Baghdad, Iraq.

Shelakhin, Pavel Ivanovich; Soviet trade union official; b. 06; ed. Moscow Labour Inst. and Moscow High Trade Union School.

Trade union work 35-36; Chief of Dept. on labour rates and wages, coal-mining trust 36-42; Asst. Head, later Head, of an Admin. of the U.S.S.R. Coal Industry 42-46; leading trade union work 46-54; Head, Organisational-Instruction Dept. of the All-Union Cen. Council of Trade Unions 54-58; Chair. Central Cttee. of the Trade Union of Geological Prospecting Workers 58-; mem. C.P.S.U. 41-; mem. Central Auditing Cttee. of Trade Unions of U.S.S.R. 68-; Red Banner of Labour, Badge of Honour, several State medals.

Central Committee of the Trade Union of Geological Prospecting Workers, 42 Leninsky Prospekt, Moscow, U.S.S.R.

Shelepin, Alexandr Nikolaevich; Soviet politician and trade union official; b. 1918; ed. Moscow Inst. of History, Philosophy and Literature.

Held exec. positions in Moscow City Cttee. of Young Communist League 43-52; Sec. Central Cttee. of Young Communist League, and also mem. U.S.S.R. Cttee. for Physical Culture and Sports under U.S.S.R. Council of Ministers 45-53; First Sec., Central Cttee. of the Lenin Young Communist League 52; mem. Central Cttee. C.P.S.U. 52-; Deputy to U.S.S.R. Supreme Soviet; mem. U.S.S.R. Slav Cttee.; Chair. State Security Cttee. Dec. 58-61; mem. Secr. of the Presidium of the Central Cttee. of C.P.S.U. 61-64, 66-Sept. 67, of Presidium 64-66, of Politburo 66-; Chair. C.P. Cttee. of Party State Control 62-65; Deputy Chair. Council of Ministers 62-65; Chair. All-Union Council of Trade Unions July 67-; awarded Order of Lenin, Order of the Red Star, and other decorations.

All-Union Council of Trade Unions, 42 Leninsky Prospekt, Moscow, U.S.S.R.

Shelest, Pyotr Yefimovich; Soviet politician; b. 1908; ed. Mariupol Metallurgical Inst.

Member C.P.S.U. 28-; Engineer, Mariupol and Kharkov 32-41; party work, Chelyabinsk, Moscow, Suratov, Leningrad and Kiev 41-54; Second Sec., Kiev City Cttee., Ukraine C.P., later Second Sec. Kiev Regional Cttee. 54-57, First Sec. 57-62; mem. Presidium Central Cttee. of Ukraine C.P. 61, Sec. Central Cttee. 62-63, First Sec. 63-65, 66-; mem. Cen. Cttee. of C.P.S.U. 61-, Candidate mem. 63-64, Presidium mem. 64-66, mem. Politburo 66-; mem. Presidium of Supreme Soviet of U.S.S.R. 66-; Hero of Socialist Labour 68, and other decorations.

Central Committee of the Ukrainian C.P., Kiev, U.S.S.R.

Shemyakin, Mikhail Mikhailovich; Soviet chemist; b. 08; ed. Moscow State Univ.

Dozent, Analytical Chemistry, Moscow Inst. of Fine Chemicals Technology 30-37; Senior Scientific Worker, later Head of Laboratory, All Union Inst. of Experimental Medicine 35-45; Prof. of Organic Chemistry, Inst. of Biological and Medicinal Chemistry, Acad. of Medical Sciences of U.S.S.R. 45-60; mem. U.S.S.R. Acad. of Sciences 53-; Prof. Chemistry of Antibiotics, Inst. of Organic Chemistry, U.S.S.R. Acad. of Sciences 57-60; Dir. Inst. for Chemistry of Natural Products, U.S.S.R. Acad. of Sciences 59-; Deputy Head Div. of Chemical Sciences, U.S.S.R. Acad. of Sciences 57-63; mem. of Presidium and Academician-Sec. Dept. of Bioorganic Chemistry, Biochemistry and Biophysics, U.S.S.R. Acad. of Sciences 63-.

Publs. *Mechanism of Pyrolysis of Carboxylic Acid Salts* 34, 36, 48, *Hydrolytic Cleavage of Carbon Bonds* 41, *Oxido-Hydrolytic Reactions of Organic Molecules* 48, 49, 51, 52, 56, 57, *Theory of Amino Acid Metabolitic Processes Catalysed by Pyridoxal Enzymes* 52, 53, *The Chemistry and Mode of Action of Chloramphenico-* 50, 52-56, 59, 67, *The Chemistry of Sarcomycin* 57-59; *The Chemistry and Total Synthesis of Tetracyclines* 53, 57-67, *The Chemistry of α-Substituted α-Amino Acids and Peptides* 55, 56, 59-61, *The Chemistry of Depsipeptides* 60-67, *The Chemistry of Antibiotics* 49, 53, 61, *Mechanism of Osazone Formation* 59, 65, *Mechanism and Stereochemistry of the Wittig Reaction* 62-67, *Rearrangements in Peptide Systems, Cyclol Formation, Hydroxy- and Amino-Acyl Incorporation in Peptides* 61-67, *Mass Spectrometric Determination of the Amino Acid Sequence in Peptides and Proteins* 65-67, *Topochemical Approach to the Structure-Activity Relations of Peptides and Depsipeptides* 66-67, *The Chemistry of Olivomycins and Chromomycins* 64-67.

Institute for Chemistry of Natural Products, Ul. Vavilova 18, Moscow, U.S.S.R.

Telephone: 13-7-25-51.

Shen Chih-yuan; Chinese economist; b. 02.
Lectured at Sharyhat Legal Coll., Peking Univ., North-
east Univ.; Rep. in C.P.P.C.C. 49; mem. Cultural and
Educational Comm., State Council 49; Prof. Yenching
Univ.; on Cttee. Democratic League 49; mem. East
China Mil. Administration Council 49-53; East China
Administrative Council 53-; Shanghai del. to N.P.C. 54;
mem. Shanghai City Council 55; mem. Cttee. Dept. of
Philosophy and Social Sciences, Academia Sinica 55;
mem. Standing Cttee. Democratic League 56.
The Department of Philosophy and Social Sciences,
Chinese Academy of Sciences, Peking, China.

Shen, Yen-ping (*see* Mao Tun).

Shepard, Commander Alan Bartlett, Jr.; American
aviator and astronaut; b. 18 Nov. 1923; ed. Naval
Acad., Annapolis, Naval War Coll., Newport, R.I.
On destroyer *Cogswell* in Pacific, Second World War;
flying training Texas and Florida; wings 47; high
altitude experiments, test pilot school, Maryland;
operations officer night fighter unit, California; test
pilot and project test pilot numerous models; on staff
of C.-in-C., Atlantic; training for space flight 60-61;
first American to enter space 5th May, 61; in charge of
Apollo Program, Astronaut Office, National Aeronautics
and Space Admin.; NASA Distinguished Service Medal.
National Aeronautics and Space Administration,
Manned Spacecraft Center, Houston 1, Texas, U.S.A.

Shepard, Horace Armor; American business executive;
b. 15 Nov. 1912; ed. Murphy High School and Auburn
Univ.
U.S. Air Force 35-51, Brig. Gen. 47; Dir. of Procurement
and Engineering U.S.A.F. Headquarters 50-51; Vice-
Pres., Asst. to Gen. Manager, Thompson Ramo Wool-
dridge Inc. 51-57, Vice-Pres. and Gen. Manager 61-62,
Pres. 62-; Legion of Merit.
Thompson Ramo Wooldridge Inc., 23555 Euclid
Avenue, Cleveland, Ohio 44117, U.S.A.

Shepardson, Charles Noah; American banker; b. 7 Jan.
1896; ed. Colorado State Univ. and Iowa State Coll.
Captain, U.S. Army 17-19; Animal Husbandman,
Extension Dept., Univ. of Wyoming 19-20; Assoc.
Prof., Colorado State Univ. 20-28; Head of Dairy
Husbandry Dept., Texas Agricultural and Mechanical
Coll. 28-44, Dean of Agriculture 44-55; mem. Board of
Govs., Fed. Reserve System 55-April 67; official of
agricultural and educational orgs.
Home: 2475 Virginia Avenue, N.W., Washington, D.C.
20037, U.S.A.
Telephone: FE 7-2472 (Home).

Shepilov, Dmitri Trofimovitch; Soviet journalist and
politician.
Dir. Propaganda and Agitation Dept., Central Cttee. of
the Communist Party 49, full mem. Central Cttee. 52,
and one of its Secs. 54; Chief Editor *Pravda* 52-56; mem.
Supreme Soviet Council of Nationalities 54 and Chair.
Foreign Affairs Comm.; mem. Soviet Del. to China 54,
to Yugoslavia 55, and to Egypt 55 and 56; Minister of
Foreign Affairs 56-57; Dir. Inst. of Econ. Acad. of
Sciences of Kirghiz S.S.R. 57-62; engaged in scientific
work 62-.
Academy of Sciences, Moscow, U.S.S.R.

Shepstone, Hon. Denis Gem; South African adminis-
trator and university official; b. 7 Feb. 1888; ed. Natal
Univ. Coll.
Served First World War; mem. Durban City Council 40,
later Chair. of its Finance Cttee.; apptd. Senator to
represent non-European people 43; Administrator of
Natal 48-58; Chancellor, Univ. of Natal 49-65; Knight of
Order of St. John; Freeman of Durban and Pieter-
maritzburg; Pres. Y.M.C.A. of South Africa, Boy
Scouts of South Africa.
3 Fallodon Court, 727 Musgrave Road, Durban, South
Africa.

Sherfield, 1st Baron, cr. 64; **Roger Mellor Makins,**
G.C.B., G.C.M.G.; British diplomatist, public servant and
business executive; b. 3 Feb. 1904; ed. Winchester and
Christ Church, Oxford.
Barrister 27; Foreign Service 28, Washington and Oslo;
mem. Staff Resident Minister in W. Africa 42, of
Resident Minister, Allied Force H.Q. Mediterranean
43-44; Minister in Washington 45-47; Asst. Under-Sec.
of State for Foreign Affairs 47-48, Deputy Under-Sec.
48-52; Ambassador to U.S.A. 52-56; Joint Perm. Sec. to
Treasury 56-59; Chair. U.K. Atomic Energy Authority
60-64; Chair. Industrial and Commercial Finance
Corpn. 64-, Estate Duties Investment Trust 66, Ship
Mortgage Finance Co. 66-, Hill, Samuel & Co. Ltd.
66-, Technical Devt. Capital Ltd. 66-, A.C. Cossor Ltd.
68-; Fellow All Souls Coll., Oxford; Fellow Winchester
Coll.; Chair. Governing Body Imperial Coll. of Science
and Technology; Chair. Marshall Aid Commemoration
Comm.; Trustee, Kennedy Memorial Trust; Hon. D.C.L.
(Oxford), Hon. M.I.C.E.
Sherfield Court, Basingstoke, Hants., England.

Sheridan, Clare; British sculptor and author; b. 86;
ed. Convent de l'Assomption, Auteuil, Paris, and private
school at Darmstadt Germany; studied with John
Tweed and at S. Kensington Coll. of Art.
Invited to Moscow 20 and worked on busts of Lenin,
Trotsky, etc., in studio in Kremlin; Lecturer in U.S.A.
21; *New York World* news corresp. in Europe 22,
sculpture exhibition in New York; exhibited Paris 34-36;
has lived in Turkey, Biskra (Sahara) and Paris.
Publs. *Nuda Veritas* 28, *Without End* 38, *The Mask* 40,
My Crowded Sanctuary 43, *To the Four Winds* 54.
M'cid, Biskra, Algeria.

Sherman, Charles Dunbar; Liberian politician; b.
27 Sept. 1918; ed. Coll. of West Africa, Howard Univ.,
Wharton School of Finance, Univ. of Pennsylvania,
School of Public Affairs, The American Univ.
Government Economist 48-51; Prof. of Econs. Liberia
Coll. and Univ. 48-53; Govt. Econ. Adviser 51-57,
Financial Adviser 55-57; Chair. Nat. Production
Council 56-; Sec. of the Treasury 57-Oct. 66; Pres.
World's Alliance of YMCA 55-; Hon. LL.D. (Oberlin
Coll., Morehouse Coll., George Wilson's Coll.); Hon.
D.C.L. (Univ. of Liberia); numerous decorations.
Monrovia, Liberia.

Sherman, Frank (Howard); Canadian iron and steel
executive; b. 4 Oct. 1917; ed. Westdale Secondary
School, Hamilton, Ont. and Queen's Univ.
Metallurgical Asst., Dominion Foundries and Steel,
Ltd. (Dofasco) 39-40, in Devt. and Operation of Arma-
ments Dept. 40-44, Asst. Works Man. 45-44, Works
Man. 47-49, Vice-Pres. and Works Man. 49-52, Exec.
Vice-Pres. 52-57, Gen. Man. 57-59, Pres. and Gen. Man.
59-64, Pres. and Chief Exec. Officer 64-; Directorships
include American Iron and Steel Inst., Bank of Nova
Scotia, Crown Life Insurance Co., Dominion Foundries
and Steel Ltd., Nat. Trust Co. Ltd., Polymer Corpn.
Ltd. and Wabush Lake Railway Co. Ltd.; mem. Exec.
Council; Canadian Manufacturers' Assocn.; Board of
Govs.: Ontario Research Foundation, McMaster Univ.
and Art Gallery of Hamilton; Board of Trustees:
Queen's Univ.
Dominion Foundries and Steel Limited, Hamilton;
Home: 9 Turner Avenue, Hamilton, Ont., Canada.

Sherman George Flamma, D.S.O., B.A.; Liberian
educationalist and diplomatist; b. 28 Aug. 1913; ed.
Coll. of West Africa and Liberia Coll.
Teacher Bassa High School 39-41, Principal 42-44;
Supervisor of Schools 44-52, Gov. Grand Bassa County
52-56; Asst. Sec. Public Works and Utilities 56; Consul-
Gen. London 56-60; Ambassador to Ghana 60-; Chief,
Special Mission to the Congo 60-61; Dean of Diplo-

matic Corps 63-; Order of the Pioneers, Grand Commdr. Star of Africa, Order of African Redemption.
Embassy of Liberia, P.O. Box 895, Accra, Ghana.

Shermarke, Abdi Rashid, D.SC.; Somali politician; b. 19.
Former member Somali Nat. Liberation Movement; mem. Somali Nat. Assembly 59-; Prime Minister of Somalia July 60-64; Pres. of Somalia June 67-.
President's Residence, Villa Somalia, Mogadishu, Somalia.

Sherriff, Robert Cedric; British writer; b. 6 June 1896; ed. New Coll., Oxford.
Entered Sun Insurance Office 14; Capt. East Surrey Regt. 17; wrote first play for performance in aid School Chapel Restoration Fund; first London production Dec. 28 when *Journey's End* was produced by Stage Society; first public performance at Savoy Theatre Jan. 29.
Publs. *Badger's Green* 30, *The Fortnight in September* (novel) 31, *Windfall* 34, *Greengates* (novel) 36, *St. Helena* (in collaboration) 36, *The Hopkins Manuscript* (novel) 38, *Chedworth* (novel) 44, *Another Year* (novel) 46, *King John's Treasure* (novel 55), *The Wells of St. Mary's* (novel) 61, *Miss Mabel* 48, *Home at Seven* 50, *The White Carnation* 53, *The Long Sunset* 55, *The Telescope* 57, *Shred of Evidence* 60 (plays); *No Leading Lady* (autobiog.) 68; numerous film adaptations, including *Goodbye Mr. Chips, The Four Feathers, Lady Hamilton, Odd Man Out, The Dam Busters,* etc.
Rosebriars, Esher, Surrey, England.

Sherrill, Rt. Rev. Henry Knox, D.D.; American ecclesiastic; b. 6 Nov. 1890; ed. Hotchkiss School, Yale Univ. and Episcopal Theological School, Cambridge, Mass.
Deacon 14, Priest 15, Protestant Episcopal Church; Asst. Minister, Trinity Church, Boston 14-17; Red Cross and U.S. Army Chaplain in France 17-19; received Medal of Merit (U.S.); Rector Church of Our Saviour, Brookline, Mass. 19-23; Trinity Church, Boston 23-30; Bishop of Mass. 30-47; Presiding Bishop 47-58; Pres. Nat. Council of Churches of Christ in U.S.A. 50-52; Pres. World Council of Churches 54-61; mem. President's Comm. on Civil Rights 47; Fellow Corpn., Yale Univ.; Fellow American Acad. Arts and Sciences; Trustee Boston Univ.; Hon. LL.D. (Boston); Hon. D.D. (Harvard, Trinity Coll., Philadelphia Divinity School, Princeton, Columbia, Hobart Coll., Univs. of Edinburgh and Rochester, Seabury Western Theological Seminary); Hon. S.T.D. (Gen. Theological Seminary); Hon. D.C.L. (Union Coll.).
Publs. *William Lawrence—Later Years of a Happy Life, The Church's Ministry in Our Time* 48, *Among Friends* 62.
Boxford, Mass., U.S.A.

Sherrill, William Wayne, B.B.A., M.B.A.; American government official; b. 23 Aug. 1926; ed. Univ. of Houston and Harvard Graduate School of Business.
Served in Second World War with U.S. Marine Corps; with Southwestern Bell Telephone Co. until 54; Admin., City Court System of City of Houston; Exec. Asst. to the Mayor; Chief Admin. Officer and City Treas.; Investment Analyst; Pres. of Homestead Bank and Exec. Vice-Pres. of Jamaica Corpn. in Houston 63; Dir. Fed. Deposit Insurance Corpn. 66-67; mem. Board of Govs., Fed. Reserve System April 67-.
1101 Savile Lane, McLean, Virginia 22101, U.S.A.

Sherrod, Robert Lee, A.B.; American writer; b. 8 Feb. 1909; ed. Univ. of Georgia.
Newspaper reporter 29-35; Corresp. *Time* and *Life* 35-52; Far East Corresp. *Saturday Evening Post* 52-55, Managing Editor 55-62, Editor 62-63, Editor-at-Large 63-65; Vice-Pres. and Editorial Coordinator, Curtis Publishing Co. 65-66; contract writer, *Life* 67-; Benjamin Franklin award 55.
Publs. *Tarawa, The Story of a Battle* 44, *On to Westward*

45, *'Life's' Picture History of World War II* 50, *History of Marine Corps Aviation* 52, *Kobunsha's History of the Pacific War* 50.
c/o Curtis Publishing Company, 641 Lexington Avenue, New York 22, N.Y., U.S.A.

Sherwood, Thomas Kilgore, S.M., SC.D.; American chemical engineer; b. 25 July 1903; ed. McGill Univ. and Mass. Inst. of Technology.
Assistant and Research Asst., Mass. Inst. of Technology 24-28; Asst. Prof. Worcester Polytechnic Inst. 28-30; Asst. Prof. Mass. Inst. of Technology 30-33, Assoc. Prof. 33-41, Prof. of Chem. Eng. 41-46, Dean of Eng. 46-52, Prof. of Chem. Eng. 52-66, Lamont DuPont Prof. 66-; Visiting Prof. Univ. of Calif. (Berkeley) 58-59, 66-67; Technical Aide, Section Chief, Div. Mem. Nat. Defence Research Cttee. 40-46; Consultant, Baruch Cttee. 42, War Dept. 44; Trustee Assoc. Univs. Inc. 48-52; Priestley Lecturer Pennsylvania State Univ. 59; Fellow American Acad. of Arts and Sciences; mem. American Chemical Soc., American Inst. of Chemical Engineers, American Soc. Mechanical Engineers, Nat. Acad. of Sciences (Chair. Sec. of Eng. 62-65), etc.; Founder and mem. Nat. Acad. of Eng.; William H. Walker Award 41; Founders' Award, American Inst. of Chemical Engineers 64; U.S. Medal for Merit 48; Hon. D.Eng. (Northeastern Univ.), Hon. D.Sc. (McGill Univ.).
Publs. *Absorption and Extraction* 37, 2nd edn. (with R. L. Pigford) 52, *Applied Mathematics in Chemical Engineering,* 2nd edn. (with H. S. Mickley and C. E. Reed) 57, *Properties of Gases and Liquids* (with R. C. Reid) 58, 68, *The Role of Diffusion in Catalysis* (with C. N. Satterfield) 64, *Process Design* 64.
Room 12-186, Massachusetts Institute of Technology, Cambridge; and Lowell Road, Concord, Mass., U.S.A.
Telephone: 617-869-6900.

Shevchenko, Sergei Timofeevich; Soviet (Ukraine) government official and diplomatist; ed. Kiev Econ. Inst.
Commissariat of Educ., Ukraine 37; Soviet Army, Second World War, later Econ. teacher, Kiev State Inst.; Ukrainian Govt. posts 54-64; Perm. Rep. of Ukraine to United Nations 64-.
Permanent Mission of the Ukrainian Soviet Socialist Republic to the United Nations, 136 East 67th Street, New York 21, N.Y., U.S.A.

Shevchenko, Vladimir Vasilevich; Soviet politician; b. 18; ed. Pedagogical Inst., Lugansk.
Party and Soviet work 37-; mem. C.P.S.U. 40-; Soviet Army 38-40; Partisan Lugansk 42-43; First Sec. Kandiev City Cttee., Ukraine C.P. 52-56; Second Sec., Lugansk Regional Cttee., Ukraine C.P. 56-61, First Sec. 61-64; First Sec. Lugansk District Cttee., Ukraine Communist Party 64-; mem. Central Cttee. C.P.S.U. 61-; Deputy to U.S.S.R. Supreme Soviet; mem. of Mandate Comm.; U.S.S.R. Supreme Soviet.
Lugansk Regional Committee of C.P.S.U., Lugansk, Ukrainian S.S.R., U.S.S.R.

Shevliagin, Dmitri Petrovich; Soviet politician and diplomatist; b. 1913; ed. Moscow Law Inst. Higher Law Courses at Foreign Trade Academy.
Official, People's Commissariat for Foreign Trade 36-37; Legal Adviser to Soviet Trade Representation in Italy 37-41; on staff C.P.S.U. Cen. Cttee. 45-68, Deputy Head of Dept. 53, Head of Dept. 65-68; Amb. to the Algerian People's Democratic Repub. 68-; mem. Central Auditing Comm. C.P.S.U.
U.S.S.R. Embassy, Algiers, Algeria.

Shibata, Shukichi; Japanese chemical executive; b. 15 Dec. 1897; ed. Tohoku Univ.
Mitsubishi Joint Stock Co. 28-32, Mitsubishi Mining Co. 32-42, Mitsubishi Chemical Industries Ltd. 42-; Man. Dir. and Gen. Man. of Kurosaki Plant, Mitsubishi

Chemical Industries Ltd. 50-58, Dir. 52-, Pres. 58-63, Chair. Board of Dirs. 63-; Chair. Board of Dirs. Kasei Mizushima Petrochemical Co. Ltd.; Dir. Amagasaki Coke Industry Co., Mitsubishi Vonnel Co.
Mitsubishi Chemical Industries Ltd., Mitsubishi Main Building, No. 4, 2-chome, Marunouchi, Chiyoda-ku, Tokyo, Japan.
Telephone: 212-6411.

Shibata, Yuji; Japanese inorganic chemist; b. 28 Jan. 1882; ed. Imperial Univ. of Tokyo, Univs. of Leipzig, Zürich and Paris.
Professor of Inorganic Chemistry, Univ. of Tokyo 13-42; Prof. Univ. of Nagoya 42-48; Rector Tokyo Metropolitan Univ. 49-57; mem. Japan. Acad. 44, Pres. 62-; Hon. mem. Rumanian Acad.; Sakurai Medal, Japan Chemical Soc. 19, Imperial Medal of Japan Acad. 27.
Major works include: study of colour change of salt solutions, study of absorption spectra of the metal complex, works on spectrochemistry, co-ordination chemistry and geochemistry.
1-30-8 Ookayama, Megurogu, Tokyo, Japan.

Shibayev, Alexei Ivanovich; Soviet politician; b. 15; ed. Gorki State University.
Member C.P.S.U. 40-; Engineer, Dep. Head then Head of workshop, Gorki 40-43; Cen. Cttee. C.P.S.U. organiser Novosibirsk 43-47; Factory Dir., Rostov-on-Don, later Saratov 47-55; Second Sec., Saratov Regional Cttee. C.P.S.U. 55-59; First Sec. Saratov Industrial District Cttee. C.P.S.U. 59-64, Saratov District Cttee. 64-; mem. Central Cttee. of C.P.S.U. 61-; Deputy to U.S.S.R. Supreme Soviet; mem. Legislative Proposals Comm. of Union Soviet, U.S.S.R. Supreme Soviet.
Saratov District Committee of C.P.S.U., Saratov, U.S.S.R.

Shiga, Yoshio; Japanese journalist; b. 8 Jan. 1901; ed. Imperial Univ., Tokyo.
Joined Communist Party 23, becoming editor of *Marxism*; elected mem. of Central Cttee. of Communist Party 27; imprisoned for political reasons 28-45; re-elected mem. of Central Cttee. 45; mem. of House of Representatives 46-47 and 49-50; removed from public office by Gen. MacArthur, June 50; underground activity 50-54; re-elected mem. House of Reps. 55-; mem. Presidium Central Cttee. Japanese Communist Party, expelled from Party 64; founded the Voice of Japan Party; Chief Editor newspaper *Nichon-no-Koe;* mem. editorial Cttee. Moscow Peace Manifesto 57.
Publs. *Eighteen Years of Imprisonment* 47, *On the State* 49, *Japanese Revolutionaries* 56, *On Japan* 60, *I Appeal to You* 64.
26-15, Minamicho-3, Kichijoji, Musashino City, Tokyo, Japan.

Shigemashi, Seishi; Japanese politician; b. 97; ed. Tokyo Univ.
Ministry of Agriculture 23; three times Vice-Minister of Agriculture and Forestry, Minister of Agriculture and Forestry 62-63; mem. House of Councillors; Vice-Pres., Meiji Bakery Co.; Liberal Democrat.
House of Councillors, Tokyo, Japan.

Shigemune, Yuzo; Japanese business executive and politician; b. 11 Feb. 1894; ed. Technical High School, Tokyo.
Member House of Peers 46-47; mem. House of Councillors 47-, Vice-Pres. 53-56, Speaker 62-; Minister of Transport April-June 59; Pres. Tanakura Denki (Electric) Co. Ltd., Patent Right Holding Co. Ltd., Meiden Shoji (Commercial) Co. Ltd., Shigemune Sangyo (Industry) Co. Ltd., Meiden Suisho (Crystal) Co. Ltd.; Chair. Meidensha Electric Mfg. Co. Ltd. 62-; Governing Dir. Japan Fed. of Employers' Asscns.; Dir. Fed. of Economic Orgs.; Dir. Japan Electric Machine Industry.
226 3-chome Higashi-Osaki, Shinagawa-ku, Tokyo.

Shiina, Etsusaburo, LL.D.; Japanese politician; b. 98; ed. Tokyo Univ.
Former Pres. Tohoku Wool Manufacturing Co. and Dir. Toho Bussan Trading Co.; mem. House of Reps.; Sec.-Gen. of Cabinet 59-60; Minister of Int. Trade and Industry 60-61, Nov. 67-; Minister of Foreign Affairs 64-Dec. 66; Chair. Liberal Dem. Party Exec. Board Dec. 66-; Liberal Democrat.
14 Hanezawa-cho, Shibuya-ku, Tokyo, Japan.

Shikin, Iosif Vasilievich; Soviet politician and diplomatist; b. 06; ed. Krupskaya Communist Acad.
Member C.P.S.U. 27-; party work, Gorki 34-39; Political Officer, Soviet army 39-45, Chief Political Officer, Soviet army 45-46, Armed Forces 46-49; Head, Lenin Mil. Political Acad. 49-50; on staff of Central Cttee. C.P.S.U. 50-61; Ambassador to Albania 61-62; First Dep. Chair. Party-State Control Cttee., Central Cttee. of C.P.S.U. and Council of Ministers 62-65, People's Control Cttee. 65-; mem. Central Auditing Comm. of C.P.S.U. 52-.
Control Committee, Ul. Kuibysheva 21, Moscow. U.S.S.R.

Shima, Shigenobu; Japanese diplomatist; b. 07; ed. Univ. of Tokyo.
Entered diplomatic service 30; served London 31-35; Private Sec. to Foreign Minister 36; Peking 37; Consul at Tientsin and Tsingtao 38-41; Foreign Office, later Ministry of the Greater East Asiatic Affairs 41-44; served Army, interned in Siberia 45-47; Dir. Osaka Liaison Office 48-51; Special Asst. (European Affairs) to Vice-Minister for Foreign Affairs 52-53; Minister in Washington 54-57; Ambassador to Sweden 57-59; Deputy Vice-Minister for Foreign Affairs 59-62, Vice-Minister 63-64; Amb. to U.K. 64-68.
450 Shiba Shirokane Sankocho, Minato-ku, Tokyo, Japan.

Shimada, Eiichi; Japanese textile executive; b. 29 Sept. 1902; ed. Tokyo Foreign Languages Coll.
Nihon Industrial Bank 24-57; President, Nitto Boseki (Spinning) Co. 57-.
2-50 Shimoumachi, Setagaya-ku, Tokyo, Japan.

Shimoda, Takeso; Japanese diplomatist; b. 07; ed. Tokyo Imperial Univ.
Entered Japanese Diplomatic Service 31, served Nanking, Moscow, The Hague; Dir. Treaties Bureau Ministry of Foreign Affairs 52-57; Minister to U.S.A. 57-60; Adviser to Minister of Foreign Affairs 60-61; Ambassador to Belgium and Chief of Japanese Del. to European Communities 60-63; Ambassador to U.S.S.R. 63-65; Vice Minister of Foreign Affairs 65-67; Amb. to U.S.A. 67-; numerous foreign decorations.
Embassy of Japan, 2520 Massachusetts Avenue, N.W., Washington, U.S.A.

Shinde, Annasaheb P., B.A., LL.B.; Indian lawyer and agriculturist; b. 21 Jan. 1922; ed. Law Colls., Poona and Ahmedabad.
Political imprisonment 44; organized landowning farmers who had leased land to private sugar factories for nominal rents; Chair. Maharashtra State Co-operative Sugar Factories Fed., Poona; Vice-Chair. Pravara Co-operative Sugar Factory, Pravaranagar, Pravara Agricultural and Industrial Devt. Co-operative Soc. Ltd.; mem. Man. Cttees., All India Co-operative Sugar Factories Fed., New Delhi, Maharashtra State Co-operative Union; Dir. Land Mortgage Bank, Ahmednagar; mem. All India Congress Cttee. and Maharashtra Pradesh Congress Cttee.; Parl. Sec. to Minister of Food and Agriculture 62-63, to Minister for Community Devt. and Co-operation 64-65; Deputy Minister for Food, Agriculture, Community Devt. and Co-operation 65-67; Minister of State for Food, Agriculture, Community Devt. and Co-operation March 67-.
Publs. *Problems of Indian Agriculture and Food, The Indo-Pakistan Conflict.*
P.O. Shriampur, Ahmednagar, Maharashtra, India.

Shindo, Koji; Japanese shipping executive; b. 25 Sept. 1902; ed. Otaru Higher Commercial Coll.
Mitsui Bussan Kaisha 25-42; Mitsui Steamship Co. Ltd. 42-, Man., Admin. Dept. 45-46, Man. Dir. 46-56, Senior Man. Dir. 56-60, Pres. 60-; Pres. Japanese Shipowners' Asscn. 62-; Dir. Japanese Nat. Railways 62-63, Mitsui OSK Lines 64-; Exec. Dir. Fed. of Econ. Orgs. 60-; Gov. Dir. Japan Fed. of Employers' Asscns. 61-; Commr. Nat. Policy Research Asscn. of Japan 61-. 1436 3-chome, Ikebukuro, Toshima-ku, Tokyo, Japan.

Shinoda, Kosaku; Japanese politician; b. 99; ed. Waseda Univ.
Journalist, *Asahi Shimbun*, Yamagata and Chiba; fmr. Parl. Vice-Minister of Agriculture and Forestry; Minister of State, Chair. Nat. Public Safety Comm. and Dir. of Autonomy Agency until 63; Liberal Democrat. House of Councillors, Tokyo, Japan.

Shinojima, Hideo; Japanese chemical executive; b. 21 Jan. 1910; ed. Tokyo Univ. Law Dept.
Member Board Tanabe Pharmaceuticals Co. 41-45; with Mitsubishi Chemical Industries Ltd. 45-, mem. Board 50-, Man. Dir. 57-61, Senior Man. Dir. 61-64, Exec. Vice-Pres. 61-64, Pres. 64-; mem. Board Mitsubishi-Monsanto Chemical Co. 60-; Pres. Kasei Mizushima Petrochemical Co. 64-; mem. Board Mitsubishi Vonnel Co., Mitsubishi Petrochemical Co., and Amagasaki Coke Industry Ltd. 65-.
24-21, 2-chome, Kakinokizaka, Meguro-ku, Tokyo, Japan.

Shintani, Torasaburo, LL.B.; Japanese politician; b. 30 Oct. 1902; ed. Tokyo Imperial Univ.
Director, Bureau of Shipping, Ministry of Transportation and Communications 43-44; Vice-Pres. Board of Communications 45-46; mem. House of Councillors 47-; Parl. Vice-Minister of Labour 49-50; Minister of Posts and Telecommunications 66-67.
3-13, 1-chome, Kita-Senzoku, Ota-ku, Tokyo, Japan.

Shirer, William Lawrence, B.A., LITT.D.; American author, journalist and radio commentator; b. 23 Feb. 1904; ed. Coe Coll.
Foreign corresp. various American newspapers, Europe, Near East and India 25-45; Pres. Authors' Guild 56-57; contrib. various publs.; Légion d'Honneur.
Publs. *Berlin Diary* 41, *End of a Berlin Diary* 47, *The Traitor* (novel) 50, *Midcentury Journey* 52, *Stranger Come Home* (novel) 54, *The Challenge of Scandinavia* 55, *The Consul's Wife* (novel) 56, *The Rise and Fall of the Third Reich* 60, *The Rise and Fall of Adolf Hitler* 61, *The Sinking of the Bismarck* 62.
7 West 43rd Street, New York City, N.Y., U.S.A.

Shiryaev, Nikolai Pavlovich; Soviet foreign trade official; b. 1913; ed. Moscow Inst. of Mines and Acad. of Foreign Trade.
Member C.P.S.U. 39-; Vice-Chair. *Raznoimport* Trust 42-43; U.S.S.R. Commercial Rep. in China 43-47; Deputy Chief of Dept., Ministry of Foreign Trade 50-53; Official, Research Inst. of Conjuncture 48-50; U.S.S.R. Commercial Rep. in India 58-62; Chief of Dept., Ministry of Foreign Trade 62-; Order of Red Banner of Labour (three times).
Ministry of Foreign Trade, 32-34 Smolenskaya-Sennaya Square, Moscow, U.S.S.R.

Shitikov, Alexei Pavlovich; Soviet politician; b. 1912; ed. Gorki Agricultural Inst. and Higher Party School.
Member C.P.S.U. 39-; party work, Soviet army 41-45; Apparatus, Khabarovsk Territorial Cttee. C.P.S.U. 45-48, 50-52; Sec. Kamchatka Regional Cttee. C.P.S.U., then First Sec. Jewish Autonomous Region 48-55; Sec. Khabarovsk Territorial Cttee. C.P.S.U. 55-57, First Sec. 57-; mem. Central Cttee. C.P.S.U. 61-; Deputy to U.S.S.R. Supreme Soviet; mem. Cttee. for Foreign Affairs, Soviet of Union.
Khabarovsk Regional Committee of C.P.S.U., Khabarovsk, U.S.S.R.

Shklovsky, Josif Samuilovich; Soviet astrophysicist; b. 16; ed. Moscow Univ.
Head, Dept. of Radio Astronomy, Shternberg Astronomical Inst., Moscow 53-; Prof. Moscow Univ.; Lenin Prize 60.
Publs. *The Solar Corona* 51, *The Nature of the Aurora Polaris' Radiance* 52, *The Origin of Cosmic Rays and Radio Astronomy* 53, *The Origin of the Crab Nebula's Radiance* 53, *Radio Astronomy* 55, *Cosmic Radio-Frequency Emission* 56, *The Nature of the Earth's Third Radiation Belt* 60, *On the Distant Planet of Venus* 61, *The Universe, Life and Reason* 62.
Moscow State University, Lenin Hills, Moscow, U.S.S.R.

Shkuratov, Ivan Fyodorovich; Soviet trade union official; b. 19 Jan. 1912; ed. Moscow Zootechnical Inst.
State-Farm Zootechnician 35-40; Soviet Army 41-46; State Farm Dir. 46-49; U.S.S.R. Ministry of State Farms 49-56; Dep. Chair. Cen. Cttee. of Agricultural and Procurement Workers' Union 56-58, Sec. 58-62, Chair. 62-; Sec. All-Union Central Council of Trade Unions 64-68; mem. Presidium All-Union Central Council of Trade Unions 68-; mem. C.P.S.U.; Order of Red Star, Order of the Red Banner of Labour, Badge of Honour, etc.
Central Committee of Agricultural and Procurement Workers' Union, 42 Leninsky Prospekt, Moscow, U.S.S.R.

Shoaib, Mohammad, M.A., LL.B.; Pakistani diplomatist and banker; b. 5 Sept. 1905; ed. Allahabad Univ.
Appointed to Provincial Admin. Service 26, to Indian Mil. Accounts Dept. 29; Chief Controller Army Factory Accounts, Govt. of India 42; after Partition appointed Adviser on Mil. Finance; Special Del. Sterling Accounts Settlement Confs.; Exec. Dir. Int. Bank for Reconstruction and Devt. representing Pakistan, U.A.R., Ethiopia, Iran and Middle Eastern countries 52-58; Minister of Finance, Govt. of Pakistan Nov. 58-62; Minister of Econ. Co-ordination Feb.-May 62; Exec. Dir. World Bank June 62-Feb. 63, Vice-Pres. Sept. 66-; Minister of Finance (Pakistan) Dec. 62-66; Fellow Inst. of Cost and Works Accountants (London), Inst. of Costs and Works Accountants (India), Inst. of Industrial Accountants (Pakistan); mem. Nat. Asscn of Accountants, New York.
International Bank for Reconstruction and Development, Washington; Home: 2920 Northampton Street, N.W., Washington, D.C., U.S.A.
Telephone: DU1-2006 (Office); 244-3975 (Home).

Shockley, William (Bradford), B.SC., PH.D.; American scientist; b. 13 Feb. 1910; ed. California Inst. of Technology, Massachusetts Inst. of Technology.
Mem. Technical Staff 36-42, Research Physicist 45-54 and Dir. Transistor Physics Research 54-55, Bell Telephone Laboratories; Dir. of Research, anti-submarine Warfare Operations Research Group US. Navy 42-44; Expert Consultant, Office of the Sec. of War 44-45; Visiting Lecturer Princeton Univ. 46; Scientific Adviser, Policy Council, Joint Research and Development Board 47-49; Scientific Advisory Panel, U.S. Army 51-60; Visiting Prof. California Inst. of Technology 54; Deputy Dir. and Dir. of Research, Weapons Systems Evaluation Group, Dept. of Defence 54-55; Dir. Semiconductor Laboratory of Beckman Instruments Inc. 55-58; Pres. Shockley Transistor Corpn. 58-60; Dir. Shockley Transistor (unit of Clevite Transistor) 60-63; Alexander M. Poniatoff Prof. of Engineering Science, Stanford Univ. 63-; Air Force Scientific Advisory Board 59-61; Medal for Merit 46; Morris Liebmann Prize 51, O. E. Buckley Prize 53, Cyrus B. Comstock Award, of Nat. Acad. of Sciences 54; Nobel Prize in Physics 56, etc.;

Hon. Sc.D. (Princeton and Rutgers Univs., Gustavus Adolphus Coll., Minnesota, U.S.A.).
Publs. *Electrons and Holes in Semi-conductors* 50, and many articles.
23466 Corta Via, Los Altos, California, U.S.A.

Shoda, Kenjiro; Japanese mathematician; b. 02; ed. Tokyo Univ.
Professor, Osaka Univ. 33-54, Pres. 54-60; mem. Japan Acad. 53-; Japan Acad. Prize 49.
Publs. *Abstract Algebra, A Manual of Algebra,* etc.
186, Ohara-cho, Ashiya-shi, Hyogo-ken, Japan.

Shoemaker, George Albert; American mining executive; b. 26 Aug. 1901; ed. Pennsylvania State Coll.
Apprentice Engineer, Babcock and Wilcox Co., New York City 23-25, Service Engineer 25-30; Union Collieries Co., Renton, Pa. 30-33, Oakmont, Pa. 33-45; Vice-Pres. Consolidation Coal Co., Oakmont 45-46, Pittsburgh Coal Co. 46-48, Pres. 48-51; Vice-Pres. Pittsburgh Consolidation Coal Co. 51-52, Exec. Vice-Pres. 52-60, Pres. 60-66; Exec. Adviser, coal, to Continental Oil Co. 66-; official of other companies.
Continental Oil Co., Kopper Building, Pittsburgh, Pa. 15219, U.S.A.

Shokin, Alexandr Ivanovich; Soviet politician; b. 1909; ed. Bauman Higher Technical School, Moscow.
Engineer, Ministry of Shipbuilding Industry 32-38, Chief Engineer, Ministry of Shipbuilding Industries 38-43; State work 43-49; Dep. Minister, U.S.S.R. Communications Industry 49-53, First Dep. Minister 54-57; First Dep. Chair. State Cttee. of Council of Ministers for Electronics 58-61, Chair. 61-65; U.S.S.R. Minister of Electronics Industries 65-; Cand. mem. Central Cttee. of C.P.S.U. 61-66, mem. 66-; Deputy to U.S.S.R. Supreme Soviet; State Prize 52, 53.
U.S.S.R. Ministry of Electronics Industries, Moscow, U.S.S.R.

Sholokhov, Michail Alexandrovich; Soviet novelist; b. 24 May 1905.
Member Acad. of Sciences of U.S.S.R.; awarded State Prize 41; corresp., broadcaster; Deputy to Supreme Soviet 46-; mem. Presidium Union of Soviet Writers 54-; mem. C.P.S.U. Central Cttee.; Nobel Prize for Literature 65; Hero of Socialist Labour 67; Lenin Prize; Order of Lenin (three times); Hon. D.Iur. (St. Andrews).
Publs. *Dvukhmuznaya* (Woman with two husbands) 25, *Alyoshkino Serdtse* (The Heart of Alyoshka) 25, *Donskiye Razkzzy* (Stories of the Don) 26, *Tikhy Don* (And Quiet Flows the Don) (4 vols.) 28-40, *Podnyataya Tselina* (Virgin Soil Upturned) 32-33, 2nd vol. 59, *They Fought for Their Country* 66, *One Man's Destiny* 67; Short stories: *Smertelnyi Vrag* (The Mortal Enemy), *Chervotochina* (Dry Rot), *Semeynyi Chelovek* (The Family Man), *Zherebyonok* (The Colt), *Collected Works* (Vols. 1-8) 59-62.
Union of Soviet Writers, 52 Vorovsky Street, Moscow, U.S.S.R.

Shoman, Abdul Hameed; Palestinian-Arab banker; b. 88; ed. privately.
Migrated to the U.S.A. 11; commenced business as a manufacturer 17; estab. Arab Bank Ltd. Jerusalem 30; Gen. Man. Arab Bank Ltd. 30-43, Chair. Board and Gen. Man. Arab Bank Ltd. 43-.
c/o The Arab Bank Ltd., King Faisal Street, Amman, Jordan.

Shone, Sir Robert Minshull, C.B.E., M.A., M.ENG.; British economist; b. 06; ed. Sedbergh School, Liverpool Univ. and Univ. of Chicago.
Industrial work 28-32; Commonwealth Fellow (U.S.A.) 32-34; Lecturer, London School of Econs. 35-36; Gen. Dir. Ministry of Supply, Iron and Steel Control 39-45; Dir. British Iron and Steel Fed. 50-53; exec. mem. Iron and Steel Board 53-61; Dir.-Gen. Nat. Econ. Devt.

Council 62-66; Dir. White Drummond Co. Ltd. 66-; Fellow, Nuffield Coll., Oxford 66-67; Visiting Prof. of Applied Econs., City Univ. (London) 67-.
Publs. *Some Modern Business Problems* (with others) 37, *The Industrial Future of Great Britain* 48, *Large-Scale Organisation* 50.
7 Windmill Hill, London, N.W.3, England.
Telephone: 01-435-1930.

Shore, Rt. Hon. Peter (David), P.C., M.P.; British politician; b. 20 May 1924; ed. Quarry Bank High School, Liverpool, and King's Coll., Cambridge.
Member Labour Party 48-; Head of Research Dept., Labour Party 59-64; M.P. for Stepney 64-; Parl. Private Sec. to Prime Minister 65-66; Joint Parl. Sec., Ministry of Technology 66-67; Sec. of State for Econ. Affairs 67-.
Publ. *Entitled to Know* 66.
House of Commons, London, S.W.1, England.

Shore, Thomas Spencer, A.B., B.J., M.B.A.; American industrialist; b. 24 June 1903; ed. Univ. of Missouri and Harvard Univ.
With Goldman, Sachs & Co. N.Y. (Investment Bankers) 26-31; Vice-Pres. and Treas. The General Tire & Rubber Co., Akron, Ohio 31-43; Gen. Partner, Goldman, Sachs & Co. N.Y. 43-48; Pres. The Eagle-Picher Co., Cincinnati, Ohio 49-; Dir. Central Trust Co., Cincinnati, Gas and Electric Co., Cluett, Peabody & Co., Kroger Co., Federated Dept. Stores Inc., Cincinnati Reds Inc., Armco Steel Corpn., Middletown, Ohio.
Home: Edwards and Walsh Roads, Cincinnati, Ohio; Office: American Bldg., Cincinnati, Ohio, U.S.A.

Shores, Louis, A.B., B.S. in L.S., M.S., PH.D.; American librarian, editor and writer; b. 14 Sept. 1904; ed. Toledo, Columbia Univs., City of New York Coll., Chicago Univ. and George Peabody Coll.
Served in New York Public Library 26-28; Fisk Univ. 28-33; Dir. and Prof., Library School, George Peabody Coll. 33-46; Dean, Library School, Florida State Univ. 46-47, Dean Emer. 67-; Visiting Prof. Univ. of Southern Ill. 68; Editor-in-Chief, *Colliers Encyclopedia* 60-; Fulbright Fellow, U.K. 51-52.
Publs. *Origins of the American College Library* 34, *Bibliographies and Summaries in Education* (with another) 36, *Basic Reference Books* 37, *How to Study* (with another) 48, *General Education* (with others) 49, *Highways in the Sky* 47, *Challenges to Librarianship* 53, *Basic Reference Sources* 54, *Instructional Materials* 60, *Mark Hopkins Log* 65, *The Library College* (with others) 66.
Florida State University, Tallahassee, Florida; 2013 W. Randolph Circle, Tallahassee, Florida, 32303 U.S.A.
Telephone: 599-3132 (Office); 385-12704 (Home).

Short, Rt. Hon. Edward Watson, P.C., M.P.; British politician; b. 17 Dec. 1912; ed. Bede College, Durham.
Served Second World War and became Capt. in Durham Light Infantry; Headmaster, Princess Louise County Secondary School, Blyth, Northumberland 47; Leader Labour Group, Newcastle City Council 50; M.P. for Newcastle upon Tyne Central 51-; Opposition Whip (N. Area) 55-62; Deputy Chief Opposition Whip 62-64; Parl. Sec. to Treasury and Govt. Chief Whip 64-66; Postmaster-Gen. 66-April 68; Sec. of State for Educ. and Science April 68-; Labour.
House of Commons, London, S.W.1, England.

Shostakovich, Dmitry Dmitryevich; Soviet pianist and composer; b. 26 Sept. 1906; ed. Leningrad Conservatoire; studied under L. N. Nikolaev and M. O. Steinberg.
Former mem. Leningrad Conservatoire; artistic advisor, Bolshoi Theatre, Moscow 54-; 1st Sec. Soviet Union of Composers 60-68; mem. editorial board *Sovietskaya Muzyka;* State prizes for piano quintet 41, 7th Symphony 42, piano trio 46; People's Artist of U.S.S.R. 54;

concert tour in Italy 58; mem. U.S.S.R. Supreme Soviet 59-; Hon. mem. St. Cecilia Acad. of Music Jan. 58; Diploma of Honour, St. Cecilia Acad. May 58; Hon. D. Mus. (Oxon.) 58; Lenin Prize for 11th Symphony 58; Hero of Socialist Labour, Order of Lenin 66; Gold Medal, Royal Philharmonic Soc. (U.K.) 66.

Works include: twelve symphonies, three ballets (*Golden Age, Bolt, Clear Stream*), three operas (*Nose, Lady Macbeth of Mtsensk, Katerina Izamilova*), symphonic suites, piano concertos, violin concertos, two cello concertos, three cantata-oratorios, six string quartets, music for films and theatrical productions, oratorio *Song of the Forest* 49, oratorio *Execution of Stepan Razin* 66, operetta *Cheryomushki* 58, symphonic poem *October* 67.

U.S.S.R. Union of Composers, 8-10 Ulitsa Nezhdanovoy, Moscow, U.S.S.R.

Shoukry, Mohammed Anwar; United Arab Republic (Egyptian) egyptologist; b. 05; ed. Cairo Univ. Inst. of Egyptology and Univ. of Göttingen.

Asst. Prof. of Egyptology Cairo Univ. 48-52, Prof. 52-; Chief Archæologist Cen. of Documentation of Egyptian Art and Civilisation 56-59; Dir.-Gen. Dept. of Egyptian Antiquities 59-66; Asst. Under-Sec. of State, Ministry of Culture and Nat. Guidance 61-.

Publ. *Die Grabstatue im Alten Reich*.

c/o Department of Egyptian Antiquities, Cairo, U.A.R.

Shpedko, Ivan Fadeevich; Soviet diplomatist; b. 11 Sept. 1918; ed. Kharkov Pedagogical Inst.

U.S.S.R. Diplomatic Service 41-, Iran 41-45, Counsellor of U.S.S.R. Embassy, Afghanistan 49-53; with Ministry of Foreign Affairs 53-56; U.S.S.R. Ambassador to Pakistan 56-60; Deputy Head, South Asian Dept. of U.S.S.R. Ministry of Foreign Affairs 61-63; Ambassador to Canada 63-; four Soviet decorations.

U.S.S.R. Embassy, 285 Charlotte Street, Ottawa, Canada.

Shrimali, Kalu Lal, M.A., PH.D.; Indian educationist and politician; b. 30 Dec. 1909; ed. Banaras Hindu Univ., Calcutta Univ. and Columbia Univ., New York. Life mem. Vidya Bhawan Soc. 31-; Dean, Faculty of Educ. Univ. of Rajputana 51-54; Parl. Sec. Ministry of Educ. New Delhi 53-55, Dep. Minister for Educ. 55-57, Minister of State in Ministry of Educ. and Scientific Research 57-58, Minister of Education 58-63; Vice-Chancellor Univ. of Mysore 64-.

Publs. *Bachon Ki Kuch Samasyayen* (Hindi), *Shiksha aur Bhartiya Loktantra* (Hindi), *The Wardha Scheme, Adventures in Education, Problems of Education in India*.

Vidya Bhawan Society, Udaipur, India.

Shrinagesh, Gen. Satyavant Mallannah; Indian army officer; b. 11 May 1903; ed. Sandhurst and Cambridge Univ.

Commissioned 23; Overall Commdr. of Indian Forces in Jammu and Kashmir 48; G.O.C.-in-C. Western Command, India 49-53; G.O.C.-in-C. Southern Command, Poona 53-55; Chief of Army Staff 55-57; Principal Admin. Staff Coll. of India 57-59; Gov. of Assam 59-62, concurrently of Nagaland 61-62; Governor of Andhra Pradesh 62-64; Gov. of Mysore 64-65.

12A Friends' Colony, New Delhi, India.

Shriver, Robert Sargent, Jr., B.S., LL.D.; American executive and public servant; b. 9 Nov. 1915; ed. Yale Univ.

Admitted to New York Bar 41; served U.S. Navy 14-45; Asst. Editor *Newsweek* 45-46; Exec. Dir. The Joseph P. Kennedy, Jr. Foundation 55-; Asst. Gen. Man. The Merchandise Mart 48-61; mem. Chicago Board of Educ. 55-60 (Pres. 56-60); Dir. The Peace Corps 61-66, Office of Econ. Opportunity 64-68; Special Asst. to the Pres. 64-68; Amb. to France 68-; Official of numerous educational bodies; Hon. LL.D., Hon. L.H.D., Hon. D.C.L. (all of very many Univs.);

Golden Heart Presidential Award (Philippines), and many national awards.

American Embassy, avenue Gabriel 2, Paris 8e, France.

Shroff, K. R. P.; Indian financier; b. 27 July 1878; ed. Bombay New High School and Byramjee Jeejeebhoy Commercial Coll.

School teacher 1900; joined his father's firm on Bombay Stock Exchange 02; mem. Bombay Stock Exchange 16, Dir. 20-, First Joint Hon. Sec. and Treas. 21, Hon. Sec. and Treas. 22, Hon. Pres. 23-39, Trustee 23-, Pres. 39-66; Patron and Principal Adviser 66-; fmr. Chair. Zoroastrian Co-operative Credit Bank Union Bank of India Ltd. 62; Padma Bhusan 67.

Sunshine, Churchgate Reclamation, Bombay 1, India.

Shtylla, Behar; Albanian politician; b. 18; ed. Kortcha secondary school and in Italy.

Fought in the resistance during Nazi occupation; after the war held important posts in the Ministry of the Interior, the Secretariat of the Albanian Democratic Front and the Ministry of Foreign Affairs; later Minister in France and Italy; Minister of Foreign Affairs 53-65.

c/o Ministry of Foreign Affairs, Tirana, Albania.

Shubnikov, Alexei Vasilyevich; Soviet crystallographer; b. 1887; ed. Moscow Univ.

Assistant, Moscow People's Univ. 13-20; Prof. of Crystallography, Ural Mining Inst. 20-25; Senior Scientific Worker, Mineralogical Inst. of U.S.S.R. Acad. of Sciences 25-37; Dir. of Laboratory, Inst. of Crystallography of U.S.S.R. Acad. of Sciences 37-45, Dir. of Inst. of Crystallography of U.S.S.R. Acad. of Sciences 45-63; mem. U.S.S.R. Acad. of Sciences; Order of Lenin, Order of Red Banner of Labour, State Prize (twice), Fedorov Prize; Ed. *Crystallography* (U.S.S.R. Acad. of Sciences).

Publs. *How Crystals Grow* 35, *Symmetry* 40, *Quartz and its Applications* 40, *Piezoelectrical Textures* 46, *Symmetry and Antisymmetry of Finite Figures* 52, *Principles of Optical Crystallography* 58, *Symmetry of Similarity* 60, *Problem of the Dissymmetry of Material Objects* 61.

Institute of Crystallography of U.S.S.R. Academy of Sciences, 59 Leninsky Prospekt, Moscow, U.S.S.R.

Shuckburgh, Sir Evelyn, G.C.M.G., C.B.; British diplomatist; b. 26 May 1909; ed. Winchester Coll. and King's Coll., Cambridge.

Joined Foreign Office 33; served Cairo 37-39, Ottawa 40-42, Buenos Aires 42-45, Prague 45-47; Head of South American Dept., Foreign Office 47-48, Western Dept., Western Organisations Dept. 49-51; Private Sec. to Sec. of State for Foreign Affairs 51-54; Asst. Under-Sec. of State, Foreign Office 54-56; seconded to Imperial Defence College as civilian instructor 56-58; Asst. Sec.-Gen. (Political Affairs) NATO 58-60; Dep. Under-Sec. Foreign Office, responsible for NATO, Western European Union, Council of Europe and West European Countries 60-62; Perm. Rep. to NATO 62-66; Amb. to Italy 66-.

British Embassy, Via Conte Rosso 25, Rome, Italy.

Shukairy, Ahmed; Saudi Arabian politician and diplomatist.

Minister of State for United Nations Affairs; Perm. Rep. to the United Nations until 63; Chair. Palestine Liberation Org. 63-Dec. 67.

Amman, Jordan.

Shuleikin, Vasily Vladimirovich; Soviet geophysicist; b. 95; ed. St. Petersburg Polytechnic Inst.

Research devoted to problems of marine physics; founded the Black Sea Hydrophysical station in the Crimea 29, the Hydrophysical Marine Laboratory 35, the Chair of Marine Physics at Moscow Univ. 45; mem. U.S.S.R. Acad. of Sciences 46-; State prizewinner 42; awarded Order of Lenin (twice), Semyonov-Tyanshan Medal of Geographical Soc. of the U.S.S.R.

Publs. *Outline of Marine Physics* 49, *Marine Physics* 53,

Theory of Marine Waves 56, *Short Course of Marine Physics* 59, *Physical Investigation of Oceans and Seas* 60. Moscow State University, Lenin Hills, Moscow, U.S.S.R.

Shuman, Charles B.; American farmer and agricultural executive; b. 27 April 1907; ed. Coll. of Agriculture, Univ. of Illinois.
Engaged in farming, Ill. 29-; mem. Board of Dirs., Ill. Agricultural Asscn. 40-45, Pres. 45-54; Pres. American Farm Bureau 54-; mem. President's Highway Safety Comm. 53-61; Pres. American Agricultural Mutual Insurance Co. 54-, American Agricultural Marketing Asscn. 60-, Farm Bureau Trade Development Corpn. 60-; mem. Nat. Livestock and Meat Board 55-, Comm. on Money and Credit 59-61.
Home: Sullivan, Ill.; Office: 1000 Merchandise Mart, Chicago, Ill., U.S.A.

Shumauskas, Moteyus Yuozo; Soviet politician; b. 1905; ed. Int. Lenin School.
Member Communist Party 24; forced labour and concentration camps 29, 31-37, 39-40; Deputy, People's Seym, Lithuania 40-; Deputy-Chair. Council of Lithuanian People's Commissariat; Chair. Lithuanian Planning Cttee. 45-50; Deputy, U.S.S.R. Supreme Soviet 46-; mem. Lithuanian S.S.R. Supreme Soviet 47-; First Sec. Sjauljay Party Cttee. 50-53; First Deputy-Chair., Lithuanian Council of Ministers 53, Chair. 56-67; Pres. of Presidium of Supreme Soviet of Lithuanian S.S.R. 67-; Deputy Chair. Presidium of Supreme Soviet of U.S.S.R. 67-; Deputy to U.S.S.R. Supreme Soviet; mem. Bureau Central Cttee. Lithuanian C.P. 49-63, 66-, mem. Presidium 63-66; candidate mem. Central Cttee. C.P.S.U. 56-; Order of Lenin 43, 51, 58, 65; Order of the Red Banner of Labour; Order of the Great Patriotic War; Order (2nd class) of the Cross of Griunvald, Poland.
Council of Ministers of Lithuanian S.S.R., Vilnius, U.S.S.R.

Shumway, Forrest N.; American oil executive; b. 21 March 1927; ed. Stanford Univ.
In U.S. Marine Corps; Senior Law Clerk and Deputy County Counsel, Los Angeles until 57; joined Legal Dept., Signal Oil and Gas Co. 57, Sec. 59-60, Asst. Gen. Counsel 60-61, Vice-Pres. and Gen. Counsel 61-64, Dir. 61-, Pres. 64-; Dir. The Garrett Corpn., Standard Insurance Co., Mack Trucks Inc., American Petroleum Inst.; mem. Nat. Petroleum Council; official of civic orgs.
Signal Oil and Gas Co., 1010 Wilshire Boulevard, Los Angeles, Calif. 90017, U.S.A.

Shumway, Norman Edward, Jr., M.D.; American surgeon; b. 1923; ed. Vanderbilt Univ. and Univ. of Minnesota.
Intern, Univ. of Minnesota Hospitals 49-50, Medical Fellow in Surgery 50-51, 53, 54; Nat. Heart Inst. Research Fellow 54-56, Special Trainee 56-57; mem. Surgical Staff, Stanford Univ. Hospitals 58-, Asst. Prof. of Surgery 59-61, Assoc. Prof. 61-, Head of Div. of Cardiovascular Surgery 64-; has performed heart transplant operations.
Stanford Medical Center, Palo Alto, California, U.S.A.

Shurabassi, Ahmed Al; United Arab Republic (Egyptian) politician; b. 99; ed. Higher School of Engineering, Egypt.
With Ministry of Public Works 24-53, Inspector of Irrigation 48-53, Asst. Inspector-Gen. of Egyptian Irrigation in Sudan 53; Egyptian Minister of Public Works 53-58; Minister of Public Works, U.A.R. 58-62; mem. Presidency Council 62-64; Minister of Waqfs and Al Azhar Affairs 64-65; Deputy Prime Minister for Waqfs, Azhar and Social Affairs 65-67.
c/o Ministry of Waqfs, Cairo, United Arab Republic.

Shurygin, Viktor Alexandrovich; Soviet politician; b. 13; ed. Journalistic Inst.
Correspondent and Editor, regional press 31-52; mem. C.P.S.U. 41-; Sec., Second Sec., Orenburg Regional Cttee. C.P.S.U. 52-61, First Sec. 61-64; Sec. Volograd Regional Cttee. of C.P.S.U. 64-; mem. Central Cttee. of C.P.S.U. 61-66; fmr. Deputy to U.S.S.R. and R.S.F.S.R. Supreme Soviets.
Volgograd Regional Committee of C.P.S.U., Volgograd, U.S.S.R.

Shuster, George Nauman, A.B., A.M., C.D'APT., PH.D.; American educationist; b. 27 Aug. 1894; ed. Univ. of Notre Dame, Université de Poitiers, Colombia Univ.
Chairman, Dept. of English, Univ. of Notre Dame 20-24; Man. Ed. *Commonweal* 25-37; Fellow, Carl Schurz Foundation 33-34; Fellow, Social Science Research Council 37-38; Pres. Hunter Coll. of the Research Council 37-38; Pres. Hunter Coll. of the City of New York 39-60, Pres. Emeritus 60-; Asst. to the Pres. and Prof. of English, Univ. of Notre Dame 61-; mem. Gen. Advisory Cttee., Div. of Cultural Relations, U.S. Dept. of State 41-44; Land Comm. for Bavaria, Dept. of State 50-51; U.S. rep., Exec. Board UNESCO 58-; Trustee, Carnegie Endowment for Int. Peace; mem. Board of Editors, *Encyclopaedia Britannica*; several foreign awards and honorary degrees.
Publs. *Catholic Spirit in Modern English Literature* 22, *Catholic Spirit in America* 26, *The Germans* 31, *Strong Rules* 34, *The English Ode from Milton to Keats* 39, *Short History of Germany* (with A. Bergstraesser) 39, *Religion behind the Iron Curtain* 52, *In Silence I Speak* 58, *Education and Moral Wisdom* 60, *The Ground I Walked On* 61, *UNESCO: Assessment and Promise* 63.
2819 York Road, South Bend, Indiana, U.S.A.

Shvernik, Nikolai Mikhailovich; Soviet politician; b. 1888.
Joined Communist Party 05; underground party activity 05-17; arrested and imprisoned several times, and exiled for three years; Chair. All-Russia Cttee. of artillery factory workers 17; Chair. Donets Area Cttee. of Metal Workers' Union 23-25, also mem. Presidium, Central Control Comm. of Communist Party, and People's Commissar for Workers' and Peasants' Inspection of R.S.F.S.R.; mem. Central Cttee. of Party 30-, and mem. Organization Bureau of Central Cttee.; Sec., All Union Central Council of Trade Unions 30-34; alt. mem. Political Bureau, Central Cttee. of C.P.S.U. 39-52; Chair. Soviet Extraordinary Comm. on Nazi Crimes 42; first Vice-Chair. U.S.S.R. Supreme Soviet and Pres. Presidium of R.S.F.S.R. Supreme Soviet 44; Pres. Presidium of U.S.S.R. Supreme Soviet 46-53; alt. mem. Presidium of Central Cttee. of C.P.S.U. and Chair. All Union Central Council of Trade Unions 53-57; alt. Chair. Party Control Comm. of C.P.S.U. Central Cttee. 56-, Chair. 62-66; mem. Presidium Central Cttee. of C.P.S.U. 57-61; mem. Central Cttee. C.P.S.U.; awards include Order of Lenin (three times) and many other decorations.
Central Committee of C.P.S.U., 4 Staraya ploshchad, Moscow, U.S.S.R.

Shvets, Ivan Trofimovich, DR. NAT. SC.; Soviet scientist; b. 1901; ed. Kiev Polytechnic Inst.
Railway worker 19-21; Lecturer, Prof., Dr. Nat. Sc., Academician of Acad. of Sciences of Ukrainian S.S.R.; Deputy Dir., Head of Faculty, Dean of Faculty of Technical Energy 29-53, Rector 53-55, Kiev Polytechnic Inst.; Dir. Inst. of Energy, later Inst. of Heat Energy of Acad. of Sciences of Ukrainian S.S.R.; Deputy Head of Board for Higher Educ., Council of Ministers of Ukrainian S.S.R. 48-50; First Scientific Sec. Acad. of Sciences of Ukrainian S.S.R. 50-52; Rector Kiev T. G. Shevchenko State Univ. 55-; Hon. D.Sc. (Bratislava Univ.).
Vladimirskaya St. 64, Kiev, Ukrainian S.S.R., U.S.S.R.

Siassi, Ali-Akbar, PH.D.; Iranian educationist and politician; b. 96; ed. Persia and France.
Professor Univ. of Teheran 27-; Head Dept. of Advanced Studies of the Min. of Educ. 32; Chancellor of the Univ. of Teheran 42; Min. of Educ. 43; drafted bill and law for national compulsory free education, and took necessary measures for its enforcement 43; Min. of State without portfolio 45; Minister of Education 48-50; Minister of Foreign Affairs 50; mem. of the Supreme Council of Educ.; del. III Int. Congress of Persian Art and Archaeology 35, UN Conf. San Francisco 45; Pres. Iranian del. UNESCO Conf. Paris 49, Int. Conf. of Univs. 50, UNESCO Conf. Paris 51, Int. Conf. of Univs., Mexico City 60, Royal Soc. Tricentenary Celebrations, London 60; perm. mem. of the Persian Acad.; Hon. Pres. Univ. of Teheran; mem. Int. Cttee. Scientific and Cultural History of Humanity; Pres. Iranian Psychological Asscn., Iranian Council of Philosophy and Human Sciences; mem. Royal Cultural Council; Commdr. Légion d'Honneur; Commdr. Pales Académiques, etc.
Publs. include: *L'Education en Perse* 21, *La Perse au Contact de l'Occident* 31, *La Méthode des Tests* 31, *Le Génie et l'Art iraniens aux prises avec l'Islam* 35, *De l'Unesco à la Sorbonne* 53, *L'Iran au XIXe siècle* (all in French); *Psychology* 38, *Educational Psychology for Teachers' Colleges* 41, *Introduction to Philosophy* 47, *Logic and Philosophy* 48, *Mind and Body* 53, *The Psychology of Avicenna and its similarities with the Modern Psychology* 54, *Logic* 56, *Ethics* 57, *Logic and Philosophy* 58, *Intelligence and Reason* 62, *Criminal Psychology* 64 (all in Persian).
President Roosevelt Avenue, Namdjou Street, Teheran, Iran.
Telephone: 756776.

Sicot, Marcel; French civil servant; b. 19 Feb. 1898; ed. Lycée de St. Brieuc and Univ. of Rennes.
Commissariat de Police 20; police, French occupied territories, Germany 21-24; Principal Commr. Renseignements généraux; Div. Commr. Second World War; re-installed Deputy Dir. Police Judicaire 45; Inspector-Gen. de la Sureté Nationale 45-58, Hon. Dir. 63-; Sec.-Gen. Org. Internationale de Police Criminelle (Interpol) 51-63, Hon. Sec.-Gen. 63-; Commdr. Légion d'Honneur.
Publs. *Servitude et Grandeur policières* 59, *A la barre de l'Interpol* 61, *La Prostitution dans le monde* 64, *Weltphänomen Prostitution* 65, *Die Wahrheit über Interpol* 66, *Fausses et vraies identités* 67.
4 rue Léon Delagrange, Paris 15e, France.

Sidarouss, H.E. Cardinal Stephanos I; United Arab Republic (Egyptian) ecclesiastic; b. 04; ed. Jesuits' Coll. Cairo, Univ. de Paris à la Sorbonne, and Ecole libre des sciences politiques.
Barrister Egypt 26-32; Vincentian Priest 39-; Prof. Seminaries at Evreux, Dax and Beauvais (France); Rector Coptic Catholic Seminary, Tahta 46, Tanta 47-53, Maadi 53-58; Auxiliary Bishop to the Patriarch of Alexandria, 47-58, Patriarch 58-; created Cardinal 65.
34 Ibn Sandar Street, Koubbeh Bridge, Cairo, United Arab Republic.
Telephone: 866-840; 863-616.

Siddavanahalli, Nijalingappa, B.A., LL.B.; Indian politician and lawyer; b. 02; ed. Central Coll., Bangalore and Law Coll., Poona.
Convicted for political offences 39 and debarred from practice 40; imprisoned 42-44 and 47; mem. Mysore Congress Working Cttee. 39-51; Pres. Mysore Pradesh Congress Cttee. 45-46, 60-62; Pres. K.P.C.C. 46-54; mem. Working Cttee. and Parly. Board, Indian Nat. Congress 48-53; mem. Constituent Assembly 46-52; mem. Parl. 52-56; mem. Mysore Constituent Assembly 48-50; Leader Vishala Mysore Legislature Congress Party 56; Chief Minister Mysore State Govt. 56-58, 62-65; Leader of Congress Legislature Party 62; mem. All-India Congress Cttee.
Bangalore, Mysore State, India.

Siddiqi, M. Raziuddin, M.A., PH.D., D.S.; Pakistani educationist; b. 7 April 1905; ed. Osmania, Cambridge, Berlin, Göttingen, Leipzig, Paris Univs.
Professor of Mathematics, Dir. of Research and Vice-Chancellor, Osmania Univ. 31-50; Dir. of Research and Vice-Chancellor, Peshawar Univ. 50-58; Vice-Chancellor, Univ. of Sind 59-64; Pres. Pakistan Acad. of Sciences 61-; Vice-Chancellor, Univ. of Islamabad Dec. 65-; Joint Sec. (in charge) Scientific and Technological Research Div., President's Secretariat.
Publs. *Lectures on Quantum Mechanics* 37, *Boundary Problems in Non-linear Partial Differential Equations* 38, *Theory of Relativity* 40, *Problems of Education* 43.
77-E, Satellite Town, Rawalpindi, West Pakistan.

Sidi Baba, Dey Ould; Moroccan diplomatist; b. 1921 (in Mauretania).
Counsellor, Ministry of Foreign Affairs, Morocco 58, Head of African Div. 59; mem. Moroccan Dels. to UN Gen. Assembly 59-64; Acting Perm. Rep. of Morocco to UN 64-65, Perm. Rep. 65-67; Minister of Royal Cabinet 67.
Ministry of Royal Cabinet, Nouakchott, Mauritania.

Sidi-Touré, Gibirila; Togolese doctor and diplomatist; b. 28 Sept. 1928; ed. Univ. of Rennes.
Ambassador to France, concurrently accredited to U.K. and Belgium, and Rep. to European Econ. Community 65-; several medical publications; Officier Ordre du Mono.
Embassy of Togo, 8 rue Alfred Roll, Paris 17e, France.

Sidikou, Abdou; Niger pharmacist and diplomatist; b. 27; ed. William Ponty School and African School of Medicine and Pharmacy, Dakar, and Univ. of Paris.
Director of Laboratory, French Sudan 49-52; Seine Hospital 56-57; Chief Pharmacist, Niamey Hospital 57-59; Dir. de Cabinet to Minister of Health, Niger 59-60; later Sec.-Gen. of Foreign Affairs 61-62; Amb. to U.S.A. and Perm. Rep. to UN 62-64; Amb. to Benelux, Fed. Germany and Perm. Rep. to EEC, Brussels 64-66; Sec. of State for Foreign Affairs 67-.
Ministry of Foreign Affairs, Niamey, Niger.

Sidky, Aziz; United Arab Republic (Egyptian) politician.
Minister of Industry 62-63; Deputy Prime Minister for Industry and Mineral Wealth 64-65; Minister for Industry, Petroleum and Mineral Resources March 68-.
Ministry for Industry, Cairo, United Arab Republic.

Sidorenko, Aleksandr Vassilevich; Soviet geologist and administrator; b. 1917; ed. Voronezh State Univ.
Head, Laboratory Turkmen branch Soviet Acad. of Sciences 43-50, Kela Branch 50-61, Chair. Presidium Kola Branch 50-61; Vice-Chair. R.S.F.S.R. State Cttee. for Co-ordination of Scientific Research Work 61-62; Minister of Geology and Mineral Wealth Protection 62-63; Chair. State Cttee. for Geology 63-65; Minister of Geology 65-; Deputy to U.S.S.R. Supreme Soviet 66-; Corresp. mem. U.S.S.R. Acad. of Sciences 53-66, mem. 66-; Candidate mem. C.P.S.U. Central Cttee. 66-; Chief Editor *Geology of the U.S.S.R.* (10 vols.) 64.
Publs. numerous articles and papers on geological subjects including *Principal Characteristics of Mineral Formation in Deserts* 56, *Preglacial Erosion Crust of Kola Peninsula* 58, *To the Problem of Litological Investigation of Metamorphical Rocks* 61.
Ministry of Geology, Bolshaya Gruzinskaya ul. 4/6, Moscow, U.S.S.R.

Sieff, Baron (Life Peer), cr. 66, of Brimpton; **Israel Moses Sieff,** B.COM.; British business executive; b. 4 May 1889; ed. Manchester Grammar School and Manchester Univ.
Joined Marks and Spencer 15, Dir. 16, Vice-Chair. and Joint Man. Dir. 26-64, Chair. and Joint Man. Dir. 64-67, Pres. 67-; Sec. Zionist Comm. 18; Chair. Political and Econ. Planning (P.E.P.) 31-39, Vice-Chair. 39-64, Pres. 66-; founded Daniel Sieff Research Inst., Rehovoth 34; Vice-Pres. World Jewish Congress, Chair. European Exec.; Chair. Anglo-Israel Chamber of Commerce 50-65, Pres. 65-; Hon. Pres. Zionist Fed. of Great Britain and Ireland.
Marks and Spencer Ltd., Michael House, 47-67 Baker Street, London, W.I, England.
Telephone: 01-935-4422.

Siegbahn, Karl Manne Georg, D.SC.; Swedish physicist; b. 3 Dec. 1886; ed. Lund Univ.
Prof. of Physics, Lund Univ. 14-23, Uppsala Univ. 24-37; Dir. Nobel Inst. for Physics, Royal Acad. of Sciences 37-; mem. Swedish, Danish, Norwegian, Finnish Acads., Int. Cttee. Weights and Measures 37-59, Hon. mem. 59-; Nobel Prize for Physics 25, Hughes Medal 34, and Rumford Medal of Royal Society, London 40, for pioneer work in high-precision X-ray spectroscopy and its application; Duddel Medal, Physical Society of London 48; foreign mem. Acad. des Sciences, Paris; hon. mem. Royal Society, Edinburgh; foreign mem. Royal Soc. London; Dr. h.c. (Freiburg, Bucharest, Oslo, Paris Univs.).
Publs. *The Spectroscopy of X-rays* 25, *Spektroskopie der Röntgenstrahlen* 31.
Nobelinstitutet för Fysik, Stockholm 50, Sweden.

Siegel, Milton P.; American (U.S.A.) international official; b. 23 July 1911; ed. Drake Univ., Des Moines.
Director of Finance and Statistics, Iowa Emergency Relief Admin., Treasurer, Iowa Rural Rehabilitation Admin. 33-35; Regional Finance and Business Manager, Farm Security Admin., U.S. Dept. of Agriculture 35-41, Chief Fiscal Officer 42-44; Asst. Treasurer, Dir. Office for Far East, UNRRA 44-45; Asst. Dir., Production and Marketing Admin., U.S. Dept. of Agriculture 45-47; Asst. Dir.-Gen. World Health Org. 47-; Visiting Prof. Univ. of Michigan 67-.
World Health Organization, avenue Appia, 1211 Geneva, Switzerland.
Telephone: 34-60-61.

Siemens, Ernst Albrecht von; German industrialist; b. 9 April 1903; ed. Munich Univ.
Chairman Siemens A.G. (formerly Siemens & Halske A.G.); Dir. Klöckner-Humboldt-Deutz A.G., Allianz-Versicherungs A.G., Deutsche Bank A.G.; Hon. Dr. Eng. Munich Technical High School.
Wittelsbacherplatz 2, 8000 Munich 2, German Federal Republic.

Sierpinski, Wacław, DR.PHIL.; Polish mathematician; b. 1882; ed. Univs. of Warsaw and Cracow.
Lecturer in Mathematics, Univ. of Lwów 08-10, Prof. 10-19; Prof. Mathematics, Univ. of Warsaw 19-60; mem. Polish Acad. of Sciences and Letters 21-; Corresp. Inst. de France 48-60, mem. 60-; Pres. Warsaw Society of Science and Letters 31-52; mem. Accademia dei Lincei 48-; mem. Royal Dutch Acad. of Science 61-; corresp. mem. Deutsche Akad. der Wissenschaften, Berlin 50-; mem. Czechoslovak Acad. of Sciences 60-; mem. Int. Acad. of Philosophy of Science 61-, Vice-Pres. 62-65; Vice-Pres. Polish Acad. of Sciences 52-57, mem. of its Presidium 57-; hon. mem. London Mathematical Soc., Rumanian Acad.; Editor and Dir. of journal *Fundamenta Mathematicae* 20-52, and *Acta Arithmetica* 58-; Dr. h.c. Univs. of Lwów, Amsterdam, Tartu, Paris, Sofia, Bordeaux, Prague, Wrocław, Moscow and Lucknow; Hon. Life mem. New York Acad. of Sciences 59.

Publs. *Leçons sur les nombres transfinis* 28, *Hypothèse du continu* 34, *Introduction to General Topology* 34, *Les ensembles projectifs et analytiques* 50, *Algèbre des Ensembles* 51, *General Topology* 52, *On the Congruence of Sets and their Equivalence by Finite Decomposition* 54, *Cardinal and Ordinal Numbers* 58, *A Selection of Problems in the Theory of Numbers* 64, *Elementary Theory of Numbers* 64.
Konopczynskiego 5/7, m. 38, Warsaw, Poland.
Telephone: 273323.

Sieveking, Lancelot de Giberne, D.S.C. (Lance Sieveking); British author and playwright; b. 19 March 1896; ed. Switzerland and St. Catharine's Coll., Cambridge.
Joined Artists' Rifles 14, later commissioned R.N., served H.M.S. *Riviera*, North Sea 15, R.N. Air Service E. Africa 16, France 17; prisoner of war 17-18; propr. and editor *The New Cambridge* 19-22; commissioned Royal Air Force, India 22; Asst. to Dir. of Education, B.B.C. 24-26, invented and organised the first Running Commentaries, later drama producer and Programme Dir. for West of England 40-44; produced first television play in world 30; Drama Script Editor, B.B.C. 45-50; special adapter and producer Radio and Television.
Publs. include *Bats in the Belfry* and *Stampede* (with G. K. Chesterton), *Smite and Spare Not* 33, *Wings of the Morning, The Woman She Was, The Stuff of Radio* 34, *The Perfect Witch* 35, *Silence in Heaven* 36, *North American Binocular* 47, *A Tomb with a View* 50, *A Private Volcano* 55, *The Eye of the Beholder* 57, *Howards End* (stage version, with E. M. Forster and Richard Cottrell) 65; *A Room with a View* (stage version with E. M. Forster and Richard Cottrell) 67, *The Double Who Wouldn't Quit* (television play) 67; many radio plays and films.
The White House, Snape, Suffolk, England.
Telephone: Snape 214.

Sievers Wicke, Hugo K.; Chilean veterinary physician and politician; b. 03; ed. Colegio Alemán, Santiago and Univs. of Chile, Buenos Aires, La Plata, Rio de Janeiro, Inst. Pasteur and Inst. Curie, Paris, Inst. of Tropical Medicine, Hamburg.
Asst. at Inst. for Veterinary Research 24-27; Prof., School of Agriculture 27-28; Mil. Veterinary Physician 26-32; Dir. Inst. of Veterinary Research, Ministry of Agriculture 30-42; Dean School Veterinary Medicine, Univ. of Chile 36-61; Vice-Rector Univ. of Chile 53-61, now Prof. Emeritus; Minister of Agriculture, Lands and Colonisation 55; Perm. Del. Int. Congress of Veterinary Medicine 36-59; Pres. Chilean Soc. of Sciences 64-66; Founder mem. Soc. of Veterinary Physicians of Chile (and past Pres.); Hon. Prof. Central Univ. of Quito, and Univ. Nat. of San Marcos, Lima; Dr. h.c. Univ. Austral de Chile; Decoration of the Rising Sun Japan 59.
Publs. *La vuélta al Mundo con 10 Estudiantes, Rutas Patagonicas, Chilenos en la Amazonia, Max Westenhöfer 1871-1951* (biography), *Domingo Amunátegui Solar* (biography), *Teliatría, Nosotros y la Comunidad, Proteinas y Alimentación*.
Casilla 161, Las Condes, Santiago, Chile.

Siglienti, Sergio; Italian banker; b. 19 May 1926; ed. Univ. Degli Studi, Rome.
In Foreign Dept., Banca Commerciale Italiana 50-54, London Office 54-56; Asst. Man., Milan 56-58; Finance Div., European Coal and Steel Community (ECSC), Luxembourg 58-60, rising to Head of Credit Dept. 60; Alt. Exec. Dir. Int. Bank for Reconstruction and Devt. —IBRD (World Bank) Nov. 60-; Exec. Dir. for Italy, Greece and Spain, Int. Monetary Fund (IMF) Nov. 60-.
International Monetary Fund, Washington, D.C. 20431, U.S.A.

Siglienti, Stefano, D.IUR.; Italian lawyer and banker; b. 19 May 1898; ed. Sassari Univ.
Officer in First World War; later joined Credito Fondiario Sardo, rose to be Deputy Gen. Man.; active

in underground activities against Fascist régime; arrested by Nazis 43; escaped; Minister of Finance (Action Party), first Bonomi Cabinet, June-Oct. 44; Chair. Istituto Mobiliare Italiano 46-; Pres. Associazione Bancaria Italiana 45-; mem. Nat. Council for Economy and Labour 55-; Chair. Italconsult; Dir. European Investment Bank 58-; Pres. Associazione Sindacale tra le aziende di credito 47-; Deputy Chair. Società Finanziara Marittima "Finmare", and Italian Branch, Int. Chamber of Commerce.
Via Quintiliano 16, Rome, Italy.

Signoret, Simone (*pseudonym* of Simone Kaminker and wife of Yves Montand, *q.v.*); German-born French actress; b. 25 March 1921.
Films include *Le Couple Idéal, Dédée d'Anvers, La Ronde, Casque d'Or, Thérèse Raquin, Les Diaboliques* (The Fiends), *La Mort en ce Jardin, Les Sorcières de Salem, Room at the Top* ("Oscar" for best actress), *Adua* 61, *Term of Trial* 62, *Dragées au Poivre, Ship of Fools, The Sleeping Car Murder, Games;* played Lady Macbeth (stage) in *Macbeth*, London 66.
15 Place Dauphine, Paris 1er, France.

Sigurdsson, Niels P.; Icelandic diplomatist; b. 1926; Univ. of Iceland.
Joined Diplomatic Service 52; First Sec. Paris Embassy 56-60; Deputy Perm. Rep. to NATO and OECD 57-60; Dir. Int. Policy Div. Minister of Foreign Affairs, Reykjavik 61; Del. to the UN Gen. Assembly 65; Amb. and Iceland's Perm. Rep. to North Atlantic Council 67-.
North Atlantic Treaty Organization, Brussels 39, Belgium.

Sijthoff, Hendrik Albert Henri; Netherlands publisher; b. 15; ed. Univs. of Leipzig and Lausanne.
Pres.-Dir. of *Het Financieele Dagblad;* Pres.-Dir. of Hendrik Sijthoff's Financieele Bladen N.V.
Office: Weesperstraat 85, Amsterdam C, Netherlands; Home: 20 Mansion Place, Greenwich, Conn., U.S.A.

Sik, Endre; Hungarian diplomatist, politician and writer; b. 2 April 1891; ed. Budapest Univ.
Prisoner-of-War, First World War; teacher, Oriental Univ., Moscow 24-36; mem. staff Historical Inst., U.S.S.R. Acad. of Sciences 38-41, Ethnographic Inst. 43-45; returned to Hungary 45; First Counsellor, Hungarian Legation, later Minister, Washington 46-49; Chief of Dept., Ministry of Foreign Affairs 49-53, Deputy Minister 53-54, First Deputy Minister 54; Minister of Foreign Affairs 58-61; mem. Central Cttee. Hungarian Socialist Workers' Party 59-; Pres. Hungarian Nat. Peace Council; mem. Exec. Council Soc. Européenne de Culture; State Prize 65, Lenin Peace Prize for 1967 68.
Publs. *History of Black Africa*, and literary works.
Pentelei Molnár u. 12, Budapest II, Hungary.

Sik, Ota, DR.SC.; Czechoslovak economist; b. 11 Sept. 1919.
Director Econ. Inst. of Czechoslovak Acad. of Sciences 63-; Chair. of Scientific Collegium of Economy, Czechoslovak Acad. of Sciences 63-; Corresp. mem. Czechoslovak Acad. of Sciences 60-; mem. Central Cttee. of Communist Party of Czechoslovakia 62-; mem. Econ. Comm., Central Cttee. of Communist Party of Czechoslovakia 62-; mem. State Comm. for Management and Organization; mem. State Planning Comm.; Deputy Prime Minister 68-.
Publs. include: *Economics, Interests, Politics, On the Question of Socialist Commodity Relations.*
Czechoslovak Academy of Sciences, tř. Politických vězňů 7, Prague 1, Czechoslovakia.

Sikorski, Kazimierz; Polish composer and teacher; b. 95; ed. in Warsaw, Lwów Univ. and Paris.
Former prof. of composition in Łódź, Poznań and Warsaw; Rector Nat. Conservatoire Warsaw; Pres. Union of Polish Composers; State Music Prize 37 and

State Prize, Class I 51, Union of Polish Composers Prize 51.
Compositions include four symphonies, concertos for clarinet and horn, three string quartets, string sextet, *Stabat Mater*, symphonic poems, works for choir, film music etc.; Ed. of *Polish music from 17th and 18th century*, and orchestration of Moniuszko operas, *Straszny dwór* and *Halka.*
Publs. Handbooks: *Harmony* (3 vols.), *Counterpoint* (3 vols.), *Musical Instruments.*
Polona 40, Warsaw 10, Poland.

Sikorsky, Igor I., M.SC.; American aircraft designer; b. Russia 25 May 1889; ed. Naval Coll. St. Petersburg, Inst. of Technology, Kiev.
Aircraft designer and builder 08-11; head aviation factory, Russo-Baltic Car Works 12-18; built and flew first multi-motored plane 13; designed and built 4-motored bombers for Russian Army; commissioned by French Govt. to build Sikorsky plane for military use 18; arrived U.S.A. 19; organised Sikorsky Aero Engineering Corpn. 23, Sikorsky Manufacturing Corpn. 25, Sikorsky Aviation Corpn. 28; naturalised American 28; developed many types multi-motored aircraft including Sikorsky amphibian and Sikorsky helicopters (the only helicopters used by the American Air Forces during Second World War); Engineering Man. Sikorsky Aircraft Div. of United Aircraft Corpn. until 57, Engineering Consultant 57-; mem. American Society Mechanical Engineers, etc.; hon. degrees Yale, Wesleyan, Lehigh and Northeastern Univs., Florida Southern Coll., Rhode Island State Coll., Univ. of Pittsburgh, Univ. of Bridgeport, Colby Co.. and Trinity Coll., Hartford; many medals and awards from both U.S. and abroad, for his work in aeronautics.
Publs. *The Story of the Winged-S, The Message of the Lord's Prayer, The Invisible Encounter.*
Sikorsky Aircraft Division, United Aircraft Corporation, Stratford, Conn. 06602, U.S.A.
Telephone: 203-378-6361.

Siles Zuazo, Hernán, D.IUR.; Bolivian lawyer, politician and diplomatist; b. 14; ed. San Andres Univ.
Sergeant in Chaco War 32; legal practice in La Paz 39-; M.P. for La Paz 43-46; in exile in Argentina and Chile, where he worked as translator for U.S. news agencies 46-51; Vice-Presidential candidate 51; a leader of the revolution of 52; Vice-Pres. of Bolivia 52-56, Pres. 56-60; Ambassador to Uruguay 60-63, to Spain 63-64; in exile in Paraguay, Sept. 64-.

Silex, Karl, D.PHIL.; German journalist; b. 6 July 1896; ed. Stettin Gymnasium, Kiel and Berlin Univs.
Naval officer during both World Wars; London corresp. *Deutsche Allgemeine Zeitung* 25, Chief Editor 33; Naval officer 43; Publisher *Deutsche Kommentare* (weekly) 49, *Bücher-Kommentare* (literary quarterly) 52-; Chief Editor *Der Tagesspiegel* (Berlin) 55-63; freelance journalist 63-.
Publs. *John Bull At Home* 29, *Patriot Macdonald* 32.
1 Berlin 21, Händelallee 39, Germany.
Telephone: 405343.

Sillitoe, Alan; British author; b. 4 March 1928; ed. elementary school, Radford, Nottingham.
Worked in various factories, Nottingham 42-46; served wireless operator, R.A.F., Malaya; lived several years in France and Spain; Hawthornden Prize 60.
Publs. (novels) *Saturday Night and Sunday Morning* 58, *The General* 60, *Key to the Door* 61, *The Death of William Posters, A Tree on Fire* 67; (stories) *The Loneliness of the Long Distance Runner* 59, *The Ragman's Daughter* 63, *Guzman, Go Home* 68; (poems) *The Rats and Other Poems* 60, *A Falling Out of Love* 64, *Love in the Environs of Voronezh* 68; (travel) *Road to Volgograd* 64.
97 Larkhall Rise, London, S.W.4, England.
Telephone: 01-622-9407.

Silone, Ignazio; Italian writer; b. 1 May 1900: ed. private and public schools.
In Italian Socialist Youth Movement 17-21; mem. Central Cttee. Italian Communist Party and editor various newspapers 21-29; left Communist Party 30; exile in Switzerland 30-44; mem. Exec. Cttee. Italian Socialist Party 41; Sec. Union Independent Socialists 48; Sec. Unitary Socialist Party 50; Founder and Pres. Teatro del Popolo (People's Theatre) 45; Editor of *Avanti* (Socialist daily newspaper); hon. corresp. mem. American Acad. of Arts and Letters 50; mem. Exec. Cttee. Int. Congress for Cultural Freedom 50; Editor *Tempo Presente*; Marzotto Prize 65.
Publs. *Fontamara* (novel) 30, *Fascism* (history) 34, *Mr. Aristotle* (short stories) 35, *Bread and Wine* (novel) 37, *The School for Dictators* (dialogues) 38, *Mazzini* (essay) 39, *The Seed Beneath the Snow* (novel) 41, *And He did Hide Himself* (play) 44, *The God that Failed* (symposium) 50, *A Handful of Blackberries* (novel) 52, *The Choice of Comrade* 55, *The Fox and the Camelias* (novel) 60, *Uscita di sicurezza* 65, *L'avventura d'un povera cristiano* 68.
Via di Villa Ricotti 36, Rome, Italy.

Silsoe, 1st Baron, cr. 63, of Silsoe; **(Arthur) Malcolm Trustram Eve,** Bt., G.B.E., M.C., T.D., Q.C.; Gentleman Usher of the Purple Rod in the Order of the British Empire 60-; British lawyer and administrator; b. 8 April 1894; ed. Winchester and Christ Church, Oxford.
Served First World War, Gallipoli 15, Egypt and Palestine 16-19; Capt. Royal Welch Fusiliers; G.S.O. 53rd Div. 17; Brig. Maj. 159th Infantry Brigade 18-19; commanded 6th Battn. Royal Welch Fusiliers 27-31; Col. (T.A.) 31; Brig. 40; called to Bar 19, K.C. 35, Bencher Inner Temple 42, Reader Inner Temple 65, Treas. Inner Temple 66; Chair. Air Transport Licensing Authority 38-39, War Damage Comm. 41-49; War Works Comm. 45-49, Local Govt. Boundary Comm. 45-49, Central Land Board 47-49, Burnham Cttees. on Teachers' Salaries 50-53, St. George's Hospital Medical School 48-54, Gov. St. George's Hospital 52-54, Road Haulage Disposal Board 53-56, mem. Church Assembly 52-57; Electoral Boundaries Comm., Mauritius 57; Pres. Ski Club of Great Britain 50-54; First Church Estates Commr. 54- (Third Church Estates Commr. 53-54); First Crown Estate Commr. 55-62; Ind. Chair. Cement Makers' Fed. 51-; Pres. Cement Makers' Asscn. 52-; Dir. Yorkshire Insurance Co. 49-66; Gov. Peabody Trust 57-65; Dir. St. Martin's Property Corpn. Ltd. 61-; Pres. Kandahar Ski Club 63-; Chair. Fiji Sugar Inquiry Comm. 61, Fiji Coconut Industry Inquiry Comm. 63; Hon. Treas. Royal Coll. of Nursing 64-.
26 Walton Street, London, S.W.3; Terminal House, 52 Grosvenor Gardens, London, S.W.1, England.
Telephone: 01-730-3782.

Siluyanov, Vasily Grigorievich; Soviet trade union official; b. 1909; ed. Moscow Inst. for Mechanisation and Electrification in Agriculture.
Member C.P.S.U. 32-; Railway Worker 24-30; Designer, Shop Man. and Dir., Chelyabinsk Tractor Works 35-42; Trade Union Official 42-; Chair. Central Cttee. Transport Eng. Workers' Union 46-48; Official at H.Q. of All-Union Council of Trade Unions 48-55; Chair. U.S.S.R. Council of Scientific and Technical Socs. 55-; mem. of Presidium, All-Union Central Council of Trade Unions; Order of Red Banner of Labour (twice), Red Star and other Soviet decorations.
U.S.S.R. Council of Scientific and Technical Societies, 42 Leninsky Prospekt, Moscow, U.S.S.R.

Silva, H.E. Cardinal Augusto Alvaro da; Brazilian ecclesiastic; b. 8 April 1876; ed. Gymnasium and Seminary, Olinda.
Ordained priest 99; Bishop of Floresta 11-15, of Barra do Rio Grande 15-24; Archbishop of São Salvador da Bahia 24; created Cardinal by Pope Pius XII 53;

mem. Sacred Congregations of Sacraments, of Religious Orders and of the Fabric of St. Peter's.
Palácio Arquiepiscopal do Campo Grande, Avenida Sete de Setembro 1309, Salvador, Bahia, Brazil.

Silva, Evandro Lins e; Brazilian lawyer and politician; b. 12.
Lawyer and prof.; Brazilian Del to Int. Legal Confs.; fmr. Attorney-Gen., and Head of Pres. Goulart's Civil Household; Minister of Foreign Affairs 63; mem. Supreme Court 63-.
Supreme Court, Praça dos Três Poderes, Brasilia, Brazil.

Silva Henríquez, H.E. Cardinal Raúl; Chilean ecclesiastic; b. 3 July 1907; ed. Universidad Católica de Chile and Ateneo Salesiano, Turin.
Former Prof. Canon and Moral Law, Salesian Study Centre, La Cisterna and Pres. Fed. of Catholic Colls., Chile; Pres. Caritas, Chile, Caritas Internacional; Diocesan Bishop, Valparaiso 59-61; Archbishop of Santiago 61-, created Cardinal 62; Primate of Chile; Hon. LL.D. (Univ. of Notre Dame).
Palacio Arzobispal, Casilla 30-D, Santiago, Chile.

Silva Muñoz, Federico, LL.D.; Spanish politician; b. 1923; ed. Universidad de Madrid.
Former Prof. of Political Economy, Central Univ. and was apptd. to Nat. Lawyers' Council and Lawyers of the Council of State; fmr. Pres. Higher Coll. of San Pablo and Rector, Centre of Univ. Studies; fmr. Dir. Sociology Studies, Univ. Menéndez Pelayo, Santander, Prof., School of Taxation Studies and Prof., Santa María de la Rábida Univ.; mem. Perm. Comm. of Inst. of Political Studies and various comms. on Devt. Plans; also Vice-Pres. Third Section, Fiscal Policy and Credit of Official Chamber of Commerce, Madrid; Procurador, Cortes 61-; Minister of Public Works 66-; mem. various religious cttees.
Ministero de Obras Públicas, Madrid, Spain.

Silverstein, Abe; American aeronautical engineer; b. 15 Sept. 1908; ed. Rose Polytechnic Inst.
Junior Engineer, Langley Laboratory, Nat. Advisory Cttee. for Aeronautics (now Nat. Aeronautics and Space Admin., N.A.S.A.) 29-40, successively, Head Full-Scale Wind Tunnel, Chief Engine Installation Div., Chief Wind Tunnel and Flight Div., Chief of Research; Assoc. Dir., Lewis Flight Propulsion Lab. 40-58; Dir. of Space Flight Programs, N.A.S.A. 58-61; Dir. Lewis Research Center 61-; numerous awards.
21160 Seabury Avenue, Fairview Park, Ohio 44126; and National Aeronautics and Space Administration, Cleveland, Ohio, U.S.A.

Silvestri, Constantin; Romanian conductor and composer; b. 31 May 1913; ed. Conservatoire Porumbescu, Bucharest.
Pianist until 35; Conductor Philharmonic Orchestra of Bucharest 46; Conductor also at Opera House, Bucharest 55; Prof. Conservatoire Ciprian Porumbescu, Bucharest 49; Principal Conductor, Bournemouth Symphony Orchestra 61-; Guest Conductor of Orchestras all over the world.
Major Works: Two ballets, *Danze di Bihor* 30, *Toccata*, Preludes and Fugues, three concerti grossi and one for orchestra, three quartets, one wind trio and other compositions.
Flat 4, Addiscombe, Cranborne Road, Bournemouth, Hants., England.

Simagin, Nikolai Alexeyevich; Soviet foreign trade official; b. 1907; ed. Inst. of Foreign Trade.
Member C.P.S.U. 30-; Dir. *Sovmongoltorg* 40-47; Chair. *Dalingtorg* 47-50; Office Dir. *Vostokintorg* 50-52; Chief, *Avtovneshtrans* Office 52-55; Deputy Commercial Rep., later, Commercial Rep., of U.S.S.R. in Mongolia 55-60; Official, Ministry of Foreign Trade 60-65; U.S.S.R.

Commercial Rep. in Mongolia 65-; Order of Red Banner of Labour (twice) and Honour Badge.
U.S.S.R. Trade Representation, Ulan-Bator, Mongolian People's Republic.

Simakov, Kayum Mukhamedzhanovich; Soviet politician; b. 1904; ed. Sverdlovsk Inst. of Non-Ferrous Metals.
Member C.P.S.U. 41-; Chief Engineer, Leningrad and Chimkent; Chair. East Kazakhstan Econ. Council 34-61; Vice-Chair. Council of Kazakh S.S.R. 61-; Chair. State Planning Cttee. Kazakh S.S.R. 65-; mem. Central Cttee. of C.P., Kazakh S.S.R.; Deputy to U.S.S.R. Supreme Soviet; mem. Cttee. for Planning and Budget, Soviet of Union.
Council of Ministers of Kazakh S.S.R., Alma-Ata, U.S.S.R.

Simavi, Haldun; Turkish journalist; b. 25; ed. Kabataş Lisesi Coll., Istanbul.
Publisher and Gen. Man. of Istanbul daily newspaper *Hurriyet* 53-.
Hurriyet, Babiali C., Istanbul-Cağaloğlu, Turkey.

Simenon, Georges; Belgian novelist; b. 13 Feb. 1903; ed. Coll. St. Servais, Liège.
Mem. Acad. Royale de Langue et de Littérature Française, Brussels.
Publs. 195 novels, including 72 in the Maigret series; books translated into 41 languages and published in 31 countries.
1066 Epalinges, Vaud, Switzerland.

Simionato, Giulietta; Italian mezzo-soprano; b. 12 May 1916; ed. under Lacatelli and Palumbo.
Has sung the best-known roles of lyric opera in the principal Italian and foreign Opera Theatres; retired Feb. 66; numerous recordings.
29/c Via di Villa Grazioli, Rome, Italy.

Simkin, William E.; American government official; b. 13 Jan. 1907; ed. Earlham Coll. and Univ. of Pennsylvania.
Principal, Cen. High School, Sherwood 28-30; Teacher Brooklyn Friends School 30-32; Rep. in W. Virginia, American Friends Service Cttee. 32-37; Instructor Wharton School of Finance and Commerce, Pennsylvania Univ. 37-39; Labor Arbitrator 39-61; Assoc. Impartial Chair. Philadelphia Men's Clothing Industry 40-61, Philadelphia Dress Industry 47-59; Arbitrator, American Viscose Corpn. 47-61, Sun Shipbuilding Co. 45-49, and for many other firms; Pres. Nat. Acad. of Arbitrators 50; Dir. Fed. Mediation and Conciliation Service 61-.
Federal Mediation and Conciliation Service, Washington, D.C. 20427, U.S.A.
Telephone: 202-961-3501 (Office); 202-554-3317 (Home).

Simms, Most Rev. George Otto, PH.D., D.D.; Irish ecclesiastic; b. 4 July 1910; ed. Cheltenham Coll. and Trinity Coll., Dublin.
Ordained Deacon 35, Priest 36; Curate-Asst., St. Bartholomew's, Dublin 35-38; Chaplain, Lincoln Theological Coll. 38-39; Dean of Residence, Trinity Coll., Dublin 39-52; Chaplain, Church of Ireland Training Coll. 43-52; Dean of Cork 52; Bishop of Cork 52-56; Archbishop of Dublin, Bishop of Glendalough and Kildare, Primate of Ireland 56-; mem. Royal Irish Acad.
Publs. Joint Editor, Facsimile Edition of the *Book of Kells* 51, Facsimile Edition of the *Book of Durrow* 60.
See House, 17 Temple Road, Dublin 6, Ireland.
Telephone: 977849.

Simon, 2nd Viscount; John Gilbert Simon, C.M.G.; British shipping and port administrator; b. 2 Sept. 1902; ed. Winchester and Balliol Coll., Oxford.
Served with Mackinnon Mackenzie and Co. in India and Ceylon 24-36; joined P. and O. Steam Navigation Co. 36; Asst. Dir. Liner Division, Ministry of War Transport, Deputy Dir., Dir., and finally Shipping Adviser 40-47; Man. Dir. P. and O. Steam Navigation Co. 47-58, and Deputy Chair. 52-58; Chair. Port of London Authority 58-; Officer of Order of Orange Nassau 47; Pres. Chamber of Shipping of U.K. 57-58, Inst. of Marine Engineers 60-61, Royal Inst. of Naval Architects 61-, Dock and Harbour Authorities Asscn. 63-67, Int. Asscn. Ports and Harbours 65-67, Int. Cargo Handling Co-ordination Asscn. (I.C.H.C.A), 63-67; mem. Nat. Ports Council 67-.
Port of London Authority, Trinity Square, London, E.C.3, England.

Simon, Claude; French writer; b. 10 Oct. 1913; ed. Collège Stanislas, Paris.
Prix de l'Express for *La Route des Flandres* 60; Prix Médicis for *Histoire* 67.
Publs. *Le Tricheur* 45, *La Corde Raide* 47, *Le Vent* 57, *L'Herbe* 58, *La Route des Flandres* 60, *La Palace* 62, *Histoire* 67.
3 place Monge, Paris 5e; place Vieille, 66 Salses (Pyrénées-Orientales), France.
Telephone: 587-10-59 (Paris).

Simon, Rt. Hon. Sir Jocelyn Edward Salis, Kt., P.C., Q.C.; British judge; b. 15 Jan. 1911; ed. Gresham's School, Holt and Trinity Hall, Cambridge.
Member of Parliament (Conservative) 51-62; Joint Parl. Under-Sec. of State, Home Office 57-58; Financial Sec. to Treasury 58-59; Solicitor-Gen. 59-62; Pres. of Probate, Divorce and Admiralty Div. of High Court 62-.
Publs. Co-author of *Change is our Ally* 54, *Rule of Law* 55, *The Church and the Law of Nullity* 55.
Home: Midge Hall, Glaisdale Head, nr. Whitby, Yorkshire; Office: Royal Courts of Justice, Strand, London, W.C.2, England.

Simon, Michel; Swiss-born French actor; b. 9 April 1895; ed. Coll. de Genève.
Former boxer and photographer; began music hall career 11, later in legitimate theatre; played in more than 80 plays and 140 films; including *Jean de la Lune*, *Boudu Sauvé des Eaux* (also produced), *Quai des Brumes*, *Non Coupable*, *Rigoletto*, *Panique*, *La Beauté du Diable*, *La Poison*, *Drôle de Drame*, *L'Impossible Monsieur Pipelet*, *Les Trois font la Paire*, *Austerlitz*, *Pierrot la Tendresse*, *Candide*, *The Train*; Prize for Best Actor (for *La Beauté du Diable*) Venice, (for *Non Coupable*) Locarno Festival and Punta del Este, Paris; Prix Populiste for *Monsieur Taxi* 52.
24 rue de la Malnoue, Noisy-le-Grand (Seine-et-Oise); and 37 rue Beauregard, Paris 2e, France.
Telephone: 380 (Noisy); GUTenburg 14-16.

Simon, Norton; American industrialist; b. 5 Feb. 1907; ed. Lowell High School, San Francisco.
Steel Products, Los Angeles 27-33; Val Vita Food Products, Los Angeles 31-42, Pres. 31-42; Pres. Hunt Bros. Packing Co., San Francisco 43; Chair. Board Hunt Foods and Industries Inc. 44-60, now Chair. Finance Cttee.; official of other companies.
Hunt Foods and Industries Inc., 1645 W. Valencia Drive, Fullerton, Calif., U.S.A.
Telephone: 871-2100.

Simon, Pierre-Henri, D.LITT.; French writer; b. 16 Jan. 1903; ed. Ecole normale supérieure.
Teacher, Saint Quentin and Chartres lycées; Prof., Catholic Univ. of Lille 29-38, School of Higher Studies, Ghent 38-40; Prisoner-of-War, Second World War; Prof. of French Literature, Univ. of Fribourg 49-63; contrib. numerous journals including *Esprit*, *Sept*, *Temps présent*, *Semaines sociales*; Literary Critic, *Le Monde* 61-; mem. Académie Française 66-; Chevalier Légion d'Honneur.
Publs. include: Moral and political essays: *Les Catholiques*, *La Politique et l'Argent*, *Contre la torture*, *La France à la Fièvre*; history and literary criticism:

L'Homme en procès, Mauriac par lui-même, Le Jardin et la Ville, Le Domaine héroïque des lettres françaises; novels: *L'Affût, Les Raisins verts, Elsinfors, Portrait d'un officier, Le Somnambule, Histoire d'un bonheur;* poems: *Les Regrets et les Jours.*
4 rue de la Ronce, Ville-d'Array, S.-et-O., France.

Simonds, 1st Viscount, cr. 54, 1st Baron, cr. 44, of Sparsholt; **Gavin Turnbull Simonds,** P.C., Kt., Q.C.; British lawyer; b. 28 Nov. 1881; ed. Winchester and New Coll., Oxford.
Called to Bar 06; Bencher Lincoln's Inn 29; Judge Chancery Div. 37-44; Chair. Nat. Arbitration Tribunal 40-44; Lord of Appeal in Ordinary 44-51, 54-62; Lord High Chancellor 51-54; Hon. Fellow New Coll., Oxford.
Flat 7, 64 Rutland Gate, London, S.W.7, England.

Simonen, Aarre Edvard; Finnish politician; b. 18 Nov. 1913.
Sec. of Welfare Offices in Helsinki 36, Chief of Legal Dept. 37-42; First Sec. of Finnish Towns Fed. 42-46, Gen. Sec. 46, Chair. 47-57; Minister of Interior 48-50; mem. of Parl. 51-62; Chair. State House Admin. 51-53; Minister of Trade and Industry 54-56, of Finance 56-57; mem. Board of Govs., Bank of Finland 57-; Deputy Prime Minister 57; Minister of Justice 66-; Social Dem. Workers and Smallholders Union; mem., Sec. and Chair. of numerous municipal and State Cttees.
Rauhankatu 13.A, Helsinki 17, Finland.

Simonnet, Maurice-René, D. en D.; French economist and politician; b. 4 Oct. 1919; ed. Ecole des Sciences Politiques, Paris, Faculty of Law, Lyons.
Deputy for Drôme 46-62; Sec. of State for the Merchant Marine 57-58; Sec.-Gen. Mouvement Républicain Populaire (M.R.P.) 55-62; Conseiller général, canton of La Chapelle-en-Vercors 64-; Chevalier, Légion d'Honneur, Croix de Guerre (39-45), Croix de Combattant Volontaire de la Résistance.
65 Avenue Victor-Hugo, Valence (Drôme), France.
Telephone: 43-31-46.

Simonov, Konstantin Mikhailovich (real name Kirill); Soviet journalist and writer; b. 28 Nov. 1915; ed. M. Gorky Literary Inst., Moscow.
War corresp. for *Red Star* and *Pravda* 38; mem. C.P.S.U. 42-; Deputy to Supreme Soviet 46-54; Editor *Literaturnaya gazeta* (Literary Gazette) 50-53; Editor *Novy Mir* (New World) 46-50, 54-58; mem. Sec. Union of Soviet Writers 46-59; six State Prizes, Order of Lenin, Red Banner of Labour, Badge of Honour and other decorations.
Publs. include poems: *Real Men* 38, *Ice Blood Battle* 38, *Pavel Cherny* 38, *A Son of an Artilleryman* 42, *Friends and Enemies* 48, *Selected Poems* 60, 64, *Three Note Books* 64; plays: *A Story of Love* 40, *Fellow from Our Town* 42, *The Russians* 42, *Under the Chestnut Trees* 45, *Russian Question* 46, *Alien Shadow* 49, *The Fourth* 62; novels: *Days and Nights* 44, *Collected Works* (3 vols.) 53, *Comrades in Arms* 53, *Those Alive and Those Dead* 59, *Over there, where were once . . .* 64, *Soldiers are not Born* 64, *From Lopatin's Notes* 65.
Union of Soviet Writers, 52 Vorovsky Street, Moscow, U.S.S.R.

Simpson, Alan, M.A. D.PHIL.; American (b. British) educator and administrator; b. 23 July 1912; ed. Dame Allan's School, Newcastle-on-Tyne, Worcester Coll. and Merton College, Oxford, and Harvard Univ.
Senior Lecturer in Modern British History and American History, Univ. of St. Andrews, Scotland 38-46; Lecturer in Constitutional Law, Univ. Coll., Dundee, Scotland 38-46; Royal Artillery 41-45; Asst. Prof. of History, Univ. of Chicago 46-54, Assoc. Prof. 54-59, Thomas E. Donneley Prof. of History, and Dean of Coll., Univ. of Chicago 59-64; Pres. of Vassar Coll. 64-; L.H.D. (Nat. Coll. of Educ., Evanston, Univ. of Rochester); LL.D. (Knox College).

Publs. *The People Shall Judge: Readings in the Formation of American Policy* (2 vols.) (co-author) 49, *Puritanism in Old and New England* 55, *The Wealth of the Gentry 1540-1660: East Anglian Studies* 61.
The President's House, Vassar College, Poughkeepsie, N.Y., U.S.A.

Simpson, George Gaylord, PH.D.; American biologist, geologist and palaeontologist; b. 16 June 1902; ed. Colorado and Yale Univs.
Fellow Nat. Research Council 26-27; Asst. Curator American Museum of Natural History, New York 27-28, Assoc. Curator 29-42, Curator 42-59, Chair. Geology and Palæontology Depts. 44-58; Prof. Columbia Univ. 45-59; Alexander Agassiz Prof. of Vertebrate Palæontology, Museum of Comparative Zoology, Harvard Univ. 59-; Geology Prof., Univ. of Anzona 67-; foreign mem. Royal Soc. (London); Lewis Prize 42, Thompson Medal 43 and Elliott Medal 44, 64, Gaudry Medal 47, Penrose Medal 52, André H. Dumont Medal 53, Commemorative Medal 58, Darwin Plaquette 59; Hon. Sc.D. Yale, Princeton, Oxford, Durham, Chicago, Cambridge, New Mexico, York (Canada), Colorado Univs.; Hon. LL.D. Glasgow Univ.; Dr. h.c. (Univ. of Paris); Linnean Soc. Gold Medal 62, Royal Soc. Darwin Medal 62; Nat. Medal of Science 66.
Publs. include *American Mesozoic Mammalia* 29, *Quantitative Zoology* (with Anne Roe) 39, *Tempo and Mode in Evolution* 44, *The Meaning of Evolution* 49, *Life of the Past* 53, *The Major Features of Evolution* 53, *Evolution and Geography* 53, *Life: An Introduction to Biology* (with Beck) 57, 65, *Behavior and Evolution* (with Anne Roe) 58, *Principles of Animal Taxonomy* 61, *This View of Life* 64.
Museum of Comparative Zoology, Harvard University, Cambridge, Mass. 02138, U.S.A.

Simpson, Milward Lee; American lawyer and politician; b. 12 Nov. 1897; ed. Univ. of Wyoming and Harvard Law School.
Infantry service, First World War; private legal practice 26-; mem. Wyo. House of Reps. 26-27; Gov. of Wyo. 55-59; U.S. Senator from Wyo. 62-67; mem. various legal and civic orgs.; Hon. LL.D.; Republican.
901 Simpson Avenue, Cody, Wyoming 82414, U.S.A.
Telephone: 587-2527.

Simpson, Norman Frederick; British playwright; b. 29 Jan. 1919; ed. Emanuel School, London, and Birkbeck Coll., Univ. of London.
Teacher in adult education until 63; full-time playwright 63-.
Plays: *A Resounding Tinkle* 58, *The Hole* 58, *One Way Pendulum* (also film) 59, *The Form* 61, *The Cresta Run* 65.
c/o Curtis Brown Ltd., 13 King Street, London, W.C.2, England.

Simson, Otto von, PH.D.; German scholar and diplomatist; b. 12; ed. Arndt Gymnasium, Berlin and Munich Univ.
Professor of the History of Art, Chicago Univ. 45-57; Perm. Del. of the German Fed. Repub. to UNESCO 59-; mem. Exec. Board UNESCO 60-64; Counsellor, Embassy of the German Fed. Rep., Paris 59-; Officier, Légion d'Honneur.
Publs. *Zur Genealogie der weltlichen Apotheose im Barock* 36, *Sacred Fortress: Byzantine Art and Statecraft in Ravenna* 48, *The Gothic Cathedral* 56, 62.
Embassy of the German Federal Republic, Avenue Franklin D. Roosevelt 13 et 15, Paris 18e, France.

Šimůnek, Otakar; Czech chemical engineer and politician; b. 23 Oct. 1908; ed. Czech Technical Univ., Prague.
In resistance movement 39-45; Dep. Minister of Food Industry 49-51; Minister of Chemical Industry 51-54; Minister-Chair. State Planning Comm. 54-62; Deputy

Prime Minister 59-68; Chair. State Comm. for Econ. and Scientific Technical Co-operation 63-66; Perm. Rep. to Council for Mutual Econ. Aid 59-68; Deputy to Nat. Assembly 54, 57, 60, 64-; mem. Presidium Central Cttee. of C.P. of Czechoslovakia 58-68; Order of Klement Gottwald (for socialist construction), Order of Repub., other Czech and foreign decorations.
Prague, Czechoslovakia.

Sinatra, Frank; American singer, actor and composer; b. 12 Dec. 1917; ed. Drake Inst.
Sang with Harry James and Tommy Dorsey Bands; appeared in the films *Las Vegas Nights, Ship Ahoy*; played leading roles in the films *Higher and Higher, Anchors Aweigh, It Happened in Brooklyn, From Here to Eternity, Guys and Dolls, Not as a Stranger, The Tender Trap, The Man with the Golden Arm, Johnny Concho, The Pride and the Passion, Pal Joey, Some Came Running, Kings Go Forth, A Hole in the Head, Never So Few, The Jimmy Durante Story, Can-Can, The Devil at 4 o'clock, Sergeants Three, Robin and the Seven Hoods, Von Ryan's Express, Assault on a Queen, The Naked Runner, On the Town, High Society, The Joker is Wild, Oceans' 11, Come Blow Your Horn, Suddenly, The Manchurian Candidate, Tony Rome.* etc.; American Motion Picture Acad. Award for Best Supporting Actor for *From Here to Eternity*.
4000 Warner Boulevard, Burbank, California, U.S.A.

Sinclair, Ernest Keith, C.M.G., O.B.E., D.F.C., F.R.G.S.; Australian journalist; b. 13 Nov. 1914; ed. Melbourne High School.
Served R.A.F., Second World War; C.O. 97 Pathfinder Sqdn. 44-45; Foreign Corresp., Europe 38, 46; Editor *The Age* 59-66; Chair. Australian Assoc. Press 65-66; Dir. Gen. Television Corpn. 59-66; now Consultant to Prime Minister of Australia and to Prime Minister's Dept.; Dir. Australian Paper Manufacturers and Hecla (Australia); mem. Australian Tourist Comm., Library Council of Victoria.
c/o Prime Minister's Department, Canberra, A.C.T., Australia.
Telephone: 71604 (Canberra).

Sinclair, Ian David, Q.C., LL.B.; Canadian lawyer and railway executive; b. 13 Dec. 1927; ed. public schools, Winnipeg and Univ. of Manitoba.
Assistant Solicitor, Canadian Pacific Railway Co. 42, Solicitor 46, Asst. to Gen. Counsel 51, Gen. Solicitor 53, Vice-Pres. (Law) 60, Vice-Pres. and Dir., mem. Exec. Cttee. 61, Pres., Canadian Pacific Railway Co. May 66-; Pres. and Dir. Midland Simcoe Elevator Co. Ltd., Northern Alberta Railway Co.; Vice-Pres. and Dir. Canadian Pacific Air Lines Ltd., Canadian Pacific Investments Ltd., Canadian Pacific Oil-Gas Ltd.; Dir. Bow River Pipe Lines Ltd., Canadian Pacific Express Co., Canadian Pacific Hotels Ltd., Pacific Logging Co. Ltd., Marathon Realty Co. Ltd., Smithsons Holdings, Canadian Pacific Securities, Trans-Canada Pipelines, Cominco Ltd., Canadian Marconi Co., Royal Bank of Canada, Sun Life of Canada; Gov. Royal Victoria Hospital, Montreal; official of other orgs.
Canadian Pacific Railway Co., Windsor Station, Montreal 3, Quebec; Home: 306 Brock Avenue, North Montreal West, Quebec, Canada.
Telephone: 610-861-6811.

Sinclair, Peter T.; American paper executive; b. 25 Dec. 1906; ed. Oregon State Univ.
Port Townsend, Washington, Pulp and Paper Mill, Crown Zellerbach Corpn. 28-38, Resident Manager, Carthage (N.Y.) Mill 38-44, Asst. Resident Manager, West Linn, Oregon 44-47, Resident Manager 47-52, Asst. Vice-Pres. (Manufacturing) 52-53, Vice-Pres. (Industrial Relations) 53-54, Vice-Pres. (Manufacturing and Converting) 54-56; Pres., Chief Exec. Officer and Dir.

Crown Zellerbach Canada Ltd., Vancouver 56-59; Exec. Vice-Pres. Crown Zellerbach Corpn. 59-63, Pres. (also Dir.) 63-; Dir. St. Francisville Paper Co., Zellerbach Paper Co., Wells Fargo Bank, Crown Simpson Pulp Co., Pacific Indemnity Co., The Chubb Corpn., The Clorax Co., etc.; Dir. Nat. Asscn. of Manufacturers, Trustee Inst. of Paper Chemistry, Appleton, Wisconsin.
Crown Zellerbach Corporation, 1 Bush Street, San Francisco, California; Home: 2000 Jackson Street, San Francisco, California 94109, U.S.A.

Sinclair, Sir Ronald Ormiston, K.B.E., LL.M.; British lawyer; b. 2 May 1903; ed. Auckland Univ. Coll. and Balliol Coll., Oxford.
Joined Nigerian Administrative Service 31, Magistrate 36; Resident Magistrate, Northern Rhodesia 38; Puisne Judge, Tanganyika 46-53; Chief Justice, Nyasaland 53-56; Vice-Pres. East African Court of Appeal 56-57; Chief Justice of Kenya 57-62; Pres. H.M. Court of Appeal for Eastern Africa 62-64; Pres. Court of Appeal for the Bahamas Islands Feb. 65- and of Court of Appeal for Bermuda June 65-; Chair. Industrial Tribunals, England and Wales 65.
43 Beechcroft Manor, Oaklands Drive, Weybridge, Surrey, England.
Telephone: Weybridge 43901.

Sinclair, Upton, B.A.; American publicist and author; b. 20 Sept. 1878; ed. City Coll. of New York and Columbia Univ.
Unsuccessful candidate for Congress as Socialist, New York 06 and California 20, for U.S. Senate 22, for Governorship of California 26 and 30, and (as Democrat) 34.
Publs. *The Jungle* 06, *The Moneychangers* 08, *King Coal* 17, *Mammonmart* 25, *Oil* 27, *Boston* 29, *The Wet Parade* 31, *Candid Reminiscences* 32, *Upton Sinclair Presents William Fox, The Way Out,* I, *Governor of California* 33, *Co-op* 36, *No Pasarán!* 37, *The Flivver King* 37, *Little Steel* 38, *Our Lady* 38, *Marie Antoinette* 39, *World's End* 40, *Between Two Worlds* 41, *Dragon's Teeth* 42, *Wide Is The Gate* 43, *Presidential Agent* 44, *Dragon Harvest* 45, *A World to Win* 46, *Presidential Mission* 47, *One Clear Call* 48, *O Shepherd, Speak!* 49, *Another Pamela* 50, *The Enemy Had It Too* 50, *The Return of Lanny Budd* 53, *The Cup of Fury* 56, *It Happened to Didymus* 58, *My Lifetime in Letters* 59, *Theirs Be the Guilt* 60, *Affectionately, Eve* 61, *Autobiography* 63, *The Cry for Justice* 63.
10201 Grosvenor Place, Rockville, Maryland, U.S.A.

Sinclair of Cleeve (1st Baron, cr. 57), of Cleeve in the County of Somerset; **Robert John Sinclair,** K.C.B., K.B.E., M.A.; British industrialist; b. 29 July 1893; ed. Glasgow Acad. and Oriel Coll., Oxford.
Commissioned in 5th Battalion K.O.S.B. Aug. 14; served Gallipoli (wounded, despatches); seconded to Min. of Munitions 16, Deputy Dir., Insp. of Munitions 17-19; mem. Prime Min.'s Advisory Panel of Industrialists Jan. 39; Dir.-Gen. of Army Requirements, War Office 39-42; mem. Supply Council 39-42; mem. Army Council 40-42; Deputy for Min. of Production on Combined Production and Resources Board, Washington 42-43; Chief Exec. Min. of Production 43-45; Chair. Imperial Tobacco Co. Ltd. 47-59, Pres. 59-67; Chair. Bristol Waterworks Co. 60-; Dir. Debenture Corpn. Ltd., Gen. Accident Fire and Life Assurance Corpn. Ltd., Nat. Provincial Bank Ltd., Tobacco Securities Trust Co. Ltd., Commonwealth Devt. Finance Co. Ltd., Finance Corpn. for Industry, etc.; Pres. Fed. of British Industries 49-50, 50-51; mem. Security Comm. 65-; Pro-Chancellor Bristol Univ.; U.S. Medal of Freedom with Gold Palm; Hon. LL.D. (Bristol); Hon. Fellow Oriel Coll., Oxford 59.
Cleeve Court, Cleeve, nr. Bristol, England.
Telephone: Yatton 2124.

Sindermann, Horst; German politician; b. 5 Sept. 1915.
Member Communist Union of Youth, Saxony 29; political imprisonment 34-45 (including Sachsenhausen concentration camp); later Chief Editor *Volksstimme* (Voice of the People), Chemnitz (now Karl-Marx-Stadt); later Chief Editor, Press Service of Sozialistische Einheitspartei Deutschlands (S.E.D.); Editor S.E.D. District paper *Freiheit* (Freedom), Halle/Saale; staff of Central Cttee. S.E.D. 55-63, Cand. mem. Central Cttee. S.E.D. 58-63, mem. 63-, Cand. mem. Politburo 63-; mem. Volkskammer 63-.
Volkskammer, Berlin, Germany.

Sindona, Michele, D.IUR.; Italian financial lawyer; b. 8 May 1920; ed. Univ. of Messina.
Legal practice, Sicily 40-46, Milan (tax, company and finance) 46-; controls Fasco A.G. (int. financial group); Pres. Banca di Messina Keyes S.p.A.; Vice-Pres. Acciaierie Crucible Vanzetti, Banca Privata Finanziaria; Dir. Snia Viscosa, Remington Rand Italia, Chesebrough Pond's Italia, Stabilimenti Tessili Italiani (S.T.I.), Reeves S.p.A., Società Industriale Agricola per la Produzione di Cellulosa (S.I.A.C.E.) and other companies.
Via Turati 29, Milan, Italy.

Singh, Air Chief Marshal Arjan, D.F.C.; Indian air force officer; b. 15 April 1919; ed. Government Coll., Lahore, R.A.F. Coll., Cranwell, and Imperial Defence Coll., London.
Wing Commdr. 45, Group Capt. 47, Air Commodore 50, Air Vice Marshal 59, Air Marshal 64, Air Chief Marshal 66; Chief of Air Staff 64-; Pres. Swimming Fed. of India; Padma Vibhushan.
c/o National & Grindlays Bank Ltd., New Delhi, India.

Singh, Dinesh, B.A.; Indian diplomatist; b. 19 July 1925; ed. Doon School, Dehra Dun, and Colvin Coll., Lucknow Univ.
Member of Parl. 57-; fmr. Private Sec. to Prime Minister; fmr. Sec. to the High Commr. for India in London, to the Ambassador in Paris; mem. Indian Dels. to FAO, ECAFE and UN; Deputy Minister for External Affairs 62-Jan. 66; Minister of State for External Affairs 66-67; Minister of Commerce 67-.
Ministry of Commerce, New Delhi, India.

Singh, Gurmukh Nihal, M.SC., Bar.-at-Law; Indian politician; b. 14 March 1895; ed. London School of Economics and Middle Temple, London.
Prof. of Economics and Political Science, later Rama Varma Prof. of Political Science, Banaras Hindu Univ. 20-39; Dean of Faculty of Arts; Principal of H.L. Coll. of Commerce, Ahmedabad, India 39-43; Principal, Ramjas Coll., Delhi 43-50, S.R. Coll. of Commerce, Delhi 50-52; M.L.A. Delhi State (Congress) 52 and Speaker 52-55; Leader of Congress Party, Delhi State Legislature, and Chief Minister of Delhi 55-56; Gov. of Rajasthan 56-62; Founder mem., Sec. and Treas. 39-41 and Pres. 42, Indian Political Science Asscn.; Founder mem., Exec. mem. and Vice-Pres. Indian Council of World Affairs and Indian Inst. of Public Admin., Delhi; mem. Indian Inst. Constitutional and Parl. Studies, Delhi.
C-193, Defence Colony, New Delhi 3, India.
Telephone: 76855.

Singh, Sardar Hukam; Indian politician; b. 30 Aug. 1895; ed. Govt. High School, Montgomery, Khalsa Coll., Amritsar and Law Coll., Lahore.
Lawyer; fmr. Pres., Singh Sabha, Montgomery; Man. Khalsa High School, Montgomery 41, 43-45; Pres. Shiromani Akali Dal; imprisoned 23-25, 55; Puisne Judge, State High Court, Kapurthala 47-48; mem. Constituent Ass. 48-50, Provisional Parl. 50-52, Lok Sabha (Parl.) 52-57, 57-; Dep. Speaker, Lok Sabha 56-62,

Speaker 62-67; Gov. of Rajastan 67-; Del. to Commonwealth Parl. Confs. 59, 61, 62; mem. Congress Party.
Governor's Office, Jaipur, Rajastan, India.

Singh, Kewal, B.A., LL.B.; Indian diplomatist; b. 1 June 1915; ed. Forman Christian Coll., Lahore, Law Coll., Lahore, and Balliol Coll., Oxford.
Joined Indian Civil Service 38; Indian Civil Service appointments 40-48; First Sec. Indian Embassy, Ankara 48-49; Indian Military Mission, Berlin 49-51; Chargé d'Affaires, Lisbon 51-53; Consul-General, Pondicherry 53-54; Chief Commr., State of Pondicherry, Karaikal, Mahe and Yanan 54-57; awarded Padma Shri for distinguished services leading to merger of French Possessions with India; Ambassador to Cambodia 57-58, to Sweden, Denmark and Finland 59-62; Deputy High Commr. in U.K. 62-65; High Commr. in Pakistan 65-66; Amb. to U.S.S.R. 66-.
Indian Embassy, 6-8 ulitsa Obukha, Moscow, U.S.S.R.

Singh, Khushwant, LL.B.; Indian author; b. 15; ed. Government Coll., Lahore, King's Coll. and Inner Temple, London.
Practised, High Court, Lahore 39-47; joined Indian Ministry of External Affairs 47; Press Attaché, Canada and then Public Relations Officer, London 48-51; Ministry of Information and Broadcasting; edited *Yojana*; Dept. of Mass Communication, UNESCO 54-56; commissioned by Rockefeller Foundation and Muslim Univ., Aligarh to write a history of the Sikhs 58; Grove Press Award.
Publs. *Mark of Vishnu* 49, *The Sikhs* 51, *Train to Pakistan* 54, *Sacred Writings of the Sikhs* 60, *I shall not hear the Nightingale* 61, *Umrao Jan Ada—Courtesan of Lucknow* (trans.) 61, *History of the Sikhs (1769-1839)* Vol. I 62, *Ranjit Singh: Maharaja of the Punjab* 62, *Fall of the Sikh Kingdom* 62, *The Skeleton* (trans.) 63, *Land of the Five Rivers* (trans.) 64, *History of the Sikhs (1839-Present Day)* 65.
1A Janpath, New Delhi, India; Authors' Club, Whitehall Court, London, S.W.1, England.

Singh, Mairembam Koireng; Indian politician; b. 19 Dec. 1915; ed. Bengali High School, Imphal.
Entered active politics 38; joined Azad Hind Fauz 44-45; mem. Manipur State Legislative Assembly 48; mem. Electoral Coll., Manipur 51-56; Pres. Manipur State Congress Cttee. 56-57; mem. Manipur Territorial Council 57-62, Chair. 62-63; Chief Minister, Manipur 63-67, 68-; Chair. Adimjati Siksha Ashram, Imphal.
Moirang, B.P.O. Moirang, Manipur, India.

Singh, Raja Roy; Indian educationist; b. 5 April 1918; ed. Univ. of Allahabad.
Entered Indian Admin. Service 43; fmr. Dir. of Educ., Uttar Pradesh; fmr. Joint Sec., Fed. Ministry of Educ., New Delhi; fmr. Joint Dir. Indian Council of Educational Research and Training, Nat. Inst. of Educ.; at Office of Educational Planning, UNESCO Headquarters, Paris 64-65; Dir. UNESCO Regional Office for Educ. in Asia 65-.
UNESCO Regional Office for Education in Asia, P.O. Box 1425, Sanam Sua Pa, Bangkok, Thailand.

Singh, Ram Subhag, M.A., PH.D.; Indian politician; b. 7 July 1917; ed. Missouri Univ.
Joined Congress Party 35; mem. of Parl. 50-; Chief Whip, Parl. Congress Party 67-; Sec. Congress Parl. Party 55-62; Minister of State in the Ministry of Agriculture 62-64, in Ministry of Social Security and Cottage Industries 64-66; Minister of State for Railways 66-67; Minister of Parl. Affairs and Communications 67-.
Ministry of Parliamentary Affairs, New Delhi, India.

Singh, Sardar Swaran, M.SC., LL.B.; Indian politician; b. 19 Aug. 1907; ed. Govt. Coll., Lahore, and Lahore Law Coll.
Elected Punjab Legislative Assembly 46; Minister of

Development, Food, Civil Supplies 46-47; mem. Gov.'s Security Council, then Partition Cttee. 47; Minister of Home, Gen. Admin., Revenue, Irrigation and Electricity in first Punjab Congress Ministry 47-49; resgnd. to resume legal practice; Minister of Capital Projects and Electricity 52; Minister for Works, Housing and Supply (Central Govt.) 52-57; elected to Rajya Sabha; initiated Subsidised Industrial Housing Scheme; led Indian del. to ECOSOC in 54 and 55; Lok Sabha (Parl.) 57-; Minister for Steel, Mines and Fuel 57-62; Minister for Railways 62-Aug. 63, of Food and Agriculture Aug. 63-June 64, of Industry, Engineering and Technical Development June 64-July 64, of External Affairs July 64-Nov. 66, of Defence Nov. 66-.
Office: Ministry of Defence, New Delhi; Home: 7 Hastings Road, New Delhi, India.

Singh, Sher, M.A.; Indian agriculturalist and politician; b. 18 Sept. 1917; ed. Delhi Univ.
Former Lecturer, M.S.J. Coll., Bharatpur, and Lecturer in Mathematics, Jat Coll., Rohtak; elected to Punjab Legislative Assembly 46, 52, 57, Punjab Legislative Council 62; Parl. Sec., Punjab 48-51; Deputy Leader of Congress Legislature Party in Punjab 56-57; Minister of Irrigation and Power, Punjab 56-57; now mem. Lok Sabha; Minister of State in Ministry of Educ. 67-; Chancellor of Gurukul (system of teaching based on ancient Indian culture), Jhajjar; mem. Syndicate of Gurukul Kangri Univ.; fmr. Founder-Pres. Haryana Lok Sabha.
Ministry of Education, New Delhi, India.

Singh, Tarlok, B.A., B.SC.; Indian civil servant; b. 26 Feb. 1913; ed. St. Vincent's School and Deccan Coll., Poona, Gujarat Coll., Ahmedabad and London School of Economics.
Indian Civil Service 37-62; Colonization Officer, Nili Bar Colony, Punjab 43; Finance Dept. Govt. of India 44-46; Private Sec. to Vice-Pres. Interim Govt. and to Prime Minister 46-47; Dir.-Gen. of Rehabilitation 47-49; mem. Planning Comm. 50-67, Additional Sec. 58-62; Hon. Fellow London School of Economics; Fellow, Inst. for Int. Economic Studies, Univ. of Stockholm 67; Padma Shri 54, Padma Bhushan 62.
Publs. *Poverty and Social Change* 45, *Resettlement Manual for Displaced Persons* 52, *Towards an Integrated Society* 68.
c/o Woodrow Wilson School, Princeton, New Jersey, U.S.A.; 16-D Nizamuddin West, New Delhi 13, India.

Singhania, Lakshmipat (brother of Sir Padampat Singhania, *q.v.*); Indian businessman; b. 23 Feb. 1910.
Entered business 29; Dir.-in-charge Aluminium Corpn. of India Ltd.; former Pres. Merchants' Chamber of U.P., Kanpur 46 and 47, and Bharat Chamber of Commerce, Calcutta 48-49; mem. Coal Control Board, Bharat Chamber of Commerce, Indian Central Jute Cttee., Joint Consultative Board of Industry and Labour, Indian Inst. of Social Welfare and Business Management, All-India Board of Technical Studies in Commerce and Business Admin., etc.; Underwriter, Lloyd's Society of London; fmr. Pres. Fed. Indian Chamber of Commerce and Industry, Indian Nat. Cttee. of the Int. Chamber of Commerce (58); President All-India Organisation of Industrial Employers.
Home: J. K. House, 12 Alipore Road, Calcutta 27; Office: 7 Council House Street, Calcutta 1, India.

Singhania, Sir Padampat, Kt. (brother of Lakshmipat Singhania, *q.v.*); Indian industrialist; b. 1905; ed. privately.
President J.K. Org. (Juggilal Kamlapat Group of Mills), Kanpur; a pioneer of cotton and woollen textiles, rayon, nylon, jute, sugar, hosiery, iron and steel, aluminium, plastic, strawboard, chemical, mining and oil industries; Founder Merchants' Chamber of U.P.; fmr. Pres.

Federation of Indian Chambers of Commerce and Industries; mem. 1st Indian Parl.; Chair. Hindustan Commercial Bank Ltd.
Kamla Tower, Kanpur, India.

Singier, Gustav Heenri; Belgian-born French artist; b. 11 Feb. 1909.
Foundation mem. of the Salon de Mai 45-; has exhibited in Paris, Stockholm, Brussels, Turin and Venice; has exclusive contract with Galerie de France, Paris; works in museums at Paris, New York, Vienna, Brussels, Basle, Johannesburg, Essen, Wellington, Tate Gallery, London, etc.; tapestries executed for the French Inst. in London, the Dominican chapel at Monteils and the Cour de Cassation, Paris; teacher of painting Acad. Ranson 51-54.
203 rue de Vaugirard, Paris 15e, France.
Telephone: SEGur 64-05.

Sinha, Bhuvaneshwar Prasad, M.A., LL.B.; Indian judge; b. 1 Feb. 1899; ed. Patna Coll. and Law School.
Vakil, Patna High Court 22-27, Advocate 27-35; Lecturer, Patna Govt. Law Coll. 26-35; mem. Senate, Patna Univ. Law Faculty, Court, Benares Hindu Univ.; Govt. Pleader, Patna High Court 35-39, Asst. Govt. Advocate 40-42, Judge 43-51; Chief Justice, Nagpur High Court 51-54; Justice, Supreme Court of India 54-59; Chief Justice 59-63; Pro-Chancellor Univ. of Delhi; Founder-mem. and Pres. Indian Law Inst.; Hon. LL.D. Patna, Bhagalpur and Vikram Univs.
20 Mathura Road, New Delhi, India.

Sinha, Satya Narain; Indian politician; b. 1900; ed. Patna.
Joined Non-Violence Movement and imprisoned 20; mem. Bihar Legislature 26-30; mem. Indian Constituent Ass. 26-47, of Lok Sabha 47-; Minister of State for Parl. Affairs 49-52; Minister for Parl. Affairs 52-67, of Information and Broadcasting Sept. 63-June 64, of Civil Aviation June 64, of Communications 64-67; Minister without Portfolio 67-Nov. 67; Minister of Health, Family Planning and Urban Devt. Nov. 67-; Chief Whip Congress Party in Central Assembly and Constitutent Assembly.
Lok Sabha, New Delhi, India.

Sinitsa, Mikhail Safronovich; Soviet politician; b. 13; ed. Polytechnical Inst., Kiev.
Engineer and technological worker 36-50; mem. C.P.S.U. 42-; First Sec., Kiev City Cttee. C.P. Ukraine 50-60; Chair., Ukraine Council of Trade Unions 60-61; First Sec.. Odessa Regional Cttee. C.P. Ukraine 61-; mem. Central Cttee. of C.P.S.U. 61-; Deputy, U.S.S.R. Supreme Soviet.
Odessa District Committee of Communist Party of Ukrainian S.S.R., Odessa, Ukrainian S.S.R., U.S.S.R.

Sinitsin, Ivan Flegontyevich; Soviet politician; b. 1911; ed. Gorky Industrial Inst.
Gorky Motor Works 29-36; worker at other enterprises, Gorky 36-46; Dir. Volgograd Tractor Works 50-57; later Head of Econ. Councils, Volgograd Region 57-60; Minister of Tractor and Farm Machine Building 65-; Alternate mem. C.P.S.U. Central Cttee.; Deputy to U.S.S.R. Supreme Soviet.
Ministry of Tractor and Farm Machine Building, Moscow, U.S.S.R.

Sinker, Sir (Algernon) Paul, K.C.M.G., C.B.; British civil servant; b. 13 April 1905; ed. Haileybury Coll. and Jesus Coll., Cambridge.
Fellow of Jesus Coll. 27-49, Tutor 29-40; civil servant Admiralty 40-45; Treasury 45-50; Adviser to Egyptian Govt. on Civil Service reform 50; First Civil Service Commr. 51-54; Dir. Gen. of the British Council 54-68; Chair. Council for Small Industries in Rural Areas 68-; Hon. Fellow Jesus Coll. 55; Hon. LL.D. (Exeter) 61.
c/o Development Commission, 3 Deans Yard, London, S.W.1, England
Telephone: 01-222-1177.

Sinnott, Edmund Ware, A.M., PH.D.; American university professor; b. 5 Feb. 1888; ed. Harvard Univ.
Austin Teaching Fellow and Asst. in Botany, Harvard Univ. 08-10 and 11-12; Sheldon Travelling Fellow 10-11; Instr. Harvard Forestry School and Bussey Inst. 13-15; Prof. of Botany and Genetics, Conn. Agric. Coll. 15-28; Prof. of Botany, Barnard Coll. 28-39; Prof. of Botany, Columbia Univ. 39-40; Sterling Prof. of Botany, Yale Univ. 40-56; Chair. Dept. of Botany 40-50; Dir. Sheffield Scientific School 45-56; Dean, Graduate School 50-56; mem. Nat. Acad. of Sciences, American Phil. Society, and others; Pres. American Asscn. for Advancement of Science 48, now emeritus.
Publs. *Botany: Principles and Problems, Principles of Genetics* (with L. C. Dunn), *Cell and Psyche, Two Roads to Truth, The Biology of the Spirit, Matter, Mind and Man, Plant Morphogenesis* 60.
Home: 459 Prospect Street, New Haven, Conn., U.S.A.

Sinwa Nawng, Sama Duwa (*see* Nawng, Sama Duwa Sinwa).

Siodmak, Robert; German-born American film director; b. 8 Aug. 1900.
Settled in U.S. after the establishment of the Nazi régime; films directed include *Menschen am Sonntag, Nachts wenn der Teufel Kam, The Spiral Staircase, The Dark Mirror, The Suspect, Deported, Richer than Earth, The Crimson Pirate, The Killers, Phantom Lady, The Strange Affair of Uncle Harry, The Rough and the Smooth, Tunnel 28* 62.
Casa Daniela, Ascona, Switzerland.

Siple, Paul Allman, B.S., PH.D.; American explorer, military geographer and climatologist; b. 18 Dec. 1908; ed. Allegheny Coll. and Clark Univ.
Rep. of Boy Scouts with 1st Byrd Antarctic Expedition 28-30, Chief Biologist and Field Party Leader 2nd Expedition 33-35; Base Leader Little America III; Senior Geographer, Technical Supervisor of Logistics and Navigator U.S. Antarctic Service Expedition 39-41; mil. service 41-46; Mil. Geographer to the U.S. Gen. Staff 46-53; Dir. Basic Science Research U.S. Army General Staff 53-54; Dir. of Scientific Projects on Navy Operation Deep Freeze I 55; Deputy to Admiral Byrd, Officer in Charge of U.S. Antarctic Programme 55-57; Scientific Leader in the initial year of operation of the U.S. I.G.Y. Geographical South Pole Station; Scientific Adviser U.S. Army Chief of Research and Devt. 46-63; Scientific Attaché U.S. Embassies Canberra, Wellington 63-66; Special scientific adviser U.S. Army Chief of Research and Devt. 67-; Fellow, American Geographical Soc.; mem. Asscn. of American Geographers, Vice-Pres. 58, Pres. 59-60; three Congressional Byrd Antarctic Expedition Medals, etc.
Publs. *A Boy Scout with Byrd, Exploring at Home, From Scout to Explorer,* 90° *South.*
3454 North Edison Street, Arlington, Va. 22207, U.S.A.

Siraud, Pierre; French diplomatist; b. 11 Oct. 1907; ed. Ecole des Sciences politiques.
With Ministry of Foreign Affairs 35-40; mem. Résistance Second World War; Second Counsellor, Washington 45-51; Deputy Sec.-Gen., Rabat 51-55; Counsellor, Ankara 55-56; Deputy Dir. Personnel and Gen. Admin. Ministry of Foreign Affairs 56-59, Chief of Protocol 61-65; Head, French Embassy Guinea 59-60; Ambassador to the Netherlands 65-; Officier Légion d'Honneur, Commdr. Ordre Nat. du Mérite and foreign honours.
Embassy of France, Lange Vijvergerg 15, The Hague, Netherlands.

Siri, H.E. Cardinal Giuseppe; Italian ecclesiastic; b. 20 May 1906; ed. Episcopal Seminary, Genoa and Pontifical Gregorian Univ., Rome.
Ordained priest 28; Titular Bishop of Livias 44; Archbishop of Genoa 46-; created Cardinal by Pope Pius XII 53; Pres. Episcopal Dir. Comm., Italian Catholic Action, Episcopal Conference of Italy (C.E.I.) 59-61; Chair. Italian Episcopal Conf. 55-65; mem. Sacred Congregations of Sacraments of the Council and of Seminaries and Univs. of Study.
Publs. *Corso di Teologia per Laici* 42, *La Strada passa per Cristo* 56.
Palazzo Arcivescovile, Piazza Mateotti 4, Genoa, Italy.

Široký, Viliam; Czechoslovak politician; b. 31 May 1902.
Railway employee; mem. C.P. of Czechoslovakia 21-; Communist mem. Parl. 35-; after Munich went to France and subsequently to Soviet Union; returned to occupied Czechoslovakia and participated in Resistance movement; arrested and imprisoned in Spielberg; escaped and crossed battle front to Soviet lines; Vice-Premier 45-53; Minister of Foreign Affairs 50-Jan. 53; Vice-Premier and mem. Govt. Presidium Jan.-Mar. 53; Prime Minister Mar. 53-63; no longer active in political life or public office.
Prague, Czechoslovakia.

Sisco, Joseph John, PH.D.; American government official; b. 31 Oct. 1919; ed. Knox Coll. and Univ. of Chicago.
U.S. Army 41-45; Central Intelligence Agency 50-51; Dept. of State 51-; Officer-in-Charge, U.N. Political Affairs 51-58, Deputy Dir. Office of UN Political and Security Affairs 58-60, Dir. 60-62; Deputy Asst. Sec. 62-65; Asst. Sec. of State for Int. Org. Affairs, Dept. of State July 65-.
Department of State, Washington, D.C., U.S.A.

Šiška, Karol, M.D., D.SC.; Czechoslovak medical scientist and surgeon; b. 19 March 1906; ed. Universita Karlova, Prague.
Head, Second Surgical Clinic, Medical Faculty, Comenius Univ. Bratislava 54, Prof. of Medical Faculty 53-; Dir., Inst. of Experimental Surgery, Slovak Acad. of Sciences 64-; Academician, Slovak Acad. of Sciences 55- (Vice-Pres. 61-65), Czechoslovak Acad. of Sciences 60-; mem. of Presidium, Czechoslovak Acad. of Sciences 61-65, Slovak Acad. of Sciences 65-; mem. Central Cttee. of C.P. of Slovakia 58-62, and of Czechoslovakia 62; designed heart and lung machines for use during operations; J. E. Purkyně Medal 57, Order of Labour 61, and many other scientific honours.
Publs. Papers on chest surgery and cardiosurgery.
Institute for Experimental Surgery, Slovak Academy of Sciences, Partizánska 2, Bratislava, Czechoslovakia.

Sisowath Sirik Matak; Cambodian politician and diplomatist; b. 22 Jan. 1914; ed. Coll. of Law and Administration of Cambodia.
Vice-Gov. and Gov. 38-49; Royal Khmer Army 49-51; Gen. Sec. to Presidency of Council of Ministers 51-52; Sec. of State for Nat. Defence 52-53; Minister of Nat. Defence and Foreign Affairs 54-56, of Nat. Defence and Nat. Educ. 57-58; Insp. of Affairs of the Kingdom 58-61; Cambodian Rep. to UNESCO, Paris 61-62; Ambassador to People's Republic of China 62-64; Minister of State in charge of National Education and Fine Arts, Phnom Penh 64-66; Amb. to Japan 66-.
Embassy of Cambodia, 17 Akasaka-Aoyama-Takagicho, Minato-ku, Tokyo, Japan.

Sisulu, Walter Max; South African politician; b. 12; ed. mission school.
Worked as gold miner on the Rand; later in a Johannesburg bakery; mem. African Nat. Congress (A.N.C.) 40-, Sec.-Gen. 49-54; on trial for treason 56-61 (acquitted 61); on trial for organising national strike 61, sentenced to six years' imprisonment; found guilty of sabotage and sentenced to life imprisonment June 64.
Robben Island, nr. Capetown, South Africa.

Sithole, Rev. Ndabaningi; African (Rhodesian) clergyman and politician; b. 20; ed. Waddilove Inst., Marandellas and Newton Theological Coll., U.S.A.
Teacher 41-55; U.S.A. 55-58; Ordained at Mount Silinda Congregationalist Church 58; Principal, Chikore Cen. Primary School; Pres., African Teachers Asscn. 59-60; Treas., Nat. Dem. Party (N.D.P.) 60, Del. to Fed. Review Conf. London Dec. 60; fmr. Chair. Zimbabwe African People's Union (Z.A.P.U.) S. Rhodesia, Pres. July-Aug. 63; Leader Zimbabwe African Nat. Union (Z.A.N.U.) Rhodesia Aug. 63-; sentenced to 12 months imprisonment Dec. 63, sent to Wha Wha Restriction Camp May 65.
Publ. *African Nationalism* 59, 67.
c/o Zimbabwe African National Union (Z.A.N.U.), Dar es Salaam, Tanzania.

Sitwell, Sir Osbert (brother of Sacheverell Sitwell, *q.v.*), Bt., C.H., C.B.E., F.R.S.L.; British writer; b. 6 Dec. 1892.
Received *Sunday Times* Gold Medal and award for English Literature 47; C.Lit.; Hon. LL.D. (St. Andrews), Hon. D.Litt. (Sheffield); Hon. F.R.I.B.A.
Publs. include: *Out of the Flame, Triple Fugue and other stories, Discursions on Travel, Art and Life, Winters of Content, The Man who Lost Himself, Before the Bombardment, Dumb Animal, Miracle on Sinai, Penny Foolish, Those Were the Days, Escape with Me, Two Generations, Open the Door, A Place of One's Own, Selected Poems, Sing High—Sing Low, Left Hand—Right Hand, Letter to My Son, The True Story of Dick Whittington, The Scarlet Tree* 46, (Editor) *A Free House* (The Writings of W. R. Sickert) 47, *Great Morning* 48, *Laughter in the Next Room* 49, *Death of a God* 49, *Noble Essences* 50, *Wrack at Tidesend* 52, *Collected Stories* 53, *The Four Continents* 54, *On the Continent* (Poems) 58, *Fee Fi Fo Fum* 59, *Tales My Father Taught Me* 62, *Pound Wise* 63, *Poems about People* 65.
Montegufoni, nr. Florence, Italy.

Sitwell, Sacheverell (brother of Sir Osbert Sitwell *q.v.*); British writer; b. 1897; ed. Eton and Balliol Coll., Oxford.
Publs. include: *The People's Palace, Doctor Donne and Gargantua, The Hundred and One Harlequins, Four Essays on Baroque Art, Actor Rehearsing and Other Poems, The Thirteenth Caesar, Canons of Giant Art, Life of Liszt, Touching the Orient, Dance of the Quick and the Dead, Collected Poems, La Vie Parisienne, Narrative Picture, Roumanian Journey, Trio, Mauretania, Poltergeists* 40, *Of Sacred and Profane Love* 40, *Valse des Fleurs* 41, *Primitive Scenes and Festivals* 42, *Splendour and Miseries* 43, *British Architects and Craftsmen* 45, *Selected Poems* 48, *Cupid and the Jacaranda* 52, *Truffle Hunt with Sacheverell Sitwell* 53, *Portugal and Madeira* 54, *Denmark* 56, *Arabesque and Honeycomb* 57, *Austria* 59, *Journey to the Ends of Time,* Vol. I: *Lost in the Dark Wood* 59, *The Bridge of the Brocade Sash: Travels and Observations in Japan* 59, *Golden Wall and Mirador* 61, *The Red Chapels of Banteai Srei* 62, *Great Palaces* 64, *Monks, Nuns and Monasteries* 65, *Southern Baroque Revisited* 68.
Weston Hall, Towcester, Northants., England.

Sivadon, Paul Daniel; French psychiatrist; b. 10 Jan. 1907; ed. Lycée Blaise Pascal, Clermont Ferrand and Univ. de Paris.
Head, Clinic for Mental Illness, Faculty de Paris 35-36; Dir. Colonie Familiale, Seine 36-43; Head Dr. Psychiatric Hospital, Ville-Evrard 43-58; Prof. of Psychiatry and Medical Psychology, Univ. of Brussels 59-; Dir. Psychiatric Services for Nat. Educ. 58-; Consultant WHO 51-65; fmr. Pres. World Fed. for Mental Health 60-61; Pres. French League for Mental Hygiene 61-66; Treas. World Psychiatric Asscn. 60-66; Officier Légion d'Honneur, Officier de la Santé Publique, Commdr. Ordre de la Couronne.

Publs. include: *Psychoses puerpérales* 33, *Rééducation Corporelle des Fonctions Mentales* 65, and over 350 scientific articles.
Château de La Verrière, 78 Le Mesnil Saint-Denis, France.

Siwertz, Sigfrid; Swedish writer; b. 24 Jan. 1882; ed. Uppsala Univ.
Member Swedish Acad. and the Swedish Nobel Cttee.
Publs. about 60 books, including *Noveller* 18, *Selambs* (Downstream) 20, *En handfull dun* 22, *Lata latituder* 24, *Det stora varuhuset* (Goldman) 26, *Reskamraterna* 29; dramatic works: *Ett brott* (A Crime) 33, *En hederlig man* 35, *I Sex fribiljetter* 43, *Fortroenden* 45, *Att vara ung* 49, *Glasberget* 52, *Trådar i en vav* 57, *Minnets kapriser* 63, essays, poems, memoirs, etc.
Birgerjarlsgatan 46, Stockholm, Sweden.

Sizov, Alexander Alexandrovich; Soviet politician; b. 1913; ed. Industrial Construction Technical School and Leningrad Inst. of Construction Engineering.
Member C.P.S.U. 41-; Soviet Army service 42-45; Engineer of *Glavleningradstroi* orgs. 45-66; Chair. Exec. Cttee. Leningrad Regional Soviet of Workers' Deputies 66-; Deputy to R.S.F.S.R. Supreme Soviet; Hero of Socialist Labour.
Leningrad Regional Soviet of Workers' Deputies, Leningrad, U.S.S.R.

Sizov, Gennady Fedorovich; Soviet politician; b. 03; ed. K.A. Timiryazev Agricultural Inst.
Member C.P.S.U. 26-; Dean of Faculty and Dir. Inst. of Dairy-Cattle Breeding, Moscow 33-41, 47-52; Soviet Army 41-47; staff of Kurgan District Cttee., C.P.S.U. 52-54; Chair. Exec. Cttee. Kurgan District Council of Working People's Deputies 54-55; First Sec. Kurgan District Cttee., C.P.S.U. 55-66; Candidate mem. Central Cttee. C.P.S.U. 56-64, mem. 64-66; Chair. Central Auditing Comm. of C.P.S.U. 66-; Deputy to U.S.S.R. Supreme Soviet; mem. Mandatory Cttee., Soviet of Union.
Central Auditing Commission of C.P.S.U., 4 Staraya ploshchad, Moscow, U.S.S.R.

Sizova, Alla Ivanovna; Soviet ballet dancer; b. 1939; ed. Leningrad School of Ballet.
Joined Leningrad Kirov Theatre of Opera and Ballet 58-; honoured artist of the R.S.F.S.R.
Major roles: Masha (*Nutcracker*), Mirta (*Giselle*), Pas de trois (*Corsair*), Katerina (*Stone Flower*), Waltz and Mazurka (*Chopiniana*), Pas de trois (*Swan Lake*), Aurora (*Sleeping Beauty*), Maria (*Fountain of Bakhchisarai*), Juliet (*Romeo and Juliet*).
State Kirov Academic Theatre of Opera and Ballet, ploshchad Iskusstv 1, Leningrad, U.S.S.R.

Sjöberg, Alf Sven Erik; Swedish producer; b. 21 June 1903; ed. Royal Theatre School.
Actor, Royal Theatre 25-29; producer 30-; studied and acted abroad; Swedish radio; produced Swedish films; Grand Prix for *Miss Julie*, Cannes 52; Hon. Dr. Phil.
Theatre production include works by Shakespeare, Strindberg, Ibsen, O'Neill, Brecht, Gombrowicz.
Kungligen Dramaten Teaten, Stockholm; Andveg. 5, Stockholm, Sweden.
Telephone: 614757 (Home).

Skachkov, Semyon Andreyevich; Soviet engineer and politician; b. 07; ed. Kharkov Engineering Inst.
Worked at Kharkov Steam Locomotive Works, rising to be Chief Metallurgist 30-41; worked in the Urals during the Second World War; later dir. of Leningrad Diesel Engine Works, Nizhny-Tagil Works and Chelyabinsk Tractor Works; First Dep. Minister of Transport Machine Building Industry 54-57; Chair. Kharkov Economic Council 57-58; Chair. State Cttee. for External Econ. Relations 58-; Cand. mem. C.P.S.U. Central Cttee. 61-; Deputy to Supreme Soviet of the U.S.S.R.; Order of Lenin, four Orders of the Red

Banner of Labour, Order of the Red Star, Order of the Patriotic War and other decorations.
State Committee for External Economic Relations, Ovchinnikovskaya naberezhnaya 18/1, Moscow, U.S.S.R.

Skak-Nielsen, Niels Verner, CAND. POL.; Danish diplomatist; b. 18 Feb. 1922; ed. Univ. of Copenhagen.
Joined Foreign Service 47; Econ. Secr. of Danish Govt. 49-51; Dep. Chief of Section, Ministry of Foreign Affairs 51-53; Sec., Del. to NATO 53-56; Chief of Section, Ministry of Foreign Affairs 56-59; Counsellor, Del. to OEEC 59-60; Minister and Perm. Rep. to EFTA and European Office of UN 60-66, Amb. 63-66; Asst. Under-Sec. of State for Econ. Affairs, Ministry of Foreign Affairs 66; Chief Statistician of Denmark 66-; mem. of Board of Chairmen of Econ. Council 67-.
Danmarks/Statistik, Frederiksholms Kanal 27, Copenhagen K, Denmark.
Telephone: 01-121675.

Skaug, Arne; Norwegian economist and diplomatist; b. 6 Nov. 1906; ed. Oslo Univ.
Econs. degree 30; with Central Bureau of Statistics 30-39; Univ. Fellowship in Economics 39; during the war served as Man. of Norwegian Social Insurance Scheme in New York, and then in Norwegian Ministry of Supply in London; Commercial Counsellor to Norwegian Embassy in Washington 44-46; Dir. Central Bureau of Statistics in Oslo 46-48; Under-Sec. of State in Foreign Ministry 48; permanent del. for Norway, with rank of Minister, later Ambassador, to OEEC in Paris 49-55; concurrently perm. rep. to NATO Council in Paris, with rank of Ambassador 53-55; Minister of Commerce and Shipping 55-62; Ambassador to the United Kingdom and the Repub. of Ireland 62-68, to Denmark 68-; G.C.V.O., Kt. Commdr. with Star of Order of St. Olav.
Royal Norwegian Embassy, Borgergade 16, Copenhagen, Denmark.

Skautrup, J. Peter A., DR. PHIL.; Danish university professor; b. 21 Jan. 1896; ed. Københavns Universitet.
Editor at Great Danish Dictionary 22-28; Tutor, Univ. of Århus 28-34, Prof. of Scandinavian Languages 34-66, Rector 32-34, 53-55; Commdr. Order of Dannebrog, Cross of Honour; several prizes; Hon. Dr. Phil. (Stockholm).
Publs. *Et Hardsysselmål* Vol. I 27-29, Vol. II 30, *Hardiske mål* Vol. I 30, Vol. II 42, *Den jyske Lov* 41, *Det danske sprogs historie* Vols. I-IV 44-68, *Jysk Sinnelaw. Antologi.* 50, *Bondesind* 50, *Arv og gæld i ordenes samfund* 58, *Jyske Lov* 64.
Stationsgade 23, Risskov, Denmark.
Telephone: Århus 179514.

Skazkin, Sergey Danilovich; Soviet scientist; b. 1890.
Docent, Moscow Univ. 20-31, Prof. 34-; mem. Acad. of Pedagogy, Acad. of R.S.F.S.R. 43-; mem. Acad. of Sciences of the U.S.S.R. 58-.
Academy of Sciences of the U.S.S.R., Leninsky Prospekt 14, Moscow, U.S.S.R.

Skeat, Theodore Cressy, B.A., F.B.A.; British papyrologist; b. 15 Feb. 1907; ed. Whitgift School, Christ's Coll., Cambridge, and British School of Archaeology, Athens.
Assistant Keeper, Dept. of Manuscripts, British Museum 31-48, Deputy Keeper 48-61, Keeper 61-; Cromer Greek Prize 32.
Publs. *Fragments of an Unknown Gospel* (with H. I. Bell) 35, *Scribes and Correctors of the Codex Sinaiticus* (with H. J. M. Milne) 38, *The Reigns of the Ptolemies* 54, *Papyri from Panopolis* 64.
63 Ashbourne Road, London W.5, England.
Telephone: 01-998-1246.

Skeen, Brig. Andrew, O.B.E.; Rhodesian politician and diplomatist; b. 3 Oct. 1906; ed. Wellington Coll. and Royal Mil. Coll., Sandhurst.
British Army Service 26-47; Pres. Manicaland Publicity Asscn.; mem. Rhodesian Forestry Comm., Rhodesian Tourist Board, Labour Conciliation Boards, Umtali Odzi Road Council, Vumba Town Planning Authority; Chair. Manicaland Div. Rhodesian Front Party; High Commr. for Rhodesia in London 65; mem. Rhodesian Parl. 66-.
Publ. *Prelude to Independence.*
Las Anod, Box 277, Umtali, Rhodesia.
Telephone: Umtali 2283-13.

Skibine, George; Russian-born American dancer and choreographer; b. 17 Jan. 1920; ed. Lycée Albert de Mun.
Joined Ballet Russe de Monte Carlo 38, Ballet Theater (New York) 40; Master Sergeant, U.S. Military Intelligence during Second World War; First Dancer and Choreographer, Ballets du Marquis de Cuevas 47-57; First Dancer and Choreographer, Paris Opera Ballet 57, Ballet Master and Dir. 58-; Artistic Dir. Rebekah Harkness Foundation and Dir. Harkness Ballet Co., New York 64-; Grand Prix de la Critique 58; Bronze Star (U.S.), Nisham Iftikar (Tunisia); married to Marjorie Tallchief, the American ballerina.
Ballets. Monte Carlo: *Tragedy in Verona*; Marquis de Cuevas: *Annabel Lee, Prisoner of the Caucasus, Achille, Ange Gris, Idylle, Pastorale*; Opéra Comique: *Concerto*; Paris Opera: *Daphnis and Chloe, Atlantide, La Péri*.
Office: Harkness Foundation, 15 E. 69th Street, New York, N.Y., U.S.A.; Home: 58 rue des Fontenelles, Sèvres (Seine-et-Oise), France.

Skilling, Hugh Hildreth, A.B., S.M., PH.D.; American professor of electrical engineering; b. 2 Sept. 1905; ed. Stanford Univ. and Mass. Inst. of Technology.
Construction Dept. Southern Calif. Edison Co., Los Angeles Calif. 27-29; Instr. to Prof., Electrical Engineering Faculty, Stanford Univ. 29, 31-; Dept. Head 41-64 (act. 41-45); act. Dean of Engineering 44-46; Lecturer on electric power transmission, Mass. Inst. of Technology 34; Dir. Electrical Engineering War Research, and Electrical Engineering War Training, Stanford Univ. 41-45; Scientific Observer, atomic bomb tests, Bikini Atoll 46; Visiting Lecturer in electrical engineering Cambridge Univ. 51-52, for Consejo Superior de Investigaciones Cientificas, Madrid 52, Univ. of Chile 57; Consultant Dartmouth Coll. and Univ. of Hawaii 58; mem. review team, Univ. of the Philippines 53, King's Coll., Cambridge 51-; Consultant, Univ. of Alaska 64, Univ. of Washington 66; visiting Prof. Electrical Eng., Cambridge Univ. 65; awarded Medal for Educ. Inst. of Electrical and Electronics Engineers, N.Y. 65.
Publs. *Transient Electric Currents* 37, *Fundamentals of Electric Waves* 42, *Prelude to Bikini* 47, *Exploring Electricity* 48, *Electric Transmission Lines* 51, *Electrical Engineering Circuits* 57, *A First Course in Electromechanics* 60, *Electromechanics* 62.
672 Mirada Road, Stanford, California, U.S.A.
Telephone: 323-5638.

Skinner, Burrhus Frederic, A.B., M.A., PH.D., SC.D., LITT.D.; American professor of psychology; b. 20 March 1904; ed. Hamilton Coll. and Harvard Univ.
With Nat. Research Council, Harvard 31-33; Jr. Fellow, Harvard 33-36; Instructor, Minnesota Univ. 36-37, Asst. Prof. 37-39, Assoc. Prof. 39-45 (war research 42-43); Prof. and Chair. Dept. of Psychology, Indiana Univ. 45-48; Prof., Harvard Univ. 48-57, Edgar Pierce Prof. 58-; Fellow American Psychological Asscn., American Philosophical Soc., Nat. Acad. of Sciences, American Acad. of Arts and Sciences, Swedish Psychological Soc., British Psychological Soc.; numerous honorary degrees.

Publs. *Behavior of Organisms* 38, *Walden Two* 48, *Science and Human Behavior* 53, *Verbal Behavior* 57, *Schedules of Reinforcement* 57 (with C. B. Ferster), *Cumulative Record* 59, 61, *Analysis of Behavior* (with James G. Holland) 61, *The Technology of Teaching* 67.
Office: Department of Psychology, Harvard University, William James Hall, 33 Kirkland Street, Cambridge; Home: 11 Old Dee Road, Cambridge, Mass. 02138, U.S.A.
Telephone: 864-0848 (Home).

Skinner, Cornelia Otis; American writer and actress; ed. Bryn Mawr Coll., Sorbonne, Paris.
Studied drama in Paris; played on American stage in *Candida*, *Lady Windermere's Fan*, *The Pleasure of His Company*, etc.; wrote and produced *The Wives of Henry VIII*, *The Empress Eugénie*, *The Loves of Charles II*, *Mansion on the Hudson*; dramatised and produced *Edna, His Wife*; Hon. degrees Temple, Clark, St. Lawrence, Rochester and New York Univs., Tufts, Mills and Hofstra Colls.
Publs. *Captain Fury* (play) 25, *Tiny Garments, Excuse It, Please!*, *Dithers and Jitters*, *Soap Behind the Ears*, *Our Hearts were Young and Gay* (with Emily Kimbrough) 42, *Family Circle* 48, *That's Me All Over* (omnibus) 48, *Nuts in May* 50, *Bottoms Up* 55, *The Ape in Me* 59, *Elegant Wits and Grand Horizontals* 63, *Madame Sarah* 67.
22 East 60th Street, New York City 22, N.Y., U.S.A.

Skjerdal, Karl; Norwegian international bank official; b. 12 July 1911; ed. Universitetet i Oslo.
Deputy Judge 39-41; Sec., Ministry of Supply 41-45; Chief of Section, Ministry of Supply and Reconstruction 45; Dir., Directorate for Industrial Supply, Ministry of Supply and Reconstruction 46-49; Dir. Directorate for Supply, Ministry of Commerce 50-51; Commercial Counsellor, Norwegian Embassy, Wash. 51-53; Alternate Dir., Int. Bank for Reconstruction and Devt. 52-53; Chief of Div., Ministry of Industries 53-55, Perm. Sec. Gen., 55-56; Exec. Dir., IBRD, Int. Finance Corpn., and Int. Devt. Asscn. Nov. 66-; mem. of Board of several Norwegian industrial companies.
International Bank for Reconstruction and Development, Washington, D.C. 20433, U.S.A.

Skládal, Josef; Czechoslovak physician and physiologist; b. 16 March 1898; ed. Prague and Paris Univs.
Former Assistant at the Medical Faculty, Univ. of Paris and Brno and Prague Physiological Insts.; Lecturer in Gen. and Experimental Pathology 36; Head of Chest Dept., Bulovka Hospital, Prague 37; Lectured Royal Society of Medicine and Physiological Society London 41, Paris 47, Moscow 57; titular mem. Int. Union against Tuberculosis; fmr. Ed. *Rozhledy v tuberkulose*; Chair. Czechoslovak Health Council in London during Second World War; Prof. of Clinical Physiology, Charles Univ. Prague 45-56, of Pathological Physiology 56-; Pres. Czechoslovak Pneumological and Phthisiological Soc. 46; special mem. Czech. Soc. of Sciences 51; mem. Scientific Council, Ministry of Health 53.
Publs. *The Pleuro-subpleural Zone* (Cambridge Univ. Press) 42, *Syndrome cortico-pleural, Quelques aspects nouveaux de l'exploration physique du poumon* 47.
Office: Institute of Clinical Physiology, Ke Karlovu 4, Prague 2; Home: Londýnská 20, Prague 2, Czechoslovakia.
Telephone: 250638 (Home).

Skobeltsyn, Dmitry Vladimirovich; Soviet nuclear and cosmic ray physicist; b. 24 Nov. 1892; ed. Petrograd Univ.
Worked at the Leningrad Polytechnic and Physico-Technical Inst., Moscow Univ.; mem. U.S.S.R. Acad. of Sciences 46-; Dir. of the Inst. of Physics of the Acad. of Sciences of the U.S.S.R. 51-; Chair. of the Cttee. for

the award of Int. Lenin Peace Prizes 50-; mem. Comm. for Foreign Affairs of the U.S.S.R. 54-; State prize-winner 51; awarded Order of Lenin (three times), Vavilov Gold Medal of the Acad. of Sciences of the U.S.S.R. 52, Order of Red Banner of Labour (twice); Mendeleyev Prize of Acad. of Sciences, U.S.S.R. 36.
Publs. *Research into Recoil Effect of Scattered Gamma Rays* 25, *Cosmic Rays* 27-29, 36, *Nature of Cosmic Radiation* 50, etc.
Academy of Sciences of the U.S.S.R., Leninsky prospekt 14, Moscow, U.S.S.R.

Skochilov, Anatoly Andrianovich; Soviet politician; b. 1912; ed. Gorki Agricultural Inst. and Higher Party School.
Member C.P.S.U. 40-; Agronomist 31-38; Soviet Army service 38-40; Official, State Security Service 40-44; Party Leader 44-54; Chair. Exec. Cttee. Arzamas Regional Soviet of Working People's Deputies 54-57; Minister of Agriculture, Tatar A.S.S.R. 57; Sec., then Second Sec., Tatar Regional Cttee. of C.P. 57-61; First Sec. Ulyanovsk Regional Cttee. of C.P. 61-; Candidate mem. Central Cttee. C.P.S.U. 61-66, mem. 66-; Deputy to U.S.S.R. Supreme Soviet; mem. Mandatory Cttee. Soviet of Union.
Ulyanovsk Regional Committee of Communist Party of U.S.S.R., Ulyanovsk, U.S.S.R.

Sköld, Per Edvin, B.A.; Swedish politician, economist and agriculturist; b. 25 May 1891; ed. Lund Univ.
Deputy 18-64; Under-Sec. of State in Ministry of Agriculture 24-26; mem. editorial staffs of various labour papers; Dir. Bank of Sweden 31-32 and 36; Min. of Agriculture 32-36, of Commerce 36-38, of Defence 38-45, of Agriculture 45-48, of Economic Co-ordination 48-49, of Finance 49-55; Chair. Board of Dirs. Bank of Sweden 57-64; Social-Democrat.
Box 3335, Höör (Summer); Strandvägen 27, Stockholm O (Winter), Sweden.
Telephone: 0413-50114 (Summer); 08-618350 (Winter).

Skouras, Spyros K.; American (b. Greece) cinema executive; b. 28 March 1893.
In U.S.A. 13-; organised chain of theatres, St. Louis; successively Gen. Man., Warner Bros. Circuit, Pres. Nat. Theatres Amusement Co., Pres. Chief Exec. Twentieth Century-Fox Film Corpn. 42-62, Chair. 62-; Chair. Admiralty Enterprises Inc., Skouras Lines Inc., Prudential Lines Inc.
Office: 444 W. 56th Street, New York City, N.Y.; Home: 2 Shore Road, Rye, New York, U.S.A.

Skov, Peter Elvig Nielsen; Danish railway executive; b. 6 Aug. 1904.
Joined Danish State Railways 20; Asst. Head Clerk, Controller of Traffic 26-42, Traffic Supt. 42-46, Chief of Office 46-54, District Man. 54-55, Gen. Man. Danish State Railways 55-; honours include Commdr. Order of Dannebrog.
Danish State Railways, Sølvgade 40, 1349 Copenhagen K, Denmark.
Telephone: 01-141227.

Skriabin, Konstantin Ivanovich; Soviet helminthologist; b. 78; ed. Yuriev Veterinary Inst.
Veterinary doctor in Central Asia 05-11; Prof. at the Don Veterinary Inst. 17-20, at the Moscow Veterinary Inst. 20-; Dir. of the Inst. of Helminthology of the U.S.S.R. 31-56; mem. U.S.S.R. Acad. of Sciences 39-; Head of the Helminthology Laboratory of the Acad. of Sciences of the U.S.S.R. 42-; formed the Comm. for the study of helmintho-fauna 22, reorganised as the Soc. of Helminthologists of the Acad. of Sciences of the U.S.S.R.; has led over 300 helminthological expeditions; Pres. of the Presidium of the Kirghiz branch of the Acad. of Sciences of the U.S.S.R. 43-52; mem. U.S.S.R. Acad. of Medical Sciences, All-Union Acad. of Agricultural Sciences; Foreign mem. Czecho-

slovak Acad. of Sciences; State prizewinner; awarded Mechnikov Gold Medal 49, Lenin Prize 57, Order of Lenin (five times), Hero of Socialist Labour.
Publs. *Foundations of Helminthology* 40, *Trematoda of Animals and Man* (22 vols.) 47-64, *Definition of Parazitic Hematod* 49-54, *Foundations of Nematodology* (13 vols.) 60-64, *Principles of Helminthology (Science and Practice) in U.S.S.R.* (2 vols.) 62, *Basic Veterinary Nematodology* (co-author) 64.
Laboratory of Helminthology of Acad. of Sciences of U.S.S.R., 33 Leninsky Prospekt, Moscow, U.S.S.R.

Skriabin, Vladimir Vladimirovich; Soviet politician; b. 1908; ed. Zaporozhe Machine Building Inst.
Member C.P.S.U. 28-; design engineer, Zaporozhe 35-40; Chair. Zaporozhe City Soviet of Workers Deputies 40; army service 41-46; Sec. Zaporozhe City Cttee. C.P. Ukraine, Chair. Zaporozhe City Exec. Cttee., then Second Sec. Zaporozhe Regional Cttee. C.P. Ukraine, Chair. Exec. Cttee. Zaporozhe Regional Soviet of Workers' Deputies 46-57; First Sec. Zaporozhe Regional Cttee. C.P. Ukraine 57-62; First Sec. Rostov Rural District Cttee. C.P.S.U. 62-64; on staff of Central Cttee. of Ukraine C.P. 64-; mem. Central Cttee. of C.P.S.U. 61-66; Deputy to Ukrainian and U.S.S.R. Supreme Soviets.
Central Committee of the Communist Party of the Ukrainian S.S.R., Kiev, Ukraine, U.S.S.R.

Skrowaczewski, Stanislaw; Polish composer and conductor; b. 3 Oct. 1923; ed. Lwow and Cracow.
Conductor, Wroclaw Philharmonic Orchestra 46-47; further composition studies with Nadia Boulanger and P. Klecki, Paris 47-49; Artistic Dir. and First Conductor, Silesian Philharmonic Orch. 49-54; First Conductor, Cracow Philharmonic Orch. 55-56; Dir. Nat. Philharmonic Orch., Warsaw 57-59; Musical Dir. Minneapolis Symphony Orch. 60-; tours in Europe, N. and S. America, Israel; State Prize, First Prize, Int. Conductor's Competition, Rome 56; D.H.L. h.c. (Hamline Univ., St. Paul, Minnesota) 63.
Compositions include Symphony for String Orchestra, three other symphonies, *Muzyka Noca* (Music by Night, suite of nocturnes), four string quartets, two overtures, *Cantique des Cantiques* (voice and orch.), *Prelude, Fugue, Post-Ludium* (orch.), opera, ballet, film and theatre music.
110 Northrop Auditorium, Minneapolis, Minn. 55455, U.S.A.

Skulkov, Igor Petrovich; Soviet politician; b. 1913; ed. Higher Party School.
Executive, *Komsomol* and Communist Party 32-42; Soviet Army 42-45; Sec. and Second Sec. Altai Territorial Cttee. of C.P.S.U. 45-51; on Staff Cen. Cttee. of C.P.S.U. 51-52, 64-65; First Sec. Ulyanovsk Regional Cttee. of C.P.S.U. 52-58; Chair. Soviet Control Comm. of R.S.F.S.R. Council of Ministers 58-59; First Sec. Udmurt Regional Cttee. of C.P.S.U. 59-64, Kostroma Regional Cttee. 65-; Alt. mem. Central Cttee. of C.P.S.U.; Deputy to Supreme Soviet of U.S.S.R.; mem. Cttee. for Trade and Municipal Services, Soviet of Union; several decorations.
Kostroma Regional Committee of C.P.S.U., Kostroma, U.S.S.R.

Skytte, Karl; Danish politician and farmer; b. 31 March 1908; ed. agricultural schools.
Member Cen. Cttee. Nat. Union of Radical Youth 29-43, Chair. 33-37; mem. Cen. Cttee. Radical Party (Det radikale Venstre) 33-; mem. Govt. Cttee. on Land Settlement 42-47; mem. of Parliament 47-; Minister of Agriculture 57-64; mem. Hillerslev Parish Council, Svendborg County Council; Chair. House of Parliament 68-.
Bregnehojgaard, pr. Hojrup, Denmark.

Slaoui, Driss; Moroccan politician and banker.
Minister of Commerce and Industry 59-61; Dir. of Royal Cabinet March 62; Minister of Public Works July 62-Jan. 63; Minister of Finance Jan. 63-64, of Nat. Economy and Agriculture Nov. 63-64; Gov. Banque du Maroc Aug. 64-; Minister of Justice 68-.
Ministry of Justice, Avenue Moulay Youssef, Rabat, Morocco.

Slater, John Clarke, PH.D.; American university professor; b. 22 Dec. 1900; ed. Univ. of Rochester and Harvard Univ.
Instructor, Asst. Prof. and Assoc. Prof. of Physics, Harvard 24-30; Prof. of Physics and Head of Dept., Mass. Inst. of Technology 30-51, Inst. Prof. 51-66; Graduate Research Prof. Univ. of Florida 64-; mem. Technical Staff, Bell Telephone Laboratories Inc. (on leave from M.I.T.) 43-44; mem. staff Brookhaven Nat. Laboratory (on leave from M.I.T.) 51-52.
Publs. *Introduction to Theoretical Physics* (with N. H. Frank) 33; *Introduction to Chemical Physics* 39, *Microwave Transmission* 42, *Mechanics,* and *Electromagnetism* (with N. H. Frank) 47, *Microwave Electronics* 50, *Quantum Theory of Matter* 51 (2nd edn. 68), *Modern Physics* 55, *Quantum Theory of Atomic Structure* I and II 60, *Quantum Theory of Molecules and Solids* I, II, III, 63, 65, 67.
Office: University of Florida, Gainesville, Fla.; Home: 623 S.W. 27th Street, Gainesville, Fla. 32601, U.S.A.
Telephone: 376-7449 (Home).

Slater, Joseph Elliott; American administrator; b. 17 Aug. 1922; ed. Univ. of California.
Naval Reserve Officer, Mil. Govt. Planning Officer, London and Paris 43-46; Officer of Econ. Directorate, Allied Control Comm. for Germany; Asst. U.S. Sec. of Allied Control Council Econ. and Financial Affairs 45-48; mem. UN Affairs Planning Staff, Dept. of State, Wash. 49; Sec.-Gen. Allied High Comm. for Germany, Bonn 49-52; Exec. Sec. Office of U.S. Special Rep. in Europe, U.S. Sec. to NATO and mem. U.S. Del. to OEEC 52; Chief Economist, Creole Petroleum Corpn., Caracas 54-57; Sec. to President's Comm. on Foreign Assistance 59; Assoc. Dir., Int. Affairs Program, Program Officer (Office of Int. Relations), Ford Foundation 61-67; Asst. Man. Dir., Devt. Loan Fund, and Deputy Asst. Sec. of State on Educ. and Cultural Affairs 60-62; Pres. Salk Inst. 68-; mem. Council on Foreign Relations, New York, Center for Inter-American Affairs, New York, Inst. for Strategic Studies, London, Int. Affairs Cttee. of Nat. Planning Asscn.; Hon. LL.D.
The Salk Institute, 10010 N. Torrey Pines Road, La Jolla, California 92037; Homes: 870 UN Plaza, New York City 10017; 2670 Hidden Valley Road, La Jolla, Calif. U.S.A.
Telephone: 714-453-4100.

Slattery, Rear-Admiral Sir Matthew Sausse, K.B.E., C.B., F.R.AE.S.; British company director; b. 12 May 1902; ed. Stonyhurst Coll., and R.N. Colls. of Osborne and Dartmouth.
Joined R.N. 16; Dir. of Air Material, Admiralty 39-41; in command H.M.S. *Cleopatra* and *Danae* 41-42; Dir.-Gen. Naval Aircraft Devt. and Production (Ministry of Aircraft Production) 41, and Chief Naval Rep. 43; Vice-Controller (Air) and Chief of Naval Air Equipment (Admiralty) and Chief Naval Rep. Supply Council (Ministry of Supply) 45-48; retd. from R.N. with war service rank of Rear Admiral 48; Man. Dir. Short Bros. & Harland Ltd. 48-52, Chair. and Man. Dir. 52-60; Chair. S.B. Realisations Ltd. 52-60, Bristol Aircraft Ltd. 57-60; Dir. Bristol Aeroplane Co. Ltd. 57-60; Special Adviser to Prime Minister on Transport of Middle East Oil 57-59; Chair. B.O.A.C. 60-63, B.O.A.C./Cunard 62-63; at present Chair. R. & W. Hawthorn,

Leslie & Co. Ltd., Hawthorn Leslie (Engineers) Ltd., Hawthorn Leslie (Shipbuilders) Ltd.; Dir. The Nat. Bank Ltd., B.T.R. Industries Ltd.; Chair. B.T.R. subsidiary Palmer Aero Products Ltd.; mem. Council Air Registration Board; Hon. D.Sc.
Harvey's Farm, Warninglid, Sussex, England.
Telephone: Warninglid 291.

Slavsky, Efim Pavlovich; Soviet politician; b. 1898; ed. Moscow Inst. of Non-Ferrous Metals and Gold.
Engineer, Workshop Man., Chief Engineer, Dir., Electrozinc Plant, Odjonikidze 38-40; Dir. Dnieper Aluminium Plant 40, Urals Plant 41-45; Deputy People's Commissar of Non-Ferrous Metallurgy 45-46; at staff of U.S.S.R. Council of Ministers 46-53; Deputy Minister, First Deputy Minister of Medium Machine Building 53-57, Minister 57-; mem. C.P.S.U. 18-; mem. C.P.S.U. Central Cttee. 61-; Deputy to U.S.S.R. Supreme Soviet; State Prize 51; Hero of Socialist Labour (thrice).
U.S.S.R. Ministry of Medium Machine Building, Moscow, U.S.S.R.

Slessor, Marshal of the Royal Air Force Sir John Cotesworth, G.C.B., D.S.O., M.C.; British officer; b. 3 June 1897; ed. Haileybury.
Served with Royal Flying Corps France, Egypt, Sudan 15-18; served India 21-22; R.A.F. Staff Coll. 24-25; Commd. No. 4 Squadron 25-28; Air Staff, Air Ministry 28-30; Instructor Staff Coll. Camberley 31-34; served India 35-37, Commd. No. 3 Indian Wing Quetta and N.F.W.P.; served Waziristan Operations 36-37; Dir. of Plans Air Min. 37-41; Air Officer Commanding No. 5 (Bomber) Group 41-42; Asst. Chief of Air Staff 42; Air Officer C.-in-C. Coastal Command 43-; C.-in-C. R.A.F. Mediterranean and Middle East and Deputy to Allied Air C.-in-C. 44-45, Air Member for Personnel 45-47; Commandant Imperial Defence Coll. 48-49; Chief Air Staff Jan. 50-52; Vice-Pres. Inst. of Strategic Studies, British Atlantic Cttee., Anglo-German Soc.; mem. English-Speaking Union, R.A.F. Benevolent Fund.
Publs. *Air Power and Armies* 36, *Strategy for the West* 54, *The Central Blue* 56, *The Great Deterrent* 57, *What Price Co-existence* 62.
Rimpton Manor, Yeovil, Somerset, England.

Slessor, Kenneth, O.B.E.; Australian writer; b. 27 March 1901; ed. Sydney C.E.G.S.
Editor *Smith's Weekly* 38; Literary Editor *Sydney Sun* 44; War Corresp. 40-44; Leader-writer *Sydney Daily Telegraph* 57-; mem. Advisory Board Australian Commonwealth Literary Fund, Nat. Literature Board of Review.
Publs. *Thief of the Moon* 24, *Earth Visitors* 26, *Darlinghurst Nights* 31, *Cuckooz Country* 32, *Five Bells* 39, *One Hundred Poems* 44 (reprinted 47), *Poems* 57, Co-Editor *Penguin Book of Modern Australian Verse* 58.
c/o *Sydney Daily Telegraph*, 168 Castlereagh Street, Sydney, N.S.W.; Home: 712 Pacific Highway, Chatswood, Sydney, N.S.W., Australia.

Slim, 1st Viscount, cr. 60, of Yarralumla in the Capital Territory of Australia and of Bishopston in the City and County of Bristol; **Field Marshal William Joseph Slim,** K.G., G.C.B., G.C.M.G., G.C.V.O., G.B.E., D.S.O., M.C.; British army officer; b. 6 Aug. 1891; ed. King Edward's School, Birmingham.
Served First World War in Gallipoli, France, Mesopotamia (twice wounded, M.C.) 14-18; Instructor Staff Coll. Camberley 34-36; Imperial Defence Coll.; Commandant 7th Gurkha Rifles 37, and Senior Officers' School India 39; commanded 10th Indian Infantry Brigade (Sudan, Eritrea, wounded) 39-41; 10th Indian Div. (Iraq, Syria, Persia) 41; 1st Burma Corps 42, 15th Indian Corps 42, Fourteenth Army 43-45; C.-in-C. Allied Land Forces South-East Asia 45; Commandant Imperial Defence Coll. 46-Dec. 47; Deputy Chair. Railway Exec. 47-48; C.I.G.S. 48-52; Gov.-Gen. of

Australia 53-60; Dir., London Assurance Ltd.; Chair. British Australian Investment Trust Ltd., British Home Entertainment Ltd.; Pres. Dalgety and N.Z. Loan Ltd.; Hon. LL.D. (Cambridge, Leeds, Birmingham, Sydney, Adelaide, Melbourne, Lancaster); Hon. D.C.L. (Oxford); Hon. D.Litt. (New England); Hon. D.Sc. (N.S.W.); Hon. F.R.A.C.P., Hon. F.R.C.S. (Edin.); Governor and Constable of Windsor Castle 64-.
Publs. *Defeat into Victory, Courage and other Broadcasts, Unofficial History.*
6/8 Tokenhouse Yard, London, E.C.2; and Norman Tower, Windsor Castle, Berks., England.
Telephone: Windsor 63106.

Slim, Mongi; Tunisian diplomatist and politician; b. 15 Sept. 1908; ed. Tunis, Lycée Saint-Louis de Paris and Université de Paris.
Mem. Bureau Politique of Néo-Destour Party (Tunisian Liberal Constitutional Party) 36-. Dir. 45-; Minister of State conducting negotiations for Tunisian self-government 55-56; Minister of Interior 55-56, of State 56; Ambassador to U.S.A. and Canada 56-61; fmr. Permanent Del. to UN; Pres. Gen. Assembly of UN 61-62; Sec. of State for Foreign Affairs, Tunisia 62-64; Sec. of State, Personal Rep. of the Pres. Nov. 64-66; Sec. of State for Justice Sept. 66-.
Secrétariat d'Etat à la Justice, Place du Gouvernement, Tunis, Tunisia.

Slim, Taieb; Tunisian politician and diplomatist; b. 14; ed. Tunis Lycée and Univ. of Paris.
Member Néo-Destour Party, detained 41-43; Arab Maghreb Bureau, Cairo 46-49; Head, Tunisian Office, Cairo 49, established Tunisian offices, New Delhi, Djakarta, Karachi; Head, Foreign Affairs, Presidency of Council of Ministers 55-56; Ambassador to U.K. 56-62; Perm. Rep. to UN 62-67; Sec. of State, Personal Rep. of Pres. 67-.
c/o Office of the President, Tunis, Tunisia.

Slipyj-Kobernyckyj-Dyckowskyj, H.E. Cardinal Joyfs; Vatican ecclesiastic; b. 17 Feb. 1892.
Ordained 17; Titular Archbishop of Serre 39; Archbishop of Lviv, Metropolitan of Halyč, Major Archbishop of Ukraine 44; arrested and deported to Siberia 45, released to Vatican City 63; mem. Sacred Congregation of the Eastern Church; mem. Comm. De Ecclesiis Orientalibus, Ecumenical Council; Cardinal 65.
Palazzina Dell'Arciprete, Vatican City, Rome, Italy.

Śliwiński, Zdzisław; Polish theatre and music executive; b. 20 July 1910; ed. High School, Lwów, and Higher Coll. of Commerce, Warsaw.
Head of Section in Dept. of Music, Ministry of Art and Culture 45-46; Vice-Dir. Polish Music Publication, Cracow 46-47; Dir.-Gen. Poznań Philharmonic Orchestra 46-58, Nat. Philharmonic Orchestra, Warsaw 58-; Dir.-Gen. of Grand Opera House (Teatr Wielki), Warsaw Jan. 65-Oct. 66; mem. Organizing Cttee. of Int. Chopin Competition 49-, Presidium of "Autumn in Warsaw" Int. Festivals of Contemporary Music 58-; Pres. Organizing Cttee. Int. Henryk Wieniawski Violin Competition, Poznań 52, 57; Gold Cross of Merit; Knight Order of Polonia Restituta.
National Philharmonic House, Jasna 5, Warsaw, Poland.
Telephone: 26-56-17.

Slonimski, Antoni; Polish writer; b. 95; ed. Warsaw.
Counsellor, Head of Section of Letters, UNESCO Prep. Comm.; Dir. Polish Cultural Inst., London 49-51; returned Poland 51; Chair. Polish Writers' Union 56-59.
Publs. include poems *Harmonja, Sonety, Parada, Godzina Poezji, Okno bez krat, Alarm*; plays *Rodzina, Murzyn Warszawski, Wieza Babel, Lekarz Bezdomny*; vol. articles *Walki nad Bzdura, Heretyk na ambonie, Moja Podróz d Rosji.*
Al. Róz 6, Warsaw, Poland.

Slyussarenko, Petr Konstantinovich; Soviet diplomatist; b. 1912.
Diplomatic service 39-; fmr. First Sec. Netherlands; fmr. Counsellor, Democratic Republic of Viet-Nam; Minister Counsellor, Cairo 61-64; Ambassador to Jordan 64-.
U.S.S.R. Embassy, Amman, Jordan.

Small, Charles John; Canadian economist; b. 19 Dec. 1919; ed. Ontario Agricultural Coll. and Univ. of Toronto.
Royal Canadian Navy serving in North Atlantic, Mediterranean, Normandy and Australia; mem. Dept. of Trade and Commerce 49, serving in The Hague 50-55; Dept. of External Affairs studying Chinese Language at Univ. of Toronto; seconded to Dept. of Trade and Commerce and apptd. Canadian Govt. Trade Commr. Hong Kong 58; Counsellor, Canadian High Commission, Karachi; Perm. Rep. of Canada to Org. for Econ. Co-operation and Devt. Aug. 65-.
Organization for Economic Co-operation and Development, 2 rue André-Pascal, Paris 16e, France.
Telephone: TRO. 32-20.

Smallpeice, Sir Basil, K.C.V.O., F.C.A., B.COM.; British businessman; b. 18 Sept. 1906.
With Bullimore and Co., chartered accountants 25-30; Accountant, Hoover Ltd. 30-37; Chief Accountant and Sec., Doulton & Co. 37-48; Dir. of Costs and Statistics, British Transport Comm. 48-50; Financial Comptroller, British Overseas Airways Corpn. 50, mem. of Board 53, Deputy Chief Exec. 54, Managing Dir. 56-63; Dir. Cunard Steamship Co. and White Star Line 64-, Chair. 65-; Admin. Adviser, Queen's Household 64-; mem. Cttee. for Exports to U.S.A. 64-66; Dir. Charterhouse Group 65-; Dir. Martins Bank 65-; Chair. English-Speaking Union of the Commonwealth 65-.
The Cunard Steam-Ship Co. Ltd., Cunard Building, 15 Lower Regent Street, London, S.W.1, England.
Telephone: 01-930-7890.

Smallwood, Joseph R., D.C.L., LL.D.; Canadian politician; b. 24 Dec. 1900; ed. Bishop Field Coll., St. John's.
Journalist and author; launched and led movement to make Newfoundland a province of Canada; Premier of Newfoundland 49-, concurrently Minister of Economic Development 56-; Liberal.
Canada House, St. John's, Newfoundland, Canada.

Smart, William Marshall, M.A., D.SC., F.R.A.S.; British astronomer; b. 9 March 1909; ed. Glasgow and Cambridge Univs.
Thomson Lecturer, Aberdeen Univ. 34; fmr. John Couch Adams Astronomer, Chief Asst. in the Observatory and Lecturer in Mathematics, Cambridge Univ.; Sec. Royal Astronomical Society 31-37, Vice-Pres. 37-38, 51-53, Pres. 49-51; Regius Prof. of Astronomy Glasgow Univ. 37-59; Dean, Faculty of Science 46-49; Halley Lecturer Oxford 41; Vice-Pres. Royal Society of Edinburgh 51-53; Lorimer Medal of Edinburgh Astronomical Soc. 58; Hon. LL.D.
Publs. *Admiralty Manual of Navigation* (in co-operation), *The Sun, the Stars and the Universe, Spherical Astronomy, Astrophysics, Astronomy, Stellar Dynamics, Foundations of Astronomy, Introduction to Sea and Air Navigation, Astronomical Navigation, Handbook of Sea Navigation, John Couch Adams and the Discovery of Neptune, Some Famous Stars, The Origin of the Earth, Celestial Mechanics, Foundations of Analytical Geometry, Combinations of Observations, Stellar Kinematics.*
Westbourne House, Westbourne Road, Lancaster, England.
Telephone: Lancaster 64742.

Smathers, George A.; American lawyer and politician; b. 4 Nov. 1913; ed. Univ. of Florida.
Practising lawyer 38-; served U.S. Marine Corps 42-45;

mem. House of Reps. (Democrat, Florida) 46-50, U.S. Senator from Florida 50-; mem. Board Junior Chamber of Commerce.
Senate Office Building, Washington 25, D.C., U.S.A.

Smedley, Harold, C.M.G., M.B.E.; British diplomatist; b. 19 June 1920; ed. Aldenham School and Pembroke Coll., Cambridge.
Royal Marine Commandos, Second World War; Dominions Office 46, British High Commission in New Zealand 48-50, S. Rhodesia 51-53, India 57-60; Private Sec. to Commonwealth Sec. 54-57; later Head of News Dept., Commonwealth Relations Office; High Commr. in Ghana 64-65 and 66-67; Amb. to Laos 67-.
Sherwood, Oak End Way, Woodham, Weybridge, Surrey, England.

Smedt, Rt. Rev. Bishop Aemilius Josephus de, D.PHIL., D.THEOL.; Belgian ecclesiastic; b. 30 Oct. 1909; ed. Univ. Gregorianum, Rome.
Auxiliary Bishop, Malines 50; Bishop of Bruges 52-; Vice-Pres. Secretariat for Christian Unity, Rome; Knight, Order of Leopold.
Publs. *Le Mariage, Le grand Mystère, Le Christ dans le Quartier, Le Sacerdoce des Fidèles, L'Amour Conjugal, Pour un dialogue "Parents-Adolescents", Pour un Climat de Liberté.*
4 H. Geeststraat, Bruges, Belgium.

Smelyakov, Nikolai Nikolayevich; Soviet foreign trade official; b. 1911; ed. Moscow Engineering Inst.
Member C.P.S.U. 38-; engineering 34-55; Minister of Engineering 56-57; Chair. Gorki Econ. Council 57-58; First Sec. Gorki Regional Cttee. of C.P. 58-59; Chair. "Amtorg" Joint-Stock Soc. in U.S.A. 59; Deputy Minister of Foreign Trade 59; Order of Red Banner of Labour (thrice), Order of Red Star, Honour Badge.
U.S.S.R. Ministry of Foreign Trade, 32-34 Smolenskaya-Sennaya Square, Moscow, U.S.S.R.

Smemo, Rt. Rev. Johannes, B.A., B.D., D.D.; Norwegian bishop; b. 31 July 1898.
Chaplain in Drammen 25; Vicar of Sor-Fron 33; Pres. Practical Theological Seminary of Church Coll., Oslo 34; Bishop of Agder 46-51, Bishop of Oslo 51-68.
Publs. *Kjaerligheten hos troens apostel* 26, *Er prekenens tid forbi?* 38, *Livet ovenfra* 40, *Guds Ja* 54, *Salmer fra Søsterkirker* 64, *Gamle samler og nye* 65, *Ung Sang* 67.
St. Halvards pl. 3, Oslo, Norway.

Smetáček, Václav, PH.D.; Czechoslovak conductor and professor of music; b. 30 Sept. 1906; ed. Acad. of Music, Prague and Charles Univ., Prague.
Founder and Oboist Prague Wind Quintet 28-56; Conductor Prague Hlahol Singing Choir 34-46, Prague Broadcasting Corpn. 34-43; Artistic Dir. and First Conductor Prague Symphony Orchestra 43-; Prof. Prague Conservatoire 45-67; has conducted orchestras in all continents of the world; numerous recordings for Suprafon, Deutsche Grammophongesellschaft and Musica Sacra; Officer Order Polonia Restituta; Honoured Artist of Czechoslovakia; Prize of the City of Prague, Order of Labour 66.
Major works: *Ballet on the Eve of a Summer Day, Vivat Olympia* (Solemn March), *Wedding March* and several Wind Quintets.
Klidná 6, Prague 6, Czechoslovakia.
Telephone: 350-592.

Smirnov, Alexander Ivanovich; Soviet politician; b. 1912; ed. Agricultural Technical School, Gorki Agricultural Inst. and Higher Party School.
Member C.P.S.U. 37-; Agronomist 31-37; Chief Zootechnician, Deputy Chief, Gorki Regional Land Section 37-43; Sec. Gorki Regional Cttee. of C.P. 43; Official, Central Cttee. C.P.S.U. 43-47, 48-53; Second Sec. Chita Regional Cttee. of C.P. 53-55; Chair. Exec. Cttee. Chita Regional Soviet of Working People's Deputies 55-61;

First Sec. Chita Regional Cttee. of C.P. 61-; Candidate mem. Central Cttee. C.P.S.U. 61-; Deputy to U.S.S.R. Supreme Soviet; mem. Cttee. of Legislative Proposals. Chita Regional Committee of Communist Party of U.S.S.R., Chita, U.S.S.R.

Smirnov, Andrei Andreyevich; Soviet diplomatist; b. 1905; ed. Leningrad Planning Inst.
Joined Diplomatic Service 36; served in Germany 40-41; Amb. to Iran 41-43; at U.S.S.R. Ministry of Foreign Affairs 43-46; Deputy Minister of Foreign Affairs of R.S.F.S.R. 46-49; Amb. to Austria 56-57, to German Fed. Repub. 57-66, to Turkey 66-.
U.S.S.R. Embassy, Ankara, Turkey.

Smirnov, Leonid Vasilievich; Soviet politician; b. 16; ed. Novocherkassy Industrial Inst.
Engineer, Foreman, Head of Electrical Dept., Factory Dir. 39-61; Deputy Chair., later Chair. State Cttee. for Defence Equipment, U.S.S.R. Ministry of Defence 61-63; mem. Central Cttee. of C.P.S.U. 61-; Dep. Chair. Council of Ministers 63-; Deputy to U.S.S.R. Supreme Soviet; Hero of Socialist Labour 61, Lenin Prize 60.
Council of Ministers, Moscow, U.S.S.R.

Smirnov, Vladimir Ivanovich; Soviet geologist; b. 31 Jan. 1910; ed. Moscow Inst. of Exploration Geology.
Post-graduate Student and Asst., Moscow Inst. of Exploration Geology 34-39, Reader and Dean of Geology Faculty 39-41; Chief Geologist, Cinnabar Mines, Cen. Asia 41-44; Reader and Dir. of Research Activities, Moscow Inst. of Exploration Geology 44-46; Vice-Minister of Geology, U.S.S.R. 46-51; Prof. and Head, Dept. of Econ. Geology, Moscow State Univ. 51-; Academician, mem. Bureau, Section of Earth Sciences, U.S.S.R. Acad. of Sciences 58-; Vice-Pres. Int. Asscn. on the Genesis Ore Deposits 64; Order of Lenin.
Publs. *Ore Deposits of Central Asia* 37, *Types of the Hydrothermal Ore Deposits Connected with the Magmatic Differentiation at Tian Shan* 44, *Geology of the Cinnabar Deposits* 47, *Estimation of Ore Reserves* 50, *Geological Basis of Prospecting and Exploration of Ore Deposits* 54, *Six Types of Primary Zoning in Hydrothermal Ore Deposits* 57, *Convergence of Pyritic Ore Deposits* 60, *Metallogenesis in Geosynclines* 62, *Outlines of Metallogenesis* 63, *Geology of Economic Minerals* 65.
Geology Faculty, Moscow State University, Lenin Hills, Moscow, U.S.S.R.

Smirnov, Vladimir Ivanovich; Soviet mathematician; b. 87; ed. Petersburg Univ.
Research devoted to the theory of the functions of the complex variable and to mathematical physics; Prof. at Petersburg Univ. 15; at the Insts. of Seismology and Mathematics of the Acad. of Sciences of the U.S.S.R. 29-35; mem. Acad. of Sciences of the U.S.S.R. 43-; State prizewinner 48; awarded Order of Lenin (thrice); Hero of Socialist Labour.
Publs. *Higher Mathematics Course* (6 vols.) 24-57, *Sur les formules de Cauchy et de Green* 32, *Solving Limited Problems of the Theory of Elasticity in the Case of Circle and Sphere* 37, *On Conjugate Functions in Manifold Euclidian Space* 57, *Constructure Theory of Functions of Complex Variable Value* 64, etc.
c/o University of Leningrad, Leningrad, U.S.S.R.

Smirnovsky, Mikhail Nikolayevich; Soviet engineer and diplomatist; b. 7 Aug. 1921; ed. secondary school, Kalinin, and Moscow Aviation Inst.
Former engineer, Moscow; Diplomatic Service 48-; joined staff of U.S.S.R. Representation in Far East Comm. 49; later Third and First Sec., Washington; Asst., later Deputy Head, U.S. Dept., Ministry of Foreign Affairs 55-58; Counsellor, later Counsellor-Minister, Washington 58-62; Head of U.S. Dept., Ministry of Foreign Affairs, and mem. Collegium of Ministry of Foreign Affairs 62-66; Ambassador to U.K.

66-, and to Malta 67-; mem. Central Auditing Comm. of C.P.S.U. 66-; numerous awards.
U.S.S.R. Embassy, 13 Kensington Palace Gardens, London, W.8, England.

Smith, Arnold Cantwell, B.A., D.C.L., LL.D.; Canadian diplomatist; b. 18 Jan. 1915; ed. Upper Canada Coll., Toronto, Lycée Champoléon, Grenoble, Univs. of Toronto, Oxford (Christ Church) and Gray's Inn, London.
Journalist and univ. lecturer; diplomatic service 39-, Tallinn 39-40, Cairo 40-43, Moscow 43-45, Brussels 50-53; mem. Del. to UN 47, 49, 51, 54; Alt. Rep. UN Security Council and Atomic Energy Comm. and Senior Adviser to Perm. Del. 49-50; Int. Truce Commr. Cambodia 55-56; Minister to U.K. 56-58; Ambassador to U.A.R. 58-61, to U.S.S.R. 61-63; Asst. Under-Sec. of State for External Affairs 63-65; apptd. first Sec.-Gen. of the Commonwealth June 65-.
Commonwealth Secretariat, Marlborough House, London, S.W.1; Home: 5 Carlton Gardens, London, S.W.1, England.

Smith, Bromley Keables; American government official; b. 21 April 1911; ed. Leland Stanford Univ.
Newspaper reporter 35-38, News Editor 38-40; entered Foreign Service 40; Vice-Consul Montreal 40; Third Sec. La Paz 41-45; Office of Sec. of State 45-48; Special Asst. to Asst. Sec. of State 49, to Sec. of State 50; Senior mem. Nat. Security Council Special Staff 53-58; Exec. Officer, Operations Co-ordinating Board 59-61; Exec. Sec. Nat. Security Council 61-.
Office: National Security Council, The White House, Washington, D.C.; Home: 2328 Massachusetts Avenue, N.W., Washington, D.C., U.S.A.

Smith, Cyril, F.R.C.M.; British concert pianist; b. 11 Aug. 1909; ed. Middlesbrough High School and Royal Coll. of Music, London.
Prof. Royal Coll. of Music 34-; played at Promenade Concert, Queen's Hall, London 29; first broadcast 29; toured Scandinavia and Central Europe 37 and has since appeared in most European countries and in India, Ceylon, Middle East and Bermuda; mem. British musical del. to U.S.S.R. 56; Royal Concert, played on two pianos, three hands, with Phyllis Sellick 58; toured New Zealand (with Phyllis Sellick) 65; mem. Jury, Munich Int. Piano Competition Sept. 65, Sept. 67; Hon. R.A.M. 61.
Publ. *Duet for Three Hands* 58.
Oak Lodge, 33 Fife Road, East Sheen, London, S.W.14, England.
Telephone: 01-876-5143.

Smith, Cyril Stanley, D.SC., D.LITT.; British-born American metallurgist and historian of technology; b. 4 Oct. 1903; ed. Univ. of Birmingham and Mass. Inst. of Technology.
Research Assoc. Mass. Inst. of Technology 26-27; Research Metallurgist American Brass Co. 27-42; Research Supervisor Nat. Defense Research Cttee. 42-43; Assoc. Div. Leader (Metallurgy) Los Alamos Scientific Laboratory 43-46; Dir. Inst. for the Study of Metals, Chicago Univ. 46-57, Prof. of Metallurgy 46-61; Inst. Prof. Mass. Inst. of Technology 61-; mem. Gen. Advisory Cttee., U.S. Atomic Energy Comm. 46-52; mem. Materials Advisory Board 54-56, President's Science Advisory Cttee. 59, Cttee. on Science and Public Policy of Nat. Acad. of Sciences 65-67; Visiting Fellow, St. Catherine's Coll. Oxford 68; Pres. Soc. for the History of Technology 63-64; mem. American Philosophical Soc., Nat. Acad. of Sciences; Medal of Merit 46, Clamer Medal (Franklin Inst.) 52, American Soc. of Metals Gold Medal 62, American Inst. Mining and Metallurgical Engineers Douglas Medal 63; naturalized U.S. citizen 40-.
Publs. *A History of Metallography* 60, *Sources for the*

History of the Science of Steel; translations (in collaboration) of *Pirotechnia* (Biringuccio) 42, 59, 66, *Treatise on Ores and Assaying* (Lazarus Ercker) 51, *On Divers Arts* (Theophilus) 63; Editor *Sorby Centennial Symposium on the History of Metallurgy* 65.
Department of Humanities, Massachusetts Institute of Technology, Cambridge, Mass. 02139, U.S.A.

Smith, Cyrus R.; American airline executive; b. 9 Sept. 1899; ed. Univ. of Texas.
Public Accountant, Peat, Marwick Mitchell and Co. 21-26; Asst. Treas. Texas-Louisiana Power Co., Fort Worth 26-28; Vice-Pres. Texas Air Transport Inc., Fort Worth 29-30; Vice-Pres. American Airlines Inc. 34-42; U.S. Army Air Force, rising to Maj.-Gen. 42-45; Pres. American Airlines Inc. until 64, Chair. and Chief Exec. 64-68; U.S. Sec. of Commerce 68-; D.S.M., Legion of Merit, Hon. C.B.E. (U.K.).
Home: 510 Park Avenue, New York City, N.Y., U.S.A.

Smith, Dodie, (Mrs. Alec Beesley); (*pseudonym* C. L. Anthony); British dramatist and novelist; ed. St. Paul's School for Girls and Royal Acad. of Dramatic Art.
Fmr. actress; buyer at Heal and Son until 31.
Plays: As C. L. Anthony: *Autumn Crocus* 31, *Service* 32, *Touch Wood* 34; As Dodie Smith: *Call It a Day* 35, *Bonnet Over the Windmill* 37, *Dear Octopus* 38, *Lovers and Friends* 43, *Letter from Paris* 52, *I Capture the Castle* 54, *These People—Those Books* 58; Novels: *I Capture the Castle* 48, *The Hundred and One Dalmatians* 56, *The New Moon with the Old* 63, *The Town in Bloom* 65, *It Ends with Revelations* 67, *The Starlight Barking* 67.
The Barretts, Finchingfield, Essex, England.
Telephone: Great Bardfield 260.

Smith, George Ivan, M.A.; Australian United Nations administrator; b. 15; ed. Sydney Univ.
Editor of Talks, Australian Broadcasting Comm. 37-39; Dir. Australian Short-Wave Service 39-41; Dir. BBC Pacific Service 41-45; Int. Affairs Films 45-47; UN Information Services, Lake Success 47-49; UN Dir. Information Centre, London 49-58; Dir. External Relations, UN, New York; Sen. Dir. of Public Information, UN 61-62; UN Rep. Katanga 61-62; Personal Rep. of UN Sec.-Gen. in East and Central Africa; Regional Dir. UN Technical Assistance Programmes in Central Africa; Visiting Prof. Princeton Univ. and Fletcher School of Law and Diplomacy Boston (on special leave from UN) 66-68; Dir. UN Office, London 68-.
97 Cadogan Gardens, London, S.W.3, England.

Smith, Howard Kingsbury, B.A.; American journalist; b. 12 May 1914; ed. Tulane Univ., New Orleans, Heidelberg Summer School, and Oxford Univ.
Reported for *New Orleans Item* 36-39; in United Press, London then Berlin 39-41; Columbia Broadcasting System (Berlin, Berne, 9th U.S. Army, Germany, and finally as Chief European Corresp. in London 46-57) 41-59; C.B.S. Washington Corresp. 57-61; News Commentator, American Broadcasting Co. (A.B.C.), Wash. 62-; Hon. LL.D. (Tulane, Roosevelt Univs.), D.Litt. (St. Norbert's Coll.), Dr. of Humane Letters (Alfred Univ. and Thiel Coll.); recipient of many awards for radio and television, including Overseas Press Award for best radio and TV reporting from abroad 52, 53, 54 and 55, George Polk Memorial and Emmy awards for documentary "The Population Explosion", and *Radio-TV Daily* award as Commentator of the Year 60, Overseas Press Award, best radio interpretation of foreign affairs 61, Du Pont award 56, 63.
Publs. *Last Train from Berlin* 42, *The State of Europe* 49, *Washington D.C.* 67.
Office: American Broadcasting Co., 1124 Connecticut Avenue, Washington, D.C.; Home: 6450 Brooks Lane, Washington, D.C. 20016, U.S.A.
Telephone: 301-OL6-3634.

Smith, Ian Douglas; Rhodesian politician; b. 8 April 1919; ed. Chaplin School, Gwelo, Rhodesia and Rhodes Univ., Grahamstown, S. Africa.
Royal Air Force 41-46; farmer; mem. S. Rhodesia Legislative Assembly 48-53, 62-, Parl. of Fed. of Rhodesia and Nyasaland 53-61; fmr. Chief Whip United Fed. Party; foundation mem. and Vice-Pres. Rhodesian Front 62, Pres. 64-; Deputy Prime Minister and Minister of Treasury S. Rhodesia Dec. 62-April 64; Prime Minister of Rhodesia April 64-.
Office of the Prime Minister, Salisbury, Rhodesia.

Smith, Maj.-Gen. James Desmond Blaise, C.B.E., D.S.O., C.D.; Canadian army officer; b. 7 Oct. 1911; ed. Univ. of Ottawa, Royal Military Coll., Canada, Staff Coll., Camberley, Imperial Defence Coll.
Joined Royal Canadian Dragoons 33; served Defence H.Q. Ottawa and 1st Infantry Div. 40; War Course, Staff Coll. Camberley 40; Directing Staff, first Canadian Army Staff Course 40-41; Brigade Major 41-42; C.O. Royal Canadian Dragoons 42; G.S.O. I, 5th Armoured Div. 42-43; Commanded 4th Armoured Brigade 43-44, 5th Gen. Staff, 1st Canadian Corps, Italy 44; Commdr. 1st Canadian Infantry Div. 44-45; Commdt. Royal Mil. Coll. 45-46; Hon. A.D.C. to the Gov.-Gen. 46; I.D.C. 46-47; Sec. Chiefs of Staff Cttee. and Mil. Sec. Cabinet Defence Cttee. 48-50; Quartermaster Gen. 50-51; Chair. Joint Staff, Canadian Mil. Rep. at SHAPE and Permanent Canadian Rep. to NATO Council 51-54; Commandant, Nat. Defence Coll., Canada 54-58; Adjutant-Gen. 58-62; Col., H.M. Regiment of Canadian Guards 61-66; Man. Dir. Pillar Eng. Ltd.; Dir. Pillar Holdings Ltd., Peak Eng. Co. Ltd., Air Engine Services Ltd., and numerous other cos.; Légion d'Honneur, Croix de Guerre, Legion of Merit (U.S.A.), Italian, Greek and Canadian decorations.
20 Eaton Place, Belgravia, London, S.W.1, England.
Telephone: 01-235-4453.

Smith, John F., Jr.; American business executive; b. 3 July 1908; ed. Tilden Technical High School, Chicago.
Apprentice mechanic, Illinois Bell Telephone Co. 28; clerk, Indiana Harbor steel plant, Inland Steel Co. 29-30, Order Div., H.Q., Chicago 30-32, 33-37, Asst. Man. 37-40, Man. 40; Inland Contact between War Production Bd. and Production Directive Cttee. 41-45; Asst. Man. Sheet and Strip Sales, Inland Steel Co. 46-48, Gen. Man. 48-51, Vice-Pres. (Sales) 52-59, Dir. 56-, mem. Finance Cttee. 59-, Pres. 59-66, Asst. to Chair. 66-; served Nat. Production Authority 51-52; official of numerous business and philanthropic orgs.
Inland Steel Company, 30 West Monroe Street, Chicago 3, U.S.A.

Smith, Lloyd Bruce; American business executive; b. 13 Oct. 1920; ed. Sheffield Science School, Yale.
With A. O. Smith Corpn., Milwaukee 42-, successively Vice-Pres., Dir., Asst. to Pres., Pres., Chair. and Chief Exec. Officer 67-; Chair., A. O. Smith of Texas; Dir. A. O. Smith Harvestore Products Inc.; mem. Business Council 60-; Board of Dirs. YMCA; Trustee Milwaukee Univ. School; Dir. First Wisconsin Nat. Bank of Milwaukee, Goodyear Tyre and Rubber Co.
A. O. Smith Corporation, P.O. Box 584, Milwaukee 1, Wisconsin 53201, U.S.A.

Smith, Margaret Chase; American politician; b. 14 Dec. 1897; ed. Skowhegan High School.
Began career as teacher; with *Independent Reporter* 19-28, Daniel E. Cummings Co. 28-30; Treasurer, New England Process Co. 28-30; mem. House of Reps. 40-48; Senator from Maine 48-; mem. Senate Appropriations, Armed Services, and Aeronautical and Space Sciences Cttees.; Republican.
Norridgewock Avenue, Skowhegan, Maine, U.S.A.

Smith, Robert Paterson; British oil executive; b. 29 Jan. 1903; ed. The Ewart, Newton Stewart.
Qualified as chartered accountant 25; joined Asiatic Petroleum Co., Calcutta 26; with Burmah-Shell, India 28-52; joined Burmah Oil Co. Ltd., London 52, mem. Board of Dirs. 55-56, Asst. Man. Dir. 56-57, Man. Dir. 57-, Chair. 65-.
Christmas Place, Edenbridge, Kent, England.

Smith, Sylvester Richard; American government official; b. 30 Aug. 1906; ed. State Univ. of Montana and Univ. of California.
Economic Analyst, Dept. of Agriculture 34-38; Chief Citrus Section, Fruit and Vegetable Div., Surplus Marketing Admin. 38-40; Chief Econ. Analysis Section, Fruit and Vegetable Div. 40-42, Asst. Chief Fruit and Vegetable Div. 42; Asst. Chief Fruit and Vegetable Branch, Agricultural Marketing Admin., U.S. Dept. of Agriculture 42-43; Asst Deputy Dir. Food Distribution Admin., War Food Admin. 43, Deputy Dir. Office of Distribution 43-44; Deputy Dir. Civilian Programs, Office Marketing Services 45; Assoc. Dir. Fruit and Vegetable Branch, Production and Marketing Admin., Dept. of Agriculture 45-46, Dir. 46-53; Dir. Fruit and Vegetable Div. Agricultural Marketing Service 53-61; Admin., Agricultural Marketing Service 61-65, Consumer and Marketing Service 65-; Distinguished Service Award, U.S. Dept. of Agriculture 56; Univ. of Montana Alumni Asscn. Distinguished Service Award 65.
Office: Consumer and Marketing Service, U.S. Department of Agriculture, Washington, D.C. 20250; Home: 4507 31st Street South, Arlington, Va. 22206, U.S.A. Telephone: 931-2409 (Home).

Smith, Wilfred Cantwell, M.A., PH.D., D.D.; Canadian university professor; b. 21 July 1916; ed. Upper Canada Coll., Univ. of Grenoble, Univ. of Madrid, American Univ. Cairo, Univ. of Toronto, Cambridge and Princeton Univs.
Served as rep. among Muslims of the Canadian Overseas Missions Council, chiefly in Lahore 40-49; Lecturer in Indian and Islamic History, Univ. of the Punjab, Lahore 41-45; Prof. of Comparative Religion 49-63, and Dir. Inst. of Islamic Studies, McGill Univ. 51-63; Pres. American Soc. for the Study of Religion 66-; Visiting Prof., London Univ. 60, Princeton Univ. 65, Toronto 68; now Prof. of World Religions and Dir. Center for the Study of World Religions, Harvard Univ.; Fellow, Royal Soc. of Canada, American Acad. of Arts and Sciences.
Publs. *Modern Islam in India* 43 (revised edns. 47, 65), *Islam in Modern History* 57, *Meaning and End of Religion* 63, *Faith of Other Men* 63, *Questions of Religious Truth* 67.
42 Francis Avenue, Cambridge, Mass. 02138, U.S.A. Telephone: 617-868-8458 (Home); 617-868-7600 (Office).

Smith-Rose, Reginald Leslie, C.B.E., D.SC., PH.D., F.C.G.I., F.I.C., A.R.C.S., C.ENG., F.I.E.E., F.I.E.E.E.; British scientist; b. 2 April 1894; ed. Imperial Coll. of Science and Technology, Univ. of London.
Asst. Engineer, Messrs. Siemens Bros. 15-19; Scientific Officer Electricity Div., Nat. Physical Laboratory 19-33, Principal Scientific Officer, Radio Div. 33-39, Superintendent, Radio Div. 39-47; Dir. of Radio Research, Dept. of Scientific and Industrial Research, London 47-60; Fellow of Inst. of Radio Engineers, New York, Vice-Pres. 48; Vice-Pres. Inst. of Electrical Engineers, London 61-65; Pres. Int. Scientific Radio Union 60-63; Radio Soc. of Great Britain 59; Sec.-Gen. Inter-Union Comm. on Frequency Allocations for Radio Astronomy and Space Science 60-; awarded Coronation Medals 37, 53, U.S. Medal of Freedom with Silver Palm 47; conducted research into problems fundamental to radio applications including electrical measurements, radio

direction finding, and the propagation of radio waves. Publs. *James Clerk Maxwell*; many scientific papers. 21 Tumblewood Road, Banstead, Surrey, England. Telephone: Burgh Heath 51697.

Smithers, Peter Henry Berry Otway, D.PHIL.; British politician and international civil servant; b. 9 Dec. 1913; ed. Harrow School and Magdalen Coll., Oxford.
Called to Bar, Inner Temple 36, joined Lincoln's Inn 37; Naval Service 39-45; M.P. 50-64; Parl. Private Sec. to Minister of State for Colonies 52-56, to Sec. of State for Colonies 56-59; Vice-Chair. Conservative Parl. Foreign Affairs Cttee. 58-62; Parl. Under-Sec. of State, Foreign Office 62-64; U.K. Del. to UN Gen. Assembly 60-63; Consultative Assembly, Council of Europe 52-56, 60; Vice-Pres. European Assembly of Local Authorities 59-62; Sec.-Gen., Council of Europe 64-; Conservative. Publ. *Life of Joseph Addison*.
Council of Europe, Strasbourg, France.

Smoktunovsky, Innokenty Mikhailovich; Soviet actor; b. 1925; ed. Pushkin Dramatic Theatre Studio, Krasnoyarsk.
Soviet Army 43-45; Leningrad Gorky Bolshoi State Drama Theatre 57-; worked in cinema 60-; Honoured Artist of R.S.F.S.R., Lenin Prize 65.
Principal stage roles: Prince Muskin in *The Idiot*, Sergei in *Irkutsky Story*.
Films include: *9 Days in One Year*, *Hamlet* 64, *Be Aware of a Car* 66.
Bolshoi State Drama Theatre, Leningrad, U.S.S.R.

Smolin, Nikolai Vasilyevich; Soviet diplomatist; b. 1914; ed. Univ. of Leningrad.
Joined Diplomatic Service 46; First Sec., Berne 50-54; at Ministry of Foreign Affairs 46-50, 54-56, 60-62; First Sec., Paris 56-57; Counsellor, Phnom Penh 57-59; Counsellor, Tunis 62-66; Amb. to Togo 66-.
U.S.S.R. Embassy, P.O. Box 634, Ataklama Street, Lome, Togo.

Smrkovsky, Josef; Czechoslovak politician; 26 Feb. 1911.
Secretary Red Trade Union Movement 32-33, Communist Youth Org. 33-35; underground C.P. Sec. 37-40; C.P. Sec. 44-45; Deputy Chair. Czech Nat. Council and Chair. Prague Nat. Cttee. 45; Deputy Minister of Agriculture and Gen. Dir. of State Farms 48-51; political imprisonment 51-55; Chair. co-operative farm 56-63; Deputy Minister-Chair. of Central Comm. of People's Control and Statistics 63-65; Minister-Chair. of Central Board of Water Resources 66; Minister of Forestry and Water Resources 67-68; Pres. Czechoslovak Nat. Assembly April 68-; Deputy to Nat. Assembly 46-51, 64-; mem. Central Cttee. and Politburo of C.P. of Czechoslovakia 45, of Central Cttee. 46-51, 66-; Order of 25th Feb. 1948 49; Order of the Repub. 66. National Assembly, Prague, Czechoslovakia.

Smuul, Juhan; Soviet poet; b. 18 Feb. 1922.
Member Communist Party 50-; Deputy Supreme Soviet of U.S.S.R.; State Prize 51, Lenin Prize 61, Merited Writer of Estonia S.S.R.; Order of Red Banner of Labour 59, of Lenin 67.
Publs. *Grim Youth* 46, *Son of Storm* 47, *Team of Chaps of Yarvesuu* 48, *Estonian Poem* 49, *Poems* 51, *I am a Member of the Komsomol* 53, *Atlantic Ocean* (play) 56, *The Ice-Book* 59, (stories) *Murka the Sailor* 61, *The Sea of Japan* 63, *Sea Songs* 63, *The Wild Captain* (play) 64, *Colonel's Widow* (play) 66.
Union of Estonian Writers, Tallinn, Estonian S.S.R., U.S.S.R.

Smyth, Henry DeWolf, A.M., PH.D.; American physicist; b. 1 May 1898; ed. Princeton and Cambridge Univs.
Nat. Research Council Fellow Cambridge Univ. 21-23, Princeton Univ. 23-24; Instructor in Physics Princeton Univ. 24-25, Asst. Prof. 25-29, Assoc. Prof. 29-36,

Prof. 36-, Chair. Dept. of Physics 35-49; consultant on war research projects to Nat. Research Council and to Office of Scientific Research and Development 40-45; consultant U.S. Manhattan District project (atomic bombs) 43-45; mem. U.S. Atomic Energy Comm. (by Presidential appointment) 49-54; Chair. Scientific and Engineering Research Board, Princeton Univ. 54-; Fellow American Physical Society, mem. Council 40-44, Vice-Pres. 55, Pres. 57-; U.S. Rep., Int. Atomic Energy Agency 61-; mem. Nat. Acad. of Sciences; mem. American Philosophical Soc.; Hon. Sc.D. (Drexel Inst. of Technology 50, Case Inst. of Technology 53).
Home: 5 Lafayette Road W., Princeton, N.J.; Office: Princeton University, Princeton, N.J., U.S.A.

Snechkus, Antanas Yuozovich; Soviet politician; b. 1903; ed. Int. Lenin School.
Member C.P.S.U. 20-; worked for the Foreign Bureau of the Central Cttee. of the Lithuanian C.P. 21-25; Sec. 26, First Sec. Central Cttee. of the Lithuanian C.P. 36, 40-; had various prison terms; after establishment of Soviet power, Dir. of State Security Dept. of Soviet Lithuania 40; mem. Central Cttee. of the C.P.S.U. 52-; Deputy to U.S.S.R. Supreme Soviet; mem. Cttee. for Foreign Affairs, Soviet of Union; awarded Order of Lenin, Order of the Red Banner of Labour (twice), Order of the Patriotic War, 1st Class.
Central Committee of the Lithuanian C.P., Vilnius, Lithuania, U.S.S.R.

Snedden, Hon. Billy Mackie, Q.C., M.P.; Australian lawyer and politician; b. 31 Dec. 1926.
Admitted to Supreme Court, W.A. 51, Victoria 55, Victorian Bar 55; Migration Officer Italy, England 52-54; mem. House of Reps. Bruce, Victoria 55-; Commonwealth Attorney-Gen. 63-66; appointed Q.C. 64; Chair. First Commonwealth Law Ministers Conf., Canberra 65; Australian Rep. Second Commonwealth Law Ministers Conf. London 66; Fed. Minister for Immigration Dec. 66-.
22 Pine Crescent, Ringwood, Victoria, Australia.

Snedden, Sir Richard, Kt., C.V.O., C.B.E., M.A., LL.B., LL.D.; British barrister-at-law; b. 18 April 1900; ed. George Watson's Coll., Edinburgh, and Edinburgh Univ.
Joint Sec. British Employers' Confed. 26-29; Asst. Sec. British Shipping Fed. 29, Sec. 33, Gen. Manager 36, Dir. 57-62; Gen. Manager Int. Shipping Fed. 36-; mem. Nat. Maritime Board 36-62, Merchant Navy Welfare Board 48-62; Vice-Chair. Merchant Navy Training Board 48-62; Chair. Nat. Sea Training Schools 44-60; mem. Gov. Body of ILO 52-60; Chair. Shipowner Group Int. Maritime Confs. 45, 46, 56, 58; British Employers del. to Int. Labour Conf. 53-59, Vice-Pres. 55, Pres. Int. Organisation of Employers 57, 58; Chair. Shipowners side of Joint Maritime Comm. of I.L.O.; mem. of the Queen's Bodyguard for Scotland; Commdr. Orders of Dannebrog (Denmark), Lion (Finland), St. Olav (Norway), and Vasa (Sweden), Crown (Belgium) and Orange Nassau (Netherlands); Grand Officer of the Order of Christ (Portugal).
Aldwick Grange, Boars Head, Crowborough, Sussex, England.
Telephone: Crowborough 2851.

Snegirev, Vladimir Vsevolodovich, M.SC.; Soviet diplomatist; b. 1923.
Joined Diplomatic Service 55; Counsellor, Paris 61-63; Deputy Head First European Dept. of U.S.S.R. Ministry of Foreign Affairs 63-64; Ambassador to Cameroon 64-.
U.S.S.R. Embassy, Yaoundé, Cameroon.

Sneh (fmrly. Kleinbaum), **Moshe,** M.D.; Israeli physician, editor and politician; b. 6 Jan. 1909; ed. Free Polish Univ. and Univ. of Warsaw.
Leader of Jewish Radical Party (Leftist Zionists)

in Poland, opposed to Pilsudski regime; Editor *Haint* (daily), *Opinia* and *Ster* (weeklies), mem. Gen. Council World Zionist Organisation 31-39; took part in Polish War against Nazi Germany Sept. 39; later escaped to Palestine; mem. Hagana 40-, Chief Hagana High Commd. 40-46; headed Jewish Resistance Movement against the British after Second World War; escaped to Paris and headed Jewish illegal immigration to Palestine 47; Head European Branch of Exec. Cttee. of Jewish Agency for Palestine 47; resgnd. Dec. 47 and joined United Workers' Party (Mapam) which was established in Feb. 48; mem. Central Political Cttee. Mapam 48-52; after Mapam split headed Left Socialist group which joined Communist party 54; mem. Central Cttee., Political Bureau, Israeli Communist Party; Chief Editor daily *Kol-Haam*; mem. Israeli Parl. (Knesset); mem. Editorial Board of daily *Al-Hamishmar* 48-52.
Kol-Haam, Eilath Street, P.O. Box 2675, Tel-Aviv, Israel.

Snell, Bruno, DR.PHIL.; German Hellenist; b. 18 June 1896; ed. Lüneburg Johanneum and Univs. of Edinburgh, Leiden, Berlin, Munich and Göttingen.
Lector Pisa Univ. 25; Privatdozent Hamburg Univ. 25, Prof. 31-60.
Publs. *Die Entdeckung des Geistes* 46 (3rd edn. 55), *Der Aufbau der Sprache* 52. 61, *Griechische Metrik* 55 (3rd edn. 62), *Poetry and Society* 61, *Scenes from Greek Drama* 64; Editions of Bacchylides 34 (4th edn. 61) and Pindar 53, 59, 63, 64.
Heimhuderstrasse 80, 2 Hamburg 13, German Federal Republic.
Telephone: 440756.

Snell, Foster Dee, B.S., M.A., PH.D.; American chemist and chemical engineer; b. 29 June 1898; ed. Colgate Univ. and Columbia Univ.
Teacher of Chemistry Columbia Univ. 19-20; Teacher of Chemistry Coll. of City of N.Y. 20-23; in charge of Technical Chemistry Pratt Inst. 23-28; Office of Production Research and Devt. 41-45; Chair. Emer. Board Foster D. Snell Inc., Chemists Building Co., Chair. of Board 29 West 15th St. Corpn. 64-, etc.; fmr. Vice-Pres. Soc. of Chemical Industry; Vice-Chair. American Section 40-42, Chair. 42-44; Pres. American Inst. of Chemists 46-48; Vice-Pres. American Oil Chemists' Soc. 40-43; Vice-Pres. Fat and Oil Comm. of Int. Union of Pure and Applied Chemistry 47-51, Pres. 51-53; Pres. Asscn. Consulting Chemists and Chemical Engineers 52-54; Vice-Pres. Chemists' Club (New York) 56-57, Pres. 62-64; Trustee Columbia Univ. 64; Soc. of Chemical Industry Medal for 1949; New York Inst. of Chemists Award 52, etc.; Hon. mem. American Inst. of Chemists 59; Hon. Sc.D. Colgate Univ. 63.
Publs. *Colorimetric Methods of Analysis* 23 (3rd edn. in 4 vols. 49-54, supplementary vols. 59, 61, 67), *Chemicals of Commerce* 39 and 52, *Chemistry Made Easy* (4 vols.) 43, 59, 60 (all with Dr. Cornelia T. Snell), *Commercial Methods of Analysis* (with Frank M. Biffen), *Dictionary of Commercial Chemicals* 62; Editor-in-Chief *Encyclopedia of Industrial Chemical Analysis*, 20 vols. first 3 vols. 66, 2 vols. 67, 2 vols. 68.
Home: 2 Fifth Avenue, New York, N.Y. 10011; Office: 29 West 15th Street, New York, N.Y. 10011, U.S.A.
Telephone: 477-2118 (Home); 924-8800 (Office).

Snelling, Sir Arthur Wendell, K.C.M.G., K.C.V.O.; British civil servant and diplomatist; b. 7 May 1914; ed. Univ. Coll., London.
Study Group Sec. Royal Inst. of Int. Affairs 34-36; appointed to Dominions Office 36; Private Sec. to Parliamentary Under-Sec. of State 39; Joint Sec. U.K. Del. Int. Monetary Conf., Bretton Woods 44; Dep. High Commr. in New Zealand 47-50, in South Africa 53-55; Asst. Under-Sec. of State, Commonwealth

Relations Office 56-59; High Commr. in Ghana 59-61; Dep. Under-Sec., Commonwealth Relations Office 61-. Commonwealth Office, Downing Street, London, S.W.1, England.
Telephone: 01-930-2323.

Snodgrass, William DeWitt, B.A., M.A., M.F.A.; American poet, critic and teacher; b. 5 Jan. 1926; ed. State Univ. of Iowa.
Instructor, English Dept., Cornell Univ., Ithaca 55-57, Univ. of Rochester 57-58; Prof. English Dept., Wayne State Univ. 59-; Leader, Poetry Workshop, Morehead, Kentucky 55, Yellow Springs, Ohio 58, 59; Pulitzer Prize for Poetry 60, and other awards.
Publ. *Heart's Needle* 51.
23805 Oxford Street, Dearborn, Mich.; Home: 669 W. Canfield, Detroit, Mich. 48201, U.S.A.
Telephone: 831-7018 (Home).

Snow, Baron (Life Peer), cr. 64, of Leicester; **Charles Percy Snow** (husband of Pamela Hansford Johnson, *q.v.*), Kt., C.B.E., PH.D.; British writer; b. 15 Oct. 1905; ed. Univ. Coll., Leicester, and Christ's Coll., Cambridge. Fellow of Christ's Coll., Cambridge 30-50 (in residence 30-40), Hon. Fellow 66-; Technical Dir. Ministry of Labour 40-44; Civil Service Commr. 45-60; Dir. English Electric Co. Ltd. 47-64; Parl. Sec. Ministry of Technology 64-66; Hon. LL.D. (Leicester, Liverpool, St. Andrews, Brooklyn Polytechnic Inst., Bridgeport, York), Hon. D.Litt. (Dartmouth, Bard, Temple, Syracuse, Pittsburgh, Ithaca Colls.); Hon. D.H.L. (Kenyon Coll., Wash. Univ., Mich. Univ.); Hon. D.Sc. (Pa. Mil. Coll.); Dr. of Phil. Sc. (Rostov-on-Don); Hon. mem. American Acad. Inst.; foreign hon. mem. American Acad. of Arts and Sciences; Extraordinary Fellow Churchill Coll., Cambridge; Fellow Morse Coll., Yale Univ.; Diamond Jubilee Medal, Catholic Univ. of America; Centennial Eng. Medal, Pa. Mil. Coll.; Resolution of Esteem, Congressional Cttee. on Science and Astronautics.
Publs. Novels: *Death Under Sail* 32, *New Lives for Old* 33, *The Search* 34, *Strangers and Brothers* 40, *The Light and the Dark* 47, *Time of Hope* 49, *The Masters* 51, *The New Men* 54, *Homecomings* 56, *The Conscience of the Rich* 58, *The Affair* 60, *Corridors of Power* 64. Lectures: *The Two Cultures and the Scientific Revolution* (Rede Lecture) 59, *Science and Government* (Godkin Lectures) 61; *Variety of Men* (biographical portraits) 67. Plays: *View over the Park* 50, *The Affair, The New Men, The Masters* (adapted by Ronald Millar) 61, 62, 63.
199 Cromwell Road, London, S.W.5, England.
Telephone: 01-373-5235.

Snow, Edgar Parks; American journalist; b. 19 July 1905; ed. Kansas City Junior Coll. and Univ. of Missouri.
Asst. Editor *China Weekly Review* Shanghai 29-30; Asst. China Corresp. *Chicago Tribune* 29; corresp. of Consolidated Press Asscn. India, China and Manchuria 30-34; Special Corresp. *New York Sun* 34-37; Special Corresp. *Daily Herald* London 32-39; Lecturer Yenching Univ. Peiping 34-35; accredited U.S. and British War Corresp. Russia, India, N. Africa, Britain, France, Germany, Austria, China, Japan 42-46; corresp. Europe, Middle East, India 47-48, Mexico 50, U.S.A. 51-; Assoc. Ed. for *Saturday Evening Post* 43-52; special res. consultant Harvard 56; special corresp. to mainland China for *Look* magazine 60; corresp. in China for *Le Nouveau Candide*, Paris 64-65; mem. American Acad. Political Science, Nat. Press Club, Overseas Press Club. Publs. *Far Eastern Front* 34, *Red Star Over China* 37, *Living China* (edited and compiled) 36, *Scorched Earth* 41, *People on Our Side* 44, *The Pattern of Soviet Power* 45, *Stalin Must Have Peace* 47, *Random Notes on Red China* 57, *Journey to the Beginning* 58, *The Great Change in China* 62.
c/o Random House, 457 Madison Avenue, N.Y., U.S.A.

Snoy et d'Oppuers, Baron Jean-Charles; Belgian economist; b. 2 July 1907; ed. Univ. of Louvain and Harvard Univ.
Entered banking business in Belgium 31; became Attaché to Minister for Economic Affairs 34, Dir., Int. Treaty Section, Ministry of Economic Affairs 36, Sec.-Gen. of the Ministry 39; dismissed from post by the Germans and active in Resistance Movement during Second World War; re-assumed duties after Liberation and became Pres. Four Party Supply Cttee. of Belgium; played prominent part in creation of Benelux Economic Union and was Chair. Council for Econ. Union; also contributed to work leading to creation of O.E.E.C. in 48; Chair. O.E.E.C. Council 48-50, Steering Board for Trade O.E.E.C. 52, 60; Chief Belgian del. 55 to Int. Cttee. set up at Messina Conf., which later became Int. Conf. for Common European Market and Euratom; Pres. Interim Cttee. for European Common Market and Euratom 57; Sec.-Gen. Ministry of Economic Affairs until 60; Perm. Rep. to European Economic Community 58-59; Managing Dir. Cie. d'Outremer pour l'Industrie et la Finance 60; Managing Partner Banque Lambert 65; Minister of Finance June 68-; several Belgian and foreign decorations including Commdr. Order of Leopold and Grand Officer Order of the Crown (Belgium); Grand Cross Order of Crown of Oak (Luxembourg), Royal Order George I (Greece), Order of Merit (Italy), Grand Cross Order of Orange Nassau (Neths.), Hon. O.B.E. (U.K.), Grand Cross Order of Merit (German Fed. Republic).
Château de et à Bois-Seigneur-Isaac, Brabant, Belgium.
Telephone: 067-222-27.

Snyder, John Wesley; American banker; b. 21 June 1895; ed. Vanderbilt Univ.
Banker in Arkansas and Missouri 19-30; Bank Receiver and Conservator, Office of Comptroller of the Currency, St. Louis 31-37; Man. St. Louis Agency, Reconstruction Finance Corpn. 37-43; Exec. Vice-Pres. and Dir. Defense Plant Corpn., Washington 40-43; Asst. to Board of Dirs. R.F.C. 40-44; Vice-Pres. First Nat. Bank of St. Louis 43-45; Fed. Loan Administrator 45; Dir. Office of War Mobilization and Reconversion 45; Sec. of Treasury 46-53; Chair. Nat. Advisory Council on Int. Monetary and Financial Problems 46-53; U.S. Gov. of Int. Monetary Fund and Int. Bank for Reconstruction 46-53; Senior U.S. Financial Rep. in admin. of Anglo-American Financial Agreement 46, and financial, rehabilitation and aid programmes, Philippines, France, Italy, Austria, Turkey, Greece, Germany, Japan and Marshall Plan operations; mem. U.S. Nat. Security Council 51-52, NATO Council 49-53; del to numerous Int. Financial Confs.; Pres. Overland Corpn., Toledo 53-; Medal for Merit 47; Hon. LL.D. (Ouachita Coll., George Washington Univ., Univ. of Arkansas, Univ. of Toledo, Georgetown Univ.), Hon. D.Sc. (Bryant Coll.).
Home: 8109 Kerry Lane, Chevy Chase, Md.; Office: Overland Corporation, Investment Bankers, 500 Security Building, Toledo, Ohio, U.S.A.

Snyder, Laurence Hasbrouck, M.S., S.D., H.H.D., D.SC.; American university president; b. 23 July 1901; ed. Rutgers Univ. and Harvard.
Instructor in Zoology, N. Carolina State Coll. of Agriculture and Eng. 24-25, Asst. Prof. 25-27, Assoc. Prof. 27-30; Assoc. Prof. of Zoology, Ohio State Univ. 30-33, Prof. 33-47; Prof. of Medical Genetics, Ohio State Univ. Coll. of Medicine 33-47, Chair., Dept. of Zoology and Entomology 42-47; Dean of Graduate Coll. Univ. of Okla. 47-58; Pres. Univ. of Hawaii 58-66, Emeritus 66-; mem. Nat. Research Council, Eugenics Research Asscn., American Soc. of Zoologists, A.A.A.S. (Pres. 57), Genetics Soc. of America (Pres. 48), American Soc. Human Genetics (Pres. 50).

Publs. include *Medical Genetics* 41, *Genetics, Medicine and Man* (with Muller and Little) 47, *Principles of Heredity*, 5th edn. 57.
2885 Oahu Avenue, Honolulu, Hawaii 96822, U.S.A.

Soames, Rt. Hon. Christopher, C.B.E.; British politician and diplomatist; b. 12 Oct. 1920; ed. Eton Coll. and Royal Mil. Coll., Sandhurst.
Captain Coldstream Guards, served in France, Italy and Middle East 39-45; Asst. Mil. Attaché, Paris 46-47; Conservative M.P. for Bedford 50-66; Parl. Private Sec. to the Prime Minister 52-55; Parl. Under-Sec. of State to Air Ministry 55-57, and to Admiralty 57-58; Sec. of State for War 58-60; Minister of Agriculture, Fisheries and Food 60-64; Amb. to France 68-; Croix de Guerre.
British Embassy, rue du Faubourg-St-Honoré, Paris, France; and Hamsell Manor, Eridge Green, Tunbridge Wells, Kent, England.

Soares e Silva, General Edmundo de Macedo; Brazilian engineer and politician; b. 9 June 1901; ed. Colégio Militar, Rio de Janeiro and Escola Militar do Realengo. Commissioned into Army 21; mem. Mil. Comm. for Metallurgical Studies, Nat. Steel Mill Comm. 31; Brazilian Rep. Geneva Disarmament Conf. 32; Sub-Chief, Cabinet of Minister of Justice 37; Technical Dir. Nat. Steel Co. 41-54, Pres. 54-; Minister of Transport and Public Works 46; Gov. of State of Rio de Janeiro 47; Prof. of Metallurgy, Polytechnic School of the Pontifíca Catholic Univ. of Rio de Janeiro 53; Exec. Pres. Comm. of Industrial Devt. 54; Pres. Advisory Council of São Paulo Steel Co. 59; Pres. Latin American Inst. of Iron and Steel 59; Vice-Pres. Mercedes Benz (Brazil) 60, now Pres.; Pres. Nat. Confederation of Industry 64, 66; Minister of Industry and Commerce 67-; Aliança Renovadora Nacional.
Ministry of Industry and Commerce, Brasilia, Brazil.

Sobakin, Vadim Konstantinovich, D.IUR.; Soviet diplomatist; b. 1927; ed. Moscow Inst. of International Relations.
Lecturer, Instructor, Prof., Dept. of Int. Law, Moscow State Inst. of Int. Relations, Asst. Dean, Dean of Dept. 60-65; Perm. Rep. of U.S.S.R. to UNESCO 65-.
Permanent Representation of the U.S.S.R. to UNESCO, 7 and 9 place de Fontenoy, Paris 7e, France.

Sobol, Nikolai Alexandrovich; Soviet politician; b. 10; ed. Mechanical and Machine Building Inst., Kharkov.
Member C.P.S.U. 39-; party work in Industry 36-58; Chair., Kharkov Nat. Econ. Council 58-60, Ukraine Nat. Econ. Council 60-61; First Sec., Kharkov Regional Cttee. C.P. Ukraine 61-63; Second Sec. Central Cttee. Ukraine C.P. 63-; mem. Central Cttee. of C.P.S.U. 61-; mem. Political Bureau Central Cttee. of Ukrainian C.P.; Deputy to U.S.S.R. Supreme Soviet; mem. Cttee. for Foreign Affairs, Soviet of Union; State Prize 51.
Central Committee of the Communist Party of the Ukraine, Kiev, Ukrainian S.S.R., U.S.S.R.

Sobolev, Sergei Lvovich; Soviet mathematician; b. 08; ed. Leningrad Univ.
Research devoted to mechanics, the dynamics of the resilient body and theoretical mathematics; mem. Acad. of Sciences of U.S.S.R.; Dir. Inst. of Mathematics and Computing Centre of the Siberian Dept. of the Acad. of Sciences of the U.S.S.R. 59-; Prof. at Moscow Univ. 35, awarded Order of Lenin; Editor-in-Chief *Bulletin of Siberian Department of U.S.S.R. Academy of Sciences*; Hon. Fellow Royal Soc. of Edinburgh 63.
Publs. *Some Applications of Functional Analysis in Mathematical Physics* 50, *Equations of Mathematical Physics* 54, *Lectures on Theory of Cubic Formulae* 64.
Institute of Mathematics, Siberian Department of Academy of Sciences of U.S.S.R., Akademgorodok, Novosibirsk, U.S.S.R.

Sobolev, Vladimir Alexeyevich; Soviet foreign trade official; b. 1912; ed. Moscow Textile Inst.
Member C.P.S.U. 46-; official, foreign trade orgs. 40-48; Dir. of Office, *Exportlyon* 48-50, 53-63; U.S.S.R. Commercial Rep. in Iran 50-51; official, Ministry of Agriculture 51-53; Deputy, later Commercial Rep. of U.S.S.R. in India 63-; Order of Red Banner of Labour.
U.S.S.R. Trade Representation, New Delhi, India.

Sobolev, Vladimir Stepanovich; Soviet geologist; b. 30 May 1908; ed. Leningrad Inst. of Mines.
Geologist, Cen. Scientific Research Exploration, Inst. of Mines, Leningrad 29-41, Prof. of Inst. 39-45; Prof. Univ. of Lvov 45-58; Dep. Dir. Inst. of Geology and Geophysics, Novosibirsk 58-; mem. Acad. of Sciences, U.S.S.R., Ukrainian S.S.R., Mineralogical Socs. of the U.S.S.R., Hungary and Czechoslovakia, Soc. géologique de France; State Prize 50.
Publs. *Petrology of Traps of the Siberian Platform, Petrology of Korosten Pluton, Introduction into Mineralogy of Silicates, Geology of Diamond Deposits, Phedorov's Method, Petrography of Igneous rocks of the Soviet Carpathians, Physical-Chemical Principles of Petrography of Igneous Rocks, Map of Metamorphic Facies of U.S.S.R.*; Ed. *Diamond Deposits of Jakutiya.*
Academicheskaya 14, Novosibirsk-90, R.S.F.S.R., U.S.S.R.
Telephone: 50625.

Sobukwe, Robert Maugatiso; South African politician; b. 24; ed. Univ. Coll. of Fort Hare.
Former Lecturer, Witwatersrand Univ., Johannesburg; fmr. mem. African Nat. Congress; Pres. South African Pan Africanist Congress 59-; in detention March 60-63, 63-.
Robben Island Prison, nr. Cape Town, South Africa.

Söderberg, Ragnar; Swedish businessman; b. 13 April 1900; ed. Stockholm Univ. of Commerce.
Chairman, The Stockholm Chamber of Commerce, AB Electrolux, Holmens Bruks och Fabriks AB, AB Sveriges Litografiska Tryckerier, Soderberg & Haak AB; Försäkringsaktiebolaget Skandia; Vice-Chair. ASEA, mem. Board Stockholms Enskilda Bank.
Djurgårdsvägen 150, Stockholm NO, Sweden.

Söderstrom, Elisabeth Anna; Swedish soprano opera singer; b. 7 May 1927; studied singing under Andrejewa de Skilonz and Opera School, Stockholm.
Engaged at Royal Opera, Stockholm 50-; appearances at Salzburg 55, Glyndebourne 57, 59, 61, 63, 64, Metropolitan Opera, New York 59, 60, 62, 63; frequent concert and TV appearances in Europe and U.S.A.; toured U.S.S.R. 66; mem. Royal Acad. of Music; Singer of the Court (Sweden) 59; Order of Vasa; Stelle della Solidarieta dell'Italia; Prize for Best Acting, Royal Swedish Acad. 65.
Roles include: Fiordiligi (*Cosi Fan Tutte*), Countess and Susanna (*Figaro*), Countess (*Capriccio*); sang three leading roles in *Der Rosenkavalier* 59.
c/o Royal Opera House, Stockholm, Sweden.

Søe, Niels; Danish university professor; b. 29 Nov. 1895; ed. Denmark, Germany and England.
Minister of the Danish Church in Hvidovre 25-30, Shanghai 30-33; Extraordinary Prof. Univ. of Copenhagen 34-39, Ordinary Prof. of Christian Ethics and Philosophy of Religion 39-66; Chair. of Danish Bible School (for training of Laymen); Chair. of Søren Kierkegaard Soc.; Co-Editor of *Dansk teologisk Tidsskrift* and of *Illustreret Religionsleksikon*; Knight of the Order of Dannebrog.
Publs. *Kristelig Gudstro og videnskabelig Verdensforklaring* 25, *Karl Barth's Bibelopfattelse* 39, *Kristelig Etik* 42, *Fra Renæssancen til vore Dage* 45, *Karl Marx og Marxismen* 51, *Religions filosofi* 55, *C. G. Jung* 55, *Dansk teologi siden 1900* 55.
Gentoftegade 8, Gentofte, Denmark.

Soe Tin, U.; Burmese lawyer and diplomatist; b. 1919. Judicial Service 42-45; legal practice 45-46; Burma Civil Service 47-48, Foreign Service 48-; Exec. Sec. Ministry of Foreign Affairs 57-62, Dir. Foreign Exchange Control Econ. and Social Boards 55-58, Perm. Sec. 62-66; Perm. Rep. of Burma to the UN 66-; mem. numerous int. delegations.
Permanent Mission of Burma to the United Nations, 10 East 77th Street, New York, N.Y. 10021, U.S.A.

Sofonov, Georgi Petrovich; Soviet trade union official; b. 15 Sept. 1919; ed. Rostov Inst. of Railway Engineering.
Mechanical Engineer, Dep. Shop Superintendent, Chair. Trade Union Factory Cttee. Moscow Likhachov Motor Works 42-62; Sec.-Gen. Cttee. Engineering Workers Trade Union 62-63, Chair. Central Cttee. 63-; mem. Presidium All-Union Central Cttee. of Trade Unions; mem. C.P.S.U.; Order of Red Banner of Labour.
Central Committee of Engineering Workers Trade Union, 42 Leninski Prospekt, Moscow, U.S.S.R.

Soglo, Gen. Christophe; Dahomeyan army officer and politician; b. 1909.
Joined French Army 31, 2nd Lt. Second World War, later fought in Indo-China becoming Capt. 50, Maj. 56; Col. of Armed Forces of Dahomey 61, Gen. 64; Head of Provisional Govt. Oct. 63-Jan. 64; Chief of Staff, Dahomeyan Army Jan. 64-Dec. 65; Pres. of the Repub. and Prime Minister Dec. 65-67, also Minister of Defence and for Rural Devt. Dec. 66-67.
Cotonou, Dahomey.

Sohl, Hans-Günther, DIPL.ING.; German businessman; b. 2 Feb. 1906; ed. Technical Univ. Berlin-Charlottenburg.
Pres. August Thyssen-Hütte A.G., Duisburg-Hamborn; Pres. Wirtschaftsvereinigung Eisen und Stahlindustrie, Düsseldorf; mem. of numerous boards in steel industry and other firms; Grosses Verdienstkreuz; Dr. Ing. e.h. Technische Hochschule, Aachen.
August Thyssen-Hütte AG, Kaiser-Wilhelm-Strasse 100, Duisburg-Hamborn 41, German Federal Republic.

Söhngen, Werner; German industrialist; b. 12 July 1906.
Chairman Rheinische Stahlwerke, Essen; Admin. Board, Unternehmensverband Ruhrbergbau, Essen; Chair. Supervisory Board, Rheinstahl Bergbau A.G., Essen, Rheinstahl Hüttenwerke A.G., Essen, Rheinstahl Henschel A.G., Kassel, Rheinstahl Wagner Werkzeugmaschinenfabriken m.b.H., Dortmund; Deputy Chair. Supervisory Board, Farbenfabriken Bayer A.G., Leverkusen; Chair. Advisory Board Rhineland and Westphalia subsidiary Allianz Versicherungs-A.G., Munich; Deputy Chair. Advisory Board, Rheinstahl Handel G.m.b.H., Duisburg; mem. Supervisory Board, Brown, Boveri & Cie, A.G., Mannheim, Gelsenkirchener Bergwerks-A.G., Essen, Münchener Rückversicherungs-Gesellschaft, Munich, Westfälische Transport-Aktien-Gesellschaft, Dortmund; mem. Advisory Board Rhein/Ruhr Ingenieur-Gesellschaft G.m.b.H., Dortmund, Ruhrgas A.G., Essen; mem. Advisory Cttee. Deutsche Bank A.G., Bergische Stahl-Industrie K.G., Romscheid c/o Rheinische Stahlwerke, Postfach 1364, Essen, German Federal Republic.

Sokhey, Major-Gen. Sir Sahib Singh, Kt., M.A., B.SC., M.D., D.T.M.; Indian administrator; b. 15 Dec. 1887; ed. Government Coll., Lahore, Edinburgh Univ., London Hospital Medical Coll., Trinity Coll., Cambridge, Johns Hopkins, Harvard and Toronto Univs.
Joined Indian Medical Service 13; served in First World War 15-21; Rockefeller Foundation Fellow 23-25; Asst. Dir. Haffkine Inst. 25-32, Dir. 32-49, Dir. (Production) 49-50; Asst. Dir.-Gen. WHO 50-52; Pres. Asscn. of Scientific Workers of India 52; nominated mem. Rajya Sabha 52-56; mem. Panel of Scientists, Indian Planning Comm. 56-; Hon. Adviser to Dir.-Gen. of Scientific and Industrial Research 62-; Fellow Indian Acad. of Sciences; Fellow Nat. Inst. of Sciences of India; mem. Lenin Peace Prize Cttee.; Int. Lenin Peace Prize 53.
c/o Council of Scientific and Industrial Research, Haffkine Inst., Bombay, India.

Sokolov, Tikhon Ivanovich; Soviet politician; b. 13; ed. Agricultural Inst., Leningrad.
Member C.P.S.U. 40-; party and Soviet work, Perm Region 41-45; Chair. Exec. Cttee. Novosibirsk Regional Soviet of Workers' Deputies 45-46; mem. Presidium and Head of Dept., Council for Collective Farm Affairs, U.S.S.R. Govt. 46-50; Chair. Council for Collective Farm Affairs, Ukrainian Govt. 50-53; Chair. Exec. Cttee. Smolensk Regional Soviet of Workers' Deputies 54-56; on staff of Central Cttee. of C.P.S.U. 56; First Sec., Novgorod Regional Cttee. of C.P.S.U. 56-58, Perm 58-60; First Sec. Tselinny Territory Cttee. of Kazakh C.P. and Sec. Central Cttee. of Kazakh C.P. 60-63; First Deputy Chair. Vladimir Rural Regional Soviet of Working People's Deputies 63-64; Sec. Vladimir District Cttee. C.P.S.U. 64-65; First Sec. Orel Regional Cttee. of C.P.S.U. 65-; Deputy to Supreme Soviet of U.S.S.R. and R.S.F.S.R.; mem. Agricultural Cttee. Soviet of Union; Candidate mem. Central Cttee. of C.P.S.U. 56-61, mem. 61-.
Orel Regional Committee of C.P.S.U., Orel, U.S.S.R..

Sokorski, Włodzimierz; Polish journalist; b. 2 July 1908; ed. Univ. of Warsaw.
General Sec. Polish Socialist Party "Left Wing" 29-31; Col., Polish Army Second World War; Vice-Minister and Minister of Culture and Arts 48-56; Pres., Cttee. for Radio and Television 56-; Vice-Pres. Polish UNESCO Cttee.; numerous Govt. and Army awards.
Publs. *The Torn Pavement* (novel) 36, *Problems of Cultural Policy* 47, *Arts for Socialism* 50, *The Journey Diary* 54, *Drawing Thick Lines* (essay) 58, *Curves* (play) 59, *Crumbs* (short stories) 61, *Escapes* (play) 61; numerous radio and television plays.
Committee for Radio and Television, Noakowskiego 20, Warsaw, Poland.

Sol Castellanos, Dr. Jorge; Salvadorean economist; b. 24 July 1915; ed. Univ. of El Salvador and Harvard Univ.
Minister of Nat. Econ., El Salvador 49-53; Alt. Exec. Dir. Int. Monetary Fund 54-56, Exec. Dir. 56-58; lawyer and Dean of School of Economics, Univ. of El Salvador 58-60; Special Rep. of Sec.-Gen. of Org. of American States (O.A.S.) for Econ. and Social Affairs 60, later Sec., Alliance for Progress; mem. for Central America, Inter-American Cttee. for Alliance for Progress 64-66; Dir. Central American Bank for Econ. Integration, Tegucigalpa 66-.
Banco Centroamericano de Integración Económica, Tegucigalpa, Honduras; Home: 11 Avenida Norte 517, San Salvador, El Salvador.
Telephone: 2-22-34 (Tegucigalpa); 21-70-44 (San Salvador).

Solá, Alberto; Argentine economist; b. 24; ed. Univ. of Buenos Aires and Univ. of Madrid.
Director, Ministry of Commerce 55-56; Nat. Dir. Politics and Finance 56-57; Under-Sec. of Finance 57-58; Prof. of Political Economy, Univ. of Buenos Aires 57-59; Dep. Dir. of Trade Affairs, Econ. Comm. for Latin America (ECLA) 58-62; Asst. Exec. Sec. Latin American Free Trade Asscn. (LAFTA) 62, Exec. Sec. 62-66; Sec. Industry and Commerce (Argentina) 67-.
Julio A. Roca 651 2° piso, Buenos Aires, Argentina.
Telephone: 34-3768.

Solages, Mgr. Bruno de, L. ès L., D.THEOL., DR.JUR. CANONICI; Docteur h.c. (Univ. of Montreal); French ecclesiastic; b. 8 Aug. 1895; ed. Inst. Catholique de Paris, Séminaire de Saint-Sulpice and Ecole Biblique Jerusalem.

Ordained 22; Chaplain of St. Louis des Français, Rome 22; Prof. of Rhetoric 25 and of Philosophy 28 Petit Séminaire de Saint-Sulpice; Editor-in-Chief *Revue Apologétique* 26; Rector Inst. Catholique de Toulouse and Apostolic Protonotary 32-64, Hon. Rector 64-; Vice-Pres. des Semaines Sociales de France 45-56; mem. Higher Council of Nat. Education 46-54.
Publs. *Camille Dupin* 18, *Le Procès de la Scolastique* 28, *Le Problème de l'Apostolat dans le monde moderne* 32, *Le Christianisme dans la Vie Publique* 35, *Pour rebâtir une chrétienté* 38, *Discours interdits* 46, *Dialogue sur l'analogie* 46, *La Théologie de la guerre juste* 47, *Essai sur l'ordre politique national et international* 47, *Billets de Christianus* 48, *L'âme, Dieu, la destinée* 55, *Synopse grècque des Evangiles* 58, *Initiation Métaphysique* 62, *Teilhard de Chardin* 67.
31 rue Fondeville, Pouvourville, 31 Toulouse (Haute-Garonne), France.
Telephone: 85-31-54.

Solaiman, Mohammed Sidky; United Arab Republic (Egyptian) engineer and politician; b. 1919.
Studied eng. and mil. science; rose to Col. in Egyptian Army; Minister of Aswan High Dam 62-66; Prime Minister 66-June 67; Deputy Prime Minister and Minister of Industry, Electricity and the Aswan Dam June 67-; Pres. Soviet-Egyptian Friendship Soc.; Order of Lenin.
Ministry of Industry, Electricity and the Aswan Dam, Cairo, United Arab Republic.

Solandt, Omond McKillop, O.B.E., M.D., D.SC., LL.D., M.R.C.P., F.R.S.C.; Canadian physiologist; b. 2 Sept. 1909; ed. Univ. of Toronto.
Lecturer in Physiology, Univ. of Cambridge 39; Dir. S.W. London Blood Supply Depot 40; Dir. Physiological Laboratory, Armoured Fighting Vehicle School 41; Dir. Tank Section, Army Operational Research Group 42; Deputy Superintendent, Army Operational Research Group 43, Superintendent 44; Chair. Defence Research Board 46-; Asst. Vice-Pres., Research and Development, Canadian Nat. Railways 56, Vice-Pres. 57; fmr. Vice-Pres. Research and Devt. and Dir. de Havilland Aircraft of Canada Ltd.; Dir. other companies; Chair. Science Council of Canada 66-; Dir. Expo 67; Chancellor Univ. of Toronto; Fellow Royal Soc. of Canada, Royal Coll. of Physicians (London); hon. mem. Engineering Inst. of Canada; Hon. D.Sc. (British Columbia, Manitoba, Laval, McGill and St. Francis Xavier, Royal Mil. Coll., Sir George Williams Univ.), Hon. LL.D. (Toronto, Dalhousie); Medal of Freedom (with Bronze Palm).
36 Hawthorn Avenue, Toronto 5, Ontario, Canada.
Telephone: 921-3954.

Solano López, Miguel; Paraguayan diplomatist; b. 16 May 1911.
Director-Gen. of Culture, Paraguay 44-45; Dir. Dept. of Organisations and Treaties, Ministry of Foreign Affairs 54; mem. Paraguayan Dels. to UN Gen. Assembly 55-; Rep. of Paraguay to UN Trusteeship Council 59-61; Alt. Rep. to UN 57-65, Perm. Rep. of Paraguay to UN 65-.
Permanent Mission of Paraguay to the United Nations, 211 East 43rd Street, New York 17, N.Y., U.S.A.

Solberg, Halvor Skappel, DR. PHIL.; Norwegian meteorologist; b. 5 Feb. 1895; ed. Univ. of Oslo.
Meteorologist in Norwegian Meteorological Service 18; Lecturer in Applied Mathematics, Univ. of Oslo 22, Prof. of Theoretical Meteorology 30-64; Dean Faculty of Science 42-46; Pres. Norwegian Cttee. of Geodesy and Geophysics 46-58; Norwegian Cttee. of Mechanics 50-55, Norwegian Cttee. of Int. Geophysical Year, Norwegian Cttee. of Computing Machinery; mem. Int. Council of Scientific Unions 46-49, Vice-Pres. 49-55; mem. Norwegian Acad. of Sciences and Letters (Gen. Sec. 46-53), Royal Danish Soc. of Sciences; Hon. mem.

American Meteorological Soc., Polish Meteorological and Hydrological Soc.
Publ. *Hydrodynamique physique* 33.
Jonas Reinsgate 6, Oslo 3, Norway.
Telephone: 46-93-80.

Soldati, Mario, D.LITT.; Italian writer, film director and actor; b. 17 Nov. 1906; ed. Turin and Columbia Univs.
Former corresp. of *Il Lavoro*; essays on art, articles in various papers and magazines, column in *Il Giorno*, Milan; films include *Piccolo mondo antico*, *Eugenia Grandet*, *Malombra*, *La Provinciale*, *La Donna del Fiume*, *La Mano dello Straniero*, *Policarpo*; TV appearances.
Publs. include *America Primo Amore*, *Racconti*, *A Cena col Commendatore*, *Lettere da Capri*, *La Messa dei Villeggianti*, *Il Vero Silvestri*, *La Confessione*. *Storie di Spettri*, *La Busta Arancione*, *Le due Città* 64.
Via Cappuccio 14, 20123 Milan, Italy.
Telephone: 865417.

Soldatov, Aleksandr Alexeevich; Soviet diplomatist; b. 1915; ed. Liebknecht Pedagogical Inst., Moscow.
Formerly Counsellor, Canberra, Senior Political Adviser to Soviet Del. to UN, Rep. to UN Trusteeship Council; mem. del. to UN 52-55; Dir. American Dept. Ministry of Foreign Affairs 55-60; Dep. Del. Geneva Foreign Ministers Conf. 59; Ambassador to United Kingdom 60-66; Deputy Minister of Foreign Affairs 66-68; Amb. to Cuba 68-; mem. C.P.S.U. Central Auditing Comm. 66-.
U.S.S.R. Embassy, Havana, Cuba.

Soldevila Zubiburu, Ferran; Spanish writer; b. 24 Oct. 1894; ed. Univs. of Barcelona and Madrid.
Secretary-Editor Historical Section Institut d'Estudis Catalans 14-20; mem. Archives, Libraries and Museums 22-38, and 54-64; Lecturer in Spanish Liverpool Univ. 26-28; Prof. of Catalan History at School of Librarianship, Barcelona 29-38, at Univ. of Barcelona 31-38, and at Estudis Universitaris Catalans 43-; mem. Inst. d'Estudis Catalans; mem. Acad. de Buenas Letras, Centro Int. di Studi Sardi, etc.; Archiviste de la Corona de Aragon; Premi Patxot, Premi de l'Escola Catalana d'Art Dramatic; corresp. mem. Int. Inst. Arts and Letters; Dr. H.C. Univ. Montpellier.
Publs. *Pere II el Gran: el desafiament amb Carles d'Anjou* 19, *Historia de Catalunya* (in collab. with F. Valls-Taberner) 22-23, *La Reina Maria*, *Muller del Magnanim* 28, *Historia de Catalunya* (3 vols.) 34-35 (2nd edn. 62-63), *Barcelona sense Universitat 1714-1836* 38, *Pere el Gran* (4 vols.) 49-, *Els almogàvers* 52, *L'almirall Ramon Marquet* 53, *Jaume I i Pere el Gran* 55, *Ramon Berenguer IV* 55, *Resum d'Historia de Catalunya* 56, *Historia de España* (8 vols.) 52-57 (2nd edn. 61-64), *Vida de Jaume I el Conqueridor* 58, *Un Segle de Vida Catalana 1814-1930* (2 vols.; ed. and part author), *Vida de Pere el Gran i Alfons el Liberal* 63; Belles-Lettres: *Poema de l'Amor Perdut*, *Exili*, *Càntics*, *La Ruta Invisible*, *Hores Angleses*, *Matilde d'Anglaterra*, *Guifré*, *l'Hostal de l'Amor*, *Albert i Francina*, *Don Joan*, *L'Aprenent de Suicida*, *L'Amador de la Gentilesa*.
Teodora Lamadrid 34, Barcelona, Spain.

Solis Ruiz, José; Spanish politician and trade unionist; b. 13.
Barrister and military lawyer; fmr. mem. Falange labour and trade union organisations, organised First Nat. Congress of Workers 46; fmr. Civil Gov., Pontevedra and Guipuzcoa; Nat. Delegate of Syndicates 51-57; Minister and Sec.-Gen. of Falange 57-.
Alcalá 44, Madrid, Spain.

Solle, Horst; German politician; b. 3 June 1924; ed. Karl Marx Univ., Leipzig.
Official, Ministry of Transport of D.D.R.; later mem. staff Central Cttee. of Socialist Unity Party (S.E.D.);

later Sec. of State, Ministry of Foreign and Inter-German Trade of D.D.R.; now Minister of External Econ. Relations, D.D.R.; Medal of Merit of D.D.R.; Patriotic Order of Merit in Silver.
Ministerium für Aussenwirtschaft, 108 Berlin, Unter den Linden 46/60, Germany.

Sollero, Lauro; Brazilian pharmacologist; b. 23 Jan. 1916; ed. Ginásio Raul Soares, Ubá, Minas Gerais, and Universidade do Brasil.
Professor in Dept. of Pharmacology, School of Medicine and Surgery, Rio de Janeiro 53-, Faculty of Medicine, Univ. of Brazil 63-; Fellow, Guggenheim Foundation, Rockefeller Foundation.
Publs. include: *Curarização, Orgão elétrico do Electrophorus electricus, Serotonina, Bloqueadores A – drenérgicos.*
Laboratório de Farmacologia, Faculdade Nacional de Medicina, Avda. Pasteur 458, Rio de Janeiro, Brazil.

Solodovnikov, Alexander Vasiljevich; Soviet theatrical director and journalist; b. 1 Aug. 1904; ed. Moscow Inst. of Literature, Philosophy and History.
Designer in shoe factory 24-30; editor of local paper 30-34; student 34-37; on staff of *Pravda* 37-38; Deputy Chair. Art Cttee. U.S.S.R. Council of Ministers 38-45; with Tass Agency 45-48; Dir. Bolshoi Theatre Moscow 48-51; Deputy Editor *Sovietskaya Kultura* 51-54; with Ministry of Culture 54-55; Dir. Moscow Arts Theatre 55-63; Adviser to Ministry of Culture 63-67; Dir. Malyi Theatre 67-; mem. Collegium, Ministry of Culture; mem. C.P. of the Soviet Union; Order of the Red Banner of Labour; three medals.
Malyi State Academic Theatre, 1/6 Ploshchad Sverdlova, Moscow, U.S.S.R.

Solomentsev, Mikhail Sergeyevich; Soviet politician; b. 13; ed. Leningrad Polytechnic Inst.
Member C.P.S.U. 40-; Engineer, Workshop Foreman, Chief Engineer, Factory Dir., Lipetsk and Chelyabinsk Regions 40-54; Sec., later Second Sec. Chelyabinsk Regional Cttee. of C.P.S.U. 54-57; Chair. Chelyabinsk Nat. Econ. Council 57-59; First Sec. Karaganda Regional Cttee., C.P. of Kazakhstan 59-64; First Sec. Rostov District Cttee. of C.P.S.U. 64-66; Sec. C.P.S.U. Central Cttee. 66-67; Head of Dept. of Heavy Industry, C.P.S.U. Central Cttee. 67-; mem. Central Cttee. of C.P.S.U. 61-; Deputy to U.S.S.R. Supreme Soviets.
Central Committee of C.P.S.U., 4 Staraya ploshchad, Moscow, U.S.S.R.

Solomon, Patrick Vincent Joseph; Trinidadian physician, politician and diplomatist; b. 12 April 1910; ed. Univs. of Belfast and Edinburgh.
Practised medicine in Scotland, Ireland, Wales, Leeward Islands and Trinidad 34-43; mem. Legislative Council, Trinidad 46-50, 56-61; Deputy Pol. Leader, People's Nat. Movement 56-66; Minister of Educ. and Culture 56-60; Minister of Home Affairs 60-64; Deputy Prime Minister 62-66; Minister of Foreign Affairs 64-66; Perm. Rep. of Trinidad and Tobago to UN 66-.
Permanent Mission ot Trinidad and Tobago to the United Nations, 801 Second Avenue, New York, N.Y. 10017, U.S.A.

Soloukhin, Vladimir Alexeyevich; Soviet writer; b. 1924; ed. Gorky Inst. of Literature.
Publs. verse: *Rain in the Steppe* 53, *Saxifrage, Streamlets on the Asphalt* 59, *Tale of the Steppes* 60, *How to Drink the Sun* 61, *Postcards from Viet-Nam* 62; novels: *Birth of Zernograd* 55, *The Goldmine* 56, *Beyond the Blue Seas* 57, *Country Roads of Vladimir* (lyrical diary) 58, *The Drop of Dew* 63, *A Lyrical Story* 64, *Mother—Stepmother;* short stories: *The Loaf of Bread* 65; poetry: *Don't seek shelter from the rain* 67.
Union of Soviet Writers, 52 Vorovsky Street, Moscow, U.S.S.R.

Solovyov, Leonid Nikolaevich; Soviet trade union official and diplomatist; b. 06; ed. Leningrad Inst. of Water Transport Engineers.
Former Technical Inspector, Cen. Cttee. of Trade Union of Heavy Machine Building Workers 37-42; Chair. Kirov Plant Trade Union Cttee., Head, Org. Dept. All-Union Cen. Trade Union Council 42-44; Sec. All-Union Central Council of Trade Unions 44-54, 59-63, Dep. Chair. 54-59; Ambassador to Mongolian People's Repub. 63-68; at Ministry of Foreign Affairs 68-; mem. Central Cttee. C.P.S.U. 61-, Deputy to Supreme Soviet, U.S.S.R.
Ministry of Foreign Affairs, 32-34 Smolenskaya-Sennaya ploshchad, Moscow, U.S.S.R.

Solovyov, Yury Vladimirovich; Soviet ballet dancer; b. 1940; ed. Leningrad School of Ballet.
Joined Kirov State Theatre of Opera and Ballet 58; Honoured Artist of the R.S.F.S.R.
Principal roles include: Prince Desiré (*Sleeping Beauty*), Siegfried (*Swan Lake*), Frondoso (*Laurencia*), The Poet (*Chopiniana*), Andrei (*Taras Bulba*), Danila (*Stone Flower*), Farkhad (*Legend of Love*), Prince (*Nutcracker*), Albert (*Giselle*), Prince Charming (*Cinderella*).
Kirov State Academic Theatre of Opera and Ballet, ploshchad Iskusstv 1, Leningrad, U.S.S.R.

Solovyov-Sedoy, Vasily Pavlovich; Soviet composer; b. 1907; ed. Central School of Music and Leningrad Conservatoire.
Honoured Worker of the Arts of R.S.F.S.R. 56, People's Artist of the R.S.F.S.R. 57, of the U.S.S.R. 67; Sec. R.S.F.S.R. Composers' Union.
Principal compositions: *Taras Bulba* (ballet) 40, revised 45, *True Friend* (operetta) 45, *The Russian Enters Port* (ballet) 62; and a great many songs, including *Moscow Nights.*
Leningrad Branch of R.S.F.S.R. Composers' Union, 45 Herzen Street, Leningrad, U.S.S.R.

Solow, Robert Merton, PH.D.; American economist; b. 23 Aug. 1924; ed. Harvard Univ.
Assistant Prof. of Statistics, Mass. Inst. of Technology 49-53, Assoc. Prof. of Econs. 54-57, Prof. of Econs. 58-; Senior Economist, Council of Econ. Advisers 61-62; Marshall Lecturer, Cambridge Univ. 63-64; Eastman Visiting Prof., Oxford Univ. 68-69; mem. Nat. Comm. on Technology, Automation and Econ. Progress 64-65; Presidential Comm. on Income Maintenance 68-; Fellow Center for Advanced Study in Behavioral Sciences 57-58; Vice-Pres. American Econ. Asscn. 68; Pres. Econometric Soc. 64; mem. American Acad. of Arts and Sciences; David A. Wells Prize, Harvard Univ. 51, John Bates Clark Medal, American Econ. Asscn. 61; Hon. LL.D. (Univ. of Chicago) 67.
Publs. *Linear Programming and Economic Analysis* 58, *Capital Theory and the Rate of Return* 63, *Sources of Unemployment in the United States* 64.
Department of Economics, Massachusetts Institute of Technology, Cambridge, Mass.; Home: 8 Martha's Point Road, Concord, Mass., U.S.A.
Telephone: 864-6900-5268; 369-9092.

Solti, Georg; Hungarian musician; b. 21 Oct. 1912; ed. High School of Music, Budapest, and studied with Zoltan Kodaly, Bela Bartok and Ernst von Dohnanyi.
General Music Dir., Munich State Opera 46-52; Gen. Music Dir., Frankfurt Opera, Permanent Conductor of Museum Concerts 52-61; Music Dir., Royal Opera House, Covent Garden 61-; has also appeared as Guest Conductor in Europe with Berlin and Vienna Philharmonic Orchestras, Vienna Symphony Orchestra, Orchestre Nationale and Conservatoire Orchestra, Paris, at Salzburg Festival, with London Philharmonic Orchestra, London Symphony Orchestra, at Edinburgh Festival, at Glyndebourne Festival, at Covent Garden; has appeared in U.S.A. with San Francisco Opera, Philadelphia Orchestra, New York Philharmonic

Orchestra, Chicago Lyric Opera, Los Angeles Symphony Orchestra, Chicago Symphony Orchestra, and at Metropolitan Opera; First Prize as a pianist, Concours International, Geneva 42; Grand Prix du Disque 59, and numerous other record awards; Hon. C.B.E. 68.
c/o The Royal Opera House, Covent Garden, London, W.C. 2, England.

Sølvhøj, Hans, M.A.; Danish politician and radio administrator; b. 11 July 1919; ed. Elsinore Public School, Univ. of Copenhagen.
Teacher at Elsinore Public School 45-47; Producer, Radio Denmark 47. Dir., Talks and Current Affairs Dept. 53-61, Dir.-Gen. 61-64; Sec. of State for Cultural Affairs 64-66, Joint Minister of State for Foreign Affairs 66-; Knight of the Danish Order of Dannebrog.
Rødelms, Mørdrup, Espergaerde, Denmark.
Telephone: 03232115.

Sommer, Charles H., B.S.; American chemical executive; b. 24 Sept. 1910; ed. Univ. of Michigan and Univ. of Arizona.
Joined Monsanto Co. 34, Man. Plasticizer and Intermediate Sales 39-51, Gen. Man., Merrimac Div. 51-54, Gen. Man. and Vice-Pres. Organic Chemicals Div. 54-59, mem. Exec. Cttee. 59-, Dir. 59-, Exec. Vice-Pres. 59-60, Pres. 60-; official of other business orgs.
Monsanto Company, P.O.B. 526, St. Louis, Mo. 63166, U.S.A.
Telephone: 314-OX4-3013.

Sommerfelt, Sören Christian; Norwegian diplomatist; b. 9 May 1916; ed. Oslo Economic High School and Oslo Univ.
Entered Norwegian Foreign Service 41; UN Secr. Div. for Refugees and Displaced Persons 46-48; First Sec., Copenhagen 48-50; Counsellor, Norwegian Perm. Del. to NATO 51-52; Dep. Head, Politico-Econ. Dept., Norwegian Ministry of Foreign Affairs 53-56, Head 56-60; Leader, numerous Norwegian trade dels. 53-60; Ambassador, Head, Norwegian Perm. Del. to EFTA, European Office of UN and other int. orgs. at Geneva 60-; Chair. GATT Perm. Council 63-64; Chair. GATT Contracting Parties 68; Norwegian Rep., CERN Council 68; Order of St. Olav (Norway), North Star (Sweden), Dannebrog (Denmark), Falcon (Iceland), Leopold II (Belgium), Ethiopian Star.
10 Parc du Château Banquet, Geneva, Switzerland.

Sommers, Davidson, LL.B.; American lawyer and financial adviser; b. 15 Feb. 1905; ed. Harvard Univ. and Harvard Law School.
Entered legal practice in New York City 30-37; Asst. Corpn. Counsel of City of New York 38; returned to general law practice 39; served in U.S. Army Air Forces, first with Army Air Force Technical Service Command, and later as Asst. Exec. to Asst. Sec. of War in Washington 42-45; Special Asst. to Sec. of War 45-46; joined Legal Dept. International Bank for Reconstruction and Development 46; General Counsel of the Bank 49-60, Vice-Pres. 56-60; apptd. Gen. Counsel of Int. Finance Corpn. July 56-60; Senior Vice-Pres. Gen. Counsel, Dir., The Equitable Life Assurance Soc. of the U.S. 60-.
24 Fifth Avenue, New York City, N.Y. 10011, U.S.A.
Telephone: GR3-6400.

Somoza Debayle, General Anastasio; Nicaraguan army officer and politician; b. 5 Dec. 1925; ed. Inst. Pedagógico de Managua, La Salle Military Acad., New York, and U.S. Military Acad., West Point.
Son of late Gen. Anastasio Somoza Garcia, Pres. of Nicaragua, and brother of late Col. Luis Somoza Debayle, Pres. of Nicaragua 56-63; entered Guardia Nacional (Nicaraguan Army) 41, rose progressively to Gen. of Div. 41-64; Head of Nat. Guard; Special envoy of Nicaragua on several Diplomatic Missions; Chair. Board Nicaragua Merchant Marine; Pres. Board LANICA Airlines; Pres. several commercial enterprises

(cotton textiles, cement, real estate, etc.); Pres. of Nicaragua May 67-; several Nicaraguan decorations, and decorations from Panama, Mexico, Peru, Repub. of China, Dominican Repub., Haiti and Brazil.
Casa Presidencial, Managua, Nicaragua.

Son Sann; Cambodian financial administrator; b. 11; ed. Ecole des Hautes Etudes Commerciales de Paris.
Deputy Gov. Provinces of Battambang and Prey-Veng 35-39; Head of Yuvan Kampuchearath (Youth Movement); Minister of Finance 46-47; Vice-Pres. Council of Ministers 49; Minister of Foreign Affairs 50; Mem. of Parl. for Phnom-Penh and Pres. Cambodian Nat. Assembly 51-52; Gov. of Nat. Bank of Cambodia 54-67; Minister of State (Finance and Nat. Economy) 61-62; Vice-Pres., in charge of Economy, Finance and Planning 65-67; Prime Minister 67; now First Vice-Pres. in charge of Econ. and Financial Affairs; Grand Officier de l'Ordre Royal du Cambodge, Commdr. du Sowathara (Mérite économique), Légion d'Honneur, Commdr. du Monisaraphon, Médaille d'or du Règne, Grand Officier du Million d'Eléphants (Laos).
29 Vithei Preah Bat Suramarit, Phnom-Penh, Cambodia.

Song Yo Chan, Gen.; Korean army officer and politician; b. 19.
Former Commander 1st Field Army and Army Chief of Staff; Martial Law Commdr. April 60; Minister of Defence June-July 61; Prime Minister July 61-62, Minister of Foreign Affairs Aug.-Oct. 61, Chair. of Econ. Planning Board 62-.
Economic Planning Board, Seoul, Republic of Korea.

Sönmez, Nejat, B.A., M.A.; Turkish journalist and diplomatist; b. 15; ed. Robert Coll. and Columbia Univ., New York.
Standardization Dept. Ministry of Commerce 38-39; Rep. of Information, Broadcasting and Tourism, Ankara and Istanbul 45-49; Press Attaché, London 49-55; Dep. Dir.-Gen. of Information, Broadcasting and Tourism 55-56, 60-61; Dir. Turkish Information Office, San Francisco 56-60; Dir.-Gen. of Information, Broadcasting and Tourism 61-63; Under-Sec. Min. of Information, Broadcasting and Tourism; Press Counsellor, Turkish Embassy, London 63-.
Basin, Yayin ve Turizm Bakanliği, Mithat Paşa Caddesi, Yenişehir, Ankara, Turkey.

Sonn, Voeunsai; Cambodian diplomatist; b. 11; ed. Ecole Centrale des Arts et Manufactures, Paris.
Former Minister of Defence and Interior, Cambodia; fmr. Minister for Finance and Economy; fmr. Minister for Foreign Affairs; fmr. Chair. of Cttee. for Co-ordination of Investigations of Lower Mekong Basin; Perm. Rep. to UN 64-65; Ambassador to France, also accred. to Spain and U.K. 65-.
Ambassade Royale du Cambodge, 21 rue Franklin, Paris 16e, France.

Sonne, Karl-Heinz, DR. ECON.; German business executive; b. 3 June 1915; ed. Wirtschaftschochschule Berlin.
Member of Management Board Concordia Electrizitäts A.G., Dortmund 48-56, Chair. of Management Board 56-62; Chair. of Management Board Bayrische Motore Werke A.G., Munich 62-65; Chair. Management Board Klöckner-Humboldt-Deutz A.G. (tractors and engines) 65-.
4600 Dortmund-Lücklemberg, Heideblick 70, German Federal Republic.

Sonneborn, Tracy M., A.B., PH.D.; American zoologist; b. 19 Oct. 1905; ed. Johns Hopkins Univ.
Fellow of Nat. Research Council, Johns Hopkins Univ. 28-30, Research Asst. 30-31, Research Assoc. 31-33, Assoc. in Zoology 33-39; Assoc. Prof. of Zoology, Indiana Univ. 39-43; Prof. of Zoology, Indiana Univ. 43-53, Distinguished Service Prof. 53-, Chair. Div. of

Biological Sciences 63-64; mem. Editorial Board *Journal of Experimental Zoology* 48-64, *Genetics* 42-61, *Journal of Morphology* 46-49, *Annual Review of Microbiology* 54-58, *Physiological Zoology* 48-60, *Cytologia*, *Experimental Cell Research* 53-63; Treas. American Soc. of Naturalists 45-47, Vice-Pres. 48, Pres. 49; Vice-Pres. Genetics Soc. of America 48-, Pres. 49; Pres. American Soc. of Zoologists 56; Vice-Pres. Soc. for Study of Evolution 58; Pres. American Inst. of Biological Science 61; hon. mem. Faculty of Biology and Medical Science, Univ. of Chile, Visiting Prof. 51; mem. Exec. Cttee. American Soc. of Cell Biology 63-65, Council Nat. Acad. of Sciences 63-66; Foreign mem. Royal Soc. 64; Hon. D.Sc. (Johns Hopkins Univ.); co-winner of Annual $1,000 Prize for Research, A.A.A.S. 46; Kimber Genetics Award of the Nat. Acad. of Sciences 59; Mendel Centennial Medal, Czechoslovak Acad. of Sciences 65.

Publs. Over 200 papers and abstracts, chiefly on genetics of paramecium.

Office: Department of Zoology, 220 Jordan Hall, Indiana University, Bloomington, Ind. 47401; Home: 1305 Maxwell Lane, Bloomington, Ind. 47401, U.S.A.

Telephone: 812-336-5796 (Home).

Sontag, Raymond James, B.S., A.M., PH.D.; American university professor; b. 2 Oct. 1897; ed. Univs. of Illinois and Pennsylvania.

Served in U.S. Infantry 18; Instructor, Univ. of Iowa 21-22; Instructor of History, Princeton Univ. 24-25, Asst. Prof. 25-30, Assoc. Prof. 30-39, Henry Charles Lea Prof. and Chair. Dept. of History 39-41; Sidney Hellman Ehrman Prof. in European History Univ. of Calif. 41-65, Emer. recalled 65-; Chief, German War Documents Project, Dept. of State 46-49; mem. American Philosophical Soc., American Historical Asscn., and Council on Foreign Relations; Pres. American Catholic Historical Asscn. 53.

Publs. *The Middle Ages* (with D. C. Munro) 28, *European Diplomatic History 1871-1932* 33, *Germany and England—Background of Conflict* 38, *Nazi-Soviet Relations* (with J. S. Beddie) 48; American Editor-in-Chief *Documents on German Foreign Policy, 1918-1945* 49.

Department of History, University of California, Berkeley 4, Calif., U.S.A.

Soong Ching-Ling (*see* Sun Yat-Sen, Madame).

Soper, Baron (Life Peer) cr. 65, of Kingsway; **Rev. Donald O. Soper,** M.A., PH.D.; British Methodist minister; b. 31 Jan. 1903; ed. St. Catharine's Coll., Cambridge, Wesley House, Cambridge, and London Univ.

Minister to the South London Mission 26-29, to the Central London Mission 29-36; Superintendent of the West London Mission 36-; Pres. of the Methodist Conf. 53; Alderman, L.C.C. 58-65; Hon. Fellow St. Catharine's Coll., Cambridge 66.

Publs. *Christ and Tower Hill, Question Time on Tower Hill, Answer Time on Tower Hill, Christianity and its Critics, Popular Fallacies about the Christian Faith, Will Christianity Work?, Practical Christianity To-Day, Questions and Answers in Ceylon, Children's Prayertime, All His Grace, It is Hard to Work for God, The Advocacy of the Gospel, Tower Hill, 12.30.*

West London Mission, Kingsway Hall, London, W.C.2, England.

Telephone: 01-405-3246.

Sophiaan, Manai; Indonesian teacher, politician and diplomatist; b. 5 Sept. 1915; ed. Djogjakarta Teachers Coll.

Teacher 37-42; Town Councillor 39-42, 44-45; mem. Parl. 46-64; mem. Young Indonesia, Chair. 33-36; Vice-Chair. Great Indonesia Party 37-42; mem. Exec. Board Indonesian Nat. Party 45-50, Sec.-Gen. 50-53; mem. Exec. Board Indonesian Nat. Party 53-; mem. Indonesian Del. to UN 60-61; Chief Del. to Brussels Conf. of

Interparl. Union 61; Chief Del. to Belgrade Conf. of Interparl. Union 63; Amb. to U.S.S.R. 64-67.

Ministry of Foreign Affairs, Djakarta, Indonesia.

Sopwith, Sir Thomas Octave Murdoch, Kt., C.B.E.; British aeronautical engineer; b. 88.

Founded Sopwith Aviation Co. 12; now Pres. Hawker Siddeley Group Ltd.; Hon. F.R.Ae.S.

Compton Manor, Kings Somborne, Hampshire, England.

Sørensen, Max, DR. JUR.; Danish university professor; b. 19 Feb. 1913; ed. Univ. of Copenhagen and Geneva, Post-graduate Inst. for International Studies.

Entered Danish Foreign Office 38; Attaché, Danish Legation, Berne 43-44, Sec., London 44-45; Asst. Chief of Section, Foreign Office, Copenhagen 45-47; Prof. of Int., Constitutional and Administrative Law, Univ. of Aarhus 47-; Rep. of Danish Govt. on Human Rights Comm. of U.N. 48-51, and Comm. on Int. Criminal Jurisdiction 51; Adviser to Danish Minister for Foreign Affairs at meetings of Cttee. of Ministers, Council of Europe 49-50; lecturer, Acad. of Int. Law, The Hague 52, 60; Chair. U.N. Sub-Cttee. on Prevention of Discrimination and Protection of Minorities 54-55; mem. of European Comm. on Human Rights, and of I.L.O. Cttee. on Application of Int. Labour Conventions 54-62; mem. Permanent Court of Arbitration, The Hague; Assoc. Inst. de Droit Int.; Legal Adviser to Danish Ministry for Foreign Affairs; Dr. Jur. h.c. (Univ. of Kiel) 64.

Publs. *Les sources du droit international* 46 *Elements of International Organization* (in Danish) 52, *Denmark and the United Nations* 56, *Manual of Public International Law* 68.

Tretommervej 21, Risskov, Denmark.

Telephone: Århus 06-17-82-64.

Sorensen, Theodore Chalkin, B.S.L., LL.B.; American lawyer and government official; b. 5 Aug. 1928; ed. Univ. of Nebraska.

Attorney, Federal Security Agency 51-52; Staff Researcher, Joint Cttee. on Railroad Retirement 52-53; Asst. to Senator John F. Kennedy 53-61; Special Counsel to Presidents Kennedy and Johnson 61-64; now lawyer, Paul, Weiss, Rifkind, Wharton & Garrison, New York City; Editor-at-Large *Saturday Review* 66-; Democrat.

Publs. *Decision-Making in The White House* 63, *Kennedy* 64.

525 Madison Avenue, New York City, N.Y., U.S.A.

Sørenson, Holger R., Kt.; Danish editor; b. 8 Sept. 1909.

Journalist since 29; with *Fyns Tidende* 32-39; Parl. Reporter and Copenhagen Editor 36-39; mem. of staff of Editors of Danish Broadcasting News Service 39-45; act. Chief Ed. 45; Press Agent, Provincial Chamber of Commerce 42-; Venstres Landsorganisation 45-56; Sec. Parl. Group of Liberal Party, Cttee. of Reps. and Exec. Cttee. of party organisation; mem. of Exec. Cttee. of Information Organisation, mem. Party Central Board 57-; Chair. Propaganda Cttee. 45-56; Ed. *Venstres Maanedsblad* (monthly) and *Den Liberale Almanak* (yearly) 45-56, Chief Ed. *Ringkjöbing Amts Dagblad* 56-62; mem. Danish Press Council 64.

Fisketorvet 12, Odense, Denmark.

Sorgenfrei, Theodor, M.SC., D.SC.; Danish geologist; b. 8 Dec. 1915; ed. Københavns Universitet.

Section Geologist, Geological Survey of Denmark 42-54, State Geologist 54-61; Prof. of Econ. Geology, Technical Univ. of Copenhagen 61-; Sec.-Gen. Int. Geological Congress, Norden 60, Int. Union of Geological Sciences 61-64; mem. Comm. on Stratigraphy, Int. Geological Congress 52-, Council of Paläontologische Gesellschaft, Germany 57-59, Council of Royal Danish Geographical Soc. 57-, Exec. Cttee. Int. Council of Scientific Unions 62-63, Royal Danish Acad. of Sciences and Letters 65-,

Council of Geologische Vereinigung (Fed. Germany) 66-; Special Lecturer Univs. of Amsterdam, Leiden and Utrecht 57, Univ. of London 61, Univ. of Stockholm 64; Visiting Prof. Louisiana State Univ. (U.S.A.) 65; Knight, Order of Dannebrog (Denmark); Chevalier Ordre des Palmes Académiques (France).

Publs. *Marine Middle-Miocene at Klintinghoved on Als* 40, *Geology and Water Well Drilling* (co-author) 54, *Geoelectrical Surveys in Denmark and Scania* 53, *Lexique Stratigraphique International: Danemark* 57, *Molluscan Assemblages from the Marine Middle Miocene of South Jutland and their Environments* 58, *Deep Tests in Denmark* 35-59.

Office: Instituttet for Teknisk Geologi, Danmarks Tekniske Højskole, Lyngby; Home: Kvædevej 71, Virum, Denmark.

Telephone: 01-882222.

Soriano, Raphael S., B.ARCH.; American architect; b. 1 Aug. 1907; ed. Coll. St. Jean, Rhodes and Univ. of Southern California.

Went to U.S. 24; naturalised 30; engaged on City Planning Project with Neutra 33; carried out special projects for Los Angeles County Regional Planning Comm. 35; private architectural practice 36-; Prof. Washington Univ. 62-63; developed industrialised packaged structures of aluminium, steel and plastic, steel houses; works exhibited at Paris Int. Exhbn. 37, New York Museum of Modern Art, 52, VII Pan-American Congress, Havana, VIII, Mexico City, São Paulo Int. Exhbn. 53, Munich Int. Exhbn. 55, Toledo (Ohio) Museum of Art 56, Moscow Int. Congress 58; Fellow American Inst. of Architects; mem. American Asscn. Univ. Profs.; VII Pan-American Congress Award 51, American Inst. of Architects Nat. Awards 51, 56, 58, 60, Progressive Architecture Award, A.I.A. Sunset Awards 57, 59, *Architectural Record* Award 56, S. Calif. A.I.A. Awards 49, 51, 57, *House and Home* Award 60, Life-A.I.A. Award 62; Speaker World Design Conf. Tokyo 60.

Projects: Site planning, apartments, hospitals, harbour facilities, research laboratories, office and medical buildings, community centres, horticultural centres and shops.

P.O. Box 128, Belvedere, Tiburon, Calif., U.S.A.

Šorm, František, D.SC., DR. TECH. ING.; Czechoslovak scientist; b. 28 Feb. 1913.

Professor of Organic Chemistry, Charles Univ., Prague; mem. Czechoslovak Acad. of Sciences 52-, Gen. Scientific Sec. 52-60, Vice-Pres. 61, Pres. of the Acad. 62-, Dir. of the Academy's Inst. of Organic Chemistry and Biochemistry; hon. mem. Romanian and Hungarian Acads. of Sciences; mem. U.S.S.R., German, Leopoldina, Bulgarian, Polish, Bavarian and Royal Danish Acads. of Sciences; hon. mem. British and Belgian Chemical Socs.; Laureate of the State Prize 50, 52, 58; Fritzsche Medal, American Chemical Soc. 59; Stas Medal, Belgian Chemical Soc. 62, etc.; Dr. h.c. (Univ. Libre de Bruxelles, Lomonosov Univ. Moscow); Order of Labour 58, 63.

Institute of Organic Chemistry and Biochemistry, Flemingovo nám. 2, Prague 6, Czechoslovakia.

Soronics, Franz; Austrian politician; b. 28 July 1920; ed. primary, secondary and trade schools, Eisenstadt.

Local Govt. work, Eisenstadt 50-62; mem. Bundesrat 56-66, State Sec. Ministry of Interior 63-66; State Sec. Ministry for Social Affairs 66-68; Minister of Interior 68-; Provincial Head of Austrian League of Workers and Employees 64-; Head of Burgenland Section of Austrian People's Party 68-, Grosses Silbernes Ehrenzeichen am Bande and other decorations.

7000 Eisenstadt, Meierhofgasse 4, Austria.

Telephone: 02682/2865; 63-17-41.

Sorsby, Arnold, C.B.E., M.D., F.R.C.S.; British surgeon and ophthalmologist; b. 10 June 1900; ed. Leeds, London and Edinburgh Univs.

Dean Medical School Royal Eye Hospital 34-38; Ophthalmic Surgeon London Jewish Hospital 27-43; Hampstead Gen. Hospital 28-43; and West End Hospital for Nervous Diseases 33-38; Hunterian Prof. Royal Coll. of Surgeons 33 and 41; Pres. London Jewish Hospital Medical Society 37; Middlemore Prize, British Medical Asscn. 36; Montgomery Lecturer, Royal Coll. of Surgeons, Dublin 41; Surgeon Royal Eye Hospital 31-66; Research Prof. Ophthalmology, Royal Coll. of Surgeons and Royal Eye Hospital 43-66; Vice-Pres. Int. League against Trachoma; mem. Expert Advisory Panel on Trachoma, WHO; Hon. Dir. Werner Group for Research in Ophthalmological Genetics Research, Medical Research Council 53-66; Dir. Medical Ophthalmology Unit, Lambeth Hospital 63-66; Hon. Adviser in Ophthalmology, Royal Nat. Inst. for the Blind 63-66; Emer. Research Prof. in Ophthalmology, Royal Coll. of Surgeons 67-; Consultant Adviser, Ministry of Health.

Publs. *A Short History of Ophthalmology* 33, 48, *Modern Trends in Ophthalmology* Vol. I 40, Vol. II 48, Vol. III 55, Vol. IV 67, *Medicine and Mankind* 42, 50, *Ophthalmia Neonatorum* 45, *The Causes of Blindness in England and Wales* 50, *Genetics in Ophthalmology* 51, *Systemic Ophthalmology* 51, 58, *Clinical Genetics* 53, *The Causes of Blindness in England 1948-1950* 53, *The Causes of Blindness in England 1951-1954* 56, *Emmetropia and its Aberrations* 57, *Antibiotics and Sulphonamides in Ophthalmology* 60, *Refraction and its Components during the Growth of the Eye* 61, *Refraction and its Components in Twins* 62, *Modern Ophthalmology* (4 vols.) 63-64, *The Incidence and Causes of Blindness in England and Wales 1948-1962* 66.

19 Parham Court, Grand Avenue, Worthing, Sussex, England.

Telephone: Worthing 40607.

Sosa, Arturo, Jr., DR.RER.POL., D.ECON.; Venezuelan economist; b. 24; ed. Colegio de San Ignacio de Loyola, Central Univ. of Venezuela.

Asst. Nat. Economic Council; Sec. Ministry of Finance 47-48; Dir.-Gen. C. A. La Nacional, Pres. Financiadora Nacional, Finalven; Dir. Compañia de Seguros La Seguridad, Cervecería Nacional, Central El Palmar, C.A. Ron Santa Teresa, Industrias Integradas S.A.; Minister of Finance Jan.-May 58, mem. Gov. Junta of Venezuela May 58-Feb. 59.

Edificio Polar, piso 13, Plaza Venezuela, Caracas, Venezuela.

Sosa-Rodríguez, Carlos; Venezuelan lawyer and diplomatist; b. 30 April 1912; ed. Colegio la Salle, Caracas, Univ. of Paris and Central Univ. of Venezuela.

Law Practice, Caracas 36-49; Lawyer, Creole Petroleum Corpn. 43-49, Comptroller-Gen. 49; Ambassador to U.K. 50-52; Perm. Rep. to UN 58-66; Pres. UN Security Council March 62, Feb. 63; Pres. UN Gen. Assembly 63.

Publ. *Le Droit Fluvial International et les Fleuves de l'Amérique Latine*.

c/o Ministry of Foreign Affairs, Caracas, Venezuela.

Sőtér, István; Hungarian university professor, literary historian and novelist; b. 13; ed. Budapest, Univ. de Paris à la Sorbonne and Ecole Normale Supérieure, Paris.

President Hungarian PEN Club; Dir. Inst. of Literary History, Hungarian Acad. of Sciences 57-; Rector Lóránd Eötvös Univ. Budapest 63-66; mem. Hungarian Acad. of Sciences; Kossuth Prize.

Publs. novels and short stories *Fellegjárás* (Walking in the Clouds) 39, *A templomrabló* (The Robber of the Church) 42, *A Kísértet* (The Ghost) 45, *Bünbeesés* (The Fall) 47, *Hidszakadás* (The Broken Bridge) 48, *Edenkert* (The Eden) 61; critical essays and historical monographs *Jókai Mór* 40, *Játék és valóság* (Play and Reality) 46, *Eötvös József* 53, *Világtájek* 57, *Nadártávlat*

59, *Nemzet és haladás* (Nation and Progress) 63, *Romantika és realizmus* 65, *Aspects et parallélismes de la littérature hongroise* 66, *Tisztule tükrök* 66.
Hungarian Academy of Sciences, Roosevelt tér 9, Budapest V, Hungary.

Soteriades, Antis; Cypriot lawyer and diplomatist; b. 10 Sept. 1924; ed. London Univ. and Gray's Inn, London.
In legal practice, Nicosia 51-56; detained on suspicion of assisting EOKA 56; escaped and became EOKA leader for Kyrenia district; mem. Exec., Edma Party May 59; Ambassador to U.K. Oct. 60-Feb. 61, High Commr. Feb. 61-66; Amb. to U.A.R. 66-.
Embassy of Cyprus, 3 Badrawi Ashour Street, Dokki, Cairo, U.A.R.

Soto, Jesús-Rafael; Venezuelan artist; b. 5 June 1923; ed. School of Fine Arts, Caracas.
Director, School of Fine Arts, Maracaibo, Venezuela 47-50; in Paris since 50; early exponent of "optical art"; various films made on works in field of kinetic art and vibrations since 58; one-man exhbns. at Caracas 49, 57, 61, Paris 56, 59, 62, 65, Brussels 57, Essen 61, Antwerp 62, Stuttgart 64, New York 65, Retrospective Exhbn., Signals, London 65; represented in perm. collections including: Tate Gallery, London, Museum of Fine Arts, Caracas, Albright-Knox Art Gallery, Buffalo, Cali Inst. of Fine Arts, Cali, Colombia, Stedelijk Museum, Amsterdam, Museum of Contemporary Arts, São Paulo, Moderna Museet, Stockholm, Kaiser Foundation, Cordoba, Argentina, Palace of Fine Arts, Brussels, Kröller-Müller Museum, Otterlo, Holland, Museum of Modern Art, Jerusalem; numerous prizes including Wolf Prize, São Paulo Bienal 63, David Bright Foundation Prize, Venice Biennale 64.
Major works include: sculpture for garden of School of Architecture, Univ. City of Caracas, two murals and sculpture for Venezuelan pavilion, Brussels Exhbn. 58.
68 rue de Turenne, Paris 3e, France.

Sotomayor, Antonio; Bolivian painter; b. 04; ed. La Paz School of Applied Arts.
Awarded first prize of Nat. Exposition of Painting 21; F.R.S.A.
Publs. *Pinturas interpretativas de indigenas de Bolivia* 29, *Pinturas con motivos mejicanos* 30, *Khasa Goes to the Fiesta* 67.
Works include *El Crucifijo, Copacabana, Lavanderas, Funeral Aimara, Alacitas, Madre, Rezando Reposo,* Historical Murals Palace Hotel and Sharon Building, San Francisco, Murals at Sonoma Mission Inn, Calif., Mural *El Tigero*, Hillsborough, Calif.; murals Peruvian Pavilion and terra cotta fountain Pacific Area, Theme Building, Golden Gate, Int. Exposition 39-40, Murals, Stage Door Canteen, S.F.; American Women's Voluntary Services Canteen; Art Faculty, Mills Coll. and California School of Fine Arts; Mural Altarpiece St. Augustine Church, Pleasanton, Calif., Glass Mosaic Facade, Hillsdale Methodist Church, Calif.; Mural, Matson Navigation Co., San Francisco, Calif.; backdrop for San Francisco Civic Auditorium Concerts.
3 Le Roy Place, San Francisco, Calif. 94109, U.S.A.
Telephone: 415-673-6193.

Soulages, Pierre; French painter; b. 24 Dec. 1919; ed. Lycée de Rodez.
Exhibited abstract painting since 47 in Salon des Surindépendants, Salon de Mai et Réalités Nouvelles; one-man exhbn., Lydia Conti Gallery, Paris 49, Birch Gallery, Copenhagen 51, Stangl Gallery, Munich 52, Kootz Gallery, New York 54-65; Gimpel Gallery, London 55, Galerie de France, Paris 56, 60, 63, exhibited in int. festivals including Biennales of Venice and São Paulo, and the itinerary of the Guggenheim Collection, the Carnegie Inst., Pittsburgh, The New Decade at the Museum of Modern Art, New York,

Tate Gallery, London, etc.; also décors for theatres and ballet; also lithographs and engravings.
Works in Museums of Modern Art, Paris, and N.Y., Tate Gallery, London, Guggenheim Museum, N.Y., Phillips Gallery, Washington, Museum of Modern Art, Rio de Janeiro, museums in many American cities and in Europe; retrospective exhbns. Hanover, Essen, The Hague, Zürich 60-61, Massachusetts Inst. of Technology 62, Copenhagen Glyptothek 63, Fine Arts Museum, Houston 66, Musée Nat. d'Art Moderne, Paris 67; retrospective exhbn. of engravings Ljubljana 61; Carnegie Prize 64.
18 rue des Trois-Portes, Paris 5e, France.

Soule, George Henry, Jr., A.B.; American author and editor; b. 11 June 1887; ed. Yale Univ.
Joined Frederick A. Stokes Co. 08; joined editorial staff *The New Republic* Dec. 14; Coast Artillery 18; joined editorial staff *New York Evening Post* 19; investigator for Inter-Church World Movement Comm. on Steel Strike 19; Dir.-at-large Nat. Bureau of Economic Research 22-; Editor *The New Republic* 24-46; Prof. of Economics, Bennington Coll. 49-57; Research Dir. Effect of Vertical Integration in Agriculture on Small Business 59-60.
Publs. *The New Unionism in the Clothing Industry* (with J. M. Budish) 20, *The Useful Art of Economics* 29, *A Planned Society* 32, *The Coming American Revolution* 34, *Sydney Hillman, Labour Statesman* 39, *The Strength of Nations* 42, *America's Stake in Britain's Future* 45, *Prosperity Decade* 47, *Introduction to Economic Science* 48, *Economic Forces in American History* 52, *Ideas of the Great Economists* 52, *Men, Wages and Employment in the Modern U.S. Economy* 54, *Time for Living* 55, *American Economic History* (with Vincent Caroso) 57, *Longer Life* 58, *The Shape of Tomorrow* 58, *Economics-Measurement, Theories, Case Studies* 61, *Economics for Living* 61, *The New Science of Economics* 64.
South Kent, Connecticut, U.S.A.

Soupault, Philippe; French writer; b. 2 Aug. 1897; ed. Univ. de Paris à la Sorbonne.
Winner of Strassburger Prize 32, Prix Italia 58, 63; fmr. Prof. Swarthmore Coll., Pa., U.S.A.
Publs. Poetry: *Les Champs Magnétiques* 19, *Westwego* 22, *Georgia* 26, *Poésies completes* 37, *L'arme secrète* 47, *Message de l'ile déserte* 48, *Chansons* 50, *Sans phrases* 53; novels: *Le Bon apôtre* 23, *Les frères Durandeau* 25, *En joue!* 25, *Le Coeur d'or* 27, *Le Négre* 27, *Les Moribonds* 34, biographies of *Henri Rousseau, Charles Baudelaire* 27, *Paolo Uccello* 28, *William Blake* 29, *Lautréamont* 31, *Souvenirs de James Joyce* 43; plays: *La fille qui faisait des miracles* 51, *Comment dresser une Garce* 54, *Tous ensemble au bout du monde* 55, *Rendezvous* 57, *La nuit du temps* 62, *Profils Perdus* 63, *Eugène Labiche* 64.
19 quai Voltaire, Paris 7e, France.

Souphanouvong, Prince; Laotian politician; b. 02; ed. Lycée Saint-Louis (Paris), Ecole Nationale des Ponts et Chaussées.
Studied engineering in France; returned to Laos 38 and became active in the Nationalist Movement; joined Pathet Lao and fought against the French; formed Nationalist Party (Neo Leo Hak Xat) in Bangkok 50; Leader of the Patriotic Front; Minister of Planning, Reconstruction and Urbanism 58; arrested 59, escaped May 60 and rejoined Pathet Lao Forces; Pathet Lao del., Geneva Conf. on Laos 61-62; Vice-Premier and Minister of Econ. Planning 62-, now absent.
Office of the Vice Premier, Vientiane, Laos.

Souphantha-Rangsi, Prince; Laotian diplomatist; b. 6 July 1912; ed. Luang Prabang, Laos.
Civil Admin. 37-40; Private Sec. to King 40-45; Provincial Gov. 45-50; mem. King's Council 50-57; Sec.-Gen. of Palace 57-63; Amb. to U.K. 63-67; Grand Officier du Million Eléphants, Medaille de la Résistance

Franco-Laotienne, Chevalier de la Légion d'Honneur and other decorations.
Ministry of Foreign Affairs, Vientiane, Laos.

Souriau, Michel, D. ès L.; French university professor; b. 13 March 1891; ed. Ecole Normale Supérieure, Paris and Fondation Thiers, Paris.
Taught in Madrid and Lycées of Annecy and Nancy 21-29; lecturer at Nancy Univ. 29-38, Dean, Faculty of Letters 38-39; Rector of Rennes Univ. 41-43, of Lille Univ. 46-55; Dir. Résidence Univ. Jean Zay and Administrator Centre Univ. Int. of Paris 55-; Dir. Permanent Mission on Higher Education; Officier, Légion d'Honneur, Ordre de Léopold I and of Instruction Publique, Commdr. Crown of Belgium, Croix de Guerre.
Publs. *La Fonction pratique de la Finalité* 27, *Le Jugement réfléchissant dans la Philosophie critique de Kant* 27, *Le Temps* 37, *Ethique transréelle* 61; contributor to *Recherches philosophiques*.
6 rue Jean Giraudoux, Sceaux (Seine), France.
Telephone: ROB-66-84.

Soustelle, Jacques, D. ès L.; French scientist and politician; b. 3 Feb. 1912; ed. Ecole normale supérieure.
Various scientific missions to Mexico 32-34, 35-36 and 39; Asst. Dir. Musée de l'Homme Paris 37; French Nat. Cttee. Del. in Central America, Mexico and West Indies 41-42; Nat. Commr. for Information 42-43; Minister of Information 45; Minister for the Colonies 45; mem. Constituent Assembly 45-46; Sec. Gen. of Rassemblement du Peuple Français; mem. French Parl. for Lyon 51-59; Gov.-Gen. of Algeria 55-56; leader, Gaullist group in Nat. Assembly 56-58; returned to Algeria May 58; Minister of Information July 58-Jan. 59; Minister attached to Prime Minister as Minister for Sahara and Atomic Questions 59-60; mem. Central Cttee. U.N.R. 58-60; Political Dir. *Voici Pourquoi* 60; Officier Légion d'Honneur; Hon. C.B.E.; living out of France 61-, expelled from Italy Aug. 62; lives mainly in Italy and Switzerland.
Publs. *La Vie quotidienne des Aztèques* 55, 62, *Aimée et souffrante Algérie* 56, *L'espérance Trahie* 62, *Sur une route nouvelle* 64, *La Page n'est pas tournée* 65, *L'Art du Mexique ancien* 66, *Les Quatre Soleils* 67.
c/o 25 rue du Président-Edouard-Herriot, Lyons 1er, (Rhône), France.

Southam, Gordon Hamilton, B.A.; Canadian civil servant; b. 19 Dec. 1916; ed. Ashbury Coll. School, Trinity Coll., Toronto and Christ Church Oxford.
Officer, Second World War, British and Canadian Armies; Reporter *The Times*, London 45-46; Editorial Writer *Ottawa Citizen* 46-47; joined Ministry of External Affairs 48; Second Sec., Stockholm 49-Aug. 53, Ottawa 53-59; Chargé d'Affaires, Warsaw Mar. 59-60, Amb. May 60-62; Head, Information Div., Ministry of External Affairs Aug. 62-64; Dir. Southam Press Ltd. 64-; Co-ordinator, Nat. Arts Centre 64-67, Dir. Gen. 67-.
327 Buena Vista Road, Rockcliffe, Ottawa, Canada.

Southard, Frank Allan, Jr., B.A., PH.D.; American economist; b. 17 Jan. 1907; ed. Pomona Coll., and Univ. of Calif.
Instructor in Economics, Univ. of Calif. 30-31, Asst. Prof. of Economics, Cornell Univ. 31-39, Prof. 39-48, Chair. of Dept. of Economics 46-48; Researcher in Int. Finance, Carnegie Endowment 34; Senior Economic Analyst, U.S. Tariff Comm. 35; Guggenheim Fellow, Latin America 40; Asst. Dir., Div. of Monetary Research, Treasury Dept. 41-42; served U.S. Naval Reserve, principally as Financial Adviser, Allied Force H.Q. Mediterranean 42-46; Dir. Office of Int. Finance, Treasury Dept. 47-48; Assoc. Dir. of Research and Statistics, in charge of int. work, Board of Govs. Federal Reserve System 48-49; Special Asst. to Sec. of Treasury and U.S. Exec. Dir. Int. Monetary Fund 49-62; Dep. Man. Dir. I.M.F. 62-; Alt. Gov. I.M.F. and I.B.R.D. 48-62; Officer Legion of Merit; Hon. O.B.E.

Publs. *American Industry in Europe* 31, *Canadian-American Industry* (with others) 36, *Foreign Exchange Practice and Policy* (with others) 40, *Some European Currency and Exchange Experiences* 43-46, 47, *Finances of European Liberation—With Special Reference to Italy* 46.
Office: International Monetary Fund, 19th and H Streets N.W., Washington, D.C. 20431; Home: 4328 Van Ness Street, N.W., Washington, D.C. 20016, U.S.A.
Telephone: DU1-3004.

Southborough, 3rd Baron, cr. 17; **Francis John Hopwood,** Kt.; British company director; b. 7 March 1897; ed. Westminster School.
Sub-Lieut., R.N.V.R. in First World War, served at Admiralty and Foreign Office, seconded to staff of Irish Convention, Dublin 17; later Sec. to War Trade Advisory Cttee.; joined Royal Dutch Shell Group 19; Pres. Asiatic Petroleum Corpn., in U.S.A. (also rep. Petroleum Board) 42-46; Man.-Dir. Shell Petroleum Co. Ltd. and N. V. de Bataafsche Petroleum Maatschappij 46-57; Chair. Shell Oil Co. 51-57; Dir. The Shell Transport and Trading Co. Ltd. 46-, Man.-Dir. 51-; Dir. The Shell Petroleum Co. Ltd., Bataafsche Petroleum Nij., Shell Overseas Exploration Co. Ltd.; Commdr. of the Order of Orange Nassau.
Bingham's Melcombe, Near Dorchester, Dorset, England.

Southwell, Sir Richard Vynne, Kt., M.A., F.R.S., British engineer; b. 2 July 1888; ed. Norwich School and Trinity Coll., Cambridge.
Fellow Trinity Coll. Cambridge 12, Lecturer 14; served First World War; Supt. Aerodynamics Dept. Nat. Physical Laboratory 20-25; Fellow Trinity Coll. and Univ. Lecturer in Mathematics, Cambridge 25-29; Prof. of Engineering Science Oxford Univ. 29-42; Rector Imperial Coll. London 42-48; Foreign Assoc. U.S. Nat. Acad. Science; Hon. Fellow Inst. Aeronautical Sciences, U.S.A.; Pres. Int. Union of Theoretical and Applied Mechanics 46-48, Int. Congress of Applied Mechanics 48-52, Treas. 52-56; Gen. Sec. British Asscn. 48-56; Hon. Fellow, Brasenose Coll., Oxford, Trinity Coll., Cambridge, Imperial Coll., London, Royal Aeronautical Soc.; Hon. LL.D. (St. Andrews, Glasgow), Hon. D.Sc. (Bristol, Belfast and Brussels), Hon. D.Eng. (Sheffield), Hon. M.I.Mech.E.; Clayton Prize 47; Worcester Read Warner Medal 54; Timoshenko Medal of Amer. Soc. Mech.E. 59; James Alfred Ewing Medal, Inst. C.E. 46.
Publs. *Introduction to the Theory of Elasticity* 36, *Relaxation Methods in Engineering Science* 40, *Relaxation Methods in Theoretical Physics* Vol. I 46, Vol. II 56.
The Old House, 20 Church Lane, Trumpington, Cambridge, England.

Soutou, Jean Marie Léon; French diplomatist; b. 18 Sept. 1912; ed. Univ. de Paris à la Sorbonne.
Entered Ministry of Foreign Affairs 43, served Switzerland 43-44, Yugoslavia 45; Administrator to Minister of Foreign Affairs 50; Sec. of Foreign Affairs 51; Asst. Dir. Cabinet of M. Mendès-France 54-55; E. European Sub-Dir. to Minister of Foreign Affairs 55-56; Minister-Counsellor, Moscow 56-58; Consul-Gen., Milan 58-61; Dir. European Affairs, Ministry of Foreign Affairs 61-62, Dir. African Affairs 62-66; Insp.-Gen. Diplomatic and Consular Corps 66-; Chevalier, Légion d'Honneur.
Ministère des Affaires étrangères, 37 Quai d'Orsay, Paris 7e; and 23 avenue de Bretteville, Neuilly-sur-Seine, Seine, France.

Souvanlasy, Khamking, L. en D.; Laotian government official and diplomatist; b. 14 Sept. 1926; ed. Collège Pavie, Vientiane, and Univ. of Paris.
Head of Dept., Ministry of Foreign Affairs 53-54, Ministry of Nat. Educ. 54-55; Under-Sec. to Pres. of Council of Ministers 55-56; Counsellor, Laotian Embassy, Tokyo 56-58, Chargé d'Affaires a.i. 58-59; Sec. of State in Presidency of Council of Ministers (in charge

of Foreign Affairs and Nat. Information) 59; Sec. of State for Foreign Affairs 60; Adviser, Ministry of Foreign Affairs 61-62; Ambassador to People's Republic of China 63-65, to U.S.A. 66-; Perm. Rep. of Kingdom of Laos in U.S.A. 66-.
Royal Laotian Embassy, 2222 S Street, N.W., Washington., D.C. 20008, U.S.A.
Telephone: DE2-6416-17 (Office); CO5-0403 (Home).

Souvanna Phouma, H.H. Prince; Laotian engineer and politician; b. 7 Oct. 1901; ed. Coll. Paul Bert and Lycée Albert Sarraut, Hanoi, Univs. of Paris and Grenoble.
Entered Public Works Service of Indo-China 31; Engineer at Phoukhoun 40-41, at Luang Prabang 41-44; Chief Engineer, Bureau à la Circonscription Territoriale des Travaux Publics du Laos 44-45; Principal Engineer (1st Class) of the Public Works Service of Indo-China; Minister of Public Works 50-51; Prime Minister, Pres. of the Council, Minister of Public Works and of Planning 51-54; Vice-Pres. of the Council and Minister of Nat. Defence and Ex-Servicemen 54-56; Prime Minister, Pres. of the Council, Minister of Nat. Defence and Ex-Servicemen, of Foreign Affairs and of Information 56-57, Prime Minister 57-58; Ambassador to France 58-59; Pres. National Assembly 60; Prime Minister, Minister of Defence and Foreign Affairs Aug.-Dec. 60; Leader of Neutralist Govt. 60-62; Prime Minister, Minister of Defence and Veterans and Social Affairs 62-, Minister of Foreign Affairs 64-; Grand Cross Order of a Million Elephants, Commdr. Légion d'Honneur, etc.
Domaine du Nongthévada, Vientiane, Laos.

Souza, Francis N.; Indian painter; b. 12 April 1904; ed. Sir J. J. School of Art, Bombay.
In London 49-; one man exhibitions London, Paris, Stockholm, Frankfurt, Stuttgart, Bombay, New Delhi, Newcastle upon Tyne, and Johannesburg; represented in Baroda Museum, Nat. Gallery, New Delhi, Tate Gallery, London, Wakefield Gallery, Haifa Museum, Nat. Gallery, Melbourne, etc.; several awards.
Publ. *Words and Lines* (autobiography) 59.
c/o Grosvenor Gallery, 30 Davies Street, London, W.1, England.

Souza Lopes, Hugo; Brazilian entomologist; b. 5 Jan. 1909; ed. Escola Nacional de Veterinaria da Universidade Rural do Brasil.
Qualified Veterinary Practitioner 33; Asst. Prof. Univ. Rural do Brasil 33-38, Prof. of Parasitology 38-64, Prof. Emer. 64-; Biologist, Instituto Oswaldo Cruz 50-, Chief of Entomology Section 61-64; mem. Brazilian Acad. of Sciences; Premio Costa Lima (Brazilian Acad. of Sciences).
Publs. research into insects (Diptera: Sarcophagidae, Calliphoridae, Acalypteratae and Memestrinidae) and molluscs.
Instituto Oswaldo Cruz, Caixa Postal 926-ZC 00, Rio de Janeiro, Brazil.

Souzay, Gérard (Gérard Marcel Tisserand); French singer; b. 8 Dec. 1920; ed. Coll. de Chinon, Lycée Hoche (Versailles), Lycée Carnot (Paris).
Debut 45; since then numerous tours and appearances in Europe, North and South America, South Africa, Australia and Japan; radio and television performances; Premier Prix d'Excellence, Paris Conservatoire.
26 rue Freycinet, Paris 16e, France.

Sowerby, Leo, MUS.D.; American composer and organist; b. 1 May 1895; ed. American Conservatory of Music, Chicago, and American Acad., Rome.
Professor American Conservatory of Music, Chicago 25-62; Organist and Choirmaster St. James' Church, Chicago 27-62; Dir. Coll. of Church Musicians, Washington Cathedral, D.C. 62-; Pulitzer prize for Musical Composition 46.
Compositions: Five Symphonies for Orchestra; Orches-

tral Concertos for Organ, Piano, Violin and Cello; Chamber and Pianoforte works, Symphony for Organ, *Canticle of the Sun;* much music for solo organ and for chorus.
[*Died July* 1968]

Soyinka, Wole, B.A.; Nigerian playwright and lecturer; b. 13 July 1935; ed. Univ. of Ibadan, Nigeria, and Univ. of Leeds, England.
Worked at Royal Court Theatre, London; Research Fellow in Drama, Univ. of Ibadan 60-61; Lecturer in English, Univ. of Ife 62-63; Senior Lecturer in English, Univ. of Lagos 65-; Artistic Dir. Orisun Theatre, 1960 Masks; Literary Editor Orisun Acting Editions.
Publs. plays: *The Lion and the Jewel* 59, *The Swamp Dwellers* 59, *A Dance of the Forests* 60, *The Trials of Brother Jero* 61, *The Strong Breed* 62, *The Road* 64, *Kongi's Harvest* 65; novel: *The Interpreters* 64; *Indandre and Other Poems* 67.
Department of English, University of Lagos, Lagos, Nigeria.

Spaak, Fernand Paul Jules, D. en D., B.A.; Belgian international civil servant; b. 8 Aug. 1923; ed. Univs. of Brussels and Cambridge.
National Bank of Belgium 50-52; Sec. Econ. Div., High Authority of European Coal and Steel Community 52-54, Exec. Asst. to Pres. of High Authority 54-58, Dir. Cartels and Concentration Div. 58-60; Gen. Dir. Supply Agency and Dir. a.i. Safeguards and Controls Euratom 66-68; Dir. Gen. for Energy, Comm. of EEC.
170 rue de la Loi, Brussels 4, Belgium.
Telephone: 35-80-40.

Spaak, Paul-Henri; Belgian lawyer and politician; b. 25 Jan. 1899.
Socialist Deputy 32-56, 61-66, Minister of Transport, Posts and Telegraphs in Van Zeeland Cabinet 35-36, of Foreign Affairs and Trade 36-38; Prime Minister May 38-Feb. 39; Minister of Foreign Affairs Sept. 39-45; deputy Prime Minister in Van Acker's Govt. Feb. 45-46; Prime Minister March 46; Minister of Foreign Affairs April 46-50; Prime Minister March 47-50; Minister of Foreign Affairs 54-57; Pres. of U.N. Assembly 46; Pres. O.E.E.C. April 48-50; Chair. Council of European Recovery 48; Pres. Consultative Assembly of Council of Europe 49-51; Chair. Int. Council of the European Movement 50-55; Minister of State for Belgium 49-; Sec.-Gen. to NATO, Paris 57-61; Dep. Prime Minister, Minister of Foreign and African Affairs 61-65; Minister of Foreign Affairs and Co-ordination of External Policy 65-66; post with I.T.T.-Europe, Brussels 66-; Chair. Special NATO working group for ensuring closer relations between the 15 member states 67-; mem. Acad. Royale de Langue et de Littérature Françaises de Belgique; Charlemagne Prize 57; Hon. Companion of Honour (C.H.) Great Britain 63.
c/o I.T.T. Belgium Ltd., 11 boulevard de l'Empereur, Brussels, Belgium.

Spaatz, Gen. Carl, D.F.C., D.S.C., D.S.M., with 3 Oak Leaf Clusters, American officer (retd.); b. 28 June 1891; ed. U.S. Mil. Acad., San Diego Aviation School, Tactical School, Command and Gen. Staff School.
2nd Lieut. 14, promoted through ranks to Brig.-Gen. 40; served with 25th Infantry Hawaii 14-15, 1st Aero Squadron N.M. 15, with punitive expeditions in Mexico and on borders; Major, 31st Aero Squadron A.E.F. 17; commander Issondan Air Training School (France) 17-18; Flight Commdr. 13th Pursuit Squadron (officially credited 3 enemy planes); Asst. Air Officer Western Dept. San Francisco 19-20; Command Mather Field Calif. 20, Kelly Field Tex. 20-21; Air Officer 8th Corps Area 21; Commander 1st Pursuit Group Selfridge Field Mich. 22-24; attached Office of Chief of Air Service 25-29; established record refuelling flight Los Angeles 29; Command 7th Bombardment Group Rock-

well Field Calif., later Commanding Officer 29-31; Commanding Officer 1st Bombardment Wing March Field Calif. 31-33; Chief of Training and Operations Div. Office of Chief of Air Corps 33-35; Exec. Officer 2nd Wing Air Force 36-39; Chief of Plans Div. Air Corps 40; Chief of Air Staff 41; Commanding Gen. U.S. Army Air Forces European Theatre of Operations 42-43; Commanding Gen. Northwest African Air Forces 43; Commanding U.S. Strategic Air Forces in Europe 44; U.S. Strategic Air Forces in the Pacific 45-46; Commanding Gen. of Army Air Forces Mar. 1st 46; Chief of Staff, U.S. Air Force, 47-48; retd. with rank of General 48; Legion of Merit, Bronze Star, Grand Officer of French Legion of Honour, French Croix de Guerre with Palm, Hon. G.B.E. (U.K.), Russian Second Order of Suvorov, Order Polonia Restituta, Commanders' Cross with Star, Grand Cordon Order of the Nile (Egypt), Order of Orange Nassau (Netherlands), Order of Crown with Palm (Belgium), etc.
5 Grafton Street, Chevy Chase Village, Md., U.S.A.

Špaček, Josef; Czechoslovak politician; b. 7 Aug. 1927; ed. School of Political Studies, Central Committee of Communist Party of Czechoslovakia.
Chief Sec. Kutná Hora District Cttee. Czechoslovak Union of Youth 46-47; Sec. District Cttee. C.P. of Czechoslovakia, Ledeč n.S. 47-50; Chief Sec. Jihlava District C.P. of Czechoslovakia 50-52; instructor, Jihlava Regional Cttee. C.P. of Czechoslovakia 54-55; Chief Sec. Pelhřimov District Cttee. C.P. 55-56; Dept. Head, Jihlava Regional Cttee. C.P. 56-59; Dept. Head, Central Cttee. C.P. of Czechoslovakia, Prague 60-61; Dept. Head, later Sec. and Chief Sec. South Moravian Regional Cttee. C.P. of Czechoslovakia, Brno 61-; mem. Central Cttee. C.P. of Czechoslovakia 66-; mem. Presidium of Central Cttee. C.P. of Czechoslovakia 68-; Order of 25 February 1948 49; Award for Merit in Construction 58.
Office: Regional Committee of Communist Party of Czechoslovakia, Brno, Burešova 20, Czechoslovakia.

Spadavekkia, Antonio Emmanuilovich; Soviet composer; b. 1907; ed. Moscow Conservatoire.
Honoured Worker of the Arts of the R.S.F.S.R. 63; Order of Badge of Honour 67.
Principal compositions: *Djangar* (symphonic suite) 40, Concerto for Piano and Orchestra 44; Operas: *The Hotel Mistress* 47, *Calvary* 53, *The Gadfly* 59, *Brave Soldier Schweik* 61; Ballet: *Coast of Happiness* 48; Incidental music for films: *Cinderella* 46, *For Those at Sea* 47, *India-rubber Boy* 50, *The Brave* 50, *Mountain Halt* 52, *The Unsubdued* 59; Music for plays: *The Minor, Katrine Lefevre, The Tamer Tamed, Fairy Kiss, The Green Trunk, The Tale of a Tale, Adventures of Chipollino, Buratino, Three Muskateers, The Great Wizard;* romances, songs, instrumental music.
Moscow Branch of R.S.F.S.R. Composers' Union, 4/6 Third Miusskaya Street, Moscow, U.S.S.R.

Spaght, Monroe Edward, PH.D.; American oil executive; b. 9 Dec. 1909; ed. Stanford Univ.
Research Chemist, Technologist, Shell Oil Co., Martinez and Wilmington, Calif. 33-40, Man. (Development and Mfg.) 40-45; Vice-Pres. Shell Development Co., New York City 46-49, Pres. Emeryville, Calif. 49-53; Exec. Vice-Pres. and Dir., Shell Oil Co. 53-60, Pres. and Dir. 60-65, Chair. 65-; a Man. Dir. Royal Dutch Petroleum Co., Shell Petroleum N.V., Shell Petroleum Co. Ltd. 65-; official scientific and educational orgs.
Shell Centre, London, S.E.1, England.

Spagnolli, Giovanni; Italian politician; b. 26 Oct. 1907; ed. Univ. Cattolica del Sacro Cuore, Milan.
Former official, Banca Commerciale Italiana; fmr. Sec. Nat. Cttee. of Liberation, Milan; Sec. Christian Democrat Party 45-48; Senator 53-, Under-Sec. for Foreign Trade 58-60, Vice-Pres. Finance and Treasury Comm. of Senate 60-63, Minister of Merchant Marine 63-66;

Minister of Posts and Telecommunications 66-68, of Merchant Marine 68-; Christian Democrat.
Via dei Monti Parioli 53/A, Rome, Italy.
Telephone: 874588.

Spahr, Charles Eugene, B.S.; American oil executive; b. 8 Oct. 1913; ed. Univ. of Kansas and Harvard Univ. Business School.
Joined Standard Oil Co. (Ohio) 39, Vice-Pres. (Transportation) 51, Exec. Vice-Pres. and Dir. 55, Pres. 57-; Major in Army Corps of Engineers 42-45; Dir. Supply and Distribution Div. Petroleum Admin. for Defense 52, White Motor Corpn., Cleveland, Electric Illuminating Co., Nat. City Bank of Cleveland, American Petroleum Inst., Cleveland and Ohio Chambers of Commerce, Ohio Bell Telephone Co.; Trustee Lutheran Hospital. Cleveland Development Foundation; mem. Exec. Cttee. Board of Trustees Case Inst. of Technology; Chair. Board of Trustees Baldwin-Wallace Coll.; mem. Exec. Cttee. of the Greater Cleveland Growth Board; mem. Nat. Petroleum Council; Chair. Plans for Progress Advisory Council; Dir. Repub. Steel Corpn.; Hon. Dr. Ing. (Fenn Coll.), Hon. LL.D. (Baldwin-Wallace Coll.), Citation for Distinguished Service (Univ. of Kansas).
The Standard Oil Co., 1750 Midland Bldg., Cleveland, Ohio 44115, U.S.A.
Telephone: 216-621-7400.

Spaldoni, Giovanni, LL.D.; Italian journalist; b. 21 June 1925.
Writer for *Il Messaggero;* Political Editor *Gazzetta del Popolo* 50-52, of *Corriere della Sera* 53-55; Editor *Resto del Carlino* 55-68; Editor *Corriere della Sera* Feb. 68-; Teacher of Contemporary History, Faculty of Political Science, Florence; Uff. della Legion d'Onore; Cavaliere di Gran Groce dell'Ordine al Merito della Repubblica.
Publs. *Sorel* 47, *Il 1848 realtà e leggenda di una rivoluzione* 48, *Ritratto dell'Italia moderna* 49, *Lotte sociali in Italia* 49, *Il papato socialista* 50, *L'opposizione cattolica da Porta Pia al '98* 54, *Giolitti e i cattolici* 60, *I radicali dell'Ottocento* 62, *I repubblicani dopo l'Unità* 62, *Un dissidente del Risorgimento* 62, *Firenze Capitale* 67, *Il Tevere più largo* 67, *Storia Fiorentina, Carducci nella storia d'Italia.*
Corriere della Sera, Via IV Novembre 149, Milan, Italy.

Spandaryan, Victor Borisovich; Soviet foreign trade official; b. 1921; ed. Moscow State Univ., Academy of Foreign Trade.
Member C.P.S.U. 44-; Chief Section, later Chief, Dept., Ministry of Foreign Trade, 50-54; Chief, Dept., Ministry of Foreign Trade 55-68; Trade Representative in Japan 68-; Order of Red Banner of Labour (twice), Order of Red Star.
U.S.S.R. Trade Representation, Tokyo, Japan.

Spanides, Vice Admiral Athanassios; Greek civil servant and retired naval officer; b. 31 July 1906; ed. Naval Cadet School, Piraeus and Naval War Coll., Athens.
Graduated as Ensign 26; served in cruisers, destroyers and submarines; C.O. Greek submarines and L.S.T.s operating in Mediterranean, Second World War; Naval Officer in charge W. Greece 45-47; Chief of Naval Personnel 47-49; Dir. War Naval Acad. 49-51; Capt. of Destroyers 51-52; Rear-Admiral 52; Nat. Military Rep. to SHAPE, Paris 53-55; Dep. Chief, Nat. Defence Staff 55-57; retd. 58; Pres. Greek Atomic Energy Comm. 55-64; Sec.-Gen. Radical Union Party (E.R.E.); Lecturer, Nat. Defence Coll. of Greece and NATO War Coll.; Medal of Bravery, War Cross (twice), D.S.O., Knight Commdr. Royal Order of George.
Charilaou Trikoupi 40, Kiffissia, Athens; and Nikis 4, Athens, Greece.

Spark, Muriel Sarah, O.B.E.; British author; ed. James Gillespie's High School for Girls, Edinburgh.
Won *The Observer* story prize 51, Italia Prize 62, James

Tait Black Memorial Prize for *The Mandelbaum Gate* 66.
Publs. *The Comforters* 57, *Robinson* 58, *Memento Mori* 59, *The Bachelors* 60, *The Ballad of Peckham Rye, The Prime of Miss Jean Brodie* 61 (play 66), (stories) *The Go-Away Bird* 58, (stories and radio plays) *Voices at Play* 61, (play) *John Masefield* 62, *Doctors of Philosophy* 63, *The Girls of Slender Means* 63, *The Mandelbaum Gate* 65, *Collected Stories* Vol. I 67, *Collected Poems* Vol. I 67, *The Public Image* 68.
c/o Macmillan & Co. Ltd., Little Essex Street, London, W.C.2, England.

Sparkman, John J., LL.B., A.M.; American politician; b. 20 Dec. 1899; ed. Univ. of Alabama.
Admitted to Alabama Bar 25; Y.M.C.A. Sec., Univ. of Alabama 23-25; Instructor, Huntsville Coll. 25-28; practised as attorney, Huntsville 25-36; U.S. Commr. 30-31; mem. Congress 37-47; U.S. Senator from Alabama 46-; Democratic nomination for Vice-Presidency 52.
Home: Huntsville, Ala.; Office: Senate Office Building, Washington, D.C., U.S.A.

Spasowski, Romuald; Polish diplomatist; b. 20; ed. Coll. of Mechanics.
Former Asst. Instructor, Coll. of Mechanics; served army; mem. Polish Mil. Mission to investigate War Crimes in Germany 46; Consul-Gen., Düsseldorf 48-49; Ministry of Foreign Affairs, Warsaw 49-51; served London 51-53; Minister to Argentina 53-55; Ambassador to U.S.A. 55-61; Dir. of Political Dept., Ministry of Foreign Affairs 61-.
Ministry of Foreign Affairs, Warsaw, Poland.

Spater, George Alexander, J.D.; American airline company executive; b. 3 May 1909; ed. Univ. of Michigan.
Admitted to N.Y. Bar 35; practised privately in New York until 58; partner Chadbourne, Wallace, Park and Whiteside 42-58; Exec. Vice-Pres., Gen. Counsel, Dir. American Airlines Inc. 59-67, Vice-Chair., Board of Dirs. 67-68, Pres. and Chief Exec. Officer 68-; mem. American Bar Asscn., Bar Asscn. City of New York.
Office: 633 Third Avenue, New York, N.Y. 10017; Home: Ardsley-on-Hudson, N.Y., U.S.A.
Telephone: 212-867-1234 (Office).

Speaight, Robert William, C.B.E., M.A., F.R.S.L.; British actor, critic, theatre director and author; b. 14 Jan. 1904; ed. Haileybury Coll. and Lincoln Coll., Oxford.
Principal parts: Becket in T. S. Eliot's *Murder in the Cathedral* leading Shakespearian parts for the Old Vic.; Christ in Dorothy Sayers' *Man Born to be King*. More in *A Man for All Seasons*; principal productions: *Antony and Cleopatra*, Geneva; *The Madwoman of Chaillot*, London; *Murder in the Cathedral*, Montreal; guest artist with Australian Broadcasting Comm. 53 and with Australian Elizabethan Theatre Trust 60, 62-63.
Publs. *The Lost Hero* 34, *The Angel in the Mist* 36, *The Unbroken Heart* 39; Biography: *Thomas Becket* 38, *William Poel and the Elizabethan Revival* 54, *Hilaire Belloc* 57, *Letters of Hilaire Belloc* 58, *William Rothenstein* 63, *Eric Gill* 66, *Teilhard de Chardin* 67; Criticism: *Acting* 39, *Drama Since 1939* 48, *George Eliot* 54, *Nature in Shakespearian Tragedy* 55, *Christian Theatre* 60.
Campion House, Benenden, Kent, England.
Telephone: Benenden 617.

Spear, Ruskin, R.A., A.R.C.A.; British artist; b. 30 June 1911; ed. Royal Coll. of Art.
Elected London Group 42, Pres. 50; Visiting Teacher of Painting, Royal Coll. of Art and St. Martin's School of Art; paintings exhibited in many English and Australian art galleries: works purchased by The Chantrey Trustees, The British Council, The Arts Council, Stratford Memorial Theatre, St. Clement Dane's R.A.F. Memorial Church; executed murals for liner *Canberra*; numerous portraits incl. Lord Adrian, Lord Rothermere, Archbishop of Canterbury, Dowager Duchess of Devonshire,

Sir Aubrey Lewis, Sir Ian Jacob, Sir Laurence Olivier, Mrs. Barbara Castle; travelling exhbns. in U.S.; exhbn. in Pushkin Museum, Moscow 57.
20 Fielding Road, London, W.4, England.
Telephone: 01-995-9736.

Spears, Maj.-Gen. Sir Edward Louis, Bt., K.B.E., C.B., M.C.; British officer, company director, author and politician; b. 7 Aug. 1886; ed. privately.
Entered Army 03; Head of British Military Mission, Paris 17-20; Conservative M.P. 22-24, 31-45; Personal Liaison Officer between Prime Minister and French Prime Minister 40; Head of Spears Mission, London 40-42, also Syria, Cairo, Brazzaville; Minister to Syria and Lebanon and mem. Middle East War Council 42-44, resigned; Chair. Ashanti Goldfields Ltd.; Chancellor Inst. of Dirs.; Pres. British Bata Shoe Co. Ltd., United Service Corps.
Publs. *Lessons of the Russo-Japanese War, Cavalry Tactical Schemes, Liaison, 1914, Prelude to Victory, Assignment to Catastrophe, Two Men Who Saved France, The Picnic Basket.*
164 St. Stephens House, London, S.W.1. England.

Specht, Charles Alfred, B.B.A.; American business executive; b. 31 July 1914; ed. Univ. Coll. Rutgers Univ. and New York Graduate School of Business Admin.
Controller, Chas. Pfizer & Co. Inc. 50-52, Dir. 52-55; Pres. Pfizer Int. Inc. 52-55; Pres. and Dir. Horizons Titanium Corpn. 55-57; Vice-Pres. and Dir. Horizons Inc. 55-56; Pres., Dir. Chief Exec. Officer, Minerals and Chemicals, Philipp Corpn. 56-63; Pres. and Dir. Macmillan Bloedel Ltd. 63-; Dir. Int. Pipe and Ceramics Corpn.
Publ. *Financing Foreign Chemical and Pharmaceutical Operations.*
Macmillian, Bloedel Ltd., 1199 W. Pender Street, Vancouver 1, B.C.; Home: 1416 Acadia Road, Vancouver 8, B.C., Canada.
Telephone: 683-6711 (Office); 224-3424 (Home).

Speidel, Gen. Hans, DR.PHIL.; German army officer; b. 28 Oct. 1897; ed. Univs. of Tübingen and Berlin, Technische Hochschule Stuttgart, Kriegsakademie.
Regular army officer 14-45; served 14-18 war in König Karl Grenadier Regt. and 39-45 war mainly in staff appts., finally as Chief of Staff to an Army Group under Rommel; arrested by the Gestapo Sept. 44; Lecturer, Univ. of Tübingen 49-55; Mil. Adviser to Fed. Govt. 51-55; C.-in-C. German Armed Forces 55-57; Commdr. Allied Land Forces Central Europe 57-63; Special Counsellor to Fed. Govt.; Pres. of Foundation, Sciences and Politics (Wissenschaft und Politik) 64-; Ritterkreuz Königlich-Württembergischen Militärverdienstordens (14-18), Ritterkreuz des Eisernen Kreuzes (39-45), Grosses Verdienstkreuz mit Stern und Schulterband 63.
Publs. *Invasion 1944—Ein Beitrag zu Rommels und des Reiches Schicksal* 49 (also publ. in France, Great Britain, U.S.A., Sweden, Italy, Greece, Japan); edited Beck's *Studien* 55; essays on Theodor Heuss, Neidhart von Gneisenau, etc.
Am Spitzenbach 15, 534 Bad Honnef/Rhein, German Federal Republic.
Telephone: Bad Honnef 3150.

Spence, Sir Basil Urwin, Kt., O.M., O.B.E., T.D., R.A., R.D.I., P.P.R.I.B.A.; British architect; b. 13 Aug. 1907; ed. George Watson's Coll., Edinburgh, schools of architecture in London and Edinburgh Univs.
Silver medallist R.I.B.A. 31; Arthur Cates Prizeman (Town Planning) 32; Pugin student 33; R.I.B.A. Distinction in Town Planning 61; served in army 39-45 war; built large country houses before war, since then housing estates, theatres, schools, university buildings, churches and factories; Adviser to Board of Trade for B.I.F. 47, 48 and 49; won competition for new Coventry Cathedral 51; Saltire Award for fishermen's

houses, Dunbar 52; Newhaven 61; Planning Consultant for Edinburgh Univ. 54, Southampton Univ. 55; apptd. to design new Town Halls for Slough, Basildon and Hampstead, new Univ. of Sussex, and various univ. science buildings, British Embassy, Rome, Hyde Park Cavalry Barracks, Civic Centre, Kensington, London, British Pavilion *Expo 67*, Montreal; Consultant architect for extension to Palais des Nations, Geneva, and int. airport at Baghdad; R.I.B.A. Council mem. 52-63, Vice-Pres. 54-55, Hon. Sec. 56; mem. Fine Art Comm. 56-; first Hoffman Wood Prof. of Architecture, Royal Acad. 61-; Pres. R.I.B.A. 58-60; Pres. Building Centre 60-67; Festival of Britain 1951 Award for Sunbury-on-Thames Housing Estate; Hon. Fellow, American Inst. of Architects, Royal Architectural Inst. of Canada, Inst. of South African Architects, Royal Coll. of Art; Hon. D.Litt. (Leicester, Southampton); Hon. LL.D. (Manitoba).

Publ. *Phoenix at Coventry* 62.

1 Canonbury Place, London, N.1, England.

Telephone: 01-226-7175.

Spence, Robert, C.B., D.SC., F.R.S.; British atomic scientist; b. 7 Oct. 1905; ed. Westoe Secondary School, South Shields, Armstrong Coll., Univ. of Durham, and Princeton Univ.

Lecturer in Physical Chemistry, Leeds Univ. 31-46; Scientific Adviser, H.Q., R.A.F., Middle East 42-44; Anglo-Canadian Atomic Energy Laboratory, Montreal 45; Head, U.K. Chemical Group, Chalk River Laboratory, Canada 45-47; Head of Chemistry Div., Atomic Energy Research Establishment, Harwell 47-60, Dep. Dir. 60-64, Dir. 64-68; Master Keynes Coll. and Prof. of Applied Chemistry 68-.

The Master's Lodge, Keynes College, The University of Kent, Canterbury, Kent, England.

Telephone: Canterbury 66822.

Spencer-Chapman, Lt.-Col. Frederick, D.S.O. and Bar, T.D.; British schoolmaster, lecturer and author; b. 10 May 1907; ed. Sedbergh School and St. John's Coll., Cambridge.

Mem. British Arctic Air Route Expedition Greenland 30-31; mem. Pan-American Arctic Airways Expedition 31-32; Master Aysgarth School, Bedale, Yorks 33-35; mem. Marco Pallis' Himalayan Expedition 36; Private Sec. to Political Officer Sikkim; first ascent Chomolhari (24,000 ft.) 37; accompanied Diplomatic Mission to Lhasa, Tibet 36-37; Housemaster Gordonstoun School, Elgin, Morayshire 38-39; trained Commando troops in Scotland 39, Australia 40, Singapore 41; Capt., later Lieut.-Col., 5th Battalion Seaforth Highlanders; entered Malayan jungle in charge of Left-behind parties Jan. 42; emerged from jungle by submarine May 45; returned by parachute Aug. 45; Exec. Officer, Outward Bound Trust 47-48; first Headmaster, King Alfred School, Plön, Schleswig-Holstein, Germany 48-52; Headmaster, St. Andrew's Coll. Grahamstown, S. Africa 56-62; Warden, Pestalozzi Children's Village, Sussex 62-66, Warden, Wantage Hall, Univ. of Reading 66-; Artic Medal 31, Gill Memorial Medal (R.G.S.) 41, Mungo Park Memorial Medal (R.S.G.S.) 48, *Sunday Times* Gold Medal and Literary Award 49.

Publs. *Northern Lights* 32, *Watkins' Last Expedition* 33, *Lhasa The Holy City* 38, *Helvellyn to Himalaya* 40, *Memories of a Mountaineer* (reprint) 45, *The Jungle is Neutral* 48, *Living Dangerously* 53, *Lightest Africa* 55.

Wantage Hall, The University, Reading, Berks., England.

Telephone: Reading 81198 (Office); Reading 81933 (Home).

Spender, Sir Percy Claude, K.C.V.O., K.B.E., KT.ST.J., Q.C., B.A., LL.B.; Australian diplomatist and international judge; b. 5 Oct. 1897; ed. Sydney Univ.

Entered public service as Clerk, Sydney Town Hall 15;

enlisted A.I.F. 18; called to N.S.W. Bar 23; K.C. 35; mem. House of Reps. for Warringah N.S.W. 37-51; mem. Fed. Exec. Council 39, Vice-Pres. Exec. Council 40; Minister without Portfolio 39; Acting Treas. 39, Treas. 40; Minister for Army 40-41; mem. Australian War Cabinet 40-41; mem. of Govt. and later Opposition mem. Australian Advisory War Council 41-45; Lieut.-Col. Active List, Australian Mil. Forces 42-45; Minister for External Affairs 49-51; Ambassador to U.S.A. 51-58; Chair. Australian del. to British Commonwealth Foreign Ministers Conf., Colombo 50, and to UN 50; Vice-Pres. Fifth Gen. Assembly 50-51; Vice-Chair. Australian del. to Seventh, Eighth, Ninth, Tenth and Eleventh Gen. Assemblies, later Chair. 52-56; Vice-Pres. Japanese Peace Treaty Conf. San Francisco 51; Chair. Australian del. to Twelve Power Conf. to settle Draft Statute for Int. Atomic Energy Agency 56 and to several other int. confs.; Australian Gov. Int. Monetary Fund and Int. Bank 51-53 and 56, Alternate Gov. Int. Monetary Fund 54-55; Judge of the Int. Court of Justice 58-67, Pres. 64-67; mem. Int. Diplomatic Acad., etc.; Hon. LL.D., D.C.L., Litt.D.

Publs. *Company Law and Practice* 39, *Foreign Policy—the Next Phase* 44.

Headingley House, 11 Wellington Street, Woollahra, Sydney, N.S.W., Australia.

Spender, Stephen, C.B.E.; British writer; b. 28 Feb. 1909; ed. Univ. Coll. School, London, and Univ. Coll., Oxford.

Poet and critic; Co-editor *Horizon* 39-41; Counsellor, Section of Letters UNESCO 47; Co-editor *Encounter* 53-66, Corresp. Editor 66-67; Consultant in Poetry in English to U.S. Library of Congress 65-; Hon. D.Litt. Montpelier Univ.

Publs. Poems in *New Signatures* 33, *Poems* (2 editions), *The Destructive Element* 34, *The Burning Cactus* (stories), *Forward From Liberalism* 36, *The Trial of a Judge* 37, *The Still Centre* 39, trans. Ernst Toller's *Pastor Hall* 39, *The Backward Son* 40, *Ruins and Visions* 42, *Life and the Poet* 42, *Citizens in War and After* 44, *European Witness* 46, *Poems of Dedication* 46, *The Edge of Being* 49, *World Within World* (autobiography) 51, *The Creative Element* 53, *Collected Poems* 55, *Engaged in Writing* 57; translation of Schiller's *Mary Stuart* 58, *The Struggle for the Modern* 62, *Selected Poems* 64.

c/o Library of Congress, Washington, D.C. 20540, U.S.A.

Sperti, George Speri, E.E., SC.D.; American scientist; b. 17 Jan. 1900; ed. Univ. of Cincinnati.

Asst. Chief Meter Laboratories U.G. & E., Cincinnati 22; Asst. Research Dir. Duncan Electrical and Manufacturing Co., Lafayette 23; Research Asst. Univ. of Cincinnati 24-25; Research Prof. and Dir. of Research (also co-founder) Basic Science Research Laboratory, Univ. of Cincinnati 25-35; mem. Board of Dirs. Gen. Development Laboratories Inc. New York 30-35, Sperti Lamp Corpn. Delaware 30-40, Dir. 35-, Research Prof., Dir. of Research, mem. Board of Trustees, mem. Board of Regents, President of the Institutum Divi Thomae Foundation; mem. Board of Trustees, Newman Foundation; Principal Consultant War Production Board 42; mem. Pontifical Acad. Science, American Asscn. for Advancement of Science, American Physical Society; mem. Royal Soc. of Arts, London; Founding mem. American Soc. for the Aged and mem. of its Medical & Scientific Cttee.; Board of Dirs. American Council for Int. Promotion of Democracy under God Inc. 59; Dir. Franklin Corpn.; mem. Emeritus Hall; Hon. mem. Società Italiana de Fisica; mem. Academia de Doctores, Madrid; Catholic Action Medal 42, Mendel Medal 43, Christian Culture Award 47; Star of Solidarity Third Class of the Italian Repub. 56; Gold Medal Univ. Int. degli Studi Sociali "Pro Deo" 58; developed type of therapeutic lamp; other developments with selective irradiation and on fluorescent lighting; discovered biological substances Biodynes; specialist in cancer research.

Publs. Co-author *Quantum Theory in Biology* 27, and *Correlated Investigations in the Basic Sciences*; Editor *Studies Inst. Divi Thomae.*

Institutum Divi Thomae, 1842 Madison Road, Cincinnati, Ohio 45206, U.S.A.

Telephone: 513-861-3460.

Spicer, Sir John Armstrong, Kt., Q.C.; Australian lawyer; b. 5 March 1899; ed. in Torquay (England) and Melbourne.

Admitted Barrister and Solicitor 21; K.C. 48; Senator Commonwealth Parl. 40-44, and 49-56; Attorney-Gen. 49-56; Chief Judge, Commonwealth Industrial Court 56-.

153 Glen Iris Road, Glen Iris, Melbourne, Victoria, Australia.

Telephone: 25-2882.

Spiegel, Modie Joseph, Jr., B.S.; American merchant; b. 29 Jan. 1901; ed. Dartmouth Coll.

Chair. and Chief Exec. Officer, Spiegel Inc.; Pres. Mail Order Assen. of America 42-; Hon. M.A. Grinnell Coll.

2511 West 23rd Street, Chicago 8, Ill., U.S.A.

Spiegel, Samuel P.; American film producer (born in Austria); b. 11 Nov. 1904; ed. Univ. of Vienna.

Went to U.S.A. 39; Pres. Horizon American Pictures Inc. 48-; two Academy Awards (*Oscars*); films produced include *Tales of Manhattan, The Stranger, African Queen, We Were Strangers, On the Waterfront, The Strange One, The Bridge on the River Kwai, The Chase, Suddenly Last Summer, Lawrence of Arabia, Mister Innocence, The Night of the Generals, The Swimmer.*

475 Park Avenue, New York City, N.Y., U.S.A.

Spiegelman, Sol, PH.D., D.SC.; American microbiologist; b. 14 Dec. 1914; ed. Coll. of City of New York, Columbia Univ. and Washington Univ., St. Louis.

Lecturer in Physics at Wash. Univ. 42-44, in Applied Mathematics 43-44, Bacteriology 45-46; Asst. Prof. in Bacteriology, School of Medicine, Wash. Univ. 46-48; Special Fellow U.S. Public Health Service 48-49; Prof. of Microbiology, Univ. of Ill. 49-63; Prof. of Microbiology and in Center of Advanced Study, Univ. of Ill. 64-; Pasteur Award, Ill. Soc. for Microbiology 63; Fellow Nat. Acad. of Sciences 65, American Acad. Arts and Sciences 66; Alumni Citation Award, Wash. Univ. 66; Hon. D.Sc. Rensselaer Polytechnic Inst. and Northwestern Univ. 66; Bertner Award, M.D. Anderson Hospital 68; Dyer Lecturer, Nat. Inst. of Health 68.

Publs: author and co-author of 182 publications on cell physiology, genetics, developmental biology and molecular biology.

University of Illinois, Department of Microbiology, 302 Burrill Hall, Urbana, Illinois 61801, U.S.A.

Telephone: 217-333-6229; 217-333-3753.

Spierenburg, Dirk P.; Netherlands international official; b. 4 Feb. 1909; ed. Netherlands School of Economics, Rotterdam.

Mem. Netherlands Ministry for Economic Affairs 35-; Dir. Netherlands Bureau for Repartition of Metals and Metal Products during the war; Dir. for trade agreements with Western European countries 45-47, Head, Permanent Mission to O.E.E.C., Paris 47-48; Dir.-Gen. of Foreign Trade and Deputy Govt. Commr. for American Aid 48; Netherlands mem. of Council of Presidents of Benelux; Pres. Council of O.E.E.C. 50 and 51; Netherlands mem. 52-, and Vice-Pres. E.C.S.C. High Authority 58-63; Head, Perm. Rep. of Netherlands to European Economic Community and EURATOM 63-.

Permanent Representation of the Netherlands to the European Communities, 62 rue Belliard, Brussels, Belgium.

Telephone: Brussels 136570.

Spilhaus, Athelstan Frederick, M.S., D.SC.; American meteorologist and oceanographer; b. 25 Nov. 1911; ed. Univ. of Cape Town and Mass. Inst. of Technology.

Research Asst. M.I.T. 34-35; Asst. Dir. of Technical Services, Union of South Africa Defence Forces 35-36, Woods Hole Oceanographic Inst. 36-37; Investigator in Physical Oceanography 38-; Asst. Prof. 37-38, Assoc. Prof. 39-41; Prof. of Meteorology New York Univ. 42-48; Capt. U.S.A.F. 43, Major 44, Lieut.-Col. 46; Dir. of Research New York Univ. 46-48; Meteorological Adviser to Govt. of Union of South Africa 47; Dean and Prof. Inst. of Technology, Univ. of Minnesota 49-66; Prof. School of Physics, Univ. of Minnesota 66-; Fellow, Royal Meteorological Society, American Inst. of Aeronautics and Astronautics, A.A.A.S.; mem. L'Université à l'Usine Cttee., American Meteorological Soc., Royal Soc. of S. Africa, American Geophysical Union; mem. U.S. Nat. Cttee., Int. Geophysical Year; mem. Nat. Science Board, Cttee. on Science and Astronautics, House of Reps.; Trustee Woods Hole Oceanographic Inst., Int. Oceanographic Foundation; U.S. Rep. UNESCO Exec. Board 55-58; U.S. Commr. Seattle World's Fair 61-62; Chair. American Editorial Board, Commonwealth and Int. Library of Science, Technology and Eng.; inventor of bathythermograph 38; Hon. D.Sc. (Coe Coll.) 61.

Publs. *A Study of the Aspiration Psychrometer, A Bathythermograph, A Detailed Study of the Surface Layers of the Ocean in the Neighbourhood of the Gulf Stream with the Aid of Rapid Measuring Hydrographic Instruments, Workbook in Meteorology* (textbook), *Weathercraft* (for children), etc., *Meteorological Instruments* (with W. E. K. Middleton), *Satellite of the Sun, Turn to the Sea, The Ocean Laboratory, Our New Age* (daily and Sunday feature).

School of Physics and Astronomy, University of Minnesota, Minn. 55455, U.S.A.

Telephone: 373-3272.

Spiljak, Mija; Yugoslav politician; b. 1916; ed. in Sisak.

Various jobs in Underground Resistance Movement in Yugoslavia during Second World War; then Sec. of Town Cttee. of League of Communists of Zagreb; mem. Exec. Cttee. of League of Communists of Croatia; fmr. Vice-Pres. Confederation of Trade Unions of Yugoslavia; Pres. of Exec. Council of Croatia 63-67, of Fed. Exec. Council of Yugoslavia 67-; mem. Croatian Assembly; mem. Central Cttee. League of Communists of Croatia; mem. of Central Cttee., and of the Presidency, of League of Communists of Yugoslavia; Deputy of Fed. Assembly; Partisan Remembrance Medal 41, and numerous other Yugoslav decorations.

Federal Executive Council, Belgrade, Yugoslavia.

Spinelli, Pier Pasquale, LL.D.; Italian diplomat; b. 8 Sept. 1902; ed. Univ. of Naples.

Vice-Consul, N.Y.C. 28 and Buffalo 30; Consul N.Y.C. 33; First Sec. Italian Legation, Havana, Cuba 38-40 and China 40-47; Chief of Economic Division, Italian Ministry of Foreign Affairs, Rome 47-50; Dir. Diplomatic Cabinet of the Administrator of Italian Somaliland 50-53; Sec.-Gen. Italian Somaliland 53-55; Alternate Dir.-Gen. of Emigration, Italian Ministry of Foreign Affairs, Rome 55; Under-Sec., Dir. of the European Office of the UN 58-66, Dir.-Gen. UN Office, Geneva Jan. 66-; Special Rep. of Sec.-Gen. of UN, Middle East 58; Special Rep. of Sec.-Gen. of UN, Yemen 63; Personal Rep. of Sec.-Gen. UN, Cyprus 64; Special Rep. of Sec.-Gen. to 18 Nations Disarmament Conf.; Under Sec.-Gen. of UN 68-.

Palais des Nations, Geneva; and Villa "Les Feuillantines", 4 Route de Ferney, Geneva, Switzerland.

Spinoy, André; Belgian politician; b. 06; ed. L'Athénée de Malines.

Secretary, Fed. of Malines 30-36; Provincial Counsellor,

Antwerp 36-44; fmr. Mayor of Malines; M.P. 44-; Minister of Nat. Defence 54-58, of Econ. Affairs 61-65; Deputy Prime Minister and Co-ordinator of Econ. Policy 65-66; Socialist.
100 ave. Reine Astrid, Malines, Belgium.

Spiridonov, Ivan Vasilevich; Soviet politician; b. 05; ed. Leningrad Industrial Inst.
Fitter, Leningrad 25-27; Man. of Workshop, Plant, Leningrad, Orel, Kuznetsk 27-50; Party work, Leningrad 50-54; Sec. Leningrad Regional Party Cttee. 54-56; First Sec. Leningrad Regional and City Party Cttee. 56-62; Sec. Central Cttee. of C.P.S.U. 61-62, mem. 61-; Chair. Soviet of the Union, Supreme Soviet of U.S.S.R. 62-; Deputy to U.S.S.R. Supreme Soviet; Chair. Parliamentary Group; mem. C.P.S.U. Central Cttee.
Presidium of the Union, Supreme Soviet of U.S.S.R., The Kremlin, Moscow, U.S.S.R.

Spiropoulos, Jean, D.IUR.; Greek international lawyer; b. 16 Oct. 1896.
Greek del. Int. Law Codification Conf. 30, Balkan Confs. 30-33, Washington Cttee. (convened to draw up Statute for Int. Court of Justice) 45, Sessions of U.N. Gen. Assembly 46-56; Legal Adviser, Greek Del. San Francisco Conf. 45, Paris Conf. 46; twice Rapporteur, Sixth Cttee. U.N. Gen. Assembly; Judge Int. Court of Justice 58-67; fmr. Prof. of Int. Law and Rector, Athens Univ.; Dir. Ministry of Foreign Affairs Legal Dept.; mem., former Pres., U.N. Int. Law Comm.; mem. Permanent Court of Arbitration; mem. Acad. of Athens.
Publs. *Théorie Générale du Droit international* 30, *L'Individu en Droit international* 32, *Private International Law* 39, *Public International Law* (3rd edn.) 40.
The University, Odos Academias, Athens, Greece.

Spitskiy, Ivan Stepanovich; Soviet diplomatist; b. 1920; ed. Moscow Pedagogical Inst. of Foreign Languages.
Diplomatic Service 43-; Counsellor, Afghanistan 55-57; Deputy Head, First African Dept., U.S.S.R. Ministry for Foreign Affairs 60-63; Minister-Counsellor, Paris 63-64; Amb. to Congo Repub. (Brazzaville) 64-.
U.S.S.R. Embassy, Brazzaville, Congo Republic.

Spitsyn, Victor Ivanovich; Soviet (Russian) scientist; b. 1902; ed. Moscow State Univ.
Worked at chemical plant 18; Instructor, Inorganic Chemistry, Moscow State Univ. 23-31; Research Chemist, Moscow Electrical Plant 23-28; Senior Research Chemist, Inst. of Applied Mineralogy and Non-ferrous Metallurgy 28-31; Prof. Inorganic Chemistry, Moscow State C. Liebknecht Pedagogical Inst. 32-42; Prof. Inorganic Chemistry, Moscow State Lomonossov Univ. 42-, Vice-Rector 42-48; Vice-Dir. Inst. of Physical Chemistry, Acad. of Sciences of the U.S.S.R. 49-53, Dir. 53-; mem. Acad. of Sciences of the U.S.S.R. 58-;Hon. Fellow, Polish Chemical Soc.; Order of Lenin (twice), Order of the Red Banner of Labour.
Publs. *The Reduction of Tungstates* 25, *The Chlorination of Oxydes* 30, *The Organisation of Soviet Beryllium Production* 33, *The Methods of Use of Radioactive Tracers* 55, *The Migration of Radioelements in Soil* 58, 60, *The Action of Radioactive Radiation of Solids on their Physico-Chemical Properties* 58, *Soviet Chemistry Today* 61, *Investigations in the Chemistry of Uranium* 61, *Radioactive Catalysts* 63.
U.S.S.R. Academy of Sciences, 14 Lenin Prospekt, Moscow, U.S.S.R.

Spitzer, Lyman, Jr., B.A., PH.D.; American astronomer; b. 26 June 1914; ed. Phillips Acad., Andover, Mass., and Yale, Cambridge, Princeton and Harvard Univs.
Instructor in Physics and Astronomy Yale Univ. 39; Scientist Special Studies Group 42, and Dir. Sonar Analysis Group 44, Columbia Univ., Division of War Research; Associate Prof. of Astrophysics Yale Univ.

46; Prof. of Astronomy, Chair. of Dept. and Dir. of Observatory, Princeton Univ. 47-, Charles A. Young Prof. of Astronomy 52-; Dir. Project Matterhorn 53-61; Chair. Exec. Cttee. Plasma Physics Laboratory 61-66; Chair. Univ. Research Board 67-; mem. Nat. Acad. of Sciences 52-, Royal Astronomical Soc., American Astronomical Soc., Physical Soc., American Acad. of Arts and Sciences, American Philosophical Soc., American Alpine Club; Pres. American Astronomical Soc. 60-62.
Publs. *Physics of Sound in the Sea* (Editor) 46, *Physics of Fully Ionized Gases* 56, 62, *Diffuse Matter in Space* 68, and many articles.
Princeton University, Princeton, N.J. 08540, U.S.A. Telephone: 609-452-3800.

Spivakovsky, Tossy; Russian-born American violinist; b. 4 Feb. 1907; ed. Hochschule für Musik, Berlin.
Brought to Berlin 09; concert debut 17; recitals and solo performances in Europe 17-33; concert tour, Australia and New Zealand 33; settled in Melbourne, taught at Melbourne Univ. Conservatory Master Class; settled in U.S.A. 43-; yearly concert tours U.S.A., Canada and Europe; apart from classical and romantic repertoire, is well known for his performances of concertos by Bartok, Stravinsky, Menotti, Miklos Rozsa, Leonard Bernstein and Roger Sessions; numerous recordings.
American Manager: Columbia Artists Management, 165 West 57th Street, New York 19, N.Y., U.S.A.; European Manager: Wilfred Van Wyck, 80 Wigmore Street, London, W.1, England; Home: Westport, Conn., U.S.A.

Spock, Benjamin, B.A., M.D.; American physician; b. 2 May 1903; ed. Yale Coll., Coll. of Physicians and Surgeons, Columbia Univ.
Pediatrical practice, Cornell Medical Coll., New York Hospital and New York City Health Department 33-47; served in U.S. Navy 44-46; mem. staff, Rochester (Minn.) Child Health Inst., Mayo Clinic and Univ. of Minnesota; organised teaching programme in child psychiatry and development, Pittsburgh Univ. Medical School 51-55; Prof. of Child Development, Western Reserve Univ. 55-67; specialises in application of psychoanalytic principles to pediatric practice; Co-Chair. Cttee. for Sane Nuclear Policy (SANE) until Oct. 67, Dir. Oct. 67-.
Publs. *The Common Sense Book of Baby and Child Care* (reprinted as *The Pocket Book of Baby and Child Care*) 46, revised edition 57, *A Baby's First Year* (with John Reinhart and Wayne Miller) 55, *Feeding Your Baby and Child* (with Miriam E. Lowenberg) 55, *Dr. Spock Talks with Mothers* 61, *Problems of Parents* 62.
538 Madison Avenue, New York, N.Y. 10022, U.S.A.

Spohr, Arnold Theodore; Canadian ballet director, teacher and choreographer; b. 26 Dec. 1927; ed. St. John's High School and Winnipeg Teachers Coll.
Piano Teacher 46-51; Principal Dancer Royal Winnipeg Ballet 47-54; Canadian Broadcasting Corpn. Television Choreographer 55-56, Choreographer Rainbow Stage 57-60; Dir. Royal Winnipeg Ballet 58-; Dir.-Teacher Royal Winnipeg Ballet School; Nelson School of Fine Arts Dance Dept.; mem. Board of Dirs. Canadian Theatre Centre.
Choreography: *Ballet Premier* 50, *Intermede* 51, *E Minor* 59, *Hansel and Gretel* 60, and 18 musicals for Rainbow Stage.
322 Smith Street, 3rd Floor, Winnipeg, Manitoba, Canada.

Spong, William Belser, Jr., LL.B.; American lawyer and politician; b. 29 Sept. 1920; ed. Hampden-Sydney Coll., Virginia and Univs. of Virginia and Edinburgh.
Admitted to the Bar, Va. 47; Lecturer in Law and Govt., Coll. of William and Mary, Williamsburg, Va. 48-49;

mem. Va. House of Delegates 54-55, Va. State Senate 56-66, United States Senate 67-; Democrat. United States Senate, Washington, D.C., U.S.A.

Sporn, Philip; American engineer and executive; b. 25 Nov. 1896; ed. Columbia Univ. School of Engineering. Joined American Electric Power Co. 20, Chief Electrical Engineer 27, Chief Engineer 33, Vice-Pres. (Engineering) 34, Exec. Vice-Pres. (and Exec. Vice-Pres. American Electric Power Service Corpn.) 45, Pres. American Electric Power Co. and all subsidiaries 47-61; Pres. Ohio Valley Electric Corpn. 62-67, Indiana-Kentucky Electric Corpn. 52-; Chair. East Central Nuclear Group Research and Devt. Cttee. 58-67, U.S. Nat. Cttee. C.I.G.R.E.; Chair. Seawater Conversion Comm. Israel Govt. 59-; Chair. System Development Cttee., Dir. and mem. Exec. Cttee. American Electric Power Co. 61-67, Dir. and Consultant 67-; Chair. Exec. Advisory Cttee. Fed. Power Comm. Nat. Power Survey 62-65; Chair. Nat. Acad. of Sciences Advisory Board on Hardened Power Systems 62-; visiting Prof. Cornell Univ. 63, 65; mem. Nat. Comm. on Technology, Automation and Econ. Progress 64-66; Lecturer, Mass. Inst. of Technology 67; Gov. Weizmann Inst. of Science; Trustee and mem. Research and Policy Cttee., Cttee. for Econ. Devt.; mem. Advisory Councils Columbia Graduate School of Business, Columbia School of Engineering and Applied Science, Cornell Coll. of Engineering; mem. Visiting Comm., Dept. of Electrical Engineering M.I.T.; Fellow and Hon. mem. American Inst. of Electrical and Electronic Engineers; Fellow and Hon. mem. American Soc. of Mechanical Engineers; Fellow American Soc. of Civil Engineers; mem. Nat. Acad. of Sciences; mem. Nat. Acad. of Eng.; awards include Edison Medal 45, John Fritz Medal 56; Hon. degrees from Stevens Inst. of Technology, Ill. Inst. of Technology, Univ. of Grenoble, Ohio State Univ., Haifa Technion, Columbia Univ. 66, and other insts.; Chevalier Légion d'Honneur.
Publs. *Heat Pumps* (with Ambrose and Baumeister) 47, *The Integrated Power System* 50, *Energy—Its Prodction, Conversion and Use in the Service of Man* 63, *Foundations of Engineering* 64, *Fresh Water from Saline Waters* 66.
320 East 72nd Street, New York City, N.Y. 10021, U.S.A. Telephone: REgent 4-1883.

Spriggs, Sir Frank Spencer, K.B.E.; British aircraft manufacturer; b. 29 March 1895; ed. Westbourne. With Sopwith Aviation Co. Ltd. 13-20; Hawker Aircraft Ltd. 20-34; Man. Dir. Hawker Siddeley Group Ltd. 36-58; fmr. Chair. Armstrong Siddeley Ltd. and Development Co. Ltd., Sir W. G. Armstrong Whitworth Aircraft Ltd., Armstrong Siddeley Motors Ltd., A. V. Roe and Co. Ltd., Air Service Training Ltd., Gloster Aircraft Ltd.; Pres. Society of British Aircraft Constructors 39-41; fmr. Chair. High Duty Alloys Ltd.; A. W. Hawksley Ltd.; Hawker Sanders Ltd.; Hawker Aircraft Ltd.; Self-Changing Gears Co. Ltd.; Gears Investment Trust Ltd.; Kelvin Construction Co. Ltd., fmr. Dir. A. V. Roe (Canada) Ltd., Canadian Car and Foundry Co. Ltd., Racair Ltd. and Brockworth Building Co. Ltd.; Hon. Fellow Royal Aeronautical Society. Steepway, Broom Close, Esher, Surrey, England.

Springer, Axel Cäsar; German newspaper publisher; b. 2 May 1912; ed. Realgymnasium Hamburg-Altona. Printing and publishing apprenticeship with provincial papers and in his father's newspaper business in Hamburg-Altona; after 45 published the broadcasting paper *Hör zu*; *Kristall, Hamburger Abendblatt* 48-; *10 Pfennig-BILD-Zeitung* 52-; also *Die Welt, Die Welt am Sonntag, Das Neue Blatt, Bild am Sonntag* 54-; also majority owner Ullstein Verlag (Berlin) and several other book and magazine publishing firms.
Kaiser-Wilhelm-Strasse 6, 2 Hamburg 36, German Federal Republic.

Springer, Hugh Worrell, C.B.E., M.A., D.SC. SOC.; Barbadian Barrister-at-Law and educationist; b. 1913; ed. Harrison Coll., Barbados, Hertford Coll., Oxford and Inner Temple, London.
Practised at Bar of Barbados 39-47; mem. House of Assembly, Barbados 40-47; mem. Exec. Council, Barbados 44-47; mem. Educ. Board, Barbados 44-47; Gen. Sec. Barbados Labour Party 40-47; Organizer and first Gen. Sec. Barbados Workers' Union 41-47; Registrar, Univ. of West Indies 47-63; mem. Educ. Authority of Jamaica 50-56, ILO Cttee. of Experts on Social Policy in Non-Metropolitan Territories 53-58, W. Indies Trade and Tariff Comm. 57-58, Univ. Grants Cttee., Ghana 59, Jamaica Public Service Comm. 59-63, W. Indies Fed. Service Comm. 60-61; Guggenheim Fellow and Fellow Harvard Centre for Int. Affairs 61-62; Senior Visiting Fellow, All Souls Coll., Oxford 62-63; Acting Gov. of Barbados 64; Dir. Inst. of Educ. of Univ. of W. Indies 63- (on leave); Chair. Cttee. for Medical Research in the Caribbean 65-; Sec. Commonwealth Educ. Liaison Cttee. and Dir. Commonwealth Educ. Liaison Unit 66-67; Asst. Commonwealth Sec.-Gen. (Educ.), 67-; Fellow Royal Soc. of Arts 68-.
Publs. *Reflections on the Failure of the First West Indian Federation* 62, *Problems of National Development in the West Indies* 65, *Barbados as a Sovereign State* 67.
Commonwealth Secretariat, Education Division, Marlborough House, Pall Mall, London, S.W.1; Home: 123 Gloucester Place, London, W.1, England.
Telephone: 01-930-9883 and 01-839-1071 (Office); 01-935-9853 (Home).

Springer, Konrad Ferdinand, DR. PHIL.; German publisher; b. 25; ed. Staatliches Kaiserin Augusta-Gymnasium, Berlin, Staatliches Kant-Gymnasium, Berlin, and Univ. of Zürich.
Partner Springer Verlag, Berlin, Heidelberg and New York 63-, J. F. Bergmanns Verlagsbuchhandlung, Munich 63-, Lange and Springer Scientific Bookshop, Berlin 63-, Springer-Verlag, Minerva Wissenschaftl. Buchhandlung, Vienna 65.
Neuenheimer Landstrasse 28-39, 69 Heidelberg 1, German Federal Republic.
Telephone: 4-91-01.

Spry, Major-General Daniel Charles, C.B.E., D.S.O., C.D.; Canadian army officer and Boy Scout official; b. 4 Feb. 1913; ed. public schools, Calgary and Halifax, Canada, Ashford School, England, and Dalhousie Univ. Served Princess Louise Fusiliers and Royal Canadian Regt.; Commdr. 3rd Canadian Infantry Div. 44, Canadian Repatriation Units in Great Britain 45; Vice-Chief of Gen. Staff, Canadian Army 46; Chief Exec. Commr. Boy Scouts Asscn., Canada 47-53; Dep. Dir. Boy Scouts Int. Bureau 51-53, Dir. Boy Scouts World Bureau 53-65; Pres. Overseas Inst. of Canada; Pres. Glenland Ltd.; mem. Board of Governors, Ashbury Coll. Ottawa.
4 Rock Avenue, Ottawa 2, Canada.
Telephone: 749-2878.

Spühler, Willy; Swiss economist and politician; b. 31 Jan. 1902; ed. Gymnasium of Zürich and Univs. of Zürich and Paris.
Statistician, Zürich 31-34; Head of Employment Bureau, Zürich 35-42; Head, Cen. Office of War Economy 39-48; mem. Zürich Town Council 42-59; mem. Nat. Council (Fed. Parl.) 38-55, mem. Standerat (Fed. Parl.) 55-59; mem. Swiss Fed. Council and Minister of Transport, Communications and Power 59-65; Minister of Fed. Political Dept. (Foreign Affairs) 66-; Pres. Swiss Confederation 63, 68, Vice-Pres. 67.
Laubeggstrasse 39, Berne, Switzerland.

Spuler, Bertold, DR. PHIL.; German university professor; b. 5 Dec. 1911; ed. Univs. of Heidelberg, Munich, Hamburg and Breslau.
Collaborator, Society for Silesian History 34-35; Asst.

Dept. of East European History, Univ. of Berlin and Co-editor *Jahrbücher für Geschichte Osteuropas* 35-37; Asst. Dept. of Near Eastern Studies, Univ. of Göttingen 37-38, Dozent 38-41; Full Prof. Univ. of Munich 42, Göttingen 45, Hamburg 48-; Hon. Dr. Theol. (Berne), Hon. D. ès Lettres (Bordeaux).

Publs. include *Die europäische Diplomatie in Konstantinopel bis 1739* 35, *Die Minderheitenschulen der europäischen Türkei von der Reformzeit bis zum Weltkriege* 36, *Die Mongolen in Iran: Politik, Verwaltung und Kultur der Ilchanzeit 1220-1350*, 3rd edn. 68, *Die Goldene Horde, Die Mongolen in Russland, 1223-1302* 43, 2nd edn. 65, *Die Gegenwartslage der Ostkirchen in ihrer staatlichen und volklichen Umwelt* 48, *Geschichte der islamischen Länder im Überblick I: Chalifenzeit; II: Mongolenzeit* 52-53, *Iran in fruhislamischer Zeit: Politik, Kulturt Verwaltung und öffentliches Leben 633-1055* 52, *Regenten und Regierungen der Welt* 53, 2nd edn. 3 vols. 62-66, *Wissenschaftl, Forschungsbericht: Der Yordere Orient in islamischer Zeit* 54, *The Age of the Caliphs* 60, *The Age of the Mongols* 60, *Geschichte der Morgenländischen Kirchen* 61, *Innerasien seit dem Aufkommen der Türken* 66, *Les Mongols et l'Europe* 61, *Wüstenfeld-Mahlersche Vergleichungstabellen zur muslimischen, iranischen und orient-christlichen Zeitrechnung*, 3rd edn. 61, *Die islamische Welt* (Saeculum Weltgeschichte III-IV, 67-69), *Die Orthodoxen Kirchen 1-56* 39-68, *Geschichte der Mongolen anhand der Quellen* 68.

Mittelweg 90, 2 Hamburg 13; Rothenbaumchaussee 36, 2 Hamburg 13, German Federal Republic.

Spychalski, Marian; Polish architect and politician; b. 06; ed. Warsaw Polytechnic.

Joined Polish Communist Party 31; awarded Grand Prix at Paris Int. Exhibition for his plan for development of Warsaw 37; during occupation of Poland, became leader in left-wing of resistance movement; mem. Polish Workers' Party 42-48; Mayor of Warsaw 45; mem. Exec. Cttee. P.W.P. 45-48; Deputy Minister of Nat. Defence 45-48; mem. Politburo, Polish United Workers' Party 48-49, 56-; expelled from Party 49, rehabilitated 56; Minister of Nat. Defence 56-68; Marshal of Poland 63-, Pres. of Council of State 68-.

1 Klonowa, Warsaw, Poland.

Spyridakis, Constantinos, PH.D.; Cypriot politician; b. 21 May 1903; ed. Pancyprian Gymnasium, Nicosia, and Univs. of Athens and Berlin.

Teacher, Pancyprian Gymnasium, Nicosia 23-31, 34-35, Asst Headmaster 35-36, Principal 36-60; Chair. Greek Board of Educ. 59-60; Pres. Greek Communal Chamber 60-65; Minister of Educ. 65-; mem. and official of numerous Academic and Scientific orgs.; Greek Grand Cross of Royal Order of Phoenix and other decorations. Publs. *Evagoras the First, King of Salamis* (German 35, Greek 45), *An Outline of the History of Cyprus* 58, *The Kings of Cyprus* (Greek) 63, *A Brief History of Cyprus* (English 63, Greek 64), etc.

St. Helen Street 10, Nicosia, Cyprus.

Spyropoulos, Jannis; Greek artist; b. 12 March 1912; ed. School of Fine Arts, Athens, and Ecole des Beaux Arts.

Numerous one-man exhibitions in Europe and U.S.A. 50-; on touring exhibitions of Greek Art, Rome 53, Belgrade 54, Malmö and Gothenburg 59, Canada 59, Cyprus 60, Helsinki 61; participated in Alexandria Biennale 55, São Paulo Bienal 57, Venice Biennale 60, Carnegie Internationals 61, 64; Documenta III (Kassel) 64, etc.; represented in Guggenheim Museum, New York, Museum of Contemporary Art, Dallas, Bezallel Nat. Museum, Jerusalem, Museum of Contemporary Art, Belgrade, Museum of Fine Arts, Ostend, Toronto Art Gallery, Nat. Art Gallery of Athens, Museum of Modern Art, Paris, Israel Museum, Jerusalem, Museum of Modern Art, Brussels, etc.; represented at EXPO,

Montreal 67; Commdr. Royal Order of Phoenix; UNESCO Prize 60.

11 Sarantaporou Street, Athens 905, Greece. Telephone: 281-182.

Sridharmadhibes, Chao Phya; Thai politician and jurist; b. 30 Oct. 1885.

President Supreme Court 27-28; Minister of Justice 28-32, 37-38, 44-45, and 46; mem. Assembly of People's Reps. 33-44, and 46; Minister of Finance 33-34; Pres. Assembly of People's Reps. 34-36; mem. Perm. Court of Arbitration, The Hague 35-41, 48-66; Minister of Foreign Affairs 38-39; Minister of Public Health 44-45; Senator and Pres. of Senate 47-51, mem. and Pres. Constituent Assembly 48-49; Privy Councillor 52-; Exec. Vice-Pres. Thai Red Cross 60-64.

Villa Chittasukh, Silom Road, Bangkok, Thailand.

Staats, Elmer Boyd, PH.D.; American economist and government official; b. 6 June 1914; ed. McPherson Coll., and Univs. of Kansas and Minnesota.

Research Asst., Kansas Legislative Council 36; mem. Staff, Public Admin. Service, Chicago 37-38; Fellow, Brookings Inst. 38-39; Asst. to Dir., Bureau of the Budget 47, Asst. Dir. (Legis. Reference) 47-49, Exec. Asst. Dir. 49-50, Asst. Dir. 58-59, Deputy Dir. 50-53, 59-66; Research Dir., Marshall Field & Co., Chicago 53; Exec. Officer Operations Co-ordinating Board, Nat. Security Council 53-58; Comptroller Gen. of the United States 66-; mem. numerous public orgs. including Pres. American Soc. for Public Admin. 61-62; mem. Board of Dirs. of American Acad. of Political and Social Science 66-, Research Advisory Cttee. of Council of State Governments 66-, President's Comm. on Budget Concepts; Rockefeller Public Service Award 61; Hon. LL.D. (McPherson Coll.) 66.

Publ. *Personnel Standards in the Social Security Program* 39.

5011 Overlook Road, N.W., Washington, D.C. 20016, U.S.A.

Stacey, Col. Charles Perry, O.B.E., C.D., A.M., PH.D., LL.D., F.R.S.C.; Canadian army officer; b. 30 July 1906; ed. Univs. of Toronto, Oxford and Princeton.

On Canadian Army Reserve 29-40; mem. Princeton Univ. History Dept. 34-40; Historical Officer, Canadian Mil. Headquarters, London 40-45; Pres. Canadian Historical Asscn. 52-53; Pres. Canadian Writers' Foundation 58-59; Dir. Historical Section, Canadian Army Gen. Staff 45-59; Hon. Sec. Royal Soc. of Canada 57-59, Hon. Editor 64-68; Special Lecturer History Toronto Univ. 59-60, Prof. 60-; on leave while acting as Dir. of History, Canadian Forces H.Q., Ottawa 65-66.

Publs. *Canada and the British Army 1846-1871* 36 (2nd edn. 63), *The Military Problems of Canada* 40, *The Canadian Army 1939-1945: an Official Summary* 48, *Introduction to the Study of Military History for Canadian Students* 55, *Six Years of War* 55, *Quebec 1759: The Siege and the Battle* 59, *Records of the Nile Voyageurs 1884-1885* 59, *The Victory Campaign* 60.

Department of History, University of Toronto, Toronto 5, Ontario; 89 Tranmer Avenue, Toronto 7, Canada.

Telephone: 928-3370 (Office); 481-4885 (Home).

Stacey, James J., F.C.I.S.; Irish company secretary; b. 19; ed. Synge St. Christian Brothers School, Dublin. Assistant Sec., Fed. of Irish Industries 47-49, Sec. 49-54, Dir.-Gen. 54-; Chair. Irish Branch Chartered Inst. of Secs. 60-62; founder-mem. Irish Nat. Productivity Cttee.; mem. Irish Nat. Industrial Econ. Council.

9 Ely Place, Dublin 2, Ireland. Telephone: Dublin 60366.

Staebler, Neil; American businessman and politician; b. 11 July 1905; ed. Univ. of Michigan.

Treasurer, Staebler-Kempf Oil Co. 26-51; Partner, Staebler and Son 26-; Chief, Building Materials Branch,

Office of Price Admin. 42-43; U.S. Navy Service 43-45; Chair. Dem. State Central Cttee. of Mich. 50-61, Dem. Nat. Ctteeman from Mich. 61-64, 65-; Visiting Prof. of Govt., Univ. of Mass. 62; mem. U.S. House of Reps. 62-64; Hon. LL.D. Univ. of Mich.
Publ. *How to Argue with a Conservative* (co-author) 66. 408 Wolverine Building, Ann Arbor, Michigan 48108, U.S.A.
Telephone: 313-662-4406.

Staehelin, Ernst, DR.THEOL. h.c. (Berne, Lausanne); DR.PHIL. h.c. (Basle); Swiss ecclesiastic; b. 3 Oct. 1889; ed. Basle, Göttingen, Berlin and Marburg Univs.
Pastor of Reformed Church, Thalheim (Aargau) 20; Extra. Prof. of Church History and Dogmatics Basle Univ. 24, Prof. 27-, Rector Univ. 33, 39 and 60; Pastor Olten 26.
Publs. include: *Der Jesuitenorden und die Schweiz* 23, *Das Buch der Basler Reformation* 29, *Das theologische Lebenswerk Johannes Oekolampads* 39, *Johann Caspar Lavaters ausgewählte Werke* 43, *Alexandre Vinets ausgewählte Werke* 44-45, *Johann Ludwig Frey, Johannes Grynaeus und das Frey-Grynaeische Institut in Basel* 47, *Die Stimme der schweizerischen Kirchen zum Sonderbundskrieg und zur Gründung des schweizerischen Bundesstaates* 48, *Die Verkündigung des Reiches Gottes in der Kirche Jesu Christi* (7 vols. 51, 53, 55, 57, 59, 63, 65), *Die Jesuitenfrage* 55, *Dewettiana, Forschungen und Texte zu Deswettes Leben und Werk* 56, *Die Wiederbringung aller Dinge* 60, *Overbeckiana: Übersicht über die auf der Universitätsbibliothek Basel aufbewahrte Korrespondenz Franz Overbecks* 62, *Professor Friedrich Lachenal* 65, *Die Korrespondenz des Basler Professors Jakob Christoph Beck 1711-1785* 68.
Ob. Heuberg 33, Basle, Switzerland.
Telephone: 061-241363.

Staempfli, George W., PH.D.; American painter, sculptor and art dealer; b. 6 Dec. 1910; ed. Univs. of Bonn, Rostock, Freiburg and Erlangen.
Worked for M. Knoedler and Co., New York 36-39; served with U.S. Army 42-46; one-man shows in N.Y. 41 and 53; Curator, Museum of Fine Arts, Houston, Texas 55-57; Foreign Service of U.S. State Dept. 57-59, and Co-ordinator, Fine Arts Program, U.S. Pavilion, Brussels World Fair 58; Pres. Staempfli Gallery Inc. New York 59-.
Publs. *Rainer Maria Rilke* 35 and critical essays on art in magazines 52-.
Office: 47 East 77th Street, New York; Home: 40 East 78th Street, New York, N.Y. 10021, U.S.A.
Telephone: 744-6696 (Home).

Staercke, André Marie de, DR.JUR.; Belgian diplomatist; b. 13; ed. Coll. St. Barbe, Ghent, and Univs. of Namur, Louvain and Paris.
Sec. to Prime Minister and Cabinet 43, to Prince Regent 45-50; Rep. to Council of NATO 51, Permanent Rep. 52-; Head Belgian Del. to EDC Conf. Paris 51; awards include Commdr. Légion d'Honneur, Ordre du Christ, Ordre du Chêne, Medal of Freedom (U.S.A.) and Grand Cross Order of Orange Nassau; Officer Order of Leopold.
14 rue Vaneau, Paris 7e, France.

Staerke, Roger De (*see* De Staercke).

Staf, Cornelis; Netherlands agricultural engineer; b. 23 April 1905; ed. Agricultural Univ.
Assistant Prof. Zunker, Breslau; Inspector Neths. Heath Soc. 34; Deputy Dir. of Bureau for Removal of Agricultural Produce from Inundated Areas 38; Man. Dir. Neths. Heath Society 40; Gen. Man. Dir. Utilisation of Ground and Agricultural Recovery 45; Permanent Under-Sec. of State, Ministry of Agriculture 46; Minister of War and Marine 51-58, of Defence, and *a.i.* of Agriculture, Fisheries and Food 58-59; Pres. Netherlands Heath Reclamation Society 60-; Chair. Agri-

cultural Economic Inst., Fruit Growers' Org.; Hon. Pres. European Plant Protection Organisation; Commdr. Order of Netherlands Lion.
Koninklijke Nederlandsche Heidemaatschappij, Lovinklaan 1, Arnhem, Netherlands.
Telephone: 08300-30711.

Staffa, H.E. Cardinal Dino; Vatican ecclesiastic; b. 14 Aug. 1906.
Ordained 29; Titular Bishop of Caesarea 60-; Sec. of Sacred Congregation of Seminars and Univs.; cr. Cardinal by Pope Paul VI 67.
Supreme Tribunal of Signatura Apostolica, Vatican City, Rome, Italy.

Ståhle, Anders Nils Oscar Kåse, LL.B.; Swedish diplomatist and public servant; b. 12 June 1901; ed. Univ. of Lund.
Entered Swedish Foreign Service 27; served home and abroad until 48; Executive Dir. Nobel Foundation 48-; represented Sweden in post-war int. confs. on shipping and trade; Del. Maritime Transport Cttee., OEEC Paris 47-59; board mem. several banking and industrial companies; holds Swedish and foreign decorations; Dr.Iur. h.c.; Steward Swedish Jockey Club.
Nobel House, Sturegatan 14, Stockholm Ö, Sweden.
Telephone: 630920 (Office); 633787 (Residence).

Stahle, Hans, M.A., M.B.A.; Swedish business executive; b. 8 Aug. 1923; ed. Uppsala Univ., Stockholm School of Economics and IMEDE Management Devt. Inst., Lausanne.
Deputy Managing Dir. Alfa-Laval AB (machinery) until 60, Managing Dir. 60-.
Hamra, Tumba, Sweden.

Stahlman, James Geddes, A.B.; American journalist; b. 28 Feb. 1893; ed. Webb School, Bell Buckle, Tenn., Vanderbilt Univ., Nashville, Tenn., and Univ. of Chicago.
President and Publisher *Nashville Banner*; Chair. of Board Newspaper Printing Corpn.; private U.S. Army, First World War; Captain, U.S.N.R., Second World War; Pres. Southern Newspaper Publishers' Assn. 32-33, Chair. of Board 33-34; Pres. American Newspaper Publishers' Assn. 37-39, Inter American Press Assn. 55-56; Trustee, Vanderbilt Univ.; mem. Nat. Council Boy Scouts of America; Hon. LL.D. (Atlanta Law School).
Home: 815 Tyne Boulevard, Nashville, Tenn.; Office: 1100 Broadway, Nashville, Tenn. 1, U.S.A.

Stahr, Elvis J., Jr., M.A., B.C.L.; American lawyer and university official; b. 9 March 1916; ed. Univ. of Kentucky, Oxford Univ., Yale Univ.
With New York law firm; served U.S. Army, Second World War; Assoc. Prof. of Law, Univ. of Kentucky 47-48, Prof. and Dean of Law Coll. 48-54; served Dept. of Army in Korean War; Provost, Univ. of Kentucky 54-56; Exec. Dir. President's Cttee. on Educ. Beyond Secondary School Level 56-57; Vice-Chancellor, Univ. of Pittsburgh 57-59; Pres. West Virginia Univ. 59-61; Sec. of the Army 61-62; Pres. Indiana Univ. 62-; Hon. LL.D. (Univ. of Maryland, Univ. of Pittsburgh, Louisiana State Univ., Texas Christian Univ., Univ. of Kentucky, Univ. of Notre Dame, West Virginia Wesleyan Coll., Concord Coll., Waynesburg Coll., Rose Polytechnic Inst.), Hon. D.Mil. Sc. (Northeastern Univ.), Hon. D.Pub. Admin. (Bethany Coll.), Hon. D.H.L. (de Pauw Univ.), and other hon. degrees.
President's Office, Indiana University, Bloomington, Ind. 47401, U.S.A.
Telephone : 812-337-4613.

Staiger, Emil, D.PHIL.; Swiss university professor and writer; b. 8 Feb. 1908; ed. Univs. of Geneva, Zürich and Munich.
Professor of German Literature, Zürich Univ. 43-; mem.

Deutsche Akad. and Vetenskaps-Societeten, Lund, Finnish Acad. of Sciences; hon. mem. Modern Language Asscn. of America.
Publs. *Die Zeit als Einbildungskraft des Dichters* 39, *Meisterwerke deutscher Sprache* 43, *Grundbegriffe der Poetik* 46, *Goethe* Vol. I 52, Vol. II 56, Vol. III 59, *Die Kunste der Interpretation* 55, *Stilwandel* 63, *Geist und Zeitgeist* 64, *Schiller* 67; trans. (into German) *Sophokles Tragödien* 44, *Griechische Epigramme* 46, *Euripides Ion* 47; (Greek and German with E. Howald) *Callimachi opera omnia* 56, *Aischylos Orestie* 59.
Witikonerstrasse 77, 8032-Zürich, Switzerland.
Telephone: 051-53-00-62.

Staikov, Entcho; Bulgarian politician; b. 01; ed. Sofia State Univ.
Member Bulgarian Communist Party 19-; Sec. District Cttee. of Communist Party, Plovdiv 34-35; political imprisonment 29-31, 30-44; Deputy Editor-in-Chief, later Editor-in-Chief *Rabotnitchesko Delo* and Dir. Bulgarian Telegraph Agency 44-52; Sec. Central Cttee. Bulgarian C.P. 52-, mem. Politburo 54-66; Chair. Exec. Council of Fatherland Front 57-; Hero of Socialist Labour.
Central Committee of Bulgarian Communist Party, Sofia, Bulgaria.

Staley, Edward, A.B.; American businessman; b. 22 Oct. 1903; ed. Miami and Harvard Univs.
With W. T. Grant Co. 26; Regional Man. and Asst. Gen. Merchandising Man. Montgomery Ward 33; Merchandising Dir. W. T. Grant Co. 40, Vice-Pres. 43, Gen. Man. and Dir. 50, Pres. 52, Vice-Chair. 55-, Chief Exec. Officer 59-; Pres. New York City Commerce and Industry Asscn. 56-58, Dir. 59-; Trustee Grant Foundation 54-.
Home: 3 Chalford Lane, Scarsdale, N.Y.; Office: 1441 Broadway, New York City, N.Y., U.S.A.

Stambolić, Petar; Yugoslav politician; b. 12 July 1912; ed. Univ. of Belgrade.
Member Young Communist League 33, C.P. of Yugoslavia 35-; organized resistance in Serbia 41; Sec. Central Cttee. of National Liberation for Serbia 41; Commdr H.Q. Nat. Liberation Army and partisan units for Serbia 43; Deputy and mem. Presidium, Antifascist Council of Nat. Liberation of Yugoslavia 43; mem. Central Cttee. of C.P. of Serbia 45, Sec. 48-57; First. Vice-Chair. Council of Ministers, Serbia 45-47; Pres Exec. Council, Serbia 48-53, Pres. Serbian Assembly 53-57; Minister of Agriculture and Forests, Yugoslavia 47-48; Pres. Fed. People's Assembly 57-63; Pres. Fed. Exec. Council 63-67; mem. Central Cttee. of C.P. of Yugoslavia 48-, mem. Politbureau 51-, and Exec. Cttee. 52-. Central Cttee. League of Communists of Yugoslavia, Chair. Ideological Comm. 48-63, mem. Presidium of Central Cttee. of League of Communists of Yugoslavia 66-; mem. Council of Fed. 63-; Pres. Central Cttee. L.C. of Serbia 68-; Order of Hero of People and other decorations.
League of Communists of Serbia, Bulevar Lenjina 6, Belgrade, Yugoslavia.

Stammberger, Dr. Wolfgang; German politician; b. 14 July 1920; ed. Univs. of Halle, Frankfurt, Prague, Vienna and Erlangen.
Private law practice, Coburg 49-; mem. Bundestag 53-; Chair. Public Health Cttee. 53-61; Fed. Minister of Justice 61-62; Social Democrat.
Sauerbruchstrasse 5, 863 Coburg Ofr., German Federal Republic.
Telephone: 09561-8858.

Stamp, Hon. Arthur Maxwell, M.A.; British economic consultant; b. 20 Sept. 1915; ed. Leys School, Cambridge, Zürich and Lausanne, and Clare Coll., Cambridge.
Called to the Bar (Inner Temple) 39; war service as Lieut.-Col. in Intelligence Corps 40-46; Financial

Adviser and Dir. John Lewis Partnership Ltd. 47-50; Acting Adviser to Bank of England 50-53; Alternate Exec. Dir. for the U.K. Int. Monetary Fund 51-53; Dir. of European Dept., Int. Monetary Fund 53-54; Adviser to Bank of England 54-57; Chair. Combined Engineering and Econ. Studies Ltd.; Dir. Philip Hill, Higginson, Erlangers Ltd. 58-65, Hill Samuel & Co. Ltd. 65-, The De La Rue Co. Ltd. 60-, Triplex Holdings Ltd. 63-; Man. Dir. Maxwell Stamp Associates Ltd.
5 Loudoun Road, London, N.W.8, England.

Stamprech, Franz, DR.PHIL.; Austrian journalist; b. 30 May 1906; ed. Vienna Univ.
Editor *Kleines Volksblatt* 29-55; Chief Editor *Wiener Zeitung* 55-.
Publs. *Tierhotel* (for children) 46, *Hans Kudlich* 47, *Frühlingsstimmen* 48, *Leopold Kunschak* (biography) 52, *Der Grosse Schlosser* (publ. in newspaper).
Rotenturmstrasse 27, Vienna, Austria.

Stancu, Zaharia, M.A.; Romanian writer; b. 1902; ed. Univ. of Bucharest.
Began career as journalist and poet 20; Editor review *Azi* (Today) 32-40, *Lumea Românească* (Romanian World) 37-39, review *Gazeta Literară* 54-62, 67-; Gen. Man. I. L. Caragiale Nat. Theatre, Bucharest 46-52 and 58-; Chair. Writers' Union of Socialist Republic of Romania 49-52 and 66-; mem. Acad. of Socialist Repub. of Romania 55-; Deputy Nat. Assembly; State Prize 54.
Publs. incl.: poetry: *Simple Poems* 28, *Whites* 37, *The Golden Bell* 39, *The Red Tree* 40; an *Anthology of Young Poets* 34; prose (novels): *Typhoon* 37, *Barefooted* 48 (translated in 32 countries), *The Mastiffs* 52, *Roots are Bitter* (5 vols.) 58-59, *Play with Death* 62, *Fools Wood* 63.
Uniunea Scriitorilor din Republica Socialistâ România, Şoseaua Kiseleff 10, Bucharest; Home: Str. Helesteu 30A, Bucharest, Romania.
Telephone: 330237.

Stanfield, Hon. Robert Lorne, B.A., LL.B., Q.C., LL.D.; Canadian politician; b. 11 April 1914; ed. Ashbury Coll., Ottawa, Dalhousie and Harvard Univs.
Governor, Dalhousie Univ. 49-56; Premier, Minister of Education, Nova Scotia 56-; Leader Progressive Conservatives, Nova Scotia; Leader Nat. Progressive Conservative Party of Canada Sept. 67-.
The Oaks, Gorsebrook Avenue, Halifax, Nova Scotia, Canada.

Stankiewicz, Witold, DR.HIST.SC.; Polish librarian and historian; b. 30 Aug. 1919; ed. Warsaw University.
Official in co-operative societies; mem. History Inst. Polish Acad. of Sciences; Chief Dir. Nat. Library 62-; Chief Editor *The National Library Yearbook* 65.
Publs. *People's Newspaper Publications in the Polish Kingdom 1905-1914* 57; co-author *History of the Polish People's Movement in Outline* 63; *Social Conflicts in Rural Poland 1918-1920* 63, *Source Materials to the History of the Peasant Movement* (co-author) 66.
39 Krasinski Street, Warsaw, Poland.

Stanley, Wendell Meredith, PH.D.; American biochemist; b. 16 Aug. 1904; ed. Earlham Coll. and Univ. of Ill.
Assoc. Univ. of Ill. 29-30, Instructor 30; Nat. Research Council Fellow in Chemistry Munich 30-31; Rockefeller Inst., New York 31-32; Princeton 32-48, mem. 40-48; Prof. of Biochemistry and Dir. Virus Laboratory, Univ. of Calif. 48-; Chair. Dept. of Biochemistry 48-53; Prof. of Virology, Chair. Dept. of Virology 58-64; Prof. of Molecular Biology 64-; Consultant, Sec. of War 45-46; WHO Expert Advisory Panel on Virus Diseases 51-; Trustee, Mills Coll. 51-58; Nat. Advisory Cancer Council, U.S. Public Health Service 52-56; Bd. of Scientific Counsellors, Nat. Cancer Inst. 57-61, Chair. 57-58; mem. Editorial Boards *Proceedings of the Society of Experimental Biology and Medicine* 51-56, *Archive für die gesamte Virusforschung* 51-;

Chair. Section of Biochemistry, Nat. Acad. of Sciences 55-58; Chair. Editorial Bd. of *Proceedings of National Academy of Sciences* 55-60; Dir.-at-Large, American Cancer Soc. 55-61, Hon. Life mem. 61-; President's Panel on Mental Retardation 61-62; Scientific Advisory Board, the Robert A. Welch Foundation 64-; mem. Nat. Acad. Sciences, American Philosophical Soc., American Asscn. Advancement of Science, Editorial Board *Cancer*; awards include Isaac Adler Award, Harvard Univ. 38; Rosenberger Medal, Univ. of Chicago 38; Nichols Medal 46 and Gibbs Medal 47, American Chemical Society; Nobel Prize in Chemistry 46; Franklin Medal, Franklin Inst., 48; Presidential Certificate of Merit 48; American Cancer Soc. Nat. Award 63; American Medical Asscn. Scientific Achievement Award 66; Hon. Sc.D. (Earlham Coll., Harvard, Yale, Princeton, Pittsburgh, Illinois, Pennsylvania and Gustavus Adolphus Coll.), LL.D. (Calif., Ind., Jewish Theological Seminary, Mills Coll.), Dr. h.c. (Paris); Order of Rising Sun (2nd Class) Japan 66.
Virus Laboratory, University of California, Berkeley, Calif. 94720, U.S.A.
Telephone: 415-848-1851.

Stanovnik, Janez; Yugoslav politician and international official; b. 4 Aug. 1922; ed. Faculty of Law, Ljubljana Univ., and Inst. for Social Sciences, Belgrade.
Took part in National Liberation Struggle 41-45; fmr. Counsellor, Perm. Mission of Yugoslavia to UN; mem. numerous Yugoslav Dels. to UN; mem. Fed. Exec. Council of Yugoslavia; Exec. Sec. of Econ. Comm. for Europe (ECE) 68-.
Economic Commission for Europe, Palais des Nations, Geneva, Switzerland.
Telephone : 33-10-00, Extension 2670.

Stans, Maurice Hubert, C.P.A., LL.D.; American investment banker; b. 22 March 1908; ed. Northwestern Univ., Columbia Univ.
Joined Alexander Grant and Co., Chicago 28; exec. partner 40-55; Dir. ten other business corpns. 35-55; Financial Consultant to U.S. Postmaster General 53-55; Deputy Postmaster General 55-57; Dir. Bureau of the Budget, U.S. Govt. 58-61; Pres. Western Bancorporation 61-62; Vice-Chair. United California Bank 61-62; Senior partner, William R. Staats & Co. 63-65; Pres. Glore Forgan, Wm. R. Staats Inc. 65-; Pres. American Inst. of Certified Public Accountants 54; Outstanding Service citation, American Inst. of C.P.A.'s and American Accounting Asscn. 52; elected Accounting Hall of Fame 60-62; Republican; Tax Foundation Public Service Award 59, Great Living American Award of U.S. Chamber of Commerce 61; several honorary degrees.
45 Wall Street, New York, N.Y. 10005, U.S.A.
Telephone: 212-944-1600.

Stanton, Frank, PH.D.; American administrator; b. 20 March 1908; ed. Ohio State Univ.
President (also Dir.) Columbia Broadcasting System Inc. 46-; Dir. New York Life Insurance Co., Holt-Rinehart and Winston Inc., New York Yankees Inc.; Trustee Center for Advanced Study in the Behavioral Sciences, Rockefeller Foundation, The Rand Corpn.; Chair. Carnegie Inst. of Washington, U.S. Advisory Comm. on Information; Dir. Lincoln Center for the Performing Arts, Stanford Research Inst.; mem. The Business Council; Fellow, American Asscn. for the Advancement of Science, American Psychological Asscn., American Acad. Arts and Sciences; mem. Architectural League of N.Y., Council on Foreign Relations Inc., Inst. of Electrical and Electronic Engineers, Nat. Acad. of Television Arts and Sciences, Radio-Television News Dirs. Asscn.
Office: 51 West 52nd Street, New York, N.Y. 10019, U.S.A.
Telephone 212-765-4321.

Stapledon, Sir Robert de Stapeldon, K.C.M.G., C.B.E., B.A.; British overseas administrator; b. 6 Feb. 1909; ed. Trinity Coll., Cambridge.
Served Provincial Admin. Nigeria 31; Sec. West African Govs. Conf. 40; Resident Minister's Office, West Africa 42; Financial Sec. Western Pacific High Comm. 46; Economic Sec. East Africa High Comm. 48; Chief Sec. Tanganyika 54-56; Gov. of Eastern Nigeria 56-60; Gov. of Bahamas 60-64.
The Old Rectory, Littleham, North Devon, England.
Telephone: Bideford 3752.

Stapp, Col. John Paul, B.A., M.A., PH.D., M.D., SC.D.; American air force officer and aerospace scientist; b. 11 July 1910; ed. Baylor Univ. (Texas), Univs. of Texas and Minnesota and School of Aviation Medicine.
Joined U.S. Air Force Medical Corps 44; pioneer of research on effects of mechanical force on living tissues, especially with regard to high-speed flight and space flight; conducted rocket sled deceleration tests on himself; planned and directed high-altitude (102,000 feet) manned balloon flights 57; organised Aeromedical Facility (Edwards Air Force Base, Calif.) and Aeromedical Field Laboratory (Holloman Air Force Base, N.M.); Chief Aerospace Medical Laboratory, Wright Air Development Div. (Wright-Patterson Air Force Base, Ohio) 58-; Special Asst. Advanced Studies, Aerospace Medical Center (Brooks Air Force Base, Tex.) 60-61, Chief Scientist 61-65; Chief of Impact Injury, Armed Forces Inst. of Pathology 65-67; Vice-Pres. Int. Astronautical Fed. 60-; Chair. Annual Stapp Car Crash Conf. 55-; Pres. Civil Aviation Medical Asscn. 68; Fellow, American Inst. Aeronautics and Astronautics, British Inter-planetary Soc.; mem. Int. Acad. Astronautics, Int. Acad. Aviation and Space Medicine, American Medical Asscn., Nat. Research Council, Int. Acad. Aviation Medicine, etc.; many awards include: John Jefferies Award 53, Cheney Award 55, Liljenkrantz Award 57, Gorgas Medal 57; Commdr. Legion of Merit 55.
Publs. *Human Exposure to Linear Deceleration* (Journal of Aviation Medicine) 50, *Crash Protection in Air Force Transports* (Aeronautical Engineering Review) 53, *Effects of Mechanical Force on Living Tissue* (Journal of Aviation Medicine) 55, 56 and 58, *Space Cabin Landing Impact Vector Effects on Human Physiology* 64.
Office: Armed Forces Institute of Pathology, Washington, D.C. 20305; and 8803 Montgomery Avenue, Chevy Chase, Md. 20015; Home: 5008 Rodman Road, Bethesda, Md. 20016, U.S.A.
Telephone: 202-576-2969 (Office).

Star Busmann, Eduard, LL.D.; Netherlands diplomatist; b. 04; ed. Utrecht Univ.
Attaché, Berlin 29; Second Sec., Paris 32; Second Sec., Berlin 35, First Sec. 36; First Sec., Copenhagen 37; First Sec., Pretoria 38, Counsellor 40; Head, Legal Dept., Neths. Foreign Office, London, also Neths. rep. with Fighting French and Judge Neths. Maritime Court 41; Head of Political Dept., Neths. Foreign Office 45; Minister at Embassy, Paris 46; Sec.-Gen. Brussels Treaty Organisation, London 48-53; Ambassador to Austria 53-58; Ambassador to U.A.R., concurrently accred. to Libya 58-63, to U.S.S.R. 63-65, to Switzerland 66-; Del. San Francisco Conf. 45, Paris Conf. 46, Geneva Conf. on Law of the Sea 58; Officer, Order of Orange Nassau (Neths.); Grand Officier, Légion d'Honneur (France); Commdr. Order of St. Olav (Norway); Grand Officer Order of Leopold II (Belgium); Chevalier, Order of Netherlands Lion; Grand Cross, Order of Merit (Austria) and Order of the Oak Crown (Luxembourg).
Netherlands Embassy, Kollerweg 11, Berne, Switzerland.

Starcke, Viggo, M.D.; Danish physician and politician; b. 13 March 1895.
Demonstrator in Anatomy Copenhagen Univ. 17; Asst., Pharmacological Inst. of Copenhagen Univ. 23; appointments at various Hospitals, Copenhagen 21-26; Chief Medical Officer, Sanatorium, Silkeborg 26-46; College Doctor, Int. Gymnastic Inst., Silkeborg 26-46; Pres. of "Danmarks Retsforbund" (Danish League of Justice) 38; M.P. 45-60; Leader of "Danmarks Retsforbund" in Parl. 46; mem. Cttee. for Foreign Affairs 47; Del. to Nordic Council; mem. Defence Cttee. 55; Minister without Portfolio 57-60.
Publs. *Diktatur? Kommunisme? eller Retsstat?* 34, *Folket og Retfærdigheden* 43, *Danmark i Verdenshistorien* 46, *The Viking Danes* 49, *Denmark in World History* 62, *Centuries of Experience with Land Taxation in Denmark* 66.
Egegården, Ørholm pr. Lyngby, Denmark.
Telephone: 06-87-80-32.

Starewicz, Artur; Polish politician; b. 20 March 1917; ed. Lvov Technical Univ.
Member revolutionary youth orgs., inc. Communist Union of Polish Youth (K.Z.M.P.); arrested 36; studied in France 37-38; chemical engineer in Soviet electrotechnical industry 43-44; mem. Polish Workers Party (P.P.R.) 44-48, Polish United Workers Party (P.Z.P.R.) 48; worked in P.P.R. Voivodship Cttee. at Rzeszow, then Cracow and Warsaw, First Sec. of P.P.R. Voivodship Cttee. in Wrocław 46-48; Head of Propaganda, P.Z.P.R. Central Cttee. 48-53; Sec. of Central Council of Trade Unions 54-56; Deputy Editor-in-Chief of daily *Trybuna Ludu* 56; Alt. mem. P.Z.P.R. Central Cttee. 54-59, mem. 59-, Head of Press Office 57-63, Sec. 63-; mem. Seym 57-; Order of the Banner of Labour, First Class 54, 64, and others.
Polska Zjednoczona Partia Robotnicza, Nowy Šwiat 6, Warsaw, Poland.

Stark, Freya Madeline, C.B.E.; British explorer and writer; ed. School of Oriental Studies and privately.
Travelled in Middle East and Iran 27-39 and in South Arabia 34-35, 37-38; joined Min. of Information Sept. 39, sent to Aden 39, Cairo 40, Baghdad 42, U.S.A. and Canada 44; Hon. LL.D. (Glasgow Univ.) 52; Founder's Medal, Royal Geographical Society, Mungo Park Medal, Royal Scottish Geographical Society, Sir Percy Sykes Medal, Royal Central Asian Society, Burton Medal, Royal Asiatic Society.
Publs. *The Valleys of the Assassins* 34, *The Southern Gates of Arabia* 36, *Baghdad Sketches* 37, *Seen in the Hadhramaut* 38, *A Winter in Arabia* 40, *Letters from Syria* 42, *East is West* 45, *Perseus in the Wind* 48, *Traveller's Prelude* 50, *Beyond Euphrates* 51, *The Coast of Incense* 53, *Ionia: A Quest* 54, *The Lycian Shore* 56, *Alexander's Path* 58, *Riding to the Tigris* 59, *Dust in the Lion's Paw* 61, *The Journey's Echo* 63, *Romans on the Euphrates* 66, *The Zodiac Arch* 68.
Montoria, San Zenone degli Ezzelini, Treviso, Italy; and c/o John Murray, 50 Albemarle Street, London, W.1, England.
Telephone: San Zenone 57073.

Starke, H. F. Gerhard, DR. PHIL.; German newspaper editor; b. 16 Aug. 1916; ed. Univs. of Leipzig and Geneva.
Editor *Deutsche Allgemeine Zeitung*, Berlin 39-45; Editor *Prisma* and *Thema* (cultural periodicals), Munich and Gauting 46-49; Chief Editor and Chief Political Dept., Nordwestdeutscher Rundfunk (NWDR), Hamburg 49-61; Dir. Deutschlandfunk, Cologne 61-66; Chief Editor *Die Welt*, Hamburg Sept. 66-.
Die Welt, 2 Hamburg 36, Kaiser-Wilhelm-Strasse 1; Hamburg 13, 48 Magdalenenstrasse, German Federal Republic.

Starke, Dr. Heinz; German politician; b. 27 Feb. 1911; ed. Univs. of Berlin, Breslau and Jena.
Worked for Econ. Admin. Body of British Zone of Occupation; fmr. Dir. Bayreuth Chamber of Commerce; mem. European Assembly 58-; mem. German Bundestag 53-; Minister of Finance 61-62; Free Democrat.
Europastrasse 6, Bad Godesberg, German Federal Republic.
Telephone: Godesberg 75049.

Starker, Janos; American (b. Hungarian) cellist; b. 5 July 1924; ed. Franz Liszt Acad. of Music, Budapest.
Solo cellist Budapest Opera House and Philharmonic Orchestra 45-46; Solo cellist Dallas Symphony Orchestra 48-49, Metropolitan Opera Orchestra 49-53, Chicago Symphony Orchestra 53-58; Resident cellist Indiana Univ. 58-, Prof. of Music 61-; Grand Prix du Disque 48; World-wide concert tours, numerous recordings and magazine articles.
Publ. *Method* 64.
Indiana University Music Department, Bloomington, Indiana, U.S.A.

Starkie, Enid Mary, C.B.E., M.A., D.LITT., Docteur de l'Université de Paris; British lecturer and writer; ed. Alexandra Coll. Dublin, Somerville Coll. Oxford, and La Sorbonne, Paris.
Assistant Lecturer in French Literature Univ. Coll. Exeter 26-29; Lecturer in French Literature Somerville Coll. Oxford 29-35; Lecturer French Literature Oxford Univ. 33-39; Fellow and Tutor Somerville Coll. Oxford 35-45; Reader in French Literature at Univ. of Oxford and Professional Fellow of Somerville Coll. 45-65; Reader Emeritus in French Literature, Univ. of Oxford; Hon. Fellow Somerville Coll.; mem. Irish Acad.; F.R.S.L.; Officier de la Légion d'Honneur, Hon. D.Litt. (Exeter), Hon. Litt.D. (Dublin); Hon. D. ès L. (Aix en Provence).
Publs. *Verhaeren* (couronné par l'Académie Française) 29, *Baudelaire* 33, *Rimbaud in Abyssinia* 37, *Arthur Rimbaud* 38, *Rimbaud en Abyssinie* 38, *A Lady's Child* (autobiography) 41, *Petrus Borel en Algérie* 50, *André Gide* 54, *Petrus Borel* 54, *Baudelaire* 57, *From Gautier to Eliot* 60, *Arthur Rimbaud* 61, *Flaubert* 67, and other books.
23 Walton Street, Oxford, England.
Telephone: Oxford 57110.

Starkie, Walter Fitzwilliam, C.M.G., C.B.E., M.A., LITT.D., M.R.I.A., F.R.S.A., F.R.S.L.; British literary historian; b. 9 Aug. 1894; ed. Shrewsbury and Trinity Coll., Dublin.
Served First World War; Lecturer in Romance Languages, Trinity Coll., 20, in Modern Spanish Drama, King's Coll., London 23; Fellow Trinity Coll., Dublin 24-47; Dir. Irish National (Abbey) Theatre 27-42; Lectured Madrid 24, 28, Florence 26, Sweden 26, U.S.A. and Canada 29, 30, France 31, 32, Italy, Austria 48, Portugal 49, Central and S. America 50; Visiting Prof. of Romance Languages, Univ. of Chicago 30; Lord Northcliffe Lecturer in Literature, Univ. Coll., London 36; Prof. of Spanish and Lecturer in Italian Literature, Dublin Univ. 26-47; Dir. British Inst. Madrid 40-54; Visiting Prof. Univ. of Texas 57, 58, New York Univ. 59, Univ. of Kansas 60, Colorado 61; Prof. in Residence, Univ. of California (Los Angeles) 64-68; Rep. of British Council in Spain 40-54; Chevalier Légion d'Honneur.
Publs. *Jacinto Benavente* 25, *Raggle-Taggle* 33, *Spanish Raggle-Taggle* 34, *Luigi Pirandello* 37, *The Waveless Plain* 38, *Grand Inquisitor* 40, *In Sara's Tents* 53, *The Road to Santiago* 57, *Spain: A Musician's Journey through Time and Space* (2 vols., with four L.P. records in English, French and German) 58, *The Dukes of Alba* 68, *Scholars and Gypsies* 63, *Six Exemplary*

Novels of Cervantes 64, *Eight Plays of the Spanish Golden Age* 64.
10805 Ashton Avenue, Los Angeles, California 90024, U.S.A.; and The Athenaeum, London, S.W.1, England.
Telephone: 474-8137 (Los Angeles).

Starnes, John Kennett; Canadian diplomatist; b. 5 Feb. 1918; ed. Trinity Coll. School, Port Hope, Institut Sillig, Switzerland, Univ. of Munich and Bishop's Univ.
Canadian Army 40-44; Dept. of External Affairs 44-; Adviser, Canadian Del. to UN 48-50; First Sec., later Counsellor, Bonn 53-56; Deputy Exec. Sec. North Atlantic Council, Paris 56-58; Ambassador to German Fed. Repub. and Head of Canadian Mil. Mission, Berlin 62-66; Amb. to United Arab Repub. 66-67, and to Repub. of Sudan 67; Asst. Under Sec. of State for External Affairs 67-.
Fleury Road, Chelsea, P.Q., Canada.
Telephone: 827-0889 (Home); 992-7590 (Office).

Starovsky, Vladimir Nikonovich, DR. ECON. SC.; Soviet economist and statistician; b. 3 May 1905; ed. Moscow State Univ. and Postgraduate Inst. of Economics, Moscow.
Joined Central Statistical Board 25; Dir. of Board and Deputy Chair. State Plan for U.S.S.R. 40-48; Dir. of Central Statistics Board, Council of Ministers, U.S.S.R. 48-; has taught at higher educational establishments 27-, Prof. of Statistics 34-; mem. Council of Ministers of U.S.S.R. 57-; mem. Supreme Soviet of the U.S.S.R. (Nationality Chamber) 62-; Corresp. mem. of the Acad. of Sciences of U.S.S.R. 58-; three Orders of Lenin, Order of the Red Banner of Labour (twice), Badge of Honour and several medals; mem. C.P. 39-; mem. of the Central Auditing Comm. of the C.P.S.U.
Publs. Numerous scientific works on political economy, economic statistics, mathematical statistics and demography.
Central Statistical Board, Ul. Kirova 39, Moscow, U.S.S.R.

Starr, Isaac, B.S., M.D.; American university medical scientist; b. 6 March 1895; ed. Princeton Univ. and Univ. of Pennsylvania.
House Officer Mass. Gen. Hospital 20-22; Instr. in Pharmacology Univ. of Pennsylvania 22-28, Asst. Prof. of Clinical Pharmacology 28-33; Hartzell Research Prof. of Therapeutics 33-45 and 48-61; Prof. of Therapeutic Research, Univ. of Pennsylvania 45-48; Dean of the School of Medicine 45-48, Emeritus Prof. Therapeutic Research 61-; during the Second World War served as Chair. Sub-Cttee. on Pharmacy, Sec. Sub-Committee on Essential Drugs, Committee on Medical Supplies, Nat. Research Council; Responsible Investigator, O.S.R.D.; Project on Convalescence. Investigator Aviation Medicine and Anti-malarials; mem. Cttee. on Narcotics and Drug Addiction (Chair. 47-60), Cttee. on Problems of Alcohol, National Research Council; Chair. Council on Drugs, American Medical Asscn. 60-63; mem. Cardiovascular Study Section, Nat. Inst. of Health 46-51; Consultant U.S. Navy A.M.A.L. 49-64, U.S. Army Chemical, Biological and Radiological Agency 62-66; Editor Board *Circulation* 49-53, 55-59; Selective Service Medal; Lasker Award, American Heart Asscn. 57; Kober Medal, Asscn. American Physicians 67.
Publs. Over 100 publications on renal physiology, drug action in man, cardiac output in man, action of derivatives of choline in man, peripheral vascular disease and its treatment, the ballistocardiogram and its utility.
851 Gates Memorial Pavilion, University Hospital, 36th and Spruce Streets, Philadelphia, Pa. 19104, U.S.A.
Telephone: 215-EV2-46000.

Starr, Hon. Michael, M.P.; Canadian politician; b. 14 Nov. 1910; ed. Oshawa High School.
With firm of Pedlar People Ltd. 28-52; Chair. Board of Works, City of Oshawa 45-49; Mayor 49-53; mem. Canadian House of Commons 52-; Minister of Labour 57-63; Progressive Conservative.
House of Commons, Ottawa, Ont., Canada.

Starrenburg, Willem F. G. L.; Netherlands oil executive; b. 1908; ed. Technische Hogeschool Te Delft.
Joined Royal Dutch/Shell 32, early service as exploitation engineer; Man. Western Div. Venezuela 50-56; Head, Production Dept. The Hague 56-57, Co-ordinator Exploration and Production 57-60; Regional Coordinator (Oil), Caribbean, Central and S. America 60-61; Dir. of Co-ordination (Chemical) 61-62; Asst. Man. Dir. Royal Dutch Petroleum Co. 62-63, Man. Dir. 63-; Principal Dir. Bataafse Petroleum Maatschappij N.V. 63-; Dir. Shell Research N.V. 64-.
Wassenaarseslag 2, Wassenaar, Netherlands.

Starý, Oldrich, M.D., D.SC.; Czechoslovak neurologist; b. 15 June 1914; ed. Charles Univ., Prague.
First Internal Clinic, Prague 39-41; Neurological Clinic, Prague 41-52; Asst. Prof. of Neurology 55-61, Prof. 61-, Dean, Faculty for Gen. Medicine, Charles Univ., Prague 61-63, Rector, Charles Univ., Prague 66-; Chief Editor *Czechoslovak Neurology;* Corresp. mem. Czechoslovak Acad. of Sciences 60-; mem. Ideological Comm. Central Cttee. C.P. of Czechoslovakia 62-, mem. Central Cttee. C.P. of Czechoslovakia 66-; mem., Pres. State Cttee. for Univs. 66-; Pres., mem. Scientific Council, Ministry of Health 67-; mem. Neurological Cttee., J. E. Purkyně Medical Soc. 53-, Soc. Française de Neurologie 65-, U.S.S.R. Acad. of Medical Sciences, Advisory Cttee. for Rehabilitation of WHO 67-.
Publs. *Some Problems of the Pathogenesis of Disorders due to Changes in an Intervertebral Disc* 59, and 110 papers on vertebrogenous disorders, the objective substrate of the regularity in the central analysis of pain, neurological problems, especially immunological pathogenesis of multiple sclerosis and problems of allergical and non-allergical migraines, reflex therapy of spastic paralysis.
Rector's Office, Charles University, Prague 1, Czechoslovakia.

Starzynski, Juliusz, PH.D.; Polish art historian; b. 06; ed. Warsaw Univ.
Dozent, Warsaw Univ. 35-39; Prof., State Inst. of Theatrical Art, Curator in Nat. Museum, Warsaw 37-39; Prof. Warsaw Univ. 49-; Dir. State Inst. of Art 59-; mem. Polish Acad. of Sciences, Chair. Theory and History of Art Cttee. 59-.
Publs. Numerous works in the field of art history, especially painting and sculpture of the XIX and XX centuries.
Polish Academy of Sciences, Palace of Culture and Sciences, Warsaw, Poland.

Stassen, Harold E., A.B., LL.B.; American lawyer and politician; b. 13 April 1907; ed. Univ. of Minnesota.
Member law firm of Stassen & Ryan, South St. Paul, Minn. 30-38; County Attorney, Dakota Co. 31-38; Gov. of Minn. 38-42; Chair. Nat. Governors' Conf. 41 and 42; Chair. Council of State Govts. 40-41; resgnd. as Gov. to enter U.S. Navy as Lieut.-Commdr. 43; served on staff of Admiral Halsey in Pacific Theatre as Halsey's Flag Sec. and later as Asst. Chief of Staff for Admin. of Third Fleet 43-45; mem. U.S. del. to San Francisco Conf. 45; Pres. Univ. of Pa. 48-53; Dir. Foreign Operations Admin. 53-55; Special Asst. to Pres. on Disarmament Problems (with cabinet rank) 55-58; partner Stassen, Kephart, Sarkis and Scullin 58-; Pres. Int. Council of Religious Educ. 42-50; Vice-Pres. Nat. Council of Churches 50-52; Pres. American Baptist

Convention 63-64; Hon. LL.D., Hon. L.H.D.; Legion of Merit; Bronze Star; Republican.
Publs. *Where I Stand* 47, *Man was Meant to be Free* 51.
Office: Fidelity Bldg., Philadelphia, Pa. 19109; Home: Penn Towers, Philadelphia, Pa. 19103, U.S.A.

Stassinopoulos, Michael; Greek university professor and politician; b. 05; ed. Athens Univ.
Lecturer in Admin. Law, Athens Univ. 37; Prof. Admin. Law, High School of Political Sciences, Athens 39-, Dean 51-; State Council Adviser 43-; Political Adviser to Dodecanese Gov. 47; Chair. Cttee. for the Civil Servants Code 48; Minister of the Press and subsequently Minister of Labour 52; Chair. Hellenic Nat. Broadcasting Inst. Admin. Board 53; Chair. Nat. Opera Admin. Board 53-; Dr. h.c. (Univ. of Bordeaux) 57, Order of St. George (First Class).
Publs. *The States' Civil Responsibility* 49, *Administrative Acts Law* 50, *Civil Service Laws* 51, *Administrative Disputes Laws* 53, *Principles of Administrative Law* 54, *Principles of Public Finance* 56, *Traité des actes administratifs* (in French), *Poems* 49, *The Land of the Blue Lakes* 50, *Harmonia* (poems).
High School of Political Sciences, Athens, Greece.

Staub, Marshal Gerald; American business executive; b. 19 June 1922; ed. LaSalle Extension Univ.
Merritt-Chapman and Scott Corpn. 44-, Treas. 51-61, Exec. Vice-Pres. 55-61, Pres. 61-, Dir. 55-, mem. Exec. Cttee. 57-; official of affiliated and other companies.
Merritt-Chapman and Scott Corporation, 277 Park Avenue, New York City, N.Y. 10017, U.S.A.

Stavropoulos, Constantin Anghelos; Greek lawyer and United Nations official; b. 15 Aug. 1905; ed. Univ. of Athens and London School of Economics.
Private legal practice 29-33, 36-39; Sec.-Gen. and Acting Gov. Epirus 33-36; Legal Adviser, Royal Greek Embassy, London 41-46, Pres. Greek Maritime Court in U.K. 42-46; with UN 43-, Legal Dept. 46-; Under-Sec., Legal Counsel, Office of Legal Affairs 55-; Acting Commr. for South West Africa; Commdr. Order of George I (Greece).
United Nations, New York 17, N.Y., U.S.A.

Stawiński, Eugeniusz; Polish politician; b. 05.
Former textile worker; fmr. mem. Communist Party of Poland; Gen. Sec. Trade Union of Textile Workers 45-48; Mayor of Łódź 49; Minister of Light Industry 49-; mem. Central Cttee. of Polish United Workers' Party 56-.
20 Hoza Street, Warsaw, Poland.

Stearns, Robert Lawrence, B.A., LL.B.; American corporation executive; b. 3 Oct. 1892; ed. Univ. of Colorado and Columbia Univ.
Admitted to Colorado Bar 16; mem. Lewis and Grant, Denver 22-35; Asst. in History Univ. of Colorado 13-14; Instr. in History, Univ. of Denver, summer 21; mem. Faculty of Univ. of Denver Law School 20-31; Prof. of Law, Univ. of Colo. 31-39, Act. Dean of Law School 31-33, Dean 35-39, Pres. of Univ. 39-53; mem. Educ. Council U.S. Navy 42-46; Operations Analyst U.S. Air Forces 42-46; mem. Board of Visitors U.S. Air Forces Air Univ.; Chair. American Council on Educ. 52; Pres. Boettcher Foundation 53-62; Pres. Webb-Waring Inst. for Medical Research 63-; Hon. LL.D. (Columbia Univ. and Univs. of Denver, New Mexico, Colorado and Colorado Coll.); medals include U.S. Medal of Freedom and U.S. Air Force Exceptional Civilian Service medal.
Publ. Compiler *Colorado Law of Wills and Estates* 38.
918 Race Street, Denver, Colo., U.S.A.
Telephone: 333-4635.

Stearns, Russell Bangs; American executive; b. 9 Feb. 1894; ed. Univ. of Mich.
With North America Co. 16-17, with Arthur Perry & Co. 20, Partner 26-30, Pres. 30-38; Chair. of Board and

Chair. Exec. Cttee. Colonial Stores Inc.; Pres., Dir. Nat. Food Products Corpn.; Dir. of numerous other companies.
Office: 24 Federal Street, Boston, Mass. 02110; Home: 50 Haven Street, Dedham, Mass. 02026, U.S.A.
Telephone: 617-326-1329 (Home); 617-542-3435 (Office).

Stebbins, Henry Endicott, A.B.; American diplomatist; b. 16 June 1905; ed. Harvard Univ.
Joined Foreign Service, Berne, Istanbul, London, Ottawa, Vienna, Paris, London 29-50; Nat. War. Coll. 50-51; Consul-Gen., Melbourne, Australia 51-54; Foreign Service Inspector, Dept. of State 54-59; Ambassador to Nepal 59-66, to Uganda 66-.
American Embassy, Kampala, Uganda and 43 Canton Avenue, Milton, Mass. 02187, U.S.A.

Stechkin, Boris Sergeevich; Soviet combustion engineer; b. 91; ed. Moscow Higher Technical School.
Instructor, Moscow Higher Technical Acad. 18-29; Prof. Moscow Air Force Acad. 21-; Prof. Moscow Aviation Inst. 33-37; Corresp. mem. U.S.S.R. Acad. of Sciences 46-53, mem. 53-; Head, Motors Lab., U.S.S.R. Acad. of Sciences 54-63; in Moscow Automobile Transport Inst. 63-; Order of Lenin, Order of Red Banner of Labour, Order of Red Star, State Prize, Hero of Socialist Labour.
Publs. *Aircraft Engines* 22, *The Thermal Calculation of an Engine* 27, *Summary of Lectures on the Theory of Aircraft Turbo-Compressors* 44, *Theory of Aviation Jet Engines* 45, *Gas Turbines* 56, *Theory of Jet Engines* (co-author, 2 vols.) 56-58.
Moscow Automobile Transport Institute, 64 Lenin Prospekt, Moscow, U.S.S.R.

Stedeford, Sir Ivan Arthur Rice, G.B.E.; British company director; b. 28 Jan. 1897; ed. Shebbear Coll., N. Devon and King Edward VI Grammar School, Birmingham.
Engineer Apprentice, Vickers Ltd. 13-16; served in R.N.A.S., First World War 17-19; motor trade 19-28; Dir. Tubes Ltd. 28; Dir. Tube Investments Ltd. 35, Man. Dir. 39, Chair. and Man. Dir. 44-61, Exec. Chair. 61-62, Life Pres. and Dir. 63-; Dir. Nat. Provincial Bank Ltd. 48-, Deputy Chair. 64-; Dir. Atlas Insurance Co. Ltd. 48-59, Rank Org. and subsidiaries 63-, Tube Investments of India 49, District Bank Ltd. 63; mem. Cttee. of Enquiry into British Broadcasting Corpn. 49; Gov. of B.B.C. 51-55; Dir. Commonwealth Devt. Finance Co. Ltd. 53-66; mem. U.K. Atomic Energy Authority 54-59; Chair. Advisory Group on British Transport Comm. 60; Life Gov. Birmingham Univ.
Witchcraft Hill, Little Gaddesden, Herts., England.
Telephone: Little Gaddesden 3234.

Steel, Sir Christopher Eden, G.C.M.G., M.V.O.; British diplomatist; b. 12 Feb. 1903; ed. Wellington and Hertford Coll., Oxford.
Entered diplomatic service 27; served Foreign Office 27-29, Rio de Janiero 29-31, Paris 31-34 and The Hague 34-35; Asst. Private Sec. to H.R.H. The Prince of Wales 35-36; served Berlin 36-39, Foreign Office 39-42; Political Adviser to Minister of State in Cairo 44, at A.F.H.Q. 44 and at SHAEF 45; Chief of Political Division, Control Commission for Germany 45-46, Political Adviser to C.-in-C. 47-49 and Deputy High Commissioner 49; Minister in Washington 50-53; Permanent Representative on Council of NATO, Paris 53-57; Ambassador to German Federal Republic 57-63; retired.
Southrop Lodge, nr. Lechlade, Gloucestershire, England.

Steel, David Edward Charles, D.S.O., M.C.; British company director; b. 29 Nov. 1916; ed. Rugby School and Univ. Coll., Oxford.
Officer, Q.R. Lancers, serving in France, the Middle East, N. Africa and Italy 40-45; admitted as Solicitor 48; worked for Linklaters and Paines 48-50; in Legal

Dept., British Petroleum Co. Ltd. 50-56; Pres. British Petroleum (N. America) Ltd. 59-61, Regional Co-ordinator, Western Hemisphere, B.P. Co. Ltd. 61-62; Managing Dir., Kuwait Oil Co. Ltd. 62-65, Dir. 65-; a Managing Dir. British Petroleum Co. 65-.
37 Ormonde Gate, London, S.W.3, England.
Telephone: 01-352-0592

Steel, Sir (Joseph) Lincoln (Spedding), Kt., F.R.S.A., M.A., J.P.; British business executive; b. 24 March 1900; ed. Christ's Hospital and St. John's Coll., Oxford.
Joined Brunner Mond and Co. Ltd. 22; Del. Dir. I.C.I. (Alkali) Ltd. 32, Managing Dir. Alkali Div. of I.C.I. Ltd. 42, Chair. Alkali Div. of I.C.I. Ltd. 43; Dir. Imperial Chemical Industries Ltd. (I.C.I.) 45-60; Dep. Chair. Triplex Holdings Ltd. 60-61, Chair. 61-66; Chair. British Nat. Cttee., Int. Chamber of Commerce 51-63, Pres. Int. Chamber of Commerce 63-65; Dir. Charter-house Investment Trust Ltd. 60-; Chair. Overseas Cttee. Fed. of British Industries 50-65; Fellow, British Inst. of Management.
The Warren, Chesham Bois, Bucks., England.
Telephone: Amersham 406.

Steen, Marguerite, F.R.S.L.; British novelist; b. 12 May 1894.
Former schoolteacher, dancer, actress.
Publs. *The Gilt Cage, Duel in the Dark, The Reluctant Madonna, They that Go Down, Where the Wind Blows, The Wise and the Foolish Virgins, Unicorn, Stallion, Spider, Spanish Trilogy: Matador, The One-Eyed Moon, The Tavern, Return of a Heroine, The Lost One, Hugh Walpole* (belles lettres), *Who Would Have Daughters?, The Marriage Will Not Take Place, Family Ties, A Kind of Insolence, The Sun is My Undoing, French for Love* (play, with Derek Patmore), *William Nichol-son: a biography, Rose Timson, Twilight on the Floods, Granada Window, The Swan, Phoenix Rising* 52, *Anna Fitzalan* 53, *The Unquiet Spirit* 55, *Little White King* 56, *The Woman in the Back Seat, The Tower* 59, *A Pride of Terrys* 62, *A Candle in the Sun* 64, *Looking Glass I* (autobiog.) 66.
Little Triton, Blewbury, Berks., England.
Telephone: Blewbury 294.

Steenbeck, Max, DR. PHIL.; German scientist; b. 21 March 1904; ed. Realgymnasium, Kiel and Univ. of Kiel.
Siemens-Schuckert, Berlin 27-45, in Soviet Union 45-56; returned to Jena 56; Dir. of Inst. for Magneto-Hydrodynamics, Jena 56-, Chief of Atomic Reactor building 57-63; Prof. Jena Univ.; mem. German Acad. of Sciences, Berlin, U.S.S.R. Acad. of Sciences; Hon. Dr. rer. nat.
Kernbergstrasse 3, Jena, German Democratic Republic.

Steeves, John Milton, B.A., M.A.; American diplomatist; b. 6 May 1905; ed. Walla Walla Coll. and Univ. of Washington.
Educational Work, India 27-43; Dept. of State 45-, served New Delhi, Tokyo, Djakarta 48-55; Foreign Relations Consultant to High Commr. of Ryuku Islands, Consul Gen. in Naha, Counsellor in Tokyo 55-57; Political Adviser to C.-in-C. Pacific 57-59; Consul-Gen. in Hong Kong 59; Dep. Asst. Sec. of State for Far Eastern Affairs 59-62; Amb. to Afghanistan 62-66; Dir.-Gen. Foreign Service, Dept. of State 66-.
Department of State, Washington, U.S.A.

Stefański, Witold, DR.RER.NAT.; Polish zoologist; ed. Univ. de Genève.
Professor Warsaw Univ. 25, Central School of Farming 52-; Vice-Pres. Polish Acad. of Sciences 62-; Pres. Nat. Cttee. Int. Union of Biological Sciences (IUBS); Corresp. mem. Veterinary Acad. of France.
Publs. include *Recherches sur la faune des Nématodes libres du bassin du Léman* 14, *Contribution à l'étude de l'excrétion chez les Nématodes libres* 17, *Zaraza stadnicza*

(Dourine) w Polsce w latach 1944-48 48, *Rozmieszczenie gza bydlecego (Hypoderma sp.) na terytorium Rzeczypos-politeej Polskiej* 49, *Parazytologia weterynaryjna* (vol. 1) 63.
Sewerynow-str., Warsaw 6, Poland.

Steiger, Rod; American actor; b. 14 April 1925; ed. Public schools.
Berlin Film Festival Award 64; Academy Award (Oscar) Best Actor 67.
Stage appearances include *Night Music* 51, *An Enemy of the People* 53, *Rashomon* 59; numerous film appearances include *On the Waterfront* 53, *Big Knife* 55, *Oklahoma* 56, *Jubal* 57, *Across the Bridge* 58, *Al Capone* 59, *Seven Thieves* 59, *The Mark* 60, *The World in my Pocket* 60, *The Tiger Among Us* 61, *The Longest Day* 61, *Convicts 4* 61, *The Time of Indifference* 62, *Hands on the City* 63, *The Pawnbroker* 64, *The Loved Ones* 64, *Doctor Zhivago* 66, *In the Heat of the Night* 67, *No Way to Treat a Lady* 68.
c/o A. Morgan Maree, Jr., and Associates, 6363 Wilshire Boulevard, Los Angeles 48, U.S.A.

Stein, Clarence S.; American architect and town planner; b. 19 June 1882; ed. School of Architecture, Columbia Univ. and Ecole des Beaux Arts, Paris.
Secretary, Cttee. on Housing, Reconstruction Comm., New York State 20; Chair., Comm. on Housing and Regional Planning, New York State 23-26; Pres., Regional Planning Council of America 25-48; Pres., Civic Films Inc. 38-58; Pres., Regional Development Council of America 48-; Chief Architect and Planner, Sunnyside Gardens, New York City 24, Radburn, New Jersey 29, Hillside Homes, Bronx 35; Architect of Calif. Inst. of Technology 27, Wichita (Kansas)Art Inst. 35, Temple Emanuel, New York City 29; Architectural and Planning Consultant Chatham Village, Pittsburgh; Greenbelt, Maryland; Greendale, Wis.; Greenhills, Ohio, etc.; Planning Dir. and Co-ordinator of Kitimat, British Columbia, Canada 51; Hon. mem. American Inst. of Planners 64; American Soc. of Planning Officials award 55, Gold Medal of Honor 56, American Inst. of Architects 56, Distinguished Service Award, American Inst. of Planners 58, Sir Ebenezer Howard Memorial Medal 60, N.J. Home Builders' Asscn. Distinguished Service Award 65.
Publ. *Towards New Towns for America* 51.
1 West 64th Street, New York City, N.Y. 10023, U.S.A.
Telephone: -ENdicott 2-8021265.

Stein, Louis, LL.B.; American lawyer and businessman; b. 29 Jan. 1906; ed. Fordham Univ. Law School.
Gen. Counsel Food Fair Stores Inc. 29-40, Vice-Pres. 40-52, Asst. to Pres. 52-53, Pres. 53-67, Chair., Chief Exec. Officer 67-; Chair. Finance Cttee. Food Fair Properties; Senior Partner law firm of Stein, Stein and Engel; Dir. Progress Manufacturing Co., Nat. State Bank of Newark, Fidelity Philadelphia Trust Co., Fed. of Jewish Agencies of Philadelphia, United Fund of Philadelphia, Nat. Conf. of Christians and Jews (mem. Finance Cttee.); Treas. Food Fair Stores Foundation, Commonwealth Mental Health Research Foundation of Philadelphia, American-Israel Soc.; Chair. Philadelphia Lyric Opera Co.; Dir. Nat. Board of Trustees, mem. Exec. Cttee. Eleanor Roosevelt Inst. for Cancer Research; Fellow Universal Brotherhood Movement (Jewish Theological Seminary) 57; awards include Distinguished Leadership Award (Teaneck Bonds for Israel) 56, Brotherhood Award (Nat. Conf. of Christians and Jews) 59; Hon. LL.D. Lasalle Coll. 57.
Food Fair Building, 3175 W. Pennsylvania Boulevard, Philadelphia 4, Pa., U.S.A.

Steinbeck, John Ernst; American writer; b. 27 Feb. 1902; ed. Stanford Univ.
Pulitzer Prize 40, Nobel Prize for Literature 62.
Publs. *Cup of Gold* 29, *To a God Unknown* 33, *Tortilla Flat* 35, *In Dubious Battle* 36, *Of Mice and Men,*

Red Pony 37, *The Grapes of Wrath* 39, *Forgotten Village* 41, *Sea of Cortez* 41, *The Moon is Down* 42, *Cannery Row* 45, *The Wayward Bus* 47, *The Pearl* 47, *The Russian Journal* 48, *Burning Bright* 50, *East of Eden* 52, *Sweet Thursday* 54, *Pipe Dream* 54, *Short Reign of Pippin IV* 57, *Once there was a War*, *The Log from the Sea of Cortez* 58, *The Winter of Our Discontent* 61, *Travels with Charley* 62, *America and the Americans* 66.
c/o McIntosh and Otis Inc., 18 East 41st Street, New York 17, N.Y., U.S.A.

Steinberg, Saul; American (b. Romanian) artist and architect; b. 15 June 1914; ed. Milan Polytechnic School.
Cartoonist 36-39; practising architect 39-41; moved to U.S. 42; illustrator for the *New Yorker* 42-; represented in museum of Modern Art N.Y.
Publs. *All in Line* 45, *The Art of Living* 49, *The Passport* 54, *The Labyrinth* 60.
179 East 71st Street, New York City, N.Y., U.S.A.

Steinberg, William; American conductor; b. 1 Aug. 1899; ed. School of Higher Musical Studies, Univ. of Cologne, and privately.
Conductor Cologne Opera House 20-25; Opera Dir. German Theatre, Prague 25-29; later Gen. Musical Dir. Frankfurt Opera House and Museumsgesellschaft Frankfurt; guest conductor Berlin State Opera House and Czech Philharmonic Prague; founder conductor Palestine Orchestra 36-38; went to U.S.A. 38; regular conductor of N.B.C.; guest conductor N.Y. Philharmonic, Philadelphia, Chicago, and other U.S. and Canadian cities; guest conductor Mexican Nat. Opera; conductor with San Francisco Opera 44-; music dir. Buffalo Philharmonic Orchestra 45-52; Musical Dir. Pittsburgh Symphony Orchestra 52-, London Philharmonic Orchestra 58-59.
11C Gateway Towers, Pittsburgh, Pa. 15222, U.S.A.

Steiner, George, B.ès L., B.A., M.A., D.PHIL.; American writer and scholar; b. 23 April 1929; ed. Univs. of Paris and Chicago, Harvard Univ. and Balliol Coll. Oxford.
Editorial Staff *The Economist*, London 52-56; Fellow, Inst. for Advanced Study, Princeton 56-58; Gauss Lecturer, Princeton Univ. 59-60; Fellow and Dir. of English Studies, Churchill Coll., Cambridge 61-; Albert Schweitzer Visiting Prof., New York Univ. 66-67; O. Henry Award 58.
Publs. *Tolstoy or Dostoevsky* 59, *The Death of Tragedy* 61, *Anno Domini: Three Stories* 64, *Language and Silence* 67; Editor *Penguin Book of Modern Verse Translation* 67.
32 Barrow Road, Cambridge, England; Harvard Club, New York City, U.S.A.

Steinhaus, Hugo, DR. MATH., PH.D., Polish mathematician; b. 14 Jan. 1887; ed. Göttingen Univ.
Prof. Lwow Univ. 20-45; Prof. Wrocław Univ. 45-; mem. Polish Acad. of Sciences; Dr. h.c. Warsaw Univ. 58, Poznań 63, Wrocław 65; Dr. med. h.c. Wrocław Acad. Med. 61.
Publs. *Theory of Games and Pursuit* 25, *Sur les Fonctions indépendantes* 36-53, *The Establishment of Paternity* 54, *Quelques Applications de Principes Topologiques à la Géométrie des Corps Convexes* 55, *A Mathematical Axiom Contradicting the Axiom of Choice* (in collaboration) 62; *Mathematical Snapshots* and various works in the field of applied mathematics.
Orłowskiego 15, Wrocław 12, Poland.

Steiniger, Edward Leo; American businessman; b. 11 Nov. 1902; ed. Pace Coll. and New York Univ.
Joined Sinclair Oil Corpn. and subsidiaries 25, resident Venezuela 28-36, 40-50, Pres. and Dir. Venezuelan Petroleum Co. 50-55, Vice-Pres., Dir. and mem. Exec. Cttee. Sinclair Oil Corpn. 55-57, Exec. Vice-Pres. 57-58, Pres. 58-64, Chair. and Chief Exec. Officer 64-; Dir. and

mem. Exec. Cttee. of American Petroleum Inst.; Dir. Richfield Oil Corpn., Kennecott Copper Corpn., American Council for Int. Promotion of Democracy under God; mem. Nat. Industrial Conf. Board, Nat. Petroleum Council, Chemical Bank N.Y. Trust Co. Advisory Bd. on Int. Business, Advisory Council of President's Associates of Pace Coll.; Trustee Fordham Univ., Emigrant Industrial Savings Bank; Knight Grand Cross Order of the Holy Sepulchre, Knight of Malta, Officer of the Royal Order of the Crown, Hon. D.S.C., Hon. LL.D., Hon. D.S.
Office: 600 Fifth Avenue, New York City 20, N.Y., U.S.A.

Steinitz, Wolfgang, DR.PHIL.; German philologist; b. 28 Feb. 1905; ed. Breslau Gymnasium and Berlin Univ.
Scientific collaborator, Museum für Völkerkunde 24-26; Asst. Hungarian Inst., Univ. of Berlin 28-33; Prof. of Finno-Ugric Languages, Inst. of Nordic Peoples, Leningrad 34-37; Visiting Prof., Univ. of Stockholm 38-45; Prof. of Finno-Ugric Philology, Dir. Finno-Ugric Inst., Humboldt Univ., Berlin 46-, Dean of Students 49-50, Dean of Philosophy Faculty 50-51, Pro-Rector 51-53; mem. Deutsche Akad. der Wissenschaften 51-, Vice-Pres. 54-63; Dir. Inst. für deutsche Volkskunde; Vice-Pres. Int. Union of Anthropological and Ethnological Sciences 60-; mem. Perm. Int. Cttee. of Linguists 61-; Vice-Pres. Societas Linguistica Europaea 66-; Hon. mem. Hungarian Acad. of Sciences and Hungarian Ethnological Soc.; Nat. Prize 50, 65; Euler Medal of U.S.S.R. Acad. of Sciences 57; Medal for Fighters against Fascism 1933-45 59.
Biberpelzstrasse 49, 1167 Berlin-Hessenwinkel, German Democratic Republic.
Telephone: 64-92-79.

Steinmetz, Maurice; Luxembourg diplomatist; b. 16 June 1904; ed. Commercial Inst., Antwerp.
Luxembourg Legation, Brussels 45-61; Perm. Rep. to UN 61-64; Ambassador to U.S.A., Canada and Mexico 64-; Luxembourg and foreign awards.
Embassy of Luxembourg, 2200 Massachusetts Avenue, N.W., Washington, D.C. 20008, U.S.A.
Telephone: 265-4171.

Stelling-Michaud, Sven, DR. ès L.; Swiss historian; b. 15 Aug. 1905; ed. Univs. of Zürich and Lausanne, Sorbonne and Ecole des Chartes, Paris.
Archaeological expeditions in Persia 29, Turkey 32; Int. Affairs Editor for *Journal de Genève* 42-47; Prof. of Modern History and History of Political Theories, Univ. of Geneva 43-58, Principal Interpreters' School 51-, Prof. of Modern History 58-, Prof. of Philosophy of History 62-.
Publs. *Visage de la Perse* 30, *St. Saphorin et la politique étrangère de la Suisse pendant la guerre de succession d'Espagne* 35, *Unbekannte schweizer Landschaften aus dem 17 Jahrhundert* 37, *Les partis politiques et la guerre* 45, *L'Université de Bologne et la Suisse aux XIII° et XIV° siècles*, 2 vols. 55, 60; ed. *Livre du Recteur de l'Académie de Genève 1559-1878* Vol. I 59, Vol. II 66, *Journal politique du Comte Ciano 1939-1943* 2 vols. 46, Jacob Burckhardt *Considérations sur l'histoire universelle* 65 (translation), *Etudes d'histoire diplomatique* 43, etc.
11 avenue Bertrand, Geneva, Switzerland.

Stelmakh, Mikhail Afanasyevich; Soviet writer; b. 1912; ed. Vinnitsa Pedagogical Inst.
Began literary work 36; Deputy to Supreme Soviet U.S.S.R.; Lenin and State Prizes 51, 61; Order of Lenin (twice), of Red Banner of Labour 62.
Publs. (trilogy) *Bread and Salt, Blood is Thicker than Water, The Big Family, Truth and Falsehood* (novel) 61, *Collected* Works (5 vols.) 62, *Goose-swans are flying*

(children's story) 64, *Against Golden Gods* 66, *Truth and Falsehood* 67.
Union of Ukrainian Writers, Kiev, Ukrainian S.S.R., U.S.S.R.

Stempels, Alexander, LL.M.; Netherlands journalist; b. 5 Feb. 1912; ed. Univ. of Utrecht.
Ed. *Nieuwe Rotterdamse Courant,* Rotterdam 35-40; during war worked in juridical admin.; parl. ed. *Nieuwe Rotterdamse Courant* 45, later also Deputy Editor-in-Chief, Editor-in-Chief 58-; Pres. Rotterdam Journalists' Org., Netherlands Asscn. of Editors-in-Chief, The Applied Linguistics Foundation; mem. Board Genootschap Onze Taal; Vice-Pres. Nat. Adoption Council; mem. Govt. Comm. for testing conscientious objectors; Officer, Order of Orange-Nassau.
Publs. *De parlementaire geschiedenis van het Indonesische vraagstuk* 50, *Adoptie* 53, *De Europese Smides* 56.
S. de Braystraat 19, Rotterdam 14, Netherlands.

Stengel, Edmund Ernst, PH.D.; German historian; b. 24 Dec. 1879; ed. Lausanne, Greifswald and Berlin Univs.
Lecturer, Marburg Univ., Prof. 14; fmr. Dir. Inst. of Medieval History, Hessisches Amt für Landesgeschichte; fmr. Pres. German Inst. for Ancient German History, *Monumenta Germaniae historica* and Historical Comm. for Hesse and Waldeck; Dir. German Historical Inst. of Rome 37-42; Editor *Marburger Studien zur älteren Deutschen Geschichte* 25-, *Schriften des Hessischen Amts für geschichtliche Landeskunde* 25-, *Quellen und Studien zur Verfassungsgeschichte des Deutschen Reiches* 28-, *Deutsches Archiv für Geschichte des Mittelalters* 38-42, *Archiv für Diplomatik, Schriftgeschichte, Sphragistik und Heraldik* 55-.
Publs. *Diplomatik der deutschen Immunitätsprivilegien* 10, *Den Kaiser macht das Heer* 10, *Urkundenbuch des Klosters Fulda I* 13-58, *Nova Alamanniae* 21-30, *Das geschichtliche Recht der hessischen Landschaft* 29, *Avignon und Rhens* 30, *Regnum und Imperium* 30, *Baldewin von Luxemburg* 37, *Hochmeister und Reich* 38, *Kaisertitel und Suveränitätsidee* 39, *Der Stamm der Hessen und das "Herzogtum" Franken* 40, *Die Reichsabtei Fulda und das Reich* 48, *Zwölf mittelhochdeutsche Minnelieder und Reimreden* (with F. Vogt) 56, *Abhandlungen und Untersuchungen zur mittelalterlichen Geschichte* 60, *Zür hessischen Geschichte* 60, *Zür Geschichte des Kaisergedankens, Das imperiale Königstum und die Königskanzerlei Ottos des Grossen,* etc.
Renthof 20, Marburg, German Federal Republic.

Stennis, John Cornelius, B.S., LL.B.; American politician; b. 3 Aug. 1901; ed. Mississippi State Coll. and Univ. of Virginia Law School.
Mem. Miss. House of Reps. from Kemper County 28-32; District Prosecuting Attorney, Sixteenth Judicial District 31 and 35; apptd. Circuit Judge, Sixteenth Judicial District 37 and elected 38, 46; U.S. Senator from Mississippi 47-; Democrat.
Senate Office Building, Washington, D.C., U.S.A.

Stensiö, Erik Helge Oswald; Swedish university professor; b. 2 Oct. 1891; ed. Univ. of Uppsala.
Professor of Palaeozoology at the Swedish Museum of Natural History, Stockholm 23-59, Emer. 59-; Foreign mem. of Royal Soc. of London; Hon. mem. Royal Soc. of Edinburgh; Hon. mem. Acad. Sciences, New York; Foreign mem. Acad. Sciences, Moscow; etc.; Wollaston Medal, Gold Medal of Linnean Soc., London, Daniel Elliott Giraud Medal, Washington; Darwin-Wallace Medal, Linnean Soc., Gold Medal, Royal Acad. of Science, Stockholm, Dumont Medal, Belgian Geological Soc.; Dr. h.c. Paris, Copenhagen, Oslo and Tübingen.
Swedish Museum of Natural History, Stockholm 50, Sweden.
Telephone: 313990.

Stepakov, Vladimir Ilich, M.SC.; Soviet journalist and politician; b. 1912; ed. Lenin Pedagogical Inst., Moscow and Acad. of Social Sciences of C.P.S.U. Central Cttee.
Former metal craftsman and wood cutter; Soviet Army 35-37; mem. C.P.S.U. 37-; staff of People's Commissariat for Means of Communication 37-40; in machine-building factory 41-45; party and political work, Moscow 44-59; Head of Dept., Central Cttee. of C.P.S.U. 59-61; Head of Ideological Dept., Communist Party of R.S.F.S.R. 61-64; Chief Editor *Izvestia* 64-65; Head of Propaganda and Agitation Dept. of Central Cttee. of C.P.S.U. 65-; mem. Central Cttee. of C.P.S.U.; Deputy to U.S.S.R. Supreme Soviet.
Propaganda and Agitation Department of Central Committee of C.P.S.U., Moscow, U.S.S.R.

Stephan, Frederick Franklin, B.A., M.A.; American university professor; b. 17 May 1903; ed. Univs. of Illinois and Chicago.
Instructor, Univ. of Pittsburgh 27-30, Asst. Prof. of Sociology 30; Dir. of Bureau of Social Research 31; Sec.-Treas. and Editor American Statistical Asscn. 35-40; Prof. of Sociology and Statistics, Cornell Univ. 40; Research adviser and chief of various statistical services in war agencies 41-45; Asst. Dir. for Social Sciences, Rockefeller Foundation 45; Dir. of Study of Sampling 46; now Prof. of Social Statistics, Princeton Univ., Dir. Office for Survey Research and Statistical Studies; mem. Central Statistical Board 35-40; Vice-Pres. American Asscn. for the Advancement of Science 47, 61; mem. Int. Statistical Inst.; Editor *Public Opinion Quarterly* 58-64; Pres. American Asscn. for Public Opinion Research 57-58; Trustee Rand Corpn. 48-61; Vice-Pres. Nat. Opinion Research Center; mem. President's Cttee. to Appraise Employment/Unemployment Statistics 61-62; Senior Demographic Consultant, the Population Council 64-66; Pres. American Statistical Asscn. 66.
24 Maclean Circle, Princeton, N.J., U.S.A.

Stephanopoulos, Stephanos; Greek lawyer and politician; b. 98; ed. Univs. of Athens and Paris.
Deputy for Elis 30; Under-Sec. in Ministry of Economy and Labour in 1st Populist Govt., Minister of Nat. Econ. in 2nd; resistance in Greece during 41-44 occupation; Minister of Transport in 1st Nat. Govt. 44, of Economic Co-ordination in Populist Govt. 46; left Populist Party 50, formed independent group which joined Kanellopoulos' Unionist-Populist Party, formed and disbanded (on Papagos' election) 51; joined Greek Rally Party 51; Minister of Foreign Affairs 52-55; Second Dep. Prime Minister Dec. 63-Feb. 64; Deputy Prime Minister Feb. 64-65, also Minister of Co-ordination June 64-65; Prime Minister Sept. 65-Dec. 66; Leader Social Populist Party 59 (later mem. Central Union Party), founded Liberal Democratic Centre Party Dec. 65.
Publs. include *Social Insurance* 32, *Economic and Social Studies* 35, *Philosophy and Social Systems* 36.
Athens, Greece.

Stephansky, Ben Solomon, M.A., PH.D.; American (b. Russian) diplomatist; b. 10 Nov. 1913; ed. Univ. of Wisconsin.
Emigrated to U.S.A. 15; teaching posts 38-42, 45-56; Foreign Service Officer 56-; Labor Attaché, Mexico City 56-59; Labor Adviser, Bureau of Inter-American Affairs, Dept. of State 59-61; Ambassador to Bolivia 61-63; Bureau of Inter-American Affairs 63-; Exec. Sec. U.S.A.-Puerto Rico Comm. on the status of Puerto Rico 64-.
Department of State, Washington, D.C., U.S.A.

Stephens, Frederick James; British oil executive; b. 30 July 1903; ed. Marlborough Coll., Grenoble Univ., France, and Pembroke Coll., Cambridge.
Joined Royal Dutch Shell Group of Companies 26, served Venezuela, London and U.S.A.; Dir. and Exec. Vice-Pres. Asiatic Petroleum Corpn., New York 46-48; returned to London 48; Managing Dir. Shell Petroleum

Co. 51-61; Managing Dir. Shell Transport and Trading Co. Ltd. 57-67, Chair. 61-67, Dir. 67-; Chair. Shell Petroleum Co. Ltd. 61-; Man. Dir. Shell Int. Petroleum Co. Ltd. 59-61; Dir. Bataafse Petroleum Maatshappij N.V.

c/o Shell Centre, London, S.E.1; and Crossacres, Pyrford Woods, Woking, Surrey, England.

Stephens, William J.; American steel executive; b. 16 Dec. 1906; ed. Brooklyn Polytechnic Inst. and Newark Coll. of Engineering.

Bethlehem Steel Corpn. 22-62, Messenger, Salesman, Tin Mills Products Manager, Asst. Gen. Manager (Sales) 51-60, Asst. Vice-Pres. and Dir. 60-62; Exec. Vice-Pres. Jones & Laughlin Steel Corpn. 62-63, Pres. 63-; Dir. Pittsburgh Nat. Bank, Equitable Gas Co., Pittsburgh Regional Industrial Devt. Corpn. etc.; mem. Advisory Council, Pittsburgh Graduate School of Business; mem. Pittsburgh Chamber of Commerce; Trustee, Duquesne Univ. Foundation.

Jones & Laughlin Steel Corporation, 3 Gateway Center, Pittsburgh 30, Pennsylvania, U.S.A.

Stephenson, Gordon, C.B.E., M.C.P., B.ARCH., F.R.A.I.A., F.R.I.B.A., F.I.L.A., M.T.P.I.; British architect and town planner; b. 6 June 1908; ed. Liverpool Inst., Univs. of Liverpool and Paris, and Massachusetts Inst. of Technology.

With Le Corbusier and Pierre Jeanneret 30-32; Lecturer, Univ. of Liverpool 32-36; Commonwealth Fellow, Mass. Inst. of Technology 36-38; Master, Architectural Assn. School of Architecture 39-40; Div. Architect, Royal Ordinance Factory and War Hostels 40-42; Snr. Research Officer and Chief Planning Officer, Ministry of Town and Country Planning 42-47; Prof. of Civic Design and Editor *Town Planning Review,* Univ. of Liverpool 48-53; Consultant to Govt. of W. Australia, City of Perth and Univ. of W. Australia 54-55; Prof. of Town and Regional Planning, Univ. of Toronto 55-60; Consultant Architect and Prof. Univ. of W. Australia 60-, and Dean, School of Architecture 66-; mem. Nat. Capital Planning Cttee., Canberra 67-.

Publs. (with Flora C. Stephenson) *Community Centres* 40, (with J. A. Hepburn) *Plan for the Metropolitan Region of Perth and Fremantle* 55, *A Redevelopment Study of Halifax, Nova Scotia* 57, (with G. G. Muirhead) *A Planning Study of Kingston, Ontario* 59.

6 Bay View Terrace, Peppermint Grove, Western Australia 6011; University of Western Australia, Nedlands, Western Australia 6009.

Telephone: 3-1966; 86-2481.

Sterky, Håkan Karl August, DR. TECH.; Swedish electrical engineer; b. 7 April 1900; ed. Royal Inst. of Technology, Stockholm, and Harvard Univ.

Radio engineer, ASEA 23-24; Transmission engineer, Royal Board of Swedish Waterfalls 26-27, Svenska Radio AB 27-31, and L.M. Ericsson Telephone Co. 31-33; Head of Design Dept., L.M. Ericsson Telephone Co. 33-37; Asst. Prof. of Telegraphy and Telephony 34-37; Prof. *pro tem.* 37-39, Ord. Prof. 39-42, and Vice-Principal 42 of Royal Inst. of Technology, Stockholm; Dir.-Gen. Royal Board of Swedish Telecommunications 42-65; Pres. Swedish Nat. Comm. Int. Scientific Radio Union, Board of Trustees, Swedish Nat. Comm. of Int. Electrotechnical Comm.; mem. Board of Atomic Energy Co., Pripp Breweries Co., Scania Vabis Co., IBM Swedish Co., Inter-Union Cttee. on Frequency Allocations for Radio Astronomy and Space Sciences (I.C.S.U.); mem. Royal Swedish Acad. Engineering Sciences, Royal Swedish Acad. of Sciences, Royal Swedish Acad. of Mil. Sciences, Science Soc. of Uppsala and Danish Acad. of Technical Sciences; Polhem Gold Medal and Hon. mem. Swedish Asscn. of Engineers and Architects.

Publs. *The Use of Thermionic Valves for Generating Multiple Frequencies* 30, *Methods of Computing and Improving the Complex Effective Attenuation, Load*

Impedances, and Reflexion Coefficients of Electric Wave Filters 33, *Frequency Multiplication and Division* 37, *Puissance et affaiblissement dans les circuits électriques* 40, *Fernwirkbetrieb in Stromversorgungsnetzen* 41, *Uebertragungsverhältnisse auf bespülten und wahlrufs betriebenen Fernsprechleitungen* 43, *Telecommunication- in Sweden, present and future* 50, *Past, Present and Future Telecommunication Standardization* 54, *The First Century of Swedish Telecommunications and what we can learn from it* 56, *The Foundation of Agriculture and Industry in Modern Sweden* 57, *Trends of Development in the Swedish Telecommunication Services* 60, *Swedish Telecommunications* 65.

Sibyllegatan 43-45, Stockholm Ö, Sweden.

Telephone: 08-600606.

Stern, Gladys Bertha; British novelist; b. 17 June 1890; ed. Notting Hill High School and Acad. of Dramatic Art.

Publs. include: *Mosaic, The Back Seat, The Dark Gentleman, The Matriarch Little Red Horses, Shining and Free, Monogram, Oleander River, The Ugly Dachshund, The Woman in the Hall, Tents of Israel, A Lion in the Garden, Another Part of the Forest, The Young Matriarch, The Reasonable Shores* 46, *No Son of Mine* 48, *Benefits Forgot* 49, *A Duck to Water* 49, *Ten Days of Christmas* 50, *The Donkey Shoe* 52, *A Name to Conjure With* 53, *Johnny Forsaken* 54, *For All We Know* 55, *Seventy Times Seven* 57, *The Patience of a Saint* 58, *And Did he Stop and Speak to You?* 58, *Unless I Marry* 59, *Bernadette* 60, *Dolphin Cottage* 62, *Promise Not to Tell* 64.

c/o A. D. Peters, 10 Buckingham Street, Adelphi, London, W.C.2, England.

Stern, Isaac; American violinist; b. Russia 21 July 1920; studied San Francisco, notably with Naoum Blinder.

Debut, San Francisco Symphony 35; New York debut 37; world tours every year 47-; appearances with major orchestras; extensive recordings; frequent appearances major festivals—Edinburgh, Casals, Berkshire, etc.; Pres. Carnegie Hall; Pres. America-Israel Cultural Foundation; mem. Nat. Arts Council.

c/o S. Hurok, 730 Fifth Avenue, New York 19, N.Y., U.S.A.

Stern, Leo, DR. RER. POL.; German (b. Austrian) historian and university professor; b. 27 March 1901; ed. Universität Wien.

Emigrated from Austria to Czechoslovakia and U.S.S.R. 34; fought in Spanish Civil War; Prof. of History, Moscow 40; Officer in Red Army 41-45; Guest Prof., Univ. of Vienna 45; Prof. of Modern History, Martin Luther-Universität, Halle-Wittenberg 50-, Rector 53-59; Vice-Pres. German Acad. of Sciences; Nat. Prize; several hon. degrees.

Publs. include: *Archivalische Forschungen zur Geschichte der deutschen Arbeiterbewegung* (14 vols.); *Philipp Melanchthon—Humanist, Reformator, Praeceptor Germaniae; Oktoberrevolution und Wissenschaft; 450 Jahre Reformation.*

Martin Luther-Universität Halle-Wittenberg, Halle (Saale), German Democratic Republic.

Stern, Otto; American (b. German) physicist; b. 17 Feb. 1888; ed. Univ. of Breslau.

Privatdozent, Technical Hochschule, Zürich 13-14, Frankfurt 14-21; Prof., Rostock Univ. 21-22, Hamburg 23-33; Research Prof. of Physics, Carnegie Inst. of Technology 33; Nobel Prize, Physics 43.

1060 Morewood Avenue, Pittsburgh, Pennsylvania, U.S.A.

Sternberger, Dolf, DR. PHIL.; German writer and professor of political science; b. 28 July 1907.

Professor of Political Science, Heidelberg Univ.; Dir. Inst. für Politische Wissenschaft; fmr. Chair. German Asscn. of Political Science; Pres. German PEN Club;

Vice-Pres. German Acad. of Language and Literature; mem. German UNESCO Comm.

Publs. *Der verstandebe Tod, eine Untersuchung zu Martin Heideggers Existential-Ontologie* 34, *Panorama oder Ansichten vom 19, Jahrhundert* 38, 55, *13 Politische Radioreden* 47, *Figuren der Fabel* 50, *Aus dem Wörterbuch des Unmenschen* 55, 68, *Lebende Verfassung*, *Studien über Koalition und Opposition* 56, *Über den Jugendstil und andere Essays* 56, *Indische Miniaturen* 57, *Begriff des Politischen* 61, *Grund und Abgrund der Macht* 62, *Ekel an der Freiheit* 64, *Die Grosse Wahlreform* 64, *Kriterien Ein Lesebuch* 65, *Ich wünschte ein Bürger zu sein* 67.

Friedrich-Ebert-Anlage 6-10, Heidelberg, German Federal Republic.

Telephone: 27091.

Stern-Rubarth, Edgar, PH.D.; Anglo-German journalist and historian; b. 15 Aug. 1883; ed. German and French univs.

Study and travel, while publishing poetry and essays 05-14; Officer in German Army in Turkey and on Western Front 14-18; Chief Editor, Ullstein, Berlin 19-25; spokesman of Weimar Govt. 25-33; Editor-in-Chief Wolffs Telegraph Bureau 25-33, Co-Dir. 29-33; dismissed by Nazi régime; emigrated to Great Britain 36; editor of periodicals in London 36-39; special war service 39-45; contributor to leading newspapers and periodicals in London 25-; British corresp. of leading German papers 47-; lecturer at German and American univs. 20-; Founder, European Customs Union 24; Co-Founder, Féd. Int. des Journalistes, Paris 26, Franco-German Soc. 27; Grosses Bundesverdienstkreuz mit Stern, war decorations.

Publs. *Propaganda as Political Instrument* 21, 22, *Count Brockdorff-Rantzau, Wanderer between Two Worlds* 29, *Stresemann the European* 30 (French edn. 32), *Three Men Tried: Stresemann's, Briand's and Austen Chamberlain's Struggle for Peace* 39 (German edn. 47), *Exit Prussia: A Plan for Europe* 40, *Short History of the Germans* (3rd edn.) 46, *Europa: Great Power or "Kleinstaaterei"?* 51, etc.; autobiography . . . *aus zuverlässiger Quelle verlautet . . .* 64.

43 Church Crescent, London, N.3, England.

Telephone: 01-346-4350.

Stevenius-Nielsen, Hans Henrik, M.SC.; Danish company director; b. 02; ed. Univ. of Copenhagen and Royal Danish Technical Coll.

Chemical Asst. Danish Sulphuric Acid and Superphosphate Works Ltd. 25-26; Asst. Royal Veterinary and Agricultural Coll. 26-27; Chief of Research Laboratory, Danish Sulphuric Acid and Superphosphate Works Ltd. 27-33, Asst. to Technical Dir. 33-40, Technical Dir. 40-45, Man. Dir. 45-64, Dir. 64; mem. Board Dirs. Hellesens Ltd. 52-, The Great Northern Telegraph Co. Ltd. 54- (Chair. 60-), Kastrup Glass Works Ltd. 61-, The Cryolite Co. Oeresund Ltd. 63-; mem. Advisory Committee Royal Greenland Trade Dept. 50-65, Chair. 63-65; mem. Atomic Energy Comm. 55-, Brewery Advisory Committee of the Carlsberg Foundation 55-; Pres. Asscn. of Chemical Industries in Denmark 45-52; Pres. Fed. of Danish Industries 52-56; Pres. Int. Superphosphate Manufacturers' Asscn. 59-62; mem. Acad. of Technical Sciences 41-, Vice-Pres. 43-48; mem. Royal Physiographical Society, Sweden 45-, Royal Swedish Acad. of Engineering Sciences 53-; Hon. Foreign mem. Society of Chemical Industry (U.K.) 56-, The Fertiliser Soc. (U.K.) 58-; mem. High Court (*Rigsretten*) 54-; Commdr. 1st Class Order of Dannebrog (Denmark), Commdr. de la Légion d'Honneur (France), Commdr. Order of Vasa (Sweden), Commdr. Order of Ouissam Alaouite (Morocco), Commdr. Order of the Belgian Crown.

Palaegade 4, 1261 Copenhagen K, Denmark.

Telephone: BYEN 2235.

Stevens, George; American film producer; b. 20 Feb. 1904; ed. Sonoma High School, Calif.

Film cameraman 21; Dir. 30-38, Producer and Dir. 38-; Second World War service with signal corps and motion picture unit; Pres. Screen Dirs. Guild 42-45; Acad. Award (twice).

Films include: *Quality Street* 37, *Vivacious Lady* 38, *Gunga Din* 39, *Penny Serenade* 41, *Woman of the Year* 42, *The More the Merrier* 43, *I Remember Mama* 48, *A Place in the Sun* 51, *Shane* 52, *Giant* 56, *The Diary of Anne Frank* 59, *The Greatest Story Ever Told* 61.

c/o Desilu Studio, 9336 W. Washington Boulevard, Culver City, California, U.S.A.

Stevens, Maj.-Gen. Sir Jack Edwin Stawell, K.B.E., C.B., D.S.O., E.D., F.A.S.A.; Australian company director; b. 7 Sept. 1896.

Enlisted A.I.F. 15; served France and Egypt; Lieut. 17; regimental soldiering 21-39; Lieut.-Col. 26, Brigadier 40; commanded 6th Australian Divisional Signals 39, 21st Australian Infantry Brigade 40; served Middle East and New Guinea; Maj.-Gen. 42; commanded 4th Division, Northern Territory Force and 6th Australian Division 43-45; Col. Commandant Royal Australian Corps of Signals 55-60; Gen. Man. and Chief Exec. Officer Overseas Telecommunications Comms. 46-50; Sec. Dept. of Nat. Development 50-51, Dept. of Supply 51-52; Chair. and Exec. Officer Australian Atomic Energy Comm. 52-56; Chair. Australian Electrical Industries Ltd. 56-64; Dir. Mount Isa Mines, Commonwealth Industrial Gases Ltd., Wood Hall Holdings Ltd., Custom Credit Corpn. Ltd., N.S.W. Board of Trustees, Executors and Agency Co., Devt. Underwriting Ltd., N.S.W. Board of Nat. Bank, British Automotive Industries Pty. Ltd.

109 Darling Point Road, Darling Point, N.S.W., Australia.

Telephone: 32-1322.

Stevens, Sir John Melior, K.C.M.G., D.S.O., O.B.E.; British banker; b. 7 Nov. 1913; ed. Winchester Coll.

Solicitor 37; Mil. Service 39-45; Adviser, Bank of England 46; Dir. European Dept. Int. Monetary Fund 54-56; Exec. Dir. Bank of England 57-65; Econ. Minister in Washington and Exec. Dir. Int. Monetary Fund and Int. Bank for Reconstruction and Devt. (World Bank) Jan. 65-67; mem. Council of Foreign Bondholders 57-64, B.B.C. Advisory Council 63-64; Sheriff, County of London 64; Man. Dir. Morgan Grenfell & Co. Ltd. 67-; Dir. Bank of England 68-.

62 Bedford Gardens, London, W.8, England.

Telephone: 01-727-6206.

Stevens, Robert T., B.A.; American executive; b. 31 July 1899; ed. Philipps Acad., Andover, Mass. and Yale Univ.

Entered employment of J.P. Stevens & Co., Inc. 21; Admin. Rep. in industry section of Nat. Recovery Admin. 33; Head of Textile Section, Nat. Defence Advisory Comm. 40; District Co-ordinator of defence contract service, Office of Production Management N.Y. area 41; Class B. Dir. Fed. Reserve Bank of N.Y. 34-42, Class C. Dir. and Chair. 48-53; Chair. Business Advisory Council of U.S. Dept. of Commerce 51-52; Secretary of the Army Feb. 53-55; served in both World Wars, Col. 42, serving in Procurement Div., Office of Quartermaster Gen., Washington, D.C. 42-45, temporary duty, European Theatre 45; Chair. Board J. P. Stevens & Co., Inc. 45-53, 62-64, Pres. 55-; Dir. Gen. Electric Co., Morgan Guaranty Trust Co. of New York; Trustee Mutual Life Ins. Co. of New York; Pres. American Textile Manufrs. Inst., Inc.; mem. Business Council; D.S.M.; Legion of Merit; Hon. LL.D. (Presbyterian Coll.); Hon. D.C.S. (New York Univ.); Hon. D.H.D. (Lafayette Coll.); Hon. Dr. Textile Industries (Clemson Agricultural Coll.).

Route 1, Woodland Ave., South Plainfield, N.J., U.S.A

Stevens, Sir Roger Bentham, G.C.M.G.; British diplomatist; b. 8 June 1906; ed. Wellington Coll. and Queen's Coll., Oxford.

Entered Consular Service 28; served Buenos Aires, New York, Antwerp; Ministry of Information 39-42; Consul in Denver, U.S.A. 42-44; Sec. British Civil Secretariat, Washington 44-46; Foreign Office 46-51; Ambassador to Sweden 51-54, to Iran 54-58; Dep. Under-Sec. Foreign Office 58-63; Vice-Chancellor, Leeds Univ. 63-; Chair. Yorks. and Humberside Economic Planning Council 65-.

Publ. *The Land of the Great Sophy* 62.

Vice-Chancellor's Lodge, Grosvenor Road, Leeds 6, England.

Telephone: Leeds 51523.

Stevens, Siaka Probyn; Sierra Leone politician; b. 24 Aug. 1905; ed. Albert Acad., Freetown, and Ruskin Coll. Oxford (47-48).

Court Messenger Force 23-30; railway worker, rising to Station Master, later mine worker with Sierra Leone Devt. Co. (DELCO) 30-43; Sec. Marampa Mineworkers Union 43, later Gen. Sec. United Mineworkers Union; mem. Protectorate Assembly, Bo 45; at Ruskin Coll. Oxford 47-48; mem. Legis. Council 51-57, Minister of Lands, Mines and Labour 51; Founder mem. Sierra Leone Org. Soc., later Sierra Leone People's Party; Deputy Leader People's Nat. Party 58-60; Leader All People's Congress 60-; political imprisonment 61; Mayor of Freetown 64-65; Prime Minister March 67; in exile 67-68; Prime Minister April 68-.

Office of the Prime Minister, Freetown, Sierra Leone.

Stevens, S(tanley) Smith, A.B., PH.D.; American psychophysicist; b. 4 Nov. 1906; ed. Stanford Univ. and Harvard Univ.

NRC Fellow in Physiology, Harvard Univ. 34-35; Research Fellow in Physics 35-36, Instr. 36-38, Asst. Prof. 38-44, Assoc. Prof. 44-46, Prof. 46-; Dir. of Psycho-Acoustic Lab. 44-62, of Psychological Labs., Harvard Univ. 49-62, of Lab. of Psychophysics 62-; Chair. Div. of Anthropology and Psychology, Nat. Research Council 49-52; mem. Nat. Acad. of Sciences, American Philosophical Soc.

Publs. *Hearing: its Psychology and Physiology* (with Hallowell Davis) 38, *The Varieties of Human Physique* (with W. H. Sheldon and W. B. Tucker) 40, *The Varieties of Temperament* (with W. H. Sheldon) 42, *Handbook of Experimental Psychology* (Editor) 51, *Sound and Hearing* (with Fred Warshofsky) 65.

William James Hall, Harvard University, Cambridge, Mass. 02138, U.S.A.

Telephone: 868-7600.

Stevens, Wayne Mackenzie, B.S., M.B.A., PH.D., C.P.A.; American economist, business consultant and executive; ed. Univ. of Ill., Northwestern and American Univs.

Sales Man., chain store supervisor, govt. marketing specialist; Prof. Marketing and Financial Management, La. State Univ. 28-37; Dean, Coll. of Business Admin. Univ. of Md. 37-42; Partner, Mackenzie Stevens & Co., Int. Business Consultants 38-; Pres. Int. Div. Assoc. Manufacturers, Inc. 46-49; adviser and consultant to Govt. and commercial organisations in U.S. and abroad 34-; Economic Commr., Korea, and ECA Dir. Trade and Finance Div. 49-50; mem. State Dept. Far-Eastern Conf., Tokyo, and Dir. Trade Mission in fifteen countries of Asia, Australia and Far East 50; Dir. School of World Business and Consultant on Int. Development, San Francisco State Coll. 50-; Chair. World Investment and Trade Corpn. 53-; mem. U.S. Sec. of Commerce Regional Export Expansion Council 62-65, Int. Economist and Project Evaluator, Nat. Planning Office, Govt. of Nicaragua Nat. Econ. Council 65-67.

Publs. *Financial Organization and Administration* 34, *Practical Accounting* 35, *Effective Structural Organization for Cooperatives* 36, *Warehousing and Storage of Agricultural Products* 37, *Cooperative Sugar Association,*

A Basis for Democratizing Tropical Agriculture 38, *Production and Marketing of Industrial Goods Co-operatively* 42, *Management Analysis Applied to Industrial Cooperation* 43, *Effective Utilization of Private Capital in Foreign Economic Development* 44, *Training of Chinese Technicians in American Methods* 45, *The So-Called Dollar Shortage* 47, *Trade, Not Aid* 48, *Currency Exchange and Pricing Policies* 50, *Public Finance* (co-author) 59.

3 Skyline Drive, Daly City, Calif. 94015, U.S.A.

Telephone: 415-755-0600; and 415-755-2100.

Stevenson, Alexander; American (b. British) banking official; b. 9 Dec. 1916; ed. Aberdeen Univ., Universität Zürich, and Univ. of Calif., Berkeley.

Research Assoc., Carnegie Endowment for Int. Peace 43-44; U.S. Army 45, later U.S. Treasury and Dept. of Justice; Int. Bank for Reconstruction and Development 47-, Senior Loan Officer, later Asst. Dir. of Dept. for Operational Relationships with South Asian Countries 59-64, Dir. South Asia Dept. 65-66.

International Bank for Reconstruction and Development, 1818 H Street N.W., Washington, D.C., U.S.A.

Stevenson, Robert S., A.B., LL.D.; American businessman; b. 10 Nov. 1906; ed. Whitworth Coll., Washington State Coll., and Lawrence Univ.

With Allis-Chalmers Manufacturing Co. 33-, Vice-Pres. and Dir. 51, Pres. and Chair. Exec. Cttee. 55-, Chair. 66-; Pres. Farm Equipment Inst. 57-58; Dir. Marshall and Ilsley Bank, Universal Oil Products Co., Nat. Cttee. on Boys and Girls Club Work (4-H); Trustee, Northwestern Mutual Life Insurance Co., Carroll Coll.

1205 Lakeside Drive, Elm Grove, Wis., U.S.A.

Stewart, Andrew, B.S.A., M.A.; Scottish-born Canadian educator and radio administrator; b. 17 Jan. 1904; ed. Daniel Stewart's Coll., East of Scotland Agricultural Coll., Edinburgh and Manitoba Univ.

Lecturer in Agricultural Economics, Manitoba Univ. 32-33; Lecturer in Political Economy, Alberta Univ. 35, Prof. of Political Economy 46, Dean of Business Affairs 49, Pres. 50-59; Chair. Board of Broadcast Govs. 59-; mem. Royal Comm. on Natural Gas (Province of Alberta) 48, on Economic Prospects (Canada) 55-57; Chair. Royal Comm. (Canada) on Price Spreads of Food Products 58-59; Fellow, Royal Soc. of Canada, Agricultural Inst. of Canada; Hon. LL.D. (Manitoba, New Brunswick, Melbourne and Alberta Univs.), Hon. D.Econ. (Laval Univ.).

Office: 48 Rideau Street, Ottawa; Home: 382 Ashbury Road, Ottawa 2, Canada.

Stewart, Freeman Kenneth, B.A., M.A., M.ED., LL.D.; Canadian educationist; b. 23 May 1913; ed. Dalhousie Univ., Oxford Univ., Ontario Coll. of Education, Univ. of Toronto.

National Dir. Canadian Legion Educ. Services 44-46; Industrial Relations Officer, Canadian Int. Paper Co. 46-47; Exec. Sec. Canadian Educ. Asscn. 47-63, 66-; Sec. Standing Cttee. of Ministers of Educ. (Canada) 60-63, 66-67; Lecturer in Comparative Educ., Univ. of Toronto 58-63; Sec. Commonwealth Educ. Liaison Cttee. and Dir. Commonwealth Educ. Liaison Unit, London 63-66.

Publs. *Inter-Provincial Co-operation in Education* 57, *The Superintendent of Schools in Canada* 58.

Canadian Education Association, 151 Bloor Street West, Toronto; Apartment 1623, Park Tower East, 400 Walmer Road, Toronto 10, Ontario, Canada.

Telephone: 924-1135; 922-5595 (Home).

Stewart, Sir Herbert Ray, Kt., C.I.E., M.SC., F.R.C.SC.I., D.I.C., N.D.A.; British international agricultural adviser; b. 10 July 1890; ed. Royal Coll. of Science for Ireland and Imperial Coll. of Science and Technology, London.

Served in France First World War 15-19; apptd. to Indian Agricultural Service 20; Prof. of Agriculture

Punjab 21-27; Asst. Dir. of Agriculture Punjab 27-32, Dir. of Agriculture 32-43; Fellow Univ. of Punjab 27-43, Dean of Faculty of Agriculture 32-43; Agricultural Commr. with Govt. of India 43-46; Vice-Chair. Imperial Council of Agricultural Research India, Pres. Board of Agriculture and Animal Husbandry India; Chair. All-India Central Cttees. for Cotton, Jute, Lac, Sugar-cane, Tobacco, Coconuts and Pres. Indian Coffee Board 44-46; Agricultural Adviser British Middle East Office Cairo 46-51; Agricultural Adviser, U.N. Economic Survey Mission for the Middle East 49, U.N. Relief and Works Agency for Palestine Refugees 50-51; Chief, Agricultural Mission of Int. Bank for Reconstruction and Development to Colombia 55-56; Agricultural Consultant, Economic Missions of Int. Bank to Pakistan 56 and 58, Italy 57, Yugoslavia 60, Uganda 60-61, Kenya 61-62.
29 Alyth Road, Bournemouth, Hants., England.
Telephone: Westbourne 64782.

Stewart, James, C.B.E., LL.D.; Canadian banker; b. 94; ed. Kinnoull School and Perth Acad., Scotland.
Dir. Imperial Life Assurance Co. of Canada, Maple Leaf Gardens Ltd., Toronto, Caledonian-Canadian Insurance Co., Montreal, Falconbridge Nickel Mines Ltd., Toronto, Atomic Energy of Canada Ltd. Ottawa, Canadian Imperial Bank of Commerce, Alexander and Alexander Services Ltd., Canadian Land & Investment Co. Ltd., Dominion Realty Co. Ltd., Guardian Insurance Co. of Canada; Dir. and Treas. Corpn. of Presbyterian Synod of Toronto; Commr. The Toronto Harbour Commissioners; mem. Canadian Advisory Board, Guardian Assurance Co.; mem. Finance Comm. Nat. Inst. for the Blind; Trustee Nat. Sanitarium Asscn., Toronto.
Office: 25 King Street West, Suite 1100, Toronto 1; Home: 10 Benvenuto Place, Apt. 503, Toronto 7, Ont., Canada.

Stewart, James, D.F.C., B.S.; American actor; b. 20 May 1908; ed. Mercersburg Acad. and Princeton Univ.
Films since 35 include *You Can't Take It With You, Made for Each Other, Mr. Smith Goes to Washington, Destry Rides Again, Philadelphia Story, Pot O' Gold, The Stratton Story, Winchester 73, Broken Arrow, Harvey, No Highway, Rear Window, The Greatest Show on Earth, Rope, Naked Spur, The Glenn Miller Story, The Man from Laramie, Strategic Air Command, Spirit of St. Louis, Anatomy of a Murder, The FBI Story, Two Rode Together, Cheyenne Autumn, Shenandoah, The Rare Breed,* etc.; American Motion Picture Acad. Award for *Philadelphia Story,* New York Critics Award for *Mr. Smith Goes to Washington,* Volpi Cup, Venice 59, for performance in *Anatomy of a Murder.*
P.O. Box 550, Beverly Hills, Calif., U.S.A.

Stewart, Rt. Hon. Michael (*see* Stewart, R. M. M.).

Stewart, Sir Michael (Norman Francis), K.C.M.G., O.B.E.; British diplomatist; b. 18 Jan. 1911; ed. Shrewsbury and Trinity Coll., Cambridge.
Assistant Keeper, Victoria and Albert Museum 35-39; Ministry of Information 39-41; Press Attaché, British Embassy, Lisbon 41-44, Rome 44-48; Foreign Office 48-51; Counsellor, Office of Commr.-Gen. for U.K. in S.E. Asia 51-54; Counsellor, Ankara 54-59; Chargé d'Affaires, Peking 59-62; Senior Civilian Instructor, Imperial Defence Coll. 62-64; Minister, Washington 64-67; Amb. to Greece 67-.
British Embassy, Athens, Greece.

Stewart, Potter, B.A., LL.B.; American judge; b. 23 Jan. 1915; ed. Hotchkiss School, Cambridge (England) and Yale Univ.
Admitted to Ohio Bar 41, New York Bar 42; Assoc. Debevoise, Stevenson, Plimpton and Page (New York) 41-42, 45-47; Assoc., Dinsmore, Shohl, Sawyer and Dinsmore (Cincinnati) 47, Partner 51-54; service in

U.S. Naval Reserve 41-45; mem. Cincinnati City Council 50-53, Vice-Mayor 52-53; Judge, U.S. Court of Appeals (Sixth Circuit) 54-58; Assoc. Justice, U.S. Supreme Court 58-; mem. Court Admin. Cttee., Judicial Conf. of the U.S. 55-58; mem. American, Ohio, Cincinnati, City of New York Bar Asscns., American Law Inst., American Judicature Soc., etc.
Supreme Court of the United States, Washington, D.C. 20543; Home: 5136 Palisade Lane, N.W., Washington, D.C. 20016, U.S.A.

Stewart, Rt. Hon. (Robert) Michael Maitland, P.C., M.P.; British politician and author; b. 6 Nov. 1906; ed. Brownhill Road L.C.C. School, Christ's Hospital and St. John's Coll., Oxford.
Member of Parl. 45-, Govt. Whip 45-47, Under-Sec. of State for War 47-51, Parl. Sec. Ministry of Supply 51; Sec. of State for Education and Science Oct. 64-Jan. 65; Sec. of State for Foreign Affairs Jan. 65-Aug. 66, March 68-; First Sec. of State 66-; Sec. for Econ. Affairs Aug. 66-Aug. 67; Labour.
Publs. *The British Approach to Politics* 38, *Modern Forms of Government* 59.
1 Carlton Gardens, London, S.W.1, England.

Steyn, Lucus Cornelius, B.A., LL.D.; South African judge; b. 21 Dec. 1903; ed. Kroonstad Secondary School and Stellenbosch Univ.
Attorney-General, South West Africa 31; Senior Law Adviser, Union Govt. 44; Judge of Appeal 55; Chief Justice of South Africa 59-.
Publ. *Uitleg van Wette.*
The Supreme Court of South Africa, Blomfontein, Orange Free State, Republic of South Africa.

Steytler, Johannes (Jan) Van Aswegen, M.R.C.S., L.R.C.P.; South African doctor, farmer and politician; b. 26 Oct. 1910; ed. Paarl Boys' High School, Grootfontein Agricultural School and Guy's Hospital, London.
M.P. for Queenstown; Chair. Cape Province United Party 58-59; resigned from United Party August 59; Leader of Progressive Party 59-.
Mountain Range, Queenstown, Cape Province, South Africa.

Stikker, Dirk Uipko, DR.JUR.; Netherlands politician and diplomatist; b. 5 Feb. 1897; ed. Univ. of Groningen.
Former Man. Dii. of branches of Twentsche Bank at Leyden and Haarlem; Man. Dir. of Heineken Lagerbeer Brewery Co. Ltd. 35-48; Dir. of S.A. des Bières Bomonti & Pyramides, Cairo; mem. of board of Société Internationale de Brasserie, Brussels; Founder and Chair. Neths. Foundation of Labour; Founder (46) and Pres. of Party of Freedom and Democracy; mem. of Senate; Minister of Foreign Affairs 48-52; Political Conciliator, later Chair., OEEC 50-52; Amb. to Great Britain 52-58; Minister, later Amb., to Iceland 54-58; Head, combined Dutch perm. representation to North Atlantic Council and OEEC with rank of Amb. 58-61, Sec.-Gen. of NATO 61-64; Dir. Royal Dutch Shell Group 64-; Consultant to UNCTAD; Hon. LL.D. (Brown Univ.); Hon. G.C.V.O., Hon. G.B.E.
Publ. *Men of Responsibility* 66.
Villa "Belfaggio", Menaggio-Loveno, Lago di Como, Italy.
Telephone: 2361.

Stinson, George Arthur, A.B., LL.B.; American lawyer and business executive; b. 11 Feb. 1915; ed. Northwestern Univ. and Columbia Univ.
U.S. Air Force 41-45; Special Asst. to Attorney-Gen., Washington, D.C. 47-48; Partner in law firm Cleary, Gottlieb, Friendly and Hamilton, New York, Washington, D.C., and Paris 48-61; Nat. Steel Corpn., Pittsburgh 61-, Pres. and Dir. 63-, Chief Exec. Officer 66-; Legion of Merit.
Office: National Steel Corporation, Grant Building, Pittsburgh, Pennsylvania 15219; Home: 420 Oliver Road, Sewickley, Pennsylvania, U.S.A.

Stirling, Alfred, C.B.E., M.A., LL.B.; Australian diplomatist; b. 8 Sept. 1892; ed. Scotch Coll., Melbourne, Univ. of Melbourne, and Univ. Coll., Oxford.
Head, Pol. Div., Australian Dept. of External Affairs 36; External Affairs Officer, London 36-45; Counsellor, Australian Legation to Netherlands 43-45; Australian High Commr. to Canada 45-47; Minister, Australian Embassy, Washington 47-48; Australian High Commr. in S. Africa 48-50; Amb. to the Netherlands 50-55, to France 55-59, to Philippines 59-62, to Italy 62-67 (also to Greece 64-65).
Publ. *Victorian* (with John Oldham) 34.
Australian Embassy, Rome, Italy.

Stirling, Duncan Alexander; British banker; b. 6 Oct. 1899; ed. Harrow and New Coll., Oxford.
Partner with H. S. Lefevre and Co. 29-49; Dir. Westminster Bank 35-, Deputy Chair. 48-61, Chair. 62-; Chair. Cttee. of London Clearing Bankers 66-; Dir. London Life Asscn. 35-, Pres. 52-66; fmr. Pres. Inst. of Bankers; Dir. Mercantile Investment Trust.
Westminster Bank Ltd., 41 Lothbury, London, E.C.2, England.
Telephone: 01-606-6060.

Stockhausen, Karlheinz; German composer; b. 28; ed. Cologne State Music High School, Univs. of Cologne and Bonn.
Worked with Oliver Messiaen and with the "Musique Concrète" Group in Paris 52-53; with Westdeutscher Rundfunk Electronic Music Studio, Cologne 53-, Artistic Dir. 63-; Co-editor *Die Reihe* (Universal Edn.) 55-58; Dozent for composition and analysis at the Int. Summer School for New Music, Darmstadt 57-; concert tours throughout the world since 58; Composition classes in *Kölner Kurse für Neue Musik* 63-.
Compositions: *Kreuzspiel* 51, *Schlagquartett, Spiel für Orchester, Punkte für Orchester* (new version 62) 52, *Klavierstücke I-IV, Kontra-Punkte* 52-53, *Elektronische Studien I und II* 53-54, *Klavierstücke V-X* 54-61, *Zeitmasse* 55-56, *Gruppen für 3 Orchester* 55-57, *Klavierstück XI* 56, *Gesang der Jünglinge* (electronic music) 55-56, *Zyklus für einen Schlagzeuger, Refrain für 3 Spieler* 59, *Carré für 4 Orchester und Chöre, Kontakte* (piano, percussion and electronic sounds) 59-60, *Originale-Musikalisches Theater* 61, *Momente für Sopran, 4 Chorgruppen und 13 Instrumentalisten* 62-64, *Plus Minus, 2 × 7 Seiten für Ausarbeitungen* 63, *Mikrophonie I für Tamtam, 2 Mikrophone 2 Filter und Regler, Mixtur für Orchester, 4 Sinusgeneratoren und Ringmodulatoren* 64, *Mikrophonie II für Chor, Hammondorgel und Ringmodulatoren* 65, *Telemusik* (electronic music) 66, *Solo für Melodieinstrument mit Rückkopplung* 66, *Adieu für Bläserquintett* 66, *Hymnen—elektronische und konkrete Musik mit Solisten* 66-67, *Prozession für Tamtam, Viola, Elektronium, Klavier, 2 Filter und Regler* 67, *Sextette für Sänger* 68, *Kurzwellen für 6 Spieler* 68.
Publs. *Texte* (2 vols.) 63-64.
Office: Studio für Elektronische Musik, Westdeutscher Rundfunk, Wallrafplaz 5, Cologne 5, German Federal Republic.

Stockwood, Rt. Rev. Arthur Mervyn; British ecclesiastic; b. 27 May 1913; ed. Christ's Coll. and Westcott House, Cambridge.
Ordained 36; Curate, St. Matthew Moorfields, Bristol 36-41, Vicar 41-55; Hon. Canon, Bristol 53-55; Vicar, St. Mary the Great, Cambridge 55-59; Bishop of Southwark 59-; Labour mem. Bristol City Council 46-55, Cambridge City Council 56-59.
38 Tooting Bec Gardens, London, S W.16, England.

Stoica, Chivu; Romanian politician; b. 1908.
Member Romanian Communist Party 31-; active in leading struggles of rail workers at Grivița works, Bucharest 33; sentenced to 12 years hard labour for political activities; took part in armed insurrection Aug. 44; mem. Central Cttee. Romanian Communist Party and Party Political Bureau 45-65, Sec. Central Cttee. 61-65; mem. Exec. Cttee. and Perm. Presidium 65-; mem. Parl. 46-48, Deputy Grand Nat. Assembly 48-; Deputy Chair. Gen. Labour Confed. of Romania 45-46; Gen. Man. Gen. Dept., Romanian Railways 46-48; Minister of Industry and Trade, then of Metallurgical and Chemical Industries 48-52; Deputy Chair. Council of Ministers 50-54, First Deputy Chair. 54-55, Chair. 55-61; Pres. State Council of Socialist Republic of Romania 65-Dec. 67; mem. Secr. Romania C.P. 67-; awarded various Romanian and foreign orders and medals; Hero of Socialist Labour (Romania) 58.
Secretariat of Romanian Communist Party, Bucharest, Romania.

Stokes, Sir Donald Gresham, Kt., T.D., M.I.MECH.E.; British engineer and business executive; b. 22 March 1914; ed. Blundell's School and Harris Inst. of Technology.
Student Engineer, Leyland Motors 30-33, Technical Asst. 33-39; Mil. Service 39-45; Export Manager Leyland Motors 46-52, Dir. and Gen. Sales Manager 52-63; Managing Dir. and Deputy Chair. Leyland Motor Corpn. 63-67, Chair. and Man. Dir. 67-; Chief Exec. and Dep. Chair. British Leyland Motor Corpn 68-; Man. Dir. Scammell Lorries Ltd. 60-; Chair. (Exec.) Standard Triumph Motor Car Co. 63-; Chair. Albion Motors Ltd. 63-, Leyland Motor Corpn. of South Africa Ltd. 63-, Self-Changing Gear Co. 63-; Pres. Leyland Motor Corpn.-U.S. 67-; Dir. District Bank Ltd. 63: mem. Council Soc. of Motor Manufacturers and Traders, Pres. 62, Deputy Pres. 63; Adviser to British Govt. on Export of British Arms 65; Chair. Econ. Devt. Cttee. for Electronics Industry 66-; mem. Board Industrial Reorganization Corpn. 66-; Hon. LL.D. (Lancaster).
25 St. James's Place, London, S.W.1, England.
Telephone: 01-493-7450.

Stokowski, Leopold Boleslawowicz Stanislaw Antoni, MUS.B. (Oxon.); American musician; b. London April 1887; ed. Royal Coll. Music, London.
Conductor Cincinnati Orchestra 09-12 and Philadelphia Orchestra 13-36, resgnd.; became American citizen 15; appeared in film *A Hundred Men and a Girl* 37, *Big Broadcast of 1937*; made film *Fantasia* with Walt Disney 40; Conductor Houston (Tex.) Symphony Orchestra 55-60; Founder-Conductor American Symphony Orchestra, New York 62-; Fellow Royal Coll. Music London; Hon. D.Mus. (Pennsylvania), LL.D. (Calif.).
Publ. *Music for All of Us* 43.
1067 Fifth Avenue, New York 28, N.Y., U.S.A.

Stoll, Arthur, D.SC.; Swiss chemist; b. 87; ed. Fed. Inst. of Technology, Zürich, Kaiser Wilhelm Inst. Chemistry, Berlin, and Munich Univ.
Asst. to Prof. Willstaetter, Fed. Inst. Technology, Zürich 09; Chief Asst. Kaiser Wilhelm Inst. Chemistry, Berlin 12-16; First Asst. Chemical Inst., Munich Univ. 17; founder Pharmaceutical Dept., Sandoz Ltd., Basle 17, President Board of Dirs. 34-, Pres. of Man. Cttee. 48-56; Pres. Comité Suisse de la Chimie 50-56; Vice-Pres. Int. Union of Pure and Applied Chemistry 51, Pres. 55-59; Vice-Pres. Int. Council of Scientific Unions 58-61; Foreign mem. Royal Soc. (U.K.); honours include: Marcel Benoist Prize 42, Flueckiger Gold Medal 43, Chevreul Medal, Paris 46, Pasteur Medal, Paris 48; Hon. M.D. (Basle, Geneva, Munich), D.Sc. (Pharm.) (Berne, Warsaw, Florence, Turin), D.Sc.(Tech.) (Zürich, Delft, Darmstadt), D.Sc. (Sorbonne, Guatemala, Würzburg, Toulouse, Strasbourg, Madrid); Chevalier de la Légion d'Honneur.
Publs. approx 200 works including: *Untersuchungen über Chlorophyll* 13, *Zusammenhänge zwischen der Chemie des Chlorophylls und seiner Funktion in der Photosynthese* 33, *Ein Gang durch biochemische Forschungsarbeiten* 33, *The Cardiac Glycosides* 36, *Altes*

und über Mutterkorn 43, *Les alcaloides de l'ergot* 45, *Ueber Ergotamin* 45, *Einführung in die Chemie der Hämine* 48, *The Cardioactive Glycosides* 49, *Ueber die Isomerie von Lysergsäure und Isolysergsäure* 49, *Ueber die herzwirksamen Glykoside der Digitalisgruppe* 50, *Über spezifische Inhaltsstoffe des Knoblauchs: Alliin, Alliinase und Allicin* 50, *Recent Investigations on Ergot Alkaloids* 50, *Die Konstitution der Sennoside* 50, *Synthese der optischaktiven Dihydro-lysergsäuren* 50, *Die Konstitution der Mutterkornalkaloide* 51.
Bildstockliweg 11, Arlesheim, nr. Basle, Switzerland.

Stoll, George Engman; American aviation executive; b. 2 Nov. 1906; ed. Goshen Coll.
Metallurgist, Engman Range Co., Goshen, Ind. 26-27, Long Manufacturing Co., Goshen 27-28; The Bendix Corpn. (fmrly. Bendix Aviation Corpn.) 29-, Products Div., South Bend, Ind. 29-33, 41; Gen. Man. Owosso (Mich.) Plant 43-46; Gen. Man. Bendix Products Div. 46-49; Vice-Pres. Bendix Corpn. 49-50, Exec. Vice-Pres. 60-65, Pres. and Chief Operating Officer 65-, Dir. 50-; Dir. W. A. Sheaffer Pen Co.; mem. Soc. Automative Engineers.
Bendix Corporation, 1104 Fisher Building, Detroit, Mich. 48202; Home: 32020 Franklin Road, Franklin Village, Mich., U.S.A.

Stoltenberg, Gerhard, DR. PHIL.; German scientist and politician; b. 29 Sept. 1928; ed. Grammar School, Bad Oldesloe, and Kiel Univ.
Scientific Asst., Kiel Univ. 54-60, Lecturer 60-65; Deputy Chair. Christian Democratic Union, Schleswig-Holstein 55; Fed. Chair. "Junge Union" 55-61; mem. Schleswig-Holstein Parl. 54-57; mem. Bundestag 57-; mem. Board of Management Fried. Krupp, Essen 65; Fed. Minister for Scientific Research Oct. 65-.
5300 Bonn 9, Heussallee 2-10, German Federal Republic.

Stone, Dewey D.; American businessman; b. 31 Aug. 1900; ed. Brockton Grammar School, Brockton High School and Coll. of Business Admin., Boston Univ.
Sergeant-Major, American Army, First World War; Pres. Harodite Finishing Co., N. Dighton, Mass. 52-; Chair. Bd. of Govs., Weizmann Inst. of Science, Rehovoth, Israel 45-; Dir. Converse Rubber Co., Crosby Valve & Gage Co., Ashton Valve Co., T. Toonan Sons Co., Trusteed Funds, Raimond Silver Mfg. Co., Leumi Financial Corpn., and foreign companies; Chair. Jewish Agency for Israel, Inc.; Nat. Chair. United Israel Appeal, United Jewish Appeal; official of many Israeli orgs. in America and Israel; Hon. D.Hum. (Boston Univ.), Hon. LL.D. (Stonehill Coll.); Hon. Fellow Weizmann Inst. of Science.
53 Arlington Street, Brockton 8; North Dighton, Mass., U.S.A.

Stone, Donald Crawford, A.B., M.S., LL.D.; American government official and educator; b. 17 June 1903; ed. Colgate, Syracuse, Cincinnati and Columbia Univs.
Staff mem. Cincinnati Bureau of Governmental Research 27-28, Inst. of Public Administration N.Y. 29-30; Dir. of Research, Int. City Managers' Asscn., Chicago 30-33; Exec. Dir., Public Administration Service, Chicago 33-39; Asst. Dir. Bureau of the Budget, Exec. Office of the Pres., Washington 39-48; Dir. of Admin., E.C.A., Washington, D.C. 48-51, M.S.A. 51-53; Pres. Springfield Coll. 53-57; Adviser to U.S. Del., to UN Conf., San Francisco 45, to Gen. Assembly of UN London 46, and New York 47, to U.S. Rep. to Economic and Social Council N.Y. 46; U.S. Rep. to UNESCO Preparatory Commission, London 46; mem. UN Standing Cttee. on Administration and Budgetary Affairs 46-48; Chair. Cttee. Int. Inst. of Administrative Sciences 49-; Dean, Graduate School of Public and Int. Affairs, Pittsburgh Univ. 57-; mem. Commission on Int. Affairs, Nat. Council of Churches 58-; Chair. Cttee. on Leaders and Specialists and mem. Cttee. on Educ. and Int. Affairs, American Council on Educ. 55-61; Advisory assignments or studies in approx. 25 countries.
University of Pittsburgh, Pittsburgh, Pa. 15213, U.S.A.

Stone, Edward Durell, B.A., D.F.A.; American architect; b. 9 March 1902; ed. Harvard Univ. and M.I.T. Architecture Schools.
Architectural practice 35-; Instructor Advanced Design for New York Univ. 37-42; served in U.S. Army 42-45; Assoc. Prof. of Architecture, Yale Univ. 46-52; Visiting Critic, Yale Univ. 51-52; mem. Architectural Advisory Cttee., Fed. Public Housing Authority; Rotch Travelling Scholarship in Architecture; Architectural League Silver Medal for Domestic Architecture 50, Gold Medal for Museum of Modern Art 50, Gold Medal for Hotel El Panama 50; Honourable Mention for Univ. of Arkansas Fine Arts Center 52; Amer. Inst. of Architects Honor Award for Univ. of Arkansas Medical Center 52, New York Chapter Medal of Honor 55, First Honor Award for Stuart Company California 58, Award of Merit for U.S. Pavilion, World's Fair, Brussels 58, A.I.A. Awards for U.S. Embassy, New Delhi 61 and Peninsula Community Hosp., Calif. 63, John F. Kennedy Award, Inst. of North American Studies, Barcelona 66; elected Nat. Inst. of Arts and Letters 58, American Acad. of Arts and Sciences 60, Royal Soc. of Arts 60-.
Principal works include: Museum of Modern Art 37 (Philip Goodwin, Associate); El Panama Hotel, Panama City 51; Univ. of Arkansas Fine Arts Center 51; Hospital for Peruvian Government Lima 57; Graf Residence, Dallas 57; U.S. pavilion, Brussels 58; U.S. Embassy, New Delhi 59; The Stuart Company, California 58; Huntington Hartford Gallery of Modern Art, New York; Stanford-Palo Alto Medical Center 60; Akron Downtown Redevelopment, Akron, Ohio; Univ. of Chicago Center for Continuing Education, Chicago 61; Nat. Cultural Center, Washington, D.C.; Pakistan Inst. of Nuclear Science and Technology, Islamabad, Pakistan 61; Nat. Geographic Soc. Office Building, Washington, D.C. 61; Int. Coll., Beirut 61; Perpetual Savings and Loan Asscn. Building, Los Angeles 61; Peninsula Community Hosp., Carmel, Calif. 63; John F. Kennedy Center for the Performing Arts, Washington, D.C. 63; N.Y. State Univ. at Albany 63, N.Y. Civic Center (Eggers and Higgins Assoc.) 63; General Motors Building, N.Y.C. (Emery Roth and Sons, Assoc.) 64; NASA Electronics Research Centre, Cambridge, Mass. (Giffels, Maguire Associates) 64; Projects in U.S., Saudi Arabia, Nicaragua and Pakistan 66.
7 East 67th Street, New York City, N.Y., U.S.A.

Stone, Rear-Admiral Ellery Wheeler; American communications executive and naval officer (Reserve); b. 14 Jan. 1894; ed. Univ. of California.
U.S. radio inspector 14-17; Lieut. U.S. Naval Reserve and district Communications supt. 17-19; Pres. Fed. Telegraph Co. 24-31; operating Vice-Pres. and Dir. Mackay Radio and Telegraph Co. 31-37; Vice-Pres. All-American Cables and Radio Inc. 37-38; Pres. and Dir. Postal Telegraph Inc. and Postal Telegraph-Cable Co. 42-; Pres. and Dir. Postal Telegraph Sales Corpn. 40; Commdr. U.S. Naval Reserve 39; Capt. 42; Rear-Admiral 43; mem. Tech. Cttees. Defence Communications Board 40; Chief Commr. Allied Comm. for Italy 44-47; Chief of Italian Mil. Affairs Section of A.F.H.Q. 47; Vice-Pres. and Dir. Int. Telephone and Telegraph Corpn.; Chair. of Board American Cable and Radio Corpn., Commercial Cable Co., Mackay Radio & Tel. Co., All-American Cables & Radio Inc.; Pres. ITT Europe Inc., Brussels 61-65, Vice-Chair. 65-; awarded U.S. Army and U.S. Navy D.S.M.s; K.B.E.; Grand Cross St. Maurice and St. Lazarus and Grand Officer Crown of Italy (Italy); Grand Cross of San Marino; Cross of Merit, 1st Class, with Crown, Knights of Malta; Chevalier, Légion d'Honneur; Commdr. Order

of Leopold II; Campaign Medals World Wars I and II; Fellow U.S. Inst. of Radio Engineers and U.S. Naval Inst.; F.R.S.A.
Publ. *Elements of Radio Communication* (3rd edn.) 26. 320 Park Avenue, New York, N.Y. 10022, U.S.A. Telephone: PLaza 2-6000.

Stone, Irving, A.B., M.A., CAND. PH.D.; American writer; b. 14 July 1903; ed. Univ. of California, Univ. of Southern California.
Teaching Fellow, Univ. of Southern California 23-24, Univ. of California 24-26; Creative Writing, Indiana 48, Washington 61, Univ. of Southern California 66; Lecturer California State Colleges 66; book reviews, magazine contributions; mem. numerous cultural, literary socs.; founder Irving and Jean Stone prizes for biog. and historical novels -68; Hon. D.Lit. (Univ. of S. Calif.) 65, (Coe Coll.) 67.
Publs. *Pageant of Youth* 33, *Lust for Life* (Vincent Van Gogh) 34, *Dear Theo* (Van Gogh's autobiography) 37, *Sailor on Horseback* (Jack London) 38, *False Witness* 40, *Clarence Darrow for the Defense* 41, *They also Ran* (Defeated Presidential Candidates) 43, *Immortal Wife* (Jessie and John Fremont) 44, *Adversary in the House* (Eugene Debs) 47, *Earl Warren* 48, *The Passionate Journey* (John Noble) 49, *We Speak for Ourselves* (A Self-Portrait of America) 50, *The President's Lady* (Rachel and Andrew Jackson) 51, *Love is Eternal* (Mary Todd Lincoln) 54, *Men to Match My Mountains* (opening of the Far West) 56, *The Biographical Novel* 57, *The Agony and the Ecstasy* (Michelangelo) 61, *Lincoln, A Contemporary Portrait* (Editor) 62, *I, Michelangelo, Sculptor* (Michelangelo's Letters) 62, *The Irving Stone Reader* 63, *Story of Michelangelo's Pietà* 64, *The Great Adventures of Michelangelo* 65, *Those Who Love* (Abigail and John Adams) 65.
c/o Doubleday & Co. Inc., 501 Franklin Avenue, Garden City, New York, N.Y. 11530, U.S.A.

Stone, J. O., B.SC., B.A.; Australian financial executive; b. 31 Jan. 1929; ed. Univ. of Western Australia and New Coll., Oxford.
Assistant to Australian Treasury Rep. in London 54-56, Australian Treasury Rep. in London 58-61; in Research and Information Div., Gen. Financial and Econ. Policy Branch, Dept. of Treasury, Canberra 56-57, in Home Finance Div. 61-62, Asst. Sec. Econ. and Financial Surveys Div. 62-66; Exec. Dir. for Australia, New Zealand and South Africa, Int. Monetary Fund (IMF) and Int. Bank for Reconstruction and Devt. (IBRD—World Bank) 67-; mem. Australian Dels. to Gen. Agreement on Tariffs and Trade (GATT) and IMF annual meetings, etc.
International Monetary Fund, 19th and H Streets, N.W., Washington, D.C. 20431, U.S.A. Telephone: 202-381-3853.

Stone, J. R. N. (*see* Stone, Richard).

Stone, Lyndes Ballard; American insurance executive; b. 27 June 1905; ed. Univ. of Kansas and Yale Law School.
Yancey, Spillers and Fist (Attorneys), Tulsa, Oklahoma 30-31; Phoenix Mutual Life Insurance Co. 31-, Second Vice-Pres. 50-54, Vice-Pres. 54-56, Dir. 56-, Exec. Vice-Pres. 56-61, Pres. 61-; Dir. Connecticut Bank and Trust Co., Inst. of Life Insurance; Trustee, Mechanics Savings Bank; Dir. Mount Sinai Hospital, Hartford; Regent, Univ. of Hartford.
Phoenix Mutual Life Insurance Company, One American Row, Hartford, Conn. 06115, U.S.A.

Stone, (John) Richard (Nicholas), C.B.E.; British economist; b. 30 Aug. 1913; ed. Westminster School and Gonville and Caius Coll., Cambridge.
With C. E. Heath and Co. (Lloyd's Brokers) 36-39; Ministry of Economic Warfare 39-40; offices of War Cabinet, Central Statistical Office 40-45; Dir. Dept. of

Applied Economics, Cambridge 45-55; Leake Prof. of Finance and Accounting, Cambridge 55-; Fellow of King's Coll., Cambridge 45, Econometric Soc. (fmr. Pres.); mem. Int. Statistical Inst.; hon. mem. Soc. of Inc. Accountants and Auditors 54; Fellow British Acad. 56.
Publs. *The Role of Measurement in Economics* 51, (with others) *The Measurement of Consumers' Expenditure and Behaviour in the United Kingdom 1920-1938* 54, *Quantity and Price Indexes in National Accounts* 56, *Social Accounting and Economic Models* (with Giovanna Croft-Murray) 59, *Input-Output and National Accounts* 61, *National Income and Expenditure* (with Giovanna Stone) 61, 64, *A Programme for Growth* (with others) 65.
13 Millington Road, Cambridge, England.

Stone, Walker; American newspaper editor; b. 8 May 1904; ed. Oklahoma State Univ. and George Washington Univ.
Writer and executive with Scripps-Howard newspapers, Washington 27-, Editor, Scripps-Howard Newspaper Alliance 43-52, Editor-in-Chief, Scripps-Howard Newspapers 53-.
Scripps-Howard Newspaper Alliance, 1013 13th Street, N.W., Washington, D.C. 20005, U.S.A. Telephone: DI7-7750.

Stoneman, William H., A.B.; American journalist; b. 15 March 1904; ed. Univ. of Mich.
Scandinavian Correspondent *Chicago Daily News* 28, Rome 29-32, Moscow 32-35, corresp. with Ethiopian forces 35-36, Berlin 36, Chief London Corresp. 36-46, 58-, War Corresp. France 39-40, Tunisia 42-43, Italy 43-44, N.W. Europe 44-45; Pres. Asscn. of American corresps. in London 39, 40-41; Personal Adviser to Sec.-Gen. of UN 46-49.
Publ. *The Life and Death of Ivar Kreuger* 32.
Chicago Daily News, 69 Fleet Street, London, E.C.4, England; and 23 rue de la Paix, Paris 2, France.

Stoner, Edmund Clifton, B.A., SC.D., F.R.S., F.INST.P.; British physicist; b. 2 Oct. 1899; ed. Bolton School and Emmanuel Coll., Cambridge.
Research Fellow Emmanuel Coll. Cambridge 28-31; Lecturer in Physics Leeds Univ. 24; Reader in Physics Leeds Univ. 27-39, Prof. of Theoretical Physics 39-51, Cavendish Prof. of Physics 51-63, Emeritus Prof. 63-; Kelvin Lecturer (Inst. of Electrical Engineers) 44, Guthrie Lecturer (Physical Society) 55.
Publs. *Magnetism and Atomic Structure* 26, *Magnetism and Matter* 34, *Magnetism* 30, 36, 46, 55.
12 St. Chad's Drive, Headingley, Leeds 6, England. Telephone: Leeds 53927.

Stopford, Rt. Rev. and Rt. Hon. Robert Wright, P.C., C.B.E., D.D., D.C.L., M.A.; British ecclesiastic; b. 20 Feb. 1901; ed. Liverpool Coll. and Hertford Coll., Oxford.
Senior History Master and Chaplain, Oundle School 25-34; Principal, Trinity Coll., Kandy, Ceylon 35-40, Achimota Coll., Gold Coast 41-45; Rector of Barnet 46-47; Moderator, Church Training Colls. 47-55; Chaplain to H.M. Queen Elizabeth 52-55; Bishop of Fulham 55-56 (also Rep. of Archbishop of Canterbury in North and Central Europe); Sec. of Schools Council and Nat. Soc. 52-55; Chair. Schools Council 56-58; Hon. Canon of Canterbury 51-55; Bishop of Peterborough 56-61, of London 61-; Chair. Church of England Board of Educ. 58-; Chair. Joint Comm. for Anglican-Methodist Union 65; Hon. Fellow Hertford Coll., Oxford; Fellow King's Coll., London.
Publs. include *None of us Liveth to Himself* 64.
Fulham Palace, London, S.W.6, England. Telephone: 01-736-5821.

Stoph, Willi; German politician; b. 9 July 1914.
Worked as a mason and foreman bricklayer, later as a technical architect, following extra-mural studies; mem. Communist Party of Germany 31-; active anti-fascist

resistance 33-45; mem. Central Cttee. Socialist Unity Party 50-, mem. Political Bureau of S.E.D. Central Cttee. 53-; mem. People's Chamber 50-; mem. Council of State 63-, Deputy Chair. 64-; Minister of the Interior 52-55; Minister of Nat. Defence (rank of Gen. of Army) 56-60; Deputy Chair. Council of Ministers 54-64, Chair. Council of Ministers of German Democratic Republic Sept. 64-; Patriotic Order of Merit (Gold); hon. title of Hero of Labour, Order of Banner of Labour, etc.
Klosterstrasse 47, 102 Berlin, Germany.

Stopper, Edwin, DR.ECON.SC.; Swiss banker; b. 14 Aug. 1912; ed. Univs. of St. Gall, London, Paris and Geneva.
Formerly in export trade and banking; Asst. to Dir. Commercial Dept., Swiss Fed. Ministry for Econ. Affairs 39-45; Sec. Central Office of Swiss Asscn. for Trade and Industry, Zürich; Acting Man. and Deputy to Central Man. for Finance, Nestlé Alimentana Ltd., Vévey 52-53; Del. for Trade Agreements, Commercial Dept. of Fed. Ministry for Econ. Affairs 54-60, rank of Minister 55-60; Dir. Swiss Fed. Finance Dept. 60-61; Dir. Swiss Fed. Commercial Dept. (rank of Amb.) 61-66; Pres. Board of Gen. Management and Chief of Dept. I, Swiss Nat. Bank 66-; Hon. Lecturer in Econs., Basle Univ.
Swiss National Bank, Börsenstrasse 15, 8022 Zürich, Switzerland.
Telephone: 051-23-47-40.

Storey, Robert Gerald, B.A.; American lawyer; b. 4 Dec. 1893; ed. Univ. of Texas and Southern Methodist Univ.
Partner Storey, Armstrong & Steger (Dallas) 34-; Dean Southern Methodist Univ. Law School 47-59; Pres. Southwestern Legal Foundation 47-; Asst. Attorney Gen. of Texas 21-23; Regent Univ. of Texas 24-30; U.S. Exec. Trial Counsel, Nuremberg Major Axis War Crimes Trials 45-46; mem. Hoover Comm. 53-55; Adviser to Govt. of South Korea 54; Rep. of State Dept. in Far and Middle East 54-55; Chair. Board of Foreign Scholarships (Int. Education Exchange) 56-62; Vice-Chair. Civil Rights Comm. 57-63; Pres. Dallas Bar Asscn. 34, State Bar of Texas 48-49; American Bar Asscn. 52-53, Inter-American Bar Asscn. 54-56; mem. Int. Bar Asscn. 52-; Vice-Chair. and mem. U.S. Sea Level Canal Study Comm.; mem. President's Comm. on Law Enforcement and Improvement in Admin. of Justice; Chair. Lakewood State Bank; Dir. Southwestern Bell Telephone Co.; Dir. and Gen. Counsel United Fidelity and Universal Life Insurance Cos., Sabine Royalty Corpn.; Chair. Texas Constitutional Revision Comm.; 2nd Lieut. in Heavy Artillery during First World War, Col. in Air Corps during Second World War; Gold Medal American Bar Asscn. 56; decorations include Legion of Merit, Medal of Freedom, Légion d'Honneur, Bronze Star; Democrat.
Publs. *Professional Responsibility* 58, *Our Unalienable Rights* 65, *The Final Judgment: Pearl Harbour to Nuremberg*; numerous articles and reviews.
4100 Republic Bank Tower, Dallas, Texas, U.S.A.

Storheill, Rear-Admiral Skule Valentin; Norwegian naval officer; b. 17 Aug. 1907; ed. Norwegian Naval Coll. and Royal Naval Staff Coll., Greenwich.
Sub-Lieut. 28, Lieut. 31, Commdr. 41, Commodore 46, Vice-Admiral 51; served in submarines 31-36; Instructor Royal Norwegian Naval Coll. 36-40; active service during Second World War 40-45; staff appt., Norwegian Admiralty 45; Chief of Staff 46-49; C.-in-C. Norwegian Training Squadron 49-51; C.-in-C. Norwegian Navy Oct. 51-54; mem. Mil. Reps. Cttee. NATO 54-58; Commdr. Allied Task Force North Norway 58-; War Cross with Sword, Commdr. with Star, Royal Order of St. Olav, St. Olav Medal with Oak Leaf and Norwegian War Medal; D.S.C. with 2 bars (U.K.); Commdr. de la

Légion d'Honneur, Croix de Guerre (France), Grand Cross, Orange Nassau, Hausorder (Netherlands), Officer Legion of Merit (U.S.A.).
Comtaskfornon, boks 357, Bodø, Norway.

Storti, Bruno; Italian trade unionist; b. 9 July 1913. Former mem. of the directing Cttee. Confederazione Generale Italiana del Lavoro; co-founder Confederazione Italiana Sindicati Lavoratori (C.I.S.L.) 50, Sec.-Gen. C.I.S.L. 59-; Chair. Int. Confed. of Trade Unions 65-; mem. Chamber of Deputies 58-; mem. Parl. of Europe 59.
Confederazione Italiana Sindicati Lavoratori, Via Po 21, Rome, Italy.

Storz, Gerhard, DR.PHIL.; German university professor; b. 19 Aug. 1898; ed. Humanistisches Gymnasium, Esslingen, and Eberhard-Karls-Universität, Tübingen. Actor and producer in various German theatres, particularly Nationaltheater, Mannheim 23-35; schoolteacher 35-45, Headmaster 45-58; Minister of Culture, Baden-Württemberg 58-64; Hon. Prof. Univ. of Tübingen 64-; Pres. Deutsche Akad. für Sprache und Dichtung, Darmstadt 66-; Grosses Bundesverdienstkreuz 63; Konrad Duden Prize, City of Mannheim 66; Hon. D.Litt. (Middleburg Coll., U.S.A.) 65.
Publs. *Umgang mit der Sprache* 37, *Das Drama Schillers* 38, *Das Wörterbuch des Unmenschen* (with Dolf Sternberger and W. E. Süskind) 45-48, *Goethe—Vigilien* 53, *Sprache und Dichtung, Versuch einer Poetik* 53, *Der Dichter Friedrich Schiller* 59, *Figuren und Prospekte* 63, *Eduard Mörike* 67, *Schwäbische Romantik* 67.
725 Leonberg bei Stuttgart, German Federal Republic.

Stow, Sir John Montague, G.C.M.G., K.C.V.O.; British retired colonial governor; b. 3 Oct. 1911; ed. Harrov and Cambridge Univ.
Administrative Officer, Nigeria 34-38, Gambia 38-44; Chief Sec., Windward Islands 44-47; Admin., St. Lucia 47-52; Dir. of Establishments, Kenya 52-55; Chief Sec., Jamaica 55-59; Gov. of Barbados 59-66, Gov.-Gen. 66-67; Chair. Regional Council of Ministers Eastern Caribbean 62-66; retd. 67.
c/o Caledonian Club, 9 Halkin Street, London, S.W.1, England.

Stowe, Leland, M.A.; American journalist; b. 10 Nov. 1899; ed. Wesleyan Univ.
Member staff *Worcester Telegram* 21; Foreign Editor Pathé News 24; Paris corresp. *New York Herald Tribune* 26-35; Pres. Anglo-American Press Club of Paris 34-35; awarded Pulitzer Prize for best foreign correspondence 30; reporter in North and South America for *New York Herald Tribune* 35-38; war corresp. *Chicago Daily News* Scandinavia, Russia, Balkans, Egypt and Far East 39-42, Europe 44-45; News Analyst, American Broadcasting Co. 44-45; Greek Mil. Cross 45; Lecturer-Writer N.Y. Post Syndicate; Foreign Editor *The Reporter Magazine* 48-50; Dir. News and Information Service, Radio Free Europe, Munich 52-54; Roving Editor *The Reader's Digest* 55-; Prof. of Journalism, Univ. of Michigan 57-; Hon. D.Litt. (Wesleyan Univ., Hobart Coll.).
Publs. *Nazi Means War* 33, *No Other Road to Freedom* 41, *They Shall Not Sleep* 44, *While Time Remains* 46, *Target: You* 49, *Conquest by Terror: The Story of Satellite Europe* 52, *Crusoe of Lonesome Lake* 57.
University of Michigan, Ann Arbor, Mich., U.S.A.

Strachan, Douglas Alan; American (b. British) international official; b. 6 Aug. 1903; ed. Paddington Technical Inst. and Willesden Polytechnic, London.
Apprentice, British Thompson-Houston Co., London 19-26; emigrated to U.S. 26; toolmaker, automobile industry, Detroit 26-37; Sec. Michigan Labor Non-Partisan League 37-39; Field Rep., Fed. Cttee. on Apprenticeship, U.S. Dept. of Labor 39-40; Dir. United Automobile Workers Union, Willow Run Bomber Plant 42-43; Deputy Vice-Chair., Office of Labor

Production, War Production Board 43-45; Dir. United Automobile Workers Union Office, Washington 45-47; Labor Adviser, American Mission for Aid to Greece (later known as Marshall Plan) 47-53; Chief, Labor Training Div., Office Labor Affairs, Agency for Int. Devt. (AID), Washington 54-59; Provincial Dir., Lahore, AID Mission, Pakistan 59-62; Deputy Dir. AID Mission, Cairo 62-64; Asst. to Dir. for Special Projects, AID, Saigon 65; Dir. Colombo Plan Bureau March 66-.
Colombo Plan Bureau, P.O. Box 596, Colombo, Ceylon.

Stradling, Rt. Rev. Leslie Edward, M.A.; British ecclesiastic; b. 11 Feb. 1908; ed. Oxford Univ., Westcott House, Cambridge.
Curate in London 33-38, Vicar 38-45; Bishop of Masasi 45-52, of S.W. Tanganyika 52-61, of Johannesburg, South Africa 61-.
Publs. *A Bishop on Safari* 60, *"The Acts" through Modern Eyes* 63, *An Open Door* 66.
Bishop's House, 4 Crescent Drive, P.O. Box 1131, Westcliff, Johannesburg, South Africa.
Telephone: 23-2537.

Straight, Whitney Williard, C.B.E., M.C., D.F.C.; British company director; b. 6 Nov. 1912; ed. Lincoln School, U.S.A., Dartington Hall, Devon, and Trinity Coll. Cambridge.
Former professional motor car driver; gave up motor racing to enter civil aviation 34; started a number of companies; served in Auxiliary Air Force Second World War 39-45; Additional Air A.D.C. to the King 44; Deputy Chair. British European Airways 46; Man. Dir. (Chief Exec.) British Overseas Airways Corpn. 47, Deputy Chair. B.O.A.C. 49-56; Dir. Midland Bank and Midland Bank Executor and Trustee Co. 56-; Exec. Deputy Chair. Rolls-Royce Ltd. 57-; Vice-Pres. Royal Air Force Asscn.; mem. Insts. of Transport, Navigation and Directors; Chair. Contemporary Arts Soc.; Companion Royal Aeronautical Soc.; Chair. Exec. Cttee. Alexandra Rose Day; Fellow Royal Soc. of Arts.
The Aviary, Windmill Lane, Southall, Middx., England.
Telephone: Southall 2711.

Strakhov, Nikolai Mikhailovich; Soviet (Russian) geologist; b. 1900; ed. Moscow State Univ.
Assistant, Moscow Geological Prospecting Inst. 30-31, Asst. Prof. 31-37, Prof. 44-46; Prof. Moscow State Univ. 51-53; Geological Inst. of U.S.S.R. Acad. of Sciences 34-; Corresp. mem. U.S.S.R. Acad. of Sciences 47-53, mem. 53-; Man. Lithological Dept. of Geological Inst. of U.S.S.R. Acad. of Sciences 37-59, Man. Laboratory of Geochemistry and Sedimentary Rocks, Geological Inst. 59-; Chief Editor *Lithology and Mineral Resources*; State Prize 48, Lenin Prize 61.
Publs. *Principles of Historical Geology* (2 vols.) 37, 38, 48, *Iron-ore Facies and their Analogues in the History of the Earth* 47, *Calcareous-dolomitic Facies in Modern and Ancient Basins* 54, *On the Geochemistry of Upper Paleozoic Deposits of Humidic Type* (with Glagoleva and Zalmanzon) 59, *Principles of the Theory of Lithogenesis* (Vols. 1-3) 60-62 (English edn. 67), *Lithogenetical Types and Their Evolution in the History of Earth* 63.
Geological Institute of the U.S.S.R. Academy of Sciences, Pyzhevsky per. 7, Moscow B-17, U.S.S.R.

Strang, 1st Baron, cr. 54; **William Strang,** G.C., B. G.C.M.G., M.B.E.; British diplomatist; b. 2 Jan. 1893; ed. Palmer's School, Univ. Coll., London, Sorbonne.
Served First World War; entered Foreign Office 19, 3rd Sec. Belgrade 19, 2nd Sec. 20, Foreign Office 22, 1st Sec. 25, Counsellor Moscow Embassy 30, Foreign Office 33; Asst. Under-Sec. of State Foreign Office 39-43; United Kingdom rep. with rank of Ambassador, European Advisory Comm. 43-45; Political Adviser to C.-in-C., British Zone, Germany 45-47; Permanent Under-Sec., Foreign Office (German Section) 47-49; Permanent Under-Sec. Foreign Office 49-53; Chair. Nat.

Parks Comm. 54-66; Chair. Food Hygiene Advisory Council 55-; Chair. Royal Inst. of Int. Affairs 58-66.
Publs. *The Foreign Office* 55, *Home and Abroad* 56, *Britain in World Affairs* 61, *The Diplomatic Career* 62.
41A Ennismore Gardens, London, S.W.7, England.

Sträng, Gunnar Georg Emmanuel; Swedish politician; b. 23 Dec. 1906; ed. Stockholm.
Labourer 21-27; rep. on Workers' Asscn. 27-32; official, T.U.C.; Chair. Agricultural Workers' Union; Minister without portfolio 45-47; Minister of Supply 47; Minister of Agriculture 48-51; Minister of Social Affairs 51-55; Minister of Finance 55-; Social Democratic Labour.
Finansdepartementet, Stockholm, Sweden.

Stranger, Rolf; Norwegian lawyer and company director; b. 15 Jan. 1891.
Chair. of Board, Confektionsfabrikanternes Landsforbund for 20 years; Chair. Norwegian Industries Fair 24-; mem. Oslo City Council 26-; Mayor of Oslo 56-59, Deputy Mayor 60-62, Mayor 62-64; M.P. 45-53; mem. Norges Industriforbund, Board of Representatives Oslo Sparebank, Bergens Privatbank, Bergen and Oslo, etc.; Man. Dir. Hanssen & Bergh A/S; Chair. of Board, Kommunes Filmcentral A/S; Conservative.
c/o Raadhuset, Oslo, Norway.

Strasberg, Lee; American theatrical director; b. 17 Nov. 1901.
Emigrated to U.S. from Austria 09; first directed and acted N.Y. 25, becoming professional 25; Actor and Asst. State Man. with Theatre Guild 25; founded Group Theatre N.Y. 30 and acted in many productions including *House of Connelly, Night over Taos, Success Story, Men in White, Gold Eagle Guy, Johnny Johnson*; directed *All the Living, Clash by Night, Fifth Column, Skipper next to God, The Big Knife*; Artistic Dir. Actors Studio, N.Y. 48-, Actors Studio Theatre Inc. 63-; lecturer on the theatre at various univs.; Pulitzer Prize for *Men in White*; Kelcey Allen Award 61; Centennial Gold Medal Award for Excellence in Dramatic Arts, Boston Coll. 63.
135 Central Park West, N.Y.C. 10023, U.S.A.

Strasser, Otto, DR. RER. POL.; German politician; b. 10 Sept. 1897; ed. Univs. of Munich, Berlin and Würzburg.
Served in German Army in First World War; Rapporteur in Reich Ministry of Food 21-23; Sec.-Gen. of an industrial concern 23-26; joined National Socialist Party 25; founded, with his brother Gregor, a revolutionary wing of the Party which came into conflict with the official policy of the Party; founded the Fighting Union of Revolutionary National-Socialists and also the Black Front; Chair. League for Germany's Renewal; in exile 33-55; returned to Germany 55; editor and publisher *Vorschau* (weekly) 57-.
Publs. *Aufbau des Deutschen Sozialismus* 31, *Wir rufen Deutschland* 32, *Die Deutsche Bartholomäusnacht* 34, *Europa von Morgen* 39, *Hitler and I* 40, *History in my Time* 41, *Germany Tomorrow* 41, *L'Aigle Prussien sur l'Allemagne* 42, *Deutschlands Erneuerung* 47, *Exil* 59, *Deutschland und der 3 Weltkrieg* 61, *Der Faschismus* 66, *Hitler II ante portas* 67.
Munich 13, Ainmillerstrasse 46, German Federal Republic.
Telephone: 399481.

Strassman, Fritz, DR.ING.; German chemist; b. 22 Feb. 1902; ed. Oberrealschule an der Scharnhorststrasse, Düsseldorf, Technische Hochschule, Hanover, and Kaiser Wilhelm Institut für Chemie, Berlin-Dahlem.
Assistant, Inst. for Physical Chemistry, Technische Hochschule, Hanover 29; scholar, Kaiser Wilhelm Inst. for Chemistry, Berlin-Dahlem 29; worked with Prof. O. Hahn and L. Meitner, Kaiser Wilhelm Inst. for Chemistry, Berlin 34; Head of Chemistry Dept., Kaiser Wilhelm Inst. for Chemistry, Tailfingen 46, Mainz

46-52; Dir. Inst. of Inorganic Chemistry and Nuclear Chemistry, Univ. of Mainz 46-, Dir. Inst. for Training and Research in Nuclear Chemistry, Univ. of Mainz 67-; Enrico Fermi Prize 66.
Mainz, Johann Friedrich von Pfeifferweg 6, German Federal Republic.

Straten-Waillet, Francois-Xavier van der; Belgian politician and diplomatist; b. 22 Jan. 1910; ed. Collège de St. André and Univ. of Louvain.
Barrister 34-38; Dir. Employers Organisation 39-45; mem. of Parl. 46-52; Minister of Commerce 47-48 and of Public Health 48-49; Pres. Christian Social Party 49-50; Del. to various sessions of the U.N., UNESCO, etc.; Minister to Argentina 52, Amb. 53-55; Amb. to Netherlands 55-66; Dir.-Gen. Political Affairs, Foreign Office, Brussels 66-; Grand Cross of Orange Nassau, Commdr. de la Couronne, Grand Cross, Orden al Merito (Argentina), Grand Officier, Order of Leopold II, etc.
Office: 254 avenue Winston Churchill, Brussels 18; Home: Duindak, Stadbroek (Anvers), Belgium.
Telephone: 43-93-02 (Office); 03-736673 (Home).

Strath, Sir William, K.C.B.; British business executive; b. 16 Nov. 1906; ed. Glasgow Univ.
Former civil servant; Inland Revenue 29-38; Air Ministry 38-40; Ministry of Aircraft Production 40-45; Ministry of Supply 45-47; Central Econ. Planning Staff 47-55; Treasury 48-55; mem. Econ. Planning Board 49-55; Full-time mem. U.K. Atomic Energy Authority 55-59; Perm. Sec. Ministry of Supply 59, Ministry of Aviation 59-60; Dir. Tube Investments Ltd. 61-, British Aluminium Co. 61-; Joint Managing Dir. Tube Investments Ltd. 61-, and Deputy Chair. 68-; Chair. British Aluminium Co. 62-; Dir. Legal and Gen. Assurance Soc. 62-.
C6 Albany, Piccadilly, London, W.1, England.

Stratton, Julius A., SC.D.; American physicist; b. 18 May 1901; ed. Univ. of Washington, Mass. Inst. of Technology, Eidgenössische Technische Hochschule, Zürich.
With M.I.T. 24-; Asst. Prof. Dept. of Electrical Engineering 28-30, Asst. Prof. of Physics 30-35, Assoc. Prof. 35-41, Prof. 41-49, Dir. Research Laboratory of Electronics 45-49, Provost, M.I.T. 49-56, Vice-Pres. 51-56, Chancellor 56-59, Acting Pres. 57-59, Pres. 59-66, Pres. Emer. 66-; Chair. of Board, The Ford Foundation Jan. 66-; Dir. American Soc. for Friendship with Switzerland, Near East Emergency Donations Cttee. (NEED, Inc.), Standard Oil Co. of New Jersey, Westinghouse Electric Corpn.; Chair. Comm. on Marine Science, Engineering and Resources 67; numerous hon. degrees and awards and decorations.
Publs. *Electromagnetic Theory* 41, *Science and the Educated Man* 66, also numerous papers.
The Ford Foundation, 320 East 43rd Street, New York, N.Y. 10017; Home: 800 Park Avenue, New York, N.Y. 10021, U.S.A.

Straub, F. Bruno; Hungarian biochemist; b. 1914.
University prof.; Vice-Pres. Nat. Peace Council 58-62; mem. Hungarian Acad. of Sciences; Sec. Dept. for Biological Studies, Hungarian Acad. of Sciences; work mainly concerns studies of muscle function, cell respiration and protein synthesis; Kossuth Prize 48, 50.
Publs. *Inorganic and Analytical Chemistry* 50, *Organic Chemistry* 52.
Hungarian Academy of Sciences, Roosevelt tér 9, Budapest V; Home: Endrödi Sándor-u. 18/a, Budapest II, Hungary.

Straus, Jack I., B.A.; American merchant; b. 13 Jan. 1900; ed. Harvard Coll.
Entered R. H. Macy & Co. Inc., Training Squad 21, Exec. Vice-Pres. 26-33, Sec. 29-33, Vice-Pres. 33-39, Acting Pres. 39-40, Pres. 40-56, Chair. 56-; mem. Board

of Trustees, Greenwich Savings Bank; fmr. mem. Board of Overseers Harvard Coll.; fmr. Dir. L.I. Railroad, Mutual Broadcasting System Inc., Gen. Teleradio Inc.; Dir. Greater N.Y. Fund, Safeway Stores Inc., Continental Can Co., Fidelity Union Trust Co.; Chair. of the Board, Roosevelt Hospital 65-; Public Gov., N.Y. Stock Exchange; Officer Order of Leopold II (Belgium); Chevalier de la Légion d'Honneur (France); Star of Italian Solidarity; Hon. LL.D. Adelphi Coll. 55; Hon. Dr. Comm. Sc. New York Univ. 58.
Home: 19 East 72nd Street, New York 21, N.Y.; Office: R. H. Macy & Co., Inc., Herald Square, New York 1, N.Y., U.S.A.

Strauss, Franz Josef; German politician; b. 6 Sept. 1915; ed. Univ. of Munich.
Served Second World War 39-45; mem. Bavarian Christian Social Union Party (C.S.U.) 45-, Deputy Chair. and Chair. until 67; mem. Bundestag (Fed. Parl.) 49-; Fed. Minister for Special Tasks 53-55, for Atomic Questions 55-56, of Defence 56-62; Fed. Sec. of the Treasury 66-.
Publ. *The Grand Design* 65.
8093 Rott am Inn, German Federal Republic.

Strauss, Hon. Jacobus Gideon Nel, Q.C., B.A., LL.B.; South African lawyer and politician; b. 17 Dec. 1900; ed. Univ. of Cape Town.
Private Sec. to Prime Minister 23-24; admitted to Johannesburg Bar 26; M.P. for Germiston District 32-57; Minister of Agriculture and Forests in Smuts Cabinet 44; Leader of Opposition 50-56; resigned from United Party 59.
Schöne-Brunnen Stud Farm, Box 509, Krugersdorp, Republic of South Africa.
Telephone: 622-2118.

Strauss, Lewis Lichtenstein; American banker; b. 31 Jan. 1896.
Fmr. mem. firm of Kuhn Loeb & Co.; fmr. Consultant and Financial Adviser to Messrs. Rockefeller; Dir.-Gen. American Transportation Corpn., Radio Corpn. of America, Nat. Broadcasting Co., Inland Steel Co.; Pres. Inst. for Advanced Study, Princeton; mem. U.S. Atomic Energy Comm. 46-50, Chair. 53-58, Special Adviser to Pres. 58-59; Sec. of Commerce 58-59; Rear Admiral U.S.N.R. (retd.); Republican.
Publ. *Men and Decisions* 63.
Brandy Station, Va., U.S.A.

Stravinsky, Igor; American composer; b. St. Petersburg 5 June 1882.
Naturalized French subject 34; naturalized American subject 45; Pres. English Bach Festival; Royal Philharmonic Soc. Gold Medal 54; Sibelius Gold Medal 55; mem. American Acad. of Arts and Letters.
Compositions include *L'Oiseau de Feu* 10, *Petrouchka* 11, *Le sacre du Printemps* 13, *Rossignol* 14, *Renard* 16, *Les Noces* 17-23, *L'Histoire du Soldat* 18, *Pulcinella* 19, *Symphonies d'Instruments à vent* 20, *Mavra* 22, *Octour* 23, *Concerto for Piano and Orchestra* 24, *Oedipus-Rex* 26, *Apollon Musagète* 27, *Le Baiser de la Fée* 28, *Capriccio for Piano and Orchestra* 29, *Symphonie de Psaumes* 30, *Concerto for Violin and Orchestra* 31, *Perséphone* 33-34, *Concerto for Two Pianos* 35, *Jeu de Cartes* 36-37, *Concerto for Chamber Ensemble* 37-38, *Symphony in C* 40, *Danses Concertantes* 42, *Scènes de Ballet* 44, *Symphony in 3 movements* 45, *Orpheus* 47, *Mass* 48, *The Rake's Progress* 51, *Cantata* 52, *Septet* 53, *Three Songs from William Shakespeare* 54, *In Memoriam Dylan Thomas* 54, *Canticum Sacrum* 56, *Agon* 57, *Threni* 58, *Movements for Piano and Orchestra* 59, *Gesualdo Monumentum* 60, *The Flood* (opera) 62, *Abraham and Isaac* 64, *Elegy for J.F.K.* 64, *Variation in Memory of Aldous Huxley* 65, *Requiem Canticles* 66, *The Song of the Nightingale* 67.
1260 N. Wetherly Drive, Hollywood, Calif., U.S.A.

Streat, Sir Edward Raymond, K.B.E.; British industrialist; b. 7 Feb. 1897; ed. Manchester Grammar School.
Served First World War (Lieut., 10th Manchester Regt.); Asst. Sec. Manchester Chamber of Commerce 19; Dir. and Sec. 20-40; Hon. Dir. Lancashire Industrial Development Council 31-40; Pres. Manchester Statistical Soc. 36-38; Sec. Export Council, Board of Trade 40; Pres. Textile Institute 46-48; Chair. Cotton Board Manchester 40-57; mem. Advisory Council D.S.I.R. 42-47; Chair. Manchester Joint Research Council 48-51; Treasurer of Council of Manchester Univ. 50-57, Chair. 57-65; Chair. North Western Electricity Consultative Council and mem. North Western Electricity Board 60-68; Vice-Pres. Lancashire and Merseyside Industrial Devt. Asscn.; Visiting Fellow Nuffield Coll., Oxford 44-59, Hon. Fellow 59.
2 Avenue Lodge, Alderley Edge, Cheshire, England.
Telephone: Alderley Edge 4212.

Street, Hon. Sir Kenneth Whistler, K.C.M.G., B.A., LL.B., K.ST.J.; Australian lawyer; b. 28 Jan. 1890; ed. Sydney Grammar School and Sydney Univ.
Called to the Bar of N.S.W. 15; mem. Industrial Comm. of N.S.W. with rank, title, and status of Supreme Court Judge 27-31; Judge of Supreme Court of N.S.W. 31-49, Chief Justice 50-60; Lieut.-Gov. of N.S.W. 50-; Lecturer, Univ. Law School 21-27; Hon. LL.D.
2 Greenoaks Avenue, Edgecliff, Sydney, New South Wales, Australia.
Telephone: 32-2203.

Streich, Rita; German singer; b. 18 Dec. 1926.
Studied with Erna Berger and Maria Ivogün; with Berlin State Opera, first important role Olympia (*Tales of Hoffmann*) 47; with Städtische Oper, Berlin 50-53, with Vienna Staatsoper 53-; sang at Bayreuth Festival 51, 52, Salzburg 54-61 and 65-, Aix-en-Provence 55, Glyndebourne 58; guest appearances in Europe, U.S.A. and Buenos Aires; concerts in Europe and U.S.A., Japan, Australia and New Zealand; numerous recordings and broadcasts; has appeared on television in Germany, Great Britain, in the Ed Sullivan Show (New York), etc.; notable roles include the Queen of the Night (*The Magic Flute*), Konstanze (*Il Seraglio*), Susanna (*The Marriage of Figaro*), Zerbinetta (*Ariadne auf Naxos*), Sophie (*Der Rosenkavalier*), Gilda (*Rigoletto*), Rosina (*The Barber of Seville*), etc.
Rathausstrasse 15, Vienna I, Austria; and Palazzo Olimpo, Ascona, Switzerland.

Streit, Clarence K.; American journalist; b. 21 Jan. 1896; ed. Montana and Oxford Univs.
Rhodes Scholar Oxford 20; Foreign Corresp. 21-; fmr. *New York Times* Corresp. for L.N.; Pres. Int. Asscn. of Journalists accredited to the League 32; Pres. Federal Union Inc. 39-; Editor *Freedom and Union* 46-; Pres. Int. Movement for Atlantic Union 59.
Publs. *Where Iron Is, There Is the Fatherland* 20, *Hafiz: The Tongue of the Hidden* 28, *Union Now* 39, *Union Now with Britain* 41, *Union Now* (post-war edn.) 48, *The New Federalist* (in collaboration) 50, *Freedom Against Itself* 54, *Freedom's Frontier—Atlantic Union Now* 61.
Home: Ontario Apartments, Washington 20009; Office: Federal Union Inc., 1736 Columbia Road, Washington, D.C. 20009, U.S.A.
Telephone: 202-AD4-2211 (Office); 202-AD4-3232 (Home).

Streit, Josef; German lawyer; b. 9 June 1911.
In Czechoslovakia until 45; mem. Czechoslovak Communist Party 38-45, Sozialistische Einheitspartei Deutschlands 45-; Area Youth Leader, Schönberg/Mecklenburg 45; Chief Adviser, Ministry of Justice 49; Public Prosecutor, Office of Public Prosecutor-Gen. of D.D.R. 51-53; staff of Central Cttee., S.E.D. 53-62, mem. Central Cttee. S.E.D. 63-; Public Prosecutor-

Gen. of D.D.R. 62-; Vaterländischer Verdienstorden in Silber.
Generalstaatsanwalt der Deutschen Demokratischen Republik, Berlin N.4, Scharnhorststrasse 37, Germany.

Stretch, David Albert; American lawyer and business executive; b. 12 Oct. 1908; ed. U.S. Naval Acad. and Harvard Univ.
Admitted to Massachusetts Bar 34; in private law firms 33-55; Exec. Vice-Pres. Atlas Corpn. 56-58, Pres. 58-59, Pres. and Chief Exec. Officer 60-65; Chair. Exec. Cttee. Texas Industries Inc. 65-; Dir. Northeast Airlines Inc. and official of other companies.
4819 Walnut Hill Lane, Dallas, Texas 75229, U.S.A.
Telephone: EM3-8035.

Streuli, Hans, DR. h.c.; Swiss architect and politician; b. 13 July 1892; ed. Swiss Federal Inst. of Technology, Zürich.
Began architectural practice 19; Pres. Communal Council of Richterswil 28; Councillor of State, Zürich 35; Federal Councillor 54-59; Pres. of the Swiss Confederacy 57; Head of the Federal Dept. of Finance and Customs until 59; Pres. Federal Banking Comm. 65-66; mem. Swiss Radical-Democratic Party.
Hornstrasse 50, Richterswil, Switzerland.

Strickland, The Hon. Mabel Edeline, O.B.E., O.ST.J.; Maltese journalist and politician; b. 8 Jan. 1899; ed. St. Mary's Coll., Hobart, Tasmania.
With Naval Cypher Office, Malta 17-18; Asst. Sec. Constitutional Party 21-45, mem. Maltese Nat. Ass. 44, Malta Legislative Assembly 50, 51-53, 62-64; Malta Chamber of Commerce 54; Managing Dir. Allied Malta Newspapers Ltd. 38-55, Chair. 66-; Editor *Times of Malta* 35-50, *Sunday Times of Malta* 35-56; Chair. Xara Palace Hotel 49-61, 66-; Leader Progressive Constitutional Party 53-; mem. House of Reps. 64-66.
Publs. *A Collection of Essays on Malta* 55, *Maltese Constitutional and Economic Issues 1955-59* 59.
Villa Parisio, Lija, Malta.
Telephone: 25742.

Strobel, Frau Käte; German housewife and politician; b. 23 July 1907; ed. primary and technical schools, Nuremberg.
Member Social Democrat Party (S.P.D.) 25-; mem. Bundestag 49-; Fed. Minister of Health 66-.
Nuremberg, 108 Julius Lossmann Strasse, German Federal Republic.

Stroessner, Gen. Alfredo; Paraguayan army officer and politician; b. 1912; ed. Military Coll., Asunción.
Entered Paraguayan army; commissioned 32, served through all ranks to Gen.; C.-in-C. of Armed Forces 51; Pres. of Paraguay 54-; mem. Partido Rojo; Cruz del Chaco, Cruz del Defensor, decorations from Argentina and Brazil.
Casa Presidencial, Avenida Mariscal López, Asunción, Paraguay.

Strong, Most Rev. Philip Nigel Warrington, C.M.G., M.A., TH.D.; British ecclesiastic; b. 11 July 1899; ed. King's School, Worcester, Selwyn Coll., Cambridge, and Bishop's Coll., Cheshunt.
Served with Royal Engineers (Signal Service) 18-19; Deacon 22, Priest 23; Curate of St. Mary's, Tyne Dock 22-26; Vicar of Christ Church, Leeds 26-31, of St. Ignatius the Martyr, Sunderland 31-36; Proctor of Convocation of York and mem. Church Assembly for Archdeaconry of Durham 36; Bishop of New Guinea 36-63; mem. Legislative Council, Territory of Papua and New Guinea 55-63; Archbishop of Brisbane and Metropolitan of Queensland, Australia 63-66; Primate of Australia and Tasmania 66-; Senior Chaplain to the Forces (Australian Army) 43-45; Hon. Fellow Selwyn Coll., Cambridge 66-; Sub-Prelate Order of St. John of Jerusalem 67-.

Publ. *Out of Great Tribulation* 47.
Bishopsbourne, 39 Eldernell Terrace, Hamilton, Brisbane, Queensland 4007, Australia.
Telephone: Brisbane 68-2706.

Stronge, Rt. Hon. Sir Charles Norman Lockhart, Bt., P.C. (Northern Ireland), M.C., M.P.; British (Northern Ireland) politician; b. 23 July 1894; ed. Eton.
War service 14-19; M.P. for Mid-Armagh, N. Ireland Parl. 38-; Asst. Parl. Sec., Ministry of Finance 41-42; Parl. Sec. and Chief Whip 42-44; Speaker N. Ireland House of Commons 45-; Dir. Commercial Insurance Co. of Ireland Ltd.; Chair. Armagh County Council 45-56; Lord Lieut. Co. Armagh 39-; Commdr. Order of Leopold (Belgium) 46; mem. of Unionist Party.
Tynan Abbey, Tynan, Co. Armagh, N. Ireland.

Štrougal, Lubomír, LL.D.; Czechoslovak politician; b. 19 Oct. 1924; ed. Universita Karlova, Prague.
Member C.P. of Czechoslovakia 45-; Sec. České Budějovice Regional Cttee., C.P. of Czechoslovakia 55-57, Chief Sec. 57-59; mem. Central Cttee., C.P. of Czechoslovakia 58-, Secr. of Central Cttee. 59-61; Minister of Agriculture and Forestry 59-61, of the Interior 61-65; Deputy, Nat. Assembly 60-; Sec. Central Cttee., C.P. of Czechoslovakia 65-68; Deputy Prime Minister 68-; mem. Comm. for Questions on Living Standards, Central Cttee. 66-, Chair. 67-68; Chair. Econ. Council 68-.
Central Committee, Communist Party of Czechoslovakia, nábr. Kyjevské brigády 12, Prague 1, Czechoslovakia.

Strouse, Norman H.; American advertising executive; b. 4 Nov. 1906; ed. Olympia High School, Washington State, U.S.A.
Advertising salesman *Seattle Post-Intelligencer* 25-29; with J. Walter Thompson Co. 29-, Dir. 52-, Pres. 55-64, Chair. 64-, Chief Exec. Officer 60-; U.S. Army Second World War (Major); Hon. LL.D. (Colgate Univ.); Legion of Merit; Medal of Merit (Philippines).
Publs. *How to Build a Poor Man's Morgan Library* 59, *The Lengthened Shadow* 60, *The Contemptible Horse* 62, *The Passionate Pirate* 64, *The Silverado Episode* 66.
2 Beekman Place, New York, N.Y., U.S.A.
Telephone: MUrray Hill 6-7000.

Stroux, Karl-Heinz; German theatre director; b. 25 Feb. 1908; ed. Landfermanngymnasium Duisburg, Universität Berlin, and Drama School of Volksbühne, Berlin.
Actor and Asst. Dir. Volksbühne, Berlin 27-30; freelance Dir. various Berlin theatres 30-38; at Burgtheater, Vienna 38-40, Staatstheater Berlin 40-45; founded Heidelberger Kammerspiele 45; Dramatic Dir. Landestheater Darmstadt 46; Dramatic Dir. Staatstheater Wiesbaden 47-49, also Film Producer and Dir. (Nova-Film) 47-49; Dramatic Dir. Hebbeltheater, Berlin 49-51; freelance Dir. Hamburg, Vienna and Düsseldorf, and Dramatic Dir. Schiller Theater, Berlin 52-55; Gen. Supt. Schauspielhaus, Düsseldorf 55-.
Schauspielhaus, 4 Düsseldorf, Jahnstrasse 1B, German Federal Republic.

Struchkova, Raisa Stepanovna; Soviet ballerina; b. 5 Oct. 1925; ed. Moscow Choreographic School.
Soloist, Bolshoi Theatre Ballet Group 44-; People's Artist of U.S.S.R.
Principal roles include: Cinderella (*Cinderella*, Prokofiev), Juliet (*Romeo and Juliet*, Prokofiev), Giselle (*Giselle*, Adan), Princess Aurora (*Sleeping Beauty*, Tchaikovsky), Odette-Odile (*Swan Lake*, Tchaikovsky), Kitri (*Don Quixote*), Parasha (*Copper Rider*, Glier), Tao Khoa (*Red Poppy*, Glier), Maria (*Fountain of Bakshisarai*, Asafyev), Janne, also Diana de Mirrel (*Flames of Paris*, Asafyev), Gayane (*Gayane*, Khachaturyan), Vakchanka (*Walpurgisnacht*, Gounod), etc.
State Academic Bolshoi Theatre, Ploshchad Sverdlova, Moscow, U.S.S.R.

Struminsky, Vladimir Vasislievich, D.SC.(ENG.); Soviet scientist (Mechanics); b. 1914; ed. Moscow State Univ.
Scientific work in Central Inst. of Aerohydrodynamics 41-66; Prof. Moscow Physical-Technical Inst. 47-66; Dir. U.S.S.R. Acad. of Sciences Siberian Dept. Inst. of theoretical and applied mechanics 66-; corresp. mem. U.S.S.R. Acad. of Sciences 58-66, mem. 66-; State Prize (twice) and Lenin Prize.
U.S.S.R. Academy of Sciences, 14 Leninsky Prospekt, Moscow, U.S.S.R.

Struycken, Antonie Arnold Marie, LL.D.; Netherlands lawyer and politician; b. 27 Dec. 1906; ed. Catholic Univ. of Nijmegen.
Solicitor in Breda 32; Alderman of Breda and mem. Prov. States 38; Head Social Services of N.V. Hollandse Kunstzijde Unie 41-45; Deputy Burgomaster Breda 45-50; Minister of Justice 50-51, 58-59, 66-67; Gov. Netherlands Antilles 51-56; Deputy Prime Minister and Minister of the Interior 56-59; mem. Council of State; Knight Order of Netherlands Lion; Grand Cross British Empire, Grand Cordon Simon Bolívar; Grand Officer Order of Orange Nassau; Catholic People's Party.
Van Alkemadelaan 342, The Hague, Netherlands.
Telephone: 245240.

Struye, Paul; Belgian lawyer; b. 96; ed. Collège Ste. Barbe, Ghent, and Univ. of Ghent.
Advocate at Court of Cassation; Senator Feb. 46-; Minister of Justice 47-48; Pres. Senate 50-54, 58-62, 63-; Minister of State 58-; mem. Parti Social Chrétien.
Publs. *Précis des Brevets Inventions* (co-author) 35, *L'évolution du sentiment public sous l'occupation allemande* 44, *Taine* 47, *Nouveaux propos du Conseiller Eudoxe* 45, *Mélanges—Mengelingen* 66.
79 rue Washington, Brussels, Belgium.
Telephone: 32-36-80.

Struyev, Alexandr Ivanovich; Soviet politician; b. 1906.
Soviet and party work 25-; mem. C.P.S.U. 27-; Chair. Exec. Cttee. Donets Regional Soviet of Workers' Deputies C.P. of Ukraine 44-47, First Sec. Donets Regional Cttee. 47-53; First Sec. Perm Regional Cttee., C.P.S.U. 54-58; Deputy Chair. Council of Ministers of R.S.F.S.R. 58-63; Chair. Council of Ministers of U.S.S.R. State Cttee. for Trade 63-65. Minister of Trade 65-; mem. Central Auditing Comm., C.P.S.U. 52-56, mem. Central Cttee. of C.P.S.U. 56-61, 66-, Cand. mem. 61-66; Deputy to U.S.S.R. Supreme Soviet.
Ministry of Trade, Council of Ministers of U.S.S.R., 28 ulitsa Razina, Moscow, U.S.S.R.

Strzelecki, Pyszard; Polish politician; b. 31 Jan. 1907.
Metal worker in Warsaw factories; mem. Metal Workers' Trade Union; mem. Asscn. of Teachers of Vocational Schools 36-39; during the occupation was an organizer of the Polish Workers Party (P.P.R.) and Peoples Guard (G.L.); Co-organizer and head of Technical Section of P.P.R. Central Cttee. 43-; fought in Warsaw uprising; mem. political leadership of Peoples Army (A.L.), Chief of Staff of A.L. Units in Central Warsaw district 44; Deputy Head of Organizational Dept. of P.P.R. Central Cttee., Second Sec. P.P.R. Voivodship Cttee. in Katowice 45-46, First Sec. P.P.R. Voivodship Cttee. in Cracow 46-48, in Katowice 48; Vice-Minister of Communications 49-51, Minister 51-61; mem. P.P.R. 42-48, Polish United Workers Party (P.Z.P.R.) 48-; Sec. P.Z.P.R. Central Cttee. 60-; Alt. mem. Political Bureau 61-64, mem. 64; Deputy to Nat. Home Council (K.R.N.) and Seym 47-56, 61-; mem. Council of State 61-; Grunwald Cross, second class 48, Order of the Banner of Labour (twice) and others.
Polska Zjednoczona Partia Robotnicza Nowy Świat 6, Warsaw, Poland.

Stuart, Sir Campbell, G.C.M.G., K.B.E., K.ST.J.; British newspaper director; b. Montreal 1885; ed. private schools.
Served Canadian Army First World War; Asst. Mil. Attaché British Embassy Washington 17; Mil. Sec. to British War Mission to U.S.A. 17; Deputy Dir. of Propaganda in Enemy Countries 18; Dir. *The Times* 19-60, Man. Dir. 20-24; Dir. of Propaganda in Enemy Countries 39-40; Chair. Beit Cttee. for Scientific Research; Gov. Imperial Coll. of Science and Technology, and London House; fmr. Chair. The Pilgrims; Treasurer Franklin Roosevelt Memorial Cttee.; Chair. and Treasurer King George's Fields Foundation; Dir. Employers' Liability Assurance Corpn., Clerical, Medical and Gen. Life Assurance Society, General Reversionary Investment Co.; one of H.M. Lieuts. for City of London; Hon. LL.D. (Coll. of William and Mary, Va., and Univ. of Melbourne).
Publs. *Secrets of Crewe House* (the official record of enemy propaganda in the War of 1914-18); *Opportunity Knocks Once, Memorial to a King.*
4 The Grove, Highgate Village, London, N.6, England.

Stuart, Jesse Hilton, B.A.; American writer; b. 8 Aug. 1907; ed. Lincoln Memorial and Vanderbilt Univs. and Peabody Coll., Nashville.
Teacher, Secondary Schools; Coll. and Univ. Lecturer; Officer U.S. Naval Reserve; Visiting Prof. American Univ. Cairo.
Publs. 25 books, 279 short stories, over 1,600 poems.
Route 1, W-Hollow, Greenup, Kentucky, U.S.A.

Stuart, R(obert) Douglas; American businessman and diplomatist; b. 20 Jan. 1886; ed. Princeton Univ.
With Quaker Oats Company 06-, Chair. Board of Dirs. 56-62, Dir. and mem. Exec. Cttee. 62-; fmr. Dir. Chicago, Burlington & Quincy Railroad; Continental Casualty Co.; Continental Assurance Co.; Dir. Canadian Corporate Management Corpn., Foundation for American Agriculture; mem. The Business Council; Treas. Republican Nat. Cttee. 49-53; Amb. to Canada 53-56; mem. Canadian American Cttee. Nat. Planning Asscn.; Hon. LL.D. (Lake Forest Coll., Coe Coll., Northwestern Univ., Univ. of Pittsburgh).
345 Merchandise Mart, Chicago 54, Ill., U.S.A.

Stubbe, Hans, DR.AGR.; German geneticist; b. 7 March 1902; ed. Landwirtschaftliche Hochschule, Berlin, and Univ. of Göttingen.
Agricultural employment 22-25; asst. at Inst. für Vererbungsforschung, Berlin 27; asst. and departmental dir. Kaiser-Wilhelm-Inst. für Züchtungsforschung, Müncheberg 29-36; Kaiser-Wilhelm-Inst. für Biologie 36-43; Dir. Kaiser-Wilhelm-Inst. für Kulturpflanzenforschung, Vienna 43-45; Prof. of General and Special Genetics and Dir. Inst. of Genetics, Univ. of Halle; Pres. Deutsche Akad. der Landwirtschaftswissenschaften, Berlin; mem. Deutsche Akad. der Wissenschaften and Dir. of its Inst. für Kulturpflanzenforschung, Gatersleben; mem. other acads. and research bodies; Nat. Prize 49. 60, Vaterländischer Verdienstorden (silver) 54, (gold) 61; Dr. h.c., Dr. Agr. h.c., Dr. Sc. h.c.
Institut für Kulturpflanzenforschung, 4325 Gatersleben, German Democratic Republic.

Stubblefield, Sir (Cyril) James, Kt., F.R.S., D.SC., A.R.C.S.; British geologist; b. 6 Sept. 1901; ed. Perse School (Cambridge), Chelsea Polytechnic and Royal Coll. of Science, London.
Demonstrator Geology Dept. Imperial Coll. of Science and Technology 23-28; with Geological Survey of Great Britain and Museum of Practical Geology 28-66, Chief Palaeontologist 47-53, Asst. Dir. 53-60, Dir. 60-66; Dir. Geological Survey of N. Ireland 60-66; Pres. 6th Int. Congress Carboniferous Stratigraphy and Geology, Sheffield 67; Pres. Geological Soc., London 58-60; Pres.

Palaeontographical Soc. 66-; Corresp. mem. Paleontological Soc., U.S.A., Geological Soc., Stockholm, Geological Soc. of France, Senckenbergischen Naturforschenden Gesellschaft; Hon. Fellow, Palaeontological Soc. of India; Fellow Imperial Coll.
Publs. *Handbook of Geology of Great Britain* (co-editor) 29, *Introduction to Palaeontology* (revised, 3rd edn.) 61.
35 Kent Avenue, Ealing, London, W.13, England.
Telephone: 01-997-5051.

Stücklen, Richard; German electrical engineer and politician; b. 20 Aug. 1916; ed. primary school and engineering school.
Former Industrial Dept. Man.; Army Service 40-44; then Man. in family business; mem. Bundestag 49-; Deputy Chair. Christian Democratic Union/Christian Socialist Union (C.S.U.) Group and Parl. Leader of C.S.U. until 57 and 67-; Fed. Minister of Posts and Telegraphs 57-66; awards include Grosskreuz des Verdienstordens der Bundesrepublik Deutschland, Bayerische Verdienstorden.
Bundeshaus, 53 Bonn; Home: Weissenburg, Eichstätter Strasse, German Federal Republic.

Studebaker, John Ward, A.M., LL.D.; American educationist; b. 10 June 1887; ed. Leander Clark Coll., Toledo, Univ. of Iowa and Columbia Univ.
Principal high school and athletic coach Guthrie Center (Ia.) 10; Principal elementary and junior high school and Superintendent Mason City 11-14; Asst. Supt. of Schools Des Moines 14-20, Supt. 20-36; U.S. Commr. of Educ. 34-48; Vice-Pres. Scholastic Magazines, New York 48-67; mem. Nat. Educ. Asscn., American Asscn. for Adult Educ., etc.
Publs. *Plain Talk, The American Way.*
50 West 44th Street, New York, N.Y. 10036; and 1971 Golden Rain Road, Walnut Creek, Calif. 94529, U.S.A.

Stummvoll, Josef Leopold, M.SC., SC.D., PH.D.; Austrian librarian; b. 19 Aug. 1902; ed. Univs. of Vienna, Kiel and Leipzig.
Research Librarian and Dir. Reading Dept., Deutsche Bücherei, Leipzig 25-33, 37-39; Dir. and organiser, Library of Coll. of Agriculture and Veterinary Medicine (Yüksek Ziraat Enstitüsü), Ankara 33-37; Research librarian, Library of the Patent Office, Berlin 39-43; non-combatant war service 43-45, P.O.W. 45; Librarian (Oberstaatsbibliothekar), Austrian Nat. Library May 46, Deputy Dir.-Gen. Sept. 46, Dir.-Gen. Oct. 49-; on leave as UNESCO Expert for development of Persian libraries 52-53; on leave as Dir. U.N. Library, New York 59-63; Chair. Fed. Bd. of Examination in Library Science; Chair. Fed. Advisory Cttee. on Librarianship; Austrian del. of Int. Fed. of Library Asscns., Vice-Pres. Asscn. of Austrian Librarians; Pres. Int. Inst. for Children's Literature 65, Österr. Inst. für Bibliotheksforschung 66; merit awards from Austria and Italy; Chief Editor *Biblos (Österreichische Zeitschrift für Buch- und Bibliothekswesen, Dokumentation, Bibliographie und Bibliophilie)* and *Biblos-Schriften* (50 vols.), *Denkmäler des Theaters, Anton Bruckner Collected Works* (19 vols.), *Museion* Publications of the Austrian Nat. Library (18 vols.), *Corpus Papyrorum Raineri, Mitteilungen aus der Papyrussammlung* (5 vols.).
Publs. Books on librarianship, history of science, documentation, etc., *Festschrift J. Stummvoll zum 50. Geburtstag* 52, *Festschrift J. Stummvoll zum 65. Geburtstag* 68.
Home: Flamminggasse 36, A 2500 Baden; Office: Josefplatz 1, 1014 Vienna, Austria.
Telephone: 02252-36565 (Home); 022-52-52-55 (Office).

Sturtevant, Alfred Henry, A.B., PH.D.; American zoologist; b. 21 Nov. 1891; ed. Columbia Univ.
Research Asst. Carnegie Inst. Washington 15-28; Prof. of Genetics California Inst. of Technology 28-47, Thomas H. Morgan Prof. of Biology 47-62, Emeritus

62-; Visiting Prof. Birmingham 32, Leeds and Durham 33, Washington 60, Texas 62, Princeton 63, Wisconsin 64; Oregon 66, Calif. (Santa Cruz) 66; Fellow American Asscn. for the Advancement of Science, Pres. Pacific Div. 54; American Soc. of Zoologists (Pres. 34), Nat. Acad. of Science, Genetics Soc. of America (Pres. 44), American Philosophical Soc.; Trustee Emer. Marine Biological Laboratory; Visiting Lecturer Harvard Univ. 40; Hon. mem. British and Japanese Genetical Societies; Hon. Sc.D. (Princeton 47, Pennsylvania 49, Yale 51); Kimber Medal Nat. Acad. Sciences 57; Carty Medal, Nat. Acad. of Sciences 65; Nat. Medal of Science for 1967.
California Institute of Technology, Pasadena, Calif. 91109, U.S.A.

Styrikovich, Mikhail Adolfovich, D.SC.(ENG.); Soviet specialist in heat engineering; b. 1902; ed. Leningrad Technical Inst.
Engineer, Leningrad optical glass factory 26-28; scientific worker of Central Turbine and Boiler Inst. 28-46; U.S.S.R. Acad. of Sciences Inst. of Energetics 38-60; Head, Laboratory of Research Inst. of High Temperatures 61-; Corresp. mem. U.S.S.R. Acad. of Sciences 46-64, mem. 64-; Academician-Sec. of the U.S.S.R. Acad. of Science Dept. for Physical Engineering Problems and for Energetics.
U.S.S.R. Academy of Sciences, 14 Leninsky prospekt, Moscow, U.S.S.R.

Styron, William, A.B.; American writer; b. 11 June 1925; ed. Davidson Coll., Duke Univ.
Member Nat. Inst. of Arts and Letters; Fellow, Silliman Coll., Yale Univ.; Pulitzer Prize for best novel 68; Hon. D.Hum. (Wilberforce Univ.) 67, Hon. D.Litt. (New School for Social Research) 68, (Tufts Univ.) 68.
Publs. *Lie Down in Darkness* 51, *The Long March* 55, *Set this House on Fire* 60, *The Confessions of Nat Turner* 67.
R.F.D., Roxbury, Conn. 06783; Summer: Vineyard Haven, Mass. 02568, U.S.A.
Telephone: 203-354-5939.

Su Yü; Chinese army officer; b. 09.
Joined Students' Brigade of 4th Army, later entered C.C.P. 26; after defeat of Nanchang Msing, served under Chu Teh at Chinkangshan 27; organised peasants of Kiangsi, Commdr. Univ. Student Corps under Lin Piao (4th Army) 31; served under Fang Chuh-min, engaged in guerilla activity in Chekiang, Hunan and Fukien Provinces, succeeded Fang; Deputy Chief of Staff, North Kiangsu Section, New 4th Army 39; Vice-Chair. East China Mil. Council 49; Vice-Chair. East China Admin. 53; del. N.P.C. 54; Chief of Staff until Oct. 58; decorated and appointed General, People's Liberation Army.
National Council of Defence, Peking, China.

Suárez, Eduardo, LL.D.; Mexican lawyer and diplomatist; b. 3 Jan. 1895; ed. Colegio Municipal de Texcoco, Colegio Inglés, Tacubaya, Escuela Nacional Preparatoria, and Escuela de Jurisprudencia de la Univ. Nac. Autónoma de México.
Superintending Under-Sec., State of Hidalgo; Pres. Central Conciliation and Arbitration Board, Mexico City; Prof. of Jurisprudence, Nat. Univ. of Mexico, various times 16-48; Counsel for Mexico in claims between Mexico and U.S.A. 26-27, in claims between Mexico and the U.K. 28; mem. Arbitration Tribunal between Mexico and France; Head of Legal Dept., Ministry of Foreign Affairs 29-31, 31-34, 35; Minister of Finance and Public Credit 35-46; Amb. to U.K. 65-; Chevalier Légion d'Honneur; Grand Cross Order of Merit (Chile); Dr. h.c. (Nat. Univ. of Mexico).
Mexican Embassy, 48 Belgrave Square, London, S.W.1, England; Paseo de la Reforma 645, Lomas, México 10, D.F., Mexico.

Suárez, Facundo Roberto; Argentine lawyer and oil executive; b. 5 Nov. 1923; ed. Agustín Alvarez National High School, Mendoza, and Law School, Univ. of La Plata.
Principal of Political Studies School, Univ. of Cuyo 56-58; mem. Chamber of Deputies 58-62; Chair. Yacimientos Petrolíferos Fiscales (Argentine Govt. Oil Fields) 63-; Unión Cívica Radical del Pueblo.
Publ. *Fondos Comunes de Inversión* 61.
Avenida Presidente Roque Sáenz Peña 777, Buenos Aires, Argentina.

Subandrio, Dr.; Indonesian politician, diplomatist and surgeon; b. 14; ed. Medical Univ., Jakarta.
Active in Nat. Movement as student and gen. practitioner; worked with underground anti-Japanese Forces during Second World War; forced to leave post at Djakarta Central Hospital and then established a private practice at Semarang; following Declaration of Independence abandoned practice to become Sec.-Gen., Ministry of Information and was later sent by Indonesian Govt. as special envoy to Europe; established Information Office, London 47; Chargé d'Affaires, London 49, Ambassador to Great Britain 50-54, to U.S.S.R. 54-56; Foreign Minister 57-66; Second Deputy First Minister 60-66, concurrently Minister for Foreign Econ. Relations 62-66; sentenced to death Oct. 66.
Djakarta, Indonesia.

Subba Rao, K.; Indian judge; b. 02; ed. Govt. Arts Coll., Rajahmundry and Madras Law Coll.
Practice at Madras Bar 26-48; Judge, Madras High Court 48-54; Chief Justice, Andhra High Court 54-56, Andhra Pradesh High Court 56-58; Justice, Supreme Court of India 58-67, Chief Justice 66-67; Chancellor, Venkateswara Univ. 54, Pro-Chancellor Delhi Univ. 66-67.
7 Rest House Crescent, Bangalore 1, India.
Telephone: 27774.

Subbulakshmi, Madurai Shanmugavadivu (Mrs. T. Sadasivam); Indian singer; b. 16; ed. privately.
Recitals with mother Veena Shanmugavadivu 28-32, independent concerts and recitals in India 32-, and at Edinburgh Int. Festival; in London, Frankfurt, Geneva and Cairo; concert tour U.S.A. 66; numerous recordings and film appearances; Padma Bhushan decoration (Govt. of India) 54; Pres. Award for Classical Carnatic Music 56.
c/o Mr. T. Sadasivam, Editor *Kalki*, Kilpauk, Madras 10, South India.
Telephone: 61324.

Subramaniam, C., B.A., B.L.; Indian politician; b. 30 Jan. 1910; ed. Madras Univ.
Joined Satyagraha Movement and imprisoned; started Satyagraha in Coimbatore 36, imprisoned 41, 43; Pres. Coimbatore District Congress, mem. All India Congress Cttee.; mem. Constituent Assembly of India 46-51, Madras Legislative Assembly 52-62; Minister of Finance, Educ. and Law, Madras State 57-62; mem. Lok Sabha 62-67, Minister of Steel and Heavy Industry, Central Govt. 62-63, of Steel, Mines and Heavy Eng. Nov. 63-June 64, of Food and Agriculture June 64-67, also of Community Devt. and Co-operation 66-67.
Publs. Travelogues in Tamil: *Countries I Visited, Around the World.*
New Delhi, India.

Suchan, Franz, DR. RER. POL.; German banker; b. 19 Jan. 1911; ed. Realgymnasium Hamburg-Harburg, Univs. of Leipzig, Heidelberg, Hamburg and Berlin.
Administrator of Husum, Schleswig-Holstein 45-47; Landesdirektor of Fed. Land Schleswig-Holstein 47-49; Plenipotentiary of Schleswig-Holstein to Fed. Govt., Bonn 49-50; mem. Board of Dirs. Berliner Zentralbank 50-54, Vice-Pres. 54-57; Pres. Landeszentralbank in

Berlin, mem. Central Bank Council, Frankfurt/Main 59-.
Landeszentralbank in Berlin, Leibnizstrasse 7-10, 1 Berlin 12, Germany.
Telephone: 34-04-51.

Sucharda, Bohumil; Czechoslovak politician; b. 20 April 1914; ed. Coll. of Commerce, Prague.
Executive Dir., Int. Monetary Fund, Washington 48-50; First Deputy Minister of Finance 51-62; Deputy Minister-Chair., Central Office of State Control and Statistics 62-63; Deputy Minister-Chair., Central Comm. of People's Control and Statistics 63-65; mem. State Planning Comm. 64-65; Minister-Chair. State Comm. for Finance, Prices and Wages 65-67; mem. Central Control and Auditing Comm., Central Cttee. of C.P. of Czechoslovakia 62-, mem. Comm. for Questions of Living Standards 66-; Minister of Finance 67-; Chair. State Comm. for Finance, Prices and Wages 67-.
Ministry of Finance, Letenská 15, Prague 1, Czechoslovakia.

Sucharitakul, Chitti; Thai diplomatist; b. 08; ed. Royal Pages Coll., Thailand, Dulwich Coll., England, Queen's Coll., Oxford, and Inner Temple, London.
Ministry of Justice, Thailand 34; Judge attached to Ministry 34; Judge of High Court, Nakorn Rajsima 37-42; Official, Court of Appeal 42-49; Ministry of Foreign Affairs 49-, Chief of Gen. Services Div., Dept. of UN Affairs 50-53; Minister to Philippines 53-56, Ambassador 56-58; Ambassador attached to Ministry of Foreign Affairs 58; mem. Constituent Assembly 59; Ambassador to Switzerland 59-63, concurrently accred. to Yugoslavia and Austria 59-63; Perm. Rep. to European Office of UN, Geneva 63; Ambassador to India, concurrently accred. to Ceylon, Afghanistan and Nepal 63-; numerous Thai and other decorations.
Royal Thai Embassy, 56-N Nyaya Marg, Chankyapuri, New Delhi, India.

Suchodolski, Bogdan, PH.D.; Polish educator; b. 27 Dec. 1903.
Prof. of Education, Warsaw Univ.; mem. Polish Acad. of Sciences.
Publs. *Uspolecznienie Kultury* (Dissemination of Culture) 36, *Wychowanie dla Przyszlosci* (Education for the Future) 48, *Pedagogika na Miare Naszych Czasów* (Education for our Times) 58, *La Pédagogie et les Grands Courants Philosophiques* 60, *Grundlagen der marxistischen Erziehungstheorie* 61, *Narodziny Nowozytnej Filozofii Czlowieka* (Origins of Modern Philosophy of Man) 63, *Trattato di Pedagogia* 64, *Teoría marxista de la educación* 66, *Rozwoj Nowozytnej Filosofii Cztowieka* (Devt. of Modern Philosophy of Man) 68.
Smiala 63A, Warsaw 77, Poland.
Telephone: 33-19-00.

Suchoň, Eugen; Czechoslovak composer; b. 25 Sept. 1908; ed. Acad. of Music and Drama, Bratislava and Prague Conservatoire.
Professor of Composition Acad. of Music and Drama, Bratislava 33; Prof. at the Dept. of Musicology and Music Pedagogy, Bratislava Univ. 49-; mem. Cttee. Union of Czechoslovak Composers; founder of the Slovak Nat. Opera; Czechoslovak State Prize (3 times), Nat. Artist 58.
Works—opera: *Krútnava* (The Vortex) 41-49, *Svätopluk* 37-59; orchestra: *A Serenade for String Orchestra* 32, *Fantasy and Burlesque for Violin and Orchestra* 33, 48, *King Svätopluk* (overture for full orchestra) 34, *Ballad Suite* 36, *Metamorphoses* 51-52, *Sinfonietta Rustica* 56, *Six Pieces for String Orchestras* 63, *Partita rapsodica* (piano and orchestra) 65; chamber music: *Sonata for Violin and Piano* 30, *String Quartet* 31, *Serenade for the Wind Quintet* 31, *Piano Quartet* 33, *Sonatina for Violin and Piano* 37, *Six Pieces for String Quartet* 63, *Nox et Solitudo* (mezzo-soprano and orchestra) 32, *Ad Astra*

(soprano and orchestra) 61, *Psalm of Carpathian Country* (chorus and orchestra) 38, *From the Hills* (4 men's choirs a capella) 40, *Five Songs of Men* (mixed chorus a capella) 62, *Poème Macabre* (violin and piano) 63, *Contemplazioni* (recitator and piano) 64, *Kaleidoskop* (6 cycles for piano) 67-68, *Concertino* (for organ and string orchestra) 68.
Union of Czechoslovak Composers, Valdštejnské nám. 4, Prague I, Czechoslovakia.

Sucksdorff, Arne Edvard; Swedish film producer; b. 3 Feb. 1917; ed. Stockholm.
Films include the documentaries *Shadow over the Snow, Cliff Face, The Open Road, Rhythm of a City, Summer Interlude, Indian Village,* and *The Divided World;* also the feature films *The Great Adventure, The Flute and the Arrow, The Boy in the Tree.*
Copacabana, Casa Cabardi, Alghero, Sardinia, Italy.

Sudrabkain, Ian (real name Arvid) **Karlovich;** Soviet (Latvian) poet; b. 94.
State prizewinner 47; People's Poet of the Latvian S.S.R.; mem. Central Cttee. Latvian C.P.; Deputy to U.S.S.R. Supreme Soviet; Order of Lenin (twice).
Publs. *Lantern to the Wind* 42, *Food for the Road* 44, *Family of Brothers* 47, *Swallow Return* 51, *Collected Works* (5 vols.) 59-60, *Poetry* 64.
Writers' Union of Latvia, Riga, Latvia, U.S.S.R.

Sudreau, Pierre Robert, L. en D.; French politician; b. 13 May 1919; ed. Ecole des Sciences Politiques, Law and Letters Faculties, Paris Univ.
Served 2nd World War, prisoner in Buchenwald; with Ministry of the Interior 43; Dir. de Cabinet, Sec. d'Etat à la Présidence du Conseil 46; Joint Dir. Gen., Dir. of Admin. and Gen. Affairs, Sûreté Nationale 47; Dir. Financial Services, Ministry of the Interior 49; Prefect, Loire-et-Cher 52-55; Sec. Gen. Seine Préfecture, Commr. for Reconstruction and Urbanisation, Paris Region 55-58; Minister of Housing (De Gaulle cabinet) June 58-Jan. 59; Minister of Construction (Debré cabinet) Jan. 59-62, of Educ. (Pompidou cabinet) 62-Dec. 62; Deputy for Loir et Cher; Pres. Fédération des Industries Ferroviaires; Commdr. Légion d'Honneur, Croix de Guerre, Médaille de la Résistance.
12 rue Bixio, Paris 7e, France.

Sudyets, Marshal Vladimir Alexandrovich; Soviet army officer; b. 1904; ed. Soviet Armed Forces Technical School and Acad. of General Staff.
Member C.P.S.U. 24-; Soviet Army 25-, held successively command posts in Soviet Fighter and Bomber Commands; Chief of Gen. Staff and Dep. C.-in-C. Soviet Air Forces 46-49; Head, Officer Training, then Commdr. Air Army 51-55; Deputy C.-in-C. Soviet Air Force, Commdr. Long Range Bomber Force 58-62; C.-in-C. Anti-Aircraft Defences and Dep. Minister of Defence U.S.S.R. 62-66; Insp.-Gen. Ministry of Defence 66-; Candidate mem. Central Cttee. C.P.S.U. 61-66; Deputy to U.S.S.R. Supreme Soviet 61-66; Hero of the Soviet Union 45, Orders of Lenin (4), Suvorov (2), Kutuzov, Red Banner (4), Red Star; Hon. K.B.E.; Marshal of Aviation 55-.
Ministry of Defence, 34 Maurice Thorez Embankment, Moscow, U.S.S.R.

Suenens, H.E. Cardinal Leon-Joseph, D.D., PH.D., B.C.L.; Belgian ecclesiastic; b. 16 July 1904; ed. Pontifical Gregorian Univ., Rome.
Ordained Priest 27; Teacher, Institut Sainte-Marie, Brussels 29; Lecturer in Philosophy, Malines Seminary 30-40; Vice-Rector, Louvain Univ. 40-45; Private Chamberlain to Pope 41; Auxiliary Bishop and Vicar-Gen. of Archdiocese of Malines 45-61; Archbishop of Malines-Brussels and Primate of Belgium 61-; Created Cardinal 62; Moderator of Vatican Council 62-65; mem. Pontifical Comm. for Revision of Canon Law 62-; Pres. Belgian Bishops' Conf. 66-.

Publs. *Theology of the Legion of Mary, Edel-Mary Quinn, The Right View on Moral Re-armament, The Gospel to Every Creature, Mary the Mother of God, Love and Control, The Nun in the World, Christian Life Day by Day.*
Aartbisdom, Wollemarkt 15, Mechelen, Belgium.
Telephone: 015-165-01.

Sugai, Kumi; Japanese painter; b. 19; ed. Osaka School of Fine Arts.
One-man shows, Galerie Cruen, Paris, Palais des Beaux Arts, Brussels 54, St. George's Gallery, London 55, Galerie Legendre, Paris 57; rep. at Pittsburgh Carnegie Int. Exhbn. 55, and Salon des Réalités Nouvelles 56, 57, Salon de Mai 57, 58, Salon Biennale 57 (all Paris) and Dunn Int. Exhbn., London 63; Int. Painting Prize, São Paulo Bienal 65.
Publ. *La Quête sans Fin.*
37 rue de la Tombe Issoire, Paris 14e, France.

Suharto, Lt.-Gen.; Indonesian army officer and politician; b. 8 June 1921.
Officer in Japanese-sponsored Indonesian Army 43; Battalion, later Regimental, Commdr. Jogjakarta 45-50; Regimental Commdr., Central Java 53; Brig.-Gen. 60; Deputy Chief of Army Staff 60-65; Chief of Army Staff 65-68, Supreme Commdr. 68-; Minister of Army 65; Deputy Prime Minister for Defence and Security 66; Chair. of Presidium of Cabinet July 66-; in charge of Defence and Security, also Minister of Army July 66; Full Gen. 66; Acting Pres. of Indonesia and First Minister for Defence and Security 67-; Full Pres. March 68-.
Presidium Office, 15 Djl. Merdeka Barat; Home: 8 Djl. Tjendana, Djakarta, Indonesia.

Suhrbier, Max, DR. IUR.; German lawyer and politician; b. 12 Oct. 1902; ed. Realgymnasium and Univ. Rostock.
Councillor for Finance, Govt. of Mecklenburg 45-48, Minister of Finance, Mecklenburg 48-52; Deputy Chair. Council of Schwerin District 52-59; mem. Länderkammer 49-50; mem. Volkskammer 50-58, 63-; Deputy Minister of Finance of German Dem. Repub. (D.D.R.) 59-60; Chair. Liberal-Demokratische Partei 60-67, Hon. Chair. 67-; Deputy Chair. Council of Ministers of D.D.R. 60-65; mem. Council of Nat. Front; Ehrenspange zum Vaterländischer Verdienstorden in Gold, Banner der Arbeit.
Liberal-Demokratische Partei Deutschlands, Taubenstrasse 48-49, Berlin, W.8, Germany.

Suitner, Prof. Otmar; Austrian conductor; b. 16 May 1922; ed. Pädagogium Innsbrück, Mozarteum Salzburg.
Music Dir. in Remscheid 52-57; Gen. Dir. of Pfalzorchester in Ludwigshafen/Rh. 57-60; Gen. Dir. of State Opera Dresden 60-64; Gen. Dir. German State Opera Berlin 64-.
Berlin-Niederschönhausen, Platanenstr. 13, Germany; and Innsbrück, Stamserfeldstr. 1, Austria.

Suits, Chauncey Guy, B.A., D.SC.; American physicist; b. 12 March 1905; ed. Univ. of Wisconsin and Swiss Fed. Inst. of Technology.
Physics Consultant, U.S. Forest Products Laboratory, Madison, Wis. 29-30; Research Physicist, Gen. Electric Co., Research Laboratory, Schenectady, N.Y. 30-40, Asst. to Dir. 40-45; Vice-Pres. and Dir. of Research 45-66; Chief, Div. 15 of Nat. Defence Research Cttee. of Office of Scientific Research and Development, Govt., and mem. Div. 14 of N.D.R.C. of O.S.R.D. 42-46; mem. Naval Research Advisory Cttee. 56-64 (Chair. 58-61); mem. Nat. Acad. of Sciences, American Philosophical Soc., Nat. Acad. of Engineering; Silliman Lecturer, Yale Univ. 52; H.M. Medal for Service in the Cause of Freedom 48; Medal for Merit 48; Procter Prize Award—RESA 58, Hon. D.Sc. (Union and Hamilton Colls.,

Drexel Inst. of Technology, Marquette Univ.), Hon. D.Eng. (Rensselaer Polytechnic Inst.) 50.
Home: Crosswinds, Pilot Knob, N.Y. 12844, U.S.A.

Sükan, Faruk; Turkish physician and politician; b. 1921.
Mayor of Eregli 58-60; Deputy Chair. and mem. Exec., Justice Party; mem. Nat. Assembly 61-; fmr. Minister of Health and Social Assistance; Minister of Interior 65-.
Ministry of Interior, Ankara, Turkey.

Sukarno, Achmed, DR.ENG.; Indonesian politician; b. 6 June 1901; ed. Bandung Univ.
Started Nationalist and non-co-operative activities 27; leader, later Pres., Partai Nasional Indonesia; activities of this Party were forbidden and he was arrested 29; tried, and sentenced to four years' imprisonment 30; granted free amnesty and released 32; joined the Partai Indonesia, later becoming its Pres.; activities of Party forbidden, arrested and exiled to Flores 33; later transferred to Sumatra and released by Japanese 42; formulated principles of Free Indonesian State (Pantja Sila) July 45; proclaimed Republic of Indonesia Aug. 45; Pres. of Republic of Indonesia 45-49; Pres. of United States of Indonesia (re-constituted Aug. 50 as unitary Repub. of Indonesia) 49-March 67, Head of State 63-66; concurrently Prime Minister 59-66; Hon. LL.D. (Gadjahmada (Jogjakarta) Far, Eastern Univ., Manila, Columbia, Michigan, McGill, Belgrade, Prague, Moscow, etc.); Lenin Peace Prize 60.
Publ. *Sarinah* 48.
Bogor, Indonesia.

Sukhadia, Mohanlal, L.E.E.; Indian politician; b. 16; ed. Nathdwara (Udaipur) and Bombay Univ.
Active mem. Praja Mandal organisation in former Mewar State 39-; interned during "Quit India" movement 42; fmr. Minister for Civil Supplies, Post-War Development, Relief and Rehabilitation, Mewar State 46; Minister of Development when State of Rajasthan was first formed; mem. Rajasthan Legislative Ass.; Minister for Civil Supplies, Agriculture and Irrigation 51-52, Minister for Revenue (except Forests and Co-operation) and Famine Relief 52-54; Chief Minister, Rajasthan 54-; Congress Party.
8 Civil Lines, Jaipur, Rajasthan, India.

Sukselainen, Vieno Johannes; Finnish economist and politician; b. 12 Oct. 1906.
Lecturer, School of Social Sciences Helsinki 39; Sec. to Prime Minister 41-45; teacher of political economics, Univ. of Turku 45-47; Prof. School of Social Sciences 47-54; Pres. of the Agrarian Union 45-64; mem. Finnish Parl. 48-, Speaker 56-57, 58-59, 68-; Minister of Finance 50-51 and 54; Minister of Interior 51-53; Gen. Dir. People's Pension Inst. 54-; Prime Minister May-Nov. 57, Jan. 59-July 61.
Tapiola, Finland.
Telephone: Helsinki 462189.

Sukthankar, Yeshwant Narayan, C.I.E., M.A., LL.B., BAR.-AT-LAW; Indian civil servant and government administrator; b. 24 Aug. 1897; ed. Bombay and Cambridge Univs.
Joined Indian civil service 22; Asst. Commr. Central Provinces, Officiating Deputy Commr. 27; Under-Sec. to Government, Central Provinces 32; Officiating Revenue Sec. 33; Deputy Indian Trade Commr. 34 and Acting Indian Trade Commr. 34 and 35; Deputy Sec. Commerce Dept. Government of India 37; Deputy Commr. 37; Tea Controller for India 39; Sec. Commerce Dept. 46-47; Sec. Ministry of Transport 47-51; Sec. Ministry of Commerce and Industry 51-52; Special Sec. Cabinet and Sec. Planning Comm. 52-53; Cabinet Sec. and Sec. Planning Comm. Government of India 53-57; Gov. of Orissa 57-62; Pres. Maritime Freight Comm. 62-67;

Gov. Dir., Board of Dirs., Indian Shipping companies 65-67.

Flat 7, Silver Foil, N. Gamadia Road, Bombay 26; and Commerce House, Ballard Estate, Bombay, India. Telephone: 361-922.

Sulaiman, Ali Haider; Iraqi diplomatist and businessman; b. 1905; ed. American Univ., Beirut.

Government official at Ministries of Education, Interior and Foreign Affairs 30-47; Minister of Social Affairs 47-48, of Public Works and Communications 49-50, of Development 53-54, of Economics 54; Ambassador to W. Germany 56-59; to United States 59-64, concurrently to Canada 61-64, also Minister to Cuba June 60-64; Under-Sec. of State for Foreign Affairs 59; Vice-Chair. del. to UN 56, 59, 60, 61, 62, 63; Under-Sec. of State for Foreign Affairs 64; Ambassador to Switzerland 64-66, to Italy 66-68; retd. to private business 68. Publ. *History of Modern European Civilisation* (Arabic) 31.

c/o Ministry of Foreign Affairs, Baghdad, Iraq.

Sulek, Miroslav; Czechoslovak journalist; b. 15 March 1918; ed. Universita Karlova, Prague.

Imprisoned and in underground movement 40-45; worked in youth and students orgs. 45-46; posts in District Orgs. of Communist Party of Czechoslovakia, later Central Cttee. 46-62; Gen. Dir. Czechoslovak News Agency 62-; mem. Presidium, Central Cttee. Union of Czechoslovak Journalists 63-; Chair. of Board, Photo Int. 65-; Order of 25th Feb. 1948, Resistance Award, Award for Merit in Construction 65, Order of Labour 68, Bulgarian Order of Labour.

Czechoslovak News Agency, Opletalova 5, Prague 1, Czechoslovakia.

Suleyman, Hikmet Sami; Iraqi diplomatist; b. 17 Aug. 1912; ed. Baghdad Coll., American Univ. of Beirut and Georgetown Univ., Washington D.C.

With Ministry for Foreign Affairs 33-; Attaché Ankara 36-39; Acting-Consul Istanbul 39; Sec. in charge of Foreign Exchange Control, Nat. Bank of Iraq 46-49; Attaché Beirut 49-50, Washington 50-54, Karachi 54-55; Consul-Gen. Jerusalem 55-58, Damascus 58-60; Deputy Under-Sec. Ministry for Foreign Affairs 60-61; Minister Bonn 61-63; Ambassador to France 63-66, to Morocco 66-; awarded Grosses Bundesverdienstkreuz. Publs. *Oil in Iraq, Rules of Diplomacy and Protocol* 61. Embassy of Iraq, 6 Avenue Victoire, Rabat, Morocco.

Sullivan, Ed(ward) Vincent; American journalist and radio and television compère; b. 28 Sept. 1902; ed. Port Chester High School.

Reporter Port Chester *Daily Item* 18-19, *Hartford Post* 19; sports writer New York *Evening Main* 20-24, *World* 24-25, *Morning Telegraph* and *Philadelphia Ledger* 25-27; Sports Editor *Evening Graphic* 27-29; columnist *Daily News* 32-; radio compère 32-; played vaudeville Loewe's State Theater, New York, Roxy, Capitol, Chicago 33-50, *Ed. Sullivan Entertains* programme, CBS 42-; compère *The Ed. Sullivan Show* CBS-TV 48-; LaSalle Coll. journalism award.

Publs. *Mister Lee, The Story of the Shuberts* 48; TV biographies of Rodgers and Hammerstein, Helen Hayes, Beatrice Lillie, Walt Disney, Cole Porter; *The Story of Ascap, The Story of Samuel Goldwyn, The Story of Robert E. Sherwood;* film scripts *There Goes my Heart* 38, *Ma, He's Making Eyes at Me;* TV play *Big Town Czar.*

c/o C.B.S. Television, 485 Madison Avenue, New York City 22, N.Y., U.S.A.

Sullivan, John Lawrence, A.B., LL.B.; American lawyer; b. 16 June 1899; ed. Dartmouth Coll. and Harvard Univ.

Served in U.S. Navy, First World War 18; admitted to New Hampshire Bar 23; began practice in Manchester, N.H., as mem. of firm Sullivan and White 24;

County Solicitor Hillsborough County 29-33; Partner, Sullivan and Sullivan 30; became sole owner 31; now senior partner Sullivan & Wynot, Manchester, N.H., and Sullivan, Shea & Kenney, Washington, D.C.; Asst. to Commr. of Internal Revenue Sept. 39; Asst. Sec. of the Treasury Jan. 40-Nov. 44; Asst. Sec. of Navy for Air July 45-June 46; Under-Sec. of the Navy June 46-47; Sec. of the Navy 47-49; Dir. Aluminium Ltd., The Martin Marietta Corpn., Brown Co., Nat. Savings and Trust Co., M.G.M., Naval Historical Foundation, Navy League of the U.S.; Trustee, Dartmouth Coll.; mem. Nat. Advisory Council, Foundation for Religious Action in Social and Civil Order; mem. Advisory Board, Inst. of Contemporary Russian Studies, Fordham Univ.; Hon. LL.D. (Duquesne, New Hampshire, Portland Univs., Dartmouth, Loyola Colls.); Democrat.

1330 Union Street, Manchester, N.H., U.S.A. Telephone: 338-1000 (Washington, D.C.).

Sullivan, Walter Seager; American journalist and author; b. 12 Jan. 1918; ed. Groton School and Yale Univ.

Field Work, Alaska, American Museum of Natural History 35; *New York Times* 40-; U.S. Navy 40-46; Foreign Corresp., Far East, *New York Times* 48-50, UN 50-52, Germany and Berlin 52-56, U.S. Antarctic Expeditions 46-47, 54-55, 56-57, Science News Editor 60-63, Science Editor 64-; Gov. Arctic Inst. of North America 59-66; Councillor, American Geographical Soc. 59-; Westinghouse Award of American Asscn. for Advancement of Science 63; George Polk Memorial Award, New York 59; Int. Non-Fiction Book Prize, Frankfurt 65.

Publs. *Quest for a Continent* 57, *White Land of Adventure* 57, *Assault on the Unknown* 61, *We Are Not Alone* 64. Office: *New York Times,* Times Square, New York; Home: 66 Indian Head Road, Riverside, Conn., U.S.A. Telephone: 203-637-3318.

Sullivan, William Healy; American diplomatist; b. 12 Oct. 1922; ed. Brown Univ. and Fletcher School of Law and Diplomacy.

U.S. Navy 43-46; Foreign Service 47-, served Bangkok 47-49, Calcutta 49-50, Tokyo 50-52, Rome 52-55, The Hague 55-58; Officer-in-Charge, Burma Affairs, Dept. of State 58-59; Foreign Affairs Officer 59; UN Adviser, Bureau of Far Eastern Affairs 60-63; Special Asst. to Under-Sec. for Political Affairs 63-64; Ambassador to Laos 64-.

American Embassy, Vientiane, Laos.

Sullo, Fiorentino; Italian politician; b. 29 March 1921. Member of Chamber of Deputies 48-; fmr. Under-Sec. for Defence, Under-Sec. for Industry and Commerce; Under-Sec. for State Participation; Minister of Transport 60; Minister of Labour and Social Insurance 60-62; of Public Works 62-63; Christian Democrat.

Chamber of Deputies, Montecitorio, Rome, Italy.

Sulman Al Khalifah, H.H. Shaikh Isa Bin; Ruler of the State of Bahrain; b. 33.

Appointed heir-apparent by his father, H.H. Shaikh Sulman bin Hamad al Khalifah 58; succeeded as Shaikh on the death of his father Nov. 61.

The Palace, Manama, Bahrain, Persian Gulf.

Sulzberger, Arthur Hays (father of Arthur Ochs Sulzberger, *q.v.*), B.S.; American newspaper proprietor; b. 12 Sept. 1891; ed. Horace Mann High School and Columbia Univ.

Started work in textile business in New York; attended Business Men's Training Camp, Plattsburg, N.Y. 16; commd 2nd Lieutenant, Field Artillery 17; in newspaper business 19-; publisher of *New York Times* 35-61; Pres. New York Times Co. 35-57; Dir. and Chair. of Board New York Times Co., Interstate Broadcasting Co.; Pres. and Publisher *Chattanooga Times* 55-57; Dir. and Chair. of Board of Times Printing Co., Chattanooga

57-; Chair. Chattanooga Publishing Co.; Dir. Spruce Falls Power and Paper Co., Ltd., Toronto 26-61; Dir. The Associated Press 43-52, The Woodrow Wilson Foundation 54-57, and other orgs.; Trustee, Columbia Univ. 44-59, The Rockefeller Foundation 38-57, Metropolitan Museum of Art, N.Y. Foundation 32-60, etc.; Gov. Thomas Jefferson Memorial Foundation; Fellow, New York Acad. of Arts and Sciences; Hon. LL.D. Rollins, Union, Dartmouth, Knox, Colby Colls., Harvard, Fairleigh Dickinson, Pittsburgh, Columbia, Colgate Univs.; Litt.D. Brown, Chattanooga, John Carroll Univs., Jewish Theological Seminary, etc.
Home: 1115 Fifth Avenue, New York 28, N.Y.; "Hillandale", 1233 Rock Rimmon Road, Stamford, Conn.; Office: *The New York Times*, 229 West 43rd Street, New York, N.Y. 10036, U.S.A.

Sulzberger, Arthur Ochs (son of Arthur Hays Sulzberger, *q.v.*); American newspaper executive; b. 5 Feb. 1926; ed. Columbia Univ.
U.S. Marine Corps., Second World War and Korean War; The New York Times Co., New York City 51-, Asst. Treas. 58-63, Pres. and Publisher 63-; Dir., Times Printing Co., Chattanooga, Spruce Falls Power and Paper Co. Ltd., Gaspesia Pulp and Paper Co. Ltd. of Canada; Chair. Teaching Systems and Resources Corpn.; Trustee Columbia Univ., mem. Coll. Council.
229 West 43rd Street, New York City, N.Y. 10036, U.S.A.
Telephone: 556-1234.

Sulzberger, Cyrus Leo, B.S.; American journalist; b. 27 Oct. 1912; ed. Harvard Univ.
Columnist for *New York Times*.
Publs. *Sit Down with John L. Lewis* 38, *The Big Thaw* 56, *What's Wrong with U.S. Foreign Policy* 59, *My Brother Death* 61, *The Test: de Gaulle and Algeria* 62, *Unfinished Revolution* 65, *History of World War II* 66.
New York Times, Times Square, New York City, N.Y., U.S.A.

Sulzer, Georg; Swiss mechanical engineer and business executive; b. 29 Dec. 1909; ed. Kantonsschule, Winterthur, and Eidgenössiche Technische Hochschule, Zürich.
Direct descendant (fourth generation) of founders of Sulzer Brothers; joined Sulzer Brothers 34, started in Technical Draftsman's School, spent three years with Sulzer Brothers, Paris; Man. Diesel Engine Sales Dept., Sulzer Brothers 45-48, Man. Dir., Sulzer Brothers 48-, Chair. of Board 59-; mem. Swiss Chamber of Commerce, Inst. für Auslandforschung, Board of Swiss Nat. Bank.
Gebrüder Sulzer Aktiengesellschaft, Winterthur, Switzerland.

Sumitra, The Most Reverend, B.A.; Indian ecclesiastic; b. 13 Nov. 1888; ed. Central Coll., Bangalore, Madras Univ., United Theological Coll., Bangalore.
Tutor Union Kanarese Seminary Tumkur 16-18; Pastor South India United Church Bangalore City 18, Bellary 21; Prof. United Theological Coll., Bangalore 34; Bishop of the Diocese of Cuddapah 47; Bishop of the Diocese of Rayalaseema 50-63; Moderator of the Church of South India 54-62; Hon. D.D. Serampore Coll.
Publs. *Notes on Revelation Ch.* 2-3, *The Restoration of Israel: Isaiah* 40-66 (in Kanarese).
XXV 2 (3), Fort, Bellary, South India.

Summerfield, Arthur Ellsworth; American businessman; b. 17 March 1899; ed. public schools at Bay City and Flint, Mich.
Entered real estate business 18; became an oil distributor 24; formed Summerfield Chevrolet Co., Flint, Mich., Pres. 29, Pres. Bryant Properties Corporation 38-; during Second World War served as Michigan Chair. of Automobile Cttee. of Nat. Automobile Dealers' Asscn. in charge of recruitment for Ordnance Dept., U.S. Army; Mich. Dir. of Nat. Automobile

Dealers Asscn. 42-49; Regional Vice-Pres. of Asscn. and Chair. Post-war Planning Cttee.; Finance Dir. Republican State Central Cttee. of Mich. 43-44; Republican Nat. Committeeman from Mich. 44-52; Regional Vice-Chair. Republican Nat. Finance Cttee. for N. Central States 46; Acting Chair. "Strategy Cttee." of Republican Party 49; Chair. Republican Nat. Cttee. 52-53; Postmaster-Gen. of U.S. Jan. 53-61; Hon. LL.D. (Michigan Univ., Defiance Coll., Ohio, Illinois Inst. of Technology).
Publ. *U.S. Mail: The Story of United States Postal Service* 60.
2952 Parkside Drive, Flint 3, Mich., U.S.A.

Summers, Sir Richard Felix, Kt., B.A., M.INST.T.; British steel executive; b. 10 Dec. 1902; ed. Shrewsbury School and Clare Coll., Cambridge.
John Summers and Sons Ltd. 25-, Dir. 31-, Man. Dir. 36-38, Chair. 38-; Dir. The Steetley Co. Ltd., District Bank Ltd. (Chair. 67-), Royal Insurance Co. Ltd., Liverpool London and Globe Co. Ltd.
Denna Hall, Burton Point, Wirral, Cheshire, England.

Summers, Sir Spencer, B.A., M.P.; British industrialist; b. 27 Oct. 1902; ed. Wellington Coll., Trinity Coll. Cambridge and Armstrong Coll. Newcastle-on-Tyne.
Joined John Summers & Sons Ltd. 26, Dir. 31-; Pres. Int. Sheets Comptoirs, Int. Steel Cartel 36-39; Chair. Sheet Makers' Conf. 38-39; Dir. of Sheets, Iron and Steel Control 39-40; Cons. M.P. for Northampton 40-45, for Aylesbury 50-; Dir.-Gen. Regional Org., Ministry of Supply 41-44; Parl. Sec. Dept. of Overseas Trade May-July 45; Chair. Management Cttee. Outward Bound Trust.
Thenford House, nr. Banbury, Oxon., England.

Summerskill, Baroness (Life Peeress) cr. 61, of Ken Wood in the County of London; **Edith Clara Summerskill**, P.C., C.H.; British physician and politician; b. 1901; ed. King's Coll. London and Charing Cross Hospital.
Qualified Doctor 24; Vice-Pres. Socialist Medical Asscn.; Labour M.P. for West Fulham 38-55, Warrington 55-61; mem. Middlesex County Council for Green Lanes Div. of Tottenham; mem. Cttee. on Women's Services 42, Women's Consultative Cttee. to Ministry of Labour, Women-Power Cttee.; Pres. Married Women's Asscn.; Parl. Sec. Ministry of Food 45-50; Minister of Nat. Insurance 50-51.
Publs. *Women, Fall In* 41, *Babies Without Tears* 41, *The Ignoble Art* 56, *Letters to my Daughter* 58, *A Woman's World* 67.
Pond House, Millfield Lane, Highgate, London, N.6, England.

Summerson, Sir John Newenham, C.B.E., F.B.A., F.S.A., A.R.I.B.A.; British architectural historian; b. 25 Nov. 1904; ed. Univ. Coll., London.
Served in architects' offices and taught Edinburgh Coll. of Art 29-30, took up architectural journalism; on staff *Architect and Building News* 34-40; Deputy Dir. Nat. Buildings Record 40-45; Curator Sir John Soane's Museum 45-; mem. Royal Comm. on Historical Monuments, Historic Buildings Council (Ministry of Works), Architectural and Historic Buildings Cttee. (Ministry of Housing), Chair. Nat. Council for Diplomas in Art and Design; Lecturer in History of Architecture, Birkbeck Coll.; Slade Prof. of Fine Art, Oxford 58-59; Ferens Prof. of Fine Art, Hull 60-61, Slade Prof. of Fine Art, Cambridge 66-67; Bampton Lecturer, Columbia 67-68; Hon. D. Litt. (Leicester and Oxford), Hon. D.Sc. (Edinburgh).
Publs. *John Nash* 34, *Georgian London* 45, *Heavenly Mansions* 49, *Sir John Soane* 52, *Sir Christopher Wren* 53, *Architecture in Britain 1530-1830* (Pelican History of Art) 53, *The Classical Language of Architecture* 64. *Book of John Thorpe* (Walpole Soc., Vol. XL) 66, *Inigo Jones* 66.
1 Eton Villas, London, N.W.3, England.
Telephone: 01-722-6247.

Sun Yat-sen, Madame (Soong Ching-Ling); Chinese politician and welfare worker; b. 90; ed. Wesleyan Coll. for Women, Macon, Georgia, U.S.A.

Sec. to Pres. Sun Yat-sen when he headed the Provisional Govt. at Nanking in 12; after failure of second revolution she fled to Japan with Sun Yat-sen and married him there in 14; after death of Sun Yat-sen in 25 she led the extreme left wing of the Kuomintang; founded China Defence League in 38 (reorganised in 45 as China Welfare Fund and in 50 changed title to China Welfare Institute); Vice-Chair. Cen. People's Govt. 49; Vice-Pres. Sino-Soviet Friendship Asscn. 49; awarded Stalin Peace Prize 51; Pres. Chinese People's Nat. Cttee. in Defence of Children 51-; Hon. Pres. All-China Democratic Women's Fed. 51-; Chair. China Welfare Inst. 51-; Vice-Chair. Standing Cttee. N.P.C. 54-59; Vice-Chair. Second Nat. Cttee. C.P.P.C.C. 54-59; Pres. Sino-Soviet Friendship Asscn. 54-; Vice-Chair. Chinese People's Republic 59-.

Publ. *The Struggle for New China* 52.

Office of the Vice-Chairman, Chinese People's Republic, Peking, China.

Sunario, Dr.; Indonesian diplomatist and university principal; b. 28 Aug. 1902; ed. Univ. of Leiden, Netherlands.

Judicial Officer, District Court, Madiun and Ponorogo 23-24; Solicitor and barrister in Djakarta, Makasar and Medan 27-41; Chief Ed. *Sedya-Tama*, Jogjakarta 41-42; Senior Official, Dept. of Justice, Djakarta 42-45; co-founder, later Dean of Law Faculty and Lecturer in Political Sciences, Gadjah Mada Univ., Jogjakarta 46-47; Political Sec. Del. of Republic of Indonesia for Indonesia-Dutch negotiations 47-48; Deputy Chief Ed. *Pemandangan*, Djakarta 49-50; mem. Provisional Parl., Djakarta 50-53; Chair. Parl. Mission to U.K. 51; Chair. Indonesian U.N. Asscn., Djakarta 51-53; Chair. Indonesian Nat. Group of the Interparl. Union 51-53; Foreign Minister 53-55 and Leader of Del. to Republic of Indonesia to Gen. Assembly of U.N. in N.Y. 53 and 54; Chair. Indonesian Del. Colombo Plan Conf., Ottawa 54; Deputy Chair. Indonesian Del. Asian-African Conf., Bandung 55; Extraordinary Prof. in Constitutional and Diplomatic History, Univ. of Indonesia 55-56; Ambassador Extraordinary and Plenipotentiary, London 56-61; Prof. of Political Science and Int. Law and Relations, President of Diponegoro State University, Semirang 63-; founder mem. Nationalist Party (P.N.I.).

Universitas Diponegoro, Djalan Hajam Wuruk, Semirang, Java, Indonesia.

Sunay, Gen. Cevdet; Turkish army officer and politician; b. 10 Feb. 1900; ed. Kuleli Military High School, Military Coll., Istanbul, and Turkish Military Staff Acad.

With Turkish Army 16-66, Gen. 59; Chief of Operations, Gen. Staff 59-60; C.-in-C. Land Forces 60, Chief of Staff Aug. 60-66; Senator 66; Pres. of Turkey 66-.

Office of the President, Ankara, Turkey.

Sundara Rajan, K. S.; Indian civil servant and international bank official; b. 14; ed. Univ. of Madras.

Defence Accounts Dept., Govt. of India 38-44, Asst. Financial Adviser (Defence) 44-47, Dep. Financial Adviser, Defence Budget 47-51, Commnr. of Income Tax 51-56, mem. Central Board of Revenue 56-60; Joint Sec. (External Finance), Govt. of India 60-63; Minister (Economic) Indian Embassy, Washington 63-; Exec. Dir. for India, Int. Bank for Reconstruction and Development (World Bank) 63-.

Embassy of India, Washington, D.C., U.S.A.

Sunderland, Sydney, C.M.G., D.SC., M.D., B.S., F.R.A.C.P., F.R.A.C.S., F.A.A.; Australian anatomist; b. 31 Dec. 1910; ed. Melbourne Univ.

Senior Lecturer in Anatomy Melbourne Univ. 36-37; Asst. Neurologist Alfred Hospital Melbourne 36-37; Demonstrator Dept. of Human Anatomy Oxford 38,

Prof. of Anatomy and Histology Melbourne Univ. 38-61, of Experimental Neurology 61-, Dean Medical Faculty 53-; Visiting Specialist, injuries of the peripheral nervous system, Australian General Military Hospital 41-45; Visiting Prof. of Anatomy, Johns Hopkins Univ. 53-54; mem. Nat. Health and Medical Research Council of Australia 53-; Foundation Fellow and Sec. for Biological Sciences, Australian Acad. of Sciences 55-58; Trustee Nat. Museum of Victoria 54-; mem. Zool. Board of Victoria 44-65; Deputy Chair. Advisory Cttee. of Victorian Mental Hygiene Authority 52-63; rep. Pacific Science Council 57-; mem. Defence Research and Development Policy Cttee. 57-, Medical Services Cttee. 57-, Commonwealth Dept. of Defence; Nat. Radiation Advisory Cttee. 57-64, Chair. 58-64; Chair Safety Review Cttee. 61-, Australian Atomic Energy Comm.; Medical Research Advisory Cttee. of Nat. Health and Medical Research Council 53-, Chair. 64-; Chair. Protective Chemistry Research Advisory Cttee., Dept. of Supply 64-; mem. Scientific Advisory Cttee. Australian Atomic Energy Comm. 62-63; Australian Univs. Comm. 62-, Cttee. of Management Royal Melbourne Hospital 63-.

Publ. *Nerves and Nerve Injuries* 68.

Department of Experimental Neurology, University of Melbourne, Parkville 3052, Victoria, Australia.

Telephone: 340484.

Sunderland, Thomas Elbert, A.B., LL.B., J.D.; American lawyer and business executive; b. 28 April 1907; ed. Univs. of Michigan and California.

Legal practice, Detroit 30-31, New York City 31-48, Chicago 48-59; U.S. Air Force 42-46; Gen. Counsel Pan American Petroleum and Transport Co., American Oil Co. 40-48; Dir., mem. Exec. Cttee. Pan American Petroleum and Transport Co. 47-54; Gen. Counsel, Dir. Standard Oil Co. (Ind.) 48-59; Vice-Pres., mem. Exec. Cttee. 54-59; Pres. and Dir. United Fruit Co. 60-65, Chair. of Board and Dir. 65-; Dir. Nat. Cash Register Co., Johns-Manville Corpn., Liberty Mutual Insurance Co., First Nat. Bank of Boston.

Office: United Fruit Company, Prudential Center, Boston, Mass. 02199; Home: 66 Fernwood Road, Chestnut Hill, Mass. 02167, U.S.A.

Sunesen, Frede; Danish banker; b. 11 May 1915; ed. Commercial Coll., Århus.

Bank official 31-50; Manager Veile Bank 50-57; mem. Board of Govs., Nat. Bank of Denmark 57-; mem. Boards of Mortgage Fund for Danish Agriculture 60, Scandinavian Airlines System 57 and Manufacturing and Manual Industries Finance Corpn. 58; Knight Order of Dannebrog, First Grade.

Øresundshoj 24, DK 2920 Charlottenlund, Denmark.

Sung Jen-chiung; Chinese soldier and administrator; b. 03.

Joined Chinese Communist Army in 27 and was engaged on political work in various army units; entered Central Party School of C.C.P. 43; commanded Central Hopeh Mil. Region 47; commissar in People's Liberation Army 49; Vice-Chair. Yunnan Mil. and Admin. Council and Sec. Yunnan Provincial Committee of C.C.P. 50; Vice-Chair. South-West Mil. and Admin. Council 52; mem. of Council for Nat. Defence 54; decorated for war service 55; appointed Lieut.-Gen. in People's Liberation Army 56; Asst. Sec.-Gen. Central Cttee. of C.C.P. 56; Minister, Third Ministry of Machine Building 56-59, Second Ministry 59-61; First Sec. Northeast Bureau, Chinese C.P. 61-; Dep. Chair. Chinese People's Political Consultative Conference (C.P.P.C.C.) 65-.

Northeast Bureau of Chinese Communist Party, Peking, China.

Sung Shao-wen; Chinese administrator; b. 06; ed. Peking Univ.

Arrested and imprisoned for anti-Japanese activity 36; guerilla activity, Wu-tai Mountains 37; Chair. Border

Govt. 38; mem. North China Govt. 48; del. for liberated areas of North China to C.P.P.C.C. 49; joined Ministry of Finance; Sec.-Gen. Finance and Economic Comm., State Council 53; Vice-Minister of Light Industry 54; Vice-Chair. Nat. Economic Comm. 56, State Planning Comm. 62-.
State Planning Commission, Peking, China.

Suomela, Vilho Samuli, PH.D.; Finnish agricultural economist; b. 27 July 1918; ed. Helsinki Univ.
Fellow, Helsinki Univ. 46-50; Manager of Experimental Farm, Helsinki Univ. 50-52; Dir. of Research Inst. of Agric. Econs. 52-; Sec. Finnish Acad. 57-59; Minister of Agriculture 63-64.
Publs. *On the Influence of the Location of Fields on Farming* 50, *Development of Productivity in Finnish Agriculture* 58.
Rukkila, Helsinki 10, Finland.
Telephone: Helsinki 434842.

Suontausta, Tauno Erland, DR. JUR.; Finnish lawyer; b. 18 Feb. 1907.
Worked in Ministry of Foreign Affairs, finally Chief of the Legal Dept. 34-47; Gen. Sec. of SOTEVA (War Reparations Supervisory Board) 48-50; Lecturer in Int. Law, Helsinki Univ. 48-58; Minister of Justice 48-50; mem. of Permanent Court of Arbitration 49-; mem. Supreme Admin. Court 50-55; mem. High Court of Impeachment 57-; Man. Dir. Fed. Finnish Insurance Companies 55; Commdr. Finnish Lion, etc.
Publs. *Valtion alueellisesta puolueettomuudesta* (Territorial Neutrality) 44, *Yhdistyneet Kansakunnat* (United Nations) 46, *La Souveraineté des Etats* 55, *Sananvapaus* (Freedom of Speech) 59.
Professorintie 10A, Helsinki 33, Finland.
Telephone: 48-66-74.

Suphamongkhon, Konthi, LL.B.; Thai lawyer and diplomatist; b. 3 Aug. 1916; ed. Univs. of Bangkok and Paris.
Chief of Section, Political Div., Ministry of Foreign Affairs 40-42; Second Sec., Tokyo 42-44; Chief of Political Div., Western Affairs Dept., Ministry of Foreign Affairs 44-48, Dir.-Gen. Western Affairs Dept. 48-50, Dir.-Gen. United Nations Dept. 50-52; Minister to Australia 52-56, Ambassador to Australia, concurrently to New Zealand 56-59; Dir.-Gen. Dept. of Int. Orgs., Ministry of Foreign Affairs 59-63; Adviser on Foreign Affairs to Prime Minister 62-64; Sec.-Gen. South East Asia Treaty Organisation (SEATO) 64-65; Ambassador to German Fed. Republic 65-; numerous decorations.
Publ. *Thailand and Her Relations with France* 40.
Royal Thai Embassy, Ubierstrasse 65, Bad Godesberg, German Federal Republic.
Telephone: Bad Godesberg 65966.

Suppes, Patrick, B.S., PH.D.; American educator; b. 17 March 1922; ed. Univ. of Chicago and Columbia Univ.
Instructor, Stanford Univ. 50-52, Asst. Prof. Dept. of Philosophy, Stanford Univ. 52-55, Assoc. Prof. 55-59, Assoc. Dean, School of Humanities and Sciences 58-61, Dir. Honors Program in Quantitative Methods in the Behavioral Sciences 58-, Prof. Dept. of Philosophy 59-, Prof. of Philosophy and Statistics 60- also of Educ. 67-, Dir. Inst. for Mathematical Studies in the Social Sciences, Stanford 59-, Chair. Dept. of Philosophy 63-; Fellow American Asscn. for Advancement of Science, American Psychological Asscn.; mem. Nat. Acad. of Educ. 65; Palmer O. Johnson Memorial Award 67.
Publs. *Introduction to Logic* 57, *Decision Making: An Experimental Approach* (with D. Davidson and S. Siegel) 57, *Axiomatic Set Theory* 60, *Markov Learning Models for Multiperson Interactions* (with R. C. Atkinson) 60, *First Course in Mathematical Logic* 64, *Experiments in Second-Language Acquisition* (with E. Crothers)

67, *Computer Assisted Instruction: Stanford's 1965-66 Arithmetic Program* (with M. Jerman and D. Brian) 68.
Ventura Hall, Stanford University, Stanford, Calif. 94305, U.S.A.
Telephone: 415-321-2300, Ext. 3111.

Surganov, Fyodor Anisimovich; Soviet politician; b. 7 June 1911; ed. Byelorussian Agricultural Inst.
Komsomol and Partisan work 39-45; Mem. staff of Cen. Cttee. of Communist Party of Byelorussia 45-47; Second Sec., Minsk Regional Cttee., C.P. of Byelorussia 47-54, First Sec. 55-56; Chair. Exec. Cttee. of Minsk Regional Soviet of Workers' Deputies 54-55; Sec. Central Cttee. of Communist Party of Byelorussia 56-65, Second Sec. 65-; Cand. mem. Central Cttee. of C.P.S.U. 56-61, mem. 61-; Deputy to Supreme Soviet, U.S.S.R., Chair. Cttee. for Agriculture, Soviet of Union.
Central Committee of the Communist Party of Byelorussia, Minsk, Byelorussian S.S.R., U.S.S.R.

Surkov, Alexei Alexandrovich; Soviet poet; b. 99; ed. Inst. of Red Professors, Moscow.
Alternative mem. Central Cttee. of the C.P.S.U. 56; first Sec. Writers' Union of the U.S.S.R. until 59, Sec. 59-; Pres. U.S.S.R.-Great Britain Soc. 58-; Deputy to U.S.S.R. Supreme Soviet; State Prizewinner 46, 51; awarded Orders of Lenin (twice), Red Banner, Red Star (twice), Badge of Honour.
Publs. *Let's Sing* 30, *Peace to the World* 50; poems: *Moscow is at our Backs, Flame Beats in the Small Stove* 42, *Victory!* 43; *Collected Works* (two vols.) 54, 59, *Songs of Mankind* 58-61, *Bullet is Frightened by Brave Man* 64, *The Voice of Time* 65.
Writers' Union of the U.S.S.R., 52 Vorovsky Street, Moscow, U.S.S.R.

Suromihardjo, Maj.-Gen. Suadi; Indonesian army officer and diplomatist; b. 1921; ed. Staff Coll., Quetta, Pakistan, Fort Bliss, U.S.A.
Department of Interior 39; 1st. Lieutenant Indonesian Army 42; C.O. (Lt.-Col.) 1st Regiment 10th Div. 45; mem. U.N. Comm. for Indonesia 47; Dep. Chief of Staff Diponegoro Div., Central Java 50; C.O. 21st Regiment, VI Div., South Kalimantan 51; C.O. 23rd Regiment VII Div. South Sulawesi 54; C.O. Indonesian Contingent U.N.E.F. Egypt 57; Commandant Indonesian Command and General Staff Coll., Bandung 59; Ambassador to Australia 61-64, to Ethiopia 64-.
Kedutaan Besar Republik Indonesia, P.O.B. 1004, Addis Ababa, Ethiopia; and Tjipinang Tjempedak 1/22, Polonia, Djakarta, Indonesia.

Surrey, Stanley Sterling; American lawyer, professor and government official; b. 3 Oct. 1910; ed. Coll. of City of New York and Columbia Univ. Law School.
Admitted to New York Bar 33; Research Asst., Columbia Univ. Law School 32-33; Attorney, Proskauer, Rose and Paskus, New York 33; Nat. Recovery Admin. Wash. 33-35; Nat. Labor Relations Board, Wash. 35-37; U.S. Treasury Dept. 38-44, 46-47; Prof. Univ. of Calif. Law School 47-49, Harvard Univ. School of Law 50-61; Asst. Sec. for Tax Policy, U.S. Treasury Dept. 61-; mem. American Acad. of Arts and Sciences.
Publs. Co-Editor *Federal Income Taxation, Cases and Materials* 61, *Federal Estate and Gift Taxation, Cases and Materials* 61, *Legislation, Cases and Materials* 55.
Office: U.S. Treasury Department, Washington, D.C.; Home: 54 Buckingham Street, Cambridge, Mass., U.S.A.
Telephone: WO 4-5363.

Süskind, W. E.; German writer and radio commentator; b. 10 June 1901.
Editor *Die Literatur* 33-42; mem. Editorial Board *Süddeutsche Zeitung* 47-; mem. Deutsche Akademie für Sprache und Dichtung.
Publs. *Das Morgenlicht* 25, *Tordis* 27, *Jugend* 29, *Mary und ihr Knecht* 32, *Vom ABC zum Sprachkunstwerk* 40,

Pferderennen 50, *Aus dem Wörterbuch des Unmenschen* (with Sternberger and Storz) 57, *Wer hätte das von uns gedacht, 10 Jahre Bundesrepublik Deutschland* 59, *Die Mächtigen vor Gericht* (Nuremberg Trials) 63, *Abziehbilder* 63, *Der nicht ganz Eiserne Kanzler* 65; trans. some of Melville's stories, E. M. Forster's *Howards End*, Lin Yutang's *My Country and My People*, short stories by Karen Blixen.
Seeheim 20, Post Ammerland, Starnbergersee, Bavaria, German Federal Republic.
Telephone: 08177-286.

Suslov, Mikhail Andreevich; Soviet politician; b. 1902; ed. Moscow Inst. of Nat. Economy.
Joined Communist Party 21; lecturer at Moscow Univ. and at Industrial Acad. 29-31; exec. post, Central Control Comm. of C.P.S.U. and People's Commissariat for Workers' and Peasants' Inspection 31-36; Sec. Rostov Regional Cttee. of Party 37-39; First Sec. Stavropol Territorial and City Cttee. of C.P.S.U. 39-44; during war, mem. Mil. Council for North Caucasus front and Chief of Staff, Stavropol Territory partisan detachments; Chair. C.P.S.U. Central Cttee. Bureau for Lithuania 44; held executive positions in Central Cttee. of Party during 46; Sec. of Central Cttee. 47-; Ed.-in-Chief *Pravda* 49-50; mem. Presidium of U.S.S.R. Supreme Soviet 50-54; Deputy of U.S.S.R. Supreme Soviet; Chair. Foreign Comm., Soviet of Union of Supreme Soviet of U.S.S.R. 54; mem. Presidium, Central Cttee. of C.P.S.U. 55-66, Politburo 66-; awarded Order of Lenin (twice), Order of the Patriotic War (1st Class), Hero of Socialist Labour; and other decorations.
C.P.S.U. Central Committee, 4 Staraya ploshchad, Moscow, U.S.S.R.

Suslov, Vladimir Pavlovich; Soviet diplomatist; b. 1923.
Member Soviet Delegation to UN 53-55, 57-61; Senior Asst. and Adviser to U.S.S.R. Foreign Minister 61-63; UN Under-Sec. for Political and Security Council Affairs until 65; at staff, Ministry of Foreign Affairs 48-57, 65-.
Ministry of Foreign Affairs, 32-34 Smolenskaya-Sennaya ploshchad, Moscow, U.S.S.R.

Sussekind, Arnaldo Lopes; Brazilian lawyer and public servant; b. 9 July 1917; ed. Colégio Mallet Soares, Rio de Janeiro, and Univ. do Brasil, Rio de Janeiro.
Federal Public Service 38-, Asst., Nat. Council of Labour; Regional Attorney, São Paulo 41-44, Rio de Janeiro 44-51; mem. Comm. on Labour Laws 42-43; Dir. of Recreation and Cultural Assistance 51-53; Dir. Dept. of Nat. Security, Minister of Labour 55-61; Pres. Perm. Comm. on Social Laws 60-61; Legal Counsel, Ministry of Labour 61-62; Minister of Labour and Social Welfare 64-65; Minister of Higher Tribunal of Labour Dec. 65-; several decorations.
Publs. numerous works on labour laws.
Avenida Roderigo Otávio 177, ap. 401, Rio de Janeiro, Brazil.

Susskind, David Howard; American television producer; b. 19 Dec. 1920; ed. Harvard Univ.
Publicity Dept., Warner Bros. also with Universal Picture Corpn. 46-48; Talent Agent, Century Artists, and Music Corpn. of America 49-52; Co-owner and Pres., Talent Assocs. Ltd., New York 52-; Chair., T.V. Discussion programme *Open End* 58-; producer T.V. programmes including duPont Show of the Month, Philco Playhouse, and Kraft Theater; numerous T.V. awards.
Produced Broadway plays *A Very Special Baby* 56, *Rashomon* 59, *Handful of Fire* 58, *Kelly* 65, *All in Good Time* 65.
Films *Edge of the City* 56, *Raisin in the Sun* 60, *Requiem*

for a Heavyweight 61, *All the Way Home* 63, T.V. programmes *Festival of Performing Arts*, *Play of the Week*, *East Side*, *West Side*.
444 Madison Avenue, New York City, N.Y., U.S.A.

Susskind, (Jan) Walter; British (born Czechoslovak) musician; b. 1 May 1913; ed. State Acad. of Music, Prague.
Conductor German Opera, Prague 33-38; pianist London Czech Trio 33-42; Principal Conductor, Royal Carl Rosa Opera Co., England 43-45; Principal Guest Conductor, Sadler's Wells Opera Co. and Glyndebourne Opera (at First Edinburgh Festival) 45-47; Principal Conductor, Scottish Nat. Orchestra 46-52; Principal Conductor, Victorian Symphony Orchestra, Melbourne 53-55; Musical Dir. and First Conductor, Toronto Symphony Orchestra, Toronto, Canada 56-65; Music Dir. Aspen, Colo., Music Festival 61-; Music Dir. St. Louis Symphony Orchestra 68-; also Guest Conductor of many leading orchestras in the world.
Works include various compositions for piano, violin and orchestra, also songs, instrumental music to films and plays.
c/o Powell Symphony Hall, St. Louis, Missouri, U.S.A.

Sutermeister, Henry; Swiss composer; b. 12 Aug. 1910. Studied philology at Paris and Munich, and music at the Acad. of Music at Munich.
Professor, Hochschule für Musik, Hanover 63-; Pres. Schweizerische Mechaulizenz; Salzburg Opera Prize 65. Operas include: *L'araignée noire*, *Romeo and Juliet*, *The Tempest*, *Niobe*, *Raskolnikoff* (Stockholm and Scala, Milan), *Botte Rouge*, *Titus Feuerfuchs* (opera burlesque) (Basle and Brussels) 58, *Seraphine*, *The Canterville Ghost* (for television) *Madame Bovary* (Zürich) 67; other works: *Missa da Requiem* 53, three piano concertos 54, cello concerto 55; two divertimenti, eight cantatas.
Vaux-sur-Morges, Switzerland.

Sutherland, Sir Gordon Brims Black McIvor, Kt., M.A., B.SC., PH.D., SC.D., F.R.S.; British scientist; b. 8 April 1907; ed. St. Andrews Univ. and Trinity and Pembroke Colls., Cambridge.
Fellow Pembroke Coll. 35-49; Leverhulme Fellow 39; Asst. to Dir. of Scientific Research in Ministry of Supply 40-41; head of group doing infra-red research for various Govt. depts. 41-45; Asst. Dir. in Colloid Science, Cambridge Univ. 44-47; mem. Council of Senate, Cambridge Univ. 46-49; Reader in Spectroscopy, Cambridge Univ. 47-49; Prof. of Physics, Univ. of Michigan 49-56; Guggenheim Fellow 56; Dir. Nat. Physical Laboratory, Teddington Sept. 56-64; Master of Emmanuel Coll., Cambridge 64-; Gov. London School of Econs. 57-65, Northampton Coll. of Advanced Technology 60-65; mem. Governing Body Coll. of Aeronautics 57-63; Pres. Triple Comm. for Spectroscopy 62-63; Vice-Pres. Int. Org. for Biophysics 61-, Royal Soc. 61-63, Int. Union of Pure and Applied Physics 63-; Pres. Inst. of Physics and the Physical Soc. 64-66; mem. of Council for Scientific Policy 65-; Hon. Fellow Pembroke Coll., Cambridge; Hon. LL.D. (St. Andrews), Hon. D.Sc. (Strathclyde).
Publs. include *Infra-red and Raman Spectra* 35.
The Master's Lodge, Emmanuel College, Cambridge, England.
Telephone: Cambridge 58356.

Sutherland, Graham Vivian, O.M.; British artist; b. 24 Aug. 1903; ed. Epsom Coll., Goldsmiths Coll. School of Art and London Univ.
Exhibited XXI Gallery 25 and 28, First Int. Surrealist Exhibition London; Exhibition Rosenberg and Helft Gallery 38, Leicester Galleries 40, Curt Valentin, Buchholz Gallery New York 46, Musée Nat. de l'Art Moderne, Paris 52, Stedelijk Museum, Amsterdam, Kunsthaus, Zürich, Tate Gallery, London 53, Galleria d'Arte Moderna, Turin 65, Haus der Kunst, Munich

67, Cologne 67; works in Tate Gallery, British Museum, Victoria and Albert Museum, London, Museum of Modern Art, New York, Musée de l'Art Moderne, Paris, Musée des Beaux-Arts, Brussels, Albertina, Vienna; Official War Artist during Second World War; Trustee, Tate Gallery 48-54; designed tapestry *Christ in Majesty* for Coventry Cathedral 62; Hon. D.Litt. (Oxford) 62, (Leicester) 65.
White House, Trottiscliffe, W. Malling, Kent, England.

Sutherland, Joan, C.B.E.; Australian opera singer; b. 7 Nov. 1926; ed. St. Catherine's School, Waverley, Sydney.
Début as Dido in Purcell's *Dido and Aeneas*, Sydney 47; Royal Opera Co., Covent Garden, London 52-; has sung leading soprano roles at the Vienna State Opera, La Scala, Milan, Teatro Fenice, Venice, the Paris Opera, Glyndebourne, San Francisco and Chicago Operas, The Metropolitan, New York, etc.
c/o Ingpen & Williams Ltd., 14 Kensington Court, London, W.8, England.

Sutherland, Lucy Stuart, C.B.E., F.R.S.A., F.B.A., M.A., D.LITT.; British university professor and public servant; b. 21 June 1903; ed. Univ. of Witwatersrand, South Africa, and Somerville Coll., Oxford.
Fellow and Tutor in Economic History and Politics, Somerville Coll., Oxford 27-45; Principal and then Asst. Sec. Board of Trade 41-45; Principal, Lady Margaret Hall, Oxford 45-; Chair. Lace Working Party 46; mem. Royal Comm. on Taxation, Profits and Income 51-55, mem. Univ. Grants Cttee.; Hon. Litt.D. (Cantab.) 63, (Kent) 67, Hon. LL.B. (Smith Coll. Northampton, Mass.) 64, Hon. D.Litt. (Glasgow) 66.
Publs. *A London Merchant (1695-1774)* 33, *The East India Company in Eighteenth-Century Politics* 52; edited (with M. McKisack) *Mediaeval Representation and Consent* 36, ed. *The Correspondence of Edmund Burke,* Vol. II 60, etc.
Lady Margaret Hall, Oxford, England.

Sutton, George Paul, A.A., B.S., M.S.; American engineer; b. 5 Sept. 1920; ed. Los Angeles City Coll. and California Inst. of Technology.
Man. of Advanced Design, Rocketdyne (North American Aviation Inc.), Canoga Park, Calif. 46-58; Hunsaker Prof. of Aeronautical Engineering, Mass. Inst. of Technology 58; Chief Scientist Advanced Research Projects Agency (Dept. of Defense) 59-60; Dir. Advanced Research Projects Div. (Inst. of Defense Analyses) 59-60; Asst. to Pres. North American Rockwell Corpn. 60-; Fellow American Inst. of Aeronautics and Astronautics; mem. Deutsche Gesellschaft für Raketentechnik und Raumfahrt, etc.; E. G. Pendray Award, American Rocket Soc. 51.
Publs. *Rocket Propulsion Elements* 49, 54, 63, *Advanced Propulsion Systems* (co-editor) 59.
Rocketdyne, 6633 Canoga Avenue, Canoga Park, Calif., U.S.A.
Telephone: 213-884-2427 (Office).

Sutton, Sir (Oliver) Graham, C.B.E., D.SC., LL.D., F.R.S.; British mathematical physicist; b. 4 Feb. 1903; ed. Univ. Coll. of Wales, Aberystwyth, and Jesus Coll., Oxford.
Lecturer, Univ. Coll. of Wales, Aberystwyth 26-28; Professional Asst., Meteorological Office 28-41; Supt. of Research, Chemical Defence Experimental Establishment, Porton 42-43; Supt. Tank Armament Research 43-45; Chief Supt., Radar Research and Development Establishment, Malvern 45-47; Chair. Atmospheric Pollution Research Cttee. 50-55; Scientific Adviser to the Army Council 51; Dean of Royal Mil. Coll. of Science, Shrivenham 52-53; Bashforth Prof. of Mathematical Physics 47-53; Pres. Royal Meteorological Society 53-55; mem. Exec. Cttee. World Meteorological Organisation 53-65, Chair. Nat. Cttee. Geodesy and Geophysics 60-66,

Natural Environment Research Council 65-; Dir.-Gen. of British Meteorological Office 53-65; Vice-Pres. Univ. Coll. of Wales 67.
Publs. *Atmospheric Turbulence* 48, *The Science of Flight* 49, *Micrometeorology* 53, *Mathematics in Action* 54, *A Compendium of Mathematics and Physics* (with D. S. Meyler) 58, *Understanding Weather* 60, *The Challenge of the Atmosphere* 61, *Mastery of the Air* 66.
c/o Natural Environment Research Council, Alhambra House, Charing Cross Road, London, W.C.2, England.

Suwayyil, Ibrahim Al-; Saudi Arabian diplomatist; b. 16; ed. Saudi Inst., Mecca, and Coll. of Sciences, Cairo.
Minister of Foreign Affairs 60-62; Adviser to King Saud and Head of Political Office in Royal Diwan Jan-Nov. 62; Minister of Agriculture Nov. 62-Aug. 64; Ambassador to United States Aug. 64-.
Embassy of Saudi Arabia, 2800 Woodland Avenue, N.W., Washington, D.C., U.S.A.

Suzuki, Gengo; Japanese financial executive; b. 11 Feb. 1904; ed. Government College of Commerce, Taiho-ku and Univ. of Wisconisn.
Lecturer and Professor in Econ. Govt. Coll. of Commerce, Taiho-ku, Taiwan 31-49, concurrently, Civil Administration Official, Govt.-Gen. Taiwan 44-45, Prof. of Econs., Taiwan Province School of Law and Commerce 45-47, Prof. of Econ. Nat. Univ. of Taiwan 47-48; Dep. Financial Commr., Ministry of Finance, Japanese Govt. 49-51, Financial Commr. 51-57; Financial Minister, Embassy of Japan, Wash. D.C. 57-60; Special Asst. to Minister for Foreign Affairs, and to Minister of Finance 60-; Exec. Dir. Int. Monetary Fund and Int. Bank for Reconstruction and Development 60-.
International Bank for Reconstruction and Development, 1818 H Street N.W., Washington, D.C., U.S.A.

Svart, Anker; Danish diplomatist; b. 15 Sept. 1918; ed. Aarhus Universitet and Univ. of Sheffield, England.
Danish Foreign Ministry 44-; Attaché, Iceland 44-46; Ministry of Foreign Affairs, Copenhagen 46-52; Sec. Danish Legation, Canada 52-55; Counsellor, Moscow 56-60, Bonn 60-62; Amb. to Repub. of China 62-65; Head of Section, Econ. and Political Dept., Ministry of Foreign Affairs 65-66; Amb. to U.S.S.R. 66-.
Danish Embassy, per. Ostrovskovo 9, Moscow, U.S.S.R.

Svedberg, Theodor (The), PH.D., DR. MED., D.SC. h.c.; Swedish scientist; b. 30 Aug. 1884; ed. Uppsala Univ.
Lecturer in Chemistry, Uppsala Univ. 07 and Prof. 12-49; mem. Swedish Acad. of Science, Halle Acad., Chemical Society London, Indian Acad. of Science, American Philosophical Society, Philadelphia, New York Acad. Sciences, Royal Society London, Nat. Acad. Sciences, Washington, etc.; Nobel Prize for Chemistry 26.
c/o Gustaf Werner Inst., Kemikum, Uppsala, Sweden.
Telephone: 018-139460.

Sveinsson, Einar Olafur, DR. PHIL.; Icelandic university professor; b. 12 Dec. 1899; ed. Univs. of Copenhagen and Iceland.
Various posts at Univ. of Iceland 31-, Head of Univ. Library 40-45, Prof. of Icelandic Literature 45-; Head of Manuscript Inst. of Iceland 62-; mem. various Cttees.; Editor *Skírnir* 44-53; Editor in Chief *Islenzk Fornrit* 52-62; Co-Editor *Arv,* Uppsala 53-; Chair. Icelandic Presidium *Kulturhistorisk leksikon for nordisk Middelalder* 62-; Hon. Fil. dr. (Uppsala); Hon. D.Litt. (Dublin); Commdr. Order of Falcon (Iceland), Royal Swedish Nordstjärna Order; Chevalier Ordre des Arts et Lettres.
Publs. *Verzeichnis isländischer Märchenvarianten* 29, *Um Njálu* 33, *Sagnaritun Oddaverja* 37, *Um íslenzkar thjóðsögur* 40, *Sturlungaöld* 40, *A Njálsbúd* 43, *Landnám íSkaftafellspingi* 48, *Studies in the Manuscript Tradition*

of *Njálssaga* 53, *The Age of the Sturlungs* 53, *Vid uppspretturnar* 56, *Dating the Icelandic Sagas* 58, *Handritamálid* 59, *Njáls saga* 59, *Les sagas islandaises* 61, *Islenzkar bókmenntir í fornöld I* 62, *Ferd og förunautar* 63, *Ritunartími Islendingasagna* 65; also worked as editor and translator.
Oddagötu 6, Reykjavik, Iceland.
Telephone: 13431.

Svenningsen, Nils Thomas; Danish diplomatist; b. 28 March 1894; ed. Univ. of Copenhagen.
Ministry of Justice 18; Ministry of Foreign Affairs 20; Sec., Berlin 24-30; various depts., Ministry of Foreign Affairs 30-41; Sec.-Gen., Ministry of Foreign Affairs 41-45; Ambassador to Sweden 45-50, to France 50-51; Sec.-Gen. Ministry of Foreign Affairs 51-61; Ambassador to Great Britain 61-64; Head of Swedish-Norwegian Commission on Research of Reindeer Grazing in North Scandinavia 64-67; Grand Cross Order of Dannebrog (Denmark), Hon. G.B.E. (U.K.) and other foreign orders.
Overgaden oven Vandet 50, Copenhagen K, Denmark.
Telephone: Asta 15-66.

Sveshnikov, Mefodii Naumovich; Soviet economist and banker; b. 1911; ed. Financial and Econ. Inst.
State Bank of U.S.S.R. 29-, Branch Manager, Office Manager, Dir. of Dept., mem. Board of Dirs., Dep. Chair. Board of Dirs.; Chair. Board of Dirs. of Bank for Foreign Trade of U.S.S.R. 57-.
The Bank for Foreign Trade of the U.S.S.R., Neglinnaya 12, Moscow, U.S.S.R.

Švestka, Oldřich; Czechoslovak journalist; b. 24 March 1922.
Member of underground movement 38-45; joined *Rudé Právo* 45, fmr. Deputy-Editor, Editor 58-; mem. Central Cttee. Communist Party of Czechoslovakia 62-; mem. Ideological Comm. Central Cttee. C.P. of Czecho-slovakia 62-.
Rudé Právo, Na Poříčí 30, Prague I, Czechoslovakia.

Svetlanov, Evgeni Fyodorovich; Soviet composer and conductor; b. 1928; ed. Gnesiny Music Education Inst. and Moscow Conservatoire.
Conductor, Moscow Radio 53; Conductor, Bolshoi Theatre, Moscow 54-62, Chief Conductor 62-65; Conductor U.S.S.R. State Symphony Orchestra 65-; People's Artist of R.S.F.S.R.
Compositions include: Symphony, Tone-Poems *Festival* 50, *Daugava* 53, *Siberian Fantasy* 53, Rhapsody 54, Cantata *Home Fields* 49, Concerto 51, five Sonatas 46-52, five Sonatinas 46-51, Preludes 45-51; about 50 Romances and Songs.
Has conducted *Rusalka* (Dargomyshski), *Pskovityanka*, *The Czar's Bride*, *Sadko*, *Snow-Maiden* (Rimsky-Korsakov), *Prince Igor* (Borodin), *The Sorceress* (Tchaikovsky), *Not Only Love* (Shchedrin), *Boris Godunov* (Mussorgsky), *October* (Muradelya), *Storm Along the Path* (Karaev), *Paganini* (Rachmaninov), *Swan Lake* (Tchaikovsky), *Night Town* (Bartok), *Pages of Life* (Belanchivadze), *Chopiniana* (Chopin).
U.S.S.R. State Symphony Orchestra, Moscow, U.S.S.R.

Svetzov, Nikolai Pavlovich; Soviet engineer and trade union official; b. 1912; ed. Novocherkask Indus-trial Inst.
Member C.P. of Soviet Union; Chair. Central Cttee. of Oil and Chemical Workers' Union 65-; mem. All-Union Council of Trade Unions; Order of Red Star.
Central Committee of Oil and Chemical Workers' Union, 42 Leninsky Prospekt, Moscow, U.S.S.R.

Sviridov, Georgy Vasilievich; Soviet composer; b. 16 Dec. 1915; ed. Leningrad Conservatoire.
Secretary Union of Composers of U.S.S.R.; State prizewinner 46, Lenin prizewinner 60, People's Artist of R.S.F.S.R. 63; Order of Lenin 63.
Works: romances set to pieces by A. Pushkin 35, M.

Lermontov 38, songs to words by Shakespeare 44, a song cycle *My Homeland* 50, songs to poems by Burns 55, a symphonic poem *In Memory of Sergei Esenin* 56, *A Pathetic Oratory* (words by Mayakovsky) 60, *Kursk Songs* for chorus and symphony orchestra 63, also composed a trio for piano, violin and 'cello, and music for films and theatre.
Union of Soviet Composers, 8-10 Nezhdanova Street, Moscow, U.S.S.R.

Svoboda, Josef; Czechoslovak architect and stage designer; b. 10 May 1920; ed. Special School for Interior Architecture, Prague and School of Fine and Applied Arts, Prague.
Stage designer, Nat. Theatre, Prague 47, Head Designer 51-; created over 320 stage sets in Czechoslovakia and for theatres in Belgium, France, Italy, Germany, U.S.S.R., U.K., U.S.A., etc.; State Prize 54, Order of Labour 63, Honoured Artist 66; Best Stage Designer, Art Biennale, São Paulo 61, London Theatre Critics' Award for Best Stage Set (*The Insect Comedy*, Čapek and *Tempest*, Ostrovsky) 66.
National Theatre, Divadelni 6, Prague I; Home: Na-Kvčinici 850/6, Prague-Nusle, Czechoslovakia.
Telephone: 27-72-69 (Office); 43-22-60 (Home).

Svoboda, Gen. Ludvík; Czechoslovak Head of State; b. 25 Nov. 1895.
Fought in Czechoslovak Legions in First World War 15-20; in Czechoslovak Army 22-39, Company Commdr. 36, later Infantry Battalion Commdr., teacher at Mil. Acad.; fought in U.S.S.R. in Second World War; organized and commanded Czechoslovak Army Unit 39-45; Minister of Nat. Defence and organized new Czechoslovak People's Army 45-50; Deputy Premier 50-51; Chief of Mil. Acad. 55-59, retd. 59; Pres. of Republic 68-; mem. Nat. Assembly 48-, mem. Presidium Nat. Assembly 60-64; mem. Presidium Czechoslovak-Soviet Friendship Union 45-; mem. Presidium and Deputy Chair. Central Cttee. of Union of Anti-Fascist Fighters 48-; numerous Czechoslovak decorations and decorations from U.S.S.R., Poland, Romania, Hungary, U.S.A., U.K. and France.
Publ. *From Buzuluk to Prague* 60.
Prague-Hrad, Czechoslovakia.

Svoboda, Ludvík, PH.D., DR. SC.; Czechoslovak philo-sopher; b. 4 May 1903.
Professor of Philosophy Charles Univ., Prague; Corresp. mem. Czechoslovak Acad. of Sciences 52-; Order of Labour 63.
Publs. include several works on Marxism and Leninism and aesthetic questions.
Czechoslovak Academy of Sciences, Národsní tř. 3, Prague I, Czechoslovakia.

Svolinský, Karel; Czechoslovak painter and graphic artist; b. 14 Jan. 1896; ed. School of Fine and Applied Arts, Prague.
Professor, Coll. of Fine and Applied Arts, Prague 45-; Grand Prix, Paris 25, 37, Milan 40, Brussels 58; Gold Medals, Paris 37 and two at Leipzig 65; State Prize 52; Honoured Artist 56; Nat. Artist 61.
Works include stained glass windows and mosaics in St. Vitus Cathedral, Prague; work for Paris Exhbn. 37, Brussels Exhbn. 58; book illustrations and layout; costumes and stage sets, Nat. and other Theatres Prague, Vienna and Moscow; at int. exhbns. in Lugano 54, Leipzig 27, 59, 65, Venice 56, São Paulo 60, Paris 63, Belgrade 65, Mainz 65, etc., one-man shows Kassel 64, Vienna 65, Offenbach/M. 66, Olomouc 66, Prague 67.
Na Zátorce 13, Prague 6, Czechoslovakia.
Telephone: 372-676.

Swai, Asanterabi Zephaniah Nsilo; Tanzanian politician and diplomatist; b. 20 April 1925; ed. Makerere Coll. and Univs. of Bombay and Delhi.
Assistant Warden, Makerere Coll. 52-54; Gen. Man.

Meru Co-operative Union 58-60; Provincial Chair., Tanganyika African National Union (T.A.N.U.), Northern Province 58-60; Chair. T.A.N.U. Economics and Social Development Cttee. 60-62, Nat. Treas. 62-; mem. Legislative Council 60-; Minister of Commerce and Industry 60; Minister of Health and Labour Jan.-Mar. 62; Minister without Portfolio and Perm. Rep. to UN 62; Minister of Development Planning, Tanganyika 62-63, Minister of State, President's Office, Directorate of Devt. and Planning 64-65; Minister of Industries, Mineral Resources and Power Sept. 65-March 67; Minister of Econ. Affairs and Devt. Planning, Chair. Nat. Devt. Corpn. March 67-June 67; Minister to E. African Community June 67-.
c/o Ministry of Economic Affairs and Development Planning, P.O. Box 9242, Dar es Salaam, Tanzania.

Swain, Robert Cuthbertson, A.B., PH.D.; American chemist; b. 14 Sept. 1907; ed. Stanford Univ., California, and Univs. of Heidelberg and Berlin.
With American Cyanamid Co. 34-, Dir. 46-; Research Chemist, Warners, N.J. 34-36, at Stamford, Conn. 37-42, Dir. of Research Div. at Stamford Labs. 42-45, Research Dir. N.Y. Office 45-46, Vice-Pres. 46-65; Dir.-Gen. Cyanamid Int. 59-65, Exec. Vice-Pres. 65-; Dir. Perkin-Elmer Corpn., Norwalk, Conn.; Consultant Office Scientific Research and Devt. 54-45; mem. and Chair. Chemical Warfare Cttee. of U.S. Dept. of Defense Research and Devt. Board 50-51; mem. Council Int. Congress Pure and Applied Chemistry, London 47; mem. various U.S. and int. chemistry comms.; Castner Memorial Award Soc. of Chemical Industry, London 53; James Turner Morehead Medal 58.
Office: American Cyanamid Company, 859 Berdan Avenue, Wayne, N.J. 07470; Home: Meadow Road, Riverside, Conn., U.S.A.
Telephone: 201-831-1234 (Office).

Swaminathan, Jagdish; Indian painter; b. 21 June 1928; ed. Delhi Polytechnic and Acad. of Fine Arts, Warsaw.
Early career of freedom fighter, trade unionist, journalist, and writer of children's books; mem. Delhi State Cttee. of Congress Socialist Party and Editor of its weekly organ, *Mazdoor Awaz*; Senior Art Teacher, Cambridge School, New Delhi; Founder-mem. *Group 1890* (avante-garde group of Indian artists); mem., Nat. Cttee., Int. Asscn. of the Arts 67-, Exec. Cttee. Delhi Slipi Chakra 67-, also Founder-Editor monthly journal, *Contra 66* and full-time painter; one-man exhbns. in New Delhi 62, 63, 64, 65, 66, in Bombay 66; in group shows Warsaw 61, Saigon 63, Tokyo Biennale 65, *Art Now in India*, London, Newcastle and Brussels 65-66, *Seven Indian Painters*, London 67; represented in various public and private collections in India and abroad.
c/o Gallery Chemould, Jahangir Art Gallery, Mahatma Gandhi Road, Bombay 1; and 6/17 W.E.A., New Delhi 5, India.

Swann, Donald Ibrahim, M.A.; British composer and actor; b. 30 Sept. 1923; ed. Westminster School and Christ Church Oxford.
Musical contributor to London revues, including *Airs on a Shoestring* 53-54; joint leader writer, musical play *Wild Thyme* 55; with Michael Flanders (*q.v.*) in two-man revues, *At the Drop of a Hat,* and *At the Drop of Another Hat* (singer and accompanist of own songs); toured Australia, New Zealand, America and Canada; other works include *London Sketches* 58, *Festival Matins* 62, *Perelandra* (opera) 61-62, settings of John Betjeman's poems 64.
Publs. *Sing Round the Year* (carols for children) 65, *The Road goes ever on* (with J. R. R. Tolkien).
13 Albert Bridge Road, London, S.W.11, England.

Swann, Michael Meredith, M.A., PH.D., F.R.S., F.R.S.E., F.R.C.S.(E.); British university principal; b. 1 Mar. 1920; ed. Winchester and Gonville and Caius Coll., Cambridge.
Army Service 40-46; Demonstrator, Dept. of Zoology, Univ. of Cambridge 46-52; Prof. of Natural History, Univ. of Edinburgh 52-62; Dean of Faculty of Science, Univ. of Edinburgh 62-65; Principal and Vice-Chancellor, Univ. of Edinburgh 65-; mem. Medical Research Council 62-65; mem. Cttee. on Manpower Resources 65-; Vice-Chair. Council for Scientific Policy 65-.
The Old College, Edinburgh 8; Home: Ormsacre, 41 Barnton Avenue, Edinburgh 4, Scotland.
Telephone: 031-NEW-1011; 031-DAV-1325.

Swart, Charles Robberts, B.A., LL.B., LL.D. (h.c.); South African lawyer, journalist and politician; b. 5 Dec. 1894; ed. Grey University College, Bloemfontein, Univ. of South Africa and Columbia Univ., New York.
Advocate Supreme Court of South Africa 19-48; fmr. Organising Sec. Nat. Party of Orange Free State 19-28; Leader Nat. Party of O.F.S. 40-59; fmr. mem. Federal Nat. Party Council; fmr. Lecturer in Law and Agricultural Legislation; M.P. for Ladybrand 23-38, Winburg 41-59; Minister of Education, Arts and Science 49-50; Minister of Justice 48-59; Deputy Prime Minister and Leader, House of Ass. 54-59; Gov.-Gen. 60-61; State Pres. Republic of South Africa 61-67; Chancellor, Univ. of Orange Free State 51-; Hon. Col. Oos-Vrystaat Regt. 53-, Regt. Univ. Oranje-Vrystaat 62-; Hon. LL.D. (Univ. of Orange Free State, Rhodes Univ. and Potchefstroom Univ.); Hon. Fellow Coll. of Physicians, Surgeons and Gynæcologists of S. Africa; hon. mem. S. Africa Acad. of Science and Art.
Publs. *Kinders van Suid-Afrika* 33, *Die Agterryer* 39.
P.O. Box 135, Brandfort, Orange Free State, Republic of South Africa.

Swartz, Col. Hon. Reginald William Cole, M.B.E., E.D., M.P.; Australian politician; b. 14 April 1911; ed. Toowoomba and Brisbane Grammar Schools.
Parliamentary Under-Sec. Ministry of Commerce and Agriculture 52-56; Parl. Sec. Ministry of Trade 56-61; Minister for Repatriation 61-64; Minister for Health 64-66; Minister for Social Services 65-66, for Civil Aviation 66-; Liberal.
22 Catto Street, Toowoomba, Queensland, Australia.
Telephone: Toowoomba 24904, 51060.

Swe, Ba; Burmese politician; b. 15; ed. Rangoon Univ.
One of founders of People's Revolutionary Party 39, Exec. Mem. of Party in Mergui District during Japanese occupation; Chief of Civil Defence in the "Kebotai" 42-45; one of leaders of Anti-Japanese Resistance Movement, in charge of Rangoon, Hanthawaddy and Insein districts 44-45, arrested and detained by Japanese; Pres. Socialist Party (originally People's Revolutionary Party) 45, later Sec.-Gen.; Sec.-Gen. Anti-Fascist People's Freedom League 47-58; Leader of "Stable" Group 58; fmr. mem. Parl. from Taikkyi; Minister of Defence 52-57, concurrently Prime Minister 56; Deputy Prime Minister 57-58.
84 Innes Road, Rangoon, Burma.

Swearingen, John Eldred, M.S.; American businessman; b. 7 Sept. 1918; ed. Univ. of South Carolina and Carnegie Mellon Univ.
Chemical Engineer, Standard Oil Co. (Indiana) 39-; various positions Stanolind Oil and Gas Co. (now Pan American Petroleum Corpn.) 47-51 and Dir. 51-; Gen. Man. Production, Standard Oil Co. (Indiana) 51, Dir. 52, Vice-Pres. 54, Exec. Vice-Pres. 56, Pres. 58-65, Chair of Board 65-; Dir. Chase Manhattan Bank, First Nat. Bank of Chicago; Dir. American Petroleum Inst., Passavant Hospital, Chicago, Council for Financial Aid to Educ.; Trustee Carnegie Inst. of Technology,

Automotive Safety Foundation, DePauw Univ.; mem. Nat. Petroleum Council; Hon. D.Eng. (S.D. School of Mines and Technology), Hon. LL.D. (DePauw Univ., Univ. of S. Carolina, Knox Coll.).

Home: 811 Normandy Lane, Glenview, Ill.; Office: 910 South Michigan Avenue, Chicago, Ill. 60680, U.S.A.

Sweden, King of (*see* Gustaf VI).

Sweeney, James Johnson, A.B.; American museum director; b. 30 May 1900; ed. Georgetown Univ., Jesus Coll. Cambridge (England), Sorbonne (Paris) and Siena Univs.

Lecturer New York Univ. Inst. of Fine Arts 35-40, Salzburg Seminar in American Studies 47 and 49; Visiting Scholar Univ. of Georgia 50-51; Dir. of Painting and Sculpture New York Museum of Modern Art 45-46, Solomon R. Guggenheim Museum, New York 52-60; Dir. Houston Museum of Fine Arts 61-68, Consultant Dir. 68-; Dir. Iran America Soc. 64-; Lecturer Harvard Univ. 61; Vice-Pres. Int. Art Critics Asscn. 48-57, Pres. 57-63; Vice-Pres. Edward MacDowell Asscn. 53-54, Pres. 55-62, Counsellor 62-; Trustee American Acad. in Rome 62-, Nat. Council of the Arts 65-, Mediaeval Acad. of America, Councillor 66; mem. American Acad. of Arts and Sciences; Art in America Award 63; Chevalier Légion d'Honneur, Officier Ordre des Arts et des Lettres.

Publs. *Plastic Redirections in XXth Century Painting* 34, *African Negro Art* (editor) 35, *Joan Miró* 41, *Alexander Calder* 43, 51, 66, *Stuart Davis* 45, *Marc Chagall* 45, *African Folk Tales and Sculpture* (with Paul Radin) 52, 64, *Burri* 55, *The Miró Atmosphere* 59, *Antoni Gaudi* (with José Luis Sert) 60, *Irish Illuminated Manuscripts* 65, *Vision and Image* 68, *Calder* 68, *Pierre Soulages* 68.

120 East End Avenue, New York City 28, N.Y., U.S.A. Telephone: BU8-0206.

Swietoslawski, Wojciech; Polish university professor; b. 1881.

Assistant in Chemistry, Inst. of Technology, Kiev 08-10; Asst. in Chemistry, Lecturer, Univ. of Moscow 10-18; Prof. of Physical Chemistry, Inst. of Technology, Warsaw 18-47; Prof. of Physical Chemistry, Univ. of Warsaw 47-61; Minister of Education 35-39; Visiting Prof., Univ. of Pittsburgh 40; Lecturer, Univ. of Iowa 41; Senior Fellow, Mellon Inst. Industrial Research 41-46; Chair. Int. Cttee. on Physical Chemistry Data; mem. Cttee. on Thermochemistry of Sub-cttee. on Themometry and Calorimetry; Head of Section of Physical Chemistry, Inst. of Engineering Chemistry, Warsaw; former Vice-Pres. of Int. Union of Chemistry; Dir. Inst. of Physical Chemistry, Polish Acad. of Sciences 55-61; mem. Polish Acad. of Sciences.

Publs. *Physical Chemistry* (4 vols. in Polish) 23-31, *Thermochemistry* (German edition 28, French edition 33), *Coke Formation Process, and Physiochemical Properties of Coals* 42, *Ebulliometric Measurements* 45, *Microcalorimetry* 46, *Physical Chemistry of Coal Tar* 56 (Russian edn. 58, German edn. 59), *Azeotropy and Poliazeotropy*, 57 (English edn. 63).

Brzozowa 10 m. 7, Warsaw 40, Poland.

Swing, Raymond; American journalist; b. 25 March 1887; ed. Oberlin Coll.

Newspaper work in Ohio and Indiana 06-12; Berlin Correspondent *Chicago Daily News* 13-17; Examiner of War Labour Board 18; Correspondent in Berlin for American newspapers 19-22; Dir. foreign service of *Wall Street Journal* 22-24; London Correspondent *New York Evening Post* and *Philadelphia Public Ledger* 24-34 and Washington Correspondent 34; mem. Editorial Board *Nation* 35-36; United States Correspondent for London *News Chronicle* 36-37; News Commentator on American Affairs for B.B.C. 35-45, on Foreign Affairs for Mutual Broadcasting Corpn. 36-42, Blue Network

42-46, for WOR, New York 50, and on American Affairs for Canadian Broadcasting Corpn. 38; commentator with Liberty Network 50-51, with Voice of America 51-53; Political Commentator 59-64; Chair. Council for Democracy 40-41; Chair. Board Americans United for World Government 46.

Publs. *Forerunners of American Fascism* 35, *How War Came* 40, *Preview of History* 44, *In the Name of Sanity* 46, *Good Evening* 64.

3116 Rodman Street, N.W., Washington, D.C., U.S.A. Telephone: WO6-2055.

Swings, Pol, PH.D., D.SC.; Belgian university professor; b. 24 Sept. 1906; Univ. of Liège.

Assistant in Astronomy, Univ. of Liège 28-32, Asst. Prof. 32-36, Prof. 36-; Visiting Prof. Univ. of Chicago 39-43, 46-52; War Research Assignment U.S.A. 43-45; mem. Royal Acad. of Belgium, American Acad. Arts and Sciences, American Philosophical Soc., Nat. Acad. of Sciences U.S.A., Bavarian Acad. of Sciences; Assoc. Inst. de France; Pres. Int. Astronomical Union 64-67; Francqui Prize 48; Decennial Physics Prize 60; Hon. D.Sc. Aix-Marseille Univ., Bordeaux Univ., Charles Univ. Prague.

Office: Department of Astrophysics, University of Liège, Sclessin; Home: 23 Avenue Léon Souguenet, 23 Esneux, Belgium.

Telephone: 04-711135 (Home).

Swinnerton, Frank Arthur; British novelist and literary critic; b. 12 Aug. 1884.

Publs. include: *Nocturne* 17, *The Georgian House, The Georgian Literary Scene* 36, *Swinnerton: An Autobiography* 37, *The Bookman's London* 51, *Background with Chorus* 56, *Death of a Highbrow* 61, *Figures in the Foreground* 63, *Quadrille* 65, *A Galaxy of Fathers* 66, *Sanctuary* 66, *The Bright Lights* 68.

Old Tokefield, Cranleigh, Surrey, England. Telephone: Cranleigh 3732.

Swinton, 1st Earl, cr. 56, 1st Viscount, cr. 35, of Masham; **Philip Cunliffe-Lister,** P.C., G.B.E., C.H., M.C.; British politician; b. 1 May 1884; ed. Winchester Coll. and Univ. Coll. Oxford.

Conservative M.P. for Hendon Div. of Middlesex 18-35; Chair. Permanent Labour Cttee. of War Cabinet-Priorities Cttee. 18; mem. Select Cttees. on Nat. Expenditure and on High Prices and Profits 19; Parl. Sec. to Board of Trade 20-21; Sec. to Overseas Trade Dept. 21-22; Chair. Imperial Economic Conf. 23; Pres. Board of Trade 22-23, 25-29 and Aug.-Nov. 31; Sec. of State for Colonies 31-35, for Air 35-38; Hon. Air Commodore No. 608 (North Riding) Squadron, Auxiliary Air Force 36-; Minister Resident in West Africa 42-44; Minister of Civil Aviation 44-45; Chancellor Duchy of Lancaster also Minister of Materials 51-53; Sec. of State for Commonwealth Relations 53-55; Chair. Swinton Conservative Coll. 58-; Hon. LL.D. (Liverpool Univ.); Hon. Fellow Univ. Coll. Oxford; Officer, Order of Leopold.

Publs. *I Remember* 48, *Sixty Years of Power* 65.

16 Kingston House, London, S.W.7; Swinton, Ripon, Yorks., England.

Telephone: Masham 310 (Yorks.).

Sydow, Erik von, B.L.; Swedish diplomatist; b. 2 Sept. 1912; ed. Uppsala Univ.

Ministry of Foreign Affairs 36; early service Germany and Baltic States; Sec. Legation to Japan 40, Chargé d'Affaires 45-46; Head of Div., Ministry of Foreign Affairs 47-49; Perm. Rep. to OEEC 49-53; Counsellor, U.S.A. 54-56; Asst. Under-Sec. Commercial and Econ. Affairs, Ministry of Foreign Affairs 59-63; Ambassador and Perm. Rep. to EFTA and other Int. Orgs. in Geneva 64-; Chair. numerous bilateral and multilateral trade negotiations.

Swedish Delegation, 91-93 rue de la Servette, 1211 Geneva, Switzerland.

Sydow, Max von; Swedish actor; b. 10 April 1929; ed. Royal Dramatic Theatre School, Stockholm.
Norrköping-Linköping Theatre 51-53, Hälsingborg Theatre 53-55, Malmö Theatre 55-60, Royal Dramatic Theatre, Stockholm 60-.
Plays acted in include: *Hamlet, Peer Gynt, Henry IV* (Pirandello), *The Tempest, Lea och Rachel, Le Misanthrope, Faust, Ett Drömspel, La Valse des Toréadors, Les Sequestrés d'Altona, King John, After the Fall, Troilus and Cressida.*
Films acted in include: *Bara en mor* 49, *Miss Julie* 50, *Det sjunde inseglet* (The Seventh Seal) 57, *Wild Strawberries* 57, *Prästen i Uddarbo* 57, *Close to Life* 57, *Ansiktet* (The Face) 58, *The Virgin Spring* 60, *Brollopsdagen* 60, *Såsom i en spegel* (Through a Glass Darkly) 61, *Älskarinnan* (The Mistress) 62, *Nattvardsgästerna* (Winter Light) 63, *The Greatest Story Ever Told* 63, *The Reward* 64, *4×4* 65, *Hawaii* 65, *Quiller Memorandum* 66, *The Hour of the Wolf* 66, *The Shame* 67.
c/o Svenska Filminstitutet, Kungsgatan 48, Stockholm C, Sweden.

Syed Putra bin Syed Hassan Jamalullail (*see* Perlis).

Syme, Sir Colin York, Kt., LL.B.; Australian businessman; b. 22 April 1903; ed. Perth and Melbourne Univs.
Partner firm of Hedderwick, Fookes and Alston 28-66; Dir. Broken Hill Pty. Co. Ltd. 37-, Chair. 52-, Dir. of Admin. 66-; Chair. Tubemakers of Australia Ltd. 66-; Pres. Walter and Eliza Hall Inst. of Medical Research; Dir. Elder Smith Goldsbrough Mort Ltd., I.C.I.A.N.Z. Ltd.; mem. Int. Advisory Cttee., The Chase Manhattan Bank, N.Y.; Hon. D.Sc.
500 Bourke Street, Melbourne, Victoria, Australia.
Telephone: 60-0701.

Syme, Sir Ronald, Kt., F.B.A.; British university professor; b. 11 March 1903; ed. New Zealand and Oriel Coll. Oxford.
Fellow and Tutor, Trinity Coll., Oxford 29-49; Press Attaché, British Legation, Belgrade 40-41, Ankara 41-42; Prof. of Classical Philology Univ. of Istanbul 42-45; Camden Prof. of Ancient History Univ. of Oxford 49-; Pres. Int. Fed. of Classical Societies 51; Pres. Society for the Promotion of Roman Studies 48-52; Sec.-Gen. Int. Council for Philosophy and the Humanities 52-; Foreign mem. Royal Danish Acad., Amer. Phil. Soc., American Acad. of Arts and Sciences, American Historical Soc.; mem. Lund Soc. of Letters, etc.; Hon. D.Litt. (N.Z.) 49, Durham 52, Belfast 59, Emory 62, Graz 62; Hon. D. ès. L. Paris 62; Hon. Fellow Oriel Coll. 58.
Publs. *The Roman Revolution* 39, *Tacitus* 58, *Colonial Elites* 58, *Sallust* 64, *Ammianus and the Historia Augusta* 68.
Brasenose College, Oxford, England.

Symington, William Stuart; American politician; b. 26 June 1901; ed. Yale Univ. and Int. Correspondence School.
With Symington companies, Rochester, N.Y. 23-30; Pres. Colonial Radio Co., Rochester 30-35, Rustless Iron & Steel Co., Baltimore 35-37; Pres. and Chair. Board Emerson Electric Manufacturing Co., St. Louis 38-45; Surplus Property Admin., Washington, D.C. 45-46; Asst. Sec. of War for Air 46-47; Sec. of Air Force, Nat. Defense 47-50; later Chair. Nat. Security Resources Board and Admin. Reconstruction Finance Corpn.; U.S. Senator from Missouri 53-; Democrat.
Senate Office Building, Washington, D.C., U.S.A.

Symonds, Henry Gardiner; American executive; b. 15 Oct. 1903; ed. Stanford Univ. and Harvard Univ.
With Ill. Merchants Trust Co., Chicago 27-30; Asst. Treas. Chicago Corpn. 30-32, Vice-Pres. 32-38, Vice-Pres., Dir. 38-45; Pres., Dir. Tenn. Gas Transmission Co. (now Tenneco), Houston 43-58, Chair. Pres. 58-60, Chair. 60-; Chair. Tenn. Gas Pipeline Co., Midwestern Gas Transmission Co., Tenneco Corpn., Tenneco

Chemicals Inc., Tenn. Life Insurance Co., Tenn. Gas Building Corpn., etc.; Dir.-Gen. Telephone and Electronics Corpn., Southern Pacific Co.
Home: 3359 Chevy Chase Drive, Houston 19; Office: Tennessee Building, Houston, Texas, U.S.A.

Symonette, Sir Roland Theodore, Kt.; Bahamas business executive and politician; b. 16 Dec. 1898; ed. Current Eleuthera, Bahamas.
Shipyard Owner and Contractor; mem. House of Assembly 35-, Exec. Council 49-64; Parl. Leader United Bahamian Party; Prime Minister of Bahamas 64-67.
601 Bay Street, Nassau, Bahamas.

Synge, John Lighton, M.A., SC.D., F.R.S., M.R.I.A., F.R.S.C.; Irish mathematician; b. 23 March 1897; ed. Trinity Coll., Dublin.
Lecturer in Mathematics Trinity Coll. Dublin 20; Asst. Prof. of Mathematics, Univ. Toronto 20-25; Fellow and Univ. Prof. of Natural Philosophy, Trinity Coll. Dublin 25-30; Prof. of Applied Mathematics, Toronto Univ. 30-43; Prof. of Mathematics Ohio State Univ. 43-46; Prof. of Mathematics Carnegie Inst. of Technology 46-48; Prof. Inst. for Advanced Studies, Dublin 48-; Visiting Lecturer Princeton 39, Visiting Prof. Brown Univ. 41, Univ. of Maryland 51; Pres. Royal Irish Acad. 61-64; Hon. Fellow Trinity Coll. Dublin.
Publs. *Mathematical Papers of Sir W. R. Hamilton, Vol. I* (Editor, with A. W. Conway) 31, *Geometrical Optics* 37, *Principles of Mechanics* (with B. A. Griffith) 42, *Tensor Calculus* (with A. Schild) 49, *Science: Sense and Nonsense* 51, *Geometrical Mechanics and de Broglie Waves* 54, *Relativity: the Special Theory* 56, *The Relativistic Gas, Kandelman's Krim, The Hypercircle in Mathematical Physics* 57, *Relativity: The General Theory* 60.
Torfan, Stillorgan Park, Blackrock, Co. Dublin; Institute for Advanced Studies, 64 Merrion Square, Dublin, Ireland.

Synge, Richard Laurence Millington, B.A., PH.D., F.R.I.C., F.R.S.E., F.R.S.; British biochemist; b. 28 Oct. 1914; ed. Winchester Coll. and Trinity Coll., Cambridge.
International Wool Secretariat Student in Biochemistry, Univ. of Cambridge 38 (transferred to Wool Industries Research Asscn., Leeds 39); Biochemist, Wool Industries Research Asscn., Leeds 41-43; Staff Biochemist, Lister Inst. of Preventive Medicine, London 43-48 (studied at Inst. of Physical Chemistry, Uppsala 46-47); Head of Dept. of Protein Chemistry, Rowett Research Inst., Bucksburn, Aberdeen, Scotland 48-67; Biochemist, Food Research Inst., Norwich 67-; shared Nobel Prize for Chemistry with A. J. P. Martin 52 (for invention of partition chromatography 41); mem. Editorial Board *Biochemical Journal* 49-55; Visiting biochemist Ruakura Animal Research Station, Hamilton, N.Z. 58-59; John Price Wetherill Medal, Franklin Inst. Philadelphia, U.S.A. (with others) 59.
Food Research Institute, Earlham Laboratory, Recreation Road, Norwich NOR 26 G, England.
Telephone: Norwich 53271.

Syrkin, Yakov Kivovich; Soviet physical chemist; b. 1894; ed. Ivanovo-Vosnessensky Polytechnical Inst.
Lecturer Ivanovo-Vosnessensky Polytechnical Inst. 19-31; Prof. 25-; Head, Laboratory Man. U.S.S.R. Acad. of Sciences Karpov Physical-chemical Inst. 31-52; Prof. Inst. of Fine Chemical Technology 31-; Head, Laboratory, U.S.S.R. Acad. of Sciences N. S. Kurnakov Inst. of Gen. and Inorganic Chemistry 61-; Corresp. mem. U.S.S.R. Acad. of Sciences 43-64, mem. 64-; State Prize.
Publs. Basic works on investigating molecular structures and chemical bonds—chemical thermodynamics, kynetics, reactions in solvents.
U.S.S.R. Academy of Sciences, 14 Leninsky prospekt, Moscow, U.S.S.R.

Sytenko, Mikhail Dmitrievich; Soviet diplomatist; b. 18; ed. Moscow Pedagogical Inst. for Foreign Languages.

Attaché, Soviet Embassy London 43; Counsellor and Chargé d'Affaires, Prague 55-56; Asst. Deputy Head, 4th European Dept., Ministry of Foreign Affairs; Amb. to Ghana 59-62; Head, Second African Dept., Ministry of Foreign Affairs 62-65; Amb. to Indonesia 65-.

U.S.S.R. Embassy, Djakarta, Indonesia.

Szabó, Ferenc; Hungarian composer; b. 27 Dec. 1902; ed. Budapest Conservatoire.

In U.S.S.R. 30-45; Prof. of Composition 45; Dir.-in-Chief Franz Liszt Musical Acad. 58-67; Kossuth Prize (twice), Outstanding Artist of the Hungarian People's Republic.

Works include: *First String-Quartet* 26, *String Trio* 27, *Toccata for Piano* 28, *Solo Sonata for Violoncello* 29, *Two Sonatas for Violin* 30, *Lyrical Suite* 36, *Homecoming* (Concerto) 45, Trilogy—*The Sea Has Arisen*, *Ludas Matyi*, *Memento*; *Third Piano Sonata* 61, *Second String Quartet* 62, *Sonata alla Rapsodia, for Clarinet and Piano* 64, *Three Songs to Verses of Miklos Radnoti* 65.

XIII Fürst Sándor-u. 33, Budapest, Hungary.
Telephone: 295-251.

Szabó, Magda; Hungarian authoress; b. 5 Oct. 1917. Graduated as a teacher 40; worked in secondary schools 40-44, 50-59; started literary career as poetess and has since written novels, plays, radio dramas and film scripts; works have been translated into many languages including English, French, German, Italian, Russian, Polish.

Publs. include *Mondják meg Zsófikának* (Tell Sally), *Az őz* (The Deer); novels include *Alarcosbál* (Fancy Ball), *Születésnap* (Birthday).

Budapest II, Julia-utca 3, Hungary.

Szabó, Pál; Hungarian novelist; b. 5 April 1893; ed. Biharugra elementary school.

Began as farm labourer; served in First World War; took part in Hungarian Revolution 18-19; began writing in thirties; mem. first of Smallholders' Party, later of Nat. Peasant Party, of which he became Pres. after Second World War; mem. of Parl. and Pres. of the Patriotic People's Front 56, Vice-Pres. 57-; mem. Hungarian Writers' Asscn. 59-; Vice-Pres. PEN Club 60-; Kossuth Prize 51, 54.

Publs. *Emberek, Békalencse, Papok, vasarnapok, Csodavárás, Anyaföld, Szakadékban, Öszivetés, Legények, Szomszédok, Macska az asztalon, Politika, Tiz esztendő, A nagy temető, Lakodalom, keresztelő, bölcső, Leánykérők. Magyarok, Most és mindörökké, Harangoznak, Isten malmai, Két okos meg a bolondos, Uj Föld* 53, *Legények Vagyunk* 55, *Munkák és Napok* 55, *Prágai Élmények* 55, *This Side of the Tisza: Beyond the Danube* 60.

Diana u. 6/c Budapest XII, Hungary.

Szabó, Zoltán, M.D.; Hungarian physician and politician; b. 17 Feb. 1914; ed. Pécs Univ.

Assistant Lecturer, Univ. Medical School, Pécs 45, Univ. Medical Clinic, Budapest 57, Asst. Prof. 63; Pres. Physicians and Health Workers Union 52, Gen. Sec. 63; First Deputy Minister of Health 63; Minister of Health 64-; mem. Central Cttee. Hungarian Socialist Workers' Party 62-.

Ministry of Health, Budapest, Hungary.

Szabolcsi, Bence; Hungarian musicologist; b. 2 Aug. 1899; ed. Budapest Acad. of Music and Leipzig Univ. Professor Budapest Acad. of Music 45-; fmr. Pres. Union of Hungarian Musicians; mem. Hungarian Acad. of Sciences (Dir. Bartók Archives); Editor (with Aladár Tóth) *Zenei Lexicon* (Hungarian musical encyclopaedia) 30; Kossuth Prize 51, 65; Editor *Musicological Studies* (10 vols.) 52-62.

Publs. incl. *An Introduction to the History of Music* 36, *The History of Music* 40, *The History of Hungarian Music* 47 (English edn. 64), *Beethoven* 47, *The History of Melody* 50 (English edn. 65), *Folk Music and History* 54, *The Twilight of Ferenc Liszt* 56 (English edn. 59), *Poem and Melody* 59, *Béla Bartók* 60 (English edn. 64), *Daybreak in Europe* (18th cent. music) 48, *Centuries of Hungarian Music* (2 vols.) 59, 61, *The Crossroad* (studies) 63, *The Artist and His Audience* 64, *Common Language in Music* 68.

Academy of Music, Budapest; and Pozsonyi út 40, Budapest XIII, Hungary.
Telephone: 409-826 (Home).

Szádeczky-Kardoss, Elemér; Hungarian geochemist and geologist; b. 1903.

University prof.; mem. Hungarian Acad. of Sciences and Sec. Dept. for Geology and Mining Science; made fundamental discoveries in fields of sediment formation, carbon petrology, magmatic rock genesis and geochemistry; Kossuth Prize 49, 52.

Publs. *Carbon Petrology* 52, *Geochemistry* 55.

Hungarian Academy of Sciences, Budapest, Hungary.

Szafer, Wladyslaw; Polish botanist; b. 86; ed. Vienna Univ.

Lecturer, Lwów Univ. 10, Prof. of Botany 14; Prof. of Botany, Cracow Univ. 18-, Dean 31-32, Rector 36-38; Dir. Botanical Garden, Cracow; Editor-in-Chief and Publisher *Ochrona Przyrody* (Nature Conservation) 20-; mem. fmr. Polish Acad. of Learning; Vice-Pres. Polish Acad. of Sciences 57-; mem. numerous foreign scientific socs.; State Prize, First Class 49.

Publs. *Flora Polska* (10 vols.) 19-, *Rosliny Polski* (The Plants of Poland), with S. Kulczynski and B. Pawlowski 24-, *Zarys Ogolnej Geografii Roslin* (An Outline of the General Geography of Plants) (3rd edn.) 64, *Zarys Paleobotaniki* (Outline of Palaeobotany, with M. Kostyniuk) (2nd edn.) 62, *Pliocene from Czorsztyn* (*West Carpathians*) 54, *Szata roslinna Polski* (Vegetation of Poland) 59, *Miocene Flora from Stare Gliwice in Upper Silesia* 61, *Ochrona Przyrody* (Conservation of Nature) (2 vols.) 65.

Kopernika 27, Cracow, Poland.

Szakács, Ödön, LL.D.; Hungarian judge; b. 1912.

Graduated as Doctor of Law and Political Science 42; Judge of district court Makó 42, County Court Szeged; Pres. County Court Debrecen 51-53, Szeged 53-55; leader Criminal Dept., Ministry of Justice 55-56; Pres. Budapest Metropolitan Court 57-62; Vice-Pres. 62-68, then Pres. of Supreme Court of Justice 68-.

c/o Supreme Court of Justice of the Hungarian People's Republic, Budapest 1, Fö-utca 1, Hungary.
Telephone: 160-075.

Szalay, József, LL.D.; Hungarian lawyer; b. 1908; ed. Budapest Univ. of Sciences.

Former law clerk; fmr. Pres. of Attorney's Office, Gyula, later Szeged; First Dep. to Attorney-Gen. 55-60; First Dep. Minister of Justice 60-63; Pres. of Supreme Court 63-68; mem. C.P. 47-.

c/o Supreme Court of Justice, Budapest, Hungary.

Szalay, Sándor, B.A., M.A., PH.D., D.SC.; Hungarian physicist; b. 4 Oct. 1909; ed. Budapest and Leipzig Univs.

Fellow of the Hungarian Acad. of Sciences 65-; Prof. Experimental Physics, Kossuth Univ.; Head, Inst. Nuclear Research of Hungary; Hungarian Nat. Kossuth Award 52.

Institute of Nuclear Research, 18c, Bem tér Debrecen, Hungary.
Telephone: Debrecen 33-87.

Szaniawski, Jerzy; Polish writer; b. 86.
First works publ. in *Kurier Warszawski* in 12; first comedy *Murzyn* (The Negro) presented in the Teatr Polski, Warsaw, in 17; plays presented at Reduta Theatre were *Papierowy kochanek* (The Paper Lover) 20,

Ewa 21, and *Lekkoduch* (The Frivolous One) 23; other works of this period incl. *Ptak* (The Bird) 24, *Zeglarz* (The Sailor) 25, *Most* (The Bridge) 27, *Fortepian* (The Piano) 28, and *Dziewczyna z lasu* (The Girl from the Forest) 39; collection of short stories *Lgarze pod "Zlota Kotwica"* (The Liars at the "Golden Anchor") 28; arrested during World War II by Gestapo; publ. *Dwa teatry* (Two Theatres) 45; other post-war works incl. *Kowal, pieniadze i gwiazdy* (The Smith, Money and Stars) 50, and *Latajacy ehlopiec* (The Flying Boy) 49 (revised 57), *Professor Tutka* (stories) 55.
Union of Polish Writers, Krakowskie Przedmieście 87-89, Warsaw, Poland.

Szczepanski, Jan, PH.D.; Polish sociologist; b. 14 Sept. 1913; ed. Univ. of Poznań.
Teaching Asst. Univ. of Poznań 37-39; later Prof. Univ. of Łódź, Rector 52-56; mem. of Parl. 57-60; Deputy Dir. Inst. of Philosophy and Sociology, Polish Acad. of Sciences 61-; Pres. Int. Sociological Asscn. 66-.
Publs. *History of Sociology* (in Polish) 61, *Sociological Problems of Higher Education* (in Polish) 63, edited *Studies in Polish Class Structure* (26 vols.).
Warsaw, Hoża 40 m 65, Poland.

Szell, George; American (born Hungarian) conductor, pianist and composer; b. 7 June 1897; ed. privately and State Acad. Vienna.
First public appearance with orchestra as pianist and composer, Vienna 08; concert tours England, Germany 09-12; début as Conductor Berlin 14; Coach and Asst. Conductor Royal Opera, Berlin 15-17; Principal Conductor, Municipal Opera, Strasbourg 17-18; concert tours 18-20; Conductor State Opera, Darmstadt 21-22; Municipal Opera, Düsseldorf 22-24; Chief Conductor State Opera, Berlin 24-29; Conductor Berlin Broadcasting Symphony Orchestra and Prof. State Acad. of Music 24-29; Gen. Music Dir. German Opera House and Philharmonic Concerts, Prague and Prof. Acad. of Music and Dramatic Arts, Prague 29-37; concert tours Europe and America 33-37; Conductor Scottish Orchestra, Glasgow and The Hague 37-39; settled in U.S. 39; Guest Conductor many American and European Orchestras; Regular guest conductor Salzburg Festivals 49-; Principal Conductor Metropolitan Opera House 42-46; Musical Dir. and Conductor, Cleveland Orchestra 46-; co-conductor Concertgebouw Orchestra, Amsterdam 58-61; Chevalier of the Legion of Honour; Laurel Leaf Award of the American Composers' Alliance; Award of Honor, Nat. Music Council; Hon. Dr. Western Reserve Univ., Cleveland, Ohio and Oberlin Coll., Ohio; Commdr. Orange Nassau; Hon. C.B.E. (U.K.); Grosses Verdienstkreuz.
Compositions: Piano Quintet, Variations on an Original Theme for orchestra, *Lyric Overture*, etc.
The Cleveland Orchestra, Severance Hall, Cleveland, Ohio 44106, U.S.A.

Szénási, Géza; Hungarian jurist; b. 1919.
Administrative econ. positions 45-56; mem. Hungarian Socialist Workers' Party 45-; mem. Central Cttee. 62-; Chief Public Prosecutor 56-.
Office of the Chief Public Prosecutor, Budapest, Hungary.

Szent-Györgyi, Albert, M.D., PH.D.; Hungarian-born American biochemist; b. 16 Sept. 1893; ed. Univ. of Budapest and Cambridge Univ.
Prof. of Medical Chemistry Szeged Univ. 31-45; Prof. of Biochemistry Univ. of Budapest 45-47; Dir. of Research Inst. of Muscle Research, Marine Biological Laboratories 47-; Prof. of Biophysics, Dartmouth Medical School 62-66; Prof. of Biology, Brandeis Univ. 66-; fmr. Pres. Acad. of Sciences, Budapest; fmr. Vice-Pres. Nat. Acad., Budapest; awarded Nobel Prize for Medicine 37.
Publs. *Oxidation, Fermentation, Vitamins, Health and*

Disease 39, *Muscular Contraction* 47, 51, 53, *The Nature of Life* 47, *Bioenergetics* 57, *Submolecular Biology* 60.
Marine Biological Laboratories, Woods Hole, Mass., U.S.A.

Szeryng, Henryk; Mexican (b. Polish) violinist; b. 22 Sept. 1921; studied with Carl Flesch, Berlin, and Gabriel Bouillon, Paris Conservatoire, and with Nadia Boulanger.
Liaison officer Polish Govt. in exile, London and translator for Gen. Sikorski 39-45; played over 300 concerts for Allied Armed Forces during this period in Britain, Canada, U.S.A., Mexico, Panama, Trinidad, Brazil, Persian Gulf, N. Africa, Italy and France; apptd. Prof. Faculty of Music, Mexican Nat. Univ. Dec. 45; Mexican citizen 46-; global concerts and goodwill tours 56-; apptd. Goodwill Ambassador by Mexican Govt. 56; Grand Prix du Disque 55, 57, 60, 61, 67; Knight Polish Order Polonia Restituta 56, Romanian Cultural Merit (First Class) 64, Officier des Arts et Lettres (France), etc.
c/o Hurok, 730 Fifth Avenue, New York City, N.Y. 10019, U.S.A.

Szigeti, Joseph; Hungarian violinist; b. 5 Sept. 1892.
Has made two round-the-world concert tours, and has appeared in recitals and with almost every major symphony orchestra in the world; appeared in film *Hollywood Canteen*.
Publs. *With Strings Attached* (autobiography) 49, *A Violinist's Notebook* 64, *The Violin Sonatas of Beethoven* 65.
Le Crépon, Baugy-sur-Clarens, Vaud, Switzerland.

Szilágyi, Béla; Hungarian diplomatist; b. 30 Oct. 1908; ed. Gymnasium and High School for Textile Industry.
Financial Director, State Coal Mines 46; Dir. State Textile Industries 48; Commercial Counsellor in India 50; Head of inter-state Depts. (Western Countries), Ministry of Foreign Trade 52; Minister to U.K. 59-63, Dep. Minister of Foreign Affairs Dec. 63-; Distinguished Worker of Foreign Trade 57, Order of Labour 56, 58, 61, 65, Order of Freedom 57, Order of Hungarian People's Republic 49, Order for the Socialist Fatherland 67.
Ministry of Foreign Affairs, Bem rakpart 47, Budapest II, Hungary.
Telephone: 350-100.

Szipka, József; Hungarian diplomatist; b. 1908.
Ambassador to Finland 54-63, to U.S.S.R. 63-; mem. Central Cttee. Hungarian Socialist Workers Party 62-; Great Cross, Finnish Order of Lion.
Hungarian Embassy, Moscow, U.S.S.R.

Szirmai, István, D.IUR.; Hungarian journalist and politician; b. 13 April 1906; ed. Univ. of Cluj, Romania.
Communist Party worker, Transylvania; mem. illegal Hungarian C.P. Central Cttee. 39-45, arrested several times; Chief of Hungarian C.P. Secr. for South Hungary 45-46; mem. Central Board Hungarian C.P. 46-49; Chair. Hungarian Broadcasting Office 49-53; Chief Ed. *Esti Budapest* (daily) 56; Chair. Govt. Information Office 57; mem. Central Cttee. Hungarian Socialist Workers' Party 57-; Alt. mem. Politburo, Sec. (Propaganda) of Central Cttee. 59-, full mem. Politburo 62-; Order of Liberty 45, "For the Workers' and Peasants' Power" Hon. Order 57.
MSzMP Központi Bizottsága, Jászai Mari tér 16, Budapest XV, Hungary.

Szokolay, Sándor; Hungarian composer; b. 1931; ed. Budapest Music Academy.
Has won prizes in Warsaw, Moscow, Vienna.
Works include: *Blood Wedding* (opera) 63, *Az iszonyat balladája* (The Ballad of Horror), *Tetemrehivds* (Ordeal of the Bier); Oratorios: *A tüz márciusa* (March Fire), *Istár pokoljárása* (Ishtar's Descent to Hell); has also

written cantatas, songs, chamber music and choral works.
Budapest XI, Villányi ut. 9, Hungary.
Telephone: 259-730.

Sztachelski, Jerzy; Polish physician and politician; b. 11; ed. Stephen Batory Univ., Vilno.
Member Communist Union of Polish Youth until 39; Officer, Polish Army, later Gen. Sec. Union of Patriots in U.S.S.R., Second World War; government posts 44-51; Minister of Health 51-56; Minister without Portfolio 57-60; Minister of Health and Social Welfare 61-; mem. Polish Workers' Party 45-, mem. Cen. Cttee. Polish United Workers' Party 48-; mem. Seym.
15 Miodowa Street, Warsaw, Poland.

Szurdi, István; Hungarian politician; b. 1911.
Manual industrial worker, later technician until 45; mem. Hungarian Socialist Workers' Party 36-, full time party functionary 46-; mem. Nat. Assembly 48-; Sec. Central Cttee. Hungarian Socialist Workers' Party 63-; Minister of Home Trade 66-.
Ministry of Home Trade, Budapest, Hungary.

Szyr, Eugeniusz; Polish economist and politician; b. 14 April 1915.
Member Union of Polish Communist Youth 30, later Polish Communist Party; Spanish Civil War 36-38; Polish Army, U.S.S.R. 43; Under-Sec. in Ministry of Industry and Commerce 46; Deputy Chair. State Comm. for Econ. Planning 49, Chair. 53-56; Sec. of Econ. Cttee., Council of Ministers 57; Deputy Chair. Council of Ministers 59-; Chair. Cttee. of Science and Technology 63-; mem. Central Cttee. Polish United Workers' Party; mem. Politburo 64-.
Council of Ministers, Warsaw, Poland.
Telephone: 280-708.

Szyszlo, Fernando de; Peruvian painter; b. 5 July 1925; ed. School of Fine Arts, Catholic Univ., Lima.
Professor of Art, Catholic Univ. of Lima and Coll. of Architecture, Nat. Univ. of Engineering; Visiting Critic Cornell Univ. 62-63; Visiting Lecturer Yale Univ. 66; First one-man exhbn., Lima 47, later in New York, Washington, Ithaca, Rio de Janeiro, São Paulo, Mexico, Buenos Aires, Santiago de Chile, Bogotá, Caracas, Florence and Paris; group exhbns. include Biennali at Venice and São Paulo; represented in museums and public collections in North and South America; Carnegie Prize 58, Guggenheim Int. Prize 64.
Avenida Diagonal 550, Miraflores, Lima, Peru.

T

Taba, Abdol Hossein, M.D.; Iranian physician; b. 12; ed. Birmingham and London Univs.
Former Dir.-Gen. of Health, Teheran; Vice-Pres. WHO Exec. Board 51, Dep. Regional Dir. Eastern Mediterranean Regional Office 52-57, Regional Dir. 57-.
World Health Organization Eastern Mediterranean Regional Office, P.O. Box 1517, Alexandria, United Arab Republic.

Tabard de Grièges, (Léon Maurice) Dominique; French former Inspector of Finances; b. 16 Feb. 1911; ed. Lycée Condorcet.
With Ministry of Finance, Budget Dept. 35-46; joined Compagnie Universelle du Canal Maritime de Suez 46, then Compagnie Financière de Suez, Dir.-Gen. 57-; now Admin. Dir.-Gen. Cie. Financière de Suez et de l'Union Parisienne; Chair. Suez Finance Co. (London) Ltd.; Dir. numerous financial companies including Banque de Suez et de l'Union des Mines, Banque de l'Union Parisienne (C.F.C.B.), Soc. d'Investissements Mobiliers, Cie. Générale d'Assurances contre les Accidents, Cie. Industrielle Maritime; Officier Légion d'Honneur, Hon. C.B.E. (U.K.).
1 rue d'Astorg, Paris 8e, France.

Tabeyev, Fikriat Akhmedzhanovich; Soviet politician; b. 1928; ed. Kazan State Univ.
Member C.P.S.U. 51-; Teacher of Political Economy, Kazan State Univ. 52-57; party work 57-59; Sec. Tartar Regional Cttee., C.P.S.U. 59-60, First Sec. 60-; mem. Central Cttee. of C.P.S.U. 61-; mem. Presidium of Supreme Soviet of U.S.S.R. 62-; mem. Cttee of U.S.S.R. Parliamentary Group; Deputy to U.S.S.R. and Tartar A.S.S.R. Supreme Soviets.
District Committee of C.P.S.U., Kazan, Tartar A.S.S.R., U.S.S.R.

Tabor, Hans Rasmussen, DR.RER.POL.; Danish diplomatist; b. 25 April 1922; ed. Birkerød Statsskole and Univ. of Copenhagen.
Secretary, Gen. Secr. Organisation for European Economic Co-operation (OEEC), Paris 48-50; Sec. Ministry of Foreign Affairs, Copenhagen 50-52; Asst. Head Danish Del. to OEEC 52-56; Branch Head Ministry of Foreign Affairs 56, 57-59; Dep. Sec.-Gen. Suez Canal Users' Asscn., London 57; Econ. Counsellor, Asst. Head Danish Mission to the European Communities 59-61, Minister and Head 61-64, Ambassador 63-64; Perm. Rep. to the UN 64-67; Minister of Foreign Affairs 67-68; Rep. of Denmark on the UN Security Council 67-68.
Publs. *Danmark og Marshallplanen* (Denmark and the Marshall Plan) 61, *De Seks og det økonomiske samarbejde i Vesten* (The Six and Economic Co-operation in the Western World).
c/o Ministry of Foreign Affairs, Copenhagen, Denmark.

Tabor, Peder; Danish editor; b. 23 Nov. 1891.
Journalist on staff of *Social-Demokraten* Fredericia 07-10; with *Social-Demokraten* Silkeborg 10-23; ed. of Social Dem. papers in Silkeborg, Herning and Skanderborg 23-30; editor of Sunday edition of *Social-Demokraten* 30; co-editor of *Social-Demokraten* (now *Aktuelt*) 34; Chief Ed. 41-59; Pres. Jutland Soc. for Modern Art 24-30; mem. exec. cttee. of Copenhagen Editors' Soc. (Pres. 43-45), of Danish-British Society 46; mem. Joint Representative Council of Danish Daily Newspapers; mem. Broadcasting Council 42-; Pres. Danish nat. news agency Ritzaus Bureau 55-59.
Publs. *Malurt* (a vol. of aphorisms) 19, *Naerbilleder*

(memoirs) 61, *Randbemaerkninger* (political aphorisms) 63.
Hans Egedes Gade 23, Copenhagen N., Denmark.
Telephone: 398093.

Taft, Charles Phelps, B.A., LL.B., LL.D., D.C.L.; American lawyer; b. 20 Sept. 1897; ed. Yale Univ.
Prosecuting Attorney, Hamilton County, Ohio 27-28; Govt. Arbitrator Toledo strikes 34; mem. Cincinnati City Council 38-42, 48-51, 55-, Mayor 55-57; Dir. Community War Services, Fed. Security Agency 41-43; Dir. War-time Economic Affairs, Dept. of State 44-45; Pres. Fed. Council of Churches 47-48; mem. Central Cttee. World Council of Churches 48-54; Partner, Taft and Luken; Medal for Merit 46; Republican.
Publs. *City Management—The Cincinnati Experiment* 33, *You and I—and Roosevelt* 36, *Why I am for the Church* 47, *Democracy in Politics and Economics* 50.
1003 First National Bank Building, Cincinnati, Ohio 45202, U.S.A.
Telephone: 513-241-2383.

Tai Ai-lien; Chinese actress; b. 16; ed. London.
Returned to China 39; travelled in West China, combined western dance and local Chinese dances, studied Aighur dancing; taught in Chungking; Kwangtung del. to N.P.C. 54; director, Peking Acad. of Dancing 55; mem. Central Cttee. Democratic League 56.
Peking Academy of Dancing, Peking, China.

Tairova, Taira Akperovna, M.SC. (ENG.); Soviet engineer and politician; b. 1913; ed. Baku Industrial Inst.
Engineer, Oil Industry, then Dir. Azerbaijan Research Inst. of Oil 36-40; Deputy Sec., then Sec. Azerbaijan C.P. Central Cttee. 42-49; Chair. Azerbaijan Council of Trade Unions 49-57; Sec. Azerbaijan Peace Cttee. 48; Deputy Supreme Soviet of the U.S.S.R. 54-; del. World Women Congress, Lausanne 55; mem. Soviet Parl. Dels. to Czechoslovakia 55, Belgium 56; Chair. Azerbaijan Scientific Technical Cttee. 57-62; mem. Soviet Del. to 13th Session of UN Gen. Assembly 59; Minister of Foreign Affairs, Azerbaijan S.S.R. 59; Deputy Chair. Azerbaijan Council of Ministers 63-; Deputy Supreme Soviet of Azerbaijan S.S.R. 59-; mem. Soviet Del. to India, Burma, Indonesia, Afghanistan 60, to Tunisia 62; Order of Red Banner of Labour (twice), Badge of Honour and other awards.
Council of Ministers of Azerbaijan S.S.R., Baku, Azerbaijan S.S.R., U.S.S.R.

Tajima, Michiji; Japanese business executive; b. 2 July 1885; ed. Tokyo Univ.
Aichi Bank 10; later Chief Personnel Section, Railway Board; Man. Dir. Showa Bank 27-36, Pres. 36; Pres. Tokyo Inquiry Office, then Pres. Japan Scholarship Soc.; Dir-Gen. Imperial Household Board 46-59; Chair. Sony Ltd. 59-.
Sony Ltd., 6-351 Kitashinagawa, Shinagawa-ku, Tokyo, Japan.

Tajitsu, Wataru; Japanese banker; b. 25 March 1902; ed. Tokyo Univ.
Joined Mitsubishi Bank 26, Pres. and Chair. of the Board 64-.
Mitsubishi Bank, 5, 2-chome, Marunouchi, Chiyoda-ku, Tokyo; Home: 6-41, 7-chome, Akasaka, Minato-ku, Tokyo, Japan.

Takagaki, Katsujiro; Japanese business executive; b. 26 Oct. 1893; ed. Tokyo Imperial Univ.
Director Mitsubishi Shoji Kaisha Ltd. 44-45, Man. Dir. 45-47, Pres. 47, Liquidator 47-49, Pres. (newly formed)

54-60, Chair. 60-; Dir. Mitsubishi Rayon Co. 53-, Mitsubishi Warehouse Co. 54-, Mitsubishi Cement Co. 55-, Dai-Nippon Paint Co. 58-; Exec. Dir. Fed. of Econ. Orgs. 52-63, Hon. mem. 63-; Vice-Pres. Tokyo Chamber of Commerce and Industry 64-65; official of numerous other business orgs.; Blue Ribbon Medal 58.
622, 7-chome, Hiratsuka, Shinagawa-ku, Tokyo, Japan.

Takahashi, Hitoshi; Japanese politician; b. 03; ed. Tokyo Univ.
Former Adviser to Japan War Bereaved Families Welfare Asscn.; fmr. Parl. Vice-Defence Minister; mem. House of Representatives; Minister of Justice 64-65; Liberal-Democrat.
c/o Ministry of Justice, Tokyo, Japan.

Takahashi, Mamoru; Japanese politician; b. 03; ed. Tokyo Univ.
Governor of Taihoku Province of Formosa 45-46; Dir. of Tax Admin. Agency 49-52; mem. House of Councillors 53-; Minister of State in charge of Econ. Planning Agency 64-65; Liberal-Democrat.
25-2 Kamiyama-cho, Shibuya-ku, Tokyo, Japan.

Takahashi, Satoru; Japanese diplomatist; b. 13.
Diplomatic Service 36-, France, Italy, Ministry of Foreign Affairs; Dir. of United Nations Bureau, Ministry of Foreign Affairs 62-63; Amb to Repub. of o! Viet-Nam 63-66, to Chile 66-.
Embassy of Japan, Callao 3796, Santiago, Chile.

Takahashi, Yusai, LL.D.; Japanese newspaper executive; b. 89; ed. Hokuyo Middle School.
Studied police systems 20-22; Asst. Sec. Home Ministry 23-24; Gov. Kagawa Prefecture 31-32; Foreign News Editor *Yomiuri Shimbun* 33-38, Gen. Man. 33-43, Vice-Pres. 42-45, Exec. Vice-Pres. and Editor 55; Chair. Board of Dirs. *Osaka Yomiuri Shimbun* 55; Pres. Japan Newspaper Asscn. 61; Hon. Prof. Police Coll. 60; Italian Order of Merit 59.
Publs. *A Study of the British Police System* 56, *A Study of the Japanese Police System of the Meiji Era*, Vol. I 60, Vol. II 61, Vol. III 63.
c/o *Yomiuri Shimbun*, 1 3-chome, Ginza Nishi, Chuo-ku, Tokyo, Japan.

Takamusa, Yosizaka; Japanese architect and town planner; b. 13 Feb. 1917; ed. Waseda Univ., Tokyo.
Lecturer, Japan Women's Coll. 42-50, Tokyo Agricultural School 45-48, Yamanasi Univ. 56-57, Tucumán Nat. Univ., Argentina 61-62; Asst. Prof. Waseda Univ. 50, Prof. 59, Head of Dept. of Architecture 64-; Man. Waseda Univ. Expedition to Equatorial Africa 58, and Leader of its MacKinley Alaska Expedition 60; Vice-Pres. Architectural Inst. of Japan; Dir. Japanese Asscn. of Architects.
Principal works: Japanese Pavilion, Venice Biennale 56, Maison Franco-Japonais 59, Athénée Français 62, Gotu City Hall 62, Univ. Seminar House 65; Projects: Redevelopment Plans for Tokada-no Baba District and Izu, Oosima.
Publs. *Form and Environment* 55, *Primitive Country to Civilized Country* 61, *Study on Dwelling* 65.
3-317 Hyakunintyo, Sinzi-ku, Tokyo, Japan.

Takeda, Chobei; Japanese business executive; b. 29 April 1905; ed. Keio Gijuku Univ.
President, Takeda Chemical Industries Ltd.
27 Doshomachi 2-chome, Higashi-ku, Osaka, Japan.

Takeuchi, Shunichi; Japanese oil executive; b. 17 Jan. 1896; ed. Tokyo Higher Commercial School.
Mitsubishi Holding Co. 17; Mitsubishi Trading Co. Ltd. 18-40, Manager, Produce Dept., London Branch 21-29, Asst. Gen. Manager, New York Branch 34-35, Gen. Manager, San Francisco and Seattle Branches 35-40; Gen. Manager, Mitsubishi Oil Co. Ltd. 41, Dir. and Pres. 46-61, Chair. of Board 61-66, Senior Adviser 66-; Dir. Japan Productivity Centre 58-; Pres. Japan

Management School 58-; Chair. of Board of Dirs. The English Language Educ. Council Inc. 63-; Vice-Pres. The Japan-British Soc., Tokyo 64-; Blue Ribbon Award 59, Order of the Rising Sun (Third Class) 66.
19-10 Nakane, 2-chome, Meguro-ku, Tokyo, Japan.

Takiguchi, Yukuo; Japanese business executive; b. 6 Aug. 1907; ed. Keio Univ.
NTN Manufacturing Co. 26-59; Pres. Toyo Bearing Co. Ltd. 59-.
3-28, Koraibashi, Higashi-ku, Osaka, Japan.

Takla, Philippe; Lebanese politician and banker; b. 3 Feb. 1915; ed. Univ. Law School, Beirut.
Law practice, Beirut 35-45; M.P. 45, 47-; Minister of Nat. Economy and Communications 45-46; Minister of Foreign Affairs 49, 61-63, 64-65, 66-Nov. 66; Gov. Bank of Lebanon 63-66, Nov. 66-67; Perm. Rep. to UN 67-.
Permanent Mission of Lebanon to the United Nations, 866 United Nations Plaza, Room 533-535, New York, N.Y. 10017, U.S.A.

Talagrand, Jacques Louis André (Thierry Maulnier); French writer; b. 1 Oct. 1909; ed. Lycée Louis-le-Grand, Paris, and Ecole Normale Supérieure.
Journalist on *l'Action Française*, later *Figaro* 30-; playwright 42-; dramatic critic *Combat* and *La Revue de Paris*; founded (with François Mauriac) *La Table Ronde*; mem. Académie Française 64-; Officier, Légion d'Honneur, Grand Prix de Littérature de l'Académie Française 59, Prix Pelman de la presse 59.
Plays: *Antigone* 44, *La Course des rois* 47, *Jeanne et les Juges* 49, *Le Profanateur* 52, *Oedipe-Roi* (adaptation) 52, *La Maison de la Nuit* 53, *La Condition humaine* (adaptation) 54, *Procès à Jésus* (adaptation) 58, *Le Sexe et le Néant* 60, *Signe du feu* (adaptation) 60.
Prose works inc. *La crise est dans l'Homme* 32, *Nietzsche* 33, *Racine* 34, *Introduction à la poésie française* 39, *Violence et Conscience* 45, *La Face de méduse du communisme* 52.
3 rue de Vaucresson, Marnes-la-Coquette (Hauts-de-Seine), France.

Talbot, Philips; American government official; b. 7 June 1915; ed. Univs. of Illinois, Chicago, London Univ., and Aligarh Muslim Univ., India.
Newspaper reporter 36-38; Fellow London Univ. 38-39; U.S. Naval service 41-46; Foreign Corresp. 46-48, 49-50; Visiting Asst. Prof. of Political Science, Chicago Univ. 48; Exec. Dir. American Univs. Field Staff Inc. 51-61; Asst. Sec. of State for Near Eastern and South Asian Affairs, Dept. of State 61-65; Amb. to Greece 65-; Ph.D. (Univ. of Chicago) 54, Hon. LL.D. (Mills Coll.) 63.
American Embassy, Athens, Greece.

Talboys, Brian Edward, M.P.; New Zealand farmer and politician; b. 7 July 1921; ed. Wanganui Collegiate School, and Victoria Univ., Wellington.
Served R.N.Z.A.F. in Second World War; joined *New Zealand Dairy Exporter* 50, later Asst. Ed.; has 500-acre farm, Heddon Bush, Southland; M.P. 57-, Parl. Under-Sec. 60-62; Minister of Agriculture 62-, Minister of Science 64-; National Party.
Parliament House, Wellington, New Zealand.

Taleghani, Khalil, B.SC.; Iranian civil engineer and politician; b. 13 Sept. 1913; ed. American Coll. of Teheran, and Univ. of Birmingham.
Junior engineer, England 37-39; Engineer, Persian Army 39-41; Chief Engineer, Technical Dir., Dir. of Ebtekar and other construction companies and Golpayegan Water Co. 41-51; Minister of Agriculture Dec. 51-June 52, July 52-March 53 and 55-56; Minister of State 56-59; Dir. Taleghani-Tashakori Co. (consulting engineers); Manager Karaj Dam Authority 54-59; Chair. Industrial and Mining Development Bank of Iran 60-63; Dir. Taleghani-Daftari (consulting engineers); Chair. B. F. Goodrich Tyre Manufacturing Co., Iran;

Chair. Pars Paper Manuf. Co.; Pres. Iranian Engineers Asscn.; Fellow, A.S.C.E.
Home: Baghe-Bank Street, Golhak, Teheran; Office: 42 Khoshbin Street, Fisher Abad, Teheran, Iran.
Telephone: 81984 (Home); 66358 (Office).

Talhouni, Bajhat; Jordanian lawyer and politician; b. 05; ed. Damascus Univ.
Former Pres. Court of Appeal; Minister of Interior, Minister of Justice and Chief of Royal Court 55-60; Prime Minister 60-62, 64-65 Oct. 67-, Minister of Foreign Affairs 61-62; Chief of Royal Cabinet 63-64.
Office of the Prime Minister, Amman, Jordan.

Tali, Alhaji Yakubu, Tolon Na; Ghanaian Chief and diplomatist; ed. Achimota.
Teacher, Northern Territories 38-47; Tali Na (Chief of Tali) 47-53; Tolon Na (Chief of Tolon) 53-; Chair. Dagomba Native Authority Council 49, later Dagomba District Council; mem. Gold Coast Legislative Assembly, later Ghana Legislative Assembly 51-, fmr. Deputy Speaker; Pres. Northern Territories Council 53-; High Commr. of Ghana in Nigeria 65-; Northern People's Party.
High Commission of Ghana, 21-23 King George V Road, Lagos, Nigeria.

Taliaferro, Paul E., A.B., LL.B.; American oil executive; b. 15 Oct. 1905; ed. Univs. of North Texas and Tulsa.
Admitted to Bar 30; Gen. Attorney, Sunray Oil Corpn. 31-37, Vice-Pres. 37-50, Dir. 46-, Vice-Pres. and Asst. to Pres. 50-52, Exec. Vice-Pres. 52-59, Pres., Chief Exec. Officer 59-64, Chair. of the Board, Chief Exec. Officer 64 (now called Sunray DX Oil Co.); Pres. and Dir. Sunray overseas cos.; Chair. and Dir. Liberia Refining Co.; Dir. numerous cos.; Exec. Dir. Int. Petroleum Exposition; Vice-Chair. Board of Trustees Univ. of Tulsa.
2735 East 57th Street South, Tulsa, Oklahoma 74105; and 1313 Sunray Building, Tulsa, Oklahoma 74120, U.S.A.
Telephone: 918-RIverside 2-4528 (Home); 918-LUther 3-4300 (Office).

Talib, Maj.-Gen. Naji; Iraqi army officer and politician; b. 1917; ed. Iraqi Staff Coll. and Sandhurst, England.
Military Attaché, London 54-55; Commdr. Basra Garrison 57-58; Minister of Social Affairs 58-59; lived abroad 59-62; Minister of Industry March 63-Nov. 64; mem. U.A.R.-Iraq Joint Presidency Council 64-65; Minister of Foreign Affairs Nov. 64-Sept. 65; Prime Minister and Minister of Petroleum Affairs Aug. 66-May 67.
Baghdad, Iraq.

Tallchief, Marjorie; American ballerina; b. 27; ed. Beverly Hills High School, Calif.
Daughter of the Chief of the Osages Indians; studied with Bronislava Nijinska; joined American Ballet Theatre; created role of Medusa in *Undertow*; Prima Ballerina, Ballet de Monte Carlo 48, American Ballet Theater 60; created leading roles in *Somnambula*, *Concerto Barrocco*, *Les Biches*, *Bolévo*, *Idylle*, *Prisoner of the Caucasus* and *Annabel Lee*; Première Danseuse Étoile, Paris Opera 57-, leading roles in *The Firebird*, *Les Noces Fantastiques*, *Giselle*, *Conte Cruel*, *Concerto* and numerous other ballets; Prima Ballerina, Hamburg State Opera 65-; Chevalier du Nicham-Iftikar.
c/o Harkness Foundation, 15 East 69 Street, New York, N.Y., U.S.A.

Talley, Lee, B.S.; American soft drink executive; b. 26 June 1901; ed. Emory Univ., Atlanta, Georgia.
Joined the Coca-Cola Co. 23, Vice-Pres., The Coca-Cola Co. Atlanta 50-52; Pres. and Dir. Coca-Cola Ltd., Toronto 52-54; Chair. Bd. Coca-Cola, Cuba 54-58; Pres. The Coca-Cola Export Corpn., New York City 54-58; Pres. The Coca-Cola Co., Atlanta 58-62, Chair. Board 61-.
The Coca-Cola Co., P.O. Drawer 1734, Atlanta, Ga. 30301, U.S.A.

Talmadge, Herman Eugene; American politician; b. 9 Aug. 1913; ed. Univ. of Georgia.
Practised law in Atlanta 36-41; served with U.S. Navy 41-45 with rank of Lieut.-Commdr.; Gov. of Georgia 48-55; U.S. Senator from Georgia 57-; Democrat.
Publ. *You and Segregation* 55.
347 Senate Office Building, Washington, D.C., U.S.A.
Telephone: 225-3643.

Tamayo, Rufino; Mexican painter; b. 99; ed. Mexico City Acad. of Fine Arts.
Executed murals for Mexico City Conservatoire 33, Smith Coll., Massachusetts 43, costumes and décor in *Antigone* (ballet) 59; rep. at numerous int. exhbns., including Dunn Int. Exhbn., London 63; Hon. mem. American Acad. of Arts and Letters; Chevalier de la Légion d'Honneur; numerous prizes.
Malintzin 20, Coyoacan, Mexico, D.F., Mexico.

Tambo, Oliver; South African politician; b. 17; ed. Anglican mission schools and Univ. Coll. of Fort Hare, Cape Province.
Teacher, Secondary School; Solicitor, Johannesburg, 51-60; banned from attending meetings 54-56 and for five years 59-; arrested on treason charges 56, charges withdrawn 57; Dep.-Pres. African Nat. Congress 58-67, Pres. 67-; escaped to London 60; mem. del. of exiled reps. of S. African parties to Third Conf. of Independent African States, Addis Ababa 60; attended UN Gen. Assembly (15th Session) 60; Head, External Mission of African Nat. Congress of South Africa.
African National Congress of South Africa, P.O. Box 2239, Dar es Salaam, Tanzania; and Africa Unity House, 3 Collingham Gardens, London, S.W.5, England.

Tamboura, Amadou, L. en D.; Upper Voltan international civil servant; b. 31 Dec. 1933; ed. primary schools in Djibo and Ouahigouya, Bamako Lycée in Mali, and Univs. of Dakar and Paris.
Customs Inspector 62; envoy to GATT 63; Div. Inspector of Customs and First Counsellor to Embassy of Upper Volta in Brussels 64; Chief, Third Div. Ouagadougou Customs; now Sec.-Gen. Customs Union of States of West Africa.
Secrétaire Général de l'Union Douanière des Etats de l'Afrique de l'Ouest, B.P. 28, Ouagadougou, Upper Volta.
Telephone: 25-79.

Tamiya, Hiroshi, D.SC.; Japanese biologist; b. 5 Jan. 1903; ed. Imperial Univ. of Tokyo.
Professor of Botany, Univ. of Tokyo 39-55; Dir. of Inst. of Applied Microbiology, Univ. of Tokyo 55-63; Dir. The Tokugawa Inst. for Biological Research 46-; mem. Special Cttee. of Int. Biological Programme 64-, Vice-Pres. 67-; Chair. Japanese Nat. Cttee. for Int. Biological Programme 64-; Editor *Biochemica et Biophysica Acta*, *Archiv für Mikrobiologie*, *Journal of Biochemistry*, *Plant and Cell Physiology*, *Journal of General and Applied Microbiology*; mem. Deutsche Akademie der Naturforscher; Foreign Assoc. U.S. Nat. Acad. of Sciences; Prize and Medal from Fujiwara Foundation; Acad. Prize from Acad. of Japan.
Publs. scientific works on metabolism of fungi, action mechanisms of respiratory enzymes, kinetics of enzyme action, mass-cultures of algae, mechanism of photosynthesis, growth physiology of micro-algae.
The Tokugawa Institute for Biological Research, Toshima-ku, Mejiro, Tokyo; Home: Shinjuku-ku, Shimo-ochiai 1-363, Tokyo, Japan.

Tamm, Igor Evgenievich; Soviet physicist; b. 8 July 1895; ed. Moscow Univ.
At Moscow Univ. 24-41, 56-58; at Lebedev Physical

Inst. of U.S.S.R. Acad. of Sciences 34-; mem. U.S.S.R. Acad. of Sciences 53-; Foreign mem. Polish Acad. of Sciences, Boston Acad. of Sciences and Art; produced the quantum theory of acoustical vibrations and scattering of light in solid bodies, developed the theory of interactions of light with electrons 30; indicated the existence of surface states (Tamm's Levels) of electrons in semiconductors 33; produced the first field theory of exchange nuclear forces (β-forces) 34; produced jointly the theory of Cherenkov Radiation 37; suggested jointly a way of obtaining controlled thermo-nuclear reaction 50; Hero of Socialist Labour; State Prizewinner; Nobel Prize for Physics (with Cherenkov and Frank) 58; Lomonosov Gold Medal, U.S.S.R. Acad. of Sciences 68; Order of Lenin, Order of Red Banner of Labour.
Publs. *Exchange Forces Between Neutrons and Protons* 34, *Relativistic Interaction of Elementary Particles* 45, *General Properties of Radiation of Systems with Superlight Speeds and Some Applications to Physics of Plazma* 59, *Electrodynamical Interaction of Electrons in Accelerators* 62.
P. N. Lebedev Physical Institute, Leninsky prospekt 53, Moscow, U.S.S.R.

Tan Chen-lin; Chinese politician; b. 03; ed. Red Army School, Junchu Kiangsi and Red Army Acad., Moscow.
Chairman, Kiangsu Prov. People's Govt. 32-54; Vice-Chair. Southwest Fukien Mil. and Admin. Cttee. 35; Commdr. Kiangnan Anti-Japanese Volunteers 38; Political Commissar 43; Sec. C.C.P., Chekiang Prov. Cttee. and Chair. Hangchow Mil. Control Comm. 49; Chair. Chekiang Prov. People's Govt. 50-52; Vice-Chair. East China Admin. Cttee. 52-54; mem. Standing Cttee., Nat. Cttee. People's Political Consultative Conf. 54-; mem. C.C.P. Central Cttee. 54-, Secretariat 56-, Politburo 58-; Dep. from Shanghai, Nat. People's Congress 58-; Vice-Premier State Council 59-, Dep. Chair. State Planning Comm. 62-; Dir., Gen. Office for Agriculture and Forestry, State Council.
State Council, Peking, People's Republic of China.

Tan Cheng; Chinese soldier; b. 1900.
Commissar on staff of 18th Army Group 42; additional mem. Central Cttee. C.C.P. at 7th Congress 45; posts in Political Dept. of army in Northern Command, later Tientsin, Wuhan and South China 49-; Vice-Chair. Ministry of Nat. Defence 54-65; decorated 55; Vice-Chair. N.P.C. 56; on Central Cttee. C.C.P. at 8th Congress 56; Dir. Political Section of People's Liberation Army 56.
c/o Ministry of National Defence, Peking, China.

Tan Chi-lung; Chinese administrator; b. 11.
Farmer; fought with Communist guerillas in Kiangsi and Chekiang Provs.; Political Commissar, People's Liberation Army 46-49; Vice-Political Commissar, Chekiang Mil. District 49-52; Vice-Chair. Chekiang Prov. People's Govt. 51-52, Chair. 52-54; Sec., C.C.P. Chekiang Prov. Cttee. 52-54; Political Commissar, Shantung Mil. District 54; Second Sec., C.C.P. Shantung Prov. Cttee. 54-56, Sec. 56-58, First Sec. 61-; mem. Shantung Prov. People's Govt. 55-; Gov. Shantung 58-61; Dep. from Shantung, Nat. People's Congress 58-; Alternate mem. C.C.P. Central Cttee. 56-.
Shantung Province Chinese Communist Party Committee, Tsinan, Shantung, People's Republic of China.

Tan Siew Sin; Malayan businessman and politician; b. 16; ed. Malacca and Raffles Coll. Singapore.
Malacca Municipal Commr. 46-49; mem. Fed. Legislative Council 48-, mem. Standing Cttee. on Finance 49-55; mem. Rubber Producers' Council 51-57, Vice-Chair. 57; mem. Rubber Industry Replanting Board 52-57, Vice-Chair. 57; Pres. Malayan Estate Owners' Asscn. 56, 57; mem. Malacca Chinese Advisory Board 50-55; Hon. Sec. Malacca Branch, Malayan Chinese Asscn. 49-57, Chair. Malacca Branch 57-, Vice-Pres. Malayan Chinese Asscn. 57-61, Pres. 61-; Fed. Minister of Commerce and Industry 57-59, Minister of Finance, Malaya 59-63, Malaysia 63-; Dir. Unitac Ltd., Malaka Pinda Rubber Estates Ltd., United Malacca Rubber Estate Ltd., Leong Hin San Ltd.
Ministry of Finance, Kuala Lumpur, Malaya, Malaysia.

Tanaka, Kakuei; Japanese politician; b. 18; ed. Chuo Technical School, Tokyo and Tokyo Univ.
Member, Lower House of Parl. 47-; Minister of Posts and Telecommunications (Kishi Cabinet) 57; Chair. Policy Board of Liberal Dem. Party 61-65, Sec.-Gen. Liberal Democratic Party 65-Nov. 66; Minister of Finance 62-65.
House of Representatives, Tokyo, Japan.

Tanaka, Paul Kotaro, LL.D.; Japanese international judge; b. 90; ed. Tokyo Imperial Univ.
Asst. Prof., Tokyo Imperial Univ. 17-23, Prof. 23-48, Emeritus 48-, Dean of Faculty of Law 37; Minister of Education 46; mem. House of Peers 46; mem. House of Councillors 47-; mem. Science Council 49; Chief Justice, Japanese Supreme Court 50-61; Judge, Int. Court of Justice 61-; mem. Japanese Acad. 41-; Hon. LL.D. (Fordham and Georgetown Univs., Boston Coll., Catholic Univ. of Chile, Univs. of Rome and Brazil).
Publs. *Theory of World Law, History of Latin-America, Education and Authority, Travel in Italy, Greece and Palestine, Seeking Truth and Peace, Treaties on Commercial Laws and Legal Philosophy.*
International Court of Justice, The Hague, Netherlands.

Tanaka, Shigematsu; Japanese business executive; b. 13 March 1898; ed. Osaka Higher Technical School.
Entered Shipbuilding Dept. Mitsui and Co., joined Mitsui Shipbuilding and Engineering Co. 37, Dir. Chief of Personnel 46, later Senior Managing Dir., Vice-Pres. 58-60, Pres. 60-; Pres. Obayame Prefectural Employers' Asscn.; Manager Tamano Shipyard 47-.
2-1-1 Muromachi, Nihonbashi, Chuo-ku, Tokyo, Japan.

Tananayev, Ivan Vladimirovich; Soviet inorganic and analytical chemist; b. 1904; ed. Dept. of Chemistry, Polytechnical Inst., Kiev.
Assistant in Analytical Chemistry, Kiev Polytechnical Inst. 25-30, Docent 30-34; Chief of Analytical Chemistry Laboratory, Acad. of Sciences of Georgian S.S.R., Tbilisi 34-35; Science worker, Inst. of Gen. and Inorganic Chemistry of Acad. of Sciences of U.S.S.R., Moscow 35-39, Doctor and Prof. 39-, Head, Analytical Laboratory and Rare Elements Laboratory 39-48, Deputy Dir. 48-54; mem. C.P.S.U. 42; Corresp. mem. U.S.S.R. Acad. of Sciences 46-58, mem. 58-; mem. Inorganic Chemistry Section of IUPAC 59-63; Lecturer, Inst. of Chemical Technology 62-; Editor-in-Chief *Inorganic Materials* 64-.
Publs. *The Physico-Chemical Analysis Method in Analytical Chemistry* 50, 56, 59, 61, *The Chemistry of Metal Fluorides* (13 editions 38-62), *Ferrocyanides of Metals* (9 editions 38-58), *Rare Elements Chemistry* 54, 55, 57, 59, 62, *Phosphates of Metals* 62, 63, *Interaction of Gadolinium Phosphate with Phospic Acid* 64.
Institute of General and Inorganic Chemistry of Academy of Sciences of U.S.S.R., Lenin Prospekt 31, Moscow U.S.S.R.

Tange, Sir Arthur Harold, Kt., C.B.E., B.A.; Australian diplomatist; b. 18 Aug. 1914; ed. Univ. of W. Australia.
Economist, various Australian Govt. Depts., Canberra 42-45; First Sec., Dept. of External Affairs 45; First Sec., Australian Mission to U.N., N.Y. 46-48; Counsellor, U.N. Div., Canberra 48-50; Asst. Sec. Dept. of External Affairs 51-53; Minister, Australian Embassy, Washington, D.C. 53-54; Sec. External Affairs 54-65; High Commr. to India and Amb. to Nepal 65-; mem. Australian del. Bretton Woods Monetary Conf., UN Preparatory Conf. UN Gen. Assembly 46, 47, 50, 51 and Econ. and Social Council, Reparations Conf., Paris;

ILO, Paris, Montreal and San Francisco; British Commonwealth Confs., London, Colombo, Sydney 49-63, etc.
Australian High Commission, Shanti Path, New Delhi, India.
Telephone: 70337.

Tange, Kenzo, DR. ENG.; Japanese architect; b. 4 Sept. 1913; ed. Tokyo Univ.
Member Japanese Architects Asscn., Hon. mem. American Acad. of Arts and Letters, Akad. der Künste, Germany; Hon. Fellow American Inst. of Architects; Royal Gold Medal, Royal Inst. of British Architects 65; AIA Gold Medal, American Inst. of Architects 66; Hon. Dr. Fine Arts, Univ. of Buffalo, N.Y.; Hon. Dr.-Ing., Technische Hochschule, Stuttgart; Hon. Dr. Arch., Politecnico di Milano, Italy.
Buildings include: Peace Memorial Park and Buildings, Hiroshima, Tokyo City Hall, Tokyo, Kurashiki City Hall, Kurashiki, Kagawa Prefectural Govt. Office, Yakamatsu, Roman Catholic Cathedral, Tokyo, Nat. Gymnasiums for 1964 Olympic Games, Tokyo, Skopje City Centre Reconstruction Project, Skopje, Yugoslavia, Yamanashi Press and Broadcasting Centre, Yamahashi.
689 Seijo Setagaya, Tokyo, Japan.
Telephone: Tokyo 482-0255.

Tangley, Baron, cr. 63 (Life Peer); **Edwin Savory Herbert,** K.B.E., LL.B., LL.D.; British solicitor and business executive; b. 29 June 1899; ed. Queen's Coll., Taunton, and Law Society's School.
R.N.V.R. 17-19; admitted solicitor 20, joined firm of Sydney Morse and Co., Senior Partner 29-; Dir.-Gen. Postal and Telegraph Censorship Dept. 40-45; Chair. Cttee. on Intermediaries 49, Cttee. of Enquiry into Electricity Supply Industry 54; mem. Council Law Soc. 35-, Pres. 56-57; Chair. Ultramar Co. Ltd., The Industrial and Gen. Trust Ltd., Trustees Corpn. Ltd., Imperial Continental Gas Asscn., and other companies; Dep. Chair. Yorkshire Insurance Co. Ltd., Rediffusion Television Ltd., Rediffusion Ltd.; Pres. Arbitration Comm., Int. Chamber of Commerce, Vice-Pres. Court of Arbitration; Chair. Royal Comm. on Local Govt. in Greater London 57; mem. Royal Comm. on Trade Unions and Employers' Asscns. 65-68; Hon. LL.D. (Montreal) 56; Medal for Merit (U.S.A.); King Haakon's Liberty Cross (Norway) 47.
Tangley Way, Blackheath, nr. Guildford, Surrey, England.

Tangney, Dorothy Margaret, B.A.; Australian politician; b. 11; ed. Univ. of W. Australia.
Teaching staff Education Dept. Western Australia; hon. Life Associate Univ. of Australia; mem. Standing Cttee. of Convocation Univ. of W. Australia; mem. Federal Exec. Australian Labour Party; Senator for W. Australia since 43 (first woman to be elected to Commonwealth Senate).
The Senate, Canberra, A.C.T., Australia.

Tanguy-Prigent, François; French politician; b. 11 Oct. 1909.
Mem. Conféd. Nat. Paysanne and active in co-operative agricultural organisations; Socialist (S.F.I.O.) Deputy 36-40, 46-58; voted against Pétain 40; a founder of the Peasant Resistance Movement, organised clandestine *Resistance Paysanne;* joined Maquis 42; Minister for Agriculture 44-47, for Ex-Servicemen 56-57; mem. S.F.I.O. Dir. Cttee; Conseiller Général for Lammeur (Finistère); Chevalier Légion d'Honneur.
1 rue Haute, Morlaix (Nord-Finistère), France.

Tanida, Toshio; Japanese shipping executive; b. 97; ed. Tokyo Higher Commercial School.
Joined Mitsubishi Goshi Kaisha 18, Mitsubishi Trading Co. 18, Man. Steamship Dept. (Kobe branch) 40, Man. Kobe branch 42, Taipeh (Formosa) branch 42, Dir. Mitsubishi Steamship Co. Ltd. 46, Man. Dir. 46; Man. Dir.

Kyokuto Shipping Co. Ltd. 49; Man. Dir. Mitsubishi Shipping Co. Ltd. 49, Senior Man. Dir. 49, Vice-Pres. 57, Pres. 58-; Chair. Japan Tanker Owners' Asscn. 54-; Dir. Japanese Shipowners' Asscn. 59-.
2-20 Marunouchi, Chiyoda-ku, Tokyo, Japan.

Taniguchi, Toyosaburo; Japanese textile executive; b. 29 July 1901; ed. Tokyo Univ.
Director Osaka Godo Spinning Co. Ltd. 29-, Toyobo Co. Ltd. 31-, Japan Rayon Textile Export Promotion Co. Ltd. 60-; Auditor Japan Exlan Co. Ltd. 56-; Exec. Vice-Pres. Toyobo Co. Ltd. 51-59, Pres. 59-, Chair. of Board 66-; Rep. Dir. Kansai Cttee. for Econ. Devt. 59-60, Standing Dir. Kansai Econ. Fed. 59-; Pres. Toyobo-Howa Textile Eng. Co. Ltd. 61-; Junior Vice-Pres. IFCATI 64-66, Senior Vice-Pres. 66-; Chair. Japan Spinners Asscns. 66-.
283 Gunge Kakiuchi, Mikage-cho, Higashinada-ku, Kobe, Japan.

Tannous, Afif I, B.A., M.A., PH.D.; American government official; b. 25 Sept. 1905; ed. American Univ. of Beirut, St. Lawrence Univ., Canton, N.Y., and Cornell Univ.
Admin. position with British Govt. in Sudan 29-31; with Education Dept., Govt. of Palestine and Rural Improvement Programme 31-33; taught Social Science at American Univ. of Beirut and directed rural improvement work 33-37; taught Social Science at Univ. of Minn., U.S.A. 40-43; joined U.S. Dept. of Agriculture, as Middle East specialist, later Head of Middle East Div.; Advisory Editor, *Middle East Journal* 47-; Lecturer on Middle East, School of Advanced Int. Studies, Washington, D.C. 48-51; Deputy Dir. U.S. Technical Co-operation Service for Lebanon 51-54; Co-ordinator, Dept. of Agriculture Services to Technical Co-operation Admin. 54-61; mem. U.S. Agricultural Mission to Middle East 46; FAO Agricultural Mission, Greece 46, UN Economic Survey Mission Middle East 49; Chief Africa and Middle East Branch, Foreign Agric. Service 56-61; Area Officer, Near East and Africa 61-; Deputy Dir. U.S. Exhibit, Cairo Int. Agricultural Exhbn. 61; Founder-mem. Soc. for Int. Devt.; Fellow, American Asscn. for Advancement of Science, American Geographical Soc., American Sociological Asscn., American Agric. Econ. Asscn.; U.S. Citizen 43-.
6912 Oak Court, Annandale, Va., U.S.A.

Tanoe, Appagny; Ivory Coast diplomatist; b. 1 Oct. 1929; ed. Univ. de Bordeaux.
Former Head Doctor, Centre Hospitalier, Abidjan; Vice-Pres. Econ. and Social Council of the Ivory Coast 61-64; Ambassador to France 65-.
Embassy of the Ivory Coast, 102 Avenue Raymond-Poincaré, Paris 16e, France.

Tans, Jean Guillaume Hubert; Netherlands politician; b. 19 Jan. 1912; ed. Univ.
Teacher in Secondary schools; mem. Second Chamber of Parl. 54; mem. Municipal Council of Maastricht 55-66; mem. Provincial States of Limburg 58-66; mem. Party Cttee. Netherlands Labour Party 61-, Chair. 65-; Knight of Order of the Lion (Netherlands).
Office: Partij van de Arbeid, Tesselschadestr. 31, Amsterdam (W); Home: Schweibergetweg 25a, Mechelen-Wittem, Netherlands.
Telephone: 04455-273; 020-87731.

Tao Chu; Chinese politician; b. 1903.
Former mem. Kuomintang; Communist guerrilla, S.E. and Central China 27-47; took part in occupation of Peking 49; in Central-South China 49-66; Senior Sec. Kwangtung C.P. 55; mem. Central Cttee. Chinese C.P. 56-; Political Commissar Canton Military Region (Kwangtung, Kwangsi and Hunan Provinces) 57-61; First Sec. Central-South Party Bureau 61-66; Head of Propaganda Dept., Central Cttee. of C.C.P. 66-; Vice-Premier 65-.
Propaganda Dept. of Central Committee of C.C.P., Peking, People's Republic of China.

Tape, Gerald Frederick, M.S., PH.D.; American physicist and scientific administrator; b. 29 May 1915; ed. Eastern Michigan Univ., and Michigan Univ.
Assistant in Physics, Eastern Mich. Univ. 33-35, Univ. of Mich. 36-39; Instructor in Physics, Cornell Univ. 39-42; Staff mem. Radiation Laboratory, Mass. Inst. of Technology 42-46; Asst., later Assoc. Prof. of Physics Univ. of Ill. 46-50; Asst. to Dir., Dep. Dir., Brookhaven Nat. Laboratory 51-62; Vice-Pres. Associated Univs. Inc. 62, Pres. 62-63; U.S. Atomic Energy Commr. 63-; Fellow American Physical Soc., mem. American Asscn. for Advancement of Science; Hon. D.Sc. (E. Michigan Univ. 64).
Publs. co-author with L. J. Haworth *Relay Radar Chapter of Massachusetts Institute of Technology Radiation Laboratory Technical Series*; co-author with Dr. F. K. Pittman and M. F. Searl *Future Energy Needs and the Role of Nuclear Power* 64.
7705 Winterberry Place, Bethesda, Maryland, U.S.A.

Tàpies, Antoni; Spanish painter; b. 13 Dec. 1923; self-taught.
First one-man exhbn., Barcelona 48, later in Paris, New York, London, Zürich, Rome, Milan, Munich, Stockholm, Hanover, Washington, Pasadena, Buenos Aires, Caracas, Düsseldorf, Bilbao, Madrid and Barcelona; French Govt. Scholarship 50; UNESCO Prize, Venice Biennale and Pittsburgh International Prize 58, Guggenheim Prize 64.
C. Zatagoza 57, Barcelona, Spain.

Tarabanov, Milko; Bulgarian diplomatist.
Former Dep. Mayor of Sofia, later First Dep. Minister for Foreign Affairs, Bulgaria; Perm. Rep. to UN 63-.
Permanent Mission of Bulgaria to the United Nations, 22 East 73rd Street, New York City 22, N.Y., U.S.A.

Taranczewski, Waclaw; Polish painter; b. 03; ed. Poznań, Cracow and Warsaw.
Organised Poznań Higher School of Art 45; Prof. of Monumental Painting, Cracow Acad. of Arts 47-; works exhibited Brussels Int. Exhibition 35, Paris Exhbn. of Modern Art 46, XXIX Venice Biennale 58, etc.; Guggenheim Foundation Nat. Prize 58 and numerous other awards; easel and mural paintings, also cycles: *Mala Malarka* (The Little Painter), *Koncert w atelier* (Concert in the Studio), *Martwa natura z swiętkiem* (Still Life with Seated Christ), *Martwa natura z wiolenczela* (Still Life with Cello).
13/6 Siemaszki, Cracow, Poland.

Tarasov, Aleksandr Michailovich; Soviet government official; b. 1912; ed. Lomonosov Mechanical Inst., Moscow.
Former Manager of Tractor Plants; Chair. Council of Nat. Econ., Byelorussian S.S.R. 58-63; Cand. mem. C.P.S.U. Central Cttee. 61-; Deputy Chair. Supreme Council of Nat. Econ., U.S.S.R. Council of Ministers 63-65; Minister of Motor Industry 65-; Deputy to U.S.S.R. Supreme Soviet.
Ministry of Motor Industry, Moscow, U.S.S.R.

Tarasov, Nikolai Nikiforovich; Soviet politician; b. 11; ed. Moscow Textile Inst.
Foreman, Shop Superintendent, Dir. of Spinning Mill, Deputy Head of Cotton Mill, Orethovo-Zuevo 35-42; Soviet Army 42-45; Factory Head Engineer, Head Engineer, Cotton Industry Central Admin. of Moscow Region, Head, Cotton Industry Central Admin. of Ivanovo Region 45-52; Dep. Minister of Light Industry of U.S.S.R. 52-53; Head, Consumer Goods Dept., U.S.S.R. Council of Ministers 53-55; Dep. Chair., U.S.S.R. State Planning Cttee. 55-57; Dep. Chair. Vladimir Econ. Council 58-60; Dep. Chair. All Russian Econ. Council 60-62; Chair. State Cttee. of U.S.S.R. State Planning Cttee. for Light Industry 62-65; Minister of Light Industry 65-; mem. C.P.S.U. 42-; Cand. mem.

Central Cttee. C.P.S.U.; Deputy to U.S.S.R. Supreme Soviet.
Ministry of Light Industry, 15 Verkhnyaya Krasnoselskaya, Moscow, U.S.S.R.

Tarasova, Alla Konstantinovna; Soviet actress; b. 1898; ed. Moscow Art Theatre Studio School.
Actress at the Moscow Art Theatre 16-; mem. C.P.S.U. 54-; People's Artist of the U.S.S.R. 37; State prize-winner.
Principal roles: Anna Karenina (*Anna Karenina*), Tatyana (*Enemies*), Masha (*Three Sisters*), Elena Andreevna (*Uncle Vanya*), Tugina (*Last Sacrifice*), Mary (*Mary Stewart*); film roles: Katherina (*Thunderstorm*), Kruchinina (*Guilty without Guilt*).
Moscow Arts Theatre, 3 Proyezd Khudozhestvennogo teatra 3, Moscow, U.S.S.R.

Tarazi, Salah El Dine, L. en D., D. en D.; Syrian diplomatist; b. 19; ed. Coll. des Frères, Damascus and Faculté Française de Droit, Beirut.
Lawyer 40-47; Lecturer and Asst. Prof. of Law, Damascus Univ. 46-48; Ministry of Foreign Affairs 49-50; Chargé d'Affaires, Brussels 51-53; Alt. Perm. Rep. to UN 53-56; Sec.-Gen., Ministry of Foreign Affairs 56-57; Ambassador to U.S.S.R. 57-58; Ambassador of U.A.R. to Czechoslovakia 58-59, to People's Repub. of China 59-61; Perm. Rep. of Syria to UN 62-64; Ambassador to U.S.S.R., concurrently accred. to Poland 65-; Syrian, Belgian and Czech awards.
Publ. *Les Services Publics Libano-Syriens* 46.
Syrian Embassy, Moscow, Mansourovsky per. 4, U.S.S.R.

Tardieu, Jean; French writer; b. 1 Nov. 1903; ed. Lycée Condorcet and Univ. de Paris à la Sorbonne.
With Radiodiffusion Télévision Française (O.R.T.F.) 44-, Head Drama Section 44-45, Dir. Club d'essai-centre 46-60, Dir. France musique O.R.T.F. 54-64, Admin. Counsellor 64-; Chevalier Légion d'Honneur.
Publs. *Accents, Le Témoin invisible, Figures, Monsieur Monsieur, Un Mot pout un autre, La Première Personne du singulier, Une voix sans personne, Théâtre de chambre, L'Espace et la Flûte, Poèmes à jouer, De la peinture abstraite, Choix de poèmes, Histoires obscures, Il était une fois, deux fois, trois fois* (Children's Book), *Pages d'écritures*; translations of many foreign plays including Goethe.
71 boulevard Arago, Paris 13e, France.

Tariki, Abdallah; Saudi Arabian oil executive; b. 19; ed. Univs. of Cairo and Texas.
Studied at Univ. of Texas and worked as trainee with Texaco Inc. in W. Texas and Calif. 45-49; Dir. Oil Supervision Office, Eastern Province, Saudi Arabia (under Ministry of Finance) 49-55; Dir.-Gen. of Oil and Mineral Affairs (Saudi Arabia) 55-60; Minister of Oil and Mineral Resources 60; Dir. Arabian American Oil Co. 59-62; Leader Saudi Arabian Del. at Arab Oil Congresses 59, 60.
c/o Ministry of Oil and Minerals, Riyadh, Saudi Arabia.

Tarjanne, Päivö Kaukomieli; Finnish diplomatist; b. 4 May 1903; ed. Univs of Helsinki and Paris, and Inst. Int. des Hautes Etudes, Paris.
Attaché, Ministry of Foreign Affairs 28; Attaché, Stockholm 29-30; Sec. Ministry of Foreign Affairs 30-32; First Sec. Berne and Geneva (mem. of permanent del. to League of Nations) 32-34; Counsellor, Stockholm 34-38; Dir. of the Administrative Section of the Ministry of Foreign Affairs 39-45 (rank of Minister 42); Minister to Norway 45-50, to Iceland 47-50; Sec.-Gen. of Ministry of Foreign Affairs 50-53; Minister to Denmark 53-55, Ambassador 55-56; Ambassador to Sweden 56-61, to Denmark 61-.
Finnish Embassy, Hammerensgade 5, Copenhagen K, Denmark.
Telephone: Mi 4304.

Tarjanne, Toivo, M.A., LL.M.; Finnish jurist; b. 8 Feb. 1893; ed. Helsinki Univ.
Sec. Ministry of Commerce and Industry 31-32, to Chancellor of Justice 32-42; Judge, Supreme Administrative Court 43; Governor of Province of Vasa 43-44; Chancellor of Justice 44-50; Pres. Supreme Court 50-63; Chancellor, Order of Finnish White Rose and Order of Finnish Lion 63-.
Pohjoiskaari 40, Helsinki 20, Finland.
Telephone: Helsinki 67-5160.

Tarkington, Andrew Wilson; American oil executive; b. 7 Aug. 1911; ed. Southern Methodist Univ., Dallas, Texas.
Credit Man. Bethlehem Supply Co., Tulsa, Oklahoma 37-39, Asst. Treas. 39-48; Treas. Continental Oil Co., Ponca City, Oklahoma 48-50, Vice-Pres. and Central Regional Gen. Man. 51-53, Vice-Pres. and Southwestern Regional Gen. Man. 54-56, Senior Vice-Pres., Continental Oil Co., Houston, Texas 56-63, Exec. Vice-Pres., New York 63-64, Pres. 64-, Pres. and Chief Exec. Officer 67-.
Continental Oil Co., 30 Rockefeller Plaza, New York, N.Y. 10020; Home: Highland Farm Road, Greenwich, Conn., U.S.A.
Telephone: NO1-9767.

Tarski, Alfred, PH.D.; American (b. Polish) professor of mathematics; b. 14 Jan. 1902; ed. Univ. of Warsaw.
Instructor, Polish Pedagogical Inst., Warsaw 22-25; Prof. Zeromski's Lycée, Warsaw 25-39; Docent and Adjoint Prof. Univ. of Warsaw 25-39; Research Assoc. Harvard Univ. 39-41; Visiting Prof. Coll. of City of New York 40-41; mem. Inst. for Advanced Study, Princeton 41-42; Lecturer, Univ. of Calif., Berkeley 42-45, Assoc. Prof. 45-46, Prof. of Mathematics 46-; Visiting Prof. Nat. Univ. of Mexico 57; Research Prof. Miller Inst. for Basic Research in Science 58-60; mem. U.S. Nat. Acad. of Sciences; Corresp. Fellow British Acad.; Foreign mem. Royal Netherlands Acad. of Sciences and Letters; Past Pres. Asscn. for Symbolic Logic, Int. Union for History and Philosophy of Science; Past Chair. U.S. Nat. Cttee. Int. Union for History and Philosophy of Science.
Publs. *The Concept of Truth in the Language of Deductive Sciences* 33, *Geometry* (with Z. Chwiałkowski and W. Schayer) 35, *Introduction to Logic and the Methodology of Deductive Sciences* 36, *Direct Decompositions of Finite Algebraic Systems* (with B. Jónsson) 47, *A Decision Method for Elementary Algebra and Geometry* 48, *Cardinal Algebras* 49, *Undecidable Theories* (with A. Mostowski and R. M. Robinson) 53, *Logic, Semantics, Metamathematics* 56, *Ordinal Algebras* 56.
Home: 462 Michigan Avenue, Berkeley, Calif. 94707; Office: Department of Mathematics, University of California, Berkeley, Calif. 94720, U.S.A.
Telephone: 415-524-2094 (Home); 415-642-2721 (Office).

Tartakower, Arie, DR. IUR., D.RER.POL.; Israeli (b. Polish) university professor; b. 24 Sept. 1897; ed. Univ. of Vienna.
Co-founder Zionist Labour Movement and Chair. Zionist Labour Party, Poland 22-29; Lecturer, Inst. of Jewish Sciences, Warsaw 32-39; Dir. Dept. of Relief and Rehabilitation of World Jewish Congress (U.S.A.) 39-46; fmr. Professor, Lecturer and Head, Dept. of Sociology of the Jews, Hebrew Univ., Jerusalem; Chair. Israel Exec., World Jewish Congress; Dep. mem. General Council World Zionist Org.; mem. World Secr., Zionist Labour Movement; Chair. World Asscn. for Hebrew Language and Culture; Co-founder and fmr. Pres. Israel Asscn. for UN.
Publs. include: *History of the Jewish Labour Movement, Jewish Emigration and Jewish Policy of Migration, The Jewish Refugee, Jewish Wanderings in the World, The Wandering Man, The Jewish Society, The Israeli Society, History of Colonization, Jewish Colonization in the Diaspora, History of Jewish Nationalism, The Tribes of Israel* (2 vols.).
1 Ben Yehuda Road, Jerusalem, Israel.
Telephone: Jerusalem 22889.

Taschereau, Robert, P.C., LL.D.; Canadian judge; b. 10 Sept. 1896; ed. Laval Univ.
Admitted to Quebec Bar 20; Prof. of Criminal Law, Laval Univ. 29-40; Prof. of Civil Law, Univ. of Ottawa 35-; Judge, Canadian Supreme Court 40-63; Chief Justice of Canada 63-67; various hon. degrees.
150 Driveway, Apt. 109, Ottawa 4, Ontario, Canada.
Telephone: 233-1860.

Tashiro, Shigeki; Japanese business executive; b. 5th Dec. 1890; ed. Meiji Univ.
Formerly with Mitsui Bussan Co., Moji, New York, Tokyo, London, Nagoya; Dir. Toyo Rayon Co. 36-, Man. Dir. 42-45, Pres. 45-50, Chair. 50-; Chair. Japan Chemical Fibre Asscn.
2-2 Muromachi, Nihonbashi, Chuo-ku, Tokyo, Japan.

Tashmuhamedov, Musa (*see* Aibek).

Tassara Gonzàlez, Gen. Luis; Chilean army officer; b. 26 Feb. 1908.
Infantry and Staff Officer; a UN Mil. Observer in Kashmir 51-52, 56-57; fmr. Instructor, Nat. Defence Acad., Chile; later Chief of Joint Operations, Armed Forces Staff; later Dir. of Army War Acad. 61; C.-in-C. Southern Reg. 61-64; Chief Mil. Observer, UN Mil. Observer Group in India and Pakistan (UNMOGIP) 66-.
c/o UNMOGIP, United Nations, New York City, N.Y., U.S.A.

Taswell, Harold Langmead Taylor, M.COM.; South African diplomatist; b. 14 Feb. 1910; ed. Christian Brothers Coll., Pretoria, and Univ. of Cape Town.
Department of External Affairs 37-, Berlin 37-39, London 39, The Hague 40, New York 40-46; Consul, Elisabethville 46-49; Int. Trade and Econ. Section, Dept. of External Affairs, Pretoria 49-51; First Sec., Wash. 51-56; Consul-Gen., Luanda, Angola 56-59; High Commr. of S. Africa in Fed. of Rhodesia and Nyasaland 59-61, Accredited Diplomatic Rep. 61-63, Accredited Diplomatic Rep. in S. Rhodesia 63-64; Head, Africa Div., Dept. of Foreign Affairs, Pretoria 64; Ambassador to U.S.A. 65-.
South African Embassy, 3051 Massachusetts Avenue, N.W., Washington, D.C. 20008, U.S.A.

Tata, Jehangir R. D.; Indian industrialist; b. 29 July 1904.
Began career as Asst. with Tata Sons Ltd. 22; Dir. 26; Chair. 38; Chair. Tata Industries Private Ltd.; Chair. or Dir. Companies managed by or assoc. with Tata Industries (Prvt.) Ltd., inc. Tata Iron & Steel Co. Ltd., Tata Oil Mills Co. Ltd., Tata Engineering & Locomotive Co. Ltd., Tata Chemicals Ltd., New India Assurance Co. Ltd.; Chair. Air-India Int., Tata Inst. of Fundamental Research, J. N. Tata Endowment for Higher Educ. of Indians; Pres. Court, Indian Inst. of Science; mem. The Indian Airlines Corpn., Exec. Cttee. IATA, Central Advisory Council of Industries, Nat. Council of Applied Econ. Research, Atomic Energy Comm., Governing Body, Council of Scientific and Industrial Research; del. to 3rd Session UN Gen. Assembly 48; Hon. mem. Iron and Steel Inst. (London); Officer of the Legion of Honour, Padma Vibhushan, Knight Commdr. Order of St. Gregory the Great.
Tata Sons Private, Ltd., Bombay House, Bruce Street, Fort, Bombay, India.

Tatarkiewicz, Władysław, PH.D.; Polish philosopher; b. 86; ed. Warsaw, Zürich, Paris, Berlin and Marburg Univs.
Former Prof. Warsaw Univ.; mem. fmr. Polish Acad. of Learning; mem. Polish Acad. of Sciences and several other Polish and foreign scientific and learned socs.
Publs. *Historia filozofii* (History of Philosophy) 31, 55,

(5th edn. 58), *Les trois morales d'Aristote* 32, *Skupienie i marzenie* (Concentration and Dreaming) 35, *O szczesciu* (On Happiness) 48, *Dominik Merlini, Historia Estetyki* (History of Aesthetics) 60.
Chocimska 35, Warsaw, Poland.

Tatay, Sándor; Hungarian writer; b. 10; ed. Sopron, Pécs.
Journalist *Kelet Népe* 37-.
Publs. *Thunderstorm* 41, *The Simeon Family* (5 vols.) 55-59, *White Carriage* 60; *The House under the Rocks* (film) 58; children's books and short stories.
Gyöngyösi, u. 53, Budapest XIII, Hungary.
Telephone: 409-523.

Tate, Allen, LITT.D.; American writer and university professor; b. 19 Nov. 1899; ed. Georgetown Preparatory School, and Vanderbilt Univ.
Guggenheim Foundation Fellow 28-30; Prof. of English, Univ. of North Carolina 38-39; Resident Fellow in Poetry, Princeton Univ. 39-42; Ed. of *The Sewanee Review* 44-47; Visiting Prof., Univ. of Chicago 49; Prof. of English, Univ. of Minnesota 51-; Visiting Prof., Univ. of Rome 53-54; American Acad. of Arts and Letters Award 48; Bollingen Prize for Poetry 56, Acad. of American Poets Award 63; Gold Medal Società Dante Alighieri 62; mem. Univ. of Oxford 58-59, Nat. Inst. of Arts and Letters, American Acad. of Arts and Letters 64.
Publs. *The Fathers* 38, *Poems 1922-1947* 48, *On the Limits of Poetry* 48, *The Hovering Fly* 48, *The Forlorn Demon* 53, *Collected Essays* 59, *Poems* 60, *Essays of Four Decades* 68.
University of the South, Sewanee, Tenn. 37375, U.S.A.

Tate, James Hugh Joseph, LL.D.; American politician; b. 10; ed. Northeast Evening High School, Strayer's Business Coll., Tucker Inst., St. Joseph's Coll. and Temple Univ. Law School.
Member Pennsylvania Legislature 40-46; Vice-Chair. Democratic City Cttee., Philadelphia 52-; mem. Philadelphia City Council 51-55, Pres. 55-62, Acting Mayor of Philadelphia 62-63, Mayor 64-; Chair. Delaware River Port Authority 62-63; mem. Exec. Cttee. American Municipal Asscn. 62-.
4029 N. 7th Street, Philadelphia 40, Pennsylvania, U.S.A.

Tati, Jacques (Jacques Tatischeff); French actor and film director; b. 9 Oct. 1908.
Formerly music-hall artist; films directed include *Gai Dimanche, L'Ecole des Facteurs, Soigne ton Gauche, Jour de Fête, Les Vacances de Monsieur Hulot, Mon Oncle, Tati No. 4, Playtime;* Scenario Prize, Venice Film Festival 49 and Grand Prix du Cinéma Français 50 for *Jour de Fête*, Int. Critics' Prize, Cannes Film Festival and Prix Louis Delluc for *Les Vacances de Monsieur Hulot* 53; Special Prize, Cannes Film Festival for *Mon Oncle* 58; "Oscar" and New York Critics' Award for best foreign film; French Cinema Acad. Grand Prix for *Playtime* 68.
44 avenue des Champs-Elysées, Paris 8e, France.

Taton, (André) René, D. ès L.; French historian; b. 4 April 1915; ed. Faculté des Sciences, Nancy and Paris, Ecole Normale Supérieure de St. Cloud.
Research Asst., Nat. Centre of Scientific Research 46, rising to Scientific Dir. 64-; Dir. of Studies Ecole pratique des Hautes Etudes 64-, Dir. Centre for Research into History of Science, Ecole des Hautes Etudes 64-; mem. Acad. Int. d'Histoire des Sciences; Laureat Académie des Sciences; Sec.-Gen. of Int. Union of the History and Philosophy of Sciences 55-.
Publs.: *L'oeuvre scientifique de Gaspard Monge* 51, *L'oeuvre mathématique de G. Desarques* 51, *Causalités et Accidents de la Decouverte Scientifique* 58 (translated into English, Spanish, Japanese), ed. *Histoire Générale des Sciences* (4 vols.), (translated into English, Italian,

Spanish, Portuguese), numerous articles on the history of mathematics and the history of sciences in general.
Centre de Recherches d'Histoire des Sciences, 12 rue Colbert, Paris 2e, France.
Telephone: 742-44-79.

Tátrai, Vilmos; Hungarian violinist; b. 1912; ed. National Conservatoire, Budapest.
Teacher 46-53; First Violinist, Budapest Symphony Orchestra 33; mem. Radio Orchestra 38; Leading Violinist Metropolitan State Concert Orchestra 40-; Founder-Leader Tátrai String Quartet 46, and led it on tours throughout Europe 52-; Founder-Leader Hungarian Chamber Orchestra 57-; Prof. of Music, Budapest Acad. of Music 65-; First prize, Bela Bartok Competition 48, Liszt Prize 52, Kossuth Prize 58, Merited Artist of Hungarian People's Republic.
Raoul Wallenberg u. 4; and Zenemüvészeti Föiskola, Liszt Ferenc tér. 2, Budapest XIII, Hungary.
Telephone: 110-529.

Tatum, Edward L(awrie), A.B., M.S., PH.D.; American biologist; b. 14 Dec. 1909; ed. Univ. of Wisconsin.
Research Asst. in Biology, Stanford Univ. 37-42, Asst. Prof. 42-45; Assoc. Prof. of Botany, Yale Univ. 45-46, Prof. of Microbiology 46-48; Prof. of Biology, Stanford Univ. 48-57; Prof. Rockefeller Univ., New York City 57-; mem. Nat. Acad. of Sciences, American Philosophical Soc., Nat. Science Board, Editorial Board *Biochemica et Biophysica Acta*; Nobel Prize for Medicine (with Beadle and Lederberg) 58.
450 East 63rd Street, New York, N.Y. 10021, U.S.A.
Telephone: 838-5645.

Taubman, (Hyman) Howard, A.B.; American journalist, author and critic; b. 4 July 1907; ed. Cornell Univ.
Journalist 29-; with *New York Times* 30-, Drama Critic 60-65, Critic-at-Large 65-; Hon. Mus.D. (Cornell Univ. and Oberlin Coll.); mem. Philadelphia Music Acad. 59-.
Publs. *Opera Front and Back* 38, *Music as a Profession* 39, *Music on My Beat* 43, *The Maestro, The Life of Arturo Toscanini* 51, *How to Build a Record Library* 53, *How to Bring up Your Child to Enjoy Music* 58, *The Making of the American Theatre* 65.
New York Times, Times Square, New York City, N.Y., Home: 41 W. 83rd Street, N.Y., U.S.A.

Tautscher, Anton, DR.RER.POL., DR.JUR.; Austrian university professor; b. 06; ed. Univ. of Graz.
Lecturer in Nat. Economy and Finance at Univ. of Graz 40-48, Asst. Prof. 48-55, Prof. 55-; Rector of Karl Franzens Univ. of Graz 57-58, 65-66.
Publs. *Ernst Ludwig Carl, Der Begründer der Volkswirtschaftslehre* 39, *Bankenverstaatlichung, Zur Frage des gestuften Zinses* 46, *Staatswirtschaftslehre des Kameralismus* 47, *Wirtschaft, Schicksal oder Aufgabe des Menschen* 49, *Geschichte der Volkswirtschaftslehre* 50, *Die Öffentliche Wirtschaft* 53, *Die Grenzen der Besteuerung* 54, *Einkommenspolitik und Genossenschaften* 55, *Wirtschaftsethik* 57, *Vom Arbeiter zum Mitarbeiter, Quantitative und qualitative Sozialpolitik* 61, *Handbuch der Oesterreichischen Wirtschaftspolitik* 61, *Grundsätze der modernen Sozialpolitik* 61, *Lebensstandard und Lebensglück* 63, *Die Wirtschaft als Schicksal und Aufgabe, Ges. Aufsätze* 65, *Die Elite aus Geist und Verantwortung zur gegenwärtigen Wirtschaftsordnung* 65, *Steigender Steuerdruck bei sinkenden Geldwert* 67.
Schröttergasse 7, Graz, Austria.

Tavares, Amandio Joaquim, M.D.; Portuguese university professor; b. 1900; ed. Univ. of Oporto.
Lecturer Univ. of Oporto 22-27; Asst. Prof. of Anatomy, Histology and Embryology 27-29; Asst. Prof. of Pathological Anatomy 29-32, Prof. 32-, Vice-Pres. Inst. of High Culture 42-52; Rector of the Univ. of Oporto 46-61; hon. Rector 61; Pres. Portuguese Asscn. for the Advancement of Sciences 50-64; Pres. Scientific Re-

search Council (Inst. of Higher Culture) 52-65; Pres. Legal Medicine Council of Oporto 59-; Dir., Dept. of Pathology, Hospital Escolar de S. João, Oporto 62-; Pres. Portuguese Pathology Soc. 63-; Vice-Pres. First Section, Nat. Education Junta 65-.
Publs. About 190 books and articles on anatomy, anthropology, pathological anatomy and education.
Rua dos Lagos 48, Senhora da Hora, Portugal.

Tavares de Sá, Hernane; Brazilian UN official; b. 7 Jan. 1911; ed. Brazil, Italy and Univ. of Louvain, Belgium.
Special Assistant to Sec.-Gen. Org. American States 48-51; Prof. Journalism, Catholic Univ., Rio de Janeiro 52-56; Editor *Visão* news magazine 57-60; Under-Sec. Public Information, UN 60-; Principal Adviser to Sec.-Gen. UN 61.
Publ. *The Brazilian People of Tomorrow* 47.
United Nations, New York City, N.Y., U.S.A.

Taverner, Sonia; Canadian ballerina; b. 18 May 1936; ed. Elmhurst Ballet School, and Royal Ballet School, London, and ballet school in New York.
Joined Royal Ballet 55, toured U.S.A. and Canada; joined Royal Winnipeg Ballet 56, leading dancer 57, ballerina 62-66; joined "Les Grands Ballets Canadiens" Spring 66, as principal dancer; appeared as guest artist with the Boston Ballet Co., in Swan Lake 67; guest artist with Toronto, Winnipeg and Vancouver Symphony Orchestras; has toured extensively over North America, Jamaica and U.K.
3431 Drummond Street, Apt. 13, Montreal, Quebec, Canada.
Telephone: 849-4841.

Taviani, Paolo Emilio; Italian politician; b. 6 Nov. 1912; ed. Univ. of Genoa.
Professor in History of Economic Theory at Genoa Univ.; leader Partisan War 43-45; organiser of Christian Democratic Party (in Genoa area) 43; mem. Constituent Assembly 46-48; mem. Parl. 48-; Deputy Sec. Christian Democratic Party 46-49, Sec. 49-50; Editor *Civitas* 50-; Italian Rep. to Schuman Plan Conf. 51 and to later E.D.C. Confs.; Under-Sec. for Foreign Affairs 51-53; Minister of Defence 53-58, of Finance 59-60, of Treasury 60-62, of Interior 62-68.
Publs. include *Social Reformers of the Italian Risorgimento* 40, *Social Prospects* 45, *Ownership* 46, *The Schuman Plan* 52, *Atlantic Solidarity and European Community* 57, *Defence of Peace* 58, *Christian Principles and Democratic System* 65.
Via di Fontanegli 33, Bavari, Genoa, Italy.

Tavolaro, Silvio, D.IUR.; Italian jurist; b. 28 Oct. 1900; ed. Univ. degli Studi, Rome.
Judge 22; Justice of Court of Appeals 41-47; Justice of Supreme Court of Italy 47-55, Presiding Judge 55-58; Chief Justice of Court of Appeals, Rome 58-62; Chief Justice of Supreme Court 62-; Perm. mem. Supreme Council of Judiciary; mem. Acad. of Biological and Moral Sciences; Hon. mem. Roman Asscn. of Legal Medicine; Knight Grand Cross Order of Malta; Medal for Social Redemption, Sacred Treasure of Japan; Grand Cross of Merit (Fed. German Repub.).
Publs. Essays and articles on constitutional law, judicial order and family law.
Office: Palazzo di Giustizia, Rome; Home: 38 Via Casperia, Rome, Italy.

Távora, Virgilio de Moraes Fernandes; Brazilian politician; b. 29 Sept. 1919; ed. Colégio Militar de Fortaleza, and Rio de Janeiro.
Military career: 2nd Lt. 39, Lt. 41, Capt. 44, Major 50, Lt.-Col. 55; Head of Partido Democrático Cristão (P.D.C.) 50; mem. Chamber of Deputies 50, Cand. for

Gov. of Ceará 58; Minister of Transport, Communications and Public Works Sept. 61-June 62; Gov. of Ceará 63-66.
c/o Palácio do Govêrno, Casa Civil do Govêrno, Fortaleza, Ceará, Brazil.

Tawes, J. Millard; American banker and politician; b. 8 April 1894; ed. Wilmington Conf. Acad., and Sadler's, Bryant and Stratton Business Coll.
Clerk of Court, Somerset County, Md. 30-38; State Comptroller 38-47; State Bank Commr. 47-50, Comptroller 50-58; Gov. of Maryland 59-66; fmr. Sec.-Treas. Crisfield Shipbuilding Co.; fmr. Pres. Nat. Asscn. of State Auditors, Comptrollers and Treasurers, Maryland State Firemen's Asscn.; mem. Board of Visitors and Govs., Washington Coll., Board of Trustees, Wesley Junior Coll., Dickinson Coll., Board of Dirs., McCready Memorial Hospital; Democrat.
State Office, Annapolis, Md., U.S.A.

Tax, Sol, PH.D., PH.B.; American university professor; b. 30 Oct. 1907; ed. Univs. of Wisconsin and Chicago.
Member Logan Museum North African Expedition 30; field research, Apache Indians 31, Fox Indians 32-34; Investigator, and later Ethnologist, Carnegie Inst. 34-48; field research in Guatemala and Chiapas (Mexico) 34-43; Research Assoc. in Anthropology, Univ. of Chicago 40-44, Assoc. Prof. 44-48, Prof. of Anthropology 48-; Assoc. Dean Div. of Social Sciences 48-53, Chair. Anthropology Dept. 55-58; Dean Univ. Extension 63-; Assoc. Editor *American Anthropologist* 48-52, Editor 53-56; Fellow American Anthropological Asscn. (Pres. 58-59); Man. Nature Project in Chiapas, Mexico 56-59; Chair. Cttee. on Darwin Centenary (1859-1959) 56-59; Editor *Current Anthropology* 57-, Viking Fund Publications in Anthropology 59-; U.S. Nat. Comm. for UNESCO 59-65, Exec. Cttee. 65-; Consultant, U.S. Office of Educ. 65-; Special Adviser, Smithsonian Inst. 65-; mem. Board of Advisors, Council on Int. Communication 66-; Viking Medallist 61.
Publs. *Heritage of Conquest: The Ethnology of Middle America* 52, *Penny Capitalism* 53, *A Guatemalan Indian Economy* 53, 63; Editor for 29th Int. Congress of Americanists Proceedings 49-52, *Civilizations of Ancient America* 51, *Acculturation in the Americas* 52, *Indian Tribes of Aboriginal America* 52, *Evolution After Darwin* (3 vols.) 60, *Anthropology Today—Selections* 62, *Horizons of Anthropology* 63.
5537 Woodlawn Avenue, Chicago, Ill. 60637, U.S.A.
Telephone: DO3-0990.

Taylor, A. Thomas; American executive; b. 18 March 1908; ed. Yale Univ.
With Swift and Co., Chicago 35-39; with Cía. Swift Internacional, S.A.C. 39-, Vice-Pres., Dir. 42-; Vice-Pres., Dir. Int. Packers Ltd. 50, Chair. of Board 54-; official of other companies.
Home: Shoreacres Grounds, Lake Bluff, Ill.; Office: 135 S. La Salle Street, Chicago, Ill. 60611, U.S.A.

Taylor, Alan John Percivale, M.A.; British historian; b. 25 March 1906; ed. Oriel Coll., Oxford.
Rockefeller Fellow in Social Sciences 29-30; Lecturer in History, Univ. of Manchester 30-38; Fellow of Magdalen Coll., Oxford; fmr. Univ. Lecturer in Int. History; Librarian, Beaverbrook Library.
Publs. *The Italian Problem in European Diplomacy 1847-49* 34, *Germany's First Bid for Colonies* 38, *The Course of German History* 45, *The Habsburg Monarchy 1809-1918* 48, *From Napoleon to Stalin* 50, *Rumours of Wars* 52, *The Struggle for Mastery in Europe 1848-1918* 54, *Bismarck* 55, *Englishmen and Others* 56, *The Trouble-Makers* 57, *The Russian Revolution of 1917* (TV lectures) 58, *The Origins of the Second World War* 61, *The First World War* 63, *Politics in Wartime* 64,

English History 1914-1945 65, *From Sarajevo to Yalta* 66.
Beaverbrook Library, 33 St. Bride Street, London, E.C.4, England.
Telephone: 01-353-2444.

Taylor, Edward Plunket, C.M.G., B.SC.; Canadian industrialist; b. 29 Jan. 1901; ed. Ashbury Coll., Ottawa Collegiate Inst., and McGill Univ., Montreal.
President Argus Corpn. Ltd., Lyford Cay Co. Ltd., New Providence Devt. Co. Ltd., Taylor McDougald & Co. Ltd., Windfields Farm Ltd.; Chair. Canadian Equity and Devt. Co. Ltd., Don Mills Devts. Ltd., Greater Hamilton Shopping Centre Ltd., The Jockey Club Ltd., Trust Corpn. of Bahamas Ltd., Exec. Cttee. Howard Smith Paper Mills Ltd., Massey-Ferguson Ltd., Canadian Breweries Ltd., Dominion Tar & Chemical Co. Ltd.; Deputy Chair. Charrington United Breweries Ltd.; Dir. Beamish & Crawford Ltd., Canadian Breweries (G.B.) Ltd., Charrington & Co. Ltd., Dominion Stores Ltd., Hedges and Butler Ltd., The Royal Bank of Canada, etc.; joint Dir.-Gen. Munitions Production 40; Exec. Asst. to Ministry of Munitions and Supply 41; Pres. War Supplies Ltd., Washington, D.C. 41; Pres. and Vice-Chair. British Supply Council in North America Sept. 41; Dir.-Gen. British Ministry of Supply Mission Feb. 42; Canadian Dep. mem. on Combined Production and Resources Board Nov. 42; Canadian Chair. Joint War Aid Cttee. U.S.-Canada Sept. 43.
Birch Hall, Windlesham, Surrey, England; and Lyford Cay, New Providence, Bahamas.

Taylor, Elizabeth (married to Richard Burton, *q.v.*); British film actress; b. 27 Feb. 1932; ed. Byron House, Hawthorne School, and Metro-Goldwyn-Mayer School.
Films include *Lassie Come Home, National Velvet, Little Women, A Place in the Sun, Ivanhoe, Elephant Walk, Rhapsody, Beau Brummel, The Last Time I Saw Paris, Giant, Raintree County, Cat on a Hot Tin Roof, Butterfield 8, Cleopatra, The V.I.P.s, The Sandpiper, Who's Afraid of Virginia Woolf, The Taming of the Shrew, Dr. Faustus, Go Forth, Reflections in a Golden Eye, The Comedians*; Acad. Award for Best Actress (*Butterfield* 8) 60; Oscar for *Who's Afraid of Virginia Woolf* 67.
c/o Publicity and Allied Interests, 72 Brook Street, London, W.1, England.

Taylor, Sir Geoffrey Ingram, Kt., F.R.S.; British scientist; b. 7 March 1886; ed. Univ. Coll. School, Cambridge Univ.
Fellow of Trinity Coll. Cambridge 10; Meteorologist Scotia Expedition to North Atlantic 13; experimental aeronautics and meteorology First World War; Yarrow Research Prof. of Royal Soc.; awarded Royal Medal of Royal Soc. 33; mem. Civil Defence Research Cttee. 39-; mem. Ministry of Supply Advisory Council 39-45; awarded Royal Society Copley Medal 44; Corresp. mem. Académie des Sciences, Paris, Nat. Acad. of Sciences, Washington, Amsterdam, Oslo, Swedish Royal Acad. of Sciences and Accad. dei Lincei; Hon. Fellow Indian Acad. of Sciences, Royal Society, Edinburgh, Royal Aeronautical Society, Manchester Coll. of Science and Technology, Inst. of Mathematics and its Applications; Foreign mem. U.S.S.R. Acad. of Sciences; Hon. D.Sc. Univ. of Bristol 59; U.S. Medal for Merit 47; Gold Medal Royal Aeronautical Soc. 54, Exner Medal Österreichischer Gewerbeverein 54; First Award Int. Panetti Prize and Medal of the Accad. delle Scienze di Torino 58; Timoshenko Medal, American Soc. of Mechanical Engineers 58; Kelvin Medal Inst. of Civil Engineers 59; Franklin Medal 62; Rice Univ. Semi-Centennial Medal of Honor 62; hon. Dr., Univ. of Paris 61; Médaille Trasenster of Univ. of Liège 62; Platinum

Medal, Inst. of Metals 64; James Watt Int. Medal of Inst. of Mechanical Engineers 65.
Trinity College, Cambridge, England.

Taylor, George William, B.S., PH.D.; American educator; b. 10 July 1901; ed. Univ. of Pennsylvania.
Instructor in Industry, Univ. Pennsylvania 23, Research Associate, Industrial Research Dept. 30-48; Associate Prof. and Prof. of Labor Relations, Wharton School 37-64; Head Business Admin. Dept., Albright Coll., Reading, Pa. 24-29; Impartial Chair. for Hosiery Industry 31-41, for Men's Clothing Industry, Philadelphia 35-60, for Women's Dress Industry, Philadelphia 47-60; Acting Chair. Philadelphia Regional Labor Board 34-35; public rep. Textile Industry Cttee. of Fair Labor Standards Act; Chair. Hosiery Industry Cttee., Vice-Chair. Wool Industry Cttee.; Impartial Umpire Gen. Motors Corpn. and United Automobile Workers of America, Congress of Industrial Organisations 41; Vice-Chair. Nat. War Labor Board 42-45, Chair. 45; Sec. President's National Labor Management Conf. 45; Chair. Advisory Board, Office of War Mobilization and Reconversion 46-47; Pres. Industrial Relations Research Asscn. 50; Chair. Nat. Wage Stabilisation Board 51; Jurisdictional Disputes Arbitrator, C.I.O. 52; Chair. Presidential Board of Inquiry, Steel Industry 59; mem. President's Advisory Cttee. on Labor Management Policy 61-; Chair. Presidential Cttee. on Aerospace Industry 63; Harnwell Prof., Univ. of Pennsylvania 64-; Presidential Mediator, Railroad Industry 64; Chair. Governors' Cttee. on Public Employee Relations 66-, Mediation Board of Copper Industry 68; Philadelphia Award 63; Pennsylvania Medal of Merit 56; Presidential Medal of Freedom 64; Pa. Award for Excellence 66.
Publs. *Full Fashioned Hosiery Industry* 29, *Vertical Integration of the Textile Industries* (with others) 37, *Inventory Policies* (with others) 39, *Government Regulation of Industrial Relations* 48; edited series on *Labor Arbitration* 55, *New Concepts in Wages Determination* (with others) 57.
Dietrich Hall, University of Pennsylvania; and 1900 Rittenhouse Square, Philadelphia, Pa. 19103, U.S.A.
Telephones: (215) 594-7722; and (215) Ki 6-0254.

Taylor, Harold McCarter, C.B.E., T.D., M.SC.(NZ), M.A., PH.D.; British university official; b. 13 May 1907; ed. Otago Boys' High School, Dunedin, New Zealand, Univ. of Otago and Clare Coll., Cambridge.
University Lecturer in Mathematics, Univ. of Cambridge 33-45; Treasurer, Univ. of Cambridge 45-53, Sec.-Gen. of the Faculties 53-61; Vice-Chancellor Univ. of Keele Oct. 61-67, retd.; Rede Lecturer, Univ. of Cambridge 66; Lt.-Col., Royal Artillery 39-45; Smith's Prize, Univ. of Cambridge 32, Fellow Society of Antiquaries 61.
Publ. *Anglo-Saxon Architecture* (with Joan Taylor) 65.
192 Huntingdon Road, Cambridge, England.

Taylor, Henry J., D.LITT.; American diplomatist, author, journalist, economist; b. 2 Sept. 1902; ed. Lawrenceville School, N.J., and Univ. of Virginia.
Entered newspaper profession 18; war correspondent in Second World War; Ambassador to Switzerland 57-61; columnist United Features Syndicate 61-; Chair. of Board, Silicone Paper Company of New York, Inc., etc.
Publs. *Germany's Economy of Coercion, Time Runs Out, Men in Motion, Men and Power, An American Speaks His Mind, The Big Man* (novel), *Men and Moments*, etc.
1 Ivy Lane, (Farmington), Charlottesville, Virginia, U.S.A.
Telephone: 703-293-2022.

Taylor, Hobart, Jr.; American lawyer and government official; b. 17 Dec. 1920; ed. Prairie View State Coll., Texas, Howard Univ., and Univ. of Michigan.
Admitted to Michigan Bar 44; Research Asst. Michigan

Supreme Court 44-45; Private Law Practice, Detroit 45-48; Asst. Prosecuting Attorney, Wayne County 49-50, Corpn. Counsel 51-61; Senior Partner Taylor, Patrick, Bailer, Wexler and Brookins (law firm) 58-61; Special Counsel, Pres. of U.S.'s Cttee. on Equal Employment Opportunity 61-62, Exec. Vice-Chair. 62-65; Special Asst. to Vice-Pres. Lyndon B. Johnson 61-63; Assoc. Counsel to Pres. Johnson 64-65; Dir. Export-Import Bank.
Office: 811 Vermont Avenue, N.W., Washington 20571; Home: 2500 Virginia Avenue, N.W., Washington 20037, U.S.A.

Taylor, Sir Hugh S., K.B.E., D.SC., F.R.S.; British chemist; b. 6 Feb. 1890; ed. Liverpool Univ., Nobel Inst. Stockholm, and Hanover Technical High School.
Instructor, Asst. Prof., Associate Prof. and Prof. of Chemistry Princeton Univ. 14-27, Chair. Dept. of Chemistry 26-51, and David B. Jones Prof. of Chemistry 27-58, Dean Graduate School 45-58; Munitions Inventions Dept., London 17-19; F.R.S. 32; mem. Pontifical Acad. of Sciences, Vatican City 37; Hon. Fellow Chemical Society, London 49; Assoc. Acad. of Sciences, Belgium; foreign mem. Accad. dei Lincei, etc.; Pres. Faraday Society 52-53; Pres. Woodrow Wilson Nat. Fellowship Foundation 58-; Mendel Medal, Villanova Coll. 33; Research award and plaque, Research Corpn., N.Y. 39, Franklin Medal, American Philosophical Society 41; Longstaff Medal, Chemical Society, London 42; Franklin Medal, Franklin Inst. 57; Procter Prize, Research Soc. of America 64; Commdr. Order of Leopold II of Belgium; Knight Commdr. Order of St. Gregory the Great (Vatican) 53; numerous honorary degrees in U.S.A., Canada, England, Ireland and Belgium.
Publs. *Industrial Hydrogen, Catalysis in Theory and Practice, Elementary Physical Chemistry, Treatise on Physical Chemistry.*
P.O.B. 642, Princeton, N.J.; 191 Library Place, Princeton, N.J. 08540, U.S.A.
Telephone: 609-924-2211.

Taylor, John Wilkinson, A.B., A.M., PH.D.; American educationist; b. 26 Sept. 1906; ed. Columbia Coll., Columbia Univ., Vanderbilt Univ., Univs. of Berlin, Paris, London and Vienna.
Teacher 29-30; Asst. Teachers Coll., Columbia Univ. 27-30, Instructor in Education 30-36; Teacher, Kaiser Friedrich Realgymnasium, Berlin 30-31; Broughton High School, Raleigh, N.C. 31-32; Educational Adviser to Pres. John Day Publ. Co. 32-33; Asst. in Education and Dir. Foreign Study, Columbia Univ. 34-35; Asst. to Chair. New Coll., Columbia Univ. 35-37, Chair. of Admissions, Scholarships, Loans, Curriculum and Personnel Guidance Cttees. 37-38; Assoc. Prof. of Comparative Education and Admin. Asst. to Pres. Louisiana State Univ. 38-40, Dir. Bureau of Educational Research 41-43; served as Capt. to Lieut.-Col. U.S. Army 43-46; Dir. of Studies, Mil. Govt. School and Holding Centre, Natousa, N. Africa 42-43; Chief Education and Religious Affairs Branch, U.S. Mil. Govt. for Germany 44-47 and U.S. Rep. Quadripartite Education Cttee. for Germany 45-47; Pres. Univ. of Louisville, Ky. 47-50; Deputy Dir.-Gen. of UNESCO 51-54, Acting Dir.-Gen. 52-53; Exec. Dir. Chicago Educational Television Asscn. 54-; Chicago Council on Foreign Relations 54; Pres. and mem. Board of Dirs., Learning Resources Inst. 63-; mem. Board of Dirs. Midwest Educational T.V. Network, Inc. 64-; mem. Film Industry Advisory Board, Chicago Int. Film Festival 65-; mem. numerous commissions and advisory cttees.; U.S. Legion of Merit; Légion d'Honneur.
Publ. *Youth Welfare in Germany* 36.
Office: 5400 North St. Louis Avenue, Chicago, Illinois 60625; Home: 1244 North State Street, Chicago, Ill. 60610, U.S.A.

Taylor, Lauriston Sale, A.B., D.SC.; American physicist; b. 1 June 1902; ed. Stevens Inst. of Technology, Cornell, Columbia Univs.
Bell Telephone Labs., New York City 22-; Nat. Bureau of Standards (N.B.S.) 27-64, Chair. Nat. Comm. Radiation, Protection and Measurements 29-64, Pres. Nat. Council 64-; Chair. Int. Comm. on Radiological Protection 28-; Eighth Fighter Command, Ninth Air Force, Europe 43-45; Chief Biophysics Branch A.E.C. 47-48; Chair. Int. Comm. on Radiological Units and Measurements 56-; Chief Atomic and Radiation Physics Div. 51-60, Radiation Physics Div. 60-62, Assoc. Dir. N.B.S. 62-64; Special Asst. to Pres. Nat. Acad. of Sciences 65-; Hon. D.Sc. (Univ. of Pennsylvania and St. Procopius Coll.).
Publs. about 140 papers principally on X-radiation measurement and protection.
7407 Denton Road, Bethesda, Md. 20014, U.S.A.
Telephone: 301-652-5096.

Taylor, Gen. Maxwell Davenport; American army officer; b. 26 Aug. 1901; ed. U.S. Military Acad., West Point.
Commissioned Second Lieut. Corps of Engineers 22; various assignments in U.S. and abroad; Instructor in French and later Asst. Prof. of Spanish, U.S. Mil. Acad., West Point 27-32; attended Field Artillery School and Commd. and Gen. Staff School 32-35; with American Embassy, Tokyo 35-37 and 37-39; Asst. Mil. Attaché, Peking 37; at Army War Coll., Washington, D.C. 39-40; special mission to Latin American countries 40; commd. 12th Field Artillery Battn. 40-41; duty at Office of Sec. of Gen. Staff 41-42; Chief of Staff and Artillery Commdr. 82nd Infantry Div. 42; served overseas in Sicilian and Italian campaigns 43-44; commd. 101st Airborne Div., invasions of Normandy and Holland, Ardennes and Central European campaigns 44-45; Supt. U.S. Mil. Acad., West Point 45-49; Chief of Staff, European Commd. H.Q., Heidelberg 49; U.S. Commdr. Berlin 49-51; Asst. Chief of Staff for Operations, Dept. of the Army 51, Deputy Chief of Staff for Operations and Admin. of Army 51-53; Commdr. 8th Army Feb. 53-55, General, June 53 and U.S. Army Forces, Far East Nov. 54-April 55; C.-in-C. U.N. Command and Far East Command Apr. 55; Chief of Staff U.S. Army 55-59; Pres. Lincoln Center for the Performing Arts 61; Mil. Rep. of President 61-62; Chair. Jt. Chiefs of Staff 62-64, Ambassador to Republic of Viet-Nam 64-65; mem. Foreign Intelligence Advisory Board 65-68, Chair. 68-; decorations include D.S.C., D.S.M. (thrice), Silver Star; D.S.O. (U.K.), Hon. C.B. (U.K.); Commdr. de la Légion d'Honneur (France); French and Belgian Croix de Guerre, etc.; Hon. D.Eng. (N.Y. Univ.); Hon. LL.D. (Bowdoin Coll., Williams Coll., Univ. of Mo., Pa. Mil. Coll., Trinity Coll., Yale Univ., Lafayette Coll., Seoul Nat. Univ., Philips Univ.).
Publs. *The Uncertain Trumpet* 60, *Responsibility and Response* 67.
c/o The Pentagon, Washington 25, D.C., U.S.A.

Taylor, Paul Schuster, M.A., PH.D., LL.D.; American economist; b. 9 June 1895; ed. Wisconsin and California Univs.
Member staff Calif. Univ. 22-62 and Prof. of Economics 39-62, Chair. of Dept. 52-56, Emer. 62-; Chair. Inst. Int. Studies 56-62; Chief Investigator of Mexican Labour in U.S. for Social Science Research Council 27-29; Consultant Nat. Comm. on Law Observance and Enforcement 30-31; Latin-American Fellow of Guggenheim Foundation 31; Regional Labour Adviser Resettlement Administration 35-36; Pres. California Rural Rehabilitation Corpn. 36-43; Consultant Social Security Board 36-40, U.S. Dept. of Interior 43-52, Export-Import Bank 52, Int. Co-operation Admin. (now U.S. Agency for Int. Development) 55, 58, 59, 61, 62, 63, 66,

67, 68, UN 60, 63; Visiting Prof. Inst. of Land Reclamation, Univ. of Alexandria 62-63.
Publs. *Sailors' Union of the Pacific* 23, *Mexican Labour in the U.S.* 28-32, *A Spanish-Mexican Peasant Community* 33, *An American-Mexican Frontier* 34, *An American Exodus* (with Dorothea Lange) 39.
1163 Euclid Avenue, Berkeley, 8, Calif., U.S.A.
Telephone: 415-524-3880.

Taylor, Robert L., PH.B., LL.B.; American judge; b. 20 Sept. 1899; ed. Milligan Coll., Vanderbilt Law School, and Yale Univ.
Admitted to Tenn. Bar 23, private legal practice, Johnson City 24-49; U.S. Dist. Judge, Eastern Dist. of Tennessee 49-, now Chief Judge.
Federal Building, Knoxville, Tennessee, U.S.A.

Taylor, Robert Thomas, TH.B., D.D.; American clergyman and church executive; b. 29 Aug. 1904; ed. James Millikin Univ., Princeton Theological Seminary and Union Theological School.
Ordained, Presbyterian Church 29, Asst. Pastor, Old First Church, Newark, N.J. 29-31, Pastor, First Reformed Church, Old Dutch Church of Sleepy Hollow, Tarrytown, N.Y. 31-41; Exec. Sec. Chicago Bible Soc. 41-49; Sec., Northwestern District, American Bible Soc. 41-43, Gen. Sec. American Bible Soc. 44-.
Publ. *Bible Baseball* 49, 52, 54.
1865 Broadway, New York, N.Y. 10023, U.S.A.

Taylor, Vice-Admiral Rufus L., B.S.; American naval officer; b. 6 Jan. 1910; ed. U.S. Naval Acad., Annapolis, Maryland and Armed Forces Staff Coll., Norfolk, Virginia.
Graduated Naval Acad. 33; served Naval Forces, Philippines 41-42; Staff, Allied Naval Forces, South West Pacific 42-43; Office of the Chief of Naval Operations 43-44, Staff, Commdr.-in-Chief, Pacific Fleet 44-46; various Intelligence posts 46-63; Rear Admiral and Dir. of Naval Intelligence 63-66; promoted to Vice-Admiral and appointed Deputy Dir. of Defense Intelligence Agency 66, of Central Intelligence Oct. 66-; Army and Navy decorations.
Quarters V, Navy Yard, Washington, D.C. 20390, U.S.A.

Tazi, Abderrahman; Moroccan industrial engineer and international banking official; b. 29; ed. Univ. of Lille.
Industrial Engineer 49-53; Dir. of Industrial Production, Ministry of Commerce and Industry 56; Econ. Counsellor, Moroccan Embassy, Bonn 57-58; First Counsellor, Perm. Moroccan Mission to UN 61, Moroccan Rep. to Econ. Comm. to UN 61; Dir.-Gen. of Econ. Affairs, Ministry of Foreign Affairs, Rabat 62; Exec. Dir. for Afghanistan, Ghana, Indonesia, Laos, Libya, Malaya, Morocco, Tunisia, Int. Bank for Reconstruction and Development (World Bank) 62-.
International Bank for Reconstruction and Development, 1818 H Street, Washington, D.C. 20433, U.S.A.

Tcherina, Ludmila; French actress and dancer; b. 10 Oct. 1925; ed. privately and studied under Yvan Clustine.
First dancer and choreographer, Ballets de Monte Carlo 40-44, Ballets de Paris 51-58; founded Compagnie de Ballets Ludmila Tcherina 58.
Chief appearances include: Ballets: *Romeo and Juliet* (with Serge Lifar) Paris 42, *Giselle* La Scala Milan 54, Bolshoi Theatre Moscow 59, *Le Martyre de Saint Sébastian* Paris Opéra 57, *Les Amants de Teruel* Théâtre Sarah Bernhardt Paris 59, *Gala* (by Salvador Dali and Maurice Béjart) Venice 61, Brussels and Paris 62, etc. Films: *The Red Shoes, The Tales of Hoffmann, Clara de Montargis, La Légende de Parsifal, La Nuit s'achève, Oh! Rosalinda, A la Mémoire d'un Héros, La Fille de Mata-Hari, Honeymoon, Les Amants de Teruel* (Cannes Film Festival, French Entry 62), etc.
Exhibited drawings and gouaches in Paris and New York; Prize for Best Feminine Performance, Vichy Film Festival for *La Nuit s'achève* 50, First Prize, Dance Film Festival, Buenos Aires for *A la Mémoire d'un Héros* 52, 'Oscar' for Best Feminine Performance by a Foreign Actress in *Tales of Hoffmann* 52, Paris Gold Medal 59, Chevalier de l'Ordre des Arts et des Lettres 62; Oscar Italien de la Popularité.
24-26 Cours Albert 1er, 75 Paris 8, France.
Telephone: 359-24-55.

Tchichellé, Stéphané; Congolese (Brazzaville) politician; b. 15; ed. Loango Mission School.
Railway worker 30, Station Master, Pointe Noire 36; mem. Railway Workers Trade Union; a leader of Parti Progressiste Congolais (P.P.C.); mem. Grand Council for French Equatorial Africa 47-57, Pres. Council's Perm. Comm. 47-48; mem. Territorial Ass. 46-56; Mayor of Pointe Noire; mem. Union Démocratique de Défense des Intérêts Africains (U.D.D.I.A.) 56-; Minister of Social Affairs, Health and Labour 57-58, Vice-Pres., Minister of Interior and Social Affairs 58-61, of Foreign Affairs 60-61, First Vice-Pres. with responsibility for Foreign Affairs 61-63.
Brazzaville, Republic of Congo.

Tchoungui, Simon Pierre; Cameroonian doctor and politician; b. 28 Oct. 1916; ed. Ecole Primaire Supérieure, Centre Médicale, Ayos, Ecole de Médecine, Dakar, and Univ. de Paris à la Sorbonne.
Former Dir. of Office, Ministry of Public Health and Population, then of Ministry of Public Works; Dir. Int. Relations, Ministry of Public Health and Population 59-60; Dir. of Public Health for Cameroon 61-; Minister of Public Health and Population 61-64; Minister of Nat. Economy 64-65; Sec. of State to the Presidency 65; Prime Minister of East Cameroon 65-; numerous decorations.
B.P. 1057, Yaoundé, Cameroon.

Tebaldi, Renata; Italian soprano opera singer; b. 1 Feb. 1922; ed. Arrigo Boito Conservatory, Parma, Gioacchino Rossini Conservatory, Pesaro, then pupil of Carmen Melis and Guiseppe Pais.
Début Rovigo 44; has sung the principal soprano operatic roles in America and Europe.
1 Piazza Guastalla, Milan, Italy.

Tebbutt, Arthur Rothwell, M.A., PH.D.; American statistician; b. 10 Nov. 1906; ed. Brown and Harvard Univs.
Harvard Econ. Soc. 27-28; Asst. Editor *Review of Economic Statistics* 29-30; Instr. in Statistics, Harvard Graduate School of Business Admin. 30-35; Asst. Prof. of Econs., Brown Univ., and Dir. Bureau of Business Research 35-40; Prof. of Statistics, Northwestern Univ. 40-, Dean of the Graduate School 45-51; Vice-Pres. American Asscn. of Graduate Schools 49, Pres. 50; Educational Consultant to French Ministry of Economic Affairs 56-57; Consultant to business firms; Republican.
Publs. *Behavior of Consumption in Business Depression* 33, *Introduction to Economic Statistics* (with W. L. Crum and A. C. Patton) 38, *Government Regulation of Sugar in World War II* 44.
822 Monticello Place, Evanston, Illinois, U.S.A.
Telephone: 328-3484.

Teillet, Roger; Canadian politician; b. 21 Aug. 1912; ed. St. Boniface Coll., St. Boniface.
Life Assurance Co., St. Boniface 35-40; Royal Canadian Air Force Second World War; mem. Manitoba Legislative Ass. 53-59, Canadian House of Commons 62-; Minister of Veterans' Affairs 63-; Liberal.
Ministry of Veterans' Affairs, Ottawa, Canada.

Teixeira, Anisio Spinola; Brazilian educationist; b. 12 July 1900; ed. Univ. of Rio de Janeiro, and Columbia Univ., New York.
Director General of Public Education, State of Bahia

24-28; Dir. Dept. of Educ. and Culture, Fed. District 31-35, Sec.-Gen. Educ. and Culture, Fed. District 35; Prof. of Philosophy of Educ., Teachers Training School of State of Bahia 28-31, Teachers Training School of Univ. of Fed. District 32-36; Adviser on Higher Educ., UNESCO 46-47; Sec. of Educ. and Health, State of Bahia 47-51; Dir. Nat. Inst. of Pedagogical Studies (INEP) 52-64, Brazilian Centre for Educ. Research (Ministry of Education) 54-64; Sec.-Gen. Comm. on Higher Educ. (CAPES) 51-64; fmr. Prof. of Philosophy of Educ., Inst. of Educ. of the Fed. District; Prof. of School Admin., Nat. Faculty of Philosophy, Univ. of Brazil 57-65; Pres. Univ. of Brasilia 63-64; Visiting Prof. Columbia Univ. 64, Univ. of Calif. (Los Angeles) 65-; mem. Fed. Council of Educ. 62-68.

Publs. *American Aspects of Education* 28, *Life and Education: An Introduction on the Pedagogy of J. Dewey* 29, *Progressive Education: An Introduction to a Philosophy of Education* 34, *Marching Toward Democracy* 34, *Public Education in Rio de Janeiro* 34, *Education for Democracy: Introduction to the Administration of a School System, Rio de Janeiro* 36, *The University and Human Liberty* 54, *Education and the Brazilian Crisis* 56, *Education is not a Privilege* 57, *Education is a Right* 67, *Education in Brazil* 68, *Education and the Modern World* 68.

Rua Benjamin Constant 32 and Rua Raul Pompeia 58 ap. 803, Rio de Janeiro, Brazil.
Telephone: 222903 (Office); 476788 (Home).

Teixeira Pinto, Luis Maria, PH.D.; Portuguese economist and politician; b. 27; ed. Instituto Superior de Ciências Econômicas e Financeiras, Technical Univ. of Lisbon, and Univ. of Paris.
Assistant Prof. Instituto Superior de Ciências Econômicas e Financeiras 48-62; Sec. Econ. Studies Dept. Portuguese Industrial Asscn. 50-52; mem. Centre for Econ. Studies, Nat. Statistical Inst. 52-55; Adviser, Commercial Dept., Export Development Fund, Paris 55-56; Prof. Instituto de Altos Estudos Militares 57-62; Dir. Dept. of Econ. Studies and Projects, Nat. Development Bank 60-62, Vice-Pres. Nat. Development Bank 62-; Minister of Econ. 62-March 65.
Publs. *Algumas notas sobre o Equilíbrio Keynesiano* 57, *L'évolution de la théorie de la croissance économique* 57, *Alguns Aspectos da Teoria do Crescimento Econômico* 57, *Portugal e a Integração Econômica Europeia* 60, *The Economic Growth of Small Nations: the Portuguese Case* 60, *A Unidade Econômica Nacional* 60, *Políticas de Desenvolvimento Econômico* 62, *O Comércio Internacional e os preços dos factores produtivos, L'Economie Portugaise, Problemas do Desenvolvimento Econômico Africano*.
Avenida Infante Santo, 66-7 C. Esq., Lisbon, Portugal.

Tejchma, Jozef; Polish politician; b. 14 July 1927; ed. Acad. of Political Sciences, Higher School of Social Sciences.
Active leader of Rural Youth Union (Wici Z.M.W.); instructor for school youth problems, Central Board of Polish Youth Union (Z.M.P.) 48; plenipotentiary, Central Board of Z.M.P. at Nowa Huta 51-54; Deputy Head of the Organizational Dept. Central Board of Z.M.P. 54-55; Co-organizer Z.M.W., Chair. Organizational Cttee., Provisional Board and later Central Board 56-63; Head of Agricultural Dept. Polish United Workers Party (P.Z.P.R.) Central Cttee. 63-64; mem. P.Z.P.R. 52-; Alt. mem. Central Cttee. and Sec. of P.Z.P.R. Central Cttee. 64-; mem. Seym 59-; Order of the Banner of Labour 1st Class 64 and others.
Polska Zjednoczona Partia Robotnicza, Nowy Šwiat 6, Warsaw, Poland.

Tejera Paris, Dr. Enrique; Venezuelan lawyer, economist and diplomatist; b. 29 April 1919; ed. National Pedagogical Inst., and Central Univ. of Venezuela.
Insurance Superintendent 41-45; Admin. Dir., Ministry

of Agriculture 45-46; Pres. Immigration Comm. 45-46; Minister Counsellor, Venezuelan Embassy, Rome 48; mem. UN staff 51-57; fmr. Prof., Central Univ., Caracas; fmr. Alt. Pres. Venezuelan Petroleum Corpn.; Gov. State of Sucre 59-61; fmr. Founder and Chair. Central Office for Co-ordinating and Planning, Caracas; Pres. of Industrial Bank, Caracas 62-63; Amb. of Venezuela to U.S.A. 63-, and to Council of Org. of American States (O.A.S.) 63-66; Exec, Dir, IMF 65-66.
Publs. *Public Administration, Theory of Development Structures* 53, *Problems of Installation* 54, *Two Elements of Government* 60.
Office: Embassy of Venezuela, Washington D.C. 20006, U.S.A.; Home: Apartado 10, 512, Caracas, Venezuela.

Tejima, Yukei; Japanese calligraphic artist; b. 01; ed. Tokyo.
Prize at Nippon Shodo Bijutsuin Exhibition 37; mem. Jury for same exhbn. 38; one of the group of Japanese calligraphists whose work was shown in a European travelling exhbn. 55; rep. at other exhbns. including São Paulo Biennale 57, Seattle 21st Century Exhibition 62; perm. display "Accademia del Giappone" Rome 62; Gold Star, Brussels Int. Exhibition 58.
1147 Yoyogi-Uehara, Shibuya-ku, Tokyo, Japan.

Tekoah, Yosef; Israeli diplomatist; b. 4 March 1925; ed. Université L'Aurore, China, and Harvard Univ.
Instructor in Int. Relations, Harvard Univ. 47-48; Dep. Legal Adviser, Ministry of Foreign Affairs 49-53; Dir. Armistice Affairs, and Head Israeli Dels. to Armistice Comms. with Egypt, Jordan, Syria and Lebanon 53-58; Dep. Perm. Rep. to UN 58, Acting Perm. Rep. 59-60; Amb. to Brazil 60-62, to U.S.S.R. 62-65; Asst. Dir.-Gen. Ministry of Foreign Affairs 66-68; Perm. Rep. to UN 68-.
Permanent Mission of Israel to the United Nations, 15 East 70th Street, New York, N.Y. 10021, U.S.A.
Telephone: TR 9-7600.

Tell, Wasfi El; Jordanian politician; b. 20; ed. American Univ. of Beirut.
Teacher 41-46; British Army Officer 46-49; Dept. of Statistics 49; Asst. Dir. Income Tax Dept. 49-55; Dir. of Press Bureau 55; Counsellor, Jordan Embassy, Bonn 55-57; Chief of Royal Protocol 57-58; Chargé d'Affaires, Teheran 58-59; Chief of Nat. Guidance 59-61; Prime Minister and Minister of Defence 62-63, 65-67; Chief of Royal Cabinet March 67- June 67; mem. Consultative Council Aug. 67-.
Amman, Jordan.

Tellenbach, Gerd, PH.D.; German university professor; b. 17 Sept. 1903; ed. Univs. of Freiburg and Munich.
Asst., Prussian Historical Inst. in Rome 28-33; Lecturer, Heidelberg, Giessen, and Würzburg Univs. 33-38; Prof., Giessen 38-42, Münster 42-44; Prof. of Medieval and Modern History, Univ. of Freiburg, and Dir. Historical School 44-63; Dir. German Historical Inst. Rome 63-; D. h.c. Ph. et Litt. (Louvain), Hon. D.Litt. (Glasgow).
Publs. include: *Römischer und christlicher Reichsgedanke in der Liturgie des früheren Mittelalters* 34, *Libertas, Kirche und Weltordnung im Zeitalter des Investiturstreites* 36, *Church, State and Christian Society* 40, *Die Entstehung des deutschen Reiches* 40, *Goethes geschichtlicher Sinn* 49, *Europa im Zeitalter der Karolinger, Historia Mundi V* 56, *Studien und Vorarbeiten zur Geschichte des grossfränkischen und frühdeutschen Adels* 57, *Zur Bedeutung der Personenforschung für die Erkenntnis des früheren Mittelalters* 57, *Kaisertum, Papstum und Europa im hohen Mittelalter, Historia Mundi VI* 58, *Neue Forschung über Cluny und die Cluniacenser* 59, *Repertorium Germanicum II* 33-61.
Istituto Storico Germanico, Corso Vittorio Emanuele 209, Rome; Casal Palocco, Viale Alessandro Magno 94, Rome, Italy.

Teller, Edward, PH.D.; Hungarian-born American scientist; b. 15 Jan. 1908; ed. Karlsruhe Technical Inst., and Univs. of Munich and Leipzig.

Research Assoc., Leipzig 29-31, Göttingen 31-33; Rockefeller Fellow, Copenhagen 34; Lecturer, Univ. of London 34-35; Prof. of Physics, George Washington Univ. 35-41, Columbia Univ. 41-42; Physicist, Manhattan Engineer District 42-46; Prof. of Physics, Univ. of Chicago 46-52; Physicist, and Asst. Dir. Los Alamos Scientific Laboratory 49-52; Consultant, Univ. of Calif. Radiation Laboratory, Livermore 52-53, Assoc. Dir. Lawrence Radiation Laboratory 54-58, Dir. 58-60; Prof. of Physics Univ. of Calif. 53-60, Prof. of Physics at Large 60-; mem. Nat. Acad. of Sciences, American Acad. of Arts and Sciences, U.S.A.F. Scientific Advisory Board, etc., Fellow American Nuclear Soc.; Joseph Priestley Memorial Award 57, Albert Einstein Award 59, Midwest Research Inst. Award, Living History Award 60; Enrico Fermi Award 62; Hon. D.Sc. (Yale, Alaska, Fordham, George Washington, S. Calif., St. Louis); Hon. LL.D. (Mount Mary).

Publs. *The Structure of Matter* (with F. O. Rice) 49, *Magneto-Hydrodynamic Shocks* (with F. de Hoffmann) 50, *Theory of Origin of Cosmic Rays* 54, *Our Nuclear Future* (with A. Latter) 58, *Legacy of Hiroshima* 62, *The Reluctant Revolutionary* 64.

University of California Radiation Laboratory, P.O. Box 808, Livermore, Calif., U.S.A.

Telles, Raymond L., Jr.; American diplomatist; b. 5 Sept. 1915.

Served U.S. Army 41-42, Air Force 43-47, 51-52; Accountant Dept. of Justice 34-41, 47-48; County Clerk 48-51, 52-56; Major of El Paso 57-61; Amb. to Costa Rica 61-67; Amb. and Chair. U.S. Section, U.S.-Mexico Comm. for Border Devt. and Friendship 67-.

Department of State, Washington, D.C., U.S.A.

Telli Boubacar, Diallo; Guinean diplomatist; b. 25; ed. Ecole William Ponty, Dakar, Ecole Nationale de France Outremer and Univ. de Paris.

Former Judge, Senegal; served on staff of French High Commissioner, Dakar; Sec.-Gen. Grand Council, French West Africa 57-58; Ambassador to U.S.A. and Perm. Rep. to the UN 58-61; Vice-Pres. 17th Session of UN Gen. Assembly 61-62; Chair. special Cttee. on Apartheid of UN Gen. Assembly 63-64; Sec.-Gen. Org. of African Unity Aug. 64-.

Organization of African Unity, P.O. Box 3243, Addis Ababa, Ethiopia.

Tello, Manuel; Mexican diplomatist; b. 99.

Entered Mexican Foreign Service 24; Vice-Consul, Brownsville and Laredo, U.S.A. 24-25, Antwerp 25-27; Consul, Hamburg and Berlin 27-29, Yokohama 30-33; mem. Mexican Permanent Del. to L.N. 33-40; Dir.-Gen. Dept. of Political Affairs and of Diplomatic Service, Secretariat of External Relations 42, Asst. Sec. of State 43; Under-Sec. of State 44; Acting Sec. of External Relations 48; Sec. of State for External Relations Aug. 51-52; Del. to San Francisco Conf. 45; Sec.-Gen. Inter-American Conf. on Problems of War and Peace, Mexico City 45; Chair. Mexican Del. to Fourth Meeting of Ministers of Foreign Affairs of American Republics, Washington, D.C. 51; Ambassador to the U.S.A. 55-58; Minister of Foreign Affairs 58-64; Senator 64-.

The Senate, Mexico City, D.F., Mexico.

Tempel, Frederik Jan; Netherlands businessman; b. 26 Dec. 1900; ed. Rotterdam School of Economics.

Joined Van den Bergh's Fabr. N.V., Rotterdam 23; Man. local Unilever cos. in France, Italy and Germany 29-40; in Holland during war and Germany 45-47; mem. Board of Unilever N.V. and Unilever Ltd. 47; Vice-Chair. Unilever Ltd. 54; Chair. Unilever N.V. 56-66; retd.

De Valkenburcht 108, Oosterbeek, Netherlands.

Telephone: 08307-4935.

Temple, George, C.B.E., F.R.S.; British mathematician; b. 2 Sept. 1901; ed. Birkbeck Coll., and Trinity Coll., Cambridge.

Asst. at Birkbeck Coll. 22-24; Asst. Lecturer in Mathematics City and Guilds Coll. 24-28; Asst. Prof. Royal Coll. of Science 30-32; Prof. of Mathematics King's Coll. London 32-53; Chief Scientific Adviser to Min. of Civil Aviation July 47-49; Sedleian Prof. of Natural Philosophy, Oxford Univ. 53-; Chair. Aeronautical Research Council 61-64.

Publs. *Introduction to Quantum Theory* 31, *Rayleigh's Principle* 33, *General Principles of Quantum Theory* 34, *An Introduction to Fluid Dynamics* 58, *Cartesian Tensors* 60.

341 Woodstock Road, Oxford, England.

Templer, Field Marshal Sir Gerald Walter Robert, K.G., G.C.B., G.C.M.G., K.B.E., D.S.O.; British army officer; b. 11 Sept. 1898; ed. Wellington Coll., and Royal Military Coll., Sandhurst.

Joined Royal Irish Fusiliers 16; served in First World War, operations in North-West Persia and Mesopotamia 19-21, operations in Palestine 36; Brevet Major 35, Brevet Lieut.-Col. 38; commd. 2nd Corps, 47th (London) Div., 1st Div., 56th (London) Div. and 6th Armoured Div. between 42 and 44; Dir. Mil. Govt. 21st Army Group 45-46; Dir. Mil. Intelligence, War Office 46-48; Vice-Chief Imperial Gen. Staff 48-50; G.O.C.-in-C. Eastern Commd. 50-52; High Commr. and Dir. of Operations, Fed. of Malaya 52-54; Chief Imperial Gen. Staff 55-58; Col. Royal Horse Guards and Gold Stick to H.M. The Queen 63-; H.M. Lieut. for Greater London 66-; Trustee Nat. Portrait Gallery 58-, Historic Churches Preservation Trust; Exec. Cttee. Nat. Trust; mem. Nat. Army Museum Council 60-; Constable of Tower of London 65-; mem. Cttee. of Inquiry into Security Procedures and Practices 61; Hon. D.C.L. (Oxford).

12 Wilton Street, London, S.W.1, England.

Tendryakov, Vladimir Fedorovich; Soviet writer; b. 23; ed. Gorki Literary Inst., Moscow.

Army service 41-43; Corresp. *Ogonyok* 51-54; admitted to Union of Soviet Writers 54; mem. Communist Party of the U.S.S.R. 48-.

Publs. *Sredi Lesov* (In the Fields) (short stories), *Padenie Ivana Chuprova* (The Fall of Ivan Chuprov) (novel) 53, *Ne ko Dvoru* (Ill Suited) 54, *Tugoi Uzel* (The Tight Knot) 56 (stories), *Uchabvi* (Pits and Bumps) 57, *Chudotvornaya* (The Wonder-Worker) 58 (novels); scenarios: *Alien In-Laws* 55, *Miracle Worker* 60, *Short Circuit* 61, *The Trial* 62; *Hahodka* (The Find) (short novel) 64, *Svidanie s Nefertiti* (Meeting with Nefertiti) (novel) 64, etc.

Writers' Union of the U.S.S.R., 52 Ulitsa Vorovskogo, Moscow, U.S.S.R.

Teng Hsiao-ping; Chinese politician and financial administrator; b. 02; ed. France.

Joined C.C.P. in France; Commissar in Eighth Route Army; Vice-Chair. Cttee. of Financial and Economic Affairs 53-54; Minister of Finance 53-54; Sec.-Gen. of Central Cttee. of C.C.P. 54-; Vice-Premier 54-; Vice-Chair. Council of Nat. Defence 54-; mem. Standing Cttee. of Political Bureau 56-; Leader, Chinese Del. to talks with Soviet C.P., Moscow, July 63; Acting Prime Minister Dec. 63-April 65.

Central Committee, C.P. of China, Peking, China.

Teng Pao-shan; Chinese administrator; b. 87; ed. Ili Military Acad., Sinkiang.

Deputy Pacification Commissioner of Shensi 30; Dep. C.-in-C., 12th War Area, Sino-Japanese War; Chair. Kansu Prov. People's Govt. 49-54; Gov. Kansu 49-67; Dep. from Kansu, Nat. People's Congress 54-, mem. Budget Cttee. 54-; mem. Nat. Defence Council 54-;

Vice-Chair. Cen. Cttee., Revolutionary Council of Kuomintang 56-.
Lanchow, Kansu, People's Republic of China.

Teng To; Chinese journalist and politician; b. 1901. Formerly editor of *New China Daily*; mem. Council of Asscn. for Cultural Relations with Foreign Countries 54; Editor-in-chief of *People's Daily* 54-57; Sec. Peking C.C.P. Cttee. 59-; Alt. Sec. North China Bureau 65-; Pres. All-China Journalists' Asscn. 55-; mem. Cttee. of Dept. of Philosophy and Social Sciences of Academia Sinica 55; Vice-Chair. Int. Asscn. of Journalists 56.
Peking Chinese Communist Party Committee, Peking, China.

Teng Tzu-hui; Chinese administrator and Marxist theoretician; b. 93; ed. Tokyo and Whampoa Mil. Acad. Joined Kuomintang 25; joined C.C.P. 26; worked under Chu Teh to set up Fukien Soviet Area 27; Chair. West Fukien Soviet 30; thereafter various political and admin. posts; Chair. Provisional People's Govt. at Chungyüan 49; mem. Central People's Govt. Council 49; Vice-Chair. Central-South Admin. Council 53; Head of Dept. of Rural Work of Central Cttee. of C.C.P. 53-56; Vice-Chair. Financial and Economic Cttee. 53-54; Vice-Premier 54-64; Vice-Chair. Chinese People's Political Consultative Conference (C.P.P.C.C.) 64-; Deputy Chair. State Planning Comm. 62-; mem. Central Cttee. of C.C.P.
Chinese People's Political Consultative Conference, Peking, China.

Teng Ying-chao, (Mme. Chou En-lai); Chinese politician; b. 02; ed. Tientsin Women's Normal Coll. Arrested for her part in the Fourth of May Movement 19; married Chou En-lai 25; next two decades active in political and women's work; C.C.P. del. to C.P.P.C.C. 46; Vice-Chair. Nat. Women's Fed. of China 49-; Vice-Chair. Cttee. for Implementation of Marriage Law 53; mem. Standing Cttee. of First N.P.C. 54; mem. Exec. Cttee. of Int. Democratic Women's Fed. 55; mem. Central Cttee. of C.C.P. 56; Vice-Chair. Chinese People's Nat. Cttee. in Defence of Children; Vice-Pres. All-China Democratic Women's Fed.
National Women's Federation of China, Peking, China.

Tengbom, Ivar Justus, DR.TECH.; Swedish architect; b. 7 April 1878; ed. Chalmers Technical Inst., and Acad. of Fine Arts.
Prof. Architectural School, Stockholm Acad. of Fine Arts 16-20; architect Royal Palaces Stockholm and Drottningholm; Dir.-Gen. Royal Board for Public Works 24-36; Pres. Royal Acad. of Fine Arts 43-53, Royal Swedish Inst. for Engineering Research, Royal Acad. Letters, History and Antiquities; mem. or corresp. mem. Central Asscn. of Austrian Architects, Architectural League of New York, Soviet Acad. of Architecture, Prussian Acad. of Arts, Royal Inst. of British Architects; Hon. Acad. of R.A., London, Accademia di San Luca, Rome; mem. American Inst. of Architects; awarded Royal Gold Medal Royal Inst. of British Architects 38; Buildings include: Stockholm's Enskilda Bank 15, Högalid Church, Stockholm 23, Concert Hall Stockholm 26, Head Office of Swedish Match Co., Stockholm 28, Johnson-Line Office 32, City Palace, Stockholm 33, Esselte building (Lithographics Factory) 33, Swedish Archaeological Acad. Rome 40, Atvidabergs house 44, High Court of Justice, Stockholm 49, Arvfurstens Palats, Foreign Office, Stockholm 52; Hon. Dr. Techn. (Darmstadt and Stuttgart Techn. High Schools).
Drottningholm, Sweden.
Telephone: Stockholm 7720146.

ten Holt, Friso; Netherlands painter and etcher; b. 6 April 1921; ed. Rijksakademie van Beeldende Kunsten, Amsterdam.
Paintings mainly of swimmers, landscapes and nude figures; Teacher Academy of Art, Haarlem; one-man exhbns. in Netherlands since 52, London 59, 62, 63, 65; Group exhbns. at Beaverbrook Art Gallery, Canada 63, Biennale Salzburg 64, Carnegie Inst., Pittsburgh 64, Netherlands travelling exhbn. 57-58; works in collections in Netherlands, Sweden, U.K., France and America.
Major works: stained-glass windows for churches in Amsterdam and The Hague.
Keizersgracht 614, Amsterdam, Netherlands.

Tennyson, Sir Charles Bruce Locker, Kt., C.M.G., M.A., F.R.S.L.; b. 8 Nov. 1879; ed. Eton Coll., and King's Coll., Cambridge.
Called to Bar 06; Asst. Legal Adviser Colonial Office 11; Deputy Dir. Federation of British Industries 19; Sec. Dunlop Rubber Co. Ltd. 28-48; Vice-Pres. Fed. of British Industries; Hon. Fellow King's Coll., Cambridge, Royal Coll. of Art, Bedford Coll., Hon. LL.D. (Cambridge).
Publs. *Cambridge from Within* 12, *Alfred Tennyson* 49; (Editor) *Shorter Poems of Frederick Tennyson* 13, *The Devil and the Lady* (by Alfred Lord Tennyson) 30, *Unpublished Poems of Alfred Tennyson* 31; *Life's All a Fragment* 53, *Six Tennyson Essays* 54, *Stars and Markets* 57.
23 The Park, London, N.W.11, England.

Tenzing, Norgay, G.M.; Nepalese climber; b. about 1914 in eastern Nepal, migrated to Bengal 32.
Took part (as porter) in expeditions under Shipton 35, Ruttledge 36 and Tilman 38; joined small expedition to Karakoram 50, and French expedition to Nanda Devi 51, when he and one Frenchman climbed the east peak; Sirdar to both Swiss expeditions 52, joining assault parties and reaching about 28,000 feet; Sirdar to British Everest expedition 53, when he and Hillary reached the summit on May 29th; Dir. of Field Training, Himalayan Mountaineering Inst., Darjeeling 54-.
1 Tonga Road, Darjeeling, West Bengal, India.

Teplov, Leonid Fyodorovich; Soviet diplomatist; b. 1909; ed. in the humanities.
Joined Diplomatic Service 41; Deputy Head Fourth European Dept., Ministry of Foreign Affairs 46-48; Consul-Gen. Bratislava 48-49; Counsellor, Prague 49-50; Chargé d'Affaires, Canada 50-54; Deputy Head, Protocol Dept., Ministry of Foreign Affairs 55-56, 62-65; Ambassador to the Sudan 56-61; Ambassador to Ethiopia 65-.
U.S.S.R. Embassy, Fikremaria Street, Addis Ababa, Ethiopia.

Terao, Takeo; Japanese banker; b. 5 April 1905; ed. Tokyo Univ.
Nomura (now Daiwa) Bank 29-, Dir. 47-, later Managing Dir., Pres. 50-; Vice-Pres. Fed. of Bankers Asscn. of Japan and Osaka Bankers' Asscn.
Daiwa Bank Ltd., 21 Bingomachi, 2-chome, Higashi-ku, Osaka, Japan.

Terebilov, Vladimir Ivanovich; Soviet lawyer; b. 1916; ed. Leningrad Inst. of Law.
Regional Public Procurator 39-49; Senior Scientific Worker and Scientific Sec., Inst. of Criminology 49-57; Deputy Head of Board of Public Procurators, U.S.S.R. 57-61; mem. U.S.S.R. Coll. of Public Procurators 61-62; Deputy Chair. of U.S.S.R. Supreme Court 62-. Supreme Court of U.S.S.R., Moscow, U.S.S.R.

Tereshkova-Nikolaeva, Valentina Vladimirovna (wife of Andriyan Nikolaev, *q.v.*); Soviet cosmonaut; b. 6 March 1937; ed. Yaroslavl Textile Coll. and Zhukovsky Air Force Engineering Acad.
Former textile worker, Krasny Perekop textile mill, Yaroslavl, and textile mill Sec., Young Communist League; mem. C.P. of the Soviet Union March 62-; cosmonaut training March 62-; made 48 orbital flights of the earth in spaceship *Vostok VI* 16th June to 19th

June 63; first woman in world to enter space; Deputy to U.S.S.R. Supreme Soviet; Chair. Soviet Women's Cttee. 68-; Pilot-Cosmonaut of U.S.S.R., Hero of Soviet Union, Joliot-Curie Gold Medal, World Peace Council 66.

Zvezdny Gorodok, Moscow, U.S.S.R.

Terkelsen, Terkel M.; Danish journalist; b. 8 Nov. 1904.
London Ed. of *Berlingske Tidende* 37-40 and 45-46; Political Intelligence Dept. of the Foreign Office, and Commentator B.B.C. Danish Service 41-45; mem. of the Danish Council London (Free Danes) 40-45; Chief Ed. *Berlingske Tidende* and *Berlingske Aftenavis* 46-; a Gov. of Fondation Européenne de la Culture.
Holck Winterfeldts Alle 6, Hellerup; Office: *Berlingske Tidende*, Pilestraede 34, Copenhagen, Denmark.
Telephone: Copenhagen 157575 (Office), HE 7227 (Home).

Terman, Frederick Emmons, A.B., SC.D.; American electrical and radio engineer; b. 6 June 1900; ed. Stanford Univ., Mass. Inst. of Technology.
Instructor Electrical Eng., Stanford Univ. 25-27, Asst. Prof. 27-30, Assoc. Prof. 30-37, Prof. and Exec. Head Dept. 37-45; Dir. Harvard Univ. Radio Research Laboratory 42-45; mem. Vacuum Tube Development Cttee. NDRC and JCB 43-46; mem. Divs. 14 and 15 of Nat. Defence Research Cttee. 42-45, Naval Research Advisory Cttee. 56-64, Chair. 57-58; Dean of School of Engineering, Stanford Univ. 45-58, Provost 55-65, Vice-Pres. 59-65, Emeritus 65-; Pres. SMU Foundation for Science and Engineering 65-; mem. Nat. Acad. of Sciences, Chair. Engineering Section 53-56, Council 56-59; Founder mem. Nat. Acad. of Engineering; mem. American Philosophical Soc.; Vice-Pres. Inst. Radio Engineers 40, Pres. 41, Dir. 40-43, 48-49, Medal of Honor 50, Founders Award 62; Vice-Pres. American Soc. of Eng. Educ. 49-51; mem. Board of Foreign Scholarships 60-66, Medal for Merit 48; Lamme Medal 64; Hon. Sc.D. (Harvard, B.C. and Syracuse Univs.).
Publs. *Transmission-Line Theory* (with W. S. Franklin) 27, *Radio Engineering* 32, 37, 47, *Measurements in Radio Engineering* 35, *Fundamentals of Radio* 38, *Radio and Vacuum Tube Theory* (in collaboration with U.S. Mil. Acad. staff) 40, *Radio Engineers' Handbook* 43, *Electronic Measurements* (with J. M. Pettit) 52, *Electronic and Radio Engineering* 55.
445 El Escarpado, Stanford, Calif., U.S.A.

Termer, Karl Ferdinand Franz, PH.D.; German university professor; b. 94; ed. Univs. of Berlin and Würzburg.
Ethnological, geographical, and historical studies; special studies in American Anthropology and Linguistics; Asst., Geographical Inst. Würzburg 21-25; Lecturer in Geography and Ethnology, Würzburg 23, Asst. Prof. 29, Prof. 32; Prof. of Ethnology, Univ. of Hamburg, and Dir. of Ethnological Museum, Hamburg 35-62, Prof. Emer. 62-.
Publs. *Zur Ethnologie und Ethnographie des nördlichen Mittelamerika* 30, *Zur Archaeologie von Guatemala* 31, *Zur Geographie der Republik Guatemala* (2 vols.) 36 and 41, *Durch Urwälder und Sümpfe Mittelamerikas* 41, *Quañhtemallan und Cuzcatlan* 48, *Der Paricutin-Vulkan in Michoacan, Mexico* 52, *Die Mayaforschung* 52, *Die Halbinsel Yucatan* 54, *Der Hund bei den Kulturvölkern Altamerikas, Etnologia y Etnografia de Guatemala* 57, *El viaje de John Cockburn a Centroamérica* 62, *Die Schiffbrüche des Cabeza de Vaca* 63.
Friedensweg 22, 2 Hamburg 52 (Hochkamp), German Federal Republic.

Terracini, Umberto Elia, Doctor of Laws; Italian journalist; b. 27 July 1895; ed. law school.
Convicted many times in early twenties for activity in the workers' movement; sentenced by special Fascist Tribunal to 23 years' imprisonment June 25; released after the overthrow of Mussolini Aug. 43; Pres. of Constituent Assembly until April 48; Senator May 48-; mem. of Italian Communist Party; collaborator on *Ordine Nuovo* (founded 1919).
Via Dogana Vecchia 29, Rome, Italy.

Terray, Jean Pierre; French banker; b. 28 July 1906.
President and Dir.-Gen. Banque de l'Union Européenne Industrielle et Financière; Dir. and mem. Directing Cttee. Schneider S.A.; Dir. Soc. des Forges et Ateliers du Creusot, Soc. Métallurgique d'Imphy, Lille-Bonnières-Colombes, Roussel Uclaf, Soc. des Automobiles SIMCA, Tréfimetaux G.P.; Auditor Compagnie Bancaire; Vice-Pres. Scodimex; Dir. Electrorail, Eurinvest, Eurofin, North American Holdings Ltd., Sparmont; mem. Supervisory Council, Interfonds.
29 avenue Georges Mandel, Paris 16e, France.

Terrenoire, Louis; French journalist and politician; b. 10 Nov. 1908.
Former trade union Sec.; Editor *La Voix Sociale, Nouveau Journal de Lyon* 30-31, Editorial Sec. *L'Aube* 32-39, later Editor; Sec. Conseil Nat. de la Résistance 44; captured and deported; Deputy to Nat. Ass. from Orne 45-51; Sec.-Gen. Rassemblement du Peuple Français (R.P.F.) 51-54; Dir. News and Information, Radiodiffusion-Télévision Française July-Nov. 58; Dep. to Nat. Ass. from Orne 58-; Minister of Information Feb. 60-Aug. 61; Minister attached to Office of Prime Minister Aug. 61-Apr. 62; Sec.-Gen. Union pour la Nouvelle République 62; mem. European Parl. 63-; mem. Union pour la Nouvelle République (U.N.R.), Pres. Assembly Group 59-60; Officier Légion d'Honneur, Croix de Guerre, Rosette de la Résistance.
6 rue de Rémusat, Paris 16e, France.

Terry, Luther Leonidas; American physician and public health administrator; b. 15 Sept. 1911; ed. Birmingham-Southern Coll., and Tulane Univ.
Chief, Medical Services, Public Health Service Hospital Baltimore 42-53, Chief Cardiovascular Clinic 50-53, Chief. Gen. Medicine and Experimental Therapeutics at P.H.S. Nat. Heart Inst. 50-58, Asst. Dir. 58-61; Surgeon-Gen. U.S. Public Health Service 61-65; Vice-Pres. for Medical Affairs, Univ. of Pennsylvania Oct. 65-; Chief U.S. Del., WHO 61-65; Lecturer, Johns Hopkins Univ. School of Medicine; fmr. Gov. American Coll. of Physicians; mem. Board of Overseers, Harvard Univ. School of Public Health; mem. and officer numerous professional orgs.; Hon. D.Sc. (Birmingham-Southern Coll., Jefferson Medical Coll., Tulane Univ., Univ. of Rhode Island and Rose Polytechnic Inst.), Hon. LL.D. (Calif. Coll. of Medicine and Univ. of Alaska), Hon. M.D. (Woman's Medical Coll. of Pennsylvania); numerous Hon. Fellowships and awards.
121 College Hall, Univ. of Pennsylvania, Philadelphia, Pa. 19104, U.S.A.
Telephone: 215-594-7231.

Terwagne, Richard; Belgian mining executive; b. 31 Oct. 1900; ed. Lycée Janson, Paris, and Brussels Univ.
Managing Dir., Union Minière, Brussels 46-; Man. Dir. Société Métallurgie Hoboken 50-60, Vice-Chair. 61-; Chair. Sogemet, Brussels; Dir. Société Minerais et Métaux, Paris, Compagnie d'Electrolyse du Palais, Paris; Officier, Ordre de Léopold, Belgium, Order Royal du Lion, Belgium.
6 rue Montagne du Parc, Brussels 1, Belgium.
Telephone: 13-60-90.

Terzakis, Anghelos; Greek novelist and dramatist; b. 16 Feb. 1907; ed. Univ. of Athens.
Sec. Nat. Theatre 37, and later apptd. Dir. of Repertory, Artistic Dir. and Gen. Dir.; Theatre Critic and Literary Contributor to Athens daily newspaper *Vima*; editor *Epoches* magazine 63-67; Cultural Adviser to Ministry of Foreign Affairs; Commdr. Order of King George.

Publs. include: (novels) *The Violet City* 37, *Princess Izabo* 45, *Without a God* 51, *Secret Life* 57; (plays) *Emperor Michael* 36, *The Cross and the Sword* 39, *Theophano* 56, *The Mediterranean Night* 58, *The Lady in White Gloves* 62, *Thomas the Apostle* 62; (history) *Greek Epic* 64.
40 Odos Pipinou, Athens (813), Greece.
Telephone: 830-984.

Tesauro, Giuseppe, M.D.; Italian gynaecologist; b. 21 June 1898; ed. Univ. of Naples.
Assistant and Chief of Service, Inst. of Clinical Obstetrics and Gynaecology, Univ. of Naples 21-35; Titular Prof. of Obstetrics and Gynaecology, Univ. of Sassari 35-36, Univ. of Messina 36-43, Dean Faculty of Medicine, Messina 39-43; Titular Prof. of Obstetrics and Gynaecology and Dir. of Clinical Obstetrics and Gynaecology, Univ. of Naples 43-; Rector, Univ. of Naples 59-; Pres. Società Italiana di Ostetricia e Ginecologia 59-61; Dir. School of Midwives and Pres. School of Professional Nurses, Naples; Pres. Int. Fertility Asscn. 62-66, Pres. Int. Fed. of Gynaecology and Obstetrics 64-67; official of numerous medical and govt. orgs.
Publs. *Cancer du col de l'utérus sur moignon d'hystérectomie subtotale* 28, *Sur le développement de tumeurs dans les ovaires soumis à l'action des rayons X* 28, *Über Erzeugung von Ehrlich-Adeno-Carcinomen-Tieren* 32, *Die Bewertung des eklamptischen Anfalls* 32, *La sterilità femminile* 39, *Conceptions actuelles sur le diagnostic et le traitement du cancer de l'utérus* 53, *Le dépistage du cancer de l'uterus par la méthode cytologique* 54, *Les isotopes radioactifs dans l'étude de la circulation amniotique* 58, *L'influence de l'isoimmunisation Rh sur la mortalité du nouveau-né* 59, *Déséquilibres métaboliques hormonaux gravidiques et anomalies congénitales* 60, *Thalassemia and Fertility* 62, *Arteriografia pelvica dopo isterectomia radicale* 63, *Trattato Italiano di Ginecologia* 64.
51 Via S. Brigida, Naples, Italy.
Telephone: 320421.

Tesemma, Getahoun; Ethiopian diplomatist; b. 1911; ed. Ethiopia, Egypt, Lebanon.
Fought with guerrillas during Italian occupation; Dir.-Gen. Ministry of Pensions 41-42; Dir.-Gen. Ministry of Interior 42-43; First Sec. Washington 43-47; Perm. Rep. U.N. 47-48; Vice-Minister, Commerce and Industry 48-58, Agriculture 58; Minister of Public Health 58; Ambassador to U.S.S.R. 59-60, to India 60-62; Minister of Nat. Community Devt. 62-, concurrently Minister of Social Affairs 66-; Pres. ILO Conf. 67; Grand Officer of the Collar of Ethiopia, Liberation Medal, Patriots Medal.
Ministry of National Community Development, Addis Ababa, Ethiopia.

Teshigawara, Sofu (Koichi); Japanese artist in flower arrangement; b. 1900.
Originated own style called *Sogetsu* (Grass of Moon), Head of the Sogetsu School.
Publ. *Flower Arrangement of the Sogetsu School.*
1, Aoyama-omote-machi, Akasaka, Minato-ku, Tokyo, Japan.

Testa, H.E. Cardinal Gustavo; Vatican ecclesiastic; b. 18 July 1886; ed. Pontifical Roman Seminary.
Ordained priest 10; seminary teacher 14-20; entered Vatican diplomatic service 20, served in Austria, Germany, Peru, Italy and Egypt; Titular Bishop of Amasea 34; attached to Secretariat of State at the Vatican 42-48; Apostolic Del. Jerusalem 48-53; Apostolic Nuncio in Switzerland 53-59; created Cardinal by Pope John XXIII 59; Pro-Pres. Comm. for Admin. of Properties of the Holy See 61; mem. Sacred Congregations for the Oriental Church, of Extraordinary Ecclesiastical Affairs and for the Reverend Fabric of St. Peter's; Sec. Sacred Congregation for the Oriental Church 62-68.
Vatican City, Rome, Italy.

Tett, Sir Hugh Charles, Kt., A.R.C.S., B.SC., D.I.C., F.INST.P., A.M.I.MECH.E.; British oil executive; b. 28 Oct. 1906; ed. Univ. Coll., Exeter and Royal Coll. of Science, London.
Esso Petroleum Co. 28-, Man., Technical Dept. 35-39; Man.-Dir. Esso Research Ltd. 47-49; Dir. Esso Petroleum Co., Ltd. 51-56, Man.-Dir. 56-59, Chair. and Man. Dir. 59-63, Chair. 59-Dec. 67; Dir. Esso Europe 66-; a Gov. London Graduate School of Business Studies; mem. Council Manchester Business School; pro-Chancellor Univ. of Southampton 67-; Fellow Imperial Coll., London 64; Hon. D.Sc. (Southampton).
Tor Point, St. George's Hill, Weybridge, Surrey, England.

Tévoédjré, Albert, D. ès SC. ECON. et SOC., L. ès L.; Dahomeyan politician and regional administrator; b. 1929; ed. Toulouse Univ., Fribourg Univ., and Institut Universitaire des Hautes Etudes Internationales, Geneva.
Assistant teacher, Lycée Delafosse, Dakar 52-54; teacher in France 57-58, teacher Lycée Victor Ballot, Porto Novo 59-; Asst. Sec.-Gen. Nat. Syndicate of Teachers, Dahomey 59, Dahomeyan Democratic Resettlement Oct. 60-; Sec. of State for Information 61-; Sec.-Gen. Union Africaine et Malgache (U.A.M.) 62-63; founder-mem. Promotion Africaine (society to combat poverty in Africa); Prof. in charge of researches at Harvard Univ. 64-65; fmr. Chief Editor *L'Etudiant d'Afrique Noire.*
Publs. *L'Afrique Revoltée* 58, *Pan-Africanism in Action* 65, *L'Afrique face aux problèmes du socialisme et de l'aide étrangère* 66, etc.
Secrétariat d'Etat à l'Information, Porto-Novo, Dahomey, West Africa.

Tewfik, Zakaria; Egyptian cotton executive; b. 1920; ed. Cairo Univ.
With Bank Misr; then Commercial Attaché, Belgium, Spain; Dir.-Gen. Exchange Control Office 61; Under-Sec. for Cotton Affairs, Ministry of Economy 61-; Dir.-Gen. Cotton Org. 61-; U.A.R. Del. to many int. cotton confs.
General Organization for Cotton, 151 Mohamed Farid Street, Cairo, United Arab Republic.

Tewson, Sir Vincent, C.B.E., M.C.; British trade union official; b. 4 Feb. 1898; ed. Bradford.
Served First World War; Sec. Organisation Dept. of T.U.C. 25-31; Asst. Gen. Sec. 31-46; Gen. Sec. 46-Sept. 60; mem. Econ. Planning Board July 47-60; Vice-Chair. *Daily Herald* 46-60; Pres. Int. Confed. of Free Trade Unions (ICFTU) 51-53; Part-time mem. London Electricity Board 60-; mem. Independent Television Authority 64-.
Kelmscott, Leecroft Road, Barnet, Hertfordshire, England.

Teymour, Mahmoud; United Arab Republic (Egyptian) writer and playwright; b. 94; ed. Egyptian schools.
Mem. Acad. for the Arabic Language, Cairo; State Prize for Literature 60, 64; Decoration of Merit, Decoration of Arts and Sciences.
Publs. in Arabic: Some sixty works, including collections of short stories, novels, plays, memoirs, essays, etc.; in French: *La Fille du Diable* 42, *Le Courtier de la Mort* 51, *La Belle aux lèvres charnues* 52, *La Fleur du Cabaret* 53, *Bonne Fête* 54, *L'Amour par-delà l'Inconnu* 55; in English: *Tales from Egyptian Life* 48, *The Call of the Unknown* 65; collections of short stories in German, Yugoslav, Hungarian, Russian and Chinese.
6 Yahia Ibrahim Street, Zamalek, Cairo, U.A.R.
Telephone: Cairo 806665.

Tezenas du Montcel, Robert; French civil servant; b. 22 Sept. 1902; ed. St. Etienne, Univs. of Lyons and Paris.
Auditor, Cour des Comptes 30; Colonial Inspector 34; Overseas Inspector-Gen. 48; Dir.-Gen. Ministry for Relations with Associated States 50; Pres. Admin. Council, Institut d'émission de l'A.O.F. et de Togo 55; Pres. Overseas Tourist Office 55; Pres. Central Bank of West African States 59-64; Dir. of Gen. Inspection of Overseas Affairs 64-; Pres. Cie. Financière France-Afrique 65; Grand Officier de la Légion d'Honneur, Croix de Guerre, foreign honours.
77 Boulevard Général-Koenig, Neuilly-sur-Seine, France.

Thacker, Maneklal Sankalchand; Indian engineer; b. 3 Dec. 1904; ed. Univ. of Bristol, England.
Worked for Bristol Corpn. Electricity Dept. 27-31; worked with Calcutta Electric Supply Corpn. 31-47; Prof. of Electrical Technology and Power Engineering, Indian Inst. of Science 47-49; Dir. Indian Inst. of Science 49-55; Dir. Scientific and Industrial Research and Additional Sec. to the Ministry of Natural Resources and Scientific Research 55-57; Sec. to Govt. of India in Ministry of Scientific Research and Cultural Affairs and Dir.-Gen. Council of Scientific and Industrial Research 57-62, mem. Planning Comm. 62-; Chair. Commonwealth Scientific Cttee. 61-; Pres. UN Conf. on the Application of Science and Technology 63, 65; Hon. D.Sc., D.Eng., D.Litt.; numerous gold medals; Padma Bhushan 55.
4 Kushak Road, New Delhi, India.

Thalmann, Ernest A., DR. IUR.; Swiss diplomatist; b. 14 Jan. 1914; ed. Univ. of Zürich.
Lawyer, District Court of Zürich 40; Fed. Dept. of Public Economy 41; Attaché, Swiss Fed. Political Dept. 45; Sec. Extraordinary Powers Cttee. and the Cttee. of Foreign Affairs of the Nat. Council 46; Second Sec. of Legation 47; Dep. Chief, Press and Information Service, Swiss Fed. Political Dept. 47; Sec. Swiss del. UN Conf. for Freedom of Press and Information, Geneva 48; Swiss Legation, Paris 49, First Sec. 51; Swiss Legation, Prague 52; Dep. Chief, Division of Organisation and Admin. Affairs, Swiss Political Dept. 54-57; Counsellor and Dep. Chief of Mission, Swiss Embassy in U.S.A. 57-60, Minister-Counsellor 60-61; Perm. Observer and Ambassador to UN 61-66; Chief, Div. for Int. Organizations, Swiss Political Dept. 66-.
Swiss Political Department, 3003 Berne, Switzerland.

Thant, U; Burmese civil servant and United Nations official; b. 22 Jan. 1909; ed. Pantanaw Nat. High School and Univ. Coll., Rangoon.
Senior Master, National High School, Pantanaw 28, Headmaster 31; Sec. Education Reorganisation Board 42; Press Dir. Burma 47; Dir. of Broadcasting, Burma 48; Sec. to Govt. of Burma (Ministry of Information) 49-57; Chair. Burmese Film Award Board 52-57; Sec. for Projects, Office of Prime Minister 53; Exec. Sec. Econ. and Social Board; Perm. Rep. of Burma to UN 57-61; Chair. UN Congo Conciliation Comm. 61; Acting Sec.-Gen. of UN Nov. 61-Nov. 62, Sec.-Gen. Nov. 62-; Hon. LL.D. from numerous U.S. univs. and Moscow Univ.
Publs. include: *Cities and their Stories* 30, *League of Nations* 33, *Towards a New Education* 46, *Democracy in Schools* 52, *History of Post-War Burma* (2 vols.) 61.
United Nations, New York City, N.Y., U.S.A.

Thapa, Surya Bahadur; Nepalese politician; b. 20 March 1928; ed. Allahabad Univ., India.
House Speaker, Advisory Assembly to King of Nepal 58; mem. Upper House of Parl. 59; Minister of Forest, Agriculture, Commerce and Industry 60; Minister of Finance and Econ. Affairs 62; Vice-Chair. Council of Ministers, Minister of Finance, Econ. Planning, Law

and Justice 63; Vice-Chair. Council of Ministers, Minister of Finance, Law and Gen. Admin. 64-65; Chair. Council of Ministers, Minister of Palace Affairs, 65-; Tri-Shakti-Patta 63, Gorkha Dakshinbahu I 65.
Naxal, Katmandu, Nepal.

Thapa, Vishwa Bandhu, B.A.; Nepalese agriculturist and politician; b. 27; ed. Adaisha, Vidyalaya, Biratnagar, Nepal; Central Hindu Coll., Benares Hindu Univ. India.
Executive Cttee. Nepali Congress Party 51-, Gen. Sec. 58; mem. Lower House of Parl. 59-, Chief Govt. Whip 59-60; mem. Council of Ministers 60-; Minister of Nat. Guidance, Home and Panchayats 60-64; Vice-Chief, Council of Ministers, Minister of Home and Panchayat Devt. 64-65.
Bharatpur, Chitwan, Nepal.

Thapar, Gen. Pran Nath; Indian army officer; b. 8 May 1906; ed. Govt. Coll., Lahore, Sandhurst.
First Punjab Regt.; war service in Burma 41, Middle East and Italy 43; Asst. Mil. Sec. G.H.Q., India 45; mem. Army Re-Organisation Cttee.; Commanded 1st Battalion 1st Punjab Regt., Indonesia 46; Mil. Sec. 48-49; Master-Gen. of Ordnance 49-50; Imperial Defence Coll. 56; G.O.C. Southern Command 57-59; Chief of Army Staff 61-62; Ambassador to Afghanistan 64-.
c/o Ministry of External Affairs, New Delhi, India.

Thatcher, (Wilbert) Ross; Canadian politician; b. 24 May 1917; ed. Moose Jaw Central Coll. and Queen's Univ.
Member House of Commons, Ottawa 45-57; Leader Liberal Party, Saskatchewan 59-; mem. Saskatchewan Legislative Assembly 60-; Premier of Saskatchewan 64-; mem. Co-operative Commonwealth Fed. 45-55; Independent 55, Liberal 56-.
Office of the Premier, Regina, Saskatchewan, Canada.

Theiler, Max, L.R.C.P., M.R.C.S., D.T.M. & H.; South African research physician; b. 30 Jan. 1899; ed. Univ. of Cape Town, St. Thomas's Hospital, London and London School of Tropical Medicine.
Assistant, later Instructor Dept. of Tropical Medicine, Harvard Medical School 22-30; staff mem. The Rockefeller Foundation 30-; Dir. of Laboratories, Div. of Medicine and Public Health of Rockefeller Foundation, N.Y. 51-; awarded Nobel Prize in Physiology and Medicine for development of vaccine against Yellow Fever.
The Rockefeller Foundation, Virus Laboratories, 66th Street and York Avenue, New York 21, N.Y., U.S.A.

Thein Maung, U, M.A., LL.B.; Burmese lawyer; b. 1890; ed. Calcutta and Cambridge Univs.
Called to the Bar (Lincoln's Inn); mem. Burma Deputation to U.K. 19-20, Burma Del. to U.K. 33-34; rep. Burma in Indian Legislative Assembly 34-36; Minister of Education Burma 36; mem. Public Service Comm. 37-38; Advocate-Gen. 38-42; Minister for Judicial Affairs 42-45; Judge, High Court of Judicature, Rangoon 45-48; Chief Justice, High Court of Union of Burma 48-50; Judge Supreme Court 50-52; Chief Justice of the Union 52-57; Deputy Prime Minister, Minister of Foreign Affairs, Religious Affairs, Health and Social Welfare, Oct. 58-60; mem. Govt. Advisory Cttee. 60.
Rangoon, Burma.

Theocharis, Reghinos D., D.PHIL.; Cypriot economist and banker; b. 10 Feb. 1929; ed. Graduate School of Economics, Athens, Univ. of Aberdeen, and London School of Economics.
Inspector of Commercial Education, Cyprus 53-56; at London School of Economics 56-58; Chief, Economic Development Unit, Bank of Greece, Athens 58-59; Minister of Finance in Cyprus Provisional Govt.

March 59-Aug. 60; Minister of Finance Aug. 60-62; Gov. of Bank of Cyprus 62-.
Publ. *Early Developments in Mathematical Economics* 61.
c/o Bank of Cyprus Ltd., P.O.B. 117, Phaneromeni Street, Nicosia, Cyprus.

Theodorakopoulos, Ioannis, PH.D.; Greek philosopher; b. 1900; ed. Univs. of Athens, Vienna and Heidelberg. Prof. of Philosophy Univ. of Salonika 25-33, Univ. of Athens 39-, Panteios School of Political Science 50-; Minister of Education 45; Chair. Greek Nat. Theatre Cttee.; mem. Acad. of Athens, Pres. 63; cttee. mem. Int. Inst. of Philosophy; hon. mem. Goethehaus (Frankfurt); Editor *Archives of Philosophy* and *Theory of Science* 29-41; Hon. LL.D. (Univ. of Athens, Ohio).
Publs. *Platons Dialektik des Seins* 27, *Plotins Metaphysik des Seins* 29, *Theory of Knowledge* 28, *The Philosophy of Kant* 30, *Philosophy and Psychology* 29, *The Philosophy of Heraclitus* 30, *Philosophy of Art* 31, *Philosophy of Education* 32, *The Problem of the Philosophy of History* 32, *History and Life* 36, *An Introduction to Plato* 40, *Plato's Phaedrus* 48, *System of Ethics* 48, *Studies of Christian and Philosophical Thought* 52, *A Philosophical Interpretation of Goethe's Faust* 56, *Plato, Plotinus, Origenis* 59, *Plato's Theory of Ideas* 60, *Dialogue, Dialectic and our Times* 61, *The Place of Hellenism in the Contemporary World* 61, *Greece and Europe* 63, *The Hundred Years of the Greek Dynasty* 63.
Odos Skoufas 19, Athens, Greece.

Theodosios VI; Greek ecclesiastic; born in Lebanon; ed. theological school of Halki, Istanbul and Univ. of Athens.
Greek Orthodox Patriarch of Antioch (Antyarka) and of All the East 59-.
The Patriarchate, P.O. Box 9, Damascus, Syria.

Theorell, Hugo, M.D.; Swedish biochemist; b. 6 July 1903; ed. Royal Caroline Medico-Surgical Inst., Stockholm.
Asst. Prof. of Chemistry, Uppsala Univ. 32; Head Biochemistry Dept., Nobel Inst. Stockholm 37-; Sec.-Gen. Swedish Society of Physicians and Surgeons 40-45, Chair. 46-47, 57-58, Hon. mem. 56-; mem. State Research Council for Natural Sciences 50-54, for Medical Sciences 58-64; Chair. Swedish Chemical Soc. 47-48; mem.Royal Swedish Acads. of Science, Engineering Sciences and of Music, Royal Danish Acad. of Sciences and Letters, Norwegian Acad. of Science and Letters, Accad. dei XL, Rome, American Acad. of Arts and Letters, Nat. Acad. of Sciences, American Philosophical Soc.; hon. mem. New York Acad. of Sciences; foreign mem. Royal Society, Polish Acad. of Sciences, Indian Acad. of Sciences, Acad. Royale de Médecine, Belgium; Nobel Prize in Physiology or Medicine 55; Commdr. Royal Order of the Northern Star, 1st Class; Commdr. Royal Norwegian Order of St. Olaf; Officer, Brazilian Order of Southern Cross; Commdr. Légion d'Honneur; principal research in field of enzymes; Dr.h.c. (Paris, Philadelphia, Louvain, Brussels, Rio de Janeiro, Kentucky and Michigan).
Home: Wenner-Gren Centre, 11346 Stockholm; Office: Nobel Medical Institute, Department of Biochemistry, Solnavägen 1, 10401 Stockholm 60, Sweden.
Telephone: 235480.

Theotokis, Spyros; Greek politician; b. 08; ed. Univs. of Athens, Paris and Lausanne.
Member of the Chamber of Deputies 34; Minister of Food 44, of Foreign Affairs 55-56, of Agriculture 57, of Finance 61-63, of Interior April 67.
c/o Ministry of Interior, Athens, Greece.

Theotonio Pereira, Pedro; Portuguese politician and diplomatist; b. 7 Nov. 1902; ed. Univ. of Lisbon.
Under-Sec. of State for Labour 33-35; Ambassador to Spain 38-45, to Brazil 45-46, to U.S.A. 47-50, 61-63, to U.K. 53-58; Minister to the Presidency 58-61; Life

mem., Portuguese Council of State 56-; Trustee, Calouste Gulbenkian Foundation 56-; Grand Cross of Carlos III, Military Order of Christ, Order of Infante Don Henrique (Portugal), Cruzeiro do Sul (Brazil), George I (Greece); Mérito Naval, Mérito Militar, Yugo y Flechas (Spain), Hon. G.C.V.O.
Dafundo, Portugal.

Thesiger, Wilfred, D.S.O., M.A.; British traveller; b. 3 Jan. 1910; ed. Eton and Magdalen Coll., Oxford. Explored Danakil country of Abyssinia 33-34; Sudan Political Service, Darfur and Upper Nile Provinces 35-39; served in Ethiopia, Syria and Western Desert with Sudan Defence Force and Special Air Service, Second World War; explored the Empty Quarter of Arabia 45-50; lived with the Madan in the Marshes of Southern Iraq 50-58; awarded Back Grant, Royal Geographical Soc. 36, Founders Medal 48; Lawrence of Arabia Medal, Royal Central Asian Soc. 55; David Livingstone Medal, Royal Scottish Geographical Soc. 61; W. H. Heinemann Bequest, Royal Soc. of Literature 64; Burton Medal, Royal Asiatic Soc. 66; Hon. D.Litt. (Leicester).
Publs. *Arabian Sands* 58, *The Marsh Arabs* 64.
15 Shelley Court, Tite Street, London, S.W.3, England.

Thi Han, Thiri Pyanchi U; Burmese politician; b. 1912; ed. Rangoon Univ.
General Sec. Rangoon Univ. Students' Union 36; Asst. Quarter-Master Gen., War Office (Burma); Deputy Controller of Civil Supplies 49, later Dir. of Procurement and Dir. of Defence Industries, Ministry of Defence; Minister of Trade Devt., Commodity Distribution and Co-operatives 59; Minister of Foreign Affairs 62-, also of Public Works and Housing, Mines and Labour 62-64, also of Nat. Planning 64-, Vice-Chair. Socialist Economy Planning Cttee. 67-.
Ministry of Foreign Affairs, Rangoon, Burma.
Telephone: 16333.

Thiam, Doudou; Senegalese politician; b. 3 Feb. 1926; ed. Lycée Van Vollenhoven, Dakar, and Poitiers Univ. Former Magistrate, Senegal; helped draft Constitutions of Republic of Senegal and of Mali Fed.; fmr. Minister of Finance, Economic Affairs and Planning, Mali Fed. Minister of Foreign Affairs, Senegal Aug. 60-; State Minister in Charge of Foreign Affairs and Relations with the Assemblies 62-; Mayor of Mbake.
68 rue Wagane Diouf, Dakar, Senegal, W. Africa.

Thiel, Frans Joseph Frits Marie Van; Netherlands politician; b. 1906; ed. Univ. of Nijmegen.
Former lawyer; M.P. 48-52, 56-; Minister of Social Works 52-56; Speaker Second Chamber of Parl. 63-; Catholic.
Warandelaan 11A, Helmond, Netherlands.
Telephone: 2010.

Thiele, Ilse; German politician; b. 4 Nov. 1920; ed. secondary school.
Shorthand typist; mem. Communist Party 45, SED 46; founder mem. Democratic Women's League (DFD), first Pres. 53-; mem. Central Cttee. SED; mem. Volkskammer.
Democratic Women's League (DFD), Clara-Zetkin-Strasse 16, Berlin W 8, Germany.

Thielicke, Helmut, D.THEOL., D.PHIL.; German theologian; b. 4 Dec. 1908; ed. Univs. of Greifswald, Marburg, Erlangen and Bonn.
Prof. at Heidelberg 36-40; Parish Priest Ravensburg 40-42; head of Theological Office of Württemberg Church 43-45; Prof. of Systematic Theology at Univ. of Tübingen 45-54; Rector Univ. of Tübingen and Pres. Conf. of Rectors, German Fed. Republic 51; Prof. of Systematic Theology, Univ. of Hamburg 54-, Rector 60; Hon. Dr.Theol. (Heidelberg Univ.), Hon. D.D. (Glasgow Univ.).

Publs. *Das Verhältnis zwischen dem Ethischen und dem Asthetischen* 32, *Geschichte und Existenz* 35, 64, *Fragen des Christentums an die moderne Welt* 47, *Tod und Leben* 46, *Theologie der Anfechtung* 49, *Der Nihilismus* 50 (Japanese trans.), *Der Glaube der Christenheit* 47, *Zwischen Gott und Satan* 46 (English trans.), *Theologische Ethik* (English trans.), 4 vols., 51, 55, 58, 64, *Das Gebet, das die Welt umspannt* 46, *Das Leben kann noch einmal beginnen* 56, *Das Bilderbuch Gottes* 57 (U.S.. Norwegian, Danish, Swedish, Dutch and Japanese trans.), *Wie die Welt begann* 60 (English trans.), *Zwischen Himmel und Erde: Begegnungen in U.S.A.* 64 (U.S. trans.), *Leiden an der Kirche* 65 (U.S. trans.) 65. 2 Hamburg 13, v-Melle-Park 6, German Federal Republic.

Thier, Jacques de, LL.D.; Belgian lawyer and diplomatist; b. 15 Sept. 1900; ed. Univ. of Liège.
Mem. of the Bar, Liège and Verviers 23; attached to the Prime Minister's Cabinet, Brussels 29-32; Diplomatic Service 30-; Attaché, Berlin 32; Chargé d'Affaires, Athens 35, Teheran 36; First Sec., Berlin 37-38; First Sec., then Counsellor, Washington 38-44; Chargé d'Affaires, Madrid 44-46; Political Dept., Ministry of Foreign Affairs 47; Asst. Head of Belgian Mission in Berlin 47-48; Consul-Gen., New York 48-55; mem. Belgian Dels. to UN 56-60; Ambassador to Mexico 55-58, to Canada 58-61, to United Kingdom 61-65; Perm. Rep. to Western European Union (W.E.U.) 61-65, retd.; Dir. several cos.; Hon. G.C.V.O., Grand Officier Ordre Léopold II (Belgium), and numerous other decorations.
5 rue Emile Claus, Brussels, Belgium. Telephone: 49-07-58.

Thiess, Frank, DR.PHIL.; German author; b. 13 March 1890; ed. Univs. of Berlin and Tübingen.
War service 15; on editorial staff of *Berliner Tageblatt* 15-19; theatrical producer in Stuttgart 20-21; dramatic critic in Hanover 21-23; Mem. Akademie der Wissenschaften und der Literatur, Mainz, PEN Club of Austria; Knight of Mark Twain Soc., U.S.A.
Publs. *Der Tod von Falern, Angelika ten Swaart, Die Verdammten, Das Gesicht des Jahrhunderts, Abschied vom Paradies, Das Tor zur Welt, Der Leibhaftige, Der Zentaur, Der Kampf mit dem Engel, Marren, Geschichte eines unruhigen Sommers, Erziehung zur Freiheit, Die Zeit ist reif, Der Weg zu Isabelle, Stürmischer Frühling, Der ewige Taugenichts, Wir werden es nie wissen, Tsushima, Das Reich der Dämonen, Caruso, Puccini, Ideen zur Natur-und Leidensgeschichte der Völker, Katharina Winter, Die Blüten welken, aber der Baum wächst, Der heilige Dämon, Die Strassen des Labyrinths, Tödlicher Karneval, Don Juans letzte Tage, Die Herzogin von Langeais, Die Wirklichkeit des Unwirklichen, Theater ohne Rampe, Geister werfen keinen Schatten, Gäa, Ursprung und Sinn des Ost-West Gegensatzes, Die griechischen Kaiser, Sturz nach oben, Das Gesicht unseres Jahrhunderts-heute, Theater ohne Vorhang, Verbrannte Erde, Freiheit bis Mitternacht, Plädoyer für Peking, Der Schwarze Engel, Zauber und Schrecken (Die Welt der Kinder).*
Rosenhöhpark, Darmstadt, German Federal Republic.

Thiessen, Peter Adolf, DR. PHIL. HABIL.; German chemist; b. 6 April 1899; ed. Univs. of Breslau, Freiburg and Göttingen.
Dozent, Univ. of Göttingen 26, Head of its Inst. of Inorganic Chemistry; Extraordinary Prof. 32; Univ. of Frankfurt 34, Münster 35, Berlin 35; Dir. Kaiser-Wilhelm-Inst. of Physical Chemistry 35; scientific work in U.S.S.R. 45-56; Prof. of Physical Chemistry, Humboldt Univ., Berlin 56-64, Prof. Emeritus 64-; mem. Deutsche Akad. der Wissenchaften zu Berlin, Dir. of its Inst. of Physical Chemistry, Emer. 64-; Hon. Chair. Research Council of D.D.R.; mem. Exec. Council Deutscher Kulturbund; Hon. mem. Chamber of Tech-

nology; non-resident mem. of Acad. of Sciences, U.S.S.R. 66; Hon. Dr. rer. nat. 59; U.S.S.R. State Prize (1st Class) 51, Order of Lenin 51, Order of Red Labour Banner 56, Nat. Prize 1st class 58, Order of Banner of Labour 59, Fatherland Gold Order of Merit 59, Distinguished People's Scientist 64.
Wissler Strasse 9, 1162 Berlin-Friedrichschagen; Forschungzentrum Adlershof, Rudower Chaussee 5, 1199 Berlin-Adlershof, German Democratic Republic. Telephone: 67-701-05.

Thieu, Lt.-Gen. Nguyen Van; Viet-Namese army officer and politician; b. 5 April 1923; ed. Catholic Pellerin School, Hué, and Nat. Military Acad., Hué.
Viet-Nam Nat. Army 48-54; Republic of Viet-Nam Army 54-; Commdr. First Infantry Div. 60-62, Fifth Infantry Div. 62-64; Deputy Premier and Minister of Defence 64-65; Chair. Nat. Leadership Cttee. and Head of State 65-; Pres. of Republic of Viet-Nam Sept. 67-; numerous decorations.
General Staff Headquarters, Saigon; Home: 184 Votanh Street, Saigon, Republic of Viet-Nam.

Thieulin, Gustave Léon Pierre; French dairy research scientist; b. 20 July 1903; ed. Ecole Nat. Vétérinaire d'Alfort, Inst. Pasteur, Inst. Nat. Agromomique.
On staff of Paris and Seine Veterinary Service 28-, in charge of Milk Research and Control Laboratory 41-, Deputy-Dir. 46; Deputy Prof. of Production, Hygiene and Control of Milk, Ecole Nat. Vétérinaire d'Alfort 32, Inst. Nat. Agronomique 38; Director of Service Vétérinaire Sanitaire (Paris and Seine Dept.) 61-; Controlêur-Gén. Services Vétérinaires 65-; Dir. and Editor-in-Chief of *Le Lait*; Consultant F.A.O.; mem. (and fmr. Pres.) Acad. Vétérinaire; mem. Acad. Nat. de Médecine; Higher Council d'Hygiene Publique; Laureate of the Acad. des Sciences, Acad. Nat. de Médecine, Acad. d'Agriculture and Acad. Vétérinaire; Officier de la Légion d'Honneur, Chevalier du Mérite Social, Officier du Mérite Agricole; Officier des Palmes Académiques; Officier de la Santé Publique, Officier du Mérite Militaire.
Publs. *Manuel d'Analyse du Lait, des Oeufs et des Produits Laitiers*, and 160 scientific and technical papers.
113 avenue Victor Hugo, Paris 16e; 48 avenue Président Wilson, Paris 16e; and Tourny (Eure), France. Telephone: 727-7924 and 727-5398.

Thijsse, Johannes Theodoor; Netherlands civil engineer; b. 93; ed. High School, Haarlem, and Technological Univ. of Delft.
Asst. Sec. State Cttee. for enclosure of Zuiderzee 18-26; Engineer (Chief Engineer 26-58) on Govt. service for enclosing and reclaiming Zuiderzee 20-58; Dir. Hydraulics Laboratory 27-60; Prof. Hydraulics Technical Univ. of Delft 36-63; mem. Royal Netherlands Acad. of Sciences 48-, Delta Comm., preparing a scheme for the enclosure of estuaries in south-west Netherlands 53-60; Sec. Int. Asscn. for Hydraulic Research 53-59; Pres. Int. Asscn. for Scientific Hydrology 51-57; Hon. mem. Royal Dutch Geographical Soc.; William Bowie Medal of American Geophysical Union.
15 A. Noordewierstraat, The Hague, Netherlands. Telephone: 070-683441.

Thimann, Kenneth Vivian, B.SC., A.R.C.S., D.I.C., PH.D.; American biologist and educationist; b. 5 Aug. 1904; ed. Caterham School, and Imperial Coll., London.
Instructor in Biochemistry, California Inst. of Technology 30-35; Lecturer, Harvard Univ. 35-36, Asst. Prof. 36-39, Assoc. Prof. 39-46, Prof. of Biology 46-62, Higgins Prof. of Biology 62-65; Prof. of Biology and Provost Crown Coll., Univ. of Calif. at Santa Cruz 65-, Acting Dean of Natural Sciences 65-66; Pres. Soc. of Gen. Physiologists 49-50, American Soc. of Plant Physiologists 50, American Soc. of Naturalists 55,

Botanical Soc. of America 60, American Inst. of Biological Sciences 65; Frank Hatton Prize for Chemistry 24, Stepehen Hales Prize, American Soc. of Plant Physiologists 36; Dr. h.c. Univs, of Basle and Clermont-Ferrand.,
Publs. *Phytohormones* (with F. W. Went) 37, *Les Auxines* 55, *The Action of Hormones in Plants and Invertebrates* (with B. Scharrer and F. Brown) 48, *The Life of Bacteria* 55, 63 (German trans. 64), and about 200 papers in scientific journals; Editor *Vitamins and Hormones* vols. 1-20, 43-62, *The Hormones* vols. 1-5, 48-63.
Division of Natural Sciences, University of California, Santa Cruz, Calif. 95060, U.S.A.
Telephone: 408-426-7300, Extn. 550.

Thiry, Marcel, D. en D.; Belgian writer; b. 13 March 1897; ed. Univ. of Liège.
Awarded Prix Verhaeren 26, Prix triennal de Poésie 35, Grand Prix Quinquennal de Poésie 58, Prix Bernheim 63, Grand Prix quinquennal de littérature 65; elected to Belgian Acad. royale de langue et de littérature françaises 39, Perpetual Sec. 60-.
Publs. Poetry: *Toi qui pâlis au nom de Vancouver* 24, *Plongeantes Proues* 25, *L'Enfant Prodigue* 27, *Statue de la Fatigue* 34, *La Mer de la Tranquillité* 38, *Ages* 50, *Poésie* 58, *Vie Poésie* 61, *Le Festin d'Attente* 63; Prose: *Marchands* 37, *Echec au Temps* 45, *La Belgique pendant la Guerre* 47, *Juste* 53, *Simul* 57, *Comme si* 59, *Le grand Possible* 60, *Le Tour du monde en guerre* 65, *Nondum Jam non* 66, *Le poème et la langue* 67.
Vaux-sous-Chèvremont, Belgium.
Telephone: 04-65-09-27.

Thode, Henry George, C.C., M.B.E., D.SC., PH.D., F.R.S., F.R.S.C., F.C.I.C.; Canadian university president; b. 10 Sept. 1910; ed. Univs. of Saskatchewan and Chicago, and Columbia Univ.
Instructor, Pennsylvania Coll. for Women 35-36; Research Asst., Columbia Univ. 36-38; Research Chemist U.S. Rubber Co., N.J. 38-39; Asst. Prof., of Chemistry, Hamilton Coll., McMaster Univ. 39-42, Assoc. Prof. 42-44, Prof. 44, Vice-Pres. 57-61, Dir. of Research 47-61, Pres. and Vice-Chancellor 61-; Research Chemist, Atomic Energy Project 43-46, Consultant 45-51; Consultant Atomic Energy of Canada Ltd. 51-; Dir. Hamilton Health Asscn. 48-68, Western New York Nuclear Research Centre, Atomic Energy of Canada Ltd.; mem. Royal Society of Canada (Pres. Section III 50-51), Pres. 59-60; Pres. Chemical Inst. of Canada 51-52; mem. Nat. Research Council 55-61, Defence Research Board 55-61, Board of Govs., Ontario Research Foundation 56-; Hon. LL.D. Univ. of Saskatchewan; Hon. D.Sc. Univ. of Toronto, Univ. of British Columbia, Acadia Univ., Laval Univ., McGill Univ., Queen's Univ., and Royal Military Coll., Canada; Chemical Inst. of Canada Medal 57; Royal Soc. of Canada Tory Medal 59.
Publs. numerous papers on electrical discharges in gases, magnetic susceptibilities, separation of isotopes, vapour pressures, isotopic abundances, and nuclear chemistry.
President's House, McMaster University, Hamilton, Ontario, Canada.
Telephone: 527-7250.

Thomale, Wolfgang; German business official; b. 25 Feb. 1900; ed. Humanistisches Gymnasium und Realgymnasium Kadettenanstalt, Berlin-Lichterfelde.
Army Officer until 45, latterly Chief of Staff to Gen. Inspector of Panzer troops; wool salesman 47-59; Pres. of Fed. of Automobile Industry 60-; mem. Management Board, Fed. of German Industries; several decorations.
638 Bad Homberg v.d.H., Herderstrasse 9, and 6 Frankfurt Main, Westendstr. 61, German Federal Republic.
Telephone: Frankfurt 72-53-47.

Thomas, A. V.; Indian businessman; b. 8 Aug. 1891; ed. Tirunelveli District.
Man. Dir. A. V. Thomas & Co. Ltd. and allied concerns; controls a number of plantation companies; Chair. Indian Rubber Board 47-49; mem. Lok Sabha (Fed. Parl.) 52-57; Madras Legislative Assembly 57-61; Chair. Cashew Export Promotion Council 61-.
P.B. No. 1603, Madras 1, India.

Thomas, Sir Ben Bowen, Kt., B.A., M.A., LL.D.; former British civil servant; b. 1899; ed. Rhondda Grammar School, Univ. Coll. of Wales, Aberystwyth, and Jesus Coll., Oxford.
Lecturer in Adult Education, Univ. of Wales 22-27; Warden of Colegharlech 27-40; Dir. of Extra Mural Studies, Univ. of Wales 40-45; Chair. South Wales Manpower Board 41-45; Permanent Sec., Welsh Dept., Ministry of Education 45-63; mem. Exec. Board UNESCO 54-62, Chair. 58-60; Pres. Nat. Inst. of Adult Education 64-, Univ. Coll. of Wales, Aberystwyth 64-, Welsh Council of UN Asscn. 64-; mem. Governing Bodies Univ. of Wales, Nat. Museum of Wales, Nat. Library of Wales, Independent Television Authority, etc.; Knight Bachelor 50; Hon. Fellow Jesus Coll. Oxford 63; Hon. LL.D. (Wales).
Publs. *Economic History of Wales* (in Welsh), *The Old Order* (in English) 40, *The Ballads of Glamorgan* 52, *The Balladmonger's Mirror* 58 (both in Welsh); numerous articles in learned journals on Welsh literary and historical subjects.
Wern, Bodlonseb, Bangor, North Wales.

Thomas, Charles Allen, A.B., M.S.; American executive; b. 15 Feb. 1900; ed. Transylvania Coll., and Mass. Inst. of Technology.
Research Chemist, Gen. Motors Research Corpn. 23-24; Research Chemist and co-owner Thomas & Hochwalt Laboratories 26-36; Dir. Central Research Dept., Monsanto Co. 36-45, Vice-Pres. and Technical Dir. 45-47, Exec. Vice-Pres. 47-51, Pres. 51-60, Chair. of Board 60-65, Chair. Finance Cttee. 65-; Chair. Board of Dirs. American Chemical Soc.; mem. Manhattan Project, in charge Clinton Laboratories, Oak Ridge, Tenn. 45-48; Chair. Scientific Manpower Advisory Cttee. to Nat. Security Resources Board; co-author Acheson-Lilienthal Report on Control of Atomic Energy; mem. Nat. Acad. of Sciences, American Philosophical Soc., American Asscn. for Advancement of Science, American Inst. of Chemical Engineers, American Inst. of Chemists, The Chemical Soc., Soc. of Chemical Industries; mem. Business Council; Medal for Merit 46; Industrial Research Inst. Medal 47; American Inst. of Chemists' Gold Medal 48; Perkin Medal 53; Priestley Medal 55; Order of Leopold 62; Palladium Medal 63; Deeds-Kettering Memorial Award 64.
Publ. *Anhydrous Aluminum Chloride in Organic Chemistry* 41.
Home: 609 S. Warson Road, St. Louis 24; Office: Monsanto Co., 800 N. Lindbergh Boulevard, St. Louis, Mo. 63166, U.S.A.

Thomas, David Winton, M.A.; British Hebraist; b. 26 Jan. 1901; ed. Merchant Taylors' School, and St. John's Coll., Oxford.
Examiner O.T. and Semitics Oxford, Liverpool, Bristol, Birmingham, Durham, Leeds, London, Manchester; Special Asst. Oriental Dept. Bodleian Library 24; Senior Scholar and Lecturer in Oriental Languages, St. John's Coll., Oxford 24; Lecturer in Arabic, Gordon Coll., Khartoum, Sudan 26; Fellow Oriental Inst. of Univ. of Chicago 29; Prof. of Hebrew and Oriental Languages, Durham Univ. 30-38; Regius Prof. of Hebrew, Cambridge Univ. 38-; Fellow St. Catharine's Coll., Cambridge 43, Pres. 65-68; Pres. Society for Old Testament Study 53-; Hon. D.D., Durham, F.B.A.
Publs. *The Recovery of the Ancient Hebrew Language* 39, *The Prophet in the Lachish Ostraca;* Editor: *Essays and*

Studies Presented to Stanley Arthur Cook 50; Editor (with M. Noth): *Wisdom in Israel and in the Ancient Near East* 55; Editor: *Documents from Old Testament Times* 58; Editor (with W. D. McHardy) *Hebrew and Semitic Studies presented to G. R. Driver* 63; Editor *Archaeology and Old Testament Study* 67.
4 Grantchester Road, Cambridge, England.
Telephone: Cambridge 54640.

Thomas, Edwin Joel; American manufacturer; b. 27 April 1899; ed. Univ. of Akron.
Joined Goodyear Tire & Rubber Co., Akron, O. 26, Supt. Production, Calif. plant 28-30, Asst. to Factory Man., Akron 30-32, Gen. Supt. 32-35, Man. Dir., England 35-36, Asst. to Pres., Akron 36-37, Exec. Vice-Pres. 37-40, Pres. 40-63, Chief Exec. Officer 56-64, Chair. of Policy Cttee. 56-58, Chair. Board 58-64, now Chair. Exec. and Finance Cttees.
Home: 812 Mayfair Road; Office: 3 East Market Street, Akron, Ohio, U.S.A.

Thomas, Rt. Hon. (Thomas) George, P.C., M.P.; British politician; b. 1909; ed. Tonypandy Grammar School and Univ. Coll. of Southampton.
M.P. for Central Cardiff 45-50, W. Cardiff 50-; Parl. Under-Sec. of State, Home Office 64-66; Minister of State, Welsh Office 66-67, Commonwealth Office 67-68; Sec. of State for Wales 68-; Vice-Pres. Methodist Conf. 59-60; Labour.
Publ. *The Christian Heritage in Politics.*
Tilbury, 173 King George V Drive, Heath, Cardiff, Glamorgan, Wales.

Thomas, Henri, L. ès L.; French writer and poet; b. 7 Dec. 1912; ed. Strasbourg Univ.
Teacher till 39; Forces 40-47; Programme Asst. B.B.C. French Section 47-58; Lecturer in French, Brandeis Univ. Mass., U.S.A. 56-60; in charge German Dept. Gallimard's Publishing House 60-; Prix Sainte-Beuve 56, Prix Medicis 60; Prix Femina 61.
Publs. Verse: *Travaux d'Aveugle, Signe de Vie, Le Monde Absent, Nul Désordre*; Novels: *Le Seau à Charbon, La Vie Ensemble, Les Déserteurs, La Nuit de Londres, La Dernière Année, John Perkins, Le Promontoire, La Chasse aux trésors, Le Parjure*; Short stories: *La Cible, Histoire de Pierrot.*
Editions Gallimard, 5 rue Sébastien-Bottin, Paris 7e, France.

Thomas, Ivor Bulmer-, M.A.; British writer and politician; b. 30 Nov. 1905; ed. St. John's and Magdalen Colls., Oxford.
Editorial staff of *The Times* 30-37; Chief Leader writer *News Chronicle* 37-39, on staff *Daily Telegraph* 52-54; served R. Fusiliers 39-42; Labour M.P. for Keighley 42-48, Independent, later Cons. 48-50; Parly. Sec. Ministry of Civil Aviation 45-46; Parly. Under-Sec. of State Colonial Office 46-47; mem. House of Laity of Church Assembly; Chair. Exec. Cttee. Historic Churches Preservation Trust 52-56; Sec. Ancient Monuments Society 57-; Hon. Dir. Friends of Friendless Churches 57-; Convener British Group Inst. Int. des Civilisations Différentes 59-.
Publs. *Coal in the New Era* 34, *Gladstone of Hawarden* 36, *Top Sawyer* 38, *Greek Mathematics* 39-42, *The Problem of Italy* 46, *The Socialist Tragedy* 49, *The Party System in Great Britain* 53, *Growth of the British Party System* 65.
12 Edwardes Square, London, W.8, England.
Telephone: 01-937-1414.

Thomas, Jean; French educationist; b. 10 Dec. 1900; ed. Ecole Normale Supérieure.
Répétiteur Ecole Normale Supérieure; Prof. Poitiers and Lyon Univs.; Chef de Service, Ministry of Nat. Education; Dir. Cultural Activities UNESCO 46-54; Asst. Dir. Gen. 54-60; Inspecteur-Gén. de l'Instruction Publique; Commdr. Légion d'Honneur, Médaille de la

Résistance, Commdr. des Palmes Académiques, Ordre des Arts et Lettres.
Publs. include *Le Romantisme Contemporain, L' Humanisme de Diderot, Sainte-Beuve et l'Ecole Normale, Le Vrai Système de Dom Deschamps, UNESCO, Education en Europe: Tendances Actuelles et Problèmes Communs.*
8 *bis* boulevard de Courcelles, Paris 17e, France.
Telephone: 622-34-49.

Thomas, Sir Miles, Kt., D.F.C.; British industrialist; b. 2 March 1897; ed. Bromsgrove School.
Served armoured car squadrons, R.F.C. and R.A.F., First World War; Man. Dir. Wolseley Motors Ltd. 36-40; Vice-Chair. Morris Motors Ltd. Wolseley Motors Ltd., Morris Commercial Cars Ltd., M.G. Car Co. Ltd., Riley Motor Co. Ltd., Morris Industries (Exports) Ltd., S.U. Carburettor Co. Ltd., Mechanisations and Aero Ltd. 40-47; Pres. Motor Trades Asscn. 34; Chair. Cruiser Tank Production Group; mem. Advisory Panel on Tank Production 41-45; Chair. British Tank Engine Mission to U.S. 42; Pres. Soc. Motor Manufacturers and Traders 47; Dir. Colonial Development Corpn. 47-51, Deritend Stamping Co. 62-; Chair. S. Rhodesian Govt. Development Comm. 47-50; Dep. Chair. BOAC 48-June 49, Chair. 49-56; Pres. IATA 51-52; Chair. Monsanto Chemicals Ltd. 56-63, Dir. Monsanto Europe Ltd. 63-65; Chair. British Productivity Council 59, Devt. Corpn. for Wales 58-67; Chair. Agricultural Central Trading Ltd. 62-67, Nat. Savings Movement 65-.
Publ. *Out on a Wing* (autobiography) 64.
Remenham Court, Henley-on-Thames, Oxfordshire, England.
Telephone: Henley 5400.

Thomas, Norman, A.B., B.D., LIT.D.; American sociologist; b. 20 Nov. 1884; ed. Princeton Univ.
Presbyterian Minister 11-18; founder and Editor *World To-morrow* 18-21; Exec. Dir. League for Industrial Democracy 22-37; Chair. Post-War World Council; Socialist Candidate for Gov. and Mayor of New York 24, 25 and 29, and for Pres. of U.S. 28, 32, 36, 40, 44, 48; Chair. Inst. for Int. Labor Research; contrib. to Socialist and Labour press.
Publs. *The Conscientious Objector in America* 23, *America's Way Out: a Program for Democracy* 30, *As I See It* 32, *What's the Matter with New York?* 32, *Human Exploitation* 34, *War—No Glory, No Profit, No Need, After the New Deal, What?* 36, *We have a Future* 39, *What is Our Destiny?* 44, *Appeal to the Nations* 47, *A Socialist's Faith* 51, *The Test of Freedom* 54, *Mr. Chairman, Ladies and Gentlemen* 55, *The Prerequisites for Peace* 59, *The Great Dissenter* 61, *Socialism Re-examined* 63.
112 East 19th Street, New York, N.Y., U.S.A.

Thomas, Orlando Pendleton, B.S., M.B.A.; American oil executive; b. 14 June 1914; ed. East Texas State Coll., Univ. of Texas, Wharton School of Univ. of Pennsylvania, New York Univ., and Harvard School of Business Admin.
U.S. Navy, Second World War; Sinclair Oil Corpn. 45-, Asst. Comptroller 54-57, Vice-Pres. 57-60, Dir. 60-, Exec. Vice-Pres. 60-64, Pres. 64-; Dir. of Bristol-Myers Co., Koppers Co. Inc.; mem. American Petroleum Inst., Econ. Club of New York, Newcomen Soc. in N. America.
Sinclair Oil Corporation, 600 Fifth Avenue, New York, N.Y. 10020, U.S.A.
Telephone: 212-246-3600.

Thomas, Rt. Hon. Peter John Mitchell, P.C., Q.C., J.P.; British politician; b. 31 July 1920; ed. Epworth Coll., Rhyl, and Jesus Coll., Oxford.
R.A.F. Service 39-45, Prisoner of War 41-45; Called to Bar 47; M.P. 51-66, Parl. Private Sec. to Solicitor-Gen. 54-59, Parl. Sec., Ministry of Labour 59-61, Parl.

Under-Sec. of State, Foreign Office 61-63, Minister of State for Foreign Affairs 63-64, Conservative.
28 Kennington Palace Court, Sancroft Street, London, S.E.11, England; and Bath, Llanbedr-y-Cennin, Conway, N. Wales.

Thomas, Rev. Ronald Stuart; British clergyman and poet; ed. Univ. of Wales and St. Michael's Coll., Llandaff.
Ordained Deacon 36, Priest 37; Curate of Chirk 36-40, of Hanmer 40-42; Rector of Manafon 42-54; Vicar of St. Michael's, Eglwysfach 54-; Heinemann Award of Royal Soc. of Literature 56 for *Song at the Year's Turning*; Sovereign's Gold Medal for Poetry 64.
Publs. *Stones of the Field* (privately published) 47, *Song at the Year's Turning* 55, *Poetry for Supper* 58, *Tares* 61, *The Bread of Truth* 63, *Pieta* 66.
Eglwysfach Vicarage, Machynlleth, Cardiganshire, Wales.

Thomas, Tracy Yerkes, A.B., M.A., PH.D.; American mathematician; b. 8 Jan. 1899; ed. Rice Inst., and Princeton Univ.
National Research Fellow in Physics, Univ. of Chicago 23-24, in Mathematics Zürich Univ. 24-25, Harvard and Princeton Univs. 25-26; Asst. Prof. of Maths. Princeton Univ. 26-31, Assoc. Prof. 31-38; Prof. of Maths. Univ. of Calif. 38-44; Prof. of Maths. Indiana Univ. 44, Chair. of Dept. 44-54, Head Graduate Inst. for Applied Maths. 50-54, Dir. Graduate Inst. for Maths. and Mechanics 54-56, Distinguished Service Prof. of Maths. 56-; Visiting Prof. Univ. of Calif., San Diego, at La Jolla 62-63, at Los Angeles 65-66, 67-68; Fellow Indiana Acad. of Sciences, Royal Astronomical Soc., Soc. Eng. Science, American Math. Soc., Math. Asscn. of America; mem. Nat. Acad. of Sciences.
Publs. *The Elementary Theory of Tensors* 31, *The Differential Invariants of Generalised Spaces* 34, *Concepts from Tensor Analysis and Differential Geometry* 61 (2nd edn. 65), *Plastic Flow and Fracture in Solids* 61.
Mathematics Department, Indiana University, Bloomington, Indiana, U.S.A.
Telephone: 332-7360.

Thomaz, Admiral Américo; Portuguese naval officer and politician; b. 19 Nov. 1894; ed. Naval Coll., Lisbon.
Midshipman 14; served on convoy duty to Great Britain and France during the First World War in the cruiser *Pedro Nunes* and the destroyers *Douro* and *Tejo* 2nd-Lieut. 18; transferred to Hydrographic Board 19; served on board the hydrographic vessel *Cinco de Outubro* 20-36; 1st-Lieut. 22, Lieut.-Commdr. 31; Sec. Ministry of Marine 36-44, in charge of hydrographic survey of Portuguese coast; Commdr. 39; Pres. Nat. Mercantile Marine Board 40-44; Capt. 41; Minister of Marine 44-58; Rear-Admiral 51; mem. Int. Council for the Exploration of the Sea, Fisheries Comm. and numerous other Portuguese and int. nautical, hydrographical and meteorological cttees.; Pres. of Portugal June 58-; Grand Cross Military Order of Christ, Grand Officer Order of Aviz, Officer Order of Santiago (Portugal), Grand Cross of the Spanish, Brazilian and Argentine Orders of Naval Merit, Grand Cross Order of Isabel the Catholic (Spain), Grand Order of the Crown of Belgium, Ordem Cruzeiro do Sul (with Collar), Order Crown (Italy), Band and Collar Queen Saba (Ethiopia), Legion of Merit (U.S.A.), Knight-Grand Commdr. of Order of Rama (Thailand), Grand Cross Order of "El Erl" of Peru, Grand Master of the Portuguese Orders.
Palácio de Belem, Lisbon; and Casa de Santa Maria, Cascais, Portugal.

Thompson, Sir Edward Hugh Dudley, Kt., M.B.E., T.D.; British company executive; b. 12 May 1907; ed. Uppingham and Lincoln Coll., Oxford.
Solicitor 31-36; Asst. Managing Dir. Ind. Coope and Allsopp Ltd. 36-39, Managing Dir. 39; Army Service 39-

45; Managing Dir. Ind Coope Ltd. 45-55, Chair. 55-62; Chair. Brewers' Soc. 59-61; Chair. and Chief Exec. Allied Breweries Ltd. 61-; Dir. Sun Alliance and London Ltd., Sun Insurance Office Ltd., P. E. Holdings Ltd.; High Sheriff of Derbyshire 64; Fellow British Inst. of Management; Assoc. mem. Parl. Group for World Government.
Culland Hall, Brailsford, Derbyshire, England.
Telephone: Brailsford 247.

Thompson, Edward K(ramer), A.B., D.HUM.LITT.; American editor; b. 17 Sept. 1907; ed. Univ. of North Dakota.
Editor Foster Co. *Independent*, Carrington, N.D. 27; City Ed. *Fargo* (N.D.) *Morning Forum* 27; Picture Ed., Asst. News Ed. *Milwaukee Journal* 27-37; Assoc. Ed. *Life* 37-42, Asst. Man. Ed. 45-49, Man. Ed., later Ed. 49-67; served with U.S. Armed Forces 42-45; decorated Legion of Merit, Hon. O.B.E.
135 Central Park W., New York, N.Y. 10023, U.S.A.
Telephone: Trafalgar 7-8734.

Thompson, Floyd LaVerne; American aeronautical engineer and research administrator; b. 25 Nov. 1898; ed. South Lyon High School, Salem, Michigan, and Univ. of Michigan.
Langley Research Center, Nat. Aeronautics and Space Admin. (NASA) 26-, Aeronautical Engineer 26-45, Chief of Research 45-52, Assoc. Dir. 52-60, Dir. 60-; Fellow American Inst. of Aeronautics and Astronautics, mem. American Asscn. for the Advancement of Science; NASA Award for Outstanding Leadership 63; Hon. D.Sc. Univ. of Mich., Coll. of William and Mary, Virginia.
NASA Langley Research Center, Langley Station, Hampton, Virginia, U.S.A.

Thompson, Sir Harold (Warris), Kt., C.B.E., F.R.S.; British chemist; b. 15 Feb. 1908; ed. King Edward VII School, Sheffield, Trinity Coll., Oxford, and Kaiser Wilhelm Inst. for Physical Chemistry, Berlin-Dahlem.
Fellow of St. John's Coll., Oxford 30-; Reader in Spectroscopy, Oxford Univ. 54-, Prof. of Physical Chemistry 64-; mem. Council Royal Soc. 59-60, 61-64, 65-, Vice-Pres. 63-64, 65-, Foreign Sec. 65-; Chair. British Nat. Cttee. for Chemistry 60-66; mem. Bureau Int. Union of Pure and Applied Chemistry (IUPAC) 63-, Pres. Int. Council of Scientific Unions (ICSU) 63-66; mem. U.K. UNESCO Comm.; Vice-Chair. Football Asscn.; Editor *Spectrochimica Acta* 57-, *Advances in Spectroscopy* Vol. I 59, Vol. II 61.
St. John's College, Oxford; Home: 33 Linton Road, Oxford, England.
Telephone: Oxford 58925.

Thompson, Homer Armstrong, B.A., M.A., PH.D.; Canadian-born American classical archaeologist; b. 7 Sept. 1906; ed. Univs. of British Columbia and Michigan.
Staff mem., American School of Classical Studies excavations of the Athenian Agora 29-, Field Dir. 45-67; Prof. of Classical Archaeology, Toronto Univ. 33-47, Head of Dept. of Art and Archaeology 46-47; Prof., Princeton Inst. for Advanced Study 47-; Asst. Dir., Curator of Classical Collection, Royal Ont. Museum, Toronto 33-47; George Eastman Visiting Prof., Oxford Univ. 59-60; Geddes-Harrower Prof. of Greek Archaeology and Art, Aberdeen Univ. 64-65; Corresp. Fellow British Acad.; Hon. mem. German Archaeological Inst., Soc. for Promotion of Hellenic Studies, Greek Archaeological Soc., Royal Soc. of Arts and Letters (Gothenburg), Acad. of Sciences (Heidelberg), Royal Swedish Acad.; mem. American Philosophical Soc., American Acad. of Arts and Sciences; Commdr. Order of the Phoenix (Greece); Hon. LL.D. (Univs. of Toronto and British Columbia); Litt.D (Univ. of Michigan); L.H.D. (Dartmouth Coll., Univs. of Athens, Lyons, Freiburg).

Publs. Studies in topography, architecture, sculpture and ceramics of ancient Athens (chiefly in *Hesperia*) 34-. Institute for Advanced Study, Princeton, N.J.; and Cherry Valley Road, Princeton, N.J. 08540, U.S.A. Telephone: 609-924-4400.

Thompson, Llewellyn E.; American diplomatist; b. 24 Aug. 1904; ed. Univ. of Colorado, Foreign Service School, and Army War Coll.

Entered Foreign Service 29; served Colombo 29, Geneva 33; Advisory mem. American Comm., Int. Inst. of Agriculture 39; served Moscow 41; Sec. in London 44; Chief, Division of Eastern European Affairs, Dept. of State 46; Deputy Dir., Office of European Affairs 47, Deputy Asst. Sec. of State 49; Counsellor (personal rank of Minister) Rome 50; High Commr. in Austria 52-55, Amb. 55-57; Amb. to U.S.S.R. 57-62, 66-; Amb.-at-Large 62-66; Rockefeller Public Service Award 62; President's Award for Distinguished Civilian Service 62. c/o Department of State, 2201 C Street, N.W., Washington, D.C., U.S.A.

Thompson, Robert Henry Stewart, M.A., D.SC., D.M., B.CH., F.C. PATH.; British chemical pathologist; b. 2 Feb. 1912; ed. Trinity Coll., Oxford, and Guy's Hospital Medical School, London.

Adrian Stokes Travelling Fellowship to Hospital of Rockefeller Inst. for Medical Research, N.Y. 37-38; Gillson Research Scholar in Pathology, Society of Apothecaries, London 38; Fellow and Tutor, Univ. Coll., Oxford 38-47; Demonstrator in Biochemistry, Oxford Univ. 38-47; served as Major in R.A.M.C. 44-46; Dean of Medical School, Oxford 46-47; Prof. of Chemical Pathology, Guy's Hospital Medical School, Univ. of London, and Consulting Chemical Pathologist to Guy's Hospital 47-65; Courtauld Prof. of Biochemistry, Middlesex Hospital Medical School, Univ. of London 65-; Trustee, Wellcome Trust 63-; awarded Radcliffe Prize for Medical Research, Oxford 43; mem. Biochemical Society, Physiological Society; Fellow, Royal Society of Medicine; Sec.-Gen. Int. Union of Biochemistry 55-64; Chair. British Nat. Cttee. for Biochemistry 67-.

Publs. *Biochemistry in Relation to Medicine* (with C. W. Carter) 53, *Biochemical Disorders in Human Disease* (with E. J. King) 57; numerous papers in medical and scientific journals.

Brockenhurst, Rockfield Road, Oxted, Surrey, England. Telephone: Oxted 3526.

Thompson, Robert Norman, M.P.; Canadian politician; b. 17 May 1914; ed. Provincial Normal School, Calgary, Bob Jones Univ., Greenville, Univ. of British Columbia, and Palmer Coll. of Chiropractic.

Public school teacher, Alberta 34-36; chiropractor 39-40; service in Second World War 40-43; Asst. Headmaster Haile Selassie Secondary School, Ethiopia 44-46, Dir. of Educ. Kaffa Province, Ethiopia 46, Dir. of Provincial Educ. Ministry of Educ., Ethiopia 47-51; Headmaster Haile Selassie Secondary School, Addis Ababa 47-51; diplomatic missions for Ethiopian Govt. 46-52; Educ. Dir. Sudan Interior Mission 52-58; Pres. Social Credit Asscn. Canada 60-61, Nat. Leader, Social Credit Party 61-; Fellow, Royal Geographical Society, London; Knight Order of St. Lazarus of Jerusalem; mem. Inter-Parl. Union.

House of Commons, Ottawa; 2 Sunnyside Crescent, Red Deer, Alberta, Canada.

Telephone: (613) 992-2940 (Office); (403) 347-6082 (Home).

Thompson, Rupert Campbell, Jr., A.B., LL.B.; American businessman; b. 5 July 1905; ed. Dartmouth Coll., and Suffolk Law School 34.

Newton Trust Co. 28-37; Joined Providence Nat. Bank 37, Pres. 43-51; Exec. Vice-Pres. Providence Union Nat. Bank 51-54; Exec. Vice-Pres. Industrial Nat. Bank

54-56; Joined Textron Inc. as Chair. Exec. Cttee. 56, Pres. 57-60, Chair. of Board 60-; Hon. D.C.S.; Dir. numerous companies.

10 Dorrance Street, Providence 3, R.I., U.S.A.

Thompson, Thomas Miller, B.A., B.S.; American transportation executive; b. 25 July 1917; ed. Western Reserve Univ., Cleveland, Ohio.

General American Transportation Corpn. 39-, East Chicago 39-41, Union Refrigerator Transit Div. 41, Office Manager, Cleveland 45-52, Asst. Vice-Pres. Chicago 52-58, Dir. and Vice-Pres. 58-60, Pres. 60-61, Chair. of Board and Chief Exec. Officer 61-, Chair. of Exec. Cttee. 63-; U.S. Marine Corps 42-45; official of other companies and civic orgs.

Home: 1616 Sheridan Road, Wilmette, Ill.; Office: General American Transportation Corporation, 120 South Riverside Plaza, Chicago, Ill. 60680, U.S.A. Telephone: 621-6200.

Thompson, Tyler; American government official; b. 21 Sept. 1907; ed. Princeton Univ.

Vice-Consul Cherbourg, France 31-33, Marseille 33-37; Sec. of Embassy and Vice-Consul, Paris 37-41; Vice-Consul, Zürich 41; Vichy, France 41-42; interned 42-44; Consul, Oran, Algeria June-Sept. 44, Marseille Oct.-Dec. 44; Sec. of Embassy and Consul, Paris 44-46; Dept. of State 46; Chief Div. of Foreign Service Planning 46-49; Student Nat. War Coll. 49-50; Counsellor, Prague 50-51; Exec. Dir. Bureau of European Affairs, Dept. of State 52-55; Minister to Canada 55-60; Ambassador to Iceland 60-61; Dir.-Gen. of Foreign Service 61-64; Ambassador to Finland 64-.

American Embassy, It. Kaivopuisto 21, Helsinki, Finland.

Telephone: 11931.

Thompson, W. Stuart; American architect; b. 25 Jan. 1890; ed. Graduate School of Architecture, Columbia Univ.

Graduate study in south-eastern Europe 13-16; Architectural Fellow, American School of Classical Studies, 13-15, Critic of Architectural Design, Cooper Union 17-20; architectural practice in New York City 18-; architect (with Phelps Barnum) for restoration of Stoa of Attalos, Athens; airport designer for U.S. Govt. 42-43; mem. Board, Near East Foundation; Hon. Citizen of Athens; Hon. mem. Athens Archaeological Soc.; Fellow, New York Acad. of Sciences; Sec. American Friends of Greece; mem. American Inst. of Architects, Archaeological Inst. of America; Order of the Saviour, Order of the Phoenix (Greece).

Projects: Gennadious Library and Loring Hall, Athens (with J. Van Pelt), Pearce Coll., Corinth Museum, Manisa (Turkey) Hospital (with H. S. Churchill), American Hospital, Istanbul; numerous buildings in Greece and Near East; private houses, apartments and office buildings in U.S.A., buildings Rio de Janeiro, Cali (Colombia), Durban, Byzantine Church, Greek Orthodox Church of the Archangels, Stamford, Conn.

60 East 42nd Street, New York 17, N.Y.; North Street and Loch Lane, Greenwich, Conn., U.S.A.

Thomsen, (Laurits) Christian Marinus; Danish horticulturalist and politician; b. 6 Jan. 1909.

Chief Gardener, Brostrøm Nursery 30-38; City Gardener, Viborg 38-; mem. Folketing 53-; mem. Council of Europe 62-64; Minister of Agriculture 64-68; Social Democrat.

Folketinget, Christiansborg, 1218 Copenhagen K; and Johs. Ewaldsvej 14, Viborg, Denmark.

Thomsen, Roszel C.; American judge; b. 17 Aug. 1900; ed. Boys Latin School, Baltimore, Johns Hopkins Univ., and Univ. of Maryland.

Legal practice, Soper, Bowie and Clark 22-27, partner, Clark, Thomsen and Smith 27-54; Chair. Board of Trustees, Goucher Coll. 54-67; U.S. Dist. Judge, Mary-

land Dist. 54-55, Chief Judge 55-; Instructor in Commercial Law, Johns Hopkins Univ. 33-43, Law School, Univ. of Maryland 52-55; mem. Judicial Conf. of United States 58-64; mem. Advisory Cttee. on Civil Rules 60-, Co-ordinating Cttee. for Multiple Litigation 62-, Cttee. to Implement the Criminal Justice Act of 1964 64-.
506 Post Office Building, Baltimore, Maryland 21202, U.S.A.
Telephone: Mulberry 5-3522.

Thomson, David, M.A., PH.D.; British historian; b. 13 Jan. 1912; ed. Sir George Monoux Grammar School, and Sidney Sussex Coll., Cambridge.
Research Fellow, Sidney Sussex Coll., Cambridge 38-45, Fellow and Senior Tutor 45-53; Univ. Lecturer in History, Cambridge 48-; mem. Inst. for Advanced Study, Princeton, N.J. 50; mem. Council of Senate, Cambridge Univ. 50-58, Chair. Faculty Board of History 58-60; Chair. Cambridge Inst. of Education 63-; Master of Sidney Sussex Coll., Cambridge 57-.
Publs. *Democracy in France* 46, *The Babeuf Plot* 47, *Equality* 49, *England in the 19th Century* 50, *Two Frenchmen: Pierre Laval and Charles de Gaulle* 51, *World History 1914-50* 54, *Europe since Napoleon* 57, *England in the 20th Century* 64, *Political Ideas* (Editor) 66, *The Proposal for Anglo-French Union in 1940* (Zaharoff Lecture) 66.
The Master's Lodge, Sidney Sussex College, Cambridge, England.
Telephone: Cambridge 55860.

Thomson, Hon. David Spence, M.C., M.P.; New Zealand dairy farmer and politician; b. 14 Nov. 1915; ed. Stratford Primary and High School.
Territorial Army 31-59, served Middle East 39-45, Prisoner of war 42, Brigadier (Reserve of Officers); Chair. Federated Farmers Sub-provincial Exec. 59-63; M.P. for Stratford 63-; Minister of Defence, Minister in charge of Tourism, Minister in charge of Publicity 66-Feb. 67; Minister of Defence, Minister Asst. to Prime Minister, Minister in charge of War Pensions, Minister in charge of Rehabilitation Feb.-March 67; Minister of Defence, Minister of Tourism, Minister Asst. to Prime Minister, Minister in charge of Publicity, Minister in charge of War Pensions, Minister in charge of Rehabilitation March 67-; National Party.
Ministry of Defence, Wellington, New Zealand.

Thomson, Rt. Hon. George Morgan, P.C., M.P.; British journalist and politician; b. 16 Jan. 1921; ed. Grove Acad., Dundee.
Royal Air Force 41-46; Editor *Forward* 46-53; M.P. 52-; Chair. Commonwealth Educ. Council 60-64; Chair. Parl. Group for World Govt. 62-64; Minister of State, Foreign Office Oct. 64-66; Chancellor of Duchy of Lancaster 66-67; Minister of State for Foreign Affairs 67-Aug. 67; Sec. of State for Commonwealth Affairs Aug. 67-; Labour.
House of Commons, London, S.W.1, England.
Telephone: 01-930-6240.

Thomson, Sir George Paget, Kt., M.A., D.SC. F.R.S., (son of late Sir J. J. Thomson); British physicist; b. 3 May 1892; ed. Trinity Coll., Cambridge.
Fellow and Lecturer Corpus Christi Coll. Cambridge 14; served First Queen's France 14-15; attached to Royal Air Force 15-19; worked on various problems of aeronautical research; Prof. of Natural Philosophy Aberdeen Univ. 22-30; Prof. of Physics Imperial Coll. of Science and Technology, London Univ. 30-52; Master of Corpus Christi Coll., Cambridge 52-62; Nobel Prize for Physics 37 for experimental discovery of interference phenomena in the irradiation of crystals by electrons; awarded Hughes Medal Royal Society 39, Royal Medal 49, Faraday Medal 60; Chair. Cttee. on Atomic Energy 40-41; Scientific Adviser Air Min. 43-44;

Scientific Adviser to British Del. to U.N. Atomic Comm. 46-47; Chair. Scientific Advisory Council, Ministry of Fuel and Power 53-57; mem. Gov. Board, Nat. Inst. for Nuclear Research 57-60; mem. Univ. Grants Cttee. 55-59; Pres. Inst. of Physics 58-6c British Asscn. for Advancement of Science 59-60; Foreign mem. American Acad. of Arts and Sciences, Lisbon Acad.; corresp. mem. Austrian Acad of Sciences; Foreign mem. Czechoslovak Acad. of Sciences; Hon. mem. Royal Soc. of New Zealand; Hon. Fellow Corpus Christi Coll. and Trinity Coll., Cambridge; Hon. D.Sc. (Lisbon), Hon. LL.D. (Aberdeen), Hon. Sc.D. (Dublin, Sheffield, Wales, Reading, Fulton and Missouri), Hon. D.Hum.Litt. (Ursinus Coll., Pennsylvania).
Publs. *Applied Aerodynamics, The Atom, Wave Mechanics of the Free Electron. Conduction of Electricity Through Gases* (with Sir J. J. Thomson) (3rd edn.), *Theory and Practice of Electron Diffraction* (with W. Cochrane), *The Foreseeable Future, The Inspiration of Science, J. J. Thomson and the Cavendish Laboratory.*
Little Howe, Mount Pleasant, Cambridge, England.
Telephone: Cambridge 54790.

Thomson, Very Rev. James Sutherland, M.A., D.D., LL.D., F.R.S.C.; Canadian theologian; b. Scotland 30 April 1892; ed. Glasgow Univ., and Trinity Coll., Glasgow.
John Clarke Fellow Glasgow Univ. 14; served with Cameron Highlanders, Rifle Brigade, First World War; Min. Middlechurch, Coatbridge, Scotland 20-24; Sec. for Education, Church of Scotland 24-30; Prof. of Systematic Theology Halifax 30-37; Pres. Univ. of Saskatchewan 37-39; Dean Faculty of Divinity McGill Univ. 49-57, Prof. of Philosophy of Religion 57-60, Lecturer in Philosophy of Religion 60-66, Prof. Emer. 66-; Moderator, United Church of Canada 56-58.
Publs. *Studies in the Life of Jesus* 27, *The Way of Revelation* 28, *War and Human Nature* 32, *With the Fifth Army in Retreat* 33, *The Unbinding of Prometheus* 45, *The Hope of the Gospel* 55, *The Divine Mission* 57, *The Word of God* 59, *God and His Purpose* 64, *Religion and Theology in Literary History of Canada* 65.
4544 Kensington Avenue, Montreal 28, P.Q., Canada.
Telephone: 489-4783.

Thomson, John, T.D., M.A.; British banker; b. 08; ed. Winchester Coll. and Magdalen Coll. Oxford.
High Sheriff of Oxfordshire 57; Vice-Chair. Barclays Bank Ltd. 56-58, Deputy Chair. 58-62, Chair. 62-; Chair. Nuffield Medical Trustees; Pres. British Bankers Asscn. 64-66; Dir. Union Discount Co. of London; Lord Lieut. of Oxfordshire 63-; mem. Royal Comm. on Trade Unions and Employers Asscns. 65-; Hon. D.C.L. (Oxon.); Deputy High Steward, Oxford Univ.; Curator Oxford Univ. Chest.
Woodperry, Oxford, England.

Thomson, Hon. Kenneth (Roy), B.A., M.A. (son of Lord Thomson of Fleet, *q.v.*); Canadian newspaperman; b. 1 Sept. 1923; ed. Upper Canada Coll. and Cambridge Univ.
Served with Canadian Air Force during Second World War; in Editorial Dept., *Timmins Daily Press*, Timmins, Ont. 47; Advertising Dept. *Galt Daily Reporter* 48-50, Gen. Man. 50-53; directed U.S. and Canadian Operations of Thomson Newspapers in Toronto 53-68; Deputy Chair. Times Newspapers Ltd. 66-67, Chair. 68-; Chair., Pres. and Dir. Thomson Newspapers Ltd., Thomson Newspapers Inc.; Dir. many companies including Dominion Freightways Co. Ltd. and Thomson Television Ltd.; Vice-Pres. Northern Broadcasting Ltd.; Vice-Pres. and Dir. Quebec Newspapers Ltd. and other companies; Pres. and Dir. Canadian Newspapers, Northern Broadcasting Co. Ltd. and other companies; Chair. of Board and Dir. Central Canada Insurance Service Ltd., Scottish and York

Holdings Ltd.; Pres., Man. Dir. and Dir. Thomson Television (Int.) Ltd.; Deputy Chair. *The Times*; Chair. Board, Pres. and Dir. *The Independent* Inc.; Pres. and Dir. Thomson Newspapers Inc.; Chair. of Board, Pres. and Dir. Thomson Newspapers Ltd.; Dir. Boys' Clubs of Canada.
Office: Times Newspapers Ltd., Printing House Square, London, E.C.4.; Home: 8 Kensington Palace Gardens, London, W.8., England.

Thomson, Virgil, A.B.; American composer and critic; b. 25 Nov. 1896; ed. Harvard Univ., and studied under Nadia Boulanger and Rosario Scalero.
Asst. Instructor in Music, Harvard Univ. 21-25; Organist, King's Chapel, Boston 22-23; lived in Paris 25-40; Music Critic *N.Y. Herald Tribune* 40-54; Pulitzer Prize in Music 49; Gold Medal Nat. Inst. of Arts and Letters 66; Brandeis Award 68; mem. American Acad. of Arts and Letters; American Acad. Arts and Sciences; Officier Légion d'Honneur; Hon. D.F.A. (Syracuse Univ.), Hon. Litt.D. (Rutgers Univ.), Litt. Hum. Doc. (Park Coll., Roosevelt Univ., Fairfield Univ.).
Publs. *The State of Music* 39, *The Musical Scene* 45, *The Art of Judging Music* 48, *Music Right and Left* 51, *Virgil Thomson* (memoirs) 66, *Music Reviewed 1940-54* 67.
Compositions include: two operas: *Four Saints in Three Acts* 28, *The Mother of Us All* 47; incidental music for plays and films, including: *The Plow that Broke the Plains* 36, *The River* 37, *Louisiana Story* 48, *The Goddess* 57, *Power Among Men* 57, *Journey to America* 64; two Symphonies and many shorter works for orchestra, a Cello Concerto, a Flute Concerto, two String Quartets, and other chamber music; four Piano Sonatas and many short piano pieces, songs and choruses; Requiem Mass.
222 West 23rd Street, New York, N.Y. 10011, U.S.A. Telephone: CH3-3700.

Thomson of Fleet, 1st Baron (cr. 64), of Northbridge in the City of Edinburgh; **Roy Herbert Thomson** (father of Kenneth Thomson, *q.v.*); British newspaperman; b. 5 June 1894; ed. Canada.
Chair. The Scotsman Publications Ltd., Scottish Television Ltd., Thomson Organisation of Great Britain Ltd., Thomson Newspapers Ltd. (Toronto), Northern Broadcasting Co. Ltd., Thomson Newspapers Inc. (U.S.A.) and other companies; Dir. The Royal Bank of Canada; Chancellor, Memorial Univ. of Newfoundland 61-.
Offices: Thomson Organisation of Great Britain Limited, Thomson House, 200 Gray's Inn Road, London, W.C.1, England; Home: Alderbourne Arches, Fulmer, Bucks., England.

Thondaman, Savumiamoorthy; Ceylonese agriculturalist; b. 30 Aug. 1913; ed. St. Andrew's Coll., Gampola.
Member Ceylon Parl. 47-51, 60-; mem. ILO Asian Advisory Cttee., Substitute Deputy mem. Governing Body of ILO; Leader, Ceylon Workers' Congress; Leader of struggle for political and econ. rights by one million persons of Indian origin in Ceylon.
Wavendon Group, Rambod, Ceylon.

Thonemann, Peter Clive, M.SC., D.PHIL., F.P.S.; British physicist; b. 3 June 1917; ed. Univs. of Melbourne and Sydney and Trinity Coll., Oxford.
Commonwealth Research Scholar (Sydney Univ.) 44-46; I.C.I. Fellow, Clarendon Laboratory, Oxford, 46-49; Head of Controlled Thermonuclear Research A.E.R.E., Harwell 49-60, Deputy Dir., Culham Laboratory of the Atomic Energy Authority 65-66; Prof. of Physics and Head of Dept., Univ. Coll., Swansea 68-.
33 Cumnor Hill, Oxford, England.
Telephone: Cumnor 2009.

Thor, Vilhjalmur; Icelandic international banking official; b. 1 Sept. 1899.
Joined Eyfiroinga Co-op Soc. 12, Asst. Gen. Man. 18-23, Gen. Man. 23-36; Chair. Board of Co-operative Factories, Akureyri 36-38; mem. Board of Dirs. Fed. of Iceland Co-operative Socs. 36-47; Commr.-Gen. for Iceland, New York World's Fair 38, Iceland Govt. Trade Commr., New York 39; Consul-Gen. of Iceland in U.S.A. 40; Gen. Man., Nat. Bank of Iceland 40-42, 44-46, 55; Minister of Foreign Affairs and Industries 42-44; Gen. Man. Fed. of Iceland Co-operative Socs. 46-54; Dir. Union of Iceland Fish Producers 46-52, Nat. Bank of Iceland 47; Chair. Board of Dirs. Fertilizer Plant Inc. 51-63; Gov. Central Bank of Iceland 57, mem. Board of Govs. 61-; Alt. Gov. for Iceland, Int. Bank for Reconstruction and Devt. (IBRD) 60-64; Exec. Dir. IBRD, IFC and Int. Devt. Asscn. 64-; numerous decorations.
International Bank for Reconstruction and Development, 1818 H. Street, N.W., Washington, D.C., U.S.A.

Thorn, George Widmer, M.D.; American physician; b. 15 Jan. 1906; ed. Coll. of Wooster, Ohio.
House Officer, Millard Fillmore Hospital, Buffalo (N.Y.) 29-30; Asst. Univ. of Buffalo 31-34; Rockefeller Fellow in Medicine, Harvard Medical School and Mass. Gen. Hospital 34-35; Asst. Prof. Dept. of Physiology, Ohio State Univ. 35-36; Assoc. Prof. of Medicine, Johns Hopkins Medical School, Assoc. Physician Johns Hopkins Hospital 36-42; Physician-in-Chief, Peter Bent Brigham Hospital, Hersey Prof. of Theory and Practice of Physic, Harvard Univ. 42-; Consultant U.S. Public Health Service, etc.; Fellow, Royal Coll. of Physicians, London; mem. Nat. Advisory Cttee. on Radiation; Trustee, Diabetic Fund; numerous awards including John Philips Memorial Award (American Coll. of Physicians) 55, Modern Medicine Award 61, George Minot Award (American Medical Asscn.) 63; Hon. mem. Soc. Colombiana de Endocrinología (Bogotá), Royal Soc. of Medicine (Great Britain); mem. Royal Acad. of Medicine (Belgium), Norwegian Medical Soc.; First Lilly Lecturer, Royal Coll. of Physicians, London 66; Commdr. Order of Hipólito Unanue (Peru).
Peter Bent Brigham Hospital, Boston, Mass. 02115; 983 Memorial Drive, Cambridge, Mass. 02138, U.S.A. Telephone: 617-876-6410 (Home).

Thorn, Sir Jules, Kt.; British business executive.
Chairman and Managing Dir. Thorn Electrical Industries Ltd. 37-; Chair. British Lighting Industries Ltd., Smart and Brown (Engineers) Ltd., Thorn-A.E.I. Radio Valves and Tubes Ltd.; Pres. British Radio Equipment Manufacturers Asscn. 64-; Chair. Radio Industry Council; Dir. African Lamps (Pty.) Ltd., Thorn Electrical Industries (Central Africa) Pty. Ltd., Thorn Electrical Industries (South Africa) Pty. Ltd.; Fellow of British Inst. of Management.
Thorn Electrical Industries Ltd., Thorn House, Upper St. Martin's Lane, London, W.C.2, England.

Thornbrough, Albert A.; American business executive; b. 1912; ed. Kansas State Coll.
President, Dir., Massey-Ferguson Ltd., Toronto.
200 University Avenue, Toronto, Ontario, Canada.

Thorndike, Dame Sybil, D.B.E. (wife of Sir Lewis Casson, *q.v.*); British actress; b. 1882; ed. Rochester High School.
Began theatrical career touring U.S.A. in Shakespearian repertory 03; with Miss Horniman's Co., Manchester 08-09, leading parts 11-13; management in London 22-27; South African tour 28; toured Middle East, Australia and New Zealand 32-33; several tours with Old Vic 40-42; tour of Belgium, France and Germany 45-46; recital tour of Australasia, Africa, Far East, Israel and Turkey 54-56.
Recent plays include: *A Family Reunion* 56, *The*

Potting Shed (London and New York) 56, *The Chalk Garden* (London and Australia) 57-58, *Eighty in the Shade* 59, *Waiting in the Wings* 60-61, *Vanity Fair* 62, *Uncle Vanya* 62, *The Reluctant Peer* 64, *Season of Goodwill* 64, *Return Ticket* 65, *Arsenic and Old Lace* 66, *The Viaduct* 67, *Night Must Fall* 68; Films: *Dawn* (Nurse Cavell) and *The Sleeping Prince*; Hon. LL.D. Manchester and Edinburgh Univs.
Publs. *Religion and the Stage, Lillian Baylis* (with Russell Thorndike).
98 Swan Court, London, S.W.3, England.

Thorneycroft, Baron (Life Peer), cr. 67, of Dunston in the County of Stafford; (**George Edward**) **Peter Thorneycroft,** P.C.; British barrister and politician; b. 26 July 1909; ed. Eton and Royal Military Acad., Woolwich.
Commissioned service in Royal Artillery 30-33; called to Bar, Inner Temple 35; practised in Birmingham; served Royal Artillery in Second World War; Conservative M.P. for Stafford 38-45, for Monmouth 45-66; Parl. Sec., Ministry of War Transport 45; Pres. of the Board of Trade 51-57, Chancellor of the Exchequer 57-58; Minister of Aviation 60-62, of Defence 62-64; Sec. of State for Defence April-Oct. 64; Dir. Pirelli Ltd. Dec. 64-, Chair. Pirelli Gen. Cable Works Ltd. 67-, Pye of Cambridge Ltd. 67-, Pye Holdings Ltd. 67-.
42c Eaton Square, London, S.W.1, England.

Thornton, Charles Bates, B.C.S.; American business executive; b. 22 July 1913; ed. Texas Technological Coll., George Washington Univ., and Columbus Univ.
U.S. Army Air Force, Second World War, Consultant to Commdg. Gen. A.A.F. 46, to Under-Sec. Dept. of State 47; Dir. of Planning, Ford Motor Co. 46-48; Vice-Pres., Chair., Exec. Cttee., Hughes Aircraft Co. 48, Asst. Gen. Man. 48-53; Vice-Pres. Hughes Tool Co. 48-53; Chair. and Pres. Litton Industries Inc. 53-61, now Chair. of the Board and Chief Exec. Officer; Dir. and mem. Exec. Cttee. United Calif. Bank, Cyprus Mines, Inc.; Dir. and mem. Finance Cttee. Trans World Airlines, Inc., Union Oil Co. of Calif.; many other directorships; mem. President's Special Comm. on Civil Disorders, The Business Council, and of other asscns. and cttees.; Trustee, Univ. of S. Calif.; Hon. D.C.S., George Washington Univ., Hon. D.Iur., Texas Technological Coll.
Office: 9370 Santa Monica Boulevard, Beverly Hills, Calif. 90213; Home: 130 Ashdale Avenue, Los Angeles 49, Calif., U.S.A.

Thorp, Willard Long, A.M., PH.D.; American economist; b. 24 May 1899; ed. Amherst Coll., Univ. of Michigan, and Columbia Univ.
Taught Econs. at Univ. of Michigan and Amherst Coll. 26-34; Research Staff of the Nat. Bureau of Econ. Research 23-33; Chief Statistician N.Y. State Board of Housing 25-26; Dir. U.S. Bureau of Foreign and Domestic Commerce 33-34; Dir. Econ. Research, Dun & Bradstreet Inc. and Editor of *Dun's Review* 35-40; Econ. Adviser to Sec. of Commerce 39-40; Chair. of Board of Gen. Public Utilities Corpn. 40-46; Dep. to Asst. Sec. of State for Econ. Affairs 45-46; Asst. Sec. of State for Econ. Affairs 46-52; U.S. rep. UN Econ. and Social Council 46-50; Prof. of Econs., Amherst Coll. and Dir. Merrill Center for Econs. 52-65; Fellow American Acad. of Arts and Sciences; Dir. Nat. Bureau Econ. Research 56-; Trustee Associated Gas and Electric Corpn. 40-46, Brandeis Univ. 56-62; American Asscn. Univ. Profs. Council 57-60; Foreign Bondholders Protective Council 58-63; Nat. Comm. on Money and Credit 58-61; Acting Pres. Amherst Coll. 57; Chief UN Econ. Survey Mission to Cyprus 60; Chief, President's Special Econ. Mission to Bolivia 61; Chair. Development Assistance Cttee. O.E.C.D. 63-67; Senior Fellow, Council on Foreign Relations, N.Y.C. 68-; Hon. LL.D.

(Marietta, Amherst, Albright Colls., Univs. of Mass., Michigan).
Publs. *The Integration of Industrial Operation* 24, *Business Annals* 26, *Economic Institutions* 28, *The Structure of Industry* (co-author) 41, *Trade, Aid or What?* 54, *The New Inflation* (co-author) 59; contrib. to *Recent Economic Changes*; Editor: *Economic Problems in a Changing World* 39, *The United States and the Far East* (American Assembly series) 56), 62, *Development Assistance Efforts and Policies* 63, 64, 65.
Harkness Road, Amherst, Mass., U.S.A.

Thorpe, Rt. Hon. (John) Jeremy, P.C., M.P.; British politician; b. 29 April 1929; ed. Rectory School, Conn., Eton Coll. and Trinity Coll., Oxford.
Barrister, Inner Temple 54; mem. Devon Sessions; mem. Parl. 59-, B.B.C. Nat. Advisory Cttee. 62; Treas. UN Parl. Group 62-67; Hon. Treas. Liberal Party 65-67, Leader 67-.
Publ. *To all Who Are Interested in Democracy* 51.
House of Commons, London, S.W.1, England.
Telephone: 01-930 6240.

Thorson, Gunnar Axel Wright; Danish marine biologist; b. 31 Dec. 1906; ed. Københavns Universitet.
Zoologist for Danish East-Greenland Expeditions 31-33; marine biological research work: Persian Gulf 37, Canary Islands 47, S. Calif. 49, W. Africa 52, Florida 56, Thailand 66; founded Marine Laboratories on Island of Ven (Sweden) 36, and Elsinore 41; Lecturer in Marine Biology, Copenhagen Univ. 46-57, Prof. 57-; Dir. Elsinore Marine Biology Laboratory 58-; Pres. Danish Natural History Soc. 52-55; Pres. Nordic Council for Marine Biology 60-; mem. Danish Nat. Council for Oceanography 59-; mem. Royal Danish Acad. of Science 55; Corresp. or Hon. mem. of scientific socs. in Finland, France, Italy, Spain, Sweden, U.K. and U.S.A.; mem. Advisory Board of Marine Insts. in Miami, Paris and Naples; Danish Science Prize 47.
Publs. *Reproduction and Larval Development of Danish Marine Bottom Invertebrates* 46, *Bottom Communities (Sublittoral on Shallow Shelf)* 57, *Larval Transport by Ocean Currents* 61, *Light as an Ecological Factor in the Dispersal of Larvae of Marine Bottom Invertebrates* 64, *Some Factors influencing the Recruitment and Establishment of Marine Benthic Communities* 66.
Marine Biological Laboratory, Groennehave, Elsinore; Home: Nationernes Allé 28, Elsinore, Denmark.
Telephone: 21 33 44, 21 66 44 (Office); 21 39 39 (Home).

Thorson, Joseph Thorarinn, P.C., B.A., LL.B., J.D., LL.D.; Canadian judge; b. 15 March 1889; ed. Winnipeg Collegiate Inst., Manitoba Coll., and New Coll., Oxford.
Barrister (Middle Temple) 13, Manitoba 13; served with B.E.F. France First World War, Capt. 16-19; Dean, Manitoba Law School 21-26; law practice 27-41; K.C. 30; Canadian del. to L.N. Assembly 38; mem. House of Commons for Winnipeg South Centre 26-30, for Selkirk 35 and 40; Liberal; Chair. War Expenditures Cttee. 41; mem. Privy Council for Canada and Ministry for Nat. War Services 41-42; Pres. Exchequer Court of Canada 42-; Pres. Int. Congress of Jurists, Berlin 52, Athens 55.
20 Crescent Road, Rockcliffe, Ottawa, Canada.

Thorsteinsson, Eggert G.; Icelandic politician; b. 6 July 1925; ed. technical school and private studies.
Mason, Reykjavík 47-53; mem. Central Cttee. Labour Party 48-; mem. Althing 53-; Asst. Man. State Housing Inst. 61-65; Minister of Social Affairs and Fisheries 65-.
Ministry of Social Affairs and Fisheries, Reykjavík, Iceland.

Thorsteinsson, Pétur; Icelandic diplomatist; b. 1917; ed. Univ. of Iceland.
Entered Ministry of Foreign Affairs 44; served Moscow 44, Ministry of Foreign Affairs 47; Del. to F.A.O. Assembly, Washington 49; Sec. Icelandic F.A.O. Cttee.

48-51; Chief of Div., Ministry of Foreign Affairs 51, Head, Commercial Division 50-53; Chair. Inter-Bank Cttee. on Foreign Exchange 52-63; Minister to U.S.S.R. 53-56, Ambassador 56-61 (concurrently Minister to Hungary 55-61 and to Rumania 56-61); Ambassador to German Fed. Republic (concurrently Ambassador to Greece and Minister to Switzerland and Yugoslavia) 61-62, to France (concurrently Perm. Rep. to NATO and OECD) 62-65, concurrently Amb. to Belgium 62-65, to Luxembourg 62-65, to EEC 63-65; Amb. to U.S.A. 65-, concurrently accred. to Argentina, Brazil, Canada and Mexico, and Minister to Cuba; Commdr. Order of the Icelandic Falcon; Belgian, French and Luxembourg decorations.
Embassy of Iceland, 2022 Connecticut Avenue, N.W. Washington, D.C. 20008; and 2443 Kalorama Road, N.W., Washington, D.C. 20008, U.S.A.
Telephone: 265-6653 (Embassy); 332-3040 (Home).

Thrane, Hans Erik, M.ECON.; Danish diplomatist; b. 14 April 1918; ed. Københavns Universitet.
Danish Foreign Service 45-; Econ. Attaché, Paris 48-52; Ministry of Foreign Affairs, Copenhagen 52-56; Econ. Counsellor, Washington 56-59; Alt. Exec. Dir., Int. Bank for Reconstruction and Devt. 58-59; Ministry of Foreign Affairs, Copenhagen 59-66, Minister 62, Asst. Undersec. of State for Econ. Affairs 64; Amb. and Perm. Rep. to European Free Trade Asscn. (EFTA), and Perm. Rep. to European Office of UN and other int. orgs. in Geneva 66-.
Mission du Danemark, 58 rue de Moillebeau, 1211 Geneva; Private: Villa "La Coudira", 59 chemin de Pregny, 1292 Chambésy, Geneva, Switzerland.
Telephone: 33-71-50 (Office); 58-13-73 (Private).

Thunberg, Lt.-Gen. Lage Gustaf Harald; Swedish officer; b. 22 March 1905.
Army commission 26, flight training 28, transferred to Air Force 34, Commdr. of Bråvalla Wing 43, Lieut.-Col. 44, Col. 47; Chief of Equipment Dept. Royal Swedish Air Bd. 47; Chief of Aircraft Dept. R.S.A.B. 49, Commdr. No. 3 Group 56; Maj.-Gen. 57; Vice-Chief R.A.S.F.B. 60; C.-in-C. Swedish Air Force 61-; Lieut.-Gen. 61.
Commander-in-Chief, Swedish Air Force, Fack, Stockholm 80, Sweden.

Thurmond, Strom; American lawyer, farmer and politician; b. 5 Dec. 1902; ed. Clemson Coll.
Teacher, South Carolina Schools 23-29, Superintendent 29-33; admitted to the Bar 30, served as City and County Attorney; State Senator 33-38; Circuit Judge 38-46; Governor of South Carolina 47-51; Trustee, Bob Jones Univ.; past Trustee, Winthrop Coll. and Baptist Coll. at Charleston; States' Rights Democratic Cand. for U.S. Presidency 48 (39 electoral votes); Chair. South Carolina Democratic Del. and mem. Nat. Exec. Cttee. 48: mem. American Bar Asscn., Clemson Alumni Asscn.; decorations include Legion of Merit, Bronze Star with "V", Purple Heart, Croix de Guerre, Croix de la Couronne, Army Commendation Ribbon; Hon. LL.D., Hon. D.M.S., Hon. L.H.D.; U.S. Senator from South Carolina 54-; active service in Europe and Pacific 42-46; fmr. Maj.-Gen. in U.S. Army Reserve (now retd.); Republican.
Box 981, Aiken, South Carolina, U.S.A.

Thurston, Raymond LeRoy, PH.D., M.A.; American diplomatist; b. 4 Feb. 1913; ed. Washington Univ., and Univs. of Texas and Wisconsin.
Diplomatic Service, Toronto, Naples, Bombay 37-45; Asst. Chief, S. Asian Affairs, Dept. of State 45-49; First Sec./Counsellor Moscow 49-51; Dir. E. European Affairs, Dept. of State 52-55; Counsellor, Athens 55-57, Paris 57-61; Minister to NATO 61; Dep. Dir. Operations

Center, Dept. of State 61; Ambassador to Haiti 61-63, to Somalia Sept. 65-; State Dept. Adviser to Commdr., Air Univ. 63-65.
American Embassy, Magadiscio, Somali Republic.

Thygesen, Jacob Christoffer, M.A.; Danish industrialist; b. 11 April 1901; ed. Copenhagen Univ.
Worked in Danish Foreign Service 26-30; joined The Danish Distilleries Ltd. 30, Man. Dir. 53; Barrister, High Court 39; Chair. Fed. of Danish Industries 61-66; Pres. Nat. Cttee. Int. Chamber of Commerce 59-66; mem. Acad. of Technical Science 56-, Atomic Energy Comm. 64-; Vice Pres. Business and Industry Advisory Comm. to OECD (BIAC), Paris 66-; Chair. The National Bank of Denmark, Danish Sulphuric Acid and Superphosphate Works Ltd., The United Paper Mills Ltd., The Royal Chartered General Fire Insurance Company Ltd., Otto Mønsted A/S; Dir. Scandinavian Tobacco Co. Ltd., Synthetic Ltd., and other industrial cos. and foundations; Commdr. 1st Grade Order of Dannebrog; Knight, Order of Orange Nassau (Netherlands), Grand Officer, Order of the Crown (Belgium).
Amaliegade 22, Copenhagen K, Denmark.

Thyssen-Bornemisza de Kaszon, Baron Hans Heinrich; Swiss industrialist and administrator; b. 13 April 1921; ed. Real Gymnasium, The Hague, Fribourg Univ.
Positions held: Pres. Thyssengas A.G., Duisburg-Hamborn; Niederrheinische Gas und Wasserwerke G.m.b.H., Duisburg-Hamborn; Bergwerksgesellschaft Walsum A.G., Walsum/Ndrrh.; Pintsch Bamag A.G., Berlin/Butzbach; Stahl- und Röhrenwerk Reisholz, Düsseldorf; August Thyssen Bank, Düsseldorf; Bremer Vulkan Schiffbau und Maschinenfabrik, Bremen-Vegesack; Havenbedrijf, Vlaardingen-Oost; del. of Board of Bank voor Handel en Scheepvaart, Rotterdam; Del. N.V. Hollandsch-Amerikaansche Beleggingsmaatschappij-Rotterdam; Pres. of Handels-en-Transport-Mij. Vulcaan, Rotterdam; Halycon Lijn, Rotterdam; mem. Verwaltungsrates, later Pres. St. Gotthard Schiffahrts A.G., Chur, Switzerland; Berliner Handels Gesellschaft, Frankfurt am Main; Affida Verwaltungsgesellschaft, Zürich; picture collection (*Collection Schloss Rohoncz*) housed and exhibited in Villa Favorita, exhibited at Nat. Gallery, London 61.
Villa Favorita, Lugano-Castagnola, Ticino, Switzerland.

Tibandebage, Andrew Kajungu; Tanzanian diplomatist; b. c. 21; ed. Makerere Coll. and London Univ. Inst. of Education.
Schoolteacher Tabora 45-54, Headmaster Bugene Middle School, Karagwe 55, Head of Mathematics Section, St. Thomas More Secondary School, Ihungo, Bukoba 56-61; Ministry of External Affairs 62-; Counsellor in London 62; Head Tanganyika Embassy to Fed. Germany 62-63, Ambassador 63-64; Ambassador of Tanzania to the Congo (Kinshasa).
c/o Ministry of External Affairs, P.O. Box 9000, Dar-es-Salaam, Tanzania.

Tibbetts, Margaret Joy, M.A., PH.D.; American diplomatist; b. 26 Aug. 1919; ed. Wheaton Coll., Norton, and Bryn Mawr Coll.
Department of State 45-49, London, Belgian Congo 49-56; Int. Cooperation Admin. 59-61; First Sec. Brussels 61-64; Ambassador to Norway 64-.
American Embassy, 18 Drammensveien, Oslo, Norway; Bethel, Maine, U.S.A.

Tidemand, Otto Grieg; Norwegian shipping executive and politician; b. 1921; ed. Commercial High School, Oslo.
Royal Norwegian Air Force, Canada, England 41-45; shipping business 45-65, mem. Stove Shipping, and Christian Smith Shipping Co., Oslo; Minister of Defence 65-; Chair. Finance Cttee. Conservative Party 52-.
Ministry of Defence, Oslo, Norway.

Tien Han; Chinese dramatist; b. 98; ed. Tokyo Normal Coll.
Worked in Chung Hwa Publ. Co.; pioneer in promoting modern stage play in China; for a time in the Creation Society; lectured on theatre at Tsinan and Futan Univs.; with Hsu Pei-hung founded a college of fine arts in Shanghai; during civil war took on tour company acting modern Peking drama; del. for Szechuan to First N.P.C. 54; Head of Central Drama Advancement Office; Chancellor, Experimental Drama School.
Publs. Plays, essays, translations.
Chinese Writers' Association, Peking, China.

Tierney, Michael, D.LITT.; Irish university official; b. 30 Sept. 1894; ed. St. Joseph's Coll., Ballinasloe, Univ. Coll., Dublin, Univs. of Paris and Berlin, and British School at Athens.
Professor of Greek, Univ. Coll., Dublin 23-47; mem. Dáil Éireann 25-32; Vice-Chair. Seanad Éireann 38-44; Pres., Univ. Coll., Dublin 47-64; Vice-Chancellor, Nat. Univ. of Ireland 62-64; mem. Irish Folklore Comm.
Alloon, Taney Road, Dundrum, Dublin 14, Ireland.
Telephone: Dublin 984996.

Tietjens, Norman Orwig, PH.B., M.A., J.D.; American judge; b. 8 July 1903; ed. Brown Univ. and Univ. of Michigan.
Admitted to Ohio Bar; Assoc., Williams, Eversmans and Morgan, Toledo 30-32, private legal practice 32-33; Special Counsel, Fed. Emergency Admin. of Public Works 33-37; Counsel, U.S. Maritime Comm. 37-38; Attorney, Office of Gen. Counsel, U.S. Treasury Dept. 38-39, Asst. Gen. Counsel 39-50; Judge, Tax Court of the U.S. 50-61, Chief Judge 61-67.
Office: Tax Court of the United States, Washington, D.C.; Home: 3509 Overlook Lane, Washington, D.C., U.S.A.

Tikhonov, Andrei Nikolaevich; Soviet mathematician and geophysicist; b. 1906; ed. Moscow State Univ.
Postgraduate, Junior Scientific Worker, Moscow State Univ. 27-35; Senior Scientific Worker, Dept. of U.S.S.R. Acad. of Sciences Inst. of Theoretical Physics 35-58; Deputy Dir. U.S.S.R. Acad. of Sciences Inst. of Applied Mathematics 53-; Prof. Moscow State Univ. 36; Corresp. mem. U.S.S.R. Acad. of Sciences 39-66, mem. 66-; Lenin Prize.
Publs. Works on theoretical pluralistic topology, on mathematical physics, and on geophysics.
U.S.S.R. Academy of Sciences, 14 Leninsky prospekt, Moscow, U.S.S.R.

Tikhonov, Nikolai Alexandrovich; Soviet engineer and politician; b. 1905; ed. Dniepropetrovsk Metallurgical Inst.
Assistant locomotive driver, technician and student 27-30; engineer, later Chief Engineer and Dir. Metallurgical plant, Dniepropetrovsk; Chief, main board of U.S.S.R. Ministry of Ferrous Metallurgy 30-55; Deputy Minister of Ferrous Metallurgy 55-57; Chair. Council of Dniepropetrovsk Econ. Region 57-60; Vice-Chair. U.S.S.R. Scientific Econ. Council 60-65; Vice-Chair. U.S.S.R. Council of Ministers 65.
U.S.S.R. Council of Ministers, Moscow, U.S.S.R.

Tikhonov, Nikolai Semyonovich; Soviet writer and poet; b. 1896.
First work published 18; del. Paris Conf. for Defence of Culture 35; Chair. Soviet Peace Cttee. 50; Chair. Cttee. for Literature and the Arts, Lenin Prize Cttee.; Deputy to U.S.S.R. Supreme Soviet; State Prizes 41, 48, 51, Int. Lenin Peace Prize 58; Hero of Socialist Labour 66, Order of Lenin (twice).
Publs. Poetry: *The Horde, Mead* 22, *Poems of Kakhetia* 35, *Friend's Shadow* 35-36, *Kirov is with us* 41, *Year of Fire* 42, *Poems of Yugoslavia* 47, *Georgian Spring, Two Streams* 51, *At the Second World Congress of Supporters of Peace* 61, *May Morning* 61, *Poems* 61, *The Morning*

of Peace 62; also *Leningrad Stories* 42, *Novels and Stories* 48, *Stories of Pakistan* 50, *White Miracle* (travels) 56, *Collected Works* (6 vols.) 59, *Selected Lyrics* 64, *Stories* 64, *Double Rainbow* 64, *From the View of Friends* 67, *The Green Darkness* 67, *Novels* 67.
Writers' Union of the U.S.S.R., 52 Vorovsky Street, Moscow, U.S.S.R.

Tilley, Cecil Edgar, PH.D., F.R.S.; British mineralogist; b. 14 May 1894; ed. Univs. of Adelaide, Sydney and Cambridge.
Professor of Mineralogy and Petrology, Univ. of Cambridge 31-61; Fellow of Emmanuel Coll., Cambridge 31-; Pres. Geological Soc. of London 49-50; Pres. Mineralogical Soc. 48-51, 57-60; Research Assoc. Carnegie Inst. of Washington 56-; Pres. Int. Mineralogical Asscn. 64-68; Foreign Assoc. Nat. Acad. of Sciences, U.S.A.; Foreign mem. Royal Swedish Acad. of Sciences; Foreign Hon. mem. American Acad. of Arts and Sciences.
Publs. Researches in the fields of mineralogy, igneous and metamorphic petrology and in experimental mineral and rock synthesis.
30 Tenison Avenue, Cambridge, England.

Tillinghast, Charles C., Jr., PH.B., LL.B.; American lawyer and corporation executive; b. 30 Jan. 1911; ed. Brown and Columbia Univs.
Admitted New York Bar 35; Dep. Asst. District Attorney N.Y. County 38-40; partner, Hughes, Hubbard & Ewing and successor firm of Hughes, Hubbard, Blair & Reed 42-57; Vice-Pres. and Dir. Bendix Corpn. 57-61; Dir. of several cos.; Pres., Chief Exec. Officer and Dir. Trans World Airlines, Inc. 61-; mem. Nat. Industrial Conf. Board 65-; Hon. L.H.D., S. Dakota School of Mines and Technology 59, Franklin Coll. 63, Redlands Univ. 64, Hon. LL.B., Columbia Univ.
Office: 605 3rd Avenue, New York, N.Y. 10016; Home: 101 Warwick Road, Bronxville, New York, N.Y. 10708, U.S.A.

Timakov, Vladimir Dmitriyevich; Soviet microbiologist; b. 1905; ed. Tomsk Univ.
Postgraduate Tomsk Univ. 29-31; Research Assoc. Tomsk Medical Inst. 31-34; Research Assoc., Asst. Prof., Head of Chair, Medical Inst., Inst. of Epidemiology and Microbiology, Ashkhabad 34-41; People's Commissar of Public Health, Turkmen S.S.R.; Scientific Dir. Inst. of Microbiology and Epidemiology 41-45; Dir. Gamaleya Inst. of Epidemiology and Microbiology 45-53, Head of Dept. 63-; Head of Chair, Second Moscow Medical Inst. 49-; Corresp. mem. U.S.S.R. Acad. of Medical Sciences 48, now mem., Acad. Sec. 57-63; Pres. U.S.S.R. Acad. of Medical Sciences 68-; Chair. Board U.S.S.R. Soc. of Epidemiologists, Microbiologists and Infectionists; Deputy Editor *Big Medical Encyclopaedia*; mem. Exec. Int. Asscn. of Microbiologists, Turkish Med. Soc., Purkinyě Soc., Czechoslovakia; numerous decorations.
Gamaleya Institute of Epidemiology and Microbiology, 2 Gamaleya Street, Moscow, U.S.S.R.

Timár, Dr. Mátyás; Hungarian politician; b. 23; ed. evening classes.
Former leather worker; Hungarian Communist Party 43-; fmr. teacher Faculty of State and Legal Sciences, Loránd Eötvös Univ. of Sciences; now Head Finance Faculty, Karl Marx Univ. of Econs., Budapest; Ministry of Finance 49-, Deputy Minister of Finance 55-57, 60-62, Minister of Finance 62-67; Deputy Chair. Council of Ministers 67-; mem. Central Cttee. Hungarian Socialist Workers' Party 66-.
Office of the Deputy Chairman of the Council of Ministers, Budapest, Hungary.

Timken, William Robert; American business executive; b. 5 March 1910; ed. Harvard Univ., and Graduate School of Business Admin.

President, Timken Roller Bearing Co. 60-.
The Timken Roller Bearing Co., 1835 Dueber Avenue, S.W., Canton, Ohio 44706; Home: 6551 Hills and Dales Road, Canton, Ohio 44708, U.S.A.

Timm, Bernhard, DR. PHIL. NAT.; German business executive; b. 1909; ed. Reformrealgymnasium Altona and Ruprecht-Karl-Universität, Heidelberg.
Worked in private laboratory of Dr. Prof. Carl Bosch, Heidelberg 34-36; joined Badische Anilin-& Soda-Fabrik A.G. (B.A.S.F.) (chemicals) 36, Dir. 50-, Deputy Chair. of Management Board 52-65, Chair. 65-; Deputy Chair. Supervisory Board Mannheimer Versicherungs-gesellschaft, Mannheim, Fendel Schiffahrts A.G., Mannheim; mem. Supervisory Board Allgemeine Elektricitäts-Gesellschaft Telefunken, Berlin/Frankfurt, Continental Gummi-Werke A.G., Hanover, Deutsche Shell A.G., Hamburg, Preussag A.G., Hanover; Pres. Soc. for Promotion of Inst. of World Commerce, Univ. of Kiel; Chair. of Univ. Soc., Heidelberg; mem. Presidium of Asscn. of German Chemical Industry; mem. Curatorium Max-Planck Inst. for Physics and Astrophysics; Hon. Prof. Univ. of Heidelberg 66.
Badische Anilin-& Soda-Fabrik A.G., Ludwigshafen am Rhein, German Federal Republic.

Timmermans, Jean, DR.CHEM.; Belgian chemist; b. 82; ed. Brussels Univ.
Dir. Bureau of Physico-Chemical Standards, Int. Union of Chemistry 20-; Prof. of Physical Chemistry Brussels Univ. 20-52; Emeritus; Pres. Belgian Chemical Soc. 27-28; Pres. first Belgian Nat. Science Congress 30; Pres. Asscn. Allied Univ. Profs. in Great Britain 43; mem. Comité Consultatif de Thermométrie, Bureau Int. des Poids et Mesures, Sèvres 46; Sec. Emeritus, Inst. Int. de Chimie, Solvay 47; Pres. Emeritus, Comité Nat. Belge de Chimie 50; hon. mem. Royal Inst. of Great Britain 31; mem. Acad. Royale de Belgique 45; hon. mem. Société de Chimie Industrielle, Paris 46; Polish Chemical Society 48; Swiss Chemical Society 52; French Chemical Society 57; Hon. Pres. Soc. de Chimie Physique 58; Corresp. mem. Acad. des Sciences 55; Hon. Pres. Belgian Chemical Soc. 62; Dr. h.c. (Dijon) 49.
Publs. *Notion d'espèce en chimie* 28 (also English, Spanish, and Russian translations), *Solutions concentrées: théorie et application aux mélanges binaires de composés organiques* 36, *Polymorphisme des composés organiques* 39, *Histoire de la Chimie* 47, *Les Constantes Physiques des Composés Organiques Cristallisés* 50 (2nd vol. 63), *Physico-Chemical Constants of Binary Systems* 59-64.
35 avenue Emile van Becealacre, Boitsfort, Brussels, Belgium.

Timmons, Benson E. L. III; American diplomatist; b. 2 March 1916; ed. Univ. of Georgia, and Balliol Coll., Oxford.
Instructor in Economics, Univ. of Georgia 37-38; Asst. to Dir. for Funds Control, U.S. Treasury 40-42, Exec. Asst. to Sec. of Treasury 46-48; U.S. Army 42-46; on staff of E.C.A. mission in Paris 48-53; Deputy Dir., then Dir. U.S. Operations Mission 53-55; Dir. Office of European Regional Affairs, Dept. of State 55-58; Counsellor and Consul-Gen., Stockholm 59-61, New Delhi 61-63; Amb. to Haiti 63-67; Deputy Sec.-Gen. OECD, Paris 67-.
Organization for Economic Co-operation and Development, 2 rue André Pascal, Paris 16e, France.
Telephone: TRO-7600.

Timofeyev, Ivan Yakovlevich; Soviet trade corporation official; b. 02; ed. Bauman Mechanical Engineering Inst., Mosocw.
Soviet Army 24-25; confectionery plant 25-29; engineer 34-39; Soviet Trade Mission in Germany 39-41; Soviet Army 41-42; executive *Stankoimport* (machine tools) 43-54; Soviet organisations in Germany 45-49; U.S.S.R.

Ministry of Foreign Trade 50; Vice-Chair. *Stankoimport* 51-55, Chair. 55-64; Soviet Trade Rep. in Austria 64-; mem. C.P.S.U.; Order of Red Banner of Labour, Badge of Honour, etc.
U.S.S.R. Trade Mission, Vienna, Austria.

Timofeyev, Nikolai Vladimirovich; Soviet politician; b. 1913; ed. Urals Forestry Engineering Inst.
Former stevedore, Siberia; later Chief Engineer and Dir. timber enterprise 35-50; Chief Engineer East Siberian Timber Trust 50-55; Deputy Minister of Paper and Woodworking Industry 55-56, Minister 56-57; Chair. Econ. Council, Kostroma 57-62, North West 62-65; Minister of Timber, Paper, Pulp and Woodworking Industry, U.S.S.R. 65-; mem. C.P.S.U. 43-; mem. Central Auditing Comm. 66-; Deputy to U.S.S.R. Supreme Soviet 66-; awarded Orders of Red Star, Badge of Honour and other decorations.
U.S.S.R. Ministry of Timber, Paper, Pulp and Woodworking Industry, 2/16 Ul. Gritsevets, Moscow, U.S.S.R.

Timofeyeva, Nina Vladimirovna; Soviet ballet dancer; b. 11 June 1935; ed. Leningrad Ballet School.
With Ballet Company of the Leningrad Kirov State Academic Theatre of Opera and Ballet 53-56; Deputy to Supreme Soviet of the U.S.S.R.; mem. Bolshoi Theatre 56-; has toured with Bolshoi Ballet in U.S.A., Fed. German Repub. and other countries; People's Artist of the R.S.F.S.R. 63; prizewinner at three int. classic dance competitions.
Principal roles: Odette-Odile (*Swan Lake*), Marta (*Giselle*), Laurensia (*Laurensia*), Phrygia (*Spartacus*), Kitri (*Don Quixote*), Mistress of the Copper Mountain (*Stone Flower*), Diane Mireille (*Flames of Paris*), Gayane (*Gayane*), Raymonda (*Raymonda*), Princess Aurora (*Sleeping Beauty*), Leili (*Leili and Medjnun*), Mekhmene Banu (*Legend of Love*), Giselle (*Giselle*), Asel (*Asel*), Bacchante (*Faust*), Masha (*Nutcracker*), Shoperiana.
State Academic Bolshoi Theatre of the U.S.S.R., Ploshchad Sverdlova 1, Moscow, U.S.S.R.
Telephone: K-9-58-71 (Home).

Timoshchenko, Andrei Mikhailovich; Soviet diplomatist; b. 10; ed. Moscow Inst. of Energy.
Diplomatic service 41-; Minister to Ethiopia 46-47; Asst. to Chief of Econ. Dept., Ministry of Foreign Affairs 48-50; Dep. Political Rep. of U.S.S.R. to Govt. of Austria 50-53, Counsellor-Minister to Austria 54-57; Consultant, Dept. of Int. Econ. Orgs., Ministry of Foreign Affairs 57-59; Counsellor-Minister to German Federal Republic 59-62; Ambassador to Tanganyika 62-64, to Tanzania 64-, concurrently to Mauritius 68-.
U.S.S.R. Embassy, P.O. Box 1905, Dar es Salaam, Tanzania.

Timoshenko, Marshal Semion Konstantinovich; Soviet officer; b. 18 Feb. 1895; ed. High Military Acad.
Joined Army 15, machine-gunner, served 4th Cavalry Div. First World War; joined Communist Party 19, served Revolution; Commdr. 3rd Cavalry Corps 25; Asst. Commdr. White Russia Mil. District 35, Kiev 35-37; Commander N. Caucasian Military Area June-Sept. 37; Commdr. and mem. Military Council Kharkov Military District 37-38, Kiev 38-40; served W. Ukraine 39, Bessarabia 40; C.-in-C. Western (Central) Front July-Nov. 41; Commissar for Defence to 41, Deputy Commissar 41; in command operations on S.W. and S. Fronts 41-42, operations Demyansk (N. Front) 43, 2nd and 3rd Ukrainian Fronts 44; Commdr. several Military Districts 46-60; Insp.-Gen. Ministry of Defence 60-; Chair. Soviet Cttee. of Veterans 61-; Deputy to U.S.S.R. Supreme Soviet; Alt. mem. C.P.S.U. Central Cttee.; Hero of the Soviet Union (twice); Order of Suvorov (three times), Order of Lenin (four times), Order of Victory 45, Order of the Red Banner (five times), and other awards.
Ministry of Defence, 34 Maurice Thorez Embankment, Moscow, U.S.S.R.

Tin Pe, Brigadier; Burmese army officer and politician. Member Burmese Revolutionary Council 62-, also Acting Chair.; Minister of Agriculture and Forests, Co-operatives, Commodity Distribution, and Land Nationalization 62-64, of Supplies, Co-operatives, and Trade Devt. 64-.
Ministry of Supplies, Rangoon, Burma.

Tinbergen, Jan; Netherlands economist; b. 12 April 1903; ed. Leiden Univ. (Doctor of Physics).
Staff of Central Bureau of Statistics, The Hague 29-36, 38-45; Business cycle research expert, League of Nations, Geneva 36-38; Dir. Central Planning Bureau, The Hague 45-55; Prof. of Development Planning, Rotterdam School of Economics 33-; mem. Neths. Acad. of Sciences; Erasmus Prize 67.
Publs. *Business Cycles in the U.S.A. 1919-1939* 39, *On The Theory of Economic Policy* 52, *Economic Policy: Principles and Design* 56, *Selected Papers* 59, *Shaping the World Economy* 62, *Development Planning* 68.
Haviklaan 31, The Hague, Netherlands.
Telephone: 070-394884.

Ting Hsi-lin, M.SC.; Chinese playwright and physicist; b. 93; ed. Birmingham.
Prof. of Physics at Nat. Univ., Peking, then Nat. Central Univ., Nanking 28-45; Dir. Research Inst. of Physics, Academia Sinica 28; after war Prof. of Physics, Shantung Univ.; Vice-Pres. Chinese People's Asscn. for Cultural Relations with Foreign Countries 53; Vice-Chair. All-China Asscn. for the Dissemination of Scientific and Technical Knowledge, to 56; Kiangsu del. to First N.P.C. 54; Non-Party Democrat in the Second C.P.P.C.C.; Dir. Nat. Library, Peking 55-; Vice-Chair. Comm. for Cultural Relations with Foreign Countries 58-.
Publs. A number of one-act plays.
Commission for Cultural Relations with Foreign Countries, Peking, People's Republic of China.

Ting Lai-fu; Chinese politician.
Former Political Commissar Tientsin Garrison; First Sec. Cttee. of Broadcasting Administrative Bureau 65-.
Broadcasting Administrative Bureau, Peking, People's Republic of China.

Ting Ling (Chiang Ping-chih); Chinese authoress; b. 07; ed. National Peking Univ., Common People's Univ., Shanghai.
Began to publish short stories in Hsiao-shuo yueh-pao 26; edited literary magazines in Shanghai 28; joined League of Left Writers 30; arrested in Shanghai 33, released 34; Dir. Central Literary Research Inst. 49-57, dismissed for "revisionism"; Shantung del. to First N.P.C. 54-58, dismissed; U.S.S.R. State Prize.
Publs. Novels and stories: *Sun Shines on the Sangkan River*, etc.
Chinese Writers' Union, Peking, China.

Tingsten, Herbert, PH.D.; Swedish political scientist; b. 17 March 1896; ed. Uppsala Univ.
Attached to Foreign Office 23-24; Asst. Prof. Uppsala Univ. 24; Prof. of Political Science Stockholm Univ. 35-46; Chief Editor *Dagens Nyheter* 46-59.
Publs. *Folkomröstningsinstitutet i U.S.A., Konstitutionella fullmaktslagar i modern parlamentarism, Studier över konstitutionsutskottets dechargeförfarande, Studier rörande ministerstyrelse, Amerikansk demokrati, Regeringsmaktens expansion under och efter världskriget, Fran parlamentarism till diktatur, Demokratiens seger och kris, Utskottsväsendet, Den nationella diktaturen, Political Behaviour, Les pleins pouvoirs, De Konservativa idéerna, Svensk utrikesdebatt mellan världskrigen, Demokratiens problem, Argument, Problem i U.S.A., Revolutionernas arvtagare, Västtysklands problem, Idéer och genier, Problemet Sydafrika, Japan, Det hotade Israel, På marknadstorget, På krigsstigen, Mitt Liv* 61-64, etc.
Villa Gerbert, Roquebrune, Cap Martin (A.M.), France.

Tinoco, Luis Demetrio; Costa Rican diplomatist; b. 1905; ed. Law School, Costa Rica, and Georgetown and Columbia Univs., U.S.A.
Under-Secretary for Finance and Commerce, Costa Rica 30; Minister for Public Educ. 40-44; mem. Costa Rican Del. to San Francisco Conf. 45; Amb. to France and Belgium and Special Amb. to Pope 46; Presidential Minister in charge of Ministry of Foreign Affairs 58-61; Amb. to German Fed. Repub., Sweden and Norway 61-66; Prof. of Finance and Econs., Law School, Costa Rica 36-61; Perm. Rep. of Costa Rica to the UN 66-; mem. Bar Asscn. of Costa Rica, Costa Rican Language Acad., Costa Rican Acad. of History.
Publ. *Treatise on Costa Rican Public Finance and Fiscal Law.*
Permanent Mission of Costa Rica to the United Nations, 211 East 43rd Street, New York, N.Y. 10017, U.S.A.

Tioulong, Gen. Nhiek; Cambodian politician and diplomatist; b. 10; ed. Lycée Chasseloup Laubat, Saigon, and Ecole d'Administration, Phnom Penh.
Entered Govt. service 31; Provincial Gov., Pursat 37, Kompong Cham 39; Gov., Phnom Penh city 45, also Minister of Education; Minister of Finance 45; accompanied King Norodom Sihanouk on mission to Paris; led Cambodian Del. at Dalat Conf. (Aug. 46); Royal Del. on several missions; Minister of Finance, later of Information 51, of Public Works 52-53; Vice-Pres. Cambodian Del. Franco-Khmer independence negotiations; Gov. Phnom Penh and Minister of Foreign Affairs 54, subsequently Minister of Nat. Defence; apptd. Gen. and Chief of Staff, Cambodian Armed Forces; directed operations until Geneva agreement; signed cease-fire agreement (July 54); as Royal Del. and High Commr. for Cambodia in Paris, presided over Cambodian Del. to Quadripartite Conf. (July 54-Mar. 55); Ambassador to Japan 55-57; Ambassador to U.S.S.R. (also Minister to Poland and Czechoslovakia) 57-58; fmr. Deputy Prime Minister, Minister of the Interior, Planning and Tourism; Minister of State, in charge of Foreign Affairs, the Interior and Tourism 61-63; mem. Cambodian del. UN Gen. Assembly 56-57; Commdr. de la Légion d'Honneur, Médaille de la Reconnaissance Française, Chevalier de l'Ordre des Million Eléphants du Laos, Officier du Dragon d' Annam, Gold Medals, King Sisowath Monivong and King Norodom Sihanouk, etc.
c/o Ministry of Foreign Affairs, Phnom Penh, Cambodia.

Tippett, Sir Michael Kemp, K.B., C.B.E.; British composer; b. 2 Jan. 1905; ed. Royal Coll. of Music.
Taught at Hazlewood School until 31; Dir. of Music, Morley Coll. 40-52; Hon. D.Mus. (Cantab.) 64, (Leeds) 64, (Dublin) 65, (Oxford) 67; Hon. Dr. Univ. (York) 66.
Works include: *String Quartet No. 1* 35, *Piano Sonata* 37, *Concerto for Double String Orchestra* 39, *A Child of Our Time* 41, *Variations for Piano and Orchestra* 42, *String Quartet No. 2* 43, *Symphony No. 1* 45, *String Quartet No. 3* 46, *Little Music for Strings* 46, *Suite in D* 48, *The Heart's Assurance* 51, *The Midsummer Marriage* 52, *Fantasia Concertante on a Theme of Corelli for String Orchestra* 53, *Concerto for Piano and Orchestra* 55, *Sonata for Four Horns* 55, *Symphony No. 2* 57, *Crown of the Year* 58, *King Priam* (opera) 61, *Magnificat and Nunc Dimittis* 62, *Piano Sonata No. 2* 62, *Incidental Music to The Tempest* 62, *Praeludium for Brass* 62, *Concerto for Orchestra* 63, *The Vision of St. Augustine* 66.
Publ. *Moving into Aquarius* 59.
c/o Schott & Co., 48 Great Marlborough Street, London, W.1, England.

Tiselius, Arne Wilhelm Kaurin, D.SC.; Swedish university professor; b. 10 Aug. 1902; ed. Uppsala Univ.
Asst. in Physical Chemistry, Uppsala Univ. 25-32, Lecturer in Chemistry 30-38, Prof. of Biochemistry

38-, now Emer. Prof.; Chair. Swedish Nat. Science Research Council 46-50; Vice-Pres. Nobel Foundation 47-60, Pres. 60-64; mem. Govt. Scientific Advisory Council 62-; Chair. Nobel Cttee. for Chemistry 65-; Head, Nobel Inst., Royal Swedish Acad. of Science 68; mem. Royal Swedish Acad. of Sciences, Royal Swedish Acad. of Engineering Sciences, Royal Scientific Societies, Uppsala, Gothenburg and Copenhagen, etc.; hon. mem. of Royal Inst. of Great Britain, Harvey Society, N.Y. Acad. of Sciences, N.Y. Acad. of Medicine; Society of Chemical Industry, London, Royal Inst. of Chemistry, London, Chemical Soc. London; foreign assoc. Nat. Acad. of Sciences, Washington; Pres. Int. Union of Pure and Applied Chemistry 51-55; awarded Nobel Prize for Chemistry 48; hon. degrees Stockholm, Paris, Cambridge, Bologna, Glasgow, Madrid, Oxford, Oslo, Lyon, Michigan, Minnesota and Berkeley; foreign mem. Royal Soc., London, and of numerous European and American scientific socs.

Institute of Biochemistry, University of Uppsala, Uppsala; Home: Thubergsvagen 22, Uppsala, Sweden. Telephone: 135554.

Tison, Léon Jean-Baptiste Hubert; Belgian university professor; b. 1895.
Engineer, roads and bridges 21; Chief Engineer, Inter-Allied Control Mission for factories and mines in the Ruhr 23; Lecturer, Univ. of Ghent 25, Ord. Prof. of Hydraulics and Aerodynamics 30-, Dir. Laboratory of Hydraulic Research; Sec.-Gen. Int. Hydrological Asscn.; Chair. Belgian Nat. Cttee. of Geodesy and Geophysics, Nat. Cttee. of Mechanics; mem. Council, Asscn. for Hydraulic Research; Del. to Consultative Cttee. for Arid Zones of UNESCO, mem. Hydrological Panel of WMO, etc.
Braamstraat 61, Gentbrugge, Belgium.
Telephone: 254648.

Tisserant, H.E. Cardinal Eugène; French ecclesiastic; b. 24 March 1884; ed. Grand Séminaire de Nancy, Ecole Biblique de Jérusalem, Ecole des Hautes-Etudes de la Sorbonne, Ecole des Langues Orientales Vivantes and Institut Catholique de Paris.
Ordained priest 07; Curator of Oriental Manuscripts Vatican Library 08; Prof. of Assyrian, Apollinarium Univ. Rome 08-13; served French Army 14-19; Asst. Prefect of Vatican Library 19-30; Adviser of the Sacred Congregation for Eastern Church Affairs 26; Prelate of His Holiness 29; Pro-Prefect of the Vatican Library 30; Protonotary Apostolic 36; Sec. of Congregation for the Eastern Church 36-59; Cardinal-Deacon 36; consecrated Bishop 37; Cardinal-Priest 37; Cardinal-Bishop of Porto and Santa-Rufina 46-66, Bishop of Ostia 51-66, Hon. Bishop 66-; Sub-Dean of the Sacred Coll. 48, Dean 51-; Prefect, Ceremonial Congregation; Pres. Comm. on Biblical Studies; mem. of Comm. on Eastern Canon Law; Librarian and Archivist of Holy Roman Church; mem. of Sacred Congregation for Extraordinary Affairs; mem. Institut de France, Académie Française 61-; Grand Croix de la Légion d'Honneur.
Publs. *Ascension d'Isaïe* 09, *Codex Zuquinensis Rescriptus Veteris Testamenti* 11, *Specimina Codicum Orientalum* 14, *Codices Armeni Bibliothecae Vaticanae* 27, *Luigi Maria Grignion de Montfort: le Scuole di Carità e le Origini dei Fratelli di San Gabriele* 49, etc.
La Curia Vescovile di Ostia, Porto e Santa-Rufina, 94, Via della Dataria, Rome; Home: 4 Via Giovanni Prati, Rome, Italy.

Titmuss, Richard Morris, C.B.E.; British university professor; b. 16 Oct. 1907; ed. privately.
Industrial and commercial work 22-42; Historian, Cabt. offices 42-49; Social Medicine Research Unit, Medical Research Council 49-50; Prof. of Social Admin., London School of Econs., London Univ. 50-; Hon. D.Sc. (Univ. of Wales), Hon. LL.D. (Edinburgh Univ., Toronto Univ.).

Publs. *Poverty and Population* 38, *Our Food Problem* (with F. Le Gros Clark) 39, *Parents Revolt* (with K. C. Titmuss) 42, *Birth, Poverty and Wealth* 43, *Problems of Social Policy* (official War History) 50, *The Cost of the National Health* (with B. Abel Smith) 55, *The Social Division of Welfare* 56, *Essays on the Welfare State* 58, *Health in Law and Opinion in England in the Twentieth Century* (editor M. Ginsberg) 59, *Social Policy and Population Growth in Mauritius* (with B. Abel Smith and T. Lynes) 61, *Income Distribution and Social Change* 62, *The Health Services of Tanganyika* (Editor) 64, *Introduction to R. H. Tawney's "Equality"* 64, *Choice and the Welfare State* 67, *Commitment to Welfare* 68.
32 Twyford Avenue, London, W.3, England.

Tito, Marshal (Josip Broz); Yugoslav politician; b. 25 May 1892.
Mechanic; served in Austro-Hungarian Army 14-15; imprisoned in Russian concentration camps 15-17; participated in the Russian revolution; returned to Yugoslavia and worked as machinist and mechanic until 27; Dist. Sec. of trade union of metal workers 27-28; took active part in illegal Yugoslav Communist Party; sentenced to six years' imprisonment for conspiracy 28; after release left the country, helped recruit Yugoslavs for the Int. Brigade in Spanish Civil War 36-38; returned to Yugoslavia before Second World War; after the German invasion organised Partisan Forces; elected Marshal of Yugoslavia and Pres. Nat. Liberation Cttee. 43; Prime Minister and Minister of Nat. Defence 45-53; Pres. of the Republic 53-; Gen. Sec. C.P. Secr. 53-66, Chair. League of Communists 66-, and Supreme Commdr. of the Armed Forces 53-.
Offices of the President of the Republic, Belgrade, Yugoslavia.

Titov, Fyodr Yegorovich; Soviet politician; b. 10; ed. Kostroma Textile Inst.
Member C.P.S.U. 30-; party work 41-65; Sec., then Second Sec. Cen. Cttee. C.P. Latvia 44-52; First Sec. Ivanova Regional Cttee. C.P.S.U. 52-59; Second Sec. Cen. Cttee. C.P. Uzbekistan 59-62; First Sec. Chechen-Ingush District Cttee. of C.P.S.U. 63-65; mem. Central Cttee. C.P.S.U. 52-66; Ambassador to Hungary 66-.
U.S.S.R. Embassy, 35 Baiza Street, Budapest 6, Hungary.

Titov, Col. Herman Stepanovich; Soviet air force officer and cosmonaut; b. 11 Sept. 1935; ed. secondary school, Volgograd Pilots' School and Zhukovsky Air Force Eng. Acad.
Training for space flight 60-61; in space-ship *Vostok II* circled earth 17 times during a journey of 25 hours Aug. 6-7, 61; mem. Young Communists' League; Candidate mem. Communist Party until 61, Full mem. 61-; student, Zhukovsky Air Force Engineering Acad. 68; Deputy, Supreme Soviet of U.S.S.R.; Pres. Viet-Nam-Soviet Friendship Soc.; Hero Soviet Union 61, Hero Order of Lenin, and other awards.
Zvezdny Gorodok, Moscow, U.S.S.R.

Titov, Vitali Nikolayevich; Soviet politician; b. 07; ed. Kharkov Building and Engineering Inst.
Worker, later Dir. State Farm 23-35; Teacher, Kharkov Building and Eng. Inst. 36-41; mem. C.P.S.U. 38-; teacher, later party organiser, Kazahkstan 41-44; party work, Ukraine 44-62; Sec. Dist. Cttee., then Sec., Second Sec. Kharkov Regional Cttee., Ukraine C.P. 44-50; Sec., Second Sec. Kharkov Regional Cttee. 50-53, First Sec. 53-61; mem. Central Cttee. of C.P.S.U. 56-, mem. Secr. of Presidium of Central Cttee. of C.P.S.U. 61-65; Chair. C.P.S.U. Comm. on Ideological Questions 62-65, Second Sec. Communist Party of Kazakhstan 65-; Deputy to U.S.S.R. Supreme Soviet, mem. Cttee. for Foreign Affairs.
c/o Central Committee of Communist Party of Kazakh S.S.R., Alma-Ata, Kazakh S.S.R., U.S.S.R.

Tittmann, Edward McLanahan; American mining engineer; b. 27 March 1906; ed. Storm King School, and Massachusetts Inst. of Technology.
Manager, Western Smelters, American Smelting and Refining Co. 41-51, Gen. Manager 51-55, Vice-Pres. and Dir. American Smelting and Refining Co. 58-59, Exec. Vice-Pres. 59-63, Chair. of the Board 63-; Pres. Southern Peru Copper Corpn. 55-58, Chair. Exec. Cttee. 63-.
120 Broadway, New York 5; and 45 Sutton Place South, New York, N.Y. 10022, U.S.A.

Tixier, Claude, L. ès L., D. ès D.; French economist; b. 22 Nov. 1913; ed. Arts and Law Faculties and Ecole des Sciences Politiques, Univ. of Paris.
Deputy Inspector of Finances 39, Inspector of Finances 42; Deputy Dir. to Ministry of Nat. Economy 45; Chief, Service of Economic Survey 46; Dir. Cabinet of Sec. of State for the budget 47; Deputy Dir. Cabinet of Minister of Finances 48; Dir. Cabinet of Prime Minister (Finances) 48; Dir. Cabinet of Minister of Finances 49; Dir.-Gen. of Finances to the Algerian Ministry. Algiers 49-58; Vice-Pres. European Investment Bank July 58-62; Pres. and Dir. Gen. Banque Industrielle de Financement et Crédit 62-67; Pres. Banque Industrielle de l'Algérie et de la Méditerranée 63-; Vice-Pres. Banque Worms et Cie. 67; Chevalier de la Légion d'Honneur.
45 boulevard Haussmann, Paris 9e; and 23 rue de Civry, Paris 16e, France.
Telephone: Paris 224-62-55.

Tobey, Mark; American artist; b. 11 Dec. 1890; ed. public schools.
Fashion artist, Chicago 17-22; teacher Seattle 22; travelled in Europe and Near East 25-27; taught at Dartington Hall, England 31-37; studied art in China and Japan 34; worked on Fed. Art Project; Exhibitions in Paris (Musée des Arts Decoratifs 61), London (Whitechapel Gallery 61), Berne, then Amsterdam 66, Düsseldorf 66, London (Hanover Gallery) 68; works in Kunstmuseum, Basle, Tate Gallery, London and in several American galleries and museums, including Museum of Modern Art, N.Y., Cleveland Art Museum, Inst. of Chicago.
4710 University Way, Seattle 5, U.S.A.

Tobin, Austin J(oseph), A.B., LL.B.; American lawyer and ports executive; b. 25 May 1903; ed. Holy Cross Coll., Mass., and Fordham Univ.
Admitted to New York Bar 28; Asst. Gen. Counsel, Port of New York Authority 35-42, Exec. Dir. 42-; Pres. Port Authority, Trans Hudson 62-; Port Consultant, Thailand Govt. and World Bank, on organization of Israel Ports Authority; mem. Board of Trustees Stevens Inst. of Technology, N.J. and U.S. Council, Int. Chamber of Commerce; mem. Board of Dirs. Tri-Continental Corpn. and other companies, Acad. of Political Sciences, and legal asscns.; awards include Chevalier Légion d'Honneur and Cavaliere Ordine al Merito; Hon. LL.D., Adelphi Coll. and Tuskegee Inst.; Hon. D.Eng., Stevens Inst. of Technology.
Port of New York Authority, 111 Eighth Avenue, New York, N.Y. 10011; Homes: 200 East 66th Street, New York, N.Y. 10021, and Bay Road, Quogue, N.Y. 11959, U.S.A.

Tobin, James, M.A., PH.D.; American economist; b. 5 March 1918; ed. Harvard Univ.
U.S. Navy 42-46; Teaching Fellow in Economics, Harvard Univ. 46-47, Junior Fellow 47-50; Assoc. Prof. of Economics, Yale Univ. 50-55, Prof. 55-57; Dir. Cowles Foundation for Research in Economics, Yale Univ. 55-61; Sterling Prof. of Economics, Yale Univ. 57- (on leave 61-62); mem. President's Council of Economic Advisers 61-62.
117 Alden Avenue, New Haven 15, Conn.; and Yale University, New Haven, Conn., U.S.A.

Tobriner, Walter N.; American lawyer; b. 2 July 1902; ed. Friends School, Washington, Princeton Univ., and Harvard Univ. Law School.
Legal practice, Washington 26-61; Prof. of Law, Nat. Univ. Law School 30-50; Army Service 43-46; mem. Board of Education 52-57, Pres. 57-61; Pres., Board of Commissioners, District of Columbia 61-67; Amb. to Jamaica 67-; Chair., Nat. Capital Housing Authority, mem. D.C. Armory Board.
6100 Thirty-third Street, N.W., Washington, D.C., U.S.A.

Todd, Baron cr. 62 (Life Peer), of Trumpington in the County of Cambridge; **Alexander Robertus Todd,** D.SC., D.PHIL., F.R.S.; British chemist; b. 2 Oct. 1907; ed. Glasgow Univ.
Assistant in Medical Chemistry 34-35, Beit Memorial Research Fellow 35-36. Edinburgh Univ.; mem. staff Lister Inst. Preventive Medicine, London 36-38; Sir Samuel Hall Prof. of Chemistry and Dir. Chemical Laboratories Manchester Univ. 38-44; Prof. Organic Chemistry Cambridge Univ. 44-; Master, Christ's Coll., Cambridge 63-; Managing Trustee, Nuffield Foundation 50-; Chair. Advisory Council on Scientific Policy 52-64; Pres. Chemical Soc. 60-62; Master, Salters' Co. 61-62; Chancellor, Univ. of Strathclyde 65-; Chair. Royal Commission on Medical Education 65-; Trustee Ciba Foundation; awarded Meldola Medal 36, Lavoisier Medal, French Chemical Soc. 48, Davy Medal of Royal Soc. 49, Royal Medal 55; Cannizzaro Medal, Italian Chemical Soc. 58; Longstaff Medal, Chemical Soc. of London 63; foreign mem. Nat. Acad. of Sciences, U.S.A., Österreichische Akad. der Wissenschaften, Ghana Acad. of Sciences, Akad. Naturf. Halle; Hon. mem. Royal Australian Chemical Inst.; Hon. LL.D. (Glasgow and Edinburgh); Hon. Dr. rer. nat. (Kiel); Nobel Prize for Chemistry 57; Hon. D.Sc. (London, Madrid, Exeter, Leicester, Melbourne, Aligarh, Wales, Yale, Sheffield, Harvard and Strasbourg).
The Master's Lodge, Christ's College, Cambridge, England.

Todd, Reginald Stephen Garfield; Rhodesian rancher and politician; b. 13 July 1908 in New Zealand; ed. Otago Univ., Univ. of Witwatersrand, and Glen Leith Theological Coll.
Worked with Thomas Todd & Sons Ltd., Invercargill, N.Z.; Superintendent Dadaya Mission, Southern Rhodesia 34-53; M.P. 46-58; Pres. United Rhodesia Party 53-58; Prime Minister 53-58; Minister of Labour 54-58; Minister of Native Education 55-57; Minister of Labour and Social Welfare 58; founded (with Sir John Moffat) Central Africa Party 59, Pres. 59-60; founded New African Party, July 61; Dir. Hokonui Ranching Co. Ltd.; restricted to his ranch for 12 months Oct. 65.
P.O. Dadaya, Rhodesia.
Telephone: 01222 Shabami.

Todorov, Stanko; Bulgarian politician; b. 20.
Active in Resistance Movement 41-44; mem. Nat. Assembly: Minister of Agriculture 52-58; Sec. Central Cttee. Bulgarian C.P. 58-59, 66-; Full mem. Politburo 61-; First Deputy Prime Minister 59-60, Deputy Prime Minister 60-66; Perm. Bulgarian Rep. to Council for Mutual Econ. Aid (COMECON) 62-66.
Central Committee of Bulgarian Communist Party, Sofia, Bulgaria.

Todorović, Mijalko; Yugoslav politician; b. 25 Sept. 1913; ed. Belgrade Univ.
In Nat. Liberation Movement 41-45; first as Political Commissar of Brigade, then of Division, and Corps, and finally of First Yugoslav Army; Asst. Minister of Nat. Defence and Head of Provisional Administration for Supplies 45-48; Minister of Agriculture and Forestry 48-53; Pres. of Econ. Cttee., Fed. Exec. Council 53-58; Vice-Pres. Fed. Exec. Council 58-63; Vice-Pres. Fed.

Assembly and Pres. of Fed. Chamber 63-66; mem. Exec. Cttee. Yugoslav League of Communists, Sec. 66-; Orders of Nat. Hero, Nat. Liberation, Partisan Star, etc.

Publs. *Disalienation of Labour, Socio-Political Foundations of the Equality of the Republics and Peoples of Yugoslavia, Reorganization of the League of Communists —an Objective Need of the Working Class, Some Questions of Our Economic System.*
League of Communists, Belgrade, Yugoslavia.

Toeplitz, Jerzy; Polish film critic and historian; b. 24 Sept. 1909; ed. Warsaw.
Co-founder "Start" (film asscn.) 29, Sec. and Vice-Pres. 30-34; film work in England and Italy 35-37; mem. Cen. Council for Film Industry 38; Rector and Prof. Cinematic High School 48-; Dir. Inst. of Art, Polish Acad. of Science 60-; Pres. Int. Fed. of Film Archives (FIAF) 48-; Vice-Pres. Int. Film and Television Council; mem. Int. Bureau of Historical Research 52-; mem, Jury, Int. Film Festival, Karlovy Vary 51, 52 and 56. Venice Documentary Film Festival 57, 62, Cannes 58, 65, Venice 60, 64, Mar del Plata 61, Moscow 59, 61, Bergamo 63, 64, Florence 65, Cracow 64, 65, San Sebastian 66.
Publs. *Historia Sztuki Filmowej (History of Cinematographic Art)* Vol. I 55, Vol. II 56, Vol. III 59, *Film i telewizja w U.S.A. (Film and T.V. in U.S.A.)* 64, etc.
Aleja Armii Ludowej 6/165, Warsaw, Poland.
Telephone: 21-63-65.

Togan, Zeki Velidi; Turkish university professor; b. 91; ed. Univ. of Vienna.
Teacher of history, Kazan, Russia 10, Ufa, Bashkurdistan 14-15; rep. Moslems of Ufa province for Moslem fraction of Russian Duma 16-17; mem. Russian Constituent Assembly 17; Chief of War Dept. Nat. Republic of Bashkurdistan 17-19; Commissar for War. Soviet Bashkurdistan 19-20; head of Govt. of Bashkurdistan 20; Pres. Nat. Cttee. Turkestan 20-23; left Russia 23; Prof. of Turkish History, Univ. of Istanbul 25-; Dir. Inst. for Islamic Studies, Univ. of Istanbul; Pres Turkish Oriental Soc. and editor of its review 63; mem. various orientalist societies and of Finnish Acad.; Hon. prof. of various German Univs.; Order of the Ferhang (1st Class) (Persia).
Publs. *The History of the Turco-Tartars* (Tatar) 11, *Collaboration scientifique entre l'orient islamique et l'Europe* 35; *Die Schwerter der Germanen nach arabischen Quellen des 9-11 Jh.* 36; *Ibn Fadlan's Reisebericht* 39; *Biruni's Picture of the World* (Arabic and English) 40; *Turkestan Today and its Recent History* (Turkish) 42; *Introduction to the General History of the Turks* (Turkish) 46; *Methodology of History* (Turkish) 50; *Khorezmian Glossary of Muqaddimat al-adab of Zamakhshari* 51; *Rise of the Turkish Empire* (English) 52; *Kritische Geschichtsauffassung in der islamischen Welt des Mittelalters* 52; *Symbolae Togan* (bio-bibliography) 55; Editor *Proceedings of 22nd Int. Congress of Orientalists* (53, 57), *Miniatures of the Istanbul Libraries* 63; *Cultural Relations Between the Irkhanides and the Byzantines* 66.
Turgutreis Sok, 21 Küçükyali, Istanbul, Turkey.

Togni, Giuseppe; Italian politician; b. 5 Dec. 1903; ed. Spoleto Technical Inst., Univs. of Pisa and Rome.
Dir. of "Gruppo Marmi" of Soc. Montecatini; mem. Consultative Council 45; deputy to Constituent Ass. 46; deputy to Parliament 46-; Under-Sec. of State, Ministry of Labour and Social Security (3rd De Gasperi Cabinet), Minister of Industry and Commerce (4th De Gasperi Cabinet), Minister for Economic Co-ordination (5th De Gasperi Cabinet), Minister of Industry (6th De Gasperi Cabinet), Minister of Transport (8th De Gasperi Cabinet), Minister of State Participation (1st Segni Cabinet); Minister of Public Works July 58-60; rep. to ECSC 52-58; Grand Cross of Sovereign Military Order of Malta, Vatican Order of St. Gregory the Great, Order of Merit Fed. German Republic, Grand Officier de la Légion d'Honneur; Christian Democrat.
Via Savoia 40, Rome, Italy.

Toh Chin Chye; Singapore physiologist and politician; b. 10 Dec. 1921; ed. Raffles Coll., Singapore, Univ. Coll., London Univ., and National Inst. for Medical Research, London.
Chair. People's Action Party 54-; Reader in Physiology, Univ. of Singapore 58-64; Deputy Prime Minister of Singapore 59-68; Minister for Science and Technology 68-; Founder of People's Action Party, now Chair.; mem. Parl. Singapore 59-; Chair, Board of Govs., Singapore Polytechnic 59-; Vice-Chancellor, Univ. of Singapore 68-;.
23 Greenview Crescent, Singapore 11, Singapore.

Toiv, Luvsandorjiin; Mongolian diplomatist; b. 15; ed. Pedagogical Coll. and Mongolian State Univ., Ulan Bator.
Chief of Educ. Dept., Mongolian Ministry of Educ. 35-36; Editor *Youth* (newspaper) 36-37, *Ulaan Od* (army newspaper) 37-47; Pres. Mongolian Writers' Union 47-50; Deputy to Great People's Khural 50-54; Counsellor, Mongolian Embassy, Moscow 53-57; Head of Dept., Ministry of Foreign Affairs, Ulan Bator 57-60; Counsellor, Peking 60-62; Perm. Rep. to United Nations 64-66.
c/o Ministry of Foreign Affairs, Ulan-Bator, Mongolian People's Republic.

Toka, Salchak Kalbakkhorekovich; Soviet (Tuva) politician; b. 1901; ed. Communist Univ. of Eastern Workers', Moscow.
Farm worker 15-21, Govt. staff, Tuva People's Republic 21-25; Sec.-Gen. Central Cttee. Tuva People's Revolutionary Party 31-44; First Sec. Tuva Regional Cttee. of C.P.S.U. 44-; Deputy to Supreme Soviet, U.S.S.R., mem. Cttee. for Planning and Budget; Alt. mem. C.P.S.U. Central Cttee.; State Prize for *The Word of Arat* 51; other decorations.
Publ. *The Word of Arat* (trilogy) 51.
Tuva Regional Committee of C.P.S.U., Kyzil, Tuva A.S.S.R., U.S.S.R.

Tokarski, Julian; Polish politician; b. 03.
Former metallurgical worker; Polish Army in U.S.S.R., Second World War; mem. Polish Workers' Party, later Polish United Workers' Party, mem. Central Cttee.; Minister of Heavy Machine Industry 50-65; Deputy Chair. Council of Ministers 59-65; mem. Council of State 65-; mem. Seym.
1/3 Ujazdowskie-alleys, Warsaw, Poland.

Tokaryev, Alexander Maximovich; Soviet politician; b. 1921; ed. Kuibyshev Inst. of Construction Engineers.
Member C.P.S.U. 42-; Soviet Army service 40-45; Konsomol Leader 49-51; Sec. Stavropol, later First Sec. Novo Kuibyshev City Cttees. of C.P. 51-55; Sec. Kuibyshev Regional Cttee. of C.P. 58-59; Chair. Exec. Cttee. Kuibyshev Regional Soviet of Working People's Deputies 59-63; First Sec. Kuibyshev Regional Cttee. of C.P. 63-67; Minister of Industrial Construction, U.S.S.R. 67-; mem. Central Cttee. C.P.S.U. 66-; Deputy to U.S.S.R. Supreme Soviet, mem. Cttee. for Construction and Bldg. Materials Industry.
U.S.S.R. Ministry of Industrial Construction, Moscow, U.S.S.R.

Tokikuni, Masuo; Japanese business executive; b. 1893; ed. Tokyo Imperial Univ.
Kirin Brewery Co. Ltd. 17-, Brewery Man. Sendai Brewery 33-42, Yokohama Brewery 42-46, Dir. 40-43, 51-, Auditor 43-51, Planning Man. 46-53, Man. Dir. 53-56, Production Man. 56-58, Exec. Man. Dir. 58-66, Pres. 66-; Chair. Japanese Brewers' Asscn. 53; Yellow Ribbon Medal 58; Decoration 3rd Class Zuiho-sho 67.
Kirin Brewery Company Ltd., Kashiwabara Building, Kyobashi, Tokyo, Japan.

Tokuyasu, Jitsuzo; Japanese politician; b. 1900.
Former Pres. *Unyu* and *Unyu Tsúshin* (transport papers); fmr. mem. Tokyo Municipal Assembly; mem. House of Reps. 53-; Parl.-Vice-Minister of Construction 58; Minister of Postal Services 64-66; Liberal-Democrat.
c/o Ministry of Postal Services, Tokyo, Japan.

Tolbert, William Richard, Jr.; Liberian politician; b. 13 May 1913; ed. Liberia Coll. (now Univ. of Liberia). Liberian Treasury 35-, Disbursing Officer 36-43; mem. of House of Reps. 43-51; Vice-Pres. of Liberia 51-; Pres. of the Senate; Pres. Baptist World Alliance 65-66, Hon. mem. American Int. Acad., Hon. D.C.L. (Liberia); numerous Liberian and foreign decorations.
The Senate, Monrovia, Liberia.

Toledo Piza, Arthur Luiz de; Brazilian painter and print-maker; b. 28.
Painter and exhibitor 43-; moved to Paris 52; regular exhibitor at Bienal of São Paulo and of Ljubljana since 51; Triennali of Grenchen since 58; One-man exhibitions in Brazil, Germany, Yugoslavia, U.S.A. and Paris; works in many important museums and private collections; Purchase Prize 53, and Nat. Prize for Prints São Paulo Biennale 59, Prizes at biennales at Ljubljana 61, Santiago 66, Venice 66, and Grenchen Triennale 61.
16 rue Dauphine, Paris 6e, France.

Tolkien, John Ronald Reuel, M.A.; British writer; b. 3 Jan. 1892; ed. Oxford Univ.
Lancashire Fusiliers 15-18; Reader, Univ. of Leeds 20, Prof. of English Language 24-25; Prof. of Anglo-Saxon, Oxford 25-45; Merton Prof. of English Language and Literature 45-49; Hon. Fellow Exeter Coll., Oxford; Benson Medal, Royal Soc. of Literature 67.
Publs. *Sir Gawain and the Green Knight, Beowulf: The Monsters and the Critics* 37, *The Hobbit* 37, *Fairy Stories: A Critical Study* 46, *Farmer Giles of Ham* 47, *The Fellowship of the Ring* 54 and 55, *Ancrene Wisse* 62, *The Adventures of Tom Bombadil* (poems) 62, *Tree and Leaf* 64, *Smith of Wootton Major* 67.
76 Sandfield Road, Headington, Oxford, England.

Tolkunov, Lev Nikolayevich; Soviet journalist; b. 1919; ed. Gorky Inst. of Literature, Moscow and Higher Party School of C.P.S.U.
Sub-Editor and Military Correspondent *Pravda* 38-44; Deputy Exec. Sec. and Head of Dept. *For a Lasting Peace, For a People's Democracy* 47-51; Deputy Editor, later Editor, People's Democracies Dept. *Pravda* 51-57; Deputy Chief of Central Cttee. of C.P.S.U. Dept. for Liaison with Communist and Workers' Parties in other Communist Countries 61-65; Editor-in-Chief *Izvestia* 65-; Alt. mem. C.P.S.U. Central Cttee. 66-; Deputy to U.S.S.R. Supreme Soviet.
Izvestia, Pushkinskaya pl. 5, Moscow, U.S.S.R.

Tolloy, Giusto; Italian politician; b. 3 Nov. 1907; ed. Accad. Militare, Modena and Scuola di Guerra.
Major in Second World War, then founded anti-fascist Partito Italiano del Lavoro, later merged with Partito Socialistà Italiano (P.S.I.); mem. Cttee. P.S.I. 47-, Organising Chief 50-54; mem. Chamber of Deputies 48-58; Senator 58-; Pres. of P.S.I. Group in the Senate; Vice-Pres. Foreign Comm. and Italian section Inter-Parliamentary Union; Minister of Foreign Trade 66-68.
The Senate, Rome, Italy.

Tolstikov, Evgeniy Ivanovich, D.SC.; Soviet Polar explorer; b. 03; ed. Moscow Hydro-meteorological Inst.
Head of the Soviet drifting station SP-4 in the Arctic 54-55; head of the Soviet Int. Geophysical Year Antarctic Expedition to Mirny 58-59; Dep. Chief, Main Dept. of Northern Sea Route of Ministry of Merchant Marine 55-57, 59-63; Deputy Head Main Board for Hydrometeorological Services for U.S.S.R. Council of Ministers 63-; mem. C.P.S.U.
Main Board for Hydrometeorological Services for U.S.S.R. Council of Ministers, Pereulok Pavlika Morzova 12, Moscow, U.S.S.R.

Tolstikov, Vasili Sergeyevich; Soviet politician; b. 17; ed. Leningrad Inst. of Railway Engineering.
Soviet Army 41-46; construction orgs., Leningrad 46-52; mem. C.P.S.U. 48-; party and Soviet work 52-57; First Deputy Chair. Exec. Cttee. Leningrad Soviet of Workers' Deputies 57-60; Sec., later Second Sec. Leningrad Regional Cttee., C.P.S.U. 60-62, First Sec. 62-; mem. Presidium of U.S.S.R. Supreme Soviet 62-; mem. Central Cttee. of C.P.S.U. 61-; Deputy to U.S.S.R. and R.S.F.S.R. Supreme Soviets.
Leningrad Regional Committee of C.P.S.U., Leningrad, U.S.S.R.

Tomasi, Henri; French conductor and composer; b. 17 Aug. 1901; ed. Conservatoire national de Musique, Paris.
Conductor French National Orchestra and at Théâtre de Monte-Carlo; numerous tours all over the world.
Major works: Operas: *L'Atlantide, Miguel Manara, Sampiero Corso, Il Poverello, L'Eloge de la Folie, L'Elixir du R. P. Gaucher, Le Silence de la mer,* etc.; Ballets: *Noces de Cendre, Rosière du village, Les Santons, Nana,* etc.; Concerti for all instruments; Symphony: *Symphonie du Tiers Monde.*
24 rue Victor-Massé, Paris 9e, France.

Tomasini, René François; French civil servant and politician; b. 14 April 1919; ed. Univ. de Strasbourg.
Early service in Provincial Prefectures; Technical Counsellor to French Resident-Gen. Morocco 54, Dir. of Work and Social Questions 55-57; Dir. Centre for re-orientation of French repatriated from Morocco and Tunisia 57; Deputy 58-; Sec.-Gen. Nat. Council of Union pour la Nouvelle République (U.N.R.) 61-, Asst. Sec.-Gen. of U.N.R. 61; mem. European Parl. Assembly 62; Vice-Pres. U.N.R.-U.D.T. in Nat. Assembly 62; Pres. Higher Council of Electricity and Gas; Mayor of Les Andelys 61-; Chevalier Légion d'Honneur, Croix de Guerre, Médaille de la Résistance, Assemblée nationale, Paris 7e; and Le Clan, Noyers-les-Andelys, Eure, France.

Tombalbaye, François; Chad politician; b. 15 June 1918.
Former businessman, school official; Territorial Councillor 52, 57-59; mem. Grand Conseil 57-59, Vice-Pres. 57-58; Prime Minister 59-, Minister of Justice 59-62, of Defence 60-62; Pres. of Council of State 60-; Pres. of the Republic 60-, also Minister of Interior and Minister of Information.
Office of the President, Fort-Lamy, Chad.

Tombaugh, Clyde William, M.A.; American astronomer; b. 4 Feb. 1906; ed. Univ. of Kansas.
Assistant Astronomer, Lowell Observatory, Flagstaff, Arizona; Science Instructor, Arizona State Coll. 43-45; Optical Physicist and Astronomer, White Sands Missile Range 46-55; Astronomer, New Mexico State Univ. 55-59; Assoc. Prof. Dept. of Earth Sciences and Astronomy, New Mexico State Univ. 61-65, Prof. 65-; mem. Int. Astronomical Union Comm. on Planets and Satellites; planetary searches and observations, including the Moon, Mars, Venus, Jupiter and Saturn; discovered ninth planet, Pluto 30, and several new galactic star clusters; Hon. D.Sc. (Univ. of Arizona), Fellow, American Inst. of Aeronautics and Astronautics, numerous awards.
Publs. *The Search for Small Natural Earth Satellites* 59 (co-author), *Lectures in Aerospace Medicine* 60, 61,

The Trans-Neptunian Planet Search 61 and over 30 other papers.

P.O. Box 306, Mesilla Park, New Mexico 88047; and Research Center, Box 756, New Mexico State University, University Park, New Mexico, U.S.A.

Telephone: (505) 526-9274 (Home); 646-2107 (Office).

Tomeh, Georges J., M.A., PH.D.; Syrian university professor and diplomatist; b. 1 March 1921; ed. American Univ. of Beirut and Georgetown Univ.

Attaché, London, and Alt. Del. to UNESCO 45-46; Syrian Embassy, Washington 47-52; Alt. Gov. Int. Monetary Fund 50; Dir. UN and Treaties Dept., Ministry of Foreign Affairs, Damascus 53-54; Asst. Prof. of Philosophy and Asst. to Dean of Arts and Sciences, American Univ. of Beirut 54-56; Dir. Research Dept., Ministry of Foreign Affairs, Damascus 56-57; Consul-Gen., New York 57-58, Consul-Gen. of United Arab Republic in New York 58, Minister, New York 61; Consul-Gen. and Deputy Perm. Rep. of Syria to UN 61-63; Minister of Economy, Syrian Arab Republic 63; Prof. of Philosophy, Syrian Univ. 64-65; Perm. Rep. to UN 65-.

Publs. *The Climax of Philosophical Conflict in Islam* 53, *Islam* 57, *The Constitution and Electoral Laws of Syria, Where Islam and Christianity Meet* 60, *The Dynamics of Neutralism in the Arab World* 64.

Permanent Mission of Syrian Arab Republic to the United Nations, 757 Third Avenue, N.Y. 10017, U.S.A.

Tomic, Radomiro; Chilean lawyer, politician and diplomatist; b. 7 May 1914; ed. Universidad Catolica de Chile.

Newspaper Editor 37-41; mem. Chamber of Deputies 41-45, 45-49, Senate 50-53, 61-65; founded Christian Democratic Party of Chile 35, Chair. of Youth Movement 35-37, Nat. Chair. of Party 46-47, 52-53; Ambassador to U.S.A. 65-.

Publs. numerous politicial essays and *The Inter-American System and the Regional Market* 58.

Embassy of Chile, 1736 Massachusetts Avenue, Washington, D.C., U.S.A.

Tomkins, Rt. Rev. Oliver Stratford, M.A., D.D.; British theologian; b. 9 June 1908; ed. Trent Coll., Christ's Coll., and Westcott House, Cambridge.

Asst. Gen. Sec. Student Christian Movement 33-36; editor *Student Movement* Magazine 36-40; Vicar Holy Trinity Church, Millhouses, Sheffield 40-45; Assoc. Gen. Sec. World Council of Churches and Sec. of its Comm. on Faith and Order 45-52; Warden of Theological Coll., Lincoln 53-59; Bishop of Bristol 59-; Editor: *Lund 1952: The Report of the Third World Conference on Faith and Order* 53.

Publs. *The Wholeness of the Church* 49, *The Church in the Purpose of God* 50, *The Life of Edward Woods* 57, *A Time for Unity* 64.

Bishop's House, Clifton Hill, Bristol 8, England.

Tomlinson, Sir Frank Stanley, K.C.M.G.; British diplomatist; b. 21 March 1912; ed. High Pavement School, Nottingham, and Univ. College, Nottingham.

Consular Service in Japan 35-41; Vice-Consul, Thailand 41-43; served in U.S.A. 43-45, Consul, Washington 45; Acting Consul-Gen., Manila 45-46, Chargé d'Affaires 46-47; First Sec., Foreign Office 47-51; Counsellor, Washington 51-54; Head of S.E. Asia Dept., Foreign Office 54-59; served Berlin 59-61; Deputy Perm. U.K. Rep. to North Atlantic Treaty Org. (NATO) 61-64; Consul-Gen., New York 64-66; High Commr. in Ceylon 66-.

British High Commission, Galle Road, Kollupitiya, Colombo, Ceylon.

Tomonaga, Sin-itiro, D.SC.; Japanese physicist; b. 31 March 1906; ed. Third High School, Kyoto, and Kyoto Imperial Univ.

Research student, Inst. of Physical and Chemical

Research 32-39; studies, Univ. of Leipzig 37-39; Asst., Inst. of Physical and Chemical Research 39-40; Lecturer, Tokyo Bunrika Univ. (absorbed into Tokyo Univ. of Educ. 49) 40, Prof. of Physics 41-, Dir. of Inst. of Optical Research, Kyoiku Univ. (Tokyo Univ. of Educ.) 63-; Pres. Tokyo Univ. of Educ. 56-62; Pres. Science Council of Japan 63-; Japan Academy Prize 48, Order of Culture 52, Lomonosov Medal (U.S.S.R.) 64; Nobel Prize for Physics 65.

Publs. *On the photo-electric production of positive and negative electrons* 34, *Innere Reibung und Wärmeleitfähigkeit der Kernmaterie* 38, *On a Relativistically Invariant Formulation of the Quantum Theory of Wave Fields* 46, *On the Effect of the Field Reactions on the Interaction of Mesotrons and Nuclear Particles I, II, III, IV* 46-47, *A Self-Consistent Subtraction Method in Quantum Field Theory I, II* 48, *Remarks on Bloch's Method of Sound Waves to Many-Fermion Problems* 50.

3-17-12, Kyonan-cho, Musashino City, Tokyo, Japan.

Tomorowicz, Bohdan; Polish diplomatist; b. 1 April 1923; ed. higher education.

In Polish Air Force in U.K. in Second World War; Editor, Polish radio 46-47; party posts, staff of Central Cttee. of Polish United Workers' Party 47-57; Foreign Service 57-; Counsellor, Polish Embassy, London 57; Deputy Dir. Dept. of Int. Orgs., Ministry of Foreign Affairs, Warsaw 63-66; Amb. and Perm. Rep. to UN, New York 66-.

Permanent Mission of the Polish People's Republic to the United Nations, 9 East 66th Street, New York, N.Y. 10021, U.S.A.

Tomsky, Nikolai Vassilievitch; Soviet sculptor; b. 1900; ed. Leningrad Technical School of Fine Arts.

Represented at exhibitions in the U.S.S.R., India, China, Indonesia, Finland, Paris Universal Exhibition 37, New York World's Fair 39, 28th Venice Biennale, Brussels Int. Exhibition 58; mem. of U.S.S.R. Acad. of Fine Arts 49-; State Prizewinner, 40, 48, 50, 52; People's Artist of the U.S.S.R.

Works include: Monuments to Kirov (Leningrad) 38, Lenin (Voronezh, Saransk and Kuibyshev) 40, 58, 63, Apanasenko (Belgorod) 49, Chernyakovsky (Vilnius) 50, Gogol (Moscow) 52, Nakhimov (Sebastopol) 59, Hero of the Soviet Union, Young Partisan, Len Golikov (Novgorod) 64.

U.S.S.R. Academy of Arts, 21 Kropotkin Street, Moscow, U.S.S.R.

Tončić-Sorinj, Lujo, LL.D.; Austrian landowner and politician; b. 12 April 1915; ed. Grammar School, Salzburg, and Univs. of Vienna and Zagreb.

Assistant to Chair. S.E. Europe Dept., Berlin Univ. 40-44; Military Service 41-44; Head of Political Dept., Austrian Research Inst. for Econs. and Politics 46-49, Editor *Berichte und Informationen* 46-49; mem. Parl. for Land Salzburg 49-66; Chair. Legal Cttee. of Austrian Parl. 53-56, Foreign Affairs Cttee. 56-59; in charge of Foreign Affairs questions, Austrian People's Party 59-; Austrian Parl. Observer to Consultative Assembly of Council of Europe 56-66, Vice-Pres. Political Comm.; Vice-Pres. Council of Europe 61-62; Minister of Foreign Affairs 66-68; Austrian mem. Interparl. Union; Sec.-Gen. Christian Democrat Group, Council of Europe; Vice-Pres. Austrian League to UN; Grosses Silberes Ehrenzeichen (Austria) and other decorations.

Home: Vienna IV, Südtiroler Platz 6, Austria.

Toom, Lieut.-Gen. Willem den; Netherlands air force officer and politician; b. 11 July 1911; ed. Royal Military Acad., Breda, Netherlands, and General Staff Coll.

Cadet, Netherlands Royal Mil. Acad. 30-33; Air training 36-37; Prisoner of war 42-45; Maj. 49, Col. 53; Asst. Chief-of-Staff, Air Force 53-55; C.O. Airbase, Ypenburg

55-56; C.O. Air Force Training Centre, Arnhem 56-58; Netherlands Mil. Rep., SHAPE, and Mil. Adviser of Netherlands Perm. Rep., NATO, Paris 58-60; Deputy Chief-of-Staff, Air Force 60-63; Dir. Air Force Procurement 63; State Sec. of Defence (Air Force) 63-65; Chair. NATO Air Defence Ground Environment System Policy Board, Paris 65-67; Minister of Defence 67-; several decorations.
Ministry of Defence, The Hague, Netherlands.

Tootell, Robert Ballard; American government official; b. 20 Sept. 1904; ed. Montana State Coll., Univ. of Calif., and Harvard Univ.
Instructor, Agricultural Econs., Montana State Coll. 28-30; Land Economist, Montana State Extension Service 31-34, 43-46, Dir. 46-53; Fed. Land Bank of Spokane, Wash. 34-43; Dir. Wash. State Agricultural Extension Service 53-54; Gov. Farm Credit Admin 54-. Farm Credit Administration, 14th Street and Independence Avenue, Washington, D.C. 20578; Home: 5104 Marlyn Drive, Sumner, Maryland, Washington, D.C. 20016, U.S.A.

Toothill, Sir John Norman, Kt., C.B.E.; British engineering executive; b. 14 Nov. 1908; ed. Beaminster Grammar School, Dorset.
Engineering apprentice, Tilling Stevens, Maidstone 30; Chief Cost Accountant Ferranti Ltd., Hollinwood, Lancs. 34-43, Gen. Man. (Scotland) 43-58, Dir. Ferranti Co. 58-; Chair. E.D.C. Vehicle Distribution and Repair; Chair. Cttee. of Inquiry into Scottish Economy 61; Vice-Pres. Scottish Council, Devt. and Industry Council; Gov. Coll. Aeronautics, Cranfield; Hon. LL.D., Hon. D.Sc.
St. Germain's, Longhiddry, East Lothian, Scotland.

Topentcharov, Vladimir; Bulgarian diplomatist; b. 06. Correspondent in Paris for Bulgarian newspapers 37-38; fmr. Deputy Minister of Foreign Affairs; fmr. Editor-in-Chief *Otetchestven Front*; fmr. Prof. of Journalism and Modern History, Univ. of Sofia; Ambassador to France 65-.
Publs. Many works about Bulgaria, China, Syria, Egypt, and one about France *Cent cinquante ans*.
Bulgarian Embassy, avenue Rapp 1, Paris 7e, France.

Töplitz, Heinrich, LL.D.; German judge; b. 5 June 1914; ed. König-Wilhelm Gymnasium, Breslau, Univs. of Breslau and Leipzig.
Military service 40; enforced labour, France and Netherlands 44-45; Junior Barrister, Berlin 45-47; Dept. of Justice, Town Council, Gross-Berlin 47-50; Sec. of State in D.D.R. Ministry of Justice 50-60; Pres. of Supreme Court of D.D.R. 60-; mem. Volkskammer 51-; mem. Presidium of Governing Body of Christlich-Demokratische Union Deutschlands (C.D.U.) 52-; Vaterländischer Verdienstorden in Silber.
Oberster Gerichtshof der Deutschen Demokratischen Republik, Scharnhorststrasse 37, 104 Berlin N.4, Germany.

Topolski, Feliks; British (born Polish) painter; b. 14 Aug. 1907; ed. Acad. of Art, Warsaw, Paris and Italy.
Came to England 35; official war artist from 40 to 45; works in British Museum, Victoria and Albert Museum, Tate Gallery, Imperial War Museum, Glasgow, Nottingham, Edinburgh, Toronto, Brooklyn, Texas Univ., Melbourne, Tel Aviv, Delhi, Warsaw, Singapore and in Buckingham Palace, London; exhibitions in Europe, Canada, U.S., India and Australia.
Publs. *The London Spectacle* 35; illustrated Bernard Shaw's *Geneva* 39, *In Good King Charles's Golden Days* 39, *Pygmalion* 41; *Penguin Prints* 41, *Britain in Peace and War* 41, *Russia in War* 42, *Three Continents* 44-45, *Portrait of G.B.S.* 46, *Confessions of a Congress Delegate* 49, *88 Pictures* 51, *Topolski's Chronicle* 53-, *Sketches of Gandhi* 54, *The Blue Conventions* 56, *Topolski's Chronicle*

for Students of World Events 58, *Topolski's Legal London* 61, *Face to Face* 64, *The United Nations: Sacred Drama* (with Conor Cruise O'Brien) 68, *Holy China* 68.
14 Hanover Terrace, London, N.W.1, England.

Torbert, Horace Gates, Jr.; American diplomatist; b. 7 Oct. 1911; ed. Yale and Harvard Univs., and U.S.A. National War Coll.
Industrial firm 34-46; army service 42-46; U.S. Foreign Service Officer 47-, Second Sec., Spain 47-50, Second Sec., Austria 50-51, First Sec. 51, Asst. Dep. Commr. 52; Consul, Salzburg 54; Officer-in-Charge Italian-Austrian Affairs, Dept. of State 56; Dep. Dir. Office of Western European Affairs, Dept. of State 57-58; Counsellor of American Embassy, Italy 58-61, Chargé d'Affaires, Hungary 61-62, Ambassador to Repub. of Somalia 62-65; Deputy Asst. Sec. of State (Congressional Relations) 65-; Legion of Merit, M.B.E. (mil.), Superior Honor Medal.
State Department, Washington, D.C. 20520, U.S.A.

Torbov, Zeko, DR. JUR., DR. PHIL.; Bulgarian university professor; b. 99; ed. Univs. of Berlin, Göttingen, Paris and Rome.
Prof. War Acad. 39; Priv. doz. Sofia State Univ. 42; Prof. Univ. for Finance and Administrative Sciences, Sofia 44; Prof. of Philosophy of Law, Sofia State Univ. 45, Dean of the Faculty of Law 48; mem. and Sec. of Bulgarian Philosophical Society, Sofia, and of Sociological Asscn., Sofia.
Publs. *Die Sozialgesetzgebung in Bulgarien* 23, *Über die Friessche Lehre vom Wahrheitsgefühl* 29, *Rationalismus und Empirismus in der Rechtswissenschaft* 43, *Naturrecht und Rechtsphilosophie* 47, Bulgarian translation of Kant's *Kritik der reinen Vernunft* 67; and several books in Bulgarian on philosophy and law.
Ul. Giovanni Gorini 7, Sofia V, Bulgaria.

Torre, H.E. Cardinal Carlos María de la; Ecuadorean ecclesiastic; b. 15 Nov. 1873.
Ordained priest 96; Bishop of Loja 12-19, of Riobamba 19-26, of Guayaquil 26-33; Archbishop of Quito 33-67; created Cardinal by Pope Pius XII 53; mem. of the Sacred Congregations of the Council, of Seminaries and Univs., and of the Reverend Fabric of Saint Peter's.
Casilla 106, Quito, Ecuador.
Telephone: 210703.

Torre, Xavier; French diplomatist and government official; b. 11 Sept. 1910; ed. Lycée de Bastia, Lycées Saint-Louis and Louis-le-Grand, Paris, and Faculty of Law, Univ. of Paris.
Department of Economic Affairs, Central Admin. Ministry of French Overseas Territories 36, successively Deputy Head, Head Office of Production and Trade; Deputy Dir. in Charge of Overseas Plan 48, Joint Dir. 52; Sec.-Gen. of Government Gen., French West Africa 54; High Commr. to Cameroun 58-60; Head European Economic Community Fact Finding Mission in Congo 62-63; Administrator French New Hebrides Soc. 61-; Admin. Optorg 64-; mem. Admin. Council Inst. des Huiles et Oléagineux Tropicaux; Officier, Légion d'Honneur.
18 rue Ernest-Cresson, Paris 14e, France.

Torre Nilsson, Leopoldo; Argentine film director; b. 24. Films include: Co-Director with Leopoldo Torres Ríos: *El Crimen de Oribe* 50, *El Hijo del Crack* 53; Director: *El Muro* 47, *Días de Odio la Tigra* 54, *Para Vestir Santos* 55, *Graciela el Protegido* 56, *La Casa del Angel* 57, *Precursores de la Pintura Argentina* 57, *El Secuestrador* 58, *Fin de Fiesta* 60, *Un Guapo del 900* 60, *La Mano en la Trampa* (Grand Prix of Int. Film Press Federation, Cannes) 61, *Piel de Verano* 61, *70 veces 7* 62, *Homenaje a la hora de la Siesta* 62, *La Terraza* 63, *Four Women for One Hero* 64, *El ojo la cerradura* 65, *The Eavesdropper* 66, *Monday's Child* 67.
Av. Santa Fé 836, 12°, Buenos Aires, Argentina.

Torres, José Garrido; Brazilian economist; b. 15; ed. New York Univ.
Head Brazilian Trade Bureau, New York 47-52; Commercial Attaché, Washington 47-52; Pres. Nat. Econ. Council 57-58; Exec.-Dir. Superintendency of Currency and Credit (S.U.M.O.C.) 58-59; mem. Nat. Econ. Council 54-58, and 59-64; Pres. Banco Nacional do Desenvolvimento Econômico 64-66; mem. numerous national dels. to international conferences; Editor *Conjuntura Econômica,* and writer of several papers on Brazilian economic problems and foreign trade; mem. Technical Council of Nat. Trade Confederation and Econ. Council of Nat. Confederation of Industry; Fellow Royal Econ. Soc.; mem. American Econ. Asscn.; Charter-mem. Catholic Econ. Asscn. U.S.A.
c/o Banco Nacional do Desenvolvimento Econômico, Rua Sete de Setembro 48, Rio de Janeiro; and Rua Humberto de Campos 1003, Rio de Janeiro, Brazil.

Torres Bodet, Jaime; Mexican diplomatist and writer; b. 17 April 1902; ed. Univ. of Mexico.
Head Dept. of Libraries of Secretariat of Public Education 22-24; Prof. French Literature Univ. of Mexico 24-28; Sec. of Legation Spain 29-31; Chargé d'Affaires in Holland 32; Sec. of Legation France 32-34; Sec. Embassy Buenos Aires 34; First Sec. Legation Paris 35; Chief Diplomatic Dept. Ministry of Foreign Affairs 36-37; Chargé d'Affaires Brussels 38-40; Under Sec. for Foreign Affairs 40-45; Minister of Education 45-46; Minister of Foreign Relations 46-48; Dir. Gen. of UNESCO 48-52; Ambassador to France 54-58; Sec. for Education, Mexico, Dec. 58-64.
Publs. include: poems: *Fervor* 18, *Canciones* 22, *Nuevas Canciones* 23, *Los Días* 23, *La Casa* 23, *Poemas* 24, *Biombo* 25, *Destierro* 30, *Cripta* 37, *Sonetos* 49, *Sin Tregua* 57, *Trébol de Cuatro Hojas* 58; novels: *Margarita de Niebla* 27, *La Educación Sentimental* 31, *Estrella de Día* 33, *Primero de Enero* 34, *Sombras* 37, *Obras Escogidas* 61, etc.; many essays.
c/o Ministry of Education, Mexico City, Mexico.

Torresi, François; French public servant; b. 23 Oct. 1898; ed. Ecole Centrale des Arts et Manufactures, Ecole Supérieure d'Electricité, and Univ. de Paris à la Sorbonne.
Former Asst. Head Central Technical Service, Compagnie Parisienne de Distribution d'Electricité; fmr. Asst.-Dir. of Production and Transport, Electricité de France, later Head of Thermic Production, now Hon. Dir.; Del.-Gen. Association Technique pour l'Energie Nucléaire 63-; Sec.-Gen. European Atomic Forum 63-; Officier Légion d'Honneur.
26 rue de Clichy, Paris 9e, France.
Telephone: 526-01-30.

Tortelier, Paul; French cellist and composer; b. 21 March 1914; ed. Conservatoire Nat. de Musique de Paris.
1st Cellist Monte Carlo 35-37; 3rd Cellist Boston Symphony Orch. 37-40; 1st Cellist Soc. des Concerts du Conservatoire de Paris 46-47; solo Cellist with leading orchs. (Europe, U.S.A., Israel, etc.) 47-56; Prof. Conservatoire Nat. Supérieur de Musique de Paris 56-; mem. Soc. des Auteurs compositeurs et éditeurs de musique; Hon. mem. Royal Acad. of Music, London.
Works: Two Cello Concertos, Concerto for Two Cellos, *Symphonie Israélienne,* Cello Sonata, Suite for Unaccompanied Cello, *Trois P'tits Tours* (cello and piano), *Spirales* (cello and piano), *Elegie,* *Toccata* (cello and piano), duos for two cellos; Cadenzas for Haydn, Schumann, Boccherini and K. P. E. Bach concertos; edition of Sammartini Sonata; Six Studies for Cello and Piano; Concerto for Violin and Orchestra.
14 rue Léon Cogniet, Paris 17e, France.

Tory, Sir Geofroy William, K.C.M.G., B.A., F.R.A.S.; British diplomat; b. 31 July 1912; ed. Queens' Coll., Cambridge.

Entered Dominions Office 35; Private Sec. to Permanent Under-Sec. of State 38-39; war service 39-43; Private Sec. to Sec. of State 45-46; Senior Sec. Office of the U.K. High Commr. Canada 46-49; Principal Sec. and Counsellor, British Embassy, Dublin 49-52; Imperial Defence Coll. 52; Deputy High Commr. in Pakistan (Peshawar) 53-54; Deputy High Commr. for U.K. in Australia 54-57; British High Commr. in Fed. of Malaya 57-63; British Amb. to Ireland 64-66; British High Commr. in Malta 67-.
British High Commission, Valletta, Malta G.C.

Tosar, Hector A.; Uruguayan composer and pianist; b. 23; ed. Montevideo, and Conservatoire Nationale de Musique, Paris, and Ecole Normale de Musique, Paris (under D. Milhaud, J. Rivier and A. Honegger).
Professor of History of Music and Musical Analysis, Conservatorio de Música, Montevideo 51-60; Prof. of Harmony, Composition and Analysis, and Chief of Theory Dept., Conservatorio de Música de Puerto Rico Oct. 61-; Guggenheim Fellowships, U.S.A. 46-47, 60-61.
Principal works: *Symphony for Strings* 59, *Te Deum* for bass, chorus and orchestra 59, *Sinfonia Concertante* for piano and orchestra 61.
Conservatorio de Música de Puerto Rico, Av. Roosevelt y Lamar, Hato Rey, Puerto Rico.

Toshima, Kenkichi, B.S.; Japanese metallurgical engineer and business executive; b. 30 June 1902; ed. Kyoto Univ.
Kobe Steel Ltd., Kobe 32-, Dir. 49-53, Man. Dir. 53-56, Senior Man. Dir. 56-58, Pres. 58-; Blue Ribbon Medal.
Office: Kobe Steel Ltd., 36-1, 1-Chome, Wakinohama-cho, Fukiai-ku, Kobe; Home: 77 Rokurokusu-cho, Ashiya City, Hyogo Prefecture, Japan.
Telephone: Kobe 22-4101 (Office); Ashiya 2-4561 (Home).

Tóth, Aladár, PH.D. (husband of Annie Fischer, *q.v.*); Hungarian music critic; b. 1898; ed. Budapest Univ. and Hungarian Acad. of Music.
Fmr. critic of *Pesti Napló;* in Stockholm during Second World War; Dir. Hungarian State Opera House 46-56; joint editor of *Zenei Lexikon;* Kossuth Prize 52, Order of Merit of the Red Banner of Labour 58, Eminent Artist, Gold Class of the Order of Labour 68.
Szt. István Park 14, Budapest, Hungary.

Toudouze, Georges G.; French historian, novelist and playwright; b. 22 June 1877.
Fmr. mem. French Archæological School at Athens; Hon. Prof. Conservatoire National de Paris; Pres. Société de l'Histoire du Costume; mem. Acad. de Marine; Laureate of Acad. Française and Inst. de France; Prof. at École des Hautes Etudes Sociales et Internationales; Sec.-Gen. Société Mutualiste des Auteurs et Compositeurs Dramatiques; Commdr. de la Légion d'Honneur.
Publs. include: *Les grandes manifestations de l'art grec, La Défense des Côtes de France, de Dunkerque à Bayonne, au XVIIe siècle, L'Homme qui volait le Gulf-Stream, L'éveilleur de volcans, Carnaval en mer, Les compagnons de l'Ice-berg en feu, Drames et gloires de la Mer, De Morgane à Le Brix, La Grèce au visage d'énigme, Le secret de l'Ile d'Acier, Le Maître de la Mort Froide, Le Voltigeur hollandais, Aux Feux Tournants des Phares, Anne de Bretagne Duchesse et Reine, Du Guesclin, Clisson Richemont et la Fin de la Guerre de Cent Ans, Dieux et Héros de la Grèce Antique, Le Secret des Argonautes, Les Derniers Jours d'Ys-la-Maudite, Molière bourgeois de Paris et tapissier du Roy, La Presqu'Ile de Crozon, La Dernière des Spartiates, Les Chercheurs d'Espace, Tanguy Homme de la Mer, Gait la Mystérieuse, Le costume français, La Belle Catalane, Mona fille des Iles, Fille de proscrit, Fille des Sirènes, Anne et le Mystère Breton, Héritière de Neptune, Les Compagnons de la Tour Dorée, Monsieur de Vauban, Contrebandière de*

Sicile, Cinq Jeunes Filles sur l'Aréthuse, Camaret, grand' garde du littoral de l'Armorique, La Filleule de Merlin, Cinq Jeunes Filles à Venise, Cinq Jeunes Filles à Capri, Cinq Jeunes Filles chez les pirates, Le Premier des Globe-Trotters, La Financée du Loup-de-la-Mer, Cinq Jeunes Filles aux Açores, La Bretagne, Chevaliers et Châtelaines de la Mer, Cinq jeunes filles sur la Tamise.
Plays: *Parmi les Loups, Les rayons du Soleil, Le fait du Prince, Les derniers Fâcheux, La Baronne à le mal de mer, Bataille de Marraines, Equinoxe, La tragique histoire d'Œdipe, Le Secret des Argonautes, Cinq jeunes filles à Majorque,* etc.
50 rue de Moscou, Paris 8e; and "Dirag-ar-Mor", Camaret-sur-Mer, Finistère, France.

Touffait, Adolphe Auguste; French lawyer; b. 29 March 1907.
Director Research into War Crimes, Ministry of Justice; Civil Dir. Ministry of Armed Forces 47-48; Minister of State for Information 49-50; Dir. of Cabt. of Vice-Pres. of Council 53-54; Minister of French Overseas Territories 55-56; Dir. of Cabt. Ministry of Justice 57-58; First Dep. Attorney for the Repub., later Attorney 58; Counsellor, Court of Cassation 61; Dir. of Personnel and Gen. Admin., Insp. Gen. of Judicial Services, Ministry of Justice April-Nov. 62; First Pres. Court of Appeal of Paris, now Solicitor-Gen., Court of Cassation; Commandeur, Légion d'Honneur.
8 boulevard Julien-Potin, Neuilly-sur-Seine (Seine), France.

Toukan, Baha'ud-din; Jordanian diplomatist; b. 10; ed. American Univ. of Beirut.
Secretary to Officer Commdg. Arab Legion 32-37; Court of Amir of Transjordan 37-42; B.B.C., London 42; Income Tax Assessor, Transjordan 45-46; Gov. of Belqa Dist. 46-47; Consul-Gen. of Transjordan in Jerusalem 47-48; Minister of Jordan to Egypt 48-51, to Turkey 51-54; Under-Sec. Ministry of Foreign Affairs 54-56, 62-; Ambassador to U.K. 56-58; Perm. Rep. to UN 58; Order of Nichan Iftikhar, First Order of Istiqlal.
Ministry of Foreign Affairs, Amman, Jordan.

Toulemon, Robert, L.en D.; French civil servant; b. 2 July 1927; ed. Univs. of Toulouse and Paris, Institut d'Etudes Politiques de Paris and Ecole Nationale d'Administration.
Inspector of Finance 54-57; Special Mission, Ministry of Finance 58; Head of Lectures, Institut d'Etudes Politiques de Paris 58-60; Technical Adviser, Office of Sec. of State for Econ. Affairs and Foreign Trade 58-60; Special Mission, Foreign Econ. Affairs Nov. 58; Head, second section, Service of Econ. Expansion 60-62; Chef de Cabinet to M. Marjolin, Vice-Pres. of Comm. of EEC 62-67; Dir. of Section in Foreign Dept. of EEC 63-.
Office: 244 rue de la Loi, Brussels; Home: avenue du Parc de Woluwe, Brussels 16, Belgium.

Toumbas, Vice-Admiral John, D.S.O.; Greek naval officer and politician; b. 24 Feb. 1901; ed. naval and military schools.
Distinguished Naval service, Second World War; Commdr. Salamis Dockyard 45; Naval Attaché Washington 46; Commdr., Naval Cadet School 46-47; Dir. of Personnel, Admiralty 47-49; Supreme Commdr. Coastal Defence Forces 49-51; C.-in-C. Coastal Defences 50-52; Nat. Military Rep., NATO Command HQ, Paris 52; C.-in-C. of the Fleet 52-53; Liberal M.P. 56-, Centre Union 58-64; Minister of State 63; Minister of Interior 64; Minister of Interior and Public Order (Security) 65, Industry Sept. 65-66, of Foreign Affairs 66; Gold Medal for Outstanding Bravery; Grand Commander of Phoenix; War Cross (four awards); other awards.
Publ. *Enemy in Sight* (memories of World War II) 54 (Academy Award.)
10 Alopekis Street, Athens, Greece.
Telephone: 714-048.

Touré, Ismaël; Guinean politician; b. 25; ed. in France.
Head, Kankan Meteorological station; mem. Kankan Municipal Council 56; mem. Faranah Territorial Assembly; Minister of Works 57-59, of Posts, Telegraphs and Transport 59-61; Minister of Public Works and Transport 61-62; Minister of Econ. Development 63-; led Guinea del. to All-African People's Conf. 60; del. to UN 60, 61; mem. Political Bureau Parti Democratique de Guinée.
Ministry of Economic Development, Conakry, Guinea.

Touré, Mamadou; Mauritanian diplomatist and administrator; b. 26; ed. Univ. of Paris.
Former Ambassador of Mauritania to France, U.K., German Fed. Repub., Belgium, Spain and EEC; Sec.-Gen. Comm. for Technical Co-operation in Africa (C.C.T.A.) 62-63; Dir. E.C.A. Inst. of Devt. and Planning, Dakar; now Amb. to German Fed. Republic, Belgium, Luxembourg and Netherlands.
Embassy of Mauritania, Bad Godesberg, Friedrichstrasse 8, German Federal Republic.

Touré, Sekou; Guinean trade unionist and politician; b. 9 Jan. 1922; ed. Ecole Coranique, French Guinea Primary Schools, Ecole Professionnelle Georges Poiret, Conakry.
Entered Post and Telecommunications Service, French Guinea 41; Sec.-Gen. Syndicat du Personnel des P.T.T., mem. Comm. Consultative Fédérale du Travail, mem. Guinea Comm. Consultative Territoriale, Comms. Mixtes Paritaires et Administratives 45; Comptable, Trésoreries (Cadre Supérieur), Sec.-Gen. Syndicat des Employés du Trésor 46: founder-mem. Rassemblement Démocratique Africain (RDA) 46; Sec.-Gen. Union Territoriale, Confédération Générale du Travail (CGT) 48; Sec.-Gen. CGT Co-ordination Cttee., French West Africa and Togoland 50; Sec.-Gen. Guinea Democratic Party 52; Territorial Counsellor 53; Pres. Confédération Générale des Travailleurs d'Afrique Noire (CGTA) 56, Mayor of Conakry, Deputy from Guinea to French Nat. Assembly 56; mem. Comité Directeur Fédéral, Union Générale des Travailleurs de l'Afrique Noire (UGTAN) Jan. 57-; Territorial Counsellor, Conakry, Grand Counsellor, French West Africa, Vice-Président du Conseil, Govt. of Guinea May 57; Vice-Prés. RDA Oct. 57; Président du Gouvernement (Head of State), Republic of Guinea (upon declaration of independence following referendum) Oct. 58- (re-elected 61, 63); Lenin Peace Prize 60.
Présidence de la République, Conakry, Guinea.

Tournier, Gilbert Edouard; French business executive and writer; b. 18 July 1901; ed. Lycée Janson de Sailly, and Univ. de Paris à la Sorbonne.
With Compagnie nationale du Rhône since its foundation in 33, fmr. Sec.-Gen., now Dir.; Admin. Dir.-Gen. Soc. d'Etudes Mer du Nord-Méditerranée; Pres. Editorial Cttee. *Delta*; Officier Légion d'Honneur, Commdr. des Palmes académiques, Officier de l'Economie nationale et du Mérite commercial.
Publs. *Rhône, dieu conquis, Le Rhône, fleuve-dieu, vous parle, Babel ou le vertige technique, Je n'ai pas de métier, Le Coeur des Hommes;* writer of film scripts: *Fleuve-dieu, Sont morts les bâtisseurs, Confluent sans âge, Suite magique, Quatuor élémentaire.*
28 boulevard Raspail, Paris 7e; and 95 rue Pierre-Brunier, Caluire, Rhône, France.

Tovar Llorente, Antonio, DR. EN FIL. Y LET.; Spanish university professor; b. 17 May 1911; ed. Univs. of Valladolid and Madrid, Sorbonne and Univ. of Berlin.
Under-Sec. for Press Affairs 40; Prof. of Latin, Univ. of Salamanca 42-63, Rector of Univ. 51-56; Visiting Prof. Univ. of Buenos Aires 48-49; Univ. Nac. Tucumán 58-59; Visiting Prof. Univ. of Illinois 60-61, Prof. of Classics 63-67; Prof. Univ. of Tübingen 67-; Hon. D.Phil. (Munich, Buenos Aires).

Publs. *Virgilio Eglogas* (with commentary) 36, *En el Primer Giro: Estudios sobre la antigüedad* 41, *Lingüística y filología clásica, su situación actual* 44, *Lengua gótica* 46, *Gramática histórica latina: Sintaxis* 46, *Vida de Sócrates* 47, *Estudios sobre las primitivas lenguas hispánicas* 49, *Antiguo eslavo* 49, *La lengua vasca* 50, *Aristóteles Retórica* (text and trans.) 53, *Socrate, sa vie et son temps* 54, *Euripides, Alcestis y Andromaca* (text and translation) 55, *Un Libro sobre Platón* 56, *The Basque Language* 57, *El Euskera y sus Parientes* 59, *Platón el Sofista* (text and trans.) 59, *Euripides, Bacantes y Hécuba* (text and trans.) 60, *Ensayos y peregrinaciones* 60, *The Ancient Languages of Spain and Portugal* 61, *Catálogo de las Lenguas de América del Sur* 61, *Propercio* (text and trans.) 63.
Seminar Vergl. Sprachwiss, Universität Tübingen, Mohlstr. 54, Tübingen, German Federal Republic.

Tovmasyan, Suren Akopovich; Soviet diplomatist; b. 09; ed. Erevan State Univ.
Member of C.P.S.U. 30-; Army service 41-46; First Sec., Central Cttee., C.P.S.U. of Armenia 53-60; Deputy of the Supreme Soviet 54-62; Ambassador to Democratic Republic of Viet-Nam 61-64; on staff of U.S.S.R. Ministry of Foreign Affairs 64-65; Ambassador to Libya 65-; mem. Central Cttee. C.P.S.U. 56-61.
U.S.S.R. Embassy, Tripoli, Libya.

Tovstonogov, Georgi Aleksandrovich; Soviet producer and former actor; b. 28 Sept. 1915; ed. Lunacharsky Inst. of Theatrical Art.
Actor and Asst. Dir. Tbilisi 31; studied at Lunacharsky Inst. 33-38; Dir. Griboyedov Theatre Russian Drama, Tbilisi 38 46; produced in Central Theatre for Children, Moscow 46-49; Actor, Producer Leningrad Komsomol Theatre 49-56; Chief Dir. Leningrad State Bolshoi Drama Theatre (Gorki) 56-; State and Lenin prize-winner, People's Artist of U.S.S.R.
Productions include *Even a Wise Man Stumbles*, *The Storm* (Ostrovsky), *An Optimistic Tragedy* (Vishnievsky), *On the Road to Immortality*, *The Sixth Floor* (from the French of A. Jeri), *Acacia in Blossom*, *Fox and Grapes*, *The Idiot* (Dostoievsky), *Sorrow from the Mind* (Griboyedov), *Quarters* (Simonov), *Virgin Soil Upturned* (Sholokhov), *Three Sisters* (Chekhov), *Barbarians* (Gorky), etc.
Leningrad State Bolshoi Drama Theatre, 1 Ploshchad Iskuss tv, Leningrad; Petrovskaya Embankment, d.4/2 kv. 70, Leningrad, U.S.S.R.

Tower, John; American politician; b. 29 Sept. 1925; ed. Southwestern Univ., Texas, Southern Methodist Univ., and London School of Economics, England.
Radio Announcer, Beaumont, Texas 48, Taylor, Texas 48-49; Insurance Agent, Dallas 50-51; Assistant Professor of Political Science, Midwestern University Texas 51-61; U.S. Senator from Texas (elected to fill vacancy caused by election of Lyndon Johnson as Vice-President of U.S.A.; re-elected 66) May 61-; Republican.
Senate Office Building, Washington, D.C., U.S.A.

Towers, Graham Ford, C.M.G., B.A.; Canadian banker; b. 29 Sept. 1897; ed. Montreal High School, St. Andrews Coll., and McGill Univ.
Lieut. Canadian Army 15-19; joined Royal Bank of Canada Montreal 20, Accountant Havana Branch 22, Inspector Foreign Dept. 24, Chief Inspector 29, Asst. Gen. Man. 33; Gov. Bank of Canada 34-54; Chair. Foreign Exchange Control Board 39-51; Chair. Nat. War Finance Cttee. 43-45; Pres. Industrial Development Bank 44-54; Alternate Gov. Int. Monetary Fund, Washington, D.C. 46-54; Dir. Bell Telephone Co. of Canada, Moore Corpn., Hudson's Bay Co.; Chair. Canada Life Assurance Ltd., B.P. Canada Ltd., Canadian Investment Fund Ltd.; Hon. LL.D. (McGill 44, Queen's 54).
Publ. *Financing Foreign Trade* 21.
260 Park Road, Rockcliffe, Ont., Canada.

Towl, E. Clinton; American aerospace executive; b. 05; ed. St. Paul's School, Garden City, New York, and Cornell Univ.
Assistant Treas., Grumman Aircraft Engineering Corpn. 37-40, Asst. Corporate Sec. and Vice-Pres. 40-54, Vice-Pres. (Admin.) 54-60, Pres. 60-, now Chair. and Chief Exec. Officer; Chair. of Board Grumman Allied Industries 63-; Pres. and Dir. Aerobilt Bodies Inc. 48-63; Pres. and Dir. Grumman Boats Inc. 56-63; mem. Exec. Cttee. and Board of Govs., Aerospace Industries Asscn.
Split Rock Road, Syosset, New York, U.S.A.

Townes, Charles Hard, M.A., PH.D.; American physicist; b. 28 July 1915; ed. Furman and Duke Univs., California Inst. of Technology.
Assistant Calif. Inst. of Technology 37-39; mem. Technical staff, Bell Telephone Laboratories 39-47; Assoc. Prof. of Physics, Columbia Univ. 48-50, Prof. 50-61; Exec. Dir. Radiation Laboratory 50-52, Chair. Dept. of Physics 52-55; Vice-Pres. and Dir. of Research, Inst. for Defense Analyses 59-61; Provost and Prof. of Physics, Mass. Inst. of Technology 61-66, Inst. Prof. 66-67; Trustee Salk Inst. for Biological Studies 63-, Carnegie Inst. of Washington 65-, Rand Corpn. 65-, Board of Dirs. Perkin-Elmer Corpn. 66-; Chair. Science and Technology Advisory Comm. for Manned Space Flight, Nat. Aeronautics and Space Admin. 64-; Guggenheim Fellow 55-56; Fulbright Lecturer, Paris 55-56, Tokyo 56; Scott Lecturer, Cambridge 63; mem. Scientific Advisory Board, U.S.A.F. 58-61, President's Science Advisory Cttee. 66-, Vice-Chair. 67-; mem. Editorial Board *Review of Scientific Instruments* 50-52, *Physical Review* 51-53, *Journal of Molecular Spectroscopy* 57-60, etc.; Fellow American Physical Soc. (Council mem. 59-62, 65-, Pres. 67), Optical Soc. of America, Inst. of Electrical and Electronics Engineers; mem. Soc. Française de Physique (Council mem. 56-58), Nat. Acad. of Sciences, Physical Soc. of Japan, American Acad. of Arts and Sciences, American Philosophical Soc., American Astronomical Soc., Instrument Soc. of America; awards include Research Corpn. Annual Award 58, Morris Leibmann Memorial Prize (Inst. of Radio Engineers) 58, Comstock Award (Nat. Acad. of Sciences) 59, Stuart Ballantine Medal (Franklin Inst.) 59, 62, Exceptional Service Award (U.S.A.F.) 59, Rumford Premium (American Acad. of Arts and Sciences) 61, David Sarnoff Award in Electronics (American Inst. of Electrical Engineers) 61, John A. Carty Medal (Nat. Acad. of Sciences) 62, Thomas Young Medal and Prize (Inst. of Physics and Physical Soc., England) 63, Nobel Prize for Physics 64, Joseph Priestley Award (Dickinson Coll.) 66; Distinguished Service Award, Calif. Inst. of Technology 66; Medal of Honor, Inst. of Electrical and Electronics Engineers 67; Hon. D.Litt.; Alumni; holder of patents in electronics, including fundamental patents on masers and lasers, etc.
Publs. *Microwave Spectroscopy* 55, *Quantum Electronics* (editor) 60, *Quantum Electronics and Coherent Light* (editor) 65; other scientific papers on microwave spectroscopy, molecular and nuclear structures, radio astronomy, masers and lasers, etc.
Massachusetts Institute of Technology, Cambridge, Mass. 02139, U.S.A.

Townsend, Lynn A.; American motor car executive; b. 12 May 1919; ed. Univ. of Michigan.
Accountants, Briggs and Icerman 39-41, Ernst and Ernst 41-44, 46-47; Supervisory Accountant and Partner, Touche, Niven, Bailey and Smart 47-57; Comptroller, Chrysler Corpn. 57-58, Group Vice-Pres. (Int. Operations) 58-60, Dir. 59-, Admin. Vice-Pres. 60-61, Pres. 61-66, Chair. of the Board 67-.
Chrysler Corporation, 341 Massachusetts Avenue, Detroit, Mich. 48231; and Bloomfield Hills, Michigan 48013, U.S.A.

Toxopeus, E.H.; Netherlands politician; b. 1918; ed. Utrecht Univ.
Member Lower Chamber, States General 56-59, 65-; Minister of Home Affairs May 59-65; Liberal.
Waalsdorperweg 161, The Hague, Netherlands.

Toyama, Genichi; Japanese business executive; b. 90; ed. elementary school.
Entered Securities Bureau, Tokyo; Pres. Kawashima Securities Co.; Pres., now Chair. Nikko Securities; Chair. Board of Dirs., Tokyo Stock Exchange; Sec. Fed. of Econ. Orgs.
New Marunouchi Building, 1-4 Marunou-chi, Chiyoda-ku, Tokyo, Japan.

Toynbee, Arnold Joseph, C.H.; British historian; b. 14 April 1889; ed. Winchester Coll., and Balliol Coll., Oxford.
Fellow and Tutor Balliol Coll. 12-15; mem. staff Political Intelligence Dept. of Foreign Office 18; mem. Middle Eastern Section of British Del. to Peace Conf.; Koraes Prof. of Byzantine and Modern Greek Language, Literature and History in London Univ. 19-24; Dir. of Studies Royal Inst. of Int. Affairs 25-55, Dir. its Foreign Research and Press Service 39-43; Research Prof. of Int. History London School of Economics 25-55, Prof. Emer. 55; Dir. Research Dept. Foreign Office 43-46; mem. Académie des Sciences Morales et Politiques, France; Hon. D.Litt. (Oxford, Cambridge, Birmingham), Hon. D.C.L. (Princeton, Columbia).
Publs. *Nationality and the War* 15, *The Western Question in Greece and Turkey* 22, *A Survey of International Affairs* (with V. M. Boulter) 24-58, *A Journey to China* 31, *Study of History* (12 vols.) 34-61, *Civilisation on Trial* 48, *The World and the West* 53, *An Historian's Approach to Religion* 56, *Christianity Among the Religions of the World, East to West: A Journey Round the World* 58, *Hellenism* 59, *Between Oxus and Jumna* (travel) 61, *The Present Day Experiment in Western Civilisation* 62, *The Economy of the Western Hemisphere* 62, *Conversation with Philip Toynbee* 62, *Hannibal's Legacy* (2 vols.) 65, *Between Niger and Nile* 65, *Acquaintances* 67, *Between Maule and Amazon* 67.
Office: Chatham House, 10 St. James's Square, London, S.W.1; Home: 95 Oakwood Court, London, W.14, England.
Telephone: 01-930-2233 (Office); 01-937-3957 (Home).

Trabucchi, Alberto, LL.D.; Italian lawyer; b. 26 July 1907; ed. Liceo "Maffei", Verona, and Univ. of Padua.
Assistant, Istituto di Filosofia del Diritto, Padua 29-35; Lecturer in Civil Law, Univ. of Ferrara 36-40; Prof. of Private Law, Univ. of Venice 38-52; Prof. of Civil Law, Univ. of Padua 42-, of Roman Law 43-45, of Private Comparative Law 49-60; Judge, Court of Justice of European Communities 62-; Dir. of *Jurisprudenza Italiana* and *Rivisto diritto civile*.
Publs. *Il Matrimonio putativo* 36, *Il Dolo nella teoria dei vizi del volere* 37, *Istituzioni di Diritto civile* 62, *Codice delle Communità Europee* 62, *Commentario Trattato C.E.E.* 65.
Via Rudena 23, Padua, Italy; and 3 rue Lavandier, Luxembourg.
Telephone: 20-615 (Padua).

Trabucchi, Giuseppe; Italian lawyer and politician; b. 04.
Former President, Nat. Agricultural Fair Corpn.; fmr. mem. Council of the company for the colonisation of the Paedano Delta; Senator for Verona 53-60; Minister of Finance 60-63; Minister for Foreign Trade 63; Christian Democrat.
c/o Ministry for Foreign Trade, Rome, Italy.

Tracy, Honor Lilbush Wingfield; British authoress; b. 19 Oct. 1913; ed. Grove School, Highgate, London.
Foreign Corresp. *The Observer* 47-50.
Publs. Travel: *Kakemono: A Sketchbook of Postwar Japan* 50, *Mind You, I've Said Nothing* 53, *Silk Hats and No Breakfast* 57, *Spanish Leaves* 64; Fiction: *The Deserters* 54, *The Straight and Narrow Path* 56, *The Prospects are Pleasing* 58, *A Number of Things* 59, *A Season of Mists* 61, *The First Day of Friday* 63, *Men at Work* 66, *The Beauty of the World* 67.
Four Chimneys, Achill Sound, Co. Mayo, Ireland.
Telephone: Achill Sound 45.

Traglia, H.E. Cardinal Luigi; Vatican ecclesiastic; b. 95.
Ordained priest 17; Titular Bishop of Caesarea in Palestine 37; fmr. Dep. Vicar-Gen. of Rome and Consultor to the Supreme Sacred Congregation of the Holy Office; Chair. Preparatory Cttee. Roman Diocesan Synod 59-60; created Cardinal by Pope John XXIII 60; Pro-Vicar General of The Pope for Rome and district until 65, Vicar-Gen. 65-68, Chancellor 68-; Chair. Episcopal Comm. directing Activities of Italian Catholic Action Movement 61-; mem. Sacred Congregations of the Holy Office, of Eastern Church, of the Sacraments and the Propaganda Fide.
Palazzo del S. Offizio, Rome, Italy.

Traikov, Georgi; Bulgarian agriculturist and politician; b. 98.
Peasant Movement 19-; Varna Agrarian Union Org. 20-43; Varna Dist. Cttee., Patriotic Front 43; Sec. Nat. Council of Patriotic Front 45; Dep. Chair. Nat. Ass. 45; Minister of Agriculture 46-49; First Dep. Prime Minister 49-64; Pres. of the Presidium of Nat. Assembly of People's Republic of Bulgaria April 64-; Chair. Council for Agriculture 62-64; Sec. Bulgarian People's Agrarian Union 47-; Lenin Peace Prize 63.
Office of the President, Sofia, Bulgaria.

Trampczynski, Witold; Polish economist; b. 09; ed. European and American Univs.
Rockefeller Fellow, Univ. of Vienna 34-35; Asst. at Univ. of Poznań 35-38; Rockefeller Fellow, Harvard Univ., Univ. of Chicago, Berkeley Univ., and London School of Econs. 38-39; Lecturer and Asst. Prof., Univ. of Poznań 39; working in Bank Emisyjny (Issue Bank) in Cracow 39-45; Prof., Univ. of Cracow 45-46; Gen. Man. of the Nat. Bank of Poland 45-53, Pres. 54-56; Minister of Foreign Trade Dec. 56-; Prof. High School of Planning, Warsaw 60-.
Publs. *Notion of Capital* 36, *Capitalisation* 39.
14 Wiejska, Warsaw, Poland.
Telephone: 21-16-08.

Tran Van Chuong, S.J.D.; Viet-Namese lawyer and diplomatist; b. 98; ed. Univ. of Paris.
Lawyer, South and North Viet-Nam 25-47; Vice-Pres. Grand Council for Econ. and Financial Interests of Indo-China 38; mem. Fed. Council of Indo-China 40; Minister of Foreign Affairs and Vice-Premier 45; Judge, Franco-Viet-Namese Court of Cassation and Council of State 53-54; Minister of State, Republic of Viet-Nam 54; Ambassador to United States 54-63, to Brazil 59-63, to Mexico 62-63; Minister to Argentina 60-63.
Publ. *Essai sur l'Esprit du Droit Sino-Annamite* 22.
5601 Western Avenue, N.W., Washington D.C. 20015, U.S.A.

Trapesnikov, Vadim Aleksandrovich; Soviet power engineer; b. 28 Nov. 1905; ed. Moscow Higher Technical School.
Power Engineer, All-Union Electrotechnical Inst. 28-33; Instructor, Moscow Power Eng. Inst. 30-39, Prof. of Automation and Electrical Machine Building 39-41; Inst. of Automation and Telemechanics, U.S.S.R. Acad. of Sciences 41-, Dir. 51-; mem. U.S.S.R. Acad. of Sciences 60-; mem. Communist Party 51-; Chief Editor *Automation and Telemechanics*, U.S.S.R. Acad. of Sciences; Deputy Minister, State Cttee. for Science and Technology; mem. Exec. Cttee., Int. Fed. of Automatic Control; Hero of Socialist Labour; Order of Red Banner of Labour, State Prize.

Publs. *Design Principles for a Series of Asynchronous Machines* 37, *Automatic Checking of Linear Dimensions in Manufactured Articles* 47, *Generalised Conditions of Proportionality and Optimum Geometry of Transformers* 48, *Cybernetics and Automatic Control* 62, *Problems of Technical Cybernetics in Institute of Automation and Telemechanics* 64.
Institute of Automation and Telemechanics, Kalanchevskaya 15a, Moscow, U.S.S.R.

Trautmann, Rezsö; Hungarian politician; b. 1907. Structural engineer; Deputy Minister of Building Industry 51-53, Minister 57-68.
Ministry of Building Industry, Budapest, Hungary.

Travell, Janet; American physician; b. 17 Dec. 1901. Former practice in New York; Assoc. Prof. of Clinical Pharmacology, Cornell Univ. Medical Coll. 51-63; Official Physician to the White House 61-65; Assoc. Clinical Prof. of Medicine, George Washington Univ. School of Medicine 61-; Special Consultant to Surgeon-Gen., U.S.A.F. 62-64; Chair. Inaugural Medical Care and Public Health Cttee., Washington, D.C. 65; mem. N.Y. Acad. of Medicine, etc.; Founder, American Coll. of Clinical Pharmacology and Chemotherapy; Pres.-elect North American Acad. of Manipulative Medicine; Hon. Dr. of Medical Sciences (Woman's Medical Coll. of Pa.) 61; Hon. D.Sc. (Wilson Coll.) 62.
4525 Cathedral Ave., N.W., Washington D.C. 20016, U.S.A.
Telephone: 202-363-9090.

Tredgold, Rt. Hon. Sir Robert Clarkson, P.C., K.C.M.G., Q.C.; Rhodesian lawyer and politician; b. 99; ed. Hertford Coll., Oxford.
Served First World War; called to Bar, Inner Temple 23; practised Southern and Northern Rhodesia; M.P. for Insiza District 34-43; Minister of Justice and Defence S. Rhodesia 35-43, Minister of Native Affairs 41-43; High Court Judge 43-50; Chief Justice 50-55; Chief Justice Fed. of Rhodesia and Nyasaland 55-60; mem. Commonwealth Judicial Cttee. Privy Council.
Tynwald South, Salisbury, Rhodesia.

Tree, Marietta P.; American diplomatist; b. 12 April 1917; ed. Shady Hill School, Chestnut Hill, Pennsylvania, St. Timothy's, Catonsville, Maryland, La Petite Ecole Florentine, Florence, Italy, and Univ. of Pennsylvania.
Hospitality Div., Office of Co-ordinator Inter-American Affairs 42-43; Researcher *Life* Magazine 43-45; mem. Fair Housing Practices Panel, New York City 58; mem. Board of Commrs. New York City Comm. on Human Rights 59-61; U.S. Rep to UN Human Rights Comm. 61-64; U.S. Rep to UN Trusteeship Council 64-65; Personal Rep. of UN Sec.-Gen. to UN Int. School Devt. Fund Jan. 66-; Hon. D.Hum.Litt. (Russell Sage Coll.); Hon. LL.D. (Univ. of Pennsylvania).
123 E. 79th Street, New York City 22, N.Y., U.S.A.
Telephone: RH4-3386.

Tréfouël, Jacques; French scientist; b. 9 Nov. 1897; ed. Univ. of Paris.
Worked at the Institut Pasteur 20-40, Dir. 40-65; mem. Acad. des Sciences, Acad. Nat. de Médecine, Acad. de Chirurgie, Acad. de Pharmacie, etc.; Dr. h.c. (Oxford, Cambridge, Laval, Rio de Janeiro, Rutgers, Athens, Uppsala, Liège, Oslo, Brussels Univs.); Hon. Dir. Institut Pasteur; Grand Officier de la Légion d'Honneur; author of many scientific studies, particularly on Sulfamides and Sulfones, some jointly with Madame Thérèse Tréfouel.
207 rue de Vaugirard, Paris 15e; and Institut Pasteur, 28 rue du Dr. Roux, Paris 15e, France.
Telephone: 734-53-40.

Tréhin, Robert Pierre-Marie; French university official; b. 8 June 1895; ed. Poitiers Univ., Sorbonne, Paris.
Teaching posts at schools at Poitiers, Orléans, Toulouse

and Paris 14-37; Prof. Rennes Univ., Head of Faculty of Science, Head, Dept. of Physical Medicine, Medical School, Rennes; Rector, Grenoble Acad. 56-; Pres. Grenoble Univ. Council; Officier, Légion d'Honneur.
Publs. *Recherches sur les cotons poudre* 18, *Mesure de chaleurs spécifiques* 21, *Etude des vibrations des membranes capillaires* 28, *Spectres d'Absorption dans l'ultra-violet de solutions* 35, *Applications de certaines méthodes physiques à la recherche des complexes en solutions* 36, *Spectres d'Absorption dans l'ultra-violet des solutions et des cristaux de sulfate de nickel* 44.
7 Place Bir Hakeim, Grenoble, France.

Trejos, Fernández, José Joaquin; Costa Rican university professor and politician; b. 18 April 1916; ed. Univ. of Michigan.
Former Prof. of Statistical Theory and Dean, Faculty of Econ., Univ. of Costa Rica; Pres. of Costa Rica 66-; Partido de Unificación Nacional (PUN).
Office of the President, San José, Costa Rica.

Trelles, Dr. Oscar; Peruvian physician and politician. Psychiatric practice, Lima; fmr. Minister of Public Health; Prime Minister and Minister of Interior July 63-Jan. 64; Ambassador to France 64-65; Sec.-Gen. Partido Acción Popular 65-.
Partido Acción Popular, Nicolás de Piérola 677, Lima, Peru.

Tremblay, Paul, B.A., LL.B., L.SC.SOC.; Canadian diplomatist; b. 6 July 1914; ed. Univ. of Montreal, McGill and George Washington Univs.
Department of External Affairs 40-; Second Sec. Washington 43-46, Santiago 46-49; Dept. of External Affairs, Ottawa 49-51; Second Sec. The Hague 51-54; Del. to NATO and OEEC, Paris 54-57; Dept. of External Affairs, Ottawa 57-59; Ambassador to Chile 59-62; Perm. Rep. to UN, New York 62-66; Ambassador to Belgium and Luxembourg 66-.
Canadian Embassy, Brussels, Belgium.

Tremelloni, Roberto; Italian political economist and politician; b. 30 Oct. 1900; ed. Univs. of Turin and Geneva.
Under Sec. Ministry for Industry 46, Minister 47; Deputy to Parl. 48-; Minister for European Economic Co-operation 48 and Del. to O.E.E.C. 49; Pres. Parl. Comm. on Unemployment and Milan Electricity Authority 52; Minister of Finance 54-55; Pres. Parl. Cttee. on Free Competition Limits 61; Treasury Minister 62-63; Minister of Finance 64-65, of Defence 66-68; Social Democrat.
Publs. include: *La Storia dell'Industria Italiana Contemporanea, L'Industria Tessile Italiana, L'Italia in un' Economia Aperta* and *Il Danaro Pubblico.*
Via Pellegrini 18, Milan, Italy.

Trench, Sir David, K.C.M.G., M.C.; British colonial administrator; b. 2 June 1915; ed. Tonbridge, and Jesus Coll., Cambridge.
Colonial Admin. Service, British Solomon Islands 38, mil. service there 42-46, later held several posts in Pacific; Hong Kong 50, Dep. Colonial Sec. 59-61; High Commr. for Western Pacific 61-64; Gov. and C.-in-C. Hong Kong April 64-.
Government House, Hong Kong.

Trend, Sir Burke St. John, G.C.B., C.V.O.; British civil servant; b. 2 Jan. 1914; ed. Whitgift School, and Merton Coll., Oxford.
Entered Civil Service (Ministry of Education) 36, Treasury 37, Asst. Private Sec. to Chancellor of the Exchequer 39-41, Principal Private Sec. 45-49, Under-Sec. to Treasury 49-55, Office of Lord Privy Seal 55-56, Dep. Sec. of the Cabinet 56-59, Third Sec. Treasury 59-60, Second Sec. Treasury 60-62, Sec. of the Cabinet 63-.
Cabinet Office, Whitehall, London, S.W.1, England.

Trengganu, H.H. The Sultan of; Tunku Ismail Nasiruddin Shah ibni Almarhum Sultan Zainal Abidin, D.K., D.M.N., K.C.M.G.; Malaysian Head of State; b. 24 Jan. 1907.
Joined Trengganu Civil Service 29, later served as High Court Registrar and Chief Magistrate; acceded to throne of Trengganu 45, installed 49; Timbalan Yang di-Pertuan Agong (Deputy Head of State) of Malaya, later Malaysia 60-66, Yang di-Pertuan Agong (Head of State) 66-.
The Sultan's Palace, Kuala Trengganu, Trengganu, Malaya, Malaysia.

Trettner, General Heinz; German army officer; b. 19 Sept. 1907; ed. Dresden Infantry School, Hanover Cavalry School, Air Force Acad. and Bonn. Univ.
Second Lieut. 29; transferred to Air Force; commanded Paratroop Div. 44-45; Prisoner of War 45-48; studied Economics and Law, Bonn Univ. 53-56; rejoined army 56; Dep. Asst. Chief of Staff, Logistics, NATO Headquarters 56-59; Commander-in-Chief, 1 Corps 60-63; Chief of Staff, Armed Forces of German Federal Republic 64-66.
c/o Zeppelinstr. 52, Bonn 53, German Federal Republic. Telephone: Bonn 27-111.

Trevaskis, Sir (Gerald) Kennedy (Nicholas), K.C.M.G., O.B.E.; British diplomatist; b. 1 Jan. 1915; ed. Marlborough and King's Coll., Cambridge.
Colonial Admin. Service 38, Cadet, N. Rhodesia; British Mil. Admin., Eritrea 41-48, British Admin. 48-50; Dist. Officer, N. Rhodesia 50-51; Political Officer, Western Aden Protectorate 51-52, Dep. British Agent 52-54, Adviser and British Agent 54-Jan. 63; Dep. High Commr. for Aden and the Protectorate of South Arabia Jan.-June 63, High Commr. June 63-Dec. 64; Dir. Mackenzie, King, Thompson Int. 65-.
Publ. *A Colony in Transition: the British Occupation of Eritrea* 60, *Shades of Amber* 68.
Nash Court Farmhouse, Marnhull, Dorset, England.

Trevelyan, Baron (Life Peer), cr. 68, of St. Veep, in the County of Cornwall; **Humphrey Trevelyan,** G.C.M.G., C.I.E., O.B.E.; retired British diplomatist; b. 27 Nov. 1905; ed. Lancing Coll., and Jesus Coll., Cambridge.
Joined Indian Civil Service 29; Indian Political Service 32-47; Political Agent in Indian States; Sec. to Agent-Gen. for India in Washington, D.C. 44-46; Joint Sec., Ministry of External Affairs, New Delhi 46-47; entered H.M. Foreign Service 47; Counsellor, Baghdad Embassy 48; Economic and Financial Adviser to U.K. High Commr. in Germany 51-53; Chargé d'Affaires, Peking, 53-55; Ambassador to Egypt 55-56; Under-Sec. U.N. 58; Ambassador to Iraq 58-61; Dep. Under-Sec. Foreign Office 62; Ambassador to U.S.S.R. 62-65; High Commr. in Aden 67; Pres. Council of Foreign Bondholders 67-; Dir. Matheson & Co., English Electric Co. Ltd., Marconi Co., British Petroleum Co. Ltd., British Bank of the Middle East.
English Electric House, Strand, London, W.C.2, England.
Telephone: 01-240-1234.

Trevethin, 3rd Baron, cr. 21, **and Oaksey,** 1st Baron, cr. 47, of Oaksey; **Geoffrey Lawrence,** P.C., Kt., Q.C., D.S.O., T.D., M.A.; British lawyer; b. 80; ed. Haileybury, New Coll. Oxford.
Called to the Bar 06, took Silk 25; Counsel to Jockey Club 22-32; Recorder of Oxford 24-32; Examiner in Ecclesiastical Causes 27-32; Attorney-Gen. to Prince of Wales 28-32; Judge High Court of Justice (King's Bench Div.) 32-44; a Lord Justice of Appeal 44-47; Lord of Appeal in Ordinary Mar. 47-57; British Pres. Int. Mil. Tribunal Nuremberg 45-46; Vice-Lieut. Wiltshire 54-; Hon. Fellow New Coll. Oxford 44; Hon. D.C.L. (Oxford).
Hill Farm, Oaksey, Malmesbury, Wilts., England.

Trevor-Roper, Hugh Redwald; British historian; b. 15 Jan. 1914; ed. Charterhouse and Christ Church, Oxford.
Research Fellow, Merton Coll., Oxford 37-39; Student of Christ Church, Oxford 45-57; Regius Prof. of Modern History in the Univ. of Oxford 57-.
Publs. *Archbishop Laud* 40, *The Last Days of Hitler* 47, *Hitler's Table Talk* (Editor) 53, *The Gentry 1540-1640* 54, *The Poems of Richard Corbett* (Editor, with J. A. W. Bennett) 55, *Historical Essays* 57 (American title, *Men and Events* 58), *Hitler's War Directives* (Editor) 64, *The Rise of Christian Europe* 63, *Religion, the Reformation and Social Change* 67.
Oriel College, Oxford; and 8 St. Aldate's, Oxford, England.
Telephone: 43388.

Trezise, Philip H.; American analyst and diplomatist; b. 27 May 1912; ed. Univ. of Michigan.
Research Assoc. Univ. of Michigan until 41; Analyst, Office of Defense Transportation 42; Office of Strategic Services, U.S. Navy 43-46; Chief Research Analyst, then Chief of Div. of Research for Far East, State Dept. 46, Chief of Div. of Research for Near East and Africa, later Deputy Dir. Office of Intelligence and Research, mem. Policy Planning Staff; Nat. War Coll. 49-50; Minister for Econ. Affairs, U.S. Embassy, and Dir. of Agency for Int. Devt. (AID) Mission, Tokyo 57-61; Deputy Asst. Sec. of State for Econ. Affairs 61-65; Head of U.S. Del. to Org. for Econ. Co-operation and Devt. (OECD) Jan. 66-; President's Award for Distinguished Fed. Civilian Service 65.
Organization for Economic Co-operation and Development, 2 rue André-Pascal, Paris 16e, France.

Triboulet, Raymond, L. EN DROIT, L. ès L.; French politician; b. 3 Oct. 1906; ed. Univ. of Paris.
Active in French Resistance 41-44; Sous-Préfet for Bayeux region 44-46; Regional Inspector for Rhine-Palatinate 46; Mem. Parl. 46-58; founder of Federalist group in French Parl.; Pres. of Gaullist Parl. group (Social Republicans) 54-58; Minister of War Veterans Jan.-Oct. 55; mem. ECSC Common Assembly 57; Pres. Union of New Republic (U.N.R.) 58; Minister of War Veterans 59-63, of Co-operation 63-66; Chevalier Légion d'Honneur; Croix de Guerre; Resistance Medal; O.B.E.
Publs. *Les Billets du Négus* 39, *Sens dessus dessous* 51, *Des Vessies pour des Lanternes* 58.
119 rue Brancas, Sèvres (S.-et-O.), France.

Tricart, Jean Léon François; French university professor; b. 16 Sept. 1920; ed. Lycée Rollin, Paris, and Univ. de Paris à la Sorbonne.
Assistant Lecturer, Univ. de Paris 45-48; Lecturer Univ. of Strasbourg 48-49, Asst. Prof. 49-55, Prof. 55-; Vice-Dean, mem. of Univ. Senate 67-; Principal Asst., Geological Map of France 60; Founder-Dir. Centre of Applied Geography, Strasbourg 56-; Pres. Applied Geomorphology Comm. of Int. Geographical Union 60-; Head of numerous technical co-operation missions in Senegal, Mauritania, Ivory Coast, Guinea, Togo, Mali, Brazil, Chile, Venezuela, Peru, Panama, El Salvador, Colombia and I.I.C.A.
Publs. include numerous scientific articles and *Principes et Méthodes de la Géomorphologie* 65, *Traité de Géomorphologie* (with A. Cailleux), 5 vols. to date.
Centre de Géographie Appliquée, Université de Strasbourg, 43 rue Goethe, 67 Strasbourg; and 85 route de la Meinau, Strasbourg-Meinau 67, France.
Telephone: 35-59-40, ext. 449.

Tricornot de Rose, Comte François de; French diplomatist; b. 3 Nov. 1910; ed. Ecole Libre des Sciences Politiques, Paris.
Secretary Embassy to U.K. 37-40, Italy 45-46; mem. French del. to UN 46-50; Minister to Spain 52-56; Ministry of Foreign Affairs, Paris 56-60; mem. Atomic

Energy Comm. (Paris) 50-64; Pres. European Nuclear Research Org. (CERN) 58-60; Deputy Chief of Staff, Nat. Defence 61-62; mem. Board Institut Français d'Etudes Stratégiques 62-64; Ambassador to Portugal 64-; Officier Légion d'Honneur.

Embassy of France, Palais d'Abiantes, rua dos Santos-o-Velho 5, Lisbon, Portugal.

Triffin, Robert, LL.D., PH.D.ECON.; American (born Belgian) economist; b. 10 June 1911; ed. Kain-lez Tournai, Louvain Univ., Harvard Univ.

Instructor, Harvard 39-42; Chief Latin American Div., Bd. of Govs. Fed. Reserve System 42-46; Int. Monetary Fund, Chief Exchange Control Div. 46-48, Chief Rep. in Europe 48-49; Special Policy Adviser, Econ. Co-operation Admin. and Alternate U.S. Rep. European Payments Union 49-51; Pelatiah Perit Prof. of Political and Social Science (Econ.) Yale Univ. 51-; headed numerous monetary and banking reorganisation missions to Latin American countries, Iran, etc.; Consultant to UN 52; Council of Econ. Advisers (U.S.) 53-54, 61; Consultant OEEC 57-58, EEC 58-; Vice-Pres. American Economic Assen. 66-67; mem. Council of Economic Advisers, Société d'Econ. Pol. (Paris); mem. American Acad. of Arts and Sciences, Assoc. Acad. Royale de Belgique; Wells Prize, Harvard 39.

Publs. *Monopolistic Competition and General Equilibrium Theory* 40, *Monetary and Banking Reform in Paraguay* 46, *Europe and the Money Muddle* 57, *Gold and the Dollar Crisis* 60, *The Evolution of the International Monetary System: Historical Reappraisal and Future Perspectives* 64, *The World Money Maze: National Currencies in International Payments* 66, *Our International Monetary System: Yesterday, Today and Tomorrow* 68.

Office: 37 Hillhouse Avenue, Yale University, New Haven, Conn. 06520; Home: 97 Loomis Place, New Haven, Conn. 06511, U.S.A.

Telephone: 787-3131, ext. 2087 (Office); 777-4380 (Home).

Trigo de Negreiros, Joaquim; Portuguese politician; b. 1900.

Pres. Municipal Chamber, Vila Flora 26; Asst. to Attorney Gen. of the Republic 36; Civil Gov. of Oporto 38; Under Sec. of State for Corporations and Social Security 40, for Social Welfare 44; Minister of the Interior 55-57; Pres. Supreme Administrative Court 58-; awards include Grand Cross Order of Christ, of the Southern Cross, of Civil Merit (Spain), of St. Gregory (Vatican), of Orange Nassau (Neths.), of Order of Greece; Commdr. Order of the Crown (Italy); Hon. C.B.E. (U.K.).

Publs. *Crédito Agricola, Assistência Social, Madeira e Açores, Pensamento e Acção.*

Rua Rodrigo da Fonseca 143-1°, Lisbon, Portugal.

Trilling, Lionel, PH.D.; American writer and university professor; b. 4 July 1905; ed. Columbia Univ.

Instructor Univ. of Wisconsin 26-27, Hunter Coll. 27-30; Instructor in English, Columbia Univ. 31, Asst. Prof. 38, Assoc. Prof. 43, Prof. 48-65; George Edward Woodberry Prof. of Literature and Criticism, Columbia Univ. 65-; Eastman Prof., Oxford Univ. 64; mem. Nat. Inst. of Arts and Letters, American Acad. of Arts and Sciences; Senior Fellow, School of Letters, Indiana Univ.; Hon. Litt.D. (Trinity Coll., Hartford, and Harvard Univ.).

Publs. *Matthew Arnold* 39, *E. M. Forster* 43, *The Middle of the Journey* 47, *The Liberal Imagination* 50, *The Opposing Self* 55, *Freud and the Crisis of our Culture* 56, *A Gathering of Fugitives* 56, *Beyond Culture* 66.

Hamilton Hall, Columbia University, New York 27, N.Y., U.S.A.

Trillo Pays, Dionisio Martin Enrique; Uruguayan author and librarian; b. 09; ed. Univ. of the Republic, Montevideo.

Dir. Nat. Library of Uruguay 47-; mem. Nat. Comm. for Archives of Artigas 47; mem. Council on Legal Rights of Authors 47; Editor *Asir*, literary review 49-.

Publs. *Mediodía* (play) 40, *Pompeyo Amargo* 42, *Zarzas* (stories) 44, *Estas hojas no caen en otoño* 46, *El patio de los naranjos* (play) 50.

Biblioteca Nacional, Guayabo 1793, Montevideo, Uruguay.

Tripathy, Sadasiba; Indian politician; b. 10; ed. High School, Jeypore.

Member Orissa Legislative Assembly 37; Minister of Revenue, Orissa 48-56, 61-65; mem. All-India Congress Cttee. 38-55; Exec. mem. Pradesh Congress Cttee. 38-55; Sec. Orissa Bhoodan Yagna 59-61; Chief Minister of Orissa 65-Feb. 67.

Bhuvaneshwar, Orissa, India.

Trippe, Juan Terry; American airline executive; b. 27 June 1899; ed. Yale Univ.

With Lee Higginson Co. 21-22; Pres. L. I. Airways Inc. 22-23; Man. Dir. Colonial Air Transport Inc. 24-26; Pres., Dir. Pan American World Airways Inc. 27-64, Chair. and Chief Exec. Officer 64-68; official of numerous other companies and civic orgs., recipient of numerous awards.

10 Gracie Square, New York City 28, U.S.A.

Tritton, Arthur Stanley, M.A., D.LITT.; British orientalist; b. 81; ed. Mansfield Coll. and St. Catherine's Soc., Oxford, and Univ. of Göttingen.

Asst., Edinburgh Univ. 11, Glasgow Univ. 19; Prof. of Arabic, Univ. of Aligarh, India 21; School of Oriental Studies 31, Prof. of Arabic 38-47.

Publs. *Rise of the Imams of Sanaa* 25, *Caliphs and their non-Muslim Subjects* 30, *Teach Yourself Arabic* 43, *Muslim Theology* 47, *Islam, Belief and Practices* 50, *Materials on Muslim Education* 57.

44 Kensington Gardens Square, London, W.2, England.

Trivedi, Sir Chandulal Madhavlal, K.C.S.I., C.I.E., O.B.E., B.A.; Indian civil servant; b. 2 July 1893; ed. Bombay Univ., Elphinstone Coll., Bombay, and St. John's Coll., Oxford.

Entered I.C.S. 17; served as Asst. Commr., Central Provinces 17-21; after serving in various capacities, posted as Dep. Sec. to Govt. of India Home Dept. 32-35 (Act. Joint Sec. April-Sept. 34); Sec. to Govt. of India Secretariat Organisation Cttee. 35-36; Commr. Berar 36, Chattisgarh Div. 36-37; Chief Sec. to Govt. C.P. and Berar 37-Mar. 42; Sec. to Govt. of India War Dept. July 42-Jan. 46; Gov. of Orissa April 46-Aug. 47; Gov. of Punjab from Aug. 15th 47-53; Gov. of Andhra 53-56; Gov. of Andhra Pradesh 56-57; mem. Planning Comm. Govt. of India 57-63; Chair. Madhya Pradesh Police Comm. 64-65; Hon. LL.D. (Punjab Univ.); Hon. D.Litt. (Andhra Univ.); Padma Vibhushan award 56; Chancellor Gujarat Ayurveda Univ. Nov. 66-.

Chandra-Bhuvan, Kapadwanj, Gujarat, India.

Trivedi, Vishnuprasad Chunilal, B.A., M.A.; Indian diplomatist; b. 12 Feb. 1916; ed. Bombay and Cambridge Univs.

Joined Govt. service 40; posts in different economic depts.; Under-Sec. Dept. of Commerce 45-47, Deputy Sec. 47-50, 53-55; Joined Indian Foreign Service 48; First Sec., Tokyo 50-53; Counsellor London 55-59, Deputy High Commr. East Pakistan 59-60, and High Commr. Karachi, Pakistan 60-61; Joint Sec. Ministry of External Affairs 61-64; Ambassador to Switzerland, concurrently accred. to the Vatican, and 18-nation Cttee. on Disarmament 64-67; Amb. to Japan 67-; Alt. Rep. ECOSOC 62, 63 and 65, Rep. to UN Gen. Assembly 63 and 65.

Embassy of India, 1-2 chome, Kodan, Chiyoda-ku, Tokyo, Japan.

Trnka, Jiří; Czechoslovak painter, stage designer and creator of cartoon and puppet films; b. 24 Feb. 1912; ed. School of Fine and Applied Arts, Prague.

Worked as illustrator of children's books and theatrical stage designer 35-45; created puppet and cartoon films 45-; awards from film festivals at Venice, Edinburgh, Locarno, etc.; Laureate of the State Prize 54, Czechoslovak Peace Prize 58, Nat. Artist 65.

Films: *Spaliček* 47, *Bajaja* 50, *Ancient Czech Legends* 53, *The Emperor's Nightingale* 48, *A Midsummer Night's Dream*, etc.

Office: Cartoon Film Studio, Konviktská ul., Prague 1; Home: Kampa Hroznová 500, Malá Straner, Prague 1, Czechoslovakia.

Troadec, René; French overseas governor; b. 6 July 1908; ed. Paris Univ. Law Faculty, and Ecole Nat. de la France d'Outre-Mer, Paris.

Admin., Middle Congo 34-39; officer in War 39-45; Dir. of Recruitment, Ecole Nat. de la France d'Outre-Mer 45-48; Sec.-Gen. French West African Ex-Servicemen's Office 48-53; Commdr., Cercle Dimbroko, Ivory Coast 54; Sec.-Gen. French Somaliland Govt. 54-56; Sec.-Gen. Ivory Coast 56; Gov. and High Comm., Chad 56-59; Sec.-Gen. French Equatorial Africa Govt. 59-60; First Councillor of Gen. High Comm. in Brazzaville 59-60; Man. attached to the Gen. Management of C.S.F.; Commdr. Légion d'Honneur, Compagnon de la Libération, Rosette de la Résistance, Croix de Guerre. Compagnie Générale de Telegraphie sans Fil, B.P. 2000, 78 Versailles and 6 rue Montmorency, Boulogne 92, France.

Telephone: 950-92-00 (Office); 605-31-37 (Home).

Troast, Paul L.; American engineer; b. 19 Nov. 1894. Engineer, Francisco & Jacobus 17-28; Chair. of the Board Mahony-Troast Construction Co., Clifton, N.J., and Camden, N.J. 28-; official of other companies. Home: 324 Dwasline Road, Clifton; Office: 790 Bloomfield Avenue, Clifton, N.J., U.S.A.

Telephone: 201-779-4803 (Home).

Troclet, Léon-Eli; Belgian barrister and politician; b. 02; ed. Univ. of Liège.

Leader of Socialist youth movement 18; Provincial Councillor Liège 28-32; Prof. and Dir. Ecole de Droit Admin. et de Police 32-45; Belgian Del. to L. of N. 31; Senator 44; Min. of Labour and Social Insurance 45-49; Vice-Pres. of Bourse du Travail (Labour Exchange) and of Unemployment Claims Comm. 34; juridical assessor to Arbitration Tribunal of Liège 27-45; mem. of clandestine Walloon Economic Council and Cttee. of Walloon Congress 43-44; Prof. of Law and Social Legislation, Univ. of Brussels; mem. European Parliament and Pres. of its Social Affairs Cttee.; Chair. I.L.O. 50-51; Minister of Labour and Social Welfare 54-58; Govt. del. to I.L.O. 45-66; Socialist.

Publs. *La réglementation de l'assurance chômage* 38, *La Wallonie et les Allocations familiales* 39, *L'influence de la guerre sur les contrats de travail et d'emploi* (2 vols.) 41, *Guide pratique de législation sociale* 42, *Problèmes belges de la sécurité sociale* 49, 62, *Signification sociale du déficit de l'Assurance-maladie* 50, 63, *Législation Sociale Internationale* (3 vols.) 52-62, *Droit Social Européen* 64, *Statut Juridique des représentants de Commerce* 64, *La loi sur la protection des rénumérations* 65.

Rue de Sclessin 4, Liège, Belgium.

Troeger, Heinrich, DR. IUR.; German banker; b. 4 March 1901; ed. Univs. of Breslau, Würzburg and Halle.

Mayor of Neusalz/Oder 26; Currency and Tax Law Consultant, Berlin 34-45; Lord Mayor of Jena 45-46; Sec.-Gen. Bizonal Länder Council 47-50; Ministerial Dir. and Deputy Minister of Finance, North-Rhine Westphalia 50; Minister of Finance, Hesse 51-56; Pres., Hesse Central Bank, Frankfurt 56-57; Vice-Pres. Deutsche Bundesbank, Frankfurt 58-; Grosses Bundesverdienstkreuz 66.

Publs. *Steuerstrafrecht, Finanzpolitische Fragen der Gegenwart, Mitarbeit am Gutachten über die Finanzreform.*

Taunusanlage 4-6, Frankfurt/Main, German Federal Republic.

Telephone: 2682 Frankfurt.

Troendle, Max, LL.D.; Swiss diplomatist; b. 15 Jan. 1905; ed. Univs. of Basle and Paris.

Swiss Diplomatic Service 31-, Munich, Zagreb, Warsaw, Riga and Rome; Del. of Swiss Govt. for Economic Negotiations and Pres. of Swiss Claims Comm. for Nationalisation 45-54; Minister to Japan 54-59, Ambassador to Japan 59-61; Ambassador to U.S.S.R. 61-64; Ambassador to German Federal Republic 64-. Embassy of Switzerland, Bayenthalgürtel 15, 5 Köln-Bayenthal, German Federal Republic.

Telephone: 38-14-41.

Trofimuk, Andrei Alexeevich; Soviet petroleum geologist; b. 16 Aug. 1911; ed. State Univ. of Kazan. Head Geologist and Scientific Leader of Central Research Laboratory of the "Vostokneft" Trust 34-40; Chief Geologist "Ishimbaineft" Trust 40-42, "Bashneft" Soc. 42-50; Chief Geologist, Main Oil and Gas Exploration Dept., Ministry of Oil Industry of U.S.S.R. 50-53; Dep. Dir. All-Union Oil and Gas Scientific Research Inst. 53-55, Dir. 55-58; Dir. Inst. of Geology and Geophysics, Siberian Branch, U.S.S.R. Acad. of Sciences 58-; mem. U.S.S.R. Acad. of Sciences 58-; mem. U.S.S.R. Acad. of Sciences Presidium, First Vice-Chair. Siberian Branch; Editor *Geology and Geophysics*; Hero of Socialist Labour 44, State Prizes 46, 50, Hon. Scientist of R.S.F.S.R. 57, Order of Lenin 50, Order of Red Banner of Labour 59, 61.

Publs. *On the Nature of Ishimbaevo Oil-Bearing Massifs* 36, *An Outline of Tectonics and Oil Content of Volga-Ural Region* 39, *Oil Content of Paleozoic Beds of Bashkiria* 50, *Conditions of Formation of Oil Deposits of Ural-Volga Oil-Bearing Region* 55, *Gas Resources of the U.S.S.R.* 59, *Oil and Gas Content of Siberian Platform* 60, *Gas-Bearing Prospects of the U.S.S.R.* 63, *Geology and Oil and Gas Content of West Siberian Lowland, a New Oil-Bearing Province of the U.S.S.R.* 63, *Oil- and Gas-Bearing Basins of the U.S.S.R.* 64, *Tectonics and Oil and Gas-Bearing prospects of Platform Regions of Siberia* (with Yu. A. Kosygin) 65, *Some Questions on the Theory of Organic Origin of Oil and the problem of Diagnostics of Oil-Source Beds* (with A. E. Kontorovich) 65, *On the Methods of Calculation of Prognostic Reserves of Oil* 66.

87 Zolotodolinskaya Street, Novosibirsk 90, U.S.S.R.

Troll, Carl, PH.D.; German professor of geography; b. 24 Dec. 1899; ed. Univ. of Munich.

Asst. in Geographical Inst., Univ. of Munich 22; Lecturer in Geography 25; Prof. of Geography, Univ. of Berlin 30; Prof. of Econ. Geography 36; Prof. of Geography and Dir. of Geographical Inst., Univ. of Bonn 38-; Rector Bonn Univ. 60-61; scientific expeditions to South America 26-29; expedition to East Africa 33-34; scientific leader of the German Himalaya expedition to Nanga Parbat 37; expedition to Abyssinia 37, to Mexico 54; mem. Acads. of Berlin, Munich, Halle, Bucharest, Mainz, Vienna, Helsinki, Rome, Venice, Buenos Aires, etc.; Pres. Int. Geographical Union 60; Carus Medal 38, Vega Medal 51, Ritter Medal 59, Victoria Medal 62, Martin Behaim Medal 59, Penck Medal 64; Dr.Sc.h.c., Dr.Phil.h.c., and other awards.

Publs. *Diluvial Geology* 24, *Bolivian Andes* 29, *Geography of South America* 30, *Vegetation of N.W. Himalaya* 39, *Colonial Land Planning of Africa* 41, *Glaciology* 42, *Geomorphology* 44, *Periglacial Geomorphology* 47-48, *Geography in Germany 1933-1945* 47, *Tropical Mountains* 59, *Physiognomy of Tropical Plants* 59, *Gr. Herder Atlas* 58, *Seasonal Climates of the Earth* 64, *Landscape Ecology and High Mountain Research* 66, *Air Photo Interpretation* 66, *Plural Societies of Developing*

Countries 66; Editor of *Erdkunde* 47-; Editor of *Bonner Geogr. Abhandl.* 47-, of *Colloquium Geographicum* 50-, of *Arbeiten zur Rheinischen Landeskunde* 52-.
Rheinbacherstrasse 55, 53 Bonn/Rhein, German Federal Republic.
Telephone: 36036.

Trollip, Alfred Ernest; South African lawyer and politician; b. 16 July 1895; ed. Jeppe High School, Johannesburg, and Witwatersrand Univ.
Deputy Speaker and Chairman of Cttees., Union Parl. 43-48; Administrator of Natal 58-61; Minister of Labour and Immigration Nov. 61-66, of Immigration and Indian Affairs 66-.
Ministry of Immigration, Pretoria, South Africa.

Trowbridge, Alexander B.; American government official; b. 1930; ed. Phillips Acad., Andover, Mass., and Princeton Univ.
U.S. Marine Corps during Korean War; with overseas operations of several petroleum companies in Cuba, El Salvador, Panama and Philippines; Pres. and Div. Man. Esso Standard Oil Co. of Puerto Rico until 65; Asst. Sec. of Commerce for Domestic and Int. Business 65-67; Acting Sec. of Commerce Feb. 67-May 67, Sec. of Commerce May 67-68.
4311 Garfield Street, N.W., Washington, D.C. 20007, U.S.A.

Troyanovsky, Oleg Alexandrovich; Soviet diplomatist; b. 1919; ed. Moscow Foreign Languages Inst., Moscow Inst. of Philosophy, Literature and History.
Diplomatic service 44; took part in many important confs.; Amb. to Japan 68-.
U.S.S.R. Embassy, 1 Azabu-Mamianacho, Minato-ku, Tokyo, Japan.

Troyat, Henri (*pseudonym* of Tarasoff); French writer; b. 1 Nov. 1911; ed. Lycée Pasteur, and Law Faculty, Univ. of Paris.
Mem. Acad. Française 59-; Légion d'Honneur.
Publs. *Faux-Jour* (Prix Populiste) 35, *L'Araigne* (Prix Goncourt) 38, *La Neige en Deuil* (Grand prix litteraire de Monaco) 52, *Tant que la terre durera* (three vols.) 47-50, *Les semailles et les moissons* (five vols.) 53-58, *La Lumière des Justes* (five vols.) 60-, *Les Eygletière* 65, *La Malandre* 67, *Les Méritiers de l'avenir* 68, etc.; biographies: *Dostoïevsky, Pouchkine, Tolstoi.*
5 rue Bonaparte, Paris 6e, France.

Trucco Gaete, Manuel; Chilean journalist, politician and diplomatist; b. 14; ed. Instituto Nacional de Santiago, Univ. of Chile, and Univ. of Georgetown, Washington.
Official of firm Salitre y Yodo, Santiago, Iquique and New York 39-43; Head Spanish Broadcasting Dept., Co-ordinator of Inter-American Affairs, New York 44-46; Under-Sec. of Foreign Affairs, Chile 46-52; Pres. Chilean Treaty Comm. 47-52; Dir. Línea Aérea Nacional 46-52; Editor *La Nación*, Santiago 46-52; Exec. Sec. Chilean Nat. Press Asscn. 54-59; Pres. of Int. Comm. and Dir. of Dept. of Int. Affairs, Radical Party 54-59; Chilean Ambassador to Bolivia 59-62; Ambassador to Organization of American States (OAS) 62-64.
Santiago, Chile.

Trudeau, Hon. Pierre Elliott, M.P.; Canadian lawyer and politician; b. 1921; ed. Collège Jean-de-Brébeuf, Montreal, Univ. of Montreal, Harvard Univ., Univ. of Paris, and London School of Economics.
Called to Bar, Province of Quebec 43, then studied at Harvard, Paris and London; subsequently employed with Cabinet Secr., Ottawa; later practised law, Province of Quebec; one of founders of *Cité Libre* (Quebec review); Assoc. Prof. of Law, Univ. of Montreal 61; mem. House of Commons 65-; Parl. Sec. to Prime Minister Jan. 66-April 67; Minister of Justice and Attorney-Gen. April 67-July 68; Leader of Liberal Party and Prime Minister of Canada April 68-.
Publs. *La Grève de l'Amiante, Deux Innocents en Chine*

(co-author), *La Fédéralisme et la Société canadienne-française* 67; and numerous articles in Canadian and foreign journals.
Prime Minister's Residence, 34 Sussex Drive, Ottawa, Canada.

Trueta, Joseph, M.A., M.D., F.R.C.S.; b. 27 Oct. 1897; Spanish-born British surgeon; ed. Barcelona Inst. and Univ.
House Surgeon Santa Creu Hospital Barcelona 21, Asst. Surgeon 28; Auxiliary Prof. Barcelona Univ. 32; Dir. of Surgery Gen. Hospital of Catalonia, Barcelona Univ. 35; Acting Surgeon-in-Charge Accident Service, Radcliffe Infirmary Oxford 42-44; Nuffield Prof. of Orthopaedic Surgery, Oxford 49-66, Prof. Emer. 66-; Hon. mem. British Orthopaedic Asscn. 40; Hon. F.R.C.S. (Canada); Hon. Fellow American Coll. of Surgeons; Hon. mem. Italian, French, German and S. American socs. of Orthopaedics and Traumatology, Portuguese Orthopaedic Soc., Scandinavian Orthopaedic Soc., Foreign Assoc., French Acad. of Surgery; Hon. Pres. Int. Soc. Surgery and Traumatology; Dr. h.c. (Oxford, Buenos Aires, Rio de Janeiro, Bogotá, Gothenburg Univs.); Commdr. Southern Cross, Officier Légion d'Honneur.
Publs. *Els tumors Malignes Primitius dels Ossos* 35, *La Hidatidosi Ossia* 36, *Tractament de les Fractures de Guerra* 38, *Treatment of War Wounds and Fractures* 39, *Principles and Practice of War Surgery* 43, *The Spirit of Catalonia* 46, *Studies of the Renal Circulation* (in collaboration) 47, *Atlas of Traumatic Surgery* 49, *Handbook on Poliomyelitis* (in collaboration) 56.
Overmead, Jack Straw's Lane, Headington Hill, Oxford, England.

Truffaut, François; French film director; b. 6 Feb. 1932; ed. secondary school.
Former journalist, cinema critic, publisher of *Cahiers du Cinéma* and *Arts*; Film Dir. 57-; First Prize Cannes Festival for *Les 400 Coups* 59.
Films: *Les Mistons, Les 400 Coups, Tirez sur le Pianiste, Jules et Jim, L'Amour à Vingt Ans, La Peau Douce, Fahrenheit 451, La Mariée était en Noir* 67.
Publ. (with Helen G. Scott) *Hitchcock* 67.
5 rue Robert-Estienne, Paris 8, France.

Trujillo Molina, General Hector Bienvenido; Dominican army officer and politician; b. 08; ed. Univ. of Santo Domingo.
Entered Army 26; Chief of Staff of Army 36; Supervisor-Gen. of National Police 38-43; Secretary of War, C.-in-C. of Army and Navy 44; succeeded his brother as Pres. of the Dominican Republic 52-60; Prof. American Int. Acad., Washington; corresp. mem. Nat. Athenaeum Arts and Sciences, Mexico; holds numerous military and other decorations of his own and foreign countries.
Living abroad.

Truman, Harry S.; American politician; b. 8 May 1884; ed. Kansas City School of Law.
Operated family farm 06-17; served U.S. Army (Artillery) in First World War 17-18; discharged with rank of Major in Reserve Corps, Col. Reserve Corps 27-52; Judge, Jackson County (Mo.) Court 22-24; Presiding Judge 26-34; Senator from Missouri 34-44; served on Appropriations, Enrolled Bills, Mil. Affairs, Printing, Interstate Commerce, and Public Buildings and Grounds Cttees., and as Chair. Special Cttee. to investigate Nat. Defence Programme; Vice-Pres. of U.S.A. Jan.-April 45; succeeded Pres. Roosevelt as Pres. of U.S.A. 12th April 45; elected for second term 49-53; awarded some fourteen hon. degrees by various institutions; Woodrow Wilson Award for distinguished services on behalf of UN 50; New York City Medal of Honor 50; Democrat.
Publs. *Autobiography: Vol. I, Years of Decisions* 55, Vol. II, *Years of Trial and Hope* 56, *Mr. Citizen* 60.
219 North Delaware Street, Independence, Missouri, U.S.A.

Trusov, Alexei Alexeyevich; Soviet trade corporation official; b. 07; ed. Leningrad Motor Highway Inst. and Leningrad Inst. of Oriental Studies.
Assistant Soviet Trade Rep. in Mongolian People's Republic 39-46, Rep. 47-50, in Korea 50-51, in Poland 56-61; Ministry of Foreign Trade 52, 54-56; Chair. *Mashinoexport* (mining, electrical machines and railway stock) 54-56, *Vostokintorg* 61-65; Trade Rep. to Turkey 65-; mem. Communist Party of Soviet Union; Order of Red Banner of Labour, etc.
U.S.S.R. Trade Mission, Ankara, Turkey.

Tryoshnikov, Alexey Fyodorovich, D.SC.; Soviet Polar explorer; b. 14 April 1914; ed. Leningrad Univ.
Head of the Soviet drifting station SP-3 in the Arctic 54-55; Head Soviet Int. Geophysical Year Antarctic Expedition to Mirny 56-58; Dir. Arctic and Antarctic Scientific Research Inst., Leningrad 60-; Hero of Socialist Labour.
Ul. Kuibysheva 1/5, kv. 121, Leningrad; and The Arctic and Antarctic Research Institute, Leningrad, U.S.S.R.

Trypanis, Constantine Athanasius, M.A., D.PHIL.; Greek university professor; b. 22 Jan. 1909; ed. Univs. of Athens, Berlin and Munich.
Lecturer in Classical Literature Athens Univ. 39; Bywater and Sotheby Prof. of Byzantine and Modern Greek, Univ. of Oxford 47-68; Prof. of Classics, Univ. of Chicago 68; Emeritus Fellow of Exeter Coll., Oxford; Fellow Royal Soc. of Literature, Int. Inst. of Arts and Letters; Archon Hieromnemon of the Oekumenical Patriarchate; Visiting Prof., U.S. univs. 63, 64, 65, 66; Visiting mem. Inst. for Advanced Study, Princeton 59-60; Corresp. mem. of Inst. for Balkan Studies, Salonica, and of Center for Neo-Hellenic Studies, Austin, Texas.
Publs. *The Influence of Hesiod upon the Homeric Hymn to Hermes* 39, *Alexandrian Poetry* 43, *Tartessos, Phanagorea, Alexandria eschate* 45, *Medieval and Modern Greek Poetry* 51, *Pedasus* 55, *The Stones of Troy* 57, *Callimachus* 58, *The Cocks of Hades* 58, *Sancti Romani Melodi Cantica* 63, *Pompeian Dog* 64, *Fourteen Early Byzantine Cantica* 68.
Exeter College, Oxford, England; and Dept. of Classics, Univ. of Chicago, Chicago, Ill., U.S.A.

Tsai Chang (Mme. Li Fu-chun); Chinese politician; b. *c.* 99; ed. France.
Joined C.C.P. in France 22; married Li Fu-chun 23; propaganda work in North Expedition 25-27; organised women in Wuhan; in Moscow for Sixth Congress, Third International; underground work in Kuomintang areas; organised women in Shensi-Kansu-Ningsia border areas 41; Cttee. of All-China Trade Unions 48; Chair. Nat. Women's Fed. of China 49-; Hunan del. to First N.P.C. and on Standing Cttee. 54; Vice-Chair. Women's International Democratic Fed.
National Women's Federation of China, Peking, People's Republic of China.

Ts'ao Chu-ju; Chinese economist and financial expert.
Mem. of Cttee. of Financial and Economic Affairs 49; Deputy Dir. Central Financial and Economic Planning Bureau 50, Dir. 52; Deputy Dir. People's Bank of China 53, Dir. 54-67.
c/o People's Bank of China, 37 Hsi Chiao Min Hsiang, Peking, China.

Tsao Yü (Wan Chia-pao); Chinese dramatist; b. 10; ed. Tsinghua Univ.
Lectured Acad. Dramatic Art; mem. of Nankai Dramatic Club 26-30; mem. of Chinese Society for the Study of Drama; in war, Dir. National Acad. Dramatic Art, Chungking; visited U.S. at invitation of State Dept.; attended All-China Fed. of Literary and Art Circles; Dir. Peking People's Acad. of Dramatic Art 52-55;

Hupeh del. to First N.P.C.; on Peking City Council 55; Vice-Chair. Peking Fed. of Literary and Art Circles; Vice-Chair. Union of Chinese Drama Workers 60-; Sec. Chinese Writers' Asscn. 56.
Publs. Plays: *Thunderstorm, Sunrise, Peking Man,* etc. (some translated into English).
Union of Chinese Drama Workers, Peking, China.

Tsarapkin, Semyon Konstantinovich; Soviet diplomatist; b. 1906; ed. Moscow Oriental Inst.
Worker in smelting plant; transferred for advanced political training; Deputy Head, Head, Second Eastern Dept., later Far Eastern Dept., Ministry of Foreign Affairs 37-44; Head, U.S.A. Dept. 44-47; Minister, Soviet Embassy, Washington 47-49; Deputy Perm. Rep. to UN Security Council 49-54; Head of Div. for Int. Organizations, Moscow 54-66; Head Soviet del. to Geneva Disarmament Talks 61-66; Amb. to German Fed. Republic 66-; Orders of Red Banner of Labour, Badge of Honour, Great Patriotic War (1st Class), etc.
U.S.S.R. Embassy, Bonn, German Federal Republic.

Tsatsos, Constantine; Greek lawyer and politician; b. 99; ed. School of Law, Athens Univ. and Univ. of Heidelberg.
Practised law 21; Assoc. Prof. of Law, Athens Univ. 30-32, Prof. of Law 32; Minister of the Interior and of Press and Air 45; Mem. Parl. for Athens 46-50; Minister of Education 49; Under-Sec. of State for Economic Co-ordination 50-51; Minister attached to Prime Minister 56-61; M.P. for Athens 61-; Pres. Acad. of Athens; Del. to Inter-Parl. Congress, Cairo 47, Rome 48.
Publs. *Der Begriff der Positiven Rechts* 28; in Greek *The Problem of Interpreting the Law* 32, *The Problem of the Sources of the Law* 41, *Social Philosophy of the Ancient Greeks* 38, *Palamas* 35, *Dialogues on Poetry* 39, *Greece on the March* 53, *At the Roots of American Democracy* 55.
9 Kydathinaion Street, Athens, Greece

Tsatsos, Vice-Admiral Constantinos: Greek naval officer; b. 01; ed. Naval Cadet College
Sub-Lieut. 23; served in destroyers as Exec. Officer and Commanding Officer; Commr. 40; Commanding Officer H.H.M.S. *Aspis,* sunk through enemy action; taken prisoner while attempting escape to Middle East 43; condemned to death but sentence commuted to 15 years; liberated by U.S. Forces May 45; served with SHAEF, Frankfurt, and as Naval Attaché, Paris, before returning Greece; A.D.C. to the King 46; Capt. 47; held various naval appointments, including Chief of Naval Personnel, Ministry of the Navy; Rear-Admiral 52; Chief Naval Training, C.-in-C. Royal Arsenal 53; C.-in-C. Fleet 53-57; Deputy Chief of Naval Operations 57-58, Chief and NATO Commdr. Eastern Mediterranean 58; C.-in-C. Naval Operations 58-59; Minister of Justice April 67.
Vassileos Constantinou 61, Kifissia, Athens, Greece.

Tschudi, Hans Peter, LL.D.; Swiss politician; b. 22 Oct. 1913; ed. Basle Univ.
Professor of Labour Law, Basle Univ. 52-59; Head of Home Dept. Govt. of Basle 53-59; Mem. of Fed. Parl. 56-59; Head of Home Dept. Swiss Govt. 59-; Vice-Pres. Swiss Confederation 64, Pres. 65; Socialist.
Publs. *Die Ferien im schweizerischen Arbeitsrecht* 48, *Koalitionsfreiheit und Koalitionszwang* 48, *Die Sicherung des Arbeitsfriedens durch das schweizerische Recht* 52, *Gesamtarbeitsvertrag und Aussenseiter* 53.
Departement des Innern, Bundeshaus-Inselgasse, 3003 Berne; Matterstrasse 6, Berne, Switzerland.
Telephone: 031-61-24-05 (Office).

Tselikov, Alexander Ivanovich; Soviet metallurgist; b. 1904; ed. Bauman Higher Technical School, Moscow.
Designer, Engineer, metallurgical plants 25-35; Lecturer, Higher Schools 35-45; Research Work, U.S.S.R. Research and Designing Inst. for Metallurgical Eng.

45-, Dir. 59-; mem. C.P.S.U. 45-; mem. U.S.S.R. Acad. of Sciences 64-; State Prize (thrice) and Lenin Prize; Hero of Socialist Labour.
Publs. Basic works on designing and developing of new metallurgical and foundry equipment.
U.S.S.R. Academy of Sciences, 14 Lenin Prospekt, Moscow, U.S.S.R.

Tsendenbal, Yumzhagiin; Mongolian politician.
Chairman of the Council of Ministers of the Mongolian People's Republic; First Secretary of the Political Bureau of the Mongolian People's Revolutionary Party.
Council of Ministers, Ulan-Bator, Mongolian People's Republic.

Tseng Shan; Chinese administrator; b. 04.
Mem. of the Soviet Govt. established at Juichin 31; Chair. Kiangsi Soviet; Chief of Organisation Dept., C.C.P.; Central Cttee. mem. at Seventh Congress C.C.P. 45; again Chief, Organisation Dept.; Minister of Textile Industry 49; posts in North China Admin.; Vice-Dir. Financial and Economic Commission, State Council and Minister of Commerce 52; Minister of Internal Affairs 60-; del to C.P.P.C.C. for C.C.P. 54; Central Cttee. mem. Eighth Congress, C.C.P. 56.
Ministry of Internal Affairs, Peking, China.

Tsevegmid, Dondogiin; Mongolian biologist and diplomatist; b. 26 March 1915; ed. Moscow Univ.
Teacher 30-45; Chancellor Ulan-Bator Univ., and Chair. Cttee. of Sciences 51-60; Deputy Minister of Foreign Affairs 60-62; Ambassador to People's Republic of China 62-; Del. to UN 61; Corresp. mem. Mongolian Acad. of Sciences.
Publs. *The Ecological and Morphological Analyses of the Duplicidentate* 50, *Fauna of the Transaltai* 63, *Selected Works* 46, 56.
Embassy of Mongolia, Peking, People's Republic of China; Department of Zoology, University of Ulan-Bator, Ulan-Bator, Mongolia.

Tshombe, Moise; Congolese (Katangan) politician; b. 10 Nov. 1919; ed. Methodist Mission School, Belgian Congo.
Joined father's business of trading stores and hotel, Elisabethville, took over business 51; fmr. Pres. African Chamber of Commerce, Elisabethville; Pres. Lunda Tribal Asscn. 56; Pres. Conakat Party 59-; Premier, Katanga Province, Congolese Republic 60-62, of South Katanga 62-June 63; Prime Minister, Minister of Foreign Affairs Information and External Commerce, Congo Republic July 64-65, also Minister of Posts and Telegraphs, Economic Development and Planning, Labour and Social Security, Interior and Civil Service Administration; detained Coquihatville and Léopold-ville 61; ousted from Congolese Parl. May 66; detained in Algiers July 67-.
Publ. *Quinze mois de gouvernement au Congo* (memoirs) 66.
c/o Ministry of Justice, Algiers, Algeria.

Tsiebo, Calvin; Madagascan politician; b. 12 July 1902; ed. Mission schools.
Lieutenant-Governor Native Admin. 25-37, Local Admin. 37-49, Gov. 49-56; Admin. Sec. Madagascar 56-57; Provincial Counsellor Tuléar 57-58; Deputy Provincial Govt. 58-60; Vice-Pres. Madagascar 60-, concurrently Minister of Social Affairs and Admin. Co-ordination 65-; Ministry of Labour; several honours.
Office of the Vice-President, Tananarive, Madagascar.
Telephone: 234-11.

Tsien Hsue-shen; Chinese atomic scientist; b. 2 Sept. 1909; ed. Chiaotung Univ., Massachusetts Inst. of Technology and California Inst. of Technology.
Research worker and teacher Calif. Inst. of Technology 41-48; returned to China 48, then returned to Calif. Inst. of Technology; later Goddard Prof. of Jet Propulsion and Dir. Rocket Section, Nat. Defense Scientific

Advisory Board (U.S.A.); returned to China after trial as Communist 55; mem. Chinese Acad. of Sciences 55; mem. Chinese C.P. 56-; believed to have worked on China's atomic bomb and hydrogen bomb.
c/o Chinese Academy of Sciences, Peking, People's Republic of China.

Tsiranana, Philibert; Madagascan politician; b. 1910; ed. Univ. of Montpellier.
Member Majunga Provincial Assembly; mem. fmr. Madagascan Representative Assembly; Deputy from Madagascar to French Nat. Assembly; Prime Minister, Malagasy Republic 58-April 59, Pres. of the Cabinet May 59-; Pres. (Head of State) 60-; Minister Counsellor, French Community 59-60.
Présidence de la République, Tananarive, Madagascar.

Tsirimokos, Elie; Greek politician; b. 1907; ed. Univ. of Athens and Univ. de Paris à la Sorbonne.
Greek Govt. Rep., Mixed Arbitration Tribunals 29-30; Barrister 31-; Liberal Deputy 36; founded Democratic Popular Union 41; Sec. for Justice, Political Cttee. for Nat. Liberation 44; Minister of Nat. Economy 44; Sec.-Gen. Socialist Party of Democratic Popular Union 45-53; Deputy, Democratic Popular Union 50-58, independent 58, later Democratic Union, later Centre Union; Pres. Nat. Assembly 63; Minister of Interior 64; Prime Minister Aug. 65; Deputy Prime Minister and Minister of Foreign Affairs Sept. 65-April 66; Vice-Pres. Int. Fed. for the Rights of Man.
Publs. *Antifascistes* 45, *Mémoire* 53, *Alexandros Svolos* 62.
8 rue Irodotou, Athens 139, Greece.

Tsitsin, Nikolay Vasiljevich; Soviet (Russian) botanist and geneticist; b. 18 Dec. 1898; ed. State Agricultural Inst., Saratov on Volga.
Worked on selection and genetics of Spring and Winter wheat, Scientific-Research Inst. of Drought, Saratov 27-32, Head, Selection Dept. 32; later Dir. Scientific Research Inst. of Grain Econ., Omsk; Dir. All-Union Agricultural Exhibition, Moscow 37-57; mem. and Vice-Pres. Lenin All Union Acad. of Agricultural Science 57-; mem. C.P.S.U. 38-; mem. U.S.S.R. Acad. of Sciences 39-, Yugoslav Acad. of Science and Arts; Dir. Main Botanical Garden, U.S.S.R. Acad. of Sciences 46-; Dr. h.c. Jena Univ.; Hon. mem. Romanian Acad. of Sciences; Corresp. mem. German Acad. of Agricultural Sciences; Chair. U.S.S.R.-India Friendship Soc.; State Prize 43.
Publs. *Problem of Winter and Perennial Wheats* 35, *Advancement of Winter Crops to East* 40, *Pyrethrum* 41, *Transformation of Cultivated Plants* 43, *Investigations in the Field of Vegative-Reproductive Hybridization* 46, *Problem of Grains: Leading Link in Agriculture* 46, *Remote Hybridization of Plants* 53, *Darwin and Problems of Modern Biology* 57, *Activated Creoline* 57, *Representatives of the New Species of Wheat, Triticum Agropyrotriticum Perenne (Cicin)* 58, *New Species and Varieties of Wheat Obtained Experimentally* 59, *New Varieties of Branchy Wheats* 60, *Remote Hybridization and the Origination of New Species* 60, *New Varieties of Winter Rye* 61, *Hybrids Triticum × Elymus (gig. and arenarius)* 61, *Wheat-elymus Amphidiploids* 63, *Hybridization of Rye with Couch-Grass* 63.
Main Botanical Garden of U.S.S.R., Academy of Sciences, Bolshaya Botanicheskaya 4, Moscow, U.S.S.R.

Tsolov, Tano; Bulgarian politician; b. 18; ed. Sofia Univ.
Young Communist League 34-40, Communist Party 40-; local Communist orgs. 44-50; Industry and Transport Section, Central Cttee. of Communist Party 50-52; Minister of Heavy Industry 52-62; mem. Central Cttee. of Communist Party 57-, Sec. 59-, Cand. mem. Political Bureau 62-66, mem. 66-; Deputy Prime Minister and Chair. of Cttee. for Industry 62-.
Committee for Industry, Sofia, Bulgaria.

Tsuchikawa, Motoo; Japanese business executive; b. 20 June 1903; ed. Kyoto Univ.

President, Nagoya Railroad.

223, 1-chome Sasashima-cho, Nakamura-ku, Nagoya, Japan.

Tsukasa, Tadashi; Japanese publisher and book executive; b. 5 Oct. 1893.

With Maruzen Co. 06-, Dir. 40-, Pres. 46-; Vice-Pres. Tokyo Chamber of Commerce and Industry; Chair. Tokyo Stationery Industrial Asscn., Japan Book Importers Asscn.

Maruzen Co. Ltd., 6 Tori-Nichome, Nihonbashi, Tokyo; and 1-15, 1-chone, Kitazawa, Setagaya-ku, Tokyo, Japan.

Tsur, Yaakov; Israeli diplomatist; b. 18 Oct. 1906; ed. Hebrew Coll., Jerusalem, Univ. of Florence and Sorbonne.

Mem. staff daily newspaper *Haaretz,* Tel Aviv 29; Dir. French Dept. and later Co-Dir. Propaganda Dept. Jewish Nat. Fund Jerusalem 30; special Zionist missions, Belgium, Greece, France 34-35, Bulgaria and Greece 40; Liaison officer with G.H.Q. British Troops in Egypt 43-45; Head del. to Greece 45; Pres. Israeli Army Recruiting Cttee. Jerusalem 48; Minister to Argentina 49-53, Uruguay 49-53, Chile 50-53, and Paraguay 50-53; Ambassador to France 53-59; Chair. Jewish National Fund 59-; Chair. Zionist Gen. Council 61-; Pres. Central Inst. for Relations with Ibero-America, Grand Officier Légion d'Honneur.

Publs. *Juifs en Guerre* 47, *The Birth of Israel* 49, *Shacharit Shel Etmol* (Autobiography) 65 (French Translation—*Prière du Matin*) 67, *Ambassador's Diary* (Hebrew) 67.

P.O. Box 283, Jerusalem; and c/o Jewish National Fund, Jerusalem, Israel.

Telephone: 39013 (Office); 33811 (Home).

Tsuruoka, Senjin; Japanese diplomatist; b. 2 June 1907; ed. Tokyo Imperial Univ.

Attaché, Paris 32; Sec. of Office of Jap. Govt. for Int. Confs., Geneva 39; First Sec., Switzerland 45; Chief of Legal Section, Ministry of Foreign Affairs 46; Deputy Dir. of Immigration Bureau, Ministry of Justice 52; Chief Japanese Del. to numerous int. confs. 55-58; Amb. to Vatican 58-59; Dir. UN Bureau, Ministry of Foreign Affairs 59-62; Amb. to Sweden 62-66, to Switzerland 66-67; Perm. Rep. to UN 67-.

Permanent Mission of Japan to the United Nations, 866 UN Plaza, Suite 520-1, New York, N.Y. 10017, U.S.A.

Tuan Chun-yi; Chinese politician; ed. School of Engineering, Tsinan Univ.

Former Secretary, C.C.P. Hupeh-Honan Regional Cttee.; mem. Southwest China Mil. and Admin. Cttee.; Vice-Chair. Cttee. of Finance and Economic Affairs, Dir. Industry Dept. 49-53; Vice-Minister, First Ministry of Machine Building State Council 52-58, Minister 58-; Dep. from Shantung, Nat. People's Congress 54-. First Ministry of Machine Building, Peking, People's Republic of China.

Tubby, Roger W.; American publisher and government official; b. 30 Dec. 1910; ed. Choate School, Yale Univ., and London School of Economics.

Newspaperman 38-42, Board of Econ. Warfare 42-44; Asst. to Administrator, Foreign Economic Admin. 44-45; Dir. Information Office Int. Trade, Dept. of Commerce 45-46, Press Officer, Dept. of State 45-50; Asst. Press Sec. The White House 50-52, Acting Press Sec. Oct.-Dec. 52, Press Sec. Dec. 52; Personal Asst. Democratic Pres. Candidate 56; Editor and Publisher, *Adirondack Daily Enterprise,* Saranac Lake 53-61; Dir. Public Relations, Democratic Nat. Cttee. 60; Asst. Sec. for Public Affairs, Dept. of State 61-62; Perm. Rep. to UN, etc., Geneva 62-; Democrat.

U.S. Mission to International Organizations, Geneva, Switzerland.

Tubman, William Vacanarat Shadrach; Liberian lawyer and politician; b. 29 Nov. 1895; ed. Cape Palmas Seminary and Cuttington Inst.

Called to Bar 17; Collector of Internal Revenue Maryland County 19-22; Senator 23-31 and 34-37; Associate Justice Supreme Court 37-44; Pres. of Republic 44-; Papal Gold Medal 59.

Office of the President, Monrovia, Liberia.

Tucci, Giuseppe, PH.D.; Italian orientalist; b. 5 June 1894; ed. Rome Univ.

Lieut. 15-19; leader scientific expeditions to Tibet and Nepal; Prof. of Religions and Philosophy of India and the Far East, Rome Univ. 33-; mem. Royal Italian Acad.; hon. mem. Soc. Asiatique (Paris), and Delhi Univ.; leader expeditions in Pakistan, Afghanistan and Iran 56-; Pres. Middle and Far East Inst.; Hon. Prof. Univ. of Kolosvar, Delhi, Univ. of Louvain.

Publs. *Storia della filosofia cinese antica* 22, *Il Buddhismo* 26, *Doctrines of Maitreyanatha, Secrets of Tibet, Predinnaga Buddhist Logic, Indo-Tibetica* (7 vols.), *Tibetan Painted Scrolls* 49, *Asia Religiosa* 46, *Tibetan Folksongs* 49, *The Tombs of the Tibetan Kings* 50, *A Lhasa e Oltre* 50, *Tra Giungle e Pagode* 54, *Preliminary Report of two Scientific Expeditions in Nepal* 56, *Minor Buddhist Texts,* Part I 56, Part II 58, *Storia della Filosofia Indiana* 58, *Nepal* 60, *Theory and Practice of the Mandala* 61.

Piazza Vescovio 21, Rome, Italy.

Tuchman, Barbara W., B.A.; American writer; b. 30 Jan. 1912; ed. Radcliffe Coll., Cambridge, Mass.

Research Asst., Inst. of Pacific Relations, New York City 34, Tokyo 35; Editorial Asst. *The Nation,* New York City 36, Spain 37; Staff writer *War in Spain,* London 37-38; American Correspondent *New Statesman,* London 39; with Far East News Desk, Office of War Information, New York City 34-45; Trustee, Radcliffe Coll. 60-; Pulitzer Prize 63.

Publs. *The Lost British Policy* 38, *Bible and Sword* 56, *The Zimmermann Telegram* 58, *The Guns of August* 62, *The Proud Tower* 66.

875 Park Avenue, New York 21, N.Y., U.S.A.

Tuck, James Leslie, M.SC., M.A., O.B.E.; British-born American physicist; b. 9 Jan. 1910; ed. Manchester Central Grammar School, Manchester and Oxford Univs.

Dalton Scholar and Demonstrator, Manchester Univ. 32-37; Salter Research Fellow, Oxford Univ. 37-39; Adviser to Lord Cherwell on Prime Minister's Staff 39-42; Principal Scientific Adviser, Ministry of Defence 42-44; Principal Scientific Officer, British Mission to Manhattan Project (Atom Bomb), Los Alamos, New Mexico 44-46; Supervisor, Dept. of Advanced Studies, Clarendon Laboratory, Oxford 46-49; Research Assoc., Chicago Univ. Inst. for Nuclear Studies 49-50; Assoc. Division Leader, Physics Div., Los Alamos Scientific Laboratory, Univ. of California 50-; Fellow American Physical Soc., Guggenheim Fellow.

Publs. Numerous papers on Accelerators, Physics of Explosives (Munroe Effect), Nuclear Cross Sections and Thermonuclear Research.

2502 35th Street, Los Alamos, New Mexico 87544, U.S.A.

Telephone: 7-5111 (Lab.); 2-6323 (Home).

Tucker, Richard; American opera singer; b. 15; ed. public schools, N.Y.

Début at Metropolitan Opera House, New York 45, leading tenor 45-; concert tours throughout U.S.A. and abroad; guest star Teatro Colon, Buenos Aires, Vienna Staatsoper, Covent Garden, London, Teatro Liceo, Barcelona, Rome Opera, Teatro Comunale, Florence, etc.; recordings for Columbia, Victor and Angel.

Columbia Artists Management Inc., 113 West 57th Street, New York City 19, N.Y., U.S.A.

Tudlik; Canadian Eskimo sculptor; b. 90.
A hunter and trapper on Baffin Island; exhibited in Canada, U.S.A., and London.
Cape Dorset, Baffin Island, Northwest Territories, Canada.

Tugwell, Rexford Guy, B.S., M.A., PH.D., LITT.D., LL.D.; American political scientist; b. 10 July 1891; ed. Univ. of Pennsylvania.
Instructor and Asst. Prof. of Economics, Columbia Univ. 20-31, Prof. 31-37; Asst. Sec. Dept. of Agriculture 33, Under-Sec. and Admin. Resettlement Admin. 34-37; Chair. New York City Planning Comm. 38-41; Chancellor Univ. of Puerto Rico 41-42; Gov. of Puerto Rico 41-46; Dir. Inst. of Planning, Univ. of Chicago 46-52; Prof. of Political Science 46-57, Prof. Emeritus 57-; Development Consultant, Univ. of Puerto Rico 61-64; Research Prof. Political Science, Univ. of S. Illinois, Carbondale 65-; Visiting Prof. London School of Econs. 49-50; Woodrow Wilson Award of American Political Science Asscn.
Publs. *The Economic Basis of Public Interest* 22, *American Economic Life* 25, *Industry's Coming of Age* 27, *The Industrial Discipline* 33, *The Battle for Democracy* 35, *Redirecting Education* 35, *The Fourth Power* 39, *Changing the Colonial Climate* 42, *The Stricken Land* 46, *The Place of Planning in Society*: *with Special Reference to Puerto Rico* 54, *A Chronicle of Jeopardy* 55, *Great Cities of the World* (co-author) 55, *The Democratic Roosevelt* (Woodrow Wilson Award) 57, *The Art of Politics* 58, *Early American Contributors* (co-author) 60, *The Enlargement of the Presidency* 60, *The Light of Other Days* 62.
Southern Illinois University, Carbondale, Illinois, U.S.A.

Tuke, Anthony William; British banker; b. 24 Feb. 1897; ed. Winchester Coll.
With Barclays Bank since 19; Local Dir. Luton District 23-31; Gen. Man. 31-46, Vice-Chair. 46-47, Deputy Chair. 47-51, Chair. 51-62; Fellow of Winchester Coll. (Warden 62-); Chair. D'Oyly Carte Opera Trust; Officer Order of St. John of Jerusalem.
Publ. *History of Barclays Bank Limited* (with P. W. Matthews) 26.
Freelands, Wherwell, Hants., England.

Tukey, Harold Bradford, B.S., PH.D.; American horticulturist; b. 30 Sept. 1896; ed. Illinois Univ., and Univ. of Chicago.
Horticulturist in charge of Hudson Valley Fruit Investigations 23-27; Chief in Research New York State Agricultural Experimental Station and Prof. of Pomology Cornell Univ. 27-45; Head Dept. of Hort. Mich. State Coll. 45-63, Prof. Emeritus 63; awarded Jackson Dawson Memorial Medal 48; Fellow American Asscn. for the Advancement of Science, American Soc. Hort. Science, Royal Horticultural Soc., London, Vice-Pres. 65-; hon. mem. Société Nat. d'Horticulture de France; Sec. American Soc. for Horticultural Science 27-47, Pres. 47; Ed. *Proceedings* 27-49; Pres. American Pomological Soc. 51-53, Int. Soc. for Horticultural Science 62-66; Pres. XVII Int. Hort. Congress 66; mem. Exec. and Editorial Staff *Rural New Yorker* 20-64; Assoc. Editor *American Fruit Grower*; Editorial Board *Review of Plant Physiology*; Marshall P. Wilder Medal 46, Norman Jay Coleman Award 56; American Horticultural Council Citation 57; Gold Medal Award 67; Liberty Hyde Bailey Medal 67; Hon. D.Hort.Sc. (Hanover Inst. of Technology).
Publs. *The Pears of New York* 21, *The Pear and its Culture* 29, *Plant Regulators in Agriculture* 54, *Dwarfed Fruit Trees* 64.
The Maples, Woodland, Mich. 48897, U.S.A.

Tuluy, Turan; Turkish diplomatist; b. 7 June 1918; ed. Galatasaray Lycée, Istanbul, and Ankara Univ.
Entered Diplomatic Service 44, served Ankara 44-47;

Second Sec., then First Sec., Rome 47-51; Chief of Section, NATO Dept., Ministry of Foreign Affairs 51-54; First Sec. and Counsellor, Athens 54-60; Head of First Political Dept., Ministry of Foreign Affairs 60-64; Ambassador to Denmark 64-65, to Greece 65-; Greek and Spanish decorations.
Turkish Embassy, King George II Street No. 8, Athens, Greece.

Tun Shein, U, B.A.; Burmese civil servant and diplomatist; b. 19; ed. Univs. of Rangoon and London.
Entered Burma Civil Service 42; joined Foreign Office 49; became its Permanent Sec. 50; Burmese Del. to many sessions of UN Gen. Assembly, beginning with sixth; Alt. Leader Burmese Del. to UN Gen. Assembly 65; Burmese Del. at Bandung and other int. confs.; Amb. to Japan 57-66; Sec., Ministry of Foreign Affairs 66-; awarded titles Thiripyanchi 55, Sithu 60.
Ministry of Foreign Affairs, Rangoon, Burma.

Tunaligil, Danis; Turkish diplomatist; b. 15 April 1915; ed. Galatasaray Lyceum, Istanbul, and Univ. of Istanbul.
Ministry of Foreign Affairs 39-, Milan, Berne, Rome, Moscow 41-53; Dir.-Gen. Ministry of Foreign Affairs, Ankara 57, Dep. Sec.-Gen. 58; Ambassador to Jordan 60-64, to Yugoslavia 64-.
Embassy of Turkey, Belgrade, Proleterskih brigada 3, Yugoslavia.

Tung Pi-wu; Chinese politician and administrator; b. 86; ed. Tokyo Law School, Soviet Union.
Joined Tung-meng-hui at time of Wuchang rising 11; clandestine revolutionary activity; taught the new written colloquial at Wuhan Middle School 20; founder of Hupeh C.C.P. and in 21, at First C.C.P. Congress, Shanghai; Dir. Agricultural and Industrial Dept. Hupeh Provincial Govt.; Del. to San Francisco Conf.; Communist Rep. in Chungking and Nanking; at C.P.P.C.C. 49; mem. Political Bureau, C.C.P. 53-; Chair. Second C.P.P.C.C. 54; Hupeh del. to First N.P.C.; Sec. Central Control Commission, C.C.P. 56; Vice-Chair. of the Republic 59-.
Office of the Vice-Chairmen of the Republic, Peking, China.

Tung Tien-chien (Tien Chien); Chinese poet; b. 17; ed. Kwang-hwa Univ., Shanghai.
Edited the periodical *New Songs and Poems* 35-36; for a long period he was engaged in political work in the Liberated Areas of North China; Dir. of Propaganda Dept. in Changchiakou 43; mem. of Cttee. of All-China Fed. of Literary and Art Circles 49; of mem. Council of Union of Chinese Writers 53; mem. of Cttee. for Appraisal of Popular Songs 54; mem. of Central Inst. of Literature 55.
Publs. Many poems describing peasant life, war, etc.
Union of Chinese Writers, Peking, China.

Tunney, James Joseph (Gene); American boxer and businessman; b. 25 May 1897; ed. La Salle Acad.
With Ocean Steamship Co., New York 12-17; served with U.S. Marine Corps 18-19; won light heavyweight championship of American Expeditionary Forces, Paris 19; professional boxer 19-28, won World Heavyweight Championship 26, retired undefeated 28; Dir. Brown Co. (Berlin, N.H.), Eversharp Inc. (Chicago), Globe and Mail (Toronto), Industrial Bank of Commerce, New York City, Pittston Co., New York City; Chair. McCandless Corpn.; Commdr. U.S.N.R. to direct athletic and physical fitness programme for the U.S. Navy 41; Capt. 45; LL.D. h.c. (Ithaca Coll.).
Publs. *A Man Must Fight, Arms For Living.*
Stamford, Connecticut, U.S.A.; Office: 200 Park Avenue, New York City 10017, N.Y., U.S.A.

Tuominen, Leo Olavi, M.A.; Finnish diplomatist; b. 19 Jan. 1911; ed. Univ. of Turku.
Joined Foreign Service 34; served Paris 34-38, Riga

38-39, and Warsaw 39, Ministry of Foreign Affairs 40; Sec. of Section, Ministry of Foreign Affairs 41-43, Chief of Section 43-46; served Antwerp 46-47; First Sec. Legation, Brussels 47-48; Asst. Dir. of Commercial Division, Ministry of Foreign Affairs 48-50; Permanent Del. to Int. Organisations, Geneva 50-52; Minister to Argentina, Chile and Uruguay 52-55; Dir. Commercial Division, Ministry of Foreign Affairs 55-56; Sec. of State, Min. of Foreign Affairs 56-57; Ambassador to Great Britain 57-; Grand Officer, Orders White Rose (Finland), of Merit (Argentina); Grand Cross Icelandic Order of the Falcon; K.B.E.; Commdr., Léopold II (Belgium), the Crown (Italy), the Oak Crown (Luxembourg), Orange Nassau (Neths.); Officer the Lion (Finland); Officier Légion d'Honneur.
Finnish Embassy, 66 Chester Square, London, S.W.1, England.
Telephone: 01-730-0771.

Tupini, Giorgio; Italian industrial executive; b. 26 June 1922; ed. Rome Univ.
Member of Parl. 48-53; fmr. Under-Sec. Prime Minister's Office; with Istituto per la Ricostruzione Industriale (I.R.I.) 53-; fmr. Pres. and Managing Dir. Navalmeccanica of Naples; fmr. Dir. and mem. Exec. Cttee. Finmeccanica; Pres. Società Finanziaria Cantieri Navali (FINCANTIERI) 59-67; Chair. and Man. Dir. Società Finanziaria Meccanica (FINMECCANICA) 68-.
Società Finanziaria Meccanica "Finmeccanica", Viale Pilsudski 92, Rome, Italy.
Telephone: 8777.

Tupitsyn, Nikolai Kuzmich; Soviet diplomatist; b. 1910; ed. Univ. of Tomsk.
Former worker in metal industry in Urals and Siberia; Ministry of Foreign Affairs 44-, served Warsaw, later Belgrade 55-58, Ministry of Foreign Affairs 58-59; Consultant, Ministry of Foreign Affairs 59-63; Amb. to Iceland 63-66; Deputy Head, Ministry of Foreign Affairs 66-.
Ministry of Foreign Affairs, 32-34 Smolenskanya-Sennaya ploshchad, Moscow, U.S.S.R.

Tupolev, Andrei Nikolaevich; Soviet aircraft designer; b. 11 Nov. 1888; ed. Moscow Higher Technical School.
Lieut.-Gen. in the Engineering-Technical Service; with Zhukovsky he organised the Central Aerodynamic Inst. (TsAGI) 18; Asst. Dir. of TsAGI 18-35; Head of the Designing Bureau 22-; Designer-Gen. to Ministry of Aircraft Industry; Pres. of the Soviet-Bulgarian Friendship Soc. 57; Hero of Socialist Labour (twice); mem. of Acad. of Sciences of U.S.S.R. 53; State prize-winner; awarded Lenin Prize 57, Order of Lenin; Gold Medal, Int. Aviation Fed. 59.
Principal designs: TB-1, ANT-9, TB-3, ANT-25, TU-2, TU-104, TU104A, TU-110, TU-114, TU-124, TU-134, TU-157, TU-144 (supersonic passenger aircraft), naval torpedo boats, aero-sleighs, gliders.
Ministry of Aircraft Industry, Moscow, U.S.S.R.

Turagay, Seyfi; Turkish air force officer and diplomatist; b. 06; ed. Military School, Air Force Coll., Military Acad. (Staff Coll.).
Graduated from Air Force Coll. 27, Staff Coll. 36; Air Attaché in London 42-43; Gen. 50; fmr. Commdr. Air Force Div., Chief of Staff of Air Acad., Commdr. of Air Force Supply and Maintenance Command, Chief of Operations and Logistics Dept., Chief of Staff of Turkish Air Force, Chief of Operations and Logistics Dept. (Gen. Staff Headquarters), Second Chief of Staff of the Turkish Gen. Staff; retd. as Lieut.-Gen. 60; Ambassador to Iraq 60-64, to Austria 64-.
Turkish Embassy, Vienna, Prinz Eugen Strasse 40, Austria.

Tureck, Rosalyn; American concert artist; b. 14 Dec. 1914; ed. Juilliard School of Music, New York.
Taught at Philadelphia Conservatory, and Mannes

Music School, New York; Lecturer, Columbia Univ. and Juilliard Music School, New York; concert tours U.S.A. and Canada 36-, Europe 47-, South America 63-, Israel 63-; performed at Venice, Holland, Edinburgh and other international festivals; specializes in the Keyboard works of J. S. Bach, played on the piano, harpsichord and clavichord; conductor 57-; formed Tureck Bach Players 59, Int. Bach Soc. 66; Regents' Professorship, Univ. of Calif., San Diego 66; D.Mus. (Colby) 64.
Publ. *Introduction to Bach Performance* (3 vols.) 60, Editor of *Sarabande, C Minor, Bach* 60.
Tillett and Holt, 124 Wigmore Street, London W.1, England.

Türler, Charles; Swiss banker; b. 96.
Gen. Man. Swiss Bank Corpn.; Chair. Alpina Versicherungs-Aktiengesellschaft, Zürich; Dir. S. A. Leu & Co. Zürich, Motor Columbus S.A., Baden, Société Int. de Placement, Basle, Kraftwerk Laufenburg S.A., Neuchâtel, Société Gén. de l'Horlogerie Suisse S.A. "Asuag", Neuchâtel, Société des Fabriques de Spiraux Réunies, Chaux-de-Fonds, Forces Motrices Bernoises S.A., Société de Participations, Berne, Société Suisse d'Electricité et de Traction, Basle, Oel & Fettwerke "Sais", Zürich.
c/o Schweizerischer Bankverein, 1 Aeschenvorstadt, Basle, Switzerland.

Turnbull, Sir Richard Gordon, G.C.M.G.; British overseas administrator; b. 7 July 1909; ed. Univ. Coll., London, and Magdalene Coll., Cambridge.
With Colonial Admin. Service Kenya, District Officer 31-48, Provincial Commr. 48-53, Minister for Internal Security and Defence 54; Chief. Sec. of Kenya 55-58; Gov., Tanganyika 58-61; Gov.-Gen. 61-62; Chair. Cen. Land Board, Kenya 63-64; High Commr. for Aden and the Protectorate of South Arabia 65-67; Fellow, Univ. Coll., London.
c/o D.S.A.O., King Charles Street, London, S.W.1, England.

Turner, Sir Michael William, Kt., C.B.E., M.A., F.Z.S.; British banker; b. 25 April 1905; ed. Marlborough Coll., and Univ. Coll., Oxford.
Joined Hongkong and Shanghai Banking Corpn. 26, Chair. and Chief Man. 53-62; interned in Singapore 42-45; Chair. British Bank of the Middle East 64-67, British Bank of the Middle East (Morocco) S.A.; Dir. Westminster Bank Ltd. and various companies; Colonial Police Medal 56; Commdr. Order of Prince Henry the Navigator (Portugal) 63; Hon. LL.D. (Hong Kong).
Whispers, Riversdale, Bourne End, Bucks., England.
Telephone: Bourne End 23965.

Turner, Sir Ralph Lilley, M.C., M.A., LITT.D., F.B.A.; British oriental scholar; b. 5 Oct. 1888; ed. Perse School, and Christ's Coll., Cambridge.
Fellow of Christ's Coll. Cambridge 12, Hon. Fellow 50; Lecturer in English and Sanskrit Queen's Coll. Benares 13; attached 2/3rd Gurkha Rifles, Indian Army Reserve of Officers 15-19; Prof. of Indian Linguistics Hindu Univ. of Benares 20; Prof. of Sanskrit London Univ. 22-54, Emeritus 54-; Dir. School of Oriental and African Studies Sept. 37-57; mem. Advisory Cttee. on Education of the Colonies and other cttees.; Hon. Fellow School of Oriental and African Studies (London) 57, Deccan Coll. (Poona) 58; hon. mem. Soc. Asiatique (Paris), Deutsche Morgenländische Gesellschaft, American Oriental Soc., Linguistic Soc. of America, Linguistic Soc. of India, etc.; corresp. mem. Norske Videnskaps-Akademi; foreign corresp. Institut de France (Acad. des Inscriptions et Belles Lettres); Hon. Fellow Ceylon Acad. of Letters; Hon. D.Litt. (Banaras), Hon. D.Lit. (Ceylon), Hon. D.Lit. (London).
Publs. *Gujarati Phonology* 21, *The Position of Romani in Indo-Aryan, A Comparative and Etymological*

Dictionary of the Nepali Language 31, *The Gavimath Inscription of Asoka, Report to the Nuffield Foundation on a Visit to Nigeria* (with J. T. Saunders and D. Veale), *Some Problems in Sound Change in Indo-Aryan* 60, *A Comparative Dictionary of the Indo-Aryan Languages* 66, *Indexes volume* 68.
Haverbrack, Bishop's Stortford, Herts., England.
Telephone: Bishop's Stortford 4135.

Turner, Sir Ronald Mark Cunliffe, Kt.; British banker; b. 29 March 1906; ed. Wellington Coll.
Entered the City, with M. Samuel & Co. Ltd. (merchant bankers) 24; with Robert Benson. Lonsdale & Co. Ltd. (merchant bankers) 34-39; Ministry of Economic Warfare 39-44; Foreign Office 44-45; Under-Sec. Control Office for Germany and Austria 45-47; now Dep. Chair. Kleinwort Benson Ltd., Rio Tinto-Zinc Corpn. Ltd.; Chair. British Home Stores Ltd., Mercantile Credit Co. Ltd.; Dir. Commercial Union Assurance, Wm. Mallinson & Sons Ltd., Calico Printers' Asscn. Ltd., Tunnel Portland Cement Co. Ltd., Nat. Cash Register Co., Midland & Int. Banks Ltd. and several overseas directorships incl. The Toronto-Dominion Bank Ltd.
St. Albans House, Goldsmith Street, London, E.C.2; and 3 The Grove, Highgate Village, London, N.6, England.
Telephone: 01-626-1531 (Office); 01-340-3421 (Home).

Turski, Stanisław, PH.D., D.SC.; Polish mathematician; b. 15 May 1906; ed. Jagiellonian Univ., Cracow.
Professor and Pres. Gdańsk Polytechnic School 45-49; mem. of Parl. 47-52; Prof., Warsaw Polytechnic School 49-51; Dir. of Dept., Ministry of Educ. for Higher Learning 49-51; Prof., Warsaw Univ. 51-, Pres. 52-; Pres. Polish Cybernetical Soc. 66-.
5/7 Konopczynski Street, Warsaw, Poland.
Telephone: 271307.

Turski, Zbigniew; Polish composer and conductor; b. 08; ed. in Warsaw.
Musical Dir. of Polish Radio 36-39; Dir. of Baltic Philharmonic Orchestra 45-46; Gold Medal Olympic Arts Contest, London 48; Prize at 2nd Festival of Polish Music 55.
Works include three Symphonies, Sinfonia de Camera, Violin Concerto, two String Quartets, cantatas *The Airs* and *The Vistula* on poems by Broniewski and Fiszer, theatre and film music.
c/o Union of Polish Composers, Rynek Starego Miasta 27, Warsaw, Poland.

Turyn, Alexander, PH.D.; Polish-American philologist; b. 26 Dec. 1900; ed. Warsaw and Berlin Univs.
Instructor Warsaw Univ. 25, Docent 29, Prof. Extra. of Classical Philology 35-39; Lecturer Univ. of Michigan 41; Assoc. Prof. New School for Social Research New York 42-45; Prof. Univ. of Illinois 45-, mem. Center for Advanced Studies 62-; corresp. mem. Polish Acad. Cracow, Acad. of Athens; research collaborator, Vatican Library; hon. mem. Epistemonike Hetaireia, Athens; Fellow Guggenheim Foundation 59; Award of Merit, American Philological Asscn. 60; Hon. Ph.D. (Athens Univ.).
Publs. *Observationes metricae* 23, *Studia Sapphica* 29, *De Aelii Aristidis codice Varsoviensi atque de Andrea Taranowski et Theodosio Zygomala* 29, *De codicibus Pindaricis* 32, *The Manuscript Tradition of the Tragedies of Aeschylus* 43, *Pindari Epinicia* 44, *The Manuscripts of Sophocles* 44, *Pindari Carmina cum fragmentis* 48, *The Sophocles Recension of Manuel Moschopulus* 49, *Studies in the Manuscript Tradition of the Tragedies of Sophocles* 52, *The Byzantine Manuscript Tradition of the Tragedies of Euripides* 57, *Codices graeci Vaticani saeculis XIII et XIV scripti annorumque notis instructi* 64.
801 South Maple Street, Urbana, Illinois 61801, U.S.A.
Telephone: 217-367-3911.

Turzún-Zadé, Mirzo; Soviet writer and poet; b. 1911; ed. Tadzhik Education Inst.
Member Acad. of Sciences of the Tadzhik S.S.R. 51-; Deputy Supreme Soviet 47-; Chair. Soviet Afro-Asian Solidarity Cttee. 56-; First Sec. Union of Writers of Tadzhik S.S.R.; State prizewinner 47; Lenin Prize 60; awarded Order of Lenin (three times); Hero of Socialist Labour 67.
Publs. Play: *The Sentence* 34; poems: *Spring and Autumn* 37, *Indian Songs* 48, *Hissar Valley, Child of his Fatherland, Tahir and Zukhra, I am from the Free East* 51, *Hasan Arobakesh* 54, *Voice of Asia* 57, *My Dear* 60, *Selected Works* (3 vols.) 60, *Path of a Sun Ray* 64, *Epoch, Life and Creative Work* 65, *The Globe* 66.
Union of Soviet Writers, 52 Vorovsky Street, Moscow, U.S.S.R.

Tuthill, John Wills; American diplomatist; b. 10 Nov. 1910; ed. Coll. of William and Mary, New York Univ., and Harvard Univ.
Private banking 32-36; Investment Counsel 36-37; Instructor and Asst. Prof. Northeastern Univ. 37-40; Foreign Service Officer 40-, Canada, Mexico, SHAEF, U.S. Military Govt., Berlin, Dept. of State, Stockholm, London, Bonn, Paris, Dept. of State 59-60; American Ambassador to Organisation for Economic Co-operation and Development (OECD) 61-62, to the European Communities 62-66, to Brazil 66-.
American Embassy, Rio de Janeiro, Brazil; Home: 394 Roger Williams Avenue, Highland Park, Ill., U.S.A.

Tutin, Dorothy, C.B.E.; British actress; b. 8 April 1930; ed. St. Catherine's, Bramley, Surrey, and Royal Acad. of Dramatic Art, London.
Appeared at Stratford Festival 58, 60; took part in Shakespeare Memorial Theatre tour of Russia 58; Shakespeare recital before Pope, Vatican 64; *Evening Standard* Award as Best Actress 60.
Principal roles: Rose (*The Living Room*), Katherine (*Henry V*), Sally Bowles (*I am a Camera*), St. Joan (*The Lark*), Catherine (*The Gates of Summer*), Hedwig (*The Wild Duck*), Viola (*Twelfth Night*), Juliet (*Romeo and Juliet*), Ophelia (*Hamlet*), Dolly (*Once More, With Feeling*), Portia (*The Merchant of Venice*), Cressida (*Troilus and Cressida*), Sister Jeanne (*The Devils*) 61, 62, Juliet (*Romeo and Juliet*) and Desdemona (*Othello*), Stratford-on-Avon 61, Varya (*The Cherry Orchard*) 61, Prioress (*The Devils*), Edinburgh 62, Polly Peachum (*The Beggar's Opera*) 63, *Hollow Crown*, New York 63, Queen Victoria (*Portrait of a Queen*) 65, Rosalind (*As You Like It*), Stratford on Avon 67, Los Angeles 68, Queen Victoria (*Portrait of a Queen*), New York 68.
Films include: *The Beggar's Opera, The Importance of Being Earnest, A Tale of Two Cities.*
8 Chester Close, Queens Ride, London, S.W.13, England.
Telephone: 01-789-3330.

Tuttle, Elbert Parr; American judge; b. 17 July 1897; ed. Punahou School, Hawaii, and Cornell Univ.
Private practice, Sutherland, Tuttle and Brennan, Washington and Atlanta 23-53; Gen. Counsel, U.S. Treasury Dept. 53-54; Circuit Judge, U.S. Court of Appeals, 5th Circuit 54-, Chief Judge 60-67; Hon. D.Iur., Emory Univ., Atlanta, Hon. LL.D., Harvard Univ.
United States Court of Appeals, Atlanta 1, Ga.; Home: 101 Peachtree Circle, N.E., Atlanta, Ga., U.S.A.

Tutuola, Amos; Nigerian writer; b. 20; ed. Mission Schools.
Worked on father's farm; trained as coppersmith; served with R.A.F. Second World War; Nigerian Broadcasting Corpn., Ibadan 45-.
Publs. *The Palm-Wine Drinkard* 52, *My Life in the Bush of Ghosts* 54, *Simbi and the Satyr of the Jungle* 55,

The Brave African Huntress 58, *The Feather Woman of the Jungle* 62, *Ajaiyi and His Inherited Poverty* 67.
c/o Nigerian Broadcasting Corporation, Broadcasting House, Ibadan, Nigeria.
Telephone: 22661/26.

Tuve, Merle Antony, B.S., M.A., PH.D.; American research physicist; b. 27 June 1901; ed. Univ. of Minnesota, Princeton Univ., and Johns Hopkins Univ.
Instructor in Physics Princeton Univ. 23-24, Johns Hopkins Univ. 24-26; Physicist and Staff mem. Carnegie Inst. of Washington 26-46, Dir. Dept. of Terrestrial Magnetism 46-66; Chair. Section T, Nat. Defence Research Cttee. and Office of Scientific Research and Devt. 40-45; Chair. Advisory Panel on Radio Astronomy, Nat. Science Foundation 53-; U.S. Comm. for the Int. Geophysical Year; Editor *Journal of Geophysical Research* 49-58; Trustee Johns Hopkins Univ.; Fellow American Physical Soc., Inst. of Radio Engineers, American Asscn. for the Advancement of Science; mem. Nat. Acad. of Sciences, Home Sec. 66-, American Acad. of Arts and Sciences and American Philosophical Soc.; Presidential Medal for Merit 46, C.B.E. 48, Bowie Medal 63, and many other awards; Hon. Sc.D. (Case, Kenyon, Williams, Johns Hopkins, Univ. of Alaska), Hon. LL.D. (Augustana and Carleton).
Publs. *Exploration of the Upper Atmosphere (Ionosphere) by Radio Pulse Methods* 25-29, *High Voltage Techniques for Nuclear Physics* 30-35, *Resonance Levels in the Atomic Nucleus* 35-37, etc.
Home: 135 Hesketh Street, Chevy Chase, Md.; Office: 5241 Broad Branch Road, N.W. Washington 15, D.C., U.S.A.

Tvardovsky, Alexandr Trifonovich; Soviet poet; b. 21 June 1910; ed. Moscow Inst. of History, Philosophy and Literature.
Editor *Novy Mir*; mem. Presidium Union of Soviet Writers; mem. Central Cttee. of C.P.S.U. until 67; State prizewinner 41, 46, 47; Lenin Prize 61; Order of Lenin (twice) and other decorations.
Publs. Anthologies: *The Road* 34, *Village Chronicles* 39, *Zagorye* 41; *Muravia* 36, *Vasili Tyorkin* 41-45, *House by the Roadside* 43-46, *Beyond the Beyond* 53-57, *Articles and Notes on Literature Home and Abroad* (prose) 60, *Selected Poems* 64, *Tyorkin in the Other World* 64, Complete works (5 vols.) 67.
Union of Soviet Writers, 52 Vorovsky Street, Moscow; and Kotelnicheskaja nab. 1/15, 125 Moscow, U.S.S.R.
Telephone: K4-57-01.

Tweter, Clifford; American banker; b. 6 Oct. 1907; ed. Northwestern School of Commerce.
With Continental-Ill. Nat. Bank & Trust Co., Chicago 25-41; with California Bank, Los Angeles 41-, Asst. Vice-Pres. 43-45, Vice-Pres. 45-54, Exec. Vice-Pres., Dir. 54-, Pres. 59-; Pres. and Dir. United California Bank; Pres. and Dir. Western Bancorporation (fmrly. Firstamerica Corpn.); Dir. United Calif. Int. Bank; official of other companies.
Home: 1489 Carla Ridge, Beverly Hills, Calif.; Office: 600 S. Spring Street, Los Angeles, Calif. 90014, U.S.A.

Twigt, Bernard Tieleman, DR. ECON.; Netherlands transport economist; b. 3 Dec. 1912; ed. Rotterdam Univ. of Economics.
Deputy Chief of Administration and Finance, International Civil Aviation Org. (ICAO), Montreal 49-56; Asst. Dir. of Admin. and Gen. Services, United Nations Relief and Works Agency for Palestine, Beirut 56-59; Sec. UN Joint Staff Pension Fund, New York 59-60; Chief Admin. Officer, UN Emergency Force, Gaza 60-62; Chief Admin. Officer, UN Operation in the Congo, Léopoldville 62-63; Assoc. Dir., Joint Admin. Div., Technical Asst. Board, UN, New York 63-64;

Sec.-Gen. Int. Civil Aviation Org. (ICAO), Montreal Aug. 64-.
ICAO Headquarters, 1080 University Street, Montreal 3, Quebec, Canada.

Twining, Gen. Nathan F.; American air force officer; b. 11 Oct. 1897; ed. U.S. Military Acad., Infantry School, Air Corps Tactical School, Commd. and Gen. Staff School.
Commissioned Second Lieut. Infantry 18; transferred to Air Corps 24; advanced through grades to Lieut.-Gen. 45, Gen. 50; Chief of Staff to Commdg. Gen. S. Pacific 42-43; Commdg. Gen. 13th Air Force, Solomon Islands 43, 15th Air Force, Italy 44-45, 20th Air Force, Pacific 45, Alaska 47-50; Vice-Chief of Staff U.S.A.F. 50-53, Chief of Staff 53-57; Chair. Joint Chiefs of Staff 57-60 (retd.); Vice-Chair. Holt, Rinehart and Winston 61-; awarded D.S.M. (Army and Navy), Legion of Merit with oak leaf cluster, D.F.C., Air Medal, etc.; Hon. K.B.E. (U.K.).
4731 Berkeley Terrace, Washington, D.C., U.S.A.

Twisleton-Wykeham-Fiennes, Sir Maurice Alberic, Kt.; British company director; b. 1 March 1907; ed. Repton School, Derbyshire, and Armstrong Coll., Newcastle.
Manager, Pneumatic Tool Dept., Sir. W. G. Armstrong Whitworth and Co. 30-37; Commercial Asst. to Man. Dir. United Steel Companies Ltd.; Gen. Works Dir. Brush Electrical Engineering Co. Ltd. 42-45; Managing Dir. Davy and United Engineering Co. Ltd., Sheffield 45-60; Managing Dir. Davy-Ashmore Group 60-, Chair. 61-; Dir. Continuous Casting Co. Ltd. 57-, Clyde Crane and Booth Ltd. 61-, Simon Engineering Ltd. 62-, North Sea Marine Engineering Construction Co. Ltd. 64-, Metallurgical Equipment Export Co. Ltd. 64-; Pres. Iron and Steel Inst. 62-63; Hon. Vice-Pres. Indian Inst. of Metals; Hon. mem. American Iron and Steel Inst.
Hill Top Farm, Dronfield, nr. Sheffield, Yorkshire, England.
Telephone: Dronfield 2274.

Tyabji, Badr-ud-Din Faiz Hasan Badr-ud-Din, B.A.; Indian diplomatist; b. 12 Nov. 1907; ed. St. Xavier's School and Coll., Bombay, and Balliol Coll., Oxford.
Under-Secretary Finance, Home and Political Affairs 32-38; Under-Sec. Defence Dept. 38-39; Deputy Commr. Punjab 40-42; Controller of Supplies, Karachi and Bombay 42-44; Deputy Sec. Planning and Development 44-46; Deputy Sec. and Joint Sec. Constituent Assembly Secretariat and Ministry of External Affairs and Commonwealth Relations 46-48; Minister and Chargé d'Affaires of India in Belgium and Luxemburg 48-50; Joint Sec. Ministry of External Affairs, New Delhi 50-52; Commonwealth Sec. Government of India 52-53; Ambassador to Indonesia 54-56; mem. of the five Sponsoring Powers Joint Secretariat which organised the Bandung Conf. 55 and a mem. of the Indian Del. which participated in it; Ambassador to Iran 56-58; Ambassador to German Fed. Republic 58-60; Special Sec. Ministry of External Affairs 61-62; Vice-Chancellor Aligarh Muslim Univ. 62-65; Amb. to Japan 65-67.
c/o Ministry of External Affairs, New Delhi, India.

Tyagi, Mahavir; Indian politician; b. 1900; ed. privately.
Member All-India Congress Cttee.; Minister of Revenue and Expenditure 51-53, of Defence Org. 53-57; mem. Lok Sabha 52-, fmr. Chair. Public Accounts Cttee., Lok Sabha; Minister of Rehabilitation April 64-66.
c/o Ministry of Rehabilitation, New Delhi, India.

Tyazhelnikov, Evgeny; Soviet politician; b. 1928.
Sec. Chelyabinsk Regional Party Cttee., C.P.S.U. 64; First Sec. Komsomol June 68-.
Central Committee of Komsomol, Ulitsa Bogdana Khmelnitskova 3/13, Moscow, U.S.S.R.

Tydings, Joseph Davies, LL.B.; American lawyer and politician; b. 4 May 1928; ed. Aberdeen Public Schools and McDonogh School, Maryland, and Univ. of Maryland.

Member Maryland House of Del. 55-61; U.S. District Attorney 61-63; U.S. Senator from Maryland 64-; Pres. Junior Bar Asscn. Baltimore City 62-63; Democrat.

New Senate Office Building, Washington, D.C.; and Oakington, Havre de Grace, Maryland, U.S.A.

Tyerman, Donald; British journalist; b. 1 March 1908; ed. Brasenose Coll., Oxford.

Lecturer Univ. Coll. Southampton 30-36; Asst. and later Deputy Editor *The Economist* 37-44; Deputy Editor *The Observer* 43-44; Asst. Editor *The Times* 44-55; Editor *The Economist* 56-65; Chair. Exec. Board Int. Press Inst. 61-62; mem. Exec. Cttee. Overseas Devt. Inst., Nat. Inst. of Econ. and Social Research; Dir. Economist Newspaper Ltd., United City Merchants Ltd.; Editorial Adviser to Hodder and Stoughton Ltd.; mem. Council of Commonwealth Press Union, Univ. of Sussex; Gov. London School of Econs.; mem. Press Council 64-.

41 Buckingham Mansions, West End Lane, London, N.W.6; and Holly Cottage, Westleton, nr. Saxmundham, Suffolk, England.

Telephone: 01-435-1030 (London); 0728-73-261 (Suffolk).

Tyler, William Royall; American government official; b. 17 Oct. 1910; ed. Oxford and Harvard Univs.

Guaranty Trust Co., New York City 34-38; Programme Manager Short Wave Radio Station Boston 40-42; Office of War Information, New York 42, North Africa 43-44, France 44-45; Dept. of State 45-, Counsellor, Paris 48-52, Consul 52-54; Dep. Dir. Office of Western European Affairs, Washington 54-57, Dir. 57-58; Political Counsellor, Bonn 58-61; Deputy Asst. Sec. of State for European Affairs, Dept. of State 61-62, Asst. Sec. of State 62-65; Ambassador to Netherlands 65-; Fellow American Acad. of Arts and Sciences; Medal of Freedom.

American Embassy, The Hague, Netherlands.

Tynan, Kenneth, B.A., F.R.S.L.; British writer; b. 2 April 1927; ed. Magdalen Coll., Oxford.

Director of Repertory Theatre, Lichfield 49; directed plays in and around London and on television 50-51; Drama Critic *The Spectator* 51; Drama Critic *Evening Standard* 52-53; Drama Critic *Daily Sketch* 53-54; Drama Critic of *The Observer* 54-63; Script Editor of Ealing Films 56-58; Drama Critic of *The New Yorker* 58-60; TV. producer 61-62; Literary Manager Nat. Theatre 63-; Film Critic *The Observer* 64-66, Arts Columnist 68-.

Publs. *He that Plays the King* 50, *Persona Grata* (with Cecil Beaton) 53, *Alec Guinness* 53, *Bull Fever* 55; B.B.C. play: *The Quest for Corbett* (with Harold Lang) 56; *Curtains* 61, *Tynan Right and Left* 67.

20 Thurloe Square, London, S.W.7, England.

Tyson, Charles Roebling; American insurance executive; b. 22 Feb. 1914; ed. Episcopal Acad., and Princeton Univ.

John A. Roebling's Sons Co. 35-53, Treas. and Dir. 36-40, Sec. Treas. 40-44, Pres. 44-53; Dir. Colorado Fuel and Iron Corpn. (which took over John A. Roebling's Sons Co. 53) 53-, Exec. Vice-Pres. 58-59; Exec. Vice-Pres. Penn Mutual Life Insurance Co. 59-61, Pres. and Chief Exec. Officer 61-; Dir. of several other companies.

Penn Mutual Life Insurance Co., Independence Square, Philadelphia 5, Pa., U.S.A.

Tyson, Robert Carroll, B.A.; American steel executive; b. 13 Aug. 1905; ed. Mercersburg Acad., and Princeton Univ.

With Remington Rand Inc. 27-29; with Price, Waterhouse and Co. 29-39; Asst. Supervisor, U.S. Steel Corpn. 39-41, Gen. Account 41-47, Asst. Comptroller 47-50, Comptroller 50-52, Dir. 50-, Vice-Chair. Finance Cttee. 52-56, Chair. Finance Cttee. 56-; mem. and official of numerous business, civic and educational organisations.

United States Steel Corporation, 71 Broadway, New York 6, and 888 Park Avenue, N.Y., U.S.A.

U

Ubac, Raoul; Belgian painter; b. 10; ed. Sorbonne and Ateliers de la Grande Chaumière.

Settled in Paris 32; work in surrealist photography 32-39; abandoned photography for pen-drawing, gouache, painting and sculpture of slates; exhbns. Paris 43, London and Brussels 46, Galerie Maeght (Paris) 50, 55, 58, 64, 66, Basel Kunsthalle 54, Zürich and Sao Paulo 57, Carnegie Inst. (Pittsburgh) 58, Dokumenta (Kassel and Geneva) 59, Dunn Int. Exhibition, London 63; works in New York Museum of Modern Art, Kunstmuseum, Basle, Carnegie Foundation, Pittsburgh and in numerous private collections.

Publs. Illustrations for poems of André Frénaud and for *Pierre Ecrite* by Yves Bonnefoy, etc.

c/o Galerie Maeght, 13 rue de Téhéran, Paris 8e, France.

Udall, Stewart Lee; American politician; b. 31 Jan. 1920; ed. Univ. of Arizona.

Served U.S. Air Force, Second World War; admitted to Arizona Bar 48, practised law, Tucson 48-54; mem. House of Reps. 55-61, mem. Interior and Insular Affairs Cttee., Labor and Education Cttee.; Sec. of the Interior 61-; Democrat.

Publ. *The Quiet Crisis*.

Office of the Secretary of the Interior, Washington, D.C. 20240, U.S.A.

Udink, B. J.; Netherlands politician; b. 12 Feb. 1926; ed. School of Economics, Rotterdam, and Ecole des Hautes Etudes Commerciales, Univ. of Lausanne.

Deputy Sec. Rotterdam Chamber of Commerce 53-58, Sec. 58-62; Lecturer, School of Econs., Rotterdam 50-63; Dir. of Central Chamber of Netherlands for Export Promotion 62-67; mem. Nat. Advisory Council for Aid to Developing Countries 65-; Minister for Aid to Developing Countries 67-.

Ministry for Aid to Developing Countries, The Hague, Netherlands.

Udochi, Julius Momo, B.A.; Nigerian lawyer and diplomatist; b. 3 June 1914; ed. Govt. School, Auchi and Catholic School, Ubiaja.

Teacher 31-38; Civil Service 38-47; Prov. Sec. Nigerian Civil Service and co-ed. *The Nigerian Civil Servant* 42-46; Hon. Sec. Etsako Union 34-54; mem. House of Reps. 54-59; Hon. Sec. Nigerian Bar Assoc. 55-59; Amb. to U.S.A. 60-66.

c/o Ministry of Foreign Affairs, Lagos, Nigeria.

Udovichenko, Petr Platonovich; Soviet (Ukrainian) diplomatist; b. 1914; ed. Novomoskovsky Pedagogical Inst.

Professor of History, Teachers Inst., Dneprodzerhinski 34-39; Asst. to Minister, Head of Dept. of Political Affairs, Ministry of Foreign Affairs, Ukraine 44-52; Pro-Rector, Kiev State Univ. 52-58; Ukrainian Perm. Rep. to UN 58-61; teacher, Kiev State Univ. 61-67; Minister of Educ. of Ukrainian S.S.R. 67-.

Ministry of Education, Kiev, Ukrainian S.S.R., U.S.S.R.

Ueda, Kazuo; Japanese banker; b. 20 Jan. 1903; ed. Tokyo Univ.

Joined 34th Bank 25; Pres. Sanwa Bank 60-.

Sanwa Bank, 4-10 Fushimimachi, Higashi-ku, Osaka; and 857 Kitamachi, Takamatsu City, Kagawa Prefecture, Japan.

Uehara, Shokichi; Japanese politician; b. 26 Dec. 1897; ed. Meiji Pharmaceutical School.

President Taisho Pharmaceutical Co. Ltd.; mem. House of Councillors 50-; fmr. Parl. Vice-Minister for Prices, and for Economic Research; fmr. Parl. Vice-Minister for Capital City Construction; fmr. Minister of State; Chair. Atomic Energy Comm.; Liberal Democrat.

c/o House of Councillors, Tokyo; Home: 5-chome, 5 Nogata, Nakano-ku, Tokyo, Japan.

Telephone: Tokyo 330-115123.

Ugarteche Tizón, Pedro; Peruvian diplomatist; b. 02; ed. Colegio de la Inmaculada, Universidad Mayor de San Marcos, Lima and Universidad de Barcelona.

Secretary to the Presidency of the Republic 31, Sec.-Gen. for External Relations 33; Head, Perm. Office at League of Nations 33; Del. to Int. Labour Office; Minister to Belgium 49; Ambassador to Bolivia 59-61, to Venezuela 61-62, to Argentina 62-; Pres., Nat. Asscn. of Writers and Artists, Peruvian Inst. of Genealogists; Founder, Peruvian Acad. of Diplomacy 55, Dir. 65-; Gran Cruz de la Orden del Sol del Peru, Gran Cruz de la Orden de Mayo (Argentina) and other orders.

Publs. *Política Exterior del Perú* 25, *El Perú en la vida internacional americana* 27, *Páginas Universitarias y Diplomáticas* 28, *Proyecto de Ley Orgánica de Relaciones Exteriores* 41, *La Comisión Consultiva de Relaciones Exteriores* 44, *Formación del Diplomático Peruano* 55, *Diplomacia y Literatura* 61, *Academia Diplomática y Aula Internacional* 62, *Educación Diplomática Antigua y Moderna* 64, *Valija Diplomática* 65, *La Orden de El Sol del Peru* 66.

Embassy of Peru, Avenida del Libertador General San Martín 1728, Buenos Aires, Argentina.

Uhlmann, Hans; German engineer and sculptor; b. 27 Nov. 1900; ed. Berlin Technical Inst.

First exhibition of metallic sculptures 45; Prof. Berlin Acad. of Fine Arts 50-; German Prize, Unknown Political Prisoner Monument Competition 53; rep. at many int. exhbns. including Brussels Int. Exhbn. 58.

Schorlemer Allee 21, Berlin 33, Germany.

Uijl, Johannes Marten den; Netherlands politician; b. 19; ed. Christenlijk Lyceum, Hilversum, and Universiteit van Amsterdam.

Former Social Editor *Het Parool*; formerly with *Vrij Nederland*; Dir. Wiardi Beckman Organisation 49-62; mem. Second Chamber 56-63; Alderman of Amsterdam; Minister of Econ. Affairs 65-66; Labour.

Publs. *De weg naar vrijheid* 52, *Socialisme en Liberalisme* 56, *Om de kwaliteit van het bestaan* 63.

c/o Ministerie van Economische Zaken, Bezuidenhoutsweg 30, The Hague, Netherlands.

Ulanfu (Wu-lan-fu); Chinese (Mongolian) politician; b. 05; ed. Far Eastern Univ., Moscow.

Joined revolutionary movement in West Mongolia; worked to arm Suiyuan Mongolian Defence Corps 37; went to Yenan at outbreak of Japanese War, studied at Army Political Acad., lectured at Inst. of Nationalities; additional mem. of 7th Congress, C.C.P. 45; Chair., formerly established Inner Mongolian Autonomous Govt. 47; on Standing Cttee. 1st C.P.P.C.C. 49; Cttee. for Nationality Questions; local govt. posts in Suiyuan to 54; North China Admin. Council 53-54; Vice-Premier State Council 54-; Chair. Nationalities Affairs Comm.; Head of Minorities Inst.; del. for Inner Mongolia at 1st N.P.C.; First Sec. of C.P. of Inner Mongolia until 67; Alt. mem. Politburo of Chinese Communist Party; Council of Nat. Defence.

Nationalities Affairs Commission, Peking, China.

Ulanova, Galina Sergeevna; Soviet ballerina; b. 10 Jan. 1910; ed. Leningrad Choreographic School.

Debut in Kirov Theatre 28, dancing the Chopin Suite (produced as *Les Sylphides* by Diaghilev Ballet); became star at the Kirov Theatre and then of the Bolshoi Ballet and danced many leading parts; has also made musical

films including *Etoiles du Ballet Russe* shown at Int. Film Festival, Cannes 54; now teaches ballet at Bolshoi Choreographic School; People's Artist of the U.S.S.R; four State Prizes, Lenin Prize 57.
Principal roles: Odette-Odile (*Swan Lake*), Aurora (*Sleeping Beauty*), Masha (*The Nutcracker*), Giselle (*Giselle*), Maria (*Bakhchisarai Fountain*), Cinderella (*Cinderella*), Juliet (*Romeo and Juliet*), Parasha (*The Copper Hoseman*), Tao Khoa (*The Red Flower*).
Publ. *Ballets Soviétiques* (The making of a ballerina).
State Academic Bolshoi Theatre, 1 Ploshchad Sverdlova, Moscow, U.S.S.R.

Ulbricht, Walter; German politician; b. 30 June 1893; ed. elementary school.
Woodworker by trade; Trade Unionist since 10; mem. Communist Party since 19; mem. of Reichstag 28-33; went to Moscow and became Head of Political Dept. of Communist Party; mem. Nat. Cttee. for Free Germany; elected to Central Secretariat of Socialist Unity Party (SED) May 46; mem. of Saxony-Anhalt Diet Oct. 46; Pres. Economic Cttee. of German People's Council April 48; First Vice-Minister-Pres. Oct. 49-60; Chair. Council of State 60-; First Sec. Socialist Unity Party.
Lothringerstrasse 1, Berlin, N.54, Germany.

Ullastres Calvo, Alberto, LL.D.; Spanish economic historian and politician; b. 14; ed. Madrid Univ.
Captain in Engineers (in reserve) of army; Prof. of Political Economy and Finance, Madrid Univ., Prof. of Econ. History, Leo XIII Inst.; Minister of Commerce 57-65; Ambassador to EEC (European Econ. Communities) 65-.
Spanish Delegation to EEC, Brussels, Belgium.

Ulrich, Franz Heinrich; German business executive; b. 6 July 1910; ed. German univs.
Member Board of Managing Dirs. Deutsche Bank AG; Chair. Supervisory Board Deutsche Erdöl-AG., Hamburg, Deutsche Gesellschaft für Wirtschaftliche Zusammenarbeit (Entwicklungsgesellschaft) mbH, Cologne; Mannesmann AG, Düsseldorf, Otto Wolff AG, Cologne; mem. Board German Bankers' Asscn.; Vice-Chair. and Treas. German Group of Int. Chamber of Commerce; Dir. Allianz Versicherungs-AG, Munich, Berlin, etc.
Deutsche Bank A.G., Königsallee 45, Düsseldorf, German Federal Republic.

Ulveling, Ralph A., PH.B., B.S., L.H.D.; American librarian; b. 9 May 1902; ed. De Paul, Columbia and Wayne State Univs.
Librarian, Public Library, Amarillo, Texas 26-27; Detroit Public Library, Chief of Branches 28-34, Assoc. Dir. 34-41, Dir. 41-; Pres. American Library Asscn. 45-46; mem. U.S. Nat. Comm. to UNESCO 46-49; Editorial Advisory Board World Book Encyclopedia 52-; Joseph W. Lippincott Award for distinguished librarianship 56.
20434 Lichfield Road, Detroit 21, Michigan, U.S.A.

Umakhnov, Magomed-Salam Ilyasovich; Soviet politician; b. 1918; ed. Higher Party School.
Member C.P.S.U. 39-; Soviet Army service 38-48; Chief of Section, Regional Cttee. of C.P. 48-52; Chair. Exec. Cttee. Territorial Soviet of Working People's Deputies; Minister of Light Industry, then Minister of Consumer Goods Industry, Daghestan A.S.S.R.; Sec. Karabudakhkentsky District Cttee. of C.P. 52-56; Chair. Council of Ministers, Daghestan A.S.S.R. 56-; Deputy to U.S.S.R. Supreme Soviet; mem. Cttee. for Planning and Budget, Soviet of Nationalities.
Council of Ministers of Daghestan A.S.S.R., Makhachkala, U.S.S.R.

Umari, Nathir Akram; Iraqi diplomatist; b. 17; ed. School of Languages, Baghdad, Liverpool Univ. and Columbia Univ.
Entered Foreign Service 45; with Iraq del. to U.N. 46-54; with U.N. Secretariat 51; Pres. Grain Board of Iraq, Acting Dir.-Gen. Dates Assoc., Oil Affairs, Econs.

and Tobacco Monopoly; Counsellor and Charge of Embassy, Delhi 58-60; Minister to U.K. 60-62; left diplomatic service for banking 63-64; Ambassador to Lebanon 64-67, to France 67-.
Embassy of Iraq, rue Pierret 1-3, Neuilly, Paris, France.

Umemura, Sakae; Japanese shipbuilder; b. 7 Jan. 1898; ed. Tokyo Univ.
Former Chief of Accountancy Dept. and Chief of Gen. Affairs Dept., Fujinagata Shipbuilding and Eng. Co. Ltd., now Pres. and Rep. Dir; Dir. Mitsui Shipbuilding and Eng. Co. Ltd.
24-3, 1-Chome, Aioidori, Abeno-ku, Osaka, Japan.
Telephone: (661)9869.

Umri, Gen. Hassan; Yemen Republican politician.
Took part in revolution against Imamate 62; Minister of Transport Sept.-Oct. 62, of Communications Oct. 62-April 63; mem. Council of Revolutionary Command 62-63; Vice-Pres. of Yemen 63-66; mem. Political Bureau 63-; Prime Minister Jan.-April 65, July 65-Sept. 66, Dec. 67-, also C.-in-C. of Army.
Office of the Prime Minister, Sana'a, Yemen.

Undén, Bo Östen, LL.D.; Swedish jurist and politician; b. 25 Aug. 1886; ed. Lund Univ.
Former Prof. of Civil and Private Int. Law Uppsala Univ.; Minister without Portfolio 17-20; Minister of Justice 20, of Foreign Affairs 24-26; Swedish mem. LN Council 24-26; Del. to LN Ass. 21-26, 28, 30-31, 33-35, 37-39; Legal Adviser to Foreign Office on Int. Law; Rector of Uppsala Univ. 29-32; Min. without Portfolio in Hanson Cabinet 32-36; Chancellor Swedish Univs. 37; mem. Parl.; Chair. Foreign Affairs Cttee.; Min. of Foreign Affairs 45-62; Del. to UN Assembly 46-61.
Publs. *Kollektivavtalet* 12, *Panträtt i rättigheter* 15, *Internationell äktenskapsrätt* 22, *Svensk sakrätt* (3 vols.) 27, 36, 40, *L'Affaire Martini, une sentence arbitrale internationale* 30, *L'article 181 du traité de Neuilly—une sentence arbitrale internationale* 33, *Tankar om Utrikespolitik* 63.
c/o Ministry of Foreign Affairs, Stockholm, Sweden.

Underhill, Lt.-Gen. Edward H.; American air force officer; b. 2 March 1907; ed. Mechanical Arts School, Boston and Lowell Inst.
U.S. Air Force 27-, Dir. of Flying, Air Corps Advanced Flying School, Brooks Field, Texas 39-42, Exec. Officer 42; Commdr., A.A.F. Glider School, Dalhart 42-43; Dir. of Training, A.A.F. Central Instruments School, Randolph Field 43; Commdr. Liberal (Kansas) Army Air Field 44; Asst. Chief of Staff, Fifth Air Force, South Pacific Theater 45; Commdr., Third Bomber Group 46-47; National War Coll., 48-49; Dep. Dir. for Military Personnel, Air Force H.Q., 49, Dir. 50; Dep. for Personnel, Far Eastern Air Forces 51-52; Dep. Commdr., Fifth Air Force 52-53; Dir., Joint Air Tactical Support Board, Fort Bragg 53-54; Dep. Commdr. Air Training Commd. 54-57; Commdr. Eastern Air Force 57-59; Senior Air Force mem. Military Studies and Liaison Div., Weapons Systems Evaluation Group 59-60; Chief of Staff, U.S. European Commd. 60-; Chair. Inter-American Defense Board 63-64; Distinguished Service Medal, Legion of Merit, UN Service Medal, National Defense Service Medal and numerous other decorations.
3625 Gunston Road, Alexandria, Va., U.S.A.

Underwood, Cecil H., M.A., LL.D.; American politician; b. 5 Nov. 1922; ed. Salem Coll., West Virginia Univ.
U.S. Army Reserve Corps. 42-43; high-school teacher 43-56; mem. staff Marietta Coll. 46-50; Vice-Pres. Salem Coll. 50-56; Vice-Pres. Island Creek Coal Co. 61-64; Public Relations Counsellor 64-; mem. West Virginia House of Delegates 44-56 and Minority Floor Leader 49-54; Gov. of West Virginia 57-61; Temp. Chair. Republican Nat. Convention 60; Dir. Civic Affairs, Monsanto Co. 65-; eight hon. degrees.
1930 S. Englewood Road, Huntington, W. Va., U.S.A.

Ungaretti, Giuseppe; Italian poet; b. 10 Feb. 1888; ed. Univ. of Paris.
Former Man. Editor of review *Mesures*; teacher of Italian Literature, São Paulo, Brazil 37-42; Prof. of Italian Literature, Univ. of Rome 42-59; Pres. European Community of Writers, European Soc. of Culture. Publs. include *L'allegria, Sentimento del tempo, Il dolore, La terra promessa, Un grido e paesaggi, Il taccuino del vecchio, Apocalissi, Il deserto e dopo,* trans. of *Visions* of William Blake.
1 Via della Sierra Nevada (EUR), Rome, Italy.

Unger, Leonard, A.B.; American diplomatist; b. 17 Dec. 1917; ed. Harvard Univ.
National Resources Planning Board 39-41; Dept. of State 41-, served Trieste, Naples; Officer in Charge of Politico-Military Affairs, European Regional Affairs Div., State Dept. 53-57; Dep. Chief of Mission, American Embassy, Bangkok, Thailand 58-62; Ambassador to Laos 62-64; Deputy Asst. Sec. of State for Far Eastern Affairs 65-67; Amb. to Thailand 67-.
c/o Department of State, Washington, D.C.; Home: 12701 Circle Drive, Rockville, Md., U.S.A.

Unruh, Fritz von; German-born American dramatist, poet and novelist; b. 10 May 1885.
Capt. First World War; mem. German Acad. of Art and Literature until 33; emigrated to France 33, then to America; returned to Germany 48; numerous awards including Kleist Prize, Goethe Prize, One World Award, Carl von Ossietzky Medal, Berlin.
Publs. *Offiziere* 11, *Prinz Louis Ferdinand* 13, *Vor der Entscheidung* 14, *Opfergang* (The first description of the battle of Verdun) 16, *Ein Geschlecht* 16, *Platz* 20, *Rosengarten* 22, *Reden an die Jugend* 23, *Stürme* 23, *Flügel der Nike* 24, *Heinrich aus Andernach* 25, *Bonaparte* 26, *Hauptmann von Werner, Zwei Feldsoldaten, Das Massengrab von Champien, Phaea* 30, *Zero* 31, *Politeia* 33, *Charlotte Corday* 35, *Gandha* 36, *Europa, Erwache?* 36, *Der nie verlor* 47 (American edn. *The End is Not Yet* 46), *Paulskirchen-Rede und Goethe-Rede* 48, *Fürchtet nichts* 52, *Die Heilige* (American edn. *The Saint*), *Mächtig seid ihr nicht in Waffen, Redenband* 57, *Wilhelmus* 53, *Duell an der Havel* 54, *Der Sohn des Generals* 58, 1st Vol. of Collected Works with 5 plays 60, *Rebell und Verkünder* 60, *Ein Traum* 60, *Pax Anima* 60, *Mahnruf* 60, *Brüder* 61, *Offenbach Rede* 61, *Die Lebendigen rufe ich* 61, *Rede an die Frankfurter Jugend* 63, *Meine Begegnung mit Trotski* 64, *Im Haus der Prinzen* 64, *Bolivar* 65, *Eine Juli-Nacht* 65, *Kalypso* (play) 66.
Hof Oranien, Diez/Lahn, German Federal Republic.

Unruh, Walther K. G., DIPL.ING.; German consulting engineer; b. 10 Jan. 1898; ed. Leipzig Univ. and Technische Hochschule, Dresden.
Technical Dir., Staatstheater, Karlsruhe 24-25, National-theater, Mannheim 25-34, Staatsoper, Hamburg 34-45; independent consultant and planner for theatres and stage equipment in Europe and U.S.A., including Berlin, Cologne, Salzburg, Brussels, Barcelona, Sydney and New Metropolitan Opera Houses and more than twenty-five German theatres 45-; Prof., West Berlin Technical Univ.; Editor and Dir. *Bühnentechnische Rundschau* (bi-monthly); Chair. Deutsche Theater-technische Gesellschaft; Dir. German Section, Int. Theatre Inst. Paris.
Publs. *ABC der Theatertechnik, Hilfsbuch der Bühnentechnik* (with F. Hansing).
Haydn Strasse 8, D-62 Wiesbaden, German Federal Republic.
Telephone: (06121) 370414.

Unsöld, Albrecht Otto Johannes, DR. PHIL.; German university professor; b. 20 April 1905; ed. Univs. of Tübingen and Munich.
Asst. Inst. of Theoretical Physics, Univ. of Munich 27; Fellow, Int. Education Board 28; Lecturer, Univ. of Munich 29, Univ. of Hamburg 30; Prof. of Theoretical Physics, Dir. Inst. of Theoretical Physics and Observatory, Univ. of Kiel 32-; corresp. mem. Bavarian Acad. of Sciences, Göttingen Acad. of Sciences; Assoc. Royal Astronomical Society, London; Hon. mem. Royal Astronomical Society of Canada; Copernicus Prize 43, Catherine Wolfe Bruce Gold Medal Astronomical Society of the Pacific 56; Gold Medal of Royal Astronomical Society 57; Editor *Zeitschrift für Astrophysik;* Dr. rer. nat. h.c. Utrecht State Univ. 61; foreign mem. Provinciaal Utrechts Genootschap van Kunsten en Wetenschappen, Utrecht 61; mem. Int. Acad. of Astronautics, Paris, Deutsche Akademie der Naturforscher Leopoldina, Halle, Kungliga Fysiografiska Sällskapet i Lund.
Publs. *Physik der Sternatmosphären* 38 (2nd edn. 55), *Der neue Kosmos* 67.
Sternwartenweg 17, Kiel 23, German Federal Republic.
Telephone: 44205.

Unterman, Rabbi Iser Jehudah; Israeli Rabbi; b. 86; ed. Rabbinical Colls. in Poland and Lithuania.
Rabbinical posts in Poland 13-23; Rabbi of Liverpool and District 23; Pres. Mizrachi Fed. of Great Britain and Ireland 43-46; Chief Rabbi, Tel-Aviv and District 46-; Chief Rabbi of Israel; Pres. Rabbinical Courts, Tel-Aviv; Pres. Union of Rabbinical Colls.; mem. Exec. Cttee., Chief Rabbinate of Holy Land.
Publ. *Shevet Myehuda* 55; contrib. rabbinical publs. in Israel, Great Britain and U.S.A.
Home: 6 Engel Street, Tel-Aviv; Office: Office of the Chief Rabbinate, 33 King David Boulevard, Tel-Aviv, Israel.

Untermeyer, Mrs. Jean Starr; American author; b. 13 May 1886; ed. Columbia Univ.
Lieder singer Vienna and London 24-25; mem. teaching staff Writers' Congress Olivet Coll. Mich. 36-37; Ford Madox Ford Prof. of Creative Literature 40; lecturer and teacher, New School of Social Research New York, Yale Univ., etc.; mem. Author's League, P.E.N.; received fellowship at Huntington Hartford Foundation, Calif. (3 times).
Publs. *Growing Pains* 18, *Dreams Out Of Darkness* 22, *Steep Ascent* 27, *Winged Child* 36, *Love and Need* (poems) 40; *Private Collection* (memoir) 65; *Job's Daughter* (poems) 67; translated Oscar Bie's *Schubert the Man,* Hermann Broch's *The Death of Virgil* 45.
235 East 73rd Street, New York, N.Y. 10021, U.S.A.
Telephone: REgent 7-4417.

Untermeyer, Louis; American author; b. 1 Oct. 1885.
Contrib. Editor *The Liberator* and *The Seven Arts;* Lecturer Amherst, Knox, Michigan and other univs.
Publs. include: *Roast Leviathan* 23, *Food and Drink* 32, *Chip—My Life and Times* 33, *Poetry—Its Appreciation and Enjoyment, The Donkey of God* 33, *Selected Poems and Parodies* 35, *Rainbow in the Sky* 35, *Play in Poetry* 37, *Heinrich Heine: Paradox and Poet* (2 vols.) 37, *From Another World* (autobiography) 39, *Stars to Steer By* 40, *Modern American and British Poetry* (revised) 42, *A Treasury of Great Poems* 42, *A Treasury of Laughter* 46, *The Book of Noble Thoughts* 46, *The Love Poems of Robert and Elizabeth Browning* 47, *An Anthology of the New England Poets* 48, *The Inner Sanctum, Walt Whitman* 49, *The New Modern American and British Poetry* 50, *The Best Humor Annual* 50, 51, 52, *The Magic Circle* 52, *Makers of the Modern World* 55, *A Treasury of Ribaldry* 56, *Lives of the Poets* 59, *Britannica Library of Great American Writing* 60, *Long Feud: Selected Poems* 62, *The Letters of Robert Frost to Louis Untermeyer* 63, *The World's Great Stories* 64, *Labyrinth of Love* 65, *Bygones: An Autobiography* 65, *The Paths of Poetry* 66, *The Firebringer and Other Stories* 68.
Great Hill Road, Newtown, Conn., U.S.A.
Telephone: 203-426-2383.

Unverzagt, Wilhelm, DR. PHIL.; German archaeologist; b. 21 May 1892; ed. Univs. of Bonn, Munich, Berlin and Frankfurt-am-Main.

Asst. Provincial Museum of Antiquities, Wiesbaden 18-20; Asst., and later Curator and Head, State Museum for Prehistory and Protohistory, Berlin 25, Dir. 26; Hon. Prof. Univ. of Berlin 32; Ordinary mem., German Acad. of Sciences, Berlin 49, fmr. Dir. of Inst. of Prehistory and Protohistory; mem. Comité d'Honneur Permanent Int. Union of Prehistoric and Protohistoric Sciences 32-; mem. Comité d'Honneur Perm. Union Int. d'Archéologie Slave 66; Hon. mem. Spanish Soc. of Anthropology, Ethnography and Prehistory, Jydsk Arkaeologisk Selskab, Aarhus; Hon. F.S.A. (London); publisher of *Prähistorische Zeitschrift* 27-, *Ausgrabungen und Funde* 56-.

Publs. *Die Keramik des Kastells Alzey* 16, *Terra sigillata mit Rädchenverzierung* 19, *Der Burgwall von Lossow* 30, *Zantoch, eine Burg im deutschen Osten,* Vol. I 36, *Der Burgwall von Kliestow* 40, *Landschaft, Burgen und Bodenfunde als Quellen nordostdeutscher Frühgeschichte* 42.

Sybelstrasse 38, Berlin-Charlottenburg 12, Germany. Telephone: 8877321.

Unwin, Sir Stanley, K.C.M.G., Kt., F.R.S.L.; British publisher; b. 19 Dec. 1884.

Chair. George Allen & Unwin Ltd.; Dir. Equitable Life Assurance Society; Past Pres. Int. Publishers' Asscn.; Past Pres. Publishers' Asscn. of Great Britain and Ireland; mem. Exec. British Council; mem. Royal Inst.; Patron, Royal Institute of International Affairs; Fellow, Royal Society of Literature; foreign hon. mem. American Acad. of Arts and Sciences; Palmes en or de l'ordre de la Couronne; Palmes d'officier d'Académie Française; Order of White Lion (Czechoslovakia), Officer, Order of Orange Nassau (Neths.), Knight Commdr. Order of Falcon (Iceland); Hon. LL.D. (Aberdeen).

Publs. *The Truth About Publishing, Two Young Men See the World, How Governments Treat Books, The Truth about a Publisher.*

4 Oak Hill Park, London, N.W.3, England.

Updike, John Hoyer, A.B.; American writer; b. 18 March 1932; ed. Shillington High School, Pennsylvania, and Harvard Coll.

Reporter on the magazine *New Yorker* 55-57.

Publs. *The Carpentered Hen* (poems) 58, *The Poorhouse Fair* (novel) 59, *The Same Door* (short stories) 59, *Rabbit, Run* (novel) 60, *Pigeon Feathers and Other Stories* 62, *The Centaur* (novel) 63, *Telephone Poles and Other Poems* 63, *Assorted Prose* 65, *Of the Farm* (novel) 65, *The Music School* (short stories) 66, *Couples* (novel).

26 East Street, Ipswich, Mass., U.S.A.

Upit, Andrei Martynovich; Soviet professor, writer and literary critic; b. 1877.

Member C.P.S.U. 40-; mem. Latvian Acad. of Sciences; M.Sc. (Philology); People's Writer of Latvia 43, State Prize 46, Hero of Socialist Labour 67, Orders of Lenin (twice), of Red Banner of Labour (three times).

Publs. include: Novels: *Robezhnieki* (trilogy, *New Sources* 08, *The Silken Web* 12, *North Wind* 21), *Return of Jan Robezhnieki* 32, *Death of Jan Robezhnieki* 33, *The Green Land* 45, *First Night* 49, *The Smiling Fox, The Story of the Life of O. Kurya* (two vols.) 62; *Collected Works* (22 vols.) 46-54, *History of Latvian Literature* (six vols.) 59, *Lads from Zamsheloye Village* 64, *Renegades* 65, *Sister Gertruda's Mystery* 67.

U.S.S.R. Writers' Union, 52 Vorovsky Street, Moscow, U.S.S.R.

Upmark, Erik Gustaf Johan; Swedish administrator; b. 04; ed. Uppsala Hoegre Allmaenna Laeroverk, War Acad., Karlberg, and Technical Univ., Stockholm.

With Vattenbyggnadsbyraan A.B. 27; with Messrs.

Rendel, Palmer and Tritton 28; Sec. Swedish Water Power Asscn. 35; Chair. State Fuel and Power Comm. 47; Gen. Manager Swedish State Rlys. 49-; mem. Royal Swedish Acad. of Engineering Sciences; Pres. Int. Union of Railways.

Office: Statens Jaernvaeger, Centralplan, Stockholm C; Home: Karlaplan 18, Stockholm NO, Sweden.
Telephone: 08-101836 (Office); 08-603247 (Home).

Upton, Thomas Graydon, A.B.; American banker; b. 26 March 1908; ed. Harvard Univ., Harvard Business School.

European Rep. Bank of the Manhattan Co. 36-40; military service 41-46; investment counsellor, New York 46-50; Vice-Pres. Foreign Dept. Philadelphia Nat. Bank 50-58; Asst. Sec. of the Treasury 58; U.S. Exec. Dir. World Bank 59-; Exec. Vice-Pres. Inter-American Development Bank 61-.

Inter-American Development Bank, 808 17th Street, N.W., Washington, D.C. 20577; and 817 Bulls Neck Road, McLean, Va. 22101, U.S.A.
Telephone: 893-9154.

Uquaili, Nabi Baksh Mohammed Sidiq, S.PK.; Pakistani chartered accountant and government official; b. 11 Aug. 1913.

Experience of agricultural banking, commercial banking, central banking, exchange control and industrial and investment banking for over thirty years; Controller of Foreign Exchange, State Bank of Pakistan 51-58; Man. Dir. Pakistan Industrial Credit and Investment Corpn. 58-66; Minister of Finance 67-; Vice-Pres. Pakistan Inst. of Chartered Accountants; Grosses Bundesverdienstkreuz.

Office: Ministry of Finance, Rawalpindi, West Pakistan; Home: 53 Muslimabad, Karachi, West Pakistan.

Urabe, Shizutaro; Japanese architect; b. 31 March 1909; ed. Kyoto Univ.

Kurashiki Rayon Co. Ltd. 34-64; Lecturer (part-time) in Architecture, Osaka Univ. Technical Course 54-55; Lecturer (part-time) in Architecture, Kyoto Univ. Technical Course 62-66; Pres. K.K., S. Urabe & Assoc. Architects 62-; Prize of *Mainichi Shuppan Bunka Sho* (publication) 61; Osaka Prefecture Architectural Contest Prize 62; Annual of Architecture Prize 63; Architectural Inst. of Japan Prize 64; Osaka Prefecture Order of Merit 65.

Buildings include: Ohara Museum (Annex) 61, Suita Service Area 63 and other offices of Japan Road Corpn. 65, Kurashiki Int. Hotel 63, Aizenbashi Hospital and Nursery School, etc. 65, Asahi Broadcasting Co. Ltd. (consultant) 61; Tokyo Zokei Univ. 66, Tokyo Women's Christian Coll., Research Inst. 67.

Offices: S. Urabe and Assoc. Architects, 7th Floor, New Hankyu Building, 8, Umeda, Kita-ku, Osaka; Shin-Nihonbashi Building, 3-1, Nihonbashi-dori, Chuo-ku, Tokyo; Home: 1-181, Kotoen, Nishinomiya Hyogo, Japan.

Urbain, Yves, PH.D.; Belgian university professor and politician; b. 2 Feb. 1914; ed. Université Catholique de Louvain.

Professor specializing in regional economy, Univ. of Louvain 45-63; Provincial Senator for Hainaut 63-65; mem. Chamber of Reps. 65-; Minister of Communications 65-66; Asst. to Prime Minister for affairs concerning regional economy 66; Christian Socialist.

c/o Prime Minister's Office, Brussels, Belgium.

Urbani, H.E. Cardinal Giovanni; Italian ecclesiastic; b. 1900.

Ordained priest 22; Titular Bishop of Assume 46; Titular Archbishop of Sardis 48; Bishop of Verona 55-58; Patriarch of Venice 58-; created Cardinal by Pope John XXIII 58; mem. Sacred Congregations of the Consistory, of Religious, of the Council and of Rites; Pres. Italian Episcopal Conf. 66-; mem. Papal Comm.

for Revision of Canon Law; elected by Italian Episcopate to First Synod of Bishops.
Palazzo Patriarcale, San Marco 318, 30124 Venice, Italy.
Telephone: 25-6-94.

Urbanski, Tadeusz; Polish university professor; b. 26 Oct. 1901.
Professor of Organic Technology, Warsaw Technical Univ. 34-39, 46-; Chemist C.N.R.S., Paris 40; Principal Exp. Officer Ministry of Supply, London 40-46; Dir. Inst. Organic Chemistry Polish Acad. Sciences 58-68; Senior Foreign Fellow N.S.F., U.S.A. and Visiting Prof. Univs. Illinois and Maryland 65-66; Pres. Polish Chemical Soc. 50; mem. Presidium, Polish Acad. of Sciences; foreign mem. German Acad. Leopoldina; mem. IUPAC Bureau 57-61; Sec. Div. Cttee. of Organic Chemistry IUPAC 61-65; Nat. Rep. Comm. on Molecular Structure and Spectroscopy IUPAC 61-; State Prizes 49 and 52; Sniadecki Medal, Polish Chemical Soc. 65.
Publs. *Theory of Nitration* (in Polish) 54, *Chemie und Technologie der Explosivstoffe*, 3 vols. 61-64 (English trans. 64-67), *Nitro Compounds* (Editor) 64.
Koszykowa 75, Warsaw 10, Poland.

Urey, Harold Clayton, B.S., PH.D., D.SC.; American chemist; b. 29 April 1893; ed. Univs. of Montana and California.
Research chemist, Barrett Chemical Co. 18-19; Instructor, Univ. of Montana 19-21; American-Scandinavian Foundation Fellow, Copenhagen 23-24; Assoc. in Chemistry, Johns Hopkins Univ. 24-29; Assoc. Prof. Columbia Univ. 29-34, Prof. 34-45; Dir. of War Research, SAM Laboratories 40-45; Distinguished Service Prof. of Chemistry, The Enrico Fermi Inst. for Nuclear Studies, Univ. of Chicago 45-52, Martin A. Ryerson Prof. 52-58; Visiting Prof. Oxford 56-57; Prof. at large, California 58-; mem. Nat. Acad. of Sciences, etc.; foreign mem. Royal Society (London), and Swedish, Belgian, Irish, Indian and American Scientific Societies; Hon. D.Sc. (Princeton, Montana, Newark, Columbia, Oxford, Washington and Lee, Athens, Yale, MacMaster, Indiana, Durham, Birmingham, Saskatchewan, Pittsburgh, Chicago, Manchester, Israel Inst. of Technology and Gustavus Adolphus Coll.); Hon. LL.D. (Calif., Wayne, Notre Dame Univs.); D.Hum. (Hebrew Union Coll.); Nobel Prize for Chemistry 34, Willard Gibbs Medal (American Chemical Soc.) 34, Davy Medal (Royal Soc., London) 40, Franklin Medal 43, Medal for Merit 46, Cordoza Award 54, Joseph Priestley Award (Dickinson Coll.) 55; Alexander Hamilton Award (Columbia Univ.) 61; J. Lawrence Smith Medal 62; Univ. of Paris Medal 64, Nat. Medal for Sciences 64; Royal Astronomical Soc. Gold Medal 66.
Publs. *Atoms, Molecules and Quanta* (with A. E. Ruark) 30, *The Planets* 52.
Revelle College, University of California, San Diego, La Jolla, Calif., Home: 7890 Torrey Lane, La Jolla, Calif. 92037, U.S.A.

Ürgüplü, Ali Suat Hayri; Turkish politician; b. 1903; ed. Lycée Galatasaray and Univ. of Istanbul.
Turkish Sec. Mixed Courts of Arbitration 26-29; Magistrate Supreme Commercial Court, Istanbul 29-32; Lawyer at Courts of Istanbul and mem. Admin. Council; mem. Turkish Nat. Assembly 39-46; Minister of Customs and Monopolies 43-46; resigned and left People's Party 46; re-elected to Grand Nat. Assembly 50 and joined Democratic Party; mem. and Vice-Chair. Council of Europe 50-52; Ambassador to Fed. German Republic 52-55, to U.K. 55-57, to U.S.A. 57-60, to Spain 60; Senator (Independent) and Speaker of Senate 61-63; Prime Minister Jan.-Oct. 65.
The Senate, Ankara, Turkey.

Uri, Pierre Emmanuel; French economic consultant; b. 11 Nov. 1911; ed. Lycée Henri IV, Ecole Normale Supérieure and Princeton Univ.
Professor of Philosophy 36-40; Research Economist 44-47; Econ. and Financial Adviser to French Planning Comm. 47-52; Prof. Nat. School of Public Admin. 47-51; Econ. Dir. European Coal and Steel Community (ECSC) 52-59, Econ. Adviser, Common Market 58-59; European Rep., Lehman Brothers 59-61; Econ. Consultant, particularly Counsellor for Studies, Atlantic Inst. 62-; Chair. Experts' Group on Long Term Development in European Economic Community 60-64; Chevalier de la Légion d'Honneur, Croix de Guerre, etc.
Publs. *La réforme de l'enseignement* 37, *Le fonds monétaire international* 45, *French National Economic Budgets* 47-48, *Report of French Delegation on Treaty of Paris Instituting the Coal and Steel Community* 51, *Report of the Inter-Governmental Committee on the Common Market and Euratom* 56, *Report on the Economic Situation of the European Community Countries* 58, *Dialogue des Continents* 63, *Une Politique Monétaire pour L'Amérique Latine* 65, *Pour gouverner* 67, *From Commonwealth to Common Market* 68.
1 avenue du Président Wilson, Paris 16e, France.
Telephone: KLeber 97-42.

Urien, César, LL.D.; Argentine lawyer and diplomatist; ed. Univ. de Buenos Aires.
Former Judiciary Official and Sec. of Sentencing Tribunal; mem. Chamber of Deputies 42; Prof. of Law and Forensic Practice; then Prof. of History; Dir. of Records, Acad. of Econ. Sciences; Minister of Agriculture and Livestock; mem. Gen. Arbitration Tribunal of Chamber of Commerce, Buenos Aires; Amb. to Spain 66-; several decorations.
Publs. on cattle-raising, milk production and agricultural co-operatives.
Embajada de la República Argentina, Paseo de la Castellana 63, Madrid, Spain.

Uris, Leon Marcus; American writer; b. 3 Aug. 1924; ed. High School.
Served with the United States Marine Corps 42-45.
Publs. *Battle Cry* 53 (novel and screenplay), *The Angry Hills* 55, *Exodus* 57, *Mila 18* 60, *Gunfight at the OK Corral* (screenplay), *Armageddon* 64, *Topaz* 67; with others *Exodus Revisited* (Photo essay) 59.
c/o McGraw Hill Book Co., 330 West 42nd Street, New York, N.Y. 10036, U.S.A.

Urquhart, Alastair Hugh, C.B.E.; Australian stockbroker; b. 3 Nov. 1919; ed. Sydney Church of England Grammar School.
Senior Partner, Australian stockbroking firm; mem. Sydney Stock Exchange 49-, Chair. 59-66; Vice-Pres. Australian Associated Stock Exchanges 60-63, Pres. 59, 64-66; Army Service 40-45; official of commercial and civic orgs.
52 Anzac Avenue, Collaroy, N.S.W., Australia.

Urrutia, Francisco; Colombian diplomatist; b. 10; ed. Ecole des sciences politiques, Paris, and Universidad Nacional de Colombia.
Sec., Quito 32; accredited corresp. of League of Nations in Colombia 32-45; elected rep. to Departmental Assembly of Cundinamarca 41; Prof. of Int. Law and Diplomatic History, Universidad del Rosario, Bogotá 40-46; Minister to Belgium 46-47; rep. of Colombia UN Security Council, Balkan Inquiry Comm. 47; Ambassador to Argentina 48-50, to UN 50-51, to Venezuela 52-53, to U.S.A. 55-57; Perm. Rep. to UN 53-57; Personal Rep. of UN Sec.-Gen. Mount Scopus 58; UN High Commrs. Rep. for Latin America 60-62, Regional Rep. for Americas 62-; Pres. Inter-American Inst. of Int. Legal Studies 66.
177 East 75 Street, New York, N.Y., U.S.A.

Urrutia Aparicio, Carlos, PH.D.; Guatemalan internationalist; b. 6 Jan. 1927; ed. Colegio de Infantes Guatemala, Univ. of Dayton, Ohio, George Washington Univ., Washington, D.C., and American Univ., Washington, D.C.
Pan American Union 55-58; Alt. Perm. Rep. of Guatemala to UN 58; Consul-Gen. of Guatemala in New York 58-60; Ambassador of Guatemala to Organization of American States (OAS) and Perm. Rep. to Council of OAS 60-63; special OAS envoy to Uruguay and Paraguay 63; Chief, OAS Div. of Gen. Information 63-65, Technical Dir. of the OAS Chronicle, and Special Asst. to Dept. of Information and Public Affairs 65-; Order of Rubén Dario (Nicaragua) and Order of El Quetzal (Guatemala).
Publs. *Juridical Aspects of the Anglo-Guatemalan Controversy: in Re Belize* 51, *Opusculo sobre el Derecho de Asilo Diplomático* 52, *Puerto Rico, América y las Naciones Unidas* 54, *Diplomatic Asylum in Latin America* 60, *Páginas internacionales de la vida democrática de Guatemala* 61.
Pan American Union, Washington 6, D.C.; Home: 8608 Rayburn Road, Bethesda, Md., U.S.A.
Telephone: 654-3282.

Ursi, H.E. Cardinal Corrado; Italian ecclesiastic; b. 26 July 1908.
Ordained Priest 31; Archbishop of Naples 51-; created Cardinal by Pope Paul VI 67.
Largo Donnaregina 23, Naples, Italy.

Urwick, Lt.-Col. Lyndall, O.B.E., M.C., M.A., F.B.I.M., M.I.P.E., C.I.MECH.E.; British industrial management consultant; b. 3 March 1891; ed. New Coll., Oxford.
Mem. staff Rowntree and Co. Ltd. 22-28; Dir. Int. Management Inst. Geneva 28-33; Chair. Urwick, Orr and Partners Ltd. (management consultants) 34-63; Consultant H.M. Treasury 40-42; G.S.O.1. Petroleum Warfare Dept. 42-44; Chair. Cttee. on Education for Management 47; Vice-Chair. British Inst. of Management 47; Gold Medal Int. Cttee. for Scientific Management 51; Wallace Clark Int. Management Award 55; Henry Laurence Gantt Gold Medal 61: The Taylor Key 63; Bowie Medal 68; Knight of St. Olaf (Norway) 48.
Publs. *The Meaning of Rationalisation* 29, *Distribution in Europe and the U.S.A.* 31, *Management of To-morrow* 33, *Organising a Sales Office* 37, *Committees in Organization* 37, *The Development of Scientific Management in Great Britain* 38, *Dynamic Administration* 41, *The Elements of Administration* 44, *The Making of Scientific Management*, Vol. I, *Thirteen Pioneers* 45, Vol. II, *British Industry* 45, Vol. III, *The Hawthorne Experiments* 48, *Freedom and Co-ordination* 49, *Management Education in American Business* 54, *The Pattern of Management* 56, *Leadership in the XX Century* 57, *Organisation* 66.
Urwick Orr & Partners Ltd., 14 Hobart Place, London, S.W.1, England; and 83 Kenneth Street, Longueville, N.S.W. 2066, Australia.
Telephone: 01-235-2494; and Sydney 422102.

Urzaiz y de Silva, Mariano; Spanish naval officer and public administrator; b. 04; ed. Instituto y Escuela Naval.
Naval Attaché, Rome, Berlin and London during Second World War, retd. from active naval list 62; Dir.-Gen. of Tourism 52-62; mem. of Spanish nobility; Gran Cruz Isabel la Católica, Gran Cruz Mérito Civil.
c/o Dirección General del Turismo, Medinaceli 2, Madrid, Spain.

Usami, Makoto; Japanese banker; b. 5 Feb. 1901; ed. Keio Univ.
Entered Mitsubishi Bank, Ltd. 24, Man. Econ. Research Dept. 47, Man. Gen. Affairs Dept. 49, Dir. 50, Dir. and Man. Head Office 51-54, Man. Dir. 54-59, Dep. Pres. 59-61, Pres. 61-64; Governor Bank of Japan 64-; Alt. Gov. for Japan, Int. Monetary Fund, Int. Bank for Reconstruction and Devt.; Chair. Fed. of the Bankers' Asscn. of Japan 62-63.
Bank of Japan, 2-1, 1 Hongoku-cho, Nihonbashi, Chuo-ku, Tokyo; Home: 24-15, 1 Minami-Aoyama, Minato-ku, Tokyo, Japan.
Telephone: 279-1111 (Office).

Usher, Arsène Assouan, M.A.; Ivory Coast lawyer and politician; b. 30; ed. Bordeaux and Poitiers Univs.
Lawyer, Court of Appeals, Poitiers 55-56; Cabinet attaché of M. Houphouet-Boigny 56; Asst. Dir. Caisse des Allocations Familiales 57-59; Conseiller Général 57-59; Dep. Vice-Pres. Nat. Assembly 59-60; Lawyer, Court of Appeals, Abidjan 59; Head, Ivory Coast Perm. Mission to UN 61-67; Minister of Foreign Affairs 67-; mem. UN Security Council 64-67.
Ministry of Foreign Affairs, Abidjan; and Cocody-Abidjan, Ivory Coast, West Africa.

Usherwood, Kenneth Ascough, C.B.E.; British insurance executive; b. 19 Aug. 1904; ed. City of London School and St. John's Coll., Cambridge.
Prudential Assurance Co. Ltd. 25-, South Africa 32-34, Near East 34-37, Deputy Gen. Man. 47-60, Gen. Man. 61-67; Dir. of Statistics, Ministry of Supply 41-45; Dir. Prudential Assurance Co. Ltd.; Pres. Inst. of Actuaries 62-64.
24 Litchfield Way, London, N.W.11, England.
Telephone: 01-455-7915.

Usinger, Robert Leslie, B.S., PH.D.; American entomologist; b. 24 Oct. 1912; ed. Univs. of California and Hawaii.
Entomologist Bishop Museum, Honolulu 35-36; Asst. Curator of Entomology, Calif. Acad. of Sciences 36-39; Instructor in Entomology, Univ. of Calif. 39-44, Asst. Prof. 44-50, Assoc. Prof. 50-53, Prof. 53, Chair. Div. of Entomology 63-; Research Assoc. Calif. Acad. of Sciences 42-, Bishop Museum, Honolulu 53-; U.S. Public Health Service, Malaria Control 43-46; Special Research Fellow, Nat. Inst. of Health (British Museum, London) 48-49; mem. Int. Comm. on Zoological Nomenclature, Paris 48, Copenhagen 53; Chair. Pacific Science Board, Nat. Acad. of Sciences 62-; Fellow Royal Entomological Soc. (London), A.A.A.S.; mem. Perm. Cttee. Int. Cong. of Entomology, Int. Union of Biological Sciences; Dir. Galapagos Int. Scientific Project 64; Editor *Pan-Pacific Entomologist* 39-49; mem. Editorial Board *General Catalogue of Hemiptera of the World;* King Frederick of Denmark Galathea Exp. Gold Medal 55; Award of Merit, Ecuador 64, Hon. Citizen, Guayaquil 64.
Publs. *The Genus Nysius and Allies in the Hawaiian Islands* 42, *Methods and Principles of Systematic Zoology* 53, *Elements of Zoology* 55, *Aquatic Insects of California* 56, *General Zoology* 57, *Classification of the Aradidae* 59, *Sierra Nevada Natural History* 63, *Monograph of Cimicidae* 66, *Life in Rivers and Streams* 66.
4 Yale Circle, Berkeley 8, and University of California, Berkeley 4, California, U.S.A.
Telephone: 526-0771 (Home).

Uslar-Pietri, Arturo; Venezuelan writer and politician; b. 06; ed. Universidad Central de Venezuela.
Professor of Political Economy, Universidad Central de Venezuela 37-41; Minister of Nat. Education, Venezuela 39-41, Minister of Finance 43, of Foreign Affairs 45; Prof. of Latin American Literature, Columbia Univ., New York 47; Prof. of Venezuelan Literature, Universidad Central, Caracas; mem. Senate, Academia Venezolana de la Lengua; Independent Candidate for Pres. Dec. 63; Head of Frente Nacional Democrático.
Publs. inc.; novels: *Las lanzas coloradas* 31, *El camino de El Dorado* 47; biography: *Apuntes para retratos* 52, *Valores Humanos I* 55, *II* 56, *III* 58; travel: *Imágenes del occidente venezolano* 40, *Las visiones del camino* 45,

Tierra venezolana 53, *El otoño en Europa* 54, *La ciudad de nadie* 60; plays: *Teatro* 58, *Chúo Gil y las tejedoras* 60. Apartado 12.551, Galerías Bolívar, Caracas, Venezuela.

Usmani, Ishrat Husain, PH.D.; Pakistani scientist and administrator; b. 15 April 1917; ed. Aligarh Univ., Bombay Univ. and Imperial Coll. of Science and Technology, London.
Joined Madras Cadre of Indian Civil Service 42; fmr. Chief Controller of Imports and Exports, Pakistan; fmr. Chair. W. Pakistan Mineral Development Corpn.; Chair. Pakistan Atomic Energy Comm. 60-; Chair. Pakistan Power Comm. 61-62; Chair. Board of Govs., IAEA Vienna 62-63; mem.-Sec. Scientific Comm., Pakistan 59-61; mem. Nat. Science Council, Pakistan; Hon. Consultant to UN Sec.-Gen. on Nuclear Non-proliferation Treaty.
Pakistan Atomic Energy Commission, P.O. Box No. 3112, Karachi, Pakistan.
Telephone: 41003 and 471292.

Usmanov, Gumer Ismagilovich; Soviet politician; b. 1932; ed. Kazan Agricultural Inst.
Member C.P.S.U. 53-; Teacher, First Sec. District Cttee. of Young Communist League 50-56; Sec., later, Second, and then First Sec. Chistopolsk City Cttee. of C.P., then Chief, Production Collective State Farm Dept. 56-65; First Sec. Buinsky District Cttee. of C.P. 65-66; Chair. Council of Ministers, Tatar A.S.S.R. 66-; Deputy to U.S.S.R. Supreme Soviet; mem. Cttee. for Construction and Building Material Industry.
Council of Ministers of Tatar A.S.S.R., Kazan, U.S.S.R.

Usmanov, Saidmakhmud Nogmanovich, M.SC.; Soviet politician; b. 1929; ed. Tashkent Agricultural Inst. and Cotton Research Inst.
Member C.P.S.U. 55-; Technician, post-graduate student 51-55; scientific worker 55-56; Teacher, Tashkent Higher Party School 56-58; Official, Central Cttee. of C.P. Uzbekistan 58-59; Sec. Surkhandaryinsk Regional Cttee. of C.P. Uzbekistan 59-61; Chair. Exec. Cttee. Surkhandaryinsk Regional Soviet of Working People's Deputies 61-62; Sec. Central Cttee. of C.P. Uzbekistan 62-63; First Deputy Minister of Production and Provision of Agricultural Produce Uzbekistan 63-64; First Sec. Samarkand Regional Cttee. of C.P. Uzbek S.S.R. 64-; mem. Central Revision Comm. of C.P.S.U. 66-; Deputy to U.S.S.R. Supreme Soviet; mem. Cttee. for Agriculture, Soviet of Union.
Samarkand Regional Committee of Communist Party of Uzbekistan, Samarkand, U.S.S.R.

Ussoskin, Moshe; Israeli foundation official; b. 8 March 1899; ed. Cernauti Univ.
Zionist work in Bessarabia 17; Rep. of Joint Distribution Cttee. and Jewish Colonisation Asscn., Balkans, Turkey and Hungary, and Dir. Central Bank for Jewish Co-operative Socs. in Rumania 28-41; in Israel 41-; Dir.-Gen. *Keren Hayesod* (Jewish Agency Foundation Fund); mem. Board Hevrat Hachsharat Hayishuv, Jerusalem Economic Corpn., Tel-Aviv Development Co., and other companies.
16 Arlosoroff Street, Jerusalem, Israel.

Ustinov, Dmitri Fedorovich; Soviet politician and administrator; b. 08; ed. Military Inst. of Mechanics.
Worked in Research Inst. 34-37; Construction Engineer later Dep. Head of Construction Bolshevik plant 35-40, Dir. 41; People's Commissar for Armaments 41-46; Minister of Armaments 46-53; Minister of Defence Industries 53-57; Dep. Chair. Council of Ministers, U.S.S.R. 57-63, First Dep. Chair. 63-65; Chair. Supreme Council of Nat. Economy 63-65; Sec. Central Cttee. of Communist Party of Soviet Union 65-, Alt. mem. Politburo 66-; Deputy to U.S.S.R. and R.S.F.S.R. Supreme Soviets; Hero of Socialist Labour (twice),

Four Orders of Lenin, Order of Kutuzov, Order of Suvorov, U.S.S.R. State Prizewinner.
Central Committee of Communist Party of Soviet Union, Moscow, U.S.S.R.

Ustinov, Peter Alexander, F.R.S.A.; British dramatist and actor; b. 16 April 1921; ed. Westminster School and London Theatre Studio.
Entered theatre as actor 39; first appearance in revue writing own material, Ambassador's Theatre, London 40; first appearance in films 40; served in army 42-46; wrote and directed films: *School for Secrets* 47, *Vice-Versa* 48, *Private Angelo* 49, *Billy Budd* 62, *Lady L* 65; collaborated on screenplay *The Way Ahead* 44; appeared in plays: *Crime and Punishment* 46, *Frenzy* 48, *Love in Albania* 49, *The Love of Four Colonels* 51; appeared in films: *Odette* 50, *Hôtel Sahara* 51, *Quo Vadis* 51, *Beau Brummel* 54, *The Egyptian* 54, *We're no Angels* 55, *Spartacus, Billy Budd* 62, *Topkapi* 63, *John Goldfarb* 64, *Lady L* 65, *Blackbeard's Ghost* 66, *Les Comédiens* 67; mem. British Film Acad.; Rector, Univ. of Dundee 68.
Plays: *House of Regrets* 42, *Blow Your Own Trumpet* 43, *The Banbury Nose* 44, *The Tragedy of Good Intentions* 45, *The Indifferent Shepherd* 48, *The Man in the Raincoat* 49, *The Love of Four Colonels* 51, *The Moment of Truth* 51, *No Sign of the Dove* 53, *Romanoff and Juliet* 56, *Photo Finish* 62, *The Life in My Hands* 63, *Half Way up the Tree, The Unknown Soldier and his Wife* 67; short stories: *Add a Dash of Pity* 59, *The Loser* (novel) 60, *The Frontiers of the Sea* 66.
c/o Film Rights Ltd., 113 Wardour Street, London, W.1, England; and La Datcha, Les Diablerets, Vaud, Switzerland.

Usubaliev, Turdakun; Soviet politician; b. 1919; ed. Kirghiz State Teaching Inst. and Higher Party School.
Teacher, Kirghiz S.S.R. 37-39; mem. C.P.S.U. 41-; party work Kirghiz S.S.R. 41-43; on staff of Central Cttee. of C.P.S.U. 45-55; Editor *Sovettik Kirgizstan*; Head, Dept. of Central Cttee. of C.P. of Kirghizstan; First Sec. Frunze City Cttee., C.P. of Kirghizstan 55-61; First Sec. Central Cttee. of Kirghiz C.P. 61-; mem. Central Cttee. of C.P.S.U. 61-; Deputy to U.S.S.R. and Kirghiz S.S.R. Supreme Soviets; mem. Cttee. for Planning and Budget, Soviet of Union.
Central Committee of the Communist Party of Kirghizstan, Frunze, Kirghiz S.S.R., U.S.S.R.

Utchenko, Sergei Lvovich; Soviet historian; b. 1 Dec. 1908; ed. Leningrad State Univ.
Assistant Prof. Leningrad State Univ. 39-41; served in Soviet Army 41-46; Prof. of Ancient History, Moscow State Univ. 50-54, Moscow Inst. of Historical Archives 54-; Head Ancient History Section, Inst. of History, Soviet Acad. of Sciences 50-; mem. C.P.S.U. 31-; Order of the Red Star and military medals.
Publs. More than 70 works including *The Law of Licinius Sextus 'De Modo Agrorum'* 47, *Sallust's Letter to Caesar* 50, *The Ideological and Political Struggle at Rome on the Eve of the Fall of the Republic* 52, *The Crisis of the Polis and the Political Views of the Roman Stoics* 55, several chapters in *World History*, Vol. II 56, *The Crisis of the Roman Comitiae* 59, *The Concept of Popular Sovereignty in Republican Rome* 60, *From the Caesar's Consulate to the Tribunate of Claudius* 61, *The Roman Army in the First Century B.C.* 62, *The Crisis and the Fall of the Roman Republic* 65, *As One Historian Sees It* 66.
Institute of History, ul. Dm. Ulyanova, Moscow; Leninsky Prospekt 61/1, kv. 162, Moscow, U.S.S.R.

Utzerath, Hansjörg; German theatre director; b. 20 March 1926; ed. Kepler Oberschule, Tübingen.
Began as actor, later in theatre management in Düsseldorf, and then in production; Chief Stage Man., Düsseldorfer Kammerspiele 55-59, Dir. 59-66; Intendant, Freie Volksbühne, Berlin Jan. 67-; Guest Producer

at Staatstheater Stuttgart, Münchener Kammerspiele and Schiller-Theater, Berlin 59-.
c/o Freie Volksbühne, Berlin 15, Schaperstrasse 24, Germany.

Uvalić, Radivoj; Yugoslav diplomat; b. 20 April 1912; ed. Univ. of Paris.
Fought in Int. Brigade in Spain 37; in Yugoslav Nat. Liberation Movement 41-45; Prof. of Political Economy, Belgrade Univ., 47-53; Minister to Norway 53-56; Ambassador to Austria 56-57; Ambassador to France 57-60; Dir. Inst. for Social Sciences 60-62; Corresp. mem. Serbian Acad. of Science 62; Ambassador to India 62-67; Merit of Nation 11, Order of Unity and Fraternity 1, Yugoslav Decoration for Labour with Red Flag, Partisan Commemoration Medal, Grand Officer, Legion of Honour, Order of Great Cross of St. Olaf (Norway), Croix de Guerre (France).
Publs. *L'Evolution des prix sur les grands marchés mondiaux de 1933 à 1939* 39, *Cours d'économie politique du socialisme* 50.
c/o Ministry of Foreign Affairs, Belgrade, Yugoslavia.

Uvarov, Sir Boris Petrovich, K.C.M.G., D.SC., F.R.S.; British entomologist; b. Russia 5 Nov. 1889; ed. Petrograd Univ.
Entomologist Murgab Crown Estate Transcaspia 10, Dept. of Agriculture Petrograd 11; Dir. Stavropol Bureau of Entomology 12; Dir. Bureau for Pest Control Tiflis 15; Lecturer in Zoology and Entomology State Univ. of Georgia, Tiflis 19; Entomologist, Imperial Inst. of Entomology 20-45; Dir. Anti-Locust Research Centre London 45-59.
Publs. *Acrididae of Middle Asia* 27, *Locusts and Grass-hoppers* 27, *Insects and Climate* 30, *Locust Research and Control* 51, *Grasshoppers and Locusts* 65.
Anti-Locust Research Centre, Wrights Lane, London, W.8; Home: 36 Kingsley Avenue, London, W.13, England.

Uys, Dirk Cornelis Hermanus; South African farmer and politician; b. 15 May 1909; ed. Bredasdorp High School and Stellenbosch Univ.
Farmer 31-; former Director, several Agricultural Co-operatives; fmr. mem. Wheat Industries Control Board; M.P. 53-, Minister of Agricultural Economics and Marketing 58-, and Lands 64-66.
Ministry of Agricultural Economics, Private Bag 250, Pretoria, Republic of South Africa.
Telephone: Pretoria 21233.

Uys, Johann Kunz, B.COMM.; South African diplomatist; b. 14 June 1907; ed. Stellenbosch Univ.
Entered Dept. of External Affairs 28; served Washington 33-37, Dept. of External Affairs 37-38, The Hague 38-40, Netherlands Govt., London 40-41; Sec. Industrial and Agricultural Requirements Comm., South Africa 41-43; Consul Elisabethville, Belgian Congo 43-46, during which time also served as Acting Consul-Gen. Léopoldville and Acting Commr. Nairobi; First Sec. The Hague 46-49; Counsellor Dept. of External Affairs, Head of Economic, Int. Trade and Gen. Sections, Dept. of External Affairs 49-54; High Commr. in Australia 54-57; Ambassador to German Federal Republic 57-60; Deputy Sec. for Foreign Affairs 60-65; Ambassador to German Fed. Republic 65-.
c/o South African Embassy, Heumarkt 1, Cologne, German Federal Republic.

V

Vadász, Elemér; Hungarian geologist; b. 1885.
Appointed Univ. Prof. under Repub. of Councils and
discharged same year 19, reinstalled after Second
World War; Academician 48-52; Pres. Hungarian-
Soviet Friendship Soc. 57, Vice-Pres. 60-; palaeontology,
stratigraphy, structural geology, bauxite and carbon
geology research; Kossuth Prize 48, 52.
Publs. include: *Analytic Geology* 55, *Earth History and
Evolution* 57, *Hungary's Geology* 60.
Muzeum körut 4/a, Budapest VIII, Hungary.

Vadim, Roger (Roger Vadim Plemiannikov); French
film director; b. 26 Jan. 1928.
Actor; script-writer and Asst. Dir. with Marc Allegret;
reporter *Paris-Match* 52-54; independent film dir. 55-;
writer and dialogue for *Futures Vedettes, Cette Sacrée
Gamine, En Effeuillant la Marguerite*; dir. and dialogue
*Et Dieu Créa la Femme, Sait-on Jamais, Les Bijoutiers
du Clair de Lune, Les Liaisons Dangereuses, Et Mourir
de Plaisir, Le Repos du Guerrier, Le Vice et la Vertu,
La Ronde, La Sonate à Kreutzer, La Curée.*
7 Avenue Ingres, Paris 16e, France.

Vagnozzi, H.E. Cardinal Egidio; Vatican diplomatist;
b. 2 Feb. 1906; ed. Lateran Pontifical Seminary and
Lateran Pontifical Univ.
Papal Secretariat of State, Vatican City 30-32; Sec.,
then Auditor and Counsellor, Apostolic Delegation,
Washington, D.C. 32-42; Counsellor, Lisbon 42, Vatican
42-46, Paris 46-48; Chargé d'Affaires, Counsellor, Papal
Internunciature, India 48-49; Apostolic Del., then
Papal Nuncio to Philippines 49-58; Apostolic Del.,
Washington, D.C. 58-67; mem. Consistorial and Extra-
ordinary Ecclesiastical Affairs Congregation 67-; cr.
Cardinal 67; Pres. Comm. of Cardinals for the Prefecture
of Econ. Affairs of the Holy See 68; Commandeur
Légion d'Honneur, Grand Cross of Order of Holy
Sepulchre.
Prefettura degli Affari Economici della Santa Sede,
Vatican City, Italy.
Telephone: 6982.

Vago, Pierre; French architect and town planner; b.
30 Aug. 1910; ed. Ecole spéciale d'Architecture, Paris.
Editor-in-Chief revue *Architecture d'Aujourd'hui* 32-48,
Pres. of Cttee. 48-; Founder and Sec.-Gen. Int. Reunions
of Architects 32-48 and Int. Union of Architects 48-67;
Head Architect for Reconstruction 48-56; Pres. Int.
Council, Soc. of Industrial Design 63-65; fmr. Vice-
Pres. Confed. of French Architects; mem. Jury of many
Int. Competitions; architect and town planner in
France, Germany, Tunisia, Luxembourg, Iran, Israel,
and Italy; Prof. and Dir. of Studies Ecole Supérieure
d'Architecture St. Luc de Belgique; honours include
membership of numerous architectural socs. and
Chevalier Légion d'Honneur.
Major works include: Basilica St. Pius X, Lourdes and
other churches, Central Bank of Tunis, Library of
Univ. of Bonn, several buildings in Algiers, France and
Fed. Rep. of Germany.
17 quai Voltaire, Paris 7e, France.
Telephone: LIT 73-90 and 91.

Vahervuori, T. Oskar, M.A.; Finnish diplomatist; b.
8 Jan. 1901; ed. Univ. of Helsinki, Sorbonne, Ecole
Libre des Sciences Politiques, Paris.
Attaché Ministry of Foreign Affairs 26; Sec. Rio de
Janeiro 29-34; Chargé d'Affaires a.i. Buenos Aires 32-34;
Sec. Bureau of Commercial Treaties Ministry of Foreign
Affairs 34-35, Chief of Bureau 35-39; Consul-Gen. N.Y.
39-42; Counsellor Washington 42-44; Ministry of For-
eign Affairs 44; Dir. Administrative Affairs 46; Dir.

Political Affairs 48-50; Minister to Brazil 50-56,
Amb. to Denmark 56-57; Perm. Under-Sec. of State,
Ministry of Foreign Affairs 57-61; Amb. to Italy 61-.
Piazzale delle Belle Arte 3, Rome, Italy.

Vail, Derrick Tilton, B.A., M.D., D.O. (OXON.); American
ophthalmologist; b. 15 May 1898; ed. Yale and Harvard
Univs.
Instructor in Ophthalmology, Coll. of Medicine, Univ. of
Cincinnati 26-37, Prof. of Ophthalmology and Dir. of
Dept. 37-45 and at Northwestern Univ. Medical School
45-66, Emer. Prof. 66-; attending Ophthalmologist,
Christ Hospital and Good Samaritan Hospital, Cincin-
nati 26-45; Dir. Eye Dept., Children's Hospital and
Cincinnati Gen. Hospital 37-45; Senior Consultant in
Ophthalmology, U.S. Army Medical Corps in the
European Theater 42-45; attending Ophthalmologist
and Head of Dept. of Ophthalmology, Passavant
Memorial Hospital, Chicago 45-66, Cook County
Hospital, Chicago 46-52; Editor-in-Chief *American
Journal of Ophthalmology* 40-65; Editor *Year Book of
Ophthalmology* 49-59; Assoc. Editor *Excerpta Medica*
59-66; mem. American Board of Ophthalmology 46-52
(Pres. 52), American Medical Asscn. (mem. Council on
Physical Medicine 46-61, Chair. Section on Ophthal-
mology 46), American Ophthalmological Soc. (Pres. 59),
Int. Fed. and Council of Ophthalmology (Pres. 62-66)
and numerous other socs.; awards include Gold Medal
for outstanding contributions of the Section on Ophthal-
mology, American Medical Asscn., Lucien Howe Gold
Medal, American Ophthalmological Soc., Leslie Dana
Medal for Prevention of Blindness, Doyne Medal Oxford
Congress Ophthal.; Hon. F.R.C.S. (Eng.); Commdr.
(Assoc.) Most Venerable Order of the Hospital of St.
John of Jerusalem.
Publs. *Gifford's Ocular Therapeutics* 42, *Truth About
Your Eyes*, 11 papers on ophthalmology.
2450 Lakeview Avenue, Chicago, Ill. 60614, U.S.A.
Telephone: LI 9-1120.

Vaillancourt, Emile; Canadian diplomatist and
author; b. 89; ed. Coll. Sainte-Marie, Montreal.
Former Alderman Outremont, P.Q., fmr. Dir.-Gen. of
Tourism P.Q., and Man. Dir. Montreal Tourist and Con-
vention Bureau; Canadian Minister to Cuba 45-48, to
Yugoslavia 48-50; Ambassador to Peru 50-55; rep. P.Q.
Govt. and Univ. of Montreal, Fifth Centenary Univ. of
Caen 32; Chief Canadian Del. and Chair. Drafting
Comm. Diplomatic Conf., Geneva 49; Special Ambassa-
dor to Panama for inauguration of Pres. 52; formerly
Dir. Health League of Canada (P.Q. Div.); mem. Acad.
of Rouen; Officer and Laureate French Acad.; Officier de
l'Instruction Publique (France), Knight Grand Officer
Order of the Holy Sepulchre of Jerusalem, of the
Nichan Iftikhar of Tunis; hon. citizen of Dieppe and
St.-Nicolas d'Aliermont, Normandy and New Orleans,
La.; Dr. h.c. (Caen) 32; Hon. LL.D. (Laval) 51, Dr. h.c.
(Montreal).
Publs. *Fine Arts in Canada, La Conquête du Canada
par les Normands, Broadside, Knots*, etc.
Montreal 25, Canada.

Vaizey, John Ernest, M.A.; British economist and
writer; b. 1 Oct. 1929; ed. Cambridge Univ.
United Nations, Geneva 52-53; Fellow, St. Catharine's
Coll., Cambridge 53-56; Lecturer in Econ. History,
Oxford Univ. 56-59; Dir. Research Unit in Econs. of
Educ., Univ. of London 60-61; Fellow and Tutor,
Worcester Coll., Oxford 62-66; Prof. of Econs., Brunel
Univ., London 66-; Visiting Prof. Univ. of Calif. 66-67;
Consultant to OECD, UN, ILO; Fellow Int. Inst. for

Educational Planning; Dir. Acton Soc. Trust 61-; mem. Public Schools Comm.; Gladstone Prizeman, Univ. of Cambridge 54; Eleanor Rathbone Lecturer, Univ. of Liverpool 66.

Publs. *The Costs of Education* 58, *Scenes from Institutional Life* 59, *The Brewing Industry 1886-1951* 60, *Some Economic Aspects of Educational Development in Europe* (with Michel Debeauvais) 60, *Guinness's Brewery in the Irish Economy 1759-1876* (with Patrick Lynch) 61, *The Economics of Education* 62, *Education for Tomorrow* 62, revised 66, *The Control of Education* 63, *The Residual Factor and Economic Growth* (Editor) 65, *Economics of Education* (Editor, with E. A. G. Robinson) 66, *Barometer Man* 67, *Resources for Education* (with John Sheehan) 68, *The Sleepless Lunch* 68; numerous pamphlets and articles.

Brunel University, Woodlands Avenue, Acton, London, W.3; Home: 24 Heathfield Terrace, London, W.4, England.

Telephone: 01-994-7994 (Home).

Vajda, Georges; French professor; b. 18 Nov. 1908; ed. Séminaire Rabbinique, Budapest, and Paris, and Ecole des Langues Orientales, Sorbonne.

Prof., Séminaire Israélite de France 36-; Lecturer, Ecole Pratique des Hautes Etudes, Sorbonne 37, Dir. 54-; Head of Oriental Section, Institut de Recherche et d'Histoire des Textes 40-; Sec. Société des Etudes Juives.

Publs. *Introduction à la Pensée Juive du Moyen Age* 47, *La Théologie ascétique de Bahya ibn Paquda* 47, *Répertoire des Catalogues et Inventaires de Manuscrits Arabes* 49, *Un Recueil de Textes Historiques Judéo-Marocains* 51, *Index Général des Manuscrits Arabes Musulmans de la Bibliothèque Nationale* 53, *Juda ben Nissim Ibn Malka, Philosophe juif marocain* 54, *Les certificats de lecture dans les manuscrits arabes de la B.N. de Paris, L'amour de Dieu dans la Théologie juive du moyen age* 57, *Album de Paléographie Arabe* 58, *Isaac Albalag, averroïste juif* 60, *Recherches sur la Philosophie et la Kabbale* 62, *Le Dictionnaire des Autorités d'Ad-Dimyati* 62, *Revue des Etudes Juives* (Editor).

Institut de Recherche et d'Histoire des Textes, 40 avenue d'Iéna, Paris; and 35 rue du Pré St. Gervais, Paris 19e, France.

Vakil, Dr. Mehdi; Iranian diplomatist; b. 10 Sept. 1907; ed. Teheran Law School and Faculté de Droit, Paris.

Former Professor of Diplomatic History, Teheran Univ., Dir. in Ministry of Education Cabinet, Cultural Counsellor Iranian Embassy, Paris, Minister Plenipotentiary; joined U.N. Secretariat 50, Sec. Econ. and Social Council 53-59; Perm. Iranian Rep. to U.N. 59-; mem. and fmr. Sec.-Gen. Soc. des Etudes Iraniennes et de l'Art Persan; Order of Crown (Iran); Légion d'Honneur, Order of the Crown of Iran, Order of Merit Argentina, Order of Merit Paraguay.

Publs. *Les Recours contre l'Administration* 35, *Neutrality in Time of War* 36.

Permanent Mission of Iran to the United Nations, 777 Third Avenue, New York, N.Y. 10017, U.S.A.

Valcárcel Vizcarra, Luis Eduardo, D.PHIL., LL.D.; Peruvian ethnologist; b. 91; ed. Univ. del Cuzco and Col. Peruano del Cuzco.

Prof. of Peruvian History, Univ. del Cuzco 17-30, Dir. Univ. Archæological Museum 23-30; Dir. Peruvian Archæological Museum, Lima 30-44; Dir. Bolivar Museum, Lima 30; Dir. National History Museum, Lima 44-65, Dir. Emer. 65-; Prof. Univ. of Lima 31-63; fmr. Dir. Ethnological Inst., Lima 46; Minister of Educ. 45-47; Prof. Emeritus Univ. of San Marcos; Order of Aztec Eagle (Mexico); Order of the Sun (Peru).

Publs. *Historia Incaica* 25, *Tempestad en los Andes*, 27 *Mirador Indio* (essays) 37, *Cuentos y Leyendas Incas* 38,

Historia de la Cultura Antigua del Perú 43, *Ruta Cultural del Peru* 45, *Historia del Perú Antiguo* 3 vols. 64, etc.

Lord Cochrane 456, Miraflores, Lima, Peru. Telephone: 22764.

Valcke, Eugène; Belgian civil engineer; b. 12; ed. Athénée Royal of Ghent, and Univ. of Ghent.

Engineer of Roads and Bridges for Limbourg 36-37; Engineer in Civil Aviation 37-40; Engineer for Roads and Bridges 40-46; Engineer-in-Chief 46-55; Dir. *Voies Hydrauliques* (Dept. of Roads and Bridges) 55-; Chief Engineer for the Gen. Commissariat for Universal and Int. Exhibition in Brussels 53, 58; lecturer at Ecole technique supérieure de l'Etat 49-; Chevalier Ordre de Léopold, Officier Ordre de Léopold II, Officier Ordre de la Couronne.

266D Ave. de Tervueren, Woluwé St. Pierre, Belgium.

Valdés Subercaseaux, Gabriel; Chilean lawyer and politician; b. 19.

Former Professor of Law, Universidad Católica; fmr. Vice-President Christian Democrat Party; Minister of Foreign Affairs Nov. 64-.

Ministry of Foreign Affairs, Santiago, Chile.

Valencia, Dr. Guillermo León; Colombian diplomatist and politician; b. 09; ed. Univ. of Popayan.

Former Permanent Representative to UN; fmr. Ambassador to Spain; Pres. of Colombia Aug. 62-Aug. 66; Amb. to Spain 67-; Conservative.

Embassy of Colombia, Martinez Campos 48, Madrid, Spain.

Valenti, Jack; American advertising executive and government official; b. 22; ed. High School, Houston, Univ. of Houston and Harvard Business School.

Former office boy, oil company; U.S. Air Force, Second World War; runs own Advertising Agency, Houston, Texas; Special Asst. to President Johnson 63-66; Pres. Motion Picture Asscn. of America 66-.

Motion Picture Association of America, Inc., 522 Fifth Avenue, New York 36, N.Y., U.S.A.

Valentine, Alan, M.A.; American administrator; b. 23 Feb. 1901; ed. Swarthmore Coll., Univ. of Pennsylvania, and Oxford Univ. (Balliol Coll.).

Instructor, Univ. of Pennsylvania 21-22; with Oxford Univ. Press in U.K. and U.S. 25-28; Asst. Prof. of English and Dean of Men, Swarthmore Coll. 28-32; Prof. in History, Arts and Letters Dept., Yale Univ., and Chair. of Board of Admissions and Master of Pierson Coll. 32-35; Pres. Univ. of Rochester 35-50; Chief of Mission to Netherlands for Econ. Co-operation Admin. 48-49; Econ. Stabilisation Dir. 50-51; Grand Officer Order of Orange-Nassau (Neths.); Hon. LL.D. (Syracuse Univ., Amherst Coll., Union Coll., Rutgers Univ., Swarthmore Coll., Denison Univ., Lake Forest Coll., Allegheny Coll., Colgate Univ.), Hon. L.H.D. (Hobart Coll., Univ. of Rochester), Hon. Litt.D. (Alfred Univ.); Fellow Int. Inst. of Arts and Letters.

Publs. *The English Novel* 27, *Biography* 27, *Dusty Answers* 41, *the Age of Conformity* 53, *Vigilante Justice* 55, *Trial Balance* 56, *Education of an American* 58, *Lord George Germain* 62, *1913: Year of Transition* 62, *Fathers to Sons* 63, *Lord North* (2 vols.) 67.

7 Lafayette Road, Princeton, N.J.; and Northaven, Maine, U.S.A.

Valenzuela, Ing. Gilberto; Mexican engineer; b. 1 Dec. 1922; ed. Escuela Nacional de Ingeniería, Univ. Nacional Autónoma de México.

Civil Engineer 47; with Nat. Railways of Mexico; worked for engineering consultants, Ford Bacon and Davis on various projects; later started his own business in Mexico City; Consulting Engineer, Dept. of Fed. District June 53; Chief, Highways Section, Dept.

of Public Works July 53-55, Deputy Dir. Construction and Conservation July 55, Dir.-Gen. of Public Works 59-64, Sec. for Public Works 64-.
Secretaría de Obras Públicas, México 12, D.F., Mexico.

Valerio, Giorgio; Italian engineer and industrialist; b. 20 March 1904; ed. Milan Engineering Univ.
With Società Edison Milan (now Montecatini Edison S.p.A.) 27-, Man. Dir. 52-, Vice-Chair., Man. Dir. 61-65, Chair. and Chief Exec. Officer 65-; Vice-Chair. Sincat, Palermo, Chatillon, Milan; Dir. Soc. Italiana per le Strade Ferrate Meridionale, Florence, Riunione Adriatica de Sicurtà, Trieste, La Fondiaria, Florence.
Foro Bonaparte, 31, Milan, Italy.

Valéry, François; French diplomatist; b. 17 July 1916; ed. Univ. of Paris.
Auditor, Cour des Comptes 44; Technical Counsellor at the Peace Conf. 46; mem. French del. to Council of Ministers for Foreign Affairs on the Marshall Plan and to Tripartite Confs. on Germany 46-50; Head of Section of Econ. Co-operation and Integration, Ministry of Foreign Affairs 48; Conseiller Référendaire, Cour des Comptes 50; Perm. Del. of France to OEEC 56-61, to OECD 61-; Vice-Pres. Exec. Cttee of OECD 67-; Chevalier de la Légion d'Honneur.
Organization for Economic Co-operation and Development, 2 rue André-Pascal, Paris 16e, France.

Valeš, Václav; Czechoslovak politician; b. 7 April 1922; ed. Commercial Acad., Slaný.
Deputy Man. of Chemical Works, Zálůzí until 55; Man. of Main Admin. of Sales affiliated to Ministry of Chemical Industry 55-56; Deputy Minister of Chemical Industry, Prague 56-62, First Deputy Minister 62-65, Minister of Chemical Industry 65-68; Minister of Foreign Trade 68-; Award for Merit in Construction 64.
Ministry of Foreign Trade, Prague 1, tř. Politických vězňů 20, Czechoslovakia.

Valkó, Márton; Hungarian engineer and diplomatist; b. 1911; ed. Technical Univ., Budapest.
Iron turner; lived in France 30-36; Dir. Budapest Underground Railway Construction 51-53, Lenin Foundry Works, Diósgyör 53-64; Amb. to France 64-; Kossuth Prize 49.
Embassy of Hungary, 5 bis square de l'Avenue Foch, Paris 16e, France.
Telephone: PAS 41-45.

Valle, Jorge González del; Guatemalan economist and financial official; b. 24 Jan. 1929; ed. Univ. de San Carlos de Guatemala, Graduate School of Business, Columbia Univ., New York, and School of Economics, Yale Univ.
Director of Credit and Econ. Adviser, Nat. Mortgage Bank, Guatemala City 52-56; Economist, Nat. Council of Econ. Planning, Guatemala City 56-59; Economist, W. Hemisphere Dept., Int. Monetary Fund, Washington, D.C. 59-61; Dir., Vice-Pres. Central American Bank for Econ. Integration, and Exec. Dir. Central American Clearing House, Tegucigalpa, Honduras 61-63; Dir. of Econ. Research, Bank of Guatemala, and Prof. of Econs., Univ. of Guatemala 63-64; Alt. Exec. Dir. Int. Monetary Fund (IMF) 64-66, Exec. Dir. 66-.
Publs. (co-author) *Payments Problems of Latin America* 63, *Integration of Latin America—Experiences and Projections* 64.
International Monetary Fund, Washington, D.C. 20431, U.S.A.

Vallejo Arbeláez, Joaquín; Colombian civil engineer and politician; b. 4 Oct. 1912; ed. Escuela Nacional de Minas.
Director of Public Educ., Antioquia 36-38; Prof. of Mathematics, Physical Sciences and Philosophy, Univ. of Antioquia and Nat. School of Mines 35-39; Deputy to Provincial Assembly, Antioquia 37-39; mem. Nat.

Assembly 39-; Pres. of Aliados McKesson Laboratories 44-64; Minister of Works 57; Minister of Finance and Public Credit 65-66; mem. Board of Dirs. of the Railway, Public Works, Polytechnic and Univ. of Antioquia.
c/o Ministerio de Hacienda y Crédito, Bogotá, Colombia.

Vallentin, Maxim; German actor and producer; b. 9 Oct. 1904.
Actor in Schlossparktheater, Berlin, and Max Reinhardt Theater, Berlin until 33; in Czechoslovakia and U.S.S.R. 33-45, Announcer, German Dept. of Moscow Radio; in D.D.R. 45-, founded Deutsches Theaterinstitut and Junges Ensemble, Weimar; Dir. Maxim-Gorki-Theater, E. Berlin 51-, also Dir. Volksbühne (People's Stage), E. Berlin 63-; mem. Central Cttee. Sozialistische Einheitspartei Deutschlands (S.E.D.) 63-.
Maxim-Gorki-Theater, Berlin, Germany.

Vallindas, Petros G., LL.D., POL. SC.M.; Greek university professor; b. 12; ed. Univs. of Athens and Berlin.
Attorney-at-Law 34-; Asst. Prof. Univ. of Athens 38-44; Prof. School of Pol. Science 38-46; Dir. of Legislative Studies, Ministry of Justice 38-41; Prof. of Private Int. and Comparative Law Univ. of Thessalonica 44-61; Dir. Hellenic Inst. of Int. and Foreign Law 39-60; Hon. Legal Adviser to Ministry of Foreign Affairs 47-, mem. Hague Permanent Court of Arbitration; mem. Council Int. Association of Legal Science; mem. Governing Council, Rome Int. Inst. for Unification of Private Law; Assoc. mem. Inst. of Int. Law; Legis. Counsellor in charge gen. codification of Greek laws; mem. Int. Acad. of Comparative Law, Council Int. Faculty of Comparative Law at Luxembourg.
Publs. *Studies on Private Law*, Editor: *Uniformity of Interpretation of Conventions on Private International Law* 32, *Greek Private International Law During the First Half of the 19th Century* 35, *Public Policy in Private International Law* 37, *Private International Law* (two Vols. with G. Streit) 37, *Theoretical Principles of Private International Law of the Greek Civil Code* 42, *Introduction to Private International Law* 43, *Nationality Law* 43, *Contributions to the Law of Leases in Ancient Greek Law* (with N. Pantazopoulos) 48, *Introduction to Comparative Law* 51, *Introduction to English Private Law* 51, *Vocabulary of the Charter of the United Nations and of the Statute of the International Court of Justice* 53, *Cases on the General Principles of Civil Law* 56, *Nationality Code of 1955* 57, *Introduction to the Science of Law* (5th edn.) 58.
4 Sekeri, Athens, Greece.

Vallois, Henri Victor, D.M., D.SC.; French anthropologist; b. 11 April 1889.
Prosector, Faculty of Medicine, Univ. of Montpellier 14; Prof. of Anatomy Univ. of Toulouse 22; Dir. Institut de Paléontologie humaine 43; Prof. Natural History Museum 47; Hon. Dir. Musée de l'Homme 61-; mem. Acad. Nat. de Médicine France, Akad. der Wissenschaften Vienna, Akad. der Wissenschaften und der Litteratur Fed. Germany, etc.; Huxley Medal Royal Anthrop. Inst. England, Viking Medal Wenner-Gren Inst. U.S.A.; Officier Légion d'Honneur; many hon. degrees.
Publs. *Traité d'Arthrologie* 26, *Anthropologie de France* 42, *Les Races Humaines* 44, *Les Hommes Fossiles* 46, *Les Primates* 55; editor *L'Anthropologie, Archives de l'Institut de Paléontologie humaine, Bulletins de la Société d'Anthropologie de Paris*.
57 rue Cuvier, Paris 5e, France.
Telephone: 535-42-12.

Valluy, Général d'Armeé Jean Etienne; French army officer; b. 15 May 1899; ed. Lycée de Lyon and Ecole Saint Cyr.
Served First World War; service in Syria, Morocco, Far East, Africa; Dir. Colonial Troops; Chief of Staff to

Gen. de Lattre 43; Commdr. 9th Infantry Div., Indo-China 44-45; Mil. Commdr., later Supreme Commdr., Indo-China; Dep. Chief of Staff SHAPE 52; NATO Standing Group, Washington 53-56; C.-in-C. Allied Forces, Cen. Europe 56-60; Grand Croix Légion d'Honneur, Croix de Guerre.
56 rue de la Rochefoucauld, Paris, France.

Valous, Guy de, Marquis; French historian; b. 1 Nov. 1891; ed. Austria, Univ. de Lyon, Ecole des Chartes, and the Sorbonne (Docteur-ès-lettres).
Librarian, Faculty of Law, Paris 21-39; Dir. Bibliothèque Ste. Geneviève Paris 40-62, Hon. Dir. 62-; Vice-Pres. Association d'Entr'aide de la Noblesse Française; Sec.-Gen. French branch, Soc. des Cincinnati; Grand Prix Gobert 37; Officer Legion of Honour.
Publs. *Le domaine de l'abbaye de Cluny aux Xe et XIe siècles* 23, *Avec les Rouges aux Iles du Vent* 30, *Sur les routes de l'Emigration, mémoires de la duchesse de Saulx-Tavanes* 34, *Le monachisme clunisien* (3 vols.) 35, *Jean de Bourbon* 49, *Divertissements de clercs: Littérature amoureuse en langue latine au Moyen-age* 57.
95 avenue de Versailles, Paris 16e, France.
Telephone: BAG 87-95.

Vályi, Péter; Hungarian economist and politician; b. 1919; ed. Budapest Technical Univ.
Member Hungarian C.P. 45-; First Deputy Pres. of Nat. Planning Office 61-66; Minister of Finance 67-.
Ministry of Finance, Budapest, Hungary.

Van Allen, James Alfred, B.S., M.S., PH.D.; American physicist; b. 7 Sept. 1914; ed. Iowa Wesleyan Coll. and State Univ. of Iowa.
Research Fellow, Carnegie Inst., Washington 39-41, Physicist 41-42; Physics Laboratory, Johns Hopkins Univ. 42, 46-50; Lieut.-Commdr. in U.S. Navy 42-46; Head of Dept. and Prof. of Physics and Astronomy, Univ. of Iowa 51-; Guggenheim Research Fellow at Brookhaven Nat. Laboratory 51; Research Associate Princeton Univ. Project Matterhorn 53-54; Dir. expeditions to study cosmic radiation Central Pacific 49, Alaska 50, Arctic 52, 57; mem. Rocket and Satellite Research Panel 46, Chair. 47-58, Exec. Cttee. 58-; mem. Advisory Cttee. on Nuclear Physics, Office of Naval Research 57-; mem. Space Science Board, Nat. Acad. of Sciences 58-; Consultant President's Science Advisory Cttee.; mem. Cosmic Radiation, Rocket Research and Earth Satellite Panel, Int. Geophysical Year; Fellow, American Physical Soc., American Geophysical Union, American Rocket Soc., Inst. of Radio Engineers, American Astronautical Soc.; mem. Nat. Acad. of Sciences, Royal Astronomical Soc. (U.K.); founder mem. Int. Acad. of Astronautics; Assoc. Editor *Physics of Fluids* 58-62, *Journal of Geophysical Research* 59-; Hickman Medal, American Rocket Soc. 49; Physics Award, Washington Acad. of Science 49; Space Flight Award, American Astronautical Soc. 58, Int. Acad. of Astronautics 61; Distinguished Civilian Service Medal (U.S. Army) 59, Guggenheim Int. Astronautics Award 62; John A. Fleming Award, American Geophysical Union 63, 64; numerous Hon. D.Scs.; discoverer of the "Van Allen Belt" of radiation around the earth and a pioneer of high-altitude rocket research.
Publs. *Physics and Medicine of the Upper Atmosphere, Rocket Exploration of the Upper Atmosphere,* etc.; Editor *Scientific Use of Earth Satellites.*
Department of Physics and Astronomy, University of Iowa, Iowa City, and 5 Woodland Mounds Road, R.F.D. 5, Iowa City, Iowa, U.S.A.

Van Atta, C(hester) M(urray), PH.D.; American physicist; b. 25 May 1906; ed. Reed Coll., and New York Univ.
Nat. Research Fellow, Mass. Inst. of Technology 33-35, Research Associate 35-38, Asst. Prof. 38-40; Physicist Naval Ordinance Laboratory 40-43; Physicist Lawrence

Radiation Laboratory Univ. of California 43-46; Prof. of Physics and Chair. Division Physical Sciences and Mathematics, Southern California 46-50; Physicist Lawrence Radiation Laboratory, Univ. of California 50-; Consultant on Vacuum Technology to the Kinney Vacuum Division of the New York Air Brake Co. 37-65; Head Project for controlled thermonuclear research programme at the Berkeley and Livermore sites of the Lawrence Radiation Laboratory; Assoc. Dir. Univ. of Californian Lawrence Radiation Laboratory, Livermore 58-; Fellow American Physical Soc. and American Asscn. for the Advancement of Science; mem. Fed. of American Scientists and American Vacuum Soc.
Publs. *The Design of High Vacuum Systems, Vacuum Science and Engineering* 65, and research papers in the fields of nuclear physics and particle accelerators.
University of California, Lawrence Radiation Laboratory, Berkeley 4, Calif. 94720; Home: Livermore, Calif. 94550, U.S.A.
Telephone: 415-525-7586.

van der Kemp, Gerald, M.V.O.; French museum curator; b. 5 May 1912; ed. Institut d'Art et d'Archéologie, Sorbonne.
With Musée du Louvre 36-41; Asst. Musée National d'Art Moderne 41-45; Curator of the Museums of Versailles, Trianons and Jeu de Paume 45-53, Chief Curator 53-; Officier de la Légion d'Honneur.
Château de Versailles, Seine-et-Oise, France.

Van der Post, Laurens Jan, C.B.E.; British writer and explorer; b. 13 Dec. 1906.
War service in Syria, Africa and the Far East 39-45; prisoner of war 43-45; Asst. to British Minister, Batavia 45-47; leader of several expeditions in Africa for British Govt. and on his own account; produced the film *The Lost World of the Kalahari* 56.
Publs. *In a Province* 34, *Venture to the Interior, A Bar of Shadow* 52, *The Face Beside the Fire* 53, *Flamingo Feather, The Dark Eye in Africa* 55, *The Lost World of the Kalahari* 58, *The Heart of the Hunter* 61, *The Seed and the Sower* 62, *Journey into Russia* 64, *A Portrait of All the Russias* 67, *The Hunter and the Whale* 67.
13 Cadogan Street, London, S.W.3, England.

Van Doren, Mark; American poet and critic; b. 13 June 1894; ed. Illinois and Columbia Univs.
Prof. of English Columbia Univ. 20-59; Literary Editor *The Nation* 24-28.
Publs. *Henry David Thoreau: a Critical Study* 16, *The Poetry of John Dryden* 20, *Spring Thunder and Other Poems* 24, *7 p.m. and Other Poems* 26, *Now the Sky and Other Poems* 28, *Anthology of World Poetry* 28, *An Autobiography of America* 29, *Jonathan Gentry* 31, *A Winter Diary and Other Poems* 35, *The Transients* (novel) 35, *The Last Look and Other Poems* 37, *Collected Poems* 39, *Shakespeare* 39, *Windless Cabins* (novel) 40, *The Mayfield Deer* 41, *The Private Reader* 42, *Our Lady Peace and other War Poems* 42, *Tilda* (novel) 43, *Liberal Education* 43, *The Seven Sleepers and other poems* 44, *The Noble Voice* 46, *New Poems* 48, *Nathaniel Hawthorne* 49, *The Short Stories of Mark Van Doren* 50, *Introduction to Poetry* 51, *Mortal Summer* 53, *Spring Birth and Other Poems* 53, *Nobody Say a Word* 53, *Selected Poems* 54, *Home with Hazel* 57, *The Autobiography of Mark Van Doren, Don Quixote's Profession* 58, *The Last Days of Lincoln* (play) 59, *Morning Worship and Other Poems* 60, *The Happy Critic* 61, *Collected Stories* 62, *Collected and New Poems* 63, *The Narrative Poems of Mark Van Doren* 64, *Collected Stories,* Vol. 2 65, *Three Plays* 66, *Somebody Came* (juvenile) 66, *100 Poems* 67, *Collected Stories,* Vol. 3 68.
Falls Village, Conn. 06031, U.S.A.

van Lare, William Bedford, C.M.G., LL.B.; Ghanaian judge and diplomatist; b. 7 Sept. 1904; ed. Mfantsipim School, Cape Coast, and Univ. Coll. London.
Master, Mfantsipim School, Cape Coast 25-27; School

teacher, Educ. Dept., Gold Coast 28-32; called to Bar, Lincoln's Inn, London 37; Legal Practitioner, Supreme Court, Gold Coast 37-43; District Magistrate 43-52; Acting Chief Registrar, Supreme Court, and Acting Registrar, W. Africa Court of Appeal 48, 50; Acting Puisne Judge, Supreme Court 50-51, Puisne Judge 52-57; Judge of Supreme Court of Ghana 57-63, Acting Chief Justice 57-58, and on several occasions 59-63; Acting Gov.-Gen. and C.-in-C., Ghana Jan. 58; Leader, Goodwill Mission to neighbouring French-speaking States 66; Chair. Conf. of Neighbouring States for re-establishment of friendly relationship and reopening of borders May 66; High Commr. in Canada June 66-; mem. Ghana's Del. to 21st and 22nd Sessions of UN Gen. Assembly.
Ghana High Commission, 85 Range Road, Ottawa, Canada.

Van Slyke, Donald Dexter, A.B., PH.D.; American research chemist; b. 29 March 1883; ed. Univ. of Michigan and Univ. of Berlin.
Rockefeller Inst. for Medical Research N.Y. 07-49; Chemist, The Hospital of The Rockefeller Inst. N.Y. 14-49; Visiting Prof. Peking Union Medical School China 22; Dir. of Research in Biology and Medicine Brookhaven Nat. Laboratory 49-51, Research Chemist 51-; Counsellor Lilly Research Grants 51-56; mem. American Nat. Acad. of Sciences; hon. mem. Royal Acad. of Uppsala, Sweden, Physiological Society of Great Britain, Acad. of Sciences of India, Società Lombarda di Medicina of Italy, Société de Pathologie Renale, France, Renal Asscn., London, Royal Society of Arts, London, Asscn. of Clinical Biochemists, London, Danish Society of Internal Medicine, Royal Danish Acad. of Sciences and Letters, Accademia Nazionale dei Lincei, Italy; numerous hon. degrees.
Publs. *Cyanosis* (with C. Lundsgaard) 23, *Factors affecting the Distribution of Electrolytes, Water and Gases in the Animal Body* 26, *The Course of Bright's Disease* (with E. Stillman and others) 30, *Quantitative Clinical Chemistry*, 2 vols. (with J. P. Peters) 31, *Micromanometric Analyses* 61.
Brookhaven National Laboratory, Upton, Long Island, New York 11973, U.S.A.

Van Vleck, John Hasbrouck, A.M., PH.D.; American professor; b. 13 March 1899; ed. Univ. of Wisconsin and Harvard Univ.
Instr. in Physics, Harvard Univ. 22-23; Asst. Prof. Minnesota 23-26, Assoc. Prof. 26-27, Prof. 27-28; Prof. Wisconsin Univ. 28-34; Prof. Harvard Univ. 34-, Hollis Prof. of Mathematics and Natural Philosophy 51-; Dean of Engineering and Applied Physics 51-57; Guggenheim Foundation Fellow 30; Lorentz Prof., Leiden Univ. 60; Eastman Prof., Oxford Univ. 61-62; Pres. American Physical Soc. 52; mem. Nat. Acad. of Sciences, American Philosophical Soc., American Acad. of Arts and Sciences; corresp. mem. Académie des Sciences; Hon. mem. Soc. Française de Physique; foreign mem. Royal Neths. Acad. of Sciences, Acad. of Sciences, Uppsala, Swedish Acad. of Sciences, Royal Soc. (U.K.); Hon. Sc.D. (Wesleyan, Wisconsin, Maryland, Oxford, Paris, Grenoble, Nancy and Harvard Univs. and Rockford Coll.); Albert A. Michelson Award, Case Inst. 63; Irving Langmuir Prize 65; Nat. Medal of Science 66.
Publs. *Quantum Principles and Line Spectra* 26, *Theory of Electric and Magnetic Susceptibilities* 32.
Lyman Laboratory of Physics, Harvard University, Cambridge, Mass. 02138, U.S.A.

Van Zandt, John Parker, B.S., PH.D.; American economist; b. 16 Jan. 1894; ed. Univs. of Chicago, Washington and Calif.
Capt. U.S. Air Service 18-26; Pres. Scenic Airways 27-29; European Aviation Rep., Ford Motor Co. 29-31; Pacific Rep., Pan-American Airways 35-38; Consultant,

Civil Aeronautics Board 39-42; Senior Staff member, The Brookings Inst. 42-47; Pres. Aviation Research Inst. 47-50; Deputy to Asst. Sec. of the Air Force 50-53; Aviation mem. U.N. Transport Survey Mission to Central America 52-53; Aircraft Section NATO 53-59; Pres. European Technical Services 59-.
Publs. *European Air Transport on the Eve of War* 40, *Geography of World Air Transport* 44, *Civil Aviation and Peace* 44, *World Aviation Annual* (Editor-in-Chief) 48.
725 15th Street, N.W., Washington, D.C. 20005; 3900 Cathedral Avenue, N.W., Washington, D.C. 20016, U.S.A.
Telephone: 338-3044.

Vanag, Yan Fritsevich; Soviet agriculturalist and economist.
Ministry of Agriculture, Latvian S.S.R. 48-62; fmr. Rector Latvian Acad. of Agriculture; Chair. Latvian Supreme Soviet 57-63; Minister of Agriculture, Latvian S.S.R. 61-62; mem. Central Cttee. of Latvian Communist Party 60-63; Corresp. mem. Lenin Acad. of Agriculture, U.S.S.R. 56-; Prof. Latvian Acad. of Agriculture 64-.
Publs. include: *The Agricultural System and the Increase in the Production of Livestock Produce* 57, *Measures for Boosting Agriculture in the Latvian S.S.R.* 57, *The Agricultural System of the "Rituaem" Kolkhoz* 60, *Twenty Years of Agriculture in Soviet Latvia* 60, *The Economy of Agriculture* 62, *Reserves for Raising Agricultural Production* 64, *The Agricultural Encyclopaedia* (in Latvian) 62-.
Ministry of Agriculture, Riga, Latvian S.S.R., U.S.S.R.

Vanamo, Jorma Jaakko, L. en D.; Finnish diplomatist; b. 30 Oct. 1913; ed. Univ. of Helsinki.
Diplomatic Service 39-, Moscow 40-41, Ministry of Foreign Affairs 41-45, Moscow 45-48, Ministry of Foreign Affairs 49-51; Counsellor, Stockholm 51-53, Washington 54-56; Dir. of Admin. Div., Ministry of Foreign Affairs 56-58; Ambassador to Poland 58-62, Minister to Romania 58-60, to Bulgaria 58-62; Ambassador to U.S.S.R., also accred. to Afghanistan and Mongolia 63-67; Sec. of State, Ministry of Foreign Affairs 67-.
Office: Ritarikatu 2, Helsinki 17; Home: Myllytie 3 A 4, Helsinki 14, Finland.
Telephone: 14311/279 (Office); 62-66-70 (Home).

Vance, Cyrus Roberts, B.A., LL.B.; American lawyer and government official; b. 27 March 1917; ed. Kent School and Yale Univ.
Lieutenant, U.S. Navy 42-46; Asst. to Pres. The Mead Corpn. 46-47; Simpson, Thacher and Bartlett, N.Y. (law firm) 47-61, Partner 56-61; Special Counsel, Preparedness Investigating Subcttee., Cttee. on Armed Services of the U.S. Senate 57-60; Consulting Counsel to Special Cttee. on Space and Astronautics, U.S. Senate 58; Gen. Counsel, Dept. of Defense 61-62; Chair. Cttee. Adjudication of Claims of the Admin. Conf. of the U.S. 61-62; Sec. of the Army 62-64; Dep. Sec. of Defense 64-67; Pres. Johnson's Special Envoy on Cyprus Situation 67, on Korean Situation 68; negotiator at Paris talks on Viet-Nam 68; mem. U.S. Supreme Court, American Bar Asscn., N.Y., State Bar Asscn., Asscn. of the Bar of the City of N.Y.; Fellow American Coll. Trial Lawyers.
3060 Foxhall Road, Washington, D.C. 16, U.S.A.

Vandeputte, Robert M. A. C., D. en D., D. en SC. POL. ET SOC.; Belgian banker and university professor; b. 08; ed. Univs. of Louvain, Nijmegen, Paris, Berlin and Berne.
Called to Antwerp Bar 30; Prof. Univ. of Louvain 36-; Cabinet Chief, Ministry of Econ. Affairs 39-40; Sec.-Gen. Asscn. Belge des Banques 40-42; Dir. Banque Nat. de Belgique 43-44; Man. Dir. Société Nat. de Crédit à l'Industrie 44-48, Pres. 48-; Dir. and mem. Exec. Cttee.

Société de Credit au Colonat 47-61; Regent Banque Nat. de Belgique 54-; Pres. Office Nat. de Sécurité Sociale 59-62; mem. Caisse Générale d'Epargne et de Retraite 58-; Dir. and mem. Directing Cttee. Société Nat. d'Investissement 62-; Dir. Palais des Beaux-Arts de Belgique 66-; Commdr. Order of the Crown and Knight Order of Léopold (Belgium); Officer Order of Merit (Italian Repub.); Commdr. Order of St. Gregory the Great (Holy See), and other awards.
Publs. in Dutch: *Beginselen van Nijverheidsrecht, Handboek voor Verzekeringen en Verzekeringsrecht*; in French: *Quelques aspects de l'Activité de la Société Nationale de Crédit à l'Industrie, Le Statut de l'Entreprise.*
16 Boulevard de Waterloo, Brussels 1; 282 Avenue de Tervueren, Brussels 15, Belgium.
Telephone: 13-62-80.

Vanderpoorten, Herman, LL.D.; Belgian politician; b. 25 Aug. 1922; ed. Atheneum Berchem-Antwerp and Rijksuniversiteit te Gent.
Attorney 45; County Councillor, Antwerp 49-58; Town Councillor and Deputy Justice of the Peace, Lier 59; mem. Chamber of Representatives 61-65; Senator 65; Minister of Interior 66-68; Pres. Liberal Flemish Asscn. 57-66.
Antwerpsesteenweg 2, Lier, Belgium.

Vanistendael, August Albert Joseph; Belgian trade unionist and social worker; b. 1917; ed. Secondary School of the Fathers of Don Bosco.
Factory Worker, Belgium 34-36; Bank Employee, Brussels 36-37; Local Branch Trade Union Sec. 38; Sec.-Gen. Nat. Federation of Christian Trade Unions in Hotel Trade, Brussels 38-40; Public Admin. 40-44; Nat. Sec. Hotel Trade Section, Nat. Fed. of Christian T.U.s of Food Industry 44-45; Sec. Nat. Fed. of Clerical Employees, Brussels 45-47; Asst. Sec.-Gen., Int. Fed. of Christian Trade Unions (IFCTU), Utrecht 47-52, Sec.-Gen. Brussels 52-, Pres. Co-operation and Solidarity; Lecturer, Univ. of Louvain 63; Lay auditor at Ecumenical Council Vatican II 66; mem. Pontifical Comm. Justice and Peace 67; mem. Joint Exploratory Cttee. of Roman Catholic Church and World Council of Churches on Justice, Devt. and Peace 67; Sec.-Gen. of Int. Co-operation for Socio-Econ. Devt. (CIDSE).
Publs. poetry: *Schakel Der Ziel* 45, *Pool en Tegenpool* 51; novel: *Barbara.*
CIDSE, 6 rue de la Limite, Brussels 3; Co-operation and Solidarity, 158 rue Joseph II, Brussels 4; Home: Prinses Lydialaan 16, Heverlee, Belgium.
Telephone: 17-53-59 and 18-05-87 (CIDSE); 34-42-60 (Co-operation and Solidarity).

Vanrullen, Emile Joseph Jules, L. ès sc.; French politician; b. 7 March 1903.
Senator from Pas de Calais 46-; Gen. Counsellor, Béthune 45-61; Quaestor, Conseil de la République 46-53; Vice-Pres. E.C.S.C. Assembly 56-58, European Parl. 58-64; Officier Palmes Académiques.
103 boulevard Thiers, Béthune (Pas de Calais), France.

Varagnac, André, D. ès L.; French archaeologist; b. 12 Jan. 1894; ed. Ecole du Louvre, Univ. de Paris.
Honorary Curator, Musée des Antiquités Nationales; Professor, Ecole pratique des Hautes Etudes; Founder-Pres. Société française d'Archéocivilisation et de Folklore; Dir. Institut Int. Archéocivilisation.
Publs. *Définition du Folklore* 38, *Costumes nationaux* 39, *Costumes français* 39, *Civilisation traditionnelle et genres de vie* 48, *Forces culturelles de l'Europe unie* 52, *De la Préhistoire au Monde Moderne* 54, *L'Art Gaulois* 56, *L'Homme avant l'Ecriture* 59, *La Religion des Celtes* 66.
54 rue de Varenne, Paris 6e, France.
Telephone: BAB 68-20.

Varda, Agnés (Mme Jacques Demy); French film writer and director; b. 30 May 1928; ed. Séte, Herault, and Univ. de Paris à la Sorbonne.
Official Photographer, Théâtre National Populaire 51-61; Reporter and Photographer for *Réalités, Plaisir de France, Marie-France* and other magazines; Prix Méliés 62 (*Cleo de 5 à 7*), Prix Louis Delluc 65 (*Le Bonheur*), Bronze Lion, Venice Festival 64 (*Salut les Cubains*), Silver Bear, Berlin Festival 65 (*Le Bonheur*).
Full-length films: *La Pointe-Courte* 54, *Cleo de 5 à 7* 61, *Le Bonheur* 64, *Les Créatures* 65; Short-length films: *O Saisons, O Châteaux* 57, *L'Opéra-Mouffe* 58, *Du côté de la Côte* 58, *Salut les Cubains* 63.
86 rue Daguerre, Paris 14e, France.

Vargas, Lt.-Gen. Jesus Miranda; Philippine army officer and international official; b. 22 March 1905; ed. Manila North High School and Philippine Constabulary Acad.
Philippine Constabulary 30-36; Philippine Army 37-51; Artillery training U.S.A. 39-40; U.S. Army 41-45, in Japanese P.O.W. Camp; Command and Gen. Staff Coll., Fort Leavenworth, U.S.A. 46-47; C.O. 5th Battalion Combat Team 50-51; Vice-Chief of Staff 51-53, Chief of Staff 54-56; Mil. Adviser to SEATO 54-56; retired from armed forces 56; Sec. of Nat. Defence 57-59; Chair. Board of Dirs. Nat. Waterworks and Sewerage Authority 57-59; Vice-Pres. Philippine-American Life Assurance Co. 59-; Pres. Philippine-American Management and Financing Co. 60-; Chair. Board of Trustees Ramon Magsaysay Award Foundation 62-65; Sec.-Gen. South East Asia Treaty Org. (SEATO) 65-; many decorations.
SEATO H.Q., P.O.B. 517, Bangkok, Thailand.
Telephone: 811322.

Vargas Fernandes, Alfredo; Costa Rican politician; b. 12; ed. Univ. of Costa Rica.
Former university teacher; fmr. Attorney-General of Costa Rica; has led Costa Rican dels. to Organisation of American States; Minister of Foreign Affairs 58-62; numerous foreign decorations.
c/o Ministry of Foreign Affairs, San José, Costa Rica.

Vargas Llosa, Mario; Peruvian writer; b. 28 March 1936; ed. Cochabamba (Bolivia), Universidad de San Marcos, Lima, and Universidad de Madrid.
Former journalist *La Crónica* Lima, *La Industria*, Piura, and La Radio Panamericana, Lima, Agence-France Presse, Paris; broadcaster on Latin American services of Radiodiffusion Télévision Française; Lecturer in Latin American Literature, Queen Mary Coll., London Univ.; Prix Leopoldo Alas 58; Prix Biblioteca Breve 62, *Critica Española* Prize 63, Romulo Gallegos Prize 67.
Publs. include: *Los Jefes* 58, *The City and The Dogs* 62, *La Casa Verde* 65, *Los Cachorros* 66.
7 Philbeach Gardens, London, S.W.5, England.
Telephone: 01-373-9567.

Vargas Ugarte, Rubén, PH.D.; Peruvian educationist; b. 86; ed. Colegio de la Inmaculada, Lima, Colegio Máximo de Granada and Colegio Máximo de Sarriá, Barcelona.
Taught in colls. at Malaga, Madrid, Lima, La Paz, Sucre 12-17, 22-34; Prof. Catholic Univ. of Lima 31-32, Gregorian Univ., Rome 32-33; Dean of Faculty of Letters, Catholic Univ. of Peru 34-44; Adviser, Peruvian Embassy to the Holy See 47; Vice-Rector, Catholic Univ. of Peru 47, Rector 47-53, then Prof. of Peruvian History; Pres. Nat. Council of Historic and Artistic Monuments; Dir. Nat. Library; Dr. h.c. (Univs. of Cuzco and Trujillo).
Publs. *Historia del Culto de María en América* 31, *El Episcopado en los Tiempos de la Emancipación* 32, *Jesuitas Peruanos desterrados a Italia* 34, *Biblioteca Peruana, Manuscritos e Impresos* (12 vols.) 35-57; *Los Jesuitas del Perú* 41, *Historia del Perú, Virreinato,*

S. XVII-XIX (5 vols.) 49-58; *Historia de la Iglesia en el Perú* (5 vols.) 53-61. *Los Jesuitas del Perú y el Arte* 63, *Historia de la compañía de Jesús en el Perú (1568-1767)* (4 vols). *D. Pedro Fernández de Castro, Conde de Lemos, Virrey del Perú* 65, *Historia General del Perú 1524-1825* 6 vols. 66.
Azángaro 468, Apdo. 387, Lima, Peru.
Telephone: 83010.

Várnai, Zseni; Hungarian poetess; b. 25 May 1890.
Awarded Silver Degree of Order of Liberty for work in movement of nat. resistance during German occupation, and First Degree of the József Attila Prize 56; awarded Munka erdemrend (Degree of Works) 58, 60, Golden Degree of Order of Works 65.
Publs. *Katonafiamnak (To My Soldier Son)*, *Vörös tavasz (Red Spring)*, *Anyasziv (Mother Heart)*, *A fájdalom könyve (Book of Grief)*, *Gracchusok anyja (Mother of the Gracchi)*, *Furulyaszó, Örömök kertje (Garden of Joys)*, *A mesélő erdö (The Forest of Tales)*, *Im itt az irás (Lo, Here is the Writing)*, *Kórus szopránban (Soprano Choir)*, *Fekete bárány (Black Lamb)*, *Én mondom és te add tovább, Legyen meg a Te akaratod!, Ég és föld között (Between Earth and Heaven)*, *Mint viharban a falevél (Like a Leaf in the Tempest)*, *Egy asszony a milliók közül (A Woman of the Millions)*, Vols. I and II, *Áldott asszonyok (Blessed Women)*, *Száz vers a szabadságért (Hundred Poems for Liberty)*, *Várnai Zseni válogatott versei* 55, *Fényben, viharban (In Light and Lightning)* (novel), *Igy égtem, énekeltem (In Flames I Sang)* 58, *Feltámadás (Resurrection)* (Dramatic poems) 59, *Peace!* (poems), *Légy boldog te Világ! (O World, Be Happy)* (poems) 61, *Élök, vigyázzatok! (People, be on your guard!)* (poems) 62, *Nem volt hiába . . . (It was not in vain)* 62, *A Woman of the Millions* (autobiography) 63, *Nyugtalan madár (Restless Bird)* (poems) 66, *Ének az anyáról (Songs upon the Mother)* 68, *Tündérkert (Fairyland)* (poems for children) 68.
Keleti Károly u. 27, Budapest II, Hungary.
Telephone: 357-759.

Vas, Istvan; Hungarian poet; b. 24 Sept. 1910.
Publisher's Reader 46, wrote poems and essays for the Press; noted as translator of plays by Shakespeare, Racine, Schiller, Molière, and novels from French and English; Kossuth Prize 62.
Publs. *Tristan* (play), *Egy szerelem három éjszakája (Three Nights of a Love—musical)*, *Évek és munkák (Years and Works—essays)*; poems: *Rapszódia egy öszi kertben (Rhapsody in an Autumn Garden)*, *Menekülö muzsa (Fleeting Muse)*.
c/o Hungarian Writers Federation, Budapest VI, Bajza-utca 18; Home: Budapest I, Groza Péter rakpart 17, Hungary.
Telephone: 229-073 (Writers Fed.); 151-856 (Home).

Vasan, S. S.; Indian editor and film producer; b. 03.
Entered journalism; founded *Ananda Vikatan*, a Tamil journal 28; entered film business 39; founded Gemini Studios 41; Editor *Ananda Vikatan*; Chair. Gemini Pictures Circuit Ltd.; elected to Parliament; mem. Indian and Eastern Newspaper Soc.
Gemini House, Edward Elliot Road, Mylapore, Madras 4, India.

Vasarely, Victor; French (b. Hungarian) artist; b. 1908; ed. Padolini-Volkmann Acad., Budapest, and Budapest Bauhaus.
Studied medicine; settled in Paris 30; one-man exhbns. Budapest 29-33, Europe 45-56, Rose Fried Gallery, New York City 58, World House Gallery, N.Y.C. 61, 62, Montevideo 58, Hanover Gallery, London 62, Pace Gallery, Boston 62; group exhbns. in Paris, Stedelijk Museum, Amsterdam, Documenta III, Kassel, Gallery Chalette, N.Y.C., Sidney Janis Gallery, N.Y.C., Solomon R. Guggenheim Museum, New York, and in São Paulo,

Rio de Janeiro and Montevideo, Tate Gallery, London 64; permanently represented in Museum of Modern Art, New York, Musée St. Etienne, Paris, Albright Knox Gallery, Harvard, Tate Gallery, London, Stedelijk Museum, Amsterdam, and in Buenos Aires, Montevideo, Brussels, Reykjavik, São Paulo, Helsinki, etc.; Guggenheim Int. Award for Merit 64.
64 rue aux Reliques, Annet-sur-Marne, nr. Paris, France.

Vásáry, Tamás; Hungarian concert pianist; b. 11 Aug. 1933; ed. Franz Liszt Univ. of Music, Budapest under Lajos Hernadi, Jozsef Gat and Zoltan Kodàly.
First solo performance at age of eight; studied at Franz Liszt Acad. until 54; remained at Franz Liszt Acad. to teach theory; recitals in Leningrad, Moscow and Warsaw; settled in Switzerland 58; London debut 61, New York 62; has since appeared in Europe, S. Africa, S. America, U.S.A., Canada, India, Thailand, Hong Kong, Australia, Japan and Mexico; records for Deutsche Grammophon; Liszt Prizes: Queen Elizabeth (Belgium), Marguerite Longue (Paris); Chopin Prizes: Int. Competition, Warsaw, Int. Competition, Brazil; Bach and Paderewski Medals (London).
Principal recordings: three records of works of F. Liszt; nine records of works of Chopin.
Villa Vásáry, Chardonne sur Vevey (Vaude), Switzerland.
Telephone: 51-04-44.

Vasconcellos Motta, H.E. Cardinal Carlos Carmelo de; Brazilian ecclesiastic; b. 90.
Ordained priest 18; Titular Bishop of Algiza 32; Bishop of São Luis do Maranhão 35-44; Archbishop of São Paulo 44-64, of Aparecida 64-; created Cardinal by Pope Pius XII 46; mem. Sacred Congregations of Religious, of Ceremonies and of Seminaries and Univs.
Praça N. Sra. Aparecida 273, Aparecida, São Paulo, Brazil.

Vasey, Sir Ernest Albert, K.B.E., C.M.G.; British financial administrator; b. 27 Aug. 1901.
Nairobi Town Council 39-50; mem. Kenya Legislative Council 45, mem. for Health and Local Govt. 50-51, for Education, Health and Local Govt. 51-52; Minister for Finance and Development 52-59; Minister for Finance, Tanganyika 60-62, Financial and Econ. Adviser, World Bank Development Service 62-66, Resident Rep., IBRD in Pakistan 62-66; mem. E. African Common Market Tribunal; 2nd Class Brilliant Star of Zanzibar, Hilal-i-Quaid-i-Azam of Pakistan 66.
Publs. *Report on African Housing* 50, *Economic and Political Trends in Kenya* 56.
P.O. Box 14235, Nairobi, Kenya.
Telephone: 25208 (Office); 53461 (Home).

Vashchenko, Grigory Ivanovich; Soviet politician; b. 1920; ed. Kharkov Engineering Coll. and U.S.S.R. Polytechnic Inst.
Factory worker in Kharkov and Nizhny Tagil 38-58; Party Official 58-63; First Sec. Kharkov Regional Cttee. C.P. of Ukraine July 63-; Alt. mem. Political Bureau, Central Cttee. C.P. Ukraine; mem. C.P.S.U. Central Cttee.; Deputy to U.S.S.R. Supreme Soviet; mem. C.P.S.U. 43-.
Kharkov Regional Committee, Communist Party of the Ukraine, Kharkov, U.S.S.R.

Vasilevsky, Marshal Alexander Mikhailovich; Soviet army officer and politician; b. 95; ed. Military Academy of General Staff.
Served 14-18 war and Civil War; various posts in People's Commissariat of Defence and Volga Mil. Area 31-36; Deputy Chief of Staff, U.S.S.R. Armed Forces 41-42, Chief of Staff 42-45, 46-49; Deputy Commissar for Defence 42-44; C.-in-C. Byelorussian Front and Far East 45; Minister of Defence 49-53, Dep. Minister of Defence 53-57, Insp.-Gen., Ministry of Defence 59-;

Hero of Soviet Union (twice), Order of Lenin (six times), Order of Red Banner of Labour (twice) and numerous other decorations.
c/o Ministry of Defence, 34 Maurice Thorez Embankment, Moscow, U.S.S.R.

Vasiliev, Anatoli Vasilievich; Soviet trade corporation official; b. 24; ed. Moscow Inst. of Communication Engineers and Higher Party School of Central Cttee. of C.P.S.U.
Soviet Army 42-46; Technician, Scientific Research Dept., later Chief of Laboratory. Moscow Power Inst. 46-50; Communist Party official, Moscow 50-58; Dir. State Publishing House of Communications and Radio Literature of U.S.S.R. Ministry of Communications 58-61; Chair. *Vsesojuznoe Objedinenie Vneshtorgizdat* 61-64; Chair. *Vsesojuznoje Objedinenije Vneshtorgreclama* (Foreign Trade Advertising Asscn.) 65-; mem. C.P.S.U.; several decorations.
V/O Vneshtorgreclama, 32-34 Smolenskaya-Sennaya ploshchad, Moscow, G-200, U.S.S.R.

Vasiliev, Nikolai Vasilievich; Soviet trade corporation official; b. 10; ed. Moscow Mechanical Machine Building Inst.
Technological Engineer, Chief, Technical Control Dept. Stankokonstruktsia Machine Tool Plant 35-39; Trade Mission, Germany 39-41, Austria 46-47, Sweden 53-59; Exec. *Stankoimport* (Machine Tools) 41-44; Chair. *Tekhnopromimport* (Equipment for Industry) 44-46; Ministry of Foreign Trade 48-50; Chair. *Mashpriborintorg* (Precision Engineering and Electrical Equipment) 59-; mem. Communist Party 39-; Order of Lenin (twice) and other awards.
V/O Mashpriborintorg, Ministry of Foreign Trade, 32-34 Smolenskaya-Sennaya ploshchad, Moscow, U.S.S.R.

Vasiliev, Vladimir Victorovich; Soviet ballet dancer; b. 1940; ed. Bolshoi Ballet School.
With Bolshoi Theatre Ballet 58-; Honoured Artist of the R.S.F.S.R.
Principal roles: The Prince (*Nutcracker*), Pan (*Valpurgis Night*), The Poet (*Chopiniana*), Danila (*Stone Flower*), Prince Charming (*Cinderella*), Batyr (*Shurale*), Andrei (*A Page of Life*), Basil (*Don Quixote*), Albert (*Giselle*), Frondoso (*Laurencia*), Medjnun (*Leili and Medjnun*).
State Academic Bolshoi Theatre of the U.S.S.R., 1 Ploshchad Sverdlova, Moscow, U.S.S.R.

Vasmadzidis, Christos; Greek politician; b. 23 Sept. 1901; ed. Athens Coll. of Agriculture.
Head of Macedonian Farm Co-operatives 24, Head of Chalkidiki Settlement Office 24-30; Insp. for Macedonia, Agrarian Bank 30-35, Dir. of Agrarian Bank 35-61, Gov. 63; Centre Union Deputy 63-; Minister of Agriculture July 65-66.
Publs. *Greek Dairy Farming Problems* 35, *The Economics and Technique of Goat-Rearing* 39.
Ministry of Agriculture, Athens, Greece.

Vass, Mrs. István; Hungarian politician; b. 15.
Worker in Rubber Factory, later welder; mem. Communist Party 39; mem. Presidium Hungarian Peace Council; M.P. 53-, Dep. Speaker 55-63, Speaker 63-67, Deputy Speaker 67-; Sec. Patriotic People's Front 56-60; Gen. Sec. Democratic Fed. of Hungarian Women 50-56, Pres. 56-57.
The National Assembly, Budapest, Hungary.

Vasseur, Pierre Marie Louis; French international administrator; b. 13 Oct. 1893; ed. Univ. of Paris.
Law practice 20-23; Sec. economic and social research section of Comité National d'Etudes 23-26; Asst. Sec. Gen. of Int. Confed. of Intellectual Workers 27; Dir. with Int. Chamber of Commerce 26-33; Sec.-Gen. 33-58, Hon. Sec.-Gen. 58-; Vice-Pres. Union of Int. Asscns.;

Officier de la Légion d'Honneur, and other decorations.
La Pastorale, Méré-Montfort l'Amaury (Seine et Oise), France.
Telephone: 214 Montfort l'Amoury.

Vassilyev, Nikolai Vassilyevich; Soviet foreign trade official; b. 1910; ed. Moscow Inst. of Mechanical Engineering.
Member C.P.S.U. 38-; Official, U.S.S.R. Trade Representation in Germany 39-41; Deputy Dir., then Vice-Chair., later Chair. *Stankoimport* Trust 41-44; Official of foreign trace orgs. of U.S.S.R. in Austria, Romania, Germany 46-50; Chair. *Tekhnoexport* Trust 50-53; U.S.S.R. Commercial Rep. in Sweden 53-59; Chair. *Mashpriborintorg* Trust 59-; Order of Lenin (twice), Order of Red Banner of Labour, Honour Badge. *Mashpriborintorg* Trust, 32-34 Smolenskaya-Sennaya Square, Moscow, U.S.S.R.

Vassy, Etienne Joseph; French physicist; b. 14 Nov. 1905; ed. Univs. of Lyons and Paris.
Assistant, Faculty of Sciences, Univ. of Paris 37-42, Asst. Prof. 42-50, Prof. 50-; Chair. Joint Comm. on Upper Atmosphere, Int. Union for Geodesy and Geophysics 57, French Cttee. Scientific Radio-electricity 62, Ionospheric Research Cttee., Advisory Group for Aeronautical Research 62; mem. Advisory Cttee. World Meteorological Org. 63; Hon. mem. Int. Television Cttee. 65-; Hon. mem. New York Acad. of Sciences; Hon. Chair. French Cttee. Scientific Radio-electricity 68; mem. Int. Astronautical Acad., and several other socs.
Publ. *Atmospheric Physics* (3 vols.) 56, 59, 66.
110 quai Louis-Blériot, 75 Paris 16e, France.
Telephone: MIR 60-74.

Vatchenko, Alexei Fedoseyevich; Soviet politician; b. 14; ed. Dniepropetrovsk Univ.
Member C.P.S.U. 40-; party work 48-; Sec. then Second Sec. Dniepropetrovsk Regional Cttee. of C.P.S.U. 54-59; First Sec. Khmelnitsky Regional Cttee., C.P. of Ukraine 59-64; First Sec. Cherkassy District Cttee. C.P. of Ukraine 64-65; First Sec. Dniepropetrovsk District Cttee. 65-; Cand. mem. Central Cttee. of C.P.S.U. 61-66, mem. 66-; mem. Political Bureau, Central Cttee. C.P. of Ukraine; Deputy to U.S.S.R. and Ukrainian S.S.R. Supreme Soviets.
Dniepropetrovsk District Committee of C.P. of Ukraine, Dniepropetrovsk, Ukrainian S.S.R., U.S.S.R.

Vaubourdolle, René Victor; French publishing executive; b. 11 July 1894; ed. Lycée Louis-le-Grand, Paris and Ecole normale supérieure.
With Librairie Hachette 20-, Editor of their Classics Series; Editor of *Classiques illustrés Vaubourdolle;* Dir. Alliance française; Commdr. Légion d'Honneur, Commdr. des Palmes académiques, Croix de Guerre.
Publs. author of several books in *Classiques illustrés Vaubourdolle* series.
Librairie Hachette, 79 boulevard Saint-Germain, Paris 6e; and 22 boulevard Saint-Michel, Paris 6e, France.
Telephone: DAN 56-74 (Home).

Vaucelles, Count Pierre Louis Joseph de; French diplomatist; b. 13 Feb. 1907; ed. Ecole Fénelon, Lycée Condorcet and Institut catholique de Paris.
Foreign Service 32-; Attaché Bucharest 32-37; Sec. Berlin 37-40, Budapest 40-43; Sec. Brussels 44-46, Counsellor 46-48; at Ministry of Foreign Affairs 48-50; Counsellor Brussels 50-52, Minister 52-54; Ambassador to Iraq 54-56; Asst. Perm. Rep. to UN 57-60; Dir. diplomatic section Institut des hautes études de défense nationale 60-63; Ambassador to Venezuela 63-68, to Norway 68-; Officier Légion d'Honneur, Commdr. Etoile noire, Grand Officier Ordre de la Couronne (Belgium), Commdr. Ordre de

Léopold, Grand Cross, Orders of Francisco de Miranda and Libertador (Venezuela).
5 rue du Dôme, Paris 16e, France; French Embassy, Oslo, Norway.
Telephone: 727-6027 (Paris).

Vaughan, David Borders; American United Nations official; b. 6 Aug. 1910; ed. New York Univ., Columbus Law School and American Univ., Washington, D.C.
With Irving Trust Co. 28-35; Asst. Dir. Finance, Farm Security Administration 35-39; Dir. Personnel, Surplus Marketing Admin. 39-40; Dir. Admin. Management, UNRRA London and Washington 42-44; Asst. Admin. Foreign Economic Admin. 42-44; Exec. Officer of Int. Trade, Dept. of Commerce; Dir. of Confs. and Gen. Services, UN 46; now Dir. with status of Under-Sec., Office of General Services, UN; Rep. of Sec.-Gen. of UN on Appointments and Promotion Board; UN mem. Jt. Staff Pensions Board; mem. Advisory UN Board on Compensation Claims.
225 Steamboat Road, Great Neck, L.I., N.Y., U.S.A.

Vaughan, Sir (George) Edgar, K.B.E.; British professor and former diplomatist; b. 24 Feb. 1907; ed. Cheltenham Grammar School and Jesus Coll., Oxford.
Vice-Consul, Hamburg 31; Second Sec. and Vice-Consul, La Paz 32-35; Vice-Consul, Barcelona 35-38, Buenos Aires 38-44; Chargé d'Affaires and Consul-Gen., Monrovia 45-46; Consul, Seattle 46-49; Consul-Gen., Lourenço Marques 49-53, Amsterdam 53-56; Minister and Consul-Gen., Buenos Aires 56-60; Ambassador to Panama 60-63, to Colombia 64-66; Special Lecturer in History, Univ. of Saskatchewan (Regina Campus) 66-67, Prof. of History 67-; Fellow, Royal Historical Soc. 65-; Foreign Corresp. mem. Colombian Acad. of History 66-; Hon. Fellow, Jesus Coll., Oxford 66-.
50 Academy Park Road, Regina, Sask., Canada.
Telephone: Regina 536-9188.

Vaughan, Hilda (Mrs. Charles Morgan); British writer; ed. privately.
Publs. *The Battle to the Weak, Here Are Lovers, The Invader, Her Father's House, The Soldier and the Gentlewoman, A Thing of Nought, The Curtain Rises, Harvest Home, Pardon and Peace, The Fair Woman, Iron and Gold, The Candle and the Light*; plays: *She, too, was Young, Forsaking All Other* (with Laurier Lister).
16 Campden Hill Square, London, W.8, England.

Vaughan, Hilton Augustus, Q.C.; Barbados judge and diplomatist; b. 23 Nov. 1901; ed. Harrison Coll., Barbados, and Middle Temple, London.
Senior mem. House of Assembly, for Bridgetown 36; Editor *Barbados Recorder* 40-41; Magistrate 41, Judge of Bridgetown Petty Debt Court 49, Acting Puisne Judge 56-60; Minister without Portfolio, Barbados Govt. 61-64; Attorney-Gen. and mem. Judicial Advisory Council 64; Minister of State and Leader of Senate 66-68; Perm. Rep. to UN 68-.
Permanent Mission of Barbados to the United Nations, 801 Second Avenue, 2nd Floor, N.Y. 10017, U.S.A.

Vaughan, Dame Janet Maria, D.B.E., D.M., F.R.C.P., M.A.; British doctor and university official; b. 18 Oct. 1899; ed. Univ. Coll. Hospital and Somerville Coll., Oxford.
Asst. Clinical Pathologist, Univ. Coll. Hospital 27-29; Rockefeller Travelling Fellow 29-30; Beit Memorial Fellow 31-34; Leverhulme Fellow Royal Coll. of Physicians 34-35; Clinical Pathologist British Post-Graduate Medical School 35-39; Dir. N.W. London Blood Supply Depot 39-45; Principal Somerville Coll. 45-67, Hon. Fellow 67-; Chair. Oxford Regional Hospital Board 50-51; Dir. Medical Research Unit for Research on Bone-Seeking Isotopes 50-; mem. Royal Comm. for Equal Pay 44-45, Phillips Cttee. on Econs. and Problems of the Provision for Old Age 53, Common-

wealth Scholarship Comm. 64-, Cttee. on Libraries of Univ. Grants Cttee. 65-67; Trustee Nuffield Foundation.
Publs. *The Anaemias* 34, and numerous scientific papers.
1 Fairlawn End, First Turn, Wolvercote, Oxford, England.
Telephone: Oxford 54111.

Vaughan, (John) Keith, C.B.E.; British painter, designer and illustrator; b. 23 Aug. 1912; ed. Christ's Hospital.
Lecturer in Painting Central School of Art, London 52-56, Slade School 57-; Resident Painter State Univ. of Iowa 60; first one-man exhbn. London 44, others in New York, London, Buenos Aires, São Paulo, retrospective exhbn. Whitechapel Art Gallery, London 62; represented in public galleries: Tate Gallery, Victoria and Albert Museum, etc., London, Fitzwilliam Museum, Cambridge and provincial museums in U.K.; Nat. Gallery of Scotland; Nat. Gallery of New South Wales; Toronto Museum; Albright-Knox Museum, Buffalo, Wadsworth Atheneum, Conn., Art Inst. of Chicago, Yale Univ., Iowa Univ.; Hon. A.R.C.A.; Design of the Year Award, Council of Industrial Design 58.
Major works: Central Mural for Dome of Discovery, Festival of Britain 51, Ceramic Mural Corby New Town 54, Mural for L.C.C. Aboyne Estate 63; Illustrated Books: *Une Saison en Enfer*, Rimbaud 49, *Tom Sawyer*, Twain 51.
Publ. *Journal and Drawings* 66.
9 Belsize Park, London, N.W.3, England.
Telephone: SWIss Cottage 4966.

Vaughn, Jack Hood, M.A.; American diplomatist; b. 18 Aug. 1920; ed. Univs. of Michigan, Pennsylvania and Mexico.
U.S. Marine Corps 43-46; Univ. Instr. 46-49; U.S. Information Service, Costa Rica and Bolivia 49-51; Agency for Int. Development, Panama, Bolivia, Washington, Senegal 52-61; Regional Dir. for Latin America, Peace Corps 61-64; Ambassador to Panama 64-65; Asst. Sec. for Latin American Affairs 65-66; Dir. The Peace Corps 66-.
Home: 502 Wolfe Street, Alexandria, Va.; Office: 806 Connecticut Avenue, Washington, D.C., U.S.A.

Vaughn, William Scott; American business executive; b. 8 Dec. 1902; ed. Vanderbilt Univ., Rice Inst. and Oxford Univ., England.
Eastman Kodak Co. 28-, Asst. to Gen. Manager, Kodak European Companies, Kodak Ltd., London 34-35, Asst. to Gen. Manager, Eastman Kodak Co., Rochester 46, Asst. Vice-Pres. 49, Vice-Pres. and Asst. Gen. Manager 50, First Vice-Pres. Tennessee Eastman Co. and Texas Eastman Co. 52, First Vice-Pres. Eastman Chemical Products Inc. 53, Pres. and Dir. 56, Vice-Pres. and Gen. Manager, Eastman Kodak Co. 58, Dir. 59, Pres. 60-66, Chair. 67-; Dir. Kodak Ltd., London, Kodak-Pathé, Paris, Canadian Kodak Co. Ltd., Kodak A.G., Stuttgart, The Proctor and Gamble Co., Lincoln Rochester Trust Co., Rochester Gas and Electric Corpn., Thompson Ramo Wooldridge Inc. (now TRW Inc.); Trustee of several educational orgs.
Eastman Kodak Co., 343 State Street, Rochester, New York, 14650, U.S.A.
Telephone: 716-325-2000.

Vaux, Roland de, Doctor of Theology; French ecclesiastic and archaeologist; b. 17 Dec. 1903; ed. Paris.
Professor French Biblical and Archaeological School Jerusalem 33, Dir. 45-65; Chief of the Archaeological Missions at Tell el Far'ah and Khirbet Qumrân; Co-Dir. British-French Archaeological Expedition, Jerusalem; corresp. fellow British Acad.; mem. de l'Acad. des Inscriptions et Belles Lettres (Paris).
Ecole Biblique et Archéologique Française, P.O.B. 53, Jerusalem, Jordan.

Vaz Pinto, Alfredo de Queiroz Ribeiro; Portuguese civil servant; b. 05; ed. Oporto Univ.
Sec. to Min. of Commerce and Communications 30; Inspector Armazens Gerais Industriais 32; Asst. Administrator-Gen. of Posts and Telegraghs 33; Man. Dir. Cia. Portuguesa Radio Marconi 37-, Chair. 41-; Chair. Transportes Aéreos Portugueses 59-.
Casa Bem Haja, Av. das Acacias, Estoril, Portugal.

Vázquez Carrizosa, Alfredo, LL.D.; Colombian lawyer and diplomatist; ed. Université Catholique de Louvain, Belgium.
Former lecturer in Public International Law and Constitutional Law, Bogotá; fmr. Secretary-Gen., Ministry of Foreign Affairs; fmr. Acting Head, Ministry of Foreign Affairs; fmr. Asst. Publisher *La República* (daily); fmr. Sec.-General of Presidency; fmr. Ambassador to Belgium; Rep. to Org. of American States 64-.
Publs. *Lectures on Public International Law* (2 vols.) 59-60.
Representation of Colombia to Organization of American States, 1609 Twenty-second Street, N.W., Washington D.C. 20008, U.S.A.

Vázquez del Mercado, Admiral Antonio; Mexican naval officer and politician; b. 2 Nov. 1903; ed. Escuela Naval Militar.
Second Officer, Commdr., Commdt. various Navy vessels 21-23; Ship's Lieut., Insp. of Mexican naval shipbuilding exports to Spain 33-35; Commdt. gunboat *Potosí* 36; Asst. Dir.-Gen. Merchant Navy, Ports and Lighthouses 37; Sec.-Gen. Autonomous Marine Dept. 40; Dir. Naval Mil. School 41; Marine Man. Petróleos Mexicanos 41-47; Dir.-Gen. Merchant Navy 47; Naval Attaché, Washington Embassy 48-54; Commdt. First Naval Zone 55; Commdt.-Gen. of Fleet 55-59; now Dir. of Central Fisheries Office 60- and Sec. of State for Navy; Naval mem. Interamerican Joint Defence Comm. and Mexican-U.S. Defence Comm.; Mil. Merit Medal and Spanish Naval Merit Medal.
Secretaría de Marina, Mexico City, Mexico.

Vázquez Salas, J. Jorge, LL.D., D.SC.POL.; Peruvian lawyer and politician; b. 29 April 1904; ed. Univ. del Gran Padre San Augustín, Arequipa and Univ. Nac. de San Marcos, Lima.
Chief Prof. Int. Public Law, Maritime and Aeronautic Law 35-60; Legal Adviser, Amb. of Ministry of Foreign Affairs of Peru 45-48; Mayor of Arequipa 60-61; Senator 63-; Minister of Foreign Affairs 65-67; Del. of Peru to First UN Gen. Assembly 46; Dr. h.c. Univ. of Guanabara; Grand Cross of the Order of the Sun (Peru), Grand Cross of the Order of Ruben Darío (Nicaragua), Order of the Aztec Eagle, First Class (Mexico), Grand Order of the Crown (Belgium), Grand Cross (German Fed. Repub.).
Manuel Fuentes 951, San Isidro, Lima, Peru.

Vedel, Vice-Admiral A. H.; Danish naval officer; b. 1 Sept. 1894.
Lieutenant 16, Lieut.-Commander 23, Commander 32, Captain 39, Vice-Admiral 41; Chair. Danish Del. to Scandinavian Defence Cttee. 48-49; C.-in-C. Danish Navy 41-58; fmr. Lecturer in Strategy, Danish Naval Acad.; fmr. Chair. Danish Naval Scientific Society; Vice-Pres. Danish Royal Geographical Society; Chair. Danish Pearyland Expedition to Greenland, Cttee. for navigation in Greenland Waters 59; Pres. UNESCO Intergovt. Conf. on Oceanographic Research, Copenhagen 60; mem. of Cttee. Danish Galathea Expedition round the World; Board mem. East Asiatic Co. Ltd.; mem. Danish Nat. Council for Oceanology and for Geography; Dr. h.c. (Univ. of Copenhagen).
Rypevej 13, Hellerup, Copenhagen, Denmark.
Telephone: Hellerup 4302.

Veen, Thijs Willem van, DR.IUR.; Netherlands journalist; b. 18 March 1920; ed. Utrecht and Groningen Univs.
Assistant at Groningen Univ. (Criminal Law) 45-47; Man. Editor Groningen edition of *Het Vrije Volk* 47-48, Asst. to Editor-in-Chief 48-51, Asst. Editor-in-Chief 51-61, Editor-in-Chief 61-.
Het Vrije Volk, Hekelveld 15, Amsterdam, Netherlands.

Veibel, Stig, DR. PHIL.; Danish university professor; b. 19 April 1898; ed. Royal Technical Coll., Copenhagen.
Assistant, Dept. of Organic Chemistry, Univ. of Copenhagen 20-31; Lecturer in Organic Chemistry, Royal Technical Coll., Copenhagen 32-44, Prof. 44-68; mem. of Acad. of Technical Sciences 43, of Danish Royal Acad. of Sciences 55; Pres. Danske Kemiske Foreningers Faellesrad for Internationalt Samarbejde (Danish Nat. Council of Chemistry) 46; Chair. Danish Chemical Society 47-50; mem. of Bureau of Int. Union of Chemistry 47-51; Hon. mem. French Chemical Society 57, Polish Chemical Soc. 59; Hon. Dr. Univ. of Bordeaux 61; Corresp. mem. Acad. of Sciences, Paris 61.
Publs. *Vejledning i organiske stoffers identification* 26, 37, 47, *Studier over nitreringsprocessen* 29, *Kemiens Historie i Danmark* 39, *Dansk kemisk bibliografi 1800-1935* 43, *Organisk Kemi I-II* 51, 58-59, *The Identification of Organic Compounds* 54, 61, 66, *Identification des substances organiques* 57, Russian edn. 57, German edn. 60, Czechoslovak edn. 64.
4 Enighedsvej, Charlottenlund, Denmark.
Telephone: OR 5776.

Vejvoda, Ivan; Yugoslav diplomat; 13 Nov. 1911; ed. Technical Univ., Prague and Zagreb.
Member Int. Brigade 37-39; arrested for political activities several times 35-41; volunteer in the French Army 39-40; joined the Nat. Liberation Movement 41 and held several political appointments; Asst. Minister for Foreign Affairs after Liberation; Ambassador to Brazil 52-55; Ambassador to Czechoslovakia 55-56; Ambassador to Great Britain 56-60; Asst.-Sec. for Foreign Affairs 60-62; Ambassador to Italy 62-67, to France 67-; Order of Yugoslav Star 1st Class, Order of Brotherhood and Unity 1st Class; Order of the Partisan Star, 2nd Class, etc.
Yugoslav Embassy, rue de la Faisanderie 54, Paris 16e, France.

Vekshinsky, Sergei Arkadevich; Soviet metallurgical engineer; b. 96; ed. Leningrad and Don Polytechnic Insts.
Chief Engineer, Leningrad Electrovacuum Plant 22-28; Head, Branch Vacuum Laboratory, "Svetlana" Electrovacuum Plant, Leningrad 28-36, Chief Engineer 36-39, Consultant 39-41; Dir. Vacuum Research Inst. 47-; Mem. U.S.S.R. Acad. of Sciences 53-; mem. Communist Party 40-; Order of Lenin (three times), State Prize 46, 51, Hero of Socialist Labour, Red Banner of Labour (three times).
Publs. *A New Method of Metallographic Study of Alloys* 44, *High Vacuum Pumps and Aggregates* 58.
U.S.S.R. Academy of Sciences, 14 Lenin Prospekt, Moscow, U.S.S.R.

Vekua, Ilya Nestorovich; Soviet mathematician; b. 1907; ed. Georgian State Univ., Tbilisi.
Former Prof. Tbilisi-Stalin Univ.; Prof. Moscow Univ. 52-57; corresp. mem. U.S.S.R. Acad. of Sciences 46-58; mem. 58-; mem. Presidium Siberian Dept. of U.S.S.R. Acad. of Sciences 58-; Rector, Novosibirsk Univ. 59-65; Vice-President, Acad. of Sciences of Georgian S.S.R. 65-66; Rector Tbilisi Univ. 66-; mem. Editorial Board U.S.S.R. Acad. of Sciences 59-; State Prize 50, Lenin Prize 63.

Publs. *New Methods of Solving Elliptical Equations* 48, *Systems of First Order Differential Equations of the Elliptical Type and Boundary Problems with an Application to the Theory of Shells* 52, *Generalised Analytic Functions* 59, *Fixed Special Points of Generalised Analytical Functions* 62, *New Methods in Mathematical Shell Theory* 65.

The University, Prospekt Tchavtchavadze 1, Tbilisi, Georgia, U.S.S.R.

Velasco Ibarra, José Maria, DR.JUR.; Ecuadorean politician; b. 93; ed. Central Univ. of Quito.
Deputy to Nat. Congress; Pres. of Republic 34-35, 44-47; elected Constitutional Pres. of Republic for term 52-56, 60-64 (resigned Nov. 61); Leader of Federación Nacional Velasquista (FNV); mem. Academia Ecuatoriana; decorated by Venezuela, Colombia, Bolivia, Chile, Argentina, El Salvador, France, etc.
Publs. *Conciencia o Barnarie, Tragedia Humana y Cristanismo, Experiencias Jurídicas Hispano-americanas, Derecho Internacional del Futuro,* etc.
Federación Nacional Velasquista, Quito, Ecuador.

Velázquez, Carlos Maria, LL.D.; Uruguayan lawyer and diplomatist; b. 29 Nov. 1918; ed. Univ. of the Republic, Montevideo.
Former teacher, intermediate schools and Mil. Inst.; Perm. Rep. of Uruguay to UN 61-65; Ambassador to U.K. 65-; Rep. of Uruguay to Security Council 65.
Publs. *La Protección Internacional de la Libertad de Enseñanza* 57, *Repertorio de la Jurisprudencia del Tribunal de lo Contencioso-Administrativo* 57-58, *El Derecho Natural y la Misión del Jurista* 57, *Sobre la Naturaleza Jurídica del Asilo en las Legaciones* 58, *La Invalidez de los Tratados Inconstitucionales* 60, *Some Legal Aspects of the Colonial Problem in Latin America* 65, *Changing Emphases at the United Nations* 66.
Embassy of Uruguay, 48 Lennox Gardens, London, S.W.1, England.
Telephone: 01-589-8835/6.

Veldkamp, Dr. G. M. J.; Netherlands politician; b. 27 June 1921; ed. Tilburg Catholic Economic Univ.
Board of Labour, Breda 41-50; Scientific Adviser, Social Insurance Section, Ministry of Social Affairs and Public Health 50-52; Lecturer, Coll. for Social Service Work, and at Technical Coll. 47-52; Chair. for Diocese and mem. Nat. Social Charitable Centre 47-52; Chair. Roman Catholic Party, Municipal Council of Breda 50-52; Sec. of State for Econ. Affairs 52-61; Minister of Social Affairs and Public Health 61-67; mem. Second Chamber of States-Gen.; Catholic Party.
c/o Ministry of Social Affairs and Public Health, 73 Zeestraat, The Hague, Netherlands.
Telephone: 070-18-32-20.

Velebit, Vladimir, LL.D.; Yugoslav politician; b. 07.
Mem. Nat. Liberation underground movement in Zagreb, then at Supreme H.Q. of Nat. Liberation Army and Partisan Units; with Nat. Liberation Movement's H.Q. in Egypt 43; Head Mil. Mission, London 44; Asst. Minister Foreign Affairs, Belgrade after Liberation; Asst. Minister for Foreign Trade; Ambassador to Italy; Ambassador to Great Britain; Under-Sec. of State for Foreign Affairs 56-58; State Under-Sec. in the Foreign Trade Cttee. 58-60; Exec. Sec. UN Econ. Comm. for Europe (ECE) 60-67; Order of Partisan Star, 1st Class, etc.
c/o Economic Commission for Europe, Palais des Nations, Geneva, Switzerland.

Veltchev, Boris Lazarov; Bulgarian politician; b. 14; ed. secondary-technical education.
Sofia Municipality 33-41; mem. First District Cttee., Bulgarian Communist Party, Sofia 40, Sec. 41; political imprisonment 41-44; successively mem. Sofia Council of Syndicalists, Sec. Municipal Employees Trade Union, Instructor at Regional Cttee. of C.P., Sofia, Sec. Sofia

City Cttee. of C.P.; Dep. Head, Trade Union and Youth Dept., Central Cttee. of Bulgarian Communist Party 52-54, Head 54-59; Sec. Central Cttee. of Bulgarian Communist Party 59-, mem. Politburo 62-; Chair. of Party and State Control Cttee. of the Party and Council of Ministers 62-; Dep. National Assembly.
Central Committee of Bulgarian Communist Party, Sofia, Bulgaria.

Venezis, Ilias; Greek writer; b. 4 March 1904; ed. Mytilene Coll.
Administrative Dir. Nat. Theatre of Greece 64-66; Awarded Acad. of Athens and State Literary prizes; mem. Athens Acad.
Publs. Fiction: *Serenity* 39, *Aeolia* 44, *Ocean* 56; Short Stories: *Aegean* 40, *Defeated* 54; History: *Archbishop Damaskinos* 52, *The Bank of Greece* 55, *Argonautes* 62, *The Prime Minister of Crete's Battle* 66; Play: *Block C* 45.
Odos Herodotou 5, Athens, Greece.
Telephone: 712-862.

Venkataraman, Krishnasami, PH.D., D.SC., F.N.I.; Indian university professor; b. 7 June 1901; ed. Univs. of Madras and Manchester.
Prof. of Organic Chemistry, Forman Christian Coll., Lahore 29-34; Reader, Dept. of Chemical Technology, Univ. of Bombay 35-38, Prof. and Dir. Chemical Tech. Dept. 38-57; Dir. Nat. Chemical Laboratory, Poona 57-66; mem. Deutsche Akademie der Naturforscher Leopoldina 60; Padma Bhushan 61; Hon. Dr. of D. E. Mendeleev Inst. of Chemical Technology, Moscow 62; Visiting Prof. Purdue Univ. Feb.-June 62; Reilly Lecturer, Univ. of Notre Dame March 62.
Publs. *The Chemistry of Synthetic Dyes,* Vols. I and II 52; articles on pure and applied organic chemistry in *Review of Textile Progress,* Kirk-Othmer's *Encyclopædia of Chemical Technology,* Zechmeister's *Progress in the Chemistry of Organic Natural Product, Pointers and Pathways in Research* 63, etc.
National Chemical Laboratory, Poona 8, India.
Telephone: Poona 54818.

Venot de Noisy, Jack; French international lawyer; b. 29 July 1916; ed. Ecole Saint-Grégoire, Pithiviers.
Honorary Pres. Int. Fed. of Judicial and Fiscal Counsellors; Sec.-Gen. Int. Council of Space Law 61-; Vice-Pres. Fed. of Latin Nations 62-; Pres. Order of Int. Lawyers of France 63-; Vice-Pres. Int. Confed. of Asscns. of Experts and Advisers; Chevalier Légion d'Honneur; Croix de Guerre.
2 avenue Foch, Paris 16e, France.

Ventslova, Antanas Tomasovich; Soviet writer; b. 7 Jan. 1906; ed. Kaunas Univ.
People's Commissar of Educ. of the Lithuanian S.S.R. 40-43; mem. C.P.S.U. 50-; Chair. of the Cttee. of the Union of Lithuanian Writers 54-59; Corresp. mem. Lithuanian Acad. of Sciences 49; People's Writer of the Lithuanian S.S.R.; State Prize 51.
Publs. novels: *Friendship* 36, *The Day of Birth* 58, *Spring River* 64; anthologies: *There the High Apple Tree* 45, *The Country's Youth* 47, *To Fight, to Burn, Not to Rest* 53, *The Earth is Good* 63, *Have you known this Land* 64; selected short stories: *The Birches in the Wind* 30, *Night* 39, *The Tree and its Shoots* 47; literary criticism: *The Time and Writers* 58, *The Wind of Epoch* 62; a book of sketches: *Journey Through China* 55, *North Silver* 62, *Selected Works* 3 vols. 56, *The Spring River* 67.
Writers' Union, Vilnius, Lithuanian S.S.R., U.S.S.R.

Ventura, Raúl Jorge Rodrigues, DR.HIST., DR. JUR.SC.; Portuguese university professor and politician; b. 19; ed. Univ. of Lisbon.
Former Public Prosecutor, Setubal and later Chief of Dept. Inst. Nacional de Trabalho e Providencia and Sec. to Under-Sec. of Corporations and Social Assist-

ance; Under-Sec. of State for Overseas Territories 53-55, Minister for Overseas Territories 55-58; corresp. mem. Inst. of Law, Nat. Univ. of Argentina, Inst. of Labour, Univ. of São Paulo and Inst. of Social Law, Lisbon.
Rua Fernão Mendes Pinto 34, Lisbon, Portugal.

Venzo, Mario, S.J.; Italian painter; b. 14 Feb. 1900; ed. Accademia di Belle Arti, Venice.
Painter in Paris 26-39; entered Society of Jesus 40; exhibitions in Milan 51-53, Rio de Janeiro 55, Turin 58, Trieste 61, Zürich 54, Munich and Berne 65, Monte Carlo and Padua 66, Turin and Milan 67; First Prize Ucai, Vicenza 50, Monte Carlo 66, Nat. Exhbn. Prize, Milan 66.
Major works: *Via Crucis* (Lonigo) 60, *Crocefissione* (Coll. Pio-Latino-Americano, Rome) 62, *Via Crucis* (Villa Cavalletti, Frascati) 64, *Crocefissione* (Alte, Vicenza) 65, *Via Crucis* (Prospiano) 67.
Aloysianum, Gallarate, Varese, Italy.
Telephone: 72244.

Vercors (*pseudonym* of Jean Bruller); French writer, graphic artist and engraver; b. 26 Feb. 1902; ed. Ecole alsacienne, Paris.
Early career as graphic artist and engraver; Founder *Editions de Minuit* with Pierre de Lescure 41; Del. to many conferences throughout the world since 45; mem. PEN Club; Hon. Pres. National Cttee. of Writers.
Major works (graphic art and engraving): *21 recettes de mort violente* 26, *Hypothèses sur les amateurs de peinture* 27, *Un homme coupé en tranches* 29, *Nouvelle clé des songes* 34, *L'Enfer* 35, *Images rassurantes de la guerre* 36, *Silence* 37, *La Danse des vivants* (160 prints) 38, *Hamlet* (French adaptation, with aqua-forte illustrations) 65.
Publications: *Le Silence de la Mer* 41, *La Marche à l'Etoile* 43, *La Sable du Temps* 45, *Les Armes de la Nuit* 46, *Les Yeux et la Lumière* 48, *Plus ou moins homme* 50, *La Puissance du jour* 51, *Les Animaux dénaturés* 52, *Les pas dans le sable, Portrait d'une amitié* 54, *Divagations d'un Français en Chine* 56, *Colères* 56, *P.P.C.* 57, *Sur ce rivage* vol. 1 58, vol. 2 58, vol. 3 60, *Sylva* 61, *Zoo ou l'Assassin philanthrope* (play) 63, *Les Chemins de l'Etre* (with P. Misraki) 65, *Quota ou les Pléthoriens* (with P. Coronel) 66, *La Bataille du Silence* 67.
Moulin des Iles, Faremoutiers, Seine-et-Marne, France.

Verdet, Ilie; Romanian politician; b. 10 May 1925.
Member Romanian C.P. 45-; worked in the Party local organs of Banat Region 48-54; Head of Section in Central Cttee. Romanian C.P., First Sec. Hunedoara Regional Party Cttee. 54-65; mem. Central Cttee. Romanian C.P. 60-; Deputy to Grand Nat. Assembly 61; Alt. mem. Exec. Cttee. of Central Cttee. of R.C.P. 65-66; First Vice-Pres. Council of Ministers of Socialist Rep. of Romania 67-; Licentiate Inst. Econ. Sciences, Bucharest.
Council of Ministers of Socialist Republic of Romania, Bucharest, Romania.

Verdier, Abel; French diplomatist; b. 15 March 1901; ed. Lycées Lakanal et Janson de Sailly and Université de Paris à la Sorbonne.
Assistant Consul, London 30-35; Consul, Saarbrücken 35-39; mem. French Mission for Economic Warfare, England 39-40; Ministry of Foreign Affairs 41-50; Ambassador to Colombia 50-55, to UNRWA, Beirut 55-57, to Finland 60-64; Ministry of Foreign Affairs 64-; Officier Légion d'Honneur, Médaille de la Résistance, Croix de Guerre (39-45) and foreign decorations.
Publs. *La Constitution fédérale de la République d'Autriche* 24, *Manuel Pratique des Consulats* 33, 47, 57, 63, *Formulaire à l'Usage des Consulats* 47, 57, 63, *Les Amours italiennes de Lamartine—Graziella et Lena* 63.
Château de la Roderie, Cerelles (S.-et-L.), France.

Verdon Smith, Sir (William) Reginald, Kt.; British business executive; b. 5 Nov. 1912; ed. Repton School and Brasenose Coll., Oxford.

President, Soc. of British Aircraft Constructors 46-48; now Vice-Chair. Rolls-Royce Ltd., Chair. Bristol Aeroplane Co. Ltd., Dir. assoc. companies in U.K. and overseas, including Bristol Siddeley Engines Ltd., British Aircraft Corpn.; Vice-Chair. Lloyds Bank Ltd.; Dep. Chair. Babcock & Wilcox Ltd., Northern and Employers Assurance Co. Ltd.
Old Manor, Littlehemptson, Totnes, S. Devon, England.

Verdoorn, Frans, PH.D.; Netherlands scientist and editor; b. 06; ed. Univs. of Utrecht, Vienna and Geneva.
Asst. Botanic Gardens Buitenzorg 30; Founder and Man. Editor The Chronica Botanica Co. 33-37; Botany Sec., Int. Union of Biological Science 35-53; Research Assoc., Harvard Univ. 40-; Technical Adviser, Neth. Indies Govt. 43-49; Organising Dir. Los Angeles Arboretum 48-49; Dir. Biohistorical Inst., Utrecht Univ. 57-; Gen. Sec., Int. Biohistorical Comm. 48-; mem. Zeeuwsch Genootschap; hon. foreign mem. Royal Botanical Society, Edinburgh; hon. staff mem. Kebun Raya Indonesia; Fellow, American Acad. Boston; Fellow, Linnean Society, London; honoured at 6th-10th Int. Botanical Congresses; corresp. mem. Botanical Soc. of America; First Mary Soper Pope Medal 46; Centenary Medal, French Botanical Soc. 54; Netherlands Soc. for History of Science Medal 63; Editor *Annales Bryologici* 28-39, *Annales Cryptogamici et Phytopathologici* 42-, *Biologia* 46-, *Bryophyta Arduennae Exsiccata* 27-29, *Chronica Botanica* 35-, *Hepaticae Selectae et Criticae* 30-39, *Lotsya* 48-, *Musci Selecti et Critici* 38-40, *"A New Series of Plant Science Books"* 38-, *Pallas* 48-.
Publs. *De Frullaniaceis* 1-18, *Manual of Bryology* 32, *Manual of Pteridology* 38, *Aims and Methods of Biological History* 44, *Plants and Plant Science in Latin America* 45, *Science and Scientists in Neth. Indies* (with P. Honig) 45, *The Modern Arboretum* 48.
Biohistorical Institute, University of Utrecht, 187 Nieuwe Gracht, Utrecht, Netherlands.

Verdross, Alfred, DR.IUR.; Austrian jurist; b. 90; ed. Vienna, Munich and Lausanne Univs.
Prof. Vienna Consular Acad. 22-38; Prof. of Int. Law and Philosophy of Law Vienna Univ. 24-, Dean of Law Faculty 31-32, 47-48 and 58-59, Rector of the Univ. 51-52; mem. UN Int. Law Comm. 57-66; Hague Perm. Court of Arbitration 58-; Judge, European Court of Human Rights 59-; mem. Austrian Acad. of Sciences; mem. Inst. of Int. Law, Vice-Pres. 52, Pres. 59-61; Pres. Int. Conf. in Vienna for the codification of the law of diplomatic relations 61; Dr. h.c. Univs. of Salamanca, Paris, Frankfurt, Vienna, Salzburg and Salonika; Austrian Hon. Medal for Arts and Sciences, Grand Cross of St. Sylvester and Order of Malta.
Publs. *Die Einheit des rechtlichen Weltbildes* 23, *Die Verfassung der Völkerrechtsgemeinschaft* 26, *Grundlinien der antiken Rechts- und Staatsphilosophie* (2nd edn.) 48, *Abendländische Rechtsphilosophie* 58 (2nd edn. 63), *Völkerrecht* (5th edn.) 64; important papers in the *Recueil des Cours de l'Académie de droit international* include *Le Fondement du Droit International* 27, *Les Règles Générales du Droit International de la Paix* 29, *Idées Directrices de l'Organisation des Nations Unies* 53.
Pokornygasse 23, 1190 Vienna, Austria.
Telephone: 36-32-96.

Veres, József; Hungarian engineer and politician; b. 1906.
Resistance Movement, Second World War; party, state, and econ. official 45-; Mayor of Budapest 58; mem. Central Cttee. of Hungarian Socialist Workers' Party 59-; Minister of Labour 63-.
Ministry of Labour, Budapest, Hungary.

Veres, Péter; Hungarian politician and writer; b. 97; ed. elementary school.
Railway labourer; imprisoned for political offences; wrote first book in prison; Pres. of Nat. Peasant Party; Pres. of Nat. Land Council 45; Minister of Construction

and Public Works 47; of Nat. Defence 47-48; fmr. Pres. Hungarian Writers Asscn.; Kossuth Prize twice.
Publs. *Számadas, Mit ér az ember, ha magyar, Falusi krónika, Ember és irás, Gyepsor, Paraszti jövendö, Próbatétel, Pályamunkások, Ukrajna földjén, Szolgaság, Szegények szerelme, Almáskert, Utközben.*
Gárdonyi Géza ut. 6o, Budapest II, Hungary.

Vereshchagin, Leonid Fedorovich; Soviet physicist; b. 1909; ed. Odessa Inst. of People's Education.
Postgraduate 30-33; Chief Engineer Research Bureau, Kharkov Turbogenerator Factory 33-34; Chief Engineer Ukrainian Physical-Technical Inst., Kharkov 34-39; Dir. Lab. Inst. of Organic Chemistry, U.S.S.R. Acad. of Sciences 39-54; Dir. Lab. of Physics of Superhigh Pressures, U.S.S.R. Acad. of Sciences 54-58; Dir. Inst. Physics of High Pressures, U.S.S.R. Acad. of Sciences 58-; Prof. Moscow State Univ. 53-; Corresp. mem. U.S.S.R. Acad. of Sciences 60-66; mem 66-; U.S.S.R. State Prize; Hero of Socialist Labour.
Publs. Basic works on problems of superhigh pressures and roentgen-structural analysis of crystals.
U.S.S.R. Academy of Sciences, 14 Lenin Prospekt, Moscow, U.S.S.R.

Verghese, Rev. Thadikkal Paul, B.A., B.D., S.T.M.; Indian ecclesiastic; b. 9 Aug. 1922; ed. Goshen Coll., Princeton and Yale Univs., Keble Coll., Oxford.
General Secretary, Orthodox Christian Student Movement of India 55-57; Hon. Lecturer in Religion, Union Christian Coll., Alwaye 54-56; Special Staff Asst. H.I.M. Haile Selassie I 56-59; Chief Adviser, Haile Selassie Foundation 59; Assoc. Gen. Sec. and Dir. of the Div. of Ecumenical Action, World Council of Churches, Geneva 62-67; Principal, Syrian Orthodox Theological Seminary, Kottayam, Kerala 67-.
Syrian Orthodox Seminary, Kottayam, Kerala, India.

Veringa, G. H.; Netherlands professor of law and politician; b. 13 April 1924; ed. Groningen Univ. and in U.S.
Lecturer, Groningen and New York 48-49; at Ministry of Justice, The Hague 50; Prof. of Penal Law, Roman Catholic Univ., Nijmegen 65-67; Minister of Educ. and Science 67-.
Ministry of Education and Science, The Hague, Netherlands.

Verissimo, Erico Lopes; Brazilian writer; b. 17 Dec. 1905; ed. Collegio Cruzeiro do Sul, Porto Alegre.
Chief Editor *Revista do Globo*, Porto Alegre 31-40; Literary Adviser Editôra Globo (publishers) 35-50; Visiting Prof. to Univ. of Calif. (Berkeley) 43-44, to summer sessions of Mills Coll., Oakland, Calif. 44-45; Dir. Dept. of Cultural Affairs, Pan American Union of Org. of American States (OAS), Washington, D.C. 53-56; Free-lance writer 56-; Hon. D.Litt. Mills Coll.; Graça Aranha Prize for *Crossroads* 35, Machado de Assís Prize for *Música ao Longe* 35.
Publs. include: (novels) *Crossroads* 35, *The Rest is Silence* 46, *Consider the Lilies of the Field* 47, *Time and the Wind* 52, *Night* 54, *His Excellency the Ambassador* 66, and *Brazilian Literature* (written in English) 45, *Mexico* 59.
Rua Felipe de Oliveira 1415, Porto Alegre, Rio Grande do Sul, Brazil.

Verity, Calvin William, Jr., B.A.; American steel executive; b. 26 Jan. 1917; ed. Phillips Exeter Acad. and Yale Univ.
With Armco Steel Corpn., Middletown, Ohio 40-, Dir. of Public Relations 61-62, Asst. to Pres. 62-63, Vice-Pres. and Gen. Man. 63-65, Exec. Vice-Pres. 65-66, Pres. 67-; Dir. Harding-Jones Paper Co., Middletown, First Nat. Bank, Middletown, Catahoula Co.
Armco Steel Corporation, Middletown, Ohio; Home: 600 Thorn Hill Lane, Middletown, Ohio, U.S.A.

VerLoren van Themaat, Pieter; Netherlands politician; b. 16; ed. Univ. of Leiden, Netherlands.
Posts in Ministry of Economic Affairs 42-52, Sub-Dir. for Economic Org. 52-54, Dir. 54-58; Head O.E.C.D. Mission to the U.S.A. with cartel experts from 10 European countries 58; Dir.-Gen. for Competition European Economic Comm. (E.E.C.) 58-; Officer Order of Orange-Nassau; numerous legal papers.
88 Chaussée de Tervueren Auderghem, Brussels, Belgium.

Vernadsky, George, M.A.; American (b. Russian) historian; b. 20 Aug. 1887; ed. Univ. of Moscow.
Lecturer, Univ. of Petrograd 14-17; acting Prof. Univ. of Perm 17-18; Prof. Univ. of Simferopol 18-20; Prof. Russian School of Law, Prague 22-27; Research Assoc. in History, Yale Univ. 27-46; Lecturer, Harvard Univ. 31-32; Lecturer, Columbia Univ. 44-45; Prof. of Russian History, Yale Univ. 46-56; Visiting Prof. Columbia Univ. 49-50; Prof. Emeritus of Russian History, Yale Univ. 56-; Hon. Pres. American Asscn. for the Advancement of Slavic Studies 65-; special award American Council of Learned Societies 58; Hon. H.L.D. Columbia Univ. 59.
Publs. *A History of Russia* 29, 61, *Lenin, Red Dictator* 31, *The Russian Revolution* 32, *Political and Diplomatic History of Russia* 36, *Bogdan, Hetman of Ukraine* 41, *Ancient Russia* 43, *Medieval Russian Laws* 47, *Kievan Russia* 48, *The Mongols and Russia* 53, *The Origins of Russia* 59 (French edn. *Essai sur les Origines Russes* 59, Italian edn. *Le Origini della Russia* 65), *Russia at the Dawn of the Modern Age* 59, *The Tsardom of Moscow* 68.
625 Orange Street, New Haven 11, Conn., U.S.A.

Verne, Claude Marie Jean, D.MED., D.SC.; French physiologist; b. 4 Oct. 1890; ed. Paris Univ.
Professeur sans chaire, Univ. de Paris 32, of Biology 46, of Histology 55-62, Hon. Prof. 62-; Dir. Institut d'Histochimie; Gen. Sec. Asscn. Française pour l'Avancement des Sciences 26-; Pres. de l'Académie de Médicine; mem. the European Tissue Culture Club; Founder-Pres. Soc. française d'Histochimie.
Publs. *Les pigments dans l'organisme animal* 19-29, *Recherches histophysiologiques sur poumon et graisses* 23-26, *Recherches sur les cultures des tissus* 30, 46, *Histochimie des graisses* 28-36, 38-42, *Précis d'histologie* 60, *La vie cellulaire hors de l'organisme* 37, *Recherches histochimiques sur les enzymes* 46-61, *sur les glandes surrénales et le pancréas* 50-57, *sur l'auto-historadiographie avec S.35* 56-58, *Etudes sur les Cellules hépatiques cultivées in vitro* 60-66, *L'Histologie* 66, *La Culture de Tissus* (with Hébert) 67.
38 rue de Varenne, Paris 7e, France.

Verner, Paul; German politician; b. 26 April 1911.
Former metal worker; mem. Kommunistische Partei Deutschlands 29-39; Editor-in-Chief *Junge Garde* 33; in Spanish Civil War 36-39; prison in Sweden 39-43, fitter in Sweden 43-45; Co-founder Freie Deutsche Jugend (F.D.J.); mem. Secretariat Central Council of F.D.J. 46-49; mem. Central Cttee. Sozialistische Einheitspartei Deutschlands (S.E.D.) 50-, mem. Secretariat 50-53, 58-; mem. Volkskammer 58-; Sec. Greater Berlin District S.E.D. 59-; mem. Politburo, S.E.D. 63-; Vaterländischer Verdienstorden in Silber.
Sozialistische Einheitspartei Deutschlands, Am Wederschen Markt, Berlin C.2, Germany.

Vernier-Palliez, Bernard Maurice Alexandre, L. ès D.; French business executive; b. 2 March 1918; ed. Ecole Libre des Sciences Politiques, Ecole des Hautes Etudes Commerciales.
Head of Welfare, Régie Nationale des Usines Renault 45-47, Sec. to Sec.-Gen. 47-48, Sec.-Gen. 48-; Chevalier de la Légion d'Honneur, Croix de Guerre, Médaille de la Résistance.
14 Rue Carnot, Rueil-Malmaison (Seine-et-Oise), France.

Vernov, Sergei Nikolaevich; Soviet physicist; b. 1910; ed. Leningrad Polytechnic Institute.
Corresponding mem. U.S.S.R. Acad. of Sciences; mem. I.G.Y. Cttee. of the U.S.S.R. 57; in Radium Inst., U.S.S.R. Acad. of Sciences 31-; Prof. Moscow Univ. 44-; State prizewinner 49; Lenin Prize 60.
Publs. *Latitudinal Effect of Cosmic Rays in the Stratosphere and Verification of Cascade Theory* 45, *Study of Interaction of Primary Components of Cosmic Rays with Matter in the Stratosphere* 49, *Study of Cosmic Rays* 58, *Discovery of Research on Radiation Belt of the Earth* 60, *Investigation of the Earth's Radiation Belts at Altitude of 0-400 kilometres* 64, *On the Assymmetry of Intensity of Fast Electrons in Conjugated Points at Certain Heights* 64, *A Study of Cosmic Rays at Altitudes of 200-409 km.* 65.
Moscow State University, Lenin Hills, Moscow B.234, U.S.S.R.

Veronese, Vittorino, D.IUR.; Italian administrator; b. 1 March 1910.
Formerly Editor *Studium*; fmr. Gen. Sec. Catholic Movement of Univ. Graduates, Prof. Inst. of Social Sciences, Athenaeum Angelicum, Rome, Pres. Catholic Action, Pius XII Foundation, Cen. Inst. of Credit, Consorzio di Credito per le Opere Publiche; Sec. Perm. Int. Congress of Lay Apostolate, Rome; mem. Italian Del to UNESCO 48-58; mem. Italian Nat. UNESCO Comm.; mem. UNESCO Exec. Board 52-56, Pres. 56-58; Dir.-Gen. UNESCO 58-61; resigned Nov. 61; Pres. Banco di Roma 61-; Dir. and mem. Exec. Cttee. of Fondazione Cini, Venice; Dir. Societá Italiana per l'Organizzazione Internazionale; Chair. Italian Cttee. for Human Rights; mem. Pontifical Comm. for Justice and Peace, Vatican City 67.
Banco di Roma, 307 Via del Corso, Rome, Italy.

Verosta, Stephan Eduard, LL.D.; Austrian lawyer and diplomatist; b. 16 Oct. 1909; ed. Gymnasium, Vienna, Univ. of Vienna and studied in Paris, Geneva and Acad. of International Law, The Hague.
Legal practice 32-35, Judge 36-; Legal Dept., Austrian Foreign Office 35-38, Deputy Legal Adviser 45-48, 49-51; Counsellor, Austrian Legation, Rome, Minister, Budapest 51-52; Head of Legal Dept., Foreign Office 53-56; Ambassador to Poland 56-61; Austrian Del. to various int. confs.; mem. Perm. Court of Arbitration, The Hague 57-; Consultant to Foreign Office 62-; Dozent in Int. Law, Univ. of Vienna 46-, Prof. of Int. Law, Jurisprudence and Int. Relations 62-; Chair. U.S.-Finnish Comm. of Conciliation 64-; mem. Austrian Acad. of Science 64; numerous decorations.
Publs. *Les Avis consultatifs de la Cour Permanente de Justice Internationale*, etc. 32, *Jean Dumont und seine Bedeutung für das Völkerrecht* 34, *Liberale und planwirtschaftliche Handelspolitik* (with Gottfried Haberler) 34, *Richterliches Gewohnheitsrecht in Österreich* 42, *Die Satzung der Vereinten Nationen* 46, *Die internationale Stellung Österreichs von 1938-1947* 47, *Die geschichtliche Kontinuität des österreichischen Staates und seine europäische Funktion* 54, *Johannes Chrysostomus, Staatsphilosoph* 60, *Geschichte des Völkerrechts* 64, *International Law in Europe and Western Asia between 100-650 A.D.* 66, *Dauernde Neutralität* 67.
1180 Vienna, Hockegasse 15, Austria.
Telephone: 47-13-48.

Verret, (Louis Joseph) Alexandre, B.A., B.S., LL.L.; Haitian journalist, teacher and diplomatist; b. 5 June 1914; ed. Inst. St. Louis de Gonzague, Port au Prince, and Faculté de Droit, Port au Prince.
Assistant Dir. of *La Tribune* (newspaper) 42; Prof. of Social Sciences, Univ. of Haiti 46-58; Consul-Gen. of Haiti 50, Attaché 58-59, Second Sec. 59-60, First Sec. 60; Alt. Rep. to UN Gen. Assembly 60-61, Rep. 61-; Senior mem. Inter-American Bar Asscn.

Publs. Poetry and literary and scientific articles in newspapers and periodicals.
Permanent Mission of Haiti to the United Nations, 801 Second Avenue, New York, N.Y. 10017, U.S.A.

Vershinin, Air Chief Marshal Konstantin Andreyevich; Soviet airman; b. 1900; ed. Zhukovsky Air Force Acad. Moscow.
Joined Red Army 19; Air Force Commdr. 41-45; Chief Air Marshal; Deputy Minister of Defence 57-, C.-in-C. of the Air Forces 46-49, 57-; mem. Central Cttee. of C.P. of the Soviet Union 61-; Deputy to Supreme Soviet; Hero of the Soviet Union; Order of Lenin (5 times), Suvorov (4 times); Order of the Red Banner (3 times); Virtuti military, etc.
Ministry of Defence, 34 Maurice Thorez Embankment, Moscow, U.S.S.R.

Verulam, 6th Earl of, cr. 1815; **John Grimston,** D.L.; British industrialist; b. 17 July 1912; ed. Oundle School and Christ Church, Oxford.
Reserve of Air Force Officers 30-36; Auxiliary Air Force 37; Conservative M.P. for St. Albans and Mid-Herts. 43-45, 50-59; Chair. Enfield Rolling Mills 60; Chair. Delta Metal Co. Ltd. 68-; Pres. London Chamber of Commerce 63-66; Pres. Wrought Non-Ferrous Council 63; Deputy Lieut. Herts. 63.
Gorhambury, St. Albans, Hertfordshire, England.
Telephone: St. Albans 55000.

Verykios, Dr. Panaghiotis Andrew; Greek diplomatist; b. 24 July 1910; ed. Univ. de Paris, Ecole Libre des Sciences Politiques, and Acad. of Int. Law, The Hague.
Greek Diplomatic Service 35-; Army Service 39-40; Vice-Consul, Bourgas, Bulgaria 40-41; Sec. and Acting Consul-Gen., Lisbon 42-45; First Sec. Ministry of Foreign Affairs, Athens 45-47; First Sec., London 47-50; Counsellor, Athens 50-52; Deputy Perm. Rep. at NATO, Paris 52-54; Counsellor, Paris 54-56; Head of NATO Dept., Athens 56-60; Amb. to Netherlands 60-64, to Denmark, also accred. to Norway and Iceland 64-67; Amb. to U.K. 67-; Greek Mil. Cross; Knight Commdr. Royal Orders of George I and Phoenix (Greece) and several foreign decorations.
Greek Embassy, 51 Upper Brook Street, London, W.1, England; Home: Iras 6, Ekali, nr. Athens, Greece.
Telephone: 01-629-0694/5 (Office); 01-629-8500 (Residence); Athens 019-216 (Home).

Veselinov, Jovan; Yugoslav (Serbian) politician; b. 06; ed. Communist Univ., Moscow.
Former metal worker; Communist Youth of Yugoslavia 30, imprisoned 31-41, later Sec. Regional Cttee. Vojvodina, later Vice-Pres. Govt. of Serbia; Pres. of People's Assembly, People's Republic of Serbia, Sec. of Central Cttee. of League of Communists of Serbia, mem. Exec. Cttee. of League of Communists of Yugoslavia 57-; Order of National Hero, etc.
Uižčka 32, Belgrade, Yugoslavia.

Vesey-FitzGerald, Brian Seymour; British naturalist; b. 1900; ed. Dover Coll. and Keble Coll., Oxford.
Editor *The Field* 38-46; mem. Honourable Soc. of Cymmrodorion; Vice-Pres. Gamekeepers' Asscn.; Editor County Books 46-; Pres. British Fairground Soc. 55-63.
Publs. *A Book of British Waders* 38, *Hampshire Scene* 40, *The Noctule* 41, *Farming in Britain* 42, *Field Fare* 42, *A County Chronicle* 42, *Hedgerow and Field* 43, *Gypsies of Britain* 44, *British Game* 46, *The Book of the Horse, It's My Delight* 47, *The Book of the Dog, A Child's Biology, Hampshire, British Bats* 48, *Bird Biology for Beginners* 49, *Background to Birds* 49, *Rivermouth* 49, *The River Avon* 51, *Borrow in Britain* 53, *Winchester* 53, *Cats* 55, *Nature Recognition* 55, *The Domestic Dog* 57, *Historic Towns* 57, *The Beauty of Cats* 58, *The Beauty of Dogs* 60, *Your Book of Dogs* 62, *Cat Owner's Encyclopaedia* 63, *Foxes in Britain* 64, *Dog Owner's Encyclo-*

paedia 65, *Animal Anthology* 65, *Portrait of the New Forest* 66, *Enquire Within About Animals* 67, *Garden Alive* 67.
Long Croft, Wrecclesham, Farnham, Surrey, England.

Vestijk, Simon; Netherlands physician and writer; b. 17 Oct. 1898; ed. high schools at Harlingen and Leeuwarden, and Univ. of Amsterdam.
Medical practice 27-32; travelled as ship's doctor to Indonesia; has worked on journals and literary periodicals; Officer Order of Orange Nassau, Knight Order of Netherlands Lion.
Publs. novels include: *Terug tot Ina Damman, Het Vijfde Zegel, De Koperen tuin*; also short stories, essays, poetry and musicological works.
Torenlaan 4, Doorn, Netherlands.

Vialar, Paul; French writer; b. 18 Sept. 1898.
Former Pres. Société des Gens de Lettres; Hon. Pres. Syndicat des Ecrivains Français; Hon. Pres. Fed. Nat. des Sociétés d'Auteurs; Pres. Asscn. des Ecrivains Sportifs, Conseil des Lettres, R.T.F.; mem. PEN Club Cttee.; Pres. Syndicat National des Auteurs et Compositeurs; Commandeur de la Légion d'Honneur, Ordre des Arts et Lettres; Croix de Guerre; and numerous foreign awards.
Publs. 15 plays and 80 novels including *La rose de la mer* (Prix Femina) 39, *La mort est un commencement* (8 vols.) (Grand Prix de la Ville de Paris) 48, *Chronique française du XXème Siècle* (10 vols. completed).
34 Av. Victor Hugo, Boulogne sur Seine, France.

Viana Filho, Luiz, LL.D.; Brazilian lawyer and writer; b. 08; ed. Aldridge School, Rio de Janeiro, and Faculty of Law, Univ. of Bahia.
Professor of International Law, Univ. of Bahia 40, Prof. of History of Brazil 43; Dep. to Fed. Congress 35-37, 46-; mem. of Historical and Geographical Soc. of Brazil 38-; mem. Brazilian Acad. of Letters 54-, Sec.-Gen. 56-64; Head of President's Civil Household 64-66; Minister of Justice *ad interim* 66; Gov. of Bahia 66-.
Publs. *O Negro na Bahia* 38, *A Vida de Rui Barbosa* 41, *A Sabinada* 40, *A Verdade na Biografia* 43, *Rui & Nabuco* 49, *A Vida de Joaquim Nabuco* 51, *A Lingua do Brasil* 38, *A Vida do Barão do Rio Branco* 59, *A Vida de Machado de Assis* 65.
Office of the Governor, Salvador, Bahia, Brazil.

Viaut, André Jules Armand, B. ès SC.; French meteorologist; b. 16 Oct. 1899; ed. Coll. de Tonnerre.
Joined French Nat. Meteorological Office 21, Chef de Section 36, Chef du Service de l'Exploitation 39, Deputy Dir. 42, Dir. 45-64, Hon. Dir. 64-; First Vice-Pres. World Meteorological Organisation 51-55, Pres. 55-63; Prix Léon Grelaud 50, Prix Hirn of Académie des Sciences 65, and several other awards; Commdr. Légion d'Honneur, Commdr. Mérite Touristique, Médaille de l'Aéronautique, Médaille d'or Aéro Club de France 65, Order of the Cedar of Lebanon, Order of Cambodia.
Publs. *Aspects du Temps en Europe Occidentale, La Météorologie, La Météorologie du Navigant, Manuel du Vol à Voile, Le Temps et les Travaux des Champs, Le Givrage, La Mer et le Vent—Météorologie Nautique.*
1 Av. Victor Hugo, 92 Meudon, Hauts-de-Seine, France.
Telephone: OBservatoire 12-63.

Vicchi, Adolfo Angel; Argentine diplomatist, politician and university professor; b. 19 April 1900.
Former Professor Admin. Law, National Univ., Cuyo; fmr. Prof. History of Civilisation Agustín Alvarez Nat. Coll., Mendoza; mem. Council Mendoza 26-28, Minister of Public Welfare 37-40, Gov. 41-43, Provincial Senator 61-62; Pres. Federación de Partidos del Centro 51-53 and 62; Ambassador to U.S.A. 55-57; Ambassador to U.K. 64-65.
Publs. *Política Económica, Federalismo y Libertad,*

Servidumbres Administrativas, La Revolución de 1955: antecedentes y consecuencias.
Avenida España 596, Mendoza, Argentina.

Vicente Vilanova, José; Salvadorean judge; b. 10; ed. Universidad Autónoma de El Salvador.
Former Counsellor, Faculty of Jurisprudence, Higher University, Sec.-Gen. of Univ., Dean of Faculty of Jurisprudence and Social Sciences, Rector of Univ. of El Salvador; Third Judge of First Instance, San Salvador Criminal Court, Magistrate, Chamber of Second Instance, Civil Court, San Salvador; now Pres. of Supreme Court, of Higher Council of Public Safety; Pres. Lawyers Asscn. of El Salvador.
Supreme Court of Justice, San Salvador, El Salvador.

Vick, Francis Arthur, O.B.E., PH.D.; British physicist; b. 5 June 1911; ed. Waverley Grammar School and Birmingham Univ.
Assistant Lecturer in Physics, Univ. Coll., London 36, Lecturer 39-44; Asst. Dir. of Scientific Research, Ministry of Supply 39-44; Lecturer in Physics, Manchester Univ. 44, Senior Lecturer 47-50; Prof. of Physics, Univ. of North Staffordshire 50-59, Vice-Principal 50-54; Dep. Dir. Atomic Energy Research Establishment, Harwell 59-60, Dir. 60-64, Dir. Research Group 61-64, mem. for Research U.K. Atomic Energy Authority 64-66; mem. Advisory Council on Research and Devt., Ministry of Power 60-63; mem. Governing body, Nat. Inst. for Research in Nuclear Science 64-65; mem. Nuclear Safety Advisory Cttee., Ministry of Power 60-66, Univ. Grants Cttee. 59-66; Pres. Asscn. of Teachers in Colls. and Depts. of Education 64-; Pres. and Vice-Chancellor, Queen's Univ., Belfast Oct. 66-; Knight Commdr., Liberian Humane Order of African Redemption 62.
Vice-Chancellor's Lodge, Lennoxvale, Belfast BT9 5BY, Northern Ireland.
Telephone: Belfast 665370.

Vickers, Harry Franklin; American executive; b. 10 Oct. 1898.
Organiser, Engineering and Mfg. Business H. F. Vickers Mfg. Co., Los Angeles 21, inc. in Calif. as Vickers Inc. 27, moved to Detroit 29, Pres. 36; company merged with Sperry Corpn. 37; continued as Pres. Vickers Inc. and became Exec. Vice-Pres. (Operations) Sperry Corpn. 47, Pres. 52-55; company merged with Remington Rand 55, Pres. Chief Exec. Officer, Dir. Sperry Rand Corpn. 55-, now Chair. and Chief Exec. Officer.
Sperry Rand Corporation, 1290 Avenue of Americas, New York City, N.Y., U.S.A.

Vickers, Jon; Canadian tenor; 29 Oct. 1926.
Began career as concert and opera singer in Canada; joined Royal Opera House, Covent Garden (London) 57; sang at Bayreuth Festival, Vienna State Opera, San Francisco, Chicago Lyric Opera, Metropolitan Opera, New York, La Scala, Milan, Paris Opera, Athens Festival, Salzburg Festival, etc.; Hon. LL.D. Univ. of Saskatchewan; Hon. C.L.D. Bishop's Univ.
c/o Metropolitan Opera Co., New York City, N.Y., U.S.A.

Vickery, Hubert Bradford, M.SC., PH.D.; American chemist; b. 28 Feb. 1893; ed. Yarmouth Acad., Dalhousie Univ., and Yale Univ.
Teacher of Science, Halifax, Nova Scotia 15-17; Chemist for Imperial Oil Ltd., Halifax 17-19; Teacher, Normal School, Truro, Nova Scotia 19-20; 1851 Exhibition Fellow 20-22; Research Chemist Connecticut Agric. Experiment Stn., New Haven 22-26, Asst. Biochemist 26-28, Biochemist in charge 28-63; Research Assoc., Carnegie Inst. of Washington 28-38; Lecturer, Yale Univ. 24-63; rank of Prof. 44; Stephen Hales Prize 33; mem. of Nat. Acad. of Sciences 43; mem. of Ed. Board of *Journal of Biological Chemistry* 41-; Assoc. Ed. *Journal of the American Chemical Society* 39-48; mem. Ed. Board of *Plant Physiology* 47-57; civilian scientific

observer at atomic bomb experiments at Bikini, Marshall Islands 46; Vice-Pres. American Society of Biological Chemists 49-50, Pres. 50-51; hon. life mem. American Society Plant Physiology 56; Hon. D.Sc. (Yale) 48.

415 Whitney Avenue, New Haven, Conn., U.S.A.

Victor, Paul-Emile, Lic.-ès-Sc., Dipl. d'Ethnologie; French explorer; b. 28 June 1907; ed. Lycée Rouget de Lisle (Lons le Saulnier), Ecole Centrale de Lyon, Faculty of Science and Letters and Inst. of Ethnology, Paris.

Greenland Expedition 34-35; crossed Greenland by dog sleigh 36; wintered on east coast of Greenland 36-37; trans-Alpine crossing by dog sleigh Nice-Chamonix 38; expedition to Lapland 39; has organised and directed the Expeditions Polaires Françaises (missions Paul-Emile Victor—Arctic and Antarctic expeditions) since 47; Pres. French Antarctic Cttee. Int. Geophysical Year; Head of Int. Glaciological Expedition to Greenland; Officier de la Légion d'Honneur, Grand Croix de l'Etoile d'Anjouan, Officier of the Orders of Vasa and Dannebrog; Gold Medal of the Royal Geographical Soc. (London), Vega Gold Medal (Sweden), Médaille spéciale de l'Administration des Monnaies.

Expéditions Polaires Françaises, 47 Avenue du Maréchal Fayolle, Paris 16e, France.

Vidal, Gore; American writer; b. 3 Oct. 1925; ed. Phillips Acad., Exeter, N.H.

Served in U.S. Army 43-46; Edgar Allen Poe award for Televison 55; Drama Critic *Reporter* (magazine) 59.

Publs. Novels: *Williwaw* 46, *In a Yellow Wood* 47, *The City and the Pillar* 48, *The Season of Comfort* 49, *A Search for the King* 50, *Dark Green, Bright Red* 50, *The Judgement of Paris* 52, *Messiah* 54, *Julian* 64, *Washington, D.C.* 67, *Myra Breckinredge* 68; short stories: *A Thirsty Evil* 56; plays: *Visit to a Small Planet* 56 (on Broadway 57-58), *The Best Man* (on Broadway 60-61); film scripts and adaptations: *Wedding Breakfast, I Accuse, Ben Hur, Suddenly Last Summer, Rocking the Boat* (political and literary commentary) 63; criticism in *Partisan Review, The Nation, The Reporter, Esquire,* etc.

Edgewater, Barrytown, New York City, N.Y., U.S.A.

Vidic, Dobrivoje; Yugoslav diplomatist; b. 27 Dec. 1918.

Joined Nat. Liberation Movement 41; mem. Central Cttee. of Yugoslav League of Communists; joined Diplomatic Service 51; Counsellor in Yugoslav Embassy, London; Ambassador to Burma; Ambassador to U.S.S.R. 54-56, 65-; Under-Sec. of State for Foreign Affairs 56-58; Yugoslav Perm. Del. at UN 58-60; Pres. Socialist Alliance Cttee. for Foreign Relations; Order of Yugoslav Flag, 1st Class, etc.

Yugoslav Embassy, Moscow, U.S.S.R.

Vidor, King Wallis; American film director; b. 8 Feb. 1895; ed. Galveston High School and Peacock Military Acad. San Antonio, Texas.

Productions include *The Big Parade, The Crowd, Hallelujah, The Citadel, Duel in the Sun, H. M. Pulham Esq., The Fountainhead, War and Peace, Solomon and Sheba.*

Publ. *A Tree is a Tree* (autobiography) 53.

Suite 104, 201 Lasky Drive, Beverly Hills, Calif., U.S.A.

Vieillard, Roger; French artist; b. 9 Feb. 1907; ed. University of Paris.

Studied under S. W. Hayter 35; took part in exhibitions by Jeune Gravure Contemporaine, Société des Peintres Graveurs, Salon de Mai, Biennales of Venice, and São Paulo; works exhibited in Paris (Galeries de France, la Hune, Adrien Maeght, Galerie Coard), London (Hanover Gallery), Rotterdam (Boymans Museum), Berne (Musée de Berne), Galerie d'Art Moderne, Basle; has specialised in line engraving; prints in French and

foreign museums and private collections; Vice-Pres., Comité Nat. de la Gravure Française, Comité National du Livre Illustré français; Chevalier de la Légion d'Honneur, Officier des Arts et des Lettres.

Principal works: Illustrations for: *La Fable de Phaeton d'Ovide* 39, *Hommage à Rimbaud* 44, *Poèmes de Jean Tardieu* 45, *Discours de la Méthode* 48, *L'Ecclésiaste* 51, *Le Banquet de Platon* 52, *Poèmes d'André Frenaud* 56, *Eléments* 56.

7 rue de l'Estrapade, Paris 5e, France.

Telephone: Odéon 40-78.

Vienne, Robert, (Baron de); French industrialist; b. 23 Jan. 1904.

President, Dir.-Gen., Constructions mécaniques et électriques Capri-Codec S.A.; mem. Soc. of French Civil Engineers; Chevalier, Légion d'Honneur.

32 rue Ernest-Renan, Colombes (Seine), France.

Vieira da Silva, Marie-Hélène (Mme Arpad Szenes); French artist; b. 13 June 1908; ed. Acad. de la Grande Chaumière under Bourdelle and Despiau.

Sculptor 19-28; influenced by Siennese school of painting 28; studied painting under Dufresne, Friesz, Fernand Léger and Bissière, also engraving under Hayter at *L'Atelier 17* 29; first one-man exh. 32; in Portugal 39, Brazil 40-47, settled in Paris 47; one-man exhbns. at Galerie Pierre 48, 51, 55, Galerie Knoedler, New York 61, 63, 66; Retrospective Exhbns. at Kestner-Gesellschaft 58, Musée de Grenoble 64, Galleria Civica d'Arte Moderna, Turin 64; works in the major galleries of the world; 1st Prize São Paulo Biennal 61; Commdr. des Arts et Lettres.

c/o Guy Weelon, 8 avenue Frochot, Paris 9e, France.

Viereck, Peter, B.S., M.A., PH.D.; American poet, historian and dramatist; b. 5 Aug. 1916; ed. Harvard Univ. and Christ Church, Oxford.

Teaching Asst., Harvard Univ. 41-42, Instructor in German Literature and tutor 46-47; History Instructor, U.S. Army, Univ. of Florence, Italy 45; Asst. Prof. History, Smith Coll. 47-48; Assoc. Prof. Mount Holyoke Coll. 48-55, Prof. of European and Russian History 55-; U.S. State Dept. mission of cultural exchange to U.S.S.R Sept.-Oct. 61; mem. Exec. Cttee. American Cttee. for Cultural Freedom; awarded Tietjens Prize for Poetry 48, Pulitzer Prize for Poetry 49; Guggenheim Fellow, Rome 49-50; Visiting Lecturer Univ. of Paris, American Univ., Beirut, and American Univ. Cairo 66; L.H.D. Olivet Coll. 59.

Publs. *Metapolitics—from the Romantics to Hitler* 41, *Terror and Decorum* (poems) 48, *Who Killed the Universe* 48, *Conservatism Revisited—The Revolt Against Revolt 1815-1849* 49, *Strike Through the Mask: New Lyrical Poems* 50, *The First Morning: New Poems* 52, *Shame and Glory of the Intellectuals* 53, *Dream and Responsibility: The Tension Between Poetry and Society* 53, *The Unadjusted Man: a New Hero for Americans* 56, 62, *Conservatism: From John Adams to Churchill* 56, *The Persimmon Tree* (poems) 56, *The Tree Witch: A Poem and Play* 61, *Metapolitics: The Roots of the Nazi Mind* 61, *Conservatism Revisited and the New Conservatism: What Went Wrong?* 62, *New and Selected Poems* 66.

Mount Holyoke College, South Hadley, Mass., U.S.A.

Vietoris, Leopold, PH.D.; Austrian professor of mathematics; b. 4 June 1891; ed. Technische Hochschule, and Univ. of Vienna.

Lecturer, Staatserziehungsanstalt, Vienna 19-20; Asst. in Maths., Technische Hochschule, Graz 20-22; Asst. in Maths., Univ. of Vienna 22-27; Rockefeller Fellowship, Amsterdam 25-26; Prof. of Maths., Univ. of Innsbruck 27-28; Technische Hochschule, Vienna 28-30, Univ. of Innsbruck 30-61, Emeritus Prof. 61-; mem. Acad. of Science, Vienna 60; Hon. mem. Austrian Mathematical Soc. 65.

Kaiserjägerstr. 40, A-6020 Innsbruck, Austria.

Telephone: 245354.

Vigón Suerodíaz, Gen. Jorge; Spanish army officer; b. 93; ed. Jesuit Coll., Gijón, and Acad. de Artillería.
Army career from age of 16; Minister of Public Works 57-July 65; recipient of numerous awards.
Publs. *Estampa de Capitanes, Milicia y Política, El espíritu Militar español* (Nat. Literature Award 50), *El Gran Capitán*, etc.
c/o Ministerio de Obras Públicas, Madrid; Home: Casado del Alisal 4, Madrid, Spain.

Vigorelli, Giancarlo; Italian writer and literary critic; b. 13.
Secretary-General European Community of Writers 60.
Publs. Essays: *Bandello* 42, *Eloquenza dei Sentimenti* 42, *Il Manzoni e il Silenzio dell'Amore* 54, *Gronchi: Battaglia di Ieri e di Oggi* 56, *Domande e Risposte per la Nuova Cina* 59, *Carte Francesi* 59, *Il Gesuita Proibito: P. Teilhard de Chardin* 63, etc.
Via Archimede 35, Rome, Italy.

Vila, George Raymond, A.B., S.M., A.M.P.; American business executive; b. 3 March 1909; ed. Wesleyan Univ., Massachusetts Inst. of Technology, Harvard Graduate School of Business Administration.
Vice-President and Gen. Man. Naugatuck Chemical Div., Uniroyal, Inc. 57, Group Exec. Vice-Pres. Uniroyal, Inc. 57-60, Pres. 60-, Chair. 65-; Chair. Uniroyal Ltd. (Canada, Scotland); Dir. Rubber Manufacturers' Asscn., ACF Industries Inc., Chemical Bank New York Trust Co., Economic Club of New York, etc.
Publs. *Critical Analysis of T-50 Test* 39, *Action of Organic Acceleration in Buna S* 42, *Plastication and Processing of GR-S* 43, *Approach of Statistical Methods to Manufacture of Synthetic Rubber* 44, *A New Era in Synthetics in Rubber to Match Plastics?* 55, *Tires: An Expanding Market for Chemicals* 56, *1960 Outlook for In-Process Materials* 59, *Economics and Trends in Rubber and the Newer Rubber-Like Materials* 59.
Uniroyal Inc., 1230 Avenue of the Americas, New York City 10020, N.Y.; Home: Windy Hill Farm, Far Hills, New Jersey 07931, U.S.A.

Vilar, Jean Louis Côme; French actor and producer; b. 25 March 1912; ed. Collège Paul Valéry and Univ. of Paris.
Director Théâtre Nat. Populaire 51-63; Dir. Avignon Festival 47-.
Acted and produced many works including: *Le Cid, Richard II, Don Juan, Meurtre dans la Cathédrale, Henrico IV, Danse de Mort, Mère Courage, L'Avare, La Ville, Ce fou de Platonov, Le Faiseur, Oedipe, Ubu, Les Caprices de Marianne, Antigone, Roses Rouges pour moi, Turcaret, L'Alcade de Zalamea, Arturo Ui, La Guerre de Troie n'aura pas Lieu, Le Dossier Oppenheimer, Le Mariage de Figaro, Macbeth, Jerusalem,* and the film *Les Portes de la Nuit.*
Publs. *Ce que je crois* 63, *De la tradition théâtrale* 63.
7 rue de l'Estrapade, Paris 5e, France.

Viljoen, Hon. Marais; South African politician; b. 2 Dec. 1915; ed. Jan Van Riebeeck High School, Cape Town, and Univ. of Cape Town.
Member Transvaal Provincial Council for Pretoria 49-53; mem. Parl. for Alberton, Transvaal 53-; Deputy Minister of Labour and of Mines 58-62; Deputy Minister of Interior, Educ., Arts and Science, of Labour and of Immigration 62-66; Minister of Labour and of Coloured Affairs 66-.
Office: Private Bag 117, Pretoria; Home: Bryntirion 18, Pretoria, South Africa.

Villa, José Garcia, A.B.; Philippine poet and critic; b. 5 Aug. 1914; ed. Univs. of the Philippines, of New Mexico and Columbia Univ.
Associate Editor New Directions Books 49; Cultural Attaché Philippine Mission to UN 53-63; Dir. N.Y. City Coll. Poetry Workshop 52-63, Prof. of Poetry, New

School for Social Research 64-; Guggenheim Fellowship 43, Bollingen Fellowship 51, Rockefeller Grant 64; American Acad. of Arts and Letters Award 42, Shelley Memorial Award 59, Pro Patria Award 61, Philippines Cultural Heritage Award 62; Hon. D.Litt.
Publs. *Footnote to Youth* (stories) 33, *Many Voices* 39, *Poems by Doveglion* 41, *Have Come, Am Here* 42, *Volume Two* 49, *Selected Poems and New* 58, *Poems Fifty-five* 62, *Poems in Praise of Love* 62, *Selected Stories* 62, *The Portable Villa* 63, *The Essential Villa* 65.
780 Greenwich Street, New York City 14, N.Y., U.S.A.

Villacieros, Antonio; Spanish diplomatist; b. 1900; ed. Colegio de la Concepción, Madrid, and Univ. Madrid.
Attaché, Spanish Embassy, Holy See 22; transferred to Ministry of State Madrid 25; Third Sec. Ministry of State 27; Second Sec. Berne 29, Ministry of State Madrid 31; during Spanish Civil War served in Burgos and Salamanca and later became Head of Diplomatic Cabinet, Ministry of Foreign Affairs 36-39; First Sec., Holy See 39-50; Minister 50; Ambassador to Ecuador 51-55; Dir.-Gen. Cultural Relations, Ministry of Foreign Affairs 55-58; Ambassador to Japan 58-, concurrently to Korea till 67; Commdr. Isabel la Católica (Spain), St. Gregory (Vatican), St. Maurice and St. Lazarus (Italy), and other Spanish and foreign decorations.
Spanish Embassy, Tokyo, Japan.

Villalba, Jovito; Venezuelan politician; b. 08; ed. Liceo Caracas, Universidad Central de Venezuela and Universidad Libre, Colombia.
Former Prof. of Constitutional Rights and Political Theory, Universidad Central, Venezuela; Sec., Federation of Venezuelan Students 28; imprisoned 28-34; Sec.-Gen. Nat. Democratic Party 36; exile in Colombia 36-38; Founder, Unión Republicana Democrática 46, now leader; exiled 52-57; Leader, Junta Patriótica 58; Presidential Candidate 63.
Unión Republicana Democrática, Caracas, Venezuela.

Villanueva, Carlos Raúl; Venezuelan architect; b. 30 May 1900; ed. Lycée Condorcet, Paris, and School of Architecture, Ecole Nationale des Beaux Arts, Paris.
Founding Professor, Faculty of Architecture, Univ. of Venezuela, Caracas; mem. Acad. of Natural Sciences, Venezuela; Hon. mem. Soc. of Architects of Colombia, American Inst. of Architects, Royal Inst. of Architects (U.K.); Corresp. mem. UNESCO Int. Cttee. for Monuments, Arts Sites, History and Archaeological Excavations; numerous awards and architectural prizes; D.Arch. h.c. Univ. of Venezuela.
Major works: Plaza de Toros, Maracay; Los Caobos Museum, Caracas; Gran Colombia School, Caracas; urban renewal of el Silencio, Caracas; low cost settlements, Maracaibo and Caracas; Inst. for Petroleum Engineering, Universidad Nacional del Zulia, Maracaibo; Univerisity City, Caracas; office building, Fundación La Salle, Caracas.
Quinta Caoma, 27 avenida de los Jabillos, La Florida, Caracas, Venezuela.
Telephone: 72-72-53.

Villaseñor, Eduardo, B.A.; Mexican economist; b. 96; ed. Univ. Michoacana, Univ. of Mexico, London School of Economics.
Prof. Political Economy Nat. School of Agriculture 21-25; Head Dept. of Co-operative Societies, Nat. Bank of Agricultural Credit 26-28; Sec. Mexican-British Claims Comm. 28-29; Commercial Attaché Legation London 29-31; Head Consular Div. Dept. of Foreign Affairs 31-32; Head Div. of Publs., Dept. of Finance and Public Credit 32; mem. Nat. Banking Comm. 32-33; Prof. of Int. Trade, Faculty of Economics, Univ. Mexico; Sec. Board Nat. Mortgage Bank of Urban and Public Works; Sec. Nat. Council Economy 32-34; Consul-Gen. New York 35; Pres. Nat. Agricultural Bank 36-37; Under-Sec. for Finance and Public Credit 38-40; Dir.-Gen.

Banco de México, S.A. 40-46; Pres. Banco del Atlántico 49-65; Chair. of Board Banco de la Ciudad de México, S.A. 66-; Commdr. de la Légion d'Honneur.
Publs. *Extasis, novela de aventuras* 28, *Nuestro Industria Textil de Algodón* 34, *Inter-American Trade and Financial Problems* 41, *The Inter-American Bank: Prospects and Dangers* 41, *Some Aspects of Mexico's War Economy* 43, *Ensayos Interamericanos Reflexiones de un economista* 44, *De la Curiosidad y otros papeles* 45, *Episodio* 52, *The English are they Human?* 53, *La Farce et la Mort au Mexique* 57, *Stabilité ou Développement de l'Economie Mexicaine* 57, *Los Recuerdos y los Dias* 60.
Reyna 39, Mexico 20, D.F., Mexico.
Telephone: 48-20-13.

Villeda Morales, Ramón; Honduran politician; b. 09. Formerly Ambassador to U.S.A.; elected Pres. of Honduras for a six-year term Sept. 57- Oct. 63; Partido Liberal.
Tegucigalpa, Honduras.

Villiers, Alan John, D.S.C., F.R.G.S.; Australian author and sailor; b. 23 Sept. 1903; ed. State schools in Melbourne.
Went to sea in sailing ships 20; mem. pioneer pelagic whaling voyage into Ross Sea, Antarctica 23-24; part-owner Finnish 4-mast barque 30-34; master-owner full-rigged ship *Joseph Conrad* 34-36; sailed Arab deep-sea dhows 38-39; Royal Navy 40-46; Master, Outward-Bound Sea Schools' training ships 49-50; voyage in Portuguese 4-mast schooner Grand Banks and Greenland 50; Commanded barque *Mayflower II* 57; Trustee Nat; Maritime Museum, Gov. Cutty Sark Soc., Chairman Soc. for Nautical Research, mem. Technical Cttee., H.M.S. *Victory*; Commdr. Portuguese Order of Santiago; Camões Prize for Literature 54.
Publs. *Falmouth for Orders* 29, *By Way of Cape Horn* 30, *Cruise of the Conrad* 37, *Sons of Sinbad* 40, *The Way of a Ship* 50, *The Quest of the Schooner Argus* 57, *The Western Ocean* 57, *Give me a Ship to Sail* 58, *Oceans of the World* 63, *Captain Cook, the Seaman's Seaman* 67.
1A Lucerne Road, Oxford, England; Cosmos Club, Washington, D.C. 20036, U.S.A.
Telephone: Oxford 55632.

Villiers, Georges; French commercial administrator; b. 15 June 1899; ed. Lycée de Lyon, Ecole nationale supérieure des Mines, Saint-Etienne.
Mayor of Lyon 41-42, deported to Germany 43-45; Pres. Nat. Council of French Employers 46-66; Pres. Council of Industrial Federations in Europe; Pres. French Cttee. of the International Chamber of Commerce; Gov. European Cultural Foundation; Officier Légion d'Honneur, Croix de Guerre (39-45) and other European international awards.
31 avenue Pierre Ier-de-Serbie, Paris 16e; and 45 avenue Hoche, Paris 8e, France.

Villot, H.E. Cardinal Jean; French ecclesiastic; b. 11 Oct. 1905; ed. Séminaire de l'Institut Catholique, Paris and Collège Angélique, Rome.
Ordained priest 30; Vice-Rector Catholic faculties of Lyon 42-50; Sec.-Gen. of the French Episcopate 50; Bishop of Vinda and Auxiliary to Cardinal Feltin 53-59; Coadjutor Archbishop of Lyon 59-65; Under-Sec. Ecumenical Council 62-65; Archbishop of Lyon 65-67; Prefect of the Sacred Congregation of the Council 67-; created Cardinal 65.
Archbishop's House, 1 Place de Fourvière, Lyon, Rhône, France.

Vimond, Paul Marcel; French architect; b. 20 June 1922; ed. Lycée de Coutances, Ecole préparatoire des beaux-arts de Rennes and Ecole nationale supérieure des beaux-arts, Paris.
Member Jury of Nat. School of Fine Arts; mem. Diocesan Comm. on Sacred Art, Paris; Chevalier des Arts et des Lettres and of Pontifical Order of Merit; Premier Grand Prix de Rome 49.

Major architectural works include: Architect in charge of Int. Exhbn. of Sacred Art, Rome 53; responsible for films and architectural reconstructions of tomb of Saint Peter, Rome; Buildings in Paris for: Assemblé de l'Union française, Conseil économique et social, Union de l'Europe occidentale, Organisation de co-opération et de développement économiques; planner and architect for Palais d'Iéna, Paris; town planner for Cherbourg; Atomic Power Station, The Hague; two theatres, three churches in Paris, hotels, restaurants, hospitals, and numerous lycées in France.
Office: 5 rue Faustin-Hélie, Paris 16e; and 91 avenue Niel, Paris 17e, France.
Telephone- 924-87-84 (Home); 870-24-82 and 870-92-84 (Office).

Vincent, Daniel, D. ès SC., M.D. PHARM.D.; French doctor and pharmacologist; b. 12 Oct. 1907; ed. Univ. of Lyon.
Head medical chemist, Faculty of Medicine and Pharmacy, Univ. of Lyon, and Head of Medical Clinic 38-39; Prof. Faculty of Medicine and Pharmacy, Toulouse 43 and Lyon 65; Regional Inspector of Pharmacy 42-45 and Principal Inspector 55; mem. Regional Council Ordre des Pharmaciens, Toulouse 50-65, New York Acad. of Sciences 61; Lauréat de l'Inst. de France, Prix Pourat 39; Lauréat de l'Acad. de Médecine, Prix Marc Sée 45, Prix Jansen 61.
Les Crètes, 54 avenue Valioud, 69 Ste. Foy-Les-Lyon, France.
Telephone: 51-93-56.

Vincent, Eric R. P., C.B.E., LITT.D., D.PHIL., M.A.; British university professor (emeritus); b. 10 Dec. 1894; ed. Berkhamsted School and Christ Church, Oxford.
Interned in Germany as civil prisoner of war 14-18; Lecturer in Italian, King's Coll., Univ. of London 22; Univ. Lecturer in Italian Language and Literature Oxford 27-34; Prof. of Italian, Cambridge 35-62, Emeritus 62-; Life Fellow of Corpus Christi Coll., Cambridge, Pres. 54-59; served Foreign Office 39-45; Commendatore Ordine Al Merito della Repubblica Italiana; fmr. Pres. of Asscn. Int. di Studi Italiani; mem. Italian Arcadian Acad.
Publs. *Ardengo Soffici, Six Essays on Modern Art, Preface and Notes* 22, *Gabriele Rossetti in England* 36, *The Commemoration of the Dead* (Foscolo's *Sepolcri*) 36, *Byron, Hobhouse and Foscolo* 49, *Ugo Foscolo, An Italian in Regency England* 53; and other works.
Corpus Christi College, Cambridge; Home: Fulford Grange, Kingston St. Mary, Taunton, Somerset, England.
Telephone: Kingston St. Mary 373.

Vinci, Piero; Italian diplomatist; b. 12; ed. University of Rome.
Diplomatic Service 38-, Switzerland, Bulgaria 38-47; Head of Press Section, Ministry of Foreign Affairs, Rome 47-49; First Sec. Beirut 49-53; Consul-Gen. London 53-55; Head of Political Office for Relations with Africa and the Middle East, Ministry of Foreign Affairs, Rome 55-59, Head of UN Division 59-60; Chief of Cabinet to Deputy Prime Minister and Minister of Foreign Affairs 60-63; Perm. Rep. to UN 64-.
Permanent Mission of Italy to the United Nations, 527 Madison Avenue, New York 22, N.Y., U.S.A.

Vinde, Victor; Swedish editor; b. 23 March 1903; ed. Caen and Paris.
Foreign Correspondent in Paris, London, New York; Editor-in-Chief *Stockholms-Tidningen* 59-65; Officier de la Légion d'Honneur.
Publs. *Eine Grossmacht fällt* 43, *America at War* 44, *Revolution in Algeria* 58.
Vattugatan 12, Stockholm, Sweden.

Viner, Jacob, PH.D.; American economist; b. 3 May 1892; ed. McGill and Harvard Univs.
Instructor in Economics Univ. of Chicago 16-17;

Special Expert U.S. Tariff Comm. and Shipping Board 17-19; Asst. Prof. of Economics 19-23, Associate Prof. 23-25, Prof. of Economics Univ. of Chicago 25-46; Prof. of Economics Princeton Univ. 46-60, Emer. 60-; Visiting Prof. Inst. Universitaire de Hautes Etudes Internationales Geneva 30-31, 33-34; Asst. to Sec. of Treasury 34; Consultant Expert U.S. Treasury 36-42; Consultant U.S. State Dept. 43-52; Visiting Prof. Yale Univ. 42-43; Univ. of California 45; London School of Econs. 46; Nat. Univ. Brazil 50; Harvard Univ. 61-62; Marshall Lecturer Cambridge Univ. 46; Ed. *Journal of Political Economy* 28-46; thirteen hon. degrees.
Publs. *Dumping* 23, *Canada's Balance of International Indebtedness* 24, *Studies in the Theory of International Trade* 37, *Trade Relations between Free-Market and Controlled Economies* 43, *The Customs Union Issue* 49, *International Economics: Studies* 51, *International Trade and Economic Development* 52, *The Long View and the Short* 58.
13 Newlin Road, Princeton, N.J. 08540, U.S.A.
Telephone: 609-924-3695.

Vines, William Joshua; Australian business executive; b. 27 May 1916; ed. Haileybury Coll., Victoria.
Army service, Middle East, New Guinea and Borneo 39-45; Sec. Alexander Fergusson Pty. Ltd. 38-47; Dir. Goodlass Wall and Co. Pty. Ltd. 47-49, Lewis Berger and Sons (Australia) Pty. Ltd. and Sherwin Williams Co. (Aust.) Pty. Ltd. 52-55; Man. Dir. Lewis Berger and Sons (Victoria) Pty. Ltd. 49-55; Managing Dir. Lewis Berger & Sons Ltd. 55-60; Managing Dir. Berger, Jensen & Nicholson Ltd. 60-61; Managing Dir. Int. Wool Secretariat 61-.
5 Carlton Gardens, London, S.W.1, England.
Telephone: 930-4654.

Vinogradov, Alexandr Pavlovich; Soviet geo-chemist; b. 96; ed. Mil. Medical Acad. and Leningrad Univ.
Member Acad. of Sciences of the U.S.S.R. 53-; Academician-Sec. Dept. of Sciences of the Earth, U.S.S.R. Acad. of Sciences, Vice-Pres. 66-; Dir. Vernadsky Inst. of Geochemistry and Analytical Chemistry, U.S.S.R. Acad. of Sciences; mem. Serbian Acad. of Sciences; Vice-Pres. Int. Geochemical Cttee.; Hero of Socialist Labour, State prizewinner 49, 51.
Publs. *Geo-chemistry of Dispersed Elements of Water* 44, *Geo-chemistry of Rare and Dispersed Chemical Elements in Soils* 50, *Elementary chemical composition of Marine organisms, Chemical evolution of the Earth, Basic Problems of Radiochemistry* 59, *Isotopes of Oxygen and Photosynthesis* 63.
Department of Sciences of the Earth, Academy of Sciences of the U.S.S.R., Moscow, U.S.S.R.

Vinogradov, Ivan Metveyevich; Soviet mathematician; b. 14 Sept. 1891; ed. Leningrad Univ.
Lecturer and later Prof. Perm Univ. 18-20; Prof. Leningrad Polytechnical Inst. and Leningrad Univ. 20-34 (founded Chair. of Numbers, Leningrad Univ.); mem. U.S.S.R. Acad. of Sciences 29-, Dir. Steklov Inst. of Mathematics 32-; hon. mem. London Mathematical Society, Netherlands Mathematical Society, American Philosophical Society, Royal Society, London, American Acad. of Arts. and Sciences, Royal Danish Acad. of Sciences, Indian Mathematical Society, Hungarian Acad. of Sciences, Italian Acad. of Sciences; foreign mem. Serbian Acad. of Sciences 59-; mem. Royal Soc., London 60-; Corresp. mem. French Acad. of Sciences, German Acad. of Sciences; Hero of Socialist Labour 45; State Prize 41; four Orders of Lenin; Hon. Ph.D. (Oslo Univ.) 50.
Publ. *New Methods in Analytic Theory of Numbers.*
Steklov Mathematics Institute, U.S.S.R. Academy of Sciences, Vavilov str. 28, Moscow B-333, U.S.S.R.
Telephone: AB7-27-91.

Vinogradov, Sergei Alexandrovich; Soviet historian and diplomatist; b. 1907; ed. Leningrad Univ.
Former Prof. of History; Diplomatic Service 39-; Counsellor, Turkey 40, Ambassador 40-48; Head, Dept. of UN Affairs, Ministry of Foreign Affairs 48-50; Chair. U.S.S.R. Council of Ministers Radio Cttee. 50-53; Ambassador to France 53-65; on staff of Ministry of Foreign Affairs 65-67; Amb. to United Arab Republic 67-; mem. Central Auditing Comm. of C.P.S.U. 62-66; Grand Croix Légion d'Honneur.
U.S.S.R. Embassy, Cairo, United Arab Republic.

Vinogradov, Victor Vladimirovich; Soviet philologist; b. 95.
Professor Univ. of Leningrad 22-29, Moscow Univ. 45-; mem. U.S.S.R. Acad. of Sciences 46-; Sec. Language and Literature Section 50-63; Dir. Inst. of Linguistics, U.S.S.R. Acad. of Sciences 50-53; Dir. Inst. of Russian Language 58-; Editor-in-Chief *Voprosi jazykoznanija* 50-; Dep. to Supreme Soviet 51-59; mem. Bulgarian, German, Danish, Polish, Rumanian, Serbian and French Acads.; Dr. h.c. Charles Univ., Prague; Lomonosov Prize 47, State Prize 51.
Publs. *Yazyk Pushkina* 35, *Ocherki po istorii russkogo literaturnogo yazyka XVII-XIX* 34, 38, *Russki yazyk: Grammatischeskoe uchenie o slove* 47, *O yazyke hudozhestvennoy literaturi* 59, *Problema avtorstva i teoria stiley* 61, *Stilistica, Teoria poeticheskoy rechy. Poetica* 63, *Sjuget i Stil* 63, etc.
Institute of Russian Language, Ulitsa Volhonka 18/2, Moscow, U.S.S.R.

Vinogradov, Vladimir Mikhailovich; Soviet diplomatist; b. 1921; ed. Mendeleyev Chemical and Technical Inst., Moscow, and Acad. of Foreign Trade.
Former chief, West European Bureau, U.S.S.R. Ministry of Trade; Ambassador to Japan 62-67; Deputy Foreign Minister of U.S.S.R. 67-; Chair. U.S.S.R. Comm. for UNESCO 68-.
Ministry of Foreign Affairs, Moscow, U.S.S.R.

Vira, Dharma; Indian civil servant and diplomatist; b. 20 Jan. 1906; ed. Lucknow and Allahabad Univs., and London School of Economics and Political Science.
Joined Civil Service 30; Joint Magistrate Aligarh 30-34, Almora 34-36, Bareilly 36; Joint Sec. Industries and Agricultural Exhibition, Lucknow 36-37; Officiating District Magistrate, Bareilly 37; District Magistrate, Etah 37-38, Almora 38-41; with Commerce Dept., Govt. of India 41-44, Deputy Sec. Industries and Civil Supplies Dept. 44-45, Textile Commr. 45-47, Joint Sec. to Cabinet 47-50; Principal Private Sec. to Prime Minister 50-51; Commercial Adviser, High Comm. London 51-53; Ambassador to Czechoslovakia 54-56; Sec. Ministry of Works, Housing and Rehabilitation 56-63; Chief Commr. for Delhi 63-64; Cabinet Sec. and Sec. to the Council of Ministers 64-66; Chair. Atomic Energy Comm. and Sec. Dept. of Atomic Energy 66; Gov., Punjab and Haryana 66-67; Gov. of W. Bengal 68-.
Dharmanyri Farm, Bignor, U.P., India.

Virden, John Closey; American business executive; b. 27 Feb. 1897; ed. Univ. School, Cleveland, Ohio.
Aviation Corps 17-19; Pres. Virden Co., Cleveland 19-27; Vice-Pres. Gill-Virden Co., Philadelphia 27-28; Pres. John C. Virden Co., Cleveland 29-36; Dir. War Production Board 42-45; Liquidation Comms. Cairo and Paris 45-46; U.S. Dept. of Commerce 48; mem. Business Council 47-; Chair. Federal Reserve Bank, Cleveland 51-56; Dir. Interlake Steel Corpn., Cleveland 49-, Cleveland Electric Illuminating Co. 50-; Diamond Alkali Co. 53-; Goodyear Tire & Rubber Co. 54-; Youngstown Steel Door Co. 54-; Chair. Eaton Yale and Towne, Inc. 57-67, Chair. Exec. Cttee. 67-.
Eaton, Yale & Towne Inc., 100 Erieview Plaza, Cleveland, Ohio 44114, U.S.A.

Virolainen, Johannes; Finnish politician and farmer; b. 31 Jan. 1914; ed. Helsinki Univ. (Agriculture and Forestry).
Vice-Chair. Agrarian Party 46-64, Chair. 65- (name of party changed to Centre Party 65); Second Minister of Interior 50-51; Second Minister of Prime Minister's Office 51; Minister of Educ. 53, 54 and 56-57; Minister of Foreign Affairs 54-56, 57 and 58; Minister of Agriculture 61-63; Deputy Prime Minister 57-58, 62-63; Prime Minister 64-66; Speaker of Parl. 66-; Chair. Nat. Planning Council 56-66; Grand Crosses Orders of Merit (Argentina), Leopold (Belgium), Dannebrog (Denmark), Hawk (Iceland); Grand Officer Order of Polonia Restituta (Poland).
Kirkniemi, Lohja, Finland.

Virolleaud, Charles, D. ès L.; French university professor; b. 2 July 1879.
Dir. of Dept. of Antiquities, French mandates in Levant 20-29; Prof. Inst. of Art and Archæology, Univ. of Paris 29-36; Prof. Ecole des Hautes Etudes (Sorbonne) 36-; mem. of Inst. de France; Officier de la Légion d'Honneur.
Publs. *Babyloniaca* 06-45, *L'astrologie chaldéenne* 08-12, *Les Poèmes phéniciens de Ras Shamra* 30-56, *Le Théâtre Persan ou le Drame de Kerbela* 50.
6 avenue Constant-Coquelin, Paris 7e, France.

Virsky, Pavel Pavlovich; Soviet ballet master; b. 1905; ed. Odessa and Moscow Ballet Schools.
Dancer with Odessa Opera and Ballet Theatre 23-31, Choreographer 32-33; Artistic Dir. Kharkov, Dniepropetrovsk and Kiev Opera and Ballet Theatres 33-37; organised Folk Dance Ensemble of the Ukrainian S.S.R. 37; choreographer with Kiev Mil. District and Soviet Army Song and Dance Ensembles 40-53; Artistic Dir. State Folk Dance Ensemble of the Ukrainian S.S.R. 55-; choreographic creations include *On the Maize Field, Dolls, The Zaporezhye Cossacks, Needle-women;* State Prize 50; People's Artist of U.S.S.R., Order of Red Banner of Labour.
Kiev State Philharmonic Society, Kiev, Ukrainian S.S.R., U.S.S.R.

Virta, Nikolai Evgenievich; Soviet writer; b. 06.
Journalist 23-35; State prizewinner (4 times).
Publs. plays *Earth* 37, *Slander* 39, *Our Daily Bread* 47, *Plot of the Doomed* 48, *Endless Horizons* 57, *In Summer the Sky is High* 60, *Three Stones of Faith* 60, *Operation Czech Forest* 61, *Thirst* 61, *Golgotha* 61, *Winds Blew and Blew* 62, *Niagara Falls* 62; novels: *Loneliness* 35, *The Adventurer* 37, *Evening Bells* 51, *Steep Hills* 55, *Soil Returned* 60, *The One We don't Know* 60, *Our Bertha* 60, *Field Marshal* 61, *Aksushka* 62, *Two Days of their Life* 62, *Fast Running Days* (novel) 65, *Novels of Last Years* 65, *Secret of Clemance and Son* (play) 64, *The End of a Career* 67.
Writers' Union, 52 Vorovsky Street, Moscow, U.S.S.R.

Virtanen, Artturi Ilmari, PH.D.; Finnish scientist; b. 15 Jan. 1895; ed. Univs. of Helsinki, Zürich, Münster and Stockholm.
First Asst. of the Central Laboratory of Industry 16-17; Chemical Asst. of the State Butter and Cheese Control Station 19; Chemist of the Laboratory of Valio Finnish Co-operative Dairies' Asscn. 19-20, and Dir. 21-; Dir. Biochemical Inst., Helsinki 31-; Lecturer in Chemistry Univ. of Helsinki 24-39; Prof. of Biochemistry Finland Inst. of Technology, Helsinki 31-39; Prof. of Biochemistry, Univ. of Helsinki 39-48; mem. Acad. of Finland 48-65 (Pres. 48-63), mem. Emer. 65-; mem. numerous other Finnish and foreign socs.; Fellow American Asscn. for the Advancement of Science; on editorial staff of various periodicals; many hon. degrees, honours and awards; Nobel Prize for Chemistry 45.
Publs. *Cattle Fodder and Human Nutrition* 38, *AIV-System as the basis of cattle-feeding* 43, *Plant Physiology*

(with J. K. Miettinen) 63, and over 600 papers mostly in the fields of pure and applied chemistry.
Biochemical Research Institute, Kalevankatu 56b, Helsinki 18, Finland.
Telephone: 646211.

Viryasov, Konstantin Sergeyevich; Soviet foreign trade official; b. 1916; ed. Kharkov Inst. of Mechanical Engineering and Acad. of Foreign Trade.
Member C.P.S.U. 43-; Chief of Section, later Deputy Chief of Dept., Ministry of Foreign Trade 47-56; U.S.S.R. Commercial Rep. in Albania 56-62; Deputy Chief of Dept., Ministry of Foreign Trade 62-63; in Cttee. of Party and State Control, later Cttee. of People's Control, Council of Ministers and Central Cttee. C.P.S.U. 63-66; U.S.S.R. Commercial Rep. in Yugoslavia 66-; Order of Red Banner of Labour.
U.S.S.R. Trade Representation, Belgrade, Yugoslavia.

Visconti, Luchino; Italian film and theatre director; b. 2 Nov. 1906; ed. Classical School.
Jean Renoir's Asst. Dir. for *Une Partie de Campagne* 35; Films directed: *La Terra Trema* (Leone d'Argento in Venice) 48, *Bellissima* 51, *Senso* 55, *Le Notti Bianche* (Leone d'Argento in Venice) 57, *Rocco and His Brothers* 61, episode in *Boccacio 70* 61, *Il Gattopardo* 62, *Vaghe Stelle Dell' Orsa* 65, *The Stranger* 67; theatre productions of Shakespeare, Chekhov, Cocteau, Sartre, etc.; operas: *La Traviata, Sonnambula, Anna Bolena* all at La Scala; *Don Carlos* at Covent Garden 58; *Il Trovatore* at Covent Garden 64; *Falstaff* in Vienna 66; *Der Rosenkavalier* at Covent Garden 66; *La Traviata* at Covent Garden 67; ballet: *Marathon* at Berlin State Opera House; now Dir. Morelli-Stoppa Co., with whom he produced at Paris Int. Drama Festival *The Impresario from Smyrna* 58, *Figli d'Arte* 59.
366 Via Salaria, Rome, Italy.

Visentini, Bruno, D.IUR.; Italian lawyer, politician and business executive; b. 1 Aug. 1914; ed. Univ. of Padua.
Vice-Chairman Istituto per la Ricostruzione Industriale (I.R.I.); Chair. Olivetti e C., S.p.A.; Dir. Montecatini-Edison; Lecturer in Business Law, Univ. of Rome; Radical Republican.
Olivetti and Co., 11 Via Jervis, Ivrea, Turin; Home: 15 Piazza di Spagna, Rome, Italy.
Telephone: Ivrea 40254; Rome 689-788 (Home).

Vishnevskaya, Galina Pavlovna; Soviet singer; b. 1926.
Studied with Vera Garina 42-52; Leningrad Musical Theatres 44-52; joined Bolshoi Theatre 52-; numerous parts in operas, notably Leonora in *Fidelio*, and Tatiana in *Eugene Onegin* (also in the film), Aida (*Aida*), Kupava (*Snow Maiden*), Liza (*Dance of Spades*), Chio-Sio-San (*Madame Butterfly*), Margaret (*Faust*), Natasha (*War and Peace*), Cherubino (*Marriage of Figaro*); concert tours with her husband; People's Artist of R.S.F.S.R.
State Academic Bolshoi Theatre of U.S.S.R., 1 Ploshchad Sverdlova, Moscow, U.S.S.R.

Vishnevsky, Alexander Alexandrovich; Soviet surgeon; b. 1906; ed. Kazan Univ.
Lecturer Kazan Univ. 29-31; Mil. Medical Acad. 31-33; Assoc., U.S.S.R. Inst. of Experimental Medicine 33-37; Head of Surgical Dept. U.S.S.R. Inst. of Experimental Medicine, Central Medical Refresher Inst. 37-41; Chief Surgeon of Army and Group of Armies 41-46; Deputy Dir. of Clinic, Inst. of Neurology 46-48; Dir. Inst. of Surgery 48-; Corresp. mem. U.S.S.R. Acad. of Medical Sciences 52-57, mem. 57-; Chair. All-Russia Soc. of Surgeons; Hon. Chair. Moscow Surgeons' Soc.; mem. Int. Surgeons' Asscn.; Hon. mem. Czechoslovak Medical Soc., Swedish Medical Soc., Piedmont Medical Soc.; Order of Lenin (three times), Red Banner (three times), Patriotic War (twice), Red Star, Hero of Socialist

Labour, Merited Scientist of R.S.F.S.R., Lenin Prize 60, Int. Leriche Prize 55.

Publs. Over 230 works on thoracic, general and field surgery, anaesthesiology and application of cybernetics in medicine.

A. V. Vishnevsky Institute of Surgery, 27 Bolshaya Serpukhovakaya Street, Moscow, U.S.S.R.

Visscher, Charles De; Belgian judge and university professor; b. 2 Aug. 1884; ed. Univ. of Ghent.
Professor of Law Louvain Univ. 11; Adviser Belgian Dept. of Foreign Affairs 19; Editor *Revue de Droit International* 20-39; mem. Int. Court of Arbitration 23-; Sec.-Gen. Inst. de Droit International 25-37; Hon. Pres. 54; Judge Permanent Court of Int. Justice 37-45, Court of Int. Justice 45-52; Pres. Inst. des Relations Internationales; hon. mem. American Society of Int. Law; mem. Acad. Royale; associate mem. Inst. de France; Hon. Dr. (Paris, Nancy, Montpellier, Poitiers); Grand Cross Order of the Crown, War Cross (with Palms).
Publs. include *Théories et Réalités en Droit international public* 53, 55, 60, *Problèmes d'interprétation judiciares* 63, *Aspects récents du droit procédural de la Cour international de Justice* 66.
200 avenue Winston Churchill, Brussels, Belgium.
Telephone: 44-65-88.

Visser 't Hooft, Willem Adolph, DR.THEOL., D.D.; Netherlands ecclesiastic; b. 20 Sept. 1900; ed. Univ. of Leiden.
Member of the staff of World Cttee. of Y.M.C.A. 24; Gen. Sec. World Student Christian Fed. 29; Gen. Sec. World Council of Churches 38-66; Editor of *The Student World* 28-38; Editor *The Ecumenical Review* 48-66; Grand Cross of the Order of Merit, German Fed. Repub. 57; Officer Legion of Honour 59; Wateler Peace Prize 62; Cross of the Great Commdr. of the Holy Sepulchre 63; Commdr. Order of St. Andrew 63; Order of St. Vladimir 64; Commdr. Order of the Netherlands Lion 65; Hon. Knight Order of St. John 66; Peace Prize of German Book Trade 66; Award of Family of Man 66; Grotius Medal 66; Sonning Prize, Copenhagen 67; Hon. D.D. (Aberdeen, Princeton, Toronto, Geneva, Yale, Oberlin, Oxford, Harvard, Tokyo, Paris, Brown Univ., Berlin, Zürich, Louvain), Hon. Prof. of Theological Faculty of Budapest 47, and Theological Acad. in Moscow 64.
Publs. *The Background of the Social Gospel in America* 28, *Anglo-Catholicism and Orthodoxy* 33, *None Other Gods* 37, *The Church and its Function in Society* (with Dr. Oldham) 39, *Wretchedness and Greatness of the Church* 44, *The Struggle of the Dutch Church* 46, *Le Conseil oecuménique des Eglises, sa nature et ses limites* 46, *Rembrandt et la Bible* 47, *The Kingship of Christ* 47, *La Renovacion de la Iglesia* 52, *The Meaning of Ecumenical* 53, *The Ecumenical Movement and the Racial Problem* 54, *The Renewal of the Church* 57, *Rembrandt and the Gospel* 58, *The Pressure of our Common Calling* 59, *No Other Name* 63, *Peace among Christians* 67.
150 Route de Ferney, 1211 Geneva 20, Switzerland.

Viswanathan, Venkata; Indian civil servant; b. 25 Jan. 1909; ed. Central Coll., Bangalore, Univ. Coll., London, and Balliol Coll., Oxford.
Indian Civil Service 30-; Asst. and Joint Magistrate, Agra, Azamgarth, Banaras 31-36; District Magistrate, Banaras 36; Asst. Settlement Officer and Settlement Officer, Bahraich, Kheri 36-40; Under-Sec., Govt. of India 40, Deputy Sec. 42; Sec. to Rep. of Govt. of India in Ceylon 43; Additional Deputy Sec. and Sec. to Rep. of Govt. of India with Govt. of Burma 44; Registrar of Co-operative Socs. U.P. 46; District Magistrate, Dehra Dun 47; Indian Alt. Del. on UN Comm., Palestine 47; Deputy High Commr. in Pakistan 47-48; Chief Sec. and Adviser Madhya Bharat 48-50; Chief Commr., Bhopal 50-52; Joint Sec. Ministry of States and Ministry of Home Affairs 52-58; Special Sec. Ministry of Home Affairs 58, Sec. 61-64; Chief Commr., Delhi 64-67; Gov. of Kerala 67-.
Office of the Governor, Trivandrum, Kerala, India.

Vital Brazil, Alvaro; Brazilian civil engineer and architect; b. 09; ed. School of Polytechnic and Fine Arts, Rio de Janeiro.
Former Prof. of Colegio Santo Antonio Maria Zacarias and of the French Lycée; Mem. Inst. of Brazilian Architects; two first awards in competitions for architectural design (São Paulo and Minas Gerais); mem. of the Executive Council of Inst. of Brazilian Architects.
Rua Buenos-Aires 24-1°, Rio de Janeiro, Brazil.

Vitali, Felice Antonio; Swiss radio and television official; b. 1907; ed. St. Gall Gymnasium and Commercial Coll.
Editor *Die Presse* 28; Radio Berne 29; Editor *Schweizer Radio Zeitung* 30; Dir. Radio Svizzera Italiana 31-47; corresp. Swiss Radio in Berlin 48-57; Project-leader UNESCO Radio Advisory Mission to Libya 57-58; Head of Information Services, Swiss Television (Zürich) 58-67; Programme Liaison of Swiss Television, Lugano 67-; Prix Pisa of the Prix Italia 62 (for TV documentary).
Radio plays: *I tre amici, La capanna del Bertuli, Idol und Masse, Kraftwerk Mittelmeer, Flut ohne Ebbe, Kampf um die öffentliche Meinung* 55, *Atome für die Politik* 56, *Die sieben Kiesel* 61; Television plays: *Der Alte Mensch was war der Generalstreik?*
Publs. *Reporter erleben England, Confidenze del Microfono, Radiohörer das geht dich an*, etc.
Ronco Nuovo, 6911 Comano-Lugano, Switzerland.
Telephone: (091)- 2-27-50; and 3-50-76.

Viteles, Morris Simon, A.M., PH.D.; American psychologist; b. 21 March 1898; ed. Univs. of Pennsylvania and Paris.
Appointed to Dept. of Psychology, Univ. of Pa. 18-; Prof. of Psychology 40-; Prof. of Psychology in Physical Medicine and Rehabilitation, Medical School 55-; Consultant to Yellow Cab Co., Philadelphia 24-65; Dir. of Personnel Research and Training, Philadelphia Electric Co. 31-64; Consultant, Bell Telephone Co., Pa. 51-, and other firms; Chair. Nat. Research Council Cttee. on Aviation Psychology 42-51; organised first psychological clinic in vocational guidance, Univ. of Pa. 21; mem. Applied Psychology Panel, Nat. Defence Research Cttee. during Second World War; Pres. Int. Congress Applied Psychology 58-; Dean, Graduate School of Education, Univ. of Pennsylvania 63-; hon. corresp. Nat. Inst. Industrial Psychology of Great Britain; Hon. mem. Soc. of Scientific Psychology of Italy, and Spanish Psychological Soc.; Editorial Board *Journal of Applied Psychology* 44-54, *Personnel Abstracts* 55-; mem. hon. ed. cttee. *Archives of Applied Psychology* 44-54, *Personal Abstracts* 55-; mem. hon. ed. cttee. *Archives of Applied Psychology of Greece* 60-.
Publs. *Industrial Psychology* 32, *The Science of Work* 34, *Vocational Guidance throughout the World* 37, *Motivation and Morale in Industry* 53, *Psychological Perspectives in Vocational Guidance* 61, Autobiographical chapter in *History of Psychology in Autobiography* (Vol. V) 67.
Home: 529 Broad Acres Road, Penn Valley, Narberth, Pa.; Business: 106 College Hall, University of Pennsylvania, Philadelphia 4, Pa., U.S.A.

Vitolo, Alfredo Roque; Argentine politician; b. 1910; ed. Univ. of Córdoba.
Joined Radical Party (Unión Cívica Radical), provincial Deputy 35-38, 39-42, and concurrently Chair. of Party in Mendoza; mem. Provincial Constituent 43; mem. Nat. Congress 48-; Minister of the Interior 58-62; founded newspapers *Proa* and *Proceso*.
Paraguay 1353, Buenos Aires, Argentina.

Vitry d'Avaucourt, Raoul (Joseph Marie), Comte de; French industrialist; b. 28 June 1895; ed. Lycée Janson-de-Sailly, Ecole Polytechnique, Ecole Nat. Supérieure des Mines de Paris.
With firm of Pechiney since 28, Man. 31-36, Gen. Man. 36-38, Dir. 38-44, Vice-Chair. and Gen. Man. 44-58, Chair. 58-; Chair. Seichime, Fria; Dir. Banque de Paris et des Pays-Bas, Cie. Gén. d'Electricité, Cie. Gén. de T.S.F., Cie. Française des Pétroles 40-, Electricité de France, and other companies; Commandeur Légion d'Honneur, Croix de Guerre (14-18), Resistance Medal.
Office: 23 rue Balzac, Paris 8e; Home: 69 avenue Victor Hugo, Paris 16e, France.

Vivian, Robert Evans, M.A., PH.D.; American university dean; b. 20 April 1893; ed. Univ. of Southern Calif. and Columbia Univ.
Engineering Dept., Home Telephone Co., Los Angeles 12-14; Teacher High School and Junior Coll. and Chief of Assay Office, Kern County, Calif. 18-28; Asst. to Prof. Columbia Univ. 29; electrochemical engineer in charge pilot plant operations Int. Agricultural Corpn. 30-31; research Chemist, later Development Engineer, Gen. Chemical Co., N.Y. 31-35; Dir. of Research, Metals Disintegrating Co., Elizabeth, N.J. 35-37; Prof. and Head of Dept. Chemical Engineering Univ. of Southern Calif. 37-42, Dean of School of Eng. 42-58, Emeritus 58-; Chair. Eng. Div., Long Beach State Coll. 58-64, Emeritus Dean 64-; mem., Sec. and Chair. several chemical asscns.; mem. Eng. Coll. Admin. Council 48-51, George Westinghouse Award Cttee. 49-51; Chemical Production Specialist, M.S.A., U.S. Govt. Mission to Italy 52, Technical Consultant M.S.A., U.S. Govt. in S.E. Asia 53; Educational Consultant Northrop Inst. of Technology, Calif. 64-.
862 Victoria Avenue, Los Angeles 5, Calif., U.S.A.

Vizcaino-Leal, Humberto; Guatemalan diplomatist; b. 11; ed. Universidad de San Carlos de Guatemala and Universidad de Madrid.
Former Judge, Civil and Penal Courts, Guatemala; Congressman, Guatemala 51-54; Ambassador to Spain 55-59, to Repub. of China 61-63; Perm. Rep. of Guatemala to UN 63-66.
c/o Ministry of Foreign Affairs, Guatemala City, Guatemala.

Vladimirsky, Vladimir Alexandrovich; Soviet foreign trade official; b. 1919; ed. Moscow Bauman Higher Technical Coll.
Member C.P.S.U. 45-; Deputy Trade Attaché of U.S.S.R. in India 50-52; Section Chief, Ministry of Foreign Trade 52-54, 59-63; Commercial Counsellor, later Commercial Rep. of U.S.S.R. in Pakistan; Deputy Chair. Chamber of Commerce 63-66; U.S.S.R. Commercial Rep., Cuba 66-; Order of Red Banner of Labour.
U.S.S.R. Trade Representation, Havana, Cuba.

Vladychenko, Ivan Maximovich; Soviet trade union official; b. 1924; ed. Donetsk Industrial Inst.
Soviet Army 41-45; mem. C.P.S.U. 43-; miner, Donbuas 51-52; Second Sec. Chistiakov City Cttee., then First Sec. Sniezhnansk Dist. Cttee., Ukraine C.P. 52-59; Chair. Central Cttee. Miners' Union 59-63; Sec. All-Union Central Council of Trade Unions 63-; mem. Central Auditing Comm. of C.P.S.U. 61-66; mem. Central Cttee. of C.P.S.U. 66-.
All-Union Central Council of Trade Unions, Leninsky prospekt 42, Moscow, U.S.S.R.

Vlahović, Veljko; Yugoslav politician; b. 14; ed. in Belgrade, Prague, Paris and Moscow.
Member, Union of Communist Youth of Yugoslavia (S.K.O.J.) 33; Representative of S.K.O.J. to Comintern (K.I.M.) later Secretary of K.I.M. 39-44; First Executive Director Slobodna Jugoslavija Radio Station, Moscow; Head, Commission for Propaganda, Central Cttee. Communist Party of Yugoslavia 44-48; mem.

Executive Central Cttee. 48-; Deputy Minister of Foreign Affairs; mem. Presidency, Socialist Alliance of the Working People of Yugoslavia; mem. Fed. Assembly; Sec. League of Communists of Yugoslavia 64-66; Nat. Hero of Yugoslavia.
League of Communists of Yugoslavia, Trg. Marksa i Engelsa 11, Belgrade, Yugoslavia.

Vlasák, František, DR. RER. NAT.; Czechoslovak scientist and politician; b. 30 Aug. 1912; ed. Universita Karlova, Prague.
Former chemical geologist and teacher in secondary scnool; Deputy Chair. Research and Technical Devt. Centre, later Deputy Chair. State Planning Comm. 50-55; Minister of Power 55-58, of Transport 58-60, of Transport and Communications 60-63; Chair. State Social Security Office 63; Minister-Chair. State Comm. for Devt. and Co-operation of Science and Technology 63-65; Chair. State Comm. for Management and Org. 63-65; Minister-Chair. State Comm. for Technology 63-68; Minister-Chair. State Planning Comm. 68-; mem. Econ. Comm., Central Cttee. of C.P. of Czechoslovakia 63-66; Order of Labour 58, Order of Republic 62.
State Planning Commission, Prague, Czechoslovakia.

Vo Nguyen Giap, Gen.; (see Giap, Gen. Vo Nguyen).

Vočadlo, Otakar, PH.D.; Czechoslovak philologist and literary historian; b. 2 Oct. 1895; ed. Charles Univ. Prague and Univ. Coll. London.
Lecturer King's Coll. London 22-28 and Workers' Educational Asscn. Tutorial Classes 27-30; lecture tour U.S.A.; Lecturer Masaryk Inst. Prague 30-; Prof. of English Language and Literature Komensky Univ. Bratislava 33-39, Charles Univ. Prague 39, Head Dept. of English Literature 45-48; Pres. Literary Section American Inst. Prague 31-37; in German concentration camps at Auschwitz and Buchenwald 42-45; Visiting Prof. King's Coll. Cambridge 45-46, mem. Šafárík Soc., Philological Soc., Czechoslovak Acad., Royal Bohemian Soc. and King's Coll. Cambridge; Founder Acad. Shakespearean Comm.; Hon. M.A. (Cantab.).
Publs. *Slovanská nesvornost* 23 and 35, *V zajetí babylonském* 24, *Anglická literatura* XX *století I* 32, 2nd edn. 47, *Současná literatura Spojených států* 34, *Basic English* 34, 36 and 40, *The Theatre and Drama in Czechoslovakia* (in *The Theatre in a Changing Europe*) 36, *Basic Step by Step* (with Ogden), Editor first Czech complete annotated edn. *Shakespeare's Works* 59-64; also essays on Shakespeare and the Slavs, lexicological studies, etc.
Legerova 36, Prague, Czechoslovakia.
Telephone: 2479175.

Vocke, Wilhelm, DR. JUR.; German banker; b. 9 Feb. 1886; ed. Erlangen, Rostock, Berlin, and Göttingen Univs.
With Ministry of Interior 13; mem. of Reichsbank Directorate, Berlin 19-39; dismissed by Hitler 39; Deputy mem. Board Bank for Int. Settlements, Basle 30-39, mem. 50-57; Dep. Chair. Reichsbank Leitstelle Hamburg 45-48; Pres. Board of Mans. and Vice-Pres. Board of Dirs., Bank Deutscher Länder and Pres. Deutsche Bundesbank, Frankfurt a/Main 48-57; German Gov. Int. Monetary Fund, Washington 52-57; Econ. Adviser to Pakistan Govt. 58-59; Hon. Dr. rer. Pol.
Georg Speyer Strasse 9, Frankfurt am Main, German Federal Republic.

Vogel, Friedrich, DR.OEC.PUBL.; German publisher; b. 23 Feb. 1902; ed. Hindenburg-Gymnasium, Düsseldorf and Univs. of Greifswald, Cologne and Munich.
Owner and Man. Dir. Verlag Handelsblatt G.m.b.H.; Man. Dir. ECON-Verlag G.m.b.H.; Handelsblatt publications include *Handelsblatt, Chemische Industrie, Technik International, Der Betrieb, Der Schrottbetrieb,*

Wirtschaft und Wettbewerb, Die Absatzwirtschaft, Die Atomwirtschaft, Plus-Zeitschrift für Unternehmens-führung, Zeitschrift für Verkehrswissenschaft; Chair. Special Comm. for Int. Collaboration, Zentralausschuss der Werbewirtschaft; mem. Board Verein Rheinisch-Westfälischer Zeitungsverleger e.V.; mem. Board Deutsch-Französischer Kreis, Advisory Body Deutsch-Englische Gesellschaft; Pres. Union of European Econ. and Financial Press.
Handelsblatt G.m.b.H., Handelsblatthaus, Kreuzstrasse 21, Düsseldorf, German Federal Republic.
Telephone: 83881.

Vogel, Brig.-Gen. Herbert Davis, DR. ING., M.S., C.E., B.S.; American civil servant; b. 26 Aug. 1900; ed. Univs. of Michigan and California, U.S. Mil. Acad. and Berlin Technical Univ.
Commissioned U.S. army 24, served through all ranks to Brigadier-Gen.; Builder and Dir. Waterways Experiment Station 30-34; District Engineer, Pittsburgh, Pa. 40-43; S.W. Pacific Theatre 44-45; District Engineer, Buffalo, N.Y. 45-49; Maintenance Engineer and Lieut.-Gov., Panama Canal 49-52; Engineer S.W. Division, Dallas 52-54; Chair. Tennessee Valley Authority 54-62; mem. Beach Erosion Board 46-49, Mississippi River Comm. 52-54, Board of Engineers for Rivers and Harbours 52-54; Hon. mem. Perm. Int. Council of Perm. Int. Asscn. of Navigation Congresses 57-64; Engineer Adviser, Int. Bank for Reconstruction and Devt. 63-67; Consulting Engineer, Principal of Herbert D. Vogel Associates 68-; mem. U.S. Cttee. Int. Comm. on Large Dams; Fellow A.S.C.E.; Nat. Dir. S.A.M.E.; mem. Nat. Soc. of Professional Engineers, R.S.A., London, Industrial Cttee., American Power Conf.; Legion of Merit; Distinguished Service Medal.
Washington Building, Washington, D.C. 20005, U.S.A. Telephone: 638-0010.

Vogel, Rudolf, DR.PHIL.; German politician and diplomatist; b. 18 April 1906; ed. Universities of Berlin and Leipzig.
Journalist 30-40; war service 40-45; Head of labour office 45-47; Dept. Head, German Bureau for Peace Questions 48; mem. Economic Council, Frankfurt 48; mem. Bundestag 49-64, Budget Expert for C.D.U. Group; Head of German Del. to Organisation for Economic Co-operation and Development (O.E.C.D.) 64-; numerous decorations.
5 rue Léonard de Vinci, Paris 16e, France.
Telephone: KLEber 03-44.

Voghel, Franz de; Belgian banker; b. 03; ed. Univ. of Louvain.
Dir. of Banking Comm. 33-45; Prof. Univ. of Louvain, mem. Conseil Central de l'Economie, Banque Centrale du Congo, Fonds des Rentes, Commission Bancaire; Minister of Finance Aug. 45-July 46; Deputy Gov. Nat. Bank of Belgium; mem. Monetary Cttee. E.E.C. 58-; awarded U.S. Medal of Freedom.
Publs. *Contrôle des banques, Statut légal des banques.*
5 boulevard de Berlaimont, Brussels, Belgium.

Vogt, Ernst, S.T.L., S.S.D.; Swiss ecclesiastic; b. 30 Jan. 1903; ed. Innsbruck Univ.
Professor of Sacred Scripture, Theological Faculty São Leopoldo 39-48; Prof. of Old Testament Exegesis 48-; Rector, Pontifical Biblical Inst., Rome 49-63.
Publ. *Os Salmos Traduzidos e Explicados* 51.
25 Via della Pilotta, Rome, Italy.

Vogt, Hersleb; Norwegian diplomatist; b. 12; ed. Univ. of Oslo.
Entered Diplomatic Service and served Ministry of Foreign Affairs 36, Paris and Luxembourg 37, Rome 38; Ministry of Foreign Affairs London 44, Oslo 45, Brussels and Luxembourg 48, London and Dublin 49; Minister to Japan 53-58, Ambassador 58; Ambassador

to German Fed. Repub. 58-63, to Denmark 63-67, to France 67-; Commdr. Order of St. Olav; Norwegian War Participation Medal (with Star); C.V.O.; Commdr. Order of Phoenix (Greece); Grand Cross Order of Rising Sun (Japan); Grand Cross (First Class), Order of Merit of the German Fed. Repub.; Grand Cross, Order of Dannebrog (Denmark).
Royal Norwegian Embassy, 28 rue Bayard, Paris 8e, France.

Voguë, Comte Arnaud de; French businessman; b. 11 June 1904.
Pres. Cie. de Saint-Gobain, Cie. de Commerce et de Navigation d'Extrème Orient :Dir. Banque de Paris et des Pays-Bas, Panhard et Levassor, Soudières Réunies-La Madeleine-Varangeville and of other concerns; Officier Légion d'Honneur, Croix de Guerre, Commdr. Palmes Académiques.
Home: 48 rue du Docteur-Blanche, Paris 16e; Office: 62 boulevard Victor Hugo, Neuilly-sur-Seine, France.

Voitec, Stefan; Romanian politician; b. 1900; ed. Bucharest Polytechnic and Bucharest Univ.
Former Leader, Social-Democratic Party of Romania; Minister of Nat. Educ. 44-48; mem. Cen. Cttee. and Act. mem. Political Bureau, Romanian Workers' Party 55-; Minister of Home Trade 55-56, of Consumer Goods Industry 57-59; Dep. Chair. Council of Ministers 57-61; Pres. Grand Nat. Assembly 61-, Vice-Pres. State Council 61-65.
Grand National Assembly, Bucharest, Romania.

Volchkov, Evgeny Petrovich; Soviet foreign trade official; b. 1913; ed. Moscow Inst. of Steel and Acad. of Foreign Trade.
Member C.P.S.U. 43-; Official, Ministry of Foreign Trade 47-48, Official, Commercial Representation of U.S.S.R. in Yugoslavia 48-50; Vice-Chair. *Promcyrye-import* Trust 50-51; Deputy Chief of Dept., Ministry of Foreign Trade 51-56, Chair. 56-66; U.S.S.R. Commercial Rep. in German Fed. Repub. 66-; Order of Red Banner of Labour, Honour Badge.
U.S.S.R. Commercial Representation, Cologne, German Federal Republic.

Volfkovich, Semyon Isaakovich; Soviet inorganic chemist and technologist; b. 1896; ed. Moscow Inst. of Nat. Econ.
Professor at Moscow Univ. 47; Pres. All-Union Mendeleyev Soc.; mem. Acad. of Sciences of the U.S.S.R.; Mendeleyev prizewinner 32, State prizewinner 41; awarded three Orders of Lenin, Order of the Red Banner of Labour, Mendeleyev Gold Medal 66.
Publs. *New Cycle of Wet Processing of Phosphorites* 28, *Technology of Nitrogen Fertilizers* 35, *General Chemical Technology* 59 (2 vols), *The Role of Physical and Chemical Analysis in the Technology of Fertilizers* 61, *Chemistry in Agriculture, Hydrothermal Treatment of the Phosphates* 64.
Scientific Research Institute of Fertilizers and Insecto-fungicides, Leninsky prospekt 55, Moscow, U.S.S.R.

Volkenshtein, Mikhail Vladimirovich; Soviet chemist; b. 1912; ed. Moscow Univ.
Research Assoc. Karpov Physico-Chemical Inst., Acad. of Sciences 33-41, Optical Inst. 42-48, Inst. of High Molecular Compounds 48-; Corresp. mem. U.S.S.R. Acad. of Sciences 66-.
U.S.S.R. Academy of Sciences, 14 Lenin Prospekt, Moscow, U.S.S.R.

Volkov, Alexander Petrovich; Soviet government official; b. 1910.
Secretary Moscow Regional Party Committee 50-52, Chair. Moscow Region Exec. Cttee. (Mayor of Moscow) 52-56; Chair. State Cttee. for Labour and Wages of U.S.S.R. Council of Ministers 56-; mem. U.S.S.R. Council of Ministers 56-; mem. C.P.S.U. Central Cttee. 56-; Deputy to U.S.S.R. Supreme Soviet; Order of

Lenin (twice), Red Banner of Labour, Badge of Honour and other awards.
State Committee for Labour and Wages, 1 Kuibyshev Square, Moscow, U.S.S.R.

Volovchenko, Ivan Platonovich; Soviet agronomist and politician; b. 17; ed. Voronezh Agricultural Coll.
Soviet Army 42-46; agronomist 46; Chief Agronomist, State Beet Farm, Lvov 46-48; various managerial posts in State Farms 48-51; Dir. Petrovsky State Farm 61-63; U.S.S.R. Minister of Agriculture 63-65; First Deputy Minister of Agriculture 65-; fmr. Deputy to U.S.S.R. Supreme Soviet; Hero of Socialist Labour 61-.
Ministry of Agriculture, 1-11 Orlikov pereulok, Moscow, U.S.S.R.

Volpe, John Anthony; American engineer and politician; b. 8 Dec. 1908; ed. Wentworth Inst., Boston, Mass.
President, John A. Volpe Construction Co.; Comm. of Public Works, Mass. 53-56; Federal Highway Administrator 56-59; Gov. of Mass. 60-62, 64-; Chair. Nat. Governors' Conf.; Republican; Grand Officer, Order of Merit (Italy) 57, Knight of Malta 60.
State Capitol, Boston, Mass.; Home: 10 Everett Avenue, Winchester, Mass., U.S.A.

Volski, Yuri Ivanovich, M.SC.; Soviet diplomatist; b. 1922.
Cultural Counsellor, Washington 59-62; Deputy Minister of Foreign Affairs, R.S.F.S.R. 62-66; Ambassador to Argentina 66-.
U.S.S.R. Embassy, Buenos Aires, Argentina.

Volwiler, Ernest Henry, PH.D.; American chemist; b. 22 Aug. 1893; ed. Miami Univ. and Univ. of Illinois.
Teacher, public school, Ohio 10-11; Teaching Asst., Miami Univ. 13-14, Univ. of Illinois 14-17; Fellow in Chemistry, Univ. of Ill. 17-18: Research Chemist, Abbott Laboratories 18-20, Chief Chemist 20-30, Dir. of Research 30-33, Vice-Pres. in charge of Research and Development 33-46, Exec. Vice-Pres. 46-50, Pres. and Gen. Man. 50-58, Chair. 58-61, Consultant 61-; Councillor 26-, Dir.-at-Large 44-49, and Pres. American Chemical Society 50, Dir. 52-56, Board Chair. 54-56, Pres. American Drug Manufacturers' Asscn. 56-58; Major, U.S. Army Chemical Warfare Reserve 25-38; Lecturer in Chemistry, Northwestern Univ. Medical School 40-61; mem. Board of Dirs. Health Information Foundation 50-61, American Foundation for Pharmaceutical Educ., Board of Grants 59-; Council for Basic Educ. 60-, Pres. 62; Chair. Chemical Div., Nat. Research Council 58-60; Pres. Board of Trustees, Lake Forest Coll. 62-66; mem. Board of Regents Nat. Library of Medicine 57-60; Nat. Science Foundation Board 58-64, Indiana Technical Asscn. 58-63; Modern Pioneers Award 40; Honor Scroll Award, American Inst. of Chemists 47, hon. mem. 52, Gold Medal Award 60; Chemical Industry Soc. Medal 54, Industrial Research Inst. Medal 55, Priestley Medal 58, Sesquicentennial Medal, Miami Univ. 59, etc.; Hon. D.Sc., LL.D., D.Med.Sc.
Home: 900 Lake Road, Lake Forest, Ill.; Office: Abbott Laboratories, North Chicago, Ill., U.S.A.
Telephone: 312-234-5370.

Von Beckh, Harald J., M.D.; Austrian-born Argentine medical scientist; b. 17 Nov. 1917; ed. Theresianum High School, Vienna and Vienna Univ.
Career devoted to aviation and later to space medicine, and in particular to weightlessness and its effects on living organisms; Lecturer Aeromedical Acad. Berlin 41, Buenos Aires Nat. Inst. of Aviation Medicine 47; joined staff of U.S. Air Force Aeromedical Field Laboratory, Holloman Air Force Base, N.M. 56, Scientific Dir. Oct. 58-64; Chief Scientist 64-; Prof. of Human Physiology, New Mexico State Univ. 59-; mem. Armed Forces/Nat. Research Council Cttee. on Bio-

Astronautics 58-61; mem. Space Medicine Cttee. of Int. Astronautical Fed. 61-, Int. Acad. of Astronautics; hon. mem. German Rocket Soc., Medical Asscn. of Armed Forces of Argentina, Portuguese Centre of Astronautical Studies, Spanish Soc. of Aerospace Medicine; Fellow British Interplanetary Soc.; Assoc. Fellow American Inst. of Aeronautics and Astronautics; Senior mem. American Rocket Soc. (Pres. Holloman Section 59-61), mem. Int. Acad. of Aviation Medicine.
Publs. *Fisiología del Vuelo* 55, *Basic Principles of Aerospace Medicine* 60; numerous papers in *Journal of Aviation Medicine* and *Journal of the British Interplanetary Society* and other aeronautical and aeromedical journals in U.S.A., Great Britain, Germany, Argentina and Spain.
P.O. Box 696, Holloman Air Force Base, New Mexico, U.S.A.

von Békésy, Georg, PH.D.; American (b. Hungarian) physicist; b. 3 June 1899; ed. Univs. of Berne and Budapest.
Research Laboratories, Hungarian Telephone System 23-46; Cen. Lab., Siemens & Halske A.G., Berlin 26-27; Privatdozent, Univ. of Budapest 32-39, Prof. 39-40, Senior Prof. 40-46; Karolinska Inst., Stockholm 46-47, Research Prof. 47-49; Research Lecturer, Psycho-Acoustic Laboratory, Harvard Univ. 47-49, Senior Research Fellow in Psycho-Physics, Harvard Univ. 49-66; Nobel Prize for Medicine 61.
Publs. *Experiments in Hearing* 60, *Sensory Inhibition* 67.
Laboratory of Sensory Sciences, 1993 East-West Rd., University of Hawaii, Honolulu, Hawaii 96822, U.S.A.
Telephone: 944-8001.

Vondeling, Anne; Netherlands politician; b. 2 March 1916; ed. Agricultural Univ., Wageningen.
Agricultural expert with the Provincial Authorities of Friesland 40-45; Dir. of an Accountancy Bureau, adviser on taxes 45-58; mem. Parl. (Socialist) 46-58, 59-65, 67-; Minister of Agriculture Jan.-Dec. 58; Deputy Prime Minister and Minister of Finance 65-Dec. 66; fmr. Prof. of Int. Econ. Orgs., Univ. of Groningen.
31 Harlingerstraatweg, Leeuwarden, The Netherlands.
Telephone: 05100-23496.

Von Euler, Ulf Svante, M.D.; Swedish professor; b. 7 Feb. 1905; ed. School of Medicine, Stockholm.
Professor of Physiology, Royal Caroline Inst., Stockholm 39-; mem. Medical Research Council of Sweden 55-61; Nobel Cttee. for Physiology and Medicine 53-65; Pres. Nobel Foundation 65-; Dr. (h.c.) Rio de Janeiro, Umeå, Dijon, Ghent and Tübingen.
Publ. *Noradrenaline* and many medical papers.
Physiology Department, Karolinska Institutet, Stockholm 60; Karlaplan 14, Stockholm No., Sweden.

von Koerber, Hans Nordewin, PH.D.; American educationist and orientalist; b. 23 July 1886; ed. Berlin and Marburg Univs.
Ethnographical Expedition, Central Africa 05-07; Linguistic Research, Central Africa 07-08; Ethnographic and Linguistic Research, Siberia, Central Asia, West China and Tibet 09-10 and 12-14; Lecturer in Oriental Linguistics, Bonn 11-12; Linguistic Research and Instruction, British India 14-20; Lecturer Marburg Univ. 20-21; Linguistic Research, Dutch Indies 21-22; Lecturer in Comparative Religion, Stralsund, Germany 23-24; Lecturer in Comparative Religion and Prof. of Oriental Linguistics, Univ. of Amoy, China 24-25; Prof. of Oriental Linguistics and Lecturer in German and French, Univ. of the Philippines 26-28; Prof. of Asiatic Studies and Dir. Foundation of Asiatic Studies, Univ. of S. Calif. 28-52, Prof. Emeritus 52-; Guest Prof. in Asian Studies and the great religions of the world in Colls. and Univs. of S. Calif. 52-66; Grand Prior, Order of St. John of Jerusalem, and other orders.
Publs. *Das Tibetische Verbalsystem* 19, *Die Morphologie*

des Tibetischen 21, *Tibetan Literature—Its Contribution Through Western Explorers* 35, *Morphology of the Tibetan Language* 35, *A Word on Philology* (Hewett Memorial) 37, *Kuan Yin: The Buddhist Madonna* 41, *About Basic Concepts and Words in Languages* 46, compiler and translator of Chinese, Japanese and German sections in *Aviation Dictionary in Nine Languages* (Lanz) 44, *Reminiscences in Education* 58, *The Cosmic Mystery* 63, *A New Revelation, Why?* 65, *The Significance of Matter* 68.
Warner Springs, Calif. 92086, U.S.A.
Telephone: 782-3361.

Vonsovsky, Sergei Vasilievich; Soviet physicist; b. 1910; ed. Leningrad State Univ.
Engineer, Chief Engineer, Ural Physical-Technical Inst. 32-39; Junior Scientific Worker, Senior Scientific Worker, Inst. for Investigation of Metals, for Metallophysics and Metallurgy, Urals Branch of U.S.S.R. Acad. of Sciences 39-47; Chief Dept., Deputy Dir. Inst. of Physics of Metals, U.S.S.R. Acad. of Sciences 47-; Corresp. mem. U.S.S.R. Acad. of Sciences 53-66, mem. 66-.
U.S.S.R. Academy of Sciences, 14 Lenin Prospekt, Moscow, U.S.S.R.

von Sternberg, Josef; American (b. Austrian) film director; b. 29 May 1894; ed. Vienna Gymnasium and New York Public Library.
Lecturer, Univ. of S. Calif. 47; Guest Lecturer, Dartmouth Coll., Univ. of Minnesota, Univ. of Ill., Notre Dame Univ., Univ. of Chicago, Iowa City Univ., Univ. of Bogotá, Congress of Theoreticians, Buenos Aires, and Univ. of Calif. (Berkeley); Lecturer, Univ. of Calif. 65, 66; Extraordinary mem. Akad. der Künste, Berlin; Förderer Austrian Kunststelle.
Films include: *Underworld* 27, *Docks of New York* 29, *Blue Angel* 30, *Morocco* 30, *Shanghai Express* 31, *American Tragedy* 31, *Scarlet Empress* 34, *Devil is a Woman* 34, *Shanghai Gesture* 41, *Saga of Anatahan* 53.
Publs. *Fun in a Chinese Laundry* (autobiog.) 65, *Souvenirs d'Montreur d'Ombres* 66.
10516 Lindbrook Drive, Los Angeles 90024, Calif., U.S.A.

Voorst tot Voorst, Baron Sweder van, LL.D.; Netherlands diplomatist; b. 5 May 1910; ed. Univ. of Leiden.
Joined Ministry of Foreign Affairs 34; Attaché Brussels 34-40, Paris 40; Netherlands Ministry of Foreign Affairs, London 40-44; First Sec. Brussels 44-46, Chargé d'Affaires Madrid 46-48; Dept. Head Netherlands Military Mission, Berlin 48-50; European Dept., Ministry of Foreign Affairs 50-52; Perm. Rep. to Council of Europe, Strasbourg 52-54; Minister Washington 54-59; Ambassador to Yugoslavia 59-64; Ambassador to Luxembourg 64-67; Knight Order of the Netherlands Lion; Officer Order of Orange-Nassau; Grand Cross Order of the Yugoslavian Flag and other awards.
c/o Ministry of Foreign Affairs, The Hague, The Netherlands.

Vorobiev, Vitaly Andreevich; Soviet banker; b. 1918; ed. Financial and Economic Institute.
Former worker in food industry; banking 42-; Man. of Primorskaya Territorial Office, Gosbank; Vice-Chair. Gosbank 54-.
Gosbank, 12 Neglinnaya ulitsa, Moscow, U.S.S.R.

Voronin, Alexei Leonidovitch; Soviet diplomatist; b. 22 Dec. 1917; ed. Leningrad State Univ.
Early career at Ministry of Foreign Affairs and Embassies abroad 44-57; Counsellor Iran 57-60; Counsellor Middle East Division, Ministry of Foreign Affairs 60-62; Counsellor Ankara 62-64; Ambassador to Guinea 64-.
Embassy of the U.S.S.R., 7ème avenue, B.P. 329, Conakry, Guinea.

Voronov, Gennadi Ivanovich; Soviet politician; b. 1910; ed. Tomsk Industrial Inst.
First Secretary, Chita Communist Party 48-55; Dep. to Supreme Soviet 50-54, mem. Central Cttee. of Supreme Soviet 52-54; U.S.S.R. Dep. Minister of Agriculture 55-57; First Sec. Orenburg Regional Party Cttee. 57-61; First Dep. Chair. Bureau for the R.S.F.S.R. 61-62; Chair. of Council of Ministers of R.S.F.S.R. 62-; Cand. mem. Presidium of Central Cttee. of C.P.S.U. 61, mem. Oct. 61-66, mem. Politburo 66-; Deputy to Supreme Soviet of U.S.S.R.
Council of Ministers of R.S.F.S.R., Delegatskaya 3, Moscow, U.S.S.R.

Voroshilov, Marshal Kliment Yefremovich; Soviet politician and army leader; b. 4 Feb. 1881; ed. country school.
Former fitter; active participant in revolutionary movement; mem. Communist Party 03-; Chair. Lugansk Soviet of Workers Deputies 17; Commdr. Tsaritsin Front and 10th Army 18; mem. Military Council of 1st Cavalry Army and several military districts 19-25; People's Commissar of Defence of U.S.S.R. 25; mem. Political Bureau of Cen. Cttee. C.P.S.U. 26-, mem. Presidium 52-60; Dep. Chair. U.S.S.R. Council of People's Commissars 40; mem. State Defence Cttee. 41-45; Dep. Chair. U.S.S.R. Council of Ministers 46-53; Pres. Presidium Supreme Soviet U.S.S.R. 53-60, mem. 60-; mem. Central Cttee. C.P.S.U.; Hero of the Soviet Union (twice); Hero of Socialist Labour; awarded eight Orders of Lenin, six Orders of the Red Banner, Order of Red Banner of Labour (thrice) and several other orders and medals.
Presidium of U.S.S.R. Supreme Soviet, Moscow, U.S.S.R.

Vorozhtsov, Nikolai Nikolaevich; Soviet chemist; b. 1907; ed. Bauman Higher Technical School, Moscow.
Member Staff U.S.S.R. Comm. for Investigation of Natural Resources 28-30; Scientific Worker State Inst. of High Pressures 30-38; Chief Dept. Kazakh State Univ. 38-43; Scientific Supervisor, Research Inst. for Organic By-products and Dyestuffs 43-47; Chief Dept. Mendeleev Chemical-Technical Inst. Moscow 45-60; Dir. Novosibirsk Inst. of Organic Chemistry of Siberian Dept. of U.S.S.R. Acad. of Sciences; Corresp. mem. U.S.S.R. Acad. of Sciences 58-66, mem. 66-; State Prize.
Publs. Works on technology of organic dyestuffs and intermediate products.
U.S.S.R. Academy of Sciences, 14 Lenin Prospekt, Moscow, U.S.S.R.

Vorster, Balthazar Johannes, B.A., LL.B.; South African lawyer and politician; b. 13 Dec. 1915; ed. Sterkstroom High School and Stellenbosch Univ.
M.P. for Nigel 53; Dep. Minister of Education, Arts, Science, Social Welfare and Pensions 58-61; Minister of Justice Aug. 61-66; Minister of Justice, Police and Prisons 66; Prime Minister 66-; Leader National Party 66-.
Union Buildings, Pretoria, Republic of South Africa.
Telephone: 20851.

Voss, August Edwardovich; Soviet politician; b. 1916; ed. Teacher-Training Inst., C.P.S.U. Higher Party School and C.P.S.U. Acad. of Social Sciences.
Soviet Army service 40-45; Party Official in Latvia 45-49; Head of Dept. of Science and Culture, Central Cttee., Latvian C.P. 53-54; Party Official at Central Cttee., Latvian C.P. 54-60; Sec. Central Cttee., Latvian C.P. 60-66, First Sec. 66-; Deputy to U.S.S.R. Supreme Soviet and Latvian Supreme Soviet.
Central Committee, Communist Party of Latvia, Riga, U.S.S.R.

Vourdoumbas, Demetrios; Greek politician; b. 1898; ed. Army Officer Cadet School and Athens Univ. Law School.

Artillery Officer 18-23; Lawyer, Thebes 27-42, Athens 42-; mem. Populist Party 35-52, Greek Rally 52-56, Nat. Radical Union 56-; mem. Parl. 35-; Under-Sec. for Army 46-47; Minister of Educ. 48-49, of Posts and Telecommunications 49-50; Under-Sec. for Nat. Defence 54-56; Minister of Industry 56, of Agriculture 62-63; Minister without Portfolio 65-67, of N. Greece 67. Chamber of Deputies, Athens, Greece.

Voutov, Peter G.; Bulgarian diplomatist; b. 17; ed. Sofia State Univ.
President Bulgarian Dem. Youth 44-46; Ministry of Foreign Affairs 47-48; Chargé d'Affaires, Washington 49-50; First Dep., Ministry of Culture 54; Minister to India 55-56; Perm. Rep. to UN 56-59; Ambassador to U.S.A. 60-62; First Deputy Minister for Foreign Affairs 63; Minister of Culture 63-66; Amb. to U.K. 66-. Bulgarian Embassy, 24 Queen's Gate Gardens, London, S.W.7, England.

Voznessenski, Andrei Andreevich; Soviet poet; b. 33; ed. Moscow Architectural Institute.
Member Union of Soviet Writers.
Publs. poems: *The Masters* 59, *Longjumeau* 64, *Antiworlds* 64; collections: *Parabola* 60, *Mosaic* 60.
U.S.S.R. Writers' Union, Ulitsa Vorovsky 52, Moscow, U.S.S.R.

Vranckx, Alfons, LL.D.; Belgian university professor and politician; b. 24 Jan. 1907.
Formerly Prof. of Constitutional Law, Univ. of Ghent; mem. Chamber of Reps. 36-47, 65-; mem. Council of State 47-65; Minister of Interior 65, of Justice June 68-; Socialist.
Ministry of Justice, Brussels, Belgium.

Vratusa, Anton; Yugoslav diplomatist; b. 21 Feb. 1915; ed. Univ. of Ljubljana.
Colonel in Yugoslav People's Army 41-45; various appointments in Ministry of Foreign Affairs and Fed. Exec. Council 45-; mem. Fed. Assembly 65-; mem. numerous dels. to UN; Pres. Yugoslav Nat. Comm. for UNESCO; Dir. Inst. for Social Sciences; Prof. at School of Political Sciences, Belgrade; Perm. Rep. to UN 67-.
Permanent Mission of Yugoslavia to the United Nations, 854 Fifth Avenue, New York, N.Y. 10017, U.S.A.

Vredenburch, Jonkheer Hendrik Frederik Lodewijk Karel van; Netherlands diplomatist; b. 05; ed. Utrecht Univ.
Entered foreign service 32; served Hamburg, Buenos Aires, Madrid, London and Washington 32-45; Political Dir. Netherlands Foreign Office 45; Royal Commr. in Indonesia 48; Administrator Int. Zone of Tangiers 48-51; Chair. Netherlands Del. Paris Conf. 51-52; Deputy Sec.-Gen. NATO 52-56; Chief Rep. in the United Kingdom of the High Authority of the European Coal and Steel Community 56-58; Dir.-Gen. for European Co-operation 58-59; Ambassador to German Fed. Republic 59-62, to Italy 62-; Knight Order of the Netherlands Lion; Commdr. Order of Orange Nassau, etc.
Via Michele Mercati 8, Rome, Italy.

Vredenburgh, Dorothy McElroy, (Mrs. Dorothy Bush), B.S.; American politician; b. 8 Dec. 1916; ed. Mississippi State Coll. for Women and George Washington Univ.
U.S. Steel Corpn., Birmingham, Alabama 37-40; Nat. Committee woman, Alabama Young Democrats 41-50; Asst. Sec. Young Democrats of America 41-43; Co-Chair. Jackson Day, Ala. 44; Vice-Pres. Young Democrats of America 43-48, Act. Pres. 44-45; Sec. Democratic Nat. Convention, Washington, D.C. (first woman to hold this position) 44, 48, 52, 56, 60, 64; Vice-Pres. Mississippi State Coll. for Women Alumnae Asscn. 58-60; Democrat.
Democratic National Committee, 1730 K Street, N.W., Washington 6, D.C., U.S.A.

Vrethem, Åke Toruif; Swedish engineer and businessman; b. 25 March 1912; ed. Royal Inst. of Technology.
Joined State Power Board 34, Chief Engineer 44-48; Asst. Man. Dir. ASEA 48, Man. Dir. 49-61, Chief Exec. Dir. Asea Group 61-; Dir. Fed. of Swedish Industries 53-; Gen. Export Asscn. of Sweden 54-; Chair. Arosmässan Cttee. 55-; Chair. Swedish Asscn. of Electrical Industries 67-; mem. Council Int. Chamber of Commerce 57-; mem. Nat. Ind. Conf. Board (U.S.A.) 61-; Pres. of Swedish Council of the European Movement 61-; Pres. Swedish Standards Asscn. 62-; Official Del. Geneva Int. Atomic Energy Conf. 58 and 64; Knight Order of the North Star, Commdr. (First Class) Order of Vasa; Officer, Order of Merit, United Arab Republic.
ASEA Group Office, P.O.B. 3281, Stockholm 3; Home: Strandvägen 33, Djursholm, Sweden.
Telephone: 7-55-42-43.

Vries, Egbert de, DR. AGR.; Netherlands economist; b. 29 Jan. 1901; ed. Univ. of Wageningen.
Govt. service in Neths. East Indies 24-41, Head of Div. for Gen. Economic Affairs in Dept. of Economic Affairs 38-41; Prof. of Agricultural Economics and Dean of Agricultural Faculty, Univ. of Batavia 41-46; returned to Neths. 46; Prof. of Tropical Agricultural Economics, Univ. of Wageningen, and adviser to Neths. Ministry of Overseas Affairs 47-50; Chief of Economic Resources Div. of Economic Dept. of Int. Bank for Reconstruction and Development 50-52; Chief of Economic Div. of Technical Operations Dept. 52-53, Agricultural Div. 53-56; Chair. Working Cttee. of Dept. of Studies, Div. Church and Society, World Council of Churches 54-61; mem. of Cttee. on Devt. Countries, World Council of Churches 62; Rector Inst. of Social Studies, The Hague 56-66; Dir. Netherlands Univs. Foundation for Int. Co-operation 56-66; Chair. Nat. Org. for Int. Aid 56-61, Vice-Chair. 61-66; Prof. of Int. Devt., Univ. of Pittsburgh 66-; Fellow, Inst. of Social Studies 66; Knight, Order of Netherlands Lion; Commdr. Order of Orange-Nassau.
Deerlake Park, Chalkhill, Pa. 15421, U.S.A.
Telephone: 412-438-4776.

Vries, Henry Lucien de; Surinam governor; b. 12 Dec. 1909.
Import-export business, Paramaribo 30-41; Army Service (Major) 41-45; Man. Dir. Surinam Bank 46-49; Chair. Staten of Surinam 46-49; Commr. for Econ. and Financial Affairs of Surinam in Netherlands 46-61; Man. Dir. Surinam Aluminium Co. (Suralco) 61-65; Vice-Chair. Advisory Council 63-65; Gov. of Surinam 65-.
Governor's House, Oranjeplein, Paramaribo, Surinam.
Telephone: Paramaribo 2841.

Vriesland, Victor Emanuel van; Netherlands writer; b. 92; ed. Gymnasium, The Hague, and Univ. of Dijon.
Arts and Literary Editor of *Nieuwe Rotterdamsche Courant*; Dir. of *De Groene Amsterdammer*; Editor of *De Vrije Bladen*, *Forum*, *Kroniek van Kunst en Kultuur*, and at present of *De Nieuwe Stem*; Pres. C. V. De Bezige Bij GA; Hon. mem. of Society of Authors; mem. of Arts Council; Vice-Pres. Bd. of Bureau of Musical Authors' Rights; fmr. Pres. Netherlands P.E.N. Centre, Dir. of Bureau of Authors' Rights, Vice-Pres. Int. Fed. of P.E.N. Clubs, now Int. Pres.; Editor several publishing houses; Order of Leopold II (Belgium); Légion d'Honneur; Order of Orange-Nassau; Hon. D.Litt. (Leyden); Constantyn Huyghens Prize, Prize Kunstenaarsverzet.
Publs. Essays: *De Cultureele Noodtoestand van het Joodsche Volk* 15, *Herman Hana* 20, *Grondslag van Verstandhouding* 46, *Vereenvoudigingen* 52, *Onderzoek en Vertoog* (2 vols.) 58, etc.; verse: *Voorwaardelijk Uitzicht* 29, *Vooronderzoek* 46, *Le Vent se couche* 49, *Jegengif* 59,

etc.; plays: *Der verlorene Sohn* 25, *Havenstad* 33; novel: *Het Afscheid van de Wereld in drie Dagen* 26; anthologies: *Winterboek W.B.*, *Spiegel van de Ned. Poezie door alle eeuwen* (3 vols. 39, 53, 54), *In den Hof van Eros* 40, *Werk en de Mens Nico van Suchtelen* 48, *De Vergetenen* 55, etc.; also short stories and many translations.
Weesperzÿde 25, Amsterdam, Netherlands.

Vrigny, Roger, L. ès L.; French writer; b. 19 May 1920; ed. Collège oratorien de Rocroy-Saint-Léon, Paris, Lycée Condorcet, Paris, and Univ. of Paris.
Professor of Literature, Collège Rocroy-Saint-Léon; Founder of *Le Miroir* Theatre Co. 50; broadcaster and radio producer; Prix Femina 63.
Publs. novels: *Arban, Lauréna, Barbegal, La Nuit de Mougins* (Prix Femina); farce: *Marute*; sketches: *L'Enlèvement d'Arabelle, l'Impromptu du réverbère*; comedy: *Les Irascibles*; mystery: *La Dame d'Onfrède*.
4 rue Jean-Ferrandi, Paris 6e, France.

Vrolijk, Maarten; Netherlands journalist and politician; b. 19.
Editorial work with *De Nederlander* 36-38; studying and writing 38-46; with *De Nieuwe Nederlander* and *Regionale Dagbladpers*, and Parl. Editor *Het Vrije Volk* until 56; mem. Second Chamber 56-63; worked for *Friese Koerier, Het Haags Dagblad* and *Het Parool-Nieuwe Pers* until 61; Alderman, The Hague 62-65; Minister of Culture, Recreation and Social Welfare 65-66; mem. Second Chamber 67-; Labour.
Pomonaplein 3, The Hague, Netherlands.

Vuchetich, Yevgeni Viktorovich; Soviet sculptor; b. 08; ed. Rostov Art School and Leningrad Arts Acad.
Member U.S.S.R. Acad. of Arts 53-; works include statue of Marshal Voroshilov 36, Partisan Girl (exhibited at the Soviet Pavilion, Paris World Fair), portrait busts: Gen. Chernyakhovsky (State Prize) 45, V. I. Chuikov 47, N. Niyazov 48, T. T. Khryukin 48, S. Kitchlew 56, V. I. Lenin 57; monuments: Gen. M. G. Yefremov at Vyazma (State Prize) 46, Gen. N. F. Vatutin in Kiev 44-47, to Soviet Army Men in Berlin 46-49, V. G. Belinsky at Penza, A. T. Matrosov at Velikie Luki, Gen. L. N. Gurtiev in Orel 54, sculpture *Let us Beat Swords into Ploughshares* 57; memorial complex in Volgograd 67; State Prizewinner 46, 47, 48, 49, 50; Grand Prix, Brussels 58; People's Artist of the U.S.S.R.; mem. of C.P. of Soviet Union.
U.S.S.R. Academy of Arts, 21 Kropotkinskaya, Moscow, U.S.S.R.

Vujanović, Nikola; Yugoslav politician, journalist and diplomatist; b. 11; ed. Law Univ., Belgrade.
Prisoner of War, German Concentration Camps 41-45; Press Managerial Functions 45-51; Dir. High Political School, Yugoslav Communist Party Cen. Cttee. 51-52; Sec. Trades Union Cen. Council 52-53; Ambassador to Rumania 54-58; Chief Ed. *Communist* (organ of League of Communists of Yugoslavia) 58-61; Ambassador, State Secr. for Foreign Affairs 61, Ambassador to Czechoslovakia 61-65; mem. League of Communist Central Cttee. of Repub. of Montenegro; Memoria 1941 Award, Nat. Order of Merit with Gold Star.
Publs. Monographs on socialist development and international policy.
c/o Ministry of Foreign Affairs, Belgrade, Yugoslavia.

Vukmanović, Svetozar N.; Yugoslav politician; b. 12; ed. Belgrade Univ.
Mem. Communist Party 33-; mem. Exec. Cttee. Central Cttee.; active in resistance movement during 39-45 war, mem. H.Q. Nat. Liberation Army; Deputy Minister of Nat. Defence 45-48; Minister of Mining 48; Chair. Council for Industry, Council for Nat. Economy; Vice-Pres. Federal Exec. Council; Pres. Central Council of the Confederation of Trade Unions of Yugoslavia; decorations include: People's Hero, Nat. Liberation Order, Partisan Star, Order of Merit for the People, Brotherhood and Unity Order, Socialist Labour Hero.

Publs. include *Trade Unions in New Conditions* 62, *Socialist Construction and Economic System* 64, *Problems of Agriculture* 65.
Central Council of the Confederation of Trade Unions of Yugoslavia, Trg. Marksa i Engelsa 5, Dom Sindikata, Belgrade, Yugoslavia.

Vulliamy, Colwyn Edward; British writer; b. 20 June 1886; ed. privately.
Served France, Macedonia, Turkey, First World War.
Publs. include *Prehistoric Forerunners* 25, *Unknown Cornwall* 25, *Immortal Man* 26, *Letters of Tsar Nicholas II* 29, *Red Archives* 29, *Archaeology of Middlesex and London* 30, *Voltaire* 30, *Rousseau* 31, *John Wesley* 31, *The Vicar's Experiments* 32, *Lobelia Grove* 32, *James Boswell* 32, *William Penn* 33, *Family Matters* 34, *Judas Maccabeus* 34, *Aspasia* 35, *Mrs. Thrale of Streatham* 36, *Royal George* 37, *Outlanders: Imperial Expansion in South Africa* 38, *Crimea: the Campaign of 1854-56* 39, *Calico Pie* (autobiography) 40, *A Short History of the Montagu-Puffins* 41, *The Polderoy Papers* 43, *Doctor Philligo* 44, *English Letter Writers, Edwin and Eleanor* 45, *Ursa Major: Dr. Johnson and his Friends* 46, *Man and the Atom* 47, *Byron* 48, *Prodwit's Guide to Writing* 49, *The Anatomy of Satire* 50, *Rocking Horse Journey* 52, *Don Among the Dead Men* 52, *The Onslow Family* 53, *Jones: A Gentleman of Wales* 54, *The Proud Walkers* 55, *Body in the Boudoir* 56, *Cakes for your Birthday* 59, *Justice for Judy* 60, *Little Arthur's Guide to Humbug* 60, *Tea at the Abbey* 61, *Floral Tribute* 63.
c/o National Provincial Bank Ltd., Guildford, Surrey, England.

Vu Van Mau, LL.B., LL.D.; Viet-Namese lawyer, diplomatist and politician; b. 25 July 1914; ed. Univ. of Hanoi and Univ. of Paris.
Lawyer, Hanoi 49; Dean, Faculty of Law, Univ. of Saigon 55-58; First Pres. Viet-Namese Supreme Court of Appeal 55; Minister of Foreign Affairs 55; Sec. of State for Foreign Affairs 56-63 (resgnd.); Pres. Viet-Namese Nat. Asscn. of Comparative Law; Ambassador to United Kingdom, Belgium and Netherlands 64-65.
Publs. Legal Works in French and Viet-Namese.
University of Saigon, 3 Công-Trúóng Chiên-si, Saigon, Republic of Viet-Nam.

Vu Van Thai; Viet-Namese diplomatist; b. 1919; ed. high school, Viet-Nam, Ecole Centrale des Arts et Manufactures, Paris, and Univ. de Paris à la Sorbonne.
Director-General of Planning, Republic of Viet-Nam 54-55; Administrator of Foreign Aid 55-57; Dir.-Gen. of Budget and Foreign Aid 57-61; Consultant to Fiscal and Financial Branch, UN Secretariat 61-62; UN Technical Assistance Adviser to Govt. of Togo and UNTA Resident Rep. in Togo 62-64; Ambassador to U.S.A. 64, 65-67; Inter-Regional Econ. Adviser, Dept. of Econ. and Social Affairs, UN 64-65.
Embassy of Viet-Nam, 2251 R Street, N.W., Washington, D.C. 20008, U.S.A.

Vvedensky, Boris Alexeevich; Soviet scientist; b. 93.
Specialist in the field of radio-physics and radiotechnics, especially ultra-short waves; Chair. Scientific Council of the Scientific Publishing House "Soviet Encyclopædia"; mem. Acad. of Sciences of the U.S.S.R. 43; corresp. mem. German Acad. of Sciences; State Prizewinner 52; awarded Order of Lenin 45, 53, 63; Hero of Socialist Labour 63; Red Banner of Labour 53, 62, Hero of Socialist Labour, Gold Medal of Hammer and Sickle, A. S. Popov gold medal 49.
Publs. *Fundamentals of Theory of Propagation of Radio Waves, Propagation of Ultra-short Waves* 34, 38, jointly with A. G. Arenberg *Problems of Propagation of Ultra-short Radio Waves* 48, *Distant Tropospheric Propagation of Ultra-short Waves* 57, etc.
Radio Engineering and Electronics Institute, U.S.S.R. Academy of Sciences, 18 Marx Avenue, Moscow, U.S.S.R.

W

Wächter, Eberhard; Austrian opera-singer; b. 8 July 1929; studied singing with Elisabeth Rado, Vienna.
Début with Volksoper, Vienna; mem. State Opera, Vienna 55-; has sung in Germany, France, Holland, England, Spain, U.S.A. and Italy, Bayreuth Festival, Salzburg Festival, etc.
Vienna XIX, 46 Fel. Mottlstrasse, Austria.
Telephone: 3417-212.

Wachuku, Jaja Anucha; Nigerian lawyer and politician; b. 18; ed. Nigeria, Gold Coast People's Coll., Trinity Coll., Dublin.
Law practice Eire 44-47; returned to Nigeria 47; mem. Ngwa Native Authority Council 49-52; mem. E. House of Ass. 51, Fed. House of Reps. 52-; Minister of Econ. Development 60-61, of Foreign and Commonwealth Affairs 61-63, of Foreign Affairs 63-65, of Aviation 65-66; Head, Nigerian Del. to UN 60-61; Chair. UN Conciliation Comm. in the Congo; mem. N.C.N.C.
Lagos, Nigeria.

Wacker, Alfred, LL.B.; Swiss lawyer and diplomatist; b. 1918; ed. Universität Bern.
Swiss Foreign Office 45-50, 58-60; at Embassy, German Fed. Repub. 50-55, Budapest 55-57; Counsellor, Mexico 61-64; Deputy Head, Swiss Mission to European Econ. Community (EEC) 64-66; Deputy Sec.-Gen. European Free Trade Asscn. (EFTA) 66-.
European Free Trade Association, 32 chemin des Colombettes, Geneva, Switzerland.
Telephone: 022-3490-00.

Wada, Haruo; Japanese trade unionist; b. 19; ed. Toba Mercantile Marine School.
Joined Yamashita Shipping Co. 39, Navigator with Yamashita Coastal Shipping Co. 45, resigned to become full-time mem. All Japan Seamen's Union 46; founder-mem. SOHYO (General Council of Japanese Trade Unions) 49-52; Gen. Sec. Japanese T.U.C. 54-64; mem. Exec. Board ICFTU 62-65; Vice-Pres. All Japan Seamen's Union 64-; Vice-Pres. Japanese Confederation of Labour (DOMEI) 64-67; Pres. ICFTU-ARO 65-.
Publ. *Introduction to the Trade Union Movement* 58.
Office: 15-26, Roppongi 7-chome, Minato-ku, Tokyo; Home: 712-5 Shofukuji, Aza Gokurakuji, Kamakura-shi, Kanagawa-ken, Japan.
Telephone: 403-6251 (Office); Kamakura 2-3524 (Home).

Wada, Tsunesuke; Japanese business executive; b. 3 Nov. 1887; ed. Kobe Univ.
Furukawa Mining Co.; later with Furukawa Trading Co.; fmr. Man. Dir. and Pres. Fujitsu Ltd., Chair. 58-; fmr. Man. Dir., Pres. and Chair. Fuji Electric Co. Ltd., Adviser 65-.
Fuji Electric Co. Ltd., 1-1 Marunouchi, Chiyoda-ku, Tokyo; 268 Chojamaru Kami-osaki, Shinagawa-ku, Tokyo, Japan.

Wadachi, Kiyoo; Japanese meteorologist; b. 02; ed. Tokyo Univ.
Entered Meteorological Observatory; has conducted research into earthquakes, tidal waves etc.; fmr. Pres. Osaka Meteorological Observatory; Dir. of Gen. Meteorological Observatory 46-; Pres. Meteorological Soc. of Japan; Vice-Pres. Science Council of Japan.
Publs. *Earthquakes, Akumade Kibo Are.*
c/o Director's House, Kishocho, Takehira-cho, Chiyoda-ku, Tokyo, Japan.

Waddington, Conrad Hal, C.B.E., SC.D., F.R.S.; British biologist; b. 8 Nov. 1905; ed. Clifton Coll., and Cambridge Univ.

Scientific research work Strangeways Laboratory and Dept. of Zoology Cambridge 30-33; Rockefeller Fellow Germany 32, U.S.A. 38; awarded Brachet Prize for Embryology Belgian Royal Acad. 34; Lecturer in Zoology Cambridge Univ. and Embryologist Strangeways Laboratory 33-45; Fellow Christ's Coll. Cambridge 34-45; Scientific Adviser to C.-in-C. Coastal Command R.A.F. 44-45; Prof. Animal Genetics, Edinburgh Univ. 46-; Hon. Dir. Unit of Animal Genetics (Agricultural Research Council) 57-; Pres. Int. Union of Biological Sciences 61-67; Hon. Dir. Epigenetics Research Group (Medical Research Council) 62; Hon. D.Sc., Montreal, Dublin and Prague; Hon. LL.D., Aberdeen; Hon. foreign mem., American Acad. of Arts and Sciences, Finnish Acad., Japanese Genetical Soc.
Publs. *The Ethical Animal* 60, *The Nature of Life* 61, *New Patterns in Genetics and Development* 62, *Towards a Theoretical Biology* (Editor) 68, *Behind Appearance* 68.
Institute of Animal Genetics, West Mains Road, Edinburgh, Scotland.
Telephone: NEWington 1011, extension 3536.

Wade, Emlyn Capel Stewart, Q.C., LL.D., F.B.A., J.P.; British barrister; b. 31 Aug. 1895; ed. St. Lawrence Coll., Ramsgate and Gonville and Caius Coll., Cambridge.
Principal, Law Society's School of Law 26-28; Fellow of St. John's Coll. Cambridge 28-31; Tutor, Gonville and Caius Coll. Cambridge 31-39, Fellow 31-; Downing Prof. of Laws of England, Univ. of Cambridge 45-62; Reader in Constitutional Law, Council of Legal Education 45-66; U.K. Del. to Cttee. on European Unity, Paris 48-49; mem. of Departmental Cttees. on Law of Defamation 39, Electoral Law 44, Law of Limitations 48, Law Reform 52-63; Pres. Soc. of Public Teachers of Law 50-51; served in Army 15-19 and 39-42; Hon. D.C.L. Durham Univ.
Publs. *Constitutional Law* (with G. Godfrey Phillips), 31 (7th edn. 65), (Editor) *Dicey; The Law of the Constitution,* 10th edn. (with new Introduction) 59.
14 Sculthorpe Road, Fakenham, Norfolk, England.
Telephone: Fakenham 2565.

Wade-Gery, Henry Theodore, M.C., F.B.A.; British historian; b. 2 April 1888; ed. Winchester and New Coll., Oxford.
Member staff Admiralty 12-13; Asst. Master Sherborne School 13-14; served First World War France and Belgium; Fellow, Wadham Coll., Oxford 14-39; mem. Inst. for Advanced Study, Princeton 37-38, 47-48, 56-58; Sather Lecturer, California Univ. 38; Wykeham Prof. of Ancient History, Oxford Univ. 39-53, Emeritus 53-; Senior Research Fellow, Merton Coll., Oxford 53-58; Hon. Litt.D. (Dublin Univ.) 51.
Publs. *Pindar's Pythian Odes* (with C. M. Bowra) 28, *The Athenian Tribute Lists* (in collaboration), Vol. I 38, Vol. II 49, Vol. III 50, Vol. IV 53; *The Poet of the Iliad* 52, *Essays in Greek History*; chapters in *Cambridge Ancient History* II and III.
The Cottage, Upton, Berks., England.

Wadia, Ardeshir Ruttonji, BAR.-AT-LAW; Indian educationist; b. 4 June 1888; ed. Wilson Coll., Bombay, London, Cambridge and Oxford.
Professor of English and Philosophy Wilson Coll. Bombay 14; Lecturer in Psychology Bombay Univ. 14-16; Prof. of Philosophy Mysore Univ. 17-42, Dean Faculty of Arts 27-30; Dir. of Public Instruction Mysore 42-43; Sec. Inter-Univ. Board 32-37; Pres. All-India Fed. of Teachers' Asscns. 26, Indian Philosophical Congress 30, Mysore State Educ. League 33; Editor

Mysore University Journal 40-42; Principal Victoria Coll. Gwalior, C.I.; Stephanos Nirmalendu Ghosh Lecturer Calcutta Univ. 45-46; Dir. of Educ. Madhya Bharat 48-49; Pro-Vice-Chancellor Maharaja Sayajirao Univ. Baroda 49-52; Dir. Tata Inst. of Social Sciences, Bombay; Editor Indian Journal of Social Work 53-62; mem. Council of States 54-66; Pres. Indian Council of Social Welfare 68-69; mem. Univ. Grants Comm.; Hon. D.Litt.; Padma Bhushan 61.
Publs. *The Ethics of Feminism, Handbook of Moral Instruction for Teachers, Civilisation as a Co-operative Adventure, Zoroaster, Pragmatic Idealism* (in *Contemporary Indian Philosophy*), *Religion as a Quest for Values, The Future of English in India, The Philosophy of Mahatma Gandhi and other Essays Philosophical and Sociological, History and Philosophy of Social Work in India* (editor), *Democracy and Society*.
96 Marine Drive, Bombay 2, India.

Wadia, Drashaw Nosherwan, M.A., D.SC., F.G.S., F.N.I., F.R.S.; Indian geologist; b. 25 Oct. 1883; ed. Baroda Coll., Bombay Univ.
Professor of Geology, Prince of Wales Coll., Kashmir 07-20; Geological Survey of India 21-39; Mineral Adviser, Govt. of Ceylon 39-44; Dir. Bureau of Mines, India 48; Geological Adviser, Govt. of India 45-, Dept. of Atomic Energy 50-; Nat. Prof. of Geology 62-; Award of Royal Geographical Soc., London; Lyell Medal, Geol. Soc., London; Leopold von Buch Medal, Germany; Padma Bhushan (India).
Publs. *Geology of India* 19, *Geology of Kashmir and North-Western Punjab* 29-34, *Syntaxis of North-Western Himalayas* 32; papers on India's mineral resources, atomic minerals, etc. 48-65, Himalayan Geosyncline 66.
10 King George's Avenue, New Delhi, India.

Wadia, Sophia; Indian editor; b. 13 Sept. 1901; ed. Lycée Molière, Paris, Columbia Univ., New York, School of Oriental and African Studies, London.
Lecturer; founder-organiser P.E.N. All-India Centre; Pres. Indian Inst. of World Culture, Bangalore; assoc. United Lodge of Theosophists; Editor *Aryan Path* 29- and *The Indian P.E.N.* 34-, Bombay; also worker in women's social, educational and cultural movements.
Publs. *The Brotherhood of Religions, Preparation for Citizenship.*
Theosophy Hall, 40 New Marine Lines, Bombay 1, India.
Telephone: 243203.

Wadsworth, James Jeremiah, A.B., LL.D.; American politician and administrator; b. 12 June 1905; ed. Yale Univ.
Member, New York State Assembly 31-41, Asst. Industrial Relations Man., Curtiss Wright Corpn. 41-45; Dir. Public Interest Div., War Assets Corpn. 45-46; Dir. Govt. Liaison, Air Transport Asscn. of America 46-48; Special Asst. to Administrator, ECA (Marshall Plan) 48-50; Dep. later Acting Admin. Fed. Civil Defense Admin. 50-53; Dep. U.S. Rep. to U.N. 53-60, U.S. Rep. 60-61; Pres. Peace Research Inst. 61-62; Board of Trustees, Freedom House 61-63; mem. Exec. Cttee. of Dag Hammarskjöld Foundation 62-65, Fed. Communications Cttee. 65-.
Publs. *The Price of Peace* 62, *Power and Order* 63, *A Warless World* 63, *The Glass House* 66.
6717 Tulip Tree Terrace, Washington, D.C. 20016, U.S.A.

Waeyenbergh, Mgr. Honoré van, DR.LITT.PHIL.; Retd. Belgian university professor; b. 25 Nov. 1891; ed. Catholic Univ. of Louvain, and Grand Séminaire, Malines.
Prof., St. Gummar's Coll., Lier 20-24, Head 24-27; Head of St. John's Coll. Antwerp 27-36; Vice-Rector Catholic Univ. of Louvain 36-40, Rector magnificus 40-64, Hon.

Rector 64-; Titular Bishop of Gilba and Auxiliary Bishop of Malines-Brussels; Chair. Int. Fed. Catholic Univs. 49-60, Hon. Chair. 60-; Dr. Litt., h.c. (Laval, Quebec), Dr. Jur. (Washington, Durham, Edinburgh), Dr. Canon & Civil Law (Dublin), Dr.Theol. (Prague, Münster, Strasbourg, Lublin), D.Phil. (Univ. Católica de Chile, Santiago); mem. Acad. Royale Flamande des Sciences, des Lettres et des Beaux-Arts de Belgique, Société Scientifique de Bruxelles; hon. mem. Consejo Superior de Investigaciones Cientificas (Spain); Founder and Chair. Univ. Lovanium de Léopoldville 48-60, Hon. Chair. 60-; decorations and awards include: Officer Order of Leopold II with palms and swords, Belgian Croix de Guerre, Grand Officer Order of Adolph of Nassau, Grand Officer Order of Leopold, Grand Officer Crown Order, Officier de la Légion d'Honneur, Commdr. Order of Orange Nassau, Order of Merit (Italy), Grand Cross Alfonso el Sabio (Spain), Order of Merit (Germany), Commdr. Order of Merit of Senegal, Order of Malta.
354 Bd. Lambermont, Brussels 3, Belgium.
Telephone: 02-154238.

Wagenhöfer, Carl Friedrich; German banker; b. 24 Feb. 1910; ed. Univs. of Erlangen, Vienna, Kiel and Munich.
Department of Finance, Bavaria 37-39; Army Service 39-45; Chief of Section for Interministerial and Superregional Questions, Dept. of Finance, Bavaria 47-52; Sec. of State, Senate of Free and Hanseatic City of Hamburg 52-56; Pres. of Landeszentralbank in Bavaria 56-; mem. Central Bank Council of Deutsche Bundesbank 56-.
Publs. *Der Föderalismus und die Notenbankverfassung* 57, *Währungspolitik in der Sozialen Marktwirtschaft* 61.
Landeszentralbank, Ludwigstrasse 13, 8 Munich 22; Gellerstrasse 6, 8 Munich 81, German Federal Republic.

Wagner, Sir Anthony Richard, K.C.V.O., D.LITT.; British genealogist; b. 6 Sept. 1908; ed. Eton and Balliol Coll., Oxford.
Portcullis Pursuivant 31-43; Richmond Herald 43-61; War Office 39-43; Private Sec. to Minister of Town and Country Planning 44-45; mem. Advisory Cttee. on Historic Buildings 47-; Registrar, Coll. of Arms 53-60; Sec. of Order of the Garter 52-61; Jt. Register of Court of Chivalry 54-; Garter Principal King of Arms 61-; Inspector of Regimental Colours 61-; Genealogist of the Order of the Bath 61-, of the Order of St. John 61-.
Publs. *Historic Heraldry of Britain* 39, *Heralds and Heraldry in the Middle Ages* 39, *Heraldry in England* 46, *Catalogue of English Mediaeval Rolls of Arms* 50, *The Records and Collections of the College of Arms* 52, *English Genealogy* 60, *English Ancestry* 61, *Heralds of England* 67.
College of Arms, Queen Victoria Street, London, E.C.4; 68 Chelsea Square, London, S.W.3; Wyndham Cottage, Aldeburgh, Suffolk, England.
Telephone: 01-248-4300.

Wagner, Aubrey Joseph; American engineer; b. 12 Jan. 1912; ed. Univ. of Wisconsin.
Tennessee Valley Authority 34-, successively Junior Hydraulic Engineer, Asst. Hydraulic Engineer, Assoc. Navigation Engineer, Asst. Chief, River Transportation Div., Act. Chief, later Chief Navigation and Transportation Bureau, Asst. Gen. Man. 51-54, Gen. Man. 54-61, Dir. 61-62, Chair. 62-; Hon. LL.B. (Newbery Coll.).
Publs. Articles in various journals and magazines.
Tennessee Valley Authority, New Sprankle Building, Knoxville, Tennessee 37902; Home: 1600 Cedar Lane, Knoxville, Tennessee 37918, U.S.A.
Telephone: 615-522-7181 (Office); 615-689-5667 (Home).

Wagner, Carl, PH.D.; German physical chemist; b. 25 May 1901; ed. Univ. of Leipzig.
Professor, Technische Hochschule, Darmstadt 34-45; Scientific Adviser, Ordnance Research and Devt. Div., Fort Bliss, U.S.A. 45-49; Visiting Prof. of Metallurgy, Mass. Inst. of Technology, U.S.A. 49-55, Prof. of Metallurgy 55-58; Head Max-Planck-Inst. für physikalische Chemie, Göttingen 58-66, Staff mem. 67-; Palladium Medal, Electrochemical Soc. 51, Willis R. Whitney Award, Nat. Asscn. of Corrosion Engineers 57, Bunsen Medal, Deutsche Bunsengesellschaft 61, Gauss Medal, Braunschweigische Wissenschaftliche Gesellschaft 64; Dr. rer. nat. h.c. (Technische Hochschule, Darmstadt), Dr. Ing. E.h. (Bergakademie Clausthal-Technische Hochschule).
Publ. *Thermodynamics of Alloys* 62.
Home: 63 Nikolausberger Weg, Göttingen; Office: Max-Planck-Institut für physikalische Chemie, 34 Göttingen, Bunsenstrasse 10, German Federal Republic.

Wagner, Gerrit A.; Netherlands oil executive; b. 21 Oct. 1916; ed. Rijksuniversiteit te Leiden.
Royal Dutch/Shell Group 46-, working in various parts of world; Vice-Pres. Compañia Shell de Venezuela 59-61, Pres. 61-64; Man. Dir. N.V. Koninklijke Nederlandsche Petroleum Maatschappij, Shell Petroleum Co. 64-; mem. Presidium of Board of Dirs. of Shell Petroleum N.V. 64-; Order of Francisco de Miranda, Second Class (Venezuela); Hon. C.B.E. (U.K.).
N.V. Koninklijke Nederlandsche Petroleum Maatschappij, 30 Carel van Bylandtlaan, The Hague, Netherlands.

Wagner, Hellmuth, DR. IUR.; German lawyer and industrial official; b. 17; ed. Staatliches Kaiserin-Augusta-Gymnasium, Berlin, and Münster Univ.
Compulsory labour service 36; apprenticeship in textile industry 36-38; Military Service 38-45; legal and political science studies, Münster Univ. 48-51; Legal Adviser to Gütersloh Town Council 51-52, Federation of German Industries 52-; Managing Dir., Federation of German Industries 63-.
Publs. articles on business management.
Bundesverband der Deutschen Industrie, Habsburger Ring 2-12, 5 Cologne, German Federal Republic.

Wagner, Philip Marshall; American newspaper columnist and viticulturist; b. 18 Feb. 1904; ed. Kent School, and Univ. of Michigan.
With General Electric Co. 25-30; Editorial Writer, *Baltimore Evening Sun* 30-36, London Correspondent *Baltimore Sun* 36-37, Editor *Evening Sun* 38-43, Editor *Baltimore Sun* 43-64; writer of syndicated newspaper column on public affairs 64-; with wife has introduced new grape varieties into American viticulture; American del. Fédération Nat. de la Viticulture Nouvelle.
Publs. *American Wines and How to Make Them* 33, *Wine Grapes and How to Grow Them* 37, *The Wine-Grower's Guide* 45, *American Wines and Wine Making* 56, *H. L. Mencken* (American Writers Series) 66; Edited (with Dr. Stanford V. Larkey) *Turner on Wines* 41.
Boordy Vineyard, Box 38, Riderwood, Md., U.S.A.

Wagner, Robert F., B.A., LL.B.; American lawyer and public official; b. 20 April 1910; ed. Yale Univ., Harvard School of Business Administration, School of Int. Relations, Geneva, and Yale Law School.
Mem. N.Y. State Assembly 38-41; served American Air Force 41-45; Tax Commr., N.Y. City 46; Commr. Dept. of Housing and Buildings, N.Y. City 46-47; Chair. N.Y. Planning Comm. 47-49; Borough Pres. of Manhattan 50-53; Mayor of New York 54-65; Amb. to Spain 68-; Chair. Nationalities Div., Dem. Nat. Cttee. 62; Bronze Star, Presidential Unit Citation, Croix de

Guerre and six battle stars; Hon. LL.D. (Long Island Univ., Fordham Univ. and Brooklyn Law School).
American Embassy, Madrid, Spain.

Wagner, Wolfgang Manfred Martin, (brother of late Wieland Wagner); German festival director; b. 30 Aug. 1919.
Director, Bayreuth Festival.
Festspielhügel 3, Bayreuth, German Federal Republic.

Wagner-Régeny, Rudolf; German composer; b. 28 Aug. 1903; ed. Hochschule für Musik, Berlin.
Répétiteur Grosse Volksoper, Berlin 24-26; composer and conductor with Rudolf von Laban 26-30; composer and teacher 28-; Rector Hochschule für Musik, Rostock 47-50; Prof. of Composition Deutsche Hochschule für Musik, Berlin 50-; mem. Deutsche Akad. der Künste, Akad. der Künste Berlin-Hanseatenweg, Bayerische Akad. der Schönen Künste, Nat. Prize 55.
Principal works, opera: *Der Günstling* 35, *Die Bürger von Calais* 39, *Johanna Balk* 41, *Prometheus* 58; ballet: *Der Zerbrochene Krug;* operas: *Das Bergwerk zu Falun* 61, *Persische Episode* 63; also chamber music, etc.
Adlergestell 255, Aldershof, Berlin, Germany.

Wahi, Prem Nath, M.D., F.R.C.P.; Indian doctor; b. 10 April 1908; ed. K.G. Medical Coll., Lucknow, London Hospital Medical School, London, and New England Deaconess Hospital, Boston, U.S.A.
Professor of Pathology, S.N. Medical Coll., Agra 41-; Principal, S.N. Medical Coll., Agra 60-; Dean, Faculty of Medicine, Agra Univ. 61-64; Dir. WHO Int. Reference Centre and Cancer Registry 63-; mem. Expert Panel of WHO on Cancer, Lyon, France 65-; has attended numerous int. conferences on cancer; Lady Brahamachari Readership, Calcutta Univ. 65; Fellow, Nat. Inst. of Sciences, India; Founder Fellow, Coll. of Pathologists, London 63; Founder Fellow, Indian Acad. of Medical Sciences 64.
S.N. Medical College, Agra (U.P.), India.

Wahlen, Friedrich Traugott; Swiss agriculturalist and politician; b. 10 April 1899; ed. Swiss Fed. Inst. of Technology, Zürich.
Asst. Inst. of Agronomy, Fed. Inst. of Technology, Zürich 20-22; Supervising Analyst Dominion Seed Laboratory, Quebec, then Chief Analyst Dominion Dept. of Agriculture, Ottawa with Canadian Civil Service 22-29; Dir. Swiss Experiment Station of Agriculture, Oerlikon, Zürich 29-43; Prof. of Agronomy, Fed. Inst. of Technology, Zürich 43-49; Chief of the Section of Agricultural Production and Home Economics in the Swiss War Food Office and Commr. for Food Production 38-42 and 42-45, organising the Wahlen Plan for assuring Switzerland's food supplies during the Second World War; mem. Swiss Council of States (Senate) 42-49; Dir. Agriculture Division, F.A.O., Washington 49-50, Rome 51-57; Chief Expanded Tech. Asst. Programme F.A.O. 50-52; Deputy Dir.-Gen. F.A.O. 57-59; Federal Councillor (Justice and Police) 59, (Public Economy) 60-June 61, (Political Dept.) July 61-65; Pres. Swiss Confederation 61; mem. Royal Swedish Acad.; Marcel Benoist Prize 40, etc.; Hon. Dr. of Medicine, Univ. of Zürich 46; Hon. Dr. of Agricultural Sciences, Univ. of Göttingen, and Laval Univ., Quebec.
39 Humboldtstrasse, Berne, Switzerland.
Telephone: 031-41-23-55.

Wahrhaftig, Zorach, DR.JUR.; Israeli lawyer and politician; b. Warsaw 2 Feb. 1906; ed. Univ. of Warsaw.
Private law practice, Warsaw 32-39; Vice-Pres. Mizrachi, Poland 26-39; mem. of exec., Keren Hayesod, Hechalutz Hamizrachi, World Jewish Congress; Deputy Dir., Inst. of Jewish Affairs, New York 43-47; Vice-Pres. Hapoel Hamizrachi, U.S.A. 43-47; Dir. Vaad Leumi Law Dept. 47; mem. Provisional Council, Govt. of Israel 49; mem. of Knesset; Deputy Minister for

Religious Affairs 56-59; Minister of Religious Affairs 61-; mem. Jewish Law Research Inst., Ministry of Justice 48; Lecturer on Talmudic Law, Hebrew Univ. Publs. *Starvation over Europe* 43, *Relief and Rehabilitation* 44, *Where Shall they Go?* 46, *Uprooted* 46, *Hazaka in Jewish Law* 64, and many publs. in Hebrew on Israeli Law and Religion.
Ministry of Religious Affairs, Jerusalem, Israel.
Telephone: 26756.

Wain, John Barrington, M.A.; British writer; b. 14 March 1925; ed. St. John's Coll., Oxford.
Lecturer in English Literature, Univ. of Reading 47-55; resigned 55 to become free-lance writer and literary critic; many lectures at Univs. in Europe, America and India; Dir. 1st "Poetry at the Mermaid" Festival, London 61.
Publs. poetry: *Mixed Feelings* 51, *A Word Carved on a Sill* 56, *Weep Before God* 61, *Wildtrack* 65; novels: *Hurry on Down* 53, *Living in the Present* 55, *The Contenders* 58, *A Travelling Woman* 59, *Strike the Father Dead* 62, *The Young Visitors* 65, *The Smaller Sky* 67; criticism: *Preliminary Essays* 57, *Essays on Literature and Ideas* 63, *The Living World of Shakespeare* 64; stories: *Nuncle and other Stories* 60, *Death of the Hind Legs* 66; autobiography: *Sprightly Running* 62.
c/o Macmillan and Co. Ltd., Little Essex Street, London, W.C.2, England.

Wajda, Andrzej; Polish film director; b. 1926; ed. Acad. of Fine Arts, Cracow, and Film Acad., Łódź.
Asst. Stage Man. 53; Film Dir. 54-; Polish State prize for film *Pokolenie* (Generation), Silver Palm for *Kanal*, Cannes.
Films: *Pokolenie* (Generation) 54, *I'm Going to the Sun* 55, *Kanal* (Canal) 56, *Popiol i diament* (Ashes and Diamonds) 58, *Lotna* 59, *Niewinni czarodzieje* (Innocent Sorcerers) 59, *Samson* 60, *Syberian Lady Macbeth* 61, *Love at 20* 61, *Ashes* 65, *Gates of Paradise* 67, *Everything to Sell* 68; directed and made scenography for play *Hatful of Rain* 59, *The Devils* 63.
Z.A.F. Kamera, 21 Chetmska Street, Warsaw, Poland.

Wakabayashi, Tenjiro; Japanese textile executive; b. 29 Jan. 1907; ed. Tohoku Univ.
Wakabayashi Seishi (silk-reeling) Co. 31-, Senior Man. Dir. 56, Pres. 58; now Pres. Toho Rayon Co.; mem. Japan Chemical Fibers Asscn.
Nishikawa Building, 3-6 Nihonbashi-Tori, Chuo-ku, Tokyo, Japan.

Wakehurst, 2nd Baron, cr. 34, of Ardingly; **Capt. John de Vere Loder,** K.G., K.C.M.G.; British public servant and parliamentarian; b. 5 Feb. 1895; ed. Eton Coll.
Capt. Royal Sussex Regt. 14-18, served Gallipoli, Egypt, Palestine; Clerk in Foreign Office 19-21; Conservative M.P. for Leicester East 24-29 and for Lewes Div. of Sussex 31-36; succeeded to title April 36; Governor of New South Wales 37-46; Prior of Order of St. John of Jerusalem 48-; Chair. English-Speaking Union of the Commonwealth 46-51; Trustee Covent Garden Opera House 49-57; Gov. of Northern Ireland 52-64; Governor, The Royal Ballet 57-.
Publs. *The Truth About Mesopotamia, Syria and Palestine* 23, *Industry and the State, Bolshevism in Perspective* 31, *Colonsay and Oronsay* 35, *Our Second Chance* 44, *Preparation for Peace* 45.
31 Lennox Gardens, London S.W.1, England.
Telephone: 01-589-0956.

Wakeley, Sir Cecil (Pembrey Grey), Bt., K.B.E., C.B., M.CH., D.SC., F.R.S. (Edin.), F.R.C.S., K.ST.J; British surgeon; b. 5 May 1892; ed. Dulwich Coll., and London Univ.
Surgical Specialist Royal Navy 15-19, Surgeon Rear-Admiral 39-46; Arris and Gale Lecturer 24-25, Arnot

Demonstrator 34, Hunterian Prof. 29, 34, 37, 40, 42, Hunterian Orator 55, Thomas Vickary Lecturer 57; Erasmus Wilson Lecturer 28, 30-33, 35-38, Bradshaw Lecturer 47; Hunter Prof. and Orator, Royal Coll. of Surgeons 55, Hunterian Orator, Hunterian Soc. 61; Examiner in Surgery 33-43, Pres. Royal Coll. of Surgeons 49-54; at present Consulting Surgeon Kings' College Hospital, Senior Surgeon Royal Masonic Hospital and Belgrave Hospital for Children, Consulting Surgeon West End Hospital for Nervous Diseases and to Royal Navy 30-; Lecturer in Anatomy, London Univ. 19-; fmr. mem. and Treas. of the Gen. Medical Council; mem. Exam. Board R.N.; Vice-Pres. and Chair. Council Imperial Cancer Research Fund; Vice-Pres. British Empire Cancer Campaign; Editorial Sec. *British Journal of Surgery*; Editor *Annals of R.C.S.* 47-; Editor *Medical Press* 33-; Chair. Medical Sickness Finance Corpn., Int. Exhibition Co-operative Wine Society Ltd; Vice-Chair. Medical Sickness Society; Chair. Wakeley Bros.; Legion of Merit U.S.A.; Order of the Nile 2nd Class, Chevalier de la Légion d'Honneur, Order of Southern Cross (Brazil); Hon. F.A.C.S., Hon. F.R.A.C.S.; Hon. F.R.C.S. (Edin. and Ireland); Hon. LL.D. (Glasgow, Lahore, Leeds), Hon. D.Sc. (Delhi and Colombo).
Publs. *Modern Treatment Yearbook* 35-, *A Textbook of Surgical Pathology*; Editor: Rose and Carless' *Manual of Surgery* 22-, *Surgical Diagnosis*, Treves and Wakeley's *Handbook of Surgical Operations, Aids to Surgery, The Pineal Gland, Synopsis of Surgery, Surgery for Nurses and Medical Dictionary*.
Woodlands, Cold Ash Hill, Liphook, Hants., England.
Telephone: Liphook 3343.

Wakolbinger, Alfred, LL.D.; Austrian commercial executive; b. 17; ed. High School, Salzburg, and Univ. of Vienna.
War Service 39-45; Head of Tourism Dept., Salzburg Chamber of Commerce 45-50; mem. Salzburg Municipal Council 48-50; Dir. Carinthian Chamber of Commerce 51-63; Sec.-Gen. Austrian Federal Economic Chamber 63-67.
Gärtnergasse 2, Vienna III, Austria.

Waksman, Selman A., M.SC., PH.D.; American university professor; b. Ukraine 22 July 1888; ed. Rutgers Coll., and Univ. of Calif.
Research Asst. in Soil Microbiology, N.J. Agricultural Experiment Station 15; American citizen 16; Microbiologist, Experiment Station and Lecturer in Soil Microbiology, Rutgers Univ. 18, Assoc. Prof. 25, Prof. 30, Prof. of Microbiology and Head of Dept. 40-58, Dir. Inst. of Microbiology 49-58, Prof. Emeritus 58-; Marine Bacteriologist, Woods Hole Oceanographic Inst. 31-42, Life Trustee 42; Pres. Comm. III on Soil Microbiology, Int. Soc. of Soil Science 27-35; awards include Leeuwenhoek Medal from Netherlands Acad. of Sciences 50, Amory Award, American Acad. of Arts and Sciences 48, Nobel Prize in Physiology and Medicine 52; Commdr. de la Légion d'Honneur (France); Order of Merit of Rising Sun (Japan); Hon. Sc.D. (Rutgers, Brandeis, Princeton Univs., R.I. State Coll., etc.), Hon. LL.D. (Yeshiva Univ., and Keio Univ., Japan); Hon. D.H.L. (Hebrew Union Coll.), Hon. M.D. (Liège and Athens Univs.), Dr. h.c. (Madrid, Göttingen and Strasbourg Univs.).
Publs. 28 books alone or with others, including: *Enzymes* 26, *Principles of Soil Microbiology* 27, *The Soil and the Microbe* 32, *Humus* 36, *Microbial Antagonisms and Antibiotic Substances* 45, *The Actinomycetes* 50, *Soil Microbiology* 52, *S. N. Winogradsky, Guide to the Actinomycetes and Their Antibiotics* 53, *My Life with Microbes* 54, *The Actinomycetes*, Vol. I 59, Vol. II 61, Vol. III 62, *The Brilliant and Tragic Life of W. M. W. Haffkine, Bacteriologist* 64, *The Conquest of Tuberculosis* 64; Editor: *The Literature on Streptomycin* 48, *Strepto-*

mycin—Nature and Practical Applications 49, *Neomycin* 56, *Actinomycin* 68.
Institute of Microbiology, Rutgers University, New Brunswick, N.J., U.S.A.
Telephone: 201-247-1766.

Wal, Gerrit Van der; Netherlands airline executive; b. 4 July 1905.
Former Financial Adviser to Anthony Fokker (aircraft manufacturer); fmr. Economic Adviser to City of Rotterdam; fmr. retail executive; Chair. Royal Netherlands Industries Fair 57-63; Dep. President Koninklijke Luchtvaart Maatschappij, N.V. (K.L.M.) 63-65, President 65-.
Koninklijke Luchtvaart Maatschappij, N.V., P.O. Box 7700 Schiphoh Airport, Amsterdam, Netherlands.

Walcha, Helmut; German organist; b. 27 Oct. 1907; ed. Leipzig Inst. of Music.
Organist and Prof. of Music Frankfurt/Main 29-; Prof. Music Inst., Frankfurt/Main; Organist, Dreikönigs Kirche, Frankfurt/Main.
Hasselhorstweg 27, Frankfurt/Main, German Federal Republic.
Telephone: 16-15524.

Walczak, Stanisław, LL.D.; Polish lawyer and politician; b. 9 April 1913; ed. Uniwersytet Jagiellonski, Cracow.
Assistant Prof., Wrocław Univ. 49, Lecturer, Dept. of Penal Law 57-64, Vice-Dean of Wrocław Univ. 53-54; Assoc. Prof. of Penal Law, Warsaw Univ. 64-; Deputy Minister of Justice 57-64, Minister of Justice 65-; UN Expert in Prevention and Treatment of Offenders 61; Dir. of Research into Juvenile Delinquency, European Co-ordination Centre for Research and Documentation in Social Science, UNESCO 64; Golden Order of Merit (Poland) (twice) and other decorations.
Publs. Works on penal law and the history of social thought.
Al. I Armii Wojska Polskiego Nr. 16 ap. 6, Warsaw, Poland.

Wald, George, PH.D.; American university professor; b. 18 Nov. 1906; ed. New York Univ. and Columbia Univ., New York.
National Research Council Fellow, Kaiser Wilhelm Inst., Berlin and Heidelberg, Univ. of Zurich and Univ. of Chicago 32-34; Tutor in Biochemical Sciences, Harvard Univ. 34-35, Instructor in Biology 35-39, Faculty Instructor 39-44, Assoc. Prof. of Biology 44-48, Prof. 48-; Visiting Prof. of Biochemistry, Univ. of Calif., Berkeley 56; Nat. Sigma Xi Lecturer 52; Chair. Div. Cttee. on Biology and Medical Sciences, Nat. Science Foundation 54-56; Guggenheim Fellow 63-64; Overseas Fellow, Churchill Coll., Cambridge 63-64; mem. Nat. Acad. of Sciences; Eli Lilly Prize, American Chemical Soc. 39; Lasker Award, Public Health Asscn. 53; Procter Award, Asscn. for Research in Ophthalmology 55; Rumford Medal, American Acad. of Arts and Sciences 59; Ives Medal, Optical Soc. of America 66; Paul Karrer Medal in Chemistry, Univ. of Zürich 67; co-recipient Nobel Prize for Medicine 67.
21 Lakeview Avenue, Cambridge, Mass. 02138, U.S.A.

Waldbrunner, Karl; Austrian engineer and politician; b. 25 Nov. 1906; ed. Vienna Technical Univ.
Engaged in construction of power stations and plants in U.S.S.R. after completion of engineering studies; returned to Austria to become chief engineer of a steel works 37; active mem. of Social Democratic Party since student days; illegal political activity during German occupation; State Sec. for Commerce, Business, Industry, and Transport 45; transferred to Federal Ministry of Insurance and Economic Planning; Minister to U.S.S.R. 46; participated in Austrian Treaty negotiations in London 47-49; Sec. Socialist Party of Austria 46-56; Minister of Transport and Nationalised Industries

49-56, of Communications and of Electric Power Development 56-62; Dep. Pres. of National Council 62-.
Bickellgasse 12, Vienna 1120, Austria.
Telephone: 42-15-25.

Walden, Juuso Walfrid; Finnish company director; b. 5 April 1907; ed. Helsinki School of Economics.
Managing Dir. and Vice-Chair. United Paper Mills Ltd.; Chair. Supervisory Board of Finnish Paper Mills Asscn.; Vice-Chair. Central Asscn. of Finnish Woodworking Industries; Dir. Oulujoki Oy, Pohjolan Voima Oy, and other companies; mem. Supervisory Boards of Kansallis-Osake-Pankki, Kemijoki Oy.
Box 40, Valkeakoski, Finland.

Waldenström, Erland; Swedish civil engineer and company director; b. 4 June 1911; ed. Royal Inst. of Technology.
Engineer, Korsnäs Sågverks AB (Korsnäs Sawmill Co.) 36-40; Technical Sec., Sveriges Industriförbund (Fed. of Swedish Industries) 40-42; Expert and Sec. of govt. investigations into technical research 41-42; Dir. of Development and Research, The Swedish Cellulose Co. 42-49; Industrial Adviser E.C.E. (UN) 48; Man. Dir. Luossavaara-Kiirunavaara Aktiebolag 50-57, Trafikaktiebolaget Grängesberg-Oxelösund (The Grängesberg Co.) 50-; Dir. Skandinaviska Banken, AB Bofors, Espérance-Longdoz (Liège), Liberian American-Swedish Minerals Co., Liberian Iron Ore Ltd., Canada; Chair. Swedish Lamco Syndicate; mem. Board Fed. Swedish Industries, Swedish Employers' Confed., etc.; mem. Royal Swedish Acad. of Engineering Sciences, Royal Swedish Opera, The Concert Asscn. of Stockholm.
Publs. *Till Frågan om det industriella framåtskridandet i Sverige* (Industrial Progress in Sweden—some comments) 42, *Avfalls-och biprodukter i skogsindustrin* (Waste and By-Products in Forest Industries) 42, *Utvecklingslinjer inom skogsindustrin* (Trends of Development in Forest Industries) 46, *The Lamco Project: A Commercial Contribution to African Economic Development* 63.
Gröndal, Djurgården, Stockholm, Sweden.

Waldheim, Kurt, LL.D.; Austrian diplomatist; b. 18; ed. Consular Acad. of Vienna, Univ. of Vienna.
Entered foreign service 45; served Ministry of Foreign Affairs; mem. Austrian Del. to Paris, London and Moscow for negotiations on Austrian State Treaty; served Paris 48-51; Head of Personnel Division, Ministry of Foreign Affairs 51-55; Permanent Austrian Observer to UN 55-56; Minister to Canada 56-58, Ambassador to Canada 58-60; Dir.-Gen. for Political Affairs, Ministry for Foreign Affairs 60-64; Permanent Rep. to UN 64-; Chair. Outer Space Cttee. of UN 65-; Fed. Minister for Foreign Affairs 68-; Commandeur Légion d'Honneur, Commandeur de l'Ordre Grand Ducal de la Couronne de Chêne, Grand Officer of the Order of Orange-Nassau, Commdr. of the Dannebrog Order, Commdr. of German Order of Merit.
1014 Vienna 1, Ballhausplatz 2, Austria.
Telephone: 63-56-31.

Waldock, Sir (Claud) Humphrey (Meredith), Kt., C.M.G., O.B.E., Q.C., D.C.L.; British university professor; b. 13 Aug. 1904; ed. Uppingham School, and Brasenose Coll., Oxford.
Barrister-at-Law 28; Fellow of Brasenose Coll. 30-47; Principal Admiralty 40; Asst. Sec. 43; Principal Asst. Sec. 44-45; U.K. Commr., Italo-Yugoslav Boundary Comm. 46; attached as Under-Sec. to Foreign Office; U.K. Rep. on Comm. for Statute of Free Territory of Trieste, Paris Conf. 46; Chichele Prof. of Public Int. Law Oxford 47-; Assoc. Inst. of Int. Law 50-61, mem. 61-; mem. European Comm. of Human Rights 54, Pres. 55-61, Judge 66-; mem. Int. Law Comm. 61-; mem. Swedish-Finnish, Swedish-Swiss, Swedish-Turkish, German-Swiss, American-Danish and Chilean-Italian

Conciliation Comms.; Fellow of All Souls Coll., Oxford; Bencher Gray's Inn; Hon. Fellow Brasenose Coll.

Publs. *English Law of Mortgages* 38; Editor *The British Year Book of International Law* 56, 6th Edn. of Brierley's *Law of Nations* 63.

6 Lathbury Road, Oxford, England.

Telephone: 58227.

Wales, Prince of, and Earl of Chester (cr. 58), H.R.H. The Prince Charles Philip Arthur George, K.G., Duke of Cornwall, Duke of Rothesay, Earl of Carrick and Baron Renfrew, Lord of the Isles and Great Steward of Scotland (cr. 52); eldest son of Queen Elizabeth II and Prince Philip, Duke of Edinburgh and heir apparent to the throne of the United Kingdom of Great Britain and N. Ireland; b. 14 Nov. 1948; ed. Cheam School, Gordonstoun School and Trinity Coll., Cambridge.

Spent six months in Australia at Timbertop, branch of Geelong Church of England Grammar School 66; Counsellor of State 67; began studies at Trinity Coll., Cambridge Oct. 67; represented H.M. The Queen at memorial service for Mr. Harold Holt Dec. 67; invested and installed as Knight of the Garter, Windsor June 68; to be invested as Prince of Wales July 69.

Buckingham Palace, London, S.W.1, England.

Walgreen, Charles Rudolph, Jr.; American businessman; b. 4 March 1906; ed. Univ. of Michigan.

Druggists' Apprentice, Walgreen Co. 25, Vice-Pres. 33-39, Dir. 34-, Pres. 39-63, Chair. 63-; Dir. Sanborn Hnos., Mexico City 46-.

4300 W. Peterson Avenue, Chicago 60646, Ill., U.S.A.

Walk, Josef, D.IUR.; Austrian business executive; b. 22 May 1902; ed. High School, Linz, and Univ. of Vienna.

Private law practice, official at Directorate of Finance, Linz, later Pres.; Mayor and Financial Dir., City of Steyr 34-38; County Govt., Upper Austria 38-45; Town Councillor, Linz 49-55, Vice-Mayor 55-59; Dep. Gen. Manager and Dep. Chair. Board of Dirs. Vereinigte Österreichische Eisen-und Stahlwerke A.G., Linz (Voest) 59-; mem. Supervisory Board Bank für Oberösterreich und Salzburg, Linz; Dep. Chair. Board of Dirs. several other companies; Grosses Ehrenzeichen für Verdienste um die Republik Österreich.

Freinbergstrasse 10, 4020 Linz/Donau, Austria.

Telephone: 07222-27164.

Walker, Ardis Manly, B.S.; American engineer, poet and writer; b. 1 April 1901; ed. Univ. of California, and Univ. of Southern California.

Mem. Technical Staff Bell Telephone Laboratories, New York City 27-32; poet and writer on American-Indian lore and early Californian history; also lecturer.

Publs. *Quatrains* (verse), *Muse, American Lyric Poetry, Sierra Prologue, Poets on Parade, Poetry Digest, The Winged Word, Mission Sonnets, Francisco Garces, Man and Missionary, Pioneer Padre, The Manly Story, Judas on the Kern, Sierra Sonnets, Last Gunmen, Freeman Junction, Walker Pass, Borax Smith: an Evaluation, Kern River Vignettes, The Rough and the Righteous.*

P.O. Box 37, Kernville, Calif., U.S.A.

Telephone: 376-6296.

Walker, Edwin Hodges, B.I.E., LL.D.; Canadian engineer; b. 27 April 1909; ed. Delta Collegiate Inst., Hamilton, Ontario, and General Motors Inst., Flint, Michigan.

Asst. to Gen. Man., McKinnon Industries Ltd., St. Catharines, Ontario 51-53, Pres. and Gen. Man. 53-57; Pres. and Gen. Man. General Motors of Canada Ltd., Oshawa, Ontario; Vice-Pres. and mem. Admin. Cttee. General Motors Corpn. 64-; Canadian and Overseas Policy Cttee.; Hon. Dr. (Univ. of Montreal).

124 Park Road North, Oshawa, Ontario, Canada.

Walker, Eric Anderson, M.A.; British historian; b. 6 Sept. 1886; ed. Mill Hill School, and Merton Coll., Oxford.

Lecturer in History Bristol Univ. 08-11; Prof. Cape Town 11-36; Fellow St. John's Coll. Cambridge 36-; Vere Harmsworth Prof. of History, Cambridge Univ. 36-51, Emeritus 51-; Adviser to the Editors of *Cambridge History of the British Empire*, Vol. VIII, *South Africa*, Joint Editor *C.H.B.E.*, Vol. III and Vol. VIII (2nd edn.); Hon. Dr. Litt. (Witwatersrand).

Publs. *Historical Atlas of S. Africa* 22, *Lord de Villiers and His Times* 25, *Modern History for S. Africans, A History of South Africa* 28, 40, *The S.A. College and the University of Cape Town* 29, *The Frontier Tradition in South Africa* 30, *The Great Trek* 60, *C.H.B.E., Vol VIII*, Chaps. xv, xxii, xxviii 36, *W. P. Schreiner: A South African* 37, *C.H.B.E., Vol. II, Chap. xv* 40, *South Africa* 40, 41, *Britain and South Africa* 41, *The British Empire: Its Structure and Spirit* 43, *Colonies* 44, *A History of Southern Africa* 57.

St. John's College, Cambridge, England.

Walker, John, B.A.; American art museum director; b. 24 Dec. 1906; ed. Harvard Univ., and with Berenson in Florence.

Assoc. in charge of Fine Arts, American Acad. in Rome 35-39; Chief Curator, Nat. Gallery of Art, Washington 39-, and Dir. 56-; Trustee American Acad. in Rome, American Fed. of Arts, Nat. Trust for Historic Preservation, A. W. Mellon Educational & Charitable Trust, Los Angeles County Museum of Arts; mem. Advisory Council, Inst. of Fine Arts of New York Univ., Fed. Council on Arts and Humanities, Comm. for the Nat. Portrait Gallery, Ctee. for Preservation of the White House, Art Cttee. of the N.Y. Hospital; Board of Advisers of Dumbarton Oaks; Treas. White House Historical Asscn.; Hon. D.F.A. (Tufts, Brown Univs., La Salle Coll.); Hon. D.Litt. (Notre Dame, Washington and Jefferson Univs.), and other hon. degrees; Officier de la Légion d'Honneur.

Publs. *A Guide to the Gardens and Villas of Italy* (with Amey Aldrich) 38; edited: *Great American Paintings from Smibert to Bellows 1729-1924* (with Macgill James) 43, *Masterpieces of Painting from the National Gallery of Art* (with Huntington Cairns) 44, *Great Paintings from the National Gallery of Art* (with Huntington Cairns) 52; *Paintings from America* 51, *Bellini and Titian at Ferrara* 56, *The National Gallery of Art, Washington* 56, *Treasures from the National Gallery of Art* (with Huntington Cairns) 62, *The National Gallery of Art, Washington, D.C.* 63, *Pageant of Painting* 66.

Office: National Gallery of Art, Constitution Avenue, Washington 20565, D.C.; Home: 2806 N. Street, N.W., Washington, D.C. 20007, U.S.A.

Walker, John Charles, M.S., PH.D.; American plant pathologist; b. 6 July 1893; ed. Univ. of Wisconsin.

Asst. in Plant Pathology, Univ. of Wisconsin 14-17, Instr. 19, Asst. Prof. 19-25, Assoc. Prof. 25-28, Prof. 28-64, Prof. Emer. 64-; Scientific Asst., U.S. Dept. of Agriculture 17-19, Asst. Pathologist 19-25, Agent 25-45, Collaborator 45-; mem. Nat. Acad. of Sciences, American Phytopathological Soc., Botanical Soc. of America, American Soc. of Naturalists.

Publs. *Diseases of Vegetable Crops* 52, *Plant Pathology* 50 (3rd edn. 68).

Home: 809 Oneida Place, Madison, Wis. 53711; Office: Russell Laboratories, Madison, Wis. 53706, U.S.A.

Telephone: 233-1071.

Walker, Sir (Charles) Michael, K.C.M.G.; British diplomatist; b. 22 Nov. 1916; ed. Charterhouse, and New Coll., Oxford.

Army service 39-45; Dominions Office 47-49; First Sec. British Embassy, Washington 49-51; Office of High Commr., Calcutta and New Delhi 52-55; Establishment

Officer Commonwealth Relations Office 55-58; Imperial Defence Coll. 58-59; Asst. Under-Sec. of State and Dir. of Establishments and Org., Commonwealth Relations Office 59-62; High Commr. in Ceylon 62-65, in Malaysia 66-.
c/o D.S.A.O. (Kuala Lumpur Bag), King Charles Street, London, S.W.1; and Long Tarrant, Burwood Park, Walton-on-Thames, Surrey, England.

Walker, Ralph; American architect; b. 28 Nov. 1889; ed. Mass. Inst. of Technology.
Joined staff of Voorhees, Walker, Smith, Smith and Haines (now named Smith, Haines, Lundberg and Waehler) 19, assoc. mem. 20, partner 26, consultant 59; served in First World War; American Inst. of Architects (Pres. 49-51, Centennial Gold Medal, Gold Medal of Honor N.Y. and Philadelphia Chapters); mem. Nat. Inst. Arts and Letters; Academician Nat. Acad. of Design; hon. corresp. mem. R.I.B.A., B.D.A., and Philippine Inst. of Architects; Union Int. des Architectes (V.-P. 48-56); Allied Professional mem. Nat. Sculpture Society; mem. American Inst. of Planners, American Soc. of Planning Officials, Comm. of Fine Arts, Washington, D.C. 59-63, etc.; Consultant, N.Y. City Housing Authority 33; Chevalier Légion d'Honneur; Officer Order of the Crown (Belgium).
Works include: N.Y. Telephone Headquarters Building, Western Union Telegraph Building, Irving Trust Co. Building, N.Y. City, Bell Telephone Laboratories, Murray Hill, N.J., Library, Mass. Inst. Technology, town for Nicaro Nickel Co., Cuba, etc.
Publs. *London* 43, *Humans-Materials-Architectures* 48, *Vidi* 51, *Ralph Walker, Architect* 57, *The Fly in the Amber* 57.
2 Park Avenue, New York, N.Y. 10016, U.S.A.

Walker, Robert B.; American tobacco executive; b. 27 Oct. 1913; ed. Cape Vincent High School.
The American Tobacco Co. 37-, Exec. Sales Manager 53-55, Dir. of Sales 55-57, mem. Board of Dirs. 55-, Vice-Pres. (Sales) 57-61, Vice-Pres. (Advertising and Sales) 61-62, Exec. Vice-Pres. 62-63, Pres. and Chief Exec. Officer 63-, Chair. of Board 65-.
The American Tobacco Co., 245 Park Avenue, New York, N.Y. 10017, U.S.A.
Telephone: 557-7000.

Walker, Sir (Edward) Ronald, C.B.E., M.A., PH.D., LITT.D.; Australian economist and diplomatist; b. 26 Jan. 1907; ed. Univ. of Sydney, and Cambridge Univ.
Lecturer in Economics, Univ. of Sydney 27-38; Prof. of Economics, Univ. of Tasmania 39-46; Economic Adviser, N.S.W. Treasury 38-39, Govt. of Tasmania 39-42; Deputy Dir.-Gen. Australian Dept. of War Organisation of Industry 42-45; Economic Counsellor for Europe and Counsellor, Australian Embassy, Paris 45-50; Exec. mem. Australian Nat. Security Resources Board 50-52; Ambassador to Japan 52-55, to U.N. 56-59; and Australian Rep. on the Security Council 56-57; Chair. UNESCO Exec. Board 47-48, Pres. UNESCO Gen. Conf. 49; Chair. U.N. Experts on Full Employment 49; Australian Rep. on Disarmament Comm. 56-58, on Econ. and Social Council 62-64, (Pres. 64), Advisory Cttee. on Application of Science and Technology 64-; Amb. to France 59-68, to German Fed. Repub. 68-.
Publs. *An Outline of Australian Economics* 31, *Australia in the World Depression* 33, *Money* (co-author) 35, *Unemployment Policy* 36, *War-time Economics* 39, *From Economic Theory to Policy* 42, *The Australian Economy in War and Reconstruction* 47, *National and International Measures for Full Employment* (in collab.) 50.
Australian Embassy, Bonn, German Federal Republic.

Wallace, Col. the Hon. Clarence, K.ST.J., C.B.E., LL.D.; Canadian company director; b. 22 June 1894; ed. St. Andrew's Coll., Toronto.
Sec. Treas. Burrard Dry Dock Co. Ltd. 21-28, Pres. 29; Vice-Pres. Cassiar Packing Co. Ltd.; Pres. Yarrows Ltd., Victoria B.C.; Dir. British Pacific Properties Ltd., Park Royal Shopping Centre Ltd., Canada Trust Co., Ocean Cement and Supplies Ltd., Canadian Western Pipe Mills Ltd., Consolidated Properties Ltd.; Lt.-Gov. British Columbia 50-55.
508-700 Chilco Street, Vancouver 5, B.C., Canada.
Telephone: MU2-2300 (Home).

Wallace, Dan(iel Philip), B.A., M.A.; Canadian government officer; b. 27 Sept. 1910; ed. St. Mary's Coll., Dalhousie Univ., Halifax, Nova Scotia, Oxford Univ., St. Francis Xavier Univ., Nova Scotia and Harvard Univ.
Associate Prof. of English, St. Francis Xavier Univ. 36-38; Chief Instructor, St. Frances Xavier Contingent, Canadian Army 39-40; Research Editor, Wartime Information Board, Ottawa 42; Sec. Nat. Film Board, Ottawa 42-47; Exec. Asst. to Minister, Dept. of Nat. Health and Welfare, Ottawa 47-54; Chief Sec. Dept. of Nat. Defence, Ottawa 54-56; Exec. Officer to Prime Minister 57; Dir. of Travel and Information, Province of Nova Scotia, Halifax 58-61; Asst. Dir. Canadian Govt. Travel Bureau, Ottawa 61-65, Dir. 65-; Dir. Canadian Tourist Asscn.; Del. to int. travel confs. in France, Germany, Bulgaria, Mexico, Australia and India.
Canadian Government Travel Bureau, 150 Kent Street, Kent Building, Ottawa; Home: 1823 Beattie Avenue, Ottawa, Ont., Canada.

Wallace, DeWitt; American publisher; b. 12 Nov. 1889; ed. California Univ.
With Webb publishing Co. 11-15, Brown and Bigelow 16; sergeant in U.S. Army 17-19; Founder-Editor *Reader's Digest* 21-65, relinquished some control to Pres. 65.
Mount Kisco, N.Y., U.S.A.

Wallace, Doreen (Mrs. D. E. A. Rash), M.A.; British writer; b. 18 June 1897; ed. Malvern Girls' Coll., and Somerville Coll., Oxford.
Fmr. teacher; anti-tithe publicist; novelist and reviewer.
Publs. *Esques* (with E. F. A. Geach) 18, *A Little Learning, The Gentle Heart, The Portion of the Levites, Creatures of an Hour, Even Such is Time, The Tithe War* 33, *Barnham Rectory* 34, *Latter Howe* 35, *Going to Sea* 36, *Old Father Antic* 37, *The Faithful Compass* 37, *The Time of Wild Roses* 38, *A Handful of Silver* 39, *East Anglia* 39, *English Lakeland* 40, *The Spring Returns* 40, *Green Acres* 41, *Land from the Waters* 44, *Carlotta Green* 44, *The Noble Savage* 45, *Billy Potter* 46, *Willow Farm* 48, *How Little We Know* 49, *Only One Life* 50, *In a Green Shade* 50, *Root of Evil* 52, *Sons of Gentlemen* 53, *The Younger Son* 54, *Daughters* 55, *The Interloper* 56, *The Money Field* 57, *Forty Years On* 58, *Richard and Lucy* 59, *Mayland Hall* 60, *Lindsay Langton and Wives* 61, *Woman with a Mirror* 63, *The Mill Pond* 66, *Ashbury People* 68.
Wortham Manor, Diss, Norfolk, England.
Telephone: Diss 2763.

Wallace, George Corley; American lawyer and politician; b. 25 Aug. 1919; ed. Univ. of Alabama.
Former state judge, Alabama; fmr. mem. Alabama State Legislature; Gov. of Alabama 63-67; Democrat.
142 S. Peny Street, Montgomery, Alabama, U.S.A.

Wallace, William Stewart, M.A., LL.D., F.R.S.C.; Canadian historian; b. 23 June 1884; ed. Toronto and Oxford Univs.
Professor of English and History Western Univ. 06-07; Prof. of History McMaster Univ. Toronto 09-20; Asst.

and Associate Librarian Univ. of Toronto 20-23, Librarian 23-54, Librarian Emer. 54-; Hon. Sec. Champlain Soc. 21-43, Pres. 43-47; Hon. Editor 48-51; Editor *Canadian Historical Review* 20-30; Gen. Editor *Encyclopaedia of Canada* (6 vols.) 35-37; Fellow Royal Soc. of Canada (Pres. Section 2, 38-39); Pres. Canadian Library Asscn. 50-51.

Publs. *Dictionary of Canadian Biography* 26, *History of the University of Toronto* 27, *Murders and Mysteries* 31, *Memoirs of Sir G. Foster* 33; Edited *Documents Relating to the North-West Company* 34, *Dictionary of Canadian Biography* (new and revised edn.) 48, *Royal Canadian Institute Centennial Volume* 49, *Dictionary of North American Authors* 51, *The Pedlars from Quebec and Other Papers on the Nor' Westers* 54, *The Ryerson Imprint* 55, Umfreville's *The Present State of Hudson's Bay* 55, *The Knight of Dundurn* 60.

16 Rosedene Road, Toronto, Ont., Canada.

Wallef, Louis; Belgian engineer and business executive; b. 13 Sept. 1901; ed. Université Catholique de Louvain.

Union Minière 26-, Pres. of Perm. Cttee. 63-, Chair. 65-; Chair. Compagnie du Congo pour le Commerce et l'Industrie 64-; Dir. Soc. Générale de Belgique 57-; Officier Ordre Royal du Lion, Chevalier Ordre de la Couronne, Commdr. Ordre de Léopold II.

6 rue Montagne du Parc, Brussels 1, Belgium.
Telephone: 13-60-90.

Wallenberg, Jacob; Swedish banker; b. 27 Sept. 1892; ed. School of Economics Stockholm.

Asst. Man. Stockholms Enskilda Bank 18, Vice-Man. Dir. and mem. Board 20, Man. Dir. 27-46, Vice-Chair. of Board 46-50, Chair. 50-; Chair. Förvaltnings AB Providentia, AB Investor, Stora Kopparbergs Bergslags AB, AB Svenska Kullagerfabriken, Alfa-Laval AB, AB Astra, Orkla Grube AB, Svenska Tändsticks AB; Bergvik och Ala AB; mem. Board Nobel Foundation 52-; Chair. of Board, Knut and Alice Wallenberg Foundation 66-; Dr. h.c. (Econ.) and Dr. med. h.c.; Hon. mem. Royal Swedish Acad. of Eng. Sciences; Commdr. Grand Cross Order of Vasa, Commdr. Grand Cross Order of Polar Star.

Strandvägen 27, Stockholm; Office: Kungsträdgårdsgatan 8, Stockholm C, Sweden.
Telephone: 22-19-00.

Wallenberg, Marc, Jr.; Swedish banker; b. 28 June 1924; ed. Harvard Graduate Business School.

Assistant Vice-President, Stockholms Enskilda Bank 53-55, Vice-Pres. and mem. Board 55, Vice Managing Dir. 56-58, Managing Dir. 58-; Chair. A.B. Nordströms Linbanor, Svenska Dataregister A.B.; Dir. Atlas Copco A.B., Orkla Grube A.B., A.B. Papyrus, Aug. Stenman A.B., A.B. Svenska Järnvägsverkstäderna, Wikmanshytte Bruks A.B., Goodyear Gummifabriks A.B., A.B. Svenska Ostasiatiska Kompaniet; Chair. British-Swedish Chamber of Commerce 64-66, Hon. Vice-Pres. 66-; Treas. Swedish Nat. Cttee. of Int. Chamber of Commerce 64-, Stockholm School of Econs. 66-; mem. of Board, Knut and Alice Wallenberg Foundation; Knight of Royal Order of Vasa (Sweden) and other foreign decorations.

Stockholms Enskilda Bank, Stockholm 16; Home:. Strandvägen 63, II Stockholm No, Sweden.
Telephone: 22-19-00 (Office).

Wallenberg, Marcus; Swedish banker and financier; b. 5 Oct. 1899.

Assistant Managing-Dir. Stockholms Enskilda Bank 25, Dep. Managing Dir. 27-46, Managing Dir. 46-58, Vice-Chair. 58-; Swedish Del. trade negotiations with Great Britain 39-43, Finland 40-44, and Great Britain and U.S.A. 43-44; Chair. and Dir. of many companies; Chair. Swedish Banks Asscn. 49-51 and 55-57, Industrial Inst. for Econ. and Social Research 50-; Vice-

Chair. and Chair. Fed. of Swedish Industries 59-64; Chair. Council of European Industrial Feds. (C.E.I.F.) 60-63, Business and Industrial Advisory Cttee. to O.E.C.D. (B.I.A.C.) 62-64; Chair. Swedish Nat. Cttee. Int. Chamber of Commerce 51-64, Hon. Chair. 64-; Pres. Int. Chamber of Commerce 65-67; mem. of Board, Knut and Alice Wallenberg Foundation; Dr. h.c. (Royal Inst. of Technology, Stockholm).

Stockholms Enskilda Bank, 8 Kungsträdgårdsgatan, Stockholm, Sweden.

Wallenreiter, Christian; German broadcasting official; b. 1900; ed. Augsburger Gymnasium St. Stephans and Universitäten München and Marburg.

Provincial Government of Rhineland-Palatinate, later with Bavarian local authorities, later with Govt. at Augsburg 27-51; Adviser on Educational Arts, Bavarian Ministry of Culture 52-58, Head of Dept. of Elementary, High and Vocational Schools and Teachers' and Adults' Training Colleges, Bavarian Ministry of Culture 58-60; Dir.-General of Bayerischer Rundfunk 60-; Pres. ARD (Arbeitsgemeinschaft der öffentlich-rechtlichen Rundfunkanstalten der Bundesrepublik Deutschland) 67-.

Rundfunkplatz 1, 8 Munich 2, German Federal Republic.
Telephone: 59001.

Waller, Ivar, PH.D.; Swedish physicist; b. 11 June 1898; ed. Uppsala Univ.

Lecturer Uppsala Univ. 25, Prof. and Dir. Inst. for Theoretical Physics 34-64, Emeritus 64-; mem. Swedish Acad. of Sciences, Reg. Soc. Uppsala, Royal Physiographical Soc. Lund, Det Norske Videnskapsakademie, Oslo; Dr. h.c., Leiden 65.

Publ. *Theoretische Studien zur Interferenz- und Dispersionstheorie der Röntgenstrahlen* 25.

Institute for Theoretical Physics, Uppsala; Trädgårdsgatan 10, Uppsala, Sweden.
Telephone: 018-115159 (Office); 018-136075 (Home).

Waller, Sir John Keith, Kt., C.B.E.; Australian diplomatist; b. 19 Feb. 1914; ed. Scotch Coll., Melbourne, and Univ. of Melbourne.

Mem. Dept. of External Affairs 36-37; Personal Sec. W. M. Hughes 37-40; Second Sec. Australian Legation Chungking 41; Sec.-Gen. Australian del. San Francisco Conf. 45; First Sec. Australian Legation Rio de Janiero 45; Chargé d'Affaires 46 and First Sec. 47 Washington; Consul-Gen. Manila 48; Officer in charge Political Intelligence Division Canberra 50; External Affairs Officer, London 51; Ambassador to Thailand 57-60, to U.S.S.R. 60-62; First Asst. Sec. Dept. of External Affairs 62-64; Ambassador to U.S.A. 64-.

Australian Embassy, 1700 Massachusetts Avenue, N.W., Washington, D.C., U.S.A.

Wallgren, Arvid Johan, F.R.C.P.; Swedish professor of pediatrics; b. 5 Oct. 1889; ed. Uppsala Univ.

Assistant Professor of Internal Medicine, Uppsala Univ. 21; Head, Children's Hospital, Gothenburg 21-43; Prof. of Pediatrics, Royal Caroline Medical School 43-56; Head, Norrtull Children's Hospital 43-51, of Pediatric Clinic Karol Sjukh 51-56; Pres. WHO Scientific Cttee. of Medical Research 59-63; Hon. Dr. (Zürich, Paris, Algiers, Santiago, Cardiff, Havana Univs.).

Pediatric Clinic, Karolinska Sjukhuset, Stockholm 60, Sweden.
Telephone: 33-91-43.

Wallinger, Sir Geoffrey Arnold, G.B.E., K.C.M.G., British diplomatist; b. 2 May 1903; ed. Sherborne School, and Clare Coll., Cambridge.

Entered Diplomatic Service 26; Sec., Cairo 27-29; Vienna 29-31; Foreign Office 31-34; on staff of U.K. High Commr. in S. Africa 35-38; Head of Chancery, Buenos Aires 38-42; First Sec., Foreign Office 43;

Counsellor, China 43-47 (local rank of Min. 45); Head of Southern Dept., Foreign Office 47-49; Minister to Hungary 49-51; Ambassador to Thailand 51-54, to Austria 54-58; Ambassador to Brazil 58-63; Dir. Bank of London and South America.
10 Moore Street, London, S.W.3, England.
Telephone: 01-584-2035.

Wallis, Sir Barnes Neville, Kt., C.B.E., F.R.S., M.I.C.E.; British aeronautical engineer; b. 26 Sept. 1887; ed. Christ's Hospital.
Trained as Marine Engineer with J. S. White and Co. Ltd.; Asst. Chief Designer, Vickers Ltd. 13-15; Army and R.N. A.S. 15; Chief Designer, Airship Dept., Vickers Ltd. 16-21; Chief Engineer, Airship Guarantee Co. (responsible for design and construction of R.100) 23-30; Chief Designer, Structures, Vickers Aviation Ltd. 30-37; Asst. Chief Designer, Vickers-Armstrongs Ltd., Aviation Section 37-45; Chief of Dept. of Aeronautical Research and Development, British Aircraft Corpn. (Operating) Ltd. 45-; Royal Designer for Industry; R.Ae.S. Silver Medal 28, 37; Ewing Medal, I.C.E. 45; Founder's Medal, Air League 62; Hon. Fellow Churchill Coll., Cambridge; Inst. of Science & Technology, Univ. of Manchester; Senior Fellow Royal Coll. of Art; Hon. D.Sc. (Bristol, London, Cambridge, Loughborough, Oxford); Hon. M.I.M.E., F.S.E., F.S.I.A., F.R.AE.S.
White Hill House, Effingham, Surrey, England.
Telephone: Weybridge 45555.

Wallis, Mieczyslaw, PH.D.; Polish writer and professor of history of art; b. 16 June 1895; ed. Univs. of Heidelberg and Warsaw.
Art Critic of *Robotnik* (The Worker) 19-34, of the *Wiadomości Literackie* (The Literary News) 34-39; Lecturer, Nat. Inst. of Theatrical Art in Warsaw 36-37; fought against the Germans 39; German prisoner of war 39-45; Chief, Section for Int. Co-operation, Polish Ministry of Culture and Art 45; Prof. of Aesthetics, Univ. of Łódź 45-51, Prof. of History of Art 51-65; Prof. of the Nat. Higher Theatrical School, Łódź 46-49; Prof. Nat. Higher Film School, Łódź 49-50; Dean Faculty of History 55-56; mem. Łódź Scientific Society.
Publs. *Expression and Mental Life* 39, *Canaletto, the Painter of Warsaw* 54, *A History of the Mirror* 56, *Polish Art between the Two Wars* 59, *Stanislaw Noakowski's Land of Childhood* 60, *Painters and Cities* 61, *Self-portrait* 64, *Noakowski* 65; *Self-portraits of Polish Artists* 66, *Art Nouveau* 67; monographs on Polish painters, etc.
Brzozowa 12, Warsaw, Poland.
Telephone: 31-60-54.

Walrath, Laurence Kaye; American lawyer and government official; b. 16 Aug. 1909; ed. Emory Univ. Acad., and Univ. of Florida.
Admitted to Florida Bar 34, Assoc. Albion W. Knight, Jacksonville 34-39; Assoc. Knight and Knight 39-41, Partner 41-45, Knight, Knight, Walrath and Pegues 46-53, Knight, Walrath, Kincaid and Young 53-56; Commr. Interstate Commerce Comm. 56-63, Chair. 63-; U.S. Naval Service 42-45.
Interstate Commerce Commission, Twelfth Street and Constitution Avenue, N.W., Washington, D.C. 20423; Home: The Berkshire, 4201 Massachusetts Avenue, N.W., Washington, D.C. 20016, U.S.A.

Walser, Martin, DR. PHIL.; German writer; b. 24 March 1927; ed. Theologisch-Philosophische Hochschule, Regensburg, and Univ. of Tübingen.
Writer 51-; Group 47 Prize 55, Hermann-Hesse Prize 57, Gerhart-Hauptmann Prize 62, Schiller Prize 65.
Publs. short stories: *Ein Flugzeug über dem Haus* 55, *Lügengeschichten* 64; novels: *Ehen in Philippsburg* 57, *Halbzeit* 60, *Das Einhorn* 66; plays: *Der Abstecher* 61, *Eiche und Angora* 62, *Überlebensgross Herr Krott* 63, *Der Schwarze Schwan* 64, *Die Zimmerschlacht* 67; essays:

Beschreibung einer Form, Versuch über Franz Kafka 61, *Erfahrungen und Leseerfahrungen* 65.
Zeppelinstrasse 18, 799 Friedrichshafen/Bodensee, German Federal Republic.
Telephone 3477.

Walsh, Lieut.-Commdr. Don; American naval officer; b. 31; ed. San Diego State Coll. and U.S. Naval Acad.
Entered navy 50, submarine service 56; became Officer-in-Charge Submersible Test Group and Bathyscaph *Trieste* 59, made record dive to 35,780 ft., Jan. 60; Submarine service 62-64; at Dept. of Oceanography, Texas A. & M. Univ. 65-; mem. American Geophysical Union, American Asscn. for Advancement of Science etc.; Dir. American Soc. for Oceanography; Legion of Merit; Gold Medals from City of Trieste and Chicago Socs. and other awards.
Department of Oceanography, Texas A. & M. University College Station, Texas 77843, U.S.A.
Telephone: 713-846-4791.

Walsh, Joseph Leonard, S.M., PH.D.; American mathematician; b. 21 Sept. 1895; ed. Harvard Univ., and Wisconsin Univ.
Asst. in Maths., Harvard Univ. 15-16, Instr. 17, 19-20, 21-24, Asst. Prof. 24-30, Assoc. Prof. 30-35, Prof. 35-66; Ensign U.S.N.R.F. 18, Lieut. (j.g.) 19, Lieut.-Commdr. U.S.N.R. 42, Commdr. 44, Capt. 52, retd. 55; Perkins Prof. Mathematics, Harvard Univ. 46-66, emeritus 66-; Prof. of Mathematics, Univ. of Maryland 65-; Consultant Nat. Bureau of Standards 51-52; mem. American Acad. of Arts and Sciences, Nat. Acad. of Sciences; Vice-Pres. American Asscn. for Advancement of Science 44, 61; Pres. American Mathematical Society 49-50.
Publs. *Interpolation and Approximation by Polynomials* 35, *Interpolation and Approximation by Rational Functions* 35, *The Location of Critical Points* 50, *The Theory of Splines and Their Application* 57, *Interpolation by Bounded Analytic Functions* 60.
Department of Mathematics, University of Maryland, College Park, Md. 20740, U.S.A.
Telephone: 779-0434.

Walston, Baron, cr. 61 (Life Peer) of Newton, Cambridge; **Henry David Leonard George Walston,** J.P., M.A.; British farmer and politician; b. 6 June 1912; ed. Eton, and King's Coll., Cambridge.
Research Fellow in Bacteriology, Harvard Univ. 34-35; mem. Hunts. War Agricultural Cttee. 39-45, Cambs. Agricultural Cttee. 48-50; Dir. of Agriculture, British Zone of Germany 46-47; Agricultural Adviser for Germany to Foreign Office 47-48; Counsellor of Duchy of Lancaster 48-54; Trustee Rural Industries Bureau; mem. Home Office Cttee. on Experiments on Living Animals May 63-64; Deputy Chair. Council of Royal Commonwealth Soc. April 63-64; Parliamentary Under-Sec. of State for Foreign Affairs 64-67; Parl. Sec., Board of Trade Jan.-Aug. 67; Labour.
Publs. *From Forces to Farming* 44, *Our Daily Bread* 52, *No More Bread* 54, *Life on the Land* (with John Mackie) 54, *Land Nationalisation, For and Against* 58, *Agriculture under Communism* 61, *The Farmer and Europe* 62.
Newton Hall, Newton, Cambridge, England.
Telephone: Harston 461.

Waltari, Mika; Finnish writer; b. 19 Sept. 1908; ed. Helsinki Univ.
Literary Critic *Maaseudun Tulevaisuus* 32-42, Finnish Radio 37-38; Editor *Suomen Kuvalehti* 36-38, State Information Office 39-40, 41-44; mem. Finnish Acad.; Pro Finlandia award 52, Commdr. Finnish Lion 60, etc.
Publs. *The Egyptian* 49, *Michael the Finn* 50, *The Sultan's Renegade* 51, *The Dark Angel* 53, *A Nail-Merchant at Nightfall* 55, *Moonscape* 56, *The Etruscan* 56, *The Tongue of Fire* 58, *The Secret of the Kingdom* 61, *The Tree of Dreams* 65, *The Roman* 66.
Tunturikatu 13, Helsinki 10, Finland.

Walter, John, M.A.; British newspaper proprietor; b. 73; ed. Eton and Christ Church, Oxford.
Co-chief proprietor *The Times*, Chair. 10-23.
69 The Drive, Hove, Sussex, England.

Walter, William Grey, M.A., SC.D.; British neuro-physiologist; b. 19 Feb. 1910; ed. Westminster School, and King's Coll., Cambridge.
Director Physiological Dept. Burden Neurological Inst., Bristol 39-; founder and Foreign Sec. Electroen-cephalographical Soc. 42; co-founder Int. Fed. of Socs. for Electroencephalography and Clinical Neurophysio-logy (Hon. Pres.), *Electroencephalography and Clinical Neurophysiology* (co-editor) 47; mem. WHO Study Group on Psychobiological Development of the Child 53-56; co-founder and Council mem. Int. Asscn. of Cybernetics 56; mem. UNESCO Study Group for Establishment of Int. Brain Research Org. 59-60.
Publs. *The Living Brain* 53, *Further Outlook* (*The Curve of the Snowflake*) 56; numerous papers.
35 Mariner's Drive, Bristol 9, England.
Telephone: 68-2412.

Walters, Basil L.; American journalist; b. 3 May 1896; ed. Indiana Univ.
Editor U.S. Army newspaper Italy 18; corresp. and telegraph editor *Milwaukee Journal* 19-28; Man. Editor *Des Moines Register-Tribune* 28-37; Exec. Editor *Minneapolis Star Journal* and *Tribune* 37-44; Exec. Editor Knight newspapers, *Detroit Free Press*, *Akron Beacon Journal*, *Chicago Daily News*, and *Miami Herald* 44-59; Ed. *Chicago Daily News* 59-61; Pres. Newspaper Research Asscn., Chicago 61-; Pres. Managing Editors' Asscn. 35, 42, 43; Pres. American Soc. of Newspaper Editors 53-54.
Route 3, Frankfort, Ind., U.S.A.
Telephone: 654-4310.

Walters, Herbert Sanford; American banker and politician; b. 17 Nov. 1891; ed. Carson Newman Coll., Castle Heights, and Tennessee Univ.
Engineering Dept., Chicago, Milwaukee and St. Paul Railway 11-14, Ill. Central Rail Road, Chicago 14-16; Partner, Harrison, Walters and Prater 26-, Pres. Walters and Prater Inc., Gen. Contractors 22-; Pres. Hamilton Nat. Bank, Morristown 46-; Commr. State Dept. Highways and Public Works, Nashville 34-35; Pres., Dir. Cherokee Broadcasting Corpn. 47-; Dir. Nashville Gas and Heating Co., E. Tennessee Natural Gas Co. 47-, Hamilton Nat. Bank, Knoxville 47-; mem. Nat. Dem. Cttee. from Tenn. 45-47, 56, Chair. State Dem. Exec. Cttee. 40-44, 53-; U.S. Senator from Tenn. Aug. 63-65 (apptd. to fill remainder of term of the late Senator Estes Kefauver).
Hamilton National Bank Building, Morristown, Tennessee; and 620 W. 2nd North Street, Morristown, Tennessee, U.S.A.
Telephone: 586-7321 (Office); 586-9309 (Home).

Walther, Gebhardt von; German diplomatist; b. 19 Dec. 1902; ed. Univs. of Cologne and Göttingen.
Attaché, Foreign Office, Berlin 29-32; Vice-Consul, Beirut 32-34; Consulate-Gen., Memel 34-36; Sec. Moscow 36-41; Consul Tripoli 41-43; Counsellor, Ankara 43-45; worked in German machine tool industry 45-51; Minister, Paris 51-56; Ambassador to Mexico 56-58, to Brazil 58-59; Perm. German Rep. to NATO 59-62; Amb. to Turkey 62-66, to U.S.S.R. 66-68.
c/o Ministry of Foreign Affairs, Bonn, German Federal Republic.

Walther, Henri; Swiss lawyer; b. 6 Feb. 1904; ed. Univ. of Lausanne.
Member of Secretariat, Central Comm. for the Naviga-tion of the Rhine 29-40, Sec.-Gen. 46-; Lawyer, Laus-anne 41-43; mem. Foreign Affairs Dept., Federal Political Dept. 43-45; Pres. Study Cttee. for River Law at Int. Inst. for Unification of Private Law, Rome 62.

Publs. *L'affaire du Lotus ou de l'abordage hauturier en droit pénal international* 29, *La jurisprudence de la Commission Centrale du Rhin de 1832 à 1939* 48, and legal articles on Rhine navigation.
Palais du Rhin, 2 Place de la République, Strasbourg, France.
Telephone: 32-35-84.

Walton, Ernest Thomas Sinton, M.A., M.SC., PH.D.; Irish university professor; b. 6 Oct. 1903; ed. Methodist Coll., Belfast, Trinity Coll., Dublin, and Cambridge Univ.
Fellow Trinity Coll. Dublin 34-, Erasmus Smith's Prof. of Natural and Experimental Philosophy 46-; awarded Hughes Medal, Royal Society (jointly with Sir John Cockcroft) 38; Nobel Prize in Physics (jointly with Sir John Cockcroft) 51, for pioneer work in the field of nuclear physics; Hon. D.Sc. (Belfast Univ.) 59.
26 St. Kevin's Park, Dartry Road, Dublin, Ireland.
Telephone: 971-328.

Walton, Sir William Turner, Kt., O.M.; British composer; b. 29 March 1902; ed. Cathedral School, and Christ Church, Oxford.
Gold Medal Royal Philharmonic Soc. 47; Hon. Mus. Dr. (Oxford, Cambridge, London, Durham, Manchester and Trinity Coll. Dublin); Hon. F.R.C.M., F.R.A.M.
Works include Pianoforte Quartet (Carnegie award) 18, String Quartet (unpublished) 21, *Façade* (with Edith Sitwell) 23 and 26, *Siesta* for small orchestra 26, *Portsmouth Point* 26. Sinfonia Concertante for piano and orchestra 28, Viola Concerto 29, *Belshazzar's Feast* 31, three Songs for Soprano 32, Symphony 35, *Crown Imperial* (Coronation March 1937), *In Honour of the City of London* 37. Violin Concerto 39, *Music for Children* 40, *Scapino* (comedy overture) 41, incidental music to film *The Foreman Went to France* 42, to Gielgud production *Macbeth* 42, to Olivier's *Henry V* 44-45, *Quartet* 47, *Hamlet* (film) 47, Violin Sonata 49, *Orb and Sceptre* (Coronation March) 53, *Te Deum* 53, *Troilus and Cressida* 54, *Richard III* (film music) 55, 'Cello Concerto 56, *Partita* 57, *Anon in Love*, Second Symphony 60, *Gloria* 61, *Variations on a Theme by Hindemith* 63, *The Twelve* (anthem) 65, *Missa Brevis* 66, *The Bear* 67.
c/o Oxford University Press, 44 Conduit Street, London, W.1, England.

Wan Waithayakon, Prince Krommun Naradhip Bongsprabandh, M.A.; Thai diplomatist and politician; b. 25 Aug. 1891; ed. Marlborough Coll., Balliol Coll., Oxford, and Ecole des Sciences Politiques, Paris.
Sec. Thai Legation, Paris 17-19; Private Sec. to Minister of Foreign Affairs 19-24; Under-Sec. of State for Foreign Affairs 24-26; Minister to London 26-30; Adviser to Premier's Office and Foreign Office, Bang-kok 33-46; Ambassador to U.S.A. 47-52; Permanent Del. to U.N. 47-59; Pres. U.N. Gen. Assembly 56-57, Conf. on Law of the Sea 58, 60; Minister of Foreign Affairs 52-58; Deputy Prime Minister 59-; Rector, Thammasat Univ. 63-; Rapporteur, Asian-African Conf., Bandung 55; Hon. D.Litt. (Chulalongkorn), Hon. D.Pol.Sc. (Thammasat, Hon. D.Law (Columbia, New York, Fairleigh Dickinson), Hon. D.C.L. (Oxford); Knight of the Most Illustrious Order of the Royal House of Chakri.
Deputy Prime Minister's Office, Bangkok; and 26 Soi 20, Sukhumvit Road, Bangkok, Thailand.
Telephone: 913346.

Wanamaker, Pearl Anderson, B.A.; American educa-tor; b. 18 Jan. 1899; ed. Western Washington Coll. of Education, Univ. of Washington.
Rural teacher 17-21; High School teacher 22-23, 28-41; County Supt. of Schools 23-27; mem. Wash. State House of Reps. 29, 33, 35, Wash. State Senate 37, 39; Supt. of Public Instruction, State of Wash. 41-57; Pres. Nat.

Educational Asscn. 46-47; Pres. Nat. Council of Chief State School Officers 50; Gov. American Nat. Red Cross 52-55; N.W. Regional Dir., Scholastic Magazines 59-; Altrusa Int. Distinguished Service Award for 45-47; American Education Award 49, and Achievement Award, Women's Nat. Press Club 50, Quota Club of Seattle 51; Woman of the Year Award, Seattle B'nai B'r'ith 55; Hon. LL.D. (Miami Univ., Ohio, Mills Coll.), Hon. L.H.D. (Columbia Univ., Smith Coll.).
415 W. Mercer Street, Seattle 98119, Washington, U.S.A.

Wanamaker, Sam; American actor and film and theatre director; b. 14 June 1919; ed. Drake Univ., Iowa, and Goodman Theatres, Chicago.
Dir. Jewish Peoples' Inst., Chicago 39-40; radio acting New York 40-41; acted in *Café Crown* 41 and *Counterattack* 42, Broadway; U.S. Army 42-45; actor and dir. 46-; Artistic Dir. New Shakespeare Theatre, Liverpool 57-59; acted in and directed *Joan of Lorraine* (Broadway) 46; acted in *My Girl Tisa* 47, *Christ in Concrete* 49, *Denning Drives North* 51; directed *Gentleman from Athens* 48, *Goodbye my Fancy* 49, *Caesar and Cleopatra, Revival of Guardsman*; acted in and/or directed *Winter Journey, The Shrike, The Rainmaker, Threepenny Opera, The Big Knife, A Hatful of Rain, A View from the Bridge, Reclining Figure, Othello, The Rose Tattoo* 59, *A Far Country* 61; acted in film *Taras Bulba* 62; directed on Broadway plays *Children from Their Games* (Irwin Shaw) 62, *Case of Libel* (Louis Nizer) 63, *A Murderer Among Us* (Louis Nizer) 63; directed at Covent Garden opera *King Priam* (Tippett) 63, *Forza del Destino* (Verdi) 63; acted in film *Those Magnificent Men in their Flying Machines* 64; directed and acted in *Macbeth*, Goodman Theatre, Chicago 64; acted in film *The Spy Who Came in From the Cold* 65; directed or acted in TV films *The Defenders, For the People, Gunsmoke, The Baron* 62-66; acted in and/or directed *The Day the Fish Came Out* 66, *Warning Shot* 66, *The Eliminator* 67, *Custer*, and TV films *The Hawk, Lassiter, Cimmarron Strip, Court Martial, The Champions, Lancer* 66-67; director *The Chinese Visitor* 68.
Canada House, Norfolk Street, The Strand, London, W.C.2, England.

Wanchoo, Kailas Nath; Indian judge; b. 25 Feb. 1903; ed. Pandit Pirthi Nath High School, Kanpur, Muir Central Coll., Allahabad, and Wadham Coll., Oxford.
Magistrate and Judge, United Provinces (later Uttar Pradesh) 26-51; Judge, Allahabad High Court 47-51; Chief Justice, Rajastan High Court 51-58; Judge, Supreme Court of India 58-67; Chief Justice of India 67-68.
6 Motilal Nehru Place, New Delhi, India.
Telephone: 46222.

Wand, Rt. Rev. and Rt. Hon. John William Charles, K.C.V.O., P.C., M.A.; British ecclesiastic; b. 25 Jan. 1885; ed. King's School, Grantham, St. Edmund Hall, Oxford, and Bishop Jacob Hostel, Newcastle-on-Tyne.
Curate of Benwell 08-11, Lancaster 11-14; Vicar-Choral of Sarum 14-19; Lecturer Sarum Theological Coll. 14-20; Tutor 20-24; Temporary Chaplain to the Forces 15-19; Hon. Chaplain 19-22 and 25-; Chaplain to the R.A.F. 22-25; Vicar of St. Mark, Sarum 19-25; Fellow, Dean, and Tutor Oriel Coll. Oxford 25-34; Lecturer in Theology St. Edmund Hall 28-31; Univ. Lecturer in Church History 31-34; Archbishop of Brisbane and Metropolitan of Queensland 34-43; Senior Chaplain (Anglican), 1st Military District, Australian Military Forces 35-43; Bishop of Bath and Wells 43-45; Bishop of London 45-55, Canon Residentiary of St. Paul's 56; Dean of the Chapels Royal 45-55; Hon. Chaplain R.N.V.R. 47-; Editor *Church Quarterly Review* 56-68; Hon. Fellow St. Edmund Hall, Oxford 38, Oriel Coll. 41, King's Coll. London 56; Hon. D.D. (Oxford), S.T.P. (Columbia), S.T.D. (Toronto), D.Litt. (Ripon, U.S.A., W. Ontario).

Publs. *The Golden String* 26, *The Development of Sacramentalism* 28, *History of the Modern Church* 30, *The Old Faith and the New Age* 33, *History of the Early Church* 35, *New Testament Letters* 44, *God and Goodness* 47, *The Spirit of Church History* 48, *The Latin Doctors* 48, *The Authority of the Scriptures* 49, *White of Carpentaria* 49, *The Greek Doctors* 50, *The High Church Schism* 51, *What Paul said* 52, (Editor) *The Anglican Communion* 48, (Joint Author) *Oxford and the Groups* 34, *Westminster Commentary* 34, *First-Century Christianity* 37, *European Civilisation* 37, *Union of Christendom* 38, *The Four Councils* 51, *What the Church of England Stands For* 51, *The Second Reform* 53, *The Mystery of the Kingdom* 53, *The Life of Jesus Christ* 55, *The Four Great Heresies* 55, *Seven Steps to Heaven* 56, *The Road to Happiness* 57, *True Lights* 58, *The Church Today* 60, *The Anglican Communion in History and Today* 61, *Doctors and Councils* 62, *St. Augustine's City of God* 63, *The Atonement* 63, *The Temptation of Jesus* 65, *Reflections on the Collects* 65, *Reflections on the Epistles* 66, *Transfiguration* 67.
3 Amen Court, London, E.C.4, England.
Telephone: 01-248-1817.

Wandel, Paul, DR. h.c.; German journalist and diplomatist; b. 16 Feb. 1905.
Engineer; mem. Communist Party 23; Pres. Communist Group, Mannheim City Council; Chief Ed. Communist *Deutsche Volks-Zeitung* after 45; Minister of Education; fmr. Sec. Central Cttee. Socialist Unity Party (S.E.D.); Ambassador to People's Republic of China 58-60; Deputy Minister of Foreign Affairs 60-63; Pres. Liga für Völkerfreundschaft 64-.
Berlin, W.8, Thalmannplatz 8-9, Germany.

Wanderley, Brig. Nelson Freire Lavenère; Brazilian air force officer; b. 09.
Miltary Air Service 30-; Liaison Officer, Italy, Second World War; fmr. Military Attaché, Uruguay and Argentina; Chief of Air Command School 60; later Commdr. 4th and 5th Air Zones; Dir.-Gen. of Civil Aeronautics 64-.
Ministry for Air, Brasilia, Brazil.

Wang Chen; Chinese soldier and administrator; b. 08.
Joined C.C.P. 27; at that time he was on the Exec. Cttee. of the Changsha Union of Railwaymen; mem. Exec. Cttee. of Communist Youth League 27; fled to Hankow in 28 and organised New First Detachment of Guerilla Forces at Liuyang; Commissar to First Independent Division of Hunan-Kiangsi Soviet; played prominent part in Japanese War; Commissar to First Field Army 49; mem. North-West Admin. Council 53; Commanded Railway Corps of People's Liberation Army; mem. Council of Nat. Defence 54; decorated for war service 55; appointed Lieut.-Gen. 56; Minister of State Farms and Land Reclamation 56-65; 4th Minister of Machine Building 65-; mem. Central Cttee. of C.C.P. 56.
Fourth Ministry of Machine Building, Peking, China.

Wang Chia-chi; Chinese biologist.
Mem. of Central Cttee. of Chiu San Society 52-; Shantung del. to First N.P.C. 54; mem. of Cttee. of Dept. of Biology, Geology and Geography of Academia Sinica 55; Dir. of Inst. of Hydrobiology of Chinese Acad. of Sciences 60-.
Institute of Hydrobiology, Wuhan, China.

Wang Chia-hsiang; Chinese Communist leader; b. 07; ed. Shanghai Univ. and U.S.S.R.
Leading party official; Commissar in Anti-Japanese War; towards end of war in Secretariat of Political Dept. of C.C.P.; cttee. mem. at 7th Congress C.C.P. 45; Chargé d'Affaires to U.S.S.R. 50; mem. Secretariat of Central Committee, C.C.P. 56-
Central Committee of Chinese Communist Party, Peking, People's Republic of China.

Wang Ho-shou; Chinese industrial administrator. Minister of Industry in North-East People's Govt. 49; Minister of Heavy Industry in Central People's Govt. 52 and under Govt. Administration Council 54; Minister of Metallurgical Industry 56-67; Chair. National Construction Commission 56.
Ministry of Metallurgical Industry, Peking, China.

Wang Hung-kun; Chinese soldier; b. 09. Various positions in Red Army and People's Liberation Army from 34; Vice-Admiral in Navy at its establishment 51; del. for E. China area People's Liberation Army to N.P.C. 54; mem. of Council of National Defence 54; decorated for war services 55.
Council of National Defence, Peking, China.

Wang Jen-chung; Chinese administrator; b. *c.* 06. Veteran C.C.P. mem.; was in Kiangsi Soviet Area and went to Yenan as commissar; posts in administration and propaganda depts. of Border Areas 38; Vice-Chair. Honan Provincial Govt. 49; Vice-Mayor Wuhan 52; on South Central Mil. and Admin. Council 53; Mayor of Wuhan 54; del. for Wuhan to N.P.C. 54; on Honan Provincial Council 55; 1st Sec. Hupeh Province Cttee. of C.C.P. 54-.
Central Committee of Hupeh Province Communist Party, Tientsin, People's Republic of China.

Wang Kan-chang; Chinese atomic scientist; b. 1906; trained in Germany and U.S.A.
Deputy Dir., Atomic Energy Inst., Acad. of Sciences, Peking 54-; mem. Standing Cttee. N.P.C. 65-.
National Academy of Sciences, Peking, China.

Wang Kuo-chuan; Chinese diplomatist.
Ambassador to German Democratic Republic 57-64, to Poland 64-.
Embassy of the People's Republic of China, Bonifraterska, Warsaw, Poland.

Wang Ling, M.A., PH.D.; Chinese historian; b. 23 Dec. 1918; ed. National Central Univ., China, and Trinity Coll. Cambridge.
Junior Research Fellow, Inst. of History and Philology, Academia Sinica 41-44; Senior Lecturer, Nat. Fu-tan Univ. 44-45, Assoc. Prof. 45-46; Collaborator to J. Needham, F.R.S. Cambridge Univ. 46-57; Visiting Lecturer, Cambridge Univ. 53, Canberra Univ. Coll., Melbourne Univ. 57-59, Cornell Univ. 65-66; Assoc. Fellow, Nat. Acad. of Science, Academia Sinica 55-57; Senior Lecturer Univ. Coll., Australian Nat. Univ., Canberra 60-61, Assoc. Prof. 61-63; Professorial Fellow, Inst. of Advanced Studies, Australian Nat. Univ. 63-; Visiting Prof. of Chinese Literature, Cornell Univ.; Visiting Prof. of Chinese Classics, Wisconsin Univ.; mem. Comm. for the History of the Social Relations of Science of the Int. Union for the History of Science 48-56; corresp. mem. Int. Acad. of History of Science, Paris 64-.
Publs. *Science and Civilisation in China* (with Dr. J. Needham, F.R.S.) Vol. I 54, Vol. II 56, Vol. III 59, Vol. IVa 62, Vol. IVb 64, *Heavenly Clockwork* (with Dr. J. Needham, F.R.S.) 60, *A Study on the Chiu Chang Suan Shu* 62.
Institute of Advanced Studies, Australian National University, Canberra, Australia.
Telephone: Canberra 495111.

Wang Ping-Chang; Chinese politician.
Former Deputy Commdr. Air Force; mem. Nat. Defence Council; 7th Minister of Machine Building 65-.
7th Ministry of Machine Building, Peking, People's Republic of China.

Wang Ping-nan; Chinese diplomatist; ed. Germany.
Joined Berlin branch of Comintern; joined C.C.P. 25; diplomatic liaison work for Eighth Route Army during Japanese War; Deputy Head of Foreign Affairs Section of Central Cttee. of C.C.P. 46; Chief of Secretariat of Ministry of Foreign Affairs 49; Mem. of Council of Institute of Foreign Affairs 51-55; Asst. to Minister of Foreign Affairs 54; Ambassador to People's Republic of Poland 55-64; Vice-Foreign Minister 64-.
Ministry of Foreign Affairs, Peking, China.

Wang Shou-tao; Chinese Communist leader; b. 07; ed. Hunan Provincial Agricultural School.
Joined Communist Youth 23; entered Kwangtung Peasants School directed by Mao Tse-tung; joined C.C.P. 25; active in peasant rising and guerila activity; Chair. Hunan Soviet 30; directed to underground work in Shanghai 32; during move to north-west, in political bureau; Additional mem. Central Cttee. C.C.P. 45; Chair. Hunan Govt. 49; Minister of Communications 53-54, 59-; Rep. of C.C.P. on C.P.P.C.C. and on Standing Cttee. 54; on Central Cttee. C.C.P. 8th Congress.
Ministry of Communications, Peking, China.

Wang Ya-nan; Chinese economist; b. *c.* 03. Professor at Tsinghua Univ.; on Fukien Provincial Council and Professor at Amoy Univ. 50; Pres. Amoy Univ.; Fukien del. to N.P.C. 54; Fukien del. and Vice-Chair. at C.P.P.C.C. 55; on Cttee. Dept. of Philosophy and Social Sciences, Chinese Acad. of Sciences 55, on Standing Cttee. of same 55.
Publs. large number of books and articles on the Chinese economy and economic history.
Amoy University, Amoy, Fukien, China.

Wang Yu-chuan; Chinese museum curator.
Fmr. Curator, Far Eastern Collection, Museum of American Numismatic Society, New York; now Curator, Historical Museum, Peking.
Historical Museum, Peking, China.

Wang Yun-sheng; Chinese journalist; b. 99.
Formerly editor of *Ta Kung Pao*; worked as a journalist in Liberated Areas 48; mem. of East China Mil. and Admin. Council 49; mem. North China Admin. Council 53-54; mem. of Exec. Cttee. of All-China Fed. of Industry and Commerce 53; mem. of Council of Asscn. for Cultural Relations with Foreign Countries 54; Vice-Pres. All-China Journalists' Asscn. 54-; mem. of Council of Institute of Foreign Affairs 55; mem. of Executive Cttee. of All-China Fed. of Industry and Commerce 56.
Publs. *Sixty Years of Sino-Japanese Relations*, etc.
All-China Journalists' Association, Peking, China.

Wang Yun-wu; Chinese writer, editor and government official; b. 88; ed. privately.
Managing Director and Editor-in-Chief Commercial Press Shanghai 21-36; mem. Presidium People's Political Council 38-46; Minister of Econ. Affairs 46-47; Vice-Pres. Exec. Yuan 47-48 and 58-63; Vice-Pres. Examination Yuan 54-58; Minister of Finance 48; Chair. Presidential Comm. on Admin. Reform 58-59; Prof. Nat. Cheng-chi Univ., Taiwan 54-; Senior Adviser to Pres. of the Republic 64-; inventor of the Wang System of Chinese Lexicography.
Publs. Works on education, scientific management, international relations, etc.
8 Lane 19, Sec. IV, South Hsin Hseng Road, Taipei, Republic of China (Taiwan).

Wangensteen, Owen Harding, B.A., B.S., M.D., PH.D.; American surgeon; b. 21 Sept. 1898; ed. Univ. of Minnesota.
Interne Univ. Hospital Minneapolis 22; Fellow in Medicine Univ. of Minnesota 23; Fellow in Surgery Mayo Clinic 24; Resident Surgeon Univ. Hospital 25; Instructor in Surgery Univ. of Minnesota 26, Asst. Prof. 27; Asst. Surgical Clinic and Physiological Inst., Berne 27-28; Assoc. Prof. of Surgery, Univ. of Minnesota 28, Dir. Dept. of Surgery 30-, Prof. of Surgery 31-66, Regents' Prof. of Surgery 66-; co-Editor *Surgery* 37-; Pres. Minn. Pathological Soc., Halsted Surgical Soc., Minn. Medical Foundation 48-54, Minn. Acad. of

Medicine 53, Heart Council 54-57, American Coll. of Surgeons 59, Research Facilities Council 59; Consultant to U.S.P.H.S.; awarded Samuel D. Gross Prize Philadelphia Acad. of Surgery 35, John Scott Award 41, Alvarenga Prize Philadelphia Coll. of Medicine 49, American Cancer Soc. Award 49, Pittsburgh Surgical Soc. Award 58, Distinguished Service Award, Univ. of Minn. 60, Passano Award 61, American Cancer Soc. Special Citation 62; Hon. mem. Hellenic Surgical Soc., Athens 61, Norwegian Acad. of Science 64, Royal Coll. of Surgeons of Edinburgh 65; mem. Nat. Acad. of Sciences 66-; Pres. American Surgical Asscn. 68-; Quinquennial Lannelongue Prize, French Acad. of Surgery 67; Distinguished Service Award, American Medical Asscn. 68; Hon. Fellow, Royal Coll. of Surgeons, London 62; Dr. h.c., Sorbonne 62; Hon. LL.D. Univ. of Buffalo 46; D.Sc. (Univ. of Chicago 56, St. Olav Coll. 58, Temple Univ. 61, Hamline Univ. 63).
Publs. *The Therapeutic Problem in Bowel Obstruction* 37, 42, 55, *Cancer of the Esophagus and Stomach* 51, 56.
2832 W. River Road, Minneapolis 55406, Minn., U.S.A.

Waniolka, Fransiszck; Polish politician; b. 12.
Former fitter; mem. Communist Party 45-; graduated from Mining Inst. 48; mem. Seym 52-; Dep. Chair. State Planning Agency 52-54; Dep. Minister of Power 54-56, Minister of Power 56-59; Minister of Heavy Industry 59-62; Dep. Prime Minister 62-; mem. Politburo, Polish United Workers' Party 64-.
Office of the Deputy Prime Minister, Warsaw, Poland.

Wank, Roland Anthony; American architectural engineer; b. 2 Oct. 1898; ed. Royal Polytechnicum, Budapest, and Technical Univ., Brno.
Designer of industrial plant and buildings, houses, community and public buildings, railroad terminals; Chief Architect Greenhills Project Resettlement Admin.; Chief Consulting Architect Rural Electrification Admin.; Head Architect Tennessee Valley Authority 33-44, Consultant to TVA 44-; Chief Designer, Albert Kahn Associates 44-45; mem. of firm Fellheimer and Wagner Dec. 45, Partner 58-; Architectural Consultant, U.N. Headquarters Comm. 46; Architectural Consultant, New Jersey Turnpike Authority 50-53, U.S. Corps of Engineers 57; Planning Consultant, New Jersey Meadowlands Regional Planning Authority 56-57; Fellow American Inst. of Architects.
Office: 155 E. 42nd Street, New York 17, N.Y.; Home: 35 Highview Avenue, New Rochelle, N.Y., U.S.A.

Wańkowicz, Melchior; Polish writer; b. 10 Jan. 1892; ed. Cracow Univ.
Lived in Great Britain and U.S.A. 39-57.
Publs. *Strzepy epopei* (Fragments of an Epopee), *Szpital w Cichiniczach* (The Hospital at Cichinicze), *Opierzona rewolucia* (Revolution Fledged), *Szczeniece lata* (Early Years), *Na tropach Smetka* (In the Steps of Smetek), *Sztafeta* (The Courier), *Monte Cassino, Ziele na kraterze* (Herb on the Crater), *Wrzesień Żagwiący* (Burning September), *Kundlizm* (Mongrelism), *Tworzywo* (Creative Material), *Droga do Urzedowa* (Road to Urzedow), *Westerplatte, Hubalczycy, Golgotha Road, Tedy i Owedy, Walczacy Gryf, Klub 3 Miejsca, Polacy i Ameryka, Storia di una Famiglia, La Litanie de la Faim, Prosto od Krowy* (Straight from the Horse's Mouth), *Zupa na gwozdziu* (Nail-Soup), *Atlantyk-Pacyfik, Madry Puhacz* (The Wise Owl).
Pulawska 10 m. 35, Warsaw, Poland.
Telephone: 45-36-77.

Wansbrough, George, M.A., C.I.E.E., M.S.A.E.; British company director; b. 23 April 1904; ed. Cheam School, Eton Coll., and King's Coll., Cambridge (Scholar).
Selfridge and Co. Ltd. 25-27; Robert Benson and Co. Ltd. (Merchant Bankers) 27-35; Dir. 32; Dir. British Power and Light Corpn. 35-48; Dir. A. Reyrolle and Co. Ltd. 34-49, Dep. Chair. 42, Chair. 45; Chair. Jowett Cars Ltd. 47-50; Dir. Bank of England 46-49; Chair.

Morphy-Richards Ltd. 44-54; Dir. of Mercantile Credit Co. Ltd. and other companies.
Hinton House, Kings Worthy, Hants., England.
Telephone: Winchester 2932.

Wansbrough-Jones, Sir Owen Haddon, K.B.E., C.B., M.A., PH.D., F.R.I.C.; British scientist; b. 25 March 1905; ed. Gresham's School, Holt, and Trinity Hall, Cambridge.
Chemical research Univ. of Cambridge 26-30; Berlin 31; Fellow of Trinity Hall 30-46; Asst. Tutor 32, Tutor 34, Hon. Fellow 56; Departmental Demonstrator, Dept. of Colloid Science, Cambridge 31-39; granted Emergency Comm. in Army 40; miscellaneous Gen. Staff and technical appointments 40-46; Dir. of Special Weapons and Vehicles 46; demobilized as Brig. April 46; Scientific Adviser to Army Council 46-50; Principal Dir. of Scientific Research (Defence), Ministry of Supply 51-53, Chief Scientist, Ministry of Supply 53-59; Treas. Faraday Society 49-60; Dir. Albright and Wilson Ltd. 59-65, Exec. Vice-Chair. 65-67, Chair. June 67-.
7 King Street, St. James's, London, S.W.1, England.
Telephone: 01-930-8608.

Warburg, Frederick Marcus; American banker; b. 14 Oct. 1897; ed. Harvard Univ.
American International Corpn. 19-21; M. M. Warburg and Co., Hamburg 21-22; Kuhn, Loeb and Co. 22-27; Lehman Bros. 27-30; Partner, Kuhn, Loeb and Co. 31-; official of several cos. and philanthropic orgs.
40 Wall Street, New York City, N.Y. 10005, U.S.A.

Warburg, James Paul, B.A.; American banker and author; b. 18 Aug. 1896; ed. Harvard Univ.
With Baltimore and Ohio Railroad Co. 16-17, First Nat. Bank of Boston 19-21; Vice-Pres. Int. Acceptance Bank New York City 21-29; Pres. Int. Manhattan Co. Inc. 29-31, Int. Acceptance Bank, also Vice-Chair. Bank of Manhattan 31-35; Dir. Polaroid Corpn.; Pres. and Dir. Fontenay Corpn., Bydale Co.; Dir. American Acad. of Political and Social Science, Philadelphia, Inst. for Policy Studies, Washington; Dep. Dir. Office of War Information 42-44.
Publs. *The Money Muddle* 34, *It's Up To Us* 34, *Hell Bent for Election* 35, *Still Hell Bent* 36, *Peace In Our Time?* 40, *Our War and Our Peace* 41, *Man's Enemy and Man* (Verse) 42, *Foreign Policy Begins at Home* 44, *Unwritten Treaty* 45, *Report on Germany* 46, *Germany—Bridge or Battleground* 47, *Put Yourself in Marshall's Place* 48, *Last Call for Common Sense* 49, *Faith, Purpose and Power* 50, *Victory Without War* 51, *How to Co-Exist* 52, *Germany—Key to Peace* 53, *The United States in a Changing World* 54, *Turning Point Toward Peace* 55, *Danger and Opportunity* 56, *Agenda for Action—Peace through Disengagement* 57, *The West in Crisis* 59, *Reveille for Rebels* 60, *Disarmament—the Challenge of the 1960s* 61, *What To Do About Berlin* 62, *Farewell to the Postwar Period* 63, *Toward a Strategy for Peace* 63, *The Long Road Home* (autobiography) 64, *Time for Statesmanship* 65, *The U.S. in the Postwar World* 66, *America's Role in the Far East* 67.
Home: Bydale, Greenwich, Conn.; Office: 60 East 42nd Street, New York City, N.Y. 10017, U.S.A.

Warburg, Otto Heinrich, M.D., DR.CHEM.; German biochemist; b. 8 Oct. 1883; ed. Berlin and Heidelberg Univs.
Served Prussian Horse Guards, First World War; Dir. Max Planck Inst. for Cell-Physiology, Berlin-Dahlem; Nobel Prize for Medicine 31; mem. German Acad. of Sciences, Berlin; foreign mem. Royal Society, London; mem. Danish Acad. of Sciences, Italian Acad. of Sciences, Indian Acad. of Sciences; Order of Merit 52; Grand Cross of Merit, with Star and Shoulder Ribbon, of the German Federal Republic.
Pulbs. *Stoffwechsel der Tumoren* 26, *Katalytische Wirkungen der lebendigen Substanz* 28, *Schwermetalle*

als Wirkungsgruppen von Fermenten 46, *Wasserstoff-übertragende Fermente* 48, *Energetik der Photosynthese* (with Dean Burk) 52, *New Methods of Cell Physiology* 62.
Garystrasse 18, Berlin-Dahlem, Germany.
Telephone: Berlin 763592.

Warburg, Sir Siegmund George, Kt.; German-born British merchant banker; b. 30 Sept. 1902; ed. Reutlingen Gymnasium, and Urach Humanistic Seminary.
Partner, M. M. Warburg and Co., Hamburg 30-38; Dir. New Trading Co., London 38-46, Kuhn Loeb and Co., New York 56-64, S. G. Warburg and Co., London 46-.
95 Eaton Square, London, S.W.1, England.

Ward, Barbara, B.A. (Lady Robert Jackson); British journalist; b. 14; ed. The Convent, Felixstowe, Lycée Molière and Sorbonne Paris, Germany, and Somerville Coll. Oxford.
University Extension Lecturer 36-39; Asst. Editor of *The Economist* 40; Gov. of Sadler's Wells and Old Vic Theatres 44-53, Trustee 43-; Gov. of B.B.C. 46-50; Hon. mem. American Acad. of Arts and Sciences; mem. Pontifical Comm. for Justice and Peace; Visiting Scholar and Carnegie Fellow, Harvard Univ. 57-68, Albert Schweitzer Prof. of Int. Econ. Devt. 68-; hon. degrees from Fordham, Smith, Columbia, Harvard, Georgetown, Utah and Boston Univs., Canisius, Lake Forest and Kenyon Colls.; Labour.
Publs. *The International Share-Out* 38, *Turkey* 41, (part-author) *Hitler's Route to Baghdad* 39, *A Christian Basis for the Post-War World* 41, *The West at Bay* 48, *A Policy for the West* 51, *Faith and Freedom* 54, *The Interplay of East and West* 57, *Five Ideas that Change the World* 59, *India and the West* 61, *The Rich Nations and the Poor Nations* 62, *Nationalism and Ideology* 66, *Spaceship Earth* 66, *The Lopsided World* 68.
c/o The Economist, 25 St. James' Street, London, S.W.1, England.

Ward, John Harris; American utilities executive; b. 17 March 1908; ed. Harvard Univ.
National Recovery Admin., Wash. 33-35; Asst. Treas. Marshall Field and Co., Chicago 37; Commonwealth Edison Co., Chicago 38-, Sec. 48-55, Vice-Pres. 51-55, Exec. Vice-Pres. 55-59, Pres. 59-64, Chair. 61-; Dir. Union Carbide Corpn., New York Life Insurance Co., Int. Harvester Co., Northern Trust Co.
Commonwealth Edison Co., 72 W. Adams Street, Chicago, Illinois; Home: 1596 Green Bay Road, Lake Forest, Ill., U.S.A.
Telephone: Cedar 4-2269 (Home).

Waring, Sir Bertram, Kt., D.L.; British business executive; b. 12 June 1893.
Joseph Lucas Ltd. 22-, now Chair. Joseph Lucas (Industries) Ltd.; Dir. Lloyds Bank Ltd. 52-64; Past Pres. Motor Industry Research Asscn., Soc. of Motor Manufacturers and Traders, Birmingham and District Engineering and Allied Employers' Asscn., Birmingham Chamber of Commerce, Inst. of Industrial Supervisors, Inst. of Works Managers; Chair. British Productivity Council 61.
Heath Lodge, Ullenhall, Warwickshire; Great King Street, Birmingham 19, England.
Telephone: NOR 5252.

Waring, Frank Walter, B.A., B.COM.; South African politician; b. 7 Nov. 1908; ed. S. African Coll. School and Cape Town Univ.
Grain Broker; M.P. for Orange Grove, Johannesburg; Minister of Information 61, Minister of Information and Tourism 63-66, Minister of Forestry, Tourism, Sport and Recreation 66-; Nat. Party.
Box 2090, Johannesburg, South Africa.

Waris, Klaus, PH.D.; Finnish economist; b. 17 March 1914; ed. Turku, Helsinki Univ.
Chief, Economic Affairs Division, Ministry of Finance 46-49; Prof. Economics Finnish Inst. of Technology 49-52; mem. Man. Board Bank of Finland 52-57; Gov. Bank of Finland 57-67; Chancellor, Helsinki School of Econs. 67-; Gov. for Finland, Int. Monetary Fund.
Kartanontie 12, Helsinki 33, Finland.

Wark, Ian William, C.M.G., C.B.E., D.SC., PH.D.; Australian physical chemist; b. 8 May 1899; ed. Scotch Coll., Melbourne, and Univs. of Melbourne, London and Calif. (Berkeley).
Exhibition of 1851 Science Research Scholarship 21-24; Lecturer in Chemistry, Univ. of Sydney 25; Research Chemist, Electrolytic Zinc Co. of Australasia Ltd. 26-39; Commonwealth Scientific and Industrial Research Organisation, Chief, Div. of Industrial Chemistry 40-58, Dir. Chemical Research Laboratories 58-60, mem. of Exec. 61-65; Chair. Commonwealth Advisory Cttee. on Advanced Educ. 65-; Gen. Pres. Royal Australian Chemical Inst. 57-58; Fellow, Australian Acad. of Science 54-, Treas. 59-63; hon. mem. Australasian Inst. Mining and Metallurgy 60-, Fellow Univ. Coll. London 65.
Publ. *Principles of Flotation* (monograph) 38, (revised with K. L. Sutherland 55).
16 Churchill Street, Mont Albert, E.10, Melbourne, Victoria, Australia.

Warner, Jack L.; American film executive; b. 92; ed. Public Schools, Youngstown, Ohio.
Former singer; pioneer, with brothers, of talking films 26-28; Pres. and Dir. Warner Bros. Pictures Inc.; numerous awards.
c/o Warner Bros. Pictures Inc., 666 Fifth Avenue, New York City, N.Y., U.S.A.

Warner, Leslie Harry; American telephone executive; b. 11; ed. Univ. of Wichita and Harvard Univ.
General Telephone System 37-; Man. Dir. Automatic Electric do Brasil, S.A., São Paulo 38-42; Vice-Pres. Automatic Electric Sales Corpn., New York City 42-46; Commercial Man., Automatic Electric Co., Chicago 46-47; Pres. Automatic Electric Sales Corpn., Automatic Electric Int., Chicago 47-54; Leich Electric Co., Genoa, Ill., Leich Sales Corpn., Chicago 54-55, Automatic Electric Co. 55-57; Exec. Vice-Pres. (Mfg.), Gen. Telephone and Electronics Corpn., New York City 57-61, Pres. 61-; Dir. numerous subsidiary and other cos.
General Telephone and Electronics Corporation, 730 Third Avenue, New York 17, N.Y., U.S.A.

Warner, Rawleigh (father of Rawleigh Warner, Jr., *q.v.*); American executive (retd.); b. 14 May 1891; ed. Princeton Univ.
With Central Trust Co. of Ill. 13; mem. Earle & Warner (Sugar Brokers) 14-17; Treas. Central Sugar Co. 15-17; Vice-Pres., Dir. Dawes Bros. Inc. 19-39; Vice-Pres., Treas., Dir. The Pure Oil Co. 26-47, Chair. Board 47-63, Chair. Exec. Cttee. 63-65.
Home: 1359 Tower Road, Winnetka, Ill.; Office: 2605 Prudential Plaza, Chicago, Illinois, U.S.A.

Warner, Rawleigh, Jr., A.B. (son of Rawleigh Warner, *q.v.*); American business executive; b. 13 Feb. 1921 ed. Lawrenceville School and Princeton Univ.
Mobil Oil Corpn. 53-; Asst. to Financial Dir. Socony-Vacuum Overseas Supply Co. 53-56; Man. Econs. Dept., Mobil Oil Corpn. 56-58, Man. Middle East Affairs Dept. 58-59, Regional Vice-Pres. for Middle East 59-60; Exec. Vice-Pres. Mobil Int. Oil Co. 60-63, Pres. 63; Dir. Exec. Vice-Pres. and mem. Exec. Cttee. Mobil Oil Corpn., with responsibility for Mobil Int. and Mobil Petroleum Corpn. Inc. 64-65, Pres. Mobil Oil Corpn. 65-; Trustee, Lawrenceville School, Industrial Relations Counselors Inc., Council for Latin America Inc., The Freedom Fund Inc., Center for Inter-American Relations.
Mobil Oil Corporation, 150 East 42nd Street, New York, N.Y. 10017, U.S.A.

Warner, Rex; British writer; b. 9 March 1905; ed. Wadham Coll., Oxford.

Schoolmaster in Egypt; Classics Master at Raynes Park County School; Dir. British Inst., Athens 45-47; Prof. Univ. of Connecticut 64-.

Publs. *Poems* 37, *The Wild-Goose Chase* 37, *The Professor* 38, *The Aerodrome* 41, *Why Was I Killed?* 43, *Poems and Contradictions* 45, *The Cult of Power* 46, *Men of Stones* 49, *John Milton* (biography) 50, *Men and Gods* 50, *Greeks and Trojans* 51, *Views of Attica* (travel) 51, *Escapade* 53, *Eternal Greece* 53, *The Vengeance of the Gods* 54, *The Greek Philosophers*, *The Young Caesar* 58, *Imperial Caesar* 60, *Pericles the Athenian* 63; translations of *Medea, Hippolytus* and *Helen* (Euripides), *Prometheus Bound* (Aeschylus), *Anabasis* (Xenophon, entitled *The Persian Expedition*), *The Peloponnesian War* (Thucydides), *The Fall of the Roman Republic* (Plutarch) 58, *Caesar's War Commentaries* 59, *Confessions of St. Augustine* 63, *Pericles the Athenian* 63, *Poems* and *The Greek Style* (Seferis) 63 and 66, *History of My Times* (Xenophon) 66, *The Converts* (novel) 67.

Department of English, University of Connecticut, Storrs, Conn., U.S.A.; and Savile Club, 69 Brook Street, London, W.1, England.

Warner, W. Lloyd, A.B., M.A.; American anthropologist and sociologist; b. 26 Oct. 1898; ed. Univ. of California and Harvard Univ.

Instructor and Asst· Prof., Harvard Univ. and Radcliffe Coll. 29-31; Assoc. Prof. Univ. of Chicago 35-41, Prof. 41-49, 59; Prof. of Social Research, Michigan State Univ. 59-.

Publs. *A Black Civilisation* 37, *Color and Human Nature* (with others) 41, *The Social Life of a Modern Community* (with Paul S. Lunt) 41, *The Status System of a Modern Community* (with Paul S. Lunt) 42, *The Social Systems of American Ethnic Groups* (with Leo Srole) 45, *Who Shall be Educated?* (with others) 45, *The Social System of the Modern Factory* (with J. O. Low) 47, *Social Class in America* (with others) 49, *Democracy in Jonesville* 49, *Structure of American Life* 52, *American Life: Dream and Reality* 53, *Big Business Leaders in America* (with James Abegglen) 55, *Occupational Mobility in American Business and Industry* (with James Abegglen) 55, *The Living and the Dead* 59, *Industrial Man* (with N. H. Martin) 59, *The Family of God* 61, *The Corporation in the Emergent American Society* 62, *The American Federal Executive* (with others) 63, *The Emergent Society: Large Scale Organizations* (with others) 67.

22 Summit Drive, Dune Acres, Chesterton, Indiana, U.S.A.

Telephone: 926-1223.

Warnke, Herbert; German trade unionist; b. 02; ed. elementary school.

Shipyard worker in Hamburg; mem. Communist Party 23, mem. Politburo; illegal anti-fascist activity 39-44; Pres. Free German Trade Union League, Mecklenburg 46; Chair. Free German Trade Union Confed. (F.D.G.B.) 48-; Vice-Pres. World Fed. of Trade Unions; mem. Volkskammer; Vaterländischer Verdienstorden (gold), Lenin Peace Prize 67, etc.

F.D.G.B., Fritz-Heckert-Strasse 70, 102 Berlin 2, Germany.

Warnock, Maurice John; American business executive; b. 28 Dec. 1902; ed. Oregon High School, Silverton and Univ. of Oregon.

With Armstrong Cork Co., Lancaster, Pennsylvania 26-, Salesman, Floor Div., Seattle 27-29, District Manager 29-30, Asst. Sales Manager, Floor Div., Lancaster 30-41, Asst. Gen. Sales Manager, Lancaster 41, Dir. of Advertising and Promotion, Lancaster 41-43, Treas. 43-59, Vice-Pres. and Treas. 50-59, Dir. 59-, Senior Vice-Pres. 59-61, First Senior Vice-Pres. 61-62, Exec. Vice-Pres. 62, Pres. 62-68, Chair. of Board 68-; Vice-Pres. and Dir.

Armstrong Cork Canada Ltd. 62-, Dir. Armstrong Cork Co. Ltd., England 62-; Dir., Pennsylvania Power and Light Co.

Armstrong Cork Co., Liberty and Charlotte Streets, Lancaster, Pa.; Home: 515 Hamilton Road, Lancaster, Pa., U.S.A.

Warnock, William, B.A., LL.D.; Irish diplomatist; b. 22 Sept. 1911; ed. The High School, Dublin, Trinity Coll., Dublin, and Hochschule für Politik, Berlin.

Entered Dept. of External Affairs as Cadet 35; Sec., Berlin 38, Chargé d'Affaires a.i., Berlin 39-44; Head of Section; Dept. of External Affairs, Dublin 44-47; Chargé d'Affaires, Stockholm 47-50; Minister to Switzerland Feb. 50-54, also accredited to Austria March 52-54; Asst. Sec. Dept. of External Affairs 54-56; Minister to Fed. Republic of Germany 56-59, Ambassador 59-62, Ambassador to Switzerland and Austria 62-64, to India 64-67; Gustav V Medal (Sweden), Grand Cross of Order of Merit (German Federal Republic).

Irish Embassy, New Delhi, India.

Warren, Earl, B.L., J.D.; American lawyer and politician; b. 19 March 1891; ed. Univ. of Calif.

Admitted to Calif. Bar 14; practised in San Francisco and Oakland 14-17; served U.S. Army 17-18; Clerk of Assembly, Judiciary Cttee. Calif. Legislature 19; Deputy City Attorney, Oakland 19-20; Deputy District Attorney, Alameda County 20-25, District Attorney 25-39; Attorney-Gen. of Calif. 39-43; Gov. of Calif. 43-53; Chief Justice of U.S. 53-68; Pres. Nat. Asscn. of Attorneys-Gen. 40-41; Chair. Republican State Central Cttee. 34-36; Republican nominee for Vice-Pres. of U.S. 48; Chancellor Board of Regents Smithsonian Inst. 53-; Chair. Board of Trustees Nat. Gallery of Art 53-; decorations include Grand Cross Order of North Star (Sweden); Commdr. de la Légion d'Honneur, etc.; Hon. degrees from Univ. of Calif. and other univs. and colls.

c/o Supreme Court Building, 1 First Street, N.E., Washington, D.C. 20543, U.S.A.

Warren, John E.; American business executive; b. 1900; ed. Univ. of Washington.

Petroleum Engineer, U.S. Bureau of Mines and U.S. Geol. Survey 25-26; Production and Dist. Supt., Continental Oil Co. 26-34; Pres. Carl B. King Drilling Co. 34-; fmr. Chair. Exec. Cttee., Cities Service Co., Pres. 59-, Chief Exec. Officer 64-.

Cities Service Co., 60 Wall Tower, New York City, N.Y., U.S.A.

Warren, Robert Penn, B.A., B.LITT.; American university professor and writer; b. 05; ed. Vanderbilt, Oxford and Yale Univs. and Univ. of California.

Asst. Prof., Southwestern Coll. 30-31, Vanderbilt Univ. 31-34; Asst. Prof. Louisiana State Univ. 34-36, Assoc. Prof. 36-42; Prof. Univ. of Minnesota 42-50; Lecturer Yale Univ. 50-51, Prof. of Playwriting 51-56, of English 61-; Poetry, Library of Congress 44-45; a Founder and Editor *Southern Review* 35-42; Rhodes Scholarship, Houghton Mifflin Literary Fellowship 36, Guggenheim Fellowship 39-40 and 47-48; Levinson Prize 36, Caroline Sinker Prize 36, 37, 38, Shelley Memorial Award 42, Pulitzer Prize for Fiction 47, Southern Prize 47, Robert Melzer Award (Screen Writer's Guild) 49, Millay Award (American Poetry Soc.), Nat. Book Award, Pulitzer Prize for Poetry 58, Sidney Hillman Award for Journalism 59, Irita Van Doren Award (*New York Herald Tribune*) 65; Bollingen Prize in Poetry 67; Hon. Litt.D., LL.D.

Publs. *John Brown: The Making of a Martyr* 29, *XXXVI Poems* 36, *An Approach to Literature* (with Cleanth Brooks and John Purser) 37, *Understanding Poetry* (with Cleanth Brooks) 38, *Night Rider* (novel) 39, *At Heaven's Gate* (novel) 43, *Eleven Poems on the Same Theme* 42, *Selected Poems* 44, *All the King's Men* (novel) 46, *Circus in the Attic* (stories) 48, *World Enough and Time* (novel)

50, *Brother to Dragons* 53, *Band of Angels* (novel) 55, *Segregation: The Inner Conflict of the South* 56, *Promises* (verse) 57, *Selected Essays* 58, *The Cave* 59, *You, Emperors and Others* (verse) 60, *The Legacy of the Civil War* 61, *Wilderness* (novel) 61, *Flood* (novel) 64, *Who Speaks for the Negro?* 65, *Selected Poems, New and Old* 66.
2495 Redding Road, Fairfield, Conn., U.S.A.

Warren, Shields, A.B., M.D.; American physician; b. 98; ed. Boston Univ., Harvard Medical School.
Professor of Pathology, Harvard Medical School (New England Deaconess Hospital) 48-65, Prof. of Pathology, Emeritus 65-; Chair. Corpn. and Trustees, Boston Univ. 61-; U.S. Rep. UN Scientific Cttee. on the Effects of Atomic Radiation 55-63; Consultant, U.S. Atomic Energy Comm. 59-; Special Consultant, Dept. of Defense (Health and Medical) 59-62; Chair. Cttee. on Pathological Effects of Atomic Radiation 55-; mem. Nat. Acad. of Sciences 62-; Hon. D.Sc., Hon. S.D., Hon. LL.D.; many awards.
Publs. *Medical Science for Everyday Use* 27, *Pathology of Diabetes Mellitus* 30, 4th edn. 66, *A Handbook for the Diagnosis of Cancer of the Uterus* (with O. Gates) 47, 48, 49, *Introduction to Neuropathology* (with S. P. Hicks) 50, *Medical Effects of the Atomic Bomb in Japan* (with A.W. Oughterson) 56, *Pathology of Ionizing Radiation* 61.
194 Pilgrim Road, Boston, Mass. 02215, U.S.A.

Wartburg, Walther von, DR. PHIL.; Swiss philologist; b. 18 May 1888; ed. Gymnasium Solothurn, Universitäten Bern und Zürich, Università degli Studi, Florence, Université de Paris à la Sorbonne, and Ecole des Hautes Etudes, Paris.
Teacher at Gymnasium Chur 10-12, Teachers' Training Coll., Wettingen (Aargau) 12-19, Gymnasium Aarau (Aargau) 19-28; Prof. Université de Lausanne 28, Universität Leipzig 29; Visiting Prof. Univ. of Chicago 35-40; Prof. Universität Basel 39-59, Emer. 59-; mem. Académie des Inscriptions et Belles-Lettres (Institut de France), British Acad., Akademien von Wien, Leipzig, Berlin, Accademia della Crusca (Florence), Accademia dei Lincei (Rome), Acad. of Sciences of Sweden, Finland, Netherlands and Barcelona.
Publs. *Französisches Etymologisches Wörterbuch, Evolution et Structure de la langue française, Ausgliederung der romanischen Sprachen, Entstehung der romanischen Völker, La posizione della lingua italiana, Einführung in Problematik und Methodik der Sprachwissenschaft.*
Predigerhofstrasse 25, Basle, Switzerland.

Washington, Walter E.; American government official; ed. Howard Univ. and Howard Law School.
Executive Dir. Nat. Capital Housing Authority, Washington, D.C. until Nov. 66; Chair. New York City Housing Authority Nov. 66-67; Commr. of District of Columbia 67-.
408 T Street, Washington, D.C. 20001, U.S.A.

Watanabe, Tadao; Japanese banker; b. 3 Sept. 1898; ed. Tokyo Univ.
Joined Bank of Japan 24; transferred to Sanwa Bank 45, Man. Dir. 45-46, Senior Man. Dir. 46-47, Pres. 47-60, Chair. 60-; Dir. Mainichi Broadcasting Co. Ltd.; Man. Dir. Kansai Econ. Fed.; Adviser Fed. of Econ. Orgs.; Adviser Japan Fed. of Employers' Asscns.
4-10 Fushimimachi, Higashi-ku, Osaka; 111 Yamatecho, Ashiyashi, Hyogo Prefecture; 5-16-35, Roppongi, Minato-ku, Tokyo, Japan.
Telephone: 0797-2-2910 (Hyogo); 03-583-2715 (Tokyo).

Watanabe, Takejiro; Japanese business executive; b. 98; ed. Tokyo Coll. of Commerce.
Land Section, Mitsubishi Co. 18-; Chief Accounting Section, Mitsubishi Land Co. 37, Dir. 47-, Auditor 48, Man. Dir. 49-51, Senior Man. Dir. 51-52, Pres. 52-.
Mitsubishi Estate Co., 2-2 Marunouchi, Chiyoda-ku, Tokyo, Japan.

Watanabe, Takeshi; Japanese banker and financial consultant; b. 15 Feb. 1906; ed. Law School of Tokyo Imperial Univ.
Ministry of Finance, Japan 30, serving as Chief Liaison Officer, Chief of the Minister's Secr. and Financial Commr.; Minister, Japanese Embassy in Washington 52-56; Exec. Dir. for Japan, Int. Bank for Reconstruction and Devt.—IBRD (World Bank) and Int. Monetary Fund (IMF) 56-60; Int. Financial Consultant 60-65; Adviser to Minister of Finance, Japan, in charge of preparatory work for the establishment of the Asian Devt. Bank 65; Pres. Asian Devt. Bank, Manila Nov. 66-.
Publ. *Japanese Finance in Early Post-War Years* (in Japanese) 66.
1266 Acacia Rd., Dasmariñas, Makati, Rizal, Philippines.

Waterhouse, Ellis Kirkham, C.B.E.; British professor of fine arts; b. 16 Feb. 1905; ed. Marlborough Coll., New Coll., Oxford, and Princeton Univ., New Jersey.
Assistant, Nat. Gallery, London 29-33; Librarian, British School at Rome 33-36; Fellow Magdalen Coll., Oxford 38-47; Dir. Nat. Galleries of Scotland 49-52; Barber Prof. of Fine Arts and Dir. of Barber Inst., Univ. of Birmingham 52-; Officer Orange-Nassau, Ordine al Merito della Repubblica Italiana.
Publs. *Roman Baroque Painting* 37, *Reynolds* 41, *British Painting 1530-1790* 53, *Gainsborough* 58, *Italian Baroque Painting* 62.
43 Calthorpe Road, Birmingham 15, England.
Telephone: 021-554-1594.

Waterink, Jan, D.D.; Netherlands clergyman and educationist; b. 90; ed. Theological Seminary, Kampen, and Free Univ. of Amsterdam.
Clergyman Reformed Church, Appelscha 14, Zutphen 17, Amsterdam 24; Extraordinary Prof. in Education 26, Ordinary Prof. in Psychology and Education 29, Vice-Chancellor 36-37 and 54-55, Free University, Amsterdam; Dir. Laboratory for applied psychology 27-61, Pedagogical Inst. 31-61, Laboratory for psychological research 55-61, Free Univ., Amsterdam; Pres. Int. Asscn. for the education of maladjusted children 47-51; Commdr. Order of the House of Orange; Knight, Order of Netherlands Lion; Officer, Order of Crown of Belgium; Hon. Dr. Ed. (Univ. of Potchefstroom, S. Africa), Hon. Ph.D. (Univ. of Ghent).
Publs. *Paedagogiek als wetenschap* 30, *Geschiedenis der paedagogiek* 40, *Ons zieleleven* 54, *De mens in het bedrijf* 55, *Puberteit* 56, *Brieven aan jonge mensen* 57, *De schooljaren, onzer kinderen* 57, *Aan moeders hand tot Jesus* 57, *Theorie der opvoeding* 58, *Sexuele voorlichting* 58, *Principe en gezag* 61, *Grondslagen der didactiek* 62, *De wet Gods en de opvoeding* 63, *Opvoeding tot Persoonlijkheid* 64.
Keizer Karelweg 487, Amstelveen, Netherlands.

Waterman, R. Lee; American glass executive; b. 06; ed. Bates College, Lewiston, Maine.
W. T. Grant Co. 26-33, 41-50; Montgomery Ward & Co. 33-41; President Sloane Blabon Corpn. 50-53; Administrative Vice-Pres. Alexander Smith Inc. 53-55; Vice-Pres. Corning Glass Works 55-64, Dir. 62-, Pres. 64-; Chair. Corning Glass Works of Canada 64-; Trustee Corning Glass Works Foundation 64-; Dir. other companies.
Corning Glass Works, Corning, N.Y.; Home: 52 East Fifth Street, Corning, N.Y. 14832, U.S.A.
Telephone: 607-962-5195 (Home).

Waters, Herbert J.; American government official; b. 14 June 1912; ed. Santa Rosa Junior Coll.
Newspaperman 28-48; Consultant, U.S. Office of Housing Expediter 49; Information Specialist U.S. Dept. of Agriculture 49-51, Asst. to Sec. 51-53; Agricultural Specialist and Press Sec. to U.S. Senator 53-55, Admin. Asst. 55-61; Asst. to Dir. Int. Co-operation

Admin. Feb.-Nov. 61; Asst. Admin. for Material Resources, Agency for Int. Devt. 62-67; Asst. Admin. for War on Hunger 67-.
5721 Little Falls Road, Arlington, Va. 22207, U.S.A.

Watkins, Arthur Vivian, LL.B.; American lawyer; b. 86; ed. Brigham Young Univ., New York Univ., and Columbia Univ.
Admitted to practice of Law in Utah 12; Ed. of *Vernal Express* 14; Asst. County Attorney, Salt Lake County 14-15; elected District Judge of Fourth Judicial District, Utah 28-32; Pres. of Sharon Stake, L.D.S. Church 29-46; Chair. of Cttee. to organise water users in Central Utah 34; U.S. Senator from Utah 47-58; Chief Commr. Indian Claims Comm. 60-; Republican.
1433 North Inglewood Street, Arlington, Va., U.S.A.

Watkinson, 1st Viscount (cr. 64), of Woking in the County of Surrey; **Harold Arthur Watkinson,** P.C., C.H.; British politician and business executive; b. 25 Jan. 1910; ed. King's Coll., London.
Conservative M.P. 50-64; Parl. Sec. Ministry of Labour 52-55; Minister of Transport and Civil Aviation 55-59, Minister of Defence 59-62; Dir. Consolidated Trust 62-, Midland Bank 64-; Group Man. Dir. Schweppes Ltd. 63-69, Exec. Chair. Jan. 69-; Chair. Cttee. for Exports to U.S.A. 64-67.
Dibbles, West Clandon, nr. Guildford, Surrey, England.

Watson, Arthur Kittredge (brother of Thomas J. Watson, *q.v.*); American business executive; b. 23 April 1919; ed. Yale Univ.
Salesman, Int. Business Machines Corpn. 47-48, Asst. to Manager, World Trade Div. 48; Dir., mem. Executive Cttee. IBM World Trade Corpn. 49, Vice-Pres. 49-54, Gen. Manager 52-54, Pres. 54-63, Chair. of Board 63-; Dir. IBM 59-, Vice-Pres. 59-61, mem. Exec. and Finance Cttees. 61-, Head of Corporate Staff 63-64, Senior Vice-Pres. 64-; Dir American Brake Shoe Co., Chemical Bank of New York Trust Co., Continental Insurance Co., Pres. Int. Chamber of Commerce 67, etc.; Trustee several public orgs.; numerous decorations.
Office: Old Orchard Road, Armonk, N.Y. 10504; Home: 751 Weed Street, New Canaan, Connecticut, U.S.A.

Watson, David Meredith Seares, D.SC., F.R.S.; British palaeontologist; b. 18 June 1886; ed. Manchester Grammar School and Manchester Univ.
Professor of Zoology and Comparative Anatomy, Univ. Coll., London 21-51, Emeritus 51-; mem. Agricultural Research Council 33-43, Acting Sec. 39-40; Sec. Scientific Food Policy Sub-Cttee., Food Policy Cttee. of War Cabinet 40-42; Trustee, British Museum 46-63; Alexander Agassiz Prof., Harvard Univ. 52; Lecturer numerous Univs.; Hon. mem. or Foreign Correspondent Acad. of Sciences of U.S.S.R., American Soc. of Herpetologists and Ichthyologists, N.Y. Acad. of Sciences, Bavarian Acad. of Sciences, Nat. Acad. of Sciences (U.S.A.), Leopoldin.-Carolin. Deutsche Akademie der Naturforscher, Indian Acad. of Sciences, American Museum of Natural History, Palaeontological Soc. of U.S.A., Soc. Géologique de France (Vice-Pres. 48), Royal Swedish Acad. of Sciences, Calif. Acad. of Sciences, Acad. Royale de Belgique, Royal Soc. of Sciences Uppsala, Soc. of Vertebrate Palaeontology, Royal Physiographical Soc. of Lund, Royal Soc. of Edinburgh, Geological Soc. of America, American Acad. of Arts and Sciences; Hon. Fellow, Univ. Coll., London; Erzhertzog Rainer Medal, K.K. biologischen Gesellschaft zu Wien 28; Lyell Medal, Geological Soc. of London 37; Mary Clarke Thompson Medal, Nat. Acad. of Sciences (U.S.A.) 41; Darwin Medal, Royal Soc. (U.K.) 42; Linnean Medal, Linnean Soc. of London 49; Darwin-Wallace Commemorative Medal, Linnean Soc. 58; Wollaston Medal, Geol. Soc. of London 65.

Publs. Over 130 papers on palaeontology and allied subjects.
2 The Knoll, Knoll Road, Godalming, Surrey, England. Telephone: Godalming 3754.

Watson, Francis John Bagott, C.V.O., F.S.A.; British museum director and civil servant; b. 24 Aug. 1907; ed. Shrewsbury School, and St. John's Coll., Cambridge.
Registrar Courtauld Inst. of Art 34-38; Asst. Keeper, later Asst. Dir. Wallace Collection 38-63, Dir. 63-; Asst. Surveyor of the King's (later the Queen's) Works of Art 47-63, Surveyor 63-; Trustee, Whitechapel Art Gallery 49-; Chair. Furniture History Soc. 66-.
Publs. *Canaletto* 49 (2nd edn. 54), *Southill, A Regency House* (with others) 51, *Catalogue of the Furniture in the Wallace Collection* 56, *Louis XVI Furniture* 59 (revised French edn. 63), *The Choiseul Gold Box* 63, *Wrightsman Catalogue* (vols. I, II) 66, *Eighteenth Century Gold Boxes of Europe* (with others), *The Guardi Family of Painters* 66-, *Tiepolo* 66, *Fragonard* 67.
8 Groom Place, Belgrave Square, London, S.W.1, England.

Watson, James Dewey, B.S., PH.D.; American biologist; b. 6 April 1928; ed. Univ. of Chicago, and Univ. of Indiana.
Research Fellow, U.S. Nat. Research Council, Univ. of Copenhagen 50-51; Fellow U.S. Nat. Foundation, Cavendish Laboratory, Univ. of Cambridge, England 51-53; Senior Research Fellow in Biology, Calif. Inst. of Technology 53-55; Asst. Prof. of Biology, Harvard Univ. 55-58, Assoc. Prof. 58-61, Prof. 61-; Consultant, President's Scientific Advisory Council 61-; Dir. Cold Spring Harbor Laboratory of Quantitative Biology 68-; mem. Nat. Acad. of Sciences, Danish Acad. of Arts and Sciences, American Acad. of Arts and Sciences, American Soc. of Biological Chemists; Senior Fellow, Soc. of Fellows, Harvard Univ. 64; Hon. Fellow of Clare Coll., Univ. of Cambridge 67; Lasker Award 60, Nobel Prize for Medicine (with F. H. C. Crick and M. F. H. Wilkins) 62, and other awards; Hon. D.Sc. (Chicago, Indiana), Hon. LL.D. (Notre Dame Univ.).
Publs. *Molecular Biology of the Gene* 65, *The Double Helix* 68; papers on structure of deoxyribonucleic acid (DNA), and viruses, and on protein synthesis.
Biological Laboratories, Harvard University, 16 Divinity Avenue, Cambridge, Mass.; Home: 10 Appian Way, Cambridge, Mass. 02138, U.S.A.
Telephone: 876-7414.

Watson, John Hugh Adam, C.M.G., M.A.; British diplomatist; b. 10 Aug. 1914; ed. Rugby, and King's Coll., Cambridge.
Entered Diplomatic Service 37; British Legation Bucharest 39, British Embassy, Cairo 40-44, Moscow 44-47; Foreign Office 47-50; British Embassy, Washington 50-56; Head of African Dept., Foreign Office 56-59; Minister and Consul-General, Senegal 59-60, Ambassador to Mali Fed. 60, to Senegal, Togo and Mauritania 60-62, to Cuba 63-66; Asst. Under-Sec. of State, Foreign Office 66-68; Diplomatic Adviser to British Leyland Motor Corpn. 68-; Fellow, Nuffield Coll., Oxford 62-63.
53 Hamilton Terrace, London, N.W.8; and Sharnden Old Manor, Mayfield, Sussex, England.
Telephone: 01-286-6330.

Watson, Thomas J., Jr. (brother of Arthur K. Watson, *q.v.*); American business executive; b. 8 Jan. 1914; ed. Brown Univ.
With International Business Machines Corpn. 37-40; with U.S. Air Force 40-45; Dir. International Business Machines Corpn. 46-, Pres. 52-61, Chief Exec. Officer 56-, Chair. of Board 61-; Dir. Bankers Trust Co.; Trustee, Rockefeller Foundation, Brown Univ., Calif. Inst. of Technology, Sarah Lawrence Coll., Airforce

Aid Soc.; U.S. Air Medal, Presidential Medal of Freedom, Légion d'Honneur, other foreign awards.
Home: Meadowcroft Lane, Greenwich, Conn.; Office: Old Orchard Road, Armonk, New York, N.Y. 10504, U.S.A.

Watson-Jones, Sir Reginald, Kt., B.SC., M.CH.ORTH., F.R.C.S.; British orthopaedic surgeon; b. 4 March 1902; ed. Liverpool Univ., London and Continental Univs.
Liverpool Royal Infirmary 27-43; Robert Jones and Agnes Hunt Orthopædic Hospital 28; Birkenhead Gen. Hospital 29-40; Consulting Orthopædic Surgeon N. Wales Sanatorium 27-40; Civilian Consultant in Orthopædic Surgery to the R.A.F. 40-: Dir. Orthopædic and Accident Service, London Hospital 43-; Lecturer in Orthopædic Pathology and Clinical Lecturer in Orthopædic Surgery, Liverpool Univ. 27-43; Hon. Lecturer in War Surgery, British Postgraduate Medical School 41-45; Pres. British Orthopædic Asscn.; Fellow, Royal Society of Medicine; Extra Orthopædic Surgeon to H.M. the Queen; fmr. Orthopædic Surgeon to H.M. the King; Arthur Sims Commonwealth Prof. of Surgery for 50-55; British Editor *Journal of Bone and Joint Surgery*.
Publs. *Fractures and Joint Injuries* 40 (4th edn. 56), *Pye's Surgical Handicraft* 14th edn. (jointly) 44, *Rheumatic Diseases* 47, *Medicine and Surgery for the Attorney* 59.
82 Portland Place, London, W.1; and House-in-the-Wood, Golden Valley, Hindhead, Surrey, England.
Telephone: LANgham 1378.

Watson-Watt, Sir Robert (Alexander), Kt., C.B., F.R.S.; British scientist; b. 92; ed. Brechin High School, Univ. Coll., Dundee and St. Andrews Univ.
Various posts in meteorology, radio and radar in Meteorological Office, Dept. of Scientific and Industrial Research, Air Ministry, Ministries of Aircraft Production, Supply, Civil Aviation and Transport 15-52; Deputy Chair. Radio Board of War Cabinet 43-45; writer, lecturer and consultant; fmr. Adviser on Radar and Electronics, Defence Research Board, Nat. Defence H.Q., Canada 52; fmr. Pres. Royal Meteorological Soc. and Inst. of Navigation; Vice-Pres. Inst. of Radio Engineers, N.Y.; U.S. Medal for Merit 46; Valdemar Poulsen Medal of Danish Acad. Technical Sciences, Hughes Medal of Royal Soc.; Cresson Medal, Franklin Inst., 57; Gold Medal, French Soc. for Encouragement of Progress 67; Hon. LL.D. (St. Andrews), D.Sc. (Toronto and Laval).
Publs. *The Cathode Ray Oscillograph in Radio Research* 33, *Through the Weather House* 35, *Three Steps to Victory* 58, *The Pulse of Radar* 59, *Man's Means to His End* 61.
7 Crescent Place, London, S.W.3, England.
Telephone: 01-589-9982.

Watters, Gustav F.; American businessman; b. 20 June 1903; ed. Bordentown Military Inst.
With Schoellkopf-Hutton & Pomeroy Doolittle & Co., investment bankers, Buffalo 28-35; Utility business under name of Niagara Lockport & Ontario Power Co., Buffalo 35-; Vice-Pres. Dir. Niagara Mohawk Power Corpn. 50-55, Exec. Vice-Pres., Dir. 55-; Vice-Pres., Dir. Niagara Falls Power Co. 47-.
Home: 215 Scarborough Drive; Office: 300 Erie Boulevard West, Syracuse, N.Y., U.S.A.

Waugh, Alec; British novelist; b. 8 July 1898; ed. Sherborne and Royal Military Coll. Sandhurst.
Served with Dorset Regt. First World War, rejoined Regt. 39, served with B.E.F. France 40; Staff Capt. Mines Dept. 40, M.E.F. 41-42, P.A.I.C. 43-45, retd. with rank of Major 45.
Publs. *The Loom of Youth* 17, *Kept* 25, *Nor Many Waters* 28, *Hot Countries* 30, *Most Women ... 31*, *So Lovers Dream* 31, *Wheels Within Wheels* 33, *The Balliols* 34, *Jill Somerset* 36, *Going Their Own Ways* 38,

No Truce with Time 41, *His Second War* 44, *Unclouded Summer* 48, *The Lipton Story* 50, *Where the Clocks Chime Twice* 52, *Guy Renton* 53, *Island in the Sun* 56, *The Sugar Islands* 58, *In Praise of Wine* 59, *Fuel for the Flame* 60, *My Place in the Bazaar* 61, *The Early Years of Alec Waugh* 62, *A Family of Islands* 64, *The Mule on the Minaret* 65, *My Brother Evelyn and Other Profiles* 67.
c/o Brandt-Brandt, 101 Park Avenue, New York 17, N.Y., U.S.A.

Waugh, Samuel Clark; American government official; b. 28 April 1890; ed. Univ. of Nebraska.
With First Trust Co., Lincoln, Nebraska 13-53, Dir. 18, and Pres. 46-53; Asst. Sec. of State for Economic Affairs, Dept. of State 53-55, Deputy Under-Sec. of State for Economic Affairs Aug.-Oct. 55; Pres. and Chair. of Board, Export-Import Bank of Washington 55-61; U.S. Alternate Gov. Int. Monetary Fund and Bank of Reconstruction and Devt. 53-55; Consultant, Department of State 64-; Int. Consultant The Bank of New York, The Blaw-Knox Co. 61-; Dir. Atlantic Council of the U.S. 65-; decorations from Mexico, Chile, Spain, Japan, Brazil, Italy, Philippines and China (Taiwan).
2101 Connecticut Avenue, Washington, D.C. 20008, U.S.A.
Telephone: 332-8298.

Wayne, John (Marion Michael Morrison); American film actor; b. 24 June 1924; ed. Univ. of S. California.
Films include: *Stagecoach* 39, *The Long Voyage Home* 40, *Reap The Wild Wind* 42, *A Lady Takes a Chance* 43, *Tall in the Saddle* 44, *They Were Expendable* 45, *Red River* 46, *Wake of the Red Witch* 48, *Sands of Iwo Jima* 49, *Operation Pacific* 50, *The Quiet Man, Jet Pilot, Big Jim McLain* 51-52, *Fort Apache, Island in the Sky, Hondo, The High and the Mighty, The Searchers, Blood Alley, The Conqueror* 55, *Wings of Eagles* 56, *Barbarian and Geisha* 58, *Horse Soldiers* 59, *North to Alaska, Hatari, McLintock* 64, *The Sons of Katie Elder* 65, *El Dorado* 67.
c/o Batjac Productions Inc., Paramount Studios, Hollywood, California, U.S.A.

Wazir, Janki Nath, B.A., LL.B., Barr.-at-Law; Indian judge; b. 05; ed. S. P. Coll., Srinagar, Kashmir, Punjab Univ., London Univ., and Middle Temple, London.
Advocate of Lahore High Court 31; part-time law lecturer Law Coll., Lahore 33-36; Judge High Court, Jammu and Kashmir State 36-48 and Chief Justice 48-; Vice-Chancellor Univ. of Jammu and Kashmir 50-57.
High Court of Jammu and Kashmir, Srinagar, Kashmir, India.

Wazyk, Adam; Polish poet; b. 17 Nov. 1905.
Co-editor *Kuznica* (weekly) 45-50; Editor *Tworczosc* (monthly) 50-54.
Publs. Verse: *Wiersze zebrane (Collected Poems)*, *Poemat dla doroslych (Poems for Adults)*, *Labirynt (Labyrinth)*, *Wagon (The Wagon)*; Novels: *Mity rodzinne (Family Myths)*, *Epizod (Episode)*; Essays: *W strone humanizmu (On the Side of Humanism)*, *Mickiewicz i wersfikacja (Mickiewicz and National Versification)*, *Kwestia gustu* (Matter of Taste) 67; numerous translations of French and Russian poets.
Aleja Róż 8, Warsaw, Poland.
Telephone: 287878.

Weatherhead, Rev. Leslie Dixon, C.B.E., M.A., PH.D., D.LITT., D.D.; British minister of religion; b. 14 Oct. 1893; ed. Manchester and London Univs.
Minister, Oxford Road Methodist Church, Manchester 22-25; Minister of Brunswick Methodist Church, Leeds 25-36; Minister of the City Temple, London 36-60, Minister Emeritus 60-; Pres. Methodist Conf. 55-56; Pres. Inst. Religion and Medicine 66-67; Hon. Chaplain H.M. Forces; Hon. Mem. Soc. of Psychotherapists; mem. Soc. for Psychical Research; Lyman-Beecher Lecturer, Yale Univ.; Selected Preacher, Univ. of Cambridge.

Publs. include *Psychology, Religion and Healing, His Life and Ours, How Can I Find God?, Psychology and Life, It Happened in Palestine, A Shepherd Remembers, Thinking Aloud in Wartime, This is the Victory, Personalities of the Passion, In Quest of a Kingdom, When the Lamp Flickers, Prescription for Anxiety, A Private House of Prayer, After Death, The Afterworld of the Poets, The Transforming Friendship, Jesus and Ourselves, Psychology in Service of the Soul, The Will of God, The Significance of Silence, The Resurrection and the Life, That Immortal Sea, Over His Own Signature, The Mastery of Sex Through Psychology and Religion, Why Do Men Suffer?, Discipleship, The Eternal Voice, A Plain Man Looks at the Cross, Key Next Door and other City Temple Sermons* 60, *Salute to a Sufferer* 62, *Wounded Spirits* 62, *The Christian Agnostic* 65, *Time For God* 67.

c/o The City Temple, Holborn Viaduct, London, E.C.1; Home: 20 Richmond Grove, Bexhill-on-Sea, Sussex, England.

Telephone: Bexhill-on-Sea 1719.

Weaver, Robert C., B.S., M.A., PH.D.; American economist and government official; b. 29 Dec. 1907; ed. Harvard Univ.

Adviser on Negro Affairs (Dept. of the Interior) 33-37; Consultant (Housing Div., Public Works Admin.) 34-37; Special Asst. to Admin., U.S. Housing Authority 37-40; Chief, Negro Employment and Training (Office of Production Man. and later War Production Board) 40-44; Visiting Prof. New York Univ. 48-50; Dir. Opportunity Fellowships (J. H. Whitney Foundation) 50-55; Dep. Commr. of Housing, N.Y. State 55, Rent Admin. 55-59; Consultant, Ford Foundation 59-60; Vice-Chair. Housing and Redevelopment Board, N.Y. City 60-61; Admin. Housing and Home Finance Agency 61-66; fmr. Chair. Nat. Asscn. for the Advancement of Colored People, mem. Advisory Comm. U.S. Housing Census for 1960, Nat. Comm. for Selection (Fulbright Fellowships), Exec. Cttee. of Action; Dir. Lavenburg Foundation; Sec. Dept. of Housing and Urban Devt. 66-; Chair. of Board FNMA 61-68; LL.D. (Harvard).

Publs. *Negro Labor: A National Problem* 46, *The Negro Ghetto* 48, *The Urban Complex* 64, *Dilemmas of Urban America* 65.

1626 K Street, N.W., Washington, D.C.; 4501 Connecticut Avenue, Washington, D.C. 20008, U.S.A.
Telephone: 382-4417.

Weaver, Warren, B.S., C.B., PH.D.; American scientific executive; b. 17 July 1894; ed. Univ. of Wisconsin.

Assistant Prof. of Maths., Throop Coll. 17-18, Calif. Inst. of Technology 19-20; Asst. Prof. of Maths., Univ. of Wisconsin 20-25, Assoc. Prof. 25-28, Prof. and Chair. of Dept. 28-32; Dir. Div. of Natural Sciences and Agriculture, Rockefeller Foundation 32-55, Vice-Pres. for Natural and Medical Sciences 55-59; Air Service, U.S. Army 17-19; Chair. Section D-2 40-42, and Chief of Applied Mathematics Panel, Nat. Defense Research Cttee. of Office of Scientific Research and Development 43-46; Fellow, Exec. Cttee. American Asscn. for Advancement of Science 50-52, Pres. 54, Chair. Board of Dirs. 55; mem. Board Scientific Consultants, Sloan-Kettering Inst. for Cancer Research 51-54, Chair. Scientific Policy Cttee. 55-59, Trustee 54-, Vice-Pres. 58-59, Chair. 59-60; Vice-Chair. Memorial Sloan-Kettering Cancer Center 60-, Chair. Scientific Policy Cttee. 60-; Chair. Basic Research Group, Research and Development Board 52-53; mem. American Philosophical Soc. 44-, Councillor 57-60; mem. Board Nat. Science Foundation 56-60; Vice-Pres. Alfred P. Sloan Foundation 59-64, Trustee 56-, Consultant on Scientific Affairs 64-; mem. Nat. Advisory Cancer Council, U.S. Public Health Service 57-60; Vice-Chair. Health Research Council, City of New York 58-60; Pres. Public Health Research Inst. of City of New York Inc. 61-63;

Chair. Board of Trustees and Fellow, Salk Inst. for Biological Studies 62-; mem. Board of Dirs. Scientists' Inst. for Public Information 63-; Fellow American Acad. of Arts and Sciences; mem. New York Acad. of Sciences 63-, Fellow 64-; King's Medal for Service in the Cause of Freedom; Medal for Merit (U.S.A.); Officier Légion d'Honneur (France); Public Welfare Medal, Nat. Acad. of Sciences 57; Hon. LL.D. (Wis.), Hon. D.Sc. (Drexel Inst. of Technology, São Paulo, Pittsburgh, New York Univs.), D.Eng. (Rensselaer Polytechnic Institute), D.Hum. Litt. (Univ. of Rochester); UNESCO Kalinga Prize 65, Arches of Science Award 65.

Publs. *The Electromagnetic Field* (with Max Mason) 29, *Mathematical Theory of Communication* (with Claude Shannon) 49, *Lady Luck—The Theory of Probability* 63, *Alice in Many Tongues* 64; Editor *The Scientist Speaks.*

Alfred P. Sloan Foundation, 630 Fifth Avenue, New York City, N.Y. 10020; Second Hill, New Milford, Connecticut 06776, U.S.A.

Webb, James Edwin, A.B.; American government official and industrialist; b. 06; ed. Univ. of N. Carolina and Washington Univ. Law School.

Employed R. G. Lassiter & Co., Raleigh, N.C. 24-25; Bureau Educational Research, Univ. of N.C. 28-29; Parham & Lassiter, Attorneys, Oxford, N.C. 29-30; Sec. to Congressman Edward W. Pou 32-34; O. Max Gardner, Attorney, Washington, D.C. 34-36; Personnel Dir. and Asst. to Pres. Sperry Gyroscope Co. Inc., Brooklyn N.Y. 36-41, Sec. and Treas. 41-43, Vice-Pres. 43-44; Gardner, Morrison & Rogers, Attorneys, Washington, D.C. 45-46; Exec. Asst. to Under-Sec. of Treasury 46; Dir. Bureau of Budget 46-49; Under-Sec. of State 49-52; Dir. Kerr-McGee Oil Industries Inc. 52-61, McDonnell Aircraft Corpn. 52-61; Admin. Nat. Aeronautics and Space Admin. 61-; Trustee George Washington Univ. 51-63, Cttee. for Econ. Devt. 53-61, Nat. Geographic Soc. 66-; Chair. Meridian House Foundation, Washington; Hon. LL.D. (Univ. of N.C. 49, Syracuse Univ. 50, Colorado Coll. 57, George Washington Univ. 61); Hon. Sc.D. (Notre Dame Univ. 61, Washington Univ. 62), Hon. D.Hum. (Wayne State Univ. 65).

National Aeronautics and Space Administration (N.A.S.A.), Washington 25, D.C.; Home: 2800 36th Street, N.W., Washington, D.C. 20007, U.S.A.

Weber, Edouard, D.IUR.; Swiss international civil servant; b. 2 Oct. 1901; ed. Univs. of Lausanne, Berne and Paris.

Former lawyer; fmr. Sec. Court of Admin., Berne Canton; Gen. Sec. Fed. Dept. of Posts and Railroads 41-49; Dir.-Gen. Swiss Posts, Telegraphs and Telephones 50-60; Dir.-Gen. Int. Bureau, Universal Postal Union, Berne 61-66; Pres. Radio Suisse Ltd.; Founder-Pres. Conf. of European Postal and Telecommunications Admins.; fmr. mem. Board of Dirs. Swiss Broadcasting Corpn., Swissair.

Publ. *Das System der festen Pfandstelle.*

Egelbergstrasse 26, 3000 Berne 15, Switzerland.
Telephone: 44-34-22.

Weber, Ernst, D.SC., D.PHIL., D.ENG.; Austrian engineer; b. 6 Sept. 1901; ed. Vienna Technical Univ.

Research Engineer Oesterreichische Siemens-Schuckert Co. Vienna 24-29; Design Engineer Siemens-Schuckert Co. Berlin 29-30; Visiting Prof. Polytechnic Inst. of Brooklyn, N.Y. 30-31, Research Prof. of Electrical Engineering 31-41, Head Research and Graduate Study in Electrical Engineering 42-45; Head Dept. of Electrical Engineering and Dir. of Microwave Research Inst. 45-57, Vice-Pres. for Research 57-63; Pres. Polytechnic Inst. of Brooklyn 57-; mem. Army Scientific Advisory Panel; Founding mem. Nat. Acad. of Eng.; mem. Nat. Acad. of Sciences; Pres. Inst. Radio Engineers 59; Pres. Inst. of Electrical and Electronics Engineers 63.

159 Lorraine Avenue, Mount Vernon, N.Y., U.S.A.
Telephone: 914-MO8-7541.

Weber, Gerhard, Prof.; German architect; b. 11 June 1909; ed. Kunstgewerbeakademie, Dresden, and Bauhaus, Dessau.
Buildings: Industriebauten Konzertsaal Hess. Rundfunk, Staatsoper Hamburg, Nationaltheater, Mannheim, Forschungsreaktor Garching.
8131 Oberallmannshausen, Post Assenhausen -Obb., German Federal Republic.
Telephone: Starnberg 58-16.

Weber, Karl, D.IUR; German lawyer and politician; b. 8 March 1898; ed. Gymnasium Koblenz, Universität Hamburg and Rheinische Friedrich-Wilhelms-Universität, Bonn.
Lawyer in Koblenz 27; Chair. Koblenz Law Society 47; Presiding mem. German Law Asscn. 52; mem. Bundestag 49-65; Minister of Justice 65; Christian Democrat.
Coblenz, Lennéstrasse 4, German Federal Republic.

Webster, David L., PH.D.; American physicist; b. 6 Nov. 1888; ed. Harvard Univ.
Asst. Instructor Harvard Univ. 09-17; Asst. Prof. of Physics Univ. of Michigan 17-19, Mass. Inst. of Technology 19-20; Prof. of Physics Stanford Univ. 20-54, Emeritus 54-; Vice-Pres. Section B of American Asscn. for Advancement of Science 32; Pres. American Asscn. of Physics Teachers 35 and 36; Co-ordinator Civilian Pilot Training, Stanford Univ. 39-41; Head Physicist, Signal Corps, U.S. Army 42; Chief Physicist, Ordnance Dept., U.S. Army 43-45; revised *Civilian Pilot Training Manual* and *Flight Instructor's Manual* for Civil Aeronautics Admin. 41; part-time Consultant, Hawaii Inst. of Geophysics 61-63; Ames Research Center, N.A.S.A. 62-.
Publs. *General Physics* (with H. W. Farwell and E. R. Drew) 23, *Roentgenray Physics (The Science of Radiology)* 33, *Electricity* in *Encyclopaedia Britannica* 55 edn.
1830 Cowper Street, Palo Alto, Calif. 94301, U.S.A.
Telephone: 415-323-6645.

Webster, Sir David Lumsden, Kt., F.R.C.M., B.A.; British opera and ballet administrator; b. 03; ed. Holt School, Liverpool Univ. and Oxford Univ.
Gen. Man. Bon Marché (Liverpool) Ltd. 32-40, Gen. Man. Lewis Ltd. (Liverpool) 40-41; Ministry of Supply Ordnance Factories, engaged on special methods of developing production 42-44; Administrator Covent Garden Preliminary Cttee. 44-46, Gen. Administrator Royal Opera House, Covent Garden 46-; Chair. Liverpool Philharmonic Soc. Ltd. 40-45; Chair. Orchestral Employers Asscn. 48-65, London Orchestral Concerts Board 65-; Gov. and Treas. Royal Ballet School 55-; Gov. The Royal Ballet 57-; Dir. Southern Television 57-, Commonwealth Festival Arts Soc. 62-; Gov. and Gen. Admin. of London Opera Centre 62-; Officier Légion d'Honneur, Commdr. Order of the North Star (Sweden), Commdr. Military Order of Christ (Portugal), Commdr. Order of Merit (Italy), Hon. R.A.M.
39 Weymouth Street, London, W.1, England.
Telephone: WELbeck 1636.

Weber, Margaret; American actress; b. 15 March 1905; ed. Queen Anne.s School, Caversham, England.
First professional engagements with Sybil Thorndike in *Trojan Women* and John Barrymore in *Hamlet* London 25; with Macdona Players, J. B. Fagan's Oxford Players, Ben Greet Shakespeare Co. and Old Vic Co. 26-30; appeared in and produced many plays for Stage Society, Repertory Players, Gate, Embassy and Q Theatres and played in West End; staged *Richard II, Hamlet, Henry IV, Twelfth Night, Macbeth, Othello* and *The Tempest* in New York; Man. Dir. American Repertory Theatre, N.Y. 46-47, directed or played in Broadway productions, including *The Seagull, Family Portrait, The Aspern Papers* and *The Cherry Orchard*; founded the Margaret Webster Shakespeare Co., playing through schools and colls. of America 48-50; staged *Don Carlo* 50, *Aida* 51, *Simon Boccanegra* 60 for Metropolitan Opera House N.Y.; produced William Walton's opera *Troilus and Cressida* (New York) 55, *The Merchant of Venice* (Stratford-on-Avon) 56; directed *Measure for Measure, Taming of the Shrew, Waiting in the Wings, 12 Angry Men, The Trojan Women*, etc.; appeared in one woman recitals of Shakespeare, Shaw and The Brontës, England, U.S.A. and South Africa; Hon. D.LL. (Lawrence Coll., Appleton, Wis. 42, Russell Sage Coll., Troy, N.Y. 44, Rutgers Univ. 47), D.H.L. (Smith Coll. 45, Fairfield Univ. 64, Boston Univ. 65).
Publs. *Shakespeare without Tears* 42, *Shakespeare Today* 56; adapted two plays *Girl Unknown* (New Theatre, London) 36, *Royal Highness* (Lyric Theatre, Hammersmith, London) 49.
c/o Spotlight, 43 Cranbourne Street, London, W.C.2, England.

Wechsler, James A.; American editor; b. 15; ed. Columbia Univ.
Editor *Columbia Spectator* 34-35; Student Advocate 36-37; Asst. Editor *Nation* magazine 38-39; Labour Editor, PM newspaper 40-41; Washington Bureau Chief, *New York Post* 42-44, Washington Correspondent 46-49, Editor, Editorial Page 49-61; Editorial Page Columnist and Editor 61-; U.S. Army 45.
Publs. *Revolt on the Campus* 35, *Labor Baron* 44, *The Age of Suspicion* 53, with Harold Levine *War, Propaganda and the United States.*
Home: 420 West End Avenue, New York City; Office: 75 West Street, New York City, N.Y., U.S.A.

Wedgwood, Dame Cicely Veronica (sister of Sir John Wedgwood, *q.v.*), D.B.E., M.A., F.R.HIST.S., F.R.S.L.; British author and historian; b. 20 July 1910; ed. Oxford Univ.
Pres. English Centre Int. P.E.N. Club 51-57; Pres. English Association 55-56; Clark Lecturer, Cambridge 57-58; Northcliffe Lecturer, University of London 59; mem. Arts Council 58-61, 66-67; mem. Royal Comm. on Historical MSS 53-, Inst. of Advanced Study, Princeton 52-68; Trustee Nat. Gallery, London 63-68; Officer, Order of Orange-Nassau; mem. American Acad.; Hon. D.Litt. (Oxford, Sheffield, Keele, Smith Coll. and Harvard), Hon. LL.D. (Glasgow).
Publs. *Strafford* 35, *The Thirty Years' War* 38, *Oliver Cromwell* 39, *William the Silent* 44, *Velvet Studies* 46, *Richelieu* 49, *English Literature in the Seventeenth Century* 50, *The Last of the Radicals* 51, *Montrose* 52, *The King's Peace* 55, *The King's War* 58, *Truth and Opinion* 60, *Poetry and Politics Under the Stuarts* 60, *Thomas Wentworth: A Revaluation* 61, *The Trial of Charles I* 64.
c/o Department of History, University College, London, W.C.1, England.

Wedgwood, Sir John Hamilton (brother of C. V. Wedgwood, *q.v.*), Bt.; British master potter; b. 1907; ed. Winchester Coll., and Trinity Coll., Cambridge.
Joined Josiah Wedgwood and Sons Ltd. 31, Dir. 35 and Deputy Chair. 55-66; mem. British Nat. Export Council 64-66; mem. Metropolitan Board of Friends' Provident and Century Life Office.
24 Rutland Court, London, S.W.7; White House, Clare, Suffolk, England.

Weed, Clyde E.; American mining executive; b. 90; ed. Michigan State Coll. and Michigan Technological Univ.
Gen. Man. (Mines) Anaconda Copper Mining Co. 38-42, Vice-Pres. (Mining Operations) 42-52, Vice-Pres. (Operations) 52-56 (name changed to Anaconda Co.), Pres. Anaconda Co. 56-58, Chair. Board of Dirs. 58-65.
Home: 435 E. 52nd Street, New York City 22; Office: 25 Broadway, New York City, N.Y., U.S.A.

Weeks, Edward A., B.S., LITT.D.; American journalist; b. 98; ed. Cornell, Harvard and Cambridge Univs.
MSS. reader and salesman with Horace Liveright. Inc.,

N.Y. City 23; Assoc. Editor *Atlantic Monthly* 24-28, Editor 38-66; Editor Atlantic Monthly Press 28-37, Senior Editor 66-; Overseer, Harvard Univ. 45-51; Trustee, Wellesley Coll. 47-65, Colonial Williamsburg 58-, Pittsburgh and Rochester Univs. 60-; Dir. Magazine Publishers' Asscn. 61-63; Dir. American Field Service 63-; Vice-Chair. United Negro Coll. Fund 63-; Fellow American Acad. Arts and Sciences.
Publs. *This Trade of Writing* 35, *Great Short Novels* (Ed.) 41, *The Pocket Atlantic* (Ed.) 46, *The Open Heart* 55, *Jubilee—One Hundred Years of the Atlantic* (Ed. with Emily Flint) 57, *In Friendly Candor* 59, *Breaking into Print* 62, *Boston: Cradle of Liberty* 65, *The Lowells and Their Institute* 66.
Home: 59 Chestnut Street, Boston, Mass., U.S.A.; Office: 8 Arlington Street, Boston, Mass. 02116, U.S.A.

Weeks, Sinclair; American manufacturer and public servant; b. 93; ed. Newton (Mass.) High School and Harvard Univ.
Employed by First National Bank of Boston 14-23; served World War I; subsequently Pres. and Chair. Reed & Barton Corpn. (silversmiths), and Chair., Exec. Cttee. United-Carr Fastener Corpn; Dir. First Nat. Bank, Boston, John Hancock Mutual Life Ins. Co.; West Point Manufacturing Co.; Senator from Mass. (locum for Henry Cabot Lodge) Feb.-Dec. 44; mem. Republican Nat. Cttee. 40-52; Treasurer 41-44; Sec. of Commerce 53-58; mem. Business Advisory Council to Sec. of Commerce.
Presidential Centre, Boston 02199, Mass., U.S.A.

Weerasinghe, Oliver, O.B.E., F.R.I.B.A., M.T.P.I.; Ceylonese city planner and diplomatist; b. 29 Sept. 1907; ed. Royal Coll., Colombo, Ceylon, and Univ. of Liverpool, England.
Directed planning and development of new city of Anuradhapura, Ceylon 40-56; Head, Town and Country Planning Dept., Ceylon 47-56; Chair. Board of Improvement Commrs., Colombo 53-56; Chief, Planning and Urbanization Section, Dept. of Econ. and Social Affairs, UN, New York 56-64; Exec. Sec. UN Seminar on Regional Planning, Tokyo 58, UN Expert Group on Metropolitan Planning, Stockholm 61, UN Symposium on New Towns, Moscow 64; Deputy Dir. Centre for Housing, Building and Planning, UN, New York 65; Ambassador of Ceylon to the U.S.A. 65-; Distinction in Town Planning, Royal Inst. of British Architects 46.
Publ. *Town Planning in Ceylon* 47.
Embassy of Ceylon, 2148 Wyoming Avenue, N.W., Washington, D.C.; Home: 2503 30th Street, N.W., Washington, D.C., U.S.A.
Telephone: DU7-0601 (Home).

Weese, Harry; American architect; b. 30 June 1915; ed. Yale Univ. School of Architecture, Mass. Inst. of Technology, Cranbrook Acad. of Art.
Research Asst. Bemis Housing Foundation, Mass. Inst. Technology (prefabricated and low-cost housing) 39; Principal, Baldwin, & Weese (architects) 40-42; U.S. Navy 42-46; Senior Designer, Chicago office Skidmore, Owings & Merrill 46-47; independent practice 47-; manufacturing plant for Cummins Engine Co., Columbus, Indiana 50-64.
Principal works: U.S. Embassy, Accra, Ghana, Hyde Park Redevelopment Project, Chicago, Arena Stage, Washington D.C., Physics Complex, Univ. of Colorado, Elvehjem Art Center, Univ. of Wisconsin, Milwaukee Center for the Performing Arts, Wisconsin, Time Inc., Chicago, Subway, Nat. Capital Transport Agency, Washington D.C., IBM Building, Milwaukee, Time & Life Building, Chicago, Research Centre, Cummins Engine Co., Columbus, Kentucky Centre for Performing Arts, Louisville.
Office: 10 West Hubbard Street, Chicago, Ill. 60610;

Home: 1235 North Astor Street, Chicago, Ill. 60610, U.S.A.
Telephone: 467-7030 (Office); MI-2-1498 (Home).

Wehner, Herbert; German journalist and politician; b. 11 July 1906; ed. Realschule.
Mem. Saxon Provincial Parl. 30-32; resistance movement 30-; emigrated to various countries including U.S.S.R. and Sweden 35-46; later Editor, Hamburg; Chair. Hamburg Union, Sozialdemokratische Partei Deutschlands (S.P.D.), Dep. Chair. Federal S.P.D. Party 58-; mem. Bundestag 49-; Minister of All-German Affairs 66-.
Beim Schlump 36, Hamburg, German Federal Republic.

Wei Heng; Chinese politician and administrator. Governor, Shansi Province 58-67, 1st Sec. Shansi Province Cttee. C.C.P. 65-; mem. Chinese Communist Party, Peking.
Taiyuan, Shansi Province (N.W. China), People's Republic of China.

Wei Kuo-ching; Chinese administrator; b. 14.
Former Political Commissar; Vice-Chair. Commission on Nationalities Affairs, Govt. Administrative Council 54; mem. Standing Cttee., Nat. People's Congress 54-56, Deputy for Kwangsi Chuang Autonomous Region 54-; Gov. Kwangsi Chuang Autonomous Region 55-; Chair. People's Council, Kwangsi Chuang Autonomous Region 58-; mem. Nat. Defence Council 54-; Alternate mem., C.C.P. Central Cttee. 56-.
Governor's Residence, Kwangsi Chuang Autonomous Region (Southern China), People's Republic of China.

Wei Tao-ming, LL.D.; Chinese diplomatist and politician; b. 1899; ed. Univ. de Paris à la Sorbonne.
Minister of Justice 28-29; Mayor of Nanking 30-32; Sec.-Gen. Executive Yuan 37-41; Amb. to France 41-42, to U.S.A. 42-46; Vice-Pres. Legislative Yuan 46-47; Gov. Taiwan Province 47-49; Adviser to Pres. 49-64; Amb. to Japan 64-66; Minister of Foreign Affairs 66-.
Publ. *Le Cheque en Chine.*
No. 10, Lane 119, Roosevelt Road, Sec. I, Taipei, Taiwan, Republic of China.

Weichmann, Herbert; German politician; b. 23 Feb. 1896; ed. Univs. of Breslau, Frankfurt (Main), Heidelberg and New York.
Provincial Judge, Breslau 26-27; Prussian Govt. posts 27-33; emigrated to France and Spain 33-40, U.S.A. 41-48; President, Hamburg Treasury 48-57; Senator for Finance, Hamburg 57-65; Chief Burgomaster of Hamburg 65-; mem. Bundesrat; Social Democrat.
Rathaus, Hamburg 1, German Federal Republic.

Weidlein, Edward Ray, M.A.; American scientist; b. 14 July 1887; ed. Univ. of Kansas.
Industrial Fellow, Univ. of Kansas 10-12; Senior Fellow, Mellon Inst., Pittsburgh 12-16, Asst. Dir. and later Assoc. Dir. 16, Acting Dir. 17-18, Dir. 21-51, Pres. 51-56 (retd.); Chair. Board of Trustees Mellon Inst. 51-55; Emer. Trustee Univ. of Pittsburgh 21-; Chief of Chemicals Branch W.P.B. 40-42, and Head Technical Consultant, W.P.B. 42-46; Pres. Regional Industrial Devt. Corpn. Fund 62-; Fellow, American Asscn. for Advancement of Science, N.Y. Acad. of Sciences, Royal Soc. of Arts; mem. American Chemical Soc. (Pres. 37, Dir. 38-47), awards include Chemical Industry Medal 35, Naval Ordnance Devt. Award 47, Priestley Medal 48, Certificate of Appreciation (Depts. of Army and Navy) 48; William Proctor Prize from Scientific Research Soc. of America 61; Richard Beatly Mellon Award 61; Founder's Award American Inst. of Chemical Engineers 66; Hon. D.Sc. (Tufts Coll. 24, Rutgers Univ. 37, Waynesburg Coll. 39, Univ. of Wichita 45, Southwestern Coll. 52, Philadelphia Coll. of Pharmacy and Science, Univ. of Miami); LL.D. (Univ. of Pittsburgh

30, Washington and Jefferson Coll. 47), D.Eng.
(Rensselnaer Polytechnic Inst. 49).
Publs. with William A. Hamor: *Science in Action,
Glances at Industrial Research.*
"Weidacres" P.O. Box 45, Rector, Pa. 15677, U.S.A.
Telephone: 238-2202.

Weidman, Rodolfo Alberto, LL.D.; Argentine lawyer
and diplomatist; b. 09; ed. School of Juridical and
Social Sciences, National Littoral Univ., Santa Fé.
Professor of Admin. Law, School of Juridical and Social
Sciences, Nat. Littoral Univ.; mem. Santa Fé Legislature 49-52; Nat. Congressman for Province of Santa Fé
52-55; Nat. Senator for Province of Santa Fé 58-, Chair.
Senate Cttee. on Constitutional Affairs; Ambassador to
Organization of American States (OAS) 62-64.
c/o Ministry of Foreign Affairs, Buenos Aires, Argentina.

Weigel, Helene, actress; b. Vienna, 12 May 1900.
Married Bertolt Brecht; began her career at the Neues
Theater, Frankfurt, Germany 18-20, appearing as
Marie in *Woyzek,* The Wife in *Weibsteufel,* and Piper-
karcka in *Die Ratten;* Schauspielhaus, Frankfurt 21-23,
Meroe in *Penthesilea,* Armgard in *Wilhelm Tell,* guest
performances as Flora Severin in *Judas,* Mannheim;
Staatstheater, Berlin 23-24, *Trommeln in der Nacht;*
she subsequently appeared at the Deutsches Theater,
Berlin 25-26 (where she met her husband) as Martha
Bernick in *Stützen der Gesellschaft* (Pillars of Society),
etc.; Renaissance Theater, Berlin 26, played Alte
Amme in *Das Leben das ich dir gab,* and Klara in *Maria
Magdalena,* etc.; Junge Bühne, Berlin 26-27 played
Jüngere Schwester in *Fegefeuer in Ingoldstadt,* and
Zigarettenverkäuferin in Brecht's *Im Dickicht der
Städte;* Lady Macbeth on radio, Berlin, March 27;
played Witwe Begbick in Brecht's *Mann ist Mann,*
Volksbühne, Berlin, Sept. 27; played Zofe Claudine
in *Georges Dandin,* and Grete in *Hinkemann* 27;
Staatstheater, Berlin 28-29, played Witwe Begbick in
Brecht's *Mann ist Mann,* Dienerin in *Ödipus,* and
Konstanze in *König Johann* (King John); Grosses
Schauspielhaus, Berlin, Dec. 30, appeared in Brecht's
Massnahme; Komödienhaus, Berlin, Jan. 32; played
the title part in Brecht's *Die Mutter* and Dienstmädchen
in *Der Fremde;* Paris, France, Oct. 37 appeared as
Guest Artist in the part of Teresa Carrar in *Die
Gewehre der Frau Carrar;* Copenhagen, Denmark 38,
Teresa Carrar in *Die Gewehre der Frau Carrar;* Chur,
Switzerland 48, appeared in the title part of *Antigone.*
Since the creation of the Berliner Ensemble in 1949,
she has appeared with that company in the following
parts: Mutter Courage in *Mutter Courage und ihre
Kinder* 49; Mutter in *Die Mutter* 51; Teresa in *Die
Gewehre der Frau Carrar* 52; Natella in *Der Kaukasische
Kreidekreis* (The Caucasian Chalk Circle) 54; Wassilissa
in *Ziehtochter* 55; Judith Keith in *Furcht und Elend des
Dritten Reiches* 57; Martha Flinz in *Frau Flinz* 61;
made her first London appearance at the Palace Theatre,
Aug. 56, with the Berliner Ensemble in *Mother Courage
and Her Children,* and subsequently as Natella in *The
Caucasian Chalk Circle;* at the Old Vic, Aug. 65, played
Volumnia in *Coriolanus* with the Berliner Ensemble;
appeared in Paris as Mutter Courage in *Mutter Courage*
54, 57, 60, Natella in *Der Kaukasische Kreidekreis* 55,
Mutter in *Die Mutter* 60; films in which she has appeared
include: *Das Siebte Kreuz* (U.S.A.) 41, and *Mutter
Courage und ihre Kinder;* television performance as
Madame Soupeau in *Die Geschichte der Simone Machard.*
c/o The Berliner Ensemble, Am Bertolt Brecht Platz,
Berlin N4, Germany.

Weigelt, Kurt, DR. JUR.; German banker; b. 84; ed.
Univs. of Berlin, Freiburg and Jena.
Barrister 08; Junior Judge 12; with Lehigh Coke Co.,
Bethlehem, Pa. 13; Chief of German War Organisation
for Supply of Oils and Fats 14-18; Pres. German

Margarine Industry 18-33; Man. Dir. Deutsche Petro-
leum A.G. 18-22; Dir. 22 and rep. mem. Board of Dirs.
27, Deutsche Bank, Berlin; engaged in negotiations on
sale of German railways in Asia Minor 26-29; German
Del. Ottoman Public Debt 27-45; Founder-Vice-Pres.
Deutsche Lufthansa 26; Pres. Deutscher Aerolloyd 28;
Pres. Air Transport Cttee., Int. Chamber of Commerce,
Paris 31-39; re-organisation German colonial companies
in Tanganyika Territory and Indonesia 24-32; Pres.
Corpn. of German Colonial Enterprises; Hon. Pres.
Deutsche Lufthansa A.G.; Baumwollspinnerei Ger-
mania; Vice-Pres. New Guinea Co., Moenus Maschinen-
fabrik A.G.; mem. of Board Deutsche Schlafwagen-
Gesellschaft; awarded Red Eagle of Prussia, Iron
Cross 14, Grand Cross with Star, Order of Merit, etc.
Hölderlinweg 29, Bad Homburg, German Federal
Republic.
Telephone: 22007.

Weigl, Henry, B.A., LL.B.; American business execu-
tive; b. 6 July 1912; ed. New York Univ., and Harvard
Univ.
Standard Brands Inc. 43-, Gen. Counsel 48-56, Vice-
Pres. 54-56, Exec. Vice-Pres. 56-60, Dir. 56-, Pres. and
mem. Exec. Cttee. 60-, Chief Exec. Officer 64-.
Standard Brands Inc., 625 Madison Avenue, New York
City, N.Y. 10022; Home: 30 Ivy Hill Road, Chappaqua,
New York, U.S.A.

Weikop, Ove Vilhelm; Danish businessman and politi-
cian; b. 21 April 1897.
Began career as retail dealer in textiles 16; Pres.
Danish Textile Retailers' Asscn. (Dansk Textil Union)
38-50; Pres. Mogensen & Dessau, Odense, Ove Weikop
& Son, Østerbros Messe; mem. Maritime and Commer-
cial Court 40-50; mem. City Council, Copenhagen 33-41;
Alderman 41-50; mem. Parl. 47; Minister of Trade 50-51;
Burgomaster of Copenhagen 51-; Commdr. Order of
Dannebrog; Grand Officer Order of Orange Nassau
(Netherlands), Order of the Crown; Knight Commdr. of
Victorian Order; Commdr. Crown of Thailand.
Home: Borgmester Jensens Alle 22, Copenhagen; Office:
Town Hall, Copenhagen, Denmark.

Weil, André; American (b. French) mathematician;
ed. Ecole Normale Supérieure, Paris, and Univs. of
Rome, Göttingen and Paris.
Professor, Aligarh Muslim Univ. 30-32; Faculty of
Science, Univ. of Strasbourg 33-39; Faculty of Philo-
sophy, Univ. of São Paulo 45-47; Prof., Dept. of
Mathematics, Univ. of Chicago 47-58; Prof. Inst. for
Advanced Study, Princeton 58-; Foreign mem. Royal
Soc. (U.K.) 66.
Institute for Advanced Study, Princeton, N.J., U.S.A.

Weilenmann, Hermann, DR.PHIL., Dr. h.c.; Swiss
historian and writer; b. 9 May 1893; ed. Univs. of
Zürich, Kiel and Geneva.
Sec., Nouvelle Société Helvétique 20-21; Sec., later Dir.
and Vice-Pres. Zürich Inst. for Adult Education 24-64;
Vice-Pres. Swiss Writers Asscn. 42-50; Int. Con-
gress of Historical Sciences 38, First World Con-
gress of Sociology 54, Int. Political Science Asscn. 61;
Pres. Swiss Schiller Foundation 54-62, Swiss Fed. for
Adult Education 51-63.
Publs. *Der Befreier* 18, *Die vielsprachige Schweiz, eine
Lösung des Nationalitätenproblems* 25, *Zusammenschluss
zur Eidgenossenschaft* 40, *Pax Helvetica oder die
Demokratie der kleinen Gruppen* 51, *Erwachsenenbildung
in der Schweiz* 55.
Kirchgasse 33, Zürich, Switzerland.

Weinberg, Alvin M., M.S., PH.D.; American physicist;
b. 20 April 1915; ed. Univ. of Chicago.
Biophysics research Univ. of Chicago 39-42; Hanford
reactor design Univ. of Chicago Metallurgical Laboratory 42-45; Section Chief Physics Division, Oak Ridge
Nat. Laboratory 45-48, Dir. 48, Research Dir. 48-55;

Dir. Oak Ridge Nat. Laboratory 55-; Fellow American Nuclear Soc., Pres. 59-60; Fellow American Physical Soc.; mem. Scientific Advisory Board to the Air Force 56-59; mem. President's Science Advisory Cttee. 60-63; mem. American Acad. of Arts and Sciences, Nat. Acad. of Sciences, mem. Cttee. on Science and Public Policy, Nat. Acad. of Sciences; co-recipient Atoms for Peace Award 60, Ernest O. Lawrence Memorial Award (Atomic Energy Comm.) 60.
Publ. *Physical Theory of Neutron Chain Reactors* (with Eugene P. Wigner) 58, *Reflections on Big Science* 67.
111 Moylan Lane, Oak Ridge; and Oak Ridge National Laboratory, P.O.B. X, Oak Ridge, Tennessee 37830, U.S.A.
Telephone: 615-483-6045.

Weinberg, Sidney James; American investment banker; b. 12 Oct. 1891; ed. Browne's Business Coll.
Goldman, Sachs and Co. 07-, Partner 27-; U.S. Naval service 17-18; Dir. Gen. Cigar Co., Ford Motor Co.; mem. Business Council 33-; Asst. Dir. of Purchases, Office of Production Management 41; Asst. to Chair. War Productivity Board 42-43, Vice-Chair. 44; Asst. to Admin. Office of Defense Mobilisation 50-51; Trustee, Cttee. for Econ. Devt., Eisenhower Exchange Fellowships, etc.; Fellow, Inst. for Judicial Administration; Medal for Merit; Hon. LL.D., Harvard Univ., etc.
Office: 55 Broad Street, New York City, N.Y. 10004; Home: 781 Fifth Avenue, New York City, N.Y. 10022, U.S.A.

Weinkauff, Hermann; German lawyer; b. 94; ed. Law Schools in Munich, Heidelberg, Würzburg and Paris.
Served in Bavarian Ministry of Justice 23-24; Legal Adviser to High Court, Leipzig 25-29; study in France on behalf of German Ministry of Justice 29-31; head of Legal Services, Leipzig High Court 32-33, Justice 33-45; Pres. Bamberg *Landesgericht* 46-49, *Oberlandesgericht* 49-50; Pres. Federal High Court Karlsruhe 50-60; Pres. of German Section of the Int. Union for Law and Social Philosophy; Dr. h.c. (Heidelberg).
Publs. *Französische Justizreform, Naturrecht in evangelischer Sicht, Richtertum und Rechtsfindung in Deutschland, Über das Widerstandsrecht.*
Graf-Ebersteinstrasse 9, Karlsruhe, German Federal Republic.

Weinstock, Arnold, B.SC. (ECON.); British business executive; b. 29 July 1924; ed. Univ. of London.
Junior Admin. Officer, Admiralty 44-47; with Private Group of Companies engaged in finance and property development 47-54; Man. Dir. Radio and Allied Industries Ltd. (now Radio and Allied Holdings Ltd.) 54-63; Dir. General Electric Co. Ltd. 61-, Man. Dir. 63-.
7 Grosvenor Square, London, W.1, England.

Weir, Major-General Sir Stephen Cyril Ettrick, K.B.E., C.B., D.S.O.; New Zealand army officer; b. 04; ed. Otago Boys' High School, Victoria Coll. and Royal Mil. Acad., Woolwich.
Commissioned Royal Artillery 27; mil. posts in New Zealand 29-39; Regt. Commdr. N.Z.E.F. 40-41; New Zealand Division 42-44, 10 Corps 44; G.O.C. 46th British Infantry Division 44-46, Southern Mil. District 48-49; Imperial Defence Coll., London 50; War Office 51; Q.M.G. 52-55; Chief N.Z. Gen. Staff 55-60; Military Adviser to N.Z. Govt. 60-61; Ambassador to Thailand 61-67, concurrently Amb. to Thailand, Laos and S. Vietnam and Rep. to South East Asia Treaty Org. (SEATO) 61-67; Legion of Merit, Greek Cross for Valour.
c/o Ministry of Foreign Affairs, Wellington, New Zealand.

Weir, Hon. Walter C.; Canadian politician; b. 7 Jan. 1929; ed. elementary and secondary education, Portage la Prairie, Manitoba.
Private business (funeral director), Minnedosa, Manitoba 53-63; Minister of Municipal Affairs, Manitoba 61-63, Acting Minister of Public Works 62, full Minister of Public Works Nov. 62-66; Minister of Highways 65-; Leader of Manitoba Progressive Conservative Party and Premier of Manitoba Nov. 67-.
Office: Room 204, Legislative Building, Winnipeg 1; Home: 670 Wellington Crescent, Winnipeg 9, Manitoba, Canada.
Telephone: 946-7201 (Office); 284-2175 (Home).

Weisgal, Meyer Wolf; American journalist and executive; b. 11 Oct. 1894; ed. Columbia Univ.
National Sec. Zionist Org. of America 21-30; Dir.-Gen. Palestine Pavilion, World's Fair, New York 39-40; Personal Political Rep. Dr. Weizmann in U.S.A. 40-48; Organiser, American Section Jewish Agency for Palestine, Sec.-Gen. 43-46; Organiser and Exec. Vice-Chair. American Cttee. Weizmann Inst. 46-59; Chair. Exec. Council Weizmann Inst. of Science, Israel 49-, Pres. 66-; del. World Zionist Congress 24-; fmr. Editor *The New Palestine* (New York) 21-30, *Jewish Standard* (Toronto) 30-32.
Publs. *Chaim Weizmann: Statesman, Scientist, Builder of the Jewish Commonwealth* 44, *Chaim Weizmann, A Biography by Several Hands* (Editor) 63, and numerous Jewish and Zionist pamphlets.
14 Neveh Weizmann, Rehovoth, Israel; and 240 Central Park South, New York 19, N.Y., U.S.A.
Telephone: 103-951721 (Israel); CI-7-3753 (New York).

Weiss, Ludwig; Austrian politician; b. 25 Aug. 1902; ed. Technische Hochschule, Vienna.
Employee Austrian Fed. Railways 27-45, then Pres. of Villach Branch; mem. Nationalrat; mem. Advisory Assembly, Council of Europe; Minister of Transport and Nationalized Undertakings April 66-; People's Party.
Ministry of Transport and Nationalized Undertakings. Vienna, Austria.

Weiss, Paul Alfred, PH.D.; American biologist; b. 21 March 18, 1898; ed. Univ. of Vienna.
Asst. Dir. Biology Research Inst., Acad. of Sciences, Vienna 22-29; Sterling Fellow, Yale Univ. 30-32; Prof. of Zoology, Univ. of Chicago 33-54; Prof., Rockefeller Inst., New York 54-64; Prof. and Dean Graduate School of Biomedical Sciences, Univ. of Texas 64-66; Prof. Emer. Rockefeller Univ. 66-; Visiting Prof. at many Univs.; mem. Science Advisory Cttee. of Pres. of U.S.A. 58-60; Chair. Div. Biology and Agriculture, Nat. Research Council 51-55, Biology Council, Nat. Acad. Sciences 53-58, U.S.A. Nat. Comm., Int. Union Biological Sciences 53-64; Consultant, U.S. Dept. of State; mem. U.S. Nat. Acad. Sciences, mem. Council 64-67; mem. Royal Swedish Acad. Science, Serbian Acad. Science, German Acad. of Science, Leopoldina, American Philosophical Soc., American Acad. Arts and Science; Pres. Growth Soc. 41, Harvey Soc. 62-63; Pres. Int. Soc. Cell Biology 65-68; Vice-Pres. American Asscn. for Advancement of Science 52-53; Hon. M.D., Hon. Sc.D., Hon. Dr. med. and surg.
Publs. *Principles of Development* 39; three books and 300 scientific papers on growth, development, nervous system, etc.
201 East 66th Street, New York, N.Y. 10021, U.S.A.
Telephone: 249-8269.

Weiss, Peter; Swedish (b. German) writer; b. 16; ed. Art Academy, Prague.
Emigrated from Germany 34, lived in England 34-36, in Czechoslovakia 36-38, in Sweden 39-; painter, film producer and writer; Charles Veillon Prize for Literature 63; Heinrich-Mann-Preis, Akademie der Künste (E. Berlin) 66.
Publs. Prose: *Der Schatten des Körpers des Kutschers* 60, *Abschied von den Eltern* 61, *Fluchtpunkt* 62, *Das Gespräch der drei Gehenden* 63; Plays: *Nacht mit gästen* 63, *Die Verfolgung und Ermordung Jean Paul Marats* 64 (film 67), *Die Ermittlung* 65, *Gesang vom Lusa-it nischen Popanz* 66, *Viet-Nam Dialogue* 67, *Wie dein*

Herrn Mockinpott das Leiden ausgetrieben wird 68, *Sangen om Utysket* (The Song of the Scarecrow) 68. Storgatan 18, Stockholm, Sweden.

Weisskopf, Victor Frederick, PH.D.; American (b. Austrian) physicist; b. 1908; ed. Vienna and Göttingen Univs.
Research Associate, Zürich Inst. of Technology 22-26, Berlin 31-32; Rockefeller Foundation Fellow, Copenhagen and Cambridge 36-37; Instructor of Physics, Univ. of Rochester 37-40, Asst. Prof. 40-43; Group Leader, Los Alamos Scientific Laboratory 43-47; Prof. of Physics, Mass. Inst. of Technology 45-; mem. Directorate, European Org. for Nuclear Research 60-61, Dir.-Gen. 61-65; Pres. American Physical Soc. 60; Max Planck Medal 56; corresp. mem. French, Scottish, Austrian and Bavarian Acads. of Sciences; foreign mem. Danish Soc. of Sciences; Hon. Fellow French Soc. of Physics, Royal Soc. of Edinburgh, Weizmann Inst., Israel; several hon. degrees.
Publs. *Theoretical Nuclear Physics* (Blatt and Weisskopf) 52, *Knowledge and Wonder* 62.
36 Arlington Street, Cambridge, Mass. 02139, U.S.A. Telephone: 617-868-2390.

Weissman, George; American tobacco executive; b. 12 July 1919; ed. Coll. of City of New York, New York Univ. and Univ. of Illinois.
United States Navy 42-46; Samuel Goldwyn 46-48; Account Exec., Benjamin Sonnenberg 48-52; Asst. to Pres. and Dir. of Public Relations, Philip Morris Inc. 52, Vice-Pres. and Dir. of Marketing 57-59, Dir. 58-, Exec. Vice-Pres. 59-; Chair. of Board and Chief Exec. Officer, Philip Morris International 60-64, Pres. 64-, Pres. and Chief Operating Officer 67-.
Philip Morris International, 100 Park Avenue, New York City, N.Y. 10017; Home: 81 Manursing Way, Rye, New York 10580, U.S.A.
Telephone: 212-679-1800 (Office); 914-WO 7-5845.

Weitz, Raanan; Israeli agriculturist; b. 27 July 1913; ed. Hebrew Gymnasia, Jerusalem, Hebrew Univ., and Univ. of Florence.
Agricultural Settlement Dept., Jewish Agency 37-, fmr. Village Instructor now Head of Dept.; Chair. Nat. and Univ. Institutes of Agriculture 60-66; Head Settlement Study Centre 63-; service with Intelligence Corps, British 8th Army, Second World War; fmr. mem. Hagana; mem. Exec., Zionist Org. 63-.
Publs. *Agriculture and Rural Development in Israel: Project and Planning* 63, *Rural Planning in Development Counties* (editor) 65, *Agricultural Development—Planning and Implementation* 68, and papers on problems of comprehensive planning.
Zionist Organisation, Jerusalem; Home: 16 Hechalutz Street, Beit-Hekerem, Jerusalem, Israel.
Telephone: 02-55086 (Home); 03-951787 (Office).

Weizsäcker, Carl-Friedrich von, DR.PHIL.; German university professor; b. 12; ed. Univs. of Berlin, Göttingen and Leipzig.
Asst. Univ. of Leipzig 33-36, Kaiser-Wilhelm-Inst. für Physik, Berlin-Dahlem 36-41; Prof. Univ. of Strasbourg 42-45; Dir. of Dept. Max-Planck-Inst. für Physik, Göttingen 46-57; Prof. of Philosophy, Hamburg 57-; Goethe Prize 58, Orden Pour le Mérite, Arnold-Raymond Prize.
Publs. *Zum Weltbild der Physik* 44, *Die Geschichte der Natur* 48, *Die Verantwortung der Wissenschaft im Atomzeitalter* 57, *Atomenergie und Atomzeitalter* 57, *Physik der Gegenwart* (with J. Juilfs) 58, *The Relevance of Science* 64.
Schwarzbuchenweg 40, Hamburg 64, German Federal Republic.

Wejchert, Kazimierz, DR.TECH.SC.; Polish architect; b. 12; ed. Warsaw.
Professor Warsaw Polytechnic 46-; Chief Planner,

Tychy New Town 51-; (Wejchert works in permanent collaboration with Dr. H. Adamczewska-Wejchert, his wife); Dir. Polish Town Planning Asscn. (Chair. 52-54); numerous prizes in town planning and architectonic competitions including First Prize for Warsaw Town Center 58.
Major projects include plans for many towns in Olsztyn and Szczecin districts 47-49, for towns, Garwolin 48, Olsztyn, Starachowice 50, regional plan for industrial towns in Upper Silesia, plan for Katowice town centre.
Publs. *Miasteczko polskie jako zagadnienie urbanstyczne* (A Small Polish Town as an Urbanistic Problem) 47, *Tereny sportowe w osiedlach* (Sports Grounds in Housing Estates) 54, *Nowe Tychy* (Tychy New Town) 60, *Miasto na Warsztacie* (sociological and town planning study) 68.
75/6 Koszykowa, Warsaw; Norwida 57, Nowe Tychy, Poland.

Welbeck, Nathanial Azarco; Ghanaian journalist and politician; b. 1915; ed. Teachers Training Coll., Kumasi.
Sec., District Education Cttee. Ahanta-Nzima 49; Deputy Gen. Sec., Convention People's Party 50; Nat. Propaganda Sec. 51; Acting Gen.-Sec. 52, Gen.-Sec. 52-53; mem. Legislative Assembly 53; Minister of Works 54-57; Minister of Labour 57-59; Minister of Guinea Affairs 59-Aug. 59, of Labour Aug. 59-Mar. 60; Minister of State March 60-61; Liaison Officer Convention People's Party 61-64, Exec. Sec. 64-66, Minister of State for Party Propaganda 65.
c/o P.O.B. 821, Accra, Ghana.

Welch, Leo D.; American oil executive; b. 22 April 1898; ed. Univ. of Rochester.
National City Bank of New York 19-44; Vice-Pres. 43-44; Dir. Cen. Bank of Argentina 36-40; Pres. Argentine Trade Promotion Corpn. 41-43; Treas. Standard Oil Co. (N.J.) 44-54, Dir. 53-63, Vice-Pres. 56-63, Exec. Vice-Pres. 57-63, Chair. Board and Vice-Chair. Exec. Cttee 60-63; Chair. Communications Satellite Corpn. 63-65, Dir. 63-; Dir. First Nat. City Bank; mem. numerous cttees.; Hon. LL.D., Georgetown Univ. 65; Commdr. Order of Merit, Chile, Argentina.
Home: Hill and Dale Farms, Benyville, Va.; Jericho Oyster Bay Road, Muttontown, L.I., N.Y.; Office: Rockefeller Plaza, N.Y.C., New York, U.S.A.

Welensky, Rt. Hon. Sir Roy (Roland), K.C.M.G.; Rhodesian politician; b. 20 Jan. 1907; ed. Primary School, Salisbury.
Worked for Rhodesia Railways (beginning as fireman and engine driver) 24-53; M.L.C. Northern Rhodesia 38-53; mem. Exec. Council 40-53; Dir. of Manpower 41-46; Leader of the Unofficial Mems. 46-53; Dep. Prime Minister Fed. Govt. of Rhodesia and Nyasaland 53-56, Min. of Transport 53-56, of Posts 53-56, Prime Minister and Minister of External Affairs 56-63, of Defence 56-59; Pres. United Federal Party 56-63; Leader New Rhodesia Party Aug.-Dec. 64.
Publ. *Welensky's 4,000 Days* 64.
82 Queen Elizabeth Road, Greendale, P.O.B. 804, Salisbury, Rhodesia.
Telephone: 23338.

Weller, Thomas Huckle, A.B., M.S., M.D.; American scientist and university professor; b. 15; ed. Harvard Univ. and Univ. of Michigan.
Teaching Fellow, Harvard Medical School 40-42; served Medical Corps, U.S. Army 42-45; Asst. Resident, Children's Hospital, Boston 46-47; Research Fellow Harvard Medical School 47-48, Instructor 48-49, Assistant Prof. Tropical Public Health, Harvard School of Public Health 49, Assoc. Prof. 50-54, Richard Pearson Strong Prof. and Head of Dept. 54-; Asst. Dir. Research Div. of Infectious Diseases, Children's Medical Center, Boston 49-55; Dir. Comm. on Parasitic Diseases, Armed Forces Epidemiological Board 53-59; Consultant on Tropical Diseases, U.S. Public Health

Service; mem. Nat. Acad. of Sciences; winner (jointly) of E. Mead Johnson Award 53, Kimble Methodology Award 54, Nobel Prize in Medicine and Physiology 54; Ledlie Prize 63; Hon. LL.D.

Publs. Papers on infectious diseases, tropical medicine, virus cultivation (especially poliomyelitis and mumps), the etiology of varicella, cytomegalic inclusion disease and rubella, herpes zoster, laboratory diagnosis of schistosomiasis.

Home: 56 Winding River Road, Needham, Mass.; Office: Harvard School of Public Health, 25 Shattuck Street, Boston, Mass., U.S.A.

Welles, (George) Orson; American actor and producer; b. 6 May 1915; ed. Todd School, Woodstock, Ill.

Fmr. actor Gate Theatre, Dublin; founded Mercury Theatre 37, now Vice-Pres.; Producer, Writer and Dir. R.K.O. Radio Pictures 39-40; mem. Actors Equity Asscn., American Fed. Radio Artists; Claire Senie Award for foremost achievement in American Theatre 38; Associate Editor *Free World Magazine.*

Directed plays: *Horse Eats Hat* 36, *Dr. Faustus, Cradle Will Rock* 37, *Julius Caesar* 37, *Shoemaker's Holiday, Heartbreak House, Danton's Death* 38; produced and acted in *Othello* (London) 51, *Moby Dick* (London) 55, *King Lear* (New York) 56; wrote and acted in *Chimes at Midnight* 60; Films: wrote, produced, directed and acted in *Citizen Kane* 40, *The Lady from Shanghai* 46; adapted, directed and acted in *Macbeth* 47, *Othello* 56; wrote, directed and produced *The Magnificent Ambersons* 42; wrote, produced and acted in *Journey into Fear* 42; wrote, directed and acted in *Confidential Report* 55; acted in *Jane Eyre* 43, *Tomorrow is For Ever* 45, *Cagliostro* 47, *The Third Man* 49, *The Black Rose* 50, *Versailles* 55, *Moby Dick* 56, *The Long Hot Summer* 58, *Compulsion* 59, *Ferry to Hong Kong* 59, *Crack in the Mirror* 60, *David and Goliath* 61, *The Trial, The V.I.P.s* 63, *I'll Never Forget What's 'Isname* 67, *A Man for All Seasons* 67.

Publs. *Mr. Arkadin* 57; Editor with Roger Hill: *Everybody's Shakespeare* 33, *Mercury Shakespeare* 39; Play: *Chimes at Midnight* (film 64).

10464 Bellago Road, Bel Air, California, U.S.A.

Wellesz, Egon, C.B.E., PH.D., M.A. and MUS. DOC. h.c. (Oxon.); Austrian musician; b. 85; ed. Vienna Univ.

Composer; Lecturer on Theory and History of Music Vienna Univ. 13; Prof. 29-38; Mus.Doc.h.c. Oxford Univ. 32; Editor *Monumenta Musica Byzantinæ* 33-; Lecturer on History of Music, Cambridge Univ. 38; Fellow, Lincoln Coll., Oxford Univ. 39-; Univ. Lecturer in History of Music 44-48; mem. Board Faculty of Music 44-; Univ. Reader in Byzantine Music 48-56; Fellow Royal Danish Acad. 46, British Acad. 53; Harvard Visiting Scholar 54 and 56-57; corresp. American Musicological Soc.; Grand Golden Cross of Merit (Austria) 60; "Pro Musica Austriaca" Medal 61; Knight Commdr. of the Apostolic Order of S. Gregory 61, First Vice-Pres. of Consociatio Internationalis Musicae Sacrae, Rome.

Compositions include Operas: *Alkestis* 24, *Die Opferung des Gefangenen* 26, *Die Bakchantinen* 31, *Incognita* 51; string quartets; *Cantate* 32; piano concerto 33, *Sonnets for soprano and strings* 34, *Prospero's Incantation* 35, *Mass in F Minor* 37, *Symphony in C* 45, *Symphony in E flat* 48, *Octet* 49, *Symphony in A* 51, *Symphony in G* 52, *Fifth Symphony* 56, *Clarinet Quintet* 59, *Violin Concerto* 61, *String Trio* 62, *Duineser Elegie* 63, *Music for Strings* 64, *Sixth Symphony* 65, *Vision for Soprano and Orchestra* 66, *Seventh Symphony* 67.

Publs. *Byzantinische Musik* 17, *Arnold Schoenberg* 21, *Aufgaben und Probleme der Orientalischen Kirchenmusik* 23, *Die moderne Instrumentation* 28-29, *Trésor de Musique Byzantine* 34, *Die Hymnen des Sticherarium* 36, *Eastern Elements in Western Chant* 44, *History of Byzantine Hymnography and Music* 49 (enlarged edn.

61), *Essays on Opera* 49, *The Akathistos Hymn* 56; Ed. *The New Oxford History of Music*, Vol. I, *The Music of the Byzantine Church, Anthology of Music*, Vol. I 59. 51 Woodstock Road, Oxford, England.
Telephone: 59857.

Wells, Everett F.; American oil executive; b. 18 Jan. 1905; ed. Univ. of Illinois.

Sales Trainee, Ashland Oil and Refining Co. 26, Salesman 27-29, Gen. Sales Man. 30-39, Vice-Pres. (Sales) 40-49, Exec. Vice-Pres. 50-57, Pres. 57-65, Chair. Exec. Cttee. 65-; Dir. Ashland Oil and Refining Co.; Chair. of Board and Dir. Nat. Refining Co.; Dir. American Independent Oil Co.; Pres. and Dir. Valvoline Oil Co.; official of several oil and commercial orgs.

Ashland Oil and Refining Co., 1401 Winchester Avenue, Ashland, Kentucky, U.S.A.

Wells, Herman B., B.S., A.M., LL.D.; American educationist; 7 June 1902; ed. Univs. of Illinois and Wisconsin, and Indiana Univ.

Asst. Cashier, First Nat. Bank, Lebanon, Ind. 24-26; Asst., Dept. of Economics, Univ. of Wisconsin 27-28; Field Sec. Indiana Bankers' Asscn. 28-31; Sec. and Research Dir. Study Comm. for Indiana Financial Instns. 31-33; Instr. in Economics Indiana Univ. 31-33, Asst. Prof. 33-35; Supervisor Div. of Banks and Trust Cos. and Div. of Research and Statistics, Dept. of Financial Instns. State of Indiana 33-35, Sec. Comm. for Financial Instns. 33-36; Dean School of Business Admin. Indiana Univ. 35-37, Pres. of Univ. 38-62, Chancellor 62-; Pres. Indiana Univ. Foundation 62; Chair. American Council on Education 44-45; Trustee Carnegie Foundation for Advancement of Teaching; adviser cultural affairs Mil. Govt., U.S. Zone, Germany 47-48; mem. UNESCO Comm. of Experts on German Questions 49-50; U.S. Nat. Comm. for UNESCO 51-55, Vice-Chair. 53-54; mem. U.S. del. to UN 57; adviser to Pakistan Minister of Educ. 59; Vice-Pres. Int. Asscn. of Univs. 55-60; Head U.S. Del. SEATO Preparatory Comm. on Universal Problems 60; Chair. Board of Trustees, Educ. and World Affairs 63; mem. President's Cttee. on U.S.-Soviet Trade Relations 65; Hon. LL.D. from eighteen univs. and colls.; Hon. L.H.D. Ohio State Univ.; Commander's Cross of Order of Merit, Fed. Repub. of Germany.

1321 East 10th Street, Bloomington, Ind.; Indiana University, Bloomington, Ind., U.S.A.
Telephone: 812-336-6275 (Home); 812-337-6647 (Office).

Wells, Oris (Vernon); American agricultural economist; b. 18 Dec. 1903; ed. New Mexico State Coll., Univ. of Minnesota and Harvard Univ.

United States Dept. of Agriculture 29-61, Adviser, War Food Admin. 42-45, Chief, Bureau of Agricultural Economics 46-53, mem. Board of Dirs. Commodity Credit Corpn. 51-61, Admin., Agricultural Marketing Service 53-61, Liaison Representative, Food and Nutrition Board, Nat. Research Council 52-61; Asst. Dir. Gen., UN Food and Agriculture Org. (FAO), Rome 61-63, Dep. Dir. Gen. 63-; Fellow, American Statistical Asscn., American Farm Econ. Asscn.

c/o UN Food and Agricultural Org., Via delle Terme di Caracalla, Rome; Via Aventina 24, Rome 00153, Italy.

Welsh, Edward Cristy, A.B., M.A., PH.D., LITT.D., LL.D.; American economist and government official; b. 20 March 1909; ed. Lafayette Coll., Tufts, and Ohio State Univs.

University Teacher of Economics; Nat. Resources Cttee. 37; Office of Price Administration 42-47; Dept. of Army 47-50; Nat. Security Resources Board 50-51; R.F.C. 51-53; Office of U.S. Senator 53-61; Exec. Sec. Nat. Aeronautics and Space Council 61-; Democrat.

Office: The White House, Washington, D.C.; Home: 1500 Arlington Boulevard, Arlington, Va., U.S.A.
Telephone: JA4-2140.

Welsh, Matthew E., B.S.ECON., DR.JUR.; American politician; b. 15 Sept. 1912; ed. Wharton School of Commerce (Univ. of Pennsylvania), Indiana Univ., and Univ. of Chicago.
State Rep., Indiana Gen. Assembly 40-43; served U.S. Navy 44-46; U.S. Attorney, S. District of Indiana 50-52; private law practice 52-60; Democratic candidate for Gov. 56; State Senator 54-61; Gov. of Indiana 61-65; Chair. U.S. Section, Int. Joint Comm., U.S. and Canada 65-; official of numerous legal, educational and religious bodies; received six hon. degrees.
600 Circle Tower Building, Indianapolis, Indiana 46204, U.S.A.
Telephone: 317-635-8900.

Welty, Eudora, B.A.; American writer; b. 09; ed. Mississippi State Coll. for Women, Univ. of Wisconsin and Columbia Univ.
Publs. *A Curtain of Green* 41, *Robber Bridegroom* 42, *The Wide Net* 43, *Delta Wedding* 46, *The Golden Apples* 49, *The Ponder Heart* 54, *The Bride of Innisfallen* 55.
1119 Pinehurst Street, Jackson, Miss., U.S.A.

Wende, Jan Karol; Polish politician; b. 1910; ed. Uniwersytet Warsazawski.
Former writer, critic and political journalist; Democratic Clubs and Democratic Party 37-39; educational activity in Polish emigration centres in U.S.S.R. 39-43; Mil. Service in Polish Army in U.S.S.R. 43-44; successively Gen. Sec. Polish Cttee. of Nat. Liberation; Vice-Minister of Culture and Fine Arts, Amb. to Yugoslavia and Pres. Cttee. for Cultural Co-operation with Foreign Countries; leading posts in Democratic Party 44-, Gen. Sec. 61-; Vice-Marshal Seym 61-.
Publs. novels: *Drogi cztowiecze* (Human Roads) 37, *Pokolonie 1905 roku* (The Generation of 1905) 39.
16 Aleja I Armii Wojska Polskiego, Warsaw, Poland.

Wendel, Henri de; French industrialist; b. 9 Sept. 1913; ed. Ecole centrale des arts et manufactures.
Director, Société Les Petits-Fils de François de Wendel and Co.; Vice-Pres. Dir.-Gen. S. A. Wendel and Co.; Admin. of Metallurgical Soc. of Senelle-Maubeuge, Slate Quarries of Angers, J. J. Carnaud Establishments and Forges de Basse-Indre; now Chair. de Wendel-Sidelor-Mosellane; Chevalier, Légion d'Honneur.
9 avenue du Maréchal-Manoury, Paris 16e, France.

Wendt, Frantz; Danish civil servant; b. 24 Feb. 1905; ed. Univs. of Copenhagen, Harvard and the Sorbonne.
Assistant Professor of Modern History and Civics, Univ. of Copenhagen 35-43; Sec.-Gen. Inst. of Econs. and History, Copenhagen 36-43; Exec. Dir. Danish Div., Norden Asscn. 43-53; Sec.-Gen. Danish Secr. of the Nordic Council 52-.
Publs. include *The Nordic Council and Co-operation in Scandinavia* 59.
The Danish Secretariat of the Nordic Council, Folketinget, Copenhagen K; Home: Ahlmanns allé 11, Hellerup, Denmark.

Wenger, Antoine, Rév. Père; French theologian, journalist and historian; b. 2 Sept. 1919; ed. Sorbonne, Strasbourg Univ.
Director of Oriental Theology, Univ. Catholique de Lyon 48-56, Prof. 56; Chief Editor *La Croix* 57-; Pres. Fédération Internationale des Directeurs de Journaux Catholiques 57-65; mem. Pontifical Marian Acad., Rome 59.
Publs. *L'Assomption dans la tradition orientale* 55, *Homelies Baptismales inédites de St. Jean Chrysostome* 57, *La Russie de Khrouchtchev* 59, *Vatican II, Première Session* 63, *Vatican II, Deuxième Session* 64., *Vatican II, Troisième Session* 65, *Quatrième Session* 66.
22 Cours Albert 1er., Paris 8e, France.
Telephone: BAL 73-05.

Werner, Charles, PH.D.; Swiss philosopher; b. 26 Feb. 1878; ed. Geneva, Jena, Paris and Berlin Univs.
Prof. of Philosophy and History of Philosophy Geneva

Univ. 09, Dean of the Philosophical Faculty 14-20, Rector of the Univ. 28-30, Hon. Prof. 53; mem. Cttee. Int. Inst. of Philosophy and Int. Fed. of Philosophical Societies; Dr. h.c. (Aix-Marseille).
Publs. *Aristote et l'idéalisme platonicien* 10, *Etudes de philosophie morale* 17, *La philosophie grecque* 38 (2nd edn. 46, pocket edn. 62), German and Spanish edn., *Le problème du mal dans la pensée humaine* 44 (2nd edn. 46) (German edn. 47), *La philosophie moderne* 54, *Essai d'une nouvelle monadologie* 59, *L'Ame et la Liberté* 60.
4 route de Florissant, Geneva, Switzerland.

Werner, Pierre; Luxembourg lawyer and politician; b. 29 Dec. 1913; ed. Univ. of Paris and Luxembourg.
Practising lawyer 38-39 and 44-45; with Banque Générale du Luxembourg 39-44; with Ministry of Finance 45; Commr. of Bank Control 45-48 and of Nat. Savings 48-49; Sec. to the Council of Govt. 49-53; Minister of Finance and of the Armed Forces 53-58; Prime Minister and Minister of Finance 59-64; Prime Minister, Min. of Foreign Affairs, of Treasury, and of Justice 64-66; Prime Minister, Minister of Treasury and of Civil Service 67-; Gov. European Investment Bank 58-62; Christian Social Party; Grand Cross of Orange Nassau (Neths.), Grand Cross of Leopold (Belgium), Order of Merit (Italy and Germany), Grand Cross Order of the White Elephant (Thailand), Grand Cross Royal Order of King George I (Greece), Grand Cross Order of Pius IX (Vatican), Grand Cross of Gold (Austria), Grand Cross Royal Order St. Olav (Norway), Grand Cross Order of Merit (Central African Repub.), Grand Cross Order of the Cross of the South (Brazil), Grand Cross of the Tunisian Repub.
2, rond-point Robert Schuman, Luxembourg.

Werth, Alexander, M.A.; British author and journalist; b. 4 Feb. 1901; ed. St. Petersburg, and Glasgow Univ.
Paris corresp. *Glasgow Herald* 29-31, *Manchester Guardian* 31-40, *Sunday Times* 37-40; Moscow corresp. *Sunday Times* 41-46, *Manchester Guardian* 46-49; Paris corresp. *The Nation* (N.Y.), etc.; Simon Research Fellow, Manchester Univ. 53-55; Visiting Prof. of History, Ohio State Univ. 57.
Publs. *France in Ferment* 34, *The Destiny of France* 37, *France and Munich* 39, *The Last Days of Paris* 40, *Moscow 41* 42, *Leningrad* 44, *The Year of Stalingrad* 46, *Musical Uproar in Moscow* 49, *France 1940-55* 56, *The Strange History of Pierre Mendès-France* 57, *America in Doubt* 59, *The de Gaulle Revolution* 60, *The Khrushchev Phase* 61, *Russia at War 1941-45* 64, *de Gaulle* 65, *Russia at Peace* 68.
13 rue Herold, Paris 1er, France.

Wesker, Arnold; British playwright; b. 24 May 1932; ed. mixed elementary schools and Upton House Central School, Hackney, London.
Left school 48, worked as furniture maker's apprentice, carpenter's mate, bookseller's assistant; R.A.F. 50-52 (ran drama group); plumber's mate, road labourer, farm labourer, seed sorter, kitchen porter and pastry-cook; studied nine months, London School of Film Technique; Arts Council Bursary 59; Dir. Centre 42, 61-; 1st Prize, Encyclopaedia Britannica Competition (for *Chicken Soup with Barley*), Premio Marzotto Drama Prize (for *Their Very Own and Golden City*) 64.
Plays: *The Kitchen* 57, The trilogy—*Chicken Soup with Barley* 58, *Roots* 59, *I'm Talking about Jerusalem* 60; *Chips with Everything* 62, *Menace* 63, *Their Very Own and Golden City* 64, *The Four Seasons* 65.
27 Bishops Road, London N.6, England.
Telephone: 01-340-5125.

West, Morris (Langlo); Australian author; b. 26 April 1916; ed. Univ. of Melbourne.
Teacher of Modern Languages and Mathematics, New South Wales and Tasmania 33-39; Army service 39-43; Nat. Brotherhood Award, Nat. Council of Christians

and Jews 60, James Tait Black Memorial Prize 60, Royal Soc. of Literature Heinemann Award 60 (All prizes for *The Devil's Advocate*); Fellow, Royal Soc. of Literature, World Acad. of Arts and Sciences; Hon. D. Litt. (Santa Clara Univ., Calif.).
Publs. *Gallows on the Sand* 55, *Kundu* 56, *Children of the Sun* 57, *The Crooked Road* (English title *The Big Story*) 57, *Backlash* (English title *Second Victory*) 58, *The Devil's Advocate* 59, *Daughter of Silence* 61, *The Shoes of the Fisherman* 63, *The Ambassador* 65, *The Tower of Babel* 68.
Box 36, P.O., St. Ives, New South Wales, Australia; c/o Paul R. Reynolds and Son, 599 Fifth Avenue, New York City 17, N.Y., U.S.A.

West, Rebecca, D.B.E.; British novelist and journalist; b. 21 Dec. 1892; ed. George Watson's Ladies' Coll., Edinburgh.
Contributor to leading British and American journals *The Daily Telegraph, Sunday Times, N.Y. Herald Tribune, Harper's Magazine, Atlantic Monthly, Sunday Telegraph*; mem. American Acad. Arts and Sciences; D.Litt. New York Univ. U.S.A.; Order of St. Sava; Chevalier Légion d'Honneur 57; A. C. Benson Silver Medal for Literature 66.
Publs. include *Henry James* 16, *The Return of the Soldier* 18, *The Judge* 22, *The Strange Necessity* 28, *Harriet Hume* 29, *D. H. Lawrence: An Elegy* 30, *St. Augustine* 33, *The Rake's Progress* (with David Low) 34, *The Harsh Voice* 35, *The Thinking Reed* 36, *Black Lamb and Grey Falcon* 42, *The Meaning of Treason* 49, *A Train of Powder* 55, *The Fountain Overflows* 57, *The Court and the Castle* 58, *The Vassall Affair* 63, *The New Meaning of Treason* 64, *The Birds Fall Down* 66.
Ibstone House, Ibstone, High Wycombe, Bucks., England.
Telephone: Turville Heath 310.

Westall, Bernard Clement, C.B.E., M.A.; British business executive; b. 28 Nov. 1893; ed. Newbury Grammar School, and Queens' Coll., Cambridge.
Director, Thomas De La Rue & Co. Ltd., London 28-31, Jt. Managing Dir. 31-34, Sole Managing Dir. 34-44, Chair. Thomas De La Rue & Co. (now The De La Rue Co. Ltd.) 44-63, Pres. 64-; Pres. English Bridge Union 63-.
Publs. (with Hubert Phillips) *The Book of Indoor Games* 32, *The Complete Book of Card Games* 33.
2 St. Swithun's College, East Grinstead, Sussex, England.

Westgren, Arne Frederik; Swedish scientist and administrator; b. 11 July 1889; ed. Univ. of Uppsala.
Lecturer of Physical Chemistry Univ. of Uppsala 17-19; Metallographer S.K.F. Ball-Bearing Co., Göteborg 18-20; Lecturer of Metallography Univ. of Stockholm 21-27; Prof. of General and Inorganic Chemistry, Univ. of Stockholm 27-43; Permanent Sec. of Swedish Royal Acad. of Sciences 43-59.
Eriksbergsgatan 3, Stockholm, Sweden.
Telephone: 11-22-18.

Westmoreland, Gen. William Childs; American army officer; b. 26 March 1914; ed. U.S. Military Acad.
U.S. Army 36-, Maj.-Gen. 56, Lieut.-Gen. 63, Gen. 64; Battery Officer, Oklahoma and Hawaii 36-41; Commdg. Officer, 34th Field Artillery Battalion 42-44; Chief of Staff, 9th Infantry Div. 44-45; Commdr. 60th Infantry Regiment, Germany 45, 504th Parachute Infantry Regiment, Fort Bragg 46-47; Chief of Staff, 82nd Airborne Div. 47-50; Instructor, Command and Gen. Staff Coll., and Army War Coll. 50-52; Commdr. 187th Airborne Regimental Combat Team, Korea and Japan 52-53; Dep. Asst. Chief of Staff (Manpower), Dept. of Army 53-54, Sec. Gen. Staff 55-58; Supt. U.S. Military Acad., West Point 60-63; Commdr. 18th Airborne Corps, Fort Bragg 63-64; Dep. Commdr. U.S. Military

Assistance Command Vietnam 64; Commdr. U.S. Mil Assistance Command, Vietnam 64-68; Chief of Staff, U.S. Army, The Pentagon 68-.
The Pentagon, Washington, D.C.; 120 South Waccamaw Avenue, Columbia, South Carolina 29205, U.S.A.

Weston, Garry Howard, B.A. (son of Willard Garfield Weston, q.v.); business executive; b. 1927; ed. Sir William Borlase School, Marlow, New Coll. Oxford, and Harvard Univ.
Director, Allied Bakeries Ltd. (U.K.) 50-; Man. Dir. Ryvita Co. Ltd. (U.K.) 50-56, and Ryvita Co. (Australia) Pty. Ltd. 54; Dir. Fortnum and Mason 52; Chair. of Directors Weston Holdings (Australia) Pty. Ltd. 54, and Man. Dir. Weston Biscuit Co. (Australia) Pty. Ltd. 54; Vice-Chair. Assoc. British Foods Ltd. (U.K.) 60-68, Chair. 68-; Dir. George Weston Foods Ltd. (Australia) 62-.
11 Upper Phillimore Gardens, London W.8, England.

Weston, Willard Garfield (father of Gary Howard Weston, q.v.); Canadian businessman; b. Canada 1898; ed. Harbord Collegiate Inst., Toronto.
Served with Canadian Engineers First World War; joined George Weston Ltd. Toronto 19-, Vice-Pres. 21, Man. 22, now Chair.; founder and Chair. George Weston Holdings Ltd., Weston Biscuits Co., Allied Bakeries Ltd.; Chair. George Weston Ltd., Toronto, and Weston Biscuit Co. New Jersey; Pres. Assoc. British Foods Ltd. 67-; Cons. M.P. for Macclesfield, England 39-45.
Weston Centre, 40 Berkeley Square, London W.1, England.

Westphal, Rev. Charles, L en TH.; French ecclesiastic; b. 24 Nov. 1896; ed. Paris, New York and Edinburgh Univs.
Secretary Gen. Féd. Française des Etudiants Chrétiens 28-39; Pastor Grenoble 39-45, Eglise Réformée du Saint-Esprit, Paris 45-; Vice-Pres. Féd. Protestante de France 53-61, Pres. 61-; mem. Central Cttee. World Council of Churches; Officier Légion d'Honneur, Croix de Guerre (1914-18).
47 rue de Clichy, Paris 9e, France.

Westrick, Ludger, D.IUR.; German politician; b. 23 Oct. 1894.
Balkan branch of Vereinigte Stahlwerke A.G., later Dir.-Gen. Vereinigte Aluminium-Werke A.G.; Public Trustee, VIAG concern 45-48; Financial Dir. Deutsche Kohlenbergbau-Leitung 48-51; Sec. of State to Minister of Economy 51-63, to Federal Chancellor 63-64; Minister for Special Missions; Minister for Chancellery Affairs 64-66; Grosses Bundesverdienstkreuz, etc.
Petersbergstrasse 44, Bad Godesberg, German Federal Republic.

Westrup, Sir Jack Allan, Kt., M.A., B.MUS., HON.D.MUS. (Oxon.), F.B.A.; British professor of music; b. 26 July 1904; ed. Dulwich Coll., and Balliol Coll., Oxford (Nettleship scholar).
Asst. master (classics) Dulwich Coll. 28-34; Editor, *Monthly Musical Record* 33-45; Asst. music critic, *Daily Telegraph* 34-40; Lecturer in Music, King's Coll., Newcastle-on-Tyne 41-44; Peyton and Barber Prof. of Music, Univ. of Birmingham 44-46; Heather Prof. of Music, Univ. of Oxford 47-.
Publs. *Purcell* 37, *Sharps and Flats* 40, *British Music* 43, 3rd edn. of Ernest Walker's *History of Music in England* 52, *Introduction to Musical History* 55, *Collins Music Encyclopedia* (with F. Ll. Harrison) 59, *Bach Cantatas* 66.
Faculty of Music, 32 Holywell, Oxford, England.
Telephone: Oxford 47069.

Wetmore, Alexander, M.S., PH.D., D.SC.; American biologist and ornithologist; b. 18 June 1886; ed. Kansas and George Washington Univs.
Asst. Biologist and Biologist, Biological Survey Dept. of

Agriculture 10-24; Asst. Sec. Smithsonian Inst., Dir. U.S. Nat. Museum 25-44, Sec. 45-52, Research Assoc. 53-; Trustee Textile Museum, Washington, George Washington Univ., Research Corpn. 47-53, Pacific War Memorial, Wildlife Inst.; Dir. Gorgas Memorial Inst. for Tropical Medicine; mem. Advisory Cttee., Int. Wildlife Protection; mem. Int. Comm. Bird Protection, Joint Latin-American Study 45-47; Sec.-Gen., 8th American Science Congress 40; Vice-Chair. Nat. Advisory Cttee. for Aeronautics 45-52; Trustee Nat. Gallery of Art 45-52; Dir. Canal Zone Biological Area 40-46; Past Pres. Explorers' Club; Pres. X Int. Ornithological Congress, Sweden 50; Chair. Cttee. on Classification and Nomenclature for 5th edn. *Check-list of North American Birds* publ. 57.
Publs. *The Migration of Birds* 27, *Birds of Porto Rico and the Virgin Islands* 27, *Fossil Birds of North America* 31, *Birds of Haiti and the Dominican Republic* 31, *Book of Birds* 37, *Check-List of the Fossil and Prehistoric Birds of North America and the West Indies* 56, *Birds of Coiba Island Panama* 57, *Revised Classification for Birds of the World* 60, *Song and Garden Birds* 64, *Water, Game and Prey Birds* 65, *Birds of Panama*, Part I 65.
5901 Osceola Road, Washington 20016, D.C., U.S.A.; and c/o Smithsonian Institution, Washington 20560, D.C., U.S.A.
Telephone: 656-5693 (Home); 381-5291 (Office).

Wetmore, Robert Bernard Norton, M.B.E.; Rhodesian civil servant and diplomatist; b. 31 Aug. 1911; ed. Prince Edward School, Salisbury.
Government Service (Treasury) 29-37; Manager Southern Rhodesia Publicity Office, Johannesburg 37-42, Supply Office 42-46; Assistant Food Controller, Salisbury 47-50; Secretary at High Comm., Pretoria 51-55; Consul-Gen. in Mozambique 55-57; Counsellor for Rhodesia and Nyasaland Affairs, British Embassy, U.S.A. 57-62; Under-Sec. External Affairs, Salisbury 62-64; Accredited Diplomatic Representative for Rhodesia in South Africa 64-65; Sec. for External Affairs 65-.
Ministry of External Affairs, Private Bag 185H, Salisbury; Home: 2 Wetmore Close, Highlands, Rhodesia.
Telephone: 27005 (Office); 42656 (Home).

Wetter, Rear-Admiral (Sten) Erik P:son; Swedish naval officer and businessman; b. 4 April 1889; ed. Swedish and Leghorn Naval Academies.
Lt. Commdr. Royal Swedish Navy 18, Commdr. 31, Rear-Admiral 43, Dep. Dir. Navy Board 43-45; mem. (Liberal) First Chamber of Riksdag 45-47; Vice-Pres. Board Swedish Ballbearing Co. (SKF) 54-62; Pres. Board A. B. Bofors 46-66; Pres. Board Home Lines Inc. 53-; Man. Dir. Swedish Orient Line 31-51; A.D.C. to H.R.H. the Crown Prince 27, Chief A.D.C. to H.M. the King 50, First Marshal of the Court to H.M. the King of Sweden 52-62; 3 Swedish orders and 12 foreign orders.
Villa Beylon, Ulriksdal, S 17190 Solna, Sweden.
Telephone: Stockholm 85-62-62.

Wever, Ernest Glen, A.M., PH.D.; American psychologist; b. 16 Oct. 1902; ed. Illinois Coll., and Harvard Univ.
Instr. Univ. of Calif. 26-27, Princeton Univ. 27-29; Asst. Prof. Princeton Univ. 29-31, Assoc. Prof. 31-41; Prof. of Psychology 41-49, Higgins Prof. of Experimental Psychology 50-; mem. American Psychological Assen.
Publs. *Theory of Hearing* 49, *Physiological Acoustics* (with M. Lawrence) 54.
29 Snowdon Lane, Princeton, New Jersey, U.S.A.

Weyerhaeuser, Frederick King; American timber executive; b. 16 Jan. 1895; ed. Yale Univ.
President Weyerhaeuser Sales Co., St. Paul, Minn. 29-59, Weyerhaeuser Co. 56-60, Chair. 55-56 and 60-66; Dir.

First Trust Co. of St. Paul 31-, Rock Island Corpn. 46-, First Nat. Bank of St. Paul 46-, Great Northern Railway Co. 46-; Trustee, Minnesota Mutual Life Insurance Co. 39-.
Home: 294 Summit Avenue, St. Paul 2; Office: First National Bank Building, St. Paul 1, Minn., U.S.A.

Weyerhaeuser, George Hunt, B.S.; American timber executive; b. 8 July 1926; ed. Yale Univ.
Served in U.S. Navy 44-46; Weyerhaeuser Co. 49-, serving respectively as: Shift Superintendent 50, Wood Products Man. 54, Asst. to Exec. Vice-Pres. 57-, Man., Wood Products Group, later Vice-Pres. 58; elected to Board of Dirs. 60; Exec. Vice-Pres. for Wood Products, Timber and Lands 61-, Exec. Vice-Pres. for Operations 64-, Pres. and Chief Exec. Officer 66-; Pres. Weyerhaeuser Int. Inc., Weyerhaeuser Int. S.A., Weyerhaeuser Properties Inc.; Dir. Boeing Co., Puget Sound Nat. Bank, Caribbean Container Co. and others.
Weyerhaeuser Company, Tacoma Building, Tacoma, Washington, U.S.A.
Telephone: FU3-3361.

Weymann, Gert; German theatre director and playwright; b. 31 March 1919; ed. Grammar School, Berlin, and Berlin Univ.
Assistant Dir., later Dir. Berlin theatre; worked as Dir. in several W. German cities and New York; Lecturer in Drama Dept., American universities 63-; Gerhart Hauptmann Prize for *Generationen* 54.
Plays: *Generationen, Eh die Brücken verbrennen*; TV Plays: *Das Liebesmahl eines Wucherers, Familie*; Radio Plays: *Der Anhalter, Die Übergabe*.
1 Berlin 31, Karlsruherstrasse 7, Germany.
Telephone: 8871861.

Weynen, Wolfgang, LL.D.; German Press Agency executive; b. 5 July 1913; ed. Univs. of Bonn, Paris, Königsberg and Leipzig.
Legal adviser and Deputy Gen. Man. Chamber of Industries and Commerce, Wiesbaden 46-48, Gen. Man. 48-55; Gen. Man. Deutsche Presse-Agentur 55-; mem. Presidency of Alliance Européenne des Agences de Presse 56, Chair. Satellite Sub-Cttee. of Int. Press Telecommunications Cttee. (IPTC) 65, mem. Presidency Cultural Cttee. of German-Korean Friendship Assen., Vice-Pres. IPTC 67; Grosses Verdienstkreuz der Republik Österreich, Chevalier Légion d'Honneur.
Publs. *Die Arbeitszeitregelung in kontinuierlichen Betrieben* 38.
dpa-Deutsche Presse-Agentur, 2 Hamburg 13, Mittelweg 38; Home: 2 Hamburg 20, Brabandstrasse 7, German Federal Republic.
Telephone: 44-12-01 (Office): 51-59-82 (Home).

Weyrauch, Wolfgang Karl Joseph; German writer; b. 15 Oct. 1907; ed. Humanistisches Gymnasium, Johann Wolfgang Goethe-Universität, Frankfurt, and Humboldt Universität zu Berlin.
Publisher's Reader *Berliner Tageblatt* 34-38, Deutscher Verlag, Berlin 38-39; Editor *Ulenspiegel*, Berlin 46-48; Publisher's Reader, Rowohlt Verlag, Hamburg 50-58; Hörspielpreis der Kriegsblinden for *Totentanz* 62.
Publs. *Der Main* (legend) 34, *Auf der bewegten Erde* (story) 46, *Von des Glücks Barmherzigkeit* (poems) 47, *Die Davidsbündler* (story) 48, *Tausend Gramm* (anthology) 49, *An die Wand geschreiben* (poems) 50, *Woher kennen wir uns bloss?* (radio play) 52, *Die Minute des Negers* (ballad) 53, *Bericht an die Regierung* (story) 53, *Die japanischen Fischer* (radio play) 55, *Gesang, um nicht zu sterben* (poems) 56, *Mein Schiff, das heisst Taifun* (stories) 59, *Anabasis* (radio play) 59, *Expeditionen* (anthology) 59, *Ich lebe in der Bundesrepublik* (anthology) 60, *Totentanz* (radio play) 61, *Dialog mit dem Unsichtbaren* (radio play) 62, *Das tapfere Schneiderlein* (radio play) 63, *Alle diese Strassen* (anthology) 65,

Etwas geschicht (stories) 66, *Das erste Haus heiss Frieden* 66, *Ausnahmezustand* (anthology) 66.
Gauting vor München, Leo Putz-Weg 9, German Federal Republic.
Telephone: 861361.

Whang, Jong Ryul; Korean politician; b. 6 Sept. 1909; ed. Law Coll., Kyushu Imperial Univ., Japan.
Professor Econ. and Finance, Commerce and Economy Coll., Ionsei Univ. 45-56; Dir. of Supply and Procurement 52-53; Prof. Econs. and Finance, Dong Kuk Univ. 58-59; Gov. of Chung Chong Buk Do Province 59-60; Econ. Counsellor, Supreme Council of Nat. Reconstruction 61-63; Minister of Finance 63; Chair. Monetary Board, Bank of Korea 63-, The Econ. and Scientific Council R.O.K. 66; Minister without Portfolio 67.
262-40 Sa Jik Dong, Chong Ro Ku, Seoul, Republic of Korea.
Telephone: 73-2871.

Wheare, Sir Kenneth Clinton, Kt., C.M.G., F.B.A., D.LITT.; British (b. Australian) college principal; b. 26 March 1907; ed. Scotch Coll., Melbourne, Univ. of Melbourne, and Oriel Coll., Oxford.
Lecturer Christ Church, Oxford 34-39; Beit Lecturer in Colonial History, Oxford 35-44; Fellow of Univ. Coll. Oxford 39-44, Dean 42-45; Gladstone Prof. of Govt. and Public Admin., Univ. of Oxford, Fellow of All Souls Coll. 44-57, Fellow of Nuffield Coll. 44-58; Rector Exeter Coll. Oxford 56-; Pro-Vice-Chancellor Oxford Univ. 58-64, 66-, Vice-Chancellor 64-66; Pres. British Acad. 67-; Constitutional Adviser to Nat. Convention of Newfoundland 46-47, to Confs. on Central African Fed. 51, 52, 53; Rhodes Trustee 48-; mem. Univ. Grants Cttee. 59-; Hon. L.H.D. (Columbia).
Publs. *The Statute of Westminster* 31, 33, *The Statute of Westminster and Dominion Status* 38 (5th edn. 53), *Federal Government* 46 (3rd edn. 53), *Abraham Lincoln and the United States* 48, *Modern Constitutions* 51, *Government by Committee* 55, *The Constitutional Structure of the Commonwealth* 60, *Legislatures* 63.
Exeter College, Oxford, England.

Wheatley, Dennis Yeats, F.R.S.A., F.R.S.L.; British author; b. 8 Jan. 1897; ed. H.M.S. *Worcester*, and privately in Germany.
Served in army in First World War 14-19; entered father's Mayfair wine business becoming sole owner 26; Dir. of numerous companies; Liveryman of Vintners Company 18, Distillers Company 22; sold business 31; gave up active wine business for writing 32; re-commissioned in R.A.F.V.R. 41 and appointed to Joint Planning Staff; worked in Office of War Cabinet 41-45; Bronze Star (Mil.), U.S.A.
Publs. *The Forbidden Territory* 33, *Black August* 34, *The Devil Rides Out, The Eunuch of Stamboul* 35, *They Found Atlantis, Murder off Miami* 36, *Red Eagle* 37, *The Golden Spaniard* 38, *The Scarlet Impostor, Faked Passports* 40, *The Black Baroness* 41, *Come into my Parlour* 46, *The Launching of Roger Brook* 47, *The Shadow of Tyburn Tree* 48, *The Rising Storm* 49, *The Second Seal* 50, *The Man Who Killed the King* 51, *To the Devil a Daughter* 54, *The Island where Time Stands Still* 55, *The Ka of Gifford Hillary* 56, *The Prisoner in the Mask* 57, *Traitor's Gate* 58, *Stranger than Fiction, The Rape of Venice* 59, *The Satanist* 60, *Saturdays with Bricks, Vendetta in Spain* 61, *Mayhem in Greece* 62, *The Sultan's Daughter* 63, *Bill for the Use of a Body* 64, *They Used Dark Forces* 64, *Dangerous Inheritance* 65, *The Wanton Princess* 66, *Unholy Crusade* 67, *The White Witch of the South Seas* 68.
Grove Place, Lymington, Hampshire; and 60 Cadogan Square, London, S.W.1, England.
Telephone: Lymington 3115; and 01-584-2332.

Wheeler, Sir Charles, K.C.V.O., C.B.E., PP.R.A., PP.R.B.S.; British sculptor; b. 1892; ed. Royal Coll. of Art, London.
Exhibitor Royal Acad. 14-; A.R.A. 34, R.A. 40; mem. Royal Fine Art Comm. 46-52; Pres. Royal Acad. 56-66; Hon. F.R.I.B.A., Hon. D.C.L. (Oxford), Hon. LL.D. (Trinity Coll. Dublin) 60; Gold Medal, Royal Soc. British Sculptors 49; Officier, Légion d'Honneur, Knight Crown of Siam, Order of Merit of Italian Republic.
Works include: R.A.F. Memorial, Malta, Jellicoe Fountain, Trafalgar Square, sculptures on Winchester Coll. War Memorial Cloisters, Bishop Jacob Memorial Church, Ilford, Indian Memorial, Neuve Chapelle, India House, South Africa House, Rhodes House, Oxford, Haileybury Coll. Chapel, Royal Empire Society, Bank of England (*Ariel*, R.B.S. Medal 37), Church House; bust, *Infant Christ*, bronze statue, *Spring*, and *Aphrodite II* (stone), purchased for nation under Chantrey Bequest; Merchant Navy Memorial, Tower Hill; sculpture, Queen's Park, Invercargill, N.Z.
Publs. *High Relief* (autobiography).
22 Cathcart Road, London, S.W.10, and Weavers, nr. Merstham, Surrey, England.

Wheeler, Sir Charles Reginald, K.B.E.; British business executive; b. 5 Dec. 1904; ed. St. Paul's School.
London Man. Baldwins Ltd. 22-29; Commercial Man. Guest Keen Baldwins 30-39; Iron and Steel Control 39-45, Controller 45; Jt. Man. Dir. Guest Keen Iron and Steel Co. 46-59, Chair. 60; Vice-Chair. Associated Electrical Industries Ltd. 61, Deputy Chair. 62-63, Chair. 63-67, Pres. 67-; Dir. Steel Co. of Wales Ltd., George Wimpey and Co. Ltd., Guest Keen and Nettlefolds Ltd., Phoenix Assurance Co. Ltd., G.E.C.; Pres. British Iron and Steel Fed. 61, Iron and Steel Inst. 58-59; Pres. Electrical Research Asscn. 66-.
The Old Croft, Bellingdon, nr. Chesham, Bucks., England.
Telephone: Cholesbury 273.

Wheeler, General Earle Gilmore; American army officer; b. 13 Jan. 1908; ed. U.S. Military Acad.
U.S. Army 32-, Gen. 62-; Chief of Staff, 63rd Infantry Div. 43-45; with Allied Forces Southern Europe 52-55; on Gen. Staff 55-57; Asst. Dep. Chief of Staff for Mil. Operations, Army Dept. 57-58; Commdg. Gen. 2nd Armoured Div. 58-60; Dir. Jt. Staff Org., Jt. Chiefs of Staff 60-62; Army Chief of Staff 62-64; Chair. Jt. Chiefs of Staff 64-; Distinguished Service Medal, Legion of Merit, Croix de Guerre with Palm (French), and many other foreign decorations; Hon. LL.D. (Univ. of Akron 64, Rhode Island 65, Washington and Jefferson Coll. 65), Hon. D.Sc. (Norwich Univ. 66).
U.S. Army Headquarters, Washington, D.C. 20301, U.S.A.

Wheeler, Sir (Robert Eric) Mortimer, Kt., C.H., C.I.E., M.C., T.D., M.A., D.LIT. (London), F.B.A., F.S.A.; British archaeologist; b. 10 Sept. 1890.
Served France, Italy and Germany in First World War; Keeper Archaeological Dept., Nat. Museum of Wales 20-24, Dir. Museum 24-26; Lecturer in Archaeology Univ. of Wales 20-24; Keeper and Sec. London Museum 26-44; Lecturer in British Archaeology and Hon. Dir. Inst. of Archaeology Univ. of London 34-44; Dir.-Gen. of Archaeology India 44-48; Prof. Archaeology of Roman Provinces, Univ. of London 48-55; Archaeological Adviser to Govt. of Pakistan 48-50; Prof. of Ancient History to Royal Acad. of Arts 65-; directed archaeological excavations Colchester 17 and 20, Caernarvon 21-23, Brecon 24-25, Caerleon 26-27, Lydney 28-29, St. Albans 30-33, Maiden Castle, Dorset 34-37, Brittany 38, Normandy 39, India 44-48, Pakistan 50, 58, etc.; Pres. Cambrian Archaeological Asscn. 31, South-Eastern Union of Scientific Societies 32, British Asscn. Conf. of

Dels. 33, Museums Asscn. 37-38, Indian Museums Asscn. 47-48, Pakistan Museums Asscn. 49; Royal Archæological Inst. 50; Vice-Pres. Society of Antiquaries 35-39, Sec. 39-40, Dir. 40-44, 49-54, Pres. 54-59; Trustee, British Museum 54-59 and 63-; Sec. British Acad. 49-; Commr. Royal Comm. on Historical Monuments (England) 39-58; Fellow, Univ. Coll., London; Lieut.-Col. R.A. 39-43, Brig. 43; served in Africa and Italy 41-43; Hon. D.Litt. (Oxford, Bristol, Delhi, Wales, Ireland); Gold Medal Soc. of Antiquaries 44; Petrie Medal, Univ. of London 51; Lucy Wharton Drexel Medal, Univ. of Pennsylvania 62.

Publs. Books on Roman London, Prehistoric and Roman Wales, London and the Saxons, the Belgic and Roman cities of Verulamium, Maiden Castle, Ancient Pakistan; *The Indus Civilisation, Archaeology from the Earth, Rome beyond the Imperial Frontiers, Early India and Pakistan, Still Digging* (autobiography), *Charsada, Roman Art and Architecture, Splendours of the East, Civilizations of the Indus Valley and Beyond, Alms for Oblivion* (collected papers.)

British Academy, Burlington Gardens, London, W.I.

Wheeler-Bennett, Sir John Wheeler, K.C.V.O., C.M.G., O.B.E., M.A., F.R.S.L.; British historian; b. 13 Oct. 1902; ed. Malvern Coll.

Asst. Publicity Sec. L.N. Union 23-24; founder and Hon. Sec. Information Service on Int. Affairs 24-30; mem. of Council and Deputy Chair. Information Cttee. of Royal Inst. of Int. Affairs 27-36; founder *Bulletin of International News* and Editor 24-32; Lecturer in Int. Law and Relations Univ. of Virginia 37-39; Asst. Dir. British Press Service, New York 39-41; Special Asst. to Dir.-Gen. British Information Service U.S.A. 41-42; Head, New York Office, Brit. Pol. Warfare Mission, U.S.A. 42-44; European Adviser Political Intelligence Dept. of Foreign Office 44; Asst. Dir.-Gen. 45; Asst. to British Political Adviser to SHAEF 44-45; attached to British prosecuting team Nuremberg trials 46; British Editor-in-Chief of captured German Foreign Office Archives 46-48, Historical Adviser to Editor-in-Chief 48-56; Lecturer in Int. Politics, New Coll. Oxford 46-50; Fellow St. Antony's Coll., Oxford 50-57, Hon. Fellow 62-; Historical Adviser Royal Archives 59-; Trustee Imperial War Museum 61-; Visiting Prof. of Int. Politics, Univ. of Arizona 64, 66, 68; Visiting Prof. of Modern History, New York Univ. 67, 68-69; Scholar in Residence, Univ. of Virginia 67-68; Hon. D.C.L. (Oxford) 60.

Publs. *Information on the Permanent Court of International Justice, The Problem of Security, The Reparations Settlement, Disarmament and Security since Locarno, The Wreck of Reparations, The Disarmament Deadlock, The Pipe Dream of Peace, Hindenburg the Wooden Titan, Brest-Litovsk: the Forgotten Peace, Munich, Prologue to Tragedy, Nemesis of Power: The German Army in Politics, King George VI: His Life and Times, John Anderson, Viscount Waverley, A Wreath to Clio.*

Garsington Manor, near Oxford, England.
Telephone: Garsington 234.

Wheelock, John Hall; American poet; b. 9 Sept. 1886; ed. Harvard, Göttingen and Berlin Univs.

Member staff Charles Scribner's Sons 11, Editor 26, Dir. 32, Sec. 32-42, Treas. 42-57, retd.; mem. The American Acad. of Arts and Letters; Hon. Consultant in American Letters to the Library of Congress; hon. mem. Poetry Soc. of America; Chancellor Acad. of American Poets; Bollingen Prize for Poetry (co-winner) 61.

Publs. *Verses by Two Undergraduates* (with Van Wyck Brooks) 05, *The Human Fantasy* 11, *The Belovèd Adventure* 12, *Love and Liberation* 13, *Alan Seeger, Poet of the Foreign Legion* 18, *Dust and Light* 19, *Theodore Roosevelt: a Bibliography* 20, *The Black Panther* 22, *The Bright Doom* 27, *Collected Poems* 36, *Poems Old and New* 56, *The Two Knowledges: An Essay on a Certain Resistance* 58, *The Gardener and other Poems* 61, *What is Poetry?* 63, *Dear Men and Women: New Poems* 66; Editor: *The Face of a Nation, Poetical Passages from the Writings of Thomas Wolfe* 39, *Editor to Author, The Letters of Maxwell E. Perkins* 50, *Poets of Today* (annually) 53-61.

350 East 57th Street, New York City, N.Y., U.S.A.
Telephone: Plaza 8-3322.

Whipple, Fred Lawrence, A.B., PH.D.; American astronomer; b. 5 Nov. 1906; ed. Univ. of California.

Mem. Staff Harvard Coll. Observatory 31; in charge of Oak Ridge Station 32-37; Instructor 32-38, Lecturer 38-45, Associate Prof. 45-50, Prof. of Astronomy 50-; Chair. Cttee. on Concentration in the Physical Sciences 47-49; Chair. Dept. Astronomy, Harvard Univ. 49-56; Research Associate Radio Research Laboratory 42-45, in charge of Confusion Reflectors "Window" (radar countermeasure); Dir. Smithsonian Inst. Astrophysical Observatory 55-; mem. Rocket and Satellite Research Panel 46-, U.S. Nat. Advisory Cttee. on Aeronautics Sub-Cttee. 46-52, U.S. Research and Development Board Panel 47-52, U.S. Nat. Cttee. I.G.Y. 55-59, Advisory Panel on Astronomy to the Nat. Science Foundation 52-55 and Chair. 54-55, mem. Div. Cttee. for Mathematical and Physical Sciences 64-, many other scientific cttees., etc.; Project Leader Harvard Radio Meteor Project 58-; Phillips Prof. of Astronomy, Harvard Univ. 68-; Voting Rep. of U.S.A. in Int. Astronomical Union 52 and 55; Associate Ed. *Astrophysical Journal* 52-54, *Astronomical Journal* 54-56, 64-; Ed. *Planetary and Space Science* 58-; Ed. *Harvard's Announcement Cards* 52-60; Ed. *Smithsonian Contributions to Astrophysics* 56-; Lowell Lecturer, Lowell Inst., Boston 47; Vice-Pres. American Astronomical Soc. 48-50, 60-, Cttee. on Space Research (COSPAR) 61-; Ed. Board *Space Science Reviews* 61-; Ed. Cttee. *Annual Review of Astronomy and Astrophysics* 65-; Donohue Medals, Pres. Certificate of Merit, J. Lawrence Smith Medal of Nat. Acad. of Sciences, Exceptional Service Award (U.S.A.F.), Liège Univ. Medal, Space Flight Award, Commr. of Order of Merit for Research and Invention; Distinguished Federal Civilian Service Award from President Kennedy and other awards; Hon. M.A., Hon. D.Sc., Hon. D.Litt., Hon. LL.D.

Publs. *Earth, Moon and Planets* 42, 63, and many scientific papers.

Smithsonian Astrophysical Observatory, 60 Garden Street, Cambridge; and 35 Elizabeth Road, Belmont 02178, Mass., U.S.A.

Whipple, George Hoyt, B.A., M.D.; American pathologist; b. 28 Aug. 1878; ed. Yale Univ., and Johns Hopkins Univ.

Assoc. Prof. of Pathology, Johns Hopkins Univ. 09-14; Resident Pathologist, Johns Hopkins Hospital 10-14; Prof. of Research Medicine, Univ. of California 14-21; Dean, Univ. of Rochester 21-53, Prof. 21-55; joint recipient of Nobel Medicine Prize for research in the treatment of anæmia 34; Trustee Rockefeller Foundation 27-43; Trustee Gen. Education Board 36-43; mem. Board of Scientific Dir. Rockefeller Inst. 36-53, Trustee 39-60, Trustee Emeritus 60; mem. Nat. Acad. of Sciences and American Philosophical Society; hon. mem. Pathological Society of Great Britain and Ireland 45-, Int. Asscn. for Dental Research 60-; foreign corresp. mem. British Medical Asscn.; Hon. Fellow, American Acad. of Oral Pathology; awarded William Wood Gerhard Medal 34, Kober Medal 39; Charles Mickle Fellow, Univ. of Toronto 38; Gold-headed cane award (American Asscn. of Pathologists and Bacteriologists) 61, Kovalenko Medal (Nat. Acad.

of Sciences) 62, Distinguished Fed. Civilian Service
Award from Pres. Kennedy 63.
56-D Manor Parkway, Rochester, N.Y. 14620, U.S.A.;
260 Crittenden Boulevard, Rochester, N.Y. 14620,
U.S.A.

Whitaker, Howard E.; American business executive;
b. 9 Oct. 1903; ed. Massachusetts Inst. of Technology.
Mead Corpn., Dayton, Ohio 25-, Dir. 50-, Pres. 52-57,
Chair. Board 57-; Chair. and Dir. Brunswick P.P. Co.;
Dir. other companies.
Mead Corporation, Dayton, Ohio; Home: 132 West
Second Street, Chillicothe, Ohio 45601, U.S.A.

Whitby, G. Stafford, A.R.C.SC., M.SC., PH.D., D.SC.,
LL.D., F.R.S.C.; British chemist; b. 26 May 1887; ed.
Royal Coll. of Science.
Demonstrator Imperial Coll. of Science and Technology
06; Chemist Société Financière des Caoutchoucs Malay
States 10; Asst. Prof. of Chemistry McGill Univ.
Montreal 20, Prof. of Organic Chemistry 23; Pres.
Canadian Inst. Chemistry 27; Pres. Canadian Chemical
Asscn. 28; Dir. Div. of Chemistry Nat. Research Council
Ottawa 29; Dir. Chemical Research Laboratory Dept.
of Scientific and Industrial Research (Great Britain)
39-42; Prof. of Rubber Chemistry Akron Univ. 42-54;
Foundation Lecturer, Inst. Rubber Industry 62;
Colwyn Gold Medal, Inst. Rubber Industry 28; Charles
Goodyear Medal 54.
Publs. *Plantation Rubber and the Testing of Rubber* 20,
Joint Ed. *High Polymers Series of Monographs, Advances
in Colloid Science*, Vol. II 46; Editor *Synthetic Rubber* 54.
c/o Akron University, Akron, Ohio 44304, U.S.A.
Telephone: 762-2441.

White, Byron R.; American lawyer and government
official; b. 8 June 1917; ed. Univ. of Colorado, Oxford
Univ., and Yale Univ.
Served U.S. Naval Intelligence, Second World War;
Yale Univ. after war; Clerk to Chief Justice of U.S.
Supreme Court 46-47; law practice in Denver, Colo.
47-61; Deputy Attorney-Gen. 61-62 Justice of U.S.
Supreme Court 62-.
U.S. Supreme Court, Washington, D.C. 20543, U.S.A.

White, Charles McElroy; American steel executive;
b. 13 June 1891; ed. Univ. of Maryland, and Carnegie
Inst. of Technology.
Joined Jones & Laughlin Steel Co. as Millwright helper
13, Gen. Supt. Aliquippa Works 29; Asst. Vice-Pres.
Republic Steel Corpn. 30-35, Vice-Pres. (Operations)
35-45, Pres. 45-56, Chief Exec. Officer 55-60; Chair.
Board 56-60, Hon. Chair. 60-; Trustee Nat. Industrial
Conference Board 46-, Chair. 59-61, Councillor 62-;
Chair. Policy Board, Business Council for Int. Under-
standing 59-62; Dir. Cleveland Trust Co., Sherwin-
Williams Co.; Hon. Vice-Pres. Amer. Iron and Steel Inst.
61-; Vice-Chair. Republican Nat. Finance Comm. 62-.
Home: 16670 South Park Boulevard, Shaker Heights,
Cleveland; Office: Republic Building, Cleveland, Ohio,
U.S.A.

White, Mrs. Eirene Lloyd, M.P.; British politician; b.
9 Nov. 1909; ed. St. Paul's Girls' School, and Somerville
Coll., Oxford.
Ministry of Labour 41-45; Parl. journalist 45-49; Labour
M.P. for East Flintshire 50-; Parl. Under-Sec. of State,
Colonial Office 64-66; Minister of State, Foreign Office
66-67; Minister of State for Wales 67-; mem. Nat.
Exec. Cttee., Labour Party 47-53, 57-.
3 Well Road, London, N.W.3, England.
Telephone: 01-435-1282.

White, Elwyn Brooks, B.A.; American writer and
editor; b. 11 July 1899; ed. Cornell Univ.
Comment writer, reporter, and contributor to *The
New Yorker* magazine; also contributed monthly
department called "One Man's Meat" to *Harper's* 38-43;

Presidential Medal of Freedom 63; Hon. Litt.D. (Dart-
mouth Coll., Hamilton Coll., Univs. of Maine, Yale,
Harvard; Bowdoin Coll., Colby Coll.).
Publs. *The Lady is Cold* 29, *Is Sex Necessary?* (with
James Thurber) 29, *Every Day is Saturday* 34, *The
Fox of Peapack* 38, *Quo Vadimus?* 39, *One Man's Meat*
42, enlarged 44, *Stuart Little* 45, *The Wild Flag* 46,
Here is New York 49, *Charlotte's Web* 52, *The Second
Tree from the Corner* 54, *The Points of My Compass* 62;
editor (with Katharine S. White) *A Subtreasury of
American Humor* 41.
North Brooklin, Maine, U.S.A.

White, Sir Frederick William George, K.B.E., M.SC.,
PH.D., F.A.A., F.R.S.; Australian physicist; b. 1905; ed.
Victoria Univ. Coll., New Zealand, and Cambridge
Univ.
Post-graduate work at Cavendish Laboratory, Cam-
bridge 29-31; Demonstrator in Physics, Lecturer in
Physics, King's Coll. London 31-37; Prof. of Physics,
Canterbury Univ. Coll. New Zealand 37; seconded to
Council for Scientific and Industrial Research as Chair.
Radiophysics Advisory Board 41; Chief Div. of Radio-
physics 42; Exec. Officer C.S.I.R. 45, mem. Exec.
Cttee. 46, Chief Exec. Officer Commonwealth Scientific
and Industrial Research Organisation (CSIRO) 49-56;
Dep. Chair. CSIRO 57-59, Chair. 59-.
Publ. *Electromagnetic Waves* 34.
57 Investigator Street, Red Hill, Canberra, A.C.T.,
Australia.

White, Harold Leslie, C.B.E., M.A., F.L.A.A.; Australian
librarian; b. 14 June 1905, ed. Wesley Coll., Melbourne,
and Queen's Coll. of Melbourne Univ.
Commonwealth Parl. Library 23-67, Parl. Librarian
until 67; Nat. Librarian, Nat. Library of Australia 47-;
Chair. Standing Cttee. Australian Advisory Council
on Bibliographical Services 60-; mem. Australian Cttees.
for UNESCO, Australian Nat. Film Board; mem.
UNESCO Int. Cttee. on Bibliography, Documentation
and Terminology 61-65.
Publs. (ed.) *Canberra: A Nation's Capital*.
National Library of Australia, Canberra, A.C.T. 2600;
Home: 27 Mugga Way, Red Hill, Canberra, A.C.T.
2600, Australia.

White, Katharine Elkus; American diplomatist;
b. 25 Nov. 1906; ed. Vassar Coll.
Mayor, Red Bank, New Jersey 50-56; Chair., New
Jersey Highway Authority 55-64; Treas., State of New
Jersey, June-Dec. 61; Chair. Advisory Council to
President's Cttee. for Traffic Safety 61-64; Ambassador
to Denmark 64-; Hon. LL.D. (Rutgers Univ.) 67.
American Embassy, Dag Hammarskjölds Allé 24,
Copenhagen Ø, Denmark; and Elkridge, Harding Road,
Red Bank, New Jersey 07701, U.S.A.

White, Lee Calvin, B.S., LL.B.; American lawyer and
government official; b. 1 Sept. 1923; ed. Univ. of
Nebraska, and Lehigh Univ.
Lawyer, Div. of Law, Tennessee Valley Authority
50-54; Legislative Asst. on staff of Senator John F.
Kennedy 54, 55-57; Counsel to Senate Small Business
Cttee. 57-58; Admin. Asst. to Senator Cooper of
Kentucky 58-61; Asst. Special Counsel to Pres. Kennedy
61-64; Special Counsel to President Johnson March
65-66; Chair. Fed. Power Comm. March 66-.
3216 W. Coquelin Terrace, Chevy Chase, Md. 20015,
U.S.A.
Telephone: OL6-4502.

White, Patrick, B.A.; Australian writer; b. 28 May
1912; ed. Cheltenham Coll., and King's Coll., Cam-
bridge.
Intelligence officer, R.A.F., World War II; W. H. Smith
& Son Award 59.
Publs. *Happy Valley* 39, *The Living and the Dead* 41,
The Aunt's Story 48, *The Tree of Man* 55, *Voss* 57,

Riders in the Chariot 61, *The Burnt Ones* 64, *Four Plays* 65, *The Solid Mandala* 66.
20 Martin Road, Centennial Park, Sydney, N.S.W., Australia.

White, Paul Dudley, A.B., M.D.; American physician; b. 6 June 1886; ed. Harvard Univ.
Intern, Mass. Gen. Hospital 11-13, Resident in Medicine 14-17 and 19-20, Consultant 20-; Teaching Fellow and later Clinical Prof. of Medicine, Harvard Univ. 14-56; engaged in research, practice and teaching of medicine, specialising in heart diseases; Chair. Comm. on Cardiovascular Disease, Nat. Research Council 40-46; Chair. American Medical Teaching Mission to Czechoslovakia 46, Greece and Italy 48, to Pakistan, India, Israel and Greece 52, to the Near East 57; Physician to Pres. Eisenhower; Exec. Dir. Nat. Advisory Heart Council 48-56; awarded Lasker Prize; Dist. Service Award of American Medical Asscn., Légion d'Honneur (France), etc.; hon. degrees from Harvard Univ., Boston Univ., Univ. of Massachusetts, Ithaca Univ., St. John's Univ. New York, Univ. of S. California, Univ. do Brasil, Univ. of Montreal, Jagiellonian Univ., Cracow.
Publs. *Heart Disease* 31, *Heart Disease in General Practice* 37, *Clues in the Diagnosis and Treatment of Heart Diseases* 55; jointly *Electrocardiography in Practice* 41, *Coronary Heart Disease in Young Adults, A Multi-disciplinary Study* 54.
Home: 115 Juniper Road, Belmont, Mass.; Office: 264 Beacon Street, Boston, U.S.A.

White, Robert M., II; American journalist; b. 6 April 1915; ed. Missouri Military Acad., and Washington and Lee Univ.
With United Press 39; Army service 40-45; Pres., Co-Ed. and Co-Publisher *Mexico* (Missouri) *Ledger* 45-; Ed. and Pres. *New York Herald Tribune* Aug. 59-Feb. 61; Dir. American Newspaper Publishers' Asscn. 55-63, Treas. 62-63; Dir. New York World's Fair (64-65); fmr. Chair. Associated Press Nominating Cttee.; fmr. Chair. and Pres. of Board Inland Daily Press Asscn.; Dir. Stephen's Coll.; Pres. See TV Co.; American Cttee. Int. Press Inst.; Dir. American Soc. of Newspaper Editors 68-; Dir. Missouri Mil. Acad.; Pres. Sigma Delta Chi (Nat. Soc. of Journalists) 67-68; mem. Pulitzer Prize Jury for Journalism 64-66; Univ. of Missouri Journalism Distinguished Service Award 67.
3 Park Circle, Mexico, Mo. 65265; Office: 300 N. Washington St., Mexico, Mo., 65265, U.S.A.
Telephone: 314-JU-1-1111 (Office); 314-JU-1-2522 (Home).

White, Robert Mayer, SC.D.; American meteorologist; b. 13 Feb. 1923; ed. Harvard Univ., and Massachusetts Inst. of Technology.
War Service with U.S. Air Force; executive at Atmospheric Analysis Laboratory, Geophysics Research Directorate, Air Force Cambridge Research Center 52-58, Chief of Meteorological Devt. Laboratory 58; Research Assoc. Massachusetts Inst. of Technology 59; Travelers Insurance Companies 59-60, Pres. Travelers Research Center, Hartford 60-63; Chief of Weather Bureau, U.S. Dept. of Commerce 63-; mem. Research Soc. of America, Royal Meteorological Soc.; mem. of numerous weather research cttees. and Chair. U.S. Cttee. of World Meteorological Organisation.
Publs. numerous technical articles.
U.S. Weather Bureau, Washington 24, D.C.; 8306 Melody Court, Bethesda, Maryland 20034, U.S.A.
Telephone: 301-496-8111 (Office); 301-365-3927 (Home).

White, Theodore H., A.B.; American writer; b. 6 May 1915; ed. Boston Latin School and Harvard Univ.
Far Eastern Correspondent, *Time* magazine 39-45; Ed. *New Republic* 47; European Corresp.-in-Chief, Overseas News Agency 48-50; Chief European Corresp. *The Reporter* magazine 50-53, Nat. Corresp. 54-55; Nat. Corresp. *Colliers* 55-56; Consultant to Columbia Broad-

casting System 61-64; Air Medal 44; Ben Franklin Award; Overseas Press Club Award; Pulitzer Prize 62, Emmy Award 64, 67.
Publs. *Thunder out of China* 46, *Stilwell Papers* 48, *Fire in the Ashes* 53, *The Mountain Road* 58, *The View from the Fortieth Floor* 60, *The Making of the President 1960* 61, *The Making of the President 1964* 65, *Caesar at the Rubicon* 68.
168 East 64th Street, New York 21, N.Y., U.S.A.

White, William Lindsay, A.B.; American writer; b. 17 June 1900; ed. Kansas State Univ., and Harvard. Reporter on *Emporia Gazette* 14, later Circulation Man., Man. Editor, Editorial Writer, Assoc. Editor, Publisher, and Editor; staff *Washington Post* 35, *Fortune Magazine* 37; war corresp. for 40 American daily newspapers, also rep. Columbia Broadcasting System, European Corresp. 39-40; rep. North American newspaper Alliance and *Reader's Digest*, London, winter 40-41; Roving Editor, *Reader's Digest* 42-; mem. Kansas State Legislature 31-32; mem. Board Overseers Harvard Univ. 50-56.
Publs. *What People Said* (novel) 38; co-author *Zero Hour* (foreign affairs) 40; *Journey for Margaret* (war-time travel) 41, *They Were Expendable* 42, *Queens Die Proudly* 43, *Report on the Russians* 45, *Report on the Germans* 47, *Lost Boundaries* 48, *Land of Milk and Honey* 49, *Bernard Baruch* 50, *Back Down the Ridge* 53, *The Captives of Korea: an unofficial White Paper* 57, *The Little Toy Dog* 62.
160 E. 66th Street, New York 21, N.Y., U.S.A.

White, William R.; American lawyer and banker; b. 24 June 1903; ed. Bucknell Univ. and Columbia Univ. Law School.
Fmr. assoc. of law firm Chadbourne, Wallace, Parke and Whiteside; fmr. Dep. Supt. and Counsel to New York State Banking Dept.; Superintendent of Banks, New York State 36-42; Pres. Nat. Asscn. of Supervisors of State Banks 37-38, Chair. Exec. Cttee. 38-42; Chair. N.Y. State Banking Board 36-42; Dir. Hennepin Paper Co.; Dir. Legal Aid Soc. 48-, mem. Exec. Cttee. 62-, Treas. 62-; Trustee and mem. Exec. Cttee. Bowery Savings Bank 43-; Vice-Pres. Guaranty Trust Co. of N.Y. (now Morgan Guaranty Trust Co. of N.Y.) 42-; Vice-Chair. War Finance Cttee. for N.Y. State for 6th War Loan 44; mem. Exec. Cttee. Banking Law Section, N.Y. State Bar Asscn. 48-51; Council of Admin. N.Y. State Bankers Asscn. 56-59; mem. Mayor's Cttee. on Transit Power Plants 57-58; Dir. Textile Banking Corpn. 59; Dir. Schick Electric Co. Inc.; Chair. Board of Trustees, Bucknell Univ.; Hon. LL.D. (Union Coll., Schenectady, Bucknell Univ.).
23 Wall Street, New York City 10015, U.S.A.

White, William Smith; American journalist; b. 20 May 1907; ed. Univ. of Texas.
Held various posts with Associated Press (News Editor, War Editor and War Corresp.); mem. Washington staff, *The New York Times* 45-57; Chief Congressional corresp. 57-58; nationally syndicated Political Columnist 58-; Regents Prof. Univ. of Calif. (Berkeley) 57-58; Contributing Editor *Harper's* Magazine 60-62; Pulitzer Prize in Letters, etc.
Publs. *The Taft Story* 54, *Citadel: The Story of the U.S. Senate* 57, *Majesty and Mischief: A Mixed Tribute to F.D.R.* 61, *The Professional: Lyndon B. Johnson* 64, *Home Place: The Story of the U.S. House of Representatives* 65.
5264 Loughborough Road, N.W., Washington 20016, U.S.A.

Whitehead, Sir Edgar Cuthbert Fremantle, K.C.M.G., O.B.E., M.A., M.P.; Rhodesian politician; b. 8 Feb. 1905; ed. Univ. Coll., Oxford.
Went to Southern Rhodesia 28; served West Africa and with Air Despatch in U.K. 39-45; M.P. for Southern Rhodesia 39-40, 46-53, 58-; Acting High Commr. for

S. Rhodesia in the U.K. 45-46; Minister of Finance and of Posts and Telegraphs, S. Rhodesia 46-53; mem. Council, Univ. of Rhodesia and Nyasaland 55-57; Minister for Rhodesia and Nyasaland Affairs, Washington 57-58; Prime Minister of Southern Rhodesia Feb. 58-Dec. 62; Leader of the Opposition 62-65; United Federal Party.
Passford House Hotel, Mount Pleasant, nr. Lymington, Hants., England.

Whitlam, Edward Gough, Q.C., B.A., LL.B., M.P.; Australian barrister and politician; b. 11 July 1916; ed. Knox Grammar School, Sydney, Canberra High School, Canberra Grammar School and Univ. of Sydney.
Royal Australian Air Force 41-45; admitted to New South Wales Bar 47; mem. House of Representatives 52-; mem. Parl. Cttee. on Constitutional Review 56-59; mem. Federal Parl. Exec. of Australian Labor Party 59-; Dep. Leader of Australian Labor Party in Federal Parliament 60-66, Leader 66-.
Publs. *The Constitution v. Labor* 57, *Australian Foreign Policy* 63, *Socialist Policies within the Constitution* 65, *Australia—Base or Bridge* (Evatt Memorial Lecture) 66.
Parliament House, Canberra, A.C.T., Australia.

Whitney, Cornelius Vanderbilt; American industrialist; b. 20 Feb. 1899; ed. Yale Univ.
Director Hudson Bay Mining and Smelting Co.; Pres. Whitney Industries Inc.; Chair. Board Marine Studios Inc.; Dir. Whitney Museum of Art.
230 Park Avenue, New York City, N.Y. 10017, U.S.A.

Whitney, Hassler, MUS.B., PH.D.; American educator; b. 23 March 1907; ed. Yale and Harvard Univs.
Nat. Research Fellow 31-33; Instr. in Maths., Harvard Univ. 33-35; Asst. Prof. 35-40; Assoc. Prof. 40-46; Prof. 46-52; Prof. Inst. for Advanced Study 52-; Research Mathematician, Nat. Defense Research Cttee, 43-45; mem. Nat. Acad. of Sciences, American Philosophical Society; Hon. S.D.
Institute for Advanced Study, Princeton, N.J., U.S.A.

Whitney, John Hay; American diplomatist and newspaper publisher; b. 17 Aug. 1904; ed. Groton School, Oxford Univ., and Yale Univ.
Senior partner, J. H. Whitney & Co., New York; Chair. Whitney Communications Corp., New York; fmr. Chair. Bd. of Freeport Sulphur Co.; Pres. John Hay Whitney Foundation; served U.S.A.F. in Second World War; special adviser on public affairs, Dept. of State; mem. Bd. of Govs. New York Hospital; Fellow of Corpn. of Yale Univ.; Trustee Museum of Modern Art; Ambassador to the U.K. 57-61; Publisher and Editor-in-Chief *New York Herald Tribune*, New York 61-67; Pres. and Publisher *New York Herald Tribune*, European Edition 61-67; Chair. *International Herald Tribune*, Paris 67-; Trustee Carnegie Endowment for Int. Peace; Nat. Gallery of Art; Chair. English Speaking Union of U.S.A.; Hon. LL.D. (Columbia).
110 West 51st Street, New York 20, N.Y., U.S.A.

Whittaker, Charles Evans, LL.B.; American judge; b. 22 Feb. 1901; ed. Univ. of Missouri.
Worked as office boy, while studying at law school, with Watson, Gage and Ess, Kansas City 20-24; admitted to Missouri Bar 23; junior partner Watson, Gage and Ess 28-32, Senior partner Watson, Ess, Whittaker, Marshall and Enggas 33-54; U.S. District Judge Mo. 54-56; Judge U.S. Court of Appeals, Eighth Circuit 56-57; Assoc. Justice of the U.S. Supreme Court 57-62 (resigned commission 65); Dealer Relations Commr., Gen. Motors Corpn. 65-; mem. Board of Govs. of Mo. Bar, Integrated 48-53 and Pres. 53-54; LL.B. h.c. Central Coll., Mo. 54.
Office: 1928 Commerce Tower, Kansas City, Mo.; Home, 6400 Aberdeen Road, Shawnee Mission, Kansas 66208: Mo., U.S.A.

Whitteridge, Sir Gordon (Coligny), K.C.M.G., O.B.E.; British diplomatist; b. 6 Nov. 1908; ed. Whitgift School, Croydon, and Univ. of Cambridge.
Joined Consular Service 32, service in Bangkok, Batavia and Medan; Foreign Office 42; 1st Sec., Moscow 48-49; Consul-Gen. Stuttgart 49-51; Counsellor and Consul-Gen. Bangkok 51-56; Consul-Gen. Seattle 56-60, Istanbul 60-62; Ambassador to Burma 62-65, to Afghanistan 65-.
British Embassy, Kabul, Afghanistan.

Whittingham, Air Marshal Sir Harold Edward, K.C.B., K.B.E., M.B., CH.B., F.R.C.P. (LOND.), F.R.C.P. (EDIN.), F.R.F.P.S., D.P.H., D.T.M. AND H., K.ST.J.; British pathologist and tropical diseases and aviation medicine specialist; b. 3 Oct. 1887; ed. Christ's Hospital, Greenock Acad., and Glasgow Univ.
Pathologist and Asst. Dir. of Research, Royal Cancer Hospital Glasgow 10-14; Scottish Nat. Red Cross 14-15; served R.A.M.C. India and Mesopotamia 15-17; Pathologist R.A.F. 18-24, Dir. of Pathology 25-30; Lecturer in Biochemistry London School of Hygiene and Tropical Medicine 26-30; Consultant in Hygiene, Pathology and Tropical Medicine R.A.F. 30-39; C.O. R.A.F. Central Medical Establishment 34-40; Dir. of Hygiene Air Ministry and Chief Exec. Officer Flying Personnel Research Cttee. 39-41; promoted Air Marshal 41; Dir.-Gen. R.A.F. Medical Services 41-46; Medical Adviser British Red Cross Society 46-48; Dir. Medical Services B.O.A.C. 48-56; Medical Adviser Commonwealth Development Corpn.; Chair. Flying Personnel Research Cttee. 49-67; Hon. Civil Consultant in aviation medicine to the R.A.F. 67-; Consultant on aviation medicine to B.E.A. 57-; mem. WHO Advisory Panel on Environmental Sanitation, Int. Acad. of Astronautics; Hon. Physician to the King 38-46; decorations include Knight Grand Cross Order of St. Olav (Norway), Commdr. U.S. Legion of Merit, North Persian Memorial Medal; Chadwick Gold Medal and Prize 25; John Jeffries Award, Inst. of Aero Sciences, U.S.A. 44; Hon. F.R.C.S. (Edinburgh) and Hon. F.R.S.M. (London); Hon. Fellow Aero-Medical Asscn., Hon. LL.D. (Glasgow).
26 Marlborough Gardens, Lovelace Road, Surbiton, Surrey, England.
Telephone: 01-399-8648.

Whittle, Air Commodore Sir Frank, K.B.E., C.B., M.A., F.R.S., C.ENG., R.A.F. (retd.); British aeronautical expert; b. 1 June 1907; ed. Leamington Coll., Royal Air Force Coll., Cranwell, and Cambridge Univ.
Posted to 111 Fighter Squadron as Pilot Officer 28; attended Flying Instructors' Course 29; Flying Instructor at No. 2 Flying Training School, Digby 30; Test Pilot, Marine Aircraft Experimental Estab., Felixstowe 31-32; attended Officers' Course of Engineering at Henlow 32-34; Cambridge Univ. 34-37; posted to Special Duty List to continue work on Whittle jet-propulsion gas turbine 37-46; Technical Adviser on Engine Design and Production to the Controller of Supplies (Air), Ministry of Supply 46-48; retd. R.A.F. 48; Technical Adviser to B.O.A.C. 48-52; consultant to Power Jets (Research and Development) Ltd. 50-53, Bataafsche Petroleum Maatschappij, The Hague 53-57; mem. Livery, Guild of Air Pilots and Air Navigators; hon. mem. Engineering Inst. of Canada; Hon. Fellow Aeronautical Society of India; Hon. M.I.Mech.E.; Hon. F.R.Ae.S.; Gold Medal (Royal Aeronautical Society); James Alfred Ewing Medal; Daniel Guggenheim Medal 46; Kelvin Gold Medal for 47; Melchett Medal 49; Rumford Medal of Royal Society 50; Gold Medal of Fed. Aéronautique Internationale 51; Churchill Medal of Soc. of Engineers; Albert Medal of Royal Soc. of Arts 52; Franklin Medal, U.S.A. 56; John Scott Award, City of Philadelphia 57; U.S. Legion of Merit; first recipient Goddard Award of American Inst. of Aeronautics and Astronautics 65;

Award of Merit City of Coventry 66; Christopher Columbus Medal and Prize (Genoa) 66; Hon. Fellow Soc. of Experimental Test Pilots (U.S.A.) 66; Hon. D.Sc. (Oxford, Manchester, Bath, Warwick and Leicester); Hon. Sc.D. (Cambridge), LL.D. (Edinburgh); Hon. D.Tech. (Technical Univ. of Norway).
Publs. *The Early History of the Whittle Jet-Propulsion Gas Turbine* (First James Clayton Lecture) 45, *Jet: The Story of a Pioneer*.
c/o The Athenæum, Pall Mall, London, S.W.1, England.

Whyatt, Sir John, Kt., q.c.; British lawyer; b. 13 April 1905; ed. Stonyhurst and Balliol Coll., Oxford.
Called to Inner Temple Bar 27; Crown Counsel, Hong Kong 37; Hong Kong Del. to Eastern Group Conf., New Delhi 40; Sec. Eastern Group Supply Council, New Delhi 41; U.K. Adviser, UNRRA Conf., Australia 45; Attorney-Gen. Barbados 48-50; Attorney-Gen. and Minister for Legal Affairs, Kenya 51-55; Chief Justice of Singapore 55-58; Dir. of Justice Research, Education and Research Trust 60; Judge of Chief Court for the Persian Gulf 61-66; Dir. of Studies, Govt. Legal Officers Course 66-.
45 Wilton Crescent, London, S.W.1, England.
Telephone: 01-235-4107.

Whyburn, William Marvin, M.A., PH.D.; American university professor; b. 12 Nov. 1901; ed. Univ. of Texas.
Teacher in Public Schools, Denton County, Texas 18-20; Instr., Maths., South Park Jr. Coll., Beaumont 23-24; Asst. Prof. of Maths., Texas Agric. and Mechanical Coll. 24-25; Assoc. Prof. Texas Technological Coll. 25-26; Nat. Research Fellow, Maths., Harvard Univ. 27-28; Asst. Prof. of Maths., Univ. of Calif., Los Angeles 28-30, Assoc. Prof. 30-38, Prof. and Chair. Dept. of Maths. 38-44; Pres. Texas Technological Coll. Lubbock 44-48; Kenan Prof. of Maths. and Head of Dept. Univ. of N.C. 48-67, Kenan Prof. Emer. 67-, Vice-Pres. for Graduate Studies and Research 56-60; Frensley Prof. of Maths., Southern Methodist Univ. 67-; Educ. supervisor, Univ. of Calif., Los Angeles, for Engineering, Science, Management War Training Programme 41-44; Chief, Operations Analysis Section, H.Q. 3rd Air Force 44; Corresp. mem. La Academie Nacional de Ciencias Exactas, Fisicas y Naturales, Lima 43; Hon. LL.D., Texas Tech. Coll. 48.
Publs. *Basic Mathematics for War and Industry* (with P. H. Daus and J. M. Gleason) 44, *First Year College Mathematics with Applications* (with P. H. Daus) 51, *Algebra for College Students* (with P. H. Daus) 55, *Introduction to Mathematical Analysis with Applications to Problems in Economics* (with P. H. Daus) 58, *Algebra with Applications to Business and Economics* (with P. H. Daus) 61.
Department of Mathematics, S. Methodist Univ., Dallas, Texas 75222; and 4 Mt. Bolus Road, Chapel Hill, N.C. 27514, U.S.A.
Telephone: EMerson 9-3096 (Dallas); 929-1658 (Chapel Hill).

Whyte, William Hollingsworth; American writer; b. 1 Oct. 1917; ed. Princeton Univ.
Worked for Vick Chemical Co. 39-41; served with U.S. Marine Corps 41-45; joined *Fortune* Magazine 46, Asst. Man. Editor 51-58; Benjamin Franklin Award 55; LL.D. h.c. Grinnell Coll.
Publs. *Is Anybody Listening?* 52, *The Organisation Man* 56, *The Exploding Metropolis* 59, *Cluster Development* 64.
175 East 94th Street, New York City 10028, U.S.A.

Wibaux, Fernand, DR.-EN-DROIT; French diplomatist; b. 21 July 1921; ed. Lycée de Lille and Faculté de Droit, Paris.
Civil Service admin., Algeria 44; Attaché to Sec. of State for Overseas Territories 49, to Minister of Merchant Marine 50-51, to High Commr., French W. Africa 52-55; Chief Asst. to Ministers for Overseas Territories 56-58;

Dir.-Gen. Niger Office 56; Consul-Gen. Bamako 60-61; Ambassador to Mali 61-64; Dir. Office de Co-opération et d'Accueil Universitaire 64-; Amb. to Chad 68-; Croix de Guerre; Officier de la Légion d'Honneur.
French Embassy, Fort-Lamy, Chad; and 14 rue de l'Abbé-Rousselot, Paris 17e, France.
Telephone: GAL-13-20.

Wibisono, Jusuf, LL.D.; Indonesian politician; b. 28 Feb. 1909; ed. Faculty of Law, Djakarta.
Vice-Chair. Working Cttee., Cen. Nat. Cttee. 45-46; Vice-Minister of Economic Affairs 46-47; Mem. of Parl. 50-56, Minister of Finance 51-52 and 56-57; mem. Exec. Council of Masjumi Party 48-59; Pres. Indonesian Islamic Trade Union S.B.I.I. (since 61 GASBIINDO) 54-66, Hon. Pres. 66-; mem. Muhammadijah Exec. Board 56-59, Provisional People's Congress 60-; mem. of Parl. 60-; mem. Exec. Board Nat. Front 60-66.
Publs. *Marriage, Polygamy and Divorce in Islam* 37, *Excursion behind the Iron Curtain* 52.
Pegangsaan Timur 40, Djarkarta, Indonesia.
Telephone: 82042.

Wicha, Władysław; Polish politician; b. 04.
Former member Communist Party of Poland; in Belgium, France and U.K. 38-45; Special Comm. for Combating Corruption 45-49; posts in Polish United Workers' Party 49-52; Vice-Minister of State Control 52-54; Minister of Interior 54-65; mem. Council of State 65-; mem. Central Cttee. of Polish United Workers' Party 54-.
2 Rakowiecka Street, Warsaw, Poland.

Wichser, Otto; Swiss railway executive; b. 29 July 1910; ed. Gymnasium, St. Gall, and Eidgenössische Technische Hochschule, Zürich.
Engineer, Chief of Section, Swiss Federal Railways 41-46, First Chief of Section 46-47, Deputy Chief Engineer 47-48, Chief Engineer 48-53, Gen. Man. 53-66, Pres. of Gen. Management 66-.
Swiss Federal Railways, 3000 Berne, 6 Hochschulstrasse; Home: 3074 Muri (Berne), 35 Gurtenweg, Switzerland.

Wichterle, Otto, D.TECH., D.SC.; Czechoslovak chemist; b. 27 Oct. 1913; ed. Czech Technical Univ., Prague, and Medical Faculty, Charles Univ., Prague.
Assistant Lecturer, Inst. of Experimental Organic Chemistry, Czech Technical Univ., Prague 35-39; Head of Polymer Dept., Bata-Zlín 40-42, 44-45; Gestapo prisoner 42-43; Asst. Prof., Faculty of Chemistry, Czech Tech. Univ., Prague 45, later Prof.; Prof. Coll. of Chemical Technology, Prague 49-; Academician, Czechoslovak Acad. of Sciences 55-; Chief of Dept. of Macromolecular Chemistry, Inst. of Chemistry 55-59, Dir. of Inst. of Macromolecular Chemistry 59-; Chair. Comm. for Macromolecular Chemistry, Czechoslovak Acad. of Sciences 56-; Deputy Chair. Scientific Collegium for Chemistry and Chemical Technology, Czechoslovak Acad. of Sciences, Prague 63; mem. Exec. Cttee. Int. Union of Pure and Applied Chemistry 67; State Prize 54; Order of Labour 66; Klement Gottwald State Prize 67.
Publs. Numerous papers and *Foundations of Preparative Organic Chemistry* (with others) 51, *Organic Chemistry* 52, 55, *Inorganic Chemistry* (with Petrů) 53, 56, *Macromolecular Chemistry* 57.
Institute of Macromolecular Chemistry, Prague 6, Na Petrinach 1888, Czechoslovakia.

Widdemer, Margaret; American poet and novelist; b. 30 Sept. 1893.
Former Vice-Pres. Board Poetry Soc. of America; Board Dirs. Pen and Brush Club; Lecturer, New York Univ. 45-48; Lecturer on fiction and co-dir. 45-65, Writers' Conf., Chautauqua, N.Y.; Hon. M.A. (Middlebury); Hon. Litt.D. (Bucknell).
Publs. *Why Not?* 16, *Factories* (poems) 17, *Old Road to*

Paradise 18 (Poetry Society Pulitzer Prize 19) *The Year of Delight* 21, *Graven Image* 23, *Gallant Lady* 26, *More Than Wife* 27, *Collected Poems* 27, *Road to Downderry* (poems) 32, *Golden Rain* 33, *Back to Virtue*, *Betty* 34, *Other Lovers* 35, *Hill Garden* (poems) 36, *Eve's Orchard* 37, *Do You Want to Write?* 37, *Hand On Her Shoulder* 38; *Ladies Go Masked* 39, *She Knew Three Brothers* 40, *Lover's Alibi* 40, *Let Me Have Wings* 41, *Angela Comes Home* 42 *Constancia Herself* 44, *Lani* 48, *Red Cloak Flying* 50, *Lady of the Mohawks* 51, *Prince in Buckskin* 52, *Basic Principles of Fiction Writing* 53, *Golden Wildcat* 54, *Great Pine's Son* 54, *Dark Cavalier: collected poems* 58, *Buckskin Baronet* 60, *Golden Friends I Had* (memoirs) 64.
c/o Doubleday and Company Inc., 277 Park Avenue, New York City, N.Y., and 1 West 67th Street, New York City 23, N.Y., U.S.A.
Telephone: TRafalgar 7-0237.

Widerberg, Bo; Swedish film director; b. 8 June 1930. Had twelve different jobs before military service; fmr. literary critic.
Films: *Barnvagnen* (The Pram) 62, *Kvarteret Korpen* (Raven's End) 63, *Kärlek 65* (Love 65) 65, *Elvira Madigan* 67.
Publs. *Kyssas* (short story) 52, *Erotikon* (novel) 57, *En stuhl, Madame* (autobiographical short story) 61, *Den gröna draken* (novel), *Visionen i svensk film* (essays).
c/o Svenska Filminstitutet, Kungsgatan 48, Stockholm C, Sweden.

Wien, Lawrence A., A.B., LL.B.; American lawyer; b. 30 May 1905; ed. Columbia Univ.
Admitted to New York Bar 27; with Wien, Lane and Klein 51-; Pres. and Dir. Real Estate Investigating Asscn., Inc. 60-, Office Maintenance Corpn. 60-, Wico Trading Corpn. 47-; founder and sponsor of Wien Int. Scholarship Program Brandeis Univ. 57, Nat. Scholarship Program Columbia Univ. Law School 59.
60 East 42nd Street, New York City 17, N.Y., U.S.A.

Wiener, Alexander S., A.B., M.D., F.A.C.P., F.C.A.P., F.A.S.C.P.; American serologist and hematologist; b. 16 March 1907; ed. Cornell Univ., and State Univ. N.Y. Coll. of Medicine.
Senior Bacteriologist (Serology) Office of Chief Medical Examiner of New York City; Attending Immunohematologist, Jewish Hospital of Brooklyn, and Adelphi Hospital 32-; Assoc. Prof. Forensic Medicine, N.Y. Univ. School of Medicine 60-; Owner Dir. of Wiener Serum Laboratory, Brooklyn, N.Y. 35-; pioneer discoverer of Rh blood types; affiliate Royal Soc. of Medicine; Lasker Award; Passano Foundation Award; Karl Landsteiner Award, etc.
Publs. *Blood Groups and Transfusion* 32 (3rd edn. 43), *An Rh-Hr Syllabus* 54 (2nd edn. 63), *The Rh-Hr Blood Types* 54, *Heredity of the Blood Groups* 58, *Advances in Blood Grouping* (vols. I, II) 61, 65.
Home: 90 Maple Street, Brooklyn, N.Y. 11225; Office: 64 Rutland Road, Brooklyn, N.Y. 11225, U.S.A.

Wiener, Paul Lester; American architect and city planner; b. 2 May 1895; ed. Leipzig, Royal Acad. of Berlin, Paris and Vienna.
Worked in Europe and America until present; co-founder Contempora, group of int. artists 28; engaged in architectural, housing and industrial design until 32; Designer U.S. Govt. building and interiors and Adviser to U.S. Comm. for Int. Exposition Paris 37; commissioned to design exhibits for Brazil and Ecuador, N.Y. World's Fair 39; Dir. of Technical Studies, New School for Social Research N.Y. 43-45; Consultant, Office of Production and Development, W.P.B. 43-45; designed many Master Plans (with J. L. Sert) for urban development in South American countries; planned urban renewal development New York City, Minneapolis and Syracuse (N.Y.); Specialist for U.S. Dept. of State Div. Int. Education 55-56; mem. American Inst. of planners;

Adj. Prof. or Urban Planning, Columbia Univ. 65-67; designed Colombian Govt. Center in New York 66; Master plan New Providence Island and City of Nassau 66-67; hon. mem. Instituto de Arquitetos do Brasil, etc.; awarded 3 Grand Prix for Public and Private Architecture by Int. Exposition of Arts and Sciences 38, etc.; Légion d'Honneur (France); Order of the Southern Cross (Brazil); Prof. h.c. Univ. San Carlos, Guatemala.
25 Washington Square North, New York City, N.Y., U.S.A.
Telephone: AL4-8453.

Wierblowski, Stefan; Polish diplomatist; b. 04.
Was a journalist prior to Second World War; Minister to Czechoslovakia 45-47, Ambassador 47-48; Sec.-Gen. to Ministry of Foreign Affairs, Warsaw 48-51; Dep. Minister 51-54; Head Del. to U.N. 49, 50, 51; Prof. Inst. of Social Sciences 54; Chair. Scientific and Editorial Council Polish Acad. of Sciences; Chair. Polish Nat. Comm. for UNESCO; mem. Exec. Council UNESCO 56-64; mem. Polish United Workers' Party.
Polish National Commission for UNESCO, Pałac Kultury i Nauki, Warsaw, Poland.
Telephone: 203355.

Wierzynski, Kazimierz; Polish poet; b. 94; ed. Cracow, Vienna and Lwów Univs.
Laureate Olympic Prize for Poetry 28; Nat. Literature Award 36; fmr. mem. Polish Acad. of Literature; now political refugee in U.S.A.
Publs. 25 books: poetry, short stories, theatrical criticism; most prominent: *Wiosna i Wino* (The Spring and Wine) 19, *Laur Olimpijski* (Olympic Laurel) 27, *Wolnosc Tragiczna* (The Tragic Freedom) 36, *Korzec Maku* 51, *Siedem Podków* 54, *Tkanka Ziemi* 60; in English: *The Forgotten Battlefield* 44, *The Life and Death of Chopin* 49, *Selected Poems* 59.
P.O. Box 525, Sag Harbor, N.Y., U.S.A.

Wiese und Kaiserwaldau, Benno von, DR.PHIL.; (son of Leopold von Wiese und Kaiserwaldau q.v.); German university professor; b. 25 Sept. 1903; ed. Univs. of Leipzig, Vienna, Heidelberg.
Lecturer in German Literature Univ. Bonn 29; Prof. Univ. Erlangen 32-43; Prof. Univ. Münster 43-57; Visiting Prof. Univ. of Indiana (Bloomington) 54-55; Princeton Univ. 55-56; Prof. Univ. Bonn 57-; Visiting Prof. Univ. of Minnesota 67-68; mem. Düsseldorfs Arbeitsgemeinschaft für Forschung des Landes Nordrhein-Westfalen; Hon. Dr. Hum. Litt., Univ. of Chicago.
Publs. *Die deutsche Tragödie von Lessing bis Hebbel* 48, *Friedrich Schiller* 59, 63, *Die deutsche Novelle von Goethe bis Kafka* Vol. I 56, Vol. II 62; *Eduard Mörike* 50, *Zwischen Utopia und Wirklichkeit* 63.
53 Bonn-Ippendorf, Bergstrasse 33, German Federal Republic.
Telephone: 282794.

Wiese und Kaiserwaldau, Leopold von (father of Benno von Wiese und Kaiserwaldau, q.v.); German sociologist; b. 2 Dec. 1876; ed. Gymnasium and Univ. of Berlin.
Former Lector, Acads. of Posen and Düsseldorf; studied in America and Asia; Prof. at Commercial High School, Cologne 15; Prof. Univ. of Cologne 15-50, Emeritus 50-; Dr. Iur. h.c., Dr. rer pol. h.c., and other honours and decorations.
Publs. *System der Allgemeine Soziologie* (4th edn.) 67, *Ethics* (2nd edn.) 60, *Introduction to General Sociology* (8th edn.) 67.
5 Köln-Lindenthal, Meister Ekkerhart-Strasse 8, German Federal Republic.

Wiesner, Jerome Bert, M.S., PH.D.; American professor and communications engineer; b. 30 May 1915; ed. Univ. of Michigan.
Chief Engineer Library of Congress, Washington 40-42; mem. staff M.I.T. Radiation Laboratory, Cambridge; Mass. 42-45; mem. staff Univ. of California, Los Alamos

Laboratory 45-46; Prof. of Electrical Eng., Assoc. Dir. and Dir. Research Lab. of Electronics, Chair. Dept. of Electrical Eng., M.I.T. 48-61; Dean of Science 64-66, Provost 66-; Special Asst. to Pres. for Science and Technology, Dir. Office of Science and Technology, White House 61-64; mem. President's Science Advisory Cttee., Inst. of Radio Engineers, Acoustical Soc. of America, Fed. of American Scientists, American Soc. for the Advancement of Science, Nat. Acad. of Science, Nat. Acad. of Eng., of American Acad. of Arts and Science.
c/o Massachusetts Institute of Technology, Cambridge 39, Mass.; Home: 61 Shattuck Road, Watertown, Mass., U.S.A.
Telephone: 617-924-1926 (Home).

Wigg, Baron (Life Peer) cr. 67, of the Borough of Dudley; **George Edward Cecil Wigg,** P.C.; British politician; b. 28 Nov. 1900; ed. Fairfields Council Schools and Queen Mary's School, Basingstoke, Hants. Army Service 19-37, 40-46; M.P. 45-67; fmr. Parl. Private Sec. to Rt. Hon. E. Shinwell; mem. Racecourse Betting Control Board 58-61, Totalisator Board 61-64; Paymaster-General 64-67; Chair. Horse Race Betting Levy Board 67-; Labour.
117 Newcastle Road, Trent Vale, Stoke-on-Trent, Staffs., England.

Wiggins, Archibald Lee Manning, B.A.; American railroad executive, banker, and newspaper publisher; b. 9 April 1891; ed. Univ. of N. Carolina.
Chairman of Board, Bank of Hartsville; Chair. Pauline and Lee Wiggins Foundation Inc.; Chair. Professional Cttee. Crippled Children Soc. of S.C.; Pres. Trust Co. of S.C.; Hartsville Publishing Co.; Trustee Coker Coll., S.C. Foundation of Independent Colls., Inc., S.C. Student Aid Council, Inc.; fmr. Chair. of Board, Atlantic Coast Line Co. 48-63, Atlantic Coastline Railroad Co. 48-61, Louisville and Nashville Railroad Co. 48-61, Clinchfield Railroad Co. 48-61, Alico Land Development Corpn. 60-63; Dir. American Telegraph and Telephone Co. 50-63; Pres. S.C. Bankers' Asscn. 31-32; Pres. American Bankers' Asscn. 43-44; mem. Advisory Council, Fed. Reserve Board 46; Under-Sec. U.S. Treasury 47-48; Dir. American Cancer Society 46-49; Treas. American Nat. Red Cross 47-48; Chair. S.C. State Reorganisation Comm. 48-50; Chair. S.C. Governor's Tax Advisory Cttee. 53-54, Fiscal Survey Comm. of S.C. 55-58, Gov. of S.C. Advisory Cttee. on Higher Education 61-62; Lecturer, Graduate School of Banking, Rutgers Univ. 44-57; Hon. LL.D. (Univs. of North and South Carolina, Duke Univ.); Democrat.
1002 Home Avenue, Hartsville, S.C., U.S.A.

Wiggins, James Russell; American newspaperman; b. 4 Dec. 1903; ed. Luverne (Minn.) High School, and USAF Air Intelligence School.
With *Rock County Star* 22-30; Editorial Writer *St. Paul Dispatch* and *St. Paul Pioneer Press* 30-33, Washington Correspondent 33-38, Man. Editor 38-42, 45-46; U.S. Army Air Force 42-45; Asst. Publisher *New York Times* 46-47; Man. Editor *The Washington Post* 47-55, Vice-Pres. 53-, Exec. Editor 55-60, Editor and Exec. Vice-Pres. 60-; Eliza Lovejoy Award 54, John Zenger Award 57, Golden Key Award 60.
1515 L Street, N.W., Washington 5, D.C., U.S.A.

Wigner, Eugene Paul, DR.ING.; American physicist; b. 17 Nov. 1902; ed. Technische Hochschule, Berlin.
Lecturer, Technische Hochschule, Berlin 28; Prof. of Math. Physics, Princeton Univ., on half-time basis 30-36; Prof. of Physics, Univ. of Wisconsin 37-38; Thomas D. Jones Prof. of Math. Physics, Princeton Univ. 38-; mem. of Visiting Cttee., Nat. Bureau of Standards 47-51, Board of Dirs., Oak Ridge Inst. of Nuclear Studies 47-50; mem. Gen. Advisory Cttee. to U.S. Atomic Energy Comm. 52-57, 59-64; on leave of absence at the Metallurgical Laboratory, Univ. of Chicago (Plutonium Project) 42-45; on leave of absence as Dir. of Research and Development of the Clinton Laboratories, Oak Ridge, Tenn. 46-47, as Lorentz Lecturer, Inst.Lorentz, Leyden, Neths. 57; mem. American Physical Soc., American Mathematical Soc., American Philosophical Society, National Acad. Sciences, American Acad. of Arts and Sciences, Franklin Society (Franklin Medal 50), Royal Netherlands Acad., American Nuclear Soc. (Dir. 60-61); corresp. mem. Akad. der Wissenschaften, Göttingen; Vice-Pres. American Physical Society 55, Pres. 56; Dir. Int. School of Physics, Enrico Fermi Course 29, Varenna 63; Dir. (on leave of absence) Civil Defense Project, Oak Ridge Nat. Laboratory 64-65; Medal for Merit 46; Fermi Award 58; Hon. D.Sc. (Univ. of Wis.) 49, (Washington Univ.) 50, (Case Inst.) 55, (Univ. of Chicago) 57, (Univ. of Alberta) 59, (Colby Coll.) 59, (Univ. of Pa.) 61; Hon. D.Litt. (Yeshiva Univ.) 63, (Thiel Coll.) 64, (Notre Dame Univ.) 65, (Technical Univ., Berlin) 66, (Swarthmore Coll) 66, (Univ. de Louvain) 67; Univ. of Liége 67, Univ. of Ill. 68; Atoms for Peace Award 60, Max Planck Medal of German Physical Soc. 61, Nobel Prize for Physics 63, George Washington Award of the American Hungarian Studies Foundation, Semmelweiss Medal of American Hungarian Medical Asscn. 65.
Publs. *Gruppentheorie und ihre Anwendungen auf die Quantenmechanik der Atomspektren* 31 (English edn. 59), *Nuclear Structure* (with L. Eisenbud) 58, *Physical Theory of Neutron Chain Reactors* (with A. M. Weinburg) 58.
Princeton Univ., Palmer Physical Laboratory, Princeton, N.J. 08540; and 8 Ober Road, Princeton, N.J., U.S.A.
Telephone: 609-452-4335.

Wigny, Pierre L. J. J.; Belgian politician; b. 18 April 1905; ed. Liège and Harvard Univs.
Sec.-Gen. Centre d'Etudes pour la Reforme de l'Etat 36-40; Minister of the Colonies 47-50; mem. (P.S.C.) Chamber of Reps.; Sec.-Gen. Int. Inst. of Differing Civilizations (Incidi) 50-; fmr. Pres. Political Economic Soc. of Belgium; mem. ECSC Common Assembly 56-58, European Parl. 58, Council of Ministers 58-; Belgian Minister of Foreign Affairs 58-61, of Justice 65-66, of Justice and French Culture 66-; Prof. of Law, Louvain Univ. and Faculty of Namur.
94 Avenue Louise, Brussels, Belgium.
Telephone: 11-16-67.

Wijemanne, A. F.; Ceylonese lawyer and politician; b. 4 Feb. 1907; ed. London Univ., and Gray's Inn, London.
Formerly active in Ceylon National Congress; mem. Senate 62-; Minister of Justice 65-; United National Party.
Ministry of Justice, Colombo; and 74 Dharmapala Mawata, Colombo 7, Ceylon.

Wijeyekoon, Hemachandra Wickrama Gerard, O.B.E., B.A.; Ceylonese army officer and diplomatist; b. 11; ed. St. Joseph's College, Colombo, Hertford College, Oxford, and Gray's Inn, London.
Officer, Ceylon Defence Force 35-39, Ceylon Army 49-63; Chief of Staff Army H.Q. 54; Commandant Ceylon Volunteer Forces 56; Commander, Ceylon Army 60-63; Sec. to Leader of House and Chief Govt. Whip 47-49; High Commissioner in Pakistan, concurrently accredited as Ambassador to Iraq and Iran 64-.
Vijaya House, 60 Clifton, Karachi, Pakistan.

Wijk, Erik Bertilsson; Swedish company director; b. 29 June 1906.
Dir. AB Svenska Telegrambyran Gothenburg 30; Man. Dir. AB Nordisk Resebureau 33; Vice-Pres. Swedish

American Line 44, Pres. 50-; mem. Bd. Rederi AB Svenska Lloyd, Eriksbergs Mekaniska Verkstads AB, Försäkrings AB Atlantica, Park Avenue Hotel AB, AB Aerotransport, Scandinavian Airlines System, Sveriges Ångfartygs Assurans Förening.
Swedish American Line, Packhusplatsen, Gothenburg C, Sweden, and Berghem, Särö, Sweden.

Wijsenbeek, Louis Jacob Florus D.D.L., D.H.A.; Netherlands museum curator; b. 21 April 1912; ed. Gymnasium Erasmianium, Rotterdam and Leiden Univ.
On staff of Ministry of Education, Arts and Sciences 39-40; Asst. Keeper Municipal Museum, The Hague 40-42; Recuperation Officer in Austria 45-47; Dir. of Delft Museums 47-51; Dir. Municipal Museum, Bredius Museum and Costume Museum, The Hague 51-; Pres. I.C.O.M. Cttee. for Museum Architecture; Vice-Pres. Royal Acad. of Arts, The Hague, Netherlands, Asscn. of Museum Dirs., Netherlands Cttee. of I.C.O.M.; Commdr. Order of Mexican Eagle, Hon. M.V.O., Officer, Royal Gurka Order of Nepal; Officer of Swedish Order of Vasa, Royal Netherlands Order of Orange Nassau, Order of Crown of Belgium, Chevalier de la Légion d'Honneur, Knight of the Order of Pius IX, Gold Medal of Merit, 1st Class (Italy).
Publs. *Het Tijdperk van de Camera Obscura* 40, *Mij spreekt de Blomme een tale* 52, *Pablo Picasso* 54, *Vraagstukken bij het Bouwen van Musea* 58, *Piet Mondriaan* 62, *Delfts Zilver* 62.
74a Anna Paulownastraat, The Hague, Netherlands.
Telephone: 608626.

Wilbur, Richard (Purdy), M.A.; American poet and university professor; b. 1 March 1921; ed. Amherst Coll., and Harvard Univ.
Asst. Prof. of English, Harvard Univ. 50-54; Assoc. Prof. Wellesley Coll. 54-57; Prof. Wesleyan Univ. 57-; mem. Nat. Inst. of Arts and Letters, American Acad. of Arts and Sciences, Soc. of Fellows of Harvard Univ. 47-50; Guggenheim Fellow 52-53; Harriet Monroe Prize 48; Oscar Blumenthal Prize 50; Prix de Rome from American Acad. of Arts and Letters 54-55; Edna St. Vincent Millay Memorial Award 56; Nat. Book Award; Pulitzer Prize 57, co-recipient Bollingen Translation Prize 63; Ford Fellow 61, Guggenheim Fellow 63.
Publs. *The Beautiful Changes and other poems* 47, *Ceremony and other poems* 50, *A Bestiary* (anthology, with Alexander Calder) 55, *The Misanthrope* (trans. from Molière) 55, *Things of this World* (poems) 56, *Poems 1943-1956* 57, *Candide* (comic opera, with Lillian Hellman and others) 57, *Poe* (edition of his poems with introduction and notes) 59, *Advice to a Prophet* (poems) 61, *Tartuffe* (trans. from Molière) 63, *The Poems of Richard Wilbur* 63, *Loudmouse* (for children) 63, *Poems of Shakespeare* (with Alfred Harbage) 66.
Portland, Connecticut, U.S.A.

Wild, John D(aniel), PH.D.; American university professor; b. 10 April 1902; ed. Univ. of Chicago, and Harvard Univ.
Instructor, Univ. of Michigan 26-27; Instructor in Philosophy, Harvard Univ. 27-34, Asst. Prof. 34-40, Assoc. Prof. 40-46, Prof. 46, on staff of Divinity School 54-61; Chair. Dept. of Philosophy, Northwestern Univ. 61-63; Prof. of Philosophy, Yale Univ. 63-; mem. Asscn. of Realistic Philosophy (Pres. 47-50), American Philosophical Asscn. (Pres. E. Div. 60), Metaphysical Soc. of America (Pres. 53).
Publs. *George Berkeley* 36, *Plato's Theory of Man* 46, *Introduction to Realistic Philosophy* 48, *Plato's Modern Enemies and the Theory of Natural Law* 53, *Challenge of Existentialism* 55.
46 Cliff Street, New Haven 11, Conn., U.S.A.

Wilder, Billy; American film writer, producer and director; b. 22 June 1906.
Former reporter, Berlin; writer *People on Sunday, Emil and the Detectives*, Germany; writer and dir. *Mauvaise Graine*, Paris; went to U.S. 34; writer in collaboration *Bluebeard's Eighth Wife, Midnight, Ninotchka, What A Life, Arise, My Love, Hold Back The Dawn, Ball of Fire*; Dir. and collaborator *The Major and the Minor, Five Graves to Cairo, Double Indemnity, The Lost Weekend, The Emperor Waltz, A Foreign Affair, Sunset Boulevard*; Producer, dir. and writer (in collaboration): *The Big Carnival, Stalag 17, Sabrina, Love in the Afternoon, Some Like It Hot, The Apartment, One, Two, Three, Irma La Douce, Kiss Me, Stupid*; co-producer, dir. and writer (in collaboration) *The Seven Year Itch*; dir., collaborator *The Spirit of St. Louis, Witness for the Prosecution*; six Academy Awards (for *Lost Weekend, Sunset Boulevard* and *The Apartment*).
Hollywood, California, U.S.A.

Wilder, Thornton Niven, M.A., LITT.D.; American novelist; b. 17 April 1897; ed. China, Yale and Princeton Univs., and American Acad. in Rome.
Lecturer in English, Univ. of Chicago 30-36; Capt. Air Force Intelligence 42, Major 43, Lt.-Col. 44; released from A.A.F. Sept. 45; awarded Legion of Merit 45, M.B.E. 45; Chevalier Légion d'Honneur 50, Orden Pour le Mérite (Bonn) 57, Presidential Medal 63, Nat. Medal of Literature 65; Litt.D. (Yale and Harvard), LL.D. (Frankfurt-am-Main) 57.
Publs. *The Cabala* 26, *The Bridge of San Luis Rey* 27, (awarded Pulitzer Prize 28), *The Angel that Troubled the Waters* (short plays) 28, *The Woman of Andros* 30, *The Long Christmas Dinner* (and other one-act plays) 31, *Heaven's My Destination* 35, *Our Town* (play, awarded Pulitzer Prize) 38, *The Merchant of Yonkers* 38, *The Skin of Our Teeth* (play, awarded Pulitzer Prize) 42, *The Ides of March* 48, *The Matchmaker* (play) 54, *A Life in the Sun* (play) 55, *Plays for Bleecker Street* 62; Opera: *The Long Christmas Dinner* 61, *The Alcestiad* 62; *The Eighth Day* (novel) 67.
50 Deepwood Drive, Hamden, Conn., 06517 U.S.A.

Wilgress, Leolyn Dana, C.C., B.A.; Canadian diplomatist; b. 20 Oct. 1892; ed. Modern School of Yokohama (Japan), Univ. School, Victoria and McGill Univ.
Junior Trade Commr. 14; Trade Commr. Omsk (Siberia) 16; transferred to Vladivostok 18; investigated trade openings in S. China 18; mem. Canadian Economic Mission to Siberia 18-20, S.E. Europe 20-21; seconded to special work in London 21-22; paid two visits of investigation to Soviet Russia 21 and 23; apptd. Canadian Trade Commr. in Hamburg 22; Dir. Commercial Intelligence Service Dept. of Trade and Commerce 32; Deputy Minister of Trade and Commerce 40; Minister (later Ambassador) to U.S.S.R. 42-47; Minister to Switzerland (with rank of Ambassador) April 47-49; High Commr. in London 49-52; Under-Sec. of State for External Affairs 52-53; Permanent Rep. of Canada to NATO and Rep. to OEEC 53-58; Chair. Canadian Section, Joint U.S.-Canadian Defence Board 59-66.
371 Mariposa Avenue, Rockcliffe Park, Ottawa, Ontario, Canada.
Telephone: 749-3440.

Wilgus, A. Curtis, M.A., PH.D.; American historian, bibliographer and university professor; b. 2 April 1897; ed. Univs. of Wisconsin and Calif.
Assistant Instr. in History, Univ. of Wisconsin 22-24; Assoc. Prof. of History, Univ. of South Carolina 24-30, George Washington Univ. 30-40, Prof. 40-51; Dir. School of Inter-American Studies, and Prof. of History, Univ. of Florida 51-63, Dir. Caribbean Conferences 50-; Vice-Chancellor Int. Inst. of Arts, San Juan, Puerto Rico and Miami 67-; organizer, charter mem. and Pres. Inter-Amer. Bibliographical and Library Asscn.;

charter mem. Soc. for Advancement of Educ.; Dir. Pan-Am. Foundation; Dir. U.S. Branch Eloy Alfaro Int. Foundation; Foreign corresp. *Panama American;* mem. Board Americas Foundation; awards include U.S., Venezuelan, French and Swedish honours; Editor *World Affairs* 40-51, *Inter-American Bibliographical Review* 40-43, *Doors to Latin America* 50-, *Latin American Monographs* 57-63, *Grandes Figures de l'Amérique* series 57-60, *Gateway to Latin America* series, *Library of Latin American History and Culture* series 65; Chair. Board of Editors *Journal of Inter-American Studies* 63.
Publs. *An Outline of Hispanic American History* 27, *A History of Hispanic America* 31, *Histories and Historians of Hispanic America* 36, 42, 65, *Outline-History of Latin America* (with Dr. Raul d'Eça) 39, *Development of Hispanic America* 41, *Latin America in Maps* 43, *Readings in Latin-American Civilization* 46, Editor *Modern Hispanic America* 33, *The Caribbean Area* 34, *Argentina, Brazil and Chile since Independence* 35, *Colonial Hispanic America* 36, *South American Dictators* 37, *Hispanic American Essays* 42, *The Caribbean at Mid-Century* 51, *The Caribbean: Peoples, Problems and Prospects* 52, *The Caribbean: Contemporary Trends* 53, *The Caribbean: Its Economy* 54, *The Caribbean: Its Culture* 55, *The Caribbean: Current Political Problems* 56, *The Caribbean: Contemporary International Relations* 57, *The Caribbean: British, Dutch, French, United States* 58, *The Caribbean: Natural Resources* 59, *The Caribbean: Education* 60, *The Caribbean: The Central American Area* 61, *The Caribbean: Contemporary Colombia* 62, *The Caribbean: Venezuelan Development* 63, *Latin American History* (with Raul d'Eça) 63, 65, 66, 67, *The Caribbean: Mexico Today* 64, *The Caribbean: Its Health Problems* 65, *The Caribbean: Current U.S. Relations* 66, *The Caribbean: Hemispheric Role of The Caribbean* 67. Home: 1140 N.E. 191st Street, North Miami Beach Fla.; Office: 8101 Biscayne Boulevard, Miami, Fla., U.S.A.

Wilhelmi, Hans, DR.IUR.; German lawyer and politician; b. 27 Aug. 1899; ed. Univs. of Göttingen and Bonn. Officer in First World War; Lawyer, Frankfurt/Main 25; political activity against Nazis 33-39; Officer in Second World War; Co-founder, Hesse Christian Democratic Union 45; mem. Bundestag 57-; mem. Law and Economic Cttee., helped draft laws for denationalisation of Volkswagen works; Federal Minister for Federal Property 60-61; Chair. Evangelical Church of Hesse and Nassau 45-; Christian Democratic Union.
Publ. *Kleine Aktienrechtsreform* 60.
Fürstenberger Str. 23, 6 Frankfurt-am-Main, German Federal Republic.

Wilkins, Fraser, PH.B.; American diplomatist; b. 30 Aug. 1908; ed. Yale Univ.
Joined Foreign Service 40, served in Iraq, Morocco, Palestine and India; Dir. Near East Affairs, Dept. of State 55-57; Minister-Counsellor, Iran 57-60; Ambassador to Cyprus 60-64; Inspector-General of the Foreign Service 64-.
4332 Garfield Street, N.W., Washington, D.C. 20007, U.S.A.

Wilkins, Maurice Hugh Frederick, C.B.E., M.A., PH.D., F.R.S.; British molecular biologist; b. 15 Dec. 1916; ed. St. John's Coll., Cambridge.
Research on luminescence of solids, Physics Dept. Birmingham Univ.; Ministry of Home Security and Aircraft Production 38; Manhattan Project (Ministry of Supply), Univ. of California 44; Lecturer in Physics, St. Andrews Univ. 45; Medical Research Council, Biophysics Research Unit, Physics Dept., King's Coll., London 46-, Dep. Dir. Biophysics Research Unit 55-, Hon. Prof. of Molecular Biology 63-; Albert Lasker Award, American Public Health Asscn. 60, Nobel Prize for Medicine 62.

Publs. Papers on luminescence and topics in biophysics e.g. molecular structure of nucleic acids.
30 St. John's Park, London S.E.3, England.
Telephone: 858-1817.

Wilkins, Roy; American administrator; b. 30 Aug. 1901; ed. Univ. of Minnesota.
Managing Editor *The Call*, Kansas City, Mo. 23-31; joined staff of Nat. Asscn. for the Advancement of Colored People (N.A.A.C.P.) as Asst. Exec. Sec. 31, Administrator 50-55, Exec. Sec. 55-64, Exec. Dir. 64-.
147-15 Village Road, Jamaica 35, N.Y., U.S.A.

Wilkinson, Denys Haigh, M.A., PH.D., SC.D., F.R.S.; British physicist and university professor; b. 5 Sept. 1922; ed. Jesus Coll., Cambridge.
Worked on British Atomic Energy Project 43-46, on Canadian Atomic Energy Project 45-46; Demonstrator 47-51, Lecturer 51-56 and Reader 56-57 Cavendish Laboratory of Univ. of Cambridge; Fellow Jesus Coll., Cambridge 44-59, Hon. Fellow 61-; Student of Christ Church, Oxford 57-; Prof. of Nuclear Physics Clarendon Laboratory of Univ. of Oxford 57-59, Prof. of Experimental Physics 59-, Head of Dept. of Nuclear Physics 62-; Rutherford Memorial Lecturer of British Physical Soc. 62; mem. Governing Board Nat. Inst. for Research in Nuclear Science 58-64; mem. Science Research Council 67-; Hon. D.Sc. Univ. of Saskatchewan; Holweck Medallist of French and British Physical Socs. 57, Hughes Medal of the Royal Soc. 65.
Publs. *Ionization Chambers and Counters* 50, and many articles in learned journals.
Nuclear Physics Laboratory, Oxford, England.
Telephone: Oxford 59911.

Wilkinson, Sir Harold, Kt., C.M.G.; British oil executive; b. 24 Feb. 1903.
Formerly: Deputy Chair. The Shell Transport and Trading Co. Ltd.; Man. Dir. The Shell Petroleum Co. Ltd., Shell Exploration Co. Ltd., Shell Int. Petroleum Co. Ltd.; Principal Dir. of Bataafse Petroleum Mij. N.V.; Chair. Canadian Shell Ltd., Shell Tankers Ltd.; Vice-Chair. Shell Caribbean Petroleum Co. (New York); Dir. Bataafse Internationale Chemie Mij. N.V., Shell Int. Chemical Co. Ltd., Shell Oil Co. (New York), retired July 64; U.S. Medal of Freedom with Bronze Palm 51, Knight Commdr. Order of Merit, Ecuador.
La Sologne en Ballëgue, Epalinges, nr. Lausanne, Switzerland.

Wilkinson, (Robert Francis) Martin; British stockbroker; b. 4 June 1911; ed. Repton School.
Partner, de Zoete and Gorton 36-; mem. London Stock Exchange 33-, mem. Council 59-, Dep. Chair. 63-65, Chairman 65-; Royal Air Force 40-45.
Kixes, Sharpthorne, Sussex; 25 Finsbury Circus, London E.C.2, England.
Telephone: 01-588-1351.

Willcocks, David Valentine, M.C., M.A., MUS.B., F.R.C.O., A.R.C.M.; British conductor; b. 30 Dec. 1919; ed. Clifton College and King's College, Cambridge.
Fellow King's College, Cambridge 47-; Organist Salisbury Cathedral 47-50, Worcester Cathedral 50-57; Conductor Worcester Three Choirs Festival and City of Birmingham Choir 50-57; Organist King's College, Cambridge 57-; Lecturer in Music, Cambridge Univ. and Cambridge Univ. Organist 57-; Conductor Cambridge Univ. Music Society 58-; Musical Director Bach Choir London 60-; Pres. Royal Coll. of Organists 66-68; Hon. R.A.M., Hon. F.R.C.C.O.
King's College, Cambridge; 13 Grange Road, Cambridge, England.
Telephone: OCA3-50411; OCA3-59559 (Home).

Willems, Jean; Belgian educationalist; b. 15 April 1895; ed. Ghent Royal State Coll., and Ghent State Univ.
Exec. Sec. Brussels Univ. 20-28; Dir. Fondation Uni-

versitaire and Fonds National de la Recherche Scientifique 28-55, Vice-Pres. 55-60, First Vice-Pres. 60-65, Pres. 65-; Dir. Francqui Foundation 32-65, Pres. 65-; Pres. Foundation for Belgian Youth Abroad 45-; Hon. Vice-Pres. Belgian-American Educational Foundation, N.Y. 45-; mem. Board of U.S. Educational Foundation in Belgium 48-; Pres. Inst. Interuniversitaire des Sciences Nucléaires 47-; Pres. Acad. Belgica, Rome 55-; mem. Council, Europe Org. for Nuclear Research 54-60, Chair. 61-63, mem. 64-, Chair. Finance Cttee. 55-57, Vice-Pres. 58-60, Pres. 60-63, Vice-Pres. 64-; Hon. C.B.E.; Commdr. Order of Leopold, Légion d'Honneur, Grand Officer Order of the Crown.
11 rue d'Egmont, Brussels 5, Belgium.
Telephone: 11-81-00.

Willey, Rt. Hon. Frederick Thomas, P.C., M.P.; British politician; b. 10; ed. Johnston School, Durham, and St. John's College, Cambridge.
Called to Bar, Middle Temple 36; M.P. 45-; Parl. Private Sec. to Rt. Hon. J. Chuter Ede 46-50; Parl. Sec. to Ministry of Food 50-51; fmr. Dir. North-Eastern Trading Estates Ltd.; fmr. River Wear Commissioner; fmr. mem. Consultative Assembly, Council of Europe and Assembly, Western European Union; Minister of Land and Natural Resources 64-67; Minister of State, Ministry of Housing and Local Govt. 67; Labour.
Publs. *Plan for Shipbuilding, Education: Today and Tomorrow.*
2 Harcourt Buildings, Temple, London, E.C.4; 11 North Square, London, N.W.11, England.

Willey, Malcolm Macdonald, A.M., PH.D.; American educational administrator; b. 13 Nov. 1897; ed. Clark Univ., and Columbia Univ.
Instr. Sociology, Dartmouth 23-24, Asst. Prof. 24-27; Assoc. Prof. Univ. of Minnesota 27-29, Prof. 29-34, Univ. Dean and Asst. to Pres. 34-43, Vice-Pres. Academic Admin. 43-63; Education Consultant, Ford Foundation Univ. of Calcutta Project 63-68; Visiting Prof. of Sociology, Maryville Coll., Tennessee 68-; fmr. Dir. American Inst. of Indian Studies; fmr. Chair. Social Science Cttee. Nat. Science Foundation; Fellow American Asscn. for Advancement of Science, American Sociological Soc.; Hon. L.H.D. (Clark), Hon. LL.D. (Maine).
Publs. *The Country Newspaper* 26, *An Introduction to Sociology* (with Jerome Davis and others) 27, *Readings in Sociology* (with same) 27, *Readings in Sociology* (with Wilson D. Wallis) 30, *Communication Agencies and Social Life* (with S. A. Rice) 33, *Depression, Recovery, and Higher Education* 37, *The Newspaper in the Contemporary Scene* (ed. with R. D. Casey) 42, *Higher Education and the War* (ed. with T. R. McConnell) 44, *Contemporary Sociology* (with S. Eldridge and others) 50, *Self-Study Manual for Indian Colleges and Universities* (with J. Arthur Branch) 68.
Maryville College, Maryville, Tennessee, U.S.A.

Williams, Sir Alan Meredith, K.C.M.G.; British diplomatist; b. 22 Aug. 1909; ed. Berkhamsted School, and Pembroke Coll., Cambridge.
Consular Service, San Francisco, Cólon (Panama), Paris, Hamburg, Rotterdam, Reykjavík, Dakar 32-43; Vice-Consul, Leopoldville 43, Acting Consul-Gen. 43, 44, Chief British Econ. Rep. 44; Consul, Vienna 45-47, Baghdad 47-49; Foreign Office 49-50; Counsellor and Deputy Consul-Gen., New York 50-53; Consul-Gen., Tunis 53-56; Foreign Office 56-60; Consul-Gen., New York 60-64; Amb. to Panama 64-66, to Spain 66-.
British Embassy, Fernando El Santo 16, Madrid, Spain.
Telephone: 219-02-00.

Williams, Albert L.; American business machine executive; b. 17 March 1911; ed. Beckley Coll.
Student Sales Rep., Int. Business Machines Corpn.

(IBM) 36, Sales Rep. 37, Controller 42-47, Treas. 47, Vice-Pres. and Treas. 48-51, mem. Board of Dirs. 51-54, Exec. Vice-Pres. 54-61, Pres. 61-66, Chair. Exec. Cttee. Board of Dirs. 66-; Dir. Mobil Oil Corpn., First Nat. City Bank (N.Y.), Gen. Foods Corpn.; Trustee, Cttee. for Econ. Devt.; mem. American Inst. C.P.A.'s.
International Business Machines Corporation, Old Orchard Road, Armonk, N.Y. 10504, U.S.A.

Williams, Arthur Leonard; British politician; b. 22 Jan. 1904; ed. Holy Trinity Church of England Elementary School, Birkenhead, and Labour Coll., London.
Member, Liverpool and N. Wales District Council, Nat. Union of Railwaymen 20-21, Sec. Birkenhead and District Jt. Cttee. 23-24; Tutor, Liverpool Labour Coll. 24-26; Tutor-Organiser, Nat. Council of Labour Colls. 26-36; Labour Parl. Candidate, Southport 29, Winchester 35; Sec. Leeds Labour Party 36-42; Regional Organiser, E. and W. Ridings of Yorkshire 42-46, Asst. Nat. Agent 46-51, Nat. Agent 51-59, Nat. Agent and Dep. Gen. Sec. 59-62, Gen. Sec. 62-68; Governor-Gen. designate Mauritius 68; Editor *Leeds Weekly Citizen* 37-44, *Labour Organiser* 52-63.
Labour Party, Transport House, Smith Square, London, S.W.1, England.

Williams, Emlyn, C.B.E., M.A.; British actor and dramatist; b. 26 Nov. 1905; ed. County School, Holywell, and Christ Church, Oxford.
First London stage appearance in *And So To Bed*, Savoy Theatre 27; since then has appeared in most of his own plays and also in *The Winslow Boy* 47, *Montserrat* 50, *The Wild Duck* 55, *Shadow of Heroes* 58, *A Man for All Seasons* (New York) 62-63, *The Deputy* (New York) 64, *A Month in the Country* 65-66, and at the Old Vic and the Memorial Theatre, Stratford-on-Avon; solo theatrical performances as Charles Dickens 51, 52, 61 and as Dylan Thomas (*A Boy Growing Up*) 55, 57 and 58; has played in the films *The Last Days of Dolwyn, Another Man's Poison, Ivanhoe, The Deep Blue Sea, I Accuse, Beyond This Place, The Wreck of the Mary Deare, The L-Shaped Room, The Eye of the Devil*; Hon. LL.D. (Bangor).
Plays: *A Murder Has Been Arranged* 31, *Glamour, Full Moon, Vessels Departing, Spring 1600, Night Must Fall* 35, *He Was Born Gay* 37, *The Corn is Green* 38, *The Light of Heart* 40, *The Morning Star* 41, *The Druids' Rest* 44, *The Wind of Heaven* 45, *Trespass* 47, *Accolade* 50, *Someone Waiting* 53, *Beth* 58; adapted *The Late Christopher Bean, A Month in the Country;* autobiography *George* 61; study of murder *Beyond Belief* 67; wrote, directed and played in the film *The Last Days of Dolwyn* 48.
123 Dovehouse Street, London, S.W.3, England.

Williams, Rt. Hon. Eric Eustace, P.C., B.A., D.PHIL.; Trinidadian politician; b. 25 Sept. 1911; ed. Tranquillity Intermediate School, Queen's Royal Coll., Port of Spain, and Oxford Univ.
Professor Social and Political Science Howard Univ., Washington 39; Julius Rosenwald Fellowships 40 and 42; Consultant British Section Anglo-American Caribbean Comm. 43-44; Sec. Agricultural Cttee. Caribbean Comm. 44-46; Consultant Caribbean Comm. 46-48; Deputy Chair. Caribbean Research Council, Caribbean Comm. 48-55; Chief Minister and Minister of Finance, Planning and Development, Trinidad 56-61, Premier 59; Minister of External Affairs 61-64; Prime Minister independent state of Trinidad and Tobago Sept. 62-, also Minister of Finance, Planning and Devt. April 67-; Pro-Chancellor Univ. of W. Indies; Hon. LL.D. (Univ. of New Brunswick) 65; Hon. D.C.L. (Oxford).
Publs. *The Negro in the Caribbean* 42, *Capitalism and Slavery* 44, *Education in the West Indies* 50; Editor

Caribbean Historical Review; Documents on British West Indian History, 1807-1833 52, *The British West Indies at Westminster, Pt. I 1789-1823* 53, *A History of the People of Trinidad and Tobago* 62, *Documents of West Indian History* 63, *Capitalism and Slavery* 64, *British Historians and the West Indies* 65.

Office of the Prime Minister, Port-of-Spain, Trinidad.

Williams, G. Mennen, A.B., J.D.; American lawyer and politician; b. 23 Feb. 1911; ed. Princeton Univ., and Univ. of Michigan Law School.

Attorney, Social Security Board, Washington, D.C. 36-37; Asst. Attorney Gen., State of Michigan 38-39; Exec. Asst. to U.S. Attorney Gen. 39-40, Special Asst., Criminal Division 40-41; served U.S. Navy 42-46; Deputy Dir., Office of Price Admin., Michigan 46-47; Democratic mem. Michigan Liquor Control Comm. 47-48; former mem. law firm of Griffiths, Williams & Griffiths; Gov. of Michigan 49-60; Sec. of State for African Affairs 61-66; Amb. to Philippines 68-; Legion of Merit; Grand Officer Order of Orange-Nassau (Netherlands); Grand Commdr. Royal Order of Phoenix (Greece); Humane Band of African Redemption (Liberia), Polonia Restituta (Polish Govt. in Exile); Hon. LL.D. (Wilberforce, Michigan, Michigan State, Western Michigan, Liberia, Lincoln Univs., Aquinas Coll., St. Augustine's Coll., Ferris Inst.); Dr. of Humanities (Lawrence Inst. of Technology); Democrat.

American Embassy, Manila, Philippines; and 25 Tonnancour Place, Grosse Pointe Farms, Michigan 48236, U.S.A.

Williams, Harrison Arlington, Jr., B.A., LL.D.; American lawyer and politician; b. 10 Dec. 1919; ed. Oberlin Coll., Ohio, Columbia Univ. Law School, and Georgetown Univ. Foreign Service School.

Seaman on a minesweeper and Navy pilot during Second World War; mem. U.S. House of Reps. 53-56; U.S. Senator from New Jersey 59-; Democrat.

Home: 231 Elizabeth Avenue, Westfield, N.J.; Office: 125 Broad Street, Elizabeth, N.J.; also Senate Office Building, Washington 25, D.C., U.S.A.

Williams, John; British guitarist; b. 24 April 1941; ed. Friern Barnet Grammar School, and Royal Coll. of Music, London.

Studied guitar with Segovia at Accad. Chigiana, Siena; has toured widely in Europe, America, Japan and Soviet Union; numerous transcriptions and gramophone recordings as solo guitarist and with Philadelphia Orchestra and English Chamber Orchestra.

c/o Ibbs and Tillett, 124 Wigmore Street, London, W.1, England.

Williams, John Bell, LL.B.; American lawyer and politician; b. 4 Dec. 1918; ed. Hinds Junior Coll., Raymond, Mississippi, Univ. of Mississippi and Jackson School of Law.

Admitted Miss. State Bar 40; gen. law practice, Raymond, Miss. 40-46; Prosecuting Attorney, Hinds County, Miss. 44-46; mem. U.S. House of Representatives 46-66; Governor of Miss. 67-; Democrat.

State Capitol, Jackson, Mississippi, U.S.A.

Williams, John Henry, M.A., PH.D., SC.D. (HON.); American economist; b. 21 June 1887; ed. Brown and Harvard Univs.

Instr. in English, Brown Univ. 12-15; Frederick Sheldon Travelling Fellow, Harvard to Argentina 17-18; Asst. Prof. of Econs., Princeton 19-20; Assoc. Prof. of Banking, Northwestern Univ. 20-21; Asst. Prof. of Econs., Harvard Univ. 21-25; Assoc. Prof. 25-29; Prof. 29-33; Econ. Adviser, Federal Reserve Bank of New York 33-52, Vice-Pres. 36-47, Econ. Consultant 56-64; Dean, Graduate School of Public Admin., Harvard 37-47; Nathaniel Ropes Prof. of Political Economy, Harvard 33-57, Emeritus 57-; William L. Clayton Prof.

Int. Econ. Affairs, The Fletcher School of Law and Diplomacy, Tufts Univ. 57-63, Emeritus 63-.

Publs. *Argentine International Trade Under Inconvertible Paper Money* (Wells Prize) 20, *Annual Studies of Balance of Payments of U.S.* 19-23, *Post-War Monetary Plans and Other Essays* 44, (co-author) *Financing American Prosperity* 45, *Economic Stability in the Modern World* 52, *Economic Stability in a Changing World* 53.

148 Coolidge Hill, Cambridge, Mass. 02138, U.S.A.

Telephone: 547-4698.

Williams, John James; American businessman; b. 17 May 1904; ed. Frankford High School, Frankford, Del.

Entered grain business 22; Senator from Delaware 46-; mem. Finance Cttee. 50-, Foreign Relations Cttee. 60-; Republican.

Millsboro, Delaware; and Senate Office Building, Washington, D.C., U.S.A.

Williams, Laurence Frederic Rushbrook, C.B.E., M.A., B.LITT., F.R.HIST.S., F.R.S.A., J.P.; British historian; b. 10 July 1890; ed. Univ. Coll., Oxford.

Lecturer Trinity Coll. Oxford 13; Fellow All Souls Coll. Oxford 14-21; Lecturer in Medieval History Queen's Univ. Canada 13-14; Prof. of Modern Indian History Allahabad Univ. 14-19; attached to Gen. Staff, Army Headquarters, India 18; Literary Asst. to Pres. Indian Central Publicity Board and special duty Indian Constitutional Reforms 18; Dir. Central Bureau of Information 20-36; Sec. to Indian Del. Imperial Conf. 23; Political Sec. to Maharaja of Patiala 25, to Chancellor of Princes 26-30; Foreign Min. Patiala 25-31; mem. Legislative Assembly 24-25; Joint Dir. Indian Princes Special Organisation 29-31; Adviser to Indian States Del., Round Table Conf. 30-31, 32; Dir. Eastern Services, B.B.C. 41-44; fmr. Dir. Min. of Information Middle East Section; Editorial Dept. of *The Times* 44-55; Editor Murray's *Handbook to India, Pakistan, Burma and Ceylon*; Adviser to His Highness the Maharao of Kutch.

Publs. *A Primer of Indian Administration, India's Parliament* (4 vols.), *A History of India under the Company and the Crown, An Empire Builder of the Sixteenth Century: Babur, What about India?, The State of Israel, The Black Hills, Kutch in History and Legend, The State of Pakistan* (2nd edn. 66).

West Hairshaw House, Stewarton, by Kilmarnock, Ayrshire, Scotland; and Athenaeum Club, London, S.W.1, England.

Telephone: Stewarton 2252.

Williams, Leslie Henry, F.R.I.C.; British company director; b. 26 Jan. 1903; ed. Highbury County School, and London Univ.

Imperial Chemical Industries Ltd., Paints Div. 29-, Dir. 43-46, Man. Dir. 46-48, Chair. 49-56, Dir. I.C.I. Main Board 57-60, Dep. Chair. I.C.I. Ltd., 60-67; Dir. British Nylon Spinners Ltd. 57-64, Ilford Ltd. 58-67; Chair. I.C.I. Fibres Ltd. 65-66; Pres. Royal Inst. of Chemistry 67-; part-time mem. Monopolies Comm. 67-.

Penny Green, West End Lane, Stoke Poges, Bucks., England.

Telephone: Farnham Common 3423.

Williams, Nick B.; American newspaper editor; b. 23 Aug. 1906; ed. Univ. of the South and Univ. of Texas.

Editorial worker, Texas, Tennessee and California 27-58; Man. Editor *Los Angeles Times* 58, Editor 59-; mem. American Society of Newspaper Editors.

4205 Beulah Drive, La Canada, Calif., U.S.A.

Williams, Paul Revere; American architect; b. 18 Feb. 1896; ed. Univ. of Southern California, and Beaux Arts Inst. of Design, Los Angeles.

Architect 23-; works include private houses, Los Angeles

Superior Court Building, Pearl Harbour Memorial, Honolulu, Franz Hall and Botany Building, Univ. of S. Calif.; Fellow, American Inst. of Architects; Award for Creative Planning, Los Angeles Chamber of Commerce.

Publs. *Small Homes for Tomorrow, New Homes for Today.*

Office: 3757 Wilshire Boulevard, Los Angeles 5, California; Home: 1690 Victoria Avenue, Los Angeles 19, California, U.S.A.

Williams, Raymond, M.A.; British writer and university lecturer; b. 31 Aug. 1921; ed. Abergavenny Grammar School, and Trinity Coll., Cambridge.

Army Service 41-45; Staff Tutor, Oxford Univ. Extra-Mural Delegacy 46-61; Univ. Lecturer in English and Fellow of Jesus Coll., Cambridge 61-67; Univ. Reader in Drama, Cambridge, 67-; Gen. Editor New Thinker's Library 61-.

Publs. *Drama from Ibsen to Eliot* 52, *Drama in Performance* 54, *Culture and Society* 58, *Border Country* 60, *The Long Revolution* 61, *Communications* 62, *Second Generation* 64, *Modern Tragedy* 66, *Public Enquiry* 67, *Drama from Ibsen to Brecht* 68.

White Cottage, Hardwick, Cambridge, England.

Williams, Robert Edmond, B.SC.; American steel executive; b. 7 Feb. 1913; ed. Univ. of California at Berkeley.

U.S. Steel Corpn., 35-60, Vice-Pres. Sales, Nat. Tube Div. 60-61; Vice-Pres. Sales, Youngstown Sheet and Tube Co. 61-63, Exec. Vice-Pres. 63-65, Dir. and mem. Exec. Cttee. April 64-, Pres. Nov. 65-, Chief Exec. Officer July 66-; Dir.-Gen. Fireproofing Co., Pittsburgh Nat. Bank, Dollar Savings & Trust Co. (Youngstown); Dir. and mem. Exec. Cttee. American Iron and Steel Inst.

The Youngstown Sheet and Tube Co., Youngstown, Ohio 44501; Home: 1359 Virginia Trail, Youngstown, Ohio 44505, U.S.A.

Williams, Roger J(ohn), M.S., PH.D.; American biochemist; b. 14 Aug. 1893; ed. Univs. of Redlands and Chicago.

Research Chemist, Fleischmann Co. 19-20; Asst. Prof. Univ. of Oregon 20-21, Assoc. Prof. 21-27, Prof. 28-31; Prof. Oregon State Coll. 32-39; Prof. of Chemistry, Univ. of Texas 39-; Dir. Clayton Foundation Biochemical Inst. Univ. of Texas 41-63; Research Council Food and Nutrition Board 49-53; mem. Nat. Acad. of Sciences, American Chemical Society (Pres. 57), Biochemical Society of London, etc.; Fellow American Asscn. for Advancement of Science; Mead Johnson Award 41; Chandler Medal 42; Hon. D.Sc. (Univ. of Redlands, Columbia Univ., Oregon State Coll.).

Publs. *An Introduction to Organic Chemistry* 27, *A Laboratory Manual of Organic Chemistry* (with R. Q. Brewster) 28, *An Introduction to Bio-chemistry* 31, *Textbook of Biochemistry* 38, *What to do about Vitamins* 45, *The Human Frontier* 46, *Biochemistry of B Vitamins* (with others) 50, *Nutrition and Alcoholism* 51, *Free and Unequal* 53, *Biochemical Individuality* 56, *Alcoholism: The Nutritional Approach* 59, *Nutrition in a Nutshell* 62.

Office: University of Texas, Austin, Texas; 1604 Gaston Avenue, Austin, Texas, U.S.A.

Williams, Rt. Rev. Ronald Ralph, M.A., D.D.; British ecclesiastic; b. 14 Oct. 1906; ed. Gonville and Caius Coll., and Ridley Hall, Cambridge.

Tutor, St. Aidans Coll., Birkenhead 28-29; Curate, Leyton Parish Church 29-31; Chaplain, Ridley Hall, Cambridge 31-34; Examining Chaplain to Bishop of Chelmsford 31; Home Education Sec., Church Missionary Society 34-40; with Religious Division, Ministry of Information 40-45, Dir. 43-45; Commissary to Bishop of Tasmania 44; Examining Chaplain to Bishop of Durham 45; Principal, St. John's Coll., Durham 45-53; Proctor in Convocation of York 50; Hon. Canon, Durham Cathedral 53-54; Bishop of Leicester 53-; mem. House of Lords 59-; hon. Fellow St. Peter's Coll. (Oxford).

Publs. *Religion and the English Vernacular* 40, *The Strife Goes On* 40, *The Christian Religion* 41, *Authority in the Apostolic Age* 50, *The Perfect Law of Liberty* 53, *The Acts of the Apostles* 53, *Reading Through Hebrews* 60, *The Word of Life* (Editor) 60, *Take Thou Authority* 61, *The Bible in Worship and Ministry* 62, *The Letters of John and James* 65, *What's Right with the Church of England* 66.

Bishop's Lodge, Springfield Road, Leicester LE2 3BD, England.

Telephone: Leicester 78985; after Nov. 68, 70895.

Williams, Tennessee, A.B.; American writer; b. 26 March 1914; ed. Univs. of Missouri and Iowa, and Washington Univ., St. Louis.

Awarded Pulitzer Prize 47 and 55, Drama Critics' Circle Award 61.

Publs. *Battle of Angels* 40, *The Glass Menagerie* 44, *You Touched Me* 46, *A Streetcar Named Desire* 47, *Summer and Smoke* 48, *Rose Tattoo* 50, *Roman Spring of Mrs. Stone* 50, *Camino Real* 53, *Cat on a Hot Tin Roof* 55, *Orpheus Descending* 57, *Suddenly Last Summer* 58, *Sweet Bird of Youth* 59, *Period of Adjustment* 60, *The Night of the Iguana* 61, *The Milk Train Doesn't Stop Here Any More* 62 (Revised version 63), *The Knightly Quest* (short stories) 67, *The Two Character Play* 67, *The Eccentricities of a Nightingale* 67, *The Seven Descents of Myrtle* 68.

c/o Audrey Wood, Ashley Famous Agency Inc., 1301 Avenue of the Americas, New York City, N.Y. 10019, U.S.A.

Williams, Walter Charles; American aeronautical engineer; b. 30 July 1919; ed. Louisiana State Univ.

Langley Memorial Aeronautical Laboratory, Nat. Advisory Cttee. for Aeronautics (NACA) 39-46; NACA Project Engineer for X-1 Experimental Aircraft Program 46-47; Head, NACA Flight Research Center, Edwards Air Force Base, California 47-59; Assoc. Dir. and Dep. Dir. Nat. Aeronautics and Space Admin. (NASA) Manned Spacecraft Center, Houston, Texas 59-63; Dep. Assoc. Admin. for Manned Space Flight Operations, NASA, Washington 63-64; Vice-Pres. Aerospace Corpn., Gen. Man. Manned Systems Div., El Segundo, Calif. 64-; NASA Distinguished Service Medal 62, and other awards.

4240 Reyes Drive, Tarzana, Calif., U.S.A.

Williams, Sir William Emrys, C.B.E.; British art administrator; b. 5 Oct. 1896; ed. Manchester Univ.

Tutor, Univ. of London Extra Mural Dept. 28-34; Sec. British Inst. of Adult Educ. 34-40; Dir. Army Bureau of Current Affairs 41-45, Bureau of Current Affairs 46-51; Sec.-Gen. Arts Council of Great Britain April 51-63; Sec. Nat. Art Collection Fund 63-; Pres. Welsh Nat. Theatre 68-; fmr. Dir. Penguin Books.

Grenville Paddock, Haddenham, Aylesbury, Bucks., England.

Williams-Ellis, Mrs. Amabel (wife of Clough Williams-Ellis, *q.v.*); British writer of novels and children's books.

Publs. *An Anatomy of Poetry, The Big Firm, Men who Found Out, Noah's Ark, How you are Made, To Tell the Truth, A History of English Life, Learn to Love First, Headlong Down the Years, Women in War Factories, The Art of Being a Woman, The Art of Being a Parent, A Food and People Geography, Changing the World, Seekers and Finders, Modern Scientists at Work, Darwin's Moon,* etc.

Plâs Brondanw, Penrhyndeudraeth, Merioneth, N. Wales.

Williams-Ellis, Clough (husband of Mrs. Amabel Williams-Ellis, *q.v.*), C.B.E., M.C., F.R.I.B.A., J.P., M.T.P.I., F.L.I.A.; British architect; b. 28 May 1883; ed. Oundle and Trinity Coll., Cambridge.

Authority on town-planning; founder of the Portmeirion Peninsular Colony, N. Wales; Chair. Council for Preservation of Rural Wales, Stevenage New Town Corpn., Glass Industry Working Party; fmr. Pres. Design and Industries Asscn.; mem. Town Planning Inst., Govt. Cttee. on Art and Industry, Univ. of Wales Art Cttee., Grand Council British Travel Asscn., Welsh Advisory Reconstruction Council; Govt. Cttee. on Nat. Parks; Welsh Cttee. Festival of Britain 51; mem. Ministry of Transport Highways Advisory Cttee., Nat. Trust Welsh Cttee.

Works include churches, schools, hotels, clubs, village schemes; private residences in China and South Africa; Portmeirion (see above); memorial to David Lloyd George; Town Planning Consultant to various municipalities.

Publs. *The Pleasures of Architecture, England and the Octopus, Architecture Here and Now, The Architect, The Face of the Land, Britain and the Beast, Plan for Living, The Adventure of Building, On Trust for the Nation, An Artist in North Wales, Town and Country Planning, Roads in the Landscape,* etc.

Plâs Brondanw, Penrhyndeudraeth, N. Wales.

Telephone: Penrhyndeudraeth 292.

Williamson, Henry; British novelist; b. 95.

Publs. include *The Beautiful Years* 21, *Dandelion Days* 22, *The Dream of Fair Women* 24, *The Pathway* 28 (forming a tetralogy called *The Flax of Dream), The Lone Swallows* 22, *The Peregrine's Saga* 23, *The Old Stag* 26, *Tarka the Otter* 27 (Hawthornden Prize 28), *Tales of a Devon Village* and *Life in a Devon Village* 32, *The Gold Falcon* 33, *Salar the Salmon* 35, *The Story of a Norfolk Farm* 41, *T. E. Lawrence: Genius of Friendship* 41, *The Phasian Bird* 48, *Scribbling Lark* 49, *The Dark Lantern* 51, *Donkey Boy* 52, *Tales of Moorland and Estuary* 53, *Young Phillip Maddison* 53, *How Dear is Life* 54, *A Fox under my Cloak* 55, *The Golden Virgin* 57, *A Clear Water Stream* 58, *Love and the Loveless: a Soldier's Tale of Passchendaele 1917* 58, *The Henry Williamson Animal Saga* 60, *A Test to Destruction* 60, *The Innocent Moon* 61, *It was the Nightingale* 62, *The Power of the Dead* 63, *The Phoenix Generation* 65, *A Solitary War* 66, *Lucifer Before Sunrise* 67, *The Gale of the World* 68.

c/o National Liberal Club, Whitehall Place, London, S.W.1; and Ox's Cross, Braunton, N. Devon, England.

Williamson, Hugh Ross, F.R.S.L.; British writer; b. 2 Jan. 1901.

Mem. editorial staff *Yorkshire Post* 25-30; Editor *Bookman* 30-34; Acting Editor *Strand Magazine* 34. Publs. *The Poetry of T. S. Eliot* 32, *John Hampden* 33, *King James I, Gods and Mortals in Love* 36, *George Villiers, Duke of Buckingham* 37, *Who Is For Liberty?* 38, *A.D. 33* 41, *Captain Thomas Schofield* 42, *Charles and Cromwell* 46, *The Arrow and the Sword* 47, *Were You There . . ?* 47, *The Silver Bowl* 48, *Four Stuart Portraits* 49, *The Seven Christian Virtues* 49, *The Gunpowder Plot* 51, *Sir Walter Raleigh* 51, *Jeremy Taylor* 52, *The Walled Garden* (autobiography) 53, *The Ancient Capital* 53, *Canterbury Cathedral* 53, *The Children's Book of (British, French, Italian, Spanish) Saints* 53, 54, 56, *The Great Prayer* 55, *Historical Whodunits* 55, *James by the Grace of God* 55, *Enigmas of History* 57, *The Day They Killed the King* 57, *The Beginnings of the English Reformation* 57, *The Sisters* 58, *A Wicked Pack of Cards* 61, *The Day Shakespeare Died* 62, *The Flowering Hawthorn* 63, *Guy Fawkes* 64, *The Butt of Malmsey* 67, *The Marriage Made Blood* 68; plays: *In a Glass Darkly* 31, *After the Event* 33, *Rose and Glove* 34, *The Seven Deadly Virtues, Monsieur Moi* 35, *Various Heavens, Cinderella's Grandchild* 36, *Mr. Gladstone* 37, *Stories from History* 38, *The Death of Don Juan* 43, *Paul, a Bondslave* 45, *Queen Elizabeth* 46, *The Story Without an End* 47, *Odds Beyond Arithmetic* 47, *The Pilgrim's Progress* (dramatic version) 48, *The Cardinal's Learning* 50, *Gunpowder, Treason and Plot* 51, *Conversation with a Ghost* 52, *Diamond Cut Diamond* 52, *His Eminence of England* 53, *The Elder Brother* 53, *Wild Grows the Heather* (musical version of J. M. Barrie's *Little Minister*) 56, *King Claudius* 57, *Test of Truth* 58, *The Mime of Bernadette* 58, *Heart of Bruce* 59, *Teresa of Avila* 61, *Quartet for Lovers* (with Ian Burford) 62, *Pavane for a Dead Infanta* 68.

c/o Savage Club, 86 St. James's Street, London, S.W.1; and 11a St. Barnabas Road, Cambridge, England.

Williamson, Malcolm Benjamin Graham; Australian composer, pianist and organist; b. 21 Nov. 1931; ed. Barker Coll., Hornsby, N.S.W., and Sydney Conservatorium of Music.

Assistant organist, Farm Street, London 55-58; Organist, St. Peter's, Limehouse 58-60; Lecturer in Music, Central School of Speech and Drama, London 61-62; Exec. Cttee., Composers Guild of Great Britain 64; Sir Arnold Bax Memorial Prize 63.

Compositions include: Operas: *Our Man in Havana* 63, *English Eccentrics* 64, *The Happy Prince* 64, *Julius Cæsar Jones* 65, *The Violins of St. Jacques* 66, *Dunstan and the Devil* 67, *Dream Play* 68; Ballets: *The Display* 64, *Sun into Darkness* 66; Orchestral: Piano Concertos 58, 60, 61, Organ Concerto 61, Violin Concerto 65, *Elevamini* (Symphony) 56, *Santiago de Espada* (Overture) 56, *Sinfonia Concertante* 61, *Sinfonietta* 65, *Symphonic Variations* 65; Chamber: *Variations for Cello and Piano* 64, *Concerto for Wind Quintet and Two Pianos, Eight Hands* 65; Organ: *Fons Amoris* 57, *Symphony* 60, *Vision of Christ Phoenix* 61, *Elegy JFK* 64; also choral and piano music.

32 Hertford Avenue, London, S.W.14, England.

Willier, Benjamin H(arrison), B.S., PH.D., D.SC.; American zoologist and embryologist; b. 2 Nov. 1890; ed. Coll. of Wooster and Univ. of Chicago.

Instr., Biology, Coll. of Wooster 15-16; Assoc. in Zoology, Univ. of Chicago 19-20, Instr. 20-24, Asst. Prof. 24-27, Assoc. Prof. 27-31, Prof. of Zoology 31-33; Prof. of Zoology and Head of Dept., also Chair., Div. of Biological Sciences, Univ. of Rochester 33-40; Henry Walters Prof. of Zoology 40-58, Emeritus 58-, Dir. of the Biological Laboratories, Johns Hopkins Univ. 40-55; Trustee, Marine Biological Laboratory, Woods Hole 33-50; Dir. Long Island Biological Asscn., Cold Spring Harbor 42-60; Government-Industry Oyster Research Programme 58-60; mem. Nat. Acad. of Sciences, Institut International d'Embryologie, Int. Soc. for Cell Biology; Assoc. Editor *Journal of Morphology* 32-34; mem. Editorial Board of *Physiological Zoology* 37-63, of *Growth* 40-49, of *Bios* 52-; Advisory Editor *Survey of Biological Progress* 46-; Editor of *Quarterly Review of Biology* 41-57; Visiting Prof., Coll. of Medicine, Univ. of Florida 64; mem. American Philosophical Soc., Board of Trustees of Science Service 59-65.

Publs. Co-author: *Sex and Internal Secretions* 39, *The Biology of Melanomas* 48, *La Différentiation sexuelle chez les Vertébrés* 51, *The Chick Embryo in Biological Research* 52; co-author and editor *Analysis of Development* 55; *Biographical Memoir of Frank Rattray Lillie* 57, co-author *Foundations of Experimental Embryology* 64.

6002 Roland Avenue, Baltimore, Md., U.S.A.

Willingham, Ben Hill; American business executive; b. 1 June 1914; ed. Hume Fogg High School, Nashville, Vanderbilt Univ.

Joined Genesco, Inc. 33, various admin. and exec.

positions, Dir. 53-, Vice-Pres. 56-58, Pres. 58-; Dir. Third Nat. Bank of Nashville; Tennessee Rep. to American Soc. of Sales Execs.; mem. Newcomen Soc. of N. America, Advisory Council of the Fashion Inst. of Technology; Trustee, Foundation for Research on Human Behavior.

874 Curtiswood Lane, Nashville, Tenn. 37204, U.S.A.

Willink, Rt. Hon. Sir Henry Urmston, Bart., P.C., M.C., Q.C., D.C.L., M.A.; British lawyer and college principal; b. 7 March 1894; ed. Eton, and Trinity Coll., Cambridge.

Served First World War 14-19; called to Bar Inner Temple 20; Nat. Conservative M.P. for North Croydon 40-48; Special Commr. for care and rehousing of London air-raid homeless 40-43; Minister of Health 43-45; Master of Magdalene Coll., Cambridge 48-66, Hon. Fellow 66-; Vice-Chancellor Cambridge Univ. 53-55; Chair. Royal Comm. on Gambling 49-51, on Police 60-62, Dean of the Arches 55-.

51 Madingley Road, Cambridge, England.

Willis, Baron (Life Peer), cr. 63, of Chislehurst; **Edward (Ted) Willis;** British author; b. 13 Jan. 1918; ed. Downhills Central School.

Royal Fusiliers 40-44; professional writer 45-; Chair. Screenwriters' Guild 58-; Dir. World Wide Pictures 67-; Labour.

Plays: *Woman in a Dressing Gown* 56, *Hot Summer Night* 59, *Doctor in the House* 60, *Mother* 61, *Slow Roll of Drums* 64, *Knock on any Door* 64, *Queenie* 67.

Films inc.: *Blue Lamp, Bitter Harvest, No Trees in the Street.*

T.V. Series incl.; *Dixon of Dock Green, Sergeant Cork.*

5 Shepherds Green, Chislehurst, Kent, England.

Willis, Charles Reginald; British journalist; b. 11 June 1906.

Formerly with *Tiverton Gazette, Evening Mail* (Barrow-in-Furness), *Evening Chronicle* (Newcastle-on-Tyne), *Evening Chronicle* (Manchester) and *Sunday Empire News* (London); joined *Evening News* 43, Deputy Chief Sub-Editor 44, Chief Sub-Editor 46, Asst. Editor 49, Deputy Editor 50-54, Editor 54-66; Editorial Dir. Harmsworth Publications Ltd. 67-.

133 Torrington Park, North Finchley, London, N.12; Associated Newspapers Ltd., Carmelite House, Carmelite Street, London, E.C.4, England.

Telephone: 01-353-6000 (Office); 01-445-9001 (Home).

Willits, Joseph Henry, A.M., PH.D., LL.D.; American economist; b. 16 June 1889; ed. Swarthmore Coll., and Univ. of Pennsylvania.

Instr. in Geography and Industry 12-17, Asst. Prof. 19-20, Prof. 20-39, Dean Wharton School of Finance and Commerce, Univ. of Pennsylvania 33-39; Sec. and Vice-Pres. Philadelphia Asscn. for Discussion of Employment Problems 15-21; Employment Supt. U.S. Naval Aircraft Factory 17-19; Dir. Indus. Research Dept. Univ. of Pa. 21-39; mem. President's Emergency Comm. for Employment 30-31, Pres. Nat. Bureau of Econ. Research 33 (Exec. Dir. 36-39), Dir. Div. of Social Sciences Rockefeller Foundation 39-54; Dir. The Educational Survey, Univ. of Pennsylvania 54-60; Vice-Pres. American Philosophical Soc. 59-61; Dir. Study of Excellence and Mediocrity in Colls. and Univs. 61-66.

Publs. *The Unemployed in Philadelphia* (with others) 15, *What the Coal Commission Found* (with others) 25, *Studies of Labor Relations for the U.S. Coal Commission.*

Box 441A, Bridgetown Pike, Langhorne, Pa., U.S.A.

Telephone: 215-757-6891.

Willoch, Kaare Isaachsen, CAND. OECON.; Norwegian politician; b. 3 Oct. 1928; ed. Ullern Gymnasium, and Univ. of Oslo.

Secretary, Fed. of Norwegian Shipowners 51-53, Counsellor, Fed. of Norwegian Industries 54-63; Sec.-Gen. Conservative Party 63-65; Minister of Trade and Shipping 63, 65-; mem. Storting 58-.

Publs. *Personal Savings* 55, *Price Policy in Norway* (with L. B. Bachke) 58.

Blokkaveien 6B, Oslo 2, Norway.

Wills, John Spencer, M.INST.T.; British business executive; b. 10 Aug. 1904; ed. Cleobury Mortimer Coll., Shropshire, and Merchant Taylors' School.

General Man. East Yorkshire Motor Services Ltd. 26-31; Man. Dir. and Chair. British Electric Traction Co. Ltd. 39-; Chair. and Man. Dir. Nat. Electric Construction Co. Ltd. 45-; Chair. Rediffusion Ltd. 47-, Rediffusion Television Ltd. 54-, Wembley Stadium Ltd. 65-; Deputy Chair. Monotype Corpn. Ltd. 47; Gov. Royal Shakespeare Theatre, Stratford-upon-Avon 46-; Trustee, London Symphony Orchestra Ltd. 62-; mem. Inst. of Transport (Pres. 50-51), Council of Public Transport Asscn. (Chair. 45-46); mem. of Council, Royal Opera House Soc. 62-; Vice-Patron, Theatre Royal Windsor Trust 65-; dir. of numerous other companies.

1 Campden House Terrace, London, W.8; Beech Farm, Battle, Sussex, England.

Wilson, Sir Alan Herries, F.R.S.; British industrial executive; b. 2 July 1906; ed. Wallasey Grammar School, and Emmanuel Coll., Cambridge.

Fellow, Emmanuel Coll. Cambridge 29-33, Hon. Fellow 59; Fellow and Lecturer, Trinity Coll. Cambridge 33-45; Univ. Lecturer in Mathematics, Cambridge 33-45; joined Courtaulds Ltd. 45, Man. Dir. 54, Deputy Chair. 57-62; Dir. Int. Computers and Tabulators Ltd. 62-; Chair. Cttee. on Coal Derivatives 59-60, on Problem of Noise 60-63; Chair. and Dir. Glaxo Group Ltd. 63-; Deputy Chair. Electricity Council 66-; mem. Iron and Steel Board 60-67; Hon. D.Sc. (Oxford).

Publs. *The Theory of Metals* 36, 53, *Semi-Conductors and Metals* 39, *Thermodynamics and Statistical Mechanics* 57.

Glaxo Group Ltd., 6-12 Clarges Street, London, W.1, England.

Telephone: 01-493-4060.

Wilson, Alexander (Sandy) Galbraith; British writer and composer; b. 19 May 1924; ed. Harrow School, Oxford Univ. and Old Vic Theatre School.

Contributed to revues *Slings and Arrows, Oranges and Lemons* 48; wrote revues for Watergate Theatre, London *See You Later, See You Again* 51-52; wrote musical *The Boy Friend* for Players Club Theatre 53, transferred to Wyndhams Theatre and on Broadway 54; *The Buccaneer* 55, *Valmouth* London 58, U.S.A. 60, *Divorce me Darling* 65; Dir. London revival of *The Boy Friend* 67.

Publs: *This is Sylvia* 54, *The Poodle from Rome* 62.

2 Southwell Gardens, London, S.W.7, England.

Telephone: 01-373-6172.

Wilson, Angus (Frank Johnson), C.B.E., B.A., F.R.S.L.; British writer; b. 11 Aug. 1913; ed. Westminster School, and Merton Coll., Oxford.

Asst. Keeper, Dept. of Printed Books, British Museum 36-55; full-time writer 55-; Lecturer, School of English Studies, Univ. of East Anglia 63-, Prof. 66-; mem. Arts Council 67-.

Publs. *The Wrong Set* 49, *Such Darling Dodos* 50, *Hemlock and After* 52, *For Whom the Cloche Tolls* 53, *Emile Zola* 54, *The Mulberry Bush* (a play, produced Bristol Old Vic 55, Royal Court Theatre 56, published 56), *Anglo-Saxon Attitudes* 56, *A Bit off the Map* 57, *The Middle Age of Mrs. Eliot* 58, *After the Show* (TV play) 59, *The Stranger* (TV play) 60, *The Old Men at the Zoo* 61, *The Invasion* (TV play) 63, *The Wild Garden* 63, *Late Call* 64, *Tempo* 64, *The Impact of Television on the Arts* 65, *No Laughing Matter* 67.

Felsham Woodside, Bradfield St. George, Bury St. Edmunds, Suffolk, England.

Wilson, Carroll Louis, S.B.; American scientist; b. 21 Sept. 1910; ed. Rochester, N.Y., and Mass. Inst. of Technology.
Assistant to Pres. Mass., Inst. of Technology 32-37; mem. Nat. Defense Research Cttee., Mission to Great Britain 41; Man. Instnl. Div., Research Corpn. of N.Y. 37-43; Senior Liaison Officer 40-42; Exec. Asst. to the Dir., Office of Scientific Research and Development, Washington, D.C. 42-46; Sec. Board of Consultants Dept. of State on Int. Control of Atomic Energy 46; Vice-Pres. and Dir. Nat. Research Corpn. of Boston 46-47; Gen. Manager U.S. Atomic Energy Comm. 47-50; Dir. Industrial Development Dept. Climax Molybdenum Co. 51-54; Pres. Climax Uranium Co. 51-54; Dir. Millipore Filter Co., Boston; Pres. and Gen. Manager Metals & Controls Corpn., Mass. 56-58; Prof. Mass. Inst. of Technology (M.I.T.) 59-; Dir. Rhode Island Hospital Trust Co.; Trustee Rhode Island Hospital, World Peace Foundation (Boston); mem. Rockefeller Brothers Fund Panel on Int. Security 57-58, Council on Foreign Relations, Dir. 64-; Dir. M.I.T. Fellows in Africa Program 60-, A. D. Little Research Inst., Edinburgh 62-; Chair. OECD Cttee. on Scientific Research 62-; mem. Expert Advisory Cttee. on Science and Development (ECOSOC) 64-; Fellow American Acad. of Arts and Sciences, American Soc. of Mining and Metallurgical Engineers; Medal for Merit 48; Hon. O.B.E.; Hon. Sc.D. (Williams Coll.).
Jacob's Hill, Seekonk, Mass., U.S.A.

Wilson, Sir Charles Haynes, Kt., M.A., LL.D., D.C.L., D.LITT.; British university officer; b. 16 May 1909; ed. Glasgow Univ. and Oxford Univ.
Fellow and Tutor in Modern History, Corpus Christi Coll., Oxford 39-52, Junior Proctor 45; Principal, Univ. Coll. of Leicester 52-57; Vice-Chancellor, Univ. of Leicester 57-61; Principal and Vice-Chancellor, Univ. of Glasgow 61-; Hon. Fellow, Corpus Christi Coll., Oxford 63.
The University, Glasgow, Scotland.
Telephone: West 8855.

Wilson, Colin Henry; British writer; b. 26 June 1931; ed. Gateway Secondary Technical School, Leicester.
Laboratory assistant 48-49, civil servant (taxes) 49-50; R.A.F. 50, discharged on medical grounds 50; then navvy, boot and shoe operative, dish washer, plastic moulder; lived Strasbourg 50, Paris 53; later factory hand and dish washer; writer 56-; Writer in Residence, Hollins Coll., Virginia, U.S.A. 66-67.
Publs. philosophy: *The Outsider* 56, *Religion and the Rebel* 57, *The Age of Defeat* 58, *The Strength to Dream* 61, *Origins of the Sexual Impulse* 63, *Beyond the Outsider* 65, *Introduction to the New Existentialism* 66; other non-fiction: *Encyclopaedia of Murder* 60, *Rasputin and the Fall of the Romanovs* 64, *Brandy of the Damned* (music essays) 65, *Eagle and Earwig* (literary essays) 65, *Shaw: A Reassessment* 66, *Sex and the Intelligent Teenager* 66, *Voyage to a Beginning* (autobiography) 66; novels: *Ritual in the Dark* 60, *Adrift in Soho* 61, *The World of Violence* 63, *Man Without a Shadow* 64, *Necessary Doubt* 65, *The Glass Cage* 66, *The Mind Parasites* 66, *The Back Room* 68.
Tetherdown, Trewallock Lane, Gorran Haven, Cornwall, England.

Wilson, Donald M.; American journalist and government official; b. 27 June 1925; ed. Yale Univ.
Air Corps Navigator, Second World War; magazine assignments in 35 countries 51-61; fmr. Far Eastern Corresp., *Life* magazine, Chief Washington Correspondent 57-61; Dep. Dir. U.S. Information Agency 61-65; General Man. Time-Life Int. 65-
Time-Life International, Time and Life Building, Rockefeller Center, New York, N.Y. 10020; 200 Mercer Street, Princeton, N.J. 08541, U.S.A.

Wilson, Sir (Archibald) Duncan, K.C.M.G.; British diplomatist; b. 12 Aug. 1911; ed. Winchester and Balliol Coll., Oxford.
Teacher, Westminster School 36-37; Asst. Keeper, British Museum 37-39; Ministry of Economic Warfare 39-41; Foreign Office 41-45; Control Comm., Germany 45-46; Foreign Service 47-, Berlin 47-49, Yugoslavia 51-53; Dir. of Research and Acting Librarian, Foreign Office 55-57; Chargé d'Affaires, Peking 57-59; Fellow, Center of Int. Affairs, Harvard Univ. 59-60; Asst. Under-Sec. Foreign Office 60-64; Ambassador to Yugoslavia 64-68, to U.S.S.R. 68-.
Publ. (with Elizabeth Wilson) *Federation and World Order* 39.
British Embassy, Moscow, U.S.S.R.

Wilson, Edmund, A.B.; American writer; b. 8 May 1895; ed. Princeton Univ.
Reporter *New York Evening Sun* 16-17; Man. Editor *Vanity Fair* 20-21; Associate Editor *New Republic* 26-31.
Publs. *Discordant Encounters* (dialogues and plays) 26, *I Thought of Daisy* 29, *Poets, Farewell* (verse) 29, *Axel's Castle* 31, *The American Jitters—A Year of the Slump* (English title: *Devil Take the Hindmost*) 32, *Travels in Two Democracies* 36, *This Room and This Gin and These Sandwiches* 37, *The Triple Thinkers* 38, *To the Finland Station* 40, *The Boys in the Back Room* 41, *The Wound and the Bow* 41, *Note Books of Night* 43, *The Shock of Recognition* (anthology) 43, *Memoirs of Hecate County* 46, *Europe Without Baedeker* 47, *The Little Blue Light* 50, *Classics and Commercials* 50, *The Shores of Light* 52, *Five Plays* 54, *The Scrolls from the Dead Sea* 55, *Red, Black, Blond and Olive* 55, *A Piece o, My Mind* 56, *The American Earthquake* 58, *Apologies to the Iroquois* 60, *Patriotic Gore* 62, *The Cold War and the Income Tax: A Protest* 63, *O Canada* 65, *The Bit Between My Teeth* 66, *A Prelude* 67.
Wellfleet, Cape Cod, Mass., U.S.A.

Wilson, Edward William; American business executive; b. 6 Feb. 1899; ed. Univ. of Chicago and John Marshall Law School.
Armour and Co. 22-, Vice-Pres. 49-55, Group Vice-Pres. (Non-Food Operations), Exec. Vice-Pres. 56-61, Pres. 61-, now Vice-Chair.; Dir. subsidiary and other companies.
Armour and Co., 401 N. Wabash Street, Chicago 60609, Illinois, U.S.A.

Wilson, Geoffrey Masterman; British international civil servant; b. 7 April 1910; ed. Manchester Grammar School, Oriel Coll., Oxford, and Middle Temple.
Practised law as barrister 35-39; served in British Embassy, Moscow and Russian Dept. of Foreign Office 40-45; in H.M. Treasury 47-51, 53-58; Dir. Colombo Plan Technical Co-operation Bureau 51-53; Under-Sec. Overseas Finance Div., H.M. Treasury and mem. Managing Board of European Payments Union 56-58; Financial Attaché, British Embassy, Washington and Alt. Exec. Dir. for U.K. of Int. Bank, Int. Finance Corpn. and Int. Development Asscn. 58-61; Consultant, Int. Bank Sept. 61-Dec. 61; Dir. of Operations for South Asia and the Middle East Dec. 61-62; Vice-Pres. Int. Bank Oct. 62-66; Deputy Sec. Ministry of Overseas Devt. 66-.
Ministry of Overseas Development, London, S.W.1; Home: 34 Sheffield Terrace, London, W.8, England.
Telephone: 01-229-7012 (Home).

Wilson, Georges; French theatre director; b. 16 Oct. 1921; ed. Centre d'Art Dramatique, Paris.
Acted in two plays in Grenier-Hussenot Company 47; entered Comédie de l'Ouest 50; entered Théâtre Nat. Populaire (T.N.P.) 52, played important roles in almost all the plays; Dir. *L'Ecole des Femmes*, *Le Client du Matin* (Théâtre de l'Oeuvre), *Un otage* (Théâtre de France), *La Vie de Galilée*, *Lumières de Bohème*; Dir. of

Théâtre Nat. Populaire 63-; Officier de l'Ordre du Mérite Nat., Chevalier de l'Ordre des Arts et Lettres.
Films directed include: *Une aussi longue absence, La jument verte, Le Caïd, Terrain Vague, Lucky Joe.*
Théâtre National Populaire, Palais de Chaillot, Paris 16e, France.
Telephone: KLEber 74-27.

Wilson, Rt. Hon. Harold (*see* Wilson, (J.) H.).

Wilson, Rt. Hon. (James) Harold, P.C., O.B.E., M.P.; British politician; b. 11 March 1916; ed. Milnsbridge Council School, Royds Hall School, Huddersfield, Wirral Grammar School, Cheshire, and Jesus Coll., Oxford.
Lecturer in Economics, New Coll., Oxford 37-38; Fellow of Univ. Coll., Oxford and research asst. to Sir William (later Lord) Beveridge 38-39; Economic Asst. to War Cabinet Secretariat 40-43; Mines Dept. (later a part of Ministry of Labour) 42-43; Dir. Economics and Statistics, Ministry of Fuel and Power 43-44; M.P. 45-; Parl. Sec. Ministry of Works 45-47; Sec. for Overseas Trade March-Oct. 47; Pres. of Board of Trade Oct. 47-51 (resgnd.); mem. Nat. Exec. of Labour Party 52- (Chair. 61-62), and of Parl. Cttee. 54-; Chair. Public Accounts Cttee. of House of Commons 59-63; Leader of Parl. Labour Party 63-; Prime Minister Oct. 64-; Chancellor Univ. of Bradford 66-; Hon. D.Iur. (Bridgeport, U.S.A.) 64; Hon. LL.D. (Lancaster) 64, (Liverpool) 65, (Nottingham) 66; Hon. D.C.L. (Oxford) 65; Hon. D.Tech. (Bradford) 66.
Publs. *New Deal for Coal* 45, *In Place of Dollars* 52, *War on Want, The War on World Poverty* 53, *Purpose in Politics* 64, *The Relevance of British Socialism* 64, *The New Britain* (speeches) 64, *Purpose in Power* 66.
10 Downing Street, London, S.W.1, England.

Wilson, John Dover, C.H., LITT.D., F.B.A., M.A.; British educationist and Shakespearean scholar; b. 13 July 1881; ed. Lancing Coll., and Gonville and Caius Coll., Cambridge.
English Lector Helsinki Univ. 06; Lecturer in English Goldsmith's Coll. London Univ. 09-12; Insp. for Adult Classes and Continuation Schools 12-24; Prof. of Education in London Univ. 24-35; Hon. Fellow Gonville and Caius Coll. Cambridge; Regius Prof. of Rhetoric and English Literature Edinburgh Univ. 35-45; Editor *The New Shakespeare* 21-66; Trustee Shakespeare's Birthplace 31-51, Life Trustee 51; Trustee Nat. Library of Scotland 46-; Pres. Scottish Classical Asscn. 50-51; Hon. LL.D. (Natal, Edinburgh), D.Litt. (Durham, Leicester), Hon. D.Lit. (London), etc.
Publs. *Life in Shakespeare's England* 11, *The War and Democracy* (in collaboration) 14, *The Essential Shakespeare* 32, *The Manuscript of Shakespeare's Hamlet and the Problems of its Transmission* 34, *What Happens in Hamlet* 35, *The Fortunes of Falstaff* 43. *A. W. Pollard: a Memoir* 48, *Shakespeare's Happy Comedies* 62, *Shakespeare's Sonnets* 63.
Three Beeches, Balerno, Midlothian, Scotland.

Wilson, Rt. Rev. John Leonard, K.C.M.G., M.A., D.D.; British ecclesiastic; b. 23 Nov. 1897; ed. Queen's Coll., and Wycliffe Hall, Oxford.
Ordained Deacon 24, Priest 26; Curate, St. Michael's Cathedral, Coventry 24-28; with Church Missionary Society, Egypt 28-29; Curate, St. Margaret's Durham 29-30; Vicar, St. Thomas's, Eighton Banks, Gateshead-on-Tyne 30-35, St. Andrew's, Monkwearmouth 35-38; Dean, St. John's Cathedral and Archdeacon of Hong Kong 38-41; Bishop of Singapore 41-49; Dean of Manchester and Asst. Bishop 49-53; Bishop of Birmingham 53-; interned Changi Camp, Singapore 43-45; Hon Fellow Queen's Coll., Oxford 54; Prelate, Order of St. Michael and St. George 63.
Bishop's Croft, Harborne, Birmingham 17, England.

Wilson, John Leonard; Canadian judge; b. 1 Sept. 1900; ed. Univ. of Toronto, and Osgoode Hall Law School, Toronto.

Legal Practice, Toronto 26-45; Judge of Supreme Court, Ontario 45-; Pres. High Court of Justice of Cyprus 62-64; Exec. mem. World Asscn. of Judges; Hon. mem. World Peace Through Law Center.
Apt. 1105, 9 Deer Park Crescent, Toronto 7, Ont., Canada.
Telephone: 363-4101.

Wilson, Joseph Chamberlain, B.A., M.B.A.; American business executive; b. 13 Dec. 1909; ed. Univ. of Rochester and Harvard Graduate School of Business Administration.
Xerox Corp. 33-, Asst. to Sales Man. 33-35, Sec. 36-37, Sec. and Treas. 38-39, Treas. 40-43, mem. Board of Dirs. 39-, Vice-Pres. 44-45, Pres., Gen. Man. and Chief Exec. Officer 46-66, Chair. Board of Dirs. and Chief Exec. Officer 66-; official of affiliated and other companies.
Office: 1250 Midtown Tower, Rochester, N.Y. 14603; Home: 1550 Clover Street, Rochester, N.Y., U.S.A.
Telephone: 716-546-4500 (Office).

Wilson, Kendrick, R., Jr.; American business executive; b. 2 Jan. 1913; ed. Phillips Exeter Acad., and Dartmouth Coll.
U.S. Trust Co. of New York 36-41; Lehman Bros. 46-50; Vice-Pres. (Finance), Dir. and mem. Exec. Cttee. Avco Mfg. Co., New York City 50-57, Pres. 57-61, Chair. Board and Chief Exec. Officer 61-.
Home: Shagbark Road, Wilson Point, South Norwalk, Conn.; Office: Avco Corporation, 750 Third Avenue, New York City 17, N.Y., U.S.A.

Wilson, Louis Round, B.A., M.A., PH.D., LITT.D., L.H.D., LL.D.; American librarian; b. 76; ed. Univ. of North Carolina.
Librarian Univ. of North Carolina 01-32, Associate Prof. of Library Administration 07-12, Prof. of Library Administration 12-20, Kenan Prof. 20-32; Dir. Univ. of North Carolina Bureau of Extension 12-21, Dir. Univ. of North Carolina Press 22-32; Dir. School of Library Science 31-32; Pres. American Library Asscn. 35-36; Dean Graduate Library School Univ. of Chicago, and Prof. of Library Science 32-42; Prof. of Library Science Univ. North Carolina 42-59, Prof. Emer. 59-; Pres. Asscn. of American Library Schools 38-39; mem. Exec. Cttee. of American Council on Educ. 36-39; Dir. Sesquicentenniel of Univ. of North Carolina 44-46.
Publs. *Chaucer's Relative Constructions* 06, *The Geography of Reading* 38, *Library Planning* 44, *The University Library* (with M. F. Tauber) 45, *The College Library in Instruction* (with others) 51, *The University of North Carolina 1900-1930* 57; several surveys of various libraries written in collaboration; Editor *Library Trends* 37, *The Role of the Library in Adult Education* 37, *Practice of Book Selection* 39, *The Library in General Education* 43, *Libraries of the South-east* 49, *Selected Papers of Cornelia Phillips Spencer* 53, *Harry Woodburn Chase* 60, *The Library of the First State University* 60, *The University of North Carolina Under Consolidation 1931-1963* 64, *Education and Libraries* (Selected Papers) 66, *The Research Triangle of North Carolina* 67; Gen. Editor *University of Chicago Studies in Library Science* (25 vols.) 33-43, Editor *Sesquicentennial Publications of the University of North Carolina* (18 vols.) 45-53.
607 East Rosemary Street, Chapel Hill, N.C. 27514, U.S.A.
Telephone: 942-3378.

Wilson, O(wen) Meredith, B.A., PH.D.; American educator; b. 21 Sept. 1909; ed. Brigham Young Univ., and Univ. of California (Berkeley).
Assistant Prof. Brigham Young Univ. 37-42, Univ. of Utah 42-44; Asst. Prof. of History, Univ. of Chicago 44-45; Assoc. Prof. of History, Assoc. Dean of Coll., Univ. of Chicago 45-47; Prof. and Dean of School of

Arts and Sciences, Univ. of Utah 47-52; Sec. and Treas., Fund for Advancement of Educ. 52-54; Pres. Univ. of Oregon 54-60, Univ. of Minnesota 60-67; Chair. American Council on Educ. 58-59, mem. Exec. Cttee, 60-61, Chair. Comm. on Plans and Objectives in Higher Educ. 62-65; mem. Exec. Cttee. Carnegie Foundation for Advancement of Teaching 61-, Chair. 65; mem. Board of Dirs. Center for Advanced Study in Behavioral Sciences 61-67, Dir. 67-; mem. Board of Trustees Inst. of Int. Educ. 61, Vice-Chair. 62, Chair. 63-; mem. Council on Higher Educ. in the American Republics 59-, Co-Chair. 64-; Chair. Nat. Advisory Council on Educ. of Disadvantaged Children 65-68; mem. Agency for Int. Devt., Univ. Relations 65-; mem. U.S. Nat. Comm. for UNESCO 62-64; Marshman S. Wattson Memorial Plaque 62.
Publ. (collaborator) *The People Shall Judge* 49.
456 Marlowe Avenue, Palo Alto, Calif., U.S.A.

Wilson, Peter Cecil; British art auctioneer; b. 8 March 1913; ed. Eton Coll., and New Coll., Oxford.
Director Sotheby and Co. London 38-, Chair. 58-; Chair. Parke-Bernet, New York 64-.
Garden Lodge, Logan Place, London, W.8, England.

Wilson, Ralph Frederick, M.COM.; British (New Zealand) economist and politician; b. 21 Sept. 1912; ed. Otago Boys' High School and Univ. of Otago.
Assistant Sec. Bureau of Industry 38; Private Sec. Minister of Supply and Industries and Commerce 41-47; Sec. N.Z. Board of Trade 50-54; Sec. N.Z. Retailers' Fed. 54-59; Gen. Dir. N.Z. Nat. Party 59-.
88 Cecil Road, Wadestown, Wellington, New Zealand.

Wilson, Richard Lawson; American journalist; b. 3 Sept. 1905; ed. Iowa State Coll., and State Univ.
Reporter, *Register*, Des Moines 26-29; *St. Louis Globe-Democrat* 29-30; City Editor *Register*, Des Moines 30-33, Washington D.C. Corresp. 30-43; Washington Corresp. *Minneapolis Star and Tribune* 38-43; Chief Washington Bureau, Cowles Publications, including *Look* Magazine 43-; Pres. National Press Club 40; Pres. Nat. Press Building Corpn.; Pulitzer Prize (for Distinguished Reporting of National Affairs) 54; Headliner Award for Magazine Reporting 54; Special Citation Raymond Clapper Award 58; Centennial Award Iowa State Coll. 58; Hon. LL.D. (Drake Univ.) 56; Hon. D.Litt. (Iowa Wesleyan Coll.).
Home: 2918 Garfield Street, N.W. Washington, D.C.; Office: 852 National Press Building, Washington, D.C., U.S.A.

Wilson, Rt. Rev. Roger Plumpton, M.A., D.D.; British ecclesiastic; b. 3 Aug. 1905; ed. Winchester Coll., and Keble Coll., Oxford.
Classical Master Shrewsbury School 28-30 and 32-34, St. Andrew's, Grahamstown, S. Africa 30-32; ordained Deacon 35; Curate St. Paul's, Liverpool 35-38; Curate St. John's, Westminster 38-39; Vicar of South Shore, Blackpool 39-45, Radcliffe-on-Trent, Notts. 45-49; Archdeacon of Nottingham 45-49; Bishop of Wakefield 49-58; Bishop of Chichester 58-.
The Bishop's Palace, Chichester, Sussex, England.

Wilson, Sir Roland, K.B.E., D.PHIL., PH.D.; Australian economist and company director; b. 7 April 1904; ed. Univs. of Tasmania, Oxford and Chicago.
Lecturer in Economics Tasmania Univ. 30-32; Economist in Commonwealth Statistician's Office 32-35; Commonwealth Statistician and Econ. Adviser to Treasury 36-40 and 46-51; Sec. Commonwealth Dept. of Labour and Nat. Service 41-46; Chair. U.N. Economic and Employment Comm. 48-51; Sec. to the Treasury 51-66; Chair. of Qantas Airways; Chair. Commonwealth Banking Corpn.; Chair. Qantas-Wentworth Hotel; Dir. I.C.I. (Australia & New Zealand); mem. Council Australian Nat. Univs.

Publ. *Capital Imports and the Terms of Trade* 31.
64 Empire Circuit, Forrest, Canberra, A.C.T., Australia.
Telephone: 7-1848.

Wilson, Thomas James, B.A., M.A., PH.D.; American book publisher; b. 25 Oct. 1902; ed. Univ. of North Carolina, and Oxford Univ.
Instr. in French, Univ. of N.C. 21-24; Rhodes Scholar St. John's Coll. Oxford 24-27; Asst. Prof. of French, Univ. of N.C. 27-30; Foreign Language Ed., then Vice-Pres. of Henry Holt & Co., Publishers, New York 30-39; Vice-Pres. Reynal & Hitchcock Inc., Publishers, N.Y. 40-42; U.S. Naval Reserve, Active service 42-45; Lieut. and Lieut.-Commdr. 44, Commdr. 45; Dir. Univ. of N.C. Press 46-47; Dir. Harvard Univ. Press 47-; Pres. Asscn. of American Univ. Presses 51-53; mem. Board of Dirs. American Book Publishers Council 48-51, 54-57, Franklin Publications 55-60, Chair. 60-64; mem. Board of Dirs. Beacon Press 58-61, Chair. 60-61; Gov. Mass. Historical Soc. 58-61 and 63-66; mem. U.S. Govt. Cttee. on Int. Book Programs 62-64, Science Information Council, Nat. Science Foundation 65-66; Litt.D. h.c., L.H.D. h.c.
Home: 6 Berkeley Place, Cambridge, Mass.; Office: 79 Garden Street, Cambridge, Mass., U.S.A.
Telephone: 617-864-0806 (Home); 617-868-7600, extension 2601 (Office).

Wilson, Hon. Sir Tom Ian Findlay, K.B.E., C.M.G.; Rhodesian farmer and company director; b. Scotland 15 Jan. 1904; ed. Morrison's Acad., Crieff.
Entered Southern Rhodesia Parl. 40, re-elected 46, resigned on return of previous mem. from active service; again elected to Parl. 49; elected Speaker S. Rhodesian Parl. 52 and Speaker Fed. Parl. of Rhodesia and Nyasaland 54-58, 59-63.
Zengeni, Penhalonga (P.O.B. 4), Rhodesia.

Wilson Smith, Sir Henry, K.C.B., K.B.E.; British business executive; b. 30 Dec. 1904; ed. Royal Grammar School, Newcastle-upon-Tyne, and Cambridge Univ.
Secretary's Office, Post Office 27-30; Treasury 30; Asst. Private Sec. to Chancellor of Exchequer 32-34, Principal Private Sec. 39-42; Under Sec., Treasury 42-46; Perm. Sec., Ministry of Defence 46-48; Second Sec. Treasury 48-51; Part-time mem. Nat. Coal Board 56-59; Dir. Powell Duffryn Ltd. 51-, Chair. 57-; Dep. Chair. Guest Keen and Nettlefolds Ltd. 62-; Chair. Doxford and Sunderland Shipbuilding and Engineering Co. Ltd. 62-; Dir. Bank of England 64-.
Ashton House, Ashton, Wedmore, Somerset, England.
Telephone: Wedmore 372.

Win Maung, U, B.A.; Burmese politician; b. 16; ed. Judson Coll., Rangoon.
Joined Burmah Oil Co. after leaving coll.; then entered govt. dept.; joined Army as 2nd Lieut. 40; during Second World War took active part in resistance movement of Anti-Fascist Organisation; went to India, where he received training in tactics of military and guerilla warfare at Mil. Coll., Calcutta and Mil. Camp, Colombo 44; rejoined guerilla forces in Burma 45; Vice-Pres. Karen Youth Organisation and Ed. *Taing Yin Tha* 45; mem. Constituent Assembly 47; Minister for Industry and Labour 47, of Transport and Communications 49; later Minister for Port, Marine, Civil Aviation and Coastal Shipping; mem. Burmese Parl. for Maubin South (Karen) 51-55 and 56-57; Pres. of the Union of Burma, 13th Mar. 57-62; detained after *coup d'état* Mar. 62-Oct. 67.
Rangoon, Burma.

Winchell, Walter; American journalist; b. 7 April 1897.
Fmrly. engaged in vaudeville; mem. staff *Vaudeville News* 22; Columnist, Drama Critic and Drama Editor *Evening Graphic*, New York 24-29; Columnist and

Dramatic Critic, *New York Mirror* 29-63; Radio and TV Commentator.
Publ. *Winchell's America*.
33 W. 56th Street, New York City, N.Y., U.S.A.

Windgassen, Wolfgang; German singer; b. 26 June. At Württemberg Staatstheater, Stuttgart 45-; numerous performances at Bayreuth Festivals and recitals and opera performances in Germany and abroad.
Buowaldstrasse 48, Stuttgart-Sillenbuch, German Federal Republic.

Windham, Sir Ralph, Kt., M.A., LL.B.; British judge; b. 25 March 1905; ed. Wellington Coll., Berks., and Trinity Coll., Cambridge.
Called to Lincoln's Inn Bar 30; Legal Draftsman, Palestine 35, District Court Judge 42; Puisne Judge, Supreme Court, Ceylon 47, Kenya 50; Chief Justice, Zanzibar 55-59; Judge of Court of Appeal for Eastern Africa 59-60; Chief Justice, Tanganyika 60-64, of Tanzania 64-65; Commr. on Foreign Compensation Comm. 65-.
Moreton House, Moreton, Ongar, Essex, England.
Telephone: Moreton 222.

Windle, William F., B.S., M.S., PH.D., SC.D.; American anatomist and neurologist; b. 10 Oct. 1898; ed. Denison Univ., Northwestern Univ., Medical and Graduate Schools.
Instructor, later Asst. and Assoc. Prof. of Anatomy, Northwestern Univ. 23-35; Prof. of Microscopic Anatomy, Northwestern Univ. Medical School 35-42; Prof. of Neurology and Dir. Inst. of Neurology 42-46; Prof. of Anatomy and Chair. of Dept., Univ. of Washington (Seattle) 46-47, Univ. of Pa. 47-51; Scientific Dir. Baxter Laboratories, Morton Grove (Ill.) 51-54; Chief, Neuroanatomical Sciences Laboratory, Nat. Inst. of Neurological Diseases and Blindness (Nat. Insts. of Health) 54-60, Asst. Dir. 60-61; Chief, Laboratory of Perinatal Physiology (Nat. Insts. of Health) San Juan, Puerto Rico 61-64; Hon. Prof. Anatomy, Univ. of Puerto Rico 62-64; Research Prof. and Dir. of Research, Inst. of Physical and Medical Rehabilitation, N.Y. Univ Medical Center 64-; *Symposia in Neuroanatomical Sciences* 54-64; Editor-in-Chief *Experimental Neurology* 59-; mem. Harvey Soc.; War—Navy Award 44, Sesquicentennial Medal, Univ. of Louisville 48, Max Weinstein Award 57.
Publs. *An Outline and Laboratory Guide to Neurology* 39, *Physiology of the Fetus* 40, *Textbook of Histology* 1st edn. 49, 2nd 53, 3rd 60, *Asphyxia* 50.
330 East 33rd Street, New York, N.Y. 10016, U.S.A.

Windsor, H.R.H. the Duke of; member of British Royal Family; b. 23 June 1894.
Succeeded his father, King George V, as King Edward VIII, 20th Jan. 36; abdicated 11th Dec. 36; Gov. and Commander-in-Chief of the Bahamas 40-45.
Publ. *A King's Story*.
4 Route du Champ d'Entraînement, Bois de Boulogne, Paris 16e, France.

Wingate, Henry Smith, B.A.; American business executive; b. 8 Oct. 1905; ed. Carleton Coll., and Univ. of Michigan.
Associate, Sullivan and Cromwell 29-35; Asst. to Pres. The Int. Nickel Co. Inc. 35-39; Sec. The Int. Nickel Co. of Canada Ltd. 39-52, Vice-Pres. 49-52; Pres. The Int. Nickel Co. of Canada Ltd., The Int. Nickel Co. Inc. 54-60, Chair. 60-; Dir. of numerous companies and organizations including: Bank of Montreal, Canadian Pacific Railway, Morgan Guaranty Trust Co. of New York, Int. Copper Research Asscn., U.S. Steel Corpn., Int. Nickel Benelux, S.A., Int. Nickel France, S.A., Public Health Research Inst. of the City of New York, Inc., Morgan New York State Corpn., the Downtown-Lower Manhattan Asscn., Inc., The Peoples Symphony Concerts N.Y., Huntington Purchase Inc. N.Y.,

Société de Chimie Industrielle, Paris; mem. Advisory Cttee. Int. Nickel Ltd., London; Trustee Seaman's Bank for Savings, N.Y., Carleton Coll., Annuity Fund for Congregational Ministers, The Canadian-Amer. Cttee. of the Nat. Planning Asscn. Washington, the Private Planning Asscn. of Canada, Council of the Nat. Industrial Conf. Board, The Business Council, Washington; Trustee: Retirement Fund for lay workers.
Home: Lloyd Neck, Long Island, N.Y.; and 520 E. 86th Street, New York, N.Y. 10028; Office: 67 Wall Street, New York, N.Y. 10005, U.S.A.

Wingfield Digby, George; British museum curator and author; b. 2 March 1911; ed. Harrow, Trinity Coll., Cambridge, and Univs. of Grenoble and Paris.
Keeper, Dept. of Textiles, Victoria and Albert Museum 47-.
Publs. *French Tapestries* 51, *Work of the Modern Potter in England* 52, *Meaning and Symbol in Three Modern Artists* 55, *Symbol and Image in William Blake* 57, *Elizabethan Embroidery* 63; joint-author *History of the West Indian Peoples* (4 vols. for schools) 51-56, *The Bayeux Tapestry* 57.
Victoria and Albert Museum, London, S.W.7; and 72 Palace Gardens Terrace, London, W.8, England.

Winiarski, Bohdan, LL.D.; Polish international lawyer; b. 27 April 1884; ed. Warsaw, Cracow, Paris and Heidelberg.
Adviser to Polish Del., Peace Conf. 19-20; Prof. of Public Int. Law Poznań 22-; Dean of Faculty of Law 36-39; mem. of Polish Del. to Int. Confs. and Assemblies of L. of N.; mem. and Vice-Pres. Comm. of Communications and Transit, L. of N. 21-27; Pres. L. of N. Cttee. on Law of Inland Navigation 25; Commissary of the Govt. for Liquidation of German property 24-27; Deputy to the Diet 28-35; Pres. of Bank of Poland (London) 41-46; Judge of Int. Court of Justice 46-67, Pres. 61-64; corresp. mem. of Polish and foreign learned societies.
Publs. Author of nearly 50 publs. on Int. and Constitutional Law in Polish and French incl. *Les Institutions politiques en Pologne au XIXe siècle* 21, *Security, Arbitration, Disarmament* 28, *Principes généraux du Droit fluvial International* (Recueil de l'Académie du Droit International, The Hague) 34, *Textbook for the Study of Public International Law* 38, *International Law of Communications* 38, etc.
Grodziska 18, Poznań, Poland.
Telephone: Poznań 67-26-45.

Winiewicz, Józef; Polish diplomatist; b. 05; ed. Univ. of Poznań.
Journalist, Ed. of Polish newspaper *Dziennik Poznanski* until 39; Ed. of a Polish newspaper in Budapest 40; went to London to specialise in problems relating to preparations for the Peace Conf.; Counsellor of the Polish Embassy in London 45-47; mem. of Polish Del. to Paris Peace Conf. 46, and to U.N. Gen. Assemblies; Ambassador to United States 47-55; Deputy Foreign Minister 55-.
23 Aleja I Armii W.P., Warsaw, Poland.

Winkhaus, Hermann Heinrich, DR.ING.; German businessman; b. 14 March 1897; studied engineering and mining at university level.
Held various mining positions 24-34; mem. Board Mannesmannröhren-Werke A.G., Düsseldorf 35- and Deputy Chair. 42-; mem. Board Mannesmann A.G., Düsseldorf 52- and Chair. Board 57-62 Ritterkreuz des Hausordens von Hohenzollern; Grosses Verdienstkreuz.
Sybelstrasse 26, Düsseldorf 4, German Federal Republic.

Winkler, Paul; French (b. Hungarian) newspaper executive; b. 7 July 1898; ed. Lycée Luthérien, and Univ. of Budapest.
Director-General *Lectures pour tous*; Pres. Dir.-Gen.

Opera Mundi 28-; Pres. Press Alliance 40-45; Political Corresp. *Washington Post* 43-45, with 1st Army 44-45; Founder *Société Edi-Monde* with Librairie Hachette 47; Founder Union of Press Syndicates, Pres. 35-39; Chair. Advertising Cttee., Int. Fed. of the Periodical Press 67-; Chevalier Légion d'Honneur.
Publs. *The Thousand Year Conspiracy* 43, *Paris-Underground* 43, *Allemagne secrète* 46, *Les Sources mystiques des concepts moraux de l'Occident* 57.
100 avenue Raymond-Poincaré, Paris 16e; 23 avenue Foch, Paris 16e; Domaine du Pré, Chartrettes, S.-et-M., France.

Winkler, Wilhelm, DR. JUR.; Austrian statistician and demographer; b. 29 June 1884; ed. German Branch of Karl Ferdinands Univ., Prague.
Lecturer in Statistics, Univ. of Vienna 23; founder and fmr. Dir. Statistical Inst. of Univ. of Vienna; Chief Population Division, Bundesamt für Statistik 25-38; Extraordinary Prof. 29; Prof. 47-55, Emeritus 55-; Dean Faculty of Law and Social Sciences 50-51; Hon. Prof. Hochschule für Welthandel 48-; was retired from his professorship by the Nazi regime 38-45; Founder, Hon. Chair. Österreichische Statistische Gesellschaft; fmr. Vice-Pres. Int. Union for the Scientific Study of Population; Editor *Statistische Vierteljahresschrift* 48-58; Co-Editor *Metrika*; organiser of Int. Demographic Congress, Vienna 59; Hon. mem. Int. Statistical Inst., mem. Austrian Acad. of Sciences; Hon. Dr. Oec. Publ. Munich Univ. 59, Hon. Dr. Rer. Pol., Vienna Univ. 66.
Publs. *Statistische Verhältniszahlen* 23, *Die Einkommensverschiebungen in Oesterreich während des Weltkrieges* 30, *Grundriss der Statistik* (2 vols.) 31-33, *Der Geburtenrückgang in Oesterreich* 35, *Grundfragen der Oekonometrie* 51, *Typenlehre der Demographie* 52, *International Population Conference* 59, *Mehrsprachiges Demographisches Wörterbuch* 60, *Demometrie*.
Ghelengasse 30, 1130 Vienna, Austria.
Telephone: 82-77-542.

Winnacker, Karl, DR.ING.; German chemist; b. 21 Sept. 1903; ed. Brunswick and Darmstadt Technical Univs.
Honorary Prof. Frankfurt-am-Main Univ. 53-; Pres. (Gen. Man.) Farbwerke Hoechst A.G.; Pres. Advisory Board, Knapsack A.G., Kalle A.G., Wiesbaden-Biebrich, Duisburger Kupferhütte, Ruhrchemie A.G., Oberhausen-Holten, Wacker-Chemie G.m.b.H., Munich, Münchener Rückversicherungsges.; mem. Advisory Board, Dresdner Bank, Frankfurt-am-Main, DEMAG A.G., Duisburg, Degussa, Frankfurt (M), etc.; mem. industrial and scientific orgs.; Pres. Deutsches Atom-Forum e.V., Bonn, Verband der Chemischen Industrie e.V., Dechema; Dr. Rer. Nat. h.c. (Technische Hochschule, Brunswick and Mainz Univs.), Dr. Phil. h.c. (Marburg Univ.).
Farbwerke Hoechst A.G., 623 Frankfurt (Main)-Hoechst; and Oelmühlweg 31A, 624 Königstein (Taunus), German Federal Republic.
Telephone: Frankfurt 31-64-67 (Office).

Winsnes, Andreas Hofgaard, PH.D.; Norwegian literary historian; b. 25 Oct. 1889; ed. Oslo Cathedral School, and Oslo Univ.
Prof. of History of Ideas, Oslo Univ. 36-42, escaped from Oslo Aug. 42; Dir. British-Norwegian Inst. London 42-45; Prof. of the History of Ideas, Univ. of Oslo 46-54.
Publs. *Norske Selskap* 24, *Niels Treschow, an Educator to Humanity* 27, *Den Annen Front, British Idealists* 32, *History of Norwegian Literature 1880-1919* 37, *Ibsen kontra Nietzsche* (in *Samtiden*) 46, *Sigrid Undset: A Study in Christian Realism* 49, *A Study in Christian Philosophy, Jacques Maritain* 57.
Nordraaksgate 22, Oslo, Norway.

Winspeare Guicciardi, Vittorio, M.A.; Italian diplomatist; b. 19 Aug. 1912; ed. Bocconi Univ., Milan.
Secretary Italian Embassy, London 45-49; mem. Italian Del. Paris Peace Conf. 46-47; First Sec. Italian Embassy, Bonn 51-54; Consul-Gen., Berlin 54-58; Amb. to Ireland 61-66, Czechoslovakia 66-68; Under-Sec.-Gen. UN and Dir.-Gen. UN Office at Geneva July 68-; Gr. Uff. Al Merito della Repubblica Italiana; Hon. Commdr. R.V.O.; Officier Légion d'Honneur; Commdr. Order of George I (Greece); Verdienstkreuz der Bundesrepublik Deutschland and others.
United Nations, Palais des Nations, Geneva, Switzerland.

Winter, Auguste de; Belgian barrister and politician; b. 12 May 1925.
Barrister; mem. Chamber of Representatives 63-; Mayor of Grimbergen and Pres. of P.L.P. Fed. of Brussels 62-66; Minister for External Trade 66-68; Parti pour la liberté et le progrès (P.L.P.).
180 boulevard Guillaume Van Haelen, Brussels 19, Belgium.
Telephone: 02-44-91-65.

Winter, Eduard; German historian; b. 16 Sept. 1896; ed. Univs. of Innsbruck and Prague (German University).
Professor of Church History 34-39, Doz. History of Philosophy 35-45, German Univ. of Prague; Head of Dept. of Vienna Inst. of Arts and Sciences 45-47; Prof. of East European History Univ. of Halle 47-51 and Rector 48-51; Prof. East European History Humboldt Univ., Berlin 51; Dir. Inst. of History of the Peoples of the U.S.S.R., Humboldt Univ. 53, Emer. 64-; Editor *Quellen und Studien zur Geschichte Osteuropas, Beiträge zur Geschichte des religiösen und wissenschaftlichen Denkens*; co-Editor *Deutsche Literaturzeitung für Kritik der Internationalen Wissenschaften, Zeitschrift für Geschichtswissenschaft* and *Zeitschrift für Slawistik*; mem. German Acad. of Sciences, Prague 35-45; mem. Král česká společnost nauk, Prague 34-46, Deutsche Akad. der Wissenschaften, Berlin 55-, Int. Acad. of History of Science, Paris 63-; Nat. Prize 56.
Publs. Numerous books on East European History, *Russland und das Papsttum* 60, 61, *Der Josefinismus* 62, *Fruhhumanismns in Böhmen* 64, *Frühaufklärung in Mittelund Osteuropa* 66, *Frühliberalismus in Donaumonarchie* 68.
111 Berlin-Niederschonhausen, Strasse 201, Nr. 20, Germany.

Winters, Hon. Robert, B.A., B.SC.; Canadian engineer and politician; b. 18 Aug. 1910; ed. Mount Allison Univ., and Mass. Inst. of Technology.
With Northern Electric Co., Montreal 34; with Royal Canadian Ordnance Corps 42 and later with R.C.E.M.E. until 46; Minister of Reconstruction and Supply 48, of Resources and Development 50-53, of Public Works 53-57, of Trade and Commerce 66-68; Pres. Brazilian Power and Light Co. 68-; Pres. Rio Algom Mines Ltd., etc.; Chair. British-Newfoundland Corpn.; Hon. LL.D. (Mount Allison Univ., Western New England Coll.), Hon. D.Eng. (Nova Scotia Technical Coll.), Hon. D.Sc. (Univ. of New Brunswick); Chair. Board of Trustees, York Univ., Toronto; mem. Corpn. of M.I.T.
431 Russell Hill Road, Toronto, Ontario, Canada.

Wintour, Charles Vere, M.A.; British journalist; b. 18 May 1917; ed. Oundle School, and Peterhouse, Cambridge Univ.
Royal Norfolk Regiment 40, G.S.O. Headquarters, Chief of Staff to Supreme Allied Commdr. (designate) and SHAEF (despatches); *Evening Standard* 46, Political Ed. 52; Asst. Ed. *Sunday Express* 52-54; Dep. Ed. *Evening Standard* 54-57; Man. Ed. *Daily Express* 57-59; Ed. *Evening Standard* 59-; Dir. Beaverbrook News-

papers 64-; Croix de Guerre 45; Bronze Star (U.S.) 45. *Evening Standard*, 47 Shoe Lane, London, E.C.4; and 9 Phillimore Gardens, London, W.8, England.

Winzer, Otto; German politician; b. 3 April 1902; ed. primary school, and school of printing.
Former compositor; mem. Kommunistische Partei Deutschlands (K.P.D.) 25-45, Sozialistische Einheitspartei Deutschlands (S.E.D.) 45-; emigrated to France, Holland and U.S.S.R. 35-45; returned to Germany 45; Municipal Councillor for Popular Education, Greater Berlin 45-46; mem. All-Berlin City Council of Deputies 46-49; mem. Exec. Cttee. and Central Cttee. S.E.D. 46-; Chief Editor *Neues Deutschland* 49; Sec. of State and Chief of Private Office of President of German Democratic Republic (D.D.R.) 49-56; mem. Volkskammer 50-; First Dep. Minister and Sec. of State, Ministry of Foreign Affairs 56-65; Minister of Foreign Affairs June 65-; Vaterländischer Verdienstorden in Gold 55, Verdienstmedaille der D.D.R. 59, Orden Banner der Arbeit 60, Karl-Marx Orden 62.
Ministerium für Auswärtige Angelegenheiten, Berlin, Germany.

Wiriath, Marcel Georges; French banker; b. 19 Nov. 1898; ed. Lycée Janson-de-Sailly, and Univ. de Paris à la Sorbonne.
Former Vice-Pres. Crédit Lyonnais, Pres. 62-; Dir. Soc. des Téléphones Erickson, Cie. des forges de Châtillon-Commentry et Neuves-Maisons, and Soc. française des Nouvelles Galeries Réunies; Officier Légion d'Honneur, Médaille Militaire, Croix de Guerre 14-18.
19 boulevard des Italiens, Paris 2e; and 7 rue Le Tasse, Paris 16e, France.

Wirkkala, Tapio; Finnish designer; b. 2 June 1915; ed. Industrial Art Inst., Helsinki.
Art Director, Industrial Art Inst. 51-54; designed interior, Finnish Pavilion, Brussels World Fair 58; Smithsonian Inst. Travelling Museum Exhibition in U.S. 56-58; seven Grande Premios in Triennales; four prizes for designing Olympic Games stamps 52; Italian President's Gold Medallion, Int. Ceramic Competition, Faenza 63 and many other awards.
A-Studio, A.Ahlstrom Osakeyhtio, Vilhonkatu 4b, Helsinki, Finland.

Wirtz, William Willard, A.B., LL.B.; American lawyer and government official; b. 14 March 1912; ed. Univ. of California (Berkeley), Beloit Coll., and Harvard Law School.
Teacher 33-39; Assistant Prof. School of Law, Northwestern Univ. 39-42; Asst. Gen. Counsel, Board of Econ. Warfare 42-43; served War Labor Board 43-45; Chair. Nat. Wage Stabilization Board 46; Prof. of Law, Northwestern Univ. 46-54; law practice 55-61; Under-Sec. of Labor 61-62, Sec. of Labor 62-; Hon. degrees from Michigan, Rhode Island, Northwestern, Yeshiva, and Roosevelt Univs. and Amherst, Monmouth Colls.; Democrat.
Department of Labor, Washington 25, D.C., U.S.A.

Wischnewski, Hans-Jürgen; German politician; b. 24 July 1922.
Served German Forces 40-45; worked in metal industry after war; mem. Social Democrat Party 46-; Sec. Metal Workers' Union, Cologne 52; mem. Bundestag 57-; Chair. Young Socialists 60; Fed. Minister for Econ. Co-operation 66-.
Bundesministerium für Entwicklungshilfe, Bonn, German Federal Republic.

Wise, George S.; American (b. Russian) university professor; b. 06; ed. Columbia Univ.
Former lecturer in Sociology at Columbia Univ. and Univ. of Mexico; business interests in U.S.A., Mexico and Israel; Pres. Tel Aviv Univ. 63-.
Tel Aviv University, 155 Herzl Street, Tel Aviv, Israel.

Wishart, Paul Barclay, B.S.; American business executive; b. 25 Sept. 1898; ed. U.S. Naval Acad.
In U.S. Navy 17-23; Dir. of Regions, Packard Motor Car Co., Detroit 23-32; joined War Materials Div., Minneapolis-Honeywell Regulator Co. (later Honeywell Inc.) 42, Asst. to Vice-Pres. (Mfg.) 43, Supt. of Mfg. 43-45, Factory Man. 45, Vice-Pres. (Minneapolis Mfg.) 45-52, Vice-Pres., Gen. Man., Dir. 52, Pres. 53-, Chair. of Board and Chief Exec. Officer Honeywell Inc. 61-65, Chair. Finance Cttee. 65-.
3100 Forest Lane, Minnetonka, Minnesota 55343, U.S.A.

Wiskemann, Elizabeth, M.A., M.LITT.; British writer; ed. Newnham Coll. Cambridge.
Fmr. research worker and Tutor in Modern European History, Cambridge Univ.; contrib. on German, Central, South and East European Affairs 32- to *Spectator*, *Economist*, *New Statesman and Nation*, *Fortnightly Review*, *Scotsman*, etc., and *Foreign Affairs*, *Nation*, *New York Herald Tribune*, *Geographical Review*, etc.; Asst. Press Attaché, British Legation, Berne 41-45; contributor to *The Times*, *Manchester Guardian* (now *The Guardian*), *Listener*, *Economist* 45-; Montague Burton Prof. Int. Relations, Edinburgh Univ. 58-61; Tutor in Modern European History, Univ. of Sussex 61-64; Hon. D.Litt. (Oxford).
Publs. *Czechs and Germans* 38 (2nd edn. 67), *Undeclared War* 39 (2nd edn. 67), *Italy* (*World To-day* Series 47, *The Rome-Berlin Axis* 49 (2nd edn. 66), *Central and South-East Europe 1945-48* (part author) 50, *Hitler's Europe* (part author) 54, *Germany's Eastern Neighbours* 56, *A Great Swiss Newspaper* 59, *Europe of the Dictators* 66, *The Europe I Saw*.
41 Moore Street, London, S.W.3, England.
Telephone: 01-589-2560.

Wistrand, Karl, B.C.L.; Swedish politician; b. 9 April 1889; ed. Uppsala Univ.
Fmr. Judge; mem. Stockholm County Council 31-37; mem. L.N. Sub-Cttee. for Iron and Steel Statistics 34-36; Man. Dir. Employers' Asscns. of Iron and Steel and Mining Industries 20-36; Sec. Iron Works Commercial Asscn. 20-38; Del. to many Int. Labour Confs. and L.N. Assembly 38; mem., Labour Court 29-49, 1st Chamber 37-53; Pres. Board State Hospitals in Stockholm 41-59; mem. State Cttee. on Admin. Control 42-53, Vice-Pres. 50-53; Pres. State Cttee. on Nat. Expenditure 45; mem. Cttee. for the Univs. 45-50; Pres. of the Swedish Council of the European Movement 49-61, Hon. Pres. 65-; mem. Consultative Ass. Council of Europe 49-59; Chair. Museum of Medical History 52-62; Comm. for non-represented Countries 53-59; Chair. Soc. Belgo-Suédoise 56-61; mem. W. European Advisory Cttee. 54-66, Royal Science Asscn. (Uppsala); Dr. med. h.c.
Publ. *Hört och Upplevat* (memoirs) 62.
Karlbergsvägen 40, Stockholm, Sweden.
Telephone: 32-65-63.

Withalm, Hermann, D.IUR.; Austrian lawyer and politician; b. 12; ed. Gymnasium, Kalksburg, and Univ. of Vienna.
Legal Practice, Poysdorf 36-38, dismissed on political grounds 38; Lawyer, State Autobahns 38-42; Military Service 42-45; Legal Practice, Vienna and Wolkersdorf 47; District Leader, Austrian People's Party 52; elected to Nat. Assembly 53; Econ. Rep. for Manhartsberg District 56-59; State Sec., Federal Ministry of Finance 56-59; Gen. Sec. Austrian People's Party 60-; Vice-Chancellor without Portfolio 68-; several decorations.
Bahnallee 14, Wolkersdorf am Russbach, Lower Austria, Austria.

Witkon, Alfred, DR.JUR.; Israeli judge; b. 23 Feb. 1910; ed. Univs. of Bonn, Berlin and Freiburg, and Middle Temple, London.
Called to Middle Temple Bar 36, to Palestine Bar 37;

practised law, Palestine 37-48; Pres. District Court, Jerusalem 48-54; Justice Supreme Court of Israel 54-; Lecturer, Hebrew Univ. 53-.
Publs. *Law and Society* 55, *Law of Taxation* 66, *Law and Politics* 65.
17 Shmarjahu Levin Street, Jerusalem, Israel.
Telephone: 35828.

Witkowski, Józef, PH.D., D.SC.; Polish astronomer; b. 21 Feb. 1892; ed. Odessa Univ.
Assistant, Odessa Observatory 18 and Cracow Observatory 19; Dir. Poznań Observatory; Prof. of Astronomy Poznań Univ. 29-67; Visiting Prof. Univ. of Algiers 65-66; fmr. Dean, Faculty of Sciences; fmr. Dir. Astronomical Inst. and Latitude Recording Station, Acad. of Sciences; Hon. Editor *Acta Astronomica*; Editor *Bulletin de la Société des Sciences de Poznań*; fmr. Pres. Polish Nat. Cttee. Geodesy and Geophysics; mem. Int. Astronomical Union; mem. Astronomical and Geodetic Cttee., Polish Acad. of Sciences; F.R.A.S. (U.K.).
12 Hevelius Street, Poznań, Poland.

Witteveen, Hendrikus Johannes; Netherlands economist and politician; b. 12 June 1921; ed. Netherlands School of Economics, Rotterdam.
Netherlands Central Planning Office 45-46; Lecturer, Netherlands School of Econs., Rotterdam 46-48, Prof. of Business Cycles and Econs. 48-63, Extraordinary Prof. 65-; mem. Parl. (First Chamber) 58-63, Second Chamber 65-; Minister of Finance 63-65, April 67-, also First Deputy Prime Minister April 67-; Liberal.
9 Nassaulaan, Wassenaar 2.H, Netherlands.

Wittig, Georg, DR.PHIL.; German chemist; b. 16 June 1897; ed. Wilhelms-Gymnasium, Kassel and Marburg Univ.
Dozent, Marburg Univ. 26-32; Head of Dept. Technische Hochschule, Brunswick 32-37; Special Prof. Univ. of Freiburg/Br. 37; Prof. and Inst. Dir. Tübingen Univ. 44-56; Prof. Heidelberg Univ. 56-; Baeyer Medal 53; mem. Acad. of Sciences, Munich and Heidelberg, Sociedad Química del Peru, Leopoldina Halle; hon. mem. Swiss Chemistry Asscn., New York Acad. of Sciences, Chemical Soc. (London); Dannie-Heineman-Preis 65; Otto Hahn Prize 67; Hon. Dr. of Sorbonne; Hon. Dr. Rer. Nat. (Univs. of Tübingen and Hamburg).
Publ. *Textbook on Stereochemistry* 30.
Bergstrasse 35, 69 Heidelberg, German Federal Republic.
Telephone: 40945.

Wittkower, Rudolf, PH.D.; British art historian; b. 22 June 1901; ed. Univs. of Munich and Berlin.
Member Bibliotheca Hertziana, Rome 23-33; Lecturer, Cologne Univ. 32-33; mem. Warburg Inst., London 34-56; Reader, Univ. of London 45-49, Prof. 49-56; Prof. and Chair., Dept. of Art History and Archaeology, Columbia Univ., New York 56-68, Avalon Prof. in the Humanities 68-; Hon. Fellow Max-Planck-Gesellschaft, Warburg Inst., London, Accademia di Belle Arti, Venice, Royal Inst. of British Architects (U.K.); Fellow British Acad., American Acad. of Arts and Sciences, Accad. dei Lincei; co-Editor *Journal of Warburg and Courtauld Institute* 37-56, *Studies in Architecture* 58-; Editor *Columbia Univ. Studies in Art and Archaeology* 64; Serena Medal, British Acad. 57; Sir Banister Fletcher Prize 61.
Publs. *Michelangelo-Bibliographie* 27, *Die Zeichnungen des G. L. Bernini* 31, *British Art and the Mediterranean* 48, *Architectural Principles in the Age of Humanism* 49, *The Drawings of the Carracci* 52, *Gian Lorenzo Bernini* 55, *Art and Architecture in Italy 1600-1750* 58, *Born under Saturn* 63, *The Divine Michelangelo* 64, *La cupola di San Pietro* 64.
25 Claremont Ave, New York, N.Y. 10027, U.S.A.

Wittkowski, Margarete; German politician; b. 18 Aug. 1910; ed. Univs. of Berlin and Basle.
Economic Editor, Central Planning Office, Ministry of Planning 46, later Head of Central Planning Office; Pres. Union of German Co-operative Socs. 52; Dep. Chair. State Planning Comm. 54-61; Dep. Chair. Council of Ministers, German Democratic Republic 61-.
Klosterstrasse 47, Berlin C2, Germany.

Wodak, Walter; Austrian diplomatist; b. 22 Nov. 1908; ed. Univ. of Vienna.
Labour and Press Attaché, Austrian Legation, London 46-48, First Sec. and Chargé d'Affaires 48-51; Counsellor and Chargé d'Affaires, Austrian Legation, Paris 51-53; Minister, later Ambassador to Yugoslavia 53-59; Head of Political Dept., Ministry of Foreign Affairs, Vienna 59-62; Consultant, Arbeiterbank A.G., Vienna 62-63; Head of Personnel and Administration Dept., Ministry of Foreign Affairs, Vienna 63-64; Ambassador to U.S.S.R. 64-; several decorations.
Austrian Embassy, 1 Starokonyushenny Pereulok, Moscow G-34, U.S.S.R.

Wodehouse, Pelham Grenville, HON. LITT.D. (Oxon.); American (b. British) writer and humorist; b. 15 Oct. 1881; ed. Dulwich Coll.
Began as a writer of school tales, such as *A Perfect Uncle, Tales of St. Augustin's, The Head of Kay's*; then specialised on stories of Psmith and Jeeves; part-author and writer of lyrics, many musical comedies.
Publs. incl. *Psmith in the City, Psmith Journalist, Leave it to Psmith, The Inimitable Jeeves, Carry on Jeeves, My Man Jeeves, Mr. Mulliner Speaking, Summer Lightning* (also film), *Young Men in Spats, Laughing Gas, Summer Moonshine, Uncle Fred in the Springtime, Eggs, Beans and Crumpets, Uncle Dynamite, Mating Season, The Performing Flea, Jeeves and the Feudal Spirit, French Leave, Something Fishy, Over Seventy* (autobiography), *Cocktail Time, A Few Quick Ones, Nothing Serious* 51, *Old Reliable* 51, *Angel Cake* 52, *America, I Like You* 56, *Jeeves in the Offing* 60, *Ice in the Bedroom* 61, *Service with a Smile* 62, *Stiff Upper Lip, Jeeves* 63, *Biffen's Millions* 64, *Frozen Assets* 64, *Galahad at Blandings* 65, *Plum Pie* 66, *The Purloined Paperweight* 67, *Company for Henry* 67.
c/o Herbert Jenkins Ltd., 2 Clement's Inn, London, W.C.2, England.

Woerdeman, Martinus Willem, M.D., D.SC., PH.D.; Netherlands university professor (Emer.); b. 92; ed. Univ. of Amsterdam.
Asst. in Anatomy and Histology, Univ. of Amsterdam 14-18, Lecturer in Histology 18-25, Prof. of Histology 25-26; Prof. of Anatomy and Embryology, Univ. of Groningen 26-31; Prof. of Anatomy and Embryology and Head of Dept. of Anatomy, Univ. of Amsterdam 31-62, Dean of Faculty of Medicine 46-50; Rector of Univ. 45-46; Pres. Royal Neths. Acad. of Sciences 53-60; Pres. Univ. of Amsterdam 53-59; Chief Editor *Excerpta Medica* and *Acta morphologica neerlando-scandinavica*; foreign mem. Royal Swedish Acad. Sciences, Royal Flemish Acad. of Medicine, Nat. Acad. of Sciences, Mexico; Swammerdam Medal 50; Commdr. Order of Orange Nassau; Knight Order of Neths. Lion; Officier de la Légion d'Honneur; Knight Order of St. Sava; Hon. D.Sc. (Oxford) 50, Hon. Ph.D. (S. Africa) 59.
Publs. *Atlas of Human Anatomy* 48, *Nomina anatomica Parisiensia* 57.
10 Botticellistr., Amsterdam NW. Z, Netherlands.
Telephone: 020-723700.

Wøhni, Einar Joakim; Norwegian agronomist and politician; b. 20; ed. State Training Coll. for Teachers in Smallholders' Schools.
Worked for seven years as a County Adviser and subsequently as a teacher in an agricultural school; mem.

of Kvaefjord County Board; Chair. Sør-Troms Labour Party 58-60; mem. Country Board, Norwegian Labour Party 57-60; Minister of Agriculture 60-63.
Akersgt. 42, Oslo, Norway.

Wojtyła, H.E. Cardinal Karol; Polish ecclesiastic; b. 18 May 1920.
Ordained Priest 46; fmr. Prof. of Moral Theology at Univs. of Cracow and Lublin; Archbishop of Cracow 64-; cr. Cardinal by Pope Paul VI 67.
Ul. Franciszkánska 3, Cracow 2, Poland.

Wold, Herman O. A., D.SC.; Swedish university professor; b. 25 Dec. 1908; ed. Univ. of Stockholm.
Professor of Statistics, Univ. of Uppsala 42-; Fellow Inst. Mathematical Statistics 46; Vice-Pres. Int. Inst. of Statistics 57-61; Fellow American Statistical Asscn. 51, Swedish Acad. Sciences 60; Pres. Econometric Soc. 66; Hon. Fellow Royal Statistical Soc. (U.K.) 61; Hon. Dr. Univ. of Lisbon.
Publs. *A Study in the Analysis of Stationary Time Series* 38, *Demand Analysis* 52 (Several translations), *Econometric Model Building: Essays on the Causal Chain Approach* (co-author) 64, *Bibliography on Time Series and Stochastic Processes* (Editor) 65, *Model Building in the Human Sciences* (co-author) 66, *Nonlinear estimation by iterative least square procedures* 66, *Forecasting on a Scientific Basis* (co-author) 67.
University Institute of Statistics, Sturegatan 2, Uppsala; and Vasagatan 1c, Uppsala, Sweden.

Wold, Terje; Norwegian judge; b. 23 Aug. 1899; ed. Univ. of Oslo.
Police officer; lawyer 22-36; Judge Court of Appeal 36-39; Minister of Justice 39-45; Judge, Supreme Court of Norway 45-, Pres. 58-; Mem. of Parliament and Pres. of Foreign Affairs Cttee. 45-49; Norwegian Del. to UN 45-49; Mem. Commission on War Crimes at London 45-46; mem. Norwegian del. to the Peace Conf. Paris 46; Del. Assembly of Council of Europe at Strasbourg 49; Chair. of Cttee. of Admin. Procedure 51-58; elected to European Court of Human Rights 59-; Pres. Norwegian Council of European Movement 56-65; Vice-Chair. for Europe World Asscn. of Judges; Hon. mem. World Peace Through Law Center; Commdr. with Star Order of St. Olav; mem. Int. Comm. of Jurists.
The Supreme Court, Grubbegt I, Oslo I; Gregers Grams vei 17, Oslo 3, Norway.
Telephone: 47-2-243137 (Home).

Wolf, Pierre-René; French writer and journalist; b. 19 Feb. 1899; ed. Lycée Corneille, Rouen, and Univs. of Rouen and Paris.
Has contributed to various literary periodicals; Man. Dir. and editorial writer of *Paris-Normandie*, Rouen; Pres. Syndicat des Quotidiens Régionaux; Officier de la Légion d'Honneur.
Publs. *Vous qui l'avez Connue, L'Homme au Bois Dormant, Marfa, Le Sac d'Or, Martin Roumagnac, A Leur Mesure, Rouen, Poèmes d'Exil.*
19 place du Général de Gaulle, Rouen, France.

Wolfbein, Seymour Louis; American government official; b. 8 Nov. 1915; ed. Brooklyn Coll., and Columbia Univ.
Research Assoc. U.S. Senate Comm. on Unemployment and Relief 38; Economist, Research Div., Works Project Admin. 39-42; Economist, Bureau of Labor Statistics, Dept. of Labor 42-45, Head, Occupational Outlook Div. 46-49, Head, Manpower and Productivity Div. 49-50, Manpower and Employment Div. 50-59, Dep. Asst. Sec. of Labor 59-62, Dir. Office of Manpower, Automation and Training 62-65, Economic Adviser to Secretary of Labor 65-; Visiting Prof. Univ. of Michigan 50-; Adjunct Prof. American Univ. 51-; Dean, School of Business Admin., Temple Univ. 67-; Distinguished Service Award, Dept. of Labor 55 and 61.

Publs. *Decline of a Cotton Textile City* 42, *The World of Work* 51, *Employment and Unemployment in the U.S.* 64, *Employment, Unemployment and Public Policy* 65.
Temple University, Philadelphia, Pa.; 6305 Crathie Lane, Washington 16, D.C., U.S.A.
Telephone: OLiver 2-2061 (Home).

Wolfenden, Sir John Frederick, C.B.E.; British educationist; b. 26 June 1906; ed. Wakefield School, and Queen's Coll., Oxford.
Henry Davison Scholar, Princeton Univ. 28-29; Fellow, Tutor in Philosophy, Magdalen Coll., Oxford 29-34; Headmaster Uppingham School 34-44; Dir. Air Training Corps 41; Headmaster Shrewsbury School 44-50; Vice-Chancellor Reading Univ. 50-63; Chair. Univ. Grants Cttee. 63-68; Dir.-designate British Museum (Oct. 68).
Publs. *The Approach to Philosophy* 32, *The Public Schools Today* 49, *How to Choose Your School* 52.
14 Park Crescent, London, W.1, England.

Wolfers, Arnold Oscar, J.U.D., PH.D.; American university professor; b. 14 June 1892; ed. Univs. of Lausanne, Munich, Berlin, Zürich and Giessen.
Practice of Law, St. Gallen, Switzerland 17-19; Lecturer, Univ. of Berlin 29-33; Dir. Hochschule für Politik, Berlin 30-33; Prof. Int. Relations, Yale Univ. 33, Sterling Prof. Emeritus 57; Research Assoc. (fmrly. Dir.) Johns Hopkins Washington Center Foreign Policy Research 57-; Special Adviser and Lecturer, School of Mil. Govt., Charlottesville, Va. 42-44; mem. of Faculty, Nat. War Coll., Washington, D.C. 47; Consultant, Dept. of State 60-, Dept. of the Army 60-.
Publs. *Die Verwaltungsorgane der Aktiengesellschaft* 17, *Amerikanische und Deutsche Loehne* 30, *Das Kartellproblem* 31, *Britain and France between Two Wars* 40, *The Anglo-American Tradition in Foreign Affairs* (with L. Martin) 56, ed. *Alliance Policy in the Cold War* 59, *Discord and Collaboration* 62.
1740 Massachusetts Avenue, N.W., Washington, D.C. 20036, U.S.A.

Wolff, Etienne Charles, PH.D.; French embryologist; b. 12 Feb. 1904; ed. Univ. de Strasbourg.
Assistant at Biological Laboratory of Wimereux, Univ. of Paris 27-28; Asst. at Medical Faculty, Univ. of Strasbourg 33-37; Assoc. Prof. of Biology, Univ. of Strasbourg 37-42, Prof. of Zoology and Embryology 42-55; Prof. Collège de France 55-, Pres. Admin., Coll. de France; Dir. Inst. of Embryology and Teratology, Centre Nat. de Recherche Scientifique; Dir. Laboratory of Embryology, Ecole Pratique des Hautes Etudes, Paris; mem. Acad. des Sciences, Acad. Nat. de Médecine; Assoc. mem. Acad. Royale de Belgique; Foreign mem. Royal Swedish Acad. of Sciences; Officier Légion d'Honneur; Commdr. de l'Ordre Nat. du Mérite; Commdr. des Palmes Académiques; Prix de l'Institut de France; Dr. h.c. (Univs. of Ghent, Louvain and Geneva).
Publs. *Les Changements de Sexe* 46, *La Science des Monstres* 48, *Les Chemins de la Vie* 64.
49 bis, avenue de la Belle-Gabrielle, 94-Nogent-sur-Marne, France.

Wolff von Amerongen, Otto; German industrialist; b. 6 Aug. 1918.
President Otto Wolff A.G.; Chair., Deputy Chair. or mem. Board of Dirs. of 16 industrial or insurance companies; Chair. Ost-Ausschuss der Deutschen Wirtschaft; Pres. German Group Int. Chamber of Commerce, Cologne Chamber of Commerce.
Marienburger Strasse 19, Marienburg, Cologne; and Zeughausstrasse 2, Cologne, German Federal Republic.
Telephone: Cologne 20411.

Wolfson, Sir Isaac (father of Leonard Wolfson, *q.v.*), Bart., F.R.S.; British businessman; b. 17 Sept. 1897; ed. Queen's Park School, Glasgow.

Joined The Great Universal Stores Ltd. 32, Man. Dir. 34-, Chair. 46-; Chair. Anglo-Portuguese Bank 66-; Pres. United Synagogue; mem. Worshipful Company of Pattenmakers, Grand Council British Empire Cancer Campaign; Hon. Pres. Weizmann Inst. of Science Foundation; Trustee Religious Centre, Jerusalem; Founder and Trustee the Wolfson Foundation, created 55, mainly for the advancement of health, education and youth activities in the U.K. and British Commonwealth; Einstein Award for Philanthropy 67; Lehmann Award 68; Hon. Fellow Weizmann Inst. of Science, Israel; Hon. LL.D. (London, Glasgow, Cambridge and Manchester), Hon. F.R.C.P., Hon. D.C.L. (Oxford), Hon. Fellow St. Edmund Hall, Oxford.
74 Portland Place, London, W.1, England.
Telephone: 01-580-6441.

Wolfson, Leonard G. (son of Sir Isaac Wolfson, *q.v.*); British retail executive; b. 1927; ed. Malvern Coll.
Director Great Universal Stores Ltd. 52- (in charge of Group organization and merchandise planning), Joint Man. Dir. 63-; Founder, Trustee and Deputy Chair. Wolfson Foundation; Hon. Pres. Council, Weizmann Inst. Science Foundation; Man. Solomon Wolfson School; Chief Warden Central Synagogue (London); Hon. Fellow St. Catherine's Coll., Oxford; Fellow Royal Geographical Soc.; mem. M.C.C., Pattenmakers Co.
Office: Universal House, 251/256 Tottenham Court Road, London, W.1, England.

Wolfson, Louis Elwood; American industrialist; b. 28 Jan. 1912; ed. Univ. of Georgia.
With M. Wolfson and Co. 34; officer and Dir. Fla. Pipe and Supply Co. Inc., Jacksonville, Fla. 34-49, M L and S Corpn., real estate and investments 46-56; Pres. Southern Pipe and Supply Co., Orlando, Fla. 48-57; controlling stockholder Tampa Shipbuilding Co. Inc., Fla. 45-58; Chair. of Bd. Merritt-Chapman and Scott Corpn., N.Y.C. 51-, and Pres. 53-59; Chair. of Board N.Y. Shipbuilding Corpn., Camden, N.J. 53-61, Chair. Exec. Cttee. 61-; Chair. of Board Capital Transit Co., Washington 51-56, Newport Steel Corpn. (Ky.) 54-56; Dir. Montgomery Ward and Co. 55-56, Revday Industries Inc. 65-; Dir. Ga. Student Educational Fund Inc., Boys Estate, Brunswick, Ga.; co-Trustee Wolfson Family Foundation Inc.; mem. Board of Govs. Eleanor Roosevelt Cancer Foundation Cttee. to Advance World Wide Fight against Cancer, American Cancer Soc., mem. Nat. Conf. Christians and Jews, Acad. of Political Science, Nat. Advisory Council, Synagogue Council of America, Economic Club of New York.
Home: 6466 North Bay Road, Miami Beach, Fla.; Office: P.O. Box 4, Jacksonville, Fla., U.S.A.

Wolniak, Zygfryd L.; Polish diplomatist; b. 22; ed. Inst. for Diplomatic and Consular Studies, Acad. of Political Sciences, Warsaw.
Served in Polish underground movement, Second World War; Ministry of Foreign Affairs 46-49; Consul, Montreal, Ottawa and Tel Aviv 49-54; Envoy to Israel 54; Commr. Int. Control Comm. in Indo-China 55-56; Ambassador to Burma and Cambodia 56-59; Dir. Afro-Asian Dept., Foreign Ministry 59-61; Ambassador to Canada 61-.
Polish Embassy, Ottawa, Canada; and Ministry of Foreign Affairs, Warsaw, Poland.

Wołoszin, Stefan, D.PHIL.; Polish professor; b. 19 Aug. 1911; ed. Uniwersytet Jagiellonski and Uniwersytet Mikałaja Kopernika w. Toroniu.
College teacher, Vilnius 35-41; Dir. Pedagogical Lyceum, Białystok 45-46; Research worker, Nicholas Copernicus Univ., Toruń 46-50; Head, Chair of Pedagogy, Adam Mickiewicz Univ., Poznań 50-53; Prof. Faculty of Gen. Pedagogy, Univ. of Warsaw 53-;

Prof. of Pedagogy, Acad. of Physical Educ., Warsaw 53-, Rector 60-; mem. Cttee. of Pedagogical and Psychological Sciences, Polish Acad. of Sciences 52-, Central Cttee. of Physical Culture and Tourism 60-, Supreme Council of Higher Educ. 66-.
Publs. Articles on education.
ul. Koszykowa 75 m. 16, Warsaw, Poland.

Wolters, Baron Laurent; Belgian oil executive; b. 24 July 1901.
Chairman and Managing Director of Petrofina; Dir. American Petrofina, Canadian Petrofina, Finapetro, Palmafina, Petrofina (Gt. Britain), Purfina, Purfina Française, Purfina Nederland, Socal, Socotole; Chair. Société Industrielle Belge des Pétroles, Petrocongo; Officier de l'Ordre de Léopold, Officier de l'Ordre de la Couronne, Médaille de la Résistance, Croix de guerre.
Château "Le Bisdom", Overijse (Brabant), Belgium.

Wong Lin Ken; Singapore historian and diplomatist; b. 31 July 1931; ed. Univ. of Malaya and Univ. of London.
Former Senior Lecturer in History, Univ. of Singapore; mem. Editorial Board *Journal of S.E. Asian History* 60-64; Editor *Journal of the South Seas Soc.* 59-60; Chair. Adult Educ. Board 64-67; Perm. Rep. to UN 67-.
Publs. *A Study of the Trade of Singapore 1819-1869* 60, *The Malayan Tin Industry to 1914* 65.
Permanent Mission of Singapore to the United Nations, 711 Third Avenue, 11th Floor, New York, N.Y. 10017, U.S.A.

Wontner, Hugh Walter Kingwell, M.V.O.; British hotelier; b. 22 Oct. 1908; ed. Oundle, and in France.
Mem. Secretarial Staff of London Chamber of Commerce 27-33; Gen. Sec. Hotels and Restaurants Asscn. of Great Britain 33-38; Sec. Coronation Accommodation Cttee. 36-37; Asst. to Sir George Reeves-Smith at the Savoy Hotel 38-41; Dir. of the Savoy, Claridge's and Berkeley Hotels, London 40, Man. Dir. 41-, Chair. 48-; Chair. Savoy Theatre Ltd.; Trustee D'Oyly Carte Opera Trust; Chair. Exec. Cttee. British Hotels and Restaurants Asscn. 57-59; Pres. Int. Hotel Asscn. 62-65; Chair. Nutrition Cttee., Univ. Coll. Hospital 45-52; mem. Lloyds 37-; mem. of Board British Travel and Holidays Asscn.; Chair. Coronation Accommodation Cttee. 52-53, Historic Houses Cttee. 65-; Master Worshipful Co. of Feltmakers 62; Clerk of Royal Kitchens 53-; Alderman of City of London 63.
1 Savoy Hill, London, W.C.2; and Hedsor Priory, Buckinghamshire, England.

Wood, Lee Blair, B.A.; American newspaper editor; b. 7 March 1893; ed. Corry High School, and Amherst Coll.
Reporter *Cleveland Leader* 16-17; Telegraph Ed. Cleveland Press 20-22, Night Ed. 23-24, News Ed. 24-25; Man. Ed. *Oklahoma News* 25-27; News Ed. *New York Telegram* (now *World Journal Tribune*) 27-28, Man. Editor 29-30 (*New York World-Telegram and The Sun*), Exec. Editor 31-60, Editor 60-62, Pres. 62-65.
Home: Downtown Athletic Club, 19 West Street, New York, N.Y.; Route 2, Ridgefield, Conn.; Office: c/o Scripps-Howard Newspapers, 200 Park Avenue, New York City 17, N.Y., U.S.A.

Wood, Rt. Hon. Richard Frederick, P.C., M.P.; British politician; b. 5 Oct. 1920; ed. Eton and New Coll., Oxford.
Attaché, British Embassy, Rome 40; served army 39-45; M.P. 50-; Parl. Private Sec. to Minister of Pensions 51-53, to Minister of State, Board of Trade 53-54, to Minister of Agriculture and Fisheries 54-55; Joint Parl. Sec., Ministry of Pensions and Nat. Insurance 55-58; Parl. Sec., Ministry of Labour 58-59; Minister of

Power 59-63, of Pensions and Nat. Ins. 63-64; Dir. Hargreaves (West Riding) 65-; Hon. Col., Queen's Royal Rifles; Hon. LL.D. Sheffield Univ.
Flat Top House, Bishop Wilton, York; and 14 Eaton Place, London S.W.1, England.

Woodbury, Peter, B.S., LL.B.; American judge; b. 24 Oct. 1899; ed. Phillips Exeter Acad., Harvard Coll., and Law School.
Served in U.S. Infantry, A.E.F. 18; Selectman, Bedford, N.H. 28-30; Justice, Bedford Municipal Court 28-32; Assoc. Justice, New Hampshire Superior Court 32-33, N.H. Supreme Court 33-41; Judge U.S. Court of Appeals for the First Circuit 41-64, Chief Judge 59-64, Senior Circuit Judge 64-; Fellow American Acad. of Arts and Sciences.
3 Pilgrim Drive, Bedford, New Hampshire 03102, U.S.A.

Woodcock, Rt. Hon. George, P.C., C.B.E.; British trade union official; b. 20 Oct. 1904; ed. Ruskin Coll., and New Coll., Oxford.
Cotton weaver 16-29; Sec. T.U.C. Research and Economic Dept. 36-47; Asst. Gen. Sec. T.U.C. 47-60, Gen. Sec. 60-; mem. cttee. on taxation of trading profits 45-51; mem. cttee. on taxation treatment of retirement provisions 50-54; mem. Royal Comm. on taxation of profits and income 51-55; mem. British Guiana Constitutional Comm. 54; mem. cttee. on working of the monetary system 57-59; Vice-Chair. Nat. Savings Cttee. 52-; Gov. Admin. Staff Coll. 57-; Vice-Pres. ICFTU 60; mem. Nat. Econ. Development Council (N.E.D.C.) 62-; Royal Comm. on Trade Unions and Employers' Asscns. 65-68; mem. B.B.C. Gen. Advisory Cttee.; Hon. LL.D. (Univ. of Sussex 63, Univ. of Manchester 68); Hon. D.C.L. (Oxford) 63; Hon. D.Sc. (Univ. of Aston) 67.
Trades Union Congress, 23/28 Great Russell Street, London, W.C.1, England.
Telephone: 01-636-4030.

Woodham-Smith, Mrs. Cecil B., C.B.E., M.A.; British writer; ed. St. Hilda's Coll., Oxford.
Awarded James Tait Black Memorial Prize for *Florence Nightingale* 50; Hon. D.Litt., Nat. Univ. of Ireland, Hon. LL.D., Univ. of St. Andrews.
Publs. *Florence Nightingale* 50, *Lonely Crusader* 51, *Lady in Chief* 53, *The Reason Why* 54, *The Great Hunger* 62.
44 Mount Street, London, W.1, England.

Woodhouse, Hon. Christopher Montague, D.S.O., O.B.E., M.A.; British politician; b. 11 May 1917; ed. Winchester Coll., and New Coll., Oxford.
Commissioned R.A. 40; commanded Allied Mil. Mission in German-occupied Greece 43-44; Asst. Sec. Nuffield Foundation 47; served Foreign Office in Athens 45 and Teheran 51; Fellow of Trinity Hall, Cambridge 49; Dir.-Gen. Royal Inst. of Int. Affairs 55-59; M.P. for Oxford 59-66; Parl. Sec. Ministry of Aviation 61-62, Home Office 62-64; Chief Editor Penguin Books 60; Dir. of Educ. and Training, Confederation of British Industry 66-; Visiting Fellow Nuffield Coll. 56; Fellow Royal Soc. of Literature; Legion of Merit (U.S.A.); Order of Phoenix with swords (Greece); Conservative. Publs. *Apple of Discord* 48, *One Omen* 50, *Dostoievsky* 51, *The Greek War of Independence* 52, *Britain and the Middle East* 59, *British Foreign Policy since the Second World War* 61, *Rhodes* (with J. G. Lockhart) 63, *The New Concept of Nations* 64, *The Battle of Navarino* 65, *Postwar Britain* 66, *The Story of Modern Greece*.
Bois Mill, Latimer, Bucks., England.
Telephone: Little Chalfont 2388.

Woodring, Wendell Phillips, A.B., PH.D.; American geologist and palaeontologist; b. 13 June 1891; ed. Albright Coll., and Johns Hopkins Univ.
Geologist, U.S. Geological Survey 19-27, 30-61; Prof. of

Invertebrate Palaeontology, Calif. Inst. of Technology 27-30; mem. Nat. Acad. of Sciences (Thompson Medal 67), American Philosophical Society; Pres. Geological Society of America 53 (Penrose Medal 49); Hon. Sc.D. (Albright Coll.); hon. Research Assoc. Smithsonian Inst. 61-.
Publs. *Geology of Republic of Haiti, Miocene Molluscs from Bowden, Jamaica, Geology of Kettleman Hills Oil Field, California, Geology and Palæontology of Palos Verdes Hills, California, Geology and Palæontology of Santa Maria District, California, Geology and Palæontology of the Canal Zone and adjoining parts of Panama.*
U.S. National Museum, Washington, D.C. 20560, U.S.A.
Telephone: 381-5334.

Woodroofe, Ernest George, B.SC., PH.D., F.INST.P., M.I.CHEM.E.; British business executive; b. 6 Jan. 1912; ed. Leeds Univ.
Director British Oil and Cake Mills Ltd. 51-56; Dir. Unilever Ltd. and Unilever N.V., in charge of Research 56-61, Vice-Chair. Unilever Ltd. 61-.
The Crest, Berry Lane, Worplesdon, Surrey, England.
Telephone: Worplesdon 2666.

Woodruff, John Douglas, C.B.E.; British writer and businessman; b. 8 May 1897; ed. New Coll., Oxford.
Served under Foreign Office in Holland 17-19; Lecturer in History, Sheffield Univ. 23-24; on editorial staff of *The Times* 26-38; in charge of Press Publicity for Empire Marketing Board 31-33; with B.B.C. 34-36; Editor *The Tablet* 36-67; Chair. Tablet Publishing Co. 37-; Dir. Hollis and Carter 48-62; Chair. Allied Circle 47-62, Associated Catholic Newspapers 53-, B.O.W. Holdings 59-.
Publs. *Plato's American Republic* 26, *The British Empire* 29, *Plato's Britannia* 30, *Charlemagne* 34, contributor to *Early Victorian England* 34, *Great Tudors* 35, *European Civilisation, The Grand Tour* 35, edited *Dear Sir* 36, *The Story of the British Colonial Empire* 39, *Talking at Random* 41, *More Talking at Random* 44, *Still Talking at Random* 48, *Walrus Talk* 54, *The Tichborne Claimant* 57, *Church and State* 60.
Marcham Priory, nr. Abingdon, Berks., England.

Woods, The Most Rev. Frank, M.A., D.D.; British ecclesiastic; b. 6 April 1907; ed. Marlborough Coll., Trinity Coll., Cambridge, and Westcott House Theological Coll., Cambridge.
Curate of St. Mary, Portsea 31-33; Chaplain Trinity Coll., Cambridge and Examining Chaplain to Bishop of Bristol 33-36; Vice-Principal Wells Theological Coll. 36-45; Chaplain to the Forces 39-45; Vicar of Huddersfield 45-52; Rural Dean of Huddersfield 45-52; Hon. Canon of Wakefield and Proctor in Convocation Wakefield 47-52; Chaplain to H.M. the King 51-52; Bishop Suffragan of Middleton and Canon Residentiary of Manchester Cathedral 52-57; Archbishop of Melbourne 57-.
Bishopscourt, Clarendon Street, East Melbourne, C.2, Australia.
Telephone: 41-4338.

Woods, George David; American international banker; b. 27 July 1901; ed. American Inst. of Banking, and New York Univ.
Harris Forbes and Co., N.Y. 18-34; First Boston Corpn. 34-62, Chair. of Board 51-62; Gen. Staff Corps, U.S. Army 42-45; Pres. and Chair. of Exec. Board Int. Bank for Reconstruction and Development (World Bank) 63-68, Int. Devt. Asscn., Washington, D.C. 63-68; Chair. of Board and Pres. Int. Finance Corpn. 63-68; mem. of Board Kaiser Foundation Hospitals; Dir. New York Times, Lincoln Centre for the Performing Arts, Inc.; Trustee New York Foundation, Univ. of Notre Dame, John F. Kennedy Library, Inc.; Hon. LL.D.

(Univ. of Notre Dame, Allegheny Coll., Bowdoin Coll., Harvard Univ., Columbia Univ.).
Office: 20 Exchange Place, New York City, N.Y. 10005; Home: 825 Fifth Avenue, New York City, N.Y. 10021; and Sheraton Park Hotel, Washington, D.C. 20008, U.S.A.
Telephone: 212-DI4-1515 (Office); 212-TE8-0800 (Home).

Woodward, Sir Ernest Llewellyn, Kt., M.A., F.B.A., HON. D. LITT. (Princeton); British university professor; b. 14 May 1890; ed. Merchant Taylors School, London, and Corpus Christi Coll., Oxford.
Served First World War 14-18; Fellow, All Souls Coll., Oxford 19-44, 62-; fmr. Lecturer in History New Coll., Oxford; Senior Proctor Oxford Univ. 28-29; Rhodes Travelling Fellow 31; attached Foreign Office 39-46; Prof. of Int. Relations Oxford 44-47; Prof. of Modern History, Oxford 47-51; Hon. Fellow Worcester and Corpus Christi Colls.; Prof. Inst. for Advanced Study, Princeton 51-60, Emer. 60-; mem. American Philosophical Society.
Publs. *Three Studies in European Conservatism, The Twelve-Winded Sky, Great Britain and the German Navy, The Age of Reform* (Oxford History of England), *Short Journey, History of England, British Foreign Policy in the Second World War* (Official History), Editor 44-55 (with R. Butler) *Documents on British Foreign Policy 1919-39, Great Britain and the War of 1914-18.*
The Garden House, 2A Walton Street, Oxford, England.
Telephone: Oxford 54779.

Woodward, R(obert) B(urns), A.M., B.S., PH.D.; American professor; b. 10 April 1917; ed. Massachusetts Inst. of Technology.
Post-doctoral Fellow Harvard Univ. 37-38, mem. Soc. of Fellows 38-40, Instructor in Chemistry 41-44, Asst. Prof. 44-46, Assoc. Prof. 46-50, Prof. 50-53; Morris Loeb Prof. of Chemistry 53-60; Donner Prof. of Science 60-; Dir. Woodward Research Inst., Basle 63-; Consultant, Polaroid Corpn. 42-; Cttee. on Medical Research 44-45, War Production Board 44-45, Chas. Pfizer and Co., Inc. 51-; Centenary Lecturer of Chemical Soc., London 51, Harvard Lecturer, Yale Univ. 59, Lecturer U.S.S.R. Acad. of Sciences, Leningrad 61, Weizmann Memorial Lecturer, Israel 63, etc.; mem. of Corpn. Massachusetts Inst. of Technology 66-71; Hon. degrees include: D.Sc. h.c. Manchester (England), New Brunswick (Canada), Yale, Harvard, Wesleyan, Bucknell Univs., Univ. of Southern California, Univ. of Chicago, Univ. of Cambridge (England), New England Coll. of Pharmacy, Colby Coll., Brandeis Univ., Univ. of Sheffield (England), Israel Inst. of Technology; Hon. A.M. Harvard Univ.; John Scott Medal 45, Baekeland Medal 55, Ledlie Prize 55, Research Corpn. Award 55, Nichols Medal 56, ACS Synthetic Organic Chemistry Award 57, Richards Medal 58, Davy Medal 59, ACS, Roger Adams Award 61, Pius XI Gold Medal of the Pontifical Acad. of Sciences 61, Scientific Achievement Medal 61, Priestly Medallion 62, Stas Medal of Belgian Chemical Soc. 62, Gold Medal for Creative Research in Synthetic Organic Chemistry 62, Nat. Medal of Science (U.S.A.) 64, Kirkwood Medal of Yale Dept. of Chemistry and New Haven Section of ACS 65, Nobel Prize in Chemistry 65, Willard Gibbs Medal 67; Fellow, American Acad. of Arts and Sciences; mem. Nat. Acad. of Sciences, American Philosophical Soc.; mem. various foreign Acads.; Hon. Fellow Chemical Soc., Indian Acad. of Sciences.
Department of Chemistry, Harvard University, Cambridge, Mass. 02138, U.S.A.

Woodward, Robert Forbes; American diplomatist; b. 1 Oct. 1908; ed. Univ. of Minnesota and Nat. War Coll.
Entered Foreign Service and served Winnipeg 32, Buenos Aires 33, Asunción 35, Bogotá 36, Rio de Janeiro 37, Dept. of State 38, La Paz 42, Dept. of State 44, Guatemala 44, Havana 46; Deputy Dir., American Republic Affairs, Dept. of State 47; attended Nat. War Coll., Washington, D.C. 49; Counsellor Stockholm 50; Chief, Div. of Foreign Service Personnel, Dept. of State 52, Deputy Asst. Sec. of State for Inter-American Affairs 53; Ambassador to Costa Rica 54-58, to Uruguay 58-61, to Chile 61; Asst. Sec. of State for Inter-American Affairs 61-62; Ambassador to Spain 62-65; Special Adviser on U.S.-Panama Relations 65-.
Home: 3224 Harriet Avenue, Minneapolis; 1642 Avon Place, N.W., Washington; Office: c/o Department of State, Washington, D.C., U.S.A.

Wooldridge, Dean E., M.S., PH.D.; American electronics executive; b. 30 May 1913; ed. Univ. of Oklahoma, and California Inst. of Technology.
Technical staff, Bell Telephone Labs. 36-46; Co-Dir., Research and Development Labs. Hughes Aircraft Co., Culver City 46-51, Dir. 51-52, Vice-Pres. (Research and Development) 52-53; Pres. Ramo Wooldridge Corpn., Los Angeles 53-58; Pres. Thompson Ramo Wooldridge Inc., Los Angeles and Cleveland 58-62; mem. Board of Dirs. Thompson Ramo Wooldridge 55-; Trustee Harvey Mudd Coll. 61-; Research Assoc. Calif. Inst. of Technology 62-66; Fellow American Physical Soc., Inst. of Electrical and Electronic Engineers, American Inst.of Aeronautics and Astronautics, American Acad. of Arts and Sciences; many awards.
Publs. *The Machinery of the Brain* 62, *The Machinery of Life* 66, *Mechanical Man* 68.
4545 Via Esperanza, Santa Barbara, Calif., U.S.A.

Woolf, Leonard Sidney; British writer and publisher; b. 25 Nov. 1880; ed. St. Paul's School, and Trinity Coll., Cambridge.
Member Ceylon Civil Service 04-11; Editor *The International Review* 19; Literary Editor *The Nation and Athenaeum* 22-28; Dir. The Hogarth Press Ltd.; Hon. Litt.D., Sussex Univ.
Publs. *The Village in the Jungle* 13, *International Government* 16, *Empire and Commerce in Africa* 20, *Imperialism and Civilisation* 28, *After the Deluge* (Vol. I 31, Vol. II 39), *Quack, Quack* 35, *Barbarians at the Gate* 39, *The War for Peace* 40, *Principia Politica* 53; autobiography *Sowing* 60, *Growing* 61, *Beginning Again* 64 (W. H. Smith Literary Award 65) *Downhill all the Way* 67.
Monks House, Rodmell, Lewes, Sussex, England.
Telephone: Lewes 2385.

Woolford, Harry Russell Halkerston; British art gallery director; b. 23 May 1905; ed. Edinburgh Coll. of Art; studied art in London, Paris and Italy.
Chief Restorer, Nat. Gallery of Scotland; Fellow Museums Asscn., Int. Inst. for Conservation of Historic and Artistic works.
Dean Park, Golf Course Road, Bonnyrigg, Midlothian, Scotland.

Woolley, Sir Richard van der Riet, Kt., O.B.E., SC.D., F.R.S.; British astronomer; b. 24 April 1906; ed. Univ. of Cape Town, and Gonville and Caius Coll., Cambridge.
Commonwealth Fellow, Mt. Wilson Observatory 29-31; Isaac Newton Student 31-33; Chief Asst., Royal Observatory, Greenwich 33-37; John Couch Adams Astronomer, Cambridge Univ. 37-39; Dir. Commonwealth Solar Observatory, Australia 39-55; Prof. of Astronomy, Australian Nat. Univ. 50-55; Vice-Pres. Int. Astronomical Union 52-58; Pres. Australian and New Zealand Asscn. for the Advancement of Science 55; Astronomer Royal (England) Jan. 56-; Pres. Royal Astronomical Soc. 63-65; Visiting Prof. of Astronomy, Univ. of Sussex.
Publs. *Eclipses of the Sun and Moon* (with Sir Frank Dyson) 37, *The Outer Layers of a Star* (with D. W. N. Stibbs) 53.
Herstmonceux Castle, Sussex, England.

Wootton, Baroness (Life Peer), cr. 58, of Abinger; **Barbara Frances Wootton,** M.A., L.H.D., J.P. (Mrs. George Wright); British social scientist; b. 14 April 1897; ed. Cambridge Univ.
Dir. of Studies in Economics, Girton Coll., Cambridge 20-22; Research worker, T.U.C. and Labour Party 22-26; Principal, Morley Coll. for Working Men and Women 26-27; Dir. of Studies in Adult Education, Univ. of London 27-44; Reader in Social Studies, Univ. of London 44-48; Prof. of Social Studies, Univ. of London 48-52; univ. research fellow 52-57; a Governor of the B.B.C. 50-56; Chair. Metropolitan Juvenile Courts 46-62, Nat. Parks Comm. 66-; A Deputy Speaker of the House of Lords 66-; Hon. LL.D. (York); Hon. D.Sc.
Publs. *Twos and Threes* 33, *Plan or No Plan* 34, *London's Burning* 36, *Lament for Economics* 38, *Freedom Under Planning* 45, *Testament for Social Science* 50, *Social Foundations of Wage Policy* 55, *Social Science and Social Pathology* 59, *Crime and the Criminal Law* 63, *In a world I never made* 67 (autobiog.).
High Barn, Abinger Common, Dorking, Surrey, England.
Telephone: Abinger 180.

Worboys, Sir Walter John, Kt., B.SC., D.PHIL.; British company director; b. 22 Feb. 1900; ed. Scotch Coll., Western Australia, Univ. of Western Australia, and Lincoln Coll., Oxford.
Dir. Imperial Chemical Industries Ltd. 48-59; Chair. Council of Industrial Design 53-60; Chair. Asscn. of British Chemical Manufacturers 53-56, Pres. 57-59; Gov. Radley Coll. 52-62; Dir. Westminster Bank Ltd. 56-, Westminster Foreign Bank Ltd. 56-65, Associated Portland Cement Ltd. 60-, British Portland Cement Ltd. 60-, Mercantile Credit Co. Ltd. 59-63, Forestal Land Timber and Railway Co. Ltd. 60-, Forestal Industries (U.K.) Ltd. 60-64; Chair. of BTR Industries Ltd. 60-, Man. Dir. 63-67; Chair. Bristol/BTR (G.R.P.) Ltd. 64-; Dir. British Overseas Fairs Ltd. 61-66; Chair. British Printing Corpn. Ltd. 65-, Deeglas Fibres Ltd. 65-68, Artrite Resins Ltd. 65-68; Chair. Governing Council Roedean School 62-; part-time mem. Board B.O.A.C. 60-64; mem. of Council and Academic Advisory Cttee., Univ. of East Anglia 64-; Chair. Academic Advisory Cttee. for Brunel Coll. 64-66; Fellow Royal Soc. of Arts 49, mem. Council 61-, Chair. of Council 67-, awarded Bicentenary Medal 56; mem. Council Soc. of Chemical Industry 55-59, Gold Medallist 57; F.R.I.C. 57-; Hon. A.R.I.B.A.; Hon. D.Tech. (Brunel); Hon. Fellow Lincoln Coll., Oxford 57-; Hon. Fellow Soc. of Industrial Artists 61-, Fellow British Inst. of Management 64-.
Flat 8, 69 Onslow Square, London, S.W.7; and Fiddlers Copse, Plaistow, nr. Billingshurst, Sussex, England.
Telephone: 01-589-0941.

Wormser, Olivier Boris; French diplomatist; b. 29 May 1913; ed. Ecole libre des sciences politiques.
French Embassy, Rome 33; with Cabt. of Ministry of French Overseas Territories 34; Cabt. of Under-Sec. of State for Foreign Affairs 36; Lecturer Faculty of Law, Dijon 38-39; Del. of French Cttee. for Nat. Liberation, London 43; Sec. to French Embassy, London 45; with Cen. Admin. 48, Head of Econ. Dept. 50, Sec. for Foreign Affairs 52, Dir. of Econ. and Financial Affairs, Ministry of Foreign Affairs 54-66; Amb. to the U.S.S.R. Oct. 66-; fmr. Perm. Del. to OEEC; Officier Légion d'Honneur.
Ministry of Foreign Affairs, 37 quai d'Orsay, Paris 7e, and 72 rue du Cherche-Midi, Paris 6e, France.
Telephone: Littre 72-34.

Worth, Irene; American actress; b. 23 June 1916; ed. Univ. of Calif. at Los Angeles.
Daily Mail Nat. Television Award 53-54; British Film Acad. Award for *Orders to Kill* 58; Page One Award, Newspaper Guild of New York, for *Toys in the Attic* 60;

American Theatre Wing "Tony" Award for *Tiny Alice* 65; *Evening Standard* Award for Noel Coward Trilogy 66; Whitbread Anglo-American Theatre Award 67; Variety Club of Great Britain Award 67.
First appeared as Fenella in *Escape Me Never*, New York 42; debut on Broadway as Cecily Hardern in *The Two Mrs. Carrolls* 48; London appearances in *Love Goes to Press* 46, *The Play's the Thing* 47, *Edward My Son* 48, *Home is Tomorrow* 48, *Champagne for Delilah* 49, *The Cocktail Party* 50, *Othello* 51, *A Midsummer Night's Dream* 52, *The Other Heart* 52, *The Merchant of Venice* 53, *A Day by the Sea* 53-54, *The Queen and the Rebels* 55, *Hotel Paradiso* 56, *Maria Stuart* 58, *The Potting Shed* 58, *King Lear* 62, *The Physicists* 63, *The Ides of March* 63, *A Song at Twilight* 66, *Shadows of the Evening* 66, *Come into the Garden Maud* 66, *Heartbreak House* 67, *Oedipus* 68; other appearances include: *The Cocktail Party*, New York 50, Old Vic tour of S. Africa 52, Shakespeare Festival, Stratford, Ont. 53, 59, *A Life in the Sun*, Edinburgh Festival 55, *Maria Stuart*, New York 57, *Toys in the Attic*, New York 60, Royal Shakespeare Theatre, Stratford 62, World tour of *King Lear* 64, *Tiny Alice*, New York 65; films include: *Orders to Kill* 57, *The Scapegoat* 58, *King of the Seas*.
38 Ladbroke Square, London, W.11, England.
Telephone: 01-727-6581.

Worthington, Edgar Barton, C.B.E., M.A., PH.D., F.L.S., F.R.G.S.; British scientist; b. 13 Jan. 1905; ed. Rugby School, and Gonville and Caius Coll., Cambridge.
Frank Smart Student Gonville and Caius Coll. during Fishing Surveys of African Lakes 27-30; Balfour Student Cambridge Univ. 30-33, Leader Expedition to E. African Lakes; Demonstrator in Zoology Cambridge Univ. 33-37; Scientist for African Research Survey 34-37; Dir. Freshwater Biological Asscn. of British Empire 37-46; Scientific Adviser Middle East Supply Council 43-45; Development Adviser, Uganda 46; Scientific Sec. Colonial Research Council 46-49; Seconded as Scientific Sec. East African High Comm. 47-51; Sec.-Gen. Scientific Council for Africa South of the Sahara 51-55; Deputy Dir.-Gen. (Scientific) Nature Conservancy, London 56-65; Scientific Dir. of International Biological Programme 65-.
Publs. *Fishing Survey of Lakes Albert and Kioga* 29, *Fisheries of Uganda* 32, *Inland Waters of Africa* (with Stella Worthington) 33, *Science in Africa* 38, *Middle East Science* 46, *Development Plan for Uganda* 47, *Life in Lakes and Rivers* (with T. T. Macan) 51, *Survey of Research and Scientific Services in East Africa* 52, *Science in the Development of Africa* 58.
Colin Godmans, Furner's Green, nr. Uckfield, Sussex; and International Biological Programme, 7 Marylebone Road, London, N.W.1, England.

Worthington, Leslie Berry, B.S.; American steel executive; b. 22 June 1902; ed. Univ. of Illinois.
Joined U.S. Steel Corpn. 23, various sales positions 23-46, Pres. U.S. Steel Supply Div. 46-57, Columbia-Geneva Steel Div. 57-59; Pres. United States Steel Corpn. 59-67, Dir., mem. Exec. Cttee.; Chair. American Iron and Steel Inst. 65-67; LL.D. (Bradley) 60.
525 William Penn Place, Pittsburgh, Pa. 15230, U.S.A.
Telephone: 412-391-2345.

Wortis, Sam Bernard, M.D., D.N.B., F.A.C.P.; American physician; b. 25 March 1904; ed. N.Y. Univ., Cornell Univ. Medical Coll., and Johns Hopkins Univ. and Hospital.
Instructor in Experimental Neurology, N.Y. Univ. Medical Coll. 30-32, Assoc. Prof. Neurology 33-42, Prof. Psychiatry and Neurology 42-, Dean 60-; Dir. Bellevue Psychiatric Hospital 42-49; Dir. Psychiatric and Neurologic Divs. Univ. Hospital, N.Y. Univ. Bellevue Medical Center; Consultant in Mental Hygiene, U.S. Public Health Service; Consultant to Veterans Admin., Wash.,

D.C.; Attending Neuropsychiatrist, N.Y. Neurological Inst. and consultant many hospitals; Dir. Nat. Cttee. on Mental Health; mem. Nat. Cttee. on Mental Hygiene, etc.; mem. WHO and Unitarian Cttee. Medical Teaching Mission to Austria 47, Poland and Finland 48; Fellow American Psychiatric, Neurological (Pres. 50, 52 and 67), Anthropological, Psychopathological and Psychological Asscns., N.Y. Acad. Medicine; Pres. Asscn. for Research in Nervous and Mental Diseases 51, Soc. of Biological Psychiatry 51, American Board of Psychiatry and Neurology 51; Pres. N.Y. Branch American Psychiatric Asscn.; Editor *Yearbook of Neurology, Psychiatry and Neurosurgery*.
410 East 57th Street, New York, N.Y. 10022, U.S.A. Telephone: 212-PL5-2122.

Woszczerowicz, Jacek; Polish actor; b. 1904; ed. Warsaw.
Debut at Reduta Theatre 24; played in Warsaw at Teatr Polski and Teatr Ateneum; important roles include Molière and Giraudoux roles and Joseph K (*The Trial*, Kafka), Jupiter (*Les Mouches*, Sartre), Richard (*Richard III*, Shakespeare), Colonel (*Across the River and into the Trees*, own adaptation of Hemingway), Ferrante (*La reine morte*, Montherlant).
Teatr Ateneum, ulica Jaracza 2, Warsaw, Poland.

Wotruba, Fritz; Austrian sculptor; b. 23 April 1907; pupil of Anton Hanak.
Private sculptor 27-; Prof. Acad. of Fine Arts, Vienna 45-.
Principal works: Torso (marble) 29-30, Sitting Figure (limestone) 49, Reclining Figure (conglomerate), 51, Figures in Relief (bronze) 58, Standing Figure (limestone) 57-59, Kneeling Figure 60, Large Figure (limestone) 63, Figures in Relief (marble relief at Philipps-Univ., Marburg) 64; designed scenery and costumes for *Der Ring des Nibelungen* Berlin Opera Festival 67.
Home: Blutgasse 5, Vienna I; Studio: Böcklinstrasse 1, Vienna II, Austria.
Telephone: 24-14-83 (Studio); 52-42-20 (Home).

Wouk, Herman, A.B.; American writer; b. 27 May 1915; ed. Columbia Univ.
Radio script-writer for leading comedians, New York 35-41; publicity work for U.S. Treasury 41-42; served U.S.N.R. 42-46; Visiting Prof. of English, Yeshiva Univ., New York City; Trustee, Coll. of the Virgin Islands 62-; mem. Authors' Guild Council, U.S.A., Author's League; Hon. L.H.D. (Yeshiva Univ.); Hon. D.Litt. (Clark Univ.); Pulitzer Prize for Fiction 52, Columbia Univ. Medal of Excellence 52.
Publs. *Aurora Dawn* 47, *The City Boy* 48, *Slattery's Hurricane* 49, *The Traitor* (play) 49, *The Caine Mutiny* (novel) 51, *The Caine Mutiny Court-Martial* (play) 53, *Marjorie Morningstar* 55, *Nature's Way* (play) 57, *This is my God* 59, *Youngblood Hawke* (novel) 62, *Don't Stop the Carnival* (novel) 65.
c/o H. Matson, 22 East 40 Street, New York City, N.Y. 10016, U.S.A.

Wrangham, Cuthbert Edward, C.B.E.; British business executive; b. 16 Dec. 1907; ed. Eton Coll., and King's Coll., Cambridge.
Air Ministry and Min. of Aircraft Production 39-45; Chair. Shelbourne Hotel Ltd. 50-60; Monopolies Commission 54-56; Chair. and Managing Dir. Power Gas Corpn. Ltd. 60-61; Deputy Chair. Davy-Ashmore Ltd. 60-61; Chair. Short Bros. and Harland Ltd. 61-67, Marine and General Mutual Life Assurance Society 61-, C. Tennant Sons & Co. Ltd. 67-.
1, 3 Albany, London, W.1; and Rosemary House, Catterick, Yorkshire, England.
Telephone: Old Catterick 375.

Wrenn, Charles Leslie, M.A. (Oxon); British philologist and literary historian; b. 30 Dec. 1895; ed. privately and Queen's Coll., Oxford.

Lecturer, Durham Univ. 17-20; Principal, Pachayappa's Coll., Madras 20-21; Prof. and Head Dept. of English, Dacca Univ. 21-27; Lecturer, Leeds Univ. 28-30, in English Language, Oxford Univ. 30-39; Prof. of English Language and Literature Univ. of London 39-46; Rawlinson and Bosworth Prof. of Anglo-Saxon and Fellow of Pembroke Coll., Oxford 46-63; Hon. Fellow, Pembroke Coll., Prof. Emeritus 63-; Pres. Philological Soc. 44-48; Chair. Council London Univ. School Slavonic Studies 44-49; Chair. Int. Asscn. of Univ. Profs. of English 50-53; Alexander White Visiting Prof., Chicago Univ. 57; O'Donnell Lecturer in Celtic, Oxford Univ. 58-59; Visiting Lecturer Moscow and Leningrad Univs. 60, etc.; hon. D.Litt. (N.U.I.) 61, Pres. Modern Humanities Research Asscn. 68.
Publs. *The English Language, Beowulf, Old English Grammar* (with R. Quirk), Enlarged edn. of R. W. Chambers' *Introduction to Beowulf, A Study of Old English Literature, Word and Symbol*.
259A Woodstock Road, Oxford, England.
Telephone: 59513.

Wright, Benjamin Fletcher, PH.D.; American educationist; b. 8 Feb. 1900; ed. Texas and Harvard Univs.
Teacher Univ. of Texas 22-26; Instructor to Prof. of Govt., Harvard 26-49, Chair. Dept. of Govt. 42-46, of Gen. Education 46-49; President, Smith Coll. 49-59; Fellow Center Advanced Study Behavioral Sciences 59-60; Prof. of Govt., Univ. of Texas 60-; Jefferson Lecturer, Univ. of Calif. 64; Visiting Prof. of Govt., Harvard 66-67; American Acad. of Arts and Sciences; Hon. LL.D., Litt.D.
Publs. *American Interpretations of Natural Law* 31, *Contract Clause of the Constitution* 38, *Growth of American Constitutional Law* 42, *Consensus and Continuity* 58, ed. *The Federalist*.
1415 Wathen Avenue, Austin, Texas 78703, U.S.A.

Wright, David McCord, LL.B., M.A., PH.D.; American professor; b. 1 Aug. 1909; ed. The Citadel (Military Coll. of S.C.), Architectural School, Univ. of Pennsylvania, and Law School, Virginia, and Graduate School, Harvard.
Attorney Reconstruction Finance Corpn. 36-37; Lecturer in Law Univ. of Virginia 40 and 47-55; Economic Consultant, Nat. Resources Planning Board 43; Lecturer U.S. Army School of Mil. Government 43; Asst. Prof. of Economics 39-42, Assoc. Prof. 42-46 and Prof. 46-55, Univ. of Va.; Fulbright Lecturer Oxford Univ. 53-54; Rockefeller Fellow 54-55; William Dow Prof. of Economics and Political Science McGill Univ. 55-62; Prof. of Economics, Univ. of Georgia 62-; mem. Advisory Board American Enterprise Asscn. 56-59, Exec. Cttee. American Economic Asscn. 52-55; Hon. mem. Soc. of Cincinnati, Ga. 67; Trustee Foundation for Economic Education 61-63; Econ. Adviser, Fed. Reserve Bank of Atlanta 64-66.
Publs. *Creation of Purchasing Power* 42, *Economics of Disturbance* 47, *Democracy and Progress* 48, *Capitalism* 51, *The Impact of the Labor Union* (ed.) 21, *A Key to Modern Economics* 54, *The Keynesian System* 62, *Growth and the Economy* 65, *The Trouble with Marx* 67, and many legal and economic articles in periodicals.
Department of Economics, University of Georgia, and 420 Fortson Drive, Athens, Georgia 30601, U.S.A.
Telephone: 543-2269.

Wright, Sir Denis Arthur Hepworth, K.C.M.G.; British diplomatist; b. 23 March 1911; ed. Brentwood School, and St. Edmund Hall, Oxford.
Assistant Advertising Man., Gallaher and Co. Ltd. 35-39; Vice-Consul, Constanza 40-41, Trebizond 41-43; Acting Consul, Mersin 43-45; Commercial Sec., Belgrade 46-48; Consul Chicago 49-51; Head Econ. Relations Dept. Foreign Office 51-53; Chargé d'Affaires and

Counsellor, Teheran 53-55; Asst. Under-Sec. of State, Foreign Office 55-59, 62; Amb. to Ethiopia 59-62, to Iran 63-.
British Embassy, Teheran, Iran.

Wright, Georg Henrik von, M.A., DR. PHIL.; Finnish philosopher; b. 14 June 1916; ed. Helsinki and Cambridge Univs.
Lecturer in Philosophy Univ. of Helsinki 43-46; Prof. of Philosophy Univ. of Helsinki 46-61; Prof. of Philosophy Univ. of Cambridge 48-51; sometime Fellow Trinity Coll., Cambridge; Visiting Prof. Cornell Univ. 54, 58, Univ. of Calif. 63, Univ. of Pittsburgh 66; Gifford Lecturer Univ. of St. Andrews 59-60; Research Fellow Acad. of Finland 61-; Andrew D. White Prof.-at-Large, Cornell Univ. 65-; Chancellor of Åbo Acad. 68-; Fellow Finnish Soc. of Sciences, Royal Swedish Acad. of Sciences, British Acad.; Pres. Int. Union of History and Philosophy of Science 63-65; Dr. h.c. Univ. of Helsinki, Univ. of Liverpool.
Publs. *The Logical Problem of Induction* 41 (2nd revised edn. 57), *A Treatise on Induction and Probability* 51, *An Essay in Modal Logic* 51, *Logical Studies* 57, *The Varieties of Goodness* 63, *Norm and Action* 63, *The Logic of Preference* 63.
4 Skepparegatan, Helsinki, Finland.
Telephone: 655-192.

Wright, Admiral Jerauld; American naval officer and diplomatist; b. 4 June 1898; ed. Naval Acad.
Ensign 17; served through ranks to Rear-Admiral 43, Vice-Admiral 50, Admiral 54; served Mediterranean 17-19, Atlantic 20-21, in the Far East 22-24, in presidential yacht U.S.S. *Mayflower* 24-26; in U.S.S. *Maryland* 26-29 and at Bureau of Ordnance 29-31 and 36-37; in U.S.S. *Salt Lake City* 31-34; staff Naval Acad. 34-36; Commdr. U.S.S. *Blue* 37-39; Exec. Officer U.S.S. *Mississippi* 41-42; held operational staff appts. for North African, Sicilian and Italian landings, and twice landed secretly on enemy territory; Commdr. U.S.S. *Santa Fe* in the Pacific 43, amphibious and joint service operations there 43-45; after 45 concerned with development of such operations under Chief of Naval Operations; U.S. Rep. to Standing Group of NATO 50-52; C.-in-C., U.S. Naval Forces, E. Atlantic and Mediterranean 52-54; C.-in-C. Atlantic (U.S. Unified Command) and Atlantic Fleet 54-60; Supreme Allied Commdr. Atlantic and NATO C.-in-C., Western Atlantic Area 54-60; Ambassador to Republic of China (Taiwan) 63-66; awards include D.S.M., Silver and Bronze Stars, Legion of Merit, Légion d'Honneur, numerous decorations and several honorary degrees.
2706 36th Street, N.W., Washington, D.C. 20007, U.S.A.

Wright, John David, B.A., LL.B.; American business executive; b. 25 June 1905; ed. Western Reserve Univ., and Western Reserve Univ. of Law.
Admitted Ohio bar 29; with law firm Garfield, Cross, McGregor, Daoust & Baldwin (Cleveland) 26-33; Asst. to Pres., Thompson Ramo Wooldridge Inc. (now TRW Inc.) 33-37, Sec. 37-43, Dir. 39-, Vice-Pres. 43-49, Vice-Pres. and Gen. Man. 49-53, Pres. and Gen. Man. 53-58, Chair. and Chief Exec. Officer 58-; Dir. of other companies; Order of Coif.
Home: 9610 Hobart Road, R.D.3, Willoughby, Ohio 44094; Office: 23555 Euclid Avenue, Cleveland, Ohio, U.S.A.

Wright, (John) Oliver, C.M.G., D.S.C.; British diplomatist; b. 6 March 1921; ed. Solihull School, and Christ's Coll., Cambridge.
Royal Navy 41-45; joined Foreign Office Nov. 45; served New York 46-47, Bucharest 48-50, Singapore 50-52, Berlin 54-56, Pretoria 57-58; Imperial Defence Coll. 59; Asst. Private Sec. to Foreign Sec. 60-63,

Private Sec. Jan. 63-Nov. 63; Private Sec. to Prime Minister Nov. 63-June 66; Ambassador to Denmark 66-.
British Embassy, Copenhagen, Denmark; Burstow Hall, nr. Horley, Surrey, England.

Wright, Judith Arundell (Mrs. J. P. McKinney); Australian writer; b. 15; ed. New England Girls' School, Armidale, N.S.W., and Sydney Univ.
Commonwealth Literary Fund Scholarship 49, 62; Lecturer in Australian literature at various Australian univs.; Hon. D.Litt., Univs. of Queensland and New England.
Publs. Poetry: *The Moving Image* 46, *Woman to Man* 49, *The Gateway* 53, *The Two Fires* 55, *A Book of Birds* 62, *Five Senses* 63, *The Other Half* 66; criticism: *Charles Harpur* 63, *Preoccupations in Australian Poetry* 64; anthologies: *A Book of Australian Verse* 56, *New Land, New Language* 57; biography: *The Generations of Man* 58; short stories: *The Nature of Love* 66; also books for children.
"Calanthe," Long Road, North Tamborine, Queensland, Australia.

Wright, Louis Booker, PH.D.; American librarian and historian; b. 1 March 1899; ed. Wofford Coll., and Univ. of North Carolina.
Newspaper Corresp. and Editor 18-23; Dept. of English, Univ. of N. Carolina 26-32; Guggenheim Fellow, England and Europe 28-29, 30; Visiting Scholar, Huntington Library 31-32, mem. Perm. Research Group 32-48; Visiting Prof. of Bibliography and Research Methods, Univ. of Calif., Los Angeles 34-48; Assoc. mem. of Faculty, Calif. Inst. of Technology 32-48; Dir. Folger Shakespeare Library 48-68; Chair. Advisory Board, John Simon Guggenheim Memorial Foundation 50-; Vice-Chair., Board of Dirs., Council of Library Resources 56-; mem. Board of Dirs., Henry Francis du Pont Winterthur Museum 55-, Harry S. Truman Library Inst. 56-; Vice-Chair. Board of Visitors, Tulane Univ. 58-; Trustee Nat. Geographic Soc.; numerous hon. degrees.
Publs. *Middle Class Culture in Elizabethan England* 35, 59, *The First Gentlemen of Virginia* 40, *The Secret Diary of William Byrd of Westover 1709–1712* 41, *The Atlantic Frontier* 47, 59, *The History and Present State of Virginia 1705 by Robert Beverley* 47, *Culture on the Moving Frontier* 52, *The Cultural Life of the American Colonies* 57, *William Byrd of Virginia, The London Diary 1717–1721, and Other Writings* 58, *Shakespeare for Everyman* 64, *The Dream of Prosperity in Colonial America* 65, *The Prose Works of William Byrd of Westover* (editor) 66, *Folger Library General Reader's Shakespeare* (editor).
National Geographic Society, Washington, D.C. 20036, U.S.A.
Telephone: Lincoln 6-4800.

Wright, Sir Norman Charles, Kt., C.B., M.A., D.SC., PH.D., F.R.I.C., F.R.S.E.; British scientist; b. 19 Feb, 1900; ed. Univ. Coll., Reading, Christ Church, Oxford, Gonville and Caius Coll., Cambridge, Cornell Univ.
Research Assistant, Reading Univ. 24-26; Commonwealth Fund Fellow, Cornell Univ. and U.S. Dept. of Agriculture 26-28; First Dir. Hannah Dairy Research Inst. 28-47; Hon. Lecturer, Glasgow Univ. 28-47; Chief Scientific Adviser (Food), Ministry of Agriculture, Fisheries and Food 47-59; Dep. Dir.-Gen. Food and Agriculture Org. (FAO) 59-63; Adviser to India 36-37, Middle East 44-45, Ceylon 45, Greece 46; Sec. British Asscn. for the Advancement of Science 63-.
Publs. *Report on Development of Cattle and Dairy Industries of India* 37, *Report on Development of Cattle Breeding and Milk Production in Ceylon* 46, *Economics, Supply and Distribution of Foods in the United Kingdom* 52, *Research for Plenty: All Flesh is Grass* 53, *Ecology*

of Domesticated Livestock 54, *The Current Food Supply Situation and Present Trends* 61.
65 Addison Road, London, W.14, England.
Telephone: 01-603-8383.

Wright, Oliver (*see* Wright, (J.) O.).

Wright, Sewall, B.S., M.S., D.SC.; American biologist; b. 21 Dec. 1889; ed. Lombard Coll., Univ. of Illinois, and Harvard Univ.
Ernest D. Burton Distinguished Service Prof. of Zoology, Univ. of Chicago 37-54; Fulbright Prof. Univ. of Edinburgh 49-50; Leon J. Cole Prof. of Genetics, Univ. of Wisconsin 55-60; Pres. Genetics Society of America 34; Pres. American Society of Zoologists 44; Pres. American Society of Naturalists 52, Society for the Study of Evolution 55; Pres. 10th Int. Genetics Con. 58; mem. U.S. Philosophical Society, Nat. Acad. of Sciences, American Acad. of Arts and Sciences, Foreign mem. Royal Soc. (England); Hon. F.R.S.E., Genetical Soc. Nat. Medal of Science 66.
Publs. on genetics of guinea pigs, inbreeding, cross-breeding, statistical consequences of Mendelian heredity, evolution.
3905 Council Crest, Madison, Wisconsin 53711; Department of Genetics, University of Wisconsin, Madison, Wis. 53706, U.S.A.
Telephone: 233-9409.

Wright, Stephen Junius, M.A., PH.D.; American university president; b. 8 Sept. 1910; ed. Hampton Inst., Howard and New York Univs.
Teacher Kennard High School, Maryland 34-36; Principal, Douglass High School 36-38; Dir. Student Teaching, North Carolina Coll. 39-41, Chair. Dept. of Educ., Act. Dean of Men 43-44; Prof. of Educ., Dir. Educ. Div., Hampton Inst. 44-45, Dean of Faculty of Educ. 45-53; Pres. Bluefield State Coll., West Virginia 53-57; Pres. Fisk Univ. 57-66, United Negro Coll Fund Inc.; mem. Board of Trustees Meharry Medical Coll., Hampton Inst.; mem. Board Arms Control and Disarmament Advisory Cttee, Inst. of Int. Educ. Board, Shaw Univ. Board of Trustees; Hon. LL.D. Colby Coll., Notre Dame, Michigan State and New York Univs., Morgan State Coll., Hon. D. Litt. Coll. of St. Thomas.
Home: 595 Ramapo Road, Teaneck, N.J.; Office: United Negro College Fund, 55 East 52nd Street, New York, N.Y. 10022, U.S.A.

Wrightson, Sir John (Garmondsway), Bt.; British business executive; b. 18 June 1911; ed. Eton Coll.
Sixth Airborne Div., Second World War; Chair. and Man. Dir. Head Wrightson; High Sheriff, Durham 59.
Neasham Hall, near Darlington, Co. Durham, England.

Wriston, Henry Merritt, A.M., PH.D.; American educationist; b. 4 July 1889; ed. Wesleyan and Harvard Univs.
Instructor and Prof. of History, Wesleyan Univ. 14-25; Pres. of Lawrence Coll. 25-37; Dir. Inst. of Paper Chemistry 29-37; Pres. Brown Univ., Providence, Rhode Is. 37-55; Vice-Pres. Council on Foreign Relations 50-51, Pres. 51-64, Hon. Pres. 64-; Exec. Dir. American Ass. 55-58, Pres. 58-62, Chair. 62-; Chair. Sec. of State's Public Cttee. on Personnel 54, President's Comm. on Nat. Goals 61; Pres. Asscn. of American Colls. 35-36, Asscn. of American Univs. 48-50; mem. Exec. Cttee. American Council of Educ. 41-44; Hon. C.B.E., Hon. ED.D., D.C.L., L.H.D., Litt.D., LL.D.
Publs. *War Chest Practice, Report of Connecticut State Council of Defense, Executive Agents in American Foreign Relations, The Nature of a Liberal College, Prepare for Peace, Challenge to Freedom, Strategy of Peace, Diplomacy in a Democracy, Academic Procession, Policy Perspectives.*
12 Beekman Place, New York, N.Y. 10022, U.S.A.

Wriston, Walter B., B.A., M.A.; American banker; b. 3 Aug. 1919; ed. Wesleyan Univ., The Fletcher School of Law and Diplomacy, Ecole Française and American Inst. of Banking.
Junior Insp., Comptrollers Div., First Nat. City Bank 46-48, Senior Insp. 48-49, Domestic Div. 49-50, Asst. Cashier 50-52, Asst. Vice-Pres. 52-54, Vice-Pres. 54-56, European District 56-58, Senior Vice-Pres. 58-59, in charge of Overseas Div. 59-60, Exec. Vice-Pres. 60-67, Pres. and Dir. First Nat. City Bank 67-; Hon. LL.D. (Lawrence Coll. and Tufts Univ.).
First National City Bank, 399 Park Avenue, New York, N.Y. 10022, U.S.A.

Wu Chih-pu; Chinese administrator; b. 06.
Political Officer, Sino-Japanese War; Chair. Honan-Anhwei-Kiangsu Border Area Administrative Council 47; Sec. C.C.P., Honan Prov. Cttee., Chair. Honan Prov. People's Govt. 49-55; First Sec. C.C.P. Honan Prov. Cttee., Gov. Honan Prov. 55; Deputy for Honan, mem. Credentials Cttee. Nat. People's Congress 54-; mem. C.C.P. Central Cttee. 56-; Sec. Central-South Bureau, Chinese Communist Party 62-.
Chengchow, Honan, People's Republic of China.

Wu Han; Chinese historian; b. 09; ed. Tsinghua Univ.
Lectured at Southwestern Combined Univ. and Tsinghua Univ.; research in Ming history; joined Democratic League; edited works of Wen I-to; Vice-Chair. and on Standing Cttee. C.P.P.C.C. 49; Vice-Mayor, Peking 52; Peking del. to N.P.C. 54; rep. of Federation of Democratic Youth to C.P.P.C.C. 54; on Cttee. of Dept. of Philosophy and Social Sciences, Chinese Acad. of Sciences 55-.
Publs. *Biography of Chu Yüan-Chang,* articles in *Tsinghua Journal,* etc.
Department of Philosophy and Social Sciences, Chinese Academy of Sciences, Peking, China.

Wu Hsin-yü; Chinese administrator; b. 02; ed. Peking Normal Coll. and Japan.
Formerly Principal of Chengjen Middle School at Taiynan; fought in New Army in Japanese War and became Head of Admin. Office of Shansi-Suiynan Border Region; later mem. of North China Govt. Council and Principal of School of Admin.; later Vice-Chair. of Shansi Provincial People's Govt.; Vice-Minister of Internal Affairs 49-53; Shansi del. to First N.P.C.; Dep. Sec.-Gen. Standing Cttee., Nat. People's Congress 62-, Vice-Chair. Bills Cttee.
National People's Congress, Peking, China.

Wu Hsiu-chan; Chinese diplomatist and politician; b. 09; ed. Sun Yat-Sen Univ., Moscow, and Frunze Military Acad.
Former Communist Guerila, Kangsi; fmr. Chief of Staff to Gen. Lin Piao; Head Russian and E. European Div., Ministry of Foreign Affaris 49; Dep. Foreign Minister 51-; Ambassador to Yugoslavia 56-57; mem. Central Cttee. Chinese Communist Party and Head Int. Liaison Dept. 56-.
Central Committee of Chinese Communist Party, Peking, People's Republic of China.

Wu Leng-hsi; Chinese journalist.
Dir. Hsinhua News Agency 52-; mem. Preparatory Cttee. All-China Journalists' Association; Tientsin del. to 1st N.P.C. 54; Sec.-Gen. and Vice-Pres. All-China Journalists' Association 55; Cttee. for the Standardisation of the Spoken Language.
Hsinhua News Agency, Peking, China.

Wu Mao-sun; Chinese administrator.
Mem. of Central Cttee. of Revolutionary Cttee. of the Kuomintang 49; Asst. Sec.-Gen. of Chinese People's Cttee. for World Peace 53; Sec.-Gen. of Institute of

Foreign Affairs 49-; Asst. Sec.-Gen. of Assoc. for Resistance to U.S. Aggression and Aid to Korea 53; mem. of Standing Cttee. of All-China Fed. of Democratic Youth 53; mem. of Council of Asscn. for Cultural Relations with Foreign Countries 54.
Chinese People's Institute of Foreign Affairs, Peking, China.

Wu Tso-jen; Chinese painter; b. 08.
Exhibitions Moscow 39, 50, Prague 46, Paris, Brussels 47, Leningrad 50; Dean, Central Fine Arts Acad., Peking; Vice-Chair. Union of Chinese Artists 53-.
Union of Chinese Artists, Peking, China.

Wu Yu-hsun (Woo Yui Hsun); Chinese scientist; b. 97; ed. Nanking Higher Normal School, Univ. of Chicago. Prof. of Physics North-East Univ. 26; Dir. Dept. Physics Central Univ.; Prof. at Tsinghua and Peking Univ. 28; at C.P.P.C.C. as non-party del. 49; Chair. of Chiao-tung Univ., Shanghai; educational cttees. in East China area; Vice-Chair. All-China Fed. of Scientific Societies 51; Kiangsi del to 1st N.P.C. 54; attended 2nd Session C.P.P.C.C.; Dir. Dept. of Mathematics, Physics and Chemistry, Acad. Sinica (now Chinese Acad. of Sciences), Vice-Pres. Acad. Sinica 51-.
Department of Mathematics, Physics and Chemistry, Chinese Academy of Sciences, Peking, China.

Wuermeling, Franz-Josef, DR. RER. POL.; German politician; b. 8 Nov. 1900; ed. High Schools, Berlin and Warburg, Univ. of Freiburg.
Civil Servant in Prussian Ministry of Interior 26-31; official in Finance Dept., later Fire Insurance Dept., Kassel Diet 31-38; official in Basalt Industry 39-47; Sec. to Rheinland-Pfalz Ministry of Interior 47-49; elected to Fed. Parl. 49; Minister for Family Affairs 53-57; Minister for Family and Youth Affairs 57-62; Grosskreuz des Verdienstordens; Christian Democrat.
Berliner Freiheit 7, Bonn, German Federal Republic.

Wünsche, Kurt Hermann, DR. IUR.; German lawyer and politician; b. 14 Dec. 1929; ed. Schillerschule, Dresden, and Deutsche Akademie für Staats-und Rechtswissenschaft "Walter Ulbricht", Potsdam-Babelsberg.
Secretary of Cen. Management Cttee. of Liberal Democratic Party 54-60; Deputy Sec.-Gen. of Liberal Democratic Party 60-65; Vice-Chair. of Council of Ministers of German Democratic Repub. (D.D.R.) 66-, also Minister of Justice; mem. Volkskammer 54-, Presidium of League for People's Friendship 61-, D.D.R. Peace Council 64-; Vaterländischer Verdienstorden der D.D.R. in Bronze und Silber, and other medals.
Publ. *Funktion und Entwicklung der Liberal-Demokratischen Partei Deutschlands im Mehrparteiensystem der Deutschen Demokratischen Republik* 64.
102 Berlin Klosterstrasse 47, Germany.

Wurster, Carl; German chemist; b. 2 Dec. 1900; ed. Gymnasium, Stuttgart, and Technische Hochschule, Stuttgart.
Joined Badische Anilin & Soda-Fabrik A.G. (B.A.S.F.), Ludwigshafen am Rhein 24, Dept. Head 32-34, Prokurist 34-36, Dir. 36-; Dir. I. G. Farbenindustrie A.G. 38-45; Man. Dir. B.A.S.F. 38-65, Chair. Advisory Board 65-; official of several other German companies; mem. Senate 51-, Vice-Pres. 60-; Max-Planck-Gesellschaft zur Förderung der Wissenschaften 51; mem. Senate, Deutsche Forschungsgemeinschaft 53-59; mem. Praesidium, Verband der Chemische Industrie e V. 55; Pres. Gesellschaft Deutscher Chemiker 57-59; mem. German Scientific Council 58-; mem. Advisory Board Stifter Verband für die Deutsche Wissenschaft 53-, mem. Board of Dirs. 62-; mem. Board of Curators Stiftung Volkswagenwerk 62-; Hon. Prof. Univ. of Heidelberg 52, Dr. rer. nat. h.c. Univ. of Tübingen 52, Dr. Ing.

e.h. Technische Hochschule, Munich 53; Dr. rer. pol. h.c. Univ. of Mannheim.
Badische Anilin und Soda-Fabrik A.G., Ludwigshafen am Rhein, German Federal Republic.

Wurster, William Wilson, A.B.; American architect; b. 20 Oct. 1895; ed. Univ. of California.
Practised in architectural firms 20-26; est. own practice 26; in partnership with T. C. Bernardi and D. Emmons 45-; Fellow, Graduate School of Design, Harvard Univ. 43; Dean, School of Architecture and Planning, Mass. Inst. of Technology 44-50; Dean, Calif. Univ. Coll. of Architecture 50-59; Dean, Coll. of Environmental Design 59-63, Acting Dean 65; mem. Nat. Capitol Park and Planning Comm. 48, Chair. 49-50; mem. Architectural Advisory Board, Dept. of State 58-63, consultant 64-; mem. Capitol Building and Planning Comm., Calif. 59-67, American Inst. of Planners; Fellow Danish Royal Acad. of Fine Arts, American Inst. of Architects, American Acad. of Arts and Sciences; Corresp. mem. Royal Inst. British Architects, Akademie der Künste, Berlin; Academician Nat. Acad. of Design.
Home: 1459 Greenwood Terrace, Berkeley 8, Calif. 94708; Office: 1620 Montgomery Street, San Francisco 94111, U.S.A.
Telephone: 415-848-7726 (Home).

Wurth, Pierre, D.EN.D.; Luxembourg diplomatist; b. 26; ed. Lycée de Garçons, Luxembourg, and University of Paris.
Lawyer 51-52; Ministry of Foreign Affairs, Luxembourg 53-54; Luxembourg Embassy, Paris 54-59; Dep. Chief, Political Section, Ministry of Foreign Affairs, Luxembourg, and Perm. Rep. to Council of Europe 59-64; Perm. Rep. of Luxembourg to United Nations 64-.
Home: 301 East 47th Street, New York, N.Y. 10017; and c/o Permanent Mission of Luxembourg to the United Nations, 200 East 42nd Street, New York City, N.Y., U.S.A.

Wüst, Georg, PH.D.; German oceanographer; b. 15 June 1890; ed. Berlin Univ.
Oceanographer of the *Meteor* Atlantic Expedition 25-27 and of *Altair* Gulf Stream Expedition 38; Prof. of Oceanography Kiel Univ. and Dir. Inst. for Marine Research, Kiel 46-59, Emeritus 60-; Visiting Prof. Columbia Univ. 60-64, Guest Prof. Bonn Univ. 65-67.
Publs. *Verdunstung auf dem Meere* 20, *Florida-und Antillenstrom* 23, *Schichtung und Zirkulation des Atlantischen Ozeans* 35-38, *Kuroshio und Golfstrom* 36, *Bodentemperatur und Bodenstrom in der Pazifischen Tiefsee* 37, *Kreisläufe des Wassers* 50-51, *Wechselbeziehungen zwischen Ozean und Atmosphäre* 54, *Stromgeschwindigkeiten im Tiefen-und Bodenwasser des Atlantischen Ozeans* 55, *Stromgeschwindigkeiten und Strommengen in der Atlantischen Tiefsee* 57, *Vertical Circulation in the Mediterranean Sea* 61, *Stratification and Circulation in the Carribbean Sea* 63, *Major Deep-Sea Expeditions and Research Vessels (1873-1960)* 64.
Wohnstift Rathsberger Strasse 63, 8520 Erlangen, German Federal Republic.
Telephone: Erlangen 825362.

Wyart, Jean, D. ès s.; French university professor; b. 16 Oct. 1902; ed. Ecole Normale Supérieure.
Asst. Univ. of Paris 28, Deputy Prof. 33-46; Prof. of Mineralogy, Sorbonne and Ecole de Physique et Chimie 46-; Sec. French Society of Mineralogy 31-40, Pres. 45; Dir. of Documentation Service of Nat. Centre of Scientific Research 41-; Pres. Int. Union of Crystallography 57; mem. Acad. des Sciences 59; hon. mem. Royal Inst. 60.
Université de Paris, 1 rue Victor Cousin, Paris 5e; Home: 18 rue Pierre-Curie, Paris 5e, France.
Telephone: DAN 94-29.

Wycech, Czesław; Polish politician; b. 99.
Active in popular movement and Union of Polish
Teachers before Second World War; Dir. Dept. of
Education and Culture, Polish Govt. in Exile during
German occupation; Pres. Union of Polish Teachers 45;
Minister of Education 45-47; mem. Polish Peasant
Party 45-47; one of leaders, United Peasant Party 49,
now Chair. of Supreme Exec.; Vice-Pres. Council of
State 56-57; Marshal of the Seym (Parl.) 57-; author of
several works on history of peasant movement and
education in Poland.
4/6 Wiejska, Warsaw, Poland.

Wyckoff, Ralph Walter Graystone, B.S., PH.D.; Ameri-
can scientist; b. 9 Aug. 1897; ed. Hobart Coll., and
Cornell Univ.
Instructor, analytical chemistry, Cornell Univ. 17-19;
Physical Chemist, Geophysical Laboratory, Carnegie
Inst. of Washington 19-27; Research Assoc., Calif.
Inst. of Technology 21-22; Assoc. mem. Rockefeller
Inst. for Medical Research 27-37; with Lederle Labora-
tories Inc. as scientist 37-40, as Assoc. Dir. in charge of
virus research 40-42; Technical Dir., Reichel Labora-
tories Inc. 42-43; Lecturer in epidemiology, Univ. of
Michigan 43-45; Senior Scientist, U.S. Public Health
Service 45; Scientist Dir. 46-52; Foreign Service Re-
serve Officer (Science Office), American Embassy,
London 52-54; Biophysicist, P.H.S. Nat. Inst. of
Health 54-59; Prof. of Physics and Bacteriology Univ.
of Arizona 59-; Dir. de Recherches Centre Nat. de la
Recherche Scientifique, France 58-62; Exchange Prof.
Univ. of Paris 65; mem. Nat. Acad. of Sciences,
American Acad. of Arts and Sciences; foreign mem,
Royal Netherlands Acad. of Sciences and Literature,
Royal Society, London; Corresp. Acad. des Sciences,
Paris, hon. mem. Société Française de Minéralogie et
de Crystallographie, Société Française de Microbiologie,
Royal Microscopical Society, London; Hon. Fellow
Indian Acad. of Sciences; Hon. M.D. (Masaryk Univ.);
Hon. Sc.D. (Strasbourg).
Publs. *An Analytical Expression of the Results of the
Theory of Space Groups* 22, *The Structure of Crystals* 24,
30, 34, *Crystal Structures* 48, 51, 53, 57, 58, 59, 60,
63, 64, 65, 66, 67, *Electron Microscopy* 49, *The World of
the Electron Microscope* 58.
Department of Physics, University of Arizona, Tucson,
Arizona 85721, and 4161 Camino Arco, Tucson,
Arizona, U.S.A.
Telephone: 602-884-1422.

Wyeth, Andrew N.; American artist; b. 12 July 1917;
ed. privately.
Artist, Landscape painter 36-; first one-man exhibition
William Macbeth Gallery, New York 37; exhbns., Doll
and Richard, Boston 38, 40, 42, 44; Macbeth Gallery
38, 41, 43, 45; Art Inst. of Chicago 41; Museum of
Modern Art, N.Y.C. 43; M. Knoedler and Co., N.Y.C.
53; Mass. Inst. of Technology, Cambridge 60; Dunn Int.
Exhibition, London 63; mem. Nat. Inst. of Arts and
Letters, American Acad. of Arts and Sciences; U.S.
Presidential Medal of Freedom 63; Einstein Award 67;
Hon. D.F.A. (Univ. of Maryland).
Chadds Ford, Pennsylvania, U.S.A.

Wyler, William; American film director and producer;
b. Mulhouse (Alsace) 1 July 1902; ed. Lausanne, and
Coll. de France.
Foreign Publicity for Universal Pictures one year; went
to Hollywood as Asst. Dir. 20; directed films for Uni-
versal, Twentieth-Century Fox, Samuel Goldwyn Pro-
ductions, Warner Bros., M-G-M and Paramount; served
U.S. Army 42-45; awarded Air Medal and Legion of
Merit (U.S.) and Légion d'Honneur (France); Irving
Talberg Award of American Film Acad. 66 and other
awards.
Directed films *Hell's Heroes* 31, *A House Divided* 32,
Counsellor-at-Law 33, *The Good Fairy* 34, *The Gay*

Deception 35, *These Three* 36, *Dodsworth* 36, *Come and
Get It* 37, *Dead End* 37, *Jezebel* 38, *Wuthering Heights*
39 (New York Critics' Award), *The Westerner* 39, *The
Letter* 40, *The Little Foxes* 41, *Mrs. Miniver* 42 (Acad.
Award for direction), *The Best Years of Our Lives* 46
(Acad. Award for direction and New York Critics'
Award), *The Heiress* 49, *Detective Story* 51, *Carrie* 52,
Roman Holiday 53, *The Desperate Hours* 54, *Friendly
Persuasion* 56 (Cannes Film Festival Award), *The Big
Country* 57, *Ben Hur* 58 (New York Critics' Best Film
of the Year, "Oscar" for directing), *The Children's
Hour* (*The Loudest Whisper*), *The Collector* 65, *How to
Steal a Million* 65, *Funny Girl* 67.
1121 Summit Drive, Beverley Hills, Calif., U.S.A.

Wylie, Sir Campbell, Kt., E.D., Q.C.; New Zealand
judge; b. 14 May 1905; ed. Auckland Grammar School,
and Victoria Univ. of Wellington.
Barrister and solicitor, New Zealand 28; Barrister-at-
Law, Inner Temple, London 50; private legal practice,
New Zealand until 40; New Zealand Expeditionary
Force 40-46; legal adviser, various Malay States 45-51;
Attorney-Gen. Barbados 52-55, British Guiana 55-56;
Attorney-General of West Indies 56-59; Federal
Justice, West Indies 59-63; Chief Justice, Unified
Judiciary of Sarawak, N. Borneo and Brunei 62-63;
Chief Justice, High Court in Borneo (Sarawak and
Sabah) 63-66; Law Revision Commr., Tonga 66-67;
Chief Justice of the Seychelles 67-.
Chief Justice, Victoria, Mahé, The Seychelles.

Wylie, Laurence William; American university
professor; b. 19 Nov. 1909; ed. Indiana Univ., Institut
des Etudes Politiques, Paris, and Brown Univ.
Instructor, Simmons College 36-40, Asst. Prof. 40-43;
Asst. Prof. Haverford Coll. 43-48, Assoc. Prof. 48-57,
Prof. 57-58, Chair. Dept. of Romance Languages 48-59;
C. Douglas Dillon Prof. of French Civilization, Harvard
Univ. 59-; Cultural Attaché, American Embassy, Paris
65-67.
Publs. *Saint-Marc Girardin Bourgeois* 47, *Village in the
Vaucluse* 57, *Deux Villages* 66; co-author: *In Search of
France* 62, *Youth: Change and Challenge* 63, *Chanzeaux,
A Village in Anjou* 67.
Home: 997 Memorial Drive, Cambridge 38, Mass.;
1540 William James Hall, Harvard University, Cam-
bridge, Mass. 02138, U.S.A.
Telephone: UNiversity 8-7600, Ext. 3834.

Wyn Harris, Sir Percy, K.C.M.G., M.B.E., K.ST.J., M.A.;
British administrative officer; b. 24 Aug. 1903; ed.
Gresham's School, Holt, and Caius Coll., Cambridge.
District Officer, Kenya Colony 26; Labour Commr.
Kenya 45, Provincial Commr. 45, Chief Native Commr.
47-49 and mem. for African Affairs in the Kenya
Govt.; Governor and C.-in-C. Colony and Protectorate
of the Gambia 49-58; mem. Devlin Commission in
Nyasaland 59; Administrator, Northern Cameroons
Oct. 60-61; Special Rep., Duke of Edinburgh's Award
Scheme Overseas 62-63; mem. Mt. Everest Expeditions
33, 36.
8 Theatre Street, Woodbridge, Suffolk, England.
Telephone: Woodbridge 2911.

Wyndham White, Sir Eric, K.C.M.G., LL.B., Barr.-at-
Law; British lawyer and international civil servant;
b. 26 Jan. 1913; ed. London School of Economics, Univ.
of London, and Middle Temple, London.
Practised as mem. English bar; Lecturer in Law
London School of Economics; mem. British del. Int.
Chamber of Commerce Berlin 37 and Copenhagen 39;
war service 39-45; special asst. to European Dir.
U.N.R.R.A. 45; Sec.-Gen. Emergency Economic Cttee.
for Europe 46; Exec. Sec. First Session Preparatory
Cttee. for Int. Trade Organisation, London 46, Second
Session, Geneva 47; Exec. Sec. U.N. Conf. on Trade and
Employment, Havana 47-48; Exec. Sec. G.A.T.T.

48-65, Dir.-Gen. 65-68; Dir. Int. Life Insurance (U.K.) June 68-.
Home: Les Charmilles, 105 route de Lausanne, Versoix, Geneva, Switzerland.

Wyszyński, H.E. Cardinal Stefan, DR.JUR.; Polish ecclesiastic; b. 3 Aug. 1901; ed. Univ. of Lublin.
Ordained Priest 24; Prof. of Sociology and Canon Law, Higher Seminary Włocławek 30-39; Rector of the Seminary and Canon of the Cathedral Assembly of Canons in Włocławek 45; Bishop of Lublin 46; Archbishop of Gniezno and Warsaw and Primate of Poland Nov. 48-; Cardinal 53; imprisoned 53-56; Organizer of Pastoral Great Novena of Millenium of Baptism in Poland 57-66; Pres. of Second Vatican Oecumenical Council; Pastoral Protector of Polish Emigration 64-. Publs. *Główne typy akcji Katolickiej za granicą* 31, *Dzieło Ks. Kard. Ferreri. Ideały i prace społeczno-apostolskie* 37, *Przemiany moralno-religijne pod wpływem bezrobocia* 37, *Stanowisko i zadanie duszpasterstwa wobec współczesnych ruchów społecznych* 38, *Stolica Apostolska a świat powojenny, Duch pracy ludzkiej* 46, *W światłach tysiąclecia* 61, *Wielka Nowenna Tysiąclecia* 62, *Gody w Kanie, Uswiecenie pracy zawodowej* 63, *Matka Kościoła* 66, *A Strong Man Armed* 66, *The Deeds of Faith* 66, *Per la Libertà e la pace degli Uomini* 67; works trans. into many languages.
Ul. Miodowa 17, Warsaw, Poland.

X

Xanthopoulos-Palamas, Christian; Greek diplomatist; b. 02; ed. Athens Univ.
Entered Greek Foreign Service 29; served in Balkan countries, Rome and Paris mem. Greek del. to Paris Peace Conf. 46; del. to Council of Europe 49-52; mem. of dels. to 3rd, 6th and 7th sessions of UN Gen. Assembly; Head of Dept. of Economic Affairs at Ministry for Foreign Affairs 52-54; Perm. Rep. to UN 54-60; Gen.-Dir. Ministry of Foreign Affairs 60-62; Perm. Rep. to NATO Oct. 62-67; Amb. to U.S.A. 67- (also accred. to Mexico and Panama); Minister for Foreign Affairs Jan.-Feb. 64; awarded Nat. Orders by Italy, Germany, France, Belgium, Argentina, Lebanon, U.A.R. and Yugoslavia; Commdr. Order of Phoenix; Greek Mil. Medal.
Greek Embassy, Washington, D.C., U.S.A.

Xuan Thuy; Viet-Namese politician; b. 2 Sept. 1912. In numerous nat. liberation movements until 45; later Editor *Cuu Quoc* (National Salvation—organ of the Viet-Minh); Deputy to Nat. Assembly, Democratic Repub. of Viet-Nam; mem. Presidium Fatherland Front Central Cttee.; Deputy Chair. N. Viet-Nam Del. to Geneva Conf. on Laos 61; Minister of Foreign Affairs 63-65; Minister without Portfolio to head Democratic Repub. of Viet-Nam's negotiating team, Paris 68; mem. Secr. Central Cttee. Lao Dong Party. Council of Ministers, Hanoi, Democratic Republic of Viet-Nam.

Y

Ya'acob, Tunku, D.K., P.M.N., S.P.M.S., C.M.G.; Malayan diplomat; b. 27 Dec. 1899; ed. Malay Coll., Kuala Kangsar, Queen's Coll., Cambridge, and Imperial Coll. of Agriculture, Trinidad.

Entered Dept. of Agriculture, Kedah State 30, Dir. 46; mem. Kedah State Legislature 31-49; former Deputy Dir. Fed. Dept. of Agriculture; Keeper of the Rulers' Seal 50-51; Regent of State of Kedah in Sultan's absence 51; joined Fed. Exec. Council with Portfolio of Agriculture 51-54; Keeper of Rulers' Seal 54; mem. Public Service Appointments and Promotions Board 54, Deputy Chair. 56 and Chair. (reconstituted as Public Services Comm.) 57-; High Commr. for the Fed. of Malaya in the U.K. 58-63, High Commr. for Malaysia 63-65; Amb. to Belgium 66-68; Amb. to France, Switzerland 66-; awarded Insignia Commdr. of St. Michael and St. George 47, of Panglima Mangku Negara 59; Pro-Chancellor of Univ. of Malaya 57; title of Tunku Panglima Beszr conferred by Sultan of Kedah 50; Insignia of Derjat Kerabat (D.K.) 61; Grand Cross Order of Homayoun; Hon. LL.D. Univ. of Malaya.

Ambassade de Malaisie, 48–50 rue de la Faisanderie, Paris 16e, France.

Telephone: 727-1385.

Yabuta, Teijiro; Japanese professor of agriculture; b. 89; ed. Univ. of Tokyo.

Technician, Agricultural Research Inst. Tokyo; fmr. Lecturer Univ. of Tokyo, Prof. 21; discovered gibberellin, and famous for studies on yeast and microbiological research; awarded Order of Culture 64.

c/o Univ. of Tokyo, Motofuji-cho, Bunkyo-ku, Tokyo, Japan.

Yacé, Philippe; Ivory Coast politician; b. 23 Jan. 1920; ed. William Ponty School, Dakar.

French Army 40-45; mem. Democratic Party of Ivory Coast (PDCI) 46-, Sec.-Gen. 59-; mem. Territorial Assembly, Ivory Coast 52-58; Deputy to Ivory Coast Constituent Assembly 58-59; Senator of the French Community 59-61; Pres. Nat. Assembly, Ivory Coast 60-; Pres., High Court of Justice 63-; Grand Officier, Légion d'Honneur, Grand Officier, Ordre National de la République de Côte-d'Ivoire.

National Assembly, Abidjan, Ivory Coast.

Yadin (formerly Sukenik), **Rav-Aloof Yigael,** M.A., PH.D.; Israeli soldier and archaeologist; b. 21 March 1917; ed. Hebrew Univ., Jerusalem.

Chief of Gen. Staff Branch, Hagana H.Q. 47; Chief of Operations, Gen. Staff, Israel Defence Forces 48; Chief of Gen. Staff Branch 49, Chief of Staff 49-52; Archæological Research Fellow, Hebrew Univ. 53-54; Lecturer in Archæology, Hebrew Univ. 55-59, Associate Prof. 59-63, Prof. 63-; Dir., Excavations at Hazor 55-58, Megiddo 60, 66-67, Judaean Desert Caves 60-61, Masada 63-65.

Publs. *The Scroll of the War of the Sons of Light against the Sons of Darkness* 55, 56, *The Message of the Scrolls* 57, *A Genesis Apocryphon* (with N. Avigad) 58, *Hazor I: The First Season of Excavations* 58, *Hazor II* 59, *Hazor III-IV* 61, *The Art of Warfare in Biblical Lands* 63, *Finds in the Bar-Kochba Caves* 63, *Masada: First Season of Excavations* 65, *The Ben Sirah Scroll from Masada* 65, *Herod's Fort and the Zealots Last Stand* 66.

47 Ramban Road, Jerusalem, Israel.

Yafi, Abdullah Aref al; Lebanese lawyer and politician; b. 1901; ed. Collège des Pères Jésuites, Beirut, and Univ. de Paris à la Sorbonne.

Admitted to Beirut Bar 26; Prime Minister and Minister of Justice 38-39; Lebanese del. to Preparatory Conf. for founding League of Arab States 44, to San Francisco Conf. 45; Minister of Justice and Finance 47; Prime Minister 52, 53, 54, 56, 66, 68-.

Office of the Prime Minister, Beirut, Lebanon.

Yagi, Hidetsugu, D.ENG.; Japanese engineer; b. 86; ed. Univs. of Tokyo, London and Harvard and Technische Hochschule, Dresden.

Professor, Tohoku Univ. 19-32, Osaka Univ. 32-42; Pres. Tokyo Inst. of Technology 42-44, Bureau of Technology 45, Osaka Univ. 46, Musashi Coll. of Engineering 55-60; mem. House of Councillors 53-56; Prof. Emer., Osaka Univ.; mem. Japan Acad. 51-; Order of Cultural Merit 56, Poulsen Gold Medal (Danish Technical Acad.) 59.

Publ. *Invention of Yagi Antenna* 28.

Yoyogi 5-29, Shibuya-ku, Tokyo, Japan.

Yagodin, Gennady Alexeyevich; Soviet physical chemist; b. 3 June 1927; ed. Mendeleyev Chemical Technology Inst., Moscow.

Deputy Dean, Mendeleyev Chemical Technology Inst., Moscow 56-59, Dean, Dept. of Physical Chemistry 59-63, Prof. of Chemical Technology 59-63; Dep. Dir.-Gen. (Head of Dept. of Training and Technical Information 63-64, Head of Dept. of Technical Operations 64-), International Atomic Energy Agency (I.A.E.A.), Vienna Sept. 63-66.

International Atomic Energy Agency, Kaerntnerring 11, Vienna, Austria.

Yaguchi, Rokuzo; Japanese politician and trade official; b. 02; ed. Kobe Higher Commercial School.

Foreign Ministry 24-; Ambassador to Chile 57; now Man. Dir. Japan External Trade Org.

Japan External Trade Organization, 1 Marunouchi, 1-chome, Chiyoda-ku, Tokyo, Japan.

Yagudin, Shamil Khairulovich; Soviet ballet dancer; b. 1932; ed. Moscow Ballet School of Bolshoi Theatre.

Joined Bolshoi Theatre Ballet 52; Honoured Art Worker of R.S.F.S.R. 62; with Bolshoi Ballet has toured U.K., Bulgaria, German Democratic Republic, Denmark, India, Canada, Norway, United Arab Republic, France, U.S.A. and Czechoslovakia.

Main roles: The Jester (*Romeo and Juliet*, Prokofiev), Karen (*Gayane*, Khachaturyan), Nurali (*Fountain of Bakhchisarai*, Afasyev), The Wicked Witch (*Swan Lake*, Tchaikovsky), Jester (*Cinderella*, Prokofiev), Petrushka (*Petrushka*, Stravinsky), Ibn Salom (*Leili and Medjnun*, Balasanyan).

State Academic Bolshoi Theatre of the U.S.S.R., ploshchad Sverdlova 1, Moscow, U.S.S.R.

Yahia, General Tahir; Iraqi army officer and politician; b. 13; ed. primary school, Tikrit, secondary school, Baghdad, Teachers' Training Coll., and Military Coll.

Former teacher, Mamounia School, Baghdad; mem. Nat. Movement 41; Commdr., Armoured Cars' Battalion, Palestine War 48; mem. Military Court, Habaniya 48; mem. Free Officers' Group 58, later Dir.-Gen. of Police; Chief-of-Staff, Iraqi Army Feb.-Nov. 63; Prime Minister of Iraq Nov. 63-Sept. 65, Sept. 67-; Al-Khidma Medal, Al-Chaja Medal, Al-Rafidain Medal.

Office of the Prime Minister, Baghdad, Iraq.

Yakovlev, Alexander Sergeyevich; Soviet aircraft designer; b. 1906; ed. Zhukovsky Air Force Engineering Acad.

Member C.P.S.U. 38; Deputy Minister of the Aircraft Industry of U.S.S.R. 40-56; Chief Designer to Ministry of Aircraft Industry 56-; Deputy to U.S.S.R. Supreme Soviet; designed sport, training, passenger, and bomber

aeroplanes; Corresp. mem. U.S.S.R. Acad. of Sciences 43-; State Prize 41, 43, 44, 46, 47, 48, Hero of Socialist Labour (twice) and many other awards.
Ministry of the Aircraft Industry, Moscow, U.S.S.R.

Yakovlev, Mikhail Danilovich, M.SC.; Soviet diplomatist; b. 1910; ed. Leningrad State Univ.
Diplomatic Service 59-; Minister of Foreign Affairs, R.S.F.S.R. 59-60; Ambassador to Congo (Léopoldville) 60-61, to Iraq 61-65; at staff, Ministry of Foreign Affairs 65-.
Ministry of Foreign Affairs, 32-34 Smolenskaya-Sennaya ploshchad, Moscow, U.S.S.R.

Yakubovsky, Fuad Borisovich; Soviet politician; b. 08; ed. Moscow Inst. of Energetics.
Worker in engineering Industry 30-54; U.S.S.R. Deputy Minister of Construction 54-63; First Deputy Chair. later Chair. U.S.S.R. State Production Cttee. for Installation and Special Construction Work 63-65; Minister of Erection and Special Construction Work 65-; Cand. mem. Central Cttee. of C.P.S.U. 66-; Deputy of Supreme Soviet of U.S.S.R.
Ministry of Erection and Special Construction Works, Bolshaya Sadovaya ul. 8-a, Moscow, U.S.S.R.

Yakubovsky, Marshal Ivan Ignatievich; Soviet army officer and politician; b. 1912; ed. Acad. of General Staff.
Soviet Army 32-; mem. C.P.S.U. 37-; Armoured Units, Second World War; Dep. Commdr. Tank Corps 44-46; Commdr. Tank Div. 48-52; Area Military Commdr., Armoured Forces 52-53; First Dep. C.-in-C. Soviet Forces in Germany 57-60, 61-62, C.-in-C. 60-61, 62-65; Area Mil. Commdr. 65-67; Deputy Defence Minister 67; Chief of Armed Forces of Warsaw Pact 67-; mem. Cen. Cttee. of C.P.S.U. 61-; Deputy to U.S.S.R. Supreme Soviet; mem. Political Bureau of Central Cttee. of C.P. of Ukraine; mem. Central Cttee. of C.P.S.U.; Hero of Soviet Union (twice); Order of Lenin (twice), Suvorov (twice); Order of Red Banner (four); Red Star; and other decorations.
c/o Ministry of Defence, 34 Maurice Thorez Embankment, Moscow, U.S.S.R.

Yakushin, Ivan Nesterovich; Soviet diplomatist; b. 1913; ed. Moscow Aviation Inst.
Diplomatic Service 46; Attaché, Sec., Counsellor, Iran 46-51, 52-55; Sec. Dept. of Near and Middle East Countries 51-52; Deputy Head, Protocol Dept., Ministry of Foreign Affairs 55; Minister, Ambassador Thailand 55-60; Deputy Head Middle East Div., U.S.S.R. Minister of Foreign Affairs 60-63; Amb. to Sudan 63-.
U.S.S.R. Embassy, Khartoum, Sudan.

Yalden-Thomson, William, M.A.; Canadian international civil servant; b. 11; ed. Harrow School and Cambridge Univ.
Co-ordinator of Labour Relations, Imperial Oil Ltd. (Canada) 43-51; Chief, Employers Relations Service, ILO 51-52, Chief of Operations 52, Asst. Dir.-Gen. 52-.
10 Parc du Château-Banquet, Geneva, Switzerland.

Yalman, Ahmed Emin, M.A.; PH.D.; Turkish journalist; b. 14 May 1888; ed. Istanbul Law School, and Columbia Univ., New York.
Reporter daily *Sabah* 07; Sub-Editor *Yeni Gazeta* 08-10; fmr. Associate Prof. of Sociology, Istanbul Univ.; war corresp. *Tanin* 15; part-proprietor and Editor *Vakit* 17-22; part-proprietor and Editor *Vatan* 22-26, *Tan* 36-39, *Vatan* 40-Jan. 61; Editor *Hur Vatan* Feb. 61; Chair. Turkish Press Inst.; hon. mem. International Press Inst.; Golden Pen of Freedom, Int. Fed. of Newspaper and Magazine Publishers 61, Gold Medal Brit. Inst. of Journalists 65.
c/o *Vatan*, Istanbul; Home: 116 Spor Caddesi, Beşiktaş, Istanbul, Turkey.

Yamagata, Shiro, B.ENG.; Japanese business executive; b. 26 Dec. 1902; ed. Tokyo Univ.
Osaka Refinery, Mitsubishi Metal Mining Co. Ltd. 27-, Man. Osaka Refinery 47-48, Dir. 50-, Man. Dir. 56-60, Pres. 60-67, Chair. 67-.
Mitsubishi Kinzoku Building, 1-6 Otemachi, Chiyoda-ku, Tokyo, Japan.
Telephone: 270-8451.

Yamamura, Shinjio; Japanese politician; b. 08; ed. Sawara Middle School.
Entered Fertiliser and Rice Business; fmr. Dir.-Gen. Prefectural Food Corpn., and Exec. of other food orgs.; fmr. mem. Japanese Prefectural Ass.; mem. House of Reps. 45-, fmr. Vice-Minister of Labour; Head of Admin. Agency July 63-July 64; Pres. Yamamura Shipbuilding Co., Sawara Shipbuilding Co.; Liberal Dem. Party.
House of Representatives, Tokyo, Japan.

Yamane, Harue; Japanese insurance executive; b. 3 April 1897; ed. Tokyo Commercial Coll.
Taisho Marine and Fire Insurance Co. Ltd. 21-, Manager Admin. Dept. 46, Managing Dir. 46-47, Pres. 47-62, Chair. 62-; Pres. Marine and Fire Insurance Asscn. of Japan 58-62; Dir. Asahi Tochi Kogyo Co. Ltd. 55-, Pres. 67-; Chair. Japan Housing Asscn. 61-; Dir. Mitsui Mining Co. Ltd. 64-.
43-5 Denenchofu 4-chome, Ota-ku, Tokyo, Japan.

Yamani, Ahmed Zaki; Saudi Arabian politician; b. 30; ed. Cairo Univ., New York Univ. and Harvard Univ.
Saudi Arabian Government Service; private law practice; Legal Adviser to Council of Ministers 58-60; Minister of State 60-62; mem .Council of Ministers 60-; Minister of Petroleum and Mineral Resources 62-; Dir. Arabian American Oil Company 62-; Chair. of Board of Dirs. General Petroleum and Mineral Org., Riyadh 62-, Coll. of Petroleum and Minerals, Dhahran 63-.
Ministry of Petroleum and Mineral Affairs, Riyadh, Saudi Arabia.

Yamasaki, Minoru, B.ARCH.; American architect; b. 1 Dec. 1912; ed. Univ. of Washington.
Instructor of Water Colour, New York Univ. 35-36; Designer 35-45; Instructor of Architectural Design, Columbia Univ. 43-45; Chief Architectural Designer for Smith Hirchman & Grylls, Detroit 45-49; Principal, Leinweber, Yamasaki & Hellmuth, Detroit, Mich. and St. Louis, Mo. 49-55, Yamasaki, Leinweber and Assocs. 55-59; Minoru Yamasaki and Assocs. Birmingham, Mich. 59-; mem. Nat. Council on the Arts; numerous architectural honours, including American Inst. of Architects First Honor Award for McGregor Memorial Community Conf. Center, Wayne State Univ., A.I.A. Gold Medal Award 59, American Inst. of Architects First Honor Award for Reynolds Metals Regional Building 61; Hon. D.Hum. (Wayne State Univ.), Hon. D.Arch. (Michigan Univ.), Hon. D.F.A. (Rensselaer Polytechnic Inst. and Bates Coll.).
Home: 3077 Livenois Road, Troy, Mich.; Office: 1025 East Maple Road, Birmingham, Mich., U.S.A.

Yamashita, Saburo; Japanese shipping executive; b. 25 April 1908; ed. Keio Univ.
Yamashita Steamship Co. 31-, Senior Man. Dir. 58, now Pres.
Yamashita Steamship Co., 2-6 Marunouchi, Chiyoda-ku, Tokyo, Japan.

Yamashita, Taro; Japanese oil executive; b. 24 April 1899; ed. Sapporo Agricultural Coll.
Former Importer & Exporter of rice, iron and woollen goods; joined Nichiro Gyogyo (Fishery Corpn.) 32, also Nihon Sanso (Oxygen) Co., Kanebo Spinning Co.; Dir. Korean Chemical Industries, Nissan Steamship Co.; Pres. Arabian Oil Co. Ltd.
48, Takanawa kita-cho, Shiba, Minato-ku, Tokyo, Japan.

Yaméogo, Antoine W.; Upper Volta financial official; b. 17 Jan. 1928; ed. Univ. de Bordeaux, Ecole Nationale des Impôts, Paris, and Univ. de Paris à la Sorbonne.
Inspector of publicly controlled financial bodies, France, Senegal and Upper Volta 55-59; Dir. of Treasury, later Commr. for Upper Volta Devt. Plan 59-61; Minister of Nat. Economy, Upper Volta 61-62; Exec. Dir. Int. Monetary Fund (IMF) 66-.
International Monetary Fund, Washington, D.C. 20431, U.S.A.
Telephone: DU-12867 (Office); 8826401 (Home).

Yaméogo, Maurice; Upper Volta politician; b. 31 Dec. 1921; ed. High School.
Member of Grand Council French W. Africa 47, Minister of Agriculture 55, of Interior 56, Premier 58-60; Pres. Council of Ministers 60-66, Minister of Defence 65-66; Pres. of the Republic 60-66; mem. Rassemblement Démocratique Africain (RDA).
Ouagadougou, Upper Volta, West Africa.

Yanagi, Masuo; Japanese banker; b. 22 June 1900; ed. Keio Univ., Tokyo.
Mitsui Bank 21-, branches in U.S.A. and Great Britain 31-33, Branch Man., Osaka 52, Man. Dir. 57, Pres. 59-64, Adviser 65-; Dir. Fuji Xerox Corpn. 65-; Auditor, Toyota Motor Co., Ltd. 65-, Mitsui Mutual Life Insurance Co. 65-.
Tomigaya 1-30-29, Shibuya-ku, Tokyo, Japan.

Yáñez, Agustín; Mexican journalist and politician; b. 04; ed. Univ. de Guadalajara and Univ. Nacional Autónoma de México.
Teacher 23-; Prof. of Literary Theory Nat. Univ. 42-, Dir. Literary Foundation 59-; Prof. Univ. Femenina 46-50; numerous other university and educational posts; Under-Sec., Presidency of the Republic 62-64; Secretary for Public Educ. 64-; mem. Seminario de Cultura Mexicana de la Lengua, Acad. Mexicana de la Lengua; Editor *Bandera de Provincias* 29-30, *Occidente* 44-45; Editor of Univ. series *Textos de Literatura Mexicana, Bibliotheca Scriptorum Graecorum et Romanorum Mexicana, Obras completas del Maestro Justo Sierra, Ediciones Conmemorativas del IV Centenario de la Universidad.*
Publs. *Justo Sierra* 62, *Proyección Universal de México* 63.
Secretaría de Educación Pública, Mexico D.F., Mexico.

Yang Chen Ning, PH.D.; Chinese professor; b. 22 Sept. 1922; ed. Nat. Southwest Associated Univ., Kunming, and Univ. of Chicago.
Instructor, Univ. of Chicago 48-49; mem. Inst. for Advanced Study, Princeton, N.J. 49-55, and Prof. 55-65; Albert E. Einstein Prof. of Science, New York State Univ. 65-; Visiting Prof. Univ. of Paris 57; Nobel Prize in Physics 57; A. Einstein Award 57.
New York State University, Stony Brook, N.Y., U.S.A.

Yang Cheng wu; Chinese army officer; b. 1912; ed. Officers' Acad. of Red Army, U.S.S.R.
In 115th Div. of 8th Route Army in Japanese and Civil Wars; on Peking-Tientsin Front 48; Garrison Commdr. Peking-Tientsin Area 51, later Chief of Staff and Deputy Commdr. N. China Mil. Area; Commdr. 66th, 67th and 68th Armies, Korea 51; Commdr. Air Defence Command People's Liberation Army 56-; Deputy Chief of Staff 59-66, Acting Chief of Staff 66-; mem. Nat. Defence Council 59-, Mil. Affairs Comm.; Alt. mem. Central Cttee. Chinese C.P. 56-57, mem. Politburo Jan. 67-.
Army Headquarters, Peking, People's Republic of China.

Yang Ching-jen; Chinese politician and administrator.
Member, Chinese Communist Party; Vice-Chair. Nationalities Affairs Cttee.; Vice-Chair. All China Youth Fed.; Vice-Chair. China Islamic Asscn.; Vice-

Pres. China–U.A.R. Friendship Asscn.; Chair., Ninghsia Hui Autonomous Region 60-.
Office of the Chairman of Ninghsia Hui Autonomous Region, Ninghsia, Ninghsia Hui Autonomous Region (N. China), People's Republic of China.

Yang Fang-chih; Chinese administrator.
Deputy Dir. of Central Financial and Economic Planning Bureau 51; Asst. Sec.-Gen. of Cttee. of Financial and Economic Affairs 52; Asst. Sec.-Gen. of Govt. Admin. Council 54; Dir. of Bureau of Foreign Experts Admin. 54-; Dir. of Counsellor's Office.
Bureau of Foreign Experts Administration, Peking, China.

Yang Han-sheng; Chinese writer.
Mem. of Standing Cttee. of Nat. Cttee. and Head of Welfare Dept. of All-China Fed. of Literary and Art Circles 49; mem. Cttee. of Cultural and Educational Affairs 49; mem. of Council of Union of Chinese Writers 53; Vice-Chair. All-China Federation of Literary and Art Circles 60-; Vice-Pres. Asscn. for Cultural Relations with Foreign Countries 54-; mem. of Council of Sino-Indonesian Friendship Asscn. 55; mem. of Council of China Cttee. for Asian Solidarity 56.
Union of Chinese Writers, Peking, China.

Yang Hsiu-feng; Chinese politician; b. 1900; ed. France.
Chair. Shansi-Chahar-Hopeh Border Region Govt.; Chair. Hopeh Provincial People's Govt.; Minister of Educ. 58-64; Pres. Supreme People's Court; Alt. mem. C.C.P. Central Cttee.
c/o Supreme People's Court, Peking, China.

Yang Ming-hsien; Chinese administrator.
Vice-Chair. of Shansi-Kansu-Ninghsia Border Region Govt. during Japanese War; on First Nat. Cttee. of C.P.P.C.C. 49-; mem. Central Cttee. of China Democratic League 49-; mem. of North-West Mil. and Admin. Council 49-53; mem. Shensi Provincial People's Govt. Council 50; Chair. Cultural and Educational Cttee. of North-West Mil. and Admin. Council 52; Vice-Chair. North-West Admin. Council 53; mem. Standing Cttee. of First N.P.C. 54; Dir. of *Kwangming Jihpao* (organ of non-Communist political parties in China) Nov. 57-63; Chair. China Democratic League 63-.
China Democratic League, Peking, People's Republic of China.

Yangel, Mikhail Kuzmich; Soviet engineer; b. 1911; ed. Moscow Aviation Inst. and Acad. of Aviation Industry.
Worker 27-31; student 31-37; Shop Man., Asst. Chief Engineer, Asst. Dir. of Factory, Chief Engineer, Dir. Scientific Research Inst. 37-; mem. C.P.S.U. 31-; Corresp. mem. U.S.S.R. Acad. of Sciences 58-66, mem. 66-; Corresp. mem. Ukrainian S.S.R. Acad. of Sciences; Deputy to U.S.S.R. Supreme Soviet; Hero of Socialist Labour (twice); Lenin Prize.
U.S.S.R. Academy of Sciences, 14 Lenin Prospekt, Moscow, U.S.S.R.

Yanshin, Alexander Leonidovich; Soviet geologist; b. 1911; ed. Moscow Geological Inst.
Researcher, Institute of Fertilizers 29-36, Geological Inst., U.S.S.R. Acad. of Sciences 36-56; Man. Dept. of Regional Tectonics, Geological Inst. 56-; Vice-Dir. Inst. of Geology and Geophysics, Siberian Div., U.S.S.R. Acad. of Sciences 59-; mem. U.S.S.R. Acad. of Sciences 58-; helped compile tectonic maps of U.S.S.R. 52, 56, Europe 64, Chief Editor tectonic map of Eurasia 65-; Order of the Red Banner of Labour, Badge of Honour.
Publs. Many works on the geology of the U.S.S.R.
Inst. of Geology and Geophysics, Novosibirsk, U.S.S.R.

Yanshin, Mikhail Mikhailovich; Soviet actor; b. 1902; ed. Moscow Art Theatre Studio School.
Moscow Art Theatre 24-; Artistic Dir. of Gypsy Romen Theatre 37-41; Chief Stage Dir. Moscow Stanislavsky

Drama Theatre 50-63; principal productions include *Blood Wedding, The Wonderful Woman Shoemaker* at the Romen Theatre, *Makar Chudra* at the Gorky, *Griboyedov, The Beautiful Girls* at the Moscow Stanislavsky Drama Theatre, *Front* and *The Late Love* at the Moscow Art Theatre; People's Artist of the U.S.S.R. 55, Order of Lenin, Order of the Badge of Honour, State prize.
Moscow Art Theatre, Proyezd Khudozhestvennogo teatra 3, Moscow, U.S.S.R.

Yanushkovskaya, Tamara Petrovna, M.SC.; Soviet trade union official; b. 1924; ed. Moscow State Univ.
Soviet Army 41-44; mem. Communist Party of Soviet Union 41-; teacher in institutions of higher learning 55-63; Chair. Central Cttee. of Educ., Univ. and Scientific Workers Union 63-; mem. All-Union Central Council of Trade Unions; mem. Central Auditing Comm. of C.P.S.U. 66-.
Central Committee of Educational, University and Scientific Workers' Trade Union, Leninsky Prospekt 42, Moscow, U.S.S.R.

Yao Yi-lin; Chinese politician.
North China Bureau, C.C.P. Sino-Japanese War; Dir. Commerce and Industry, North China People's Govt. 49, Vice-Minister of Trade 49, Vice Minister of Commerce 52-59; Dep. Dir. Office of Finance and Trade Affairs, State Council 59-; Minister of Commerce 60-; Dep. from Kiangsi Prov. and mem. Budget Cttee., Nat. People's Congress 54-; Alternate mem. C.C.P. Central Cttee. 58.
Ministry of Commerce, Peking, China.

Yarborough, Ralph Webster, LL.B.; American lawyer and politician; b. 8 June 1903; ed. Sam Houston State Teachers Coll., Huntsville, Texas, U.S. Military Acad., West Point, N.Y., and Univ. of Texas Law School.
Practised law, El Paso, Texas 27-30; Asst. Attorney-Gen. Texas 31-34; Dir. Lower Colorado River Authority 35-36; Lecturer, Univ. of Texas Law School 35; District Judge, Austin 36-41; served in Second World War and Lieut.-Col. 46; U.S. Senator from Texas 57-; mem. and former Pres. Travis Bar Asscn.; mem. El Paso Bar Asscn.; mem. and former Dir. State Bar of Texas; mem. American Bar Asscn., American Law Inst., Texas Board of Examiners 47-51, etc.; U.S. del. Inter-Parliamentary Union Conf., Brasilia, Oct. 62, Dublin 65, Canberra, Easter 66, Teheran Sept. 66, Palma de Mallorca Mar. 67; Democrat.
Home: 2527 Jarratt Avenue, Austin, Texas; Office: 460 Senate Office Building, Washington, D.C. 20510, U.S.A. Telephone: 202-225-5922.

Yarushevichius, Stanislovas Stanislovo; Soviet politician; b. 1925; ed. Kaunas State Univ.
Foreman, Shop Man., Dir. Kaunas Rubber Goods Combine 51-58; mem. C.P.S.U. 54-; Vice-Chair. Lithuanian S.S.R. State Cttee. for Co-ordination of Scientific Research Work 58-65; Perm. Rep. Lithuanian S.S.R. Council of Ministers to the U.S.S.R. Council of Ministers 65-.
Office of the Permanent Representative of the Lithuanian S.S.R. Council of Ministers to the U.S.S.R. Council of Ministers, Ulitsa Vorovskogo 24, Moscow, U.S.S.R.

Yashiro, Yukio; Japanese art historian and museum director; b. 5 Nov. 1890; ed. Tokyo Imperial Univ.
Studied art in Tokyo, Florence, London, Paris and Berlin; Prof. Imperial School of Fine Arts, Tokyo 17-42; Dir. Inst. of Art Research, Tokyo 30-42; Lecturer Harvard Univ., U.S.A. 33; now Dir. The Museum Yamato Bunkakan, Nara; Commdr. Ordine al Merito (Italy).
Publs. *Sandro Botticelli* (3 vols.) 25; *Japanische Malerei der Gegenwart* 31, *Principles of Japanese Art* 43, *Masterpieces of Far Eastern Arts in European and American*

Collections (2 vols.) 42, *2000 Years of Japanese Art* 58, *Art Treasures of Japan* (2 vols.) 61, *Characteristics of Japanese Art* (revised edn., 2 vols.) 65.
The Museum Yamato Bunkakan, Nara City, Nara Prefecture; Home: 1013 Kitahonmachi, Oisho-cho, Naka-gun, Kanagawa-ken, Japan.

Yasnov, Mikhail Alexeyevich; Soviet politician; b. 06; ed. Moscow Univ.
Member C.P.S.U. 25-; construction work, Moscow City Council 30-38; Dep. Chair. Exec. Cttee., Moscow City Council 38-49, Chair. 50-56; Dep. Minister of Town Construction U.S.S.R. 49-50; Chair. Council of Ministers R.S.F.S.R. 56-57, First Deputy Chair. 57-67; Chair. Presidium of Supreme Soviet of R.S.F.S.R. 67-; Deputy Chair. Presidium of Supreme Soviet of U.S.S.R. 67-; mem. Central Cttee. C.P.S.U. 52-; Deputy to U.S.S.R. and R.S.F.S.R. Supreme Soviets.
Presidium of R.S.F.S.R. Supreme Soviet, 3 Delegatskaya ulitsa, Moscow, U.S.S.R.

Yassein, Mohammed Osman, B.SC.; Sudanese civil servant; b. 15; ed. Gordon Coll. and London School of Economics.
Joined Sudanese Political Service 45; Liaison Officer in Ethiopia 52-53; Gov. Upper Nile Province 54-55; Permanent Under-Sec. of Foreign Affairs 56-; mem. Sudanese Del. to U.N. 56; Del. to Ind. African States Conf., Monrovia 59, to Accra Conf. on Positive Action for Peace and Security in Africa 60, to Independent African States Conf., Léopoldville 60; Special Adviser to UN on training of diplomatists 61-62; Special Envoy to Ethiopia and Somalia on border dispute; mem. African Unity Org. Comm. for Conciliation and Arbitration between Algeria and Morocco; Kt. Great Band of Humane Order of African Redemption, Liberia, Grand Officer, Order of Menelik II, Republican Order, U.A.R., Star of Yugoslavia.
Publs. *The Sudan Civil Service* 54, *Analysis of the Economic Situation in the Sudan* 58, *Problems of Transfer of Power—the Administration Aspect* 61, *Germany and Africa* 62.
Ministry of Foreign Affairs, P.O. Box 873, Khartoum, Sudan.

Yassin, Aziz Ahmed, PH.D.; United Arab Republic (Egyptian) engineer; b. 13 Aug. 1918; ed. Abbassia Secondary School, Cairo Univ., and Imperial Coll., London Univ.
Ministry of Housing and Public Utilities, rising to Under-Sec. of State 39-59; Chair. and Pres. Tourah Portland Cement Co., Alexandria Portland Co. 59-63; mem. Board of Dirs. Helwan Portland Cement Co., Sudan Portland Cement Co. 59-63; Chair. Egyptian Cement Companies Marketing Board 59-63; Chair. Board of Dirs. Egyptian Gen. Org. for Housing and Public Building Contracting Companies 63-65; Minister of Tourism and Antiquities Oct. 65-66, of Housing and Utilities 66-67; External Prof. in Soil Mechanics, Cairo Univ. 51-; External Prof. of Civil Engineering, Ain Shams Univ.; official of other civil engineering and building orgs.
Home: 4 Waheeb Doas Street, Maadi, Cairo, United Arab Republic.

Yasui, Kaoru, LL.D.; Japanese jurist; b. 7 April 1907; ed. Tokyo Univ.
Assistant Prof. Tokyo Univ. 32-42, Prof. 42-48; Prof. Hosei Univ. 52-, Dean Faculty of Jurisprudence 57-63; Dir. 63-; Leader (Chair. etc.) Japan Council Against Atomic and Hydrogen Bombs 54-65; Pres. Japanese Inst. for World Peace 65-; Lenin Peace Prize 58; Gold Medal (Czechoslovakia) 65.
Publs. *Outline of International Law* 39, *Banning Weapons of Mass Destruction* 55, *People and Peace* 55, *Collection of Treaties* 60, *The Materialistic Dialectics and the Science of International Law* 66.
Kamiogikubo 1-7, Suginamiku, Tokyo, Japan.

Yasui, Ken; Japanese politician; b. 11; ed. Kyoto Univ.
Formerly with S. Manchurian Railway Co., later with Chosun Railway Co. of China; fmr. Sec. to Gov. of Tokyo; mem. House of Councillors; fmr. Parl. Vice-Minister of Labour; Minister of State, Dir. of Admin. Affairs, Prime Minister's Office June 65-66; Liberal Democrat.
c/o House of Councillors, Tokyo, Japan.

Yasukawa, Daigoro; Japanese business executive; b. 2 June 1886; ed. Tokyo Univ.
Entered Hitachi Mfg. Co. 12; studied at Westinghouse Electric Co., America; established Yaskawa Electric Mfg. Co. 15; Chair. Electricity Machinery Control Board 42-45; now Chair. Yaskawa Electric Mfg. Co. Ltd., Chair. Tokyo Olympic Games Cttee. 63-65.
2346 Fujita, Yahata, Kitakyushu City, Fukuoka Prefecture; and 1052 Nakabaru, Tobata, Kitakyushu City, Fukuoka Prefecture, Japan.

Yates, Frank, C.B.E., SC.D., F.R.S.; British research scientist; b. 02; ed. Clifton Coll., and St. John's Coll., Cambridge.
Research Officer and Mathematical Adviser, Gold Coast Geodetic Survey 27-31; at Rothamsted Experimental Station 31-; Head of Dept. of Statistics 33-68, Deputy Dir. 58-68; Scientific Adviser to various Ministries 39-; Hon. Wing-Commdr., R.A.F. 43-45; Head of Agricultural Research Statistical Service 47-68; mem. UN Sub-Comm. on Statistical Sampling 47-51; mem. Governing Body Grassland Research Station 48-; mem. Int. Statistical Inst. 47-; Pres. of British Computer Soc. 61-62; Royal Medal, Royal Soc. 66; Pres. Royal Statistical Soc. 67-68.
Publs. *Design and Analysis of Factorial Experiments* 37, *Statistical Tables for Biological, Medical and Agricultural Research* (with R. A. Fisher) 38-63, *Sampling Methods for Censuses and Surveys* 49-60.
Rothamsted Experimental Station, Harpenden, Hertfordshire, England.
Telephone: Harpenden 4671.

Yazici, Bulent, M.S.; Turkish banker; b. 3 Feb. 1911; ed. Robert Coll., Istanbul and Columbia Univ.
Ministry of Finance Inspector 34-45; Financial Counsellor, Turkish Embassy, Washington 45-49; Asst. Gen. Man., Industrial Development Bank of Turkey 50-60, Chair. 60-; Dir. and Gen. Man. Türkiye İş Bankası A.S. June 60-; Chair. Turkish American Foreign Trade Bank 64-; Vice-Chair. Asscn. of Banks of Turkey 60-; Chair. Union of Chambers of Commerce, Industry and Exchanges of Turkey Sept. 60-May 62.
Türkiye İş Bankası A.S., Umum Müdür, Ankara; Riza Şah Pehlevi Caddesi 41-43, İş Bankasi Lojmani, Ankara, Turkey.
Telephone: 124383.

Ydigoras Fuentes, Gen. Miguel; Guatemalan politician and civil engineer; b. 17 Oct. 1895; ed. Mil. Acad. of Guatemala, and Guatemala Nat. Univ.
Military Attaché in Washington, Paris; Military Adviser in Peace Confs. delegation in Versailles 19; Dean of Polytecnhic School; Gov. of 4 States in Guatemala; Dir. of Public Roads 38-44; Pres. Dels. to 3rd UNRRA Congress, UNESCO Congress, U.N. Preparatory Comm. and U.N. 1st. Session, London 45-46; led repatriation Mission for Guatemalan Displaced Persons in Germany 46-47; mem. Neutral Observer Corps apptd. by Int. Court of Justice to organise referendum in French possessions in India 49; Minister to U.K. 45-50; Candidate for Presidency 50; Minister to Colombia 55, Ambassador 56-58; Pres. of Guatemala 58-63; mem. American Society for Geographical Research.
Publs. Map of boundary sections of Guatemala and Mexico, and Map of Roads of Guatemala and El Salvador; also books on military affairs and road construction.
Living in Nicaragua.

Yefanov, V. P., (*see* Efanov).

Yefimov, B. Y., (*see* Efimov).

Yeh Chien-ying, Marshal; Chinese soldier; b. 03; ed. Yunnan Military Acad. and studied military science in U.S.S.R. and Germany.
Took part in Northern Expedition 26; taught Whampoa Mil. Acad. 26; joined C.C.P. 26; Chief of Staff of 3rd Regiment of Red Army 31; Pres. Mil. Council of C.C.P. 31; Dir. Nanking Office of Red Army 37; Chief of Staff of Eighth Route Army 45; Mayor of Peking 49; same year Commdr. Kwangtung Mil. Region, mem. People's Govt. Council, Chair. Kwangtung Provincial People's Govt., Mayor of Canton, and Commdr. South China Mil. Region; Vice-Chair. People's Revolutionary Mil. Council 54; Vice-Chair. of Council of Nat. Defence 54-; mem. Central Cttee. Chinese C.P. 45-, Secr. 66-67, Politburo 67-; decorated for war service 55.
Council of National Defence, Peking, China.

Yeh, George Kung-Chao, B.A., M.A.; Chinese politician and diplomatist; b. 04; ed. Amherst Coll., Mass., U.S.A., and Cambridge Univ.
Prof. of English, Nat. Peking Univ. 26-27; Asst. Prof. Nat. Chinan Univ. 27-29; Prof. Tsing Hua Univ. 29-35; Prof. and Chair. Dept. Western Languages and Literature, Nat. Peking Univ. 35-39; Research Fellowship, China Foundation 37-39; Dir. British Malaya Office, Chinese Ministry of Information 40-41, Dir. U.K. Office 42-46; Counsellor and concurrently Dir. of European Affairs Dept., Ministry of Foreign Affairs 46-47; Admin. Vice-Minister of Foreign Affairs 47-49; Ambassador Extraordinary on Special Mission to Burma 47; Vice-Minister 49, Minister of Foreign Affairs (Taiwan) 49-58; Chair. Chinese Del., Seventh, Ninth and later Sessions UN Gen. Assembly; Ambassador to U.S.A. 58-61; Minister without Portfolio 61-; Special Grand Cordon, Order of Brilliant Star, Order of Propitious Clouds, many foreign decorations; Hon. LL.D. (Seoul, Amherst).
Publs. *Social Forces in English Literature, Introducing China, The Concept of Jen, Cultural Life in Ancient China* (Royal Soc. of Arts Medal 43), *On Ancient Chinese Poetry.*
The Executive Yuan, Taipei, Republic of China (Taiwan).

Yemelyanov (*see* Emelyanov).

Yen, Chia-Kan, B.SC.; Chinese politician; b. 23 Oct. 1905; ed. St. John's Univ. Shanghai.
Various government posts including Commr. of Reconstruction, Fukien Provincial Govt. 38-39, Finance Commr. Fukien Province, Chair. Fukien Provincial Bank 39-45; Dir. of Procurement, War Production Board 45; Communications Commr., Taiwan Provincial Govt. 45-46, Finance Commr. 46-49; Chair. Bank of Taiwan 46-49; Minister of Econ. Affairs, Republic of China (Taiwan) 50, of Finance 50-54, 58-63; Vice-Chair. Council for U.S. Aid 50, 63; Gov. of Taiwan 54-57; Minister without Portfolio 57-58; Chair. Council for U.S. Aid 57-58; Pres. Exec. Yuan (Prime Minister) 63-; Chair. Council for Int. Econ. Co-operation and Devt. 63-; Vice-Pres. Repub. of China 66-; Hon. LL.D. (Nat. Seoul Univ.) Korea 64, Hon. D.Pol. (Nat. Chulalongkorn Univ., Thailand) 68.
4 Section II, Chungking Road, South, Taipei, Taiwan, Republic of China.

Yendo, Masayoshi, B.ENG.; Japanese architect; b. 30 Nov. 1920; ed. Waseda Univ.
Murano Architect office 45-49; Pres. M. Yendo Associated Architects and Engineers 52-; Geijutsu Sensyo (Art Commendation Award) 65; Architectural Inst. of Japan Award 65.

Buildings include: 77th Bank Head Office 57, Hieizan Int. Sightseers' Hotel 59, Keio Terminal and Dept. Store Building 60, Resort Hotel Kasyoen 62, Yamaguchi Bank Head Office 62, 77th Building (77th Bank, Tokyo Branch) 63, Japan Coca-Cola Concentrating Plant 64.

M. Yendo Associated Architects and Engineers, Nakajima Building, 7, 8-chome, Ginza Nishi, Chuo-ku, Tokyo, Japan.

Telephone: 572-8321 (Tokyo).

Yerby, Frank Garvin; American novelist; b. 5 Sept. 1916; ed. Paine Coll., Fisk Univ. and Univ. of Chicago. Teacher, Florida Agricultural and Mechanical Coll. 39, Southern Univ. 40-41; Laboratory Technician, Ford Motor Co., Detroit 41-44, Ranger Aircraft, New York 44-45; writer 44-.

Publs. *The Foxes of Harrow* 46, *The Vixens* 47, *The Golden Hawk* 48, *Pride's Castle* 49, *Flood Tide* 50, *A Woman Called Fancy* 51, *The Saracen Blade* 52, *The Devil's Laughter* 53, *Benton's Row* 54, *The Treasure of Pleasant Valley* 55, *Captain Rebel* 56, *Fairoaks* 57, *The Serpent and the Staff* 58, *Jarrett's Jade* 59, *Gillian* 60, *The Garfield Honor* 61, *Griffin's Way* 62, *The Old Gods Laugh* 64, *An Odour of Sanctity* 66, *Goat Song* 67.

c/o William Morris Agency, 1740 Broadway New York City, N.Y., U.S.A.; General Mola 103, Madrid 6, Spain. Telephone: 2-61-17-11; and 2-05-03-76.

Yerovi Indaburu, Clemente; Ecuadorean economist, farmer and politician; b. 1904.
Businessman from Guayaquil; Minister of Treasury and Minister of Economy (responsible for banana growing devt. plan) 49-52; fmr. Minister of Agriculture; fmr. Ambassador to UNESCO and EEC; Pres. of Ecuador March 66-Sept. 66.
Quito, Ecuador.

Yetkin, Suut Kemal; Turkish scholar; b. 03; ed. Univs. of Paris and Rennes.
Asst. Prof. of History of Art and Aesthetics, Univ. of Istanbul 33-39; Dir.-Gen. of Fine Arts, Ministry of Education 39-41; Prof. of History of Art and Aesthetics, Ankara Univ. 41-50, of History of Turkish and Islamic Arts 50-59; Rector Ankara Univ. 59-63; mem. Académie des Sciences Morales et Politiques; Republican Party.
Publs. (in Turkish) *Philosophie de l'Art* 34, *Cours d'Esthétique* 42, *Les Doctrines Littéraires* 43, *Causeries Littéraires* 44, *L'Art de Leonardo da Vinci* 45, *Questions d'Art* 45, *Sur la Littérature* 53, *Les Peintres Célèbres* 55, *A. Gide: Choix de ses Ecrits Critiques* 55, *Histoire de l'Architecture Musulmane* 59; (in French) *Architecture Turque en Turquie* 62.
Kavaklidere Sok., Güney Apartments No. 23/5, Ankara, Turkey.

Yifru, Ketema; Ethiopian government official; b. 11 Dec. 1929; ed. Haile Selassie Secondary School, Addis Ababa and Boston Univ., U.S.A.
Italian Dept., Ministry of Foreign Affairs 52-53; Dir.-Gen. American and Asian Sections, Ministry of Foreign Affairs 53-56, Asst. Minister and Head of Dept. of Asian and American Affairs 56-58; Ministry of The Pen 58-61, Vice-Minister 60-61; Minister of State for Foreign Affairs 61-66; Minister of Foreign Affairs April 66-; Grand Officer of Order of Menelik II and other decorations.
Ministry of Foreign Affairs, P.O.B. 393, Addis Ababa, Ethiopia.

Yo Wei-fan; Chinese politician.
Former Sec. Chinese C.P. Taiyuan Municipal Cttee. and Major of Taiyuan; Sec. Chinese C.P. Nanking Municipal Cttee.; Mayor of Nanking 65-.
Office of the Mayor of Nanking, Nanking, Kiangsu Province, People's Republic of China.

Yokota, Kisaburo; Japanese judge; b. 96; ed. Law Department, Tokyo Univ.
Assistant Prof. of Int. Law, Tokyo Univ. 24; studied

Int. Law, France, U.S.A., Germany 26-28; Legal Adviser Japanese Del., London Naval Conf. 29-30; Prof. of Int. Law, Tokyo Univ. 30-57, Dean of Law Dept. 48-51; Pres. of Japanese Inst. of Int. Law 55-61; mem. Int. Law Comm. of UN 57-60; Chief Justice, Supreme Court of Japan 60-; mem. Acad. of Japan 49-, Assoc. of Inst. of Int. Law 52-.
Publs. *Elements of International Law* Vol. I 33, Vol. II 34, *Studies in International Law Cases* 33, *Legal Nature of International Arbitration* 34, *Studies on the United Nations* 47, *Renunciation of War* 47, *War Crimes* 47, *Fundamental Problems of International Law* 49, *International Security* 49, *A Commentary on the United Nations* 50, *Self-Defence in International Law* 51, *A Treatise on International Law* Vol. I 55, Vol II 58, *Law of the Sea* 59, *Law of Diplomatic Relations* 63.
39 Wakamiya-cho, Shinjuku-ku, Tokyo, Japan.

Yokota, Minoru; Japanese newspaper editor and publisher; b. 11 Feb. 1894; ed. Nippon Univ.
Chief Canton and Peiping Bureaux, Dentsu News Agency 24-36, Gen. Man. Southern China Bureau, Asian News Editor, Domei News Agency 36-46; Pres. Sekai Nippo 46-48; Dir. Japan Newspaper Publishers and Editors Asscn. 47; Dir. Kyodo News Service 48; Pres. Sekai Keizai Shinbun 48-51; Vice-Pres. Sangyo Keizai Shinbun 51-56; mem. Japan UNESCO Cttee. 56-61; Sec.-Gen. Japan Newspaper Publishers and Editors Asscn. 56-.
660, 1-chome, Kamiuma-cho, Setagaya-ku, Tokyo, Japan.

York, Archbishop of (*see* Coggan, Most Rev. Frederick Donald).

York, Herbert Frank, A.B., M.S., PH.D.; American physicist; b. 24 Nov. 1921; ed. Rochester and California Univs.
Joined staff of California Univ. Radiation Laboratory 43; attached to Y-12 Plant, Oak Ridge, Tenn. 44-45; California Univ. Graduate School 45-49; undertook, with Dr. Hugh Bradner, design and execution of major experiment in "Operation Greenhouse" (Eniwetok) 50; Asst. Prof. of Physics California Univ. 51; headed programme, Livermore weapon development laboratory 52-54, Dir. 54-58; Assoc. Dir. California Univ. Radiation Laboratory 54-58; Dir. of Research, Advanced Research Projects Division, Inst. for Defense Analyses, Chief Scientist, Dept. of Defense Advanced Research Projects Agency 58; Dir. Defense Research and Engineering, Dept. of Defense 58-61; Chancellor, Calif. Univ. at San Diego 61-64, Prof. of Physics, Calif. Univ. 61-; fmr. mem. Army and Air Force Scientific Advisory Board; Vice-Chair. President's Science Advisory Cttee. 65-67, mem. 57-58, 64-68; mem. Board of Trustees Aerospace Corpn. 61-, Board of Trustees, Inst. for Defense Analyses 64-67.
University of California, San Diego, Box 109, La Jolla, Calif., and 6110 Camino de la Costa, La Jolla, Calif., U.S.A.
Telephone: 459-2161.

Yorty, Samuel William; American lawyer and politician; b. 1 Oct. 1909; ed. Southwestern Univ. and Univ. of S. California.
Admitted to Calif. Bar 39; mem. Calif. State Ass. 36-40, 49-50; fmr. U.S. Congressman, Calif.; U.S.A.F. 42-45; Mayor of Los Angeles 61-; Democrat.
City Hall, Los Angeles 90012, California, U.S.A.

Yoshida, Isoya; Japanese architect; b. 19 Dec. 1894; ed. Tokyo Acad. of Fine Arts.
Founder-Dir. Isoya Yoshida's Architectural Inst., Tokyo 26-; Lecturer, Tokyo Acad. of Fine Arts (now Tokyo Univ. of Arts) 41-46, Prof. 46-49; Prof. Tokyo Univ. of Arts 49-61, Prof. Emeritus 62-; Councillor Establishment Cttee. of the Imperial Palace 63-; mem. Establishment Cttee. of Dept. for Foreign Affairs of Japan 52-60,

The Nat. Theatre 66, Japan Acad. of Arts; Hon. Fellow American Inst. of Architects 68-; Councillor Establishment Cttee. of Highest Court of Justice in Japan 67-; Awards include Japan Acad. of Arts Prize 52, The Order of Culture 64, Cultural Merit 64.
Principal works include: Matsushima New Park Hotel 39, The Kabuki Theatre 51, Japan Acad. of Arts, Tokyo 55, Gotoh Art Museum, Tokyo, Museum Yamato Bunkakan, Nara, Gyokudo Memorial Museum, Ome 61, Japanese Inst. of Culture in Rome, Kitazawa Hall, Suwa 62, Nat. Educ. Centre, Tokyo 63, Tokyo Hilton Hotel 63, Osaka Royal Hotel 65, The Temple Shinshoji 68, The Temple Chuguji 68.
1052 Ninomiya, Ninomiya-machi, Nakagun, Kanagawa-ken, Japan.
Telephone: 0463-7-0053.

Yoshida, Tomizo; Japanese cancer specialist; b. 10 Feb. 1903; ed. Imperial Univ. of Tokyo.
Assistant Prof. Nagasaki Medical Coll. 35-38, Prof. 38-44; Prof. Tohoku Imperial Univ. 44-52; Prof. Tokyo Univ. 52-; Dir. Sasaki Inst. 53-; Dean Faculty of Medicine, Tokyo Univ. 58; Vice-Pres. Science Council of Japan 63-65; Dir. Cancer Inst., Japanese Foundation for Cancer Research 63-; Adviser Minister of Educ. 63-; Pres. Int. Cancer Congress 66; Order of Cultural Merit 59; Imperial Prize; Japanese Acad. 31, 53, Scheele Medal 56, Koch Medal (Germany) 63.
Publs. *Outbreak of Cancer* 44, *Yoshida Sarcoma* 49, *Virchow's Cellular Pathology* 57.
Cancer Institute, 2-2615 Nishisugamo, Toshima-ku, Tokyo; and Sasaki Institute, 2-2 Kanda Surugadai, Chiyoda-ku, Tokyo, Japan.
Telephone: 917-7564 (Cancer Inst.); 292-8091 (Sasaki Inst.).

Yoshimura, Junzo; Japanese architect; b. 7 Sept. 1908; ed. Tokyo Acad. of Fine Arts.
At Architectural Office of Antonin Raymond 31-42; own architectural practice 43-; Asst. Prof. in Architecture, Tokyo Univ. of Arts 47-61, Prof. 62-; mem. Architectural Inst. of Japan, Japan Architects' Asscn.; Architectural Inst. Prize 56, Parsons Medal (New York) 56.
Works include: Int. House of Japan, Tokyo 55, Public Kambara Hospital 56, The Motel on the Mountain, New York 56, Hotel Kowakien, Hakone, 59, Mountain House for Yawata Iron and Steel Co., Kujyu 60, N.C.R. H.Q., Tokyo 62, Americana Building, Osaka 65, Prefectural Aichi Univ. of Arts, Aichi 65-, and many residences.
Home: 5-30-24 Minamidae, Nakano-ku, Tokyo, Japan.

Yoshino, Gakuzo; Japanese investment executive; b. 28 Nov. 1897; ed. Tokyo Commercial Coll.
Furukawa Trading Co. 19-20; Mitsukoshi Dept. Store 20-24, Kokaisha Co. 24-; Kawashimaya Shoten Co. 25, Dir. 34, Man. Dir. 36-39; Man. Dir. Kawashimaya Securities Co. 39-43, Senior Man. Dir. 43-44; Man. Dir. Nikko Securities Co. 44-47, Pres. 47-64, Chair. of Board 64-; Chair. Board of Govs. Tokyo Stock Exchange 60-64.
Nikko Securities, New Tokyo Building, 2-3 Marunouchi, Chiyoda-ku, Tokyo; Home: 1438 Senzuko, Meguro-ku, Tokyo, Japan.

Yoshitake, Eichi; Japanese politician; b. 03; ed. Tokyo Univ.
Former Gov., Toyama Prefecture; fmr. Vice-Minister of Labour; Minister of Labour and Welfare 51; fmr. Pres. Kanda Coal Mining Co.; Minister of Home Affairs July 64-65; Liberal Democrat.
c/o Ministry of Home Affairs, Tokyo, Japan.

Yost, Charles Woodruff, A.B.; American diplomatist; b. 6 Nov. 1907; ed. Princeton Univ. and Ecole des Hautes Etudes Internationales, Paris.
Entered foreign service 30; served Alexandria 30-32,

Warsaw 32-33; free-lance journalism 33-35; served Dept. of State 35-45; Asst. to Sec. of State, San Francisco Conf. on U.N. 45; Sec.-Gen. to U.N. Del. to Berlin Conf. 45; served Bangkok 45-46; Political Adviser to U.S. Del. to U.N. Gen. Assembly 46; served Prague 47, Vienna 47-49; Dir. Office of Eastern European Affairs, Dept. of State 49-50; Minister in Athens 50-53; Deputy High Commr. for Austria 53-54; Minister to Laos 54-55, Ambassador 55-56; Minister in Paris 56-58; Ambassador to Syria Jan.-Mar. 58 (terminated by creation of United Arab Republic); Ambassador to Morocco 58-61; Dep. Rep. to UN Security Council 61-65; Career Ambassador 64; Rockefeller Public Service Award 64; Deputy Perm. Rep. to UN 65-66; Senior Fellow, Council on Foreign Relations 66-.
Publs. *The Age of Triumph and Frustration* 64, *The Insecurity of Nations* 68.
Council on Foreign Relations, 58 East 68th Street, New York, N.Y. 10021; and 10 East End Avenue, New York, N.Y. 10021, U.S.A.
Telephone: 212-628-9197.

Yost, Don Merlin Lee, B.S., PH.D.; American inorganic chemist and teacher; b. 30 Oct. 1893; ed. Univ. of Calif., Univ. of Utah, and Calif. Inst. of Technology.
Du Pont Fellow, Calif. Inst. of Technology 24; Fellow Int. Educ. Board, Univs. of Uppsala, Sweden, and Berlin 28-29; Lieut.-Commdr. U.S.N.R. 36, retd. 40; now Prof. of Inorganic Chemistry, Calif. Inst. of Technology; A. D. Little Visiting Prof. of Chemistry, Mass. Inst. Technology; Fellow American Physical Society; mem. National Acad. of Sciences, American Acad. of Arts and Sciences; Presidential Certificate of Merit 48.
Publs. *Systematic Inorganic Chemistry* (with H. Russell, Jnr.) 44, *The Rare Earth Elements and their Compounds* (with H. Russell, Jnr. and C. S. Garner) 47.
California Institute of Technology, Pasadena, U.S.A.

Youlou, Abbé Fulbert; Congolese ecclesiastic and politician; b. 17; ed. Brazzaville seminary.
Ordained priest 46; Mayor of Brazzaville 56-Aug. 63; Minister of Agriculture, Livestock, Water and Forestry 57-58; Pres. Council of Ministers 58-60, Pres. Congo Republic 60-Aug. 63; Minister of Justice 60-61, of the Interior 60-61, of National Defence 60-Aug. 63; Pres. and founder, Democratic Movement for the Defence of African Interests; founder St.-Vincent-de-Paul Conf. Brazzaville.
Publs. *Où en Sommes-Nous pour une Afrique Meilleure, L'Art Noir ou les Croyances en Afrique Centrale, Diagnostic et Remèdes, Vers une Formule Efficace pour Construire une Afrique Meilleure, Le Matsouanisme.*
Spain.

Younes, Mahmoud; United Arab Republic (Egyptian) engineer; b. 3 April 1912; ed. Royal Coll. of Engineers, Cairo Univ. and Staff Officer's Coll.
Engineer with Mechanical and Electrical Dept., Ministry of Public Works, Cairo 37; army engineer 37; with Mil. Operations Directorate 43; Lecturer, Staff Officers' Coll. 44 and 47; Dir. Technical Affairs Office, G.H.Q. 52; mem. Permanent Board for Development of Nat. Production 53; Man. Dir. and Chair. Gen. Petroleum Authority 54; Counsellor, Ministry of Commerce and Industry and Mineral Wealth; Man. Dir. and Deputy Chair. Suez Canal Authority 56, Chair. 57-65; Deputy Prime Minister for Transport and Communications 65-67; Minister of Oil and Transport 67; Pres. Engineers' Syndicate 54-; Dir. and Chair. Cie. Orientale des Pétroles d'Egypte et Soc. Coopérative des Pétroles 58-; mem. National Assembly 64-; Order of Merit (Class I), Order of the Nile (Class III), Military Star, Liberation Medal, Palestine Medal, Grand Cordon of the Order of the Yugoslav Standard, Grand Officer of the Panamanian Nat. Order of Vasco Nuñez de Balboa, Republic Medal (Class III), Military Service Medal

(Class I), Order of The Republic (Class I), and other decorations.
151 El Sayed el Mirghani Street, Heliopolis, Cairo, United Arab Republic.

Young, Rev. Canon Andrew John, M.A.; British ecclesiastic and poet; b. 85; ed. Edinburgh Univ.
Vicar of Stonegate, Sussex 41-59; Canon of Chichester Cathedral; Queen's Gold Medal for Poetry; Hon. LL.D.
Publs. *Collected Poems* 36, *Speak to the Earth* 40, *Prospect of Flowers* 45, *Collected Poems* 48, *Retrospect of Flowers* 50, *Prospect of Britain* 56, *Out of the World and Back* 59, *The Poet and the Landscape* 62, *The New Poly-olbion*, *Quiet as Moss* 67, *Burning as Light* 67.
Park Lodge, Church Lane, Yapton, Arundel, Sussex, England.
Telephone: Yapton 210.

Young, Col. Sir Arthur Edwin, Kt., C.M.G., C.V.O.; British police officer; b. 1907; ed. Portsmouth Grammar School.
Served Portsmouth City Police 24; Chief Constable of Leamington 38; Senior Asst. Chief Constable of Birmingham 41; Chief Constable of Hertfordshire 45; Asst. Commr. Metropolitan Police 47; Commr. of Police, City of London 50-; Dir. of Public Safety, Allied Control Comm., Italy 43-45; Hon. Commr. of Police, New York; mem. Board of Govs. of the Police College; adviser on re-organisation Gold Coast Police 51; Commr. of Malaya Police 52, of Kenya Police 54; Officer (Brother) Order of St. John of Jerusalem; Chair. Life Guard Fed.; Chair. of Council B.-P. Scout Guild; Chair. Council Police Athletic Asscn.; mem. Advisory Council Nat. Police Fund, Chair. Educ. Cttee.; fmr. mem. London and Home Counties Traffic Advisory Cttee.; Vice-Pres. Police Mutual Assurance Soc.; Chair. Police Council of Great Britain 67.
26 Old Jewry, London, E.C.2, England.
Telephone: 01-606-8866.

Young, Brian Walter Mark; British foundation director; b. 23 Aug. 1922; ed. Eton Coll., and King's Coll., Cambridge.
Assistant Master, Eton Coll., 47-52; Headmaster of Charterhouse 52-64; Dir. of Nuffield Foundation Sept. 64-; mem. Central Advisory Council for Education 56-59, Chair. Centre for Curriculum Renewal and Educational Devt. Overseas and Assoc. Examining Board; mem. U.K. Nat. Comm. for UNESCO.
Publs. *Via Vertendi* 52, *Intelligent Reading* 64.
Nuffield Lodge, Regent's Park, London, N.W.1, England.
Telephone: 01-722-8871.

Young, (Charles) Kenneth, B.A., F.R.S.L.; British author and journalist; b. 27 Nov. 1916; ed. Queen Elizabeth's Grammar School, Wakefield, Coatham School, Redcar, and Leeds Univ.
Army Service, Second World War; Foreign Office 44; B.B.C. European Service 48; *Daily Mirror* 50; Perm. Under-Sec. Dept., Cabt. Office 50; *Daily Telegraph* 52-60; Editor *The Yorkshire Post* 60-64; Political and Literary Adviser, Beaverbrook Newspapers 65-; broadcaster, Editor Television series *The Book Man* 60; Gov. Welbeck Coll.
Publs. *D. H. Lawrence* 52, *John Dryden* (critical biography) 54, *Ford Madox Ford* 58, *A. J. Balfour* (authorised biography) 63, *Churchill and Beaverbrook* (a study in friendship) 66, *Rhodesia and Independence* 67, *Compton Mackenzie* 68, *Music's Great Days at the Spas and Watering Places* 68.
The Daily Express, Fleet Street, London, E.C.4; and Amberfield, Chart Sutton, Maidstone, Kent, England.
Telephone: Maidstone 43000; and 01-353-8000.

Young, Frank George, M.A., D.SC., PH.D., F.R.I.C., F.R.S.; British university professor; b. 25 March 1908; ed. Alleyn's School and Univ. Coll. London.
Bayliss-Starling Scholar, Sharpey Scholar, and Schafer Prizeman in Physiology, Univ. Coll., London 29-32; Beit Memorial Fellow at Univ. Coll., London, Univ. of Aberdeen and Univ. of Toronto 32-36; mem. of scientific staff, Medical Research Council, Nat. Inst. for Medical Research 36-42; William Julius Mickle Fellow, Univ. of London 40; Prof. of Biochemistry, St. Thomas's Hospital Medical School, Univ. of London 42-45; at Univ. Coll., Univ. of London 45-49; Sir William Dunn Prof. of Biochemistry, Univ. of Cambridge 49-; mem. Medical Research Council 50-54; Hon. Fellow of Trinity Hall, Cambridge; Master of Darwin College, Cambridge 64-; Fellow, Univ. Coll., London; Chair. Editorial Board *Biochemical Journal* 42-46; Pres. European Asscn. for the Study of Diabetes 65-; mem. Royal Comm. on Medical Educ. 65-68; Treas. Int. Union of Biochemistry 67-; mem. Int. Council of Science Unions 67-; Trustee Ciba Foundation 67-; Hon. Dr., Montpellier and Aberdeen Univs. and Catholic Univ. of Chile.
Department of Biochemistry, Tennis Court Road, Cambridge, England.

Young, George Sterling, M.S.; American business executive; b. 5 April 1899; ed. U.S. Naval Acad. and Columbia Univ.
Engineer, Columbia Engineering and Management Corpn. 30-36; Vice-Pres. and Gen. Man. Mich. Gas Transmission Corpn. Detroit 36-41 Vice-Pres. (Transmission) Columbia Engineering Corpn., New York City 42-45, Dir. 45-64, Vice-Pres. (Operations) 45-51, name changed to Columbia Gas System Service Corpn. 51, Pres. 51, Chief Exec. Officer 56-64, Chair. 60-64; Dir. Columbia Gas & Electric Corpn. 46, mem. Exec. Cttee. 47, firm name changed to Columbia Gas System Inc. 48, Exec. Vice-Pres. 49, Pres. 51-60, Chief Exec. Officer 56-64, Chair. of Board 60-64, Chair. Exec. Cttee. 64-.
Office: 120 E. 41st Street, New York City 10017, N.Y., U.S.A.

Young, John Zachary, M.A., F.R.S.; British zoologist; b. 18 March 1907; ed. Marlborough Coll. and Magdalen Coll., Oxford.
Fellow, Magdalen Coll., Oxford 31-45; Univ. Demonstrator in Zoology and Comparative Anatomy, Oxford 33-45; Prof. of Anatomy, Univ. Coll., London 45-; Rockefeller Fellow 36; B.B.C. Reith Lecturer 50; Chair. Zoology Section, Dublin Meeting British Asscn. for Advancement of Science 57; Foreign hon. mem. American Acad. of Arts and Sciences 57; Royal Medal, Royal Soc. 67; Hon. D.Sc. (Bristol Univ.) 56.
Publs. *The Life of Vertebrates* 50, *Doubt and Certainty in Science* 51, *The Life of Mammals* 57.
Albany Cottage, Park Village East, Regent's Park, London, N.W.1, England.
Telephone: 01-387-6654.

Young, Kenneth (*see* Young, C. K.)

Young, Kenneth Todd, M.A.; American diplomatist; b. 22 June 1916; ed. Lingnan Univ. (China), Univ. of Paris, and Harvard Univ.
Teaching Fellow Harvard Univ. 40-42; War Production Board 42-43, U.S. Army (Capt.) 43-46; Asst. Political Intelligence Officer, State Dept. 46-49; Far Eastern specialist, Dept. of Defense 49-52; Dir. Office of Northeast Asian Affairs, State Dept. 52-54; Act. Dir. Office of Philippine and S.E. Asian Affairs 54, Dir. 55; Dir. Office of S.E. Asian Affairs 56-58; with oil co. 58-61; Ambassador to Thailand 61-63; Pres. Asia Soc., New York City 65-68.
112 East 64th Street, New York City 10021, U.S.A.

Young, Michael, M.A., PH.D.; British sociologist; b. 9 Aug. 1915; ed. Dartington Hall School, London Univ. and Gray's Inn, London.
Director of Political and Econ. Planning 41-45; Sec. Research Dept., Labour Party 45-51; Dir. Inst. of

Community Studies 53-; Chair. Consumers' Asscn. 56-65, Pres. 65-; Chair. Advisory Centre for Educ. 59-; Lecturer in Sociology, Cambridge Univ. 61-63, Trustee, Dartington Hall 42-; Chair. Social Science Research Council 65-.

Publs. *Family and Kinship in East London* (with Peter Willmott) 57, *The Rise of the Meritocracy* 59, *Family and Class in a London Suburb* (with Peter Willmott) 61, *Innovation and Research in Education* 65.

18 Victoria Park Square, London, E.2, England.

Young, Stephen M., LL.B.; American politician; b. 4 May 1889; ed. Kenyon Coll. and Western Reserve Univ.

Army service in both World Wars; Allied Military Gov., Reggio Province, Italy 45; fmr. mem. Ohio Gen. Assembly, Chief Criminal Prosecuting Counsel, Cuyahoga County, mem. Ohio Comm. on Unemployment Insurance, Special Counsel to Attorney Gen. of Ohio; Congressman-at-large seventy-third, seventy-fourth, seventy-seventh and eighty-first Congresses; U.S. Senator from Ohio 58-; mem. Senate Cttees. on Armed Services, Aeronautical and Space Sciences, Public Works; Order of Crown of Italy, Bronze Star, etc.; Hon. Master of Civil Law, Kenyon Coll.; LL.D., Central State Coll.; Chubb Fellow, Yale Univ.; Democrat.

458 Senate Office Building, Washington 25, D.C., U.S.A.

Young, Wayland (*see* Kennet, 2nd Baron).

Young, Whitney M., Jr.; American social worker; b. 31 July 1921; ed. Kentucky State College, Massachusetts Inst. of Technology, Univ. of Minnesota and Harvard Univ.

Industrial Relations Secretary, St. Paul Urban League 48-50; Exec. Dir. Omaha Urban League 50-54; Dean, Atlanta University School of Social Work 54-61; Exec. Dir. Nat. Urban League 61-; mem. President's Cttees. on Law Enforcement and Admin. of Justice; Nat. Advisor Council of U.S. Office of Econ. Opportunity; Advisory Council on Vocational Educ., U.S. Office of Educ.; Board Trustees, Eleanor Roosevelt Memorial Foundation; Vice-Chair. Citizens Crusade against Poverty; several hon. degrees.

Office: 55 East 52nd Street, New York, N.Y. 10022; Home: 29 Mohegan Place, New Rochelle, N.Y., U.S.A.

Youngdahl, Luther Wallace, B.A., LL.B.; American lawyer and politician; b. 29 May 1896; ed. Gustavus Adolphus Coll., St. Peter and Minnesota Coll. of Law.

Admitted to Bar 21; Asst. Minneapolis City Attorney 21-23; Partner of Judge M. C. Tifft in Law Practice 23-30; apptd. municipal Judge 30, elected district Judge 36; elected Assoc. Justice, Minnesota Supreme Court 42; Gov. of Minnesota 46-51; Judge U.S. District Court for D.C. Oct. 51-, Senior Judge 66-; served on faculty of Minneapolis-Minnesota Coll. of Law; mem. President's Comm. on Law Enforcement and the Admin. of Justice 66; Grand Cross, Order of North Star (Sweden); fourteen Hon. LL.D. degrees; 1st Lieut. during First World War.

4101 Cathedral Avenue, N.W., Washington, D.C., U.S.A.

Younger, J. Arthur; American politician; b. 11 April 1893; ed. Univ. of Washington.

Army Service, First World War; Vice-Pres., Dir. and Man. Mortgage Loan Dept., Seattle Title Trust Co. 20-30; Pres. Seattle Mortgage Loan Co. 30-34; Asst. Appraiser-Adviser Home Loan Bank Board, Chief of Savings and Loan Div., Fed. Home Loan Bank Board, Wash. 34-37; Exec. Vice-Pres. Citizens Fed. Savings and Loans Asscn., San Francisco 37-; mem. U.S. House of Reps. 52-; mem. Interstate and Foreign Commerce Cttee.

House of Representatives, Washington, D.C.; and 3448 Edison, San Mateo, Calif., U.S.A.

Younger, Rt. Hon. Kenneth Gilmour; British politician and administrator; b. 15 Dec 1908; ed. Winchester Coll. and New Coll., Oxford.

Called to the Bar, Inner Temple 32; army service in Second World War; Labour M.P. for Grimsby 45-59; Parl. Under-Sec. Home Office 47-50; Minister of State for Foreign Affairs 50-51; Joint Vice-Chair. Royal Inst. of Int. Affairs 53-55, 58-59, Dir. 59-; Chair. Board of Trustees, UN Inst. for Training and Research, New York 65-66.

Publs. *Fabian International Essays* 57 (Joint Editor), *The Public Service in the New States* 59, *Changing Perspectives in British Foreign Policy* 64.

3 Clareville Grove, London, S.W.7, England.

Yourcenar, Marguerite; French writer; b. 8 June 1903. Publs. *Alexis ou le Traité du vain combat* 29, *La Nouvelle Eurydice* 31, *Pindare* 32, *La Mort conduit l'Attelage* 34, *Denier du Rêve* 34, *Feux* 36, *Les Songes et Les Sorts* 38, *Les Nouvelles Orientales* 38, *Le Coup de Grâce* 39, *Mémoires d'Hadrien* 51, *Electre ou la Chute des Masques* 54, *Les Charités d'Alcippe* 56, *Sous Bénéfice d'Inventaire* 62, *Le Mystère d'Alceste* 63; trans. *The Waves* (Virginia Woolf) 37, *What Maisie Knew* (Henry James) 47, *Poems* (Constantine Cavafy) 58, *Fleuve Profond, Sombre Rivière* (Negro Spirituals) 64.

Petite Plaisance, Northeast Harbor, Maine 04662, U.S.A.

Telephone: 816-276-3940.

Youssef, S. Mohamed; United Arab Republic (Egyptian) educationist; b. 97; ed. Tanta Primary School, Abbassia Secondary School, and Teacher Training Coll.

Successively Secondary School Teacher, Headmaster, Gen. Dir. of Personnel, Ministry of Educ., Dir. of Recruitment and Training, Civil Service Bureau, Dir.-Gen. of Secondary Educ., Minister of Educ., Asst. Under-Sec. of State, Perm. Under-Sec. of State, Ministry of Education; M.P. 57-; Minister of Education 61-67.

c/o Ministry of Education, Cairo, United Arab Republic.

Yousuf, Lieut.-Gen. Mohammed; Pakistani soldier and diplomatist; b. 08; ed. Prince of Wales's Royal Military Coll. and Royal Military Coll., Sandhurst.

Joined 7th Light Cavalry 29; Brigade Major 42; commanded 18th King Edward's Own Cavalry 47; raised 12th Div. 48; G.O.C. East Pakistan 49; led Military Mission to Iran 51; Chief of Gen. Staff 51; Commdt. Pakistan Armoured Corps 52; retd. from Army 56; High Commr. for Pakistan in Australia and New Zealand 56-59, in Great Britain 59-63; Ambassador to Afghanistan 63-; Nishani Liaqat (Iran), Légion d'Honneur.

Pakistan Embassy, Kabul, Afghanistan.

Yu Chiu-li, Lt.-Gen.; Chinese politician.

Former Chief, Finance Dept., People's Liberation Army; Political Commissar, Combined Services H.Q., People's Liberation Army 57-58; Minister of Petroleum Industry 58-.

Ministry of Petroleum Industry, Peking, People's Republic of China.

Yü Ping-po, B.A.; Chinese literary historian and man of letters; b. 8 Jan. 1900; ed. National Univ. of Peking. Taught literature at Yenching Univ., later National Univ. of Peking, Tsinghua Univ. and China Univ.; after war at National Univ. of Peking; research fellow Inst. of Literature 53-; Chekiang del. to First N.P.C. 54, Second 58, Third 64; mem. Asian Solidarity Cttee. 56; mem. Central Cttee. Chiu San Society 58-; mem. Chinese People's Cttee. for World Peace 65.

Publs. Many articles and books on *T'zu* poetry, *Shih-ching, Hung-lou meng*; collections of poems, critical essays, etc.

Chiu San Society, Peking, China.

Yuan Han-ching; Chinese scientist; b. 05; ed. Tsing-hua Univ., Illinois Univ.
Professor at National Central Univ.; Sec.-Gen. Chinese Asscn. for the Dissemination of Scientific and Technical Knowledge 54-56; attended C.P.P.C.C. 54, Vice-Sec.-General 55; on Cttee. of Dept. of Physics, Mathematics and Chemistry, Chinese Acad. of Sciences, 55-; on Cttee. Chiu San Society 56.
Chinese Academy of Sciences, Peking, China.

Yuan Jen-Yuan; Chinese politician and adminis-trator.
Former Gov. Tsinghai Province; mem. Control Comm., Central Cttee. of Chinese Communist Party 62-.
Control Committee of Central Committee of Chinese Communist Party, Peking, People's Republic of China.

Yugov, Anton; Bulgarian politician; b. 5 Aug. 1904.
As a youth worked in a tobacco factory, took an active part in the Trade Union and Workers' Movement 22; mem. Bulgarian Communist Party 28-; Party training in Moscow 34-36; elected to Party Politbureau 37, expelled from Cen. Cttee. 62; imprisoned 40, escaped 41; took an active part as Party Sec. in the Underground Movement; mem. of Gov. and Minister of the Interior 44-49, of Industry 50; later Dep. Prime Minister, Prime Minister 56-62.
Sofia, Bulgaria.

Yukawa, Hideki, D.SC.; Japanese physicist; b. 23 Jan. 1907; ed. Kyoto Univ.
Lecturer, Kyoto Univ. 32, Osaka Univ. 33; Asst. Prof. Osaka Univ. 36; Prof. of Physics, Kyoto Univ. 39- (on leave of absence 48-52); Visiting Prof., Inst. for Ad-vanced Study, Princeton 48-49; Prof. of Physics, Columbia Univ. 51-; Imperial Prize, Japan Acad. 40; Order of Decoration of Japan 43; mem. Japan Acad. 46; Foreign Assoc., Nat. Acad. of Sciences, U.S. 49; Nobel Prize for Physics 49; Prof. Emeritus (Osaka Univ.); Dir. Research Inst. for Fundamental Physics, Kyoto Univ. 53-; Hon. Citizen of Kyoto; Hon. Dr. Univ. of Paris; Hon. mem. Royal Soc. of Edinburgh, Indian Acad. of Sciences, Accademia Nazionale dei Lincei; mem. Pontificia Academia Scientiarum; foreign mem. Royal Soc. London.
Yukawa Hall, Kyoto University, Kyoto; Izumigawa, Shimogamo, Sakyo-ku, Kyoto, Japan; and 501 West 121st Street, New York, N.Y. 10027, U.S.A.

Yukawa, Morio; Japanese diplomatist; b. 23 Feb. 1908; ed. Tokyo Univ.
Entered Foreign Service 33; served U.K., Geneva; Dir. Econ. Stabilisation Board, Cabinet 50-51; Dir. Econ. Affairs Bureau, Foreign Office 51-52; Minister-Council-lor to France 52-54; Dir. Int. Co-operation Bureau, Foreign Office 54-55; Dir. Econ. Affairs Bureau,

Foreign Office 55-57; Amb. to Philippines 57-61; Deputy Vice-Minister, Foreign Office 61-63; Amb. to Belgium, Luxembourg and European Econ. Commu-nity 63-68, to U.K. 68-.
Embassy of Japan, Grosvenor Street, London W.1., England; 30-10 Gochome Denyenchofu, Ota-ku, Tokyo, Japan.

Yunak, Ivan Kharitonovich; Soviet politician; b. 18; ed. Glukhov Agricultural Inst.
Army Service 41-46; mem. C.P.S.U. 44-; Agronomist Dist. Agricultural Dept., Kiev 46-49; party work and Soviet work 49-; Chair. Dniepropetrovsk Regional Council of Workers' Deputies 54-61; First Sec. Tula Regional Cttee. C.P.S.U. 61-; mem. Central Cttee. of C.P.S.U. 61-; Deputy to U.S.S.R. Supreme Soviet; mem. Budget and Planning Comm., Soviet of Union of U.S.S.R. Supreme Soviet.
Tula Regional Committee of Communist Party of Soviet Union, Tula, U.S.S.R.

Yunich, David Lawrence, B.A., M.A.; American merchant; b. 21 May 1917; ed. Union College and Harvard Graduate School of Business Administration.
Senior Vice-Pres. Macy's, New York 51-54; Pres. Bamberger's, New Jersey 55-62; Pres. Macy's, New York 62-; Dir. R. H. Macy and Co. Inc. 59-; Dir. National Retail Merchants' Asscn. 62-, Carnegie Hall Corpn. 63-, Prudential Insurance Co. of America 65-, East River Savings Bank 65-, American Management Asscn.; Vice-Chair. Tax Comm. for State of New Jersey 60-62; Trustee Union and Skidmore Colls.; Hon. LL.D. (Union Coll.) 64.
Macy's, New York, Herald Square, New York, N.Y.; Home: Five Birches, Cooper Road, Scarsdale, N.Y., U.S.A.
Telephone: SCarsdale 3-6506 (Home).

Yusof bin Ishak; Singapore statesman and former journalist; b. 12 Aug. 1910; ed. Raffles Inst., Singapore.
Joined staff of *Warta Malaya* 32; organised Malay paper *Utusan Melayu* 39, Man. Dir. and Ed. 46-59; Chair. Public Service Comm. July-Dec. 59; Yang di-Pertuan Negara (Head of State of Singapore) 59-8 Aug. 65; became First Pres. of Republic of Singapore when made independent of Malaysia 9 Aug. 65-.
The Istana, Singapore.

Yussof, Dr. Mohammed; Afghan politician.
Former Minister of Mines and Industries; Prime Minister and Minister of Foreign Affairs March 63-Nov. 65; Amb. to German Fed. Repub. 66-.
Embassy of Afghanistan, 5301 Uckesdorf bei Bonn, Liebfrauenweg 1a, German Federal Republic.
Telephone: Bonn 53917.

Z

Zabrodin, Yevgeni Grigoryevich; Soviet diplomatist; b. 1907; ed. Moscow Inst. of Oriental Studies.
Diplomatic Service 38-; Deputy Head Second Far Eastern Dept., U.S.S.R. Ministry of Foreign Affairs 45-48; Deputy Gen. Sec. U.S.S.R. Ministry of Foreign Affairs 49-50, Head, Second Far Eastern Dept. 50-53; Counsellor, Indonesia 54-57; Counsellor-Envoy, Japan 57-58; Ambassador to Nepal 59-65; on Staff Ministry of Foreign Affairs 65-67; Consul-Gen. in Sapporo, Japan 67-.
U.S.S.R. Consulate-General, Sapporo, Japan.

Zacharias, Jerrold Reinach, B.A., PH.D.; American physicist; b. 23 Jan. 1905; ed. Columbia Univ.
Teacher, Hunter Coll., New York City 31-40; with Radiation Laboratory, Mass. Inst. of Technology 40-45, Prof. of Physics, Mass. Inst. of Technology 46-66, Inst. Prof. 66-, Dir. Nuclear Science Laboratory 46-56; Assoc. Dir. Project Lexington (nuclear-powered flight) 48; Dir. Project Hartwell (undersea warfare) 50; Assoc. Dir. Project Charles 51, Project Lincoln 51-52 (both air defence); Dir. Summer Study on Distant Early Warning Line 52; Technical Dir. Project Lamp Light (continental defence) 54; Chair. Physical Science Study Cttee. 56-; mem. Nat. Acad. of Sciences; main field of research: electric and magnetic shapes of atomic nuclei, one outgrowth of which has been the invention of what is claimed to be the world's most precise atomic clock.
32 Clifton Street, Belmont, Mass., U.S.A.
Telephone: IV-4-5461.

Zachwatowicz, Jan, DR.TECH.SC.; Polish architect; b. 1900; ed. Warsaw Technical Univ.
Asst. Warsaw Tech. Univ. 26-30, Adjunct 35-39, Prof. 39-; Conservator Gen. of Polish Republic and Dir. Gen. Department of Conservation 45-57; mem. fmr. Polish Acad. of Learning 46, Polish Acad. of Sciences 52-; conservation work includes uncovering and restoration fortified walls of Warsaw Old Town and plans for reconstruction of historical monuments in Warsaw and other cities; Hon. mem. Royal Inst. of British Architects 36; State Prize, First Class.
Publs. *Twierdza Zamosc* (*The Forts of Zamosc*) 36, *Katedra Gnieznienska* (*Gniezno Cathedral*) 47, *Dzieje architektury polskiej* (*History of Polish Architecture*) 52, 54, *Konserwacja zabytkow* (*The Conservation of Monuments*) 56, 65, *Architektura Polska X i XI w.* (*Polish Architecture of X-XI Centuries*) 61, *Architektura Polska* (*Polish Architecture*) 66.
Koszykowa 55, Warsaw, Poland.
Telephone: 284885.

Zafrulla Khan, Sir Muhammad, K.C.S.I., B.A., LL.B., HON. LL.D. (Cantab); Pakistani politician; b. 6 Feb. 1893; ed. Govt. Coll., Lahore, and King's Coll., London.
Barrister-at-Law (Lincoln's Inn); Advocate, Sialkot, Punjab 14-16; practised Lahore High Court 16-35; mem. Punjab Legislative Council 26-35; del. Indian Round Table Confs. 30, 31, 32; del. Joint Select Cttee. of Parl. on Indian Reforms 33; Pres. All-India Muslim League 31; mem. Gov.-Gen.'s Exec. Council 35-41; Leader Indian Del. to Assembly of L. of N. 39; Agent-Gen. of Govt. of India in China 42; Judge Fed. Court of India 41-June 47; Constitutional Adviser to H.H. Ruler of Bhopal June-Dec. 47; Leader Pakistan Del. to Annual Session of U.N. Gen. Assembly Sept.-Nov. 47; Minister of Foreign Affairs and Commonwealth Relations, Govt. of Pakistan Dec. 47; Leader Pakistan Del. to U.N. Security Council on India-Pakistan dispute 48-54, and to sessions of U.N. Gen. Assembly 47-54;

Leader Pakistan del. to San Francisco Conf. on Japanese Peace Treaty 51; Leader Pakistan Del. to SEATO Conf. Manila 54; Judge at the Int. Court of Justice, The Hague 54-61, Vice-Pres. April 58-61; Perm. Rep. of Pakistan to UN 61-64; Judge, Int. Court of Justice 64-; Pres. 17th session UN General Assembly Sept. 62-63.
Publ. *Islam: Its Meaning for Modern Man* 62.
International Court of Justice, The Hague, Netherlands.

Zahedi, Ardeshir, LL.B.; Iranian diplomatist; b. 17 Oct. 1928; ed. in Teheran, American Univ. of Beirut and Univ. of Utah (U.S.A.).
Civil Adjutant to His Imperial Majesty the Shah of Iran 54-; Iranian Amb. to U.S.A. 60-62, to U.K. 62-67; Minister of Foreign Affairs 67-; LL.D., Utah State Univ.
Ministry of Foreign Affairs, Teheran, Iran.

Zahedi, Dr. Hassan; Iranian banker; b. 11; ed. Teheran Univ. and Columbia Univ., U.S.A.
Entered Government Service 36, in Agricultural Bank until 45; in U.S. and posts with UN 45-48; in Ministry of Finance 58-61; Gen. Manager Agricultural Bank, Teheran 61-67; Minister of Agriculture 67-.
Ministry of Agriculture, Teheran, Iran.

Zaher, Aref, B.A.; Iraqi international civil servant; b. 1910; ed. American University of Beirut.
Ministry of Foreign Affairs, Iraq 38-41; Ministry of Finance 41-42; Ministry of Education 42-48; League of Arab States 48-, Dir. of Economic Dept. 56-63; Asst. Sec.-Gen. 63-; Cedar Medal (Lebanon) 54.
League of Arab States, Cairo, United Arab Republic.
Telephone: 819633.

Zahir Shah (*see* Mohammed Zahir Shah).

Zahn, Dr. Joachim; German business executive; b. 24 Jan. 1914.
Member Management Board Daimler-Benz A.G., Stuttgart-Untertürkheim; Chair. of Advisory Board Mercedes-Benz Argentina, Mercedes-Benz of North America, Inc., Maschinenfabrik Esslingen A.G., Maybach Mercedes-Benz-Motorenbau G.m.b.H., Mercedes-Benz (Australia) Pty. Ltd., Handelsgesellschaft für Daimler-Benz-Erzeugnisse A.G.; Deputy Chair. Advisory Board Auto Union G.m.b.H., Obermain Schuhfabrik A.G.; mem. Advisory Board Tata Engineering & Locomotive Co. Ltd., Pongs & Zahn Textilwerke A.G., Mercedes-Benz do Brazil S.A., United Car and Diesel Distributors Pty. Ltd., Frankfurter Versicherungs A.G.; Adviser for Deutsche Bank A.G., Allianz-Versicherungs A.G., Munich, Süd-West-Chemie, Neu-Ulm, External Trade, Ministry of Econs.; mem. Management Board Verband der Automobilindustrie e.V.
7000 Stuttgart 1, Gerokstrasse 13B, German Federal Republic.

Zaid bin Sultan bin Zaid, H.H. Sheikh (brother of Shakhbut, *q.v.*); Ruler of Abu Dhabi.
Former Gov. of Eastern Province; deposed his brother, Sheikh Shakhbut and succeeded to Sheikhdom 66.
Royal Diwan, Abu Dhabi, Trucial States.

Zain, Dr. Zairin; Indonesian diplomatist; b. 17 Sept. 1913.
Diplomatic Service 47-, successively Dep. Head of Mission in India, Dep. Rep. Singapore and Malaya, Head of Directorate of Econ. Affairs at Ministry of Foreign Affairs, Djakarta, Chargé d'Affaires, Bonn, Minister, Washington, London; Ambassador to German

Federal Republic 56-61, to U.S.A. 61-65, to Switzerland 65-67.
c/o Ministry of Foreign Affairs, Djakarta, Indonesia.

Zaitsev, Grigory Titovich; Soviet diplomatist; b. 19 Dec. 1902; ed. Moscow Inst. of Oriental Studies and Inst. of Red Professors.
Diplomatic work 44-; Dep. Head Near Eastern Dept., People's Commissariat for Foreign Affairs 44-45; Minister to Iraq 45-49; Dep. Head Middle East Dept., U.S.S.R. Ministry of Foreign Affairs 49-50; Ambassador to Netherlands 50-53; Head of Dept. for Near and Middle East, Ministry of Foreign Affairs 53-56, for Near East 56-58; Ambassador to Iraq 58-61; Head of Dept. for Middle East 61-63; Amb. to Iran 63-68.
c/o Ministry of Foreign Affairs, Moscow, U.S.S.R.

Zaitsev, Mikhail Vasilyevich; Soviet politician; b. 1921; ed. Chuvash Pedagogical Inst.
Member C.P.S.U. 42-; Teacher 39-42; Party Official 42-55; Vice-Chair. Council of Ministers of Chuvash Autonomous S.S.R. 55-61; First Sec. Cheboksary City Cttee. C.P.S.U. 61-62; Chair. Council of Ministers Chuvash Autonomous S.S.R. 62-; Deputy to U.S.S.R. Supreme Soviet.
Council of Ministers, Chuvash A.S.S.R., Cheboksary, U.S.S.R.

Zajączkowski, Ananiasz, DR. PHIL.; Polish university professor; b. 03; ed. Cracow Univ., Germany, France and Turkey.
Asst. Univ. of Warsaw 32, Lecturer in Turkish 33, Extra. Prof. of Turcology 35, Ord. Prof. of Turkish 45-; mem. Polish Acad. of Sciences, Polish Board of Orientology; Dir. Inst. of Oriental Studies 53-.
Publs. include *Gramatyka porownawcza jezykow tureckich* (Comparative Grammar of the Turkish Languages).
6 Sewerynów, Warsaw, Poland.

Zakharikhin, Pyotr Akimovich; Soviet foreign trade official; b. 1919; ed. Kuibyshev Industrial Inst. and Academy of Foreign Trade.
Member C.P.S.U. 41-; Dir. *Soyuzpromexport* Trust 47-48; at Ministry of Foreign Trade 48-50; Deputy Commercial Rep. of U.S.S.R. in France 50-54; Deputy Chief, later Chief, of Dept., *Raznoimport* Trust 54-57; Section Chief *Prodintorg* Trust 57-59; U.S.S.R. Commercial Rep. in Morocco 59-62; Deputy Chief, later Chief, of Dept., Ministry of Foreign Trade 62-66; U.S.S.R. Commercial Rep. in France 66-; Order of Red Banner of Labour.
U.S.S.R. Trade Representation, Paris, France.

Zakharov, Alexei Vassilevich; Soviet diplomatist; b. 1913; ed. Plekhanov Inst. of National Economy.
Chairman U.S.S.R. Purchasing Commission in U.S.A. 42; Dep. Head, Accounting and Econ. Dept., Deputy Minister of Foreign Trade 51-53; U.S.S.R. Rep., later Deputy Rep. to Council of Mutual Econ. Aid 53-56; Dep. Minister of Foreign Affairs 56-59; Ambassador to Finland 59-65; Head of Dept. of Scandinavian Affairs, Ministry of Foreign Affairs 65-67; Deputy Perm. Rep. to UN 67-.
U.S.S.R. Permanent Representation, United Nations, New York, U.S.A.

Zakharov, Marshal Matvei Vasilievich; Soviet army officer; b. 98; ed. Frunze Mil. Acad.
Took part in October Revolution; joined Gen. Staff 37; Chief of Staff 41-45; Head Mil. Acad. of Gen. Staff 45-49; Head Chief Admin. of Gen. Staff 49-52; Chief Inspector Soviet Army 52-53; Commdr. Leningrad Mil. Area 53-57; Commdr.-in-Chief Soviet troops in Germany 57-60; Chief of Gen. Staff of Soviet Army, First Dep. Minister of Defence 60-63, 64-; Head Higher Military Acad. 63-64; mem. Central Cttee. C.P.S.U. 61-; Dep. to Supreme Soviet; Hero of the Soviet Union, Order of

Lenin (4), Order of Red Banner (4), Suvorov (2), Kutuzov; many other awards.
c/o Ministry of Defence, 34 Maurice Thorez Embankment, Moscow, U.S.S.R.

Zakhava, Boris Yevgenevich; Soviet actor and producer; b. 96; ed. Moscow Commercial Inst.
Joined Vakhtangov's Drama Studio 14; taught drama since 17, directed at Shchukin Theatre School 24-; with others founded Vakhtangov State Theatre in which he has acted and produced using the Stanislavsky and Vakhtangov approach; People's Artist of R.S.F.S.R.; State Prize; Red Banner of Labour and other awards. Productions include *The Badgers* (Leonov), *The Seagull* (Chekhov), *First Joys* (Fedin), *Hamlet* (Shakespeare), *The Aristocrats* (N. Pogodin), *The Great Sovereign* (Solovyov), *The Young Guard* (Fadeyev), *Yegor Bulychev and Others* (produced with participation of the author Maxim Gorky), *The Government Inspector* (Gogol); played Field-Marshal Kutuzov in *War and Peace* (Leo Tolstoy).
Publs. *Vakhtangov and His Studio* 27, *Principles of Directing* 34, *The Creative Work of E. B. Vakhtangov* 39, *Mastership of Actor and Producer* 64.
Shchukin Theatre School of Vakhtangov Theatre, Moscow, U.S.S.R.

Zaki, Hassan Abbas; United Arab Republic (Egyptian) politician; b. 2 Jan. 1917; ed. primary and secondary schools and Cairo Univ.
Commercial Sec. U.A.R. Embassy, Wash. 52; Govt. Rep. in Stock Exchange Mina El Bassal 55; Dir.-Gen. Exchange Control Dept. Ministry of Econs.; mem. Nat. Assembly; Minister of the Treasury 58, of Economy and Supply 61; Head of Board of Dirs. Gen. Egyptian Org. for Insurance 65; Minister of Economy and Foreign Trade 66-; Order of Merit (Fourth Class); Grand Cordon of the Yugoslav Flag; Grand Cross Royal Order of Phoenix (Greece); Grand Star (Chevalier) of Somali Order; Ordinal Tuder Vladiminescu (First Class) of Romania.
Publs. Various articles on monetary, international trade and cotton policies.
Ministry of Economy and Foreign Trade, Lazogly Square, Cairo; Home: 23 Gabalia Street, Zamalek, U.A.R.
Telephone: 914222 (Office); 816719 (Home).

Žákovič, Michal, LL.D.; Czechoslovak politician; b. 27 April 1916; ed. Law Faculty, Comenius Univ., Bratislava.
Worked in Municipal Transport Enterprise, Bratislava 46-48; mem. Slovak Nat. Council 48-, Deputy Chair. 54-60, mem. Presidium 54-; Chair. Freedom Party 60-; mem. Presidium Slovak Peace Cttee. 50-; mem. Presidium Nat. Front 56-; Award for Merit in Construction 66.
Bratislava, Ul. Obrancov mieru 6/c, Czechoslovakia.

Zakythinos, Denis; Greek historian and university professor; b. 05; ed. Gymnasium of Lixouri, Univs. of Athens and Paris.
Sec. Institut Néo-hellénique, Univ. of Paris 31-32; Dir. Fondation Hellénique, Cité Universitaire de Paris 32-35; Dir. State Gen. Archives 37-46; Prof. of Byzantine History, Univ. of Athens 39-; Minister of Press and Information April-Aug. 45; Prof. of History of Civilisations, High School of Political Sciences, Athens 51-57, Prof. of Modern Greek History 57-; Dir. of review *L'Hellénisme Contemporain* 55-; Dir. Centre of Byzantine Researches 60-; Gen.-Sec. Asscn. Internationale des Etudes Byzantines 61-; Rector High School of Political Sciences 62-63; Pres. Asscn. Int. d'Etudes du Sud-Est Européen 63-; Minister attached to Prime Minister's Office Dec. 63-Feb. 64.
Publs. include *Le Despotat grec de Morée*, Vol. I 32, Vol. II 53, *Le chrysobulle d'Alexis III, empereur de Trébizonde, en faveur des Vénitiens* 32, *La Grèce et les*

Balkans 47, *Crise monétaire et Crise économique à Byzance du XIIIe au XVe siècle* 48 (all in French), *The Slavs in Greece: Contributions in the History of Medieval Hellenism* (in Greek) 45, *Byzantium: State and Society, Historical Survey* (in Greek) 51, *The Capture of Constantinople and the Turkish Domination* (Greek and French) 54, *Turkish Domination: an Introduction to Modern History of Hellenism* (in Greek) 57, *Byzantine Texts* (in Greek) 57, *The Political History of Modern Greece* (in Greek) 62, *Byzantine Greece 392-1204* (in Greek) 65.

Odos Democritou 6, Athens, Greece.

Zalokostas, Christos; Greek writer, politician and industrialist; b. 96; ed. Munich Polytechnic.
Member of Parliament 46-; Parliamentary Representative of Greece, Council of Europe 53-56; represented Greece at Olympic Games (fencing), Berlin 36; World Pistol Champion 39; Popular Party.
Publs. include *The Chronicle of Slavery* 45, *King Alexander* 46, *Poverty in the Sun* 52, *Marina* 57.
Amerikis 21, Athens, Greece.

Zamarias, Harilaos; Greek diplomatist; b. 99; ed. Univ. of Lausanne.
Attaché, Ministry of Foreign Affairs 21; High Comm., Smyrna 21-22, Sofia, Pyrgos, Alexandria, Belgrade, Berlin, Warsaw, Skopje, Cairo 23-45; Consul-Gen., Alexandria 45-50; Minister 50; Ambassador to Austria 51-54; Foreign Office 54-56; Ambassador to Belgium 56-62, to U.A.R. 62-67; Commdr. of Order of George I, Commdr. of the Phoenix, Grand Cross of Austria.
Royal Greek Embassy, Cairo, United Arab Republic.

Zambeaux, Charles; French judge; b. 96; ed. Lycée de Bordeaux and Bordeaux Univ.
Deputy to Public Prosecutor at Tribunals at Rheims, Troyes, Versailles and Paris; Dep. Public Prosecutor and Advocate-Gen. Court of Appeal, Paris, and Dir. of Cabinet of Keeper of the Seals 44-46; Counsellor, Court of Cassation 46-63, Pres. of Chamber of Court of Cassation 63-67, Hon. Pres. 67-; Commdr. Légion d'Honneur; Grand Officier, Ordre Nationale du Merite.
127 avenue Jean Baptiste Clément, Boulogne-sur-Seine (Hauts de Seine), France.
Telephone: 403-0572.

Zambrowski, Roman; Polish politician; b. 09.
Sec. Communist Youth Union 31-36 and imprisoned several times for political activities; in Soviet Union during Second World War where he became Head of Political-Educational Dept. First Polish Army; mem. Political Bureau, Polish United Workers' Party 45-63; mem. Council of State 45-55; Minister of State Control 55-56; Sec. Central Cttee. Polish United Workers' Party 45-54, 56-63; mem. of Seym (Parliament) 45-, Vice-Marshal 47-52; Vice-Pres. Supreme Board of Control 63-68.
82, Marszalkowska, Warsaw, Poland.

Zampa, Luigi; Italian film director; b. 2 Jan. 1905; studied architecture.
Studied cinematography at Centro Sperimentale di Cinematografia; has directed the following films: *Un americano in vacanza* 45, *Vivere in pace* 46, *Onorevole Angelina* 47, *Anni difficili* 48, *Campane a Martello* 49, *Signori in Carrozza!* 51, *Processo alla città* 52, *La romana* 54, *L'arte d'arrangiarsi* 55, *Ragazze d'oggi* 55, *La ragazza del Palio* 57, *Ladro lui Ladra lei* 57, *La Ragazza* 58, *Il Magistrato* 59, *Anni Ruggenti* 62.
Via Monti Parioli 44, Rome, Italy.

Zamyatin, Leonid Mitrofanovich; Soviet diplomatist; b. 1922; ed. Moscow Aviation Inst.
Member C.P. of Soviet Union 44-; at Ministry of Foreign Affairs 46-50; First Sec., Secr. of Minister of Foreign Affairs 50-52; Asst. Head, Third European Dept., Ministry of Foreign Affairs 52-53; First Sec., Counsellor on Political Questions of U.S.S.R. Mission

to UN 53-57; Soviet Deputy Rep. on Preparatory Cttee., and later on Board of Govs., Int. Atomic Energy Agency (IAEA) 57-59, Soviet Rep. on IAEA 59-60; Deputy Head, American Countries Dept., Ministry of Foreign Affairs 60-62, Head of Press Dept. 62-, mem. of Collegium of Ministry 62-; Orders and medals of U.S.S.R.
Ministry of Foreign Affairs, 32-34 Smolenskaya-Sennaya ploshchad, Moscow, U.S.S.R.

Zangen, Wilhelm; German industrialist; b. 30 Sept. 1891.
Member of Board, Schiess A.G., Düsseldorf 25-59, Demag A.G., Duisburg 29-34; Gen. Man. Mannesmann A.G., Düsseldorf 34-57, Chair. of Supervisory Board 57-67, Hon. Chair. 67-; Leader Reichsgruppe Industrie; Dr. rer. pol. h.c.
Cäciliena Allee 5/8, Düsseldorf, German Federal Republic.

Zanuck, Darryl F., American film producer; b. 5 Sept. 1902.
Fmrly. with Warner Bros. Pictures Inc., writer, producer and supervisor; Pres. in charge of production Darryl F. Zanuck Productions Inc.; Pres. 20th Century Fox 62-.
Films include: *Wilson, How Green Was My Valley, This Above All, Grapes of Wrath, The Razor's Edge, Gentleman's Agreement, The Snake Pit, Pinky, All About Eve, David and Bathsheba, Viva Zapata!, The Snows of Kilimanjaro, The Man in the Grey Flannel Suit, Island in the Sun, The Sun also Rises, Roots of Heaven, Crack in the Mirror, The Big Gamble, Compulsion, Sanctuary, The Longest Day.*
20th Century-Fox Film Corporation, Beverly Hills, California, U.S.A.

Zanuso, Marco; Italian architect; b. 14 May 1916; ed. Politecnico de Milano.
Architectural practice 45-; mem. C.I.A.M. 56-; Istituto Naz. Urbanistica 56-; City Councillor, Milan 56-60; mem. Building Comm., Milan Corpn. 61-63, 67-69; mem. City Devt. Comm., Milan 69; Lecturer, Faculty of Architecture, Milan Polytechnic; Pres. Assn. for Industrial Design 66-; numerous gold medals; Int. Plastic Exhbn. Prize, London 66; Gold Medal, Ministry of Industry and Commerce 66, etc.
Buildings include: H.Q. for American Co. 48; Olivetti buildings, Buenos Aires 54; Olivetti buildings, São Paulo 65; Brinnel buildings, Casella d'Asolo 66; Int. H.Q., S.G.S. Fairchild, Agrate 67; Olivetti buildings, Scarmagno (Ivrea) 68; Arflex factory, Brion Vega factory.
Studio; Via Laveno 6, Milan; Home: Piazza Castello 20, Milan, Italy.
Telephone: 4040312, 4040322 (Studio); 866127 (Home).

Zao Wou Ki; Chinese painter; b. 20; ed. Nat. School of Fine Arts, Hangchow.
Prof. of Design, Nat. School of Fine Arts, Hangchow 41-47; left China to live in Paris 48; exhibited in Salon de Mai, Paris 50- and in the capitals of Europe and America; Int. Prize for modern painting, Carnegie Inst., Pittsburgh 55.
Works in many collections throughout Europe.
c/o Société des Artistes Indépendants, Grand Palais des Champs-Elysées, Cour la Reine, Paris 8e, France.

Zariski, Oscar; American mathematician; b. 24 April 1899; ed. Univ. of Kiev (Ukraine), and Univ. of Rome.
Fellow Int. Educ. Board 24-26; Johnston Scholar, Johns Hopkins Univ. 27-29, Assoc. 29-32, Assoc. Prof. 32-37, Prof. of Maths. 37-45; Research Prof. of Maths., Univ. of Ill. 46-47; Prof. of Maths. and Tutor in Dept. of Maths., Harvard Univ. 47-61, Dwight Parker Robinson Prof. 61-; former Editor *Transactions of the American Mathematical Society, American Journal of Mathematics, Illinois Journal of Mathematics;* fmr.

Co-operating Ed. of *Annals of Mathematics*; mem. Nat. Acad. of Sciences, American Acad. Arts and Sciences, American Philosophical Society, Accad. Nazionale dei Lincei; Corresp. mem. Academia Nacional de Ciencias Exactas, Físicas y Naturales de Lima, Acad. Brasileira de Ciencias, hon. mem. of Sociedade de Matematica de São Paulo, London Mathematical Society; Cole Prize in Algebra 44, Nat. Medal of Science, Washington 66; Hon. D.Sc. Brandeis Univ. 65.

Publs. *Algebraic Surfaces* 35, *Some Results in the Arithmetic Theory of Algebraic Varieties* 38, *The Reduction of the Singularities of an Algebraic Surface* 39, *Local Uniformisation on Algebraic Varieties* 40, *Foundations of a General Theory of Birational Correspondences* 43, *Reduction of the Singularities of Algebraic Three-dimensional Varieties* 44, *Theory and Application of Abstract Holomorphic Functions on an Algebraic Variety* 51, *Compleet Linear Systems on Normal Varieties and a Generalisation of a Lemma of Enriques-Severi* 52, *The Problem of Minimal Models in the Theory of Algebraic Surfaces* 58, *Commutative Algebra* (2 vols.) (with P. Samuel) 58, 60.

Department of Mathematics, Harvard University, Cambridge 38, Mass.; and 27 Lancaster Street, Cambridge 40, U.S.A.

Zarkhy, Alexander Grigoryevich; Soviet film producer; b. 1908; ed. Leningrad Technicum of Dramatic Art.

Asst. Producer 28, Producer for Lenfilm 29-49, for Byelorusfilm 50-55, for Mosfilm 57-; State Prize Winner; Honoured Art Worker of Byelorussian S.S.R. People's Artist of R.S.F.S.R. 65.

Films include: *The Wind into the Face* 29, *Hot Days* 33, *The Deputy of the Baltic* 37, *The Member of the Government* 39, *His Name is Suhi Bator* 43, *Malahov Kurgan* 44, *In the Name of Life* 46, *Nesterko* 53, *The Height* 57, *The People on the Bridge* 59, *Hallo Life* 62, *Anna Karenina* 68.

Mosfilm Studio, 1 Mosfilmovskaya ulitsa, Moscow, U.S.S.R.

Zarodov, Konstantin Ivanovich; Soviet journalist; b. 1920; ed. Vologda Railway Engineering Coll., C.P.S.U. Higher Party School and C.P.S.U. Acad. of Social Sciences.

Member C.P.S.U. 40; Navy Service 39-46; Young Communist League Official 46-50; mem. staff *Komsomolskaya Pravda* 50-51, *For a Lasting Peace, for People's Democracy!* 54-56; at Central Cttee. of C.P.S.U. 56-61; Editor-in-Chief, *Sovietskaya Rossiya* 61-64; First Deputy Editor-in-Chief, *Pravda* 65-; Alt. mem. C.P.S.U. Central Cttee. 66-.

Editorial Board, *Pravda*, 24 Pravda Street, Moscow, U.S.S.R.

Zavadsky, Yuri Alexandrovich; Soviet theatrical producer; b. 94; ed. Moscow University.

At Vakhtangov Theatre 15, Moscow Art Theatre 24-31, at Gorky Theatre, Rostov 36-40; Artistic Dir. of the Red Army Theatre 32-35; Chief Stage Dir. Mossoviet Theatre 40-; Prof. Moscow State Theatrical Inst.; Pres. theatrical section of Union of Soviet Socs. for friendship and cultural relations with foreign countries; mem. C.P.S.U.; People's Artist of the U.S.S.R., State Prize 46, 51; awarded Order of Lenin (twice), Order of the Red Banner of Labour; Lenin Prize 65.

Main productions: *Death of a Squadron*, *On the Bank of the Neva*, *Enemies*, *The Philistines*, *Encounter in Darkness*, *The Moscow Character*, *The Law of Honour*, *The Storm*, *The Russian Question*, *Boundless Vistas*, *Lyubov Yarovaya*, *Fancy Ball*, *Othello*, etc.

Mossoviet Drama Theatre, Bolshaya Sadovaya ulitsa 16, Moscow, U.S.S.R.

Zavala, Silvio, D. en D.; Mexican historian; b. 09; ed. Univ. of the South-East, Nat. Univ. of Mexico and Central Univ. of Madrid.

Centre of Historical Studies, Madrid 33-36; Sec. Nat. Museum of Mexico 37-38; founder and dir. *Revista de Historia de América* (review of Pan-American Inst. of Geography and History) 38-65; Pres. Historical Comm. of Pan-American Inst. of Geography and History 46-65; mem. Col. de México 40; life mem. El Colegio Nacional 47; Visiting Prof. Univ. of Puerto Rico 45, Univ. of Havana 46; Prof. of History of Social Insts. of America, Nat. Univ. of Mexico; Visiting Prof. Mexico City Coll.; Prof. Smith Coll., Mexico; Dir. Nat. Museum of History, Chapultepec 46-54; Chief, Section of Education, Science and Culture of U.N. 47; Visiting Lecturer Harvard 53, Visiting Prof. Washington (Seattle) and Ghent 56; Perm. Del. to UNESCO 56-62, mem. Exec. Council 60-66, Vice-Pres. 62-64; Vice-Pres. Int. Council of Philosophy and Hum. (later Pres.) 59-; Ambassador to France 66-; Pres. Colegio de México 63-; mem. Exec. Council, Int. Cttee. for Historical Sciences; mem. Nat. Acad. of History and Geography, Mexican Acad. of History; corresp. mem. numerous Acads. of History, etc.; hon. mem. Historical Asscn. England 56, American Historical Asscn., Washington, D.C. 59; Prof. h.c. Colegio de San Nicolás, Morelia, Inst. of Latin American Studies, Univ. of Texas; Hon. D. Litt., Columbia Univ. 54, Ghent Univ. 57, Toulouse Univ. 65.

Publs. Many works on the Spanish colonisation of America, Latin American history, New World History, etc.

Ambassade de Mexique, rue de Longchamp 9, Paris 16e, France.

Zavala Ortiz, Miguel Angel; Argentine lawyer and politician; b. 24 Dec. 1906; ed. Univ. of Buenos Aires.

Political life 30-; Federal Dep. 48-51; imprisoned 51; fmr. Presidential Candidate; Minister of Foreign Affairs Oct. 63-June 66; Unión Cívica Radical del Pueblo.

c/o Ministry of Foreign Affairs, Arenales 761, Buenos Aires, Argentina.

Zavatt, Joseph Carmine; American judge; b. 19 Sept. 1900; ed. Columbia Univ. School of Political Science and New York Univ. Law School.

Admitted to New York State Bar 26; private legal practice, Cedarhurst, N.Y. 27-57; Instructor City Coll., N.Y. School of Business Admin. 30-33; Counsel N.Y. State Jt. Legislative Comm. to revise Mil. Law 48-53; Judge U.S. Dist. Court, Eastern Dist., N.Y. State 57, now Chief Judge; U.S. Naval Service, Second World War.

Home: 67 Hilton Avenue, Garden City, N.Y. 11530; Office: United States Courthouse, 225 Washington Street, Brooklyn, N.Y. 11201, U.S.A.

Zavoisky, Evgeny Konstantinovich; Soviet physicist; b. 1907; ed. Kazan State Univ.

Postgraduate Asst. Prof., Prof. Kazan State Univ. 30-47; Section Chief U.S.S.R. Acad. of Sciences Kurchatov Inst. of Atomic Energy 47-; Corresp. mem. U.S.S.R. Acad. of Sciences 53-64, mem. 64-; discovered and studied the paramagnetic resonance; investigated problems of use of electron-optimal converter; Lenin Prize.

U.S.S.R. Academy of Sciences, 14 Lenin Prospekt, Moscow, U.S.S.R.

Zawieyski, Jerzy; Polish dramatist, novelist and politician; b. 02.

Deputy to Seym (Parl.) 57-; Leader of Catholic Movement; mem. Council of State.

Publs. Plays: *Powrót Przeleckiego* (*The Return of Przeltecki*), *Rozdroze miłości* (*Crossroads of Love*), *Ocalenie Jakuba* (*The Salvation of Jakob*), *Maz doskonaly* (*The Perfect Husband*), *Socrates*; Novels: *Droga do domu* (*The Road Home*), *Noc Huberta* (*Hubert's Night*).

Krakowskie Przedmieście 87/89, Warsaw, Poland.

Zayyat, Mohamed Hassan El-, M.A., D.PHIL.; United Arab Republic (Egyptian) diplomatist; b. 14 Feb. 1915; ed. Cairo and Oxford Universities.

Lecturer and Asst. Professor Alexandria Univ. 42-50; Cultural Attaché, Egyptian Embassy, Washington D.C. 50-54, First Sec. and Counsellor 54; Counsellor, Egyptian Embassy, Teheran 55-57, Minister 57; Del. of Egypt on UN Advisory Council for Somaliland 58-60, Special Envoy and Ambassador of U.A.R. in Somaliland 60; Head of Dept. of Arab Affairs and Perm. Del. of U.A.R. to Arab League 60-62; Alt. Perm. Rep. of U.A.R. to UN 62-64; Ambassador to India, concurrently accred. to Nepal 64-65; Under-Sec. of State for Foreign Affairs 65-; Decorations from U.A.R., Iran, Somalia.

c/o Ministry of Foreign Affairs, Cairo, United Arab Republic.

Zbinden, Hans, DR. PHIL.; Swiss writer, lecturer, and editor; b. 26 Aug. 1893; ed. Univs. of Berne and Zürich; studied in East and West Europe.

Lecture tours in U.S.A., Guest Prof. Madison; Editor of Iris Art Books Berne 34-59; corresp. mem. Deutsche Akad. für Sprache und Dichtung and of Deutsche Gesellschaft für Soziologie; Prof. in Cultural Sociology, Univ. of Berne; Sec. Goethe-Stiftung für Kunst und Wissenschaft, Zürich; Pres. Swiss Authors Asscn. 53-67, Hon. Pres. 67-; Bundesverdienstkreuz der Bundesrepublik Deutschland.

Publs. *Die politischen Ideen des Vincenzo Gioberti* 19, *Zur geistigen Lage Amerikas* 31, *Technik und Geisteskultur* 33, *Der Kampf um den Frieden* 34, *Geist und Wirtschaft* 35, *Die Moralkrise des Abendlandes* 41, *Geistige Aufgaben unseres Landes* 42, *Der Schriftsteller in unserer Zeit* 43, *Albert Anker, Mensch und Werk* 44, *Der Flüchtling und die Humanität* 45, *Um Deutschlands Zukunft* 46, *Von der innern Freiheit* 48, *Gefahren der modernen Demokratie* 48, *Welt im Zwielicht* (essays) 51, *Giovanni Segantini* 51, *Jugend und Staat* 52, *Das Spiel um den Spoel* 52, *Vermassung und Demokratie* 53, *Schulnot und Bildungskrise* 53, *Vom Buchklima unserer Zeit* 53, *Von der Axt zum Atomwerk* (essays) 54, *Schulnoete der Gegenwart* 55, *Ueber Not und Glück des Alters* 58, *Der Bedrohte Mensch* 59, *Das freie Unternehmertum und die Wandlungen der Gesellschafts-Struktur* 60, *Soziale Grundprobleme der Erholung Fünftagewoche, Ferien und schöpferische Musse* 61, *Jugend und Alter in der Gesellschaft von heute* 61, *Albert Anker in neuer Sicht* 61, "*Ich bin ein Schweizerknabe*" 62, *Ohnmacht der Eliten?* 63, *Humanismus der Wirtschaft* 63, *Im Strom der Zeit* 64, *Schweizer Literatur in europäischer Sicht* 64, *Kulturprobleme der Wirtschaft* 66, *Mensch und Technik in unserer Zeit* 67; edited and trans.: Benjamin Constant *Über die Gewalt* 42, 48, 63, A. de Tocqueville *In der nordamerikanischen Wildnis* 54 and *Über die Demokratie in Amerika* Vol. I 59, Vol. II 62.

Alleeweg 13, Berne, CH 3000, Switzerland.

Telephone: 031-44-3074.

Zea, Germán; Colombian lawyer and politician; b. 15 April 1905; ed. Colegio de Araújo and Univ. Libre, Bogotá.

Member Congress and Senate of Colombia at various times; Mayor of Bogotá 38-41; Comptroller-Gen. of Colombia 41; Gov. of Cundinamarca 43-44; Minister of Justice 60-62; Pres. Dirección Nacional Liberal 60; Colombian Rep. at Int. Confs. and Chief of Perm. Colombian Del. to UN 62-65; Minister of Foreign Affairs 66-; Prof. of Constitutional and Admin. Law, Univ. Libre, Bogotá, Pres. of Univ.; mem. Academia Colombiana de Jurisprudencia; decorations from Colombia, Venezuela, Brazil, Chile, Mexico, Panama and Bolivia.

Ministerio de Relaciones Exteriores, Bogotá, Colombia.

Zea Aguilar, Leopoldo, PH.D.; Mexican university professor and writer; b. 30 June 1912.

Editor review *Tierra Nueva* 40; Prof. Escuela Nacional Preparatoria 42-47; Prof. Escuela Normal de Maestros 44-45; Prof., Faculty of Philosophy and Letters, Nat.

Univ. of Mexico 44; mem. El Colegio de México 40; Pres., Cttee. for the History of Ideas, Panamerican Inst. of Geography and History; Chief of Dept. of Univ. Studies, Secretariat of Public Education 53-54; research work, Univ. of Mexico 54-; mem. Société Européenne de Culture 53-; Dir.-Gen. of Cultural Relations Foreign Office; Vice-Pres. Historical Comm. of Pan American Inst. of Geography and History 61-; Dir. of Faculty of Philosophy and Letters, Nat. Univ. of Mexico 66-.

Publs. *El Positivismo en México* 43, *Apogeo y Decadencia del Positivismo en México* 44, *Ensayos sobre Filosofía en la Historia* 48, *Dos Etapas del Pensamiento en Hispanoamérica* 49, *La Filosofía como Compromiso* 52, *América como Conciencia* 52, *Conciencia y posibilidad del Mexicano* 52, *El Occidente y la Conciencia de México* 53, *La Conciencia del Hombre en la Filosofía* 52, *América en la conciencia de Europa* 55, *La Filosofía en México* 55, *Esquema para una Historia de las ideas en América* 56, *Del Liberalismo a la Revolución en la Educación Mexicana* 56, *América en la Historia* 57, *La Cultura y el Hombre de nuestros Días* 59, *Latinoamérica y el Mundo* 60, *Ensayo sobre México y Latinoamérica* 60, *Democracias y Dictaduras en Latinoamérica* 60, *El Pensamiento en Latinoamérica* 63, *The Latin American Mind* 63, *L'Amérique dans l'Histoire* 63, *El Pensamiento Latinoamericano* 65.

Ciudad Universitaria, Torre de Humanidades, Mexico, D.F., Mexico.

Zeayen, Dr. Yusif; Syrian physician and politician; b. 1931; ed. Univ. of Damascus.

Minister of Agrarian Reform 63; mem. Presidential Council 64-65; Prime Minister Sept.-Dec. 65, Feb. 66-.

Office of the Prime Minister, Damascus, Syrian Arab Republic.

Zech, Walther; German publisher; b. 12 Nov. 1918; ed. Düsseldorf Realgymnasium (Hindenburgschule).

Pupil in private bank of B. Simons & Co. (now Poensgen, Marx & Co.) Düsseldorf 37-39; war service 40-45, prisoner of war 45-46; Dept. Man. Essen branch, "Die Welt" Verlags G.m.b.H. 47-49; Editor Düsseldorfer Zeitschriftenverlag 50-52; Editor and Man. Dir. VDI-Verlag G.m.b.H., Düsseldorf 52-62; now Editor and Man. Dir. Mainzer Verlagsanstalt und Druckerei, Darmstädter Tagblatt G.m.b.H., Wiesbadener Tagblatt-Verlag, G.m.b.H., Verlags-und Verwaltungsgesellschaft m.b.H. (Mainz), and Wiesbaden Kurier Verlag und Druckerei G.m.b.H., Wiesbaden; mem. Soc. of Fed. German Newspaper Publishers, Bad Godesberg, Soc. of Fed. German Magazine Publishers, Frankfurt, Asscn. of German Graphic Trades, Presidium, Int. Fed. of the Periodical Press (FIPP), Paris, Council, Technical Comm. of German Press Agencies, Hamburg, Confed. of German Industries and Chamber of Commerce, Mainz; Adviser, Dresdner Bank AG., Rhineland-Pfalz, Zigarettenfabrik Rhenania G.m.b.H, Andernach.

Grosse Bleiche 44-50, Mainz, German Federal Republic.

Telephone: 06131-361.

Zechmeister, László, D.ING.; Hungarian-born American organic chemist; b. 14 May 1889; ed. Zürich Polytechnic.

Asst. to Prof. Willstätter, Zürich 10-12; Chief Asst. Kaiser Wilhelm Inst. Chemistry 12-14; War service 14-18; Prisoner of War in Russia 15-17; Industrial Research in Hungary 20-21; research work in Prof. Bjerrum's laboratory, Copenhagen, 21-23; Prof. of Chemistry, Univ. of Pécs Medical School 23-40; Prof. Organic Chemistry, Calif. Inst. of Technology 40-59, Prof. Emer. 59-; hon. mem. Hungarian Acad. of Science and awarded its Grand Prix 37; mem. Royal Danish Acad. of Science; awarded Pasteur Medal and Claude Bernard Medal, Paris; Ed. *Fortschritte der Chemie organischer Naturstoffe* 38-.

Publs. *Organic Chemistry* (2 vols.) 30, 32, *Carotinoide* 34, *Principles and Practice of Chromatography* (with

Dr. Cholnoky) 3rd edn. 50, *Progress in Chromatography* 50, *Cis-trans Isomeric Carotenoids, Vitamins A and Arylpolyenes* 62, and about 250 research papers.
California Institute of Technology, Pasadena, Calif. 91109, U.S.A.
Telephone: 7923909.

Zeckendorf, William; American real estate administrator; b. 30 June 1905; ed. New York Univ.
Entered real estate business 25; Partner L. Gans 30; Vice-Pres. Webb & Knapp, Inc. 37, Pres. 47-62, Chair. 62-65; Webb & Knapp (Canada) Ltd., Webb & Knapp Nat. Corpn. Washington, D.C., Chair. of Board and Dir. Gulf States Land & Industries Inc., Colmar Surinam Oil Co.; Dir. American Hydrofoil Lines Inc., Webb and Knapp (Canada) Ltd.; Real Estate Adviser to the Rockefeller family; Trustee and Dir. of many cultural and medical bodies; Hon. LL.D. (Long Island, American Univs.), Hon. D.Hum.Litt. (Wilberforce Univ.); seven foreign Awards.
Home: 30 Beekman Place, N.Y.C.; Office: Webb & Knapp, Inc., 383 Madison Avenue, New York 17, N.Y., U.S.A.

Zeckendorf, William, Jr.; American hotel executive; b. 31 Oct. 1929; ed. Lawrenceville School and Univ. of Arizona.
Webb and Knapp Inc. 50-, Vice-Pres. 55-58, Pres. 62-, Dir. 57-; Dir. Webb and Knapp (Canada) Ltd., Gulf States Land and Industries Inc., New Orleans; Pres. Zeckendorf Hotels Corpn.; U.S. Army 52-54.
Home: Croton Lake Road, Mount Kisco, N.Y.; Office: 383 Madison Avenue, New York City 10017, U.S.A.

Zeeland, Paul van, M.A., PH.D.; Belgian politician; b. 93; ed. Louvain and Princeton Univs.
Prime Minister of Belgium 35-37; fmr. Pres. Assembly, L.N.; Pres. Belgian Comm. for Study of Post-war Problems; Dir. Inst. of Economic Sciences, Univ. of Louvain; Vice-Gov. Banque Nat. de Belgique; Deputy Dir. Bank for Int. Settlements; Belgian Repatriation Commr. (rank of Ambassador); Pres. Co-ordinating Foundation for Refugees; Pres. European League for Economic Co-operation, etc.; Minister for Foreign Affairs 49-54; Minister of State 48-; Chair. The Dollar Fund 67-; mem. American Philosophical Soc., Acad. Méditerranéenne, and Inst. de France; decorations include Croix de Guerre with palm, Grand Croix de la Légion d'Honneur (France), Medal of Freedom with bronze palm (U.S.), Grand Cross Order of Vasa (Sweden), Grand Cross Order of White Eagle (Poland), Grand Cross Order of St. Olav (Norway), etc.; Hon. D.Sc.Pol. (Louvain), Hon. LL.D., D.C.H.L. (Princeton), Hon. D.L.C. (Brown), Hon. D.C.L. (Wesleyan), Dr. h.c. (Costa Rica).
Publs. *La Réforme Bancaire aux Etats-Unis d'Amérique de 1913 à 1921* 22, *Réflexions sur le plan Quinquennal* 31, *Regards sur l'Europe 1932* 33.
Château de la Houssière, Braine-le-Comte; 7 Avenue Charles-Albert, Brussels 17, Belgium.

Zeffirelli, Franco; Italian theatrical producer and designer; b. 12 Feb. 1923; ed. Liceo Artistico, Florence, and School of Agriculture, Florence.
Designer Univ. Productions Florence; actor Morelli Stoppa Company; collaborated with Salvador Dali in sets for *As You Like It* 48; sets for *A Streetcar Named Desire, Troilus and Cressida* 49; set for *Three Sisters* 51; productions at Covent Garden, London 59-61, The Old Vic, London 60, Teatro dello Cometa, Rome 60, *Much Ado About Nothing*, London and Paris 65, Verga's *La Lupe*, Florence 65; Dir. Film *The Taming of the Shrew* 66, *Romeo and Juliet* 67; Dir., sets and costumes for *Antony and Cleopatra* (New York) 66; producer and designer La Scala, Milan 52; artistic dir. and producer in Italian cinema 47-; Prix des Nations 64.
Via Due Macelli 31, Rome, Italy.

Zeghari, M'Hammed; Moroccan financial official and politician.
Governor Banque du Maroc (Central Bank) to 65; Minister of State 65-66; Deputy Prime Minister and Minister of Devt. 66-67; Minister of Agriculture and Agrarian Reform in Charge of Econ. Affairs 67-.
277 Avenue Mohammed V, Rabat, Morocco.

Zehrfuss, Bernard; French architect; b. 20 Oct. 1911; ed. Collège Stanislas.
Head, Architecture and Urbanism Services, Tunisia 43-48; mem. Conseil Nat. de la Construction 50-53; Consulting Architect, Ministry of Construction, Chief Architect of Public Buildings and Nat. Palaces 53-65.
Projects: buildings in Tunisia, Algeria and in France including UNESCO Building, Paris, Palais du Centre National des Industries et des Techniques, Paris, Renault factory at Flins, Hôtel du Mont d'Arbois, Megève, Danish Embassy in Paris, Super-Montparnasse in Paris, Science Faculty in Tunis.
11 rue Arsène Houssaye, Paris 8e, France.
Telephone: WAG 33-89.

Zeïbstein, Uri; French (b. Lithuanian) scientist; b. 10 Jan. 1912; ed. Univ. of Bordeaux.
Successively Head of Laboratory and Dir. Radio-Electronic Laboratories, fmr. Vitus Ests. 33-39; Head, Electronic Dept., D.F. Factories 40-46; Head of Electronic Research Dept., Nat. Soc. for Research and Construction of Aircraft Engines (S.N.E.C.M.A.) 46-51; Technical Dir. and Dir.-Gen. Sexta Soc. 51-58; Head of Physics and Electronics Laboratories, later Asst. to Pres. of Atomic Div., S.N.E.C.M.A. 60-; Prof. Nat. Conservatory of Arts and Craft Trade; mem. New York Acad. of Sciences, Accademia Teatina for Sciences (Italy), Accademia Tiberina (Italy); Officer of the Order of Merit for Research and Invention; mem. Unione della Legion d'Oro (Italy).
Home: 1 Villa des Iris, 92 Bagneux, Seine; Office: 22 Quai Gallièni, 92 Suresnes, France.
Telephone: 1-2536933 (Home); 1-6050208 (Office).

Zeldovich, Yakov Borisovich; Soviet physicist; b. 8 March 1914; ed. Leningrad Univ.
Associate Inst. of Chemical Physics, U.S.S.R. Acad. of Sciences 31-; Corresp. mem. U.S.S.R. Acad. of Sciences 46-58, mem. 58-; State Prize 43.
Publs. *The Theory of Combustion and Detonation by Gas* 44, *Theory of Shock Waves and an Introduction to Gas Dynamics* 46, *Development of the Anti-Particle Theory, Elementary Particle Charges and the Properties of Heavy Neutral Mesons* 56, *Experimental Investigation of Spherical Gas Detonation* 56, *Quasi-Stable States with a Strong Isotopic Spin in Light Nuclei, Spacing by Singular Potential in Turbulence Theory and in Pulse Representation* 60, *The Existence of New Light Nuclei Isotopes and Equations for the Neutron State* 60, *Higher Mathematics for Beginners* 60, 63, 65, *Physics of Shock Waves and High Temperature Hydrodynamics* 64, *Relativistic Astrophysics* 64, 65, *Survey of Modern Cosmology* 65, *Elements of Applied Mathematics* 66.
Institute of Chemical Physics of U.S.S.R. Academy of Sciences, Vorobyevskoye Chaussée 2. Moscow, U.S.S.R.

Zeller, Général d'Armée Henri; French army officer; b. 18 March 1896; ed. Lycée Victor-Hugo, Besançon, Coll. Stanislas, Paris and Ecole Supérieure de Guerre.
Deputy Chief of Staff 45; Chief of Staff to Gén. de Lattre de Tassigny 46-48; Military Gov., Metz, Commdr. 6th Military Region 48-53; Military Gov. of Paris 53-58; mem. Conseil Supérieur de la Guerre 55-56; Grand Croix, Légion d'Honneur; Hon. K.B.E., C.B.
66 avenue de Versailles, Paris 16e, France.

Zellerbach, Harold Lionel, B.S.; American business executive; b. 25 March 1894; ed. Univ. of Calif. and Univ. of Pennsylvania.
Joined Zellerbach Paper Co. 17, Dir. 28-59, Chair. Bd.

57-59, Chair. Exec. Cttee. Crown Zellerbach Corpn. 59-; Dir. Joseph Magnin Co.; Dir. Niantic Corpn. and Pacific Nat. Bank; official of cultural and educational orgs.
1 Bush Street, San Francisco, Calif. 94119, U.S.A.

Zellerbach, William Joseph; American paper industry executive; b. 15 Sept. 1920; ed. Univ. of Pennsylvania. Crown Zellerbach Corpn. 46-, Vice-Pres. (Marketing Service) 59-, Dir. 59-; Pres. Zellerbach Paper Co. 61-; mem. Gen. Advisory Cttee. on Foreign Assistance Programs of the Agency for Int. Development; official of several welfare orgs.
Home: 3540 Jackson Street, San Francisco, California, U.S.A.

Zeman, Karel; Czechoslovak film director; b. 3 Nov. 1910.
Creator of numerous puppet and trick films; State Prize 57; Grand Prix for trick film *An Invention of Destruction*, Brussels Int. Exhbn. 58; Honoured Artist of Czechoslovakia 61, State Prize 57, 59; Czechoslovak Peace Prize 59, and other awards.
Films include: *Inspiration, King Lávra, The Treasure of Bird Island, A Trip to Prehistoric Times* (State Prize), *Baron Münchhausen, The Jester's Tale* (prizes at San Francisco Film Festival).
Film Studio/Kudlov, Gottwaldov, Czechoslovakia.
Telephone: Gottwaldov 2301; Gottwaldov 3175 (Home).

Zenteno Anaya, Lieut.-Colonel Joaquín; Bolivian army officer and politician; b. 21; ed. Infantry Academy, Auvours, France, Staff College, Paris, and Staff and Command College "Mcal. Andrew", Santa Cruz, Bolivia.
Former Professor of Military Intelligence, Staff College, Bolivia, later Dir. of Studies; later Chief of Operations, Bolivian Army; Minister of Foreign Affairs Nov. 64-66.
Publ. *Manual de Inteligencia Estratégica.*
2782 Avenida 6 de Agosto, La Paz, Bolivia.

Zerba, H.E. Cardinal Cesare; Vatican ecclesiastic; b. 15 April 1892.
Ordained priest 15; consecrated Bishop of Colesse 62; Secretary of Sacred Congregation of the Discipline of the Sacraments to 65; mem. Comm. De Sacramentorum Disciplina, Ecumenical Council; created Cardinal 65.
Vatican City, Rome, Italy.

Zermatten, Maurice; Swiss writer; b. 22 Oct. 1910; ed. Desclée de Brouwer, Paris.
Teacher of French literature; Pres. Société Suisse des écrivains; awarded Prix Fondation Schiller 38, Prix Bodmer 40, Prix d'honneur Schiller 46, Grand Prix catholique de littérature, Paris 59, Grand Prix Gottfried Keller 60, French Acad. Prize 61; first work published 36.
Publs. *Le Cœur Inutile, Le Chemin difficile, Contes des Hauts-Pays du Rhône, Les Années valaisannes de Rilke, Les Chapelles Valaisannes, La Colère de Dieu, Le Sang des Morts, Christine, Le Pain Noir, L'Esprit des Tempêtes, Connaissance de Ramuz, Traversée d'un Paradis, Les Mains Pures, Isabelle de Chevron, La Montagne sans Etoiles, Le Lierre et le Figuier, La Fontaine d'Aréthuse, Un Lys de Savoie, Le Bouclier d'Or, Le Cancer des Solitudes, La Rose noire de Marignan, La Louve, Pays sans Chemin, Visages* etc.
Gravelone, Sion, Valais, Switzerland.
Telephone: 027-220-84.

Zetterling, Mai Elisabeth (Mrs. David Hughes); Swedish film director and actress; b. 24 May 1925; ed. Royal Theatre School of Drama, Stockholm.
Staff of National Theatre, Stockholm 43-45; first prize Venice Film Festival (*The War Game*) 63; under contract film director to Sandrews of Sweden.
London stage appearances include: *The Wild Duck* and *The Doll's House* (Ibsen), *Point of Departure* and *Restless Heart* (Anouilh), *The Seagull* (Chekhov), *Creditors* (Strindberg); film appearances: *Knock on Wood*

and *Only Two Can Play;* film dir. B.B.C. Television documentaries; Dir. and Co-writer films: *The War Game* 63, *Loving Couples* 65.
Publs. *The Cat's Tale* (with David Hughes) 65, *The Longing* 66 (film 66), *Night Games* (also film) 66.
c/o John Redway, 35 Davies Street, London, W.1; Berry Grove, West Liss, Hampshire, England.

Zevi, Bruno; Italian architect; b. 22 Jan. 1918; ed. Graduate School of Design, Harvard Univ. and Faculty of Architecture, Univ. of Rome.
Left Italy for political reasons 39-44; Ed. *Quaderni Italiani* (anti-Fascist magazine smuggled into Italy from U.S.A.) 41-43; Dir. technical magazines of U.S. Information Service in Italy 44-46; co-founder Asscn. for an Organic Architecture in Italy 46; co-Ed. *Metron*, an architectural magazine 45-55; Prof. History of Modern Architecture, Univ. of Rome 48-52, Prof. History of Architecture, Univ. of Venice 48-63; Prof. History of Architecture, Univ. of Rome 63-; Gen. Sec. Italian Town Planning Inst. 52-; Vice-Pres. Italian Inst. of Architecture; Editor *l'architettura—cronache e storia* 55-; Academician Venice Acad. of Art 53, Accad. di San Luca, Rome 60; Hon. mem. Royal Inst. of British Architects.
Publs. *Towards an Organic Architecture* 45 (English edn. 49), *Saper Vedere l'Architettura* 48 (English edn. *Architecture as Space* 57), *Storia dell'Architettura Moderna* 50, *Architettura e Storiografia* 51, *Poetica dell'Architettura Neoplastica* 53, *Architecture* (in *International Encyclopaedia of the Arts*) 58, *Biagio Rossetti architetto ferrarese il primo urbanista moderno europeo* 60, *Architettura in nuce* 60, *Michelangelo architetto* 64.
Via Nomentana 150, Rome, Italy.
Telephone: 8380481.

Zhamsarangin, Sambu; Mongolian politician; b. 27 June 1895.
Member, Politburo, Mongolian People's Revolutionary Party; Ministry of Finance 22-30; Diplomatic service 37-54; Deputy Minister for Foreign Affairs and Vice-Chair. Mongolian-Soviet Friendship Soc. 52-54; Chair. Presidium Great People's Khural; Head of State, Mongolian People's Republic 54-; several decorations.
Presidium of the Great People's Khural, Ulan Bator, Mongolian People's Republic.

Zhavoronkov, Nikolai Mikhailovich; Soviet chemist; b. 1907; ed. Moscow Inst. of Chemical Technology.
Instructor Moscow Inst. of Chemical Technology 30-42, Prof. 42-; Dep. Dir., later Dir. Karpov Physiochemical Inst. 44-48; Dir. Mendeleev Chemical Technological Inst. 48-62; Dir. Inst. of General and Inorganic Chemistry, U.S.S.R. Academy of Sciences 62-; Corresp. mem. U.S.S.R. Acad. of Sciences 53-62, mem. 62-; mem. Presidium Acad. of Sciences of U.S.S.R., Academician Sec. Dept. of Physical Chemistry and Technology of Inorganic Compounds 63-; mem. Communist Party 39-; numerous decorations.
Publs. *Hydraulic Principles of the Scrubber Process and Heat Transfer in Scrubbers* 44, *Nitrogen in Nature and Engineering* 51, *Sources of Industrial Bonded Nitrogen* 51, *Mass Transfer in the Pellicular Absorption Process* 51, *Determining the Separation Factor of Boron Isotopes with Equilibrium Evaporation of* BCl_3 56, *Chemical Industry and Research in the Soviet Union* 56, *K. A. Timiryazev and the Nitrogen Problem* 56, *Separating Stable Boron Isotopes* 60, *Investigation of Pellicular Absorption Process with High Speed of Gas* 61, *High Temperature Gas-Liquid Chromatography* 62, *Investigation of Hydrogen Isotopic Exchange between Water and Thiolates* 62, *Principal Directions in Development of Separation Methods of Stable Isotopes* 63, *Phase Equilibria for Mixtures Acrilonitrile—Acetonitrile* 64.
Institute of General and Inorganic Chemistry of Academy of Sciences of U.S.S.R., Leninsky prospekt 31, Moscow, U.S.S.R.

Zheludev, Ivan Stepanovich; Soviet scientist; b. 7 March 1921; ed. Moscow State Univ.
Senior Lecturer, Moscow State Univ. 55-62; Head of Laboratory of Electrical Properties of Crystals, Inst. of Crystallography, U.S.S.R. Acad. of Sciences, Moscow 61-66; Deputy Dir. (Dept. of Technical Operations), Int. Atomic Energy Agency, Vienna 66-; Visiting Prof., Indian Inst. of Science, Bangalore 62-63.
International Atomic Energy Agency, Vienna 1, Kärntnerring, Austria.

Zhigalin, Vladimir Fyodorovich; Soviet engineer and politician; b. 1907; ed. Leningrad Mechanical Inst.
Leningrad and Moscow factories 31-40; Chief of Dept. People's Commissariat of Heavy Machine-Building 40-45; Dep. People's Commissar, Dep., later First Dep. Minister, of Heavy Machine-Building 45-57; Dep., later First Dep. Chair., Moscow City Econ. Council 57-61, Chair. 61-63, First Dep. Chair. U.S.S.R. Council of National Economy 63-65; Minister of Heavy Power and Transport Engineering 65-; Alt. mem. Central Cttee. of C.P.S.U., later mem. Central Cttee. of C.P.S.U. 64-; Dep. to U.S.S.R. Supreme Soviet; several decorations.
Ministry of Heavy Power and Transport Engineering, Moscow, U.S.S.R.

Zhirmunsky, Victor Maksimovich; Soviet linguist and literary critic; b. 1891; ed. St. Petersburg Univ.
Postgraduate, Prof. Saratov Univ. 12-19, 42-44; Dept. Chief, Prof., Leningrad State Univ. 19-49; Scientific research work in State Inst. of History of Arts 20-30; Research Inst. of Language and Literature 21-25; Prof. Hertsen Pedagogical Inst. 23-31, 54-56; U.S.S.R. Acad. of Sciences Inst. of Language and Thought 34-35; U.S.S.R. Acad. of Sciences Inst. of Literature 35-50; Section Chief of folksongs of Azerbaijan Acad. of Sciences 43-44; Senior Scientific Worker, Section Chief of U.S.S.R. Acad. of Sciences Inst. of Linguistics, Leningrad 50-; Prof. Leningrad State Univ. 56-; Corresp. mem. U.S.S.R. Acad. of Sciences 39-66, mem. 66-; Corresp. mem. German Democratic Repub. Acad. of Sciences 56-, British Acad. 62-; Merited Worker of Science and Technology of Uzbek S.S.R.
Publs. Works on theory of literature and folksongs, on history and dialects of the German Language.
U.S.S.R. Academy of Sciences, 14 Lenin Prospekt, Moscow, U.S.S.R.

Zhivkov, Todor; Bulgarian politician; b. 11; ed. High School of Drawing and Engraving, Sofia.
Printing worker; joined Bulgarian Young Communist League 28, Communist Party 32; mem. Resistance against Nazis 41-44; candidate mem., Central Cttee., Communist Party 45, full mem. 48; First Sec., Sofia City Cttee. 48-49, candidate mem. Political Bureau and Sec. Central Cttee. 50, mem. Political Bureau 51-, First Sec. Central Cttee. 54-, mem. Nat. Assembly 45-, of Presidium 56-, Prime Minister Nov. 62-.
Publs. *Rural Co-operation* 57, *Report to Seventh Congress* 58, *Developing the Economy* 59, *U.N. General Assembly* 60, *Agricultural Production* 61, *The XXII Congress of the Communist Party of the Soviet Union and its Lessons for the Bulgarian Communist Party* 61.
Office of the Prime Minister, Sofia, Bulgaria.

Zhivkov, Zhivko; Bulgarian politician; b. 15; ed. Sofia Univ.
Young Communist League 31-, Communist Party 35-; imprisoned 42-44; mem. Cen. Cttee., later Sec., Young Communist League; fmr. Dep. to Foreign Minister; Minister of Foreign Trade 52-57, of Educ. and Culture 58-59, Dep. Prime Minister 59-62, First Dep. Prime Minister 62-; mem. Political Bureau, Central Cttee. of Bulgarian Communist Party 62-; mem. National Assembly.
Office of the First Deputy Prime Minister, Sofia, Bulgaria.

Zhukov, Anatoli Borisovich; Soviet biologist and forestry specialist; b. 1901; ed. Kharkov Institute of Agriculture and Forestry.
Forestry specialist, Trostjansky Experimental Forestry Station 23-28; Dept. Chief, Central Experimental Forestry Station of Ukrainian Research Inst. of Forestry 30-37; Asst. Dir. Mokhnatch Experimental Forestry Station 37-38; Asst. Dir., Dir. Byelorussian Scientific Research Inst. of Forestry; Asst. Prof. Byelorussian Forestry-Technical Inst. 31-41; Asst. Dir. U.S.S.R. Scientific Research Inst. of Forestry 42-56; Dept. Chief, U.S.S.R. Acad. of Sciences Forestry Inst. 56-59; Dir. U.S.S.R. Acad. of Sciences Siberian Dept. Inst. of Wood and Timber 59-; mem. U.S.S.R. Acad. of Sciences; Merited Worker of Science and Engineering of R.S.F.S.R.
U.S.S.R. Academy of Sciences, 14 Lenin Prospekt, Moscow, U.S.S.R.

Zhukov, Dmitri Alexandrovich; Soviet diplomatist; b. 1909; ed. Leningrad Industrial Inst.
Worked in Trams Dept., Leningrad 28-29; Engineer, Inst. of Boilers and Turbines 36-38; Dir. Russky Diesel plant, Leningrad 38-39; Asst. Head, Second Far East Dept., Ministry of Foreign Affairs 39; Counsellor Soviet Embassy, Tokyo 39-43; Deputy Head, Head of Second Far East Dept., Ministry of Foreign Affairs 43-45; Amb. to Chile 45-48; Head of Latin American Dept., Ministry of Foreign Affairs 48-53, Head of Protocol Dept. 53-54; Amb. to Indonesia 54-58; Deputy Gen. Sec. Ministry of Foreign Affairs 58-60, Gen. Sec. 65-67, Head of Latin American Dept. 67-; mem. C.P.S.U. 37-; Orders and medals of U.S.S.R.
Ministry of Foreign Affairs, 32-34 Smolenskaya-Sennaya ploshchad, Moscow, U.S.S.R.

Zhukov, Evgeny Mikhailovich; Soviet historian; b. 1907; ed. Leningrad Oriental Inst.
Lecturer Leningrad Oriental Inst. and Leningrad Univ. 29-32; Research Worker Inst. of History, Moscow 39-41; mem. C.P. 41-; Head of Pacific Inst., Moscow 43-50; Deputy Dir. Inst. of History, Moscow 54-57; Academician, Sec. of Historical Dept. U.S.S.R. Acad. of Sciences 58-, mem. Presidium 58-; mem. U.S.S.R. Acad. of Sciences 58-; Vice-Pres. Int. Union of Orientalists; Order of Red Banner of Labour (twice).
Publs. *Outlines of Oriental History in the Period of Imperialism* 34, *History of Japan* 39, *Outlines of History of Japanese Liberalism* 44, *International Relations on the Far East* 56, *New History of Eastern Countries: Outlines of Modern History of Japan* 57, *On dividing World History into Periods* 60.
Chief Editor *World History*, Vols. I-IX 55-62, *Soviet Historical Encyclopaedia*, Vols. I-VI 61-65.
Department of History of Academy of Sciences of U.S.S.R., ulitsa Dmitria Ulyanova 19, Moscow, U.S.S.R.

Zhukov, (Yuri) Georgi Alexandrovich; Soviet journalist and politician; b. 08; ed. Lomonosov Inst., Moscow.
Correspondent, local papers in Lugansk, Kharkov 27-32; Correspondent, mem. Ed. Board *Komsomolskaya Pravda* 32-38; Corresp. magazine *Nasha Strana* (Our Country) 38-40; mem. C.P.S.U. 43-; Head of Dept. *Novi Mir* (New World) 40-41; Deputy Exec. Sec. Editorial Board *Pravda* 46-47, Paris Correspondent 47-52, Foreign Ed. 52-57; Chair. U.S.S.R. Council of Ministers' State Cttee. for Cultural Relations with Foreign Countries 57-60; *Pravda* observer 62-; Dep. Supreme Soviet; Vice-Chair. Soviet Peace Cttee., Soviet-American Inst.; Pres. U.S.S.R.-France Soc.; mem. Central Auditing Comm. of C.P.S.U.; Order of Lenin, Order of the Red Banner of Labour, Order of the Red Star, Lenin Prize.
Publs. *Border* 38, *Three Months in Geneva* 54, *Soldier's Life* 46, *American Notes* (essays) 47, *The West After*

War 48, *Taming Tigers* 61, *Japan* 62, *Meetings in Transcarpathia* 62, *One MIG out of a Thousand* 63, *These Seventeen Years* 63, *Silent Art* 64, *The People of the Thirties* 65.
Pravda Editorial Office, 24 ulitsa Pravdy, Moscow U.S.S.R.

Zhukov, Georgi Konstantinovich, Marshal of Soviet Union, K.C.B.; Soviet officer; b. 1896.
Enlisted as private 15; Vice-Commissar of Defence; served against Japanese Forces Amur River 38-39; Chief of Gen. Staff Aug. 40-Oct. 41; fmr. Commander Kiev, command field forces Vyazma and Mozhaisk sectors; Commander-in-Chief Moscow Outer Defences 41; organised offensive Central and Kalinin Fronts Aug. 42 (with Gen. Koniev); Commander-in-Chief Western Front 41-42; Commander-in-Chief Southern Front; 1st Deputy Commissar for Defence 42-44; Commdr. 1st Ukrainian Front 44; Soviet head of Allied Control Comm. in Germany 45-46; C.-in-C. Land Forces 46, Deputy Minister of the Armed Forces of the Soviet Union April 46; First Deputy Minister of Defence 53-55; Minister of Defence 55-57; mem. Presidium Central Cttee. Soviet Communist Party 57; in retirement 58-; twice awarded Order of Suvorov; holds Order of Lenin (5), Order of Red Banner (3), Hero of Soviet Union; awarded Order of Victory 44, Virtuti Military (first class), Gruenwald Star (first class), and other awards.
c/o Ministry of Defence, 34 Maurice Thorez Embankment, Moscow, U.S.S.R.

Zhuravlieva, Marina Ilyinichna; Soviet politician; b. 22 Jan. 1931; ed. Herzen Pedagogical Inst., Leningrad.
Member C.P.S.U. 53-; Komsomol worker 54-57; Third Sec., Frunze (Leningrad) Regional Cttee. C.P.S.U. 57-58; Sec. Leningrad District Cttee. Komsomol 58-59; Secr. Central Cttee. Komsomol 59-; Cand. mem. Central Cttee. C.P.S.U. 61-.
Central Committee of All-Union Lenin Communist Union of Youth, ulitsa Bogdana Kmelnitskovo 3/13, Moscow, U.S.S.R.

Zhuraytis, Algis; Soviet conductor; b. 1928; ed. Vilnius and Moscow Conservatoires.
Conductor Lithuanian Opera and Ballet State Theatre 51-54; Conductor of the Bolshoi Theatre 60-; radio performances 55-.
State Academic Bolshoi Theatre of U.S.S.R., 1 Ploshchad Sverdlova, Moscow, U.S.S.R.

Ziegler, Dr. Karl; German chemist; b. 26 Nov. 1898; ed. Marburg Univ.
Assistant Prof., Marburg Univ. 23-26; Asst., Chemical Inst., Heidelberg Univ. 26-36; Prof. of Chemistry and Dir. of Chemical Inst., Univ. of Halle-Saale 36-45; Dir. Max Planck Inst. for Coal Research, Mülheim-Ruhr 43-; Hon. Prof. Technische Hochschule, Aachen 49-; Hon. D.Rer.Nat. Univ. of Heidelberg, Univ. of Giessen, Technische Hochschule Hanover; mem. Bavarian Acad. of Sciences, Acad. of Sciences Göttingen, German Acad. of Sciences, Halle Leopoldina; hon. mem. Chemical Soc. of Japan, Soc. of Chemical Industry; Nobel Prize for Chemistry 63, numerous other awards.
Max-Planck-Institut für Kohlenforschung, Kaiser-Wilhelm-Platz 1, 433 Mülheim-Ruhr, German Federal Republic.
Telephone: 34021/2.

Zielstra, Gen. Hendrik Pieter; Netherlands air force officer; b. 8 Nov. 1908; ed. Breda Royal Military Acad.
Second Lt. Infantry 30; with Army Air Corps as Observer 36, Bomber Squadron 40; P.O.W. Germany 42-45; Staff Coll. for Army and Air Force 46-47; U.S.A.F. Air Univ. 48; Dir. Air Force Staff Coll. 49-51; with SHAPE and Aircent 51-52; Personnel Dept., Ministry of Defence 52-54; Commdg. Officer Eindhoven Air Base 54-55; Deputy Chief Air Staff 55; Vice-Chief Air Staff 56-60; mem. Mil. Cttee. Perm. Session, Washington 60-61; Chief of Air Staff and C.-in-C. Netherlands Air Force 61-65; Chair. Joint Chiefs of Staff Cttee. 65-; A.D.C. Extraordinary to H.M. Queen Juliana 65-.
Ministry of Defence, Plein 4, The Hague; Home: Wassenaargseweg 115, The Hague, Netherlands.
Telephone: 070-24-73-50 (Home); 62-43-41 (Office).

Zietek, Jerzy; Polish politician; b. 10 June 1901.
Participated in Silesian uprisings 19-21; later worked in self-government; worked in Soviet military building, U.S.S.R.; joined Polish Army, Second-in-Command R. Traugutt Third Div. 44; after the Liberation Vice-Voivoda of Silesia-Dabrowa-Dabrowa Region, then Vice-Chair. of Presidium of Voivodship Peoples Council in Katowice 45-63, Chair. 64-; mem. Polish Workers Party (P.P.R.) 45-48, Polish United Workers Party (P.Z.P.R.) 48-, P.Z.P.R. Central Cttee. 64-; mem. Home Nat. Council (K.R.N.) then mem. Seym. 47-; Chair. Seym Cttee. for Building and Public Services; mem. Council of State 63-; Vice-Chair. Supreme Council of Union of Fighters for Freedom and Democracy 49-; Order of the Builders of People's Poland 64 and others.
Polska Zjednoczona Partia Robotnicza, Nowy Šwiat 6, Warsaw, Poland.

Zijlstra, Jelle, DR. ECON.SC.; Netherlands university professor, politician and banker; b. 27 Aug. 1918; ed. Rotterdam School of Economics.
Asst. Rotterdam School of Economics 45-46, Lecturer 47; Prof. of Economic Sciences, Free Univ. of Amsterdam 48-52; Minister of Economic Affairs 52-59, of Finance 59-July 63; Prof. of Economic Sciences, Free Univ. of Amsterdam 63-67; Pres. Board of Govs., European Investment Bank 62-July 63; Prime Minister 66-67; Pres. Netherlands Bank May 67-; Pres. Bank of Int. Settlements and Chair. of Board of Dirs. June 67; Gov. Int. Monetary Fund Washington 67-; Anti-Revolutionary Party.
Publ. *The Velocity of Circulation of Money and its Significance for the Value of Money and Monetary Equilibrium* 48.
Bavoylaan 14, The Hague; De Nederlandsche Bank N.V., Westeinde 1, Amsterdam, Netherlands.
Telephone: 854982 (Home); 63133 (Office).

Zimbalist, Efrem (husband of Mary Zimbalist, q.v.); American violinist and musical director; b. 9 April 1889; ed. Imperial School, St. Petersburg (pupil of Leopold Auer).
Début Berlin 07; concert performances in principal cities of Europe and America; Dir. Curtis Inst. of Music, Philadelphia 41-; composer of works for orchestra, string quartet, violin sonata, and works for voice and piano.
c/o ABC, 7 West 66th Street, New York City 10023, U.S.A.

Zimbalist, Mary Louise Curtis (wife of Efrem Zimbalist, q.v.); American music educator; b. 6 Aug. 1876; ed. Ogontz School, Temple and Pennsylvania Univs., Williams Coll., Colby Coll.
Hon. President, Settlement School of Music of Philadelphia 12-26; founded and endowed Curtis Inst. of Music 24, Pres. 24-.
The Curtis Institute of Music, Rittenhouse Square, Philadelphia, Pa., U.S.A.

Zimmerman, Charles J., B.S., M.B.A., C.L.U.; American insurance executive; b. 9 Jan. 1902; ed. Dartmouth Coll., The Amos Tuck School of Business Admin.
Exec. Man. New York Life Underwriters' Asscn. 24-26; Gen. Agent, The Conn. Mutual Life Insurance Co. 26-46; Man. Dir. Life Insurance Agency Management Asscn. 46-56; Pres. The Conn. Mutual Life Insurance Co. 56-67, Chair. 67-; Founder Univ. of Hartford 57; Trustee Dartmouth Coll., Lawrence Acad., Nat. Conf. of Christians and Jews; Chair. American Coll. of Life Under-

writers; Trustee, S. S. Huebnar Foundation for Insurance and Educ., Chair. 68; Dir. Inst. of Living, Hartford, Life Insurance Medical Research Fund (Chair. 63-), Nat. Asscn. for Mental Health, Inc., Conn. Bank and Trust Co., Hartford Gas Co., State Dime Savings Bank, Junior Achievement of Hartford Inc.; mem. Exec. Cttee. American Life Convention; John Newton Memorial Award 51.

140 Garden Street, Hartford, Conn.; and 70 Mohawk Drive, West Hartford, Conn. 06117, U.S.A.

Telephone: 203-249-0631 (Office); 203-232-1533 (Home).

Zimmermann, Gerhard; German politician; b. 1921. Former Head of Shipbuilding Industry, Rostock; Minister of Heavy Industries 65-; Order of Banner of Labour.

Ministry of Heavy Industries, Berlin, Germany.

Zimyanin, Mikhail Vasilievich; Soviet journalist; b. 14; ed. Mogilev Pedagogical Inst.

Member C.P.S.U. 39-; First Sec. Cen. Cttee., Komsomol Byelorussia 40-46; Second Sec. Gomel Regional Cttee. C.P.S.U. 46; Minister of Educ., Byelorussia 46-47; Sec. Second Sec. Cen. Cttee. C.P. Byelorussia 47-53, First Sec. 53; Ministry of Foreign Affairs 53-56, Far Eastern Dept. 57-60, Ambassador to Dem. Repub. of Viet-Nam 56-57, to Czechoslovakia 60-65; Dep. Foreign Minister 65; Editor of *Pravda* 65-; mem. Cen. Cttee. C.P.S.U. 52-56, 66-; mem. Cen. Auditing Comm. C.P.S.U. 56-66; Dep. Chair. Council of Nationalities of 'J.S S.R. Supreme Soviet 50-54.

Pravda, 24 Ulitsa Pravdy, Moscow, U.S.S.к.

Zingarelli, Italo, LL.D.; Italian journalist and writer; b. 9 July 1891.

Editor *Ora* 10; Zürich corresp. *Corriere della Sera* 16-18 and Vienna corresp. 21; mem. staff of *Epoca* 18-21; Editor *Secolo* 26 and its Vienna corresp. 26-27; Vienna corresp. *Stampa* and *Agenzia Stefani* until 38; toured Middle East, Asia and Europe 38-43; Foreign Ed. *Il Tempo* Feb.-Dec. 45, Ed. of *Libera Stampa*, Rome, Dec. 45-Mar. 46; Foreign Ed. *Il Tempo* April 46; Ed. *Il Globo* June 52-62.

Publs. *La marina nella guerra attuale* 15, *La marina italiana* 15, *Il Dominio del mare nel conflitto anglo-germanico* 15, *L'invasione* 19, *L'agonia del bolscevismo* 23, *Il volto di Vienna* 25, *Der Gross Balkan* 27, *Il risveglio dell'Islam* 28, *Das Erbe von Versailles* 30, *Vienna non imperiale* 30, *Vienna* 35, *La leggenda di Ognuno* 36, *Vecchia Austria* 37, *I paesi danubiani e balcanici* 38, *Vicino e lontano Oriente* 40, *Il terzo braccio di Regina Coeli* 44, *Questo è il giornalismo* 46, *I tre imperialismi* 49, *I Padroni del Mondo* 52, *Lo stivale delle mille leghe* 62, etc.

c/o *Il Globo*, Via Due Macelli 23, Rome; and Piazza Stefano Jacini 5, Rome, Italy.

Zinn, Georg August; German lawyer and politician; b. 27 May 1901; ed. Univs. of Göttingen and Berlin.

Municipal official, Kassel 20-31; legal practice, Kassel 31-; war service 41-45; Minister of Justice, Hesse 45-49; Dir. Hesse Personnel Office 46-49, 50-; mem. Bundestag 49-50; Pres. Bundesrat 53-54, 64-65; Minister-Pres. and Minister of Justice, Hesse 50-62, Minister-Pres. 50-; Dr. phil. h.c., Dr. agr. h.c.

Publ. *Die Verfassung des Landes Hessen* 54.

Bierstadter Strasse 2, 62 Wiesbaden, German Federal Republic.

Zinneman, Fred; American (b. Austrian) film director; b. 29 April 1907; ed. Universität Wien and School of Cinematography, Paris.

Studied techniques of camera, lighting and mechanics, Paris; went to U.S.A. 29; directed documentaries and short films until 41, major films 41-; initiated, with others, school of realism in American Cinema; several awards including 3 Academy Awards, 4 New York Film Critics Awards, 2 Directors' Guild of America

Annual Awards; Hon. Award for *A Man for All Seasons*, Moscow Film Festival 67; Contributor to *Encyclopedia Britannica* (Film Directing).

Films include: *The Wave, The Seventh Cross, The Search, Act of Violence, The Men, High Noon, Member of the Wedding, From Here to Eternity, Oklahoma, Hatful of Rain, The Nun's Story, The Sundowners, Behold a Pale Horse, A Man for All Seasons.*

35 Blomfield Road, London, W.9, England.

Telephone: 01-289-0433.

Zinner, Ernst; German astronomer; b. 2 Feb. 1886; ed. Jena, Munich and Lund Univs.

Observer to Geodetic Comm. 19-26; Dir. Remeis-Observatory, Bamberg 26-53; mem. Halle Acad. of Science; mem. Int. Acad. of History of Science; mem. Int. Astronomical Union; Dr. h.c. 61.

Publs. *Verzeichnis der astronomischen Handschriften des deutschen Kulturgebietes* 25, *Veröffentlichungen der Remeis-Sternwarte*, I-IV 26-39, *Geschichte der Sternkunde* 30, *Die fränkische Sternkunde im 11 bis 16 Jahrhundert* 34, *Der deutsche Kalender des Johannes Regiomontan* 37, *Leben und Wirken des Johannes Müller von Königsberg genannt Regiomontanus* 38, *Die ältesten Räderuhren und modernen Sonnenuhren* 39, *Geschichte und Bibliographie der astronomischen Literatur in Deutschland zur Zeit der Renaissance* 41, *Entstehung und Ausbreitung der copernicanischen Lehre* 43; *Astronomie Geschichte ihrer Probleme* 51, *Sternglaube und Sternforschung* 53, *Die Erklärung des Lichtwechsels der vermissten Sterne* 52, *Aus der Frühzeit der Räderuhr* 54, *Astronomische Instrumente des 11 bis 18 Jahrhunderts* 56, *The Stars Above Us* 57, *Alte Sonnenuhren an europäischen Gebäuden* 64.

Sternwarstr. 7, 86 Bamberg, German Federal Republic.

Telephone: Bamberg 24453.

Zinsou, Emile Derlin; Dahomeyan doctor and politician; b. 23 March 1918; ed. Ecole Primaire Supérieure, Ecole Africaine de Médecine, Dakar and Univ. de Paris à la Sorbonne.

Represented Dahomey in French Nat. Assembly; fmr. Vice-Pres. Assemblée de l'Union française, Senator, Territorial Council; fmr. Minister of Economy and of The Plan; fmr. Ambassador to France; Pres. Supreme Court of Dahomey; Minister of Foreign Affairs 61-63, 65-67; designated Pres. of Dahomey July 68; numerous decorations include: Commdr. Ordre Nat., Dahomey, Grand Officier Légion d'Honneur.

Cotonou, Dahomey.

Ziv-Av, Itzhak; Israeli administrative official; b. 4 June 1907; ed. Inst. of Pedagogy, Smolensk.

In Israel 26-; Managing Editor *Haboker* 35-48; Dir. Public Relations Div., Ministry of Defence and Gen. H.Q., Israel Defence Forces 48-52; Dir.-Gen. Israel Farmers' Federation 52-; mem. Editorial Board of *Hayiom* daily; mem. Board of Dirs. Jewish National Fund; mem. Council, State Land Authority, Habimah, The National Theatre.

Publs. *The Unknown Land, I Seek my Brethren, The Price of Freedom, Forever Ours, From Frontier to Frontier, A World to Live in, Another World.*

Israel Farmers' Federation, P.O. Box 209, Tel-Aviv, Israel.

ZoBell, Claude E., M.S., PH.D.; American microbiologist; b. 22 Aug. 1904; ed. Utah State Univ. and Univ. of California.

Principal, Rigby (Idaho) Elementary School 24-26; Instructor, Utah State Univ. 28-29; Research Asst., Hooper Foundation 29-30; Instructor, Scripps Inst. Oceanography, Univ. of Calif. 32-36, Asst. Prof. 38-42, Assoc. Prof. 42-48, Prof. 48-, Chair. Div. of Marine Biology 56-60; Research Assoc., Univ. of Wisconsin 38-39; Special Fellow, Rockefeller Foundation, Europe 48-49; Participant in Galathea Round-the-World Deep Sea Expedition; first to recover living organisms from

greatest depths of the sea; Royal Danish Navy Galathea Medal 52.
Publs. *Marine Microbiology* 46, 200 articles or papers dealing with researches on function of bacteria as geochemical agents and in origin of oil.
2404 Ellentown Road, La Jolla, Calif. 92037; Scripps Institution, Univeristy of California, La Jolla, Calif., U.S.A.

Zořka, Borek; Austrian trade unionist; b. 27; ed. Univ. Charles IV, Prague, Acad. of Int. Law, The Hague, Brussels Free Univ. and Inst. of Int. Studies, Geneva.
Assistant, International Confederation of Free Trade Unions (ICFTU), Brussels 50-57; Liaison Officer, Int. Trade Secretariats (ITS), Geneva; Order of Merit (Czechoslovakia) 45.
Publs. *The Trials of Zagreb* 54, *Czechoslovak Constitutions* 55, *The Company of Katanga* 56, *Tunisian Nationalism* 56, *Trade Unionism in Africa* 56, *ILO Industrial Committees* 61, *Assistance to Trade Unions in Developing Countries* 61.
I.T.S. Liaison Office, 18 boulevard James-Fazy, Geneva; 8a Avenue de Miremont, Geneva, Switzerland.

Zoitakis, Gen. George; Greek army officer; b. 1910; ed. Cadet School, Higher War Coll. of Greece, School of Nat. Defence, and American School of Special Arms, Germany.
Infantry 2nd Lieut. 32; 1st Lieut. 38; Major 46; Lieut. Col. 49; Col. 55; Brig. 60; Maj.-Gen. 63; Lieut.-Gen. 65; Under Sec. of State for Nat. Defence April 67; Regent of Greece Dec. 67-; mem. Mixed Greco-Bulgarian Cttee. for settling frontier incidents, then Pres. of corresp. Greek-Yugoslav Cttee.; numerous medals.
Office of the Regent, Athens, Greece.

Żółkiewski, Stefan, PH.D.; Polish university professor; b. 9 Dec. 1911; ed. Warsaw Univ.
Prof. of the History of Polish Literature, Warsaw Univ.; fmr. mem. Presidium, Polish Acad. of Sciences, Sec. for Section I of Acad. of Sciences 61-68; mem. Central Cttee. Polish United Workers Party; State Prizes 51, 53 and 64; Minister of Higher Education 55-59; Pres. Polish Semiotic Asscn.
Publs. *Stare i nowe Literaturoznawstwo* (Old and New Approaches to Literature), *Spór o Mickiewicza* (Dispute over Mickiewicz), *Kultura i Polityka* (Culture and Politics) 58, *Perspektywy Literatury XX Wieku* 60, *Przepowiednie i Wspomnienia* 63, *O Kulturze Polski* (Culture of Poland) 64, *Zagadnienia Stylu* (The Problem of Style) 65; Ed. *Kultura i Społeczeństwo*.
Aleja Róz 6/14, Warsaw, Poland.
Telephone: 21-39-92.

Zollner, Maxime-Léopold; Dahomeyan diplomatist; b. 1934; ed. Dahomey and Univ. de Paris.
Counsellor, Dahomey Perm. Mission to UN 60-63; Counsellor, Wash. 61-63; Sec.-Gen. Malagasy Union 63-64; Deputy Perm. Rep. to UN 64-67, Perm. Rep. 67-.
Permanent Mission of Dahomey to the United Nations, 4 East 73rd. Street, New York, N.Y. 10021, U.S.A.

Zolotas, Xenophon, DR.ECON.; Greek university professor; b. 26 March 1904; ed. Univs. of Athens, Leipzig and Paris.
Professor of Econs. Univ. of Salonica 28, of Athens 31-; Chair. Board of Dirs., Agricultural Bank of Greece 36-40; Jt. Gov. Bank of Greece (after Liberation) Oct. 44-45; mem. UNRRA Council 46; Gov. of Int. Monetary Fund for Greece 46-67, mem. Greek Del. to UN Gen. Ass. 48-53; Del. to Econ. Comm. for Europe 49; mem. Currency Cttee. 50, Vice-Chair. ECE 52; Minister of Co-ordination Oct. 52; Gov. Bank of Greece 55-Aug. 67; mem. "Group of Four" for remodelling of OEEC 60; Editor *Greek Review of Economics*; mem. Acad. of Athens 52-; Grand Cross of Royal Order of the Phoenix.
Publs. *Griechenland auf dem Wege zur Industrialisierung*

26, *Etalon-or en théorie et en pratique* 34, *La question de l'or et le problème monetaire* 37, *Monetary Stability and Economic Development* 58, *Economic Development and Technical Education* 59, *The Problem of the International Monetary Liquidity* 61, *Towards a Reinforced Gold Exchange Standard* 61, *Economic Development and Private Enterprise* 62, *International Monetary Order: Problems and Policies* 62, *The Role of The Banks in a Developing Country* 63, *The Multicurrency Standard and the International Monetary Fund* 63, *Monetary Equilibrium and Economic Development* 65, *Remodelling the International Monetary System* 65, *Alternative Systems for International Monetary Reform* 65, *Monetary and Economic Developments in Greece* 66, *International Labor Migration and Economic Development* 66, *The Gold Trap and the Dollar* 68; in Greek *Monetary Stability* 29, *Monetary Stabilization* 29, *Liberal Socialism* 44, *Economics* 44, *Monetary Problems and the Greek Economy* 50, *Inflationary Pressures in the Greek Economy* 51, *Regional Planning and Economic Development*.
Home: 25 Dionissiou Areopagitou Street, Athens 402; Office: 8 Vissarionos Street, Athens 135, Greece.
Telephone: 914-780 (Home); 634-647 (Office).

Zolotukhin, Grigory Sergeyevich; Soviet politician; b. 1911; ed. Agricultural Coll. and C.P.S.U. Higher Party School.
Member C.P.S.U. 39-; Exec. posts in Tambov Region 31-38; Agronomist 38-39; Young Communist League and Party Official 39-65; First Sec. Krasnodar Territory Cttee. of C.P.S.U. 66-; Alt. mem. C.P.S.U. Central Cttee. 56-66, mem. 66-; Deputy to U.S.S.R. Supreme Soviet 66-.
Krasnodar Territory Committee, Communist Party of the Soviet Union, Krasnodar, U.S.S.R.

Zondek, Herman, M.D.; Israeli physician; b. 4 Sept. 1887; ed. Gymnasium, Rogasen, Prussia, and Univs. of Göttingen and Berlin.
Lecturer, Friedrich Wilhelm Univ., Berlin 18-21; Dir. Municipal Hospital am Urban, Berlin 26; Prof. of Medicine, Berlin Univ. 34; Dir. Medical Div. Bikur Holim Hospital, 34; Visiting Prof. Hebrew Univ. Medical School, Jerusalem 40; Hcn. Pres. Scientific Council of Israel Medical Asscn., Israel Soc. of Internal Medicine, Jerusalem Acad. of Medicine; mem. Israel Acad. of Sciences and Humanities; affil. Royal Soc. of Medicine, London.
Publs. *Das Hungerödem* (Hunger Oedema) 20, *The Diseases of the Endocrine Glands* (German) 23, later revised and enlarged editions in German, English, French, Polish, Russian and Italian 26-58; about 250 papers on endocrine physio-pathology.
8 Maimon Street, Jerusalem, Israel.

Zonn, Włodzimierz, M.A., D.PH.; Polish astronomer; b. 14 Nov. 1905; ed. Wilno Univ.
Assistant Astonomer, Warsaw Observatory 38, Prof. of Astronomy 51-; Prisoner of War in Germany 39-45; Pres. Polish Astronomical Cttee. 64-; mem. Int. Astronomical Union (IAU) 48, Cttee. on Space Research (COSPAR) Bureau 58, American Astronomical Soc. 62; numerous awards.
Publs. *General Astrophysics* 55, *Stellar Astronomy* (with K. Rudnicki) 57 (Russian and English trans.), *Stellar Evolution* 58, *Interstellar Matter* (with S. Grzedzielski) 61, *Astronomy yesterday and now* 65, *Modern Cosmology* 67.
Al. Ujazdowski 4, Warsaw, Poland.
Telephone: 289935.

Zorin, Valerian Alexandrovitch; Soviet diplomatist; b. 02; ed. High Communist Inst. of Education.
Important position in Central Cttee. of Komsomol 22-32; post-graduate student High Communist Inst. of Education 33-35; party and pedagogical work 35-41; Asst. Gen. Sec. of People's Commissariat of Foreign Affairs 41-

42, Head Fourth European Dept. 43-45; Ambassador to Czechoslovakia 45-47; Deputy Minister of Foreign Affairs 47-55, 56-57, concurrently Perm. Rep. of U.S.S.R. to UN Security Council 52-53; Ambassador to the German Fed. Republic 55-60; Perm. Rep. to UN 60-62; Alt. mem. Central Cttee. C.P.S.U. 56-61, mem. 61-; Ambassador to France 65-; Rep. to Geneva Disarmament Talks 60, 64; Order of Lenin (2), Order of the Red Banner (2), Badge of Honour, Medal for Outstanding Work in the Great Patriotic War and other decorations.
U.S.S.R. Embassy, 79 rue de Grenelle, Paris 7e, France.

Zorrilla de San Martin, Alejandro; Uruguayan diplomatist; b. 09.
Formerly with Banco de la República Oriental del Uruguay, latterly Head of Commercial Dept.; mem. National Assembly 55-65; Vice-Pres. Cttee. for Public Works 55; Vice-Pres. House of Representatives 59, Pres. 60; Pres. Cttee. for the Treasury 62; Minister for Foreign Affairs 63-65; mem. National Govt. Council 65-66; mem. Partido Nacional 56-, Sec. 59-63; mem. numerous cttees. and numerous international awards.
c/o Partido Nacional, Montevideo, Uruguay.

Zotov, Vasili Petrovich; Soviet politican; b. 1899.
Economic Executive 29-38, 50-53; Dep. People's Commissar, People's Commissar, later Minister of Food Industry of U.S.S.R. 38-49; Dep. Minister of Home and Foreign Trade of U.S.S.R. 53; Minister of Foodstuffs Industry of U.S.S.R. 53-57; Dep. Chair. U.S.S.R. State Planning Cttee. (*Gosplan*) 57-62; Head of Food Industry Dept., U.S.S.R. Econ. Council 62-64; mem. Board of National Economy, U.S.S.R., Dep. Chair. Council of Nat. Economy, U.S.S.R. 64-65; Minister of Food Industry 65-; mem. C.P.S.U. 25-; Cand. mem. Central Cttee. C.P.S.U.; Dep. to U.S.S.R. Supreme Soviet; Order of Lenin (three times), Order of Red Banner of Labour, etc.
Ministry of Food Industry, Moscow, U.S.S.R.

Zoungrana, H.E. Cardinal Paul; Upper Voltan ecclesiastic; b. 3 Sept. 1917; ed. l'Institut Catholique de Paris, and Université Pontificale Gregorienne.
Ordained priest 42; mem. Missionary Soc. of the White Fathers; Archbishop of Ouagadougou 60-; created Cardinal 65; Pres. West African Episcopal Conference.
Archbishop's House, B.P. 90, Ouagadougou, Upper Volta.
Telephone: 27-92.

Žourek, Jaroslav, LL.D.; Czechoslovak international jurist; b. 29 March 1908; ed. Universita Karlova, Prague.
Former Asst., Seminary of Int. Law, Charles Univ., Prague; Legal Officer, Ministry of Foreign Affairs 37; Scientific and Teaching Work, Law Faculty of Charles Univ. 45-48, Assoc. Prof. 48-; Del. of Czechoslovakia at Conf. of Law of the Sea, Geneva 58; mem. UN Int. Law Comm. 48-61, Pres. 57-58; leading Research Assoc. in Int. Law, Czechoslovak Acad. of Sciences 54-; Judge *ad hoc*, Int. Court of Justice, The Hague 59-60; UN expert at Conf. on Consumer Regulations 63; Special Adviser to Czech. del. at Conf. on Law of Treaties Vienna 68; Assoc. mem. Inst. of Int. Law; mem. Presiding Council Int. Court of Arbitration for Maritime and Inland Navigation, Gdynia, Pres. 64, 67; Past Pres. and now Vice-Pres. Int. Law Asscn.; London; Yugoslav award for outstanding services to the country (Zaslugy Za narod).
Publs. *Definition de l'agression* 57, *Statut et Fonctions des consuls* 62; numerous studies on questions of International Law.
c/o Czechoslovak Academy of Sciences, Prague 1, Národní tr 3; Home: Prague 6-Střešovice, Lomená 5, Czechoslovakia.
Telephone 35-20-35.

Zrzavý, Jan; Czechoslovak artist; b. 5 Nov. 1890.
Member of "The Obstinates" of early 20th Century; many study trips in Italy especially Venice; worked in Brittany 23-30; painter of landscapes, figurative paintings, still lifes, also illustrator of many books; one-man exhbns. in Paris, Venice, Berlin, Dresden, Munich, Geneva and London; Nat. Artist of Czechoslovakia 66.
Malá Strana, Nové zámecké schody 6, Prague 1, Czechoslovakia.
Telephone: 53041.

Zuayter, Akram; Jordanian educationist and diplomatist; b. 09; ed. Al-Najah Coll., Nablus, American Univ. of Beirut, and School of Law, Jerusalem.
Teacher, Secondary Schools, Nablus and Acre 27-30; Chief Editor *Mira'at-al-Shark* and *Al-Hayat*, Jerusalem 30-31; Prof. of History, Training Coll., Baghdad 34-35; Sec. Palestinian Nat. Cttee. 36; exiled 37-50; Insp. of Educ., Iraq 40-41; Pres. Arab Del. to Latin America for Palestine Cause 47-48; Minister of Educ., All-Palestine Govt. 49; Counsellor, Syrian Del. to Arab League, mem. Perm. Palestine Cttee. 50; Gen. Sec. Moslem Confs., Jerusalem 60-62; Ambassador of Jordan to Syria 62-63, to Iran 63-65; Minister of Foreign Affairs, Jordan Feb. 66-Dec. 66; Senator 67-; Minister of the Royal Hashemite Court 67-; numerous decorations incl. Grand Cordon of Order of Independence (Jordan) and Knight's Cross of the Most distinguished Order of St. Michael and St. George (Great Britain).
Publs. *Our History* 35, *Arabic Readings* 39, *Recent History* 41, *Mission to a Continent* 50, *The Palestine Cause* 54, *An Essay in Federation* 55.
The Royal Hashemite Court, Amman, Jordan.
Telephone: 37341 (Office); 41783 (Home).

Zuberi, Itrat Husain, M.A., PH.D., F.R.S.L. (London); Pakistani university professor and writer; b. 10; ed. St. John's Coll., Agra, Edinburgh and Oxford Univs.
Senior Professor of English Literature and Principal Islamic Coll., Calcutta 38-47; Carnegie Fellow in English, Merton Coll., Oxford 48-50; Prof. and Head of Dept. of English, Dacca Univ. 51-53; Vice-Chancellor, Univ. of Rajshahi, East Pakistan 53-59; Adviser and Jt. Sec., Ministry of Education, Pakistan 57-59; mem. Exec. Board UNESCO 57-58; Visiting Prof. of English, Iowa Univ., U.S.A. 60-, Univ. Coll., Claremont, Calif. 61-62.
Publs. include *The Dogmatic and Mystical Theology of John Donne, The Metaphysical Poets of the Seventeenth Century, Malory to Huxley, Seventeenth Century Prose 1600-1660.*
c/o English Department, Iowa University, Iowa City, Iowa, U.S.A.

Zuckerman, Sir Solly, O.M., K.C.B., M.A., M.D., D.SC., L.R.C.P., F.R.S.; British anatomist; b. 04; ed. South African Coll. School, Cape Town Univ., and Univ. Coll. Hospital London.
Demonstrator of Anatomy Cape Town Univ. 23-25; Union Research Scholar 25; Research anatomist to London Zoological Society and Demonstrator of Anatomy, Univ. Coll., London 28-32; Research Assoc. and Rockefeller Research Fellow Yale Univ. 33-34; William Julius Mickle Fellow, London Univ. 35; Beit Memorial Research Fellow 34-37; Hunterian Prof. Royal Coll. of Surgeons 37; Univ. Demonstrator Human Anatomy Dept. Oxford 34-45; Sands Cox Prof. of Anatomy Birmingham Univ. 39-; Scientific Adviser British Military Orgs. 39-46; Group Capt. (Hon.) R.A.F. 43-46; Deputy Chair. Advisory Council on Scientific Policy 48-64; mem. Nat. Resources Technical Cttee. 51-64; mem. Agricultural Research Council 49-59; Trustee British Museum 67-; Hon. Sec. Zoological Society, London; Fellow Univ. Coll., London; Fellow Commoner, Christ's Coll., Cambridge; Gregynog Lecturer Univ. of Wales 56; Mason Lecturer Univ. of Birmingham 57, Lees Knowles Lecturer, Cambridge

Univ. 65; Scientific Adviser, Cabinet Office. 64-66, Chief Scientific Adviser to the Govt. 66-; Chief Scientific Adviser to Sec. of State for Defence until 66; Hon. Fellow Royal Coll. of Surgeons.

Publs. *The Social Life of Monkeys and Apes* 32, *Functional Affinities of Man, Monkeys and Apes* 33, *The Scientist and War* 66.

11 Hasker Street, London, S.W.3, England.

Zuckert, Eugene M., B.A., LL.B.; American lawyer and government official; b. 9 Nov. 1911; ed. Yale Univ. and Harvard Graduate School of Business Admin.

Attorney, U.S. Securities and Exchange Commission, Washington and New York City 37-40; Instructor, Asst. Prof., Asst. Dean, Harvard Graduate School of Business 40-44; Exec. Asst. to Administrator of Surplus Property Admin. 45-46; Special Asst. to Sec. of War for Air 46-47; Asst. Sec. U.S. Air Force 47-52; mem. Atomic Energy Comm. 52-54; fmr. Attorney and Man. Consulting Dir., Information for Industry Inc.; fmr. Chair. of Board, Nuclear Science and Engineering Corpn.; Sec. of the Air Force 61-65; Attorney and Management Consulting, Wash., D.C. 65-; Counsel to Lear Scoutt & Rasenberger, Wash. 67-; mem. Board, Nuclear Utility Services, Inc., Vitro Corpn. of America, Isotopes Inc.; Hon. LL.D., George Wash. Univ. 62, Hon. D.Eng. Clarkson Coll., New York.

Publ. (Joint) *Atomic Energy for Your Business* 56.

141 Hesketh Street, Chevy Chase, Maryland 20015, U.S.A.

Zuckmayer, Carl; German (naturalised American) writer; b. 27 Dec. 1896.

Playwright and poet; his first play, *Kreuzweg*, was produced at the Berlin State Theatre 20; Kleist prizewinner 25; Georg Büchner prizewinner 29; Goethe prizewinner 52.

Publs. Plays: *Der fröhliche Weinberg* 25, *Schinderhannes* 27, *Katharina Knie* 28, *Kakadu-Xakada* (for children) 29, *Der Hauptmann von Köpenick* (also film) 31, *Der Schelm von Bergen* 34, *The Moon in the South* 37, *Bellman* 38, *Second Wind* 41, *The Last Drop* 41, *Des Teufels General* 46, *Barbara Blomberg* 49, *Der Gesang im Feuerofen* 50, *Ulla Winblad* 53, *Das kalte Licht* 55, *Der trunkene Herkules* 58, *Der Schinderhannes* 66; Novels: *Magdalena von Bozen* 36, *Herr über Leben und Tod* 38, *Das Seelenbräu* 45; Verse: *Der Baum* 26; *Collected Works* (in 4 vols.) 46, 48, 50, 52; *Die langen Wege* (essay) 52; short stories, *Das Leben des Horace A. W. Tabor* 64; *Als wär 's ein Stück von mir* (memoirs) 66.

Saas-Fee, Switzerland.

Zukor, Adolph; American film producer; b. Hungary b. 7 Jan. 1873.

Fmrly. in hardware, upholstery and fur businesses New York and Chicago; founder Famous Players Film Co. 12; Chair. Board Paramount Pictures Corpn. 35- (now Chair. Emeritus).

Paramount Pictures Corpn., Paramount Bldg., New York, N.Y., U.S.A.

Zukrowski, Wojciech; Polish writer; b. 16.

Counsellor, Polish Embassy, New Delhi 56-58.

Publs. Short stories: *Z kraju milczenia* (From the Land of Silence), *Piorkiem flaminga* (With a Flamingo's Quill), *Córeczka* (Little Daughter), *Okruchy weselnego tortu* (Crumbs from the Wedding Cake); Novels: *Dni kleski* (Days of Defeat), *Bathed in Fire* (Ministry of Defence Prize 61); Travel: *Dom bez scian* (House without Walls), *Wanderings with my Guru: India, In the Kingdom of a Million Elephants: Laos, Niesmialy narzeczony* (Chinese legends); Film: *Bathed in Fire*.

Krakowskie Przedmieście 87/89, Warsaw, Poland.

Zupka, František; Czechoslovak trade union official; b. 30 June 1901.

Joined C.P. of Czechoslovakia 21; Communist mem.

Parl. 35, re-elected 64; imprisoned by Gestapo during occupation; Pres. of Slovak Trade Union movement after war; mem. Central Cttee. C.P. of Czechoslovakia 54-66; Pres. Central Council of Trade Unions 50-65; mem. Nat. Assembly; Klement Gottwald Order 55.

National Assembly, Prague, Czechoslovakia.

Zurayk, Constantine Kayser, M.A., PH.D.; Syrian educationist; b. 18 April 1909; ed. American Univ. of Beirut, Univ. of Chicago and Princeton Univ.

Asst. Prof. of History, American Univ. of Beirut 30-42, Assoc. Prof. 42-45; First Counsellor, Syrian Legation, Washington 45-46; Syrian Minister to U.S.A. 46-47; Vice-Pres. and Prof. of History, American Univ. of Beirut 47-49; Rector, Syrian Univ., Damascus 49-52; Vice-Pres. American Univ. of Beirut 52-54, Acting Pres. 54-57, Disting. Prof. of History 56-; del. U.N. Gen. Assembly and Alt. Rep. of Syria on Security Council 46-47; Pres. Int. Asscn. of Univs. 65-; mem. Int. Comm. for Scientific and Cultural History of Mankind; mem. Iraq Acad., Arab Acad., Damascus, American Historical Asscn.; Order of Merit (distinguished class) (Syria); Education Medal (First Class), Commdr. Order of Cedar (Lebanon).

Publs. *Al-Wa'y al Qawmi* (National Consciousness), *Ma'na al-Nakbah* (The Meaning of the Disaster), *Ayyu Ghadin* (Whither Tomorrow?), *Nahnu wa-l-Tarikh* (Facing History), *Hadha al-'Asr al-Mutafafajjir* (This Explosive Age), *Fi Ma'rakat al-Hadarah* (In the Battle for Culture), *Ma'na al-Nakbah Mujaddahan* (The Meaning of the Disaster Again); Editor Isma'il Beg Chol's *Al-Yazidiyyah qadiman wa hadithan* (Yazidis past and present), Ibn al-Furat's *History* Vols. VII-IX (with Najla Izzedin); Translator Miskawayh's *Tahdhib al-Akhlag* (The Refinement of Character).

American University of Beirut, Beirut, Lebanon.

Zutter, Philippe, L. en D.; Swiss diplomatist; b. 28 Jan. 1904; ed. Neuchâtel and Vienna Univs.

Entered Fed. Political Dept. 30; served successively in Bucharest, Buenos Aires, and Santiago, where he was Permanent Chargé d'Affaires with rank of Counsellor 43-46; Deputy Chief Int. Organisations Div., Fed. Political Dept. 46-48, Chief of Div. (rank of Minister) 49-52; Minister to Spain 52-57, Ambassador 57-59, Ambassador to Italy 59-67.

c/o Ministry of Foreign Affairs, Berne, Switzerland.

Zverev, Sergei Alexeyevich; Soviet politician; b. 12; ed. Leningrad Precision Mechanics and Optics Inst.

Member C.P.S.U. 42-; Designer, Head Technologist and Engineer, defence industry plants 36-47; Dep. Head, later Head, Cen. Dept. of Defence Industry 47-52; Dep. Minister of Armaments and Dep. Minister of Defence Industry 52-57; Vice-Chair., later First Vice-Chair. State Cttee. of U.S.S.R. Council of Ministers for Defence Technology 57-63, Chair. 63-65; Minister of Defence Industry of U.S.S.R. 65-; mem. Central Cttee. C.P.S.U.; Deputy to U.S.S.R. Supreme Soviet; three Orders of Lenin, two Orders of Red Banner of Labour, etc.

Ministry of Defence Industry, Moscow, U.S.S.R.

Zweig, Arnold; German novelist and playwright; b. 10 Nov. 1887; ed. Breslau, Munich, Berlin, Rostock, Göttingen and Tübingen Univs.

During First World War Private in France, Hungary and Serbia; stationed before Verdun for 13 months, later in Press Dept. of Eastern Headquarters Bialystok, Kovno and Wilna; emigré 33; deprived of German nationality 36; returned to East Germany 48; Pres. Deutsche Akad. der Künste 50-53, Hon. Pres. 57-; mem. Volkskammer; Pres. German P.E.N. Centre 58; Kleist Prize 15, Nat. Prize 50, Lenin Peace Prize 58.

Publs. *Claudia* 12, *Ritualmord in Ungarn* 15, *Caliban oder Politik und Leidenschaft* (an essay on anti-semitism) 26, *The Case of Sergeant Grischa* 27, *Young Woman of 1914* 31, *Education Before Verdun* 36, *Insulted and Exiled* 37, *The Crowning of a King* 37, *Versunkene Tage*

38, *The Axe of Wandsbek* 43, *Fahrt zum Acheron* 51, *Westlandsaga* 52, *Die Feuerpause* 54, *Soldatenspiele*, *Früchtekorb* 56, *Die Zeit ist Reif* 57, *Fünf Romanzen* 59, *Essays I* and *II* 59, 67, *Novellen I, II* 61, *Traum is Teuer* 62, *Dramen* 63, *Jahresringe* (poems) 64.
Homeyerstrasse 13, Berlin-Niederschönhausen, Germany.

Zwick, Charles John, B.S., PH.D.; American economist and government official; b. 17 July 1926; ed. Univ. of Connecticut and Harvard Univ.
Instructor, Univ. of Connecticut 51-54; Harvard Univ. 54-56; Head, Logistics Dept., the RAND Corpn. 56-63, mem. Research Council 63-65; Asst. Dir. U.S. Bureau of the Budget 65-68, Dir. Jan. 68-.
Bureau of the Budget, Washington, D.C. 20503; Home: 4612 Langdrum Lane, Chevy Chase, Maryland 20015, U.S.A.
Telephone: 202-395-3864 (Office); 301-657-2837 (Home).

Zwicky, Fritz, DR.SC.NAT.; Swiss physicist; b. 14 Feb. 1898; ed. Zürich Federal Institute of Technology.
Fellow in Physics Int. Education Board 25-27; Asst. Prof. of Theoretical Physics California Inst. of Technology 27-29, Associate Prof. 29-42, Prof. of Astrophysics 42-; Astronomer, Mt. Wilson and Palomar Observatories; mem. and Vice-Pres. Int. Acad. of Astronautics; Trustee Pestalozzi Foundation of America Inc.; Pres. Soc. for Morphological Research; U.S. Presidential Medal of Freedom.
Home: 2065 Oakdale Street, Pasadena 10, California, U.S.A.

Zwiener, Kenneth Vernon; American banker; b. 29 Aug. 1905; ed. Univ. of California.
Harris Trust and Savings Bank 29-, Asst. Vice-Pres. 46-55, Pres. 55-63, Dir. 54-, Chair. of Board 63-; Dir. Continental Casualty Co., Union Tank Car Co., Kellogg Co. and others.
Home: 1287 Sunview Lane, Winnetka, Ill.; Office: 111 West Monroe Street, Chicago 90, Ill., U.S.A.

Zwierzyński, Jan; Polish airline executive; b. 30; ed. Engineering School.
Successively Technical Dept., Polish Airlines *Lot*, Dir. Chief Mechanic's Dept.; Office of Council of Ministers; Dir. Dept. of Civil Aeronautics, Ministry of Transport; Dir. Polish Airlines *Lot* 63-.
17 Grojecka Street, Warsaw, Poland.

Zworykin, Vladimir Kosma, PH.D.; American television specialist; b. 30 July 1889; ed. Petrograd (Leningrad) Inst. of Technology, Collège de France, Pittsburgh Univ.
Went to U.S.A. 19; research with Westinghouse Electric and Manufacturing Co. 20-29; with Radio Corpn. of America 29-, Dir. of Electronic Research with RCA Manufacturing Co. 29-42, Assoc. Research Dir. RCA Laboratories 42-45, Dir. Electronic Research 46-54, Vice-Pres. and Technical Consultant 47-54 (retd.), now Hon. Vice-Pres. RCA; Technical Consultant RCA Laboratories; Fellow Inst. of Radio Engineers, American Inst. of Electrical Engineering, American Physical Soc., American Asscn. for Advancement of Science; mem. Electron Microscope Soc. of America, Nat. Acad. of Sciences, Nat. Acad. of Engineering, American Acad. of Arts and Sciences, American Philosophical Society; hon. mem. Soc. Motion Picture and TV Engineers, British Inst. of Radio Engineers; Officier d'Académie de France; many awards including Faraday Medal (British) 65, Presidential Medal of Science (U.S.A.) 66.
Publs. Co-author: *Photocells and their Applications* 32, *Television* 40, *Electron Optics and Electron Microscope* 45, *Photoelectricity and its Application* 49, *Television* 54, *Television in Science and Industry* 58.
Home: 103 Battle Road Circle, Princeton, N.J. 08540; Office: RCA Laboratories Division, Radio Corporation of America, Princeton, N.J., U.S.A.

Zygmund, Antoni, PH.D.; American university professor; b. 26 Dec. 1900; ed. Univ. of Warsaw.
Instructor, Polytechnical School, Warsaw 22-29; Docent, Univ. of Warsaw 26-30; Prof. Univ. of Wilno, Poland 30-39; Prof. Mount Holyoke Coll., South Hadley, Mass. 40-45; Prof., Univ. of Pennsylvania 45-47; Prof. Univ. of Chicago 47-; mem. Polish, American and Argentine Acads.
Publs. *Trigonometric Series* 35, 59, *Analytic Functions* (with S. Saks) 38, 65.
Department of Mathematics, University of Chicago. Chicago 37; Home: 5420 East View Park, Chicago, Ill. 60615, U.S.A.

OBITUARY

A list of persons whose deaths have been noted since the preparation of the previous edition.

* = biography still appears in this edition with the date of death noted.

** = biography still appears in this edition.

Adam, Henri Georges	27 Aug. 1967
Adcock, Sir Frank Ezra	22 Feb. 1968
Ailleret, Gen. Charles	9 March 1968
**Alegria, Ciro	17 Feb. 1967
Allport, Gordon Willard	Oct. 1967
Amer, Field Marshal Mohammed	
Abdul Hakim	14 Sept. 1967
Andreas, Willy	July 1967
Angell, Sir Norman	7 Oct. 1967
Antonov, Vasili Ivanovich	Aug. 1967
Arbuzov, Alexandr Yerminigeldovich	24 Jan. 1968
Arghezi, Tudor	14 July 1967
Arno, Peter	22 Feb. 1968
Asquith, Hon. Anthony	21 Feb. 1968
Attlee, Earl Clement Richard	8 Oct. 1967
Aymé, Marcel	14 Oct. 1967
*Azhaev, Vasilii Nikolaevich	April 1968
Babinger, Franz	23 June 1967
Baillieu, Baron; Clive Latham Baillieu	18 June 1967
Balandin, Aleksey Aleksandrovich	22 May 1967
Balfour of Burleigh, Baron; George	
John Gordon Bruce	4 June 1967
Barton, Bruce	5 June 1967
Basdevant, Jules	6 Jan. 1968
Bauer, Gérard	4 Sept. 1967
Baumgarten, Hans	24 March 1968
*Berg, Paal Olav	24 May 1968
Bergman, Bo	17 Nov. 1967
Berkner, Lloyd Viel	5 June 1967
Bicester, Baron; Randal Hugh	
Vivian Smith	15 Jan. 1968
**Blomdahl, Karl-Birger	18 June 1968
Boktor, Amir	18 July 1966
**Boring, Edward Garrigues	July 1968
Branco, Marshal Humberto Castelo	18 July 1967
Bregman, Alexander	15 Aug. 1967
**Brennan, H.E. Cardinal Francis J.	2 July 1968
Brooks, Hon. Alfred J.	Dec. 1967
Bruce of Melbourne, Viscount;	
Stanley Melbourne Bruce	25 Aug. 1967
**Cadogan, Rt. Hon. Sir Alexander	9 July 1968
Cam, Helen Maud	9 Feb. 1968
Cardijn, H.E. Cardinal Joseph	25 July 1967
Casares y Sanchez, Julio	1 July 1964
*Chardonne, Jacques	May 1968
Chateaubriand Bandeira de Mello,	
Francisco de Assis	April 1968
Chatfield, Baron; Admiral of the Fleet	
Alfred Ernle Montacute Chatfield	16 Nov. 1967
*Chaves Batista, Augusto	30 Nov. 1967
Ch'eng Ch'ien, Gen.	April 1968
Christophoros II	22 July 1967
*Chrysostomos	9 June 1968
Clausen, Mads	27 Aug. 1966
Clement, Rufus Early	7 Nov. 1967
Cluytens, André	3 June 1967
Cobban, Alfred	1 April 1968
Cockcroft, Sir John	18 Sept. 1967
*Cohen, Sir Andrew	17 June 1968
Cooper, John Cobb	22 July 1967
**Costopoulos, Stavros	23 June 1968
*Dávalos-Hurtado, Eusebio	Jan. 1968

Davies, Sydney John	25 July 1967
De Blank, Most Rev. Joost	1 Jan. 1968
Dehler, Thomas	21 July 1967
de Sabata, Victor	10 Dec. 1967
Desai, Manilal Jagdish	4 Oct. 1967
Desnica, Vladan	4 March 1967
Deutsch, Otto Erich	Nov. 1967
Deutscher, Isaac	19 Aug. 1967
**Dobson, Sir Roy	7 July 1968
Dönges, Theophilus Ebenhaezer	10 Jan. 1968
**Dorling, Capt. Henry Taprell	1 July 1968
Dreyer, Carl Theodor	20 March 1968
Dumesnil, René	24 Dec. 1967
Duncan, Patrick	4 June 1967
Duvivier, Julien	29 Oct. 1967
Ehrenburg, Ilya Grigorievich	31 Aug. 1967
Eisner, Jan	2 May 1967
Ekelöf, (Bengt) Gunnar	March 1968
Emerson, Robert Alton	March 1966
Emié, Louis	Nov. 1967
Erixon, Sigurd	18 Feb. 1968
Fabricius, Knud Frederik Krog	30 June 1967
Favreau, Guy	11 July 1967
Ferber, Edna	16 April 1968
Ferenczi, Béni	1 June 1967
Fleming, Robert Vedder	28 Nov. 1967
Florey, Baron; Howard Walter Florey	21 Feb. 1968
Forbes, Esther	12 Aug. 1967
Forbes, Rosita	30 June 1967
*Franck, Hans	11 April 1964
*Fry, Rev. Franklin C.	6 June 1968
Gagarin, Col. Yuri Alexeyevich	27 March 1968
Garçon, Maurice	29 Dec. 1967
Garner, John Nance	7 Nov. 1967
Gestido, Gen. Oscar	6 Dec. 1967
Gibbs, William Francis	7 Sept. 1967
Graf, Oskar Maria	28 June 1967
Gray, Sir Archibald Montague Henry	13 Oct. 1967
Grier, Mary Lynda Dorothea	21 Aug. 1967
Grohmann, Will	5 May 1968
Grosso, Orlando	6 Jan. 1968
Grumach, Ernst	5 Oct. 1967
Gual Villalbi, Pedro	12 Jan. 1968
*Gueye, Lamine	10 June 1968
Gyllenswärd, Ragnar Hugo Ferdinand	26 Feb. 1967
Hammes, Charles-Léon	1967
Hardwick, Charles Zachary	12 May 1967
Hartung, Karl	19 July 1967
*Hasnie, Shujaat Ali	17 March 1968
Heiler, Friedrich	24 April 1967
Henner, Kamil	1967
**Heymans, Corneille Jean F.	18 July 1968
Hinshelwood, Sir Cyril Norman	9 Oct. 1967
Hobson, Rt. Hon. Sir John Gardiner	
Sumner	4 Dec. 1967
Hochfeld, Julian	21 July 1966
**Holmes, Julius C.	13 July 1968
Holt, Rt. Hon. Harold Edward	17 Dec. 1967
*Hoskins, Halford Lancaster	Deceased
Hsu Kuang-ping	3 March 1968
Hume, Sir (Hubert) Nutcombe	22 Dec. 1967
Hurst, Fannie	23 Feb. 1968

*Husain, Altaf	25 May 1968	Maurois, André	9 Oct. 1967
*Hutton, John Henry	May 1968	May, Geoffrey	Feb. 1964
Huysmans, Camille	25 Feb. 1968	May, Morton J.	17 May 1968
		Mazon, André	14 July 1967
Ibrahim, Hafiz Mohd.	Jan. 1968	M'Ba, Léon	28 Nov. 1967
Ierusalimsky, Nikolai Dimitrievich	5 May 1967	Meigs, Merill Church	Jan. 1968
Infeld, Leopold	16 Jan. 1968	Meunier du Houssoy, Robert	3 March 1968
Irwin, Margaret	11 Dec. 1967	**Millin, Sarah Gertrude	6 July 1968
Irwin, William Andrew	22 April 1968	Millsop, Thomas E.	Sept. 1967
**Ivchenko, Alexander	July 1968	*Milyutin, Yuri Sergeevich	June 1968
Iveagh, Earl of; Rupert Edward Cecil		*Moll, Siegmund Bruno	31 Jan. 1968
Lee Guinness	14 Sept. 1967	**Morano, H.E. Cardinal Francesco	12 July 1968
		Morison, Stanley Arthur	11 Oct. 1967
Jerichow, Herbert Peter Andreas	17 Aug. 1967	Münnich, Dr. Ferenc	29 Nov. 1967
Johnson, Robert Wood	30 Jan. 1968		
Johnston, Wayne Andrew	4 Dec. 1967	*Nash, Rt. Hon. Sir Walter	4 June 1968
Jones, Daniel	4 Dec. 1967	Newman, Bernard	19 Feb. 1968
Jones, Sir Walter Benton	5 Dec. 1967	Ngileruma, Alhaji Muhammad	17 Feb. 1968
Jung, Mehdi Nawaz	28 June 1967	Nicolson, Hon. Sir Harold	1 May 1968
		Nordhoff, Heinrich	12 April 1968
Kaiser, Henry J.	24 Aug. 1967	Nye, Lt.-Gen. Sir Archibald Edward	13 Nov. 1967
Karve, Dattatreya Gopal	28 Dec. 1967		
Katju, Kailas Nath	Feb. 1968	Ovechkin, Valentin Vladimirovich	Jan. 1968
*Keller, Helen Adams	1 June 1968		
Kemsley, Viscount; James Gomer		Pacini, H.E. Cardinal Alfredo	23 Dec. 1967
Berry	6 Feb. 1968	Panofsky, Erwin	15 March 1968
Kennedy, Margaret	31 July 1967	Parran, Thomas	15 Feb. 1968
*Kennedy, Robert Francis		**Paustovsky, Konstantin Georgievich	14 July 1968
Assasinated; died 6 June 1968		Périer, Gilbert	13 March 1968
Kettner, Radim	Deceased 1967	Peries, Sir Albert	21 Sept. 1967
Kevin, J. C. G.	13 Feb. 1968	Perreux, Gabriel	29 Oct. 1967
Kiernan, Thomas Joseph	Dec. 1967	Phelan, E. J.	15 Sept. 1967
Kilgore, Bernard	14 Nov. 1967	Pincus, Gregory	22 Aug. 1967
King, Martin Luther, Jr. Assasinated	4 April 1968	Pizzetti, Ildebrando	13 Feb. 1968
Kobelt, Karl	4 Jan. 1968	**Pla y Deniel, H.E. Cardinal Enrique	5 July 1968
Korin, Pavel Dmitrievich	22 Nov. 1967	*Pode, Sir Julian	11 June 1968
Kozlov, Vasili Ivanovich	2 Dec. 1967	Poivilliers, Georges	9 March 1968
Krupp von Bohlen und Halbach,		*Prado Ugarteche, Manuel	14 Aug. 1967
Alfried	31 July 1967	Pu Yi (Henry Pu Yi)	17 Oct. 1967
Kuhn, Richard	1 Aug. 1967	Pyriev, Ivan Alexandrovich	7 Feb. 1968
Kuwatly, Shukri Ali	30 June 1967		
Kuypers, Julian Joseph	15 Nov. 1967	Quandt, Harald	22 Sept. 1967
		*Quasimodo, Salvatore	14 June 1968
Lambury of Northfield, Baron;		*Queeny, Edgar M.	7 July 1968
Leonard Percy Lord	13 Sept. 1967	Queiroz, Rachel de	18 July 1967
Landau, Lev Davidovich	1 April 1968		
Langhelle, Nils	27 Aug. 1967	*Rakotomalala, Louis	1 July 1968
Lavrovsky, Leonid Mikhailovitch	26 Nov. 1967	Randall, Clarence Belden	4 Aug. 1967
Lazurick, Robert (Maurice)	17 April 1968	Rao, Mysore Subba	Dec. 1967
Leigh, Vivien	8 July 1967	Raspletin, Alexander Andreevich	Deceased 1967
Levi Della Vida, Giorgio	Dec. 1967	*Read, Sir Herbert	12 June 1968
Lightner, Milton C.	24 March 1968	Riberi, H.E. Cardinal Antonio	16 Dec. 1967
Liljestrand, Göran	Jan. 1968	Richaud, H.E. Cardinal Paul Marie A.	5 Feb. 1968
Lindsay, Howard	11 Feb. 1968	Riphahn, Wilhelm	Deceased
Litchfield, Edward Harold	9 March 1968	Ritter, Gerhard	1 July 1967
Litchfield, Lawrence, Jr.	28 Oct. 1967	Robertson, Norman A.	16 July 1968
Locher, Arthur E.	16 Nov. 1967	**Robinson, Sir Foster Gotch	31 Oct. 1967
Lohia, Dr. Rammanohar	11 Oct. 1967	Roser, Rev. Francisco Xavier	12 Feb. 1967
*Lohr, Lenox Riley	June 1968	*Runcorn, Baron; Dennis Forwood	
Lohse, Adolf	6 Nov. 1967	Vosper	20 Jan. 1968
*Louw, The Hon. Eric Hendrik	24 June 1968		
Luce, Henry Robinson	28 Feb. 1967	Saigh, H.E. Cardinal Maximos IV	5 Nov. 1967
Luthuli, Chief Albert	21 July 1967	Sandburg, Carl	22 July 1967
Lutz, Ralph Haswell	Deceased	Sargent, Henry Barry	26 March 1967
		Sargent, Sir Malcolm	3 Oct. 1967
McCullers, Carson	29 Sept. 1967	Sassoon, Siegfried	1 Sept. 1967
Magritte, René	15 Aug. 1967	Schick Gutiérrez, René	3 Aug. 1966
Malcev, Anatolij Ivanovitch	July 1967	Schnabel, Franz	Deceased 1966
Markelov, Ivan Alexeyevich	30 Jan. 1968	Schneider, Kurt	27 Oct. 1967
*Marsh, Daniel L.	20 May 1968	Scott, Winfield Townley	May 1968
Marshall, Edison	29 Oct. 1967	Sedlmayr, Hans	22 April 1968
Martin, Joseph William, Jr.	6 March 1968	Seebohm, Hans Christoph	17 Sept. 1967
Martino, Gaetano	21 July 1967	Selvinsky, Ilya Lvovich	21 March 1968
Massey, Rt. Hon. Vincent	30 Dec. 1967	Serafin, Tullio	Deceased
*Mathiassen, Therkel	14 March 1967	Serov, Vladimir Aleksandrovich	19 Jan. 1968
Matthews, Zachariah Keodireland	May 1968		

Sheppard, Sir John Tresidder	7 May 1968	Upadhyaya, Deendayal	Feb. 1968
Sherek, Henry	23 Sept. 1967		
Sho, Kiyohiko	Deceased	Valletta, Vittorio	10 Aug. 1967
Singh, Master Tara	22 Nov. 1967	Veuillot, H.E. Cardinal Pierre	14 Feb. 1968
Sohlman, Rolf Ragnarsson	22 July 1967	Vian, Admiral of the Fleet Sir Philip L.	27 May 1968
Sokolovsky, Marshal Vasilii Danilovich	10 May 1968	Visher, Stephen Sargent	25 Oct. 1967
Sorokin, Pitirim Alexandrovitch	10 Feb. 1967	Vollgraff, (Carl) Wilhelm	20 Oct. 1967
*Sowerby, Leo	July 1968	Voronov, Chief Marshal of Artillery	
Spellman, H.E. Cardinal Francis		Nikolai Nikolaevich	28 Feb. 1968
Joseph	2 Dec. 1967		
Starnuti, Edgardo Lami	4 May 1968	Wahba, Sheikh Hafiz	23 Nov. 1967
Stern, Lina Solomonova	18 March 1968	Wallace, Mrs. Lurleen Burns	7 May 1968
Sylla, Albert	19 July 1967	Waterman, Alan Tower	30 Nov. 1967
		Watkins, Vernon Phillips	8 Oct. 1967
Tappouni, H.E. Cardinal Ignace		Wedgwood, Hon. Josiah	5 May 1968
Gabriel	29 Jan. 1968	Wehrer, Albert	Deceased
Taudière, Emile	9 Oct. 1967	Weinberger, Jaromir	9 Aug. 1967
Tecchi, Bonaventura	30 March 1968	Wenzel, Alois	20 July 1967
Tienchensin (Tien Ken sin),		Williams, Rt. Rev. Alwyn Terrell Petre	18 Feb. 1968
H.E. Cardinal Thomas	24 July 1967	Wilshaw, Sir Edward	3 March 1968
Treharne, Reginald Francis	3 July 1967	Wolfit, Sir Donald	17 Feb. 1968
Tremblay, Hon. René	22 Jan. 1968	Woodward, Lt.-Gen. Sir Eric Winslow	Dec. 1967
Tsai Ting-kai	25 April 1968		
**Tsirimokos, Elie	13 July 1968	Yeh Chi-chuang	July 1967
Twining, Baron; Edward Francis		Yudin, Pavel Fedorovich	April 1968
Twining	21 July 1967		
Tychina, Pavlo Grigorievich	16 Sept. 1667	Zadkine, Ossip	25 Nov. 1967